EUROPEAN RAIL TIMETABLE

Summer 2014

Rail and ferry services
throughout Europe

An expanded edition of the monthly
European Rail Timetable
June 2014

Published by
European Rail Timetable Limited
28 Monson Way
Oundle
Northamptonshire
PE8 4QG
United Kingdom

ISBN 978–0–9929073–0–3

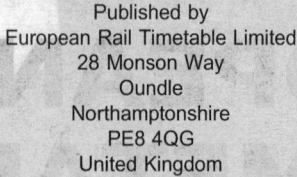

Director and Editor-in-Chief : John Potter

Editor : Chris Woodcock

Editorial team : Peter Bass, Reuben Turner, David Turpie

Commercial Manager: Keri Potter

Subscriptions: Peter Weller

Consultant : Lisa Bass

Telephone (Editorial & Sales) +44 (0)1832 270198

e-mail (Sales): sales@europeanrailtimetable.eu

e-mail (Editorial): editorial@europeanrailtimetable.eu

Website and on-line bookshop : www.europeanrailtimetable.eu

Every care has been taken to render the timetable correct in accordance with the latest information, but changes may be made by the railway authorities and the publishers cannot hold themselves responsible for the consequences of either changes or inaccuracies.

Cover created by Andrea Collins:
www.millstonecreative.co.uk
millstonecreative@btinternet.com

Printed and bound by CPI Group (UK) Ltd, Croydon, CR0 4YY

INTRODUCTION

This **Summer 2014** edition is a specially enlarged version of the monthly **European Rail Timetable**, published by European Rail Timetable Limited and recognised throughout the world as the indispensable compendium of European rail schedules. This seasonal edition appears twice yearly in Summer and Winter versions based on the June and December monthly editions.

Previously published by Thomas Cook, the European Rail Timetable is still compiled by the same dedicated team and has been the travelling companion of the tourist and business traveller, InterRailer and Eurailer for many years.

The intention of this special seasonal edition is to make the timetable more widely available to the increasing numbers of holidaymakers who are touring Europe by train, whether using InterRail, Eurail or one of the other popular European rail passes, or simply travelling point to point. It includes additional information of use to rail travellers, especially those trying this kind of holiday for the first time.

Our feature on **Rail Passes** (pages v to xi) includes full details of the InterRail Global Pass and InterRail One Country Pass schemes (for European residents), as well as latest details of the various Eurail passes for those resident outside Europe. Many other passes are also featured, including a selection of citywide tickets and visitor cards for those visiting major European cities.

The **Country-by-Country** section (pages xii to xxxii) is packed with useful information about each country, and there is a chart of visa requirements on page xxxii. In the main body of the timetable, **Newslines** on page 3 has information about the latest changes and about the particular contents of this edition. Pages 8 and 9 help you make vital preparations for your journey, whilst a little time spent reading the notes on pages 4 to 7, explaining how to read the timetable, will be amply repaid when you get down to the task of planning your travels.

Whether you intend to travel only in one or two countries, or are attempting a spectacular grand tour of Europe, the timetables in this book will cover most of the routes you will need and will enable you to pre-plan your journey, which is often half the fun. Rail timetables are, however, always liable to change and you are recommended to consult the latest monthly edition of the European Rail Timetable or local information before travelling.

BEYOND EUROPE

Our Beyond Europe section covers a different area of the world in each monthly edition. As a special bonus we are including all six areas in this special Summer edition, along with selected tables for South America as an added bonus. Further details will be found on page 577.

ACCOMMODATION

Hotels:

Europe offers an excellent choice, from five-star hotels to room only. Your main problem may lie in finding something to suit your budget. Rooms in private houses are often a good, inexpensive and friendly option (local tourist offices often have lists), but you may be expected to stay for more than one night. The quality of cheaper hotels in Eastern Europe may still be less than inspiring and you may do better with a private room. Local tourist offices are almost always your best starting point if you haven't pre-booked. If they don't handle bookings themselves (there's usually a small charge), they will re-direct you to someone who does and/or supply you with the information to do it yourself – tell them your price horizons.

Hostels:

For those on a tight budget, the best bet is to join **HI** (Hostelling International); there's no age limit. Membership of a national association will entitle you to use over 5000 HI hostels in 60 different countries and, apart from camping, they often provide the cheapest accommodation. The norm is dormitory-style, but many hostels also have single and family rooms.

Many offer excellent-value dining and many have self-catering and/or laundry facilities. Some hostels are open 24 hours, but most have lock-out times and reception's hours are usually limited; advise them if you are arriving out of hours. Reservation is advisable – many hostels fill well in advance and even those with space are likely to limit your stay to three nights if you just turn up without booking. In winter (except around Christmas) you may be able to get special price deals.

Buy the HI's directory Europe, which lists hostel addresses, contact numbers, locations and facilities; the HI website is *www.hihostels.com.*

Camping:

This is obviously the cheapest accommodation if you're prepared to carry the equipment. There are campsites right across Europe, from basic (just toilets and showers) to luxury family-oriented sites with dining-rooms, swimming pools and complexes of permanent tents. The drawback is that sites are often miles from the city centres. There's no really good pan-European guide to campsites, but most tourist offices can provide a directory for their country.

WHAT TO TAKE WITH YOU

Luggage:

Backpack (not more than 50 litres for women or 60 litres for men) plus day sack; sort your luggage into see-through polythene bags (makes fishing out your socks from the backpack much easier), plus take plastic bags for dirty clothes etc, and elastic bands for sealing them. If flying to or from your holiday you will need to check your airlines baggage regulations.

Clothing:

Lightweight clothing, preferably of a type that doesn't need ironing; smart casual clothes for evening wear, swimsuit, sun hat, long-sleeved garment to cover shoulders (essential in some churches/temples; women may need headscarves); non-slip foot-wear – and don't forget underwear! All-purpose hiking boots (useful for big walks around cities) or rubber sandals with chunky soles are good when it's hot; flip flops for the shower etc.

First Aid/Medical:

Insect repellent and antihistamine cream, sun-screen cream, after-sun lotion, water-sterilising tablets, something for headaches and tummy troubles, antiseptic spray or cream, medicated wet-wipes, plasters for blisters, bandage, contraceptives and tampons (especially if visiting Eastern Europe, where they can be sometimes difficult to get – or try the luxury shop in the city's biggest hotel). Spare spectacles/contact lenses and a copy of your prescription.

Overnight Equipment:

Lightweight sleeping-bag (optional), sheet liner (for hostelling), inflatable travel pillow, earplugs, and eyemask.

Documents:

Passport, tickets, photocopies of passport/visas (helps if you lose the passport itself) and travel insurance, travellers' cheques counterfoil, passport photos, student card, numbers of credit cards and where to phone if you lose them.

Other items:

A couple of lightweight towels, small bar of soap, water-bottle, pocket knife, torch (flashlight), sewing kit, padlock and chain (for anchoring your luggage), safety matches, mug and basic cutlery, toothbrush, travel wash, string (for a washing-line), travel adapter, mobile (cell) phone charger, universal bath plug (often missing from wash-basins), sunglasses, alarm clock, notepad and pen, pocket calculator (to convert money), a money-belt and a good book/game (for long journeys).

EUROPEAN RAIL PASSES

Rail passes represent excellent value for train travellers who are touring around Europe (or parts of it) or making a number of journeys within a short period. They can offer substantial savings over point-to-point tickets, as well as greater flexibility. Passes may cover most of Europe (e.g. InterRail or Eurail), a specific group of countries, single countries, or just a certain area. InterRail passes are only available to European residents, whereas Eurail passes are only for non-European residents. Most passes cannot be used in your country of residence.

Passes either cover a specified number of consecutive days, or are of the *flexi* type where you get so many 'travel days' within a specified period (there are boxes on the pass where you write each date). Free travel requires the use of a travel day, whereas discounted travel does not.

With InterRail and Eurail *flexi* passes, direct night trains or ferries leaving after 1900 hrs can count as the next travel day (as long as it's not the first day of validity). Free overnight ferries count as either the day of departure or the next day. Passes generally cover the ordinary services of the national rail companies, but supplements often have to be paid for travel on high-speed services, night trains, and 'global price' trains. 'Private' railways may not accept passes but may give discounts to passholders. Extra charges always apply for travel in sleeping cars or couchettes.

Passes can be purchased from appointed agents and their websites, and some may be available from principal railway stations. Your passport may be required for identification, also one or two passport-size photos.
In this feature USD = US dollars, € = euros, £ = pounds sterling.

InterRail

Europe-wide or single-country passes for European residents website: www.interrail.eu

INTERRAIL GLOBAL PASS - valid in 30 European countries:
Austria, Belgium, Bosnia-Herzegovina, Bulgaria, Croatia, Czech Republic, Denmark, Finland, France, Germany, Great Britain, Greece, Hungary, Ireland (including Northern Ireland), Italy, Luxembourg, FYR Macedonia, Montenegro, the Netherlands, Norway, Poland, Portugal, Romania, Serbia, Slovakia, Slovenia, Spain, Sweden, Switzerland and Turkey.
NOT VALID in the passholder's country of residence.

PRICES - GLOBAL PASS

Youth is 25 or under	Youth 2nd class	Adult 2nd class	Adult 1st class
5 days within 10 days (flexi)	€184	€281	€441
10 days within 22 days (flexi)	€269	€399	€628
15 days continuous	€312	€442	€694
22 days continuous	€345	€517	€812
1 month continuous	€442	€668	€1050

2014 prices in Euros. Children aged 4 - 11 pay approx 50% of the adult price. Global Pass Senior (60+) gives 10% discount (not for One Country passes).

INTERRAIL ONE COUNTRY PASS - valid in one country
Covers any one of the participating countries above (except Bosnia-Herzegovina, FYRO Macedonia or Montenegro). NOT available for the passholder's country of residence. Note that Benelux (Belgium, Luxembourg, Netherlands) counts as one country. *Greece Plus* and *Italy Plus* passes includes Italy - Greece ferry services operated by Attica Group (Superfast Ferries - some routes are run jointly with Anek Lines).

PRICES - ONE COUNTRY PASS *3, 4, 6 or 8 days within 1 month*

France, Germany, Great Britain or Italy Plus:

	Youth	2nd	1st		Youth	2nd	1st
3 days	€147	€216	€338	6 days	€199	€302	€475
4 days	€157	€237	€372	8 days	€222	€334	€525

Austria, Italy, Norway (2nd class only), Spain or Sweden:

3 days	€129	€190	€299	6 days	€184	€281	€441
4 days	€152	€216	€338	8 days	€216	€326	€512

Benelux, Denmark, Finland, Greece Plus, Ireland or Switzerland:

3 days	€83	€125	€197	6 days	€135	€212	€332
4 days	€103	€158	€248	8 days	€168	€255	€401

Croatia, Czech Republic, Greece, Hungary, Poland, Portugal, Romania, Slovakia, Slovenia or Turkey:

3 days	€54	€82	€128	6 days	€88	€133	€210
4 days	€65	€100	€157	8 days	€102	€157	€246

Bulgaria, FYR Macedonia or Serbia:

3 days	€39	€59	€94	6 days	€77	€112	€176
4 days	€54	€82	€128	8 days	€87	€134	€212

WHO CAN BUY INTERRAIL PASSES
Any national of a European country (including Russia) with a valid passport, or anyone who has lived in Europe for at least six months. Passes can be purchased up to three months before travel begins.

SUPPLEMENTS AND RESERVATION FEES
Required for certain types of high-speed or 'global price' train.

International day train examples, 2nd class (subject to change): France - Italy *TGV* €60 (€80 in 1st class); *Berlin - Warszawa Express* €4; *EC Switzerland - Italy* €10; *Eurostar* passholder fare (e.g. London - Paris from €89); *IC* Stockholm - Oslo €3; *TGV/ICE* France - Germany €13; *TGV Lyria* (France - Switzerland) €10; *Thalys* passholder fare €30 - 39; *TGV* Brussels - France €9; France - Spain €11 - 26; *SJ Snabbtåg* Stockholm - København €7. *IC bus* Klagenfurt - Venezia €9 (€13 1st class).

Domestic examples: **Croatia** *IC* €1. **Czech Republic** *SC* €8. **Finland** *Pendolino* €3 - 7. **France** *TGV* €6 (peak €21), *Intercités* with compulsory reservation €6. **Germany** free on *ICE* (*ICE Sprinter* €12). **Greece** *ICity* €7 - 20. **Hungary** *IC* €3. **Italy** *FA, FB* and *FR* €10. **Norway** long-distance trains €6.3. **Poland** *EIC/TLK* free (€2.3 if made on train), *BWE* €4. **Portugal** *AP/IC* €5. **Romania** *IC* €3. **Slovakia** *IC* €5. **Slovenia** *ICS* €3.4 (€5.1 1st class). **Spain** *AVE* €10, most other long-distance trains €6.5, *MD* €4.5. **Sweden** *Snabbtåg* €7.

Night trains: Many night trains are globally priced and fares for passholders vary widely. *Elipsos* night trains France - Spain give discounted fares, as do *Berlin Night Express* (Berlin - Malmö). Passes do not include sleeping accommodation, which is typically €19 to €75 for a couchette, and €39 to €216 for a berth in a sleeping car.

The number of seats allocated to InterRail holders may be limited (e.g. on *TGV* and *Thalys* trains). If sold out, you may have to buy an ordinary ticket. The fold-out Travel Report inside the ticket cover must be filled in. Direct night trains or ferries leaving after 1900 hrs can count as next day.

DISCOUNT IN COUNTRY OF RESIDENCE
Although the pass is not valid in the country of residence, holders of Global passes can obtain a reduction for one return ticket to the border or nearest airport. This is usually 50% (Bosnia 30%, Germany 25%, Spain 35%) but there is no discount in Czech Republic, Poland, Romania or the United Kingdom.

VALIDITY ON PRIVATE RAILWAYS
InterRail passes are valid on the national railway companies in each country, plus many privately run railways (some give discounts). For details see the InterRail Traveller's Guide or www.interrail.eu. Selected details are as follows (subject to change): **Austria**: free travel on WESTbahn and ROeEE. **Denmark**: free travel on Arriva and DSB-First, 50% discount on Hjørring - Hirtshals and Frederikshavn - Skagen. **France**: SNCF bus services included. **Germany**: free on most regional services (not Züssow - Świnoujście). **Hungary**: GySEV services are included. **Italy**: not valid on NTV's *Italo* trains. **Netherlands**: privately run regional lines are included. **Norway**: Flåmsbana (Myrdal - Flåm) gives 30% discount. **Spain**: FEVE and FGC railways give 50% discount. **Sweden**: included are Arlanda Express, Arriva, DSB First, Inlandsbanan, MerResor, Norrtåg, Øresundståg, Skånetrafiken, Tågkompaniet, Värmlandstrafik, Västtrafik, Veolia. **Switzerland**: free travel on BLS, FART/SSIF, MOB, RhB, SOB, THURBO and ZB. Many others offer 50% discount, including AB, ASM, CJ, FB, LEB, MBC, NStCM, RA, RB, RBS, SZU, TMR, TPC, TPF, TRN, WB, WSB. The MGB (Disentis - Brig - Zermatt and Göschenen - Andermatt) and Gornergratbahn offer 50% to under-26s only. Discounted fare on William Tell Express (rail and boat tour). No discounts available on BRB or narrow gauge railways in Jungfrau area (BOB, JB, WAB).

VALIDITY ON FERRY AND BUS SERVICES
The pass includes free deck passage between Italy and Greece on SuperFast Ferries and Minoan Lines (you pay port taxes €7, high-season surcharge €10 June/Sept., €20 July/Aug., and possibly a fuel surcharge); free air-seats for 1st class pass holders. Free deck passage on Scandlines. Many other ferry companies offer discounts (not on cabins), for example: Balearia 20%, Finnlines 20%, Fjord1 Fylkesbaatane 50%, Grimaldi 20%, Irish Ferries 30%, Stena Line 20% (30% on UK routes), Tallink Silja 20% (high-season), 40% (low-season), Viking Line 50%. Special fares apply on Destination Gotland.

Also valid on ÖBB Austrian lake services. Most Swiss lakes give 50% discount. Certain bus services in Scandinavia (including Luleå - Haparanda - Tornio - Kemi) and some railway museums are free or discounted. A limited number of tourist attractions, hotels, hostels and cycle hire outlets also offer discounts.

Eurail

Eurail Global Pass *For non-European residents.* website: www.eurail.com www.eurailgroup.org

Area of validity

The *Eurail Global Pass* is valid for unlimited travel on the national railways of 24 European countries, namely Austria, Belgium, Bulgaria, Croatia, Czech Republic, Denmark, Finland, France, Germany, Greece, Hungary, Ireland (including Northern Ireland), Italy, Luxembourg, the Netherlands, Norway, Portugal, Romania, Slovakia, Slovenia, Spain, Sweden, Switzerland and Turkey. Additional countries participate in the *Eurail Select Pass*, *Eurail Regional Pass* and *Eurail One Country Pass* (see below).

Who can buy the pass?

The pass can be purchased by anyone resident outside Europe (but excluding residents of Russia and CIS or Turkey). Passes are sold through official Eurail Sales Agents (see www.eurailgroup.org) and can also be bought directly from Eurail through www.eurail.com.

The option exists to buy the passes after arrival in Europe but it is much cheaper to buy them beforehand, and since you can buy them up to six months in advance, there is no point in waiting until the last minute. Pass validity cannot be changed once in Europe, and passes must be validated before first use.

Periods of validity and prices

Adult *Eurail Global Passes* are valid for first class travel (naturally you can also travel in second class), wheras the under-26 Youth version is for 2nd class travel only. Prices (from eurail.com) in US dollars are as follows:

Youth is 25 or under	Youth 2nd class	Adult 1st class	Saver * (per person)
10 days within 2 months	623 USD	955 USD	813 USD
15 days within 2 months	817 USD	1254 USD	1067 USD
15 days continuous	528 USD	812 USD	690 USD
21 days continuous	682 USD	1046 USD	891 USD
1 month continuous	838 USD	1287 USD	1095 USD
2 months continuous	1181 USD	1816 USD	1543 USD
3 months continuous	1457 USD	2240 USD	1904 USD

* Saver: two to five people travelling together (price per person).
Children (age 4-11) pay approx 50% of the adult price.

Supplements payable

Eurostar and *Thalys* charge a passholder rate, as do other 'global price' trains (see the InterRail page for further details). French *TGV* and certain *Intercités* require the reservation fee only. In Spain most long-distance trains have a supplement/reservation fee (sample 2nd class rates: regional trains €4.5, long-distance €6.5, *AVE* Turista class €10; where meal provided in 1st/Preferente class €23.50). Supplements are also payable on *ICE Sprinter*, *Freccia* services in Italy (€10), *SJ Snabbtåg* (€7) and *Icity* trains in Greece (€6-35). Further details are given in the InterRail section on the previous page. As with all passes, sleeper/couchette supplements and seat reservations are extra.

Validity on other railways

Eurail passes are valid on the principal railway companies in each country, but may not be valid on 'private' or locally run railways (some give discounts). Selected details are as follows (some require reservations): **Austria**: free travel on WESTbahn and ROeEE. **Denmark**: free travel on Arriva and DSB-First, 50% discount on Hjørring - Hirtshals and Frederikshavn - Skagen. **France**: SNCF buses included. **Hungary**: GySEV services are included. **Italy**: not valid on NTV's *Italo* trains. **Norway**: Flåmsbana (Myrdal - Flåm) gives 30% discount. **Spain**: FEVE and FGC railways give 50% discount. **Sweden**: most trains included (see under InterRail for a full list). **Switzerland**: free travel on many railways including AB, ASM, BLS, BLT, CJ, FART/SSIF, FB, LEB, MBC, MOB, NStCM, RA, RhB, SOB, SZU, THURBO, TMR, TPC, TPF, TRN, WB, WSB, ZB. There is 50% discount on Vitznau-Rigi, the Pilatus line (and cable car) offers 30%, and there is a 25% discount on railways in the Jungfrau region (BOB, JB, WAB), the MGB (Disentis-Brig-Zermatt), and the Gornergratbahn. There are reductions on some cable cars as well. A list of bonuses is included in the Traveler's Guide issued with your pass.

Ferry services

Free passage or fare reductions are available on various ferry services; the main ones are shown below. Ferry discounts usually exclude cabin accommodation, and other restrictions (such as compulsory reservation) may apply: free deck passage between Italy and Greece on SuperFast Ferries and Minoan Lines (you pay port taxes €7, high-season surcharge €10 June/Sept., €20 July/Aug., and possibly a fuel surcharge); free air-seats for 1st class pass holders. Also free deck passage on Scandlines. Many other ferry companies offer discounts (not on cabins), for example: Balearia 20%, Finnlines 20%, Grimaldi 20%, Irish Ferries 30%, Stena Line 20% (30% on UK routes), Tallink Silja 20% - 40%, Viking Line 50%. Special fares apply on Destination Gotland. Most boat services on the Swiss lakes are included, as are Austrian lake services operated by ÖBB. Bodensee ferries operated by BSB, SBS, ÖBB give 50% discount. There are also reductions on some river cruises (e.g. certain DDSG sailings); KD Line give free travel on their scheduled Rhine and Mosel boats.

Other discounts

Certain bus services in Norway offer a 50% discount. Some railway museums offer free or discounted entry and a limited number of tourist attractions, hotels and hostels offer discounts. If in doubt, ask!

Note regarding flexi passes: free travel requires the use of a 'travel day', whereas discounted travel does not, provided it is within the overall validity of the pass. For free overnight travel by ferry you can enter either the day of departure or day of arrival. A direct overnight train leaving after 1900 hrs requires only the following day to be used as a 'travel day'.

Eurail Select Pass *For non-European residents*

A *Eurail Select Pass* allows unlimited travel in 4 adjoining countries selected from the following (some are grouped together and count as one):

• Austria • Benelux (Belgium/Netherlands/Luxembourg) • Bulgaria • Croatia/Slovenia • Czech Republic • Denmark • Finland • France • Germany • Greece • Hungary • Ireland (including NIR) • Italy • Norway • Portugal • Romania • Serbia/Montenegro • Slovakia • Spain • Sweden • Switzerland • Turkey.

'Adjoining' means linked by a direct train (not through another country) or shipping line included in the Eurail scheme; for example Italy's links include Spain and Greece.

The Select Pass is available for 5, 6, 8 or 10 travel days within a two-month period. The adult pass costs 573/627/730/834 USD respectively. The *Saver* pass for 2 or more people travelling together gives 15% reduction. The Youth (under 26) pass is priced at 65% of the adult price and children aged 4 to 11 travel at half the adult fare. As with the *Eurail Global Pass*, the adult version gives 1st class travel, the youth version 2nd class. The 3 and 5 country passes are no longer available.

International Ferries: *Select/Regional/One Country* passes must be valid in both the countries of departure and arrival to obtain free travel, but only need to be valid in one of the countries to obtain discounted travel.

Eurail Regional Pass *For non-European residents*

A *Eurail Regional Pass* allows unlimited travel in any one of 24 regions as listed below (usually two countries). Conditions vary but all are available for 5, 6, 8 or 10 days within 2 months, and some also for 4, 7 or 9 days (Portugal-Spain also for 3 days). All are available in Adult and Family 1st class versions (most also in 2nd class), and there is a youth 2nd class version for all except Portugal-Spain (youth discounts vary). Passes should be obtained before travelling to Europe (some are also for sale in the countries where the pass is valid, but not to European residents). For current prices and further information see www.eurail.com. Eligibility, supplements, discounts etc. are generally as for the *Global Pass* above.

• Austria-Croatia - Slovenia • Austria-Czech Republic
• Austria-Germany • Austria-Hungary • Austria-Switzerland
• Benelux-France • Benelux-Germany • Croatia-Slovenia-Hungary
• Czech Rep-Germany • Czech Rep-Slovakia • Denmark-Germany
• Denmark-Sweden • Finland-Sweden • France-Germany
• France-Italy • France-Spain • France-Switzerland
• Germany-Poland • Germany-Switzerland • Greece-Italy
• Hungary-Romania • Italy - Spain • Norway-Sweden
• Portugal - Spain • Scandinavia (Denmark/Finland/Norway/Sweden, 2nd class only).

Eurail One Country Passes *For non-European residents*

A *Eurail One Country Pass* allows unlimited travel in a single European country as listed below (Benelux counts as one). Each pass has its own characteristics regarding class of travel, number of travel days, and availability of youth, family and child versions. A few also have discounts for seniors. For prices and further information see www.eurail.com.

• Austria • Benelux (Belgium, Luxembourg, the Netherlands)
• Bulgaria • Croatia • Czech Republic • Denmark • Finland
• Greece • Hungary • Ireland • Italy • Norway • Poland
• Portugal • Romania • Slovakia • Slovenia • Spain • Sweden

BritRail

Britrail is a pass for overseas visitors to Great Britain, allowing unlimited travel on the national rail network in England, Scotland and Wales. It is not available to residents of Great Britain, Northern Ireland, the Isle of Man or the Channel Islands. It is best to buy the pass before arriving in Britain. Prices shown are US prices for 2014 (www.britrail.net). Youth prices apply to ages 16 to 25, senior applies to 60+. Child prices (ages 5 to 15) are approx 50% of the adult fare.

BRITRAIL CONSECUTIVE PASS

Travel for a certain number of consecutive days, First or Standard class.

(USD prices)	Adult 1st cl.	Youth 1st cl.	Senior 1st cl.	Adult Std cl.	Youth Std cl.	Senior Std cl.
3 days	345	279	295	235	189	235
4 days	429	345	369	289	235	289
8 days	615	495	525	409	329	409
15 days	919	735	779	615	495	615
22 days	1165	935	989	775	625	775
1 month	1375	1105	1169	919	735	919

BRITRAIL FLEXIPASS

Flexi version gives 3, 4, 8 or 15 days travel within a two-month period.

(USD prices)	Adult 1st cl.	Youth 1st cl.	Senior 1st cl.	Adult Std cl.	Youth Std cl.	Senior Std cl.
3 days	435	349	369	295	235	295
4 days	539	435	459	365	295	365
8 days	785	629	669	525	425	525
15 days	1179	945	999	795	635	795

BRITRAIL PASS + IRELAND

Adds Northern Ireland and the Republic of Ireland. Not available to residents of the UK or Ireland.
5 days within one month: 835 USD first class, 569 USD standard.
10 days within one month: 1489 USD first class, 1005 USD standard.

BRITRAIL ENGLAND PASSES

The Britrail England Pass excludes Wales and Scotland. A Britrail South West pass is also available. Both passes are available in Consecutive and Flexi versions.

BRITRAIL LONDON PLUS PASS

This 'flexi' pass allows unlimited rail travel in London and the surrounding area. You can visit such places as Canterbury, Salisbury, Bristol, Oxford, Cambridge, King's Lynn, the whole coast from Harwich to Weymouth, and even get as far as Worcester. No youth or senior discount available.

(USD prices)	Adult 1st cl.	Adult Std cl.
2 days within 8 days	245	165
4 days within 8 days	339	259
7 days within 15 days	419	309

BRITRAIL SCOTLAND PASSES

Three different passes are available; Freedom of Scotland (available as 4 days within 8 and 8 days within 15 versions), Central Scotland (3 days within 7) and Highlands (4 days within 8).

DISCOUNTS

Reductions are available on passes as follows, but only one type of discount can be used (this includes youth and senior discounts):

Eurail Passholder Discount: Those aged 16 to 25 with valid Eurail passes pay about 50% of the normal adult fare.

Party Discount: for 3 to 9 adults travelling in a group. Passengers 3 to 9 receive a 50% discount on the cost of their passes. The passes must be of the same type and duration and the party must travel together.

Family Discount: if you purchase any adult or senior pass, one accompanying child (aged 5–15) receives a free pass of the same type and duration. Any further children travelling receive a 50% discount. All children under 5 travel free.

Guest Pass Discount: a friend or relative who is a UK resident may accompany the pass holder. Both get 25% off the adult fare and must travel together at all times. The guest must carry proof of UK residence.

Other International Passes

BALKAN FLEXIPASS

Unlimited travel in Bosnia (ŽFBH and ŽRS), Bulgaria, Greece, Macedonia, Montenegro, Romania, Serbia and Turkey for any 5/7/10/15 days in one month. 1st class €120/162/210/252, 2nd class €88/120/156/186. 40% discount for under 26s, 50% for children, 20% for over 60s. Supplements for *IC* trains. Allows travel on Attica Group (Superfast) ferries international routes and 30% discount on domestic routes. Prices from Serbian Railways. Only 1st class 5, 10 and 15 day passes are usually offered outside participating countries (with increased prices). Not available to residents of the above countries.

EUREGIO - BODENSEE TAGESKARTE

One day's unlimited travel by rail, bus and ferry in border region Austria/Germany/Switzerland surrounding Lake Constance. In Germany valid only on DB local trains. Adult 45 CHF/€31, small groups (1 or 2 adults and up to 4 children) 84 CHF/€58. Zonal versions also available for smaller areas.

EUREGIO TICKET MAAS-RHEIN

One days unlimited travel in border region Belgium/Netherlands/Germany by rail and bus (covers Liège, Hasselt, Maastricht, Heerlen, Aachen, Düren). In Germany covers only local trains and buses. Price €18. At weekends/public holidays valid as a family ticket (2 adults plus 3 children under 12).

EUROPEAN EAST PASS

Offers unlimited rail travel throughout Austria, Czech Republic, Hungary and Slovakia for any 5 to 10 days within a month. Valid also on direct services through Germany between Kufstein and Salzburg (the passholder cannot leave the train). Now available to European residents (except those from countries where the ticket is valid) as well as non-European residents. Price for 5 days: 1st class €236, 2nd class €162 (up to 5 extra days €25/21 per day 1st/2nd class). Children aged 4-11 half price. Discounts available on river cruises, Children's Railway etc. Note that the ticket is no longer valid in Poland.

ÖRESUND RUNDT

Two days unlimited travel on trains and buses in the København, Malmö and Helsingborg area (includes the metro in København), 249 SEK. Children 7-15 half price. The Öresund can only be crossed by rail in one direction; the Helsingborg - Helsingør ferry (included) must be used in the other direction. Available in Denmark from København Tourist Office and in Sweden from Skånetrafiken.

PASS ALSACE - RHEIN-NECKAR

A day ticket valid on Saturdays, Sundays and public holidays covering local trains, buses and trams in the Rhein-Neckar area (VRN) of Germany, plus local trains in the Bas Rhin area of France. Therefore covers the Mannheim, Heidelberg and Strasbourg areas. Price €17.50 for one person or €28.50 for a group of 2-5 people.

PASSBASK

Covers the area between Bayonne in France and San Sebastian in Spain on SNCF trains (includes *TGV* but not night trains) and EuskoTren services. Valid for one day in July or August, or for Saturdays and Sundays (i.e. two days) rest of the year. A barrier pass for EuskoTren should be obtained at Hendaye station. Price €11, child aged 4-12 €7.

SAAR-LOR-LUX TICKET

One day's unlimited 2nd class travel on Saturday or Sunday throughout Saarland (i.e. Saarbrücken area of Germany, local trains only), Lorraine (i.e. Metz, Nancy, Épinal area of France) and all CFL trains in Luxembourg. Price €29; for groups of 2-5 people add €14.50 per extra person. Not valid on *TGV* or *ICE* trains.

OTHER PASSES

A range of day tickets is available covering areas of the Czech Republic and adjoining countries, i.e. **Euro-Neisse Tageskarte** (Liberec, Jelenia Góra, Zittau/Görlitz; www.zvon.de), the **EgroNet-Ticket** (Cheb, Karlovy Vary, Plauen, Zwickau; www.egronet.de), the **Bayern-Böhmen Ticket** (Bavaria/Bohemia), the **Sachsen-Böhmen Ticket** (Saxony/Bohemia) and the **Elbe-Labe Ticket**. See also under Czech Republic.

Railplus

Railplus cards are valid for one year and offer a discount of 25% on cross-border rail travel (excluding supplements) between the participating countries, which are Austria, Belgium, Bulgaria, Croatia, Czech Republic, Denmark, Finland, France, Germany, Great Britain, Hungary, Italy, Latvia, Lithuania, Luxembourg, Macedonia, Montenegro, Netherlands, Norway, Poland, Portugal, Romania, Serbia, Slovakia, Slovenia, Spain, Sweden, Switzerland and Ukraine.

France, Norway, Portugal, Spain and Sweden only grant discounts to youth (12-25) and seniors (60+). Cards are not available for sale in all participating countries, and you may be required to hold a national railcard for the country where you buy the pass, in addition to the Railplus card.

Passes for Domestic Travel

Every effort has been made to show latest prices, but some may have changed. Most cities offer day tickets valid on public transport (some include local trains), and larger cities often have Visitor Cards, available from airports and tourist information offices (often also hotels and online).

AUSTRIA

European residents: see InterRail Global Pass and One Country Pass. Non-European residents: see Eurail Global Pass, Eurail Select/Regional/One Country Passes. See also European East Pass, Euregio-Bodensee Tageskarte.

Eurail Austria Pass: for non-Europeans, must be purchased outside Europe. 3 to 8 days within one month, €185/131 1st/2nd class for 3 days plus approx €20/15 per extra day. Youth (12-25) pay 65% of adult 2nd class fare. Children 6-11 half price. Group 'Saver' discount available.

Einfach-Raus-Ticket: one day's 2nd class travel on regional trains for groups of 2 to 5 people, €35. On Mons to Fris not valid before 0900 hrs.

Gruppenticket offers a discount on standard fares for groups of 2 or more. The more people travelling together, the higher the discount (5% for 2-3 persons, increasing in stages to 30% for groups of 10 or more).

Vorteilscard annual cards giving 45-50% discount; the *Classic* version (€99) is available to all but there are cheaper cards for families, seniors and those under 26.

ÖSTERREICHcard Classic gives unlimited travel for 1 year, €1,640 (1st class €2,190).

Wien metro/tram/bus: 24/48/72 hours €7.1/12.4/15.4; any 8 days (not necessarily consecutive) €35.8; weekly ticket (only available from Monday 0000 to the following Monday 0900) €15.8. For journeys from/to the airport buy an additional zone ticket (€2.1). **Wien-Karte**: unlimited travel on local transport in Vienna plus discounted museum entry, 72 hours €21.9. One child up to age 15 free.

Other visitor cards giving local travel plus museum/sights discounts for 24/48/72 hours: **Salzburg Card** €26/35/41 (reduced by €3-5 low season Nov to Apr); **Innsbruck Card** €31/39/45 (€33/41/47 from May 1). Children half price.

BELARUS

Minsk: 10-day public transport passes are available from metro stations.

BELGIUM

European residents: see InterRail Global Pass and One Country Pass. Non-European residents: see Eurail Global Pass, also Select/Regional/One Country (Benelux) Passes. See also Euregio Ticket Maas-Rhein.

Nettreinkaart/Carte Train Réseau: unlimited travel on rail network, 1 week €86 (1st class €133), 1 month €288/444. Longer periods and add-ons for city transport also available.

Discounts on SNCB point to point tickets: **Rail Pass** (age 26+) allows 10 single journeys between two specified stations (not frontier) for €76 2nd class, €117 1st class, valid 1 year. **Go Pass 10** is under 26 version, €51 2nd class. **Weekend Ticket**: 50% discount, from Friday 1900 hrs. **Senior Ticket** (65+), flat fare of €6 2nd class, €13 1st class, from 0900 Mon-Fri, not Sat/Sun in peak summer.

Brussels: **Jump ticket** gives all transport in greater Brussels (including SNCB rail, not airport) 1 day €7. **Discover Brussels**: STIB only, includes bus from/to airport; 1 day €7, 2 days €13, 3 days €17. Cards for 5 or 10 journeys also available. **Brussels Card** gives public transport (STIB only) plus museums, 24/48/72 hrs €24/36/43.

De Lijn has 1/3/5 day passes (€5/10/15 in advance or €7/12/18 if purchased from driver), includes coastal tram.

BOSNIA-HERZEGOVINA

European residents: see InterRail Global Pass. See also Balkan Flexipass.

BULGARIA

European residents: see InterRail Global Pass and One Country Pass. Non-European residents: see Eurail Global/Select/One Country Passes. See also Balkan Flexipass.

Sofia: all SKGT metro, tram and bus: 1 day 4 BGN, 10 trips 8 BGN.

CROATIA

European residents: see InterRail Global Pass and One Country Pass. Non-European residents: see Eurail Global Pass, Eurail Select/Regional/One Country passes.

Zagreb: day ticket (dnevna karta) all ZET tram/bus (zone 1): 40 HRK. **Zagreb Card** adds museums, discounts, 24 hrs 60 HRK, 72 hrs 90 HRK.

CZECH REPUBLIC

European residents: see InterRail Global Pass and One Country Pass. Non-European residents: see Eurail Global Pass, Eurail Select/Regional/One Country Passes. See also European East.

Day ticket (Celodenní Jízdenka): 2nd cl. travel on whole rail network 550 CZK (on *SC* trains 200 CZK reservation payable). 13 regional areas also available, 150-225 CZK. Certain regions also have day tickets including border areas of Germany or Poland, 250-300 CZK. Other day tickets cover specific cross-border areas: EgroNet, Labe-Elbe, Libnet+.

Group Weekend ticket (Skupinová víkendová jízdenka): 2nd cl. travel on whole network on Sat or Sun for 2 adults and up to 3 children, 650 CZK (800 CZK including local transport in Praha). Reservation fee payable on *SC* trains. Valid cross-border to first station (on local trains). 13 regional areas also available, 225-300 CZK. A version for Czech Republic plus border areas of Germany or Poland costs 700 CZK (regional areas also available, 300-350 CZK).

Praha: all public transport (including most trains): 24 hrs 110 CZK, 3 days 310 CZK. Wider areas available. **Prague Card**: 2/3/4 day admission card, includes transport when booked online, €45-68 (student €33-53). Most cities have day tickets for city transport.

DENMARK

European residents: see InterRail Global Pass and One Country Pass. Non-European residents: see Eurail Global Pass, Eurail Select/Regional/One Country Passes. See also Öresund Rundt.

Fares based on national zonal system; 30-day **Pendlerkort** aimed at commuters (photocard required) including all-zones version. 10-journey tickets also available. Discount card available for 16-25 year olds.

København: **City Pass** zones 1-4 (city + airport) on bus, metro and train 24/72 hr 80/200 DKK. **24-Hour Ticket** adds greater København, 130 DKK. **FlexCard**: 7 days; 2 zones 240 DKK, 4 zones 350 DKK. **Copenhagen Card**: greater København public transport, free entry to 72 attractions, 24/48/72/120 hrs €48/65/78/110 (2 children under 10 free).

ESTONIA

Tallinn: tram/bus 1-day €3; 3-days €5; 5-days €6 (supplement on express buses). **Tallinn Card**: adds museums etc, 24 hrs €24; 48 hrs €32; 72 hrs €40. Under 15s half price.

FINLAND

European residents: see InterRail Global Pass and One Country Pass. Non-European residents: see Eurail Global Pass, Eurail Select/Regional/One Country Passes.

Helsinki: single-charge electronic cards for all public transport including local trains: 1/2/3 days €8/12/16; 7 days €32 (1-7 days available). **Helsinki Card**: public transport plus free entry to main sights, €39/51/61 for 24/48/72 hrs, child 7-16: €17/20/23.

FRANCE

European residents: see InterRail Global Pass and One Country Pass. Non-European residents: see Eurail Global Pass, Eurail Regional Pass. See also Pass Alsace - Rhein-Neckar, Passbask, Saar-Lor-Lux.

France Railpass: only available to non-European residents, valid for 3 to 9 days within one month. Adult 3 days 312/253 USD 1st/2nd class plus approx 44/37 USD per extra day (9-day: 573/458 USD). Approx 30% discount for Youth (aged 12-25), 12% discount for Senior (60+, 1st class only). Saver version for 2-5 people: 15% discount. Children half fare. Special Passholder fare payable on *Eurostar*, *Thalys*, night trains; reservation fee payable on *TGV* (also *Intercité* if 🅁). Pass is available from RailEurope and other agents.

Annual railcards are available for children, young people (ages 12-17 or 18-27) and seniors (60+) giving 25% - 50% discount off rail fares. A **Carte Week-End** is available for all ages giving discounts at weekends.

Regional Tickets: several regions offer day tickets on TER (local) trains at weekends and holidays. Conditions vary and some only valid in summer. Details generally available on TER website www.ter-sncf.com. The 3 day **Lille City Pass** (€45) includes TER trains in Nord-Pas de Calais region, available from Lille tourist office, Place Rihour. **Alsa Plus 24h**: a zonal day pass for Alsace, €34 for the whole region; group ticket (2-5 people) available at weekends for €35.1.

Paris Visite: public transport within Paris, plus discounted entry to attractions: zones 1-3: €10.85/17.65/24.1/34.7 for 1/2/3/5 days. Zones 1-5 (includes suburbs and airports): €22.85/34.70/48.65/59.5. Children 4-11 half price. **Mobilis**: Paris one-day ticket (not available on airport services), €6.8 (zones 1-2) to €16.1 (zones 1-5).

Most cities have bus/tram day tickets, e.g. **Lyon** €5.2, **Lille** €4.1.

GERMANY

European residents: see InterRail Global Pass and One Country Pass. Non-European residents: see Eurail Global Pass, Eurail Select/Regional Passes. See also Euregio-Bodensee, Euregio Mass-Rhein, Sar-Lor-Lux.

German Rail Pass: for people resident outside Europe; 3 to 7 and 10 days unlimited travel within one month. 3 days €260/193 1st/2nd class; 4 days €280/207; 5 days €300/222; 6 days €331/225; 7 days €363/269; 10 days €457/338. Also **Youth Pass** for those under 26 (2nd class only): €154-€271. **Twin Pass** also available giving a discount of approximately 50% for second adult. Available from Deutsche Bahn London or on-line (not to European residents). No supplements on *ICE*, *IC*, *EC*. 20% discount on Romantische Strasse bus.

Passes for Domestic Travel

Schönes-Wochenende-Ticket: one day's unlimited travel on Saturday or Sunday (to 0300 following day) on local trains (IRE/RE/RB/S-Bahn), 2nd class. Price €44 from machines, €46 from ticket offices. Valid for up to 5 people, buy on the day. Also valid on trams/buses in certain areas, and on certain rail lines across the border into Poland.

Quer-durchs-Land-Ticket: one day's unlimited travel Mondays to Fridays (valid from 0900 to 0300 following day) on local trains (IRE/RE/RB/S-Bahn), 2nd class. Valid for up 5 people. €44 for one person, then add €8 for each additional person in the group (€76 for a group of five).

Regional tickets (Länder-Tickets): one day's unlimited 2nd class travel for up to 5 people on DB local trains (not before 0900 on Mon-Fri, valid to 0300 the following day). **Baden-Württemberg** €23 for one person (add €4 for each additional person). **Bayern** €23 for one person (add €4 for each additional person). **Brandenburg-Berlin** €29. **Hessen** (includes most buses) €31. **Mecklenburg-Vorpommern** €22 for one person (add €4 for each additional person). **Niedersachsen** €22 for one person (add €4 for each additional person). **Nordrhein-Westfalen** (SchönerTag Ticket) one person €28.50, 2–5 people €39.50. **Rheinland-Pfalz** plus **Saarland** €23 for one person (add €4 for each additional person). **Sachsen** including **Sachsen-Anhalt** and **Thüringen** €22 for one person (add €4 for each additional person). **Schleswig-Holstein** €27 (add €3 for each additional person; includes travel in Mecklenburg-Vorpommern and all public transport in Hamburg). All Länder tickets may be purchased on the day from ticket machines (most cost €2 more if purchased from travel centres).

Bahncard 25/50: valid for 1 year, giving discounts of 25% or 50% on all national DB trains for €62 or €255 in 2nd class (1st class €125/515). Accompanied children under 15 travel free (ticket must be issued). Both cards entitle the holder to a 25% discount for international journeys between Germany and 30 European countries (not available where global fares are charged). Lower priced Bahncards available for young people and family members of Bahncard holders. **Bahncard 100** (passport photo required) gives unlimited travel for 1 year, €4,090 in 2nd class, €6,890 in 1st class. All available from DB London.

Harz: HSB narrow gauge railway 3/5 days €70/105, child 6-11 50%.

Tageskarte (day ticket): most urban areas offer 24/48/72 hour tickets valid on most public transport; generally a zonal system operates.

Welcome Tickets: most public transport in selected cities, also includes free or reduced entry to many museums and visitor attractions. Buy from Tourist Information, main stations, some airports and hotels. Examples:

Berlin Welcome Card: one adult and up to 3 children under 15; 48 hours €20.5, 72 hours €27.5, 5 days €37.5. Covers zones A, B and C and includes DB trains. **Dresden City Card**: 1 day €9.9; family card also available for 2 adults and up to 4 children under 15 €13.9. Includes ferry trips within the Dresden tariff zone. **Frankfurt Card**: 1 day €9.9, 2 days €14.5; group ticket (up to 5) €20 (1 day)/€29.5 (2 days). Includes travel from/to the airport. **Hamburg Card**: Day Ticket €9.5. Also 3 days €22.9, 5 days €38.5. Group versions (up to 5) €15.5/39.9/64.9. **Hannover Card**: 1 day €9.5, 2 days 14.5, 3 days €17.5, group ticket (up to 5) €19.5/26.5/33.5. **Köln Welcome Card**: 24 hours €9, group ticket (up to 5) €19. Wider areas also available. **Leipzig Card**: 1 day €9.9, 3 days €19.9, 3 day group (2 adults and up to 3 children under 14) €37.9. **Nürnberg Card**: 2 days €23 (accompanied children aged 6–11 €5).

GREAT BRITAIN

European (non-UK) residents: see InterRail Global Pass and One Country Pass. Non-UK residents see also Britrail.

Railcards: annual cards giving 34% discount on most rail fares; 16-25 Railcard, Two Together, Family & Friends, Senior: all £30. Disabled Persons £20. Network Railcard gives off-peak discount in South East England, £30.

All-Line Rail Rover: covers whole National Rail network. 1st/standard class £724/£478 (7 days), £1106/£724 (14 days). 34% discount for children aged 5-15 and holders of Senior/Disabled railcard, and (standard class only) 16-25/Two Together/Family & Friends railcard. Some restrictions before 1000 Mon-Fri. Not valid on Eurostar, Heathrow Express, London Underground. Valid on Ffestiniog Railway but not other private railways.

Freedom of Scotland Travelpass: all rail services in Scotland (includes Carlisle and Berwick) plus Caledonian MacBrayne ferry services and some buses. Standard class only. Valid 4 out of 8 days (£134) or 8 out of 15 days (£179.70); not before 0915 Mon to Fri (except on Glasgow - Oban/Mallaig services and north of Inverness). 34% discount with 16-25/Two Together/Senior/Disabled railcard; 50% discount for children (5-15). 20% discount on Northlink Ferries to Orkney and Shetland; 10% off sleeper fares to/from Scotland. Smaller areas also available: **Highland Rover**, 4 days out of 8 £81.50; **Central Scotland Rover** 3 in 7 days, £36.30.

Explore Wales Flexipass: 8 days travel on most buses in Wales, plus standard-class rail travel on any 4 days out of the 8 (not before 0915 Mon to Fri), price £94, children half price, some railcard holders 34% discount. Various discounts available. Tickets available online and at most staffed stations. Other areas available: South Wales (£64), North and Mid Wales (£64).

A range of **Rover** tickets is available covering various areas, typically for 7 days, 3 in 7 days, 4 in 8 days, or 8 in 15 days. Most not valid until after the morning peak Mon to Fri. Examples: Anglia Plus, Coast and Peaks, Devon and Cornwall, East Midlands, Heart of England, Kent, North Country, North East, North West, South West, Thames.

Ranger day tickets also available: e.g. Cambrian Coast, Cheshire, Cumbria, Devon, East Midlands, Isle of Wight, Lakes, Lancashire, Lincolnshire, North Downs, Oxfordshire, Settle & Carlisle, South Pennines, Thames branches, Tyne & Tees, Valley Lines, West Midlands, West Yorkshire, Yorkshire Coast. Details: nationalrail.co.uk.

All-day tickets (some off-peak) covering local rail and most buses are available in Derbyshire, Glasgow, Greater Manchester, Merseyside, South Yorkshire, West Yorkshire, Tyneside and West Midlands.

London: Day Travelcards cover almost all transport (Underground, bus and rail) in the London area; peak version from £9 (central London, zones 1-2) to £17 (zones 1-6), off-peak version (not before 0930 Mon-Fri) from £8.90. 7-day tickets from £31.40 (central zones) to £57.20 (zones 1-6), no off-peak version. Children under 11 travel free with an Oyster photocard. Travelcard holders may take up to four children aged 11-15 for £2 each after 1000 (otherwise half fare). For single journeys, stored-value Oyster cards give best value; Visitor Oyster cards are available preloaded from £10 to £50 (plus £3 fee).

Isle of Man Explorer: most trains (not Groudle Glen), trams and buses: 1/3/5/7 days, £16/32/39/47. Children 5-15 half price (1 free).

GREECE

European residents: see InterRail Global Pass and One Country Pass (also Greece Plus). Non-European residents: see Eurail Global Pass, Eurail Select/Regional/One Country Pass. See also Balkan Flexipass.

Vergina Flexipass: unlimited first class rail travel for 3, 5 or 10 days within one month or two months, 1st or 2nd class. Prices unknown.

Athens: 24-hour ticket valid on metro (including ISAP), trams and buses €4, weekly ticket €14 (excludes the airport - single fare: €8). 3-day tourist ticket including airport €20.

HUNGARY

European residents: see InterRail Global Pass and One Country Pass. Non-European residents: see Eurail Global Pass, Eurail Select/Regional/One Country Passes. See also European East. Travel by rail and local transport is free for over-65s with an EU passport or ID card.

START Klub Card: gives 50% discount on 2nd class travel. Valid for either 6 months or one year: 19900/34900 HUF (14900/24900 HUF under 26 years). Requires passport style photograph.

Balaton Mix: rail and shipping services around Lake Balaton, Apr. 27 - Oct. 6 (2013 dates). 3-day ticket gives 1 day's unlimited travel HUF 3250, child 6-14 HUF 1890, family (2 adults + 2 children) HUF 8590. 7-day ticket gives any 2 days travel for HUF 5390/3090/14500. 50% discount on rail journey to/from the area within period of validity.

Budapest: BKV tram/metro/bus/rail, 24 hrs HUF 1650, 72 hrs HUF 4150, 7 days HUF 4950. Also 24hr group ticket (2-5 people), HUF 3300. **Budapest Card** also includes museums, walking tour and discounts: 24 hrs HUF 4500, 48 hrs HUF 7500, 72 hrs HUF 8900.

IRELAND

European residents: see InterRail Global Pass and One Country Pass. Non-European residents: see Eurail Global/Select/One Country Passes. InterRail and Eurail passes valid in the Republic of Ireland are also valid in Northern Ireland. See also Britrail + Ireland.

REPUBLIC OF IRELAND ONLY:

Irish Explorer Rail Only: any 5 days in 15 on IÉ rail services, €160 (child €80), standard class. **Trekker** gives 4 consecutive days on Irish Rail for €110. **Irish Explorer Rail and Bus**: IÉ rail plus Bus Éireann services, any 8 days in 15, €245 (child €122).

Dublin area: **Short Hop Zone** tickets: Rail only 1 day €11.1, 3 days €23.8, 7 days €40.5; Bus & Rail 1/3/7 day, €13.2/27/46.5. Also available 1 day Rail/Luas €11.8, 7 day Bus/Luas €46.5. All exclude Airlink. **Rambler** (bus only, includes Airlink): 5 days €27.5, family 1 day €11. Luas **Flexi** ticket (tram only): 1 day €6.4, 7 day €23.5 (child €2.7/8.4); **Combi** ticket also includes bus: adult 1/7 day, €8.8/36 (child €3.6/9.8). **Freedom** ticket: 3 days bus plus city tour and discounts €28, child (under 14) €12.

NORTHERN IRELAND ONLY:

iLink integrated smartcard gives unlimited bus and rail travel on Translink services (Northern Ireland Railways, Ulsterbus and Belfast Citybus). Zone 4 covers the whole of Northern Ireland: 1 day £16.50, 7 days £58, 1 month £201. Zone 1 covers Belfast city (£6.30/22/75). Children half price. Initial £1 fee for the card (free online). **Belfast Visitor Pass** includes visitor discounts: 1/2/3 days £6.30/£10.50/£14.

ITALY

European residents: see InterRail Global Pass and One Country Pass (also Italy Plus). Non-European residents: see Eurail Global Pass, Eurail Select/Regional/One Country Passes.

Passes for Domestic Travel

Roma: Roma Pass: 3-day transport pass (€34) with museum discounts. Biglietto Integrato Giornaliero (BIG) covers rail / metro / bus in urban area for one day, €6 (excludes Fiumicino airport, restrictions on rail / metro). Biglietto Turistico Integrato (BTI) valid 3 days €16.5, weekly ticket (CIS) €24. Roma & Lazio day ticket (BIRG) covers wider area (all 7 zones €14), also 3 day ticket (BTR) €8.9 to 39.2.

Milano: 24 hour ticket (abbonamento giornaliero): ATM city services plus local Trenitalia, Trenord rail services, €4.5. Also 48 hour ticket €8.25. **Lombardia**: IVOL ticket valid on most public transport (not *ES*, *IC* trains, airport services, cable cars), 1 / 2 days €15 / 25, 3 / 7 days €30 / 40.

Napoli: 'Campania > artecard' is a transport + museum visitors card, with various options. The 3 day card (€32) allows free entry to two museums with 50% off others; the 7 day version (€34) allows 5 free then 50% off.

Venezia: Travel cards for ACTV buses and boats: 12 / 24 hrs €18 / 20; 36 / 48 hrs €25 / 30; 72 hrs €35; 7 days €50. Each card is also available with airport transfer add-on (€4 each way).

Mobilcard Südtirol: regional trains, buses, funiculars and cable cars in Bolzano, Malles, Brennero area: 1 / 3 / 7 days; €15 / 23 / 28 respectively.

Day tickets available in other major cities.

LATVIA

Riga Card: public transport, bus tour, plus free / discounted museum entry; 12 / 14 / 18 LVL for 24 / 48 / 72 hours (under 16s half price).

LITHUANIA

Vilnius: local VVT buses / trolleybuses 24 hrs 13 LTL, 72 hrs 23 LTL, 10 days 46 LTL. **Vilnius Card** includes discounts, 24 / 72 hrs, 58 / 90 LTL.

LUXEMBOURG

European residents: see InterRail Global Pass and One Country Pass (Benelux). Non-European residents: see Eurail Global Pass, Eurail Select / Regional / One Country (Benelux) Passes. See also Sar-Lor-Lux Ticket.

Dagesbilljee / Billet longue durée: day ticket €4.00, unlimited 2nd class travel on all public transport throughout the country; not valid to border points; valid until 0400 hrs following morning. €6 if bought on board the train. Carnet of 5 day tickets €16. **Oeko Pass**: valid one month €50 2nd class, €75 1st class; from CFL offices.

Luxembourg Card: unlimited travel on trains and buses throughout the country, plus free entry to 50 attractions. 1 day €11; any 2 days €19, any 3 days €27 (the 2 / 3 day tickets must be used within two weeks). Family pass for 2 - 5 people (max 3 adults) for 1 / 2 / 3 days: €28 / 48 / 68.

MACEDONIA

European residents: see InterRail Global Pass and One Country Pass. See also Balkan Flexipass.

MONTENEGRO

European residents: see InterRail Global Pass. Non-European residents: see Eurail Select Pass. See also Balkan Flexipass.

NETHERLANDS

European residents: see InterRail Global Pass and One Country Pass (Benelux). Non-European residents: see Eurail Global Pass, Eurail Select / Regional / One Country (Benelux) Passes. See also Euregio Maas-Rhein.

A national stored-value OV-chipkaart is available for public transport, initial cost €7.50, which can be loaded with day tickets. Short-term cards are also available in Amsterdam as shown below.

NS Day Ticket (Dagkaart) replaces the previous paper ticket and is only available with an OV-chipkaart (see above). Allows unlimited travel on NS trains (not other companies) for one day: €49.2 2nd cl, €83.6 1st cl.

Railrunner: up to 3 children (aged 4 - 11) may accompany an adult (18 +) for a flat rate of €2.50 per day. Excludes *Thalys*.

Amsterdam: GVB tram / bus / metro: chipcards are available for 24 hrs €7.5, 48 / 72 hrs €12 / 16.5, also 4 / 5 / 6 / 7 days (€21 / 26 / 29.5 / 32). **Amsterdam & Region Day Card**: a 1-day GVB ticket including Connexxion and EBS (not valid on trains), €13.5. **I amsterdam Card**: tram / bus / metro, one free canal tour plus free / discounted entry to various attractions, 24 / 48 / 72 hrs: €47 / 57 / 67.

NORWAY

European residents: see InterRail Global Pass and One Country Pass. Non-European residents: see Eurail Global Pass, Eurail Select / Regional / One Country Passes.

Eurail Norway Pass: for non-Europeans: 3 to 8 days 2nd class travel within one month, €202 for 3 days, €304 for 8 days. Youth (under 26) get 35% reduction. Saver (group) pass available. 30% discount on Flåm Railway, various ferry discounts; not valid on Oslo Airport Express.

Oslo: 24 hour ticket for all 'Ruter' public transport in zone 1 (wider areas available): 90 NOK, 7 days 230 NOK, children half price. **Oslo Pass**: all public transport including NSB local trains (zones 1 - 2, excludes airport), free entry to attractions, discounts on sightseeing buses / boats: 24 / 48 / 72 hours 290 / 425 / 535 NOK (children pay approximately 50%).

Bergen Card: local bus travel plus free or discounted entry to various attractions, 24 / 48 hrs: 200 / 260 NOK (children aged 3-15, 75 / 100 NOK).

POLAND

European residents: see InterRail Global Pass and One Country Pass. Non-European residents: see Eurail Regional / One Country Passes.

PKP Intercity operates *EIC*, *EC*, *Ex*, *TLK* trains and offers the following passes for its trains: **Bilet Weekendowy** (weekend ticket): valid 1900 Fri to 0600 Mon (extended if Thurs or Mon is public holiday), 154 PLN 2nd class, 247 PLN 1st class; seat reservations free (but not compulsory). PLUS version adds REGIO trains (not IR, RE) for an extra 17 PLN. **Bilet Podróznika** (Traveller ticket): similar to weekend ticket but only for *TLK* trains (with seats), 74 / 104 PLN 2nd / 1st class. Both the above also available from train conductor. **Bilety Sieciowe** (network tickets): 3 months 2900 / 4050 PLN (2nd / 1st class); 6 months 5400 / 7500 PLN; annual 9900 / 14600 PLN. A version with unnamed holder is also available.

Przewozy Regionalne (PR) operates REGIO, IR and RE trains: **Bilety Sieciowe** (network tickets): weekly / monthly 159 / 369 PLN. **REGIOkarnet**: valid for any 3 days out of 2 months, 129 PLN (valid in 1st class where available); 75 PLN for REGIO trains only; validate at ticket office before travel. **Bilet Turystyczny** (tourist ticket): valid 1800 Friday to 0600 Monday, 79 PLN (valid in 1st class); 45 PLN for REGIO trains only. Both tickets valid across German border, e.g. to Görlitz, Frankfurt (Oder). **Bilet Turystyczny + Czechy** adds border area of Czech Republic. Passes valid on REGIO trains also valid on Arriva RP and Koleje Dolnoślaskie.

Warsaw ZTM tram / bus / metro / rail (zone 1, includes Chopin airport): 1 day 15 PLN. Weekend ticket valid 1900 Fri - 0800 Mon also available. **Koleje Mazowieckie** (KM) trains: wide area around Warsaw, 24 hr Bilet dobowy imienny 30 PLN.

PORTUGAL

European residents: see InterRail Global Pass and One Country Pass. Non-European residents: see Eurail Global Pass, Eurail Select / Regional / One Country Passes.

Intra-Rail: zonal (4 zones) pass with free nights at youth hostels; *Xcape* version valid 3 days in one zone €59 (€69 if aged 30 +). *Xplore* version valid 10 days in two adjacent zones €199 (€239 if aged 30 +). Not valid on *AP* trains. Buy at major stations. Prices with Youth Card: €53 / 173.

Lisboa: Carris tram / bus / metro - one-day ticket (bilhete 24h Rede) €6 in conjunction with reusable *7 Colinas* smartcard (€0.50). Includes the funiculars and lift. **Lisboa Card** includes free and discounted attractions: 24 / 48 / 72 hrs, €18.5 / 31.5 / 39 (ages 4 - 15: €11.5 / 17.5 / 20.5).

Coimbra: day ticket on SMTUC local buses €3.50.

Porto: *Andante Tour Card* gives metro + STCP bus + local rail, all zones, 24 hrs €7, 72 hrs €15. **Porto Card** also includes free / discounted entry to tourist attractions, 1 day €10.5, 2 days €17.5, 3 days €21.5.

ROMANIA

European residents: see InterRail Global Pass and One Country Pass. Non-European residents: see Eurail Global Pass, Eurail Select / Regional / One Country Passes. See also Balkan Flexipass.

Bucuresti: RATB tram, bus and trolleybus network (not express buses): 1 / 7 / 15 days, 8 / 17 / 25 RON. Metro day pass 6 RON (16 incl. RATB).

RUSSIA

Moskva: bus / tram tickets available from kiosks in strips of 10 / 20. Separate 10-trip tickets available for metro. Monthly *yediniy bilyet* covers bus / tram / metro. No tourist tickets. **St Peterburg**: bus / tram tickets available in packs of 10; multi-journey cards can be bought for the metro.

SERBIA

European residents: see InterRail Global Pass and One Country Pass. Non-European residents: see Eurail Select Pass. See Balkan Flexipass.

SLOVAKIA

European residents: see InterRail Global Pass and One Country Pass. Non-European residents: see Eurail Global Pass, Eurail One Country Pass. See also European East.

Bratislava: urban tram / bus network, 24 hrs €4.50, 48 hrs €8.30, 3 days €10, 7 days €15. **Bratislava City Card** includes many discounts, 1 day €10, 2 days €12, 3 days €15, available from tourist offices.

SLOVENIA

European residents: see InterRail Global Pass and One Country Pass. Non-European residents: see Eurail Global Pass, Eurail Select / Regional / One Country Passes.

Ljubljana: the Urbana tourist card includes city buses, castle funicular, tourist boat and museums, valid for 24, 48 or 72 hours, €23 / 30 / 35 (discounts available online).

Passes for Domestic Travel

SPAIN

European residents: see InterRail Global Pass and One Country Pass. Non-European residents: see Eurail Global Pass, Eurail Select/Regional/One Country Passes. See also Passbask.

RENFE Spain Pass: for people resident outside Spain giving 4, 6, 8, 10 or 12 individual journeys. Tickets must be obtained in advance using the pass; reservations are free. Valid 1 month from first journey. Tourist class €163-392, Business/Club €229-550, children aged 4-13 get 25% discount (2013 prices). Can be purchased online (www.renfe.com).

Barcelona T-Dia ticket: valid 1 day on metro/TMB bus/tram/local rail, from €7.6 (zone 1, includes airport) to €21.7 (all 6 zones, wide area around the city). Zone 1 travelcards also available for 2/3/4/5 days at €14/20/25.5/30.5 (cheaper online). **Barcelona Card**: adds free or disounted museums, 2 to 5 days €37/47/56/62 (children 30% off).

Madrid: Abono Turístico (Tourist Ticket) gives all public transport in Zone A, 1/2/3 days €8.4/14.2/18.4, also 5/7 days €26.8/35.4, children 50%. Available for wider area (zone T) at double the price. **Madrid Card** gives various attractions, 24/48/72/120 hrs €45/55/65/75 (cheaper online); combine with Tourist Ticket above for transport.

SWEDEN

European residents: see InterRail Global Pass and One Country Pass. Non-European residents: see Eurail Global Pass, Eurail Select/Regional/One Country Passes. See also Öresund Rundt.

Stockholm: all SL public transport in Greater Stockholm, 24/72 hours 115/230 SEK, 7 days 300 SEK, plus smartcard 20 SEK. Reduced 40% for under 20s/over 65s. **Stockholm Card** includes museums, 495/650/795/1050 SEK for 24/48/72/120 hours (50-70% less for ages 6-17).

SWITZERLAND

European residents: see InterRail Global Pass and One Country Pass. Non-European residents: see Eurail Global Pass, Eurail Select/Regional Passes. See also Euregio-Bodensee.

Swiss Pass: available to all non-Swiss residents. Consecutive days on Swiss Railways, boats and most alpine postbuses and city buses. Valid for 4, 8, 15, 22 days or 1 month. 1st class 435/629/762 CHF for 4/8/15 days, 883/971 CHF for 22 days/1 month. 2nd class 272/393/476 CHF for 4/8/15 days, 552/607 CHF for 22 days/1 month. Youth Pass gives 25% reduction for under 26s. All versions give 50% reduction on many funicular and mountain railways. Also acts as a Museum Pass - free entrance to 400 sites. Children aged 6-15 travel free with a Family Card (issued free by Switzerland Tourism, London) if accompanied by a parent (not other relatives), otherwise half fare.

Swiss Flexi Pass: as above but for 2-6 days within 1 month. Prices 1st/2nd class: 299/199 CHF, 416/260 CHF (3 days), 504/315 CHF (4 days), 582/364 CHF (5 days), 662/414 CHF (6 days). No Youth discount.

Saver Program: applies to the Swiss Pass or Flexi Pass (not 2-day Flexi and Youth Pass) - 15% reduction per person for groups travelling together.

Swiss Transfer Ticket: return ticket from any airport/border station to any other Swiss station; use within 1 month. Each journey must be completed on day of validation and on the most direct route. 1st class 222 CHF, 2nd class 139 CHF. Family Card valid, see above. Cannot be obtained in Switzerland.

Swiss Card: as Swiss Transfer Ticket but also offers unlimited half-fare tickets for 1 month and 50% reduction on many private railways. 1st/2nd class 282/199 CHF. Family card valid, see above under Swiss Pass.

Swiss Half Fare Card: 50% off most public transport, for one month 120 CHF.

The above passes are available online and from Switzerland Tourism, also from major Swiss stations (Swiss Card only at border and airport stations). Not available to Swiss residents.

GA (General-Abo): monthly (minimum 4 months) and annual passes covering most public transport are available for commuters.

Halbtax (half-fare card) gives 50% off most public transport, also 25% off travel from Switzerland to Germany or Austria. Valid 1 year, 175 CHF.

Halbtax add-ons: holders of the Halbtax half-fare card can buy day tickets online from www.sbb.ch (english version www.rail.ch) for 121/71 CHF 1st/2nd class, valid on most public transport. Version not valid before 0900 Mon-Fri: 96/58 CHF. Packs of 6 can be bought for price of 5. An add-on pass is also available for one month at 655/400 CHF.

Bernese Oberland Regional Pass: valid May to October. Available for 4, 6, 8 or 10 days unlimited travel: 230/290/330/370 CHF 2nd class, 276/348/396/444 CHF 1st class.

Regional Passes: several other areas are available including Adventure Card Valais, Graubünden Pass, Lake Geneva-Alps and Tell Pass.

Jungfrau VIP Pass: offers three days of consecutive travel on the railways and cable cars in the Jungfrau region (May to Oct) for 235 CHF (child 70 CHF). Includes one trip to the Jungfraujoch. Discounts for holders of Swiss Pass, Swiss Flexi Pass or Half Fare Card. The similar **Jungfrau Unlimited Railways Pass** is valid for six days travel, but (discounted) tickets to the Jungfraujoch must be purchased (£179, child £54). Not available in Switzerland.

Bern: day ticket for all transport in city 12 CHF. From summer 2014, the new **Bern Ticket** is issued to overnight guests offering free bus and tram travel within the inner city.

Genève: Day ticket (Carte 24 Heures) includes buses, trams, trains and boats: 10.6 CHF (valid for 2 people at weekends). **Carte 9 h** is valid from 0900 hrs, 8 CHF. Day ticket for wider regional area 18.5 CHF (13.2 CHF after 0900). The **Geneva Transport Card** is given to those staying at a hotel or youth hostel in the city and allows unrestricted travel on all public transport for the duration of the stay.

Zürich: Tageskarte gives 24 hours on all transport including SBB trains, 14/8.4 CHF 1st/2nd class (central zone only); all zones in Canton 54.8/33.2 CHF. Off-peak version is 9-UhrPass, all zones, not before 0900 Mon-Fri, 41.4/25 CHF. **Zürich Card** includes all museums: 24 hours 24 CHF, 72 hours 48 CHF (children 16/32 CHF), includes airport.

TURKEY

European residents: see InterRail Global Pass and One Country Pass. Non-European residents: see Eurail Global/Select Passes. See also Balkan Flexipass.

Tren Tur Karti: 30 day network pass. *Ekspres* version covers day trains excluding high-speed (YTL 190), *Yatakli Karti* includes night trains (YTL 500). Various *YHT* cards cover high-speed lines. Buy from main stations.

UKRAINE

Kyïv: a monthly travelcard is available but there are no tourist tickets.

Where to Buy your Pass

Sources of rail passes (and point to point tickets) include the following:

IN THE UNITED KINGDOM

ACP Rail - see www.acprail.com and www.britrail.net

Deutsche Bahn UK (German Railways)
UK Booking Centre, PO Box 687a, Surbiton, KT6 6UB
✆ 08718 808066 www.bahn.com

European Rail Ltd
17 Tileyard Studios, Tileyard Road, London, N7 9AH
✆ 020 7619 1083 www.europeanrail.com

Ffestiniog Travel
Unit 6, Snowdonia Business Park, Penrhyndeudraeth, Gwynedd LL48 6LD
✆ 01766 772030 www.ffestiniogtravel.com

International Rail
PO Box 153, Alresford, Hampshire SO24 4AQ
✆ 0871 231 0790 www.internationalrail.com

Rail Canterbury
39 Palace Street, Canterbury, Kent CT1 2DZ
✆ 01227 450088 www.rail-canterbury.co.uk

RailTourGuide
Suite 41, 7-15 Pink Lane, Newcastle upon Tyne, NE1 5DW
✆ 0191 246 0708 www.railtourguide.com

Real Russia
5 The Ivories, Northampton Street, Islington, London, N1 2HY
✆ 0207 100 7370 www.realrussia.co.uk

Trainseurope
4 Station Approach, March, Cambs PE15 8SJ
Also at St Pancras International station (East Midlands Trains ticket office). ✆ 0871 700 7722 www.trainseurope.co.uk

Voyages sncf
Voyages-sncf Travel Centre, 193 Piccadilly, London W1J 9EU
✆ 0844 848 5848 www.voyages-sncf.com

IN THE USA AND CANADA

Rail Europe Inc.
44 South Broadway, White Plains, NY 10601, USA
✆ 1-800-622-8600 www.raileurope.com

Rail Europe, Canada
✆ 1-800-361 7245 (1-800-361-RAIL) www.raileurope.ca

See also **Rick Steve's** comprehensive website: www.ricksteves.com.
For a list of **Eurail** agents worldwide see www.eurailgroup.org.

AUSTRIA

CAPITAL
Vienna (Wien).

CLIMATE
Moderate Continental climate. Warm summer; high snowfall in winter.

CURRENCY
Euro (EUR / €). 1 euro = 100 cent. For exchange rates see page 9.

EMBASSIES IN VIENNA
Australia: Mattiellistraße 2-4, ✆ 1 506 740. **Canada**: Laurenzenberg 2, ✆ 1 531 383 000. **New Zealand** Mattiellistraße 2-4/3, ✆ 1 505 3021. **UK**: Jaurèsgasse 12, ✆ 1 716 130. **USA**: Boltzmanngasse 16, ✆ 1 313 390.

EMBASSIES OVERSEAS
Australia: 12 Talbot St, Forrest, Canberra, ACT 2603, ✆ 2 629 515 33. **Canada**: 445 Wilbrod St, Ottawa ON, KIN 6M7, ✆ 613 789 1444. **UK**: 18 Belgrave Mews West, London SW1X 8HU, ✆ 020 7344 3250. **USA**: 3524 International Court NW, Washington DC 20008, ✆ 202 895 6700.

LANGUAGE
German; English is widely spoken in tourist areas.

OPENING HOURS
Banks: mostly Mon, Tues, Wed, Fri 0800–1230 and 1330–1500, Thur 0800–1230 and 1330–1730. **Shops**: Mon–Fri 0800–1830 (some closing for a 1- or 2-hour lunch), Sat 0800–1200/1300 (in larger towns often until 1700). **Museums**: check locally.

POST OFFICES
Indicated by golden horn symbol; all handle poste restante (*postlagernde Briefe*). Open mostly Mon–Fri 0800–1200 and 1400–1800. Main and station post offices in larger cities open 24 hrs. Stamps (*Briefmarke*) also sold at Tabak/Trafik shops.

PUBLIC HOLIDAYS
Jan 1, Jan 6 (Epiphany), Easter Mon, May 1, Ascension Day, Whit Mon, Corpus Christi, Aug 15 (Assumption), Oct 26 (National Day), Nov 1 (All Saints), Dec 8 (Immaculate Conception), Dec 25, 26. For dates of movable holidays see page 2.

PUBLIC TRANSPORT
Most long-distance travel is by rail (see below). Inter-urban buses operated by ÖBB-Postbus (www.postbus.at); usually based by rail stations or post offices. City transport is efficient with integrated ticketing; buy tickets from machines or Tabak/Trafik booths. Wien has an extensive metro and tram system; for day tickets see Passes section. Other cities with tram networks include Graz, Innsbruck and Linz. Taxis are metered; extra charges for luggage (fixed charges in smaller towns).

RAIL TRAVEL
See Tables **950 - 999**. Operated by Österreichische Bundesbahnen (ÖBB) (www.oebb.at). *RJ* (*Railjet*) / *EC* / *IC*) operate every 1–2 hrs on main domestic and international routes. *ICE* trains operate certain international services to / from Germany. Other train categories: *D* (ordinary fast trains); *REX* (semi-fast local trains); *R* (local stopping trains). S-Bahn services operate in major cities. Private operator *Westbahn* also operate fast trains between Wien and Salzburg. Most overnight trains convey sleeping-cars (up to three berths), couchettes (four/six berths) and 2nd-class seats. Seat reservations available on long-distance services.

TELEPHONES
Dial in: ✆ +43 then number (omit initial 0). Outgoing: ✆ 00. Phonecards are sold at post offices and tobacconists (Tabak Trafiken). Operator assistance / enquiries: ✆ 1611 (national); ✆ 1613 (rest of Europe); ✆ 1614 (rest of world). Emergency: ✆ 112. Police: ✆ 133. Fire: ✆ 122. Ambulance: ✆ 144.

TIPPING
Hotels, restaurants, cafés and bars: service charge of 10–15% but tip of around 10% still expected. Taxis 10%.

TOURIST INFORMATION
Austrian National Tourist Office (www.austria.info). Staff invariably speak some English. Tourist office opening times vary widely, particularly restricted at weekends in smaller places. Usually called *Fremdenverkehrsbüro*; look for green 'i' sign. Main tourist office in Vienna: Albertinaplatz / Maysedergasse, ✆ 01 24 555.

TOURIST OFFICES OVERSEAS
Australia: 36 Carrington St, 1st floor, Sydney NSW 2000, ✆ 02 9299 3621, info@antosyd.org.au. **Canada**: 2 Bloor St West, Suite 400, Toronto ON, M4W 3E2, ✆ 416 967 3381, travel@austria.info. **UK**: 9-11 Richmond Buildings, off Dean St., London W1D 3HF, ✆ 0845 101 18 18, holiday@austria.info. **USA**: P.O. Box 1142, New York NY 10108-1142, ✆ 212 944 6880, travel@austria.info.

VISAS
See page xxxii for visa requirements.

BELGIUM

CAPITAL
Brussels (Bruxelles/Brussel).

CLIMATE
Rain prevalent at any time; warm summers, cold winters (often with snow).

CURRENCY
Euro (EUR / €). 1 euro = 100 cent. For exchange rates see page 9.

EMBASSIES IN BRUSSELS
Australia: Ave des Arts 56, ✆ 02 286 0500. **Canada**: Avenue de Tervueren 2, ✆ 02 741 0611. **New Zealand**: Avenue des Nerviens 9/31, ✆ 02 512 1040. **UK**: Avenue d'Auderghem 10, ✆ 02 287 6211. **USA**: Boulevard du Regentlaan 27, ✆ 02 811 4000.

EMBASSIES OVERSEAS
Australia: 19 Arkana St, Yarralumla, Canberra, ACT 2600, ✆ 2 627 325 01. **Canada**: 360 Albert St, Suite 820, Ottawa ON, K1R 7X7, ✆ 613 236 7267. **UK**: 17 Grosvenor Crescent, London SW1X 7EE, ✆ 020 7470 3700. **USA**: 3330 Garfield St NW, Washington DC 20008, ✆ 202 333 6900.

LANGUAGE
Dutch (north), French (south) and German (east). Many speak both French and Dutch, plus often English and/or German.

OPENING HOURS
Many establishments close 1200–1400. **Banks**: Mon–Fri 0900–1600. **Shops**: Mon–Sat 0900/1000–1800/1900 (often later Fri). **Museums**: vary, but most open six days a week: 1000–1700 (usually Tues–Sun, Wed–Mon or Thur–Tues).

POST OFFICES
Postes / Posterijen / De Post open Mon–Fri 0900–1200 & 1400–1600 (very few open Sat morning). Brussels Post Office at Midi Station Mon–Fri 0800–1930, Sat. 1030–1630. Stamps are also sold at newsagents.

PUBLIC HOLIDAYS
Jan 1, Easter Sun/Mon, May 1, Ascension Day, Whit Sun/Mon, July 21 (National Day), Aug 15 (Assumption), Nov 1 (All Saints), Nov 11 (Armistice), Dec 25. For dates of movable holidays see page 2. Transport and places that open usually keep Sunday times on public holidays.

PUBLIC TRANSPORT

National bus companies: De Lijn (Flanders), TEC (Wallonia, i.e. the French-speaking areas); few long-distance buses. Brussels has extensive metro / tram / bus system operated by STIB with integrated ticketing; tickets can be purchased from tram / bus driver but it's cheaper to buy in advance from machines at metro stations or special kiosks (also offices labelled *Bootik*). For day tickets see Passes section. Some tram and bus stops are request stops – raise your hand. Taxis seldom pick up in the street, so find a rank or phone; double rates outside city limits.

RAIL TRAVEL

See Tables **400 - 439**. Operated by NMBS (in Dutch) / SNCB (in French) (www.b-rail.be). Rail information offices: 'B' in an oval logo. Seat reservations available for international journeys only. Some platforms serve more than one train at a time; check carefully. Left luggage and cycle hire at many stations. Timetables usually in two sets: Mondays to Fridays and weekends/holidays.

TELEPHONES

Dial in: ✆ +32 then number (omit initial 0). Outgoing: ✆ 00. Phonecards are sold at post offices, newsagents and supermarkets. Some public phones accept credit cards. Emergency: ✆ 112. Police: ✆ 101. Fire, ambulance: ✆ 100.

TIPPING

Tipping in cafés, bars, restaurants and taxis is not the norm, as service is supposed to be included in the price, but is starting to be expected in places where staff are used to serving people from the international community (who often leave generous tips): 10 to 15%. Tip hairwashers in salons, cloakroom / toilet attendants.

TOURIST INFORMATION

Toerisme Vlaanderen (www.toervl.be / www.visitflanders.co.uk). Office de Promotion du Tourisme de Wallonie et de Bruxelles (www.belgium-tourism.net). Dutch: *Dienst voor Toerisme*. French: *Office de Tourisme*. Brussels tourist office: Hôtel de Ville, Grand Place or rue Royale 2, ✆ 025 138 940. Most tourist offices have English-speaking staff and free English-language literature, but charge for walking itineraries and good street maps. Opening hours, especially in small places and off-season, are flexible.

TOURIST OFFICES OVERSEAS

UK: Tourism Flanders - Brussels, 1a Cavendish Square, London W1G 0LD. ✆ 020 7307 7738, info@visitflanders.co.uk; Belgian Tourist Office Brussels-Wallonia 217 Marsh Wall, London E14 9FJ. ✆ 020 7531 0390, ✆ 0800 954 5245 (to order brochures), info@belgiumtheplaceto.be. **USA / Canada**: 220 East 42nd St, Suite 3402, New York NY 10017, ✆ 212 758 8130, info@visitbelgium.com

VISAS

See page xxxii for visa requirements.

BULGARIA

CAPITAL

Sofia (Sofiya).

CLIMATE

Hot summers; wet spring and autumn; snow in winter (skiing popular).

CURRENCY

Lev (BGN or Lv.); 1 lev = 100 stotinki (st). Tied to euro. For exchange rates, see page 9. Credit cards are increasingly accepted.

EMBASSIES IN SOFIA

Australia *refer to Australian Embassy in Greece*.
Canada: (Consulate) 7 Pozitano St, ✆ 02 969 9710. **New Zealand**: *refer to NZ Embassy in Belgium*. **UK**: ul. Moskovska 9, ✆ 02 933 9222. **USA**: ulitsa Kozyak 16, ✆ 02 937 5100.

EMBASSIES OVERSEAS

Australia: 29 Pindary Crescent str. O'Malley, Canberra, ACT 2606, ✆ 2 628 697 11. **Canada**: 325 Steward St, Ottawa ON, K1N 6K5, ✆ 613 789 3215. **UK**: 186 - 188 Queen's Gate, London SW7 5HL, ✆ 020 7584 9400. **USA**: 1621 22nd St NW, Washington DC 20008, ✆ 202 387 0174.

LANGUAGE

Bulgarian (written in the Cyrillic alphabet); English, German, Russian and French in tourist areas. Nodding the head indicates 'no' (*ne*); shaking it means 'yes' (*da*).

OPENING HOURS

Banks: Mon–Fri 0900–1500. Some exchange offices open longer hours and weekends. **Shops**: Mon–Fri 0800–2000, closed 1200–1400 outside major towns, Sat open 1000–1200. **Museums**: vary widely, but often 0800–1200, 1400–1830. Many close Mon or Tues.

POST OFFICES

Stamps (*marki*) are sold only at post offices (*poshta*), usually open Mon–Sat 0800–1730. Some close 1200–1400.

PUBLIC HOLIDAYS

Jan 1, Mar. 3 (National Day), Orthodox Good Fri / Easter Mon, May 1 (Labour Day), May 6, May 24 (Education and Culture), Sept 6 (Unification), Sept 22 (Independence), Dec 24, 25, 26. For dates of movable holidays see page 2.

PUBLIC TRANSPORT

There is an extensive bus network but quality is variable. They are slightly more expensive than trains but both are very cheap for hard-currency travellers. In Sofia buses and trams use the same ticket; punch it at the machine after boarding, get a new ticket if you change. For day tickets see Passes section.

RAIL TRAVEL

See Tables **1500 - 1560**. Bulgarian State Railways (BDZ) (www.bdz.bg) run express, fast and stopping trains. Often crowded; reservations are recommended (obligatory for express trains). Certain long-distance trains provide a bistro / buffet service. Overnight trains convey 1st- and 2nd-class sleeping cars and seats. One platform may serve two tracks, platforms and tracks are both numbered. Signs at stations are in Cyrillic.

TELEPHONES

Dial in: ✆ +359 then number (omit initial 0). Outgoing: ✆ 00. Tokens (for local calls) and phonecards are sold at post offices and tobacconists. Emergency: ✆ 112.

TIPPING

Waiters and taxi drivers expect a tip of about 10%.

TOURIST INFORMATION

Bulgarian Tourism Authority (www.bulgariatravel.org). Main tourist informaion Centre: St Klimet Ohridski Sofia University, ✆ 02 491 83 44. tourist@info-sofia.bg. There are tourist offices in all main cities.

TOURIST OFFICES OVERSEAS

UK and **USA**: Tourist information available at the Bulgarian Embassies listed above.

VISAS

See page xxxii for visa requirements. Passports must have 3 months validity remaining. Visitors staying with friends or family (i.e. not in paid accommodation) need to register on arrival.

CROATIA

CAPITAL
Zagreb.

CLIMATE
Continental on the Adriatic coast, with very warm summers.

CURRENCY
Kuna (HRK or kn); 1 kuna = 100 lipa. For exchange rates, see page 9. Credit cards are widely accepted.

EMBASSIES IN ZAGREB
Australia: Centar Kaptol, 3rd Floor, Nova Ves 11, ✆ 1 4891 200. **Canada**: Prilaz Gjure Dezelica 4, ✆ 1 4881 200. **New Zealand** (Consulate): Vlaska ulica 50A, ✆ 1 4612 060. **UK**: Ivana Lučića 4, ✆ 1 6009 100. **USA**: Ulica Thomasa Jeffersona 2, ✆ 1 6612 200.

EMBASSIES OVERSEAS
Australia: 14 Jindalee Crescent, O'Malley, Canberra, ACT 2606, ✆ 2 6286 6988. **Canada**: 229 Chapel St, Ottawa ON, K1N 7Y6, ✆ 613 562 7820. **New Zealand** (Consulate): 131 Lincoln Rd, Henderson, PO Box 83-200, Edmonton, Auckland, ✆ 9 836 5581. **UK**: 21 Conway St, London, W1T 6BN, ✆ 020 7387 2022. **USA**: 2343 Massachusetts Ave. NW, Washington DC 20008-2803, ✆ 202 588 5899.

LANGUAGE
Croatian. English, German and Italian spoken in tourist areas.

OPENING HOURS
Banks: Mon–Fri 0700–1900, Sat 0700–1300, but may vary, some banks may open Sun in larger cities. Most **shops**: Mon–Fri 0800–2000, Sat 0800–1400/1500; many shops also open Sun, especially in summer. Some shops close 1200–1600. Most open-air **markets** daily, mornings only. **Museums**: vary.

POST OFFICES
Usual hours: Mon–Fri 0700–1900 (some post offices in larger cities open until 2200), Sat 0700–1300. Stamps (*markice*) are sold at newsstands and tobacconists (*trafika*), Post boxes are yellow.

PUBLIC HOLIDAYS
Jan 1, Jan 6 (Epiphany), Easter Sun/Mon, May 1, Corpus Christi, June 22 (Antifascist Struggle), June 25 (National Day), Aug. 5 (Nat. Thanksgiving), Aug. 15 (Assumption), Oct 8 (Independence), Nov 1 (All Saints), Dec. 25, 26. For dates of movable holidays see page 2. Many local Saints' holidays.

PUBLIC TRANSPORT
Buses and trams are cheap, regular and efficient. Zagreb and Osijek have tram networks. Jadrolinija maintains most domestic ferry lines; main office in Rijeka, ✆ +385 51 666 111.

RAIL TRAVEL
See Tables **1300 - 1359**. National railway company: Hrvatske željeznice (HŽ) (www.hzpp.hr). Zagreb is a major hub for international trains. Efficient services but there is a limited network and services can be infrequent. Daytime trains on the Zagreb - Split line are operated by modern tilting diesel trains. Station amenities: generally left luggage, a bar, and WCs.

TELEPHONES
Dial in: ✆ +385 then number (omit initial 0). Outgoing: ✆ 00. Public phones accept phonecards only (sold at post offices, newsstands and tobacconists). Police: ✆ 92. Fire: ✆ 93. Ambulance: ✆ 94.

TIPPING
Leave 10% for good service in a restaurant. It's not necessary to tip in bars.

TOURIST INFORMATION
Croatian National Tourist Board (www.croatia.hr). Main office: Iblerov trg 10/IV, 10000 Zagreb, ✆ 014 699 333, info@htz.hr. Zagreb Tourist Board, Kaptol 5, 10000 Zagreb ✆ 014 898 555.

TOURIST OFFICES OVERSEAS
UK: Elsinore House, 77 Fulham Palace Rd, London, W6 8JA, ✆ 020 8563 7979, info@croatia-london.co.uk **Germany**: Rumfordstrasse 7, 80469 Munich ✆ 089 223 344, kroatien-tourismus@online.de **USA**: 350 Fifth Ave., Suite 4003, New York NY 10118, ✆ 212 279 8672, cntony@earthlink.net or info@htz.hr

VISAS
See page xxxii for visa requirements.

CZECH REPUBLIC

CAPITAL
Prague (Praha).

CLIMATE
Mild summers and very cold winters.

CURRENCY
Czech crown or koruna (CZK or Kč); 1 koruna = 100 haléřu. For exchange rates, see page 9. Credit cards are widely accepted.

EMBASSIES IN PRAGUE
Australia (Consulate): 6th Floor, Solitaire Building, ulica Klimentska 10, ✆ 221 729 260. **Canada**: Ve Struhach 95/2, ✆ 272 101 800. **New Zealand** (Consulate): Václavské náměstí 11, ✆ 234 784 777. **UK**: Thunovská 14, ✆ 257 402 111. **USA**: Tržiště 15, ✆ 257 022 000.

EMBASSIES OVERSEAS
Australia: 8 Culgoa Circuit, O'Malley, Canberra, ACT 2606, ✆ 2 6290 1386. **Canada**: 251 Cooper St., Ottawa ON, K2P 0G2, ✆ 613 562 3875. **New Zealand** (Consulate): 110 Customs Street West, Auckland 1010, ✆ 9 306 5883. **UK**: 26–30 Kensington Palace Gardens, London W8 4QY, ✆ 020 7243 1115. **USA**: 3900 Spring of Freedom St NW, Washington DC 20008, ✆ 202 274 9100.

LANGUAGE
Czech. Czech and Slovak are closely related Slavic tongues. English, German and Russian are widely understood, but Russian is less popular.

OPENING HOURS
Banks: Mon–Fri 0800–1800. **Shops**: Mon–Fri 0900–1800, Sat 0900–1200 (often longer in Prague Sat–Sun). **Food shops**: usually open earlier plus on Sun. **Museums**: (usually) Tues–Sun 1000–1800. Most castles close Nov–Mar.

POST OFFICES
Usual opening hours are 0800–1900. Stamps also available from newsagents and tobacconists. Post boxes: orange and blue.

PUBLIC HOLIDAYS
Jan 1, Easter Sun/Mon, May 1, May 8 (Liberation), July 5 (Cyril & Methodius), July 6 (Jan Hus), Sept 28 (Statehood), Oct 28 (Founding), Nov. 17 (Freedom & Democracy), Dec 24, 25, 26. For dates of movable holidays see page 2.

PUBLIC TRANSPORT
Extensive long-distance bus network competing with the railways, run by private companies (many previously part of the nationalised ČSAD). In Prague the long-distance bus station is close to Florenc metro station. If boarding at a bus station with a ticket window, buy your ticket in advance, otherwise pay the driver. Good urban networks with integrated ticketing. Prague (Praha) has metro and tram system - see Passes feature for day tickets. Other cities with trams include Brno, Ostrava, Plzeň, Olomouc, Liberec.

RAIL TRAVEL

See Tables **1100 - 1169**. National rail company is České Dráhy (ČD) (www.cd.cz). An extensive network with many branch lines and cheap fares, but sometimes crowded trains. The best mainline trains are classified *IC*, *EC* or *Ex*. The fastest Praha - Ostrava trains are classified *SC* meaning *SuperCity* and are operated by Pendolino tilting trains - a compulsory reservation fee of CZK 200 or €7.00 applies on these. Other fast (*R* for rychlík) trains are shown in our tables with just the train number. Semi-fast trains are *Sp* or spešný, local trains (very slow) are *Os* or osobný. Some branch lines are now operated by private companies, and on the Praha - Ostrava route ČD compete with two private operators: RegioJet and Leo Express. Many long-distance trains have dining or buffet cars. Seats for express trains may be reserved at least one hour before departure at the counter marked R at stations.

TELEPHONES

Dial in: ✆+420 then number. Outgoing: ✆ 00. Payphones accept coins or phonecards (sold at post offices, tobacconists, newsstands, hotels and money exchange offices). Police: ✆ 158. Fire: ✆ 150. Ambulance: ✆ 155. Also 112

TIPPING

You should tip at pubs and restaurants, in hotels and taxis and hairdressers. In general, round up the nearest CZK 10 unless you are somewhere upmarket, when you should tip 10%.

TOURIST INFORMATION

Czech Tourism (www.czechtourism.com). Main office: Vinohradská 46, 120 41 Praha 2, Vinohrady, ✆ 221 580 611. Prague Information Service (www.praguewelcome.cz), Information centre, Old Town Hall, Staromestská námesti 1, Praha 1.

TOURIST OFFICES OVERSEAS

Canada: See USA **UK**: 13 Harley Street, London W1G 9QG, ✆ 020 7631 0427, info-uk@czechtourism.com
USA: 1109 Madison Ave., New York NY 10028, ✆ 212 288 0830, info-usa@czechtourism.com

VISAS

See page xxxii for visa requirements.

DENMARK

CAPITAL

Copenhagen (København).

CLIMATE

Maritime climate. July–Aug is warmest, May–June often very pleasant, but rainier; Oct–Mar is wettest, with periods of frost.

CURRENCY

Danish crown or krone, DKK or kr; 1 krone = 100 øre. For exchange rates, see page 9.

EMBASSIES IN COPENHAGEN

Australia: Dampfaergevej 26, ✆ 70 26 36 76. **Canada**: Kristen Bernikowsgade 1, ✆ 33 48 32 00. **New Zealand** (Consulate): Store Strandstraede 21, ✆ 33 37 77 02. **UK**: Kastelsvej 36-40, ✆ 35 44 52 00. **USA**: Dag Hammarskjölds Allé 24, ✆ 33 41 71 00.

EMBASSIES OVERSEAS

Australia: 15 Hunter St, Yarralumla, Canberra, ACT 2600, ✆ 2 6270 5333. **Canada**: 47 Clarence St, Suite 450, Ottawa ON, K1N 9K1, ✆ 613 562 1811. **New Zealand** (Consulate): 273 Bleakhouse Rd, Howick, Auckland 2014, ✆ 9 537 3099. **UK**: 55 Sloane St, London SW1X 9SR, ✆ 020 7333 0200. **USA**: 3200 Whitehaven St NW, Washington DC 20008-3683, ✆ 202 234 4300.

LANGUAGE

Danish. English is almost universally spoken.

OPENING HOURS

Banks (Copenhagen): Mon–Fri 0930–1600 (some until 1700; most until 1800 on Thur). Vary elsewhere. **Shops**: (mostly) Mon–Thur 0930–1730, Fri 0930–1900/2000, Sat 0900–1300/1400, though many in Copenhagen open until 1700 and may also open Sun. **Museums**: (mostly) daily 1000/1100–1600/1700. In winter, hours shorter and museums usually close Mon.

POST OFFICES

Mostly Mon–Fri 0900/1000–1700/1800, Sat 0900–1200 (but opening times vary greatly). Stamps also sold at newsagents.

PUBLIC HOLIDAYS

Jan 1, Maundy Thurs, Good Fri, Easter Sun/Mon, Common Prayer Day (4th Fri after Easter), Ascension, Whit Sun/Mon, June 5 (Constitution Day), Dec. 25, 26. For dates of movable holidays see page 2.

PUBLIC TRANSPORT

Long-distance travel is easiest by train (see below). Excellent regional and city bus services, many connecting with trains. Modern and efficient metro (www.m.dk) and suburban rail network in and around the capital; see Passes feature for day tickets. No trams in København; bus network can be tricky to fathom. Bridges or ferries link all the big islands. Taxis: green *Fri* sign when available; metered, and most accept major credit cards. Many cycle paths and bike hire shops; free use of City Bikes in Copenhagen central area (returnable coin required).

RAIL TRAVEL

See Tables **700 - 728**. Operator: Danske Statsbaner (DSB); (www.dsb.dk). Some independent lines, and certain former DSB services are now operated by private company ArrivaTog (www.arriva.dk). *IC* trains reach up to 200 km/h. *Re* (regionaltog) trains are frequent, but slower. Reservations are recommended (not compulsory) on *IC* and *Lyn* trains - DKK 30 in standard class; reservation included in business class. Reservations close 15 minutes before a train leaves its originating station. Nationwide reservations ✆ 70 13 14 15. Baggage lockers at most stations, usually DKK 30 per 24 hrs. Usually free trolleys, but you may need a (returnable) coin.

TELEPHONES

Dial in: ✆+45 then number. Outgoing: ✆ 00. Most operators speak English. Phonecards are available from DSB kiosks, post offices and newsstands. Directory enquiries: ✆ 118. International operator/directory: ✆ 14. Emergency services: ✆ 112. Police ✆ 114

TIPPING

At least DKK 20 in restaurants. Elsewhere (taxis, cafés, bars, hotels etc) tipping is not expected.

TOURIST INFORMATION

Danish Tourist Board (www.visitdenmark.com). Nearly every decent-sized town in Denmark has a tourist office (*turistbureau*), normally found in the town hall or central square; they distribute maps, information and advice. Some will also book accommodation for a small fee, and change money.

TOURIST OFFICES OVERSEAS

UK: 55 Sloane St, London SW1X 9SY, ✆ 020 7259 5958, london@visitdenmark.com **USA / Canada**: P.O.Box 4649, Grand Central Station New York NY 10163-4649, ✆ 212 885 9700, info@goscandinavia.com

VISAS

See page xxxii for visa requirements.

ESTONIA

CAPITAL
Tallinn.

CLIMATE
Warm summers, cold, snowy winters; rain all year, heaviest in Aug.

CURRENCY
Euro (EUR/€). 1 euro = 100 cent. For exchange rates see page 9.

EMBASSIES IN TALLINN
Australia (Consulate): c/- Standard Ltd Marja 9, ✆ 650 9308.
Canada (Consulate): Toom Kooli 13, ✆ 627 3311.
New Zealand: See Germany.
UK: Wismari 6, ✆ 667 4700.
USA: Kentmanni 20, ✆ 668 8100.

EMBASSIES OVERSEAS
Australia (Consulate): Suite 1, 144 Pacific Highway, Sydney, NSW 2060, ✆ 2 8014 8999. **Canada**: 260 Dalhousie St, Suite 210, Ottawa ON, K1N 7E4, ✆ 613 789 4222. **New Zealand** (Consulate): 3 Olliver Grove, Waikanae Beach, Wellington 5036, ✆ 4 293 1361. **UK**: 16 Hyde Park Gate, London SW7 5DG, ✆ 020 7838 5388. **USA**: 2131 Massachusetts Ave. NW, Washington DC 20008, ✆ 202 588 0101.

LANGUAGE
Estonian. Some Finnish is useful, plus Russian in Tallinn and the north-east.

OPENING HOURS
Banks: Mon–Fri 0900–1600. **Shops**: Mon–Fri 0900/1000–1800/1900, Sat 0900/1000–1500/1700; many also open Sun. **Museums**: days vary (usually closed Mon and/or Tues); hours commonly 1100–1600.

POST OFFICES
Post offices *(Eesti Post)* are generally open 0900–1800 Mon–Fri, 0930–1500 Sat. The central post office in Tallinn is located at Narva 1. Stamps are also sold at large hotels, newsstands, and tourist offices.

PUBLIC HOLIDAYS
Jan 1, Feb 24 (Independence), Good Fri, Easter Sun, Easter Mon (unofficial), May 1, Whit Sunday, June 23 (Victory), June 24 (Midsummer), Aug 20 (Restoration of Independence), Dec 24, 25, 26. For dates of movable holidays see page 2.

PUBLIC TRANSPORT
Long-distance bus services are often quicker, cleaner, and more efficient than rail, but getting pricier. The main operator is Eurolines (www.eurolines.ee). Book international journeys in advance at bus stations; pay the driver on rural and local services. Tallinn has a tram network.

RAIL TRAVEL
See Tables **1800 - 1890**. Local rail services are operated by Elron (www.elron.ee), international services by GoRail (www.gorail.ee). Comfortable overnight train to Moskva; best to take berth in 2nd-class coupé (4-berth compartments); 1st-class *luxe* compartments (2-berth) also available. Reservations are compulsory for all sleepers; entry visa to Russia may need to be shown when booking. Daytime service to St Peterburg. Very little English spoken at stations.

TELEPHONES
Dial in: ✆ +372 then number. Outgoing: ✆ 00. Pay phones take phonecards (from hotels, tourist offices, post offices, newsstands). Police: ✆ 110. Fire, ambulance: ✆ 112.

TIPPING
Not necessary to tip at the bar or counter, but tip 10% if served at your table. Round up taxi fares to a maximum of 10%.

TOURIST INFORMATION
Estonian Tourist Board: www.visitestonia.com. tourism@eas.ee. Tallinn Tourist Information: Niguliste 2/ Kullassepa 4, 10146 Tallinn, ✆ 645 7777, turismiinfo@tallinnlv.ee.

TOURIST OFFICES OVERSEAS
UK: Tourism brochures available from the Estonian Embassy (see above) mon-fri 0900 - 1700. **Germany**: Baltikum Tourismus Zentrale, Katharinenstraße 19-20, 10711 Berlin, ✆ 030 89 00 90 91, www.baltikuminfo.de. info@baltikuminfo.de.

VISAS
See page xxxii for visa requirements.

FINLAND

CAPITAL
Helsinki (Helsingfors).

CLIMATE
Extremely long summer days; spring and autumn curtailed further north; continuous daylight for 70 days north of 70th parallel. Late June to mid-August best for far north, mid-May to September for south. Ski season: mid-January to mid-April.

CURRENCY
Euro (EUR/€). 1 euro = 100 cent. For exchange rates see page 9.

EMBASSIES IN HELSINKI
Australia (Consulate): c/- Tradimex Oy, Museokatu 25B, ✆ 04 204 492. **Canada**: Pohjoisesplanadi 25B, ✆ 09 228 530. **New Zealand** (Consulate): Erottajankatu 9, ✆ 50 342 9950. **UK**: Itäinen Puistotie 17, ✆ 09 2286 5100. **USA**: Itäinen Puistotie 14B, ✆ 09 616 250.

EMBASSIES OVERSEAS
Australia: 12 Darwin Ave., Yarralumla, Canberra, ACT 2600, ✆ 2 6273 3800. **Canada**: 55 Metcalfe St, Suite 850, Ottawa ON, K1P 6L5, ✆ 613 288 2233. **New Zealand** (Consulate): 1Kimberley Rd, Epsom Auckland 1023, ✆ 9 368 5711. **UK**: 38 Chesham Place, London SW1X 8HW, ✆ 020 7838 6200. **USA**: 3301 Massachusetts Ave. NW, Washington DC 20008, ✆ 202 298 5800.

LANGUAGE
Finnish, and, in the north, Lapp/Sami. Swedish, the second language, often appears on signs after the Finnish. English is widely spoken, especially in Helsinki. German is reasonably widespread.

OPENING HOURS
Banks: Mon–Fri 0915–1615, with regional variations. **Shops**: Mon–Fri 0900–2000, Sat 0900–1500, though many shops open Mon–Fri 0700–2100, Sat 0900–1800; many shops also open Sun, June–Aug. **Stores/food shops**: Mon–Sat 0900–1800/2000. **Museums**: usually close Mon, hours vary. Many close in winter.

POST OFFICES
Most *posti* open at least Mon–Fri 0900–1700. Stamps also sold at shops, hotels and bus and train stations. Yellow postboxes.

PUBLIC HOLIDAYS
Jan 1, Jan 6 (Epiphany), Good Fri, Easter Sun/Mon, May 1, Ascension, Midsummer (Sat falling June 20–26), All Saints (Sat falling Oct 31 - Nov 6), Dec 6 (Independence), Dec 25, 26. For dates of movable holidays see page 2.

PUBLIC TRANSPORT
There are more than 300 bus services daily from Helsinki to all parts of the country. The main long-distance bus operators are Matkahuolto (www.matkahuolto.fi) and the Expressbus consortium (www.expressbus.com). Bus stations (*Linja-autoasema*) often have restaurants and shops. It is usually cheaper to buy tickets in advance. Bus stop signs show a black bus on a yellow background (local services) or a white bus on a blue background (long distance).

Helsinki has metro / tram / bus network with integrated ticketing. Taxis can be hailed in the street (for hire when the yellow *taksi* sign is lit).

RAIL TRAVEL

See Tables **790 - 799**. National rail company: VR (www.vr.fi); tilting Pendolinos (up to 220 km/h) run on certain lines. Fares depend on train type - those for *S220* (Pendolino), *IC* (InterCity) and *P* (express) trains include a seat reservation. Please note that travel classes are referred to as *Eco* (2nd class) and *Extra* (1st class). Sleeping-cars: one, two or three berths per compartment (variable supplement in addition to the appropriate *Eco* class express fare). In winter sleeping accommodation generally costs less on Mondays to Thursdays. Rail station: *Rautatieasema* or *Järnvägsstation*; virtually all have baggage lockers.

TELEPHONES

Dial in: ✆ + 358 then number (omit initial 0). Outgoing: ✆ 00. Phonecards are sold by *R-kiosk* newsstands, tourist offices, *Tele* offices, and some post offices. There are no public telephone booths in Helsinki. Directory enquiries: ✆ 020202. Emergency services: ✆ 112.

TIPPING

Service charge included in hotel and restaurant bills but leave coins for good service. Hotel and restaurant porters and sauna attendants expect a euro or two. Taxi drivers and hairdressers do not expect a tip.

TOURIST INFORMATION

Finnish Tourist Board (www.visitfinland.com). PO Box 625, Töölönkatu 11, 00101 Helsinki, ✆ 029 50 58000, mek@visitfinland.com. Every Finnish town has a tourist office *(Matkailutoimistot)* where staff speak English. English literature, mostly free.

TOURIST OFFICES OVERSEAS

USA: 297 York Street, Jersey City, NJ 07302 ✆ 917 863 5484.

VISAS

See page xxxii for visa requirements.

FRANCE

CAPITAL

Paris, divided into *arrondissements* 1 to 20 (1er, 2^e^ etc).

CLIMATE

Cool–cold winters, mild–hot summers; south coast best Oct–Mar, Alps and Pyrenees, June and early July. Paris best spring and autumn.

CURRENCY

Euro (EUR / €). 1 euro = 100 cent. For exchange rates see page 9.

EMBASSIES IN PARIS

Australia: 4 rue Jean Rey, ✆ 01 40 59 33 00. **Canada**: 35 avenue Montaigne, ✆ 01 44 43 29 00. **New Zealand**: 7 ter, rue Léonard de Vinci, ✆ 01 45 01 43 43. **UK**: 35 rue du Faubourg St Honoré, ✆ 01 44 51 31 00. **USA**: 2 avenue Gabriel, ✆ 01 43 12 22 22.

EMBASSIES OVERSEAS

Australia: 6 Perth Ave. Yarralumla, Canberra, ACT 2600, ✆ 2 6216 0100. **Canada**: 42 Sussex Drive, Ottawa ON, K1M 2C9, ✆ 613 789 1795. **New Zealand**: 34-42 Manners St, Wellington, ✆ 4 384 2555. **UK**: 58 Knightsbridge, London SW1X 7JT, ✆ 020 7073 1000. **USA**: 4101 Reservoir Rd, NW, Washington DC 20007, ✆ 202 944 6000.

LANGUAGE

French; many people can speak a little English, particularly in Paris.

OPENING HOURS

Paris and major towns: shops, banks and post offices are generally open 0900/1000–1700/1900 Mon-Fri, plus often Sat am / all day. Small shops can be open Sun am but closed Mon. **Provinces**: weekly closing is mostly Sun pm / all day and Mon; both shops and services generally close 1200–1400; services may have restricted opening times. Most **super/hypermarkets** open unti; 2100/2200. **Museums**: (mostly) 0900–1700, closing Mon and/or Tues; longer hours in summer; often free or discount rate on Sun. **Restaurants** serve 1200–1400 and 1900–2100 at least. Public holidays: services closed, food shops open am in general; check times with individual museums and tourist sights.

POST OFFICES

Called *La Poste*. Letter boxes are small, wall or pedestal-mounted, and yellow. Basic rate postage stamps (*timbres*) can also be bought from tobacconists (*Tabacs* or *Café-Tabacs*).

PUBLIC HOLIDAYS

Jan 1, Easter Mon, May 1, May 8 (Victory), Ascension Day, Whit Mon, July 14 (Bastille Day), Aug 15 (Assumption), Nov 1 (All Saints), Nov 11 (Armistice), Dec 25. For dates of movable holidays see page 2. If a holiday falls on a Tuesday or Thursday, many businesses close additionally on the Monday or Friday.

PUBLIC TRANSPORT

In Paris, use the Métro where possible: clean, fast, cheap and easy. For urban and suburban transport, *carnets* (sets of 10 tickets) are cheaper than individual tickets; for day tickets see Passes feature. Bus and train timetable leaflets (free) are available from tourist offices, bus and rail stations. Many cities have modern tram / light rail networks; Lyon, Marseille and Toulouse also have metro systems. Bus services are infrequent after 2030 and on Sundays. Sparse public transport in rural areas, and few long-distance bus services. Licensed taxis (avoid others) are metered; white roof-lights when free; surcharges for luggage, extra passengers, and journeys beyond the centre.

RAIL TRAVEL

See Tables **250 - 399**. Société Nationale des Chemins de fer Français (SNCF) (www.sncf.com), ✆ 3635 (premium rate, in French), followed by 1 for traffic status, 2 for timetables, 3 for reservations and tickets, 4 for other services. Excellent network from Paris to major cities with *TGV* trains using dedicated high-speed lines (up to 320 km/h on the *Est Européen* line to eastern France) as well as conventional track. However, some cross-country journeys can be slow and infrequent. Trains can get very full at peak times, so to avoid having to spend the journey standing, book a seat. Prior reservation is compulsory on *TGV* high-speed trains and the charge is included in the ticket price; rail pass holders will have to pay at least the reservation fee. Tickets can cost more at busy times (known as 'white' periods). Long distance trains on non-TGV routes are usually branded *Intercité* using refurbished rolling stock - some have compulsory reservation as shown in our tables. Reservation is also compulsory on all overnight trains: most convey couchettes and reclining seats only (sleeping cars are only conveyed on international trains). A certain number of couchette compartments are reserved for women only or those with small children; otherwise, couchette accommodation is mixed. There is a minimal bar/trolley service on some long-distance trains. Larger stations have 24-hour coin-operated left-luggage lockers, and sometimes pay-showers.

TELEPHONES

Dial in: ✆ + 33 then number (omit initial 0). Outgoing: ✆ 00. Most payphones have English instructions. Few accept coins; some take credit cards. Phonecards (*télécartes*) are sold by post offices, some tobacconists and certain tourist offices. Emergency: ✆ 112. Police: ✆ 17. Fire: ✆ 18. Ambulance: ✆ 15.

TIPPING

Not necessary to tip in bars or cafés although it is common practise to round up the price. In restaurants there is no obligation to tip, but if you wish to do so, leave €1–2.

TOURIST INFORMATION

Maison de la France (www.franceguide.com). 79/81 Rue de Clichy, 75009 Paris, ✆ 0 142 967 000. Local tourist offices: look for *Syndicat d'Initiative* or *Office de Tourisme*. Staff generally speak English. Many sell passes for local tourist sights or services and can organise accommodation (for a fee). Opening times are seasonal.

TOURIST OFFICES OVERSEAS

Australia: Level 13, 25 Bligh St, Sydney NSW 2000, ✆ 02 9231 6277, info.au@franceguide.com. **Canada**: 1800 avenue McGill College, Suite 1010, Montréal QC, H3A 3J6, ✆ 514 288 2026, canada@franceguide.com. **UK**: Lincoln House, 300 High Holborn, London WC1V 7JH, ✆ 0207 061 6600, info.uk@franceguide.com. **USA**: 825 Third Avenue, 29th floor, New York NY 10022, ✆ 212 838 7800, info.us@franceguide.com. Also in Los Angeles and Chicago.

VISAS

See page xxxii for visa requirements.

GERMANY

CAPITAL

Berlin.

CURRENCY

Euro (EUR/€). 1 euro = 100 cent. For exchange rates see page 9.

EMBASSIES IN BERLIN

Australia: Wallstraße 76-79, ✆ 030 88 00 880.
Canada: Leipziger Platz 17, ✆ 030 203 12 470.
New Zealand: Friedrichstraße 60, ✆ 030 206 210.
UK: Wilhelmstraße 70/71, ✆ 030 204 570.
USA: Clayallee 170, ✆ 030 830 50.

EMBASSIES OVERSEAS

Australia: 119 Empire Circuit, Yarralumla, Canberra, ACT 2600, ✆ 2 6270 1911. **Canada**: 1 Waverley St, Ottawa ON, K2P 0T8, ✆ 613 232 1101. **New Zealand**: 90-92 Hobson St, Thorndon, Wellington, ✆ 4 473 6063. **UK**: Embassy, 23 Belgrave Sq., London SW1X 8PZ, ✆ 020 7824 1300. **USA**: 2300 M Street, NW, Suite 300 Washington DC, 20037, ✆ 202 298 4000.

LANGUAGE

German; English and French widely spoken in the west, especially by young people, less so in the east.

OPENING HOURS

Vary; rule of thumb: **Banks**: Mon–Fri 0830–1300 and 1430–1600 (until 1730 Thur). **Shops**: Mon–Fri 0900–1830 (large department stores may open 0830/0900–2000) and Sat 0900–1600. **Museums**: Tues–Sun 0900–1700 (until 2100 Thur).

POST OFFICES

Mon–Fri 0800–1800, Sat 0800–1200. Main post offices have poste restante (*Postlagernd*).

PUBLIC HOLIDAYS

Jan 1, Jan 6*, Good Fri, Easter Mon, May 1, Ascension Day, Whit Mon, Corpus Christi*, Aug 15*, Oct 3 (German Unity), Nov 1* (All Saints), Dec 25, 26. For dates of movable holidays see page 2.
* Catholic feastdays, celebrated only in the south (see p. 367 for other regional holidays).

PUBLIC TRANSPORT

Most large cities have U-Bahn (U) underground railway and S-Bahn (S) urban rail service, many have trams. City travel passes cover these and other public transport, including local ferries in some cities (e.g. Hamburg). International passes usually cover S-Bahn. Single fares are expensive; a day card (*Tagesnetzkarte*) or multi-ride ticket (*Mehrfahrkarte*) pays for itself if you take more than three rides (see Passes feature for selected day tickets). Long-distance buses are not common.

RAIL TRAVEL

See Tables **800 - 949**. Deutsche Bahn (DB) (www.bahn.de). ✆ 01805 99 66 33 (20ct per call) for timetable and fares information, ticket purchase and reservations. Timetable freephone (automated): ✆ 0800 1507090. UK booking centre ✆ 08718 80 80 66 (8p per minute). *Sparpreis* are good value single fares which must be purchased at least three days in advance for travel on a fixed day/train. Long-distance day trains: *ICE* (modern high-speed trains; up to 300km/h; higher fares but no extra charge for InterRail holders), *IC*, *EC* and *D*. Regional trains: *IRE*, *RE*, *RB* (modern, comfortable and connect with long-distance network). Frequent local S-Bahn services operate in major cities. Some local services are now operated by private railways. Overnight services (*CNL*, *EN*, *D*) convey sleeping-cars (up to three berths) and/or couchettes (up to six berths), also reclining seats - reservation is generally compulsory. Most long-distance trains convey a bistro or restaurant car (an at-seat service is offered in first class). Seat reservations possible on long-distance trains. Stations are well staffed, often with left luggage and bicycle hire. Main station is *Hauptbahnhof* (Hbf).

TELEPHONES

Dial in: ✆ +49 then number (omit initial 0). Outgoing: ✆ 00. *Kartentelefon* boxes take phonecards only (available from news-agents, tobacconists and some kiosks). National directory enquiries: ✆ 11833 (11837 in English). International directory enquiries: ✆ 11834. Police: ✆ 110. Fire: ✆ 112. Ambulance: ✆ 112.

TIPPING

Not a must but customary for good service. Small sums are rounded up, while for larger sums you could add a tip of EUR 1, or up to 10% of the bill.

TOURIST INFORMATION

German National Tourist Office (www.germany-tourism.de). Main office: Beethovenstraße 69, 60325 Frankfurt am Main, ✆ 069 974 640, info@germany.travel. Tourist offices are usually near rail stations. English is widely spoken; English-language maps and leaflets available. Most offer a room-finding service.

TOURIST OFFICES OVERSEAS

Australia: c/o Gate 7 Pty Ltd, Level 1, 97 Rose St. Chippendale, Sydney NSW 2008, ✆ 02 9331 6202, germanytourism@smink.com.au. **Canada**: Vox International Inc, 2 Bloor St West, Suite 2601, Toronto ON, M4W 3E2, ✆ 416 935 1896, info@-gnto.ca. **UK**: PO Box 2695, London W1A 3TN, ✆ 020 7317 0908, office-britain@germany.travel **USA**: 122 East 42nd Street, New York NY 10168-0072, ✆ 212 661 7200, office-usa@germany.travel. Also in Chicago (✆ 773 539 6303) and Los Angeles (✆ 310 545 1350).

VISAS

See page xxxii for visa requirements.

GREECE

CAPITAL

Athens (Athína).

CLIMATE

Very hot summers, more manageable in spring or autumn.

CURRENCY

Euro (EUR/€). 1 euro = 100 cent. For exchange rates see page 9.

EMBASSIES IN ATHENS

Australia: Level 6, Thon Building, Kifisias/Alexandras, Ambelokipi, ✆ 210 870 4000. **Canada**: Ioannou Ghennadiou 4, ✆ 210 727 3400. **New Zealand** (Consulate): Kifissias Avenue 76, Ambelokipi, ✆ 210 6924 136. **UK**: Ploutarchou 1, ✆ 210 727 2600. **USA**: Vasilissis Sophias 91, ✆ 210 721 2951.

EMBASSIES OVERSEAS

Australia: 9 Turrana St, Yarralumla, Canberra, ACT 2600, ✆ 2 6273 3011. **Canada**: 76-80 MacLaren St, Ottawa ON, K2P 0K6, ✆ 613 238 6271. **New Zealand**: 38 - 42 Waring Taylor St, Wellington 6142, ✆ 4 473 7775. **UK**: 1A Holland Park, London W11 3TP, ✆ 020 7229 3850. **USA**: 2217 Massachusetts Ave. NW, Washington DC 20008, ✆ 202 939 1300.

LANGUAGE
Greek; English widely spoken in Athens and tourist areas (some German, French or Italian), less so in remote mainland areas.

OPENING HOURS
Banks: (usually) Mon–Thur 0800–1400, Fri 0830–1330, longer hours in peak holiday season. **Shops**: vary; in summer most close midday and reopen in the evening (Tue, Thu, Fri) 1700–2000. **Sites and museums**: mostly 0830–1500; Athens sites and other major archaeological sites open until 1900 or open until sunset in summer.

POST OFFICES
Normally Mon–Fri 0800–1300, Sat 0800–1200; money exchange, travellers cheques, Eurocheques. Stamps sold from vending machines outside post offices, street kiosks.

PUBLIC HOLIDAYS
Jan 1, Jan 6 (Epiphany), Shrove Mon (48 days before Easter*), Mar 25 (Independence), Easter Sun/Mon*, May 1, Whit Mon*, Aug 15 (Assumption), Oct 28 (National Day), Dec 25, 26. Everything closes for Easter. *Holidays related to Easter are according to the Orthodox calendar – dates usually differ from those of Western Easter (see page 2).

PUBLIC TRANSPORT
KTEL buses: fast, punctual, fairly comfortable long-distance services; well-organised stations in most towns (tickets available from bus terminals), website: www.ktel.org. Islands connected by ferries and hydrofoils; City transport: bus or (in Athens) trolleybus and metro; services may be crowded. Outside Athens, taxis are plentiful and good value.

RAIL TRAVEL
See Tables **1400 - 1499**. Operator: TrainOSE S.A. (OSE) (www.trainose.gr). Call centre for reservations and information (24-hour, english spoken): ✆ 1110. Limited rail network, especially away from the main Athens - Thessaloniki axis. Reservations are essential on most express trains. *ICity* trains are fast and fairly punctual, but supplements can be expensive. Stations: often no left luggage or English-speaking staff, but many have bars.

TELEPHONES
Dial in: ✆ +30 then number. Outgoing: ✆ 00. Payphones take phonecards only (on sale at most shops and street kiosks). Bars, restaurants, and kiosks often have privately owned metered phones: pay after making the call. Emergency: ✆ 112. Police: ✆ 100. Fire: ✆ 199. Ambulance: ✆ 166. Tourist police (24 hrs, English-speaking): ✆ 171.

TIPPING
Not necessary for restaurants or taxis.

TOURIST INFORMATION
Greek National Tourist Organisation (www.visitgreece.gr). Main office: Tsoha 7, 11521 Athens, ✆ 2 108 707 000. Athens information desk: Amalias 26, ✆ 2 103 310 392. Tourist offices provide sightseeing information, fact sheets, local and regional transport schedules.

TOURIST OFFICES OVERSEAS
Australia: 37-49 Pitt St, Sydney NSW 2000, ✆ 02 9241 1663, hto@tpg.com.au. **UK**: 4 Great Portland St, London W1W 8QJ, ✆ 020 7495 9300, info@gnto.co.uk. **USA**: 305 East 47th Street, New York NY10017, ✆ 212 421 5777, info@greektourism.com.

VISAS
See page xxxii for visa requirements.

HUNGARY

CAPITAL
Budapest.

CURRENCY
Forint (HUF or Ft). For exchange rates see page 9. You can buy your currency at banks and official bureaux. Credit cards and small denomination travellers cheques are widely accepted. Euros are more useful than dollars or sterling.

EMBASSIES IN BUDAPEST
Australia: *refer to Australian Embassy in Austria.* **Canada**: Ganz utca 12–14, ✆ 1 392 3360. **New Zealand** (Consulate): Nagymazö utca 47, ✆ 1 302 2484. **UK**: Harmincad utca 6, ✆ 1 266 2888. **USA**: Szabadság tér 12, ✆ 1 475 4400.

EMBASSIES OVERSEAS
Australia: 17 Beale Crescent, Deakin, Canberra, ACT 2600, ✆ 2 6282 3226. **Canada**: 299 Waverley St, Ottawa ON, K2P 0V9, ✆ 613 230 2717. **New Zealand** (Consulate): 23 Fife St, Coxs Bay, Auckland 1144, ✆ 9 376 3609. **UK**: 35 Eaton Place, London SW1X 8BY, ✆ 020 7201 3440. **USA**: 3910 Shoemaker St NW, Washington DC 20008, ✆ 202 362 6730.

LANGUAGE
Hungarian. English and German are both widely understood.

OPENING HOURS
Food/tourist shops, markets, malls open Sun. **Banks**: commercial banks Mon–Thur 0800–1500, Fri 0800–1300. **Food shops**: Mon–Fri 0700–1900, others: 1000–1800 (Thur until 1900); shops close for lunch and half-day on Sat (1300). **Museums**: usually Tues–Sun 1000–1800, free one day a week, closed public holidays.

POST OFFICES
Mostly 0800–1800 Mon–Fri, 0800–1200 Sat. Stamps also sold at tobacconists. Major post offices cash Eurocheques and change western currency; all give cash for Visa Eurocard/Mastercard, Visa Electron and Maestro cards.

PUBLIC HOLIDAYS
Jan 1, Mar 15 (Revolution), Easter Sun/Mon, May 1, Whit Sun/Mon, Aug 20 (St. Stephen's), Oct 23 (National Day), Nov 1 (All Saints), Dec 25, 26. For dates of movable holidays see page 2.

PUBLIC TRANSPORT
Long-distance buses: *Volánbusz* (www.volanbusz.hu), ✆ +36 1 382 0888. Extensive metro / tram / bus system in Budapest with integrated tickets; for day tickets see Passes section. Debrecen, Miskolc and Szeged also have trams. Ferry and hydrofoil services operate on the Danube.

RAIL TRAVEL
See Tables **1200 - 1299**. A comprehensive network operated by Hungarian State Railways (MÁV) (www.mav.hu) connects most towns and cities. Express services link Budapest to major centres and Lake Balaton: *IC* trains require compulsory reservation and supplement. Most *EC* trains require a supplement but not reservation; trains to Romania have compulsory reservation. A new fast train supplement has also been introduced (not necessary with international tickets or passes). Other trains include *gyorsvonat* (fast trains) and *sebesvonat* (semi-fast). Local trains (*személyvonat*) are very slow. Book sleepers well in advance.

TELEPHONES
Dial in: ✆ +36 then number (omit initial 06, which is only used when dialing from city to city within Hungary). Outgoing: ✆ 00. Payphones take HUF 10, 20, 50 and 100 coins or phonecards (sold at hotels, newsstands, tobacconists and post offices). Directory enquiries: ✆ 198 (International ✆ 199). Emergency: ✆ 112. Police: ✆ 107. Fire: ✆ 105. Ambulance: ✆ 104.

TIPPING
Round up by 5–15% for restaurants and taxis. People do not generally leave coins on the table; instead the usual practise is to make it clear that you are rounding up the sum. Service is included in some upmarket restaurants.

TOURIST INFORMATION

Hungarian National Tourist Office (www.gotohungary.com). Tourinform Call Centre 0800 - 2000 Mon - Fri ✆ 01 438 80 80, email info@itthon.hu
Tourinform branches throughout Hungary. English-speaking staff. The *Hungarian Tourist Card* (www.hungarycard.hu) gives various discounts.

TOURIST OFFICES OVERSEAS

UK: 46 Eaton Place, London SW1X 8AL, ✆ 020 7823 0132, htlondon@hungarytourism.hu **USA**: 470 7th Avenue, Suite 2601, New York NY 10123, ✆ 212 695 1221, info@gotohungary.com

VISAS

See page xxxii for visa requirements.

IRELAND

CAPITAL

Dublin. For Northern Ireland see under United Kingdom.

CLIMATE

Cool, wet winters, mild spring and autumn. Intermittent rain is a common feature of the Irish weather.

CURRENCY

Euro (EUR / €). 1 euro = 100 cent. For exchange rates see page 9.

EMBASSIES IN DUBLIN

Australia: Fitzwilton House, Wilton Terrace, ✆ 01 664 5300. **Canada**: 7–8 Wilton Terrace, ✆ 01 234 4000. **New Zealand** (Consulate): P.O. Box 9999, Dublin, ✆ 01 660 4233. **UK**: 29 Merrion Road, ✆ 01 205 3700. **USA**: 42 Elgin Road, ✆ 01 668 8777.

EMBASSIES OVERSEAS

Australia: 20 Arkana St, Yarralumla, Canberra, ACT 2600 ✆ 2 6214 0000. **Canada**: Suite 1105, 130 Albert St, Ottawa ON, K1P 5G4, ✆ 613 233 6281. **New Zealand** (Consulate): 205 Queen Street, Auckland 1140, ✆ 9 977 2252. **UK**: 17 Grosvenor Place, London SW1X 7HR, ✆ 020 7235 2171. **USA**: 2234 Massachusetts Ave. NW, Washington DC 20008, ✆ 202 462 3939.

LANGUAGE

Most people speak English. The Irish language (Gaeilge) is spoken in several areas (known as the Gaeltacht) scattered over seven counties and four provinces, mostly along the western seaboard. Official documents use both languages.

OPENING HOURS

Shops generally open Mon - Sat 0900 - 1730; most shopping centres stay open until 2000 on Thurs and Fri. Some shops open on Sunday, 1200 - 1800.

POST OFFICES

Postal service: *An Post*, www.anpost.ie. Most communities have a post office, usually open Mon-Fri 0900 - 1730 or 1800, Sat 0900 - 1300; often closed one hour at lunchtime (except main offices). Sub post offices often close at 1300 one day per week.

PUBLIC HOLIDAYS

Jan 1 (New Year's Day), Mar 17 (St Patrick's Day), Good Fri (bank holiday only), Easter Mon, first Mon in May, first Mon in June, first Mon in Aug, last Mon in Oct, Dec 25 (Christmas Day), Dec 26 (St Stephen's Day). Holidays falling at the weekend are generally observed on the next following weekday.

PUBLIC TRANSPORT

A modern tramway system in Dublin called *Luas* (www.luas.ie) has two unconnected lines; the red line is the most useful for visitors as it connects Connolly and Heuston stations. Dublin Bus operates an extensive network throughout the capital, but journeys can be very slow in rush-hour traffic. Almost all bus services outside Dublin are operated by Bus Éireann (www.buseireann.ie), ✆ 01 836 6111 (daily 0830–1900). Long distance services leave from the Dublin bus station (*Busáras*) in Store St, near Connolly rail station.

RAIL TRAVEL

See Tables **230 - 249**. Rail services are operated by Iarnród Éireann (IÉ) (www.irishrail.ie). Timetable and fares enquiries: ✆ 01 850 366 222 (0900–1700 Mon-Fri). The *Enterprise* express service Dublin - Belfast is operated jointly with Northern Ireland Railways. Local IÉ north-south electric line in Dublin is called DART.

TELEPHONES

Dial in: ✆ +353 then number (omit initial 0). Outgoing: ✆ 00 (048 for Northern Ireland). Pay phones take coins, phonecards or credit cards. Directory enquiries: ✆ 11811 / 11850 (International ✆ 11818). Operator assistance: ✆ 10 (International ✆ 114). Emergency services: ✆ 112 or 999.

TIPPING

A tip of 12 - 15% is expected in restaurants. Taxis 10%.

TOURIST INFORMATION

Fáilte Ireland (www.discoverireland.ie) or (www.ireland.com). Main office: 5th Floor, Bishop's Square, Redmond's Hill, Dublin 2, ✆ 014 763 400. Tourist offices offer a wide range of information, also accommodation bookings.

TOURIST OFFICES OVERSEAS

Australia: Level 5, 36 Carrington St, Sydney NSW 2000, ✆ 02 9964 6900. **Canada**: 2 Bloor St West, Suite 3403, Toronto ON, M4W 3E2, ✆ 416 925 6368. **UK**: 103 Wigmore St, London W1U 1QS, ✆ 020 7518 0800. **USA**: 345 Park Avenue, 17th floor, New York NY 10154, ✆ 212 418 0800.

VISAS

See page xxxii for visa requirements.

ITALY

CAPITAL

Rome (Roma).

CLIMATE

Very hot in July and Aug. May, June, and Sept are best for sightseeing. Holiday season ends mid Sept or Oct. Rome is crowded at Easter.

CURRENCY

Euro (EUR / €). 1 euro = 100 cent. For exchange rates see page 9.

EMBASSIES IN ROME

Australia: Via Antonio Bosio 5, ✆ 06 852 721. **Canada**: Via Zara 30, ✆ 06 85 44 42 911. **New Zealand**: Via Clitunno 44, ✆ 06 853 7501. **UK**: Via XX Settembre 80a, ✆ 06 4220 0001. **USA**: Via Vittorio Veneto 121, ✆ 06 46 741.

EMBASSIES OVERSEAS

Australia: 12 Grey St, Deakin, Canberra ACT 2600, ✆ 2 6273 3333. **Canada**: 275 Slater St, Ottawa ON, K1P 5H9, ✆ 613 232 2401. **New Zealand**: 34-38 Grant Rd, Thorndon, Wellington, ✆ 4 473 5339. **UK**: 14 Three Kings Yard, London W1K 4EH, ✆ 020 7312 2200. **USA**: 3000 Whitehaven St NW, Washington DC 20008, ✆ 202 612 4400.

LANGUAGE

Italian; standard Italian is spoken across the country though there are marked regional pronunciation differences. Some dialects in more remote areas. Many speak English in cities and tourist areas. In the south and Sicily, French is often more useful than English.

OPENING HOURS

Banks: Mon–Fri 0830–1330, 1430–1630. **Shops**: (usually) Mon–Sat 0830/0900–1230, 1530/1600–1900/1930; closed Mon am/Sat pm July/Aug. **Museums/sites**: usually Tues–Sun 0930–1900; last Sun of month free; most refuse entry within an hour of closing. Churches often close at lunchtime.

POST OFFICES

Mostly Mon–Fri 0830–1330/1350, Sat 0830–1150. Some counters (registered mail and telegrams) may differ; in main cities some open in the afternoon. Send anything urgent via express. *Posta prioritaria* stamps also guarantee a faster delivery. Stamps (*francobolli*) are available from tobacconists (*tabacchi*). Poste restante (*Fermo posta*) at most post offices.

PUBLIC HOLIDAYS

All over the country: Jan 1, Jan 6 (Epiphany), Easter Sun/Mon, Apr 25 (Liberation), May 1, June 2 (Republic), Aug 15 (Assumption, virtually nothing opens), Nov 1 (All Saints), Dec 8 (Immaculate Conception), Dec 25, 26. For dates of movable holidays see page 2.
Regional Saints' days: Apr 25 in Venice, June 24 in Florence, Genoa and Turin, June 29 in Rome, July 11 in Palermo, Sept 19 in Naples, Oct 4 in Bologna, Dec 6 in Bari, Dec 7 in Milan.

PUBLIC TRANSPORT

Buses are often crowded, but regular, and serve many areas inaccessible by rail. Services may be drastically reduced at weekends; this is not always made clear in timetables. Tickets are usually purchased from newsagents. Roma, Milano and Napoli have metro systems; most major cities have trams. Taxis (metered) can be expensive; steer clear of unofficial ones.

RAIL TRAVEL

See Tables **580 - 648**. The national operator is Trenitalia, a division of Ferrovie dello Stato (FS) (website www.trenitalia.com). National rail information ✆ 89 20 21 (+39 06 68 47 54 75 from abroad). The trunk high-speed line from Torino to Salerno via Milano, Roma and Napoli allows fast journey times between major cities. Core services are branded *Frecciarossa*, whilst tilting *Frecciargento* trains divert off the high-speed lines to serve other cities. *Frecciabianca* services are fast premium fare services which use traditional lines. Reservation is compulsory on all types of service except *EC* (EuroCity) trains to Austria operated in Italy by LeNord. Other services are classified *Regionale Veloce* (fast regional train) and *Regionale* (stops at most stations). Services are reasonably punctual. Some long-distance trains do not carry passengers short distances. Sleepers: single or double berths in 1st class, three (sometimes doubles) in 2nd. Couchettes: four berths in 1st class, six in 2nd, although there is a number of four-berth 2nd-class couchettes. Refreshments on most long-distance trains. There are often long queues at stations; buy tickets and make reservations at travel agencies (look for FS symbol).

TELEPHONES

Dial in: ✆ +39 then number. Outgoing: ✆ 00. Public phones take phonecards *(carta telefonica)* available from any newsstand, tobacconist or coffee shop. Some take coins or credit cards (mostly in tourist areas). Metered phones (*scatti*) are common in bars and restaurants; pay the attendant after use. Phone directory assistance: ✆ 12. International enquiries: ✆ 176. Carabinieri: ✆ 112. Police: ✆ 113. Fire: ✆ 115. Ambulance: ✆ 118.

TIPPING

In restaurants you need to look at the menu to see if service charge is included. If not, a tip of 10% is fine depending on how generous you feel like being. The same percentage applies to taxi drivers. A helpful porter can expect up to €2.50.

TOURIST INFORMATION

Italian State Tourist Board (www.enit.it). Main office: Via Marghera 2/6, 00185 Roma, ✆ 0 649 711, sedecentrale@enit.it. Most towns and resorts have an *Azienda Autonoma di Soggiorno e Turismo* (AAST), many with their own websites, or *Pro Loco* (local tourist board).

TOURIST OFFICES OVERSEAS

Australia: Ground Floor, 140 William St, East Sydney NSW 2011, ✆ 02 9357 2561, sydney@enlt.it. **Canada**: 110 Yonge Street, Suite 503, Toronto ON, M5C 1T4, ✆ 416 925 4882, toronto@enit.it. **UK**: 1 Princes St, London W1B 2AY, ✆ 020 7408 1254, info.london@enit.it. **USA**: 630 Fifth Avenue, Suite 1965, New York NY 10111, ✆ 212 245 5618, newyork@enit.it. Also Chicago (✆ 312 644 0996) chicago@enit.it. and Los Angeles (✆ 310 820 1898) losangeles@enit.it.

VISAS

See page xxxii for visa requirements.

LATVIA

CAPITAL

Riga.

CLIMATE

Warm summers, cold, snowy winters; rain all year, heaviest in August.

CURRENCY

Euro (EUR/€). 1 euro = 100 cent. For exchange rates see page 9. Latvia joined the Euro zone from January 1, 2014.

EMBASSIES IN RIGA

Australia: (Consulate) c/- Airtour, 7 Vilandes ✆ 6732 0509. **Canada**: Baznicas iela 20/22, ✆ 6781 3945. **New Zealand**: *refer to NZ Embassy in Germany*. **UK**: J Alunana iela 5, ✆ 6777 4700. **USA**: Samnera Velsa St. 1, ✆ 6710 7000.

EMBASSIES OVERSEAS

Australia: (Consulate) 2 Mackennel Street, Melbourne, VIC 3079, ✆ 3 9499 6920. **Canada**: 350 Sparks St, Suite 1200, Ottawa ON, K1R 7S8, ✆ 613 238 6014. **New Zealand** (Consulate): 166 St Asaphs St., Te Whare Ta Wahi, Christchurch 8140, ✆ 3 365 3505. **UK**: 45 Nottingham Place, London W1U 5LY, ✆ 020 7312 0041. **USA**: 2306 Massachusetts Ave. NW, Washington DC 20008, ✆ 202 328 2840.

LANGUAGE

Latvian is the majority language. Russian is the first language of around 30% and is widely understood. English and German can often be of use, especially in the larger towns.

OPENING HOURS

Banks: mainly Mon–Fri 0900–1700, some Sat 0900–1300. **Shops**: Mon–Fri 0900/1000–1800/1900 and Sat 0900/1000–1700. Many close on Mon. **Museums**: days vary, but usually open Tues/Wed–Sun 1100–1700.

POST OFFICES

Mon–Fri 0900–1800, Sat 0900–1300. The main post office in Riga, at Brivibas bulvaris 19, is open 24 hrs. Postboxes are yellow.

PUBLIC HOLIDAYS

Jan 1, Good Fri, Easter Mon, May 1, May 4 (Independence Day), June 23 (Ligo Day), June 24 (Saint John), Nov 18 (Republic), Dec 25, 26, 31. For dates of movable holidays see page 2.

PUBLIC TRANSPORT

Very cheap for Westerners. Taxis generally affordable (agree fare first if not metered). Beware of pickpockets on crowded buses and trams. Long-distance bus network preferred to slow domestic train service.

RAIL TRAVEL

See Tables **1800 - 1899**. Comfortable overnight trains to Moscow and St Peterburg; best to take berth in 2nd-class coupé (4-berth compartment); 1st-class *luxe* compartments (2-berth) are also available. Reservation is compulsory for all sleepers; Russian-bound ones may require proof of entry visa when booking. Very little English spoken at stations.

TELEPHONES

Dial in: ✆ +371 then number. Outgoing: ✆ 00. Public phones take coins, phonecards or credit cards. Phonecards sold by shops, kiosks, hotels and post offices; look for the *Lattelekom* sign. Emergency: ✆ 112. Police: ✆ 02. Fire: ✆ 01. Ambulance: ✆ 03.

TIPPING

Not necessary to tip at the bar or counter, but tip 10% if served at your table. Round up taxi fares to a maximum of 10%.

TOURIST INFORMATION

Latvian Tourism Development Agency (www.latvia.travel/en). Brivibas iela 55, Riga 1519, ✆ 67 229 945, info@latvia.travel Tourist Hotline: 1188

TOURIST OFFICES OVERSEAS

Germany: Baltikum Tourismus Zentrale, Katharinenstraße 19-20, 10711 Berlin, ✆ 030 89 00 90 91, info@baltikuminfo.de.

VISAS

See page xxxii for visa requirements. Applications may take up to 30 days; confirmed hotel reservations are required. Visas may also be valid for Estonia and Lithuania. Passports must be valid for at least 3 months following the stay. Visas issued on arrival at the airport (not train border crossings) are valid 10 days.

LITHUANIA

CAPITAL

Vilnius.

CLIMATE

Warm summers, cold, snowy winters; rain all year, heaviest in August.

CURRENCY

Litas (LTL or Lt); 1 litas = 100 centu (ct), singular centas. Travellers cheques and credit cards are widely accepted. For exchange rates see page 9.

EMBASSIES IN VILNIUS

Australia (Consulate): 23 Vilniaus St. ✆ 05 212 33 69. **Canada** (Consulate): Jogailos St. 4, ✆ 05 249 09 50. **New Zealand**: *refer to NZ Embassy in Germany*. **UK**: Antakalnio Str. 2, ✆ 05 246 29 00. **USA**: Akmenu gatve 6, ✆ 05 266 55 00.

EMBASSIES OVERSEAS

Australia (Consulate): 39 The Boulevarde. Doncaster, VIC 3108, ✆ 3 9840 0070. **Canada**: 150 Metcalfe St. Suite 1600, Ottawa ON, K2P 1P1, ✆ 613 567 5458. **UK**: 2 Bessborough Gardens, London SW1V 2JE, ✆ 020 7592 2840. **USA**: 2622 16 Street NW, Washington DC 20009, ✆ 202 234 5860.

LANGUAGE

Lithuanian. Russian is the first language of around 10% of the population. English and German can often be of use, especially in the larger towns.

OPENING HOURS

Banks: mostly Mon–Thur 0900–1600, Fri 0900–1500. **Shops**: (large shops) Mon–Fri 1000/1100–1900; many also open Sat until 1600. Some close for lunch 1400–1500 and also on Sun and Mon. **Museums**: days vary, most close Mon and sometimes Tues and open at least Wed and Fri; often free on Wed; hours usually at least 1100–1700, check locally.

POST OFFICES

All towns have post offices *(Lietuvos Paštas)* with an international telephone service. Offices are generally open 0800–1830 Mon–Fri and 0800–1400 Sat. Smaller offices often close for an hour at midday.

PUBLIC HOLIDAYS

Jan 1, Feb 16 (Independence Day), Mar 11 (Restoration of Statehood), Easter Mon, May 1 (not banks), July 6 (King Mindaugas), Aug. 15 (Assumption), Nov 1 (All Saints), Dec 25, 26. For dates of movable holidays see page 2.

PUBLIC TRANSPORT

Similar to Latvia (see above).

RAIL TRAVEL

See Tables **1800 - 1899**. Major routes are to St Petersburg, Moscow, Kaliningrad, Warsaw, and Minsk. Overnight trains have 54-bunk open coaches (P), 4-bed compartments (K) and (on Moscow trains only) 2-bed compartments (M-2).

TELEPHONES

Dial in: ✆ +370 then number (omit initial 8). Outgoing: ✆ 00. Phonecards (*telefono kortelė*) are sold at newsstands and supermarkets. Emergency: ✆ 112. Police: ✆ 02. Fire: ✆ 01. Ambulance: ✆ 03.

TIPPING

Not necessary to tip at the bar or counter, but tip 10% if served at your table. Round up taxi fares to a maximum of 10%.

TOURIST INFORMATION

Lithuania State Department of Tourism (www.tourism.lt and www. travel.lt). Main tourist office in Vilnius: Vilniaus g. 22, LT-01119, Vilnius, ✆ 526 296 60, tic@vilnius.lt. There are tourist offices in most towns.

TOURIST OFFICES OVERSEAS

Germany: Lituanian Tourism, Jösephspitalstr 15, 80331 Muenchen, ✆ 089 55 25 33 406, info@baltikuminfo.de. **UK**: Lithuanian National Tourism Office, 11 Blades Court, London SW15 2NU, ✆ 0208 877 4546, lithuania@representationplus.co.uk

VISAS

See page xxxii for visa requirements.

LUXEMBOURG

CAPITAL

Luxembourg City (Ville de Luxembourg).

CLIMATE

Rain prevalent at any time; warm summers, cold winters (often with snow).

CURRENCY

Euro (EUR/€). 1 euro = 100 cent. For exchange rates see page 9.

EMBASSIES IN LUXEMBOURG

Australia: *refer to Australian Embassy in Belgium*. **Canada** (Consulate): 15, rue Guillaume Schneider, ✆ 26 270 570. **New Zealand**: *refer to NZ Embassy in Belgium*. **UK**: 5 Boulevard Joseph II, ✆ 22 98 64. **USA**: 22 Boulevard Emmanuel Servais, ✆ 46 01 23.

EMBASSIES OVERSEAS

Australia (Consulate): 6 Damour Ave, Sydney, NSW 2070, ✆ 2 9880 8002. **UK**: 27 Wilton Crescent, London SW1X 8SD, ✆ 020 7235 6961 (visa info. between 1000 and 1145). **USA/Canada**: 2200 Massachusetts Ave. NW, Washington DC 20008, ✆ 202 265 4171.

LANGUAGE

Luxembourgish is the national tongue, but almost everybody also speaks fluent French and/or German, plus often at least some English.

OPENING HOURS
Many establishments take long lunch breaks. **Banks**: usually Mon–Fri 0830–1200 and 1400–1630 or later. **Shops**: Mon 1300/1400–1800; Tues–Sat 0800/0900–1800. **Museums**: most open six days a week (usually Tues–Sun).

POST OFFICES
Usually open Mon–Fri 0800–1200 and 1400–1700.

PUBLIC HOLIDAYS
Jan 1, Easter Mon, May 1, Ascension, Whit Mon, June 23 (National Day), Aug 15 (Assumption), Nov 1 (All Saints), Dec 25, 26. Many businesses and banks also observe Carnival (Feb 11 in 2012), Good Friday, Nov 2 (All Souls). For dates of movable holidays see page 2.

PUBLIC TRANSPORT
Good bus network between most towns. Taxis not allowed to pick up passengers in the street; most stations have ranks.

RAIL TRAVEL
See Table **445** for local services. Operator: Société Nationale des Chemins de fer Luxembourgeois (CFL) (www.cfl.lu), ✆ +352 2489 2489. Frequent rail services converge on Luxembourg City. Inexpensive multi-ride passes (good for one hour or up to 24 hours) are valid on trains and local buses. Most rail stations are small with few facilities.

TELEPHONES
Dial in: ✆ +352 then number. Outgoing: ✆ 00. Phonecards (*Telekaarten*) are available from post offices and stations. Police: ✆ 113. Fire and ambulance: ✆ 112.

TIPPING
In restaurants, cafés and bars service charge is usually included (round up bill to the next euro). Taxi drivers EUR 2–5; porters EUR 1–2; hairdressers EUR 2; cloakroom attendants EUR 0.50; toilet attendants EUR 0.25.

TOURIST INFORMATION
Office National du Tourisme (www.visitluxembourg.com). Gare Centrale, P.O. Box 1001, L-1010 Luxembourg, ✆ 4 282 8210, info@visitluxembourg.com. Information and hotel bookings: Luxembourg City Tourist Office, 30 Place Guillaume II, L-1648 Luxembourg, ✆ 222 809, touristinfo@lcto.lu (www.lcto.lu),

TOURIST OFFICES OVERSEAS
Germany: Klingelofer Straße 7 D 10785 Berlin, ✆ 03 2575 773, info@visitluxembourg.de. **USA**: 17 Beekman Place, New York NY 10022, ✆ 212 935 8888, info@visitluxembourg.com.

VISAS
See page xxxii for visa requirements.

NETHERLANDS

CAPITAL
Amsterdam is the capital city. The Hague (Den Haag) is the seat of government.

CLIMATE
Can be cold in winter; rain prevalent all year. Many attractions close Oct–Easter, while Apr–May is tulip time and the country is crowded; June–Sept can be pleasantly warm and is busy with tourists.

CURRENCY
Euro (EUR / €). 1 euro = 100 cent. For exchange rates see page 9.

EMBASSIES IN THE HAGUE
Australia: Carnegielaan 4, ✆ 0 70 310 8200. **Canada**: Sophialaan 7, ✆ 0 70 311 1600. **New Zealand**: Eisenhowerlaan 77N, ✆ 0 70 346 9324. **UK**: Lange Voorhout 10, ✆ 0 70 427 0427. **USA**: Lange Voorhout 102, ✆ 0 70 310 2209.

EMBASSIES OVERSEAS
Australia: 120 Empire Circuit, Yarralumla, Canberra, ACT 2600, ✆ 2 6220 9400. **Canada**: Constitution Square Building, 350 Albert St, Suite 2020, Ottawa ON, K1R 1A4, ✆ 1 877 388 2443.
New Zealand: Investment House, cnr Ballance & Featherston Streets, Wellington, ✆ 4 471 6390. **UK**: 38 Hyde Park Gate, London SW7 5DP, ✆ 020 7590 3200. **USA**: 4200 Linnean Ave. NW, Washington DC 20008, ✆ 202 244 5300.

LANGUAGE
Dutch; English is very widely spoken.

OPENING HOURS
Banks: Mon–Fri 0900–1600/1700 (later Thur or Fri). **Shops**: Mon–Fri 0900/0930–1730/1800 (until 2100 Thur or Fri), Sat 0900/0930–1600/1700. Many close Mon morning. **Museums**: vary, but usually Mon–Sat 1000–1700, Sun 1100–1700 (some close Mon). In winter many have shorter hours.

POST OFFICES
Post offices *(TPG Post)* are generally open Mon–Fri 0830–1700; some also open on Sat 0830–1200. Many shops selling postcards also sell stamps. Post international mail in the left slot, marked *overige* (other), of the red *TPG* mailboxes.

PUBLIC HOLIDAYS
Jan 1, Good Fri, Easter Sun/Mon, Apr 27 (King's Birthday), May 5 (Liberation Day), Ascension Day, Whit Sun/Mon, Dec 25, 26. For dates of movable holidays see page 2.

PUBLIC TRANSPORT
Premium rate number for all rail and bus enquiries (computerised, fast and accurate): ✆ 09 009 292 (www.9292ov.nl). Taxis are best boarded at ranks or ordered by phone as they seldom stop in the street. In many cities (not Amsterdam), shared *Treintaxis* have ranks at stations and yellow roof signs (€4.90 for anywhere within city limits; tickets from rail ticket offices). A nationwide stored value contactless Smartcard system called OV-Chipcard is being introduced for all public transport. Personalised and anonymous cards are available, and disposable cards are also available for vsitors. These can be purchased at ticket offices and also from machines (payment by cash or credit card). OV-Chipcard readers are located on railway platforms and on trams and buses etc. (remember to swipe your card at the beginning and end of your journey).

RAIL TRAVEL
See Tables **450 - 499**. National rail company Nederlandse Spoorwegen (NS) (www.ns.nl) provides most services, though private operators run local train services in some parts of the north and east. Through tickets can be purchased between all stations in the Netherlands, regardless of operator. Cycle hire and cycle and baggage storage are usually available at larger stations. Smaller stations are usually unstaffed, but all stations have ticket vending machines. Some paper tickets are being replaced by the OV-Chipcard (see previous paragraph). Travellers found to have boarded a train without a valid ticket must pay a fine of €35 plus the cost of their fare. *Intercity direct* are fast services between Amsterdam, Schiphol, Rotterdam and Breda via the high-speed line (supplement payable, except for local journeys Amsterdam - Schiphol and Rotterdam - Breda). Other fast trains, calling only at principal stations, are classified *Intercity*. Local stopping trains are known as *Sprinter* services. Seat reservations are not available except for international journeys and for travel on *Intercity direct* services.

TELEPHONES
Dial in: ✆ +31 then number (omit initial 0). Outgoing: ✆ 00. Green booths take only phonecards (*telefoonkaarten*), available from post offices, tourist offices (VVV), rail stations (NS), telecom shops (Primafoon) and major department stores (some booths also take credit cards). Orange / grey booths take coins, credit cards and *Telfort* phonecards, available from Holland Welcome Service (GWK), Wizzl shops and NS rail stations. Most information-line numbers are prefixed 0900 and are at premium rates. Operator: ✆ 0800 0410. International enquiries: ✆ 09 008 418. National enquiries: ✆ 09 008 008. Emergency services: ✆ 112.

TIPPING

Although service charges are included, it is customary in restaurants, bars and cafés to leave a tip of 5–10% if you are satisfied. Taxi drivers expect a 10% tip.

TOURIST INFORMATION

Netherlands Board of Tourism (www.holland.com), Vlietweg 15, 2260 MG Leidschendam, ✆ 070 370 5705, info@holland.com. Vereniging voor Vreemdelingenverkeer (VVV: signs show a triangle with three Vs). Tourist bureaux are all open at least Mon–Fri 0900–1700, Sat 1000–1200. The *Museumkaart* (€49.95, under 18s €25.00 plus €4.95 one-time fee) obtainable from VVV, participating museums and www.Museumkaart.nl, is valid for one year and gives free entry to over 400 museums nationwide.

TOURIST OFFICES OVERSEAS

see www.holland.com

VISAS

See page xxxii for visa requirements.

NORWAY

CAPITAL

Oslo.

CLIMATE

Surprisingly mild considering it's so far north; can be very warm in summer, particularly inland; the coast is appreciably cooler. May and June are driest months, but quite cool; summer gets warmer and wetter as it progresses, and the western fjords have high rainfall year-round. Days are very long in summer: the sun never sets in high summer in the far north. July and Aug is the busiest period; Sept can be delightful. Winter is the time to see the Northern Lights (*Aurora Borealis*). Excellent snow for skiing Dec–Apr.

CURRENCY

Norwegian crown or krone (NOK or kr); 1 krone = 100 øre. For exchange rates see page 9. On slot machines, *femkrone* means a NOK 5 coin and *tikrone* a NOK 10 coin.

EMBASSIES IN OSLO

Australia (Consulate): Wilh. Wilhelmsen ASA, Strandveien 20, Lysaker, ✆ 67 58 48 48. **Canada**: Wergelandsveien 7, ✆ 22 99 53 00. **New Zealand** (Consulate): c/o Halfdan Ditlev-Simonsen & Co AS, Strandveien 50, Lysaker. ✆ 67 11 00 30. **UK**: Thomas Heftyesgate 8, ✆ 23 13 27 00. **USA**: Henrik Ibsens gate 48, ✆ 21 30 85 40.

EMBASSIES OVERSEAS

Australia: 17 Hunter St, Yarralumla, Canberra, ACT 2600, ✆ 2 6270 5700. **Canada**: 150 Metcalfe St. Suite 1300, Ottawa ON, K2P 1P1, ✆ 613 238 6571. **New Zealand** (Consulate): 6b Wagener Place, Mt Albert, Auckland 1025, ✆ 21 780 726. **UK**: 25 Belgrave Sq., London, SW1X 8QD, ✆ 020 7591 5500. **USA**: 2720 34th St NW, Washington D.C. 20008, ✆ 202 333 6000.

LANGUAGE

Norwegian, which has two official versions: *Nynorsk* and *Bokmål*. Norwegian has three additional vowels: æ, ø, å, which (in that order) follow z. Almost everyone speaks English; if not, try German.

OPENING HOURS

Banks: Mon–Wed and Fri 0815–1500 (1530 in winter), Thur 0815–1700. In Oslo, some open later, in the country some close earlier. Many have minibank machines that accept Visa, MasterCard (Eurocard) and Cirrus. **Shops**: Mon–Fri 0900–1600/1700 (Thur 0900–1800/2000), Sat 0900–1300/1500, many open later, especially in Oslo. **Museums**: usually Tues–Sun 1000–1500/1600. Some open Mon, longer in summer and/or close completely in winter.

POST OFFICES

Usually Mon–Fri 0800/0830–1700, Sat 0830–1300. Yellow postboxes with red crown-and-posthorn symbol are for local mail; red boxes with yellow symbol for all other destinations.

PUBLIC HOLIDAYS

Jan 1, Maundy Thur, Good Fri, Easter Sun/Mon, May 1, Ascension Day, May 17 (Constitution Day), Whit Sun/Mon, Dec 25, 26. For dates of movable holidays see page 2.

PUBLIC TRANSPORT

Train, boat and bus schedules are linked to provide good connections. It is often worth using buses or boats to connect two dead-end rail lines (e.g. Bergen and Stavanger), rather than retracing your route. Rail passes sometimes offer good discounts, even free travel, on linking services. NorWay Bussekspress (www.nor-way.no), Karl Johans gate 2, N-0154 Oslo, ✆ 82 021 300 (premium rate) has the largest bus network with routes going as far north as Kirkenes. Long-distance buses are comfortable, with reclining seats, ample leg room. Tickets: buy on board or reserve, ✆ 81 544 444 (premium-rate). Taxis: metered, can be picked up at ranks or by phoning; treat independent taxis with caution.

RAIL TRAVEL

See Tables **770 - 789**. Operated by: Norges Statsbaner (NSB) (www.nsb.no). All trains convey 2nd-class seating. Most medium- and long-distance trains also convey *NSB Komfort* accommodation, a dedicated area with complimentary tea/coffee and newspapers (supplement payable). Sleeping cars have one- and two-berth compartments; a sleeper supplement is payable per compartment (for two people travelling together, or sole use for single travellers). Long-distance trains convey a bistro car serving hot and cold meals, drinks and snacks. Reservation possible (and recommended) on all long-distance trains, ✆ (within Norway) 81 500 888, then dial 9 for an english speaking operator. Reserved seats not marked, but your confirmation specifies carriage and seat/berth numbers. Carriage numbers shown by the doors, berth numbers outside compartments, seat numbers on seat-backs or luggage racks. Stations: most have baggage lockers, larger stations have baggage trolleys. Narvesen chain (at most stations; open long hours) sells English-language publications and a good range of snacks.

TELEPHONES

Dial in: ✆ +47 then number. Outgoing: ✆ 00. *Telekort* (phonecards) are available from Narvesen newsstands and post offices. Card phones are green; some accept credit cards. Coin and card phones are usually grouped together. Directory enquiries: ✆ 180 (Nordic countries), ✆ 181 (other countries). Local operator: ✆ 117. International operator: ✆ 115. Operators speak English. These are all premium-rate. Police: ✆ 112. Fire: ✆ 110. Ambulance: ✆ 113.

TIPPING

Tip 10% in restaurants (but not bars/cafés) if you are satisfied with the food, service etc. Not necessary for taxis.

TOURIST INFORMATION

Innovation Norway (www.visitnorway.com). Main office: Akersgata 13, 0158 Oslo, ✆ 2200 2500. Tourist offices (*Turistkontorer*) and bureaux (*Reiselivslag / Turistinformasjon*) exist in almost all towns and provide free maps, brochures, etc.

TOURIST OFFICES OVERSEAS

UK: Charles House, 5 Lower Regent St, London SW1Y 4LR, ✆ 020 7389 8800, infouk@innovationnorway.no. **USA**: 655 Third Avenue, 18th floor, New York NY 10017, ✆ 212 885 9700, newyork@innovationnorway.no.

VISAS

See page xxxii for visa requirements.

POLAND

CAPITAL

Warsaw (Warszawa).

CLIMATE

Temperate, with warm summers and cold winters; rain falls throughout year.

CURRENCY

Złoty (PLN or zł), divided into 100 groszy. For exchange rates see page 9. British pounds, American dollars and (especially) euros are useful. *Kantor* exchange offices sometimes give better rates than banks. Credit cards are increasingly accepted but not universal.

EMBASSIES IN WARSAW

Australia: ul. Nowogrodzka 11, ✆ 22 521 34 44. **Canada**: ul. Jana Matejki 1/5, ✆ 22 584 31 00. **New Zealand**: Aleje Ujazdowskie 51, ✆ 22 521 05 00. **UK**: ul Kawalerii 12, ✆ 22 311 00 00. **USA**: Aleje Ujazdowskie 29/31, ✆ 22 504 20 00.

EMBASSIES OVERSEAS

Australia: 7 Turrana St, Yarralumla, Canberra, ACT 2600, ✆ 2 6272 1000. **Canada**: 443 Daly Ave., Ottawa ON, K1N 6H3, ✆ 613 789 0468. **New Zealand**: 142 - 4 Featherston St, Wellington, ✆ 4 475 9453. **UK**: 47 Portland Place, London W1B 1JH, ✆ 020 7291 3520. **USA**: 2640 16th St NW, Washington DC 20009, ✆ 202 499 1700.

LANGUAGE

Polish. Many older Poles speak German; younger Poles, particularly students, are likely to understand English. Russian is widely understood, but unpopular.

OPENING HOURS

Banks: Mon–Fri 0800–1600/1800, Sat 0800–1300. **Shops**: Mon–Fri 0800/1100–1900, Sat 0900–1300. **Food shops**: Mon–Fri 0600–1900, Sat 0600–1600. **Museums**: usually Tues–Sun 1000–1600; often closed public holidays and following day.

POST OFFICES

Known as *Poczta*; Mon–Fri 0700/0800–1800/2000, Sat 0800–1400 (main offices). City post offices are numbered (main office is always 1); number should be included in the post restante address. Post boxes: green (local mail), red (long-distance).

PUBLIC HOLIDAYS

Jan 1, Jan 6 (Epiphany), Easter Sun/Mon, May 1, May 3 (Constitution), Corpus Christi, Aug 15 (Assumption), Nov 1 (All Saints), Nov 11 (Independence), Dec 25, 26. For dates of movable holidays see page 2.

PUBLIC TRANSPORT

Buses are cheap and sometimes more practical than trains. Main long-distance bus station in Warszawa is adjacent to the Zachodnia (western) station. Some services (including PolskiBus) leave from suburban metro stations. Tickets normally include seat reservations (seat number is on back), bookable from bus station. In rural areas, bus drivers will often halt between official stops if you flag them down. Extensive tram networks in Warszawa and most other cities; Warszawa also has a modern north-south metro line.

RAIL TRAVEL

See Tables **1000 - 1099**. Most long-distance trains are classified *EC, EIC, Ex* or *TLK* and are operated by PKP Intercity, www.intercity.pl. *TLK* are lower-cost daytime and overnight services. Reservation is compulsory on all trains operated by PKP Intercity. Purely local trains (*osobowy*) are classified *R* (REGIO) and are operated by a separate company, Przewozy Regionalne, which also operates longer distance *IR* (InterREGIO) and *RE* services, often in competition with PKP Intercity, and tickets are not interchangeable. In some areas local services are operated by different companies (e.g. Koleje Śląskie around Katowice). At stations, departures (*odjazdy*) are shown on yellow paper, arrivals (*przyjazdy*) on white. Note that long distance trains are shown in red on timetables at stations. Fares are about 50% higher for 1st class, but still cheap by western standards and probably worth it. Overnight trains usually have 1st and 2nd-class sleepers, plus 2nd-class couchettes and seats. Left luggage and refreshments in major stations.

TELEPHONES

Dial in: ✆ +48 then number (omit initial 0). Outgoing: ✆ 0*0 *(wait for tone after first 0)*. Older public phones take tokens (*żetony* – from post offices, hotels and Ruch kiosks). Newer phones accept phonecards. English-speaking operator: ✆ 903. Police: ✆ 997. Fire: ✆ 998. Ambulance: ✆ 999. Emergency (from mobile): ✆ 112.

TIPPING

An older system of rounding up has now been largely superseded by a flat rate 10% for table service in bars and restaurants, also for hairdressers, taxis and guides.

TOURIST INFORMATION

Polish National Tourist Office (www.poland.travel). IT tourist information office can usually help with accommodation. Also Orbis offices, for tourist information, excursions and accommodation.

TOURIST OFFICES OVERSEAS

UK: Level 3, Westgate House, West Gate, London W5 1YY, ✆ 0300 303 1812, london@poland.travel. **USA**: 5 Marine View Plaza, Hoboken NJ 07030, ✆ 201 420 9910, info.na@poland.travel.

VISAS

See page xxxii for visa requirements.
For travellers in Germany, visas are obtainable from the Polish consulate in Berlin (www.berlin.polemb.net).

PORTUGAL

CAPITAL

Lisbon (Lisboa).

CLIMATE

Hotter and drier as you go south; southern inland parts very hot in summer; spring and autumn milder, but wetter. Mountains are very cold in winter.

CURRENCY

Euro (EUR/€). 1 euro = 100 cent. For exchange rates see page 9.

EMBASSIES IN LISBON

Australia: Avenida da Liberdade 200, ✆ 21 310 1500.
Canada: Avenida da Liberdade 198–200, ✆ 21 316 4600.
New Zealand: (Consulate) Rua da Sociedade Farmaceutica 68 ✆ 213 140 780.
UK: Rua de São Bernardo 33, ✆ 21 392 4000.
USA: Avenida das Forças Armadas, ✆ 21 727 3300.

EMBASSIES OVERSEAS

Australia: 32 Thesiger Court, Deakin, ACT 2600, ✆ 2 6260 4970. **Canada**: 645 Island Park Dr., Ottawa ON, K1Y OB8, ✆ 613 729 2922. **New Zealand**: (Consulate) 21 Marion St, Wellington, ✆ 4 382 7655. **UK**: 11 Belgrave Sq., London SW1X 8PP, ✆ 020 723 5533. **USA**: 2012 Massachusetts Ave. NW, Washington DC 20036, ✆ 202 332 3007.

LANGUAGE

Portuguese. Older people often speak French as second language, young people Spanish and/or English. English, French, and German in some tourist areas.

OPENING HOURS

Banks: Mon–Fri 0830–1445/1500. **Shops**: Mon–Fri 0900/1000–1300 and 1500–1900, Sat 0900–1300. City shopping centres often daily 1000–2300 or later. **Museums**: Tues–Sun 1000–1700/1800; some close for lunch and some are free on Sun. Palaces and castles usually close on Wed.

POST OFFICES

Post offices (*Correios*) are open Mon–Fri 0900–1800. The main offices in larger towns and at airports also open on Sat 0900–1300. Stamps (*selos*) can also be bought wherever you see the *Correios* symbol: a red-and-white horseback rider.

PUBLIC HOLIDAYS

Jan 1, Good Fri, Easter Sun, Apr 25 (Freedom), May 1, Corpus Christi, June 10 (National Day), Aug 15 (Assumption), Oct 5 (Republic), Nov 1 (All Saints), Dec 1 (Independence), Dec 8 (Immaculate Conception), Dec 25. Many local Saints' holidays. For dates of movable holidays see page 2.

PUBLIC TRANSPORT

Usually buy long-distance bus tickets before boarding. Bus stops: *paragem;* extend your arm to stop a bus. Taxis: black with green roofs or beige; illuminated signs; cheap, metered in cities, elsewhere fares negotiable; drivers may ask you to pay for their return journey; surcharges for luggage over 30 kg and night travel; 10% tip. City transport: single tickets can be bought as you board, but books of tickets or passes are cheaper; on boarding, insert 1–3 tickets (according to length of journey) in the machine behind the driver.

RAIL TRAVEL

See Tables **690 - 699**. Operator: Comboios de Portugal (CP) (www.cp.pt). Cheap and generally punctual; 1st/2nd class on long-distance. Fastest trains are *IC* and *AP* (Alfa Pendular), modern, fast; supplement payable; seat reservations compulsory, buffet cars. CP information line, ✆ 808 208 208. Left-luggage lockers in most stations.

TELEPHONES

Dial in: ✆ +351 then number. Outgoing: ✆ 00. Payphones take coins or phonecards (from Portugal Telecom shops, post offices, newsstands and hotels), and occasionally credit cards. International calls are best made at post offices; pay after the call. Operator: ✆ 118. Emergency services: ✆ 112.

TIPPING

Not necessary in hotels; customary to round up taxi fares and bills in cafés/bars, though not essential. Tip 10% in restaurants.

TOURIST INFORMATION

Portuguese National Tourist Office (www.visitportugal.com). info@visitportugal.com, ✆ 211 140 200

TOURIST OFFICES OVERSEAS

UK: 11 Belgrave Square, London SW1X 8PP, ✆ 0207 201 6666, tourism.london@portugalglobal.pt. **USA**: 590 Fifth Avenue, 4th floor, New York NY 10036, ✆ 646 723 0200, tourism@iecp.pt

VISAS

See page xxxii for visa requirements.

ROMANIA

CAPITAL

Bucharest (Bucuresti).

CLIMATE

Hot inland in summer, coast cooled by breezes; milder in winter, snow inland, especially in the mountains.

CURRENCY

Leu (plural: lei). 1 leu = 100 bani. For exchange rates see page 9.

Carry pounds, euros or dollars, in small denominations, plus traveller's cheques; change cash (commission-free) at exchange kiosks or banks; as rates can vary it's wise to check a few places first. Keep hold of your exchange vouchers; avoid black market exchange (risk of theft). Credit cards are needed for car rental, and are accepted in better hotels and restaurants. *Bancomats* (automatic cash dispensers; accept most cards at good rates) in most cities.

EMBASSIES IN BUCHAREST

Australia (Consulate): The Group, Praga St 3 ✆ 21 206 22 00. **Canada**: 1-3 Tuberozelor St, ✆ 21 307 50 00. **New Zealand**: *refer to NZ Embassy in Belgium.* **UK**: Jules Michelet 24, ✆ 21 201 72 00. **USA**: Dr Liviu Librescu Blvd. 4–6, ✆ 21 200 33 00.

EMBASSIES OVERSEAS

Australia: 4 Dalman Crescent, O'Malley, Canberra ACT 2606, ✆ 2 6286 2343. **Canada**: 655 Rideau St, Ottawa ON, K1N 6A3, ✆ 613 789 3709. **New Zealand** (Consulate): 53 Homewood Ave, Karori, Wellington 6012, ✆ 4 476 6883. **UK**: Arundel House, 4 Palace Green, London W8 4QD, ✆ 020 7937 9666. **USA**: 1607 23rd St NW, Washington DC, 20008, ✆ 202 332 4846.

LANGUAGE

Romanian. English is understood by younger people, plus some French, German, and Hungarian throughout Transylvania.

OPENING HOURS

Banks: Mon–Fri 0900–1200/1300; private exchange counters open longer. **Shops**: usually 0800/0900–1800/2000, plus Sat morning or all day; often close 1300–1500. Local food shops often 0600–late. Few except in Bucharest open Sun. **Museums**: usually 0900/1000–1700/1800; open weekends, closed Mon (and maybe Tues).

POST OFFICES

There are post offices *(Posta Romana)* in all towns, open 0700-1900 Mon–Fri and until 1300 Sat. Postboxes are red. Mail usually takes five days to reach western Europe and up to two weeks to reach the US.

PUBLIC HOLIDAYS

Jan 1, 2, Easter Sun/Mon (Orthodox), May 1, Whit Mon (Orthodox), Aug 15 (St Mary's), Dec 1 (National Unity Day), Dec 25, 26. For dates of movable holidays see page 2.

PUBLIC TRANSPORT

Buy bus/tram/metro tickets in advance from kiosks (as a rule) and cancel on entry. Taxis are plentiful and inexpensive; if the meter is not in use agree price first and always pay in lei, not foreign currency. Avoid unlicensed vehicles. Trains are best for long-distance travel, although bus routes are expanding and connect important towns and cities.

RAIL TRAVEL

See Tables **1600 - 1699**. Societatea Națională de Transport Feroviar de Călători (CFR) operates an extensive network linking all major towns (www.cfrcalatori.ro). Most main lines are electrified and quite fast, but branch line services are very slow. Trains are fairly punctual and very cheap. Except for local trains, reserve and pay a speed supplement in advance (tickets issued abroad include the supplement): cheapest are *tren de persoane* (very slow), then *accelerat* (still cheap), *rapid*, and finally *IC* trains (prices approaching Western levels). Food is normally available only on *IC* trains and some *rapids*; drinks sold on some other trains. Couchette (*cuseta*) or sleeper (*vagon de dormit*) accommodation is inexpensive. An increasing number of services are now operated by private operators, such as Regiotrans, Transferoviar Grup SA, and Softrans S.R.L.

TELEPHONES

Dial in: ✆ +40 then number (omit initial 0). Outgoing: ✆ 00. Operator-connected calls from hotels and post offices: pay after making the call. Blue public phones accept coins only, Oranges' phones take phonecards available from post offices and newsstands. Emergency: ✆ 112. Police: ✆ 955. Fire: ✆ 981. Ambulance: ✆ 961.

TIPPING

Small tips are appreciated for good service at restaurants, hotels and in taxis. Only tip 10% at top-notch restaurants.

TOURIST INFORMATION

Romanian National Tourist Office (www.romaniatourism.com). Bucharest TIC: ✆ 021 305 55 00, turism@bucuresti-primaria.ro (www.tourism-bucharest.com) Regional tourist information offices in all major centres.

TOURIST OFFICES OVERSEAS

UK: 12 Harley St, London W1G 9PG, ✆ 020 7224 3692, romaniatravel@btconnect.com. **USA**: 355 Lexington Ave., 8th floor, New York NY 10017, ✆ 212 545 8484, info@romaniatourism.com.

VISAS

See page xxxii for visa requirements. Make sure you keep your visa papers when you enter – you'll pay a large fine if you don't have them when you leave Romania.

SLOVAKIA

CAPITAL

Bratislava.

CLIMATE

Mild summers and very cold winters.

CURRENCY

Euro (EUR/€). 1 euro = 100 cent. For exchange rates see page 9. Slovakia joined the Euro zone from January 1, 2009.

EMBASSIES IN BRATISLAVA

Australia: *refer to Australian Embassy in Austria.* **Canada**: Carlton Court Yard & Savoy Buildings, Mostova 2, ✆ 2 5920 4031.
New Zealand: *refer to NZ Embassy in Austria.* **UK**: Panská 16, ✆ 2 5998 2000. **USA**: Hviezdoslavovo námestie 4, ✆ 2 5443 0861.

EMBASSIES OVERSEAS

Australia: 47 Culgoa Circuit, O'Malley, Canberra, ACT 2606, ✆ 2 6290 1516. **Canada**: 50 Rideau Terrace, Ottawa ON, K1M 2A1, ✆ 613 749 4442. **New Zealand** (Consulate): 188 Quayt St, Auckland 1010, ✆ 9 366 5111. **UK**: 25 Kensington Palace Gardens, London W8 4QY, ✆ 020 7313 6470. **USA**: 3523 International Court NW, Washington DC 20008, ✆ 202 237 1054.

LANGUAGE

Slovak, a Slavic tongue closely related to Czech. Some Russian (unpopular), German, Hungarian (especially in the south), plus a little English and French.

OPENING HOURS

Banks: Mon–Fri 0800–1800. **Shops**: Mon–Fri 0900–1800, Sat 0800–1200. **Food shops** usually open 0800 and Sun.
Museums: (usually) Tues–Sun 1000–1700. Most **castles** close on national holidays and Nov–Mar.

POST OFFICES

Usual post office hours: 0800–1900. Stamps are also available from newsagents and tobacconists. Post boxes are orange.

PUBLIC HOLIDAYS

Jan 1, Jan 6 (Epiphany), Good Fri, Easter Sun/Mon, May 1, May 8 (Victory Day), July 5 (Cyril & Methodius), Aug 29 (National Day), Sept 1 (Constitution), Sept 15 (Virgin Mary), Nov 1 (All Saints), Nov 17 (Freedom and Democracy), Dec 24, 25, 26. For dates of movable holidays, see page 2.

PUBLIC TRANSPORT

There is a comprehensive long-distance bus network, often more direct than rail in upland areas. Buy tickets from the driver; priority is given to those with bookings.

RAIL TRAVEL

See Tables **1170 - 1199**. The national rail operator is Železničná spoločnost' (ŽSSK), running on the network of ŽSR. Trains are cheap, but often crowded. Apart from a small number of *EC* and *IC* trains (for which higher fares apply), the fastest trains are *expresný* (*Ex*) and *Rýchlik* (*R*). Cheaper are *zrýchlený* (semi-fast) and *osobný* (very slow). At stations, departures (*odjezdy*) are shown on yellow posters, arrivals (*prijezdy*) on white. Sleeping cars/couchettes (reserve at all main stations, well in advance in summer) are provided on most overnight trains. Seat reservations (at station counters marked R) are recommended for express trains. Reservation agency: MTA, Páričkova 29, Bratislava, ✆ 0 255 969 343.

TELEPHONES

Dial in: ✆ +421 then number (omit initial 0). Outgoing: ✆ 00. Public phones take coins or phonecards, available from post offices and selected newsstands. Information: ✆ 120 (national), ✆ 0149 (international). Emergency: ✆ 112. Police: ✆ 158. Fire: ✆ 150. Ambulance: ✆ 155.

TIPPING

Tipping is expected at hotels, hairdressers, in eateries and taxis. In general, round up to the next SKK 10, unless you are somewhere very upmarket, where you should tip 10%.

TOURIST INFORMATION

Slovak Tourist Board (www.slovakia.travel). Main office: Námestie L'. Štúra 1, P.O. Box 35, 974 05 Banská Bystrica, ✆ 0 484 136 146, sacr@sacr.sk. Bratislava Tourist Information Centre, Klobučnicka 2, 815 15 Bratislava (www.bratislava.sk), ✆ 0 216 186, touristinfo@bratislava.sk. Staff speak English and can arrange accommodation.

TOURIST OFFICES OVERSEAS

Germany: Slowakische Zentrale für Tourismus, Zimmerstr. 27, D-10969, Berlin, ✆ +49 (0) 30 2594 2640. **USA** Phorall LLC 18 Florence St. Edison NY08817 nyoffice@slovakia.travel

VISAS

See page xxxii for visa requirements.

SLOVENIA

CAPITAL

Ljubljana.

CLIMATE

Warm summers, cold winters; Mediterranean climate along coast; snow in the mountains in winter.

CURRENCY

Euro (EUR/€). 1 euro = 100 cent. For exchange rates see page 9.

EMBASSIES IN LJUBLJANA

Australia (Consulate): *refer to Australian Embassy in Austria.*
Canada (Consulate): Linhartova cesta 49a, ✆ 1 252 4444.
New Zealand: (Consulate) Lek d.d., Verovskova 57, ✆ 1 580 3055.
UK: Trg Republike 3, ✆ 1 200 3910.
USA: Prešernova 31, ✆ 1 200 5500.

EMBASSIES OVERSEAS

Australia: 26 Akame Circuit, O'Malley, Canberra, ACT 2606, ✆ 2 6290 0000. **Canada**: 150 Metcalfe St. Suite 2200, Ottawa, ON, K2P 1P1, ✆ 613 565 5781. **UK**: 10 Little College St, London SW1P 3SH, ✆ 020 7222 5700. **USA**: 2410 California St., Washington DC 20008, ✆ 202 386 6610.

LANGUAGE

Slovenian. English, German and Italian are often spoken in tourist areas.

OPENING HOURS

Banks: vary, but mostly Mon–Fri 0830–1230 and 1400–1630, Sat 0830–1200. **Shops**: mostly Mon–Fri 0800–1900, Sat 0830–1200.
Museums: larger ones 1000–1800, many smaller ones 1000–1400; some close Mon.

POST OFFICES

Mon–Fri 0800–1800, Sat 0800–1200. Main post offices in larger centres may open evenings and on Sun. Ljubljana's main post office in Trg Osvobodilne Fronte 5, by the railway station, is open 24 hrs.

PUBLIC HOLIDAYS

Jan 1, 2, Feb 8 (Culture), Easter Sun/Mon, Apr 27 (Resistance), May 1, 2, June 25 (Statehood), Aug 15 (Assumption), Oct 31 (Reformation), Nov 1 (All Saints), Dec 25, 26. For dates of movable holidays, see page 2.

PUBLIC TRANSPORT

Long-distance bus services are frequent and inexpensive; normally, buy your ticket on boarding. Information: Trg Osvobodilne Fronte 5, next to Ljubljana station, ✆ 012 344 606. On city buses pay by dropping the exact flat fare or a cheaper token (available from newsstands and post offices) into the farebox next to the driver. Daily and weekly passes are available in the main cities.

RAIL TRAVEL

See Tables **1300 - 1359**. Operator: Slovenske železnice (SŽ) (www.slo-zeleznice.si). Information: ✆ 012 913 332 (+386 1 29 13 332 from abroad). Efficient network, but fewer services on Saturdays. Reserve for *ICS* trains; supplements are payable on other express services.

TELEPHONES

Dial in: ✆ +386 then number (omit initial 0). Outgoing: ✆ 00. Public phones take phonecards, available from post offices, newspaper kiosks and tobacconists. Police: ✆ 113. Fire and ambulance: ✆ 112.

TIPPING

No need to tip bar staff or taxi drivers, although you can round sums up as you wish. In restaurants add 10%.

TOURIST INFORMATION

Slovenian Tourist Board (www.slovenia.info). Main office: Krekov trg 10, SI-1000 Ljubljana, ✆ 01 306 45 75, stic@visitljubljana.si

TOURIST OFFICES OVERSEAS

UK: Slovenian Tourist Board, 10 Little College Street, London SW1P 3SH. ✆ 0870 225 53 05, london@slovenia.info
USA: 2929 East Commercial Boulevard, Suite 201, Fort Lauderdale, FL 33308, ✆ 954 491 0112, info@slovenia.info

VISAS

See page xxxii for visa requirements.

SPAIN

CAPITAL

Madrid.

CURRENCY

Euro (EUR/€). 1 euro = 100 cent. For exchange rates see page 9.

EMBASSIES IN MADRID

Australia: Paseo de la Castellana, 259D, ✆ 913 536 600.
Canada: Paseo de la Castellana, 259D, ✆ 913 828 400.
New Zealand: Pinar 7, ✆ 915 230 226. **UK**: Paseo de la Castellana 259D, ✆ 917 146 300. **USA**: Serrano 75, ✆ 915 872 200.

EMBASSIES OVERSEAS

Australia: 15 Arkana St, Yarralumla, Canberra, ACT 2600, ✆ 2 6273 3555. **Canada**: 74 Stanley Avenue, Ottawa ON, K1M 1P4, ✆ 613 747 2252. **New Zealand**: 50 Manners St, Wellington 6142, ✆ 4 802 5665. **UK**: 39 Chesham Place, London SW1X 8SB, ✆ 020 7235 5555. **USA**: 2375 Pennsylvania Ave. NW, Washington DC 20037, ✆ 202 452 0100.

LANGUAGE

Castilian Spanish is the most widely spoken language. There are three other official languages: Catalan in the east; Galician (*Galego*) in the north-west, and Basque (*Euskera*) in the Basque country and parts of Navarre. English is fairly widely spoken in tourist areas. Note that in Spanish listings *Ch* often comes after the *C*'s, *Ll* after the *L*'s, and *Ñ* after the *N*'s.

OPENING HOURS

Banks: Mon–Thur 0930–1630; Fri 0830–1400; Sat 0830–1300 (winter); Mon–Fri 0830–1400 (summer). **Shops**: Mon–Sat 0930/1000–1400 and 1700–2000/2030; major stores do not close for lunch, food shops often open Sun. **Museums**: vary, mostly open 0900/1000, close any time from 1400 to 2030. Few open Mon and some also close (or open half day) Sun. Expect to find most places closed 1300–1500/1600, especially in the south.

POST OFFICES

Most *Oficinas de Correos* are open 0830–1430 Mon–Fri, 0930–1300 Sat, although the main offices in large cities often stay open until around 2100 on Mon–Fri. Main offices offer poste restante *(lista de correos)*. Stamps *(sellos)* are also sold at tobacconists (estancos). Post overseas mail in the slot marked *Extranjero*.

PUBLIC HOLIDAYS

Jan 1, Jan 6 (Epiphany), Maundy Thurs, Good Fri, Easter Sun, May 1, Aug 15 (Assumption), Oct 12 (National Day); Nov 1 (All Saints), Dec 6 (Constitution), Dec 8 (Immaculate Conception), Dec 25. Each region has up to four additional public holidays, usually local Saints' days (e.g. Andalucia Feb 28, Galacia July 25, Catalonia Sept 11). For the dates of movable holidays, see page 2.

PUBLIC TRANSPORT

Numerous regional bus companies provide a fairly comprehensive and cheap (if sometimes confusing) service. The largest bus operating groups are ALSA (www.alsa.es) and Avanzabus (www.avanzabus.com). City buses are efficient and there are metro systems in Madrid, Barcelona, València and Bilbao.

RAIL TRAVEL

See Tables **650 - 689**. National rail company: Red Nacional de los Ferrocarriles Españoles (RENFE) (www.renfe.es). FEVE and a number of regionally-controlled railways operate lines in coastal regions. General information: RENFE ✆ 902 320 320; FEVE ✆ 902 100 818; AVE (high-speed): ✆ 915 066 329; Grandes Líneas (other long-distance): ✆ 902 105 205; international: ✆ 934 901 122. Spain's high-speed network has expanded considerably over the last few years and the Barcelona - Madrid service has some of the fastest trains in Europe. As well as *AVE* high-speed trains, other long-distance categories include *Altaria, Euromed*, *Talgo* (light articulated trains) and IC expresses (see page 322 for further train categories). *Estrella*: night train (including sleeper and/or couchette cars). A pricier alternative for night travel is the *Trenhotel* (hotel train), offering sleeping compartments with their own shower and WC. All convey 1st and 2nd-class accommodation (*Preferente* and *Turista*; AVE also have a 'super-first' class: *Club*) and require advance reservation. *Regionales*: local stopping service; *Cercanías*: suburban trains. In remoter parts of country, services may be very infrequent. Reservation is compulsory on all services for which a train category (*Talgo, IC* etc) is shown in the timing column of this timetable. RENFE offer money back if their AVE trains on the Sevilla line arrive more than 5 minutes late.

TELEPHONES

Dial in: ✆ +34 then number. Outgoing: ✆ 00. Public phones usually have English instructions and accept coins or phonecard (*Teletarjeta*; sold in tobacconists, post offices and some shops). Payphones in bars are usually more expensive. Emergency (police / fire / ambulance): ✆ 112.

TIPPING

Not necessary to tip in bars and taxis; tipping is more common in restaurants but by no means obligatory. If you want to tip for good service, add around 5%.

TOURIST INFORMATION
Spanish Tourist Office / Turespaña www.tourspain.es (USA: www.spain.info/en_US, UK: www.spain.info/en_GB). Local *Oficinas de Turismo* can provide maps and information on accommodation and sightseeing, and generally have English-speaking staff. Regional offices stock information for the whole region, municipal offices cover only that city; larger towns have both types of office.

TOURIST OFFICES OVERSEAS
Canada: 2 Bloor Street West, Suite 3402, Toronto ON M4W 3E2, ✆ 416 961 3131, toronto@tourspain.es. **UK**: 64 North Row, 6th floor, London W1K 7DE, ✆ 0207 317 2011, londres@tourspain.es. **USA**: 60 East 42nd Street, Suite 5300 (53rd floor), New York NY 10165-0039, ✆ 212 265 8822, nuevayork@tourspain.es. Also in Chicago ✆ 312 642 1992, Los Angeles ✆ 323 658 7188, Miami ✆ 305 476 1966.

VISAS
See page xxxii for visa requirements.

SWEDEN

CAPITAL
Stockholm.

CLIMATE
Often warm (especially in summer; continuous daylight in far north). Huge range between north and south; it can be mild in Skåne (far south) in Feb, but spring comes late May in the north. Winter generally very cold everywhere.

CURRENCY
Swedish crown or krona (SEK, kr, or Skr); 1 krona = 100 öre. For exchange rates see page 9. *Växlare* machines give change. The best exchange rate is obtained from Forex, which has branches at many stations. Keep receipts so that you can reconvert at no extra cost.

EMBASSIES IN STOCKHOLM
Australia: Klarabergsviadukten 63, ✆ 08 613 2900. **Canada**: Klarabergsgatan 23, ✆ 08 453 3000. **New Zealand**: *refer to NZ Embassy in Belgium*. **UK**: Skarpögatan 6–8, ✆ 08 671 3000. **USA**: Dag Hammarskjölds Väg 31, ✆ 08 783 5300.

EMBASSIES OVERSEAS
Australia: 5 Turrana St, Yarralumla, Canberra, ACT 2600, ✆ 2 6270 2700. **Canada**: 377 Dalhousie St, Ottawa ON, K1N 9N8, ✆ 613 244 8200. **New Zealand** (Consulate): Molesworth House, 101 Molesworth Street, Wellington, ✆ 4 499 9895.
UK: 11 Montagu Pl., London W1H 2AL, ✆ 020 7917 6400.
USA: 2900 K Street NW, Washington DC 20007, ✆ 202 467 2600.

LANGUAGE
Swedish. English is widely spoken. Useful rail / bus / ferry words include *daglig* (daily), *vardagar* (Mon–Sat), and *helgdagar* (Sundays and holidays).

OPENING HOURS
Banks: Mon–Fri 0930–1500 (Thur, and Mon–Fri in some cities, until 1730). Some, especially at transport terminals, have longer hours. **Shops**: mostly Mon–Fri 0900/0930–1700/1800, Sat 0900/0930–1300/1600. In larger towns department stores open until 2000/2200; also some on Sun 1200–1600. **Museums**: vary widely. In winter, many attractions close Mon and some close altogether.

POST OFFICES
Generally Mon–Fri 0900–1800, Sat 1000–1300, but there are local variations. Stamps are also sold at newsagents and tobacconists. Post boxes: yellow (overseas), blue (local).

PUBLIC HOLIDAYS
Jan 1, Jan 6 (Epiphany), Good Fri, Easter Sun/Mon, May 1, Ascension Day, Whit Sun, June 6 (National Day), Midsummer Day (Sat falling June 20–26), All Saints Day (Sat falling Oct 31 - Nov 6), Dec 25, 26. Many places close early the previous day, or Fri if it's a long weekend. For dates of movable holidays, see page 2.

PUBLIC TRANSPORT
The transport system is highly efficient; ferries are covered (in whole or part) by rail passes and city transport cards. Swebus (www.swebus.se), ✆ 0771 218 218 (+46 771 218 218 from abroad) is the biggest operator of long-distance buses. Advance booking is essential, tickets may be purchased at sales offices, by telephone or via the website. Bus terminals usually adjoin rail stations.

RAIL TRAVEL
See Tables **730 - 769**. National rail company: SJ AB, formerly part of Statens Järnvägar (SJ) (www.sj.se or www.samtrafiken.se). Best services are operated by high-speed trains (*Snabbtåg*, shown as *Sn* in our tables) running at up to 200 km/h and using either SJ 2000 trains (formerly X2000) or the new SJ 3000 units. Supplements are required on *Snabbtåg*. Some local lines are run by regional authorities or private companies such as Veolia Transport (www.veolia.se); see page 350 for other operators. SJ information and sales line, ✆ (0) 771 757575, Veolia ✆ (0) 771 260 000. Sleeping-cars: one or two berths in 2nd class; couchettes: six berths; female-only compartment available. 1st-class sleeping-cars (en-suite shower and WC) on many overnight services; 2nd-class have wash-basins, shower and WC are at the end of the carriage. Long-distance trains have a refreshment service. Many trains have a family coach with a playroom, and facilities for the disabled. Seat reservations are compulsory on *Sn* and night trains. *Sn* services also operate between Sweden and Copenhagen via the Öresund bridge and tunnel but it is better to use the frequent local trains for short journeys. 'C' (for Central) in timetables etc. means the town's main station. *Biljetter* indicates the station ticket office, often with limited opening hours, but ticket machines are also widely in use. *Pressbyrån* kiosks (at stations) sell snacks and English-language publications.

TELEPHONES
Dial in: ✆ +46 then number (omit initial 0). Outgoing: ✆ 00. Coin-operated phones take krona or euro. Most card phones accept credit / debit cards and *Telia* phonecards (*telefonkor-ten*), available from most newsagents, tobacconists, and *Pressbyrån* kiosks). Emergency services (police / fire / ambulance): ✆ 112.

TIPPING
Restaurants include a service charge but a tip of 10–15% is appreciated. Taxis 10%. Tip hotel staff, porters, cloakroom attendants etc. at your discretion.

TOURIST INFORMATION
Swedish Travel & Tourism Council: www.visitsweden.com. info@visitsweden.com. Tourist offices, of which there are 400 throughout the country, are called *Turistbyråer*. Stockholm Visitor Centre: Kulturhuset, Sergels Torg 3, 10327 Stockholm, ✆ 085 0828 508, touristinfo@stockholm.se. also Terminal 5, Aranda Airport.

TOURIST OFFICES OVERSEAS
UK: 5 Upper Montagu St, London W1H 2AG, ✆ 020 7108 6168, uk@visitsweden.com. **USA**: PO Box 4649, Grand Central Station, New York NY10163-4649, ✆ 212 885 9700, usa@visitsweden.com.

VISAS
See page xxxii for visa requirements.

SWITZERLAND

CAPITAL
Berne (Bern).

CLIMATE
Rainfall spread throughout the year. May–Sept are best in the mountains. June or early July best for the wild flowers. Snow at high altitudes even in midsummer. Season in the lakes: Apr–Oct. July and Aug get very busy.

CURRENCY

Swiss franc (CHF or Sfr.); 1 franc = 100 centimes. For exchange rates, see page 9.

EMBASSIES IN BERNE

Australia (Consulate in Geneva): Chemin des Fins 2, Geneva, ✆ 0 22 799 91 00. **Canada**: Kirchenfeldstrasse 88, ✆ 0 31 357 32 00. **New Zealand** (Consulate in Geneva): 2 Chemin des Fins, Geneva, ✆ 0 22 929 03 50. **UK**: Thunstrasse 50, ✆ 0 31 359 77 00. **USA**: Sulgeneckstrasse 19, ✆ 0 31 357 70 11.

EMBASSIES OVERSEAS

Australia: 7 Melbourne Avenue, Forrest, Canberra, ACT 2603, ✆ 2 6162 8400. **Canada**: 5 Marlborough Avenue, Ottawa ON, K1N 8E6, ✆ 613 235 1837. **New Zealand**: 10 Customhouse Quay, Wellington 6040, ✆ 4 472 1593. **UK**: 16-18 Montagu Place, London W1H 2BQ, ✆ 020 7616 6000. **USA**: 2900 Cathedral Ave. NW, Washington DC 20008, ✆ 202 745 7900.

LANGUAGE

German, French, Italian, and Romansch are all official languages. Most Swiss people are at least bilingual. English is widespread.

OPENING HOURS

Banks: Mon–Fri 0800–1200 and 1400–1700. Money change desks in most rail stations, open longer hours. **Shops**: Mon–Fri 0800–1200 and 1330–1830, Sat 0800–1200 and 1330–1600. Many close Mon morning. In stations, shops open longer hours and on Sun. **Museums**: usually close Mon. Hours vary.

POST OFFICES

Usually Mon–Fri 0730–1200 and 1345–1830, Sat 0730–1100; longer in cities. Poste restante (*Postlagernd*) facilities are available at most post offices.

PUBLIC HOLIDAYS

Holidays vary by region. Most have Jan 1, 2, Good Fri, Easter Mon, Ascension Day, Whit Mon, Aug 1 (National Day), Dec 25, 26. Some areas also have May 1, Corpus Christi, Nov 1 (All Saints), Dec 8 (Immaculate Conception). For dates of movable holidays see page 2.

PUBLIC TRANSPORT

Swiss buses are famously punctual. Yellow postbuses call at rail stations; free timetables from post offices. Swiss Pass valid (see Passes feature), surcharge for some scenic routes. The best way to get around centres is often on foot. Most cities have efficient tram and bus networks with integrated ticketing.

RAIL TRAVEL

See Tables **500 - 579**. The principal rail carrier is Swiss Federal Railways (SBB / CFF / FFS) (www.sbb.ch). Information: ✆ 0 900 300 300 (English-speaking operator). There are also many local lines with independent operators. Services are fast and punctual, trains spotlessly clean. Reservations are required on some sightseeing trains (e.g. Glacier Express, Bernina-Express). All main stations have information offices (and usually tourist offices), shopping and eating facilities. Bicycle hire at most stations.

TELEPHONES

Dial in: ✆ +41 then number (omit initial 0). Outgoing: ✆ 00. Phonecards (*taxcard*) are available from Swisscom offices, post offices, newsagents and most rail stations in denominations of CHF 5, 10, 20, and 50. Some payphones accept Euros. National enquiries: ✆ 111. International operator: ✆ 1141. All operators speak English. Emergency: ✆ 112. Police: ✆ 117. Fire: ✆ 118. Ambulance: ✆ 114.

TIPPING

Not necessary or expected in restaurants or taxis.

TOURIST INFORMATION

Switzerland Tourism (www.myswitzerland.com). Main office: Tödistrasse 7, CH-8027 Zürich (Not open to the public). International toll-free ✆ 00800 100 200 29 (information, reservations, etc.). There are Tourist Offices in almost every town and village. The standard of information is excellent.

TOURIST OFFICES OVERSEAS

Canada: 480 University Ave, Suite 1500, Toronto ON, M5G 1V2, ✆ 800 794 7795 (toll-free), info.caen@myswitzerland.com. **UK**: 30 Bedford Street, London WC2E 9ED, ✆ 00800 100 200 29 (free-phone), info.uk@myswitzerland.com. **USA**: 608 Fifth Ave., New York NY 10020, ✆ 01 800 794 7795 (toll-free), info.usa@myswitzerland.com.

VISAS

See page xxxii for visa requirements.

TURKEY

CAPITAL

Ankara.

CLIMATE

Very hot summers, more manageable in spring or autumn. Cool Nov–Mar.

CURRENCY

New Turkish lira (TRY or YTL). 1 lira = 100 kurus. For exchange rates, see page 9. Credit cards are widely accepted.

CONSULATES IN ISTANBUL

Australia: Ritz Carlton residences, Asker Ocaği Caddesi No 15, Elmadağ 34367, ✆ 393 8542. **Canada**: 209 Buyukdere Caddesi Tekfen Tower, ✆ 385 9700. **New Zealand**: Inonu Caddesi No 48/3 Taksim, Istanbul 34437, ✆ 244 0272. **UK**: Mesrutiyet Caddesi No 34, Tepebasi Beyoglu, ✆ 334 6400. **USA**: İstinye Mahallesi, Kaplı calar Mekvii Sokak No 2, İstinye 34460, ✆ 335 9000.

EMBASSIES OVERSEAS

Australia: 6 Moonah Place, Yarralumla, Canberra, ACT 2600, ✆ 2 6234 0000. **Canada**: 197 Wurtemburg St., Ottawa ON, K1N 8L9, ✆ 613 244 2470. **New Zealand**: 17 - 17 Murphy St, Thorndon, Wellington 6011, ✆ 4 472 1290. **UK**: (Consulate) Rutland Lodge Rutland Gardens, Knightsbridge, London SW7 1BW, ✆ 020 7591 6900. **USA**: 2525 Massachusetts Ave, NW, Washington, DC 20008, ✆ 202 612 6700.

LANGUAGE

Turkish, which is written using the Latin alphabet. English and German are often understood.

OPENING HOURS

Banks: 0830–1200, 1300–1700, Mon–Fri (some private banks are open at lunchtime). Shops 0930–1900; until around 2400 in tourist areas. **Government offices**: 0830–1230, 1300–1700 (closed Sat and Sun). In Aegean and Mediterranean regions, many establishments stay open very late in summer. **Museums**: many close on Mon.

POST OFFICES

Post offices have PTT signs. Major offices: Airport, Beyoğlu and Sirkeci open 24 hrs all week (limited services at night). Small offices: 0830–1700 (some close 1230–1300).

PUBLIC HOLIDAYS

Jan 1, Apr 23, May 1, 19, Aug 30, Oct 29. Religious festivals have movable dates and can affect travel arrangements and business opening times over an extended period. The main festival periods are *Seker Bayrami* (Aug. 7 – 10 in 2013) and *Kurban Bayrami* (Oct. 14 – 17 in 2013).

PUBLIC TRANSPORT

An excellent long-distance bus system, run by competing companies (amongst the best are Varan and Ulusoy), generally provides quicker journeys than rail. *Dolmus* minibuses that pick up passengers like a taxi, but at much cheaper rates and operating along set routes, can be used for shorter journeys. Istanbul has a modern metro line, as well as a light-rail and tram route. Passenger ferries link major ports.

RAIL TRAVEL
See Tables **1570 - 1590** (also **1550** for European Turkey). Operator: TCDD (Turkish State Railways) (www.tcdd.gov.tr). Traditional routes are tortuous and journeys slow. However, new high-speed lines between Ankara and Eskisehir / Konya are now open with further lines under construction. A new tunnel under the Bosphorus has now opened resulting in the partial closure of Sirkeci station and the complete closure of Haydarpasa station for several years.

TELEPHONES
Dial in: ✆ +90 then number (omit initial 0). Outgoing: ✆ 00. Payphones take *Türk Telekom* phonecards (*Telekart*) available in 30, 60, and 100 units from post offices, shops, kiosks and some hotels. Hotels often charge very high rates. Directory enquiries: ✆ 118. International operator: ✆ 115. Emergency: ✆ 112. Police: ✆ 155. Fire: ✆ 110. Ambulance: ✆ 112.

TIPPING
A 10% tip is usual in restaurants, unless service is included. 10–20% is customary at hair salons.

TOURIST INFORMATION
Turkish National Tourist Office www.gototurkey.com. Ministry of Culture and Tourism: Atatürk Bulvarı 29, 06050 Opera, Ankara, ✆ 312 309 0850. www.kultur.gov.tr

TOURIST OFFICES OVERSEAS
UK: 4th Floor, 29-30 St James's Street, London SW1A 1HB, ✆ 020 7839 7778, info@gototurkey.co.uk. **USA**: 825 3rd Avenue 5 floor, New York NY 10022, ✆ 212 687 2194, ny@tourismturkey.org. also Los Angeles ✆ 323 937 8066, Washington ✆ 202 612 6800

VISAS
See page xxxii for visa requirements.

UNITED KINGDOM

CAPITAL
London.

CLIMATE
Cool, wet winters, mild spring and autumn, winter can be more extreme. Wetter in the west. August and Bank Holiday weekends busiest in tourist areas.

CURRENCY
Pounds Sterling (GBP or £). £1 = 100 pence (p). For exchange rates, see page 09.

EMBASSIES IN LONDON
Australia (High Commission): Australia House, The Strand, ✆ 020 7379 4334. **Canada** (High Commission) Macdonald House, 1 Grosvenor Square, ✆ 020 7258 6600. **New Zealand** (High Commission): New Zealand House, 80 Haymarket, ✆ 020 7930 8422. **USA**: 24 Grosvenor Square, ✆ 020 7499 9000.

EMBASSIES OVERSEAS
Australia (High Commission): Commonwealth Ave, Yarralumla, Canberra, ACT 2600, ✆ 2 6270 6666. **Canada** (High Commission): 80 Elgin St, Ottawa ON, K1P 5K7, ✆ 613 237 1530. **New Zealand** (High Commission): 44 Hill St, Wellington, ✆ 4 924 2888. **USA**: 3100 Massachusetts Ave. NW, Washington DC 20008, ✆ 202 588 6500.

LANGUAGE
English, plus Welsh in Wales and Gaelic in parts of Scotland.

OPENING HOURS
Banks: Mon–Fri 0930–1530 (or later); some open Sat morning. **Shops**: Mon–Sat 0900–1730. Many supermarkets and some small shops open longer, plus Sunday 1000–1600. **Museums**: usually Mon–Sat 0900/1000–1730/1800, half-day Sun.

POST OFFICES
Usually Mon–Fri 0930–1730, Sat 0930–1300; stamps sold in newsagents, supermarkets etc.

PUBLIC HOLIDAYS
Jan 1, Good Fri, Easter Mon *(not Scotland)*, Early May Bank Holiday (first Mon in May), Spring Bank Holiday (normally last Mon in May), Summer Bank Holiday (last Mon in August) *(not Scotland)*, Dec 25, 26.
Scotland: *also* Jan 2, Summer Bank Holiday (first Mon in August). Northern Ireland: *also* Mar 17 (St Patrick), July 12 (Orangemen). Holidays falling at the weekend are transferred to the following weekday. For the dates of movable holidays, see page 2.

PUBLIC TRANSPORT
Intercity express bus services (coaches) are generally cheaper, but slower, than trains, and mostly require prebooking. The main long-distance coach operator in England and Wales is National Express (www.nationalexpress.com), or Citylink (www.citylink.co.uk) in Scotland. Comprehensive local bus network; most companies belong to large groups such as Stagecoach, First or Arriva. Bus stations are rarely adjacent to railway stations. Traveline (www.traveline.org.uk) is an on-line and telephone service for all UK timetables: ✆ 0871 200 22 23 (10p per minute). Extensive 'Underground' railway network in London operated by Transport for London (www.tfl.gov.uk) who also control the bus service using private companies.
In Northern Ireland, Ulsterbus (part of Translink) is the principal bus operator. (www.translink.co.uk)

RAIL TRAVEL
See Tables **100 - 234**. Passenger services in Great Britain are provided by a number of train operating companies, working together as National Rail (www.nationalrail.co.uk). Through tickets are available to all stations in the country. If asked, booking-office staff will quote the cheapest through fare regardless of operator (time period restrictions apply to the very cheapest fares). National Rail enquiries: ✆ 08457 48 49 50. Fast trains, comfortable and frequent, have first and standard class. Other long- and medium-distance regional services are often standard-class only. Refreshments are often available on board. Sleepers: cabins are two-berth or (higher charge) single. Advance reservation (essential for sleepers) is available for most long-distance services - a fee may be charged. Travel between Saturday evening and Sunday afternoon is sometimes interrupted by engineering works and buses may replace trains. In Northern Ireland, trains are operated by Northern Ireland Railways (NIR), part of Translink. NIR enquiries: ✆ 028 90 666 630.

TELEPHONES
Dial in: ✆ +44 then number (omit initial 0). Outgoing: ✆ 00. Payphones take coins, credit or debit cards. Emergency services: ✆ 999 or 112.

TIPPING
Tip 10% in restaurants, except where service is included (becoming increasingly common), but not in pubs, self-service restaurants or bars. Tip taxis (10%) hailed in the street.

TOURIST INFORMATION
VisitBritain (www.visitbritain.com). 20 Great Smith Street, London SW1P 3BT, ✆ 020 7578 1000. There are local tourist offices in most towns and cities.

TOURIST OFFICES OVERSEAS
Australia: The Gateway, 1 Macquarie Place Sidney, NSW 2000 ✆ 2 8247 2275. **Canada**: 777 Bay Street Suite 2800 Toronto ON M5G 2G2 ✆ 664 666 77. **USA** 845 Third Avenue, 10th Floor New York NY 10022 ✆ 212 850 0349. Also in Los Angeles ✆ 310 481 2989 Intending visitors should refer to the website www.visitbritain.com

VISAS
See page xxxii for visa requirements.

Visa Requirements

The table below shows whether nationals from selected countries (shown in columns) need visas to visit countries in Europe (shown in rows) - the symbol ▲ indicates that a visa **is** required. This information applies to tourist trips for up to 30 days - different requirements may apply for longer trips or for visits for other purposes, also if you are resident in a country other than your own. To enter certain countries you may need up to three months remaining validity on your passport. Holders of biometric ordinary passports sometimes do not require a visa.

The first row and column, labelled **Schengen area**, apply to the 26 European countries which have signed the Schengen Agreement whereby border controls between the member countries have been abolished. It is possible to obtain a single Schengen visa to cover all these countries, which are:

Austria, Belgium, Czech Republic, Denmark, Estonia, Finland, France, Germany, Greece, Hungary, Iceland, Italy, Latvia, Liechtenstein, Lithuania, Luxembourg, Malta, Netherlands, Norway, Poland, Portugal, Slovakia, Slovenia, Spain, Sweden, Switzerland.

Note that the Schengen area and the European Union (EU) differ in the following respects: Iceland, Liechtenstein, Norway and Switzerland are not in the EU but have implemented the Schengen agreement, whereas the United Kingdom and the Republic of Ireland are in the EU but have opted out of Schengen. Andorra is not included in the Schengen area. Croatia, Cyprus, Romania and Bulgaria are in the EU and are legally obliged to join Schengen once certain requirements are met.

Visas should generally be applied for in advance from an Embassy or Consulate of the country you are visiting, although sometimes they are available on arrival. Transit visas may be available for those travelling through a country in order to reach another, but these may also need to be purchased in advance. The information show below is given as a guide only - entry requirements may be subject to change.

NATIONALS OF →

▲ VISA REQUIRED

TRAVELLING TO ↓	**Schengen area**	Albania	Belarus	Bosnia-Herzegovina	Bulgaria	Croatia	Cyprus	Macedonia	Moldova	Montenegro	Romania	Russia	Serbia	Switzerland	Turkey	UK / Ireland	Ukraine	Australia	Canada	Japan	New Zealand	USA
Schengen area	–	▲	▲	▲	:	:	:	:	▲	:	:	▲	:	:	▲	:	▲	:	:	:	:	:
Albania ◇	:	–	▲	:	:	:	:	:	▲	:	:	▲	:	:	:	:	▲	:	:	:	:	:
Belarus	▲	▲	–	▲	▲	▲	▲	:	:	:	▲	:	:	▲	▲	▲	:	▲	▲	▲	▲	▲
Bosnia-Herzegovina	:	▲	▲	–	:	:	:	:	▲	:	:	:	:	:	:	:	▲	:	:	:	:	:
Bulgaria	:	▲	▲	:	–	:	:	▲	▲	▲	:	▲	▲	:	▲	:	▲	:	:	:	:	:
Croatia	:	:	▲	:	:	–	:	:	▲	:	:	▲	:	:	:	:	▲	:	:	:	:	:
Cyprus △	:	▲	▲	▲	:	:	–	▲[1]	▲	▲[1]	:	▲	▲[1]	:	▲	:	▲	:	:	:	:	:
Macedonia	:	:	▲	:	:	:	:	–	▲	:	:	▲	:	:	:	:	▲	:	:	:	:	:
Moldova	:	▲	:	▲	:	▲	:	▲	–	▲	:	:	▲	:	▲	:	:	▲	:	:	▲	:
Montenegro	:	:	▲	:	:	:	:	:	▲	–	:	:	:	:	:	:	:	:	:	▲	:	:
Romania	:	▲	▲	▲	:	:	:	▲[1]	▲	▲[1]	–	▲	▲[1]	:	▲	:	▲	:	:	:	:	:
Russia	▲	▲	:	:	▲	▲	▲	:	:	:	▲	–	▲[1]	▲	:	▲	:	▲	▲	▲	▲	▲
Serbia	:	:	:	:	:	:	:	:	▲	:	:	:	–	:	:	:	:	:	:	:	:	:
Switzerland	:	▲[1]	▲	▲[1]	:	:	:	▲[1]	▲	▲[1]	:	▲	▲[1]	–	▲	:	▲	:	:	:	:	:
Turkey	●[2]	:	●	:	:	:	●	:	●	:	:	:	:	:	–	●	:	●	●	:	:	●
UK / Ireland	:	▲	▲	▲	:	:	:	▲	▲	▲	:	▲	▲	:	▲	–	▲	:	:	:	:	:
Ukraine	:	▲	:	▲	:	▲	:	▲	:	▲	:	:	▲	:	▲	:	–	▲	:	:	▲	:

NOTES

▲ – Visa required (see also general notes above table).

▲[1] – Visa not required by holders of 'biometric' passports.

● – Electronic visa required before entering the country (prices vary according to nationality). For further information and to make a visa application see www.evisa.gov.tr.

●[2] – ● applies to nationals of Austria, Belgium, Hungary, Malta, Netherlands, Norway, Poland, Portugal, Slovakia and Spain.

◇ – Tax of 10 euro may be payable on entry to Albania.

△ – Citizens of Macedonia, Moldova, Montenegro and Serbia holding a valid Schengen type 'C' visa that has been used to enter the Schengen region at least once, can enter and stay in Cyprus within the validity of their Schengen visa. If holding a single entry visa they must travel directly from the Schengen region to Cyprus.

EUROPEAN RAIL TIMETABLE

JUNE 2014

GENERAL INFORMATION

SPECIAL FEATURE

TIMETABLES

This month:
North America
Tables from **9000**
Maps: page 565 / 568

CONTACT DETAILS

Director and Editor-in-chief	John Potter
Editor	Chris Woodcock
Editorial Team	Peter Bass Reuben Turner David Turpie
Commercial Manager	Keri Potter
Subscriptions Manager	Peter Weller
Consultant	Lisa Bass
General sales enquiries	Mon-Fri 0900 - 1700 GMT +44 (0)1832 270198
e-mail	editorial@europeanrailtimetable.eu
website	www.europeanrailtimetable.eu

ISSN 1748-0817 Published monthly.
Printed and bound by CPI Group (UK) Ltd, Croydon, CR0 4YY

Cover created by Andrea Collins website: www.millstonecreative.co.uk
e-mail: millstonecreative@btinternet.com

European Rail Timetable Limited
28 Monson Way
Oundle
Northamptonshire PE8 4QG, United Kingdom

Company Number 8590554

CALENDAR

CALENDRIER CALENDARIO KALENDER CALENDARIO

2014

JANUARY

M	T	W	T	F	S	S
①	②	③	④	⑤	⑥	⑦
–	–	1	2	3	4	5
6	7	8	9	10	11	12
13	14	15	16	17	18	19
20	21	22	23	24	25	26
27	28	29	30	31	–	–

FEBRUARY

M	T	W	T	F	S	S
①	②	③	④	⑤	⑥	⑦
–	–	–	–	–	1	2
3	4	5	6	7	8	9
10	11	12	13	14	15	16
17	18	19	20	21	22	23
24	25	26	27	28	–	–

MARCH

M	T	W	T	F	S	S
①	②	③	④	⑤	⑥	⑦
31	–	–	–	–	1	2
3	4	5	6	7	8	9
10	11	12	13	14	15	16
17	18	19	20	21	22	23
24	25	26	27	28	29	30

APRIL

M	T	W	T	F	S	S
①	②	③	④	⑤	⑥	⑦
–	1	2	3	4	5	6
7	8	9	10	11	12	13
14	15	16	17	18	19	20
21	22	23	24	25	26	27
28	29	30	–	–	–	–

MAY

M	T	W	T	F	S	S
①	②	③	④	⑤	⑥	⑦
–	–	–	1	2	3	4
5	6	7	8	9	10	11
12	13	14	15	16	17	18
19	20	21	22	23	24	25
26	27	28	29	30	31	–

JUNE

M	T	W	T	F	S	S
①	②	③	④	⑤	⑥	⑦
30	–	–	–	–	–	1
2	3	4	5	6	7	8
9	10	11	12	13	14	15
16	17	18	19	20	21	22
23	24	25	26	27	28	29

JULY

M	T	W	T	F	S	S
①	②	③	④	⑤	⑥	⑦
–	1	2	3	4	5	6
7	8	9	10	11	12	13
14	15	16	17	18	19	20
21	22	23	24	25	26	27
28	29	30	31	–	–	–

AUGUST

M	T	W	T	F	S	S
①	②	③	④	⑤	⑥	⑦
–	–	–	–	1	2	3
4	5	6	7	8	9	10
11	12	13	14	15	16	17
18	19	20	21	22	23	24
25	26	27	28	29	30	31

SEPTEMBER

M	T	W	T	F	S	S
①	②	③	④	⑤	⑥	⑦
1	2	3	4	5	6	7
8	9	10	11	12	13	14
15	16	17	18	19	20	21
22	23	24	25	26	27	28
29	30	–	–	–	–	–

OCTOBER

M	T	W	T	F	S	S
①	②	③	④	⑤	⑥	⑦
–	–	1	2	3	4	5
6	7	8	9	10	11	12
13	14	15	16	17	18	19
20	21	22	23	24	25	26
27	28	29	30	31	–	–

NOVEMBER

M	T	W	T	F	S	S
①	②	③	④	⑤	⑥	⑦
–	–	–	–	–	1	2
3	4	5	6	7	8	9
10	11	12	13	14	15	16
17	18	19	20	21	22	23
24	25	26	27	28	29	30

DECEMBER

M	T	W	T	F	S	S
①	②	③	④	⑤	⑥	⑦
1	2	3	4	5	6	7
8	9	10	11	12	13	14
15	16	17	18	19	20	21
22	23	24	25	26	27	28
29	30	31	–	–	–	–

2015

JANUARY

M	T	W	T	F	S	S
①	②	③	④	⑤	⑥	⑦
–	–	–	1	2	3	4
5	6	7	8	9	10	11
12	13	14	15	16	17	18
19	20	21	22	23	24	25
26	27	28	29	30	31	–

FEBRUARY

M	T	W	T	F	S	S
①	②	③	④	⑤	⑥	⑦
–	–	–	–	–	–	1
2	3	4	5	6	7	8
9	10	11	12	13	14	15
16	17	18	19	20	21	22
23	24	25	26	27	28	–

MARCH

M	T	W	T	F	S	S
①	②	③	④	⑤	⑥	⑦
30	31	–	–	–	–	1
2	3	4	5	6	7	8
9	10	11	12	13	14	15
16	17	18	19	20	21	22
23	24	25	26	27	28	29

APRIL

M	T	W	T	F	S	S
①	②	③	④	⑤	⑥	⑦
–	–	1	2	3	4	5
6	7	8	9	10	11	12
13	14	15	16	17	18	19
20	21	22	23	24	25	26
27	28	29	30	–	–	–

MAY

M	T	W	T	F	S	S
①	②	③	④	⑤	⑥	⑦
–	–	–	–	1	2	3
4	5	6	7	8	9	10
11	12	13	14	15	16	17
18	19	20	21	22	23	24
25	26	27	28	29	30	31

JUNE

M	T	W	T	F	S	S
①	②	③	④	⑤	⑥	⑦
1	2	3	4	5	6	7
8	9	10	11	12	13	14
15	16	17	18	19	20	21
22	23	24	25	26	27	28
29	30	–	–	–	–	–

PUBLIC HOLIDAYS 2014

JOURS FÉRIÉS GIORNI FESTIVI FEIERTAGE DÍAS FESTIVOS

The dates given below are those of national public holidays. They do not include regional, half-day or unofficial holidays. Passengers intending to travel on public holidays, or on days immediately preceding or following them, are strongly recommended to reserve seats and to confirm timings locally. Further information regarding special transport conditions applying on holiday dates may be found in the introduction to each country.

Austria: Jan. 1, 6, Apr. 21, May 1, 29, June 9, 19, Aug. 15, Nov. 1, Dec. 8, 25, 26.

Belarus: Jan. 1, 7, Mar. 8, Apr. 29, May 1, 9, July 3, Nov. 7, Dec. 25.

Belgium: Jan. 1, Apr. 21, May 1, 29, June 9, July 21, Aug. 15, Nov. 1, 11, Dec. 25.

Bosnia-Herzegovina: Jan. 1, 7, 14, 27, Mar. 1, May 1, Aug. 15, Nov. 3, 25, Dec. 25. *Other religious holidays are observed in certain areas.*

Bulgaria: Jan. 1, Mar. 3, Apr. 18, 19, 21, May 1, 6, 24, Sept. 6, 22, Dec. 24, 25, 26.

Croatia: Jan. 1, 6, Apr. 21, May 1, June 19, 25, Aug. 5, 15, Oct. 8, Nov. 1, Dec. 25, 26.

Czech Republic: Jan. 1, Apr. 21, May 1, 8, July 5, Oct. 28, Nov. 17, Dec. 24, 25, 26.

Denmark: Jan. 1, Apr. 17, 18, 21, May 16, 29, June 9, Dec. 25, 26.

Estonia: Jan. 1, Feb. 24, Apr. 18, May 1, June 23, 24, Aug. 20, Dec. 24, 25, 26.

Finland: Jan. 1, 6, Apr. 18, 21, May 1, 29, June 21, Nov. 1, Dec. 6, 25, 26.

France: Jan. 1, Apr. 21, May 1, 8, 29, June 9, July 14, Aug. 15, Nov. 1, 11, Dec. 25.

Germany: Jan. 1, 6*, Apr. 18, 21, May 1, 29, June 9, 19*, Aug. 15*, Oct. 3, 31*, Nov. 1*, 19*, Dec. 25, 26.
** Observed in certain regions: see also page 367.*

Great Britain: *England & Wales*: Jan. 1, Apr. 18, 21, May 5, 26, Aug. 25, Dec. 25, 26.
Scotland: Jan. 1, 2, Apr. 18, May 5, 26, Aug. 4, Dec. 25, 26.

Greece: Jan. 1, 6, Mar. 3, 25, Apr. 18, 21, May 1, June 9, Aug. 15, Oct. 28, Dec. 25, 26.

Hungary: Jan. 1, Mar. 15, Apr. 21, May 1, June 9, Aug. 20, Oct. 23, Nov. 1, Dec. 25, 26.

Ireland (Northern): Jan. 1, Mar. 17, Apr. 18, 21, May 5, 26, July 14, Aug. 25, Dec. 25, 26.

Ireland (Republic): Jan. 1, Mar. 17, Apr. 21, May 5, June 2, Aug. 4, Oct. 27, Dec. 25, 26.

Italy: Jan. 1, 6, Apr. 21, 25, May 1, June 2, Aug. 15, Nov. 1, Dec. 8, 25, 26. *Also regional holidays.*

Latvia: Jan. 1, Apr. 18, 21, May 1, 5, June 23, 24, Nov. 18, Dec. 24, 25, 26, 31.

Lithuania: Jan. 1, Mar. 11, Apr. 21, May 1, June 24, Aug. 15, Nov. 1, Dec. 24, 25, 26.

Luxembourg: Jan. 1, Apr. 21, May 1, 29, June 9, 23, Aug. 15, Nov. 1, Dec. 25, 26.

Macedonia: Jan. 1, 7, Apr. 21, May 1, 24, Aug. 2, Sept. 8, Oct. 11, 23, Dec. 8.

Moldova: Jan. 1, 7, 8, Mar. 8, Apr. 21, May 1, 9, Aug. 27.

Netherlands: Jan. 1, Apr. 18, 21, 26, May 5, 29, June 9, Dec. 25, 26.

Norway: Jan. 1, Apr. 17, 18, 21, May 1, 17, 29, June 9, Dec. 25, 26.

Poland: Jan. 1, 6, Apr. 21, May 1, 3, June 19, Aug. 15, Nov. 1, 11, Dec. 25, 26.

Portugal: Jan. 1, Apr. 18, 25, May 1, June 10, Aug. 15, Dec. 8, 25.

Romania: Jan. 1, 2, Apr. 21, May 1, June 9, Aug. 15, Dec. 1, 25, 26.

Russia: Jan. 1, 7, Feb. 24, Mar. 8, 10, May 1, 9, June 12, Nov. 4.

Serbia: Jan. 1, 2, 7, Feb. 15, Apr. 18, 21, May 1, 2 (May 9 and June 28 also generally observed).

Slovakia: Jan. 1, 6, Apr. 18, 21, May 1, 8, July 5, Aug. 29, Sept. 1, 15, Nov. 1, 17, Dec. 24, 25, 26.

Slovenia: Jan. 1, Feb. 8, Apr. 21, May 1, 2, June 25, Aug. 15, Oct. 31, Nov. 1, Dec. 25, 26.

Spain: Jan. 1, 6*, Mar. 19*, Apr. 17*, 18, May 1, Aug. 15*, Oct. 13, Nov. 1, Dec. 6, 8, 25. *Also some local holidays. * Observed in most regions.*

Sweden: Jan. 1, 6, Apr. 18, 21, May 1, 29, June 6, 21, Nov. 1, Dec. 25, 26.

Switzerland: Jan. 1, 2•, Mar. 19•, Apr. 18*, 21*, May 1•, 29, June 9*, 19•, Aug. 1, 15•, Nov. 1•, Dec. 8•, 25, 26*. *Also some local holidays.*
** Observed in most regions; • some regions.*

Turkey: Jan. 1, Apr. 23, May 1, 19, Aug. 30, Oct. 29 (also 2014 festival periods July 29–31, Oct. 5–8).

Ukraine: Jan. 1, 7, Mar. 8, 10, Apr. 21, May 1, 2, 9, June 9, 28, 30, Aug. 25.

MOVABLE HOLIDAYS

Fêtes mobiles – Feste mobile
Bewegliche Feste – Fiestas movibles

	2014	2015
Good Friday	Apr. 18	Apr. 3•
Easter Monday	Apr. 21	Apr. 6•
Ascension Day	May 29	May 14•
Whit Monday (Pentecost)	June 9	May 25•
Corpus Christi	June 19	June 4

• *In the Orthodox calendar: Apr. 10, Apr. 13, May 21, June 1 respectively.*

TIME COMPARISON

COMPARAISON DES HEURES COMPARAZIONE DELLE ORE ZEITVERGLEICH COMPARACIÓN DE LAS HORAS

West European Time	*WINTER: GMT* *SUMMER: GMT +1*	Ireland, Portugal, United Kingdom; Iceland *(GMT all year)*
Central European Time	*WINTER: GMT +1* *SUMMER: GMT +2*	Albania, Austria, Belgium, Bosnia, Croatia, Czech Rep., Denmark, France, Germany, Hungary, Italy, Luxembourg, Macedonia, Malta, Montenegro, Netherlands, Norway, Poland, Serbia, Slovakia, Slovenia, Spain, Sweden, Switzerland
East European Time	*WINTER: GMT +2* *SUMMER: GMT +3*	Bulgaria, Estonia, Finland, Greece, Latvia, Lithuania, Moldova, Romania, Turkey, Ukraine; Belarus *(GMT+3 all year)*; Kaliningrad *(GMT+3 all year)*
Moskva Time	GMT +4 ALL YEAR	Western Russia *(except Kaliningrad)*

Daylight Saving Time ('Summer Time') applies between 0100 GMT on March 30 and 0100 GMT on October 26, 2014 *(GMT = Greenwich Mean Time = UTC)*

Time comparison for countries which appear only in the shipping section are shown on page 542

What's new this month

WELCOME

Welcome to the June edition of the *European Rail Timetable* which, for most countries, includes updated summer schedules valid from June 15 to December 13. As usual there are a number of exceptions and readers are advised to refer to the introductory text of each country to confirm timetable validity. For example, new timings in Russia, Belarus, Ukraine and the Baltic states were introduced on June 1, whilst schedules in Great Britain changed on May 18. In Sweden the summer timetable will commence on June 29 and details will be shown in the July edition.

ROUTE OF THE MONTH

Nicky Gardner and Susanne Kries return to the rails this month with a journey across the Alps on the *Bernina Railway* from Pontresina in Switzerland to the Italian town of Tirano (Table **547**). Operated by the narrow gauge Rhätische Bahn, this is a truly fascinating and particularly scenic rail journey. This month's feature will be found on page 35.

INTERNATIONAL

The number of *TGV* services between Paris and Barcelona will be increased to four in each direction from July 6 (Table **13**).

Greece has been reconnected to the European rail network with the welcome return of the Thessaloníki – Beograd and Thessaloníki – Sofia through trains. Both services were reintroduced as planned last month and full timings are now shown in Tables **61**, **1380** and **1560**.

GREAT BRITAIN

Services between Barmouth and Pwllheli have been disrupted for several months due to a combination of ongoing storm damage repairs and bridge construction work. A replacement bus service is currently running between Harlech and Pwllheli and, with no immediate prospect of the normal rail service being restored, timings have now been included in Table **148**. Readers intending to travel in this area are advised to confirm their travel arrangements with the operator as timings could change at short notice.

The First TransPennine Express service between Manchester and Scotland (Table **151**) has been enhanced following the delivery of new electric trains. There is now an hourly service between Manchester and Carlisle with alternate trains serving Edinburgh and Glasgow.

As part of the 'Northern Hub' project, the number of First TransPennine Express trains between Leeds and Manchester have been increased from four to five per hour on Mondays to Saturdays (Table **188**). The hourly Newcastle service now runs to and from Liverpool via Manchester Victoria, thus providing two direct Leeds to Liverpool services per hour (the other continuing to run via Manchester Piccadilly). The extra space required to show this expanded service has meant that Tables **190** and **192** have had to be temporarily relocated to page 337.

FRANCE

The direct service from Paris to Royan (Table **301**) will not run this summer.

From July 5 the through service between Bordeaux and Clermont Ferrand is expected to be withdrawn between Ussel and Clermont Ferrand (Table **326**).

Services to and from Genève via Bellegarde will be severely disrupted from July 15 to August 29 in the next phase of work to improve the route between Lyon and the Swiss border. During this period most cross border services will be replaced by bus between Bellegarde and Genève or, in some cases, cancelled altogether. This includes many *TGV* services between Paris and Genève, although alternative connections will be available via Lausanne.

SWITZERLAND

There are amendments to several Swiss tables from June 15. Most notable is the restructure of services via the Gotthard pass between Zürich and Milano. International services now operate every two hours 0732 - 1932 from Zürich and 0825 - 2025 from Milano Centrale. One train pair between Luzern and Milano also operates (Table **550**).

ITALY

New schedules will come into force from June 15. Only partial information was available as we went to press, but all trains shown in our tables with a train number have been checked and amended where necessary although timings around holiday dates should be verified locally. Minor alterations to local services are also expected and will be shown in subsequent editions.

SPAIN

Additional services have been introduced on the routes from Palma to sa Pobla and Manacor (Table **674**).

DENMARK

The usual plethora of engineering work is affecting several lines once again this summer.

The København to Kalundborg route is disrupted until August 17 when no direct services will operate; passengers will be required to complete part of the journey by bus between either Lejre or Hvalsø (both west of Roskilde) and Holbæk. Table **704** has been updated to show the temporary schedules.

København to Helsingør is also disrupted whilst bridge works take place. From June 21 to July 20 passengers will be required to use S-tog Line C between Østerport and Klampenborg for journeys to and from Helsingør (Table **703**).

In addition, Århus to Grenaa is partially closed until October 17 whilst work takes place in connection with construction of the new Århus light rail system (Table **728**). Replacement bus services are provided.

ICELAND

Further minor alterations have been made to summer schedules and Table **729** has been updated.

GERMANY

From June 14 to July 27 timings and stopping patterns of services between Hamburg and Hannover are subject to alteration in the latest phase of work to upgrade this particular route. During this period many *IC* services are suspended between Hannover and Hamburg, whilst *ICE* services are diverted or make additional station stops resulting in extended journey times.

AUSTRIA

A new timetable valid from May 31 has been introduced on the narrow gauge *Mariazellerbahn* between St Pölten and Mariazell (Table **994**). Most services are operated by a brand new fleet of electric multiple unit trains, although a traditional loco-hauled service continues to operate on Saturdays, with a steam service also running on selected dates.

POLAND

Retimings are expected from June 15, but unfortunately information was not available as we went to press. We hope to show updated schedules next month.

SLOVAKIA

Following a period of suspension, the international bus service between Poprad Tatry and Zakopane (Table **1183**) is expected to recommence on June 15.

HUNGARY

Summer timings for lines around Lake Balaton will be in effect from June 21 to August 31 and have been incorporated into this edition, along with further amendments from June 21. From that date the *IC* trains between Budapest and Eger (Table **1261**) will no longer carry the InterCity classification and will therefore no longer require compulsory reservation.

ALBANIA

Further changes have been made to the timetable following restructure of Hekurudha Shqiptarë (Albanian Railways) into business units (Table **1390**).

CONTINUED ON PAGE 576

EXPLANATION OF STANDARD SYMBOLS

	EXPLANATION OF SYMBOLS	*EXPLICATION DES SIGNES*	*DELUCIDAZIONE DEI SEGNI*	*ZEICHENERKLÄRUNG*	*EXPLICACIÓN DE LOS SIGNOS*
	SERVICES	**SERVICES**	**SERVIZI**	**DIENSTE**	**SERVICIOS**
12	Through service (1st and 2nd class seats)	Relation directe (places assises 1re et 2e classe)	Relazione diretta (con posti di 1a e 2a classe)	Direkte Verbindung (Sitzplätze 1. und 2. Klasse)	Relación directa (con asientos de 1a y 2a clase)
	Sleeping car	Voiture-lits	Carrozza letti	Schlafwagen	Coche-camas
	Couchette car	Voiture-couchettes	Carrozza cuccette	Liegewagen	Coche-literas
✕	Restaurant car	Voiture-restaurant	Carrozza ristorante	Speisewagen	Coche-restaurante
	Snacks and drinks available *(see page 8)*	Voiture-bar ou vente ambulante *(voir page 8)*	Carrozza bar o servizio di buffet *(vedere pagina 8)*	Imbiss und Getränke im Zug *(siehe Seite 8)*	Servicio de cafetería o bar móvil *(véase pág. 8)*
2	Second class only	Uniquement deuxième classe	Sola seconda classe	Nur zweite Klasse	Sólo segunda clase
	Bus or coach service	Service routier	Servizio automobilistico	Buslinie	Servicio de autobuses
	Shipping service	Service maritime	Servizio marittimo	Schifffahrtslinie	Servicio marítimo
	DAYS OF RUNNING	**JOURS DE CIRCULATION**	**GIORNI DI EFFETTUAZIONE**	**VERKEHRSTAGE**	**DÍAS DE CIRCULACIÓN**
⚒	Mondays to Saturdays except holidays*	Du lundi au samedi, sauf les fêtes*	Dal lunedì al sabato, salvo i giorni festivi*	Montag bis Samstag außer Feiertage*	De lunes a sábado, excepto festivos*
Ⓐ	Mondays to Fridays except holidays*	Du lundi au vendredi, sauf les fêtes*	Dal lunedì al venerdì, salvo i giorni festivi*	Montag bis Freitag außer Feiertage*	De lunes a viernes, excepto festivos*
Ⓑ	Daily except Saturdays	Tous les jours sauf les samedis	Giornalmente, salvo il sabato	Täglich außer Samstag	Diario excepto sábados
Ⓒ	Saturdays, Sundays and holidays*	Les samedis, dimanches et fêtes*	Sabato, domenica e giorni festivi*	Samstage, Sonn- und Feiertage*	Sábados, domingos y festivos*
†	Sundays and holidays*	Les dimanches et fêtes*	Domenica e giorni festivi*	Sonn- und Feiertage*	Domingos y festivos*
①②	Mondays, Tuesdays	Les lundis, mardis	Lunedì, martedì	Montag, Dienstag	Lunes, martes
③④	Wednesdays, Thurdays	Les mercredis, jeudis	Mercoledì, giovedì	Mittwoch, Donnerstag	Miércoles, jueves
⑤⑥	Fridays, Saturdays	Les vendredis, samedis	Venerdì, sabato	Freitag, Samstag	Viernes, sábados
⑦	Sundays	Les dimanches	Domenica	Sonntag	Domingos
①–④	Mondays to Thursdays	Des lundis aux jeudis	Dal lunedì al giovedì	Montag bis Donnerstag	De lunes a jueves
	OTHER SYMBOLS	**AUTRES SIGNES**	**ALTRI SIMBOLI**	**SONSTIGE SYMBOLE**	**OTROS SÍMBOLOS**
IC **29**	Train number (**bold figures** above train times)	Numéro du train (en **caractères gras** au-dessus de l'horaire du train)	Numero del treno (in **neretto** sopra gli orari del treno)	Zugnummer (über den Fahrplanzeiten in **fetter Schrift** gesetzt)	Número del tren (figura en **negrita** encima del horario del tren)
◆	See footnotes (listed by train number)	Renvoi aux notes données en bas de page (dans l'ordre numérique des trains)	Vedi in calce alla pagina l'annotazione corrispondente al numero del treno	Siehe die nach Zugnummern geordneten Fußnoten	Véase al pie de la página la nota correspondiente al número del tren
R	Reservation compulsory	Réservation obligatoire	Prenotazione obbligatoria	Reservierung erforderlich	Reserva obligatoria
	Frontier station	Gare frontalière	Stazione di frontiera	Grenzbahnhof	Estación fronteriza
	Airport	Aéroport	Aeroporto	Flughafen	Aeropuerto
|	Train does not stop	Sans arrêt	Il treno non ferma qui	Zug hält nicht	El tren no para aquí
—	Separates two trains in the same column between which no connection is possible	Sépare deux trains de la même colonne qui ne sont pas en correspondance	Separa due treni della stessa colonna che non sono in coincidenza	Trennt zwei in derselben Spalte angegebene Züge, zwischen denen kein Anschluß besteht	Separa dos trenes de la misma columna entre los cuales no hay enlace
→	Continued in later column	Suite dans une colonne à droite	Continuazione più avanti a destra	Fortsetzung weiter rechts	Continuación a la derecha
←	Continued from earlier column	Suite d'une colonne à gauche	Seguito di una colonna a sinistra	Fortsetzung von links	Continuación desde la izquierda
v.v.	Vice versa	Vice versa	Viceversa	Umgekehrt	A la inversa
	** Public holiday dates for each country are given on page 2.* *Other, special symbols are explained in table footnotes or in the introduction to each country.*	** Les dates des fêtes légales nationales sont données en page 2.* *D'autres signes particuliers sont expliqués dans les notes ou bien dans l'avant-propos relatif à chaque pays.*	** Per le date dei giorni festivi civili nei diversi paesi vedere pagina 2.* *Altri segni particolari vengono spiegati nelle note in calce ai quadri o nella introduzione attinente a ogni paese.*	** Gesetzlichen Feiertage der jeweiligen Länder finden Sie auf Seite 2.* *Besondere Symbole sind in den Fußnoten bzw. in der Einleitung zu den einzelnen Ländern erklärt.*	** Las fechas de los días festivos en cada país figuran en la página 2.* *La explicación de otros signos particulares se da en las notas o en el preámbulo correspondiente a cada país.*

What is the European Rail Timetable?

The European Rail Timetable is a concise guide to rail and ferry schedules throughout Europe, and even includes each month an area of the world outside Europe. Needless to say, it cannot be comprehensive (it would run into thousands of pages), but through our knowledge and experience, together with valuable feedback from our readers, we can select those services which we believe will satisfy the needs of most travellers.

When do the services change?

There is a major annual timetable change in mid-December affecting almost all European countries, with many countries having a second change in mid-June. There are, of course, exceptions. For example, the British summer timetable starts in late May, Sweden changes again in mid-August, whilst Russia and the other CIS countries have their main change at the end of May. Many holiday areas also have separate timetables for the high-summer period, particularly areas of France and Italy. In fact, changes can happen at any time of year, and railways issue amendments either on set dates or as and when necessary. Engineering work also causes frequent changes, and shipping schedules can change at any time.

How are the trains selected for inclusion?

People travel for many reasons, whether for leisure, business, sightseeing, visiting friends or relations, or just for the fun of it, and there are no hard and fast rules for selecting the services that we show. Naturally, major towns and inter-city services are shown as a matter of course, but the level of smaller places and local trains shown will depend on the country and even the area. It's surprising just how many minor lines we manage to squeeze in! Generally we will show a greater number of local trains in areas which are popular tourist destinations or where other services are sparse.

It is not possible to show suburban trains within cities or conurbations, or most outer-suburban routes to places close to large cities. However, where there are places of particular interest or importance in this category we do try to show brief details of frequency and journey time.

When should I use the International section?

The rail tables are divided into two sections - International (Tables **9** to **99**) and Country by Country (Tables **100** upwards). For some international services between adjacent countries (for example Stockholm - Oslo or Hamburg - Århus) it is necessary to use the relevant Country tables - the index or maps will guide you. Local trains which cross international frontiers will usually only be found in the Country sections.

Some international trains also carry passengers internally within each country and will therefore be found in the Country tables as well as the International section. Some services are primarily for international travel and will therefore only be found in the International section - this includes *Eurostar* trains (London - Paris / Brussels) and *Thalys* services (Paris - Brussels - Amsterdam / Köln), as well as certain long-distance night trains.

What about places outside Europe?

The European Rail Timetable includes the whole of Turkey and Russia. Furthermore, our **Beyond Europe** section at the back of each edition features timetables from a different area of the world each month. There are six areas (each twice yearly), covering **India** (Jan/July), **South East Asia, Australia and New Zealand** (Feb/Aug), **China** (March/Sept), **Japan** (April/Oct), **Africa and the Middle East** (May/Nov), and **North America** (June/Dec).

What else does it contain?

A summary of international sleeper services will be found on page 33, listing types of accommodation, operators and facilities on board.

A summary of European rail passes will be found on page 34. A more detailed version of this appears in our **Seasonal Summer** and **Winter** editions.

Each month a different rail journey is described in our *Route of the Month* feature, written by Nicky Gardner and Susanne Kries, editors of Hidden Europe magazine.

Our timetables and other products may be purchased from our website **www.europeanrailtimetable.eu**.

HOW TO USE THE TIMETABLE

Using the index

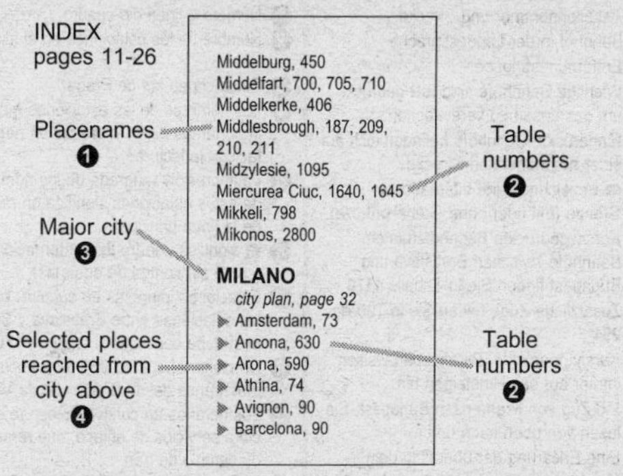

Look up the two places between which you are travelling. It can often be helpful to start your search from the *smaller* of the two locations. ❺

Using the maps

The maps can be the quickest way of finding the required table number, if you already know the geographical location of the places required. ❿

COMMENT TROUVER VOTRE TRAIN

❶ Localité.
❷ Numéros des tableaux.
❸ Grande ville.
❹ Localités sélectionnées à gagner de la grande ville en haut.
❺ Cherchez les deux bouts du parcours désiré sur la liste des villes. Commencer par la ville de moindre importance peut faciliter la recherche.
❻ Ligne principale.
❼ Ligne secondaire.
❽ Ligne à grande vitesse.
❾ Liaison en autocar.
❿ La consultation des cartes – si vous savez déjà la location géographique de vos points de départ et d'arrivée – est le moyen le plus rapide de repérer les numéros des tableaux relatifs à votre parcours.

COME TROVARE IL VOSTRO TRENO

❶ Località.
❷ Numeri dei quadri-orario.
❸ Grandi città.
❹ Principali destinazione raggiungibili dalla località in neretto sopra.
❺ Cercate le localita' tra le quali dovrete viaggiare; spesso può essere di aiuto iniziare la ricerca dalla località più piccola.
❻ Principale linea ferroviaria.
❼ Linea ferroviaria secondaria.
❽ Linea ad alta velocità.
❾ Autobus.
❿ Le mappe sono il metodo più rapido per trovare i numeri dei quadri-orario di cui avete bisogno, quando gia' siete a conoscenza della collocazione geografica delle localita' di partenza e arrivo del vostro viaggio.

WIE FINDE ICH MEINEN ZUG?

❶ Ortsname.
❷ Tabellennummer.
❸ Großstadt.
❹ Knotenpunkte erreichbar von der Großstadt oben.
❺ Suchen Sie Ihre Start- und Endbahnhof im Ortsverzeichnis. Dazu empfehlen wir, Ihre Suche aus der Richtung des *kleineren* Ortes aufzunehmen.
❻ Hauptstrecke.
❼ Nebenstrecke.
❽ Hochgeschwindigkeitsstrecke.
❾ Busverbindung.
❿ Kennen Sie die geographische Lage der Ausgangs- und Bestimmungsorte Ihrer Reise, dann empfehlen wir einen Blick in die im Kursbuch enthaltene Übersichtskarte.

COMO BUSCAR SU TREN

❶ Localidad.
❷ Números de los cuadros horarios.
❸ Gran ciudad.
❹ Principales destinos accesibles a través de esta localidad.
❺ Busque los dos lugares a través de los cuales viaja. Normalmente facilita la búsqueda empezar por la localidad más pequeña.
❻ Línea principal.
❼ Línea secundaria.
❽ Línea de alta velocidad.
❾ Línea de autobuses.
❿ Los mapas pueden ser la forma más rápida de encontrar los cuadros que debe consultar, si ya conoce el punto de inicio y conclusión de su viaje.

Numbers in circles refer to translations below

Reading the tables

Trains run daily unless otherwise shown by symbol or footnote 15

Table number and route 1

Station names in local language 2

Distance from Praha in km 3

Important stations are shown in **bold** for clarity 4

Indented station: shows a branch off the main route of the table 5

d. = depart, a. = arrive (the first time in a column is always a departure time, the last is an arrival). 14

Train category (where shown) 13

Train number (where shown) 12

Standard symbols (e.g. Ⓐ, 🄁, ✕) are explained on page 4.

Other symbols (e.g. ⊖) and letters (**E**, **r**) are explained below the table.

♦ means footnotes are listed by train number. 11

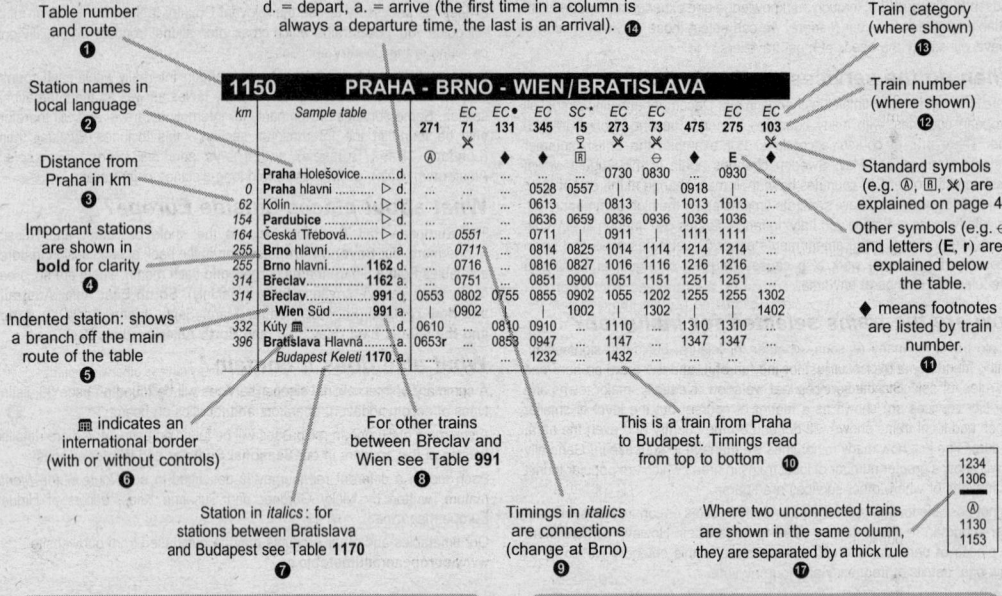

1150 PRAHA - BRNO - WIEN / BRATISLAVA

km	*Sample table*										
			EC	*EC•*	*EC*	*SC**	*EC*	*EC*		*EC*	*EC*
		271	**71**	**131**	**345**	**15**	**273**	**73**	**475**	**275**	**103**
			✕			🍷	✕	✕			✕
		Ⓐ		♦	♦	🄁		⊖	♦	**E**	♦
	Praha Holešovice .... d.	...	...	...	...	...	0730	0830	...	0930	...
0	**Praha** hlavni .... ▷ d.	...	...	...	0528	0557	|	|	0918	|	...
62	Kolín .... ▷ d.	...	...	...	0613	|	0813	|	1013	1013	...
154	**Pardubice** .... ▷ d.	...	...	...	0636	0659	0836	0936	1036	1036	...
164	Česká Třebová .... ▷ d.	...	*0551*	...	0711	|	0911	|	1111	1111	...
255	**Brno** hlavní .... a.	...	*0711*	...	0814	0825	1014	1114	1214	1214	...
255	**Brno** hlavní .... **1162** d.	...	0716	...	0816	0827	1016	1116	1216	1216	...
314	**Břeclav** .... **1162** a.	...	0751	...	0851	0900	1051	1151	1251	1251	...
314	**Břeclav** .... **991** d.	0553	0802	0755	0855	0902	1055	1202	1255	1255	1302
	Wien Süd .... **991** a.	|	0902	|	|	1002	|	1302	|	|	1402
332	Kúty 🛃 .... d.	0610	...	0810	0910	...	1110	...	1310	1310	...
396	**Bratislava** Hlavná .... a.	0653r	...	0853	0947	...	1147	...	1347	1347	...
	Budapest Keleti **1170** a.	...	...	...	1232	...	1432	...	...	...	...

🛃 indicates an international border (with or without controls) 6

For other trains between Břeclav and Wien see Table **991** 8

This is a train from Praha to Budapest. Timings read from top to bottom 10

Station in *italics*: for stations between Bratislava and Budapest see Table **1170** 7

Timings in *italics* are connections (change at Brno) 9

Where two unconnected trains are shown in the same column, they are separated by a thick rule 17

1234
1306
▬▬
Ⓐ
1130
1153

CLASSES OF TRAVEL:
Trains have 1st and 2nd class seats unless otherwise shown. However, local trains may only have 2nd class seats. 15

TIME ZONES:
Times are in local time (Russian times are in Moscow time). For time zones see page 2. Timings are given in 24 hour clock (see page 9). 16

COMMENT LIRE LES TABLEAUX

1. Numéro et parcours du tableau.
2. Nom de la gare en langue locale.
3. La distance en km de Praha.
4. Les noms de gares importantes sont imprimés en **gras** pour faciliter la lecture.
5. La mise en retrait des noms de gares indique une ligne d'embranchement.
6. 🛃 indique une frontière internationale (avec ou sans le contrôle).
7. Les noms de gares imprimés en *italique*: vous trouverez des gares sur le trajet Bratislava - Budapest en consultant le tableau **1170**.
8. Consultez le tableau **991** pour trouver des trains supplémentaires de Břeclav à Wien.
9. Les heures en *italique* indiquent une *correspondance* et supposent dans tous les cas un changement de train.
10. Ici un train de Praha à Budapest. Lire de haut en bas.
11. Les signes conventionnels sont expliqués à la page 4. Les autres signes et lettres sont expliqués en bas du tableau. Le symbole ♦ à l'en-tête d'une colonne signifie qu'il faut consulter le note qui porte le numéro du train concerné.
12. Le numéro du train (en cas échéant).
13. Indication de catégorie (en cas échéant).
14. d. = départ, a. = arrivée. Pour chaque train la *première* mention est toujours une heure de *départ*, la *dernière* toujours une heure d'*arrivée*.
15. Sauf indication contraire, les trains circulent *tous les jours* et y compris des places assises de 1ère et 2ème classe.
16. Toutes les indications horaires sont données en heures locales (voir page 2). En Russie c'est à l'heure Moskva.
17. Deux trains de la même colonne qui ne sont pas en correspondance sont separés par une règle épaisse.

COME SI CONSULTA UN QUADRO ORARIO

1. Numero del quadro e percorso.
2. Nome della stazione nella lingua locale.
3. Distanze in km da Praha.
4. I nomi delle stazioni piu' importante sono stampati in **neretto** per renderne più facile la lettura.
5. I nomi delle stazioni rientrati rispetto alla colonna principale indicano una diramazione dal percorso principale del quadro-orario in questione.
6. 🛃 indica una stazione di confine (con o senza controllo).
7. Stazioni in *corsivo*: per gli orari tra le stazione di Bratislava e Budapest bisogna consultare il quadro **1170**.
8. Consultare il quadro **991** per ulteriori treni da Břeclav a Wien.
9. Gli orari *in corsivo* si riferiscono a servizi *in coincidenza* che implicano un cambio di treno.
10. Questo e' un treno da Praha a Budapest. La lettura viene fatta dall'alto verso il basso.
11. I simboli convenzionali sono spiegate a pagina 4. Altri simboli e lettere sono spiegati sotto il quadro-orario in questione. Il simbolo ♦ all'inizio di una colonna-orario significa che bisogna fare riferimento alla nota corrispondente al numero del treno in questione.
12. Numero del treno (quando indicato).
13. Classificazione del treno (quando indicato).
14. d. = partenza, a. = arrivo. Notare che l'orario che compare per *primo* nel quadro-orario è sempre un l'orario di *partenza*, mentre quello che compare per *ultimo* è sempre l'orario di *arrivo*.
15. Se non ci sono altre indicazioni i treni si intendono giornalieri, con prima e seconda classe di viaggio.
16. Gli orari sono sempre espressi in ora locale (in Russia e' utilizzati l'ora di Mosca). Per informazioni sui fusi orari vedere a pagina 2.
17. Quando nella colonna-orario ci sono due treni che non sono in coincidenza tra loro, questo e' indicato dalla linea in grassetto che li separa.

WIE LESE ICH DIE FAHRPLÄNE

1. Tabellennummer und Strecke.
2. Bahnhof in der Landessprache.
3. Entfernungsangabe.
4. Wichtige Bahnhöfe sind **fett** gedruckt um das Lesen zu vereinfachen.
5. Eingerückte Bahnhöfe befinden sich auf einer abzweigenden Strecke.
6. 🛃 Bezeichnet eine internationale Grenze (mit oder ohne Grenzkontrolle).
7. *Kursiv* gedruckte Bahnhofsnamen: Bahnhöfe zwischen Bratislava und Budapest finden Sie in Tabelle **1170**.
8. Zusätzliche Züge finden Sie in Tabelle **991**.
9. *Kursiv* gedruckte Zeitangaben weisen immer auf das Umsteigen hin.
10. Ein Zug von Praha nach Budapest. Sie lesen von oben nach unten.
11. Eine Erklärung der überall in dem Kursbuch verwendeten konventionellen Zeichen finden Sie auf Seite 4. Anderen Zeichen und Buchstaben finden Sie unter der Fahrplantabelle. Das Zeichen ♦ im Kopf der Zugspalte bedeutet: Sehen Sie bei der Fußnote des Zuges mit der betreffenden Zugnummer nach.
12. Zugnummer (wo zutreffend).
13. Zuggattung (wo zutreffend).
14. d. = Abfahrt, a. = Ankunft. Es handelt sich stets bei der ersten für einen Zug angegebenen Zeit um eine Abfahrtzeit, bei der letzten um eine Ankunftzeit.
15. Sofern nicht anders angemeldet, verkehren die Züge *täglich*. Im Allgemeinen führen die Züge die 1. und 2. Wagenklasse.
16. Fahrzeiten sind immer in der jeweiligen Landeszeit angegeben (Seite 2). Russische Fahrzeiten sind auf Moskauer Zeit.
17. Im Falle von zwei Züge in der gleichen Spalte ohne Anschlussmöglichkeit, liegt das Zeichen ▬▬ zwischen den Zügen.

COMO LEER LOS CUADROS

1. Número y línea del cuadro.
2. Nombre de las estaciones en el idioma local.
3. Distancia en km de Praga.
4. Los nombres de las estaciones más importantes están impresas en **negrita** facilitar la lectura.
5. La impresión sangrada de los nombres de estas estaciones significa un ramal de la línea principal.
6. 🛃 significa una frontera internacional (con o sin control de aduanas).
7. Estaciones impresas en *cursiva*: para las estaciones entre Bratislava y Budapest debe consultar el cuadro **1170**.
8. Consultar el cuadro **991** para encontrar más trenes desde Břeclav hasta Viena.
9. Los horarios en cursiva, hacen referencia a servicios de enlace, que requieren un cambio de tren.
10. Esto un tren desde Praga hasta Budapest. Leer de arriba a abajo.
11. La explicación de los signos convencionales se da en la página 4. Ostros símbolos y letras se explican al pie del cuadro. El símbolo ♦ en el encabezamiento de la columna quiere decir: consulte la nota que lleva el número del tren interesado.
12. Número de tren (si se indica).
13. Tipo de tren (si se indica).
14. d. = salida, a. = llegada. Nótese que el primer horario indicado en las columnas es siempre un horario de salida, y el último un horario de llegada.
15. Salvo indicación contraria, los trenes circulan a *diario* y llevan plazas sentadas de primera y segunda clases.
16. Todas las indicaciones horarias son en horario local (Para Rusia se utiliza la hora local de Moscú). Para comprobar las franjas horarias mirar la página 2. Los horarios utilizan el sistema horario de 24h (ver página 9).
17. Cuando dos trenes que no tienen conexión aparecen en la misma columna, estos se encuentran separados por el símbolo ▬▬.

Reading the footnotes

These footnotes relate to the sample table on page 6 ❶

In certain tables, footnotes are listed by train number, shown by ♦ on relevant trains ❷

♦ – NOTES (LISTED BY TRAIN NUMBERS)

102/3 – POLONIA – [12] ✕ Warszawa - Ostrava - Břeclav - Wien and v.v.

131 – MORAVIA – [12] Bohumin - Ostrava - Břeclav - Bratislava.

345 – AVALA – [12] ✕ Praha - Bratislava - Budapest - Beograd. Conveys on ⑤ June 12 - Sept. 18 ▬ 2 cl. Praha - Beograd (335) - Thessaloniki.

475 – JADRAN – June 19 - Sept. 4. 🛏 1, 2 cl., ▬ 2 cl., [2] Praha - Bratislava - Zagreb - Split (Table 92); [12] Praha - Bratislava.

E – SLOVAN, not June 19 - Sept. 4.

r – 0659 on ©.

▷ – See also Table 1160.

⊖ – Runs 10 mins later on Aug. 15.

• – *Ex* in Slovakia.

* – Pendolino tilting train. Classified *EC* in Austria.

OTHER TRAIN NAMES:

71 – GUSTAV MAHLER

73 – FRANZ SCHUBERT

Letters and symbols may be found above the timings (e.g. **E**) or against individual times (e.g. **r**).

Symbols may also appear in the station column (e.g. ▷). ❻

Train names are sometimes listed separately. ❺

Train **345** is named 'AVALA' and runs daily from Praha to Beograd with 1st and 2nd class seats and a restaurant car. On Fridays June 12 to September 18, a through couchette car runs from Praha to Thessaloniki, attached to train **335** between Beograd and Thessaloniki. ❸

Train **475** is named 'JADRAN' and runs only from June 19 to September 4. It has a sleeper, couchettes and second class seats from Praha to Split via Bratislava and Zagreb, as well as first and second class seats only going as far as Bratislava. Further details will be found in Table **92**. ❹

Always read the footnotes; they may contain important information. Standard symbols are explained on page 4. ❼

Dates shown are where a train **starts** its journey (unless otherwise noted). Some notes show both directions of the train (e.g. **102/3**) with "and v.v." ❽

FURTHER HINTS ON READING THE TIMETABLE

- Refer to the introduction to each country for important information such as train types, supplements, compulsory reservation, and the dates of validity of the timings. Exceptions are noted in individual tables.
- For dates of public holidays see page 2.
- Please allow adequate time for changing trains, especially at large stations. Connections are not guaranteed, especially when late running occurs (connecting trains are sometimes held for late running trains).
- A Glossary of common terms appears on page 10.

LES NOTES EN BAS DU TABLEAU

❶ Ces notes se rapportent au example de tableau à la page 6.

❷ Dans certains tableaux, le symbole ♦ à l'en-tête d'une colonne signifie qu'il faut consulter le note qui porte le numéro du train concerné.

❸ Le train **345** s'appelle AVALA et circule tous les jours de Praha à Beograd avec des places assises de 1ère et 2ème classe et une voiture-restaurant. Tous les vendredis du 12 juin jusqu'au 18 sept il y a aussi une voiture-couchettes de Praha à Thessaloniki, qui se joint au train **335** entre Beograd et Thessaloniki.

❹ Le train **475** s'appelle JADRAN et circule seulement entre le 19 juin et le 4 septembre. Il compris des voitures-lits, couchettes et places assises de 2ème classe à Split via Zagreb, et des places assises de 1ère et 2ème classe jusqu'à Bratislava. Voir le tableau **92**.

❺ Les noms des trains sont parfois indiqués séparément.

❻ Les lettres et signes sont situés à l'en-tête d'une colonne ou à côté d'une heure dans la colonne. Une signe peut sortir également a côté d'un nom de gare.

❼ Les notes peuvent vous donner des informations importantes. Les signes conventionnels sont expliqués à la page 4.

❽ Sauf indication contraire, les jours et dates de circulation mentionnés sont ceux applicables à la *gare d'origine* du train (mentionnée si elle ne figure pas sur le tableau même dans les notes). Les notes peuvent expliquer les deux sens d'un train (e.g. **102/3**) utilisant "and v.v." (et vice versa).

PLUS DE CONSEILS

- Il vous est fortement recommandé de consulter aussi l'introduction à chaque section nationale: vous y trouverez des précisions concernant la classification des trains, les prestations offertes à bord des trains, les suppléments, la réservation des places, etc.
- Jours fériés - voir page 2.
- Aucune correspondance n'est garantie pourtant. N'oubliez pas non plus que dans les grandes gares les changements peuvent entraîner une longue marche et l'emprunt d'escaliers.
- Lexique - voir page 10.

NOTE ALLA FINE DEL QUADRO-ORARIO

❶ Queste note si riferiscono all' esempio a pagina 6.

❷ In certi quadri-orario, il simbolo ♦ nelle note di testa significa che bisogna fare riferimento alla nota con il numero di treno corrispondente.

❸ Il treno **345** si chiama AVALA ed e' giornaliero tra Praha a Beograd con posti di 1ª e 2ª classe e carrozza ristorante. Il venerdì dal 12 giugno fino al 18 settembre e' aggiunta a Beograd una carrozza cuccette diretta a Thessaloniki, combinandosi con il treno **335** tra Beograd e Thessaloniki.

❹ Il treno **475** si chiama JADRAN ed e' operativo solo dal 19 giugno al 4 settembre. Il treno si compone di carrozze letti, carrozze cuccette, e posti di 2ª classe tra Praha e Split, via Bratislava e Zagrabria; inoltre ci sono anche posti di 1ª e 2ª classe fino a Bratislava. Consultare anche il quadro-orario **92** al riguardo

❺ I nomi dei treni sono talvolta indicati separatamente.

❻ Lettere e simboli possono essere sia alla testa di una colonna-orario, che accanto all'orario del treno stesso. Un simbolo potrebbe anche essere accanto al nome di una stazione.

❼ E' importante leggere sempre le note a le informazioni a fine quadro. I segni convenzionali sono elencati e spiegati a pagina 4.

❽ Salvo casi in cui sia diversamente indicato, le date di circolazione dei treni si riferiscono sempre alla stazione dove il treno inizia il suo viaggio (come viene riportato nelle note a fine quadro, e Inoltre nel quadro stesso).

ALTRI CONSIGLI UTILI

- Vi consigliamo vivamente di consultare anche l'introduzione dedicata ad ogni nazione. Troverete importanti informazioni riguardanti i servizi di trasporto di ciascun paese, così come le categorie dei treni, la ristorazione, il pagamento di supplementi, le necessità di prenotazione, ecc.
- I giorni festivi suddivisi per paese sono elencati a pagina 2.
- Le coincidenze indicate non sono garantite. Tenete presente che che nelle grandi stazioni il trasferimento tra due binari potrebbe significare un lungo tratto da percorrere a piedi e con l'uso di scale.
- Il glossario si trova a pagina 10.

FUSSNOTEN

❶ Fußnoten beziehen sich auf die Beispieltabelle auf Seite 6.

❷ ♦: Sehen Sie bei der Fußnote des Zuges mit der betreffenden Zugnummer nach.

❸ Zug **345** heißt AVALA und fährt täglich zwischen Praha und Beograd mit Sitzplätzen 1. und 2. Klasse. An Freitagen vom 12. Juni bis 18. September führt dieser Zug durchgehende Liegewagen von Praha nach Thessaloniki (mit Zug **335** vereinigt von Beograd nach Thessaloniki).

❹ Zug **475** heißt JADRAN und fährt nur von 19. Juni bis 4. September. Er führt Schlaf-, Liege und Sitzwagen 2. Klasse von Praha nach Split über Zagreb, auch Sitzwagen 1. und 2. Klasse, die nur bis Bratislava fahren. Auf Tabelle **92** finden Sie weitere Informationen.

❺ Zugnamen können besonders aufgeführt sein.

❻ Zeichen und Buchstaben finden sich im Kopf der Zugspalte oder neben einer bestimmten Zeitangabe. Zeichen sind auch in der Bahnhofsspalte möglich.

❼ In Fußnoten findet man wichtige Informationen. Standardzeichen sind auf Seite 4 erklärt.

❽ Die erwähnten Tage und Zeitabschnitte für Züge, die nicht täglich verkehren, gelten für den Ausgangsbahnhof des Zuges (wenn dieser nicht in der Tabelle steht, ist er in einer Fußnote erwähnt). Fußnoten dürfen beide Richtungen erklären (z.B. **102/3**), mit "and v.v." (und umgekehrt).

WEITERE HINWEISE

- Es ist zu empfehlen, die Einleitungen zu jedem einzelnen Land zu lesen. Darin werden Sie wichtige Informationen über die Besonderheiten jedes Landes finden: Zugcharakterisierung, Services an Bord der Züge, Zuschlagpflicht, Reservierungsbedingungen usw.
- Feiertage - siehe Seite 2.
- Anschlussversäumnisse durch Verspätung oder Ausfall von Zügen sind immer möglich. Bitte beachten Sie, dass auf Großstadtbahnhöfen häufig längere Fußwege zurückgelegt bzw. Treppen benutzen werden müssen.
- Glossar - siehe Seite 10.

LAS NOTAS AL PIE DEL CUADRO

❶ Estas notas hacen referencia al ejemplo de la página 6.

❷ El símbolo ♦ ciertas tablas horarias significa: que hay que consultar la nota a pie de página con el número correspondiente.

❸ El Tren **345** se llama AVALA y circula a diario entre Praga y Belgrado con plazas sentadas de 1ra y 2da clase, además de con coche-restaurante. Los Viernes del 12 de junio al 18 de septiembre el tren lleva coches litera desde Praga hasta Tesalónica que se combinan con el tren **335** entre Belgrado y Tesalónica.

❹ El Tren **475** se llama JADRAN y circula solamente del 19 de junio al 4 de septiembre. El Tren **475** se llama JADRAN y circula solamente del 19 de junio al 4 de sept. El tren dispone de lleva vagones de coches cama, litera, y plazas sentadas de 2da clase entre Praga y Split a través de Zagreb, también plazas sentadas de 1ra y 2da clase hasta Bratislava. Consulte el cuadro **92**.

❺ Los nombres de los Trenes a veces son enumerados por separado.

❻ Las letras y signos se encuentran en el encabezamiento de las distintas columnas horarias o adyacentes a horas de salida individuales. Los símbolos también pueden aparecer en la columna de la estación.

❼ Lea siempre las notas a pie de cuadro ya que pueden contener información importante. La explicación de los signos convencionales se da en la página 4.

❽ Salvo indicación contraria los días y fechas de circulación de los trenes son aquéllos mencionados en la estación de *origen* del tren. Algunas notas muestran ambas direcciones del tren mediante la nota "and v.v." (y viceversa).

INFORMACIÓN ADICIONAL

- Se recomienda vivamente que consulte también los preámbulos al comienzo de cada sección nacional: le proporcionarán datos importantes sobre las particularidades de cada país: tipos de trenes, restauración, pago de suplementos, y necesidades de reservación anticipada.
- Días festivos - cunsulte la página 2.
- Los trasbordos no se pueden garantizar, sobretodo en el caso de retrasos. Hay que ser consciente también que el trasbordo en las estaciones de grandes ciudades puede suponer un desplazamiento bastante largo a pie y el uso de escaleras.
- Glosario - cunsulte la página 10.

The following is designed to be a concise guide to travelling in Europe by train. For more details of accommodation available, catering, supplements etc., see the introduction to each country.

BUYING YOUR TICKET

Train tickets must be purchased before travelling, either from travel agents or at the station ticket office (or machine). Where a station has neither a ticket office nor a ticket machine, the ticket may usually be purchased on the train.

Tickets which are not dated when purchased (for example in France, Italy and the Netherlands) must be validated before travel in one of the machines at the entrance to the platform.

In certain Eastern European countries foreign nationals may have to buy international rail tickets at the office of the state tourist board concerned and not at the railway station. The tickets can sometimes only be purchased in Western currency and buying tickets can take a long time.

All countries in Europe (except Albania) offer two classes of rail accommodation, usually 1st and 2nd class. 1st class is more comfortable and therefore more expensive than 2nd class. Local trains are often 2nd class only. In Southern and Eastern Europe, 1st class travel is advisable for visitors as fares are reasonable and 2nd class can be very overcrowded.

RESERVATIONS

Many express trains in Europe are restricted to passengers holding advance seat reservations, particularly in France, Sweden and Spain. This is shown by the symbol 🅁 in the tables, or by notes in the introduction to each country. All *TGV*, *Eurostar* and *Pendolino* trains require a reservation, as do all long-distance trains in Spain.

Reservations can usually be made up to two months in advance. A small fee is charged, but where a supplement is payable the reservation fee is often included. Reservations can often be made on other long-distance services and this is recommended at busy times.

SUPPLEMENTS

Many countries have faster or more luxurious train services for which an extra charge is made. This supplement is payable when the ticket is purchased and often includes the price of a seat reservation. The supplement can sometimes be paid on the train, but usually at extra cost. The introduction to each country gives further information. On certain high-speed services, the first class fare includes the provision of a meal.

RAIL PASSES

Passes are available which give unlimited travel on most trains in a given area. These range from InterRail and Eurail passes which cover most of Europe for up to one month, to local passes which cover limited areas for one day. Further details of InterRail and Eurail passes appear elsewhere in this edition, and a special feature on rail passes appears in the twice-yearly Independent Travellers Edition.

FINDING YOUR TRAIN

At most stations departures are listed on large paper sheets (often yellow), and / or on electronic departure indicators. These list trains by departure, giving principal stops, and indicate from which platform they leave.

On each platform of principal European stations, a display board can be found giving details of the main trains calling at that platform. This includes the location of individual coaches, together with their destinations and the type of accommodation provided.

A sign may be carried on the side of the carriage indicating the train name, principal stops and destination and a label or sign near the door will indicate the number allocated to the carriage, which is shown on reservation tickets. 1st class accommodation is usually indicated by a yellow band above the windows and doors and/or a figure 1 near the door or on the windows

A sign above the compartment door will indicate seat numbers and which seats are reserved. In non-compartment trains, reserved seats have labels on their headrests. In some countries, notably Sweden and Yugoslavia, reserved seats are not marked and occupants will be asked to move when the passenger who has reserved the seat boards the train.

✕ CATERING 🍸

Many higher quality and long-distance trains in Europe have restaurant cars serving full meals, usually with waiter service, or serve meals at the passenger's seat. Such trains are identified with the symbol ✕ in the tables. Full meals may only be available at set times, sometimes with separate sittings, and may only be available to passengers holding first class tickets. However, the restaurant car is often supplemented by a counter or trolley service offering light snacks and drinks.

Other types of catering are shown with the symbol 🍸. This varies from a self-service buffet car serving light meals (sometimes called bistro or café) to a trolley which is wheeled through the train, serving only drinks and sandwiches. Where possible, the introduction to each country gives further information on the level of catering to be expected on particular types of train.

The catering shown may not be available throughout the journey and may be suspended or altered at weekends or on holidays.

SLEEPING CARS 🛏

Sleeping cars are shown as 🛏 in the timetables. Standard sleeping car types have bedroom style compartments with limited washing facilities and full bedding. Toilets are located at one or both ends of the coach. An attendant travels with each car or pair of cars and will serve drinks and continental breakfast at an extra charge. 1st class sleeping compartments have one or two berths (in Britain and Norway, and in older Swedish sleeping cars, two berth compartments require only 2nd class tickets) and 2nd class compartments have three berths. Some trains convey special T2 cabins, shown as 🛏 (T2) in the tables, with one berth in 1st class and two berths in 2nd class.

Compartments are allocated for occupation exclusively by men or by women except when married couples or families occupy all berths. Children travelling alone, or who cannot be accommodated in the same compartment as their family, are placed in women's compartments. In Russia and other countries of the CIS, however, berths are allocated in strict order of booking and men and women often share the same compartments.

Some trains have communicating doors between sleeping compartments which can be opened to create a larger room if both compartments are occupied by the same family group. Berths can be reserved up to 2 months (3 months on certain trains) before the date of travel and early reservation is recommended as space is limited, especially on French ski trains and in Eastern Europe. Berths must be claimed within 15 minutes of boarding the train or they may be resold.

HOTEL TRAINS

A new generation of overnight trains known collectively as Hotel trains are now running on a selection of national and international routes. The facilities are of a higher standard than those offered in conventional sleeping cars, and special fares are payable. The trains fall into the following categories:

City Night Line : Most night trains radiating from Germany, as well as domestic overnight trains within Germany, now come under the *City Night Line* banner. They operate on 15 routes serving eight countries, and are shown as *CNL* in our tables. *Deluxe* class consists of one or two berth cabins, with one or two moveable armchairs, a table and an en suite washroom containing toilet, washbasin and shower. *Economy* compartments have two berths, the upper of which folds away against the cabin wall, and the lower becomes a seat for day use. There are also four berth family compartments as well as couchettes and reclining seats (sleeperettes). A first class ticket is required for *Deluxe* compartments (but no longer for single occupancy of a *Economy* compartment). Double deck cars, with *Deluxe* on the upper deck, are also available.

Trenhotel (Spain). These trains, of the *Talgo* type, run on the international route from Madrid to Lisboa. They also run on internal routes within Spain, from Barcelona to A Coruña, Gijon, Granada and Vigo and v.v., and Madrid to A Coruña, Ferrol and Pontevedra and v.v. The highest class of accommodation is known as *Gran Clase*, which has shower and toilet facilities in each compartment and can be used for single or double occupancy.

Compartments with showers can also now be found on a number of services in Sweden, Norway and Italy, and other international routes include Wien to Zürich and Roma and the Amsterdam - Warszawa *Jan Kiepura*.

COUCHETTES ━

Couchettes (━) are a more basic form of overnight accommodation consisting of simple bunk beds with a sheet, blanket and pillow. The couchettes are converted from ordinary seating cars for the night, and there are usually 4 berths per compartment in 1st class, 6 berths in 2nd class. On certain trains (e.g. in Austria and Italy), 4 berth compartments are available to 2nd class passengers, at a higher supplement. Washing and toilet facilities are provided at the ends of each coach. Men and women are booked into the same compartments and are expected to sleep in daytime clothes. A small number of trains in Germany, however, have women-only couchette compartments.

INTERNATIONAL OVERNIGHT SERVICES

A summary of international overnight services will be found on page 33 which specifies the various types of accommodation and catering provided on each individual service (including details of the operator).

WHEELCHAIR ACCESS ♿

High-quality main line and international trains are now often equipped to accommodate passengers in wheelchairs. Access ramps are available at many stations and some trains are fitted with special lifts. The following trains have at least one wheelchair space, often with accessible toilets:

International: all Eurostar trains, many EC and other trains. CityNightLine trains have a special compartment. *Austria:* many IC/EC trains. *Denmark:* IC and Lyn trains. *France:* all TGV trains and many other long distance services. *Germany:* all EC, ICE, IC and IR trains. *Italy:* all Pendolino and many EC or IC trains. *Netherlands:* most trains. *Sweden:* X2000 and most IC and IR trains, some sleeping cars. *Switzerland:* All IC, most EC and some regional trains. *Austria, Great Britain, Ireland, Poland:* certain trains only.

Most of these railways publish guides to accessibility, and some countries, for example France, provide special staff to help disabled travellers. Wheelchair users normally need to reserve in advance, stating their requirements. The Editor would welcome information for countries not listed.

CAR-SLEEPERS

Trains which convey motor cars operate throughout much of Europe and are shown in Table **1** for international services and Table **2** for other services. The motor cars are conveyed in special wagons while passengers travel in sleeping cars or couchettes, usually (but not always) in the same train.

LUGGAGE & BICYCLES

Luggage may be registered at many larger stations and sent separately by rail to your destination. In some countries, bicycles may also be registered in advance and certain local and some express trains will convey bicycles (there may be a charge). The relevant railways will advise exact details on request.

HEALTH REQUIREMENTS

It is not mandatory for visitors to Europe to be vaccinated against infectious diseases unless they are travelling from areas where these are endemic. For travellers' peace of mind, however, protection against the following diseases should be considered:

AIDS	Cholera
Hepatitis A	Hepatitis B
Polio	Rabies
Tetanus	Typhoid

Full information is available from the manual published by the World Health Organisation, and travellers should seek advice from their Travel Agent.

DRINKING WATER

Tap water is usually safe to drink in most parts of Europe. The water in washrooms or toilets on trains is, however, not suitable for drinking. Those who doubt the purity of the tap water are recommended to boil it, to use sterilisation tablets, or to drink bottled water.

CLIMATE

Most of Europe lies within the temperate zone but there can be considerable differences between North and South, East and West, as illustrated in the table below. Local temperatures are also affected by altitude and the difference between summer and winter temperatures tends to be less marked in coastal regions than in areas far removed from the sea.

	Bucuresti	Dublin	Madrid	Moskva
JANUARY				
Highest	2°	8°	10°	– 6°
Lowest	– 6°	3°	3°	– 12°
Rain days	6	13	9	11
APRIL				
Highest	18°	11°	18°	10°
Lowest	6°	4°	7°	2°
Rain days	7	10	11	9
JULY				
Highest	29°	19°	31°	23°
Lowest	16°	11°	18°	14°
Rain days	7	9	3	12
OCTOBER				
Highest	18°	14°	19°	8°
Lowest	6°	8°	10°	2°
Rain days	5	11	9	10

Highest = Average highest daily temperature in °C
Lowest = Average lowest daily temperature in °C
Rain days = Average number of days with recorded precipitation

Source : World Weather Information Service

FIND US ON FACEBOOK!

www.facebook.com/EuropeanRailTimetable

and on **Twitter** @EuropeanRailTT

CURRENCY CONVERSION

The information shown below is intended to be indicative only. Rates fluctuate from day to day and commercial exchange rates normally include a commission element.

Country	unit	1 GBP =	1 USD =	1 EUR =	100 JPY =
Euro zone (‡)	**euro**	**1.25**	**0.74**	**1.00**	**0.72**
Albania	lek	175.45	103.45	139.95	101.32
Belarus	rubl	17282.80	10190.00	13785.50	9980.90
Bosnia	marka	2.45	1.45	1.96	1.42
Bulgaria	lev	2.45	1.45	1.96	1.42
Croatia	kuna	9.50	5.60	7.58	5.49
Czech Republic	koruna	34.39	20.28	27.43	19.86
Denmark	krone	9.35	5.51	7.46	5.40
Georgia	lari	3.00	1.77	2.39	1.73
Hungary	forint	384.76	226.85	306.90	222.20
Iceland	krona	193.77	114.26	154.56	111.90
Lithuania	litas	4.33	2.55	3.45	2.50
Macedonia	denar	76.96	45.38	61.39	44.44
Moldova	leu	23.44	13.82	18.70	13.54
Norway	krone	10.17	6.00	8.12	5.88
Poland	złoty	5.17	3.05	4.12	2.98
Romania	leu nou	5.51	3.25	4.39	3.18
Russia	rubl	58.35	34.40	46.54	33.70
Serbia	dinar	144.56	85.24	115.31	83.49
Sweden	krona	11.27	6.65	8.99	6.51
Switzerland	franc	1.55	0.90	1.22	0.88
Turkey	yeni lira	3.60	2.12	2.87	2.08
Ukraine	hryvnya	20.01	11.80	15.96	11.56
United Kingdom	pound	1.00	0.59	0.80	0.58

‡ – Austria, Belgium, Cyprus, Estonia, Finland, France, Germany, Greece, Ireland, Italy, Latvia, Luxembourg, Malta, the Netherlands, Portugal, Slovakia, Slovenia and Spain.

The euro is also legal tender in Andorra, Kosovo, Monaco, Montenegro, San Marino, and the Vatican City.

PASSPORTS AND VISAS

Nationals of one country intending to travel to or pass through another country normally require a valid passport and will also require a visa unless a special visa-abolition agreement has been made between the countries concerned. The limit of stay permitted in each country is usually 3 months.

Applications for visas should be made well in advance of the date of travel to the local consulate of the country concerned. Consuls usually make a charge for issuing a visa. Before issuing a transit visa, a consul normally requires to see the visa of the country of destination.

The possession of a valid passport or visa does not necessarily grant the holder automatic access to all areas of the country to be visited. Certain countries have zones which are restricted or prohibited to foreign nationals.

All border controls have been abolished, however, between those countries which have signed the **Schengen Agreement** (see list below), and a visa allowing entry to any of these countries is valid in all of them.

LIST OF SCHENGEN AREA COUNTRIES

Austria, Belgium, Czech Republic, Denmark, Estonia, Finland, France, Germany, Greece, Hungary, Iceland, Italy, Latvia, Lithuania, Luxembourg, Malta, Netherlands, Norway, Poland, Portugal, Slovakia, Slovenia, Spain, Sweden, Switzerland.

METRIC CONVERSION TABLES

The Celsius system of temperature measurement, the metric system of distance measurement and the twenty-four hour clock are used throughout this book. The tables below give Fahrenheit, mile and twelve-hour clock equivalents.

TEMPERATURE

°C	°F
–20	–4
–15	5
–10	14
–5	23
0	32
5	41
10	50
15	59
20	68
25	77
30	86
35	95
40	104

Conversion formulae :

°C = (°F – 32) x 5 / 9

°F = (°C x 9 / 5) + 32

DISTANCE

km	miles	km	miles	km	miles
1	0.62	45	27.96	300	186.41
2	1.24	50	31.07	400	248.55
3	1.86	55	34.18	500	310.69
4	2.49	60	37.28	600	372.82
5	3.11	65	40.39	700	434.96
6	3.73	70	43.50	800	497.10
7	4.35	75	46.60	900	559.23
8	4.97	80	49.71	1000	621.37
9	5.59	85	52.82	1100	683.51
10	6.21	90	55.92	1200	745.65
15	9.32	95	59.03	1300	807.78
20	12.43	100	62.14	1400	869.92
25	15.53	125	77.67	1500	932.06
30	18.64	150	93.21	2000	1242.74
35	21.75	175	108.74	3000	1864.11
40	24.85	200	124.27	4000	2485.48

TIME

Midnight departure	=	0000
1 am	=	0100
5 am	=	0500
5.30 am	=	0530
11 am	=	1100
12 noon	=	1200
1 pm	=	1300
3.45 pm	=	1545
Midnight arrival	=	2400

GLOSSARY

🔑	*FRANCAIS*	*ITALIANO*	*DEUTSCH*	*ESPAÑOL*
additional trains	d'autres trains	ulteriori treni	weitere Züge	otros trenes
also	[circule] aussi	[si effettua] anche	[verkehrt] auch	[circula] también
alteration	modification	variazione	Änderung	modificación
approximately	environ	circa	ungefähr	aproximadamente
arrival, arrives (a.)	arrivée, arrive	arrivo, arriva	Ankunft, kommt an	llegada, llega
and at the same minutes past each hour until	puis toutes les heures aux mêmes minutes jusqu'à	poi ai stessi minuti di ogni ora fino a	und so weiter im Takt bis	luego a los mismos minutos de cada hora hasta
calls at	s'arrête à	ferma a	hält in	efectúa parada en
certain	déterminé	certo	bestimmt	determinado
change at	changer à	cambiare a	umsteigen in	cambiar en
composition	composition	composizione	Zugbildung	composición
confirmation	confirmation	conferma	Bestätigung	confirmación
connection	correspondance, relation	coincidenza, relazione	Anschluss, Verbindung	correspondencia, enlace
conveys	comporte, achemine	ha in composizione	befördert, führt	lleva
daily	tous les jours	giornalmente	täglich	diariamente
delay	retard	ritardo	Verspätung	retraso
departure, departs (d.)	départ, part	partenza, parte	Abfahrt, fährt ab	salida, sale
earlier	plus tôt	più presto	früher	más temprano
engineering work	travaux de voie	lavori sul binario	Bauarbeiten	obras de vía
even / uneven dates	jours pairs / impairs	giorni pari / dispari	gerade / ungerade Daten	fechas pares / impares
every 30 minutes	toutes les 30 minutes	ogni 30 minuti	alle 30 Minuten	cada 30 minutos
except	sauf	escluso	außer	excepto
fast(er)	(plus) rapide	(più) rapido	schnell(er)	(más) rápido
for	pour	per	für	para
from Rennes	(en provenance) de Rennes	(proviene) da Rennes	von Rennes	(procede) de Rennes
from Jan. 15	à partir du 15 janvier	dal 15 di gennaio	vom 15. Januar (an)	desde el 15 de enero
hourly	toutes les heures	ogni ora	stündlich	cada hora
hours (hrs)	heures	ore	Stunden	horas
journey	voyage, trajet	viaggio, percorso	Reise	viaje, trayecto
journey time	temps de parcours	tempo di tragitto	Reisezeit	duración del recorrido
later	plus tard	più tardi	später	más tarde
may	peut, peuvent	può, possono	kann, können	puede(n)
minutes (mins)	minutes	minuti	Minuten	minutos
not	ne [circule] pas	non [si effettua]	[verkehrt] nicht	no [circula]
not available	pas disponible	non disponibile	nicht erhältlich	no disponible
on the dates shown in Table **81**	les jours indiqués dans le tableau **81**	nei giorni indicati nel quadro **81**	an den in der Tabelle **81** angegebene Daten	los días indicados en el cuadro **81**
only	seulement	esclusivamente	nur	sólo
operator	entreprise de transports	azienda di trasporto	Verkehrsunternehmen	empresa de transportes
other	autre	altro	andere	otros
runs	circule	circola, si effettua	verkehrt	circula
sailing	traversée	traversata	Überfahrt	travesia
ship	bateau, navire	nave, battello	Schiff	barco
stopping trains	trains omnibus	treni regionali	Nahverkehrszüge	trenes regionales
stops	s'arrête	ferma	hält	efectúa parada
subject to	sous réserve de	soggetto a	vorbehaltlich	sujeto a
summer	été	estate	Sommer	verano
supplement payable	avec supplément	con pagamento di supplemento	zuschlagpflichtig	con pago de suplemento
then	puis	poi	dann	luego
through train	train direct	treno diretto	durchgehender Zug	tren directo
timings	horaires	orari	Zeitangaben	horarios
to York	vers, à destination de York	(diretto) a York	nach York	(continúa) a York
to / until July 23	jusqu'au 23 juillet	fino al 23 di luglio	bis zum 23. Juli	hasta el dia 23 de julio
to pick up	pour laisser monter	per viaggiatori in partenza	zum Zusteigen	para recoger viajeros
to set down	pour laisser descendre	per viaggiatori in arrivo	zum Aussteigen	para dejar viajeros
unless otherwise shown	sauf indication contraire	salvo indicazione contraria	sofern nicht anders angezeigt	salvo indicación contraria
valid	valable	valido	gültig	válido
when train **44** runs	lors de la circulation du train **44**	quando circola il treno **44**	beim Verkehren des Zuges **44**	cuando circula el tren **44**
winter	hiver	inverno	Winter	invierno

INDEX OF PLACES by table number

The BEYOND EUROPE section is indexed separately - see the back of each edition

🚆 Connection by train from the nearest station shown in this timetable.
⛴ Connection by boat from the nearest station shown in this timetable.
🚌 Connection by bus from the nearest station shown in this timetable.
10/355 Consult both indicated tables to find the best connecting services.

OSLO

P

PARIS

PARIS ✈ CHARLES DE GAULLE

POZNAŃ

CRUISE TRAINS

The services shown in the European Rail Timetable are the regular scheduled services of the railway companies concerned. However, a number of specialised operators also run luxurious cruise trains taking several days to complete their journey. Overnight accommodation is provided either on the train or in hotels. Cruise trains are bookable only through the operating company or its appointed agents and normal rail tickets are not valid on these trains. A selection of operators is shown below.

The Danube Express : Fully escorted holidays in central and eastern Europe by luxury private train based in Budapest. Operator: Danube Express, Offley Holes Farm, Charlton Road, Preston, Hitchin, SG4 7TD, UK; ✆ +44 (0)1462 441400. Website: www.danube-express.com

Belmond Royal Scotsman : Luxury tours of Scotland starting from Edinburgh. Operator: Belmond Royal Scotsman, 1st Floor, Shackleton House, 4 Battle Bridge Lane, London, SE1 2HP, UK; ✆ 0845 077 2222 (UK only) or +44 (0) 20 3117 1380. Website: www.royalscotsman.com

El Transcantábrico and **El Expreso de La Robla** : Rail cruises along Spain's northern coast. Operator: Trenes Turísticos de Lujo, Plaza de los Ferroviarios s/n., 33012 Oviedo, Asturias, Spain; ✆ +34 902 555 902, fax +34 985 981 711. Website: www.trenesturisticosdelujo.com

Trans-Siberian Express : Tours by private hotel train along the Trans-Siberian Railway. Operator: Golden Eagle Luxury Trains, Denzell House, Denzell Gardens, Dunham Road, Altrincham, WA14 4QF, UK; ✆ +44 (0)161 928 9410, fax +44 (0)161 941 6101. Website: www.goldeneagleluxurytrains.com.

Venice Simplon-Orient-Express : This well-known luxury train runs once or twice weekly from late March to early November, mostly on its established London - Paris - Venezia route. Operator: Orient-Express Hotels Ltd., 1st Floor, Shackleton House, 4 Battle Bridge Lane, London, SE1 2HP, UK; ✆ 0845 077 2222 (UK only) or +44 (0) 20 3117 1380. Website: www.vsoe.com

LIST OF ADVERTISERS

CITY STATION LOCATION PLANS

Passenger railway	Main station
Metro	Local station
Bus / tram line	Bus station
Ferry	Airport

Only those metro, bus, and tram lines which provide inter-station links or connect outlying main stations to the city centre are shown.

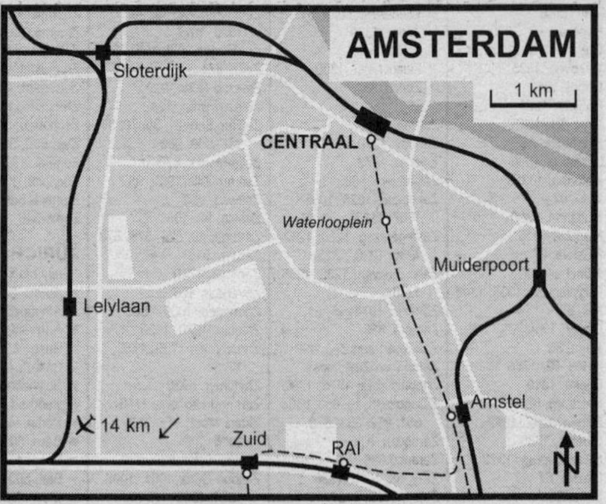

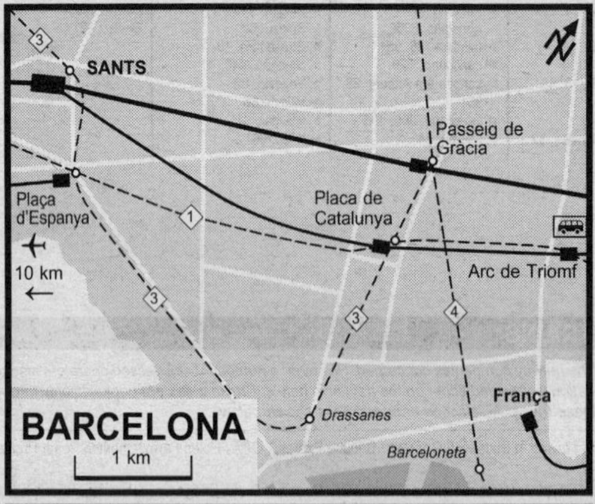

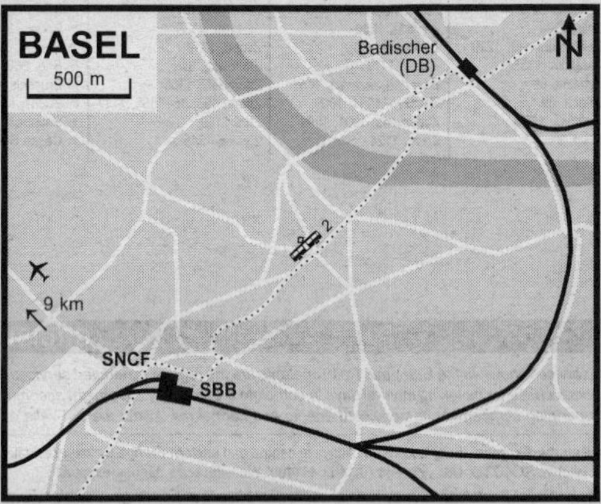

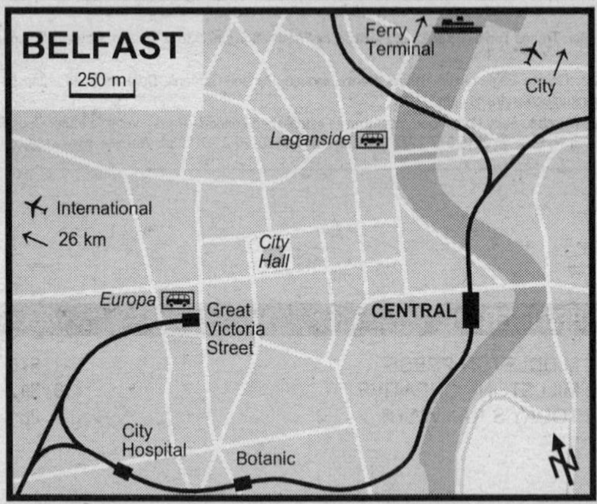

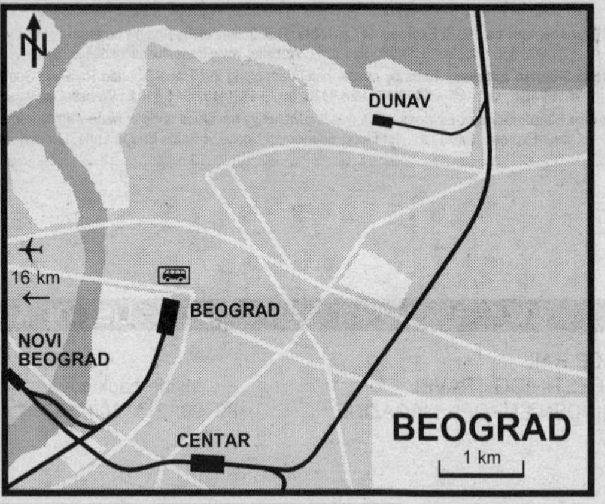

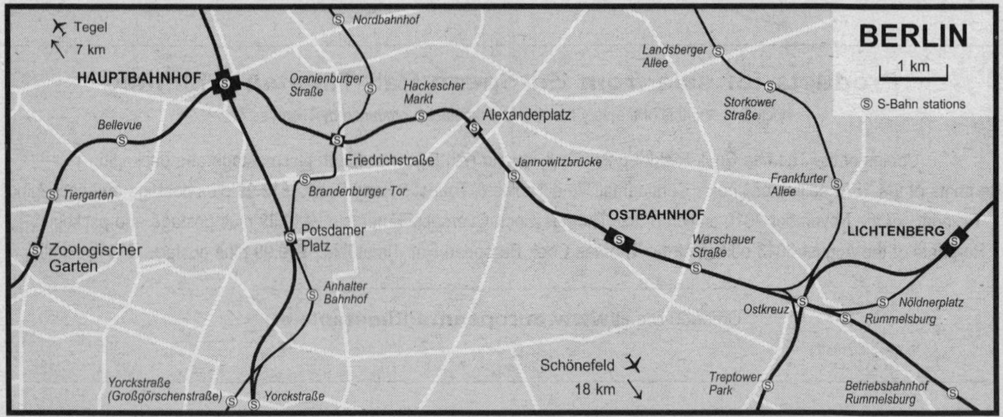

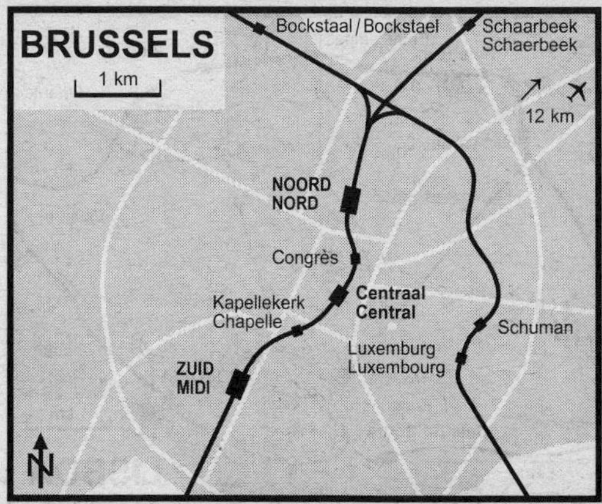
BRUSSELS
1 km
Bockstaal / Bockstael
Schaarbeek
Schaerbeek
12 km
NOORD
NORD
Congrès
Kapellekerk
Chapelle
Centraal
Central
Schuman
Luxemburg
Luxembourg
ZUID
MIDI

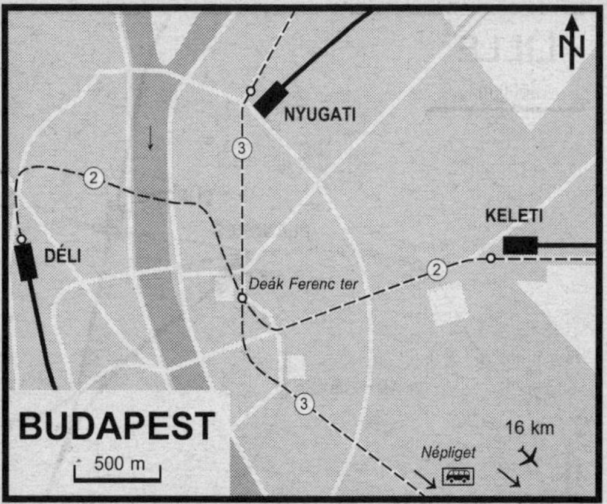
NYUGATI
KELETI
DÉLI
Deák Ferenc ter
BUDAPEST
500 m
16 km
Népliget

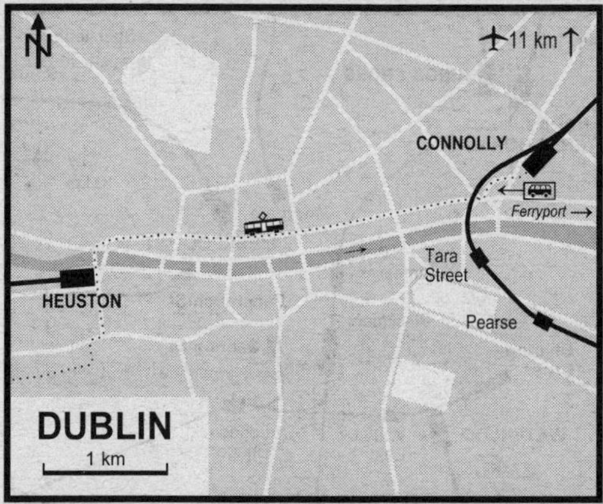
11 km
CONNOLLY
Ferryport
Tara
Street
HEUSTON
Pearse
DUBLIN
1 km

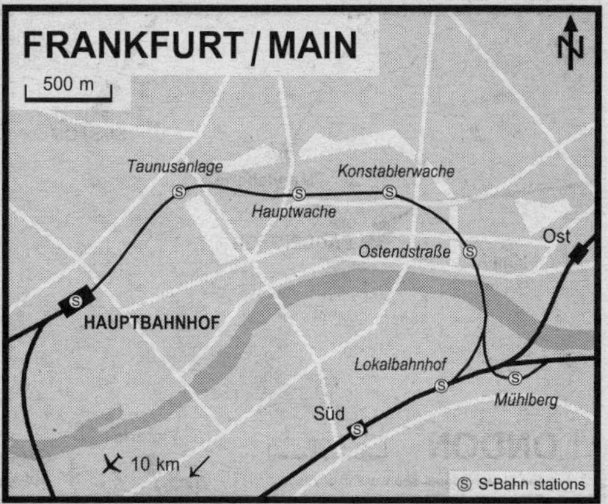
FRANKFURT / MAIN
500 m
Taunusanlage
Konstablerwache
Hauptwache
Ostendstraße
Ost
HAUPTBAHNHOF
Lokalbahnhof
Mühlberg
Süd
10 km
S-Bahn stations

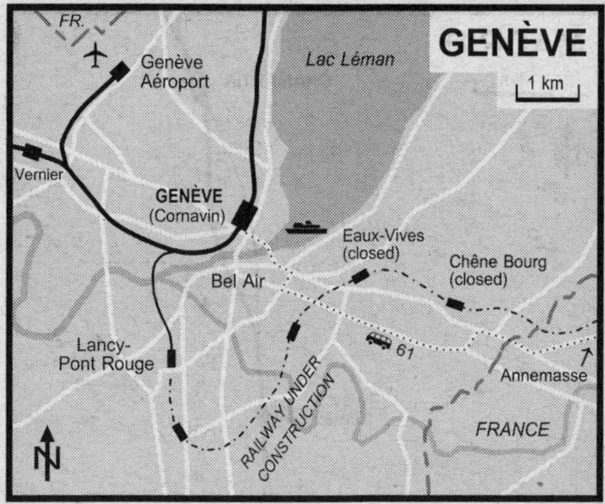
FR.
GENÈVE
Lac Léman
1 km
Genève
Aéroport
Vernier
GENÈVE
(Cornavin)
Eaux-Vives
(closed)
Chêne Bourg
(closed)
Bel Air
Lancy-
Pont Rouge
61
Annemasse
RAILWAY UNDER
CONSTRUCTION
FRANCE

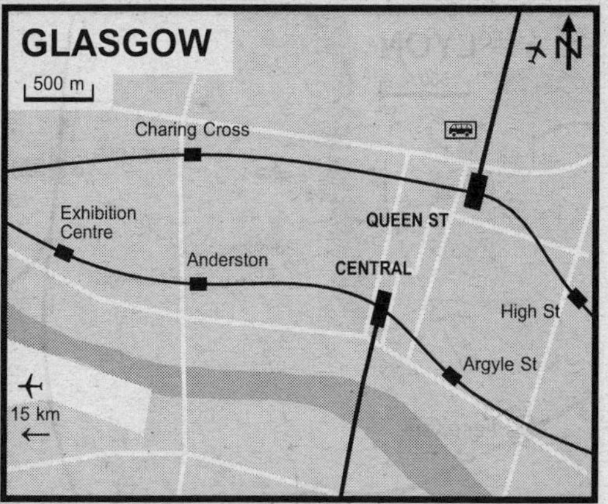
GLASGOW
500 m
Charing Cross
Exhibition
Centre
QUEEN ST
Anderston
CENTRAL
High St
Argyle St
15 km

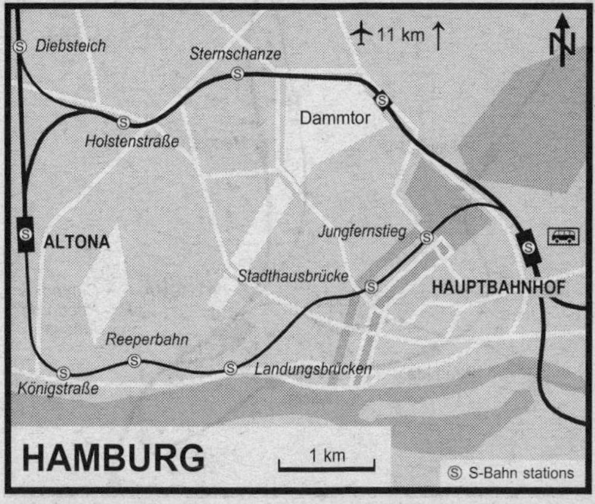
Diebsteich
11 km
Sternschanze
Dammtor
Holstenstraße
ALTONA
Jungfernstieg
Stadthausbrücke
HAUPTBAHNHOF
Reeperbahn
Landungsbrücken
Königstraße
HAMBURG
1 km
S-Bahn stations

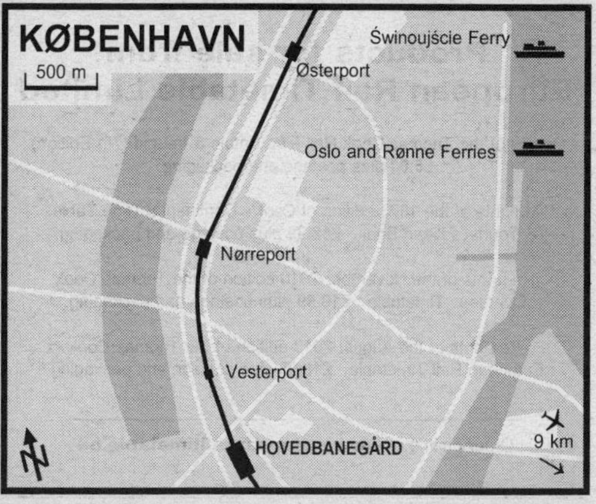
KØBENHAVN
500 m
Świnoujście Ferry
Østerport
Oslo and Rønne Ferries
Nørreport
Vesterport
HOVEDBANEGÅRD
9 km

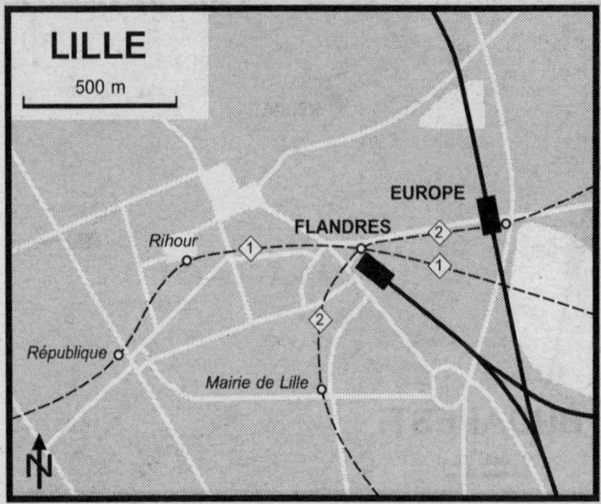
LILLE
500 m
EUROPE
FLANDRES
Rihour
1
2
République
Mairie de Lille
N

Entrecampos
Roma
Sete Rios
Roma-Areeiro
Sintra
Oriente
Areeiro
Campolide
Alameda
São Sebastião
Oriente
Marquês de Pompal
Rato
N
Restauradores
Rossio
SANTA APOLÓNIA
Baixa-Chiado
Rossio
1 km
Cascais
Cais do Sodré
Terreiro do Paço
LISBOA
Barreiro

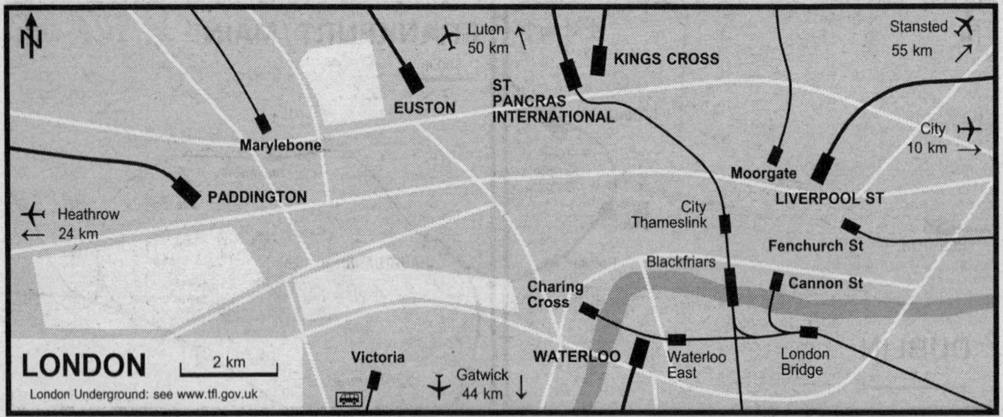
N
Luton 50 km
Stansted 55 km
KINGS CROSS
ST PANCRAS INTERNATIONAL
EUSTON
Marylebone
City 10 km
Moorgate
PADDINGTON
LIVERPOOL ST
Heathrow 24 km
City Thameslink
Fenchurch St
Blackfriars
Charing Cross
Cannon St
WATERLOO
Waterloo East
London Bridge
Victoria
Gatwick 44 km
LONDON
2 km
London Underground: see www.tfl.gov.uk

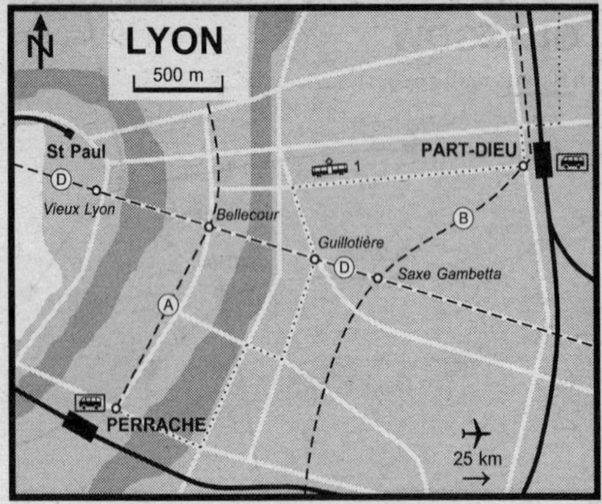
N
LYON
500 m
St Paul
PART-DIEU
1
D
Vieux Lyon
Bellecour
B
Guillotière
D
Saxe Gambetta
A
PERRACHE
25 km

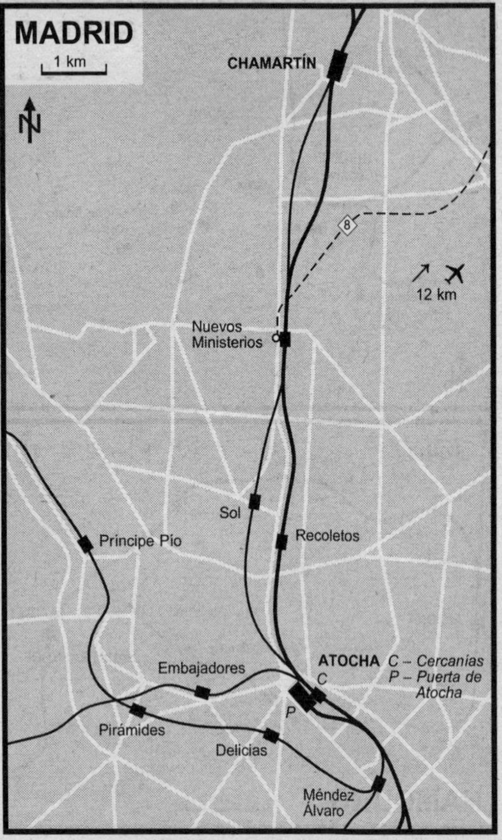
MADRID
1 km
CHAMARTÍN
N
8
12 km
Nuevos Ministerios
Sol
Principe Pío
Recoletos
Embajadores
ATOCHA C – Cercanías
P – Puerta de Atocha
C
P
Pirámides
Delicias
Méndez Álvaro

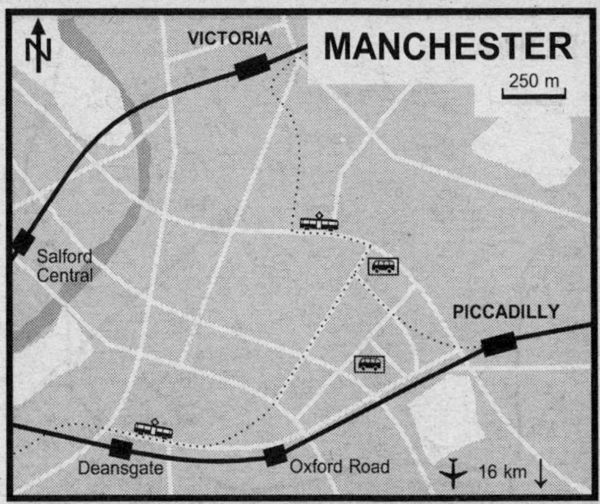
MANCHESTER
250 m
VICTORIA
Salford Central
PICCADILLY
Deansgate
Oxford Road
16 km

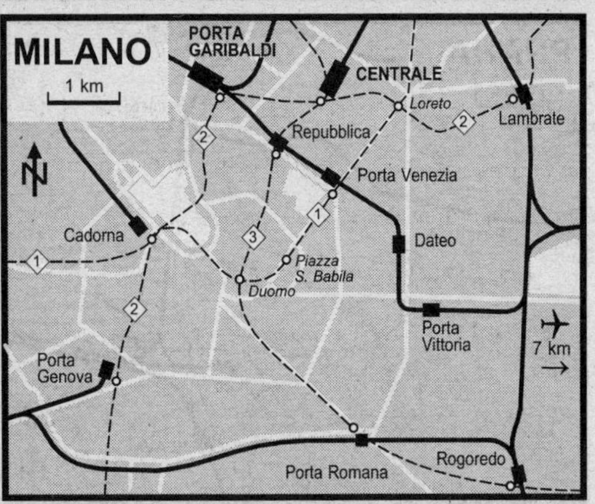
MILANO
1 km
PORTA GARIBALDI
CENTRALE
Loreto
Lambrate
Repubblica
Porta Venezia
Cadorna
Dateo
Piazza S. Babila
Duomo
Porta Vittoria
7 km
Porta Genova
Rogoredo
Porta Romana

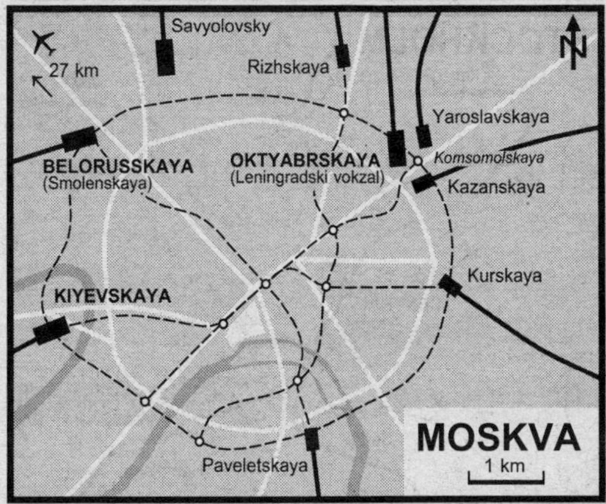
Savyolovsky
27 km
Rizhskaya
Yaroslavskaya
BELORUSSKAYA
(Smolenskaya)
OKTYABRSKAYA
(Leningradski vokzal)
Komsomolskaya
Kazanskaya
Kurskaya
KIYEVSKAYA
Paveletskaya
MOSKVA
1 km

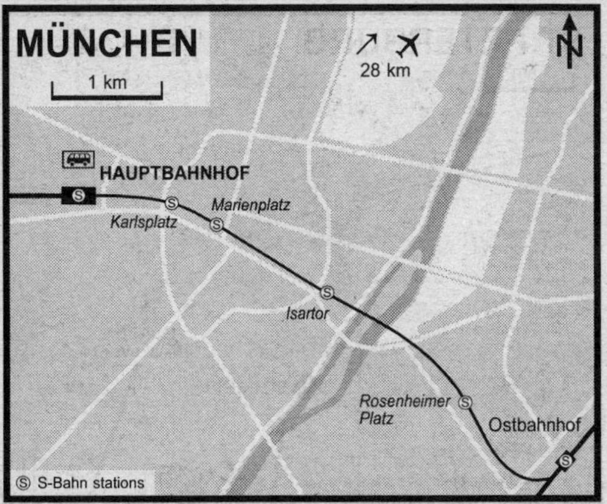
MÜNCHEN
1 km
28 km
HAUPTBAHNHOF
Karlsplatz
Marienplatz
Isartor
Rosenheimer Platz
Ostbahnhof
S-Bahn stations

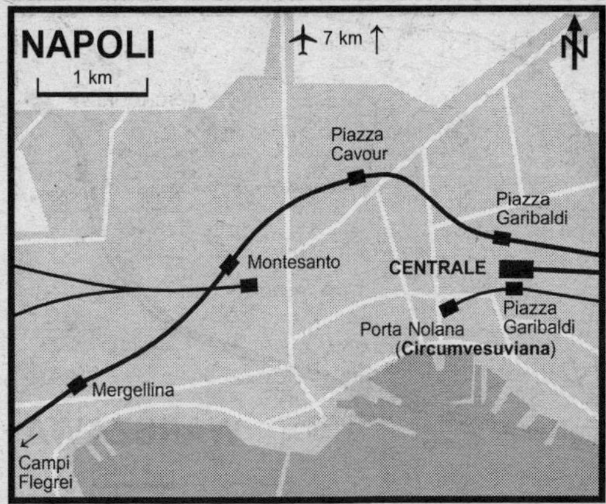
NAPOLI
1 km
7 km
Piazza Cavour
Piazza Garibaldi
Montesanto
CENTRALE
Porta Nolana
(Circumvesuviana)
Piazza Garibaldi
Mergellina
Campi Flegrei

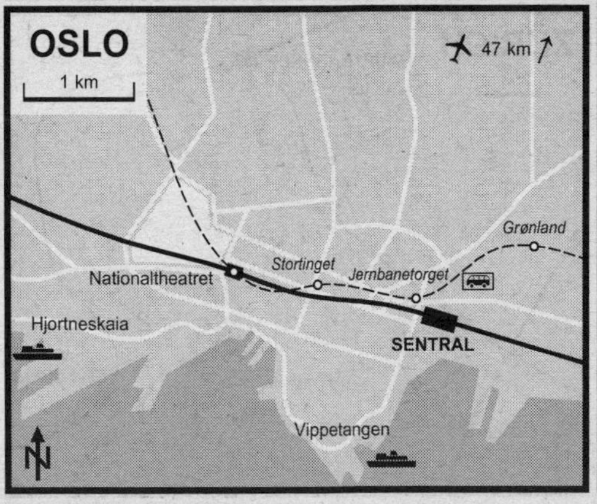
OSLO
1 km
47 km
Grønland
Nationaltheatret
Stortinget
Jernbanetorget
Hjortneskaia
SENTRAL
Vippetangen

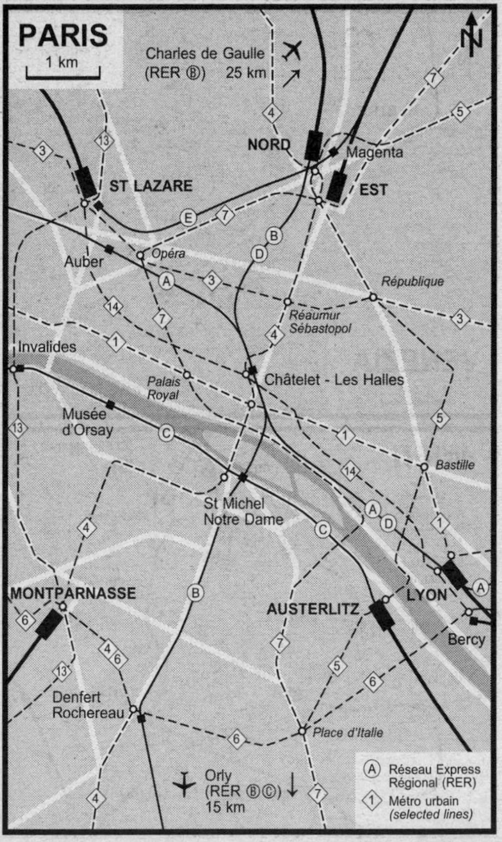
PARIS
1 km
Charles de Gaulle
(RER B) 25 km
NORD
Magenta
ST LAZARE
EST
Opéra
Auber
République
Réaumur Sébastopol
Invalides
Châtelet - Les Halles
Palais Royal
Musée d'Orsay
Bastille
St Michel Notre Dame
MONTPARNASSE
AUSTERLITZ
LYON
Bercy
Denfert Rochereau
Place d'Italie
Orly
(RER B C)
15 km
Réseau Express Régional (RER)
Métro urbain
(selected lines)

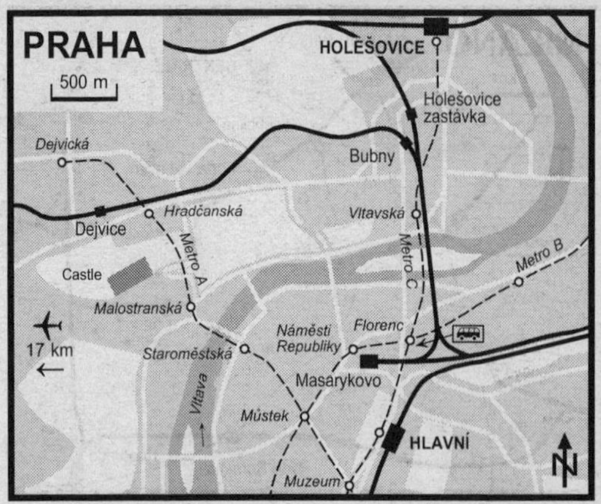
PRAHA
500 m
HOLEŠOVICE
Holešovice zastávka
Dejvická
Bubny
Hradčanská
Dejvice
Vltavská
Metro A
Metro C
Metro B
Castle
Malostranská
17 km
Náměstí Republiky
Florenc
Staroměstská
Masarykovo
Vltava
Můstek
HLAVNÍ
Muzeum

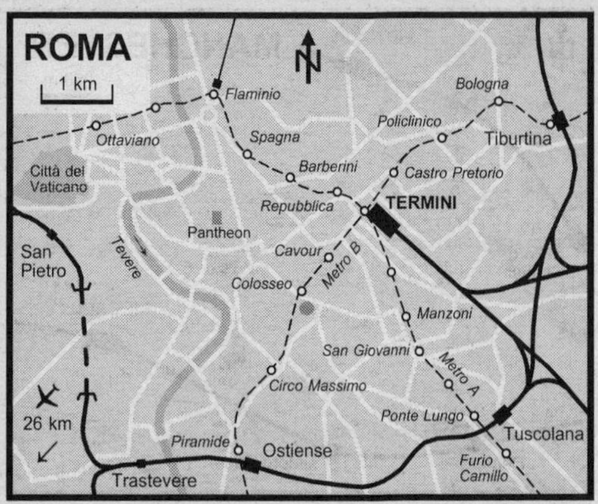
ROMA
1 km
Flaminio
Bologna
Ottaviano
Spagna
Policlinico
Tiburtina
Città del Vaticano
Barberini
Castro Pretorio
Repubblica
TERMINI
Pantheon
San Pietro
Tevere
Cavour
Metro B
Colosseo
Manzoni
San Giovanni
Metro A
Circo Massimo
26 km
Ponte Lungo
Tuscolana
Piramide
Ostiense
Furio Camillo
Trastevere

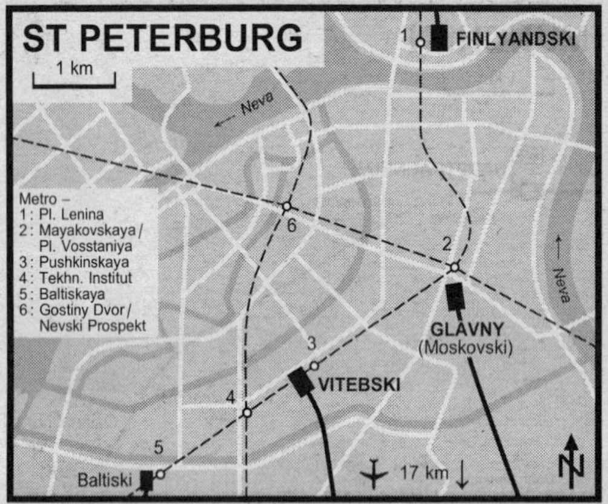
ST PETERBURG
1 km
1
FINLYANDSKI
Neva
Metro –
1: Pl. Lenina
2: Mayakovskaya / Pl. Vosstaniya
3: Pushkinskaya
4: Tekhn. Institut
5: Baltiskaya
6: Gostiny Dvor / Nevski Prospekt
6
2
Neva
GLAVNY (Moskovski)
3
VITEBSKI
4
5
Baltiski
17 km

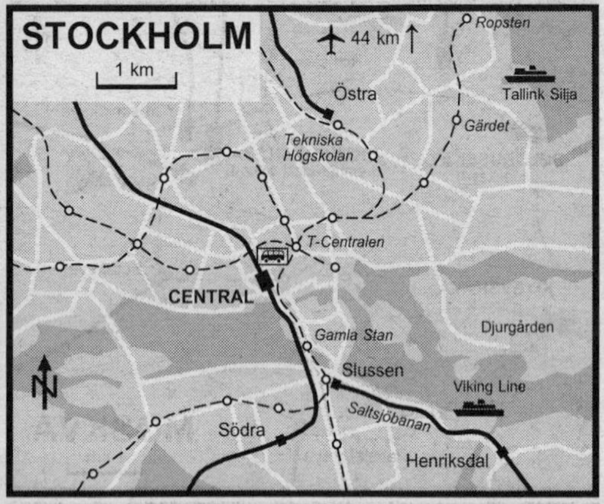
STOCKHOLM
1 km
44 km
Ropsten
Östra
Tallink Silja
Gärdet
Tekniska Högskolan
T-Centralen
CENTRAL
Djurgården
Gamla Stan
Slussen
Viking Line
Saltsjöbanan
Södra
Henriksdal

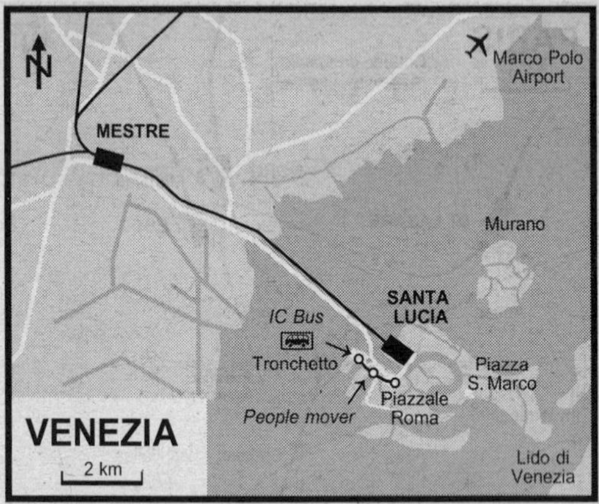
Marco Polo Airport
MESTRE
Murano
SANTA LUCIA
IC Bus
Tronchetto
Piazza S. Marco
Piazzale Roma
People mover
VENEZIA
2 km
Lido di Venezia

Gdańska
Wileńska
WSCHODNIA
Stadion
Ratusz Arsenal
Wisła
Świętokrzyska
CENTRALNA
Powiśle
10 km
Centrum
Śródmieście
Ochota
WARSZAWA
1 km

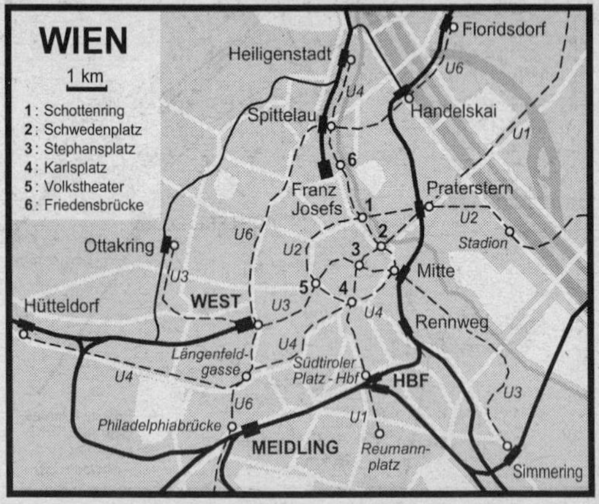
WIEN
1 km
Floridsdorf
Heiligenstadt
U6
U4
Spittelau
Handelskai
U1
1: Schottenring
2: Schwedenplatz
3: Stephansplatz
4: Karlsplatz
5: Volkstheater
6: Friedensbrücke
6
Franz Josefs
Praterstern
1
U2
2
Stadion
Ottakring
U6
U2
3
Mitte
U3
5
4
WEST
U3
U4
Hütteldorf
Rennweg
U4
Längenfeld-gasse
Südtiroler Platz - Hbf
HBF
U4
U3
U6
U1
Philadelphiabrücke
MEIDLING
Reumann-platz
Simmering

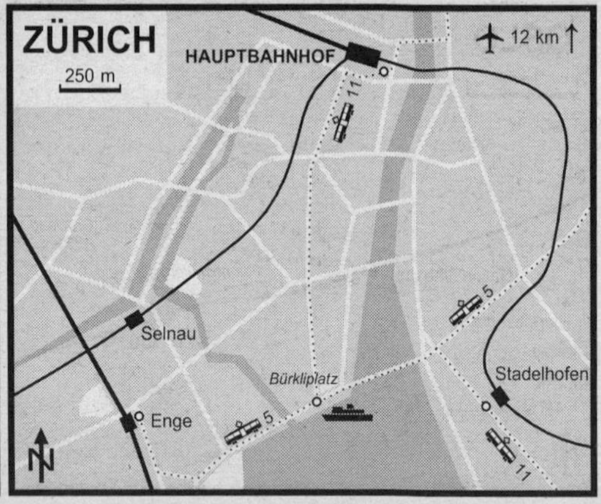
ZÜRICH
250 m
HAUPTBAHNHOF
12 km
11
5
Selnau
Stadelhofen
Bürkliplatz
Enge
5
11

SELECTED DAILY INTERNATIONAL SLEEPER SERVICES

From	To	Train Number	Brand	Facilities and owner	Train Name	International table number
Paris	Berlin	451/450	City Night Line	🛏 1, 2 cl. 🚿(cnl), ▬ 2 cl.(cnl), 🍸	Perseus	20, 30
Paris	Hamburg	50451/40479	City Night Line	🛏 1, 2 cl. 🚿(cnl), ▬ 2 cl.(cnl), 🍸	Andromeda	20
Amsterdam	Warszawa	447/446	Euro Night	🛏 1, 2 cl. 🚿(pkp), ▬ 2 cl.(db), 🍴(pkp)	Jan Kiepura	24
Köln	Wien	421/420	Euro Night	🛏 1, 2 cl. 🚿(öbb), ▬ 2 cl.(öbb)		28, 66
Amsterdam	München	419/418	City Night Line	🛏 1, 2 cl. 🚿(db), ▬ 2 cl.(sbb), 🍸	Pollux	28
Paris	München	40451/40418	City Night Line	🛏 1, 2 cl. 🚿(cnl), 🍸	Cassiopeia	32
München	Budapest	463/462	Euro Night	🛏 1, 2 cl.(mav), ▬ 2 cl.(mav)	Kálmán Imre	32
Wien	Bucuresti	347/346	Euro Night	🛏 1, 2 cl.(cfr), ▬ 2 cl.(cfr), 🍴(cfr)	Dacia (Summer)	32, 61
Budapest	Bucuresti	1347/1346	Euro Night	🛏 1, 2 cl.(cfr), ▬ 2 cl.(cfr), 🍴(cfr)	Muntenia (Winter)	32, 61
Budapest	Bucuresti	473/472	Euro Night	🛏 1, 2 cl.(cfr), ▬ 1, 2 cl.(cfr)	Ister	32, 61
Paris	Venezia	221/220	Thello Euro Night	🛏 1, 2 cl.(ti), ▬ 2 cl.(ti), 🍴(ti)		44
Irún / Hendaye	Lisboa	312/310	Trenhotel talgo	🛏 1, 2 cl. 🚿(renfe), 🍴(renfe)	Surex / Sud Expresso	46
Lisboa	Madrid	335/332	Trenhotel talgo	🛏 1, 2 cl. 🚿(renfe), 🍴(renfe)	Lusitania	46
Berlin	København	300/301	Euro Night	▬ 2 cl.(bne)	Berlin Night Express	50
Berlin	Kaliningrad	40445/40444		🛏 1, 2 cl.(rzd)	(Summer only)	51
Zürich	Praha	459/458	City Night Line	🛏 1, 2 cl. 🚿(cd), ▬ 2 cl.(sbb), 🍸	Canopus	54
Amsterdam	København	40447/40473	City Night Line	🛏 1, 2 cl. 🚿(db), ▬ 2 cl.(db), 🍸	Borealis	54
Amsterdam	Praha	457/456	City Night Line	🛏 1, 2 cl. 🚿(cd), ▬ 2 cl.(db), 🍸	Kopernikus / Phoenix	54
København	Praha	50473/40456	City Night Line	🛏 1, 2 cl. 🚿(cd), ▬ 2 cl.(cd), 🍸	Orion	54
København	Basel	473/472	City Night Line	🛏 1, 2 cl. 🚿(sbb), ▬ 2 cl.(db), 🍸	Aurora	54
Hamburg	Zürich	478/479	City Night Line	🛏 1, 2 cl. 🚿(sbb), ▬ 2 cl.(sbb), 🍸	Komet	54, 73
Warszawa	Kyïv	68/67		🛏 1, 2 cl.(uz)	Kyïv Ekspres	56
Warszawa	Moskva	10/9		🛏 1, 2 cl.(rzd)	Polonez	56
Warszawa	Minsk	115/116		🛏 1, 2 cl.(bc)		56
Nice	Moskva	18/17		🛏 1, 2 cl. 🚿(rzd), 🍴(pkp, rzd)		59
Berlin	Budapest	477/476	Euro Night	🛏 1, 2 cl.(cd), ▬ 2 cl.(mav)	Metropol	60
Berlin	Wien	477/476	Euro Night	🛏 1, 2 cl.(cd), ▬ 2 cl.(mav)	Metropol	60
Praha	Budapest	477/476	Euro Night	🛏 1, 2 cl. 🚿(cd)	Metropol	60
Bucuresti	Sofia	383/382		🛏 1, 2 cl.(cfr / bdz)	Bulgaria Express	61
Budapest	Beograd	341/340		🛏 1, 2 cl.(zs) *, ▬ 2 cl.(zs)	Beograd	61
Budapest	Sofia	341/490		🛏 1, 2 cl.(zs) *, ▬ 2 cl.(zs)	Beograd	61
Beograd	Skopje	335/334		🛏 1, 2 cl.(mz), ▬ 2 cl.(mz)	Hellas Express	61
Bucuresti	istanbul	491/490 ❖		🛏 1, 2 cl.(cfr), ▬ 2 cl.(tcdd)	Bosphor	61, 98
Beograd	istanbul	491/490		🛏 1, 2 cl.(zs), ▬ 2 cl.(tcdd)	Balkan Express	61
Beograd	Sofia	293/292		🛏 1, 2 cl.(bdz), ▬ 2 cl.(zs)	Nušić	61
Villach	Beograd	315/314		🛏 1, 2 cl.(zs), ▬ 2 cl.(zs)		62
Hamburg	Wien	491/490	Euro Night	🛏 1, 2 cl. 🚿(öbb), ▬ 2 cl.(öbb)	Hans Albers	64
München	Budapest	463/462	Euro Night	🛏 1, 2 cl.(mav), ▬ 2 cl.(mav)	Kálmán Imre	65
München	Roma	485/484	City Night Line	🛏 1, 2 cl. 🚿(db), ▬ 2 cl.(db), 🍸	Lupus	70
München	Venezia	363/358	City Night Line	🛏 1, 2 cl. 🚿(db), ▬ 2 cl.(db), 🍸	Pictor	70
Amsterdam	Zürich	40419/40478	City Night Line	🛏 1, 2 cl. 🚿(cnl), ▬ 2 cl.(cnl), 🍸	Pegasus	73
København	Basel	473/472	City Night Line	🛏 1, 2 cl. 🚿(sbb), ▬ 2 cl.(db), 🍸	Aurora	73
Zürich	Berlin	1258/1259	City Night Line	🛏 1, 2 cl. 🚿(sbb), ▬ 2 cl.(sbb), 🍸	Sirius	73
Zürich	Zagreb	465/414	Euro Night	🛏 1, 2 cl.(hz), ▬ 2 cl.(hz)		86
Zürich	Budapest	467/466	Euro Night	🛏 1, 2 cl.(mav), ▬ 2 cl.(mav)	Wiener Walzer	86
Zürich	Graz	465/464	Euro Night	🛏 1, 2 cl. 🚿(öbb), ▬ 2 cl.(öbb)	Zürichsee	86
Wien	Roma	1235/1234	Euro Night	🛏 1, 2 cl. 🚿(öbb), ▬ 2 cl.(öbb)	Tosca	88
Wien	Venezia	237/236	Euro Night	🛏 1, 2 cl. 🚿(öbb), ▬ 2 cl.(öbb)	Vienna - Venezia Express	88
Wien	Milano	1235/1234	Euro Night	🛏 1, 2 cl.(ti), ▬ 2 cl.(ti)		88
Praha	Moskva	22/21		🛏 1, 2 cl.(rzd)	Vltava	95
Cheb	Moskva	22/21		🛏 1, 2 cl.(rzd)	Vltava	95
Wien	Moskva	22/21		🛏 1, 2 cl.(rzd)	Vltava	95
Bratislava	Moskva	22/21		🛏 1, 2 cl.(rzd)		95
Wrocław	Kyïv	52/51		🛏 1, 2 cl. 🚿(pkp)		96
Beograd	Moskva	15/16		🛏 1, 2 cl.(rzd)	Tisza	97
Sofia	Moskva	60/59		🛏 1, 2 cl.(rzd)	Bolgariya Express	98
Kraków	Budapest	402/476		🛏 1, 2 cl.(pkp), ▬ 2 cl.(pkp)		99
Warszawa	Budapest	407/476		🛏 1, 2 cl.(pkp), ▬ 2 cl.(pkp)		99
Warszawa	Wien	407/406		🛏 1, 2 cl. 🚿(pkp), ▬ 2 cl.(öbb)	Chopin	99
Kraków	Wien	402/406		🛏 1, 2 cl.(pkp), ▬ 2 cl.(pkp)		99
Praha	Warszawa	443/407		🛏 1, 2 cl.(pkp), ▬ 2 cl.(pkp)		99
Praha	Kraków	403/402		🛏 1, 2 cl.(cd), ▬ 2 cl.(cd)	Silesia	99
Helsinki	Moskva	31/32	Firménny	🛏 1, 2 cl. 🚿(rzd), 🍴	Lev Tolstoi	1910
Non daily sleepers (other seasonal services operate):						
Paris	Moskva	453/452	Euro Night	🛏 1, 2 cl. 🚿(rzd), 🍴(pkp, rzd)	Trans European Express	24
Berlin	Saratov	70/69		🛏 1, 2 cl.(rzd)	Saratov Express	1980
Berlin	Novosibirsk	1249/1248		🛏 2 cl.(rzd)		1980

Key to ownership of sleeping cars:

bdz - Bulgarian, bc - Belarussian, bne - Berlin Night Express, cd - Czech, cfr - Romanian, cnl - City Night Line, db - German, hz - Croatian, mav - Hungarian, mz - Macedonain, öbb - Austrian, pkp - Polish, renfe - Spanish, rzd - Russian, sbb - Swiss, ti - Italian, uz - Ukrainian, zs - Serbian.

🚿 – shower. 🍴 – restaurant car.

* *No sleeping cars conveyed until further notice.*

❖ – The compostion of this train is subject to confirmation.

Note: This list excludes trains not shown in our International section (e.g. Czech Republic to Slovakia, Ukraine to Russia etc.).

InterRail - *for European residents.*

website: www.interrail.eu

INTERRAIL GLOBAL PASS - valid in 30 European countries:

Austria, Belgium, Bosnia-Herzegovina, Bulgaria, Croatia, Czech Republic, Denmark, Finland, France, Germany, Great Britain, Greece, Hungary, Ireland (including Northern Ireland), Italy, Luxembourg, FYR Macedonia, Montenegro, the Netherlands, Norway, Poland, Portugal, Romania, Serbia, Slovakia, Slovenia, Spain, Sweden, Switzerland and Turkey.

NOT VALID in the passholder's country of residence.

PRICES - GLOBAL PASS

Youth is 25 or under	Youth 2nd class	Adult 2nd class	Adult 1st class
5 days within 10 days (flexi)	€184	€281	€441
10 days within 22 days (flexi)	€269	€399	€628
15 days continuous	€312	€442	€694
22 days continuous	€345	€517	€812
1 month continuous	€442	€668	€1050

2014 prices in Euros. Children aged 4 - 11 pay approx 50% of the adult price. Global Pass Senior (60+) gives 10% discount (not for One Country passes).

INTERRAIL ONE COUNTRY PASS - valid in one country

Covers any one of the participating countries above (except Bosnia-Herzegovina, FYRO Macedonia or Montenegro). NOT available for the passholder's country of residence. Note that Benelux (Belgium, Luxembourg, Netherlands) counts as one country. *Greece Plus* and *Italy Plus* passes includes Italy-Greece ferry services operated by Attica Group (Superfast Ferries - some routes are run jointly with Anek Lines).

PRICES - ONE COUNTRY PASS *3, 4, 6 or 8 days within 1 month*

France, Germany, Great Britain or Italy Plus:

	youth	2nd	1st		youth	2nd	1st
3 days	€147	€216	€338	6 days	€199	€302	€475
4 days	€157	€237	€372	8 days	€222	€334	€525

Austria, Italy, Norway (2nd class only), Spain or Sweden:

3 days	€129	€190	€299	6 days	€184	€281	€441
4 days	€152	€216	€338	8 days	€216	€326	€512

Benelux, Denmark, Finland, Greece Plus, Ireland or Switzerland:

3 days	€83	€125	€197	6 days	€135	€212	€332
4 days	€103	€158	€248	8 days	€168	€255	€401

Croatia, Czech Republic, Greece, Hungary, Poland, Portugal, Romania, Slovakia, Slovenia or Turkey:

3 days	€54	€82	€128	6 days	€88	€133	€210
4 days	€65	€100	€157	8 days	€102	€157	€246

Bulgaria, FYR Macedonia or Serbia:

3 days	€39	€59	€94	6 days	€77	€112	€176
4 days	€54	€82	€128	8 days	€87	€134	€212

WHO CAN BUY INTERRAIL PASSES

Any national of a European country (including Russia) with a valid passport, or anyone who has lived in Europe for at least six months. Passes can be purchased up to three months before travel begins.

SUPPLEMENTS AND RESERVATION FEES

Required for certain types of high-speed or 'global price' train. International day train examples, 2nd class (subject to change): France - Italy *TGV* €60 (€80 in 1st class); *Berlin - Warszawa Express* €4; *EC Switzerland - Italy* €10; *Eurostar* passholder fare (e.g. London - Paris from €89); *IC* Stockholm - Oslo €3; *TGV*/*ICE* France - Germany €13; *TGV Lyria* (France - Switzerland) €10; *Thalys* passholder fare €30 - 39; *TGV* Brussels - France €9; France - Spain €11 - 26; *SJ Snabbtåg* Stockholm - København €7. *IC bus* Klagenfurt - Venezia €9 (€13 1st class). Domestic examples: **Croatia** *IC* €1. **Czech Republic** *SC* €8. **Finland** *Pendolino* €3 - 7. **France** *TGV* €6 (peak €21), *Intercités* with compulsory reservation €6. **Germany** free on *ICE* (*ICE Sprinter* €12). **Greece** *ICity* €7 - 20. **Hungary** *IC* €3. **Italy** *FA*, *FB* and *FR* €10. **Norway** long-distance trains €6.3. **Poland** *EIC*/*TLK* free (€2.3 if made on train), *BWE* €4. **Portugal** *AP*/*IC* €5. **Romania** *IC* €3. **Slovakia** *IC* €5. **Slovenia** *ICS* €3.4 (€5.1 1st class). **Spain** *AVE* €10, most other long-distance trains €6.5, *MD* €4.5. **Sweden** *Snabbtåg* €7.

Night Trains: Many night trains are globally priced and fares for passholders vary widely. *Elipsos* night trains France / Italy - Spain give discounted fares, as do *Berlin Night Express* (Berlin - Malmö). Passes do not include sleeping accommodation, which is typically €19 to €75 for a couchette, €39 to €216 for a berth in a sleeping car.

The number of seats allocated to InterRail holders may be limited (e.g. on *TGV* and *Thalys* trains). If sold out, you may have to buy an ordinary ticket. The fold-out Travel Report inside the ticket cover must be filled in. Direct night trains or ferries leaving after 1900 hrs can count as next travel day.

DISCOUNT IN COUNTRY OF RESIDENCE

Although the pass is not valid in the country of residence, passholders can obtain a reduction for one return ticket to the border or nearest airport. This is usually 50% (Bosnia 30%, Germany 25%, Spain 35%) but there is no discount in Czech Republic, Poland, Romania or the United Kingdom.

VALIDITY ON PRIVATE RAILWAYS

InterRail passes are valid on the national railway companies in each country, plus many privately run railways (some give discounts). For details see the InterRail Traveller's Guide or www.interrail.eu. Selected details are as follows: **Austria**: free travel on WESTbahn and ROeEE. **Denmark**: free travel on Arriva and DSB-First, 50% discount on Hjørring - Hirtshals and Frederikshavn - Skagen. **France**: SNCF bus services included. **Germany**: free on most regional services (not Züssow - Świnoujście). **Hungary**: GySEV services are included. **Italy**: not valid on NTV's *Italo* trains. **Netherlands**: privately run regional lines are included. **Norway**: Flåmsbana (Myrdal - Flåm) gives 30% discount. **Spain**: FEVE and FGC railways give 50% discount. **Sweden**: included are Arlanda Express, Arriva, DSB First, Inlandsbanan, MerResor, Norrtåg, Øresundståg, Skånetrafiken, Tågkompaniet, Värmlandstrafik, Västtrafik, Veolia. **Switzerland**: free travel on BLS, FART/SSIF, MOB, RhB, SOB, THURBO and ZB. Many others offer 50% discount, including AB, ASM, CJ, FB, LEB, MBC, NStCM, RA, RB, RBS, SZU, TMR, TPC, TPF, TRN, WB, WSB. The MGB (Disentis - Brig - Zermatt and Göschenen - Andermatt) and Gornergratbahn offer 50% to under-26s only. Discounted fare on William Tell Express (rail and boat tour). No discounts available on BRB or narrow gauge railways in Jungfrau area (BOB, JB, WAB).

VALIDITY ON FERRY AND BUS SERVICES

The pass includes free deck passage between Italy and Greece on SuperFast Ferries and Minoan Lines (you pay port taxes €7, high-season surcharge €10 June/Sept, €20 July/Aug, and possibly a fuel surcharge); free air-seats for 1st class pass holders. Free deck passage on Scandlines. Many other ferry companies offer discounts (not on cabins), for example: Balearia 20%, Finnlines 20%, Fjord1 Fylkesbaatane 50%, Grimaldi 20%, Irish Ferries 30%, Stena Line 20% (30% on UK routes), Tallink Silja 20% (high-season), 40% (low-season), Viking Line 50%. Special fares apply on Destination Gotland. Valid on ÖBB Austrian lake services; most Swiss lakes give 50%. A few buses, tourist attractions and cycle hire offer discounts.

Eurail - *for non-European residents.*

website: www.eurail.com www.eurailgroup.org

EURAIL GLOBAL PASS - valid in 24 European countries:

Austria, Belgium, Bulgaria, Croatia, Czech Republic, Denmark, Finland, France, Germany, Greece, Hungary, Ireland (including Northern Ireland), Italy, Luxembourg, the Netherlands, Norway, Portugal, Romania, Slovakia, Slovenia, Spain, Sweden, Switzerland, Turkey.

PRICES - GLOBAL PASS

Youth is 25 or under	Youth 2nd class	Adult 1st class	Saver * (per person)
10 days within 2 months	623 USD	955 USD	813 USD
15 days within 2 months	817 USD	1254 USD	1067 USD
15 days continuous	528 USD	812 USD	690 USD
21 days continuous	682 USD	1046 USD	891 USD
1 month continuous	838 USD	1287 USD	1095 USD
2 months continuous	1181 USD	1816 USD	1543 USD
3 months continuous	1457 USD	2240 USD	1904 USD

* Saver: two to five people travelling together (price per person).
Children (age 4 - 11) pay approx 50% of the adult price.

WHO CAN BUY EURAIL PASSES

Anyone resident outside Europe (but excluding residents of Russia and CIS or Turkey). Passes are sold through official sales agents. For prices of Select, Regional and One Country passes see www.eurail.com or agents.

EURAIL SELECT PASS - 4 adjoining countries chosen from:

Austria, Belgium / Netherlands / Luxembourg, Bulgaria, Croatia / Slovenia, Czech Republic, Denmark, Finland, France, Germany, Greece, Hungary, Ireland (including NIR), Italy, Norway, Portugal, Romania, Serbia / Montenegro, Spain, Sweden, Switzerland, Turkey. Countries grouped above count as one.

EURAIL REGIONAL PASS - choose from 24 regions:

A range of passes, generally for two adjoining countries, e.g. France-Germany, France-Italy, Benelux-Germany, Hungary-Romania, Portugal-Spain. Also includes Scandinavia (Denmark / Finland / Norway / Sweden).

EURAIL ONE COUNTRY PASSES - valid in any one of the following:

Austria, Benelux (Belgium / Netherlands / Luxembourg), Bulgaria, Croatia, Czech Republic, Denmark, Finland, Greece, Hungary, Ireland, Italy, Norway, Poland, Portugal, Romania, Slovakia, Slovenia, Spain, Sweden.

Direct night trains or ferries leaving after 1900 hrs can count as next trave[l] day. Supplements generally not required for *EC*, *IC*, *ICE* trains. French *TGV* trains require the reservation fee only. Other supplements are similar to those shown under InterRail above. Sleeper/couchette supplements and seat reservations are extra. For discounts on private railways and ferry companies see www.eurail.com (they may vary from InterRail, notably in Switzerland where the Jungfrau railways offer discounts to Eurail holders).

Table 547: The Bernina Railway

Nicky Gardner and Susanne Kries take the train over the Alps from Switzerland to Italy.

The great and the good came to Pontresina to relax and enjoy the Alpine scenery of eastern Switzerland. Hans Christian Andersen stayed in Pontresina. So did Richard Wagner. Mrs Gaskell started writing *Wives and Daughters*, her gossipy tale of scandal and intrigue in an English country town, while holidaying – with all her daughters – in Pontresina. That was 150 years ago this summer. But Pontresina's star faded as the literary crowd shifted their affections elsewhere. A certain class of English traveller stayed loyal to Pontresina, but that class dwindled and eventually there was no-one left to attend the English church in Pontresina. So in 1974 it was demolished. Pontresina has slipped out of fashion, but there is still very good reason to visit. For it lies at the northern end of one of the finest rail routes in the Alps.

ACROSS THE ALPS

Travellers from northern and central Europe heading through Switzerland to northern Italy have a choice of three possible rail itineraries that traverse the great Alpine ranges. There is the classic Gotthard Tunnel route (shown in Table 550). Further west, there is the journey through the Simplon Tunnel to Lago Maggiore and beyond (Table 590). But the third route, which strikes south from Pontresina and traverses the Bernina Pass, is by far the most impressive of the three. This is the youngest of the three Swiss Alpine rail routes to northern Italy, opened only in 1910. And it is the only one of the three that really traverses a mountain pass, and a very fine one at that.

The 55 kilometres of the Bernina railway from Pontresina to the Italian town of Tirano are almost all above ground. True, there are one or two short tunnels and some quite extensive snow sheds to protect the railway from avalanches, but this is a route that really goes *over* the mountains, rather than tunnelling through them. And, with gradients at over seven per cent and a maximum altitude of over 2000 metres, the little red trains of the metre-gauge Rhaetian Railway transport passengers from Pontresina up into a high Alpine environment of icy glaciers and rocky moraines before plunging in a great series of loops down into the Poschiavo Valley which it then follows south to the Italian Valtellina.

GLACIERS AND GORGES

Until the opening of the railway, only the most adventurous visitors to Pontresina contemplated the arduous excursion to Alp Grüm, which was commended by Baedeker for its restaurant and fine view of the Palü glacier. But now the railway transports tourists from Pontresina up to the front door of the restaurant at Alp Grüm in just forty minutes, and the view is every bit as magnificent as it was in Baedeker's day. The Palü glacier has receded a little, and Mr Baedeker might well be bemused by the signs in Japanese on the railway station platform, but otherwise it is much the same. A place for deep snow in winter with gentian, edelweiss and moss campion in summer.

This railway offers a kaleidoscope of scenery from rocky gorges to carefully tended vineyards. The descent into Italy communicates a sense of entering the sunny south. In Tirano, the train runs through the streets. Traffic waits, not always patiently, as the train moves smoothly past shops and houses, on past the great pilgrimage church of the *Madonna di Tirano* until the train comes to a halt at the Rhaetian Railway's own little station just beside the Italian station.

From Tirano, you can continue south to Milano (Table 593). In summer, there is also a useful direct bus from Tirano to Lugano (Table 543). If you are tempted to ride the Bernina Railway, take our advice and avoid the trains marked in Table 547 as Bernina Express. Opt instead for the regular slow trains that ply the route. They are often much quieter and a lot more fun. Roll down the window and breathe the fresh Bernina air.

The authors of our Route of the Month are the editors of hidden europe magazine. Find out more about the magazine, and Nicky and Susanne's other work, at www.hiddeneurope.co.uk.

The destinations of international Car Sleeper services from these terminals are shown in Table 1.

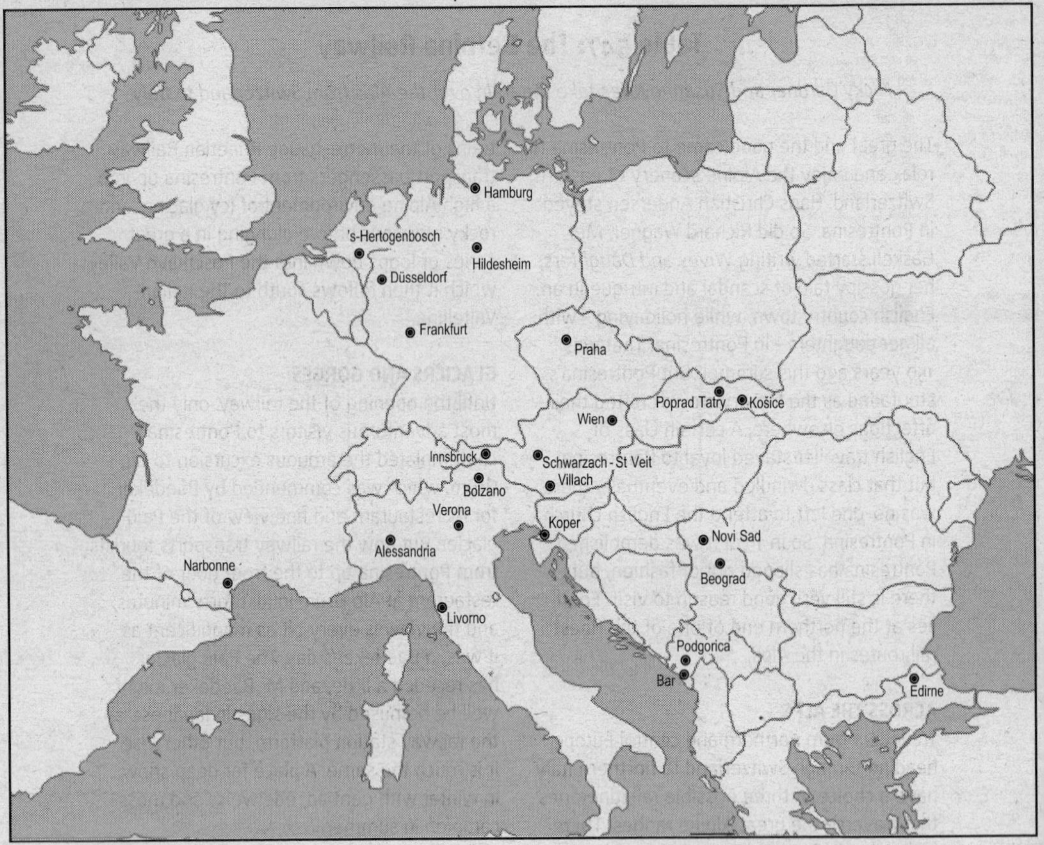

AUTO-TRAIN, AUTOREISEZÜGE, MOTORAIL

Car-carrying trains are composed of special wagons or vans for the conveyance of motorcars usually with sleeping cars and couchettes enabling the driver and passengers to travel overnight in comfort in the same train. Some services (particularly in France) convey vehicles separately allowing passengers a choice of trains for their own journey. Some shorter distance services run by day and convey seating coaches.

Cars are often loaded on the trains at separate stations from the passenger station and may be loaded some time before the passenger train departs. International car-carrying trains are shown in Table **1**, Domestic car-carrying trains in Table **2**. Some services also carry passengers without cars.

Details of Channel Tunnel shuttle services may be found on page 45. Austrian and Swiss alpine tunnel car-carrying trains are shown in the relevant country section - see pages 458 and 262 respectively for details.

Readers should be careful to check that dates refer to current schedules, as old dates may be left in the table until such time as current information is received. Loading and train times may vary on some dates, but will be confirmed by the agent when booking.

Some services shown in Table **1** are operated by organisations other than national railway companies. Contact details for these are:
Services from Germany: DB AutoZug, (UK booking centre); ✆ 08718 80 80 66.
Services from Netherlands: Euro-Express-Treincharter (EETC), Burgemeestersrand 57, 2625 NV Delft; ✆ +31 (0)15 213 36 36, fax +31 (0)15 214 07 39.
Certain Eastern European services (see table for details):
Optima Tours, Karlstrasse 56, 80333 D-München; ✆ +49 89 54880 - 111, fax +49 89 54880 - 155.

SEE MAP PAGE 36

INTERNATIONAL CAR-CARRYING TRAINS 1

ALESSANDRIA to

DÜSSELDORF:
⑥ Apr. 5 - Oct. 25, 2014.
Alessandria load 1430 - 1500, depart 1740, Düsseldorf Hbf arrive 1026.
Train **41352**: 🛏 1,2 cl., 🛌 2 cl. and ✕.

FRANKFURT:
⑥ Apr. 5 - Oct. 25, 2014.
Alessandria load 1455 - 1525, depart 1740, Frankfurt Neu Isenburg arrive 0551 - 0659.
Train **73370**: 🛏 1,2 cl., 🛌 2 cl. and ✕.

HAMBURG:
⑥ Apr. 5 - Oct. 25, 2014.
Alessandria load 1430 - 1600, depart 1740, Hamburg Altona arrive 1344 - 1435.
Train **43370**: 🛏 1,2 cl., 🛌 2 cl. and ✕.

's-HERTOGENBOSCH:
⑥ May 31 - Aug. 30, 2014.
Alessandria load 1230 - 1430, depart 1605, 's-Hertogenbosch arrive 0943.
Train **13400**: 🛏 1,2 cl., 🛌 2 cl. and ✕.
Operator: Euro-Express-Treincharter (see table heading).

BAR to

BEOGRAD:
Daily.
Bar loading times not advised, depart 2000, Beograd arrive 0753. Also daily day train.
Train **1342**: 🛏 1,2 cl., 🛌 2 cl. and 🍸.

NOVI SAD:
June 7 - Sept. 8, 2014.
Bar loading times not advised, depart 1700, Novi Sad arrive 0657.
Train **1136**: 🛏 1,2 cl., 🛌 2 cl. and 🚃2.

BEOGRAD to

BAR:
Daily.
Beograd loading times not advised, depart 2110, Bar arrive 0849. Also daily day train.
Train **1343**: 🛏 1,2 cl., 🛌 2 cl. and 🍸.

PODGORICA:
Sept. 9 - Dec. 13, 2013.
Beograd loading times not advised, depart 0910, Podgorica arrive 1923.
Train **433**: 🛏 1,2 cl., 🚃2 and 🍸.

BOLZANO to

German services may be bookable only in Germany.

DÜSSELDORF:
① May 5 - 26; ①④ May 29 - Aug. 28; ① Sept. 1 - 29, 2014.
Bolzano load 1600 - 1630, depart 1846, Düsseldorf Hbf arrive 0814 (0826⑤).
Train **43322/6**: 🛏 1,2 cl., 🛌 2 cl. and ✕.

HAMBURG:
⑥ Jan. 4 - Apr. 26; ① May 5 - 26; ①④ May 29 - Aug. 28; ① Sept. 1 - 29, 2014.
Until Apr. 26: Bolzano load 1600 - 1930, depart 1740 (2106 from Apr. 5), Hamburg Altona arrive 0912 (1138 from Apr. 6).
From May 5: Bolzano load 1715 - 1730, depart 1846, Hamburg Altona arrive 1103 - 12.38.
Train **13380/2/4/6**: 🛏 1,2 cl., 🛌 2 cl. and ✕.

HILDESHEIM:
⑥ Apr. 5 - 26; ① May 5 - 26; ①④ May 29 - Aug. 28; ① Sept. 1 - 29, 2014.
Until Apr. 26: Bolzano load 1900 - 1930, depart 2106, Bolzano arrive 0851.
From May 5: Bolzano load 1645 - 1715, depart 1846, Bolzano arrive 0851 - 0903.
Train **43380/53382/6**: 🛏 1,2 cl., 🛌 2 cl. and ✕.

DÜSSELDORF to

ALESSANDRIA:
⑤ Apr. 4 - Oct. 24, 2014.
Düsseldorf Hbf load 1445 - 1515, depart 1603, Alessandria 0906.
Train **41350**: 🛏 1,2 cl., 🛌 2 cl. and ✕.

BOLZANO:
⑦ May 4 - 25; ③⑦ May 28 - Aug. 31; ⑦ Sept. 7 - 28, 2014.
Düsseldorf Hbf load 1530 - 1645, depart 1713 (1734③), Bolzano arrive 0749.
Train **43323/7**: 🛏 1,2 cl., 🛌 2 cl. and ✕.

INNSBRUCK:
⑤ Jan. 3 - Apr. 25, 2014.
Düsseldorf Hbf load 2030 - 2115, depart 2143, Innsbruck Hbf arrive 0906.
Train **13321/5**: 🛏 1,2 cl., 🛌 2 cl. and ✕.

NARBONNE:
⑤ Apr. 4 - Oct. 24, 2014.
Düsseldorf Hbf load 1400 - 1430, depart 1603, Narbonne arrive 1100.
Train **1350**: 🛏 1,2 cl., 🛌 2 cl. and ✕.

SCHWARZACH-ST VEIT:
⑦ May 5 - Sept. 29, 2013.
Düsseldorf Hbf loading time not advised, depart 2155, Schwarzach-St Veit arrive 0917 (1009 from Aug. 4).
Train **13323**: 🛏 1,2 cl., 🛌 2 cl. and ✕.

VILLACH:
⑦ May 4 - 25; ③⑦ May 28 - Aug. 31; ⑦ Sept. 7 - 28, 2014.
Düsseldorf Hbf load 1600 - 1615, depart 1713 (1734③), Villach arrive 0742 (1151 on ① May 5 - 12).
Train **13323/27**: 🛏 1,2 cl., 🛌 2 cl. and ✕.

EDIRNE to

VILLACH:
Apr. 17, 25, May 1, 9, 15, 23, 29, June 6, 12, 20, 26, July 4, 10, 18, 22, 26, 31, Aug. 1, 7, 8, 11, 14, 15, 18, 21, 22, 25, 28, 29, Sept. 1, 4, 5, 8, 11, 12, 18, 22, 26, Oct. 2, 9, 13, 17, 23, 27, 31, Nov. 6, 10, 15.
Timings vary. 🛌 and ✕.
Contact operator for further details.
Operator: Optima Tours (see table heading).

FRANKFURT (NEU ISENBURG) to

ALESSANDRIA:
⑤ Apr. 4 - Oct. 24, 2014.
Frankfurt Neu Isenburg load 1930 - 2000, depart 2034 or 2132, Alessandria arrive 0906.
Train **73371**: 🛏 1,2 cl., 🛌 2 cl. and ✕.

NARBONNE:
⑤ Apr. 4 - Oct. 24, 2014.
Frankfurt Neu Isenburg load 1845 - 1930, depart 1946 or 2034, Narbonne arrive 1100.
Train **53371**: 🛏 1,2 cl., 🛌 2 cl. and ✕.

HAMBURG to

ALESSANDRIA:
⑤ Apr. 4 - Oct. 24, 2014.
Hamburg Altona load 1205 - 1305, depart 1319 or 1348, Alessandria arrive 0906.
Train **43371/7**: 🛏 1,2 cl., 🛌 2 cl. and ✕.

BOLZANO:
⑤ Jan. 3 - Apr. 25; ⑦ May 4 - 25; ③⑦ May 28 - Aug. 31; ⑦ Sept. 1 - 28, 2014.
Until Apr. 25: Hamburg Hbf load 1745 - 1810, depart 1837, Bolzano arrive 1048 (0949 from Apr. 5).
From May 4: Hamburg Hbf load 1230 - 1450, depart 1319 - 1523, Bolzano arrive 0749.
Train **13381/3/5/7**: 🛏 1,2 cl., 🛌 2 cl. and ✕.

INNSBRUCK:
⑤ Jan. 3 - Mar. 28, 2014.
Hamburg Altona load 1755 - 1825, depart 1857, Innsbruck Hbf arrive 0806.
Train **43385**: 🛏 1,2 cl., 🛌 2 cl. and ✕.

NARBONNE:
⑤ Apr. 4 - Oct. 24, 2014.
Hamburg Altona load 1230 - 1320, depart 1319 or 1348, Narbonne arrive 1100.
Train **13371**: 🛏 1,2 cl., 🛌 2 cl. and ✕.

VILLACH:
⑦ May 4 - 25; ③⑦ May 28 - Aug. 31; ⑦ Sept. 7 - 28, 2014.
Hamburg Altona load 1215 - 1435, depart 1319 - 1523, Villach Ost arrive 0742 (1151 on ① May 5 - 12).
Train **43383/7**: 🛏 1,2 cl., 🛌 2 cl. and ✕.

WIEN:
Daily until Oct. 31, 2014.
Hamburg Altona load 1945 - 2000, depart 2020, Wien Westbf arrive 0856.
Train **491**: 🛏 1,2 cl., 🛌 2 cl. and 🚃2.

's-HERTOGENBOSCH to

ALESSANDRIA:
⑤ May 30 - Aug. 29, 2014.
's-Hertogenbosch load 1245 - 1500, depart 1612, Alessandria arrive 1023.
Train **13401**: 🛏 1, 2 cl., ▬ 2 cl. and ✕.
Operator: Euro-Express-Treincharter (see table heading).

KOPER:
⑤ June 27 - Aug. 29, 2014.
's-Hertogenbosch load 1045 - 1300, depart 1412, Koper arrive 0855.
Train **13419**: 🛏 1, 2 cl., ▬ 2 cl. and ✕.
Operator: Euro-Express-Treincharter (see table heading).

LIVORNO:
⑤ Apr. 25 - Oct. 3, 2014.
's-Hertogenbosch load 0945 - 1200, depart 1312, Livorno arrive 1131.
Train **13409**: 🛏 1, 2 cl., ▬ 2 cl. and ✕.
Operator: Euro-Express-Treincharter (see table heading).

HILDESHEIM to

BOLZANO:
⑤ Apr. 4 - 25; ⑦ May 4 - 25; ③⑦ May 28 - Aug. 31; ⑦ Sept. 7 - 28, 2014.
Until Apr. 25: Hildesheim load 1930 - 2000, depart 2103, Bolzano arrive 0949.
From May 4: Hildesheim load 1620 - 1730, depart 1655 - 1836, Bolzano arrive 0749.
Train **43381/53383/7**: 🛏 1, 2 cl., ▬ 2 cl. and ✕.

INNSBRUCK:
⑤ Jan. 3 - Mar. 28, 2014.
Hildesheim load 1920 - 2050, depart 2157, Innsbruck Hbf arrive 0806.
Train **53385**: 🛏 1, 2 cl., ▬ 2 cl. and ✕.

VILLACH:
⑦ May 4 - 25; ③⑦ May 28 - Aug. 31; ⑦ Sept. 7 - 28, 2014.
Hildesheim load 1550 - 1700, depart 1655 - 1836, Villach Ost arrive 0742 (1151 on ① May 5 - 12).
Train **73383/7**: 🛏 1, 2 cl., ▬ 2 cl. and ✕.

INNSBRUCK to

DÜSSELDORF:
⑥ Jan. 4 - Apr. 26, 2014.
Innsbruck Hbf load 1745 - 1830, depart 1918, Düsseldorf Hbf arrive 0639.
Train **13320/4**: 🛏 1, 2 cl., ▬ 2 cl. and ✕.

HAMBURG:
⑥ Jan. 4 - Mar. 29, 2014.
Innsbruck Hbf load 1800 - 1830, depart 2013, Hamburg Altona arrive 0912.
Train **43384**: 🛏 1, 2 cl., ▬ 2 cl. and ✕.

HILDESHEIM:
⑥ Jan. 4 - Mar. 29, 2014.
Innsbruck Hbf load 1800 - 1830, depart 2013, Hildesheim arrive 0624.
Train **53384**: 🛏 1, 2 cl., ▬ 2 cl. and ✕.

KOPER

's-HERTOGENBOSCH:
⑥ June 28 - Aug. 30, 2014.
Koper load 1230 - 1430, depart 1525, 's-Hertogenbosch arrive 1043.
Train **13418**: 🛏 1, 2 cl., ▬ 2 cl. and ✕.
Operator: Euro-Express-Treincharter (see table heading).

KOŠICE

PRAHA:
Daily except Dec. 24, 31.
Košice depart 2208, Praha hlavní arrive 0737.
Train **442**: 🛏 1, 2 cl., ▬ 2 cl. and [2].

LIVORNO to

German services may be bookable only in Germany.

's-HERTOGENBOSCH:
⑥ Apr. 26 - Oct. 4, 2014.
Livorno load 1330 - 1530, depart 1703, 's-Hertogenbosch arrive 1443.
Train **13408**: 🛏 1, 2 cl., ▬ 2 cl. and ✕.
Operator: Euro-Express-Treincharter (see table heading).

WIEN:
⑥ Apr. 12 - June 14; ④⑥ June 19 - Aug. 30; ⑥ Sept. 6 - 27, 2014 (also Apr. 21, May 1, 29, June 9).
Livorno Centrale load 1630 - 1800, depart 1920, Wien Matzleinsdorf (Wien Hbf from mid-June) arrive 0834.
Train **1234**: 🛏 1, 2 cl., ▬ 2 cl. and [2].

NARBONNE to

Loading at Gare auto/train (🚌 connection)

DÜSSELDORF:
⑥ Apr. 5 - Oct. 25, 2014.
Narbonne load 1320 - 1350, depart 1558, Düsseldorf Hbf arrive 1026.
Train **1352**: 🛏 1, 2 cl., ▬ 2 cl. and ✕.

FRANKFURT:
⑥ Apr. 5 - Oct. 25, 2014.
Narbonne load 1310 - 1340, depart 1558, Frankfurt Neu Isenburg arrive 0551 - 0613.
Train **53370**: 🛏 1, 2 cl., ▬ 2 cl. and ✕.

HAMBURG:
⑥ Apr. 5 - Oct. 25, 2014.
Narbonne load 1325 - 1415, depart 1558, Hamburg Altona arrive 1344 - 1435.
Train **13370**: 🛏 1, 2 cl., ▬ 2 cl. and ✕.

NOVI SAD to

BAR:
June 6 - Sept. 7, 2014.
Novi Sad loading times not advised, depart 2117, Bar arrive 1046.
Train **1137**: 🛏 1, 2 cl., ▬ 2 cl. and [2].

PODGORICA to

BEOGRAD:
Sept. 10 - Dec. 14, 2013.
Podgorica loading times not advised, depart 2005, Beograd arrive 0603.
Train **432**: 🛏 1, 2 cl., [2] and 🍸.

POPRAD TATRY to

PRAHA:
Daily except Dec. 24, 31.
Poprad Tatry depart 2243, Praha hlavní arrive 0649.
Train **444**: 🛏 1, 2 cl., ▬ 2 cl. and [2].

PRAHA to

KOŠICE:
Daily except Dec. 24, 31.
Praha hlavní depart 2226, Košice arrive 0752.
Train **443**: 🛏 1, 2 cl., ▬ 2 cl. and [2].

POPRAD TATRY:
Daily except Dec. 24, 31.
Praha hlavní depart 2153, Poprad Tatry arrive 0612.
Train **445**: 🛏 1, 2 cl., ▬ 2 cl. and [2].

SCHWARZACH - ST VEIT to

DÜSSELDORF:
① May 6 - Sept. 30, 2013.
Schwarzach-St Veit loading time not advised, depart 1840 (1918 from Aug. 5), Düsseldorf arrive 0658 (0742 from Aug. 6).
Train **13322**: 🛏 1, 2 cl., ▬ 2 cl. and ✕.

VERONA to

WIEN:
⑤⑦ June 15 - Sept. 28, 2014.
Verona Porta Nuova load 2100 - 2200, depart 2338, Wien Hbf ARZ arrive 0850.
Train **481**: 🛏 1, 2 cl., ▬ 2 cl. and [2].

VILLACH to

DÜSSELDORF:
① May 5 - 19; ①④ May 26 - Aug. 28; ① Sept. 1 - 29, 2014.
Villach Ost load 1315 - 1640, depart 1732 (1356 on ① May 5 - 12), Düsseldorf Hbf arrive 0814 - 0826.
Train **13322/26**: 🛏 1, 2 cl., ▬ 2 cl. and ✕.

EDIRNE:
Apr. 14, 19, 23, 27, May 3, 7, 11, 17, 21, 25, 31, June 4, 8, 14, 18, 22, 28, July 2, 6, 12, 16, 20, 24, 25, 30, Aug. 2, 3, 6, 9, 10, 16, 23, 30, Sept. 6, 14, 20, 30, Oct. 5, 11, 19, 25, Nov. 2, 8, 12.
Timings vary. ▬ and ✕.
Contact operator for further details.
Operator: Optima Tours (see table heading).

HAMBURG:
① May 5 - 26; ①④ May 29 - Aug. 28; ① Sept. 1 - 29, 2014.
Villach Ost load 1315 - 1640, depart 1732 (1356 on ① May 5 - 12), Hamburg Altona arrive 1103 - 1238.
Train **43382/6**: 🛏 1, 2 cl., ▬ 2 cl. and ✕.

HILDESHEIM:
① May 5 - 26; ①④ May 29 - Aug. 28; ① Sept. 1 - 29, 2014.
Villach Ost load 1315 - 1640, depart 1732 (1356 on ① May 5 - 12), Hildesheim arrive 0851 - 0903.
Train **73382/6**: 🛏 1, 2 cl., ▬ 2 cl. and ✕.

WIEN to

HAMBURG:
Daily until Oct. 31, 2014.
Wien Westbf load 1925 - 1940, depart 2000, Hamburg Altona arrive 0804.
Train **490**: 🛏 1, 2 cl., ▬ 2 cl. and [2].

LIVORNO:
⑤ Apr. 11 - June 13; ③⑤ June 18 - Aug. 29; ⑤ Sept. 5 - 26, 2014 (also Apr. 20, Apr. 30, May 28, June 8).
Wien Matzleinsdorf (Wien Hbf from mid-June) load 1900 - 1945, depart 2021, Livorno Centrale arrive 0856.
Train **1237**: 🛏 1, 2 cl., ▬ 2 cl. and [2].

VERONA:
④⑥ June 14 - Sept. 27, 2014.
Wien Hbf ARZ loading time not advised, depart 1910, Verona Porta Nuova arrive 0645.
Train **60235**: 🛏 1, 2 cl., ▬ 2 cl. and [2].

AUSTRIA

to 13/12/14

Feldkirch - Graz: daily.
Feldkirch - Wien (Westbf): daily (day and night trains).
Graz - Feldkirch: daily.
Innsbruck - Wien (Westbf): daily (day train).
Villach - Wien (Matzleinsdorf): daily (day train).
Wien (Westbf) - Feldkirch: daily (day and night trains).
Wien (Westbf) - Innsbruck: daily (day train).
Wien - Villach (Matzleinsdorf): daily (day train).

CROATIA

to 13/12/14

Split - Zagreb: daily.
Zagreb - Split: daily.

FINLAND

to 10/08/14

Helsinki - Kemijärvi: ⑤.
Helsinki - Kolari: ③⑤⑥ June 16 - Aug. 10.
Helsinki - Oulu: daily (not July 11, Aug. 1).
Helsinki - Rovaniemi: daily.
Kemijärvi - Helsinki: ⑥.
Kolari - Helsinki: ④⑥⑦ June 16 - Aug. 10.
Kolari - Tampere: ④⑥⑦ June 16 - Aug. 10.
Kolari - Turku: *winter only.*
Oulu - Helsinki: daily (not July 12, Aug. 2).
Rovaniemi - Helsinki: daily.
Rovaniemi - Tampere: daily.
Rovaniemi - Turku: daily (not July 12, Aug. 2).
Tampere - Kolari: ③⑤⑥ June 16 - Aug. 10.
Tampere - Rovaniemi: daily.
Turku - Kolari: *winter only.*
Turku - Rovaniemi: daily (not July 11, Aug. 1).

Note: Helsinki trains load and unload at Pasila station (3 km north of Helsinki station)

FRANCE

to 13/12/14

Avignon - Paris: ⑥ Jan. 11 - Mar. 29; ④⑥ Apr. 3 - June 21; daily June 24 - Sept. 8; ④⑥ Sept. 11 - 27; ⑥ Oct. 4 - Dec. 13.
Biarritz - Paris▲: ⑥ Apr. 12 - 26; ④⑥ May 1 - June 21; ①②③④⑤⑥ June 24 - Sept. 8; ④⑥ Sept. 11 - 27.
Bordeaux - Paris: ⑥ Jan. 4 - Apr. 26; ④⑥ May 1 - June 21; ①②③④⑤⑥ June 24 - Sept. 8; ④⑥ Sept. 11 - 27; ⑥ Oct. 4 - Dec. 13.
Briançon - Paris▲: ④⑥ June 12 - 21; ②④⑥ June 24 - Sept. 6.
Brive - Paris: ⑥ Apr. 12 - 26; ④⑥ May 1 - June 21; ①②③④⑤⑥ June 24 - Sept. 8; ④⑥ Sept. 11 - 27.
Fréjus-St. Raphaël – see St. Raphaël.
Lyon - Paris: ⑥ Jan. 4 - June 21; ②⑥ June 24 - Sept. 6; ⑥ Sept. 13 - Dec. 13.
Marseille - Paris: ⑥ Jan. 4 - Mar. 29; ④⑥ Apr. 3 - June 21; daily June 24 - Sept. 8; ④⑥ Sept. 11 - 27; ⑥ Oct. 4 - Dec. 13.
Narbonne - Paris▲: ⑥ Jan. 4 - Apr. 26; ④⑥ May 1 - June 21; ①②③④⑤⑥ June 24 - Sept. 8; ④⑥ Sept. 11 - 27; ⑥ Oct. 4 - Dec. 13.
Nice - Paris▲: ⑥ Jan. 4 - Mar. 29; ④⑥ Apr. 3 - May 17; ②④⑥ May 20 - June 21; daily June 24 - Sept. 8; ②④⑥ Sept. 9 - 27; ④⑥ Oct. 2 - Nov. 1; ⑥ Nov. 8 - Dec. 13.
Paris - Avignon: ⑤ Jan. 10 - Mar. 28; ③⑤ Apr. 2 - June 20; daily June 23 - Sept. 7; ③⑤ Sept. 10 - 26; ⑤ Oct. 3 - Dec. 12.
Paris - Biarritz▲: ⑤ Apr. 11 - 25; ③⑤ Apr. 30 - June 20; ①②③④⑤⑥ June 23 - Sept. 6; ③⑤ Sept. 10 - 26.
Paris - Bordeaux: ⑤ Jan. 3 - Apr. 25; ③⑤ Apr. 30 - June 20; ①②③④⑤⑥ June 23 - Sept. 6; ③⑤ Sept. 10 - 26; ⑤ Oct. 3 - Dec. 12.
Paris - Briançon▲: ③⑤ June 11 - 20; ①③⑤ June 23 - Sept. 5.
Paris - Brive: ⑤ Apr. 11 - 25; ③⑤ Apr. 30 - June 20; ①②③④⑤⑥ June 23 - Sept. 6; ③⑤ Sept. 10 - 26.
Paris - Lyon: ⑤ Jan. 3 - June 20; ①⑤ June 23 - Sept. 5; ⑤ Sept. 12 - Dec. 12.
Paris - Marseille: ⑤ Jan. 3 - Mar. 28; ③⑤ Apr. 2 - June 20; daily June 23 - Sept. 7; ③⑤ Sept. 10 - 26; ⑤ Oct. 3 - Dec. 12.
Paris - Narbonne▲: ⑤ Jan. 3 - Apr. 25; ③⑤ Apr. 30 - June 20; ①②③④⑤⑥ June 23 - Sept. 6; ③⑤ Sept. 10 - 26; ⑤ Oct. 3 - Dec. 12.
Paris - Nice▲: ⑤ Jan. 3 - Mar. 28; ③⑤ Apr. 2 - May 16; ①③⑤ May 19 - June 20; daily June 23 - Sept. 7; ①③⑤ Sept. 8 - 26; ③⑤ Oct. 1 - 31; ⑤ Nov. 7 - Dec. 12.
Paris - St. Raphaël▲: ⑤ Jan. 3 - Mar. 28; ③⑤ Apr. 2 - May 16; ①③⑤ May 19 - June 20; daily June 23 - Sept. 7; ①③⑤ Sept. 8 - 26; ③⑤ Oct. 1 - 31; ⑤ Nov. 7 - Dec. 12.
Paris - Toulon▲: ⑤ Jan. 3 - Mar. 28; ③⑤ Apr. 2 - May 16; ①③⑤ May 19 - June 20; daily June 23 - Sept. 7; ①③⑤ Sept. 8 - 26; ③⑤ Oct. 1 - 31; ⑤ Nov. 7 - Dec. 12.
Paris - Toulouse▲: ⑤ Jan. 3 - Apr. 25; ③⑤ Apr. 30 - June 20; ①②③④⑤⑥ June 23 - Sept. 6; ③⑤ Sept. 10 - 26; ⑤ Oct. 3 - Dec. 12.

FRANCE (continued)

to 13/12/14

St. Raphaël - Paris▲: ⑥ Jan. 4 - Mar. 29; ④⑥ Apr. 3 - May 17; ②④⑥ May 20 - June 21; daily June 24 - Sept. 8; ②④⑥ Sept. 9 - 27; ④⑥ Oct. 2 - Nov. 1; ⑥ Nov. 8 - Dec. 13.
Toulon - Paris▲: ⑥ Jan. 4 - Mar. 29; ④⑥ Apr. 3 - May 17; ②④⑥ May 20 - June 21; daily June 24 - Sept. 8; ②④⑥ Sept. 9 - 27; ④⑥ Oct. 2 - Nov. 1; ⑥ Nov. 8 - Dec. 13.
Toulouse - Paris▲: ⑥ Jan. 4 - Apr. 26; ④⑥ May 1 - June 21; ①②③④⑤⑥ June 24 - Sept. 8; ④⑥ Sept. 11 - 27; ⑥ Oct. 4 - Dec. 13.

Passengers are offered a choice of departure times, mostly by day train but those noted ▲ also include night trains (Briançon night train only).

GERMANY

to 31/10/14

Basel (Lörrach) - Hamburg Altona: ⑥ Jan. 4 - 25; ①⑥ Feb. 1 - Mar. 31; ①④⑥ Apr. 3 - 28; ①④⑥⑦ May 1 - 11; ①③④⑤⑥⑦ May 12 - 31; daily June 1 - Oct. 5; ①④⑤⑥⑦ Oct. 6 - 12; ①⑤⑥⑦ Oct. 13 - 27.
Basel (Lörrach) - Hildesheim: ⑥ Jan. 4 - 25; ①⑥ Feb. 1 - Mar. 31; ①④⑥ Apr. 3 - 28; ①④⑥⑦ May 1 - 11; ①③④⑤⑥⑦ May 12 - 31; daily June 1 - Oct. 5; ①④⑤⑥⑦ Oct. 6 - 12; ①⑤⑥⑦ Oct. 13 - 27.
Berlin Wannsee - München Ost: daily. [*CNL* train].
Düsseldorf - München Ost: ⑤ Jan. 3 - Apr. 25.
Hamburg Altona - Basel (Lörrach): ⑤ Jan. 3 - 31; ⑤⑦ Feb. 2 - Mar. 30; ③⑤⑦ Apr. 2 - 30; ③⑤⑥⑦ May 2 - 11; ②③④⑤⑥⑦ May 13 - 31; daily June 1 - Sept. 30; ③④⑤⑥⑦ Oct. 1 - 12; ④⑤⑥⑦ Oct. 16 - 26 (also Oct. 31).
Hamburg Altona - München Ost: ⑤ Jan. 3 - Mar. 28; ⑤⑦ Apr. 4 - 25. Also daily *CNL* train.
Hildesheim - Basel (Lörrach): ⑤ Jan. 3 - 31; ⑤⑦ Feb. 2 - Mar. 30; ③⑤⑦ Apr. 2 - 30; ③⑤⑥⑦ May 2 - 11; ②③④⑤⑥⑦ May 13 - 31; daily June 1 - Sept. 30; ③④⑤⑥⑦ Oct. 1 - 12; ④⑤⑥⑦ Oct. 16 - 26 (also Oct. 31).
Hildesheim - München Ost: ⑤ Jan. 3 - Mar. 28; ⑤⑦ Apr. 4 - 25.
München Ost - Berlin Wannsee: daily. [*CNL* train].
München Ost - Düsseldorf: ⑥ Jan. 4 - Apr. 26.
München Ost - Hamburg Altona: ⑥ Jan. 4 - Mar. 29; ①⑥ Apr. 5 - 26. Also daily *CNL* train.
München Ost - Hildesheim: ⑥ Jan. 4 - Mar. 29; ①⑥ Apr. 5 - 26.
Niebüll - Westerland: Daily shuttle service; 18 - 28 per day in summer, 12 - 14 per day in winter.
Westerland - Niebüll: Daily shuttle service; 18 - 28 per day in summer, 12 - 14 per day in winter.

CNL – *DB City Night Line* (see page **8** for description).

GREECE

to 13/12/14

Athína - Thessaloníki: daily.
Thessaloníki - Athína: daily.

SLOVENIA

to 13/12/14

Bohinjska Bistrica - Podbrdo - Most na Soči: daily.
Most na Soči - Podbrdo - Bohinjska Bistrica: daily.

Note: service operates through the Julian Alps. Passengers remain in their vehicles. Also accepts passengers without vehicles.

Scenic Rail Routes of Europe

The following is a list of some of the most scenic rail routes of Europe, timings for most of which can be found within the timetable (the relevant table number has been specified in bold). Routes marked * are some of the editorial team's favourite journeys. Please note that this list does not include specialised mountain and tourist railways.

Types of scenery : C-Coastline, F-Forest, G-Gorge, L-Lake, M-Mountain, R-River.

ALBANIA

Elbasan - Pogradec	M L G R	**1390**

AUSTRIA

Bruck an der Mur - Villach	M R	**980**
Gmunden - Stainach Irdning*	M L	**961**
Innsbruck - Brennero	M	**595**
Innsbruck - Garmisch*	M	**895**
Innsbruck - Schwarzach-St Veit	M G	**960**
Krems - Emmersdorf	R	**991**
Landeck - Bludenz*	M	**951**
St Pölten - Mariazell*	M	**994**
Salzburg - Villach*	M G	**970**
Selzthal - Kleinreifling - Steyr	M G R	**976/977**
Wiener Neustadt - Graz	M	**980**

BELGIUM and LUXEMBOURG

Liège - Luxembourg*	R	**444**
Liège - Marloie	R	
Namur - Dinant	R	**440**

BULGARIA

Septemvri - Dobriniste	M	**1510**
Sofia - Burgas	M	**1500**
Tulovo - Gorna Oryakhovitsa	M	**1525**

CROATIA and BOSNIA

Rijeka - Ogulin	M	**1310**
Ogulin - Split	M	**1330**
Sarajevo - Ploče	M G R	**1355**

CZECH REPUBLIC

Karlovy Vary - Mariánské Lázně	R F	**1123**
Karlovy Vary - Chomutov	R	**1110**
Praha - Děčín	R	**1100**

DENMARK

Struer - Thisted	C	**716**

FINLAND

Kouvola - Joensuu	L F	**797**

FRANCE

Aurillac - Neussargues	M G	**331**
Bastia - Ajaccio	M	**369**
Bourg-en-Bresse - Bellegarde	M	**341**
Chambéry - Bourg St Maurice	M	**366**
Chambéry - Modane	M L	**367**
Chamonix - Martigny*	M G	**572**
Clermont Ferrand - Béziers	M G	**332**
Clermont Ferrand - Nîmes*	M G R	**333**
Gap - Briançon	M L	**362**
Genève - Aix les Bains	M R	**364**
Grenoble - Veynes - Marseille	M	**632**
Marseille - Ventimiglia	C	**360/361**
Mouchard - Montbéliard	R	**378**
Nice - Digne	M	**359**
Nice / Ventimiglia - Cuneo*	M G	**581**
Perpignan - Latour de Carol*	M G	**354**
Portbou - Perpignan	C	**355**
Sarlat - Bergerac	R	**318**
Toulouse - Latour de Carol	M	**312**
Valence - Veynes	M	**362**

GERMANY

Arnstadt - Meiningen	M	**870**
Dresden - Děčín	G R	**1100**
Freiburg - Donaueschingen	G F	**938**
Garmisch - Reutte - Kempten	M	**888**
Heidelberg - Neckarelz	R	**923/924**
Koblenz - Mainz*	G R	**911/914**
München - Lindau	M	**935**
Murnau - Oberammergau	M L	**897**
Naumburg - Saalfeld	R	**849/851**
Niebüll - Westerland	C	**821**
Nürnberg - Pegnitz	G R	**880**

GERMANY - continued

Offenburg - Konstanz	M F	**916**
Pforzheim - Nagold / Wildbad	F	**941**
Plattling - Bayerisch Eisenstein	F	**929**
Rosenheim - Berchtesgaden	M L	**890/891**
Rosenheim - Wörgl	M	**951**
Siegburg/Bonn - Siegen	R	**807**
Stuttgart - Singen	F	**940**
Titisee - Seebrugg	L F	**938**
Trier - Koblenz - Giessen	R	**906/915**
Ulm - Göppingen	M	**930**
Ulm - Tuttlingen	R	**938**

GREAT BRITAIN and IRELAND

Alnmouth - Dunbar	C	**180**
Barrow in Furness - Maryport	C	**159**
Coleraine - Londonderry	C	**231**
Dun Laoghaire - Wicklow	C	**237**
Edinburgh - Aberdeen	C	**224**
Exeter - Newton Abbot	C	**115/116**
Glasgow - Oban / Mallaig*	M L	**218**
Inverness - Kyle of Lochalsh*	M C	**226**
Lancaster - Carlisle - Carstairs	M G R	**151**
Liskeard - Looe	R	**118**
Llanelli - Craven Arms	M	**146**
Machynlleth - Pwllheli	M C	**148**
Perth - Inverness	M	**221**
Plymouth - Gunnislake	R	**118**
St Erth - St Ives	C	**118**
Sheffield - Chinley	M	**193/206**
Shrewsbury - Aberystwyth	M R	**147**
Skipton - Settle - Carlisle	M R	**173**

GREECE

Korinthos - Patras	C	**1450**
Diakoptó - Kalávrita	M G	**1455**

HUNGARY

Budapest - Szob	R	**1255**
Eger - Szilvásvárad	M	**1299**
Székesfehérvár - Balatonszentgyörgy	L	**1220**
Székesfehérvár - Tapolca	L	**1225**

ITALY

Bologna - Pistoia	M	**609**
Bolzano - Merano	M	**597**
Brennero - Verona*	M	**595**
Brig - Arona	M L	**590**
Domodossola - Locarno*	M G	**551**
Firenze - Viareggio	M	**614**
Fortezza - San Candido	M	**596**
Genova - Pisa	C	**610**
Genova - Ventimiglia	C	**580**
Lecco - Tirano	M L	**593**
Messina - Palermo	C	**641**
Napoli - Sorrento	C	**639**
Roma - Pescara	M	**624**
Salerno - Reggio Calabria	C	**640**
Taranto - Reggio Calabria	C	**635**
Torino - Aosta	M	**586**

NORWAY

Bergen - Oslo*	M L	**780/781**
Bodø - Trondheim	M L	**787**
Dombås - Åndalsnes	M	**785**
Drammen - Larvik	C	**783**
Myrdal - Flåm*	M C	**781**
Oslo - Kongsvinger	R	**750**
Oslo / Røros - Trondheim	M L	**784/785**
Stavanger - Kristiansand	M	**775**

POLAND

Jelenia Góra - Walbrzych	M	**1084**
Kraków - Zakopane	M	**1066**
Olsztyn - Elk	L	**1035**
Olsztyn - Morag	L	**1035**
Tarnów - Krynica	M	**1078**

PORTUGAL

Covilhã - Entroncamento	M R	**691**
Pampilhosa - Guarda	M	**692**
Porto - Coimbra	C R	**690**
Porto - Pocinho*	R	**694**
Porto - Valenca	M C	**696**

ROMANIA

Brasov - Ploesti	M	**1600**
Caransebes - Craiova	M G R	**1620**
Fetesti - Constanta	R	**1680**
Oradea - Cluj Napoca	R	**1612**

SERBIA and MONTENEGRO

Priboj - Bar	M L	**1370**

SLOVAKIA

Banská Bystrica - Brezno - Košice	M	**1192**
Žilina - Poprad Tatry	M	**1180**

SLOVENIA

Jesenice - Sežana	M R	**1302**
Maribor - Zidani Most	M	**1315**
Villa Opicina - Ljubljana - Zagreb	G R	**1305**

SPAIN

Algeciras - Ronda	M R	**673**
Barcelona - Latour de Carol	M	**656**
Bilbao - San Sebastián	M	**686**
Bilbao - Santander	M	**687**
Ferrol - Gijón*	C	**687**
Granada - Almería	M	**673**
Huesca - Canfranc	M G R	**670**
León - Monforte de Lemos	M	**682**
León - Oviedo	M	**685**
Lleida - La Pobla de Segur	M L	**655**
Málaga - Bobadilla	G	**673**
Santander - Oviedo	M C	**687**
Zaragoza - València	M R	**670**

SWEDEN

Bollnäs - Ånge - Sundsvall	M L	**76**
Borlänge - Mora	M L F	**758**
Borlänge - Ludvika - Frövi	M L F	**755**
Narvik - Kiruna	M F	**76**
Östersund - Storlien	L F	**76**

SWITZERLAND

Andermatt - Göschenen	G	**57**
Basel - Delémont - Moutier	M R	**50**
Chur - Arosa	M G	**54**
Chur - Brig - Zermatt*	M	**575/57**
Chur - St Moritz*	M G	**54**
Davos - Filisur	M G	**545**
Davos - Landquart	M	**54**
Interlaken Ost - Jungfraujoch*	M	**56**
Interlaken Ost - Luzern	M L	**56**
Interlaken West - Spiez	L	**56**
Lausanne - Brig	M L R	**57**
Lausanne - Neuchâtel - Biel	M L	**50**
Montreux - Zweisimmen - Lenk	M L G	**56**
Rorschach - Kreuzlingen	L	**53**
St Moritz - Scuol Tarasp	M	**54**
St Moritz - Tirano*	M	**54**
Spiez - Zweisimmen	G	**56**
Thun - Kandersteg - Brig*	M L	**56**
Zürich / Luzern - Chiasso	M L	**55**
Zürich - Chur	M L	**52**

City Plans are on pages 28 - 32

AIRPORT → CITY CENTRE LINKS

5

Airport code and name	City	Distance	Journey	Transport ‡	City terminal	Table
AAR Aarhus	Århus	37 km	40 mins	🚌 flybus, connects with flights	Banegårdspladsen, Central rail station	
ABZ Aberdeen, Dyce	Aberdeen	11 km	33 mins	🚌 **727**, ①–⑤ every 30 mins; ⑥⑦ hourly	Union Square bus station. Also ①–⑤ 🚌 **80** to Dyce rail station	
ALC Alacant	Alacant	12 km	30 mins	🚌 **C6**, every 20 mins 0600 - 0000	Plaza Puerta del Mar	
AMS Amsterdam, Schiphol	Amsterdam	17 km	20 mins	Train, every 10 mins (every hour 2400 - 0600)	Centraal rail station	**451, 454**
	Rotterdam	65 km	45 mins	Train, every 30 mins (every hour 2400 - 0600)	Centraal rail station	**450, 454**
	Den Haag	43 km	35 mins	Train, every 30 mins (every hour 2400 - 0600)	Centraal rail station	**450, 454**
AOI Ancona, Falconara	Ancona	16 km	30 mins	1) 🚌 Linea **J**, 2) Train hourly at peak times: 17 mins	Main rail station	
ATH Athína, Elefthérios Venizélos	Athína	27 km	39 mins	Metro (line **3**), every 30 mins 0635 - 2335	Syntagma	**1440**
	Pireás	41 km	90 mins	🚌 **X96**, 3 - 4 per hour	Platía Karaiskáki	
BCN Barcelona, Aeroport del Prat	Barcelona	14 km	19 mins	Train, 0513, 0535, 0609, then every 30 mins: 0609 - 2314	Sants. Also calls at Passeig de Gràcia rail station (26 mins)	**659**
BSL Basel - Mulhouse - Freiburg	Basel	9 km	20 mins	🚌 **50**, ①–⑤ 8 per hour; ⑥⑦ 6 per hour	SBB rail station / Kannenfeldplatz	
	Freiburg	60 km	55 mins	🚌 ①–⑤ every 1 - 2 hours; ⑥⑦ every 2 hours	Rail station	
BHD Belfast, City, George Best	Belfast	2 km	15 mins	🚌 *Airlink* **600**, ①–⑥ every 20 mins; ⑦ every 40 mins	Europa Buscentre. Also train from Sydenham rail station	
BFS Belfast, International	Belfast	26 km	40 mins	🚌 *Airbus* **300**, Ⓐ every 15 mins; ⑥ every 20; ⑦ every 30	Europa Buscentre (adjacent to Great Victoria St rail station)	
BEG Beograd, Nikola Tesla	Beograd	18 km	30 mins	🚌 **72**, every 32 minutes	Rail station	
SXF Berlin, Schönefeld	Berlin	24 km	28 mins	Train, *AirportExpress* **RE7/ RB14** 2 per hour 0631 - 2331	Hbf, also Ost, Alexanderplatz and Zoo rail stations	**847**
TXL Berlin, Tegel	Berlin	7 km	40 mins	🚌 *JetExpressBus TXL*, Ⓐ every 10 mins, Ⓒ every 20 mins	Hauptbahnhof rail station	
BIQ Biarritz - Anglet - Bayonne	Biarritz	3 km	22 mins	🚌 *STAB* **6**, every hour approx.	Town centre	
	Bayonne	7 km	28 mins	🚌 *STAB* **6**, every hour approx.	Rail station	
BIO Bilbao, Sondika	Bilbao	10 km	45 mins	🚌 Bizkaibus **A-3247**, every 20 mins 0620 - 0000	Plaza Moyúa (Metro station Moyúa)	
BHX Birmingham, International	Birmingham	12 km	11 mins	Train, ①–⑥ ± 9 per hour, ⑦ 6 per hour	New Street rail station from International	**129, 142, 143**
BLQ Bologna, Guglielmo Marconi	Bologna	8 km	25 mins	🚌 *Aerobus* BLQ, every 15 mins 0600 - 2315	Centrale rail station	
BOD Bordeaux, Mérignac	Bordeaux	12 km	45 mins	🚌 Jet' Bus, every 45 mins 0745 - 2245	St Jean rail station	
BOH Bournemouth, Hurn	Bournemouth	10 km	15 mins	🚌 **A 1** *Airport Shuttle*, hourly 0730 - 1830	Rail station, Bus station (Travel Interchange)	
BTS Bratislava, Milan Rastislav Štefánika	Bratislava	10 km	25 mins	🚌 **61**, 3 - 4 per hour	Main rail station (Hlavná stanica)	
BRE Bremen	Bremen	3 km	20 mins	Tram **6**, ①–⑥ every 10 mins, ⑦ every 20 mins	Main rail station	
VBS Brescia, Montichiari, Verona	Verona	50 km	45 mins	🚌, connects with Ryanair flights	Main rail station	
	Brescia	18 km	20 mins	🚌, connects with Ryanair flights	Main rail station	
BRS Bristol, International	Bristol	13 km	30 mins	🚌 *International Flyer*, ①–⑥ 3 - 6 per hour; ⑦ 2 - 6 per hour	Temple Meads rail station, also bus station	
BRQ Brno	Brno	8 km	20 mins	🚌 **76**, 2 per hour	Main rail station, also bus station	
BRU Brussels, Nationaal / Zaventem	Brussels	12 km	25 mins	Train, 2 - 4 per hour	Midi / Zuid rail station (also calls at Central and Nord)	**425**
	Antwerpen	38 km	34 mins	Train, hourly	Centraal	**425**
OTP Bucuresti, Henri Coanda, Otopeni	Bucuresti	16 km	45 mins	🚌 **783**, ①–⑤ every 15 - 30 mins; ⑥⑦ every 30 mins	Piata Victoriei (800m from Nord station or 1 stop on subway)	
	Bucuresti	16 km	68 mins	🚌 to P.O. Aeroport H, hourly 0845 - 1945, 2023, then train	Nord station	
BUD Budapest, Ferihegy	Budapest	16 km	40 mins	🚌 **200E**, every 10 - 20 mins	Köbánya-Kispest metro station (metro connection to city centre)	
	Budapest	18 km	25 mins	Train, 2 - 6 per hour	🚌 **200E**, to Ferihegy station then train to Nyugati rail station.	
BZG Bydgoszcz	Bydgoszcz	4 km	30 mins	🚌 **80**, 2 per hour	Main rail station	
CCF Carcassonne, Salvaza	Carcassonne	5 km	10 mins	🚌, connects with Ryanair flights	Place Davilla and Carcassonne rail station	
CWL Cardiff	Cardiff	19 km	40 mins	🚌 *Airbus Xpress* **X91**, ①–⑥ hourly, ⑦ every 2 hours	Central rail station, city centre	
	Cardiff	19 km	50 mins	🚌 to Rhoose then Train: ①–⑥ hourly, ⑦ every 2 hours	Central rail station	
CRL Charleroi, Brussels South	Brussels	55 km	60 mins	🚌 *Brussels City Shuttle*, every 30 mins	Brussels Midi (corner of Rue de France / Rue de l'Instruction)	
	Charleroi		18 mins	🚌 *Line* **A**, ①–⑤ 2 per hour, ⑥⑦ hourly	Main rail station	
ORK Cork	Cork	8 km	25 mins	🚌 **226**, ①–⑥ 2 per hour, ⑦ hourly	Rail station, also Parnell Place bus station	
LDY Derry (Londonderry)	Londonderry	11 km	30 mins	🚌 connects with flights	Foyle Street bus station	
DNR Dinard - Pleurtuit - St-Malo	St Malo	14 km	20 mins	Taxis only. Dinard 6 km 10 mins		
DSA Doncaster - Sheffield	Doncaster	10 km	25 mins	🚌 **91**, ①–⑥ 2 per hour; ⑦ hourly	Frenchgate Interchange (bus station)	
DOK Donetsk	Donetsk	13 km	40 mins	Fixed-run taxi **5**	Main rail station	
DTM Dortmund, Wickede	Dortmund	10 km	25 mins	🚌 every hour, AirportExpress	Main rail station (Hbf). Also 🚌 to Holzwickede rail station	
DRS Dresden	Dresden	15 km	21 mins	Train (S-Bahn **S2**) every 30 mins	Main rail stations (Hbf and Neustadt)	**857a**
DUB Dublin	Dublin	11 km	60 mins	🚌 *Airlink* **747**, every 10 mins (15 - 20 mins on ⑦)	Bus station (Busáras) 30min, O'Connell St., Heuston rail station	
	Belfast	157 km	130 mins	🚌 **001 / 200**, hourly 0520 - 2120 also 2320, 0120, 0320	Europa Buscentre. Also 2220, 0020, 0220, 0420 June 3 - Sept. 22	
DBV Dubrovnik, Čilipi	Dubrovnik	24 km	30 mins	🚌 *Atlas Bus*, connects with flights	Bus station	
DUS Düsseldorf, International	Düsseldorf	7 km	12 mins	Train (S - Bahn **S1**) Ⓐ every 20 mins, Ⓒ every 30 mins	Main rail station (Hauptbahnhof)	**800, 802**
EMA East Midlands, Nottingham - - Leicester - Derby	East Midlands	10 km	10 mins	Taxi shuttle	East Midlands Parkway rail station	
	Nottingham	21 km	55 mins	🚌 *Skylink*, every 30 min. 0505 - 0105, also 0205, 0305, 0405	Broadmarsh bus station	
	Derby	19 km	40 mins	🚌 *Skylink* every 30 min. 0615 - 1855; (60 mins 1945 - 0545)	Bus station	
	Loughborough	8 km	25 mins	🚌 *Skylink* every 30 min. 0715 - 2017; (60 mins 2057 - 0657)	Swan Street	
	Leicester	23 km	55 mins	🚌 *Skylink* every 30 min. 0715 - 1948; (60 mins 2057 - 0657)	St Margaret's bus station	
EDI Edinburgh, Turnhouse	Edinburgh	11 km	25 mins	🚌 *Airlink* **100**, every 10 mins. **N 22** 2400 - 0600 every 30mins.	Haymarket rail station; Waverley Bridge (next to Waverley station)	
ERF Erfurt	Erfurt	6 km	22 mins	Tram, Line 4, Ⓐ 3 - 6 per hour; Ⓒ 2 per hour	Main rail station (Hauptbahnhof)	
EBJ Esbjerg	Esbjerg	12 km	21 mins	🚌 **8**, hourly	*Bybusterminal*	
EXT Exeter	Exeter	8 km	25 mins	🚌 **56, 56A, 56B**, 1 per hour	St Davids rail station	
FAO Faro	Faro	6 km	20 mins	🚌 *EVA*, 1 per hour	Bus station	
FLR Firenze, Amerigo Vespucci	Firenze	7 km	20 mins	🚌 Ataf *Vola in bus* **62**, every 30 mins	Santa Maria Novella rail station	
HHN Frankfurt, Hahn	Frankfurt	120 km	105 mins	🚌, connects with Ryanair flights	Mannheimer Straße, adjacent to main rail station (Hauptbahnhof)	
Also 🚌 to Bingen, 60 mins; Heidelberg hbf, 140 mins; Koblenz, 70 mins; Köln hbf, 135 mins; Luxembourg, 105 mins; Mainz, 70 mins; Mannheim, 110 mins						
FRA Frankfurt	Frankfurt	10 km	15 mins	Train (S-Bahn **S8** or **S9**), 4 - 6 times hourly	Main rail station (Hauptbahnhof)	**917a**
FDH Friedrichshafen	Friedrichshafen	4 km	7 mins	1 - 2 trains per hour	Main rail station (Stadt) or Harbour (Hafen)	**933**
GDN Gdańsk, Lech Walesa	Gdańsk	10 km	26 mins	🚌 **110**, 1 - 2 per hour	Wrzeszcz rail station, then 3 stops (every 15 mins) to Główny	
GVA Genève	Genève	6 km	6 mins	Train, 5 times hourly	Cornavin rail station	**500, 570**
GOA Genova, Cristoforo Colombo	Genova	7 km	20 mins	🚌 *Volabus*, 1 - 2 per hour	Principe rail station	
GRO Girona	Girona	12 km	25 mins	🚌, hourly	Rail / Bus station (Estación autobuses)	
	Barcelona	102 km	70 mins	🚌, connects with Ryanair flights	Estacio del Nord, corner of carrer Ali Bei 80 / Sicilia	

‡ – The frequencies shown apply during daytime on weekdays and are from the airport to the city centre. There may be fewer journeys in the evenings, at weekends and during the winter months. Extended 🚌 journey times could apply during peak hours.

5 AIRPORT → CITY CENTRE LINKS

City Plans are on pages 28 - 32

Airport code and name		City	Distance	Journey	Transport ‡	City terminal	Table
GLA	Glasgow, International	Glasgow	15 km	15 mins	🚌 *GlasgowFlyer*, ①–⑥ every 10 mins, ⑦ every 15 mins.	Central rail station	
PIK	Glasgow, Prestwick	Glasgow	61 km	50 mins	Train, ①–⑥ every 30 mins, ⑦ every 60 mins	Central rail station	**216**
GSE	Göteborg, City	Göteborg	17 km	30 mins	🚌, connects with Ryanair, Air Berlin and Wizz Air flights	Nils Ericson Terminalen (bus station) / Central rail station	
GOT	Göteborg, Landvetter	Göteborg	25 km	30 mins	🚌, ①–⑤ 3 per hour, ⑥⑦ 2 - 3 per hour	Nils Ericson Terminalen (bus station) / Central rail station	
GRZ	Graz	Graz	9 km	9 mins	Train ①–⑥ 1 - 2 per hour, ⑦ every 2 hours	Main rail station (Hauptbahnhof)	**980**
GNB	Grenoble, St Geoirs	Grenoble	37 km	45 mins	🚌, connects with flights	Main rail station, also bus station	
HAM	Hamburg, Fuhlsbüttel	Hamburg	11 km	24 mins	Train (S-Bahn **S1**), every 10 mins	Main rail station (Hauptbahnhof)	
HAJ	Hannover, Langenhagen	Hannover	15 km	17 mins	Train (S-Bahn **S5**), every 30 mins	Main rail station (Hauptbahnhof)	**809**
HEL	Helsinki, Vantaa	Helsinki	19 km	35 mins	🚌 **615**, ①–⑤ every 15 mins, ⑥⑦ every 20 - 30 mins	Rail station (stop 10)	
		Tikkurila	7 km	22 mins	🚌 **61**, ①–⑤ every 10 mins, ⑥ 10 - 15 mins, ⑦ 15 - 20 mins.	Rail station for trains to Helsinki (20 mins; 16 km)	
NOC	Ireland West Airport Knock	Ballyhaunis	22 km	30 mins	🚌 **64**, 0855, 1250	Rail station	**235**
IOM	Isle of Man, Ronaldsway	Douglas	16 km	30 mins	🚌 **1**, hourly (every 30 mins in peak periods)	Lord street	
IST	İstanbul, Atatürk	İstanbul	28 km	40 mins	🚌, *Havas Airport Shuttle* hourly 0400 - 2400	Taksim	
		İstanbul	28 km	60 mins	Metro to Zeytinburnu, then over bridge for Tram **T1**	Sirkeci rail station	
SAW	İstanbul, Sabiha Gökcen	İstanbul	32 km	60 mins	🚌, 1–2 per hour, 0540 - 2040	Bus station. Also Pendik rail station is 4km from airport	
XRY	Jerez	Jerez	10 km	9 mins	Train, 11 trains per day	Jerez de la Frontera, then to Cadiz	**671**
FKB	Karlsruhe - Baden-Baden	Baden-Baden	8 km	15 mins	🚌 **205**, connects with Ryanair flights	Rail station; also 🚌 **140** to Karlsruhe Hbf, 25 mins	
KTW	Katowice, Pyrzowice	Katowice	34 km	50 mins	🚌 *Lotnisko, PKM*, 1 per hour approx	Katowice Dworzec (main rail station)	
KUN	Kaunas	Kaunas	13 km	40 mins	🚌 **120, 29**	City centre	
		Vilnius	102 km	90 mins	🚌 connects with Ryanair flights	Hotel Panorama, close to bus and rail stations	
KLU	Klagenfurt	Klagenfurt	5 km	25 mins	🚌 **45**, to Annabichl rail station, then train or 🚌 **40**	Main rail station and bus station	
CPH	København, Kastrup	København	12 km	15 mins	Train, every 10 mins	Main rail station (Hovedbanegård)	**703**
		Malmö	36 km	22 mins	Train, every 20 mins	Central rail station	**703**
CGN	Köln / Bonn, Konrad Adenauer	Bonn	25 km	32 mins	🚌 **SB60**, ①–⑤ 2 per hour; ⑥⑦ 1 - 2 per hour	Main rail station (Hauptbahnhof)	
		Köln	15 km	16 mins	Train **S13**, ①–⑤ every 20 mins, ⑥⑦ every 30 mins	Main rail station (Hbf). Also to Mönchengladbach, Koblenz	**802**
KRK	Kraków, Balice	Kraków	12 km	20 mins	Train, 2 per hour	Kraków Główny. Balice rail station is 200m from air terminal	**1099**
KBP	Kyïv, Boryspil	Kyïv	34 km	60 mins	🚌 **322** *Polit*, 2 - 3 per hour	Main rail station	
LBA	Leeds - Bradford	Leeds	16 km	40 mins	🚌 **757**, 2 per hour	Main rail station and bus station	
		Bradford	11 km	40 mins	🚌 **747**, ①–⑥ 2 per hour	Interchange rail station	
AOC	Leipzig, Altenburg - Nobitz	Leipzig	75 km	70 mins	🚌 **250** *ThüSac*, connects with Ryanair flights	Main rail station. Also stops at Altenburg rail station after 15 mins	
LEJ	Leipzig - Halle	Leipzig	20 km	14 mins	Train, 2 - 3 per hour	Main rail station (Hauptbahnhof)	**856**
		Halle	18 km	12 mins	Train, 2 per hour	Main rail station (Hauptbahnhof)	**856**
LNZ	Linz, Blue Danube	Linz	12 km	19 mins	🚌, connects with Ryanair flights	Main rail station. Also free 🚌 to Hörsching rail station, 3 mins	
LIS	Lisboa, Portela	Lisboa	3 km	9 mins	Train, Red (Vermelho) line. Every 5–9 mins	Oriente rail station. For Santa Apolónia change at São Sebastião	
LPL	Liverpool, John Lennon	Liverpool	11 km	35 mins	🚌 **500**, every 30 mins 0645 - 2345	Lime Street rail stn, Paradise St. Interchange; also 🚌 **700** to Manchester	
LJU	Ljubljana, Jože Pučnik, Brnik	Ljubljana	26 km	45 mins	🚌, Ⓐ hourly 0500 - 2000; Ⓒ 0700, every 2 hours 1000 - 2000	Bus station (Avtobusna postaja)	
LCJ	Łódź, Lublinek	Łódź	6 km	20 mins	🚌 **65**	Kaliska rail station	
LCY	London, City	London	12 km	25 mins	Train (Docklands Light Railway), every 8 - 10 mins	Bank underground (tube) station	**140**
LGW	London, Gatwick	London	44 km	30 mins	Train *Gatwick Express*, every 15 minutes	Victoria rail station	**103, 105, 140**
LHR	London, Heathrow	London	24 km	15 mins	Train *Heathrow Express*, every 15 minutes	Paddington rail station	**140**
		London	24 km	58 mins	Underground train (tube), every 6 - 12 mins	King's Cross St Pancras rail station	**140**
LTN	London, Luton	London	50 km	35 mins	6–7 per hour (🚌 between and Parkway rail station)	St Pancras International rail station	**103, 140, 170**
SEN	London, Southend	London	64 km	55 mins	Train, 3 per hour	Liverpool Street rail station	
STN	London, Stansted	London	55 km	46 mins	Train *Stansted Express*, every 15 minutes	Liverpool Street rail station	**140**
LBC	Lübeck, Blankensee	Lübeck	8 km	30 mins	🚌 **6**, every 20 mins	Bus station (bus stop 5). Also train from Flughafen 300m walk	**827**
		Hamburg	59 km	75 mins	🚌 *VHHAG*, connects with Ryanair flights	Corner Adenaueralle / Brockesstrasse (ZOB) near main rail station	
LUZ	Lublin	Lublin	10 km	15 mins	Train, ①–⑥ 5 per day, ⑦ 3 per day, connects with flights	Main rail station	
LUX	Luxembourg, Findel	Luxembourg	7 km	25 mins	🚌 **16**, every 15 mins ①–⑥, every 30 mins ⑦	Central rail station	
LWO	Lviv, Skniliv	Lvov	10 km		🚌, Taxi-bus *Marshrutka*	City Centre	
LYS	Lyon, St Exupéry	Lyon	23 km	30 mins	Tram *RhôneExpress*, 4 per hour	Part Dieu rail station	
		Chambéry	87 km	60 mins	🚌 Altibus, 4 - 5 times daily	Bus station (gare routière)	
		Grenoble	91 km	65 mins	🚌 Faure Vercors, 0630 Ⓐ, hourly 0730 - 2330	Bus station (gare routière); Place de la Résistance	
MAD	Madrid, Barajas T4	Madrid	12 km	11 mins	Train, Cercanías every 30 mins 0628 - 2258	Chamartín, also Atocha Cercanías 25 mins (see city plans p30)	
AGP	Málaga	Málaga	8 km	12 mins	Train, every 30 mins	María Zambrano (renfe) and Centro-Alameda rail stations	**662**
MMX	Malmö, Sturup	Malmö	30 km	45 mins	🚌 *flygbussarna*, 1 - 2 per hour	Central rail station	
MAN	Manchester	Manchester	16 km	14 mins	Train, up to 9 per hour (hourly through the night)	Piccadilly rail station	
MSE	Manston	Ramsgate	3 km	9 mins	🚌 **38**, ①–⑥ hourly 0943 - 1343	Rail station	
MRS	Marseille, Provence	Marseille	28 km	25 mins	🚌, every 20 mins. See also rail / bus on Table **351**	St Charles rail station; also 🚌 to Aix TGV rail stn. every 30 mins	
FMM	Memmingen	Memmingen	5 km	10 mins	🚌 **2, 810, 811**	Bus station and rail station; also 🚌 to München, 95 mins	
LIN	Milano, Linate	Milano	9 km	20 mins	1) 🚌 **73** every 10 mins; 2) 🚌 *Starfly*, every 30 mins	1) Piazza S. Babila, Metro line 1; 2) Centrale rail station	
MXP	Milano, Malpensa	Milano	45 km	40 mins	1) *Malpensa Express* train, every 30 mins; 2) 1 - 2 per hour	1) Cadorna and Bovisa rail stations; 2) Centrale rail station	**583**
				50 mins	🚌 *Bus Express*, 2 per hour / *Shuttle Air* 3 per hour	Centrale rail station. Also 🚌 to Gallarate (Table **590**)	
BGY	Milano, Orio al Serio, Bergamo	Milano	45 km	60 mins	🚌, 1 - 2 per hour	Centrale rail station (Air Terminal)	
		Bergamo	4 km	15 mins	🚌, 2 per hour	Rail station	
MSQ	Minsk	Minsk	42 km	90 mins	🚌, **112, 300**,	Vostochniy and Moskovskiy bus stations	
DME	Moskva, Domodedovo	Moskva	35 km	47 mins	Train, *Aeroexpress*, 1 - 2 per hour approx, 0600 - 0000	Paveletskaya rail station	**1901**
SVO	Moskva, Sheremetyevo	Moskva	35 km	35 mins	Train, *Aeroexpress*, 1 - 2 per hour approx, 0500 - 0030	Belorusskaya rail station	**1901**
VKO	Moskva, Vnukovo	Moskva	28 km	40 mins	Train, *Aeroexpress*, 1 per hour approx, 0600 - 0000	Kiyevskaya rail station	**1901**
MUC	München, International	München	37 km	40 mins	Train **S1**, **S8** for Hbf, every 10 mins; **S8** for Ost, every 20 mins	Main rail stations (Hauptbahnhof, Ostbahnhof)	**892**
		Freising	6 km	24 mins	🚌 *MVV* **635**, every 20 mins	Rail station for connections to Regensburg, Passau	**878, 944**
NTE	Nantes, Atlantique	Nantes	9 km	30 mins	🚌 *Tan Air*, ± hourly; connects with flights	Main rail station	
NAP	Napoli, Capodichino	Napoli	7 km	20 mins	🚌 *ANM* **3S** line, 2 per hour; *Alibus*, 2 per hour	Piazza Garibaldi (Centrale rail station)	
NCL	Newcastle, International	Newcastle	9 km	25 mins	Metro train, every 12 mins	Main rail station	

‡ – The frequencies shown apply during daytime on weekdays and are from the airport to the city centre. There may be fewer journeys in the evenings, at weekends and during the winter months. Extended 🚌 journey times could apply during peak hours.

¶ – Graz Airport - Feldkirchen rail station is located about 300 metres away from the airport.

City Plans are on pages 28-32

AIRPORT → CITY CENTRE LINKS

Airport code and name	City	Distance	Journey	Transport ‡	City terminal	Table
NCE Nice, Côte d'Azur	Nice	7 km	20 mins	🚌 **99**, 2 per hour	SNCF rail station ¶	
		7 km	20 mins	🚌 **98**, 3 per hour	City centre, Riquier	
FNI Nîmes-Arles-Camargue	Nîmes	12 km	20 mins	🚌, connects with Ryanair flights	Rail station	
NWI Norwich	Norwich	8 km	24 mins	🚌 **603**, ①–⑥ 4 per hour 0700 - 1800, 1835, 1905, 1935, 2002	Bus station	
NUE Nürnberg	Nürnberg	6 km	12 mins	Train, U-bahn **U2**, 4-6 per hour	Main rail station (Hauptbahnhof)	
ODS Odesa	Odesa	9 km	30mins	🚌 **129**	Rail station	
OSL Oslo, Gardermoen	Oslo	49 km	19 mins	Train *Flytoget*, 3-6 per hour	Central rail station	**771**
TRF Oslo, Sandefjord Torp	Oslo	123 km	116 mins	🚌 to Torp rail station (4 mins) for train to Oslo	Also 🚌 to Oslo Bus terminal	**783**
RYG Oslo, Rygge	Oslo	69 km	51 mins	🚌 connects with Ryanair flights, to Rygge rail station (4 km).	Sentral rail station (51 mins Rygge to Sentral)	**770**
PMO Palermo, Falcone-Borsellino	Palermo	24 km	45 mins	Train *Trinacria express*, ①–⑥ 2 per hour, ⑦ hourly	Centrale rail station	
PMI Palma, Mallorca	Palma	11 km	30 mins	🚌 **1**, every 15 mins	Paseo de Mallorca, Placa d'Espanya (for rail stations), the Port	
BVA Paris, Beauvais	Paris	80 km	75 mins	🚌, connects with Ryanair and WizzAir flights	Porte Maillot, Metro (Line 1) for Châtelet Les Halles, Gare de Lyon	
CDG Paris, Charles de Gaulle	Paris	25 km	35 mins	RER train, (Line B), every 7-15 mins	Nord, Châtelet Les Halles, and St Michel rail stations	**398**
	Disneyland	23 km	45 mins	🚌 **VEA** Navette / Shuttle, every 20 minutes	Disneyland Resort, Disneyland hotels	
ORY Paris, Orly	Paris	15 km	35 mins	🚌 to Pont de Rungis, then RER train, (Line C) 4 per hr.	Austerlitz, St Michel, Musée d'Orsay, and Invalides rail stns.	**398**
	Paris	15 km	33 mins	ORLYVAL shuttle to Antony then RER train, (Line B) 4 per hr.	Châlet-Les-Halles, Nord rail stations	**398**
PGF Perpignan, Rivesaltes	Perpignan	5 km	15 mins	🚌, connects with flights	Rail station, bus station (gare routière)	
PSA Pisa, Galileo Galilei	Pisa	2 km	8 mins	🚌 every 10 minutes	Centrale rail station	**613**
OPO Porto	Porto	17 km	35 mins	Metro Train, Line E, 3 per hour	Campanhã rail station	
POZ Poznań, Ławica	Poznań	6 km	20 mins	🚌 **L** *MPK*, 2 per hour	Rail station	
PRG Praha, Ruzyně	Praha	19 km	41 mins	🚌 **AE** *Airport Express*, every 5-20 mins	hlavní rail station	
	Praha	17 km	60 mins	🚌 **119**, every 10 mins	Dejvická metro station, then Metro line A to muzeum (see City Plans)	
PUY Pula	Pula	6 km	15 mins	🚌, connects with Ryanair flights	Town centre	
REU Reus	Reus	6 km	20 mins	🚌 **50**, *Hispano Igualadina*, hourly	Rail station	**652**
	Barcelona	90 km	90 mins	🚌 *Hispano Igualadina* connects with Ryanair flights	Sants rail station	
KEF Reykjavík, Keflavík	Reykjavík	50 km	45 mins	🚌 *flybus*, connects with all flights	BSÍ bus terminal	
RIX Riga	Riga	13 km	30 mins	🚌 **22**, every 10-30 mins	Abrenes iela (street) next to rail station	
RJK Rijeka	Rijeka	30 km	45 mins	🚌 *Autotrans*, connects with flights	Bus station, Jelačić Square	
CIA Roma, Ciampino	Roma	15 km	40 mins	🚌 *Terravision* 1-3 per hour	Termini rail station	**622**
FCO Roma, Fiumicino	Roma	26 km	42 mins	Train, ①–⑥ 4 per hour, ⑦ 2 per hour	Ostiense and Tiburtina rail stations	**622**
(also known as Leonardo da Vinci)		26 km	31 mins	*Leonardo Express* rail service, every 30 mins	Termini rail station	**622**
RTM Rotterdam	Rotterdam	5 km	20 mins	*Airport Shuttle* **33**, ①–⑤ every 10 mins, ⑥⑦ every 15 mins	Groot Handelsgebouw (adjacent to Centraal rail station)	
RZE Rzeszów, Jasionka	Rzeszów	15 km	20 mins	🚌 **L**, connects with flights	Main rail station and bus station	
LED St Peterburg, Pulkovo II	St Peterburg	17 km	60 mins	🚌 **13**	Moskovskaya Metro station, Line 2 for Nevski Pr. (see City Plans)	
SZG Salzburg, W. A. Mozart	Salzburg	5 km	22 mins	🚌 **2**, ①–⑥ every 10-20 mins, ⑦ every 20 mins	Main rail station	
SIP Simferopol	Simferopol	12 km	28 mins	🚌 **9** (trolleybus), every 10–15 mins	Main rail station	
SKP Skopje, Alexander the Great	Skopje	14 km	25 mins	🚌 Vardar Ekspres, connects with flights	Bus station	
AER Sochi	Adler	3 km	9 mins	Train, 17 per day, 12 of which continue to Sochi 43-49 mins.	Rail station	**1960**
SOF Sofia, International	Sofia	10 km	25 mins	🚌 **84**, **384**, every 10-20 mins	University	
SOU Southampton	Southampton	8 km	8 mins	Train, 50 metres from terminal, 4-5 trains per hour	Central rail station	**108, 129**
SPU Split, Kaštela	Split	16 km	50 mins	🚌 connects with flights	Bus station. Departs 200m from Airport terminal	
SVG Stavanger, Sola	Stavanger	14 km	30 mins	🚌, ①–⑤ every 20 mins, ⑥ 2 per hour, ⑦ hourly	Atlantic Hotel / Fiskepiren	
ARN Stockholm, Arlanda	Stockholm	44 km	20 mins	*Arlanda Express* train, every 15 mins	Central rail station	**747, 760**
NYO Stockholm, Skavsta	Stockholm	103 km	80 mins	🚌, connects with Ryanair flights	Cityterminal (bus station), also 🚌 to Nyköping rail station	
VST Stockholm, Västerås	Stockholm	107 km	75 mins	🚌, connects with Ryanair flights	Cityterminal (bus station), also 🚌 **941** to Västerås rail station	
SXB Strasbourg, Entzheim	Strasbourg	10 km	9 mins	Train from Entzheim Aéroport (300m walk) 1-4 per hour	Gare Centrale (Central rail station)	**388**
STR Stuttgart, Echterdingen	Stuttgart	20 km	27 mins	Train (S-Bahn **S2**, **S3**), 2-4 times hourly 0508-0008	Main rail station (Hauptbahnhof)	**932**
SZZ Szczecin, Goleniów	Szczecin	43 km	56 mins	Train, 0832, 1552 Ⓑ, 1905.	Szczecin Główny. Also 🚌 connects with Ryanair/Norwegian flights	
TLL Tallinn, Ülemiste	Tallinn	5 km	22 mins	🚌 **90K**, every 30 mins 0800 - 1800	Balti jaam (rail station)	
TMP Tampere, Pirkkala	Tampere	18 km	25 mins	🚌, connects with Ryanair flights	Main rail station (Rautatieasemalta)	
TBS Tbilisi	Tbilisi	19 km	30 mins	Train, 2 per day: 0845, 1805	Rail station	
TIA Tirana (Tiranë), Nënë Tereza	Tirana	12 km	45 mins	🚌 *Rinas Express*, every hour 0600 - 1800	National Museum in city centre	
TRN Torino, Caselle	Torino	16 km	20 mins	*SATTI* train every 30 mins	Torino Dora rail station, Piazza Baldissera	
	Torino	16 km	40 mins	🚌, ①–⑥ 2-3 per hour; ⑦ 1-2 per hour	Torino Porta Nuova and Porta Susa rail stations	
TLS Toulouse, Blagnac	Toulouse	8 km	20 mins	🚌 *Flybus*, every 20 minutes	Place Jeanne d'Arc / Matabiau rail / bus station (gare routière)	
TRS Trieste, Ronchi dei Legionari	Trieste	33 km	50 mins	🚌 **51**, ①–⑥ 1-2 per hour; ⑦ hourly	Bus station, next to rail station	
	Monfalcone	4 km	17 mins	🚌 **10**, ①–⑥ 1-2 per hour; ⑦ hourly	Rail station	
TRD Trondheim, Værnes	Trondheim	33 km	37 mins	Train, ①–⑤ hourly, ⑥⑦ every two hours	Rail station. Værnes rail station is 220m from Airport terminal	**787**
VLC València	València	9 km	22 mins	Train, Lines **3**, **5**, Ⓐ every 6-9 mins; ⑥⑦ every 8-12 mins	Xátiva for Nord rail station	
VCE Venezia, Marco Polo	Venezia	12 km	25 mins	🚌 **5**, 2 per hour	Piazzale Roma (see city plans p32)	
	Venezia		80 mins	Waterbus *Alilaguna* ± every 30 mins	Lido 53-63 mins / Piazza S. Marco, 72-80 mins	
TSF Venezia, Treviso	Venezia	30 km	70 mins	🚌, connects with flights	Mestre rail station, Piazzale Roma (see city plans p32)	
VRN Verona, Villafranca	Verona	12 km	20 mins	🚌, every 20 mins 0635-2335	Rail station	
VNO Vilnius	Vilnius	4 km	7 mins	Train, 0637, 0728 and every ± 40 minutes until 1944	Rail station	**1812**
WAW Warszawa, Frederic Chopin, Okęcie,	Warszawa	13 km	23 mins	SKM / KM train, 3-5 per hour	Śródmieście (2-3 per hr) or Centralna (1-2 per hr) rail stations	
WMI Warszawa, Modlin	Warszawa	44 km	47 mins	🚌, to Modlin rail stn, then train, approx hourly	Centralna rail station	**1030**
NRN Weeze, Niederhein	Düsseldorf	70 km	75 mins	🚌, connects with Ryanair flights	Main rail station (Hauptbahnhof) Worringer Street	
	Düsseldorf	74 km	82 mins	🚌 **SW1**, to Weeze rail station, then train, Table **802**	Main rail station (Hauptbahnhof)	**802**
VIE Wien, Schwechat	Wien	21 km	16 mins	*City Airport Train (CAT)*, every 30 mins; special fares	Mitte rail station	**979**
	Wien	21 km	25 mins	S-bahn, every 30 mins	Mitte rail station	**979**
	Bratislava	54 km	60 mins	🚌 *ÖBB-Postbus / Blaguss*, hourly	AS Mlynské nivy (bus station) / Einsteinnova/Petrzalka	**979**
WRO Wrocław, Copernicus	Wrocław	10 km	30 mins	🚌 **406**, ①–⑥ 2-3 per hour; ⑦ every 40 mins	Rail station, bus station	
ZAG Zagreb	Zagreb	17 km	25 mins	🚌, 1-2 per hour	Bus station (Autobusni kolodvor), Avenija Marina Drzica	
ZAZ Zaragoza	Zaragoza	10 km	30 mins	🚌, ①–⑥ 1-2 per hour 0615 - 2315; ⑦ hourly 0645 - 2245	Paseo María Agustín, 150m from Portillo rail station	
ZRH Zürich	Zürich	10 km	13 mins	Train, 7-8 per hour	Main rail station (HB)	**529**
ZQW Zweibrücken	Zweibrucken	4 km	10 mins	Taxi	Rail station. Also 🚌 **199** to Saarbrücken	**918**

‡ – The frequencies shown apply during daytime on weekdays and are from the airport to the city centre. There may be fewer journeys in the evenings, at weekends and during the winter months. Extended 🚌 journey times could apply during peak hours.

¶ – Also train, from Nice St Augustin, ± hourly; 800m from Terminal 1.

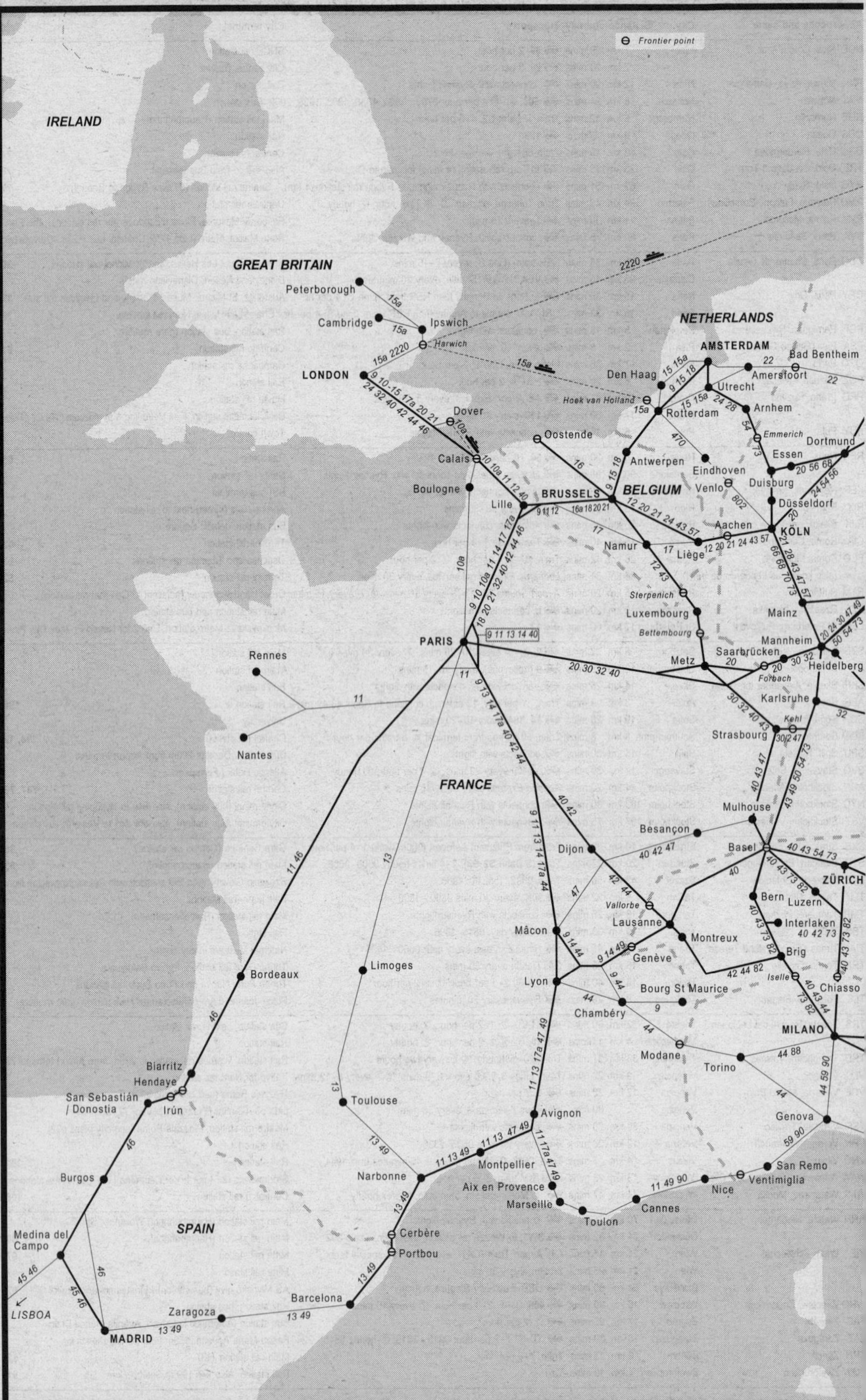
Frontier point
IRELAND
GREAT BRITAIN
NETHERLANDS
BELGIUM
FRANCE
SPAIN
Peterborough
Cambridge
Ipswich
Harwich
LONDON
Dover
Calais
Boulogne
Lille
BRUSSELS
Oostende
Antwerpen
Namur
Liège
AMSTERDAM
Den Haag
Hoek van Holland
Rotterdam
Utrecht
Amersfoort
Bad Bentheim
Arnhem
Emmerich
Eindhoven
Venlo
Essen
Dortmund
Duisburg
Düsseldorf
Aachen
KÖLN
Sterpenich
Luxembourg
Bettembourg
Mainz
Mannheim
Heidelberg
Saarbrücken
Forbach
Metz
Karlsruhe
Kehl
Strasbourg
Mulhouse
Basel
ZÜRICH
Bern
Luzern
Interlaken
Brig
Iselle
Chiasso
MILANO
Besançon
Dijon
Vallorbe
Lausanne
Montreux
Genève
Mâcon
Lyon
Bourg St Maurice
Chambéry
Modane
Torino
Genova
San Remo
Ventimiglia
Nice
Cannes
Toulon
Marseille
Aix en Provence
Avignon
Montpellier
Narbonne
Cerbère
Portbou
Barcelona
Zaragoza
MADRID
Medina del Campo
LISBOA
Burgos
San Sebastián / Donostia
Irún
Hendaye
Biarritz
Bordeaux
Toulouse
Limoges
PARIS
Rennes
Nantes
2220
15a
10a
9 11 13 14 40

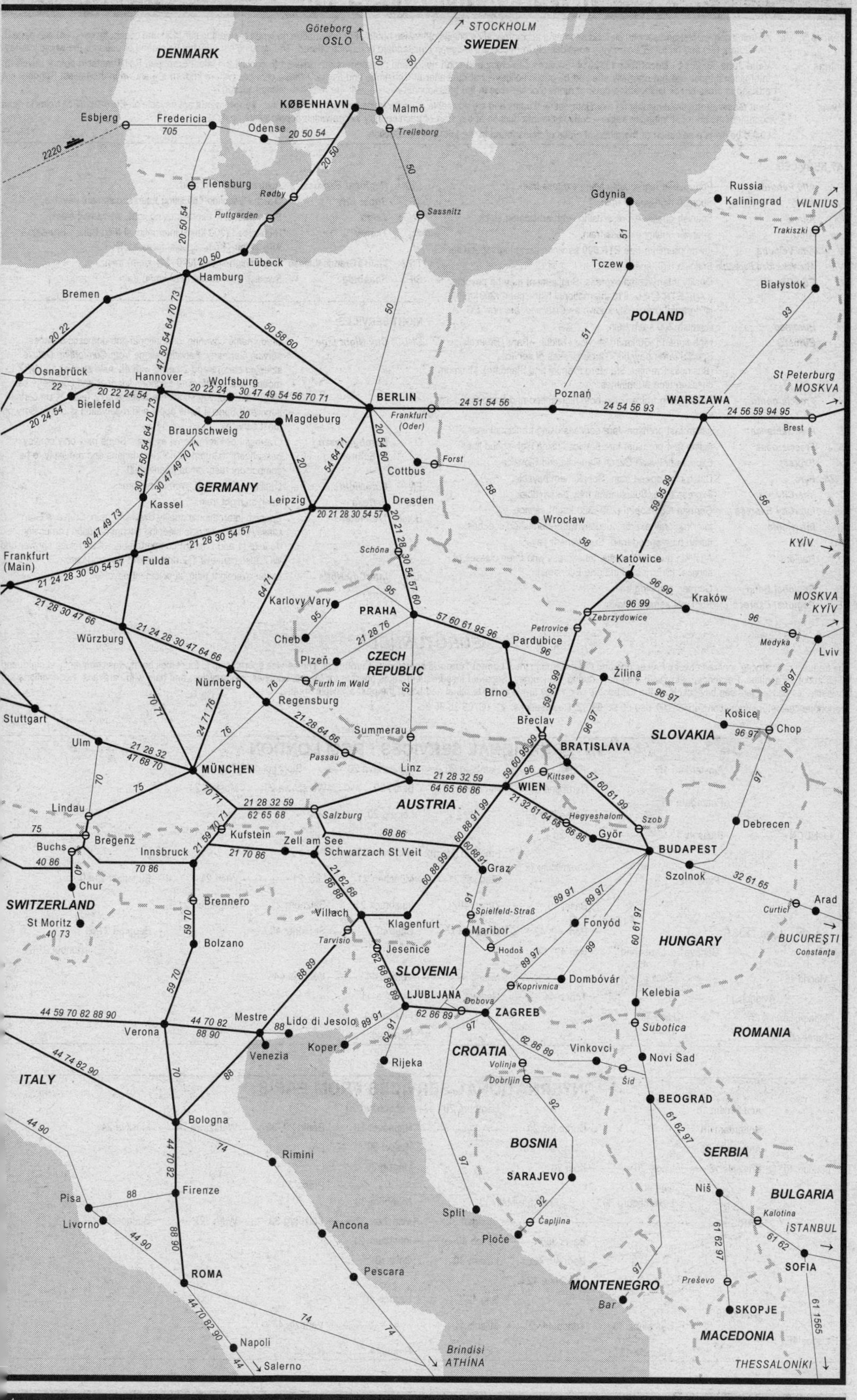

DENMARK
SWEDEN
GERMANY
POLAND
CZECH REPUBLIC
SLOVAKIA
AUSTRIA
SWITZERLAND
SLOVENIA
HUNGARY
ROMANIA
CROATIA
BOSNIA
SERBIA
BULGARIA
MONTENEGRO
MACEDONIA
ITALY
Göteborg OSLO
STOCKHOLM
Esbjerg
Fredericia
Odense
KØBENHAVN
Malmö
Trelleborg
Flensburg
Rødby
Puttgarden
Sassnitz
Lübeck
Hamburg
Bremen
Osnabrück
Hannover
Wolfsburg
Bielefeld
Braunschweig
Magdeburg
BERLIN
Frankfurt (Oder)
Cottbus
Forst
Dresden
Leipzig
Kassel
Fulda
Frankfurt (Main)
Würzburg
Nürnberg
Regensburg
Stuttgart
Ulm
MÜNCHEN
Passau
Schöna
Karlovy Vary
Cheb
Plzeň
Furth im Wald
PRAHA
Pardubice
Brno
Břeclav
Summerau
Linz
Salzburg
WIEN
Kittsee
BRATISLAVA
Hegyeshalom
Győr
Szob
BUDAPEST
Szolnok
Debrecen
Curtici
Arad
BUCUREŞTI
Constanţa
Gdynia
Tczew
Poznań
WARSZAWA
Wrocław
Katowice
Zebrzydowice
Petrovice
Kraków
Žilina
Košice
Chop
Medyka
Lviv
Russia
Kaliningrad
VILNIUS
Trakiszki
Białystok
St Peterburg
MOSKVA
Brest
KYÏV
MOSKVA KYÏV
Lindau
Bregenz
Buchs
Chur
St Moritz
Innsbruck
Kufstein
Zell am See
Schwarzach St Veit
Brennero
Bolzano
Villach
Tarvisio
Klagenfurt
Graz
Spielfeld-Straß
Maribor
Hodoš
Fonyód
Dombóvár
Koprivnica
Jesenice
LJUBLJANA
Dobova
ZAGREB
Kelebia
Subotica
Novi Sad
Vinkovci
Šid
BEOGRAD
Niš
Kalotina
İSTANBUL
SOFIA
Preševo
SKOPJE
THESSALONÍKI
Verona
Mestre
Venezia
Lido di Jesolo
Koper
Rijeka
Volinja
Dobrljin
SARAJEVO
Split
Čapljina
Ploče
Bar
Bologna
Rimini
Firenze
Pisa
Livorno
Ancona
Pescara
ROMA
Napoli
Salerno
Brindisi ATHINA

INTERNATIONAL SERVICES

Services All trains convey first and second classes of seating accommodation unless otherwise noted. For information on types of sleeping car (🛏) and couchette car (▬) see page 8. Restaurant (✕) and buffet (🍸) cars vary considerably from country to country in standard of service offered. The catering car may not be carried or open for the whole journey.

Timings **Valid June 15, 2014 - December 13, 2014**. Services can change at short notice and passengers are advised to consult the latest European Rail Timetable before travelling. International trains are not normally affected by public holidays, but may alter at Christmas and Easter - these changes (where known) are shown in the tables. Readers are advised to cross-check timings and days of running of services in the International section with the relevant country section.

Tickets **Seat reservations** are available for most international trains and are advisable as some trains can get very crowded. **Supplements** are payable on **EuroCity** (*EC*) trains in most countries and on most InterCity trains – consult the introduction at the start of each country to see which supplements apply.

Listed below is a selection of the different types of trains found in the International Section.

DAY SERVICES:

AP	***Alfa Pendular***	Portuguese high-quality tilting express train.
Alvia	***Alvia***	Spanish high-speed train.
Alta	***Altaria***	Spanish quality express using light, articulated stock.
Arco	***Arco***	Spanish quality express train.
AV	***Alta Velocità***	Italian premium fare **ETR 500** services using high-speed lines.
AVE	***Alta Velocidad Española***	Spanish high-speed train.
EC	***EuroCity***	Quality international express. Supplement may be payable. Italian **ETR 470** or **610** international high-speed (200 km/h) tilting train, previously known as *Cisalpino*, are now *EC*.
Em	***Euromed***	Spanish 200 km/h train.
☆	***Eurostar***	High-speed (300 km/h) service London - Paris / Brussels. Special fares payable. Three classes of service: (Business Premier, Standard Premier and Standard). Minimum check-in time 30 minutes.
FA	***Frecciargento***	Italian tilting trains using both high-speed and traditional lines.
FB	***Frecciabianca***	Italian fast premium fare services using traditional lines.
FR	***Frecciarossa***	Italian fast premium fare services using high-speed lines.
Ex	***Express***	Express between Czech Republic and Slovakia.
FYRA	***Fyra***	Dutch high-speed train. Supplement payable.
IC	***InterCity***	Express train. Supplement may be payable.
ICE	***InterCity Express***	German high-speed (230 - 320 km/h) service.
IR	***InterRegio***	Inter-regional express usually with refurbished coaches.
ITA	***.italo***	Italian high-speed train. Supplement payable.
RJ	***Railjet***	Austrian quality international express with three classes of service: (Business, First and Economy).
RB	***Regional Bahn***	German stopping train.
RE	***Regional Express***	Regional semi-fast train.
REX	***Regional Express***	Austrian semi-fast train.
SC	***Super City***	Czech Pendolino **680** tilting train, supplement payable.
Talgo	***Talgo***	Spanish quality express using light, articulated stock.
⇌	***Thalys***	High-speed (300 km/h) international train Paris - Brussels - Amsterdam / Köln. Special fares apply.
TGV	**Train à Grande Vitesse**	French high-speed (270 - 320 km/h) train.
Sn	***Snabbtåg***	Swedish high-speed (210 km/h) train.

NIGHT SERVICES:

CNL	***City Night Line***	Brand name covering international and domestic services serving Germany. Facilities range from *Comfortline Deluxe* sleeping cars (1 and 2 berth) with en-suite shower and WC, to modernised *Comfortline Economy* sleeper and couchette cars. Most trains convey shower facilities and 🍸 (also ✕ on certain services). Special fares apply and reservation is compulsory on most services.
D	***Durchgangszug*** or **Schnellzug**	Overnight or international express. Some may only convey passengers to international destinations and are likely to be compulsory reservation, marked Ⓡ.
EN	***EuroNight***	Quality international overnight express.
Estr	***Estrella***	Spanish night train.
Hotel	***Trenhotel***	Spanish international quality overnight train. Conveys Gran Clase / Grande Classe sleeping accommodation comprising *de luxe* (1 and 2 berth) compartments with en-suite shower and WC. Also conveys 1, 2 and 4 berth sleeping cars.
ICN	***InterCity Notte***	Italian overnight train, supplement payable.

EUROTUNNEL

The frequent car-carrying service between Folkestone and Calais through the **Channel Tunnel** is operated by Eurotunnel. The service operates up to four times hourly (less frequently at night) and takes about 35 minutes. Passengers stay with their cars during the journey. Separate less-frequent trains operate for lorries, coaches, motorcycles, and cars with caravans. Reservations are advisable but passengers can buy tickets at the toll booths when they arrive at the terminal and board the next available shuttle.

Freephone customer information service: ✆ 080 00 96 99 92. Reservations: ✆ 08705 35 35 35.

INTERNATIONAL SERVICES FROM LONDON

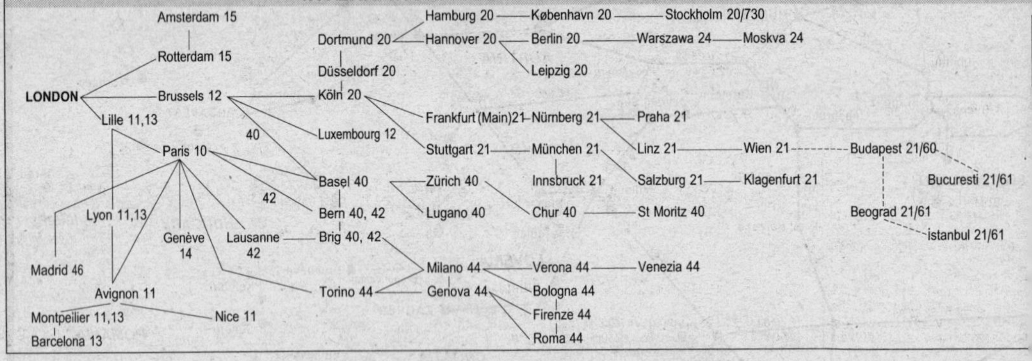

INTERNATIONAL SERVICES FROM PARIS

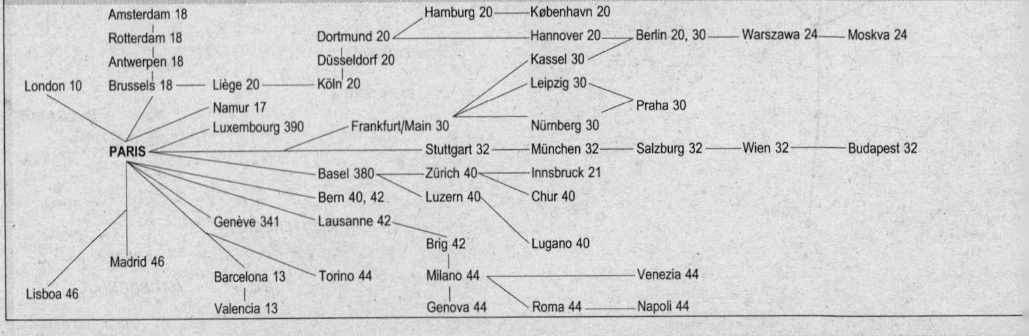

LONDON, AMSTERDAM, BRUSSELS and LILLE - ST GERVAIS and BOURG ST MAURICE 9

Other connections are available by changing in Paris (or in Lille and Lyon). Supplements are payable on TGV trains

train type	TGV		TGV			TGV	TGV		☆	TGV			⇌		☆		☆				
train number	**964**		**5108**			**962**	**5146**		**9110**	**9796**			**9920**		**9092**		**9096**				
train number	**965**		**5109**			**963**	**5147**		Ⓡ	**9797**			**9921**		**9093**		**9097**				
notes			Ⓡ🍷			Ⓡ🍷	Ⓡ🍷		✕	Ⓡ🍷			Ⓡ🍷		Ⓡ✕		Ⓡ✕				
notes	**Y**		**H**			**Y**	**H**		⑥	**C**			**A**		**M**		**R**◐				
London St Pancras d.	...	...	...	...	...	...	...	...	0657	...	...	...	...	...	0939	...	2009	...	...	...	...
Ashford International **11** a.	...	...	...	...	...	...	...	...	0724	...	...	...	...	...	1007	...	2040	...	...	...	...
Ashford International **11** d.	...	...	...	...	...	...	...	...	0728	...	...	...	...	...	1025	...	2055	...	...	...	...
Amsterdam Centraal d.	...	...	...	...	...	...	...	...	|	...	...	...	0540	...	|	...	|	...	...	...	...
Schiphol d.	...	...	...	...	...	...	...	...	|	...	...	...	0559	...	|	...	|	...	...	...	...
Den Haag HS d.	...	...	...	...	...	...	...	...	|	...	...	...	|	...	|	...	|	...	...	...	...
Rotterdam CS d.	...	...	...	...	...	...	...	...	|	...	...	...	0633	...	|	...	|	...	...	...	...
Antwerpen Centraal d.	...	...	...	...	...	...	...	...	|	...	...	...	0712	...	|	...	|	...	...	...	...
Brussels Midi/Zuid d.	...	...	...	...	...	...	...	...	|	...	...	...	0759	...	|	...	|	...	...	...	...
Lille Europe 11 d.	0605	...	0824	...	...	0953	0943	...	0926	1002	...	...	|	...	|	...	|	...	...	...	...
Douai **11** d.	|	...	|	...	...	|	1012	...	...	|	...	...	|	...	|	...	|	...	...	...	...
Arras **11** d.	|	...	|	...	...	|	1030	...	...	|	...	...	|	...	|	...	|	...	...	...	...
TGV Haute Picardie **11** d.	|	...	0900	...	...	1029	|	...	...	|	...	...	|	...	|	...	|	...	...	...	...
Paris Charles de Gaulle ✈ **11** d.	0708	...	0934	...	...	1105	1118	...	...	|	...	...	|	...	|	...	|	...	...	...	...
Marne la Valleé Chessy § **11** d.	0722	...	0948	...	...	1122	1131	...	...	|	...	...	|	...	|	...	|	...	...	...	...
Genève a.	|	...	|	...	...	|	|	...	...	1416	...	...	|	...	|	...	|	...	...	...	...
Lausanne a.	|	...	|	...	...	|	|	...	...	|	...	...	|	...	|	...	|	...	...	...	...
Aigle a.	|	...	|	...	...	|	|	...	...	1547	...	...	|	...	|	...	|	...	...	...	...
Martigny a.	|	...	|	...	...	|	|	...	...	1613	...	...	|	...	|	...	|	...	...	...	...
Sierre a.	|	...	|	...	...	|	|	...	...	1639	...	...	|	...	|	...	|	...	...	...	...
Visp a.	|	...	|	...	...	|	|	...	...	1657	...	...	|	...	|	...	|	...	...	...	...
Brig a.	|	...	|	...	...	|	|	...	...	1708	...	...	|	...	|	...	|	...	...	...	...
Cluses (Haute Savoie) a.	|	...	1410	...	...	|	|	...	...	...	...	...	|	...	|	...	|	...	...	...	...
Salanches Megève a.	|	...	1434	...	...	|	|	...	...	...	...	...	|	...	|	...	|	...	...	...	...
St Gervais a.	|	...	1442	1606	...	|	|	...	...	...	...	...	|	...	|	...	|	...	...	...	...
Chamonix a.	|	...	...	1645	...	|	|	...	...	...	...	...	|	...	|	...	|	...	...	...	...
Chambéry a.	1021	...	...	...	...	|	1438	...	...	...	...	...	1231	...	|	...	|	...	...	...	...
Albertville a.	1107	...	...	...	...	1459	1523	...	...	...	...	...	1314	...	|	...	|	...	...	...	...
Moûtiers-Salins a.	1134	...	...	...	...	1534	1601	...	...	...	...	...	1356	...	1812	...	0517	...	...	...	...
Aime la Plagne a.	1152	...	...	...	...	...	1619	...	...	...	...	...	1424	...	1830	...	0545	...	...	...	...
Landry a.	1204	...	...	...	...	...	1634	...	...	...	...	...	1434	...	|	...	|	...	...	...	...
Bourg St Maurice a.	1215	...	...	...	...	...	1652	...	...	...	...	...	1444	...	1851	...	0607	...	...	...	...

train type		☆			TGV	☆		TGV		⇌		TGV		TGV	TGV		☆				
train number		**9095**			**9278**	**9161**		**5178**		**9987**		**970**		**5174**	**972**		**9099**				
train number		**9094**			**9279**			**5179**		**9986**		**971**		**5175**	**973**		**9098**				
notes		Ⓡ✕			Ⓡ🍷	Ⓡ✕		Ⓡ🍷		Ⓡ🍷		Ⓡ🍷		Ⓡ🍷	Ⓡ🍷		Ⓡ✕				
notes		**G**			**D**	**D**		**T**		**B**		**Z**		**K**	**Z**		**G**◧				
Bourg St Maurice d.	...	0944	...	...	...	...	...	...	...	1545	...	1608	...	1738	...	...	2215	...	...	...	...
Landry d.	...	|	...	...	...	...	...	...	...	1555	...	1619	...	1748	...	...	|	...	...	...	...
Aime la Plagne d.	...	|	...	...	...	...	...	...	...	1606	...	1630	...	1759	...	...	|	...	...	...	...
Moûtiers-Salins a.	...	1010	...	...	...	...	...	...	...	|	...	|	...	|	...	...	2242	...	...	...	...
Moûtiers-Salins d.	...	1026	...	...	...	...	...	...	...	1628	...	1657	...	1815	1825	...	2254	...	...	...	...
Albertville d.	...	|	...	...	...	...	...	...	...	1716	...	1747	...	1848	1857	...	|	...	...	...	...
Chambéry d.	...	|	...	...	...	...	...	...	...	1755	...	|	...	1938	|	...	|	...	...	...	...
Chamonix d.	...	|	...	...	...	...	1411	...	...	|	...	|	...	|	|	...	|	...	...	...	...
St Gervais d.	...	|	...	...	...	...	1454	1542	...	|	...	|	...	|	|	...	|	...	...	...	...
Salanches Megève d.	...	|	...	...	...	...	...	1551	...	|	...	|	...	|	|	...	|	...	...	...	...
Cluses (Haute Savoie) d.	...	|	...	...	...	...	...	1607	...	|	...	|	...	|	|	...	|	...	...	...	...
Brig d.	...	|	...	...	1251	...	...	|	...	|	...	|	...	|	|	...	|	...	...	...	...
Visp d.	...	|	...	...	1302	...	...	|	...	|	...	|	...	|	|	...	|	...	...	...	...
Sierre d.	...	|	...	...	1318	...	...	|	...	|	...	|	...	|	|	...	|	...	...	...	...
Martigny d.	...	|	...	...	1341	...	...	|	...	|	...	|	...	|	|	...	|	...	...	...	...
Aigle d.	...	|	...	...	1401	...	...	|	...	|	...	|	...	|	|	...	|	...	...	...	...
Lausanne d.	...	|	...	...	|	...	...	|	...	|	...	|	...	|	|	...	|	...	...	...	...
Genève d.	...	|	...	...	|	...	...	|	...	|	...	|	...	|	|	...	|	...	...	...	...
Marne la Vallée Chessy § **11** a.	...	|	...	...	|	...	...	2015	...	|	...	2121	...	2229	2318	...	|	...	...	...	...
Paris Charles de Gaulle ✈ **11** a.	...	|	...	...	|	...	...	2033	...	|	...	2151	...	2243	2333	...	|	...	...	...	...
TGV Haute Picardie **11** a.	...	|	...	...	|	...	...	2104	...	|	...	|	...	2314	0005	...	|	...	...	...	...
Arras **11** a.	...	|	...	...	|	...	...	|	...	|	...	|	...	|	|	...	|	...	...	...	...
Douai **11** a.	...	|	...	...	|	...	...	|	...	|	...	|	...	|	|	...	|	...	...	...	...
Lille Flandres a.	...	|	...	...	|	...	...	|	...	|	...	2249	...	|	|	...	|	...	...	...	...
Lille Europe 11 a.	...	|	...	...	1855	2030	...	2134	...	|	...	...	...	2344	0040	...	|	...	...	...	...
Dunkerque a.	...	|	...	...	...	|	...	...	...	|	...	...	...	...	...	...	|	...	...	...	...
Brussels Midi/Zuid a.	...	|	...	...	...	|	...	...	...	2244	...	...	...	...	...	...	|	...	...	...	...
Gent Sint-Pieters a.	...	|	...	...	...	|	...	...	...	|	...	...	...	...	...	...	|	...	...	...	...
Brugge a.	...	|	...	...	...	|	...	...	...	|	...	...	...	...	...	...	|	...	...	...	...
Oostende a.	...	|	...	...	...	|	...	...	...	|	...	...	...	...	...	...	|	...	...	...	...
Antwerpen Centraal a.	...	|	...	...	...	|	...	...	...	2327	...	...	...	...	...	...	|	...	...	...	...
Rotterdam CS a.	...	|	...	...	...	|	...	...	...	0002	...	...	...	...	...	...	|	...	...	...	...
Den Haag HS a.	...	|	...	...	...	|	...	...	...	|	...	...	...	...	...	...	|	...	...	...	...
Schiphol a.	...	|	...	...	...	|	...	...	...	0022	...	...	...	...	...	...	|	...	...	...	...
Amsterdam Centraal a.	...	|	...	...	...	|	...	...	...	0041	...	...	...	...	...	...	|	...	...	...	...
Ashford International **11** a.	...	1537	...	...	...	2033	...	...	...	...	...	...	...	...	...	...	0634	...	...	...	...
London St Pancras a.	...	1611	...	...	...	2106	...	...	...	...	...	...	...	...	...	...	0716	...	...	...	...

– THALYS NEIGE – ⑥ Dec. 20 - Mar. 14: (12) 🍷 Amsterdam - Bourg St Maurice; ⑥ Dec. 20 - Apr. 4: (12) 🍷 Brussels - Bourg St Maurice.

– THALYS NEIGE – ⑥ Dec. 27 - Mar. 21: (12) 🍷 Bourg St Maurice - Amsterdam; ⑥ Dec. 20 - Apr. 11: (12) 🍷 Bourg St Maurice - Brussels.

– ⑥ Dec. 21 - Apr. 5.

– ⑥ Dec. 28 - Apr. 12.

– ⑥ Dec. 28 - Apr. 12.

– Dec. 22, 29, Feb. 16, 23.

– ⑥ Dec. 15 - Mar. 30.

– ⑥ Dec. 21 - Apr. 5.

– ⑤ Dec. 20 - Apr. 4.

– Dec. 29, Jan. 5, Feb. 23, Mar. 2.

– Feb. 16, 23.

– Feb. 23, Mar. 2.

◐ – 🍷 until 2400. ✕ after departure from Ashford. ✕ and 🍷 from 0500.

◧ – 🍷 until 2400. ✕ after departure from Moûtiers. ✕ and 🍷 from 0500.

§ – Station for Disneyland, Paris.

⇌ – *Thalys* high-speed train Ⓡ 🍷. Special fares payable.

☆ – Eurostar train. Special fares payable. Minimum check-in time 30 minutes.

10 LONDON - LILLE - PARIS and BRUSSELS *by Eurostar*

Minimum check-in time is 30 minutes, but passengers are advised to allow longer due to immigration procedures. Not available for London - Ebbsfleet - Ashford or v.v. Special fares payable that include three classes of service: business premier, standard premier and standard. All times shown are local times (France and Belgium are one hour ahead of Great Britain). All Eurostar services are 🅁, non-smoking and convey ✕ in 1st class, 🍸 in 2nd class. Service June 1 - December 13.

km	km	train number	9080	9002	9110	9110	9004	9006	9006	9008	9008	9114	9010	9010	9010	9116	9116	9012	9014	9014	9018	9018	9126	9020	9022	9060	9024
		notes	①–⑤	⑥	①–⑤	⑥	①–⑤	⑥		①–⑤	⑥	①–⑤	⑦	⑥	①–⑤	①–⑤	⑥⑦	⑥	①–⑤	⑥⑦			①–⑥	⑥			
		notes	h		f		g	Z	E				y		j	j	y	U	j	y	S	M	j	W	X	O	
0	0	**London** St Pancras d.	0540	0618	0650	0657	0701	0722	0731	0755	0801	0804	0819	0825	0831	0858	0858e	0900	0917	0922	1015	1025	1058	1101	1131	1201	1225
35	35	Ebbsfleet International d.	0558	|	0708	|	|	0742	|	0812	|	|	0838	0842	|	0915	0915	|	0935	|	1035	1042	1115	|	|	|	1242
90	90	Ashford International d.	0624	0655	0728	0728	|	|	|	|	|	|	|	|	|	|	|	|	0955	0955t	|	|	|	|	|	|	|
166	166	Calais Fréthun a.	|	|	0859	|	|	|	|	|	|	|	|	|	|	|	1059	|	|	|	|	|	|	|	|	|	|
267	267	Lille Europe a.	|	|	0930	0926	|	|	|	|	|	1026	|	|	|	1126	1130	|	|	|	|	|	1326	|	|	|	|
	373	**Brussels** Midi / Zuid a.	|	|	1007	1011	|	|	|	|	|	1105	|	|	|	1205	1208	|	|	|	|	|	1405	|	|	|	|
492		**Paris** Nord a.	0917	0947	...	...	1017	1047	1047	1117	1117	...	1147	1147	1147	...	...	1217	1247	1247	1347	1347	...	1417	1447	1517	1547

train number	9132	9026	9028	9030	9136	9032	9034	9140	9036	9038	9144	9040	9042	9148	9044	9152	9046	9152	9048	9050	9156	9158	9054	9162	9056
notes			Ⓑ	⑥		Ⓑ	⑦	Ⓑ		⑤	⑥	Ⓑ	⑥	Ⓑ		⑦	Ⓑ	①–⑤	⑤		⑥⑦	①–⑤		⑦	⑦
notes		Y		D	P		y			m						y		j	G		y	j		x	n
London St Pancras d.	1258	1301	1331	1401	1404	1431	1501	1504	1531	1601	1604	1622	1652	1704	1731	1755b	1801	1804	1831	1901	1904	1934	2001	2004	2031
Ebbsfleet International d.	1315	|	|	|	|	|	|	|	|	|	|	|	|	|	|	|	|	|	|	|	|	|	|	|	|
Ashford International d.	|	|	|	|	|	|	|	|	|	|	|	1655t	1723	|	|	1828	|	|	|	|	|	|	|	|	|
Calais Fréthun a.	1459	|	|	|	|	|	|	|	|	|	|	|	|	|	|	|	|	|	|	|	2059	2129	|	|	|
Lille Europe a.	1530	|	|	|	1626	|	|	1726	|	|	1826	|	|	1926	|	2026	|	2026	|	|	2130	2200	|	2226	|
Brussels Midi / Zuid a.	1608	|	|	|	1705	|	|	1805	|	|	1905	|	|	2005	|	2105	|	2105	|	|	2208	2238	|	2305	|
Paris Nord a.	...	1617	1647	1717	...	1747	1817	...	1847	1917	...	1947	2017	...	2047	...	2117	...	2147	2217	...	...	2317	...	2347

train number	9109	9005	9007	9113	9009	9011	9117	9013	9015	9019	9125	9023	9129	9025	9027	9029	9133	9031	9033	9035	9037	9141	9141	9039	9145	9041	9043
notes	①	①	①–⑥	①–⑥	①–⑤	⑥⑦		①–⑤			①–⑥		⑦		⑦		①–⑤		⑦	⑥⑦	⑤	⑥⑦	①–⑤				
notes	q	z	j	j	j	y		N			r		y	H	C	AA			J	m	L	y	j		P	B	Q
Paris Nord d.	...	0643	0713	...	0743	0813	...	0843	0913	1013	...	1113	...	1143	1213	1243	...	1313	1343	1413	1443	...	...	1513	...	1543	1613
Brussels Midi / Zuid d.	0656	|	|	0756	|	|	0852	|	|	|	1056	|	1156	|	|	|	1252	|	|	|	|	1452	1456	|	1556	|	|
Lille Europe d.	0736	|	|	0835	|	|	0930	|	|	|	1136	|	1236	|	|	|	1330	|	|	|	|	1530	1536	|	1636	|	|
Calais Fréthun d.	|	|	|	|	|	|	1001	|	|	|	|	|	|	|	|	|	1401	|	|	|	|	1601	|	|	|	|	|
Ashford International a.	|	|	|	|	|	|	|	|	|	1107t	|	|	|	|	|	|	|	|	|	|	|	|	|	1607t	|	|	|
Ebbsfleet International a.	|	|	|	|	|	|	|	|	1018	|	|	|	|	|	|	|	1345	1418	|	|	|	1545	1545	|	|	|	1718
London St Pancras a.	0757c	0800	0830	0857	0900	0930	0957	1000	1039	1139	1157	1230	1257	1300	1330	1400	1403	1439	1500	1530	1600	1603	1603	1639	1657	1700	1739

train number	9045	9149	9149	9149	9047	9153	9153	9051	9157	9053	9055	9055	9161	9161	9059	9061	9063
notes	⑦		⑥			①–⑤	⑦	Ⓑ	Ⓑ	⑦	⑥⑦	①–⑤	Ⓑ	⑥		⑦	Ⓑ
notes	K	F		R		j	y			V	y	j				DD	d
Paris Nord d.	1643	...	...	...	1713	...	...	1813	...	1843	1913	1913	...	...	2013	2043	2113
Brussels Midi / Zuid d.	|	1656	1656	1656	|	1756	1756	|	1856	|	|	|	1952	1952	|	|	|
Lille Europe d.	|	1736	1736	1736	|	1836	1836	|	1935	|	|	|	2030	2030	|	|	|
Calais Fréthun d.	|	|	|	|	|	|	|	|	|	|	|	|	2101	2101	|	|	|
Ashford International a.	|	1734	|	1737	|	|	1835	|	|	|	2007	2010	|	2035	|	|	|
Ebbsfleet International a.	|	|	1748	|	|	1845	|	1918	|	|	|	|	2045	|	2118	|	2218
London St Pancras a.	1800	1809	1809	1811	1830	1903	1910	1939	1957	2000	2039	2041	2103	2109	2139	2200	2239

B – ⑤ May 25 - Aug. 30.
C – ⑦ (⑤⑦ Apr. 4 - Aug. 30) also Aug. 25, Nov. 11.
D – ⑥ (⑤⑥⑦ Mar. 29 - Aug. 30) also Aug. 25.
E – ①–⑤ May 25 - Aug. 30 (not Aug. 25); ① Aug. 31 - Dec. 13.
F – ④⑤ May 25 - Aug. 30.
G – ⑤ (①–⑤ Mar. 31 - Aug. 30) also Nov. 11; not Aug. 25.
H – May 25 - Aug. 30.
J – Mar. 30 - Aug. 30.
K – ④⑤⑦ May 25 - Aug. 30 (also Aug. 25; not Aug. 24); ⑤ Aug. 31 - Dec. 13 (also Nov. 11).
L – ⑤ (①–⑤ Mar. 31 - Aug. 30) not Aug. 25.
M – Ⓑ (daily Apr. 6 - Aug. 30) not Oct. 19.
N – ①–⑤ June 1 - July 26; ①⑥ July 27 - Aug. 30; ①–⑤ Aug. 31 - Dec. 13 (not Nov. 11).
O – ①④⑤ May 29 - June 6; ①④⑤⑥ June 7 - Aug. 30 (not Aug. 25).
P – ⑤⑦ (Ⓑ Mar. 30 - Aug. 30) also Oct. 23, 27–30, Nov. 11.

Q – Not ⑤ May 25 - Aug. 30.
R – ①–③ May 25 - Aug. 30; ①–⑤ Aug. 31 - Dec. 13.
S – Oct. 19 only.
T – ⑤⑦ May 23 - Aug. 30 (also May 26, Aug. 25; not May 25).
U – ⑥ June 28 - Sept. 30.
V – Ⓑ May 25 - Aug. 30; ②③④⑤⑦ Aug. 31 - Dec. 13.
W – ⑥ (⑥⑦ Mar. 29 - Aug. 30) also Aug. 25.
X – ②③④⑤⑥ (daily Mar. 25 - Aug. 30) not Aug. 25, Nov. 10, 11.
Y – ⑦ May 25 - Aug. 30 (also Aug. 25).
Z – Feb. 1 - July 28; Sept. 20 - Dec. 13.
AA – ①–⑥ May 25 - Aug. 30 (not Aug. 25); ①–⑤ Aug. 31 - Dec. 14 (not Nov. 11).

b – 1751 on Nov. 11.
c – 0759 from July 27.
d – Not June 8.
e – 0857 ⑥ May 25 - July 26.

f – Not June 9, July 21, Aug. 15, 25, Nov. 10, 11.
g – Not Aug. 25, Nov. 11.
h – Not June 9, July 14, July 27 - Aug. 30, Nov. 10, 11.
j – Not Aug. 25, Nov. 11.
m – Also Nov. 11.
n – Also June 8, Aug. 25, Nov. 11.
q – Not June 9, July 21, Aug. 25, Nov. 10.
r – Not Nov. 11.
t – Not Oct. 19.
x – Not Aug. 24.
y – Also Aug. 25, Nov. 11.
z – Not June 9, July 14, July 27 - Aug. 30, Nov. 10, 11.

10a LONDON – PARIS *by rail–sea–rail*

Subject to alteration

Other services are available by taking normal service trains between London and Dover (Tables **100**, **101**), sailings between Dover and Calais (Table **2110**) and normal service trains betweer Calais and Paris, by changing at Boulogne (Table **261**), passengers making their own way between stations and docks at Dover and Calais, allowing at least 1 hour for connections.

French train number			🚢	TGV 7254	2	2022					🚢	2	2	2032	2032				🚢	2	2036	
sea crossing (see below)	①–⑤	⑥	①–⑥		①–⑥	①–⑥	⚡	⑦	⑥	①–⑤		①–⑥	⑦	⑥⑦	①–⑤		⑦	⑦⚡	⑦	⑦	⑦	
notes	p⚡	⚡		🅁A	f	f	p	q		p		f	h	h	f		q	q		h	h	
London St Pancras d.	0710	0712	...	...	...	...	0910	...	...	...	...	...	...	...	...	...	...	1212	...	...	...	...
London Charing Cross d.	|	|	...	...	...	...	|	0908	0910	0913	...	...	...	...	...	...	1108	|	...	...	...	...
Dover Priory ✤ a.	0818	0820	...	...	...	...	1020	1102	1101	1102	...	...	...	...	...	...	1302	1320	...	...	...	...
Dover Eastern Docks 🚌 ✤ d.	...	...	0925	...	...	...	...	...	...	...	1205	...	...	...	...	...	...	...	1445	...	...	...
Calais Port 🚌 ✤ a.	...	...	1155	...	...	...	...	...	...	...	1435	...	...	...	...	...	...	...	1715	...	...	...
Calais Ville ✤ d.	...	...	...	1325	1331	...	...	...	...	...	...	1539	1610	...	...	...	...	...	...	1807	...	...
Boulogne Ville d.	...	...	...	|	1406	1413	...	...	...	...	...	1612	1645	1704	1712	...	...	...	...	1847	1904	...
Amiens a.	...	...	...	|	...	1536	...	...	...	...	...	...	...	1836	1836	...	...	...	...	...	2036	...
Paris Nord a.	...	...	...	1514	...	1656	...	...	...	...	...	...	...	1956	1956	...	...	...	...	...	2156	...

French train number	2003	2	TGV 7223	🚢		⚡		2009	2	🚢		2	🚢			2013	2	2	2	🚢		
sea crossing (see below)	⑥	⑥		①–⑥	①–⑥	①–⑥			①–⑥			⑦		⚡			⑦	⑥	①–⑤			⚡
notes			🅁A		p	p			f			h					h		f			
Paris Nord d.	0701	...	0946	...	...	...	...	1004	...	...	...	...	...	...	...	1404	...	...	...	...	...	...
Amiens d.	0824	...	|	...	...	...	...	1121	...	...	...	...	...	...	...	1521	...	...	...	...	...	...
Boulogne Ville d.	0958	1048	|	...	...	...	...	1252	1311	...	...	1410	...	...	...	1643	1647	1651	1711	...	...	...
Calais Ville ✤ a.	...	1121	1131	...	...	...	...	...	1348	...	...	1440	...	...	...	...	1721	1724	1748	...	...	...
Calais Port 🚌 ✤ d.	...	...	...	1235	...	...	...	...	...	1520	...	...	1605	...	...	...	...	...	...	1850	...	...
Dover Eastern Docks 🚌 ✤ a.	...	...	...	1305	...	...	...	...	...	1550	...	...	1635	...	...	...	...	...	...	1920	...	...
Dover Priory ✤ d.	...	...	...	...	1425	1445	...	...	...	...	1724	...	...	1745	1825	...	...	...	...	...	2025	204
London Charing Cross a.	...	...	...	...	1624	|	...	...	...	...	1922	...	...	|	2022	...	...	...	...	...	2222	|
London St Pancras a.	...	...	...	...	...	1551	...	...	...	...	...	...	...	1851	...	...	...	...	...	...	...	215

A – ①–⑥ (not June 9, July 14, Aug. 15, Nov. 11).

f – Not June 9, July 14, Aug. 15, Nov. 11.
h – Also June 9, July 14, Aug. 15, Nov. 11.
p – Not Aug. 25.

q – Also Aug. 25.

⚡ – Supplement payable.

🚢 – Ship service, operated by P & O Ferries. ✕ on ship. One class only on ship. For additional ferry services see Table **2110**.

✤ – 🚌 service: From Dover Priory to Dover Eastern Docks (journey time 10 minutes): Every [illegible] minutes 0710 – 2050. From Dover Eastern Docks to Dover Priory: Every 20 minut 0700 – 2040. Not a guaranteed connection.

From Calais Port to Calais Ville station 1120, 1220, 1305, 1405, 1500, 1640, 174 1835. From Calais Ville station to Calais Port 1040, 1135, 1235, 1320, 1420, 151 1655, 1755. Not a guaranteed connection.

LONDON / BRUSSELS - LILLE - CHARLES DE GAULLE ✈ - WESTERN / SOUTHERN FRANCE 11

DAY TRAINS (FOR NIGHT TRAINS SEE TABLE 13). Supplements are payable on *TGV* trains. Connections at Lille are not guaranteed. Other connections available via Paris.

km	*train type*	*TGV*	*TGV*	*TGV*	*TGV*	*TGV*		*TGV*	*TGV*	*TGV*	*TGV*	*TGV*	*TGV*	⇌		☆	☆	☆	☆	*TGV*	*TGV*			
	train number	**5102**	**5104**	**5200**	**5110**	**9810**		**5214**	**5211**	**9800**	**9812**	**5202**	**5202**	**9926**		**9110**	**9110**	**9084**	**9110**	**5164**	**9826**			
	train number	**5103**	**5105**	**5201**	**9811**	**9811**	**17483**	**5215**		**9801**	**9811**	**5450**	**5450**	**9927**				**9085**		**9826**	**9827**			
	notes	Ⓡ 🍷	Ⓡ 🍷	Ⓡ 🍷	Ⓡ 🍷	Ⓡ 🍷		Ⓡ 🍷	Ⓡ 🍷	Ⓡ 🍷	Ⓡ 🍷	Ⓡ 🍷	Ⓡ 🍷	Ⓡ 🍷		Ⓡ ✕	Ⓡ ✕	Ⓡ ✕	Ⓡ ✕	Ⓡ 🍷	Ⓡ 🍷			
												①-⑤	⑥⑦			①-⑤	⑥		①-⑤					
				g					**h**			**n**	**c**	**C**		**q**		**Q**						
	London St Pancras **12** d.	...	...	...	...	...	...	...	...	...	...	...	...	...	...	0650	0657	0717	0804	...	...	...	...	...
	Ebbsfleet International **12** d.	...	...	...	...	...	...	...	...	...	...	...	...	...	...	0708	|	|	|	...	...	...	...	...
	Ashford International **12** d.	...	...	...	...	...	...	...	...	...	...	...	...	...	...	0728	0728	0755e	|	...	...	...	...	...
	Brussels Midi / Zuid **12** d.	...	...	...	...	0710	...	...	...	0817	0817	...	...	0958	...	|	|	|	|	...	1031	...	...	...
	Lille Europe **12** a.	...	...	...	...	|	...	...	...	0852	0852	...	...	|	...	0930	0926	|	1026	...	|	...	...	...
0	**Lille** Europe d.	0537‡	0537‡	0703	0654f	|	...	0836	0836	0902	0902	0921	0921	|	...	...	...	|	...	1043	|	...	...	...
	Douai d.	|	|	|	0716f	|	...	|	|	|	|	|	|	|	...	...	...	|	...	|	|	...	...	...
	Arras d.	0559	0559	|	0732	|	...	|	|	|	|	|	|	|	...	...	...	|	...	|	|	...	...	...
99	TGV Haute Picardie d.	0619	0619	0747	|	|	...	0915	0915	|	|	|	|	|	...	...	...	|	...	1115	|	...	...	...
203	Paris Charles de Gaulle ✈ a.	0648	0648	0814	0821	0826	...	0944	0944	0953	0953	1011	1011	|	...	...	...	|	...	1144	1149	...	...	...
203	Paris Charles de Gaulle ✈ d.	0658	0658	0819	0831	0831	...	0949	0949	0958	0958	1016	1016	|	...	...	...	|	...	1158	1158	...	...	...
227	Marne la Vallée § d.	0711	0711	0833	0843	0843	...	1003	1003	1011	1011	1034	1034	|	...	...	...	|	...	1211	1211	...	...	...
289	Massy TGV d.	|	|	0908	|	|	...	1038	1038	|	|	1108	1108	|	...	...	...	|	...	|	|	...	...	...
	Le Mans a.	|	|	|	|	|	...	1127	1127	|	|	|	|	|	...	...	...	|	...	|	|	...	...	...
	Rennes a.	|	|	|	|	|	...	|	1250	|	|	|	|	|	...	...	...	|	...	|	|	...	...	...
	Angers St Laud a.	|	|	|	|	|	...	1210	...	|	|	|	|	|	...	...	...	|	...	|	|	...	...	...
	Nantes a.	|	|	|	|	|	...	1248	...	|	|	|	|	|	...	...	...	|	...	|	|	...	...	...
	St Pierre des Corps a.	|	|	0959	|	|	...	...	...	|	|	1159	1159	|	...	...	...	|	...	|	|	...	...	...
	Futuroscope a.	|	|	|	|	|	...	...	...	|	|	|	1235	|	...	...	...	|	...	|	|	...	...	...
	Poitiers a.	|	|	1041	|	|	...	...	...	|	|	1241	|	|	...	...	...	|	...	|	|	...	...	...
	Angoulême a.	|	|	1133	|	|	...	...	...	|	|	1332	1332	|	...	...	...	|	...	|	|	...	...	...
	Bordeaux a.	|	|	1237	|	|	...	...	...	|	|	1437	1437	|	...	...	...	|	...	|	|	...	...	...
521	Le Creusot TGV a.	|	|	...	|	|	...	...	...	|	|	...	...	|	...	...	...	|	...	|	|	...	...	...
645	**Lyon** Part Dieu a.	0900	0900	...	1030	1030	...	...	...	1200	1200	...	...	|	...	...	...	|	...	1400	1400	...	...	...
	Lyon Perrache a.	|	|	...	|	|	...	...	...	|	|	...	...	|	...	...	...	|	...	|	|	...	...	...
	Lyon St Exupéry ✈ a.	|	|	...	|	|	...	...	...	|	|	...	...	|	...	...	...	|	...	|	|	...	...	...
	Valence TGV a.	|	0945	...	1110	1110	...	...	...	|	|	...	...	1325	...	...	...	|	...	1440	1440	...	...	...
	Avignon TGV a.	1008	|	...	1144	1144	...	...	...	1310	|	...	...	1359	...	...	...	1353k	...	|	|	...	...	...
	Nîmes a.	|	1036	...	|	|	...	...	...	|	1316	...	...	|	...	...	...	...	...	|	|	...	...	...
	Montpellier a.	|	1104	...	|	|	...	...	...	|	1350	...	...	|	...	...	...	...	...	|	|	...	...	...
	Béziers a.	|	...	...	|	|	...	...	...	|	...	...	...	|	...	...	...	...	...	|	|	...	...	...
	Narbonne a.	|	...	...	|	|	...	...	...	|	...	...	...	|	...	...	...	...	...	|	|	...	...	...
	Toulouse Matabiau a.	|	...	...	|	|	...	...	...	|	...	...	...	|	...	...	...	...	...	|	|	...	...	...
	Perpignan a.	|	...	...	|	|	...	...	...	|	...	...	...	|	...	...	...	...	...	|	|	...	...	...
	Aix en Provence TGV a.	1031	...	...	|	|	...	...	...	1333	...	...	...	1423	...	...	...	...	...	1531	1531	...	...	...
	Marseille St Charles a.	1046	...	...	1216	1216	1231	...	...	1349	...	...	...	1440	...	...	...	...	...	1546	1546	...	...	...
	Toulon a.	...	...	...	...	...	1315	...	...	1502	...	...	...	...	...	...	...	...	...	...	...	...	...	...
	St Raphaël - Valescure a.	...	...	...	...	...	1410	...	...	...	...	...	...	...	...	...	...	...	...	...	...	...	...	...
	Cannes a.	...	...	...	...	...	1434	...	...	...	...	...	...	...	...	...	...	...	...	...	...	...	...	...
	Nice a.	...	...	...	...	...	1505	...	...	...	...	...	...	...	...	...	...	...	...	...	...	...	...	...

train type	☆	*TGV*	*TGV*	☆	☆	*TGV*	*TGV*	*TGV*	☆	*TGV*	☆	*TGV*	*TGV*	*TGV*		☆	*TGV*	*TGV*	*TGV*	*TGV*				
train number	**9110**	**5226**	**5225**	**9116**	**9116**	**9828**	**6811**	**5218**	**9074**	**5218**	**9126**	**5232**	**5209**	**5222**		**9132**	**5134**	**6183**	**5119**	**6217**				
train number		**5227**				**9829**	**6810**	**5219**		**5219**		**5233**		**5223**			**5135**							
notes	Ⓡ ✕	Ⓡ 🍷	Ⓡ 🍷	Ⓡ ✕	Ⓡ ✕	Ⓡ 🍷	Ⓡ 🍷	Ⓡ 🍷	Ⓡ ✕	Ⓡ 🍷	Ⓡ ✕	Ⓡ 🍷	Ⓡ 🍷	Ⓡ 🍷		Ⓡ ✕	Ⓡ 🍷	Ⓡ 🍷	Ⓡ 🍷	Ⓡ 🍷				
	①-⑤	⊖		①-⑤	⑥⑦						①-⑥							⑤⑥⑦						
		j		**z**	**y**				**G**		**z**		**H**					**w**						
London St Pancras **12** d.	0804	...	...	0858	0858	...	...	...	1015	...	1058	...	...	...	...	1258	...	...	...	...	...	...	...	...
Ebbsfleet International **12** d.	|	...	...	0915	0915	...	...	...	1034	...	1115	...	...	...	...	1315	...	...	...	...	...	...	...	...
Ashford International **12** d.	|	...	...	|	|	...	...	...	1058	...	|	...	...	...	...	|	...	...	...	...	...	...	...	...
Brussels Midi / Zuid **12** d.	|	...	...	|	|	1217	...	...	|	...	|	...	...	...	...	|	...	...	...	...	...	...	...	...
Lille Europe **12** a.	1026	...	...	1126	1130	1253	...	...	1254s	...	1326	...	...	...	...	1530	...	...	...	...	...	...	...	...
Lille Europe d.	...	1106f	1106f	...	...	1303	...	1308f	|	...	...	1352	1352	1445f	...	...	1554	...	1554	...	...	...	...	...
Douai d.	...	1129	1129	...	...	|	...	|	|	...	...	|	|	1508	...	...	|	...	|	...	...	...	...	...
Arras d.	...	1147	1147	...	...	|	...	|	|	...	...	|	|	1525	...	...	|	...	|	...	...	...	...	...
TGV Haute Picardie d.	...	1214	1214	...	...	|	...	|	|	←	...	|	|	1549	...	...	1624	...	1624	...	...	...	...	...
Paris Charles de Gaulle ✈ a.	...	1244	1244	...	...	1353	...	1404	|	1404	...	1444	1444	1616	...	...	1653	...	1653	...	...	...	...	...
Paris Charles de Gaulle ✈ d.	...	1249	1249	...	...	1358	...	→	|	1409	...	1449	1449	1621	...	...	1658	...	1658	...	...	...	...	...
Marne la Vallée § d.	...	1303	1303	...	...	1411	...	...	1357	1433	...	1503	1503	1634	...	...	1711	...	1711	...	...	...	...	...
Massy TGV d.	...	1338	1338	...	...	|	...	...	...	1508	...	1538	1538	1708	...	...	|	...	|	...	...	...	...	...
Le Mans a.	...	1428	1428	...	...	|	...	...	...	|	...	1627	1627	|	...	...	|	...	|	...	...	...	...	...
Rennes a.	...	1546	|	...	...	|	...	...	...	|	...	1749h	|	|	...	...	|	...	|	...	...	...	...	...
Angers St Laud a.	...	...	1516	...	...	|	...	...	...	|	...	...	1715	|	...	...	|	...	|	...	...	...	...	...
Nantes a.	...	...	1559	...	...	|	...	...	...	|	...	...	1758	|	...	...	|	...	|	...	...	...	...	...
St Pierre des Corps a.	...	...	...	...	...	|	...	...	...	1559	...	...	...	1759	...	...	|	...	|	...	...	...	...	...
Futuroscope a.	...	...	...	...	...	|	...	...	...	|	...	...	...	|	...	...	|	...	|	...	...	...	...	...
Poitiers a.	...	...	...	...	...	|	...	...	...	1641	...	...	...	1841	...	...	|	...	|	...	...	...	...	...
Angoulême a.	...	...	...	...	...	|	...	...	...	1733	...	...	...	1933	...	...	|	...	|	...	...	...	...	...
Bordeaux a.	...	...	...	...	...	|	...	...	...	1837	...	...	...	2037	...	...	|	...	|	...	...	...	...	...
Le Creusot TGV a.	...	...	...	...	...	|	...	...	...	...	...	...	...	...	...	...	|	...	|	...	...	...	...	...
Lyon Part Dieu a.	...	...	...	...	...	1600	1610	...	...	...	...	...	...	...	...	...	1900	...	1900	...	...	...	...	...
Lyon Perrache a.	...	...	...	...	...	|	|	...	...	...	...	...	...	...	...	...	|	...	|	...	...	...	...	...
Lyon St Exupéry ✈ a.	...	...	...	...	...	|	|	...	...	...	...	...	...	...	...	...	|	...	|	...	...	...	...	...
Valence TGV a.	...	...	...	...	...	|	|	...	...	...	...	...	...	...	...	...	|	...	1944	...	...	...	...	...
Avignon TGV a.	...	...	...	...	...	1707	|	...	...	...	...	...	...	...	...	...	2008	...	|	...	...	...	...	...
Nîmes a.	...	...	...	...	...	|	1725	...	...	...	...	...	...	...	...	...	|	...	2029	...	...	...	...	...
Montpellier a.	...	...	...	...	...	|	1753	...	...	...	...	...	...	...	...	...	|	...	2058	2141	...	...	...	...
Béziers a.	...	...	...	...	...	|	1840	...	...	...	...	...	...	...	...	...	|	...	...	2229	...	...	...	...
Narbonne a.	...	...	...	...	...	|	1855	...	...	...	...	...	...	...	...	...	|	...	...	2245	...	...	...	...
Toulouse Matabiau a.	...	...	...	...	...	|	2012	...	...	...	...	...	...	...	...	...	|	...	...	|	...	...	...	...
Perpignan a.	...	...	...	...	...	|	...	...	...	...	...	...	...	...	...	...	|	...	...	2322	...	...	...	...
Aix en Provence TGV a.	...	...	...	...	...	1731	...	...	...	...	...	...	...	...	...	...	2031	2045	...	...	...	...	...	...
Marseille St Charles a.	...	...	...	...	...	1746	...	...	...	...	...	...	...	...	...	...	2046	|	...	...	...	...	...	...
Toulon a.	...	...	...	...	...	1844	...	...	...	...	...	...	...	...	...	...	...	2139	...	...	...	...	...	...
St Raphaël - Valescure a.	...	...	...	...	...	1937	...	...	...	...	...	...	...	...	...	...	...	2228	...	...	...	...	...	...
Cannes a.	...	...	...	...	...	2002	...	...	...	...	...	...	...	...	...	...	...	2254	...	...	...	...	...	...
Nice a.	...	...	...	...	...	2033	...	...	...	...	...	...	...	...	...	...	...	2326	...	...	...	...	...	...

C – THALYS SOLEIL – ⑥ June 28 - Aug. 30: (12) 🍷 Amsterdam (depart 0740; d. 0658 Aug. 16; d. 0725 Aug. 2; see Table **18**) - Brussels - Marseille.

G – ①③④⑤⑦ (daily May 21 - June 2; July 23 - Sept. 1; Oct. 22 - Nov. 7). On Oct. 19 depart London 1025, Ebbsfleet 1044, not call at Ashford.

H – ①②③④⑦ (not Aug. 14).

P – ⑥ July 6 - Sept. 7.

Q – ⑥ June 28 - Sept. 6.

c – Also July 14, Aug. 15; not Nov. 17.

e – Arrive 0746.

f – Lille **Flandres** (◇).

g – Not July 20.

h – Not July 13.

k – Avignon **Centre**.

n – Not July 14, Aug. 15; also Nov. 17.

q – Not June 9, July 21, Aug. 15, 25, Nov. 10, 11.

s – Calls to set down only.

w – Also July 14, Aug. 14, Nov. 11.

y – Also Aug. 25, Nov. 11.

z – Not Aug. 25, Nov. 11.

⊖ – To St Malo on dates in Table **261**.

§ – Marne la Vallée - Chessy (station for Disneyland).

‡ – 0528 on Oct. 4, 5, 6, 11, 12, 13.

☆ – Eurostar train. Special fares payable. Minimum check-in time 30 minutes. Valid June 1 - Dec. 13.

◇ – 500 metres from Lille Europe (see Lille City Plan on page 30).

11 LONDON / BRUSSELS - LILLE - CHARLES DE GAULLE ✈ - WESTERN / SOUTHERN FRANCE

DAY TRAINS (FOR NIGHT TRAINS SEE TABLE 13). Supplements payable on all *TGV* services. Connections at Lille are not guaranteed. Other connections available via Paris.

train type		☆	*TGV*	*TGV*	☆	*TGV*	*TGV*	*TGV*	☆	*TGV*	☆	*TGV*	*TGV*	*TGV*
train number		**9136**	**9836**	**5240**	**9140**	**5237**	**5230**	**5124**	**9144**	**5130**	**9148**	**5234**	**9846**	**9846**
train number			**9837**	**5241**			**5231**	**5125**		**5131**		**5235**	**9847**	**5137**
notes		Ⓡ✕	Ⓡ🍷	Ⓡ🍷	Ⓡ✕	Ⓡ🍷	Ⓡ🍷	Ⓡ🍷	Ⓡ✕	Ⓡ🍷	Ⓡ✕	Ⓡ🍷	Ⓡ🍷	Ⓡ🍷
					⑧	y			⑥	▷	⑧	⑤		⑦
		Q				△	▽					j		p
London St Pancras **12**	d.	1404	...	...	1504	...	...	...	1604	...	1704	...	...	...
Ebbsfleet International **12**	d.	│	...	...	│	...	...	...	│	...	│	...	...	...
Ashford International **12**	d.	│	...	...	│	...	...	...	│	...	│	...	...	...
Brussels Midi / Zuid **12**	d.	│	1617	...	│	...	...	...	│	...	│	...	1917	...
Lille Europe **12**	a.	1626	1653	...	1726	...	...	...	1826	...	1926	...	1952	...
Lille Europe	d.	...	1703	1709f	...	1752	1752	1826	...	1900f	...	1952	2002	2002
Douai	d.	...	│	│	...	│	│	│	...	│	...	│	│	│
Arras	d.	...	│	│	...	│	│	│	...	│	...	│	2028	2028
TGV Haute Picardie	d.	...	│	│	...	│	│	1854	...	│	...	│	│	│
Paris Charles de Gaulle ✈	a.	...	1753	1803	...	1843	1843	1923	...	1953	...	2044	2111	2111
Paris Charles de Gaulle ✈	d.	...	1758	1808	...	1848	1848	1928	...	1958	...	2049	2116	2116
Marne la Vallée §	d.	...	1811	1833	...	1901	1901	1941	...	2007	...	2103	2130	2130
Massy TGV	d.	...	│	1908	...	1938	1938	│	...	...	...	2138	│	│
Le Mans	a.	...	│	│	...	2028	2028	│	...	...	...	2228	│	│
Rennes	a.	...	│	│	...	2158	│	│	...	...	...	│	│	│
Angers St Laud	a.	...	│	│	...	...	2110	│	...	...	...	2311	│	│
Nantes	a.	...	│	│	...	...	2149	│	...	...	...	2349	│	│
St Pierre des Corps	a.	...	│	2000	...	...	...	│	...	...	...	...	│	│
Futuroscope	a.	...	│	│	...	...	...	│	...	...	...	...	│	│
Poitiers	a.	...	│	2041	...	...	...	│	...	...	...	...	│	│
Angoulême	a.	...	│	2132	...	...	...	│	...	...	...	...	│	│
Bordeaux	a.	...	│	2237	...	...	...	│	...	...	...	...	│	│
Le Creusot TGV	a.	...	│	...	...	...	...	│	...	...	...	...	2239	2239
Lyon Part Dieu	a.	...	2000	...	...	...	...	2130	...	...	...	...	2324	2324
Lyon Perrache	a.	...	│	...	...	...	...	│	...	...	...	...	2337	│
Lyon St Exupéry ✈	a.	...	│	...	...	...	...	│	...	...	...	...	...	│
Valence TGV	a.	...	2045	...	...	...	...	│	...	...	...	...	...	0008
Avignon TGV	a.	...	│	...	...	...	...	2238	...	...	...	...	...	│
Nîmes	a.	...	2130	...	...	...	...	│	...	...	...	...	...	0056
Montpellier	a.	...	2158	...	...	...	...	│	...	...	...	...	...	0122
Béziers	a.	...	2251t	...	...	...	...	│	...	...	...	...	...	...
Narbonne	a.	...	2307t	...	...	...	...	│	...	...	...	...	...	...
Toulouse Matabiau	a.	...	│	...	...	...	...	│	...	...	...	...	...	...
Perpignan	a.	...	2342t	...	...	...	...	│	...	...	...	...	...	...
Aix en Provence TGV	a.	...	...	...	...	...	...	2301	...	...	...	...	...	...
Marseille St Charles	a.	...	...	...	...	...	...	2316	...	...	...	...	...	...
Toulon	a.	...	...	...	...	...	...	...	...	...	...	...	...	...
St Raphaël - Valescure	a.	...	...	...	...	...	...	...	...	...	...	...	...	...
Cannes	a.	...	...	...	...	...	...	...	...	...	...	...	...	...
Nice	a.	...	...	...	...	...	...	...	...	...	...	...	...	...

train type		*TGV*	*TGV*	☆	*TGV*	*TGV*	*TGV*	☆	*TGV*	☆	*TGV*	*TGV*	*TGV*	☆	*TGV*	*TGV*	*TGV*	*TGV*	*TGV*	☆	☆
train number		**9809**	**9852**	**9117**	**5152**	**5254**	**5252**	**9125**	**9854**	**9129**	**5144**	**9862**	**5440**	**9133**	**9860**	**5117**	**5270**	**5272**	**5264**	**9141**	**9141**
train number			**9853**		**5153**	**5255**			**9855**		**9862**	**9863**	**5261**		**9861**		**5271**		**5265**		
notes		Ⓡ🍷	Ⓡ🍷	Ⓡ✕	Ⓡ🍷	Ⓡ🍷	Ⓡ🍷	Ⓡ✕	Ⓡ🍷	Ⓡ✕	Ⓡ🍷	Ⓡ🍷	Ⓡ🍷	Ⓡ✕	Ⓡ🍷	Ⓡ🍷	Ⓡ🍷	Ⓡ🍷	Ⓡ🍷	Ⓡ✕	Ⓡ✕
		①–⑤			▷	①–⑥	①–⑥	①–⑥		⑦				①–⑤				k		⑥⑦	①–⑤
		n				m	m	h		d			c				▽	△	c	d	
Nice	d.	...	...	...	...	...	...	...	...	...	...	...	...	...	...	...	...	...	...	...	...
Cannes	d.	...	...	...	...	...	...	...	...	...	...	...	...	...	...	...	...	...	...	...	...
St Raphaël - Valescure	d.	...	...	...	...	...	...	...	...	...	...	...	...	...	...	...	...	...	...	...	...
Toulon	d.	...	...	...	...	...	...	...	...	...	...	...	...	...	0813	0813	...	...	...	...	...
Marseille St Charles	d.	...	...	...	...	...	...	...	0644	...	0714	...	...	...	0912	0912	...	...	...	...	...
Aix en Provence TGV	d.	...	...	...	...	...	...	...	│	...	0730	...	...	...	0926	0926	...	...	...	...	...
Perpignan	d.	...	...	...	...	...	...	...	│	...	│	0518z	...	...	│	│	...	...	...	...	...
Toulouse Matabiau	d.	...	...	...	...	...	...	...	│	...	│	│	...	...	│	│	...	...	...	...	...
Narbonne	d.	...	...	...	...	...	...	...	│	...	│	0554z	...	...	│	│	...	...	...	...	...
Béziers	d.	...	...	...	...	...	...	...	│	...	│	0612z	...	...	│	│	...	...	...	...	...
Montpellier	d.	...	...	...	...	...	...	...	│	...	│	0702	...	...	│	│	...	...	...	...	...
Nîmes	d.	...	...	...	...	...	...	...	│	...	│	0729	...	...	│	│	...	...	...	...	...
Avignon TGV	d.	...	...	...	...	...	...	...	0716	...	│	│	...	...	0948	0948	...	...	...	...	...
Valence TGV	d.	...	...	...	...	...	...	...	0749	...	│	0820	...	...	│	│	...	...	...	...	...
Lyon St Exupéry ✈	d.	...	...	...	...	...	...	...	│	...	│	│	...	...	│	│	...	...	...	...	...
Lyon Perrache	d.	...	...	...	...	...	...	...	│	...	│	│	...	...	│	│	...	...	...	...	...
Lyon Part Dieu	d.	...	0550	...	...	...	...	...	0830	...	0900	0900	...	...	1100	1100	...	...	...	...	...
Le Creusot TGV	d.	...	0630	...	...	...	...	...	│	...	│	│	...	...	│	│	...	...	...	...	...
Bordeaux	d.	...	│	...	...	...	...	...	│	...	│	│	0723	...	│	│	...	...	0923	...	...
Angoulême	d.	...	│	...	...	...	...	...	│	...	│	│	0821	...	│	│	...	...	1021	...	...
Poitiers	d.	...	│	...	...	...	...	...	│	...	│	│	0912	...	│	│	...	...	1112	...	...
Futuroscope	d.	...	│	...	...	...	...	...	│	...	│	│	│	...	│	│	...	...	│	...	...
St Pierre des Corps	d.	...	│	...	...	...	...	...	│	...	│	│	1001	...	│	│	...	...	1201g	...	...
Nantes	d.	...	│	...	...	...	0605	...	│	...	│	│	│	...	│	│	1005	...	│	...	...
Angers St Laud	d.	...	│	...	...	...	0638	...	│	...	│	│	│	...	│	│	1043	...	│	...	...
Rennes	d.	...	│	...	...	0607	│	...	│	...	│	│	│	...	│	│	│	1004	│	...	...
Le Mans	d.	...	│	...	...	0733	0733	...	│	...	│	│	│	...	│	│	1133	1133	│	...	...
Massy TGV	d.	...	│	...	...	0824	0824	...	│	...	│	│	1055	...	│	│	1225	1225	1255	...	...
Marne la Vallée §	d.	...	0749	...	0852	0901	0901	...	1022	...	1052	1052	1135	...	1252	1252	1300	1300	1331	...	...
Paris Charles de Gaulle ✈	a.	...	0759	...	0903	0911	0911	...	1032	...	1102	1102	1145	...	1302	1302	1311	1311	1341	...	...
Paris Charles de Gaulle ✈	d.	...	0807	...	0908	0916	0916	...	1037	...	1107	1107	1157	...	1307	1326	1316	1316	1346	...	...
TGV Haute Picardie	d.	...	│	...	│	0949	0949	...	1107	...	│	│	1227	...	│	1356	│	│	│	...	...
Arras	a.	...	│	...	│	│	│	...	│	...	│	│	│	...	│	│	│	│	│	...	...
Douai	a.	...	│	...	│	│	│	...	│	...	│	│	│	...	│	│	│	│	│	...	...
Lille Europe	a.	...	0857	...	0957	1017	1017	...	1138	...	1157	1157	1257f	...	│	1424	1406	1406	1437	...	...
Lille Europe **12**	d.	0732	0907	0930	...	...	...	1136	1151	1236	...	1207	...	1330	│	...	...	...	...	1530	1536
Brussels Midi / Zuid **12**	a.	0807	0943	│	...	...	...	│	1226	│	...	1251	...	│	1420	...	...	...	...	│	│
Ashford International **12**	a.	...	...	│	...	...	...	│	...	│	...	...	...	│	...	...	...	...	...	│	│
Ebbsfleet International **12**	a.	...	...	│	...	...	...	│	...	│	...	...	...	1345	...	...	...	...	...	1545	1545
London St Pancras **12**	a.	...	...	0957	...	...	...	1157	...	1257	...	...	...	1403	...	...	...	...	...	1603	1603

Q – ⑤⑦ (⑧ Mar. 30 - Aug. 30) also Oct. 23, 27–30, Nov. 11.

c – Not July 20.

d – Also Aug. 25, Nov. 11.

f – Lille **Flandres** (◇).

g – Not Oct. 27 - Nov. 7.

h – Not Nov. 11.

j – Also Aug. 14; not Aug. 15.

k – Not July 13.

m – Not July 14.

n – Not Apr. 21, May 1, 29, June 9.

p – Also July 14, Nov. 11; not Sept. 7, Oct. 19.

t – ⑤⑦ (also July 14, Aug. 14, Nov. 11; not Aug. 15).

y – Not July 12, 13, Sept. 6, 13.

z – ①⑥ (also July 15, Aug. 15, Nov. 12; not July 14, Sept. 20, 27, Nov. 10).

▽ – To / from Le Croisic on dates in Table **288**.

△ – To / from Lorient or Quimper on dates in Table **285**.

▷ – To / from Dijon, Besancon and Mulhouse (Table **370**).

◇ – 500 metres from Lille Europe (see Lille City Plan on page 30).

☆ – Eurostar train. Special fares payable. Minimum check-in time 30 minutes Valid June 1 - Dec. 13.

§ – Marne la Vallée - Chessy. Station for Disneyland Paris.

SOUTHERN / WESTERN FRANCE - CHARLES DE GAULLE ✈ - LILLE - BRUSSELS / LONDON 11

DAY TRAINS (FOR NIGHT TRAINS SEE TABLE 13). Supplements payable on all *TGV* services. Connections at Lille are not guaranteed. Other connections available via Paris.

train type	*TGV*	☆		*TGV*	*TGV*	☆	☆	☆		*TGV*	*TGV*	☆	☆	☆	☆	☆		*TGV*	*TGV*	*TGV*	☆	☆	
train number	**5256**	**9145**		**5442**	**9866**	**9149**	**9149**	**9149**		**5278**	**5280**	**9153**	**9153**	**9057**	**9057**	**9057**		**6859**	**5192**	**9868**	**9161**	**9161**	
train number	**5257**			**5277**	**9867**						**5281**							**6858**	**5193**	**9869**			
notes	Ⓡ 🍷 ⑦	Ⓡ ✕		Ⓡ 🍷	Ⓡ 🍷	Ⓡ ✕	Ⓡ ✕ ⑥	Ⓡ ✕		Ⓡ 🍷	Ⓡ 🍷	Ⓡ ✕ ①–⑤	Ⓡ ✕ ⑦	Ⓡ ✕	Ⓡ ✕	Ⓡ ✕		Ⓡ 🍷	Ⓡ 🍷	Ⓡ 🍷	Ⓡ ✕ ⑧	Ⓡ ✕ ⑥	
		E				**F**		**G**		▽	▽		**k**	**R**	⑤	**S**							
Nice d.	...	...	...	...	0927r	...	...	...	...	...	...	...	...	...	...	...	...	...	...	...	...	...	...
Cannes d.	...	...	...	...	0958r	...	...	...	...	...	...	...	...	...	...	...	...	...	...	...	...	...	...
St Raphaël - Valescure d.	...	...	...	...	1023r	...	...	...	...	...	...	...	...	...	...	...	...	...	...	...	...	...	...
Toulon d.	...	...	...	...	1115r	...	...	...	...	...	...	...	...	...	...	...	...	...	...	...	...	...	...
Marseille St Charles d.	...	...	...	...	1214	...	...	...	...	...	...	...	...	...	...	...	...	...	1414	...	...	...	...
Aix en Provence TGV d.	...	...	...	...	|	...	...	...	...	...	...	...	...	...	...	...	...	...	1429	...	...	...	...
Perpignan d.	...	...	...	...	|	...	...	...	...	...	...	...	...	...	...	...	...	...	|	...	...	...	...
Toulouse Matabiau d.	...	...	...	...	|	...	...	...	...	...	...	...	...	...	...	...	...	...	|	...	...	...	...
Narbonne d.	...	...	...	...	|	...	...	...	...	...	...	...	...	...	...	...	...	...	|	...	...	...	...
Béziers d.	...	...	...	...	|	...	...	...	...	...	...	...	...	...	...	...	...	...	|	...	...	...	...
Montpellier d.	...	...	...	...	|	...	...	...	...	...	...	...	...	...	...	...	...	1302	|	1502	...	...	...
Nîmes d.	...	...	...	...	|	...	...	...	...	...	...	...	...	...	...	...	...	1329	|	1529	...	...	...
Avignon TGV d.	...	...	...	...	1245	...	...	...	...	...	...	...	...	...	...	...	...	|	1451	|	...	...	...
Valence TGV d.	...	...	...	...	1320	...	...	...	...	...	...	...	...	...	...	...	...	1417	|	1616	...	...	...
Lyon St Exupéry ✈ d.	...	...	...	...	|	...	...	...	...	...	...	...	...	...	...	...	...	|	|	|	...	...	...
Lyon Perrache d.	...	...	...	...	|	...	...	...	...	...	...	...	...	...	...	...	...	|	|	|	...	...	...
Lyon Part Dieu d.	...	...	...	...	1400	...	...	...	...	...	...	...	...	...	...	...	...	1451	1600	1700	...	...	...
Le Creusot TGV d.	...	...	...	...	|	...	...	...	...	...	...	...	...	...	...	...	...	...	|	|	...	...	...
Bordeaux d.	...	...	...	1123	|	...	...	...	...	...	...	...	...	...	...	...	...	...	|	|	...	...	...
Angoulême d.	...	...	...	1221	|	...	...	...	...	...	...	...	...	...	...	...	...	...	|	|	...	...	...
Poitiers d.	...	...	...	1312	|	...	...	...	...	...	...	...	...	...	...	...	...	...	|	|	...	...	...
Futuroscope d.	...	...	...	|	|	...	...	...	...	...	...	...	...	...	...	...	...	...	|	|	...	...	...
St Pierre des Corps d.	...	...	...	1401	|	...	...	...	...	...	...	...	...	...	...	...	...	...	|	|	...	...	...
Nantes d.	...	...	...	|	|	...	...	...	...	1404	...	...	...	...	...	...	...	...	|	|	...	...	...
Angers St Laud d.	...	...	...	|	|	...	...	...	...	1444	...	...	...	...	...	...	...	...	|	|	...	...	...
Rennes d.	1114	...	...	|	|	...	...	...	...	|	1408	...	...	...	...	...	...	...	|	|	...	...	...
Le Mans d.	1232	...	...	|	|	...	...	...	...	1532	1533	...	...	...	...	...	...	...	|	|	...	...	...
Massy TGV d.	1325	...	...	1455	|	...	...	...	...	1627	1627	...	...	...	...	...	...	...	|	|	...	...	...
Marne la Vallée § d.	1401	...	...	1535	1553	...	...	...	...	1701	1701	...	...	1654	1654	1802	...	...	1752	1853	...	...	...
Paris Charles de Gaulle ✈ a.	1411	...	...	1545	1603	...	...	...	...	1711	1711	...	...	|	|	|	...	...	1801	1903	...	...	...
Paris Charles de Gaulle ✈ d.	1416	..	...	1550	1608	...	...	...	...	1716	1716	...	...	|	|	|	...	...	1806	1908	...	...	...
TGV Haute Picardie d.	|	...	...	|	|	...	...	...	...	|	|	...	...	|	|	|	...	...	1841	|	...	...	...
Arras a.	|	...	...	|	|	...	...	...	...	|	|	...	...	|	|	|	...	...	1859	|	...	...	...
Douai a.	|	...	...	|	|	...	...	...	...	|	|	...	...	|	|	|	...	...	1917	|	...	...	...
Lille Europe a.	1507	...	...	1639	1657	...	...	...	...	1807	1807	...	...	|	|	|	...	...	1944f	1957	...	...	...
Lille Europe **12** d.	...	1636	...	...	1707	1736	1736	1736	...	...	...	1836	1836	|	|	|	...	...	...	2007	2030	2030	...
Brussels Midi / Zuid **12** a.	...	|	...	...	1743	|	|	|	...	...	...	|	|	|	|	|	...	...	...	2043	|	|	...
Ashford International **12** a.	...	|	...	...	...	1734	|	1737	...	...	...	|	1835	1803	1806	1903	...	...	...	...	|	2035	...
Ebbsfleet International **12** a.	...	|	...	...	...	|	1748	|	...	...	...	1845	|	1826	1834	1926	...	...	...	...	2045	|	...
London St Pancras **12** a.	...	1657	...	...	...	1809	1809	1811	...	...	...	1903	1910	1846	1854	1946	...	...	...	...	2103	2109	...

train type	☆		⇌			*TGV*	*TGV*	*TGV*		*TGV*	*TGV*		*TGV*		*TGV*	*TGV*		*TGV*					
train number	**9087**		**9955**			**5266**	**6861**	**5182**		**5290**	**5288**		**5284**		**5186**	**5180**		**5194**					
train number	**9086**		**9956**			**5267**	**6860**	**5017**			**5289**		**5285**		**5187**	**5186**		**5195**					
notes	Ⓡ ✕		Ⓡ 🍷			Ⓡ 🍷	Ⓡ 🍷 ①–⑥	Ⓡ 🍷		Ⓡ 🍷	Ⓡ 🍷		Ⓡ 🍷		Ⓡ 🍷	Ⓡ 🍷		Ⓡ 🍷 ⑦					
	Q		**Y**							⊖								**D**					
Nice d.	...	...	...	...	...	...	...	...	...	...	...	...	...	...	...	...	...	...	...	...	...	...	...
Cannes d.	...	...	...	...	...	...	...	...	...	...	...	...	...	...	...	...	...	...	...	...	...	...	...
St Raphaël - Valescure d.	...	...	...	...	...	...	...	...	...	...	...	...	...	...	...	...	...	...	...	...	...	...	...
Toulon d.	...	...	...	...	...	...	...	...	...	...	...	...	...	...	...	...	...	...	...	...	...	...	...
Marseille St Charles d.	...	...	1620	...	...	...	...	1714	...	...	...	...	...	...	...	1814	...	1914	...	...	...	...	...
Aix en Provence TGV d.	...	...	1636	...	...	...	...	1729	...	...	...	...	...	...	...	1829	...	1931	...	...	...	...	...
Perpignan d.	...	...	|	...	...	...	...	|	...	...	...	...	...	...	...	|	...	|	...	...	...	...	...
Toulouse Matabiau d.	...	...	|	...	...	...	1450	|	...	...	...	...	...	...	...	|	...	|	...	...	...	...	...
Narbonne d.	...	...	|	...	...	...	1604	|	...	...	...	...	...	...	...	|	...	|	...	...	...	...	...
Béziers d.	...	...	|	...	...	...	1620	|	...	...	...	...	...	...	...	|	...	|	...	...	...	...	...
Montpellier d.	...	...	|	...	...	...	1702	|	...	...	...	...	...	...	1802	|	...	|	...	...	...	...	...
Nîmes d.	...	...	|	...	...	...	1729	|	...	...	...	...	...	...	1829	|	...	|	...	...	...	...	...
Avignon TGV d.	1639t	...	1658	...	...	...	|	1751	...	...	...	...	...	...	|	1852	...	1953	...	...	...	...	...
Valence TGV d.	|	...	1735	...	...	...	|	|	...	...	...	...	...	...	1916	|	...	|	...	...	...	...	...
Lyon St Exupéry ✈ d.	|	...	|	...	...	...	|	|	...	...	...	...	...	...	|	|	...	|	...	...	...	...	...
Lyon Perrache d.	|	...	|	...	...	...	|	|	...	...	...	...	...	...	|	|	...	|	...	...	...	...	...
Lyon Part Dieu d.	|	...	|	...	...	...	1850	1900	...	...	...	...	...	...	2000	2000	...	2100	...	...	...	...	...
Le Creusot TGV d.	|	...	|	...	...	...	...	|	...	...	...	...	...	...	|	|	...	|	...	...	...	...	...
Bordeaux d.	|	...	|	...	...	1523	...	|	...	...	...	...	1723	...	|	|	...	|	...	...	...	...	...
Angoulême d.	|	...	|	...	...	1621	...	|	...	...	...	...	1821	...	|	|	...	|	...	...	...	...	...
Poitiers d.	|	...	|	...	...	1712	...	|	...	...	...	...	1912	...	|	|	...	|	...	...	...	...	...
Futuroscope d.	|	...	|	...	...	1721	...	|	...	...	...	...	|	...	|	|	...	|	...	...	...	...	...
St Pierre des Corps d.	|	...	|	...	...	1801	...	|	...	...	...	...	2001	...	|	|	...	|	...	...	...	...	...
Nantes d.	|	...	|	...	...	|	...	|	...	...	1755	...	|	...	|	|	...	|	...	...	...	...	...
Angers St Laud d.	|	...	|	...	...	|	...	|	...	...	1834	...	|	...	|	|	...	|	...	...	...	...	...
Rennes d.	|	...	|	...	...	|	...	|	...	1807	|	...	|	...	|	|	...	|	...	...	...	...	...
Le Mans d.	|	...	|	...	...	|	...	|	...	1933	1933	...	|	...	|	|	...	|	...	...	...	...	...
Massy TGV d.	|	...	|	...	...	1855	...	|	...	2025	2025	...	2055	...	|	|	...	|	...	...	...	...	...
Marne la Vallée § d.	|	...	|	...	...	1931	...	2052	...	2100	2100	...	2131	...	2152	2152	...	2253	...	...	...	...	...
Paris Charles de Gaulle ✈ a.	|	...	|	...	...	1941	...	2101	...	2111	2111	...	2141	...	2202	2202	...	2303	...	...	...	...	...
Paris Charles de Gaulle ✈ d.	|	...	|	...	...	1950	...	2106	...	2116	2116	...	2146	...	2207	2207	...	2308	...	...	...	...	...
TGV Haute Picardie d.	|	...	|	...	...	|	...	|	...	2149	2149	...	2215	...	2238	2238	...	2338	...	...	...	...	...
Arras a.	|	...	|	...	...	2033	...	|	...	2207	2207	...	|	...	|	|	...	|	...	...	...	...	...
Douai a.	|	...	|	...	...	2050	...	|	...	2226	2226	...	|	...	|	|	...	|	...	...	...	...	...
Lille Europe a.	|	...	|	...	...	2112f	...	2157g	...	2251f	2251f	...	2244	...	2304c	2304c	...	0004x	...	...	...	...	...
Lille Europe **12** d.	|	...	|	...	...	...	...	...	...	...	...	...	...	...	...	...	...	...	...	...	...	...	...
Brussels Midi / Zuid **12** a.	|	...	2112	...	...	...	...	...	...	...	...	...	...	...	...	...	...	...	...	...	...	...	...
Ashford International **12** a.	2105	...	...	...	...	...	...	...	...	...	...	...	...	...	...	...	...	...	...	...	...	...	...
Ebbsfleet International **12** a.	|	...	...	...	...	...	...	...	...	...	...	...	...	...	...	...	...	...	...	...	...	...	...
London St Pancras **12** a.	2142	...	...	...	...	...	...	...	...	...	...	...	...	...	...	...	...	...	...	...	...	...	...

A – From Marne la Vallée - Chessy (station for Disneyland). Table **17a**.
D – ⑦ Apr. 6 - Aug. 24 (also Apr. 21, June 9).
E – ⑤⑦ (⑧ Mar. 30 - Aug. 30) also Oct. 23, 27–30, Nov. 11.
F – ④⑤ May 25 - July 26.
G – ①–③ May 25 - Aug. 30; ①–⑤ Aug. 31 - Dec. 13.
Q – ⑥ July 5 - Sept. 13.
R – ⑦ (⑥⑦ July 26 - Aug. 31) also Oct. 25, Nov. 1.
S – ①③④ (①②③④ July 28 - Aug. 28) also Oct 28, Nov. 4.
Y – THALYS SOLEIL – ⑥ July 5 - Aug. 30: (12) 🍷 Marseille - Brussels - Amsterdam (arrive 2140; Table **18**). On July 19, Aug. 16 arrive Amsterdam 2359. On Aug. 2 arrive Amsterdam 2335.
c – On ①–⑤ June 23 - Aug. 1 and ①–⑤ Oct. 6–17 diverted to Lille Flandres (arrive 2307).

f – Lille **Flandres** (◇).
g – On ①–⑤ June 23 - July 4 diverted to Lille Flandres (arrive 2200).
h – Also Nov. 11.
j – Lille **Flandres** (◇). On Nov. 16, 17 arrive 2044, not call at Arras, Douai.
k – Also Aug. 25, Nov. 11.
r – Daily June 28 - Aug. 31, Sept. 20 - Oct. 12, Nov. 1 - Dec. 13 (also Sept. 13, 14, Oct. 18, 19, 25, 26).
t – Avignon **Centre**.
x – July 13–28 diverted to Lille Flandres (arrive 0008).

⊖ – From St Malo on dates in Table **261**.
☆ – Eurostar train. Special fares payable. Minimum check-in time 30 minutes. Valid June 1 - Dec. 13.
⊖ – On ①–⑤ July 29 - Aug. 23 (also Aug. 17, 18; not Aug. 16) arrive Lille Flandres 2122, not call at Douai. On Nov. 16, 17 arrive Lille Flandres 2110, not call at Arras, Douai.
▽ – Not Aug. 17, 18. On Nov. 16 arrive Lille Flandres 1940, not call at Arras, Douai.
◇ – 500 metres from Lille Europe (see Lille City Plan on page 30).
§ – Marne la Vallée - Chessy, station for Disneyland Paris.

12 LONDON - LILLE - BRUSSELS *by Eurostar*

All times shown are local times (France and Belgium are one hour ahead of Great Britain). For the complete service London - Lille see Table 10. For other services Lille - Brussels (by TGV) see Table 16a. All Eurostar services are 🅁 and convey 🍴 in 1st class, 🍷 in 2nd class.

Service June 1 - Dec. 13.

km																										
	train type	☆	*ICE*			☆				☆					☆	☆					☆	*ICE*				
	train number	**9110**	**15**			**9110**				**9114**					**9116**	**9116**					**9126**	**17**				
	notes	①–⑤	🍷		①–⑤	⑥		⑥⑦		①–⑤		①–⑤		⑥⑦	①–⑤	⑥⑦		①–⑤		⑥⑦	①–⑥	🍷		①–⑤		⑥⑦
	notes	**f z**	**K**		**p**			**q**				**p**		**q**	**j**	**y z**		**p**		**q**	**j**	**K**		**p**		**q**
0	**London** St Pancras d.	0650	...	...	...	0657	...	...	...	0804	...	...	...	...	0858	0858	...	...	...	...	1058	...	...	...	...	...
35	Ebbsfleet International d.	0708	...	...	...	|	...	...	...	|	...	...	...	...	0915	0915	...	...	...	...	1115	...	...	...	...	...
90	Ashford International d.	0728	...	...	...	0728	...	...	...	|	...	...	...	...	|	|	...	...	...	...	|	...	...	...	...	...
267	Lille Europe a.	0930	...	...	...	0926	...	...	...	1026	...	...	...	...	1126	1130	...	...	...	...	1326	...	...	...	...	...
267	Lille Europe d.	0933	...	...	...	0930	...	...	...	1030	...	...	...	...	1130	1133	...	...	...	...	1330	...	...	...	...	...
373	**Brussels** Midi / Zuid a.	1007	1025	1026	1031	1011	1033	1058	1105	1105	1126	1131	1133	1158	1205	1208	1226	1231	1233	1258	1405	1425	1426	1431	1433	1458
	Brugge a.	...	|	1124	|	...	|	|	1201	...	1224	|	|	|	...	...	1324	|	|	|	...	|	1524	|	|	|
	Leuven a.	...	|	...	1057	...	|	1125	...	...	...	1157	|	1225	...	...	...	1257	|	1325	...	|	...	1457	|	1525
	Liège Guillemins a.	...	1112	...	1155	...	|	1200	...	...	...	1255	|	1300	...	...	...	1355	|	1400	...	1512	...	1555	|	1600
	Namur a.	...	...	...	...	...	1139	...	...	...	...	...	1239	...	...	...	...	...	1339	...	...	...	...	...	1539	...
	Luxembourg a.	...	...	...	...	...	1340	...	...	...	...	...	1445	...	...	...	...	...	1540	...	...	...	...	...	1740	...

train type	☆						☆		⇌					☆	*ICE*						☆		⇌			
train number	**9132**						**9136**		**9461**					**9140**	**19**						**9144**		**9473**			
notes			①–⑤		⑥⑦					①–⑤		⑥⑦		Ⓑ	🍷		①–⑤		⑥⑦		⑥				⑥⑦	
notes	**z**		**p**		**q**		**P**		**K**			**q**			**K**		**p**		**q**				**E**		**q**	
London St Pancras d.	1258	...	...	...	...	...	1404	...	...	...	...	...	...	1504	...	...	...	...	...	...	1604	...	...	...	...	...
Ebbsfleet International d.	1315	...	...	...	...	...	|	...	...	...	...	...	...	|	...	...	...	...	...	...	|	...	...	...	...	...
Ashford International d.	|	...	...	...	...	...	|	...	...	...	...	...	...	|	...	...	...	...	...	...	|	...	...	...	...	...
Lille Europe a.	1530	...	...	...	...	...	1626	...	...	...	...	...	...	1726	...	...	...	...	...	...	1826	...	...	...	...	...
Lille Europe d.	1533	...	...	...	...	...	1630	...	...	...	...	...	...	1730	...	...	...	...	...	...	1830	...	...	...	...	...
Brussels Midi / Zuid a.	1608	1626	1631	1633	1658	...	1705	1726	1728	1731	1733	1758	...	1805	1825	1826	1831	1833	1858	...	1905	1926	1928	1933	1958	...
Brugge a.	...	1724	|	|	|	...	...	1824	|	|	|	|	...	...	|	1924	|	|	|	...	...	2024	|	|	|	...
Leuven a.	...	...	1657	|	1725	...	...	...	|	1757	|	1825	...	...	|	...	1857	|	1925	...	...	...	|	|	2025	...
Liège Guillemins a.	...	...	1755	|	1800	...	...	...	1811	1855	|	1900	...	...	1912	...	1955	|	2000	...	...	...	2011	|	2100	...
Namur a.	...	...	...	1740	...	...	...	...	...	...	1840	...	...	...	...	...	...	1939	...	...	...	...	...	2039	...	...
Luxembourg a.	...	...	...	1940	...	...	...	...	...	...	2040	...	...	...	...	...	...	2140	...	...	...	...	...	2240	...	...

train type	☆						☆	☆						☆					☆						☆	
train number	**9148**						**9152**	**9152**						**9156**					**9158**						**9162**	
notes	Ⓑ		①–⑤		⑥⑦		⑦	①–⑤		①–⑤		⑥⑦		⑥⑦		⑥⑦			①–⑤	①–⑤	⑥⑦		⑥⑦		⑦	
notes			**p**		**q**		**y**	**j**		**p**		**q**		**y z**		**q**			**j z**	**p**	**q**		**q**		**x**	
London St Pancras d.	1704	...	...	...	...	...	1755	1804	...	...	...	...	...	1904	...	...	...	...	1934	...	...	...	...	...	2004	...
Ebbsfleet International d.	|	...	...	...	...	...	|	|	...	...	...	...	...	|	...	...	...	...	|	...	...	...	...	...	|	...
Ashford International d.	|	...	...	...	...	...	1828	|	...	...	...	...	...	|	...	...	...	...	|	...	...	...	...	...	|	...
Lille Europe a.	1926	...	...	...	...	...	2026	2026	...	...	...	...	...	2130	...	...	...	...	2200	...	...	...	...	...	2226	...
Lille Europe d.	1930	...	...	...	...	...	2030	2030	...	...	...	...	...	2133	...	...	...	...	2203	...	...	...	...	...	2230	...
Brussels Midi / Zuid a.	2005	2026	2031	2033	2058	...	2105	2105	2126	2131	2133	2158	...	2208	2226	2258	2233	...	2238	2257	2258	2305	2333	...	2305	...
Brugge a.	...	2124	|	|	|	...	...	...	2224	|	|	|	...	...	2324	|	|	...	...	|	|	0001	|	...	...	...
Leuven a.	...	...	2057	|	2125	...	...	...	...	2157	|	2225	...	...	...	2327	|	...	...	2323	2327	...	|	...	...	...
Liège Guillemins a.	...	...	2155	|	2200	...	...	...	...	2255	|	2302	...	...	...	0023	|	...	...	0023	0023	...	|	...	...	...
Namur a.	...	...	...	2139	...	...	...	...	...	...	2241	...	...	...	...	...	2339	...	...	...	...	...	0046	...	...	...
Luxembourg a.	...	...	...	2340	...	...	...	...	...	...	...	...	...	...	...	...	...	...	...	...	...	...	...	...	...	...

train type				☆						☆					☆						☆					☆
train number				**9109**						**9113**					**9117**						**9125**					**9129**
notes	①–⑤		①–⑤	①		①–⑤	⑥⑦			①–⑥							①–⑤				①–⑥					⑦
notes	**p**			**h**		**p**	**q**			**j**					**z**		**p**				**j**					**y**
Luxembourg d.	...	...	...	...	...	...	...	...	...	...	...	...	...	...	...	0620	0650	...	...	...	...	0720	...	...	...	...
Namur d.	0411	...	...	...	...	...	...	0551	...	...	...	...	0651	...	...	0820	0843	...	0851	...	...	0921	...	0951	...	...
Liège Guillemins d.	|	...	0443	...	...	...	...	|	0600	...	...	...	|	0700	...	|	|	...	|	0900	...	|	...	|	1000	...
Leuven d.	|	...	0537	...	...	...	...	|	0637	...	...	...	|	0734	...	|	|	...	|	0937	...	|	...	|	1037	...
Brugge d.	|	0450	|	...	...	0557	0559	|	|	...	...	0658	|	|	...	|	|	0859	|	|	...	|	0959	|	|	...
Brussels Midi / Zuid d.	0545	0555	0603	0656	...	0655	0655	0657	0703	0756	...	0755	0757	0803	0852	0927	0945	0955	0957	1003	1056	1027	1055	1057	1103	1156
Lille Europe a.	...	...	...	0731	...	...	...	...	...	0830	...	...	...	...	0926	...	...	...	...	...	1130	...	...	...	...	1230
Lille Europe d.	...	...	...	0736	...	...	...	...	...	0836	...	...	...	...	0930	...	...	...	...	...	1136	...	...	...	...	1236
Ashford International a.	...	...	...	|	...	...	...	...	...	|	...	...	...	...	|	...	...	...	...	...	|	...	...	...	...	|
Ebbsfleet International a.	...	...	...	|	...	...	...	...	...	|	...	...	...	...	|	...	...	...	...	...	|	...	...	...	...	|
London St Pancras a.	...	...	...	0757	...	...	...	...	...	0857	...	...	...	...	0957	...	...	...	...	...	1157	...	...	...	...	1257

train type					☆					☆	☆					☆					☆	☆	☆			
train number					**9133**					**9141**	**9141**					**9145**					**9149**	**9149**	**9149**			
notes					①–⑤					⑥⑦	①–⑤											⑥				
notes					**z**					**y z**	**j**					**P**					**F**		**R**			
Luxembourg d.	0820	...	...	...	...	1020	...	...	...	...	...	1120	...	...	...	...	1220	...	...	...	...	...	...	...	...	...
Namur d.	1021	...	1051	...	...	1221	...	1251	...	...	...	1321	...	1351	...	...	1421	...	1451	...	...	...	...	...	...	...
Liège Guillemins d.	|	...	|	1100	...	|	...	|	1300	...	...	|	...	|	1400	...	|	...	|	1500	...	...	...	...	...	...
Leuven d.	|	...	|	1137	...	|	...	|	1337	...	...	|	...	|	1437	...	|	...	|	1537	...	...	...	...	...	...
Brugge d.	|	1059	|	|	...	|	1259	|	|	...	...	|	1359	|	|	...	|	1459	|	|	...	...	...	...	...	...
Brussels Midi / Zuid d.	1127	1155	1157	1203	1252	1327	1355	1357	1403	1452	1456	1427	1455	1457	1503	1556	1527	1555	1557	1603	1656	1656	1656	...	...	...
Lille Europe a.	...	...	...	...	1326	...	...	...	...	1526	1532	...	...	...	...	1630	...	...	...	...	1732	1730	1730	...	...	...
Lille Europe d.	...	...	...	...	1330	...	...	...	...	1530	1536	...	...	...	...	1636	...	...	...	...	1736	1736	1736	...	...	...
Ashford International a.	...	...	...	...	|	...	...	...	...	|	|	...	...	...	...	|	...	...	...	...	1734	|	1737	...	...	...
Ebbsfleet International a.	...	...	...	...	1345	...	...	...	...	1545	1545	...	...	...	...	|	...	...	...	...	|	1748	|	...	...	...
London St Pancras a.	...	...	...	...	1403	...	...	...	...	1603	1603	...	...	...	...	1657	...	...	...	...	1809	1809	1811	...	...	...

train type					☆	☆						☆						☆	☆							
train number					**9153**	**9153**						**9157**						**9161**	**9161**							
notes					①–⑤	⑦						Ⓑ						Ⓑ	⑥							
notes					**j**	**y**												**z**	**z**							
Luxembourg d.	1324	...	...	...	...	...	...	1420	...	...	...	...	...	1520	...	...	...	...	...	...	...	...	...	...	...	...
Namur d.	1521	...	1551	...	...	...	...	1621	...	1651	...	...	...	1721	...	1751	...	...	...	...	...	...	...	...	...	...
Liège Guillemins d.	|	...	|	1600	...	...	...	|	...	|	1700	...	...	|	...	|	1800	...	...	...	...	...	...	...	...	...
Leuven d.	|	...	|	1637	...	...	...	|	...	|	1737	...	...	|	...	|	1837	...	...	...	...	...	...	...	...	...
Brugge d.	|	1559	|	|	...	...	...	|	1659	|	|	...	...	|	1759	|	|	...	...	...	...	...	...	...	...	...
Brussels Midi / Zuid d.	1627	1655	1657	1703	1756	1756	...	1727	1755	1757	1803	1856	...	1827	1855	1857	1903	1952	1952	...	...	...	...	...	...	...
Lille Europe a.	...	...	...	...	1830	1830	...	...	...	...	...	1930	...	...	...	...	...	2026	2026	...	...	...	...	...	...	...
Lille Europe d.	...	...	...	...	1836	1836	...	...	...	...	...	1935	...	...	...	...	...	2030	2030	...	...	...	...	...	...	...
Ashford International a.	...	...	...	...	|	1835	...	...	...	...	...	|	...	...	...	...	...	|	2035	...	...	...	...	...	...	...
Ebbsfleet International a.	...	...	...	...	1845	|	...	...	...	...	...	|	...	...	...	...	...	2045	|	...	...	...	...	...	...	...
London St Pancras a.	...	...	...	...	1903	1910	...	...	...	...	...	1957	...	...	...	...	...	2103	2109	...	...	...	...	...	...	...

E – To Essen (Table **20**).
F – ④⑤ May 25 - Aug. 30.
K – To Köln (Tables **20**, **21**).
P – ⑤⑦ (Ⓑ Mar. 30 - Aug. 30) also Oct. 23, 27–30, Nov. 11.
R – ①–③ May 25 - Aug. 30; ①–⑤ Aug. 31 - Dec. 13.

f – Not June 9, July 21, Aug. 15, 25, Nov. 10, 11.
g – Not May 5, 26.
h – Not June 9, July 21, Aug. 25, Nov. 10.
j – Not Aug. 25, Nov. 11.
k – Not Apr. 21, May 1, 5, 8, 9, 26, 29.
p – Not Apr. 21, May 1, 29, June 9.
q – Also Apr. 21, May 1, 29, June 9.
x – Not Aug. 24.
y – Also Aug. 25, Nov. 11.
z – Calls at Calais Fréthun, see Table **10**.

⇌ – *Thalys* high-speed train. 🅁 🍷. Special fares payable. Valid June 1 - Aug. 30.
☆ – Eurostar train. 🅁, 🍴 in 1st class, 🍷 in 2nd class. Special fares payable. Minimum check-in time is 30 minutes, but passengers are advised to allow longer due to immigration procedures. Not available for London - Ebbsfleet - Ashford or v.v. journeys. Valid June 1 - Dec. 13.

LONDON - PARIS - BARCELONA - MADRID 13

train type	*TGV*	*AVE*		*TGV*	*AVE*		☆	*TGV*	*AVE*		☆	☆	*TGV*		☆			*AVE*	*AVE*	*AVE*	
train type/train number	**9711**	**3142**		**9713**	**3172**		**9014**	**9715**	**3212**		**9020**	**9022**	**9717**		**9044**	**3731**		**9713**	**19730**	**3122**	
notes	**9710**			**9712**				**9714**					**9716**			**3733**		**9712**			
notes				**E**							**C**	**X**	**B**			**G**	2				
notes											⑥	Ⓑ				Ⓡ					
London St Pancras **10** d.	...	...	...	...	...	...	0917**t**	...	...	...	1101	1131	...	...	1731	...	...	...	...	...	...
Paris Nord **10** a.	...	...	...	...	...	...	1247	...	...	...	1417	1447	...	...	2047	...	...	...	...	...	...
Paris Gare de Lyon d.	0715	...	...	1007	...	...	...	1407	...	...	...	...	1607	...	...	...	...	...	...	...	...
Paris Austerlitz d.	|	...	...	|	...	...	...	|	...	...	...	...	|	...	...	2157	...	...	...	...	...
Les Aubrais-Orléans d.	|	...	...	|	...	...	...	|	...	...	...	...	|	...	...	2259	...	...	...	...	...
Valence TGV d.	|	...	...	1221	...	...	...	1621	...	...	...	...	1821	...	...	|	...	...	...	...	...
Nimes d.	1009	...	...	1309	...	...	...	1709	...	...	...	...	1909	...	...	|	...	...	...	...	...
Montpellier d.	1037	...	...	1337	...	...	...	1737	...	...	...	...	1941	...	...	|	...	...	...	...	...
Béziers d.	|	...	...	1418	...	...	...	|	...	...	...	...	2031	...	...	|	...	...	...	...	...
Narbonne d.	1135	...	...	1435	...	...	...	1835	...	...	...	...	2047	...	...	0643	...	...	...	...	...
Perpignan d.	1213	...	...	1513	...	...	...	1913	...	...	...	...	2125	...	...	0724	...	1007	...	...	...
Cerbère 🛃 a.	|	...	...	|	...	...	...	|	...	...	...	...	|	...	...	0812	...	|	...	...	...
Portbou 🛃 a.	|	...	...	|	...	...	...	|	...	...	...	...	|	...	...	0822	0833	|	...	...	...
Figueres Vilafant ◇ a.	1242	...	...	1540	...	...	...	1942	...	...	...	...	2150	...	...	...	0857**x**	1031	...	...	...
Girona a.	1259	...	...	1557	...	...	...	1959	...	...	...	...	2207	...	...	...	0935	1047	...	...	...
Barcelona Sants a.	1340	1400	...	1638	1700	...	...	2040	2100	...	...	...	2248	...	...	...	1109	1127	1140	1200	...
Zaragoza Delicias a.	...	1540	...	...	1826	...	...	...	2240	...	...	...	...	...	...	...	...	|	|	1340	...
Madrid Puerta de Atocha a.	...	1710	...	...	1945	...	...	...	0002	...	...	...	...	...	...	...	...	1413	1413	1510	...

train type	*TGV*		*AVE*	*AVE*	*TGV*	☆	☆		*AVE*	*TGV*		*AVE*	*TGV*		*AVE*		*AVE*		☆		
train type/train number	**9700**		**3053**	**3061**	**9702**	**9051**	**9055**		**3093**	**9704**		**3123**	**9706**		**3333**		**9724**	**3730**	**9015**		
notes	**9701**				**9703**					**9705**			**9707**				**9725**	**3732**			
notes	**E**															2	**19724**	Ⓡ			
notes			①–⑤	①–④		Ⓑ												**H**			
Madrid Puerta de Atocha d.	...	...	0550	0610	...	...	...	...	0930	...	...	1230	...	...	1310	...	1540	...	...	...	...
Zaragoza Delicias d.	...	...	0706	|	...	...	...	...	1046	...	...	1346	...	...	1432	...	|	...	...	...	...
Barcelona Sants d.	0605	...	0855	0840	0920	...	...	...	1234	1320	...	1530	1620	...	1606	1716	1826	...	...	...	...
Girona d.	0646	...	...	...	1001	...	...	...	...	1401	...	...	1701	...	...	1848	1905	...	...	...	...
Figueres Vilafant ◇ d.	0703	...	...	...	1018	...	...	...	...	1418	...	...	1718	...	...	1927**x**	1922	...	...	...	...
Portbou 🛃 d.	|	...	...	...	|	...	...	...	...	|	...	...	|	...	...	1953	|	...	...	...	...
Cerbère 🛃 d.	|	...	...	...	|	...	...	...	...	|	...	...	|	...	...	1957	|	2016	...	...	...
Perpignan a.	0730	...	...	...	1044	...	...	...	...	1443	...	...	1744	...	...	...	1947	2107	...	...	...
Narbonne a.	0811	...	...	...	1125	...	...	...	...	1524	...	...	1824	...	...	...	...	2207	...	...	...
Béziers a.	0828	...	...	...	|	...	...	...	...	|	...	...	1841	...	...	...	...	|	...	...	...
Montpellier a.	0920	...	...	...	1218	...	...	...	...	1617	...	...	1921	...	...	...	...	|	...	...	...
Nimes a.	0949	...	...	...	1249	...	...	...	...	1649	...	...	1949	...	...	...	...	|	...	...	...
Valence TGV a.	|	...	...	...	1338	...	...	...	...	1738	...	...	|	...	...	...	...	|	...	...	...
Les Aubrais-Orléans a.	|	...	...	...	|	...	...	...	...	|	...	...	|	...	...	...	...	0620	...	...	...
Paris Austerlitz a.	|	...	...	...	|	...	...	...	...	|	...	...	|	...	...	...	...	0722	...	...	...
Paris Gare de Lyon a.	1245	...	...	...	1553	...	...	...	...	1953	...	...	2245	...	...	...	...	...	...	...	...
Paris Nord **10** d.	...	...	...	...	...	1813	1913	...	...	...	...	...	...	...	...	...	...	...	0913	...	...
London St Pancras **10** a.	...	...	...	...	...	1939	2041	...	...	...	...	...	...	...	...	...	...	...	1039	...	...

B – Calls at Sète 2001, Agde 2017.
C – ⑥ (⑥⑦ Mar. 29 - Aug. 30) also Aug. 25.
G – *Intercite de Nuit* – 🛏 1, 2 cl., [2] (reclining) Paris - Portbou.
E – From July 6.
H – *Intercite de Nuit* – 🛏 1, 2 cl., [2] (reclining) Cerbère - Paris.
X – ②③④⑤⑥ (daily Mar. 25 - Aug. 30) not Aug. 25, Nov. 10, 11.

t – 0922 on ⑥⑦ (also Aug. 25, Nov. 11).
x – Figueres.

✗ – Supplement payable.
TGV – *Train à Grande Vitesse* Ⓡ 🍸 ✗.
AVE – Alta Velocidad Española Ⓡ 🍸 ✗.

◇ – 🚌 connections available to Figueres bus station (Table **657**).
☆ – Eurostar train. Ⓡ, ✕ in 1st class, 🍸 in 2nd class. Special fares payable. Minimum check-in time 30 minutes. Additional services are shown on Table **10**. Valid June 1 - Dec. 13.

LONDON - GENÈVE 14

For the full service Paris - Genève, see Table **341**. 90 minutes (including Eurostar check-in time of 30 minutes) has been allowed from Paris **Lyon** and Paris **Austerlitz** to Paris Nord; additional Eurostar services are available, see Table **10**.

Engineering work between Bellegarde and Genève from July 15 to Aug. 29 will disrupt services. See Table 341.

train type	☆	☆	*TGV*	☆	☆	*TGV*	*TGV*	☆	*TGV*	☆	*TGV*	☆	*TGV*	☆	*TGV*	*TGV*	☆	*TGV*	☆	*TGV*	☆	☆	**5705**				
train number	**9006**	**9006**	**9773**	**9110**	**9110**	**9832**	**9750**	**9018**	**9775**	**9022**	**9777**	**9028**	**9781**	**9132**	**9834**	**9747**	**9032**	**9785**	**9036**	**9789**	**9044**	**9046**	**5594**				
notes	⑥			①–⑤	⑥						Ⓑ	Ⓑ				**9746**	Ⓑ			⑤		Ⓑ		🚌			
notes	**Z**	**E**	♥	**k**		Ⓡ	Ⓡ	**M**	♥	**X**	♥		♥		Ⓡ	Ⓡ		♥		♥			**A**				
London St Pancras **10** d.	0722	0731	...	0650	0657	...	...	1025	...	1131	...	1331	...	1258	...	...	1431	...	1531	...	1731	1801	...	...	...	...	...
Lille Europe d.	|	|	...	0930	0926	1102	...	|	...	|	...	|	...	1530	1602	...	|	...	|	...	|	|	...	...	...	...	...
Paris Nord **10** a.	1047	1047	...	...	...	|	...	1347	...	1447	...	1647	...	...	|	...	1747	...	1847	...	2047	2117	...	...	...	...	...
Paris Gare de Lyon d.	...	...	1211	...	...	|	...	...	1511	...	1611	...	1811	...	|	...	...	1911	...	2011	...	...	...	...	...	...	...
Paris Austerlitz d.	...	...	|	...	...	|	...	...	|	...	|	...	|	...	|	...	...	|	...	|	...	...	2312**c**	...	...	...	...
Lyon Part Dieu a.	...	...	|	...	...	1400	1534	...	|	...	|	...	|	...	1900	1934	...	|	...	|	...	...	|	...	...	...	...
La Roche sur Foron a.	...	...	|	...	...	...	|	...	|	...	|	...	|	...	...	|	...	|	...	|	...	...	0741	0812	...	...	...
Genève a.	...	...	1527	...	...	...	1716	...	1816	...	1927	...	2127	...	...	2116	...	2219	...	2327	...	...	...	0912**e**	...	...	...

train type	*TGV*	☆	*TGV*	*TGV*	☆	*TGV*	☆	*TGV*	☆	*TGV*	☆	*TGV*	☆	*TGV*	☆	*TGV*	*TGV*	☆	☆		**5596**	☆	☆				
train number	**9760**	**9023**	**9752**	**5144**	**9133**	**9764**	**9031**	**9768**	**9039**	**9770**	**9047**	**9772**	**9055**	**9774**	**9059**	**9744**	**9868**	**9161**	**9161**		**5706**	**9011**	**9013**				
notes	①–⑥				①–⑤	①–⑥				①–⑤		⑥⑦		①–⑤				Ⓑ	⑥	🚌		⑥⑦	①–⑤				
notes	♥**C**		Ⓡ	Ⓡ		♥**h**		♥		♥**b**		♥**p**		♥**b**		Ⓡ					**A**	**r**	**N**				
Genève d.	0612	...	0642	...	...	0742	...	0942	...	1142	...	1342	...	1429	...	1442	...	...	...	1848**v**	...	...	...	...	...	...	...
La Roche sur Foron a.	|	...	|	...	...	|	...	|	...	|	...	|	...	|	...	|	...	...	...	1941	2150**x**	...	...	...	...	...	...
Lyon Part Dieu d.	|	...	0830	0900	...	|	...	|	...	|	...	|	...	|	...	1626	1700	...	...	...	|	...	...	...	...	...	...
Paris Austerlitz a.	|	...	...	|	...	|	...	|	...	|	...	|	...	|	...	...	|	...	...	...	0618	...	...	...	...	...	...
Paris Gare de Lyon a.	0927	...	...	|	...	1049	...	1249	...	1449	...	1649	...	1749	...	...	|	...	...	...	...	...	...	...	...	...	...
Paris Nord **10** d.	...	1113	...	|	...	...	1313	...	1513	...	1713	...	1913	...	2013	...	|	...	...	...	...	0813	0843	...	...	...	...
Lille Europe d.	...	|	...	1157	1330	...	|	...	|	...	|	...	|	...	|	...	1957	2030	2030	...	...	|	|	...	...	...	...
London St Pancras **10** a.	...	1230	...	...	1403	...	1439	...	1639	...	1830	...	2041	...	2139	...	...	2103	2109	...	...	0930	1000	...	...	...	...

A – *CORAIL LUNÉA* – Ⓡ 🛏 1, 2 cl. [2] (reclining) Paris - La Roche sur Foron - St Gervais and v.v. For days of running see Table **365**.
C – ①–⑥ (daily July 20 - Aug. 17) not July 14, Nov. 11.
E – ①–⑤ May 25 - Aug. 30 (not Aug. 25); ① Aug. 31 - Dec. 13.
M – Ⓑ (daily Apr. 6 - Aug. 30).
N – ①–⑤ (① July 27 - Aug. 30) not Nov. 11.
X – ②③④⑤⑥ (daily Mar. 25 - Aug. 30) not Aug. 25, Nov. 10, 11.
Z – Feb. 1 - July 28; Sept. 20 - Dec. 13.

b – Not July 14, Aug. 15, Nov. 11.
c – 2137 on ⑦ (timings may vary).
e – Genève **Eaux Vives**. 0858 on Ⓐ.
h – Not July 14, Nov. 11.
j – Not June 9, July 14, July 27 - Aug. 30, Nov. 10, 11.
k – Not June 9, July 21, Aug. 15, 25, Nov. 10, 11.
p – Also July 14, Aug. 15, Nov. 11.
r – Also Aug. 25, Nov. 11.

v – Genève **Eaux Vives**.
x – 2025 on ⑥⑦.

🚌 – *SNCF* service; see table **366a**.
♥ – *TGV Lyria* service. Ⓡ special fares payable. At-seat meal service in first class.
☆ – Eurostar train. Ⓡ, ✕ in 1st class, 🍸 in 2nd class. Special fares payable. Minimum check-in time 30 minutes. Additional services are shown in Table **10**. Connections across Paris between *TGV* and Eurostar services are not guaranteed. Valid Feb 1 - July 26.

TRAIN NAMES: **6577** VERSAILLES **6569/6572** VOLTAIRE **6581/6568** HENRY DUNANT **6585/6564** J J ROUSSEAU

15 LONDON - ROTTERDAM - AMSTERDAM *by Eurostar*

train type	☆	☆	⇌	☆	⇌	1230	1230	☆	☆	⇌	1234	1234	☆	1242	1242	⇌
train number	9110	9110	9991	9114	9327	①-⑤	⑥⑦	9116	9116	9993	①-⑤	⑥⑦	9126	①-⑤	⑥⑦	9351
notes	A	⑥	⑥	①-⑤		✣w	✣m	E	B	T	✣w	✣m	C	✣w	✣m	
London St Pancras 12 d.	0650	0657	...	0804	...	...	...	0858	0858	...	...	...	1058	...	...	...
Ebbsfleet International 12 d.	0708	|	...	|	...	...	...	0915	0915	...	...	...	1115	...	...	...
Ashford International d.	0728	0728	...	|	...	...	...	|	|	...	...	...	|	...	...	...
Lille Europe 12 d.	0933	0930	...	1030	...	...	...	1130	1133	...	...	...	1330	...	...	...
Brussels Midi/Zuid 12 a.	1007	1011	...	1105	...	...	...	1205	1208	...	...	...	1405	...	...	...
Brussels Midi/Zuid d.	...	...	1052	...	1152	1152	1156	...	...	1252	1252	1256	...	1452	1456	1552
Antwerpen Centraal a.	...	...	1127	...	1227	1234	1238	...	...	1327	1334	1338	...	1534	1538	1627
Roosendaal 🏛 a.	...	...	|	...	|	1306	1311	...	...	|	1406	1411	...	1606	1610	|
Rotterdam Centraal a.	...	...	1202	...	1302	1352	1352	...	...	1402	1452	1452	...	1655	1652	1702
Den Haag HS a.	...	...	|	...	|	1416	1416	...	...	|	1516	1516	...	1716	1716	|
Schiphol ✈ a.	...	...	1224	...	1324	...	...	...	...	1424	...	...	...	...	...	1724
Amsterdam Centraal a.	...	...	1242	...	1342	...	...	...	...	1442	...	...	...	...	...	1742

train type	☆	⇌	1250	1250	☆	⇌	1254	1254	☆	⇌	☆	⇌	1262	1262
train number	9132	9357	①-⑤	⑥⑦	9136	9363	①-⑤	⑥⑦	9140	9369	9144	9375	①-⑤	⑥⑦
notes		⑧	✣w	✣m	P	⑤⑦g	✣w	✣m	⑧		⑥	⑤⑦g	✣w	✣m
London St Pancras 12 d.	1258	...	...	...	1404	...	...	...	1504	...	1604	...	...	...
Ebbsfleet International 12 d.	1315	...	...	...	|	...	...	...	|	...	|	...	...	...
Ashford International d.	|	...	...	...	|	...	...	...	|	...	|	...	...	...
Lille Europe 12 d.	1533	...	...	...	1630	...	...	...	1730	...	1830	...	...	...
Brussels Midi/Zuid 12 a.	1608	...	...	...	1705	...	...	...	1805	...	1905	...	...	...
Brussels Midi/Zuid d.	...	1652	1652	1656	...	1752	1752	1756	...	1852	...	1952	1952	1956
Antwerpen Centraal a.	...	1727	1734	1738	...	1827	1834	1838	...	1927	...	2027	2034	2038
Roosendaal 🏛 a.	...	|	1807	1810	...	|	1906	1911	...	|	...	|	2106	2111
Rotterdam Centraal a.	...	1802	1855	1852	...	1902	1952	1952	...	2002	...	2102	2152	2152
Den Haag HS a.	...	|	1916	1916	...	|	2016	2016	...	|	...	|	2217	2217
Schiphol ✈ a.	...	1824	...	...	...	1924	...	...	...	2024	...	2124	...	...
Amsterdam Centraal a.	...	1842	...	...	...	1942	...	...	...	2042	...	2142	...	...

train type	☆	⇌	1266	1266	☆	☆	⇌
train number	9148	9381	①-⑤	⑥⑦	9152	9152	9995
notes	⑧		✣w	✣m	⑦k	E	⑧
London St Pancras 12 d.	1704	...	...	...	1755b	1804	...
Ebbsfleet International 12 d.	|	...	...	...	|	|	...
Ashford International d.	|	...	...	...	1828	|	...
Lille Europe 12 d.	1930	...	...	...	2030	2030	...
Brussels Midi/Zuid 12 a.	2005	...	...	...	2105	2105	...
Brussels Midi/Zuid d.	...	2052	2052	2056	...	...	2152
Antwerpen Centraal a.	...	2127	2134	2138	...	...	2227
Roosendaal 🏛 a.	...	|	2206	2210	...	...	|
Rotterdam Centraal a.	...	2202	2252	2252	...	...	2302
Den Haag HS a.	...	|	2317	2317	...	...	|
Schiphol ✈ a.	...	2224	...	...	...	...	2324
Amsterdam Centraal a.	...	2242	...	...	...	...	2342

train type	⇌	☆	1209	1209	⇌	☆	1213	1213	⇌	☆	1217	1217	⇌	☆
train number	9310	9117	⑥⑦	①-⑤	9322	9125	⑥⑦	①-⑤	9328	9129	⑥⑦	①-⑤	9334	9133
notes	T		■m	■w		M	■m	■w	L	⑦k	■m	■w	⑥⑦y	①-⑤
Amsterdam Centraal d.	0618	...	...	...	0818	...	...	...	0918	...	...	...	1018	...
Schiphol ✈ △ d.	0633	...	...	...	0833	...	...	...	0933	...	...	...	1033	...
Den Haag HS d.	|	...	0743	0743	|	...	0844	0844	|	...	0944	0944	|	...
Rotterdam Centraal d.	0658	...	0808	0805	0858	...	0908	0908	0958	...	1008	1008	1058	...
Roosendaal 🏛 a.	|	...	0847	0854	|	...	0947	0954	|	...	1047	1054	|	...
Antwerpen Centraal d.	0733	...	0922	0926	0933	...	1022	1026	1033	...	1122	1126	1133	...
Brussels Midi/Zuid a.	0808	...	1004	1008	1008	...	1104	1108	1108	...	1204	1208	1208	...
Brussels Midi/Zuid 12 d.	...	0852	...	...	...	1056	...	...	...	1156	...	...	...	1252
Lille Europe 12 a.	...	0926	...	...	...	1130	...	...	...	1230	...	...	...	1330
Ashford International a.	...	|	...	...	...	|	...	...	...	|	...	...	...	|
Ebbsfleet International 12 a.	...	|	...	...	...	|	...	...	...	|	...	...	...	1345
London St Pancras 12 a.	...	0957	...	...	...	1157	...	...	...	1257	...	...	...	1403

train type	1225	1225	☆	☆	1229	1229	⇌	☆	⇌	☆	☆	☆
train number	⑥⑦	①-⑤	9141	9141	⑥⑦	①-⑤	9352	9145	9358	9149	9149	9149
notes	■m	■w	B	E	■m	■w		P	⑤⑦y	R	⑥	H
Amsterdam Centraal d.	...	...	...	...	...	...	1318	...	1418	...	...	...
Schiphol ✈ △ d.	...	...	...	...	...	...	1333	...	1433	...	...	...
Den Haag HS d.	1144	1144	...	...	1244	1244	|	...	|	...	...	...
Rotterdam Centraal d.	1208	1208	...	...	1308	1308	1358	...	1458	...	...	...
Roosendaal 🏛 a.	1247	1254	...	...	1347	1354	|	...	|	...	...	...
Antwerpen Centraal d.	1322	1326	...	...	1422	1426	1433	...	1533	...	...	...
Brussels Midi/Zuid a.	1404	1408	...	...	1504	1508	1508	...	1608	...	...	...
Brussels Midi/Zuid 12 d.	...	...	1452	1456	...	...	...	1556	...	1656	1656	1656
Lille Europe 12 a.	...	...	1526	1530	...	...	...	1632	...	1732	1732	1732
Ashford International a.	...	...	|	|	...	...	...	|	...	1734	|	1737
Ebbsfleet International 12 a.	...	...	1545	|	...	...	...	|	...	|	1748	|
London St Pancras 12 a.	...	...	1603	1557	...	...	...	1657	...	1809	1809	1811

train type	1237	1237	⇌	☆	☆	⇌	⇌	☆	1245	1245	⇌	☆	☆
train number	⑥⑦	①-⑤	9364	9153	9153	9996	9370	9157	⑥⑦	①-⑤	9376	9161	9161
notes	■m	■w		E	⑦k	D	⑤	⑧	■m	■w	⑧	⑧	⑥
Amsterdam Centraal d.	...	...	1518	...	...	1618	1618	...	...	...	1718	...	...
Schiphol ✈ △ d.	...	...	1533	...	...	1633	1633	...	...	...	1733	...	...
Den Haag HS d.	1444	1444	|	...	...	|	|	...	1644	1644	|	...	...
Rotterdam Centraal d.	1508	1508	1558	...	...	1658	1658	...	1708	1708	1758	...	...
Roosendaal 🏛 a.	1547	1554	|	...	...	|	|	...	1747	1754	|	...	...
Antwerpen Centraal d.	1622	1626	1633	...	...	1733	1733	...	1822	1826	1833	...	...
Brussels Midi/Zuid a.	1704	1708	1708	...	...	1808	1808	...	1904	1908	1908	...	...
Brussels Midi/Zuid 12 d.	...	...	...	1756	1756	...	...	1856	...	...	...	1952	1952
Lille Europe 12 a.	...	...	...	1832	1832	...	...	1930	...	...	...	2026	2026
Ashford International a.	...	...	...	|	1835	...	...	|	...	...	...	|	2035
Ebbsfleet International 12 a.	...	...	...	1845	|	...	...	|	...	...	...	2045	|
London St Pancras 12 a.	...	...	...	1903	1910	...	...	1957	...	...	...	2103	2109

A – ①-⑤ (not June 9, July 21, Aug. 15, 25, Nov. 10, 11).
B – ⑥⑦ (also Aug. 25, Nov. 11).
C – ①-⑥ (not Aug. 25, Nov. 11).
D – ①-④ (not June 9, July 14, 21).
E – ①-⑤ (not Aug. 25, Nov. 11).
H – ①-③ May 25 - Aug. 30; ①-⑤ Aug. 31 - Dec. 13.
L – ①-⑤ (①-⑥ Apr. 6 - Aug. 30) not June 9, July 14, 21.
M – ①-⑥ (not Nov. 11).
P – ⑤⑦ (⑧ Mar. 30 - Aug. 30) also Oct. 23, 27–30, Nov. 11.

R – ④⑤ May 25 - Aug. 30.
T – ①-⑤ (not June 9, July 14, 21).

b – 1751 on Nov. 11.
g – Also June 9, July 14, 21.
k – Also Aug. 25, Nov. 11.
m – Also June 9.
w – Not June 9.
y – Also June 9, July 14, 21.

△ – Trains stop to pick up only.
⇌ – *Thalys* high-speed train. 🄁 🍸. Valid June 1 - Aug. 30. Special fare payable.
☆ – Eurostar train. 🄁, ✕ in 1st class, 🍸 in 2nd class. Special fares payable. Minimum check-in time 30 minutes. Not available for London - Ebbsfleet - Ashford or v.v. journeys. Valid June 1 - Dec. 13.
✣ – Service calls at Mechelen 26 minutes after Brussels Midi/Zuid, and at Dordrecht 22-27 minutes after Roosendaal.
■ – Service calls at Dordrecht 14-15 minutes after Rotterdam Centraal and at Mechelen 18 minutes after Antwerpen Centraal.

LONDON - AMSTERDAM *by rail–sea–rail via Harwich - Hoek van Holland* 15a

notes	①–⑥	⑥	①–⑤	①–⑥				⑦	⑦	⑦	⑦	⑦		⑦	⑦	①–⑤	⑥	①–⑥	⑦	⑦	①–⑥		①–⑥			①–⑥	
				🚢						🚢												🚢					
London Liverpool Street ... d.	...	0638	0638	...	...	...	...	...	0755	...	...	...	...	1932	...	1932	1932	...	...	...	...	...	...	...	...	...	...
Peterborough ... d.	...	|	|	...	...	...	...	...	|	...	...	...	...	|	...	|	|	1750	1745	...	...	...	...	...	...	...	...
Cambridge ... d.	...	|	|	...	...	...	...	...	|	...	...	...	...	|	...	|	|	|	|	1912	1944	...	...	...	...	...	...
Colchester ... d.	...	0740	0743	...	...	...	...	...	0857	...	...	...	...	2037	2046	2025	2032	|	|	|	|	...	...	...	...	...	...
Ipswich ... d.	0659	|	|	...	...	...	...	0751	|	...	...	...	...	...	|	|	|	1928	1925	2036	2101	...	...	...	...	...	...
Manningtree ... d.	|	0748	0751	...	...	...	...	|	0905	...	...	...	...	...	2055	2034	2040	...	...	|	|	...	...	...	...	...	...
Harwich International 🏛 ... a.	0728	0809	0810	...	...	...	...	0819	0925	...	...	...	...	...	2114	2054	2056	...	...	2105	2130	...	...	...	...	...	...
Harwich International 🏛 ... d.	...	...	...	0900	...	...	...	...	...	1000	...	...	...	...	...	...	...	...	...	...	...	2315	...	...	...	...	...
Hoek van Holland Haven 🏛 . a.	...	...	...	1645	...	...	...	...	...	1800	...	...	...	...	...	...	...	...	...	...	...	0745	...	...	...	...	...
										⑦												①–⑤					
Hoek van Holland Haven 🏛 . d.	...	...	...	1726	...	...	...	...	...	1856	...	...	...	...	...	...	...	...	...	...	...	0810	...	0826	...	...	...
Schiedam Centrum ... a.	...	...	...	1751	1757	...	...	...	...	1921	1927	...	...	...	...	...	...	...	...	...	...	0835	0842	0851	...	0857	0927
Rotterdam Centraal ... a.	...	...	...	1757	|	1805	...	...	...	1927	|	1935	...	...	...	...	...	...	...	...	...	0841	|	0857	0905	|	|
Utrecht Centraal ... a.	...	...	...	...	|	1843	...	...	...	...	|	2013	...	...	...	...	...	...	...	...	...	...	|	...	0943	|	|
Amersfoort ... a.	...	...	...	...	|	1905	...	...	...	...	|	2035	...	...	...	...	...	...	...	...	...	...	|	...	1005	|	|
Den Haag HS ... a.	...	...	...	...	1811	...	...	...	...	...	1941	...	...	...	...	...	...	...	...	...	...	...	0856	...	...	0911	0941
Schiphol ✈ ... a.	...	...	...	...	1842	...	...	...	...	...	2012	...	...	...	...	...	...	...	...	...	...	...	|	...	...	0942	1012
Amsterdam Centraal ... a.	...	...	...	...	1902	...	...	...	...	...	2032	...	...	...	...	...	...	...	...	...	...	...	0948	...	...	1002	1032

notes						①–⑥	⑦	①–⑥											①–⑤	⑥	⑥	⑦	⑦	①–⑥	⑦	⑦	①–⑥
Amsterdam Centraal ... d.	1129	...	1142	...	...	...	...	...	1829	...	1842	...	...	1929	...	1942	...	...	...	...	...	...	...	...	...	...	...
Schiphol ✈ ... d.	1147	...	|	...	...	...	...	...	1847	...	|	...	...	1947	...	|	...	...	...	...	...	...	...	...	...	...	...
Den Haag HS ... d.	1219	...	1234	...	...	...	...	...	1919	...	1934	...	...	2019	...	2034	...	...	...	...	...	...	...	...	...	...	...
Amersfoort ... d.	|	...	|	1156	...	...	...	...	|	...	|	1856	...	|	...	|	1956	...	...	...	...	...	...	...	...	...	...
Utrecht ... d.	|	...	|	1217	...	...	...	...	|	...	|	1917	...	|	...	|	2017	...	...	...	...	...	...	...	...	...	...
Rotterdam Centraal ... d.	|	1232	|	1255	1302	...	...	...	|	1932	|	1955	2002	|	2032	|	2055	2102	...	...	...	...	...	...	...	...	...
Schiedam Centrum ... d.	1233	1237	1248	...	1307	...	...	...	1933	1937	1948	...	2007	2033	2037	2048	...	2107	...	...	...	...	...	...	...	...	...
Hoek van Holland Haven 🏛 ... a.	...	1301	...	...	1331	...	...	...	▬	2001		...	2031	...	2101	...	...	2131	...	...	...	...	...	...	...	...	...
													⑥⑦					①–⑤									
					🚢								🚢					🚢									
Hoek van Holland Haven 🏛 ... d.	...	...	...	...	1430	...	...	...	...	...	...	...	2130	...	...	...	...	2230	...	...	...	...	...	...	...	...	...
Harwich International 🏛 ... a.	...	...	...	...	2000	...	...	...	...	...	...	...	0630	...	...	...	...	0630	...	...	...	...	...	...	...	...	...
					⑦				①–⑥									①–⑤									
Harwich International 🏛 ... d.	...	...	...	...	2035	2045	2110	...	2138	...	...	...	...	...	...	...	...	0715	...	0720	...	0720	...	0750	0830	...	...
Manningtree ... a.	...	...	...	...	2048	2058	|	2112	|	...	...	...	...	...	...	...	...	0731	0759	0733	0755	0733	0738	|	|	...	...
Ipswich ... a.	...	...	...	...	|	|	2137	2125	2204	...	...	...	...	...	...	...	...	|	0811	|	0807	|	0750	0817	0853	0955	0958
Colchester ... a.	...	...	...	...	2057	2107	...	...	...	...	...	...	...	...	...	...	...	0741	...	0742	...	0742	...	|	|	|	|
Cambridge ... a.	...	...	...	...	|	|	...	...	...	...	...	...	...	...	...	...	...	|	...	|	...	|	...	0939	1025	|	|
Peterborough ... a.	...	...	...	...	|	|	...	...	...	...	...	...	...	...	...	...	...	|	...	|	...	|	...	...	...	1131	1139
London Liverpool Street ... a.	...	...	...	...	2202	2214	...	...	...	...	...	...	...	...	...	...	...	0854	...	0845	...	0859	...	...	...	...	...

SEA CROSSING (for rail / sea / rail journeys): 🚢 – Ship service, operated by Stena Line. Ⓡ One class only on ship. ✕ on ship. A cabin berth is necessary on night sailings.

PARIS - BRUSSELS - OOSTENDE 16

For additional services change at Brussels Midi. Table **18** Paris - Brussels. Table **400 / 401** Brussels - Gent - Brugge. Table **400** Brussels - Oostende.

	⇌	⇌	⇌	
	9313	**9333**	**9375**	
	⑥	⑦h	⑧x	
Paris Nord **18** ... d.	0801	1125	1825	...
Brussels Midi / Zuid **18** ... a.	0923	1247	1947	...
Brussels Midi / Zuid ... d.	0940	1258	1958	...
Gent Sint-Pieters ... a.	1011	1327	2027	...
Brugge ... a.	1036	1351	2051	...
Oostende ... a.	1051	1406	2106	...

	⇌	⇌	⇌	⇌
	9308	**9308**	**9370**	**9376**
	⑥j	①–⑤f	⑦h	⑥
Oostende ... d.	0609	0609	1654	1754
Brugge ... d.	0625	0625	1709	1809
Gent Sint-Pieters ... d.	0650	0653	1733	1833
Brussels Midi / Zuid ... a.	0721	0725	1802	1902
Brussels Midi / Zuid **18** ... d.	0743	0743	1813	1913
Paris Nord **18** ... a.	0905	0905	1935	2035

f – Not July 14, 21, Aug. 15.
h – Also July 14, 21.
j – Also Aug. 15.
x – Train number **9475** applies on ⑤⑦ (also July 14, 21).

⇌ – *Thalys* high-speed train. Ⓡ 🍸. Special fares payable. Valid June 1 - Aug. 30.

LILLE - BRUSSELS (Summary Table) 16a

train type	TGV	TGV	☆	☆	⇌	☆	☆	☆	TGV	⇌	TGV	☆	☆	☆	TGV	☆	☆	☆	TGV	☆	⇌	☆	☆	☆		
train number	**9809**	**9852**	**9110**	**9110**	**9991**	**9114**	**9116**	**9116**	**9854**	**9993**	**9862**	**9126**	**9132**	**9136**	**9866**	**9140**	**9144**	**9148**	**9868**	**9152**	**9995**	**9156**	**9158**	**9162**		
train number		**9853**							**9855**		**9863**				**9867**				**9869**							
notes	Ⓡ🍸	Ⓡ🍸	⑥	①–⑤	⑥	①–⑤	①–⑤	⑥⑦	Ⓡ🍸	①–⑤	Ⓡ🍸	①–⑥			Ⓡ🍸	⑧	⑥	⑧	Ⓡ🍸	⑧	⑧	⑥⑦	①–⑤	⑦		
notes	A			f	C		m	y		G C		m		Q							C	y	m	w		
Lille Europe ... d.	0732	0907	0930	0933	1006	1030	1130	1133	1151	1159	1207	1330	1533	1630	1707	1730	1830	1930	2007	2030	2106	2133	2203	2230	...	...
Brussels Midi / Zuid ... a.	0807	0943	1011	1007	1042	1105	1205	1208	1226	1235	1243	1405	1608	1705	1743	1805	1905	2005	2043	2105	2141	2208	2238	2305	...	...

train type	☆	☆	TGV	☆	⇌	☆	☆	TGV	☆		☆	☆	☆	TGV	☆	☆	☆	☆	⇌	☆	TGV	☆				
train number	**9109**	**9113**	**9800**	**9117**	**9994**	**9125**	**9129**	**9828**	**9133**		**9141**	**9141**	**9145**	**9836**	**9149**	**9149**	**9149**	**9153**	**9996**	**9157**	**9846**	**9161**				
train number			**9801**					**9829**						**9837**							**9847**					
notes	①	①–⑥	Ⓡ🍸			①–⑥	⑦	Ⓡ🍸	①–⑤		⑥⑦	①–⑤		Ⓡ🍸		⑥		⑧	①–④	⑧	Ⓡ🍸					
notes	p	f			C	m	y				y	m	Q		F		R		K C							
Brussels Midi / Zuid ... d.	0656	0756	0817	0852	0916	1056	1156	1217	1252	...	1452	1456	1556	1617	1656	1656	1656	1756	1820	1856	1917	1952	...	...	...	...
Lille Europe ... a.	0731	0830	0852	0926	0952	1130	1230	1253	1326	...	1526	1530	1630	1653	1732	1730	1730	1830	1858	1930	1952	2026	...	...	...	...

A – ①–⑤ (not June 9).
C – To / from Amsterdam (Table **18**).
F – ④⑤ May 25 - Aug. 30.
G – ①–⑤ (not June 9, July 14, 21).
K – ①–④ Apr. 12 - Aug. 30 (not June 9, July 14, 21).
Q – ⑤⑦ (⑧ Mar. 30 - Aug. 30) also Oct. 23, 27–30, Nov. 11.
R – ①–③ May 25 - Aug. 30; ①–⑤ Aug. 31 - Dec. 13.

f – Not June 9, July 21, Aug. 15, 25, Nov. 10, 11.
m – Not Aug. 25, Nov. 11.
p – Not June 9, July 21, Aug. 25, Nov. 10.
w – Not Aug. 24.
y – Also Aug. 25, Nov. 11.

☆ – Eurostar train. Ⓡ, ✕ in 1st class, 🍸 in 2nd class. Special fares payable. Minimum check-in time 30 minutes departing from Brussels. Valid June 1 - Dec. 13.
⇌ – *Thalys* high-speed train. Ⓡ 🍸. Special fares payable. Valid June 1 - Aug. 30.

PARIS - NAMUR - LIÈGE 17

km	*train type*	⇌
	train number	**9483**
	notes	
	notes	
0	**Paris** Nord ... ▲ d.	1934
282	Mons ... a.	2055
323	Charleroi Sud ... a.	2127
359	**Namur** ... a.	2157
419	**Liège** Guillemins ... ▲ a.	2241

train type	⇌
train number	**9406**
notes	
notes	
Liège Guillemins ▲ d.	0551
Namur ... d.	0635
Charleroi Sud ... d.	0705
Mons ... d.	0738
Paris Nord ... ▲ a.	0859

LONDON - AVIGNON / MARNE LA VALLÉE 17a

train type	☆		☆	
train number	**9084**		**9074**	
train number	**9085**			
notes	**J**		**A**	
London St Pancras ... d.	0717	...	1015	...
Ebbsfleet International ... d.	|	...	1034	...
Ashford International ... d.	0755**z**	...	1058	...
Lille Europe ... a.	|	...	1254**s**	...
Marne la Vallée § ... a.	|	...	1357	...
Lyon Part Dieu ... a.	|	...	...	...
Avignon Centre ... a.	1353	...	...	...
Aix en Provence TGV ... a.	...	...	...	...

train type	☆	☆	☆	☆
train number	**9057**	**9057**	**9057**	**9087**
train number				**9086**
notes	**B**	⑤	**C**	**K**
Aix en Provence TGV .. d.	...	...	...	...
Avignon Centre ... d.	...	...	...	1639
Lyon Part Dieu ... d.	...	...	...	|
Marne la Vallée § ... d.	1654	1654	1802	|
Lille Europe ... d.	|	|	|	|
Ashford International ... a.	1803	1806	1903	2105
Ebbsfleet International . a.	1826	1834	1926	|
London St Pancras ... a.	1846	1854	1946	2142

NOTES FOR TABLES 17 AND 17a

– ①③④⑤⑦ (daily May 21 - June 2; July 23 - Sept. 1; Oct. 22 - Nov. 7). On Oct. 19 depart London 1025, Ebbsfleet 1044, not call at Ashford.
– ⑦ (⑥⑦ July 26 - Aug. 31) also Oct. 25, Nov. 1.
– ①③④ (①②③④ July 28 - Aug. 28) also Oct 28, Nov. 4.
– ⑥ July 5 - Sept. 13.

K – ⑥ June 28 - Sept. 6.
s – Calls to set down only.
z – Arrive 0746.

▲ – For other trains Paris - Liège see Table **20**.

⇌ – *Thalys* high-speed train. Ⓡ 🍸. Special fares payable. Valid June 1 - Aug. 30.
☆ – Eurostar train. Ⓡ, ✕ in 1st class, 🍸 in 2nd class. Special fares payable. Minimum check-in time 30 minutes. Not available for London - Ashford or v.v. journeys. Valid June 1 - Dec. 13.
§ – Marne la Vallée - Chessy (station for Disneyland).

18 AMSTERDAM - BRUSSELS - PARIS

Brussels - Disneyland: see Table 11

For the full service London - Brussels and v.v. see Table **12**. Connections at Brussels are not guaranteed.

		train type	⇌	⇌	⇌	⇌	⇌		1205	1205	⇌	⇌		⇌	1209	1209	⇌	⇌	⇌		1213	1213	⇌	⇌	
		train number	**9300**	**9304**	**9308**	**9310**	**9412**	**910**	■	■	**9994**	**9316**	**914**	**9926/7**	■	■	**9322**	**9422**	**9424**	**918**	■	■	**9328**	**9328**	
		notes	①-④	①-⑤	①-⑥	①-⑤		①-⑥	⑥	①-⑤		①-⑥		⊕	⑥⑦	①-⑤					⑥⑦	①-⑤		⑦	
			f	k	k	k		z	c	w	R	U		A	m	w		S			m	w	L	t	
0	*0*	**Amsterdam** Centraal ...... d.	...	...	...	0618	...	0555	...	...	0718	...	0655	0740	...	...	0818	...	...	0755	...	...	0918	...	...
17	*17*	Schiphol ✈ .... ⊕ d.	...	...	...	0633	...	0609	...	...	0733	...	0709	0757	...	...	0833	...	...	0809	...	...	0933	...	...
60		Den Haag HS .... d.	...	...	...	|	...	|	0643	0643	|	...	|	|	0743	0743	|	...	...	|	0844	0844	|	...	...
82	*70*	**Rotterdam** Centraal........ d.	...	...	...	0658	...	0637	0708	0705	0758	...	0736	0833	0808	0805	0858	...	...	0836	0908	0908	0958	...	...
140		Roosendaal 🏛 .... d.	...	...	...	|	...	...	0747	0754	|	...	...	|	0847	0854	|	...	...	...	0947	0954	|	...	...
181	*165*	**Antwerpen** Centraal .... d.	...	...	...	0733	...	...	0822	0826	0833	...	...	0910	0922	0926	0933	...	...	...	1022	1026	1033	...	...
229	*212*	**Brussels** Midi / Zuid..... △ a.	...	...	...	0808	...	...	0904	0908	0908	...	...	|	1004	1008	1008	1005	...	...	1104	1108	1108	...	...
229	*212*	**Brussels** Midi / Zuid .... d.	0613	0713	0743	0813	0837	...	...	...	...	0913	...	0958	...	...	1013	1013	1037	...	...	...	1113	1113	...
541	*524*	**Paris** Nord..................... a.	0735	0835	0905	0935	0959	...	...	...	...	1035	...	...	...	...	1135	1135	1159	...	...	...	1235	1235	...

train type		1217	1217	⇌	⇌	⇌		1225	1225		1229	1229	⇌	⇌	⇌		⇌	1237	1237	⇌	⇌	⇌	⇌	⇌	⇌
train number	**922**	■	■	**9334**	**9338**	**9340**	**930**	■	■	**934**	■	■	**9352**	**9356**	**9358**	**942**	**9362**	■	■	**9364**	**9366**	**9996**	**9370**	**9370**	**9472**
notes		⑥⑦	①-⑤	⑥⑦	①-⑤			⑥⑦	①-⑤		⑥⑦	①-⑤		⑤	⑤⑦		②③④	⑥⑦	①-⑤		Ⓑ	①-④	⑤	Ⓑ	
		m	w	y	k			m	w		m	w		b	y		K	m	w		b	Y			
Amsterdam Centraal....... d.	0855	...	...	1018	...	1118	1055	...	...	1155	...	...	1318	...	1418	1355	...	...	...	1518	...	1618	1618	...	...
Schiphol ✈ .... ⊕ d.	0909	...	...	1033	...	1133	1109	...	...	1209	...	...	1333	...	1433	1409	...	...	...	1533	...	1633	1633	...	...
Den Haag HS.............. d.	|	0944	0944	|	...	|	|	1144	1144	|	1244	1244	|	...	|	|	...	1444	1444	|	...	|	|	...	...
Rotterdam Centraal .... d.	0936	1008	1008	1058	...	1158	1136	1208	1208	1236	1308	1308	1358	...	1458	1436	...	1508	1508	1558	...	1658	1658	...	...
Roosendaal 🏛 .... d.	...	1047	1054	|	...	|	...	1247	1254	▬	1347	1354	|	...	|	▬	...	1547	1554	|	...	|	|	...	...
Antwerpen Centraal........ d.	...	1122	1126	1133	...	1233	...	1322	1326	⇌	1422	1426	1433	...	1533	⇌	...	1622	1626	1633	...	1733	1733	...	...
Brussels Midi / Zuid .... △ a.	...	1204	1208	1208	...	1308	...	1404	1408	**9448**	1504	1508	1508	...	1608	**9358**	...	1704	1708	1708	...	1808	1808	...	...
Brussels Midi / Zuid .... d.	...	...	...	1213	1243	1313	...	...	...	1437	...	...	1513	1543	1613	1613	1643	...	...	1713	1737	...	1813	1813	1837
Paris Nord....................... a.	...	...	...	1335	1405	1435	...	...	...	1559	...	...	1635	1705	1735	1735	1805	...	...	1835	1859	...	1935	1935	1959

train type		1245	1245	⇌	⇌	⇌		1249	1249	⇌	⇌		1253	1253	⇌		1257	1257	⇌	⇌		1261	1261		
train number	**950**	■	■	**9376**	**9376**	**9380**	**954**	■	■	**9382**	**9484**	**958**	■	■	**9388**	**962**	■	■	**9394**	**9394**	**966**	■	■		
notes		⑥⑦	①-⑤	Ⓑ		⑤		⑥⑦	①-⑤				⑥⑦	①-⑤	Ⓑ		⑥⑦	①-⑤	①-⑤	⑦		⑥⑦	①-⑤		
		m	w			b		m	w				m	w			m	w	k	y		m	w		
Amsterdam Centraal....... d.	1555	...	...	1718	...	...	1655	...	...	1818	...	1755	...	...	1918	1855	...	...	2018	2018	1955	...	...	...	...
Schiphol ✈ .... ⊕ d.	1609	...	...	1733	...	...	1709	...	...	1833	...	1809	...	...	1933	1909	...	...	2033	2033	2009	...	...	...	...
Den Haag HS.............. d.	|	1644	1644	|	...	...	|	1744	1744	|	...	|	1844	1844	|	|	1944	1944	|	|	|	2044	2044	...	...
Rotterdam Centraal .... d.	1636	1708	1708	1758	...	...	1736	1808	1805	1858	...	1836	1908	1908	1958	1936	2008	2008	2058	2058	2036	2108	2108	...	...
Roosendaal 🏛 .... d.	...	1747	1754	|	...	...	...	1847	1854	|	...	...	1947	1954	|	...	2047	2054	|	|	...	2147	2154	...	...
Antwerpen Centraal........ d.	...	1822	1826	1833	...	...	...	1922	1926	1933	...	...	2022	2026	2033	...	2122	2126	2133	2133	...	2222	2226	...	...
Brussels Midi / Zuid .... △ a.	...	1904	1908	1908	...	...	...	2004	2008	2008	...	...	2104	2108	2108	...	2204	2208	2208	2208	...	2304	2308	...	...
Brussels Midi / Zuid .... d.	...	...	...	1913	1913	1943	...	...	...	2016	2037	...	...	...	2113	...	...	...	...	2213	...	...	...	...	...
Paris Nord....................... a.	...	...	...	2035	2035	2105	...	...	...	2138	2159	...	...	...	2235	...	...	...	...	2335	...	...	...	...	...

train type	1206	1206		⇌	1210	1210	⇌	⇌	⇌	⇌	⇌	⇌	⇌	1218	1218		⇌	⇌	1222	1222		⇌	⇌	⇌	⇌
train number	❖	❖	**911**	**9391**	❖	❖	**9401**	**9303**	**9403**	**9403**	**9305**	**9309**	**9309**	❖	❖	**923**	**9413**	**9315**	❖	❖	**927**	**9317**	**9319**	**9321**	**9991**
notes	①-⑤	⑥		①-⑤	①-⑤	⑥⑦		①-⑤	⑥⑦	①-⑤	①-④		①-⑥	①-⑤	⑥⑦				①-⑤	⑥⑦		⑥	①-⑤	⑦	⑥
	w	c		k	w	m		k	N	T	f	X	k	w	m				w	m		q	k	t	M
Paris Nord...................... d.	...	...	...	...	...	...	0601	0625	0625	0625	0655	0725	0725	...	...	...	0801	0825	...	...	...	0855	0901	0925	...
Brussels Midi / Zuid .... a.	...	...	...	...	...	...	0723	0747	0747	0747	0817	0847	0847	...	...	...	0923	0947	...	...	...	1017	1023	1047	...
Brussels Midi / Zuid .... ▽ d.	0552	0556	...	0618	0652	0656	▬	0752	0755	0805	...	0852	...	0852	0856	...	...	0952	0952	0956	...	...	...	...	1052
Antwerpen Centraal........ a.	0634	0638	...	0655	0734	0738	...	0827	...	...	...	0927	...	0934	0938	...	...	1027	1034	1038	...	...	...	...	1127
Roosendaal 🏛 .... a.	0706	0711	...	|	0806	0811	**915**	|	...	...	...	|	...	1006	1011	...	...	|	1106	1110	...	...	...	...	|
Rotterdam Centraal .... a.	0755	0752	0824	0733	0855	0852	0924	0902	...	...	...	1002	...	1052	1052	1124	...	1102	1152	1152	1224	...	...	...	1202
Den Haag HS.............. a.	0816	0816	|	|	0916	0916	|	|	...	...	...	|	...	1116	1116	|	...	|	1216	1216	|	...	...	...	|
Schiphol ✈ .... ⊗ a.	...	...	0850	0802	...	...	0950	0924	...	...	...	1024	...	...	...	1150	...	1124	...	...	1250	...	...	...	1224
Amsterdam Centraal....... a.	...	...	0906	0820	...	...	1006	0942	...	...	...	1042	...	...	...	1206	...	1142	...	...	1306	...	...	...	1242

train type	⇌	⇌	1230	1230		⇌	⇌	1234	1234		⇌	⇌	⇌	1242	1242		⇌	1246	1246		⇌	⇌	1250	1250	
train number	**9325**	**9327**	❖	❖	**935**	**9333**	**9993**	❖	❖	**939**	**9437**	**9339**	**9341**	❖	❖	**947**	**9351**	❖	❖	**951**	**9357**	**9357**	❖	❖	**955**
notes	①-⑥		①-⑤	⑥⑦			①-⑤	①-⑤	⑥⑦					①-⑤	⑥⑦			①-⑤	⑥⑦		Ⓑ	⑥	①-⑤	⑥⑦	
	U		w	m		E	V	w	m					w	m			w	m			q	w	m	
Paris Nord...................... d.	1001	1025	...	...	...	1125	...	...	...	...	1201	1225	1255	...	...	...	1425	...	...	...	1525	1525	...	...	...
Brussels Midi / Zuid .... a.	1123	1147	...	...	...	1247	...	...	...	...	1323	1347	1417	...	...	...	1547	...	...	...	1647	1647	...	...	...
Brussels Midi / Zuid .... ▽ d.	...	1152	1152	1156	...	...	1252	1252	1256	...	...	1352	...	1452	1456	...	1552	1552	1556	...	1652	...	1652	1656	...
Antwerpen Centraal........ a.	...	1227	1234	1238	...	...	1327	1334	1338	...	...	1427	...	1534	1538	...	1627	1634	1638	...	1727	...	1734	1738	...
Roosendaal 🏛 .... a.	...	|	1306	1311	...	...	|	1406	1411	...	...	|	...	1606	1610	...	|	1706	1711	...	|	...	1807	1810	...
Rotterdam Centraal .... a.	...	1302	1352	1352	1424	...	1402	1452	1452	1524	...	1502	...	1655	1652	1724	1702	1755	1752	1824	1802	...	1855	1852	1924
Den Haag HS.............. a.	...	|	1416	1416	|	...	|	1516	1516	|	...	|	...	1716	1716	|	|	1816	1816	|	|	...	1916	1916	|
Schiphol ✈ .... ⊗ a.	...	1324	...	...	1450	...	1424	...	...	1550	...	1524	...	...	...	1750	1724	...	...	1850	1824	...	...	...	1950
Amsterdam Centraal....... a.	...	1342	...	...	1506	...	1442	...	...	1606	...	1542	...	...	...	1806	1742	...	...	1906	1842	...	...	...	2006

train type	⇌	⇌	1254	1254		⇌	⇌	⇌	⇌	⇌	1262	1262		⇌	⇌	1266	1266	⇌	⇌	⇌	⇌	⇌	⇌		
train number	**9461**	**9363**	❖	❖	**959**	**9365**	**9369**	**9473**	**9375**	**9375**	❖	❖	**969**	**9377**	**9381**	❖	❖	**9955/6**	**9387**	**9995**	**9389**	**9395**	**9399**		
notes		⑤⑦	①-⑤	⑥⑦						⑤⑦	①-⑤	⑥⑦		Ⓑ		①-⑤	⑥⑦	⊗		Ⓑ			⑦		
		y	w	m		W			D	y	w	m		J		w	m	B	C	G	F	H	y		
Paris Nord...................... d.	1601	1625	...	...	...	1655	1725	1758	1825	1825	...	...	...	1855	1925	...	...	...	2025	...	2055	2155	2225	...	...
Brussels Midi / Zuid .... a.	1723	1747	...	...	...	1817	1847	1923	1947	1947	...	...	...	2017	2047	...	...	2112	2147	...	2217	2317	2347	...	...
Brussels Midi / Zuid .... ▽ d.	...	1752	1752	1756	...	...	1852	...	...	1952	1952	1956	...	...	2052	2052	2056	|	...	2152	...	...	...	...	...
Antwerpen Centraal........ a.	...	1827	1834	1838	...	...	1927	...	...	2027	2034	2038	...	...	2127	2134	2138	2200	...	2227	...	...	...	...	...
Roosendaal 🏛 .... a.	...	|	1906	1911	...	...	|	...	...	|	2106	2111	...	...	|	2206	2210	|	...	|	...	...	...	...	...
Rotterdam Centraal .... a.	...	1902	1952	1952	2024	...	2002	...	...	2102	2152	2152	2254	...	2202	2252	2252	2234	...	2302	...	...	...	...	...
Den Haag HS.............. a.	...	|	2016	2016	|	...	|	...	...	|	2217	2217	|	...	|	2317	2317	|	...	|	...	...	...	...	...
Schiphol ✈ .... ⊗ a.	...	1924	...	...	2050	...	2024	...	...	2124	...	...	2320	...	2224	...	...	2301	...	2324	...	...	...	...	...
Amsterdam Centraal....... a.	...	1942	...	...	2106	...	2042	...	...	2142	...	...	2336	...	2242	...	...	2320	...	2342	...	...	...	...	...

A – THALYS SOLEIL – ⑥ June 28 - Aug. 30: 🛏12 🍸 Amsterdam - Brussels - Marseille (Table **11**). On Aug. 2 depart Amsterdam 0725, Schipol 0742, Rotterdam 0818. On Aug. 16 depart Amsterdam 0658, Rotterdam 0833, not call Schiphol.
B – THALYS SOLEIL ⑥ July 5 - Aug. 30: 🛏12 🍸 Marseille - Valence *TGV* - Brussels - Amsterdam (Table **11**). On July 19, Aug. 16 arrive Rotterdam 2234, Amsterdam 2359, not call Schiphol. On Aug. 2 arrive Rotterdam 2249, Schiphol 2316, Amsterdam 2335.
C – ⑤⑥⑦ (⑤⑦ July 13 - Aug. 30) also June 9; not July 20.
D – ①②③④⑥ (①-④ July 13 - Aug. 30; not July 14, 21).
E – ⑤⑥⑦ (daily Apr. 6 - July 12; ②③④⑤⑥⑦ July 13 - Aug. 30).
F – ②③④⑤⑦ (Ⓑ Apr. 6 - July 12; ①②③④⑥⑦ July 13 - Aug. 30).
G – Ⓑ. From Lille Europe (Table **16a**).
H – ①-⑥ (daily Apr. 4 - July 12; not June 8; ⑤ July 13 - Aug. 30).
J – Ⓑ (①-⑤ July 13 - Aug. 30; not July 14, 21).
K – ②③④ (②③④⑤ Apr. 6 - July 12) not June 10, July 13 - Aug. 30.
L – ①-⑤ (①-⑥ Apr. 6 - Aug. 30) not June 9, July 14, 21.
M – ⑥. From Lille Europe (Table **16a**).
N – To Brussels, Nationaal / Zaventem airport, arrive 0812. Also June 9, July 21.
R – Ⓑ (daily Apr. 12 - Aug. 30). To Lille Europe (Table **16a**).
S – From Brussels, Nationaal / Zaventem airport, depart 0948.
T – To Brussels, Nationaal / Zaventem airport, arrive 0822. Not June 9, July 21.
U – ①-⑥ (⑥ July 13 - Aug. 30) not June 9.
V – ①-⑤ (not June 9, July 14, 21). From Lille Europe (Table **16a**).
W – ②③④⑤⑦ (daily Apr. 6 - July 12; not June 8; ①-⑥ July 13 - Aug. 30; not July 14, 21).
X – ①②③④⑥ (not June 9, July 14, 21).

Y – ①-④ (not June 9, July 14, 21). To Lille Europe (Table **16a**).

b – Not July 13 - Aug. 30.
c – Also May 1.
f – Not June 9, July 13 - Aug. 30.
g – Not June 8.
k – Not June 9, July 14, 21.
m – Also Apr. 21, May 1, 29, June 9.
n – Not Apr. 20, May 1, 8, 29, 30.
q – Not July 13 - Aug. 30.
t – Also June 9; not July 13 - Aug. 30.
w – Not Apr. 21, May 1, 29, June 9.
y – Also June 9, July 14, 21.
z – Not May 29, June 9.

⊗ – Calls to set down only.
⊕ – Calls to pick up only.
⇌ – *Thalys* high-speed train. Ⓡ 🍸. Special fares payable. Valid June 1 - Aug. 30.
❖ – Service calls at Mechelen 26 minutes after Brussels Midi / Zuid, and at Dordrecht 22 - 27 minutes after Roosendaal.
■ – Service calls at Dordrecht 14 - 15 minutes after Rotterdam Centraal and at Mechele[n] 18 minutes after Antwerpen Centraal.
▽ – All services except *Thalys* call at Brussels Central 3 mins. after Brussels Midi / Zuid
△ – All services except *Thalys* call at Brussels Central 4 mins. before Brussels Midi / Zui

LONDON, PARIS and BRUSSELS - KÖLN, HAMBURG and BERLIN 20

For the full service London - Brussels and v.v. see Table **12**. For Paris - Brussels and v.v. see Table **18**. Connections at Brussels are not guaranteed.

train type	ICE	ICE	IC	RE	IC	ICE	⇌	ICE	EC	IC	IC	RE	IC	ICE	ICE	⇌	RE	IC	ICE	EC	IC	IC	RE	ICE	ICE
train number	**11**	**545**	**2037**	**10508**	**2310**	**35**	**9401**	**847**	**379**	**2441**	**2159**	**10510**	**231**	**1028**	**37**	**9413**	**10514**	**133**	**859**	**179**	**2049**	**2239**	**10121**	**1122**	**39**
notes	🍷	🍷	🍷		🍷	⚡		🍷	✗	🍷	🍷		**131**	🍷	⚡			🍷	**1539**	✗	①–⑥	🍷		🍷	⚡
						C	**S**						🍷		**D**				🍷		🍷				**D**
London St Pancras ... d.	...	...	...	...	...	...	...	...	...	...	...	...	...	...	...	...	...	...	...	...	...	...	...	...	...
Ebbsfleet International d.	...	...	...	...	...	...	...	...	...	...	...	...	...	...	...	...	...	...	...	...	...	...	...	...	...
Ashford International .. d.	...	...	...	...	...	...	...	...	...	...	...	...	...	...	...	...	...	...	...	...	...	...	...	...	...
Lille Europe ... d.	...	...	...	...	...	...	...	...	...	...	...	...	...	...	...	...	...	...	...	...	...	...	...	...	...
Paris Nord ... d.	...	...	...	...	...	...	0601	...	...	...	...	...	...	...	...	0801	...	...	...	...	...	...	...	...	...
Brussels Midi/Zuid ... a.	...	...	...	...	...	...	0723	...	...	...	...	...	...	...	...	0923	...	...	...	...	...	...	...	...	...
Brussels Midi/Zuid ... d.	0625	...	...	...	...	...	0728	...	...	...	...	...	...	...	...	0928	...	...	...	...	...	...	...	...	...
Brussels Nord ... d.	0633	...	...	...	...	...	|	...	...	...	...	...	...	...	...	|	...	...	...	...	...	...	...	...	...
Liège Guillemins ... a.	0712	...	...	...	...	...	0811	...	...	...	...	...	...	...	...	1011	...	...	...	...	...	...	...	...	...
Liège Guillemins ... d.	0714	...	...	...	...	...	0814	...	...	...	...	...	...	...	...	1014	...	...	...	...	...	...	...	...	...
Aachen 🛃 ... a.	0736	...	...	...	...	...	0836	...	...	...	...	...	...	...	...	1036	...	...	...	...	...	...	1051	...	...
Köln Hbf ... a.	0815	...	...	...	...	...	0915	...	...	...	...	...	...	...	...	1115	...	...	...	...	...	...	1144	...	...
Köln Hbf ... d.	...	0828	...	0831	0908	...	0920	0928	...	...	...	0931	0946	1010	...	...	1131	1146	1148	...	...	...	1149	1210	...
Wuppertal Hbf ... a.	...	|	...	|	|	...	|	|	...	...	...	|	|	1041	...	...	|	|	1214	...	...	...	|	1241	...
Hagen Hbf ... a.	...	|	...	|	|	...	|	|	...	...	...	|	|	1059	...	...	|	|	1232	...	...	...	|	1259	...
Düsseldorf Hbf ... a.	...	0851	...	0901	0929	...	0943	0950	...	...	...	1001	1009	|	...	...	1201	1209	|	...	...	...	1219	|	...
Duisburg Hbf ... a.	...	0908	...	0918	0942	...	1001	1008	...	...	...	1018	1023	|	...	...	1218	1223	|	...	...	...	1236	|	...
Oberhausen ... a.	...	|	...	0926	|	...	|	|	...	...	...	1026	1031	|	...	...	1226	1231	|	...	...	...	|	|	...
Essen Hbf ... a.	...	0921	...	...	0957	...	1015	1021	...	...	...	...	|	|	...	...	...	|	|	...	...	...	1250	|	...
Bochum Hbf ... a.	...	0933	...	...	1008	...	...	1033	...	...	...	...	|	|	...	...	...	|	|	...	...	...	1303	|	...
Dortmund Hbf ... a.	...	0946	...	...	1021	...	...	1046	...	...	...	...	|	1121	...	...	...	|	|	...	...	...	1315	1321	...
Hamm (Westf) ... a.	...	1006	...	...	|	...	...	1106	...	...	...	...	|	|	...	...	...	|	1302	...	...	...	1336	|	...
Bielefeld Hbf ... a.	...	1036	...	...	|	...	...	1135	...	...	...	...	|	|	...	...	...	|	1335	...	...	...	...	|	...
Münster ... a.	...	|	...	...	1054	...	...	|	...	...	...	...	1127	1155	...	...	...	1327	|	...	...	...	...	1356	...
Osnabrück Hbf ... a.	...	|	...	...	1121	...	...	|	...	...	...	...	...	1221	...	...	...	...	|	...	...	...	...	1423	...
Bremen Hbf ... a.	...	|	...	...	1214	...	...	|	...	...	...	...	...	1314	...	...	...	...	|	...	...	...	...	1515	...
Hannover Hbf ... a.	...	1128	1136	...	|	...	...	1228	...	1236	...	...	...	|	...	...	...	...	1428	...	1436	...	...	|	...
Hamburg Hbf ... a.	...	|	|	...	1312	1328	...	|	...	|	...	...	...	1412	1528	...	...	...	|	...	|	...	...	1612	1728
København H ⊙ a.	...	|	|	...	...	1814	...	|	...	|	...	...	...	...	2014	...	...	...	|	...	|	...	...	...	2214
Wolfsburg ... a.	...	|	|	...	...	...	...	1302	...	|	...	...	...	...	...	...	...	...	1502	...	|	...	...	...	...
Braunschweig Hbf ... a.	...	|	1208	...	...	...	...	|	...	1309	...	...	...	...	...	...	...	...	|	...	1509	...	...	...	...
Magdeburg Hbf ... a.	...	|	1257	...	...	...	...	|	...	1355	...	...	...	...	...	...	...	...	|	...	1555	...	...	...	...
Halle Hbf ... a.	...	|	1353	...	...	...	...	|	...	1451	...	...	...	...	...	...	...	...	|	...	1651	...	...	...	...
Leipzig Hbf ... a.	...	|	1419	...	...	...	...	|	...	1518	1624	...	...	...	...	...	...	...	|	...	1718	1825	...	...	...
Berlin Hbf ... a.	...	1308	|	...	...	...	...	1408	1446	...	|	...	...	...	...	...	...	...	1609	1647	...	|	...	...	...
Berlin Ostbahnhof ... a.	...	1319	|	...	...	...	...	1419	|	...	|	...	...	...	...	...	...	...	1620	|	...	|	...	...	...
Dresden Hbf ... a.	...	...	1529	...	...	...	...	...	1652	...	1728	...	...	...	...	...	...	...	...	1852	...	1929	...	...	...
Bad Schandau 🛃 ... a.	...	...	...	...	...	...	...	...	1736	...	...	...	...	...	...	...	...	...	...	1936	...	...	...	...	...
Děčín ... a.	...	...	...	...	...	...	...	...	1753	...	...	...	...	...	...	...	...	...	...	1953	...	...	...	...	...
Praha Holešovice ... a.	...	...	...	...	...	...	...	...	1916	...	...	...	...	...	...	...	...	...	...	2116	...	...	...	...	...
Praha hlavní ... a.	...	...	...	...	...	...	...	...	1926	...	...	...	...	...	...	...	...	...	...	2126	...	...	...	...	...

train type	⇌	☆	⇌	ICE	RE	ICE	☆	☆	⇌	RE	IC	ICE	ICE	☆	⇌	ICE	RE	ICE	☆	☆	⇌	RE	ICE	EC	ICE	ICE
train number	**9315**	**9110**	**9317**	**15**	**10516**	**559**	**9116**	**9116**	**9437**	**10522**	**2004**	**953**	**943**	**9126**	**9341**	**17**	**10524**	**653**	**9132**	**9136**	**9461**	**10530**	**947**	**114**	**957**	**26**
notes		①–⑤	⑥	🍷		🍷	①–⑤	⑥⑦			**2014**	🍷	🍷	①–⑥		🍷		🍷					🍷		🍷	🍷
		p	**q**				**m**	**y**			Ⓑ	Ⓑ		**m**						**P**			**H**		⑤⑦**j**	
London St Pancras ... d.	...	0650	...	...	...	...	0858	0858	...	...	...	...	...	1058	...	...	...	...	1258	1404	...	...	...	...	...	...
Ebbsfleet International d.	...	0708	...	...	...	...	0915	0915	...	...	...	...	...	1115	...	...	...	...	1315	|	...	...	...	...	...	...
Ashford International .. d.	...	0728	...	...	...	...	|	|	...	...	...	...	...	|	...	...	...	...	|	|	...	...	...	...	...	...
Lille Europe ... d.	...	0933	...	...	...	...	1130	1133	...	...	...	...	...	1330	...	...	...	...	1533	1630	...	...	...	...	...	...
Paris Nord ... d.	0825	|	0855	...	...	...	|	|	1201	...	...	...	...	|	1255	...	...	...	|	|	1601	...	...	...	...	...
Brussels Midi/Zuid ... a.	0947	1007	1017	...	...	...	1205	1208	1323	...	...	...	...	1405	1417	...	...	...	1608	1705	1723	...	...	...	...	...
Brussels Midi/Zuid ... d.	...	...	...	1025	...	...	▬	▬	1328	...	...	...	...	▬	▬	1425	...	...	▬	▬	1728	...	...	...	...	...
Brussels Nord ... d.	...	...	...	1033	...	...	...	...	|	...	...	...	...	...	...	1433	...	...	...	...	|	...	...	...	...	...
Liège Guillemins ... a.	...	...	...	1112	...	...	*RE*	...	1411	...	...	...	...	...	...	1512	...	...	...	*EC*	1811	...	...	...	...	...
Liège Guillemins ... d.	...	...	...	1114	...	...	**10123**	*IC*	1414	...	...	...	...	...	*ICE*	1514	...	...	...	**2**	1814	...	...	...	...	...
Aachen 🛃 ... a.	...	...	...	1136	...	...	1151	**2218**	1436	...	...	...	...	*RE*	**1026**	1536	...	...	*RE*	**8**	1836	...	...	...	...	...
Köln Hbf ... a.	...	...	...	1215	...	...	1244	🍷	1515	...	...	...	...	**10129**	🍷	1615	...	...	**10131**	**B**	1915	...	...	...	...	...
Köln Hbf ... d.	...	...	...	...	1231	1248	1249	1310	1520	1531	1546	1548	...	1549	1610	...	1631	1648	1649	1710	...	1931	1926	1946	1948	2010
Wuppertal Hbf ... a.	...	...	...	...	|	1314	|	|	|	|	|	1614	...	|	1641	...	|	1714	|	|	...	|	|	|	2014	2041
Hagen ... a.	...	...	...	...	|	1332	|	|	|	|	|	1632	...	|	1659	...	|	1732	|	|	...	|	|	|	2032	2059
Düsseldorf Hbf ... a.	...	...	...	...	1301	|	1319	1331	1542	1601	1609	|	...	1619	|	...	1701	|	1719	1731	...	2001	1950	2008	|	|
Duisburg Hbf ... a.	...	...	...	...	1318	|	1336	1344	|	1618	1626	|	...	1636	|	...	1718	|	1736	1744	...	2018	2008	2022	|	|
Oberhausen ... a.	...	...	...	...	1326	|	|	|	|	1626	1631	|	...	|	|	...	1726	|	|	|	...	2026	|	|	|	|
Essen Hbf ... a.	...	...	...	...	...	|	1350	1357	1607	...	|	|	1623	1650	|	...	...	|	1750	1757	...	...	2021	2037	|	|
Bochum Hbf ... a.	...	...	...	...	...	|	1403	1408	▬	...	|	|	|	1703	|	...	...	|	1803	1808	...	...	2033	2047	|	|
Dortmund Hbf ... a.	...	...	...	...	...	|	1415	1421	...	...	|	|	|	1715	1721	...	...	|	1815	1821	...	...	2046	2100	|	2120
Hamm (Westf) ... a.	...	...	...	...	...	1402	1438	|	...	...	|	1702	1707	1736	|	...	...	1802	1836	|	...	...	2106	...	2102	|
Bielefeld ... a.	...	...	...	...	...	1436	▬	|	...	...	|	1735	1735	▬	|	...	...	1836	▬	|	...	...	2135	...	2135	|
Münster ... a.	...	...	...	...	...	|	*IC*	1456	*ICE*	...	1727	|	|	*IC*	1756	...	...	|	...	1856	...	...	|	...	|	2156
Osnabrück ... a.	...	...	...	...	...	|	**2431**	1523	**39**	...	...	|	|	**2045**	1822	...	...	|	*IC*	1923	...	...	|	...	|	2224
Bremen Hbf ... a.	...	...	...	...	...	|	🍷	1614	⚡	...	...	|	|	Ⓑ	1914	...	...	|	**2435**	2015	...	...	|	...	|	2318
Hannover Hbf ... a.	...	...	...	...	...	1528	1536	|	**D**	...	...	1828	1828	1836	|	...	...	1928	1936	|	...	...	2228	...	2228	|
Hamburg Hbf ... a.	...	...	...	...	...	|	|	1712	1728	...	...	|	|	|	2012	...	...	|	|	2112	...	...	|	...	|	0015
København H ⊙ a.	...	...	...	...	...	|	|	▬	2214	...	...	|	|	|	...	...	...	|	|	...	...	...	|	...	|	...
Wolfsburg ... a.	...	...	...	...	...	|	|	*IC*	...	...	...	1902	1902	|	...	...	...	|	|	...	...	...	2302	...	2302	...
Braunschweig Hbf ... a.	...	...	...	...	...	|	1608	**2239**	...	...	...	|	|	1909	...	...	...	|	2008	...	...	...	|	...	|	...
Magdeburg Hbf ... a.	...	...	...	...	...	|	1657	1703	...	...	...	|	|	1955	...	...	...	|	2057	...	...	...	|	...	|	...
Halle ... a.	...	...	...	...	...	|	...	1753	...	...	...	|	|	2051	...	...	...	|	2153	...	...	...	|	...	|	...
Leipzig Hbf ... a.	...	...	...	...	...	|	...	1819	...	...	...	|	|	2118	...	...	...	|	2219	...	...	...	|	...	|	...
Berlin Hbf ... a.	...	...	...	...	...	1708	...	|	...	...	...	2007	2007	...	...	...	...	2108	|	...	...	...	0008	...	0008	...
Berlin Ostbahnhof ... a.	...	...	...	...	...	1719	...	|	...	...	...	2019	2019	...	...	...	...	2121	|	...	...	...	...	...	...	...
Dresden Hbf ... a.	...	...	...	...	...	...	...	1929	...	...	...	...	...	...	...	...	...	...	2329x	...	...	...	...	...	...	...
Bad Schandau 🛃 ... a.	...	...	...	...	...	...	...	...	...	...	...	...	...	...	...	...	...	...	...	...	...	...	...	...	...	...
Děčín ... a.	...	...	...	...	...	...	...	...	...	...	...	...	...	...	...	...	...	...	...	...	...	...	...	...	...	...
Praha Holešovice ... a.	...	...	...	...	...	...	...	...	...	...	...	...	...	...	...	...	...	...	...	...	...	...	...	...	...	...
Praha hlavní ... a.	...	...	...	...	...	...	...	...	...	...	...	...	...	...	...	...	...	...	...	...	...	...	...	...	...	...

B – (12) ✗ Chur - Basel - Köln - Dortmund - Hamburg. To Kiel on dates shown in Table **912**.

C – (12) 🍷 ⚡ Berlin - Hamburg - København (Table **50**).

D – (12) 🍷 ⚡ Hamburg - København (Table **50**).

H – ①②③④⑥ (also Oct. 4; not Oct. 2).

P – ⑤⑦ (Ⓑ Mar. 30 - Aug. 30) also Oct. 23, 27–30, Nov. 11.

S – Calls at Düsseldorf Flughafen ✈ arrives 0951.

j – Also Oct. 2; not Oct. 4.

m – Not Aug. 25, Nov. 11.

p – Not June 9, July 21, Aug. 15, 25, Nov. 10, 11.

q – Not July 13 - Aug. 30.

x – ⑥ only.

y – Also Aug. 25, Nov. 11.

⇌ – *Thalys* high-speed train. Ⓡ 🍷. Special fares payable. Valid June 1 - Aug. 30.

⚡ – Supplement payable.

⊙ – 🛃 between Hamburg and København is Rødby, see Table **720**.

☆ – Eurostar train. Ⓡ, ✗ in 1st class, 🍷 in 2nd class. Special fares payable. Minimum check-in time 30 minutes. Not available for London - Ebbsfleet - Ashford or v.v. journeys. Valid June 1 - Dec. 13.

For London - Esbjerg - København by rail and sea via Harwich, see Table 200, DFDS Seaways Table 2220 and Table 705

20 LONDON, PARIS and BRUSSELS - KÖLN, HAMBURG and BERLIN

For the full service London - Brussels and v.v. see Table **12**. For Paris - Brussels and v.v. see Table **18**. Connections at Brussels are not guaranteed.

train type	☆	⇌	*ICE*	*RE*	*ICE*	*IC*	*ICE*	*ICE*	☆	⇌	*RE*	*RE*	*ICE*	*ICE*	*CNL*	*CNL*	*IC*	*EC*	*IC*		☆	*CNL*	*CNL*	*ICE*	
train number	**9140**	**9365**	**19**	**10542**	**657**	**2318**	**1102**	**102**	**9144**	**9473**	**10534**	**10141**	**1522**	**512**	**457**	**40447**	**2020**	**31**	**2241**		**9036**	**451**	**50451**	**33**	
				10532																		**471**			
notes	⑧		🍷		🍷	🍷	🍷	🍷					🍷	🍷	🅁	🅁	🍷		①–⑥						
		W			⑦	⑧	⑥	⑧	⑥	**G**					**F**	**E b**		**T K**				**A**	**B**	**K**	
London St Pancras ..... d.	1504	...	...	...	...	...	...	...	1604	...	...	...	...	...	...	...	...	...	...	...	1531	...	...	...	...
Ebbsfleet International .. d.	|	...	...	...	...	...	...	...	|	...	...	...	...	...	...	...	...	...	...	...	|	...	...	...	...
Ashford International .... d.	|	...	...	...	...	...	...	...	|	...	...	...	...	...	...	...	...	...	...	...	|	...	...	...	...
Lille Europe .... d.	1730	...	...	...	...	...	...	...	1830	...	...	...	...	...	...	...	...	...	...	...	|	...	...	...	...
Paris Nord .... d.	|	1655	...	...	...	...	...	...	|	1758	...	...	...	...	...	...	...	...	...	...	1847	2005¶	2005¶	...	...
Brussels Midi/Zuid ...... a.	1805	1817	...	...	...	...	...	...	1905	1923	...	...	...	...	...	...	...	...	...	...	...	|	|	...	...
Brussels Midi/Zuid ...... d.	...	...	1825	...	...	...	...	...	...	1928	...	...	...	...	...	...	...	...	...	...	...	|	|	...	...
Brussels Nord .... d.	...	...	1833	...	...	...	...	...	...	|	...	...	...	...	...	...	...	...	...	...	...	|	|	...	...
Liège Guillemins .... a.	...	...	1912	...	...	...	...	...	...	2011	...	...	...	...	...	...	...	...	...	...	...	|	|	...	...
Liège Guillemins .... d.	...	...	1914	...	...	...	...	...	...	2014	...	...	...	...	...	...	...	...	...	...	...	|	|	...	...
Aachen ⊞ .... a.	...	...	1936	...	...	...	...	...	...	2036	...	...	...	...	...	...	...	...	...	...	...	|	|	...	...
Köln Hbf .... a.	...	...	2015	...	...	...	...	...	...	2115	...	...	...	...	...	...	...	...	...	...	...	|	|	...	...
Köln Hbf .... d.	...	...	...	2031	2048	2110	2110	2110	...	2120	2131	2149	2210	2210	2228	2228	0210	...	...	...	...	|	|	...	...
Wuppertal Hbf .... a.	...	...	...	|	2114	|	|	2141	...	|	|	|	2241	|	2314u	2314u	|	...	...	...	...	|	|	...	...
Hagen Hbf .... a.	...	...	...	|	2132	|	|	2159	...	|	|	|	2259	|	|	|	|	...	...	...	...	|	|	...	...
Düsseldorf Hbf .... a.	...	...	...	2101	|	2131	2131	|	...	2142	2201	2219	|	2231	|	|	0233	...	...	...	...	|	|	...	...
Duisburg Hbf .... a.	...	...	...	2118	|	2144	2144	|	...	2200	2218	2236	|	2244	|	|	0250	...	...	...	...	|	|	...	...
Oberhausen .... a.	...	...	...	2126	|	|	|	|	...	|	2226	|	|	|	|	|	|	...	...	...	...	|	|	...	...
Essen Hbf .... a.	...	...	...	...	|	2157	2157	|	...	2216	...	2250	|	2257	|	|	0306	...	...	...	...	|	|	...	...
Bochum Hbf .... a.	...	...	...	...	|	2208	2208	|	...	...	...	2303	|	|	|	|	0316	...	...	...	...	|	|	...	...
Dortmund Hbf .... a.	...	...	...	...	|	2221	2221	2221	...	...	...	2315	2321	|	2356u	2356u	0329	...	...	...	...	|	|	...	...
Hamm (Westf) .... a.	...	...	...	...	2202	|	2248	2248o	...	...	...	2345	...	|	0014u	0014u	|	...	...	...	...	|	|	...	...
Bielefeld Hbf .... a.	...	...	...	...	2236	|	2318	2318o	...	...	...	...	...	|	0043u	0043u	|	...	...	...	...	|	|	...	...
Münster .... a.	...	...	...	...	|	2254j	|	|	...	...	...	...	...	2358	|	|	0415	...	0538	...	...	|	|	...	...
Osnabrück Hbf .... a.	...	...	...	...	|	...	|	|	...	...	...	...	...	...	|	|	0446	...	0602	...	...	|	|	...	...
Bremen Hbf .... a.	...	...	...	...	|	...	|	|	...	...	...	...	...	...	|	|	0552	...	|	...	...	|	|	...	...
Hannover Hbf .... a.	...	...	...	...	2328	...	0018	0018o	...	...	...	...	...	...	0240u	|	|	...	0718	...	...	0630v	0630s	...	...
Hamburg Hbf .... a.	...	...	...	...	|	...	...	...	...	...	...	...	...	...	|	0356s	0651	0725	|	...	...	|	0836n	0928	...
København H ⊙ .. a.	...	...	...	...	|	...	...	...	...	...	...	...	...	...	|	1007	...	1214	|	...	...	|	...	1414	...
Wolfsburg .... a.	...	...	...	...	0002	...	...	...	...	...	...	...	...	...	|	...	...	...	0753	...	...	|	...	...	...
Braunschweig Hbf .... a.	...	...	...	...	|	...	...	...	...	...	...	...	...	...	|	...	...	...	|	...	...	|	...	...	...
Magdeburg Hbf .... a.	...	...	...	...	|	...	...	...	...	...	...	...	...	...	|	...	...	...	|	...	...	|	...	...	...
Halle Hbf .... a.	...	...	...	...	|	...	...	...	...	...	...	...	...	...	|	...	...	...	|	...	...	|	...	...	...
Leipzig Hbf .... a.	...	...	...	...	|	...	...	...	...	...	...	...	...	...	|	...	...	...	|	...	...	|	...	...	...
Berlin Hbf .... a.	...	...	...	...	0110	...	...	...	...	...	...	...	...	...	0426	...	...	...	0921	...	...	0828v	...	...	...
Berlin Ostbahnhof .... a.	...	...	...	...	0121	...	...	...	...	...	...	...	...	...	0435	...	...	...	0932	...	...	...	...	...	...
Dresden Hbf .... a.	...	...	...	...	...	...	...	...	...	...	...	...	...	...	0658	...	...	...	...	...	...	...	...	...	...
Bad Schandau ⊞ ..... a.	...	...	...	...	...	...	...	...	...	...	...	...	...	...	0736	...	...	...	...	...	...	...	...	...	...
Děčín .... a.	...	...	...	...	...	...	...	...	...	...	...	...	...	...	0753	...	...	...	...	...	...	...	...	...	...
Praha Holešovice ..... a.	...	...	...	...	...	...	...	...	...	...	...	...	...	...	0916	...	...	...	...	...	...	...	...	...	...
Praha hlavní .... a.	...	...	...	...	...	...	...	...	...	...	...	...	...	...	0926	...	...	...	...	...	...	...	...	...	...

train type		*CNL*	*CNL*	☆		*ICE*	*EC*	*IC*	*CNL*	*CNL*	*RE*	⇌		*ICE*	*IC*	*RE*	*RE*	*ICE*	⇌	☆	☆				
train number		**40479**	**450**	**9023**		**32**	**30**	**2021**	**40473**	**456**	**10503**	**9412**		**101**	**2319**	**10106**	**10505**	**18**	**9322**	**9125**	**9129**				
		491	**470**													**10104**			**9422**						
notes								🍷	🅁	🅁	①–⑤			🍷	①–⑥			🍷		①–⑥	⑦				
		C	**D**			**K**	**S K**		**E k**	**F**	**h**									**p**	**y**				
Praha hlavní .... d.	...	...	...	...	...	...	...	...	...	1829	...	...	...	...	...	...	...	...	...	...	...	...	...	...	...
Praha Holešovice ..... d.	...	...	...	...	...	...	...	...	...	1839	...	...	...	...	...	...	...	...	...	...	...	...	...	...	...
Děčín .... d.	...	...	...	...	...	...	...	...	...	2000	...	...	...	...	...	...	...	...	...	...	...	...	...	...	...
Bad Schandau ⊞ ..... d.	...	...	...	...	...	...	...	...	...	2017	...	...	...	...	...	...	...	...	...	...	...	...	...	...	...
Dresden Hbf .... d.	...	...	...	...	...	...	...	...	...	2053	...	...	...	...	...	...	...	...	...	...	...	...	...	...	...
Berlin Ostbahnhof .... d.	...	...	...	...	...	...	...	...	...	0022	...	...	...	...	...	...	...	...	...	...	...	...	...	...	...
Berlin Hbf .... d.	...	...	2007	...	...	...	...	...	...	0032	...	...	...	...	...	...	...	...	...	...	...	...	...	...	...
Leipzig Hbf .... d.	...	...	|	...	...	...	...	...	...	|	...	...	...	...	...	...	...	...	...	...	...	...	...	...	...
Halle Hbf .... d.	...	...	|	...	...	...	...	...	...	|	...	...	...	...	...	...	...	...	...	...	...	...	...	...	...
Magdeburg Hbf .... d.	...	...	|	...	...	...	...	...	...	|	...	...	...	...	...	...	...	...	...	...	...	...	...	...	...
Braunschweig Hbf .... d.	...	...	|	...	...	...	...	...	...	|	...	...	...	...	...	...	...	...	...	...	...	...	...	...	...
Wolfsburg .... d.	...	...	|	...	...	...	...	...	...	|	...	...	...	...	...	...	...	...	...	...	...	...	...	...	...
København H ⊙ .. d.	...	...	|	...	...	1525	1742	...	1846	|	...	...	...	...	...	...	...	...	...	...	...	...	...	...	...
Hamburg Hbf .... d.	...	2034	|	...	...	2016	2216	2246	0031	|	...	...	...	...	...	...	...	...	...	...	...	...	...	...	...
Hannover Hbf .... d.	...	2216	2216	...	...	...	...	|	|	|	...	...	...	...	...	...	...	...	...	...	...	...	...	...	...
Bremen Hbf .... d.	...	|	|	...	...	...	...	2344	|	|	...	...	...	...	...	...	...	...	...	...	...	...	...	...	...
Osnabrück Hbf .... d.	...	|	|	...	...	...	...	0045	|	|	...	...	...	...	...	...	...	...	...	...	...	...	...	...	...
Münster .... d.	...	|	|	...	...	...	...	0113	|	|	...	...	...	...	0503c	...	...	...	...	...	...	...	...	...	...
Bielefeld Hbf .... d.	...	|	|	...	...	...	...	|	0355s	0355s	...	...	...	...	|	...	...	...	...	...	...	...	...	...	...
Hamm (Westf) .... d.	...	|	|	...	...	...	...	0133	0425s	0425s	...	...	...	...	|	0515	...	...	...	...	...	...	...	...	...
Dortmund Hbf .... d.	...	|	|	...	...	...	...	0152	0447s	0447s	...	...	...	0537	0537	0545	...	...	...	...	...	...	...	...	...
Bochum Hbf .... d.	...	|	|	...	...	...	...	0203	|	|	...	...	...	|	0549	0556	...	...	...	...	...	...	...	...	...
Essen Hbf .... d.	...	|	|	...	...	...	...	0215	|	|	...	0540	...	|	0600	0609	...	...	...	...	...	...	...	...	...
Oberhausen .... d.	...	|	|	...	...	...	...	|	|	|	0534	|	...	|	|	|	0634	...	...	...	...	...	...	...	...
Duisburg Hbf .... d.	...	|	|	...	...	...	...	0229	|	|	0542	0554	...	|	0612	0623	0642	...	...	...	...	...	...	...	...
Düsseldorf Hbf .... d.	...	|	|	...	...	...	...	0247	|	|	0558	0613	...	|	0627	0640	0658	...	...	...	...	...	...	...	...
Hagen Hbf .... d.	...	|	|	...	...	...	...	|	|	|	|	|	...	0557	|	|	|	...	...	...	...	...	...	...	...
Wuppertal Hbf .... d.	...	|	|	...	...	...	...	|	0538s	0538s	|	|	...	0614	|	|	|	...	...	...	...	...	...	...	...
Köln Hbf .... a.	...	|	|	...	...	...	...	0309	0614	0614	0629	0636	...	0646	0650	0712	0729	...	...	...	...	...	...	...	...
Köln Hbf .... d.	...	|	|	...	...	...	...	...	...	...	...	0645	...	...	...	...	...	0743	...	...	...	...	...	...	...
Aachen ⊞ .... d.	...	|	|	...	...	...	...	...	...	...	...	0724	...	...	...	...	...	0821	...	...	...	...	...	...	...
Liège Guillemins .... a.	...	|	|	...	...	...	...	...	...	...	...	0748	...	...	...	...	...	0844	...	...	...	...	...	...	...
Liège Guillemins .... d.	...	|	|	...	...	...	...	...	...	...	...	0751	...	...	...	...	...	0846	...	...	...	...	...	...	...
Brussels Nord .... a.	...	|	|	...	...	...	...	...	...	...	...	|	...	...	...	...	...	0927	...	...	...	...	...	...	...
Brussels Midi/Zuid ...... a.	...	|	|	...	...	...	...	...	...	...	...	0832	...	...	...	...	...	0935	...	...	...	...	...	...	...
Brussels Midi/Zuid ...... d.	...	|	|	...	...	...	...	...	...	...	...	0837	...	...	...	...	...	...	1013	1056	1156	...	...	...	...
Paris Nord .... a.	...	0924‡	0924‡	1113	...	...	...	...	...	...	...	0959	...	...	...	...	...	...	1135	|	|	...	...	...	...
Lille Europe .... a.	...	...	...	|	...	...	...	...	...	...	...	...	...	...	...	...	...	...	...	1130	1230	...	...	...	...
Ashford International .... a.	...	...	...	|	...	...	...	...	...	...	...	...	...	...	...	...	...	...	...	|	|	...	...	...	...
Ebbsfleet International. . a.	...	...	...	|	...	...	...	...	...	...	...	...	...	...	...	...	...	...	...	|	|	...	...	...	...
London St Pancras ..... a.	...	...	...	1230	...	...	...	...	...	...	...	...	...	...	...	...	...	...	...	1157	1257	...	...	...	...

NOTES FOR THIS PAGE AND THE FOLLOWING PAGE

A – *City Night Line* PERSEUS – 🛏 1, 2 cl., ▬ 2 cl. (including ladies only berths), (2) (reclining), 🍷 Paris - Metz (depart 2353) - Forbach ⊞ - Saarbrücken (0058) - Göttingen (arrive 0611) - Hannover - Berlin Spandau (arrive 0851) - Berlin Hbf - Berlin Südkreuz (0909). 🅁 Special fares apply.

B – *City Night Line* ANDROMEDA 🛏 1, 2 cl., ▬ 2 cl. (including ladies only berths), 🍷 Paris - Forbach ⊞ - Saarbrücken (0058) - Göttingen (arrive 0611) - Hannover - Hamburg Hbf - Hamburg Altona (0850) 🅁 Special fares apply.

C – *City Night Line* ANDROMEDA 🛏 1, 2 cl., ▬ 2 cl. (including ladies only berths), 🍷 Hamburg Altona (depart 2013) - Hamburg Hbf - Hannover - Göttingen (2333) - Saarbrücken (arrive 0456) - Forbach ⊞ - Paris. 🅁 Special fares apply.

D – *City Night Line* PERSEUS – 🛏 1, 2 cl., ▬ 2 cl. (including ladies only berths), (2) (reclining), 🍷 Berlin Südkreuz (depart 1944) - Berlin Hbf - Berlin Spandau (2007) - Hannover - Göttingen (2331) - Saarbrücken (arrive 0520) - Forbach ⊞ - Metz (0615) - Paris. 🅁 Special fares apply.

E – *City Night Line* BOREALIS – 🛏 1, 2 cl., ▬ 2 cl., (2) (reclining), 🍷 🅁 Amsterdam - Köln - København and v.v. Special fares apply.

F – *City Night Line* KOPERNIKUS / PHOENIX – 🛏 1, 2 cl., ▬ 2 cl., (2) (reclining), 🍷 Amsterdam - Köln - Berlin - Dresden - Praha and v.v. 🅁 Special fares apply.

G – Calls at Düsseldorf Flughafen ✈ arrives 2150.

H – Calls at Düsseldorf Flughafen ✈ departs 0604.

J – (12) 🍷 ⚡ København - Hamburg - Berlin.

K – (12) 🍷 ⚡ Hamburg - København and v.v.

P – ⑤⑦ (⑧ Mar. 30 - Aug. 30) also Oct. 23, 27–30, Nov. 11

S – May 18 - Oct. 26.

T – May 18 - Oct. 27.

NOTES CONTINUED ON NEXT PAGE →

For London - Esbjerg - København and v.v. by rail and sea via Harwich, see Table 200, DFDS Seaways Table 2220 and Table 705

BERLIN, HAMBURG and KÖLN - BRUSSELS, PARIS and LONDON 20

For the full service Brussels - London and v.v. see Table **12**. For Brussels - Paris and v.v. see Table **18**. Connections at Brussels are not guaranteed.

train type	*ICE*	*RE*	*EC*	⇌	☆	*EC*	*IC*	*IC*	*ICE*	*ICE*	⇌	*IC*	*IC*	*ICE*	*IC*	⇌	*IC*	*IC*	*ICE*	*RE*	*RE*	*ICE*	⇌	☆	☆	☆
train number	**1521**	**10110**	**115**	**9424**	**9129**	**9**	**2013**	**2434**	**654**	**16**	**9448**	**2023**	**2044**	**954**	**1936**	**9448**	**2217**	**2430**	**650**	**10126**	**10521**	**14**	**9368**	**9157**	**9161**	**9161**
notes	✕	**10108**	🍷	🍷	⑦ y	🍷	🍷			🍷	🍷	**1023** 🍷	①–⑥	①–⑥	🍷	🍷	🍷	🍷	✕			🍷	Ⓑ x 🍷	Ⓑ	Ⓑ	⑥
Praha hlavní d.	...	...	...	...	...	...	...	...	...	...	...	...	...	...	...	...	...	...	...	...	...	...	...	...	...	...
Praha Holešovice d.	...	...	...	...	...	...	...	...	...	...	...	...	...	...	...	...	...	...	...	...	...	...	...	...	...	...
Děčín d.	...	...	...	...	...	...	...	...	...	...	...	...	...	...	...	...	...	...	...	...	...	...	...	...	...	...
Bad Schandau 🛃 d.	...	...	...	...	...	...	...	...	...	...	...	...	...	...	...	...	...	...	...	...	...	...	...	...	...	...
Dresden Hbf d.	...	...	...	...	...	...	...	...	...	...	...	...	...	...	...	...	...	0823	...	...	...	...	...	...	...	...
Berlin Ostbahnhof d.	...	...	...	...	...	...	...	...	0638	...	...	...	...	0736	...	...	...	|	1038	...	...	...	...	...	...	...
Berlin Hauptbahnhof d.	...	...	...	...	...	...	...	...	0649	...	...	...	...	0747	...	...	...	|	1049	...	...	...	...	...	...	...
Leipzig Hbf d.	...	...	...	...	...	...	...	0540f	|	...	...	...	0640	|	...	...	...	0940	|	...	...	...	...	...	...	...
Halle Hbf d.	...	...	...	...	...	...	...	0607f	|	...	...	...	0707	|	...	...	...	1007	|	...	...	...	...	...	...	...
Magdeburg Hbf d.	...	...	...	...	...	...	0601f	0700	|	...	...	...	0802	|	...	...	...	1100	|	...	...	...	...	...	...	...
Braunschweig Hbf d.	...	...	...	...	...	...	0651f	0751	|	...	...	...	0851	|	...	...	...	1151	|	...	...	...	...	...	...	...
Wolfsburg d.	...	...	...	...	...	...	|	|	|	...	...	...	|	0856	...	...	...	|	|	...	...	...	...	...	...	...
København H ⊙ d.	...	...	...	...	...	...	|	|	|	...	...	...	|	|	...	...	...	|	|	...	...	...	...	...	...	...
Hamburg Hbf d.	...	...	...	...	...	0646	|	|	|	...	...	0746	|	|	...	...	1046	|	|	...	...	...	...	...	...	...
Hannover Hbf d.	...	...	...	...	...	|	0740	0823	0831	...	...	|	0923	0931	...	...	|	1223	1231	...	...	...	...	...	...	...
Bremen Hbf d.	...	...	...	...	...	0744	|	▬	|	...	...	0844	▬	|	...	...	1144	...	|	...	...	...	...	...	...	...
Osnabrück Hbf d.	...	...	...	...	...	0837	|	...	|	...	...	0937	...	|	...	...	1237	...	|	...	...	...	...	...	...	...
Münster d.	...	...	0631	...	...	0904	|	...	|	...	...	1003	*ICE*	|	1032	...	1303	...	|	...	...	...	...	...	...	...
Bielefeld Hbf d.	...	...	|	...	...	|	0842	...	0922	...	...	|	**517**	1022	|	...	|	...	1322	...	...	...	...	...	...	...
Hamm (Westf) d.	...	0615	|	...	...	|	0914	...	0954	...	...	|	✕	1054	|	...	|	...	1354	1322	...	...	...	...	...	...
Dortmund Hbf d.	0636	0645	|	...	...	0937	0952	...	|	...	...	1036	1037	|	|	...	1337	...	|	1345	...	...	...	...	...	...
Bochum Hbf d.	|	0656	|	...	...	0949	1003	*RE*	|	...	...	|	1049	|	|	...	1349	...	|	1356	...	...	...	...	...	...
Essen Hbf d.	|	0709	|	...	...	1000	1014	**10513**	|	...	...	|	1100	|	|	1125	1400	...	|	1409	...	...	...	...	...	...
Oberhausen d.	|	|	0727	...	...	|	|	1034	|	...	...	|	|	|	1127	|	|	...	|	|	1434	...	...	...	...	...
Duisburg Hbf d.	|	0723	0735	...	...	1012	1030	1042	|	...	...	|	1112	|	1136	1138	1412	...	|	1423	1442	...	...	...	...	...
Düsseldorf Hbf d.	|	0740	0751	...	...	1027	1050	1058	|	...	...	|	1127	|	1149	1154	1428	...	|	1440	1458	...	...	...	...	...
Hagen Hbf d.	0657	|	|	...	...	|	|	|	1024	...	...	1057	|	1124	|	|	|	...	1424	|	|	...	...	...	...	...
Wuppertal Hbf d.	0714	|	|	...	...	|	|	|	1041	...	...	1114	|	1141	|	|	|	...	1441	|	|	...	...	...	...	...
Köln Hbf a.	0746	0812	0815	...	...	1050	1115	1129	1109	...	...	1146	1149	1209	1212	1229	1450	...	1509	1512	1529	...	...	...	...	...
Köln Hbf d.	...	...	...	0845	...	▬	...	...	...	1143	...	▬	▬	...	...	1245	▬	...	...	...	...	1543	...	...	...	...
Aachen 🛃 d.	...	...	...	0924	...	...	...	...	...	1221	...	...	...	...	...	1324	...	...	...	...	...	1621	...	...	...	...
Liège Guillemins a.	...	...	...	0946	...	...	...	...	...	1244	...	☆	☆	...	...	1346	...	...	...	...	...	1644	...	...	...	...
Liège Guillemins d.	...	...	...	0949	...	☆	...	...	...	1246	...	**9141**	**9141**	...	...	1349	☆	...	...	...	...	1646	...	...	...	...
Brussels Nord a.	...	...	...	|	...	**9133**	...	...	...	1327	...	⑥⑦	①–⑤	...	...	|	**9145**	...	...	...	...	1727	...	...	...	...
Brussels Midi/Zuid a.	...	...	...	1032	...	①–⑤	...	...	...	1335	...	**y**	**q**	...	...	1432	**P**	...	...	...	...	1735	...	...	...	...
Brussels Midi/Zuid d.	...	...	...	1037	1156	1252	...	...	...	...	1437	1452	1456	...	...	1437	1556	...	...	...	...	...	1737	1856	1952	1952
Paris Nord a.	...	...	...	1159	|	|	...	...	...	...	1559	|	|	...	...	1559	|	...	...	...	...	...	1859	|	|	|
Lille Europe a.	...	...	...	...	1230	1326	...	...	...	...	...	1526	1532	...	...	...	1630	...	...	...	...	...	...	1930	2026	2026
Ashford International a.	...	...	...	...	|	|	...	...	...	...	...	|	|	...	...	...	|	...	...	...	...	...	...	|	|	2035
Ebbsfleet International a.	...	...	...	...	|	1345	...	...	...	...	...	1545	1545	...	...	...	|	...	...	...	...	...	...	|	2045	|
London St Pancras a.	...	...	...	...	1257	1403	...	...	...	...	...	1603	1603	...	...	...	1657	...	...	...	...	...	...	1957	2103	2109

train type	*IC*	*IC*	*EC*	*ICE*	*IC*	⇌	☆	☆	*ICE*	*IC*	*ICE*	*IC*	*EC*	*ICE*	*IC*	⇌	*ICE*	*IC*	*RE*	*ICE*	*IC*	*ICE*	*RE*	*ICE*	⇌	
train number	**2327**	**2048**	**178**	**950**	**132**	**9472**	**9161**	**9161**	**38**	**2311**	**1129**	**2440**	**176**	**858**	**130**	**9484**	**36**	**2213**	**10134**	**1558**	**2036**	**556**	**10529**	**10**	**9394**	
notes	**2027** 🍷	🍷	✕		**2019** 🍷	🍷	Ⓑ	⑥	**J**	🍷	🍷	🍷	✕	✕	🍷	🍷	**K**	🍷		🍷	🍷	✕		🍷	⑦ z	
Praha hlavní d.	...	...	0629	...	...	...	...	...	...	...	...	...	0829	...	...	...	...	...	...	...	...	...	...	...	...	...
Praha Holešovice d.	...	...	0639	...	...	...	...	...	...	...	...	...	0839	...	...	...	...	...	...	...	...	...	...	...	...	...
Děčín d.	...	...	0800	...	...	...	...	...	...	...	...	...	1000	...	...	...	...	...	...	...	...	...	...	...	...	...
Bad Schandau 🛃 d.	...	...	0817	...	...	...	...	...	...	...	...	...	1017	...	...	...	...	...	...	...	...	...	...	...	...	...
Dresden Hbf d.	...	...	0904	...	...	...	...	...	...	...	...	...	1104	...	...	...	...	...	...	1153	...	...	...	...	...	...
Berlin Ostbahnhof d.	...	...	|	1136	...	...	...	...	...	...	...	...	|	1336	...	...	...	...	...	|	...	1438	...	...	...	...
Berlin Hauptbahnhof d.	...	...	1114	1147	...	...	...	...	...	...	...	...	1315	1347	...	...	...	...	...	|	...	1449	...	...	...	...
Leipzig Hbf d.	...	1040	...	|	...	...	...	...	...	...	...	1240	...	|	...	...	...	...	...	1307	1340	|	...	...	...	...
Halle Hbf d.	...	1107	...	|	...	...	...	...	...	...	...	1307	...	|	...	...	...	...	...	...	1407	|	...	...	...	...
Magdeburg Hbf d.	...	1202	...	|	...	...	...	...	...	...	...	1402	...	|	...	...	...	...	...	...	1500	|	...	...	...	...
Braunschweig Hbf d.	...	1251	...	|	...	...	...	...	...	...	...	1451	...	|	...	...	...	...	...	...	1551	|	...	...	...	...
Wolfsburg d.	...	|	...	1256	...	...	...	...	...	...	...	|	...	1456	...	...	...	...	...	...	|	|	...	...	...	...
København H ⊙ d.	...	|	...	|	...	...	...	...	0742	...	...	|	...	|	...	...	0942	...	...	...	|	|	...	...	...	...
Hamburg Hbf d.	1146	|	...	|	...	...	...	...	1216	1246	1346	|	...	|	...	...	1416	1446	...	...	|	|	...	...	...	...
Hannover Hbf d.	|	1323	...	1331	...	...	...	...	...	|	|	1523	...	1531	...	...	...	|	...	...	1623	1631	...	...	...	...
Bremen Hbf d.	1244	...	...	|	...	...	...	...	...	1344	1444	...	...	|	...	...	...	1544	...	...	...	|	...	...	...	...
Osnabrück Hbf d.	1337	...	...	|	...	...	...	...	...	1437	1537	...	...	|	...	...	...	1637	...	...	...	|	...	...	...	...
Münster d.	1403	...	...	|	1431	...	...	...	...	1503	1602	...	...	|	1631	...	...	1703	...	...	...	|	...	...	...	...
Bielefeld Hbf d.	|	...	...	1422	|	...	...	...	...	|	|	...	...	1622	|	...	...	|	...	...	...	1722	...	...	...	...
Hamm (Westf) d.	|	...	...	1454	|	...	...	...	...	|	|	...	...	1654	|	...	...	|	1722	...	...	1754	...	...	...	...
Dortmund Hbf d.	1436	...	...	|	|	...	...	...	...	1537	1636	...	...	|	|	...	...	1737	1745	...	...	|	...	...	...	...
Bochum Hbf d.	|	...	...	|	|	...	...	...	...	1549	|	...	...	|	|	...	...	1749	1756	...	...	|	...	...	...	...
Essen Hbf d.	|	...	...	|	|	...	...	...	...	1600	|	...	...	|	|	1704	...	1800	1809	...	...	|	...	...	...	...
Oberhausen d.	|	...	...	|	1527	...	...	...	...	|	|	...	...	|	1727	|	...	|	|	...	...	|	1834	...	...	...
Duisburg Hbf d.	|	...	...	|	1536	...	...	...	...	1612	|	...	...	|	1736	|	...	1812	1823	...	...	|	1842	...	...	...
Düsseldorf Hbf d.	|	...	...	|	1549	...	...	...	...	1627	|	...	...	|	1749	1731	...	1827	1840	...	...	|	1858	...	...	...
Hagen Hbf d.	1457	...	...	1524	|	...	...	...	...	|	1657	...	...	1724	|	|	...	|	|	...	...	1824	|	...	...	...
Wuppertal Hbf d.	1514	...	...	1541	|	...	...	...	...	|	1714	...	...	1741	|	|	...	|	|	...	...	1841	|	...	...	...
Köln Hbf a.	1546	...	...	1609	1612	...	...	...	...	1650	1746	...	...	1809	1812	1829	...	1850	1912	...	...	1909	1929	...	...	...
Köln Hbf d.	...	...	...	...	...	1643	...	...	...	...	...	...	...	...	...	1843	...	...	...	...	...	...	...	1943	...	...
Aachen 🛃 d.	...	...	...	...	...	1724	...	...	...	...	...	...	...	...	...	1924	...	...	...	...	...	...	...	2021	...	...
Liège Guillemins a.	...	...	...	...	...	1746	...	...	...	...	...	...	...	...	...	1946	...	...	...	...	...	...	...	2044	...	...
Liège Guillemins d.	...	...	...	...	...	1749	...	...	...	...	...	...	...	...	...	1949	...	...	...	...	...	...	...	2046	...	...
Brussels Nord a.	...	...	...	...	...	|	...	...	...	...	...	...	...	...	...	|	...	...	...	...	...	...	...	2127	...	...
Brussels Midi/Zuid a.	...	...	...	...	...	1832	...	...	...	...	...	...	...	...	...	2032	...	...	...	...	...	...	...	2135	...	...
Brussels Midi/Zuid d.	...	...	...	...	...	1837	1952	1952	...	...	...	...	...	...	...	2037	...	...	...	...	...	...	...	...	2213	...
Paris Nord a.	...	...	...	...	...	1959	|	|	...	...	...	...	...	...	...	2159	...	...	...	...	...	...	...	...	2335	...
Lille Europe a.	...	...	...	...	...	...	2026	2026	...	...	...	...	...	...	...	...	...	...	...	...	...	...	...	...	...	...
Ashford International a.	...	...	...	...	...	...	|	2035	...	...	...	...	...	...	...	...	...	...	...	...	...	...	...	...	...	...
Ebbsfleet International a.	...	...	...	...	...	...	2045	|	...	...	...	...	...	...	...	...	...	...	...	...	...	...	...	...	...	...
London St Pancras a.	...	...	...	...	...	...	2103	2109	...	...	...	...	...	...	...	...	...	...	...	...	...	...	...	...	...	...

← NOTES CONTINUED FROM PREVIOUS PAGE

W – ②③④⑤⑦ (daily Apr. 6 - July 12; not June 8; ①–⑥ July 13 - Aug. 30; not July 14, 21).
J – Via Flensburg (0553**s**), Padborg (0607**s**) and Odense (0817**s**).
[illegible] – ① only.
[illegible] – ①–⑥.
g – Not Aug. 26.
h – Not Oct. 3.
[illegible] – ⑦ only.
K – Via Odense (2028**u**), Padborg (2224**u**) and Flensburg (2238**u**).
[illegible] – Arrive Hamburg 0821, 0833, 0835, 0844, 0845 on certain dates.

o – ①–⑤.
p – Not Nov. 11.
q – Not Aug. 25, Nov. 11.
s – Calls to set down only.
u – Calls to pick up only.
v – Arrives Hannover 0702, Berlin Hbf 0857 on certain dates.
x – Not July 13 - Aug. 30.
y – Also Aug. 25, Nov. 11.

z – Also June 9, July 14, 21.
¶ – Paris **Est**. Depart 2025 on ⑥⑦.
‡ – Paris **Est**. Arrive 1101 on July 16 - 19.
☆ – Eurostar train. Ⓡ, ✕ in 1st class, 🍷 in 2nd class. Special fares payable. Minimum check-in time 30 minutes. Not available for London - Ebbsfleet - Ashford or v.v. journeys. Valid June 1 - Dec. 13.
⇌ – *Thalys* high-speed train. Ⓡ 🍷. Special fares payable. Valid Dec. 15 - July 12.
⊙ – 🛃 between Hamburg and København is Rødby (Table **720**).

For København - Esbjerg - London by rail and sea via Harwich, see Table 705, DFDS Seaways Table 2220 and Table 200

21 LONDON and BRUSSELS - FRANKFURT, WIEN and MÜNCHEN

train type	ICE	ICE	ICE	EC	ICE	RJ	🚌	ALX	ICE	⇌	ICE	IC	ICE	ICE	IC	RJ	EC	IC	ICE	EN	🚌	⇌	ICE	ICE	IC	
train number	**11**	**11**	**529**	**89**	**91**	**67**	**42010**	**355**	**593**	**9401**	**621**	**115**	**27**	**515**	**1281**	**69**	**83**	**119**	**27**	**347**	**42014**	**9413**	**625**	**517**	**2023**	
notes	①-⑤	⑥⑦	🍷	✕	🍷	🍷	[R]		**1091**		**1121**	✕	🍷	🍷		🍷	🍷	🍷	🍷	🍷★	[R]		**825**	🍷	**1023**	
	j	y			R		🍷	J	🍷	w			S		G			C	S	A	🍷		🍷		🍷	
London St Pancras ... d.	...	...	...	...	...	...	...	...	...	...	...	...	...	...	...	...	...	...	...	...	...	...	...	...	...	...
Ebbsfleet International d.	...	...	...	...	...	...	...	...	...	...	...	...	...	...	...	...	...	...	...	...	...	...	...	...	...	...
Ashford International .. d.	...	...	...	...	...	...	...	...	...	...	...	...	...	...	...	...	...	...	...	...	...	...	...	...	...	...
Lille Europe ... d.	...	...	...	...	...	...	...	...	...	...	...	...	...	...	...	...	...	...	...	...	...	...	...	...	...	...
Paris Nord ... d.	...	...	...	...	...	...	...	...	...	0601	...	...	...	...	...	...	...	...	...	...	...	0801	...	...	...	...
Brussels Midi / Zuid ... a.	...	...	...	...	...	...	...	...	...	0723	...	...	...	...	...	...	...	...	...	...	...	0923	...	...	...	...
Brussels Midi / Zuid ... d.	0625	0625	...	...	...	...	...	...	...	0728	...	...	...	...	...	...	...	...	...	...	...	0928	...	...	...	...
Brussels Nord ... d.	0633	0633	...	...	...	...	...	...	...	|	...	...	...	...	...	...	...	...	...	...	...	|	...	...	...	...
Liège Guillemins ... a.	0712	0712	...	...	...	...	...	...	...	0811	...	...	...	...	...	...	...	...	...	...	...	1011	...	...	...	...
Liège Guillemins ... d.	0714	0714	...	...	...	...	...	...	...	0814	...	...	...	...	...	...	...	...	...	...	...	1014	...	...	...	...
Aachen Hbf ⊞ ... a.	0736	0736	...	...	...	...	...	...	...	0836	...	...	...	...	...	...	...	...	...	...	...	1036	...	...	...	...
Köln Hbf ... a.	0815	0815	...	...	...	...	...	...	...	0915	...	...	...	...	...	...	...	...	...	...	...	1115	...	...	...	...
Köln Hbf ... d.	0820	0820	...	...	...	...	...	...	...	...	0937e	...	0953	0955	...	...	...	...	...	...	...	...	1144x	1155	1153	...
Bonn Hbf ... a.	|	|	...	...	...	...	...	...	...	...	|	...	1012	|	...	...	...	...	...	...	...	...	|	|	1212	...
Koblenz Hbf ... a.	⊖	⊖	...	...	...	...	...	...	...	...	⊖	...	1046	⊖	...	...	...	...	←	...	...	...	⊖	⊖	1246	...
Mainz Hbf ... a.	|	|	...	...	...	...	...	...	...	...	|	...	1137	|	...	...	...	...	1139	...	...	...	|	|	1337	...
Frankfurt Flughafen ✈ a.	0910	0926	...	...	...	...	...	...	...	...	1026c	...	→	1050	...	...	...	...	1159	...	...	...	1234	1250	1359	...
Frankfurt (Main) Hbf . a.	0924	0941	0954	...	...	...	...	...	0950	...	1041c	...	...	|	...	...	...	...	1213	...	...	...	1248	|	1412	...
Würzburg Hbf ... a.	...	...	1102	...	...	...	...	...	|	...	1202	...	...	|	...	...	...	...	1331	...	...	...	1402	|	▬	...
Nürnberg Hbf ... a.	...	...	1159	...	1230	...	1245	...	|	...	1259	...	...	|	...	...	...	...	1427	...	1445	...	1459	|	...	...
Regensburg Hbf ... a.	...	...	|	...	1325	...	|	1421	|	...	|	...	...	|	...	...	...	...	1525	...	|	...	|	|	...	...
Praha hlavní ... a.	...	...	|	...	|	...	1622	1844	|	...	|	...	...	|	...	...	...	...	|	...	1822	...	|	|	...	...
Mannheim Hbf ... a.	...	...	|	...	|	...	...	...	1027	...	|	...	...	1123	...	...	...	1154	|	...	...	...	|	1323	...	...
Stuttgart Hbf ... a.	...	...	|	...	|	...	...	...	1108	...	|	...	...	1208	...	...	...	1246	|	...	...	...	|	1408	*EC*	...
Ulm Hbf ... a.	...	...	|	...	|	...	...	...	1207	...	|	...	...	1307	...	...	...	1401	|	...	...	...	|	1507	**189**	...
Augsburg Hbf ... a.	...	...	|	...	|	...	...	...	1253	...	|	...	...	1353	...	...	...	|	|	...	...	...	|	1553	✕	...
München Hbf ... a.	...	...	1312	1338	|	1327	...	...	1327	...	1412	1427	...	1427	1519	1527	1538	|	|	...	...	...	1613	1627	1738	...
Salzburg ... a.	...	...	...	|	|	1457	...	...	...	...	...	1609	...	...	|	1702	|	|	|	...	...	...	...	...	|	...
Kufstein ⊞ ... a.	...	...	...	1439	|	|	...	...	...	...	...	|	...	...	1622	|	1639	◧	|	...	...	...	...	...	1839	...
Wörgl ... a.	...	...	...	1449	|	|	...	...	...	...	...	|	...	...	1635	|	1649	|	|	...	...	...	...	...	1849	...
Kitzbühel ... a.	...	...	...	|	|	|	...	...	...	...	...	|	...	...	1728	|	|	|	|	...	...	...	...	...	|	...
Zell am See ... a.	...	...	...	|	|	|	...	...	...	...	...	|	...	...	1824	|	|	|	|	...	...	...	...	...	|	...
Schwarzach St Veit ... a.	...	...	...	|	|	|	...	...	...	...	...	1709	...	...	1854	|	|	|	|	...	...	...	...	...	|	...
Innsbruck Hbf ... a.	...	...	...	1523	|	|	...	...	...	...	...	|	...	...	...	|	1723	1902	|	...	...	...	...	...	1923	...
Bad Gastein ... a.	...	...	...	...	|	|	...	...	...	...	...	1741	...	...	...	|	...	...	|	...	...	...	...	...	...	...
Villach ... a.	...	...	...	...	|	|	...	...	...	...	...	1843	...	...	...	|	...	...	|	...	...	...	...	...	...	...
Klagenfurt ... a.	...	...	...	...	|	|	...	...	...	...	...	1915	...	...	...	|	...	...	|	...	...	...	...	...	...	...
Passau ⊞ ... a.	...	...	...	...	1433	|	...	...	...	...	...	...	...	...	...	|	...	...	1633	...	...	...	...	...	...	...
Linz ... a.	...	...	...	...	1542	1606	...	...	...	...	...	...	...	...	...	1806	...	...	1742	...	...	...	...	...	...	...
Wien Westbahnhof . a.	...	...	...	...	1704	1724	...	...	...	...	...	...	...	...	...	1924	...	...	1904	1948	...	...	...	...	...	...
Budapest Keleti ▲ .. a.	...	...	...	...	...	2049	...	...	...	...	...	...	...	...	...	...	...	...	...	2249	...	...	...	...	...	...

train type / number	⇌	☆	⇌	ICE	ICE	EC	ICE	ICE	🚌	ALX	EC	EC	☆	☆	⇌	ICE	ICE	ICE	CNL	⇌	☆	ICE	ICE	ICE	EN	
train number	**9315**	**9110**	**9317**	**15**	**627**	**189**	**597**	**29**	**42018**	**357**	**117**	**1217**	**9116**	**9116**	**9437**	**125**	**723**	**611**	**485**	**9341**	**9126**	**17**	**691**	**725**	**463**	
notes		①-⑤	⑥	🍷	**927**	✕	🍷	🍷	[R] 🍷		Ⓑ	⑥	①-⑤	⑥⑦		🍷	🍷	🍷	**363**		①-⑥	🍷	🍷	🍷		
		q	f		🍷					J	🍷	🍷	p	k	w		Ⓑ		D		p		Ⓑ		B	
London St Pancras ... d.	...	0650	...	...	...	...	...	...	...	...	...	...	0858	0858	...	...	...	...	...	...	1058	...	...	...	...	...
Ebbsfleet International d.	...	0708	...	...	...	...	...	...	...	...	...	...	0915	0915	...	...	...	...	...	...	1115	...	...	...	...	...
Ashford International .. d.	...	0728	...	...	...	...	...	...	...	...	...	...	|	|	...	...	...	...	...	...	|	...	...	...	...	...
Lille Europe ... d.	...	0933	...	...	...	...	...	...	...	...	...	...	1130	1133	...	...	...	...	...	...	1330	...	...	...	...	...
Paris Nord ... d.	0825	|	0855	...	...	...	...	...	...	...	...	...	|	|	1201	...	...	...	...	1255	|	...	...	...	...	...
Brussels Midi / Zuid ... a.	0947	1007	1017	...	...	...	...	...	...	...	...	...	1205	1208	1323	...	...	...	...	1417	1405	...	...	...	...	...
Brussels Midi / Zuid ... d.	...	...	...	1025	...	...	...	...	...	...	...	...	▬	...	1328	...	...	...	...	▬	...	1425	...	...	...	...
Brussels Nord ... d.	...	...	...	1033	...	...	...	...	...	...	...	...	...	...	|	...	...	...	...	...	...	1433	...	...	...	...
Liège Guillemins ... a.	...	...	...	1112	...	...	...	...	...	...	...	...	...	...	1411	...	...	...	...	*IC*	...	1512	...	...	...	...
Liège Guillemins ... d.	...	...	...	1114	...	...	...	...	...	...	...	...	*IC*	...	1414	...	...	...	...	**2027**	...	1514	...	...	...	...
Aachen Hbf ⊞ ... a.	...	...	...	1136	...	...	...	...	...	...	...	...	**2313**	...	1436	...	...	...	...	**2327**	...	1536	...	...	...	...
Köln Hbf ... a.	...	...	...	1215	...	...	...	...	...	...	...	...	🍷	...	1515	...	...	...	...	🍷	...	1615	...	...	...	...
Köln Hbf ... d.	...	...	...	1220	...	...	...	...	...	...	...	...	1253	...	...	1528	...	1555	...	1553	...	1620	...	...	...	...
Bonn Hbf ... a.	...	...	...	|	...	...	...	...	...	...	...	...	1312	...	...	|	...	|	...	1612	...	|	...	...	...	...
Koblenz Hbf ... a.	...	...	...	⊖	...	...	...	...	...	...	...	...	1346	...	...	⊖	...	⊖	...	1646	...	⊖	...	...	...	...
Mainz Hbf ... a.	...	...	...	|	...	...	...	...	...	...	...	...	1437	...	...	|	...	|	...	1737	...	|	...	...	...	...
Frankfurt Flughafen ✈ a.	...	...	...	1310	...	...	...	...	...	...	...	...	|	...	...	1616	...	1650	...	1759	...	1726	...	...	...	...
Frankfurt (Main) Hbf . a.	...	...	...	1325	1354	...	1350	1416	...	...	1420	...	|	...	...	1630	1654	|	...	1813	...	1741	1750	1754	...	...
Würzburg Hbf ... a.	...	...	...	...	1502	...	|	1531	...	...	|	...	|	...	...	...	1802	|	...	1931	...	...	|	1902	...	...
Nürnberg Hbf ... a.	...	...	...	...	1559	...	|	1627	1645	...	|	...	|	...	...	...	1859	|	...	2027	...	...	|	1959	...	...
Regensburg Hbf ... a.	...	...	...	...	|	...	|	1725	|	1835	|	...	|	...	...	...	|	|	...	2131	...	...	|	|	...	...
Praha hlavní ... a.	...	...	...	...	|	...	|	|	2022	2244	|	...	|	...	...	...	|	|	...	|	...	...	|	|	...	...
Mannheim Hbf ... a.	...	...	...	...	|	...	1427	|	...	...	|	...	1521	...	...	...	|	1723	...	|	...	...	1827	|	...	...
Stuttgart Hbf ... a.	...	...	...	...	|	...	1508	|	...	...	1554	...	1622	...	...	...	|	1808	...	|	...	...	1908	|	...	...
Ulm Hbf ... a.	...	...	...	...	|	...	1607	|	...	...	1653	...	...	...	...	...	|	1907	...	|	...	...	2007	|	...	...
Augsburg Hbf ... a.	...	...	...	...	|	...	1653	|	...	...	1740	...	...	...	...	...	|	1953	...	|	...	...	2052	|	...	...
München Hbf ... a.	...	...	...	...	1712	1738	1727	|	...	...	1811	1827	...	...	...	...	2014	2027	2103	|	...	...	2129	2112	2340	...
Salzburg ... a.	...	...	...	...	...	|	...	|	...	...	2010	2009	...	...	...	...	...	...	|	|	...	...	...	...	0118	...
Kufstein ⊞ ... a.	...	...	...	...	...	1839	...	|	...	...	|	|	...	...	...	...	...	...	2207	|	...	...	...	...	|	...
Wörgl ... a.	...	...	...	...	...	1849	...	|	...	...	|	|	...	...	...	...	...	...	2218	|	...	...	...	...	|	...
Kitzbühel ... a.	...	...	...	...	...	|	...	|	...	...	|	|	...	...	...	...	...	...	|	|	...	...	...	...	|	...
Zell am See ... a.	...	...	...	...	...	|	...	|	...	...	|	|	...	...	...	...	...	...	|	|	...	...	...	...	|	...
Schwarzach St Veit ... a.	...	...	...	...	...	|	...	|	...	...	2109	2109	...	...	...	...	...	...	|	|	...	...	...	...	|	...
Innsbruck Hbf ... a.	...	...	...	...	...	1923	...	|	...	...	|	|	...	...	...	...	...	...	2258	|	...	...	...	...	|	...
Bad Gastein ... a.	...	...	...	...	...	...	...	|	...	...	2141	2141	...	...	...	...	...	...	...	|	...	...	...	...	|	...
Villach ... a.	...	...	...	...	...	...	...	|	...	...	2246	2246	...	...	...	...	...	...	...	|	...	...	...	...	|	...
Klagenfurt ... a.	...	...	...	...	...	...	...	|	...	...	2317	2317	...	...	...	...	...	...	...	|	...	...	...	...	|	...
Passau ⊞ ... a.	...	...	...	...	...	...	...	1833	...	...	...	...	...	...	...	...	...	...	...	2242	...	...	...	...	|	...
Linz ... a.	...	...	...	...	...	...	...	1942	...	...	...	...	...	...	...	...	...	...	...	...	...	...	...	...	0338	...
Wien Westbahnhof .. a.	...	...	...	...	...	...	...	2104	...	...	...	...	...	...	...	...	...	...	...	...	...	...	...	...	0545h	...
Budapest Keleti ▲ .. a.	...	...	...	...	...	...	...	...	...	...	...	...	...	...	...	...	...	...	...	...	...	...	...	...	0854	...

A – DACIA – Apr. 23 - Oct. 1, Dec. 2 - 14: 🛏 1, 2 cl., ▬ 2 cl., (2) ✕ Wien - Budapest - Bucuresti.

B – KÁLMÁN IMRE – 🛏 1, 2 cl., ▬ 2 cl., (2) München - Wien - Budapest.

C – (12) 🍷 Munster - Köln - Stuttgart - Lindau ⊞ - Innsbruck (Table **70**).

D – *City Night Line* LUPUS / PICTOR – 🛏 1, 2 cl., ▬ 2 cl., (2) (reclining) 🍷 München - Innsbruck - Roma / Venezia. [R] Special fares apply.

G – GROSSGLOCKNER – ⑥ June 21 - Sept. 13: (12) München - Kufstein ⊞ - Wörgl - Zell am See - Schwarzach St Veit. Not Aug. 9, 16.

J – *ALX* – (12) München - Praha. *Ex* in the Czech Republic (Table **76**).

R – (12) ✕ Hamburg - Nürnberg - Wien.

S – (12) ✕ Dortmund - Köln - Nürnberg - Wien.

c – On ⑦ runs 7 - 8 minutes later.

e – Köln **Messe / Deutz** (Table **910**). 0944 on ⑦. Connections from Köln Hbf depart every 2 - 5 minutes, journey time 2 - 3 minutes.

f – Not July 13 - Aug. 30.

h – Wien **Hütteldorf**.

j – Not Oct. 3.

k – Also Aug. 25, Nov. 11.

p – Not Aug. 25, Nov. 11.

q – Not June 9, July 21, Aug. 15, 25, Nov. 10, 11.

w – To Essen (Table **20**).

x – Köln **Messe / Deutz** (Table **910**). Connections from Köln Hbf depart every 2 - 5 minutes, journey time 2 - 3 minutes.

y – Also Oct. 3.

◧ – ⊞ is at Lindau.

▲ – ⊞ is at Hegyeshalom.

⊖ – Via Köln - Frankfurt high speed line.

⇌ – *Thalys* high-speed train. [R] 🍷. Special fares payable. Valid June 1 - Aug. 30.

🚌 – **DB / ČD** *ExpressBus*. [R] 🍷. Rail tickets valid. ⊞ is Waidhaus (Germany). Timings subject to alteration from May 26 (Table **76**).

RJ – ÖBB *Railjet* service. (1) (business class), (1) (first class), (2) (economy class), ✕.

☆ – Eurostar train. [R], ✕ in 1st class, 🍷 in 2nd class. Special fares payable. Minimum check-in time 30 minutes. Not available for London - Ebbsfleet - Ashford or v.v. journeys. Valid June 1 - Dec. 13.

★ – Compulsory reservation for international journeys between Hungary and Romania.

LONDON and BRUSSELS - FRANKFURT, WIEN and MÜNCHEN 21

train type	☆	☆	⇌	*ICE*	*ICE*	*ICE*	*EN*	☆	⇌	*ICE*	*ICE*	*IC*	☆	⇌	*ICE*	*EN*	*RJ*	*CNL*	*ICE*	*IC*	*CNL*	*RJ*	*EC*	*EC*	
train number	**9132**	**9136**	**9461**	**615**	**1659**	**1029**	**421**	**9140**	**9365**	**19**	**1029**	**2315**	**9144**	**9473**	**227**	**421**	**49**	**459**	**617**	**2221**	**419**	**61**	**81**	**111**	
notes				🍷	**1625**	🍷	🅁	⑧		🍷	🍷	**2215**	⑥		🍷	🅁	🍷	🅁	🍷	**2321**	🅁	🍷	**1289**	🍷	
		Q			🍷		**B**		**W**			🍷		**w**		**B**		**A**		🍷	**P**		🍴		
London St Pancras.....d.	1258	1404	...	...	...	...	...	1504	...	...	...	...	1604	...	...	...	...	...	...	...	...	...	...	...	...
Ebbsfleet International ..d.	1315	│	...	...	...	...	...	│	...	...	...	...	│	...	...	...	...	...	...	...	...	...	...	...	...
Ashford International....d.	│	│	...	...	...	...	...	│	...	...	...	...	│	...	...	...	...	...	...	...	...	...	...	...	...
Lille Europe ....d.	1533	1630	...	...	...	...	...	1730	...	...	...	...	1830	...	...	...	...	...	...	...	...	...	...	...	...
Paris Nord ....d.	│	│	1601	...	...	...	...	│	1655	...	...	...	│	1758	...	...	...	...	...	...	...	...	...	...	...
Brussels Midi / Zuid.....a.	1608	1705	1723	...	...	...	...	1805	1817	...	...	...	1905	1923	...	...	...	...	...	...	...	...	...	...	...
Brussels Midi / Zuid.....d.	...	...	1728	...	...	...	...	...	...	1825	...	...	...	1928	...	...	...	...	...	...	...	...	...	...	...
Brussels Nord..............d.	...	...	│	...	...	...	...	...	...	1833	...	...	...	│	...	...	...	...	...	...	...	...	...	...	...
Liège Guillemins ....a.	...	...	1811	...	...	...	...	...	...	1912	...	...	...	2011	...	...	...	...	...	...	...	...	...	...	...
Liège Guillemins ....d.	...	...	1814	...	...	...	...	...	...	1914	...	...	...	2014	...	...	...	...	...	...	...	...	...	...	...
Aachen Hbf 🛃.............a.	...	...	1836	...	...	...	...	...	...	1936	...	...	...	2036	...	...	...	...	...	...	...	...	...	...	...
Köln Hbf ....a.	...	...	1915	...	...	...	...	...	...	2015	...	...	...	2115	...	...	...	...	...	...	...	...	...	...	...
Köln Hbf ....d.	...	...	...	1957	...	1953	2005	...	...	2027	...	2053	...	...	2128	...	...	...	2155	2153	2346	...	...	...	...
Bonn Hbf.......................a.	...	...	...	│	...	2012	2034**d**	...	...	│	...	2112	...	...	│	...	...	...	│	2212	0007**u**	...	...	...	...
Koblenz Hbf...................a.	...	...	...	⊖	...	2046	2113**d**	...	...	⊖	...	2146	...	...	⊖	←	...	...	⊖	2246	0040**u**	...	...	...	...
Mainz Hbf......................a.	...	...	...	│	...	2140	2207	...	...	│	...	2237	...	...	│	2209**d**	...	...	│	2337	0137**u**	...	...	...	...
Frankfurt Flughafen ✈ .a.	...	...	...	2050	2102	2159	→	...	...	2116	...	2259	...	...	2216	2233**d**	...	...	2250	2359	0156**u**	...	...	...	...
Frankfurt (Main) Hbf ...a.	...	...	...	│	2113	2213	...	...	...	2130	2218	2311	...	...	2230	2300**d**	...	0054**j**	│	0013	│	...	...	...	...
Würzburg Hbf...........a.	...	...	...	│	...	2341	...	...	...	...	2341	...	...	...	...	0224	...	│	│	...	│	...	...	...	...
Nürnberg Hbf ....a.	...	...	...	│	...	0036	...	...	...	...	0036	...	...	...	...	0321	...	│	│	...	│	...	...	...	...
Regensburg Hbf ....a.	...	...	...	│	...	...	...	...	...	...	...	...	...	...	...	0427	...	│	│	...	│	...	...	...	...
Praha hlavní ....a.	...	...	...	│	...	...	...	...	...	...	...	...	...	...	...	│	...	1029	│	...	│	...	...	...	...
Mannheim Hbf ....a.	...	...	...	2123	...	...	...	...	...	...	...	...	...	...	...	│	...	...	2337	...	0233	...	...	...	...
Stuttgart Hbf..............a.	...	...	...	2208	...	...	...	...	...	...	...	...	...	...	...	│	...	...	0056**p**	...	0417	...	...	...	...
Ulm Hbf.........................a.	...	...	...	2307	...	...	...	...	...	...	...	...	...	...	...	│	...	...	...	...	0542	...	...	...	...
Augsburg Hbf..............a.	...	...	...	2353	...	...	...	...	...	...	...	...	...	...	...	│	...	...	...	...	0633	...	...	...	...
München Hbf ....a.	...	...	...	0027	...	...	...	...	...	...	...	...	...	...	...	│	...	...	...	...	0710	0727	0731	0827	...
Salzburg...................a.	...	...	...	...	...	...	...	...	...	...	...	...	...	...	...	│	...	...	...	...	...	0857	│	1009	...
Kufstein 🛃.................a.	...	...	...	...	...	...	...	...	...	...	...	...	...	...	...	│	...	...	...	...	...	│	0832	│	...
Wörgl..........................a.	...	...	...	...	...	...	...	...	...	...	...	...	...	...	...	│	...	...	...	...	...	│	0844	│	...
Kitzbühel.......................a.	...	...	...	...	...	...	...	...	...	...	...	...	...	...	...	│	...	...	...	...	...	│	│	│	...
Zell am See ....a.	...	...	...	...	...	...	...	...	...	...	...	...	...	...	...	│	...	...	...	...	...	│	│	│	...
Schwarzach St Veit......a.	...	...	...	...	...	...	...	...	...	...	...	...	...	...	...	│	...	...	...	...	...	│	│	1109	...
Innsbruck Hbf ....a.	...	...	...	...	...	...	...	...	...	...	...	...	...	...	...	│	...	...	...	...	...	│	0923	│	...
Bad Gastein.................a.	...	...	...	...	...	...	...	...	...	...	...	...	...	...	...	│	...	...	...	...	...	│	...	1141	...
Villach..........................a.	...	...	...	...	...	...	...	...	...	...	...	...	...	...	...	│	...	...	...	...	...	│	...	1243	...
Klagenfurt ....a.	...	...	...	...	...	...	...	...	...	...	...	...	...	...	...	│	...	...	...	...	...	│	...	1315	...
Passau 🛃 ....a.	...	...	...	...	...	...	...	...	...	...	...	...	...	...	...	0532	...	...	...	...	...	│	...	...	...
Linz.........................a.	...	...	...	...	...	...	...	...	...	...	...	...	...	...	...	0648	...	...	...	...	...	1006	...	...	...
Wien Westbahnhof ....a.	...	...	...	...	...	...	...	...	...	...	...	...	...	...	...	0856	0948	...	...	...	...	1124	...	...	...
Budapest Keleti ▲....a.	...	...	...	...	...	...	...	...	...	...	...	...	...	...	...	...	1249	...	...	...	...	1449	...	...	...

train type	*EC*	*EC*	*RJ*	*CNL*	⇌	*CNL*	*IC*	*ICE*	*EN*	*ICE*	⇌	☆	*IC*	*ICE*	*ICE*	⇌	☆	*EN*	*IC*	*ICE*	*ICE*	*ICE*	⇌	☆	☆
train number	**110**	**188**	**68**	**418**	**9412**	**458**	**2212**	**618**	**420**	**18**	**9322**	**9125**	**2220**	**616**	**226**	**9424**	**9129**	**420**	**2216**	**728**	**692**	**16**	**9448**	**9141**	**9141**
notes	🍴	**1288**	🍷				🍷	**1018**	🅁	🍷	**9422**	①–⑥	**2320**	🍷	🍷	🍷	⑦	🅁	🍷	🍷	🍷	🍷	🍷	⑥⑦	①–⑤
notes		🍴		**P**	**w**	**A**		🍷	**B**			**h**	🍷				**y**	**B**						**y**	**q**
Budapest Keleti ▲....d.	...	...	1510	...	...	...	...	...	...	...	...	...	...	...	...	...	...	...	...	...	...	...	...	...	...
Wien Westbahnhof....d.	...	...	1836	...	...	...	...	...	1956	...	...	...	...	...	...	...	...	...	...	...	...	...	...	...	...
Linz.........................d.	...	...	1953	...	...	...	...	...	2158	...	...	...	...	...	...	...	...	...	...	...	...	...	...	...	...
Passau 🛃 ....d.	...	...	│	...	...	...	...	...	2306	...	...	...	...	...	...	...	...	...	...	...	...	...	...	...	...
Klagenfurt ....d.	1642	...	│	...	...	...	...	...	│	...	...	...	...	...	...	...	...	...	...	...	...	...	...	...	...
Villach..........................d.	1716	...	│	...	...	...	...	...	│	...	...	...	...	...	...	...	...	...	...	...	...	...	...	...	...
Bad Gastein.................d.	1817	...	│	...	...	...	...	...	│	...	...	...	...	...	...	...	...	...	...	...	...	...	...	...	...
Innsbruck Hbf ....d.	│	2036	│	...	...	...	...	...	│	...	...	...	...	...	...	...	...	...	...	...	...	...	...	...	...
Schwarzach St Veit......d.	1850	│	│	...	...	...	...	...	│	...	...	...	...	...	...	...	...	...	...	...	...	...	...	...	...
Zell am See ....d.	│	│	│	...	...	...	...	...	│	...	...	...	...	...	...	...	...	...	...	...	...	...	...	...	...
Kitzbühel.......................d.	│	│	│	...	...	...	...	...	│	...	...	...	...	...	...	...	...	...	...	...	...	...	...	...	...
Wörgl..........................d.	│	2114	│	...	...	...	...	...	│	...	...	...	...	...	...	...	...	...	...	...	...	...	...	...	...
Kufstein 🛃.................d.	│	2124	│	...	...	...	...	...	│	...	...	...	...	...	...	...	...	...	...	...	...	...	...	...	...
Salzburg...................d.	1951	│	2102	...	...	...	...	...	│	...	...	...	...	...	...	...	...	...	...	...	...	...	...	...	...
München Hbf ....d.	2133	2225	2232	2250	...	...	...	0038**c**	│	...	...	...	...	0325	...	...	...	...	...	0649	0632**e**	...	...	...	...
Augsburg Hbf..............d.	...	...	...	2320	...	...	...	0110**c**	│	...	...	...	...	0357	...	...	...	...	...	│	0706**e**	...	...	...	...
Ulm Hbf.........................d.	...	...	...	0010	...	...	...	0202**c**	│	...	...	...	...	0440	...	...	...	...	...	│	0751**e**	...	...	...	...
Stuttgart Hbf..............d.	...	...	...	0135	...	...	...	0305	│	...	...	...	...	0551	...	...	...	...	0737	│	0851	...	...	...	...
Mannheim Hbf ....d.	...	...	...	0256	...	...	...	0440	│	...	...	...	...	0636	...	...	...	...	0839	│	0932	...	...	...	...
Praha hlavní ....d.	...	...	...	│	...	1829	...	│	│	...	...	...	...	│	...	...	...	...	│	│	│	...	...	...	...
Regensburg Hbf ....d.	...	...	...	│	...	│	...	│	0013	...	...	...	...	│	...	...	...	...	│	│	│	...	...	...	...
Nürnberg Hbf ....d.	...	...	...	│	...	│	...	│	0115	...	...	...	...	│	...	...	...	...	│	0802	│	...	...	...	...
Würzburg Hbf...........d.	...	...	...	│	...	│	...	│	0211	...	...	...	...	│	...	...	...	←	│	0855	│	...	...	...	...
Frankfurt (Main) Hbf...d.	...	...	...	│	...	0359**j**	...	0544	0602	0625**b**	...	...	0542**n**	│	0727	...	...	0615	│	1004	1008	1016	...	...	...
Frankfurt Flughafen ✈..d.	...	...	...	0339**s**	...	...	...	0601	→	0638**b**	...	...	0558**n**	0709	0743	...	...	0626**s**	│	...	...	1032	...	...	...
Mainz Hbf......................d.	...	...	...	│	...	...	...	│	...	│	...	...	0617**n**	│	│	...	...	0646**s**	0920	...	...	│	...	...	...
Koblenz Hbf...................d.	...	...	...	0446**s**	...	...	0606	⊖	...	⊖	...	...	0713	⊖	⊖	...	...	0744**s**	1013	...	...	⊖	...	...	...
Bonn Hbf.......................d.	...	...	...	0520**s**	...	...	0644	│	...	│	...	...	0744	│	│	...	...	0819**s**	1044	...	...	│	...	...	...
Köln Hbf ....a.	...	...	...	0543	...	...	0705	0705	...	0739	...	...	0805	0805	0832	...	...	0842	1105	...	...	1139	...	...	...
Köln Hbf ....d.	...	...	...	...	0645	...	...	...	...	0743	...	...	...	...	...	0845	...	▬	...	...	...	1143	...	...	...
Aachen Hbf 🛃.............d.	...	...	...	...	0724	...	...	...	...	0821	...	...	...	...	...	0924	...	...	...	...	...	1221	...	...	...
Liège Guillemins ....a.	...	...	...	...	0748	...	...	...	...	0844	...	...	...	...	...	0946	...	...	...	...	...	1244	...	...	...
Liège Guillemins ....d.	...	...	...	...	0751	...	...	...	...	0846	...	...	...	...	...	0949	...	☆	...	...	...	1246	...	...	...
Brussels Nord..............a.	...	...	...	...	│	...	...	...	...	0927	...	...	...	...	...	│	...	**9133**	...	...	...	1327	...	...	...
Brussels Midi / Zuid.....a.	...	...	...	...	0832	...	...	...	...	0935	...	...	...	...	...	1032	...	①–⑤	...	...	...	1335	...	...	...
Brussels Midi / Zuid.....d.	...	...	...	...	0837	...	...	...	...	...	1013	1056	...	...	...	1037	1156	1252	...	...	...	...	1437	1452	1456
Paris Nord ....d.	...	...	...	...	0959	...	...	...	...	...	1135	│	...	...	...	1159	│	│	...	...	...	...	1559	│	│
Lille Europe ....a.	...	...	...	...	...	...	...	...	...	...	...	1130	...	...	...	...	1229	1326	...	...	...	...	...	1526	1532
Ashford International....a.	...	...	...	...	...	...	...	...	...	...	...	│	...	...	...	...	│	│	...	...	...	...	...	│	│
Ebbsfleet International .a.	...	...	...	...	...	...	...	...	...	...	...	│	...	...	...	...	│	1345	...	...	...	...	...	1545	1545
London St Pancras.....a.	...	...	...	...	...	...	...	...	...	...	...	1157	...	...	...	...	1257	1403	...	...	...	...	...	1603	1603

A – *City Night Line* CANOPUS – 🛏 1,2 cl., 🛌 2 cl., [2] (reclining), 🍷 Zürich - Basel - Frankfurt (Main) **Süd** - Děčín 🛃 - Praha and v.v. 🅁 Special fares apply.

B – 🛏 1, 2 cl., 🛌 2 cl. (4, 6 berth), [2] 🍷 Köln - Frankfurt - Passau 🛃 - Wien and v.v. 🅁 Special fares apply. For international journeys only.

P – *City Night Line* POLLUX – 🛏 1, 2 cl., 🛌 2 cl. (4, 6 berth), [2] (reclining), 🍷 🅁 Amsterdam - Köln - München and v.v. Special fares apply.

Q – ⑤⑦ (⑧ Mar. 30 - Aug. 30) also Oct. 23, 27–30, Nov. 11.

W – ②③④⑤⑦ (daily Apr. 6 - July 12; not June 8; ①–⑥ July 13 - Aug. 30; not July 14, 21).

b – On ①–⑤ depart Frankfurt (Main) 0629, Frankfurt Flughafen 0643.

c – ① only.

d – Departure time.

e – ①–⑤ (not Oct. 3).

h – Not Nov. 11.

j – Frankfurt (Main) **Süd**.

n – Daily (①–⑥ from Nov, 10).

p – 0040 on ①⑦ (also Oct. 4).

q – Not Aug. 25, Nov. 11.

s – Calls to set down only.

u – Calls to pick up only.

w – To / from Essen (Table **20**).

y – Also Aug. 25, Nov. 11.

▲ – 🛃 is at Hegyeshalom.

⇌ – *Thalys* high-speed train. 🅁 🍷. Special fares payable. Valid June 1 - Aug. 30.

☆ – Eurostar train. 🅁, 🍴 in 1st class, 🍷 in 2nd class. Special fares payable. Minimum check-in time 30 minutes. Not available for London - Ebbsfleet - Ashford or v.v. journeys. Valid June 1 - Dec. 13.

⊖ – Via Köln - Frankfurt high speed line.

RJ – ÖBB *Railjet* service. [1] (business class), [1] (first class), [2] (economy class), 🍴.

21 MÜNCHEN, WIEN and FRANKFURT - BRUSSELS and LONDON

train type	ICE	EN	CNL	ICE	ICE	⇌	☆	IC	ICE	IC	RJ	ALX	ICE	🚌	ICE	ICE	⇌	☆	ICE	EC	ICE	⇌	☆	☆
train number	1122	462	484	612	726	9448	9145	2024	208	2312	260	356	228	42009	720	14	9368	9157	518	218	628	9472	9161	9161
notes	🍷		358	🍷	①-⑥	🍷		🍷	✕	🍷	🍷		🍷	🅁🍷	🍷	🍷	Ⓑ	Ⓑ	🍷	🍷	🍷	🍷	Ⓑ	⑥
notes		K	C		c	w	Q					A					🍷			g				
Budapest Keleti ▲ d.	...	2110	...	...	...	...	...	...	...	...	...	...	...	...	...	...	...	...	...	...	...	...	...	...
Wien Westbahnhof d.	...	0010h	...	...	...	...	...	...	...	...	0636	...	0652	...	...	...	...	...	...	...	...	...	...	...
Linz d.	...	0201	...	...	...	...	...	...	...	...	0753	...	0818	...	...	...	...	...	...	...	...	...	...	...
Passau ▦ d.	...	|	...	...	...	...	...	0718	...	...	|	...	0924	...	...	...	...	...	...	...	...	...	...	...
Klagenfurt d.	...	|	...	...	...	...	...	|	...	...	|	...	|	...	...	...	...	...	...	...	...	...	...	...
Villach d.	...	|	...	...	...	...	...	|	...	...	|	...	|	...	...	...	...	...	...	...	...	...	...	...
Bad Gastein d.	...	|	...	...	...	...	...	|	...	...	|	...	|	...	...	...	...	...	...	...	...	...	...	...
Innsbruck Hbf d.	...	|	0436	...	...	...	...	|	0709	...	|	...	|	...	...	...	...	...	...	...	...	...	...	...
Schwarzach St Veit d.	...	|	|	...	...	...	...	|	|	...	|	...	|	...	...	...	...	...	...	...	...	...	...	...
Zell am See d.	...	|	|	...	...	...	...	|	|	...	|	...	|	...	...	...	...	...	...	...	...	...	...	...
Kitzbühel d.	...	|	|	...	...	...	...	|	|	...	|	...	|	...	...	...	...	...	...	...	...	...	...	...
Wörgl d.	...	|	0518	...	...	...	...	|	0747	...	|	...	|	...	...	...	...	...	...	...	...	...	...	...
Kufstein ▦ d.	...	|	0529	...	...	...	...	|	0758	...	|	...	|	...	...	...	...	...	...	...	...	...	...	...
Salzburg d.	...	0428	|	...	...	...	...	|	|	...	0902	...	|	...	...	...	...	...	...	0951	...	...	...	...
München Hbf d.	...	0615	0630	0728	0750	...	...	|	0900	...	1030	...	|	...	1050	...	...	...	1130	1133	1150	...	...	...
Augsburg Hbf d.	...	...	...	0803	|	...	...	|	...	...	...	...	|	...	|	...	...	...	1203	...	|	...	...	...
Ulm Hbf d.	...	...	...	0851	|	...	...	|	...	...	...	...	|	...	|	...	...	...	1251	...	|	...	...	...
Stuttgart Hbf d.	...	...	...	0951	|	...	...	|	...	1137	...	...	|	...	|	...	...	...	1351	...	|	...	...	...
Mannheim Hbf d.	...	...	...	1036	|	...	...	|	...	1239	...	...	|	...	|	...	...	...	1436	...	|	...	...	...
Praha hlavní d.	...	...	...	|	|	...	...	|	...	|	...	0515	|	0735	|	...	...	...	|	...	|	...	...	...
Regensburg Hbf d.	...	...	...	|	|	...	...	0827	...	|	...	0929	1029	|	|	...	...	...	|	...	|	...	...	...
Nürnberg Hbf d.	0729c	...	...	|	0901	...	...	0928	...	|	...	...	1128	1114	1200	...	...	...	|	...	1300	...	...	...
Würzburg Hbf d.	0827c	...	...	|	0955	...	...	1027	...	|	...	...	1227	...	1257	...	...	...	|	...	1355	...	...	...
Frankfurt (Main) Hbf. d.	0942	...	...	|	1110	...	...	1142	...	|	...	...	1340	...	1404	1429	...	...	|	...	1510	...	...	...
Frankfurt Flughafen ✈ d.	0958	...	...	1109	1125	...	...	1158	...	|	...	...	...	...	...	1443	...	...	1509	...	1525	...	...	...
Mainz Hbf d.	1020	...	...	|	|	...	...	1220	...	1320	...	...	...	...	...	|	...	...	|	...	|	...	...	...
Koblenz Hbf d.	1113	...	...	⊖	⊖	...	...	1313	...	1413	...	...	...	...	...	⊖	...	...	⊖	...	⊖	...	...	...
Bonn Hbf d.	1144	...	...	|	|	...	...	1344	...	1444	...	...	...	...	...	|	...	...	|	...	|	...	...	...
Köln Hbf a.	1205	...	...	1205	1214x	...	...	1405	...	1505	...	...	...	...	...	1539	...	...	1605	...	1614x	...	...	...
Köln Hbf d.	...	...	...	...	...	1245	...	...	...	...	...	...	...	...	...	1543	...	...	...	...	...	1643	...	...
Aachen Hbf ▦ d.	...	...	...	...	...	1324	...	...	...	...	...	...	...	...	...	1621	...	...	...	...	...	1724	...	...
Liège Guillemins a.	...	...	...	...	...	1346	...	...	...	...	...	...	...	...	...	1644	...	...	...	...	...	1746	...	...
Liège Guillemins d.	...	...	...	...	...	1349	...	...	...	...	...	...	...	...	...	1646	...	...	...	...	...	1749	...	...
Brussels Nord a.	...	...	...	...	...	|	...	...	...	...	...	...	...	...	...	1727	...	...	...	...	...	|	...	...
Brussels Midi/Zuid a.	...	...	...	...	...	1432	...	...	...	...	...	...	...	...	...	1735	...	...	...	...	...	1832	...	...
Brussels Midi/Zuid d.	...	...	...	...	...	1437	1556	...	...	...	...	...	...	...	...	...	1743	1856	...	...	...	1837	1952	1952
Paris Nord a.	...	...	...	...	...	1559	|	...	...	...	...	...	...	...	...	...	1905	|	...	...	...	1959	|	|
Lille Europe a.	...	...	...	...	...	...	1630	...	...	...	...	...	...	...	...	...	...	1930	...	...	...	...	2026	2026
Ashford International a.	...	...	...	...	...	...	|	...	...	...	...	...	...	...	...	...	...	|	...	...	...	...	|	2035
Ebbsfleet International a.	...	...	...	...	...	...	|	...	...	...	...	...	...	...	...	...	...	|	...	...	...	...	2045	|
London St Pancras a.	...	...	...	...	...	...	1657	...	...	...	...	...	...	...	...	...	...	1957	...	...	...	...	2103	2109

train type	EC	IC	ICE	ICE	EN	ICE	🚌	ICE	IC	RE	ICE	EC	ICE	⇌	RJ	ICE	IC	ICE	EC	RJ	🚌	ICE	ICE	EC	ICE	⇌
train number	218	1280	596	106	346	28	42013	826	118	79022	516	114	624	9484	60	26	1284	1090	88	60	42017	622	572	6	10	9394
notes	🍷		✕	🍷	✕	✕	🅁🍷	926		🍷	🍷	🍷	🍷	🍷	🍷	✕		594	✕	🍷	🅁🍷	1222	✕	🍷	🍷	⑦
notes	g	G			D			1226	E					w		F	H	✕				🍷				
Budapest Keleti ▲ d.	...	...	...	...	0510	...	...	...	...	...	...	...	...	...	0710	...	...	...	...	0710	...	...	...	...	...	...
Wien Westbahnhof d.	...	...	...	...	0816	0852	...	...	...	...	...	...	...	...	1012	1052	...	...	...	1036	...	...	...	...	...	...
Linz d.	...	...	...	...	▬	1018	...	...	...	...	...	...	...	...	▬	1218	...	...	...	1153	...	...	...	...	...	...
Passau ▦ d.	...	...	...	...	...	1124	...	...	...	...	...	...	...	...	...	1324	...	...	...	|	...	...	...	...	...	...
Klagenfurt d.	...	...	...	...	EC	|	...	...	...	...	...	0842	...	...	...	|	...	...	...	|	...	...	...	...	...	...
Villach d.	...	...	...	...	82	|	...	...	...	...	...	0916	...	...	...	|	...	...	...	|	...	...	...	...	...	...
Bad Gastein d.	...	...	...	...	✕	|	...	...	...	...	...	1017	...	...	...	|	...	...	...	|	...	...	...	...	...	...
Innsbruck Hbf d.	...	...	...	...	1036	|	...	...	0856	...	...	|	...	...	...	|	...	...	1236	|	...	...	...	...	...	...
Schwarzach St Veit d.	...	...	...	...	|	|	...	...	|	...	...	1051	...	...	...	|	1005	...	|	|	...	...	...	...	...	...
Zell am See d.	...	0839	...	...	|	|	...	...	|	...	...	|	...	...	...	|	1035	...	|	|	...	...	...	...	...	...
Kitzbühel d.	...	0931	...	...	|	|	...	...	|	...	...	|	...	...	...	|	1127	...	|	|	...	...	...	...	...	...
Wörgl d.	...	1024	...	...	1110	|	...	...	|	...	...	|	...	...	...	|	1222	...	1310	|	...	...	...	...	...	...
Kufstein ▦ d.	...	1044	...	...	1120	|	...	...	◧	...	...	|	...	...	...	|	1234	...	1320	|	...	...	...	...	...	...
Salzburg d.	0951	|	...	...	|	|	...	...	|	1109	...	1151	...	...	...	|	|	...	|	1302	...	...	...	...	...	...
München Hbf d.	1145	1149	1228	...	1221	|	...	1250	|	1317	1328	1333	1350	...	...	|	1333	1428	1421	1430	...	1450	...	...	...	...
Augsburg Hbf d.	1217	...	1303	...	...	|	...	|	|	...	1403	...	|	...	...	|	...	1503	...	...	...	|	...	...	...	...
Ulm Hbf d.	1304	...	1351	...	...	|	...	|	1356	...	1451	...	|	...	ALX	|	...	1551	...	...	...	|	...	...	...	...
Stuttgart Hbf d.	1405	...	1451	...	...	|	...	|	1512	...	1551	...	|	...	354	|	...	1651	...	...	...	|	1726	...	...	...
Mannheim Hbf d.	|	...	1529	1536	...	|	...	|	1606	...	1636	...	|	...	A	|	...	1732	...	...	...	|	1806	...	...	...
Praha hlavní d.	|	...	...	|	...	|	0935	|	...	...	|	...	|	...	0915	|	...	|	...	...	1135	|	|	...	...	...
Regensburg Hbf d.	|	...	...	|	...	1229	|	|	...	...	|	...	|	...	1331	1429	...	|	...	...	|	|	|	...	...	...
Nürnberg Hbf d.	|	...	...	|	...	1328	1314	1400	...	...	|	...	1500	...	...	1528	...	|	...	...	1514	1600	|	...	...	...
Würzburg Hbf d.	|	...	...	|	...	1427	...	1455	...	...	|	...	1555	...	...	1627	...	|	...	...	...	1655	|	...	...	...
Frankfurt (Main) Hbf. d.	1540	...	...	|	...	1536	...	1610	...	...	|	...	1710	...	...	1736	...	1808	...	...	...	1804	|	...	1829	...
Frankfurt Flughafen ✈ d.	...	...	...	1609	...	...	...	1623	...	...	1709	...	1725	...	...	...	...	...	...	...	...	...	1838	...	1843	...
Mainz Hbf d.	...	...	...	|	...	...	...	|	...	...	|	...	|	...	...	...	...	...	...	...	...	...	...	1720	|	...
Koblenz Hbf d.	...	...	...	⊖	...	...	...	⊖	...	...	⊖	...	⊖	...	...	...	...	...	...	...	...	...	...	1813	⊖	...
Bonn Hbf d.	...	...	...	|	...	...	...	|	...	...	|	...	|	...	...	...	...	...	...	...	...	...	...	1844	|	...
Köln Hbf a.	...	...	...	1705	...	...	...	1732e	...	...	1805	...	1813x	...	...	...	...	...	...	...	...	...	...	1905	1939	...
Köln Hbf d.	...	...	...	...	...	...	...	...	...	...	...	...	...	1843	...	...	...	...	...	...	...	...	...	...	1943	...
Aachen Hbf ▦ d.	...	...	...	...	...	...	...	...	...	...	...	...	...	1924	...	...	...	...	...	...	...	...	...	...	2021	...
Liège Guillemins a.	...	...	...	...	...	...	...	...	...	...	...	...	...	1946	...	...	...	...	...	...	...	...	...	...	2044	...
Liège Guillemins d.	...	...	...	...	...	...	...	...	...	...	...	...	...	1949	...	...	...	...	...	...	...	...	...	...	2046	...
Brussels Nord a.	...	...	...	...	...	...	...	...	...	...	...	...	...	|	...	...	...	...	...	...	...	...	...	...	2127	...
Brussels Midi/Zuid a.	...	...	...	...	...	...	...	...	...	...	...	...	...	2032	...	...	...	...	...	...	...	...	...	...	2135	...
Brussels Midi/Zuid d.	...	...	...	...	...	...	...	...	...	...	...	...	...	2037	...	...	...	...	...	...	...	...	...	...	...	2213
Paris Nord d.	...	...	...	...	...	...	...	...	...	...	...	...	...	2159	...	...	...	...	...	...	...	...	...	...	...	2335
Lille Europe a.	...	...	...	...	...	...	...	...	...	...	...	...	...	...	...	...	...	...	...	...	...	...	...	...	...	...
Ashford International a.	...	...	...	...	...	...	...	...	...	...	...	...	...	...	...	...	...	...	...	...	...	...	...	...	...	...
Ebbsfleet International a.	...	...	...	...	...	...	...	...	...	...	...	...	...	...	...	...	...	...	...	...	...	...	...	...	...	...
London St Pancras a.	...	...	...	...	...	...	...	...	...	...	...	...	...	...	...	...	...	...	...	...	...	...	...	...	...	...

A – *ALX* – 🚃 Praha - München. *Ex* in Czech Republic (Table **76**).
C – *City Night Line* LUPUS / PICTOR – 🛏 1, 2 cl., 🛌 2 cl., 🚃 (reclining) 🍷 Roma / Venezia - Innsbruck - München. 🅁 Special fares apply (Table **70**).
D – DACIA – Apr. 22 - Sept. 30, Dec. 1 - 14: 🛏 1, 2 cl., 🛌 2 cl., 🚃 ✕ Bucuresti - Budapest - Wien.
E – 🚃 🍷 Salzburg (depart 0653) - Innsbruck - Lindau ▦ - Stuttgart - Köln - Munster (Table **70**).
F – 🚃 ✕ Wien - Nürnberg - Frankfurt - Köln - Dortmund.
G – GROSSGLOCKNER – ⑥ June 28 - Sept. 13: 🚃 Zell am See - Wörgl - Kufstein ▦ - München. Not Aug. 9, 16.
H – GROSSGLOCKNER – ⑦ June 22 - Sept. 14: 🚃 Schwarzach St Veit - Zell am See - Wörgl - Kufstein ▦ - München. Not Aug. 9, 16.
K – KÁLMÁN IMRE – 🛏 1, 2 cl., 🛌 2 cl., 🚃 Budapest - Wien - München.

Q – ⑤⑦ (Ⓑ Mar. 30 - Aug. 30) also Oct. 23, 27–30, Nov. 11.
c – ①-⑥.
e – On ⑥ arrive at Köln **Messe / Deutz** at 0727, see note **x**.
g – From Graz (Table **68**).
h – Wien **Hütteldorf**.
w – From Essen, see Table **20**.
x – Köln **Messe / Deutz** (Table **910**). Connections to Köln Hbf depart every 2 - 5 minutes, journey time 2 - 3 minutes.
y – Also Aug. 26, Nov. 11.

⊖ – Via Köln - Frankfurt high speed line.
▲ – ▦ is at Hegyeshalom.
◧ – ▦ is at Lindau.

🚌 – **DB / ČD** *ExpressBus.* 🅁 🍷. Rail tickets valid. 1st and 2nd class. ▦ is Waidhaus (Germany). Timings subject to alteration from May 26 (Table **57**).
☆ – Eurostar train. 🅁, ✕ in 1st class, 🍷 in 2nd class. Special fares payable. Minimum check-in time 30 minutes. Not available for London - Ebbsfleet - Ashford or v.v. journeys. Valid June 1 - Dec. 13.
⇌ – *Thalys* high-speed train. 🅁 🍷. Special fares payable. Valid Dec. 15 - July 12.
RJ – ÖBB *Railjet* service. 🚃 (business class), 🚃 (first class), 🚃 (economy class) ✕.

AMSTERDAM - BERLIN 22

For night services between Amsterdam and Berlin, see Table **54**.

train type	IC	IC	IC	IC	IC	IC	IC	IC	ICE		RE	IC	IC	
train number	141	143	145	147	149	241	241	241	645			243	243	
notes							⑧q	⑦w	655			⑦w		
	✕	✕	✕	✕	✕	✕	✕	✕	✕			✕	✕	
Amsterdam Centraal d.	0701	0901	1101	1301	1501	1701	1701	1701	...	...	...	1901	1901	...
Hilversum d.	0722	0922	1122	1322	1522	1722	1722	1722	...	...	...	1922	1922	...
Amersfoort d.	0737	0937	1137	1337	1537	1737	1737	1737	...	...	...	1937	1937	...
Apeldoorn d.	0803	1003	1203	1403	1603	1803	1803	1803	...	...	...	2003	2003	...
Deventer d.	0817	1017	1217	1417	1617	1817	1817	1817	...	...	...	2017	2017	...
Almelo d.	0845	1045	1245	1445	1645	1845	1845	1845	...	...	...	2045	2045	...
Hengelo d.	0859	1059	1259	1459	1659	1859	1859	1859	...	...	...	2059	2059	...
Bad Bentheim 🛃 a.	0916	1116	1316	1516	1716	1916	1916	1916	...	1957	...	2116	2116	2157
Rheine a.	0940	1140	1340	1540	1740	...	1940	1940	...	2012	...	2140	...	2212
Osnabrück Hbf a.	1006	1206	1406	1606	1806	...	2006	2006	...	2046	2116	2206	...	2246
Minden a.	1047	1247	1447	1647	1847	...	2047	2047	...	...	2207	2250	...	...
Hannover Hbf a.	1118	1318	1518	1718	1918	...	2118	2118	2131	...	2251	2326	...	...
Wolfsburg a.	1153	1353	1553	1753	1953	...	...	2153	|	...	...	...	...	...
Stendal a.	1225	1425	1625	1825	2025	...	...	2225	|	...	...	...	...	...
Berlin Hauptbahnhof a.	1315	1515	1715	1915	2115	...	...	2318	2308	...	...	...	...	...
Berlin Ostbahnhof a.	1326	1526	1726	1926	2126	...	...	...	2319	...	...	...	...	...

train type	ICE	IC	IC	RE		IC	IC	IC	IC	IC	IC	IC
train number	646	242	242			240	240	148	146	144	142	140
notes	①–⑤	①–⑥				①–⑥						
	d	e✕	✕			e✕	✕	✕	✕	✕	✕	✕
Berlin Ostbahnhof d.	0411	...	...	...	...	0625	...	0825	1025	1225	1425	1625
Berlin Hauptbahnhof d.	0422	...	...	...	...	0636	...	0836	1036	1236	1436	1636
Stendal d.	0516	...	...	...	...	0734	...	0934	1134	1334	1534	1734
Wolfsburg d.	0548	...	...	...	...	0805	...	1005	1205	1405	1605	1805
Hannover Hbf d.	0618	0640	...	0709	...	0840	...	1040	1240	1440	1640	1840
Minden d.	...	0712	...	0752	...	0912	...	1112	1312	1512	1712	1912
Osnabrück Hbf d.	...	0753	...	0843	0914	0953	...	1153	1353	1553	1753	1953
Rheine d.	...	0821	...	...	0948	1021	...	1221	1421	1621	1821	2021
Bad Bentheim 🛃 d.	...	0844	0844	...	1003	1044	1044	1244	1444	1644	1844	2044
Hengelo a.	...	0901	0901	...	...	1101	1101	1301	1501	1701	1901	2101
Almelo a.	...	0914	0914	...	...	1114	1114	1314	1514	1714	1914	2114
Deventer a.	...	0940	0940	...	...	1140	1140	1340	1540	1740	1940	2140
Apeldoorn a.	...	0954	0954	...	...	1154	1154	1354	1554	1754	1954	2154
Amersfoort a.	...	1024	1024	...	...	1224	1224	1424	1624	1824	2024	2224
Hilversum a.	...	1038	1038	...	...	1238	1238	1438	1638	1838	2038	2238
Amsterdam Centraal a.	...	1100	1100	...	...	1300	1300	1500	1700	1900	2100	2300

d – Not June 9, Oct. 3. e – Not June 9. q – Not June 8. w – Also June 9; not June 8.

LONDON, AMSTERDAM, BRUSSELS and PARIS - WARSZAWA and MOSKVA 24

Russian timings liable to vary from October 26, 2014

train type	☆	ICE	ICE	24JI	☆	ICE	⇌	EN
train number	9110	15	559	453	9140	19	9473	447
notes	①–⑤	🍷	🍷	P	⑧		R	J
notes	g						🍷	R
London St Pancras d.	0650	...	...	...	1504	...	...	...
Lille Europe **12** d.	0933	...	...	...	1730	...	...	...
Paris Nord d.	|	...	...	0828x	|	...	1758	...
Strasbourg d.	|	...	...	1308	|	...	|	...
Brussels Midi / Zuid d.	1007	1025	...	|	1805	1825	1928	...
Liège Guillemins d.	...	1114	...	|	...	1914	2014	...
Aachen 🛃 d.	...	1139	...	|	...	1939	2040	...
Amsterdam Centraal d.	...	|	...	|	...	|	|	1901
Köln Hbf d.	...	1220	1248	|	...	2015	2115	2228
Dortmund Hbf d.	...	|	|	|	...	...	...	2356
Mannheim d.	...	|	|	1507	...	...	...	|
Frankfurt (Main) Hbf d.	...	1325	|	1615f	...	...	...	|
Fulda d.	...	...	|	1726	...	...	...	|
Hannover d.	...	...	1531	1913	...	...	...	|
Berlin Hbf d.	...	...	1708p	2103	...	...	...	0423a
Berlin Ostbahnhof d.	...	...	...	2136	...	...	...	0646a
Frankfurt (Oder) 🛃 d.	...	...	...	2239	...	...	...	|
Rzepin a.	...	...	...	2300	...	...	...	0805
Poznań Gł. a.	...	...	...	0030	...	...	...	0930
Warszawa Centralna a.	...	...	...	0337	...	...	...	1215
Warszawa Wschodnia a.	...	...	...	0350	...	...	...	1228
Warszawa Wschodnia d.	...	...	...	0423	...	...	...	...
Terespol a.	...	...	...	0644	...	...	...	...
Terespol d.	...	...	...	0724	...	...	...	...
Brest Tsentralny 🛃 a.	...	...	...	1012	...	...	...	...
Brest Tsentralny 🛃 d.	...	...	...	1210	...	...	...	...
Baranavichy a.	...	...	...	|	...	...	...	...
Minsk a.	...	...	...	1536	...	...	...	...
Orsha Tsentralnaya § a.	...	...	...	1811	...	...	...	...
Smolensk Tsentralny 🛃 § a.	...	...	...	2035	...	...	...	...
Vyazma a.	...	...	...	2223	...	...	...	...
Moskva Belorusskaya a.	...	...	...	0058	...	...	...	...

train type	24JI	ICE	ICE	☆	☆	EN	⇌	☆	☆
train number	452	954	14	9157	9161	446	9412	9125	9129
notes	Q	🍷	🍷	⑧	⑥	J	R	①–⑥	⑦
notes						R	🍷	k	y
Moskva Belorusskaya d.	0843	...	...	...	...	...	...	...	...
Vyazma d.	1136	...	...	...	...	...	...	...	...
Smolensk Tsentralny 🛃 § d.	1323	...	...	...	...	...	...	...	...
Orsha Tsentralnaya § d.	1347	...	...	...	...	...	...	...	...
Minsk d.	1625	...	...	...	...	...	...	...	...
Baranavichy d.	1807	...	...	...	...	...	...	...	...
Brest Tsentralny 🛃 a.	1958	...	...	...	...	...	...	...	...
Brest Tsentralny 🛃 d.	2215	...	...	...	...	...	...	...	...
Terespol a.	2033	...	...	...	...	...	...	...	...
Terespol d.	2113	...	...	...	...	...	...	...	...
Warszawa Wschodnia a.	2342	...	...	...	...	...	...	...	...
Warszawa Wschodnia d.	0012	...	...	...	...	1742	...	...	...
Warszawa Centralna d.	0025	...	...	...	...	1755	...	...	...
Poznań Gł. d.	0322	...	...	...	...	2029	...	...	...
Rzepin d.	0502	...	...	...	...	2151	...	...	...
Frankfurt (Oder) 🛃 a.	0524	...	...	...	...	|	...	...	...
Berlin Ostbahnhof a.	|	...	...	...	...	0016d	...	...	...
Berlin Hbf d.	0715	0747	...	...	...	0027	...	...	...
Hannover a.	0944	0928	...	...	...	|	...	...	...
Fulda a.	1125	|	...	...	...	|	...	...	...
Frankfurt (Main) Hbf a.	1234f	|	1429	...	...	|	...	...	...
Mannheim a.	1343	|	|	...	...	|	...	...	...
Dortmund Hbf a.	|	|	|	...	...	0447	...	...	...
Köln Hbf a.	|	1209j	1539	...	...	0614	0645	...	...
Amsterdam Centraal d.	|	...	|	...	...	0959	|	...	...
Aachen 🛃 a.	|	...	1616	...	...	...	0720	...	...
Liège Guillemins a.	|	...	1644	...	...	...	0748	...	...
Brussels Midi / Zuid a.	|	...	1735	1856	1952	...	0832	1056	1156
Strasbourg a.	1525	...	...	|	|	...	|	|	|
Paris Nord a.	2031x	...	...	|	|	...	0959	|	|
Lille Europe **12** a.	...	...	...	1930	2026	...	...	1130	1230
London St Pancras a.	...	...	...	1957	2109	...	...	1157	1257

J – JAN KIEPURA – 🛏 1, 2 cl., 🛏 2 cl., (2) (reclining): Amsterdam - Warszawa and v.v. ✕ Rzepin - Warszawa and v.v.

M – TRANSEUROPEAN EXPRESS ①②④⑥⑦ May 31 - Oct. 5; ①④⑦ Oct. 6 - Dec. 13: 🛏 1, 2 cl. Moskva (**23** *JI*) - Brest (**452**) - Berlin - Paris. ✕ (RZD) Moskva - Brest and ✕ (PKP) Warszawa - Paris.

P – TRANSEUROPEAN EXPRESS ①②③④⑥ June 1 - Oct. 5; ②③⑥ Oct. 6 - Dec. 13: 🛏 1, 2 cl. Paris (**453**) - Berlin - Brest (**24** *JI*) - Moskva. ✕ (PKP) Paris - Warszawa and ✕ (RZD) Brest - Moskva.

a – Arrival time.

d – Departure time.

f – Frankfurt (Main) **Süd**.

g – Not June 9, July 21, Aug. 15, 25, Nov. 10, 11.

j – Onward connection to Brussels and London at 1245 *Thalys* **9448**, see Table **20**.

k – Not Nov. 11.

p – Later arrival at 2007 available, see Table **20**.

s – Calls to set down only.

u – Calls to pick up only.

x – Paris **Est**.

y – Also Aug. 25, Nov. 11.

☆ – Eurostar train. R, ✕ in 1st class, 🍷 in 2nd class. Special fares payable. Minimum check-in time 30 minutes. Not available for London - Ebbsfleet - Ashford or v.v. journeys. Valid June 1 - Dec. 13. Additional services are shown in Table **10**.

§ – 🛃: Osinovka (BY) / Krasnoye (RU).

⇌ – *Thalys* high-speed train. R 🍷. Special fares payable. Valid June 1 - Aug. 30. For additional services see Tables **20**, **21**.

✕ (PKP) – Polish railways restaurant car.

✕ (RZD) – Russian railways restaurant car.

28 AMSTERDAM - FRANKFURT, WIEN and MÜNCHEN

train type		ICE	ICE	ICE		ICE	ICE	ICE	🚌		ICE	ICE	ICE	ICE	🚌		ICE	ICE	ICE		ICE	ICE	ICE		ICE	ICE
train number		121	515	623		105	595	27	42014		123	629	519	229	42022		125	723	611		127	727	613		129	615
notes	①–⑥	①–⑥	🍷	923		🍷	🍷	✕	Ⓡ 🍷		🍷	🍷	🍷	✕	Ⓡ 🍷		🍷	🍷	🍷		🍷	🍷	🍷		🍷	🍷
				✕		D			2			Ⓑ			2			Ⓑ			V	Ⓑ				
Amsterdam Centraal d.	...	0704	...	...	...	0804	...	...	...	...	1034	...	...	...	...	...	1234	...	...	...	1434	...	...	...	1634	...
Rotterdam Centraal d.	0635	|	...	...	0735	|	...	...	...	1005	|	...	...	...	...	1205	|	...	...	1405	|	...	...	1605	|	...
Utrecht Centraal d.	0713	0732	...	...	0813	0832	...	...	...	1043	1102	...	...	...	...	1243	1302	...	...	1443	1502	...	...	1643	1702	...
Arnhem ◐ d.	...	0807	...	...	...	0907	...	...	...	...	1137	...	...	...	...	...	1337	...	...	...	1537	...	...	...	1737	...
Oberhausen ◐ a.	...	0858	...	...	...	0958	...	...	...	...	1224	...	...	...	...	...	1424	...	...	...	1624	...	...	...	1824	...
Duisburg a.	...	0906	...	...	...	1006	...	...	...	...	1232	...	...	...	...	...	1432	...	...	...	1632	...	...	...	1832	...
Düsseldorf Hbf a.	...	0920	...	...	...	1020	...	...	...	...	1246	...	...	...	...	...	1446	...	...	...	1646	...	...	...	1846	...
Köln Hbf a.	...	0943t	...	...	...	1045	...	...	...	...	1312	...	...	...	...	...	1512	...	...	...	1712	...	...	...	1912	...
Köln Hbf d.	...	0945t	...	...	...	1055	...	...	...	...	1328	...	...	...	...	...	1528	...	...	...	1720	...	...	...	1920	...
Bonn Hbf a.	...	|	...	...	...	|	...	...	...	...	|	...	...	...	...	...	|	...	...	...	|	...	...	...	|	...
Koblenz a.	...	⊖	...	...	...	⊖	...	...	...	...	⊖	...	...	...	...	...	⊖	...	...	...	⊖	...	...	...	⊖	...
Mainz a.	...	|	...	...	...	|	...	...	...	...	|	...	...	...	...	...	|	...	...	...	|	...	...	...	|	...
Frankfurt Flughafen ✈ a.	...	1034	1053	1137	...	1150	...	1202	...	...	1416	...	1453	...	...	...	1616	...	1653	...	1816	...	1853	...	2016	2053
Frankfurt (Main) Hbf a.	...	1050	|	1148	...	|	...	1213	...	...	1430	1454	|	1621	...	...	1630	1654	|	...	1830	1854	|	...	2030	|
Würzburg a.	...	...	|	1302	...	|	...	1331	...	...	...	1602	|	1731	...	...	...	1802	|	...	...	2002	|	...	...	|
Nürnberg a.	...	...	|	1359	...	|	...	1427	1445	...	...	1659	|	1827	1845	...	...	1859	|	...	...	2059	|	...	...	|
Regensburg a.	...	...	|	...	...	|	...	1525	|	...	...	|	|	1925	|	...	...	|	|	...	...	|	|	...	...	|
Praha hlavní a.	...	...	|	...	...	|	...	|	1822	...	...	|	|	|	2222	...	...	|	|	...	...	|	|	...	...	|
Mannheim a.	...	...	1123	...	...	1223	1230	|	...	...	...	|	1523	|	...	...	...	|	1723	...	...	|	1923	...	...	2123
Stuttgart a.	...	...	1208	...	...	...	1308	|	...	...	...	|	1608	|	...	...	...	|	1808	...	...	|	2008	...	...	2208
Ulm a.	...	...	1307	...	...	...	1407	|	...	...	...	|	1707	|	...	...	...	|	1907	...	...	|	2107	...	...	2307
Augsburg a.	...	...	1353	...	...	...	1453	|	...	...	...	|	1753	|	...	...	...	|	1953	...	...	|	2153	...	...	2353
München Hbf a.	...	...	1427	...	...	...	1528	|	...	...	...	1812	1827	|	...	...	...	2012	2027	...	...	2213	2226	...	...	0027
Passau ▦ a.	...	...	...	...	...	...	...	1633	...	...	...	...	...	2033	...	...	...	...	...	...	...	...	...	...	...	...
Linz a.	...	...	...	...	...	...	...	1742	...	...	...	...	...	2142	...	...	...	...	...	...	...	...	...	...	...	...
Wien Westbahnhof a.	...	...	...	...	...	...	...	1904	...	...	...	...	...	2304	...	...	...	...	...	...	...	...	...	...	...	...

train type	EN	ICE	EN	CNL		CNL	CNL	RJ	ICE	IC
train number	421	227	421	459		457	419	61	223	2009
notes		🍷				Ⓡ	1319	🍷	🍷	⑦
	A		A	P		K	B		S	
Amsterdam Centraal d.	...	1834	...	...	...	1901	2031	...	2104	...
Rotterdam Centraal d.	...	*1805*	...	...	1820	|	*1950*	...	*2020*	...
Utrecht Centraal d.	...	1902	...	...	1858	1929	2059	...	2132	...
Arnhem ◐ d.	...	1937	...	...	...	2007	2137	...	2207	...
Oberhausen ◐ a.	...	2024	...	...	...	|	|	...	2256	...
Duisburg a.	...	2032	...	...	...	2146d	2257d	...	2304	...
Düsseldorf Hbf a.	...	2046	...	...	...	2202d	2313d	...	2318	...
Köln Hbf a.	...	2112	...	...	...	|	|	...	2343	...
Köln Hbf d.	2005	2128		...	...	2228	2346	...	...	2353
Bonn Hbf a.	2034d	|	...	...	...	|	0007d	...	...	0012
Koblenz a.	2113d	⊖	...	...	...	|	0040d	...	...	0046
Mainz a.	2209d	|	...	...	...	|	|	...	...	0140
Frankfurt Flughafen ✈ a.	|	2216	←	...	...	|	0156d	...	...	0202
Frankfurt (Main) Hbf a.	2243	2230	2300	0054k	...	|	|	...	...	0217
Würzburg a.	→	...	0224	|	...	|	|	...	...	...
Nürnberg a.	...	...	0321	|	...	|	|	...	...	...
Regensburg a.	...	...	0427	|	...	|	|	...	...	...
Praha hlavní a.	...	...	|	1029	...	0926	|	...	...	...
Mannheim a.	...	...	|	...	...	...	0233	...	...	...
Stuttgart a.	...	...	|	...	...	...	0417	...	...	...
Ulm a.	...	...	|	...	...	...	0542	...	...	...
Augsburg a.	...	...	|	...	...	...	0633	...	...	...
München Hbf a.	...	...	|	...	...	...	0710	0727	...	...
Innsbruck Hbf a.	...	...	|	...	...	...	0946r	|	...	...
Passau ▦ a.	...	...	0532	...	...	...	...	|	...	...
Linz a.	...	...	0648	...	...	...	...	1006	...	...
Wien Westbahnhof a.	...	...	0856	...	...	...	...	1124	...	...

train type	RJ	CNL	CNL		CNL	ICE		EN	ICE	ICE	EN
train number	68	418	456		458	222		420	616	226	420
notes	🍷	1318	Ⓡ			①–④			🍷	🍷	
		C	K		P			A			A
Wien Westbahnhof d.	1836	...	...	...	...	...	...	1956	...	...	...
Linz d.	1953	...	...	...	...	...	...	2158	...	...	...
Passau ▦ d.	|	...	...	...	...	...	...	2306	...	...	...
Innsbruck Hbf d.	|	1954r	...	...	...	...	...	|	...	...	...
München Hbf d.	2232	2250	...	...	...	...	...	|	0325	...	...
Augsburg d.	...	2320	...	...	...	...	...	|	0357	...	...
Ulm d.	...	0010	...	...	...	...	...	|	0440	...	...
Stuttgart d.	...	0135	...	...	...	...	...	|	0551	...	...
Mannheim d.	...	0256	...	...	...	...	...	|	0636	...	...
Praha hlavní d.	...	|	1829	...	1829	...	...	|	|	...	...
Regensburg d.	...	|	|	...	|	...	...	0013	|	...	...
Nürnberg d.	...	|	|	...	|	...	...	0115	|	...	...
Würzburg d.	...	|	|	...	|	...	...	0211	|	...	...
Frankfurt (Main) Hbf d.	...	|	|	...	0359k	0510	...	0602a	|	0727	...
Frankfurt Flughafen ✈ d.	...	0339a	|	...	...	0525	...	0626a	0709	0743	...
Mainz d.	...	|	|	...	...	|	...	0646a	|	|	...
Koblenz d.	...	0446a	|	...	...	⊖	...	0744a	⊖	⊖	←
Bonn Hbf d.	...	0520a	|	...	...	|	...	0819a	|	|	0819a
Köln Hbf a.	...	0543a	0614a	...	...	0640	...	→	0805	0832	0842
Köln Hbf d.	...	|	|	...	...	0646	...	...	...	0846	▬
Düsseldorf Hbf d.	...	0610a	0654a	...	...	0713	...	...	...	0913	...
Duisburg d.	...	0626a	0709a	...	...	0726	...	...	...	0926	...
Oberhausen ◐ d.	...	|	|	...	...	0734	...	...	...	0934	...
Arnhem ◐ a.	...	0745	0845	...	...	0824	...	...	...	1029	...
Utrecht Centraal a.	...	0828	0926	0947	...	0859	0917	...	...	1100	1117
Rotterdam Centraal a.	...	*0925*	|	1025	...	|	0955	...	...	|	1155
Amsterdam Centraal a.	...	0856	0959	...	...	0926	...	...	...	1126	...

train type	ICE	ICE	ICE		ICE	ICE	ICE	IC	ICE	ICE	ICE	EC	ICE	ICE	🚌	ICE	ICE		🚌	ICE	ICE	ICE	ICE	ICE	ICE	
train number	614	820	128		612	726	126	2024	610	722	124	8	28	596	42013	626	122		42017	26	1090	104	514	620	120	
notes	🍷	①–⑤	🍷		🍷	①–⑥	🍷	🍷	🍷	🍷	🍷	2	🍷	🍷	Ⓡ 🍷	926	🍷		Ⓡ 🍷	🍷	594	🍷	🍷	1220	④⑤⑦	
		g					V					🍷			2	1226			2		🍷	D		🍷		
Wien Westbahnhof d.	...	...	...	...	...	...	...	...	...	...	...	...	0852	...	...	...	...	...	...	1052	...	...	...	...	...	...
Linz d.	...	...	...	...	...	...	...	...	...	...	...	...	1018	...	...	...	...	...	...	1218	...	...	...	...	...	...
Passau ▦ d.	...	...	...	...	...	...	...	0718	...	...	...	...	1124	...	...	...	...	...	...	1324	...	...	...	...	...	...
München Hbf d.	0527	0548	...	...	0728	0750	...	|	0928	0950	...	...	|	1228	...	1250	...	...	...	|	1428	...	1528	1550	...	...
Augsburg d.	0602	|	...	...	0803	|	...	|	1003	|	...	...	|	1303	...	|	...	...	...	|	1503	...	1603	|	...	...
Ulm d.	0651	|	...	...	0851	|	...	|	1051	|	...	...	|	1351	...	|	...	...	...	|	1551	...	1651	|	...	...
Stuttgart d.	0751	|	...	...	0951	|	...	|	1151	|	...	...	|	1451	...	|	...	...	...	|	1651	...	1751	|	...	...
Mannheim d.	0836	|	...	...	1036	|	...	|	1236	|	...	1439	|	1532	...	|	...	...	...	|	1729	1736	1836	|	...	...
Praha hlavní d.	|	|	...	...	|	|	...	|	|	|	...	|	|	|	0935	|	...	...	1135	|	...	|	|	|	...	...
Regensburg d.	|	|	...	...	|	|	...	0827	|	|	...	|	1229	|	|	|	...	...	|	1429	...	|	|	|	...	...
Nürnberg d.	|	0700	...	...	|	0901	...	0928	|	1100	...	|	1328	|	1314	1400	...	...	1514	1528	...	|	|	1700	...	...
Würzburg d.	|	0755	...	...	|	0955	...	1027	|	1155	...	|	1427	|	...	1455	...	...	...	1627	...	|	|	1755	...	...
Frankfurt (Main) Hbf d.	|	0904	0929	...	|	1104	1129	1142	|	1304	1329	|	1536	1608	...	1604	1629	...	...	1742	...	|	|	1904	1929	...
Frankfurt Flughafen ✈ d.	0906	...	0943	...	1106	...	1143	1158	1306	...	1343	|	...	...	...	...	1643	...	...	1755	...	1809	1906	...	1943	...
Mainz d.	...	...	|	...	...	...	|	1220	...	...	|	1520	...	...	...	...	|	...	...	...	...	|	▬	...	|	...
Koblenz d.	...	...	⊖	...	...	...	⊖	1313	...	...	⊖	1613	...	...	...	...	⊖	...	...	...	...	⊖	...	...	⊖	...
Bonn Hbf d.	...	...	|	...	...	...	|	1344	...	...	|	1644	...	...	...	...	|	...	...	...	...	|	...	...	|	...
Köln Hbf a.	...	...	1032	...	...	...	1232	1405	...	...	1432	1705	...	...	...	...	1739	...	...	...	...	1905	...	...	2039	...
Köln Hbf d.	...	...	1046	...	...	...	1246	▬	...	...	1446	▬	...	...	...	...	1746	...	...	...	...	1917	...	...	2046	...
Düsseldorf Hbf d.	...	...	1113	...	...	...	1313	...	...	...	1514	...	...	...	...	...	1814	...	...	...	...	1940	...	...	2113	...
Duisburg d.	...	...	1126	...	...	...	1326	...	...	...	1529	...	...	...	...	...	1826	...	...	...	...	1953	...	...	2126	...
Oberhausen ◐ d.	...	...	1134	...	...	...	1334	...	...	...	1536	...	...	...	...	...	1834	...	...	...	...	2000	...	...	2134	...
Arnhem ◐ a.	...	...	1229	...	...	...	1429	...	...	...	1629	...	...	...	...	...	1929	...	...	...	...	2053	...	...	2224	...
Utrecht Centraal a.	...	...	1300	1317	...	...	1500	1517	...	...	1700	1717	...	...	...	...	2000	2017	...	...	...	2128	2147	...	2259	...
Rotterdam Centraal a.	...	...	|	1355	...	...	|	1555	...	...	|	1755	...	...	...	...	|	2055	...	...	...	|	2225	...	|	...
Amsterdam Centraal a.	...	...	1326	...	...	...	1526	...	...	...	1726	...	...	...	...	...	2026	...	...	...	...	2155	...	...	2326	...

A – 🛏 1, 2 cl., ▬ 2 cl. (4, 6 berth), (2) 🍷: Köln - Frankfurt - Passau ▦ - Wien and v.v. Ⓡ Special fares apply. For international journeys only.

B – *City Night Line* POLLUX – 🛏 1, 2 cl., ▬ 2 cl. (4, 6 berth), (2) (reclining), 🍷 Ⓡ Amsterdam - Köln - München. Special fares apply.

C – *City Night Line* POLLUX – 🛏 1, 2 cl., ▬ 2 cl. (4, 6 berth), (2) (reclining), 🍷 Ⓡ München - Köln - Amsterdam. Special fares apply.

D – (12) 🍷 Amsterdam - Mannheim - Basel and v.v. (Table **73**).

K – *City Night Line* KOPERNIKUS / PHOENIX – 🛏 1, 2 cl., ▬ 2 cl., (2) (reclining), 🍷 Amsterdam - Köln - Berlin - Dresden - Praha and v.v. Ⓡ Special fares apply.

P – *City Night Line* CANOPUS – 🛏 1, 2 cl., ▬ 2 cl., (2) (reclining), 🍷: Zürich - Basel - Frankfurt (Main) **Süd** - Děčín ▦ - Praha and v.v. Ⓡ Special fares apply.

S – ⑦ (⑤⑦ June 9 - Nov. 1).

V – Mar. 22 - Nov. 3.

a – Arrival time.

d – Departure time.

g – Not Oct. 3.

k – Frankfurt (Main) **Süd**.

t – Köln **Messe / Deutz**.

🚌 – **DB / ČD** *ExpressBus*. Ⓡ 🍷. Rail tickets valid. 2nd class only. Timings subject to alteration from May 26 (Table **76**).

RJ – ÖBB *Railjet* service. (1) (business class), (1) (first class), (2) (economy class) ✕.

◐ – ▦ between Arnhem and Oberhausen is Emmerich.

⊖ – Via Köln - Frankfurt high speed line.

PARIS - FRANKFURT - BERLIN, LEIPZIG, DRESDEN and PRAHA — 30

Alternative services Paris - Frankfurt are available via Brussels (Table **21**). Alternative services Paris - Berlin are available via Brussels (Table **20**).

train type	*ICE*	*ICE*	*ICE*	*EC*	*ICE*	*TGV*	*TGV*	*ICE*	*ICE*	*EC*	*ICE*	*ICE*	*ICE*	*ICE*	*ICE*	*ICE*	*ICE*	*ICE*	*ICE*	*ICE*	*CNL*	*CNL*	*CNL*	*CNL*		
train number	**9551**	**372**	**1559**	**379**	**623**	**9553**	**9553**	**370**	**1651**	**179**	**627**	**9555**	**276**	**296**	**1655**	**725**	**9557**	**1659**	**1029**	**9559**	**1259**	**459**	**451**	**471**		
notes	[R]★	**392**	🍷	✖	**923**	[R]★	[R]★	🍷	🍷	✖	**927**	[R]★	🍷	🍷	🍷	🍷	[R]★	🍷	🍷	[R]★						
notes	①–⑥	🍷		**K**	🍷	⑦	①–⑥	**J**		**D**	🍷		**J**	**J**	⑧		⑧	⑧			**C**	**B**	[R]	[R]		
	w	**J**										**P**	⑧	⑥									**A R**	**A S**		
Paris Est ... d.	0658**x**	...	...	...	...	0857**x**	0858**x**	...	...	...	...	1310**z**	...	...	...	...	1659**x**	...	...	1843**v**	...	...	2005	2025	...	...
Metz ... d.	|	...	...	...	...	|	|	...	...	...	...	|	...	...	...	...	|	...	...	|	...	...	|	|	...	...
Forbach 🏛 ... d.	0848	...	...	...	...	1047	|	...	...	...	...	|	...	...	...	...	|	...	...	2048	...	...	|	|	...	...
Saarbrücken ... a.	0856	...	...	...	...	1055	1055	...	...	...	...	1457	...	...	...	...	1856	...	...	2056	...	...	|	|	...	...
Kaiserslautern ... a.	0935	...	...	...	...	1133	1133	...	...	...	...	1535	...	...	...	...	1935	...	...	2134	...	...	|	|	...	...
Karlsruhe Hbf ... a.	|	...	...	...	...	|	|	...	...	...	...	|	...	...	...	...	|	...	...	|	...	...	|	|	...	...
Mannheim ... a.	1017	...	...	...	...	1215	1215	...	...	...	...	1617	...	...	...	...	2016	...	...	2217	0005	0005	|	|	...	...
Frankfurt (Main) Hbf ... a.	1058	...	...	...	...	1258	1258	...	...	...	...	1658	...	...	...	...	2058	...	...	2258	|	|	|	|	...	...
Frankfurt (Main) Hbf ... d.	...	1113	1119	...	1154	...	...	1313	1319	...	1354	...	1713	1713	1720	1754	...	2118	2218	...	0054**q**	0054**q**	|	|	...	...
Würzburg ... a.	...	|	|	...	1301	...	...	|	|	...	1502	...	|	|	|	1902	...	|	2341	...	|	|	|	|	...	...
Nürnberg ... a.	...	|	|	...	1359	...	...	|	|	...	1559	...	|	|	|	1959	...	|	0036	...	|	|	|	|	...	...
Fulda ... a.	...	1209	1212	...	...	...	...	1409	1412	...	...	...	1809	1806	1812	...	...	2212	...	...	|	|	|	|	...	...
Erfurt ... a.	...	|	1332	...	...	...	...	|	1532	...	...	...	|	1931	1932	...	...	2338	...	...	0345	0345	|	|	...	...
Leipzig Hbf ... a.	...	|	1446	...	...	...	...	|	1646	...	...	...	|	2046	2049	...	...	0059**r**	...	...	|	0642	|	|	...	...
Dresden Hbf ... a.	...	|	1604	1708	...	...	...	|	1804	1908	...	...	|	|	2206	...	...	...	...	...	|	0803	|	|	...	...
Děčín (🏛 = Schöna) ... a.	...	|	...	1753	...	...	...	|	...	1953	...	...	|	|	...	...	...	...	...	...	|	0853	|	|	...	...
Praha Holešovice ... a.	...	|	...	1916	...	...	...	|	...	2116	...	...	|	|	...	...	...	...	...	...	|	1019	|	|	...	...
Praha hlavní ... a.	...	|	...	1926	...	...	...	|	...	2126	...	...	|	|	...	...	...	...	...	...	|	1029	|	|	...	...
Kassel Wilhelmshöhe ... a.	...	1241	...	...	...	...	...	1441	...	...	...	...	1841	|	...	...	...	...	...	...	|	...	|	|	...	...
Göttingen ... a.	...	1301	...	...	...	...	...	1501	...	...	...	...	1901	|	...	...	...	...	...	...	|	...	0613	0541	...	...
Hannover Hbf ... a.	...	|	...	...	...	...	...	|	...	...	...	...	|	|	...	...	...	...	...	...	|	...	0702	0630	...	...
Braunschweig ... a.	...	1357	...	...	...	...	...	1557	...	...	...	...	1957	|	...	...	...	...	...	...	|	...	|	|	...	...
Wolfsburg ... a.	...	1415	...	...	...	...	...	1615	...	...	...	...	2015	|	...	...	...	...	...	...	|	...	|	|	...	...
Berlin Hauptbahnhof ... a.	...	1525	...	...	...	...	...	1725	...	...	...	...	2125	2204	...	...	...	...	...	...	0719	...	0858	0828	...	...
Berlin Ostbahnhof ... a.	...	1536	...	...	...	...	...	1736	...	...	...	...	2140	...	...	...	...	...	...	...	...	...	...	...	...	...

train type	*CNL*	*CNL*	*ICE*	*TGV*	*ICE*	*ICE*	*ICE*	*ICE*	*TGV*	*TGV*	*ICE*	*ICE*	*ICE*	*ICE*	*ICE*	*ICE*	*EC*	*ICE*	*TGV*	*ICE*	*EC*	*ICE*	*ICE*	*ICE*	*CNL*	
train number	**458**	**1258**	**9558**	**9568**	**1028**	**822**	**1656**	**275**	**9556**	**9556**	**724**	**1652**	**279**	**9554**	**626**	**373**	**176**	**1558**	**9552**	**622**	**378**	**1556**	**375**	**9550**	**450**	
notes			[R]★	[R]★	🍷	🍷	🍷	🍷	[R]★	[R]★	🍷	🍷	🍷	[R]★	**926**	🍷	✖	🍷	[R]★	**1222**	✖	🍷	🍷	[R]★		
notes	**B**	**C**	①–⑤	⑥		①–⑥	①–⑥	①–⑤	①–⑥	⑦					**1226**	**J**	**G**			🍷	**E**			⑧	[R]	
				Q				**j**	**T**	**T**					🍷										**H**	
Berlin Ostbahnhof ... d.	...	...	...	...	...	...	...	0407	...	...	...	...	0822	...	...	1222	...	...	...	...	...	...	1422	...	...	...
Berlin Hauptbahnhof ... d.	...	2215	...	...	...	...	...	0418	...	...	...	...	0833	...	...	1233	...	...	...	...	...	...	1433	...	2008	...
Wolfsburg ... d.	...	|	...	...	...	...	...	0533	...	...	...	...	0940	...	...	1340	...	...	...	...	...	...	1540	...	|	...
Braunschweig ... d.	...	|	...	...	...	...	...	0554	...	...	...	...	0958	...	...	1358	...	...	...	...	...	...	1558	...	|	...
Hannover Hbf ... d.	...	|	...	...	...	...	...	|	...	...	...	...	|	...	...	|	...	...	...	...	...	...	|	...	2216	...
Göttingen ... d.	...	|	...	...	...	...	...	0646	...	...	...	...	1055	...	...	1455	...	...	...	...	...	...	1655	...	2332	...
Kassel Wilhelmshöhe ... d.	...	|	...	...	...	...	...	0707	...	...	...	...	1116	...	...	1516	...	...	...	...	...	...	1716	...	|	...
Praha hlavní ... d.	1829	|	...	...	...	...	...	|	...	...	...	...	|	...	...	|	0829	...	...	...	1029	..	|	...	|	...
Praha Holešovice ... d.	1839	|	...	...	...	...	...	|	...	...	...	...	|	...	...	|	0838	...	...	...	1038	...	|	...	|	...
Děčín (🏛 = Schöna) ... d.	2000	|	...	...	...	...	...	|	...	...	...	...	|	...	...	|	1000	...	...	...	1200	...	|	...	|	...
Dresden Hbf ... d.	2104	|	...	...	...	...	...	|	...	...	...	0753	|	...	...	|	1045	1153	...	...	1245	1353	|	...	|	...
Leipzig Hbf ... d.	2226	|	...	...	...	...	0459	|	...	...	...	0911	|	...	...	|	...	1311	...	...	...	1511	|	...	|	...
Erfurt ... d.	0121	0121	...	...	...	...	0618	|	...	...	...	1025	|	...	...	|	...	1425	...	...	...	1625	|	...	|	...
Fulda ... d.	|	|	...	...	...	...	0744	0738	...	...	...	1144	1147	...	...	1547	...	1544	...	...	...	1744	1747	...	|	...
Nürnberg ... d.	|	|	...	...	0530	0600	|	|	...	...	1000	|	|	...	1400	|	...	|	...	1600	...	|	|	...	|	...
Würzburg ... d.	|	|	...	...	0626	0655	|	|	...	...	1055	|	|	...	1455	|	...	|	...	1655	...	|	|	...	|	...
Frankfurt (Main) Hbf ... a.	0359**q**	0359**q**	...	...	0736	0804	0837	0844	...	...	1204	1237	1244	...	1604	1644	...	1637	...	1804	...	1837	1844	...	|	...
Frankfurt (Main) Hbf ... d.	|	|	0600	0654	...	...	...	...	0857	0857	...	...	...	1301	...	...	...	...	1658	...	...	...	...	1901	|	...
Mannheim ... d.	0443	0443	0640	0739	...	...	...	...	0942	0942	...	...	...	1341	...	...	...	...	1743	...	...	...	...	1941	|	...
Karlsruhe Hbf ... d.	...	...	|	|	...	...	...	...	|	|	...	...	...	|	...	...	...	...	|	...	...	...	...	|	|	...
Kaiserslautern ... d.	...	...	0722	0823	...	...	...	...	1023	1023	...	...	...	1423	...	...	...	...	1824	...	...	...	...	2023	|	...
Saarbrücken ... d.	...	...	0800	0903	...	...	...	...	1102	1102	...	...	...	1502	...	...	...	...	1903	...	...	...	...	2102	|	...
Forbach 🏛 ... a.	...	...	0808	0911	...	...	...	...	|	1110	...	...	...	|	...	...	...	...	1911	...	...	...	...	|	|	...
Metz ... a.	...	...	|	|	...	...	...	...	|	|	...	...	...	|	...	...	...	...	|	...	...	...	...	|	|	...
Paris Est ... a.	...	...	1005**e**	1101**e**	...	...	...	...	1255	1302	...	...	...	1655**e**	...	...	...	...	2112**c**	...	...	...	...	2258**e**	0924	...

A – *City Night Line* PERSEUS – 🛏 1, 2 cl., ▬ 2 cl. (including ladies only berths), (2) (reclining) 🍷 Paris - Kehl 🏛 - Hannover - Berlin Spandau - Berlin Hbf - Berlin Südkreuz. [R] Special fares apply. (Table **20**).
B – *City Night Line* CANOPUS – 🛏 1,2 cl., ▬ 2 cl., (2) (reclining) 🍷 Zürich - Basel - Frankfurt (Main) **Süd** - Děčín 🏛 - Praha and v.v. [R] Special fares apply.
C – *City Night Line* SIRIUS – 🛏 1, 2 cl., 🛏 1, 2 cl. (T4), ▬ 2 cl. (4, 6 berth), (2) (reclining) 🍷 Zürich - Basel - Mannheim - Frankfurt (Main) **Süd** - Berlin and v.v. [R] Special fares apply.
D – ALOIS NEGRELLI – (12) ✖ Berlin - Dresden - Praha.
E – CARL MARIA VON WEBER – (12) ✖ Wien - Praha - Dresden - Berlin - Stralsund. To Ostseebad Binz on dates in Table **844**).
G – (12) ✖ Brno - Praha - Dresden - Berlin - Hamburg.
H – *City Night Line* PERSEUS - 🛏 1, 2 cl., ▬ 2 cl. (including ladies only berths), (2) (reclining) 🍷 Berlin Südkreuz - Berlin Hbf - Berlin Spandau - Hannover - Kehl 🏛 - Paris. [R] Special fares apply. (Table **20**).
J – (12) 🍷 Interlaken Ost - Basel - Mannheim - Berlin and v.v.
K – CARL MARIA VON WEBER – (12) ✖ Stralsund - Berlin - Dresden - Praha - Brno. From Ostseebad Binz on dates in Table **60**.
P – On ⑥ (also Apr. 20, June 8; not Apr. 19, June 7) runs as *TGV* **9565**.
Q – On Apr. 19, June 7 runs as *ICE* **9564**.
R – ⑥⑦.
S – Daily except on dates in note **R**. Calls at Göttingen 0613, Hannover 0702 and Berlin 0858 on certain dates.
T – Runs as *ICE* **9566** on certain dates.

c – 2054, 2102 on certain dates.
e – 5 - 15 minutes earlier on certain dates.
j – Not Apr. 18, 21, May 1, 29, June 9.
q – Frankfurt (Main) **Süd**.
r – ①⑥ (also Apr. 18, 22, May 1, 29, June 10; not Apr. 21).
s – Calls to set down only.
u – Calls to pick up only.
v – 1906 until Mar 3 and from Apr. 18.
w – Not Apr. 21, June 9.
x – 8 - 12 minutes later from Apr. 18.
z – 5 minutes earlier Mar 4 - Apr. 17.

★ – *Alleo* ICE / TGV service. A DB / SNCF joint enterprise.

32 LONDON - PARIS - MÜNCHEN - WIEN - BUDAPEST - BUCURESTI

Alternative services London - München and London - Wien - Budapest are available via Brussels (Table **21**)

train type	*IC*	*RJ*	*TGV*	*TGV*	*TGV*	*ICE*	*EC*	*RJ*	*TGV*	*ICE*	*EC*	☆	☆	*TGV*	*ICE*	*EC*	☆	☆	*ICE*	*ICE*	☆	☆	*TGV*	*EN*	
train number	**2265**	**65**	**9591**	**9571**	**9571**	**1091**	**115**	**69**	**9553**	**595**	**219**	**9002**	**9004**	**9573**	**597**	**117**	**9008**	**9010**	**9555**	**599**	**9018**	**9020**	**9575**	**463**	
train number/notes	🍷	🍷	★	★	★	**593**	🍷	🍷	★	🍷	🍷	⑥	①–⑤	★	🍷	**1217**	①–⑤	⑦	★	🍷		⑥	★		
notes	**E**		**B**	**C**		🍷					**x**		**g**			🍷		**y**	**P**		**A**	**W**		**K**	
London St Pancras **10** d.	...	...	...	...	...	...	...	...	...	...	...	0618	0701	...	...	...	0755	0819	...	...	1025	1101	...	...	...
Paris Nord **10** a.	...	...	...	...	...	...	...	...	...	...	...	0947	1017	...	...	...	1117	1147	...	...	1347	1417	...	...	...
Paris Est d.	...	...	0725	0725	0718	...	...	...	0858e	...	...	▬	...	1117	...	...	▬	...	1310	...	▬	...	1525	...	...
Strasbourg d.	...	...	0947	0947	0947	...	...	...	|	...	...	...	...	1347	...	...	...	...	|	...	...	...	1747	...	...
Kehl 🛃 d.	...	...	|	|	|	...	...	...	◧	...	...	...	...	|	...	...	...	...	◧	...	...	...	|	...	...
Mannheim Hbf d.	...	...	|	|	|	...	...	...	1215	1230	...	...	...	|	...	...	...	...	1617	1630	...	...	|	...	...
Karlsruhe Hbf d.	0806	...	1028	1028	1028	...	...	...	▬	|	...	...	...	1428	...	...	...	...	...	|	...	...	1828	...	...
Stuttgart Hbf d.	0853	...	|	1116	1104z	1112	1158	...	...	1312	1358	...	...	1504	1512	1558	...	...	...	1712	...	...	1919	...	...
Ulm Hbf d.	0956	...	1221	1221	...	1209	1256	...	...	1409	1456	...	...	...	1609	1656	...	...	...	1809	...	...	2017	...	...
Augsburg Hbf d.	1044	...	1306	1306	...	1255	1342	...	...	1455	1542	*RJ*	...	...	1655	1742	...	...	...	1855	*EC*	...	2103	...	...
München Pasing a.	1106	...	|	|	...	1318	|	...	...	1519	|	**261**	...	...	1718	|	*RJ*	...	...	1918	**391**	...	|	...	...
München Hbf a.	1115	...	1336	1336	...	1327	1411	...	...	1528	1611	🍷	...	...	1727	1811	**661**	...	...	1927	🍷	...	2136	...	...
München Hbf d.	...	1134	...	...	...	...	1427	1527	...	...	1627	1723	...	...	...	1827	🍷	...	...	...	2024	...	...	2340	...
Salzburg Hbf 🛃 a.	...	1302	...	...	...	...	1609	1657	*EN*	...	1809	1857	...	...	...	2009	2102	...	...	...	2212	...	...	0118	...
Linz Hbf a.	...	1415	...	...	...	...	...	1806	**347**	...	...	2006	...	...	...	...	2206	...	...	...	2330f	...	...	0338	...
St Pölten Hbf a.	...	1505	...	...	...	...	...	1858	¶	...	...	2058	...	...	...	...	2258	...	...	...	...	...	...	0458	...
Wien Westbahnhof a.	...	1530	...	...	...	...	...	1924	**M**	...	...	2124	...	...	...	...	2324	...	...	...	...	...	...	0545h	...
Wien Westbahnhof d.	...	1548	...	...	...	...	...	...	1948	...	...	...	...	...	...	...	...	...	...	...	...	...	...	0601q	...
Hegyeshalom 🛃 a.	...	1655	...	...	...	...	...	...	2055	...	...	...	...	...	...	...	...	...	...	...	...	...	...	0655	...
Györ a.	...	1721	...	...	...	...	...	...	2121	...	...	...	...	...	...	...	...	...	...	...	...	...	...	0724	...
Budapest Keleti a.	...	1849	...	...	...	...	...	...	2249	...	...	...	...	...	...	...	...	...	...	...	...	...	...	0854	...
Bucuresti Nord a.	...	...	...	...	...	...	...	...	1605	...	...	...	...	...	...	...	...	...	...	...	...	...	...	...	...

train type	☆	*TGV*	*ICE*	☆	☆	*TGV*	*ICE*	☆	☆	*CNL*	*RJ*	*EN*
train number	**9024**	**9577**	**693**	**9030**	**9032**	**9559**	**1093**	**9034**	**9036**	**40451**	**61**	**473**
train number/notes		★	🍷	⑥	Ⓑ	★	**695**	⑦		Ⓡ	🍷	¶
notes		Ⓑ		**D**				**y**		**G**		**S**
London St Pancras **10** d.	1225	...	...	1401	1431	...	...	1501	1531	...	...	...
Paris Nord **10** a.	1547	...	...	1717	1747	...	...	1817	1847	...	...	...
Paris Est d.	...	1710	...	...	...	1843j	...	...	...	2005o	...	...
Strasbourg d.	...	1947	...	...	...	|	...	...	...	|	...	...
Kehl 🛃 d.	...	|	...	...	...	◧	...	...	...	|	...	...
Mannheim Hbf d.	...	|	...	...	...	2217	2230	...	...	|	...	...
Karlsruhe Hbf d.	...	2029	...	...	...	...	|	...	...	|	...	...
Stuttgart Hbf d.	...	2105	2112	...	...	...	2308	...	...	0417s	...	...
Ulm Hbf d.	...	...	2209	...	...	...	...	...	...	0542s	...	...
Augsburg Hbf d.	...	...	2255	...	...	...	...	...	...	0633s	...	...
München Pasing a.	...	...	2318	...	...	...	...	...	...	|	...	...
München Hbf a.	...	...	2327	...	...	...	...	...	...	0710	...	...
München Hbf d.	...	...	...	...	...	...	...	...	...	...	0731	...
Innsbruck Hbf a.	...	...	...	...	...	...	...	...	...	...	|	...
Salzburg Hbf 🛃 a.	...	...	...	...	...	...	...	...	...	...	0902	...
Linz Hbf a.	...	...	...	...	...	...	...	...	...	...	1015	...
St Pölten Hbf a.	...	...	...	...	...	...	...	...	...	...	1105	...
Wien Westbahnhof a.	...	...	...	...	...	...	...	...	...	...	1130	...
Wien Westbahnhof d.	...	...	...	...	...	...	...	...	...	...	1148	...
Hegyeshalom 🛃 a.	...	...	...	...	...	...	...	...	...	...	1255	...
Györ a.	...	...	...	...	...	...	...	...	...	...	1321	...
Budapest Keleti a.	...	...	...	...	...	...	...	...	...	...	1449	1910
Bucuresti Nord a.	...	...	...	...	...	...	...	...	...	...	...	1210

train type	*EN*	*RJ*	*CNL*	*ICE*	*ICE*	☆	*TGV*	☆
train number	**472**	**66**	**40418**	**616**	**9558**	**9023**	**9568**	**9031**
train number/notes	¶	🍷	Ⓡ		★		★**Q**	
notes	**S**		**H**		①–⑤		⑥	
Bucuresti Nord d.	1725	...	...	...	...	...	...	...
Budapest Keleti d.	0850	1310	...	...	...	...	...	...
Györ d.	...	1432	...	...	...	...	...	...
Hegyeshalom 🛃 d.	...	1502	...	...	...	...	...	...
Wien Westbahnhof a.	...	1612	...	...	...	...	...	...
Wien Westbahnhof d.	...	1630	...	...	...	...	...	...
St Pölten Hbf d.	...	1654	...	...	...	...	...	...
Linz Hbf d.	...	1745	...	...	...	...	...	...
Salzburg Hbf 🛃 d.	...	1856	...	...	...	...	...	...
Innsbruck Hbf d.	...	|	...	...	...	...	...	...
München Hbf a.	...	2025	...	...	...	...	...	...
München Hbf d.	...	2045n	2250	0325	...	...	...	...
München Pasing d.	...	2051n	|	0333	...	...	...	...
Augsburg Hbf d.	...	2116n	2320u	0357	...	...	...	...
Ulm Hbf d.	...	2204n	0010u	0440	...	...	...	...
Stuttgart Hbf d.	...	2305n	0135u	0551	...	...	...	...
Karlsruhe Hbf d.	...	|	|	|	...	...	...	...
Mannheim Hbf d.	...	2344n	|	0628	0640	...	0739	...
Kehl 🛃 d.	...	...	|	...	◧	...	◧	...
Strasbourg a.	...	...	|	...	|	...	|	...
Paris Est a.	...	...	0924	...	1005r	...	1101r	...
Paris Nord **10** d.	...	...	...	...	...	1113	...	1313
London St Pancras **10** a.	...	...	...	...	...	1230	...	1439

train type	*TGV*	☆	*IC*	*EN*	*TGV*	☆	☆	*EC*	*ICE*	*TGV*	☆	*RJ*	*EC*	*TGV*	*ICE*	*TGV*	*EN*	*RJ*	*EC*	*ICE*	*TGV*	*TGV*	*TGV*	*IC*	
train number	**9578**	**9027**	**72**	**462**	**9576**	**9035**	**9039**	**390**	**598**	**9574**	**9051**	**262**	**114**	**9592**	**1090**	**9572**	**346**	**60**	**112**	**592**	**9570**	**9570**	**9550**	**2264**	
train number/notes	★	⑦	Ⓡ		★	⑥⑦		🍷	🍷	★	Ⓑ	🍷	🍷	★	**594**	★	¶	🍷	🍷	🍷	★	★	★		
notes	①–⑥	**F**	**T**	**K**		**b**								**B**	🍷	⑥⑦	**M**				①–⑤	**C**	Ⓑ	**E**	
Bucuresti Nord d.	...	...	0545	...	...	...	...	...	...	...	...	...	...	...	...	...	1300	...	...	...	...	...	...	...	...
Budapest Keleti d.	...	...	1850	2110	...	...	...	...	...	...	...	...	...	...	...	...	0510	0710	...	...	...	...	...	...	...
Györ d.	...	...	▬	2232	...	...	...	...	...	...	...	...	...	...	...	...	0632	0832	...	...	...	...	...	...	...
Hegyeshalom 🛃 d.	...	...	...	2302	...	...	...	...	...	...	...	...	...	...	...	...	0702	0902	...	...	...	...	...	...	...
Wien Westbahnhof a.	...	...	...	2356q	...	...	...	...	...	...	...	...	...	...	...	...	0816	1012	...	...	...	...	...	...	...
Wien Westbahnhof d.	...	...	...	0011h	...	...	...	...	...	...	...	0836	...	...	...	...	▬	1030	...	...	...	...	...	...	...
St Pölten Hbf d.	...	...	...	0052	...	...	...	...	...	...	...	0902	...	...	...	...	...	1054	...	...	...	...	...	...	...
Linz Hbf d.	...	...	...	0201	...	...	...	0632c	...	...	...	0953	...	...	...	...	...	1145	...	...	...	...	...	...	...
Salzburg Hbf 🛃 d.	...	...	...	0428	...	...	...	0751	...	...	...	1102	1151	...	...	...	...	1256	1351	...	...	...	...	...	...
München Hbf a.	...	...	...	0610	...	...	...	0933	...	...	...	1229	1333	...	...	...	...	1425	1533	...	...	...	...	...	...
München Hbf d.	...	...	...	▬	0627	...	...	0945	1028	...	...	...	1345	1401	1428	...	...	...	1546	1628	...	1615	...	1648	...
München Pasing d.	...	...	...	...	|	...	...	|	1036	...	...	...	|	|	1436	...	...	...	|	1636	...	|	...	1656	...
Augsburg Hbf d.	...	...	...	...	0657	...	...	1017	1103	...	...	...	1417	1432	1503	...	...	...	1617	1703	...	1646	...	1721	...
Ulm Hbf d.	...	...	...	...	0743	...	...	1104	1151	...	...	...	1504	1520	1551	...	*TGV*	...	1704	1751	...	1735	...	1804	...
Stuttgart Hbf d.	0655	...	...	...	0855	...	...	1201	1247	1255	...	...	1609	1625	1651	1655	**9552**	...	1801	1851	1855	1855	...	1911	...
Karlsruhe Hbf d.	0733	...	...	...	0933	...	...	...	...	1333	...	...	|	1719	|	1733	★	...	...	|	1933	1933	...	1953	...
Mannheim Hbf d.	|	...	...	...	|	...	...	...	...	|	...	...	1656	|	1729	|	1743	...	...	1929	|	|	1941	...	...
Kehl 🛃 d.	|	...	☆	...	|	...	...	...	...	|	...	...	...	|	...	|	◧	...	...	...	|	|	◧	...	...
Strasbourg a.	0811	...	**9029**	☆	1011	...	...	...	...	1411	...	...	...	1811	...	1811	|	...	...	...	2011	2011	|	...	...
Paris Est a.	1035	...	**J**	**9031**	1235	...	...	...	...	1635	...	...	...	2035	...	2035	2112t	...	...	...	2235	2235	2258r	...	...
Paris Nord **10** d.	...	1213	1243	1313	...	1413	1513	...	...	...	1813	...	...	...	...	...	...	...	...	...	...	...	...	...	...
London St Pancras **10** a.	...	1330	1400	1439	...	1530	1639	...	...	...	1939	...	...	...	...	...	...	...	...	...	...	...	...	...	...

A – Ⓑ (daily Apr. 6 - Aug. 30). On Oct. 19 depart 1015.
B – June 19, Sept. 26, Oct. 3.
C – June 1, 22, Aug. 17, Sept. 28, Oct. 5.
D – ⑥ (⑤⑥⑦ Mar. 29 - Aug. 30) also Aug. 25.
E – From / to Basel (Table **912**).
F – ⑦ (⑤⑦ Apr. 4 - Aug. 30) also Aug. 25, Nov. 11).
G – *City Night Line* CASSIOPEIA – 🛏 1, 2 cl., 🛌 2 cl. (including ladies only compartment), [2] 🍷 Paris - München. Ⓡ Special fares apply.
H – *City Night Line* CASSIOPEIA – 🛏 1, 2 cl., 🛌 2 cl. (including ladies only compartment), [2] 🍷 München - Paris. Ⓡ Special fares apply.
J – ①–⑥ May 25 - Aug. 30 (not Aug. 25); ①–⑤ Aug. 31 - Dec. 14 (not Nov. 11).
K – KÁLMÁN IMRE – 🛏 1, 2 cl., 🛌 2 cl., [2] München - Budapest and v.v.
M – DACIA – 🛏 1, 2 cl., 🛌 2 cl., [2] ✕ Wien - Budapest - Bucuresti and v.v.
P – On ⑥ (also June 8; not June 7) runs as *TGV* **9565**.
Q – On June 7 runs as *ICE* **9564**.
S – *EuroNight* ISTER – 🛏 1, 2 cl., 🛌 1, 2 cl., [2] ✕ Budapest - Bucuresti and v.v.
T – TRAIANUS – [12] 🍷 Bucuresti - Budapest.
W – ⑥ (⑥⑦ Mar. 29 - Aug. 30) also Aug. 25.

b – Also Nov. 11.
c – ①–⑥.
e – 0857 on ⑦. 8 - 12 minutes later from Apr. 18.
f – Not ⑥.
g – Not Aug. 25, Nov. 11.
h – Wien **Hütteldorf**.
j – 1906 from Apr. 18.
n – ⑤⑥ (also June 8, Oct. 2).
o – 2025 on dates shown in Table **30**.
q – Wien **Meidling**.
r – 5 - 15 minutes earlier on certain dates.
s – Calls to set down only.
t – 2054, 2102 on certain dates.
u – Calls to pick up only.
x – To Graz (arrive 2223; Table **68**).
y – Also Aug. 25, Nov. 11.

z – 1112 on June 1, 22, Aug. 17, Sept. 28, Oct. 5.

¶ – Compulsory reservation for internationa journeys between Hungary and Romania

◧ – 🛃 is at Forbach.

TGV – Ⓡ, supplement payable, 🍷.

☆ – Eurostar train. Ⓡ, ✕ in 1st class, 🍷 in 2nd class. Special fares payable. Minimum check-in time 30 min. Valid June 1 - Dec. 13.

★ – *Alleo* ICE / TGV service. A DB / SNCF joint enterprise.

RJ – ÖBB *Railjet* service. [1] (business class), [1] (first class), [2] (economy class), ✕.

LONDON - PARIS - BASEL - ZÜRICH, INTERLAKEN, BRIG and MILANO 40

For **Brussels - Köln - Milano** and **Brussels - Strasbourg - Milano** services see Table **43**.

train type / number	*TGV*	*IC*	*IC*	*IC*	*IC*	*ICN*	*IC*	*EC*	☆	*TGV*	*IC*	*EC*	*IC*	*IC*	*ICN*	☆	☆	☆	*TGV*	*IC*	*EC*	*IC*	*IC*	*ICN*	*ICN*	*IR*
train number	**9203**	**569**	**1069**	**969**	**620**	**1520**	**671**	**57**	**9080**	**9211**	**575**	**321**	**1075**	**1626**	**526**	**9004**	**9006**	**9006**	**9213**	**579**	**323**	**1079**	**830**	**1630**	**530**	**2181**
notes	♥ **k**							🅁 🍷	①–⑤	♥		🅁 🍷				①–⑤	⑥		♥	🍷	🅁 🍷					
	①–⑥							⊗	**h**			⊗				**g**	**Z**	**E**			⊗					
London St Pancras ....d.	...	...	...	...	...	...	...	...	0540	...	...	...	...	...	...	0701	0722	0731	...	...	...	...	...	...	...	...
Paris Nord ....a.	...	...	...	...	...	...	...	...	0917	...	...	...	...	...	...	1017	1047	1047	...	...	...	...	...	...	...	...
Paris Gare de Lyon ....d.	0711**z**	...	...	...	...	...	...	...	...	1019**z**	...	...	...	...	...	▬	▬	...	1157	...	...	...	...	...	...	...
Dijon ....d.	0846**z**	...	...	...	...	...	...	...	...	1153**z**	...	...	...	...	...	...	...	...	1351	...	...	...	...	...	...	...
Besançon TGV ⊖ ....d.	|	...	...	...	...	...	...	...	...	|	...	...	...	...	...	...	...	...	|	...	...	...	...	...	...	...
Belfort TGV ⊡ ....d.	0941	...	...	...	...	...	...	...	...	|	...	...	...	...	...	...	...	...	|	...	...	...	...	...	...	...
Mulhouse ....d.	1006	...	...	...	...	...	...	...	...	1306	...	...	...	...	...	*IR*	...	...	1506	...	...	...	...	...	...	...
Basel SBB ....a.	1026	...	...	...	...	...	...	...	...	1326	...	...	...	...	...	**2177**	...	...	1526	...	...	...	...	...	...	...
Basel SBB ....d.	1033	...	1031	1059	1103	...	1104	1231	...	1333	...	...	1331	1403	...	1404	...	...	1533	...	...	1531	...	1603	...	1604
Zürich HB ....a.	1126	1137	|	|	|	...	|	|	...	1426	1437	1532	|	|	...	|	...	...	1626	1637	1732	|	...	|	...	|
Landquart ....a.	...	1241	|	|	|	...	|	|	...	...	1541	|	|	|	...	|	...	...	...	1741	|	|	...	|	...	|
Chur ....a.	...	1252	|	|	|	...	|	|	...	...	1552	|	|	|	...	|	...	...	...	1752	|	|	...	|	...	|
Chur ....d.	...	*1258*	|	|	|	...	|	|	...	...	*1558*	|	|	|	...	|	...	...	...	*1758*	|	|	...	|	...	|
St Moritz ....a.	...	*1458*	|	|	|	...	|	|	...	...	*1758*	|	|	|	...	|	...	...	...	*1958*	|	|	...	|	...	|
Luzern ....a.	...	...	|	|	|	...	1205	|	...	...	...	|	|	|	...	1505	...	...	...	...	|	|	...	|	...	1705
Arth Goldau ....a.	...	...	|	|	|	...	1244	|	...	...	...	1614	|	|	...	1544	...	...	...	...	1814	|	...	|	...	1744
Bellinzona ....a.	...	...	|	|	|	...	1423	|	...	...	...	1757	|	|	...	1753	...	...	...	...	1957	|	...	|	...	1953
Locarno ....a.	...	...	|	|	|	...	1447	|	...	...	...	|	|	|	...	1813	...	...	...	...	|	|	...	|	...	2013
Lugano ....a.	...	...	|	|	|	...	...	|	...	...	...	1824	|	|	...	...	*IC*	...	...	...	2024	|	...	|	...	...
Chiasso 🏛 ....a.	...	...	|	|	|	...	...	|	...	...	...	1848	|	|	...	...	**826**	...	...	...	2048	|	...	|	...	...
Bern ....a.	...	...	1127	1156	|	...	...	1327	...	...	...	|	1427	|	...	...	1507	...	...	...	|	1627	1707	|	...	...
Thun ....a.	...	...	1152	1221	|	...	...	1352	...	...	...	|	1452	|	...	...	1524	...	...	...	|	1652	1724	|	...	...
Spiez ....a.	...	...	1202	1231	|	...	...	1402	...	...	...	|	1502	|	...	...	1534	...	...	...	|	1702	1734	|	...	...
Interlaken West ....a.	...	...	|	1251	|	...	...	|	...	...	...	|	1522	|	...	...	|	...	...	...	|	1722	|	|	...	...
Interlaken Ost ....a.	...	...	|	1257	|	...	...	|	...	...	...	|	1528	|	...	...	|	...	...	...	|	1728	|	|	...	...
Biel/Bienne ....a.	...	...	|	...	1210	1216	...	|	...	...	...	|	...	1510	1519	...	|	...	...	...	|	...	|	1710	1719	...
Neuchâtel ....a.	...	...	|	...	1235	1232	...	|	...	...	...	|	...	1532	1535	...	|	...	...	...	|	...	|	1732	1735	...
Lausanne ....a.	...	...	|	...	|	1315	...	|	...	...	...	|	...	1615	|	...	|	...	...	...	|	...	|	1815	|	...
Genève ....a.	...	...	|	...	1342	...	...	|	...	...	...	|	...	...	1642	...	|	...	...	...	|	...	|	...	1842	...
Brig ....a.	...	...	1240	...	...	...	...	1440	...	...	...	|	...	...	...	...	1611	...	...	...	|	...	1811	...	...	...
Como San Giovanni ....a.	...	...	...	...	...	...	...	◧	...	...	...	|	...	...	...	...	...	...	...	...	2056	...	...	...	...	...
Milano Centrale ....a.	...	...	...	...	...	...	...	1635	...	...	...	1935	...	...	...	...	...	...	...	...	2135	...	...	...	...	...

train type / number	☆	*TGV*	*EC*		*IC*	*IR*	*EC*	*ICN*	*ICN*	☆	☆	*TGV*	*IC*	*IC*	*IC*	*ICE*	*ICN*	*IR*	☆	☆	*TGV*	*RE*	*TGV*	*IC*	*ICN*	*IR*
train number	**9014**	**9215**	**59**		**585**	**2185**	**325**	**1636**	**536**	**9022**	**9022**	**9219**	**589**	**889**	**1087**	**373**	**1640**	**2540**	**9028**	**9030**	**9223**	**1795**	**9225**	**1644**	**1544**	**2197**
notes		♥	🅁 🍷		🍷		🅁 🍷			⑥		♥							Ⓑ	⑥	♥		♥			
			⊗				⊗			**W**	**X**									**D**						
London St Pancras ....d.	0917**t**	...	...	...	...	...	...	...	...	1101	1131	...	...	...	...	...	...	...	1331	1401	...	...	...	...	...	...
Paris Nord ....a.	1247	...	...	...	...	...	...	...	...	1417	1447	...	...	...	...	...	...	...	1647	1717	...	...	...	...	...	...
Paris Gare de Lyon ....d.	...	1415**e**	...	...	...	...	...	...	...	...	...	1557**c**	...	...	...	...	...	...	▬	...	1815**z**	...	1815**z**	...	...	...
Dijon ....d.	...	|	...	...	...	...	...	...	...	...	...	|	...	...	...	...	...	...	...	...	1952**z**	...	1952**z**	...	...	...
Besançon TGV ⊖ ....d.	...	|	...	...	...	...	...	...	...	...	...	|	...	...	...	...	...	...	...	...	|	...	|	...	...	...
Belfort TGV ⊡ ....d.	...	1643	...	...	...	...	...	...	...	...	...	1842	...	...	...	...	...	...	...	...	|	...	|	...	...	...
Mulhouse ....d.	...	1707	...	...	...	...	...	...	...	...	...	1907	...	...	...	...	...	...	*IR*	...	2106	...	2106	...	...	...
Basel SBB ....a.	...	1726	...	...	...	...	...	...	...	...	...	1926	...	...	...	...	...	...	**2191**	...	2126	...	2126	...	...	...
Basel SBB ....d.	...	1736	1731	...	1733	1804	...	1803	...	...	...	1933	...	...	1931	1959	2003	...	2004	...	2133	...	2136	2203	...	2202
Zürich HB ....a.	...	1835	|	...	1826	|	1932	|	...	...	...	2026	2037	2109	|	|	|	...	|	...	2226	2312	|	|	...	|
Landquart ....a.	...	...	|	...	1941	|	|	|	...	...	...	...	2141	|	|	|	|	...	|	...	...	0039	|	|	...	|
Chur ....a.	...	...	|	...	1952	|	|	|	...	...	...	...	2152	|	|	|	|	...	|	...	...	0049	|	|	...	|
Chur ....d.	...	...	|	...	*1958*	|	|	|	...	...	...	...	...	|	|	|	|	...	|	...	...	...	|	|	...	|
St Moritz ....a.	...	...	|	...	*2157*	|	|	|	...	...	...	...	...	|	|	|	|	...	|	...	...	...	|	|	...	|
Luzern ....a.	...	...	|	...	...	1905	|	|	...	...	...	...	...	|	|	|	|	...	2105	...	...	...	|	|	...	2305
Arth Goldau ....a.	...	...	|	...	...	1944	2014	|	...	...	...	...	...	2146	|	|	|	...	2144	...	...	...	|	|	...	...
Bellinzona ....a.	...	...	|	...	...	2153	2157	|	...	...	...	...	...	2323	|	|	|	...	...	...	...	...	|	|	...	...
Locarno ....a.	...	...	|	...	...	...	|	|	...	...	...	...	...	*2356*	|	|	|	...	...	...	...	...	|	|	...	...
Lugano ....a.	...	...	|	...	...	...	2224	|	...	...	...	...	...	2347	|	|	|	...	...	...	...	...	|	|	...	...
Chiasso 🏛 ....a.	...	...	|	...	...	...	2248	|	...	...	...	...	...	0012	|	|	|	...	...	...	...	...	|	|	...	...
Bern ....a.	...	...	1827	...	...	...	|	|	...	...	...	...	...	...	2027	2056	|	...	...	...	...	...	2250	|	...	...
Thun ....a.	...	...	1852	...	...	...	|	|	...	...	...	...	...	...	2052	2124	|	...	...	...	...	...	|	|	...	...
Spiez ....a.	...	...	1902	1905	...	...	|	|	...	...	...	...	...	...	2102	2134	|	...	...	...	...	...	|	|	...	...
Interlaken West ....a.	...	...	|	1923	...	...	|	|	...	...	...	...	...	...	|	2151	|	...	...	...	...	...	2348	|	...	...
Interlaken Ost ....a.	...	...	|	1928	...	...	|	|	...	...	...	...	...	...	|	2157	|	...	...	...	...	...	2353	|	...	...
Biel/Bienne ....a.	...	...	|	...	...	...	|	1910	1919	...	...	...	...	...	|	...	2110	...	...	...	...	...	...	2310	2316	...
Neuchâtel ....a.	...	...	|	...	...	...	|	1932	1935	...	...	...	...	...	|	...	2132	...	...	...	...	...	...	...	2332	...
Lausanne ....a.	...	...	|	...	...	...	|	2015	|	...	...	...	...	...	|	...	2215	2221	...	...	...	...	...	...	0015	...
Genève ....a.	...	...	|	...	...	...	|	...	2046	...	...	...	...	...	|	...	...	2305	...	...	...	...	...	...	...	...
Brig ....a.	...	...	1940	...	...	...	|	...	...	...	...	...	...	...	2140	...	...	...	...	...	...	...	...	...	...	...
Como San Giovanni ....a.	...	...	◧	...	...	...	2256	...	...	...	...	...	...	...	...	...	...	...	...	...	...	...	...	...	...	...
Milano Centrale ....a.	...	...	2135	...	...	...	2335	...	...	...	...	...	...	...	...	...	...	...	...	...	...	...	...	...	...	...

D – ⑥ (⑤⑥⑦ Mar. 29 - Aug. 30) also Aug. 25.

E – ①–⑤ May 25 - Aug. 30 (not Aug. 25); ① Aug. 31 - Dec. 13.

W – ⑥ (⑥⑦ Mar. 29 - Aug. 30) also Aug. 25.

X – ②③④⑤⑥ (daily Mar. 25 - Aug. 30) not Aug. 25, Nov. 10, 11.

Z – Feb. 1 - July 28; Sept. 20 - Dec. 13.

c – 1623 Mar. 1 - Apr. 18.

e – 1423 Mar. 1 - Apr. 18, May 28.

g – Not Aug. 25, Nov. 11.

h – Not June 9, July 14, July 27 - Aug. 30, Nov. 10, 11.

k – Not Apr. 21, June 9.

t – 0922 on ⑥⑦ (also Aug. 25, Nov. 11).

z – 4 - 8 minutes later Mar. 1 - Apr. 18.

⊖ – Full name: Besancon Franche-Comté TGV.

⊡ – Full name: Belfort Montbéliard TGV.

♥ – *TGV Lyria* service. 🅁 🍷 special fares payable. At-seat meal service in first class.

◧ – 🏛 between Brig and Milano is Domodossola. Ticket point is **Iselle**.

⊗ – **ETR 470 / 610**. Compulsory reservation for international journeys. Supplement payable for international journeys and for internal journeys within Italy.

☆ – Eurostar train. 🅁, ✕ in 1st class, 🍷 in 2nd class. Special fares payable. Minimum check-in time 30 minutes. Valid June 1 - Dec. 13.

40 MILANO, BRIG, INTERLAKEN and ZÜRICH - BASEL - PARIS - LONDON

For **Milano - Köln - Brussels** and **Milano - Strasbourg - Brussels** services see Table **43**.

train type	*ICN*	*ICN*	*IR*	*IC*	*IC*	*TGV*	☆	*IC*	*ICN*	*ICN*	*IC*	*ICN*	*IC*	*TGV*	*TGV*	☆	*EC*	*ICN*	*ICN*	*IR*	*IC*	*IC*	*TGV*	☆		
train number	**1511**	**611**	**2162**	**1060**	**560**	**9206**	**9031**	**1064**	**1517**	**617**	**1066**	**654**	**566**	**9214**	**9210**	**9039**	**50**	**1521**	**621**	**2170**	**1070**	**570**	**9218**	**9047**		
notes	✗	✗				♥			✗	✗		🍷	🍷	♥	♥		🅁 🍷 ⊗	✗	✗			🍷	♥			
Milano Centrale d.	...	...	...	...	...	...	...	...	...	...	...	...	...	...	...	...	0725	...	...	...	...	...	...	...	...	...
Como San Giovanni d.	...	...	...	...	...	...	...	...	...	...	...	...	...	...	...	...	◧	...	...	...	...	...	...	...	...	...
Brig d.	...	...	...	...	...	...	...	0720	...	...	...	...	...	...	...	...	0920	...	...	...	...	...	...	...	...	...
Genève d.	...	...	...	...	...	...	...	│	...	0714	...	...	...	...	...	...	│	...	0914	...	...	...	...	...	...	...
Lausanne d.	0539	...	...	...	...	...	...	│	0745	│	...	...	...	...	...	...	│	0945	│	...	...	...	...	...	...	...
Neuchâtel d.	0624	...	...	...	...	...	...	│	0827	0824	...	...	...	...	...	...	│	1027	1024	...	...	...	...	...	...	...
Biel/Bienne d.	0641	0649	...	...	...	...	...	│	0843	0849	...	...	...	...	...	...	│	1043	1049	...	...	...	...	...	...	...
Interlaken Ost d.	...	│	...	0627	...	...	...	│	▬	│	0830	...	...	...	...	...	│	...	│	...	1030	...	...	...	...	...
Interlaken West d.	...	│	...	0632	...	...	...	│	...	│	0835	...	...	...	...	...	│	...	│	...	1035	...	...	...	...	...
Spiez d.	...	│	...	0654	...	...	...	0754	...	│	0854	...	...	...	...	...	0954	...	│	...	1054	...	...	...	...	...
Thun d.	...	│	...	0704	...	...	...	0804	...	│	0904	...	...	...	...	...	1004	...	│	...	1104	...	...	...	...	...
Bern d.	...	│	...	0734	...	...	...	0834	...	│	0934	...	...	0910	...	...	1034	...	│	...	1134	...	...	...	...	...
Chiasso 🏛 d.	...	│	...	│	...	...	...	│	...	│	│	0546	...	│	...	...	│	...	│	0711	│	...	...	...	...	...
Lugano d.	...	│	...	│	...	...	...	│	...	│	│	0612	...	│	...	...	│	...	│	0737	│	...	...	...	...	...
Locarno d.	...	│	...	│	...	...	...	│	...	│	│	│	...	│	...	...	│	...	│	│	│	...	...	...	...	...
Bellinzona d.	...	│	...	│	...	...	...	│	*IR*	│	│	0636	...	│	...	...	│	...	│	0806	│	...	...	...	...	...
Arth Goldau d.	...	│	...	│	...	...	...	│	**2166**	│	│	0813	...	│	...	...	│	...	│	1014	│	...	...	...	...	...
Luzern d.	...	│	0654	│	...	...	...	│	0854	│	│	│	...	│	...	...	│	...	│	1054	│	...	...	...	...	...
St Moritz d.	...	│	│	│	...	...	...	│	│	│	│	│	...	│	...	...	│	...	│	│	│	*0802*	...	...	...	...
Chur a.	...	│	│	│	...	...	...	│	│	│	│	│	...	│	...	...	│	...	│	│	│	*1003*	...	...	...	...
Chur d.	...	│	│	│	0606	...	...	│	│	│	│	│	0809	│	...	...	│	...	│	│	│	1009	...	...	...	...
Davos Platz d.	...	│	│	│	│	...	...	│	│	│	│	│	*0653*	│	...	...	│	...	│	│	│	*0902*	...	...	...	...
Landquart d.	...	│	│	│	0615	...	...	│	│	│	│	│	0819	│	...	...	│	...	│	│	│	1019	...	...	...	...
Sargans d.	...	│	│	│	0625	...	...	│	│	│	│	│	0828	│	...	...	│	...	│	│	│	1028	...	...	...	...
Zürich HB d.	...	│	│	│	0723	0734	...	│	│	│	│	0851	0923	│	0934	...	│	...	│	│	│	1123	1134	...	...	...
Basel SBB a.	...	0753	0755	0829	...	0827	...	0929	0955	0953	1029	...	...	1024	1027	...	1129	...	1153	1155	1229	...	1227	...	...	...
Basel SBB d.	...	...	...	...	...	0834	...	...	...	...	...	...	...	1034	1034	...	...	...	...	...	...	...	1234	...	...	...
Basel SNCF 🏛 ▷ d.	...	...	...	...	...	│	...	...	...	...	...	...	...	│	│	...	...	...	...	...	...	...	│	...	...	...
Mulhouse a.	...	...	...	...	...	0853	...	...	...	...	...	...	...	1053	1053	...	...	...	...	...	...	...	1253	...	...	...
Belfort TGV ⊡ a.	...	...	...	...	...	0918	...	...	...	...	...	...	...	│	│	...	...	...	...	...	...	...	1318	...	...	...
Besançon TGV ⊖ a.	...	...	...	...	...	│	...	...	...	...	...	...	...	│	│	...	...	...	...	...	...	...	│	...	...	...
Dijon a.	...	...	...	...	...	│	...	...	...	...	...	...	...	1210c	1210c	...	...	...	...	...	...	...	│	...	...	...
Paris Gare de Lyon a.	...	...	...	...	...	1137e	...	...	...	...	...	...	...	1345c	1345c	...	...	...	...	...	...	...	1537r	...	...	...
Paris Nord d.	...	...	...	...	...	...	1313	...	...	...	...	...	...	...	...	1513	...	...	...	...	...	...	...	1713	...	...
London St Pancras a.	...	...	...	...	...	...	1439	...	...	...	...	...	...	...	...	1639	...	...	...	...	...	...	...	1830	...	...

train type	*IC*	*ICN*	*ICN*	*IR*	*IC*	*EC*	*IC*	*TGV*	☆	*EC*	*EC*	*EC*	*ICN*	*ICN*	*IR*	*IC*	*TGV*	☆	*EC*	*IC*	*ICN*	*ICN*	*IR*	*ICE*	*IR*	*TGV*
train number	**1072**	**1525**	**625**	**2174**	**1074**	**312**	**574**	**9222**	**9055**	**314**	**96**	**52**	**1529**	**629**	**2178**	**1078**	**9226**	**9063**	**316**	**1080**	**1535**	**635**	**2182**	**1082**	**782**	**9230**
notes		✗	✗			🅁 🍷 ⊗	🍷	♥		🅁 🍷 ⊗		🅁 🍷 ⊗	✗	✗			♥ Ⓑ f	Ⓑ	🅁 🍷 ⊗		✗	✗				♥
Milano Centrale d.	...	...	...	...	...	0825	...	...	...	1025	...	1125	...	...	...	...	...	...	1225	...	...	...	...	...	...	...
Como San Giovanni d.	...	...	...	...	...	0903	...	...	...	1103	...	◧	...	...	...	...	...	...	1303	...	...	...	...	...	...	...
Brig d.	1120	...	...	...	...	│	...	...	...	│	...	1320	...	...	...	...	...	...	│	1520	...	...	...	...	...	...
Genève d.	│	...	1114	...	...	│	...	...	...	│	...	│	...	1314	...	...	...	...	│	│	...	1514	...	...	...	...
Lausanne d.	│	1145	│	...	...	│	...	...	...	│	...	│	1345	│	...	...	...	...	│	│	1545	│	...	...	...	...
Neuchâtel d.	│	1227	1224	...	...	│	...	...	...	│	...	│	1427	1424	...	...	...	...	│	│	1627	1624	...	...	...	...
Biel/Bienne d.	│	1243	1249	...	...	│	...	...	...	│	...	│	1443	1449	...	...	...	...	│	│	1643	1649	...	...	...	...
Interlaken Ost d.	│	...	│	...	1230	│	...	...	...	│	...	│	...	│	...	1430	...	...	│	│	...	│	...	1630	...	...
Interlaken West d.	│	...	│	...	1235	│	...	...	...	│	...	│	...	│	...	1435	...	...	│	│	...	│	...	1635	...	...
Spiez d.	1154	...	│	...	1254	│	...	...	...	│	...	1354	...	│	...	1454	...	...	│	1554	...	│	...	1654	...	...
Thun d.	1204	...	│	...	1304	│	...	...	...	│	...	1404	...	│	...	1504	...	...	│	1604	...	│	...	1704	...	...
Bern d.	1234	...	│	...	1334	│	...	...	...	│	...	1434	...	│	...	1534	...	...	│	1634	...	│	...	1734	...	...
Chiasso 🏛 d.	│	...	│	...	│	0912	...	...	...	1112	...	│	...	│	...	│	...	...	1312	│	...	│	...	│	...	...
Lugano d.	│	...	│	...	│	0934	...	...	...	1134	...	│	...	│	...	│	...	...	1334	│	...	│	...	│	...	...
Locarno d.	│	...	│	0945	│	│	...	...	...	│	...	│	...	│	1145	│	...	...	│	│	...	│	1345	│	...	...
Bellinzona d.	│	...	│	1006	│	1001	...	...	...	1201	...	│	...	│	1206	│	...	...	1401	│	...	│	1406	│	...	...
Arth Goldau d.	│	...	│	1214	│	1145	...	...	...	1345	...	│	...	│	1414	│	...	...	1545	│	...	│	1614	│	...	...
Luzern d.	│	...	│	1254	│	│	...	...	...	│	...	│	...	│	1454	│	...	...	│	│	...	│	1654	│	...	...
St Moritz d.	│	...	│	│	│	│	*1002*	...	...	│	*1102*	│	...	│	│	│	...	...	│	│	...	│	│	│	*1302*	...
Chur d.	│	...	│	│	│	│	*1203*	...	...	│	*1303*	│	...	│	│	│	...	...	│	│	...	│	│	│	*1503*	...
Chur d.	│	...	│	│	│	│	1209	...	...	│	1316	│	...	│	│	│	...	...	│	│	...	│	│	│	1516	...
Davos Platz d.	│	...	│	│	│	│	*1102*	...	...	│	*1202*	│	...	│	│	│	...	...	│	│	...	│	│	│	*1402*	...
Landquart d.	│	...	│	│	│	│	1219	...	...	│	1326	│	...	│	│	│	...	...	│	│	...	│	│	│	1526	...
Sargans d.	│	...	│	│	│	│	1228	...	...	│	1339	│	...	│	│	│	...	...	│	│	...	│	│	│	1539	...
Zürich HB d.	│	...	│	│	│	1228	1323	1334	...	1428	1448	│	...	│	│	│	1534	...	1628	│	...	│	│	│	1648	1727
Basel SBB a.	1329	...	1353	1355	1429	...	...	1427	...	...	...	1529	...	1553	1555	1629	1627	...	...	1729	...	1753	1755	1829	...	1823
Basel SBB d.	...	...	...	...	...	...	...	1434	...	...	...	...	...	...	...	...	1634	...	...	...	...	...	...	...	...	1834
Basel SNCF 🏛 ▷ d.	...	...	...	...	...	...	...	│	...	...	...	...	...	...	...	...	│	...	...	...	...	...	...	...	...	│
Mulhouse a.	...	...	...	...	...	...	...	1453	...	...	...	...	...	...	...	...	1653	...	...	...	...	...	...	...	...	1854
Belfort TGV ⊡ a.	...	...	...	...	...	...	...	│	...	...	...	...	...	...	...	...	│	...	...	...	...	...	...	...	...	1919
Besançon TGV ⊖ a.	...	...	...	...	...	...	...	│	...	...	...	...	...	...	...	...	│	...	...	...	...	...	...	...	...	│
Dijon a.	...	...	...	...	...	...	...	1603v	...	...	...	...	...	...	...	...	1802	...	...	...	...	...	...	...	...	│
Paris Gare de Lyon a.	...	...	...	...	...	...	...	1737v	...	...	...	...	...	...	...	...	1937z	...	...	...	...	...	...	...	...	2137x
Paris Nord d.	...	...	...	...	...	...	...	...	1913	...	...	...	...	...	...	...	...	2113	...	...	...	...	...	...	...	...
London St Pancras a.	...	...	...	...	...	...	...	...	2041	...	...	...	...	...	...	...	...	2236	...	...	...	...	...	...	...	...

c – Arrive Dijon 1159, 1202 and arrive Paris 1337, 1340 on certain dates.

e – Arrive 1140, 1145 on certain dates.

f – Not May 1, 8, 29, June 8.

r – Arrive 1540, 1545 on certain dates.

v – Arrive Dijon 1600, 1610 and arrive Paris 1740, 1745 on certain dates.

x – Arrive 2140, 2142, 2145 on certain dates.

z – Arrive 1940, 1945, 1957 on certain dates.

⊖ – Full name: Besancon Franche-Comté TGV.

⊡ – Full name: Belfort Montbéliard TGV.

♥ – *TGV Lyria* service. 🅁 🍷 special fares payable. At-seat meal service in first class.

◧ – 🏛 between Brig and Milano is Domodossola. Ticket point is **Iselle**.

☆ – Eurostar train. 🅁 ✗. Special fares payable. Minimum check-in time 30 minutes. Valid June 1 - Dec. 13

⊗ – **ETR 470 / 610**. Compulsory reservation for international journeys. Supplement payable for internationa journeys. *ESc* supplement payable for internal journeys within Italy.

▷ – Trains arrive at SBB (Swiss) platforms and depart from SNCF (French) platforms. Minimum connectior time 10 minutes. Connections at Basel are not guaranteed.

LONDON - PARIS - LAUSANNE - BRIG 42

train type	TGV	IR	TGV		☆	☆	TGV	IR		☆	TGV	IR	☆	☆	☆	TGV	IR	TGV			☆	☆	TGV	IR
train number	9261	1717	9263		9004	9006	9269	1725		9014	9271	1733	9018	9020	9022	9273	1737	9273			9024	9028	9277	1741
notes	♥🍷		♥🍷 B		①–⑤ g	⑥ Z	♥🍷			⑦ y	♥🍷 ⑦f		M	W	X	♥🍷		♥🍷 C				Ⓑ	♥🍷	
London St Pancras **10** d.	...	...	...	...	0701	0722	...	...	...	0922	...	...	1025	1101	1131	...	...	...	...	...	1225	1331	...	...
Paris Nord **10** a.	...	...	...	...	1017	1047	...	...	...	1247	...	...	1347	1417	1447	...	...	...	...	...	1547	1647	...	...
Paris Gare de Lyon d.	0802c	...	0802	...	...	...	1157x	...	...	...	1357z	...	—	...	...	1557v	...	1557	...	...	...	...	1757e	...
Dijon d.	0935c	...	0935	...	...	...	1334x	...	...	...	1533z	...	...	...	...	1733v	...	1733	...	...	...	...	1933e	...
Frasne a.	1044	...	1044	...	...	...	1444	...	...	...	1644	...	...	...	...	1844	...	1844	...	...	...	...	2042	...
Vallorbe ◧ a.	1059	...	1059	...	...	...	1459	...	...	...	1659	...	...	...	...	1859	...	1859	...	...	...	...	2059	...
Lausanne a.	1137	...	1137	...	...	...	1537	...	...	...	1737	...	...	...	...	1937	...	1937	...	...	...	...	2137	...
Lausanne d.	...	1220	1139	...	...	...	...	1620	...	...	...	1821	...	...	...	...	2020	1939	...	...	...	...	...	2220
Montreux a.	...	1239	1213	...	...	...	...	1639	...	...	...	1840	...	...	...	...	2039	2013	...	...	...	...	...	2239
Aigle a.	...	1250	1226	...	...	...	...	1650	...	...	...	1851	...	...	...	...	2050	2026	...	...	...	...	...	2250
Martigny a.	...	1307	1251	...	...	...	...	1707	...	...	...	1908	...	...	...	...	2107	2055	...	...	...	...	...	2307
Sion a.	...	1322	1315	...	...	...	...	1722	...	...	...	1923	...	...	...	...	2122	2116	...	...	...	...	...	2322
Sierre a.	...	1333	1329	...	...	...	...	1733	...	...	...	1934	...	...	...	...	2133	2130	①–⑥	⑦	...	...	...	2333
Visp a.	...	1352	1404	1410	...	...	...	1752	1810	...	...	1951	2010	...	...	...	2152	2201	2240	2323	...	...	...	2352
Zermatt a.	...	│	│	1513	...	...	...	│	1913	...	...	│	2113	...	...	...	│	│	2344	0025	...	...	...	│
Brig a.	...	1402	1418	...	...	...	...	1802	...	...	...	2002	...	...	...	...	2202	2212	...	...	...	...	...	0002

train type	IR	IR	TGV	☆	IR	TGV	☆		IR	TGV	☆	☆		IR	EC	TGV		IR	TGV	TGV				
train number	1406	1708	9260	9025	1712	9264	9039		1720	9268	9051	9055		1728	34	9270		1732	9272	9272				
notes			♥🍷 D	H		♥🍷 A				♥🍷 E	Ⓑ	⑥⑦ y			[R]🍷 ⊗	♥🍷 ⑤⑦			♥🍷 G	♥🍷 B				
Brig d.	0428	...	...	...	0557	...	...	...	0957	...	...	...	...	1357	1420	w	...	1557	...	1551	...	...	...	...
Zermatt d.	│	...	...	...	│	...	...	0839	│	...	...	...	1239	│	│	...	1439	│	...	│	...	...	...	...
Visp d.	0436	...	...	...	0608	...	...	0947	1008	...	...	...	1347	1408	│	...	1547	1607	...	1602	...	...	...	...
Sierre d.	0455	...	...	...	0624	...	...	...	1024	...	...	...	...	1424	│	...	...	1625	...	1629	...	...	...	...
Sion d.	0506	0532	...	...	0636	...	...	...	1036	...	...	...	...	1436	1448	...	...	1637	...	1641	...	...	...	...
Martigny d.	0520	0546	...	...	0650	...	...	...	1050	...	...	...	...	1450	│	...	...	1651	...	1705	...	...	...	...
Aigle d.	0542	0608	...	...	0707	...	...	...	1107	...	...	...	...	1507	│	...	...	1708	...	1734	...	...	...	...
Montreux d.	0553	0619	...	...	0718	...	...	...	1118	...	...	...	...	1518	1525	...	...	1719	...	│	...	...	...	...
Lausanne a.	0614	0640	...	...	0739	...	...	...	1139	...	...	...	...	1539	1542	...	...	1740	...	1820	...	...	...	...
Lausanne d.	...	...	0624	...	...	0824	...	...	...	1224	...	...	...	...	...	1624	...	...	1824	1824	...	...	...	...
Vallorbe ◧ d.	...	...	0659	...	...	0859	...	...	...	1300	...	...	...	...	...	1701	...	...	1901	1901	...	...	...	...
Frasne d.	...	...	0715	...	...	0917	...	...	...	1316	...	...	...	...	...	1716	...	...	1916	1916	...	...	...	...
Dijon a.	...	...	0828	...	...	1027	...	...	...	1425	...	...	...	...	...	1827	...	...	2024	2024	...	...	...	...
Paris Gare de Lyon a.	...	...	1010	...	...	1203	...	...	...	1603	...	...	...	...	...	2019	...	...	2202	2202	...	...	...	...
Paris Nord **10** d.	...	...	...	1143	...	...	1513	...	...	...	1813	1913	...	...	...	...	...	...	...	...	...	...	...	...
London St Pancras **10** a.	...	...	...	1300	...	...	1639	...	...	...	1939	2039	...	...	...	...	...	...	...	...	...	...	...	...

A – Arrive Paris 1206, 1212, 1216, 1219, 1232 on certain dates.
B – ⑥ Feb. 1 - Mar. 8.
C – ⑤ Jan 31 - Mar 7.
D – Arrive Paris 1033 Apr. 7 - June 14.
E – Arrive Paris 1606, 1616, 1617, 1634 on certain dates.
G – Arrive Paris 2205, 2215, 2236 on certain dates.
H – May 25 - Aug. 30.
M – Ⓑ (daily Apr. 6 - Aug. 30). On Oct. 19 depart London 1015.
W – ⑥ (⑥⑦ Mar. 29 - Aug. 30) also Aug. 25.
X – ②③④⑤⑥ (daily Mar. 25 - Aug. 30) not Aug. 25, Nov. 10, 11.
Z – Feb. 1 - July 28; Sept. 20 - Dec. 13.

c – Depart Paris 0723, Dijon 0915 on certain dates.
e – Depart Paris 1724, 1733, 1741, Dijon 1928 on certain dates.
f – Also Apr. 21, June 9.
g – Not Aug. 25, Nov. 11.
v – Depart Paris 1527, 1548, Dijon 1722, 1725 on certain dates.
w – Arrive Paris 2003, 2007, 2022 on certain dates.
x – Depart Paris 1123, 1141, Dijon 1322 on certain dates.
y – Also Aug. 25, Nov. 11.

z – Depart Paris 1345, 1348 and depart Dijon 1523 on certain dates.

◇ – Stopping train. 2nd class only.
⊗ – **ETR 470/610**. See Table **82**.
♥ – *TGV Lyria* service. [R]. Special fares payable. At-seat meal service in first class.
☆ – Eurostar train. [R], ✕ in 1st class, 🍷 in 2nd class. Special fares payable. Minimum check-in time 30 mins. Valid June - Dec. 13. Additional Eurostar services are available, see Table **10**.

BRUSSELS - KÖLN - MILANO and BRUSSELS - STRASBOURG - MILANO 43

BRUSSELS - KÖLN - BASEL - MILANO

train type	⇌	CNL	EC		ICE	ICE	ICE	EC		
train number	9473	40419	315		15	107	207	59		
notes	🍷[R]		[R]✕ ⊗		🍷	⑦	①–⑥	[R]🍷 ⊗		
Brussels Midi/Zuid d.	1928	...	...	...	1025	...	...	...	...	...
Aachen ◧ d.	2040	...	...	...	1139	...	...	...	...	...
Köln Hbf d.	2115	2346	...	...	1215	1255	...	...	...	...
Frankfurt Flughafen ✈ d.	...	0156	...	...	1310	│	1353	...	...	...
Mannheim Hbf d.	...	0404	...	...	...	1434	1434	...	...	...
Basel SBB ◧ d.	...	0710	...	...	...	1647	1647	1731	...	...
Zürich HB d.	...	0834	0932	...	...	...	...	│	...	...
Bern d.	...	...	│	...	...	...	...	1834	...	...
Brig d.	...	...	│	...	...	...	...	1944	...	...
Domodossola ◧ ¶ a.	...	...	◧	...	...	...	...	2012	...	...
Milano Centrale a.	...	...	1335	...	...	...	...	2135	...	...

train type	EC	ICE	ICE	⇌	EC	EC	IC	CNL	⇌	
train number	50	278	518	9472	320	36	1090	40478	9412	
notes	[R]🍷 ⊗	🍷	🍷	🍷	[R]🍷 ⊗	[R]🍷 ⊗				
Milano Centrale d.	0725	...	...	...	1625	1725	...	...	...	...
Domodossola ◧ ¶ d.	0848	...	...	...	◧	1848	...	...	...	...
Brig d.	0920	...	...	...	│	1916	1920	...	...	...
Bern d.	1034	...	...	...	│	...	2034	...	...	...
Zürich HB d.	│	...	...	...	2028	...	│	2042	...	...
Basel SBB ◧ d.	1129	1213	...	...	...	...	2129	2213	...	...
Mannheim Hbf a.	...	1422	1436	...	...	...	...	0126	...	...
Frankfurt Flughafen ✈ a.	...	...	│	...	...	...	...	0339	...	...
Köln Hbf a.	...	...	1605	1643	...	...	...	0543	0645	...
Aachen ◧ a.	...	...	...	1720	...	...	...	...	0720	...
Brussels Midi/Zuid a.	...	...	...	1832	...	...	...	...	0832	...

BRUSSELS - STRASBOURG - BASEL - MILANO

train type/number	EC	TGV	EC		EC	IC		
train number	91	9213	323		97	791		
notes	❖ V	🍷	[R] 🍷		❖ R	🍷		
russels Midi/Zuid d.	0733	...	...	...	1309	...	...	...
amur d.	0841	...	...	...	1416	...	...	...
uxembourg ◧ d.	1047	...	...	...	1611	...	...	...
hionville d.	1110	...	...	...	1636	...	...	...
etz d.	1131	...	...	...	1657	...	...	...
trasbourg d.	1251	...	...	...	1819	...	...	...
ulhouse d.	1348	...	...	...	1915	...	...	...
asel SNCF ◧ ▷ a.	1438	...	...	...	1938	...	...	...
asel SBB d.	...	1533	...	...	...	2007	...	...
ürich HB a.	...	1626	1732	...	...	2100	...	...
hiasso ◧ a.	...	...	2048	...	...	...	...	...
rig a.	...	...	│	...	...	...	...	...
ilano Centrale a.	...	...	2135	...	...	...	...	...

train type	EC	EC		EC	EC			
train number	50	90		52	96			
notes	[R]🍷 ⊗	❖ V		[R]🍷 ⊗	❖ R			
Milano Centrale d.	0725	...	...	1125	...	...	...	...
Brig d.	0920	...	...	1320	...	...	...	...
Chiasso ◧ d.	│	...	...	│	...	...	...	...
Zürich HB d.	│	...	...	│	...	...	...	...
Basel SBB a.	1129	...	...	1529	...	...	...	...
Basel SNCF ◧ ◁ d.	...	1316	...	...	1618	...	...	...
Mulhouse d.	...	1341	...	...	1646	...	...	...
Strasbourg d.	...	1450	...	...	1750	...	...	...
Metz d.	...	1609	...	...	1910	...	...	...
Thionville d.	...	1627	...	...	1929	...	...	...
Luxembourg ◧ a.	...	1649	...	...	1949	...	...	...
Namur a.	...	1845	...	...	2142	...	...	...
Brussels Midi/Zuid a.	...	1951	...	...	2251	...	...	...

R – IRIS – 12 Brussels - Basel and v.v.
– VAUBAN – 12 Brussels - Basel and v.v.

– ◧ is Chiasso.
– Ticket point is **Iselle**.
❖ – Timings may vary on certain dates.

⇌ – *Thalys* high-speed train. [R] 🍷. Special fares payable. Valid June 1 - Aug. 30.
⊗ – **ETR 470/610**. Compulsory reservation for international journeys. Supplement payable for international journeys.
▷ – Trains arrive at SNCF (French) platforms and depart from SBB (Swiss) platforms. Minimum connection time 10 minutes. Connections at Basel are not guaranteed.
◁ – Trains arrive at SBB (Swiss) platforms and depart from SNCF (French) platforms. Minimum connection time 10 minutes. Connections at Basel are not guaranteed.

44 LONDON - PARIS - TORINO - MILANO - VENEZIA and ROMA

train type	TGV		TGV	IC	FR	ITA	FR	FB	FR	☆		TGV	ITA	FR	FB	FR	IC
train number	**9239**	**17921**	**9241**	**515**	**9569**	**9943**	**9643**	**9733**	**9545**	**9080**	**18503**	**9245**	**9955**	**9655**	**9745**	**9557**	**519**
notes	R ✕		R ✕	↯	R ✕	R ✕	R ✕	R 🍷	R ✕			R ✕	R ✕	R ✕	R 🍷	R ✕	↯
notes	♣ A		♣ B		↯	↯	↯ Ⓑ	↯	↯	①–⑤ b		♣	↯	↯	↯	↯	
London St Pancras **10 12** d.	...	...	...	...	...	...	...	...	...	0540	...	...	...	...	...	...	...
Paris Nord **10** a.	...	...	...	...	...	...	...	...	...	0917	...	...	...	...	...	...	...
Paris Gare de Lyon d.	0641	...	0749	...	...	...	...	...	...	...	...	1041	...	...	...	...	...
Lyon Part Dieu d.	|	0840	|	...	...	...	...	...	...	...	1140	|	...	...	...	...	...
Lyon St Exupéry TGV ✈ d.	0836	|	0949	...	...	...	...	...	...	...	|	1235	...	...	...	...	...
Chambéry d.	0944	0958	1050	...	...	...	...	...	...	...	1259	1342	...	...	...	...	...
Modane 🏛 d.	1055	...	1155	...	...	...	...	...	...	...	...	1455	...	...	...	...	...
Oulx ▲ a.	1123	...	1223	...	...	...	...	...	...	...	...	1523	...	...	...	...	...
Torino Porta Nuova § a.	|	...	|	...	...	...	...	...	...	...	...	|	...	...	...	...	1805
Torino Porta Susa § a.	1224	...	1328	...	1432	...	...	1419	...	...	...	1618	...	1753	1719	1802	|
Torino Porta Nuova § a.	|	...	|	1405	|	...	...	|	...	...	...	|	...	|	|	|	|
Novara a.	|	...	|	|	|	...	...	1511	...	...	...	1713	...	|	1811	|	|
Milano Porta Garibaldi a.	1351	...	1451	|	1516	1534	...	|	...	...	...	1751	1834	|	|	|	|
Milano Centrale a.	...	...	...	|	|	|	...	1550	...	...	...	...	|	1842	1852	1900	|
Milano Centrale d.	...	...	...	|	|	|	1600	1605	1615	...	...	...	|	1900	1905	1915	|
Alessandria a.	...	...	...	1500	|	|	|	|	|	...	...	...	|	|	|	|	1900
Genova Piazza Principe a.	...	...	...	1553	|	|	|	|	|	...	...	...	|	|	|	|	1953
La Spezia a.	...	...	...	...	|	|	|	|	|	...	...	...	|	|	|	|	...
Viareggio a.	...	...	...	...	|	|	|	|	|	...	...	...	|	|	|	|	...
Pisa Centrale a.	...	...	...	...	|	|	|	|	|	...	...	...	|	|	|	|	...
Livorno a.	...	...	...	...	|	|	|	|	|	...	...	...	|	|	|	|	...
Grosseto a.	...	...	...	...	|	|	|	|	|	...	...	...	|	|	|	|	...
Brescia a.	...	...	...	...	|	|	|	1651	|	...	...	...	|	|	1951	|	...
Verona Porta Nuova a.	...	...	...	...	|	|	|	1727	|	...	...	...	|	|	2027	|	...
Vicenza a.	...	...	...	...	|	|	|	1754	|	...	...	...	|	|	2054	|	...
Padova a.	...	...	...	...	|	|	|	1812	|	...	...	...	|	|	2112	|	...
Venezia Mestre a.	...	...	...	...	|	|	|	1828	|	...	...	...	|	|	2128	|	...
Venezia Santa Lucia a.	...	...	...	...	|	|	|	1840	|	...	...	...	|	|	2140	|	...
Piacenza a.	...	...	...	...	|	|	|	...	|	...	...	...	|	|	...	|	...
Parma a.	...	...	...	...	|	|	|	...	|	...	...	...	|	|	...	|	...
Reggio Emilia a.	...	...	...	...	|	|	|	...	|	...	...	...	|	|	...	|	...
Modena a.	...	...	...	...	|	|	|	...	|	...	...	...	|	|	...	|	...
Bologna Centrale a.	...	...	...	...	1632	1647	|	...	1717	...	...	...	1947	|	...	2017	...
Firenze SMN a.	...	...	...	...	1710	1725	|	...	1755	...	...	...	2025	|	...	2055	...
Roma Tiburtina a.	...	...	...	...	1839	1854	|	...	1924	...	...	...	2154	|	...	2224	...
Roma Termini a.	...	...	...	...	1850	|	1855	...	1935c	...	...	...	...	2155	...	2235	...
Napoli Centrale a.	...	...	...	...	...	2005	...	...	2055	...	...	...	...	...	...	...	...
Salerno a.	...	...	...	...	...	...	...	...	...	...	...	...	...	...	...	...	...

train type	☆			TGV	ICN		ICN	☆	☆	EN	FR ↯		IC	IC	IC	FR ↯
train number	**9014**	**18531**	**17931**	**9249**	**1911**	**10611**	**799**	**9032**	**9034**	**221**	**9505**	**2004**	**653**	**505**	**1583**	**9509**
notes				R ✕	R ↯	2	R ↯				R 🍷		R 🍷	R 🍷	R 🍷	R 🍷
notes			C	♣	H		E	Ⓑ	⑦ j	V	①–⑥ p		↯	↯	↯	
London St Pancras **10 12** d.	0917e	...	...	...	...	...	...	1431	1501	...	...	...	...	...	...	...
Paris Nord **10** a.	1247	...	...	...	...	...	...	1747	1817	...	...	...	...	...	...	...
Paris Gare de Lyon d.	...	...	...	1441	...	...	...	...	...	1959	...	...	...	...	...	...
Dijon d.	...	...	...	|	...	...	...	...	...	2241	...	...	...	...	...	...
Lyon Part Dieu d.	...	1440	1540	|	...	...	...	...	...	|	...	...	...	...	...	...
Lyon St Exupéry TGV ✈ d.	...	|	|	1635	...	...	...	...	...	|	...	...	...	...	...	...
Chambéry d.	...	1558	1658	1742	...	...	...	...	...	|	...	...	...	...	...	...
Modane 🏛 d.	...	...	...	1855	...	...	...	...	...	⊙	...	...	...	...	...	...
Oulx ▲ a.	...	...	...	1923	...	...	...	...	...	|	...	...	...	...	...	...
Torino Porta Susa § a.	...	...	...	2018	...	...	...	...	...	|	...	...	...	...	...	...
Torino Porta Nuova § a.	...	...	...	|	...	...	2155	...	...	|	...	...	...	...	...	...
Novara a.	...	...	...	|	...	...	|	...	...	|	...	...	...	...	...	...
Milano Porta Garibaldi a.	...	...	...	2151	...	...	|	...	...	|	...	...	...	...	...	...
Milano Centrale a.	...	...	...	...	...	...	|	...	...	0600	...	...	...	...	...	...
Milano Centrale d.	...	...	...	...	2320	0015	|	...	...	|	0615	0618	0705	...	0635	0715
Novara a.	...	...	...	...	|	|	|	...	...	|	|	0657	|	...	|	|
Torino Porta Susa a.	...	...	...	...	|	|	|	...	...	|	|	0758	|	...	|	|
Alessandria a.	...	...	...	...	|	|	2257	...	...	|	|	...	|	...	|	|
Genova Piazza Principe a.	...	...	...	...	|	|	2350	...	...	|	|	...	0842	0852	|	|
La Spezia a.	...	...	...	...	|	|	0124	...	...	|	|	...	...	1005	|	|
Viareggio a.	...	...	...	...	|	|	|	...	...	|	|	...	...	1041	|	|
Pisa Centrale a.	...	...	...	...	|	|	0220	...	...	|	|	...	...	1100	|	|
Livorno a.	...	...	...	...	|	|	0239	...	...	|	|	...	...	1127	|	|
Grosseto a.	...	...	...	...	|	|	0355	...	...	|	|	...	...	1233	|	|
Brescia a.	...	...	...	...	|	0133	|	...	...	0710	|	...	...	|	|	|
Verona Porta Nuova a.	...	...	...	...	|	0220	|	...	...	0752	|	...	...	|	|	|
Vicenza a.	...	...	...	...	|	...	|	...	...	0843	|	...	...	|	|	|
Padova a.	...	...	...	...	|	...	|	...	...	0906	|	...	...	|	|	|
Venezia Mestre a.	...	...	...	...	|	...	|	...	...	0923	|	...	...	|	|	|
Venezia Santa Lucia a.	...	...	...	...	|	...	|	...	...	0935	|	...	...	|	|	|
Piacenza a.	...	...	...	...	0008	...	|	...	...	...	|	...	...	|	0734	|
Parma a.	...	...	...	...	0059	...	|	...	...	...	|	...	...	|	0807	|
Reggio Emilia a.	...	...	...	...	|	...	|	...	...	...	|	...	...	|	0822	|
Modena a.	...	...	...	...	|	...	|	...	...	...	|	...	...	|	0837	|
Bologna Centrale a.	...	...	...	...	|	...	|	...	...	...	0717	...	...	|	0855	0817
Firenze SMN a.	...	...	...	...	|	...	|	...	...	...	0755	...	...	|	1017v	0855
Roma Tiburtina d.	...	...	...	...	0717	...	|	...	...	...	0924	...	...	|	1310	1024
Roma Termini a.	...	...	...	...	|	...	0555o	...	...	...	0935c	...	...	1416	|	1035c
Napoli Centrale a.	...	...	...	...	0930	...	0827	...	...	...	1055	...	...	...	1534	1155
Salerno a.	...	...	...	...	1025	...	0925	...	...	...	1144	...	...	...	...	...

A – Daily Jan. 7 - Apr. 20; ⑥⑦ Apr. 21 - June 14.
B – ①–⑤ Apr. 21 - June 14.
C – ①–⑤ (not Aug. 15, Nov. 1, 11).
E – 🛏 1, 2 cl., ▬ 2 cl., (2) Torino - Roma - Napoli - Salerno.
H – 🛏 1, 2 cl., ▬ 2 cl. (4 berth), (2) Milano - Salerno.
V – *Thello* - 🛏 1, 2 cl. (1, 2, 3 berth), ▬ 2 cl. (4, 6 berth, ladies only 4 berth), ✕ Paris - Venezia. For use by passengers making international journeys only. Special fares payable. Not Mar. 22, 29.

b – Not June 9, July 14, July 27 - Aug. 30, Nov. 10, 11.
c – Departs 10 - 19 minutes later.
e – 0922 on ⑥⑦ (also Aug. 25, Nov. 11).
f – Calls at Torino Porta Susa before Torino Porta Nuova.
j – Also Aug. 25, Nov. 11.
o – Roma **Ostiense**.

p – Not Aug. 15, Nov. 1.
v – Firenze **Rifredi**.

↯ – Supplement payable.
♣ – *TGV* France-Italy service. R ✕ Special fares payable.
▲ – Station for the resorts of Cesana, Claviere and Sestriere.
☆ – Eurostar train. R, ✕ in 1st class, 🍷 in 2nd class. Special fares payable. Minimum check-in time 30 minutes. Valid June 1 - Dec. 13. Additional Eurostar services are available, see Table **10**.
⊙ – Frontier / ticketing points 🏛 are Vallorbe and Domodossola. Ticket point for Domodossola is **Iselle**.
§ – Local train services (Tables **585**, **586**) and metro services run between Torino **Porta Susa** and Torino **Porta Nuova**.

OTHER TRAIN NAMES: **9241** – ALESSANDRO MANZONI **9249** – CARAVAGGIO

ROMA and VENEZIA - MILANO - TORINO - PARIS - LONDON 44

train type	*TGV*			☆		*ICN*		*TGV*		☆	☆		*IC*	*FB*	*FR*	*IC*	*ITA*	*FR* ⚡	*TGV*	
train number	**9240**	**83264**	**17906**	**9039**		**1910**		**9244**	**83270**	**9051**	**9055**		**666**	**9718**	**9524**	**746**	**9930**	**9630**	**9248**	**83496**
notes	[R] ✕					[R] ⚡		[R] ✕					🍷	[R] 🍷	**9526**	🍷	[R] ✕	[R] ✕	[R] ✕	
notes	♣	⑥⑦	①–⑤			**H**		♣		Ⓑ			⚡	⚡	[R] ✕	⚡	⚡	①–⑤	♣	
		y	**q**					**g**							⚡			★ **p**		
Salerno d.	...	...	...	...	...	2038	...	...	...	...	...	...	...	...	0912	...	...	...	...	...
Napoli Centrale d.	...	...	...	...	...	2130	...	...	...	...	...	...	...	...	1000	...	1045	...	...	...
Roma Termini d.	...	...	...	...	...	|	...	...	...	...	...	...	...	...	1120	...	|	1300	...	...
Roma Tiburtina d.	...	...	...	...	...	2344	...	...	...	...	...	...	...	...	1129	...	1155	|	...	...
Firenze SMN d.	...	...	...	...	...	|	...	...	...	...	...	...	...	...	1300	...	1325	|	...	...
Bologna Centrale d.	...	...	...	...	...	|	...	...	...	...	...	...	...	...	1338	...	1403	|	...	...
Modena d.	...	...	...	...	...	|	...	...	...	...	...	...	...	...	|	...	|	|	...	...
Reggio Emilia d.	...	...	...	...	...	|	...	...	...	...	...	...	...	...	|	...	|	|	...	...
Parma d.	...	...	...	...	...	0521	...	...	...	...	...	...	...	...	|	...	|	|	...	...
Piacenza d.	...	...	...	...	...	0602	...	...	...	...	...	...	...	...	|	...	|	|	...	...
Venezia Santa Lucia d.	...	...	...	...	...	|	...	...	...	...	...	...	...	1150	|	...	|	|	...	...
Venezia Mestre d.	...	...	...	...	...	|	...	...	...	...	...	...	...	1202	|	...	|	|	...	...
Padova d.	...	...	...	...	...	|	...	...	...	...	...	...	...	1217	|	...	|	|	...	...
Vicenza d.	...	...	...	...	...	|	...	...	...	...	...	...	...	1235	|	...	|	|	...	...
Verona Porta Nuova d.	...	...	...	...	...	|	0540	...	...	...	...	...	...	1302	|	...	|	|	...	...
Brescia d.	...	...	...	...	...	|	0627	...	...	...	...	...	...	1339	|	...	|	|	...	...
Grosseto d.	...	...	...	...	...	|	|	...	...	...	...	...	...	|	|	...	|	|	...	...
Livorno d.	...	...	...	...	...	|	|	...	...	...	...	...	...	|	|	...	|	|	...	...
Pisa Centrale d.	...	...	...	...	...	|	|	...	...	...	...	...	...	|	|	...	|	|	...	...
Viareggio d.	...	...	...	...	...	|	|	...	...	...	...	...	...	|	|	...	|	|	...	...
La Spezia d.	...	...	...	...	...	|	|	...	...	...	...	...	1040	|	|	...	|	|	...	...
Genova Piazza Principe d.	...	...	...	...	...	|	|	...	...	...	...	...	1219	|	|	1319	|	|	...	...
Alessandria d.	...	...	...	...	...	|	|	...	...	...	...	...	|	|	|	|	|	|	...	...
Milano Centrale d.	...	...	...	...	...	0655	0735	...	...	...	...	...	1350	1425	1440	1455	|	1555x	...	...
Milano Porta Garibaldi d.	0600	...	...	...	...	...	...	0850	...	...	...	...	...	...	...	...	1518	|	1610	...
Novara d.	0631	...	...	...	...	...	...	|	...	...	...	...	...	...	...	...	...	|	|	...
Torino Porta Nuova § d.	|	...	...	...	...	...	...	|	...	...	...	...	...	...	...	...	...	|	|	...
Torino Porta Susa § d.	0739	...	...	...	...	...	...	1015	...	...	...	...	...	...	...	...	...	1652	1735	...
Torino Porta Nuova § d.	|	...	...	...	...	...	...	|	...	...	...	...	...	...	...	...	...	...	|	...
Oulx ▲ d.	0837	...	...	...	...	...	...	1113	...	...	...	...	...	...	...	...	...	...	1842	...
Modane 🏛 a.	0905	...	...	...	...	...	...	1144	...	...	...	...	...	...	...	...	...	...	1912	...
Chambéry a.	1016	1102	1123	...	...	...	...	1248	1302	...	...	...	...	...	...	...	...	...	2017	2102
Lyon St Exupéry TGV ✈ a.	1126	|	|	...	...	...	...	|	|	...	...	...	...	...	...	...	...	...	2125	|
Lyon Part Dieu a.	|	1220	1252	...	...	...	...	|	1420	...	...	...	...	...	...	...	...	...	|	2221
Paris Gare de Lyon a.	1323z	...	...	...	...	...	...	1611	...	...	...	...	...	...	...	...	...	...	2319	...
Paris Nord **10** d.	...	...	...	1513	...	...	...	...	...	1813	1913	...	...	...	...	...	...	...	...	...
London St Pancras **10 12** a.	...	...	...	1639	...	...	...	...	...	1939	2041	...	...	...	...	...	...	...	...	...

train type	*IC*	*FR*		*FR*	*IC*	*IC*	*FB*	*EN*	☆
train number	**728**	**9552**		**9654**	**35428**	**35420**	**9826**	**220**	**9023**
notes	**722**	[R] ✕		[R] ✕	[R]	[R]	[R] ✕		
notes	[R] 🍷	⚡		⚡	⚡	⚡	⚡	**V**	
	⚡				Ⓒ	Ⓐ			
Salerno d.	1530	...	...	...	...	...	...	...	...
Napoli Centrale d.	1605	1700	...	...	...	...	...	...	...
Roma Termini d.	...	1820	...	1900	...	...	...	...	...
Roma Tiburtina d.	...	1829	...	|	...	...	...	...	...
Firenze SMN d.	...	2000	...	|	...	...	...	...	...
Bologna Centrale d.	...	2038	...	|	...	...	1918	...	...
Modena d.	...	|	...	|	...	...	1941	...	...
Reggio Emilia d.	...	|	...	|	...	...	1954	...	...
Parma d.	...	|	...	|	...	...	2010	...	...
Piacenza d.	...	|	...	|	...	...	2041	...	...
Venezia Santa Lucia d.	...	|	...	|	...	...	|	1920	...
Venezia Mestre d.	...	|	...	|	...	...	|	1932	...
Padova d.	...	|	...	|	...	...	|	1950	...
Vicenza d.	...	|	...	|	...	...	|	2013	...
Verona Porta Nuova d.	...	|	...	|	...	...	|	2050	...
Brescia d.	...	|	...	|	...	...	|	2133	...
Grosseto d.	...	|	...	|	1604	1610	|	|	...
Livorno d.	...	|	...	|	1718	1726	|	|	...
Pisa Centrale d.	...	|	...	|	1736	1744	|	|	...
Viareggio d.	...	|	...	|	1753	1802	|	|	...
La Spezia d.	...	|	...	|	1842	1842	|	|	...
Genova Piazza Principe d.	...	|	...	|	2027	2027	|	|	...
Alessandria d.	...	|	...	|	|	|	|	|	...
Torino Porta Susa d.	...	|	2002	|	|	|	|	|	...
Novara d.	...	|	2103	|	|	|	|	|	...
Milano Centrale d.	...	2140	2145	2155	2200	2200	2215	2255	...
Milano Porta Garibaldi d.	...	...	...	...	...	...	...	|	...
Novara d.	...	...	...	...	...	...	...	|	...
Torino Porta Nuova § d.	...	...	...	...	...	...	...	|	...
Torino Porta Susa § d.	...	...	...	...	...	...	...	|	...
Torino Porta Nuova § d.	...	...	...	...	...	...	...	|	...
Oulx ▲ d.	...	...	...	...	...	...	...	|	...
Modane 🏛 a.	...	...	...	...	...	...	...	⊙	...
Chambéry a.	...	...	...	...	...	...	...	|	...
Lyon St Exupéry TGV ✈ a.	...	...	...	...	...	...	...	|	...
Lyon Part Dieu a.	...	...	...	...	...	...	...	|	...
Dijon a.	...	...	...	...	...	...	...	0635	...
Paris Gare de Lyon a.	...	...	...	...	...	...	...	0930	...
Paris Nord **10** d.	...	...	...	...	...	...	...	...	1113
London St Pancras **10 12** a.	...	...	...	...	...	...	...	...	1230

H – 1, 2 cl., 2 cl. (4 berth), Salerno - Milano.

V – *Thello* – 1, 2 cl. (1, 2, 3 berth), 2 cl. (4, 6 berth, ladies only 4 berth), ✕ Venezia - Milano - Paris. For use by passengers making international journeys only. Special fares payable. Not Mar. 22, 29.

– Calls at Aix les Bains at 1304.

– Not Aug. 15, Nov. 1.

– Not Aug. 15, Nov. 1, 11.

– Calls at Torino Porta Nuova before Torino Porta Susa.

– Connection to Paris train in next column available at Torino Porta Susa.

– Also Aug. 15, Nov. 1, 11.

– 1329, 1332 on certain dates.

★ – Service offering Executive, Business, Premium and Standard class.

⚡ – Supplement payable.

♣ – *TGV* France-Italy service. [R] ✕ Special fares payable.

▲ – Station for the resorts of Cesana, Claviere and Sestriere.

☆ – Eurostar train. [R], ✕ in 1st class, 🍷 in 2nd class. Special fares payable. Minimum check-in time 30 minutes. Valid June 1 - Dec. 13. Additional Eurostar services are available, see Table **10**.

⊙ – Frontier / ticketing points 🏛 are Vallorbe and Domodossola. Ticket point for Domodossola is **Iselle**.

§ – Local train services (Tables **585, 586**) and metro services run between Torino **Porta Susa** and Torino **Porta Nuova**.

OTHER TRAIN NAMES: **9240** – CARAVAGGIO **9248** – ALESSANDRO MANZONI

45 MADRID - LISBOA

	🚌 P	🚌 Q		332 A	
Madrid Chamartín .... d.	...	...	...	2150	...
Madrid Estación Sur ❖ ..... d.	0930	1430	...	|	...
Cáceres .... d.	1300	1845	...	|	...
Badajoz .... 🛃 ES d.	1530	2000	...	|	...
Elvas .... 🛃 PT d.	|	|	...	|	...
Lisboa Oriente .... a.	1800	2230	...	0730	...

	🚌 P	🚌 Q		335 A	
Lisboa Oriente .... d.	0915	1215	...	2118	...
Elvas .... 🛃 PT d.	|	|	...	|	...
Badajoz .... 🛃 ES d.	1330	1630	...	|	...
Cáceres .... a.	1600	1800	...	|	...
Madrid Estación Sur ❖ .. a.	1930	2150	...	|	...
Madrid Chamartín .... a.	...	...	...	0820	...

A – LUSITANIA *Hotel Train* – For details see Table **46** notes.
P – 🚌 operated by Alsa, additional buses operate, rail tickets not valid; www.alsa.es
Q – 🚌 operated by Avanza, additional buses operate, rail tickets not valid; www.avanzabus.com
ES – Spain (Central European Time).
PT – Portugal (West European Time).
❖ – Madrid south bus station close to Méndez Álvaro metro (see Madrid city plan on page 30).

46 LONDON - PARIS - LISBOA, PORTO and MADRID

train type / number	*TGV*	*Alvia*	*MD*	☆	☆	*TGV*	*Hotel*	*Hotel*	*IC*		☆		*IC*	*MD*	*MD*		
train number	**8531**	**4166**	**18310**	**9008**	**9008**	**8537**	**312**	**332**	**533**		**9044**	**4053**	**18012**	**18322**	**18318**		
notes	🅁 ⚡ J		2	①–⑤	⑥	🅁 ⚡ 🍷	🅁 🍷 A	🅁 🍷 K	🅁 🍷			🅁 P		2	2		
London St Pancras 10 .... d.	...	...	...	0755	0801	...	...	...	...	...	1731	...	...	...	...	...	...
Paris Nord 10 .... a.	...	...	...	1117	1117	...	...	...	...	...	2047	...	...	...	...	...	...
Paris Montparnasse .... d.	0728	...	...	...	...	1227	...	...	...	...	...	...	...	...	...	...	...
Paris Austerlitz .... d.	|	...	...	...	...	|	...	...	...	...	...	2154	...	...	...	...	...
Les Aubrais-Orléans .... d.	|	...	...	...	...	|	...	...	...	...	...	2253	...	...	...	...	...
Blois .... d.	|	...	...	...	...	|	...	...	...	...	...	|	...	...	...	...	...
Poitiers .... d.	|	...	...	...	...	|	...	...	...	...	...	|	...	...	...	...	...
Bordeaux St Jean .... d.	1051	...	...	...	...	1551	...	...	...	...	...	|	...	...	...	...	...
Biarritz .... d.	1248	...	...	...	...	1748	...	...	...	...	...	0821	...	...	...	...	...
Hendaye .... d.	1315	...	...	...	...	1811	...	...	...	...	...	0848	...	...	...	...	...
Irún 🛃 .... d.	1321	1620	...	...	...	1820	1850	...	...	...	...	0854	1123	...	...	...	...
San Sebastián / Donostia .... a.	...	1637	...	...	...	...	1908	...	...	...	...	...	1139	...	...	...	...
Vitoria / Gasteiz .... a.	...	1812	...	...	...	...	2045	...	...	...	...	...	1333	...	...	...	...
Burgos Rosa de Lima .... a.	...	1932	...	...	...	...	2204	...	...	...	...	...	1448	...	...	...	...
Valladolid Campo Grande .... a.	...	2048	2130	...	...	...	2320	...	...	...	...	...	1616	1740	1905	...	...
Madrid Chamartín .... d.	...	|	|	...	...	...	|	2150	...	...	...	...	|	|	|	...	...
Ávila .... d.	...	|	|	...	...	...	|	2311	...	...	...	...	|	|	|	...	...
Medina del Campo .... a.	...	|	2204	...	...	...	2351	2355	...	...	...	...	|	1804	1931	...	...
Madrid Chamartín .... a.	...	2200	|	...	...	...	|	|	...	...	...	...	1910	...	|	...	...
Salamanca .... a.	...	...	2247	...	...	...	0057	0057	...	...	...	...	...	...	2028	...	...
Ciudad Rodrigo .... a.	...	...	...	...	...	...	0206	0206	...	...	...	...	...	...	...	...	...
Fuentes d'Oñoro .... 🛃 ES d.	...	...	...	...	...	...	0230	0230	...	...	...	...	...	...	...	...	...
Vilar Formoso .... 🛃 PT d.	...	...	...	...	...	...	0225	0225	...	...	...	...	...	...	...	...	...
Guarda .... a.	...	...	...	...	...	...	0252	0252	...	...	...	...	...	...	...	...	...
Mangualde .... a.	...	...	...	...	...	...	0346	0346	...	...	...	...	...	...	...	...	...
Coimbra-B .... a.	...	...	...	...	...	...	0502	0502	0520	...	...	...	...	...	...	...	...
Pombal .... a.	...	...	...	...	...	...	0530	0530	|	...	...	...	...	...	...	...	...
Entroncamento .... a.	...	...	...	...	...	...	0606	0606	|	...	...	...	...	...	...	...	...
Lisboa Oriente .... a.	...	...	...	...	...	...	0720	0720	|	...	...	...	...	...	...	...	...
Lisboa Santa Apolónia .... a.	...	...	...	...	...	...	0730	0730	|	...	...	...	...	...	...	...	...
Aveiro .... a.	...	...	...	...	...	...	...	...	0553	...	...	...	...	...	...	...	...
Porto Campanhã .... a.	...	...	...	...	...	...	...	...	0635	...	...	...	...	...	...	...	...

tra in type / number	*MD*	*Alvia*	*TGV*		☆		*IC*	*Hotel*	*Hotel*	*TGV*	☆						
train number	**18302**	**4087**	**8544**	**4052**	**9015**		**532**	**335**	**310**	**8542**	**9059**						
notes	2	🍷	🅁 ⚡ Ⓑ j	🅁 Q			🅁 🍷	🅁 🍷 K	🅁 🍷 B	🅁 ⚡ 🍷							
Porto Campanhã .... d.	...	...	...	...	...	...	2200	...	...	...	...	...	...	...	...	...	...
Aveiro .... d.	...	...	...	...	...	...	2245	...	...	...	...	...	...	...	...	...	...
Lisboa Santa Apolónia .... d.	...	...	...	...	...	...	|	2118	2118	...	...	...	...	...	...	...	...
Lisboa Oriente .... d.	...	...	...	...	...	...	|	2127	2127	...	...	...	...	...	...	...	...
Entroncamento .... d.	...	...	...	...	...	...	|	2224	2224	...	...	...	...	...	...	...	...
Pombal .... d.	...	...	...	...	...	...	|	2309	2309	...	...	...	...	...	...	...	...
Coimbra-B .... d.	...	...	...	...	...	...	2321	2337	2337	...	...	...	...	...	...	...	...
Mangualde .... d.	...	...	...	...	...	...	...	0043	0043	...	...	...	...	...	...	...	...
Guarda .... d.	...	...	...	...	...	...	...	0138	0138	...	...	...	...	...	...	...	...
Vilar Formoso .... 🛃 PT d.	...	...	...	...	...	...	...	0235	0235	...	...	...	...	...	...	...	...
Fuentes d'Oñoro .... 🛃 ES d.	...	...	...	...	...	...	...	0340	0340	...	...	...	...	...	...	...	...
Ciudad Rodrigo .... d.	...	...	...	...	...	...	...	0359	0359	...	...	...	...	...	...	...	...
Salamanca .... d.	0725	...	...	...	...	...	...	0456	0456	...	...	...	...	...	...	...	...
Madrid Chamartín .... d.	|	0800	...	...	...	...	...	|	|	...	...	...	...	...	...	...	...
Medina del Campo .... d.	0815	|	...	...	...	...	...	0556	0600	...	...	...	...	...	...	...	...
Ávila .... a.	|	|	...	...	...	...	...	0640	|	...	...	...	...	...	...	...	...
Madrid Chamartín .... a.	|	|	...	...	...	...	...	0810	|	...	...	...	...	...	...	...	...
Valladolid Campo Grande .... d.	0850	0909	...	...	...	...	...	...	0629	...	...	...	...	...	...	...	...
Burgos Rosa de Lima .... d.	...	1023	...	...	...	...	...	...	0748	...	...	...	...	...	...	...	...
Vitoria / Gasteiz .... d.	...	1141	...	...	...	...	...	...	0912	...	...	...	...	...	...	...	...
San Sebastián / Donostia .... d.	...	1320	...	...	...	...	...	...	1055	...	...	...	...	...	...	...	...
Irún .... a.	...	1345	...	...	...	...	...	...	1118	...	...	...	...	...	...	...	...
Hendaye 🛃 .... a.	...	1351	1445	1908	...	...	...	...	1128	1245	...	...	...	...	...	...	...
Biarritz .... a.	...	...	1511	1935	...	...	...	...	...	1311	...	...	...	...	...	...	...
Bordeaux St Jean .... a.	...	...	1709	|	...	...	...	...	...	1509	...	...	...	...	...	...	...
Poitiers .... a.	...	...	|	|	...	...	...	...	...	|	...	...	...	...	...	...	...
Blois .... a.	...	...	|	|	...	...	...	...	...	|	...	...	...	...	...	...	...
Les Aubrais-Orléans .... a.	...	...	|	0610	...	...	...	...	...	|	...	...	...	...	...	...	...
Paris Austerlitz .... a.	...	...	|	0718	...	...	...	...	...	|	...	...	...	...	...	...	...
Paris Montparnasse .... a.	...	...	2033	...	...	...	...	...	...	1833	...	...	...	...	...	...	...
Paris Nord 10 .... d.	...	...	...	...	0913	...	...	...	...	...	2013	...	...	...	...	...	...
London St Pancras 10 .... a.	...	...	...	...	1039	...	...	...	...	...	2139	...	...	...	...	...	...

A – SUREX / SUD EXPRESSO *Trenhotel* – 🛏 *Gran Clase / Gran Classe* (1, 2 berths), 🛏 *Preferente* (1, 2 berths), 🛏 *Turista* (4 berths), 💺 🍷 Irún (**312**) - Vilar Formoso (**313**) - Lisboa.

B – SUD EXPRESSO / SUREX *Trenhotel* – 🛏 *Gran Clase / Gran Classe* (1, 2 berths), 🛏 *Preferente* (1, 2 berths), 🛏 *Turista* (4 berths), 💺 🍷 Lisboa (**310**) - Vilar Formoso (**311**) - Hendaye.

E – CAMINO DE SANTIAGO – 💺 🍷 Irún - Burgos - A Coruña and A Coruña - Burgos - Hendaye.

J – ①–⑥ (not Aug. 15, Nov. 1, 11).

K – LUSITANIA *Hotel Train* – 🛏 *Gran Clase / Gran Classe* (1, 2 berths), 🛏 *Preferente* (1, 2 berths), 🛏 *Turista* (4 berths), 💺 🍷 🅁 Madrid (**332/3**) - Medina del Campo (**312**) - Lisboa and Lisboa (**310**) - Medina del Campo (**330/5**) - Madrid. Special fares apply.

P – *Intercite de Nuit* – for dates of running see Table **305**. 🛏 1, 2 cl. 💺 (reclining) Paris - Irún.

Q – *Intercite de Nuit* – for dates of running see Table **305**. 🛏 1, 2 cl. 💺 (reclining) Hendaye - Paris.

j – Not Aug. 15.

Alvia – *Alvia* 🅁 🍷 ⚡.
Arco – *Arco* 🅁 ⚡ 🍷.
Estr – *Estrella.* 🅁 🍷 ⚡.
AVE – *Alta Velocidad Española* 🅁 🍷 ⚡.
◐ – Via Pamplona.
⚡ – Supplement payable.
ES – Spain (Central European Time).
PT – Portugal (West European Time).
☆ – Eurostar train. 🅁, ✕ in 1st class, 🍷 in 2nd class. Specia fares payable. Minimum check-in time 30 minutes. Valid June 1 - Dec. 13. Additional Eurostar services are available, see Table **10**.

FRANKFURT - STRASBOURG - LYON - MARSEILLE 47

train type	ICE	ICE	ICE	IC	ICE			TGV	TGV	
train number	517	518	597	2068	75			9580	9836	
notes							①-⑤	9581	9837	
							w	🄡★	🄡	
Hamburg Hbf d.	...	...	...	...	1024	...	...	...	...	...
Berlin Hbf d.	...	...	0935	...	|	...	...	...	...	...
Hannover Hbf d.	...	...	|	...	1141	...	...	...	...	...
Nürnberg Hbf d.	...	...	|	1139	|	...	...	...	...	...
München Hbf d.	...	1130	|	|	|	...	...	...	...	...
Stuttgart Hbf d.	...	1351	|	1400	|	...	...	...	...	...
Dortmund Hbf d.	1037	|	|	|	|	...	...	...	...	...
Köln Hbf d.	1155	|	|	|	|	...	...	...	...	...
Frankfurt (Main) Hbf d.	|	|	1344	|	1405	...	...	1401	...	...
Mannheim d.	1323	1428	...	|	1445	...	...	1440	...	...
Karlsruhe d.	...	...	...	1453	1508	...	...	1513	...	...
Baden-Baden d.	...	...	...	...	...	...	...	1535	...	...
Offenburg d.	...	...	...	...	...	1434	1504	|	...	...
Kehl 🏛 d.	...	...	...	...	...	1452	1522	|	...	...
Strasbourg a.	...	...	...	...	...	1504	1534	1601	...	...
Mulhouse a.	...	...	...	...	...	...	...	1653	...	...
Belfort Montbéliard TGV a.	...	...	...	...	...	...	...	1725	...	...
Besançon TGV ⊖ a.	...	...	...	...	...	...	...	1748	...	...
Chalon sur Saône a.	...	...	...	...	...	...	...	1853	...	...
Mâcon Ville a.	...	...	...	...	...	...	...	|	...	...
Lyon Part Dieu a.	...	...	...	...	...	...	...	1956	2010	...
Avignon TGV a.	...	...	...	...	...	...	...	2108	|	...
Aix en Provence TGV a.	...	...	...	...	...	...	...	2131	|	...
Marseille St Charles a.	...	...	...	...	...	...	...	2146	|	...
Nimes a.	...	...	...	...	...	...	...	...	2129	...
Montpellier a.	...	...	...	...	...	...	...	...	2156	...

train type	TGV	TGV			ICE	IC	ICE	ICE	ICE
train number	9862	9582			72	2161	519	106	596
notes	9863	9583	①-⑤						
		🄡★	w						
Montpellier d.	0702	...	...	...	...	...	...	...	...
Nimes d.	0729	...	...	...	...	...	...	...	...
Marseille St Charles d.	|	0814	...	...	...	...	...	...	...
Aix en Provence TGV d.	|	0829	...	...	...	...	...	...	...
Avignon TGV d.	|	0851	...	...	...	...	...	...	...
Lyon Part Dieu d.	0854	1004	...	...	...	...	...	...	...
Mâcon Ville d.	...	|	...	...	...	...	...	...	...
Chalon sur Saône d.	...	1109	...	...	...	...	...	...	...
Besançon TGV ⊖ d.	...	1211	...	...	...	...	...	...	...
Belfort Montbéliard TGV d.	...	1235	...	...	...	...	...	...	...
Mulhouse d.	...	1305	...	...	...	...	...	...	...
Strasbourg d.	...	1355	1422	1452	...	...	...	...	...
Kehl 🏛 a.	...	|	1433	1503	...	...	...	...	...
Offenburg a.	...	|	1452	1522	...	...	...	...	...
Baden-Baden a.	...	1422	...	...	...	...	...	...	...
Karlsruhe a.	...	1446	...	...	1451	1506	...	...	...
Mannheim a.	...	1518	...	...	1514	|	1531	1536	...
Frankfurt (Main) Hbf a.	...	1558	...	...	1553	|	|	|	1613
Köln Hbf a.	...	...	...	...	|	|	|	1705	|
Dortmund Hbf a.	...	...	...	...	|	|	|	1821	|
Stuttgart Hbf a.	...	...	...	...	|	1603	1608	...	|
München Hbf a.	...	...	...	...	|	|	1827	...	|
Nürnberg Hbf a.	...	...	...	...	|	1818	...	...	|
Hannover Hbf a.	...	...	...	...	1817	...	...	...	|
Berlin Hbf a.	...	...	...	...	|	...	...	...	2021
Hamburg Hbf a.	...	...	...	...	1935	...	...	...	...

w – Not Oct. 3, Nov. 1, 11. ★ – *Alleo* ICE / TGV service. A DB / SNCF joint enterprise. ⊖ – Full name: Besançon Franche-Comté TGV.

MADRID - BARCELONA - MARSEILLE, LYON and GENÈVE 49

train type / number	TGV		AVE	AVE	AVE	TGV		AVE	AVE	AVE	AVE		AVE	TGV	TGV	AVE	TGV	AVE	AVE		AVE	AVE	
train number	9700		9734	3053	3061	9703		3463	3071	9720	9722		3093	9704	9754	3123	9707	3333	9739		9724	9726	
train number						9702				9721	9723						9706		9738		9725		
notes																					19724		
notes	E P		H	①-⑤	①-④	P	e	⑥⑦	①-⑤		H			P	e		P					H	
Madrid d.	...	...	...	0550	0610	...	...	0620	0700	...	...	...	0930	...	...	1230	...	1310	...	...	1540	...	...
Barcelona Sants d.	0609	...	0720	0855	0840	0920	...	0929	0930	1024	1024	...	1234	1320	...	1530	1620	1606	1725	...	1826	1826	...
Girona d.	0650	...	0801	...	...	1001	...	...	...	1103	1103	...	...	1401	...	...	1701	...	1804	...	1905	1905	...
Figueres Vilafant d.	0707	...	0818	...	...	1018	...	...	...	1120	1120	...	...	1418	...	...	1718	...	1821	...	1922	1922	...
Perpignan a.	0730	...	0843	...	...	1044	...	...	...	1143	1143	...	...	1443	...	...	1744	...	1844	...	1947	1947	...
Narbonne a.	0811	...	0921	...	...	1125	...	...	...	|	|	...	...	1524	...	...	1824	...	1924	...	|	|	...
Carcassonne a.	|	...	|	...	...	|	...	...	...	1246	|	...	...	|	...	...	|	...	|	...	|	2056	...
Toulouse Matabiau a.	|	...	|	...	...	|	...	...	...	1331	|	...	...	|	...	...	|	...	|	...	|	2141	...
Béziers a.	0828	...	|	...	...	|	...	...	...	...	1239	...	...	|	...	...	1841	...	|	...	2039	...	...
Montpellier a.	0920	...	1027	...	...	1218	...	...	...	...	1321	...	...	1617	1728	...	1921	...	2021	...	2121	...	...
Nîmes a.	0949	...	1055	...	...	1249	...	...	...	...	1354	...	...	1649	1753	...	1949	...	2056	...	2153	...	...
Avignon TGV a.	...	...	|	...	...	|	...	...	...	...	1413	...	...	|	|	...	...	...	|	...	2219	...	...
Aix en Provence TGV a.	...	...	|	...	...	|	...	...	...	...	1435	...	...	|	|	...	...	...	|	...	2242	...	...
Marseille St Charles a.	...	...	|	...	...	|	...	...	...	...	1450	...	...	|	|	...	...	...	|	...	2258	...	...
Nice a.	...	...	|	...	...	|	...	...	...	...	...	...	...	|	|	...	...	...	|	...	...	...	...
Valence TGV a.	...	...	1142	...	...	1338	1356	...	...	...	...	...	...	1738	1841	...	...	...	2145	...	...	...	...
Lyon Part Dieu a.	...	...	1224	...	...	...	|	...	...	...	...	...	...	...	1924	...	...	...	2224	...	...	...	...
Genève 🏛 a.	...	...	...	...	...	...	1700	...	...	...	...	...	...	...	2116	...	...	...	...	...	...	...	...

train type / number	AVE	AVE		AVE	AVE		TGV	AVE		TGV	AVE	AVE	AVE	AVE	AVE	TGV	TGV	AVE		TGV		AVE	
train number	9729	9730		9741	3132		9711	3142		9713	3172	9735	3192	9743	3202	9756	9715	3212		9717		9732	
train number		19730		9740			9710										9714					9733	
notes																							
notes	H				Ⓑ		P			E P				H		z	P		e	P		H	
Genève 🏛 d.	...	...	...	...	...	...	...	...	...	...	...	...	...	...	...	1242	...	...	1459	...	...	...	...
Lyon Part Dieu d.	...	...	...	0736	...	...	...	...	...	...	...	...	...	1430	...	1436	...	...	|	...	...	...	...
Valence TGV d.	...	...	...	0813	...	...	...	...	...	1221	...	...	...	|	...	1510	1621	...	1814	1821	...	...	...
Nice d.	...	...	...	|	...	...	...	...	...	|	...	...	...	|	...	...	|	...	...	|	...	...	...
Marseille St Charles d.	...	0710	...	|	...	...	...	...	...	|	...	...	...	|	...	...	|	...	...	|	...	1910	...
Aix en Provence TGV d.	...	0724	...	|	...	...	...	...	...	|	...	...	...	|	...	...	|	...	...	|	...	1924	...
Avignon TGV d.	...	0746	...	|	...	...	...	...	...	|	...	...	...	|	...	...	|	...	...	|	...	1946	...
Nîmes d.	...	0809	...	0905	...	...	1009	...	...	1309	...	...	...	1548	...	...	1709	...	...	1909	...	2005	...
Montpellier d.	...	0837	...	0935	...	...	1037	...	...	1337	...	...	...	1625	...	...	1737	...	...	1941	...	2037	...
Béziers d.	...	0919	...	|	...	...	|	...	...	1418	...	...	...	1719	...	...	|	...	...	2031	...	2118	...
Toulouse Matabiau d.	0816	|	...	|	...	...	|	...	...	|	...	1505	...	|	...	...	|	...	...	|	...	|	...
Carcassonne d.	0900	|	...	|	...	...	|	...	...	|	...	1608	...	|	....	...	|	....	...	|	...	|	...
Narbonne d.	|	|	...	1034	...	...	1135	...	...	1435	...	|	...	|	...	...	1835	...	...	2047	...	|	...
Perpignan d.	1007	1007	...	1110	...	...	1213	...	...	1513	...	1726x	...	1810	...	...	1913	...	...	2125	...	2207	...
Figueres Vilafant a.	1031	1031	...	1133	...	...	1242	...	...	1542	...	1746	...	1835	...	...	1942	...	...	2150	...	2230	...
Girona a.	1047	1047	...	1149	...	...	1259	...	...	1559	...	1805	...	1851	...	...	1959	...	...	2207	...	2246	...
Barcelona Sants a.	1127	1127	...	1229	1300	...	1340	1400	...	1638	1700	1845	1900	1930	2000	...	2040	2100	...	2248	...	2326	...
Madrid a.	...	1413	...	...	1545	...	...	1710	...	...	1945	...	2145	...	2310	...	...	0002	...	...	...	...	...

E – From July 6.
H – To commence on a date to be announced.
P – To / from Paris (Table **13**).
e – Not May 2, 3.
x – 1723 Mar. 31 - Apr. 3.
z – Not May 2, 3, 4.
AVE – Alta Velocidad Española 🄡 🍷 ⚡.
TGV – *Train à Grande Vitesse* 🄡 🍷 ⚡.
⚡ – Supplement payable.

50 OSLO, STOCKHOLM and KØBENHAVN - HAMBURG - BERLIN

Day Trains (for night trains see below)

train type / train number	1/3			ICE				ICE	ICE		Sn		ICE	IC		Sn		EC	IC
train number	[R]			**38**		**1033**		**36**	**1719**		**519**	**1045**	**34**	**2071**		**525**		**238**	**2073**
notes	J			🍷		①–⑤		🍷	🍷		①–⑤		🍷	🍷				🍷	🍷
notes	Ⓑ			c				c					c					Q c	
Stockholm Central d.	2125	...	...	...	...	...	...	...	...	...	0521	...	...	...	...	0821	...	...	...
Göteborg d.	|	...	...	...	...	0540	...	...	...	...	|	0740	...	...	...	|	0940	...	...
Malmö C ⊡ d.	0537	0553	0653	...	...	0853	0853	...	...	...	0958	1053	...	...	...	1250	1253	...	...
København H. ⊡ d.	...	0628	0728	0742	...	0928	0928	0942	...	...	1032	1128	1142	...	...	1323	1328	1342	...
Rødby Ferry 🛃 d.	...	...	...	0936	...	...	...	1136	...	...	...	...	1336	...	...	...	...	1536	...
Puttgarden 🛃 a.	...	...	...	1036	...	...	...	1236	...	...	...	...	1436	...	...	...	...	1636	...
Lübeck Hbf a.	...	...	...	1137	...	...	...	1337	...	...	...	...	1537	...	...	...	...	1737	...
Hamburg Hbf a.	...	...	...	1216	...	...	...	1416	1505	...	...	...	1616	1629	...	...	...	1816	1827
Berlin Hauptbahnhof a.	...	...	...	1427	...	...	...	...	1643	...	...	...	...	1834	...	...	...	...	2035

train type / train number	Sn			ICE	ICE			391		Sn	Sn				EC				
train number	**527**			**32**	**905**			**105**		**529**	**531**		**1081**		**30**				
notes	①–⑥			🍷				①–⑥		Ⓑ	Ⓑ				🍷				
notes				c											S c				
Oslo Sentral d.	...	...	...	...	...	...	...	0702	...	...	...	...	...	...	...	...	...	...	...
Stockholm Central d.	0921	...	...	...	...	...	...	|	...	1021	1121	...	...	...	...	...	...	...	...
Göteborg d.	|	...	1040	...	...	...	...	1040	1140	|	|	...	1340	...	...	...	...	...	...
Malmö C ⊡ d.	1347	1413	1353	...	...	...	...	...	1453	1500	1547	1602	1653	1653	...	...	...	...	...
København H. ⊡ d.	...	1448	1428	1525	...	...	...	...	1528	1540	...	1636	1728	1728	1742	...	...	...	...
Rødby Ferry 🛃 d.	...	...	...	1736	...	...	...	...	...	...	...	...	...	...	1931	...	...	...	...
Puttgarden 🛃 a.	...	...	...	1836	...	...	...	...	...	...	...	...	...	...	2036	...	...	...	...
Lübeck Hbf a.	...	...	...	1937	...	...	...	...	...	...	...	...	...	...	2137	...	...	...	...
Hamburg Hbf a.	...	...	...	2016	2121	...	...	...	...	...	...	...	...	...	2216	...	...	...	...
Berlin Hauptbahnhof a.	...	...	...	...	2312	...	...	...	...	...	...	...	...	...	...	...	...	...	...

train type	ICE	EC		398	Sn	Sn			ICE	ICE		Sn			ICE		Sn		
train number	**1618**	**31**	**1050**	**134**	**538**	**540**			**1616**	**33**	**1062**	**542**			**35**	**1086**	**550**		
notes	①–⑤	🍷			⑥	Ⓑ			**1706**	🍷					🍷		Ⓑ		
notes	y	T c							🍷	c					c				
Berlin Hauptbahnhof d.	0515	...	...	...	...	...	...	...	0712	...	...	...	...	...	1125	...	...	...	...
Hamburg Hbf d.	0708	0725	...	...	...	...	...	...	0853	0928	...	...	...	...	1328	...	...	...	...
Lübeck Hbf d.	...	0806	...	...	...	...	...	...	...	1006	...	...	...	...	1406	...	...	...	...
Puttgarden 🛃 d.	...	0908	...	...	...	...	...	...	...	1108	...	...	...	...	1508	...	...	...	...
Rødby Ferry 🛃 a.	...	1008	...	...	...	...	...	...	...	1208	...	...	...	...	1608	...	...	...	...
København H. ⊡ d.	...	1214	1232	...	1229	...	...	...	...	1414	1432	1429	...	...	1814	1832	1836	...	...
Malmö C ⊡ a.	...	...	1306	...	1259	1411	...	...	...	...	1506	1459	...	...	...	1906	1909	...	...
Göteborg a.	...	...	1615	1755	|	|	...	...	...	...	1815	|	...	...	...	2215	|	...	...
Stockholm Central a.	...	...	...	|	1740	1840	...	...	...	...	...	1940	...	...	...	...	2340	...	...
Oslo Sentral a.	...	...	...	2149	...	...	...	...	...	...	...	...	...	...	...	...	...	...	...

train type / train number	ICE	ICE		2				ICE	ICE					ICE	EC				
train number	**1512**	**37**	**1098**	[R]				**1510**	**39**					**892**	**239**				
notes		🍷		J					🍷						🍷				
notes		c		Ⓑ					c						Q c				
Berlin Hauptbahnhof d.	1312	...	...	...	...	...	...	1524	...	...	...	...	...	1712	...	...	...	...	...
Hamburg Hbf d.	1454	1528	...	...	...	...	...	1709	1728z	...	...	...	...	1854	1928	...	...	...	...
Lübeck Hbf d.	...	1606	...	...	...	...	...	...	1806	...	...	...	...	...	2006	...	...	...	...
Puttgarden 🛃 d.	...	1708	...	...	...	...	...	...	1908	...	...	...	...	...	2108	...	...	...	...
Rødby Ferry 🛃 a.	...	1808	...	...	...	...	...	...	2008	...	...	...	...	...	2208	...	...	...	...
København H. ⊡ d.	...	2014	2032	...	...	...	...	...	2214	2232	...	...	...	...	0019	0112	...	...	...
Malmö C ⊡ a.	...	...	2106	2237	...	...	...	...	...	2306	...	...	...	...	...	0146	...	...	...
Göteborg a.	...	...	0015	|	...	...	...	...	...	...	...	...	...	...	...	...	...	...	...
Stockholm Central a.	...	...	...	0617	...	...	...	...	...	...	...	...	...	...	...	...	...	...	...

50 KØBENHAVN - KÖLN, AMSTERDAM, BASEL and BERLIN

Night Trains (for day trains see above)

train type	391		Sn	CNL	CNL	CNL	EN				Sn	Sn	395			EN			
train number	**105**	**1081**	**533**	**50473**	**40473**	**473**	**301**				**537**	**539**	**117**	**1105**		**301**			
notes	①–⑥			[R] 🍷	[R] 🍷	[R] 🍷	①④					Ⓑ				⑥			
notes	🍷			K	A	B	G b						🍷			H b			
Oslo Sentral d.	0702	...	...	...	...	...	...	...	...	...	...	...	1302	...	...	...	...	...	...
Stockholm Central d.	|	...	1221	...	...	...	...	...	...	...	1421	1521	|	...	...	...	...	...	...
Göteborg d.	1040	1340	|	...	...	...	...	...	...	...	|	|	1650	1740	...	...	...	...	...
København H ⊡ d.	...	|	|	...	...	...	...	...	...	...	|	|	...	|	2012	...	...	...	...
Malmö C ⊡ d.	...	1653	1657	...	...	...	1735	...	...	...	1850	1950	...	2051	2046	2235	...	...	...
København H. ⊡ a.	...	1728	1731x	...	...	...	|	...	...	...	...	...	...	...	...	|	...	...	...
København H. d.	...	...	...	1846	1846	1846	|	...	...	...	...	...	...	...	...	|	...	...	...
Odense d.	...	...	...	2028	2028	2028	|	...	...	...	...	...	...	...	...	|	...	...	...
Padborg 🛃 d.	...	...	...	2224	2224	2224	|	...	...	...	...	...	...	...	...	|	...	...	...
Flensburg 🛃 d.	...	...	...	2238	2238	2238	|	...	...	...	...	...	...	...	...	|	...	...	...
Köln a.	...	...	...	|	0614	|	|	...	...	...	...	...	...	...	...	|	...	...	...
Amsterdam a.	...	...	...	|	0959	|	|	...	...	...	...	...	...	...	...	|	...	...	...
Basel SBB a.	...	...	...	|	...	1030	|	...	...	...	...	...	...	...	...	|	...	...	...
Berlin Hbf a.	...	...	...	0426	...	...	0623	...	...	...	...	...	...	...	...	0732	...	...	...

train type	EN		EN			394	S	CNL	CNL	CNL		398	Sn	Sn	EN		398		Sn
train number	**302**		**300**		**1026**	**124**	**530**	**472**	**40447**	**40456**	**1038**	**134**	**536**	**538**	**300**		**134**		**542**
notes			⑤					[R] 🍷	[R] 🍷	[R] 🍷		🍷	Ⓑ	⑥	③⑦		🍷		⑥
notes	P b		C b					B	A	K					D b				
Berlin Hbf d.	0930	...	1927	...	...	...	...	...	...	0032	...	...	...	...	2228	...	...	...	...
Basel SBB d.	|	...	|	...	...	...	...	1826	...	|	...	...	...	...	|	...	...	...	...
Amsterdam d.	|	...	|	...	...	...	...	|	1901	|	...	...	...	...	|	...	...	...	...
Köln d.	|	...	|	...	...	...	...	|	2228	|	...	...	...	...	|	...	...	...	...
Flensburg 🛃 a.	|	...	|	...	...	...	...	0553	0553	0553	...	...	...	...	|	...	...	...	...
Padborg 🛃 a.	|	...	|	...	...	...	...	0607	0607	0607	...	...	...	...	|	...	...	...	...
Odense a.	|	...	|	...	...	...	...	0817	0817	0817	...	...	...	...	|	...	...	...	...
København H. a.	|	...	|	...	...	...	...	1007	1007	1007		...	...	...	|	...	...	...	...
København H. ⊡ d.	|	...	|	...	...	...	...	...	...	...	1032	...	1115	1229	|	...	...	...	...
Malmö C ⊡ a.	1810	1833	0800	0833	0908	...	0911	...	...	...	1106	...	1156	1259	1259	1308	...	1313	1511
København H ⊡ a.	...	1908	...	0908	|	...	|	...	...	...	|	...	|	|	...	|	...	1348	|
Göteborg a.	...	...	...	...	1215	1300	|	...	...	...	1415	1755	|	|	...	1615	1755	...	|
Stockholm Central a.	...	...	...	...	...	|	1340	...	...	...	...	|	1640	1740	...	...	|	...	1940
Oslo Sentral a.	...	...	...	...	...	1652	...	...	...	...	...	2149	...	...	...	...	2149	...	...

NOTES FOR TABLE 50 ON NEXT PAGE →

BERLIN - GDYNIA 51

train type		*EC*	
train number		**55**	
notes		**H** [R]	
Berlin Hbf .... d.	...	1537	...
Berlin Ost .... d.	...	1550	...
Frankfurt (Oder) 🏛 .. d.	...	1645	...
Rzepin .... a.	...	1708	...
Poznań Gł. .... a.	...	1827	...
Gniezno .... a.	...	1857	...
Inowrocław .... a.	...	1935	...
Bydgoszcz Gł. .... a.	...	2004	...
Tczew .... a.	...	2116	...
Gdańsk Gł. .... a.	...	2134	...
Sopot .... a.	...	2149	...
Gdynia Gł. .... a.	...	2208	...

train type		*EC*	
train number		**54**	
notes		**H** [R]	
Gdynia Gł. .... d.	...	0654	...
Sopot .... d.	...	0703	...
Gdańsk Gł. .... d.	...	0721	...
Tczew .... d.	...	0739	...
Bydgoszcz Gł. .... d.	...	0851	...
Inowrocław .... d.	...	0921	...
Gniezno .... d.	...	0957	...
Poznań Gł. .... d.	...	1028	...
Rzepin .... d.	...	1151	...
Frankfurt (Oder) 🏛 ...a.	...	1206	...
Berlin Ost .... a.	...	1306	...
Berlin Hbf .... a.	...	1318	...

H – BERLIN GDANSK EXPRESS [12] ✕ [R] Berlin - Poznań - Gdynia and v.v. (Table **1020**).

PRAHA - ZÜRICH 52

train type				*CNL*
train number	**1541**	**1543**	**1545**	**458**
notes				**C**
Praha hlavní .... d.	0515	0915	1315	1829
Praha Holešovice .... d.	|	|	|	1839
Tábor .... d.	0654	1054	1454	|
Veselí nad Lužnicí .... d.	0721	1121	1521	|
České Budějovice .... d.	0809	1209	1609	|
Summerau 🏛 .... d.	0913	1313	1712	◧
Linz Hbf .... a.	1024	1424	1824	|
	RJ	*RJ*	*RJ*	|
	162	**166**	**662**	|
	🍷	🍷	🍷	|
Linz Hbf .... d.	1053	1453	1853	|
Salzburg .... a.	1158	1558	1958	|
Innsbruck Hbf .... a.	1351	1751	2145	|
Zürich HB .... a.	1720	2120	...	0917

train type	*RJ*	*RJ*		*CNL*
train number	**663**	**163**		**459**
notes	🍷	🍷		**C**
Zürich HB .... d.	...	0840	...	1942
Innsbruck Hbf .... d.	0809	1209	...	|
Salzburg .... d.	1000	1402	...	|
Linz Hbf .... a.	1106	1506	...	|
	1540	**1542**		|
Linz Hbf .... d.	1135	1535	...	|
Summerau 🏛 .... a.	1247	1644	...	◧
České Budějovice .... a.	1353	1753	...	|
Veselí nad Lužnicí .... a.	1439	1839	...	|
Tábor .... a.	1505	1905	...	|
Praha Holešovice .... a.	|	|	...	1019
Praha hlavní .... a.	1639	2039	...	1029

C – *City Night Line* CANOPUS – 🛏 1, 2 cl., ▬ 2 cl., [2] (reclining), 🍷 Praha - Frankfürt - Zürich and v.v. ✕ Frankfürt - Zürich and v.v. (Table **54**). [R] Special fares apply.

RJ – ÖBB *Railjet* service. [1] (premium class), [1] (first class), [2] (economy class), ✕.

◧ – 🏛 at Bad Schandau and Basel Bad Bf.

TRAIN NAMES: **1540 / 1541** – F A GERSTNER **1542 / 1543** – ANTON BRUCKNER

ZÜRICH and AMSTERDAM - KØBENHAVN, WARSZAWA, PRAHA and BERLIN 54

	CNL	*CNL*	*EN*	*CNL*	*CNL*	*CNL*	*CNL*	*CNL*		
	40456	**472**	**447**	**457**	**40447**	**1259**	**459**	**478**		
	[R] 🍷	[R] 🍷	[R] 🍷	[R] 🍷	[R] 🍷	[R] 🍷	[R] 🍷	[R] 🍷		
	O	**A**	**J**	**K**	**B**	**S**	**C**	**L**		
Zürich HB .... d.	...	...	...	...	...	1942	1942	2042	...	...
Basel SBB .... d.	...	1826	...	...	...	2113	2113	2213	...	...
Karlsruhe Hbf .... d.	...	2035	...	...	...	2304	2304	0029	...	...
Frankfurt (Main) Süd .... d.	...	|	...	...	...	0054	0054	|	...	...
Frankfurt (Main) Hbf .... d.	...	2219	...	...	...	|	|	|	...	...
Fulda .... d.	...	2343	...	...	...	|	|	|	...	...
Erfurt Hbf .... a.	...	|	...	...	...	0345	0345	|	...	...
Weimar .... a.	...	|	...	...	...	0457	0539	|	...	...
Leipzig Hbf .... a.	...	|	...	...	...	|	0642	|	...	...
Praha hlavní .... d.	1829	|	...	...	...	|	|	|	...	...
Dresden Hbf .... d.	2053	|	...	...	...	|	|	|	...	...
Amsterdam Centraal .... d.	|	|	1901	1901	1901	|	|	|	...	...
Utrecht Centraal .... d.	|	|	1929	1929	1929	|	|	|	...	...
Arnhem .... d.	|	|	2007	2007	2007	|	|	|	...	...
Emmerich .... d.	|	|	2050	2050	2050	|	|	|	...	...
Duisburg Hbf .... d.	|	|	2146	2146	2146	|	|	|	...	...
Düsseldorf Hbf .... d.	|	|	2202	2202	2202	|	|	|	...	...
Köln Hbf .... d.	|	|	2228	2228	2228	|	|	|	...	...
Wuppertal Hbf .... d.	|	|	2314	2314	2314	|	|	|	...	...
Dortmund Hbf .... d.	|	|	2356	2356	2356	|	|	|	...	...
Hamm (Westf) .... d.	|	|	0014	0014	0014	|	|	|	...	...
Bielefeld Hbf .... d.	|	|	0043	0043	0043	|	|	|	...	...
Berlin Ostbahnhof .... a.	2346	|	|	|	|	|	|	|	...	...
Berlin Ostbahnhof .... d.	0016	|	|	|	|	|	|	|	...	...
Berlin Hbf .... a.	0027**z**	|	0423	0423	|	0719	|	|	...	...
Berlin Ostbahnhof .... a.	|	|	0646	0435	|	...	|	|	...	...
Warszawa Centralna .... a.	|	|	1215	|	|	...	|	|	...	...
Dresden Hbf .... a.	|	|	...	0658	|	...	0803	|	...	...
Praha hlavní .... a.	|	|	...	0926	|	...	1029	|	...	...
Hannover .... a.	|	|	...	...	|	...	...	0630	...	...
Hamburg Hbf .... a.	0410	0410	...	...	0410	...	...	0835	...	...
Neumünster .... a.	0452	0452	...	...	0452	...	...	...	...	...
Flensburg .... a.	0553	0553	...	...	0553	...	...	...	...	...
Padborg .... a.	0607	0607	...	...	0607	...	...	...	...	...
Kolding .... a.	0732	0732	...	...	0732	...	...	...	...	...
Odense .... a.	0817	0817	...	...	0817	...	...	...	...	...
Ringsted .... a.	|	|	...	...	|	...	...	...	...	...
Roskilde .... a.	0944	0944	...	...	0944	...	...	...	...	...
Høje Taastrup .... a.	|	|	...	...	|	...	...	...	...	...
København H .... a.	1008	1008	...	...	1008	...	...	...	...	...

	CNL	*CNL*	*CNL*	*EN*	*CNL*	*CNL*	*CNL*	*CNL*		
	479	**458**	**1258**	**446**	**456**	**40473**	**473**	**50473**		
	[R] 🍷	[R] 🍷	[R] 🍷	[R] 🍷	[R] 🍷	[R] 🍷	[R] 🍷	[R] 🍷		
	L	**C**	**S**	**J**	**K**	**B**	**A**	**O**		
København H .... d.	...	...	...	...	...	1846	1846	1846	...	...
Høje Taastrup .... d.	...	...	...	...	...	|	|	|	...	...
Roskilde .... d.	...	...	...	...	...	1911	1911	1911	...	...
Ringsted .... d.	...	...	...	...	...	|	|	|	...	...
Odense .... d.	...	...	...	...	...	2028	2028	2028	...	...
Kolding .... d.	...	...	...	...	...	2110	2110	2110	...	...
Padborg .... d.	...	...	...	...	...	2224	2224	2224	...	...
Flensburg .... d.	...	...	...	...	...	2238	2238	2238	...	...
Neumünster .... d.	...	...	...	...	...	2339	2339	2339	...	...
Hamburg Hbf .... d.	2027	...	...	...	...	0031	0031	0031	...	...
Hannover .... d.	2216	...	...	...	...	|	|	|	...	...
Praha hlavní .... d.	|	1829	...	...	1829	|	|	|	...	...
Dresden Hbf .... d.	|	2104	...	...	2053	|	|	|	...	...
Warszawa Centralna .... d.	|	|	...	1755	|	|	|	|	...	...
Berlin Ostbahnhof .... d.	|	|	...	0016	0016	|	|	|	...	...
Berlin Hbf .... d.	|	|	2211	0027	0027	|	|	0423**a**	...	...
Berlin Ostbahnhof .... a.	|	|	|	|	|	|	|	|	...	...
Berlin Ostbahnhof .... d.	|	|	|	|	|	|	|	|	...	...
Bielefeld Hbf .... a.	|	|	|	0355	0355	0355	|	|	...	...
Hamm (Westf) .... a.	|	|	|	0425	0425	0425	|	|	...	...
Dortmund Hbf .... a.	|	|	|	0447	0447	0447	|	|	...	...
Wuppertal Hbf .... a.	|	|	|	0538	0538	0538	|	|	...	...
Köln Hbf .... a.	|	|	|	0614	0614	0614	|	|	...	...
Düsseldorf Hbf .... a.	|	|	|	0654	0654	0654	|	|	...	...
Duisburg Hbf .... a.	|	|	|	0710	0710	0710	|	|	...	...
Emmerich .... a.	|	|	|	0800	0800	0800	|	|	...	...
Arnhem .... a.	|	|	|	0845	0845	0845	|	|	...	...
Utrecht Centraal .... a.	|	|	|	0927	0927	0927	|	|	...	...
Amsterdam Centraal .... a.	|	|	|	0959	0959	0959	|	|	...	...
Dresden Hbf .... a.	|	|	|	...	...	...	|	0659	...	...
Praha hlavní .... a.	|	|	|	...	...	...	|	0927	...	...
Leipzig Hbf .... d.	|	2226	|	...	...	...	|	...	...	...
Weimar .... d.	|	2348	0039	...	...	...	|	...	...	...
Erfurt Hbf .... d.	|	0121	0121	...	...	...	|	...	...	...
Fulda .... a.	|	|	|	...	...	...	0523	...	...	...
Frankfurt (Main) Hbf .... a.	|	|	|	...	...	...	0640	...	...	...
Frankfurt (Main) Süd .... a.	|	0359	0359	...	...	...	|	...	...	...
Karlsruhe Hbf .... a.	0437	0540	0540	...	...	...	0816	...	...	...
Basel SBB .... a.	0647	0754	0754	...	...	...	1030	...	...	...
Zürich HB .... a.	0834**x**	0917	0917	...	...	...	...	...	...	...

A – *City Night Line* AURORA – 🛏 1, 2 cl., ▬ 2 cl. (4, 6 berth), [2] (reclining), 🍷 Basel - Frankfurt - København and v.v. [R] Special fares apply.

B – *City Night Line* BOREALIS – 🛏 1, 2 cl., ▬ 2 cl., [2] (reclining), 🍷 Amsterdam - Köln - København and v.v. [R] Special fares apply.

C – *City Night Line* CANOPUS – 🛏 1, 2 cl., ▬ 2 cl., [2] (reclining), 🍷 Praha hlavní - Praha Holešovice - Bad Schandau 🏛 - Dresden - Leipzig - Frankfurt (Main) Süd - Basel Bad Bf 🏛 - Zürich and v.v. [R] Special fares apply.

J – JAN KIEPURA – 🛏 1, 2 cl., ▬ 2 cl., [2] (reclining) Amsterdam - Köln - Warszawa and v.v. (Table **24**).

K – *City Night Line* KOPERNIKUS / PHOENIX – 🛏 1, 2 cl., ▬ 2 cl., [2] (reclining), 🍷 Amsterdam - Köln - Berlin - Dresden - Praha and v.v. [R] Special fares apply.

L – *City Night Line* KOMET – 🛏 1, 2 cl., 🛏 1, 2 cl. (T4), ▬ 2 cl. (4, 6 berth), [2] (reclining), 🍷 Zürich - Basel - Hamburg and v.v. [R] Special fares apply.

O – *City Night Line* ORION – 🛏 1, 2 cl., ▬ 2 cl., 🍷 Praha - Dresden - Berlin - København and v.v. [R] Special fares apply.

S – *City Night Line* SIRIUS – 🛏 1, 2 cl., 🛏 1, 2 cl. (T4), ▬ 2 cl. (4, 6 berth), [2] (reclining), 🍷 Zürich - Halle - Berlin and v.v. [R] Special fares apply.

a – Arrival time.

x – 0820 on ⑥⑦.

z – Departure time.

← NOTES FROM TABLE 50 ON PREVIOUS PAGE

A – *City Night Line* BOREALIS – 🛏 1, 2 cl., ▬ 2 cl., [2] (reclining), 🍷 København - Köln - Amsterdam and v.v. 🍷 København - Hamburg and v.v. [R] Special fares apply.

B – *City Night Line* AURORA – 🛏 1, 2 cl., ▬ 2 cl. (4, 6 berth), 🍷 København - Frankfurt - Basel and v.v. [R] Special fares apply. Conveys ORION - 🛏 1, 2 cl., ▬ 2 cl. København - Praha and v.v.

C – BERLIN NIGHT EXPRESS – ⑤ June 26 - Aug. 17: ▬ 2 cl., 🍷 (✕ on board ferry) Berlin - Malmö. [R] Special fares apply.

D – BERLIN NIGHT EXPRESS – ③⑦ June 26 - Aug. 17: ▬ 2 cl., 🍷 (✕ on board ferry) Berlin - Malmö. [R] Special fares apply.

G – BERLIN NIGHT EXPRESS – ①④ June 26 - Aug. 17 (also June 5): ▬ 2 cl., 🍷 (✕ on board ferry) Malmö - Berlin. [R] Special fares apply.

H – BERLIN NIGHT EXPRESS – ⑥ June 26 - Aug. 17: ▬ 2 cl., 🍷 (✕ on board ferry) Malmö - Berlin. [R] Special fares apply.

K – *City Night Line* ORION – 🛏 1, 2 cl., ▬ 2 cl., 🍷 København - Berlin - Dresden - Praha and v.v. [R] Special fares apply.

J – ⑧: 🛏 1, 2 cl., ▬ 2 cl., [2] 🍷 [R] Stockholm - Malmö and v.v.

P – June 8.

Q – June 10 - Aug. 24.

S – May 18 - Oct. 26.

T – May 18 - Oct. 27.

b – Train is conveyed by train-ferry Trelleborg 🏛 - Sassnitz Fährhafen 🏛 (Mukran) and v.v.

c – Passengers to / from Rødby or Puttgarden may be required to leave / board the train on board the ferry.

y – Not Oct. 3.

z – 1721 July 14 - Aug. 24.

Sn – *Snabbtåg* high speed train. [R] ✕.

⊡ – Additional services Malmö - København and v.v. are available, see Table **703**.

56 KÖLN - BERLIN - WARSZAWA - MOSKVA

Russian timings liable to vary from October 26, 2014

train type	*EC*	*ICE*	*EC*				*ICE*	*EC*			*ICE*	*EC*		*ICE*	*EC*		*ICE*			*EN*			
train number	41	541	43	10*ZH*	12010		555	45	116*BJ*		557	55		559	47		953	24*JI*		447	405	405	
notes	✕	1541	✕	11011	68*KJ*		🍷	✕	11016		🍷	✕		🍷	¶		🍷	453		Ⓡ	22*AJ*	58*AJ*	
	①–⑥	①–⑥													Ⓑ		Ⓑ				Ⓡ	Ⓡ	
	T		T	P	C		A	T	W		A	N		A	T		A	M		J	Q	H	
Köln Hbf d.	...	0429	...	...	...	...	0848	...	...	...	1048	...	...	1248	...	...	1548	...	...	2228	...	...	...
Düsseldorf Hbf d.	...	0453	...	...	...	...	0853z	...	...	...	1053z	...	...	1253z	...	...	1553z	...	...	|	...	...	...
Dortmund Hbf d.	...	0547	...	...	...	...	0948z	...	...	...	1148z	...	...	1348z	...	...	1648z	...	...	2356	...	...	...
Bielefeld Hbf d.	...	0640	...	...	...	...	1038	...	...	...	1238	...	...	1438	...	...	1737	...	...	0043	...	...	...
Hannover Hbf d.	...	0731	...	...	...	...	1131	...	...	...	1331	...	...	1531	...	...	1831	1912	...	|	...	...	...
Berlin Zoo d.	...	|	...	...	...	...	|	...	...	...	|	...	...	|	...	...	|	|	...	|	...	...	...
Berlin Hbf a.	...	0908	...	...	...	...	1308	...	...	...	1508	...	...	1708	...	...	2007	|	...	|	...	...	...
Berlin Hbf d.	0637	|	0937	...	...	...	|	1337	...	...	|	1537	...	|	1737	...	|	2129	...	0637	...	...	...
Berlin Ostbahnhof d.	0650	0919	0950	...	...	...	1319	1350	...	...	1519	1550	...	1719	1750	...	2019	2138	...	0650	...	...	...
Frankfurt (Oder) 🛃 d.	0745	...	1045	...	...	...	...	1445	...	...	...	1645	...	...	1845	...	...	2239	...	|	...	...	...
Rzepin d.	0808	...	1108	...	...	...	...	1508	...	...	...	1708	...	...	1908	...	...	2303	...	0808	...	...	...
Poznań Gł. d.	0933	...	1230	...	...	...	...	1630	...	...	...	1827	...	...	2030	...	...	0045	...	0933	...	...	...
Warszawa Centralna a.	1215	...	1505	1610	1650	...	...	1905	2120	...	...	...	...	...	2306¶	...	...	0343	...	1215	...	...	...
Warszawa Wschodnia d.	1228	...	1528	1621	1700	...	...	1933	2130	...	...	...	...	...	2319	...	...	0426	...	1228	...	1215	...
Terespol a.	...	...	...	1852	|	...	...	...	0006	...	...	...	...	...	...	...	...	0643	...	...	0455	1515	...
Brest Tsentralny 🛃 a.	...	...	...	2206	|	...	...	...	0330	...	...	...	...	...	...	...	...	0918r	...	...	0743t	1749t	...
Yahodyn 🛃 a.	...	...	...	|	2230	...	...	...	|	...	...	...	...	...	...	...	...	|	...	...	|	|	...
Kyïv a.	...	...	...	|	1035	...	...	...	|	...	...	...	...	...	...	...	...	|	...	...	|	|	...
Minsk a.	...	...	...	0255	...	...	...	...	0907	...	...	...	...	...	...	...	...	1436	...	...	1314	2313	...
Orsha Tsentralnaya § a.	...	...	...	0523	...	...	...	...	...	...	...	...	...	...	...	...	...	1712	...	...	1558	0157	...
St Peterburg Vitebski a.	...	...	...	|	...	...	...	...	...	...	...	...	...	...	...	...	...	|	...	...	|	1640	...
Smolensk Tsentralny 🛃 § a.	...	...	...	0745	...	...	...	...	...	...	...	...	...	...	...	...	...	1935	...	...	1828	...	...
Moskva Belorusskaya ‡ a.	...	...	...	1253	...	...	...	...	...	...	...	...	...	...	...	...	...	2358	...	...	2320	...	...

train type/number	*EC*	*ICE*			*EC*	*ICE*				*EC*	*ICE*		*EC*	*ICE*		*EC*	*EN*					*ICE*	
train number	46	950		115*BJ*	54	858		67*KJ*	9*JA*	44	856		42	540		40	446		49*JA*	21*JA*	23*JI*	652	
notes	✕	1530		11018	✕	🍷		21010	11012	✕	🍷		✕	🍷		✕	Ⓡ		404	404	452		
	①–⑥	🍷												⑤⑥⑦		Ⓑ			Ⓡ	Ⓡ			
	T	A		W	N			C	P	T			T	e		T	J		X	V	F	A	
Moskva Belorusskaya ‡ d.	...	...	...	...	...	...	...	...	1720	...	...	...	...	...	...	...	...	...	...	0843	0744	...	...
Smolensk Tsentralny 🛃 § d.	...	...	...	...	...	...	...	...	2220	...	...	...	...	...	...	...	...	...	...	1323	1226	...	...
St Peterburg Vitebski d.	...	...	...	...	...	...	...	...	|	...	...	...	...	...	...	...	...	...	1522	|	|	...	...
Orsha Tsentralnaya § d.	...	...	...	...	...	...	...	...	2242	...	...	...	...	...	...	...	...	...	0123	1347	1247	...	...
Minsk d.	...	...	...	2144	...	...	...	...	0110	...	...	...	...	...	...	...	...	...	0406	1625	1528	...	...
Kyïv d.	...	...	...	|	...	...	...	1552	|	...	...	...	...	...	...	...	...	...	|	|	|	...	...
Yahodyn 🛃 d.	...	...	...	|	...	...	...	0324	|	...	...	...	...	...	...	...	...	...	|	|	|	...	...
Brest Tsentralny 🛃 d.	...	...	...	0340	...	...	...	|	0632	...	...	...	...	...	...	...	...	...	1445j	2215	2115f	...	...
Terespol d.	...	...	...	0238	...	...	...	|	0530	...	...	...	...	...	...	...	...	...	1445	2033	2113	...	...
Warszawa Wschodnia a.	0542	...	...	0530	...	...	...	0735	0802	0942	...	...	1442	...	...	1742	1742	...	...	...	2342	...	...
Warszawa Centralna d.	0555	...	...	0540	...	...	...	0745	0815	0955	...	...	1455	...	...	1755	1755	...	...	...	0023s	...	...
Poznań Gł. d.	0828	...	...	...	1028	...	...	...	...	1228	...	...	1728	...	...	2029	2029	...	...	...	0341s	...	...
Rzepin d.	0951	...	...	...	1151	...	...	...	...	1351	...	...	1851	...	...	2151	2151	...	...	...	0523s	...	...
Frankfurt (Oder) 🛃 a.	1012	...	...	...	1212	...	...	...	...	1412	...	...	1912	...	...	2212	|	...	...	...	0600s	...	...
Berlin Ostbahnhof a.	1106	1136	...	...	1306	1336	...	...	...	1506	1536	...	2006	2056	...	2306	2306	...	...	...	|	0838	...
Berlin Hbf a.	1116	|	...	...	1316	|	...	...	...	1516	|	...	2016	|	...	2320	0024	...	...	...	0653	|	...
Berlin Hbf d.	...	1147	...	...	...	1347	...	...	...	...	1547	...	...	2107	...	...	|	...	...	...	|	0849	...
Berlin Zoo a.	...	|	...	...	...	|	...	...	...	...	|	...	...	|	...	...	|	...	...	...	|	|	...
Hannover Hbf a.	...	1328	...	...	...	1528	...	...	...	...	1728	...	...	2256	...	...	|	...	...	...	0944	1028	...
Bielefeld Hbf a.	...	1420	...	...	...	1620	...	...	...	...	1820	...	...	2353	...	...	0355	...	...	...	...	1120	...
Dortmund Hbf a.	...	1509z	...	...	...	1709z	...	...	...	...	1909z	...	...	0047	...	...	0447	...	...	...	...	1209z	...
Düsseldorf Hbf a.	...	1605z	...	...	...	1805z	...	...	...	...	2005z	...	...	0145	...	...	|	...	...	...	...	1305z	...
Köln Hbf a.	...	1609	...	...	...	1809	...	...	...	...	2009	...	...	0209	...	...	0614	...	...	...	...	1309	...

A – (12) ✕ Köln - Wuppertal - Hamm - Berlin and Düsseldorf - Hamm - Berlin and v.v. Table **810**.

C – KYÏV EKSPRES / KIEV EXPRESS – 🛏 1, 2 cl. Warszawa - Kyïv and v.v.

M – TRANSEUROPEAN EXPRESS ①②④⑥⑦ May 31 - Oct. 5; ①④⑦ Oct. 6 - Dec. 13: 🛏 1, 2 cl. Moskva (**23** *JI*) - Brest (**452**) - Berlin - Paris. ✕ (RZD) Moskva - Brest and ✕ (PKP) Warszawa - Paris.

H – ⑤⑥: 🛏 1, 2 cl. Praha (**445**) - Bohumín (**405**) - Brest (**22***GJ*) - Orsha (**58**) - St Peterburg (journey 2 nights).

J – JAN KIEPURA – 🛏 1, 2 cl., ▬ 2 cl., (2) (reclining) Amsterdam - Köln - Warszawa and v.v. ✕ Rzepin - Warszawa and v.v.

M – TRANSEUROPEAN EXPRESS ①②③④⑥ June 1 - Oct. 5; ②③⑥ Oct. 6 - Dec. 13: 🛏 1, 2 cl. Paris (**453**) - Berlin - Brest (**24** *JI*) - Moskva. ✕ (PKP) Paris - Warszawa and ✕ (RZD) Brest - Moskva.

N – BERLIN GDANSK EXPRESS (12) ✕ Ⓡ Berlin - Poznań - Gdynia and v.v.

P – POLONEZ – 🛏 1, 2 cl., 🍷 Warszawa - Moskva and v.v. ✕ Brest - Moskva and v.v.

Q – VLTAVA ③④⑥: 🛏 1, 2 cl. Praha (**405**) - Bohumín - Katowice - Brest (**22***AJ*) - Moskva. Also **22***EJ*, **22***GJ*..

T – BERLIN WARSZAWA EXPRESS – (12) and ✕ Berlin - Poznań - Warszawa and v.v. Ⓡ Special fares apply. Supplement payable in Poland.

V – VLTAVA ②③⑤: 🛏 1, 2 cl. Moskva (**21***JA*) - Terespol (**404**) - Katowice - Bohumín - Praha.

W – 🛏 1, 2 cl. Warszawa - Minsk and v.v.

X – ③④: 🛏 1, 2 cl. St Peterburg (**49***JA*) - Brest (**404**) - Bohumín (**444**) - Praha (journey 2 nights).

c – Berlin **Gesundbrunnen**.

d – Departure time.

e – Also Oct. 2, 3.

f – Arrive 1901.

g – Arrive 1047.

h – Arrive 0823.

j – Arrive 0824.

k – Depart 2036.

r – Depart 1110.

s – Calls to set down only.

t – Depart 0940.

u – Calls to pick up only.

v – Depart 0840.

x – Berlin **Lichtenberg**.

y – Arrive 1630.

z – For train number, days of running and possible earlier timings of Düsseldorf portion see Table **810**.

§ – 🛃: Osinovka (BY) / Krasnoye (RU).

¶ – Connections to train **1249** are possible at Warszawa Centralna.

‡ – Also known as Moskva **Smolenskaya** station.

BRUSSELS - KÖLN - FRANKFURT - LEIPZIG - DRESDEN - PRAHA 57

train type	CNL	D	EC	ICE	EC	ICE	EC	ICE	EC	⇌	ICE	ICE	EC	⇌	ICE	ICE	EC	ICE	ICE	EN	EN			
train number	459	61459	171	1553	173	1555	175	1597	177	9401	515	1559	379	9413	517	1651	179	15	1653	477	60477			
notes			✕	①–⑤	✕	🍷	✕	1557	✕	🍷	🍷	🍷	✕	🍷	🍷	🍷	✕	🍷	🍷	🍷	407			
	A	2	L	w	C		H	🍷	S				D				Q			M				
Brussels Midi / Zuid d.	...	...	...	...	...	...	...	...	...	0728	...	...	...	0928	...	...	...	1025	...	...	...	...	...	...
Köln Hbf d.	...	...	...	...	...	...	...	...	...	0915	0955	...	...	1115	1155	...	...	1220	...	...	...	...	...	...
Frankfurt Flughafen ✈ d.	...	...	...	...	...	...	...	...	...	...	1050	1102	...	...	1250	1302	...	1313	1502	...	...	...	...	...
Frankfurt (Main) Hbf d.	...	...	...	0452f	...	0720	...	0920	...	...	...	1119	...	...	...	1319	...	1325	1520	...	...	...	...	...
Frankfurt (Main) Süd d.	0054	...	...	|	...	|	...	|	...	...	...	|	...	...	...	|	...	...	|	...	...	...	...	...
Fulda d.	|	0213	...	0551f	...	0814	...	1014	...	...	...	1214	...	...	...	1414	...	...	1614	...	...	...	...	...
Erfurt Hbf d.	0345s	0523	...	0732	...	0934	...	1134	...	...	...	1334	...	...	...	1534	...	...	1734	...	...	...	...	...
Weimar d.	0539s	0542	...	0749	...	|	...	|	...	...	...	|	...	...	...	|	...	...	|	...	...	...	...	...
Leipzig d.	0642s	0651	...	0851	...	1051	...	1251	...	...	...	1451	...	...	...	1651	...	...	1851	...	...	...	...	...
Dresden Hbf d.	0803s	0808	0906	1004	1108	1204	1306	1404	1508	...	...	1604	1708	...	...	1804	1908	...	2004	2106	2106	...	...	...
Bad Schandau 🏛 ◧ d.	0836s	0838	0938	...	1138	...	1338	...	1538	...	...	...	1738	...	...	...	1938	...	...	|	|	...	...	...
Děčín 🏛 ◧ d.	0853s	0856	0955	...	1156	...	1356	...	1556	...	...	...	1756	...	...	...	1956	...	...	2156	2156	...	...	...
Praha Holešovice a.	1019	1019	1118	...	1316	...	1518	...	1716	...	...	...	1916	...	...	...	2116	...	...	2318	2318	...	...	...
Praha hlavní a.	1029	1029	1127	...	1326	...	1527	...	1726	...	...	...	1926	...	...	...	2126	...	...	2327	2327	...	...	...
Wien Meidling **1150** a.	...	...	|	...	1824	...	|	...	|	...	...	...	...	...	...	...	...	...	...	|	0617	...	...	...
Bratislava hlavná **1150** a.	...	...	1550	...	...	...	1950	...	2147	...	...	...	...	...	...	...	...	...	...	0536	...	...	...	...
Budapest Keleti **1175** a.	...	...	1835	...	...	...	2235	...	...	...	...	...	...	...	...	...	...	...	...	0835	...	...	...	...

train type	EC	ICE	ICE	⇌	EC	ICE	ICE	⇌	EC	ICE	ICE	EC	ICE	ICE	EC	ICE	EC	ICE	D	CNL	EN	EN	ICE	ICE
train number	178	1650	518	9472	176	1558	516	9484	378	1556	514	174	1554	512	172	1552	170	1740	61458	458	476	60406	1652	14
notes	✕	🍷	🍷	🍷	✕	🍷	🍷	🍷	✕	🍷	🍷	✕	🍷		✕	🍷	✕	2230			🍷	476	✕	🍷
	Q				P				F			H			C		L		2	A	M			
Budapest Keleti **1175** d.	...	...	...	...	...	...	...	...	...	...	...	0525	...	...	...	...	0925	...	...	...	2005	...	...	...
Bratislava hlavná **1150** d.	...	...	...	...	...	...	...	...	0613	...	...	0810	...	...	...	...	1213	...	...	...	2258	...	...	...
Wien Meidling **1150** d.	...	...	...	...	...	...	...	...	|	...	...	|	...	...	0932	...	|	...	...	...	|	2231	...	...
Praha hlavní d.	0629	...	...	...	0829	...	...	...	1029	...	...	1229	...	...	1429	...	1629	...	1829	1829	0429	0429	...	...
Praha Holešovice d.	0639	...	...	...	0839	...	...	...	1039	...	...	1238	...	...	1439	...	1638	...	1839	1839	0438	0438	...	...
Děčín 🏛 ◧ d.	0800	...	...	...	1000	...	...	...	1200	...	...	1400	...	...	1600	...	1800	...	2000	2000u	0602	0602	...	...
Bad Schandau 🏛 ◧ a.	0815	...	...	...	1015	...	...	...	1215	...	...	1415	...	...	1615	...	1815	...	2015	2017u	|	|	...	...
Dresden Hbf a.	0845	0953	...	...	1045	1153	...	...	1245	1353	...	1445	1553	...	1645	1753	1845	1853	2047	2104u	0649	0649	0753	...
Leipzig a.	...	1107	...	...	...	1307	...	...	...	1507	...	...	1707	...	...	1907	...	2005	2217	2226u	...	...	0907	...
Weimar a.	...	|	...	...	...	|	...	...	...	|	...	...	|	...	...	2009	...	...	2346	2348u	...	...	|	...
Erfurt Hbf a.	...	1223	...	...	...	1423	...	...	...	1623	...	...	1823	...	...	2027	...	...	0003	0121u	...	...	1023	...
Fulda a.	...	1342	...	...	...	1542	...	...	...	1742	...	...	1942	...	...	2151	...	...	...	|	...	...	1142	...
Frankfurt (Main) Süd a.	...	|	...	...	...	|	...	...	...	|	...	...	|	...	...	|	...	...	...	0359	...	...	|	...
Frankfurt (Main) Hbf a.	...	1437	...	...	...	1637	...	...	...	1837	...	...	2037	...	...	2254	...	...	...	...	...	...	1237	1429
Frankfurt Flughafen ✈ a.	...	1455	1509	...	...	1655	1709	...	...	1855	1909	...	2055	2109	...	...	...	...	...	...	...	...	1255	1440
Köln Hbf a.	...	...	1605	1643	...	...	1805	1843	...	...	2005	...	...	2205	...	...	...	...	...	...	...	...	...	1539
Brussels Midi / Zuid a.	...	...	...	1832	...	...	...	2032	...	...	...	...	...	...	...	...	...	...	...	...	...	...	...	1735

A – *City Night Line* CANOPUS – 🛏 1, 2 cl., ▬ 2 cl., (2) (reclining), 🍷: Zürich - Basel - Frankfurt (Main) Süd - Děčín 🏛 - Praha and v.v. Ⓡ Special fares apply.
C – VINDOBONA – (12) ✕ Hamburg - Berlin - Dresden - Praha - Wien - Villach and v.v.
D – CARL MARIA VON WEBER – (12) ✕ Stralsund - Berlin - Dresden - Praha - Brno. From Ostseebad Binz on dates in Table **844**.
F – SLOVENSKÁ STRELA – (12) ✕ Bratislava - Praha - Dresden - Berlin - Stralsund. To Ostseebad Binz on dates in Table **844**.
H – JAN JESENIUS / JESZENSZKY JÁNOS – (12) ✕ Hamburg - Berlin - Dresden - Praha - Budapest and v.v.
L – HUNGARIA – (12) ✕ Berlin - Dresden - Praha - Budapest and v.v.
M – METROPOL – 🛏 1, 2 cl., ▬ 2 cl., (2) Berlin Hbf - Dresden - Praha - Budapest and v.v.
P – JOHANNES BRAHMS – (12) ✕ Brno - Praha - Dresden - Berlin - Hamburg.
Q – ALOIS NEGRELLI – (12) ✕ Berlin - Dresden - Praha and v.v.
S – SLOVENSKÁ STRELA – (12) ✕ Berlin - Dresden - Praha - Bratislava.

f – ① only.
s – Calls to set down only.
u – Calls to pick up only.
w – Not Oct. 3.

⇌ – *Thalys* high-speed train. Ⓡ 🍷. Special fares payable. Valid June 9 - Dec. 14.
◧ – Ticketing point is Schöna.

HAMBURG - WROCŁAW - KRAKÓW 58

train type	EC	TLK
train number	249	63102
notes	Ⓡ ⊡	Ⓡ
	W	
Hamburg Altona d.	...	...
Hamburg Hbf d.	0658k	...
Lüneburg d.	0737k	...
Uelzen d.	0758k	...
Stendal d.	0850k	...
Berlin Hbf d.	0941	...
Berlin Ost d.	|	...
Berlin Südkreuz d.	0947	...
Cottbus d.	1115	...
Forst 🏛 d.	1134	...
Záry a.	1211	...
Węgliniec a.	1259	...
Węgliniec d.	1314	...
Bolesławiec a.	1329	...
Legnica a.	1356	...
Wrocław Gł. a.	1439	...
Wrocław Gł. d.	...	1539
Katowice a.	...	1824
Kraków Gł. a.	...	2039

train type	TLK	EC
train number	38102	248
notes	Ⓡ	Ⓡ ⊡
		X
Kraków Gł. d.	0622	...
Katowice d.	0837	...
Wrocław Gł. a.	1127	...
Wrocław Gł. d.	...	1220
Legnica d.	...	1303
Bolesławiec d.	...	1330
Węgliniec a.	...	1345
Węgliniec d.	...	1400
Záry d.	...	1447
Forst 🏛 a.	...	1525
Cottbus a.	...	1543
Berlin Südkreuz a.	...	|
Berlin Ost a.	...	1659
Berlin Hbf a.	...	1708
Stendal a.	...	1758y
Uelzen a.	...	1858y
Lüneburg a.	...	1914y
Hamburg Hbf a.	...	1944y
Hamburg Altona a.	...	2001y

W – WAWEL – (12) (Hamburg ①–⑥ **h** -) Berlin - Forst 🏛 - Wrocław.
X – WAWEL – (12) Wrocław - Forst 🏛 - Berlin (- Hamburg Ⓑ **y**).

k – ①–⑥ (not June 9, Oct. 3).
y – Ⓑ (not June 8, Oct. 2).

⊡ – Supplement payable in Poland.

NICE - MOSKVA 59

train number		18 *BJ*	18 *BJ*	
notes		⑥	⑥	
notes		S	R	
Nice d.	...	2052	2052	⑥
Monaco-Monte Carlo d.	...	2118	2118	:
Menton d.	...	2128	2128	:
Ventimiglia 🏛 d.	...	2200	2200	:
Bordighera d.	...	2209	2209	:
San Remo d.	...	2219	2219	:
Genova Piazza Principe d.	...	0048	0048	⑦
Milano Rogoredo d.	...	0228	0228	:
Verona d.	...	0420	0420	:
Bolzano / Bozen d.	...	0548	0548	:
Brennero / Brenner 🏛 d.	...	0715	0715	:
Innsbruck Hbf d.	...	0809	0809	:
Salzburg Hbf d.	...	|	|	:
Linz Hbf d.	...	1320	1320	:
Wien Hütteldorf d.	...	1518	1518	:
Břeclav 🏛 d.	...	1745	1745	:
Bohumín 🏛 d.	...	1958	1958	①
Zebrzydowice 🏛 d.	...	2019	2019	:
Katowice d.	...	2124	2124	:
Warszawa Centralna a.	...	0053	0053	:
Warszawa Wschodnia a.	...	0058	0058	:
Warszawa Wschodnia d.	...	0143	0143	:
Terespol a.	...	0415	0415	:
Terespol 🏛 PL d.	...	0455	0455	:
Brest Tsentralny 🏛 BY a.	...	0643	0743	:
Brest Tsentralny d.	...	0840	0940	:
Minsk d.	...	1229	1329	:
Orsha Tsentralnaya § BY d.	...	1516	1616	:
Smolensk Tsentralny § RU d.		1732	1832	
Vyazma d.		1946	2048	
Moskva Belorusskaya a.		2220	2320	

train number		17 *BJ*	17 *BJ*	
notes		④	④	
notes		Q	P	
Moskva Belorusskaya d.	...	1118	1240	④
Vyazma d.	...	1448	1546	:
Smolensk Tsentralny § RU d.	...	1639	1739	:
Orsha Tsentralnaya § BY d.	...	1702	1802	:
Minsk d.	...	1935	2035	:
Brest Tsentralny a.	...	2310	0010	:
Brest Tsentralny 🏛 BY d.	...	0113	0213	⑤
Terespol 🏛 PL a.	...	0031	0031	:
Terespol d.	...	0111	0111	:
Warszawa Wschodnia a.	...	0347	0347	:
Warszawa Wschodnia d.	...	0417	0417	:
Warszawa Centralna d.	...	0430	0430	:
Katowice d.	...	0819	0819	:
Zebrzydowice 🏛 d.	...	0925	0925	:
Bohumín 🏛 d.	...	1002	1002	:
Břeclav 🏛 d.	...	1218	1218	:
Wien Hütteldorf d.	...	1352	1352	:
Linz Hbf d.	...	1540	1540	:
Salzburg Hbf d.	...	|	|	:
Innsbruck Hbf d.	...	2243	2243	:
Brennero / Brenner 🏛 d.	...	2337	2337	:
Bolzano / Bozen d.	...	0042	0042	⑥
Verona d.	...	0225	0225	:
Milano Rogoredo d.	...	0352	0352	:
Genova Piazza Principe d.	...	0553	0553	:
San Remo d.	...	0814	0814	:
Bordighera d.	...	0825	0825	:
Ventimiglia 🏛 d.	...	0904	0904	:
Menton d.		0928	0928	:
Monaco-Monte Carlo d.		0937	0937	:
Nice a.		0950	0950	:

P – ④ Nov. 6, 2014 - Mar. 26, 2015: 🛏 1 cl. (lux), 🛏 1, 2 cl. Moskva - Nice. ✕ (RZD) Moskva - Brest and ✕ (PKP) Warszawa - Nice (journey two nights).
Q – ④ Apr. 3, 2014 - Oct. 30, 2014: 🛏 1 cl. (lux), 🛏 1, 2 cl. Moskva - Nice. ✕ (RZD) Moskva - Brest and ✕ (PKP) Warszawa - Nice (journey two nights).
R – ⑥ Nov. 1, 2014 - Mar. 21, 2015: 🛏 1 cl. (lux), 🛏 1, 2 cl. Nice - Moskva. ✕ (PKP) Nice - Warszawa and ✕ (RZD) Brest - Moskva (journey two nights).
S – ⑥ Mar. 29, 2014 - Oct. 25, 2014: 🛏 1 cl. (lux), 🛏 1, 2 cl. Nice - Moskva. ✕ (PKP) Nice - Warszawa and ✕ (RZD) Brest - Moskva (journey two nights).

BY – Belarus (East European Time).
PL – Poland (Central European Time).
RU – Russia (Moskva Time).

§ – 🏛 : Osinovka (BY) / Krasnoye (RU).
✕ (PKP) – Polish railways restaurant car.
✕ (RZD) – Russian railways restaurant car.

60 HAMBURG - BERLIN - PRAHA - WIEN - BUDAPEST - BEOGRAD

train type	*EC*	*EC*	*EC*	*EC*	*EC*	*EC*	*IC*	*EC*	*EC*	*EC*	*EC*	*EC*	*EC*	*EC*	*EC*	*EC*	*EC*	*EC*	*EC*	*EC*	*EN*	*EN*	*EN*
train number	**271**	**71**	**273**	**73**	**275**	**75**	**60457**	**277**	**103**	**77**	**171**	**173**	**131**	**279**	**175**	**105**	**177**	**79**	**379**	**179**	**477**	**477**	**60477**
notes	✕	🍷	✕	✕	✕	✕	2	✕	✕	🍷	✕	✕	✕	✕	✕	✕	✕	🍷	✕	✕			**407**
			J				**E**	**T**	**K**				**L**			**S**			**H**	**R**	**C**	**A**	**B**
Hamburg Altona ... d.	...	...	...	...	...	...	...	...	...	...	...	0614	...	...	0814	...	...	...	...	...	...	...	...
Hamburg Hbf ... d.	...	...	...	...	...	...	...	...	...	...	...	0628	...	...	0828	...	...	...	...	...	...	...	...
Berlin Hbf ... d.	...	...	...	...	...	...	...	...	...	...	0646	0846	...	...	1046	...	1246	...	1446	1648	...	1822	1822
Berlin Südkreuz ... d.	...	...	...	...	...	...	0459	...	...	...	0653	0853	...	...	1053	...	1253	...	1453	1655	...	1828	1828
Dresden Hbf ... d.	...	...	...	...	...	...	0706	...	...	...	0906	1108	...	...	1308	...	1508	...	1708	1906	...	2106	2106
Bad Schandau 🏛 ⊖ ... d.	...	...	...	...	...	...	0738	...	...	...	0938	1138	...	...	1338	...	1538	...	1738	1938	...	|	|
Děčín ... d.	...	...	...	...	...	...	0756	...	...	...	0955	1156	...	...	1356	...	1556	...	1756	1956	...	2156	2156
Ústí nad Labem hlavní ... d.	...	...	...	...	...	...	0813	...	...	...	1013	1213	...	...	1413	...	1613	...	1813	2013	...	2213	2213
Praha Holešovice ... d.	...	...	...	...	...	...	0917	...	...	...	1118	1317	...	...	1517	...	1717	...	1917	2117	...	2318	2318
Praha hlavní ... a.	...	...	...	...	...	...	0927	...	...	...	1127	1326	...	...	1526	...	1726	...	1926	2127	...	2327	2327
Praha hlavní ... d.	...	0439**e**	0539	0639	0739	0839	...	0939	...	1039	1139	1339	...	1439	1539	...	1739	1839	1939	...	2345	2345	2345
Pardubice ... d.	...	0541**e**	0641	0741	0841	0941	...	1041	...	1141	1241	1441	...	1541	1641	...	1841	1941	2041	...	0103	0103	0103
Brno hlavní ... d.	0622	0722	0822	0922	1022	1122	...	1222	...	1322	1422	1622	...	1722	1822	...	2022	2122	2219	...	0315	0315	0315
Břeclav ... a.	0654	0754	0854	0954	1054	1154	...	1254	...	1354	1454	1654	...	1754	1854	...	2054	2154	...	...	0354	0354	0354
Břeclav ... d.	0657	0802	0857	1002	1057	1202	...	1257	1302	1402	1457	1702	1657	1802	1857	1902	2057	2202	...	...	0440	0440	0450
Wien Meidling ... a.	|	0924	|	1124	|	1324	...	|	1424	1524	|	1824	|	1922	|	2017	|	2303**p**	...	...	|	|	0617
Wien Westbahnhof ... a.	|	|	|	|	|	|	...	|	|	|	|	|	|	...	|	2032	|	...	...	...	|	|	0632
Wiener Neustadt Hbf ... a.	|	0955	|	1155	|	1355	...	|	1454	1555	|	1854	|	...	|	...	|	...	...	...	|	|	...
Graz Hbf ... a.	|	...	|	...	|	...	...	|	|	...	|	|	|	...	|	...	|	...	...	...	|	|	...
Klagenfurt Hbf ... a.	|	...	|	...	|	...	...	|	1821	...	|	2216	|	...	|	...	|	...	...	...	|	|	...
Villach Hbf ... a.	|	...	|	...	|	...	...	|	1846	...	|	2240	|	...	|	...	|	...	...	...	|	|	...
Kúty 🏛 ... d.	0713	...	0913	...	1113	...	...	1313	...	...	1513	...	1710	...	1910	...	2110	...	...	...	0455	0455	...
Bratislava hlavná ... d.	0753	...	0953	...	1153	...	...	1353	...	...	1553	...	1750	...	1950	...	2147	...	...	...	0548	0548	...
Štúrovo 🏛 △ ... a.	0911	...	1111	...	1311	...	...	1511	...	...	1711	...	1908	...	2107	...	...	...	...	...	0710	0710	...
Budapest Keleti ... a.	1035	...	1235	...	1435	...	...	1635	...	...	1835	...	2035	...	2235	...	...	...	...	...	0835	0835	...
Budapest Keleti ... d.	...	...	1305	...	...	...	...	...	...	...	...	...	...	...	...	...	...	...	...	...	...	...	...
Subotica 🏛 ... a.	...	...	1632	...	...	...	...	...	...	...	...	...	...	...	...	...	...	...	...	...	...	...	...
Novi Sad ... a.	...	...	1913	...	...	...	...	...	...	...	...	...	...	...	...	...	...	...	...	...	...	...	...
Beograd ... a.	...	...	2050	...	...	...	...	...	...	...	...	...	...	...	...	...	...	...	...	...	...	...	...

train type/number	*EC*	*EC*	*EC*	*EC*	*EC*	*EC*	*EC*	*EC*	*EC*	*EC*	*EC*	*EC*	*EC*	*IC*	*EC*	*EC*	*EC*	*EC*	*EC*	*EC*	*EN*	*EN*	*EN*
train number	**178**	**176**	**378**	**78**	**104**	**174**	**278**	**130**	**172**	**170**	**70**	**102**	**276**	**60456**	**72**	**274**	**74**	**272**	**76**	**270**	**60406**	**476**	**476**
notes	✕	✕	✕	🍷	✕	✕	✕	✕	✕	✕	🍷	✕	✕	2	✕	✕	✕	✕	🍷	✕	**476**		**718**
	R		**Q**		**S**			**L**				**K**	**U**	**E**				**J**			**X**	**A**	**D**
Beograd ... d.	...	...	...	...	...	...	...	...	...	...	...	...	...	...	...	...	...	0645	...	...	...	...	...
Novi Sad ... d.	...	...	...	...	...	...	...	...	...	...	...	...	...	...	...	...	...	0834	...	...	...	...	...
Subotica 🏛 ... d.	...	...	...	...	...	...	...	...	...	...	...	...	...	...	...	...	...	1128	...	...	...	...	...
Budapest Keleti ... a.	...	...	...	...	...	...	...	...	...	...	...	...	...	...	...	...	...	1454	...	...	...	...	...
Budapest Keleti ... d.	...	...	...	...	...	0525	...	0725	...	0925	...	...	1125	...	...	1325	...	1525	...	1725	...	2005	2005
Štúrovo 🏛 △ ... d.	...	...	...	...	...	0652	...	0852	...	1049	...	...	1249	...	...	1449	...	1652	...	1849	...	2124	2124
Bratislava hlavná ... d.	...	...	0613	...	...	0813	...	1013	...	1213	...	...	1440	...	...	1610	...	1813	...	2010	...	2258	2258
Kúty 🏛 ... d.	...	...	0651	...	...	0850	...	1050	...	1247	...	...	1447	...	...	1647	...	1851	...	2047	...	2338	2338
Villach Hbf ... d.	...	...	|	...	...	|	...	|	0526	|	...	0914	|	...	...	|	...	|	...	|	...	|	|
Klagenfurt Hbf ... d.	...	...	|	...	...	|	...	|	0549	|	...	0939	|	...	...	|	...	|	...	|	...	|	|
Graz Hbf ... d.	...	...	|	...	...	|	0537	|	|	|	...	|	|	...	...	|	...	|	...	|	...	|	|
Wiener Neustadt Hbf ... d.	...	...	|	...	...	|	0747	|	0904	|	1204	1304	|	...	1404	|	1604	|	1804	|	...	|	|
Wien Westbahnhof ... d.	...	...	|	...	...	|	|	|	|	|	|	|	|	...	|	|	|	|	|	|	2216	|	|
Wien Meidling ... d.	...	...	|	0650**p**	0742	|	0824	|	0932	|	1232	1332	|	...	1432	|	1632	|	1832	|	2231	|	|
Břeclav ... a.	...	...	0703	0753	0853	0903	0953	1103	1053	1302	1353	1453	1502	...	1553	1702	1756	1903	1953	2102	2343	2353	2353
Břeclav ... d.	...	...	0706	0806	...	0906	1006	...	1106	1305	1406	...	1505	...	1606	1705	1806	1906	2006	2105	0018	0015	0015
Brno hlavní ... d.	...	0539	0739	0839	...	0937	1039	...	1139	1337	1439	...	1537	...	1639	1737	1839	1939	2039	2137	0110	0052	0052
Pardubice ... d.	...	0718	0918	1018	...	1117	1218	...	1318	1517	1618	...	1717	...	1818	1917	2018	2118	2218	...	0252	0244	0509
Praha hlavní ... a.	...	0821	1021	1121	...	1221	1321	...	1421	1621	1721	...	1821	...	1921	2021	2121	2221	2321	...	0409	0403	0623
Praha hlavní ... d.	0629	0829	1029	...	...	1229	...	...	1429	1629	...	...	...	1829	...	...	...	...	...	...	0429	0429	...
Praha Holešovice ... d.	0639	0839	1039	...	...	1238	...	...	1439	1638	...	...	...	1839	...	...	...	...	...	...	0439	0438	...
Ústí nad Labem hlavní ... d.	0742	0942	1142	...	...	1342	...	...	1542	1742	...	...	...	1942	...	...	...	...	...	...	0543	0543	...
Děčín ... d	0800	1000	1200	...	...	1400	...	...	1600	1800	...	...	...	2000	...	...	...	...	...	...	0604	0604	...
Bad Schandau 🏛 ⊖ ... a.	0815	1015	1215	...	...	1415	...	...	1615	1815	...	...	...	2015	...	...	...	...	...	...	|	|	...
Dresden Hbf ... a.	0849	1045	1245	...	...	1445	...	...	1645	1845	...	...	...	2047	...	...	...	...	...	...	0649	0649	...
Berlin Südkreuz ... a.	1107	1308	1508	...	...	1708	...	...	1908	2108	...	...	...	|	...	...	...	...	...	...	0901	0901	...
Berlin Hbf ... a.	1115	1315	1514	...	...	1715	...	...	1915	2115	...	...	...	2346¶	...	...	...	...	...	...	0910	0908	...
Hamburg Hbf ... a.	...	1528	...	...	...	1928	...	...	2133	...	...	...	...	...	...	...	...	...	...	...	...	...	...
Hamburg Altona ... a.	...	1541	...	...	...	1943	...	...	2148	...	...	...	...	...	...	...	...	...	...	...	...	...	...

A – METROPOL – 🛏 1, 2 cl., ▬ 2 cl., [2] Berlin - Praha - Budapest and v.v.

B – METROPOL – 🛏 1, 2 cl., ▬ 2 cl., [2] Berlin (**477**) - Praha - Břeclav (**407**) - Wien.

C – 🛏 1, 2 cl., ▬ 2 cl. (also [2] June 14 - Sept. 14) Praha - Pardubice - Břeclav - Budapest.

D – 🛏 1, 2 cl., ▬ 2 cl. (also [2] June 14 - Sept. 14) Budapest (**476**) - Břeclav - Pardubice (**718**) - Praha.

E – For additional cars see Table **54**.

H – CARL MARIA VON WEBER – [12] ✕ Stralsund (depart 1139) - Berlin - Praha - Brno (from Ostseebad Binz on dates in Table **844**).

J – AVALA – [12] ✕ Praha - Budapest - Beograd and v.v. Conveys 🛏 2 cl. Moskva - Budapest - Beograd and v.v. Conveys from Praha on ②③⑤⑥ June 13 - Sept. 5 and from Bar on ③④⑥⑦ June 14 - Sept, 6: 🛏 2 cl. Praha - Budapest - Subotica - Bar and v.v. (Table **97**).

K – POLONIA – [12] ✕ Warszawa - Břeclav - Wien - Villach and v.v. (Table **99**).

L – VARSOVIA – [12] ✕ Warszawa - Břeclav - Budapest and v.v. (Table **99**).

Q – SLOVENSKÁ STRELA – [12] ✕ Bratislava - Praha - Berlin - Stralsund (arrive 1825). To Ostseebad Binz on dates in Table **844**.

R – From / to Rostock on date shown in Table **835**.

S – SOBIESKI – [12] ✕ Warszawa - Břeclav - Wien and v.v. (Table **99**).

T – SLOVAN – [12] ✕ Praha - Břeclav - Budapest. Conveys on ②⑤ June 13 - Aug. 29: 🛏 1, 2 cl. Praha (**277**) - Budapest (**1204**) - Split (Table **89**).

U – SLOVAN – [12] ✕ Budapest - Břeclav - Praha. Conveys on ③⑥ June 14 - Aug. 30: 🛏 1, 2 cl. Split (**1205**) - Budapest (**276**) - Praha (Table **89**).

X – METROPOL – 🛏 1, 2 cl., ▬ 2 cl., [2] Wien (**406**) - Břeclav (**476**) - Praha - Berlin.

e – ①–⑥ (not Apr. 21).

p – Wien **Praterstern** (Table **982**).

△ – Routeing point for international tickets: Szob.

⊖ – Routeing point for international tickets: Schöna.

¶ – Berlin **Ostbahnhof**.

OTHER TRAIN NAMES:

70/71 –	GUSTAV MAHLER
72/73 –	SMETANA
74/75 –	FRANZ SCHUBERT
76/77 –	ANTONÍN DVOŘÁK
78/79 –	JOHANN GREGOR MENDEL
170/171 –	HUNGARIA
172/173 –	VINDOBONA
175/174 –	JÁN JESENIUS / JESZENSZKY JÁNOS
176 –	JOHANNES BRAHMS
177 –	SLOVENSKÁ STRELA
178/179 –	ALOIS NEGRELLI
270/271 –	PETROV
274/275 –	JAROSLAV HAŠEK
278/279 –	GUSTAV KLIMT

NOTES CONTINUED FROM TABLE 61 ON PAGE 79

* – Reported as not running most nights.

⊠ – *Train temporarily suspended between Beograd and Sofia.*

¶ – Train number for international bookings.

✗ – Supplement payable.

❦ – Until Aug. 12 this service is expected to be operated by bus between Gorna Oryakhovitsa and Dimitrovgra (please confirm timings locally).

♣ – 🚌 Kapikule - İstanbul and v.v. It has been reported that trains **491/490** are currently running through to Çerkezköy, see Table **1550**.

PRAHA / WIEN / BUDAPEST - BEOGRAD / BUCUREŞTI and İSTANBUL / ATHÍNA 61

Services to / from İstanbul are subject to alteration until further notice. Trains are replaced by 🚌 Kapikule - İstanbul and v.v.

train type	*IC*	*IC*	*EC*				*EN*	461	81031				341		491	81031		*EN*	1385				
train number	73	373	273	293	1481	1471	473	491	[R]	461		341	337	491	81031	[R]	337	347	383	361		335	
notes	[R]	[R]	✕				[R]	81031	🚌	[R]		[R]		⊠		🚌		[R]					
	H	P	J	N	F	L	R	[R]S	♣	W		G	M		T	♣	Y	E	A			K	
Praha hlavní d.	...	...	0539	...	...	...	...	...	...	...	...	...	...	...	...	...	...	...	...	...	...	...	...
Brno hlavní d.	...	...	0822	...	...	...	...	...	...	...	...	...	...	...	...	...	...	...	...	...	...	...	...
Wien Westbahnhof d.	...	...	|	...	...	...	...	...	...	...	...	...	...	...	...	...	...	1948	...	...	...	...	...
Bratislava hlavná d.	...	...	0953	...	...	...	...	...	...	...	...	...	...	...	...	...	...	|	...	...	...	...	...
Budapest Keleti d.	0710	0910	1305	...	1110	1110	1910	...	...	...	...	2220	2220	...	...	...	...	2330	...	...	...	...	...
Lökösháza a.	1006	1206	|	...	1406	1406	2206	...	...	...	...	|	|	...	...	...	...	0215	...	...	...	...	...
Curtici 🛃 a.	1150	1346	|	...	1547	1547	2346	...	...	...	...	|	|	...	...	...	...	0355	...	...	...	...	...
Arad a.	1231	1426	|	...	1634	1634	0028	...	...	...	...	|	|	...	...	...	...	0442	...	...	...	...	...
Timişoara a.	1326	|	|	...	|	|	|	...	...	...	...	|	|	...	...	...	...	|	...	...	...	...	...
Craiova a.	1936	|	|	...	2342	2342	|	...	...	...	...	|	|	...	...	...	...	|	...	...	...	...	...
Braşov a.	|	2235	|	...	|	|	0934	...	...	...	...	|	|	...	...	...	...	1331	...	...	...	...	...
Bucureşti Nord a.	2245	...	|	...	|	|	1210	...	...	...	...	|	|	...	...	...	...	1605	...	...	...	...	...
Bucureşti Nord d.	...	...	|	...	|	|	...	1255	...	1255	...	|	|	...	...	...	...	...	2312	...	...	...	...
Videle a.	...	...	|	...	0201	0201	...	1344	...	1344	...	|	|	...	...	...	...	...	|	...	...	...	...
Giurgiu Nord 🛃 a.	...	...	|	...	0356	0356	...	1451	...	1451	...	|	|	...	...	...	...	...	0113	...	...	...	...
Giurgiu Nord 🛃 d.	...	...	|	...	0435	0435	...	1520	...	1520	...	|	|	...	...	...	...	...	0145	...	...	...	...
Ruse 🛃 a.	...	...	|	...	0500	0500	...	1545	...	1545	...	|	|	...	...	...	...	...	0210	...	...	...	...
Ruse 🛃 d.	...	...	|	...	0540	0540	...	1620	...	1620	...	|	|	...	...	...	...	...	0315	...	...	...	...
Gorna Oryakhovitsa a.	...	...	|	...	|	|	...	1817	...	1817	...	|	|	...	...	...	...	...	0503	...	...	...	...
Varna a.	...	...	|	...	0910	|	...	|	...	|	...	|	|	...	...	...	...	...	|	...	...	...	...
Burgas a.	...	...	|	...	...	1125	...	|	...	|	...	|	|	...	...	...	...	...	|	...	...	...	...
Subotica 🛃 a.	...	...	1632	...	...	...	...	|	...	|	...	0152	0152	...	...	...	...	...	|	...	...	...	...
Novi Sad a.	...	...	1913	...	...	...	...	|	...	|	...	0451	0451	...	...	...	...	...	|	...	...	...	...
Beograd a.	...	...	2050	2150	...	...	...	|	...	|	...	0632	0632	0750	...	...	0750	...	|	...	...	1845	...
Niš a.	...	...	...	0157	...	...	...	|	...	|	...	...	1159	1217	...	...	1159	...	|	...	...	2325	...
Tabanovci 🛃 a.	...	...	...	|	...	...	...	|	...	|	...	...	1610	|	...	...	1610	...	|	...	...	0350	...
Skopje a.	...	...	...	|	...	...	...	|	...	|	...	...	1722	|	...	...	1722	...	|	...	...	0444	...
Idoméni 🛃 a.	...	...	...	|	...	...	...	|	...	|	...	...	...	|	...	...	...	...	|	...	...	1010	...
Dimitrovgrad 🛃 a.	...	...	...	0510	...	...	...	2326	...	|	...	...	...	1520	...	...	...	...	|	...	...	|	...
Kalotina Zapad 🛃 a.	...	...	...	0638	...	...	...	|	...	|	...	...	...	1626	...	...	...	...	|	...	...	|	...
Pleven a.	...	...	...	|	...	...	...	|	...	1932	...	...	...	|	...	...	...	...	0629	...	...	|	...
Mezdra a.	...	...	...	|	...	...	...	|	...	2049	...	...	...	|	...	...	...	...	0744	...	...	|	...
Sofia a.	...	...	...	0813	...	...	...	|	...	2225	...	...	...	1820	...	...	...	...	1026	...	...	|	...
Sofia d.	...	...	...	...	...	...	...	|	...	...	...	...	...	...	1830	...	...	...	...	1530	...	|	...
Svilengrad a.	...	...	...	...	...	...	...	0040	...	...	...	...	...	...	0040	...	...	...	...	|	...	|	...
Kapikule 🛃 a.	...	...	...	...	...	...	...	0150	0255	...	...	...	...	...	0150	0255	...	...	...	|	...	|	...
İstanbul Sirkeci a.	...	...	...	...	...	...	...	...	0750	...	...	...	...	...	...	0750	...	...	...	|	...	|	...
Kulata 🛃 a.	...	...	...	...	...	...	...	...	...	...	...	...	...	...	...	...	...	...	...	1853	...	|	...
Thessaloníki a.	...	...	...	...	...	...	...	...	...	...	...	...	...	...	...	...	...	...	...	2222	...	1116	...
Athína Lárisa a.	...	...	...	...	...	...	...	...	...	...	...	...	...	...	...	...	...	...	...	...	...	...	...

train type/number				1384	*EN*	81032	81032				81032	81032			336	*EN*			*EC*	*IC*	*IC*		
train number	1480	1470	360	382	346	[R]	492		460	336	[R]	492	490	340	340	472	292	334	272	372	72		
notes				[R]	[R]	🚌	460		[R]		🚌		⊠	[R]		[R]			✕	[R]	[R]		
	B	D		A	E	♣	[R]S		W	Y	♣	T		G	V	R	N	K	J	P	H		
Athína Lárisa d.	...	...	...	...	...	...	...	...	...	...	...	...	...	...	...	...	...	...	...	...	...	...	...
Thessaloníki d.	...	...	0655	...	...	...	...	...	...	...	...	...	...	...	...	...	...	1552	...	...	...	...	...
Kulata 🛃 d.	...	...	1020	...	...	...	...	...	...	...	...	...	...	...	...	...	...	|	...	...	...	...	...
İstanbul Sirkeci d.	...	...	|	...	...	2200	...	...	...	...	2200	...	...	...	...	...	...	|	...	...	...	...	...
Kapikule 🛃 d.	...	...	|	...	...	0252	0405	...	...	...	0252	0405	...	...	...	...	...	|	...	...	...	...	...
Svilengrad d.	...	...	|	...	...	...	0515	...	...	...	...	0513	...	...	...	...	...	|	...	...	...	...	...
Sofia a.	...	...	1345	...	...	...	|	...	...	...	...	1028	...	...	...	...	...	|	...	...	...	...	...
Sofia d.	...	...	...	1905	...	...	|	...	0755	...	...	...	1130	...	...	...	2030	|	...	...	...	...	...
Mezdra d.	...	...	...	2038	...	...	|	...	0925	...	...	...	|	...	...	...	|	|	...	...	...	...	...
Pleven d.	...	...	...	2151	...	...	|	...	1037	...	...	...	|	...	...	...	|	|	...	...	...	...	...
Kalotina Zapad 🛃 d.	...	...	...	|	...	...	|	...	|	...	...	...	1311	...	...	...	2152	|	...	...	...	...	...
Dimitrovgrad 🛃 d.	...	...	...	|	...	...	0629	...	|	...	...	...	1230	...	...	...	2120	|	...	...	...	...	...
Idomeni 🛃 d.	...	...	...	|	...	...	|	...	|	...	...	...	|	...	...	...	|	1732	...	...	...	...	...
Skopje d.	...	...	...	|	...	...	|	...	|	0820	...	...	|	...	0820	...	|	2010	...	...	...	...	...
Tabanovci 🛃 d.	...	...	...	|	...	...	|	...	|	0924	...	...	|	...	0924	...	|	2124	...	...	...	...	...
Niš d.	...	...	...	|	...	...	|	...	|	1321	...	...	1527	...	1321	...	0002	0121	...	...	...	...	...
Beograd d.	...	...	...	|	...	...	|	...	|	1809	...	...	1957	2145	2145	...	0454	0533	0645	...	...	...	...
Novi Sad d.	...	...	...	|	...	...	|	...	|	...	...	...	...	2319	2319	...	...	...	0834	...	...	...	...
Subotica 🛃 d.	...	...	...	|	...	...	|	...	|	...	...	...	...	0218	0218	...	...	...	1128	...	...	...	...
Burgas d.	...	1730	...	|	...	...	|	...	|	...	...	...	...	|	|	...	...	...	|	...	...	...	...
Varna d.	2030	|	...	|	...	...	|	...	|	...	...	...	...	|	|	...	...	...	|	...	...	...	...
Gorna Oryakhovitsa d.	|	|	...	2309	...	...	1158	...	1158	...	...	...	...	|	|	...	...	...	|	...	...	...	...
Ruse 🛃 a.	2355	2355	...	0107	...	...	1355	...	1355	...	...	...	...	|	|	...	...	...	|	...	...	...	...
Ruse 🛃 d.	0040	0040	...	0215	...	...	1430	...	1430	...	...	...	...	|	|	...	...	...	|	...	...	...	...
Giurgiu Nord 🛃 a.	0105	0105	...	0240	...	...	1455	...	1455	...	...	...	...	|	|	...	...	...	|	...	...	...	...
Giurgiu Nord 🛃 d.	0125	0125	...	0320	...	...	1530	...	1530	...	...	...	...	|	|	...	...	...	|	...	...	...	...
Videle d.	0254	0254	...	|	...	...	1640	...	1640	...	...	...	...	|	|	...	...	...	|	...	...	...	...
Bucureşti Nord a.	|	|	...	0528	...	...	1729	...	1729	...	...	...	...	|	|	...	...	...	|	...	...	...	...
Bucureşti Nord d.	|	|	...	...	1300	...	...	...	...	...	...	...	...	|	|	1725	...	...	|	...	0545	...	...
Braşov d.	|	|	...	...	1537	...	...	...	...	...	...	...	...	|	|	2006	...	...	|	0600	|	...	...
Craiova d.	0513	0513	...	...	|	...	...	...	...	...	...	...	...	|	|	|	...	...	|	|	0852	...	...
Timişoara d.	|	|	...	...	|	...	...	...	...	...	...	...	...	|	|	|	...	...	|	|	1425	...	...
Arad d.	1232	1232	...	...	0100	...	...	...	...	...	...	...	...	|	|	0520	...	...	|	1427	1521	...	...
Curtici 🛃 d.	1314	1314	...	...	0150	...	...	...	...	...	...	...	...	|	|	0610	...	...	|	1510	1610	...	...
Lököshaza d.	1315	1315	...	...	0130	...	...	...	...	...	...	...	...	|	|	0550	...	...	|	1450	1550	...	...
Budapest Keleti a.	1650	1650	...	...	0440	...	...	...	...	...	...	...	...	0604	0604	0850	...	...	1454	1750	1850	...	...
Bratislava hlavná a.	...	...	...	...	|	...	...	...	...	...	...	...	...	...	...	...	...	...	1810	...	...	...	...
Wien Westbahnhof a.	...	...	...	...	0816	...	...	...	...	...	...	...	...	...	...	...	...	...	|	...	...	...	...
Brno hlavní a.	...	...	...	...	...	...	...	...	...	...	...	...	...	...	...	...	...	...	1937	...	...	...	...
Praha hlavní a.	...	...	...	...	...	...	...	...	...	...	...	...	...	...	...	...	...	...	2221	...	...	...	...

A – BULGARIA EXPRESS – 🛏 1, 2 cl.*, [12] Bucureşti - Sofia and v.v. Conveys 🛏 2 cl. Moskva, Lviv, Kyïv and Minsk - Sofia and v.v. on dates shown in Table **98**.
B – ALBENA – ⑦ June 15 - Sept. 14: 🛏 1, 2 cl., ▬ 2 cl., [2] ✕ Varna - Budapest.
D – NESBAR – ③⑥ June 14 - Sept. 13: 🛏 1, 2 cl., ▬ 2 cl., [2] ✕ Burgas - Budapest.
E – DACIA – 🛏 1, 2 cl., ▬ 2 cl., [2] ✕ Wien - Bucureşti and v.v.
F – ALBENA – ⑥ June 14 - Sept. 13: 🛏 1, 2 cl., ▬ 2 cl., [2] ✕ Budapest - Varna.
G – BEOGRAD – 🛏 1, 2 cl., ▬ 2 cl., [2] Budapest - Beograd and v.v. 🛏 1, 2 cl., [12] Budapest - Beograd - Sofia and v.v. *Train temporarily suspended between Beograd and Sofia*
H – TRAIANUS – [12] 🍸 Budapest - Bucureşti and v.v.
J – AVALA – [12] ✕ Praha - Budapest - Beograd. Conveys ②③⑤⑥ June 13 - Sept. 5 🛏 1, 2 cl. Praha - Subotica - Bar. Conveys ②⑤ June 17 - Sept. 2: 🛏 2 cl. Moskva - Bar.
K – HELLAS EXPRESS – 🛏 1, 2 cl.*, ▬ 2 cl.*, [2] Beograd - Skopje and v.v. ▬ 2 cl., [2] Beograd - Skopje - Thessaloníki and v.v.
L – NESBAR – ②⑤ June 13 - Sept. 12: 🛏 1, 2 cl., ▬ 2 cl., [2] ✕ Budapest - Burgas.
M – ①④ June 19 - Aug. 28: ▬ 2 cl., [2] Budapest - Beograd - Skopje.
N – NUŠIĆ – ▬ 2 cl., [2] Beograd - Sofia and v.v.

P – TRANSSYLVANIA – [12] ✕ Budapest - Braşov and v.v.
Q – AVALA – [12] ✕ Beograd - Budapest - Praha. Conveys ①④⑤⑦ June 15 - Sept. 7 🛏 1, 2 cl. Bar - Subotica - Praha. Conveys 🛏 2 cl. ⑤⑦ June 9 - Sept. 8 🛏 2 cl. Bar - Moskva.
R – *EuroNight* ISTER – 🛏 1, 2 cl., ▬ 1, 2 cl., [2] ✕ Budapest - Bucureşti and v.v.
S – BOSPHOR – 🛏 1, 2 cl., ▬ 2 cl. Bucureşti - İstanbul and v.v. (The compostion of this train is subject to confirmation). ⚠
T – BALKAN EXPRESS – Conveys June 9 - Dec. 14: 🛏 1, 2 cl. Beograd - Sofia (**81031/2**) - İstanbul and v.v. Conveys Dec. 15 - June 14: ▬ 2 cl. Beograd - Sofia (**81031/2**) - İstanbul and v.v. Conveys June 1 - Oct. 31 from Sofia, June 2 - Nov. 1 from İstanbul: ▬ 2 cl. Sofia - İstanbul and v.v. *Train temporarily suspended between Beograd and Sofia. The compostion of this train is subject to confirmation.*
V – ③⑦ June 18 - Aug. 27: ▬ 2 cl., [2] Skopje - Beograd - Budapest.
W – ROMANIA – [2] Bucureşti - Sofia and v.v.
Y – OLYMPUS – [2] Beograd - Skopje and v.v.

←NOTES CONTINUED ON PREVIOUS PAGE 78.

62 MÜNCHEN - LJUBLJANA - ZAGREB - BEOGRAD - THESSALONÍKI

train type/number		*EC*	*EC*			*EC*113		*EC*	*D*	*D*				*D*							
train number		111	211	483		*EC*213		115	315	315	491	337	499	415	335	293					
notes		🍷				🍷◧		🍴		⊠	⊠										
			T			M		W		Y	D	K	L	F	E	H					
München Hbf d.	...	0827	...	...	...	1227	...	1427	...	...	...	...	2340	...	...	...	...	...	...	...	...
Salzburg Hbf 🛃 d.	...	1012	...	...	...	1412	...	1612	...	...	...	...	0134	...	...	...	...	...	...	...	...
Bischofshofen d.	...	1054	...	...	...	1454	...	1654	...	...	...	...	|	...	...	...	...	...	...	...	...
Schwarzach St Veit d.	...	1111	...	...	...	1511	...	1711	...	...	...	...	0226	0427	...	...	...	...	...	...	...
Bad Gastein d.	...	1142	...	...	...	1542	...	1742	...	...	...	...	|	0501	...	...	...	...	...	...	...
Villach Hbf d.	...	1243	1253	...	...	1653	...	1843	1925	1925	...	...	0415	0625	...	...	...	...	...	...	...
Jesenice 🛃 a.	...	...	1333	...	...	1733	...	...	2006	2006	...	...	0455	0705	...	...	...	...	...	...	...
Ljubljana a.	...	...	1431	1510	...	1831	...	...	2106	2106	...	...	0558	0811	...	...	...	...	...	...	...
Rijeka a.	...	...	|	1755	...	|	...	...	|	|	...	...	|	|	...	...	...	...	...	...	...
Dobova 🛃 a.	...	...	1620	...	...	2007	...	...	2249	2249	...	...	0754	0957	...	...	...	...	...	...	...
Zagreb a.	...	...	1713	...	...	2055	...	...	...	2336	...	...	0853	1044	...	...	...	...	...	...	...
Zagreb d.	...	...	1728	...	...	...	...	...	...	2355	...	...	...	1116	...	...	...	...	...	...	...
Vinkovci a.	...	...	2101	...	...	...	...	...	...	0324	...	...	...	1445	...	...	...	...	...	...	...
Šid 🛃 a.	...	...	...	...	...	...	...	...	...	0402	...	...	...	1518	...	...	...	...	...	...	...
Beograd a.	...	...	...	...	...	...	...	...	...	0651	0750	0750	...	1732	1845	2150	...	...	...	...	...
Niš a.	...	...	...	...	...	...	...	...	...	...	1159	1159	...	...	2325	0157	...	...	...	...	...
Dimitrovgrad 🛃 a.	...	...	...	...	...	...	...	...	...	...	1520	|	...	...	|	0510	...	...	...	...	...
Kalotina Zapad 🛃 a.	...	...	...	...	...	...	...	...	...	...	1626	|	...	...	|	0638	...	...	...	...	...
Sofia a.	...	...	...	...	...	...	...	...	...	...	1820	|	...	...	|	0813	...	...	...	...	...
Tabanovci 🛃 a.	...	...	...	...	...	...	...	...	...	...	...	1610	...	...	0350	...	...	...	...	...	...
Skopje a.	...	...	...	...	...	...	...	...	...	...	...	1722	...	...	0444	...	...	...	...	...	...
Idoméni 🛃 a.	...	...	...	...	...	...	...	...	...	...	...	...	...	...	1010	...	...	...	...	...	...
Thessaloníki a.	...	...	...	...	...	...	...	...	...	...	...	...	...	...	1116	...	...	...	...	...	...
Athína Lárisa a.	...	...	...	...	...	...	...	...	...	...	...	...	...	...	...	...	...	...	...	...	...

train type			*D*				*D*	*D*	*EC*		*EC*212			*EC*	*EC*						
train number	292	334	414		336	490	314	314	114		*EC*112		482	210	110						
notes				498		⊠	⊠		🍴		🍷◧				🍷						
	H	E	F	L	K	D	Y		W		M			T							
Athína Lárisa d.	...	...	...	...	...	...	...	...	...	...	...	...	...	...	...	...	...	...	...	...	...
Thessaloníki d.	...	1552	...	...	...	...	...	...	...	...	...	...	...	...	...	...	...	...	...	...	...
Idoméni 🛃 d.	...	1732	...	...	...	...	...	...	...	...	...	...	...	...	...	...	...	...	...	...	...
Skopje d.	...	2010	...	...	0820	...	...	...	...	...	...	...	...	...	...	...	...	...	...	...	...
Tabanovci 🛃 d.	...	2124	...	...	0924	...	...	...	...	...	...	...	...	...	...	...	...	...	...	...	...
Sofia d.	2030	|	...	...	|	1130	...	...	...	...	...	...	...	...	...	...	...	...	...	...	...
Kalotina Zapad 🛃 d.	2152	|	...	...	|	1311	...	...	...	...	...	...	...	...	...	...	...	...	...	...	...
Dimitrovgrad 🛃 d.	2120	|	...	...	|	1230	...	...	...	...	...	...	...	...	...	...	...	...	...	...	...
Niš d.	0002	0121	...	...	1321	1527	...	...	...	...	...	...	...	...	...	...	...	...	...	...	...
Beograd d.	0454	0533	1100	...	1809	1957	2125	...	...	...	...	...	...	...	...	...	...	...	...	...	...
Šid 🛃 d.	...	...	1355	...	...	...	0042	...	...	...	...	...	...	...	...	...	...	...	...	...	...
Vinkovci d.	...	...	1441	...	...	...	0120	...	...	...	...	...	...	0848	...	...	...	...	...	...	...
Zagreb a.	...	...	1809	...	...	...	0451	...	...	...	...	...	...	1225	...	...	...	...	...	...	...
Zagreb d.	...	...	1837	2120	...	...	0500	...	...	...	0650	...	...	1230	...	...	...	...	...	...	...
Dobova 🛃 d.	...	...	1925	2153	...	...	0530	0530	...	...	0738	...	...	1323	...	...	...	...	...	...	...
Rijeka d.	...	...	|	|	...	...	|	|	...	...	|	...	1200	|	...	...	...	...	...	...	...
Ljubljana d.	...	...	2110	2350	...	...	0703	0703	...	...	0912	...	1445	1505	...	...	...	...	...	...	...
Jesenice 🛃 d.	...	...	2205	0049	...	...	0827	0827	...	...	1009	...	...	1609	...	...	...	...	...	...	...
Villach Hbf a.	...	...	2243	0131	...	...	0908	0908	0916	...	1058	...	...	1650	1716	...	...	...	...	...	...
Bad Gastein a.	...	...	0024	|	...	...	...	...	1016	...	1216	...	...	...	1817	...	...	...	...	...	...
Schwarzach St Veit a.	...	...	0057	0318	...	...	...	...	1049	...	1248	...	...	...	1848	...	...	...	...	...	...
Bischofshofen a.	...	...	...	|	...	...	...	...	1105	...	1303	...	...	...	1903	...	...	...	...	...	...
Salzburg Hbf 🛃 a.	...	...	...	0409	...	...	...	...	1148	...	1348	...	...	...	1948	...	...	...	...	...	...
München Hbf a.	...	...	...	0615	...	...	...	...	1333	...	1533	...	...	...	2133	...	...	...	...	...	...

D – BALKAN EXPRESS – [12] Beograd - Sofia and v.v. June 9 - Dec. 14: 🛏 1, 2 cl. Beograd - Sofia - İstanbul and v.v. Dec. 15 - June 14: ▬ 2 cl. Beograd - Sofia - İstanbul and v.v. May be replaced by 🚌 for part of journey. *Train temporarily suspended between Beograd and Sofia. The compostion of this train is subject to confirmation.*
E – HELLAS EXPRESS – 🛏 1, 2 cl.*, ▬ 2 cl.*, [2] Beograd - Skopje and v.v. ▬ 2 cl., [2] Beograd - Skopje - Thessaloníki and v.v.
F – [2] Zürich (**465**) - Schwarzach St Veit (**415**) - Zagreb - Beograd and Beograd (**414**) - Zagreb - Schwarzach St Veit (**464**) - Zürich. [12] Villach - Beograd and v.v. Table **86**.
H – NUŠIĆ – ▬ 2 cl., [2] Beograd - Sofia and v.v.
K – OLYMPUS – [2] Beograd - Skopje and v.v.
L – LISINSKI – 🛏 1, 2 cl., ▬ 2 cl., [2] München - Salzburg - Zagreb and v.v.
M – [12] Frankfurt - München - Zagreb and v.v. 🍴 München - Villach and v.v.

T – SAVA – [2] Villach - Jesenice 🛃 - Ljubljana - Zagreb - Vinkovci and v.v.
W – WÖRTHERSEE – [12] 🍴 Münster - Klagenfurt and Klagenfurt - Dortmund.
Y – 🛏 1, 2 cl., ▬ 2 cl., [12] Villach - Beograd and v.v. *Temporarily suspended.*

✓ – Supplement payable.
* – Reported as not running most nights.
◧ – Supplement payable: Jesenice 🛃 - Zagreb - Beograd and v.v.
⊠ – Temporarily suspended.
RJ – ÖBB *Railjet* service. [1] (business class), [1] (first class), [2] (economy class), 🍴.

64 HAMBURG and BERLIN - WIEN - BUDAPEST

For alternative services via Břeclav see Table **60**

train type	*ICE*	*RJ*	*ICE*	*ICE*	*ICE*	*RJ*	*ICE*	*ICE*	*RJ*	*ICE*	*ICE*	*ICE*	*EN*	*ICE*	*ICE*	*ICE*	*ICE*	*ICE*	*ICE*		*EN*	*RJ*	
train number	21	63	1003	783	23	65	1005	91	67	1207	787	27	347	1509	789	29	209	881	229		491	49	
notes	🍷	🍷	①–⑥	①–⑥	🍷	🍷	1525	🍷	🍷	1707	🍷	🍷	Ⓡ		🍷	🍷	🍷	🍷	🍷			🍷	
		B				B	🍷		B	🍷			D	🍷							A	C	
Hamburg Hbf d.	...	...	...	0555	...	...	...	0803	...	...	1001	...	...	...	1201	...	...	1353	...	...	2034	...	...
Hannover Hbf d.	...	...	...	0726	...	...	...	0926	...	...	1126	...	...	...	1326	...	...	1526	...	...	2227	...	...
Berlin Hbf d.	...	...	0437	|	...	...	0639	|	...	0840	|	...	...	1040	|	...	1243	|	...	...	|	...	...
Leipzig Hbf d.	...	...	|	|	...	...	|	|	...	|	|	...	...	|	|	...	1401	|	...	...	|	...	...
Nürnberg Hbf d.	0830	...	0924	1024	1030	...	1124	1230	...	1324	1424	1430	...	1524	1624	1630	1724	1824	1830	...	0321**a**	...	...
Passau 🛃 d.	1038	...	...	...	1238	...	...	1438	...	...	...	1638	...	...	...	1838	...	...	2038	...	0532**a**	...	...
Linz Hbf a.	1142	1215	...	...	1342	1415	...	1542	1615	...	...	1742	...	...	...	1942	...	...	2142	...	0648	...	...
Wien Westbahnhof a.	1304	1330	...	...	1504	1530	...	1704	1730	...	...	1904	1948	...	...	2104	...	...	2304	...	0856	0948	...
Budapest Keleti § a.	...	1649	...	...	...	1849	...	...	2049	...	...	...	2249	...	...	...	...	...	...	...	...	1249	...

train type	*ICE*	*ICE*	*ICE*	*EN*	*ICE*	*ICE*	*ICE*	*RJ*	*ICE*	*ICE*	*ICE*	*RJ*	*ICE*	*ICE*	*RJ*	*ICE*	*ICE*	*ICE*	*RJ*	*ICE*	*RJ*	*EN*	
train number	228	880	1508	346	28	788	1506	60	26	786	1004	62	90	1502	64	22	782	1000	66	20	68	490	
notes	🍷	🍷	🍷	Ⓡ	🍷	🍷	1206	🍷	🍷	🍷	1504	🍷	🍷	🍷	🍷	🍷	1182	1600	🍷	🍷	🍷		
				D			906	B			🍷	B			B		🍷	⑤⑦j	B		B	A	
Budapest Keleti § d.	...	...	...	0510	...	...	...	0710	...	...	...	0910	∴	...	1110	...	...	...	1310	...	1510	...	...
Wien Westbahnhof d.	0652	...	...	0816	0852	...	...	1030	1052	...	...	1230	1252	...	1430	1452	...	...	1630	1652	1812	1956	...
Linz Hbf d.	0818	...	...	...	1018	...	...	1145	1218	...	...	1345	1418	...	1545	1618	...	...	1745	1818	...	2158	...
Passau 🛃 a.	0918	...	...	...	1118	...	...	...	1318	...	...	...	1518	...	...	1718	...	...	...	1918	...	2306**d**	...
Nürnberg Hbf a.	1125	1133	1234	...	1325	1333	1434	...	1525	1533	1634	...	1725	1835	...	1925	1934	1935	...	2125	...	0115**d**	...
Leipzig Hbf a.	...	|	|	...	...	|	|	...	|	|	|	...	|	2203	...	...	|	2308	...	...	...	|	...
Berlin Hbf a.	...	|	1719	...	...	|	1919	...	|	|	2120	...	|	2318	...	...	|	0025	...	...	...	|	...
Hannover Hbf a.	...	1432	...	...	...	1632	...	...	|	1832	...	...	2032	...	...	...	2232	...	...	...	...	0613	...
Hamburg Hbf a.	...	1554	...	...	...	1753	...	...	0015	1953	...	...	2153	...	...	...	0002	...	...	...	...	0748	...

A – HANS ALBERS – 🛏 1, 2 cl., ▬ 2 cl., [2] 🍷 Hamburg - Passau 🛃 - Wien and v.v.
B – ÖBB *Railjet* service. [1] (premium class), [1] (first class), [2] (economy class), 🍴 München - Wien - Budapest and v.v.
C – ÖBB *Railjet* service. [1] (business class), [1] (first class), [2] (economy class), 🍴 Wien - Budapest.
D – DACIA – 🛏 1, 2 cl., ▬ 2 cl., [12] 🍴 Wien - Budapest - Bucuresti and v.v.

a – Arrival time.
d – Departure time.
j – Also Oct. 2, 31; not Oct. 4.

§ – 🛃 is at Hegyeshalom.

MÜNCHEN - WIEN - BUDAPEST - BUCUREŞTI 65

train type	*RJ*	*EN*	*RJ*	*RJ*	*RJ*		*RJ*		*RJ*	*EN*	*RJ*		*RJ*	*RJ*	*EN*	*RJ*	*EC*	*RJ*		*EC*		*EN*	
train number	**41**	**467**	**49**	**265**	**61**		**63**		**65**	**473**	**67**		**165**	**69**	**347**	**261**	**117**	**661**		**391**		**463**	
notes	♀		♀	♀	♀		♀		♀	[R]	♀		♀	♀	[R]	♀	**1217**	♀					
		W		①-⑥						**Y**			**z**		**D**							**A**	
München Hbf ... d.	...	...	...	0624	0731	...	0934	...	1134	...	1334	...	...	1527	...	1723	1827	...	...	2024	...	2340	...
Salzburg Hbf 🏛 ... d.	...	0434	0702r	0808	0908	...	1108	...	1308	...	1508	...	1608	1702	...	1902	2010	2102	...	2215	...	0213	...
Linz Hbf ... d.	...	0607	0808r	0915	1015	...	1215	...	1415	...	1615	...	1715	1808	...	2008	...	2208	...	2330p	...	0340	...
St Pölten Hbf ... d.	...	0702	0859r	1005	1105	...	1305	...	1505	...	1705	...	1805	1859	...	2059	...	2259	...	...	...	0500	...
Wien Westbahnhof ... a.	...	0734	0924r	1030	1130	...	1330	...	1530	...	1730	...	1830	1924	...	2124	...	2324	...	...	...	0545h	...
Wien Westbahnhof ... d.	0648	0756	0948	...	1148	...	1348	...	1548	...	1748	...	1848	...	1948	...	...	...	...	...	...	0601e	...
Hegyeshalom 🏛 ... a.	0755	0855	1055	...	1255	...	1455	...	1655	...	1855	...	1955	...	2055	...	...	...	...	...	...	0655	...
Győr ... a.	0821	0921	1121	...	1321	...	1521	...	1721	...	1921	...	2024	...	2121	...	...	...	...	...	...	0726	...
Budapest Keleti ... a.	0949	1049	1249	...	1449	...	1649	...	1849	1910	2049	...	2154	...	2249	...	...	...	...	...	...	0854	...
Bucureşti Nord ... a.	...	...	...	...	...	...	...	...	...	1210	...	...	...	...	1605	...	...	...	...	...	...	...	...

train type	*EC*	*RJ*		*RJ*	*EN*	*RJ*		*RJ*	*EN*	*RJ*		*RJ*		*RJ*		*RJ*		*RJ*		*EN*	*IC*	*EN*	
train number	**390**	**260**		**262**	**346**	**162**		**60**	**472**	**62**		**64**		**66**		**68**		**42**		**466**	**72**	**462**	
notes		♀		♀	[R]	♀		♀	[R]	♀		♀		♀		♀		♀			[R]		
					D	**z**			**Y**					**F**						**W**	**H**	**A**	
Bucureşti Nord ... d.	...	...	...	...	1300	...	...	...	1725	...	...	...	...	...	...	...	...	...	...	...	0545	...	...
Budapest Keleti ... d.	...	...	...	...	0510	0605	...	0710	0850	0910	...	1110	...	1310	...	1510	...	1710	...	1910	1850	2110	...
Győr ... d.	...	...	...	...	0632	0729	...	0832	...	1032	...	1232	...	1432	...	1632	...	1832	...	2032	...	2232	...
Hegyeshalom 🏛 ... d.	...	...	...	...	0702	0802	...	0902	...	1102	...	1302	...	1502	...	1702	...	1902	...	2102	...	2302	...
Wien Westbahnhof ... a.	...	...	...	...	0816	0912	...	1012	...	1212	...	1412	...	1612	...	1812	...	2012	...	2216	...	2356e	...
Wien Westbahnhof ... d.	...	0636	...	0836	...	0930	...	1030	...	1230	...	1430	...	1630	...	1830	...	2030	...	2240	...	0011h	...
St Pölten Hbf ... d.	...	0702	...	0902	...	0954	...	1054	...	1254	...	1454	...	1654	...	1854	...	2054	...	2308	...	0051	...
Linz Hbf ... d.	0632r	0753	...	0953	...	1045	...	1145	...	1345	...	1545	...	1745	...	1945	...	2145	...	0005	...	0158	...
Salzburg Hbf 🏛 ... d.	0751	0902	...	1102	...	1152	...	1256	...	1456	...	1656	...	1856	...	2052	...	2252	...	0116	...	0428	...
München Hbf ... a.	0933	1030	...	1229	...	...	...	1425	...	1632	...	1825	...	2025	...	2226	...	...	...	...	...	0610	...

A – KÁLMÁN IMRE – 🛏 1,2 cl., ▬ 2 cl. [2] München - Wien - Budapest and v.v.
D – DACIA – 🛏 1,2 cl., ▬ 2 cl., [2] ✕ Bucureşti - Budapest - Wien and v.v.
F – From / to Frankfurt (Main) Hbf on dates shown in Table **930**.
H – TRAIANUS – [12] ♀ Bucureşti - Budapest.
W – WIENER WALZER – 🛏 1,2 cl., ▬ 2 cl., [2] Zürich - Salzburg - Wien - Budapest and v.v. [12] ✕ Wien - Budapest and v.v.
Y – *EuroNight* ISTER – 🛏 1,2 cl., ▬ 1,2 cl., [2] ✕ Budapest - Bucureşti and v.v.

e – Wien **Meidling**.
h – Wien **Hütteldorf**.
p – Not ⑥.
r – ①-⑥ (not Apr. 21, June 9).
z – From / to Zürich (Table **86**).

RJ – ÖBB *Railjet* service. [B] (business class), [1] (first class), [2] (economy class), ✕.

DORTMUND - KÖLN - FRANKFURT - WIEN - BUDAPEST 66

train type	*ICE*	*RJ*	*ICE*	*ICE*	*ICE*	*RJ*	*ICE*	*EN*	*ICE*	*ICE*	*EN*	*RJ*
train number	**21**	**63**	**23**	**1521**	**91**	**67**	**27**	**347**	**29**	**229**	**421**	**49**
notes	♀		♀		♀		♀	**D**[R]	♀	♀	**A**	
Dortmund Hbf ... d.	...	...	0437	0636	...	...	0837	...	...	...	...	...
Bochum Hbf ... d.	...	...	0448	|	...	...	0848	...	...	...	...	...
Essen Hbf ... d.	...	...	0459	|	...	...	0859	...	...	...	...	...
Duisburg Hbf ... d.	...	...	0512	⊙	...	...	0912	...	...	...	...	...
Düsseldorf Hbf ... d.	...	...	0527	|	...	...	0927	...	...	...	...	...
Köln Hbf ... d.	...	...	0553	0753	...	...	0953	...	...	...	2005	...
Bonn Hbf ... d.	...	...	0614	0814	...	...	1014	...	...	...	2034	...
Koblenz Hbf ... d.	...	...	0648	0848	...	...	1048	...	...	...	2113	...
Mainz Hbf ... d.	...	...	0739	0939	...	...	1139	...	...	...	2209	...
Frankfurt Flug. ✈ ... d.	...	...	0802	1002	...	...	1202	...	...	...	2233	...
Frankfurt (M) Hbf ... d.	0622	...	0819	1018	...	...	1221	...	1416	1621	2300	...
Würzburg Hbf ... d.	0733	...	0933	1125	1135	...	1333	...	1533	1733	0226	...
Nürnberg Hbf ... d.	0830	...	1030	▬	1230	...	1430	...	1630	1830	0324	...
Regensburg Hbf ... d.	0927	...	1127	...	1327	...	1527	...	1727	1927	0430	...
Passau Hbf 🏛 ... d.	1038	...	1238	*RJ*	1438	...	1638	...	1838	2038	0535	...
Linz ... a.	1142	...	1342	**65**	1542	...	1742	...	1942	2142	0648	...
Wien Westbf ... a.	1304	1348	1504	1548	1704	1748	1904	1948	2104	2304	0856	0948
Hegyeshalom 🏛 ... a.	...	1455	...	1655	...	1855	...	2055	...	...	...	1055
Budapest Keleti ... a.	...	1649	...	1849	...	2049	...	2249	...	...	...	1249

train type	*ICE*	*EN*	*ICE*	*RJ*	*ICE*	*RJ*	*ICE*	*RJ*	*ICE*	*RJ*	*ICE*	*RJ*	*EN*
train number	**228**	**346**	**28**	**60**	**26**	**62**	**90**	**64**	**22**	**66**	**20**	**68**	**420**
notes	♀	**D**[R]	♀		♀		♀		♀		♀		**A**
Budapest Keleti ... d.	...	0510	...	0710	...	0910	...	1110	...	1310	...	1510	...
Hegyeshalom 🏛 ... d.	...	0702	...	0902	...	1102	...	1302	...	1502	...	1702	...
Wien Westbf ... d.	0652	0816	0852	1012	1052	1212	1252	1412	1452	1612	1652	1812	1956
Linz ... d.	0818	...	1018	...	1218	...	1418	▬	1618	...	1818	...	2158
Passau Hbf 🏛 ... a.	0918	...	1118	...	1318	...	1518	*ICE*	1718	...	1918	...	2304
Regensburg Hbf ... a.	1027	...	1227	...	1427	...	1627	**1522**	1828	...	2027	...	0011
Nürnberg Hbf ... a.	1125	...	1325	...	1525	...	1725	♀	1925	...	2125	...	0112
Würzburg Hbf ... a.	1224	...	1424	...	1624	...	1822	1827	2024	...	2226	...	0209
Frankfurt (M) Hbf a.	1340	...	1536	...	1736	...	...	1936	2136	...	2339	...	0602
Frankfurt Flug. ✈ . a.	...	...	...	...	1755	...	...	1955	2157	...	...	...	0626
Mainz Hbf ... a.	...	...	...	...	1818	...	...	2018	2218	...	...	...	0646
Koblenz Hbf ... a.	...	...	...	...	1911	...	...	2111	2311	...	...	...	0744
Bonn Hbf ... a.	...	...	...	...	1942	...	...	2142	2342	...	...	...	0819
Köln Hbf ... a.	...	...	...	...	2005	...	...	2205	0005	...	...	...	0842
Düsseldorf Hbf ... a.	...	...	...	...	|	...	...	|	0032	...	...	...	...
Duisburg Hbf ... a.	...	...	...	...	|	...	...	|	0045	...	...	...	...
Essen Hbf ... a.	...	...	...	...	⊙	...	...	⊙	0057	...	...	...	...
Bochum Hbf ... a.	...	...	...	...	|	...	...	|	0109	...	...	...	...
Dortmund Hbf ... a.	...	...	...	...	2120	...	...	2321	0121	...	...	...	...

A – 🛏 1,2 cl., ▬ 2 cl. (4, 6 berth), [2] ♀ Köln - Frankfurt - Passau 🏛 - Wien and v.v. [R] Special fares apply. For international journeys only.
D – DACIA – 🛏 1,2 cl., ▬ 2 cl., [12] ✕ Wien - Budapest - Bucureşti and v.v.

RJ – ÖBB *RailJet* service. [B] (business class), [1] (first class), [2] (economy class), ✕.
⊙ – Via Hagen, Wuppertal (Table **800**).

DORTMUND - KÖLN - MÜNCHEN - GRAZ and KLAGENFURT 68

train type / number	*EC*	*EC*	*EC*	*IC*	*EC*	*EC*	*EC*	*D*	*EC*	*EC*	*EN*
train number	**111**	**211**	**217**	**690**	**113**	**113**	**115**	**315**	**219**	**117**	**499**
notes	♀	**H**	♀	♀	♀	**213**	✕		♀	**1217**	**L**
			G			**Z**	**W**			♀	
Dortmund Hbf ... d.	...	...	...	...	...	...	...	...	...	...	...
Bochum Hbf ... d.	...	...	...	...	...	...	...	...	...	...	...
Essen Hbf ... d.	...	...	...	...	...	...	...	...	...	...	...
Duisburg Hbf ... d.	...	...	...	...	...	...	0735	...	...	...	...
Düsseldorf Hbf ... d.	...	...	...	...	...	...	0751	...	...	...	...
Köln Hbf ... d.	...	...	...	...	...	...	0818	...	...	...	...
Bonn Hbf ... d.	...	...	...	...	...	...	0837	...	...	...	...
Koblenz Hbf ... d.	...	...	...	...	...	...	0918	...	...	...	...
Mainz Hbf ... d.	...	...	...	...	...	...	1017	...	...	...	...
Frankfurt (Main) Hbf ... d.	...	...	...	...	0822	0822	|	...	1220	1420t	...
Mannheim ... d.	...	...	0712	...	|	|	1102	...	|	|	...
Heidelberg ... d.	...	...	|	...	0914	0914	|	...	1314	1514t	...
Stuttgart Hbf ... d.	...	...	0758	...	0958	0958	1158	...	1358	1558	...
Ulm ... d.	...	...	0856	...	1056	1056	1256	...	1456	1656	...
Augsburg ... d.	...	...	0942	...	1142	1142	1342	...	1542	1742	...
München Hbf ... d.	0827	...	1027	...	1227	1227	1427	...	1627	1827	2340
Salzburg 🏛 ... a.	1009	...	1209	1212	1409	1409	1609	...	1809	2009	0118
Bischofshofen ... a.	1052	...	1302	1252	1452	1452	1652	...	1902	2052	|
Selzthal ... a.	|	...	1440	|	|	|	|	...	2040	|	|
Graz ... a.	|	...	1623	|	|	|	|	...	2223	|	|
Schwarzach St Veit ... a.	1109	...	...	1309	1509	1509	1709	...	...	2109	0223
Villach Hbf ... a.	1243	1253	...	1443	1643	1643	1843	1925	...	2246	0351
Klagenfurt ... a.	1315	|	...	...	1719	|	1915	|	...	2317	|
Ljubljana ... a.	...	1431	...	...	...	1831	...	2106	...	...	0558

train type / number	*EC*	*D*	*EC*	*EC*	*EC*	*EC*	*EC*	*EC*	*EN*
train number	**218**	**314**	**114**	**112**	**212**	**216**	**210**	**110**	**498**
notes	♀		✕	♀	**112**	♀	**H**	♀	**L**
			W		**Z**	**G**			
Ljubljana ... d.	...	0703	...	...	0912	...	1505	...	2350
Klagenfurt ... d.	...	|	0842	1027	|	...	|	1642	|
Villach Hbf ... d.	...	0908	0916	1116	1116	...	1650	1716	0146
Schwarzach St Veit ... d.	...	...	1051	1250	1250	...	...	1850	0320
Graz ... d.	0544	...	|	|	|	1137	...	|	|
Selzthal ... d.	0719	...	|	|	|	1319	...	|	|
Bischofshofen ... d.	0857	...	1107	1305	1305	1457	...	1905	|
Salzburg 🏛 ... d.	0951	...	1151	1351	1351	1551	...	1951	0428
München Hbf ... a.	1133	...	1333	1533	1533	1732	...	2133	0615
Augsburg ... a.	1215	...	1415	1615	1615	1815	...	...	...
Ulm ... a.	1302	...	1502	1702	1702	1902	...	...	...
Stuttgart Hbf ... a.	1401	...	1600	1801	1801	2001	...	...	...
Heidelberg ... a.	1444	...	|	1844	1844	|	...	...	...
Mannheim ... a.	|	...	1656	|	|	2048	...	...	...
Frankfurt (Main) Hbf ... a.	1540	...	|	1940	1940	...	...	...	...
Mainz Hbf ... a.	...	...	1739	...	...	...	...	...	...
Koblenz Hbf ... a.	...	...	1841	...	...	...	...	...	...
Bonn Hbf ... a.	...	...	1920	...	...	...	...	...	...
Köln Hbf ... a.	...	...	1942	...	...	...	...	...	...
Düsseldorf Hbf ... a.	...	...	2008	...	...	...	...	...	...
Duisburg Hbf ... a.	...	...	2022	...	...	...	...	...	...
Essen Hbf ... a.	...	...	2037	...	...	...	...	...	...
Bochum Hbf ... a.	...	...	2047	...	...	...	...	...	...
Dortmund Hbf ... a.	...	...	2100	...	...	...	...	...	...

G – [12] ♀ Saarbrücken - Mannheim - Graz and v.v.
H – SAVA – [2] Villach - Jesenice 🏛 - Ljubljana - Zagreb - Vinkovci and v.v. ✕ Jesenice 🏛 - Zagreb and v.v.
L – LISINSKI – 🛏 1,2 cl., ▬ 2 cl., [2] München - Ljubljana - Zagreb and v.v.
W – WÖRTHERSEE – [12] ✕ Münster (depart 0631) - Klagenfurt and Klagenfurt - Dortmund.
Z – [12] ♀ Frankfurt - Stuttgart - München - Villach - Ljubljana - Zagreb and v.v.

k – Köln **Messe / Deutz.**
t – Ⓑ.

70 DORTMUND - MÜNCHEN - INNSBRUCK - VENEZIA and MILANO

train type/number	*CNL*	*CNL*	*CNL*	*IC*	*EC*	*EC*	*IC*	*ICE*	*ICE*	*EC*	*IC*	*ICE*	*IC*
train number	**1247**	**1287**	**419**	**60419**	**1289**	**81**	**515**	**521**	**699**	**85**	**2021**	**525**	**361**
notes	🅁	🅁			✕	✕	🍷	🍷	*RJ*	✕		**925**	🍷
	P	**A**	**L**		♥**S**	♥**R**			**63**	♥		🍷	
Hamburg Hbf ... d.	...	2126**t**	...	...	...	...	...	...	...	...	2246	...	...
Berlin Hbf ... d.	2059	|	...	...	...	...	...	...	...	...	|	...	...
Dortmund Hbf ... d.	|	|	...	...	...	...	...	...	...	...	0152	0524**j**	...
Bochum Hbf ... d.	|	|	...	...	...	...	...	...	...	...	0203	0538**j**	...
Essen Hbf ... d.	|	|	...	...	...	...	...	...	...	...	0215	0553**j**	...
Duisburg Hbf ... d.	|	|	2257	...	...	...	...	...	...	...	0229	0608**j**	...
Dusseldorf Hbf ... d.	|	|	2313**u**	...	...	...	...	...	...	...	0247	0621**j**	...
Köln Messe/Deutz ... d.	|	|	|	...	...	...	...	...	...	...	|	0644**x**	...
Köln Hbf ... d.	|	|	2346**u**	...	...	...	...	0422	...	...	0351	|	...
Bonn Hbf ... d.	|	|	|	...	...	...	...	|	...	...	0416	|	...
Koblenz Hbf ... d.	|	|	|	...	...	...	...	⊖	...	...	0531	⊖	...
Mainz Hbf ... d.	|	|	|	...	...	...	...	|	...	...	0627	|	...
Frankfurt Flughafen ✈ ... d.	|	|	|	...	...	...	...	0535	...	...	0648	0737	...
Frankfurt (Main) Hbf ... d.	|	|	|	...	...	...	...	0551	...	...	0702	0754	...
Mannheim Hbf ... d.	|	|	|	...	...	...	...	|	...	...	▬	|	...
Heidelberg Hbf ... d.	|	|	|	...	...	...	...	|	...	...	...	|	...
Stuttgart Hbf ... d.	|	|	0417**a**	0435	...	...	...	|	0656	...	...	|	0853
Ulm Hbf ... d.	|	|	0542**a**	0544	...	...	...	|	0756	...	...	|	0956
Lindau 🛃 ... a.	|	|	|	|	...	...	...	|	|	...	...	|	|
Bregenz ... a.	|	|	|	|	...	...	...	|	|	...	...	|	|
Bludenz ... a.	|	|	|	|	...	...	...	◐	|	...	...	◐	|
Langen am Arlberg ... a.	|	|	|	|	...	...	...	|	|	...	...	|	|
St Anton am Arlberg ... a.	|	|	|	|	...	...	...	|	|	...	...	|	|
Landeck - Zams ... a.	|	|	|	|	...	...	...	|	|	...	...	|	|
Augsburg Hbf ... d.	0625**s**	0625**s**	0633**a**	0636	...	...	...	|	0839	...	...	|	1039
München Hbf ... d.	0705	0705	0710	0710	0738	0738	...	0912	0913	0938	...	1112	1111
München Ost ▲ ... d.	...	...	...	...	0747	0747	...	▬	▬	0947	**1509**	▬	▬
Kufstein 🛃 ... d.	...	...	...	...	0841	0841	...	...	...	1041	2	...	...
Wörgl ... d.	...	...	...	...	0851	0851	0902	...	...	1051	1137	...	...
Kitzbühel ... a.	...	...	...	...	|	|	0931	...	...	|	1217	...	...
St Johann in Tirol ... a.	...	...	...	...	|	|	0939	...	...	|	1226	...	...
Saalfelden ... a.	...	...	...	...	|	|	1007	...	...	|	1303	...	...
Zell am See ... a.	...	...	...	...	|	|	101	...	...	|	1314	...	...
Jenbach ... a.	...	...	...	...	0904	0904	▬	...	...	1104	▬	...	...
Innsbruck Hbf ... a.	...	...	...	...	0923	0923	...	...	...	1123	...	...	...
Innsbruck Hbf ... d.	...	...	...	...	0927	0927	...	*EC*	*FB*	1127	...	*FB*	*FB*
Brennero/Brenner 🛃 ... a.	...	...	...	...	1002	1002	...	**37**	**9722**	1202	...	**9727**	**9728**
Bolzano/Bozen ... a.	...	...	...	...	1117	1127	**2257**	🅁🍷	🅁	1329	...	🅁⚡	🅁
Trento ... a.	...	...	...	...	1150	1202		⊗	🍷⚡	1402	...	🍷	🍷⚡
Verona ... a.	...	...	...	...	1239	1256	1326	1329	1402	1458	*FA*	1529	1532
Padova ... a.	...	...	...	...	1326	|	|	1412	|	|	**9439**	1611	|
Venezia Santa Lucia ... a.	...	...	...	...	1356	|	|	1440	|	|	🅁⚡	1640	|
Milano Centrale ... a.	...	...	...	...	...	|	|	...	1525	|	🍷	...	1655
Bologna Centrale ... a.	...	...	...	...	...	1407**f**	1451	...	...	1620	1653	...	...
Firenze SMN ... a.	...	...	...	...	...	...	...	...	...	...	1730	...	...
Roma Termini ... a.	...	...	...	...	...	...	...	...	...	...	1905	...	...
Napoli Centrale ... a.	...	...	...	...	...	...	...	...	...	...	2030	...	...

train type/number	*EC*	*IC*	*ICE*	*EC*		*EC*	*IC*	*ICE*	*IC*	*EC*		*IC*
train number	**87**	**519**	**529**	**89**	**1513**	**115**	**1281**	**623**	**2261**	**83**	**1515**	**119**
notes	✕	🍷		✕	2	✕		**923**	🍷	✕	2	🍷
	♥			♥		**Q**	**H**	🍷		♥		**K**
Hamburg Hbf ... d.	...	...	...	...	...	...	...	...	...	...	...	...
Berlin Hbf ... d.	...	...	...	...	...	...	...	...	...	...	...	...
Dortmund Hbf ... d.	...	...	0724	...	...	...	...	...	...	...	...	...
Bochum Hbf ... d.	...	...	0738	...	...	...	...	...	...	...	...	...
Essen Hbf ... d.	...	...	0753	...	...	...	...	...	...	...	...	0823
Duisburg Hbf ... d.	...	...	0808	...	...	0735	...	...	...	...	...	0838
Dusseldorf Hbf ... d.	...	...	0821	...	...	0751	...	...	...	...	...	0852
Köln Messe/Deutz ... d.	...	...	0844	...	...	|	...	1030**y**	...	...	...	|
Köln Hbf ... d.	...	...	|	...	...	0818	...	1019**c**	...	...	...	0918
Bonn Hbf ... d.	...	...	|	...	...	0837	...	|	...	...	...	0937
Koblenz Hbf ... d.	...	...	⊖	...	...	0918	...	⊖	...	...	...	1018
Mainz Hbf ... d.	...	...	|	...	...	1017	...	|	...	...	...	1113
Frankfurt Flughafen ✈ ... d.	...	...	0937	...	...	|	...	1137	...	...	...	|
Frankfurt (Main) Hbf ... d.	...	...	0954	...	...	|	...	1154	...	...	...	|
Mannheim Hbf ... d.	...	...	|	...	...	1102	...	|	...	...	...	1154
Heidelberg Hbf ... d.	...	...	|	...	...	|	...	|	...	...	...	1206
Stuttgart Hbf ... d.	...	...	|	...	...	1158	...	|	1253	...	...	1257
Ulm Hbf ... d.	...	...	|	...	...	1256	...	|	1356	...	...	1411
Lindau 🛃 ... a.	...	...	|	...	...	|	...	|	|	...	...	1554
Bregenz ... a.	...	...	|	...	...	|	...	|	|	...	...	1610
Bludenz ... a.	...	...	◐	...	...	|	...	◐	|	...	...	1655
Langen am Arlberg ... a.	...	...	|	...	...	|	...	|	|	...	...	1725
St Anton am Arlberg ... a.	...	...	|	...	...	|	...	|	|	...	...	1736
Landeck - Zams ... a.	...	...	|	...	...	|	...	|	|	...	...	1804
Augsburg Hbf ... d.	...	...	|	...	...	1342	...	|	1439	...	...	|
München Hbf ... d.	1138	...	1312	1338	...	1411	1519	1512	1511	1538	...	|
München Ost ▲ ... d.	1147	...	▬	1347	...	▬	|	...	...	1547	...	|
Kufstein 🛃 ... d.	1241	...	...	1441	...	...	1624	...	...	1641	...	|
Wörgl ... d.	1251	1302	...	1451	1537	...	1647	...	...	1651	1745	|
Kitzbühel ... a.	|	1331	...	|	1617	...	1728	...	...	|	1820	|
St Johann in Tirol ... a.	|	1339	...	|	1626	...	1736	...	...	|	1830	|
Saalfelden ... a.	|	1407	...	|	1703	...	1812	...	...	|	1903	|
Zell am See ... a.	|	1417	...	|	1714	...	1824	...	...	|	1915	|
Jenbach ... a.	1304	▬	...	1504	▬	...	...	...	...	1704	▬	|
Innsbruck Hbf ... a.	1323	...	...	1523	...	...	...	...	...	1723	...	1902
Innsbruck Hbf ... d.	1327	*EC*	*FA*	1527	...	*FB*	...	...	...	1727	*FB*	...
Brennero/Brenner 🛃 ... a.	1402	**42**	**9483**	1602	...	**9746**	...	...	...	1802	**9749**	...
Bolzano/Bozen ... a.	1529	🅁🍷	🅁⚡	1729	**2107**	🅁⚡	...	...	...	1929	🅁	...
Trento ... a.	1602	⊗	✕	1802		✕	...	...	...	2002	🍷⚡	...
Verona ... a.	1657	1732	1750	1858	1918	1932	...	...	...	2056	2129	...
Padova ... a.	1741	|	|	...	2021	|	...	...	...	|	2212	...
Venezia Santa Lucia ... a.	1810	|	|	...	2054	|	...	...	...	|	2240	...
Milano Centrale ... a.	...	1855	|	...	...	2055	...	...	...	*2335*	...	...
Bologna Centrale ... a.	...	...	1842	...	...	...	...	...	...	...	...	...
Firenze SMN ... a.	...	...	1920¶	...	...	...	...	...	...	...	...	...
Roma Termini ... a.	...	...	2040	...	...	...	...	...	...	...	...	...
Napoli Centrale ... a.	...	...	...	...	...	...	...	...	...	...	...	...

train type/number	*ICE*	*ICE*	*EC*	*ICE*	*ICE*	*ICE*	*ICE*	*CNL*	*CNL*	*CNL*
train number	**517**	**627**	**189**	**519**	**209**	**723**	**611**	**485**	**40485**	**40363**
notes	🍷	**927**	✕	🍷	🍷	🍷	🍷			
		🍷	♥			Ⓑ		**B**	**T**	**C**
Hamburg Hbf ... d.	...	...	...	...	1051	...	...	...	...	...
Berlin Hbf ... d.	...	...	...	...	1243	...	...	...	...	...
Dortmund Hbf ... d.	1037	1103**y**	...	1237	|	...	1437	...	...	...
Bochum Hbf ... d.	1049	|	...	1249	|	...	1449	...	...	...
Essen Hbf ... d.	1100	|	...	1300	|	1453	1500	...	...	...
Duisburg Hbf ... d.	1112	|	...	1312	|	1508	1512	...	...	...
Dusseldorf Hbf ... d.	1127	|	...	1327	|	1521	1527	...	...	...
Köln Messe/Deutz ... d.	|	|	...	|	|	1544	|	...	...	...
Köln Hbf ... d.	1155	1215**q**	...	1355	|	|	1555	...	...	...
Bonn Hbf ... d.	|	|	...	|	|	|	|	...	...	...
Koblenz Hbf ... d.	⊖	⊖	...	⊖	|	⊖	⊖	...	...	...
Mainz Hbf ... d.	|	|	...	|	|	|	|	...	...	...
Frankfurt Flughafen ✈ ... d.	1253	1329	...	1453	|	1637	1653	...	...	...
Frankfurt (Main) Hbf ... d.	|	1354	...	|	|	1654	|	...	...	...
Mannheim Hbf ... d.	1331	|	...	1531	|	|	1731	...	...	...
Heidelberg Hbf ... d.	|	|	...	|	|	|	|	...	...	...
Stuttgart Hbf ... d.	1412	|	...	1612	|	|	1812	...	...	...
Ulm Hbf ... d.	1509	|	...	1709	|	|	1909	...	...	...
Lindau 🛃 ... a.	|	|	...	|	|	|	|	...	...	...
Bregenz ... a.	|	|	...	|	|	|	|	...	...	...
Bludenz ... a.	|	|	...	|	|	|	|	...	...	...
Langen am Arlberg ... a.	|	|	...	|	|	|	|	...	...	...
St Anton am Arlberg ... a.	|	|	...	|	|	|	|	...	...	...
Landeck - Zams ... a.	|	|	...	|	|	|	|	...	...	...
Augsburg Hbf ... d.	1555	|	...	1755	|	|	1955	...	...	...
München Hbf ... d.	1627	1712	1738	1827	1901	2012	2027	2103	2103	2340
München Ost ▲ ... d.	...	...	1747	▬	|	▬	▬	|	|	|
Kufstein 🛃 ... d.	...	...	1841	**E** 2	2004	**E** 2	2	2209	2209	|
Wörgl ... d.	...	...	1851	1919	2015	2000	2043	2220	2220	|
Kitzbühel ... a.	...	...	|	1952	|	2033	2117	|	|	|
St Johann in Tirol ... a.	...	...	|	2000	|	2041	2125	|	|	|
Saalfelden ... a.	...	...	|	...	|	...	2200	|	|	|
Zell am See ... a.	...	...	|	...	|	...	2213	|	|	|
Jenbach ... a.	...	...	1904	...	2029	...	...	2234	2234	|
Innsbruck Hbf ... a.	...	...	1923	...	2051	...	...	2258	2258	|
Innsbruck Hbf ... d.	...	...	...	...	...	...	...	2305	2305	|
Brennero/Brenner 🛃 ... a.	...	...	...	...	...	...	...	2342	2342	|
Bolzano/Bozen ... a.	...	...	...	...	...	...	...	0107	0107	|
Trento ... a.	...	...	...	...	...	...	...	0140	0140	|
Verona ... a.	...	...	...	...	...	...	...	0237	0237**e**	|
Padova ... a.	...	...	...	...	...	...	...	|	|	|
Venezia Santa Lucia ... a.	...	...	...	...	...	...	...	|	|	0834
Milano Centrale ... a.	...	...	...	...	...	...	...	|	0930	...
Bologna Centrale ... a.	...	...	...	...	...	...	...	0420	...	...
Firenze SMN ... a.	...	...	...	...	...	...	...	0618	...	...
Roma Termini ... a.	...	...	...	...	...	...	...	0920	...	...
Napoli Centrale ... a.	...	...	...	...	...	...	...	...	...	...

train type	**1520**	*ICE*	*EC*	*IC*	*ICE*	*IC*		*EC*	*ICE*	*IC*	*ICE*
train number	**1500**	**208**	**390**	**1280**	**596**	**118**	**1502**	**82**	**516**	**1284**	**1090**
notes	2	🍷	🍷		🍷	🍷	2	✕	🍷		**594**
				J		**G**		♥		**D**	
Napoli Centrale ... d.	...	...	...	...	...	...	...	...	...	...	...
Roma Termini ... d.	...	...	...	...	...	...	...	...	...	...	...
Firenze SMN ... d.	...	...	...	...	...	...	...	...	...	...	...
Bologna Centrale ... d.	...	...	...	...	...	...	...	...	...	...	...
Milano Centrale ... d.	...	...	...	...	...	...	...	...	...	...	...
Padova ... d.	...	...	...	...	...	...	...	...	...	...	...
Venezia Santa Lucia . d.	...	...	...	...	...	...	...	...	...	...	...
Verona ... d.	...	...	...	...	...	...	...	...	...	...	...
Trento ... d.	...	...	...	...	...	...	...	...	...	...	...
Bolzano/Bozen ... d.	...	...	...	...	...	...	...	...	...	...	...
Brennero/Brenner 🛃 ... d.	...	...	...	...	...	...	...	...	...	...	...
Innsbruck Hbf ... a.	...	...	...	...	...	...	...	...	...	...	...
Innsbruck Hbf ... d.	...	0709	...	...	...	0856	...	1036	...	...	...
Jenbach ... d.	...	0730	...	...	...	|	...	1055	...	...	...
Zell am See ... d.	0623	|	...	0839	...	|	0847	|	...	1035	...
Saalfelden ... d.	0636	|	...	0850	...	|	0858	|	...	1046	...
St Johann in Tirol ... d.	0710	|	...	0923	...	|	0934	|	...	1118	...
Kitzbühel ... d.	0718	|	...	0931	...	|	0943	|	...	1127	...
Wörgl ... d.	0752	0747	...	1023	...	|	1023	1110	...	1220	...
Kufstein 🛃 ... a.	...	0755	...	1032	...	|	...	1118	...	1232	...
München Ost ▲ ... a.	...	0848	...	|	...	|	...	1210	...	|	...
München Hbf ... a.	...	0900	0945	1149	1228	|	...	1221	1328	1341	1428
Augsburg Hbf ... a.	...	|	1015	...	1301	|	...	...	1400	...	1500
Landeck - Zams ... d.	...	|	|	...	|	0951	...	...	|	...	|
St Anton am Arlberg d.	...	|	|	...	|	1016	...	...	|	...	|
Langen am Arlberg .. d.	...	|	|	...	|	1026	...	...	|	...	|
Bludenz ... d.	...	|	|	...	|	1055	...	...	|	...	|
Bregenz ... d.	...	|	|	...	|	1144	...	...	|	...	|
Lindau 🛃 ... d.	...	|	|	...	|	1202	...	...	|	...	|
Ulm Hbf ... a.	...	|	1102	...	1349	1345	...	...	1449	...	1549
Stuttgart Hbf ... a.	...	|	1201	...	1447	1458	...	...	1547	...	1647
Heidelberg Hbf ... a.	...	|	1244	...	|	1553	...	...	|	...	|
Mannheim Hbf ... a.	...	|	|	...	1529	1606	...	...	1628	...	1729
Frankfurt (Main) Hbf. a.	...	|	1340	...	1608	|	...	...	|	...	1808
Frankfurt Flughafen ✈ . a.	...	|	...	...	|	|	...	...	1706	...	...
Mainz Hbf ... a.	...	|	...	...	|	1646	...	...	|	...	...
Koblenz Hbf ... a.	...	|	...	...	|	1741	...	...	⊖	...	...
Bonn Hbf ... a.	...	|	...	...	|	1820	...	...	|	...	...
Köln Hbf ... a.	...	|	...	...	|	1842	...	...	1805	...	...
Köln Messe/Deutz ... a.	...	|	...	...	|	|	...	...	|	...	...
Dusseldorf Hbf ... a.	...	|	...	...	|	1906	...	...	|	...	...
Duisburg Hbf ... a.	...	|	...	...	|	1922	...	...	|	...	...
Essen Hbf ... a.	...	|	...	...	|	1934	...	...	|	...	...
Bochum Hbf ... a.	...	|	...	...	|	...	...	...	|	...	...
Dortmund Hbf ... a.	...	|	...	...	|	...	...	...	1921	...	...
Berlin Hbf ... a.	...	1520	...	...	2021	...	...	...	...	...	...
Hamburg Hbf ... a.	...	...	...	...	...	...	...	...	...	...	...

FOR NOTES SEE NEXT PAGE →

MILANO and VENEZIA - INNSBRUCK - MÜNCHEN - DORTMUND 70

train type / number	*EC*	*FB*	*FB*	*EC*	*FB*	*FB*	*FB*	*FR*	*EC*	*ICE*	*FA*	*FB*	*EC*	*ICE*		*FB*	*FB*	*EC*	*EC*	*CNL*	*IC*	*CNL*	*CNL*	*CNL*	*ICE*
train number	**88**	**9712**	**9713**	**80**	**9713**	**9791**	**9714**	**9518**	**84**	**524**	**9416**	**9723**	**86**	**990**		**9729**	**9732**	**188**	**1288**	**418**	**60418**	**40462**	**484**	**40484**	**612**
notes	✕	🍷↯	🍷↯	✕	🍷↯	Ⓡ↯	🍷↯	Ⓡ↯	✕	🍷	Ⓡ↯	Ⓡ↯	✕	*RJ* **66**		Ⓡ↯	Ⓡ↯	✕	✕	**M**					🍷
	♥	Ⓡ	Ⓡ	♥	Ⓡ	⑥⑦	Ⓡ	🍷	♥				♥	**1590**				♥**R**	♥**S**			**C**	**F**	**T**	
Napoli Centrale d.	...	...	...	...	...	...	...	0800	...	...	...	...	...	...	...	...	...	...	...	...	...	...	...	...	...
Roma Termini d.	...	...	...	...	...	...	...	0925	...	...	1040	...	...	...	...	...	...	...	...	...	...	...	1912	...	...
Firenze SMN d.	...	...	...	...	...	...	...	1100	...	...	1215	...	...	...	...	...	...	...	...	...	...	...	2209	...	...
Bologna Centrale d.	*0710*h	...	...	...	...	...	...	1137	1152	...	1255	...	...	...	1410	...	...	1552f	...	...	...	...	2315	...	...
Milano Centrale d.	*0705*h	...	0905	...	0935	1035	...	▬	|	...	|	1305	...	...	|	1505	...	|	...	...	...	...	|	2135	...
Venezia Santa Lucia d.	*0658*h	0850	|	...	|	|	1050	...	|	...	|	|	1335	...	|	|	1520	|	1550	...	...	2057	|	|	...
Padova d.	*0725*	0917	|	...	|	|	1117	...	|	...	1352	|	1407	...	|	|	1547	|	1614	...	...	|	|	|	...
Verona d.	0904	1000	1027	1102	1057	1157	1200	...	1304	...	▬	1427	1502	...	1536	1627	1630	1702	1702	...	...	|	0101	0101z	...
Trento d.	0959	▬	▬	1159	▬	▬	▬	...	1359	...	...	▬	1559	...	▬	▬	▬	1759	1759	...	...	|	0156	0156	...
Bolzano / Bozen d.	1034	...	...	1234	...	...	...	...	1434	...	...	...	1634	...	...	...	...	1834	1834	...	...	|	0230	0230	...
Brennero / Brenner 🏛 d.	1200	...	...	1400	...	...	...	...	1600	...	...	...	1800	...	...	...	...	2000	2000	...	...	|	0357	0357	...
Innsbruck Hbf a.	1232	...	...	1432	...	...	...	...	1632	...	...	*IC*	1832	...	...	...	...	2032	2032	...	...	|	0431	0431	...
Innsbruck Hbf d.	1236	...	**1506**	1436	...	...	...	**1508**	1636	...	...	**518**	1836	...	...	...	**1512**	2036	2036	...	...	|	0436	0436	...
Jenbach d.	1255	...	2	1455	...	...	...	2	1655	...	...	🍷	1855	...	...	...	2	2057	2057	...	...	|	0500	0500	...
Zell am See d.	|	...	1247	|	...	...	...	1447	|	...	...	1743	|	...	...	...	1847	|	|	...	...	|	|	|	...
Saalfelden d.	|	...	1258	|	...	...	...	1458	|	...	...	1753	|	...	...	...	1858	|	|	...	...	|	|	|	...
St Johann in Tirol d.	|	...	1334	|	...	...	...	1534	|	...	...	1820	|	...	...	...	1934	|	|	...	...	|	|	|	...
Kitzbühel d.	|	...	1343	|	...	...	...	1543	|	...	*ICE*	1828	|	...	*CNL*	*CNL*	1943	|	|	...	...	|	|	|	...
Wörgl d.	1310	*ICE*	1423	1510	*IC*	*ICE*	*ICE*	1623	1710	...	**510**	1858	1910	...	**1286**	**1246**	2023	2114	2114	...	...	|	0518	0518	...
Kufstein 🏛 a.	1318	**514**	...	1518	**360**	**528**	**512**	...	1718	...	**1010**	▬	1918	...	Ⓡ	Ⓡ	...	2122	2122	...	...	|	0527	0527	...
München Ost ▲ a.	1410	🍷	...	1610	🍷	🍷	🍷	...	1810	...	**1110**	...	2010	...	**A**	**P**	...	2211	2211	...	...	|	|	|	...
München Hbf a.	1421	1528	...	1624	1648	1647	1728	...	1821	1850	1928	...	2021	2045	2213	2213	...	2221	2221	2250	2250	0615	0630	0630	0728
Augsburg Hbf a.	...	1601	...	...	1720	|	1800	...	...	|	2000	...	...	2116	2247	2247	...	...	...	2320d	2318	...	...	...	0800
Landeck - Zams d.	...	|	...	...	|	|	|	...	...	|	|	...	...	|	|	|	...	...	...	|	|	...	...	...	|
St Anton am Arlberg d.	...	|	...	...	|	|	|	...	...	|	|	...	...	|	|	|	...	...	...	|	|	...	...	...	|
Langen am Arlberg d.	...	|	...	...	|	◐	|	...	...	◐	|	...	...	|	|	|	...	...	...	|	|	...	...	...	|
Bludenz d.	...	|	...	...	|	|	|	...	...	|	|	...	...	|	|	|	...	...	...	|	|	...	...	...	|
Bregenz d.	...	|	...	...	|	|	|	...	...	|	|	...	...	|	|	|	...	...	...	|	|	...	...	...	|
Lindau 🏛 a.	...	|	...	...	|	|	|	...	...	|	|	...	...	|	|	|	...	...	...	|	|	...	...	...	|
Ulm Hbf a.	...	1649	...	...	1802	|	1849	...	...	|	2049	...	...	2202	|	|	...	...	...	0010d	0008	...	...	...	0849
Stuttgart Hbf a.	...	1747	...	...	1907	|	1947	...	...	|	2147	*IC*	...	2300	|	|	...	...	...	0135d	0116	...	...	...	0947
Heidelberg Hbf a.	...	|	...	...	...	|	|	...	...	|	|	**2020**	...	|	|	|	...	...	...	|	...	...	...	...	|
Mannheim Hbf a.	...	1828	...	...	...	|	2028	...	...	|	2229		...	2344	|	|	...	...	...	|	...	...	...	...	1028
Frankfurt (Main) Hbf a.	...	|	...	...	...	2004	|	...	...	2204	|	2324	...	0042r	|	|	...	...	...	|	...	...	...	...	|
Frankfurt Flughafen ✈ a.	...	1906	...	...	...	2022	2106	...	...	2222	2304	2336	...	0023r	|	|	...	...	...	0339	...	...	...	...	1106
Mainz Hbf a.	...	|	...	...	...	|	|	...	...	|	...	2358	...	...	|	|	...	...	...	|	...	...	...	...	|
Koblenz Hbf a.	...	⊖	...	...	...	⊖	⊖	...	...	⊖	...	0055	...	...	|	|	...	...	...	0446	...	...	...	...	⊖
Bonn Hbf a.	...	|	...	...	...	|	|	...	...	|	...	0133	...	...	|	|	...	...	...	0520	...	...	...	...	|
Köln Hbf a.	...	2005	...	...	...	|	2205	...	...	|	...	0156	...	...	|	|	...	...	...	0543	...	...	...	...	1205
Köln Messe/Deutz a.	...	|	...	...	...	2113	|	...	...	2337	...	|	...	...	|	|	...	...	...	|	...	...	...	...	|
Dusseldorf Hbf a.	...	2031	...	...	...	2137	2231	...	...	2359	...	0233	...	...	|	|	...	...	...	0610	...	...	...	...	1231
Duisburg Hbf a.	...	2044	...	...	...	2150	2244	...	...	0012	...	0250	...	...	|	|	...	...	...	0626	...	...	...	...	1244
Essen Hbf a.	...	2057	...	...	...	2202	2257	...	...	0025	...	0306	...	...	|	|	...	...	...	...	...	...	...	...	1257
Bochum Hbf a.	...	2108	...	...	...	2214	...	...	...	0036	...	0316	...	...	|	|	...	...	...	...	...	...	...	...	1308
Dortmund Hbf a.	...	2121	...	...	...	2230	...	...	...	0048	...	0329	...	...	|	|	...	...	...	...	...	...	...	...	1321
Berlin Hbf a.	...	...	...	...	...	...	...	...	...	...	...	|	...	...	|	0804	...	...	...	...	...	...	...	...	...
Hamburg Hbf a.	...	...	...	...	...	...	...	...	...	...	...	0651	...	...	0755	...	...	...	...	...	...	...	...	...	...

A – *City Night Line* PYXIS – 🛏 1, 2 cl., 🛏 1, 2 cl. (T4), ▬ 2 cl. (6 berth), [2] (reclining), 🍷 Hamburg - München and v.v. Special fares payable.
B – *City Night Line* LUPUS – 🛏 1, 2 cl., ▬ 2 cl., [2] 🍷 München - Innsbruck - Roma. Special fares apply. Ⓡ for journeys to Italy.
C – *City Night Line* PICTOR – 🛏 1, 2 cl., 🛏 1, 2 cl. (Excelsior), ▬ 2 cl., [2] 🍷 München - Tarvisio 🏛 - Venezia and v.v. Special fares apply. Ⓡ for journeys to / from Italy.
D – GROSSGLOCKNER – ⑦ June 22 - Sept. 14: [12] Schwarzach St Veit (depart 1005) - Zell am See - Wörgl - Kufstein 🏛 - München. Not Aug. 10, 17.
E – ①–⑤ (not Aug. 15, Nov. 1).
F – *City Night Line* LUPUS – 🛏 1, 2 cl., ▬ 2 cl., [2] 🍷 Roma - Innsbruck - München. Special fares apply. Ⓡ for journeys from Italy.
G – [12] 🍷 Salzburg (depart 0653) - Innsbruck - Lindau 🏛 - Stuttgart - Köln - Munster.
H – GROSSGLOCKNER – ⑥ June 21 - Sept. 13: [12] München - Kufstein 🏛 - Wörgl - Zell am See - Schwarzach St Veit (arrive 1854). Not Aug. 9, 16.
J – GROSSGLOCKNER – ⑥ June 28 - Sept. 13: [12] Zell am See - Wörgl - Kufstein 🏛 - München. Not Aug. 9, 16.
K – [12] 🍷 Munster (depart 0727) - Köln - Stuttgart - Lindau 🏛 - Innsbruck.
L – *City Night Line* POLLUX – 🛏 1, 2 cl., ▬ 2 cl. (4, 6 berth), [2] (reclining), 🍷 Ⓡ Amsterdam - Köln - München. Special fares apply.
M – *City Night Line* POLLUX – 🛏 1, 2 cl., ▬ 2 cl. (4, 6 berth), [2] (reclining), 🍷 Ⓡ München - Köln - Amsterdam. Special fares apply.
P – *City Night Line* CAPELLA – 🛏 1, 2 cl., 🛏 1, 2 cl. (T4), ▬ 2 cl. (6 berth), [2] (reclining), 🍷 Berlin - München and v.v. Special fares payable.
Q – WÖRTHERSEE – [12] ✕ Münster - Klagenfurt.
R – ①–⑤ Mar. 31 - Oct. 31; daily Nov. 3 - Dec. 13.
S – ⑥⑦ Mar. 29 - Nov. 2.
T – *City Night Line* APUS – 🛏 1, 2 cl., ▬ 2 cl., Ⓡ München - Innsbruck - Verona - Milano and v.v. Special fares apply.

a – Arrival time.
c – ①–⑥.
d – Departure time.
e – Depart 0722.
f – From Mar. 31.
g – Milano **Porta Garibaldi**.
h – Change at Verona.
j – Depart 22-32 minutes earlier on ⑥⑦ (also Oct. 3).
k – Köln **Messe / Deutz**.
q – 1227 on ①–⑥.
r – Train stops at Frankfurt Flughafen before Frankfurt (Main) Hbf.
s – Calls to set down only.
t – 2123 Mar. 2 - Aug. 22.
u – Calls to pick up only.
x – 0618 on ⑥⑦ (also Oct. 3).
y – ⑦ only.
z – Arrive 2258.

◐ – Via Nürnberg (Table **904**).
⊗ – **ETR 470 / 610**. Compulsory reservation for international journeys. Supplement payable for international journeys. *ESc* supplement payable for internal journeys within Italy.
⊖ – Via Köln - Frankfurt high speed line.
¶ – Firenze **Campo di Marte**.
↯ – Supplement payable.
‡ – Train number Milano - Verona and v.v.
▲ – Change here for München Airport (Table **892**).
♥ – DB-ÖBB EuroCity service.

BERLIN - MÜNCHEN - INNSBRUCK 71

For other services from Berlin to Innsbruck, change at München (Tables **851** and **70**).

train type	*CNL*	*ICE*	*ICE*	*ICE*	*IC*	*ICE*	*ICE*	*ICE*	
train number	**1247**	**823**	**521**	**525**	**1005**	**1207**	**1509**	**209**	
notes	**C**	①–⑤ j		**925**	**1525**	**1707**		**A**	
Berlin Hbf d.	2059	...	...	...	0639	0840	1040	1243	...
Nürnberg Hbf d.	|	0558	0802	1002	1128	1328	1528	1728	...
München Hbf a.	0705	0709	0912	1112	1312	1449	1647	1850	...
		EC **81** **E**	*EC* **85** **E**	*EC* **87** **E**	*EC* **89** **E**	*EC* **83** **E**	*EC* **189** **E**	|	
München Hbf d.	...	0738	0938	1138	1338	1538	1738	1901	...
Kufstein 🏛 a.	...	0839	1039	1239	1439	1639	1839	2001	...
Innsbruck Hbf a.	...	0923	1123	1323	1523	1723	1923	2051	...

train type	*ICE*	*EC*	*EC*	*EC*	*EC*	*EC*	*CNL*		
train number	**208**	**82**	**88**	**80**	**84**	**86**	**1246**		
notes	**B**	**E**	**E**	**E**	**E**	**E**	**C**		
Innsbruck Hbf d.	0709	1036	1236	1436	1636	1836	...	...	...
Kufstein 🏛 d.	0758	1120	1320	1520	1720	1920	...	...	...
München Hbf a.	0900	1221	1421	1621	1821	2021	...	...	...
	|	*ICE* **1206** **906f**	*ICE* **1504** **1004**	*ICE* **1502**	*ICE* **1500**	*ICE* **922** **520t**			
München Hbf d.	0916	1315	1449	1716	1916	2050	2213	...	...
Nürnberg Hbf a.	1031	1431	1628	1831	2031	2200	|	...	...
Berlin Hbf a.	1520	1919	2120	2318	...	...	0804	...	...

A – [12] ✕ Hamburg - Berlin - München - Kufstein 🏛 - Innsbruck.
B – [12] ✕ Berlin - München - Kufstein 🏛 - Innsbruck.
C – *City Night Line* CAPELLA – 🛏 1, 2 cl., ▬ 2 cl., [2] (reclining) 🍷 Berlin - München and v.v. Ⓡ. Special fares payable. See Table **851** for details of this train.

f – Train Number **1506** on certain dates.
j – Not Aug. 15, Oct. 3, Nov. 1.
t – Train Number **1620** on certain dates.

73 AMSTERDAM, BERLIN, DORTMUND and KÖLN - BASEL - ZÜRICH and MILANO

For other connections Basel - Luzern - Chiasso see Table **550**, for Basel - Bern - Interlaken and Brig see Table **560**.

train type	ICE	EC	IR	ICE	ICE	EC	IC	IR	CNL	IR	ICE	ICE	IR	ICN	IC	EC	ICE	IC	EC	ICE	ICE	ICE	IR	EC	EC
train number	3	15	1765	271	5	17	967	1769	473	1771	101	275	2173	877	573	57	71	973	7	121	515	277 297	2177	7	21
notes	🍷	🅡🍷 ⊗		M ①–⑥	🍷	🅡🍷 ⊗			🍷 C		🍷	🍷	¶		🍷	🅡🍷 ⊗	🍷		✕ B	①–⑥	🍷	🍷	¶	✕ B	🅡🍷 ⊗
København H. d.	...	...	...	...	...	...	...	...	1846	...	...	...	...	...	...	...	...	...	...	...	...	...	...	...	...
Hamburg Hbf d.	...	...	...	0025e	...	...	...	...	0031	...	...	...	...	...	...	...	0618	...	0442v	...	0541	...	...	...	...
Bremen Hbf d.	...	...	...	|	...	...	...	...	|	...	...	...	...	...	...	...	|	...	0540v	...	0639	...	...	...	...
Berlin Hbf d.	...	...	...	|	...	...	...	...	|	...	...	0433p	...	...	...	...	|	...	|	...	|	0633c	...	...	...
Hannover Hbf d.	...	...	...	0150e	...	...	...	...	|	...	...	|	...	...	...	...	0741	...	|	...	|	|	...	...	...
Dortmund Hbf d.	...	...	...	|	...	...	...	...	|	...	0537	|	...	...	...	...	|	...	0737	...	0837	|	...	...	...
Essen Hbf d.	...	...	...	|	...	...	...	...	|	...	|	|	...	...	...	...	|	...	0800	...	|	|	...	...	...
Amsterdam Centraal d.	...	...	...	|	...	...	...	...	|	...	|	|	...	...	...	...	|	...	|	0704	|	|	...	...	...
Utrecht Centraal d.	...	...	...	|	...	...	...	...	|	...	|	|	...	...	...	...	|	...	|	0732	|	|	...	...	...
Arnhem ⊙ d.	...	...	...	|	...	...	...	...	|	...	|	|	...	...	...	...	|	...	|	0807	|	|	...	...	...
Duisburg Hbf d.	...	...	...	|	...	...	...	...	|	...	h	|	...	...	...	...	|	...	0812	0908	h	|	...	...	...
Düsseldorf Hbf d.	...	...	...	|	...	...	...	...	|	...	|	|	...	...	...	...	|	...	0827	0923	|	|	...	...	...
Köln Hbf d.	...	...	...	|	...	...	...	...	|	...	0655	|	...	...	...	...	|	...	0853	0945x	0955	|	...	...	...
Bonn Hbf d.	...	...	...	|	...	...	...	...	|	...	|	|	...	...	...	...	|	...	0914	|	|	|	...	...	...
Koblenz Hbf d.	...	...	...	|	...	...	...	...	|	...	⊖	|	...	...	...	...	|	...	0948	⊖	⊖	|	...	...	...
Mainz Hbf d.	...	...	...	|	...	...	...	...	|	...	|	|	...	...	...	...	|	...	1039	|	|	|	...	...	...
Frankfurt Flughafen ✈ d.	...	...	...	0555r	...	...	...	...	|	...	0753	|	...	...	...	...	|	...	|	1034	1053	|	...	...	...
Frankfurt (Main) Hbf d.	...	...	...	0538r	0650	...	...	...	0640s	...	|	0850	...	...	...	...	1005	...	|	...	|	1050	...	...	...
Mannheim Hbf d.	...	...	...	0627	0736	...	...	...	0750s	...	0836	0936	...	...	...	...	1045	...	1123	...	1123	1136	...	...	...
Karlsruhe Hbf d.	0556p	...	...	0656	0800	...	...	...	0816s	...	0900	1000	...	...	...	...	1110	...	1149	...	...	1200	...	...	...
Freiburg (Brsg) Hbf d.	0702p	...	...	0802	0901	...	...	...	0937s	...	1004	1101	...	...	...	...	1212	...	1255	...	...	1301	...	...	...
Basel Bad Bf 🏛 a.	0735p	...	...	0835	0934	...	...	...	1014s	...	1037	1134	...	...	...	...	1245	...	1327	...	...	1334	...	←	...
Basel SBB a.	0747p	...	...	0847	0947	...	...	...	1030	...	1047	1147	...	...	...	...	1254	...	1335	...	...	1347	...	1335	...
	|			|	|						*IC* 969	|					*IC* 775		|			|		|	
Basel SBB ★ d.	0807	...	...	0859	1007	...	1000	...	...	1047	1100	1159	1204	...	1233	1231	1307	1300	1407	...	...	1359	1404	1407	...
Bern a.	|	...	...	0956	|	...	1056	...	...	|	1156	1256	|	...	|	1327	|	1356	→	...	...	1456	|	|	...
Spiez a.	|	...	...	1031	|	...	1131	...	...	|	1231	1331	|	...	|	1402	|	1431	▬	...	...	1531	|	|	...
Interlaken Ost a.	|	...	...	1057	|	...	1157	...	...	|	1257	1357	|	...	|	|	|	1457	...	...	...	1557	|	|	...
Brig a.	|	...	...	*1111*f	|	...	*1211*f	...	...	|	*1311*f	*1411*f	|	...	|	1440	|	*1511*f	*IR*	...	...	*1611*f	|	|	...
Domodossola 🏛 § a.	|	...	...	...	|	...	...	...	...	|	...	...	|	...	|	|	|	...	1775	...	...	...	|	|	...
Zürich HB a.	0900	0909	0912	...	1100	1109	...	1112	...	1152	...	...	|	1309	1326	|	1400	...	1412	...	...	...	|	1500	1509
Landquart a.	...	|	1032	...	...	|	...	1232	...	1332	...	...	|	|	1441	|	...	...	1532	...	...	...	|	1632	|
Chur a.	...	|	1043	...	...	|	...	1243	...	1343	...	...	|	|	1452	|	...	...	1543	...	...	...	|	1643	|
Chur d.	...	|	*1058*	...	...	|	...	*1258*	...	*1358*	...	...	|	|	*1458*	|	...	...	*1558*	...	...	...	|	*1658*	|
St Moritz a.	...	|	*1258*	...	...	|	...	*1458*	...	*1558*	...	...	|	|	*1658*	|	...	...	*1758*	...	...	...	|	*1858*	|
Luzern a.	...	|	...	...	...	|	...	...	...	...	...	...	1305	|	...	|	...	...	...	...	...	...	1505	...	|
Arth-Goldau a.	...	0948	...	...	...	1148	...	...	...	...	...	...	1344	1346	...	|	...	...	...	...	...	...	1544	...	1548
Bellinzona a.	...	1123	...	...	...	1323	...	...	...	...	...	...	1553	1523	...	|	...	...	...	...	...	...	1753	...	1723
Lugano a.	...	1147	...	...	...	1347	...	...	...	...	...	...	...	1547	...	|	...	...	...	...	...	...	...	...	1747
Chiasso 🏛 a.	...	1208	...	...	...	1408	...	...	...	...	...	...	...	1611	...	|	...	...	...	...	...	...	...	...	1808
Como San Giovanni a.	...	1215	...	...	...	1415	...	...	...	...	...	...	...	...	...	|	...	...	...	...	...	...	...	...	1815
Milano Centrale a.	...	1250	...	...	...	1450	...	...	...	...	...	...	...	...	...	1638	...	...	...	...	...	...	...	...	1850

train type	ICE	ICE	IR	IC	ICN	EC	ICE	EC	EC	ICE	IR	IC	ICE	EC	ICE	IR	EC	ICE	ICE	ICN	ICE	ICE	ICE	IR	EC
train number	105 505	73	1781	977	679	9	279	9	23	75	1785	981	123	59	371	2185	25	109	77 1177	689	125	987	373	2191	791
notes	🍷	🍷			🍷	✕ D	🍷	✕ D	🅡🍷 ⊗	🍷			🍷	🅡🍷 ⊗	🍷		🅡🍷 ⊗	🍷 Ⓑ	🍷	🍷	🍷	🍷	🍷		
København H. d.	...	...	...	...	...	...	...	...	...	...	...	...	...	...	...	...	...	...	...	...	...	...	...	...	...
Hamburg Hbf d.	...	0824	...	...	...	0646	...	...	...	1024	...	...	...	...	...	...	...	...	1224	...	...	...	...	...	...
Bremen Hbf d.	...	|	...	...	...	0744	...	...	...	|	...	...	...	...	...	...	...	...	|	...	...	...	...	...	...
Berlin Hbf d.	...	|	...	...	...	|	0833	...	...	|	...	...	...	...	1033	...	...	...	|	...	...	...	1233	...	...
Hannover Hbf d.	...	0941	...	...	...	|	|	...	...	1141	...	...	...	...	|	...	...	...	1341	...	...	...	|	...	...
Dortmund Hbf d.	...	|	...	...	...	0937	|	...	...	|	...	...	...	...	|	...	...	1337	|	...	...	...	|	...	...
Essen Hbf d.	...	|	...	...	...	1000	|	...	...	|	...	...	...	...	|	...	...	|	|	...	...	...	|	...	...
Amsterdam Centraal d.	0804	|	...	...	...	|	|	...	...	|	...	...	1034	...	|	...	...	|	|	...	1234	...	|	...	...
Utrecht Centraal d.	0832	|	...	...	...	|	|	...	...	|	...	...	1102	...	|	...	...	|	|	...	1302	...	|	...	...
Arnhem ⊙ d.	0907	|	...	...	...	|	|	...	...	|	...	...	1137	...	|	...	...	|	|	...	1337	...	|	...	...
Duisburg Hbf d.	1008	|	...	...	...	1012	|	...	...	|	...	...	1234	...	|	...	...	h	|	...	1434	...	|	...	...
Düsseldorf Hbf d.	1022	|	...	...	...	1027	|	...	...	|	...	...	1248	...	|	...	...	|	|	...	1448	...	|	...	...
Köln Hbf d.	1055	|	...	...	...	1053	|	...	...	|	...	...	1328	...	|	...	...	1455	|	...	1528	...	|	...	...
Bonn Hbf d.	|	|	...	...	...	1114	|	...	...	|	...	...	|	...	|	...	...	|	|	...	|	...	|	...	...
Koblenz Hbf d.	⊖	|	...	...	...	1148	|	...	...	|	...	...	⊖	...	|	...	...	⊖	|	...	⊖	...	|	...	...
Mainz Hbf d.	|	|	...	...	...	1239	|	...	...	|	...	...	|	...	|	...	...	|	|	...	|	...	|	...	...
Frankfurt Flughafen ✈ d.	1153	|	...	...	...	|	|	...	...	|	...	...	1418	...	|	...	...	1553	|	...	1618	...	|	...	...
Frankfurt (Main) Hbf d.	|	1205	...	...	...	|	1250	...	...	1405	...	...	1430	...	1450	...	...	|	1605	...	1630	...	1650	...	...
Mannheim Hbf d.	1236	1245	...	...	...	1323	1336	...	...	1445	...	...	▬	...	1536	...	...	1636	1645	...	▬	...	1736	...	...
Karlsruhe Hbf d.	1300	1310	...	...	...	1349	1400	...	...	1510	...	...	...	...	1600	...	...	1700	1710	...	...	...	1800	...	...
Freiburg (Brsg) Hbf d.	1401	1412	...	...	...	1455	1501	...	...	1612	...	...	...	...	1701	...	...	1801	1812	...	...	...	1901	...	...
Basel Bad Bf 🏛 a.	1434	1445	...	...	...	1527	1534	←	...	1645	...	...	...	...	1734	...	...	1834	1845	...	...	...	1934	...	...
Basel SBB a.	1447	1454	...	...	...	1535	1547	1535	...	1654	...	...	...	...	1747	...	...	1847	1854	...	...	...	1947	...	...
		|				|	*IC* 979	|		|			*ICN* 683 🍷		|			▬ *IC* 587	|				|		
Basel SBB ★ d.	...	1507	...	1500	1504	1607	1600	1607	...	1707	...	1700	1704	1731	1759	1804	...	1833	1907	1904	...	1900	1959	2004	2007
Bern a.	...	|	...	1556	|	→	1656	|	...	|	...	1756	|	1827	1856	|	...	|	|	|	...	1956	2056	|	|
Spiez a.	...	|	...	1631	|	...	1731	|	...	|	...	1831	|	1902	1931	|	...	|	|	|	...	2031	2134	|	|
Interlaken Ost a.	...	|	...	1657	|	...	1757	|	...	|	...	1857	|	|	1957	|	...	|	|	|	...	2054	2156	|	|
Brig a.	...	|	...	*1711*f	|	...	*1811*f	|	...	|	...	*1911*f	|	1940	*2011*f	|	...	|	|	|	*IR*	*2111*f	*2240*‡	|	|
Domodossola 🏛 § a.	...	|	...	...	|	...	...	|	...	|	...	...	|	|	...	|	...	|	|	|	1789	...	...	|	|
Zürich HB a.	...	1600	1612	...	|	...	...	1700	1709	1800	1812	...	|	|	...	|	1909	1926	2000	|	2012	...	...	|	2100
Landquart a.	...	...	1732	...	|	...	...	1832	|	...	1932	...	|	|	...	|	|	2041	...	|	2132	...	...	|	▬
Chur a.	...	...	1743	...	|	...	...	1843	|	...	1943	...	|	|	...	|	|	2052	...	|	2143	...	...	|	
Chur d.	...	...	*1758*	...	|	...	...	*1858*	|	...	*1958*	...	|	|	...	|	|	*2056*	...	|	⊠	...	...	|	*ICN*
St Moritz a.	...	...	*1958*	...	|	...	...	*2058*	|	...	*2203*	...	|	|	...	|	|	*2303*	...	|	...	...	...	|	**891**
Luzern a.	...	...	...	...	1605	...	...	...	|	...	...	...	1805	|	...	1905	|	...	...	2005	...	...	...	2105	🍷
Arth-Goldau a.	...	...	...	...	1644	...	...	...	1748	...	...	...	1844	|	...	1944	1948	...	...	2045	...	...	...	2144	2150
Bellinzona a.	...	...	...	...	1823	...	...	...	1923	...	...	...	2023	|	...	2153	2123	...	...	2223	...	...	...	...	2323
Lugano a.	...	...	...	...	1847	...	...	...	1947	...	...	...	2047	|	...	2226	2147	...	...	2247	...	...	...	...	2347
Chiasso 🏛 a.	...	...	...	...	*1926*	...	...	...	2008	...	...	...	...	|	...	2258	2208	...	...	2313	...	...	...	...	0013
Como San Giovanni a.	...	...	...	...	...	...	...	...	2015	...	...	...	...	|	...	...	2215	...	...	...	...	...	...	...	...
Milano Centrale a.	...	...	...	...	...	...	...	...	2050	...	...	...	...	2135	...	...	2250	...	...	...	...	...	...	...	...

CONTINUED ON NEXT PAGE

AMSTERDAM, BERLIN, DORTMUND and KÖLN - ZÜRICH and MILANO 73

train type	*ICE*	*IR*	*IR*	*ICE*	*ICE*	*IR*	*IC*		*IR*	*ICE*	*ICE*	*IC*	*IC*	*CNL*	*CNL*	*IR*	*EC*	*IC*	*IC*	*IC*	*CNL*	*IC*	*IC*	*IR*	*IC*
train number	**79**	**2293**	**1793**	**127**	**375**	**1797**	**993**		**2195**	**129**	**377**	**2307**	**61419**	**40419**	**479**	**2163**	**15**	**561**	**959**	**810**	**1258**	**60458**	**565**	**2165**	**1063**
notes	🍷			🍷	🍷					🍷	🍷	🍷	2		**1279**	¶	[R] 🍷	🍷	🍷	🍷	[R] 🍷		🍷	¶	
notes				**T**											**K**		⊗				**G**				
København H ... d.	...	...	...	...	...	...	...	...	...	...	...	...	...	...	...	...	...	...	...	...	...	...	...	...	...
Hamburg Hbf ... d.	1424	...	...	...	...	...	...	...	...	...	...	1846	...	...	2027	...	...	...	...	...	...	...	...	...	...
Bremen Hbf ... d.	|	...	...	...	...	...	...	...	...	...	...	1944	...	...	|	...	...	...	...	...	...	...	...	...	...
Berlin Hbf ... d.	|	...	...	...	1433	...	...	...	...	...	1633	|	...	...	|	...	...	...	...	...	2211	...	...	...	...
Hannover Hbf ... d.	1541	...	...	...	|	...	...	...	...	...	|	|	...	...	2216	...	...	...	...	...	|	...	...	...	...
Dortmund Hbf ... d.	|	...	...	...	|	...	...	...	...	...	|	2137	...	...	|	...	...	...	...	...	|	...	...	...	...
Essen Hbf ... d.	|	...	...	...	|	...	...	...	...	...	|	2200	...	...	|	...	...	...	...	...	|	...	...	...	...
Amsterdam Centraal ... d.	|	...	...	1434	|	...	...	...	...	1634	|	|	...	2031	|	...	...	...	...	...	|	...	...	...	...
Utrecht Centraal ... d.	|	...	...	1502	|	...	...	...	...	1702	|	|	...	2059**u**	|	...	...	...	...	...	|	...	...	...	...
Arnhem ⊙ ... d.	|	...	...	1537	|	...	...	...	...	1737	|	|	...	2137**u**	|	...	...	...	...	...	|	...	...	...	...
Duisburg Hbf ... d.	|	...	...	1634	|	...	...	...	...	1834	|	2212	2257	2257**u**	|	...	...	...	...	...	|	...	...	...	...
Düsseldorf Hbf ... d.	|	...	...	1648	|	...	...	...	...	1848	|	2227	2313	2313**u**	|	...	...	...	...	...	|	...	...	...	...
Köln Hbf ... d.	|	...	...	1720	|	...	...	...	...	1920	|	2250	2346	2346**u**	|	...	...	...	...	...	|	...	...	...	...
Bonn Hbf ... d.	|	...	...	|	|	...	...	...	...	|	|	...	0007	0007**u**	|	...	...	...	...	...	|	...	...	...	...
Koblenz Hbf ... d.	|	...	...	⊖	|	...	...	...	...	⊖	|	...	0040	0040**u**	|	...	...	...	...	...	|	...	...	...	...
Mainz Hbf ... d.	|	...	...	|	|	...	...	...	...	|	|	...	0137	0137**u**	|	...	...	...	...	...	|	...	...	...	...
Frankfurt Flughafen ✈ ... d.	|	...	...	1818	|	...	...	...	...	2018	|	...	0156	0156**u**	|	...	...	...	...	...	|	...	...	...	...
Frankfurt (Main) Hbf ... d.	1805	...	...	1830	1850	...	...	...	...	2030	2050	...	|	|	|	...	...	...	...	...	|	...	...	...	...
Frankfurt (Main) Süd ... d.	|	...	...	▬	|	...	...	...	...	...	|	...	|	|	|	...	...	...	...	...	0359**s**	0402	...	...	...
Mannheim Hbf ... d.	1845	...	...	...	1936	...	...	...	...	...	2136	...	0404	|	|	...	...	...	...	...	0443**s**	0445	...	...	...
Karlsruhe Hbf ... d.	1910	...	...	...	2000	...	...	...	...	...	2200	...	0439	0437**s**	0437**s**	...	...	...	...	...	0540**s**	0542	...	...	...
Freiburg (Brsg) Hbf ... d.	2012	...	...	...	2101	...	...	...	...	...	2311	...	0558	0555**s**	0555**s**	...	...	...	...	...	0705**s**	0707	...	...	...
Basel Bad Bf 🛃 ... a.	2045	...	...	...	2134	...	...	...	...	...	2346	...	0636	0636**s**	0636**s**	...	...	...	...	...	0745**s**	0745	...	...	...
Basel SBB ... a.	2054	...	...	...	2147	...	...	...	...	...	2354	...	0647	0647**s**	0647**s**	...	...	...	...	...	0754**s**	0754	...	...	...
	|			*IC* **991**	*IC* **795**						*IR* **1999**			|	|						|				
Basel SBB ★ ... d.	2107	...	...	2059	2207	...	2159	...	2205	...	0013	...	...	|	|	0704	...	...	0659	...	|	...	...	0804	0831
Bern ... a.	|	...	...	2156	|	...	2256	...	|	...	|	...	...	|	|	|	...	...	0756	0807	|	...	...	|	0927
Spiez ... a.	|	...	...	2234	|	...	2335	0012	|	...	|	...	...	|	|	|	...	...	0831	0834	|	...	...	|	1002
Interlaken Ost ... a.	|	...	...	2257	|	...	2359	|	|	...	|	...	...	|	|	|	...	...	0857	|	|	...	...	|	|
Brig ... a.	|	...	...	...	|	...	...	0120	|	...	|	...	...	|	|	|	...	...	...	0911	|	...	...	|	1040
Domodossola 🛃 § ... a.	|	...	...	...	|	...	...	...	|	...	|	...	...	|	|	|	...	...	...	...	|	...	...	|	▬
Baden ... a.	|	...	...	...	|	...	...	...	|	...	0108	...	...	0759	0759	|	...	...	...	...	0858	...	...	|	...
Zürich HB ... a.	2200	2209	2212	...	2300	2312	...	...	|	...	0124	...	...	0834	0834	|	0909	0837	...	...	0917	...	0937	|	...
Landquart ... a.	...	|	2332	...	...	0039	...	...	|	...	...	...	...	...	...	|	|	0941	...	...	...	...	1041	|	...
Chur ... a.	...	|	2343	...	...	0049	...	...	|	...	...	...	...	...	...	|	|	0952	...	...	...	...	1052	|	...
Chur ... d.	...	|	...	...	...	...	...	...	|	...	...	...	...	...	...	|	|	*0958*	...	...	...	...	*1058*	|	*EC*
St Moritz ... a.	...	|	...	...	...	...	...	...	|	...	...	...	...	...	...	|	|	*1158*	...	...	...	...	*1258*	|	**15**
Luzern ... a.	...	|	...	...	...	...	...	...	2305	...	...	...	...	...	...	0805	|	...	...	...	...	...	...	0905	[R] 🍷
Arth-Goldau ... a.	...	2246	...	...	...	...	...	...	*2345*	...	...	...	...	...	...	0844	0948	...	...	...	...	...	...	0944	0950
Bellinzona ... a.	...	0042	...	...	...	...	...	...	...	...	...	...	...	...	...	1053	1123	...	...	...	...	...	...	1153	1123
Lugano ... a.	...	0114	...	...	...	...	...	...	...	...	...	...	...	...	...	...	1137	...	...	...	...	...	...	...	1137
Chiasso 🛃 ... a.	...	0146	...	...	...	...	...	...	...	...	...	...	...	...	...	...	1208	...	...	...	...	...	...	...	1208
Como San Giovanni ... a.	...	...	...	...	...	...	...	...	...	...	...	...	...	...	...	...	1215	...	...	...	...	...	...	...	1215
Milano Centrale ... a.	...	...	...	...	...	...	...	...	...	...	...	...	...	...	...	...	1250	...	...	...	...	...	...	...	1250

A – *City Night Line* PEGASUS – 🛏 1, 2 cl., 🛏 1, 2 cl. (T4), 🛏 2 cl. (4, 6 berth), [2] (reclining), 🍷 Amsterdam - Mannheim - Basel - Zürich. [R] Special fares apply.

B – [12] 🍴 (Hamburg ①–⑥) Dortmund - Köln - Basel - Zürich - Chur.

C – *City Night Line* AURORA – 🛏 1, 2 cl., 🛏 2 cl. (4, 6 berth), [2] 🍷 København - Basel. [R] Special fares apply.

D – [12] 🍴 Hamburg - Dortmund - Köln - Basel - Zürich - Chur.

G – *City Night Line* SIRIUS – 🛏 1, 2 cl., 🛏 1, 2 cl. (T4), 🛏 2 cl. (4, 6 berth), [2] (reclining), 🍷 Berlin - Frankfurt - Basel - Zürich. [R] Special fares apply. Conveys *City Night Line* (Train **458**) CANOPUS Praha - Dresden - Frankfurt - Zürich (Table **54**).

K – *City Night Line* KOMET – 🛏 1, 2 cl., 🛏 1, 2 cl. (T4), 🛏 2 cl. (4, 6 berth), [2] (reclining), 🍷 Hamburg - Hannover - Mannheim - Basel - Zürich. [R] Special fares apply.

M – [12] 🍷 (Hamburg ①) - Frankfurt ①–⑥ - Basel - Interlaken Ost.

T – Mar. 22 - Nov. 3.

c – 0557 on ⑦.

e – ① only.

f – Change at Bern.

h – Via Hagen and Wuppertal.

p – ①–⑤ (not Oct. 3).

r – Train stops at Frankfurt (Main) Hbf before Frankfurt Flughafen.

s – Calls to set down only.

u – Calls to pick up only.

v – ①–⑥.

x – Köln **Messe / Deutz**.

¶ – To Locarno (Table **550**).

⊙ – 🛃 is at Emmerich.

§ – Ticket point is **Iselle**.

‡ – Change at Bern. 2301 on ⑦.

⊖ – Via Köln - Frankfurt high speed line.

★ – Connections at Basel are not guaranteed.

⊗ – **ETR 470 / 610**. Compulsory reservation for international journeys. Supplement payable for international journeys and for internal journeys within Italy.

⊠ – Change at Landquart for St Moritz. Landquart depart 2147, Klosters arrive 2228, change trains, depart 2232, St Moritz arrive 2344 (by connecting 🚌 Samedan - St Moritz ①–⑤ Apr. 10 - Sept. 28) see tables **545**, **546**.

Table 73 continued on next page

MILANO and ROMA - PÁTRA - ATHÍNAI 74

train type	*FB*	*FA*				*FB*		
train number	**9809**	**9355**			**2320**	**9803**		
notes	[R] 🍴 ⚡	[R] 🍴 ⚡	⛴ *SF*			[R] 🍴 ⚡	⛴ *SF*	
Milano Centrale ... d.	1035	...	...	...	...	0735	...	...
Bologna ... d.	1242	...	...	...	...	0942	...	...
Roma Termini ... d.	|	1450	...	...	0545	|	...	...
Foligno ... d.	|	|	...	...	0742	|	...	...
Ancona ... d.	1431	|	...	...	0955	1126	...	...
Ancona Marittima ... d.	|	|	...	...	...	...	1330	...
Pescara Centrale ... d.	1540	|	...	...	...	...	|	...
Caserta ... d.	|	1603	...	...	...	...	|	...
Foggia ... d.	1714	1750	...	...	...	...	|	...
Bari Centrale ... a.	1820	1848	...	...	...	...	|	...
Bari Marittima ... d.	...	...	2000	...	...	...	|	...
Pátra ... a.	...	...	1230	...	...	...	1130	...
Athína Lárisa ... a.	...	...	✣	...	...	...	✣	...

train type		*FB*		*IC*			*FB*	*IC*	*FA*	
train number		**9818**	**2327**	**541**			**9818**	**612**	**9354**	
notes	⛴ *SF*	[R] 🍴 ⚡		[R] 🍴 ⚡		⛴ *SF*	[R] 🍴 ⚡	[R] 🍴 ⚡	[R] 🍴 ⚡	
Athína Lárisa ... d.	✣	...	...	...	...	✣	...	...	...	...
Pátra ... d.	1430	...	...	...	...	1800	...	...	...	...
Bari Marittima ... a.	|	...	...	...	...	0830	...	...	...	...
Bari Centrale ... d.	|	...	...	...	...	...	0938	1204	1317	...
Foggia ... a.	|	...	...	...	...	...	1037	1319	1413	...
Caserta ... a.	|	...	...	...	...	...	|	|	1602	...
Pescara Centrale ... a.	|	...	...	...	...	...	1212	1503	|	...
Ancona Marittima ... a.	1030	...	...	...	...	...	|	|	|	...
Ancona ... a.	...	1327	1343	1530	...	...	1324	1633	|	...
Foligno ... a.	...	|	1543	1715	...	...	|	|	|	...
Roma Termini ... a.	...	|	1750	1854	...	...	|	|	1720	...
Bologna ... a.	...	1514	...	...	...	...	1514	1900	...	...
Milano Centrale ... a.	...	1725	...	...	...	...	1725	...	...	...

⚡ – Supplement payable.

✣ – For 🚌 services Pátra - Athína and v.v. see Table **1450**.

SF – **Superfast Ferries**, for days of running see Tables **2715**, **2755**.

73 MILANO and ZÜRICH - KÖLN, DORTMUND, BERLIN and AMSTERDAM

For other connections Basel - Luzern - Chiasso see Table **550**, for Basel - Bern - Interlaken and Brig see Table **560**.

train type	*ICE*	*ICE*	*IC*	*ICE*	*IR*	*ICE*	*ICE*	*IC*	*IR*	*ICN*	*ICE*	*IC*	*IR*	*ICE*	*ICE*	*ICN*	*IC*	*IC*	*ICE*	*EC*	*IR*	*EC*	*EC*	*ICE*	*EC*	
train number	**374**	**128**	**952**	**78**	**1754**	**372**	**126**	**956**	**1762**	**864**	**76**	**562**	**2166**	**370**	**124**	**668**	**962**	**566**	**74**	**12**	**2170**	**8**	**50**	**278**	**8**	
notes	🍷			🍷		**392**	🍷				🍷			🍷	🍷	🍷			🍷	🅁 🍷		**2**	🅁 🍷	🍷	**2**	
						🍷	**T**													⊗		**H**🍴	⊗		**H**🍴	
Milano Centrale d.	...	...	...	...	...	...	...	...	...	...	...	...	...	...	...	...	...	...	...	0710	...	...	0725	...	...	...
Como San Giovanni d.	...	...	...	...	...	...	...	...	...	...	...	...	...	...	...	...	...	...	...	0745	...	...	│	...	...	...
Chiasso 🏛 d.	...	...	...	...	...	...	...	...	...	0443	...	...	...	...	...	0641	...	...	...	0752	0711	...	│	...	...	...
Lugano d.	...	...	...	...	...	...	...	...	...	0508	...	...	...	...	...	0712	...	...	...	0812	0737	...	│	...	...	...
Bellinzona d.	...	...	...	...	...	...	...	...	...	0532	...	...	0606	...	...	0736	...	...	...	0836	0806	...	│	...	...	...
Arth-Goldau d.	...	...	...	...	...	...	...	...	...	0713	...	...	0814	...	...	0914	...	...	...	1013q	1014	...	│	...	...	...
Luzern d.	...	...	...	...	...	...	...	...	...	│	...	...	0854	...	...	0954	...	...	...	│	1054	...	│	...	...	...
St Moritz d.	...	...	...	...	...	...	...	...	...	│	...	...	│	...	...	│	...	*0536*k	...	│	│	*0702*	│	...	...	...
Chur a.	...	...	...	...	...	...	...	...	...	│	...	...	│	...	...	│	...	*0744*k	...	│	│	*0903*	│	...	...	...
Chur d.	...	...	...	...	0513	...	...	...	0613	│	...	0709	│	...	...	│	...	0809	...	│	│	0916	│	...	...	...
Landquart d.	...	...	...	...	0523	...	...	...	0623	│	...	0719	│	...	...	│	...	0819	...	│	│	0926	│	...	...	...
Zürich HB d.	...	...	...	0600	0700	...	...	...	0748	0751	0800	0834	│	...	...	│	...	0923	1000	1051	│	1100	│	...	...	...
Domodossola 🏛 § d.	...	...	...	│	│	...	...	...	...	...	│	│	│	...	...	│	...	...	│	...	│	│	│	...	...	...
Brig d.	...	...	...	│	│	*0547*f	...	*0649*f	...	...	│	│	│	*0749*f	...	│	*0849*f	...	│	...	│	│	0920	*0949*f	...	...
Interlaken Ost d.	...	...	...	│	│	0600	...	0700	...	...	│	│	│	0800	...	│	0900	...	│	...	│	│	│	1000	...	...
Spiez d.	...	...	0520	│	│	0622	...	0722	...	...	│	│	│	0822	...	│	0922	...	│	...	│	│	0954	1022	...	...
Bern d.	...	...	0604	│	│	0704	...	0804	...	...	│	│	│	0904	...	│	1004	...	│	...	│	│	1034	1104	←	...
Basel SBB ★ a.	...	...	0659	0653	0753	0759	...	0859	...	...	0853	0927	0955	0959	...	1055	1059	...	1053	...	1155	1153	1129	1159	1153	...
				│		│					│			│					│			│		│	│	
Basel SBB d.	0608	...	...	0706	...	0813	...	...	...	...	0906	...	...	1013	...	...	...	...	1106	...	...	1220	...	1213	1220	...
Basel Bad Bf 🏛 d.	0618	...	...	0715	...	0823	...	...	...	...	0915	...	...	1023	...	...	...	...	1115	...	...	→	...	1223	1230	...
Freiburg (Brsg) Hbf d.	0652	...	...	0749	...	0857	...	...	...	...	0949	...	...	1057	...	...	...	...	1149	...	...	...	...	1257	1304	...
Karlsruhe Hbf d.	0800	...	...	0851	...	1000	...	...	...	...	1051	...	...	1200	...	...	...	...	1251	...	...	...	...	1400	1412	...
Mannheim Hbf a.	0822	...	...	0914	...	1022	...	...	...	...	1116	...	...	1223	...	...	...	...	1314	...	...	...	...	1422	1437	...
Frankfurt (Main) Hbf a.	0908	0929	...	0952	...	1108	1129	...	...	...	1153	...	...	1308	1329	...	...	...	1353	...	...	...	...	1508	│	...
Frankfurt Flughafen ✈ a.	│	0940	...	│	...	│	1140	...	...	...	│	...	...	│	1340	...	...	...	│	...	...	...	...	│	│	...
Mainz Hbf a.	│	│	...	│	...	│	│	...	...	...	│	...	...	│	│	...	...	...	│	...	...	...	...	│	1518	...
Koblenz Hbf a.	│	⊖	...	│	...	│	⊖	...	...	...	│	...	...	│	⊖	...	...	...	│	...	...	...	...	│	1611	...
Bonn Hbf a.	│	│	...	│	...	│	│	...	...	...	│	...	...	│	│	...	...	...	│	...	...	...	...	│	1642	...
Köln Hbf a.	│	1032	...	│	...	│	1232	...	...	...	│	...	...	│	1432	...	...	...	│	...	...	...	...	│	1705	...
Düsseldorf Hbf a.	│	1111	...	│	...	│	1311	...	...	...	│	...	...	│	1511	...	...	...	│	...	...	...	...	│	1731	...
Duisburg Hbf a.	│	1124	...	│	...	│	1327	...	...	...	│	...	...	│	1527	...	...	...	│	...	...	...	...	│	1744	...
Arnhem ⊙ a.	│	1229	...	│	...	│	1429	...	...	...	│	...	...	│	1629	...	...	...	│	...	...	...	...	│	│	...
Utrecht Centraal a.	│	1300	...	│	...	│	1500	...	...	...	│	...	...	│	1700	...	...	...	│	...	...	...	...	│	│	...
Amsterdam Centraal a.	│	1326	...	│	...	│	1526	...	...	...	│	...	...	│	1726	...	...	...	│	...	...	...	...	│	│	...
Essen Hbf a.	│	...	...	│	...	│	...	...	...	...	│	...	...	│	...	...	...	...	│	...	...	...	...	│	1757	...
Dortmund Hbf a.	│	...	...	│	...	│	...	...	...	...	│	...	...	│	...	...	...	...	│	...	...	...	...	│	1821	...
Hannover Hbf a.	│	...	...	1217	...	│	...	...	...	...	1417	...	...	│	...	...	...	...	1617	...	...	...	...	│	│	...
Berlin Hbf a.	1325	...	...	│	...	1525	...	...	...	...	│	...	...	1725	...	...	...	...	│	...	...	...	...	1925	│	...
Bremen Hbf a.	...	...	...	│	...	...	...	...	...	...	│	...	...	...	...	...	...	...	│	...	...	...	...	...	2015	...
Hamburg Hbf a.	...	...	...	1335	...	...	...	...	...	...	1535	...	...	...	...	...	...	...	1735	...	...	...	...	...	2112	...
København H. a.	...	...	...	...	...	...	...	...	...	...	...	...	...	...	...	...	...	...	...	...	...	...	...	...	...	...

train type	*IC*	*ICN*	*IC*	*ICE*	*ICE*	*EC*	*EC*	*IR*	*ICE*	*EC*	*IC*	*IC*	*IC*	*ICE*	*IC*	*EC*	*EC*	*IR*	*IC*	*IC*	*IC*	*ICN*	*EC*	*IC*	*ICE*	*EC*
train number	**570**	**672**	**968**	**72**	**122**	**14**	**6**	**2174**	**276**	**6**	**574**	**774**	**974**	**104**	**576**	**16**	**52**	**2178**	**978**	**578**	**780**	**680**	**34**	**831**	**376**	**102**
notes		🍷		🍷	🍷	🅁 🍷	🍴	¶	**296**	🍴			🍷	**504**	🍷	🅁 🍷	🅁 🍷	¶					🅁 🍷	🍷	🍷	**1102**
						⊗	**G**		🍷	**G**				🍷		⊗	⊗						⊗			🍴
Milano Centrale d.	...	...	...	...	...	0910	...	...	...	...	...	...	...	...	...	1110	1125	...	...	...	...	...	1225	...	...	...
Como San Giovanni d.	...	...	...	...	...	0945	...	...	...	...	...	...	...	...	...	1145	│	...	...	...	...	...	│	...	...	...
Chiasso 🏛 d.	...	...	...	...	...	0952	...	...	...	...	...	...	...	...	...	1152	│	...	...	...	...	...	│	...	...	...
Lugano d.	...	0912	...	...	...	1012	...	...	...	...	...	...	...	...	...	1212	│	...	...	...	...	1312	│	...	...	...
Bellinzona d.	...	0936	...	...	...	1036	...	1006	...	...	...	...	...	...	...	1236	│	1206	...	...	...	1336	│	...	...	...
Arth-Goldau d.	...	1114	...	...	...	1213	...	1214	...	...	...	...	...	...	...	1409	│	1414	...	...	...	1514	│	...	...	...
Luzern d.	...	1154	...	...	...	│	...	1254	...	...	...	...	...	...	...	▬	│	1454	...	...	...	1554	│	...	...	...
St Moritz d.	*0802*	│	...	...	...	│	*0902*	│	...	...	*1002*	...	...	...	*1102*	...	│	│	...	*1202*	...	│	│	...	...	...
Chur a.	*1003*	│	...	...	...	│	*1103*	│	...	...	*1203*	...	...	...	*1303*	...	│	│	...	*1403*	...	│	│	...	...	...
Chur d.	1009	│	...	...	...	│	1116	│	...	...	1209	...	...	...	1309	*IR*	│	│	...	1409	...	│	│	...	...	...
Landquart d.	1019	│	...	...	...	│	1126	│	...	...	1219	...	...	...	1319	**96**	│	│	...	1419	...	│	│	...	...	...
Zürich HB d.	1123	│	...	1200	...	1251	1300	│	...	...	1323	1400	...	...	1434	1500	│	│	...	1523	1600	│	│	...	...	...
Domodossola 🏛 § d.	...	│	...	│	...	...	│	│	...	...	...	│	...	...	│	│	│	│	...	▬	│	│	│	...	...	...
Brig d.	...	│	*1049*f	│	...	...	│	│	*1149*f	...	...	│	*1249*f	...	│	│	1320	│	*1349*f	...	│	│	1416	1449	...	...
Interlaken Ost d.	...	│	1100	│	...	...	│	│	1200	...	...	│	1300	...	│	│	│	│	1400	...	│	│	...	│	1500	...
Spiez d.	...	│	1122	│	...	...	│	│	1222	...	...	│	1322	...	│	│	1354	│	1422	...	│	│	...	1525	1522	...
Bern d.	...	│	1204	│	...	...	│	│	1304	←	...	│	1404	...	│	│	1434	│	1504	...	│	│	...	1554	1604	...
Basel SBB ★ a.	...	1255	1259	1253	...	...	1353	1355	1359	1353	...	1453	1459	...	1527	1553	1529	1555	1559	...	1653	1655	...	...	1659	...
				│			│		│	│			*ICE* **70** 🍷						*ICE* **270** 🍷						│	
Basel SBB d.	...	...	...	1306	...	...	1420	...	1413	1420	...	...	1506	1513	...	...	...	...	1613	...	...	...	...	...	1706	1713
Basel Bad Bf 🏛 d.	...	...	...	1315	...	...	→	...	1423	1430	...	...	1515	1523	...	...	...	...	1623	*ICE*	...	...	...	...	1715	1723
Freiburg (Brsg) Hbf d.	...	...	...	1349	...	...	...	...	1457	1504	...	...	1549	1557	...	...	...	...	1656	**120**	...	...	...	...	1749	1757
Karlsruhe Hbf d.	...	...	...	1451	...	...	...	...	1600	1612	...	...	1651	1700	...	...	...	...	1801	🍷	...	...	...	...	1851	1901
Mannheim Hbf a.	...	...	...	1514	...	...	...	...	1622	1637	...	...	1714	1723	...	...	...	...	1823	④⑤⑦	...	...	...	...	1914	1924
Frankfurt (Main) Hbf a.	...	...	...	1553	1629	...	...	...	1708	│	...	...	1753	│	...	...	...	...	1908	1929	...	...	...	...	1953	│
Frankfurt Flughafen ✈ a.	...	...	...	│	1640	...	...	...	│	│	...	...	│	1806	...	...	...	...	│	1940	...	...	...	...	│	2006
Mainz Hbf a.	...	...	...	│	│	...	...	...	│	1718	...	...	│	│	...	...	...	...	│	│	...	...	...	...	│	│
Koblenz Hbf a.	...	...	...	│	⊖	...	...	...	│	1811	...	...	│	⊖	...	...	...	...	│	⊖	...	...	...	...	│	⊖
Bonn Hbf a.	...	...	...	│	│	...	...	...	│	1842	...	...	│	│	...	...	...	...	│	│	...	...	...	...	│	│
Köln Hbf a.	...	...	...	│	1739	...	...	...	│	1905	...	...	│	1905	...	...	...	...	│	2039	...	...	...	...	│	2105
Düsseldorf Hbf a.	...	...	...	│	1812	...	...	...	│	1931	...	...	│	1938	...	...	...	...	│	2111	...	...	...	...	│	│
Duisburg Hbf a.	...	...	...	│	1824	...	...	...	│	1944	...	...	│	1950	...	...	...	...	│	2124	...	...	...	...	│	**h**
Arnhem ⊙ a.	...	...	...	│	1929	...	...	...	│	│	...	...	│	2053	...	...	...	...	│	2224	...	...	...	...	│	│
Utrecht Centraal a.	...	...	...	│	2000	...	...	...	│	│	...	...	│	2128	...	...	...	...	│	2259	...	...	...	...	│	│
Amsterdam Centraal a.	...	...	...	│	2026	...	...	...	│	│	...	...	│	2155	...	...	...	...	│	2326	...	...	...	...	│	│
Essen Hbf a.	...	...	...	│	...	...	...	...	│	1957	...	...	│	...	...	...	...	...	│	...	...	...	...	...	│	│
Dortmund Hbf a.	...	...	...	│	...	...	...	...	│	2021	...	...	│	...	...	...	...	...	│	...	...	...	...	...	│	2221
Hannover Hbf a.	...	...	...	1817	...	...	...	...	│	│	...	...	2017	...	...	...	...	...	│	...	...	...	...	...	2217j	...
Berlin Hbf a.	...	...	...	│	...	...	...	...	2125b	│	...	...	│	...	...	...	...	...	2325	...	...	...	...	...	│	...
Bremen Hbf a.	...	...	...	│	...	...	...	...	...	2215x	...	...	│	...	...	...	...	...	...	...	...	...	...	...	│	...
Hamburg Hbf a.	...	...	...	1935	...	...	...	...	...	2314x	...	...	2146	...	...	...	...	...	...	...	...	...	...	...	2351j	...
København H. a.	...	...	...	...	...	...	...	...	...	...	...	...	...	...	...	...	...	...	...	...	...	...	...	...	...	...

CONTINUED ON NEXT PAGE

MILANO and ZÜRICH - KÖLN, DORTMUND, BERLIN and AMSTERDAM 73

train type	*IC*	*IR*	*IC*	*ICN*	*ICE*	*CNL*	*IC*	*ICN*	*IC*	*ICE*	*IC*	*IC*	*EC*	*ICE*	*IC*	*IC*	*CNL*	*IC*	*EC*	*IR*	*IC*	*CNL*	*CNL*	*IC*	*ICE*
train number	**1080**	**2182**	**580**	**882**	**272 292 1172**	**472**	**582**	**684**	**986**	**590 992 698**	**988**	**586**	**20**	**4**	**990**	**588**	**459 1259**	**992**	**22**	**2190**	**590**	**478**	**40478**	**60478**	**1124**
notes	🍷	¶	🍷			J	🍷	🍷	🍷		🍷	🍷	[R] 🍷 ⊗	🍷		🍷	C 🍷		[R] 🍷 ⊗	¶		K	A	2	🍷
Milano Centrale ... d.	...	...	...	...	...	...	...	...	...	...	...	...	1510	...	...	...	...	...	...	...	...	...	...	...	...
Como San Giovanni ... d.	...	...	...	...	...	...	...	...	...	...	...	...	1545	...	...	...	...	...	...	...	...	...	...	...	...
Chiasso 🏛 ... d.	...	...	...	1349	...	...	...	...	...	...	...	...	1552	...	...	...	...	...	1752	...	...	...	...	...	...
Lugano ... d.	...	...	...	1412	...	...	...	1512	...	...	...	...	1612	...	...	...	...	...	1812	...	...	...	...	...	...
Bellinzona ... d.	...	1406	...	1436	...	...	...	1536	...	...	...	...	1636	...	...	...	...	...	1836	1806	...	...	...	...	...
Arth-Goldau ... d.	...	1614	...	1613	...	...	...	1714	...	...	...	...	1813	...	...	...	...	...	2009	2014	...	...	...	...	...
Luzern ... d.	...	1654	...	|	...	...	...	1754	...	...	...	...	|	...	...	...	...	...	...	2054	...	...	...	...	...
St Moritz ... d.	...	|	*1302*	|	...	...	*1402*	|	...	...	...	*1502*	|	...	...	*1602*	...	...	...	|	*1702*	...	...	...	...
Chur ... a.	...	|	*1503*	|	...	...	*1603*	|	...	...	...	*1703*	|	...	...	*1803*	...	...	...	|	*1903*	...	...	...	...
Chur ... d.	...	|	1509	|	...	...	1609	|	...	...	...	1709	|	...	...	1809	...	...	...	|	1909	...	...	...	...
Landquart ... d.	...	|	1519	|	...	...	1619	|	...	...	...	1719	|	...	...	1819	...	...	...	|	1919	...	...	...	...
Zürich HB ... d.	...	|	1623	1651	1700	...	1734	|	...	...	...	1823	1851	1900	...	1923	1942	...	...	|	2023	2042	2042	...	...
Baden ... d.	...	|	...	▬	|	...	|	|	...	...	...	...	...	|	...	...	1958	...	...	|	...	2100	2100	...	...
Domodossola 🏛 § ... d.	1448	|	...	*IC*	|	...	|	|	...	...	...	...	...	|	...	...	|	...	...	|	...	|	|	...	...
Brig ... d.	1520	|	...	**982**	|	...	|	|	*1649*f	...	*1749*f	...	...	|	*1849*f	...	|	*1949*f	...	|	...	|	|	...	...
Interlaken Ost ... d.	|	|	...	1600	|	...	|	|	1700	...	1800	...	...	|	1900	...	|	2000	...	|	...	|	|	...	...
Spiez ... d.	1554	|	...	1622	|	...	|	|	1722	...	1822	...	...	|	1922	...	|	2022	...	|	...	|	|	...	...
Bern ... d.	1634	|	...	1704	|	...	|	|	1804	...	1904	...	...	|	2004	...	|	2104	...	|	...	|	|	...	...
Basel SBB ★ ... a.	1729	1755	...	1759	1753	...	1827	1855	1859	...	1959	...	...	1953	2059	...	|	2159	...	2155	...	|	|	...	...
					|				*ICE* **100** 🍷					|			|					|	|		
Basel SBB ... d.	...	...	...	...	1813	1826	...	...	1913	...	...	...	...	2013	...	...	2113u	...	...	...	...	2213u	2213u	2213	...
Basel Bad Bf 🏛 ... d.	...	...	...	...	1823	1839u	...	...	1923	...	...	...	...	2023	...	...	2122u	...	...	...	...	2223u	2223u	2223	...
Freiburg (Brsg) Hbf ... d.	...	...	...	...	1857	1915u	...	...	1956	...	...	...	...	2057	...	...	2158u	...	...	...	...	2300u	2300u	2300	...
Karlsruhe Hbf ... d.	...	...	...	...	2000	2035u	...	...	2101	...	...	...	...	2200	...	...	2304u	...	...	...	...	0029u	0029u	0029	...
Mannheim Hbf ... a.	...	...	...	...	2022	2104u	...	...	2124	2132	...	...	...	2222	...	...	0005u	...	...	...	...	|	|	0126	...
Frankfurt (Main) Süd ... d.	...	...	...	...	|	|	...	...	|	|	...	...	...	|	...	...	0051u	...	...	...	...	|	|	|	...
Frankfurt (Main) Hbf ... a.	...	...	...	...	2108	2219u	...	...	|	2208	...	...	...	2315	...	...	|	...	...	...	...	|	|	|	...
Frankfurt Flughafen ✈ ... a.	...	...	...	...	|	|	...	...	2206	...	...	...	...	...	...	...	|	...	...	...	...	|	0339	0339	...
Mainz Hbf ... a.	...	...	...	...	|	|	...	...	|	...	...	...	...	...	...	...	|	...	...	...	...	|	|	|	...
Koblenz Hbf ... a.	...	...	...	...	|	|	...	...	⊖	...	...	...	...	...	...	...	|	...	...	...	...	|	0446	0446	...
Bonn Hbf ... a.	...	...	...	...	|	|	...	...	|	...	...	...	...	...	...	...	|	...	...	...	...	|	0520	0520	...
Köln Hbf ... a.	...	...	...	...	|	|	...	...	2305	...	...	...	...	...	...	...	|	...	...	...	...	|	0543	0543	0609
Düsseldorf Hbf ... a.	...	...	...	...	|	|	...	...	2331	...	...	...	...	...	...	...	|	...	...	...	...	|	0610	0610	0631
Duisburg Hbf ... a.	...	...	...	...	|	|	...	...	2348	...	...	...	...	...	...	...	|	...	...	...	...	|	0626	0626	0644
Arnhem ⊙ ... a.	...	...	...	...	|	|	...	...	|	...	...	...	...	...	...	...	|	...	...	...	...	|	0745	...	|
Utrecht Centraal ... a.	...	...	...	...	|	|	...	...	|	...	...	...	...	...	...	...	|	...	...	...	...	|	0828	...	|
Amsterdam Centraal ... a.	...	...	...	...	|	|	...	...	|	...	...	...	...	...	...	...	|	...	...	...	...	|	0856	...	|
Essen Hbf ... a.	...	...	...	...	|	|	...	...	0001	...	...	...	...	...	...	...	|	...	...	...	...	|	...	...	0657
Dortmund Hbf ... a.	...	...	...	...	|	|	...	...	0024	...	...	...	...	...	...	...	|	...	...	...	...	|	...	...	0721
Hannover Hbf ... a.	...	...	...	...	0002t	|	...	...	...	...	...	...	...	...	...	...	|	...	...	...	...	0630s	...	...	|
Berlin Hbf ... a.	...	...	...	...	|	|	...	...	...	...	...	...	...	...	...	...	0719	...	...	...	...	|	...	...	|
Bremen Hbf ... a.	...	...	...	...	|	|	...	...	...	...	...	...	...	...	...	...	...	...	...	...	...	|	...	...	0914
Hamburg Hbf ... a.	...	...	...	...	0137t	0356	...	...	...	...	...	...	...	...	...	...	...	...	...	...	...	0835e	...	...	1012
København H. ... a.	...	...	...	...	...	1007	...	...	...	...	...	...	...	...	...	...	...	...	...	...	...	...	...	...	...

A – *City Night Line* PEGASUS – 🛏 1, 2 cl., 🛏 1, 2 cl. (T4), 🛏 2 cl. (4, 6 berth), [2] (reclining), 🍷 Zürich - Basel - Mannheim - Amsterdam. [R] Special fares apply.

C – *City Night Line* SIRIUS – 🛏 1, 2 cl., 🛏 1, 2 cl. (T4), 🛏 2 cl. (4, 6 berth), [2] (reclining), 🍷 Zürich - Basel - Frankfurt - Berlin [R] Special fares apply. Conveys *City Night Line* **459** CANOPUS Zürich - Frankfurt - Dresden - Praha (Table **54**).

G – [12] ✕ Chur - Basel - Köln - Dortmund (- Hamburg Ⓑ).

H – [12] ✕ Chur - Basel - Köln - Dortmund - Hamburg. To Kiel on dates shown in Table **912**.

J – *City Night Line* AURORA – 🛏 1, 2 cl., 🛏 2 cl. (4, 6 berth), [2] (reclining) 🍷 Basel - Fulda - København. [R] Special fares apply.

K – *City Night Line* KOMET – 🛏 1, 2 cl., 🛏 1, 2 cl. (T4), 🛏 2 cl. (4, 6 berth), [2] (reclining) 🍷 Zürich - Basel - Mannheim - Hannover - Hamburg. [R] Special fares apply.

T – Mar. 22 - Nov. 3.

b – 2204 on ⑥.

e – Arrive Hamburg 0821, 0833, 0844, 0845 on certain dates.

f – Change trains at Bern.

h – Via Wuppertal, Hagen.

j – ⑤⑦ (also Oct. 2; not Oct. 4).

k – On ⑦ and holidays, depart St Moritz 0557, arrive Chur 0759.

q – Arrive 4 minutes earlier.

s – Calls to set down only.

t – ②③④⑤⑥⑦.

u – Calls to pick up only.

x – Ⓑ.

⊙ – 🏛 is at Emmerich.

§ – Ticket point is **Iselle**.

¶ – From Locarno (Table **550**).

★ – Connections at Basel are not guaranteed.

⊖ – Via Köln - Frankfurt high speed line.

⊗ – **ETR 470 / 610**. Compulsory reservation for international journeys. Supplement payable for international journeys and for internal journeys within Italy.

For Table 74 see page 85

MÜNCHEN - ZÜRICH 75

train type	*EC*		*EC*		*EC*		*EC*		
train number	**196**		**194**		**192**		**190**		
notes	✕		✕		✕		✕		
München Hbf ... d.	0717	...	1233	...	1633	...	1833	...	...
Buchloe ... d.	0758	...	1317	...	1717	...	1917	...	...
Memmingen ... d.	|	...	1346	...	1746	...	1946	...	...
Kempten Hbf ... d.	0841	...	|	...	|	...	|	...	...
Lindau 🏛 ... d.	0954	...	1454	...	1855	...	2055	...	...
Bregenz 🏛 ... d.	1006	...	1506	...	1906	...	2106	...	...
St Margrethen 🏛 ... a.	1018	...	1518	...	1918	...	2118	...	...
St Gallen ... a.	1041	...	1541	...	1941	...	2141	...	...
Winterthur ... a.	1117	...	1617	...	2017	...	2217	...	...
Zürich Flughafen ✈ ... a.	1132	...	1632	...	2032	...	2232	...	...
Zürich HB ... a.	1144	...	1644	...	2044	...	2244	...	...

train type	*EC*		*EC*		*EC*		*EC*		
train number	**191**		**193**		**195**		**197**		
notes	✕		✕		✕		✕		
Zürich HB ... d.	0716	...	0916	...	1316	...	1816	...	...
Zürich Flughafen ✈ ... d.	0728	...	0928	...	1328	...	1828u	...	...
Winterthur ... d.	0742	...	0942	...	1342	...	1842u	...	...
St Gallen ... d.	0819	...	1019	...	1419	...	1919u	...	...
St Margrethen 🏛 ... d.	0842	...	1042	...	1442	...	1942u	...	...
Bregenz 🏛 ... d.	0855	...	1055	...	1455	...	1955	...	...
Lindau 🏛 ... a.	0905	...	1105	...	1505	...	2005	...	...
Kempten Hbf ... a.	|	...	|	...	|	...	2122	...	...
Memmingen ... a.	1013	...	1213	...	1613	...	|	...	...
Buchloe ... a.	1041	...	1241	...	1641	...	2203	...	...
München Hbf ... a.	1128	...	1328	...	1728	...	2245	...	...

u – Calls to pick up only.

76 MÜNCHEN and NÜRNBERG - PRAHA

train type	*RE*	*ALX*	*ALX*	🚌 P	🚌 P	🚌 Q	🚌 P	*RE*	*ALX*	🚌 P	🚌 Q	🚌 P	🚌 P	🚌 P	*RE*	*RE*	*ALX*	🚌 Q	🚌 P	🚌 P	🚌 Q	*RE*	*ALX*	🚌 P	
train number		**351**	**351**	**42002**	**42004**	**42050**	**42006**		**353**	**42008**	**42052**	**42010**	**42012**	**42014**			**355**	**42056**	**42016**	**42018**	**42058**		**357**	**42022**	
notes		①–⑥		🅁	🅁	🅁	🅁		¶	🅁	🅁	🅁	🅁	🅁	⑥⑦	①–⑤	¶	🅁	🅁	🅁	🅁		¶	🅁	
notes		**y** ¶	¶							⑤⑦				**C**	**z**	**t**	🍷				**m**		🍷	**C**	
München Hbf .... d.	...	0455	...	...	...	0800	...	...	0901	...	1000	...	...	...	...	...	1244	1400	...	...	1700	...	1702	...	...
Nürnberg Hbf .... d.	0536	|	...	0742	0842	|	0942	0948	|	1042	|	1142	1242	1342	1348	1353	|	|	1542	1742	|	1753	|	1942	...
Regensburg .... d.	|	0623	...	|	|	|	|	|	1031	|	|	|	|	|	|	|	1419	|	|	|	|	|	1835	|	...
Schwandorf .... d.	0644	0705	0705	|	|	|	|	1057	1107	|	|	|	|	|	1457	1457	1507	|	|	|	|	1857	1909	|	...
Furth im Wald 🏛 .... d.	...	0750	0750	◐	◐	|	◐	...	1150	◐	|	◐	◐	◐	...	...	1550	|	◐	◐	|	...	1952	◐	...
Plzeň hlavní .... a.	...	0857	0857	|	|	|	|	...	1257	|	|	|	|	|	...	...	1657	|	|	|	|	...	2059	|	...
Praha hlavní .... a.	...	1044	1044	1119	1219	1239	1319	...	1444	1419	1439	1519	1619	1719	...	...	1844	1839	1919	2119	2159	...	2244	2302	...

train type	*ALX*	*RE*		🚌 Q	🚌 P	🚌 P	*ALX*	*RE*	🚌 P	🚌 Q		🚌 P	*ALX*	*RE*	🚌 P	🚌 Q	🚌 P	🚌 P	🚌 Q	🚌 P	*ALX*	*RE*	🚌 P		🚌 P
train number	**356**			**42051**	**42005**	**42007**	**354**		**42009**	**42053**		**42011**	**352**		**42013**	**42055**	**42015**	**42017**	**42057**	**42019**	**350**		**42021**		**42023**
notes	¶			🅁	🅁	🅁	¶		🅁	🅁		🅁	¶		🅁	🅁	🅁	🅁	🅁	🅁	¶		🅁		🅁
notes	🍷			**r**	**D**		🍷											⑤⑦							
Praha hlavní .... d.	0515	...	...	0655	0735	0835	0915	...	1035	1015	...	1235	1315	...	1335	1415	1435	1535	1615	1635	1715	...	1735	...	1835
Plzeň hlavní .... d.	0700	...	...	|	|	|	1100	...	|	|	...	|	1500	...	|	|	|	|	|	|	1900	...	|	...	|
Furth im Wald 🏛 .... a.	0810	...	...	|	◐	◐	1210	...	◐	|	...	◐	1610	...	◐	|	◐	◐	|	◐	2012	...	◐	...	◐
Schwandorf .... a.	0854	0909	...	|	|	|	1255	1309	|	|	...	|	1657	1709	|	|	|	|	|	|	2056	2110	|	...	|
Regensburg .... a.	0929	|	...	|	|	|	1331	|	|	|	...	|	1737	|	|	|	|	|	|	|	2133	|	|	...	|
Nürnberg Hbf .... a.	|	1022	...	|	1114	1214	|	1422	1414	|	...	1614	|	1822	1714	|	1814	1914	|	2014	|	2218	2114	...	2214
München Hbf .... a.	1116	...	...	1154	...	...	1503	...	...	1454	...	...	1915	...	...	1854	...	...	2054	...	2305	...	...	...	...

C – Daily except ②.

D – Daily except ③.

P – 🚌 **DB / ČD** *IC Bus*. Rail tickets valid. 🅁 🍷. Supplement payable. 2nd class only. At Praha hlavní railway station the bus stop is located outside the old building on the upper level (access from platform one); street name is Wilsonova. At Nürnberg Hbf the bus stop is at Bahnhofvorplatz Hauptausgang (main entrance).

Q – 🚌 **DB / Czech Student Agency** *IC Bus*. Rail tickets valid. 🅁 🍷. Supplement payable. 2nd class only. At Praha hlavní railway station the bus stop is located outside the old building on the upper level (access from platform one); street name is Wilsonova. The bus stop for München is at Hackerbrücke (approx. 700 metres from München Hbf).

m – Also calls at München Flughafen Terminal 2, Halt 22 (d. 1743).

r – Calls at München Flughafen Terminal 2, Halt 22 (a. 1111).

t – Not June 9, 19, Oct. 3.

y – Not June 9, 19, Aug. 15, Oct. 3, Nov. 1.

z – Also June 9, 19, Oct. 3.

¶ – *Ex* in the Czech Republic.

◐ – 🏛 is Waidhaus (Germany).

ALX – Arriva Länderbahn Express.

CONNECTING SERVICES

Hamburg - Hannover - Nürnberg : Table **900**
Köln - Frankfurt - Nürnberg : Table **920**
Karlsruhe - Stuttgart - Nürnberg : Table **925**

GENÈVE, BASEL and ZÜRICH - MILANO, VENEZIA and ROMA 82

train type	IC	EC	FR↗	FB	IR	EC	IR	EC	FB	IC	IC	EC	FR	EC	IR	EC	FR	IR	EC	FR	IR	EC	FB	FR↗	FB
train number	**806**	**35**	**9521**	**9791**	**1405**	**51**	**2159**	**313**	**9715**	**959**	**810**	**37**	**9529**	**253**	**2165**	**315**	**9537**	**2169**	**317**	**9545**	**1417**	**57**	**9737**	**9549**	**9739**
notes		R 🍸 ⊗	9523 R ✗	R 🍸 A		R 🍸 ⊗		R 🍸 ⊗✣	R ✗ ↗		🍸	R 🍸 ⊗	R ✗ ↗	🍸 ⊗✣		R 🍸 ⊗✣	R ✗ ↗		R 🍸 ⊗✣	R ✗ ↗		R 🍸 ⊗	R 🍸 ↗	9551 R ✗	R 🍸 ↗
Genève Aéroport ✈ d.	...	...	...	...	0553	...	...	...	...	...	...	...	...	...	...	...	...	...	...	...	1153	...	...	...	...
Genève d.	...	0542	...	...	0603	...	...	...	...	...	...	0742	...	...	...	...	...	...	...	...	1203	...	...	...	...
Lausanne d.	...	0617	...	...	0646	...	...	...	...	...	...	0818	...	...	...	...	...	...	...	...	1246	...	...	...	...
Montreux d.	...	0635	...	...	0706	...	...	...	...	...	...	0836	...	...	...	...	...	...	...	...	1306	...	...	...	...
Aigle d.	...	|	...	...	0717	...	...	...	...	...	...	|	...	...	...	...	...	...	...	...	1317	...	...	...	...
Martigny d.	...	|	...	...	0739	...	...	...	...	...	...	|	...	...	...	...	...	...	...	...	1339	...	...	...	...
Sion d.	...	0713	...	...	0755	...	...	...	...	...	...	0913	...	...	...	...	...	...	...	...	1355	...	...	...	...
Zürich HB d.	...	|	...	...	|	...	...	0732	...	...	...	|	...	...	...	0932	...	...	1132	...	|	...	...	...	...
Basel SBB d.	...	|	...	...	|	0631	0604	|	...	0659	...	|	...	...	0804	|	...	1004	|	...	|	1231	...	...	...
Olten d.	...	|	...	...	|	0659	0630	|	...	0729	...	|	...	...	0830	|	...	1030	|	...	|	1259	...	...	...
Bern d.	0607	|	...	...	|	0734	|	|	...	0756	0807	|	...	...	|	|	...	|	|	...	|	1334	...	...	...
Spiez d.	0636	|	...	...	|	0805	|	|	...	...	0836	|	...	...	|	|	...	|	|	...	|	1405	...	...	...
Luzern d.	|	|	...	...	|	|	0718	|	...	...	|	|	...	0847	0918	|	...	1118	|	...	|	|	...	...	...
Arth-Goldau d.	|	|	...	...	|	|	0744	0817	...	...	|	|	...	0916	0944	1017	...	1144	1217	...	|	|	...	...	...
Bellinzona d.	|	|	...	...	|	|	...	0959	...	...	|	|	...	1059	...	1159	...	...	1359	...	|	|	...	...	...
Lugano d.	|	|	...	...	|	|	...	1026	...	...	|	|	...	1126	...	1226	...	...	1426	...	|	|	...	...	...
Chiasso 🏛 d.	|	|	...	...	|	|	...	1052	...	...	|	|	...	1211	...	1252	...	...	1452	...	|	|	...	...	...
Como San Giovanni a.	|	|	...	...	|	|	...	1026	...	...	|	|	...	1215	...	|	...	...	1456	...	|	|	...	...	...
Visp d.	0703	|	...	...	0825	0832	...	|	...	...	0903	|	...	|	...	|	...	...	|	...	1425	1432	...	...	...
Brig d.	0711	0744	...	...	0832	0844	...	|	...	...	0911	0944	...	|	...	|	...	...	|	...	1432	1444	...	...	...
Domodossola 🏛 ¶ a.	...	|	...	...	...	|	...	|	...	...	...	|	...	|	...	|	...	...	|	...	...	|	...	...	...
Stresa a.	...	0838	...	...	...	0938	...	|	...	...	...	|	...	|	...	|	...	...	|	...	...	1538	...	...	...
Gallarate a.	...	|	...	...	...	|	...	|	...	...	...	1103	...	|	...	|	...	...	|	...	...	|	...	...	...
Milano Centrale a.	...	0935	...	...	...	1035	...	1035	...	...	...	1135	...	1250	...	1335	...	...	1535	...	...	1635	...	...	...
train type		FR						FR						FR		FB			FB						
train number		**9619**						**9525**						**9533**		**9725**			**9733**						
notes		✗↗ R C						✗↗ R						✗↗ R		R 🍸 ↗			R 🍸 ↗						
Milano Centrale d.	...	1000	1015	1035	...	...	...	1115	1135	...	...	1205	1215	1315	...	1405	1415	...	1605	1615	...	...	1705	1715	1735
Verona Porta Nuova a.	...	|	|	1157	...	...	...	|	1257	...	...	1327	|	|	...	1527	|	...	1727	|	...	...	1827	|	1857
Venezia Mestre a.	...	|	|	1258	...	...	...	|	1358	...	...	1428	|	|	...	1628	|	...	1828	|	...	...	1928	|	1958
Venezia Santa Lucia a.	...	|	|	1310	...	...	...	|	1410	...	...	1440	|	|	...	1640	|	...	1840	|	...	...	...	|	2010
Bologna Centrale a.	...	|	1115	...	...	...	...	1215	...	...	...	...	1315	1415	...	...	1515	...	...	1715	...	...	...	1815	...
Firenze SMN a.	...	|	1155	...	...	...	...	1255	...	...	...	...	1355	1455	...	...	1555	...	...	1755	...	...	...	1855	...
Roma Termini a.	...	1255	1335	...	...	...	...	1435	...	...	...	...	1535	1635	...	...	1735	...	...	1935	...	...	...	2035	...
Napoli Centrale a.	...	1415	1455	...	...	...	...	1555	...	...	...	...	1655	1755	...	...	1855	...	...	2055	...	...	...	2155	...

train type	EC	IR	EC	FR↗	FB	FR	IR	EC	FB	FR↗	IR	EC	IR	EC		ICE	IC	EC	ICN	IR	EC
train number	**39**	**2173**	**319**	**9651**	**9741**	**9553**	**2177**	**321**	**9745**	**9559**	**2181**	**323**	**1427**	**59**	**2117**	**277**	**836**	**41**	**1911**	**2185**	**325**
notes	R 🍸 ⊗		R ✗ ⊗✣	R ✗ Ⓑ f	R 🍸 ↗	R ✗ ↗		R ✗ ⊗✣	R 🍸	R ✗ Ⓑ f		R ✗ ⊗✣		R 🍸 ⊗			🍸	R 🍸 ⊗	R ↗ K		R ✗ ⊗✣
Genève Aéroport ✈ d.	...	...	...	...	...	...	...	...	...	...	...	...	1653	...	...	...	...	...	...	...	...
Genève d.	1342	...	...	...	...	...	...	...	...	...	...	...	1703	...	...	...	...	1842	...	...	...
Lausanne d.	1418	...	...	...	...	...	...	...	...	...	...	...	1746	...	...	...	...	1918	...	...	...
Montreux d.	1436	...	...	...	...	...	...	...	...	...	...	...	1806	...	...	...	...	1936	...	...	...
Aigle d.	|	...	...	...	...	...	...	...	...	...	...	...	1817	...	...	...	...	|	...	...	...
Martigny d.	|	...	...	...	...	...	...	...	...	...	...	...	1839	...	...	...	...	|	...	...	...
Sion d.	1513	...	...	...	...	...	...	...	...	...	...	...	1855	...	...	...	...	2013	...	...	...
Zürich HB d.	|	...	1332	...	...	...	...	1532	...	...	...	1732	|	...	...	...	1802	|	...	...	1932
Basel SBB d.	|	1204	|	...	...	...	1404	|	...	...	1604	|	|	1731	...	1759	|	|	...	1804	|
Olten d.	|	1230	|	...	...	...	1430	|	...	...	1630	|	|	1759	...	1829	|	|	...	1830	|
Bern d.	|	|	|	...	...	...	|	|	...	...	|	|	|	1834	...	1856	1907	|	...	|	|
Spiez d.	|	|	|	...	...	...	|	|	...	...	|	|	|	1905	...	...	1936	|	...	|	|
Luzern d.	|	1318	|	...	...	...	1518	|	...	...	1718	|	|	|	...	...	|	|	...	1918	|
Arth-Goldau d.	|	1344	1417	...	...	...	1544	1617	...	...	1744	1817	|	|	...	...	|	|	...	1944	2017
Bellinzona d.	|	...	1559	...	...	...	...	1759	...	...	...	1959	|	|	...	...	|	|	...	...	2159
Lugano d.	|	...	1626	...	...	...	...	1826	...	...	...	2026	|	|	...	...	|	|	...	...	2226
Chiasso 🏛 d.	|	...	1652	...	...	...	...	1852	...	...	...	2052	|	|	...	...	|	|	...	...	2252
Como San Giovanni a.	|	...	|	...	...	...	...	|	...	...	...	2056	|	|	...	...	|	|	...	...	2256
Visp d.	|	...	|	...	...	...	...	|	...	...	...	|	1925	1932	...	...	2003	|	...	...	|
Brig d.	1544	...	|	...	...	...	...	|	...	...	...	|	1932	1944	...	...	2011	2044	...	...	|
Domodossola 🏛 ¶ a.	|	...	|	...	...	...	...	|	...	...	...	|	...	|	...	...	...	|	...	...	|
Stresa a.	1638	...	|	...	...	...	...	|	...	...	...	|	...	|	...	...	...	2138	...	...	|
Gallarate a.	|	...	|	...	...	...	...	|	...	...	...	|	...	2103	...	...	...	|	...	...	|
Milano Centrale a.	1735	...	1735	...	...	...	...	1935	...	...	...	2135	...	2135	...	...	...	2235	...	...	2335
Milano Centrale d.	...	...	...	1800	1805	1815	...	...	1905	2015	...	...	...	...	2225	...	...	...	2317	...	...
Verona Porta Nuova a.	...	...	...	|	1927	|	...	...	2027	|	...	...	...	...	0020	...	...	...	|	...	...
Venezia Mestre a.	...	...	...	|	2028	|	...	...	2128	|	...	...	...	...	...	...	...	...	|	...	...
Venezia Santa Lucia a.	...	...	...	|	...	|	...	...	2140	|	...	...	...	...	...	...	...	...	|	...	...
Bologna Centrale a.	...	...	...	|	...	1915	...	...	...	2115	...	...	...	...	...	...	...	...	|	...	...
Firenze SMN a.	...	...	...	|	...	1955	...	...	...	2155	...	...	...	...	...	...	...	...	|	...	...
Roma Termini a.	...	...	...	2055	...	2135	...	...	...	2335	...	...	...	...	...	...	...	...	0717t	...	...
Napoli Centrale a.	...	...	...	2215	...	2255	...	...	...	...	...	...	...	...	...	...	...	...	0930	...	...

A – ⑥⑦ (also Aug. 15, Dec. 8).
C – ①–⑤ (not Aug. 15, Dec. 8).
K – 🛏 1, 2 cl. (Excelsior), 🛏 1, 2 cl. (T2), 🛏 1, 2 cl., 🛌 2 cl. (4, 6 berth), (12) Milano - Napoli - Salerno.

t – Roma **Tiburtina**.
↗ – Supplement payable.
¶ – Ticket point is **Iselle**.

⊗ – **ETR 470 / 610.** Compulsory reservation for international journeys. Supplement payable for international journeys and for internal journeys within Italy.
✣ – May not be an **ETR 470 / 610** tilting train. If not, then expected to run up to 45 minutes late.

f – Not Aug. 15, Dec. 8.

82 ROMA, VENEZIA and MILANO - ZÜRICH, BASEL and GENÈVE

train type	E	IR			IR	EC	IC	IC	FR ⚡	FR ⚡	FB	EC	IR	FB	FR	FR	EC	IR	FB	FR	FR ⚡	IC	ICE	EC	IR
train number	1910	1420	2710		2176	32	823	968	9504	9606	9790	314	2178	9708	9508	9610	52	1428	9712	9512	9614	831	376	316	2182
notes	K					[R] 🍷	🍷	🍷	[R] ✕	[R] ✕	[R] ✕	[R] ✕		[R] ✕	[R] ✕	[R] ✕	[R] 🍷		[R] ✕	[R] ✕	[R] ✕	🍷	🍷	[R] ✕	
						⊗			C		⚡	⊗ ❖		A ⚡	⚡	A ⚡	⊗		⚡	⚡				⊗ ❖	
Napoli Centrale d.	2130	...	...	...	...	...	...	...	...	...	...	...	...	...	...	0640	...	...	...	0700	0740	...	...	...	...
Roma Termini d.	2344t	...	...	...	...	...	...	...	0620	0700	...	...	...	...	0720	0800	...	...	...	0820	0900	...	...	...	...
Firenze SMN d.	│	...	...	...	...	...	...	...	0800	│	...	...	...	...	0900	│	...	...	...	1000	│	...	...	...	...
Bologna Centrale d.	│	...	...	0522	...	...	...	...	0838	│	...	...	...	...	0938	│	...	...	...	1038	│	...	...	...	...
Venezia Santa Lucia d.	│	...	...	│	...	...	...	...	│	│	...	...	...	0750	│	│	...	...	0850	│	│	...	...	...	...
Venezia Mestre d.	│	...	...	│	...	...	...	...	│	│	0740	...	...	0802	│	│	...	...	0902	│	│	...	...	...	...
Verona Porta Nuova d.	│	...	0540	│	...	...	...	...	│	│	0845	...	...	0902	│	│	...	...	1002	│	│	...	...	...	...
Milano Centrale a.	0655	...	0736	0800	...	...	...	...	0940	0959	1000	...	...	1025	1040	1055	...	...	1125	1140	1155	...	...	...	...
	EC 50 [R] 🍷 ⊗			EC 312 [R] ✕ ⊗ ❖																	EC 34 [R] 🍷 ⊗				
Milano Centrale d.	0725	...	...	0825	...	0825	...	...	...	...	...	1025	...	...	...	...	1125	...	...	...	1225	...	...	1225	...
Gallarate d.	0756	...	...	│	...	│	...	...	...	...	...	│	...	...	...	...	│	...	...	...	│	...	...	│	...
Stresa d.	│	...	...	│	...	0921	...	...	...	...	...	│	...	...	...	...	1221	...	...	...	1321	...	...	│	...
Domodossola 🏛 ¶ d.	│	...	...	│	...	│	...	...	...	...	...	│	...	...	...	...	│	...	...	...	│	...	...	│	...
Brig a.	0916	0928	...	│	...	1016	1049	...	...	...	...	│	...	...	...	...	1316	1328	...	...	1416	1449	...	│	...
Visp a.	0926	0934	...	│	...	│	1055	...	...	...	...	│	...	...	...	...	1326	1334	...	...	│	1455	...	│	...
Como San Giovanni d.	│	│	...	0903	...	│	│	...	...	...	...	1103	...	...	...	...	│	│	...	...	│	│	...	│	...
Chiasso 🏛 a.	│	│	...	0908	...	│	│	...	...	...	...	1108	...	...	...	...	│	│	...	...	│	│	...	1308	...
Lugano a.	│	│	...	0932	...	│	│	...	...	...	...	1132	...	...	...	...	│	│	...	...	│	│	...	1332	...
Bellinzona a.	│	│	...	0959	...	│	│	...	...	...	...	1159	...	...	...	...	│	│	...	...	│	│	...	1359	...
Arth-Goldau a.	│	│	...	1143	1214	│	│	...	...	...	...	1343	1414	...	...	...	│	│	...	...	│	│	...	1543	1614
Luzern a.	│	│	...	│	1241	│	│	...	...	...	...	│	1441	...	...	...	│	│	...	...	│	│	...	│	1641
Spiez a.	0953	│	...	│	│	│	1124	...	...	...	...	│	│	...	...	...	1353	│	...	...	│	1524	...	│	│
Bern a.	1023	│	...	│	│	│	1154	1204	...	...	...	│	│	...	...	...	1423	│	...	...	│	1554	1604	│	│
Olten a.	1100	│	...	│	1327	│	...	1230	...	...	...	│	1527	...	...	...	1500	│	...	...	│	...	1630	│	1727
Basel SBB a.	1129	│	...	│	1355	│	...	1259	...	...	...	│	1555	...	...	...	1529	│	...	...	│	...	1659	│	1755
Zürich HB a.	...	│	...	1228	...	│	...	...	...	...	...	1428	...	...	...	...	...	│	...	...	│	...	...	1628	...
Sion a.	...	1004	...	...	...	1046	...	...	...	...	...	...	...	...	...	...	...	1404	...	...	1446	...	...	...	...
Martigny a.	...	1019	...	...	...	│	...	...	...	...	...	...	...	...	...	...	...	1419	...	...	│	...	...	...	...
Aigle a.	...	1041	...	...	...	│	...	...	...	...	...	...	...	...	...	...	...	1441	...	...	│	...	...	...	...
Montreux a.	...	1052	...	...	...	1124	...	...	...	...	...	...	...	...	...	...	...	1452	...	...	1524	...	...	...	...
Lausanne a.	...	1114	...	...	...	1142	...	...	...	...	...	...	...	...	...	...	...	1514	...	...	1542	...	...	...	...
Genève a.	...	1157	...	...	...	1218	...	...	...	...	...	...	...	...	...	...	...	1557	...	...	1618	...	...	...	...
Genève Aéroport + a.	...	1207	...	...	...	...	...	...	...	...	...	...	...	...	...	...	...	1607	...	...	...	...	...	...	...

train type/number	FB	FR	IR	FR	EC	FR	FB	IR	FR	FB	EC	IC	FR	FB	FR ⚡	IR	IR	EC	FR	FR ⚡	EC	IC	FR	FB	EC
train number	9714	9520	2184	9524	258	9528	9726	2188	9532	9728	36	1090	9536	9732	9638	1442	2540	322	9540	9642	42	1092	9544	9740	324
notes	[R] ✕	[R] ✕		[R] ✕	[R] 🍷	[R] ✕	[R] ✕		[R] ✕	[R] ✕	[R] 🍷		[R] ✕	[R] ✕	[R] ✕			[R] ✕	[R] ✕	[R] ✕	[R] 🍷		[R] ✕	[R] ✕	[R] ✕
	⚡	⚡		⚡	⊗ ❖	⚡	⚡		⚡	⚡	⊗		⚡	⚡				⊗ ❖	⚡	G	⊗		⚡	⚡	⊗ ❖
Napoli Centrale d.	...	0900	...	1000	...	1100	...	...	1200	...	...	...	1300	...	...	...	...	...	1400	1440	...	...	1500	...	...
Roma Termini d.	...	1020	...	1120	...	1220	...	...	1320	...	...	...	1420	...	1500	...	...	...	1520	1600	...	...	1620	...	...
Firenze SMN d.	...	1200	...	1300	...	1400	...	...	1500	...	...	...	1600	...	│	...	...	...	1700	│	...	...	1800	...	...
Bologna Centrale d.	...	1238	...	1338	...	1438	...	...	1538	...	...	...	1638	...	│	...	...	...	1738	│	...	...	1838	...	...
Venezia Santa Lucia d.	1050	│	...	│	...	│	1320	...	│	1420	...	...	│	1520	│	...	...	...	│	│	1620	...	│	1720	...
Venezia Mestre d.	1102	│	...	│	...	│	1332	...	│	1432	...	...	│	1532	│	...	...	...	│	│	1632	...	│	1732	...
Verona Porta Nuova d.	1202	│	...	│	...	│	1432	...	│	1532	...	...	│	1632	│	...	...	...	│	│	1732	...	│	1832	...
Milano Centrale a.	1325	1340	...	1440	...	1540	1555	...	1640	1655	...	...	1740	1755	1755	...	...	...	1840	1855	1855	...	1940	1955	...
		EC 318 [R] ✕ ⊗ ❖					EC 320 [R] 🍷 ⊗ ❖								EC 56 [R] 🍷 ⊗						│				
Milano Centrale d.	...	1425	...	...	1510	...	1625	...	...	...	1725	...	...	...	1825	...	...	1825	...	...	1925	...	...	...	2025
Gallarate d.	...	│	...	...	│	...	│	...	...	...	│	...	...	...	│	...	...	│	...	...	1958	...	...	...	│
Stresa d.	...	│	...	...	│	...	│	...	...	...	1821	...	...	...	1921	...	...	│	...	...	│	...	...	...	│
Domodossola 🏛 ¶ d.	...	│	...	...	│	...	│	...	...	...	1848	...	...	...	│	...	...	│	...	...	│	...	...	...	│
Brig a.	...	│	...	...	│	...	│	...	...	...	1916	1920	...	...	2016	2028	...	│	...	...	2116	2120	...	...	│
Visp a.	...	│	...	...	│	...	│	...	...	...	│	1926	...	...	2026	2034	...	│	...	...	│	2126	...	...	│
Como San Giovanni d.	...	│	...	...	1544	...	│	...	...	...	│	│	...	...	│	│	...	│	...	...	│	│	...	...	2103
Chiasso 🏛 a.	...	1508	...	...	1549	...	1708	...	...	...	│	│	...	...	│	│	...	1908	...	...	│	│	...	...	2108
Lugano a.	...	1532	...	...	1632	...	1732	...	...	...	│	│	...	...	│	│	...	1932	IR	...	│	│	...	...	2132
Bellinzona a.	...	1559	...	...	1659	...	1759	...	...	...	│	│	...	...	│	│	...	1959	**2192**	...	│	│	...	...	2159
Arth-Goldau a.	...	1743	1814	...	1843	...	1943	2014	...	...	│	│	...	...	│	│	...	2143	2214	...	│	│	...	...	2343
Luzern a.	...	│	1841	...	1913	...	│	2041	...	...	│	│	...	...	│	│	...	│	2241	...	│	│	...	...	│
Spiez a.	...	│	│	...	...	...	│	│	...	...	│	1953	...	...	2053	│	...	│	│	...	│	2153	...	...	│
Bern a.	...	│	│	...	...	...	│	│	...	...	│	2023	...	...	2123	│	...	│	│	...	│	2223	...	...	│
Olten a.	...	│	1928	...	...	...	│	2128	...	...	│	2100	...	...	2200	│	...	│	2327	...	│	...	...	...	│
Basel SBB a.	...	│	1955	...	...	...	│	2155	...	...	│	2129	...	...	2229	│	...	│	2359	...	│	...	...	...	│
Zürich HB a.	...	1828	...	...	...	...	2028	...	...	...	│	...	...	...	...	│	...	2228	...	...	│	...	...	...	0028
Sion a.	...	...	...	...	...	...	...	...	...	...	1948	...	...	...	...	2104	...	...	...	...	2148	...	...	...	...
Martigny a.	...	...	...	...	...	...	...	...	...	...	│	...	...	...	...	2119	...	...	...	...	│	...	...	...	...
Aigle a.	...	...	...	...	...	...	...	...	...	...	│	...	...	...	...	2141	...	...	...	...	│	...	...	...	...
Montreux a.	...	...	...	...	...	...	...	...	...	...	2024	...	...	...	...	2152	...	...	...	...	2224	...	...	...	...
Lausanne a.	...	...	...	...	...	...	...	...	...	...	2042	...	...	...	...	2214	2221	...	...	...	2242	...	...	...	...
Genève a.	...	...	...	...	...	...	...	...	...	...	2118	...	...	...	...	...	2305	...	...	...	2318	...	...	...	...
Genève Aéroport + a.	...	...	...	...	...	...	...	...	...	...	...	...	...	...	...	...	...	...	...	...	...	...	...	...	...

A – ①–⑤ (not Aug. 14, Dec. 8).

C – ①–⑥ (not Aug. 14, Dec. 8).

G – ⑧ (not Aug. 15, Dec. 8).

K – 🛏 1, 2 cl. (Excelsior), 🛏 1, 2 cl. (T2), 🛏 1, 2 cl., ▬ 2 cl. (4 berth), (12) Salerno - Napoli - Milano.

f – Not Aug. 15, Dec. 8.

q – Venezia **Mestre**.

t – Roma **Tiburtina**.

⚡ – Supplement payable.

¶ – Ticket point is **Iselle**.

⊗ – **ETR 470 / 610**. Compulsory reservation for international journeys. Supplement payable for international journeys and for internal journeys within Italy.

❖ – May not be an **ETR 470 / 610** tilting train. If not, then expected to run up to 45 minutes late.

ZÜRICH - INNSBRUCK - WIEN, GRAZ, ZAGREB and BUDAPEST 86

train type/number	RJ	RJ	IC	EC	IC	RJ	IC	EC	EC	RJ	EC	EC	RJ	EN	EC	D	IC	RJ	EC	RJ	EC	RJ	RJ	EN	EN	EN
train number	**49**	**663**	**515**	**111**	**211**	**161**	**690**	**217**	**163**	**563**	**113**	**113**	**165**	**347**	**115**	**315**	**611**	**167**	**219**	**169**	**117**	**363**	**365**	**465**	**465**	**467**
notes	🍷	🍷	🍷			🍷	🍷	🍷			✕	**213**		**D**	✕			🍷		🍷	**1217** ✕	🍷	🍷	**Z**	**415** **A**	**W**
Zürich HB d.	...	...	...	...	...	0640	...	...	0840	...	...	...	1040	...	...	...	...	1240	...	1440	...	1640	1840	2040	2040	2240
Sargans d.	...	...	...	...	...	0737	...	...	0937	...	...	...	1137	...	...	...	...	1337	...	1537	...	1737	1937	2137	2137	2337
Buchs 🏛 d.	...	...	...	...	...	0754	...	...	0959	...	...	...	1154	...	...	...	...	1354	...	1554	...	1759	1954	2208	2208	2358
Bregenz d.	...	0547	...	...	...	|	...	...	|	...	...	...	|	...	...	...	...	|	...	|	...	|	|	|	|	|
Feldkirch d.	...	0615	...	...	...	0828	...	...	1016	...	...	...	1215	...	...	...	...	1415	...	1615	...	1816	2015	2242	2242	0016
Bludenz d.	...	0628	...	...	...	0828	...	...	1029	...	...	...	1228	...	...	...	...	1428	...	1628	...	1829	2028	2258	2258	0032
Langen am Arlberg d.	...	0654	...	...	...	0854	...	...	1055	...	...	...	1254	...	...	...	...	1454	...	|	...	|	2054	2331	2331	|
St Anton am Arlberg d.	...	0705	...	...	...	0905	...	...	1105	...	...	...	1305	...	...	...	...	1505	...	1701	...	1905	2105	2341	2341	|
Landeck-Zams d.	...	0729	...	...	...	0929	...	...	1129	...	...	...	1329	...	...	...	...	1529	...	1725	...	1929	2129	0009	0009	|
Ötztal d.	...	0753	...	...	...	0953	...	...	1153	...	...	...	1353	...	...	...	...	1553	...	1753	...	1953	2153	|	|	|
Innsbruck Hbf d.	0505**x**	0820	0824	...	...	1022	...	...	1224**e**	1220	...	...	1420	...	...	...	...	1622	...	1822	...	2022	2216	0056	0056	0221
Jenbach d.	0524**x**	|	0846	...	...	|	...	...	1245	|	...	...	|	...	...	...	...	|	...	|	...	|	...	0119	0119	|
Wörgl d.	0538**x**	|	0902	...	...	|	...	...	1302	|	...	...	|	...	...	...	...	|	...	|	...	|	...	0138	0138	|
Kitzbühel d.	|	|	0932	...	...	|	...	...	1332	|	...	...	|	...	...	...	...	|	...	|	...	|	...	|	|	|
St Johann in Tirol d.	|	|	0940	...	...	|	...	...	1340	|	...	...	|	...	...	...	...	|	...	|	...	|	...	|	|	|
Saalfelden d.	|	|	1008	...	...	|	...	...	1408	|	...	...	|	...	...	...	...	|	...	|	...	|	...	|	|	|
Zell am See d.	|	|	1019	...	...	|	...	...	1419	|	...	...	|	...	...	...	...	|	...	|	...	|	...	|	|	|
Schwarzach St Veit d.	|	|	|	...	...	|	...	...	|	|	...	...	|	...	...	...	...	|	...	|	...	|	...	0324	0427	|
Salzburg Hbf d.	0708**x**	1008	|	1012	...	1208	1212	1215	|	1408	...	...	1608	...	1612	...	1615	1808	1815	2008	2012	2208	...	|	|	0434
Bischofshofen a.	|	|	|	1052	...	|	1252	1302	|	|	...	...	|	...	1652	...	1702	|	1902	|	2052	|	...	0336	|	|
Schwarzach St Veit a.	|	|	1048	1109	...	|	1309	|	1448	|	1511	1511	|	...	1709	...	|	|	|	|	2109	|	...	|	|	|
Selzthal a.	|	|	1240	|	...	|	|	1440	1640	|	|	|	|	...	|	...	1840	|	2040	|	|	|	...	0504	|	|
Graz Hbf a.	|	|	1414	|	...	|	|	1614	1814	|	|	|	|	...	|	...	2014	|	2214	|	|	|	...	0700	|	|
Villach Hbf a.	|	|	▬	1243	1253	|	1443	...	...	|	1643	1643	|	...	1843	1853	...	|	...	|	2243	|	...	...	0605	|
Klagenfurt a.	|	|	...	1315	|	|	▬	...	...	|	1718	|	|	...	1915	|	...	|	...	|	2317	|	...	...	|	|
Jesenice 🏛 a.	|	|	...	...	1333	|	...	...	...	|	▬	1733	|	...	...	1933	...	|	...	|	...	|	...	...	0705	|
Ljubljana ⊙ a.	|	|	...	...	1431	|	...	...	...	|	...	1831	|	...	...	2040	...	|	...	|	...	|	...	...	0811	|
Zagreb ⊙ a.	|	|	...	...	1713	|	...	...	...	|	...	2053	|	...	...	...	...	|	...	|	...	|	...	...	1044	|
Vinkovci ⊕ a.	|	|	...	...	2103	|	...	...	...	|	...	...	|	...	...	...	...	|	...	|	...	|	...	...	1445	|
Beograd ⊕ a.	|	|	...	...	...	|	...	...	...	|		...	|	...	...	...	...	|	...	|	...	|	...	...	1732	|
Linz Hbf a.	0813**x**	1113	...	...	...	1313	...	...	...	1513	...	...	1715	...	...	...	...	1913	...	2113	...	2313	...	...	...	0607
St Pölten a.	0903**x**	1203	*RJ*	...	...	1403	*RJ*	...	...	1603	*RJ*	...	1805	...	...	...	...	2003	...	2203	...	0003	...	...	...	0702
Wien Westbahnhof a.	0930**x**	1230	**63**	...	...	1430	**65**	...	...	1630	**67**	...	1830	...	...	...	...	2030	...	2230	...	0030	...	...	...	0734
Wien Westbahnhof d.	0948	...	1348	...	...	...	1548	...	...	...	1748	...	1848	1948	...	...	...	...	...	...	...	...	...	...	...	0756
Hegyeshalom 🏛 a.	1055	...	1455	...	...	...	1655	...	...	...	1855	...	1955	2055	...	...	...	...	...	...	...	...	...	...	...	0855
Györ a.	1121	...	1521	...	...	...	1721	...	...	...	1921	...	2024	2121	...	...	...	...	...	...	...	...	...	...	...	0921
Budapest Keleti a.	1249	...	1649	...	...	...	1849	...	...	...	2049	...	2154	2249	...	...	...	...	...	...	...	...	...	...	...	1049

train type/number	RJ	RJ	EC	IC	RJ	IC	EN	EC	RJ	EC	RJ	RJ	EC	EC	RJ	RJ	RJ	IC	RJ	IC	EC	RJ	RJ	EN	EN	EN
train number	**362**	**364**	**218**	**693**	**160**	**512**	**346**	**114**	**162**	**212**	**60**	**862**	**164**	**216**	**62**	**166**	**64**	**518**	**168**	**610**	**210**	**66**	**662**	**466**	**414**	**464**
notes	🍷	🍷	🍷	🍷	🍷	🍷	🅁 **D**	✕	🍷	**112**	🍷	🍷	🍷	🍷	🍷	🍷	🍷	🍷	🍷	🍷		🍷	🍷	**W**	**464** **A**	**Z**
Budapest Keleti d.	...	...	...	...	...	...	0510	...	0605	...	0710	...	...	...	0910	...	1110	...	...	...	...	1310	...	1910	...	...
Györ d.	...	...	...	...	...	...	0632	...	0729	...	0832	...	...	...	1032	...	1232	...	...	...	...	1432	...	2032	...	...
Hegyeshalom 🏛 d.	...	...	...	...	...	...	0702	...	0802	...	0902	...	...	...	1102	...	1302	...	...	...	...	1502	...	2102	...	...
Wien Westbahnhof a.	...	...	...	...	...	...	0816	...	0912	...	1012	...	...	...	1212	...	1412	...	...	...	...	1612	...	2216	...	...
Wien Westbahnhof d.	...	0530**x**	...	...	0730	...	▬	...	0930	...	▬	1030	...	...	▬	1330	...	...	1530	...	...	▬	1730	2240	...	...
St Pölten d.	...	0556**x**	...	...	0756	...	...	...	0954	...	...	1056	...	...	...	1356	...	...	1556	...	...	...	1756	2307	...	...
Linz Hbf d.	...	0647**x**	...	...	0847	...	...	...	1045	...	...	1147	...	...	...	1447	...	...	1647	...	...	...	1847	0002	...	...
Beograd ⊕ d.	...	|	...	...	|	...	...	...	|	...	...	|	...	...	...	|	...	...	|	...	...	...	|	|	1100	...
Vinkovci ⊕ d.	...	|	...	...	|	...	*D*	...	|	...	...	|	...	...	...	|	...	...	|	...	0901	...	|	|	1441	...
Zagreb ⊙ d.	...	|	...	...	|	...	**314**	...	|	0650	*EC*	|	...	...	...	|	...	...	|	...	1235	*EC*	|	|	1837	...
Ljubljana ⊙ d.	...	|	...	...	|	...	0727	...	|	0922	**112**	|	...	...	*IC*	|	...	...	|	...	1525	**110**	|	|	2110	...
Jesenice 🏛 d.	...	|	...	...	|	...	0827	...	|	1017	✕	|	...	...	**691**	|	...	...	|	...	1627	🍷	|	|	2205	...
Klagenfurt d.	...	|	...	0645	|	...	|	0842	|	|	1027	|	...	...	1245	|	...	...	|	...	|	1642	|	|	|	...
Villach Hbf d.	...	|	...	0716	|	...	0908	0916	|	1116	1116	|	...	...	1316	|	...	...	|	...	1709	1716	|	|	2316	...
Graz Hbf d.	...	|	0545	|	|	0745	...	|	|	|	|	|	0945	1145	|	|	...	1345	|	1545	...	|	|	|	|	2224
Selzthal d.	...	|	0719	|	|	0919	...	|	|	|	|	|	1119	1319	|	|	...	1519	|	1719	...	|	|	|	|	0029
Schwarzach St Veit d.	...	|	|	0850	|	|	...	1050	|	1218	1218	|	1312	|	1450	|	...	|	|	|	...	1850	|	|	|	|
Bischofshofen d.	...	|	0857	0905	|	1057	...	1105	|	...	...	|	|	1457	1505	|	...	1650	|	1857	...	1905	|	|	|	0158
Salzburg Hbf d.	...	0756	0944	0948	0956	1144	...	1148	1156	...	...	1300	|	1544	1548	1556	...	|	1756	1944	...	1948	1956	0140	|	|
Schwarzach St Veit d.	...	|	...	...	|	...	...	...	|	...	...	|	|	...	...	|	...	1712	|	...	...	...	|	|	0226	0226
Zell am See d.	...	|	...	...	|	...	...	...	|	...	...	|	1343	...	...	|	...	1743	|	...	...	...	|	|	|	|
Saalfelden d.	...	|	...	...	|	...	...	...	|	...	...	|	1352	...	...	|	...	1752	|	...	...	...	|	|	|	|
St Johann in Tirol d.	...	|	...	...	|	...	...	...	|	...	...	|	1420	...	...	|	...	1820	|	...	...	...	|	|	|	|
Kitzbühel d.	...	|	...	...	|	...	...	...	|	...	...	|	1428	...	...	|	...	1828	|	...	...	...	|	|	|	|
Wörgl d.	...	|	...	...	|	...	...	...	|	...	...	1423	1500	...	...	|	...	1900	|	...	...	...	|	|	|	|
Jenbach d.	...	|	...	...	|	...	...	...	|	...	...	1438	1516	...	...	|	...	1916	|	...	...	...	|	|	|	|
Innsbruck Hbf d.	0740	0944	...	...	1144	...	...	...	1344	...	...	1454	1543	...	...	1744	...	1936	1944	...	...	...	2144	0340	0453	0453
Ötztal d.	0804	1008	...	...	1208	...	...	...	1406	...	...	...	1607	...	...	1808	...	...	2008	...	...	...	2208	|	|	|
Landeck-Zams d.	0828	1034	...	...	1232	...	...	...	1430	...	...	...	1630	...	...	1832	...	...	2032	...	...	...	2232	|	0545	0545
St Anton am Arlberg d.	0852	1058	...	...	1256	...	...	...	1454	...	...	...	1654	...	...	1856	...	...	2056	...	...	...	2256	|	0610	0610
Langen am Arlberg d.	0902	1108	...	...	1306	...	...	...	1504	...	...	...	1704	...	...	1906	...	...	2106	...	...	...	2306	|	0620	0620
Bludenz d.	0930	1135	...	...	1333	...	...	...	1531	...	...	...	1731	...	...	1933	...	...	2133	...	...	...	2333	0523	0706	0706
Feldkirch d.	0943	1148	...	...	1348	...	...	...	1544	...	...	...	1744	...	...	1948	...	...	2151	...	...	...	2347	0540	0738	0738
Bregenz a.	|	|	...	...	|	...	...	...	|	...	...	...	|	...	...	|	...	...	|	...	...	...	0010	|	|	|
Buchs 🏛 a.	0958	1206	...	...	1406	...	...	...	1606	...	...	...	1758	...	...	2006	...	...	2206	...	...	...	...	0601	0753	0753
Sargans a.	1023	1223	...	...	1423	...	...	...	1623	...	...	...	1823	...	...	2023	...	...	2223	...	...	...	...	0620	0823	0823
Zürich HB a.	1120	1320	...	...	1520	...	...	...	1720	...	...	...	1920	...	...	2120	...	...	2320	...	...	...	...	0720	0920	0920

A – ALPINE PEARLS – 🛏 1, 2 cl., 🛌 2 cl. Zürich - Zagreb and v.v. [2] Zürich - Beograd and v.v. [12] Villach - Beograd and v.v.

D – DACIA – 🛏 1, 2 cl., 🛌 2 cl., [2] ✕ Wien - Budapest - Bucuresti and v.v.

W – WIENER WALZER – 🛏 1, 2 cl., 🛌 2 cl., [2] Zürich - Wien - Budapest and v.v. 🛏 1, 2 cl., 🛌 2 cl., [2] Zürich - Wien and v.v. [12] ✕ Wien - Budapest and v.v. Special fares payable.

Z – ZÜRICHSEE – 🛏 1,2 cl., 🛌 2 cl., [2] Zürich - Graz and v.v.

e – Arrive 1216.

x – ①–⑥ (not Apr. 21, June 9).

RJ – ÖBB *Railjet* service. [1] (business class), [1] (first class), [2] (economy class), ✕.

⊙ – 🏛 between Ljubljana and Zagreb is Dobova.

⊕ – 🏛 between Vinkovci and Beograd is Šid.

◧ – 🏛 is St Margrethen (Table **75**).

OTHER TRAIN NAMES: *EC* **211/212** – SAVA *EC* **960** – LISZT FERENC / FRANZ LISZT *EC* **962** – SEMMELWEIS IGNAC / IGNAZ SEMMELWEIS *EC* **967** – CSÁRDÁS

88 WIEN - KLAGENFURT - VENEZIA, MILANO and ROMA

train type/number	🚌	*REX*	*IC*	*RJ*	🚌	*RJ*	🚌	*EC*	*REX*	*EN*	*EN*	*EN*	*EN*
train number	**831**	**1881**	**31**	**531**	**835**	**533**	**837**	**103**	**1883**	**235**	**235**	**1237**	**237**
notes	[R]		🍸	✕	[R]	✕	[R]	✕		**R**	**480**	**C**	**G**
		2			**A**		**A**		2	⚡	**V**⚡	⚡	🏖⚡
Wien Meidling d.	...	...	0630	0830	...	1030	...	1830	...	1930	1930	2030	2056**r**
Bruck an der Mur d.	...	...	0815	1015	...	1215	...	2015	...	2125	2125	2222	|
Klagenfurt Hbf d.	0605	...	1023	1223	1210	1423	1410	1823	...	2338	2338	0021	|
Linz Hbf d.	|	...	|	|	|	|	|	|	...	|	|	|	2240
Salzburg Hbf d.	|	...	|	|	|	|	|	|	...	|	|	|	0134
Villach Hbf d.	0650	0945	1050	1246	1256	1446	1456	1846	1929	0006	0006	0045	0415
Tarvisio 🏛 a.	|	1013	1112	...	|	...	|	...	1957	0029	0029	0108	0508
Udine a.	0825	1130	1216	...	1430	...	1630	...	2115	|	|	0217	0623
Venezia Mestre a.	1000	...	1353	...	1605	...	1805	...	...	0256	0256**h**	|	0813
Venezia Tronchetto ★ a.	1020	...	|	...	1625	...	1825	...	...	|	|	|	|
Venezia Santa Lucia a.	...	...	1405	...	...	...	...	...	...	|	|	|	0824
Padova a.	...	...	...	...	...	...	...	...	...	|	0607	0415	...
Verona Porta Nuova a.	...	...	...	...	...	...	...	...	...	|	0657	|	...
Milano Centrale a.	...	...	...	...	...	...	...	...	...	|	0930	|	...
Bologna Centrale a.										0448	...	0541	...
Firenze SMN a.										0618	...	0655	...
Pisa Centrale a.										|	...	0836	...
Livorno Centrale a.										|	...	0856	...
Roma Termini a.										0920	...	...	...

OTHER CONNECTING SERVICES

Venezia - Roma: Table **600**
Venezia - Milano: Table **605**

train type/number	*REX*	*EC*	🚌	*RJ*	🚌	*RJ*	*REX*	*IC*	🚌	*EN*	*EN*	*EN*	*EN*
train number	**1880**	**102**	**830**	**630**	**832**	**632**	**1882**	**30**	**838**	**236**	**1236**	**481**	**234**
notes		✕	[R]	✕	[R]	✕		🍸	[R]	**H**	**D**	**234**	**R**
	2		**A**				2		**A**	🏖⚡	⚡	**W**⚡	⚡
Roma Termini d.	...	...	...	...	...	...	...	...	...	...	...	...	1912
Livorno Centrale d.	...	...	...	...	...	...	...	...	...	...	1925	...	|
Pisa Centrale d.	...	...	...	...	...	...	...	...	...	...	1946	...	|
Firenze SMN d.	...	...	...	...	...	...	...	...	...	...	2105	...	2209
Bologna Centrale d.	...	...	...	...	...	...	...	...	...	...	2224	...	2330
Torino Porta Nuova d.	...	...	...	...	...	...	...	...	...	...	|	...	|
Torino Porta Susa d.	...	...	...	...	...	...	...	...	...	...	|	...	|
Milano Centrale d.	...	...	...	...	...	...	...	...	...	...	|	2135	|
Verona Porta Nuova d.	...	...	...	...	...	...	...	...	...	...	|	2323	|
Padova d.	...	...	...	...	...	...	...	...	...	...	2349	0012	0041
Venezia Santa Lucia d.	...	...	...	...	...	...	...	1559	...	2057	|	|	|
Venezia Tronchetto ★ d.	...	...	0920	...	1120	...	...	|	1820	|	|	|	|
Venezia Mestre d.	...	...	0940	...	1140	...	...	1611	1840	2109	|	0130**g**	0130
Udine d.	0707	...	1115	...	1315	...	1717	1742	2015	2247	0157	|	|
Tarvisio 🏛 d.	0827	...	|	...	|	...	1840	1849	|	0020	0319	0352	0352
Villach Hbf a.	0854	0914	1250	1314	1450	1514	1907	1911	2150	0042	0341	0414	0414
Salzburg Hbf a.	...	|	|	|	|	|	...	|	|	0409	|	|	|
Linz Hbf a.	...	|	|	|	|	|	...	|	|	0624	|	|	|
Klagenfurt Hbf a.	...	0937	1335	1337	1535	1537	...	1937	2235	|	0407	0439	0439
Bruck an der Mur a.	...	1144	...	1544	...	1744	...	2144	...	|	0621	0639	0639
Wien Meidling a.	...	1327	...	1727	...	1927	...	2327	...	0810**r**	0904	0833	0833

A – Apr. 12 - Oct. 26.
C – TOSCANA MARE ⑤ Apr. 11 - Sept. 26 (also ③ June 18 - Aug. 27; also Apr. 20, 30, May 28, June 8): 🛏 1, 2 cl. (T2), ▬ 2 cl. (6 berth), [2] [R] Wien - Firenze - Pisa - Livorno.
D – TOSCANA MARE ⑥ Apr. 12 - Sept. 27 (also ④ June 19 - Aug. 28; also Apr. 21, May 1, 29, June 9): 🛏 1, 2 cl. (T2), ▬ 2 cl. (6 berth), [2] [R] Livorno - Pisa - Firenze - Wien.
G – VIENNA-VENEZIA EXPRESS – 🛏 1, 2 cl., 🛏 1, 2 cl. (T2), ▬ 2 cl. (6 berth), [2] Wien (**944**) - Salzburg (**499**) - Villach (**237**) - Udine - Venezia.
H – VENEZIA-VIENNA EXPRESS – 🛏 1, 2 cl., 🛏 1, 2 cl. (T2), ▬ 2 cl. (6 berth), [2] Venezia (**236**) - Udine - Villach (**498**) - Salzburg (**945**) - Wien.
R – ALLEGRO TOSCA – 🛏 1, 2 cl. (Excelsior), 🛏 1, 2 cl., ▬ 2 cl. (6 berth), [2] Wien - Roma and v.v.
V – 🛏 1, 2 cl., ▬ 2 cl. (4 berth), [2] Wien (**235**) - Venezia Mestre (**480**) - Milano. Train number **60235** also applies.
W – 🛏 1, 2 cl., ▬ 2 cl. (4 berth), [2] Milano (**481**) - Venezia Mestre (**234**) - Wien.

g – Arrive 0030.
h – Depart 0552. Train **480**.
r – Wien **Westbahnhof**.

★ – See Venezia City Plan on page 32.
🏖 – From June 1 to Sept. 15, an **ÖBB** *IC Bus* departs Venezia Mestre 0825 for Lido di Jesolo (arrives 0920). Also departs Lido di Jesolo 1945 for Venezia Mestre (arrives 2040). Rail tickets **not** valid.
⚡ – Supplement payable.
RJ – ÖBB *Railjet* service. [1] (business class), [1] (first class), [2] (economy class), ✕.
🚌 – **ÖBB** *IC Bus*. Rail tickets valid. [R]. Supplement payable. 1st and 2nd class. 🍸 in first class. Connections to/from Wien are made at Villach.

89 VENEZIA - LJUBLJANA - ZAGREB - BUDAPEST and BEOGRAD

train type	*IC*	*D*	*IC*		🚌	*EC*	**1604**			
train number	**201**	**415**	**205**		**832**	**213**	**1247**	**1205**		
notes					[R]					
notes	**A**		**Q**				**K**	**C**		
Venezia Tronchetto d.	...	...	...	...	1120	...	...	...	...	...
Venezia Mestre d.	...	...	...	...	1140	...	...	...	...	...
Villach Hbf d.	...	0625	...	...	1450	1653	...	...	...	...
Koper a.	...	|	...	...	...	|	2008	...	...	...
Ljubljana d.	0635	0825	...	...	...	1835	2230	...	...	...
Dobova 🏛 d.	0821	1012	...	...	...	2021	|	...	...	...
Split d.	|	|	...	...	...	|	|	1837	...	...
Zagreb a.	0853	1044	...	...	...	2053	|	0311	...	...
Zagreb d.	0957	1116	1434	...	...	...	|	0319	...	...
Vinkovci a.	|	1445	|	...	...	...	|	|	...	...
Šid 🏛 a.	|	1518	|	...	...	...	|	|	...	...
Beograd a.	|	1732	|	...	...	...	|	|	...	...
Koprivnica 🏛 d.	1122	...	1613	...	...	...	◧	0437	...	...
Gyékényes a.	1135	...	1626	...	...	...	|	0450	...	...
Nagykanizsa a.	1235	...	|	...	...	...	|	0559	...	...
Kaposvár a.	|	...	1802	...	...	...	|	|	...	...
Dombóvár a.	|	...	1846	...	...	...	|	|	...	...
Fonyód a.	1408	...	|	...	...	...	|	0702	...	...
Siófok a.	1459	...	|	...	...	...	|	0752	...	...
Székesfehérvár a.	1539	...	|	...	...	...	0734	0830	...	...
Budapest Déli a.	1629	...	|	...	...	...	0824	|	...	...
Budapest Keleti a.	...	...	2115	...	...	...	1035	0935	...	...

train type	*D*	*EC*	*EC*	🚌	*IC*	*D*	*IC*		**1246**	
train number	**314**	**31**	**212**	**835**	**200**	**414**	**204**	**1204**	**1605**	
notes		[R]		[R]						
notes				**T**	**B**		**P**	**D**	**J**	
Budapest Keleti a.	...	...	...	...	...	...	1445	1800	1800	...
Budapest Déli d.	...	...	...	...	0605	...	|	|	2030	...
Székesfehérvár d.	...	...	...	...	0653	...	|	1917	2118	...
Siófok d.	...	...	...	...	0739	...	|	2001	|	...
Fonyód d.	...	...	...	...	0827	...	|	2053	|	...
Dombóvár d.	...	...	...	...	|	...	1655	|	|	...
Kaposvár d.	...	...	...	...	|	...	1739	|	|	...
Nagykanizsa d.	...	...	...	...	0945	...	|	2157	|	...
Gyékényes d.	...	...	...	...	1047	...	1913	2242	|	...
Koprivnica 🏛 a.	...	...	...	...	1100	...	1926	2255	◧	...
Beograd d.	...	...	...	...	|	1100	|	|	|	...
Šid 🏛 d.	...	...	...	...	|	1355	|	|	|	...
Vinkovci d.	...	...	...	...	|	1441	|	|	|	...
Zagreb a.	...	...	...	...	1250	1809	2056	0008	|	...
Zagreb d.	...	...	0650	...	...	1837	2120	0015	|	...
Split a.	...	...	|	...	...	|	|	0848	|	...
Dobova 🏛 d.	0535	...	0738	...	...	1925	2152	...	|	...
Ljubljana d.	0727	...	0922	...	...	2110	2337	...	0623	...
Koper a.	|	...	|	...	...	|	...	...	0845	...
Villach Hbf a.	0908	1050	1058	1256	...	2243	...	...	...	...
Venezia Mestre a.	...	1353	...	1605	...	...	...	...	...	...
Venezia Tronchetto a.	...	1405	...	1625	...	...	...	...	...	...

A – AGRAM – [12] Ljubljana (**499**) - Zagreb (**201**) - Budapest.
B – AGRAM – [12] Budapest - Zagreb.
C – ADRIA ③⑥ June 14 - Aug. 30: 🛏 1, 2 cl., ▬ 2 cl., [2] 🍸 Split - Zagreb - Budapest. Conveys 🛏 1, 2 cl. Split - Budapest (**276**) - Praha (Table **60**) and 🛏 1, 2 cl. Split - Budapest (**16**) - Moskva (Table **97**).
D – ADRIA ②⑤ June 13 - Aug. 29: 🛏 1, 2 cl., ▬ 2 cl., [2] 🍸 Budapest - Zagreb - Split. Conveys 🛏 1, 2 cl. Praha (**277**) - Budapest - Split (Table **60**) and 🛏 1, 2 cl. Moskva (**15**) - Budapest - Split (Table **97**).
J – ISTRA – ①④ June 23 - Aug. 28: 🛏 1, 2 cl., ▬ 2 cl., [2] Budapest (**1246**) - Hodoš - Maribor (**1605**) - Koper.
K – ISTRA – ②⑤ June 24 - Aug. 29: 🛏 1, 2 cl., ▬ 2 cl., [2] Koper (**1604**) - Maribor (**1247**) - Hodoš - Budapest.
P – RIPPL-RÓNAI – [12] 🍸 Budapest (**204**) - Zagreb (**498**) - Ljubljana.
Q – RIPPL-RÓNAI – [12] 🍸 Zagreb - Budapest.
T – Apr. 12 - Oct. 26.

k – Budapest **Keleti**.

◧ – 🏛 is Hodoš.
🚌 – **ÖBB** *IC Bus*. [R] Rail tickets valid. Supplement payable. 1st and 2nd class. 🍸 in first class.

MARSEILLE - NICE - MILANO, ROMA and VENEZIA 90

train type		EC	IC	FB	IC	FB	FR				IC	IC	FB	FB	FR			EC	IC	IC	FR	FB		
train number		139	663	9773	511	9723	9533		17473		745	665	9777	9727	9541			145	677	673	9557	9749		
notes	◇	140	664	[R]🍷	[R]🍷	[R]🍷	[R]✕		①–⑤	◇	746	[R]	[R]✕	[R]🍷	[R]✕		◇	146	678	[R]🍷	[R]✕	[R]🍷		
notes		[R]ϟ	[R]ϟ	ϟ	ϟ	ϟ	ϟ		p		[R]ϟ	ϟ	ϟ	ϟ	ϟ			[R]ϟ	[R]ϟ	ϟ	ϟ	ϟ		
notes		Q	P															Q	P					
Marseille St Charles d.	...	...	...	...	...	...	...	...	0631	...	...	...	...	...	...	...	...	1131	...	...	...	...	...	...
Toulon d.	...	...	...	...	...	...	...	...	0716	...	...	...	...	...	...	...	...	1218	...	...	...	...	...	...
Cannes d.	0639	...	...	...	...	...	...	...	0838	0911	...	...	...	...	...	...	1310	1336	...	...	...	...	...	...
Nice d.	0722	0809	...	...	...	...	...	...	0906	0952	...	...	...	...	...	...	1355	1409	...	...	...	...	...	...
Monaco - Monte Carlo d.	0747	0824	...	...	...	...	...	...	...	1016	...	...	...	...	...	...	1419	1427	...	...	...	...	...	...
Ventimiglia 🛂 d.	0813	0902	0858	...	...	...	...	...	...	1043	1059	...	...	...	...	...	1443	1502	1459	...	...	...	...	...
San Remo a.	...	0913	0913	...	...	...	...	...	...	...	1114	...	...	...	...	...	...	1514	1514	...	...	...	...	...
Genova Piazza Principe a.	...	1106	1106	1212	1251	...	...	...	...	...	1306	1347	1452	...	...	...	...	1706	1706	1748	...	...	...	...
Milano Centrale a.	...	1250	1250	|	|	1305	1310	...	...	...	1450	|	|	1505	1510	...	...	1855	1855	|	1910	2005	...	...
Verona a.	...	...	...	|	|	1427	|	...	...	...	...	|	|	1627	|	...	...	...	...	|	|	2127	...	...
Venezia Santa Lucia a.	...	...	...	|	|	1540	|	...	...	...	...	|	|	1740	|	...	...	...	...	|	|	2240	...	...
La Spezia a.	...	...	...	1312	1407	...	|	...	...	...	...	1519	1618	...	|	...	...	...	...	1920	|	...	...	...
Pisa Centrale a.	...	...	...	1357	1506	...	|	...	...	...	...	...	1713	...	|	...	...	...	...	2018	|	...	...	...
Firenze SMN a.	...	...	...	|	|	...	1455	...	...	...	...	...	|	...	1655	...	...	...	...	...	2055	...	...	...
Roma Termini a.	...	...	...	1633	1803	...	1630	...	...	...	...	...	2003	...	1830	...	...	...	...	...	2230	...	...	...
Napoli Centrale a.	...	...	...	...	2039	...	1755	...	...	...	...	...	...	...	1955	...	...	...	...	...	...	...	...	...

train type			EC	IC	ICN	ICN			
train number	17487		147	747	799	1911			
notes		◇	148	748	[R]	[R]			
notes			[R]ϟ	[R]ϟ	ϟ	ϟ			
notes			Q	P	B	A			
Marseille St Charles d.	1431	...	1531	...	...	...	...	...	...
Toulon d.	1517	...	1619	...	...	...	...	...	...
Cannes d.	1637	1710	1736	...	...	...	...	...	...
Nice d.	1706	1755	1809	...	...	...	...	...	...
Monaco - Monte Carlo d.	...	1819	1827	...	...	...	...	...	...
Ventimiglia 🛂 d.	...	1843	1902	1859	...	...	...	...	...
San Remo a.	...	...	1914	1914	...	...	...	...	...
Genova Piazza Principe a.	...	...	2106	2106	2353	...	...	...	...
Milano Centrale a.	...	...	2250	2250	|	2320	...	...	...
Verona a.	...	...	...	...	|	|	...	...	...
Venezia Santa Lucia a.	...	...	...	...	|	|	...	...	...
La Spezia a.	...	...	...	...	0124	|	...	...	...
Pisa Centrale a.	...	...	...	...	0221	|	...	...	...
Firenze SMN a.	...	...	...	...	|	0407j	...	...	...
Roma Termini a.	...	...	...	...	0555o	0717t	...	...	...
Napoli Centrale a.	...	...	...	...	0817	0938	...	...	...

train type	ICN	IC	IC	EC					
train number	796	658	653	141		17486			
notes	[R]	[R]🍷	654	142	◇				
notes	ϟ	ϟ	[R]ϟ	[R]ϟ					
notes	A		P	Q					
Napoli Centrale d.	2140	...	...	...	...	...	...	...	...
Roma Termini d.	2358o	...	...	...	...	...	...	...	...
Firenze SMN d.	|	...	...	...	...	...	...	...	...
Pisa Centrale d.	0326	0544	...	...	...	...	...	...	...
La Spezia d.	0425	0640	...	...	...	...	...	...	...
Venezia Santa Lucia d.	|	|	...	...	...	...	...	...	...
Verona d.	|	|	...	...	...	...	...	...	...
Milano Centrale d.	|	|	0705	0705	...	...	...	...	...
Genova Piazza Principe d.	0601	0816	0855	0855	...	...	...	...	...
San Remo d.	...	...	1047	1047	...	...	...	...	...
Ventimiglia 🛂 a.	...	...	1104	1101	1150	...	...	...	...
Monaco - Monte Carlo a.	...	...	...	1136	1213	...	...	...	...
Nice a.	...	...	...	1151	1237	1355	...	...	...
Cannes a.	...	...	...	...	1320	1423	...	...	...
Toulon a.	...	...	...	...	...	1542	...	...	...
Marseille St Charles a.	...	...	...	...	...	1631	...	...	...

train type	FB	FB	FB	FR	FR	FB	IC	EC				IC	IC	FB	FR	IC	EC		FR	FB	FB	IC		
train number	9706	9708	9762	9508	9610	9710	741	143		17490		510	674	9718	9526	743	159		9532	9726	9774	675		
notes	[R]🍷	[R]	[R]🍷	[R]🍷	[R]	[R]🍷	742	144	◇			[R]🍷	[R]🍷	[R]🍷	[R]✕	744	160	◇	[R]✕	[R]🍷	[R]🍷	676	◇	
notes	ϟ	ϟ	ϟ	ϟ	ϟ	ϟ	[R]ϟ	[R]ϟ				ϟ	ϟ	ϟ	ϟ	[R]ϟ	[R]ϟ		ϟ	ϟ	ϟ	[R]ϟ	C	
notes		H			H		P	Q								P	Q							
Napoli Centrale d.	...	...	...	...	0640	...	...	...	...	...	...	0731	...	...	1000	...	...	...	1200	...	...	...	...	...
Roma Termini d.	...	...	0657	0725	0800	...	...	...	...	...	...	0957	...	...	1125	...	...	...	1325	...	1357	...	...	...
Firenze SMN d.	...	...	|	0900	|	...	...	...	...	...	...	...	...	...	1300	...	...	...	1500	...	...	...	...	...
Pisa Centrale d.	...	...	0933	|	|	...	...	...	...	...	...	1303	1344	...	|	...	...	...	|	...	1629	...	...	...
La Spezia d.	...	...	1017	|	|	...	...	...	...	...	...	1400	1440	...	|	...	...	...	|	...	1715	...	...	...
Venezia Santa Lucia d.	...	0750	|	|	|	0832q	...	...	...	...	...	|	|	1150	|	...	...	...	|	1320	|	...	...	...
Verona d.	0832	0902	|	|	|	0932	...	...	...	...	...	|	|	1302	|	...	...	...	|	1432	|	...	...	...
Milano Centrale d.	0955	1025	|	1045	1055	1055	1110	1110	...	...	...	|	|	1425	1445	1510	1510	...	1645	1555	|	1705	...	...
Genova Piazza Principe d.	...	...	1122	...	...	...	1255	1255	...	...	...	1521	1616	...	...	1655	1655	...	...	...	1816	1855	...	...
San Remo d.	...	...	...	...	...	...	1447	1447	...	...	...	...	...	...	...	1847	1847	...	...	...	...	2050	...	...
Ventimiglia 🛂 a.	...	...	...	...	...	...	1504	1501	1520	...	...	...	...	...	...	1904	1901	1920	...	...	...	2107	2120	...
Monaco - Monte Carlo a.	...	...	...	...	...	...	...	1536	1544	...	...	...	...	...	...	...	1936	1945	...	...	...	...	2143	...
Nice a.	...	...	...	...	...	...	...	1551	1608	1655	...	...	...	...	...	...	1951	2008	...	...	...	...	2204	...
Cannes a.	...	...	...	...	...	...	...	...	1653	1723	...	...	...	...	...	...	2025	2051	...	...	...	...	2251z	...
Toulon a.	...	...	...	...	...	...	...	...	...	1840	...	...	...	...	...	...	2146	...	...	...	...	...	...	...
Marseille St Charles a.	...	...	...	...	...	...	...	...	...	1929	...	...	...	...	...	...	2229	...	...	...	...	...	...	...

A – [sleeper] 1, 2 cl., [couchette] 2 cl. (4 berth), [2] Milano - Napoli - Salerno.
B – [sleeper] 1, 2 cl., [couchette] 2 cl. (4 berth), [2] Torino - Genova - Napoli - Salerno and v.v.
C – ⑧ (daily Mar. 30 - Oct. 5).
H – ①–⑤ (not Aug. 15, Dec. 8).
P – Service runs until replaced by train **Q** when through services commence.
Q – To commence on a date to be announced.

j – Firenze **Campo di Marte**.
o – Roma **Ostiense**.
p – Not July 14, Aug. 15, Nov. 1.
q – Venezia **Mestre**.
t – Roma **Tiburtina**.
z – ⑤⑥⑦ Mar. 30 - Oct. 5.

ϟ – Supplement payable.
◇ – Stopping train. Alternative services available, see Table **361**.
★ – Service offering Executive, Business, Premium and Standard class.

WIEN - LJUBLJANA and ZAGREB 91

train type	EC			EC	IC	ICS		1246	
train number	151	483	2752	159	246	23		1605	
notes	E		2	✕ϟ C	D	[R]		J	
Wien Meidling d.	0803	...	...	1603	...	...	...	...	...
Wiener Neustadt Hbf d.	0832	...	...	1632	...	...	...	...	...
Graz Hbf d.	1038	...	...	1838	...	...	...	...	...
Spielfeld-Straß 🛂 d.	1120	...	...	1920	...	...	...	...	...
Budapest Déli d.	|	...	...	|	1335	...	...	2030	...
Hodoš 🛂 d.	|	...	...	|	1757	...	...	0105	...
Maribor a.	1138	...	...	1938	1942	1945	...	0240	...
Pragersko a.	1201	...	...	2010	...	1958	...	|	...
Zidani Most a.	1306	...	...	|	...	2053	...	0506	...
Dobova 🛂 a.	|	...	...	2154	...	|	...	|	...
Zagreb a.	|	...	...	2242	...	|	...	|	...
Ljubljana a.	1406	1510	1540	...	...	2138	...	0606	...
Koper a.	...	|	1808	...	...	...	...	0845	...
Rijeka a.	...	1755	...	...	...	...	...	...	...

train type/number	IC	ICS	EC	IC			EC	1604	
train number	508	14	158	247		482	150	1247	
notes		[R]	✕ϟ C	D			E	K	
Rijeka d.	...	...	...	...	...	1200	...	...	...
Koper d.	0525	...	...	...	1003	|	...	2008	...
Ljubljana d.	0746	0805	...	...	1235	1445	1600	2230	...
Zagreb d.	...	|	0725	...	...	...	|	|	...
Dobova 🛂 d.	...	|	0812	...	...	...	|	|	...
Zidani Most d.	...	0850	|	...	...	...	1656	2327	...
Pragersko d.	...	0941	0959	...	...	...	1800	|	...
Maribor d.	...	0953	1019	1205	...	...	1819	0200	...
Hodoš 🛂 a.	...	...	|	1355	...	...	|	0330	...
Budapest Déli a.	...	...	|	1824	...	...	|	0824	...
Spielfeld-Straß 🛂 a.	...	...	1036	...	...	...	1836	...	...
Graz Hbf a.	...	...	1120	...	...	...	1920	...	...
Wiener Neustadt Hbf a.	...	...	1328	...	...	...	2128	...	...
Wien Meidling a.	...	...	1357	...	...	...	2157	...	...

C – CROATIA – [12] ✕ Wien - Zagreb and v.v.
D – CITADELLA – [12] Budapest - Hodoš - Maribor and v.v.
E – EMONA – [12] ✕ Wien - Ljubljana and v.v.
J – ISTRA – ①④ June 23 - Aug. 28: [sleeper] 1, 2 cl., [couchette] 2 cl., [2] Budapest (**1246**) - Hodoš - Maribor (**1605**) - Koper.
K – ISTRA – ②⑤ June 24 - Aug. 29: [sleeper] 1, 2 cl., [couchette] 2 cl., [2] Koper (**1604**) - Maribor (**1247**) - Hodoš - Budapest.

ϟ – Supplement payable.
◇ – Stopping train.

92 ZAGREB - SARAJEVO

train number		397	
notes		A	
Zagreb d.	...	0909	...
Sunja d.	...	1033	...
Volinja 🏛 d.	...	1120	...
Dobrljin 🏛 d.	...	1148	...
Novi Grad d.	...	1143	...
Banja Luka d.	...	1317	...
Doboj d.	...	1504	...
Zenica d.	...	1639	...
Sarajevo a.	...	1757	...
Sarajevo d.	...	...	...
Mostar d.	...	...	...
Ploče d.	...	...	...

train number		396	
notes		A	
Ploče d.	...	...	...
Mostar d.	...	...	...
Sarajevo a.	...	...	...
Sarajevo d.	...	1054	...
Zenica d.	...	1214	...
Doboj d.	...	1402	...
Banja Luka d.	...	1549	...
Novi Grad d.	...	1720	...
Dobrljin 🏛 d.	...	1750	...
Volinja 🏛 d.	...	1817	...
Sunja d.	...	1846	...
Zagreb a.	...	2009	...

A – (12) Zagreb - Sarajevo and v.v.

93 WARSZAWA - VILNIUS

train number	10011	394	818
notes	H	2	2
Warszawa Centralna d.	0723	...	...
Warszawa Wschodnia d.	|	...	...
Białystok d.	1032	...	...
Suwałki d.	1243	...	...
Šeštokai 🏛 § a.	...	...	...
Kaunas a.	...	...	1700
Vilnius a.	...	...	1816

train number	819		10012
notes	2		H
Vilnius d.	1120	...	...
Kaunas d.	1236	...	...
Šeštokai 🏛 § d.	...	...	...
Suwałki a.	...	...	1540
Białystok a.	...	...	1750
Warszawa Wschodnia a.	...	...	2110
Warszawa Centralna a.	...	...	2129

H – HAŃCZA – (12) Warszawa - Šeštokai and v.v.

g – Warszawa **Gdańska.**

§ – 🏛 at Trakiszki / Mockava.

94 MOSKVA / St PETERBURG - WARSZAWA

train number	23*JI*	23*JI*	115*BJ*	115*BJ*	9*JA*	9*JA*	19*JA*	21*JA*	21*JA*
train number	452	452	11018	11018	11012	11012	404	404	404
notes	N W	N X	Z X	Z W	R X	R W	S	P X	P W
Moskva Belorusskaya d.	0602	0744	...	...	1650	1720	...	0744	0843
Smolensk Tsentralny 🏛 § d.	1028	1226	...	...	2132	2220	...	1223	1323
St Peterburg Vitebski d.	|	|	...	...	|	|	2359	|	|
Orsha Tsentralnaya § d.	1149	1247	...	...	2154	2242	1347z	1247	1347
Minsk d.	1428	1528	2044	2144	0022	0110	1625	1525	1625
Brest Tsentralny 🏛 d.	2015	2115	0240	0340	0532	0632	2215	2115	2215
Terespol a.	2033	2033	0158	0158	0450	0450	2033	2033	2033
Warszawa Wschodnia a.	2339	2342	0530	0530	0802	0802	...	...	...
Warszawa Centralna a.	2358	0023	0540	0540	0815	0815	...	...	...

train number	405*ZH*	405*AJ*	405*AJ*	10*ZH*	10*ZH*	116*BJ*	116*BJ*	24*JI*	24*JI*
train number	22*AJ*	22*AJ*	20*GJ*	11011	11011	11016	11016	453	453
notes	Q X	Q W	T	R X	R W	Z X	Z W	M X	M W
Warszawa Centralna d.	...	...	...	1525	1610	2120	2120	0345	0345
Warszawa Wschodnia d.	...	...	...	1535	1621	2130	2130	0422	0422
Terespol d.	0455	0455	0455	1922	1922	0036	0036	0724	0724
Brest Tsentralny 🏛 a.	0643	0743	0743	2106	2206	0230	0330	0918j	1118f
Minsk a.	1214	1314	1314	0155	0255	0807	0907	1436	1636
Orsha Tsentralnaya § a.	1458	1558	1558	0423	0523	...	...	1712	1912
St Peterburg Vitebski a.	|	|	0530	|	|	...	...	|	|
Smolensk Tsentralny 🏛 § a.	1726	1828	...	0645	0745	...	...	1935	2254
Moskva Belorusskaya a.	2230	2320	...	1145	1253	...	...	2358	0330

M – TRANSEUROPEAN EXPRESS ②③⑥ (①②③④⑥ May 28 - Oct. 3) 🛏 1, 2 cl. Paris (**453**) - Berlin - Brest (**24** *JI*) - Moskva. ✕ (RZD) Brest - Moskva. Conveys passengers to Belarus and Russia only.

N – TRANSEUROPEAN EXPRESS ①④⑦ (①②④⑥⑦ May 29 - Oct. 3) 🛏 1, 2 cl. Moskva (**23** *JI*) - Brest (**452**) - Berlin - Paris. ✕ (RZD) Moskva - Brest. Conveys passengers from Belarus and Russia only.

P – VLTAVA ②③⑤: 🛏 1, 2 cl. Moskva (**21***JA*) - Terespol (**404**) - Praha (Table **95**). Conveys 🛏 1, 2 cl. Moskva - Wien.

Q – VLTAVA ③④⑥: 🛏 1, 2 cl. Praha (**405**) - Terespol - Brest (**22***AJ*) - Moskva (Table **95**). Conveys 🛏 1, 2 cl. Wien - Moskva.

R – POLONEZ – 🛏 1, 2 cl. 🍷 Warszawa - Moskva and v.v. ✕ Brest - Moskva and v.v.

S – ①②④ (②④ May 27 - Oct. 2): 🛏 1, 2 cl. St Peterburg (**19***JA*) - Orsha (**21**) - Terespol (**404**) - Praha (journey 2 nights). Conveys ①②④ (②④ May 27 - Oct. 2): 🛏 1, 2 cl. St Peterburg (**19***JA*) - Orsha (**21**) - Terespol (**404**) - Bohumín (**101**) - Wien (journey 2 nights).

T – ③④⑥ (④⑥ May 29 - Oct. 4): 🛏 1, 2 cl. Praha (**405**) - Brest (**22***GJ*) - Orsha (**20**) - St Peterburg (journey 2 nights). Conveys ③④⑥ (④⑥ May 29 - Oct. 4): 🛏 1, 2 cl. Wien (**100**) - Bohumín (**405**) - Brest (**22***GJ*) - Orsha (**20**) - St Peterburg (journey 2 nights).

W – Oct. 27, 2013 - Mar. 29, 2014.

X – Mar. 30, 2014 - Oct. 24, 2014.

Z – 🛏 1, 2 cl. Minsk - Warszawa and v.v.

f – Depart 1310.

j – Depart 1110.

x – Warszawa **Gdańska**.

z – Arrive 1045.

§ – 🏛: Osinovka (BY) / Krasnoye (RU).

95 MOSKVA / St PETERBURG - CHEB, PRAHA and WIEN

train number	19*JA*	19*JA*	21*JA*	21*JA*	21*JA*		
notes	B	Q	V	J	C	✣	
Moskva Belorusskaya d.	...	...	0843	0843	0843	0744	...
Smolensk Tsentralny 🏛 § d.	...	...	1323	1323	1323	1223	...
St Peterburg Vitebski d.	2359	2359	|	|	|	|	...
Orsha Tsentralnaya § d.	1347x	1347x	1347	1347	1347	1247	...
Minsk d.	1625	1625	1625	1625	1625	1525	...
Brest Tsentralny 🏛 d.	2215z	2215z	2215z	2215z	2215z	2115j	...
Terespol a.	2033	2033	2033	2033	2033	2033	...
Warszawa Centralna a.	|	|	|	|	|	←	...
Katowice a.	0313	0313	0313	0313	0313	...	...
Bohumín 🏛 a.	0439	0439	0439	0439	0439r	...	...
Ostrava hlavní a.	0524	0659	0524	0524	0659	...	...
Břeclav a.	|	0850	|	|	0850	...	...
Wien Westbahnhof a.	|	1038	|	|	1038	...	...
Olomouc a.	0656	...	0656	0656	...	...	...
Pardubice a.	0831	...	0831	0831	...	...	...
Praha hlavní a.	0947	...	0947	0947e	...	...	...
Karlovy Vary a.	...	...	...	1446	...	...	...
Cheb a.	...	...	...	1538	...	...	...

train number	22*IJ*	22*ZH*	22*AJ*	22*GJ*	22*GJ*		
notes	H	K	W	P	A	✣	
Cheb d.	...	1016	...	...	...	...	...
Karlovy Vary d.	...	1105	...	...	...	...	...
Praha hlavní d.	...	1647f	1647	...	1647	...	...
Pardubice d.	...	1758	1758	...	1758	...	...
Olomouc d.	...	1925	1925	...	1925	...	...
Wien Westbahnhof d.	1634	|	|	1634	|	...	...
Břeclav d.	1823	|	|	1823	|	...	...
Ostrava hlavní d.	2011	2026	2026	2026	2026	...	...
Bohumín 🏛 d.	2055	2055	2055	2055	2055	...	...
Katowice d.	2221	2221	2221	2221	2221	...	...
Warszawa Centralna d.	|	|	|	|	|	←	...
Terespol d.	0455	0455	0455	0455	0455	0455	...
Brest Tsentralny 🏛 a.	0743c	0743c	0743c	0743c	0743c	0643	...
Minsk a.	1314	1314	1314	1314	1314	1214	...
Orsha Tsentralnaya § a.	1558	1558	1558	1558t	1558t	1458	...
St Peterburg Vitebski a.	|	|	|	0530	0530	|	...
Smolensk Tsentralny 🏛 § a.	1828	1828	1828	...	...	1726	...
Moskva Belorusskaya a.	2320	2320	2320	...	...	2230	...

A – ③④⑥: 🛏 1, 2 cl. Praha (**405**) - Brest (**22***GJ*) - Orsha (**20**) - St Peterburg (journey 2 nights).

B – ①②④: 🛏 1, 2 cl. St Peterburg (**19***JA*) - Orsha (**21**) - Terespol (**404**) - Praha (journey 2 nights).

C – ②③⑤: 🛏 1, 2 cl. Moskva (**21***JA*) - Terespol (**404**) - Bohumín (**101**) - Wien.

H – ③④⑥: 🛏 1, 2 cl. Wien (**100**) - Bohumín (**405**) - Brest (**22***IJ*) - Moskva (journey 2 nights).

J – ② Dec. 17 - May 20: 🛏 1, 2 cl. Moskva (**21***JA*) - Terespol (**404**) - Praha (**608**) - Cheb. ✕ Moskva - Brest.

K – ④ Dec. 19 - May 22: 🛏 1, 2 cl. Cheb (**609**) - Praha (**405**) - Brest (**22***ZH*) - Moskva. ✕ Brest - Moskva.

P – ③④⑥: 🛏 1, 2 cl. Wien (**100**) - Bohumín (**405**) - Brest (**22***GJ*) - Orsha (**20**) - St Peterburg (journey 2 nights).

Q – ①②④: 🛏 1, 2 cl. St Peterburg (**19***JA*) - Orsha (**21**) - Terespol (**404**) - Bohumín (**101**) - Wien (journey 2 nights).

V – VLTAVA ②③⑤: 🛏 1, 2 cl. Moskva (**21***JA*) - Terespol (**404**) - Praha.

W – VLTAVA ③④⑥: 🛏 1, 2 cl. Praha (**405**) - Brest (**22***AJ*) - Moskva. Also **22***EJ*, **22***GJ*.

c – Depart 0940.

e – Depart 1129.

f – Arrive 1427.

j – Arrive 1858.

r – Depart 0652.

t – Depart 1653.

x – Arrive 1045.

z – Arrive 1958.

§ – 🏛: Osinovka (BY) / Krasnoye (RU).

✣ – Provisional timings for trains **21**/**22** in previous column in Russia Mar. 30, 2014 - Oct. 24, 2014.

PRAHA, WIEN and KRAKÓW - KYÏV 96

train number	EC	SC	EC		IR	35LJ	Sko	Ex		609
train number	172	505	130		63124	35SH	74LJ	221		16UJ
notes		R ⟋	⊡	◇	2	G		🍸		A
Praha hlavní ... d.	...	0929	...	...	...	...	...	1116	...	...
Pardubice ... d.	...	1028	...	...	...	...	...	1223	...	...
Česká Třebová ... d.	...	|	...	...	...	...	...	1304	...	...
Olomouc ... d.	...	1143	...	...	...	...	...	1349	...	...
Wien Westbahnhof ... d.	0932f	|	...	...	...	...	...	|	1221x	...
Bratislava hlavná ... d.	|	|	...	...	...	...	...	|	1327	1353
Břeclav ... d.	1053	|	1107	...	...	...	...	|	...	|
Ostrava hlavní ... d.	...	1240	1301	...	...	...	...	|	...	|
Žilina ... d.	...	...	|	...	...	...	...	1622	...	1639
Košice ... a.	...	...	|	...	...	...	...	...	...	1945
Košice ... d.	...	...	|	...	...	...	...	...	...	2010
Čierna nad Tisou 🏛 a.	...	...	|	...	...	...	...	...	...	2155
Chop 🏛 ... a.	...	...	|	...	...	...	...	...	...	0030
Bohumín 🏛 ... d.	...	...	1320	...	...	...	...	...	...	|
Zebrzydowice 🏛 ... d.	...	...	1338	...	...	...	...	...	...	|
Katowice ... d.	...	...	1433	1507	1720	...	...	...	...	|
Kraków Główny ... d.	...	...	...	1736	1929	2059	...	...	...	|
Przemyśl ... a.	...	...	...	...	...	0200	...	...	...	|
Przemysl ... d.	...	...	...	...	...	0356	...	...	...	|
Mostiska II ◐ ... d.	...	...	...	...	...	0600	...	...	...	|
Lviv ... a.	...	...	...	...	...	0715	0741	...	...	1032
Ternopil ... a.	...	...	...	...	...	...	|	...	...	1300
Kozyatyn ... a.	...	...	...	...	...	...	|	...	...	1758
Kyïv ... a.	...	...	...	....	...	...	1656	...	...	2003

train number	IC	52	TLK	EC	SC	EC	15VJ	Ex		
train number	169	36SH	36102	131	512	173	604	220		
notes		G	36103		R ⟋		B	🍸		
Kyïv ... d.	1726	...	...	...	...	...	1105	...	...	...
Kozyatyn ... d.	|	...	...	...	...	...	1332	...	...	...
Ternopil ... d.	|	...	...	...	...	...	1835	...	...	...
Lviv ... d.	2220	2259	...	...	...	...	2114	...	...	...
Mostiska II ◐ ... d.	...	0045	...	...	...	...	|	...	...	...
Przemyśl ... a.	...	0020	...	...	...	...	|	...	...	...
Przemyśl ... d.	...	0211	...	...	...	...	|	...	...	...
Kraków Główny ... a.	...	0706	0850	...	...	...	|	...	...	...
Katowice ... a.	...	...	1050	1324	...	...	|	...	...	...
Zebrzydowice 🏛 ... a.	...	...	...	1422	...	...	|	...	...	...
Bohumín 🏛 ... a.	...	...	...	1440	...	...	|	...	...	...
Chop 🏛 ... d.	...	...	...	|	...	...	0510	...	...	...
Čierna nad Tisou 🏛 d.	...	...	...	|	...	...	0553	...	...	...
Košice ... a.	...	...	...	|	...	...	0720	...	...	...
Košice ... d.	...	...	...	|	...	...	0815	...	...	...
Žilina ... a.	...	...	...	|	...	...	1121	1138	...	...
Ostrava hlavní ... a.	...	...	...	1459	1527	...	|	|	...	...
Břeclav ... a.	...	...	...	1654	|	1702	|	|	...	...
Bratislava hlavná ... a.	...	...	...	...	|	|	1407	|	1442	...
Wien Westbahnhof ... a.	...	...	...	...	|	1824f	...	|	1548x	...
Olomouc ... a.	...	...	...	...	1623	...	...	1411	...	...
Česká Třebová ... a.	...	...	...	...	|	...	...	1456	...	...
Pardubice ... a.	...	...	...	...	1738	...	...	1535	...	...
Praha hlavní ... a.	...	...	...	...	1839	...	...	1653	...	...

A – 🛏 1, 2 cl. Bratislava (**609**) - Košice (**8819**) - Čierna nad Tisou (**8860**) - Chop (**16** *UJ*) - Kyïv - Moskva (journey 2 nights; see Table **97**).
B – 🛏 1, 2 cl. Moskva (**15** *VJ*) - Kyïv - Chop (**8861**) - Čierna nad Tisou (**964**) - Košice (**604**) - Žilina - Bratislava (journey 2 nights; see Table **97**).
G – LVIV EXPRESS – 🛏 2 cl. Kraków (**33105/33114**) - Przemyśl - Lviv and v.v. See Table **1075** for dates and times of running.

f – Wien **Meidling**.
x – Wien **Hbf** (Table **996**).
⟋ – Supplement payable.
◇ – Stopping train. 2nd class only.

🚌 – Run by Przewozy Regionalne.
◐ – 🏛 at Medyka / Mostiska **II** (Table **1056**).
⊡ – Supplement payable in Poland; Reservation compulsory in Poland.

MOSKVA - BUDAPEST and BEOGRAD 97

train type/number	15FJ	204	335	15FJ	15FJ	15FJ	273	15FJ	15FJ	15FJ
notes	273			1204	1204	604	1137	273	335	335
notes	A		M	C	F	W	H	P	S	U
Moskva Kiyevskaya ... d.	2330‡	...	...	2330‡	2330‡	2330‡	...	2330‡	2330‡	...
Kyïv ... d.	1103	...	...	1103	1103	1103	...	1103	1103	1103
Lviv ... d.	2114	...	...	2114	2114	2114	...	2114	2114	2114
Chop 🏛 ... d.	0540	...	...	0540	0540	0510	...	0540	0540	0540
Bratislava hlavná ... a.	|	...	...	|	|	1405	...	|	|	|
Debrecen ... a.	0812	...	...	0812	0812	...	...	0812	0812	0812
Szolnok ... a.	0950	...	...	0950	0950	...	...	0950	0950	0950
Budapest Keleti ... a.	1120	...	...	1120	1120	...	...	1120	1120	1120
Budapest Keleti ... d.	1305	1445	...	1800	1800	...	1305	1305	1305	1305
Siófok ... a.	|	|	...	|	1959	...	|	|	|	|
Zagreb ... a.	|	2056	...	|	0003	...	|	|	|	|
Split ... a.	|	...	...	|	0932	...	|	|	|	|
Koper ... a.	|	...	...	0835	...	...	|	|	|	|
Subotica 🏛 ... a.	1632	...	...	...	...	...	1632	1632	1632	1632
Novi Sad ... a.	1913	...	...	...	...	...	2047	2047	1910	1910
Beograd ... a.	2050	...	2150	...	...	...	2237x	2237x	2052	2052
Niš ... a.	...	...	0157	...	...	...	|	|	0216	0216
Bar ... a.	...	...	|	...	...	...	1046	1046	|	|
Skopje ⊖ ... a.	...	...	0722	...	...	...	...	...	0722	0722

train type/number	201	1136	272	334	272	1205	1205	609	334	334
notes		272	16KH		16KH	16KH	16KH	16UJ	16	16
notes	R	J	Q	M	B	G	D	W	T	V
Skopje ⊖ ... d.	...	...	...	2010	...	...	...	...	2010	2010
Bar ... d.	...	1700	1700	|	...	...	...	...	|	|
Niš ... d.	...	|	|	0121	...	...	...	...	0112	0112
Beograd ... d.	...	0517x	0517x	0533	0645	...	...	...	0645	0645
Novi Sad ... d.	...	0728	0728	...	0835	...	...	...	0835	0835
Subotica 🏛 ... d.	...	1128	1128	...	1128	...	...	...	1128	1128
Koper ... d.	...	|	|	...	|	...	2017	...	|	|
Split ... d.	...	|	|	...	|	1740	|	...	|	|
Zagreb ... d.	0957	|	|	...	|	0322	|	...	|	|
Siófok ... d.	1501	|	|	...	|	0751	|	...	|	|
Budapest Keleti ... a.	1629r	1454	1454	...	1454	0940	1035	...	1454	1454
Budapest Keleti ... d.	...	...	1840	...	1840	1840	1840	...	1840	1840
Szolnok ... d.	...	...	2003	...	2003	2003	2003	...	2003	2003
Debrecen ... d.	...	...	2135	...	2135	2135	2135	...	2135	2135
Bratislava hlavná ... d.	...	...	|	...	|	|	|	1353	|	|
Chop 🏛 ... a.	...	...	0113	...	0113	0113	0113	0030	0113	0113
Lviv ... a.	...	...	1032	...	1032	1032	1032	1032	1032	1032
Kyïv ... a.	...	...	2003	...	2003	2003	2003	2003	2003	2003
Moskva Kiyevskaya ... a.	...	...	0926‡	...	0926‡	0926‡	0926‡	0926‡	0926‡	...

A – TISZA – 🛏 2 cl. Moskva (**15**) - Budapest (**273**) - Beograd (journey 2 nights).
B – TISZA – 🛏 2 cl. Beograd (**272**) - Budapest (**16**) - Moskva (journey 2 nights).
C – ②⑥ June 24 - Aug. 26: 🛏 2 cl. Moskva (**15**) - Budapest (**1246**) - Maribor (**1605**) - Koper (journey 3 nights).
D – ②⑤ June 27 - Aug. 29: 🛏 2 cl. Koper (**1604**) - Maribor (**1247**) - Budapest (**16**) - Moskva (journey 3 nights).
F – ①④ June 12 - Aug. 28: 🛏 2 cl. Moskva (**15**) - Budapest (**1204**) - Zagreb - Split (journey 3 nights).
G – ③⑥ June 15 - Aug. 31: 🛏 2 cl. Split (**1205**) - Zagreb - Budapest (**16**) - Moskva (journey 3 nights).
H – PANONIJA – ①⑤ June 14 - Sept. 6 🛏 1, 2 cl., ▬ 2 cl., 🚃2 Budapest (**273**) - Subotica (**1137**) - Bar. Conveys ②③⑤⑥ June 13 - Sept. 5 🛏 1, 2 cl. Praha (**273**) - Subotica (**1137**) - Bar.
J – PANONIJA – ②⑥ June 15 - Sept. 7 🛏 1, 2 cl., ▬ 2 cl., 🚃2 Bar (**1136**) - Subotica (**272**) - Budapest. Conveys ③④⑥⑦ June 14 - Sept. 6 🛏 1, 2 cl., ▬ 2 cl. Bar (**1136**) - Subotica (**272**) - Praha.
M – HELLAS EXPRESS – 🛏 1, 2 cl.*, ▬ 2 cl.*, 🚃2 Beograd - Skopje and v.v. 🛏 1, 2 cl.*, ▬ 2 cl.*, 🚃2 Beograd - Sofiya and v.v.
P – ②④ June 12 - Sept. 4: 🛏 2 cl. Moskva (**15**) - Budapest (**273**) - Subotica (**1137**) - Bar (journey 3 nights).
Q – ④⑥ June 14 - Sept. 7: 🛏 2 cl. Bar (**1136**) - Subotica (**272**) - Budapest (**16**) - Moskva (journey 3 nights).

S – ⑤ June 21 - Sept. 6: 🛏 2 cl. Moskva (**15**) - Budapest (**271**) - Beograd (**335**) - Skopje.
T – ① June 24 - Sept. 9: 🛏 2 cl. Skopje (**334**) - Beograd (**270**) - Budapest (**16**) - Moskva.
U – ③ June 12 - Sept. 11: 🛏 2 cl. Kyïv - Skopje (journey 2 nights).
V – ⑤ June 14 - Sept. 13: 🛏 2 cl. Skopje - Kyïv (journey 2 nights).
W – 🛏 1, 2 cl. Moskva - Bratislava and v.v., journey 2 nights (Table **96**).

r – Budapest **Déli**.
x – Novi Beograd.

⊖ – 🏛 at Preševo / Tabanovci.
⊡ – 🏛 at Gevgelija / Idomeni.
* – Reported as not running most nights.
‡ – Russian timings liable to vary from Oct. 26, 2014.

MOSKVA - BUCUREŞTI, SOFIA and İSTANBUL 98

train number	59MJ	68MZ	59MJ	59MJ	59MJ	59MJ	51JA	101BJ	461	
train number	383	383	1183	1183	383	1181	1003	1003	491	
notes	F❖	N❖	W❖	K	A	V	R	Y	M	
Moskva Kiyevskaya ... d.	...	...	...	0930§	0930§	0930§	...	...	...	...
St Peterburg Vit ‡ ... d.	...	...	...	|	|	|	1915	...	...	...
Minsk ... d.	...	0125f	...	|	|	|	1935	1935	...	...
Kyïv ... d.	...	2010	...	2010	2010	2010	|	|	...	...
Lviv ... d.	0536	|	0536	|	|	|	0741	0741	...	...
Chernivtsi ... d.	1034	1034	1034	1034	1034	1034	1241	1241	...	...
Vadul Siret 🏛 ... d.	1340	1340	1340	1340	1340	1340	1546	1545	...	...
Bucureşti Nord ... a.	2302	2302	2302	2302	2302	2302	0127	|	1230	...
Constanta ... a.	|	|	|	|	|	|	|	0319	|	...
Ruse 🏛 ... a.	0320	0320	0320	0320	0320	0320	0500	...	1525	...
Varna ... a.	|	|	|	|	|	0812	1040	...	|	...
Burgas ... a.	|	|	1045	1045	|	...	...	...	|	...
Sofia ... a.	1110	1110	...	...	1110	...	...	...	|	...
Kapikule 🏛 ... a.	...	...	...	...	...	...	...	...	0150	...
İstanbul Sirkeci ... a.	...	...	...	...	...	...	...	...	0750x	...

train number	1004	1006	382	382	1180	1182	382	1182	492	
train number	101VJ	102MZ	60KJ	60MJ	60SZ	60KH	60MJ	60MJ	460	
notes	X	Z	P❖	T❖	Q	S	B	U❖	G	
İstanbul Sirkeci ... d.	...	...	...	...	...	...	...	...	2200x	...
Kapikule 🏛 ... d.	...	...	...	...	...	...	...	...	0405	...
Sofia ... d.	...	...	1845	1845	...	...	1845	...	|	...
Burgas ... d.	...	...	|	|	...	1830	|	1900	|	...
Varna ... d.	1915	...	|	|	2115	|	|	|	|	...
Ruse 🏛 ... d.	0040	...	0200	0200	0200	0200	0200	0200	1545	...
Constanta ... d.	|	0100	|	|	|	|	|	|	|	...
Bucureşti Nord ... d.	0340	|	0600	0600	0600	0600	0600	0600	1833	...
Vadul Siret 🏛 ... a.	1330	1330	1540	1540	1540	1540	1540	1540	...	...
Chernivtsi ... a.	1640	1640	1832	1832	1832	1832	1832	1832	...	...
Lviv ... a.	2157	2157	|	2334	|	|	|	2334	...	...
Kyïv ... a.	|	|	0913z	...	0913	0913	0913	...	...	...
Minsk ... a.	1040	1040	2310	...	|	|	|	...	...	...
St Peterburg Vit ‡ ... a.	0814	...	...	...	|	|	|	...	...	...
Moskva Kiyevskaya ... a.	...	...	...	...	2143§	2143§	2143§	...	...	...

A – BOLGARIYA EXPRESS – 🛏 1, 2 cl. Moskva (**59**) - Vadul Siret (**383**) - Bucureşti - Sofia.
B – BOLGARIYA EXPRESS – 🛏 1, 2 cl. Sofia (**382**) - Bucureşti - Vadul Siret (**60**) - Moskva.
F – ②⑤⑦: 🛏 2 cl. Lviv (**59**) - Vadul Siret (**1385**) - Bucureşti - Ruse 🏛 - Sofia.
G – BOSPHOR – 🛏 1, 2 cl., ▬ 2 cl. İstanbul (**81032**) - Kapikule 🏛 (**492/464**) - Ruse 🏛 (**460**) - Bucureşti. ⇟
K – ②④⑥ June 3 - Sept. 30: 🛏 2 cl. Moskva (**59**) - Vadul Siret (**383**) - Bucureşti - Ruse 🏛 (**1183**) - Burgas.
M – BOSPHOR – 🛏 1, 2 cl., ▬ 2 cl. Bucureşti (**461**) - Ruse 🏛 (**465/491**) - Kapikule 🏛 (**81031**) - İstanbul. ⇟
N – ⑥ (②⑥ June 4 - Sept. 3): 🛏 2 cl. Minsk (**68**) - Homel (**54**) - Kyïv (**59**) - Vadul Siret (**383**) - Sofia.
P – ① (①④ June 6 - Sept. 5): 🛏 2 cl. Sofia (**382**) - Vadul Siret (**60**) - Kyïv (**54**) - Homel (**615**) - Minsk.
Q – ②③⑤⑦ June 3 - Oct. 1: 🛏 2 cl. Varna (**1180**) - Ruse 🏛 (**382**) - Bucureşti - Vadul Siret (**60**) - Moskva.
R – ②⑤ June 3 - Sept. 9: 🛏 2 cl. St Peterburg (**51***JA*) - Minsk - Varna.
S – ①④⑥ June 5 - Oct. 2: 🛏 2 cl. Burgas (**1182**) - Ruse 🏛 (**382**) - Bucureşti - Vadul Siret (**60**) - Moskva.
T – ①③⑥: 🛏 2 cl. Sofia (**382**) - Ruse 🏛 - Bucureşti - Vadul Siret (**60**) - Lviv.
U – ①⑥ June 17 - Sept. 2: 🛏 2 cl. Burgas (**1182**) - Lviv.
V – ①③⑤⑦ June 1 - Sept. 29: 🛏 2 cl. Moskva (**59**) - Vadul Siret (**383**) - Bucureşti - Ruse 🏛 (**1181**) - Varna.

W – ⑤⑦ June 14 - Aug. 30: 🛏 2 cl. Lviv (**59**) - Vadul Siret (**383**) - Burgas.
X – ①⑤ June 6 - Sept. 13: 🛏 2 cl. Varna - Minsk (**52**) - St Peterburg.
Y – ③ June 4 - Sept. 10: 🛏 2 cl. Minsk - Constanta.
Z – ⑥ June 7 - Sept. 13. 🛏 2 cl. Constanta - Minsk.

f – 0059 (train **312**) on certain dates.
x – By 🚌 from / to Çerkezköy (Table **1550**).
z – Depart 1030 (Train **54***KJ*).

§ – Russian timings liable to vary from Oct. 26, 2014.
‡ – Full name is St Peterburg Vitebski.
⇟ – Until Aug. 12 this service is expected to be operated by bus between Gorna Oryakhovitsa and Dimitrovgrad (please confirm timings locally).
❖ – Subject to confirmation.

99 WARSZAWA and KRAKÓW - PRAHA, WIEN and BUDAPEST

train type/train number		*EC*	*SC*	*EC*		*TLK*	*EC*	*SC*	*EC*		*TLK*	*EC*	*SC*	*EC*					**402**			
train number		**103**	**510**	**277**		**38100**	**131**	**512**	**173**		**37102**	**105**	**516**	**175**		**407**		**407**	**407**	**402**	**402**	
notes/train number		✕	🍷	✕		**38101**	✕	🍷	✕		**37103**	✕	🍷	✕		**477**	**407**	**444**	**477**	**407**	**442**	
notes	◇	⊡	[R]				⊡	[R]				⊡	⌿									
notes		**V**	⌿	**Z**			**T**	⌿	**H**			**Y**		**K**		**B**	**C**	**P**	**A**	**D**	**R**	
Warszawa Wschodnia ....d.	...	0607	...	...	...	...	1007	...	...	...	...	1207	...	...	...	2007	2007	2007	...	...	...	...
Warszawa Centralna ....d.	...	0620	...	...	...	...	1020	...	...	...	...	1220	...	...	...	2020	2020	2020	...	...	...	...
Kraków Główny ....d.	0623	│	...	...	...	1019	│	...	...	...	1239	│	...	...	...	│	│	│	2203	2203	2203	...
Katowice ....d.	0842	0924	...	...	...	1233	1324	...	...	...	1453	1524	...	...	...	2351	2351	2351	│	│	│	...
Zebrzydowice 🏛 ....d.	...	1023	...	...	...	...	1423	...	...	...	...	1623	...	...	...	0053	0053	0053	0102	0102	0102	...
Bohumín 🏛 ....a.	...	1040	...	...	...	...	1440	...	...	...	...	1640	...	...	...	0111	0111	0111	0119	0119	0119	...
Bohumín 🏛 ....d.	...	1052	...	...	...	...	1452	...	...	...	...	1652	...	...	...	0212	0212	0300	0212	0212	0337	...
Ostrava hlavní ....a.	...	1059	1127	...	...	...	1459	1527	...	...	...	1659	1727	...	...	0217	0217	0306	0217	0217	0344	...
Přerov ....a.	...	1150	│	...	...	...	1550	│	...	...	...	1750	│	...	...	0309	0309	│	0309	0309	│	...
Olomouc ....a.	...	│	1223	...	...	,...	│	1623	...	...	...	│	1823	...	...	│	│	0403	│	│	0449	...
Pardubice ....a.	...	│	1338	...	...	...	│	1738	...	...	...	│	1938	...	...	│	│	0526	│	│	0623	...
Praha hlavní ....a.	...	│	1439	...	...	...	│	1839	...	...	...	│	2039	...	...	│	│	0648	│	│	0737	...
Břeclav ....a.	...	1250	...	1257	...	...	1654	...	1702	...	...	1850	...	1857	...	0405	0405	...	0405	0405	...	...
Wien Meidling ....a.	...	1424	...	│	...	...	│	...	1824	...	...	2017	...	│	...	│	0617	...	│	0617	...	...
Wien Westbahnhof ....a.	...	│	...	│	...	...	│	...	│	...	...	2034	...	│	...	│	0632	...	│	0632	...	...
Wiener Neustadt Hbf ....a.	...	1454	...	│	...	...	│	...	1854	...	...	...	...	│	...	│	...	...	│	...	...	...
Klagenfurt ....a.	...	1821	...	│	...	...	│	...	2216	...	...	...	...	│	...	│	...	...	│	...	...	...
Villach Hbf ....a.	...	1846	...	│	...	...	│	...	2240	...	...	...	...	│	...	│	...	...	│	...	...	...
Kúty 🏛 ....a.	...	...	...	1311	...	...	1711	...	...	...	...	...	...	1911	...	0453	...	...	0453	...	...	...
Bratislava hlavná ....a.	...	...	...	1350	...	...	1750	...	...	...	...	...	...	1950	...	0536	...	...	0536	...	...	...
Štúrovo 🏛 △ ....a.	...	...	...	1511	...	...	1911	...	...	...	...	...	...	2111	...	0710	...	...	0710	...	...	...
Budapest Keleti ....a.	...	...	...	1635	...	...	2035	...	...	...	...	...	...	2235	...	0835	...	...	0835	...	...	...

train type/train number	*EC*	*Ex*	*EC*	*TLK*		*EC*	*SC*	*EC*	*TLK*		*EC*	*SC*	*EC*	*TLK*							**476**	
train number	**174**	**143**	**104**	**76102**		**172**	**505**	**130**	**83100**		**276**	**507**	**102**	**63102**		**443**	**445**		**406**	**476**	**406**	
notes/train number	✕	✕	✕	**73102**		✕	🍷	✕			✕	🍷	✕	**63103**		**403**	**406**	**406**	**403**	**406**	**403**	
notes			⊡				[R]	⊡				[R]	⊡									
notes	**K**		**Y**			**H**	⌿	**T**			**Z**	⌿	**V**			**S**	**Q**	**C**	**E**	**G**	**F**	
Budapest Keleti ....d.	0525	...	...	...	...	...	...	0725	...	...	1125	...	...	...	...	...	...	...	...	2005	2005	...
Štúrovo 🏛 △ ....d.	0649	...	...	...	...	...	...	0849	...	...	1249	...	...	...	...	...	...	...	...	2124	2124	...
Bratislava hlavná ....d.	0810	...	...	...	...	...	...	1010	...	...	1410	...	...	...	...	...	...	...	...	2258	2258	...
Kúty 🏛 ....d.	0847	...	...	...	...	...	...	1049	...	...	1447	...	...	...	...	...	...	...	...	2340	2340	...
Villach Hbf ....d.	│	...	...	...	...	0526	...	│	...	...	│	...	0914	...	...	...	...	...	...	│	│	...
Klagenfurt ....a.	│	...	...	...	...	0549	...	│	...	...	│	...	0939	...	...	...	...	...	...	│	│	...
Wiener Neustadt Hbf ....d.	│	...	...	...	...	0904	...	│	...	...	│	...	1304	...	...	...	...	...	...	│	│	...
Wien Westbahnhof ....d.	│	...	...	...	...	│	...	│	...	...	│	...	│	...	...	...	...	2212	2212	│	│	...
Wien Meidling ....d.	│	...	0741	...	...	0932	...	│	...	...	│	...	1332	...	...	...	...	2231	2231	│	│	...
Břeclav ....d.	0902	...	0910	...	...	1053	...	1107	...	...	1502	...	1510	...	...	...	...	0025	0025	0025	0025	...
Praha hlavní ....d.	...	0616	│	...	...	...	0929	│	...	...	...	1329	│	...	...	2216	2158	│	│	│	│	...
Pardubice ....d.	...	0723	│	...	...	...	1028	│	...	...	...	1428	│	...	...	2327	2314	│	│	│	│	...
Olomouc ....d.	...	0853	│	...	...	...	1143	│	...	...	...	1543	│	...	...	0101	0036	│	│	│	│	...
Přerov ....d.	...	│	1008	...	...	...	│	1208	...	...	...	│	1608	...	...	│	│	0119	0119	0119	0119	...
Ostrava hlavní ....d.	...	0957	1102	...	...	...	1240	1301	...	...	...	1640	1702	...	...	0207	0136	0211	0211	0211	0211	...
Bohumín 🏛 ....a.	...	...	1108	...	...	...	...	1308	...	...	...	...	1708	...	...	0214	0142	0219	0219	0219	0219	...
Bohumín 🏛 ....d.	...	...	1120	...	...	...	...	1320	...	...	...	...	1720	...	...	0307	0255	0255	0307	0255	0307	...
Zebrzydowice 🏛 ....d.	...	...	1138	...	...	...	...	1338	...	...	...	...	1738	...	...	0326	0317	0317	0326	0317	0326	...
Katowice ....a.	...	...	1233	1302	...	...	...	1433	1507	...	...	...	1833	1844	...	│	0417	0417	│	0417	│	...
Kraków Główny ....a.	...	...	│	1522	...	...	...	│	1722	...	...	...	│	2059	...	0630	│	│	0630	│	0630	...
Warszawa Centralna ....a.	...	...	1549	...	...	...	...	1750	...	...	...	...	2145	...	...	...	0805	0805	...	0805	...	...
Warszawa Wschodnia ....a.	...	...	1608	...	...	...	...	1808	...	...	...	...	2203	...	...	...	0823	0823	...	0823	...	...

A – 🛏 1, 2 cl., ▬ 2 cl. Kraków (**402**) - Bohumín (**407**) - Břeclav (**477**) - Budapest.

B – 🛏 1, 2 cl., ▬ 2 cl., [2] Warszawa (**407**) - Břeclav (**447**) - Bratislava - Budapest.

C – CHOPIN – 🛏 1, 2 cl. (Lux), 🛏 1, 2 cl., ▬ 2 cl. [2] Warszawa - Wien and v.v. Conveys 🛏 1, 2 cl. Moskva - Wien and v.v. (Table **95**).

D – 🛏 1, 2 cl. (also ▬ 2 cl. Mar. 27 - Sept. 22) Kraków (**402**) - Bohumín (**407**) - Wien.

E – 🛏 1, 2 cl. (also ▬ 2 cl. Mar. 28 - Sept. 23) Wien (**406**) - Bohumín (**403**) - Kraków.

F – 🛏 1, 2 cl., ▬ 2 cl. Budapest (**476**) - Břeclav (**406**) - Bohumín (**403**) - Kraków.

G – 🛏 1, 2 cl., ▬ 2 cl., [2] Budapest (**476**) - Bratislava - Břeclav (**406**) - Warszawa.

H – VINDOBONA – [12] ✕ Hamburg - Berlin - Praha - Wien - Villach and v.v.

K – JÁN JESENIUS / JESZENSZKY JÁNOS – [12] ✕ Hamburg - Berlin - Praha - Břeclav - Budapest and v.v.

P – 🛏 1, 2 cl., ▬ 2 cl. [2] Warszawa (**407**) - Bohumín (**444**) - Praha.

Q – 🛏 1, 2 cl., ▬ 2 cl. [2] Praha (**445**) - Bohumín (**406**) - Warszawa.

R – SILESIA – 🛏 1, 2 cl., ▬ 2 cl. [2] Kraków (**402**) - Bohumín (**442**) - Praha.

S – SILESIA – 🛏 1, 2 cl., ▬ 2 cl. [2] Praha (**443**) - Bohumín (**403**) - Kraków.

T – VARSOVIA – [12] ✕ Warszawa - Budapest and v.v.

V – POLONIA – [12] ✕ Warszawa - Wien - Villach and v.v.

Y – SOBIESKI – [12] ✕ Warszawa - Wien and v.v.

Z – SLOVAN – [12] ✕ Praha - Břeclav - Budapest and v.v.

△ – Routeing point for international tickets: Szob.

⊡ – Supplement payable in Poland; Reservation compulsory in Poland.

SC – *SUPERCITY PENDOLINO* train, 🍷 [R] ⌿; operated by tilting trains.

⌿ – [R] with supplement payable.

◇ – Stopping train. 2nd class only.

GREAT BRITAIN

SEE MAP PAGES 98/99

Operators: Passenger services are provided by a number of private passenger train companies operating the **National Rail** (www.nationalrail.co.uk) network on lines owned by the British national railway infrastructure company **Network Rail**. The following Network Rail codes are used in the table headings to indicate the operators of trains in each table:

AW	Arriva Trains Wales	GR	East Coast	ME	Merseyrail	TP	TransPennine Express
CC	c2c	GW	First Great Western	NT	Northern Rail	VT	Virgin Trains
CH	Chiltern Railways	HT	Hull Trains	SE	Southeastern	XC	Arriva Cross Country
EM	East Midlands Trains	IL	Island Line	SN	Southern		
FC	First Capital Connect	LE	Greater Anglia	SR	First ScotRail		
GC	Grand Central Railway	LM	London Midland	SW	South West Trains		

Timings: Except where indicated otherwise, timings are valid **May 18 - December 13, 2014.**
As service patterns at weekends (especially on ⑦) usually differ greatly from those applying on Mondays to Fridays, the timings in most tables are grouped by days of operation: Ⓐ = Mondays to Fridays; ⚒ = Mondays to Saturdays; ⑥ = Saturdays; ⑦ = Sundays. Track engineering work, affecting journey times, frequently takes place at weekends, so it is advisable to confirm your journey details locally if planning to travel in the period between the late evening of ⑥ and the late afternoon of ⑦. Confirm timings, too, if you intend travelling on public holidays (see page **2**) as there may be alterations to services at these times. Suburban and commuter services are the most likely to be affected; the majority of long-distance and cross-country trains marked Ⓐ and ⚒ run as normal on these dates. No trains (except limited Gatwick and Heathrow Express services) run on **December 25**, with only a limited service on certain routes on **December 26**. In Scotland only trains between Edinburgh/Glasgow and England run on **January 1**.

Services: Unless indicated otherwise (by '2' in the train column or '2nd class' in the table heading), trains convey both **first** (1st) and **standard** (2nd) classes of seated accommodation. Light refreshments (snacks, hot and cold drinks) are available from a **buffet car** or a **mobile trolley service** on board those trains marked 🍷 and ✕: the latter also convey a **restaurant car** or serve meals to passengers at their seats (this service is in some cases available to first-class ticket holders only). Note that catering facilities may not be available for the whole of a train's journey. **Sleeping-cars** (🛏) have one berth per compartment in first class and two in standard class.

Reservations: Seats on most long-distance trains and berths in sleeping-cars can be reserved in advance when purchasing travel tickets at rail stations or directly from train operating companies (quote the departure time of the train and your destination). Seat reservation is normally free of charge.

SE 2nd class — LONDON - THE SOUTH EAST via HS1 HIGH SPEED LINE — 100

Service until October 4. Special fares are payable for high-speed services. For slower services see Table 101.

LONDON - CHATHAM - FAVERSHAM

km			⑥	Ⓐ	Ⓐ	Ⓐ	⑥	Ⓑ	⚒		⚒	⑥⑦	Ⓐ	⚒			⚒								
0	**London** St Pancras	d.	0651	0655	0725	0752	0755	0825	0851	0925	0955	1022	1028	1052	...	1125	1155	1222	1252	1325	1355	1425	1455	1525	1555
9	Stratford International	d.	0658	0702	0732	0802	0802	0832	0858	0932	1002	1032	1035	1059	...	1132	1202	1232	1259	1332	1402	1432	1502	1532	1602
35	Ebbsfleet International	d.	0714	0714	0744	0814	0814	0844	0914	0944	1014	1044	1046	1114	...	1144	1214	1244	1314	1344	1414	1444	1514	1544	1614
54	**Chatham**	d.	0735	0737	0805	0835	0835	0905	0935	1005	1035	1105	1107	1135	...	1205	1235	1305	1335	1405	1435	1505	1535	1605	1635
70	Sittingbourne	d.	0752	0755	0822	0852	0852	0922	0952	1022	1052	1122	1124	1152	...	1222	1252	1322	1352	1422	1452	1522	1552	1622	1652
83	**Faversham**	a.	0803	0805	0833	0903	0903	0933	1003	1033	1103	1133	1133	1203	...	1233	1303	1333	1403	1433	1503	1533	1603	1633	1703

			⑥⑦	Ⓐ	Ⓐ	⑥⑦	⑦	Ⓐ	⑥	Ⓐ	⑥⑦			⑥⑦	Ⓐ									⚒
London St Pancras	d.	1625	1655	1658	1725	1725	1752	1755	1755	1825	1825	1855	...	1925	1928	1955	2025	2055	2125	2155	2225	2255	2325	2355
Stratford International	d.	1632	1702	1705	1732	1732	1802	1802	1802	1832	1832	1902	...	1932	1935	2002	2032	2102	2132	2202	2232	2302	2332	0002
Ebbsfleet International	d.	1644	1714	1716	1743	1744	1814	1813	1814	1844	1844	1914	...	1944	1946	2014	2044	2114	2144	2214	2244	2314	2344	0014
Chatham	d.	1705	1735	1737	1803	1805	1835	1833	1835	1905	1905	1935	...	2005	2009	2035	2105	2135	2205	2235	2305	2335	0005	0035
Sittingbourne	d.	1722	1752	1756	1822	1822	1852	1851	1852	1924	1922	1952	...	2022	2027	2052	2122	2152	2222	2252	2322	2352	0022	0052
Faversham	a.	1733	1803	1805	1831	1833	1903	1900	1903	1932	1933	2003	...	2033	2036	2103	2133	2203	2233	2303	2333	0003	0033	0103

		Ⓐ	⚒	Ⓐ	⑥	Ⓐ	⑥⑦	Ⓐ	⑥		Ⓐ		⚒		⚒			⚒						
Faversham	d.	0456	0528	0558	0628	0634	0658	0704	0728	...	0733	0758	0828	0858	0928	0958	...	1028	1058	1128	1158	1228	1258	1328
Sittingbourne	d.	0507	0537	0607	0637	0642	0707	0713	0737	...	0741	0807	0837	0907	0937	1007	...	1037	1107	1137	1207	1237	1307	1337
Chatham	d.	0524	0554	0624	0654	0700	0724	0730	0754	...	0800	0824	0854	0924	0954	1024	...	1054	1124	1154	1224	1254	1324	1354
Ebbsfleet International	a.	0546	0616	0646	0716	0717	0746	0747	0816	...	0817	0846	0916	0946	1016	1046	...	1116	1146	1216	1246	1316	1346	1416
Stratford International	a.	0559	0629	0659	0729	0730	0759	0800	0830	...	0830	0900	0930	1000	1029	1059	...	1129	1159	1230	1300	1330	1403	1429
London St Pancras	a.	0606	0636	0706	0739	0737	0806	0807	0837	...	0837	0907	0937	1007	1036	1106	...	1136	1206	1237	1307	1337	1409	1436

Faversham	d.	1358	1428	...	1458	1528	1558	...	1628	1658	...	1728	1758	1828	...	1858	1928	...	1958	2028	2058	...	2128	2158
Sittingbourne	d.	1407	1437	...	1507	1537	1607	...	1637	1707	...	1737	1807	1837	...	1907	1937	...	2007	2037	2107	...	2137	2207
Chatham	d.	1424	1454	...	1524	1554	1624	...	1654	1724	...	1754	1824	1854	...	1924	1954	...	2024	2054	2124	...	2154	2224
Ebbsfleet International	a.	1446	1516	...	1546	1616	1646	...	1716	1746	...	1818	1846	1916	...	1946	2016	...	2046	2116	2146	...	2216	2246
Stratford International	a.	1459	1530	...	1603	1629	1703	...	1729	1800	...	1830	1902	1929	...	2000	2029	...	2103	2129	2200	...	2229	2259
London St Pancras	a.	1506	1537	...	1610	1636	1709	...	1736	1807	...	1837	1909	1936	...	2007	2036	...	2109	2136	2207	...	2236	2306

LONDON - ASHFORD - DOVER and MARGATE

km			⚒	⚒	⚒	⚒																				⑥⑦	Ⓐ	Ⓐ	Ⓐ
0	**London** St Pancras	d.	0640	0710	0742	0810	0840	0910	0942	1010	1042	1112	1142	1212	1242	1312	1342	1412	1442	1512	1542	1610	1640	1640	1640	1712
9	Stratford International	d.	0647	0717	0749	0817	0847	0917	0949	1017	1049	1119	1149	1219	1249	1319	1349	1419	1449	1519	1549	1617	1647	1647	1647	1719
35	Ebbsfleet International	d.	0659	0729	0801	0829	0859	0929	1001	1029	1101	1131	1201	1231	1301	1331	1401	1431	1501	1531	1601	1629	1658	1659	1659	|
90	Ashford International	d.	0722	0750	0822	0852	0922	0952	1022	1052	1122	1152	1222	1252	1322	1352	1422	1452	1522	1552	1622	1652	1722	1723	1725	1751
112	Folkestone Central	a.	|	0807	|	0907	|	1007	|	1107	|	1207	|	1307	|	1407	|	1507	|	1607	|	1707	|	1738	|	1806
124	**Dover** Priory	a.	|	0820	|	0920	|	1020	|	1120	|	1220	|	1320	|	1420	|	1520	|	1620	|	1720	|	1749	|	1818
112	Canterbury West	a.	0738	...	0838	...	0938	...	1038	...	1138	...	1238	...	1338	...	1438	...	1538	...	1638	...	1738	...	1740	...
140	**Ramsgate**	a.	0800	...	0859	...	0959	...	1059	...	1159	...	1259	...	1359	...	1459	...	1559	...	1659	...	1759	...	1759	...
149	**Margate**	a.	0811	...	0910	...	1010	...	1110	...	1210	...	1310	...	1410	...	1510	...	1610	...	1710	...	1810	...	1812	...

		Ⓐ	⑥⑦	Ⓐ	Ⓐ	⑥⑦	Ⓐ	⑥⑦	Ⓐ	Ⓐ	Ⓐ	⑥⑦	Ⓐ	Ⓐ		⑥⑦								⑥⑦	Ⓐ	
London St Pancras	d.	1712	1712	1742	1742	1742	1812	1812	1819	1842	1842	1842	1910	1910	...	1912	1942	2012	2042	2112	2142	2212	2242	2312	2312	2342
Stratford International	d.	1719	1719	1749	1749	1749	1819	1819	1826	1849	1849	1849	1917	1917	...	1919	1949	2019	2049	2119	2149	2219	2249	2319	2319	2349
Ebbsfleet International	d.	|	1731	|	|	1801	|	1831	1837	|	|	1901	1929	1929	...	1931	2001	2031	2101	2131	2201	2231	2301	2331	2331	0001
Ashford International	d.	1754	1752	1821	1824	1822	1849	1852	1858	1920	1923	1922	1952	1955	...	1952	2022	2052	2122	2152	2222	2252	2322	2352	2352	0020
Folkestone Central	a.	|	1807	1836	|	|	|	1907	1913	1935	|	|	2007	|	...	2007	|	2107	|	2207	|	2307	|	0007	0007	...
Dover Priory	a.	|	1820	1848	|	|	|	1920	1926	1948	|	|	2020	|	...	2020	|	2120	|	2220	|	2322	|	0020	0018	...
Canterbury West	a.	1809	...	...	1839	1838	1904	...	...	...	1938	1938	...	2011	...	...	2038	...	2138	...	2238	...	2338	...	|	...
Ramsgate	a.	1829	...	...	1859	1900	1931	...	...	...	1959	2000	...	2034	...	...	2100	...	2200	...	2300	...	0001	...	0054	...
Margate	a.	1842	...	...	1912	1911	1942	...	...	...	2012	2011	...	2045	...	...	2111	...	2211	...	2311	...	...	...	...	...

		Ⓐ	Ⓐ	⑥	⚒	Ⓐ	Ⓐ	⑥	Ⓐ	Ⓐ	⑥	Ⓐ	⑦		⑥	Ⓐ	Ⓐ	Ⓐ	⑥⑦	Ⓐ	⑥⑦					
Margate	d.	...	...	...	...	0548	...	0553	...	...	...	0646	...	...	0653	...	...	...	...	0749	0753	...	0851	...	0953	...
Ramsgate	d.	...	0500	0505	...	0600	...	0605	...	0626	...	0658	...	...	0705	...	...	0730	...	0801	0805	...	0903	...	1005	...
Canterbury West	d.	...	0525	0525	...	0620	...	0625	...	0650	...	0718	...	...	0725	...	...	0750	...	0825	0825	...	0923	...	1025	...
Dover Priory	d.	...	|	|	0545	|	0612	|	0642	|	0645	|	...	...	|	0716	0742	|	0745	|	|	0845	|	0945	|	1045
Folkestone Central	d.	...	|	|	0556	|	0623	|	0653	|	0656	|	...	...	|	0727	0753	|	0756	|	|	0856	|	0956	|	1056
Ashford International	d.	0515	0543	0543	0613	0643	0643	0643	0713	0713	0713	0736	0743	...	0743	0745	0813	0813	0813	0843	0843	0913	0943	1013	1043	1113
Ebbsfleet International	a.	0534	0602	0602	0632	|	|	0702	|	|	0732	|	0802	...	0802	0804	|	|	0832	0902	0902	0932	1002	1032	1102	1132
Stratford International	a.	0546	0614	0614	0644	0712	0712	0714	0742	0742	0744	0805	0814	...	0814	0817	0842	0842	0844	0914	0914	0944	1014	1044	1114	1144
London St Pancras	a.	0553	0621	0621	0651	0719	0719	0721	0750	0750	0751	0813	0821	...	0821	0824	0849	0849	0851	0921	0921	0951	1021	1051	1121	1151

																								⚒
Margate	d.	1053	...	1153	...	1253	...	1353	...	1453	...	1553	...	1653	...	...	1753	...	1853	...	1953	...	2053	...	2153	...
Ramsgate	d.	1105	...	1205	...	1305	...	1405	...	1505	...	1605	...	1705	...	...	1805	...	1905	...	2005	...	2105	...	2205	...
Canterbury West	d.	1125	...	1225	...	1325	...	1425	...	1525	...	1625	...	1725	...	...	1825	...	1925	...	2025	...	2125	...	2225	...
Dover Priory	d.	|	1145	|	1245	|	1345	|	1445	|	1545	|	1645	|	...	1745	|	1845	|	1945	|	2045	|	2145	|	2245
Folkestone Central	d.	|	1156	|	1256	|	1356	|	1456	|	1556	|	1656	|	...	1756	|	1856	|	1956	|	2056	|	2156	|	2256
Ashford International	d.	1143	1213	1243	1313	1343	1413	1443	1513	1543	1613	1643	1713	1743	...	1813	1843	1913	1943	2013	2043	2113	2143	2213	2243	2313
Ebbsfleet International	a.	1202	1232	1302	1332	1402	1432	1502	1532	1602	1631	1702	1732	1803	...	1832	1902	1932	2002	2035	2102	2132	2202	2232	2302	2332
Stratford International	a.	1214	1244	1314	1344	1414	1444	1514	1544	1614	1644	1714	1744	1816	...	1846	1914	1946	2014	2047	2114	2144	2214	2244	2314	2344
London St Pancras	a.	1221	1251	1321	1351	1421	1451	1521	1551	1621	1651	1721	1751	1822	...	1853	1921	1953	2021	2054	2121	2151	2222	2251	2321	2351

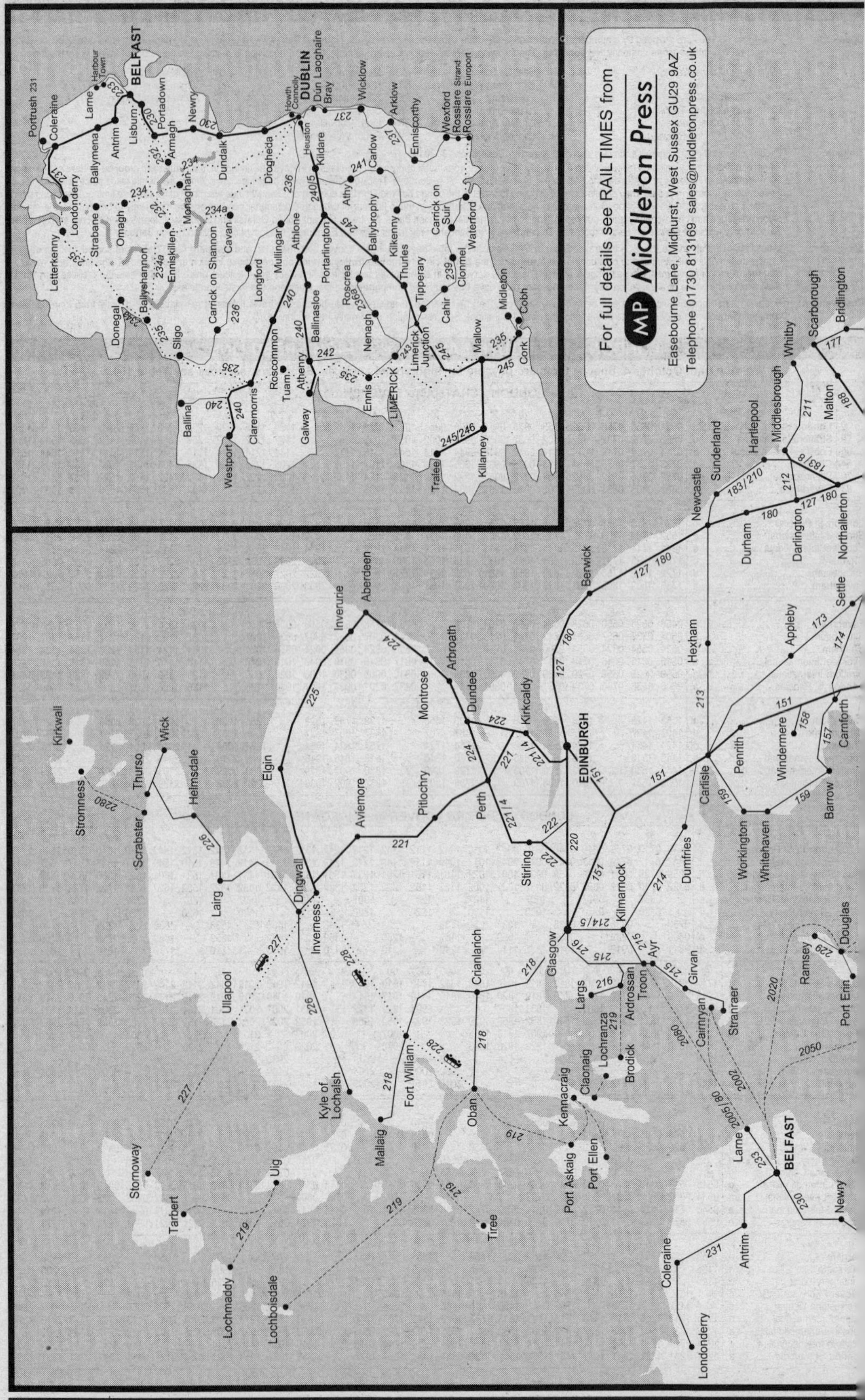
BELFAST
DUBLIN
Portrush
Coleraine
Larne
Harbour
Town
Ballymena
Antrim
Lisburn
Portadown
Newry
Armagh
Dundalk
Drogheda
Howth
Connolly
Dun Laoghaire
Bray
Wicklow
Arklow
Enniscorthy
Wexford
Rosslare Strand
Rosslare Europort
Londonderry
Letterkenny
Strabane
Omagh
Enniskillen
Monaghan
Cavan
Carrick on Shannon
Ballyshannon
Donegal
Sligo
Longford
Mullingar
Athlone
Kildare
Heuston
Athy
Carlow
Kilkenny
Carrick on Suir
Waterford
Portarlington
Ballybrophy
Thurles
Tipperary
Clonmel
Cahir
Roscrea
Nenagh
Ballinasloe
Roscommon
Claremorris
Ballina
Westport
Tuam
Athenry
Galway
Ennis
LIMERICK
Limerick Junction
Mallow
Cork
Cobh
Midleton
Killarney
Tralee
Kirkwall
Stromness
Thurso
Wick
Scrabster
Helmsdale
Lairg
Dingwall
Inverness
Elgin
Inverurie
Aberdeen
Aviemore
Pitlochry
Montrose
Arbroath
Dundee
Perth
Kirkcaldy
Stirling
EDINBURGH
Berwick
Newcastle
Sunderland
Hexham
Durham
Hartlepool
Middlesbrough
Darlington
Northallerton
Whitby
Scarborough
Bridlington
Malton
Appleby
Settle
Carlisle
Penrith
Windermere
Carnforth
Barrow
Workington
Whitehaven
Dumfries
Kilmarnock
Glasgow
Ayr
Troon
Ardrossan
Largs
Girvan
Stranraer
Cairnryan
Crianlarich
Fort William
Mallaig
Kyle of Lochalsh
Ullapool
Oban
Stornoway
Tarbert
Uig
Lochmaddy
Lochboisdale
Tiree
Port Askaig
Port Ellen
Kennacraig
Claonaig
Lochranza
Brodick
Douglas
Ramsey
Port Erin
Larne
Newry
Antrim
Coleraine
Londonderry

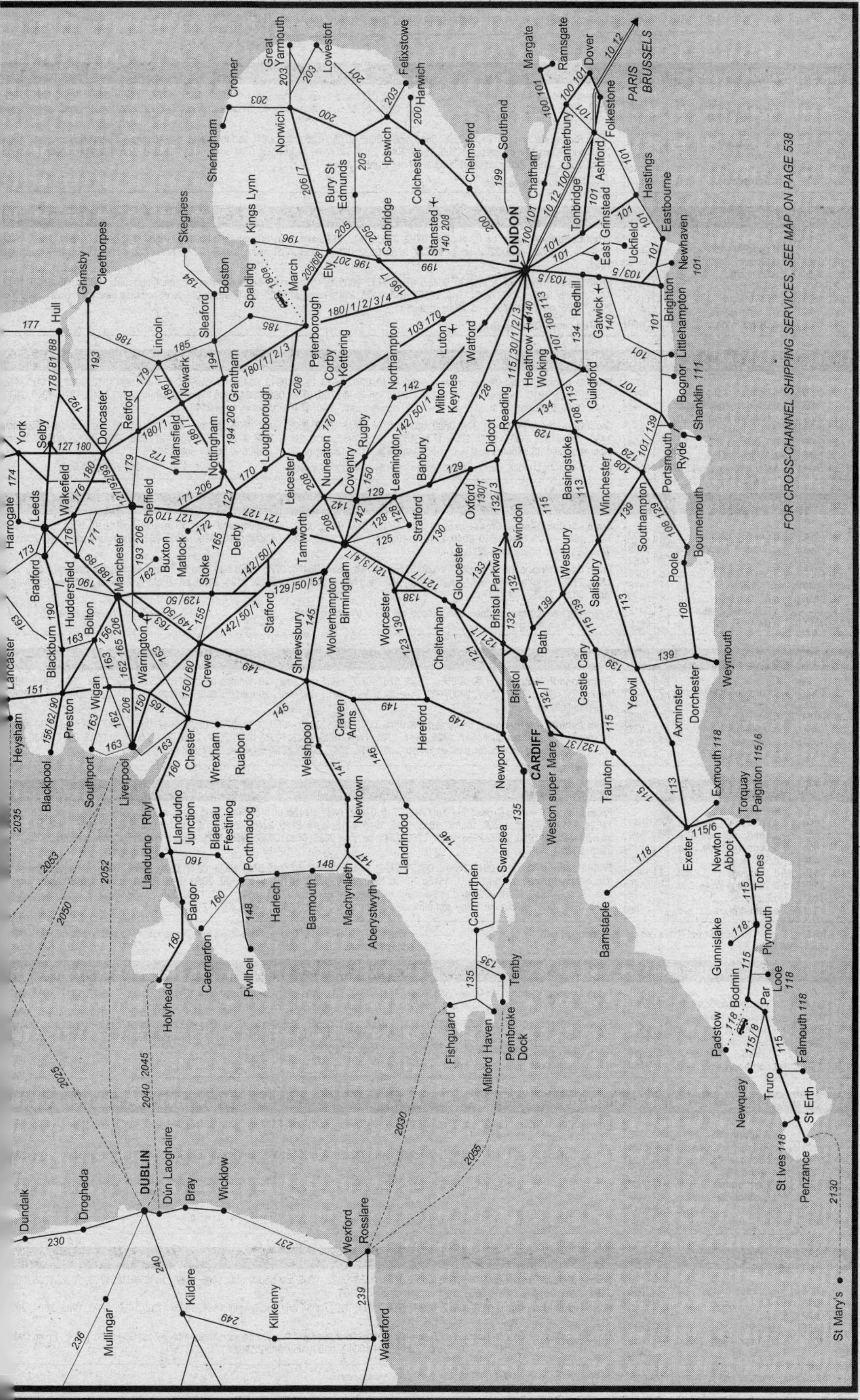

LONDON
CARDIFF
DUBLIN
FOR CROSS-CHANNEL SHIPPING SERVICES, SEE MAP ON PAGE 538
PARIS
BRUSSELS
Great Yarmouth
Lowestoft
Cromer
Sheringham
Norwich
Felixstowe
Harwich
Ipswich
Colchester
Bury St Edmunds
Cambridge
Chelmsford
Southend
Margate
Ramsgate
Dover
Folkestone
Canterbury
Chatham
Ashford
Hastings
Tonbridge
East Grinstead
Uckfield
Eastbourne
Newhaven
Brighton
Redhill
Gatwick
Stansted
Kings Lynn
Skegness
Cleethorpes
Grimsby
Hull
Boston
Spalding
March
Ely
Peterborough
Sleaford
Lincoln
Newark
Grantham
Nottingham
Mansfield
Retford
Doncaster
Selby
York
Harrogate
Leeds
Wakefield
Bradford
Huddersfield
Sheffield
Manchester
Buxton
Matlock
Derby
Stoke
Loughborough
Leicester
Corby
Kettering
Northampton
Luton
Watford
Milton Keynes
Rugby
Coventry
Nuneaton
Leamington
Banbury
Tamworth
Birmingham
Wolverhampton
Stafford
Crewe
Warrington
Wigan
Bolton
Blackburn
Preston
Lancaster
Heysham
Blackpool
Southport
Liverpool
Chester
Wrexham
Ruabon
Shrewsbury
Welshpool
Newtown
Machynlleth
Aberystwyth
Barmouth
Harlech
Porthmadog
Pwllheli
Blaenau Ffestiniog
Llandudno
Llandudno Junction
Rhyl
Bangor
Caernarfon
Holyhead
Craven Arms
Llandrindod
Hereford
Worcester
Stratford
Oxford
Didcot
Reading
Heathrow
Woking
Guildford
Basingstoke
Winchester
Southampton
Portsmouth
Ryde
Shanklin
Bognor
Littlehampton
Bournemouth
Poole
Weymouth
Dorchester
Salisbury
Westbury
Swindon
Bristol Parkway
Gloucester
Cheltenham
Bath
Bristol
Newport
Weston super Mare
Castle Cary
Yeovil
Axminster
Taunton
Exeter
Exmouth
Barnstaple
Newton Abbot
Torquay
Paignton
Totnes
Plymouth
Gunnislake
Bodmin
Padstow
Par
Looe
Newquay
Truro
Falmouth
St Erth
St Ives
Penzance
St Mary's
Swansea
Carmarthen
Tenby
Fishguard
Milford Haven
Pembroke Dock
Dundalk
Drogheda
Dun Laoghaire
Bray
Wicklow
Wexford
Rosslare
Waterford
Kilkenny
Kildare
Mullingar

101 LONDON - THE SOUTH and SOUTH EAST — SE, SN

Typical off-peak journey time in hours and minutes
READ DOWN ↓ READ UP ↑

Journey times may be extended during peak hours on Ⓐ (0600 - 0900 and 1600 - 1900) and also at weekends.
The longest journey time by any train is noted in the table heading.

LONDON VICTORIA - RAMSGATE

Valid until October 4 — Longest journey: 2 hours 10 minutes — SE

km					
0	0h00	↓	d.**London** Victoria.....a.	↑	1h57
18	0h17		d.Bromley South.......d.		1h40
55	0h50	↓	d.Chatham................d.	↑	1h10
72	1h09		d.Sittingbourne...........d.		0h50
84	1h21	↓	d.Faversham...............d.	↑	0h42
119	1h49		d.Margate..................d.		0h10
128	1h59	↓	a.**Ramsgate**...............d.	↑	0h00

From London Victoria: on Ⓐ: 0522, 0552, 0622, 0722 and every 30 minutes until 1622, 1657, 1727, 1757**m**, 1827, 1857, 1922, 1952, 2022, 2052, 2122, 2222, 2322; on ⑥ at 0522, 0622, 0722, 0752 and every 30 minutes until 2022, 2122, 2222, 2322; on ⑦ at 0805 and hourly until 2305.

From Ramsgate: on Ⓐ at 0432, 0506, 0540, 0608, 0632, 0705, 0735, 0805, 0840 and then at 05 and 40 minutes past each hour until 1505, 1535 and every 30 minutes until 1905, 1925, 2005, 2105, 2205; on ⑥ at 0505, 0540 and then at 05 and 40 minutes past each hour unti 1905, 2005, 2105, 2205; on ⑦ at 0635 and hourly until 2235.

m – To/from Margate only.

LONDON VICTORIA - DOVER

Valid until October 4 — Longest journey: 2 hours 10 minutes — SE

km					
0	0h00	↓	d.**London** Victoria.....a.	↑	2h02
18	0h17		d.Bromley South.......d.		1h43
55	0h50	↓	d.Chatham................d.	↑	1h15
72	1h09		d.Sittingbourne...........d.		0h58
84	1h21	↓	d.Faversham...............d.	↑	0h47
99	1h37		d.Canterbury East.....d.		0h27
124	1h58	↓	a.**Dover** Priory..........d.	↑	0h00

From London Victoria: on Ⓐ at 0645, 0722, 0752, 0822, 0852 and every 30 minutes until 1622, 1657, 1727, 1757, 1827, 1857, 1922, 1952, 2022, 2052, 2122, 2222; on ⑥ at 0722, 0752, 0822, 0852 and every 30 minutes until 2022, 2122, 2222; on ⑦ at 0805 and hourly unti 2205.

From Dover Priory: on Ⓐ at 0430, 0545**c**, 0705, 0735, 0805, 0845 and at the same minutes past each hour until 1505, 1539, 1605, 1639 1705, 1739, 1805, 1839, 1905, 1940, 2005, 2045, 2105, 2145; on ⑥ at 0505, 0545 and at the same minutes past each hour until 1905 2005, 2105; on ⑦ at 0735 and hourly until 2135.

c – To London **Charing Cross**.

LONDON CHARING CROSS - CANTERBURY WEST

Valid until October 4 — Longest journey: 1 hour 55 minutes — SE

km					
0	0h00	↓	d.**London** C Cross ...a.	↑	1h46
1	0h03		d.**London** Waterloo ‡ a.		1h42
3	0h09	↓	d.**London** Bridge......a.	↑	1h37
36	0h32		d.Sevenoaks.............d.		1h13
48	0h40	↓	d.Tonbridge...............d.	↑	1h04
90	1h16		a.Ashford Int'l...........d.		0h27
113	1h44	↓	a.**Canterbury** West...d.	↑	0h00

From London Charing Cross: on Ⓐ at 0630, 0710, 0740, 0813, 0833, 0913, 0940 and every 30 minutes until 1610, 1637, 1714, 1745**c** 1808**c**, 1841, 1910, 1940, 2040, 2140, 2240, 2340; on ⑥ at 0700, 0730, 0800, 0840 and every 30 minutes until 1740, 1840, 1940, 2040 2140, 2240, 2340; on ⑦ at 0810 and every 30 minutes until 1640, 1740 and hourly until 2140.

From Canterbury West: on Ⓐ at 0600, 0634**c**, 0706, 0736, 0800, 0836, 0907, 0936 and then at 07 and 36 minutes past each hour unt 1436, 1504, 1536, 1604, 1636, 1704, 1736, 1804, 1836, 1907, 1936, 2007, 2036, 2107, 2136; on ⑥ at 0556, 0704, 0736, 0807, 0836 an then at 07 and 36 minutes past each hour until 1936, 2004, 2104; on ⑦ at 0804 and hourly until 2104.

c – To/from London Cannon Street (does not call at Waterloo East). ‡ – London Waterloo East.

LONDON CHARING CROSS - DOVER

Valid until October 4 — Longest journey: 2 hours 6 minutes — SE

km					
0	0h00	↓	d.**London** C Cross ...a.	↑	2h02
1	0h03		d.**London** Waterloo ‡ a.		1h58
3	0h09	↓	d.**London** Bridge......a.	↑	1h53
36	0h32		d.Sevenoaks.............d.		1h28
48	0h40	↓	d.Tonbridge...............d.	↑	1h16
90	1h20		d.Ashford Int'l...........d.		0h39
113	1h40	↓	d.Folkstone Central...d.	↑	0h12
124	1h51		a.**Dover** Priory..........d.		0h00

From London Charing Cross: on Ⓐ at 0530, 0710, 0740, 0813, 0833, 0913, 0940 and every 30 minutes until 1610, 1637, 1724**c**, 1741 1821, 1841, 1910, 1940, 2010, 2040, 2110, 2140, 2210, 2240, 2310, 2340; on ⑥ at 0600, 0700, 0800, 0910 and hourly until 2310, 2340; o ⑦ at 0810 and hourly until 2210, 2240.

From Dover Priory: on Ⓐ at 0437, 0528, 0545**c**, 0604**c**, 0624, 0649**c**, 0725, 0758 and then at 25 and 58 minutes past each hour unt 2125, 2158; on ⑥ at 0451, 0551, 0625, 0725, 0825 and hourly until 1925, 2025, 2125, 2158; on ⑦ at 0725, 0825, 0925 and hourly unt 1925, 2025, 2125.

c – To/from London Cannon Street (does not call at Waterloo East). ‡ – London Waterloo East.

LONDON VICTORIA - ASHFORD INTERNATIONAL

Valid until October 4 — Longest journey: 1 hour 40 minutes — SE

km					
0	0h00	↓	d.**London** Victoria.....a.	↑	1h34
18	0h16		d.Bromley South.......d.		1h18
28	0h27	↓	d.Swanley.................d.	↑	1h02
64	1h03		d.Maidstone East......d.		0h31
68	1h08	↓	d.Bearsted................d.	↑	0h24
95	1h32		a.**Ashford** Int'l...........d.		0h00

From London Victoria: on Ⓐ at 0555, 0637, 0707, 0736, 0807 and every 30 minutes until 1637, 1652, 1712, 1742, 1803, 1818, 1842 1907, 1937, 2007, 2307, 2107, 22007, 2307; on ⑥ at 0607, 0707 and every 30 minutes until 2007, 2107, 2207, 2307; On ⑦ at 0745 an hourly until 2245.

From Ashford International: on Ⓐ at 0518, 0549, 0603, 0615, 0640, 0656, 0714, 0747, 0825, 0847, 0930, 0947 and then at 30 and 4 minutes past each hour until 1547, 1625, 1647, 1725, 1749, 1825, 1849, 1925, 1947, 2017, 2117, 2217; on ⑥ at 0518, 0547, 0630, 064 and then at 30 and 47 minutes past each hour until 1847, 1947, 2047, 2217; on ⑦ at 0647 and hourly until 2147.

LONDON CHARING CROSS - HASTINGS

Valid until October 4 — Longest journey: 1 hour 53 minutes — SE

km					
0	0h00	↓	d.**London** C Cross ...a.	↑	1h43
1	0h03		d.**London** Waterloo ‡ a.		1h39
3	0h08	↓	d.**London** Bridge......a.	↑	1h35
36	0h34		d.Sevenoaks.............d.		1h09
48	0h43	↓	d.Tonbridge...............d.	↑	1h00
55	0h55		d.Tunbridge Wells.....d.		0h49
89	1h33	↓	d.Battle....................d.	↑	0h16
100	1h45		a.**Hastings**.................d.		0h00

From London Charing Cross: on Ⓐ at 0645, 0715, 0746**c**, 0817, 0842**c**, 0914**c**, 0945, 1015, 1045 and every 30 minutes until 1615, 164 1702**c**, 1719*, 1737**c***, 1759*, 1828**c***, 1845, 1915, 1945, 2015, 2045, 2145, 2245, 2345; on ⑥ at 0745, 0815, 0845, 0915, 0945 and eve 30 minutes until 1915, 1955, 2055, 2155, 2255, 2345; on ⑦ at 0825, 0855, 0925, 0955, 1025, 1055 and every 30 minutes until 2025, 212 2225, 2325.

From Hastings: on Ⓐ at 0517, 0537**c**, 0605*, 0620*, 0643**c***, 0703*, 0727**c***, 0744, 0814, 0847, 0929, 0950, 1031, 1050 and at the sam minutes past each hour until 1531, 1545**c**, 1619, 1650, 1719, 1750, 1819, 1846, 1950, 2050, 2150, 2210; on ⑥ at 0550 and every minutes until 0850, 0931, 0950 and at the same minutes past each hour until 1650, 1720, 1750, 1850, 1950, 2050, 2150, 2210; on ⑦ 0720, 0750, 0831, 0850 and at the same minutes past each hour until 1850, 1950, 2050, 2150.

c – To/from London Cannon Street (does not call at Waterloo East).
‡ – London Waterloo East.
* – Does not call at London Bridge, Sevenoaks and Tonbridge. Frequent additional trains call these stations.

LONDON VICTORIA - EASTBOURNE

Longest journey: 1 hour 44 minutes — SN

km					
0	0h00	↓	d.**London** Victoria.....a.	↑	1h26
17	0h16		d.East Croydon..........d.		1h09
43	0h33	↓	d.Gatwick Airport.......d.	↑	0h53
61	0h50		d.Haywards Heath....d.		0h34
81	1h06	↓	d.Lewes....................d.	↑	0h19
106	1h27		a.**Eastbourne**............d.		0h00

From London Victoria: on Ⓐ at 0532, 0647, 0747, 0817, 0847 and every 30 minutes until 1647, 1727, 1757, 1847, 1917, 1947, 20 2047, 2117, 2147, 2247; on ⑥ at 0747 and every 30 minutes until 2147, 2247; on ⑦ at 0847 and hourly until 2247.

From Eastbourne: on Ⓐ at 0508, 0657**g**, 0732**g**, 0757, 0815, 0856, 0928, 0955, 1031, 1058 and at the same minutes past each hour u 1757, 1831, 1900, 1931, 2030, 2131, 2215; on ⑥ at 0503, 0624, 0658, 0731, 0758 and at the same minutes past each hour until 19 2301, 2131, 2218; on ⑦ at 0658, 0755, 0859 and hourly until 2059.

g – Does not call at Gatwick Airport.

ASHFORD - HASTINGS - EASTBOURNE - BRIGHTON

Longest journey: 2 hours 7 minutes — SN

km					
0	0h00	↓	d.**Ashford** Intl...........a.	↑	1h46
25	0h23		d.Rye.........................d.		1h24
42	0h42	↓	d.**Hastings**...............d.	↑	1h04
50	0h52		d.Bexhill....................d.		0h52
67	1h07	↓	a.**Eastbourne**............d.	↑	0h37
67	1h15		d.**Eastbourne**............a.		0h32
93	1h35	↓	d.Lewes....................d.	↑	0h12
106	1h48		a.**Brighton**...............d.		0h00

From Ashford International: on Ⓐ at 0614, 0717, 0833 and hourly until 2133; on ⑥ at 0615, 0733 and hourly until 2133; on ⑦ at 08 0922 and hourly until 2122.

From Brighton: on Ⓐ at 0618, 0732 and hourly until 1932, 2030; on ⑥ at 0632 and hourly until 2032; on ⑦ at 0820 and hourly until 20

LONDON BRIDGE - UCKFIELD

Longest journey: 1 hour 19 minutes — S

km					
0	0h00	↓	d.**London** Bridge......a.	↑	1h15
16	0h16		d.East Croydon..........d.		0h59
32	0h29	↓	d.Oxted.....................d.	↑	0h44
57	0h55		d.Eridge △...............d.		0h17
70	1h01	↓	d.Crowborough.........d.	↑	0h12
74	1h15		a.**Uckfield**...............d.		0h00

From London Bridge: on Ⓐ at 0608, 0638, 0703, 0758, 0903, 1008 and hourly until 1508, 1538, 1608, 1638, 1708, 1808, 1908, 20 2104, 2204, 2304; on ⑥ at 0608 and hourly until 2208, 2304.

From Uckfield: on Ⓐ at 0518, 0542, 0630, 0708, 0734, 0804, 0834 and hourly until 1534, 1633, 1732, 1832, 1900, 1933, 2004, 20 2134; on ⑥ at 0634 and hourly until 2134.

On ⑦ services run Oxted - Uckfield and v.v. only. Connections available from/to London Victoria (see East Grinstead Table). **From Oxt** at 0937⑦ and hourly until 2237⑦. **From Uckfield** at 1034⑦ and hourly until 2234⑦.

△ – **Spa Valley Railway** (Eridge - Tunbridge Wells West: *8 km*). ✆ 01892 537715. www.spavalleyrailway.co.uk

LONDON - THE SOUTH and SOUTH EAST

Typical off-peak journey time in hours and minutes
READ DOWN ↓ READ UP ↑

Journey times may be extended during peak hours on Ⓐ (0600 - 0900 and 1600 - 1900) and also at weekends.
The longest journey time by any train is noted in the table heading.

LONDON VICTORIA - EAST GRINSTEAD
Longest journey: 60 minutes SN

km					
0	0h00	↓	d.**London** Victoria.....a.	↑	0h56
17	0h17	↓	d.East Croydon.........d.	↑	0h37
33	0h37	↓	d.Oxted...................d.	↑	0h16
48	0h54	↓	a.**East Grinstead** ▽.d.	↑	0h00

From London Victoria: on Ⓐ at 0525, 0552, 0624, 0654, 0710, 0732, 0853 and every 30 minutes until 2253, 2324; on ⑥ at 0523, 0623, 0653 and every 30 minutes until 2253, 2324; on ⑦ at 0747, 0853, 0923, 0953 and every 30 minutes until 1953, 2053, 2153, 2236.

From East Grinstead: on Ⓐ at 0558, 0637, 0705, 0736, 0807 and every 30 minutes until 2237, 2254; on ⑥ at 0637 and every 30 minutes until 2237, 2254; on ⑦ at 0820, 0912, 0942 and every 30 minuts until 2012, 2112, 2212, 2309.

▽ – **Bluebell Railway** (🚂 East Grinstead - Sheffield Park: *18 km*). ✆ 01825 720800. www.bluebell-railway.com

LONDON VICTORIA - LITTLEHAMPTON
Longest journey: 1 hour 47 minutes SN

km					
0	0h00	↓	d.**London** Victoria.....a.	↑	1h42
17	0h16	↓	d.East Croydon.........a.	↑	1h25
43	0h33	↓	d.Gatwick Airport ......a.	↑	1h09
61	0h50	↓	d.Haywards Heath ....a.	↑	0h54
82	1h06	↓	d.Hove.......................a.	↑	0h35
96	1h21	↓	d.Worthing.................d.	↑	0h21
114	1h41	↓	a.**Littlehampton**.......d.	↑	0h00

From London Victoria: on Ⓐ at 0747, 0817, 0847 and every 30 minutes until 1617, 1657**bg**, 1717, 1746, 1817**g**, 1847, 1917, 1947, 2017, 2047, 2147; on ⑥ at 0747 and every 30 minutes until 2047, 2147; on ⑦ at 0817 and hourly until 2117.

From Littlehampton: on Ⓐ at 0553**b**, 0641**g**, 0702**g**, 0729, 0815 and every 30 minutes until 1815, 1913, 2015, 2115; on ⑥ at 0545, 0615 and every 30 minutes until 1815, 1915, 2015, 2115; on ⑦ at 0715 and hourly until 2015.

b – From / to **London Bridge** (not calling at Victoria).
g – Does not call at Gatwick Airport.

LONDON VICTORIA - BOGNOR REGIS
Longest journey: 1 hour 57 minutes SN

km					
0	0h00	↓	d.**London** Victoria.....a.	↑	1h50
17	0h16	↓	d.East Croydon.........d.	↑	1h30
43	0h37	↓	d.Gatwick Airport .....d.	↑	1h08
61	1h03	↓	d.Horsham.................d.	↑	0h50
94	1h30	↓	d.Arundel...................d.	↑	0h16
110	1h40	↓	d.Barnham..................d.	↑	0h07
116	1h46	↓	a.**Bognor Regis**.......d.	↑	0h00

From London Victoria: on Ⓐ at 0602, 0802 and every 30 minutes until 1632, 1702**g**, 1734**g**, 1804, 1834**g**, 1902, 1932, 2002, 2032, 2117**k**, 2217**k**; on ⑥ at 0532, 0602, 0632 and every 30 minutes until 2002, 2032, 2117**k**, 2217**k**; on ⑦ at 0702, 0802 and hourly until 2102, 2202.

From Bognor Regis: on Ⓐ at 0606, 0717**g**, 0755, 0826, 0856, 0930, 0956 an at the same minutes past each hour until 1456, 1527, 1556, 1630, 1656, 1730, 1757, 1833**k**, 1933**k**, 2033**k**; on ⑥ at 0630, 0656 and at the same minutes past each hour until 1756, 1833**k**, 1933**k**, 2033**k**; on ⑦ at 0652, 0759 and hourly until 2159.

g – Does not call at Gatwick Airport.
k – Does not call at Arundal and Horsham.

SEAFORD - BRIGHTON
Longest journey: 42 minutes SN

km					
0	0h00	↓	d.**Seaford**.................a.	↑	0h36
2	0h05	↓	d.Newhaven Harbour..d.	↑	0h30
5	0h07	↓	d.Newhaven Town ....d.	↑	0h28
15	0h19	↓	d.Lewes.....................d.	↑	0h18
22	0h26	↓	d.Falmer....................d.	↑	0h09
28	0h35	↓	a.**Brighton** ....d.	↑	0h00

From Seaford: on Ⓐ at 0545, 0630, 0716, 0759, 0856, 0925, 0958 and at the same minutes past each hour until 1658, 1720, 1758, 1823, 1859, 1917, 1958, 2028, 2058, 2128, 2158, 2220, 2258, 2325; on ⑥ at 0505, 0628, 0658, 0728, 0758, 0825, 0858 and at the same minutes past each hour until 1958, 2028, 2058, 2128, 2158, 2220, 2258, 2325; on ⑦ at 0757 and every 30 minutes until 2127, 2153, 2227, 2253

From Brighton: on Ⓐ at 0545, 0639, 0717, 0740, 0810, 0845, 0910 and every 30 minutes until 1710, 1745, 1802, 1838, 1908, 1940, 2010, 2104, 2140, 2204, 2234, 2334; on ⑥ at 0552, 0610, 0640 and every 30 minutes until 2040, 2104, 2140, 2204, 2234, 2334; on ⑦ at 0715, 0749, 0809, 0849, 0909, 0947 and at the same minutes past each hour until 2209, 2239.

BRIGHTON - PORTSMOUTH HARBOUR
Longest journey: 1 hour 49 minutes SN

km	⚒	⑦				⚒	⑦
0	0h00	0h00	↓	d.**Brighton**..............d.	↑	1h19	1h44
2	0h04	0h10		d.Hove.......................d.		1h15	1h40
16	0h22	0h31	↓	d.Worthing ....d.	↑	0h57	1h19
35	0h39	0h54		d.Barnham..................d.		0h39	0h57
45	0h47	1h02	↓	d.Chichester...............d.	↑	0h31	0h43
59	1h02	1h23		d.Havant.....................d.		0h17	0h22
71	1h14	1h37	↓	a.**Portsmouth** S ▽.d.	↑	0h04	0h04
72	1h18	1h41		a.**Portsmouth** H .....d.		0h00	0h00

From Brighton: on Ⓐ at 0553, 0635, 0715, 0737, 0803 and hourly until 1603**p**, 1703, 1800, 1900**p**, 2003, 2103, 2133, 2203; on ⑥ at 0601, 0703 and hourly until 1903, 1956, 2103, 2203; on ⑦ at 0719, 0830 and hourly until 2030, 2125.

From Portsmouth Harbour: on Ⓐ at 0533, 0604, 0720, 0829 and hourly until 1629, 1640, 1729, 1827, 1932**p**, 2032**p**, 2115**p**, 2215, 2244; on ⑥ at 0629 and hourly until 1929, 2028, 2111, 2215, 2244; on ⑦ at 0714 and hourly until 1914, 2015**p**, 2114.

p – To / from Portsmouth & Southsea only.
▽ – Portsmouth and Southsea.

BRIGHTON - SOUTHAMPTON CENTRAL
Longest journey: 2 hours 1 minute SN

km	⚒	⑦				⚒	⑦
0	0h00	0h00	↓	d.**Brighton**..............d.	↑	1h45	1h50
2	0h04	0h04		d.Hove.......................d.		1h41	1h46
16	0h22	0h25	↓	d.Worthing ....d.	↑	1h23	1h25
35	0h44	0h48		d.Barnham..................d.		1h00	1h03
45	0h52	0h56	↓	d.Chichester...............d.	↑	0h52	0h54
59	1h04	1h08		d.Havant.....................d.		0h38	0h42
75	1h23	1h25	↓	d.Fareham ....d.	↑	0h23	0h24
98	1h46	1h56		a.**Southampton** C ..d.		0h00	0h00

From Brighton: on Ⓐ at 0514, 0530, 0627, 0706, 0730, 0833 and hourly until 1733, 1828, 1930, 2030; on ⑥ at 0515, 0527, 0633 and hourly until 1833, 1929, 2030; on ⑦ at 0800 and hourly until 2100.

From Southampton Central: on Ⓐ at 0610, 0733 and hourly until 1333, 1426, 1533 and hourly until 2033, 2113; on ⑥ at 0633 and hourly until 1333, 1426, 1533 and hourly until 2033, 2113; on ⑦ at 0730, 0827, 0930 and hourly until 1930, 2029, 2130.

LONDON WATERLOO - READING
Valid until October 4 Longest journey: 1 hour 35 minutes SW

km					
0	0h00	↓	d.**London** Waterloo ..a.	↑	1h22
16	0h16	↓	d.Richmond ....d.	↑	1h03
18	0h20	↓	d.Twickenham............d.	↑	0h58
30	0h33	↓	d.Staines ....d.	↑	0h36
46	0h53	↓	d.Ascot ....d.	↑	0h28
70	1h20	↓	a.**Reading** ....d.	↑	0h00

From London Waterloo: on Ⓐ at 0505, 0550 and every 30 minutes until 2350; on ⑥ at 0505, 0550 and every 30 minutes until 2350; on ⑦ at 0709, 0809 and every 30 minutes until 2339.

From Reading: on Ⓐ at 0542 and every 30 minutes until 2312; on ⑥ at 0542 and every 30 minutes until 2312; on ⑦ at 0754 and every 30 minutes until 2254.

LONDON WATERLOO - WINDSOR
Valid until October 4 Longest journey: 1 hour 09 minutes SW

km					
0	0h00	↓	d.**London** Waterloo ..a.	↑	0h56
16	0h20	↓	d.Richmond ....d.	↑	0h34
18	0h24	↓	d.Twickenham............d.	↑	0h30
30	0h39	↓	d.Staines ....d.	↑	0h15
41	0h53	↓	a.**Windsor** ▷ ....d.	↑	0h00

From London Waterloo: on Ⓐ at 0558 and every 30 minutes until 2328; on ⑥ at 0558 and every 30 minutes until 2328; on ⑦ at 0644, 0744, 0844, 0925 and at the same minutes past each hour until 1925, 1944, 2044, 2144, 2244.

From Windsor and Eton Riverside: on Ⓐ at 0553 and every 30 minutes until 2253; on ⑥ at 0553 and every 30 minutes until 2253; on ⑦ at 0701, 0801, 0901, 1001, 1034 and at the same minutes past each hour until 2101, 2201, 2301.

▷ – Windsor and Eton Riverside.

103 BEDFORD - LUTON ✈ - LONDON - GATWICK ✈ - BRIGHTON FC

Subject to alteration on ⑦ August 3 - September 7.
Other services : Bedford - Luton Airport - London St Pancras Table 170; London Victoria - Gatwick Airport - Brighton Table 105.
London Victoria - Gatwick Airport *Gatwick Express* Table 140.

km			Ⓐ	Ⓐ	Ⓐ	Ⓐ	Ⓐ	Ⓐ	Ⓐ	Ⓐ	Ⓐ	Ⓐ	Ⓐ	Ⓐ	Ⓐ	Ⓐ	Ⓐ	Ⓐ	Ⓐ	Ⓐ	Ⓐ	Ⓐ	Ⓐ	Ⓐ	Ⓐ	
0	**Bedford** d.	Ⓐ	0042	0142	0242	0342	0408	0420	0500	0520	0540	0558	0622	0654	0658	0730	0748	0804	0824	0840	0854	0910	0924	0940	0954	and at
31	Luton d.		0106	0206	0306	0406	0432	0444	0524	0544	0604	0622	0646	0714	0722	0750	0812	0828	0848	0904	0918	0934	0948	1004	1018	the same
33	Luton Airport ✈ d.		0109	0209	0309	0409	0435	0447	0527	0546	0606	0624	0648	|	0725	|	0815	0830	0850	0906	0920	0936	0950	1006	1020	minutes
48	St Albans City d.		0121	0221	0321	0421	0447	0459	0539	0558	0618	0636	0700	0726	0738	0802	0828	0844	0902	0918	0932	0948	1002	1018	1032	past
80	**London** St Pancras d.		0154	0254	0354	0454	0512	0532	0602	0622	0638	0658	0720	0744	0756	0820	0848	0904	0922	0940	0954	1010	1024	1040	1054	each
85	**London** Bridge d.		|	|	|	|	0530	0550	0620	0642	0700	0716	0742	|	0818	|	0912	0927	0942	0957	1012	1027	1042	1057	1112	hour
101	East Croydon d.		0236	0336	0436	0532	0548	0606	0635	0655	0715	0731	0755	0826	0837	0858	0925	0941	0955	1011	1025	1041	1055	1111	1125	until
127	Gatwick Airport ✈ d.		0256	0356	0456	0548	0604	0623	0652	0711	0731	0747	0812	0842	0853	0913	0941	0957	1011	1027	1041	1057	1111	1127	1141	
145	Haywards Heath d.		...	...	0512	0602	0619	0639	0706	0726	0745	0802	0827	0858	0908	0927	0956	1011	1027	1041	1055	1111	1127	1141	1155	♣
166	**Brighton** a.		...	...	0530	0622	0640	0659	0727	0744	0805	0823	0848	0918	0925	0946	1017	1025	1047	1055	1115	1125	1147	1155	1215	

	Ⓐ	Ⓐ	Ⓐ	Ⓐ	Ⓐ	Ⓐ	Ⓐ	Ⓐ		Ⓐ	Ⓐ	Ⓐ	Ⓐ	Ⓐ	Ⓐ	Ⓐ	Ⓐ	Ⓐ		Ⓐ	Ⓐ	Ⓐ	Ⓐ	Ⓐ	Ⓐ	Ⓐ	Ⓐ
Bedford d.	1510	1524	1540	1550	1608	1624	1640	1707	...	1720	1734	1754	1810	1824	1840	1854	1925	1952	...	2022	2052	2122	2152	2222	2242	2312	2342
Luton d.	1534	1548	1604	1610	1632	1648	1702	1731	...	1744	1758	1818	1834	1848	1904	1918	1949	2016	...	2046	2116	2146	2216	2246	2306	2336	0006
Luton Airport ✈ d.	1536	1550	1606	1613	1634	1650	1704	1734	...	1746	1800	1820	1836	1850	1906	1920	1951	2018	...	2048	2118	2148	2219	2248	2309	2339	0009
St Albans City d.	1548	1602	1618	1624	1647	1702	1716	1745	...	1758	1812	1832	1848	1902	1918	1932	2003	2030	...	2100	2130	2200	2230	2300	2321	2351	002
London St Pancras d.	1610	1622	1640	1646	1708	1728	1740	1808	...	1818	1834	1854	1909	1924	1939	1954	2024	2054	...	2124	2154	2224	2254	2324	2354	0024	005
London Bridge d.	1627	1643	...	|	|	|	|	1828	...	|	1857	1912	1927	1942	1957	2012	2042	2112	...	2142	2212	2242	2312	2342	0012	0042	|
East Croydon d.	1641	1700	...	1726	1747	1809	1826	1843	...	1901	1911	1925	1941	1955	2011	2025	2055	2125	...	2155	2225	2255	2325	2357	0029	0057	013
Gatwick Airport ✈ d.	1657	1716	...	1742	1814	1824	1849	1859	...	1918	1926	1941	1957	2011	2027	2041	2111	2141	...	2211	2241	2311	2341	0019	0049	0119	015
Haywards Heath d.	1711	1732	...	1758	1831	1838	...	1915	...	1930	1942	1957	2011	2025	2041	2057	2125	2159	...	2225	2259	2325	2359	...	...	...	...
Brighton a.	1730	1754	...	1818	1853	1901	...	1934	...	1952	2001	2017	2029	2045	2057	2117	2145	2219	...	2245	2319	2345	0019	...	...	...	...

		⑥	⑥	⑥	⑥	⑥	⑥	⑥	⑥	⑥	⑥	⑥	⑥	⑥	⑥		⑥	⑥	⑥	⑥	⑥	⑥	⑥	⑥	⑥	⑥
Bedford d.	⑥	0042	0142	0242	0312	0342	0422	0452	0522	0540	0554	0610	0624	0640	0654	and at	1810	1824	1840	1854	1922	1952	2022	2052	2122	215
Luton d.		0106	0206	0306	0336	0406	0446	0516	0546	0604	0618	0634	0648	0704	0718	the same	1834	1948	1904	1918	1946	2016	2046	2116	2146	221
Luton Airport ✈ d.		0109	0209	0309	0339	0409	0449	0519	0549	0606	0620	0636	0650	0706	0720	minutes	1836	1950	1906	1920	1948	2018	2048	2118	2148	221
St Albans City d.		0121	0221	0321	0351	0421	0501	0531	0601	0618	0632	0648	0702	0718	0732	past	1948	1902	1918	1932	2000	2030	2100	2130	2200	223
London St Pancras d.		0154	0254	0354	0424	0454	0534	0553	0624	0640	0654	0710	0724	0740	0754	each	1910	1924	1940	1954	2024	2054	2124	2154	2226	225
London Bridge d.		|	|	|	|	|	0552	0612	0642	0657	0712	0727	0742	0757	0812	hour	1927	1942	1957	2012	2042	2112	2142	2212	2242	231
East Croydon d.		0236	0336	0436	0506	0532	0605	0625	0655	0711	0725	0741	0755	0811	0825	until	1941	1955	2011	2025	2055	2125	2155	2225	2255	232
Gatwick Airport ✈ d.		0256	0356	0456	0526	0554	0620	0641	0711	0727	0741	0757	0811	0827	0841		1957	2011	2027	2041	2111	2141	2211	2241	2311	234
Haywards Heath d.		...	...	...	0544	0611	0637	0655	0727	0741	0755	0811	0827	0841	0855	♣	2011	2027	2041	2057	2125	2159	2225	2259	2325	235
Brighton a.		...	...	...	0605	0631	0657	0715	0747	0755	0815	0825	0847	0855	0915		2025	2047	2055	2117	2145	2219	2245	2319	2345	001

	⑥	⑥	⑥	⑥			⑦	⑦	⑦	⑦	⑦	⑦	⑦		⑦	⑦	⑦	⑦	⑦	⑦	⑦	⑦	⑦	⑦	⑦	⑦
Bedford d.	2218	2242	2312	2342	...	⑦	0602	0607	0712	0750	0820	0850	0920	and at	1820	1850	1920	1950	2012	2042	2112	2142	2212	2242	2312	234
Luton d.	2242	2306	2336	0006	...		0634	0702	0736	0814	0844	0914	0944	the same	1844	1914	1944	2014	2036	2106	2136	2206	2236	2306	2336	000
Luton Airport ✈ d.	2244	2309	2339	0009	...		0637	0705	0739	0817	0847	0917	0947	minutes	1847	1917	1947	2017	2039	2109	2139	2209	2239	2309	2339	000
St Albans City d.	2256	2321	2351	0021	...		0649	0717	0751	0829	0859	0929	0959	past	1859	1929	1959	2029	2051	2121	2151	2221	2251	2321	2351	002
London St Pancras d.	2324	2354	0024	0054	...		0724	0750	0824	0854	0924	0954	1024	each	1924	1954	2024	2054	2124	2154	2224	2254	2324	2354	0024	005
London Bridge d.	2342	0012	0042	|	...		0741	0809	0841	0911	0941	1011	1041	hour	1941	2011	2041	2111	2141	2211	2241	2311	2341	0012	0042	|
East Croydon d.	2357	0029	0057	0136	...		0754	0821	0856	0926	0956	1026	1056	until	1956	2026	2056	2126	2156	2226	2256	2326	2357	0029	0057	013
Gatwick Airport ✈ d.	0019	0049	0119	0155	...		0818	0842	0912	0942	1012	1042	1112		2012	2042	2112	2142	2212	2242	2312	2342	0020	0049	0119	015
Haywards Heath d.	0038	0110	...	...	...		0834	0856	0926	0956	1026	1056	1126	♣	2026	2056	2126	2156	2226	2256	2326	2356	0036	...	...	...
Brighton a.	0059	0129	...	...	...		0853	0915	0947	1015	1047	1115	1147		2047	2115	2147	2215	2247	2315	2347	0015	0055	...	...	...

		Ⓐ	Ⓐ	Ⓐ	Ⓐ	Ⓐ	Ⓐ	Ⓐ	Ⓐ	Ⓐ	Ⓐ	Ⓐ	Ⓐ	Ⓐ	Ⓐ	Ⓐ	Ⓐ	Ⓐ	Ⓐ	Ⓐ	Ⓐ	Ⓐ	Ⓐ	Ⓐ	Ⓐ	
Brighton d.	Ⓐ	...	...	...	...	...	...	0510	0540	0550	0624	0702	0724	0750	0802	0816	0834	0900	0907	0934	0937	1004	1007	1034	1037	and at
Haywards Heath d.		...	...	...	...	...	...	0531	0601	0611	0645	0725	0747	0809	0825	0839	0900	0918	0931	0948	1001	1018	1031	1048	1101	the same
Gatwick Airport ✈ d.		0121	0221	0321	0421	0457	0527	0547	0617	0625	0702	0739	0801	0824	0839	0853	0917	0932	0947	1002	1017	1032	1047	1102	1117	minutes
East Croydon d.		0140	0240	0340	0440	0516	0548	0602	0632	0645	0723	0754	0823	0839	0854	0909	0932	0946	1002	1017	1032	1047	1102	1117	1132	past
London Bridge a.		|	|	|	|	0534	0602	0615	0646	0658	|	|	|	|	0908	|	0946	1000	1015	1030	1045	1100	1115	1130	1145	each
London St Pancras a.		0220	0320	0420	0518	0552	0622	0634	0702	0716	0804	0831	0904	0920	0932	0948	1004	1018	1033	1048	1103	1118	1133	1148	1203	hour
St Albans City a.		0253	0353	0453	0553	0624	0643	0657	0722	0741	0825	0852	0925	0940	0951	1009	1025	1039	1055	1109	1125	1139	1155	1209	1225	until
Luton Airport ✈ a.		0305	0405	0505	0605	0635	0655	0709	0734	0753	0837	0901	0937	0951	1000	1020	1037	1050	1106	1120	1137	1150	1207	1220	1237	
Luton a.		0308	0408	0508	0608	0638	0658	0712	0737	0756	0840	0904	0940	0954	1003	1023	1040	1053	1109	1123	1140	1153	1210	1223	1240	♣
Bedford a.		0335	0435	0535	0637	0704	0724	0740	0803	0823	0905	0926	1007	1020	1023	1049	1105	1119	1135	1149	1205	1219	1235	1249	1305	

	Ⓐ	Ⓐ	Ⓐ	Ⓐ	Ⓐ	Ⓐ	Ⓐ	Ⓐ	Ⓐ	Ⓐ	Ⓐ	Ⓐ	Ⓐ	Ⓐ	Ⓐ	Ⓐ	Ⓐ	Ⓐ	Ⓐ	Ⓐ	Ⓐ	Ⓐ	Ⓐ	Ⓐ	Ⓐ	Ⓐ	Ⓐ
Brighton d.	1504	1507	1534	1537	1604	1607	1624	1630	1703	1707	1724	1737	1803	1807	1834	1837	1907	1934	1937	2003	2007	2034	2037	2111	2137	2207	22
Haywards Heath d.	1518	1531	1548	1558	1618	1626	1638	1651	1718	1726	1746	1801	1818	1831	1848	1901	1931	1948	2001	2019	2031	2048	2101	2132	2201	2231	22
Gatwick Airport ✈ d.	1532	1547	1602	1612	1632	1642	1653	1708	1732	1739	1800	1817	1832	1847	1902	1917	1947	2002	2017	2032	2047	2102	2117	2147	2217	2247	23
East Croydon d.	1547	1602	1617	1628	1647	1658	1709	1723	1747	1758	1816	1832	1847	1902	1917	1932	2002	2017	2032	2047	2102	2117	2132	2202	2232	2302	23
London Bridge a.	1600	1616	|	|	|	|	1727	|	1813	|	|	1846	1900	1915	1930	1945	2015	2030	2045	2100	2115	2130	2145	2215	2245	2315	23
London St Pancras a.	1617	1635	1701	1705	1731	1735	1745	1801	1831	1835	1901	1905	1919	1933	1948	2003	2033	2048	2103	2118	2133	2148	2203	2231	2302	2332	00
St Albans City a.	1638	1656	1719	1725	1749	1755	1806	1819	1849	1857	1919	1928	1945	1955	2009	2025	2055	2109	2125	2138	2155	2208	2225	2256	2326	2356	00
Luton Airport ✈ a.	1652	1708	|	1738	|	1808	1820	|	|	1909	|	1939	1957	2006	2020	2038	2107	2120	2137	2150	2207	2220	2237	2308	2338	0008	00
Luton a.	1655	1711	1732	1741	1802	1811	1823	1832	1902	1912	1931	1942	2000	2009	2023	2041	2110	2123	2140	2153	2210	2223	2240	2311	2341	0011	00
Bedford a.	1720	1738	1753	1806	1823	1836	1848	1855	1923	1938	1955	2008	2026	2035	2049	2106	2135	2149	2205	2219	2236	2249	2306	2338	0008	0038	01

	Ⓐ	Ⓐ			⑥	⑥	⑥	⑥	⑥	⑥	⑥	⑥	⑥	⑥	⑥	⑥	⑥	⑥	⑥	⑥	⑥	⑥		⑥	⑥	⑥
Brighton d.	2311	2337	...	⑥	...	...	...	...	...	...	0525	0602	0625	0637	0704	0707	0734	0737	0804	0807	0834	0837	and at	2004	2007	20
Haywards Heath d.	2329	2359	...		...	...	...	...	...	...	0546	0618	0646	0701	0718	0731	0748	0801	0818	0831	0848	0901	the same	2018	2031	20
Gatwick Airport ✈ d.	2343	0015	...		0121	0221	0321	0421	0457	0527	0602	0632	0702	0717	0732	0747	0802	0817	0832	0847	0902	0917	minutes	2032	2047	21
East Croydon d.	0002	0036	...		0140	0240	0340	0440	0516	0548	0617	0647	0717	0732	0747	0802	0817	0832	0847	0902	0917	0932	past	2047	2102	21
London Bridge a.	0021	0052	...		|	|	|	|	|	0602	0630	0700	0730	0745	0800	0815	0830	0845	0900	0915	0930	0945	each	2100	2115	21
London St Pancras a.	0038	0108	...		0220	0320	0420	0520	0554	0618	0647	0717	0748	0803	0818	0833	0848	0903	0918	0933	0948	1003	hour	2118	2133	21
St Albans City a.	0111	0141	...		0253	0353	0453	0557	0625	0640	0710	0740	0809	0825	0839	0855	0909	0925	0939	0955	1009	1025	until	2139	2155	22
Luton Airport ✈ a.	0123	0153	...		0305	0405	0505	0609	0637	0652	0721	0751	0821	0837	0851	0907	0920	0937	0950	1007	1020	1037		2150	2207	22
Luton a.	0126	0156	...		0308	0408	0508	0612	0640	0655	0724	0754	0823	0840	0853	0910	0923	0940	0953	1010	1023	1040	♣	2153	2210	22
Bedford a.	0152	0222	...		0335	0435	0535	0639	0705	0720	0750	0820	0849	0905	0919	0935	0949	1005	1019	1035	1049	1105		2219	2235	22

	⑥	⑥	⑥	⑥	⑥	⑥	⑥			⑦	⑦	⑦	⑦	⑦	⑦	⑦	⑦		⑦	⑦	⑦	⑦	⑦	⑦	⑦	⑦
Brighton d.	2037	2107	2137	2207	2233	2311	2337	...	⑦	0606	0636	0704	0736	0804	0844	0914	0944	and at	2014	2044	2114	2144	2214	2244	2314	23
Haywards Heath d.	2101	2131	2201	2231	2254	2329	2359	...		0624	0654	0724	0754	0824	0903	0933	1003	the same	2033	2103	2133	2203	2233	2303	2333	00
Gatwick Airport ✈ d.	2117	2147	2217	2247	2317	2343	0015	...		0638	0708	0738	0808	0838	0917	0947	1017	minutes	2047	2117	2147	2217	2247	2317	2347	00
East Croydon d.	2132	2202	2232	2302	2332	0002	0036	...		0657	0727	0757	0827	0856	0933	1003	1033	past	2103	2133	2203	2233	2303	2333	0002	00
London Bridge a.	2145	2215	2245	2315	2344	0021	0051	...		0715	0745	0815	0845	0915	0945	1015	1045	each	2115	2145	2215	2245	2315	2345	0022	00
London St Pancras a.	2203	2232	2302	2332	0002	0038	0108	...		0734	0804	0834	0904	0934	1004	1032	1102	hour	2132	2202	2234	2304	2334	0004	0039	01
St Albans City a.	2225	2256	2326	2356	0026	0110	0141	...		0808	0838	0908	0938	1008	1038	1057	1127	until	2157	2227	2308	2338	0008	0038	0111	01
Luton Airport ✈ a.	2237	2308	2338	0008	0038	0123	0153	...		0820	0850	0920	0950	1020	1053	1109	1139		2209	2239	2320	2350	0020	0050	0123	01
Luton a.	2240	2311	2341	0011	0041	0126	0156	...		0823	0853	0923	0953	1023	1057	1112	1142	♣	2212	2242	2323	2353	0023	0053	0126	01
Bedford a.	2306	2338	0008	0038	0108	0152	0222	...		0849	0919	0949	1019	1049	1119	1138	1208		2238	2308	2349	0019	0049	0119	0152	02

♣ – Timings may vary by ± 3 minutes.

SN LONDON - GATWICK ✈ - BRIGHTON 105

For Bedford - Luton Airport - London St Pancras - Gatwick Airport - Brighton services see Table 103.
For London Victoria - Gatwick Airport *Gatwick Express* services see Table 140.

km			②–⑤	Ⓐ	Ⓐ	Ⓐ	Ⓐ	Ⓐ	Ⓐ	Ⓐ	Ⓐ	Ⓐ	Ⓐ	Ⓐ	Ⓐ	Ⓐ	and at	Ⓐ	Ⓐ	Ⓐ	Ⓐ	Ⓐ	Ⓐ	Ⓐ	Ⓐ	Ⓐ
0	**London** Victoria ....d.	Ⓐ	0005	0100	0400	0501	0606	0615	0630	0645	0736	0807	0837	0849	0906	0936	the same	1551	1606	1636	1706	1732	1744	1802	1815	1826
17	East Croydon ....d.		0027	0124	0426	0523	0623	|	|	|	0752	0823	0853	0908	0922	0952	minutes	1608	1622	1652	1723	|	|	|	|	1841
43	Gatwick Airport ✈ ....d.		0046	0149	0452	0550	0640	0648	0704	0725	0808	|	|	0923	|	|	past each	1623	|	|	|	1804	1815	1836	1847	|
61	Haywards Heath.......d.		0103	0206	0506	0606	|	0700	0716	0738	0822	0852	|	|	|	|	hour until	|	|	1720	1748	1816	1827	1849	1859	1909
82	**Brighton**.................a.		0117	0223	0521	0627	0705	0713	0735	0753	0838	0908	0928	0952	0958	1028	✣	1652	1658	1738	1810	1835	1845	1910	1917	1925

	Ⓐ	Ⓐ	Ⓐ	Ⓐ	Ⓐ	Ⓐ	Ⓐ	Ⓐ	Ⓐ	Ⓐ	Ⓐ	Ⓐ	Ⓐ	Ⓐ			⑥	⑥	⑥	⑥	⑥	⑥	⑥	⑥	and at	⑥
ondon Victoria .... d.	1832	1844	1906	1936	2006	2036	2102	2106	2136	2206	2236	2302	2306	2332	...	⑥	0005	0100	0400	0502	0532	0706	0736	0751	the same	1906
ast Croydon............ d.	|	|	1923	1953	2023	2053	2118	2123	2152	2222	2252	2320	2323	2349	...		0027	0124	0424	0524	0548	0722	0752	0808	minutes	1922
atwick Airport ✈..... d.	1907	1915	|	|	|	|	2139	|	|	|	|	2339	|	0015	...		0046	0149	0449	0553	0622	|	|	0823	past each	|
aywards Heath .... d.	1920	1927	1948	2018	2047	2117	2153	2147	2216	2247	2316	2353	2348	0032	...		0103	0206	0503	0607	0641	|	|	|	hour until	|
righton .... a.	1940	1944	2004	2033	2101	2131	2215	2201	2230	2301	2330	0015	0001	0052	...		0117	0223	0517	0627	0702	0757	0827	0852	✣	1957

	⑥	⑥	⑥	⑥	⑥	⑥	⑥	⑥	⑥	⑥	⑥	⑥			⑦	⑦	⑦	⑦	⑦	⑦	⑦	⑦	⑦	⑦	⑦	⑦	⑦
ondon Victoria .... d.	1936	1951	2006	2021	2036	2106	2136	2206	2236	2302	2306	2332	...	⑦	0005	0100	0400	0502	0547	0632	0726	0832	0927	0932	1006	1027	1032
ast Croydon............ d.	1952	2008	2022	2038	2052	2123	2153	2223	2253	2318	2323	2352	...		0027	0126	0426	0525	0610	0655	0747	0853	0942	0949	1023	1042	1049
atwick Airport ✈..... d.	|	2023	|	2053	|	|	|	|	|	2339	|	0015	...		0046	0151	0453	0550	0633	0722	0813	0913	1006	|	|	1106	|
aywards Heath .... d.	|	|	|	|	|	2147	2217	2247	2317	2353	2347	0032	...		0103	0208	0508	0604	0648	0739	0829	0930	1022	|	|	1122	|
righton .... a.	2027	2052	2057	2122	2127	2201	2231	2301	2331	0015	0001	0052	...		0117	0223	0523	0620	0709	0759	0850	0951	1043	1024	1103	1143	1124

	and at	⑦	⑦	⑦	⑦	⑦	⑦	⑦	⑦	⑦	⑦
ondon Victoria .... d.	the same	1906	1927	1932	2006	2027	2032	2106	2127	2227	2332
ast Croydon............ d.	minutes	1923	1942	1949	2023	2042	2049	2123	2142	2242	2353
atwick Airport ✈..... d.	past each	1939	2006	|	|	2106	|	|	2207	2306	0015
aywards Heath .... d.	hour until	|	2022	|	|	2122	|	|	2223	2322	0031
righton .... a.	✣	2003	2043	2024	2103	2143	2124	2203	2243	2346	0052

		Ⓐ	Ⓐ	Ⓐ	Ⓐ	Ⓐ	Ⓐ	Ⓐ	Ⓐ	Ⓐ	Ⓐ
Brighton..............d.	Ⓐ	0350	0523	0617	0630	0640	0650	0656	0714	0729	0744
Haywards Heath....d.		0425	0539	0635	0651	0703	0706	0720	0735	0751	0806
Gatwick Airport ✈ .a.		0501	0554	0652	0704	0715	|	0732	0747	0802	0818
East Croydon.........a.		0527	0610	0715	|	|	0738	|	|	|	|
London Victoria....a.		0549	0629	0732	0737	0750	0757	0806	0820	0835	0852

	Ⓐ	Ⓐ	Ⓐ	Ⓐ	Ⓐ	Ⓐ	Ⓐ	Ⓐ	and at	Ⓐ	Ⓐ	Ⓐ	Ⓐ	Ⓐ	Ⓐ	Ⓐ	Ⓐ	Ⓐ	Ⓐ	Ⓐ	Ⓐ	Ⓐ	Ⓐ	Ⓐ	Ⓐ	Ⓐ
righton .... d.	0813	0830	0845	0919	0925	0949	1019	1025	the same	1449	1519	1525	1549	1555	1619	1649	1655	1719	1749	1755	1819	1849	1858	1919	1928	1949
aywards Heath .... d.	|	0849	0858	|	|	|	|	|	minutes	|	|	|	|	|	|	|	1721	|	|	1822	|	|	1921	|	|	|
atwick Airport ✈..... a.	|	0901	0909	|	0951	|	|	1052	past each	|	|	1552	|	1622	|	|	1736	|	|	1836	|	|	1939	|	|	|
ast Croydon............ a.	|	|	0925	0952	1008	1022	1052	1108	hour until	1522	1552	1608	1624	1638	1654	1725	1753	1756	1825	1853	1856	1923	2000	1953	2008	2023
ondon Victoria .... a.	0920	0935	0943	1011	1025	1040	1110	1124	✣	1540	1610	1624	1642	1656	1712	1742	1809	1814	1842	1909	1915	1943	2020	2010	2026	2040

	Ⓐ	Ⓐ	Ⓐ	Ⓐ	Ⓐ	Ⓐ	Ⓐ	Ⓐ	Ⓐ			⑥	⑥	⑥	⑥	⑥	⑥	⑥	⑥	⑥	and at	⑥	⑥	⑥	⑥	⑥
righton .... d.	1955	2019	2049	2102	2119	2149	2203	2219	2305	...	⑥	0350	0521	0550	0556	0611	0649	0719	0724	0749	the same	1819	1824	1849	1854	1919
aywards Heath .... d.	2022	|	|	2123	|	|	2223	|	2326	...		0425	0537	0612	0615	0640	|	|	|	|	minutes	|	|	|	|	|
atwick Airport ✈..... a.	2037	|	|	2137	|	|	2237	|	2352	...		0502	0550	0626	0637	0653	|	|	0752	|	past each	|	1852	|	1922	|
ast Croydon............ a.	2059	2053	2123	2159	2153	2223	2259	2253	0017	...		0528	0610	0640	0652	0709	0722	0752	0808	0822	hour until	1852	1908	1922	1938	1952
ondon Victoria .... a.	2118	2110	2140	2217	2211	2241	2318	2313	0039	...		0556	0630	0657	0709	0727	0740	0810	0824	0840	✣	1910	1924	1940	1954	2010

	⑥	⑥	⑥	⑥	⑥		⑥	⑥	⑥	⑥			⑦	⑦	⑦	⑦	⑦	⑦	⑦	and at	⑦	⑦	⑦	⑦	⑦	⑦
righton .... d.	1949	1954	2019	2049	2100	...	2119	2149	2200	2305	...	⑦	0613	0706	0806	0838	0900	0910	0935	the same	2000	2010	2035	2104	2204	2305
aywards Heath .... d.	|	2022	|	|	2122	...	|	|	2222	2326	...		0634	0727	0826	|	0925	|	|	minutes	2025	|	|	2125	2225	2326
atwick Airport ✈..... a.	|	2037	|	|	2137	...	|	|	2237	2352	...		0647	0742	0842	|	0940	|	|	past each	2040	|	|	2140	2240	2345
ast Croydon............ a.	2022	2059	2052	2122	2209	...	2152	2222	2259	0017	...		0705	0804	0903	0915	1000	0945	1013	hour until	2100	2045	2113	2200	2300	0017
ondon Victoria .... a.	2040	2117	2110	2140	2217	...	2210	2240	2320	0041	...		0729	0825	0919	0932	1017	1003	1030	✣	2117	2105	2130	2217	2320	0039

✣ – Timings may vary by ± 3 minutes.

SW 🍸 on most trains LONDON - GUILDFORD - PORTSMOUTH 107

km			①	Ⓐ	Ⓐ	Ⓐ	Ⓐ	Ⓐ	Ⓐ	Ⓐ	Ⓐ		Ⓐ	Ⓐ	Ⓐ	Ⓐ	Ⓐ	Ⓐ	Ⓐ	Ⓐ	Ⓐ	Ⓐ	Ⓐ	Ⓐ	Ⓐ
0	**London** Waterloo....... 113 d.	Ⓐ	0050	0500	0615	0645	0730	0800	0830	0900	0930	and at	1600	1630	1700	1730	1800	1830	1900	1930	2000	2030	2100	2130	2200
39	Woking....................... 113 d.		0118	0553	0643	0713	0755	0825	0855	0925	0955	the same	1625	1655	1725	1756	|	1858	1925	1955	2025	2055	2125	2155	2225
49	Guildford.............................d.		0126s	0604	0655	0725	0804	0839	0907	0934	1004	minutes	1634	1704	1737	1808	1833	1908	1937	2004	2034	2104	2134	2204	2234
69	Haslemere...........................d.		|	0628	0720	0753	0825	0855	0925	0949	1023	past each	1651	1724	1754	1826	1852	1926	1953	2023	2055	2122	2155	2225	2255
07	Havant.................................a.		0200s	0659	0751	0826	0849	0919	0949	1015	1049	hour until	1715	1749	1819	1850	1915	1950	2016	2048	2118	2145	2218	2248	2318
18	**Portsmouth** & Southsea ...a.		0214s	0716	0807	0843	0902	0932	1002	1028	1102		1728	1802	1832	1903	1929	2004	2029	2101	2132	2158	2232	2303	2331
20	**Portsmouth** Harbour ....a.		0219	0720	0812	0848	0907	0937	1007	1033	1107	♣	1735	1809	1839	1910	1936	2010	2034	2106	2137	2202	2237	2308	2336

	Ⓐ	Ⓐ	Ⓐ			⑥	⑥	⑥	⑥	⑥	⑥	⑥	⑥	⑥		⑥	⑥	⑥	⑥	⑥	⑥	⑥	⑥	⑥	⑥
ndon Waterloo ....113 d.	2230	2315	2345	...	⑥	0520	0645	0730	0800	0830	0900	0930	1000	1030	and at	1900	1930	2000	2030	2100	2130	2200	2230	2315	2345
oking..........................113 d.	2255	2343	0013	...		0613	0713	0755	0825	0855	0925	0955	1025	1055	the same	1925	1955	2025	2055	2125	2155	2225	2255	2343	0013
uildford.............................d.	2304	2352	0025	...		0625	0725	0804	0834	0904	0934	1004	1034	1104	minutes	1934	2004	2034	2104	2134	2204	2234	2304	2352	0025
slemere.............................d.	2325	0012	0050	...		0645	0745	0821	0849	0921	0949	1021	1049	1121	past each	1949	2021	2049	2121	2155	2225	2255	2325	0012	0050
vant....................................a.	2348	0036	0121	...		0719	0816	0849	0915	0949	1015	1049	1115	1149	hour until	2015	2049	2115	2144	2218	2248	2318	2348	0036	0121
rtsmouth & Southsea ....a.	0002	0050	0137	...		0735	0832	0902	0928	1002	1028	1102	1128	1202		2028	2102	2128	2158	2232	2302	2331	0002	0049	0137
rtsmouth Harbour..........a.	0007	0054	...	...		0740	0837	0907	0933	1007	1033	1107	1133	1207	♣	2033	2107	2133	2203	2236	2308	2336	0007	0054	...

		⑦	⑦	⑦	⑦	⑦	⑦	⑦	⑦	⑦	⑦	⑦		⑦	⑦	⑦	⑦	⑦	⑦	⑦	⑦	⑦	⑦	⑦	⑦
ndon Waterloo ....113 d.	⑦	...	0800	0830	0900	0930	1000	1030	1100	1130	1200	1230	and at	1800	1830	1900	1930	2000	2030	2100	2130	2200	2230	2300	2330
oking..........................113 d.		0732	0835	0904	0935	1004	1032	1102	1132	1202	1232	1302	the same	1832	1902	1932	2002	2032	2102	2132	2202	2232	2302	2332	0003
uildford.............................d.		0741	0845	0914	0945	1014	1042	1112	1142	1212	1242	1312	minutes	1842	1912	1942	2012	2042	2112	2142	2212	2242	2312	2342	0012
slemere.............................d.		0807	0912	0929	1012	1029	1107	1127	1207	1227	1307	1327	past each	1907	1927	2007	2027	2107	2127	2207	2227	2307	2327	0007	0027
vant....................................a.		0838	0943	0952	1043	1052	1138	1150	1238	1250	1338	1350	hour until	1938	1950	2038	2050	2138	2150	2238	2250	2338	2350	0038	0050
rtsmouth & Southsea ....a.		0853	0958	1006	1058	1105	1153	1204	1253	1304	1353	1404		1953	2004	2053	2104	2153	2204	2253	2304	2353	0004	0053	0104
rtsmouth Harbour..........a.		0857	1003	1011	1103	1111	1158	1211	1258	1311	1358	1411	♣	1958	2011	2058	2109	2158	2208	2258	2309	2358	0009	0058	0109

		Ⓐ	Ⓐ	Ⓐ	Ⓐ	Ⓐ	Ⓐ	Ⓐ	Ⓐ	Ⓐ	Ⓐ	Ⓐ		Ⓐ	Ⓐ	Ⓐ	Ⓐ	Ⓐ	Ⓐ	Ⓐ	Ⓐ	Ⓐ	Ⓐ	Ⓐ	Ⓐ
rtsmouth Harbour..............d.	Ⓐ	0425	0514	0550	0615	0642	0713	0745	0815	0845	0915	0945	and at	1515	1545	1615	1645	1715	1745	1815	1845	1915	1945	2015	2045
rtsmouth & Southsea ....d.		0430	0519	0555	0620	0647	0718	0750	0820	0850	0920	0950	the same	1520	1550	1620	1650	1720	1750	1820	1850	1920	1950	2020	2050
vant.....................................d.		0446	0535	0611	0634	0700	0732	0804	0834	0904	0934	1004	minutes	1534	1604	1634	1704	1734	1804	1834	1904	1934	2004	2034	2104
slemere.............................d.		0521	0614	0647	0702	0735	0800	0832	0902	0932	1002	1032	past each	1602	1637	1702	1737	1802	1832	1902	1932	2002	2032	2102	2132
ildford...............................d.		0550	0631	0707	0717	0754	0815	0854	0917	0947	1017	1047	hour until	1617	1700	1717	1800	1817	1855	1921	1947	2017	2047	2117	2147
oking..........................113 a.		0600	0640	0715	0725	|	0826	|	0927	0959	1025	1057		1625	1711	1725	1811	|	1903	1928	1957	2025	2058	2125	2157
ndon Waterloo ....113 a.		0629	0712	0745	0754	0832	0855	0931	0955	1027	1051	1124	♣	1651	1743	1754	1843	1859	1929	1959	2024	2050	2127	2150	2227

	Ⓐ	Ⓐ			⑥	⑥	⑥	⑥	⑥	⑥	⑥	⑥		⑥	⑥	⑥	⑥	⑥	⑥	⑥	⑥	⑥	⑥	⑥	⑥
rtsmouth Harbour..........d.	2119	2219	...	⑥	0438	0514	0619	0645	0715	0745	0815	0845	and at	1615	1645	1719	1745	1815	1845	1915	1945	2015	2045	2119	2219
rtsmouth & Southsea ....d.	2124	2224	...		0443	0519	0624	0650	0720	0750	0820	0850	the same	1620	1650	1724	1750	1820	1850	1920	1950	2020	2050	2124	2224
vant.....................................d.	2140	2240	...		0459	0535	0640	0704	0734	0804	0834	0904	minutes	1634	1704	1740	1804	1834	1904	1934	2004	2034	2104	2140	2240
slemere.............................d.	2215	2315	...		0534	0613	0715	0732	0802	0832	0902	0932	past each	1702	1732	1815	1832	1902	1932	2002	2032	2102	2132	2215	2315
ildford...............................d.	2239	2339	...		0602	0634	0734	0747	0817	0847	0917	0947	hour until	1717	1747	1834	1847	1917	1947	2017	2047	2117	2149	2239	2339
king..........................113 a.	2249	2349	...		0611	0644	0744	0757	0826	0857	0925	0957		1725	1757	1844	1857	1925	1957	2025	2059	2125	2157	2249	2349
ndon Waterloo ....113 a.	2319	0033	...		0640	0713	0813	0823	0851	0923	0957	1027	♣	1751	1823	1913	1923	1951	2023	2050	2127	2150	2224	2318	0032

		⑦	⑦	⑦	⑦	⑦	⑦	⑦	⑦	⑦	⑦	⑦	⑦	⑦		⑦	⑦	⑦	⑦	⑦	⑦	⑦	⑦	⑦	⑦
rtsmouth Harbour..............d.	⑦	0643	0729	0748	0829	0848	0932	0948	1032	1048	1132	1148	1232	1248	and at	1832	1848	1932	1948	2032	2048	2132	2148	2232	2248
rtsmouth & Southsea ....d.		0648	0734	0753	0834	0853	0937	0953	1037	1053	1137	1153	1237	1253	the same	1837	1853	1937	1953	2037	2053	2137	2153	2237	2253
vant.....................................d.		0702	0747	0807	0847	0907	0950	1007	1050	1107	1150	1207	1250	1307	minutes	1850	1907	1950	2007	2050	2107	2150	2207	2250	2307
slemere.............................d.		0737	0814	0842	0914	0942	1017	1042	1117	1142	1217	1242	1317	1342	past each	1917	1942	2017	2042	2117	2142	2217	2242	2317	2342
ildford...............................d.		0805	0835	0905	0935	1005	1035	1106	1135	1206	1235	1305	1335	1405	hour until	1935	2005	2035	2105	2135	2205	2235	2305	2335	0005
king..........................113 a.		0813	0842	0915	0942	1015	1042	1113	1142	1213	1242	1313	1342	1413		1942	2013	2042	2113	2142	2213	2242	2313	2342	0013
ndon Waterloo ....113 a.		0850	0916	0948	1014	1046	1114	1149	1214	1244	1314	1344	1414	1444	♣	2014	2044	2114	2144	2214	2244	2314	2344	0014	...

s – Calls to set down only.

♣ – Timings may vary by ± 6 minutes.

108 LONDON - SOUTHAMPTON - BOURNEMOUTH - WEYMOUTH

🍷 on most trains SW

km			②-⑤	Ⓐ	Ⓐ	Ⓐ	Ⓐ	Ⓐ	Ⓐ	Ⓐ	Ⓐ	Ⓐ		Ⓐ	Ⓐ	Ⓐ	Ⓐ	Ⓐ	Ⓐ	Ⓐ	Ⓐ	Ⓐ	Ⓐ	Ⓐ
0	**London Waterloo** 113 d.	Ⓐ	0005	...	...	...	0530	0630	0735	0805	0835	0905	and	1635	1705	1735	1805	1835	1905	1935	2005	2035	2105	2135
39	Woking 113 d.		0037	...	...	...	0601	0657	0800	|	0900	|	at	1700u	|	|	|	|	|	2000	|	2100	2132	2200
77	Basingstoke 129 d.		0056	...	...	0540	0621	0718	0820	0849	|	0949	the	|	|	|	|	|	1949	|	2049	|	2152	|
107	Winchester 129 d.		0113	...	...	0559	0638	0734	0837	0905	0933	1005	same	1733	1800	1830	1900	1930	2005	2033	2105	2133	2208	2233
120	**Southampton Airport** 129 d.		0126	...	...	0613	0653	0749	0852	0914	0942	1014	minutes	1742	1809	1839	1909	1939	2014	2042	2115	2142	2222	2242
128	**Southampton Central** 129 d.		0137	...	...	0625	0701	0800	0901	0924	0951	1024	past	1753	1821	1851	1919	1951	2024	2051	2125	2151	2231	2251
149	Brockenhurst 129 d.		0153s	...	0616	0644	0718	0817	0918	0938	1005	1038	each	1808	|	|	1936	|	2038	2108	2144	2205	2250	2305
174	**Bournemouth** 129 d.		0215	0611	0644	0711	0746	0844	0945	1004	1024	1104	hour	1824	1850	1921	2007	2021	2104	2127	2212	2224	2317	2329
183	Poole d.		...	0624	0657	0724	0758	0857	0958	1014	1037	1114	until	1837	1903	1934	2019	2034	2115	2139	2223	2237	2329	2342
219	Dorchester South d.		...	0658	0731	0758	0833	0929	1026	1054	1106	1149	♠	1908	1937	2003	2054	2102	2147	2212	...	2309	...	0015
230	**Weymouth** a.		...	0714	0747	0814	0844	0940	1034	1106	1114	1200		1919	1950	2015	2107	2113	2158	2223	...	2320	...	0026

	Ⓐ	Ⓐ	Ⓐ			⑥	⑥	⑥	⑥	⑥	⑥	⑥	⑥	⑥		⑥	⑥	⑥	⑥	⑥	⑥	⑥	⑥	⑥
London Waterloo 113 d.	2205	2235	2305	...	⑥	0005	...	...	...	0530	0630	0735	0805	0835	and	1905	1935	2005	2035	2105	2135	2205	2235	2305
Woking 113 d.	2232	2300	2332	...		0037	...	...	...	0601	0657	0800	|	0900	at	|	2000	|	2100	2132	2200	2232	2300	2332
Basingstoke 129 d.	2252	|	2353	...		0056	...	...	...	0621	0718	0821	0849	|	the	1949	|	2049	|	2152	|	2252	|	2352
Winchester 129 d.	2308	2333	0012	...		0113	...	...	...	0641	0734	0838	0905	0933	same	2005	2033	2105	2133	2208	2233	2308	2333	0011
Southampton Airport 129 d.	2322	2342	0028	...		0126	...	...	...	0656	0748	0851	0914	0942	minutes	2014	2042	2114	2142	2222	2242	2322	2342	0025
Southampton Central 129 d.	2330	2351	0038	...		0137	...	...	0621	0705	0800	0900	0924	0951	past	2024	2051	2124	2151	2230	2251	2330	2351	0035
Brockenhurst 129 d.	2349	0005	0054s	...		0153s	...	0616	0640	0722	0817	0917	0938	1005	each	2038	2105	2143	2205	2249	2305	2349	0005	0051s
Bournemouth 129 d.	0016	0022	0118	...		0215	0611	0644	0711	0749	0844	0944	1004	1024	hour	2104	2124	2210	2224	2317	2329	0016	0022	0115
Poole d.	0028	0035	0130	...		...	0624	0657	0724	0802	0857	0957	1014	1037	until	2114	2137	2223	2237	2329	2342	0030	0035	0127
Dorchester South d.	...	...	...	...		...	0658	0731	0758	0834	0929	1027	1049	1105	♠	2149	2209	...	2309	...	0015	...	...	...
Weymouth a.	...	...	...	...		...	0709	0742	0809	0845	0940	1035	1100	1113		2200	2220	...	2320	...	0026	...	...	...

		⑦	⑦	⑦	⑦	⑦	⑦	⑦	⑦	⑦	⑦	⑦		⑦	⑦	⑦	⑦	⑦	⑦	⑦	⑦	⑦	⑦	⑦
London Waterloo 113 d.	⑦	0005	...	...	...	0754	0835	0854	0935	0954	1035	1054	and	1735	1754	1835	1854	1935	1954	2035	2054	2135	2154	2254
Woking 113 d.		0037	...	...	...	0828	0909	0928	1009	1028	1108	1128	at	1807	1828	1907	1928	2007	2028	2107	2128	2207	2228	2328
Basingstoke 129 d.		0056	...	0748	...	0848	0929	0948	1029	1048	1128	1148	the	1828	1848	1928	1948	2028	2048	2128	2148	2228	2248	2348
Winchester 129 d.		0113	...	0808	...	0908	0946	1008	1046	1108	1144	1208	same	1844	1908	1944	2008	2044	2108	2144	2208	2244	2308	0008
Southampton Airport 129 d.		0126	...	0827	...	0927	0955	1027	1055	1127	1153	1227	minutes	1853	1927	1953	2027	2053	2127	2153	2227	2253	2327	0027
Southampton Central 129 d.		0137	...	0835	0903	0935	1003	1035	1103	1135	1203	1235	past	1903	1935	2003	2035	2103	2135	2203	2235	2303	2335	0037
Brockenhurst 129 d.		0153s	...	0857	0917	0957	1018	1057	1118	1157	1217	1257	each	1917	1957	2017	2057	2117	2157	2217	2257	2317	2354	0053
Bournemouth 129 d.		0215	0839	0924	0939	1024	1039	1124	1139	1224	1239	1324	hour	1939	2024	2039	2124	2139	2224	2239	2324	2339	0022	0117
Poole d.		...	0851	0933	0951	1033	1051	1133	1151	1233	1251	1333	until	1951	2033	2051	2133	2151	2233	2251	2333	2351	0034	0129
Dorchester South d.		...	0924	...	1024	...	1124	...	1224	...	1324	...	♠	2025	...	2125	...	2225	...	2325	...	0025	...	...
Weymouth a.		...	0935	...	1035	...	1135	...	1235	...	1335	...		2036	...	2136	...	2236	...	2336	...	0036	...	...

		Ⓐ	Ⓐ	Ⓐ	Ⓐ	Ⓐ	Ⓐ	Ⓐ	Ⓐ	Ⓐ	Ⓐ	Ⓐ	Ⓐ		Ⓐ	Ⓐ	Ⓐ	Ⓐ	Ⓐ	Ⓐ	Ⓐ	Ⓐ	Ⓐ	Ⓐ
Weymouth d.	Ⓐ	...	...	...	0550	0620	0650	...	0725	0755	0820	0903	0920	and	1703	1720	1803	1820	1903	1920	2010	2110	2210	2310
Dorchester South d.		...	...	...	0602	0632	0702	...	0737	0807	0833	0913	0933	at	1713	1733	1813	1833	1913	1937	2022	2122	2222	2322
Poole d.		0457	0542	0608	0639	0709	0739	0755	0811	0841	0907	0940	1007	the	1740	1807	1840	1907	1940	2009	2054	2154	2254	2354
Bournemouth 129 d.		0512	0554	0625	0656	0726	0759	0810	0825	0859	0918	0955	1022	same	1759	1822	1859	1922	1959	2022	2112	2212	2312	0003
Brockenhurst 129 d.		0538	0614	|	|	|	0815	0841	0852	0915	0941	1011	1045	minutes	1815	1845	1915	1945	2015	2045	2140	2240	2340	...
Southampton Central 129 d.		0555	0630	0700	0730	0800	0830	0900	...	0930	1000	1030	1100	past	1830	1900	1930	2000	2030	2100	2200	2300	2359	...
Southampton Airport 129 a.		0602	0637	0707	0737	0807	0837	0907	...	0937	1007	1037	1107	each	1837	1907	1937	2007	2037	2108	2207	2307	0009	...
Winchester 129 a.		0617	0647	0717	0747	0817	0847	0917	...	0947	1017	1047	1117	hour	1847	1917	1947	2017	2047	2117	2217	2323	...	...
Basingstoke 129 a.		0634	|	|	|	0834	|	0935	...	|	1034	|	1134	until	|	1934	|	2034	|	2134	2234	2343	...	...
Woking 113 a.		0653	|	|	|	0853	0922	0954	...	1020	|	1119	|	♠	1925	|	2019	|	2119	|	2254	0018	...	...
London Waterloo 113 a.		0724	0747	0816	0850	0925	0953	1023	...	1049	1120	1149	1220		1952	2020	2049	2124	2149	2222	2323	0104	...	...

		⑥	⑥	⑥	⑥	⑥	⑥	⑥	⑥	⑥	⑥	⑥		⑥	⑥	⑥	⑥	⑥	⑥	⑥	⑥		⑥	⑥
Weymouth d.	⑥	...	0537	...	0650	0717	0803	0820	0903	0920	1003	1020	and	1703	1720	1803	1820	1903	1920	2010	2110	...	2210	231
Dorchester South d.		...	0547	...	0702	0733	0813	0833	0913	0933	1013	1033	at	1713	1733	1813	1833	1913	1933	2022	2122	...	2222	232
Poole d.		0528	0622	0707	0739	0807	0840	0907	0940	1007	1040	1107	the	1740	1807	1840	1907	1940	2007	2054	2154	...	2254	235
Bournemouth 129 d.		0542	0642	0722	0759	0822	0859	0922	0959	1022	1059	1122	same	1759	1822	1859	1922	1959	2022	2112	2212	...	2312	000
Brockenhurst 129 d.		0610	0710	0745	0815	0845	0915	0945	1015	1045	1115	1145	minutes	1815	1845	1915	1945	2015	2045	2140	2240	...	2340	...
Southampton Central 129 d.		0630	0730	0800	0830	0900	0930	1000	1030	1100	1130	1200	past	1830	1900	1930	2000	2030	2100	2200	2300	...	2359	...
Southampton Airport 129 a.		0637	0737	0807	0837	0907	0937	1007	1037	1107	1137	1207	each	1837	1907	1937	2007	2037	2107	2207	2307	...	0009	...
Winchester 129 a.		0651	0747	0817	0847	0917	0947	1017	1047	1117	1147	1217	hour	1847	1917	1947	2017	2047	2117	2217	2323	...	...	...
Basingstoke 129 a.		0708	|	0834	|	0934	|	1034	|	1134	|	1234	until	|	1934	|	2034	|	2134	2234	2343	...	...	...
Woking 113 a.		0727	0821	|	0919	|	1019	|	1119	|	1219	|	♠	1919	|	2019	|	2119	|	2253	0018	...	...	...
London Waterloo 113 a.		0753	0849	0920	0949	1020	1049	1120	1149	1221	1251	1321		1949	2020	2049	2124	2149	2222	2322	0104	...	...	...

		⑦	⑦	⑦	⑦	⑦	⑦	⑦	⑦	⑦	⑦	⑦	⑦	⑦	⑦		⑦	⑦	⑦	⑦	⑦	⑦	⑦	⑦
Weymouth d.	⑦	...	...	0743	...	0843	...	0948	...	1048	...	1148	...	1248	...	and	1748	...	1848	...	1958	2058	2158	225
Dorchester South d.		...	...	0755	...	0855	...	1000	...	1100	...	1200	...	1300	...	at	1800	...	1900	...	2010	2110	2210	231
Poole d.		0650	0750	0830	0855	0930	0955	1032	1055	1132	1155	1232	1255	1332	1355	the	1832	1855	1932	1955	2050	2150	2250	235
Bournemouth 129 d.		0706	0806	0850	0906	0950	1006	1050	1106	1150	1206	1250	1306	1350	1406	same	1850	1906	1950	2006	2106	2206	2306	000
Brockenhurst 129 d.		0734	0834	0909	0934	1009	1034	1109	1134	1209	1234	1309	1334	1409	1434	minutes	1909	1934	2009	2034	2134	2234	2334	...
Southampton Central 129 d.		0755	0855	0925	0955	1025	1055	1125	1155	1225	1255	1325	1355	1425	1455	past	1925	1955	2025	2055	2155	2255	2353	...
Southampton Airport 129 a.		0802	0902	0932	1002	1032	1102	1132	1202	1232	1302	1332	1402	1432	1502	each	1932	2002	2032	2102	2202	2302	...	...
Winchester 129 a.		0822	0922	0941	1022	1041	1122	1141	1222	1241	1322	1341	1422	1441	1522	hour	1941	2022	2041	2122	2222	2322	...	...
Basingstoke 129 a.		0842	0942	0958	1042	1058	1142	1158	1242	1300	1344	1358	1442	1458	1542	until	1958	2042	2058	2142	2242	2342	...	...
Woking 113 a.		0902	1002	1019	1102	1118	1202	1218	1302	1318	1402	1418	1502	1518	1602	♠	2018	2102	2118	2202	2302	0002	...	...
London Waterloo 113 a.		0941	1039	1050	1139	1150	1237	1249	1337	1349	1437	1449	1537	1549	1637		2049	2137	2149	2237	2337	0033	...	...

Brockenhurst - Lymington Pier (for ⛴ to Isle of Wight).
Journey 11 minutes. Trains call at Lymington Town 6 minutes later:
Ⓐ: 0559 and every 30 minutes until 0929, 1012 and every 30 minutes until 1812, 1848 and every 30 minutes until 2218.
⑥: 0612, 0642 and every 30 minutes until 2112, 2148, 2218.
⑦: 0859, 0929 and every 30 minutes until 2059, 2129, 2159.

Lymington Pier - Brockenhurst.
Journey 11 minutes. Trains call at Lymington Town 2 minutes later:
Ⓐ: 0614 and every 30 minutes until 0944, 1027 and every 30 minutes until 1827, 1903 a every 30 minutes until 2233.
⑥: 0627, 0657 and every 30 minutes until 2127, 2203, 2233.
⑦: 0914, 0944 and every 30 minutes until 2114, 2144, 2214.

s – Calls to set down only. u – Calls to pick up only. ♠ – Timings may vary by ± 3 minutes. ☛ For ⛴ services Weymouth / Poole - Jersey / Guernsey / St Malo and v.v., see Table **2100**.

111 PORTSMOUTH - RYDE - SHANKLIN

2nd class

Through fares including ferry travel are available. Allow 10 minutes for connections between trains and ferries. Operator: Wightlink ✆ 0871 376 4342. www.wightlink.co.

Portsmouth Harbour - Ryde Pierhead ⛴
⚒: 0515Ⓐ, 0615 and hourly until 2215 (also 0740Ⓐ, 0840Ⓐ, 1640Ⓐ, 1740Ⓐ, 1845Ⓐ).
⑦: 0715 and hourly until 2215.

Ryde Pierhead - Portsmouth Harbour Journey time: ± 20 minu
⚒: 0547Ⓐ, 0647 and hourly until 2247 (also 0710Ⓐ, 0810Ⓐ, 0910Ⓐ, 1710Ⓐ, 1810(
⑦: 0747 and hourly until 2247.

Service until December 19. Additional services operate on ⑥ Apr. 12 - Sep. 27 and on public holidays.

Ryde Pierhead - Shanklin: *14 km*
⚒: 0549, 0607, 0649, 0707, 0749, 0807, 0849, 0907, 0949, 1007, 1049*, 1107, 1149*, 1207*, 1249*, 1307*, 1349, 1407, 1449*, 1507*, 1549*, 1607*, 1649, 1707, 1749, 1807, 1849, 1907, 1949, 2007, 2045, 2145.
⑦: 0649, 0749, 0849, 0907**b**, 0949, 1007**b**, 1049*, 1107**b**, 1149*, 1207**b***, 1249*, 1307*, 1349, 1407, 1449*, 1507*, 1549*, 1607*, 1649, 1707, 1749, 1807, 1849, 1907**b**, 1949, 2045, 2145.

Shanklin - Ryde Pierhead Journey time: ± 24 minu
⚒: 0618, 0638, 0718, 0738, 0818, 0838, 0918, 0938, 1018, 1038*, 1118, 1138*, 1218 1238*, 1318*, 1338, 1418, 1438*, 1518*, 1538*, 1618*, 1638, 1718, 1738, 1818, 18 1918, 1938, 2018, 2118, 2218.
⑦: 0718, 0818, 0838**b**, 0918, 0938**b**, 1018, 1038**b***, 1118, 1138**b***, 1218*, 1238**b***, 13 1338, 1418, 1438*, 1518*, 1538*, 1618*, 1638, 1718, 1738, 1818, 1838**b**, 1918, 193 2018, 2118, 2218.

b – Until Sep. 28.
* – Also calls at Smallbrook Junction (connection with **Isle of Wight Steam Railway**, see note △) 9 minutes after Ryde / 15 minutes after Shanklin.

△ – **Isle of Wight Steam Railway** (🚂 Smallbrook Junction - Wootton: *9 km*). ✆ 019 882204. www.iwsteamrailway.co.uk

SW Most trains 🍸 LONDON - SALISBURY - EXETER 113

km			Ⓐ	Ⓐ	Ⓐ	Ⓐ	Ⓐ	Ⓐ	Ⓐ	Ⓐ **B**	Ⓐ	Ⓐ	Ⓐ **B**	Ⓐ	Ⓐ	Ⓐ	Ⓐ	Ⓐ	Ⓐ	Ⓐ	Ⓐ	Ⓐ	Ⓐ **B**	Ⓐ	Ⓐ
0	**London** Waterloo .... **108** d.	Ⓐ	...	...	...	...	...	0710	0820	0920	1020	1120	1220	1320	1420	1520	1550	1620	1650	1720	1750	1820	1920	2020	2120
39	Woking .... **108** d.		...	...	...	...	...	0736	0846	0946	1046	1146	1246	1346	1446	1546	1616	1646	1716	1746	|	1846	1946	2046	2149
77	Basingstoke .... **108** d.		...	...	...	...	0722	0757	0907	1007	1107	1207	1307	1407	1507	1607	1638	1707	1738	1807	1838	1907	2007	2107	2214
107	Andover .... d.		...	...	...	...	0744	0819	0924	1024	1124	1224	1324	1424	1524	1624	1700	1729	1800	1829	1900	1929	2029	2129	2236
134	**Salisbury** .... a.		...	...	...	...	0803	0839	0943	1042	1142	1242	1343	1442	1542	1642	1720	1748	1820	1848	1920	1948	2049	2148	2255
134	**Salisbury** .... d.		...	...	0608	0740	0808	0847	0947	1047	1147	1247	1347	1447	1547	1647	1723	1753	1823	1853	1923	1953	2053	2206	2303
169	Gillingham .... d.		...	...	0642	0811	0837	0917	1017	1117	1217	1317	1417	1517	1617	1717	1747	1820	1851	1919	1954	2022	2119	2235	2327s
190	Sherborne .... d.		...	...	0657	0826	...	0932	1025	1132	1232	1332	1432	1532	1632	1732	...	1835	1906	1934	2009	2037	2134	2250	2342s
197	**Yeovil** Junction .... a.		...	...	0703	0832	...	0938	1038	1138	1238	1338	1438	1538	1638	1738	...	1840	1914	1939	2016	2043	2140	2255	2348
197	**Yeovil** Junction .... d.		...	0615	0707	0839	...	0939	1039	1139	1239	1339	1439	1539	1639	1739	...	1842	...	1941	...	2044	2141	2257	...
211	Crewkerne .... d.		...	0624	0716	0849	...	0949	1049	1149	1249	1349	1449	1549	1649	1749	...	1851	...	1950	...	2054	2151	2306	...
233	Axminster .... d.		0552	0656	0737	0903	...	1003	1103	1203	1303	1403	1503	1603	1703	1803	...	1905	...	2004	...	2108	2205	2320	...
249	Honiton .... d.		0607	0712	0753	0916	...	1016	1116	1216	1316	1416	1516	1616	1716	1818	...	1919	...	2017	...	2120	2219	2332	...
276	**Exeter** Central .... a.		0630	0737	0817	0939	...	1037	1137	1237	1337	1437	1539	1635	1735	1837	...	1940	...	2039	...	2142	2243	2356	...
277	**Exeter** St Davids .... a.		0635	0742	0821	0944	...	1042	1142	1242	1342	1442	1544	1642	1739	1842	...	1946	...	2044	...	2147	2247	0001	...

	Ⓐ	Ⓐ			⑥	⑥	⑥	⑥	⑥	⑥	⑥ **B**	⑥	⑥	⑥ **B**	⑥	⑥	⑥	⑥	⑥	⑥	⑥ **B**	⑥	⑥	⑥	⑥
London Waterloo .... **108** d.	2220	2340	...	⑥	...	...	...	...	0710	0820	0920	1020	1120	1220	1320	1420	1520	1620	1720	1820	1920	2020	2120	2220	2340
Woking .... **108** d.	2249	0008	...		...	...	...	...	0736	0846	0946	1046	1146	1246	1346	1446	1546	1646	1746	1846	1946	2046	2149	2249	0008
Basingstoke .... **108** d.	2311	0028	...		...	...	...	...	0759	0907	1007	1107	1207	1307	1407	1507	1607	1707	1807	1907	2007	2107	2214	2311	0028
Andover .... d.	2333	0050	...		...	...	...	...	0821	0924	1024	1124	1224	1324	1424	1524	1624	1724	1824	1924	2024	2129	2236	2333	0050
Salisbury .... a.	2352	0110	...		...	...	...	...	0842	0942	1042	1142	1242	1342	1442	1542	1642	1742	1843	1943	2042	2148	2255	2353	0110
Salisbury .... d.	...	...	...		...	...	0615	0745	0847	0947	1047	1147	1247	1347	1447	1547	1647	1747	1847	1947	2047	2153	2303	...	...
Gillingham .... d.	...	...	...		...	...	0642	0811	0917	1017	1117	1217	1317	1417	1517	1617	1717	1817	1919	2017	2117	2218	2327s	...	...
Sherborne .... d.	...	...	...		...	...	0657	0826	0932	1032	1132	1232	1332	1432	1532	1632	1732	1832	1934	2032	2132	2233	2342s	...	...
Yeovil Junction .... a.	...	...	...		...	...	0703	0832	0938	1038	1138	1238	1338	1438	1538	1638	1738	1838	1939	2038	2138	2241	2348	...	...
Yeovil Junction .... d.	...	...	...		...	0615	0707	0839	0939	1039	1139	1239	1339	1439	1539	1639	1739	1839	1941	2039	2139	...	...	...	...
Crewkerne .... d.	...	...	...		...	0624	0716	0849	0949	1049	1149	1249	1349	1449	1549	1649	1749	1849	1950	2049	2149	...	...	...	...
Axminster .... d.	...	...	...		0552	0656	0738	0903	1003	1103	1203	1303	1403	1503	1603	1703	1803	1903	2005	2103	2203	...	...	...	...
Honiton .... d.	...	...	...		0607	0712	0754	0916	1016	1116	1216	1316	1416	1516	1616	1716	1817	1916	2017	2117	2217	...	...	...	...
Exeter Central .... a.	...	...	...		0630	0737	0818	0939	1037	1137	1237	1337	1437	1537	1637	1737	1837	1937	2039	2138	2241	...	...	...	...
Exeter St Davids .... a.	...	...	...		0635	0742	0822	0944	1042	1142	1242	1342	1442	1542	1642	1742	1842	1942	2043	2142	2245	...	...	...	...

		⑦	⑦	⑦		⑦	⑦	⑦		⑦ **B**	⑦	⑦		⑦	⑦	⑦		⑦ **B**	⑦	⑦	⑦		⑦	⑦	
London Waterloo .... **108** d.	⑦	...	...	0815	...	0915	1015	1115	...	1215	1315	1415	...	1515	1615	1715	...	1815	1915	2015	2115	...	2215	2335	...
Woking .... **108** d.		...	...	0847	...	0947	1046	1146	...	1246	1346	1446	...	1546	1646	1746	...	1846	1946	2046	2146	...	2246	0008	...
Basingstoke .... **108** d.		...	0805	0908	...	1008	1107	1207	...	1307	1407	1507	...	1607	1707	1807	...	1907	2007	2107	2207	...	2307	0040	...
Andover .... d.		...	0827	0930	...	1025	1129	1224	...	1329	1424	1529	...	1624	1729	1824	...	1929	2024	2129	2226	...	2329	0102	...
Salisbury .... a.		...	0846	0946	...	1045	1145	1245	...	1345	1445	1545	...	1645	1745	1845	...	1945	2045	2145	2245	...	2348	0122	...
Salisbury .... d.		0706	0851	0951	...	1051	1151	1251	...	1351	1451	1551	...	1651	1751	1851	...	1951	2051	2151	2251	...	...	...	...
Gillingham .... d.		0731	0921	1021	...	1121	1221	1321	...	1421	1521	1621	...	1721	1821	1921	...	2021	2121	2221	2322	...	...	...	...
Sherborne .... d.		0746	0936	1036	...	1136	1236	1336	...	1436	1536	1636	...	1736	1836	1936	...	2036	2136	2236	2337	...	...	...	...
Yeovil Junction .... a.		0751	0941	1041	...	1141	1241	1341	...	1441	1541	1641	...	1741	1841	1941	...	2041	2141	2242	2343	...	...	...	...
Yeovil Junction .... d.		0753	0943	1043	...	1143	1243	1343	...	1443	1543	1643	...	1743	1843	1943	...	2043	2143	...	2344	...	...	...	...
Crewkerne .... d.		0802	0952	1052	...	1152	1252	1352	...	1452	1552	1652	...	1752	1852	1952	...	2052	2152	...	2354	...	...	...	...
Axminster .... d.		0816	1006	1106	...	1206	1306	1406	...	1506	1606	1706	...	1806	1906	2006	...	2106	2206	...	0008	...	...	...	...
Honiton .... d.		0831	1018	1118	...	1218	1318	1418	...	1518	1618	1718	...	1818	1918	2018	...	2118	2220	...	0020	...	...	...	...
Exeter Central .... a.		0854	1040	1140	...	1240	1340	1440	...	1540	1640	1740	...	1840	1940	2040	...	2142	2243	...	|	...	...	...	...
Exeter St Davids .... a.		0859	1045	1145	...	1245	1345	1445	...	1545	1645	1745	...	1845	1945	2045	...	2146	2248	...	0046	...	...	...	...

		Ⓐ	Ⓐ	Ⓐ	Ⓐ	Ⓐ	Ⓐ	Ⓐ	Ⓐ	Ⓐ	Ⓐ **B**	Ⓐ	Ⓐ	Ⓐ	Ⓐ	Ⓐ	Ⓐ	Ⓐ **B**	Ⓐ	Ⓐ	Ⓐ	Ⓐ	Ⓐ	Ⓐ	Ⓐ
Exeter St Davids .... d.	Ⓐ	...	...	...	...	0510	...	0642	0725	...	0823	0925	1025	1125	1225	1325	1425	1525	1624	1725	1825	1925	2025	2125	2257
Exeter Central .... d.		...	...	...	...	0514	...	0645	0730	...	0827	0930	1030	1130	1230	1330	1430	1530	1629	1730	1830	1930	2030	2130	2301
Honiton .... d.		...	...	...	...	0541	0619	0712	0752	...	0855	0955	1055	1155	1255	1355	1455	1555	1656	1755	1859	1955	2057	2159	2332
Axminster .... d.		...	...	...	...	0552	0630	0723	0803	...	0906	1006	1106	1206	1306	1406	1506	1606	1707	1806	1910	2006	2108	2210	2343
Crewkerne .... d.		...	...	...	...	0605	0643	0736	0816	...	0919	1019	1119	1219	1319	1419	1519	1619	1720	1819	1923	2019	2121	2223	256
Yeovil Junction .... a.		...	...	...	...	0614	0652	0745	0825	...	0927	1027	1127	1227	1327	1427	1527	1627	1728	1827	1931	2028	2129	2231	0004
Yeovil Junction .... d.		...	...	0512	0550	0620	0653	0750	0829	...	0929	1029	1129	1229	1329	1429	1529	1629	1730	1829	1933	2029	2131	2233	0006
Sherborne .... d.		...	...	0518	0556	0626	0700	0756	0835	...	0935	1035	1135	1235	1335	1435	1535	1635	1736	1835	1939	2306	2137	2239	|
Gillingham .... d.		...	...	0534	0612	0642	0715	0812	0851	0918	0951	1051	1151	1251	1351	1451	1551	1651	1752	1851	1955	2051	2153	2255	|
Salisbury .... a.		...	...	0559	0639	0707	0740	0837	0916	0942	1016	1116	1216	1316	1416	1516	1616	1716	1822	1923	2022	2122	2218	2329	0043
Salisbury .... d.		0512	0540	0603	0645	0715	0745	0847	0921	0947	1021	1121	1221	1321	1421	1521	1621	1721	1827	1926	2026	2126	2226	...	...
Andover .... d.		0532	0600	0623	0705	0735	0805	0906	0938	1006	1038	1138	1238	1338	1438	1538	1638	1738	1844	1945	2045	2145	2245	...	...
Basingstoke .... **108** a.		0558	0626	0649	0728	0758	0828	0928	0955	1028	1055	1155	1255	1355	1455	1555	1655	1755	1901	2008	2108	2207	2307	...	...
Woking .... **108** a.		0618	0646	|	|	0818	0848	0949	1015	1049	1115	1215	1315	1415	1515	1615	1715	1815	1921	2029	2129	2228	*2331*	...	...
London Waterloo .... **108** a.		0649	0714	0739	0814	0846	0917	1019	1049	1119	1149	1249	1349	1449	1549	1649	1749	1849	1950	2100	2204	2258	*0009*	...	...

		⑥	⑥	⑥	⑥	⑥	⑥	⑥	⑥	⑥ **B**	⑥	⑥	⑥		⑥ **B**	⑥	⑥	⑥ **B**	⑥	⑥	⑥	⑥	⑥	⑥	⑥
Exeter St Davids .... d.	⑥	...	...	...	...	0510	...	0641	0725	0824	0925	1025	1125	...	1225	1325	1425	1525	1625	1725	1825	1925	2025	2125	2257
Exeter Central .... d.		...	...	...	...	0514	...	0645	0730	0828	0930	1030	1130	...	1230	1330	1430	1530	1630	1730	1830	1930	2030	2130	2301
Honiton .... d.		...	...	...	...	0541	0619	0713	0755	0855	9055	1055	1155	...	1255	1355	1455	1555	1655	1757	1855	1955	2056	2157	2332
Axminster .... d.		...	...	...	...	0552	0630	0724	0806	0906	1006	1106	1206	...	1306	1406	1506	1606	1706	1808	1906	2006	2107	2208	2343
Crewkerne .... d.		...	...	...	...	0605	0643	0737	0819	0919	1019	1119	1219	...	1319	1419	1519	1619	1719	1821	1919	2019	2120	2221	2356
Yeovil Junction .... a.		...	...	...	...	0614	0652	0745	0827	0927	1027	1127	1227	...	1327	1427	1527	1627	1727	1829	1927	2027	2129	2229	0004
Yeovil Junction .... d.		...	...	...	...	0620	0653	0750	0829	0929	1029	1129	1229	...	1329	1429	1529	1629	1729	1831	1929	2029	2130	2231	0006
Sherborne .... d.		...	...	...	...	0626	0700	0756	0835	0935	1035	1135	1235	...	1335	1435	1535	1635	1735	1837	1935	2035	2137	2237	|
Gillingham .... d.		...	...	...	...	0642	0715	0812	0851	0951	1051	1151	1251	...	1351	1451	1551	1651	1751	1853	1951	2051	2152	2253	|
Salisbury .... a.		...	...	...	...	0707	0740	0837	0916	1016	1116	1216	1316	...	1416	1516	1616	1716	1816	1918	2016	2116	2223	2329	0041
Salisbury .... d.		0512	0544	0618	0647	0721	0747	0847	0921	1021	1121	1221	1321	...	1421	1521	1621	1721	1821	1926	2026	2126	2227	...	...
Andover .... d.		0532	0603	0635	0706	0738	0806	0906	0938	1038	1138	1238	1338	...	1438	1538	1638	1738	1838	1945	2045	2145	2247	...	...
Basingstoke .... **108** a.		0558	0628	0655	0728	0755	0828	0928	0955	1055	1155	1255	1355	...	1455	1555	1655	1755	1855	2008	2108	2207	2309	...	...
Woking .... **108** a.		0618	0649	0715	0749	0817	0849	0949	1015	1115	1215	1315	1415	...	1515	1615	1715	1815	1915	2029	2129	2228	2332	...	...
London Waterloo .... **108** a.		0649	0719	0749	0819	0849	0919	1019	1049	1149	1249	1349	1449	...	1549	1649	1749	1849	1949	2104	2204	2257	*0003*	...	...

		⑦	⑦	⑦		⑦	⑦	⑦		⑦	⑦	⑦		⑦	⑦	⑦ **B**		⑦	⑦	⑦		⑦	⑦	⑦	⑦
Exeter St Davids .... d.	⑦	...	...	...	...	...	...	0925	...	1025	1125	1225	...	1325	1425	1525	...	1625	1725	1825	...	1925	2025	2125	2315
Exeter Central .... d.		...	...	...	...	...	...	0930	...	1030	1130	1230	...	1330	1430	1530	...	1630	1730	1830	...	1930	2030	2130	2319
Honiton .... d.		...	...	...	...	...	0858	0957	...	1057	1157	1257	...	1357	1457	1557	...	1657	1757	1857	...	1957	2057	2159	2336s
Axminster .... d.		...	...	...	...	...	0909	1009	...	1109	1209	1309	...	1409	1509	1609	...	1709	1809	1909	...	2009	2109	2210	2351s
Crewkerne .... d.		...	...	...	...	...	0922	1022	...	1122	1222	1322	...	1422	1522	1622	...	1722	1822	1922	...	2022	2122	2223	0012s
Yeovil Junction .... a.		...	...	...	...	...	0930	1030	...	1130	1230	1330	...	1430	1530	1603	...	1730	1830	1930	...	2030	2131	2232	0021s
Yeovil Junction .... d.		...	...	0732	...	...	0932	1032	...	1132	1232	1332	...	1432	1532	1632	...	1732	1832	1932	...	2032	2132	2233	0021s
Sherborne .... d.		...	...	0738	...	...	0938	1038	...	1138	1238	1338	...	1438	1538	1638	...	1738	1838	1938	...	2038	2138	2240	|
Gillingham .... d.		...	...	0754	...	0854	0954	1054	...	1154	1254	1354	...	1454	1554	1654	...	1754	1854	1954	...	2054	2154	2256	|
Salisbury .... a.		...	...	0820	...	0920	1020	1120	...	1220	1320	1420	...	1520	1620	1720	...	1820	1920	2020	...	2120	2220	2321	0057
Salisbury .... d.		0642	0724	0827	...	0927	1027	1127	...	1227	1327	1427	...	1527	1627	1727	...	1827	1927	2027	...	2127	2227	...	...
Andover .... d.		0659	0743	0846	...	0946	1044	1146	...	1244	1346	1444	...	1546	1644	1746	...	1844	1946	2044	...	2146	2246	...	...
Basingstoke .... **108** a.		0719	0808	0908	...	1002	1106	1204	...	1306	1402	1506	...	1602	1706	1802	...	1906	2002	2106	...	2203	2308	...	...
Woking .... **108** a.		0739	0828	0928	...	1028	1128	1228	...	1328	1428	1528	...	1628	1728	1828	...	1928	2028	2128	...	2228	*2350*	...	...
London Waterloo .... **108** a.		0820	0912	1011	...	1104	1204	1304	...	1359	1459	1559	...	1659	1759	1859	...	1959	2059	2159	...	2259	*0033*	...	...

ll service London Waterloo - Salisbury:
Ⓐ: 0710, 0750, 0820, 0850, 0920, 0950 and at the same minutes past each hour until 1750, 1820, 1850, 1920, 1950, 2020, 2120, 2220, 2340.
⑥: 0710, 0750, 0820, 0850, 0920, 0950 and at the same minutes past each hour until 1750, 1820, 1850, 1920, 1950, 2020, 2120, 2220, 2340.

Full service Salisbury - London Waterloo:
Ⓐ: 0512, 0540, 0603, 0645, 0715, 0745, 0815, 0847 and then at 21 and 47 minutes past each hour until 1827, 1847, 1926, 2026, 2126, 2226.
⑥: 0512, 0544, 0618, 0647, 0721, 0747, 0821, 0847, 0921, 0947 and at the same minutes past each hour until 1847, 1926, 2026, 2126, 2227.

B – Conveys (12) London - Salisbury - Bristol and v.v.
s – Stops to set down only.
u – Stops to pick up only.

115 LONDON and BRISTOL - EXETER - PAIGNTON, PLYMOUTH and PENZANCE GW, XC

Service until September 7. Service on ⑦ subject to alteration June 22 - July 27.

km			①	②–⑤	②–⑤	①	Ⓐ	Ⓐ	Ⓐ	Ⓐ	Ⓐ	Ⓐ	Ⓐ	Ⓐ	Ⓐ	Ⓐ	Ⓐ	Ⓐ	Ⓐ	Ⓐ	Ⓐ	Ⓐ	Ⓐ	Ⓐ	Ⓐ
				K		K		2	2a	2b	2b		2		A	2		B	2		a▲	b	2		C
0	**London** Paddington .... d.	Ⓐ	...	2345z	...	2350x	...	...	...	...	...	...	...	...	0706	...	...	0730	...	...	0906	0906	...	...	1006
58	Reading .... d.		...	0037u	...	0037u	...	...	...	...	...	...	...	...	0733	...	...	0759	...	...	0935u	0935u	...	...	1032u
85	Newbury .... d.		...	|	...	|	...	...	...	...	...	...	...	...	0749	...	...	|	...	...	|	|	...	...	|
154	Westbury .... d.		...	|	...	|	...	...	...	...	...	...	...	...	0826	...	...	|	...	...	|	|	...	...	|
186	Castle Cary .... d.		...	|	...	|	...	...	...	...	...	...	...	...	|	...	...	|	...	...	1031	1031	...	...	|
	Birmingham New St **127** ..... d.		...	|	...	|	...	...	...	...	...	...	...	0642	|	...	0712	|	...	0812	|	|	...	0917	|
	Bristol Temple Meads .... d.		...	|	...	|	...	...	0524	0524	...	0634	0642	0810	|	...	0844	0913	0855	0944	|	|	0955	1045	|
230	Taunton .... d.		...	0235	...	|	...	...	0618	0618	...	0707	0739	0842	0903	...	0916	0946	1002	1019	1053	1053	1100	1117	|
253	Tiverton Parkway .... d.		...	|	...	|	...	...	0633	0633	...	0719	0754	0854	0916	...	0928	|	|	1031	1106	1106	1116	1130	|
279	**Exeter** St Davids .... **116** a.		...	0306	...	0305	...	...	0651	0651	...	0732	0812	0907	0930	...	0940	1011	1033	1045	1122	1122	1133	1143	1208
279	**Exeter** St Davids .... **116** d.		...	0411	...	0435	...	0628	0655	0655	...	0734	0814	0909	0933	0935	0942	1014	1034	1046	1125	1125	1135	1145	1208
299	Dawlish .... **116** d.		...	|	...	|	...	0642	0716	0716	...	|	|	|	|	|	|	|	1050	|	|	|	|	|	|
303	Teignmouth .... **116** d.		...	|	...	|	...	0647	0721	0721	...	|	|	|	|	|	|	|	1055	|	|	|	|	|	|
311	**Newton Abbot** .... **116** d.		...	0433	...	0456	...	0655	0728	0728	...	0755	0835	0929	0956	0958	1004	1036	1103	1106	1145	1145	1157	1205	1229
321	Torquay .... **116** d.		...	|	...	|	...	|	|	|	...	|	|	0941	1009	|	|	|	1115	|	|	|	|	|	|
324	**Paignton** .... **116** a.		...	|	...	|	...	|	|	|	...	|	|	0946	1019	|	|	|	1127	|	|	|	|	|	|
325	Totnes .... d.		...	|	...	|	...	0709	0742	0742	...	0806	0849	...	...	1011	1018	1049	...	1120	1158	1158	1210	1217	|
363	**Plymouth** .... a.		...	0514	...	0535	...	0740	0811	0811	...	0833	0919	...	...	1042	1047	1117	...	1146	1227	1227	1242	1247	1306
363	**Plymouth** .... d.		0543	0543	0628	0628	0702	0753a	0814	0814	0820	...	0921	...	...	1043	...	1120	...	...	*1239*	1228	▬	...	1311
370	Saltash .... d.		|	|	|	|	0715	0802a	0824	|	0832	...	0931	...	...	1054	...	|	...	...	*1248*	1238	...	...	|
392	Liskeard .... d.		0608	0608	0651	0709	0736	0820a	0843	0839	0853	...	0950	...	...	1113	...	1144	...	...	*1307*	1258	...	...	1335
406	Bodmin Parkway .... d.		0622	0622	0703	0723	0749	0833a	0855	0851	|	...	1002	...	...	1125	...	1157	...	...	*1319*	1313	Ⓐ	...	1348
	Lostwithiel .... d.		0628	0628	0708	0729	0755	0840a	0900	0856	|	...	1007	...	...	1130	...	|	...	...	*1324*	1319	2b	...	|
419	Par .... d.		0636	0637	0715	0738	0804	0854a	0908	0917	0914	...	1015	...	...	1138	...	1209	...	...	*1332*	1329	1337	...	1400
452	**Newquay** .... a.		|	|	|	|	|	...	|	1009	|	...	|	...	...	|	...	|	...	...	|	1420	|	...	|
426	St Austell .... d.		0645	0646	0721	0746	0811	...	0916	...	0923	...	1022	...	...	1145	...	1216	...	...	*1339*	...	1344	...	1407
449	Truro .... d.		0704	0706	0738	0806	0830	...	0934	...	0940	...	1040	...	...	1203	...	1234	...	...	*1357*	...	1402	...	1425
464	Redruth .... d.		0716	0718	0749	0820	0842	...	0947	...	0953	...	1053	...	...	1216	...	1246	...	...	*1410*	...	1415	...	1437
470	Camborne .... d.		0724	0726	0755	0827	0848	...	0953	...	1000	...	1059	...	...	1222	...	1253	...	...	*1416*	...	1421	...	1445
482	St Erth .... d.		0738	0742	0807	0845	0902	...	1008	...	1014	...	1110	...	...	1233	...	1305	...	...	*1428*	...	1433	...	1459
491	**Penzance** .... a.		0752	0753	0816	0859	0912	...	1016	...	1027	...	1123	...	...	1243	...	1317	...	...	*1439*	...	1444	...	1511

	Ⓐ	Ⓐ	Ⓐ	Ⓐ	Ⓐ	Ⓐ	Ⓐ	Ⓐ	Ⓐ	Ⓐ	Ⓐ	Ⓐ	Ⓐ	⑤	Ⓐ	Ⓐ	Ⓐ	Ⓐ	Ⓐ	Ⓐ	Ⓐ	Ⓐ	Ⓐ	Ⓐ	Ⓐ
		▲	D	E		F	▲			▲			▲	c	G								H		
London Paddington .... d.	...	...	1000	1106	...	1206	...	1218	1303	...	...	1406	...	1434	1506	...	...	1606	...	1636	1703	...	1803	1733	...
Reading .... d.	...	...	1028	1133u	...	1233u	...	1249	1333u	...	...	1434u	...	1501u	1533u	...	...	1632u	...	1704	1730u	...	1831u	1801	...
Newbury .... d.	...	...	|	|	...	|	...	1313	|	...	...	|	...	|	|	...	...	|	...	1719	1748	...	|	1819	...
Westbury .... d.	...	...	|	1221	...	|	...	1358	|	...	...	|	...	1604	1623	...	...	|	...	1803	|	...	|	1901	...
Castle Cary .... d.	...	...	|	1240	...	|	...	1416	|	...	...	|	...	1624	1641	...	...	|	...	1821	|	...	|	1919	...
Birmingham New St **127** ..... d.	0942	1017	|	|	1117	|	1217	|	|	1317	1342	|	1417	|	|	1517	1542	|	1612	|	|	1712	|	|	1812
Bristol Temple Meads .... d.	1115	1144	1147	|	1245	|	1344	|	|	1445	1513	|	1544	|	|	1645	1713	|	1744	|	|	1844	|	|	1945
Taunton .... d.	1201	1215	1229	1302	1317	|	1415	1441	1448	1517	1545	1549	1615	1651	1705	1717	1745	1750	1816	1844	1852	1916	1948	1942	2018
Tiverton Parkway .... d.	1213	1227	|	1315	1330	|	1427	...	1501	1529	1557	1602	1627	1707	1718	1729	1757	1803	1828	1857	1905	1928	|	1955	2030
Exeter St Davids .... **116** a.	1226	1240	1255	1331	1343	1408	1440	...	1517	1543	1612	1618	1640	1726	1734	1742	1811	1819	1841	1914	1921	1942	2013	2009	2043
Exeter St Davids .... **116** d.	1228	1241	1257	1333	1344	1408	1441	...	1518	1544	...	1620	1641	...	1735	1743	1812	1822	1845	1914d	1922	1944	2016	2020	2045
Dawlish .... **116** d.	1240	|	1309	|	|	|	|	...	|	|	...	|	|	...	|	|	1824	|	|	|	|	|	|	2043	|
Teignmouth .... **116** d.	1245	|	1315	|	|	|	|	...	|	|	...	|	|	...	|	|	1829	|	|	|	|	|	|	2050	|
Newton Abbot .... **116** d.	1252	1301	1323	1353	1404	1429	1501	...	1539	1604	...	1640	1702	...	1757	1812	1837	1843	1908	1935d	1942	2006	2036	2058	2104
Torquay .... **116** d.	1304	|	1335	|	|	|	|	...	|	|	...	|	|	...	|	|	1848	|	|	|	|	|	|	2112	|
Paignton .... **116** a.	1310	|	1343	|	|	|	|	...	|	|	...	|	|	...	|	|	1855	|	|	|	|	|	|	2122	|
Totnes .... d.	...	1312	...	1406	1417	|	1513	...	1553	1620	...	1653	1715	...	1810	1823	...	1856	1920	|	1956	2017	2050	...	2116
Plymouth .... a.	...	1338	...	1436	1443	1506	1540	...	1622	1648	...	1721	1740	...	1838	1849	...	1926	1945	2015d	2024	2043	2118	...	2146
Plymouth .... d.	...	*1353*	...	...	...	1512	*1557*	...	1628b	*1704*	...	1723	*1755*	...	1842	1901	...	1931	1949	...	2026	2050	2120	...	...
Saltash .... d.	...	*1402*	...	...	...	|	*1611*	...	|	*1717*	...	1734	*1804*	...	|	|	...	1940	|	...	2037	|	|	...	...
Liskeard .... d.	...	*1421*	...	...	...	1536	*1632*	...	1653b	*1740*	...	1754	*1820*	...	1907	1924	...	1957	2012	...	2056	2113	2145	...	...
Bodmin Parkway .... d.	...	*1433*	...	...	...	1549	*1644a*	...	1706b	...	...	1807	*1832*	...	1919	1936	...	2010	2024	...	2109	2125	2159	...	...
Lostwithiel .... d.	...	*1438*	...	...	...	|	*1649a*	...	1712b	...	...	1813	*1837*	...	|	|	...	|	|	...	|	2131	|	...	...
Par .... d.	...	*1446*	...	...	...	1601	*1657a*	...	1721b	...	...	1822	*1845*	...	1931	1946	...	2022	2034	...	2121	2138	2211	...	...
Newquay .... a.	...	|	...	...	...	|	|	...	|	...	...	|	|	...	|	|	...	|	|	...	|	|	|	...	...
St Austell .... d.	...	*1453*	...	...	...	1608	*1706a*	...	1728b	...	...	1829	*1853*	...	1939	1952	...	2029	2041	...	2128	2144	2218	...	...
Truro .... d.	...	*1511*	...	...	...	1626	*1723a*	...	1746b	...	...	1847	*1910*	...	2000	2018	...	2047	2102	...	2146	2203	2237	...	...
Redruth .... d.	...	*1524*	...	...	...	1638	*1736a*	...	1759b	...	...	1859	*1923*	...	2010	2029	...	2059	2118	...	2158	2214	2248	...	...
Camborne .... d.	...	*1530*	...	...	...	1646	*1742a*	...	1807b	...	...	1907	*1929*	...	2018	2035	...	2107	2125	...	|	2220	|	...	...
St Erth .... d.	...	*1542*	...	...	...	1700	*1754a*	...	1822b	...	...	1921	*1942*	...	2028	2046	...	2120	2135	...	2216	2232	|	...	...
Penzance .... a.	...	*1553*	...	...	...	1712	*1806a*	...	1833b	...	...	1933	*1954*	...	2042	2054	...	2131	2143	...	2230	2241	2313	...	...

	Ⓐ	①–④	⑤	Ⓐ	Ⓐ	Ⓐ	Ⓐ	Ⓐ	Ⓐ			⑥	⑥	⑥	⑥	⑥	⑥	⑥	⑥	⑥	⑥	⑥	⑥	⑥	⑥
		J▲	J									K		▲				2							
London Paddington .... d.	1835	1903	1903	...	...	1945	...	2035	2145	...	⑥	2345z	...	...	...	...	...	...	...	0736	0730	...	0835	0906	...
Reading .... d.	1903	1933	1933u	...	...	2012	...	2102	2212	...		0037u	...	...	...	...	...	...	...	0804u	0759	...	0903u	0934u	...
Newbury .... d.	1919	1950	1950	...	...	2028	...	2119	|	...		|	...	...	...	...	...	...	...	|	|	...	0919	|	...
Westbury .... d.	2006	|	|	...	...	2106	...	2156	|	...		|	...	...	...	...	...	...	...	|	|	...	0956	|	...
Castle Cary .... d.	2024	|	|	...	...	2126	...	2215	|	...		|	...	...	...	...	...	...	...	|	|	...	1015	|	...
Birmingham New St **127** ..... d.	|	|	|	1912	1942	|	2012	|	|	...		|	...	...	...	...	0642	...	0712	|	|	0812	|	|	091
Bristol Temple Meads .... d.	|	|	|	2044	2113	|	2144	|	2335	...		|	...	*0524*	0608	0644	0812	...	0845	|	0917	0944	|	|	102
Taunton .... d.	2046	2054	2054	2116	2144	2148	2216	2237	0036s	...		0235	...	*0618*	0715	0730	0843	...	0916	|	0951	1017	1037	1050	110
Tiverton Parkway .... d.	2059	2107	2107	2128	2156	2202	2228	2250	0049s	...		|	...	*0633*	0727	0743	0855	...	0928	|	|	1030	1050	1103	111
Exeter St Davids .... **116** a.	2116	2123	2123	2141	2209	2218	2241	2306	0107	...		0306	...	*0652*	0740	0758	0907	...	0939	0952	1016	1044	1106	1119	112
Exeter St Davids .... **116** d.	2117d	2125	2125	2143	2211	2219	2242	2308	...	...		0411	...	*0656*	0741	0800	0910	0928	0942	0954	1019	1046	1108	1122	112
Dawlish .... **116** d.	|	|	|	|	|	|	|	|	...	...		|	...	*0714*	|	0818	|	|	|	|	|	1059	1124	|	|
Teignmouth .... **116** d.	|	|	|	|	|	|	|	|	...	...		|	...	*0719*	|	0824	|	|	|	|	|	1105	1131	|	|
Newton Abbot .... **116** d.	2137d	2145	2145	2206	2230	2240	2308	2328	...	...		0433	...	*0726*	0801	0832	0929	0949	1001	|	1039	1113	1139	1142	114
Torquay .... **116** d.	|	|	|	|	|	|	|	|	...	...		|	...	|	|	|	0941	|	|	|	|	1125	1151	|	|
Paignton .... **116** a.	|	|	|	|	|	|	|	|	...	...		|	...	|	|	|	0947	|	|	|	|	1133	1201	|	|
Totnes .... d.	|	2158	2158	2217	2242	2253	2320	2342	...	...		|	...	*0740*	0812	0846	...	1002	1013	|	1052	...	...	1156	120
Plymouth .... a.	2215d	2226	2226	2243	2313	2325	2345	0011	...	...		0514	...	*0813*	0838	0916	...	1032	1039	1050	1120	...	...	1224	123
Plymouth .... d.	...	*2246*	2229	...	...	...	...	...	...	...		0543	0635	0818	...	0923	...	1033	...	1053	1123	...	...	1228	123
Saltash .... d.	...	*2255*	2239	...	...	...	...	...	...	...		|	|	0828	...	0933	...	1045	...	|	|	...	...	1238	|
Liskeard .... d.	...	*2314*	2259	...	...	...	...	...	...	...		0608	0659	0847	...	0950	...	1106	...	|	1147	...	...	1255	130
Bodmin Parkway .... d.	...	*2326*	2313	...	...	...	...	...	...	...		0622	0712	0859	...	1003	...	1118	...	|	1201	...	...	1308	132
Lostwithiel .... d.	...	*2331*	2319	...	...	...	...	...	...	...		0628	0718	0904	...	1009	...	1123	...	|	|	...	...	|	|
Par .... d.	...	*2339*	2328	...	...	...	...	...	...	...		0637	0728	0912	...	1016	...	1131	...	1141	1212	...	...	|	133
Newquay .... a.	...	|	|	...	...	...	...	...	...	...		|	0818	|	...	|	...	|	...	1242	|	...	...	|	143
St Austell .... d.	...	*2346*	2335	...	...	...	...	...	...	...		0646	...	0920	...	1024	...	1139	...	...	1220	...	...	1323	...
Truro .... d.	...	*0005*	2353	...	...	...	...	...	...	...		0706	...	0937	...	1042	...	1156	...	...	1238	...	...	1341	...
Redruth .... d.	...	*0018*	0006	...	...	...	...	...	...	...		0718	...	0950	...	1054	...	1209	...	...	1250	...	...	1355	...
Camborne .... d.	...	*0024*	0014	...	...	...	...	...	...	...		0726	...	0956	...	1101	...	1215	...	...	1257	...	...	1402	...
St Erth .... d.	...	*0035*	0028	...	...	...	...	...	...	...		0742	...	1008	...	1116	...	1227	...	...	1310	...	...	1419	...
Penzance .... a.	...	*0046*	0040	...	...	...	...	...	...	...		0753	...	1018	...	1127	...	1237	...	...	1322	...	...	1428	...

A – THE DEVON EXPRESS – (12) and 🍸 London Paddington - Paignton and v.v.
B – THE MERCHANT VENTURER – (12) and 🍸 London Paddington - Penzance and v.v.
C – THE CORNISH RIVIERA – (12) and 🍸 London Paddington - Penzance and v.v.
D – THE TORBAY EXPRESS – (12) and 🍸 London Paddington - Paignton and v.v.
E – THE MAYFLOWER – (12) and 🍸 London Paddington - Plymouth and v.v.
F – THE ROYAL DUCHY – (12) and 🍸 London Paddington - Penzance and v.v.
G – THE CORNISHMAN – (12) and 🍸 London Paddington - Penzance and v.v.
H – THE GOLDEN HIND – (12) and 🍸 London Paddington - Penzance and v.v.
J – THE ARMADA – (12) and 🍸 London Paddington - Plymouth / Penzance and v.v.
K – THE NIGHT RIVIERA – 🛏 1, 2. cl and (2) London Paddington - Penzance and v.v. Passengers may occupy cabins at London Paddington from 2230 and at Penzance fror 2045⑦/2115Ⓐ.
L – THE ATLANTIC COAST EXPRESS – (12) and 🍸 London Paddington - Newquay and v.

NOTES CONTINUE ON PAGE 107

GW, XC LONDON and BRISTOL - EXETER - PAIGNTON, PLYMOUTH and PENZANCE 115

Service until September 7. Service on ⑦ subject to alteration June 22 - July 27.

	⑥	⑥	⑥	⑥	⑥	⑥	⑥	⑥	⑥	⑥	⑥	⑥	⑥	⑥	⑥	⑥	⑥	⑥	⑥	⑥	⑥	⑥	⑥	⑥	⑥
		C						L	F	2								2			2			▲	D
London Paddington .... d.	...	1006	...	...	1035	1106	...	1135	1206	...	...	1235	1306	...	...	1406	...	...	1506	...	...	1606	...	1706	1630
Reading .... d.	...	1033u	...	...	1104u	1134u	...	1204u	1233u	...	...	1305u	1332u	...	...	1433u	...	...	1532u	...	...	1633u	...	1732u	1659
Newbury .... d.	...	|	...	...	|	|	...	|	|	...	...	1322	|	...	...	|	...	...	|	...	...	|	...	|	|
Westbury .... d.	...	|	...	...	1154	|	...	|	|	...	...	1359	|	...	...	|	...	...	1623	...	...	|	...	1822	|
Castle Cary .... d.	...	|	...	...	1212	|	...	|	|	...	...	1416	|	...	...	|	...	...	1641	...	...	|	...	1841	|
Birmingham New St **127** ..... d.	0912	|	0942	1012	|	|	1112	|	|	...	1212	|	|	1312	1342	|	1412	...	|	1512	...	|	1612	|	|
Bristol Temple Meads .... d.	1044	|	1112	1144	|	|	1244	|	|	...	1344	|	|	1444	1512	|	1544	...	|	1644	...	|	1744	|	1818
Taunton .... d.	1116	|	1200	1217	1235	1250	1316	|	|	...	1417	1439	1448	1517	1543	1548	1616	...	1703	1717	...	1749	1816	1903	1907
Tiverton Parkway .... d.	1128	|	1212	1229	1249	|	1328	|	|	...	1429	|	1501	1529	1555	1601	1628	...	1716	1730	...	1802	1828	1916	1921
Exeter St Davids .... **116** a.	1140	1209	1225	1240	1304	1315	1341	1352	1409	...	1443	1503	1517	1543	1607	1617	1640	...	1731	1743	...	1818	1840	1932	1936
Exeter St Davids .... **116** d.	1143	1211	1227	1243	1308	1318	1342	1355	1411	...	1446	1506	1519	1544	1612	1618	1642	...	1734	1747	1750	1819	1846	1934	1939
Dawlish .... **116** d.	|	|	1239	|	1322	|	|	|	|	...	1504	1524	|	|	1636	|	|	...	|	|	1809	|	|	|	|
Teignmouth .... **116** d.	|	|	1244	|	1328	|	|	|	|	...	1510	1530	|	|	1641	|	|	...	|	|	1815	|	|	|	|
Newton Abbot .... **116** d.	1203	1232	1252	1306	1337	1339	1402	|	1432	...	1518	1538	1542	1604	1649	1639	1702	...	1756	1812	1824	1841	1905	1954	2000
Torquay .... **116** d.	|	|	1303	|	1350	|	|	|	|	...	1530	1551	|	|	1701	|	|	...	|	|	|	|	|	|	2013
Paignton .... **116** a.	|	|	1310	|	1400	|	|	|	|	...	1538	1558	|	|	1708	|	|	...	|	|	|	|	|	|	2023
Totnes .... d.	1214	|	...	1318	...	1352	1413	|	|	...	...	...	1556	1617	...	1652	1713	...	1808	1824	1837	1854	1917	2007	...
Plymouth .... a.	1240	1314	...	1345	...	1421	1439	1451	1509	...	...	...	1623	1643	...	1723	1739	...	1837	1851	1906	1924	1942	2035	...
Plymouth .... d.	...	1315	...	1348	...	1424	...	1454	1511	1603	...	...	1626	1650	...	1726	1742	1752	...	1855	1907	1929	1948	*2040*	...
Saltash .... d.	...	|	...	|	...	|	...	|	|	1612	...	...	|	|	...	|	|	1805	...	|	1917	|	|	*2054*	...
Liskeard .... d.	...	1340	...	1411	...	1449	...	|	1536	1633	...	...	1650	1713	...	1751	1805	1829	...	1921	1938	1954	2011	*2113*	...
Bodmin Parkway .... d.	...	1354	...	1424	...	1502	...	|	1549	1645	...	...	1703	1729	...	1803	1817	1842	...	1933	1952	2007	2023	*2125*	...
Lostwithiel .... d.	...	|	...	|	...	|	...	1532	|	1650	...	...	|	|	...	|	|	1858	...	|	|	|	2028	*2130*	...
Par .... d.	...	1406	...	1434	...	|	...	1543	1601	1656	...	...	|	1742	...	1816	1828	1857	...	1944	2003	2018	2035	*2138*	...
Newquay .... a.	...	|	...	|	...	|	...	1647	|	...	...	...	|	1838	...	|	|	|	...	|	|	|	|	|	...
St Austell .... d.	...	1414	...	1442	...	1517	...	...	1608	...	...	...	1720	...	...	1822	1834	1904	...	1952	2011	2026	2041	*2145*	...
Truro .... d.	...	1430	...	1500	...	1535	...	...	1626	...	...	...	1737	...	...	1841	1852	1923	...	2015	2029	2044	2102	*2203*	...
Redruth .... d.	...	1444	...	1512	...	1548	...	...	1638	...	...	...	1750	...	...	1852	1908	1935	...	2027	2042	2059	2113	*2217*	...
Camborne .... d.	...	1450	...	1519	...	1555	...	...	1646	...	...	...	1757	...	...	1901	1915	1943	...	2035	2049	2106	2119	*2223*	...
St Erth .... d.	...	1506	...	1532	...	1610	...	...	1658	...	...	...	1813	...	...	1911	1925	1957	...	2046	2059	2117	2131	*2234*	...
Penzance .... a.	...	1518	...	1541	...	1621	...	...	1710	...	...	...	1825	...	...	1923	1934	2007	...	2056	2111	2127	2142	*2244*	...

	⑥	⑥	⑥	⑥	⑥	⑥	⑥	⑥	⑥			⑦	⑦	⑦	⑦	⑦	⑦	⑦	⑦	⑦	⑦	⑦	⑦	⑦	⑦
													2	2		2								▲	
London Paddington .... d.	...	1806	...	1830	1906	...	2006	...	2030	...	⑦	...	...	...	...	...	...	0757	0857	...	0957	...	1057	...	1127
Reading .... d.	...	1833u	...	1859	1932	...	2033	...	2059	...		...	...	...	...	...	...	0838	0932	...	1032	...	1132	...	1208
Newbury .... d.	...	|	...	|	1949	...	2047	...	|	...		...	...	...	...	...	...	|	0948	...	|	...	|	...	|
Westbury .... d.	...	|	...	|	2027	...	2126	...	|	...		...	...	...	...	...	...	|	1021	...	|	...	|	...	1305
Castle Cary .... d.	...	|	...	|	2044	...	2144	...	|	...		...	...	...	...	...	...	|	|	...	1134	...	|	...	1323
Birmingham New St **127** ..... d.	1712	|	1812	|	|	1912	|	1942	|	...		...	...	...	...	...	...	|	|	0912	|	1030	|	1130	|
Bristol Temple Meads .... d.	1844	|	1944	2015	|	2044	|	2144	2217	...		...	...	0733	0844	0828	0948	1000	|	1044	|	1154	|	1254	|
Taunton .... d.	1916	1947	2016	2103	2107	2116	2206	2218	2318	...		...	...	0827	0915	0932	1019	1033	1057	1115	1157	1225	1247	1325	1344
Tiverton Parkway .... d.	1928	|	2028	...	2120	2129	2219	2230	2331	...		...	...	0842	0927	0948	1031	1047	1110	1127	|	1236	|	1337	|
Exeter St Davids .... **116** a.	1943	2013	2039	...	2136	2144	2235	2244	2347	...		...	...	0859	0939	1005	1044	1103	1126	1139	1222	1252	1314	1352	1410
Exeter St Davids .... **116** d.	1945	2016	2043	...	2139	2147	2339	2247	...	...		...	...	0901	0941	1006	1045	1105	1126	1141	1224	1253	1315	1353	1410
Dawlish .... **116** d.	|	|	|	...	|	|	2249	|	...	...		...	...	0914	|	1021	|	1119	|	|	|	|	|	|	1429
Teignmouth .... **116** d.	|	|	|	...	|	|	2255	|	...	...		...	...	0919	|	1026	|	1125	|	|	|	|	|	|	1435
Newton Abbot .... **116** d.	2005	2037	2101	...	2159	2210	2303	2313	...	...		...	...	0927	1000	1033	1105	1132	1147	1200	1245	1313	1336	1413	1442
Torquay .... **116** d.	|	|	|	...	|	|	|	|	...	...		...	...	|	|	|	|	|	|	|	|	|	|	|	1455
Paignton .... **116** a.	|	|	|	...	|	|	|	|	...	...		...	...	|	|	|	|	|	|	|	|	|	|	|	1502
Totnes .... d.	2016	2051	2113	...	2211	2223	2316	2329	...	...		...	...	0940	1012	1046	1116	1145	1201	1212	1258	1326	|	1426	...
Plymouth .... a.	2042	2119	2138	...	2243	2249	2346	2355	...	...		...	...	1010	1037	1115	1142	1213	1230	1237	1326	1352	1414	1452	...
Plymouth .... d.	...	2120	...	...	...	...	...	...	...	...		0901	0910	1011	...	1115	...	1215	1235	1255	1328	...	1420	*1458*	...
Saltash .... d.	...	|	...	...	...	...	...	...	...	...		|	0920	1023	...	1126	...	|	|	|	|	...	|	*1507*	...
Liskeard .... d.	...	2145	...	...	...	...	...	...	...	...		0925	0943	1044	...	1145	...	1243	1300	1318	1352	...	1444	*1526*	...
Bodmin Parkway .... d.	...	2159	...	...	...	...	...	...	...	...		0938	0955	1056	...	1157	...	1256	1313	1330	1405	...	1458	*1539*	...
Lostwithiel .... d.	...	|	...	...	...	...	...	...	...	...		|	1000	1101	...	1202	...	|	|	|	1411	...	|	*1545*	...
Par .... d.	...	2211	...	...	...	...	...	...	...	...		0955	1008	1109	...	1210	...	1308	1325	1340	1422	...	|	*1553*	...
Newquay .... a.	...	|	...	...	...	...	...	...	...	...		1100	|	|	...	|	...	|	|	|	1512	...	|	|	...
St Austell .... d.	...	2218	...	...	...	...	...	...	...	...		...	1016	1116	...	1218	...	1315	1332	1349	...	...	1514	*1600*	...
Truro .... d.	...	2236	...	...	...	...	...	...	...	...		...	1034	1138	...	1235	...	1334	1351	1407	...	...	1532	*1619*	...
Redruth .... d.	...	2248	...	...	...	...	...	...	...	...		...	1047	1152	...	1248	...	1346	1403	1418	...	...	1543	*1632*	...
Camborne .... d.	...	2256	...	...	...	...	...	...	...	...		...	1053	1158	...	1254	...	1354	1411	1428	...	...	1551	*1638*	...
St Erth .... d.	...	2309	...	...	...	...	...	...	...	...		...	1106	1208	...	1306	...	1406	1423	1435	...	...	1603	*1650*	...
Penzance .... a.	...	2322	...	...	...	...	...	...	...	...		...	1115	1219	...	1316	...	1416	1433	1449	...	...	1615	*1700*	...

	⑦	⑦	⑦	⑦	⑦	⑦	⑦	⑦	⑦	⑦	⑦	⑦	⑦	⑦	⑦	⑦	⑦	⑦	⑦	⑦	⑦	⑦	⑦	⑦	⑦
					e	2							▲												
London Paddington .... d.	1157	...	1257	...	1300	...	1357	...	...	1457	...	1500	1557	...	1657	...	1757	...	1857	...	...	1900	1957	...	2057
Reading .... d.	1232	...	1332	...	1338	...	1432	...	...	1532	...	1538	1632	...	1732	...	1832	...	1932	...	...	1938	2032	...	2132
Newbury .... d.	1248	...	|	...	|	...	1448	...	...	|	...	|	1648	...	|	...	1848	...	|	...	...	|	2048	...	|
Westbury .... d.	|	...	1419	...	|	...	|	...	...	|	...	|	1724	...	|	...	1927	...	|	...	...	|	2127	...	|
Castle Cary .... d.	|	...	|	...	|	...	1534	...	...	|	...	|	1743	...	|	...	|	...	2030	...	...	|	2145	...	|
Birmingham New St **127** ..... d.	|	1212	|	1312	|	...	|	1412	1442	|	1512	|	|	1612	|	1712	|	1812	|	1842	1912	|	|	2012	|
Bristol Temple Meads .... d.	|	1344	|	1444	1455	...	|	1544	1614	|	1644	1655	|	1744	|	1844	|	1944	|	2019	2044	2055	|	2144	|
Taunton .... d.	1354	1415	1455	1515	1530	...	1556	1613	1645	1651	1715	1752	1805	1818	1849	1916	2000	2018	2051	2059	2115	2151	2208	2215	2249s
Tiverton Parkway .... d.	|	1427	1508	1527	|	...	|	1624	1657	1704	1727	...	1818	1830	1902	1927	2015	2030	2105	2112	2127	2204	2221	2228	2302s
Exeter St Davids .... **116** a.	1419	1443	1523	1539	1554	...	1622	1640	1709	1719	1739	...	1834	1845	1918	1945	2030	2043	2121	2127	2139	2222	2236	2245	2318
Exeter St Davids .... **116** d.	1423	1444	1524	1542	1556	1610	1624	1643	1713	1721	1742	...	1835	1847	1919	1949	2031	2043	2122	2130	2141	...	2237	2246	...
Dawlish .... **116** d.	|	|	|	|	|	1625	|	|	1725	|	|	...	|	|	|	|	|	|	2135	2142	|	...	|	|	...
Teignmouth .... **116** d.	|	|	|	|	|	1630	|	|	1730	|	|	...	|	|	|	|	|	|	2141	2147	|	...	|	|	...
Newton Abbot .... **116** d.	1446	1503	1545	1601	1617	1637	1643	1703	1738	1740	1800	...	1856	1906	1938	2008	2054	2104	2148	2155	2200	...	2258	2306	...
Torquay .... **116** d.	|	|	|	|	|	|	|	|	1749	|	|	...	|	|	|	|	|	|	|	2206	|	...	|	|	...
Paignton .... **116** a.	|	|	|	|	|	|	|	|	1756	|	|	...	|	|	|	|	|	|	|	2213	|	...	|	|	...
Totnes .... d.	1500	1515	1559	1613	|	1652	1701	1716	...	1755	1813	...	|	1918	1954	2020	2107	2114	2202	...	2213	...	2311	2322	...
Plymouth .... a.	1527	1544	1627	1641	1655	1722	1730	1742	...	1821	1838	...	1936	1943	2021	2045	2134	2143	2230	...	2240	...	2341	2347	...
Plymouth .... d.	1535	...	1635	...	...	1735	...	...	...	1825	1853	...	*1943*	...	2025	2050	2140	...	...	...	...	...	...	...	...
Saltash .... d.	|	...	|	...	...	1744	...	...	...	|	|	...	*1952*	...	|	|	|	...	...	...	...	...	...	...	...
Liskeard .... d.	1557	...	1657	...	...	1805	...	...	...	1850	1916	...	*2011*	...	2049	2113	2204	...	...	...	...	...	...	...	...
Bodmin Parkway .... d.	1612	...	1710	...	...	1817	...	...	...	1904	1928	...	*2023*	...	2102	2125	2217	...	...	...	...	...	...	...	...
Lostwithiel .... d.	|	...	|	...	...	1822	...	...	...	|	|	...	*2028*	...	|	|	|	...	...	...	...	...	...	...	...
Par .... d.	1624	...	1722	...	...	1830	...	...	...	1915	1938	...	*2036*	...	2113	2135	2230	...	...	...	...	...	...	...	...
Newquay .... a.	|	...	|	...	...	|	...	...	...	|	|	...	|	...	|	|	|	...	...	...	...	...	...	...	...
St Austell .... d.	1632	...	1729	...	...	1837	...	...	...	1923	1945	...	*2043*	...	2120	2146	2238	...	...	...	...	...	...	...	...
Truro .... d.	1650	...	1747	...	...	1855	...	...	...	1940	2001	...	*2100*	...	2138	2200	2253	...	...	...	...	...	...	...	...
Redruth .... d.	1702	...	1759	...	...	1908	...	...	...	1953	2012	...	*2114*	...	2151	2211	2308	...	...	...	...	...	...	...	...
Camborne .... d.	1710	...	1807	...	...	1914	...	...	...	2004	2021	...	*2120*	...	2158	2219	2315	...	...	...	...	...	...	...	...
St Erth .... d.	1722	...	1820	...	...	1925	...	...	...	2016	2031	...	*2132*	...	2210	2229	2327	...	...	...	...	...	...	...	...
Penzance .... a.	1735	...	1832	...	...	1937	...	...	...	2028	2039	...	*2142*	...	2222	2241	2338	...	...	...	...	...	...	...	...

OTES CONTINUED FROM PAGE 106

– Until July 4 and from Sep. 1.
– July 7 - Aug. 29.
– July 11 - Aug. 29.
– ⑤ only.
– Until June 15.
– Stops to set down only.

u – Stops to pick up only.
x – From London Paddington on ⑦.
z – From London Paddington on ①–⑤.

* – Connection by 🚌.
▲ – Connecting train conveys 2 only.

115 LONDON and BRISTOL - EXETER - PAIGNTON, PLYMOUTH and PENZANCE GW, XC

Service until September 7. Service on ⑦ subject to alteration June 22 - July 27.

		Ⓐ	Ⓐ	Ⓐ	Ⓐ	Ⓐ	Ⓐ	Ⓐ	Ⓐ	Ⓐ	Ⓐ	Ⓐ	Ⓐ	Ⓐ	Ⓐ	Ⓐ	Ⓐ	Ⓐ	Ⓐ	Ⓐ	Ⓐ	Ⓐ	Ⓐ	Ⓐ	Ⓐ
						J			H	2			2							C				G	
Penzance d.	Ⓐ	...	...	...	...	...	...	...	0505	0521	...	0541	0600	0628	0645	...	...	0741	0828	0844	...	...	0940	1000	...
St Erth d.		...	...	...	...	...	...	...	|	|	...	|	0609	0636	0655	...	...	0751	0836	0854	...	...	0948	1010	...
Camborne d.		...	...	...	...	...	...	...	|	0540	...	0558	0621	0646	0706	...	...	0805	0846	0906	...	...	1001	1021	...
Redruth d.		...	...	...	...	...	...	...	0525	|	...	0605	0627	0652	0713	...	...	0812	0852	0913	...	...	1008	1028	...
Truro d.		...	...	...	...	...	...	...	0538	0555	...	0618	0639	0704	0726	...	...	0825	0904	0926	...	...	1019	1041	...
St Austell d.		...	...	...	...	...	...	...	0555	▬	...	0635	0656	0720	0744	...	...	0843	0920	0943	...	...	1035	1058	...
Newquay d.		...	...	...	...	...	...	...	|	...	...	|	|	|	|	...	...	|	|	|	...	...	|	|	...
Par d.		...	...	...	...	...	...	...	|	...	...	0643	0703	0727	0752	...	...	0851	0927	0951	...	...	1042	1107	...
Lostwithiel d.		...	...	...	...	...	...	...	|	...	...	0651	0710	|	0800	...	...	|	|	|	...	...	1049	|	...
Bodmin Parkway d.		...	...	...	...	...	...	...	0611	...	...	0657	0716	0737	0806	...	...	0903	0937	1003	...	...	1055	1119	...
Liskeard d.		...	...	...	...	...	...	...	0626	...	...	0711	0729	0753	0820	...	...	0916	0950	1016	...	...	1108	1133	...
Saltash d.		...	...	...	...	...	...	...	|	Ⓐ	...	0730	0748	|	0839	...	...	0935	|	|	...	...	|	|	...
Plymouth a.		...	...	...	...	...	...	...	0651		...	0741	0804	0820	0849	...	...	0946	1018	1041	...	...	1139	1158	...
Plymouth d.		...	0509	0520	0530	0553	0625	...	0655	0725	...	0748	0809	0825	0853	0925	...	0948	1025	1044	...	1125	1150	1201	1225
Totnes d.		...	|	0545	0558	|	0650	...	|	0750	...	0816	0840	0850	0923	0950	...	1019	1050	|	...	1150	1215	1229	1251
Paignton 116 d.		...	|	|	|	|	|	0702	|	|	0740	|	|	|	|	|	1007	|	|	|	1106	|	|	|	|
Torquay 116 d.		...	|	|	|	|	|	0708	|	|	0746	|	|	|	|	|	1013	|	|	|	1112	|	|	|	|
Newton Abbot 116 d.		...	0547	0602	0611	0631	0703	0719	0732	0803	0806	0829	0852	0905	0936	1003	1024	1032	1103	|	1126	1203	1228	1242	1304
Teignmouth 116 d.		...	0554	|	|	|	|	0726	|	|	0813	|	0859	|	|	|	1031	|	|	|	1133	|	|	|	|
Dawlish 116 d.		...	|	|	0621	|	|	0731	|	|	0819	|	0904	|	|	|	1036	|	|	|	1139	|	|	|	|
Exeter St Davids 116 a.		...	0610	0618	0633	0651	0720	0743	0752	0820	0839	0849	0918	0922	0956	1020	1048	1054	1120	1138	1152	1220	1245	1302	1322
Exeter St Davids d.		0546	0612	0624	0635	0652	0724	0745	0753	0824	0841	0851	0933	0923	0958	1024	1050	1056	1124	1140	1155	1224	1250	1304	1324
Tiverton Parkway d.		0602	0627	0637	0651	|	0737	0758	|	0837	|	0906	0950	0937	1013	1037	1103	1111	1137	|	1209	1237	1306	1319	1338
Taunton d.		0617	0654	0651	0706	0718	0751	0812	0819	0851	0905	0921	1007	0951	1028	1051	1117	1126	1151	|	1224	1251	1322	1334	1352
Bristol Temple Meads a.		|	0757	0725	|	|	0826	0852	|	0925	0957	|	1111	1025	|	1123	1151	1158	1223	|	|	1324	1355	|	1425
Birmingham New St 127 a.		|	|	0855	|	|	0956	1023	|	1055	|	|	...	1158	|	1256	1326	|	1356	|	|	1456	1523	|	1556
Castle Cary a.		0637	|	...	0726	|	...	...	|	...	|	0941	...	...	|	...	...	|	...	|	1245	...	...	|	...
Westbury a.		0659	|	...	0745	|	...	...	|	...	|	1000	...	...	1103	...	...	|	...	|	1304	...	...	|	...
Newbury a.		0745	|	...	0829	|	...	...	|	...	|	|	...	...	|	...	...	|	...	|	1350	...	...	|	...
Reading a.		0806	0914	...	0850	0832	...	...	0932	...	1108	1050	...	...	1150	...	...	1309	...	1316	1420	...	...	1450	...
London Paddington a.		0838	0944	...	0921	0900	...	...	1002	...	1138	1124	...	...	1223	...	...	1338	...	1344	1454	...	...	1521	...

	Ⓐ	Ⓐ	Ⓐ	Ⓐ	Ⓐ	Ⓐ	Ⓐ	Ⓐ	Ⓐ	Ⓐ	Ⓐ	Ⓐ	Ⓐ	Ⓐ	Ⓐ	Ⓐ	Ⓐ	⑤	Ⓐ	Ⓐ	Ⓐ	Ⓐ	①–④	①–④	⑤
	2	a▲	b			2	D		E	2		F		2a	a	2b	Lb	c				2	2		2
Penzance d.	...	*1046*	1047	...	...	1141	...	...	...	1251	...	1400	...	1449	...	1452	...	...	...	1600	...	...	1644	...	1644
St Erth d.	...	*1055*	1057	...	...	1150	...	...	...	1303	...	1410	...	1458	...	1501	...	...	...	1610	...	...	1653	...	1653
Camborne d.	...	*1107*	1111	...	...	1202	...	...	...	1315	...	1421	...	1510	...	1513	...	...	...	1620	...	...	1705	...	1705
Redruth d.	...	*1113*	1118	...	...	1208	...	...	...	1321	...	1428	...	1516	...	1519	...	...	...	1628	...	...	1711	...	1711
Truro d.	...	*1125*	1131	...	...	1219	...	...	...	1332	...	1441	...	1527	...	1530	...	...	...	1641	...	...	1724	...	1724
St Austell d.	...	*1142*	1149	...	...	1236	...	...	...	1349	...	1458	...	1544	...	1547	...	...	...	1658	...	...	1741	...	1741
Newquay d.	...	|	|	...	...	|	...	...	...	|	...	|	...	|	...	|	1506	...	...	|	...	...	|	...	|
Par d.	...	*1150*	1157	...	...	1244	...	...	...	1357	...	1506	...	1552	...	1554	1600	...	...	1707	...	...	1748	...	1748
Lostwithiel d.	...	*1156*	|	...	...	1250	...	...	...	1404	...	|	...	1558	...	...	1609	...	...	1714	...	...	1755	...	1755
Bodmin Parkway d.	...	*1202*	1208	...	...	1256	...	...	...	1410	...	1518	...	1604	...	...	1616	...	...	1721	...	...	1801	...	1801
Liskeard d.	...	*1217*	1221	...	...	1309	...	...	...	1423	...	1531	...	1617	...	...	1629	...	...	1734	...	...	1814	...	1814
Saltash d.	...	*1235*	1241	...	...	1329	...	...	...	1442	...	|	...	1638	...	...	|	...	...	|	...	...	1832	...	1832
Plymouth a.	...	*1245*	1252	...	...	1339	...	...	...	1451	...	1556	...	1652	...	...	1654	...	...	1800	...	...	1842	...	1842
Plymouth d.	...	1256	1256	1325	...	1343	...	1425	1500	1508	1525	1600	1625	...	1657	...	1657	...	1725	1803	1825	...	1844	...	1844
Totnes d.	...	1324	1324	1351	...	1413	...	1450	1528	1538	1551	1628	1650	...	1728	...	1728	...	1751	1831	1850	...	1914	...	1914
Paignton 116 d.	1248	|	|	|	1401	|	1415	|	|	|	|	|	|	...	|	...	|	...	|	|	|	1852	|	...	|
Torquay 116 d.	1254	|	|	|	1407	|	1421	|	|	|	|	|	|	...	|	...	|	...	|	|	|	1857	|	...	|
Newton Abbot 116 d.	1308	1337	1337	1404	1418	1427	1433	1503	1541	1552	1604	1641	1703	...	1741	...	1741	...	1804	1844	1903	1909	1927	...	1927
Teignmouth 116 d.	1315	|	|	|	1425	...	1440	|	|	...	|	|	|	...	|	...	|	...	|	|	|	1916	|	...	|
Dawlish 116 d.	1320	|	|	|	1430	...	1446	|	|	...	|	|	|	...	|	...	|	...	|	|	|	1921	|	...	|
Exeter St Davids 116 a.	1332	1357	1357	1422	1442	...	1459	1520	1601	...	1622	1701	1721	...	1801	...	1801	...	1823	1903	1920	1939	1949	...	1949
Exeter St Davids d.	1336	1359	1359	1424	1444	...	1501	1524	1603	...	1624	1703	1724	...	1803	...	1803	1820	1825	1906	1924	1939	...	1955	1949
Tiverton Parkway d.	1353	|	|	1438	1457	...	1516	1537	1617	...	1638	1718	1737	...	1817	...	1817	1848	1839	1921	1937	|	...	2010	2006
Taunton d.	1410	1424	1424	1452	1511	...	1531	1551	1631	...	1651	1732	1751	...	1831	...	1831	|	1853	1936	1951	2010	...	2025	2022
Bristol Temple Meads a.	1513	|	|	1525	1555	...	|	1626	|	...	1724	|	1823	...	|	...	|	|	1926	|	2024	2054	...	|	...
Birmingham New St 127 a.	...	|	|	1656	1723	...	|	1756	|	...	1856	|	1956	...	|	...	|	|	2052	|	2203	...	...	|	...
Castle Cary a.	...	1444	1444	...	...	...	1551	...	|	...	...	|	...	...	1853	...	1853	|	...	|	...	...	...	2045	...
Westbury a.	...	1502	1502	...	...	...	|	...	|	...	...	|	...	...	1912	...	1912	|	...	|	...	...	...	2104	...
Newbury a.	...	|	|	...	...	...	|	...	|	...	...	|	...	...	1949	...	1949	|	...	|	...	...	...	2142	...
Reading a.	...	1550	1550	...	...	...	1650	...	1749	...	...	1851	...	...	2006	...	2006	2020	...	2050	...	...	...	2159	...
London Paddington a.	...	1622	1622	...	...	...	1724	...	1821	...	...	1924	...	...	2039	...	2039	2052	...	2124	...	...	...	2238	...

	⑤	Ⓐ	Ⓐ	Ⓐ	Ⓐ	Ⓐ	①–⑤	Ⓐ			⑥	⑥	⑥	⑥	⑥	⑥	⑥	⑥	⑥	⑥	⑥	⑥	⑥	⑥	⑥
				2a	2b		K							2				▲				D			
Penzance d.	...	1739	...	1916	1913	2018	2145	2208	...	⑥	...	...	...	0510	...	...	...	*0526*	0630	...	0650	...	...	0718	...
St Erth d.	...	1749	...	1925	1923	2027	2155	2216	...		...	...	...	|	...	...	...	*0534*	0638	...	0700	...	...	0729	...
Camborne d.	...	1803	...	1937	1938	2041	2208	2231	...		...	...	...	0527	...	...	...	*0547*	0651	...	0711	...	...	0744	...
Redruth d.	...	1811	...	1943	1945	2049	2216	2237	...		...	...	...	0533	...	...	...	*0553*	0657	...	0718	...	...	0751	...
Truro d.	...	1823	...	1955	1958	2102	2229	2249	...		...	...	...	0545	...	...	...	*0601*	0709	...	0731	...	...	0805	...
St Austell d.	...	1840	...	2012	2015	2119	2247	2305	...		...	...	...	▬	...	...	...	*0621*	0725	...	0748	...	...	0822	...
Newquay d.	...	|	...	|	|	|	|	|	...		...	...	...	...	...	...	...	|	|	...	|	...	...	|	...
Par d.	...	1849	...	2019	2024	2127	2257	2312	...		...	...	...	...	...	...	...	*0628*	0732	...	0756	...	...	0830	...
Lostwithiel d.	...	|	...	2026	2031	2134	|	2319	...		...	...	...	...	...	...	...	*0635*	0739	...	0804	...	...	0838	...
Bodmin Parkway d.	...	1901	...	2032	2038	2140	2309	2326	...		...	...	...	...	...	...	...	*0641*	0746	...	0810	...	...	0844	...
Liskeard d.	...	1914	...	2045	2051	2153	2325	2338	...		...	...	...	...	...	...	...	*0655*	0758	...	0823	...	...	0857	...
Saltash d.	...	|	...	2105	|	2212	|	|	...		...	...	...	...	...	...	...	*0714*	|	...	|	...	...	0917	...
Plymouth a.	...	1939	...	2120	2116	2225	2349	0001	...		...	...	...	...	...	...	...	*0730*	0821	...	0849	...	...	0926	...
Plymouth d.	...	1942	...	*2125*	*2125*	▬	2355	...	...		0525	0540	0625	...	...	0655	0725	0747	0825	0839	0852	...	0920	0933	...
Totnes d.	...	2010	...	*2155*	*2155*	...	0024	...	...		0550	0607	0650	...	...	|	0750	0814	0850	0904	0919	...	0945	1002	...
Paignton 116 d.	...	|	2014	|	|	...	|	...	...		|	|	|	...	0702	|	|	|	|	|	|	0918	|	|	100
Torquay 116 d.	...	|	2020	|	|	...	|	...	...		|	|	|	...	0708	|	|	|	|	|	|	0925	|	|	101
Newton Abbot 116 d.	...	2023	2031	*2207*	*2207*	...	0037	...	...		0603	0620	0703	...	0719	0732	0803	0827	0903	0917	0932	0939	0958	1015	102
Teignmouth 116 d.	...	|	|	*2214*	*2214*	...	|	...	...		|	|	|	...	0726	|	|	|	|	|	|	0949	1005	|	103
Dawlish 116 d.	...	|	|	*2219*	*2219*	...	|	...	...		|	|	|	Ⓐ	0731	|	|	|	|	|	|	0957	1011	|	103
Exeter St Davids 116 a.	...	2043	2050	*2240*	*2240*	...	0059	...	...		0620	0640	0720		0742	0752	0820	0847	0920	0939	0952	1013	1025	1035	104
Exeter St Davids d.	...	2045	2052	...	...	Ⓐ	0106	...	...		0623	0641	0723	0729	0745	0754	0823	0849	0923	0941	0954	1015	1027	1038	105
Tiverton Parkway d.	...	2100	2104	...	...		|	...	...		0637	0656	0737	0744	0758	0809	0837	0904	0937	0954	1009	1030	1040	1103	110
Taunton d.	2027	2115	2118	...	...	2129	0142	...	...		0650	0711	0750	0759	0811	0824	0850	0919	0950	1007	1024	1045	1053	|	111
Bristol Temple Meads a.	|	2147	2152	...	...	2232	|	...	...		0722	|	0823	0857	0848	|	0924	|	1024	1052	|	1124	1126	|	115
Birmingham New St 127 a.	|	|	2343	...	...	|	|	...	...		0856	|	0955	|	1025	|	1056	|	1155	1226	|	|	1255	|	132
Castle Cary a.	2045	|	...	...	...	|	|	...	...		...	0731	...	|	...	|	...	0939	...	...	|	|	...	1123	...
Westbury a.	2104	|	...	...	...	|	|	...	...		...	0751	...	|	...	|	...	0954	...	...	1059	|	...	1142	...
Newbury a.	2142	|	...	...	...	|	|	...	...		...	0833	...	|	...	|	...	|	...	...	|	|	...	|	...
Reading a.	2159	2308	...	...	...	2353	0400s	...	...		...	0851	...	1011	...	0941	...	1054	...	...	1148	1245	...	1237	...
London Paddington a.	2230	2344	...	...	...	0034	0523	...	...		...	0921	...	1039	...	1010	...	1124	...	...	1223	1315	...	1309	...

For footnotes see pages 106 and 107.

GW, XC — LONDON and BRISTOL - EXETER - PAIGNTON, PLYMOUTH and PENZANCE — 115

Service until September 7. Service on ⑦ subject to alteration June 22 - July 27.

	⑥	⑥	⑥	⑥	⑥	⑥	⑥	⑥	⑥	⑥	⑥	⑥	⑥	⑥	⑥	⑥	⑥	⑥	⑥	⑥	⑥	⑥	⑥	⑥	⑥
		C				2			L							2									
Penzance d.	0828	0839	...	0954	...	...	1100	...	...	...	...	1158	...	...	...	1300	...	1401	...	...	1500	...	...	1552	1625
St Erth d.	0836	0850	...	1005	...	...	1111	...	...	...	...	1209	...	...	...	1309	...	1411	...	...	1510	...	...	1602	1635
Camborne d.	0846	0906	...	1020	...	...	1126	...	...	...	...	1224	...	...	...	1321	...	1422	...	...	1525	...	...	1613	1646
Redruth d.	0852	0913	...	1027	...	...	1133	...	...	...	...	1231	...	...	...	1327	...	1429	...	...	1532	...	...	1620	1653
Truro d.	0904	0926	...	1040	...	...	1146	...	...	...	...	1244	...	...	...	1338	...	1442	...	...	1545	...	...	1633	1705
St Austell d.	0920	0944	...	1058	...	...	1204	...	...	...	...	1302	...	...	...	1355	...	1459	...	...	1603	...	...	1651	1723
Newquay d.	|	|	0935	|	...	...	|	...	1130	...	...	|	...	...	1319	|	...	|	...	...	|	1530	...	|	|
Par d.	0927	0951	1031	1106	...	1125	|	...	1226	...	...	|	...	...	1414	1423	...	1507	...	...	1611	1627	...	1659	1730
Lostwithiel d.	|	|	|	|	...	1133	|	...	|	...	...	|	...	...	|	1429	...	|	...	...	1619	|	...	1706	|
Bodmin Parkway d.	0937	1002	1047	1118	...	1140	1221	...	|	...	...	1319	...	...	|	1435	...	1519	...	...	1925	1637	...	1713	1741
Liskeard d.	0950	1015	1057	1131	...	1155	1234	...	|	...	...	1332	...	...	|	1448	...	1533	...	...	1638	1651	...	1726	1755
Saltash d.	|	|	|	|	...	1220	|	...	|	...	...	|	...	...	|	1509	...	|	...	...	1700	|	...	|	|
Plymouth a.	1017	1040	1121	1156	...	1231	1258	...	1311	...	...	1356	...	...	1458	1520	...	1558	...	...	1710	1714	...	1751	1819
Plymouth d.	1025	1043	1125	1200	...	1235	1300	...	1314	1325	...	1400	1425	...	1507	...	1525	1601	...	...	...	1725	...	1754	1825
Totnes d.	1050	|	1150	1229	...	1307	1328	...	|	1350	...	|	1450	...	|	...	1550	1628	...	...	...	1750	...	1821	1851
Paignton 116 d.	|	|	|	|	1235	|	|	1307	|	|	1355	|	|	1431	|	...	|	|	1637	1703	...	|	1811	|	|
Torquay 116 d.	|	|	|	|	1242	|	|	1315	|	|	1401	|	|	1438	|	...	|	|	1644	1710	...	|	1818	|	|
Newton Abbot 116 d.	1103	|	1203	1242	1254	1321	1342	1328	|	1403	1412	1436	1503	1450	1544	...	1603	1641	1656	1722	...	1803	1830	1834	1904
Teignmouth 116 d.	|	|	|	|	1303	|	|	1337	|	|	1419	|	|	1458	|	...	|	|	1704	1730	...	|	|	|	|
Dawlish 116 d.	|	|	|	|	1310	|	|	1344	|	|	1424	|	|	1504	|	...	|	|	1710	1737	...	|	|	|	|
Exeter St Davids 116 a.	1120	1137	1220	1302	1321	1349	1402	1408	1415	1421	1435	1456	1521	1528	1605	...	1620	1701	1721	1756	...	1821	1848	1854	1922
Exeter St Davids d.	1123	1140	1223	1305	1323	...	1405	1411	1418	1423	1437	1459	1523	1532	1607	...	1623	1703	1723	1802	...	1823	1850	1856	1923
Tiverton Parkway d.	1137	|	1237	1320	1337	...	|	|	|	1437	1450	1514	1537	|	1622	...	1637	1717	1737	1817	...	1837	1904	1911	1937
Taunton d.	1150	|	1250	1335	1350	...	1430	1444	|	1450	1503	1529	1550	1557	1636	...	1650	1732	1750	1832	...	1850	1917	1926	1950
Bristol Temple Meads a.	1224	|	1323	|	1424	...	|	|	|	1524	1549	|	1624	|	|	...	1724	|	1822	|	...	1922	1954	|	2023
Birmingham New St **127** a.	1355	|	1455	|	1555	...	|	|	|	1655	1726	|	1755	|	|	...	1855	|	1958	|	...	2052	2138	|	2151
Castle Cary a.	...	|	...	|	...	...	|	1507	|	...	...	1549	...	1618	|	...	...	|	...	1852	...	...	...	1946	...
Westbury a.	...	|	...	|	...	...	|	1526	|	...	...	|	...	1636	|	...	...	|	...	1911	...	...	...	2005	...
Newbury a.	...	|	...	|	...	...	|	1605	|	...	...	|	...	|	|	...	...	|	...	1946	...	...	...	|	...
Reading a.	...	1319	...	1451	...	...	1549	1627	1554	...	...	1649	...	1734	1753	...	...	1848	...	2007	...	...	...	2058	...
London Paddington a.	...	1347	...	1521	...	...	1621	1702	1633	...	...	1721	...	1808	1823	...	...	1922	...	2037	...	...	...	2132	...

	⑥	⑥	⑥	⑥	⑥	⑥	⑥	⑥		⑦	⑦	⑦	⑦	⑦	⑦	⑦	⑦	⑦	⑦	⑦	⑦	⑦	⑦	⑦	⑦
				2	2		2																		
Penzance d.	1655	...	1740	...	1906	...	...	2132	...		...	...	...	...	...	...	0830	0930	0947	...	...	...	1100	...	1139
St Erth d.	1705	...	1750	...	1915	...	...	2141	...		...	...	...	...	...	...	0839	0938	0957	...	...	...	1110	...	1149
Camborne d.	1720	...	1804	...	1927	...	...	2152	...		...	...	...	...	...	...	0855	0948	1008	...	...	...	1123	...	1201
Redruth d.	1727	...	1811	...	1933	...	...	2159	...		...	...	...	...	...	...	0901	0954	1014	...	...	...	1129	...	1207
Truro d.	1740	...	1824	...	1944	...	...	2212	...		...	...	...	...	...	...	0915	1006	1027	...	...	...	1142	...	1221
St Austell d.	1757	...	1841	...	2001	...	...	2229	...		...	...	...	...	...	...	0931	1022	1044	...	...	...	1159	...	1237
Newquay d.	|	1726	|	...	|	2000	2121	|	...		...	...	...	...	...	...	|	|	|	...	...	...	|	1132	|
Par d.	1805	1822	1849	1900	2009	2057	2209	2236	...		...	...	...	...	...	...	0940	1029	1053	...	...	...	1207	1228	1245
Lostwithiel d.	1813	|	|	1907	2015	|	2218	|	...		...	...	...	...	...	...	|	|	|	...	...	...	|	|	|
Bodmin Parkway d.	1819	1835	1901	1913	2021	2110	2224	2247	...		...	...	...	...	...	...	0952	1039	1106	...	...	...	1219	1241	1258
Liskeard d.	1832	1848	1914	1926	2034	2123	2237	2301	...		...	...	...	...	...	...	1005	1052	1119	...	...	...	1233	1254	1311
Saltash d.	1851	|	|	1944	2054	|	2255	|	...		...	...	...	...	...	...	1024	|	|	...	...	...	|	|	|
Plymouth a.	1901	1914	1939	1955	2110	2148	2312	2325	...		...	...	...	...	...	...	1031	1115	1144	...	...	...	1258	1318	1336
Plymouth d.	1904	1948	1942	—	2115	...	...	...	...		...	0840	0925	1010	1025	...	1040	1125	1145	1200	1225	1252	1300	1325	1344
Totnes d.	1934	|	2009	...	2144	...	...	...	...		...	0907	0950	1040	1050	...	1107	1150	1215	|	1250	|	1328	1351	1411
Paignton 116 d.	|	|	|	...	|	...	...	...	...	⑦	...	|	|	|	|	1050	|	|	|	|	|	|	|	|	|
Torquay 116 d.	|	|	|	...	|	...	...	...	...		...	|	|	|	|	1056	|	|	|	|	|	|	|	|	|
Newton Abbot 116 d.	1946	1955	2022	...	2156	...	...	...	...		...	0921	1003	1054	1103	1108	1121	1203	1229	1236	1303	1327	1341	1404	1425
Teignmouth 116 d.	...	|	|	...	2203	...	...	...	...		...	0928	|	|	|	1115	|	|	|	|	|	|	|	|	|
Dawlish 116 d.	...	|	|	...	2208	...	...	...	...		...	0934	|	|	|	1120	|	|	|	|	|	|	|	|	|
Exeter St Davids 116 a.	...	2014	2042	...	2222	...	...	...	...		...	0947	1020	1114	1121	1130	1141	1220	1249	1255	1320	1345	1401	1422	1445
Exeter St Davids d.	...	2016	2044	Ⓐ	...	...	...	...	...		0839	0949	1023	1118	1123	1133	1143	1223	1250	1257	1323	1347	1403	1424	1458
Tiverton Parkway d.	...	|	2059		...	...	...	...	...		0854	|	1037	1133	1137	1147	1158	1237	|	1311	1337	|	1417	1438	|
Taunton d.	...	2042	2114	2130	...	...	...	...	...		0908	1014	1050	1148	1152	1020	1212	1250	1316	1324	1350	|	1432	1451	1512
Bristol Temple Meads a.	...	|	2147	2212	...	...	...	...	...		|	|	1121	1223	1227	1244	|	1326	|	1357	1421	1438	|	1526	|
Birmingham New St **127** a.	...	|	|	|	...	...	...	...	...		|	|	1249	|	1348	1427	|	1448	|	1527	1548	1627	|	1649	|
Castle Cary a.	...	|	|	|	...	...	...	...	...		0929	|	...	|	...	...	1232	...	|	...	...	...	|	...	1533
Westbury a.	...	|	|	|	...	...	...	...	...		0947	1047	...	|	...	...	1252	...	1354	...	...	...	|	...	1551
Newbury a.	...	|	|	|	...	...	...	...	...		1027	1126	...	|	...	...	1331	...	|	...	...	...	|	...	1631
Reading a.	...	2159	2306	2347	...	...	...	...	...		1043	1148	...	1349	...	...	1350	...	1449	...	...	...	1549	...	1650
London Paddington a.	...	2226	2342	0033	...	...	...	...	...		1121	1224	...	1422	...	...	1424	...	1524	...	...	...	1625	...	1724

	⑦	⑦	⑦	⑦	⑦	⑦	⑦	⑦	⑦	⑦	⑦	⑦	⑦	⑦	⑦	⑦	⑦	⑦	⑦	⑦	⑦	⑦	⑦	⑦	⑦
	2								2			2									2		2	2	K
Penzance d.	1205	...	1230	1256	...	...	...	...	1341	...	...	1440	1501	1530	...	1550	...	...	...	1725	1750	...	1900	2005	2115
St Erth d.	1214	...	1238	1306	...	...	...	...	1351	...	...	1450	1511	1538	...	1559	...	...	...	1734	1759	...	1909	2014	2125
Camborne d.	1225	...	1251	1319	...	...	...	...	1404	...	...	1502	1523	1549	...	1611	...	...	...	1746	1812	...	1920	2026	2138
Redruth d.	1231	...	1258	1325	...	...	...	...	1410	...	...	1508	1530	1555	...	1617	...	...	...	1753	1818	...	1926	2032	2145
Truro d.	1243	...	1309	1338	...	...	...	...	1421	...	...	1519	1542	1607	...	1631	...	...	...	1805	1830	...	1938	2044	2200
St Austell d.	1259	...	1326	1356	...	...	...	...	1438	...	...	1536	1600	1623	...	1647	...	...	...	1824	1846	...	1955	2101	2218
Newquay d.	|	...	|	|	...	...	...	...	|	...	...	|	|	|	...	|	...	1621	...	|	|	...	|	|	|
Par d.	1306	...	1332	1403	...	...	...	...	1445	...	...	1543	1608	1630	...	1655	...	1716	...	1832	1854	...	2003	2109	|
Lostwithiel d.	1313	...	1339	|	...	...	...	...	1452	...	...	1550	|	|	...	|	...	|	...	|	1900	...	2009	|	|
Bodmin Parkway d.	1319	...	1346	1416	...	...	...	...	1458	...	...	1556	1619	1640	...	1708	...	1729	...	1843	1907	...	2015	2121	2235
Liskeard d.	1333	...	1358	1429	...	...	...	...	1511	...	...	1609	1632	1652	...	1721	...	1742	...	1856	1921	...	2028	2135	2250
Saltash d.	1354	...	|	|	...	...	...	...	1529	...	...	1627	|	|	...	|	...	1800	...	|	1939	...	2047	|	|
Plymouth a.	1403	...	1421	1454	...	...	...	...	1538	...	...	1637	1658	1715	...	1745	...	1810	...	1921	1950	...	2100	2200	2315
Plymouth d.	1407	1425	1435	1454	1510	1524	...	1543	1549	1610	1625	1638	1700	1725	...	1745	...	1810	1825	1925	...	1955	2115	...	2320
Totnes d.	1436	1451	1500	1525	|	1550	...	1610	1621	1639	1648	1707	1728	1750	...	1816	...	1840	1851	1952	...	|	2142	...	2348
Paignton 116 d.	|	|	|	|	|	|	1545	|	|	|	|	|	|	|	...	|	1820	|	|	|	...	|	|	...	|
Torquay 116 d.	|	|	|	|	|	|	1551	|	|	|	|	|	|	|	...	|	1826	|	|	|	...	|	|	...	|
Newton Abbot 116 d.	1449	1504	1512	1538	1548	1603	1605	1623	1634	1652	1701	1720	1740	1802	...	1829	1837	1852	1904	2005	...	2032	2155	...	0001
Teignmouth 116 d.	1456	|	|	|	|	|	1613	|	|	|	|	1727	|	|	...	|	|	|	|	|	...	|	2202	...	|
Dawlish 116 d.	1501	|	|	|	|	|	1618	|	|	|	|	1732	|	|	...	|	|	|	|	|	...	|	2207	...	|
Exeter St Davids 116 a.	1515	1522	1530	1558	1608	1621	1632	1645	1655	1717	1721	1746	1801	1820	...	1850	1856	1914	1922	2025	...	2053	2221	...	0023
Exeter St Davids d.	...	1524	1532	1601	1610	1624	1634	1646	...	1719	1723	1751	1802	1823	...	1852	1858	1916	1924	2026	...	2055	...	...	0106
Tiverton Parkway d.	...	1537	1545	1616	1625	1637	|	1701	...	1734	1737	|	1819	1836	...	|	1911	1931	1937	2042	...	2110	...	...	|
Taunton d.	...	1551	1558	1631	1640	1651	1659	1715	...	1748	1752	1822	1834	1849	1857	1917	1924	1945	1951	2055	...	2123	...	...	|
Bristol Temple Meads a.	...	1626	1649	|	1719	1726	1756	|	...	1822	1827	1922	|	1925	1953	|	1957	|	2024	|	...	2200	...	...	|
Birmingham New St **127** a.	...	1750	1827	|	|	1848	|	|	...	|	1948	...	|	2049	|	|	2118	|	2148	|	...	|	...	...	|
Castle Cary a.	...	...	...	|	|	...	|	1736	...	|	...	...	|	...	|	|	...	2006	...	2117	...	|	...	...	|
Westbury a.	...	...	...	|	|	...	|	1754	...	|	...	...	|	...	|	1952	...	2026	...	2139	...	|	...	...	|
Newbury a.	...	...	...	|	|	...	|	1832	...	|	...	...	|	...	|	2027	...	|	...	2218	...	|	...	...	|
Reading a.	...	...	...	1748	1842	...	1914	1849	...	1944	...	...	1949	...	2115	2047	...	2114	...	2237	...	2330	...	...	0402s
London Paddington a.	...	...	...	1824	1921	...	1952	1925	...	2021	...	...	2024	...	2154	2121	...	2151	...	2322	...	0013	...	...	0509

For footnotes see pages 106 and 107.

116 EXETER - PAIGNTON

2nd class GW

Local trains. For long distance trains see Table 115.

km																									
		Ⓐ	Ⓐ	Ⓐ	Ⓐ	Ⓐ	Ⓐ	Ⓐ	Ⓐ	Ⓐ	Ⓐ	Ⓐ	Ⓐ	Ⓐ	Ⓐ	Ⓐ	Ⓐ	Ⓐ	Ⓐ	Ⓐ	Ⓐ	Ⓐ	Ⓐ	Ⓐ
0	**Exeter** St Davids .... d.	Ⓐ	0534	0611	0718	0750	0823	0858	0958	1034	1056	1156	1249	1303	1356	1502	1556	1626	1656	1728	1750	1830	1928	2129	2237
20	Dawlish .... d.		0555	0631	0738	0810	0845	0925	1019	1050	1116	1227	|	1324	1427	1522	1616	1646	1716	1754	1811	1851	1948	2149	2303
24	Teignmouth .... d.		0600	0636	0743	0815	0850	0930	1024	1055	1121	1232	|	1329	1432	1527	1621	1651	1721	1759	1816	1856	1953	2154	2308
32	Newton Abbot .... d.		0609	0645	0752	0824	0859	0939	1040	1103	1130	1240	1313	1338	1441	1536	1630	1700	1730	1810	1825	1911	2009	2203	2316
42	Torquay .... d.		0620	0656	0803	0836	0910	0950	1051	1115	1141	1252	1325	1349	1452	1547	1641	1711	1741	1821	1836	1922	2020	2214	2327
45	**Paignton** .... 🚂 a.		0628	0706	0812	0844	0917	0957	1100	1127	1151	1300	1334	1358	1500	1554	1651	1720	1751	1830	1845	1930	2029	2223	2337

		⑥	⑥	⑥	⑥	⑥	⑥	⑥	⑥	⑥	⑥	⑥	⑥		⑥	⑥	⑥	⑥	⑥	⑥	⑥	⑥	⑥	⑥
Exeter St Davids .... d.	⑥	0518	0536	0611	0750	0837	0857	0957	1035	1056	1156	1256	1357	...	1436	1456	1557	1656	1727	1827	1856	1913	2007	2056
Dawlish .... d.		0539	0557	0631	0810	0851	0928	1016	1051	1116	1216	1316	1436	...	1451	1516	1616	1716	1753	1846	1909	1933	2036	2116
Teignmouth .... d.		0544	0602	0636	0815	0856	0933	1021	1056	1121	1221	1321	1441	...	1457	1521	1621	1721	1758	1851	1914	1938	2041	2121
Newton Abbot .... d.		0552	0611	0645	0824	0906	0941	1033	1104	1132	1238	1330	1450	...	1506	1530	1630	1730	1809	1901	1922	1947	2048	2130
Torquay .... d.		0603	0622	0656	0835	0916	0953	1041	1114	1143	1248	1341	1501	...	1517	1541	1641	1741	1820	1912	1932	1958	2100	2141
Paignton .... 🚂 a.		0611	0630	0706	0844	0925	1001	1052	1123	1151	1256	1349	1509	...	1525	1551	1651	1751	1827	1921	1940	2006	2107	2148

		⑦	⑦		⑦	⑦		⑦	⑦		⑦	⑦		⑦	⑦		⑦	⑦		⑦	⑦		⑦	
Exeter St Davids .... d.	⑦	0843	0954	...	1053	1157	...	1300	1325	...	1400	1505	...	1600	1657	...	1756	1856	...	1956	2056	...	2156	...
Dawlish .... d.		0903	1014	...	1113	1217	...	1315	1338	...	1420	1517	...	1615	1710	...	1816	1916	...	2016	2109	...	2216	...
Teignmouth .... d.		0908	1019	...	1118	1222	...	1320	1343	...	1425	1522	...	1620	1715	...	1821	1921	...	2021	2114	...	2221	...
Newton Abbot .... d.		0917	1037	...	1127	1231	...	1328	1352	...	1436	1530	...	1628	1723	...	1829	1930	...	2030	2122	...	2230	...
Torquay .... d.		0928	1048	...	1138	1242	...	1339	1403	...	1447	1542	...	1639	1735	...	1840	1941	...	2041	2134	...	2241	...
Paignton .... 🚂 a.		0935	1054	...	1145	1250	...	1346	1410	...	1453	1550	...	1646	1742	...	1847	1948	...	2048	2141	...	2249	...

		Ⓐ	Ⓐ	Ⓐ	Ⓐ	Ⓐ	Ⓐ	Ⓐ	Ⓐ	Ⓐ	Ⓐ	Ⓐ	Ⓐ	Ⓐ	Ⓐ	Ⓐ	Ⓐ	Ⓐ	Ⓐ	Ⓐ	Ⓐ	Ⓐ	Ⓐ	Ⓐ
Paignton .... 🚂 d.	Ⓐ	0610	0634	0711	0823	0913	1015	1123	1213	1248	1313	1423	1513	1612	1630	1655	1726	1753	1835	1852	1933	2035	2230	2341
Torquay .... d.		0615	0639	0716	0828	0918	1023	1128	1218	1254	1318	1428	1518	1617	1635	1700	1731	1758	1840	1857	1938	2040	2235	2346
Newton Abbot .... d.		0634	0652	0737	0841	0939	1036	1141	1231	1308	1341	1441	1531	1631	1648	1713	1744	1811	1853	1909	1950	2053	2248	2359
Teignmouth .... d.		0641	0659	0745	0848	0946	1044	1148	1238	1315	1348	1448	1538	1638	1655	1720	1751	1818	1900	1916	1958	2100	2255	0006
Dawlish .... d.		0646	0704	0750	0853	0951	1049	1153	1243	1320	1353	1453	1543	1643	1700	1725	1756	1823	1905	1921	2003	2105	2300	0011
Exeter St Davids .... a.		0709	0733	0814	0915	1014	1110	1216	1313	1332	1416	1516	1613	1712	1718	1750	1818	1846	1933	1939	2026	2128	2322	0034

		⑥	⑥	⑥	⑥	⑥	⑥	⑥	⑥	⑥	⑥	⑥	⑥	⑥	⑥	⑥	⑥	⑥	⑥	⑥	⑥	⑥	⑥	⑥
Paignton .... 🚂 d.	⑥	0613	0634	0806	0904	0930	1023	1057	1113	1213	1249	1300	1413	1513	1543	1613	1713	1752	1853	1921	1950	2013	2113	2153
Torquay .... d.		0618	0639	0811	0909	0935	1028	1102	1118	1218	1254	1305	1418	1518	1548	1618	1719	1757	1858	1926	1955	2018	2118	2158
Newton Abbot .... d.		0631	0652	0834	0935	0949	1041	1123	1141	1232	1306	1317	1440	1534	1609	1631	1741	1810	1912	1940	2008	2031	2131	2211
Teignmouth .... d.		0638	0659	0841	0942	0956	1049	1130	1148	1239	1313	1324	1448	1542	1616	1638	1749	1817	1919	1947	2015	2038	2138	2218
Dawlish .... d.		0643	0704	0846	0947	1002	1054	1135	1153	1244	1318	1329	1453	1547	1621	1643	1754	1822	1924	1952	2020	2043	2143	2223
Exeter St Davids .... a.		0706	0733	0909	1010	1018	1115	1158	1216	1313	1335	1359	1515	1615	1634	1715	1818	1847	1945	2025	2037	2105	2205	2245

		⑦	⑦	⑦		⑦	⑦	⑦		⑦	⑦	⑦		⑦	⑦	⑦		⑦	⑦	⑦		⑦	⑦	
Paignton .... 🚂 d.	⑦	0949	1100	1149	...	1257	1350	1419	...	1457	1545	1555	...	1621	1655	1749	...	1855	1955	2055	...	2152	2300	...
Torquay .... d.		0954	1105	1154	...	1302	1355	1424	...	1502	1551	1600	...	1626	1700	1754	...	1900	2000	2100	...	2157	2305	...
Newton Abbot .... d.		1007	1125	1207	...	1315	1407	1437	...	1515	1605	1612	...	1638	1712	1807	...	1913	2013	2113	...	2209	2318	...
Teignmouth .... d.		1014	1132	1214	...	1322	1414	1444	...	1522	1613	1619	...	1645	1719	1814	...	1920	2020	2120	...	2216	2325	...
Dawlish .... d.		1019	1137	1219	...	1327	1419	1449	...	1527	1618	1624	...	1650	1724	1819	...	1925	2025	2125	...	2221	2330	...
Exeter St Davids .... a.		1041	1151	1242	...	1341	1440	1512	...	1541	1632	1640	...	1713	1741	1840	...	1948	2049	2139	...	2242	2352	...

🚂 – **DARTMOUTH STEAM RAILWAY** (Paignton - Kingswear and v.v. *10 km*. Daily Apr. 1 - Nov. 2). Paignton station is shared with National Rail services. Connection at Kingswear with ⛴ t Dartmouth, combined rail / ferry tickets available. ✆ (0)1803 555872. www.dartmouthrailriver.co.uk

118 BRANCH LINES and BUS CONNECTIONS IN DEVON and CORNWALL

GW

Rail tickets are generally not valid on 🚌 services shown in this table.

EXETER - EXMOUTH *'The Avocet Line'* 18 km

From **Exeter St Davids**: ⚒: 0544, 0606Ⓐ, 0629, 0711, 0736, 0816, 0848, 0918, 0950 and at the same minutes past each hour until 1718, 1747⑥, 1752Ⓐ, 1820, 1850, 1932, 2030, 2131Ⓐ, 2138⑥, 2231Ⓐ, 2236⑥, 2306⑥, 2328Ⓐ; ⑦: 0830, 0945, 1044, 1155, 1248, 1348, 1450, 1550, 1648, 1748, 1850, 1951, 2052, 2148, 2248, 2325.

From **Exmouth**: ⚒: 0612, 0645Ⓐ, 0714, 0753, 0823, 0853 and at the same minutes past each hour until 1523, 1553, 1625, 1655, 1725, 1755, 1827, 1855, 1935, 2008, 2104, 2205Ⓐ, 2211⑥, 2310Ⓐ, 2343⑥; ⑦: 0910, 1021, 1124, 1228, 1324, 1431, 1524, 1624, 1724, 1824, 1924, 2024, 2124, 2229, 2329, 2359.

Journey 37 - 40 minutes.

EXETER - BARNSTAPLE *'The Tarka Line'* 63 km

From **Exeter St Davids**: 0550Ⓐ, 0554⑥, 0648Ⓐ, 0655⑥, 0831⚒, 0843⑦, 0927⚒, 0953⑦, 1027⚒, 1127⚒, 1203⑦, 1227⚒, 1327⚒, 1408⑦, 1427⚒, 1527⚒, 1601⑦, 1657⚒, 1757⚒, 1759⑦, 1857⚒, 2001⑦, 2100⚒, 2253⑤.

From **Barnstaple**: 0700Ⓐ, 0708⑥, 0843⚒, 0943⚒, 1000⑦, 1043⚒, 1126⑦, 1143⚒, 1243⚒, 1324⑦, 1343⚒, 1443⚒, 1523⑦, 1543⚒, 1708⚒, 1720⑦, 1813⚒, 1916⚒, 1920⑦, 2024⚒, 2130⑦, 2216⚒.

Journey 65 minutes. Trains call at ***Crediton*** *(11 minutes after Exeter / 54 minutes after Barnstaple) and* ***Eggesford*** *(25 minutes after Exeter / 25 minutes after Barnstaple).*

PLYMOUTH - GUNNISLAKE *'The Tamar Valley Line'* 24 km

Plymouth dep: Ⓐ: 0506, 0641, 0840, 1054, 1254, 1454, 1638, 1823, 2131; ⑥: 0627, 0854, 1059, 1254, 1447, 1638, 1823, 2131; ⑦: 0904, 1106, 1313, 1517, 1741.

Gunnislake dep: Ⓐ: 0551, 0731, 0929, 1145, 1345, 1545, 1729, 1913, 2221; ⑥: 0717, 0945, 1153, 1345, 1545, 1729, 1917, 2221; ⑦: 1018, 1207, 1405, 1607, 1844.

Journey 45 - 50 minutes. Service on ⑥⑦ valid until Sep. 7.

LISKEARD - LOOE *'The Looe Valley Line'* 14 km

Liskeard dep: Ⓐ: 0605, 0714, 0833, 0858, 1118, 1215, 1319, 1428, 1541, 1641, 1806, 1918; ⑥: 0550, 0712, 0835, 0958, 1112, 1212, 1324, 1428, 1542, 1656, 1801, 1928, 2040; ⑦: 1012, 1126, 1250, 1400, 1503, 1610, 1735, 2015.

Looe dep: Ⓐ: 0637, 0746, 0909, 1032, 1147, 1247, 1351, 1457, 1613, 1715, 1840, 1952; ⑥: 0622, 0747, 0909, 1032, 1141, 1244, 1356, 1456, 1614, 1728, 1833, 2000, 2112; ⑦: 1045, 1158, 1322, 1432, 1535, 1642, 1815, 2015.

Journey 28 - 33 minutes. Service on ⑥⑦ valid until Sep. 7.

BODMIN PARKWAY - PADSTOW *Western Greyhound 🚌 service 555*

From **Bodmin Parkway**: 0730⚒, 0830⚒, 0930, 1030⚒, 1130, 1230⚒, 1330, 1430⚒, 1530, 1630⚒, 1730, 1830⚒, 1930⚒, 2210⚒.

From **Padstow**: 0630⚒, 0730⚒, 0830, 0930⚒, 1030, 1130⚒, 1230, 1330⚒, 1430, 1530⚒, 1630, 1730⚒, 1830⚒, 2030⚒.

Journey 57 minutes. Buses also make calls in Bodmin town centre and at Bodmin General station, and call at ***Wadebridge*** *(33 minutes after Bodmin / 25 minutes after Padstow).*

PAR - NEWQUAY *'The Atlantic Coast Line'* 33 km

Par dep: Ⓐ: 0917, 1142 **A**, 1213 **B**, 1329 **A**, 1407 **B**, 1610, 1829, 2028; ⑥: 0728, 0946, 114 1333, 1543, 1742, 2022; ⑦: 0900, 0955, 1149, 1422, 1638, 1836.

Newquay dep: Ⓐ: 1013, 1240 **A**, 1303 **B**, 1501 **B**, 1506 **A**, 1722, 1925, 2126; ⑥: 0935, 113 1319, 1530, 1726, 2000, 2121; ⑦: 0952, 1132, 1304, 1621, 1735, 1940.

See also Table ***115****. Journey 55 - 60 minutes. Service on ⑥⑦ valid until Sep. 7.*

TRURO - FALMOUTH DOCKS *'The Maritime Line'* 20 km

Truro dep: ⚒: 0604, 0631, 0714, 0747, 0820, 0851 and at the same minutes past each ho until 1620, 1651, 1727, 1759, 1831, 1902, 2004, 2105, 2206; ⑦: 0901, 1042, 1209, 130 1412, 1535, 1700, 1813, 1946, 2103, 2204.

Falmouth Docks dep: ⚒: 0631, 0715, 0747, 0820, 0850 and at the same minutes past eac hour until 1620, 1650, 1727, 1759, 1831, 1902, 1929, 2031, 2132, 2235; ⑦: 0935, 1110, 123 1335, 1439, 1602, 1730, 1840, 2013, 2130, 2233.

Trains call at ***Falmouth Town*** *22 minutes after Truro and 3 minutes after Falmouth Docks. Journey 25 minutes. Service on ⑥⑦ valid until Sep. 7.*

ST AUSTELL - EDEN PROJECT *First Devon and Cornwall 🚌 service 10*

From **St Austell railway station**: 0845⚒, 0850⑦, 0930⚒, 1035⑦, 1040⚒, 1140⑦, 1150 1205⑥, 1230Ⓑ, 1355, 1445⑦, 1502⚒, 1535⑦, 1550⑥, 1610Ⓐ, 1625⑦, 1700⑥, 1705 1710⑦.

From **Eden Project**: 0910⚒, 0950⑦, 0955⚒, 1100⑦, 1115⚒, 1200⑦, 1210Ⓐ, 1300 1305⑦, 1315⑥, 1425, 1515⑦, 1522⚒, 1605⑦, 1625⑥, 1630Ⓐ, 1650⑦, 1755⑥, 1800⑥

Journey 20 minutes.

ST ERTH - ST IVES *'The St Ives Bay Line'* 7 km

St Erth dep: Ⓐ: 0706**p**, 0801, 0905**p**, 0938, 1018, 1048 and at the same minutes past ea hour until 1618, 1648, 1717, 1748, 1818, 1848, 1918, 1948, 2018, 2048, 2123, 2158; 0650**p**, 0800, 0903**p**, 0935, 1013, 1048, 1118, 1148 and at the same minutes past each hc until 1618, 1648, 1717, 1759, 1859, 2001, 2033, 2106, 2147; ⑦: 0853**p**, 0927, 1000, 10 1113, 1143, 1213, 1242, 1311, 1341, 1411, 1441, 1511, 1541, 1611, 1641, 1726, 1826, 19

St Ives dep: Ⓐ: 0725, 0815**q**, 0922, 0953, 1033, 1103, 1133 and at the same minutes pa each hour until 1703, 1731, 1803, 1833, 1905, 1932, 2003, 2033, 2103, 2137, 2231**q**; ⑥: 07 0815**q**, 0920, 0950, 1027, 1103, 1133 and at the same minutes past each hour until 17 1732, 1817**q**, 1926, 2017, 2049, 2124, 2205**q**; ⑦: 1213, 1245, 1330, 1403, 1433, 1503, 15 1603, 1633, 1703, 1740, 1811, 1848, 1950**q**.

Journey 15 minutes. Service on ⑥⑦ valid until Sep. 7.

A – July 7 - Aug. 29.
B – Until July 4 and from Sep. 1.

p – 🚆2 Penzance - St Ives (departs Penzance 8 - 10 minutes earlier).
q – 🚆2 St Ives - Penzance (journey time St Ives - Penzance: ± 14 minutes).

CARDIFF - GLOUCESTER - BIRMINGHAM - NOTTINGHAM

No service Birmingham - Cardiff on ⑦ June 22 - July 27.

km		⚒	Ⓐ	⑥	Ⓐ	⚒	⚒	⚒	⑥	Ⓐ	⚒	Ⓐ	⑥	⚒	Ⓐ A	⑥ A	Ⓐ	⑥	⚒	Ⓐ	⑥	⚒	Ⓐ	⑥	⚒
0	**Cardiff** Central d.		...	...	...	...	...	...	...	...	...	0640	0640	...	0700	0700	0745	0745	...	0845	0845	...	0945	0945	...
19	Newport d.		...	...	...	...	...	...	...	...	...	0655	0655	...	0715	0715	0802	0800	...	0900	0900	...	1000	1000	...
91	**Gloucester** d.		...	...	...	...	...	...	0707	0710	...	0746	0746	...	|	|	0849	0849	...	0950	0950	...	1050	1050	...
101	Cheltenham d.		...	...	...	...	...	...	0718	0721	...	0757	0757	...	0840	0841	0900	0900	...	1001	1001	...	1101	1101	...
174	**Birmingham** New St. ⊕ a.		...	...	...	...	...	...	0808	0816	...	0845	0845	...	0926	0926	0945	0945	...	1045	1045	...	1145	1145	...
174	**Birmingham** New St. 127 d.		...	0619	0619	0649	0719	0749	...	...	0819	0849	0849	0919	...	...	0949	0949	1019	1049	1049	1119	1149	1149	1219
202	Tamworth 127 d.		...	0639	0639	0707	0739	0807	...	...	0836	0909	0909	0936	...	...	1007	1007	1036	1109	1109	1136	1207	1207	1235
222	Burton on Trent 127 d.		...	0651	0651	0719	0750	0819	...	...	0848	0921	0921	0948	...	...	1019	1019	1048	1121	1121	1148	1219	1219	1247
241	**Derby** 127 a.		...	0705	0704	0734	0805	0836	...	...	0900	0934	0934	1000	...	...	1034	1035	1100	1134	1134	1200	1234	1235	1300
241	**Derby** 172 d.		0600	0710	0709	0740	0810	0840	...	...	0908	0940	0940	1008	...	...	1040	1040	1108	1140	1140	1208	1240	1240	1308
267	**Nottingham** 172 a.		0622	0738	0738	0809	0834	0906	...	...	0928	1003	1004	1028	...	...	1103	1106	1128	1203	1204	1228	1303	1304	1328

	Ⓐ	⑥	⚒	Ⓐ	⑥	⚒	Ⓐ	⑥	⚒	Ⓐ	⑥	⚒	Ⓐ	⑥	⚒	Ⓐ	⑥	⚒	Ⓐ	⑥	⚒	⑥	Ⓐ	⑥	Ⓐ
Cardiff Central d.	1045	1045	...	1145	1145	...	1245	1245	...	1345	1345	...	1445	1445	...	1545	1545	...	1645	1645	...	1745	1746	1845	1845
Newport d.	1100	1100	...	1202	1200	...	1301	1300	...	1400	1400	...	1501	1500	...	1600	1600	...	1700	1700	...	1800	1800	1900	1901
Gloucester d.	1150	1150	...	1248	1248	...	1350	1350	...	1440	1450	...	1550	1550	...	1650	1650	...	1750	1750	...	1846	1846	1946	1946
Cheltenham d.	1201	1201	...	1258	1259	...	1401	1401	...	1501	1501	...	1601	1601	...	1701	1701	...	1801	1801	...	1857	1857	1957	1958
Birmingham New St ⊕ a.	1245	1245	...	1345	1345	...	1445	1445	...	1545	1545	...	1645	1645	...	1745	1745	...	1845	1845	...	1945	1945	2042	2041
Birmingham New St 127 d.	1249	1249	1319	1349	1349	1419	1449	1449	1519	1549	1549	1619	1649	1649	1719	1749	1749	1819	1849	1849	1919	1949	1949	2049	2049
Tamworth 127 d.	1309	1309	1336	1409	1409	1436	1509	1509	1536	1609	1609	1636	1709	1709	1736	1809	1809	1836	1909	1909	1936	2009	2009	2109	2109
Burton on Trent 127 d.	1319	1321	1348	1421	1421	1447	1521	1521	1548	1621	1621	1648	1721	1721	1748	1821	1821	1848	1921	1921	1948	2021	2021	2121	2121
Derby 127 a.	1334	1334	1400	1434	1435	1500	1535	1536	1600	1634	1634	1700	1734	1734	1800	1834	1836	1900	1934	1935	2000	2034	2034	2134	2133
Derby 172 d.	1340	1340	1408	1440	1440	1508	1540	1540	1608	1640	1640	1708	1740	1740	1808	1840	1840	1906	1940	1940	2008	2040	2040	2140	2140
Nottingham 172 a.	1403	1404	1428	1503	1504	1528	1603	1604	1628	1703	1704	1731	1803	1804	1831	1903	1904	1934	2003	2004	2028	2104	2103	2208	2208

	Ⓐ	Ⓐ	⑥	Ⓐ		⑥	Ⓐ	Ⓐ		⑦		⑦	⑦	⑦		⑦	⑦	⑦		⑦	⑦	⑦		⑦	⑦	⑦
Cardiff Central d.	1950	...	2000	...	...	2050	2105	2150	...		...	1045	1145	...	1245	1345	1445	...	1545	1645	1745	...	1845	1945	2045
Newport d.	2005	...	2015	...	...	2105	2121	2205	...		...	1059	1159	...	1259	1359	1459	...	1559	1659	1759	...	1859	2000	2059
Gloucester d.	2058	...	2107	...	...	2149	2204	2247	...		...	1151	1247	...	1349	1447	1547	...	1647	1747	1847	...	1952	2049	2148
Cheltenham d.	2109	...	2118	...	...	2200	2215	2258	...		...	1203	1258	...	1400	1458	1558	...	1658	1758	1858	...	2002	2100	2159
Birmingham New St ⊕ a.	2151	...	2207	...	...	2242	2305	2359	...		...	1245	1341	...	1442	1541	1641	...	1741	1841	1941	...	2044	2144	2242
Birmingham New St 127 d.	...	2203	2210	2309	...	...	...	...	...		1149	1249	1349	...	1449	1549	1649	...	1749	1849	1949	...	2049	...	...
Tamworth 127 d.	...	2227	2227	2328	...	...	...	...	...		1207	1307	1407	...	1509	1607	1707	...	1807	1909	2007	...	2106	...	...
Burton on Trent 127 d.	...	2239	2239	2340	...	...	...	...	...		1219	1319	1419	...	1521	1619	1719	...	1819	1921	2019	...	2119	...	...
Derby 127 a.	...	2252	2255	2354	...	...	...	...	...		1234	1333	1434	...	1533	1634	1764	...	1833	1933	2034	...	2133	...	...
Derby 172 d.	...	2258	2300	2358	...	...	...	...	...		1240	1340	1440	...	1540	1640	1740	...	1840	1940	2040	...	2140	...	...
Nottingham 172 a.	...	2327	2328	0017	...	...	...	...	...		1300	1400	1500	...	1600	1700	1800	...	1900	2000	2100	...	2200	...	...

	⚒	⑥	Ⓐ	Ⓐ	⑥	⑥	Ⓐ	Ⓐ B	⑥ B	⑥	Ⓐ	⚒	⑥	Ⓐ	⚒	⑥	Ⓐ	⚒	⑥	Ⓐ	⚒	⑥	Ⓐ	⚒	⑥
Nottingham 172 d.		...	...	...	...	0558	0600	0637	0637	0658	0704	0737	0812	0812	0841	0910	0910	0941	1010	1010	1041	1110	1110	1141	1210
Derby 172 a.		...	...	...	...	0629	0631	0659	0659	0729	0731	0802	0832	0833	0907	0930	0931	1007	1031	1031	1107	1129	1131	1207	1230
Derby 127 d.		...	...	...	...	0636	0636	0706	0706	0736	0736	0806	0837	0837	0910	0936	0936	1011	1037	1036	1111	1136	1137	1211	1236
Burton on Trent 127 d.		...	...	...	...	0648	0648	0717	0717	0750	0750	0818	0849	0849	0921	0950	0950	1022	1049	1049	1122	1149	1149	1222	1249
Tamworth 127 d.		...	...	...	...	0701	0701	0730	0730	0802	0803	0830	0902	0902	0933	1002	1002	1034	1102	1102	1134	1202	1202	1234	1302
Birmingham New St 127 a.		...	...	...	...	0724	0725	0754	0752	0824	0824	0854	0924	0924	0956	1024	1024	1056	1124	1124	1156	1224	1224	1256	1323
Birmingham New St ⊕ d.		0500	0500	0537	0542	0730	0730	...	...	0830	0830	...	0930	0930	...	1030	1030	...	1130	1130	...	1230	1230	...	1330
Cheltenham d.		0603	0602	0643	0642	0810	0814	...	...	0910	0910	...	1010	1010	...	1110	1110	...	1210	1210	...	1310	1310	...	1410
Gloucester a.		0612	0616	0653	0652	0820	0823	...	...	0920	0920	...	1020	1020	...	1120	1120	...	1220	1220	...	1320	1320	...	1420
Newport a.		0705	0708	0752	0748	0906	0912	...	...	1005	1011	...	1106	1111	...	1205	1210	...	1305	1311	...	1406	1410	...	1510
Cardiff Central a.		0721	0726	0808	0804	0922	0930	...	...	1021	1029	...	1124	1129	...	1223	1228	...	1321	1329	...	1422	1428	...	1526

	Ⓐ	⚒	⑥	Ⓐ	⚒	⑥	Ⓐ	⚒	⑥	Ⓐ	⚒	⑥	Ⓐ	⚒	⑥	Ⓐ	Ⓐ A	⑥ A	⚒	⑥	Ⓐ	⚒	Ⓐ	⑥	⚒
Nottingham 172 d.	1210	1241	1310	1310	1341	1410	1410	1441	1510	1510	1541	1610	1610	1641	1710	1710	...	...	1741	1810	1810	1841	1910	1910	1940
Derby 172 a.	1231	1307	1330	1331	1407	1430	1431	1507	1530	1531	1607	1630	1631	1707	1730	1731	...	...	1807	1830	1832	1907	1931	1932	2006
Derby 127 d.	1237	1311	1336	1336	1411	1436	1436	1511	1536	1537	1611	1636	1636	1711	1736	1737	...	...	1811	1836	1837	1910	1936	1936	2010
Burton on Trent 127 d.	1249	1325	1349	1349	1422	1449	1448	1525	1549	1549	1622	1649	1649	1725	1749	1749	...	...	1823	1849	1849	1921	1949	1949	2022
Tamworth 127 d.	1302	1334	1402	1402	1433	1502	1502	1534	1602	1602	1634	1702	1702	1736	1802	1802	...	...	1835	1902	1902	1933	2002	2002	2033
Birmingham New St 127 a.	1324	1356	1423	1424	1456	1524	1524	1556	1624	1624	1656	1724	1724	1756	1824	1826	...	...	1858	1922	1924	1955	2025	2024	2056
Birmingham New St ⊕ d.	1330	...	1430	1430	...	1530	1530	...	1630	1630	...	1730	1730	...	1830	1830	1842	1842	...	1930	1930	...	2030	2030	...
Cheltenham d.	1410	...	1510	1510	...	1610	1610	...	1710	1714	...	1816	1818	...	1910	1915	1925	1925	...	2010	2011	...	2110	2110	...
Gloucester a.	1423	...	1520	1520	...	1620	1620	...	1720	1723	...	1826	1829	...	1920	1924	|	|	...	2020	2020	...	2120	2120	...
Newport a.	1510	...	1606	1611	...	1708	1711	...	1806	1812	...	1911	1916	...	2003	2011	2047	2044	...	2111	2110	...	2214	2219	...
Cardiff Central a.	1530	...	1625	1629	...	1724	1730	...	1824	1830	...	1930	1933	...	2020	2029	2105	2102	...	2127	2128	...	2235	2245	...

	⑥	Ⓐ	Ⓐ	⑥		⑦	⑦	⑦		⑦	⑦		⑦	⑦		⑦	⑦		⑦	⑦		⑦	⑦		⑦
Nottingham 172 d.	2037	2040	2139	2139	...		...	...	...	1111	1210	...	1310	1410	...	1510	1610	...	1710	1810	...	1910	2010	...	2110
Derby 172 a.	2102	2104	2207	2207	...		...	...	...	1131	1230	...	1330	1429	...	1530	1630	...	1729	1830	...	1930	2029	...	2130
Derby 127 d.	2110	2110	2212	2211	...		...	1018	...	1136	1236	...	1336	1435	...	1535	1635	...	1736	1835	...	1936	2036	...	2136
Burton on Trent 127 d.	2124	2124	2223	2221	...		...	1029	...	1147	1247	...	1347	1447	...	1547	1647	...	1747	1847	...	1947	2048	...	2148
Tamworth 127 d.	2135	2135	2235	2233	...		...	1042	...	1200	1300	...	1401	1500	...	1600	1700	...	1800	1900	...	2000	2100	...	2159
Birmingham New St 127 a.	2157	2158	2301	2300	...		...	1102	...	1222	1321	...	1422	1521	...	1622	1720	...	1820	1921	...	2023	2120	...	2223
Birmingham New St ⊕ d.	...	...	...	...	...		1012	1112	...	1230	1330	...	1430	1530	...	1630	1730	...	1830	1930	...	...	...	...	...
Cheltenham d.	...	...	...	...	...		1052	1152	...	1310	1410	...	1510	1610	...	1711	1810	...	1912	2010	...	...	...	...	...
Gloucester a.	...	...	...	...	...		1102	1202	...	1321	1420	...	1521	1620	...	1720	1820	...	1926	2021	...	...	...	...	...
Newport a.	...	...	...	...	...		1148	1252	...	1406	1508	...	1606	1706	...	1806	1906	...	2011	2106	...	...	...	...	...
Cardiff Central a.	...	...	...	...	...		1208	1312	...	1426	1531	...	1626	1727	...	1828	1927	...	2031	2128	...	...	...	...	...

CARDIFF - GLOUCESTER - CHELTENHAM

2nd class AW

km		⚒	⚒	Ⓐ	⑥	⚒	⚒	⚒	⚒	⚒	⚒	⚒	⚒	Ⓐ	⑥	Ⓐ	⑥		⑦	⑦	⑦	⑦	⑦	⑦	⑦	⑦
0	**Cardiff** Central 132 d.		0612	0706	0712	0912	1012	1212	1312	1512	1612	1712	1812	2112	2112	2320	2320	...		1023	1225	1425	1623	1823	2023	2226
19	Newport 132 d.		0626	0723	0727	0926	1027	1227	1327	1527	1626	1727	1827	2127	2127	2340	2339	...		1038	1240	1440	1638	1838	2038	2249
36	Caldicot d.		0640	0740	0740	0938	1040	1240	1341	1538	1640	1740	1840	2140	2140	0001	2359	...		1058	1259	1501	1658	1858	2058	2309
47	Chepstow d.		0649	0749	0749	0948	1049	1249	1350	1547	1649	1749	1849	2149	2149	0010	0008	...		1107	1308	1510	1707	1907	2107	2318
59	Lydney Junction 🚂 d.		0658	0758	0758	0956	1058	1258	1359	1556	1658	1758	1858	2158	2158	0019	0017	...		1116	1317	1519	1716	1916	2116	2327
91	**Gloucester** 133 d.		0721	0821	0822	1021	1121	1322	1421	1621	1720	1822	1921	2223	2222	0039	0038	...		1142	1342	1541	1740	1942	2141	2348
101	**Cheltenham** 133 a.		0734	0834	0835	1035	1135	1336	...	1635	1735	1836	1934	2237	...	...	...	...		1156	1351	1551	1750	1955	...	...

	⚒	Ⓐ	⑥	⚒	⚒	⚒	⚒	⚒	⑥	Ⓐ	⚒	⚒	⚒	⚒		⑥	Ⓐ		⑦	⑦	⑦	⑦	⑦	⑦	⑦	⑦
Cheltenham 133 d.		0537	...	0745	0845	1045	1146	1345	...	...	1645	1745	1845	1945	...	...	2300	...		...	1218	1418	1618	1835	2018	...
Gloucester 133 d.		0550	0550	0758	0858	1058	1158	1358	1435	1445	1658	1758	1858	1958	...	2309	2313	...		1048	1230	1433	1637	1848	2031	2233
Lydney Junction 🚂 d.		0609	0609	0817	0917	1117	1217	1417	1454	1504	1717	1817	1917	2017	...	2328	2333	...		1107	1249	1452	1656	1907	2050	2252
Chepstow d.		0619	0619	0827	0927	1127	1227	1427	1504	1514	1727	1827	1927	2027	...	2338	2342	...		1117	1259	1502	1707	1917	2100	2302
Caldicot d.		0626	0627	0835	0935	1135	1235	1435	1512	1522	1735	1835	1934	2035	...	2346	2351	...		1125	1307	1510	1713	1925	2110	2309
Newport 132 a.		0641	0642	0850	0951	1150	1251	1450	1535	1537	1750	1850	1953	2050	...	0008	0006	...		1145	1333	1531	1737	1953	2131	2330
Cardiff Central 132 a.		0700	0700	0910	1011	1212	1308	1515	1553	1558	1810	1910	2012	2110	...	0035	0035	...		1206	1352	1547	1758	2011	2149	2350

– Via Bristol (Table 127).
– To Bournemouth (Table 129).
– Calls to set down only.

⊕ – Minimum connecting time at Birmingham New Street is 12 minutes.

🚂 – DEAN FOREST RAILWAY (Lydney Junction - Parkend. *7 km*). Lydney Junction station is 10 minutes walk from the National Rail station. ✆ 01594 845840. www.deanforestrailway.co.uk

123 BIRMINGHAM - WORCESTER - HEREFORD — 2nd class LM

km		⚒	Ⓐ	⑥	⑥	Ⓐ	Ⓐ	⑥	Ⓐ	⚒	⚒	⚒	⚒	⚒	⚒	⚒	⚒	Ⓐ	⑥	Ⓐ	⑥	Ⓐ	⑥	Ⓐ	Ⓐ
0	**Birmingham** New Street d.		...	...	0649	0659	0719	0749	0759	0849	0949	1049	1149	1249	1349	1449	1549	1619	1649	1649	1719	1719	1749	1749	1759
21	Bromsgrove d.		...	...	0710	0722	0746	0810	0823	0910	1010	1110	1210	1310	1410	1510	1610	1640	1710	1710	1740	1740	1810	|	1821
32	Droitwich Spa d.		...	...	0720	0732	0756	0820	0832	0920	1020	1120	1220	1320	1420	1520	1620	1651	1720	1720	1750	1752	1820	1817	1834
41	**Worcester** Foregate Street d.		0559	0633	0732	0742	0811	0832	0842	0932	1032	1132	1232	1332	1432	1532	1632	1709	1732	1735	1758h	1807	1835	1835	1856
54	Great Malvern d.		0611	0645	0745	0759	0822	0845	0855	0945	1045	1145	1245	1345	1445	1545	1645	1721	1745	1747	...	1819	1848	1849	1909
65	Ledbury d.		0625	0658	0759	0812	...	0859	0908	0959	1059	1159	1259	1359	1459	1559	1659	...	1759	1800	...	1831	1901	1904	...
87	**Hereford** a.		0649	0714	0819	0832	...	0919	0928	1019	1119	1219	1319	1419	1519	1619	1719	...	1816	1822	...	1851	1921	1924	...

	Ⓐ	⑥	⑥	Ⓐ	Ⓐ	Ⓐ	⑥	①–④	⑤	⑤	①–④		⑦	⑦	⑦	⑦	⑦	⑦	⑦		⑦	⑦	⑦	⑦	⑦
Birmingham New Street d.	1819	1849	1919	1919	1959	2059	2059	2145	2200	2300	2315	...		...	1000	1200	1358	1558	1758	...	1858	...	1958	2058	2205
Bromsgrove d.	1846	1910	1940	1941	2019	2120	2120	|	2220	2319	|	...		...	1020	1221	1418	1618	1818	...	1918	...	2018	2118	2225
Droitwich Spa d.	1957	1920	1950	1952	2029	2130	2130	2234	2234	2329	2358	...		...	1030	1232	1428	1628	1827	...	1928	...	2031	2129	2236
Worcester Foregate Street d.	1910h	1938	2000	2015	2036h	2141	2150	2247h	2247h	2337h	0007h	...	▽	0908	1056	1250	1453	1642	1842	...	1942	2014	2100	2143	2252
Great Malvern d.	...	1950	2025	2027	...	2154	2202	...	...	...	...	...		0920	1108	1302	1506	1703	1859	...	...	2028	...	2156	2305
Ledbury d.	...	...	2039	2041	...	2209	2215	...	...	...	...	...		0932	1121	1315	1519	1716	1912	...	...	2043	...	2209	...
Hereford a.	...	...	2102	2103	...	2229	2235	...	...	...	...	...		0948	1139	1332	1537	1734	1930	...	...	2101	...	2227	...

	⚒	Ⓐ	Ⓐ	⑥	Ⓐ	⑥	Ⓐ	Ⓐ	⑥	⑥	Ⓐ	Ⓐ	⑥	Ⓐ	⑥	Ⓐ	⚒	⚒	⚒	⚒	⚒	⚒	⑥	⚒	⚒
Hereford d.		0450	...	...	*0528*	...	...	...	0617	...	0709	0734	0740	...	0840	0849	0940	1040	1140	1240	1340	1440	...	1540	1640
Ledbury d.		|	...	...	*0545*	...	...	...	0634	...	0725	0750	0758	...	0858	0908	0958	1058	1158	1258	1358	1458	...	1558	1658
Great Malvern d.		0517	0549	...	*0559*	0621	0647	0702	0649	...	0737	0805	0810	0838	0910	0919	1010	1110	1210	1310	1410	1510	...	1610	1710
Worcester Foregate Street d.		0530	0602	0607h	0626h	0633	0700	0716	0707h	0735h	0749	0824	0824	0851	0924	0931	1024	1124	1224	1324	1424	1524	1554h	1624	1724
Droitwich Spa d.		...	0611	0615	0634	0642	0715	0734	...	0743	0805	0833	0833	0901	0933	0945	1033	1133	1233	1333	1433	1533	1603	1633	1733
Bromsgrove d.		...	0621	|	0643	0652	0725	|	...	0753	|	0843	0843	0911	0943	0954	1043	1143	1243	1343	1443	1543	1613	1643	1743
Birmingham New Street a.		...	0647	0648	0706	0716	0747	0809	...	0816	0838	0907	0911	0942	1011	1022	1111	1211	1311	1411	1511	1611	1645	1711	1811

	⚒	Ⓐ	⑥	Ⓐ	⑥	⑤	①–④	⑥	⑥	⑥	⑥	Ⓐ		⑦	⑦	⑦	⑦	⑦	⑦	⑦	⑦	⑦	⑦	⑦	⑦
Hereford d.	1740	1848	1912	1950	2000	2129	2129	...	2135	...	2250	2259	...		...	1006	1200	1405	1609	1634	...	1809	1830	...	2006
Ledbury d.	1758	1904	1928	2009	2016	2145	2145	...	2151	...	2306	2315	...		...	1022	1216	1421	1625	1652	...	1825	1848	...	2022
Great Malvern d.	1810	1915	1939	2020	2027	2156	2156	2130	2203	...	2317	2327	...		...	1034	1230	1433	1637	1705	...	1837	1911	...	2037
Worcester Foregate Street d.	1825	1928	1952	2031	2040	2210	2210	2142	2218h	2247h	2327	2339	...	▽	0902h	1046	1242	1445	1649	1726h	1757h	1849	1924	1949	2049
Droitwich Spa d.	1833	1937	2001	2045	2049	2219	2219	2202	...	2255	...	...	...		0910	1103	1303	1503	1703	...	1805	1903	...	2003	2103
Bromsgrove d.	1842	1947	|	2055	2059	2229	|	|	...	|	...	...	...		0920	1113	1313	1513	1713	...	1815	1913	...	2013	2113
Birmingham New Street a.	1912	2018	2056n	2120	2120	2251	2255	2255n	...	2336n	...	...	...		0942	1137	1337	1537	1737	...	1837	1937	...	2037	2137

h – Worcester Shrub Hill. n – Birmingham Snow Hill. ▽ – Service on ⑦ subject to alteration June 22 - Sept. 7.

124 BIRMINGHAM - KIDDERMINSTER - WORCESTER — 2nd class LM

km		⚒	Ⓐ	⑥	Ⓐ	⑥	Ⓐ	Ⓐ	⑥	Ⓐ	⑥	⚒	Ⓐ	⑥	⚒	⚒	⚒	Ⓐ	⑥	⚒	⑥	Ⓐ	Ⓐ	⑥	⑥
0	**Birmingham** Moor St d.		0604	0631	0649	0701	0717	0748	0749	0833	0845	0909	0939	0940	1009	1039	1109	1139	1139	1209	1239	1239	1309	1309	1339
1	**Birmingham** Snow Hill d.		0608	0635	0653	0705	0724	0753	0753	0843	0853	0913	0943	0943	1013	1043	1113	1143	1143	1213	1243	1243	1313	1313	1343
31	Kidderminster ▶ d.		0648	0715	0734	0745	0805	0834	0831	0920	0933	0947	1017	1017	1047	1117	1147	1217	1217	1247	1317	1317	1347	1347	1417
45	Droitwich Spa d.		0659	0728	0746	0756	0818	0847	0842	0931	0944	1000	1028	1028	1100	1128	1200	1228	1228	1300	1328	1328	1400	1400	1431
54	**Worcester** Shrub Hill a.		|	0739	|	0805	0826	|	|	0940	0952	|	|	1036	|	1136	|	1236	|	|	1336	|	1408	|	1439
54	**Worcester** Foregate St a.		0709	...	0757	0813	0832	0858	0851	...	...	1009	1037	...	1109	...	1209	...	1237	1309	...	1337	...	1409	1446

	Ⓐ	⑥	Ⓐ	⑥	Ⓐ	⑥	Ⓐ	⚒	⚒	⑥	Ⓐ	⚒	Ⓐ	⑥	Ⓐ	⑥	Ⓐ	⑥	Ⓐ	⑥	⑥	Ⓐ	⑥	Ⓐ	⑥
Birmingham Moor St d.	1339	1409	1409	1439	1439	1509	1509	1539	1609	1639	1638	1709	1732	1739	1749	1818	1839	1849	1924	1924	1952	1954	2052	2052	2152
Birmingham Snow Hill d.	1343	1413	1413	1443	1443	1513	1513	1543	1613	1643	1643	1713	1736	1743	1753	1823	1843	1853	1928	1928	1956	1958	2056	2055	2156
Kidderminster ▶ d.	1417	1447	1447	1517	1517	1547	1550	1617	1647	1717	1722	1747	1813	1820	1832	1900	1920	1934	2009	2009	2036	2039	2136	2136	2236
Droitwich Spa d.	1428	1500	1500	1528	1528	1600	1604	1628	1700	1728	1737	1801	1826	1834	1846	1913	1931	1945	2022	2022	2048	2050	2148	2147	2250
Worcester Shrub Hill a.	1438	|	1510	1536	|	|	1612	|	|	|	|	1813	|	|	|	|	|	1953	|	2032	2056	2059	2256	2200	2258
Worcester Foregate St a.	1444	1509	...	...	1537	1609	1623	1640	1709	1737	1746	...	1836	1843	1855	1922	1940	...	2031	...	2101	...	...	2207	2303

	Ⓐ	Ⓐ	⑥			⑦	⑦		⑦	⑦	⑦		⑦	⑦	⑦		⑦	⑦	⑦		⑦	⑦		⑦	⑦
Birmingham Moor St d.	2155	2256	2257	...	⑦	0926	1015	...	1115	1215	1315	...	1414	1515	1615	...	1702	1715	1815	...	1915	2015	...	2143	2252
Birmingham Snow Hill d.	2158	2300	2301	...		0930	1022	...	1122	1222	1322	...	1422	1522	1622	...	1705	1722	1822	...	1922	2022	...	2146	2255
Kidderminster ▶ d.	2238	2341	2341	...		1005	1059	...	1159	1259	1357	...	1459	1557	1657	...	1733	1757	1859	...	1957	2057	...	2220	2329
Droitwich Spa d.	2252	2352	2353	...	▷	1017	1111	...	1211	1311	1409	...	1511	1609	1709	...	1745	1809	1911	...	2009	2109	...	2231	2341
Worcester Shrub Hill a.	2300	0001	0001	...		1025	1122	...	1223	|	|	...	|	|	|	...	1752	|	1919	...	2017	2118	...	2339	2349
Worcester Foregate St a.	2308	...	...	...		1030	1135	...	...	1320	1418	...	1520	1618	1718	...	...	1818	...	...	...	2124	...	...	...

	⚒	Ⓐ	⑥	Ⓐ	Ⓐ	⑥	Ⓐ	⑥	Ⓐ	Ⓐ	⑥	Ⓐ	⑥	Ⓐ	⑥	Ⓐ	⑥	Ⓐ	⚒	⚒	Ⓐ	⑥	⚒	⚒	Ⓐ
Worcester Foregate St d.		...	...	...	...	...	...	...	0714	...	0747	0802	...	0838	0856	0903	...	...	1016	...	1116	...	1151	1216	...
Worcester Shrub Hill d.		0530	0544	0612	0635	0625	0651	0701	|	0735	|	|	0815	0844	|	|	0948	0952	|	1052	|	1117	|	|	1251
Droitwich Spa d.		0538	0552	0620	0643	0633	0704	0709	0723	0743	0756	0811	0823	0953	0905	0912	0956	1000	1025	1100	1125	1125	1200	1225	1259
Kidderminster ▶ d.		0548	0602	0633	0656	0646	0717	0722	0736	0754	0806	0824	0836	0906	0916	0925	1006	1010	1040	1110	1140	1140	1210	1240	1310
Birmingham Snow Hill d.		0632	0645	0721	0739	0732	0800	0805	0815	0835	0845	0905	0915	0945	0956	1004	1041	1045	1115	1145	1215	1215	1245	1315	1345
Birmingham Moor St a.		0637	0653	0725	0743	0739	0805	0809	0819	0839	0849	0909	0919	0949	1000	1009	1049	1049	1119	1149	1219	1219	1249	1319	1349

	⑥	⚒	⚒	⚒	⚒	Ⓐ	⑥	Ⓐ	⑥	Ⓐ	⑥	Ⓐ	⚒	⑥	Ⓐ	⑥	Ⓐ	⑥	Ⓐ	Ⓐ	⑥	Ⓐ	⑥	Ⓐ	⑥
Worcester Foregate St d.	1251	...	1351	1416	...	...	1516	1533	1546	1613	1614	1634	1647	...	1716	1747	1756	1812	...	1846	1851	1946	1952	2051	...
Worcester Shrub Hill d.	|	1317	|	|	1452	1515	|	1547	|	|	|	1640	|	1715	|	|	|	1818	1837	|	|	|	|	|	205
Droitwich Spa d.	1300	1325	1400	1425	1500	1523	1525	1555	1555	1622	1623	1648	1656	1723	1725	1756	1805	1826	1845	1855	1900	1955	2001	2100	210
Kidderminster ▶ d.	1310	1340	1410	1440	1510	1536	1540	1606	1610	1635	1636	1701	1706	1736	1738	1806	1815	1836	1855	1910	1913	2010	2014	2113	211
Birmingham Snow Hill d.	1345	1415	1445	1515	1545	1615	1615	1645	1645	1718	1715	1739	1745	1815	1817	1845	1855	1915	1935	1955	1955	2055	2056	2155	215
Birmingham Moor St a.	1349	1419	1449	1519	1549	1620	1619	1649	1649	1724	1719	1744	1749	1819	1824	1852	1859	1919	...	1959	1959	2059	2059	2159	215

	⑥	Ⓐ	Ⓐ	⑥			⑦	⑦		⑦	⑦		⑦	⑦		⑦	⑦	⑦		⑦	⑦	⑦		⑦	⑦
Worcester Foregate St d.	2142	...	2217	...	...	⑦	0920	1019	...	1109	1220	...	1326	1424	...	1528	1626	1727	...	1826	...	...	...	2118	222
Worcester Shrub Hill d.	2154	2154	2227	2247	...		0926	1025	...	1127	1226	...	|	|	...	|	|	|	...	|	1938	2036	...	2125	222
Droitwich Spa d.	2202	2202	2235	2255	...		0934	1033	...	1135	1235	...	1335	1433	...	1537	1635	1736	...	1835	1946	2044	...	2133	223
Kidderminster ▶ d.	2212	2212	2248	2305	...	▷	0944	1045	...	1145	1245	...	1345	1443	...	1547	1645	1746	...	1845	1956	2054	...	2143	224
Birmingham Snow Hill d.	2255	2255	2328	2336	...		1022	1121	...	1221	1322	...	1421	1521	...	1623	1721	1824	...	1921	2033	2130	...	2219	232
Birmingham Moor St a.	2259	2259	2336	2339	...		1028	1128	...	1229	1329	...	1429	1529	...	1629	1729	1829	...	1925	2037	2134	...	2223	...

▶ – **Kidderminster - Bridgnorth** and v.v. (*Severn Valley Railway*). *26 km*. Daily May - September and on certain other dates throughout the year. ✆ 01299 403816. www.svr.co.uk.
▷ – Service on ⑦ subject to alteration Aug. 3 - Sept. 7.

125 STRATFORD UPON AVON - BIRMINGHAM — 2nd class LM

km		⚒	Ⓐ	Ⓐ	⑥	Ⓐ	⚒	⚒	and at	⚒	⚒	Ⓐ	⑥	Ⓐ	Ⓐ	⑥	⚒	⚒	⚒	⚒			⑦	⑦	⑦
0	**Stratford upon Avon** d.		0627	0652	0700	0719	0742	0826	the same	1626	1726	1755	1808	1826	1851	1849	1926	2026	2126	2233	...	⑦	0929	1029	112
13	Henley in Arden d.		0643	0707	0715	0735	0758	0841	minutes	1641	1741	1807	1823	1841	1907	1904	1941	2041	2140	2246	...		0943	1043	114
40	**Birmingham** Moor St d.		0723	0747	0754	0807	0837	0917	past each	1717	1817	1838	1903	1917	1934	1943	2017	2117	2217	2318	...		1014	1114	121
41	**Birmingham** Snow Hill a.	♡	0726	0750	0757	0810	0841	0920	hour until	1720	1820	1841	1906	1920	1937	1946	2020	2120	2220	2322	...		1017	1117	121

	⑦	⑦ 🚂	⑦	⑦	⑦	⑦ 🚂	⑦	⑦	⑦	⑦	
Stratford upon Avon d.	1229	1236	1329	1429	1529	1613	1629	1729	1829	1929	...
Henley in Arden d.	1243	|	1343	1443	1543	|	1643	1743	1843	1943	...
Birmingham Moor St d.	1314	1336	1414	1514	1614	1708	1714	1814	1914	2014	...
Birmingham Snow Hill a.	1317	1341	1417	1517	1617	1713	1717	1817	1917	2017	...

	⚒	Ⓐ	Ⓐ	Ⓐ	⑥	Ⓐ	⚒	⚒	and at
Birmingham Snow Hill d.		0553	0629	0640	0722	0722	0828	0928	the same
Birmingham Moor St d.		0556	0632	0643	0725	0725	0831	0931	minutes
Henley in Arden d.		|	0703	0720	0802	0805	0906	1006	past each
Stratford upon Avon a.	♡	0645	0716	0735	0817	0820	0921	1021	hour until

	⚒	⚒	Ⓐ	⑥	Ⓐ	⚒	⚒	⚒	⚒	⚒	⚒			⑦	⑦	⑦ 🚂	⑦	⑦	⑦	⑦ 🚂	⑦	⑦		⑦	⑦	⑦
Birmingham Snow Hill d.	1528	1628	1703	1707	1728	1747	1828	1928	2028	2128	2228	...	⑦	0927	1026	1023	1125	1227	1327	1356	1427	1527	...	1627	1727	182
Birmingham Moor St d.	1531	1631	1706	1710	1731	1750	1831	1931	2031	2131	2231	...		0930	1029	1028	1128	1230	1330	1401	1430	1530	...	1630	1730	183
Henley in Arden d.	1606	1706	1736	1748	1806	1828	1906	2007	2107	2207	2307	...		1001	1100	1111	1159	1301	1401	1441	1501	1601	...	1702	1801	190
Stratford upon Avon a.	1621	1721	1749	1803	1821	1843	1921	2021	2121	2221	2321	...		1015	1115	1137	1214	1315	1415	1504	1515	1615	...	1716	1815	191

🚂 – THE SHAKESPEARE EXPRESS – (12) ✕ (1st class only) and 🍷. ⑦ July 20 - Sept. 7. National Rail tickets NOT valid. Vintage Trains Ltd. ✆ 0121 708 4960. www.shakespeareexpress.co
♡ – Additonal services are available Birmingham Snow Hill - Dorridge - Stratford upon Avon on ⚒.

XC Most trains 🍸 BRISTOL - BIRMINGHAM - YORK - NEWCASTLE - EDINBURGH 127

Service until September 7 (subject to alteration on ⑦ June 22 - July 27). For other services see Tables 121, 132, 170, 180 and 189.

km																								
			Ⓐ	Ⓐ	Ⓐ	Ⓐ	Ⓐ	Ⓐ	Ⓐ	Ⓐ	Ⓐ	Ⓐ	Ⓐ	Ⓐ	Ⓐ	Ⓐ	Ⓐ	Ⓐ	Ⓐ	Ⓐ	Ⓐ	Ⓐ	Ⓐ	Ⓐ
			G		G				G					C	G	W	T				ZG	S		A
	Plymouth **115**	d.	Ⓐ	...	...	...	...	...	...	...	...	...	0520	...	...	0625	...	...	0725	...	...	0825	...	...	0925
0	**Bristol** Temple Meads	d.		...	...	...	...	...	...	0627	...	0700	0730	...	0800	0830	...	0900	0930	...	1000	1030	...	1100	1130
10	**Bristol** Parkway	d.		...	...	...	...	...	...	0638	...	0709	0739	...	0809	0839	...	0909	0939	...	1009	1039	...	1109	1139
72	Cheltenham Spa	d.		...	...	...	...	...	...	0710	...	0740	0811	...	0840	0912	...	0942	1011	...	1041	1111	...	1142	1211
	Reading **129**	d.		...	...	...	...	...	...	|	0640	|	|	0741	|	|	0840	|	|	0940	|	|	1040	|	|
145	**Birmingham** New Street	a.		...	...	...	...	...	...	0756	0815	0826	0855	0918	0926	0956	1018	1023	1055	1118	1126	1158	1218	1226	1256
145	**Birmingham** New Street	d.		...	...	0600	0630	0703	0730	0803	0830	0831	0903	0930	0931	1003	1030	1031	1103	1130	1131	1203	1230	1231	1303
	Manchester Piccadilly **129**	a.		...	...	|	|	|	|	|	|	0959	|	|	1059	|	|	1159	|	|	1259	|	|	1359	|
173	Tamworth	a.		...	...	|	|	0719	|	0819	|	...	|	|	...	1019	|	...	|	|	...	1219	|	...	|
193	Burton on Trent	a.		...	...	|	|	0731	|	0829	|	...	0927	|	...	|	|	...	1126	|	...	|	|	...	1328
212	**Derby**	a.		...	0556	0633	0711	0742	0809	0841	0906	...	0939	1006	...	1038	1106	...	1138	1206	...	1238	1306	...	1340
250	Chesterfield	a.		...	0614	0653	0731	0802	0832	0902	|	...	1002	|	...	1102	|	...	1202	|	...	1302	|	...	1402
270	**Sheffield**	a.		...	0629	0706	0745	0816	0845	0917	0944	...	1017	1044	...	1117	1141	...	1217	1244	...	1317	1342	...	1418
299	Doncaster	a.		...	0657	|	0823	|	0918	|	1018	...	|	1118	...	|	1218	...	|	1318	...	|	1418	...	|
316	Wakefield Westgate	a.		...	|	0734	|	0846	|	0946	|	...	1046	|	...	1146	|	...	1246	|	...	1346	|	...	1446
332	**Leeds**	a.		...	|	0750	|	0902	|	1001	|	...	1101	|	...	1201	|	...	1301	|	...	1401	|	...	1501
344	**York**	a.		...	0723	0822	0847	0932	0940	1030	1039	...	1130	1139	...	1230	1239	...	1330	1340	...	1430	1439	...	1530
415	Darlington	a.		...	0757	0857	0916	0959	1013	1057	1113	...	1157	1213	...	1257	1313	...	1400	1413	...	1457	1513	...	1557
450	Durham	a.		...	0815	0914	0933	1017	1030	1115	1130	...	1215	1230	...	1315	1330	...	1417	1430	...	1515	1530	...	1615
473	**Newcastle**	a.		0735	0838	0927	0947	1030	1045	1129	1145	...	1229	1244	...	1329	1345	...	1430	1443	...	1529	1545	...	1629
529	Alnmouth	a.		|	...	0958	...	|	...	|	...	...	|	...	...	1401	...	...	|	...	...	1600	...	...	1700
581	Berwick upon Tweed	a.		0818	...	1019	...	|	...	1221	...	...	|	...	...	1422	...	...	|	...	...	1621	...	...	|
673	**Edinburgh** Waverley	a.		0904	...	1106	...	1203	...	1305	...	...	1410	...	...	1507	...	...	1605	...	...	1705	...	...	1807

		Ⓐ	Ⓐ	Ⓐ	Ⓐ	Ⓐ	Ⓐ	Ⓐ	Ⓐ	Ⓐ	Ⓐ	Ⓐ	Ⓐ	Ⓐ	Ⓐ	Ⓐ	Ⓐ	Ⓐ	Ⓐ	Ⓐ	Ⓐ	Ⓐ	Ⓐ	Ⓐ
			T	ZG	S		D		Z	G	S				T		S				X		S	
Plymouth **115**	d.	...	...	1025	...	...	1125	...	1150	1225	...	...	1325	...	...	1425	...	...	1525	...	...	1625	...	...
Bristol Temple Meads	d.	...	1200	1230	...	1300	1330	...	1400	1430	...	1500	1530	...	1600	1630	...	1700	1730	...	1800	1830	...	1900
Bristol Parkway	d.	...	1209	1239	...	1309	1339	...	1409	1440	...	1509	1540	...	1609	1639	...	1709	1740	...	1809	1839	...	1909
Cheltenham Spa	d.	...	1240	1311	...	1342	1410	...	1441	1511	...	1542	1611	...	1641	1711	...	1742	1811	...	1841	1911	...	1940
Reading **129**	d.	1140	|	|	1240	|	|	1340	|	|	1440	|	|	1540	|	|	1640	|	|	1740	|	|	1839	|
Birmingham New Street	a.	1318	1326	1356	1418	1424	1456	1518	1523	1556	1618	1626	1656	1718	1723	1756	1818	1824	1856	1918	1923	1956	2017	2023
Birmingham New Street	d.	1330	1331	1403	1430	1431	1503	1530	1531	1603	1630	1631	1703	1730	1731	1803	1830	1831	1903	1930	1931	2003	2030	2031
Manchester Piccadilly **129**	a.	|	1459	|	|	1559	|	|	1659	|	|	1758	|	|	1859	|	|	1959	|	|	2058	|	|	2159
Tamworth	a.	|	...	1419	|	...	|	|	...	1619	|	...	|	|	...	1819	|	...	|	|	...	2019	|	...
Burton on Trent	a.	|	...	|	|	...	1526	|	...	|	|	...	1726	|	...	|	|	...	1925	|	...	|	|	...
Derby	a.	1406	...	1440	1506	...	1540	1606	...	1640	1706	...	1739	1806	...	1838	1905	...	1940	2004	...	2038	2109	...
Chesterfield	a.	|	...	1502	|	...	1602	|	...	1703	|	...	1802	|	...	1902	1927	...	2004	|	...	2102	2137	...
Sheffield	a.	1444	...	1517	1544	...	1617	1644	...	1718	1741	...	1818	1843	...	1919	1941	...	2019	2039	...	2115	2150	...
Doncaster	a.	1518	...	|	1618	...	|	1718	...	|	|	...	|	1916	...	|	2015	...	|	2119	...	|	2229	...
Wakefield Westgate	a.	|	...	1546	|	...	1646	|	...	1748	1814	...	1847	|	...	1950	|	...	2047	|	...	2147	|	...
Leeds	a.	|	...	1601	|	...	1704	|	...	1802	1832	...	1903	|	...	2005	|	...	2110	|	...	2204	|	...
York	a.	1540	...	1630	1639	...	1730	1739	...	1831	1902	...	1930	1939	...	2030	2038	...	...	2140	...	...	2252	...
Darlington	a.	1613	...	1658	1714	...	1758	1813	...	1900	1931	...	2000	2010	...	2057	2113	...	...	2213	...	...	...	...
Durham	a.	1630	...	1715	1731	...	1815	1830	...	1918	1948	...	2018	2027	...	2114	2130	...	...	2230	...	...	...	...
Newcastle	a.	1645	...	1730	1745	...	1832	1846	...	1932	2001	...	2033	2042	...	2128	2144	...	...	2247	...	...	...	...
Alnmouth	a.	...	...	1800	...	...	|	...	...	2000	2026	...	|	...	...	2158	...	...	...	...	...	...	...	...
Berwick upon Tweed	a.	...	...	1821	...	...	1921	...	...	2023	|	...	2121	...	...	|	...	...	...	...	...	...	...	...
Edinburgh Waverley	a.	...	...	1905	...	...	2009	...	...	2108	2128	...	2213	...	...	2303	...	...	...	...	...	...	...	...

		Ⓐ	Ⓐ	Ⓐ	Ⓐ			⑥	⑥	⑥	⑥	⑥	⑥	⑥	⑥	⑥	⑥	⑥	⑥	⑥	⑥	⑥	⑥	⑥
					T			G		G				G				B	C	G	S	T		
Plymouth **115**	d.	1725	...	1825	...	...	⑥	...	...	...	...	...	...	...	...	...	0525	...	...	0625	...	...	0725	...
Bristol Temple Meads	d.	1930	2000	2030	2200	...		...	...	...	...	...	...	0615	...	0700	0730	...	0800	0830	...	0900	0930	...
Bristol Parkway	d.	1940	2009	2040	2210	...		...	...	...	...	...	...	0624	...	0709	0739	...	0809	0839	...	0909	0939	...
Cheltenham Spa	d.	2011	2056	2117	2241	...		...	...	...	...	...	...	0711	...	0741	0813	...	0841	0910	...	0941	1011	...
Reading **129**	d.	|	|	|	|	...		...	...	...	...	...	...	|	0645	|	|	0747	|	|	0840	|	|	0940
Birmingham New Street	a.	2052	2140	2203	2343	...		...	...	...	...	...	...	0756	0817	0825	0856	0918	0926	0955	1018	1025	1056	1118
Birmingham New Street	d.	2103	...	...	...	...		...	...	0557	0630	0703	0730	0803	0830	0831	0903	0930	0931	1003	1030	1031	1103	1130
Manchester Piccadilly **129**	a.	|	...	...	...	...		...	...	|	|	|	|	|	|	0959	|	|	1059	|	|	1159	|	|
Tamworth	a.	2119	...	...	...	...		...	...	0613	0646	0719	0746	0819	|	...	|	|	...	1019	|	...	|	|
Burton on Trent	a.	2130	...	...	...	...		...	...	0624	0656	0729	0756	0829	|	...	0928	|	...	|	|	...	1128	|
Derby	a.	2143	...	...	...	...		...	0555	0635	0709	0742	0809	0842	0908	...	0941	1006	...	1041	1109	...	1141	1206
Chesterfield	a.	2206	...	...	...	...		...	0630	0656	0730	0802	0830	0902	|	...	1002	|	...	1102	|	...	1202	|
Sheffield	a.	2224	...	...	...	...		...	0643	0709	0748	0816	0845	0917	0944	...	1017	1044	...	1117	1142	...	1217	1244
Doncaster	a.	|	...	...	...	...		...	0716	|	0823	|	0918	|	1017	...	|	1115	...	|	1216	...	|	1317
Wakefield Westgate	a.	2259	...	...	...	...		...	|	0739	|	0845	|	0946	|	...	1046	|	...	1146	|	...	1246	|
Leeds	a.	2315	...	...	...	...		...	|	0753	|	0903	|	1001	|	...	1101	|	...	1200	|	...	1302	|
York	a.	...	...	...	...	...		...	0744	0819	0847	0930	0940	1030	1039	...	1130	1139	...	1230	1239	...	1330	1339
Darlington	a.	...	...	...	...	...		...	0813	0857	0916	0957	1013	1057	1113	...	1157	1213	...	1258	1313	...	1358	1413
Durham	a.	...	...	...	...	...		...	0830	0913	0933	1016	1030	1115	1130	...	1215	1230	...	1315	1330	...	1415	1430
Newcastle	a.	...	...	...	...	...		0738	0845	0927	0947	1030	1044	1129	1146	...	1229	1245	...	1329	1345	...	1429	1443
Alnmouth	a.	...	...	...	...	...		|	...	0958	...	|	...	|	...	...	|	...	...	1358	...	...	|	...
Berwick upon Tweed	a.	...	...	...	...	...		0821	...	1019	...	|	...	1219	...	...	|	...	...	1419	...	...	|	...
Edinburgh Waverley	a.	...	...	....	..	...		0907	...	1103	...	1207	...	1304	...	...	1406	...	...	1504	...	...	1604	...

		⑥	⑥	⑥	⑥	⑥	⑥	⑥	⑥	⑥	⑥	⑥	⑥	⑥	⑥	⑥	⑥	⑥	⑥	⑥	⑥	⑥	⑥	⑥
			ZG	S		A		T	ZG	S		ND			TG	S				T		S		
Plymouth **115**	d.	...	0825	...	0839	0920	...	...	1025	...	...	1125	...	...	...	...	...	1325	...	...	1425	...	...	1525
Bristol Temple Meads	d.	1000	1030	...	1100	1130	...	1200	1230	...	1300	1330	...	1400	1430	...	1500	1530	...	1600	1630	...	1700	1730
Bristol Parkway	d.	1009	1039	...	1109	1139	...	1209	1239	...	1309	1339	...	1409	1440	...	1509	1539	...	1609	1639	...	1709	1739
Cheltenham Spa	d.	1041	1111	...	1141	1211	...	1241	1311	...	1341	1411	...	1441	1512	...	1540	1611	...	1640	1711	...	1741	1813
Reading **129**	d.	|	|	1039	|	|	1140	|	|	1239	|	|	1340	|	|	1439	|	|	1540	|	|	1639	|	|
Birmingham New Street	a.	1126	1155	1218	1226	1255	1318	1326	1355	1418	1426	1455	1518	1526	1555	1618	1626	1655	1718	1726	1755	1818	1826	1855
Birmingham New Street	d.	1131	1203	1230	1231	1303	1330	1331	1403	1430	1431	1503	1530	1531	1603	1630	1631	1703	1730	1731	1803	1830	1831	1903
Manchester Piccadilly **129**	a.	1259	|	|	1359	|	|	1459	|	|	1559	|	|	1659	|	|	1759	|	|	1859	|	|	1959	|
Tamworth	a.	...	1219	|	...	|	|	...	1419	|	...	|	|	...	1619	|	...	|	|	...	1819	|	...	|
Burton on Trent	a.	...	|	|	...	1327	|	...	|	|	...	1527	|	...	|	1654	...	1726	|	...	|	|	...	1927
Derby	a.	...	1241	1306	...	1341	1406	...	1441	1506	...	1540	1606	...	1640	1706	...	1741	1806	...	1841	1905	...	1939
Chesterfield	a.	...	1302	|	...	1402	|	...	1502	|	...	1603	|	...	1703	|	...	1802	|	...	1902	1930	...	2004
Sheffield	a.	...	1317	1343	...	1417	1444	...	1517	1544	...	1618	1644	...	1718	1744	...	1818	1843	...	1918	1951	...	2021
Doncaster	a.	...	|	1418	...	|	1517	...	|	1618	...	|	1716	...	|	|	...	|	1916	...	|	2018	...	|
Wakefield Westgate	a.	...	1346	|	...	1446	|	...	1546	|	...	1646	|	...	1748	1813	...	1847	|	...	1950	|	...	2048
Leeds	a.	...	1401	|	...	1501	|	...	1601	|	...	1701	|	...	1802	1831	...	1901	|	...	2004	|	...	2102
York	a.	...	1430	1439	...	1530	1539	...	1630	1639	...	1729	1737	...	1831	1902	...	1930	1939	...	2030	2039	...	2155
Darlington	a.	...	1457	1513	...	1558	1613	...	1658	1713	...	1756	1813	...	1900	1931	...	1957	2010	...	2057	2113	...	...
Durham	a.	...	1515	1530	...	1615	1630	...	1715	1730	...	1813	1830	...	1918	1948	...	2014	2027	...	2114	2130	...	...
Newcastle	a.	...	1529	1545	...	1629	1645	...	1729	1745	...	1827	1843	...	1932	2001	...	2028	2042	...	2128	2144	...	...
Alnmouth	a.	...	1558	...	...	1657	...	...	1759	...	...	|	...	...	2000	...	...	|	...	...	2155	...	...	...
Berwick upon Tweed	a.	...	1619	...	...	|	...	...	1819	...	...	1917	...	...	2023	...	...	2118	...	...	|	...	...	...
Edinburgh Waverley	a.	...	1707	...	...	1803	...	...	1906	...	...	2005	...	...	2108	...	...	2208	...	...	2257	...	...	...

– To/from Aberdeen (Table **224**).
– To/from Bournemouth (Table **129**).
– To/from Cardiff Central (Table **121**).
– To/from Dundee (Table **224**).
– To/from Glasgow Central (Table **220**).

M – From Nottingham (Table **121**).
N – To/from Newquay (Table **115**).
S – To/from Southampton Central (Table **129**).
T – To/from Paignton (Table **115**).
W – To/from Winchester (Table **129**).

Z – To/from Penzance (Table **115**).
X – To/from Exeter St Davids (Table **115**).

a – Not June 22 - July 27.
s – Calls to set down only.

127 BRISTOL - BIRMINGHAM - YORK - NEWCASTLE - EDINBURGH

Most trains 🍸 XC

Service until September 7 (subject to alteration on ⑦ June 22 - July 27). For other services see Tables 121, 132, 170, 180 and 189.

	⑥	⑥	⑥	⑥	⑥	⑥	⑥	⑥	⑥			⑦	⑦	⑦	⑦	⑦	⑦	⑦	⑦	⑦	⑦	⑦	⑦
			T	S		N	B	T	Z				G		G		A		G		T	Z	
Plymouth **115** d.	...	...	...	...	...	1725	...	...	1825	...	⑦	...	...	...	...	...	0925	...	1025	...	...	1125	...
Bristol Temple Meads d.	...	1800	1830	...	1900	1930	...	2000	2030	...		...	...	0915	1030	...	1130	...	1230	...	1300	1330	...
Bristol Parkway d.	...	1809	1839	...	1909	1940	...	2009	2039	...		...	...	0924	1039	...	1139	...	1239	...	1309	1339	...
Cheltenham Spa d.	...	1841	1911	...	1941	2011	...	2041	2111	...		...	...	1012	1110	...	1210	...	1310	...	1341	1410	...
Reading **129** d.	1740	|	|	1839	|	|	1910	|	|	...		...	...	|	|	...	|	...	|	1254	|	|	1341
Birmingham New Street a.	1918	1926	1958	2018	2026	2052	2048	2138	2154	...		...	...	1049	1148	...	1249	...	1348	1419	1427	1448	1511
Birmingham New Street d.	1930	1931	2003	2030	2031	2057	2103	...	2156	...		0903	1003	1103	1203	1230	1303	1330	1403	1430	1431	1503	1530
Manchester Piccadilly **129** a.	|	2059	|	|	2204	2235	|	...	|	...		|	|	|	|	|	|	|	|	|	1559	|	|
Tamworth a.	|	...	2019	|	...	...	2119	...	|	...		0919	1018	|	1219	|	|	|	1419	|	...	|	|
Burton on Trent a.	|	...	|	|	...	...	2130	...	|	...		0928	1029	1125	|	|	1326	|	|	|	...	1525	|
Derby a.	2006	...	2042	2124	...	...	2141	...	2231	...		0941	1040	1137	1241	1301	1337	1401	1439	1501	...	1537	1601
Chesterfield a.	2030	...	2104	2146	...	...	2203	...	2254	...		1002	1102	1201	1302	1329	1402	1429	1502	|	...	1602	|
Sheffield a.	2049	...	2119	2205	...	...	2220	...	2309	...		1016	1117	1218	1318	1343	1417	1443	1517	1547	...	1618	1648
Doncaster a.	2121	...	|	2230	...	...	2251	...	|	...		|	|	|	|	1413	|	1513	|	1615	...	|	1713
Wakefield Westgate a.	|	...	2148	|	...	...	2309	...	|	...		1044	1144	1244	1345	|	1444	|	1545	|	...	1644	|
Leeds a.	|	...	2201	|	...	...	2327	...	2350	...		1102	1201	1302	1402	|	1502	|	1602	|	...	1702	|
York a.	2143	...	...	2255	...	...	...	...	...	...		1127	1227	1327	1427	1437	1527	1542	1627	1640	...	1727	1740
Darlington a.	2213	...	...	...	...	...	...	...	...	...		1154	1254	1355	1454	1513	1554	1610	1654	1714	...	1754	1810
Durham a.	2230	...	...	...	...	...	...	...	...	...		1211	1311	1412	1512	1530	1611	1627	1711	1732	...	1811	1827
Newcastle a.	2247	...	...	...	...	...	...	...	...	...		1225	1325	1426	1526	1544	1625	1642	1725	1747	...	1825	1841
Alnmouth a.	...	...	...	...	...	...	...	...	...	...		|	1351	|	1552	...	1651	...	1751	...	...	|	...
Berwick upon Tweed a.	...	...	...	...	...	...	...	...	...	...		|	1412	|	1612	...	|	...	1812	...	...	1909	...
Edinburgh Waverley a.	...	...	...	...	...	...	...	...	...	...		1357	1456	1602	1656	...	1757	...	1856	...	...	1957	...

	⑦	⑦	⑦	⑦		⑦	⑦	⑦	⑦		⑦	⑦	⑦	⑦		⑦	⑦	⑦	⑦		⑦	⑦	⑦
		G				N						Z							Z		T		
Plymouth **115** d.	1200	1225	...	1252	...	1325	...	...	1425	...	...	1435	1524	...	...	...	1625	...	1725	...	...	1825	...
Bristol Temple Meads d.	1400	1430	...	1500	...	1530	...	1600	1630	...	...	1700	1730	...	...	1800	1830	1900	1930	...	2000	2030	2210
Bristol Parkway d.	1409	1439	...	1509	...	1540	...	1609	1640	...	...	1709	1740	...	...	1809	1839	1909	1939	...	2009	2040	2220
Cheltenham Spa d.	1441	1510	...	1541	...	1611	...	1640	1712	...	...	1741	1811	...	...	1840	1910	1941	2010	...	2040	2111	2249
Reading **129** d.	|	|	1440	|	...	|	1540	|	|	...	1641	|	|	1740	...	|	|	|	|	...	|	|	|
Birmingham New Street a.	1527	1548	1612	1627	...	1649	1712	1726	1750	...	1812	1827	1848	1912	...	1926	1948	2027	2049	...	2118	2148	2340
Birmingham New Street d.	1531	1603	1630	1631	...	1703	1730	1731	1803	...	1830	1831	1903	1931	...	1931	2003	2031	2103	...	...	2203	...
Manchester Piccadilly **129** a.	1659	|	|	1756	...	|	|	1856	|	...	|	1958	|	|	...	2100	|	2157	|	...	...	|	...
Tamworth a.	...	1619	|	...	...	|	|	...	1819	...	|	...	|	|	...	...	2019	...	2119	...	...	2219	...
Burton on Trent a.	...	|	|	...	...	1728	|	...	|	...	|	...	1926	|	...	...	|	...	2129	...	...	|	...
Derby a.	...	1638	1702	...	...	1740	1802	...	1839	...	1903	...	1940	2002	...	...	2038	...	2141	...	...	2240	...
Chesterfield a.	...	1702	|	...	...	1803	|	...	1904	...	|	...	2002	|	...	...	2102	...	2202	...	...	2304	...
Sheffield a.	...	1717	1749	...	...	1819	1845	...	1920	...	1940	...	2018	2041	...	...	2116	...	2218	...	...	2320	...
Doncaster a.	...	|	1814	...	...	|	1916	...	|	...	2016	...	|	2120	...	...	|	...	|	...	...	|	...
Wakefield Westgate a.	...	1744	1833	...	...	1847	|	...	1948	...	|	...	2049	|	...	...	2147	...	2244	...	...	|	...
Leeds a.	...	1802	1851	...	...	1904	|	...	2005	...	|	...	2106	|	...	...	2204	...	2302	...	...	0016	...
York a.	...	1827	1921	...	...	1929	1939	...	2030	...	2039	...	2131	2143	...	...	...	...	...	...	...	...	...
Darlington a.	...	1854	1948	...	...	1959	2010	...	2059	...	2113	...	...	2224	...	...	...	...	...	...	...	...	...
Durham a.	...	1911	2005	...	...	2017	2027	...	2117	...	2130	...	...	2241	...	...	...	...	...	...	...	...	...
Newcastle a.	...	1925	2019	...	...	2031	2041	...	2131	...	2144	...	...	2312	...	...	...	...	...	...	...	...	...
Alnmouth a.	...	1951	...	...	...	|	|	...	2159	...	...	...	...	...	...	...	...	...	...	...	...	...	...
Berwick upon Tweed a.	...	2012	...	...	...	2121	|	...	|	...	...	...	...	...	...	...	...	...	...	...	...	...	...
Edinburgh Waverley a.	...	2056	...	...	...	2212	2221	...	2304	...	...	...	...	...	...	...	...	...	...	...	...	...	...

		Ⓐ	Ⓐ	Ⓐ	Ⓐ	Ⓐ	Ⓐ	Ⓐ	Ⓐ	Ⓐ	Ⓐ	Ⓐ	Ⓐ	Ⓐ	Ⓐ	Ⓐ	Ⓐ	Ⓐ	Ⓐ	Ⓐ	Ⓐ	Ⓐ	Ⓐ
		T				MB		S				T		S					G	S		D	
Edinburgh Waverley d.	Ⓐ	...	...	...	...	...	...	...	...	...	...	...	...	...	...	0606	0700	...	0707	...	...	0810	...
Berwick upon Tweed d.		...	...	...	...	...	...	...	...	...	...	...	...	...	...	0647	0739	...	|	...	...	0851	...
Alnmouth d.		...	...	...	...	...	...	...	...	...	...	...	...	...	...	0708	0759	...	|	...	...	|	...
Newcastle d.		...	...	...	...	...	...	...	...	...	0625	...	0645	0725	...	0741	0835	...	0843	0935	...	0942	1035
Durham d.		...	...	...	...	...	...	...	...	...	0638	...	0658	0738	...	0755	0848	...	0856	0949	...	0956	1048
Darlington d.		...	...	...	...	...	...	...	...	...	0655	...	0715	0755	...	0812	0905	...	0913	1006	...	1013	1105
York d.		...	...	...	...	...	...	...	...	0640	0726	...	0743	0826	...	0845	0935	...	0945	1035	...	1045	1135
Leeds d.		...	...	...	...	...	0600	0616	...	0705	|	...	0811	|	...	0911	|	...	1011	|	...	1111	|
Wakefield Westgate d.		...	...	...	...	...	0612	0628	...	0719	|	...	0823	|	...	0923	|	...	1023	|	...	1124	|
Doncaster d.		...	...	...	...	...	|	0646	...	|	0756	...	|	0851	...	|	0958	...	|	1059	...	|	1158
Sheffield d.		...	...	0601	...	...	0652	0718	...	0753	0820	...	0856	0924	...	0955	1024	...	1055	1124	...	1155	1224
Chesterfield d.		...	...	0626	...	...	0706	0730	...	0806	0832	...	0908	|	...	1006	|	...	1107	|	...	1206	|
Derby d.		...	0610	0648	...	0706	0727	0750	...	0828	0853	...	0928	0953	...	1028	1053	...	1128	1153	...	1228	1253
Burton on Trent d.		...	0620	0658	...	0717	0738	0800	...	0838	|	...	0938	|	...	|	|	...	|	|	...	|	|
Tamworth d.		...	0631	0709	...	0730	0750	0811	...	0850	|	...	|	|	...	1048	|	...	|	|	...	1248	|
Manchester Piccadilly **129** d.		...	|	|	0600	|	|	|	0707	|	|	0807	|	|	0907	|	|	1007	|	|	1107	|	|
Birmingham New Street a.		...	0652	0727	0733	0754	0808	0827	0834	0910	0926	0933	1006	1027	1033	1109	1127	1133	1207	1227	1233	1308	1327
Birmingham New Street d.		0642	0712	0733	0742	0804	0812	0833	0842	0917	0933	0942	1017	1033	1042	1117	1133	1142	1217	1233	1242	1317	1333
Reading **129** a.		|	|	0908	|	0939	|	1011	|	|	1109	|	|	1211	|	|	1307	|	|	1411	|	|	1508
Cheltenham Spa a.		0721	0750	...	0824	...	0849	...	0924	0958	...	1024	1059	...	1124	1157	...	1224	1259	...	1324	1357	...
Bristol Parkway a.		0754	0826	...	0853	...	0925	...	0953	1030	...	1053	1130	...	1153	1229	...	1253	1330	...	1357	1429	...
Bristol Temple Meads a.		0805	0839	...	0914	...	0938	...	1008	1042	...	1110	1140	...	1205	1242	...	1309	1341	...	1408	1442	...
Plymouth **115** a.		...	1047	...	...	...	1146	...	...	1247	...	...	1338	...	...	1443	...	...	1540	...	...	1648	...

	Ⓐ	Ⓐ	Ⓐ	Ⓐ	Ⓐ	Ⓐ	Ⓐ	Ⓐ	Ⓐ	Ⓐ	Ⓐ	Ⓐ	Ⓐ	Ⓐ	Ⓐ	Ⓐ	Ⓐ	Ⓐ	Ⓐ	Ⓐ	Ⓐ	Ⓐ	Ⓐ
	X	G	S		GZ		T	AZ			GZ					C	G				S		G
Edinburgh Waverley d.	...	0908	...	...	1010	...	...	1106	...	...	1208	...	...	1306	...	...	1408	...	...	1508	...	...	1605
Berwick upon Tweed d.	...	0951	...	...	1049	...	...	1149	...	...	1248	...	...	|	...	...	1450	...	...	|	...	...	|
Alnmouth d.	...	|	...	...	|	...	...	1209	...	...	|	...	...	1409	...	...	|	...	...	|	...	...	1701
Newcastle d.	...	1044	1135	...	1144	1235	...	1241	1335	...	1342	1435	...	1442	1505	...	1541	1635	...	1641	1732	...	1741
Durham d.	...	1056	1149	...	1156	1248	...	1254	1349	...	1355	1448	...	1456	1518	...	1554	1648	...	1652	1748	...	1754
Darlington d.	...	1113	1206	...	1213	1305	...	1313	1406	...	1413	1505	...	1513	1535	...	1613	1705	...	1711	1805	...	1813
York d.	...	1145	1235	...	1245	1335	...	1345	1435	...	1445	1534	...	1545	1606	...	1645	1735	...	1745	1834	...	1845
Leeds d.	...	1211	|	...	1311	|	...	1411	|	...	1511	|	...	1611	1640	...	1711	|	...	1811	|	...	1911
Wakefield Westgate d.	...	1223	|	...	1323	|	...	1423	|	...	1523	|	...	1623	1652	...	1723	|	...	1823	|	...	1923
Doncaster d.	...	|	1259	...	|	1358	...	|	1459	...	|	1558	...	|	|	...	|	1759	...	|	1858	...	|
Sheffield d.	...	1255	1324	...	1355	1424	...	1455	1524	...	1555	1624	...	1654	1724	...	1758	1824	...	1858	1924	...	1954
Chesterfield d.	...	1307	|	...	1407	|	...	1507	|	...	1607	|	...	1707	|	...	1810	|	...	1910	|	...	2006
Derby d.	...	1328	1353	...	1428	1453	...	1528	1553	...	1628	1653	...	1728	1753	...	1829	1853	...	1929	1954	...	2028
Burton on Trent d.	...	1339	|	...	|	|	...	1538	|	...	|	|	...	1738	|	...	|	|	...	1938	|	...	|
Tamworth d.	...	|	|	...	1447	|	...	|	|	...	1647	|	...	|	|	...	1848	|	...	|	|	...	2047
Manchester Piccadilly **129** d.	1207	|	|	1307	|	|	1407	|	|	1507	|	|	1607	|	|	1705	|	|	1805	|	|	1907	|
Birmingham New Street a.	1333	1407	1427	1433	1507	1527	1533	1603	1627	1633	1709	1727	1733	1805	1827	1833	1908	1927	1933	2007	2027	2034	2107
Birmingham New Street d.	1342	1417	1433	1442	1517	1533	1542	1612	1633	1642	1712	1733	1742	1812	1833	1842	1912	1933	1942	2012	2033	2042	2112
Reading **129** a.	|	|	1611	|	|	1708	|	|	1808	|	|	1910	|	|	2008	|	|	2107	|	|	2217	|	|
Cheltenham Spa a.	1424	1458	...	1524	1558	...	1624	1651	...	1724	1751	...	1824	1852	...	1924	1950	...	2024	2051	...	2126	2151
Bristol Parkway a.	1453	1530	...	1555	1630	...	1653	1725	...	1754	1828	...	1853	1932	...	1958	2027	...	2055	2125	...	2201	223[illegible]
Bristol Temple Meads a.	1510	1541	...	1610	1641	...	1710	1739	...	1807	1841	...	1905	1943	...	2009	2041	...	2105	2136	...	2213	2243
Plymouth **115** a.	...	1740	...	...	1849	...	...	1945	...	...	2043	...	...	2146	...	...	2243	...	2313	2345	...	...	...

For footnotes see page 113.

XC Most trains 🍷 EDINBURGH - NEWCASTLE - YORK - BIRMINGHAM - BRISTOL 127

Service until September 7 (subject to alteration on ⑦ June 22 - July 27). For other services see Tables 121, 132, 170, 180 and 189.

		Ⓐ	Ⓐ	Ⓐ	Ⓐ G	Ⓐ G			⑥ T	⑥	⑥	⑥	⑥ MB	⑥ T	⑥ S	⑥ N	⑥	⑥	⑥ T	⑥ Z	⑥ S	⑥	⑥	⑥
Edinburgh Waverley	d.	...	1708	...	1805	2002	...	⑥	...	...	...	...	...	...	...	...	...	...	...	...	...	...	0608	0700
Berwick upon Tweed	d.	...	1751	...	1849	2045	...		...	...	...	...	...	...	...	...	...	...	...	...	...	...	0647	0740
Alnmouth	d.	...	|	...	1910	2105	...		...	...	...	...	...	...	...	...	...	...	...	...	...	...	0707	0800
Newcastle	d.	1835	1843	1935	1942	2134	...		...	...	...	...	...	...	...	...	...	0623	...	...	0735	...	0741	0835
Durham	d.	1848	1856	1950	1955	...	...		...	...	...	...	...	...	...	...	...	0638	...	...	0748	...	0754	0848
Darlington	d.	1906	1913	2007	2013	...	...		...	...	...	...	...	...	...	...	...	0655	...	...	0805	...	0813	0905
York	d.	1935	1945	2035	2045	...	...		...	...	...	...	...	...	...	...	0645	0727	...	0745	0835	...	0845	0935
Leeds	d.	|	2011	|	2111	...	...		...	...	...	...	...	0600	0616	...	0710	|	...	0811	|	...	0911	|
Wakefield Westgate	d.	|	2023	|	2123	...	...		...	...	...	...	...	0612	0629	...	0722	|	...	0824	|	...	0924	|
Doncaster	d.	1959	|	2102	|	...	...		...	...	...	...	...	|	0647	...	|	0756	...	|	0859	...	|	0958
Sheffield	d.	2024	2057	2129	2200	...	...		...	...	0545	...	...	0650	0718	...	0756	0820	...	0854	0923	...	0954	1023
Chesterfield	d.	|	2109	2141	2224	...	...		...	...	0557	...	...	0704	0730	...	0808	0832	...	0906	|	...	1006	|
Derby	d.	2054	2129	2202	2245	...	...		...	0610	0648	...	0706	0726	0750	...	0828	0853	...	0927	0952	...	1027	1052
Burton on Trent	d.	|	2140	|	2255	...	...		...	0620	0659	...	0717	0737	0800	...	0838	|	...	0941	|	...	|	|
Tamworth	d.	|	2150	|	2306	...	...		...	0631	0709	...	0730	0748	0811	...	0849	|	...	|	|	...	1048	|
Manchester Piccadilly **129**	d.	|	|	|	|	...	...		...	|	|	0600	|	|	|	0707	|	|	0807	|	|	0907	|	|
Birmingham New Street	a.	2129	2209	2251	2325	...	...		...	0650	0727	0733	0752	0808	0828	0834	0908	0927	0933	1003	1027	1033	1104	1127
Birmingham New Street	d.	...	2212	...	...	...	...		0642	0712	0733	0742	0804	0812	0833	0842	0912	0933	0942	1012	1033	1042	1112	1133
Reading **129**	a.	...	|	...	...	...	...		|	|	0907	|	0939	|	1006	|	|	1111	|	|	1207	|	|	1307
Cheltenham Spa	a.	...	2251	...	...	...	...		0724	0751	...	0824	...	0851	...	0924	0951	...	1024	1051	...	1124	1151	...
Bristol Parkway	a.	...	2320	...	...	...	...		0753	0824	...	0853	...	0924	...	0953	1029	...	1054	1125	...	1153	1229	...
Bristol Temple Meads	a.	...	2340	...	...	...	...		0805	0838	...	0906	...	0938	...	1004	1042	...	1109	1138	...	1204	1242	...
Plymouth **115**	a.	...	...	...	...	...	...		...	1039	...	...	...	...	...	1231	1240	...	...	1345	...	...	1439	...

		⑥	⑥ GT	⑥ S	⑥	⑥ DN	⑥	⑥ T	⑥ GZ	⑥ S	⑥	⑥ GZ	⑥	⑥	⑥ AZ	⑥	⑥	⑥ G	⑥	⑥	⑥	⑥	⑥ C	⑥ G
Edinburgh Waverley	d.	...	0707	...	...	0805	...	...	0908	...	...	1005	...	...	1108	...	...	1205	...	...	1309	...	...	1405
Berwick upon Tweed	d.	...	|	...	...	0847	...	...	0951	...	...	1047	...	...	1151	...	...	1246	...	...	|	...	...	1447
Alnmouth	d.	...	|	...	...	0909	...	...	|	...	...	|	...	...	1211	...	...	|	...	...	1409	...	...	|
Newcastle	d.	...	0842	0935	...	0942	1035	...	1044	1135	...	1142	1235	...	1243	1335	...	1344	1435	...	1444	1505	...	1541
Durham	d.	...	0856	0949	...	0956	1048	...	1056	1149	...	1155	1248	...	1256	1349	...	1356	1448	...	1456	1518	...	1554
Darlington	d.	...	0913	1006	...	1013	1105	...	1113	1206	...	1212	1305	...	1313	1406	...	1413	1505	...	1513	1535	...	1613
York	d.	...	0945	1035	...	1045	1135	...	1145	1235	...	1245	1335	...	1345	1435	...	1445	1535	...	1545	1606	...	1645
Leeds	d.	...	1011	|	...	1111	|	...	1211	|	...	1311	|	...	1411	|	...	1511	|	...	1611	1640	...	1711
Wakefield Westgate	d.	...	1024	|	...	1124	|	...	1224	|	...	1323	|	...	1424	|	...	1524	|	...	1624	1652	...	1723
Doncaster	d.	...	|	1059	...	|	1159	...	|	1259	...	|	1358	...	|	1459	...	|	1559	...	|	|	...	|
Sheffield	d.	...	1054	1123	...	1154	1223	...	1254	1323	...	1354	1423	...	1454	1523	...	1554	1623	...	1654	1723	...	1754
Chesterfield	d.	...	1106	|	...	1207	|	...	1306	|	...	1407	|	...	1506	|	...	1607	|	...	1706	|	...	1807
Derby	d.	...	1130	1152	...	1229	1252	...	1327	1352	...	1430	1453	...	1527	1552	...	1627	1653	...	1727	1752	...	1827
Burton on Trent	d.	...	1141	|	...	|	|	...	1338	|	...	|	|	...	1538	|	...	|	|	...	1738	|	...	|
Tamworth	d.	...	|	|	...	1249	|	...	|	|	...	1449	|	...	|	|	...	1648	|	...	|	|	...	1846
Manchester Piccadilly **129**	d.	1007	|	|	1107	|	|	1207	|	|	1307	|	|	1407	|	|	1507	|	|	1607	|	|	1706	|
Birmingham New Street	a.	1133	1207	1227	1233	1308	1326	1332	1404	1425	1433	1508	1527	1533	1604	1627	1633	1707	1727	1733	1807	1827	1833	1906
Birmingham New Street	d.	1142	1212	1233	1242	1312	1333	1342	1412	1433	1442	1512	1533	1542	1612	1633	1642	1712	1733	1742	1812	1833	1842	1912
Reading **129**	a.	|	|	1409	|	|	1508	|	|	1609	|	|	1708	|	|	1808	|	|	1908	|	|	2008	|	|
Cheltenham Spa	a.	1224	1249	...	1325	1351	...	1424	1451	...	1524	1551	...	1624	1650	...	1724	1751	...	1824	1851	...	1924	1951
Bristol Parkway	a.	1253	1324	...	1355	1426	...	1457	1524	...	1554	1629	...	1653	1725	...	1753	1829	...	1853	1925	...	1955	2029
Bristol Temple Meads	a.	1307	1338	...	1405	1440	...	1509	1538	...	1607	1642	...	1707	1738	...	1807	1842	...	1904	1938	...	2005	2042
Plymouth **115**	a.	...	...	...	...	1643	...	...	1739	...	...	1851	...	...	1942	...	...	2042	...	...	2138	...	...	2249

		⑥	⑥	⑥	⑥ S	⑥	⑥ G	⑥	⑥	⑥	⑥ G			⑦ Z	⑦	⑦	⑦	⑦	⑦	⑦	⑦	⑦ T	⑦ Z	⑦
Edinburgh Waverley	d.	...	...	1508	...	...	1605	...	1708	...	1808	...	⑦	...	...	...	...	...	...	0908	...	...	1008	...
Berwick upon Tweed	d.	...	...	|	...	...	|	...	1751	...	1851	...		...	...	...	...	...	...	0949	...	...	|	...
Alnmouth	d.	...	...	|	...	...	1703	...	|	...	1911	...		...	...	...	...	...	...	|	...	...	1105	...
Newcastle	d.	1635	...	1642	1732	...	1744	1835	1844	1935	1945	...		...	...	...	...	0935	...	1039	...	...	1140	...
Durham	d.	1648	...	1655	1748	...	1756	1849	1857	1950	1957	...		...	...	...	...	0948	...	1053	...	...	1153	...
Darlington	d.	1705	...	1713	1805	...	1813	1906	1914	2007	2014	...		...	...	...	...	1005	...	1110	...	...	1210	...
York	d.	1735	...	1745	1834	...	1845	1935	1945	2035	2045	...		...	...	...	0933	1033	...	1141	...	...	1241	...
Leeds	d.	|	...	1811	|	...	1911	|	2011	|	2111	...		...	0810	0900	1000	1100	...	1211	...	...	1311	...
Wakefield Westgate	d.	|	...	1823	|	...	1924	|	2023	|	2123	...		...	0823	0911	1012	1112	...	1224	...	...	1324	...
Doncaster	d.	1759	...	|	1859	...	|	1959	|	2059	|	...		...	|	0932	1030	1130	...	|	...	...	|	...
Sheffield	d.	1823	...	1858	1924	...	1954	2023	2054	2125	2154	...		...	0854	0957	1057	1157	...	1257	...	...	1359	1422
Chesterfield	d.	|	...	1910	|	...	2006	|	2106	2137	2206	...		...	0907	1009	1109	1209	...	1309	...	...	1409	1432
Derby	d.	1852	...	1929	1953	...	2027	2052	2127	2156	2226	...		...	0928	1033	1129	1229	...	1332	1355	...	|	1453
Burton on Trent	d.	|	...	1937	|	...	|	|	2138	|	2237	...		...	|	|	1140	|	...	1343	|	...	1448	|
Tamworth	d.	|	...	|	|	...	2046	|	2149	|	2247	...		...	|	1053	|	1248	...	|	|	...	|	|
Manchester Piccadilly **129**	d.	|	1805	|	|	1907	|	|	|	|	|	...		...	|	|	|	|	...	|	|	1307	|	|
Birmingham New Street	a.	1926	1933	2006	2027	2033	2103	2125	2206	2244	2306	...		...	1019	1121	1205	1306	...	1409	1427	1431	1505	1526
Birmingham New Street	d.	1933	1942	2012	2033	2042	2112	...	...	...	...	...		0912	1030	1130	1212	1312	1342	1412	1433	1442	1512	1533
Reading **129**	a.	2108	|	|	2212	|	|	...	...	...	...	...		|	|	|	|	|	|	|	1610	|	|	1701
Cheltenham Spa	a.	...	2024	2051	...	2124	2150	...	...	...	...	...		0950	1109	1209	1251	1351	1423	1450	...	1524	1551	...
Bristol Parkway	a.	...	2053	2120	...	2158	2230	...	...	...	...	...		1022	1139	1240	1320	1420	1453	1523	...	1559	1620	...
Bristol Temple Meads	a.	...	2104	2135	...	2212	2241	...	...	...	...	...		1033	1151	1251	1331	1431	1508	1534	...	1611	1635	...
Plymouth **115**	a.	...	...	2355	...	...	...	...	...	...	...	...		1237	1352	1452	1541	1641	...	1742	...	...	1838	...

		⑦	⑦	⑦	⑦	⑦ GZ	⑦	⑦	⑦ G	⑦	⑦ T	⑦ A		⑦	⑦	⑦ G	⑦	⑦	⑦ G	⑦	⑦	⑦	⑦	⑦ G
Edinburgh Waverley	d.	...	1105	...	...	1208	...	...	1308	1355	...	1410	...	...	...	1508	...	...	1608	...	...	1708	...	1808
Berwick upon Tweed	d.	...	1148	...	...	1248	...	...	|	1434	...	1449	...	...	...	|	...	...	|	...	...	1751	...	1851
Alnmouth	d.	...	1208	...	...	|	...	...	1408	|	...	|	...	...	...	|	...	...	1705	...	...	|	...	|
Newcastle	d.	...	1240	1335	...	1340	1435	...	1440	1523	...	1540	...	1635	...	1640	1735	...	1740	1825	...	1840	1926	1940
Durham	d.	...	1253	1348	...	1353	1449	...	1454	1536	...	1553	...	1648	...	1653	1748	...	1754	1837	...	1853	1939	1953
Darlington	d.	...	1310	1406	...	1410	1506	...	1511	1553	...	1610	...	1705	...	1710	1806	...	1811	1854	...	1910	1956	2010
York	d.	...	1341	1435	...	1441	1535	...	1541	1624	...	1641	...	1733	...	1741	1835	...	1841	1924	...	1941	2024	2041
Leeds	d.	...	1411	|	...	1511	|	...	1611	|	...	1711	...	|	...	1811	|	...	1911	|	...	2011	|	2111
Wakefield Westgate	d.	...	1423	|	...	1523	|	...	1623	|	...	1723	...	|	...	1823	|	...	1922	|	...	2023	|	2123
Doncaster	d.	...	|	1459	...	|	1559	...	|	1652	...	|	...	1759	...	|	1859	...	|	1954	...	|	2051	|
Sheffield	d.	...	1454	1524	...	1554	1624	...	1654	1724	...	1754	...	1824	...	1854	1924	...	1954	2021	...	2054	2120	2154
Chesterfield	d.	...	1506	|	...	1606	|	...	1706	|	...	1806	...	|	...	1906	|	...	2006	|	...	2106	2132	2206
Derby	d.	...	1526	1553	...	1627	1654	...	1726	1754	...	1826	...	1854	...	1927	1956	...	2027	2054	...	2126	2153	2226
Burton on Trent	d.	...	1537	|	...	|	|	...	1737	|	...	|	...	|	...	1938	|	...	|	|	...	2137	2203	2237
Tamworth	d.	...	|	|	...	1648	|	...	|	|	...	1845	...	|	...	|	|	...	2045	|	...	2147	2214	2247
Manchester Piccadilly **129**	d.	1407	|	|	1507	|	|	1607	|	|	1707	|	...	|	1807	|	|	1907	|	|	2007	|	|	|
Birmingham New Street	a.	1531	1602	1626	1631	1705	1726	1731	1802	1826	1831	1904	...	1928	1931	2005	2027	2031	2103	2126	2139	2205	2231	2305
Birmingham New Street	d.	1542	1612	1633	1642	1712	1733	1742	1812	1833	1842	1912	...	1933	1942	2012	2033	2042	2112	...	2142	2212	...	...
Reading **129**	a.	|	|	1809	|	|	1901	|	|	2009	|	|	...	2109	|	|	2208	|	|	...	|	|	...	...
Cheltenham Spa	a.	1624	1650	...	1724	1751	...	1824	1851	...	1924	1951	...	...	2024	2051	...	2124	2151	...	2223	2252	...	...
Bristol Parkway	a.	1654	1720	...	1802	1820	...	1854	1921	...	2003	2020	...	...	2056	2120	...	2159	2233	...	2252	2322	...	...
Bristol Temple Meads	a.	1708	1733	...	1813	1836	...	1908	1932	...	2014	2031	...	...	2106	2129	...	2210	2244	...	2306	2333	...	...
Plymouth **115**	a.	...	1943	...	...	2045	...	...	2141	...	...	2238	...	...	...	2347	...	...	...	...	...	...	...	...

or footnotes see pages 113 and 114.

128 LONDON - STRATFORD and BIRMINGHAM

2nd class CH

km	Ⓐ		Ⓐ	Ⓐ	Ⓐ	Ⓐ	Ⓐ	Ⓐ	Ⓐ	Ⓐ▲	Ⓐ	Ⓐ	Ⓐ	Ⓐ▲	Ⓐ	Ⓐ	Ⓐ	Ⓐ	Ⓐ	Ⓐ	Ⓐ▲	Ⓐ	Ⓐ	Ⓐ
0	**London** Marylebone ◇	d.	...	...	0605	0645	0715	0745	0815	0845	0915	0910	0945	1015	1045	1115	1145	1215	1218	1245	1315	1345	1415	1445
45	High Wycombe ◇	d.	...	...	|	0716	|	0809	|	0910	|	0944	1009	|	1109	|	1209	|	1241	1309	|	1409	|	1509
111	Banbury 129	d.	0605	...	0703	0800	0807	0844	0906	0946	1007	1024	1043	1107	1145	1206	1243	1307	1321	1343	1407	1444	1506	1544
143	**Leamington Spa** 129	d.	0624	0652	0721	0818	0824	0904	0925	1004	1025	1042	1101	1125	1204	1223	1301	1325	1339	1401	1425	1502	1523	1602
146	Warwick	d.	0629	0657	0726	0823	0829	0909	0930	1010	1032p	1047	1106	1132p	1209	1229p	1306	1332p	1343	1406	1431p	1506	1529p	1606
167	**Stratford upon Avon**	a.	|	0727	|	0857	|	|	|	|	|	1116	|	|	|	|	|	|	1418	|	|	|	|	|
169	Solihull	d.	0649	...	0751	...	0845	0931	0946	1032	1045	...	1124	1145	1231	1243	1324	1345	...	1426	1444	1525	1543	1626
180	**Birmingham** Moor Street	a.	0658	...	0802	...	0853	0942	0954	1044	1053	...	1132	1159	1241	1259	1332	1359	...	1434	1459	1533	1559	1634

		Ⓐ	Ⓐ	Ⓐ	Ⓐ	Ⓐ	Ⓐ▲	Ⓐ	Ⓐ▲	Ⓐ	Ⓐ	Ⓐ▲	Ⓐ	Ⓐ	Ⓐ	Ⓐ	Ⓐ	Ⓐ	Ⓐ	Ⓐ	Ⓐ	Ⓐ	Ⓐ	Ⓐ	Ⓐ
London Marylebone ◇	d.	1515	1518	1545	1615	1618	1647	...	1715	1718	1747	1815	1818	1847	1915	1945	2015	2018	2045	2115	2145	2215	2245	2307	2320
High Wycombe ◇	d.	|	1546	1609	|	|	|	...	|	|	|	|	|	|	|	2009	|	2045	2109	|	2209	|	2309	|	2355
Banbury 129	d.	1607	1631	1643	|	1720	1745	...	|	1820	1845	1910	1925	1945	2009	2043	2112	2137	2147	2214	2247	2313	2347	2350	0046
Leamington Spa 129	d.	1625	1652	1701	1722	1737	1803	1817	1822	1837	1903	1928	1943	2003	2027	2101	2130	2156	2205	2232	2305	2331	0005	0003	...
Warwick	d.	1632p	1657	1705	1728p	1741	1809p	1822	1828p	1841	1909p	1934p	1947	2008	2033p	2106	2135p	2201	2210	2238p	2309	2337p	0009	0025	...
Stratford upon Avon	a.	|	1732	|	|	|	|	1852	|	|	|	|	2017	|	|	|	|	2235	|	|	|	|	|	|	...
Solihull	d.	1645	...	1724	1741	1801	1825	...	1841	1901	1926	1951	...	2028	2049	2132	2151	...	2229	2254	2338	2353	0029	0041	...
Birmingham Moor Street	a.	1653	...	1735	1751	1810	1840	...	1849	1916	1938	1958	...	2036	2103	2140	2159	...	2237	2302	2346	0007	0043	0055	...

⑥		⑥	⑥	⑥	⑥	⑥	⑥	⑥	⑥	⑥	⑥	⑥	⑥	⑥	⑥	⑥	⑥	⑥	⑥	⑥	⑥	⑥	⑥	⑥
London Marylebone ◇	d.	...	0700	...	0800	0827	0906	0909	0936	1006	1036	1106	1109	1136	1206	1236	1306	1309	1336	1406	1436	1506	1509	1536
High Wycombe ◇	d.	0612	0724	...	0824	0856	|	0941	0959	|	1101	|	1141	1159	|	1301	|	1341	1359	|	1501	|	1541	1559
Banbury 129	d.	0702	0805	...	0908	0941	1002	1029	1039	1102	1141	1204	1232	1241	1302	1341	1402	1431	1441	1502	1541	1602	1632	1641
Leamington Spa 129	d.	0721	0823	0830	0926	0959	1021	1047	1059	1121	1159	1224	1251	1259	1321	1359	1421	1449	1459	1521	1559	1621	1651	1659
Warwick	d.	0725	0829p	0834	0930	1003	1027p	1051	1103	1127p	1203	1231p	1256	1303	1327p	1403	1427p	1454	1503	1527p	1603	1627p	1656	1703
Stratford upon Avon	a.	|	|	0909	|	|	|	1115	|	|	|	|	1333	|	|	|	|	1533	|	|	|	|	1732	|
Solihull	d.	0748	0845	...	0950	1023	1042	...	1123	1142	1223	1245	...	1323	1342	1423	1442	...	1523	1542	1623	1642	...	1723
Birmingham Moor Street	a.	0803	0859	...	1001	1033	1055	...	1133	1155	1233	1256	...	1333	1355	1433	1455	...	1533	1555	1633	1655	...	1733

		⑥	⑥	⑥	⑥	⑥	⑥	⑥	⑥	⑥	⑥	⑥	⑥	⑥	⑥		⑦	⑦	⑦	⑦	⑦	⑦	⑦	⑦	⑦
London Marylebone ◇	d.	1606	1636	1706	1709	1736	1806	1836	1906	1909	1936	2000	2036	2106	2208	...		0815	0906	0930	1006	1036	1106	1109	1136
High Wycombe ◇	d.	|	1701	|	1741	1759	|	1900	|	1941	2001	2025	2100	2129	|	...		0844	0934	|	|	1101	|	1143	1201
Banbury 129	d.	1702	1741	1803	1832	1841	1903	1941	2002	2034	2043	2105	2140	2212	2304	...		0928	1016	1031	1103	1141	1203	1231	1241
Leamington Spa 129	d.	1721	1759	1823	1851	1859	1923	1959	2021	2053	2100	2123	2157	2230	2323	...		0946	1034	1050	1121	1159	1221	1250	1258
Warwick	d.	1727p	1803	1829p	1856	1903	1929p	2003	2027p	2058	2105	2127	2202	2234	2327	...		0951	1038	1054	1125	1203	1227p	1254	1302
Stratford upon Avon	a.	|	|	|	1932	|	|	|	|	2132	|	|	|	|	|	...		|	|	1129	|	|	|	1329	|
Solihull	d.	1742	1823	1843	...	1923	1943	2029	2042	...	2124	2148	2222	2300	2348	...		1016	1058	...	1145	1229	1243	...	1323
Birmingham Moor Street	a.	1753	1835	1853	...	1935	1955	2039	2055	...	2135	2157	2234	2308	2359	...		1024	1106	...	1153	1204	1257	...	1331

		⑦	⑦	⑦	⑦	⑦	⑦	⑦	⑦	⑦	⑦	⑦	⑦	⑦	⑦	⑦	⑦	⑦	⑦	⑦	⑦	⑦	⑦	⑦	⑦
London Marylebone ◇	d.	1206	1236	1306	1309	1336	1406	1436	1506	1509	1536	1606	1636	1706	1709	1736	1806	1836	1906	1930	2006	2030	2100	2208	2310
High Wycombe ◇	d.	|	1301	|	1343	1401	|	1501	|	1543	1601	|	1701	|	1743	1801	|	1901	|	2001	2031	2101	2130	|	2344
Banbury 129	d.	1303	1341	1403	1431	1459	1503	1559	1603	1632	1641	1703	1741	1803	1845	1841	1904	1941	2003	2041	2105	2141	2210	2308	0035
Leamington Spa 129	d.	1321	1359	1421	1450	1503	1521	1603	1621	1651	1659	1721	1759	1821	1905	1859	1923	1959	2021	2059	2123	2159	2228	2326	...
Warwick	d.	1327p	1403	1427p	1454	1507	1527p	1607	1627p	1655	1703	1727p	1803	1827p	1909	1903	1929p	2003	2027p	2103	2127	2203	2232	2330	...
Stratford upon Avon	a.	|	|	|	1529	|	|	|	|	1730	|	|	|	|	1939	|	|	|	|	|	|	|	|	|	...
Solihull	d.	1343	1429	1443	...	1523	1543	1629	1643	...	1723	1743	1829	1843	...	1924	1946	2024	2043	2130	2147	2223	2258	2350	...
Birmingham Moor Street	a.	1357	1437	1457	...	1531	1557	1637	1657	...	1731	1757	1838	1857	...	1933	2000	2033	2057	2138	2203	2231	2307	2358	...

Ⓐ		Ⓐ	Ⓐ	Ⓐ	Ⓐ	Ⓐ	Ⓐ	Ⓐ	Ⓐ	Ⓐ	Ⓐ▲	Ⓐ	Ⓐ▲	Ⓐ	Ⓐ	Ⓐ	Ⓐ	Ⓐ	Ⓐ	Ⓐ	Ⓐ	Ⓐ	Ⓐ	Ⓐ▲
Birmingham Moor Street	d.	...	0515	...	...	0546	0610	...	...	0628	0655	...	0711	...	...	0755	0810	0825	0855	0915	...	0955	1015	1055
Solihull	d.	...	0524	...	...	0555	0619	...	...	0638	0704	...	0720	...	...	0805	0819	0837	0907	0924	...	1004	1024	1104
Stratford upon Avon	d.	...	|	...	...	|	|	...	0608	|	|	...	|	...	0733	|	|	|	|	|	0914	|	|	|
Warwick	d.	...	0536p	...	0555p	0609p	0634p	...	0640	0702	0717p	...	0737p	...	0803	0818p	0837	0906	0921p	0944	0948	1016p	1042	1116p
Leamington Spa 129	d.	...	0541	...	0603	0615	0640	...	0645	0706	0723	...	0744	...	0808	0824	0842	0911	0927	0949	0953	1022	1046	1122
Banbury 129	d.	0520	0559	...	0621	0633	0658	...	...	0724	|	0744	0803	0807	0825	|	0900	0930	|	1007	1013	1040	1104	1140
High Wycombe ◇	d.	0558	|	0708	|	|	|	0742	...	|	|	0830	|	0854	|	|	|	1006	|	1040	1102	|	1137	|
London Marylebone ◇	a.	0631	0701	0746	0732	0735	0800	0819	...	0828	0829	0902	0903	0928	0932	0936	0959	1036	1039	1108	1129	1134	1208	1234

		Ⓐ	Ⓐ	Ⓐ	Ⓐ	Ⓐ▲	Ⓐ	Ⓐ	Ⓐ	Ⓐ	Ⓐ	Ⓐ	Ⓐ▲	Ⓐ	Ⓐ	Ⓐ	Ⓐ	Ⓐ	Ⓐ	Ⓐ	Ⓐ	Ⓐ	Ⓐ	Ⓐ	Ⓐ
Birmingham Moor Street	d.	1115	...	1155	1215	1255	1315	1355	1415	...	1455	1515	1555	1615	1655	1710	...	1755	1815	1843	1914	2018	...	2118	...
Solihull	d.	1124	...	1203	1224	1304	1324	1404	1424	...	1504	1524	1604	1624	1703	1718	...	1805	1824	1852	1926	2027	...	2127	...
Stratford upon Avon	d.	|	1135	|	|	|	|	|	|	1435	|	|	|	|	|	|	1735	|	|	|	|	|	2049	|	2315
Warwick	d.	1142	1202	1215p	1242	1316p	1343	1416p	1442	1503	1516p	1543	1617p	1643	1718	1739	1802	1822p	1849	1906p	1949	2047	2116	2151	2334
Leamington Spa 129	d.	1146	1207	1220	1246	1322	1348	1422	1446	1508	1522	1547	1623	1648	1723	1743	1808	1828	1854	1912	1954	2052	2121	2156	2339
Banbury 129	d.	1204	1225	1238	1305	1340	1406	1440	1504	1526	1540	1605	1641	1706	1741	1802	1827	1846	1913	1932	2012	2113	2146	2214	2358
High Wycombe ◇	d.	1237	1305	|	1338	|	1439	|	1537	1605	|	1638	|	1739	|	1839	1913	1925	1958	2014	2045	2145	2226	2248	...
London Marylebone ◇	a.	1308	1333	1334	1408	1434	1508	1534	1608	1634	1636	1708	1742	1810	1847	1908	1949	1950	2030	2048	2112	2213	2301	2313	...

⑥		⑥	⑥	⑥	⑥	⑥	⑥	⑥	⑥	⑥	⑥	⑥	⑥	⑥	⑥	⑥	⑥	⑥	⑥	⑥	⑥	⑥	⑥	⑥
Birmingham Moor Street	d.	...	...	0615	0642	0715	0755	...	0815	0855	0915	...	0955	1015	1055	1115	...	1155	1215	1255	1315	...	1355	1415
Solihull	d.	...	...	0624	0651	0724	0805	...	0824	0905	0924	...	1005	1024	1104	1124	...	1205	1224	1305	1324	...	1405	1424
Stratford upon Avon	d.	...	...	|	|	|	|	0756	|	|	|	0914	|	|	|	|	1137	|	|	|	|	1337	|	|
Warwick	d.	...	...	0647	0705p	0743	0818p	0824	0844	0919p	0942	0948	1019p	1044	1115p	1144	1204	1221p	1244	1319p	1344	1404	1419p	1444
Leamington Spa 129	d.	...	...	0652	0711	0748	0824	0829	0849	0925	0948	0953	1025	1049	1121	1149	1209	1227	1249	1325	1349	1409	1425	1449
Banbury 129	d.	0604	0629	0710	0729	0807	0844	0850	0910	0945	1006	1013	1045	1110	1140	1210	1227	1245	1310	1343	1410	1427	1443	1510
High Wycombe ◇	d.	0649	0711	0751	|	|	|	0938	0951	|	1047	1106	|	1150	|	1250	1312	|	1350	|	1450	1512	|	1550
London Marylebone ◇	a.	0726	0742	0823	0830	0911	0947	1017	1020	1042	1114	1141	1147	1217	1244	1317	1347	1350	1417	1447	1517	1547	1550	1617

		⑥	⑥	⑥	⑥	⑥	⑥	⑥	⑥	⑥	⑥	⑥	⑥	⑥	⑥	⑥		⑦	⑦	⑦	⑦	⑦	⑦	⑦	⑦
Birmingham Moor Street	d.	1455	1515	...	1555	1615	1655	1715	...	1755	1845	...	1945	2045	...	2125	...		0825	0855	0915	...	0955	1015	1055
Solihull	d.	1505	1524	...	1605	1624	1705	1724	...	1805	1854	...	1954	2054	...	2134	...		0834	0904	0924	...	1004	1024	1104
Stratford upon Avon	d.	|	|	1537	|	|	|	|	1735	|	|	1937	|	|	2135	|	...		|	|	|	0938	|	|	|
Warwick	d.	1519p	1544	1604	1619p	1644	1719p	1744	1803	1820	1911	2009	2017	2117	2155	2201	...		0852	0919p	0942	1001	1019p	1047	1120p
Leamington Spa 129	d.	1525	1549	1609	1625	1649	1725	1749	1808	1825	1917	2017	2023	2122	2204	2205	...		0958	0925	0948	1006	1025	1052	1126
Banbury 129	d.	1543	1610	1627	1644	1710	1744	1810	1826	1844	1935	...	2046	2148	...	2223	...		0916	0943	1006	1024	1043	1110	1144
High Wycombe ◇	d.	|	1650	1712	|	1750	|	1850	|	|	2014	...	2126	2227	...	2306	...		|	|	1047	1106	|	1149	|
London Marylebone ◇	a.	1648	1722	1744	1747	1818	1847	1917	1924	1950	2040	...	2158	2300	...	2335	...		1021	1044	1117	1141	1144	1217	1244

		⑦	⑦	⑦	⑦	⑦	⑦	⑦	⑦	⑦	⑦	⑦	⑦	⑦	⑦	⑦	⑦	⑦	⑦	⑦	⑦	⑦	⑦	⑦	⑦
Birmingham Moor Street	d.	1115	...	1155	1215	1255	1315	...	1355	1415	1455	1515	...	1555	1615	1655	1715	...	1755	1815	1855	1918	...	2018	2118
Solihull	d.	1124	...	1204	1224	1304	1324	...	1404	1424	1504	1524	...	1604	1624	1704	1724	...	1804	1824	1904	1926	...	2027	2127
Stratford upon Avon	d.	|	1138	|	|	|	|	1338	|	|	|	|	1538	|	|	|	|	1738	|	|	|	|	2000	|	|
Warwick	d.	1142	1201	1219p	1247	1319p	1342	1401	1419p	1447	1519p	1542	1601	1619p	1647	1719p	1742	1801	1819p	1842	1919p	1951	2023	2046	2147
Leamington Spa 129	d.	1148	1206	1225	1252	1325	1348	1406	1425	1452	1525	1548	1606	1625	1652	1725	1748	1806	1825	1848	1925	1957	2028	2051	2152
Banbury 129	d.	1206	1224	1243	1310	1343	1406	1424	1443	1510	1543	1606	1624	1643	1710	1743	1810	1824	1843	1910	1943	2015	2048	2109	2215
High Wycombe ◇	d.	1247	1306	|	1349	|	1447	1506	|	1549	|	1647	1706	|	1749	|	1849	1906	|	1949	|	2100	2132	2153	2301
London Marylebone ◇	a.	1317	1341	1344	1417	1444	1517	1541	1544	1617	1644	1717	1740	1743	1817	1844	1917	1941	1944	2017	2043	2150	2208	2241	2347

LONDON - AYLESBURY

Subject to alteration from October 5

From **London Marylebone**:

Ⓐ: 0633, 0703, 0724, 0757, 0827, 0857, 0927, 0942, 1012 and every 30 minutes until 1612, 1627, 1642, 1711, 1730, 1742, 1759, 1811, 1832, 1843, 1859, 1918, 1933, 1955, 2021, 2042, 2112, 2142, 2212, 2242, 2312, 2357.

⑥: 0712, 0742 and every 30 minutes until 2012, 2112, 2212, 2312, 2357.

⑦: 0812, 0912, 1012, 1112, 1212, 1312, 1412, 1442, 1512, 1542, 1612, 1642, 1712, 1742, 1812, 1842, 1912, 1942, 2012, 2042, 2112, 2142, 2227, 2327.

From **Aylesbury**: Journey time: ± 55 - 60 minutes. *61 km*

Ⓐ: 0520, 0549, 0607, 0624, 0638, 0656, 0710, 0728, 0742, 0800, 0813, 0833, 0905, 093 and every 30 minutes until 1705, 1732, 1803, 1830, 1903, 1935, 2005, 2035, 2105, 2135, 2235.

⑥: 0605, 0705, 0735 and every 30 minutes until 1905, 2005, 2105, 2205.

⑦: 0735, 0835, 0905, 0935, 1005, 1035, 1135, 1235, 1335, 1435, 1505, 1535, 1605, 163 1705, 1735, 1805, 1835, 1905, 1935, 2005, 2035, 2105, 2135, 2235.

p – Warwick Parkway.
▲ – Conveys 'Business Zone' (supplement payable).
◇ – Frequent additional services are available between these stations.

XC Most services 🍸 BOURNEMOUTH - READING - BIRMINGHAM - MANCHESTER 129

Service until September 7 (subject to alteration on ⑦ June 22 - July 27).

Ⓐ

km		Ⓐ	Ⓐ	Ⓐ	Ⓐ	Ⓐ	Ⓐ	Ⓐ	Ⓐ	Ⓐ	Ⓐ	Ⓐ	Ⓐ	Ⓐ	Ⓐ	Ⓐ	Ⓐ	Ⓐ	Ⓐ	Ⓐ	Ⓐ	Ⓐ	Ⓐ
											C			T									T
0	**Bournemouth** 108 d.	...	...	...	...	...	...	...	...	...	...	0630	...	...	0730	...	...	0845	...	...	0945	...	...
25	Brockenhurst 108 d.	...	...	...	...	...	...	...	...	...	...	0649	...	...	0749	...	...	0900	...	...	1000	...	...
46	**Southampton** Central 108 d.	...	...	...	...	0515	...	...	0615	...	...	0715	...	...	0815	...	...	0915	0946	...	1014	...	...
54	**Southampton** Airport 108 d.	...	...	...	...	0522	...	...	0622	...	...	0722	...	...	0822	...	...	0922	0955	...	1022	...	...
67	Winchester 108 d.	...	...	...	...	0531	...	...	0631	...	...	0731	0801	...	0831	...	...	0931	1003	...	1031	...	...
97	Basingstoke 108 d.	...	...	...	...	0547	...	...	0647	...	...	0747	0818	...	0847	...	...	0947	1019	...	1047	...	...
122	**Reading** 131 d.	...	...	...	...	0610	0640	...	0709	0741	...	0809	0840	...	0909	0940	...	1010	1040	...	1110	1140	...
166	Oxford 131 d.	...	...	...	...	0636	0708	...	0736	0809	...	0836	0907	...	0936	1007	...	1036	1107	...	1136	1207	...
203	Banbury 128 d.	...	...	...	...	0654	0726	...	0756	0827	...	0854	0926	...	0956	1029	...	1054	1125	...	1153	1225	...
235	Leamington Spa 128 d.	...	...	...	...	0712	0743	...	0814	0844	...	0912	0943	...	1013	1047	...	1112	1143	...	1211	1243	...
250	Coventry 150 d.	...	...	...	...	0727	|	...	0826	|	...	0927	|	...	1027	|	...	1127	|	...	1227	|	...
267	Birmingham Intl 150 d.	...	...	...	...	0738	|	...	0838	|	...	0938	|	...	1038	|	...	1138	|	...	1238	|	...
	Bristol Temple Meads 127 d.	...	...	...	...	|	|	0700	|	|	0800	|	|	0900	|	|	1000	|	|	1100	|	|	1200
280	**Birmingham** New St 150 a.	...	...	...	...	0748	0815	0826	0848	0918	0926	0948	1018	1023	1048	1118	1126	1148	1218	1226	1248	1318	1326
280	**Birmingham** New St 150 d.	0557	0622	0657	0731	0757	0830	0831	0857	0930	0931	0957	1030	1031	1057	1130	1131	1157	1230	1231	1257	1330	1331
	York 127 a.	|	|	|	|	|	1039	|	|	1139	|	|	1239	|	|	1340	|	|	1439	|	|	1540	|
	Newcastle 127 a.	|	|	|	|	|	1145	|	|	1244	|	|	1345	|	|	1443	|	|	1545	|	|	1645	|
300	Wolverhampton 150 a.	0616	0641	0715	0749	0815	...	0849	0915	...	0949	1015	...	1049	1115	...	1149	1215	...	1249	1315	...	1349
326	Stafford 150 a.	0629	0653	0729	0800	0829	...	0900	0929	...	1000	1029	...	1100	1128	...	1200	1229	...	1300	1329	...	1400
352	Stoke on Trent 150 a.	0650	0713	|	0819	0854	...	0919	0954	...	1019	1054	...	1119	1154	...	1219	1254	...	1319	1354	...	1419
384	Macclesfield 150 a.	0711	0730	|	0836	0911	...	|	1011	...	|	1111	...	|	1211	...	|	1311	...	|	1411	...	|
403	Stockport 150 a.	0725	0745	0820	0850	0924	...	0949	1024	...	1049	1124	...	1149	1224	...	1249	1324	...	1349	1424	...	1449
412	**Manchester** Piccadilly 150 a.	0734	0759	0834	0859	0934	...	0959	1035	...	1059	1135	...	1159	1235	...	1259	1335	...	1359	1435	...	1459

	Ⓐ	Ⓐ	Ⓐ	Ⓐ	Ⓐ	Ⓐ	Ⓐ	Ⓐ	Ⓐ	Ⓐ	Ⓐ	Ⓐ	Ⓐ	Ⓐ	Ⓐ	Ⓐ	Ⓐ	Ⓐ	Ⓐ	Ⓐ	Ⓐ	Ⓐ	Ⓐ	Ⓐ
						Z		E				T						X						
Bournemouth 108 d.	1045	...	...	1145	...	...	1245	...	...	1345	...	...	1445	...	...	1545	...	...	1645	...	...	1745	...	1845
Brockenhurst 108 d.	1100	...	...	1200	...	...	1300	...	...	1400	...	...	1500	...	...	1600	...	...	1700	...	...	1800	...	1900
Southampton Central 108 d.	1115	1146	...	1215	...	...	1315	1346	...	1415	...	...	1515	1546	...	1615	...	...	1715	1746	...	1815	...	1915
Southampton Airport 108 d.	1122	1153	...	1222	...	...	1322	1353	...	1422	...	...	1522	1553	...	1622	...	...	1722	1753	...	1822	...	1922
Winchester 108 d.	1131	1202	...	1231	...	...	1331	1403	...	1431	...	...	1531	1602	...	1631	...	...	1731	1802	...	1831	...	1931
Basingstoke 108 d.	1147	1218	...	1247	...	...	1347	1419	...	1447	...	...	1547	1618	...	1647	...	...	1747	1818	...	1847	...	1947
Reading 131 d.	1210	1240	...	1310	1340	...	1410	1440	...	1509	1540	...	1610	1640	...	1709	1740	...	1810	1839	...	1909	1940	2010
Oxford 131 d.	1236	1307	...	1336	1407	...	1436	1507	...	1536	1607	...	1636	1707	...	1736	1807	...	1836	1913	...	1936	2007	2036
Banbury 128 d.	1254	1326	...	1354	1425	...	1457	1525	...	1555	1624	...	1655	1729	...	1755	1826	...	1855	1931	...	1956	2028	2054
Leamington Spa 128 d.	1312	1344	...	1412	1442	...	1514	1543	...	1612	1643	...	1713	1747	...	1812	1846	...	1912	1950	...	2013	2046	2112
Coventry 150 d.	1328	|	...	1427	|	...	1527	|	...	1627	|	...	1728	|	...	1827	|	...	1927	|	...	2027	|	2128
Birmingham Intl 150 d.	1339	|	...	1438	|	...	1538	|	...	1638	|	...	1739	|	...	1838	|	...	1938	|	...	2038	|	2139
Bristol Temple Meads 127 d.	|	|	1300	|	|	1400	|	|	1500	|	|	1600	|	|	1700	|	|	1800	|	|	1900	|	|	|
Birmingham New St 150 a.	1349	1418	1424	1448	1518	1423	1548	1618	1623	1648	1718	1723	1748	1818	1824	1849	1918	1923	1948	2017	2023	2048	2123	2148
Birmingham New St 150 d.	1357	1430	1431	1457	1530	1431	1557	1630	1631	1657	1730	1731	1757	1830	1831	1857	1930	1931	1957	2030	2031	2057	...	2157
York 127 a.	|	1639	|	|	1739	|	|	1902	|	|	1939	|	|	2038	|	|	2140	|	|	2252	|	|	...	|
Newcastle 127 a.	|	1745	|	|	1846	|	|	2001	|	|	2042	|	|	2144	|	|	2247	|	|	...	|	|	...	|
Wolverhampton 150 a.	1415	...	1449	1515	...	1550	1615	...	1649	1715	...	1750	1815	...	1849	1915	...	1949	2016	...	2049	2116	...	2216
Stafford 150 a.	1429	...	1500	1529	...	1601	1630	...	1700	1729	...	1801	1829	...	1900	1927	...	2000	2029	...	|	2131	...	2229
Stoke on Trent 150 a.	1454	...	1519	1554	...	1620	1654	...	1718	1754	...	1820	1854	...	1919	1954	...	2019	2054	...	2118	2154	...	2249
Macclesfield 150 a.	1511	...	|	1611	...	|	1711	...	|	1811	...	|	1911	...	|	2011	...	|	2111	...	|	2211	...	2307
Stockport 150 a.	1524	...	1549	1624	...	1649	1724	...	1749	1824	...	1849	1924	...	1948	2024	...	2048	2124	...	2147	2224	...	2321
Manchester Piccadilly 150 a.	1535	...	1559	1635	...	1659	1735	...	1758	1835	...	1859	1935	...	1959	2035	...	2058	2135	...	2159	2235	...	2335

	Ⓐ	Ⓐ	Ⓐ	Ⓐ		⑥	⑥	⑥	⑥	⑥	⑥	⑥	⑥	⑥	⑥	⑥	⑥	⑥	⑥	⑥	⑥	⑥	⑥
															C			T					
Bournemouth 108 d.	...	...	1945	...	...	...	...	...	...	...	...	...	...	0625	...	0637	...	...	0745	...	...	0845	...
Brockenhurst 108 d.	...	...	2000	...	...	...	...	...	...	...	...	...	...	0639	...	0655	...	...	0800	...	...	0900	...
Southampton Central 108 d.	...	...	2015	...	...	...	...	...	...	0509	...	...	0615	0653	...	0715	0747	...	0815	...	...	0915	0947
Southampton Airport 108 d.	...	...	2022	...	...	...	...	...	...	0516	...	...	0622	0701	...	0722	0754	...	0821	...	...	0922	0954
Winchester 108 d.	...	...	2031	...	...	...	...	...	...	0525	...	...	0631	0709	...	0731	0803	...	0831	...	...	0931	1003
Basingstoke 108 d.	...	...	2047	...	...	...	...	...	...	0541	...	...	0647	0725	...	0747	0819	...	0847	...	...	0947	1019
Reading 131 d.	2040	...	2110	2146	...	...	...	...	...	0610	0645	...	0710	0747	...	0810	0840	...	0910	0940	...	1010	1039
Oxford 131 d.	2109	...	2136	2230	...	...	...	...	...	0638	0712	...	0736	0815	...	0836	0907	...	0936	1007	...	1036	1107
Banbury 128 d.	2133	...	2154	2253	...	...	...	...	...	0656	0733	...	0754	0833	...	0854	0924	...	0954	1024	...	1054	1124
Leamington Spa 128 d.	2152	...	2211	2311	...	...	...	...	...	0714	0751	...	0812	0850	...	0912	0942	...	1012	1042	...	1112	1142
Coventry 150 d.	|	...	2224	2325	...	...	...	...	...	0727	|	...	0827	|	...	0927	|	...	1027	|	...	1127	|
Birmingham Intl 150 d.	|	...	2234	2336	...	...	...	...	...	0738	|	...	0838	|	...	0938	|	...	1038	|	...	1138	|
Bristol Temple Meads 127 d.	|	...	|	|	...	...	...	...	...	|	|	0700	|	|	0800	|	|	0900	|	|	1000	|	|
Birmingham New St 150 a.	2217	...	2245	0002	...	...	...	...	...	0748	0817	0825	0848	0918	0926	0948	1018	1025	1048	1118	1126	1148	1218
Birmingham New St 150 d.	...	2230	...	...	...	0557	0631	0657	0731	0757	0830	0831	0857	0930	0931	0957	1030	1031	1057	1130	1131	1157	1230
York 127 a.	...	|	...	...	...	|	|	|	|	|	1039	|	|	1139	|	|	1239	|	|	1339	|	|	1439
Newcastle 127 a.	...	|	...	...	...	|	|	|	|	|	1146	|	|	1245	|	|	1345	|	|	1443	|	|	1545
Wolverhampton 150 a.	...	2248	...	...	...	0616	0649	0715	0749	0815	...	0849	0915	...	0949	1015	...	1049	1115	...	1149	1215	...
Stafford 150 a.	...	2300	...	...	...	0629	0700	0729	0800	0829	...	0900	0929	...	1000	1029	...	1100	1129	...	1200	1229	...
Stoke on Trent 150 a.	...	2320	...	...	...	0650	0718	|	0819	0854	...	0919	0954	...	1019	1054	...	1119	1154	...	1219	1254	...
Macclesfield 150 a.	...	|	...	...	...	0711	0736	|	0836	0911	...	|	1011	...	|	1111	...	|	1211	...	|	1311	...
Stockport 150 a.	...	|	...	...	...	0725	0749	0820	0849	0924	...	0949	1024	...	1049	1124	...	1149	1224	...	1249	1324	...
Manchester Piccadilly 150 a.	...	0012	...	...	...	0734	0759	0834	0859	0935	...	0959	1035	...	1059	1135	...	1159	1235	...	1259	1335	...

	⑥	⑥	⑥	⑥	⑥	⑥	⑥	⑥	⑥	⑥	⑥	⑥	⑥	⑥	⑥	⑥	⑥	⑥	⑥	⑥	⑥	⑥	⑥	⑥
	P			T												T								
Bournemouth 108 d.	...	0945	...	...	1045	...	...	1145	...	...	1245	...	...	1345	...	...	1445	...	...	1545	...	...	1645	...
Brockenhurst 108 d.	...	1000	...	...	1100	...	...	1200	...	...	1300	...	...	1400	...	...	1500	...	...	1600	...	...	1700	...
Southampton Central 108 d.	...	1015	...	...	1115	1147	...	1215	...	...	1315	1347	...	1415	...	...	1515	1547	...	1615	...	...	1715	1747
Southampton Airport 108 d.	...	1022	...	...	1122	1154	...	1222	...	...	1322	1354	...	1422	...	...	1522	1554	...	1622	...	...	1722	1754
Winchester 108 d.	...	1031	...	...	1131	1203	...	1231	...	...	1331	1403	...	1431	...	...	1531	1603	...	1631	...	...	1731	1803
Basingstoke 108 d.	...	1047	...	...	1147	1219	...	1247	...	...	1347	1419	...	1447	...	...	1547	1618	...	1647	...	...	1747	1818
Reading 131 d.	...	1109	1140	...	1209	1239	...	1310	1340	...	1410	1439	...	1509	1540	...	1610	1639	...	1709	1740	...	1809	1839
Oxford 131 d.	...	1136	1207	...	1236	1307	...	1336	1407	...	1434	1507	...	1534	1607	...	1636	1707	...	1736	1807	...	1836	1907
Banbury 128 d.	...	1154	1224	...	1254	1324	...	1354	1424	...	1454	1524	...	1554	1624	...	1654	1724	...	1754	1824	...	1854	1924
Leamington Spa 128 d.	...	1212	1242	...	1312	1342	...	1412	1442	...	1512	1542	...	1612	1642	...	1712	1742	...	1812	1842	...	1912	1942
Coventry 150 d.	...	1227	|	...	1327	|	...	1427	|	...	1527	|	...	1627	|	...	1727	|	...	1827	|	...	1927	|
Birmingham Intl 150 d.	...	1238	|	...	1338	|	...	1438	|	...	1538	|	...	1638	|	...	1738	|	...	1838	|	...	1938	|
Bristol Temple Meads 127 d.	1100	|	|	1200	|	|	1300	|	|	1400	|	|	1500	|	|	1600	|	|	1700	|	|	1800	|	|
Birmingham New St 150 a.	1226	1248	1318	1326	1348	1418	1426	1448	1518	1526	1548	1618	1626	1648	1718	1726	1748	1818	1826	1848	1918	1926	1948	2018
Birmingham New St 150 d.	1231	1357	1330	1331	1357	1430	1431	1457	1530	1531	1557	1630	1631	1657	1730	1731	1757	1830	1831	1857	1930	1931	1957	2030
York 127 a.	|	|	1539	|	|	1639	|	|	1737	|	|	1902	|	|	1939	|	|	2039	|	|	2143	|	|	2255
Newcastle 127 a.	|	|	1645	|	|	1745	|	|	1843	|	|	2001	|	|	2042	|	|	2144	|	|	2247	|	|	...
Wolverhampton 150 a.	1249	1315	...	1349	1415	...	1449	1515	...	1549	1615	...	1649	1715	...	1749	1815	...	1849	1915	...	1949	2015	...
Stafford 150 a.	1300	1329	...	1400	1429	...	1500	1529	...	1600	1629	...	1700	1729	...	1800	1829	...	1900	1929	...	2000	2029	...
Stoke on Trent 150 a.	1318	1354	...	1419	1454	...	1519	1554	...	1619	1654	...	1719	1754	...	1819	1854	...	1919	1954	...	2019	2054	...
Macclesfield 150 a.	|	1411	...	|	1511	...	|	1611	...	|	1711	...	|	1811	...	|	1911	...	|	2011	...	2036	2111	...
Stockport 150 a.	1349	1424	...	1449	1524	...	1549	1624	...	1649	1724	...	1749	1824	...	1849	1924	...	1949	2024	...	2049	2124	...
Manchester Piccadilly 150 a.	1359	1435	...	1459	1535	...	1559	1635	...	1659	1735	...	1759	1835	...	1859	1935	...	1959	2035	...	2059	2135	...

– From/to Cardiff Central (Table **121**).
– From/to Derby (Table **127**).
– From/to Edinburgh (Table **127**).
– From/to Leeds (Table **127**).
M – From/to Nottingham (Table **121**).
N – From/to Newquay (Tables **115** and **127**).
P – From/to Plymouth (Tables **115** and **127**).
S – From/to Sheffield (Table **127**).
T – From/to Paignton (Tables **115** and **127**).
X – From/to Exeter (Tables **115** and **127**).
Z – From/to Penzance (Tables **115** and **127**).

129 BOURNEMOUTH - READING - BIRMINGHAM - MANCHESTER

Most services 🍸 XC

Service until September 7 (subject to alteration on ⑦ June 22 - July 27).

	⑥	⑥	⑥	⑥	⑥	⑥	⑥	⑥	⑥			⑦	⑦	⑦	⑦	⑦	⑦	⑦	⑦	⑦	⑦	⑦	⑦	⑦
		L	N																	T			P	
Bournemouth 108 d.	...	1745	...	...	1845	...	...	1945	...	...	⑦	...	...	...	...	0940	...	1040	...	...	1140	...	...	1240
Brockenhurst 108 d.	...	1800	...	...	1900	...	...	2000	...	...		...	...	...	...	0957	...	1057	...	...	1157	...	...	1257
Southampton Central 108 d.	...	1815	...	...	1915	...	...	2015	...	...		...	...	...	0915	1015	...	1115	...	...	1215	...	...	1315
Southampton Airport 108 d.	...	1822	...	...	1922	...	...	2022	...	...		...	...	...	0922	1022	...	1122	...	...	1222	...	...	1322
Winchester 108 d.	...	1831	...	...	1931	...	...	2031	...	...		...	...	...	0931	1031	...	1131	...	...	1231	...	...	1331
Basingstoke 108 d.	...	1847	...	...	1947	...	...	2047	...	...		...	...	...	0947	1047	...	1147	...	...	1247	...	...	1347
Reading 131 d.	...	1910	...	1940	2009	2040	...	2109	2140	...		...	...	0911	1011	1111	...	1211	1254	...	1311	1341	...	1411
Oxford 131 d.	...	1936	...	2007	2036	2107	...	2136	2207	...		...	...	0937	1037	1137	...	1237	1317	...	1337	1406	...	1437
Banbury 128 d.	...	1954	...	2029	2054	2125	...	2155	2229	...		...	...	0955	1055	1155	...	1255	1335	...	1355	1424	...	1455
Leamington Spa 128 d.	...	2012	...	2046	2112	2144	...	2212	2246	...		...	...	1012	1112	1212	...	1312	1352	...	1412	1442	...	1512
Coventry 150 d.	...	2027	...	|	2127	2156	...	2227	|	...		...	...	1028	1129	1228	...	1326	|	...	1426	|	...	1526
Birmingham Intl 150 d.	...	2038	...	|	2138	2211	...	2238	|	...		...	...	1040	1140	1240	...	1338	|	...	1438	|	...	1538
Bristol Temple Meads 127 d.	1900	|	1930	|	|	|	...	|	|	...		...	...	|	|	|	...	|	|	1300	|	|	1400	|
Birmingham New St 150 a.	2026	2048	2052	2116	2148	2221	...	2248	2317	...		...	...	1050	1151	1250	...	1348	1419	1427	1448	1511	1527	1548
Birmingham New St 150 d.	2031	...	2057	...	2157	...	2231	...	...	...		0901	1001	1101	1201	1301	1331	1401	1430	1431	1501	1530	1531	1601
York 127 a.	|	...	|	...	|	...	|	...	...	...		|	|	|	|	|	|	|	1640	|	|	1740	|	|
Newcastle 127 a.	|	...	|	...	|	...	|	...	...	...		|	|	|	|	|	|	|	1747	|	|	1841	|	|
Wolverhampton 150 a.	2049	...	2115	...	2215	...	2249	...	...	...		0919	1019	1119	1219	1319	1349	1419	...	1449	1519	...	1549	1619
Stafford 150 a.	2100	...	2130	...	2229	...	2301	...	...	...		0932	1032	1132	1232	1333	|	1433	...	|	1533	...	|	1634
Stoke on Trent 150 a.	2120	...	2153	...	2250	...	2320	...	...	...		|	1051	1151	1252	1356	1419	1456	...	1519	1556	...	1619	1656
Macclesfield 150 a.	2138	...	2211	...	2307	...	2338	...	...	...		|	1108	1209	1310	1414	|	1514	...	|	1614	...	|	1714
Stockport 150 a.	2153	...	2224	...	2320	...	2353	...	...	...		1021	1122	1222	1328	1428	|	1528	...	|	1628	...	|	1728
Manchester Piccadilly 150 a.	2204	...	2235	...	2330	...	0010	...	...	...		1037	1131	1240	1340	1440	1457	1540	...	1559	1640	...	1659	1740

	⑦	⑦	⑦	⑦		⑦	⑦	⑦	⑦		⑦	⑦	⑦	⑦		⑦	⑦	⑦	⑦		⑦	⑦	⑦	⑦
		P							Z															
Bournemouth 108 d.	...	...	1340	...	...	...	1440	...	...	...	1540	...	...	1640	...	...	...	1740	...	...	1840	...	1940	...
Brockenhurst 108 d.	...	...	1357	...	...	...	1457	...	...	...	1557	...	...	1657	...	...	...	1757	...	...	1857	...	1957	...
Southampton Central 108 d.	...	...	1415	...	...	...	1515	...	...	...	1615	...	...	1715	...	...	...	1815	...	...	1915	...	2015	...
Southampton Airport 108 d.	...	...	1422	...	...	...	1522	...	...	...	1622	...	...	1722	...	...	...	1822	...	...	1922	...	2022	...
Winchester 108 d.	...	...	1431	...	...	...	1531	...	...	...	1631	...	...	1731	...	...	...	1831	...	...	1931	...	2031	...
Basingstoke 108 d.	...	...	1447	...	...	...	1547	...	...	...	1647	...	...	1747	...	...	...	1847	...	...	1947	...	2047	...
Reading 131 d.	1440	...	1511	1540	...	...	1611	1641	...	...	1709	1740	...	1810	...	1841	...	1911	1940	...	2011	2040	2111	2134
Oxford 131 d.	1506	...	1537	1606	...	...	1637	1706	...	...	1737	1807	...	1837	...	1906	...	1937	2006	...	2037	2106	2137	2206
Banbury 128 d.	1525	...	1555	1625	...	...	1655	1725	...	...	1754	1825	...	1855	...	1924	...	1955	2024	...	2155	2124	2154	2224
Leamington Spa 128 d.	1543	...	1612	1643	...	...	1712	1743	...	...	1812	1843	...	1912	...	1942	...	2012	2042	...	2112	2141	2212	2242
Coventry 150 d.	|	...	1626	|	...	...	1726	|	...	...	1826	|	...	1926	...	1954	...	2026	2054	...	2126	2153	2223	2253
Birmingham Intl 150 d.	|	...	1638	|	...	...	1738	|	...	...	1838	|	...	1938	...	2004	...	2038	2104	...	2138	2203	2233	2303
Bristol Temple Meads 127 d.	|	1500	|	|	...	1600	|	|	1700	...	|	|	1800	|	...	|	1900	|	|	...	|	|	|	|
Birmingham New St 150 a.	1612	1627	1648	1712	...	1726	1748	1812	1827	...	1848	1912	1926	1948	...	2015	2027	2048	2115	...	2148	2214	2243	2313
Birmingham New St 150 d.	1630	1631	1701	1730	...	1731	1801	1830	1831	...	1901	2131	1931	2001	...	...	2031	2101	...	...	2201	...	...	...
York 127 a.	1921	|	|	1939	...	|	|	2039	|	...	|	2143	|	|	...	...	|	|	...	...	|	...	...	...
Newcastle 127 a.	2019	|	|	2041	...	|	|	2144	|	...	|	2312	|	|	...	...	|	|	...	...	|	...	...	...
Wolverhampton 150 a.	...	1649	1719	...	...	1749	1819	...	1849	...	1919	...	1949	2019	...	...	2053	2119	...	...	2220	...	...	...
Stafford 150 a.	...	|	1735	...	...	|	1835	...	|	...	1937	...	|	2036	...	...	|	2136	...	...	2236	...	...	...
Stoke on Trent 150 a.	...	1719	1756	...	...	1819	1856	...	1919	...	1956	...	2019	2056	...	...	2120	2156	...	...	2255	...	...	...
Macclesfield 150 a.	...	|	1814	...	...	|	1915	...	|	...	2014	...	|	2115	...	...	|	2214	...	...	2312	...	...	...
Stockport 150 a.	...	|	1828	...	...	|	1928	...	|	...	2028	...	|	2128	...	...	|	2227	...	...	2327	...	...	...
Manchester Piccadilly 150 a.	...	1756	1840	...	...	1856	1940	...	1958	...	2040	...	2100	2140	...	...	2157	2239	...	...	2341	...	...	...

		Ⓐ	Ⓐ	Ⓐ	Ⓐ	Ⓐ	Ⓐ	Ⓐ	Ⓐ	Ⓐ	Ⓐ	Ⓐ	Ⓐ	Ⓐ	Ⓐ	Ⓐ	Ⓐ	Ⓐ	Ⓐ	Ⓐ	Ⓐ	Ⓐ	Ⓐ	Ⓐ
					S		M	L				T					E							X
Manchester Piccadilly 150 d.	Ⓐ	...	...	0511	...	0600	...	...	0707	0727	...	0807	0827	...	0907	0927	...	1007	1027	...	1107	1127	...	1207
Stockport 150 d.		...	...	|	...	0608	...	...	0716	0735	...	0816	0835	...	0916	0935	...	1016	1035	...	1116	1135	...	1216
Macclesfield 150 d.		...	...	|	...	|	...	...	|	0749	...	|	0849	...	|	0949	...	|	1049	...	|	1149	...	|
Stoke on Trent 150 d.		...	...	0607	...	|	...	...	0744	0807	...	0844	0907	...	0944	1007	...	1044	1107	...	1144	1207	...	1244
Stafford 150 d.		...	...	0625	...	0700	...	...	0801	0826	...	0903	0926	...	1003	1026	...	1102	1125	...	1203	1226	...	1302
Wolverhampton 150 d.		...	...	0641	...	0716	...	...	0816	0841	...	0917	0941	...	1017	1041	...	1117	1141	...	1216	1241	...	1317
Newcastle 127 d.		...	...	|	...	|	...	...	|	|	0625	|	|	0725	|	|	0835	|	|	0935	|	|	1035	|
York 127 d.		...	...	|	...	|	...	...	|	|	0726	|	|	0826	|	|	0935	|	|	1035	|	|	1135	|
Birmingham New St 150 a.		...	...	0657	...	0733	...	...	0834	0858	0926	0933	0958	1027	1033	1058	1127	1133	1158	1227	1233	1258	1327	1333
Birmingham New St 150 d.		0604	0633	0704	0733	0742	0804	0833	0842	0904	0933	0942	1004	1033	1042	1104	1133	1142	1204	1233	1242	1304	1333	1342
Bristol Temple Meads 127 a.		|	|	|	|	0914	|	|	1008	|	|	1110	|	|	1205	|	|	1309	|	|	1408	|	|	1510
Birmingham Intl 150 d.		0614	|	0714	|	...	0814	|	...	0914	|	...	1014	|	...	1114	|	...	1214	|	...	1314	|	...
Coventry 150 d.		0625	|	0725	|	...	0825	|	...	0925	|	...	1025	|	...	1125	|	...	1225	|	...	1325	|	...
Leamington Spa 128 d.		0637	0700	0738	0759	...	0838	0900	...	0938	1000	...	1038	1100	...	1138	1201	...	1238	1300	...	1338	1400	...
Banbury 128 a.		0653	0718	0755	0815	...	0854	0918	...	0954	1017	...	1054	1117	...	1154	1217	...	1254	1321	...	1354	1417	...
Oxford 131 a.		0714	0741	0814	0839	...	0914	0941	...	1013	1041	...	1114	1141	...	1214	1241	...	1314	1341	...	1413	1440	...
Reading 131 a.		0741	0813	0839	0908	...	0939	1011	...	1039	1109	...	1139	1211	...	1239	1307	...	1339	1411	...	1439	1508	...
Basingstoke 108 a.		0808	0840	0908	...	...	1008	1038	...	1108	...	...	1208	1239	...	1308	...	...	1408	1439	...	1508	...	...
Winchester 108 a.		0824	0856	0924	...	...	1024	1054	...	1124	...	...	1224	1254	...	1324	...	...	1424	1454	...	1524	...	...
Southampton Airport 108 a.		0832	0908	0932	...	...	1032	1107	...	1132	...	...	1232	1308	...	1332	...	...	1434	1508	...	1532	...	...
Southampton Central 108 a.		0844	0917	0941	...	...	1043	1117	...	1143	...	...	1241	1317	...	1341	...	...	1442	1517	...	1541	...	...
Brockenhurst 108 a.		0859	...	0956	...	...	1058	...	...	1158	...	...	1256	...	...	1356	...	...	1456	...	...	1556	...	...
Bournemouth 108 a.		0914	...	1012	...	...	1112	...	...	1212	...	...	1310	...	...	1410	...	...	1511	...	...	1610	...	...

	Ⓐ	Ⓐ	Ⓐ	Ⓐ	Ⓐ	Ⓐ	Ⓐ	Ⓐ	Ⓐ	Ⓐ	Ⓐ	Ⓐ	Ⓐ	Ⓐ	Ⓐ	Ⓐ	Ⓐ	Ⓐ	Ⓐ	Ⓐ	Ⓐ	Ⓐ	Ⓐ	Ⓐ
						T									C			P						
Manchester Piccadilly 150 d.	1227	...	1307	1327	...	1407	1427	...	1507	1527	...	1607	1627	...	1705	1727	...	1805	1827	...	1907	1927	2007	...
Stockport 150 d.	1235	...	1316	1335	...	1416	1435	...	1516	1535	...	1616	1635	...	1713	1735	...	1813	1835	...	1916	1935	2016	...
Macclesfield 150 d.	1249	...	|	1349	...	|	1449	...	|	1549	...	|	1649	...	1727	|	...	1826	1854	...	|	1949	|	...
Stoke on Trent 150 d.	1307	...	1344	1407	...	1444	1508	...	1544	1607	...	1644	1707	...	1744	|	...	1844	1907	...	1944	2007	2044	...
Stafford 150 d.	1326	...	1402	1426	...	1503	1526	...	1603	1626	...	1703	1726	...	1804	1828	...	1902	1926	...	2004	2028	2103	...
Wolverhampton 150 d.	1341	...	1416	1441	...	1517	1541	...	1616	1641	...	1716	1741	...	1816	1841	...	1916	1941	...	2018	2044	2116	...
Newcastle 127 d.	|	1135	|	|	1235	|	|	1335	|	|	1435	|	|	1505	|	|	1635	|	|	1732	|	|	|	...
York 127 d.	|	1235	|	|	1335	|	|	1435	|	|	1534	|	|	1606	|	|	1735	|	|	1834	|	|	|	...
Birmingham New St 150 a.	1358	1427	1433	1458	1527	1533	1558	1627	1633	1658	1727	1733	1758	1827	1833	1858	1927	1933	1958	2027	2034	2100	2133	...
Birmingham New St 150 d.	1404	1433	1442	1504	1533	1542	1604	1633	1642	1704	1733	1742	1804	1833	1842	1904	1933	1942	2004	2033	2042	2104	...	2204
Bristol Temple Meads 127 a.	|	|	1610	|	|	1710	|	|	1807	|	|	1905	|	|	2009	|	|	2105	|	|	2213	|	...	|
Birmingham Intl 150 d.	1414	|	...	1514	|	...	1614	|	...	1714	|	...	1814	|	...	1914	|	...	2014	|	...	2114	...	2214
Coventry 150 d.	1424	|	...	1524	|	...	1624	|	...	1724	|	...	1824	|	...	1924	|	...	2024	|	...	2124	...	2225
Leamington Spa 128 d.	1438	1500	...	1538	1601	...	1638	1700	...	1738	1800	...	1837	1900	...	1938	2004	...	2038	2100	...	2138	...	2238
Banbury 128 a.	1454	1517	...	1554	1617	...	1654	1717	...	1754	1818	...	1854	1917	...	1954	2021	...	2054	2117	...	2154	...	2254
Oxford 131 a.	1513	1541	...	1613	1640	...	1713	1740	...	1815	1840	...	1913	1939	...	2013	2039	...	2113	2140	...	2214	...	2314
Reading 131 a.	1540	1611	...	1639	1708	...	1739	1808	...	1840	1910	...	1941	2008	...	2039	2107	...	2141	2217	...	2241	...	2349
Basingstoke 108 a.	1608	1639	...	1708	...	...	1808	...	...	1908	...	...	2009	...	...	2109	...	...	2209	2239	...	2305	...	...
Winchester 108 a.	1624	1659	...	1724	...	...	1824	...	...	1924	...	...	2024	...	...	2124	...	...	2224	2256	...	2324	...	...
Southampton Airport 108 a.	1632	1707	...	1732	...	...	1832	...	...	1932	...	...	2032	...	...	2132	...	...	2232	2312	...	2336	...	...
Southampton Central 108 a.	1641	1717	...	1741	...	...	1844	...	...	1941	...	...	2041	...	...	2140	...	...	2242	2320	...	2343	...	...
Brockenhurst 108 a.	1656	...	...	1756	...	...	1858	...	...	1956	...	...	2058	...	...	2155	...	...	2256	...	...	...	...	...
Bournemouth 108 a.	1710	...	...	1815	...	...	1913	...	...	2012	...	...	2115	...	...	2215	...	...	2321	...	...	...	...	...

For footnotes see page 117.

XC Most services 🍷 **BOURNEMOUTH - READING - BIRMINGHAM - MANCHESTER** **129**

Service until September 7 (subject to alteration on ⑦ June 22 - July 27).

	Ⓐ	Ⓐ	Ⓐ			⑥	⑥	⑥	⑥ S	⑥	⑥ M	⑥ L	⑥ N	⑥	⑥	⑥ T	⑥	⑥	⑥	⑥	⑥ E	⑥	⑥	⑥
Manchester Piccadilly .... 150 d.	2027	2127	2207	...	⑥	...	...	0511	...	0600	...	...	0707	0727	...	0807	0827	...	0907	0927	...	1007	1027	...
Stockport .... 150 d.	2035	2135	2216	...		...	...	|	...	0608	...	...	0716	0735	...	0816	0835	...	0916	0935	...	1016	1035	...
Macclesfield .... 150 d.	2049	2149	2229	...		...	...	|	...	0621	...	...	|	0749	...	|	0849	...	|	0949	...	|	1049	...
Stoke on Trent .... 150 d.	2107	2208	2247	...		...	...	0608	...	0639	...	...	0744	0807	...	0844	0907	...	0944	1007	...	1044	1107	...
Stafford .... 150 d.	2125	2226	2309	...		...	...	0626	...	0658	...	...	0803	0826	...	0903	0926	...	1003	1026	...	1103	1126	...
Wolverhampton .... 150 d.	2141	2241	2322	...		...	...	0641	...	0716	...	...	0816	0841	...	0916	0941	...	1016	1041	...	1116	1141	...
Newcastle 127 .... d.	|	|	|	...		...	...	|	...	|	...	...	|	|	0623	|	|	0735	|	|	0835	|	|	0935
York 127 .... d.	|	|	|	...		...	...	|	...	|	...	...	|	|	0727	|	|	0835	|	|	0935	|	|	1035
Birmingham New St ...... 150 a.	2200	2258	2339	...		...	...	0657	...	0733	...	...	0834	0858	0927	0933	0958	1027	1033	1058	1127	1133	1159	1227
Birmingham New St ...... 150 d.	...	...	...	...		0604	0633	0704	0733	0742	0804	0833	0842	0904	0933	0942	1004	1033	1042	1104	1133	1142	1204	1233
Bristol Temple Meads 127 .. a.	...	...	...	...		|	|	|	|	0906	|	|	1004	|	|	1109	|	|	1204	|	|	1307	|	|
Birmingham Intl .... 150 d.	...	...	...	...		0614	|	0714	|	...	0814	|	...	0914	|	...	1014	|	...	1114	|	...	1214	|
Coventry .... 150 d.	...	...	...	...		0625	|	0725	|	...	0825	|	...	0925	|	...	1025	|	...	1125	|	...	1225	|
Leamington Spa .... 128 d.	...	...	...	...		0638	0700	0738	0800	...	0838	0900	...	0938	1000	...	1038	1100	...	1138	1200	...	1238	1302
Banbury .... 128 a.	...	...	...	...		0654	0717	0754	0817	...	0854	0917	...	0954	1017	...	1054	1117	...	1154	1217	...	1254	1319
Oxford .... 131 a.	...	...	...	...		0714	0740	0814	0840	...	0914	0940	...	1014	1040	...	1114	1140	...	1214	1240	...	1314	1340
Reading .... 131 a.	...	...	...	...		0739	0806	0839	0907	...	0939	1006	...	1041	1111	...	1139	1207	...	1240	1307	...	1339	1409
Basingstoke .... 108 a.	...	...	...	...		0808	0839	0908	...	...	1008	1039	...	1108	...	...	1208	1240	...	1308	...	...	1408	1440
Winchester .... 108 a.	...	...	...	...		0824	0854	0924	...	...	1024	1054	...	1124	...	...	1224	1255	...	1324	...	...	1424	1455
Southampton Airport ..... 108 a.	...	...	...	...		0832	0908	0932	...	...	1032	1108	...	1132	...	...	1232	1308	...	1332	...	...	1432	1508
Southampton Central .... 108 a.	...	...	...	...		0841	0917	0939	...	...	1041	1117	...	1141	...	...	1241	1317	...	1341	...	...	1441	1517
Brockenhurst .... 108 a.	...	...	...	...		0856	...	0957	...	...	1057	...	...	1157	...	...	1257	...	...	1357	...	...	1457	...
Bournemouth .... 108 a.	...	...	...	...		0914	...	1011	...	...	1112	...	...	1211	...	...	1311	...	...	1411	...	...	1511	...

	⑥	⑥	⑥	⑥ T	⑥	⑥	⑥	⑥	⑥	⑥	⑥	⑥	⑥	⑥	⑥	⑥	⑥	⑥	⑥ C	⑥	⑥	⑥	⑥	⑥
Manchester Piccadilly .... 150 d.	1107	1127	...	1207	1227	...	1307	1327	...	1407	1427	...	1507	1527	...	1607	1627	...	1706	1727	...	1805	1827	...
Stockport .... 150 d.	1116	1135	...	1216	1235	...	1316	1335	...	1416	1435	...	1516	1535	...	1616	1635	...	1715	1736	...	1813	1835	...
Macclesfield .... 150 d.	|	1149	...	|	1249	...	|	1349	...	|	1449	...	|	1549	...	|	1649	...	1727	|	...	1826	|	...
Stoke on Trent .... 150 d.	1144	1207	...	1244	1307	...	1344	1407	...	1444	1507	...	1544	1607	...	1644	1707	...	1745	1807	...	1844	1907	...
Stafford .... 150 d.	1203	1225	...	1303	1326	...	1403	1426	...	1503	1526	...	1603	1625	...	1703	1726	...	1804	1826	...	1903	1926	...
Wolverhampton .... 150 d.	1216	1241	...	1316	1341	...	1416	1441	...	1516	1541	...	1617	1641	...	1717	1741	...	1816	1841	...	1916	1941	...
Newcastle 127 .... d.	|	|	1035	|	|	1135	|	|	1235	|	|	1335	|	|	1435	|	|	1505	|	|	1635	|	|	1732
York 127 .... d.	|	|	1135	|	|	1235	|	|	1335	|	|	1435	|	|	1535	|	|	1606	|	|	1735	|	|	1834
Birmingham New St ...... 150 a.	1233	1258	1326	1333	1358	1425	1433	1458	1527	1533	1558	1627	1633	1658	1727	1733	1758	1827	1833	1858	1926	1933	1959	2027
Birmingham New St ...... 150 d.	1242	1304	1333	1342	1404	1433	1442	1504	1533	1542	1604	1633	1642	1704	1733	1742	1804	1833	1842	1904	1933	1942	2004	2033
Bristol Temple Meads 127 .. a.	1405	|	|	1509	|	|	1607	|	|	1707	|	|	1807	|	|	1904	|	|	2005	|	|	2104	|	|
Birmingham Intl .... 150 d.	...	1314	|	...	1414	|	...	1514	|	...	1614	|	...	1714	|	...	1814	|	...	1914	|	...	2014	|
Coventry .... 150 d.	...	1325	|	...	1425	|	...	1525	|	...	1625	|	...	1725	|	...	1825	|	...	1925	|	...	2025	|
Leamington Spa .... 128 d.	...	1338	1400	...	1438	1500	...	1538	1602	...	1638	1700	...	1738	1802	...	1838	1900	...	1938	2003	...	2038	2100
Banbury .... 128 a.	...	1354	1416	...	1454	1519	...	1554	1619	...	1654	1717	...	1754	1818	...	1854	1917	...	1954	2018	...	2054	2119
Oxford .... 131 a.	...	1414	1440	...	1514	1540	...	1614	1640	...	1714	1741	...	1814	1840	...	1914	1940	...	2014	2040	...	2114	2141
Reading .... 131 a.	...	1440	1508	...	1539	1609	...	1640	1708	...	1739	1808	...	1840	1908	...	1939	2008	...	2040	2108	...	2138	2209
Basingstoke .... 108 a.	...	1508	...	...	1608	1640	...	1708	...	...	1808	...	...	1908	...	...	2008	...	...	2108	...	...	2209	2239
Winchester .... 108 a.	...	1524	...	...	1624	1655	...	1724	...	...	1824	...	...	1924	...	...	2024	...	...	2124	...	...	2224	2256
Southampton Airport ..... 108 a.	...	1532	...	...	1632	1708	...	1732	...	...	1832	...	...	1932	...	...	2032	...	...	2132	...	...	2232	2312
Southampton Central .... 108 a.	...	1541	...	...	1641	1717	...	1741	...	...	1841	...	...	1941	...	...	2041	...	...	2141	...	...	2240	2320
Brockenhurst .... 108 a.	...	1557	...	...	1657	...	...	1757	...	...	1857	...	...	1957	...	...	2057	...	...	2157	...	...	2256	...
Bournemouth .... 108 a.	...	1611	...	...	1711	...	...	1811	...	...	1911	...	...	2011	...	...	2111	...	...	2215	...	...	2320	...

	⑥	⑥	⑥	⑥	⑥	⑥			⑦	⑦	⑦	⑦	⑦	⑦	⑦	⑦	⑦ D	⑦ T	⑦	⑦ S	⑦	⑦	⑦	⑦
Manchester Piccadilly .... 150 d.	1907	1927	2007	2027	2107	2127	...	⑦	...	0827	0927	1027	...	1127	...	1226	...	1307	1327	...	1407	1427	...	1507
Stockport .... 150 d.	1916	1935	2016	2035	|	2135	...		...	0836	0936	1036	...	1136	...	1235	...	|	1336	...	|	1436	...	|
Macclesfield .... 150 d.	|	1949	|	2049	|	2149	...		...	|	0949	1049	...	1149	...	1249	...	|	1349	...	|	1449	...	|
Stoke on Trent .... 150 d.	1944	2007	2044	2107	2144	2207	...		...	|	1007	1107	...	1207	...	1307	...	1343	1407	...	1443	1507	...	1543
Stafford .... 150 d.	2003	2026	2103	2127	2203	2229	...		...	0926	1027	1128	...	1225	...	1325	...	|	1425	...	|	1525	...	|
Wolverhampton .... 150 d.	2016	2041	2116	2142	2216	2244	...		...	0941	1043	1142	...	1241	...	1341	...	1415	1441	...	1515	1541	...	1615
Newcastle 127 .... d.	|	|	|	|	|	|	...		...	|	|	|	...	|	...	|	...	|	|	...	|	|	1335	|
York 127 .... d.	|	|	|	|	|	|	...		...	|	|	|	...	|	...	|	...	|	|	...	|	|	1435	|
Birmingham New St ...... 150 a.	2033	2058	2132	2159	2232	2301	...		...	0958	1059	1158	...	1258	...	1358	...	1431	1458	...	1531	1558	1626	1631
Birmingham New St ...... 150 d.	2042	2104	...	...	...	...	...		0904	1004	1104	1204	1233	1304	1333	1404	1433	1442	1504	1533	1542	1604	1633	1642
Bristol Temple Meads 127 .. a.	2212	|	...	...	...	...	...		|	|	|	|	|	|	|	|	|	1611	|	|	1708	|	|	1813
Birmingham Intl .... 150 d.	...	2114	...	...	...	...	...		0914	1014	1114	1214	|	1314	|	1414	|	...	1514	|	...	1614	|	...
Coventry .... 150 d.	...	2125	...	...	...	...	...		0925	1025	1125	1225	|	1325	|	1425	|	...	1525	|	...	1625	|	...
Leamington Spa .... 128 d.	...	2138	...	...	...	...	...		0938	1038	1138	1238	1307	1338	1359	1438	1507	...	1538	1559	...	1638	1707	...
Banbury .... 128 a.	...	2154	...	...	...	...	...		0954	1054	1154	1254	1323	1354	1415	1454	1525	...	1554	1615	...	1654	1712	...
Oxford .... 131 a.	...	2216	...	...	...	...	...		1014	1114	1214	1314	1343	1414	1435	1514	1546	...	1614	1635	...	1714	1743	...
Reading .... 131 a.	...	2241	...	...	...	...	...		1047	1139	1240	1345	1409	1441	1501	1539	1610	...	1646	1701	...	1738	1809	...
Basingstoke .... 108 a.	...	2307	...	...	...	...	...		1109	1209	1309	1409	...	1509	...	1609	...	...	1709	...	...	1809	...	...
Winchester .... 108 a.	...	2324	...	...	...	...	...		1124	1224	1324	1424	...	1524	...	1624	...	...	1724	...	...	1824	...	...
Southampton Airport ..... 108 a.	...	2332	...	...	...	...	...		1133	1233	1333	1433	...	1533	...	1633	...	...	1733	...	...	1833	...	...
Southampton Central .... 108 a.	...	2341	...	...	...	...	...		1142	1242	1342	1442	...	1542	...	1642	...	...	1740	...	...	1842	...	...
Brockenhurst .... 108 a.	...	...	...	...	...	...	...		1202	1302	1401	1503	...	1602	...	1702	...	...	1802	...	...	1901	...	...
Bournemouth .... 108 a.	...	...	...	...	...	...	...		1226	1326	1426	1526	...	1626	...	1726	...	...	1826	...	...	1926	...	...

	⑦	⑦	⑦		⑦	⑦ E	⑦ T		⑦	⑦	⑦		⑦		⑦	⑦	⑦		⑦	⑦	⑦			
Manchester Piccadilly .... 150 d.	1527	...	1607	...	1627	...	1707	...	1727	...	1807	...	1827	...	...	1907	1927	...	2007	2107	2207	...	...	...
Stockport .... 150 d.	1536	...	|	...	1636	...	|	...	1736	...	|	...	1836	...	...	|	1936	...	2016	2116	2216	...	...	...
Macclesfield .... 150 d.	1549	...	|	...	1649	...	|	...	1749	...	|	...	1849	...	...	|	1949	...	2029	2129	2229	...	...	...
Stoke on Trent .... 150 d.	1607	...	1643	...	1708	...	1743	...	1808	...	1843	...	1907	...	...	1943	2007	...	2047	2147	2247	...	...	...
Stafford .... 150 d.	1625	...	|	...	1726	...	|	...	1827	...	|	...	1925	...	...	|	2027	...	2109	2206	2305	...	...	...
Wolverhampton .... 150 d.	1641	...	1715	...	1741	...	1815	...	1841	...	1915	...	1941	...	...	2015	2041	...	2122	2222	2319	...	...	...
Newcastle 127 .... d.	|	1435	|	...	|	1523	|	...	|	1635	|	...	|	...	1735	|	|	...	|	|	|	...	...	...
York 127 .... d.	|	1535	|	...	|	1624	|	...	|	1733	|	...	|	...	1835	|	|	...	|	|	|	...	...	...
Birmingham New St ...... 150 a.	1658	1726	1731	...	1758	1826	1831	...	1858	1928	1931	...	1958	...	2027	2031	2058	...	2139	2240	2336	...	...	...
Birmingham New St ...... 150 d.	1704	1733	1742	...	1804	1833	1842	...	1904	1933	1942	...	2004	...	2033	2042	2104	...	2142	...	...	...	...	...
Bristol Temple Meads 127 .. a.	|	|	1908	...	|	|	2014	...	|	|	2106	...	|	...	|	2210	|	...	2306	...	...	...	...	...
Birmingham Intl .... 150 d.	1714	|	...	...	1814	|	...	...	1914	|	...	...	2014	...	|	...	2114	...	...	...	...	...	...	...
Coventry .... 150 d.	1725	|	...	...	1825	|	...	...	1925	|	...	...	2025	...	|	...	2124	...	...	...	...	...	...	...
Leamington Spa .... 128 d.	1738	1759	...	...	1838	1907	...	...	1938	2007	...	...	2038	...	2100	...	2135	...	...	...	...	...	...	...
Banbury .... 128 a.	1754	1816	...	...	1854	1923	...	...	1954	2024	...	...	2054	...	2117	...	...	...	...	...	...	...	...	...
Oxford .... 131 a.	1814	1935	...	...	1914	1943	...	...	2014	2043	...	...	2114	...	2137	...	2208	...	...	...	...	...	...	...
Reading .... 131 a.	1839	1901	...	...	1939	2009	...	...	2039	2109	...	...	2142	...	2208	...	2233	...	...	...	...	...	...	...
Basingstoke .... 108 a.	1909	...	...	...	2009	...	...	...	2109	...	...	...	2209	...	...	...	...	...	...	...	...	...	...	...
Winchester .... 108 a.	1924	...	...	...	2024	...	...	...	2124	...	...	...	2224	...	...	...	...	...	...	...	...	...	...	...
Southampton Airport ..... 108 a.	1933	...	...	...	2033	...	...	...	2133	...	...	...	2233	...	...	...	...	...	...	...	...	...	...	...
Southampton Central .... 108 a.	1940	...	...	...	2041	...	...	...	2143	...	...	...	2242	...	...	...	...	...	...	...	...	...	...	...
Brockenhurst .... 108 a.	2002	...	...	...	2102	...	...	...	2202	...	...	...	...	...	...	...	...	...	...	...	...	...	...	...
Bournemouth .... 108 a.	2026	...	...	...	2126	...	...	...	2226	...	...	...	...	...	...	...	...	...	...	...	...	...	...	...

For footnotes see page 117.

130 LONDON - WORCESTER - HEREFORD GW

Subject to alteration on ⑥ September 13 - October 18, and on ⑦ August 3 - September 7.

km		Ⓐ	Ⓐ	Ⓐ	Ⓐ	Ⓐ	Ⓐ	Ⓐ	Ⓐ	Ⓐ	Ⓐ	Ⓐ	Ⓐ	Ⓐ	Ⓐ	Ⓐ	Ⓐ	Ⓐ	Ⓐ	
0	**London** Paddington ..... 131 d.	0545	0648	0822	0921	0950	1022	1120	1221	1321	1421	1552	...	1722	1749	1822	1922	2022	2148	...
58	Reading ..... 131 d.	0617	0719	0852	0952	1022	1052	1152	1252	1352	1452	1622u	...	1750	1822	1851	1952	2053	2225	...
103	**Oxford** ..... 131 d.	0651	0804	0921	1025	1048	1119	1219	1325	1419	1520	1649	1732	1817	1849	1923	2020a	2121	2253	...
148	Moreton in Marsh ..... d.	0728	0839	0958	1100	1122	1156	1254	1359	1454	1554	1727	1818	1855	1928	2002	2057a	2157	2334	...
172	Evesham ..... a.	0746	0855	1018	1115	...	1216	1312	1417	...	1612	1748	1837	1915	1944	2021	2117a	2217	2353	...
172	Evesham ..... d.	0753	0856	1025	1115	...	1225	1312	1426	...	1621	1749	1837	1915	1945	2022	2121	2218	2354	...
194	**Worcester** Shrub Hill .... 123 a.	0812	0915	1045	1135	...	1244	1332	1446	...	1640	1809	1859	1935	2005	2041	2147	2240	0013	...
195	**Worcester** Foregate St. 123 a.	0816	0919	1049	1141	...	1249	1336	1452	...	1644	*1821*	1911	1939	*2014*	2045	2151	2244	...	...
208	Great Malvern ..... 123 a.	*0854*	0930	1108	*1233*	...	1303	1356	1511	...	*1721*	*1836*	1925	1953	*2027*	2059	2207	2259	...	...
219	Ledbury ..... 123 a.	*0907*	*0957*	1122	*1257*	...	1324	*1457*	*1557*	...	*1759*	*1902*	...	2008	*2004*	2114	2235	...	...	...
241	**Hereford** ..... 123 a.	*0928*	*1017*	1143	*1319*	...	1348	*1519*	*1619*	...	*1822*	*1924*	...	2029	*2103*	2134	2255	...	...	...

	⑥	⑥	⑥
London Paddington ..... 131 d.	0521	0621	0721
Reading ..... 131 d.	0554	0654	0754
Oxford ..... 131 d.	0623	0723	0823
Moreton in Marsh ..... d.	0700	0757	0857
Evesham ..... a.	0720	0816	0916
Evesham ..... d.	0725	0821	0921
Worcester Shrub Hill .... 123 a.	0744	0840	0940
Worcester Foregate St. 123 a.	0749	0844	0944
Great Malvern ..... 123 a.	0803	0901	1000
Ledbury ..... 123 a.	*0857*	*0957*	*1057*
Hereford ..... 123 a.	*0919*	*1019*	*1119*

	⑥	⑥	⑥	⑥	⑥	⑥	⑥	⑥	⑥	⑥	⑥	
London Paddington ..... 131 d.	0821	1021	1121	1321	1421	1521	1621	1721	1821	1950	2148	...
Reading ..... 131 d.	0854	1054	1154	1354	1454	1554	1654	1754	1854	2022	2221	...
Oxford ..... 131 d.	0923	1123	1223	1423	1523	1623	1723	1823	1923	2049	2250	...
Moreton in Marsh ..... d.	1000	1159	1259	1459	1557	1657	1803	1859	1959	2125	2327	...
Evesham ..... a.	1020	1219	1317	1518	1616	1716	1823	1919	2019	2143	2345	...
Evesham ..... d.	1025	1220	1321	1521	1621	1721	1824	1921	2023	2143	2345	...
Worcester Shrub Hill .... 123 a.	1044	1240	1340	1540	1640	1740	1844	1941	2043	2202	0007	...
Worcester Foregate St. 123 a.	1049	1249	1344	1544	1644	1744	1855	1945	2049	2206	...	...
Great Malvern ..... 123 a.	1102	1303	1400	1600	1700	1801	1909	*2013*	2102	2222	...	...
Ledbury ..... 123 a.	1120	1321	*1457*	*1657*	*1757*	*1900*	1923	*2038*	2116	...	...	...
Hereford ..... 123 a.	1139	1339	*1519*	*1719*	*1816*	*1921*	1945	*2102*	2135	...	...	...

	⑦	⑦	⑦	⑦	⑦	⑦	⑦	⑦	⑦	⑦	⑦	⑦
London Paddington ..... 131 d.	0803	0935	1042	1242	1342	1442	1542	1642	1742	1842	1942	2142
Reading ..... 131 d.	0846	1017	1120	1320	1421	1519	1621	1721	1822	1921	2022	2219
Oxford ..... 131 d.	0918	1047	1151	1352	1452	1554	1655	1755	1850	1955	2052	2253
Moreton in Marsh ..... d.	0952	1125	1227	1429	1525	1632	1728	1832	1928	2029	2129	2332
Evesham ..... a.	1010	1144	1248	1447	1547	1648	1743	1850	1945	2048	2149	2350
Evesham ..... d.	1012	1148	1248	1447	1547	1648	1745	1851	1949	2048	2149	2352
Worcester Shrub Hill .... 123 a.	1032	1207	1309	1507	1607	1709	1804	1910	2009	2108	2211	0012
Worcester Foregate St. 123 a.	1036	1210	1312	1511	*1642*	1712	1807	1913	2013	*2124*	2214	...
Great Malvern ..... 123 a.	1054	1223	1326	1523	*1654*	1726	*1854*	1925	2026	*2137*	2228	...
Ledbury ..... 123 a.	*1120*	1239	1341	1539	*1716*	1739	*1911*	...	2041	*2208*	...	...
Hereford ..... 123 a.	*1139*	1258	1408	1557	*1734*	1755	*1930*	...	2101	*2227*	...	...

	Ⓐ	Ⓐ	Ⓐ	Ⓐ	Ⓐ	Ⓐ	Ⓐ	Ⓐ	Ⓐ	Ⓐ	Ⓐ	Ⓐ	Ⓐ	Ⓐ	Ⓐ	Ⓐ	Ⓐ	Ⓐ	Ⓐ	
Hereford ..... 123 d.	...	0450	0528	...	0642	*0734*	...	*0849*	...	*1040*	1314	*1343*	...	1514	*1540*	*1740*	*1848*	*1950*	2151	...
Ledbury ..... 123 d.	...	|	0545	...	0659	*0750*	...	*0908*	...	*1058*	1331	*1400*	...	1531	*1558*	*1758*	*1904*	*2009*	2209	...
Great Malvern ..... 123 d.	...	0517	0559	...	0712	*0805*	...	0954	...	*1134*	1345	1426	...	1545	*1648*	*1810*	1944	*2020*	2222	...
Worcester Foregate St. 123 d.	...	0531	0614	0653	0728	0826	...	1006	...	1206	1401	1438	...	1601	1728	1849	1956	2059	2234	...
Worcester Shrub Hill .... 123 d.	0511	0536	0630	0655	0732	0838	...	1009	...	1208	1409	1441	...	1605	1731	1852	2004	2103	2243	...
Evesham ..... a.	0525	0553	0646	0712	0749	0854	...	1026	...	1225	1427	1458	...	1622	1748	1908	2020	2120	2300	...
Evesham ..... d.	0527	0553	0649	0712	0750	0904	...	1030	...	1231	1428	1505	...	1623	1748	1908	2020	2121	2301	...
Moreton in Marsh ..... d.	0547	0609	0709	0727	0811	0923	0950	1049	1150	1250	1448	1524	1553	1645	1807	1926	2047	2141	2326	...
Oxford ..... 131 a.	0624	0649	0747	0812	0849	0959	1028	1128	1229	1326	1525	1559	1628	1729	1855	2000	2127	2227	2358	...
Reading ..... 131 a.	0653	0725	0822	...	0914	1025	1054	1155	1255	1354	1555	1625	1656	1754	1931	2024	2155	2253	0041	...
London Paddington ..... 131 a.	0728	0759	0851	...	0947	1100	1129	1230	1330	1430	1629	1700	1734	1828	2006	2059	2241	2338	0121	...

	⑥	⑥	⑥
Hereford ..... 123 d.	...	0617	0710
Ledbury ..... 123 d.	...	0634	0730
Great Malvern ..... 123 d.	0556	0649	0744
Worcester Foregate St. 123 d.	0609	0704	0759
Worcester Shrub Hill .... 123 d.	0612	0708	0804
Evesham ..... a.	0629	0725	0821
Evesham ..... d.	0629	0726	0825
Moreton in Marsh ..... d.	0648	0745	0845
Oxford ..... 131 a.	0723	0826	0925
Reading ..... 131 a.	0755	0856	0954
London Paddington ..... 131 a.	0829	0929	1029

	⑥	⑥	⑥	⑥	⑥	⑥	⑥	⑥	⑥	⑥	⑥	⑥	
Hereford ..... 123 d.	*0740*	*0840*	*0940*	1213	*1340*	1513	*1540*	*1640*	*1740*	*1912*	2020	*2135*	...
Ledbury ..... 123 d.	*0758*	*0858*	*0958*	1231	*1358*	1531	*1558*	*1658*	*1758*	*1928*	2040	*2151*	...
Great Malvern ..... 123 d.	0843	0951	1058	1244	1434	1544	1634	1749	1835	*1939*	2053	2241	...
Worcester Foregate St. 123 d.	0858	1004	1111	1259	1457	1559	1655	1802	1849	2002	2111	2253	...
Worcester Shrub Hill .... 123 d.	0902	1008	1115	1304	1501	1604	1702	1806	1902	2006	2115	2259	...
Evesham ..... a.	0919	1024	1131	1321	1518	1620	1718	1823	1918	2023	2132	2317	...
Evesham ..... d.	0932	1031	1132	1330	1526	1621	1726	1827	1927	2024	2133	...	...
Moreton in Marsh ..... d.	0951	1050	1150	1349	1545	1641	1744	1845	1945	2043	2152	...	...
Oxford ..... 131 a.	1028	1126	1228	1427	1621	1721	1821	1921	2021	2126	2234	...	...
Reading ..... 131 a.	1056	1157	1256	1453	1655	1756	1855	1955	2055	2159	2307	...	...
London Paddington ..... 131 a.	1130	1232	1332	1527	1729	1829	1929	2029	2129	2238	2351	...	...

	⑦	⑦	⑦	⑦	⑦	⑦	⑦	⑦	⑦	⑦	⑦
Hereford ..... 123 d.	...	*1006*	*1200*	1332	1435	...	1634	...	1830	...	*2006*
Ledbury ..... 123 d.	...	*1022*	*1216*	1351	1455	...	1652	...	1848	...	*2022*
Great Malvern ..... 123 d.	0920	1115	1315	1411	1508	...	1705	...	1911	2015	*2037*
Worcester Foregate St. 123 d.	0932	1128	1327	1426	1523	...	1722	1825	1929	2028	*2118*
Worcester Shrub Hill .... 123 d.	0935	1131	1331	1430	1527	1628	1726	1830	1932	2031	2128
Evesham ..... a.	0951	1149	1347	1448	1545	1645	1742	1845	1949	2048	2145
Evesham ..... d.	0952	1149	1349	1449	1548	1648	1748	1848	1949	2049	2149
Moreton in Marsh ..... d.	1011	1208	1408	1508	1608	1708	1808	1909	2010	2108	2208
Oxford ..... 131 a.	1049	1246	1448	1547	1649	1749	1849	1952	2048	2148	2242
Reading ..... 131 a.	1126	1325	1522	1617	1724	1825	1919	2025	2120	2219	2318
London Paddington ..... 131 a.	1204	1407	1607	1655	1804	1907	1959	2102	2204	2304	0007

a – On ⑤: Oxford d. 2024, Moreton d. 2101, Evesham a. 2121.

u – Calls to pick up only.

131 LONDON - OXFORD GW

Subject to alteration on ⑥ September 13 - October 18, and on ⑦ August 3 - September 7. Frequent additional slower services are available.

km		②–⑤	Ⓐ	Ⓐ	Ⓐ	Ⓐ	Ⓐ	Ⓐ	Ⓐ	Ⓐ	Ⓐ	Ⓐ	Ⓐ	Ⓐ	Ⓐ	Ⓐ	Ⓐ	Ⓐ	Ⓐ	Ⓐ	Ⓐ	Ⓐ	Ⓐ	Ⓐ	Ⓐ
0	**London** P ◇ 130 132 d.	0022	0512	0545	0620	0648	0721	0750	0822	0851	0921	0950	1022	1050	1120	1150	1221	1250	1321	1350	1421	1450	1522	1552	1622
58	Reading ..... 130 132 d.	0101	0550	0617	0651	0721	0752	0822	0852	0922	0952	1022	1052	1121	1152	1222	1252	1322	1352	1422	1452	1522	1552	1622u	1653
102	**Oxford** ..... 130 a.	0134	0620	0651	0722	0802	0819	0849	0920	0953	1020	1047	1118	1150	1218	1248	1320	1350	1418	1448	1518	1550	1618	1647	1722

	Ⓐ	Ⓐ	Ⓐ	Ⓐ	Ⓐ	Ⓐ	Ⓐ	Ⓐ	Ⓐ	Ⓐ	Ⓐ	Ⓐ	Ⓐ	Ⓐ	⑤	Ⓐ	
London P ◇ 130 132 d.	1649	1722	1749	1822	1850	1922	1950	2022	2048	2118	2148	2218	2248	2318	2342	2333	...
Reading ..... 130 132 d.	1721	1750	1822	1851	1923	1952	2022	2053	2120	2151	2225	2256	2328	0004	0025	0027	...
Oxford ..... 130 a.	1751	1815	1847	1920	1949	2021	2052	2118	2151	2218	2247	2329	0001	0035	0102	0118	...

	⑥	⑥	⑥	⑥	⑥	⑥	⑥	⑥
London P ◇ 130 132 d.	0022	0521	0550	0621	0650	0721	0750	0821
Reading ..... 130 132 d.	0101	0554	0622	0654	0722	0754	0822	0852
Oxford ..... 130 a.	0134	0622	0652	0720	0748	0819	0848	0919

	⑥	⑥	⑥	⑥	⑥	⑥	⑥	⑥	⑥	⑥	⑥	⑥	⑥	⑥	⑥	⑥	⑥	⑥	⑥	⑥	⑥	⑥	⑥	⑥	⑥	⑥
London P ◇ 130 132 d.	0850	0921	0950	1021	1050	1121	1150	1221	1250	1321	1350	1421	1450	1521	1550	1621	1650	1721	1750	1821	1850	1921	1950	2018	2050	2118
Reading ..... 130 132 d.	0922	0954	1022	1054	1122	1154	1222	1254	1322	1354	1422	1454	1522	1554	1622	1654	1722	1754	1822	1854	1922	1954	2022	2051	2123	2151
Oxford ..... 130 a.	0948	1019	1048	1119	1148	1220	1248	1319	1348	1419	1448	1518	1548	1619	1648	1718	1748	1818	1848	1918	1948	2020	2047	2118	2154	2227

	⑥	⑥	⑥	⑥	
London P ◇ 130 132 d.	2148	2218	2248	2333	...
Reading ..... 130 132 d.	2221	2254	2330	0012	...
Oxford ..... 130 a.	2248	2335	0001	0057	...

	⑦	⑦	⑦	⑦		⑦	⑦	⑦	⑦	⑦		⑦	⑦	⑦	⑦		⑦	⑦	⑦	⑦
London P ◇ 130 132 d.	0803	0842	0935	1042	...	1142	1242	1342	1442	1542	...	1642	1742	1842	1942	...	2042	2142	2242	2347
Reading ..... 130 132 d.	0844	0920	1017	1120	...	1219	1320	1421	1520	1621	...	1721	1822	1921	2022	...	2117	2220	2322	0030
Oxford ..... 130 a.	0912	0952	1043	1150	...	1251	1351	1451	1549	1650	...	1750	1848	1950	2050	...	2147	2251	2349	0102

	②–⑤	②–⑤	Ⓐ	Ⓐ	Ⓐ	Ⓐ	Ⓐ	Ⓐ	Ⓐ	Ⓐ	Ⓐ	Ⓐ	Ⓐ	Ⓐ	Ⓐ	Ⓐ	Ⓐ	Ⓐ	Ⓐ	Ⓐ	Ⓐ	Ⓐ	Ⓐ	Ⓐ	Ⓐ
Oxford ..... 130 d.	0007	0400	0503	0543	0559	0630	0655	0734	0752	0807	0851	0901	0931	1001	1031	1101	1131	1201	1231	1301	1331	1401	1431	1501	1531
Reading ..... 130 132 a.	0113	0438	0543	0616	0626	0653	0725	0756	0822	0835	0916	0936	0954	1025	1054	1124	1155	1225	1255	1325	1354	1425	1455	1524	1555
London P ◇ 130 132 a.	0207	0541	0646	0654	0708	0728	0759	0831	0851	0908	0947	1008	1029	1100	1129	1159	1230	1309	1330	1359	1430	1501	1530	1601	1629

	Ⓐ	Ⓐ	Ⓐ	Ⓐ	Ⓐ	Ⓐ	Ⓐ	Ⓐ	Ⓐ	Ⓐ	Ⓐ	Ⓐ	Ⓐ	Ⓐ	Ⓐ	
Oxford ..... 130 d.	1601	1631	1701	1731	1801	1831	1906	1931	2001	2031	2101	2132	2211	2230	2309	...
Reading ..... 130 132 a.	1625	1656	1726	1754	1824	1855	1931	1954	2024	2055	2124	2155	2244	2253	2341	...
London P ◇ 130 132 a.	1700	1734	1759	1828	1859	1930	2006	2030	2059	2131	2200	2241	2325	2338	0027	...

	⑥	⑥	⑥	⑥	⑥	⑥	⑥	⑥	⑥
Oxford ..... 130 d.	0007	0027	0359	0514	0549	0631	0701	0731	0801
Reading ..... 130 132 a.	0041	0113	0430	0557	0627	0657	0727	0755	0825
London P ◇ 130 132 a.	0121	0207	0531	0701	0731	0737	0801	0829	0859

	⑥	⑥	⑥	⑥	⑥	⑥	⑥	⑥	⑥	⑥	⑥	⑥	⑥	⑥	⑥	⑥	⑥	⑥	⑥	⑥	⑥	⑥	⑥	⑥	⑥	⑥
Oxford ..... 130 d.	0831	0901	0931	1001	1032	1101	1130	1201	1231	1301	1331	1401	1431	1501	1531	1601	1631	1701	1731	1801	1831	1901	1931	2001	2031	2101
Reading ..... 130 132 a.	0856	0924	0954	1027	1056	1124	1157	1226	1256	1326	1354	1426	1453	1525	1555	1625	1655	1725	1756	1825	1855	1925	1955	2025	2055	2127
London P ◇ 130 132 a.	0929	0959	1029	1101	1130	1159	1232	1259	1332	1359	1429	1459	1527	1559	1630	1659	1729	1759	1829	1859	1929	1959	2029	2059	2129	2201

	⑥	⑥	⑥	⑥	⑥	
Oxford ..... 130 d.	2131	2201	2235	2301	2307	...
Reading ..... 130 132 a.	2159	2231	2307	2330	0001	...
London P ◇ 130 132 a.	2238	2308	2352	0016	0105	...

	⑦	⑦	⑦	⑦		⑦	⑦	⑦	⑦		⑦	⑦	⑦	⑦		⑦	⑦	⑦	⑦
Oxford ..... 130 d.	0855	0950	1055	1150	...	1250	1350	1452	1550	...	1650	1750	1850	1953	...	2050	2150	2246	2315
Reading ..... 130 132 a.	0925	1019	1126	1218	...	1321	1418	1522	1617	...	1718	1819	1919	2023	...	2118	2219	2318	2352
London P ◇ 130 132 a.	0959	1055	1201	1257	...	1357	1456	1600	1655	...	1800	1857	1955	2100	...	2158	2304	0007	0051

◇ – London Paddington.

GW Most trains 🍷 LONDON - BRISTOL - CARDIFF - SWANSEA 132

Service until September 7 (subject to alteration on ⑦ from June 22).

km			Ⓐ	Ⓐ	Ⓐ	Ⓐ	Ⓐ	Ⓐ A	Ⓐ B	Ⓐ	Ⓐ	Ⓐ	Ⓐ	Ⓐ	Ⓐ	Ⓐ	Ⓐ	Ⓐ C	Ⓐ	Ⓐ	Ⓐ	Ⓐ	Ⓐ	Ⓐ
0	**London** Paddington 115 d.	Ⓐ	0519	0630	0645	0700	0715	0730	0745	0800	0815	0830	0845	0900	0915	0930	0945	1000	1015	1030	1045	1100	1115	1130
58	Reading 115 d.		0554	0657	0712	0730	0742	0759	0813	0828	0845	0859	0912	0928	0942	0959	1012	1028	1043	1059	1112	1128	1144	1159
85	Didcot Parkway d.		0609	0712	|	0744	0757	|	|	0841	0858	0913	|	|	0957	1013	|	|	1058	1113	|	|	1158	1213
124	**Swindon** d.		0627	0730	0742	0801	0815	0827	0842	0900	0916	0933	0942	0955	1015	1030	1042	1055	1115	1130	1142	1155	1215	1230
151	Chippenham d.		0641	0744	|	0817	|	0842	|	0915	|	0945	|	1009	|	1044	|	1109	|	1144	|	1209	|	1244
172	Bath a.		0654	0757	|	0829	|	0855	|	0929	|	0959	|	1024	|	1059	|	1124	|	1159	|	1223	|	1259
180	**Bristol** Parkway a.		|	|	0806	|	0840	|	0906	|	0942	|	1006	|	1040	|	1106	|	1142	|	1206	|	1242	|
190	**Bristol** Temple Meads 137 a.		0709	0817	|	0845	|	0910	|	0945	|	1015	|	1039	|	1115	|	1140	|	1215	|	1239	|	1315
221	Weston super Mare 137 a.		|	...	|	...	|	...	|	...	|	...	|	...	|	...	|	1206	|	...	|	...	|	...
215	Newport a.		0747	...	0832	...	0907	...	0929	...	1006	...	1031	...	1106	...	1131	...	1204	...	1231	...	1305	...
234	**Cardiff** Central a.		0802	...	0849	...	0923	...	0948	...	1023	...	1046	...	1123	...	1146	...	1221	...	1246	...	1322	...
	Swansea **135** a.		0859	...	0947	...	...	...	1044	...	...	...	1143	...	...	...	1243	...	...	...	1344	...	...	...

	Ⓐ	Ⓐ	Ⓐ	Ⓐ	Ⓐ	Ⓐ	Ⓐ	Ⓐ	Ⓐ	Ⓐ	Ⓐ	Ⓐ	Ⓐ	Ⓐ	Ⓐ	Ⓐ	Ⓐ	Ⓐ	Ⓐ	Ⓐ □	Ⓐ D	Ⓐ	Ⓐ E¶
London Paddington 115 d.	1145	1200	1215	1230	1245	1300	1315	1330	1345	1400	1415	1430	1445	1500	1515	1530	1545	1600	1615	1630	1645	1700	1715
Reading 115 d.	1212	1228	1242	1259	1312	1327	1342	1359	1412	1428	1444	1459	1512	1528	1543	1558	1612	1628	1644	1659	1712	1727	1742
Didcot Parkway d.	|	|	1258	1312	|	|	1357	1413	|	|	1458	1513	|	|	1558	1612	|	|	1701	1712	|	1742	1758
Swindon d.	1242	1255	1315	1330	1340	1355	1415	1430	1442	1455	1517	1530	1541	1555	1616	1629	1642	1657	1719	1730	1741	1800	1815
Chippenham d.	|	1309	|	1344	|	1409	|	1444	|	1509	|	1544	|	1610	|	1644	|	1714	|	1745	|	1814	|
Bath a.	|	1324	|	1359	|	1423	|	1459	|	1524	|	1600	|	1624	|	1658	|	1726	|	1759	|	1827	|
Bristol Parkway a.	1306	|	1342	|	1406	|	1440	|	1506	|	1544	|	1606	|	1640	|	1706	|	1743	|	1806	|	1840
Bristol Temple Meads 137 a.	|	1344	|	1415	|	1439	|	1515	|	1540	|	1615	|	1639	|	1714	|	1741	|	1814	|	1844	|
Weston super Mare 137 a.	|	...	|	...	|	...	|	...	|	...	|	1652	|	...	|	1752	|	...	|	1851	|	...	|
Newport a.	1331	...	1404	...	1430	...	1505	...	1531	...	1606	...	1630	...	1706	...	1731	...	1807	...	1830	...	1911
Cardiff Central a.	1346	...	1422	...	1446	...	1522	...	1546	...	1622	...	1646	...	1724	...	1748	...	1822	...	1848	...	1926
Swansea **135** a.	1443	...	...	...	1543	...	...	...	1643	...	...	...	1743	...	...	...	1845	...	1922	...	1945	...	2022

	Ⓐ □	Ⓐ	Ⓐ F	Ⓐ	Ⓐ	Ⓐ	Ⓐ	①-④	⑤	Ⓐ	Ⓐ	Ⓐ	Ⓐ	Ⓐ	Ⓐ △	⑤	①-④	⑤	①-④	Ⓐ			⑥
London Paddington 115 d.	1730	1745	1800	1815	1830	1845	1900	1915	1915	1930	2000	2015	2045	2115	2145	2215	2215	2245	2245	2330	...	⑥	...
Reading 115 d.	1757	1812	1828	1842	1857	1912	1928	1942	1948u	1959	2029	2041	2114	2141	2212	2243	2255	2311	2323	0010	...		...
Didcot Parkway d.	1811	|	1842	1858	1912	|	1942	1957	|	2012	2042	2057	2128	2201	2231	2303	2314	2332	2343	0029	...		...
Swindon d.	1830	1845	1900	1916	1929	1941	2001	2016	2016	2030	2100	2115	2145	2219	2249	2322	2333	2350	0001	0048	...		...
Chippenham d.	1844	|	1914	|	1945	|	2016	|	|	2044	2116	|	2200	|	2303	2336	2346	|	|	0103	...		...
Bath a.	1857	|	1928	|	1958	|	2029	|	|	2059	2129	|	2214	|	2317	2349	2358	|	|	0115	...		...
Bristol Parkway a.	|	1909	|	1941	|	2005	|	2040	2042	|	|	2140	|	2246	|	|	|	0015	0025	|	...		0658b
Bristol Temple Meads 137 a.	1912	|	1943	|	2013	|	2044	|	|	2115	2144	|	2229	|	2332	0004	0014	|	|	0130	...		0646b
Weston super Mare 137 a.	1948	|	...	|	2053	|	...	|	|	2150	...	|	...	|	0005	...	...	|	|	|	...		|
Newport a.	...	1933	...	2005	...	2031	...	2104	2105	...	...	2203	...	2319	...	...	...	0038	0055	0211s	...		0731
Cardiff Central a.	...	1949	...	2022	...	2048	...	2119	2119	...	...	2223	...	2340	...	...	...	0054	0115	0232	...		0747
Swansea **135** a.	...	2047	...	2119	...	2150	...	2220	2220	...	...	2322	...	0039	...	...	...	0155	0216	...	...		0844

	⑥	⑥	⑥ ♤	⑥	⑥	⑥	⑥ H♧	⑥	⑥	⑥	⑥	⑥	⑥	⑥	⑥	⑥	⑥	⑥	⑥	⑥	⑥	⑥	⑥
London Paddington 115 d.	0630	0700	0730	0745	0800	0830	0845	0900	0930	0945	1000	1030	1045	1100	1130	1145	1200	1230	1245	1300	1330	1345	1400
Reading 115 d.	0659	0729	0759	0814	0828	0859	0912	0928	0959	1014	1028	1059	1112	1128	1159	1214	1228	1259	1314	1328	1359	1414	1428
Didcot Parkway d.	0712	|	0812	|	|	0912	|	|	1012	|	|	1112	|	|	1212	|	|	1312	|	|	1412	|	|
Swindon d.	0730	0755	0830	0841	0855	0930	0940	0955	1030	1041	1055	1130	1139	1155	1230	1241	1255	1330	1341	1355	1430	1441	1455
Chippenham d.	0744	0809	0844	|	0909	0944	|	1009	1044	|	1109	1144	|	1209	1244	|	1309	1344	|	1409	1444	|	1509
Bath a.	0800	0824	0900	|	0924	1000	|	1024	1100	|	1124	1200	|	1224	1259	|	1324	1400	|	1424	1500	|	1524
Bristol Parkway a.	|	|	|	0905	|	|	1007	|	|	1106	|	|	1205	|	|	1306	|	|	1406	|	|	1506	|
Bristol Temple Meads 137 a.	0815	0839	0915	|	0939	1015	|	1039	1115	|	1139	1215	|	1239	1314	|	1342	1415	|	1439	1515	|	1541
Weston super Mare 137 a.	...	...	...	|	...	...	|	1106	...	|	...	1235	|	...	...	|	...	1435	|	...	...	|	...
Newport a.	...	...	...	0929	...	...	1031	...	...	1131	...	...	1231	...	...	1331	...	...	1431	...	...	1531	...
Cardiff Central a.	...	...	...	0946	...	...	1047	...	...	1146	...	...	1246	...	...	1347	...	...	1446	...	...	1545	...
Swansea **135** a.	...	...	...	1043	...	...	1143	...	...	1243	...	...	1343	...	...	1443	...	...	1543	...	...	1643	...

	⑥	⑥	⑥	⑥	⑥	⑥	⑥ C	⑥	⑥	⑥	⑥ ¶	⑥	⑥ □	⑥	⑥ □	⑥	⑥	⑥	⑥ △	⑥	⑥	⑥	⑥ e
London Paddington 115 d.	1430	1445	1500	1530	1545	1600	1630	1645	1700	1730	1745	1800	1830	1845	1900	1930	1945	2000	2030	2045	2130	2200	2235
Reading 115 d.	1459	1512	1528	1559	1614	1628	1659	1712	1728	1759	1812	1828	1859	1912	1928	1959	2012	2028	2059	2113	2159	2228	2304
Didcot Parkway d.	1512	|	|	1612	|	|	1712	|	|	1812	|	|	1912	|	|	2012	|	2042	2112	|	2212	2242	2325
Swindon d.	1530	1539	1555	1630	1641	1655	1730	1740	1755	1830	1839	1855	1930	1939	1955	2030	2040	2100	2130	2142	2231	2259	2342
Chippenham d.	1544	|	1609	1644	|	1709	1744	|	1809	1844	|	1909	1944	|	2009	2045	|	2114	2145	|	2246	|	2356
Bath a.	1600	|	1624	1700	|	1724	1800	|	1824	1900	|	1924	2000	|	2024	2100	|	2129	2200	|	2301	|	0011
Bristol Parkway a.	|	1605	|	|	1706	|	|	1806	|	|	1907	|	|	2006	|	|	2106	|	|	2206	|	2326	|
Bristol Temple Meads 137 a.	1615	|	1639	1715	|	1739	1815	|	1839	1915	|	1938	2015	|	2040	2116	|	2145	2214	|	2315	|	0031
Weston super Mare 137 a.	1635	|	...	1735	|	...	1836	|	...	1950	|	...	2036	|	2126	...	|	...	2247	|	...	|	...
Newport a.	...	1630	...	...	1729	...	...	1830	...	...	1930	...	...	2030	...	...	2131	...	...	2246	...	2357	...
Cardiff Central a.	...	1646	...	...	1746	...	...	1846	...	...	1946	...	...	2044	...	...	2147	...	...	2307	...	0018	...
Swansea **135** a.	...	1743	...	...	1846	...	...	1943	...	...	2043	...	...	2143	...	...	2245	...	...	0005	...	...	...

	⑥ f	⑥ 🚌 f	⑥ e	⑥ f	⑥ 🚌 f			⑦ ♤	⑦	⑦	⑦ ¶	⑦	⑦	⑦	⑦ ¶	⑦	⑦	⑦ ▽	⑦ ¶	⑦	⑦	⑦ □	⑦
London Paddington 115 d.	2235	...	2330	2330	...	...	⑦	0757	0835	0900	0927	1000	1037	1100	1137	1200	1237	1300	1337	1400	1437	1500	1537
Reading 115 d.	2302	...	0006	0003	...	...		0838	0915	0938	1000	1038	1112	1138	1214	1238	1312	1338	1412	1438	1512	1538	1612
Didcot Parkway d.	2317	...	0021	0019	...	...		0855	0932	0954	1018	1052	1128	1152	1228	1252	1329	1352	1428	1452	1528	1552	1628
Swindon d.	2334	2350	0041	0038	0047	...		0914	0949	1013	1037	1111	1147	1211	1247	1311	1347	1411	1445	1511	1547	1611	1647
Chippenham d.	|	0035	0057	|	0122	...		0929	|	1028	|	1125	|	1226	|	1326	|	1426	|	1526	|	1626	|
Bath a.	|	0108	0111	|	0157	...		0942	|	1041	|	1138	|	1239	|	1339	|	1439	|	1539	|	1639	|
Bristol Parkway a.	|	|	|	|	|	...		|	1016	|	1103	|	1213	|	1312	|	1412	|	1511	|	1613	|	1713
Bristol Temple Meads 137 a.	0009	0138	0125	0111	0227	...		0957	|	1056	|	1153	|	1253	|	1353	|	1452	|	1553	|	1653	|
Weston super Mare 137 a.	...	...	...	...	...	...		...	|	1117	|	1231	|	...	|	1428	|	...	|	...	|	1726	|
Newport a.	...	...	...	...	...	...		...	1041	...	1132	...	1240	...	1338	...	1438	...	1537	...	1640	...	1740
Cardiff Central a.	...	...	...	...	...	...		...	1102	...	1150	...	1259	...	1357	...	1500	...	1557	...	1700	...	1800
Swansea **135** a.	...	...	...	...	...	...		...	1158	...	1247	...	1354	...	1454	...	1556	...	1653	...	1758	...	1858

	⑦	⑦	⑦		⑦	⑦	⑦		⑦	⑦ △	⑦		⑦	⑦	⑦		⑦	⑦	⑦		⑦	⑦	
London Paddington 115 d.	1600	1637	1700	...	1727	1737	1800	...	1837	1900	1927	...	1937	2000	2037	...	2100	2137	2200	...	2303	2337	...
Reading 115 d.	1638	1712	1738	...	1803	1812	1838	...	1912	1938	2006	...	2012	2038	2112	...	2138	2212	2245	...	2345	0017	...
Didcot Parkway d.	1652	1728	1752	...	|	1828	1852	...	1928	1952	|	...	2028	2052	2128	...	2154	2228	2303	...	0002s	0034s	...
Swindon d.	1711	1747	1811	...	1832	1847	1911	...	1946	2011	2033	...	2046	2111	2146	...	2213	2247	2323	...	0020s	0052s	...
Chippenham d.	1726	|	1826	...	1847	|	1926	...	|	2026	2049	...	|	2126	|	...	2228	|	2338	...	0036s	0107s	...
Bath a.	1739	|	1839	...	1902	|	1939	...	|	2039	2102	...	|	2139	|	...	2241	|	2351	...	0050s	0122s	...
Bristol Parkway a.	|	1813	|	...	|	1913	|	...	2010	|	|	...	2110	|	2210	...	|	2313	|	...	|	|	...
Bristol Temple Meads 137 a.	1756	|	1853	...	1920	|	1954	...	|	2054	2116	...	|	2153	|	...	2258	|	0007	...	0106	0136	...
Weston super Mare 137 a.	...	|	...	...	1957	|	...	...	|	2126	...	...	|	2230	|	...	...	|	...	...	...	...	...
Newport a.	...	1840	...	...	...	1940	...	...	2038	...	...	...	2138	...	2240	...	...	2341	...	...	...	...	...
Cardiff Central a.	...	1900	...	...	...	2000	...	...	2056	...	...	...	2156	...	2259	...	...	0006	...	...	...	...	...
Swansea **135** a.	...	1955	...	...	...	2055	...	...	2153	...	...	...	2255	...	2359	...	...	0102	...	...	...	...	...

A – THE MERCHANT VENTURER – 12 and 🍷 London Paddington - Penzance and v.v.
B – THE ST DAVID – 12 and 🍷 London Paddington - Swansea and v.v.
C – THE TORBAY EXPRESS – 12 and 🍷 London Paddington - Paignton and v.v.
D – THE CAPITALS UNITED – 12 and 🍷 London Paddington - Swansea and v.v.
E – THE RED DRAGON – 12 and 🍷 London Paddington - Carmarthen and v.v.
F – THE BRISTOLIAN – 12 and 🍷 London Paddington - Bristol Temple Meads.
G – THE BRISTOLIAN – 12 and 🍷 Weston super Mare - London Paddington.
H – THE PEMBROKE COAST EXPRESS – 12 and 🍷 London Paddington - Pembroke Dock and v.v.

NOTES CONTINUE ON PAGE 122

132 LONDON - BRISTOL - CARDIFF - SWANSEA

Most trains 🍸 GW

Service until September 7 (subject to alteration on ⑦ from June 22).

		Ⓐ	Ⓐ	Ⓐ	Ⓐ	Ⓐ	Ⓐ	Ⓐ	Ⓐ	Ⓐ	Ⓐ	Ⓐ	Ⓐ	Ⓐ	Ⓐ	Ⓐ	Ⓐ	Ⓐ	Ⓐ	Ⓐ	Ⓐ	Ⓐ	Ⓐ
										D	G		▽		□					E¶	♡		
Swansea 135 d.	Ⓐ	...	...	0352	...	0458	...	0527	...	0558	...	0628	...	0658	...	0728	...	0758	...	0828	...	...	...
Cardiff Central d.		...	...	0512	...	0555	...	0624	...	0655	...	0725	...	0755	...	0825	...	0855	...	0925	...	0955	...
Newport d.		...	...	0530	...	0609	...	0638	...	0709	...	0739	...	0809	...	0839	...	0909	...	0939	...	1009	...
Weston super Mare 137 d.		...	...	|	...	|	...	|	0620	|	0648	|	0725	|	0749	|	...	|	...	|	0929	|	...
Bristol Temple Meads 137 d.		0447	0529	|	0600	|	0635	|	0700	|	0730	|	0800	|	0830	|	0900	|	0930	|	1000	|	1030
Bristol Parkway d.		0457u	|	0600	|	0631	|	0701	|	0731	|	0801	|	0831	|	0901	|	0931	|	1001	|	1031	|
Bath d.		|	0541	|	0613	|	0648	|	0713	|	0743	|	0813	|	0843	|	0913	|	0943	|	1013	|	1043
Chippenham d.		|	0554	|	0625	|	0700	|	0725	|	0755	|	0825	|	0855	|	0925	|	0955	|	1025	|	1055
Swindon a.		0522	0608	0626	0640	0657	0715	0727	0740	0757	0810	0827	0840	0857	0910	0926	0940	0957	1010	1027	1040	1057	1110
Didcot Parkway a.		0541	0627	0645	0658	|	|	0745	0801	|	0828	0845	0858	|	0928	|	|	1016	1028	1046	|	1116	1128
Reading 115 a.		0556	0641	0659	0713	0728	0743	0800	0816	|	0843	0900	0914	0925	0944	0957	1012	1030	1043	1100	1108	1130	1145
London Paddington 115 a.		0624	0716	0732	0744	0802	0814	0833	0845	0854	0914	0929	0944	0958	1015	1032	1042	1107	1114	1132	1138	1202	1214

	Ⓐ	Ⓐ	Ⓐ	Ⓐ	Ⓐ	Ⓐ	Ⓐ	Ⓐ	Ⓐ	Ⓐ	Ⓐ	Ⓐ	Ⓐ	Ⓐ	Ⓐ	Ⓐ	Ⓐ	Ⓐ	Ⓐ	Ⓐ	Ⓐ	Ⓐ	Ⓐ
						♤			B													A	
Swansea 135 d.	0928	...	...	...	1028	...	...	...	1128	...	...	...	1228	...	...	...	1328	...	...	...	1428	...	...
Cardiff Central d.	1025	...	1055	...	1125	...	1155	...	1225	...	1255	...	1325	...	1355	...	1425	...	1455	...	1525	...	1555
Newport d.	1039	...	1109	...	1139	...	1209	...	1239	...	1309	...	1339	...	1409	...	1439	...	1509	...	1539	...	1609
Weston super Mare 137 d.	|	...	|	...	|	...	|	...	|	...	|	...	|	...	|	...	|	...	|	...	|	...	|
Bristol Temple Meads 137 d.	|	1100	|	1130	|	1200	|	1230	|	1300	|	1330	|	1400	|	1430	|	1500	|	1530	|	1600	|
Bristol Parkway d.	1101	|	1131	|	1201	|	1231	|	1301	|	1331	|	1401	|	1431	|	1501	|	1531	|	1601	|	1631
Bath d.	|	1113	|	1143	|	1213	|	1243	|	1313	|	1343	|	1413	|	1443	|	1513	|	1543	|	1613	|
Chippenham d.	|	1125	|	1155	|	1225	|	1255	|	1325	|	1355	|	1425	|	1455	|	1525	|	1555	|	1625	|
Swindon a.	1128	1140	1157	1210	1227	1240	1257	1310	1327	1340	1357	1410	1427	1440	1457	1510	1527	1539	1557	1610	1627	1640	1657
Didcot Parkway a.	|	|	1216	1228	1246	|	1316	1328	|	|	1415	1428	1446	|	1516	1528	|	|	1616	1628	1646	|	1716
Reading 115 a.	1202	1212	1230	1243	1300	1309	1330	1343	1358	1411	1430	1443	1500	1509	1530	1543	1559	1612	1629	1643	1700	1708	1731
London Paddington 115 a.	1233	1244	1300	1314	1333	1338	1406	1414	1433	1440	1508	1514	1533	1544	1608	1614	1632	1644	1708	1714	1730	1738	1802

	Ⓐ	Ⓐ	Ⓐ	Ⓐ	Ⓐ	Ⓐ	Ⓐ	Ⓐ	Ⓐ	Ⓐ	Ⓐ	Ⓐ	Ⓐ	Ⓐ	①-④	⑤	Ⓐ	Ⓐ			⑥	⑥	⑥
																	♤	□					
Swansea 135 d.	...	1528	...	...	...	1628	...	...	...	1728	...	1828	...	1929	2028	2028	...	...	...	⑥	...	0358	0458
Cardiff Central d.	...	1625	...	1655	...	1725	...	1755	...	1825	...	1925	...	2025	2125	2125	...	...	...		...	0455	0555
Newport d.	...	1639	...	1709	...	1739	...	1809	...	1839	...	1939	...	2039	2139	2139	...	...	...		...	0509	0609
Weston super Mare 137 d.	...	|	...	|	1710	|	...	|	1808	|	...	|	...	|	|	|	...	2201	...		...	|	|
Bristol Temple Meads 137 d.	1630	|	1700	|	1730	|	1800	|	1830	|	1930	|	2030	|	|	|	2150	2235	...		0530	0600d	|
Bristol Parkway d.	|	1701	|	1731	|	1801	|	1831	|	1901	|	2001	|	2101	2201	2201	|	|	...		|	0542d	0631
Bath d.	1643	|	1713	|	1743	|	1813	|	1843	|	1943	|	2043	|	|	|	2202	2247	...		0543	0613	|
Chippenham d.	1655	|	1725	|	1755	|	1825	|	1855	|	1955	|	2055	|	|	|	2215	2300	...		0555	0625	|
Swindon a.	1710	1727	1740	1757	1810	1827	1840	1857	1910	1927	2010	2027	2110	2129	2225	2227	2231	2314	...		0609	0640	0657
Didcot Parkway a.	1728	|	|	1816	1828	1846	|	|	1928	1946	2028	2046	2130	2152	...	|	2250	2333	...		0628	0658	0716
Reading 115 a.	1743	1758	1810	1830	1845	1900	1910	1925	1943	2000	2043	2100	2146	2211	...	2302	2306	2353	...		0643	0714	0731
London Paddington 115 a.	1815	1830	1844	1902	1916	1932	1939	1954	2014	2037	2114	2132	2216	2244	...	2338	2344	0034	...		0714	0744	0807

	⑥	⑥	⑥	⑥	⑥	⑥	⑥	⑥	⑥	⑥	⑥	⑥	⑥	⑥	⑥	⑥	⑥	⑥	⑥	⑥	⑥	⑥	⑥
							□				△							♡	¶				
Swansea 135 d.	...	0528	...	0558	...	0628	...	0658	...	0728	...	...	0828	...	...	0928	...	...	1028	...	...	1128	...
Cardiff Central d.	...	0625	...	0655	...	0725	...	0755	...	0825	...	...	0925	...	...	1025	...	...	1125	...	...	1225	...
Newport d.	...	0639	...	0709	...	0739	...	0809	...	0839	...	...	0939	...	...	1039	...	...	1139	...	...	1239	...
Weston super Mare 137 d.	...	|	0624	|	...	|	0724	|	...	|	0830	...	|	...	...	|	...	...	|	1131	...	|	...
Bristol Temple Meads 137 d.	0630	|	0700	|	0730	|	0800	|	0830	|	0900	0930	|	1000	1030	|	1100	1130	|	1200	1230	|	1300
Bristol Parkway d.	|	0701	|	0731	|	0801	|	0831	|	0901	|	|	1001	|	|	1101	|	|	1201	|	|	1301	|
Bath d.	0643	|	0713	|	0743	|	0813	|	0843	|	0913	0943	|	1013	1043	|	1113	1143	|	1213	1243	|	1313
Chippenham d.	0655	|	0725	|	0755	|	0825	|	0855	|	0925	0955	|	1025	1055	|	1125	1155	|	1225	1255	|	1325
Swindon a.	0709	0727	0740	0757	0809	0827	0840	0858	0909	0927	0940	1010	1028	1039	1110	1127	1139	1209	1227	1240	1309	1327	1339
Didcot Parkway a.	0728	0746	0759	0816	0828	0846	0859	0916	0928	0946	|	1028	1047	|	1128	1146	|	1228	1246	|	1328	1346	|
Reading 115 a.	0744	0800	0815	0832	0844	0900	0914	0931	0947	1000	1011	1046	1101	1112	1144	1201	1212	1245	1301	1311	1344	1400	1412
London Paddington 115 a.	0814	0832	0844	0902	0914	0938	0944	1002	1015	1032	1039	1114	1133	1140	1214	1237	1241	1315	1338	1342	1414	1432	1440

	⑥	⑥	⑥	⑥	⑥	⑥	⑥	⑥	⑥	⑥	⑥	⑥	⑥	⑥	⑥	⑥	⑥	⑥	⑥	⑥	⑥	⑥	⑥
		H♧															♧					♤	□
Swansea 135 d.	...	1228	...	...	1328	...	...	1428	...	...	1528	...	...	1628	...	...	1728	...	1828	...	1928	...	...
Cardiff Central d.	...	1325	...	...	1425	...	...	1525	...	...	1625	...	...	1725	...	...	1825	...	1925	...	2025	...	...
Newport d.	...	1339	...	...	1439	...	...	1539	...	...	1639	...	...	1739	...	...	1839	...	1939	...	2039	...	...
Weston super Mare 137 d.	1301	|	...	...	|	...	1501	|	...	...	|	...	1701	|	...	1801	|	...	|	2010	|	...	2153
Bristol Temple Meads 137 d.	1330	|	1400	1430	|	1500	1530	|	1600	1630	|	1700	1730	|	1800	1830	|	1930	|	2033	|	2147	2230
Bristol Parkway d.	|	1401	|	|	1501	|	|	1601	|	|	1701	|	|	1801	|	|	1901	|	2001	|	2101	|	|
Bath d.	1343	|	1413	1443	|	1513	1543	|	1613	1643	|	1713	1743	|	1813	1843	|	1943	|	2046	|	2202	2243
Chippenham d.	1355	|	1425	1455	|	1525	1555	|	1625	1655	|	1725	1755	|	1825	1855	|	1955	|	2058	|	2215	2255
Swindon a.	1410	1427	1439	1509	1527	1539	1609	1627	1639	1710	1727	1739	1809	1827	1839	1909	1927	2009	2027	2113	2129	2229	2310
Didcot Parkway a.	1428	1446	|	1528	1546	|	1628	1646	|	1728	1746	|	1828	1846	|	1928	1946	2028	2046	2131	2147	2248	2330
Reading 115 a.	1444	1500	1510	1544	1600	1611	1644	1700	1710	1743	1758	1813	1843	1900	1910	1946	2000	2044	2106	2148	2205	2305	2347
London Paddington 115 a.	1514	1530	1541	1614	1638	1640	1714	1732	1738	1814	1832	1841	1914	1932	1939	2014	2032	2114	2137	2216	2241	2342	0033

		⑦	⑦		⑦	⑦	⑦		⑦	⑦	⑦		⑦	⑦	⑦		⑦	⑦	⑦		⑦	⑦	⑦
																	▽						
Swansea 135 d.	⑦	...	...	...	...	...	0810	...	...	...	0921	...	...	1021	...	...	...	1121	...	...	1221	...	1321
Cardiff Central d.		...	...	...	0800	...	0905	...	...	...	1015	...	...	1115	...	...	...	1215	...	...	1315	...	1415
Newport d.		...	...	...	0818	...	0920	...	...	...	1032	...	...	1132	...	...	...	1232	...	...	1332	...	1432
Weston super Mare 137 d.		...	...	...	|	0811	|	...	...	0956	|	...	...	|	1138	...	...	|	1251	...	|	...	|
Bristol Temple Meads 137 d.		0740	0815	...	|	0845	|	...	0948	1030	|	...	1130	|	1200	...	1230	|	1330	...	|	1430	|
Bristol Parkway d.		|	|	...	0846	|	0949	...	|	|	1101	...	|	1201	|	...	|	1301	|	...	1401	|	1501
Bath d.		0753	0828	...	|	0858	|	...	1001	1043	|	...	1143	|	1213	...	1243	|	1343	...	|	1443	|
Chippenham d.		|	0840	...	|	0910	|	...	1013	1055	|	...	1155	|	1226	...	1255	|	1355	...	|	1455	|
Swindon a.		|	0855	...	0913	0924	1014	...	1029	1110	1126	...	1210	1226	1240	...	1310	1326	1410	...	1426	1510	1526
Didcot Parkway a.		|	0913	...	|	0944	|	...	1047	1128	1146	...	1227	1246	1301	...	1328	1346	1427	...	1446	1528	1546
Reading 115 a.		0900	0930	...	0948	1002	1052	...	1103	1143	1202	...	1244	1302	1315	...	1349	1402	1443	...	1502	1543	1602
London Paddington 115 a.		0941	1006	...	1021	1037	1126	...	1140	1221	1236	...	1320	1336	1351	...	1422	1436	1512	...	1536	1621	1636

	⑦	⑦	⑦		⑦	⑦	⑦		⑦	⑦	⑦		⑦	⑦	⑦		⑦	⑦	⑦		⑦	⑦	⑦
									▽	¶	♡			▽			¶	□				¶	▽
Swansea 135 d.	...	1421	...	...	...	1521	...	...	...	1621	...	...	1651	...	...	...	1751	...	1851	...	...	1955	...
Cardiff Central d.	...	1515	...	...	...	1615	...	...	...	1715	...	...	1750	...	...	...	1850	...	1950	...	...	2055	...
Newport d.	...	1532	...	...	...	1632	...	...	...	1731	...	...	1804	...	...	...	1904	...	2004	...	...	2109	...
Weston super Mare 137 d.	1451	|	...	...	...	|	...	...	1702	|	1729	...	|	...	...	...	|	1927	|	...	2026	|	...
Bristol Temple Meads 137 d.	1530	|	1600	...	1630	|	1700	...	1730	|	1800	...	|	1830	1900	...	|	2000	|	...	2100	|	2210
Bristol Parkway d.	|	1601	|	...	|	1701	|	...	|	1801	|	...	1833	|	|	...	1933	|	2033	...	|	2138	|
Bath d.	1543	|	1613	...	1640	|	1713	...	1743	|	1813	...	|	1843	1913	...	|	2013	|	...	2113	|	2223
Chippenham d.	1555	|	1625	...	1655	|	1725	...	1755	|	1825	...	|	1855	1925	...	|	2025	|	...	2125	|	2235
Swindon a.	1610	1626	1640	...	1710	1726	1740	...	1810	1825	1840	...	1857	1910	1940	...	1957	2040	2057	...	2140	2204	2250
Didcot Parkway a.	1628	1646	1658	...	1728	1745	1758	...	|	1846	1858	...	1915	|	1957	...	2015	2058	|	...	2201	|	2311
Reading 115 a.	1644	1702	|	...	1744	1802	1812	...	1842	1900	1914	...	1933	1944	2014	...	2033	2115	2128	...	2219	2243	2330
London Paddington 115 a.	1722	1738	1753	...	1821	1836	1852	...	1921	1936	1952	...	2012	2021	2051	...	2106	2154	2201	...	2258	2326	0013

NOTES CONTINUED FROM PAGE 121

b – Calls at Bristol Temple Meads, then Bristol Parkway.
d – Calls at Bristol Parkway, then Bristol Temple Meads.
e – Until July 26.
f – Aug. 2 - Sep. 6.
s – Stops to set down only.
u – Stops to pick up only.
△ – To / from Exeter (Table **115**).
▽ – To / from Plymouth (Table **115**).
□ – To / from Taunton (Table **115**).
♡ – To / from Paignton (Table **115**).
¶ – To / from Carmarthen (Table **135**).
♤ – To / from Penzance (Table **115**).
♧ – To / from Pembroke Dock (Table **135**).

GW 2nd class — SWINDON - WESTBURY — 132a

Service until September 7 (subject to alteration on ⑦ from June 22).

km		Ⓐ	⑥	Ⓐ	⑦	⑥	Ⓐ	⑦	⑥		Ⓐ	⑥	⑦	Ⓐ	⑥	⑦		⑥	Ⓐ	⑦	Ⓐ	⑥	⑦	Ⓐ	⑥
0	**Swindon** 132 d.	0612	0836	0849	0926	1036	1047	1141	1236	...	1247	1436	1451	1514	1522	1728	...	1736	1736	1824	1852	1936	1953	2012	2108
27	Chippenham 132 d.	0629	0853	0906	0943	1053	1104	1158	1253	...	1304	1453	1508	1539	1539	1745	...	1753	1753	1841	1909	1953	2010	2029	2125
46	Trowbridge 139 d.	0647	0911	0931	1001	1111	1123	1216	1311	...	1322	1511	1526	1602	1558	1803	...	1811	1812	1859	1927	2011	2028	2047	2143
52	**Westbury** 139 a.	0655	0920	0942	1008	1120	1133	1223	1320	...	1333	1520	1533	1610	1605	1810	...	1818	1821	1907	1935	2020	2036	2055	2152

	Ⓐ	Ⓐ	⑥	⑥	⑦	⑥	Ⓐ	⑦		⑥	Ⓐ	⑦	⑥	Ⓐ	⑥		Ⓐ	⑦	⑥	⑦	✕	⑦	Ⓐ	⑦
Westbury 139 d.	0704	0732	0732	0822	0835	0932	0948	1032	...	1132	1147	1332	1332	1414	1506	...	1615	1629	1632	1720	1832	1850	1932	1940
Trowbridge 139 d.	0710	0738	0738	0828	0840	0938	0954	1037	...	1138	1153	1337	1338	1420	1512	...	1621	1634	1638	1725	1838	1856	1938	1945
Chippenham 132 d.	0731	0759	0800	0848	0900	1000	1014	1101	...	1200	1213	1401	1400	1441	1529	...	1642	1700	1700	|	1900	1915	2001	2007
Swindon 132 a.	0748	0818	0820	0906	0920	1020	1034	1119	...	1220	1236	1419	1420	1503	1550	...	1703	1717	1722	1804	1923	1933	2021	2024

GW Most London trains convey ⚲ — LONDON - CHELTENHAM — 133

Service until September 7 (subject to alteration on ⑦ from June 22).

km			Ⓐ ▽	Ⓐ 2	Ⓐ	Ⓐ 2	Ⓐ	Ⓐ 2	Ⓐ	Ⓐ 2	Ⓐ	Ⓐ 2	Ⓐ	Ⓐ 2	Ⓐ A	Ⓐ	Ⓐ 2	Ⓐ	Ⓐ 2▽	Ⓐ 2			⑥ 2	⑥	⑥ 2	⑥
0	**London** Paddington d.	Ⓐ	...	...	0736	...	0936	...	1136	...	1336	...	1536	...	1742	1847	...	1948	...	...	...	⑥	...	0815	...	1015
58	Reading d.		...	...	0802	...	1003	...	1203	...	1404	...	1602	...	|	1919	...	2018	...	...	...		...	0842	...	1042
85	Didcot Parkway d.		...	...	0817	...	1018	...	1218	...	1418	...	1617	...	1821	1934	...	2034	...	...	...		...	0856	...	1056
124	**Swindon** d.		0653	0750	0840	0938	1039	1138	1239	1338	1439	1538	1638	1754	1841	1955	2025	2055	2204	2336	...		0716	0915	1014	1115
164	Stroud d.		0723	0820	0908	1007	1107	1207	1307	1407	1507	1607	1706	1822	1909	2023	2053	2123	2236	0006	...		0745	0945	1043	1145
183	Gloucester a.		0744	0846	0929	1029	1130	1228	1330	1428	1530	1629	1729	1849	1945	2046	2115	2146	2256	0027	...		0806	1006	1105	1207
194	**Cheltenham** Spa a.		0803	0905	0952	1048	1152	1246	1352	1447	1552	1647	1752	1905	2001	2102	2133	2202	2310	...	...		0824	1022	1123	1222
	Worcester Shrub Hill a.		...	...	...	...	...	...	...	...	...	...	...	...	...	...	...	2224	...	...	...		...	...	...	...

	⑥ 2	⑥	⑥ 2	⑥	⑥ 2	⑥	⑥ 2	⑥	⑥ 2	⑥	⑥ 2			⑦	⑦ 2	⑦	⑦	⑦ 2	⑦	⑦	⑦ 2	⑦	⑦ 2	⑦	⑦ 2
London Paddington d.	...	1215	...	1415	...	1615	...	1815	...	2015	...	...	⑦	0827	...	1027	1227	...	1427	1627	...	1827	...	2027	...
Reading d.	...	1242	...	1442	...	1642	...	1842	...	2042	...	...		0905	...	1102	1303	...	1501	1705	...	1905	...	2105	...
Didcot Parkway d.	...	1256	...	1456	...	1656	...	1856	...	2056	...	...		|	...	|	|	...	|	|	...	|	...	|	...
Swindon d.	1214	1315	1414	1515	1614	1715	1814	1915	2000	2115	2241	...		0940	1047	1134	1334	1432	1534	1734	1838	1934	2030	2134	2257
Stroud d.	1243	1345	1443	1545	1643	1745	1843	1945	2030	2145	2310	...		1007	1116	1202	1402	1503	1602	1802	1906	2002	2059	2204	2326
Gloucester a.	1303	1406	1503	1606	1703	1806	1903	2006	2050	2206	2331	...		1028	1136	1223	1426	1522	1626	1824	1929	2024	2119	2224	2351
Cheltenham Spa a.	1324	1422	1525	1622	1725	1822	1925	2022	2103	2221	...	...		1050	1147	1240	1446	1534	1644	1844	...	2045	2133	2240	0006
Worcester Shrub Hill a.	...	...	...	...	...	...	...	...	...	...	...	...		...	...	...	...	...	...	...	...	...	...	...	...

		Ⓐ 2	Ⓐ	Ⓐ	Ⓐ	Ⓐ	Ⓐ 2	Ⓐ	Ⓐ 2	Ⓐ		Ⓐ 2	Ⓐ A	Ⓐ 2	Ⓐ	Ⓐ 2	Ⓐ	Ⓐ 2	Ⓐ 2	Ⓐ 2		⑥ 2	⑥	⑥
Worcester Shrub Hill d.	Ⓐ	...	0521	...	0706	...	...	...	...	...	...	...	...	...	...	...	...	...	...	...	⑥	...	...	0836
Cheltenham Spa d.		...	0553	0630	0729	0820	0918	1020	1120	1220	...	1320	1420	1520	1620	1739	1834	2001	2100	2201		0530	0731	0900
Gloucester d.		0517	0608	0645	0745	0846	0933	1044	1133	1244	...	1333	1444	1533	1643	1754	1849	2012	2121	2214		0542	0746	0914
Stroud d.		0535	0629	0705	0804	0905	0952	1105	1152	1305	...	1352	1505	1552	1704	1812	1911	2030	2139	2233		0601	0804	0935
Swindon a.		0605	0658	0735	0833	0936	1023	1134	1224	1333	...	1424	1533	1624	1733	1850	1939	2104	2210	2305		0632	0835	1003
Didcot Parkway a.		...	0719	0753	0852	0954	...	1154	...	1352	...	...	1552	...	1752	...	1958	...	...	...		...	0852	1022
Reading a.		...	0734	0811	0907	1008	...	1208	...	1406	...	...	1606	...	1806	...	2014	...	...	...		...	0908	1034
London Paddington a.		...	0807	0840	0940	1037	...	1238	...	1437	...	...	1639	...	1839	...	2046	...	...	...		...	0941	1109

	⑥ 2	⑥	⑥ 2	⑥	⑥ 2	⑥	⑥ 2	⑥	⑥ 2	⑥	⑥ 2	⑥ 2			⑦ 2	⑦	⑦ 2	⑦	⑦		⑦ 2	⑦	⑦ 2	⑦	⑦
Worcester Shrub Hill d.	...	...	...	...	...	...	...	...	...	...	...	...	...	⑦	...	...	...	...	...	...	...	...	...	...	...
Cheltenham Spa d.	1001	1100	1201	1300	1401	1500	1601	1700	1801	1900	2001	2120	...		0924	1133	1303	1333	1533	...	1632	1733	...	2001	2146
Gloucester d.	1013	1115	1213	1315	1413	1514	1613	1715	1813	1915	2013	2134	...		0937	1150	1315	1347	1547	...	1645	1747	1938	2017	2159
Stroud d.	1032	1135	1232	1336	1432	1535	1632	1735	1832	1936	2032	2153	...		0955	1210	1333	1407	1607	...	1703	1808	1955	2037	2218
Swindon a.	1104	1203	1304	1404	1504	1603	1704	1803	1904	2004	2103	2225	...		1024	1238	1402	1438	1638	...	1733	1838	2029	2108	2247
Didcot Parkway a.	...	1222	...	1423	...	1622	...	1822	...	2023	...	...	...		...	|	...	|	|	...	...	|	...	2128	...
Reading a.	...	1238	...	1439	...	1638	...	1837	...	2038	...	...	...		...	1307	...	1506	1706	...	...	1906	...	2148	...
London Paddington a.	...	1306	...	1509	...	1707	...	1907	...	2107	...	...	...		...	1340	...	1540	1741	...	...	1942	...	2227	...

A – THE CHELTENHAM SPA EXPRESS – (12) and ⚲ London Paddington - Cheltenham Spa and v.v.

▽ – Subject to alteration from Sep. 1

GW — GATWICK AIRPORT ✈ - READING — 134

km			Ⓐ	Ⓐ	Ⓐ	Ⓐ	Ⓐ	Ⓐ		Ⓐ	Ⓐ	Ⓐ	Ⓐ	Ⓐ	Ⓐ	Ⓐ	Ⓐ	Ⓐ			⑥	⑥	⑥	
0	**Gatwick** Airport ✈ d.	Ⓐ	0531	0556	0658	0758	0907	1003	and	1503	1603	1703	1803	1913	2003	2103	2222	2318	...	⑥	0531	0603	0703	and
10	Redhill d.		0543	0613	0710	0808	0923	1013	hourly	1513	1613	1713	1813	1926	2013	2113	2233	2334	...		0541	0613	0713	hourly
43	Guildford d.		0613	0643	0743	0838	0954	1044	until	1544	1644	1744	1847	1955	2044	2144	2314	0002	...		0612	0644	0744	until
84	**Reading** a.		0658	0729	0828	0917	1023	1119		1624	1719	1824	1925	2032	2119	2219	0001	0043	...		0701	0719	0819	

	⑥	⑥	⑥	⑥	⑥			⑦	⑦	⑦	⑦	⑦	⑦	⑦	⑦	⑦		⑦	⑦	⑦	⑦	⑦	⑦	⑦	⑦	⑦
Gatwick Airport ✈ d.	1903	2003	2103	2222	2318	...	⑦	0610	0710	0810	0908	1008	1108	1208	1308	1408	...	1508	1608	1708	1808	1908	2008	2108	2208	2308
Redhill d.	1913	2013	2113	2233	2328	...		0620	0720	0819	0920	1019	1120	1219	1320	1419	...	1520	1619	1720	1819	1920	2019	2120	2219	2320
Guildford d.	1944	2044	2144	2314	0002	...		0651	0752	0859	0952	1059	1152	1259	1352	1459	...	1552	1659	1752	1859	1952	2059	2152	2259	2352
Reading a.	2019	2119	2219	0001	0037	...		0726	0835	0937	1035	1135	1235	1335	1435	1535	...	1635	1735	1835	1935	2035	2136	2236	2339	0037

		Ⓐ	Ⓐ	Ⓐ	Ⓐ	Ⓐ	Ⓐ		Ⓐ	Ⓐ	Ⓐ	Ⓐ	Ⓐ	Ⓐ	Ⓐ	Ⓐ	Ⓐ	Ⓐ			⑥	⑥	⑥	
Reading d.	Ⓐ	0434	0524	0634	0734	0834	0934	and	1434	1528	1634	1734	1834	1934	2034	2134	2234	2334	...	⑥	0434	0534	0634	and
Guildford d.		0510	0600	0710	0818	0913	1010	hourly	1510	1610	1710	1818	1910	2010	2110	2218	2318	0021	...		0510	0610	0710	hourly
Redhill a.		0539	0629	0738	0846	0942	1038	until	1538	1642	1738	1847	1940	2038	2149	2248	2358	0049	...		0539	0639	0739	until
Gatwick Airport ✈ a.		0555	0641	0750	0859	0959	1050		1550	1659	1754	1900	1956	2050	2204	2304	0011	0103	...		0558	0650	0750	

	⑥	⑥	⑥	⑥	⑥			⑦	⑦	⑦	⑦	⑦	⑦	⑦	⑦	⑦		⑦	⑦	⑦	⑦	⑦	⑦	⑦	⑦	⑦
Reading d.	1934	2034	2134	2234	2334	...	⑦	0603	0703	0818	0918	1018	1118	1218	1318	1418	...	1518	1618	1718	1818	1918	2018	2118	2218	2315
Guildford d.	2010	2110	2218	2318	0021	...		0640	0747	0856	1002	1056	1202	1256	1402	1456	...	1602	1656	1802	1856	2002	2056	2202	2256	2359
Redhill a.	2038	2144	2252	2358	0049	...		0709	0818	0936	1036	1136	1236	1336	1436	1536	...	1636	1736	1836	1936	2036	2136	2236	2336	0030
Gatwick Airport ✈ a.	2050	2159	2305	0010	0100	...		0729	0831	0947	1048	1147	1248	1347	1448	1547	...	1648	1747	1848	1947	2048	2147	2248	2347	0041

135 CARDIFF - SWANSEA - SOUTH WEST WALES

Most London trains convey 🍷 — AW, GW

Service until September 7. For ⛴ services to Ireland see Table 2030.

km		⚒ 2	⚒ 2	⚒ 2	⚒ 2	⚒ 2	⚒ 2	Ⓐ 2	⑥ 2	⑥ 2	⑦ 2	Ⓐ 2	⑥ 2	Ⓐ 2	⑥	⑦ 2	⑥	⑦ 2	Ⓐ 2	⑥ 2	Ⓐ	Ⓐ	Ⓐ 2	⑥ 2	Ⓐ
	London Paddington **132** d.	...	...	...	...	...	...	...	...	...	...	...	...	...	...	...	...	...	...	...	0519	0645	...	...	0745
	Manchester Piccadilly **149** d.	...	...	...	...	...	...	...	...	...	...	...	...	...	...	...	...	...	...	...	|	|	...	...	|
0	**Cardiff** Central d.	...	...	...	...	...	...	0537	0536	...	...	0642	0642	0642	...	0710	0748	...	0750	0758	0804	0850	0904	0904	0946
32	Bridgend d.	...	...	...	...	...	...	0607	0607	...	...	0702	0702	0702	...	0731	0809	...	0809	0817	0825	0911	0923	0923	1007
52	Port Talbot d.	...	...	...	...	...	...	0623	0623	...	...	0718	0718	0718	...	0745	0822	...	0825	0830	0838	0927	0936	0938	1020
61	Neath d.	...	...	...	...	...	...	0634	0634	...	...	0729	0729	0729	...	0753	0830	...	0835	0837	0846	0933	0943	0945	1028
73	**Swansea** a.	...	...	...	...	...	...	0651	0651	...	...	0745	0745	0745	...	0806	0844	...	0851	0854	0859	0947	0955	0957	1042
73	**Swansea** d.	...	...	...	...	...	0545	0653	0653	0724	...	0750	0750	0750	0815	0815	▬	...	0901	0900	*0915*	▬	1000	1004	...
91	Llanelli d.	...	...	...	...	...	0604	0711	0711	0741	...	0808	0808	0808	0836	0835	⑥	...	0920	0919	*0934*	⑦	1019	1022	...
124	**Carmarthen** a.	...	...	...	...	...	0638	0743	0743	0809	...	0840	0840	0840	0908	0907	2	...	0950	0948	...	2	1051	1051	...
124	**Carmarthen** d.	0450	0530	0550	0558	...	0638	0746	0746	0819	0820	0843	0845	0843	...	0910	0940	0955	0959	0957	...	1019	*1058*	*1056*	...
147	Whitland d.	0503	0546	0605	0613	...	0656	0800	0800	0838	0836	0902	0900	0907	...	0926	0954	1011	1014	1014	...	1034	*1113*	*1111*	...
172	Tenby d.	|	0624	|	|	...	0732	|	|	0911	|	0943	|	|	...	0956	1024	|	|	|	...	1111	*1149*	*1145*	...
191	**Pembroke Dock** a.	|	0659	|	|	...	0807	|	|	0944	|	1018	|	|	...	1027	...	|	|	|	...	1141	*1223*	*1220*	...
166	Clarbeston Road d.	0518x	...	0620x	0627x	0734	...	0814x	0815x	...	0852x	...	0915x	0922x	...	...	...	1027x	1028x	1028x	...	...	...	...	...
174	Haverfordwest d.	0529	...	|	0635	|	...	0823	0823	...	0900	...	|	|	...	...	...	1035	1036	1036	...	...	...	...	...
189	**Milford Haven** a.	0553	...	|	0658	|	...	0843	0849	...	0920	...	|	|	...	...	...	1055	1057	1058	...	...	...	...	...
191	**Fishguard** Harbour a.	...	...	0646	...	0758	...	...	...	...	...	...	0943	0947	...	...	...	...	...	...	...	...	...	...	...

	⑥	⑦ 2	⚒ 2	Ⓐ 2	Ⓐ	⑥ H	⑥ 2	Ⓐ 2	⑥ 2	Ⓐ 2	⑦	⑥ 2	⑦ 2	Ⓐ 2	⚒	⑦	⑥ 2	⑦ 2	⑥ 2	Ⓐ 2	⑥	Ⓐ	Ⓐ 2	⑦	⑥ 2
London Paddington **132** d.	0745	...	...	...	0845	0845	...	...	...	...	0835	...	...	...	0945	0927	...	...	...	...	1045	1045	...	1037	...
Manchester Piccadilly **149** d.	|	...	0630	0730	|	|	...	...	...	...	|	0730	...	0830	|	|	0830	...	...	0930	|	|	...	|	0930
Cardiff Central d.	0947	0950	1004	1042	1048	1048	1057	1057	...	...	1102	1104	1120	1138	1148	1154	1204	1205	...	1239	1248	1248	...	1300	1304
Bridgend d.	1008	1020	1023	1101	1109	1109	1120	1119	...	...	1124	1123	1140	1159	1209	1214	1223	1235	...	1258	1309	1309	...	1321	1323
Port Talbot d.	1021	1037	1035	1114	1122	1122	|	|	...	...	1137	1136	1154	1211	1222	1227	1236	1252	...	1311	1322	1322	...	1334	1336
Neath d.	1029	1045	1042	1121	1130	1130	|	|	...	...	1144	1143	1202	1218	1230	1235	1243	|	...	1318	1330	1330	...	1342	1343
Swansea a.	1043	1058	1055	1134	1143	1143	|	|	...	...	1158	1156	1214	1234	1243	1247	1255	|	...	1333	1343	1344	...	1354	1355
Swansea d.	...	1101	1100	1137	...	1150	|	|	1150	1200	...	1205	1217	1240	...	1258	1303	|	1335	1337	...	...	1400	...	1405
Llanelli d.	...	1121	1118	1154	...	1208	1201	1203	1207	1219	...	1224	1235	1259	...	1316	1322	1324	1351	1356	...	...	1416	...	1424
Carmarthen a.	...	1154	1145	1226	...	1239	|	|	1239	1248	...	1253	1306	1322	...	1344	1347	1359	1420	1430	...	...	1445	...	1453
Carmarthen d.	...	1206	1148	...	...	1246	|	|	1258	1251	...	...	1308	1330	...	...	1351	1405	1438	...	...	...	1451	...	...
Whitland d.	...	1222	1201	...	...	1305	1237	1245	1312	1306	...	...	1324	1345	...	...	1406	1421	1454	...	...	...	1506	...	...
Tenby d.	...	|	|	...	...	1341	|	|	1345	1345	...	...	|	|	...	...	|	|	1534	...	...	...	1545	...	...
Pembroke Dock a.	...	|	|	...	...	1414	|	|	1419	1419	...	...	|	|	...	...	|	|	1609	...	...	...	1619	...	...
Clarbeston Road d.	...	1238x	1215x	...	...	...	|	|	...	...	...	...	|	1359x	...	...	1420x	1437x	...	...	...	...	...	...	...
Haverfordwest d.	...	1246	1223	...	...	...	|	|	...	...	...	...	|	1408	...	...	1429	1445	...	...	...	...	...	...	...
Milford Haven a.	...	1306	1248	...	...	...	|	|	...	...	...	...	|	1431	...	...	1452	1509	...	...	...	...	...	...	...
Fishguard Harbour a.	...	...	...	...	...	...	1319	1327	...	...	...	...	1400	...	...	...	...	...	...	...	...	...	...	...	...

	⑦ 2	Ⓐ 2	⚒	⑦	⑥ 2	⑦ 2	Ⓐ 2	⚒	Ⓐ	⑦	⑥ 2	⑥ 2	⑦ 2	Ⓐ 2	⑥ 2	⚒	⑦	⑥ 2	Ⓐ 2	⑦ 2	Ⓐ 2	⚒	⑥ 2	⑦	⑥ 2
London Paddington **132** d.	...	...	1145	1137	...	...	...	1245	...	1237	...	...	...	...	...	1345	1337	...	...	...	...	1445	...	1437	...
Manchester Piccadilly **149** d.	...	1030	|	|	1030	1030	1130	|	...	|	1130	...	...	1230	1230	|	|	...	...	1230	...	|	...	|	1330
Cardiff Central d.	...	1341	1348	1357	1404	1405	1443	1448	...	1500	1504	...	...	1539	1540	1548	1558	1604	1604	1609	...	1648	...	1701	1704
Bridgend d.	...	1404	1409	1418	1423	1435	1502	1509	...	1520	1523	...	...	1601	1559	1609	1619	1624	1625	1639	...	1709	...	1724	1725
Port Talbot d.	...	1418	1422	1430	1436	1451	1515	1522	...	1533	1536	...	...	1614	1616	1622	1632	1640	1641	1656	...	1722	...	1737	1740
Neath d.	...	1425	1430	1440	1443	1459	1522	1530	...	1541	1543	...	...	1621	1623	1630	1640	1648	1649	1704	...	1730	...	1745	1750
Swansea a.	...	1434	1443	1454	1455	1512	1534	1543	...	1556	1555	...	...	1633	1635	1643	1653	1701	1702	1723	...	1743	...	1758	1805
Swansea d.	1413	1437	...	1459	1500	1514	1537	...	1600	...	1600	1605	1638	1640	1640	...	1700	1706	1705	1725	1735	...	1750	...	1809
Llanelli d.	1433	1456	...	1516	1520	1533	1556	...	1618	...	1619	1628	1658	1659	1659	...	1717	1724	1724	1744	1754	...	1809	...	1828
Carmarthen a.	1506	1522	...	1545	1545	1603	1630	...	1647	...	1653	1701	1730	1728	1728	...	1745	1755	1755	1815	1830	...	1847	...	1857
Carmarthen d.	1508	1528	...	...	1549	1609	...	...	1651	...	...	1708	1732	1731	1731	...	...	1757	1757	1820	...	...	...	...	1902
Whitland d.	1523	1543	...	...	1604	1627	...	...	1706	...	...	1732	1748	1746	1746	...	...	1813	1813	1837	...	...	...	...	1918
Tenby d.	1555	|	...	...	|	|	...	...	1745	...	...	1805	1819	|	|	...	...	|	|	|	...	...	...	...	1950
Pembroke Dock a.	1630	|	...	...	|	|	...	...	1819	...	...	1840	1855	|	|	...	...	|	|	|	...	...	...	...	2020
Clarbeston Road d.	...	1557x	...	...	1618x	1642x	...	...	...	...	...	...	...	1800x	1800x	...	...	1827x	1827x	1853x	...	...	...	...	...
Haverfordwest d.	...	1606	...	...	1626	1651	...	...	...	...	...	...	...	1808	1808	...	...	|	|	1901	...	...	...	...	...
Milford Haven a.	...	1629	...	...	1649	1711	...	...	...	...	...	...	...	1831	1831	...	...	|	|	1925	...	...	...	...	...
Fishguard Harbour a.	...	...	...	...	...	...	...	...	...	...	...	...	...	...	...	...	...	1851	1856	...	...	...	...	...	...

	Ⓐ 2	⑦ 2	Ⓐ 2	Ⓐ 2	Ⓐ	⑥	⑦	⑥ 2	⑥ 2	⑦ 2	⑦ 2	Ⓐ	⚒ 2	⑥	Ⓐ	⑦	Ⓐ 2	⑥ 2	Ⓐ	⑦ 2	Ⓐ 2	⑥	Ⓐ	⑦	⑥ 2
London Paddington **132** d.	...	...	...	...	1545	1545	1537	...	...	...	...	1615	...	1645	1645	1637	...	...	1715	...	...	1745	1745	1737	...
Manchester Piccadilly **149** d.	1330	...	1430	...	|	|	|	1430	...	1430	...	|	...	|	|	|	1530	1530	|	...	1630	|	|	|	1630
Cardiff Central d.	1704	...	1740	...	1750	1748	1801	1804	...	1806	...	1827	...	1848	1850	1901	1904	1904	1929	...	1946	1948	1952	2001	2001
Bridgend d.	1725	...	1800	...	1812	1809	1820	1825	...	1838	...	1849	...	1909	1909	1920	1923	1924	1950	...	2005	2009	2011	2020	2023
Port Talbot d.	1740	...	1817	...	1825	1822	1833	1841	...	1854	...	1902	...	1922	1922	1933	1938	1939	2003	...	2021	2022	2026	2033	2036
Neath d.	1750	...	1825	...	1831	1830	1840	1849	...	1902	...	1910	...	1930	1930	1940	1948	1949	2010	...	2028	2030	2034	2040	|
Swansea a.	1805	...	1838	...	1845	1846	1858	1902	...	1918	...	1922	...	1943	1945	1955	2004	2005	2021	...	2042	2043	2047	2055	|
Swansea d.	1809	1837	1841	...	...	...	...	1905	...	1920	...	...	1934	...	...	...	2011	2013	2033	2035	2052	2100	...	...	|
Llanelli d.	1828	1857	1900	...	...	...	...	1924	...	1939	...	...	1954	...	...	...	2030	2032	2050	2055	2111	2116	...	...	2106
Carmarthen a.	1857	1929	1927	...	...	...	...	1951	...	2008	...	...	2029	...	...	...	2055	2057	2122	2127	2139	2148	...	...	2134
Carmarthen d.	1902	1932	1930	...	...	...	...	1955	...	2008	...	...	...	...	...	...	*2110*	2100	...	...	2141	...	...	...	2205
Whitland d.	1918	1948	1946	...	...	...	...	2010	...	2030	2037	...	...	...	...	...	*2125*	2115	...	...	2156	...	...	...	2220
Tenby d.	1952	|	|	...	...	...	...	|	...	|	2106	...	...	...	...	...	*2154*	2143	...	...	|	...	...	...	|
Pembroke Dock a.	*2035*	|	|	...	...	...	...	|	...	|	2136	...	...	...	...	...	*2226*	2218	...	...	|	...	...	...	|
Clarbeston Road d.	...	2004x	2000x	2005	...	...	...	2025x	2030	2046x	...	...	...	...	...	...	...	...	...	...	2210x	...	...	...	2234x
Haverfordwest d.	...	2012	2009	|	...	...	...	2033	|	2054	...	...	...	...	...	...	...	...	...	...	2223	...	...	...	2242
Milford Haven a.	...	...	2032	|	...	...	...	2056	|	2122	...	...	...	...	...	...	...	...	...	...	2246	...	...	...	2305
Fishguard Harbour a.	...	...	...	2029	...	...	...	...	2054	...	...	...	...	...	...	...	...	...	...	...	...	...	...	...	...

	⑦ 2	Ⓐ	⑥	Ⓐ	⑦	Ⓐ 2	⑥ 2		Ⓐ	⑥	⑦	①–④ 2	⑤⑥ 2	Ⓐ	⑦ 2	⚒ 2	⑥ 2		⑦	⑥	Ⓐ 2	Ⓐ	⑦	⑤	①–④
London Paddington **132** d.	...	1815	1845	1845	1837	...	...	...	1915	1945	1937	...	...	2015	...	...	...	...	2037	2045	...	2115	2137	2245	2245
Manchester Piccadilly **149** d.	...	|	|	|	|	...	...	...	|	|	|	1830	1830	|	...	...	...	...	|	|	1930	|	|	|	|
Cardiff Central d.	2015	2025	2048	2054	2057	2104	2104	...	2124	2148	2157	2209	2207	2226	2230	...	2244	...	2259	2308	2315	2343	0006	0055	0117
Bridgend d.	2037	2046	2109	2115	2119	2127	2123	...	2146	2210	2219	2235	2233	2248	2251	...	2314	...	2321	2330	2345	0005	0028	0121	0142
Port Talbot d.	2054	2059	2122	2128	2131	2145	2139	...	2159	2223	2231	2247	2245	2301	2305	...	2331	...	2335	2343	0001	0018	0041	0134	0155
Neath d.	2102	2107	2130	2136	2139	2152	2146	...	2207	2231	2239	|	2252	2309	2313	...	2342	...	2343	2351	0013	0026	0050	0142	0203
Swansea a.	2114	2119	2143	2150	2153	2204	2157	...	2220	2245	2255	|	2307	2322	2325	...	2358	...	0059	0005	0028	0039	0102	0155	0216
Swansea d.	2118	...	...	...	...	2227	2225	...	...	...	...	|	2310	...	2338	2345	0010	...	...	...	0045	...	...	...	...
Llanelli d.	2137	...	...	...	...	2246	2244	...	...	...	...	2321	2329	...	2358	0002	0029s	...	...	...	0102s	...	...	...	...
Carmarthen a.	2206	...	...	...	...	2315	2318	...	...	...	...	2357	0007	...	0030	0028	0105	...	...	...	0140	...	...	...	...
Carmarthen d.	2210	...	...	...	...	2320	...	...	...	...	...	...	...	...	0034	0031	...	...	...	...	...	...	...	...	...
Whitland d.	2226	...	...	...	...	2335	...	...	...	...	...	...	...	...	0050	0046	...	...	...	...	...	...	...	...	...
Tenby d.	|	...	...	...	...	|	...	...	...	...	...	...	...	...	|	|	...	...	...	...	...	...	...	...	...
Pembroke Dock a.	|	...	...	...	...	|	...	...	...	...	...	...	...	...	|	|	...	...	...	...	...	...	...	...	...
Clarbeston Road d.	2242x	...	...	...	...	2350x	...	...	...	...	...	...	...	...	0103x	0100x	...	...	...	...	...	...	...	...	...
Haverfordwest d.	2250	...	...	...	...	2358	...	...	...	...	...	...	...	...	|	|	...	...	...	...	...	...	...	...	...
Milford Haven a.	2310	...	...	...	...	0021	...	...	...	...	...	...	...	...	|	|	...	...	...	...	...	...	...	...	...
Fishguard Harbour a.	...	...	...	...	...	...	...	...	...	...	...	...	...	...	0132	0128	...	...	...	...	...	...	...	...	...

H – THE PEMBROKE COAST EXPRESS – (12) and 🍷 London Paddington - Pembroke Dock and v.v. (see Table **132**).
a – ⑤ only (to Swindon on ①–④).
s – Calls to set down only.
x – Calls on request.

△ – Connects with train in previous column.
☆ – Connecting train conveys (2) only.

AW, GW Most London trains convey 🍸

SOUTH WEST WALES - SWANSEA - CARDIFF 135

Service until September 7. For 🚢 services to Ireland see Table 2030.

	②–⑥ 2	⑦ 2	⑦ 🚌	Ⓐ ☆	⑥ ☆	Ⓐ	⑥	Ⓐ	⑥	⚒ 2	Ⓐ	⑥	Ⓐ	⑥	Ⓐ 2	⑥ 2	Ⓐ	⑥	Ⓐ 2	⑥ 2	⚒	⚒ 2	Ⓐ	⑦	Ⓐ
Fishguard Harbour d.	...	0150	...	*0150*	*0150*	...	...	...	...	...	...	...	...	...	...	...	...	...	...	...	...	...	...	...	...
Milford Haven d.	0018	|	...	|	|	...	...	...	...	...	...	...	...	...	...	...	...	...	...	...	...	0555	...	...	...
Haverfordwest d.	0033	|	...	|	|	...	...	...	...	...	...	...	...	...	...	...	...	...	...	...	...	0610	...	...	...
Clarbeston Road d.	0041x	|	...	*0212x*	*0212x*	...	...	...	...	...	...	...	...	...	...	...	...	...	...	...	...	0618x	...	...	...
Pembroke Dock d.	|	|	...	|	|	...	...	...	...	...	...	...	...	...	...	...	...	...	...	...	...	|	...	...	...
Tenby d.	|	|	...	|	|	...	...	...	...	...	...	...	...	...	...	...	...	...	...	...	...	|	...	...	...
Whitland d.	0054	0224s	...	*0224*	*0224*	...	...	...	...	...	...	...	...	...	...	...	...	...	...	...	...	0631	...	...	...
Carmarthen a.	0116	0242s	...	*0241*	*0241*	...	...	...	...	...	...	...	...	...	...	...	...	...	...	...	...	0647	...	...	...
Carmarthen d.	...	0245s	0250	*0303*	*0244*	...	...	...	...	0503	...	...	...	...	0547	0555	...	...	0615	0620	...	0650	...	...	0730
Llanelli d.	...	0308s	|	*0325*	*0306*	...	...	...	...	0528	...	...	...	...	0615	0624	...	...	0644	0648	...	0719	...	...	0805
Swansea a.	...	|	0350	*0347*	*0329*	...	...	...	...	|	...	...	...	...	0635	0643	...	...	0704	0708	...	0738	...	...	0821
Swansea d.	...	|	...	0352	0358	0458	0458	0527	0528	|	0558	0558	0628	0628	0640	0647	0658	0658	0706	0711	0728	0744	0758	0810	0828
Neath d.	...	|	...	0404	0410	0510	0510	0539	0540	|	0610	0610	0640	0640	0653	0658	0710	0710	0717	0726	0740	0755	0810	0822	0840
Port Talbot d.	...	|	...	0412	0418	0518	0518	0547	0548	0601	0618	0618	0648	0648	0704	0705	0718	0718	0724	0737	0748	0802	0818	0829	0848
Bridgend d.	...	|	...	0425	0430	0531	0531	0600	0601	0616	0631	0631	0701	0701	0720	0720	0731	0731	0740	0753	0801	0817	0831	0842	0901
Cardiff Central a.	...	0410	...	0501	0452	0552	0552	0621	0622	0643	0652	0652	0722	0722	0748	0742	0752	0752	0802	0834	0822	0842	0852	0905	0922
Manchester Piccadilly **149** a.	...	...	...	|	|	|	|	|	|	1014	|	|	|	|	...	1115	|	|	1115	...	|	1215	|	|	|
London Paddington **132** a.	...	...	...	0732	0744	0802	0807	0833	0832	...	0854	0902	0929	0938	...	...	0958	1002	...	...	1032	...	1107	1126	1132

	⚒ 2	⚒ 2	⚒ 2	⑦	Ⓐ	⑥	⑦ 2	⚒ 2	⑦	Ⓐ	⑥	⑦ 2	⚒ 2	⑦	⑦ 2△	⑥ 2	Ⓐ 2	⚒	Ⓐ 2	⑥ 2	Ⓐ 2	⑥ 2	⑦ ☆	Ⓐ	⑥ H
Fishguard Harbour d.	0653	...	...	...	...	...	...	0804	...	...	...	...	...	...	...	...	...	...	0954	0953	...	...	...	...	...
Milford Haven d.	|	0705	...	...	...	...	...	|	...	...	...	...	0908	...	0928	...	...	...	|	|	...	...	...	...	...
Haverfordwest d.	|	0720	...	...	...	...	...	|	...	...	...	...	0923	...	0943	...	...	...	|	|	...	...	...	...	...
Clarbeston Road d.	0717	0728x	...	...	...	...	...	0825x	...	...	...	...	0931x	...	0952x	...	...	...	1017x	1014x	...	...	...	...	...
Pembroke Dock d.	▬	|	0659	...	...	...	...	|	...	...	...	...	|	...	|	...	0909	...	|	|	...	...	...	...	1001
Tenby d.	...	|	0729	...	...	...	...	|	...	...	...	...	|	...	|	...	0938	...	|	|	...	...	...	...	1037
Whitland d.	...	0741	0756	...	...	...	...	0838	...	...	...	...	0944	...	1008	1005	1007	...	1032	1029	...	...	...	...	1108
Carmarthen a.	...	0755	0815	...	...	...	...	0857	...	...	...	...	1003	...	1024	1025	1024	...	1049	1046	...	...	...	...	1126
Carmarthen d.	...	0801	0818	...	...	...	0840	0900	...	...	0935	0940	1004	...	1030	1027	1031	...	...	...	1103	1109	*1053*	...	1135
Llanelli d.	⑥	0830	0848	...	...	...	0907	0925	...	...	1003	1010	1031	...	1057	1053	1057	...	...	...	1131	1137	*1123*	...	1203
Swansea a.	...	0849	0907	...	...	...	0927	0951	...	...	1021	1032	1049	...	1116	1120	1123	...	...	...	1152	1156	*1147*	...	1219
Swansea d.	0828	0855	0910	0921	0928	0928	0932	0955	1021	1028	1028	...	1055	1121	1132	...	...	1128	...	...	1155	1200	1221	1228	1228
Neath d.	0840	0906	0925	0933	0940	0940	0943	1006	1033	1040	1040	...	1106	1133	1143	...	...	1140	...	...	1206	1211	1233	1240	1240
Port Talbot d.	0848	0913	0936	0940	0948	0948	0950	1013	1040	1048	1048	...	1113	1140	1150	...	...	1148	...	...	1213	1218	1240	1248	1248
Bridgend d.	0901	0926	0953	0953	1001	1001	1005	1026	1053	1101	1101	...	1126	1153	1205	...	...	1201	...	...	1226	1231	1253	1301	1301
Cardiff Central a.	0922	0948	1018	1014	1022	1022	1029	1048	1114	1122	1122	...	1148	1214	1234	...	...	1222	...	...	1248	1252	1314	1322	1322
Manchester Piccadilly **149** a.	|	1315	...	|	|	|	1419	1415	|	|	|	...	1515	|	1615	...	...	|	...	...	1615	1615	|	|	|
London Paddington **132** a.	1133	...	...	1236	1233	1237	...	...	1336	1333	1338	...	...	1436	...	...	...	1433	...	...	...	...	1536	1533	1530

	⚒ 2	⑥ 2	⑦	⑦ 2	⑥ 2	Ⓐ 2	Ⓐ	⑥	⑦ 2	Ⓐ 2	⑥ 2	⑦ ☆	Ⓐ	⑥	Ⓐ 2	⑥ 2	Ⓐ 2	⑥ 2	⑦	⑥ 2	Ⓐ 2	Ⓐ	⑥	⑦ 2	⚒ 2
Fishguard Harbour d.	...	...	...	...	...	...	...	...	...	...	...	...	...	...	...	...	1329	1330	...	...	...	...	...	...	...
Milford Haven d.	1108	...	...	...	...	...	...	...	1128	...	...	...	...	...	1308	1308	|	|	...	...	...	...	...	1323	...
Haverfordwest d.	1123	...	...	...	...	...	...	...	1143	...	...	...	...	...	1323	1323	|	|	...	...	...	...	...	1336	...
Clarbeston Road d.	1131x	...	...	...	...	...	...	...	1152x	...	...	...	...	...	1331x	1331x	|	|	...	...	...	...	...	1345x	...
Pembroke Dock d.	|	...	...	1040	...	1109	...	...	|	...	...	*1155*	...	...	|	|	|	|	...	1309	1309	...	...	|	...
Tenby d.	|	...	...	1114	1141	1143	...	...	|	...	...	*1223*	...	...	|	|	|	|	...	1342	1341	...	...	|	...
Whitland d.	1144	...	...	1145	1209	1211	...	...	1208	...	...	*1254*	...	...	1344	1344	1404	1404	...	1411	1409	...	...	1402	...
Carmarthen a.	1200	...	...	1205	1227	1229	...	...	1226	...	...	*1315*	...	...	1400	1400	1421	1420	...	1428	1430	...	...	1420	...
Carmarthen d.	1205	...	...	...	1231	1233	...	...	1229	1302	1302	*1318*	...	...	1405	1405	1428	1424	...	1433	1438	...	...	1430	1503
Llanelli d.	1230	1235	...	...	1257	1259	...	...	1255	1330	1330	*1348*	...	...	1430	1430	1450	1447	...	1458	1503	...	...	1456	1532
Swansea a.	1249	1304	...	...	1322	1322	...	...	1318	1351	1349	*1413*	...	...	1449	1449	|	|	...	1522	1523	...	...	1521	1551
Swansea d.	1253	1310	1321	...	...	...	1328	1328	1342	1355	1400	1421	1428	1428	1455	1455	|	|	1521	...	...	1528	1528	1533	1555
Neath d.	1304	1325	1333	...	...	...	1340	1340	1353	1406	1411	1433	1440	1440	1506	1506	|	|	1533	...	...	1540	1540	1544	1606
Port Talbot d.	1311	1336	1340	...	...	...	1348	1348	1400	1413	1418	1440	1448	1448	1513	1513	|	|	1540	...	...	1548	1548	1551	1613
Bridgend d.	1325	1353	1353	...	...	...	1401	1401	1416	1426	1431	1453	1501	1501	1526	1526	1537	1531	1553	...	...	1601	1601	1606	1626
Cardiff Central a.	1348	1415	1414	...	...	...	1422	1422	1445	1447	1452	1514	1522	1522	1547	1551	1558	1558	1614	...	...	1622	1622	1636	1648
Manchester Piccadilly **149** a.	1714	...	|	...	...	...	|	|	1817	1813	1815	|	|	|	1915	1915	...	...	|	...	...	|	|	2017	2015
London Paddington **132** a.	...	...	1636	...	...	...	1632	1638	...	...	...	1738	1730	1732	...	...	...	...	1836	...	...	1830	1832	...	...

	⑦	Ⓐ	⑥	⑦ ☆	Ⓐ 2	⑥ 2	⑥	Ⓐ 2	Ⓐ	⑦ 2	⑦	Ⓐ 2	⑥ 2	Ⓐ	⑥	⑦	⑥ 2	Ⓐ 2	⑥ 2	⑦ 2	Ⓐ 2	⑥	⑦ 2	Ⓐ	Ⓐ 2
Fishguard Harbour d.	...	...	...	*1422*	...	...	...	...	...	...	...	...	...	...	...	...	...	...	...	...	...	...	...	...	...
Milford Haven d.	...	...	...	|	1508	1508	...	...	...	1528	...	...	...	...	...	...	1708	1708	...	...	...	...	1730	...	...
Haverfordwest d.	...	...	...	|	1523	1523	...	...	...	1543	...	...	...	...	...	...	1723	1723	...	...	...	...	1745	...	...
Clarbeston Road d.	...	...	...	|	1531x	1531x	...	...	...	1552x	...	...	...	...	...	...	1731x	1731x	...	...	...	...	1753x	...	...
Pembroke Dock d.	...	...	...	|	|	|	1455	1509	...	|	...	...	...	...	...	...	|	|	1625	1645	1709	...	|	...	...
Tenby d.	...	...	...	|	|	|	1536	1541	...	|	...	...	...	...	...	...	|	|	1655	1713	1738	...	|	...	...
Whitland d.	...	...	...	*1457*	1544	1544	1609	1609	...	1609	...	...	...	...	...	...	1745	1745	1726	1744	1807	...	1808	...	...
Carmarthen a.	...	...	...	*1514*	1600	1600	1627	1627	...	1626	...	...	...	...	...	...	1803	1802	1744	1804	1824	...	1829	...	...
Carmarthen d.	1526	...	...	*1540*	1605	1605	1633	1631	...	1631	1655	1658	1702	...	...	...	1807	1806	1833	1807	1831	...	...	...	1850
Llanelli d.	1559	...	...	*1610*	1630	1630	1705	1656	...	1701	1722	1726	1730	...	...	...	1836	1835	1859	1838	1857	...	...	...	1921
Swansea a.	1614	...	...	*1635*	1649	1649	1721	1722	...	1723	1739	1746	1749	...	...	...	1856	1855	1923	1906	1919	...	...	...	1943
Swansea d.	1621	1628	1628	1651	1655	1658	1728	...	1728	1730	1751	1749	1754	1828	1828	1851	1900	1858	...	...	...	1928	...	1929	1951
Neath d.	1633	1640	1640	1703	1706	1709	1740	...	1740	1741	1803	1803	1805	1840	1840	1903	1911	1913	...	...	...	1940	...	1940	2002
Port Talbot d.	1640	1648	1648	1710	1713	1716	1748	...	1748	1748	1810	1814	1812	1848	1848	1910	1919	1924	...	...	...	1948	...	1948	2009
Bridgend d.	1653	1701	1701	1723	1726	1731	1801	...	1801	1803	1823	1829	1827	1901	1901	1923	1933	1940	...	...	...	2001	...	2001	2023
Cardiff Central a.	1714	1722	1722	1745	1746	1751	1822	...	1822	1832	1845	1849	1847	1922	1922	1945	1956	2003	...	...	...	2023	...	2022	2046
Manchester Piccadilly **149** a.	|	|	|	|	2106	2116	|	...	|	2219	|	2214	2213	|	|	|	...	...	...	...	...	|	...	|	...
London Paddington **132** a.	1936	1932	1932	2012	...	...	2032	...	2037	...	2106	...	...	2132	2137	2201	...	...	...	...	...	2241	...	2247	...

	⑥ 2	⑦	Ⓐ	⚒ 2	Ⓐ 2	⑥ 2	⑦ 2	⑦ 2	⑥ 2	Ⓐ 2	⑦ 2	⑥ 2	Ⓐ 2	Ⓐ 2	Ⓐ 2	⑥ 2	⑥ 2	⑦ 2	⑥ 2	Ⓐ 2	⑦ 2	⑥ 2	Ⓐ 2	⑦ 2	⚒ 2
Fishguard Harbour d.	...	...	...	1900	...	...	...	...	...	...	...	...	...	...	2050	2100	...	...	...	...	...	...	...	...	...
Milford Haven d.	...	...	...	|	1908	1908	...	1938	...	...	...	...	...	2036	|	|	2116	2135	...	...	...	...	...	2315	2318
Haverfordwest d.	...	...	...	|	1923	1923	...	1953	...	...	...	...	...	2051	|	|	2131	2151	...	...	...	...	...	2330	2333
Clarbeston Road d.	...	...	...	1922	1931x	1931x	...	2001x	...	...	...	...	...	2059x	2112x	2122x	2139x	2159x	...	...	...	...	...	2339x	2341x
Pembroke Dock d.	...	...	...	▬	|	|	1900	|	1909	*1919*	...	...	...	|	|	|	|	|	2109	2109	2145	2218	2228	|	|
Tenby d.	...	...	...	...	|	|	1928	|	1951	1957	...	...	...	|	|	|	|	|	2142	2153	2213	2245	2255	|	|
Whitland d.	...	...	...	...	1944	1944	1959	2017	2021	2027	...	...	...	2112	2126	2136	2152	2214	2211	2221	2244	2315	2325	2353	2354
Carmarthen a.	...	...	...	⑦	2000	2004	2016	2036	2039	2045	...	...	...	2134	2146	2157	2214	2231	2228	2239	2305	2334	2344	0014	0016
Carmarthen d.	1854	1905	...	2	2005	2007	2019	...	2047	2047	2115	...	...	...	...	...	...	2234	2235	2244	...	...	...	...	...
Llanelli d.	1925	1932	...	1958	2029	2031	2051	...	2117	2117	2141	*2144*	*2139*	...	...	...	...	2304	2305	2314	...	...	...	...	...
Swansea a.	1947	1949	...	2025	2049	2051	2117	...	2142	2142	2204	*2212*	*2212*	...	...	...	...	2327	2330	2343	...	...	...	...	...
Swansea d.	1952	1955	2028	2040	2056	2055	...	...	2143	2143	2210	2220	2232	...	...	...	...	2331	...	...	...	...	...	...	...
Neath d.	2003	2007	2040	2051	2107	2106	...	...	2159	2158	2221	2235	2247	...	...	...	...	2343	...	...	...	...	...	...	...
Port Talbot d.	2010	2014	2048	2058	2114	2113	...	...	2210	2209	2228	2246	2258	...	...	...	...	2350	...	...	...	...	...	...	...
Bridgend d.	2024	2028	2101	2111	2127	2126	...	...	2226	2225	2245	2302	2314	...	...	...	...	0006	...	...	...	...	...	...	...
Cardiff Central a.	2047	2050	2122	2135	2150	2146	...	...	2250	2247	2307	2326	2338	...	...	...	...	0030	...	...	...	...	...	...	...
Manchester Piccadilly **149** a.	...	|	|	...	...	...	...	...	...	...	...	...	...	...	...	...	...	...	...	...	...	...	...	...	...
London Paddington **132** a.	...	2326	2338a	...	...	...	...	...	...	...	...	...	...	...	...	...	...	...	...	...	...	...	...	...	...

For footnotes see previous page.

136 CARDIFF - BRISTOL — 2nd class GW

On ①–⑥ most trains continue to Taunton (Table 137) or Portsmouth (Table 139).

km																							
			Ⓐ	Ⓐ	Ⓐ	Ⓐ	Ⓐ	Ⓐ	Ⓐ	Ⓐ	Ⓐ		Ⓐ	Ⓐ	Ⓐ	Ⓐ	Ⓐ	Ⓐ	Ⓐ	Ⓐ	Ⓐ	Ⓐ	Ⓐ	Ⓐ
0	**Cardiff** Central .... d.	Ⓐ	0628	0700	0730	0800	0830	0900	0930	1000	1030	and at the same	1600	1630	1700	1730	1800	1830	1900	1930	2000	2030	2100	2130
19	Newport .... d.		0642	0715	0744	0815	0844	0915	0944	1015	1044	minutes past	1615	1644	1715	1744	1815	1844	1915	1944	2015	2044	2115	2143
61	**Bristol** T Meads .... a.		0718	0751	0818	0853	0918	0953	1019	1051	1118	each hour until	1651	1718	1753	1818	1851	1918	1951	2017	2053	2119	2152	2222

	Ⓐ	Ⓐ	Ⓐ	Ⓐ			⑥	⑥	⑥	⑥	⑥	⑥	⑥	⑥	⑥	⑥		⑥	⑥	⑥	⑥	⑥	⑥	⑥
Cardiff Central .... d.	2140	2204	2236	2327	...	⑥	0455	0628	0700	0730	0800	0830	0900	0930	1000	1030	and at the same	1600	1630	1700	1730	1800	1830	1900
Newport .... d.	2156	2218	2253	2345	...		0509	0644	0715	0744	0815	0844	0915	0944	1015	1044	minutes past	1615	1644	1715	1744	1815	1844	1915
Bristol T Meads .... a.	2229	2305	2337	0033	...		0554	0718	0751	0819	0853	0919	0951	1018	1052	1119	each hour until	1651	1719	1751	1819	1851	1919	1951

	⑥	⑥	⑥	⑥	⑥	⑥			⑦	⑦	⑦	⑦	⑦	⑦	⑦	⑦		⑦	⑦	⑦	⑦		⑦	⑦	⑦	⑦
Cardiff Central .... d.	1930	2000	2030	2100	2130	2204	...	⑦	0805	0913	1008	1108	1208	1308	1408	1508	...	1608	1635	1708	1740	...	1808	1908	2018	2200
Newport .... d.	1944	2015	2044	2115	2144	2218	...		0823	0927	1022	1122	1221	1322	1422	1522	...	1622	1649	1722	1754	...	1822	1922	2031	2219
Bristol T Meads .... a.	2019	2053	2119	2151	2224	2305	...		0904	1013	1102	1203	1304	1402	1503	1604	...	1703	1727	1804	1833	...	1906	2006	2111	2300

		Ⓐ	Ⓐ	Ⓐ	Ⓐ	Ⓐ	Ⓐ	Ⓐ	Ⓐ	Ⓐ	Ⓐ	Ⓐ	Ⓐ	Ⓐ		Ⓐ	Ⓐ	Ⓐ	Ⓐ	Ⓐ	Ⓐ	Ⓐ	Ⓐ	Ⓐ
Bristol T Meads .... d.	Ⓐ	0520	0554	0619	0650	0716	0720	0754	0824	0854	0921	0956	1021	1054	and at the same	1624	1654	1721	1754	1821	1854	1921	1954	2015
Newport .... a.		0608	0628	0659	0725	0747	0807	0827	0902	0924	0958	1026	1102	1126	minutes past	1700	1727	1758	1825	1906	1926	2001	2027	2047
Cardiff Central .... a.		0624	0648	0718	0744	0802	0824	0846	0924	0943	1019	1043	1123	1145	each hour until	1727	1744	1817	1843	1924	1946	2021	2046	2105

	Ⓐ	Ⓐ	Ⓐ	Ⓐ			⑥	⑥	⑥	⑥	⑥	⑥	⑥	⑥	⑥	⑥		⑥	⑥	⑥	⑥	⑥	⑥	⑥
Bristol T Meads .... d.	2054	2119	2154	2254	...	⑥	0646	0650	0721	0754	0820	0854	0921	0954	1021	1054	and at the same	1621	1654	1721	1754	1821	1854	1921
Newport .... a.	2126	2158	2236	2334	...		0731	0726	0758	0826	0901	0925	0958	1024	1100	1124	minutes past	1700	1726	1758	1825	1901	1924	1956
Cardiff Central .... a.	2145	2218	2300	2356	...		0747	0744	0817	0843	0922	0943	1018	1043	1121	1143	each hour until	1718	1744	1818	1843	1918	1943	2016

	⑥	⑥	⑥	⑥	⑥	⑥			⑦	⑦		⑦	⑦		⑦	⑦		⑦	⑦		⑦	⑦		⑦	⑦	
Bristol T Meads .... d.	1954	2010	2054	2129	2154	2254	...	⑦	0948	1148	...	1348	1448	...	1548	1648	...	1748	1848	...	1948	2048	...	2148	2248	...
Newport .... a.	2025	2044	2125	2211	2241	2335	...		1025	1230	...	1426	1524	...	1626	1729	...	1826	1926	...	2028	2126	...	2231	2325	...
Cardiff Central .... a.	2043	2102	2143	2230	2301	2355	...		1041	1245	...	1446	1541	...	1644	1746	...	1844	1942	...	2046	2142	...	2253	2347	...

137 BRISTOL - TAUNTON — 2nd class GW

Service until September 7. On ①–⑥ most trains continue to / from Cardiff Central (Table 136).

km																											
			Ⓐ	Ⓐ	Ⓐ	Ⓐ	Ⓐ	Ⓐ	Ⓐ	Ⓐ	Ⓐ	Ⓐ	Ⓐ	Ⓐ	Ⓐ	Ⓐ	Ⓐ	Ⓐ	Ⓐ	Ⓐ	Ⓐ	Ⓐ	Ⓐ			⑥	⑥
0	**Bristol** TM ...... d.	Ⓐ	0524	0642	0718	0826	0855	0955	1053	1153	1253	1357	1453	1553	1653	1755	1820	1856	1955	2055	2156	2306	2335	...	⑥	0524	0618
31	Weston ⊙ .... d.		0545	0706	0749	0901	0929	1023	1123	1222	1322	1425	1528	1627	1728	1830	1855	1930	2029	2133	2229	2342	0005s	...		0545	0646
43	Highbridge ⊖ .. d.		0555	0717	0800	0911	0940	1034	1134	1233	1333	1436	1538	1637	1738	1841	1909	1940	2039	2144	2240	2354	0016s	...		0555	0657
53	Bridgwater .... d.		0603	0725	0808	0919	0948	1042	1142	1241	1341	1444	1546	1645	1746	1849	1917	1948	2047	2152	2248	0002	0024s	...		0603	0705
72	**Taunton** .... a.		0616	0738	0824	0933	1001	1059	1157	1257	1358	1457	1601	1700	1801	1903	1928	2004	2102	2207	2301	0014	0036	...		0616	0719

	⑥	⑥	⑥	⑥	⑥	⑥	⑥	⑥	⑥	⑥	⑥	⑥	⑥	⑥	⑥	⑥			⑦	⑦	⑦	⑦	⑦	⑦	⑦	⑦	⑦
Bristol TM .... d.	0718	0857	0955	1053	1153	1253	1355	1453	1553	1653	1753	1853	1953	2055	2159	2217	...	⑦	0733	0828	1023	1111	1304	1555	1807	1905	2025
Weston ⊙ .... d.	0751	0932	1023	1123	1222	1323	1423	1523	1623	1723	1823	1923	2024	2128	2233	2247s	...		0756	0859	1058	1140	1332	1628	1835	1940	2058
Highbridge ⊖ .... d.	0802	0944	1034	1134	1233	1334	1434	1535	1634	1734	1834	1934	2034	2139	2244	2258s	...		|	0910	1109	1150	1343	1643	1846	1951	2109
Bridgwater .... d.	0810	0952	1042	1142	1241	1342	1442	1543	1642	1742	1842	1942	2042	2147	2252	2305s	...		0812	0918	1117	1158	1351	1651	1854	1959	2117
Taunton .... a.	0824	1006	1059	1156	1257	1359	1501	1559	1657	1759	1856	1959	2059	2159	2305	2317	...		0825	0931	1131	1212	1405	1706	1908	2013	2133

		Ⓐ	Ⓐ	Ⓐ	Ⓐ	Ⓐ	Ⓐ	Ⓐ	Ⓐ	Ⓐ	Ⓐ	Ⓐ	Ⓐ	Ⓐ	Ⓐ	Ⓐ	Ⓐ	Ⓐ	Ⓐ	Ⓐ	Ⓐ			⑥	⑥	⑥	⑥
Taunton .... d.	Ⓐ	0512	0602	0634	0654	0736	0836	0938	1007	1104	1207	1307	1410	1515	1607	1706	1808	1910	2030	2129	2245	...	⑥	0528	0634	0654	0735
Bridgwater .... d.		0524	0614	0646	0705	0748	0848	0950	1019	1116	1219	1319	1422	1527	1619	1717	1819	1922	2042	2140	2257	...		0540	0646	0705	0747
Highbridge ⊖ .... d.		0532	0621	0654	0713	0756	0856	0957	1027	1124	1227	1327	1430	1534	1627	1725	1827	1929	2050	2147	2305	...		0548	0654	0712	0755
Weston ⊙ .... a.		0543	0632	0704	0724	0806	0908	1008	1038	1134	1238	1338	1441	1545	1637	1737	1838	1940	2100	2159	2315	...		0559	0705	0724	0805
Bristol TM .... a.		0620	0709	0741	0757	0841	0943	1042	1111	1212	1309	1411	1513	1615	1711	1814	1913	2019	2135	2232	2351	...		0634	0741	0758	0840

	⑥	⑥	⑥	⑥	⑥	⑥	⑥	⑥	⑥	⑥	⑥	⑥	⑥	⑥			⑦	⑦	⑦	⑦	⑦	⑦	⑦	⑦	⑦	⑦	⑦
Taunton .... d.	0759	0910	1012	1107	1207	1307	1407	1507	1607	1707	1807	1907	2017	2135	...	⑦	0835	1011	1136	1311	1518	1659	1719	1822	1857	2025	2135
Bridgwater .... d.	0810	0922	1024	1119	1219	1319	1419	1519	1619	1719	1819	1919	2029	2147	...		0847	1023	1148	1323	1530	1710	1730	1834	1907	2037	2148
Highbridge ⊖ .... d.	0817	0930	1032	1127	1227	1327	1427	1527	1627	1727	1827	1927	2037	2155	...		0855	1031	1155	1330	1537	1718	1737	1841	1914	2045	2155
Weston ⊙ .... a.	0827	0942	1042	1137	1237	1337	1437	1537	1637	1737	1837	1937	2048	2205	...		0906	1041	1205	1341	1547	1728	1748	1852	1925	2056	2205
Bristol TM .... a.	0857	1013	1113	1210	1309	1411	1510	1609	1711	1811	1910	2009	2124	2242	...		0938	1111	1242	1413	1619	1756	1819	1922	1953	2131	2237

s – Calls to set down only. ⊖ – Highbridge and Burnham. ⊙ – Weston super Mare.

138 WORCESTER - GLOUCESTER - BRISTOL — 2nd class GW

Service on ⑦ valid until September 7. Most trains from Worcester continue to / from Weymouth (Table 139).

km																										
			Ⓐ	Ⓐ	Ⓐ	Ⓐ	Ⓐ	Ⓐ	Ⓐ	Ⓐ	Ⓐ	Ⓐ	Ⓐ	Ⓐ	Ⓐ	Ⓐ	Ⓐ	Ⓐ	Ⓐ	Ⓐ	Ⓐ	Ⓐ			⑥	⑥
0	**Worcester** Shrub Hill d.	Ⓐ	*0521*	...	...	0649	*0708*	0906	...	1106	...	1306	...	1506	...	1706	...	1907	...	...	2132	2228	...	⑥	...	...
24	Ashchurch ♤ .... d.		*0540*	...	*0627*	0705	|	0924	...	1124	...	1324	...	1524	...	1724	...	1924	...	...	2152	2251	...		...	...
36	Cheltenham Spa **121** d.		*0548*	0624	*0643*	0716	*0727*	0933	...	1132	...	1332	...	1533	...	1732	...	1933	2048	2152	2205	2304	...		...	0648
46	**Gloucester** .... **121** a.		*0602*	0634	*0653*	0726	*0738*	0942	...	1145	...	1344	...	1544	...	1744	...	1942	2058	2201	2221	2317	...		...	0658
46	**Gloucester** .... d.		0616	0642	0705	0739	0841	0945	1041	1147	1241	1346	1441	1546	1640	1746	1841	1945	2115	2206	2228	...	...		0620	0702
97	**Bristol** Parkway .... a.		0654	0722	0748	0819	0920	1023	1119	1223	1318	1422	1518	1622	1719	1823	1920	2023	2150	2232	2304	...	...		0701	0739
108	**Bristol** T Meads .... a.		0712	0740	0800	0836	0936	1039	1135	1235	1335	1439	1536	1638	1736	1838	1935	2039	2211	2243	2319	...	...		0713	0755

	⑥	⑥	⑥	⑥	⑥	⑥	⑥	⑥	⑥	⑥	⑥	⑥	⑥	⑥	⑥	⑥			⑦	⑦		⑦	⑦		⑦	⑦
Worcester Shrub Hill . d.	0647	...	0908	...	1106	...	1254	...	1506	...	1706	...	1906	...	...	2131	...	⑦	...	...	...	1436	1640	...	1840	2038
Ashchurch ♤ .... d.	0703	...	0924	...	1124	...	1310	...	1524	...	1724	*1807*	1924	...	...	2151	...		...	...	...	1451	1657	...	1855	2054
Cheltenham Spa .. **121** d.	0713	...	0934	...	1133	...	1320	...	1533	...	1733	*1816*	1933	2102	2150	2201	...		1007	1203	...	1500	1706	...	1904	2102
Gloucester .... **121** a.	0725	...	0945	...	1145	...	1332	...	1544	...	1745	*1826*	1945	2112	2159	2211	...		1017	1214	...	1511	1716	...	1918	2113
Gloucester .... d.	0740	0841	0946	1041	1146	1241	1342	1441	1546	1641	1746	1841	1946	2114	2205	...	...		1018	1216	...	1514	1719	...	1920	2115
Bristol Parkway .... a.	0818	0919	1024	1120	1224	1319	1421	1519	1624	1719	1824	1920	2024	2152	2230	...	...		1053	1254	...	1552	1756	...	1957	2153
Bristol T Meads .... a.	0834	0936	1039	1135	1239	1334	1437	1535	1640	1734	1839	1935	2039	2204	2241	...	...		1107	1308	...	1608	1809	...	2011	2207

		Ⓐ	Ⓐ	Ⓐ	Ⓐ	Ⓐ	Ⓐ	Ⓐ	Ⓐ	Ⓐ	Ⓐ	Ⓐ	Ⓐ	Ⓐ	Ⓐ	Ⓐ	Ⓐ	Ⓐ	Ⓐ	Ⓐ			⑥	⑥	⑥	⑥
Bristol T Meads .... d.	Ⓐ	...	...	0734	0841	0941	1041	1141	1241	1341	1441	1541	1641	1741	1841	1941	2000	2041	...	2211	...	⑥	...	0615	...	0741
Bristol Parkway .... d.		...	...	0748	0852	0952	1055	1152	1252	1352	1452	1552	1652	1753	1852	1952	2009	2052	...	2223	...		...	0624	...	0752
Gloucester .... a.		...	...	0832	0933	1032	1134	1233	1334	1433	1534	1633	1734	1833	1930	2032	2035	2132	...	2303	...		...	0652	...	0833
Gloucester .... **121** d.		0600	0714	...	0937	...	1136	...	1337	...	1536	...	1736	...	1938	2035	2046	2133	2152	...	...		0550	0700	0715	...
Cheltenham Spa .. **121** a.		0610	0724	...	0946	...	1146	...	1346	...	1546	...	1747	...	1949	2048	2054	2144	2202	...	...		0559	0709	0724	...
Ashchurch ♤ .... a.		0620	0734	...	0956	...	1156	...	1356	...	1556	...	1756	...	1959	...	...	2154	|	...	...		0609	...	0734	...
Worcester Shrub Hill . a.		0641	0754	...	1014	...	1213	...	1414	...	1614	...	1816	...	2015	...	...	2214	2224	...	...		0633	...	0752	...

	⑥	⑥	⑥	⑥	⑥	⑥	⑥	⑥	⑥	⑥	⑥	⑥	⑥	⑥			⑦		⑦A	B	⑦		⑦	⑦		⑦
Bristol T Meads .... d.	0841	0941	1041	1141	1241	1341	1441	1541	1641	1741	1841	1941	2043	2206	...	⑦	0941	...	1211	1211	1441	...	1641	1841	...	2041
Bristol Parkway .... d.	0852	0952	1052	1152	1252	1352	1452	1552	1652	1752	1852	1952	2052	2218	...		0953	...	1221	1221	1451	...	1650	1850	...	2050
Gloucester .... a.	0933	1032	1132	1233	1335	1433	1533	1633	1733	1833	1933	2033	2134	2301	...		1034	...	1302	1302	1534	...	1732	1932	...	2133
Gloucester .... **121** d.	0937	...	1136	...	1337	...	1537	...	1737	...	1937	2037	2137	...	...		1036	...	1306	1318	1552	...	1735	1937	...	2136
Cheltenham Spa .. **121** a.	0947	...	1147	...	1347	...	1547	...	1747	...	1948	2049	2148	...	...		1046	...	1317	1330	1602	...	1745	1947	...	2146
Ashchurch ♤ .... a.	0957	...	1157	...	1357	...	1557	...	1757	...	1957	...	2157	...	...		...	...	1325	1339	1612	...	1755	1957	...	...
Worcester Shrub Hill . a.	1014	...	1215	...	1415	...	1614	...	1815	...	2015	...	2218	...	...		...	...	1345	1358	1632	...	1815	2027	...	...

A – Until June 15 and from Aug. 3. **B** – June 22 - July 27. ♤ – Ashchurch for Tewkesbury.

GW 2nd class BRISTOL - WEYMOUTH, SOUTHAMPTON and PORTSMOUTH 139

Service on ⑦ valid until September 7. Frequent additional trains are available Bristol Temple Meads - Westbury and v.v.

BRISTOL - WESTBURY - WEYMOUTH

km		Ⓐ	⑥	⑦	⑥	Ⓐ	⑥B	⑦		⚒	⚒	⑦	⚒	Ⓐ	⑥	⑥C	Ⓐ	⑥B		⑦	⚒	⚒	⑦	⚒	⑥D	Ⓐ
0	**Bristol** T Meads .... d.	0544	0549	...	0839	0841	0906	0925	...	0949	1149	1310	1349	1448	1449	1649	1649	1649	...	1743	1749	1949	2049	2049	2311	2320
19	Bath .... d.	0603	0607	...	0857	0859	0927	0944	...	1007	1207	1327	1407	1506	1507	1707	1707	1707	...	1801	1807	2007	2106	2107	2329	2338
34	Bradford on Avon...... d.	0619	0623	...	0913	0915	0941	0959	...	1023	1223	1340	1423	1522	1523	1723	1724	1723	...	1817	1823	2023	2123	2123	2344	2354
39	Trowbridge............... d.	0626	0629	...	0919	0921	0948	1007	...	1029	1229	1347	1429	1528	1529	1729	1731	1729	...	1824	1829	2029	2129	2129	2350	2359
49	**Westbury** .... a.	0631	0636	...	0926	0928	0955	1014	...	1036	1236	1355	1436	1535	1536	1736	1736	1736	...	1831	1836	2036	2136	2136	2357	0007
49	**Westbury** .... d.	0647	0647	0912	0927	0932	1002	1017	...	1037	1237	1425	1437	1538	1537	1738	1739	1740	...	1831	1840	2037	2140	2139	2358	0008
58	Frome....................... d.	0656	0656	0922	0936	0941	1016	1031	...	1046	1247	1434	1451	1547	1546	1747	1749	1750	...	1839	1849	2048	2149	2150	0008	0019
81	Castle Cary............... d.	0714	0715	0940	0953	1000	1037	1049	...	1103	1304	1451	...	1609	1602	1805	1806	1809	...	1858	1906	...	2206	2208	...	...
100	Yeovil Pen Mill .... d.	0735	0729	0954	1007	1014	1053	1103	...	1117	1317	1505	...	1624	1617	1821	1822	1823	...	1912	1919	...	2220	2223	...	...
133	Dorchester West .... d.	0809	0803	1026	1038	1048	1133	1141	...	1154	1354	1540	...	1658	1658	1854	1858	1911	...	1947	1954	...	2254	2258	...	...
144	**Weymouth** .... a.	0824	0817	1042	1057	1103	1145	1154	...	1209	1409	1554	...	1710	1710	1910	1912	1927	...	2001	2010	...	2309	2313	...	...

		Ⓐ	⑥	Ⓐ	⑥	Ⓐ	⑥	Ⓐ	⑦	⑥	Ⓐ	Ⓐ	⑥	⑦	⑥C	Ⓐ	⑥B	⑦	⑥B	⑥C	Ⓐ	⑦	⑥B	⑦	Ⓐ	⑥
Weymouth............... d.	...	...	...	0533	0638	0640	0846	0853	1105	1110	1110	1310	1310	1415	1508	1508	1608	1610	1728	1728	1730	1756	1828	2009	2021	2021
Dorchester West........ d.	...	...	...	0545	0651	0653	0859	0906	1118	1126	1123	1323	1323	1428	1521	1521	1623	1623	1740	1741	1743	1809	1841	2022	2034	2034
Yeovil Pen Mill.......... d.	...	...	...	0620	0730	0730	0934	0941	1154	1205	1205	1408	1406	1504	1556	1556	1705	1658	1722	1818	1823	1844	1919	2057	2106	2109
Castle Cary............... d.	...	...	...	0645	0744	0744	0948	0955	1208	1222	1223	1422	1420	1518	1610	1610	1719	1713	1843	1832	1837	1859	1933	2110	2118	2123
Frome....................... d.	...	0645	0649	0704	0802	0802	1007	1015	1227	1239	1242	1441	1439	1537	1629	1629	1738	1731	1905	1857	1906	1918	1958	2134	2137	2142
Westbury................ a.	...	0654	0658	0712	0811	0809	1016	1024	1236	1248	1250	1446	1448	1546	1638	1638	1747	1740	1916	1905	1917	1927	2009	2143	2146	2151
Westbury................ d.	...	0655	0709	0718	0817	0817	1038	1038	1258	1249	1252	1451	1448	1547	1638	1638	1748	1741	1918	1917	1919	1930	2014	2145	2155	2155
Trowbridge .... d.	...	0702	0715	0724	0823	0823	1044	1044	1304	1256	1258	1457	1455	1553	1644	1644	1754	1748	1925	1923	1925	1936	2021	2151	2202	2202
Bradford on Avon....... d.	...	0707	0721	0730	0829	0829	1050	1050	1310	1302	1304	1503	1501	1559	1650	1650	1800	1753	1932	1929	1931	1942	2029	2157	2207	2208
Bath .... d.	...	0725	0735	0748	0847	0847	1108	1108	1325	1319	1322	1521	1518	1617	1708	1708	1818	1811	1949	1947	1949	2000	2047	2215	2225	2225
Bristol T Meads........ a.	...	0746	0752	0806	0905	0905	1129	1128	1343	1337	1341	1534	1536	1635	1727	1729	1836	1833	2009	2005	2008	2018	2105	2233	2243	2244

BRISTOL - WESTBURY - SOUTHAMPTON - PORTSMOUTH

km		Ⓐ	⑥	Ⓐ	⑥	⚒	⚒	⚒A	⑦	⑥	Ⓐ	⑦	⚒	⑦	⚒	⑦	⚒	Ⓐ	⑥	⑥A	ⒶA	⑦	⚒	⑦	⚒	⑦
0	**Bristol** T Meads .... d.	...	...	0544	0549	0722	0822	0851	0910	0922	0922	1015	1022	1110	1122	1210	1222	1239	1243	1251	1251	1310	1322	1415	1422	1510
19	Bath Spa.................. d.	...	...	0603	0607	0735	0835	0907	0927	0935	0936	1026	1035	1127	1135	1223	1235	1257	1300	1307	1307	1327	1335	1427	1435	1527
34	Bradford on Avon...... d.	...	...	0619	0623	0747	0847	0920	0940	0947	|	1043	1047	1140	1147	1240	1247	1312	1313	1320	1320	1340	1347	1444	1447	1540
39	Trowbridge................ d.	...	...	0626	0629	0753	0853	0927	0946	0953	0951	1049	1053	1147	1153	1246	1253	1319	1320	1327	1327	1347	1353	1451	1453	1547
46	**Westbury** .... a.	...	...	0631	0636	0801	0901	0934	0953	1000	0958	1057	1101	1155	1201	1252	1301	1326	1327	1333	1333	1355	1401	1458	1501	1557
46	**Westbury** .... d.	0549	0601	0640	0643	0801	0901	0939	0959	1000	0959	1059	1101	1201	1201	1301	1301	1327	1328	1339	1339	1401	1401	1501	1501	1605
53	Warminster .... a.	0556	0609	0647	0650	0809	0909	0946	1008	1009	1007	1107	1109	1210	1209	1307	1309	1336	1337	1346	1346	1410	1409	1508	1509	1614
85	Salisbury.................. a.	0618	0631	0710	0712	0832	0932	1009	1032	1031	1029	1130	1132	1232	1232	1332	1332	1358	1359	1410	1410	1434	1432	1532	1532	1635
112	Romsey .... a.	0637	0650	0729	0742	0850	0950	...	1050	1050	1048	1149	1150	1250	1250	1351	1350	1418	1418	...	...	1505	1450	1550	1550	1651
123	**Southampton** C .... a.	0649	0702	0740	0802	0904	1004	...	1103	1103	1104	1201	1204	1303	1304	1403	1404	1432	1432	...	...	1515	1504	1603	1604	1703
147	Fareham .... a.	0715	0727	0805	0827	0927	1027	...	1126	1127	1127	1224	1227	...	1327	1426	1427	...	...	...	...	...	1527	1626	1627	1726
	Portsmouth & S....... a.	0738	0746	0824	0846	0946	1046	...	1145	1146	1146	1243	1246	...	1346	1445	1446	...	...	...	...	...	1546	1645	1646	1745
165	**Portsmouth** H.......... a.	0745	0752	0830	0852	0955	1054	...	1152	1152	1154	1251	1254	...	1354	1455	1454	...	...	...	...	...	1554	1652	1654	1755

	⚒	⚒A	⑦A	⑦	⑥	Ⓐ	Ⓐ	⑦	⑥	Ⓐ	⑦	⑦	⚒	⑦	⑦	⚒	⑦	⑥	Ⓐ	⑦	⑥	Ⓐ	⑦	Ⓐ	Ⓐ	⑦
Bristol T Meads........ d.	1522	1551	1604	1611	1622	1622	1708	1715	1722	1723	1740	1809	1822	1850	1910	1922	2015	2022	2022	2125	2122	2123	2135	2204	2223	2310
Bath Spa .... d.	1535	1607	1620	1624	1635	1635	1726	1733	1735	1736	1752	1827	1835	1902	1927	1935	2027	2035	2036	2138	2136	2136	2149	2221	2236	2322
Bradford on Avon....... d.	1547	1624	1631	1641	1647	1647	1740	1744	1747	1748	1805	1839	1847	1915	1940	1947	2044	2047	2047	2150	2148	2148	2200	2237	2247	2335
Trowbridge .... d.	1553	1630	1637	1648	1653	1653	1747	1751	1753	1754	1812	1847	1853	1922	1947	1953	2051	2053	2053	2157	2154	2155	2206	2243	2253	2342
Westbury................. a.	1601	1637	1644	1655	1701	1700	1754	1800	1801	1802	1819	1853	1901	1929	1954	2001	2058	2101	2100	2204	2201	2203	2213	2350	2300	2349
Westbury................. d.	1601	1639	1646	1701	1701	1701	1755	1801	1801	1805	1820	1901	1901	1931	1959	2001	2101	2101	2101	2205	2201	2203	2215	...	2305	2350
Warminster............... a.	1609	1646	1653	1710	1709	1709	1806	1808	1809	1812	1829	1908	1909	1936	2008	2009	2108	2109	2109	2212	2209	2211	2222	...	2312	2359
Salisbury.................. a.	1632	1709	1716	1732	1732	1732	...	1832	1832	1835	1852	1929	1932	2000	2030	2032	2132	2132	2132	2234	2232	2232	2246	...	2335	...
Romsey.................... a.	1650	...	...	1750	1751	1750	...	1850	1850	1854	1914	1950	1950	2018	2050	2050	2151	2150	2150	2254	2250	2253	...	...	...	...
Southampton C .... a.	1704	...	...	1803	1803	1804	...	1903	1903	1904	1925	2003	2004	2029	2103	2104	2203	2203	2202	2305	2303	2304	...	...	...	...
Fareham.................... a.	1727	...	...	1826	1827	1827	...	1926	1927	1927	...	2026	2027	2054	2126	2127	2226	2226	2242	2329	2326	2327	...	...	...	...
Portsmouth & S .... a.	1746	...	...	1845	1845	1852	...	1945	1946	1946	...	2046	2046	2115	2144	2146	2245	2246	2259	2346	2344	2348	...	...	...	...
Portsmouth H.......... a.	1754	...	...	1853	1853	1900	...	1952	1952	1954	...	2051	2054	2126	2151	2152	2252	2252	2304	2354	2352	2354	...	...	...	...

	Ⓐ	⚒	⚒	⚒	Ⓐ	⑥	Ⓐ	⑥	⚒	⚒	⑦	⚒	⚒A	Ⓐ	⑥	⚒	⑦	⚒	⑥	Ⓐ	⑦	⚒	⚒A	⑦A	⑦	⚒
Portsmouth H.......... d.	...	...	...	...	0600	0600	0705	0723	...	0823	0908	0923	...	...	...	1023	1108	1123	...	...	...	1223	...	...	1308	1323
Portsmouth & S .... d.	...	...	...	...	0604	0604	0709	0727	...	0827	0912	0927	...	...	...	1027	1112	1127	...	...	...	1227	...	...	1312	1327
Fareham.................... d.	...	...	...	...	0624	0628	0729	0747	...	0847	0932	0947	...	...	...	1047	1132	1147	...	...	...	1247	...	...	1332	1347
Southampton Central d.	...	...	...	...	0646	0653	0752	0810	0823	0910	0954	1010	...	1042	1042	1110	1154	1210	1227	1227	1254	1310	...	...	1354	1410
Romsey..................... d.	...	...	...	...	0700	0711	0811	0821	0835	0921	1006	1021	...	1054	1053	1121	1206	1221	1238	1239	1306	1321	...	...	1406	1421
Salisbury.................. d.	...	...	0640	...	0719	0730	0830	0840	0901	0940	1025	1040	1052	1114	1113	1140	1225	1240	1304	1306	1327	1340	1352	1355	1427	1440
Warminster .... d.	...	...	0700	0723	0739	0750	0852	0901	0923	1001	1045	1101	1112	1133	1135	1201	1244	1301	1326	1334	1347	1401	1412	1415	1448	1501
Westbury................. a.	...	...	0708	0732	0747	0759	0901	0909	0935	1009	1053	1109	1120	1141	1143	1209	1254	1309	1334	1342	1356	1409	1420	1423	1456	1509
Westbury................. d.	0558	0638	0709	0738	0753	0802	0910	0910	0938	1010	1100	1110	1121	1142	1147	1210	1258	1310	1338	1344	1356	1410	1421	1424	1500	1510
Trowbridge .... d.	0604	0644	0715	0744	0800	0808	0916	0916	0948	1016	1106	1116	1127	1149	1153	1216	1304	1316	1344	1350	1402	1416	1427	1430	1508	1516
Bradford on Avon....... d.	0610	0650	0721	0750	0806	0814	0922	0922	0950	1022	1112	1122	1133	1155	1159	1222	1310	1322	1350	1356	1408	1422	1433	1436	1514	1522
Bath .... a.	0628	0708	0735	0808	0822	0830	0936	0936	1008	1036	1126	1136	1147	1212	1217	1236	1325	1336	1408	1414	1425	1436	1447	1451	1528	1536
Bristol T Meads........ a.	0646	0727	0752	0829	0841	0844	0952	0948	1029	1048	1145	1148	1205	1233	1235	1248	1343	1348	1429	1435	1444	1448	1505	1506	1540	1549

	⚒	⑦	⚒	⑦	⚒	Ⓐ	⑦	⚒	⑦	⑦	⚒	Ⓐ	⑥	⑦	⚒	⑦A	⑦	⑦	⚒	⚒A	⑦	⚒	Ⓐ	⑥	Ⓐ	⑦
Portsmouth H.......... d.	...	1408	1423	1508	1523	...	1608	1623	...	1708	1723	...	...	1808	1823	...	...	1908	1923	...	2008	2023	...	...	2123	2205
Portsmouth & S .... d.	...	1412	1427	1512	1527	...	1612	1627	...	1712	1727	...	...	1812	1827	...	...	1912	1927	...	2012	2027	...	...	2127	2212
Fareham.................... d.	...	1432	1447	1532	1547	...	1632	1647	1703	1732	1747	...	...	1832	1847	...	1905	1932	1947	...	2032	2047	...	...	2148	2232
Southampton Central d.	...	1454	1510	1554	1610	...	1654	1710	1726	1754	1810	1842	1845	1854	1910	...	1928	1954	2010	...	2054	2110	2120	2127	2222	2257
Romsey..................... d.	...	1506	1521	1606	1621	...	1706	1721	1739	1806	1821	1854	1856	1906	1921	...	1940	2006	2021	...	2106	2121	2131	2138	2234	2309
Salisbury.................. d.	...	1527	1540	1627	1640	...	1725	1740	1801	1827	1840	1913	1915	1925	1940	1955	2001	2027	2040	2057	2127	2140	2153	2204	2300	2328
Warminster................ d.	1528	1548	1601	1648	1701	1728	1746	1801	1821	1848	1901	1932	1936	1948	2001	2015	2021	2048	2101	2117	2148	2201	2215	2226	2320	2348
Westbury................. a.	1536	1556	1609	1656	1709	1736	1752	1809	1830	1856	1909	1940	1945	1955	2009	2023	2030	2056	2109	2125	2156	2210	2226	2234	2331	2357
Westbury................. d.	1538	1600	1610	1700	1710	1738	1758	1810	1832	1900	1910	1941	1946	2000	2010	2023	2039	2100	2110	2125	2200	2210	2232	2238	...	...
Trowbridge .... d.	1544	1606	1616	1706	1716	1744	1805	1816	1838	1906	1916	1948	1952	2006	2016	2029	2045	2106	2116	2131	2206	2216	2238	2244	...	...
Bradford on Avon....... d.	1550	1612	1622	1712	1722	1750	1810	1822	1844	1912	1922	1953	1958	2012	2022	2035	2051	2112	2122	2137	2213	2222	2244	2250	...	...
Bath .... a.	1608	1628	1636	1726	1736	1808	1829	1836	1858	1925	1936	2008	2016	2025	2036	2049	2109	2125	2136	2151	2227	2236	2302	2308	...	...
Bristol T Meads........ a.	1629	1642	1648	1744	1748	1828	1843	1849	1916	1939	1948	2026	2033	2039	2048	2104	2127	2139	2151	2206	2240	2250	2323	2331	...	...

A – (12) Bristol Temple Meads - London Waterloo and v.v. (Table **113**).
B – Until Sep. 6.
C – From Sep. 13.
D – Until Oct. 18.

140 LONDON AIRPORT LINKS

Gatwick ✈

GATWICK EXPRESS: Daily non-stop rail service from / to **London Victoria**. Journey time: 30 minutes (35 minutes on ⑦).

From **London** Victoria: 0001, 0032, 0330, 0430, 0500 and every 15 minutes until 2345.

From **Gatwick Airport**: 0035, 0050, 0135, 0435, 0520, 0550 and every 15 minutes until 2350.

Other rail services via Gatwick Airport: London Victoria - Eastbourne Table **101**; Bedford - Brighton Table **103**; London Victoria - Brighton Table **105**; Reading - Gatwick Airport Table **134**.

Heathrow ✈

HEATHROW EXPRESS: Daily non-stop rail service **London** Paddington - **Heathrow** Terminal 5 and v.v. Journey times: Heathrow Central ♣ 15 minutes, Heathrow Terminal 5 21 minutes.
From **London** Paddington: 0510⚒/0625⑦ and every 15 minutes until 2325.
From **Heathrow** Terminal 5 (6 minutes later from Heathrow Central): 0512⚒/0618⑦ and every 15 minutes until 2348.

HEATHROW CONNECT: Daily rail service **London** Paddington - **Heathrow** Central and v.v. Journey time 32 minutes.
From **London** Paddington: on ⚒ at 0442, 0513, 0533 and every 30 minutes until 2103 (additional later trains on ⑤⑥); on ⑦ at 0627, 0712 and hourly until 2312.
From **Heathrow** Central ♣: on ⚒ at 0529, 0557 and every 30 minutes until 2127 (additional later trains on ⑤⑥); on ⑦ at 0713 and hourly until 2313.

♣ – Heathrow Central serves Terminals 1, 2 and 3. A free rail transfer service operates every 15 minutes Heathrow Central - Heathrow Terminals 4 and 5 and v.v.

PICCADILLY LINE: London Underground service between **Kings Cross St Pancras** and all Heathrow terminals via Central London. Journey time: 50 - 58 minutes.
Frequent trains (every 4 - 10 minutes) 0530⚒/0730⑦ - 2300⚒/2330⑦.

RAILAIR LINK 🚌 **Reading** railway station - **Heathrow Airport** (Service **X25**).
From **Reading**: Services call at Heathrow Terminal 5 (±40 minutes), Heathrow Terminal 1 (±50 minutes) and Heathrow Terminal 3 (±56 minutes):
On Ⓐ at 0400, 0500, 0530, 0555, 0608, 0620, 0640, 0700, 0720, 0740, 0800, 0820, 0840, 0905 and every 20 minutes until 1805, 1835, 1905, 1935, 2005, 2035, 2105, 2205, 2305.
On Ⓒ at 0400, 0500, 0545, 0615, 0645 and every 30 minutes until 1915, 1945, 2025, 2055, 2205, 2305.
From **Heathrow Airport** Bus Station: Services call at Heathrow Terminal 5 (±10 minutes) and Reading Railway Station (±50 minutes).
On Ⓐ at 0005, 0500, 0600, 0630, 0657, 0720 and every 20 minutes until 1000, 1015, and every 20 minutes until 1755, 1815, 1835, 1855, 1915, 1940, 2010, 2040, 2110, 2140, 2215, 2305.
On Ⓒ at 0005, 0500, 0600, 0700, 0730 and every 30 minutes until 1900, 1920, 1950, 2020, 2050, 2130, 2200, 2305.

RAILAIR LINK 🚌 **Woking** rail station - **Heathrow Airport** (Service **701**).
From **Woking**: Services call at Heathrow Terminal 5 (±25 - 45 minutes) and Heathrow Central Bus Station (±40 - 60 minutes).
0520Ⓐ, 0550Ⓐ, 0620, 0650, 0720, 0750, 0820, 0850, 0935 and every 30 minutes until 2105, 2205.
From **Heathrow** Central Bus Station: Services call at Heathrow Terminal 5 (±15 minutes) and Woking (±45 - 65 minutes).
0545Ⓐ, 0615Ⓐ, 0645, 0715, 0745, 0830 and every 30 minutes until 2030, 2115, 2215, 2315.

Luton ✈

First Capital Connect services Brighton - Gatwick Airport - London St Pancras - Luton Airport Parkway ◧ - Luton ◧ - Bedford: Table **103**.
East Midlands Trains services London St Pancras - Luton Airport Parkway ◧ - Luton ◧ - Leicester - Nottingham / Derby / Sheffield: Table **170**.

◧ – A frequent shuttle 🚌 service operates between each of the rail stations and the airport terminal.

🚌 service **Milton Keynes** - **Luton Airport** and v.v. (Stagecoach route **99**. Journey 55 minutes) for connections from / to **Birmingham** (Table **143**), **Liverpool** and **Manchester** (Table **150**).
From **Milton Keynes** railway station: 0630⚒, 0750⚒, 0855⚒, 0920⑦, 0955⚒, 1020⑦, 1055⚒ and at the same minutes past each hour until 2020⑦, 2055⚒, 2120⑦, 2155Ⓐ.
From **Luton Airport**: 0540⚒, 0650⚒, 0750⚒, 0820⑦, 0905⚒, 0920⑦ and at the same minutes past each hour until 1805⚒, 1820⑦, 1905⚒, 1920⑦, 2005⚒, 2020⑦, 2105Ⓐ.

Stansted ✈

STANSTED EXPRESS: Daily rail service from / to **London** Liverpool St. Journey time ± 45 minutes.
From **London** Liverpool Street: on ⚒ at 0440, 0510 and every 15 minutes until 2255, 2325; on ⑦ at 0440, 0510, 0540, 0610 and every 15 minutes until 2255, 2325.
From **Stansted Airport**: on ⚒ at 0600 and every 15 minutes until 2345, 2359; on ⑦ at 0530, 0600, 0630, 0700 and every 15 minutes until 2345, 2359.

Most trains call at **Tottenham Hale** for London Underground (Victoria Line) connections to / from Kings Cross, St Pancras, Euston, and Victoria stations.
For *Cross Country* services to / from Cambridge, Peterborough, Leicester and Birmingham see Table **208**.

City ✈

DOCKLANDS LIGHT RAILWAY from / to **Bank** (interchange with London Underground: Central, Circle, District, Northern, and Waterloo & City Lines).
Trains run every 7 - 10 minutes 0530 - 0030 on ⚒, 0700 - 2330 on ⑦. Journey time: ± 22 minutes.

Inter - Airport 🚌 links

Operator: National Express ✆ 08717 818178. www.nationalexpress.com

Gatwick North Terminal - **Heathrow** Central. Journey 1½ hours
0005, 0025, 0230, 0330, 0525, 0610, 0710Ⓐ, 0725Ⓒ, 0825, 0855, 0925, 1015, 1025, 1110, 1125, 1225, 1235, 1325, 1330, 1425, 1445, 1525, 1535, 1625, 1710, 1725, 1825, 1910, 1925, 1940, 2025, 2120, 2155, 2255.

Heathrow Central - **Gatwick** North Terminal.
0055, 0155, 0320, 0440, 0540, 0640, 0700, 0740, 0825, 0840, 0925, 0955, 1025, 1055, 1125, 1155, 1225, 1255, 1325, 1355, 1425, 1455, 1525, 1555, 1655, 1735, 1755Ⓒ, 1805Ⓐ, 1825, 1955Ⓒ, 2005Ⓐ, 2055, 2200, 2255, 2355.

Gatwick North Terminal - **Stansted**. Journey 3 hours
0340, 0535, 0720, 0735, 0935, 1135, 1335, 1535, 1735, 1935, 2205.

Stansted - **Gatwick** North Terminal.
0140, 0405, 0605, 0615, 1015, 1215, 1415, 1615Ⓒ, 1625Ⓐ, 1815Ⓒ, 1825Ⓐ, 2115.

Heathrow Central - **Luton**. Journey 2 hours
0515Ⓐ, 0530Ⓒ, 0715Ⓐ, 0730Ⓒ, 0930, 1130, 1330, 1530, 1730, 1930, 2130, 2330.

From **Luton** to **Heathrow** Central.
0355, 0555, 0740Ⓐ, 0755Ⓒ, 0955, 1155, 1355, 1555, 1755, 1955, 2155.

Heathrow Central - **Stansted**. Journey 1½ hours
0505, 0705, 0905, 1105, 1305, 1505, 1705, 1905, 2105, 2335.

Stansted - **Heathrow** Central.
0140, 0405, 0605, 0815, 1015, 1215, 1415, 1615Ⓒ, 1625Ⓐ, 1815Ⓒ, 1825Ⓐ, 2115.

141 EAST CROYDON - MILTON KEYNES

SN

km			Ⓐ	Ⓐ	Ⓐ	Ⓐ	Ⓐ	Ⓐ	Ⓐ	Ⓐ	Ⓐ	Ⓐ		Ⓐ	Ⓐ	Ⓐ	Ⓐ	Ⓐ	Ⓐ			⑥	⑥
0	**East Croydon** d.	Ⓐ	...	...	...	...	...	...	0750	0807	0908	1010	and at	1710	1810	1910	...	...	...	...	⑥	...	...
12	Clapham Junction d.		0501	0530	0555	0620	0638	0739	0819	0839	0939	1039	the same	1739	1839	1939	2039	2139	2239	...		0508	0538
18	Kensington Olympia d.		0512	0544	0607	0630	0649	0750	0831	0850	0950	1050	minutes	1750	1850	1950	2050	2150	2250	...		0519	0549
	Wembley Central d.		|	0600	0623	0647	0707	0807	0847	0907	1007	1107	past each	1808	1907	2007	2107	|	|	...		|	0605
40	Watford Junction 142 a.		0540	0615	0636	0657	0719	0819	0902	0919	1019	1119	hour until	1819	1919	2019	2119	2223	2332	...		0547	0617
88	**Milton Keynes** 142 a.		...	0656	...	...	0803	0901	...	1001	1101	1201	❖	1901	2001	2101	2201	...	...	...		...	0700

	⑥	⑥		⑥	⑥	⑥	⑥	⑥	⑥			⑦	⑦	⑦	⑦	⑦	⑦		⑦	⑦	⑦	⑦
East Croydon d.	...	0610	and at	1710	1810	1910	...	...	...	...	⑦	...	...	...	...	...	...	and at	...	...	...	...
Clapham Junction d.	0609	0636	the same	1739	1839	1938	2025	2139	2239	...		0815	0915	1015	1115	1205	1305	the same	1905	2005	2115	2215
Kensington Olympia d.	0620	0647	minutes	1750	1850	1948	2036	2150	2250	...		0826	0926	1026	1126	1216	1316	minutes	1916	2016	2125	2226
Wembley Central d.	0636	0707	past each	1807	1908	|	|	|	|	...		|	|	|	|	|	|	past each	|	|	|	|
Watford Junction 142 a.	0650	0719	hour until	1819	1921	2014	2109	2220	2319	...		0855	0957	1055	1154	1242	1342	hour until	1942	2042	2153	2256
Milton Keynes 142 a.	...	0800	❖	1900	...	...	...	...	...	...		...	...	...	...	...	...	❖	...	...	...	...

		Ⓐ	Ⓐ	Ⓐ	Ⓐ	Ⓐ	Ⓐ	Ⓐ	Ⓐ		Ⓐ	Ⓐ	Ⓐ	Ⓐ	Ⓐ	Ⓐ	Ⓐ	Ⓐ			⑥	⑥	⑥
Milton Keynes 142 d.	Ⓐ	...	...	...	0701	0813	...	0913	1013	and at	1713	1813	1917	2013	2113	...	2211	...	...	⑥	...	...	0713
Watford Junction 142 d.		0554	0653	0723	0738	0852	0915	0953	1053	the same	1751	1852	1954	2051	2152	2227	2254	2336	...		0552	0655	0751
Wembley Central d.		0605	0704	0735	0749	0903	0927	1005	1105	minutes	1803	1904	2006	2104	|	|	|	|	...		|	0706	0803
Kensington Olympia a.		0623	0722	0757	0807	0921	0946	1024	1121	past each	1821	1921	2023	2124	2221	2254	2323	0007	...		0623	0724	0821
Clapham Junction a.		0633	0732	0807	0817	0931	0957	1034	1134	hour until	1833	1931	2033	2132	2231	2305	2335	0017	...		0633	0734	0832
East Croydon a.		...	...	...	0902	0956	...	1056	1156	❖	1902	...	...	...	...	...	2359	...	...		0656	0756	0856

		⑥	⑥	⑥	⑥	⑥	⑥	⑥	⑥			⑦	⑦	⑦	⑦	⑦		⑦	⑦	⑦	⑦	⑦
Milton Keynes 142 d.	and at	1713	1813	...	1914	...	...	...	...	...	⑦	...	...	...	...	...	and at	...	...	...	...	...
Watford Junction 142 d.	the same	1751	1851	1931	1951	2043	2144	2248	2325	...		0917	1017	1122	1222	1322	the same	1922	2022	2117	2217	2317
Wembley Central d.	minutes	1803	1903	1942	|	|	|	|	|	...		|	|	|	|	|	minutes	|	|	|	|	|
Kensington Olympia a.	past each	1821	1921	1957	2022	2111	2211	2316	2352	...		0947	1047	1149	1250	1349	past each	1950	2049	2147	2247	2344
Clapham Junction a.	hour until	1831	1932	2010	2032	2120	2220	2326	0002	...		0958	1058	1159	1259	1359	hour until	1959	2059	2200	2257	2354
East Croydon a.	❖	1856	1957	...	2059	...	...	...	...	...		...	...	...	...	...	❖	...	...	...	...	0015

❖ – Timings may vary by up to 5 minutes.

LM LONDON - NORTHAMPTON - BIRMINGHAM and CREWE 142

LONDON - NORTHAMPTON - BIRMINGHAM

km			Ⓐ	Ⓐ	Ⓐ	Ⓐ	Ⓐ	Ⓐ	Ⓐ	Ⓐ	Ⓐ	Ⓐ	Ⓐ	Ⓐ	Ⓐ	Ⓐ		Ⓐ	Ⓐ	Ⓐ	Ⓐ	Ⓐ	Ⓐ	Ⓐ	Ⓐ
0	**London** Euston d.	Ⓐ	...	...	...	0534	...	0624	0634	0713	0749	0754	0813	0849	0854	0913	and	1449	1454	1513	1549	1554	1613	1650	1713
28	Watford Junction d.		...	...	...	0555	...	0641	0653	|	0803	0812	|	0903	0911	|	at	1503	1511	|	1603	1611	|	|	|
64	Leighton Buzzard d.		...	...	...	0628	...	0717	0725	0742	|	0837	0842	|	0936	0942	the	|	1536	1542	|	1636	1642	1720	1742
75	Bletchley d.		...	...	...	0634	...	0722	0732	0750	|	0844	0850	|	0943	0950	same	|	1543	1550	|	1643	1650	1727	|
80	Milton Keynes d.		...	0537	...	0640	...	0726	0737	0754	0824	0850	0854	0925	0949	0954	minutes	1524	1549	1554	1625	1649	1654	1732	1752
106	**Northampton** a.		...	0553	...	0656	...	0738	0753	0811	0841	0907	0910	0941	1005	1011	past	1544	1605	1611	1641	1705	1713	1748	1811
106	**Northampton** d.		0516	0555	0616	0658	0716	0745	0755	0813	0855	0916	*0925*	0955	*1025*z	1016	each	1555	...	1616	1655	1716	...	1755	1820
136	Rugby d.		0538	0617	0638	0720	0738	0804	0817	0835	0917	0938	*0947*	1017	*1047*z	1038	hour	1617	...	1638	1717	1738	...	1817	1842
154	Coventry d.		0550	0630	0650	0733	0750	...	0829	0850	0930	0950	*1011*	1030	*1111*	1050	until	1630	...	1650	1730	1750	...	1830	1854
171	**Birmingham** I ✈ d.		0605	0646	0705	0749	0805	...	0845	0905	0946	1005	*1029*	1046	*1129*	1105	△	1646	...	1705	1746	1805	...	1846	1909
185	**Birmingham** New St. a.		0616	0701	0717	0806	0817	...	0901	0917	1001	1017	*1042*	1101	*1142*	1117		1702	...	1717	1801	1817	...	1901	1920

	Ⓐ	Ⓐ	Ⓐ	Ⓐ	Ⓐ	Ⓐ	Ⓐ	Ⓐ	Ⓐ	Ⓐ	Ⓐ	Ⓐ	Ⓐ	Ⓐ	Ⓐ	Ⓐ	Ⓐ	Ⓐ			⑥	⑥	⑥	⑥	⑥	⑥
London Euston d.	1724	1746	1751	1813	1829	1849	1913	1946	1954	2013	2046	2054	2113	2146	2154	2224	2304	2324	...	⑥	...	...	0534	...	...	0624
Watford Junction d.	1744	|	1811	|	1847	|	|	|	2011	|	|	2111	|	|	2215	2241	2329	2340	...		...	...	0552	...	...	0641
Leighton Buzzard d.	1809	1820	|	1842	|	1920	1943	2018	2036	2042	2118	2136	2144	2218	2247	2306	0002	0007	...		...	...	0625	...	...	0709
Bletchley d.	1816	|	1841	|	1918	1926	|	|	2043	2050	|	2143	2152	|	2254	2314	0009	0014	...		0531	...	0632	...	...	0716
Milton Keynes d.	1821	1831	1845	1854	1923	1932	1956	2029	2049	2055	2129	2149	2157	2232	2202	2323	0018	0023	...		0537	...	0637	...	...	0723
Northampton a.	1837	1848	1904	1911	1939	1950	2011	2046	2106	2113	2146	2208	2214	2250	2319	2342	0036	0040	...		0553	...	0653	...	...	0739
Northampton d.	1846	1857	...	1920	...	1955	2020	2055	2116	2126	2156	...	2217	2255	...	...	...	...	...		0555	0616	0655	0716	0737	*0755*
Rugby d.	1908	1919	...	1942	...	2017	2042	2117	2138	2145	2217	...	2240	2317	...	...	...	...	...		0617	0638	0717	0738	0759	*0817*
Coventry d.	...	1932	...	1954	...	2030	2054	2130	2150	...	2230	...	2251	2330	...	...	...	...	...		0630	0650	0730	0750	0811	*0830*
Birmingham I ✈ d.	...	1948	...	2009	...	2046	2109	2146	2205	...	2246	...	2309	2348	...	...	...	...	...		0646	0705	0746	0805	0829	*0846*
Birmingham New St. a.	...	2003	...	2021	...	2101	2120	2201	2217	...	2302	...	2321	0004	...	...	...	...	...		0701	0716	0801	0817	0842	*0901*

	⑥	⑥	⑥	⑥	⑥	⑥	⑥	⑥	⑥		⑥	⑥	⑥	⑥	⑥	⑥	⑥	⑥	⑥	⑥	⑥	⑥	⑥	⑥	⑥
London Euston d.	...	0705	0749	0754	...	0849	0854	0913	0949	and	1754	1813	1849	1854	1913	...	1946	2035	...	2108	2128	2154	2234	2304	2344
Watford Junction d.	...	0726	0803	0811	...	0903	0911	|	1003	at	1811	|	1903	1911	|	...	2002	2051	...	2125	2144	2215	2250	2324	0002
Leighton Buzzard d.	...	0758	|	0836	...	|	0936	0942	|	the	1836	1842	|	1936	1942	...	2035	2116	...	2150	2207	2247	2313	2356	0034
Bletchley d.	...	0804	|	0843	...	|	0943	0950	|	same	1843	1850	|	1943	1950	...	2042	2123	...	2157	2214	2254	2320	0003	0041
Milton Keynes d.	...	0810	0826	0849	...	0926	0949	0954	1026	minutes	1849	1854	1926	1949	1954	...	2049	2131	...	2206	2222	2303	2328	0011	0048
Northampton a.	...	0826	0841	0905	...	0942	1005	1012	1042	past	1905	1912	1944	2005	2012	...	2107	2150	...	2227	2243	2320	2349	0028	0110
Northampton d.	0816	0835	0855	0916	0935	0955	*1025*	1016	1055	each	*1935*	1916	1955	...	2022	2055	2116	2159	2216	...	2255	...	...	...	...
Rugby d.	0838	0857	0917	0938	0957	1017	*1047*	1038	1117	hour	*1957*	1938	2017	...	2044	2117	2138	2221	2238	...	2317	...	...	...	...
Coventry d.	0850	0911	0930	0950	1011	1030	*1111*	1050	1130	until	*2011*	1950	2030	...	2056	2130	2150	2233	2250	...	2330	...	...	...	...
Birmingham I ✈ d.	0905	0929	0946	1005	1029	1046	*1129*	1105	1146	△	*2029*	2005	2046	...	2114	2146	2205	2249	2305	...	2348	...	...	...	...
Birmingham New St. a.	0917	0942	1001	1017	1042	1101	*1142*	1117	1201		*2042*	2018	2101	...	2125	2201	2216	2304	2316	...	0004	...	...	...	...

		⑦	⑦	⑦	⑦	⑦	⑦	⑦	⑦	⑦	⑦	⑦	⑦	⑦	⑦		⑦	⑦	⑦	⑦	⑦	⑦	⑦	⑦	⑦
London Euston d.	⑦	0653	0723	0752	0823	0854	0924	0954	1001	1028	1053	1124	1153	1234	1250	and	1934	1950	2034	2106	2130	2200	2228	2258	2334
Watford Junction d.		0712	0744	0810	0843	0912	0944	1010	1019	1046	1114	1142	1214	1250	1306	at	1950	2006	2050	2123	2150	2219	2249	2317	2355
Leighton Buzzard d.		0740	0813	0839	0912	0940	1012	1035	1047	1115	1143	1212	1243	1315	1327	the	2015	2027	2115	2149	2219	2247	2318	2349	0027
Bletchley d.		0747	0820	0845	0919	0947	1019	1042	|	|	1150	1219	1250	1322	|	same	2022	|	2122	2156	2226	2254	2325	2356	0034
Milton Keynes d.		0756	0828	0851	0924	0956	1027	1050	1059	1128	1158	1228	1258	1328	1337	minutes	2028	2037	2128	2205	2234	2303	2333	0005	0043
Northampton a.		0813	0845	0909	0944	1013	1044	1106	1116	1145	1215	1245	1315	1344	1351	past	2044	2054	2145	2222	2250	2320	2350	0022	0100
Northampton d.		...	...	0926	1000	...	1100	1108	...	1158	...	1255	...	1355	1402	each	2055	2106	2155	...	2252	2332	...	...	...
Rugby d.		...	...	0948	1022	...	1122	1130	...	1220	...	1317	...	1417	1426	hour	2117	2130	2217	...	2314	2354	...	...	...
Coventry d.		...	...	1000	1034	...	1134	...	...	1232	...	1330	...	1430	...	until	2130	...	2230	...	2338	0005	...	...	...
Birmingham I ✈ d.		...	...	1009	1052	...	1152	...	...	1250	...	1348	...	1448	...	△	2148	...	2248	...	2356	...	...	...	...
Birmingham New St. a.		...	...	1026	1103	...	1203	...	...	1301	...	1359	...	1459	...		2159	...	2259	...	0007	...	...	...	...

		Ⓐ	Ⓐ	Ⓐ	Ⓐ	Ⓐ	Ⓐ	Ⓐ	Ⓐ	Ⓐ	Ⓐ	Ⓐ	Ⓐ	Ⓐ	Ⓐ	Ⓐ	Ⓐ	Ⓐ	Ⓐ	Ⓐ		Ⓐ	Ⓐ	Ⓐ	Ⓐ
Birmingham New St d.	Ⓐ	...	...	...	...	...	...	*0553*	...	*0614*	...	0654	0714	0733	0754	*0814*	0833	0854	0914	0933	and	1554	...	1633	1654
Birmingham I ✈ d.		...	...	...	...	...	...	*0605*	...	*0630*	...	0705	0730	0745	0805	*0830*	0845	0905	0930	0945	at	1605	...	1645	1705
Coventry d.		...	...	...	...	...	0557	*0620*	...	*0647*	...	0721	0742	0804	0821	*0848*	0900	0921	0948	1000	the	1621	...	1700	1721
Rugby d.		...	...	...	0516	...	0613	*0632*	0643	*0659*	...	0732	0753	0815	0839	*0859*	0912	0932	0959	1012	same	1632	...	1716	1732
Northampton a.		...	...	...	0537	...	0634	*0654*	0705	*0724*	...	0754	0817	0837	0900	*0918*	0934	0954	1020	1034	minutes	1657	...	1737	1756
Northampton d.		0415	0449	0505	0546	0618	0638	0700	0714	0732	0738	0805	0825	0847	0905	0925	0950	1005	1025	1050	past	1705	1725	1750	1805
Milton Keynes d.		0431	0505	0521	0602	0635	0655	0717	0732	0747	0754	0822	0841	0904	0922	0941	1006	1022	1041	1106	each	1722	1741	1806	1822
Bletchley d.		0436	0509	0526	0607	0640	0700	|	|	0752	|	0827	0846	|	0927	0946	|	1027	1046	|	hour	1727	1746	|	1827
Leighton Buzzard d.		0442	0516	0533	0614	0647	0707	0726	0741	0758	0806	0833	0853	|	0933	0953	|	1033	1053	|	until	1733	1753	|	1833
Watford Junction d.		0511	0550	0601	0635	0705	|	|	|	0827	|	|	|	0928	0959	|	1030	1059	|	1130	△	1759	|	1830	1859
London Euston a.		0533	0612	0619	0652	0722	0739	0802	0811	0849	0839	0910	0927	0945	1018	1027	1046	1117	1127	1146		1818	1827	1846	1918

	Ⓐ	Ⓐ	Ⓐ	Ⓐ	Ⓐ	Ⓐ	Ⓐ	Ⓐ	Ⓐ	Ⓐ	Ⓐ	Ⓐ	Ⓐ	Ⓐ	Ⓐ			⑥	⑥	⑥	⑥	⑥	⑥	⑥	⑥	⑥
Birmingham New St d.	1713	1733	1754	...	1833	1854	...	1933	1954	2033	2054	2134	2154	...	2254	...	⑥	...	...	...	0614	0714	0733	0754	0814	0833
Birmingham I ✈ d.	1725	1745	1805	...	1845	1905	...	1945	2005	2045	2105	2145	2205	...	2305	...		...	...	...	0630	0730	0745	0805	0830	0845
Coventry d.	1740	1800	1821	...	1900	1921	...	2000	2021	2100	2121	2200	2221	...	2321	...		...	...	...	0648	0748	0800	0821	0848	0900
Rugby d.	1756	1812	1832	...	1918	1932	...	2012	2032	2114	2132	2212	2232	...	2332	...		...	...	...	0659	0759	0812	0832	0859	0912
Northampton a.	1817	1834	1852	...	1945	1954	...	2038	2053	2135	2154	2234	2253	...	2354	...		...	...	...	0720	0820	0834	0856	0920	0934
Northampton d.	1825	1850	1905	1925	1950	2005	2025	...	2105	2137	2205	...	2255	2335	...	...		0516	0605	0705	0733	0825	0850	0905	0925	0950
Milton Keynes d.	1841	1906	1921	1941	2006	2022	2041	...	2122	2153	2222	...	2313	2353	...	...		0532	0622	0722	0749	0841	0906	0922	0941	1006
Bletchley d.	1846	|	1927	1946	|	2027	2046	...	2127	2158	2227	...	2318	2358	...	...		0537	0627	0727	0754	0846	|	0927	0946	|
Leighton Buzzard d.	1853	|	1933	1953	|	2033	2053	...	2133	2204	2233	...	2324	0004	...	...		0543	0633	0733	0801	0853	|	0933	0953	|
Watford Junction d.	|	1930	1959	|	2030	2059	|	...	2159	2233	2259	...	2359	0032	...	...		0616	0701	0759	0823	|	|	0959	|	1030
London Euston a.	1929	1946	2019	2027	2045	2117	2129	...	2222	2252	2321	...	0021	0055	...	...		0638	0720	0818	0840	0927	0947	1017	1027	1046

	⑥	⑥	⑥		⑥	⑥	⑥	⑥	⑥	⑥	⑥	⑥		⑥	⑥	⑥	⑥	⑥	⑥	⑥	⑥	⑥	⑥	⑥	⑥
Birmingham New St d.	0854	0914	0933	and	1554	1614	1633	1654	1714	1733	1754	1814	...	1833	1854	1914	1933	1954	...	2033	2054	2134	2154	2214	2254
Birmingham I ✈ d.	0905	0930	0945	at	1605	1630	1645	1705	1731	1745	1805	1830	...	1845	1905	1930	1945	2005	...	2045	2105	2145	2205	2230	2305
Coventry d.	0921	0948	1000	the	1621	1648	1700	1721	1749	1800	1821	1848	...	1900	1921	1948	2000	2021	...	2100	2121	2200	2221	2248	2321
Rugby d.	0932	0959	1012	same	1632	1659	1712	1732	1800	1812	1832	1859	...	1912	1932	1959	2012	2032	...	2112	2132	2212	2232	2259	2332
Northampton a.	0955	1020	1034	minutes	1653	1721	1734	1753	1821	1834	1853	1920	...	1934	1953	2020	2035	2053	...	2134	2153	2233	2253	2321	2355
Northampton d.	1005	1025	1050	past	1705	1725	1750	1805	1831	1850	1905	1931	...	...	2000	2032	...	2102	2120	...	2205	2243	...	2330	...
Milton Keynes d.	1022	1041	1106	each	1722	1741	1806	1822	1847	1906	1922	1947	...	...	2016	2047	...	2118	2134	...	2221	2259	...	2346	...
Bletchley d.	1027	1046	|	hour	1727	1746	|	1827	1852	|	1927	1952	...	...	2021	|	...	|	2139	...	2226	2304	...	2351	...
Leighton Buzzard d.	1033	1053	|	until	1733	1753	|	1833	1858	|	1933	1958	...	...	2027	2056	...	|	2146	...	2232	2310	...	2357	...
Watford Junction d.	1059	|	1130	△	1759	|	1830	1859	1927	1930	1959	2027	...	...	2051	2126	...	2152	2219	...	2307	2345	...	0020	...
London Euston a.	1117	1127	1146		1817	1827	1846	1917	1946	1945	2018	2045	...	...	2109	2146	...	2212	2237	...	2327	0005	...	0040	...

		⑦	⑦	⑦		⑦	⑦	⑦	⑦	⑦	⑦	⑦	⑦	⑦		⑦	⑦	⑦	⑦	⑦	⑦		⑦	⑦	⑦
Birmingham New St d.	⑦	...	...	...	...	...	...	...	...	0914	...	1014	...	1114	and	...	1914	...	...	2014	...	...	2114	...	2214
Birmingham I ✈ d.		...	...	...	...	...	...	...	...	0925	...	1025	...	1125	at	...	1925	...	...	2025	...	...	2125	...	2225
Coventry d.		...	...	...	...	...	...	...	...	0944	...	1044	...	1144	the	...	1944	...	...	2044	...	...	2144	...	2244
Rugby d.		...	...	...	...	...	...	...	...	0955	...	1055	1120	1155	same	1920	1955	2014	...	2055	2120	...	2155	*2200*	2255
Northampton a.		...	...	...	...	...	...	...	...	1017	...	1117	1141	1217	minutes	1941	2017	2035	...	2117	2141	...	2217	*2243*	2317
Northampton d.		...	_0620_*	0753	...	0822	0853	0931	1008	1037	1108	1125	1148	1225	past	1950	2025	2050	...	2129	2155	...	2225	2300	...
Milton Keynes d.		0642	0711	0809	...	0840	0909	0947	1024	1055	1124	1142	1203	1241	each	2007	2041	2107	2115	2145	2211	...	2241	2316	...
Bletchley d.		0647	0716	0914	...	0845	0914	0952	1029	1100	1129	1146	|	1246	hour	|	2046	|	2120	2145	2216	...	2246	2321	...
Leighton Buzzard d.		0653	0722	0920	...	0851	0920	0958	1035	1106	1135	1153	1211	1252	until	2015	2052	2114	2126	2156	2222	...	2252	2327	...
Watford Junction d.		0724	0753	0859	...	0922	0953	1029	1105	1137	1206	1217	1233	1317	△	2035	2122	2137	2156	2226	2253	...	2323	2359	...
London Euston a.		0744	0813	0913	...	0944	1013	1051	1125	1200	1225	1237	1253	1338		2053	2142	2155	2219	2248	2315	...	2343	0021	...

– 15xx train: Northampton d. 1537, Rugby d. 1559 then in pattern to Birmingham New St.

△ – Timings may vary by up to 3 minutes.

– Connection by 🚌.

142 LONDON - NORTHAMPTON - BIRMINGHAM and CREWE LM

LONDON - CREWE

km			Ⓐ	Ⓐ	Ⓐ	Ⓐ	Ⓐ	Ⓐ	Ⓐ	Ⓐ	Ⓐ	Ⓐ	Ⓐ	Ⓐ	Ⓐ	Ⓐ	Ⓐ	Ⓐ			⑥	⑥	⑥	⑥	⑥
0	**London** Euston ... 150 d.	Ⓐ	...	...	0624	0746	0846	0946	1046	1146	1246	1346	1446	1546	1646	1724	1805	2013	...	⑥	...	...	0624	0746	0846
27	Watford Junction ... 150 d.		...	...	0641	|	|	|	|	|	|	|	|	|	|	1744	1826	|	...		...	...	0641	|	|
78	Milton Keynes ... 150 d.		...	...	0722	0819	0919	1019	1119	1219	1319	1419	1519	1619	1719	1821	1907	2055	...		...	...	0723	0819	0919
104	Northampton ... d.		0545	0635	0745	|	|	|	|	|	|	|	|	|	|	1846	1945	2126	...		0542	0638	0745	|	|
135	Rugby ... d.		0604	0659	0804	0842	0942	1042	1142	1242	1342	1442	1542	1642	1747	1908	2004	2145	...		0602	0658	0804	0842	0942
158	Nuneaton ... d.		0620	0712	0816	0854	0954	1054	1154	1254	1354	1454	1554	1654	1800	1924	2017	2159	...		0614	0712	0816	0854	0954
178	Tamworth (Low Level) ... d.		0635	0729	0830	0909	1009	1109	1209	1309	1409	1509	1609	1700	1815	1939	2031	2215	...		0629	0729	0830	0909	1009
188	Lichfield Trent Valley ... d.		0641	0735	0836	0917	1017	1117	1217	1317	1417	1517	1617	1709	1822	1945	2037	2221	...		0635	0735	0836	0917	1017
217	Stafford ... 150 d.		0659	0754	0854	0939	1039	1139	1239	1339	1439	1539	1639	1739	1844	|	2053	2241	...		0654	0754	0854	0939	1039
243	Stoke on Trent ... 150 d.		0718	0815	0915	1002	1102	1202	1302	1402	1502	1602	1702	1802	1904	2014	2114	|	...		0714	0815	0915	1002	1102
268	**Crewe** ... 150 a.		0740	0838	0938	1024	1124	1224	1324	1424	1524	1624	1724	1824	1927	2037	2137	2300	...		0737	0838	0938	1024	1124

	⑥	⑥	⑥	⑥	⑥	⑥	⑥	⑥	⑥	⑥			⑦	⑦	⑦	⑦	⑦	⑦		⑦	⑦	⑦	⑦	⑦	⑦
London Euston ... 150 d.	0946	1046	1146	1246	1346	1446	1546	1646	1746	1846	...	⑦	*0752*	0954	1024	1124	1250	1350	...	1450	1550	1650	1750	1850	1950
Watford Junction ... 150 d.	|	|	|	|	|	|	|	|	|	|	...		*0810*	1010	1040	1142	1306	1406	...	1506	1606	1706	1806	1906	2006
Milton Keynes ... 150 d.	1019	1119	1219	1319	1419	1519	1619	1719	1819	1919	...		*0851*	1050	1120	1228	1337	1437	...	1537	1637	1737	1837	1937	2037
Northampton ... d.	|	|	|	|	|	|	|	|	|	|	...		0938	1108	1140	1302	1402	1502	...	1602	1702	1802	1902	2002	2106
Rugby ... d.	1042	1142	1242	1342	1442	1542	1642	1742	1842	1942	...		1000	1130	1203	1326	1426	1526	...	1626	1726	1826	1926	2026	2130
Nuneaton ... d.	1054	1154	1254	1354	1454	1554	1654	1754	1854	1958	...		1014	1143	1217	1340	1440	1540	...	1640	1740	1840	1940	2040	2143
Tamworth (Low Level) ... d.	1109	1209	1309	1409	1509	1609	1709	1809	1909	2014	...		1029	1157	1232	1355	1455	1555	...	1655	1755	1855	1955	2055	2158
Lichfield Trent Valley ... d.	1117	1217	1317	1417	1517	1617	1717	1817	1917	2021	...		1035	1204	1238	1401	1501	1601	...	1701	1801	1901	2001	2101	2204
Stafford ... 150 d.	1139	1239	1339	1439	1539	1639	1739	1839	1939	2042	...		1057	1221	1300	1419	1520	1620	...	1720	1820	1920	2020	2120	2226
Stoke on Trent ... 150 d.	1202	1302	1402	1502	1602	1702	1802	1902	2002	2102	...		1116	1240	1320	1437	1541	1641	...	1741	1845	1945	2045	2145	2245
Crewe ... 150 a.	1224	1324	1424	1524	1624	1724	1824	1927	2024	2124	...		1143	1302	1343	1500	1603	1703	...	1803	1907	2007	2107	2207	2307

		Ⓐ	Ⓐ	Ⓐ	Ⓐ	Ⓐ	Ⓐ	Ⓐ		Ⓐ	Ⓐ	Ⓐ	Ⓐ	Ⓐ	Ⓐ	Ⓐ	Ⓐ			⑥	⑥	⑥	⑥	⑥	⑥
Crewe ... 150 d.	Ⓐ	0518	0652	0755	0902	1002	1102	1202	...	1302	1402	1502	1602	1702	1802	1902	2015	...	⑥	0700	0802	0902	1002	1102	1202
Stoke on Trent ... 150 d.		|	0719	0818	0928	1028	1128	1228	...	1328	1428	1528	1628	1728	1828	1928	2037	...		0721	0828	0928	1028	1128	1228
Stafford ... 150 d.		|	0740	0837	0956	1056	1156	1256	...	1356	1456	1556	1656	1756	1855	1951	2104	...		0748	0856	0956	1056	1156	1256
Lichfield Trent Valley ... d.		0605	0756	0904	1013	1113	1213	1313	...	1413	1513	1613	1713	1813	1913	2008	2120	...		0805	0913	1013	1113	12123	1313
Tamworth (Low Level) ... d.		0612	0803	0912	1020	1120	1220	1320	...	1420	1520	1620	1720	1820	1920	2015	2127	...		0811	0920	1020	1120	1220	1320
Nuneaton ... d.		0628	0818	0928	1036	1136	1236	1336	...	1436	1536	1636	1736	1836	1936	2031	2142	...		0827	0936	1036	1136	1236	1336
Rugby ... 150 d.		0643	0834	0953	1053	1153	1253	1353	...	1453	1553	1653	1753	1853	1953	2047	2158	...		0843	0953	1053	1153	1253	1353
Northampton ... d.		0705	|	|	|	|	|	|	...	|	|	|	|	|	|	2107	2216	...		|	|	|	|	|	|
Milton Keynes ... 150 d.		0730	0855	1014	1114	1214	1314	1414	...	1514	1614	1714	1815	1914	2014	...	...	...		0905	1014	1114	1214	1314	1414
Watford Junction ... 150 d.		|	|	|	|	|	|	|	...	|	|	|	|	|	|	...	...	...		|	|	|	|	|	|
London Euston ... 150 a.		0811	0937	1050	1150	1250	1350	1450	...	1550	1650	1750	1851	1950	2050	...	...	...		0950	1050	1150	1250	1350	1450

	⑥	⑥	⑥	⑥		⑥	⑥	⑥			⑦	⑦	⑦		⑦	⑦	⑦		⑦	⑦	⑦		⑦	⑦	⑦
Crewe ... 150 d.	1302	1402	1502	1602	...	1702	1802	1902	...	⑦	0930	1037	1137	...	1237	1337	1433	...	1537	1633	1737	...	1837	1937	2044
Stoke on Trent ... 150 d.	1328	1428	1528	1628	...	1728	1828	1928	...		0951	1059	1159	...	1259	1359	1455	...	1559	1655	1759	...	1859	1959	2106
Stafford ... 150 d.	1356	1456	1556	1656	...	1756	1856	1951	...		1018	1118	1218	...	1318	1418	1518	...	1618	1718	1818	...	1918	2018	2125
Lichfield Trent Valley ... d.	1413	1513	1613	1713	...	1813	1913	2008	...		1035	1135	1235	...	1335	1435	1535	...	1635	1735	1835	...	1935	2035	2142
Tamworth (Low Level) ... d.	1420	1520	1620	1720	...	1820	1920	2015	...		1042	1142	1242	...	1342	1442	1542	...	1642	1742	1842	...	1942	2042	2149
Nuneaton ... d.	1436	1536	1636	1736	...	1836	1936	2031	...		1058	1158	1258	...	1358	1458	1558	...	1658	1758	1858	...	1958	2058	2205
Rugby ... 150 d.	1453	1553	1653	1753	...	1853	1952	2047	...		1120	1220	1320	...	1420	1520	1620	...	1720	1820	1920	...	2014	2120	2220
Northampton ... d.	|	|	|	|	...	|	2012	2107	...		1141	1241	1341	...	1441	1541	1641	...	1741	1841	1941	...	2035	2141	2243
Milton Keynes ... 150 d.	1514	1614	1714	1814	...	1914	...	...	...		1202	1034	1404	...	1504	1604	1704	...	1804	1904	2006	...	2106	2210	...
Watford Junction ... 150 d.	|	|	|	|	...	|	...	...	...		1232	1334	1434	...	1534	1634	1734	...	1834	1934	2034	...	2136	2252	...
London Euston ... 150 a.	1550	1650	1750	1850	...	1950	...	...	...		1251	1353	1453	...	1553	1653	1753	...	1853	1953	2053	...	2155	2315	...

BIRMINGHAM - CREWE - LIVERPOOL

km			Ⓐ	Ⓐ	Ⓐ	Ⓐ	Ⓐ	Ⓐ		Ⓐ	Ⓐ	Ⓐ	Ⓐ	Ⓐ	Ⓐ	Ⓐ	Ⓐ	Ⓐ	Ⓐ			⑥	⑥	⑥	⑥
0	**Birmingham** New St. d.	Ⓐ	...	...	0601	0636	0701	0736	and at	1701	1736	1801	1836	1901	1936	2036	2136	2238	2309	...	⑥	...	...	0601	0636
19	Wolverhampton ... d.		...	...	0620	0652	0720	0754	the same	1720	1754	1820	1854	1920	1953	2054	2154	2304	2336	...		...	...	0620	0652
43	Stafford ... d.		...	...	0636	0709	0736	0810	minutes	1736	1810	1836	1910	1937	2010	2110	2210	2320	2353	...		...	...	0636	0709
82	**Crewe** ... d.		0602	0632	0658	0734	0758	0832	past each	1757	1832	1901	1932	1958	2032	2132	2242	2349	0013	...		0612	0632	0658	0731
118	Runcorn ... d.		0629	0659	0724	0801	0822	0850	hour until	1825	1857	1922	1956	...	2056	2154	2307	...	...	...		0631	0659	0724	0757
	Liverpool SP ‡ ... d.		0638	0708	0732	0809	0831	0859	★	1833	1905	1930	2005	...	2105	2203	2317	...	...	...		0640	0708	0732	0806
140	**Liverpool** Lime St ... a.		0650	0722	0744	0821	0844	0910		1845	1916	1941	2016	...	2116	2215	2330	...	...	...		0652	0720	0744	0817

	⑥	⑥	⑥	⑥		⑥	⑥	⑥	⑥	⑥	⑥	⑥	⑥	⑥			⑦	⑦	⑦	⑦		⑦	⑦	⑦
Birmingham New St . d.	0701	0736	0801	0836	and at	1701	1736	1801	1836	1901	2001	2036	2136	2238	...	⑦	0942	1042	1142	1235	and at	1835	1935	2135
Wolverhampton ... d.	0720	0754	0820	0854	the same	1720	1754	1820	1854	1920	2022	2054	2159	2304	...		1000	1100	1200	1253	the same	1853	1953	2159
Stafford ... d.	0736	0810	0836	0910	minutes	1736	1810	1836	1910	1936	2038	2110	2216	2320	...		1017	1117	1217	1309	minutes	1909	2009	2216
Crewe ... d.	0800	0832	0858	0932	past each	1757	1832	1859	1930	1958	2106	2130	2238	2340	...		1038	1138	1238	1331	past each	1931	2031	2238
Runcorn ... a.	0825	0850	0922	0950	hour until	1825	1853	1922	...	2025	2130	...	...	...	...		1101	1201	1301	1354	hour until	1954	2054	...
Liverpool SP ‡ ... a.	0833	0859	0930	0959	★	1833	1902	1931	...	2033	2138	...	...	...	...		1109	1210	1310	1403	★	2002	2103	...
Liverpool Lime St ... a.	0846	0910	0942	1010		1845	1914	1944	...	2046	2150	...	...	...	...		1121	1221	1321	1414		2014	2114	...

		Ⓐ	Ⓐ	Ⓐ	Ⓐ	Ⓐ	Ⓐ	Ⓐ		Ⓐ	Ⓐ	Ⓐ	Ⓐ	Ⓐ	Ⓐ	Ⓐ	Ⓐ	Ⓐ	Ⓐ	Ⓐ			⑥	⑥	⑥
Liverpool Lime St ... d.	Ⓐ	...	...	0630	0704	0734	0804	0834	and at	1704	1734	1804	1834	1911	1934	2004	2034	2134	2234	2335	...	⑥	...	...	0632
Liverpool SP ‡ ... d.		...	...	0640	0714	0745	0815	0844	the same	1715	1744	1815	1844	1921	1944	2015	2044	2144	2245	2346	...		...	...	0642
Runcorn ... d.		...	...	0648	0722	0753	0824	0852	minutes	1725	1752	1825	1852	1929	1952	2025	2052	2152	2254	2354	...		...	...	0650
Crewe ... d.		0620	0647	0716	0749	0819	0849	0919	past each	1749	1819	1849	1919	1955	2018	2047	2118	2218	2321	0023	...		0611	0649	0716
Stafford ... d.		0641	0709	0737	0810	0841	0910	0946	hour until	1810	1844	1910	1943	2016	2041	2110	2141	2241	...	...	...		0635	0710	0741
Wolverhampton ... a.		0657	0725	0753	0826	0856	0927	0959	★	1827	1854	1927	1955	2029	2057	2126	2157	2300	...	...	...		0652	0726	0757
Birmingham New St . a.		0720	0750	0817	0847	0917	0947	1017		1848	1917	1948	2017	2047	2117	2147	2217	2327	...	...	...		0719	0750	0817

	⑥	⑥	⑥	⑥		⑥	⑥	⑥	⑥	⑥	⑥	⑥	⑥	⑥			⑦	⑦	⑦	⑦		⑦	⑦	⑦
Liverpool Lime St ... d.	0704	0734	0804	0834	and at	1704	1734	1804	1834	1904	1934	2034	2134	2204	...	⑦	...	1134	1234	1334	and at	1934	2034	2134
Liverpool SP ‡ ... d.	0714	0744	0815	0844	the same	1715	1744	1815	1844	1914	1944	2044	2144	2214	...		...	1144	1244	1344	the same	1944	2044	2144
Runcorn ... d.	0722	0752	0824	0852	minutes	1725	1752	1824	1852	1923	1952	2052	2152	2223	...		...	1152	1252	1352	minutes	1952	2052	2152
Crewe ... d.	0749	0819	0849	0919	past each	1749	1822	1849	1919	1951	2018	2118	2224	2249	...		1020	1219	1319	1419	past each	2018	2119	2222
Stafford ... d.	0810	0845	0910	0942	hour until	1810	1843	1910	1941	2012	2043	2139	2245	...	...		1042	1240	1340	1440	hour until	2040	2140	2243
Wolverhampton ... a.	0826	0855	0926	0955	★	1827	1856	1927	1958	2028	2059	2158	2301	...	...		1059	1256	1356	1456	★	2056	2156	2259
Birmingham New St . a.	0848	0917	0947	1017		1847	1917	1947	2016	2048	2117	2220	2320	...	...		1118	1315	1415	1515		2116	2217	2316

NUNEATON - COVENTRY

From Nuneaton: 2nd class Journey ± 20 minutes *16 km*

Ⓐ: 0637, 0737, 0828, 1015, 1117, 1215 and hourly until 1815, 1915, 2015, 2115, 2220.
⑥: 0647, 0814, 0915, 1015, 1115, 1215 and hourly until 1815, 1946, 2115, 2215.
⑦: 1230, 1411, 1511, 1611, 1711, 1811, 2011, 2200.

From Coventry:

Ⓐ: 0612, 0706, 0804, 0906, 1042 and hourly until 1842, 1942, 2042, 2142.
⑥: 0616, 0716, 0842, 0942, 1042 and hourly until 1742, 1842, 2015, 2145.
⑦: 1155, 1346, 1446, 1546, 1646, 1746, 1946, 2135.

BEDFORD - BLETCHLEY

From Bedford: 2nd class Journey ± 44 minutes *26 kr*

Trains call at **Woburn Sands** 30 minutes later:

Ⓐ: 0625, 0731, 0831, 0933, 1055, 1155, 1255, 1355, 1455, 1555, 1639, 1737, 1821, 1921 2055, 2156.
⑥: 0631, 0731, 0831, 0933, 1055, 1155, 1255, 1355, 1455, 1555, 1637, 1737, 1821, 1921 2055, 2156.

From Bletchley:

Trains call at **Woburn Sands** 11 minutes later:

Ⓐ: 0531, 0642, 0732, 0822, 1005, 1105, 1201, 1301, 1401, 1501, 1549, 1647, 1731, 183 2001, 2101.
⑥: 0541, 0634, 0732, 0839, 1005, 1105, 1201, 1301, 1401, 1501, 1547, 1647, 1731, 183 2001, 2101.

s – Calls to set down only.
u – Calls to pick up only.

‡ – Liverpool South Parkway. 🚌 connections available to / from John Lennon Airport.
★ – Timings may vary by ± 3 minutes.

AW 2nd class **BIRMINGHAM - SHREWSBURY - CHESTER** **145**

km			⑥	Ⓐ	⑥	Ⓐ	Ⓐ	⑥	Ⓐ	Ⓐ	⑥	Ⓐ	⑥	⑥	⚒	Ⓐ	⚒	⚒	⚒	⚒	⚒	⚒	⚒	⚒
		⚒					A			L		L												
0	**Birmingham** International ✈ .d.		...	...	...	...	...	...	...	...	...	0708	0709	...	0808	...	0909	...	1008	1108	...	1208	1308	1408
13	**Birmingham** New Street .. △ d.		...	...	...	...	...	0623	0625	...	...	0723	0722	...	0823	...	0923	...	1023	1123	...	1223	1323	1423
34	Wolverhampton △ d.		...	...	...	...	...	0642	0643	...	...	0742	0741	...	0842	...	0942	...	1043	1142	...	1242	1342	1442
59	Telford Central △ d.		...	...	...	...	...	0659	0659	...	...	0759	0757	...	0859	...	0958	...	1059	1158	...	1258	1359	1458
65	Wellington △ d.		...	...	...	...	...	0705	0706	...	...	0805	0805	...	0905	...	1005	...	1106	1205	...	1306	1405	1506
	Cardiff Central **149** d.		...	...	...	...	...	|	|	0510	0520	|	|	0721	|	0721	|	0921	|	|	1121	|	|	|
81	**Shrewsbury** △ a.		...	...	...	...	...	0718	0718	0720	0722	0819	0820	0919	0920	0919	1019	1120	1120	1219	1320	1323	1419	1519
81	**Shrewsbury** d.		0520	0520	0610	0610	...	0727	0727	0724	0724	0821	0821	0924	0927	0924	1023	1124	1127	1222	1324	1327	1422	1527
	Aberystwyth **147** a.		|	|	|	|	...	0925	0925	|	|	|	|	|	1125	|	|	|	1325	|	|	1525	|	1725
110	Gobowen d.		0539	0539	0630	0630	...	...	...	0743	0743	0840	0840	0943	...	0943	1042	1143	...	1242	1343	...	1441	...
122	Ruabon d.		0551	0551	0642	0642	...	...	...	0754	0754	0852	0852	0954	...	0954	1054	1154	...	1254	1354	...	1453	...
129	Wrexham General d.		0558	0604	0650	0649	0700	...	...	0802	0801	0900	0900	1002	...	1002	1101	1202	...	1300	1402	...	1500	...
149	**Chester** a.		0616	0624	0708	...	0716	...	...	0820	0818	0917	0917	1019	...	1019	1121	1219	...	1319	1419	...	1520	...
	Holyhead **165** a.		...	...	...	...	...	...	...	...	1014	...	1105	1209	...	1223	1313	1413	...	1508	1615	...	1715	...

	⚒	⚒	⚒	⚒	Ⓐ	⑥	Ⓐ	Ⓐ	⚒	⑥	Ⓐ	Ⓐ	⑥	Ⓐ	⑥	Ⓐ	⑥	Ⓐ	⑥	⚒	⑥	⑥	Ⓐ	Ⓐ
							L										J							
Birmingham International ✈ .d.	...	1508	1609	...	...	1709	1708	...	1809	...	...	1904	1909	2004	2009	...	...	2104	2109	...	...	...	...	...
Birmingham New Street .. △ d.	...	1523	1623	...	...	1723	1723	...	1823	...	...	1923	1923	2023	2023	...	...	2123	2123	...	2205	...	2212	...
Wolverhampton △ d.	...	1542	1642	...	...	1742	1742	...	1842	...	...	1942	1942	2042	2042	...	...	2142	2141	...	2225	...	2243	...
Telford Central △ d.	...	1558	1658	...	...	1758	1801	...	1858	...	...	1959	1959	2058	2058	...	...	2158	2158	...	2252	...	2310	...
Wellington △ d.	...	1605	1705	...	...	1806	1806	...	1905	...	...	2006	2005	2105	2105	...	...	2206	2204	...	2300	...	2318	...
Cardiff Central **149** d.	1321	|	|	1521	1621	|	|	1716	|	1721	1821	|	|	|	|	1934	1934	|	|	2055	|	...	|	...
Shrewsbury △ a.	1519	1619	1719	1719	1809	1819	1820	1908	1919	1919	2009	2019	2019	2118	2119	2137	2135	2218	2221	2257	2315	...	2330	...
Shrewsbury d.	1524	1622	1727	1724	1810	1822	1824	1909	1930	1924	2010	2024	2024	2142	2142	2139	2137	2224	2223	2306	...	2333	...	2337
Aberystwyth **147** a.	|	|	1925	|	|	|	|	|	2125	|	|	|	|	2344	2341	|	|	|	|	|	...	|	...	|
Gobowen d.	1543	1641	...	1743	|	1842	1843	|	...	1943	|	2043	2043	...	...	2158	2156	2243	2242	|	...	2352	...	2357
Ruabon d.	1554	1654	...	1754	|	1854	1855	|	...	1954	|	2055	2055	...	...	2209	2207	2255	2254	|	...	0004	...	0009
Wrexham General d.	1602	1702	...	1802	|	1902	1905	1943	...	2002	|	2102	2102	...	...	2214	2213	2301	2301	|	...	0014	...	0015
Chester a.	1622	1721	...	1821	1905	1920	1921	2001	...	2021	2101	2119	2121	...	...	2234	2231	2319	2320	0027	...	0033	...	0035
Holyhead **165** a.	1820	1916	...	2018	...	2131	...	2145	...	2225	...	...	...	...	...	0048	...	...	...	...	...	...	...	...

	⑥	Ⓐ	⑥		⑦	⑦	⑦	⑦	⑦	⑦	⑦	⑦	⑦	⑦	⑦	⑦	⑦	⑦	⑦	⑦	⑦	⑦	⑦	⑦
Birmingham International ✈ .d.	...	...	...	...		...	0951	1048	1208	1307	...	1407	1507	1607	...	1707	1807	1907	2007	...	2108	...	2211	2308
Birmingham New Street .. △ d.	2255	2332	2335	...		...	1004	1105	1224	1324	...	1424	1524	1624	...	1724	1824	1924	2024	...	2124	...	2224	2324
Wolverhampton △ d.	2313	0002	2354	...		...	1022	1127	1242	1342	...	1443	1543	1643	...	1743	1843	1943	2043	...	2143	...	2242	2346
Telford Central △ d.	2329	0029	0022	...		...	1049	1154	1259	1358	...	1459	1559	1659	...	1759	1859	1959	2059	...	2210	...	2309	0013
Wellington △ d.	2336	0036	0030	...		...	1057	1201	1305	1404	...	1506	1606	1706	...	1805	1906	2006	2106	...	2217	...	2316	0020
Cardiff Central **149** d.	|	|	|	...		...	|	|	|	|	1322	|	|	|	1522	|	|	|	|	...	|	2104	|	|
Shrewsbury △ a.	2349	0053	0043	...		...	1112	1215	1318	1418	1521	1519	1622	1719	1723	1819	1919	2019	2119	...	2230	2314	2332	0035
Shrewsbury d.	...	...	...	...		1016	...	1217	1327	1420	1522	1527	1624	1727	1730	1820	1927	2022	2130	...	2232	2319	...	...
Aberystwyth **147** a.	...	...	...	...		|	...	|	1525	|	|	1725	|	1925	|	|	2125	|	2326	...	|	|	...	...
Gobowen d.	...	...	...	...		1035	...	1237	...	1439	1542	...	1643	...	1749	1840	...	2042	...	...	|	|	...	...
Ruabon d.	...	...	...	...		1047	...	1249	...	1451	1554	...	1655	...	1801	1851	...	2054	...	...	|	|	...	...
Wrexham General d.	...	...	...	...	⑦	1054	...	1256	...	1458	1600	...	1706	...	1808	1858	...	2101	...	2235	|	|	...	...
Chester a.	...	...	...	...		1113	...	1320	...	1518	1618	...	1726	...	1825	1917	...	2120	...	2253	2331	0033	...	...
Holyhead **165** a.	...	...	...	...		...	...	...	...	...	1837	...	...	...	2018	2130	...	...	...	...	...	...	...	...

		Ⓐ	⑥	Ⓐ	⑥	Ⓐ	⑥	Ⓐ	⚒	Ⓐ	Ⓐ	Ⓐ	⑥	Ⓐ	⑥	⚒	Ⓐ	Ⓐ	⑥	Ⓐ	⑥	⚒	⚒	Ⓐ
Holyhead **165** d.	⚒	...	...	...	...	...	0425	0425	...	0533	...	0514	0522	0628	0635	...	...	0715	0715	0805	0820	...	0923	1040
Chester d.		...	...	0530	0537	0545	0612	0618	...	0715	...	0702	0721	0819	0819	...	0926	0919	0920	1020	1019	...	1130	1219
Wrexham General d.		...	...	0546	0555	0603	0638	0637	...	0732	0747	|	0737	0834	0834	...	0942	|	0936	1036	1035	...	1145	1234
Ruabon d.		...	...	0553	▬	...	0645	0644	...	|	0755	|	0744	0841	0841	...	0949	|	0943	1042	1042	...	1153	1241
Gobowen d.		...	...	0605	...	...	0657	0656	...	|	0807	|	0756	0853	0853	...	1001	|	0955	1054	1054	...	1205	1253
Aberystwyth **147** d.		...	...	|	...	...	|	|	0514	|	|	|	|	|	|	0730	|	|	|	|	|	0930	|	|
Shrewsbury a.		...	...	0626	⑥	...	0717	0716	0711	0807	0828	0825	0820	0913	0913	0926	1022	1026	1029	1114	1114	1126	1227	1314
Shrewsbury △ d.		0518	0522	0633	0633	...	0719	0718	0731	0810	...	0832	0833	0914	0915	0933	1024	1032	1033	1116	1115	1133	1233	1315
Cardiff Central **149** a.		|	|	|	|	...	0922	0921	|	0958	...	|	|	1115	1114	|	1209	|	|	1322	1315	|	|	1511
Wellington △ d.		0531	0535	0646	0646	...	...	...	0744	...	...	0845	0846	...	...	0946	...	1046	1046	...	...	1146	1246	...
Telford Central △ d.		0538	0542	0653	0653	...	...	...	0751	...	...	0852	0853	...	...	0953	...	1052	1053	...	...	1153	1253	...
Wolverhampton △ d.		0559	0602	0712	0712	...	...	...	0809	...	...	0911	0912	...	...	1010	...	1109	1111	...	...	1211	1310	...
Birmingham New Street .. △ a.		0615	0620	0730	0728	...	...	...	0829	...	...	0929	0927	...	...	1030	...	1130	1128	...	...	1230	1329	...
Birmingham International ✈ .a.		0650	0649	0750	0750	...	...	...	0850	...	...	0949	0949	...	...	1050	...	1149	1150	...	...	1250	1350	...

	⑥	⚒	⑥	Ⓐ	Ⓐ	⑥	⚒	Ⓐ	⑥	⑥	Ⓐ	⚒	⑥	Ⓐ	⚒	⚒	Ⓐ	⑥	Ⓐ	Ⓐ	⑥	⚒	Ⓐ	⑥
																			A					
Holyhead **165** d.	1033	...	1123	1127	1232	1238	...	1328	1328	1423	1434	...	1523	1544	1650	...	1730	1730	...	...	...	...	1921	1921
Chester d.	1219	...	1330	1330	1419	1419	...	1530	1530	1619	1619	...	1728	1730	1828	...	1917	1928	2022	...	2027	...	2121	2120
Wrexham General d.	1234	...	1346	1346	1434	1434	...	1546	1546	1635	1635	...	1744	1748	1845	...	1933	1944	2038	2049	2043	...	2137	2137
Ruabon d.	1241	...	1353	1353	1441	1441	...	1553	1553	1642	1642	...	1751	1755	1851	...	1840	1951	...	2057	2051	...	2144	2144
Gobowen d.	1253	...	1405	1405	1453	1453	...	1605	1605	1654	1654	...	1803	1807	1903	...	1952	2003	...	2108	2102	...	2156	2157
Aberystwyth **147** d.	|	1130	|	|	|	|	1330	|	|	|	|	1530	|	|	|	1730	|	|	...	|	|	1930	|	|
Shrewsbury a.	1313	1326	1428	1427	1513	1513	1526	1627	1627	1714	1714	1727	1824	1827	1924	1926	2014	2026	...	2128	2122	2128	2216	2217
Shrewsbury △ d.	1315	1333	1433	1433	1515	1515	1533	1632	1632	1716	1716	1733	1833	1833	1925	1933	...	...	...	...	...	2133	2218	2231
Cardiff Central **149** a.	1524	|	|	|	1715	1708	|	|	|	1915	1921	|	|	|	2143	|	...	...	...	...	...	|	|	|
Wellington △ d.	...	1346	1446	1446	...	...	1546	1645	1645	...	...	1746	1846	1846	...	1946	...	...	...	...	...	2146	2232	2245
Telford Central △ d.	...	1353	1453	1453	...	...	1553	1652	1652	...	...	1753	1853	1853	...	1953	...	...	...	...	...	2153	2238	2251
Wolverhampton △ d.	...	1410	1511	1511	...	...	1611	1709	1707	...	...	1811	1911	1911	...	2010	...	...	...	...	...	2209	2255	2308
Birmingham New Street .. △ a.	...	1430	1528	1530	...	...	1630	1730	1726	...	...	1830	1928	1930	...	2029	...	...	...	...	...	2233	2328	2329
Birmingham International ✈ .a.	...	1450	1549	1549	...	...	1650	1749	1749	...	...	1850	1950	1950	...	2050	...	...	...	...	...	...	...	...

	⑥	Ⓐ			⑦	⑦	⑦	⑦	⑦	⑦	⑦	⑦	⑦	⑦	⑦	⑦	⑦	⑦	⑦	⑦	⑦	⑦	⑦	⑦
Holyhead **165** d.	...	...	...	⑦	...	...	...	...	...	...	1020	...	...	...	...	...	...	1625	...	...	...	...	...	...
Chester d.	2228	2228	...		0808	...	...	0922	...	1131	1221	...	1331	...	1531	...	1731	1824	...	1926	...	2126	2204	2300
Wrexham General d.	2244	2244	...		0826	...	...	0938	...	1148	1238	...	1348	...	1548	...	1748	1841	...	1942	...	2144	2222	|
Ruabon d.	2251	2251	...		...	...	...	0945	...	1155	1245	...	1355	...	1555	...	1755	1847	...	1949	...	2151	...	|
Gobowen d.	2303	2303	...		...	...	...	0957	...	1207	1257	...	1407	...	1607	...	1807	1859	...	2001	...	2202	...	|
Aberystwyth **147** d.	|	|	...		...	...	...	|	0930	|	|	1130	|	1330	|	1530	|	|	1730	|	1930	|	...	|
Shrewsbury a.	2323	2323	...		...	...	...	1018	1125	1227	1318	1325	1427	1526	1627	1727	1827	1920	1925	2021	2125	2222	...	0014
Shrewsbury △ d.	2326	2326	...		...	0810	0909	1020	1140	1231	1319	1331	1431	1533	1640	1733	1831	1921	1931	2023	2131	2223	...	...
Cardiff Central **149** a.	|	|	...		...	|	|	|	|	|	1531	|	|	|	|	|	|	2136	|	|	|	|	...	...
Wellington △ d.	2340	2340	...		...	0824	0923	1034	1154	1245	...	1345	1445	1547	1654	1747	1845	...	1945	2037	2145	2237	...	...
Telford Central △ d.	2347	2347	...		...	0831	0930	1040	1200	1251	...	1351	1451	1553	1700	1753	1851	...	1951	2044	2151	2245	...	...
Wolverhampton △ d.	0016	0017	...		...	0900	0959	1057	1217	1308	...	1408	1509	1609	1719	1809	1908	...	2008	2112	2209	2314	...	...
Birmingham New Street .. △ a.	...	...	...		...	0915	1014	1113	1232	1323	...	1423	1524	1624	1735	1827	1925	...	2023	2129	2228	...	...	...
Birmingham International ✈ .a.	...	...	...		...	0931	1032	1131	1256	1355	...	1455	1558	1655	1756	1855	1955	...	2058	2156	2258	...	...	...

A – [12] and 🍷 Wrexham - London Euston and v.v. (Table **150**).
J – To/from Llandudno Junction (Table **165**).
L – To/from Llandudno (Table **165**).

△ – Additional services are available Birmingham New Street - Shrewsbury and v.v. on ⚒.

146 SHREWSBURY - SWANSEA
2nd class AW

km		⚒	⚒	⑦	⚒	⑦	⚒				
0	**Shrewsbury** 149 d.	0516	0900	1204	1358	1618	1801	...	...	...	...
20	Church Stretton 149 d.	0533	0918	1222	1416	1636	1819	...	...	...	...
32	Craven Arms 149 d.	0547	0928	1233	1426	1647	1831	...	...	...	...
52	Knighton d.	0609	0952	1257	1455	1711	1855	...	...	...	...
84	**Llandrindod** a.	0643	1030	1335	1533	1749	1933	...	...	...	...
84	**Llandrindod** d.	0652	1031	1341	1540	1801	1935	...	...	...	...
110	Llanwrtyd d.	0721	1107	1412	1611	1830	2016	...	...	...	...
128	Llandovery d.	0745	1132	1437	1636	1855	2040	...	...	...	...
146	Llandeilo d.	0806	1154	1459	1658	1917	2101	...	...	...	...
159	Pantyffynnon d.	0823	1211	1516	1715	1934	2119	...	...	...	...
178	Llanelli 135 d.	0855	1242	1541	1740	2003	2144	...	...	...	...
196	**Swansea** 135 a.	0923	1304	1602	1805	2025	2212	...	...	...	...

	⚒	⚒	⑦	⚒	⑦c	⑦d	⚒			
Swansea 135 d.	0431	0915	1108	1312	1526	1535	1820	...	...	...
Llanelli 135 d.	0450	0934	1129	1332	1551	1555	1840	...	...	...
Pantyffynnon d.	0510	0955	1150	1353	1611	1615	1858	...	...	...
Llandeilo d.	0529	1015	1210	1413	1631	1635	1918	...	...	...
Llandovery d.	0551	1037	1232	1435	1653	1657	1940	...	...	...
Llanwrtyd d.	0616	1105	1257	1501	1719	1723	2010	...	...	...
Llandrindod a.	0644	1136	1328	1531	1749	1753	2040	...	...	...
Llandrindod d.	0655	1140	1343	1542	1800	1800	2044	...	...	...
Knighton d.	0732	1218	1422	1621	1839	1839	2121	...	...	...
Craven Arms 149 d.	0754	1239	1444	1643	1903	1903	2142	...	...	...
Church Stretton 149 d.	0807	1253	1457	1656	1916	1916	2155	...	...	...
Shrewsbury 149 a.	0822	1309	1512	1711	1931	1931	2212	...	...	...

c – Until Oct. 19.

d – From Oct. 26.

147 SHREWSBURY - ABERYSTWYTH
2nd class AW

km		⚒	⚒	Ⓐ	⑦	⑥	Ⓐ	⑦a	⚒	⑦	⑦a	⚒	⑦b	⚒	⑦	⚒	⑦	⚒	⑦	⚒	⑦	⑥	Ⓐ	⑦
	Birmingham New St 145 d.	...	...	...	...	0623	0625	...	0823	...	...	1023	...	1223	1224	1423	1424	1623	1624	1823	1824	2023	2023	2024
0	**Shrewsbury** d.	...	...	...	...	0727	0727	0845	0927	...	...	1127	1126	1327	1327	1527	1527	1727	1727	1930	1927	2142	2142	2130
32	Welshpool d.	...	...	...	...	0749	0749	0907	0949	...	...	1149	1149	1349	1349	1549	1549	1749	1749	1952	1949	2204	2204	2152
54	Newtown d.	...	...	...	...	0804	0804	0923	1004	...	...	1204	1205	1404	1404	1604	1604	1804	1804	2007	2004	2220	2220	2207
63	Caersws d.	...	...	...	...	0813	0813	0932	1013	...	...	1213	1214	1413	1413	1613	1613	1813	1813	2016	2013	2229	2229	2216
98	Machynlleth d.	0435	0635	0807	0850	0848	0848	1005	1051	1050	1232	1251	1248	1451	1448	1651	1648	1851	1851	2046	2048	2259	2307	2247
104	Dovey Junction ‡ d.	0442	0642	0814	0857	0855	0855	1012	1058	1057	1239	1258	1255	1458	1455	1658	1655	1858	1858	2058	2055	2311	2314	2256
118	Borth d.	0453	0653	0825	0908	0906	0906	1022	1106	1108	1250	1309	1306	1509	1506	1709	1706	1909	1909	2109	2106	2322	2325	2307
131	**Aberystwyth** a.	0512	0710	0844	0925	0925	0925	1041	1125	1125	1304	1325	1325	1525	1525	1725	1725	1925	1925	2125	2125	2341	2344	2326

		⚒	⚒	⚒	⑦		⑦	⚒	⑦	⚒		⑦	⚒	⑦	⚒		⑦	⚒	⑦	⚒		⑦	⑥	Ⓐ
Aberystwyth d.	...	0514	0730	0930	0930	...	1130	1130	1330	1330	...	1530	1530	1730	1730	...	1930	1930	2130	2136	...	2330	2346	2353
Borth d.	...	0527	0743	0943	0943	...	1143	1143	1343	1343	...	1543	1543	1743	1743	...	1943	1943	2143	2149	...	2343	2359	0006
Dovey Junction ‡ d.	...	0538	0754	0954	0954	...	1154	1154	1354	1354	...	1554	1554	1754	1754	...	1954	1954	2154	2200	...	2354	0010	0017
Machynlleth d.	...	0547	0807	1007	1007	...	1207	1207	1407	1407	...	1607	1607	1807	1807	...	2007	2007	2201	2207	...	0001	0017	0024
Caersws d.	...	0613	0833	1033	1033	...	1233	1233	1433	1433	...	1633	1633	1833	1833	...	2033	2036	...	...	...	...	...	...
Newtown d.	...	0625	0846	1046	1045	...	1245	1246	1445	1446	...	1645	1646	1845	1846	...	2046	2048	...	...	...	...	...	...
Welshpool d.	...	0641	0901	1101	1101	...	1301	1301	1501	1501	...	1701	1701	1901	1901	...	2101	2104	...	...	...	...	...	...
Shrewsbury a.	...	0711	0926	1126	1125	...	1325	1326	1526	1526	...	1727	1727	1925	1926	...	2125	2128	...	...	...	...	...	...
Birmingham New St 145 a.	...	0829	1030	1230	1232	...	1423	1430	1624	1630	...	1827	1830	2023	2029	...	2228	2233	...	...	...	...	...	...

a – Until Sep. 7.

b – From Sep. 14.

‡ – Trains call on request.

148 MACHYNLLETH - PWLLHELI
2nd class AW

Due to engineering work, buses replace trains Harlech - Pwllheli and v.v. until further notice.
Please confirm all services with operator or National Rail Enquiries.

km		⚒	⚒	⚒	⚒	⚒	⚒	⚒	⑤	⚒	
0	**Machynlleth** d.	0507	0647	0857	1055	1255	1456	1705	1859	2120	...
6	Dovey Junction d.	0514	0654	0904	1102	1302	1503	1712	1906	2127	...
16	Aberdovey d.	0527	0706	0916	1115	1314	1515	1724	1919	2139	...
22	Tywyn d.	0534	0716	0929	1132	1324	1525	1735	1930	2149	...
37	Fairbourne d.	0552	0734	0947	1150	1343	1543	1753	1948	2207	...
41	Barmouth d.	0604	0747	1001	1202	1356	1557	1805	2000	2221	...
58	**Harlech** a.	0629	0812	1026	1226	1421	1622	1830	...	2245	...
		⚒ 🚌	⚒ 🚌	⚒ 🚌	⚒ 🚌	⚒ 🚌	⚒ 🚌	⚒ 🚌		⚒ 🚌	...
	Harlech d.	0639	0822	1035	1237	1431	1632	1840	...	2256	...
	Penrhyndeudraeth d.	0714	0857	1110	1312	1506	1707	1915	...	2331	...
	Minffordd 160 d.	0719	0902	1115	1317	1511	1712	1920	...	2336	...
	Porthmadog 160 d.	0729	0912	1125	1327	1521	1722	1930	...	2346	...
	Criccieth d.	0739	0922	1135	1337	1531	1732	1940	...	2356	...
	Pwllheli bus station a.	0759	0942	1155	1357	1551	1752	2000	...	0016	...

	⚒	⚒ 🚌	⚒ 🚌	⚒ 🚌	⚒ 🚌	⚒ 🚌	⚒ 🚌	⚒ 🚌	⚒ 🚌	⑤
Pwllheli bus station d.	...	0545	0650	0900	1050	1255	1500	1700	1920	...
Criccieth d.	...	0605	0710	0920	1110	1315	1520	1720	1940	...
Porthmadog 160 d.	...	0615	0720	0930	1120	1325	1530	1730	1950	...
Minffordd 160 d.	...	0625	0730	0940	1130	1335	1540	1740	2000	...
Penrhyndeudraeth d.	...	0630	0735	0945	1135	1340	1545	1745	2005	...
Harlech a.	...	0705	0810	1020	1210	1415	1620	1820	2040	...
		⚒	⚒	⚒	⚒	⚒	⚒	⚒	⚒	
Harlech d.	...	0717	0821	1030	1231	1428	1629	1835	2053	...
Barmouth d.	0646	0750	0852	1103	1256	1455	1656	1900	2120	2225
Fairbourne d.	0654	0758	0900	1111	1304	1503	1704	1908	2128	2233
Tywyn d.	0717	0817	0927	1132	1325	1526	1735	1929	2150	2252
Aberdovey d.	0723	0823	0933	1138	1331	1532	1741	1935	2156	2258
Dovey Junction d.	0738	0838	0948	1153	1346	1547	1950	1950	2211	2317
Machynlleth a.	0745	0844	0955	1200	1353	1554	1957	1957	2218	2324

149 CARDIFF - HEREFORD - CREWE - MANCHESTER
2nd class AW

Most Manchester trains continue to / from destinations on Table 135.

km			Ⓐ	Ⓐ J	Ⓐ	Ⓐ	Ⓐ	Ⓐ	Ⓐ	Ⓐ	Ⓐ	Ⓐ	Ⓐ	Ⓐ	Ⓐ	Ⓐ	Ⓐ	Ⓐ	Ⓐ	Ⓐ	Ⓐ	Ⓐ	Ⓐ	Ⓐ	Ⓐ	Ⓐ
0	**Cardiff** Central 132 d.	Ⓐ	0435	0508	0540	0650	0721	0805	0850	0921	1005	1050	1121	1205	1250	1321	1405	1450	1521	1550	1621	1650	1716	1750	1821	1850
19	Newport 132 d.		0453	0528	0558	0704	0736	0819	0905	0936	1019	1104	1136	1219	1304	1336	1419	1504	1536	1604	1635	1704	1731	1804	1835	1904
30	Cwmbrân d.		0505	0538	0608	0714	0746	0829	0915	0946	1029	1114	1146	1229	1314	1346	1429	1514	1546	1614	1644	1714	1742	1814	|	1915
35	Pontypool & New Inn d.		0511	0544	0614	|	0752	|	|	0952	|	|	1152	|	|	1352	|	|	1552	1619	|	|	1749	1819	|	1920
50	Abergavenny d.		0518	0553	0623	0727	0801	0842	0928	1001	1042	1127	1201	1242	1326	1401	1443	1527	1601	1629	1657	1727	1800	1829	1857	1929
89	**Hereford** d.		0547	0625	0649	0753	0827	0908	0954	1027	1106	1153	1227	1308	1355	1426	1508	1553	1627	1654	1724	1753	1825	1854	1922	1955
109	Leominster d.		0600	0638	0702	0806	|	0921	1007	|	1121	1206	|	1321	1408	|	1521	1606	1640	1707	|	1806	|	1907	|	2008
127	Ludlow d.		0611	0649	0713	0817	0848	0932	1018	1048	1132	1217	1248	1332	1419	1447	1532	1617	1651	1718	|	1817	|	1918	1943	2019
138	Craven Arms 146 d.		0620	0657	0721	0825	0856	|	1026	1056	|	1225	1256	|	1427	1455	|	1625	|	1727	|	1825	|	1927	|	2027
150	Church Stretton 146 d.		0629	0706	0730	0834	0905	|	1039	1105	|	1238	1305	|	1436	1504	|	|	1706	1736	|	1834	|	1936	|	2036
170	**Shrewsbury** 146 a.		0643	0720	0744	0848	0919	0958	1052	1119	1158	1252	1319	1358	1450	1519	1558	1648	1720	1750	1809	1848	1908	1950	2009	2051
170	**Shrewsbury** ¶ d.		0644	0724	0746	0850	0924	1000	1053	1124	1159	1254	1324	1359	1452	1524	1559	1650	1724	1751	1810	1850	1909	1951	2010	2052
200	Whitchurch ¶ d.		0704	|	0806	0906	|	|	1112	|	|	1310	|	|	1508	|	|	1710	|	1809	|	1906	|	|	|	2110
223	**Crewe** ¶ a.		0724	|	0824	0927	|	1029	1129	|	1229	1328	|	1429	1528	|	1629	1728	|	1828	1843	1925	|	2022	2040	2129
	Chester 160 a.		|	0820	|	|	1019	|	|	1219	|	|	1419	|	|	1620	|	|	1820	|	1905	|	2001	|	2101	|
	Holyhead 160 a.		|	...	|	|	1223	|	|	1413	|	|	1615	|	|	1819	|	|	2018	|	...	|	2145	|	...	|
263	Stockport a.		0754	...	0859	0957	...	1058	1158	...	1258	1358	...	1458	1558	...	1658	1757	...	1858	...	1958	...	2051	...	2158
273	**Manchester** P'dilly a.		0810	...	0914	1014	...	1115	1215	...	1315	1415	...	1515	1615	...	1714	1813	...	1915	...	2015	...	2106	...	2214

For continuation of Table and footnotes see next page ▶ ▶ ▶

AW 2nd class — CARDIFF - HEREFORD - CREWE - MANCHESTER — 149

Most Manchester trains continue to / from destinations on Table 135.

	Ⓐ	Ⓐ	Ⓐ	Ⓐ			⑥	⑥	⑥	⑥	⑥	⑥	⑥	⑥	⑥	⑥	⑥	⑥	⑥	⑥	⑥	⑥	⑥	⑥	⑥	⑥
Cardiff Central 132 d.	1934	2017	2055	2155	...	⑥	0435	0520	0540	0650	0721	0750	0850	0921	0955	1055	1121	1155	1255	1321	1355	1455	1521	1555	1655	1721
Newport 132 d.	1948	2031	2112	2212	...		0452	0535	0557	0704	0736	0804	0904	0936	1009	1109	1136	1209	1309	1336	1409	1509	1536	1609	1709	1735
Cwmbrân d.	1958	2041	2122	2224	...		0503	0545	0608	0714	0746	0814	0914	0946	1019	1119	1146	1219	1319	1346	1419	1519	1546	1619	1719	1746
Pontypool & New Inn d.	2003	2047	|	2230	...		0509	0551	0613	|	0751	|	|	0952	|	|	1150	|	|	1352	|	|	1552	1624	|	1752
Abergavenny d.	2012	2056	2135	2240	...		0518	0600	0623	0727	0801	0827	0927	1001	1032	1132	1200	1232	1332	1401	1432	1532	1601	1634	1732	1801
Hereford d.	2039	2122	2201	2308	...		0547	0625	0649	0753	0827	0853	0953	1027	1058	1158	1228	1258	1358	1426	1458	1558	1627	1659	1758	1827
Leominster d.	2052	2135	2214	2321	...		0600	0638	0702	0806	|	0906	1006	|	1111	1211	|	1311	1411	|	1511	1611	1640	1712	1811	|
Ludlow d.	2103	2146	2225	2332	...		0611	0649	0713	0817	0848	0917	1017	1048	1122	1222	1249	1322	1422	1447	1522	1622	1651	1723	1822	1848
Craven Arms 146 d.	2112	2154	2233	2342	...		0620	0657	0721	0825	0856	|	1025	1056	|	1230	1257	|	1430	1455	|	1630	|	|	1830	1856
Church Stretton 146 d.	2121	2203	2242	2351	...		0629	0706	0730	0834	0905	|	1034	1105	|	1238	1306	|	1440	1504	|	1639	1705	|	1839	1905
Shrewsbury 146 a.	2137	2217	2256	0007	...		0643	0720	0744	0851	0919	0943	1048	1120	1148	1252	1320	1348	1453	1518	1548	1653	1719	1749	1853	1919
Shrewsbury ¶ d.	2139	2219	2306	0012	...		0644	0724	0746	0852	0924	0944	1050	1124	1149	1254	1324	1349	1455	1524	1549	1655	1724	1751	1855	1924
Whitchurch ¶ d.	|	2242	2332	0038	...		0704	|	0806	0909	|	1001	1106	|	1206	|	|	1406	|	|	1606	|	|	1807	|	|
Crewe ¶ a.	|	2303	2353	0106	...		0722	|	0824	0927	|	1020	1125	|	1224	1326	|	1429	1525	|	1624	1726	|	1828	1926	|
Chester **160** a.	2234	|	0018	...	...		|	0818	|	|	1019	|	|	1219	|	|	1419	|	|	1622	|	|	1821	|	|	2021
Holyhead **160** a.	0048	|	...	...	...		|	1014	|	|	1209	|	|	1413	|	|	1613	|	|	1820	|	|	2018	|	|	2225
Stockport a.	...	2340	...	...	...		0754	...	0859	0957	...	1058	1158	...	1258	1358	...	1458	1558	...	1658	1758	...	1858	1958	...
Manchester P'dilly a.	...	2348	...	...	...		0810	...	0915	1015	...	1115	1215	...	1315	1415	...	1515	1615	...	1714	1815	...	1915	2015	...

	⑥	⑥	⑥ J	⑥	⑥	⑥			⑦	⑦	⑦	⑦	⑦	⑦	⑦	⑦	⑦	⑦	⑦	⑦	⑦	⑦	⑦	⑦	⑦	⑦
Cardiff Central 132 d.	1756	1850	1934	2010	2055	2154	...	⑦	...	0830	0920	1035	1135	1240	1322	1340	1456	1522	1556	1640	1735	1840	1940	...	2104	2315
Newport 132 d.	1810	1904	1948	2026	2110	2212	...		...	0849	0941	1051	1151	1254	1336	1354	1514	1536	1614	1654	1749	1854	1955	...	2119	2335
Cwmbrân d.	1820	1915	1958	2037	2121	2224	...		...	0900	0951	1102	1205	1309	1347	1409	1524	1547	1624	1709	1804	1909	2010	...	2130	2346
Pontypool & New Inn d.	1825	1920	2003	2042	|	2229	...		...	0906	0957	1108	1211	1315	|	|	|	1552	|	1715	1810	|	2016	...	2136	2352
Abergavenny d.	1835	1929	2012	2052	2134	2239	...		...	0915	1008	1118	1222	1325	1400	1422	1538	1602	1637	1725	1820	1922	2026	...	2146	0002
Hereford d.	1900	1955	2039	2120	2200	2303	...		...	0941	1036	1150	1254	1355	1426	1448	1604	1628	1704	1753	1849	1949	2054	...	2214	0030
Leominster d.	1913	2008	2052	2133	2214	▬	...		...	0955	1050	1203	1308	1408	|	1501	|	1641	|	1807	1903	2003	2108	...	2227	...
Ludlow d.	1924	2019	2103	2144	2225	...	...		...	1006	1101	1214	1319	1419	1448	1512	1625	1652	1726	1818	1914	2014	2119	...	2238	...
Craven Arms 146 d.	|	2027	2112	2154	2233	...	...		...	1014	|	1224	|	1428	|	|	|	1700	|	1826	|	2022	2129	...	2248	...
Church Stretton 146 d.	|	2036	2121	2203	2242	⑥	...		...	1023	|	1233	|	1437	|	|	|	1709	|	1835	|	2031	2138	...	2257	...
Shrewsbury 146 a.	1950	2053	2135	2217	2257		...		...	1037	1130	1248	1348	1451	1521	1538	1651	1723	1752	1849	1940	2045	2155	...	2314	...
Shrewsbury ¶ d.	1952	2057	2137	2219	2306	2349	...		0955	1039	1131	1251	1350	1453	1522	1540	1653	1730	1754	1854	1941	2048	...	2232	2319	...
Whitchurch ¶ d.	2008	|	|	2244	2331	0015	...		|	1100	1158	|	|	|	|	1606	|	|	|	|	2006	|	...	|	2346	...
Crewe ¶ a.	2027	2128	|	2304	2353	0038	...		1025	1122	1222	1326	1425	1525	|	1627	1725	|	1825	1924	2027	2123	...	2304	0009	...
Chester **160** a.	|	|	2231	|	0018	...	...		|	|	|	|	|	|	1618a	|	|	1825	|	|	|	|	...	2331	0033	...
Holyhead **160** a.	|	|	...	|	...	...	...		|	|	|	|	|	|	1837	|	|	2018	|	|	|	|	...	...	...	...
Stockport a.	2059	2158	...	2332	...	...	...		1058	|	1258	1400	1500	1558	...	1658	1758	...	1858	1958	2057	2158	...	...	...	...
Manchester P'dilly a.	2116	2213	...	2349	...	...	...		1112	1202	1315	1419	1515	1615	...	1715	1817	...	1915	2017	2114	2219	...	...	...	...

		Ⓐ	Ⓐ	Ⓐ	Ⓐ	Ⓐ	Ⓐ	Ⓐ	Ⓐ	Ⓐ	Ⓐ	Ⓐ J	Ⓐ	Ⓐ	Ⓐ	Ⓐ	Ⓐ	Ⓐ	Ⓐ	Ⓐ	Ⓐ	Ⓐ	Ⓐ	Ⓐ	Ⓐ	Ⓐ
Manchester P'dilly d.	Ⓐ	...	...	...	...	...	0630	...	...	0730	...	0830	...	0930	...	1030	1130	...	1230	1330	...	1430	1530	...	1630	1730
Stockport d.		...	...	...	...	...	0639	...	...	0739	...	0839	...	0939	...	1039	1139	...	1239	1339	...	1439	1539	...	1639	1739
Holyhead **160** d.		...	...	...	...	0425	|	0533	0514	|	0628	|	...	|	0805	|	|	1040	|	|	1232	|	|	1434	|	|
Chester **160** d.		...	...	...	...	0618	|	0715	0702	|	0819	|	0926	|	1020	|	|	1219	|	|	1419	|	|	1619	|	|
Crewe ¶ d.		...	0454	...	0555	|	0708	|	0734	0808	|	0908	|	1008	|	1108	1208	|	1308	1408	|	1508	1608	|	1708	1809
Whitchurch ¶ d.		...	0513	...	0616	|	|	|	0754	|	|	|	|	|	|	|	|	|	|	1428	|	|	1628	|	|	1829
Shrewsbury ¶ a.		...	0533	...	0642	0716	0742	0807	0825	0837	0913	0937	1022	1037	1114	1137	1237	1314	1337	1445	1513	1537	1647	1714	1737	1848
Shrewsbury 146 d.		...	0540	0610	0644	0718	0744	0810	...	0840	0914	0940	1024	1039	1116	1139	1239	1315	1340	1450	1515	1540	1650	1716	1740	1850
Church Stretton 146 d.		...	0555	0626	0659	|	0759	|	...	|	0930	|	|	1054	|	1154	|	1330	|	1505	1530	|	1706	1731	|	1905
Craven Arms 146 d.		...	0603	0634	0707	|	0807	|	...	|	0938	|	|	|	1137	|	|	1338	|	1513	1538	|	1714	1739	|	1913
Ludlow d.		...	0610	0643	0714	0744	0815	|	...	0906	0945	1006	|	1108	1144	1208	1305	1345	1406	1520	1546	1606	1721	1746	1806	1920
Leominster d.		...	0621	0654	0725	0754	0826	|	...	0916	|	1016	|	1118	|	1218	1315	|	1416	1531	|	1616	1732	1757	1816	1931
Hereford d.		0526	0641	0710	0745	0811	0842	0856	...	0933	1010	1033	|	1135	1208	1235	1332	1411	1433	1551	1611	1633	1751	1814	1833	1948
Abergavenny d.		0551	0704	0734	0808	0834	0905	|	...	0956	1033	1056	|	1158	1231	1258	1355	1433	1456	1614	1634	1656	1814	1837	1856	2011
Pontypool & New Inn d.		0602	0714	0745	0817	0844	|	|	...	|	1043	|	|	|	1242	|	1450	|	|	1623	1644	|	1824	|	|	2021
Cwmbrân d.		0607	0719	0750	0822	0849	0917	|	...	1009	1048	1109	|	1211	1247	1311	1410	|	1509	1628	1649	1709	1829	1849	1909	2026
Newport 132 a.		0619	0729	0800	0837	0900	0934	0940	...	1020	1101	1120	1153	1222	1256	1322	1420	1454	1521	1639	1659	1721	1839	1900	1922	2037
Cardiff Central 132 a.		0641	0749	0818	0853	0922	0956	0958	...	1039	1117	1137	1211	1237	1322	1339	1437	1510	1537	1657	1715	1739	1855	1920	1943	2103

	Ⓐ	Ⓐ	Ⓐ	Ⓐ	Ⓐ	Ⓐ		⑥	⑥	⑥	⑥	⑥	⑥	⑥	⑥	⑥	⑥	⑥	⑥	⑥	⑥	⑥	⑥	⑥	⑥	⑥
Manchester P'dilly d.	...	1830	1930	2030	*2135*	2236	⑥	...	...	...	...	...	0630	0730	...	0830	0930	...	1030	1130	...	1230	1330	...	1430	1530
Stockport d.	...	1839	1939	2039	*2144*	2244		...	...	...	...	...	0639	0739	...	0839	0939	...	1039	1139	...	1239	1339	...	1439	1539
Holyhead **160** d.	1650	|	|	|	|	|		...	...	...	...	0425	|	|	0635	|	|	0820	|	|	1033	|	|	1238	|	|
Chester **160** d.	1828	|	|	|	|	|		...	...	...	...	0612	|	|	0819	|	|	1019	|	|	1219	|	|	1419	|	|
Crewe ¶ d.	|	1908	2009	2121	*2212*	2314		...	0454	...	0555	|	0708	0808	|	0908	1008	|	1108	1208	|	1308	1408	|	1508	1608
Whitchurch ¶ d.	|	1929	2029	2142	*2233*	2334		...	0513	...	0616	|	0728	0827	|	|	|	|	|	1227	|	|	1427	|	|	1627
Shrewsbury ¶ a.	1924	1955	2048	2208	*2301*	0003		...	0533	...	0642	0717	0747	0845	0913	0937	1036	1114	1137	1245	1313	1337	1443	1513	1537	1643
Shrewsbury 146 d.	1925	1956	2050	2209	2308	...		...	0540	0613	0644	0719	0750	0850	0915	0940	1038	1115	1140	1250	1315	1340	1445	1515	1540	1645
Church Stretton 146 d.	|	2011	2105	2244	2324	...		...	0555	0628	0659	|	0805	0905	|	0955	1054	|	1155	1305	1330	|	1500	|	1555	1700
Craven Arms 146 d.	|	2019	2113	2232	2332	...		...	0603	0636	0707	|	0813	0913	|	1003	1102	|	1203	1313	1338	|	1508	|	1603	1708
Ludlow d.	1951	2027	2120	2240	2341	...		...	0610	0644	0714	0745	0820	0920	0942	1010	1109	1141	1210	1320	1344	1406	1515	1541	1610	1715
Leominster d.	|	2037	2131	2250	2352	...		...	0621	0655	0725	0755	0831	0931	|	1021	1120	|	1221	1331	|	1416	1526	|	1621	1726
Hereford d.	2017	2054	2150	2311	0009	...		0542	0642	0711	0744	0812	0851	0951	1007	1038	1146	1206	1238	1351	1410	1433	1546	1606	1638	1746
Abergavenny d.	2040	2122	2216	2334	0033	...		0607	0705	0734	0807	0835	0914	1014	1030	1101	1209	1229	1301	1414	1432	1456	1609	1629	1701	1809
Pontypool & New Inn d.	|	2132	|	2343	|	...		0618	0715	0744	0816	0845	|	|	1040	|	|	1239	|	|	1443	|	|	1639	|	|
Cwmbrân d.	2053	2137	2228	2348	0046	...		0623	0720	0749	0821	0850	0926	1026	1045	1113	1221	1244	1313	1426	1448	1509	1621	1644	1713	1821
Newport 132 a.	2115	2150	2241	2359	0059	...		0634	0737	0800	0831	0901	0937	1037	1055	1127	1235	1254	1328	1436	1504	1521	1633	1654	1733	1833
Cardiff Central 132 a.	2142	2206	2304	0015	0120	...		0654	0754	0820	0850	0922	0959	1101	1115	1153	1253	1317	1353	1453	1524	1537	1653	1708	1753	1853

	⑥	⑥	⑥	⑥	⑥	⑥	⑥	⑥	⑥			⑦	⑦	⑦	⑦	⑦	⑦	⑦	⑦	⑦	⑦	⑦	⑦	⑦	⑦	⑦
Manchester P'dilly d.	...	1630	1730	...	1830	1930	2030	2135	2235	...	⑦	...	0930	1030	1124	...	1230	1330	1430	1530	1630	1730	...	1830	1930	2030
Stockport d.	...	1639	1739	...	1839	1939	2039	2144	2244	...		...	0939	1039	1140	...	1240	1340	1439	1539	1639	1739	...	1839	1939	2039
Holyhead **160** d.	1423	|	|	1650	|	|	|	|	|	...		...	|	|	|	1020	|	|	|	|	|	|	1625	|	|	|
Chester **160** d.	1619	|	|	1829	|	|	|	|	|	...		...	|	|	|	1221	|	|	|	|	|	|	1824	|	|	|
Crewe ¶ d.	|	1708	1809	|	1910	2009	2109	2212	2314	...		...	1013	1111	1213	|	1313	1413	1510	1613	1713	1813	|	1913	2010	2113
Whitchurch ¶ d.	|	1727	1828	|	1931	2028	2130	2233	2334	...		...	1035	|	|	|	1334	|	|	|	1734	|	|	1934	|	2135
Shrewsbury ¶ a.	1714	1743	1846	1924	1956	2048	2153	2301	0003	...		...	1101	1141	1243	1318	1359	1443	1544	1643	1800	1843	1920	2000	2044	2203
Shrewsbury 146 d.	1716	1745	1850	1926	1958	2050	2155	▬	...	...		0750*	1103	1145	1244	1319	1401	1444	1547	1644	1801	1844	1921	2001	2045	2204
Church Stretton 146 d.	|	1800	1905	|	2013	2105	2210	...	...	...		0815*	1119	|	|	1335	|	1500	|	1700	|	|	1937	|	2101	2220
Craven Arms 146 d.	|	1808	1913	|	2021	2113	2218	...	...	...		0835*	1127	|	|	1343	|	1508	|	1708	|	|	1945	|	2110	2229
Ludlow d.	1742	1815	1920	1951	2028	2120	2226	⑥	...	...		0855*	1136	1213	1313	1351	1428	1516	1617	1716	1829	1912	1953	2029	2118	2237
Leominster d.	|	1826	1931	|	2039	2131	2237		...	...		0920*	1147	1223	1324	1402	1439	1526	1628	1726	1839	|	2004	2039	2130	2249
Hereford d.	1807	1843	1951	2017	2056	2148	2253	2315	...	...		1009	1203	1239	1340	1419	1456	1543	1644	1743	1857	1936	2021	2055	2146	2305
Abergavenny d.	1830	1906	2014	2040	2119	2211	2316	2338	...	...		1033	1227	1302	1403	1442	1519	1606	1708	1806	1920	1959	2046	2118	2210	2329
Pontypool & New Inn d.	1840	|	2023	|	2128	|	2325	|	...	...		1043	|	1312	|	1452	|	1616	|	1816	|	|	2056	|	2221	2339
Cwmbrân d.	1845	1918	2028	2052	2133	2223	2330	2350	...	...		1048	1240	1317	1416	1457	1531	1621	1721	1821	1933	2011	2101	2131	2226	2344
Newport 132 a.	1855	1934	2040	2114	2144	2236	2346	0006	...	...		1059	1251	1328	1431	1507	1548	1631	1733	1831	1948	2026	2114	2144	2235	2354
Cardiff Central 132 a.	1915	1958	2100	2143	2204	2256	0006	0037	...	...		1118	1313	1346	1452	1531	1605	1652	1751	1852	2008	2045	2143	2205	2257	0020

– To / from Llandudno Junction.
– Arrives 1629 June 22 - July 27.
– Connection by 🚌.

¶ – Additional trains Shrewsbury - Crewe at 0544⚒, 0757⚒, 1018⚒, 1224⚒, 1424⚒, 1624⚒, 1825⚒, 2032⚒; Crewe - Shrewsbury at 0640Ⓐ, 0720⑥, 0734Ⓐ, 0920⚒, 1120⚒, 1320⚒, 1520⚒, 1720⚒.

150 LONDON - BIRMINGHAM, CHESTER, HOLYHEAD, MANCHESTER and LIVERPOOL VT

Certain Wolverhampton services continue to / from destinations on Table 151.
For Birmingham - Manchester trains see Table 129. For London - Northampton - Birmingham - Crewe/Liverpool trains see Table 142.

LONDON - BIRMINGHAM - WOLVERHAMPTON

km		⚒	Ⓐ	⑥	Ⓐ	⚒	⚒	⚒	⚒	⚒	⚒		⚒	⚒	⚒	⚒	Ⓐ	⑥	Ⓐ	⑥	⚒	⚒	⚒
0	**London** Euston d.		0620	0623	0643	0703	0723	0743	0803	0823	0843	and	1603	1623	1643	1703	1723	1723	1743	1743	1803	1823	1843
28	Watford Junction △ d.		0634	0637	|	|	0737	|	|	0837	|	at the	|	1637	|	|	1737	1737	|	|	|	1837	|
80	Milton Keynes d.		|	|	0713	|	|	0813	|	|	0913	same	|	|	1713	|	|	|	1813u	1813	|	|	1913
133	Rugby d.		0713	|	|	0751	|	|	0851	|	|	minutes	1651	|	|	1751	|	|	|	|	1851	|	|
151	Coventry a.		0722	0722	0742	0802	0822	0842	0902	0922	0942	past	1702	1722	1742	1802	1822	1822	1842	1842	1902	1922	1942
168	**Birmingham** International ✈ a.		0733	0733	0753	0813	0833	0853	0913	0933	0953	each	1713	1733	1753	1813	1833	1833	1856	1853	1913	1933	1953
182	**Birmingham** New St a.		0745	0747	0808	0827	0845	0908	0927	0945	1008	hour	1727	1745	1808	1827	1845	1845	1908	1908	1927	1945	2008
190	Sandwell & Dudley a.		...	...	0824	...	...	0924	...	...	1024	until	...	...	1824	...	...	1858	1924	1924	...	2058	2024
202	**Wolverhampton** a.		...	...	0837	...	...	0937	...	...	1037		...	...	1837	...	...	1911	1937	1937	...	2011	2036

	⑥	Ⓐ	⚒	Ⓐ	⑥	Ⓐ	Ⓐ	⑥	Ⓐ	Ⓐ	⑥	Ⓐ	⑥A	⑥B	Ⓐ	Ⓐ		⑦	⑦	⑦	⑦	⑦	⑦	⑦
London Euston d.	1903	1903	1923	1943	1943	2003	2023	2025	2043	2103	2103	2143	2143	2143	2230	2330	...		0850	0950	1050	1150	1220	1240
Watford Junction △ d.	|	|	1937	|	|	|	2307	2040	|	|	2118	2158	2158	2158	2245	|	...		0905	1005	1105	1205	1234	|
Milton Keynes d.	|	|	|	2013	2021	|	|	|	2113	2134	2150	2217	2230	2230	2329	0028	...		0938	1038	1138	1230	|	1313
Rugby d.	1951	1951	|	|	|	2051	|	|	|	2157	2212	|	2253	2306	0001	0100	...		1014	1114	1214	1250	|	|
Coventry a.	2002	2002	2022	2042	2050	2102	2124	2136	2142	2206	2222	2246	2302	2315	0010	0118	...		1023	1123	1223	1259	1322	1342
Birmingham International ✈ a.	2013	2013	2033	2053	2101	2113	2134	2150	2153	2218	2233	2300	2313	2326	0021	0129	...		1034	1134	1234	1310	1333	1353
Birmingham New St a.	2027	2027	2045	2108	2113	2127	2146	2204	2204	2229	2245	2316	2325	2338	0032	0141	...		1047	1147	1247	1325	1345	1408
Sandwell & Dudley a.	2053	...	2058	2124	|	|	2159	2224	2215	2241	2256	2333	2336	2349	|	|	...		1058	1158	1258	...	1356	1424
Wolverhampton a.	2108	...	2111	2137	2138	2156	2212	2238	2230	2256	2310	2347	2350	0003	0103	0210	...		1113	1213	1312	...	1410	1437

	⑦	⑦	⑦		⑦	⑥	⑦	⑦	⑦	⑦	⑦	⑦	⑦	⑦	⑦	⑦	⑦	⑦	⑦	⑦	⑦	⑦	⑦
London Euston d.	1300	1320	1340	and	1600	1620	1640	1700	1720	1740	1800	1820	1840	1900	1920	1940	2000	2018	2038	2054	2155	2225	2325
Watford Junction △ d.	|	1334	|	at the	|	1634	|	|	1734	|	|	1834	|	|	1934	|	|	2032	|	2110	2209	2239	2339
Milton Keynes d.	|	|	1413	same	|	|	1713	|	|	1813	|	|	1913	|	|	2013	|	|	2116	2143	2245	2312	0012
Rugby d.	1351	|	|	minutes	1651	|	|	1751	|	|	1851	|	|	1951	|	|	2051	|	|	2207	2323	2348	0046s
Coventry a.	1402	1422	1442	past	1702	1722	1742	1802	1822	1842	1902	1922	1942	2003	2022	2042	2103	2120	2146	2216	2333	2357	0058s
Birmingham International ✈ a.	1413	1433	1453	each	1713	1733	1753	1813	1833	1853	1913	1933	1953	2013	2033	2053	2113	2131	2157	2227	2344	0008	0109s
Birmingham New St a.	1425	1445	1508	hour	1725	1745	1808	1825	1844	1908	1925	1945	2008	2025	2045	2108	2125	2144	2209	2239	2356	0021	0122s
Sandwell & Dudley a.	...	...	1524	until	...	...	1824	...	...	1924	1948	...	2024	2035	2056	2124	...	2156	2224	2251	|	|	|
Wolverhampton a.	...	...	1537		...	...	1837	...	...	1937	2002	...	2037	2047	2110	2137	...	2210	2238	2306	0017	0043	0144

	⚒	Ⓐ	Ⓐ	⑥	Ⓐ	⑥	Ⓐ	⑥	Ⓐ	⑥	Ⓐ	⑥	Ⓐ	Ⓐ	⑥	Ⓐ	⑥	Ⓐ	⑥	Ⓐ	⑥	⚒	⚒	⚒
Wolverhampton d.		0500	0524	...	0545	0545	0604	0606	0627	0627	0645	0645	0705	...	0705	0724	0725	0745	0745	...	...	...	0845	...
Sandwell & Dudley d.		|	0534	...	0555	0556	0615	0617	0638	0637	0656	0656	0715	...	0714	|	|	0757	0755	...	...	...	0855	...
Birmingham New St d.		0529	0550	0550	0610	0610	0630	0630	0650	0650	0710	0710	0730	...	0730	0750	0750	0810	0810	0830	0830	0850	0910	0930
Birmingham International ✈ d.		0540	0600	0600	0620	0620	0640	0640	0700	0700	0720	0720	|	0741	0740	0800	0800	0820	0820	0840	0840	0900	0920	0940
Coventry d.		0551	0611	0611	0631	0631	0651	0651	0711	0711	0731	0731	|	0752	0751	0811	0811	0831	0830	0851	0851	0911	0931	0951
Rugby a.		0601	|	0623	|	|	|	|	|	0721	|	|	|	|	|	0821	0822	|	|	|	|	0922	|	|
Milton Keynes a.		0622	0638	|	0659	0659	|	|	0740s	|	|	0758	|	|	|	|	|	|	0858	0918	|	|	0958	|
Watford Junction ▽ a.		0645	|	|	|	0719	0737	0736	|	|	|	|	|	|	0837	|	|	0916	|	|	0939	|	|	1039
London Euston a.		0704	0715	0717	0734	0738	0753	0755	0815	0817	0831	0835	0843	0850	0856	0915	0915	0934	0935	0955	0959	1015	1035	1055

		⚒	⚒	⚒	Ⓐ	⑥	Ⓐ	⑥	Ⓐ	Ⓐ	⑥	Ⓐ	⑥	Ⓐ	⑥A	⑥B	Ⓐ	Ⓐ			⑦	⑦	⑦
Wolverhampton d.	and	...	1745	...	...	...	1845	1845	...	1945	1945	...	2045	2047	2107	2107	2145	2245	...		0805	0905	1005
Sandwell & Dudley d.	at the	...	1755	...	...	...	1855	1855	...	1955	1955	...	2055	2057	2117	2117	2156	2255	...		0815	0915	1015
Birmingham New St d.	same	1750	1810	1830	1850	1850	1910	1910	1930	2010	2010	2050	2110	2110	2130	2130	2210	2310	...		0830	0930	1030
Birmingham International ✈ d.	minutes	1800	1820	1840	1900	1900	1920	1920	1940	2020	2020	2100	2120	2120	2140	2140	2220	2320	...		0840	0940	1040
Coventry d.	past	1811	1831	1851	1911	1911	1931	1931	1951	2031	2031	2111	2131	2131	2151	2151	2231	2331	...		0851	0951	1051
Rugby a.	each	1822	|	|	1922	1921	|	1942	2002	|	2042	2122	2142	|	2201	2201	2243	2343	...	⑦	0902	1002	1102
Milton Keynes a.	hour	|	1858	|	|	|	1958	2005	|	2058	2104	|	2204	2158	2225	2236	2306	0023	...		0937	1037	1137
Watford Junction ▽ a.	until	|	|	1939	|	|	|	2034	2041	2119	2135	|	2234	2220	2311	2311	2339	0052	...		1007	1111	1208
London Euston a.		1917	1932	1956	2015	2023	2034	2055	2058	2139	2157	2213	2255	2243	2330	2330	0006	0115	...		1028	1131	1227

	⑦		⑦	⑦	⑦	⑦	⑦		⑦	⑦	⑦	⑦	⑦	⑦	⑦	⑦	⑦	⑦	⑦		⑦	⑦	⑦
Wolverhampton d.	1105	...	1145	...	...	1245	...	and	...	1645	...	...	1745	...	...	1845	...	1942	...	...	2105	2205	2237
Sandwell & Dudley d.	1115	...	1157	...	...	1255	...	at the	...	1656	...	...	1756	...	...	1856	...	1956	...	...	2117	2216	2248
Birmingham New St d.	1130	1150	1210	1230	1250	1310	1330	same	1650	1710	1730	1750	1810	1830	1850	1910	1930	2010	2030	...	2130	2230	2300
Birmingham International ✈ d.	1140	1200	1220	1240	1300	1320	1340	minutes	1700	1720	1740	1800	1820	1840	1900	1920	1940	2020	2040	...	2140	2240	2310
Coventry d.	1151	1211	1231	1251	1311	1331	1351	past	1711	1729	1751	1811	1831	1851	1914	1931	1951	2031	2051	...	2151	2251	2321
Rugby a.	1203	1223	|	|	1323	|	|	each	1723	|	|	1823	|	|	1924	|	|	|	2103	...	2202	2303	2334
Milton Keynes a.	1226	|	1300	|	|	1358	|	hour	|	1758	|	|	1858	|	|	1958	|	2059	2126	...	2235	2336	0013s
Watford Junction ▽ a.	|	|	|	1338	|	|	1438	until	|	|	1838	|	|	1938	|	|	2038	|	2202	...	2305	0006	0043
London Euston a.	1306	1320	1338	1357	1418	1438	1457		1818	1838	1857	1917	1939	1957	2018	2039	2057	2148	2223	...	2325	0027	0105

LONDON - CHESTER (- HOLYHEAD)

km		Ⓐ	⑥	Ⓐ	⚒	⚒	⚒	⚒	⚒	⑥	Ⓐ	⑦	⚒	⑦	Ⓐ	⑥	⑦	⑥	Ⓐ	⑦	⑥	ⒶL	⑦	Ⓐ	Ⓐ
0	**London** Euston d.	0710	0810	0810	0910	1010	1110	1210	1310	1410	1410	1508	1510	1608	1610	1610	1708	1710	1710	1808	1810	1810	1908	1910	2010
80	Milton Keynes d.	0741	0841	0843	0941	1041	1141	1241	1341	1441	1441	1542	1541	1642	1641u	1641	1742	1741	1741u	1842	1841	1841u	1942	1941	2041
254	Crewe d.	0849	0949	0953	1049	1149	1249	1349	1449	1549	1549	1652	1649	1752	1749	1749	1856	1852	1857	1952	1949	1956	2055	2049	2149
288	**Chester** a.	0913	1013	1013	1113	1213	1313	1413	1513	1610	1612	1713	1713	1813	1808	1809	1913	1912	1916	2013	2013	2015	2113	2113	2213
	Bangor **160** a.	...	...	1127	1216	...	...	...	...	1717	...	...	...	...	1921	1921	2027	2024	2028	2123	...	2125	2222	2222	...
	Holyhead **160** a.	...	...	*1223*	1250	...	...	...	...	1751	...	...	...	...	*2018*	1955	2059	2058	2059	2154	...	2159	2256	2256	...

		Ⓐ	⑥	ⒶL	⑥	Ⓐ	Ⓐ	⑥	⚒	⑦	⚒	⚒	⑦	Ⓐ	⑥	⑦	⚒	⑦	⚒	⑦	⚒	Ⓐ	⑦	⑦	Ⓐ
Holyhead **160** d.	...	0448	...	0551	0652	0655	...	0755	0855	...	...	...	1055	*1127*	...	1150	...	1250	1358	1355	...	...	...	...	...
Bangor **160** d.	...	0514	...	0618	0720	0722	...	0822	0922	...	...	...	1122	1224	...	1217	...	1318	1425	1422	...	...	...	...	...
Chester d.	...	0626	0717	0735	0835	0835	0935	0935	1035	1128	1135	1235	1232	1335	1335	1330	1435	1433	1535	1533	1635	1735	1735	1835	1935
Crewe a.	...	0647	0736	0754	0854	0854	0954	0954	1054	1147	1154	1254	1253	1354	1354	1350	1454	1453	1554	1552	1654	1754	1753	1853	1954
Milton Keynes a.	...	|	0852	|	1002	1002	1102	1102	1202	1304	1302	1402	1403	1502	1502	1503	1602	1603	1702	1703	1802	1901	1903	2003	2104
London Euston a.	...	0834	0930	0941	1039	1039	1139	1139	1239	1346	1339	1439	1444	1539	1539	1545	1639	1644	1739	1744	1839	1939	1945	2046	2143

BIRMINGHAM - STAFFORD - CHESTER (- HOLYHEAD)

km		⚒	Ⓐ2	⑦2						
0	**Birmingham New Street** d.	0530	2252	2255	...	...	...	...	...	...
19	Wolverhampton d.	0548	2327	2315	...	...	...	...	...	...
43	Stafford d.	0601	2343	2331	...	...	...	...	...	...
82	Crewe d.	0623	0010	0001	...	...	...	...	...	...
116	**Chester** a.	0643	0032	0022	...	...	...	...	...	...
	Bangor **160** a.	0749	0146	0144	...	...	...	...	...	...
	Holyhead **160** a.	0823	0215	0220	...	...	...	...	...	...

	⑥	Ⓐ	⑦2	Ⓐ					
Holyhead **160** d.	...	...	1825	*1921*	...	...	...	...	...
Bangor **160** d.	...	...	1904	2020	...	...	...	...	...
Chester d.	0422	0422	2027	2135	...	...	...	...	...
Crewe d.	0500	0500	2052	2156	...	...	...	...	...
Stafford d.	0525	0525	2116	|	...	...	...	...	...
Wolverhampton d.	0540	0540	2135	2228	...	...	...	...	...
Birmingham New Street a.	0558	0608	2152	2250	...	...	...	...	...

A – Until June 14 and from Sep. 13.
B – June 21 - Sep. 6.
C – Aug. 2 - Sep. 6 and from Oct. 25.
D – ①②③④⑥.
L – Conveys [12] London Euston - Wrexham General and v.v. (Table 145).

a – On Ⓐ calls to pick up only.
s – Calls to set down only.
u – Calls to pick up only.
y – On Ⓐ calls to set down only.

△ – Trains stop here to pick up only.
▽ – Trains stop here to set down only.
□ – London Euston - Manchester: *304* km via Crewe.

VT LONDON - BIRMINGHAM, CHESTER, HOLYHEAD, MANCHESTER and LIVERPOOL 150

For Birmingham - Manchester trains see Table 129. For London - Northampton - Birmingham - Crewe / Liverpool trains see Table 142.

LONDON - MANCHESTER AND LIVERPOOL

km□		⚒	Ⓐ	Ⓐ	⚒	⚒	⚒	⚒	⚒	⚒	Ⓐ	⑥	⚒	⚒	⚒	⚒		⚒	⑥	⚒	⚒	Ⓐ	⑥	⚒	Ⓐ
0	**London** Euston d.		0526	0616	0636	0655	0707	0720	0735	0800	0807	0807	0820	0840	0900	0907	and	1620	1633	1640	1700	1707	1707	1720	1733
80	Milton Keynes d.		0615	0646	|	0727	|	0750	0806	|	0838	|	0850	|	|	|	at	1650	|	|	|	|	|	1750a	|
155	Nuneaton d.		0645	|	|	|	|	|	|	|	|	|	|	|	|	|	the	|	|	|	|	|	1803	|	|
215	Stafford d.		0708	|	|	|	0823	|	|	|	0927	0923	|	|	|	1023		|	1759	|	|	1823	1827	|	1856
235	Stoke on Trent d.		|	0745	|	0825	|	0848	|	0925	|	|	0948	|	1025	|	same	1748	|	|	1825	|	|	1848	|
267	Macclesfield d.		|	0802	|	0841	|	|	|	0941	|	|	|	|	1041	|	minutes	|	|	|	1841	|	|	|	|
254	Crewe d.		0725	|	0811	|	0843	|	0911	|	|	0943	|	1011	|	1043	past	|	|	1811	|	1843	1847	|	1916
287	Stockport d.		|	0817	0837	0856	|	0917	0937	0956	|	|	1017	1037	1056	|	each	1817	|	1837	1856	|	|	1917	|
296	**Manchester** P'dilly a.		|	0828	0849	0907	|	0928	0949	1007	|	|	1028	1049	1107	|	hour	1828	|	1849	1907	|	|	1928	|
290	Runcorn d.		0745	...	...	...	0900	...	...	...	1000	1001	...	...	...	1100	until	...	1831	...	...	1900	1904	...	1933
312	**Liverpool** Lime St a.		0805	...	...	...	0921	...	...	...	1021	1021	...	...	...	1121		...	1852	...	...	1921	1923	...	1952

	⚒	⚒	⚒	⚒	⑥	Ⓐ	⚒	⚒	Ⓐ	⑥	⚒	⑥	Ⓐ	Ⓐ	Ⓐ	⑥	⑥	⑥C	Ⓐ	Ⓐ	⑥	Ⓐ	Ⓐ	Ⓐ	⑤	D
London Euston d.	1740	1800	1807	1820	1833	1833	1840	1900	1907	1907	1920	1940	1940	2000	2007	2011	2020	2031	2040	2100	2100	2107	2140	2200	2300	2300
Milton Keynes d.	|	|	|	1850a	|	|	|	|	|	|	1950	|	|	|	|	|	2105	|	|	2131	2145	2138	|	2239	|	|
Nuneaton d.	|	|	|	|	|	|	|	|	2003	2003	|	|	|	|	2103	|	2133	|	|	|	|	2207	|	2314s	|	|
Stafford d.	|	|	1923	|	1959	1957	|	|	2027	2027	|	|	2104	|	2127	2146	|	|	|	|	2234	|	|	2352s	|	|
Stoke on Trent d.	|	1925	|	1948	|	|	|	2025	|	|	2048	|	|	2125	|	|	2205	|	|	2228	|	|	2312	|	0114s	0118s
Macclesfield d.	|	1941	|	|	|	|	|	2041	|	|	|	|	|	2141	|	|	2221	|	|	2244	|	|	2328	|	0131s	0135s
Crewe d.	1911	|	1943	|	|	2017	2011	|	|	2047	|	2119	2123	|	2148	2206	|	2237	2213	|	2259	2254	|	0018	|	|
Stockport d.	1937	1956	|	2017	|	|	2037	2056	|	|	2117	2145	|	2154	|	|	2236	|	2239	2259	2325	|	2343	...	0145s	0149s
Manchester P'dilly a.	1949	2007	|	2028	|	|	2049	2110	|	|	2128	2153	2157	2207	|	|	2251	2311	2248	2311	2338	|	2351	...	0156	0200
Runcorn d.	...	...	2000	...	2032	2034	...	...	2101	2105	...	...	...	...	2205	2224	...	...	...	...	...	2311	...	...	...	...
Liverpool Lime St a.	...	...	2021	...	2052	2053	...	...	2121	2125	...	...	...	...	2225	2246	...	...	...	...	...	2334	...	...	...	...

	⑦	⑦	⑦	⑦	⑦	⑦	⑦	⑦	⑦	⑦	⑦	⑦	⑦	⑦	⑦	⑦	⑦	⑦	⑦	⑦	⑦	⑦	⑦	⑦	⑦	⑦
London Euston d.		0810	0815	0820	0915	0920	1015	1020	1115	1120	1205	1217	1237	1257	1305	1317	1337	1357	1405	1417	1437	1457	1505	1517	1537	1557
Milton Keynes d.		0856	|	0906	|	1007	|	1107	1204	1208	|	1250	|	|	|	1350	|	|	|	1450	|	|	|	1550	|	|
Nuneaton d.		|	0944	|	1045	|	1147	|	|	|	|	|	|	|	|	|	|	|	|	|	|	|	|	|	|	|
Stafford d.		|	1008	|	1109	|	1214	|	1253	|	1325	|	|	|	1425	|	|	|	1525	|	|	|	1625	|	|	|
Stoke on Trent d.		|	|	1021	|	1122	|	1225	|	1311	|	1350	|	1426	|	1450	|	1526	|	1550	|	1626	|	1650	|	1726
Macclesfield d.		|	|	1038	|	1138	|	1242	|	1328	|	|	|	1442	|	|	|	1542	|	|	|	1642	|	|	|	1742
Crewe d.		1019	1030	|	1132	|	1234	|	1315	|	1345	|	1413	|	1445	|	1513	|	1545	|	1613	|	1645	|	1713	|
Stockport d.		1044	|	1052	|	1153	|	1256	|	1342	|	1419	1439	1457	|	1519	1539	1557	|	1619	1639	1657	|	1719	1739	1757
Manchester P'dilly a.		1055	|	1103	|	1204	|	1308	|	1353	|	1429	1450	1509	|	1529	1550	1609	|	1629	1650	1709	|	1729	1750	1809
Runcorn d.		...	1047	...	1149	...	1251	...	1332	...	1402	...	...	...	1502	...	...	...	1602	...	...	...	1702	...	...	...
Liverpool Lime St a.		...	1109	...	1210	...	1312	...	1354	...	1424	...	...	...	1522	...	...	...	1622	...	...	...	1722	...	...	...

	⑦	⑦	⑦	⑦		⑦	⑦	⑦	⑦	⑦	⑦	⑦	⑦		⑦	⑦	⑦	⑦	⑦	⑦	⑦	⑦		⑦	⑦	⑦
London Euston d.	1605	1617	1637	1657	...	1705	1717	1737	1757	1805	1817	1837	1857	...	1905	1917	1937	1957	2005	2008	2015	2035	...	2121	2125	2151
Milton Keynes d.	|	1650	|	|	...	|	1750	|	|	|	1850	|	|	...	|	1950	|	|	|	2041	2048	|	...	|	2214	2239
Nuneaton d.	|	|	|	|	...	1804	|	|	|	|	|	|	|	...	2004	|	|	|	2104	|	|	|	...	2253	|	2330
Stafford d.	1725	|	|	|	...	|	|	|	|	1925	|	|	|	...	2029	|	|	|	|	2133	|	2200	...	2318	|	2355s
Stoke on Trent d.	|	1750	|	1826	...	|	1850	|	1926	|	1950	|	2026	...	|	2050	|	2126	|	|	2150	|	...	|	2329	|
Macclesfield d.	|	|	|	1842	...	|	|	|	1942	|	|	|	2042	...	|	|	|	2142	|	|	|	|	...	|	2346	|
Crewe d.	1745	|	1813	|	...	1846	|	1913	|	1945	|	2013	|	...	2049	|	2113	|	2146	2155	|	2221	...	2343	|	0018s
Stockport d.	|	1819	1839	1857	...	|	1919	1939	1957	|	2019	2039	2057	...	|	2119	2139	2157	|	|	2219	2246	...	|	0001	0040s
Manchester P'dilly a.	|	1829	1850	1909	...	|	1929	1950	2009	|	2029	2050	2109	...	|	2129	2150	2209	|	|	2229	2257	...	|	0012	0050
Runcorn d.	1802	...	...	...	...	1902	...	...	...	2002	...	...	...	...	2106	...	...	...	2203	2212	...	...	...	0005	...	...
Liverpool Lime St a.	1822	...	...	...	...	1922	...	...	...	2022	...	...	...	...	2127	...	...	...	2223	2233	...	...	...	0028	...	...

	⚒	Ⓐ	Ⓐ	⑥	⑥	Ⓐ	⑥	Ⓐ	⚒	⚒	Ⓐ	⑥	⑥	Ⓐ	Ⓐ	⚒	⑥	⑥	Ⓐ	Ⓐ	⑥	⚒	⚒	⚒	⚒	⚒
Liverpool Lime St d.		...	0527	...	0547	...	...	0605	...	...	...	0645	...	...	0700	...	...	0719	...	0747	0747	...	...	...	0847	...
Runcorn d.		...	0543	...	0603	...	...	0621	...	...	...	0701	...	...	0715u	...	...	0736	...	0803	0803	...	...	...	0903	...
Manchester P'dilly d.		0505	|	0525	|	0555	0555	|	0610	0635	0643	|	0655	0700	|	0715	0735	|	0735	|	|	0755	0815	0835	|	0855
Stockport d.		0513	|	0534	|	0603	0603	|	0618	0643	0651	|	0704	0707u	|	0723	0743	|	0743	|	|	0804	0823	0843	|	0904
Crewe d.		0534	0600	0557	|	0627	0627	|	|	|	0715	0718	0727	|	|	|	|	0752	|	0821	0821	0827	|	|	0921	0929
Macclesfield d.		|	|	|	|	|	|	|	0631	0656	|	|	|	|	|	|	0756	|	0756	|	|	|	|	0856	|	|
Stoke on Trent d.		|	|	|	|	|	|	|	0648	0712	|	|	|	|	|	0750	0812	|	0812	|	|	|	0850	0912	|	|
Stafford a.		0554	0620	0618	0634	|	|	0652	|	|	0735	0738	|	|	|	|	|	0815	|	0840	0840	|	|	|	0943	|
Nuneaton a.		0617	|	0658	0706	|	|	|	|	|	|	|	|	|	|	|	|	|	0844	|	0904	|	|	|	|	|
Milton Keynes a.		0651	0713	0711	|	|	0731	|	|	|	|	|	|	|	|	0846	|	|	|	|	|	|	0946	|	|	|
London Euston a.		0729	0751	0753	0805	0808	0810	0823	0828	0846	0854	0900	0905	0901	0904	0924	0943	0947	0952	1001	1006	1011	1024	1043	1105	1108

	⚒	⚒	⚒	⚒		⚒	⚒	⑥	Ⓐ	⚒	⚒	⚒	⑥	Ⓐ	⑥	Ⓐ	Ⓐ	⑥	Ⓐ	⑥	Ⓐ	Ⓐ	⑥	⑥	Ⓐ
Liverpool Lime St d.	...	...	0947	...		...	...	1647	1647	...	...	...	1747	1747	...	...	...	...	...	...	1847	...	1847	...	...
Runcorn d.	...	...	1003	...	and	...	...	1703	1703	...	...	...	1803	1803	...	...	...	...	...	...	1903	...	1903	...	...
Manchester P'dilly d.	0915	0935	|	0955	at	1615	1635	|	|	1655	1715	1735	|	|	1755	1755	1815	1815	1835	1835	|	1855	|	1855	1915
Stockport d.	0923	0943	|	1004	the	1623	1643	|	|	1704	1723	1743	|	|	1804	1804	1823	1823	1843	1843	|	1904	|	1904	1923
Crewe d.	|	|	1021	1027	same	|	|	1722	|	1727	|	|	|	1822	1827	1828	|	|	|	|	1921	1927	1921	1927	|
Macclesfield d.	|	0956	|	|	minutes	|	1656	|	|	|	|	1756	|	|	|	|	|	|	1856	1856	|	|	|	|	1936
Stoke on Trent d.	0950	1012	|	|	past	1650	1712	|	|	|	1750	1812	|	|	|	|	1850	1849	1912	1912	|	|	|	|	1952
Stafford a.	|	|	1040	|	each	|	|	1741	1734	|	|	|	1836	1842	|	|	|	|	|	|	1940	|	19341	|	|
Nuneaton a.	|	|	|	|	hour	|	|	|	|	|	|	|	|	|	|	|	|	|	|	|	|	|	|	|	|
Milton Keynes a.	1046	|	|	|	until	1746	|	|	1823	|	1849	|	|	|	|	1933	1946	1945	|	|	|	2031	|	|	2048
London Euston a.	1124	1143	1159	1205		1824	1843	1901	1902	1912	1926	1943	1959	2007	2005	2008	2024	2034	2042	2059	2104	2106	2116	2120	2126

	⑥	Ⓐ	Ⓐ	⑥	Ⓐ	⑥	Ⓐ	Ⓐ		⑦	⑦	⑦	⑦	⑦	⑦	⑦	⑦	⑦	⑦	⑦	⑦	⑦	⑦	⑦	⑦	⑦
Liverpool Lime St d.	...	1948	...	1948	...	...	2048	...	...		...	...	0815	0838	...	0938	...	...	1038	...	...	1147	...	...	...	1247
Runcorn d.	...	2004	...	2004	...	...	2104	...	...		...	...	0835	0854	...	0954	...	...	1054	...	...	1203	...	...	...	1303
Manchester P'dilly d.	1935	|	1955	|	2015	2035	|	2115	...		0805	0820	|	|	0920	|	1020	1035	|	1115	1135	|	1155	1215	1235	|
Stockport d.	1943	|	2004	|	2023	2043	|	2123	...		0814	0828	|	|	0927	|	1029	1043	|	1123	1143	|	1205	1223	1243	|
Crewe d.	|	2022	2027	2021	|	|	2121	|	...		0839	|	0852	0911	|	1012	1053	|	1112	|	|	1221	1228	|	|	1321
Macclesfield d.	1956	|	|	|	2036	2056	|	2136	...		|	0842	|	|	0940	|	|	1055	|	|	1156	|	|	|	1257	|
Stoke on Trent d.	2012	|	|	|	2053	2112	|	2153	...		|	0859	|	|	0957	|	|	1113	|	1151	1213	|	|	1251	1314	|
Stafford a.	|	|	2047	2041	|	|	2143	|	...		0901	|	|	0931	|	1032	|	|	1135	|	|	1242	|	|	|	1342
Nuneaton a.	|	2104	|	|	|	|	2217	|	...		|	|	|	0955	|	1056	|	|	1158	|	|	|	|	|	|	|
Milton Keynes a.	2110	|	2135	|	2152	2210	2254	2300	...		|	|	1018	|	1116	1146	|	1221	|	1250	|	|	|	1347	|	|
London Euston a.	2201	2209	2213	2215	2233	2302	2346	2351	...		1058	1102	1106	1137	1209	1232	1257	1300	1313	1328	1348	1404	1410	1428	1448	1504

	⑦	⑦	⑦	⑦		⑦	⑦	⑦	⑦	⑦	⑦	⑦	⑦	⑦	⑦	⑦	⑦	⑦	⑦	⑦	⑦	⑦	⑦	⑦	⑦
Liverpool Lime St d.	...	...	...	1347		...	...	1618	...	1647	...	...	...	1747	...	...	...	1847	...	...	...	1947	...	...	2047
Runcorn d.	...	...	...	1403	and	...	...	1634	...	1703	...	...	...	1803	...	...	...	1903	...	...	...	2003	...	...	2103
Manchester P'dilly d.	1255	1315	1335	|	at	1555	1615	|	1635	|	1655	1715	1735	|	1755	1815	1835	|	1855	1915	1935	|	2021	2055	|
Stockport d.	1304	1322	1342	|	the	1604	1623	|	1642	|	1704	1722	1742	|	1804	1822	1842	|	1904	1922	1941	|	2027	2103	|
Crewe d.	1327	|	|	1421	same	1627	|	1651	|	1721	1727	|	|	1821	1827	|	|	1921	1927	|	|	2022	|	|	2121
Macclesfield d.	|	|	1355	|	minutes	|	|	|	1655	|	|	|	1755	|	|	|	1855	|	|	|	1954	|	2040	2115	|
Stoke on Trent d.	|	1350	1412	|	past	|	1650	|	1712	|	|	1750	1812	|	|	1850	1912	|	|	1950	2011	|	2057	2133	|
Stafford a.	|	|	|	1442	each	|	|	|	|	1742	|	|	|	1842	|	|	|	1942	|	|	|	2042	|	|	2142
Nuneaton a.	|	|	|	|	hour	|	|	|	|	|	|	|	|	|	|	|	|	|	|	|	|	|	|	|	2217
Milton Keynes a.	|	1448	|	|	until	|	1749	1803	|	|	|	1849	|	|	|	1948	|	|	|	2046	|	2136	2203	2246	2304
London Euston a.	1508	1526	1548	1604		1809	1827	1844	1848	1904	1907	1927	1948	2005	2008	2027	2048	2103	2110	2131	2158	2228	2257	2349	2354

For notes see previous page.

151 LONDON and BIRMINGHAM - PRESTON - EDINBURGH and GLASGOW

Most trains 🍸 TP, VT

km	km		⚒	Ⓐ	⚒	⚒	⚒	Ⓐ	⑥	Ⓐ	⚒	⑥	⚒	⚒	Ⓐ ◐	⑥	⚒	⚒	⚒ ◐	⚒	⚒	⚒ ◐	⚒
0		**London Euston** 150 d.		...	...	...	...	...	...	0530	...	0605	...	0730	0643	...	...	0830	0743	...	0930	0843	...
80		Milton Keynes 150 d.		...	...	...	...	...	...	0623	...	0641	...	|	0713	...	...	|	0813	...	|	0913	...
		Birmingham New St 150 d.		...	...	...	0615	...	...	|	...	|	0715	|	0815	0815	...	|	0915	...	|	1015	...
		Wolverhampton 150 d.		...	...	...	0637	...	...	|	...	|	0737	|	0837	0837	...	|	0937	...	|	1037	...
253		Crewe 150 d.		...	0557	...	0709	...	...	0732	...	0755	0809	|	0909	0909	...	|	1009	...	|	1109	...
291		Warrington Bank Quay d.		...	0615	...	0727	...	...	0749	...	0812	0827	0914	0927	0927	...	1014	1027	...	1114	1127	...
	0	**Manchester** Airport ✈ d.		...	|	0558	|	0700	0700	|	0725	|	|	|	|	|	0900	|	|	1000	|	|	1100
	16	**Manchester** Piccadilly d.		0500	|	0613	|	0716	0716	|	0745	|	|	|	|	|	0916	|	|	1016	|	|	1116
310	47	Wigan North Western d.		|	0625	0642	0738	0743	0743	0800	0811	0823	0837	0925	0938	0938	0943	1025	1038	1043	1125	1138	1143
334	71	**Preston** a.		0542	0638	0658	0751	0758	0758	0813	0826	0836	0851	0938	0951	0951	0958	1038	1051	1058	1138	1151	1158
368	105	Lancaster a.		0558	0654	0714	0807	0814	0814	0829	0842	0852	0908	0954	1007	1007	1014	1054	1107	1114	1154	1207	1214
398	135	Oxenholme a.		0612	0707	0728	0821	|	0828	0843	0856	0905	|	|	1021	1021	1028	1108	|	|	|	1220	1228
450	187	Penrith a.		|	0733	0753	|	0851	0853	|	0921	0931	0945	1030	|	|	1053	|	1144	|	1229	|	|
478	215	Carlisle a.		0652	0749	0811	0900	0910	0911	0921	0938	0947	1000	1046	1059	1059	1111	1146	1200	1206	1246	1259	1308
519	256	Lockerbie a.		0711	0809	0830	|	0929	0929	|	0957	|	|	|	|	|	1129	|	|	|	|	|	1327
641	378	**Edinburgh** Waverley a.		|	|	0937	1022	|	|	|	1102	|	|	|	1222	|	|	|	|	1326	|	1422	|
643	380	**Glasgow** Central a.		0817	0913	...	...	1029	1029	1036	...	1059	1116	1201	...	1222	1229	1301	1317	...	1401	...	1429

	Ⓐ	⑥	⚒ ◐	⚒	⚒	⚒ ◐	Ⓐ	⑥	⚒	⚒ ◐	⚒	Ⓐ	⑥	⚒ ◐	⚒	⑥	Ⓐ	⑥ ◐	Ⓐ ◐	⚒	⚒	⚒ ◐	⚒
London Euston 150 d.	1030	1030	0943	...	1130	1043	...	...	1230	1143	...	1330	1330	1243	...	1430	1430	1343	1343	...	1530	1443	...
Milton Keynes 150 d.	|	|	1013	...	|	1113	...	...	|	1213	...	|	|	1313	...	|	|	1413	1413	...	|	1513	...
Birmingham New St 150 d.	|	|	1115	...	|	1215	...	...	|	1315	...	|	|	1415	...	|	|	1515	1515	...	|	1615	...
Wolverhampton 150 d.	|	|	1137	...	|	1237	...	...	|	1337	...	|	|	1437	...	|	|	1537	1537	...	|	1637	...
Crewe 150 d.	|	|	1209	...	|	1309	...	...	|	1409	...	|	|	1509	...	|	|	1609	1609	...	|	1709	...
Warrington Bank Quay d.	1216	1214	1227	...	1314	1327	...	...	1415	1427	...	1514	1514	1527	...	1614	1614	1627	1627	...	1714	1726	...
Manchester Airport ✈ d.	|	|	|	1200	|	|	1300	1300	|	|	1400	|	|	|	1500	|	|	|	|	1600	|	|	1700
Manchester Piccadilly d.	|	|	|	1216	|	|	1316	1316	|	|	1416	|	|	|	1516	|	|	|	|	1616	|	|	1715
Wigan North Western d.	1225	1225	1238	1243	1325	1338	1343	1343	1426	1438	1443	1525	1525	1538	1543	1625	1625	1638	1638	1643	1725	1737	|
Preston a.	1238	1238	1251	1258	1338	1351	1358	1358	1439	1451	1458	1538	1538	1551	1558	1638	1648	1651	1651	1658	1738	1751	1758
Lancaster a.	|	1254	1307	1314	1354	1407	1414	1415	1455	1507	1514	|	1554	1608	1614	1654	1659	1708	1708	1714	1754	1807	1814
Oxenholme a.	1305	1308	1321	1328	1408	|	|	|	|	1521	1528	1604	1608	|	1628	|	1715	1721	1721	1728	1808	1821	1828
Penrith a.	|	|	|	1353	|	1442	1451	|	1529	|	1553	1630	|	1644	|	1729	1740	|	1746	1753	|	1846	1853
Carlisle a.	1346	1346	1400	1411	1446	1458	1508	1508	1546	1600	1611	1646	1646	1700	1711	1746	1759	1800	1805	1811	1846	1902	1911
Lockerbie a.	|	|	|	1429	|	|	1527	1526	|	|	1630	|	|	|	1729	|	|	|	|	1830	|	|	1930
Edinburgh Waverley a.	|	|	|	1539	|	1622	|	|	|	|	1735	|	|	1822	|	|	|	|	|	1940	|	2023	|
Glasgow Central a.	1501	1501	1517	...	1601	...	1630	1630	1705	1717	...	1801	1801	...	1830	1901	1915	1916	1923	...	2001	...	2034

	Ⓐ	⑥	⚒ ◐	⚒	Ⓐ	Ⓐ	Ⓐ	⑥	Ⓐ ◐	⑥ ◐	Ⓐ	Ⓐ	Ⓐ ◐	⑥ ◐	Ⓐ	Ⓐ	⑥	⚒ ◐	⑤	Ⓐ	⑥ A	Ⓐ ◐	Ⓐ
London Euston 150 d.	1630	1630	1543	...	1633	1657	1730	1730	1643	1643	1757	1830	1743	1743	...	1930	1930	1843	1846	2030	2031	1943	2110
Milton Keynes 150 d.	|	|	1613	...	|	|	|	|	1713	1713	|	|	1813u	1813	...	|	|	1913	|	|	|	2013	|
Birmingham New St 150 d.	|	|	1715	...	|	|	|	|	1815	1815	|	|	1915	1915	...	|	|	2015	|	|	|	2115	|
Wolverhampton 150 d.	|	|	1737	...	|	|	|	|	1837	1837	|	|	1937	1937	...	|	|	2037	|	|	|	2137	|
Crewe 150 d.	|	|	1809	...	1818	|	|	|	1909	1909	|	|	2009	2009	...	|	2105	2116	2057s	|	2237	2155	|
Warrington Bank Quay d.	|	1814	1827	...	1836	1850	1914	1914	1927	1927	1950	2014	2027	2027	...	2117	2122	...	2121s	2223	2254	2218	2315
Manchester Airport ✈ d.	|	|	|	1800	|	|	|	|	|	|	|	|	|	|	2000	|	|	...	|	|	|	|	|
Manchester Piccadilly d.	|	|	|	1816	|	|	|	|	|	|	|	|	|	|	2016	|	|	...	|	|	|	|	|
Wigan North Western d.	|	1825	1838	1843	1847	1901	1925	1925	1938	1938	2001	2025	2038	2038	2043	2128	2133	...	2132s	2234	2305	2235	2326
Preston a.	1830	1838	1851	1858	1901	1914	1938	1938	1951	1954	2014	2038	2051	2059	2059	2140	2149	...	2147	2253	2319	2246	2342
Lancaster a.	|	1854	1907	1914	...	1930	1954	1954	2008	...	2033	2054	2107	...	2114	2156	...	...	...	...	...	2300	...
Oxenholme a.	|	1908	1921	1928	...	1943	2008	2008	|	...	...	2108	2121	...	2128	2210	...	...	...	...	...	...	...
Penrith a.	|	1933	|	1953	...	2009	|	2033	2044	...	...	2133	|	...	2153	2235	...	...	...	...	...	...	...
Carlisle a.	|	1949	2000	2011	...	2025	2046	2049	2100	...	...	2149	2200	...	2211	2251	...	...	...	...	...	...	...
Lockerbie a.	|	|	|	|	...	2043	|	|	|	...	...	2209	|	...	2230	|	...	...	...	...	...	...	...
Edinburgh Waverley a.	|	|	|	2138	...	|	|	|	2222	...	...	|	|	...	2336	|	...	...	...	...	...	...	...
Glasgow Central a.	2038	2101	2117	...	...	2148	2202	2201	...	...	...	2311	2318	...	...	0005	...	...	...	...	...	...	...

	⑦	⑦ B	⑦	⑦ B	⑦ C	⑦ B	⑦ B	⑦ C	⑦ C	⑦	⑦	⑦ C	⑦	⑦	⑦	⑦	⑦	⑦	⑦	⑦	⑦	⑦	⑦ ◐
London Euston 150 d.		...	...	...	...	...	...	...	...	0845	...	...	0945	...	...	1045	...	...	1228	...	...	1328	1240
Milton Keynes 150 d.		...	...	...	...	...	...	...	...	0932	...	...	1033	...	...	1133	...	...	|	...	...	|	1313
Birmingham New St 150 d.		...	0845	0920	0920	...	...	...	...	|	1020	...	|	1120	...	|	1220	...	|	1320	...	|	1415
Wolverhampton 150 d.		...	0904	0937	0937	...	...	...	...	|	1037	...	|	1137	...	|	1237	...	|	1337	...	|	1437
Crewe 150 d.		...	0937	1009	1009	...	1021	1021	...	1057	1109	...	1157	1209	...	1258	1309	...	|	1409	...	|	1509
Warrington Bank Quay d.		...	0954	1027	1027	...	1037	1037	...	1114	1127	...	1214	1227	...	1315	1327	...	1416	1427	...	1516	1527
Manchester Airport ✈ d.		0900	|	|	|	1000	|	|	1000	|	|	1100	|	|	1200	|	|	1300	|	|	1400	|	|
Manchester Piccadilly d.		0916	|	|	|	1016	|	|	1016	|	|	1116	|	|	1216	|	|	1316	|	|	1416	|	|
Wigan North Western d.		0943	1005	1038	1038	1043	1048	1048	1043	1125	1138	1143	1225	1238	1243	1326	1338	1343	1427	1438	1443	1527	1538
Preston a.	⑦	0958	1022	1051	1051	1058	1104	1104	1110	1138	1151	1158	1238	1251	1258	1340	1351	1358	1440	1450	1458	1540	1551
Lancaster a.		1014	...	1108	1116	1114	1124	1135	1126	1154	1208	1214	1254	1307	1314	1356	1408	1414	1456	1508	1514	1556	1608
Oxenholme a.		1028	...	1122	1132	1128	...	...	1144	1208	1222	1228	1308	1321	1328	1410	|	1428	|	1522	1528	1610	|
Penrith a.		1053	...	|	|	|	...	...	|	1233	|	|	1333	|	1353	1435	1444	1453	1531	|	1553	|	1644
Carlisle a.		1111	...	1159	1210	1208	...	...	1224	1249	1301	1308	1349	1400	1411	1451	1500	1510	1547	1601	1611	1648	1700
Lockerbie a.		1129	...	|	|	1226	...	...	1242	|	|	1326	|	|	1430	|	|	|	|	|	1629	|	|
Edinburgh Waverley a.		1234	...	|	|	|	...	...	1348	|	1419	|	|	|	1534	|	1619	|	|	|	1734	|	1818
Glasgow Central a.		...	...	1320	1329	1328	...	...	...	1402	...	1428	1502	1516	...	1603	...	1628	1700	1717	...	1801	...

	⑦	⑦	⑦ ◐	⑦		⑦	⑦ ◐	⑦	⑦		⑦ ◐	⑦	⑦		⑦ ◐	⑦	⑦ ◐	⑦ ◐		⑦	⑦	⑦ ◐	⑦
London Euston 150 d.	...	1428	1340	...	...	1528	1440	...	1628	...	1540	...	1728	...	1640	1828	1740	1840	...	1928	2025	1940	2050
Milton Keynes 150 d.	...	|	1413	...	...	|	1513	...	|	...	1613	...	|	...	1713	|	1813	1913	...	|	|	2013	2137
Birmingham New St 150 d.	...	|	1515	...	...	|	1615	...	|	...	1715	...	|	...	1815	|	1915	2015	...	|	|	2115	|
Wolverhampton 150 d.	...	|	1637	...	...	|	1637	...	|	...	1737	...	|	...	1837	|	1937	2037	...	|	|	2137	|
Crewe 150 d.	...	|	1609	...	...	|	1709	...	|	...	1809		|		1909	|	2009	2110	...	|	2213	2217	2251
Warrington Bank Quay d.	...	1616	1627	...	...	1716	1727	...	1816	...	1827	...	1916	...	1927	2016	2027	...	...	|	2230	2236	2308
Manchester Airport ✈ d.	1500	|	|	1600	...	|	|	1700	|	...	|	1800	|	...	|	|	|	...	...	|	|	|	|
Manchester Piccadilly d.	1516	|	|	1616	...	|	|	1716	|	...	|	1816	|	...	|	|	|	...	...	|	|	|	|
Wigan North Western d.	1543	1627	1638	1643	...	1727	1738	1743	1827	...	1838	1843	1927	...	1938	2027	2038	...	...	2116	2241	2247	2319
Preston a.	1558	1640	1651	1658	...	1740	1751	1758	1840	...	1851	1858	1940	...	1951	2040	2051	...	...	2127	2258	2306	2339
Lancaster a.	1614	1656	1708	1714	...	1756	1807	1814	1856	...	1907	1914	1956	...	2007	2056	2108	...	...	2140	...	...	...
Oxenholme a.	1628	|	1721	1728	...	1810	1821	1828	1910	...	1921	1928	2010	...	|	2110	2122	...	...	2156	...	...	...
Penrith a.	|	1731	|	1753	...	|	1846	1853	1935	...	|	1953	2035	...	2044	2135	|	...	...	2210	...	...	...
Carlisle a.	1708	1747	1801	1811	...	1848	1903	1917	1951	...	2000	2011	2051	...	2059	2151	2201	...	...	2235	...	...	...
Lockerbie a.	1727	|	|	1829	...	|	|	1936	|	...	|	2029	|	...	|	|	2220	...	...	2251	...	...	...
Edinburgh Waverley a.	|	|	|	1934	...	|	2021	|	|	...	|	2134	|	...	|	|	2305	...	...	|	...	...	...
Glasgow Central a.	1828	1900	1916	...	...	2001	...	2038	2104	...	2115	...	2202	...	2220	2305	2322	...	...	0002	...	...	...

A – Until July 26 and Sep. 13 - Oct. 18.
B – June 22 - Sep. 7.
C – Until June 15 and from Sep. 14.
D – Until Sep. 7.
E – From Sep. 14.
◐ – Via Table **150** (page 134).

TP, VT Most trains 🍷 GLASGOW and EDINBURGH - PRESTON - BIRMINGHAM and LONDON 151

km			Ⓐ	⑥	Ⓐ	Ⓐ	Ⓐ	⑥	⑥ ◐	Ⓐ	Ⓐ	⑥	⚒ ◐	⚒	⚒ ◐	⚒	⚒	⚒ ◐	⚒	⑤	⚒ ◐	⚒	⚒
	Glasgow Central d.	⚒	...	...	...	...	0428	0426	...	0422	0540	0540	...	...	0550	0630	0710	...	0735	...	0800	...	0840
	Edinburgh Waverley d.		...	...	...	...	|	|	...	|	|	|	...	0615	|	|	|	0652	|	...	|	0812	|
	Lockerbie d.		...	...	...	...	|	|	...	0550	|	|	...	|	|	0725	0808	|	|	...	|	0911	|
	Carlisle d.		...	...	...	...	0543	0544	...	0622	0649	0649	...	0733	0702	0746	0833	0806	0849	...	0910	0933	0949
	Penrith d.		...	...	...	...	0558	0558	...	0642	|	|	...	0748	0718	0800	0848	0821	|	...	|	0948	1003
	Oxenholme d.		...	...	...	...	0621	0621	...	0709	0724	0724	...	0812	0742	0823	0912	|	0923	...	|	1012	|
	Lancaster d.		...	0538	0535	...	0636	0636	...	0724	0738	0738	0658	0827	0757	0838	0927	0857	0938	...	0956	1027	1038
	Preston d.		0533	0558	0600	0616	0656	0657	0617	0742	0754	0758	0717	0845	0817	0858	0945	0917	0958	0952	1017	1045	1058
	Wigan North Western d.		0545	0609	0611	0627	0708	0709	0628	0755	0809	0809	0728	0857	0828	0909	0958	0928	1009	1004	1028	1058	1109
	Manchester Piccadilly a.		|	|	|	|	|	|	|	0827	|	|	|	0929	|	|	1027	|	|	|	|	1127	|
	Manchester Airport ✈ a.		|	|	|	|	|	|	|	0847	|	|	|	0947	|	|	1047	|	|	|	|	1147	|
	Warrington Bank Quay d.		0556	0620	0622	0638	0718	0719	0639	...	0820	0820	0739	...	0839	0920	...	0939	1020	1016	1039	...	1120
0	Crewe 150 a.		|	|	0642	0658	|	|	0658	...	|	|	0758	...	0858	|	...	0958	|	1035	1058	...	|
63	Wolverhampton 150 a.		|	|	|	0736	|	|	0731	...	|	|	0833	...	0933	|	...	1033	|	|	1134	...	|
82	**Birmingham** New St 150 a.		|	|	|	0801	|	|	0805	...	|	|	0905	...	1005	|	...	1105	|	|	1205	...	|
	Milton Keynes 150 a.		|	0738	|	...	|	|	0858	...	|	|	0958	...	1058	|	...	1159	|	|	1258	...	|
	London Euston 150 a.		0758	0817	0834	...	0907	0913	0935	...	1013	1016	1035	...	1134	1116	...	1234	1213	1229	1334	...	1313

	⚒ ◐	⑥	Ⓐ	⚒	⚒ ◐	Ⓐ	⑥	⚒	⚒ ◐	⚒	⚒	⚒ ◐	Ⓐ	⑥	⚒	⚒ ◐	⚒	⚒	⚒ ◐	⚒	⚒	Ⓐ ◐	⑥ ◐
Glasgow Central d.	...	0907	0907	0940	1000	...	...	1040	...	1109	1140	1200	...	...	1240	...	1309	1340	1400	...	1440	...	...
Edinburgh Waverley d.	0852	|	|	|	|	1008	1012	|	1051	|	|	|	1212	1212	|	1251	|	|	|	1416	|	1451	1452
Lockerbie d.	|	1007	1010	|	|	1106	1110	|	|	1207	|	|	1311	1311	|	|	1407	|	|	1516	|	|	|
Carlisle d.	1008	1030	1033	1049	1110	1133	1133	1149	1208	1230	1249	1310	1333	1333	1349	1408	1430	1449	1510	1539	1549	1608	1608
Penrith d.	|	1045	1048	|	1125	1148	1148	|	|	1245	1303	|	|	1348	|	1422	1445	|	|	|	|	1621	1622
Oxenholme d.	1042	1109	|	1123	|	1212	1212	1223	1243	1309	|	|	1410	1412	1424	|	1509	1523	1544	1615	1624	|	|
Lancaster d.	1057	1124	1124	1138	|	1227	1227	1238	1257	1325	1338	1356	1425	1427	1439	1456	1525	1538	|	1629	1638	1657	1657
Preston d.	1117	1142	1145	1158	1217	1245	1246	1258	1317	1345	1358	1417	1444	1446	1458	1516	1545	1558	1617	1648	1658	1717	1716
Wigan North Western d.	1128	|	1158	1209	1228	1258	1258	1309	1328	1358	1409	1428	1458	1458	1509	1528	1558	1609	1628	|	1709	1728	1727
Manchester Piccadilly a.	|	1227	1227	|	|	1327	1327	|	|	1427	|	|	1528	1527	|	|	1627	|	|	1729	|	|	|
Manchester Airport ✈ a.	|	1247	1247	|	|	1347	1347	|	|	1447	|	|	1547	1547	|	|	1651	|	|	1747	|	|	|
Warrington Bank Quay d.	1139	...	...	1220	1239	...	...	1320	1339	...	1420	1439	...	...	1520	1539	...	1620	1639	...	1720	1739	1738
Crewe 150 a.	1158	...	...	|	1258	...	...	|	1358	...	|	1459	...	...	|	1558	...	|	1658	...	|	1759	1759
Wolverhampton 150 a.	1233	...	...	|	1333	...	...	|	1433	...	|	1534	...	...	|	1633	...	|	1733	...	|	1833	1832
Birmingham New St 150 a.	1305	...	...	|	1405	...	...	|	1505	...	|	1605	...	...	|	1705	...	|	1805	...	|	1905	1905
Milton Keynes 150 a.	1358	...	...	|	1458	...	...	|	1558	...	|	1658	...	...	|	1758	...	|	1858	...	|	1958	2005
London Euston 150 a.	1433	...	...	1413	1534	...	...	1516	1634	...	1613	1734	...	...	1713	1834	...	1813	1932	...	1918	2034	2055

	Ⓐ	⑥	Ⓐ	⑥	⚒	Ⓐ ◐	⑥ ◐	Ⓐ	⑥	Ⓐ ◐	⑥ ◐	⚒	Ⓐ	⑥	Ⓐ	⑥	⚒	Ⓐ	⑥	Ⓐ	⑥	Ⓐ	Ⓐ
Glasgow Central d.	1449	1509	1540	1540	...	1600	1600	1640	1640	...	...	1706	1730	1740	1740	1800	...	1840	1840	...	...	2010	...
Edinburgh Waverley d.	|	|	|	|	1612	|	|	|	|	1652	1652	|	|	|	|	|	1813	|	|	1852	1852	|	2014
Lockerbie d.	1558	1607	|	|	1710	|	|	|	|	|	|	1806	|	1832	1835	|	1912	|	|	|	|	2105	2112
Carlisle d.	1621	1630	1648	1649	1733	1709	1709	1752	1752	1808	1807	1830	1846	1852	1857	1909	1934	1949	1948	2006	2007	2126	2135
Penrith d.	1640	1645	1703	1703	1748	|	|	1806	|	|	|	1845	1900	1906	|	|	1949	|	2002	|	2022	2139	|
Oxenholme d.	1715	1710	|	|	1812	1744	1744	1830	1826	1842	1843	1909	1923	1929	1932	|	2013	2024	2025	2041	2045	2203	2212
Lancaster d.	1729	1725	1737	1738	1827	|	|	1844	1841	1857	1858	1925	1937	1944	1947	1957	2028	2038	2040	2056	2100	2218	2227
Preston d.	1748	1745	1758	1758	1845	1817	1817	1905	1901	1916	1917	1945	1958	2004	2007	2017	2047	2058	2100	2116	2121	2240	2245
Wigan North Western d.	1801	1758	1809	1809	1858	1828	1828	1916	1912	1929	1929	1958	2009	2015	2019	2028	2057	2109	2111	2128	2132	2252	2258
Manchester Piccadilly a.	1827	1827	|	|	1927	|	|	|	|	|	|	2027	|	|	|	|	2127	|	|	|	|	|	2328
Manchester Airport ✈ a.	1847	1847	|	|	1947	|	|	|	|	|	|	2047	|	|	|	|	2147	|	|	|	|	|	2346
Warrington Bank Quay d.	...	...	1820	1820	...	1839	1839	1927	1923	1939	1940	...	2020	2026	2031	2039	...	2120	2122	2139	2143	2303	...
Crewe 150 a.	...	...	|	|	...	1858	1858	|	|	1959	1959	...	2039	2045	2050	2059	...	|	2141	2159	2202	2324	...
Wolverhampton 150 a.	...	...	|	|	...	1932	1932	|	|	2039	2032	...	|	|	2130	2132	...	|	2222	2232	2240	...	...
Birmingham New St 150 a.	...	...	|	|	...	2005	2005	|	|	2105	2105	...	|	|	2150	2155	...	|	2246	2257	2259	...	...
Milton Keynes 150 a.	...	...	|	|	...	2058	2104	2045	2042	2158	2204	...	2148	2151	...	...	...	2240	...	...	...	...	...
London Euston 150 a.	...	...	2012	2020	...	2139	2157	2125	2138	2243	2255	...	2225	2245	...	...	...	2339	...	...	...	...	...

		⑦	⑦	⑦	⑦	⑦	⑦ D	⑦ E	⑦ ◐	⑦	⑦	⑦ ◐	⑦	⑦	⑦ ◐	⑦	⑦	⑦ ◐	⑦	⑦	⑦ ◐	⑦	⑦
Glasgow Central d.	⑦	...	...	...	...	...	0937	0937	...	...	1034	1051	1106	1136	1158	...	1242	...	1306	1336	1355	...	1436
Edinburgh Waverley d.		...	...	...	...	...	|	|	...	1012	|	|	|	|	|	1212	|	1251	|	|	|	1412	|
Lockerbie d.		...	...	...	...	...	|	|	...	1110	|	|	1208	|	|	1310	|	|	1411	|	|	1510	|
Carlisle d.		...	...	...	...	...	1046	1056	...	1133	1146	1207	1233	1249	1310	1333	1354	1407	1433	1449	1511	1533	1549
Penrith d.		...	...	...	...	...	1100	1110	...	1148	1200	|	1248	|	|	1348	|	1422	1448	|	|	1548	|
Oxenholme d.		...	...	...	...	...	1123	1133	...	1212	1224	1243	1312	1323	|	1412	1428	|	1512	1523	1545	1612	1623
Lancaster d.		...	...	...	...	...	1138	1148	1158	1227	1238	1257	1327	1338	1358	1427	1443	1457	1527	1538	|	1627	1638
Preston d.		0900	1000	1017	1058	1117	1158	1208	1217	1245	1258	1317	1346	1358	1417	1445	1503	1517	1546	1558	1617	1645	1658
Wigan North Western d.		0911	1011	1028	1109	1128	1209	1219	1228	1258	1309	1328	1359	1409	1428	1458	1514	1528	1559	1609	1629	1658	1709
Manchester Piccadilly a.		|	|	|	|	|	|	|	|	1327	|	|	1427	|	|	1527	|	|	1627	|	|	1727	|
Manchester Airport ✈ a.		|	|	|	|	|	|	|	|	1347	|	|	1447	|	|	1547	|	|	1647	|	|	1747	|
Warrington Bank Quay d.		0922	1022	1039	1120	1139	1220	1230	1239	...	1320	1339	...	1420	1439	...	1525	1539	...	1620	1640	...	1720
Crewe 150 a.		0941	1041	1059	|	1159	|	|	1259	...	|	1359	...	|	1458	...	|	1558	...	|	1659	...	|
Wolverhampton 150 a.		|	|	1131	|	1232	|	|	|	...	|	1431	...	|	1534	...	|	1632	...	|	1732	...	|
Birmingham New St 150 a.		|	|	1155	|	1254	|	|	1406	...	|	1506	...	|	1607	...	|	1706	...	|	1807	...	|
Milton Keynes 150 a.		1107	1207	...	|	...	|	|	1458	...	|	1558	...	|	1658	...	|	1758	...	|	1858	...	|
London Euston 150 a.		1206	1246	...	1322	...	1417	1425	1539	...	1513	1639	...	1613	1738	...	1721	1838	...	1814	1938	...	1911

	⑦ ◐	⑦		⑦	⑦ ◐			⑦	⑦			⑦	⑦		⑦	⑦			⑦	⑦		⑦	⑦
Glasgow Central d.	...	1506	...	1536	1557	...	...	...	1640	...	...	...	1706	...	1736	...	...	...	1830	...	...	...	2008
Edinburgh Waverley d.	1451	|	...	|	|	...	...	1612	|	...	...	1651	|	...	|	1812	...	...	|	1851	...	1957	|
Lockerbie d.	|	1605	...	|	|	...	...	1710	|	...	...	|	1807	...	1832	1910	...	...	|	|	...	2055	2103
Carlisle d.	1607	1633	...	1649	1709	...	...	1733	1751	...	...	1807	1833	...	1852	1933	...	...	1944	2007	...	2117	2124
Penrith d.	1622	1648	...	1703	|	...	...	1748	1805	...	...	|	1848	...	1906	1948	...	...	|	2022	...	|	2139
Oxenholme d.	|	1712	...	|	1744	...	...	1812	1828	...	...	1842	1912	...	1929	2012	...	...	2020	|	...	2153	2203
Lancaster d.	1657	1727	...	1738	|	...	...	1827	1843	...	...	1857	1927	...	1944	2027	...	...	2034	2057	...	2208	2218
Preston d.	1718	1746	...	1758	1817	...	...	1845	1903	...	...	1917	1946	...	2004	2045	...	...	2055	2117	...	2227	2238
Wigan North Western d.	1729	1759	...	1809	1828	...	...	1858	1914	...	...	1928	1959	...	2015	2058	...	...	2107	2129	...	2240	2250
Manchester Piccadilly a.	|	1827	...	|	|	...	...	1927	|	...	...	|	2027	...	|	2127	...	...	|	|	...	2308	|
Manchester Airport ✈ a.	|	1847	...	|	|	...	...	1947	|	...	...	|	2047	...	|	2146	...	...	|	|	...	2327	|
Warrington Bank Quay d.	1740	...	...	1820	1839	...	...	...	1925	...	...	1939	...	...	2026	...	...	...	2118	2139	...	...	2301
Crewe 150 a.	1759	...	...	|	1858	...	...	...	|	...	...	1959	...	...	2045	...	...	...	2138	2159	...	...	2320
Wolverhampton 150 a.	1833	...	...	|	1934	...	...	...	|	...	...	2033	...	...	|	...	...	...	2217	2232	...	...	...
Birmingham New St 150 a.	1906	...	...	|	2006	...	...	...	|	...	...	2051	...	...	|	...	...	...	2235	2255	...	...	...
Milton Keynes 150 a.	1958	...	...	|	2059	...	...	...	|	...	...	...	...	...	2152	...	...	...	...	...	...	...	...
London Euston 150 a.	2039	...	...	2013	2148	...	...	...	2122	...	...	...	...	...	2255	...	...	...	...	...	...	...	...

For footnotes and return service see previous page.

155 CREWE - STOKE - DERBY
2nd class EM

km			⚒	Ⓐ	⑥	⚒	⚒	⚒		⚒	⚒	⚒	⚒	⚒			⑦	⑦	⑦	⑦	⑦	⑦	⑦	⑦
0	Crewe 150 d.	⚒	0607	0658	0707	0807	0907	1007	and at	1607	1707	1807	1907	2045	...	⑦	1404	1505	1608	1708	1808	1908	2015	2116
24	Stoke on Trent 150 d.		0633	0724	0733	0833	0933	1033	the same	1633	1733	1833	1933	2118	...		1429	1532	1635	1735	1835	1935	2040	2142
33	Blythe Bridge d.		0645	0736	0745	0845	0945	1045	minutes	1645	1745	1845	1945	2130	...		1441	1544	1647	1747	1847	1947	2052	2154
51	Uttoxeter d.		0658	0749	0758	0858	0958	1058	past each	1658	1758	1858	1958	2142	...		1454	1556	1659	1759	1859	1959	2105	2206
82	Derby a.		0725	0816	0825	0926	1026	1126	hour until	1726	1826	1926	2027	2211	...		1519	1624	1727	1828	1928	2028	2134	2236

		⚒	⚒	⚒	⚒	⚒		⚒	⚒	⚒	⚒	⚒	⚒			⑦	⑦	⑦	⑦		⑦	⑦	⑦
Derby d.	⚒	0640	0740	0842	0942	1042	and at	1542	1642	1742	1842	1942	2040	...	⑦	1438	1538	1638	1742	...	1842	1941	2040
Uttoxeter d.		0705	0807	0907	1007	1107	the same	1607	1706	1807	1907	2007	2107	...		1503	1603	1703	1806	...	1906	2006	2105
Blythe Bridge d.		0719	0821	0921	1021	1121	minutes	1621	1721	1821	1921	2021	2121	...		1517	1617	1717	1821	...	1920	2020	2119
Stoke on Trent 150 a.		0734	0834	0934	1034	1134	past each	1634	1734	1834	1934	2034	2134	...		1530	1631	1730	1835	...	1934	2034	2133
Crewe 150 a.		0759	0859	1001	1101	1201	hour until	1701	1801	1901	2001	2101	2201	...		1600	1700	1802	1902	...	2003	2100	2200

156 MANCHESTER - PRESTON - BLACKPOOL
NT, TP

Subject to alteration July 19 - August 31. For services during this period please contact operator of National Rail (www.nationalrail.co.uk).

km			⚒	⚒	⚒2	⚒	⚒2	⚒	⚒2	Ⓐ	⑥	⚒2	⚒		⚒2	⚒	⚒2	Ⓐ	⑥	⚒2	⚒	Ⓐ2	⑥2	⚒	Ⓐ2
0	Manchester Airport d.		0001	0527	...	*0618*	...	0756	...	0825	...	...	0929	and at	...	1529	...	1629	1629	...	1729	...	...	1829	...
16	Manchester P'dilly d.	⚒	0016	0544	...	*0633*	...	0815	...	0846	0912	...	0946	the same	...	1546	...	1646	1646	...	1746	...	...	1846	...
	Manchester V'toria d.		|	|	0619	|	0723	|	0823	|	|	0923	|	minutes	1523	|	1623	|	|	1723	|	1823	1823	|	1918
34	Bolton d.		0030s	0603	0634	*0652*	0741	0833	0841	0907	0935	0941	1007	past each	1541	1607	1641	1706	1707	1741	1807	1841	1841	1907	1936
66	Preston a.		0101s	0632	0712	*0718*	0818	0859	0917	0933	1002	1017	1033	hour until	1619	1633	1719	1730	1733	1817	1836	1918	1921	1935	2014
66	Preston d.		|	0635	0713	0738	0819	0859	0919	0936	1005	1019	1035	★	...	1636	1719	1732	1738	1819	1840	1919	1924	1935	2015
94	Blackpool North a.		0127	0705	0742	0808	0848	0927	0947	1002	1029	1050	1102		...	1708	1747	1802	1807	1847	1910	1949	1952	2002	2044

	⑥2	⚒	⚒2	⚒	⚒2	⚒	⚒2	⚒	⑥2	Ⓐ2			⑦△	⑦△	⑦	⑦2	⑦	⑦2	⑦		⑦2	⑦	⑦2	⑦	⑦
Manchester Airport d.	...	1929	...	2029	...	2129	...	2229	...	...	...		0005	0530	...	...	0847	...	0929	and at	...	2029	...	2129	2230
Manchester P'dilly d.	...	1946	...	2046	...	2146	...	2246	...	...	...	⑦	0030	0555	0802	...	0903	...	0946	the same	...	2046	...	2146	2246
Manchester V'toria d.	1923	|	2023	|	2123	|	2223	|	2323	2323	...		|	|	|	0823	|	0923	|	minutes	2023	|	2123	|	|
Bolton d.	1941	2007	2041	2107	2139	2207	2241	2307	2341	2341	...		0055s	0620s	0824	0841	0924	0941	1007	past each	2041	2107	2141	2205	2305
Preston a.	2020	2033	2117	2133	2218	2233	2317	2334	0017	0019	...		0130s	0655s	0851	0917	0950	1017	1033	hour until	2117	2133	2217	2228	2340
Preston d.	2022	2035	2119	2135	2218	2235	2319	2335	0019	0021	...		|	|	0853	0919	1000	1019	1035	★	2119	2135	2219	2229	2347
Blackpool North a.	2050	2101	2147	2202	2248	2301	2347	0003	0047	0049	...		0210	0735	0919	0949	1026	1047	1101		2147	2203	2247	2255	0015

		⚒	⚒	Ⓐ2	⚒2	⚒	⚒2	⑥2	Ⓐ	⑥	⚒2	⑥	Ⓐ	⚒2	⚒	⚒2	⚒		⚒2	⚒	⚒2	⚒	Ⓐ	⑥	⚒2
Blackpool North d.		0337	0447	0539	0619	0639	0654	0721	0736	0744	0821	0840	0844	0921	0940	1021	1040	and at	1521	1540	1621	1640	1717	1740	1821
Preston a.		|	0510	0603	0649	0706	0716	0749	0803	0811	0849	0907	0908	0949	1004	1049	1108	the same	1549	1604	1649	1708	1744	1808	1849
Preston d.	⚒	0402u	0512	0605	0649	0708	0718	0750	0812	0812	0850	0909	0909	0950	1012	1050	1109	minutes	1550	1609	1650	1709	1746	1809	1850
Bolton d.		0431u	0540	0640	0725	0734	0755	0826	0835	0835	0926	0935	0935	1026	1035	1126	1135	past each	1626	1635	1726	1735	1814	1835	1926
Manchester V'toria a.		|	|	0700	0749	|	|	0847	|	|	0947	|	|	1047	|	1147	|	hour until	1647	|	1747	|	|	|	1947
Manchester P'dilly a.		0446	0600	...	...	0757	0818	...	0856	0856	...	0956	0956	...	1056	...	1156	★	...	1656	...	1756	1836	1856	...
Manchester Airport a.		0506	0617	...	...	0817	...	...	0917	0917	...	1017	1017	...	1117	...	1217		...	1717	...	1817	1853	1917	...

	⚒	⚒2	⚒	⚒2	⚒	⚒2	⚒	⚒2	⚒	⑥2	Ⓐ2			⑦△	⑦△	⑦	⑦2	⑦	⑦2		⑦2	⑦	⑦2	⑦	⑦
Blackpool North d.	1840	1921	1944	2021	2044	2121	2144	2221	2245	2306	2313	...		0320	0520	0748	0821	0844	0921	and at	2021	2044	2121	2144	2306
Preston a.	1905	1949	2008	2049	2108	2149	2208	2250	2309	2334	2341	...	⑦	|	|	0812	0849	0908	0949	the same	2049	2108	2149	2208	2332
Preston d.	1910	1950	2009	2050	2109	2150	2209	2250	2310	2335	2342	...		0400u	0600u	0813	0850	0909	0950	minutes	2050	2109	2150	2209	2333
Bolton d.	1935	2026	2035	2126	2135	2226	2235	2326	2336	|	0017	...		0435u	0635u	0837	0926	0935	1026	past each	2126	2135	2226	2235	0005
Manchester V'toria a.	|	2047	|	2147	|	2247	|	2348	|	0029	0034	...		|	|	|	0945	|	1045	hour until	2145	|	2245	|	|
Manchester P'dilly a.	1957	...	2057	...	2156	...	2256	...	2353	...	...	...		0500u	0700u	0859	...	0956	...	★	...	2156	...	2256	0021
Manchester Airport a.	2025	...	2119	...	2217	...	2317	...	0020	...	...	...		0525	0725	0920	...	1017	...		...	2217	...	2317	0037

s – Calls to set down only.
u – Calls to pick up only.
△ – By 🚌.
★ – Timings may vary by up to 5 minutes.

157 MANCHESTER - PRESTON - BARROW IN FURNESS
NT, TP

km			Ⓐ2	⚒a	Ⓐ2	⑥2	Ⓐa	⑥	Ⓐ2	Ⓐ2	⑥2	Ⓐ	⑥	Ⓐ	⑥2	⑥	Ⓐ2	⑥2	Ⓐ2	⚒a	Ⓐ2	⑥2	Ⓐ2	⑥2	Ⓐ2a	⑥a
0	Manchester A. 156 d.	⚒	...	0618	...	...	...	...	...	...	...	...	...	...	...	...	...	...	...	1429	...	...	...	...	...	1629
16	Manchester P. 156 d.		...	0633	...	...	...	...	...	...	...	...	...	...	...	...	...	...	...	1446	...	...	...	...	1627	1646
34	Bolton 151 d.		...	0652	...	...	0852	...	...	...	...	...	...	...	...	...	...	...	...	1507	...	...	...	...	1649	1707
66	Preston 151 d.		0519	0720	...	...	0930	0945	...	...	...	1203	...	...	...	1407	...	...	...	1546	...	...	...	...	1728	1745
100	Lancaster 151 d.		0541	0736	0848	0902	0946	1001	1024	1123	1128	1220	1223	1334	1332	1423	1421	1520	1533	1602	1646	1700	1721	1736	1748	1801
110	Carnforth d.		0551	0744	0857	0911	0954	1019	1034	1133	1137	1228	1231	1342	1341	1431	1431	1530	1543	1610	1655	1710	1730	1745	1758	1809
119	Arnside d.		0601	0754	0908	0921	1004	1019	1044	1144	1148	1238	1241	1351	1352	1440	1441	1540	1554	1620	1706	1721	1741	1756	1809	1819
124	Grange over Sands d.		0607	0800	0914	0927	1010	1025	1050	1150	1154	1244	1247	1356	1358	1445	1447	1546	1600	1626	1712	1727	1747	1802	1815	1825
140	Ulverston d.		0624	0816	0931	0944	1026	1041	1107	1206	1210	1300	1303	1409	1414	1458	1504	1603	1617	1642	1729	1744	1803	1818	1831	1841
156	Barrow in Furness a.		0647	0839	0953	1006	1049	1104	1128	1228	1232	1323	1326	1429	1435	1518	1526	1626	1639	1705	1753	1808	1825	1840	1856	1904

	Ⓐ	⚒a	Ⓐa	⑥2	⑥a	Ⓐ2	Ⓐ	⑥b	⑥c	⑥d	⑥e	Ⓐ			⑦j	⑦m	⑦j	⑦2	⑦	⑦2	⑦f	⑦a	⑦	⑦2	⑦a
Manchester Airport 156 d.	...	1729	1900	...	2000	...	...	...	2200	...	2200	2200	...	⑦	...	...	1100	...	...	...	...	1729	...	...	2029
Manchester Piccadilly 156 d.	...	1746	1916	...	2016	...	...	...	2216	...	2216	2216	...		...	...	1116	...	...	...	...	1746	...	...	2046
Bolton 151 d.	...	1807	1933	...	2033	...	...	...	2232	...	2232	2235	...		...	...	|	...	...	...	...	1807	...	...	2107
Preston 151 d.	...	1843	2001	2003	2059	...	2147	2125*	2255	...	2304	2313	...		1010	1115	1158	1404	1604	...	1804	1845	2000	...	2152
Lancaster 151 d.	1823	1859	2017	2023	2115	2120	2203	2245*	2311	2311	2320	2330	...		1026	1131	1214	1420	1620	1720	1820	1901	2016	2103	2208
Carnforth d.	1831	1907	2025	2033	2123	2130	2211	2320	2320	2320	2329	2338	...		1034	1139	1223	1428	1628	1730	1828	1909	2024	2128	2216
Arnside d.	1841	1917	2035	2044	2133	2141	2221	2330	2330	2330	2339	2348	...		1044	1149	1233	1438	1638	1741	1838	1919	2034	2138	2226
Grange over Sands d.	1847	1923	2041	2050	2139	2147	2227	2335	2335	2335	2345	2353	...		1050	1155	1239	1444	1644	1747	1844	1925	2040	2144	2232
Ulverston d.	1903	1939	2057	2106	2155	2203	2243	2351	2351	2351	0002	0009	...		1106	1211	1255	1500	1700	1802	1900	1941	2056	2200	2248
Barrow in Furness a.	1929	2004	2120	2128	2218	2227	2306	0016	0016	0016	0026	0032	...		1129	1234	1318	1523	1723	1826	1923	2004	2119	2224	2311

		⚒	Ⓐa	⑥a	⚒	Ⓐa	Ⓐ2	⑥a	Ⓐ2	⑥2	Ⓐa	⑥a	⑥2	Ⓐ2	Ⓐ	⑥	⚒2	⚒a	⑥2	Ⓐa	Ⓐ2	⑥	Ⓐ2	⑥2	⑥
Barrow in Furness d.	⚒	0435	0532	0532	0615	0648	0714	0733	0800	0808	0850	0850	1009	1009	1120	1120	1211	1333	1427	1440	1518	1525	1610	1629	1720
Ulverston d.		0451	0547	0547	0634	0707	0731	0752	0818	0826	0907	0907	1028	1028	1137	1137	1229	1352	1446	1456	1537	1541	1628	1647	1737
Grange over Sands d.		0503	0600	0600	0650	0723	0745	0808	0835	0842	0922	0922	1044	1048	1152	1152	1245	1408	1502	1508	1553	1553	1644	1703	1752
Arnside d.		0509	0606	0606	0656	0729	0751	0814	0841	0848	0928	0928	1050	1050	1158	1158	1251	1414	1508	1514	1559	1559	1650	1709	1758
Carnforth d.		0519	0616	0616	0707	0740	0803	0825	0854	0859	0939	0939	1102	1108	1209	1209	1303	1425	1520	1524	1611	1609	1702	1721	1809
Lancaster 151 a.		0529	0623	0624	0715	0748	0813	0833	0905	0912	0946	0947	1112	1118	1217	1219	1315	1433	1532	1532	1622	1617	1714	1733	1817
Preston 151 a.		...	0642	0642	0734	0807	...	0852	0930	...	1005	1007	...	...	1237	...	...	1453	...	1552	...	1637	...	...	1837
Bolton 156 a.		...	0707	0707	...	0834	...	0934	...	...	1034	1034	...	...	...	...	...	1534	...	1634	...	...	...	...	...
Manchester Piccadilly 156 a.		...	0727	0727	...	0856	...	0956	...	...	1056	1056	...	...	...	...	...	1556	...	1656	...	...	...	...	...
Manchester Airport 156 a.		...	0747	0747	...	0917	...	1017	...	...	1115	1115	...	...	...	...	...	1617	...	1717	...	...	...	...	...

	Ⓐ	⑥2	Ⓐ2	⑥a	Ⓐ	Ⓐ2	⑥2g	⑥2d	⑥2b			⑦h	⑦j	⑦k		⑦2j	⑦a	⑦2h		⑦	⑦2k		⑦	⑦	⑦
Barrow in Furness d.	1720	1803	1803	1917	2015	2143	2143	2143	2143	...	⑦	0917	0917	0917	...	1005	1025	1054	...	1217	1310	...	1417	1617	1817
Ulverston d.	1737	1821	1821	1936	2034	2201	2201	2201	2201	...		0936	0936	0936	...	1020	1044	1109	...	1236	1329	...	1436	1636	1836
Grange over Sands d.	1752	1837	1837	1952	2049	2217	2217	2217	2217	...		0952	0952	0952	...	1033	1100	1122	...	1252	1345	...	1452	1652	1852
Arnside d.	1758	1843	1843	1958	2055	2223	2223	2223	2223	...		0958	0958	0958	...	1039	1106	1128	...	1258	1351	...	1458	1658	1858
Carnforth d.	1809	1855	1855	2009	2107	2235	2235	2235	2235	...		1009	1009	1009	...	1049	1117	1138	...	1309	1403	...	1509	1709	1909
Lancaster 151 a.	1819	1906	1906	2017	2114	2245	2246	2246	2310*	...		1045*	1017	1018	...	1101	1125	1150	...	1317	1415	...	1517	1717	1917
Preston 151 a.	...	1931	1932	2037	2135	2311	2311	2340*	0001*	...		...	1041	...	...	...	1144	...	...	1337	...	...	1537	1737	1937
Bolton 156 a.	...	...	...	...	...	...	...	...	...	...		...	1108	...	...	...	1208	...	...	...	...	...	...	...	...
Manchester Piccadilly 156 a.	...	...	...	...	...	...	...	...	...	...		...	1127	...	...	...	1227	...	...	...	...	...	...	...	...
Manchester Airport 156 a.	...	...	...	...	...	...	...	...	...	...		...	1147	...	...	...	1247	...	...	...	...	...	...	...	...

a – Subject to alteration July 19 - Aug. 31.
b – Until June 14.
c – June 21 - July 12 (also Sep. 6).
d – From Sep. 13.
e – July 19 - Aug. 30.
f – From Sep. 14.
g – June 21 - Sep. 6.
h – Until June 15.
j – June 22 - Sep. 7.
k – From Sep. 14.
m – Until June 15 and from Sep. 14.

TP PRESTON - OXENHOLME - WINDERMERE 158

km		⚒	⑥	Ⓐ	⚒	⚒	⑥	⑥	Ⓐ	Ⓐ	⑥	⚒	Ⓐ	⑥	⚒	⑥	Ⓐ	Ⓐ	⑥	Ⓐ	⑥	Ⓐ	⑥
							a	b		△			△										
	Manchester Airport ✈ .... 151 d.	...	...	...	...	...	0825	0825	...	0929	...	...	1129	...	...	1329	...	...	...	...	...	...	...
	Manchester Piccadilly .... 151 d.	...	...	...	...	...	0846	0846	...	0946	...	...	1146	...	...	1346	...	...	...	...	...	...	...
	Bolton .... d.	...	...	...	...	...	0907	0907	...	1007	...	...	1207	...	...	1407	...	...	...	...	...	...	...
0	Preston .... 151 d.	...	...	...	...	...	0932	0945	...	1045	1045	...	1245	...	...	1445	...	...	...	...	1704	1804	1809
34	Lancaster .... 151 d.	0546	...	...	...	...	0948	1001	...	1101	1101	...	1301	...	...	1501	...	...	...	...	1720	1820	1825
68	**Oxenholme** .... 151 d.	0621	0722	0733	0827	0911	1005	1018	1033	1118	1118	1233	1318	1318	1417	1518	1536	1622	1634	1733	1737	1837	1842
72	Kendal .... d.	0626	0726	0737	0831	0915	1009	1023	1037	1122	1122	1237	1322	1322	1421	1522	1540	1626	1638	1737	1741	1841	1846
84	**Windermere** .... a.	0641	0741	0752	0846	0930	1026	1040	1049	1139	1139	1252	1339	1339	1436	1539	1556	1641	1653	1752	1758	1901	1904

	⚒	⚒	Ⓐ	⑥	⑥	Ⓐ		⑦	⑦	⑦	⑦		⑦	⑦	⑦	⑦		⑦	⑦	⑦	⑦		⑦
				c	d 🚌			e	f 🚌	e	f												
Manchester Airport ✈ .... 151 d.	...	...	...	...	...	...	...	0847	...	...	...	...	...	...	...	...	...	...	...	...	...	...	...
Manchester Piccadilly .... 151 d.	...	...	...	...	...	...	...	0903	...	...	...	...	...	...	...	...	...	...	...	...	...	...	...
Bolton .... d.	...	...	...	...	...	...	...	0924	...	...	...	...	...	...	...	...	...	...	...	...	...	...	...
Preston .... 151 d.	...	...	...	...	...	...	...	1005	...	...	...	...	...	...	...	...	...	...	...	1804j	...	...	...
Lancaster .... 151 d.	...	...	...	...	...	...	...	1021	0955	...	1122	...	...	...	...	...	...	...	...	1820j	...	...	...
Oxenholme .... 151 d.	1934	2022	2115	2115	2120	2200	...	1038	1040	1135	1139	...	1227	1335	1421	1535	...	1621	1733	1837	1928	...	2016
Kendal .... d.	1938	2026	2119	2119	2130	2224	...	1042	1050	1139	1144	...	1231	1339	1425	1539	...	1625	1737	1841	1932	...	2020
Windermere .... a.	1953	2041	2132	2134	2205	2239	...	1056	1125	1154	1158	...	1246	1354	1440	1554	...	1640	1752	1856	1944	...	2035

	Ⓐ	⑥	⑥	Ⓐ	⚒	⑥	Ⓐ	⑥	Ⓐ	⚒	Ⓐ	⑥	⚒	⑥	Ⓐ	⑥	Ⓐ	Ⓐ	⑥	Ⓐ	⑥	Ⓐ	⑥
																				△	△		
Windermere .... d.	0644	0658	0747	0756	0850	0937	0947	1040	1054	1147	1254	1256	1344	1441	1458	1550	1600	1651	1708	1803	1803	1904	1906
Kendal .... d.	0658	0712	0801	0811	0902	0951	1001	1054	1105	1201	1306	1310	1358	1455	1503	1604	1612	1705	1722	1817	1817	1918	1918
Oxenholme .... 151 d.	0703	0717	0806	0816	0907	0956	1006	1059	1111	1206	1311	1315	1403	1502	1517	1609	1617	1710	1727	1822	1822	1923	1923
Lancaster .... 151 d.	...	...	...	...	...	1014	...	1117	1131	...	1329	...	...	1518a	...	...	...	...	1745	1840	1847	...	...
Preston .... 151 a.	...	...	...	...	...	1034	...	1136	1150	...	...	...	...	1537a	...	...	...	...	1803	1858	1907	...	...
Bolton .... a.	...	...	...	...	...	...	...	|	...	...	...	...	...	...	...	...	...	...	...	1935	1935	...	...
Manchester Piccadilly .... 151 a.	...	...	...	...	...	...	...	1227	...	...	...	...	...	...	...	...	...	...	...	1957	1956	...	...
Manchester Airport ✈ .... 151 a.	...	...	...	...	...	...	...	1247	...	...	...	...	...	...	...	...	...	...	...	2024	2025	...	...

	⚒	⑥	Ⓐ	⑥	Ⓐ	⑥	⑥	Ⓐ		⑦	⑦	⑦	⑦	⑦	⑦	⑦	⑦	⑦	⑦	⑦	⑦	⑦	⑦
		d		c		k	d 🚌			g 🚌	h 🚌	e	e	f						△			
Windermere .... d.	1958	2045	2050	2050	2140	2140	2140	2245	...	1038	1048	1100	1159	1202	1250	1358	1447	1558	1648	1803	1902	1948	2040
Kendal .... d.	2012	2056	2104	2104	2154	2154	2215	2259	...	1103	1113	1112	1213	1213	1302	1412	1501	1612	1702	1817	1914	2002	2054
Oxenholme .... 151 d.	2017	2102	2109	2109	2159	2159	2225	2304	...	1113	1123	1117	1218	1218	1307	1417	1506	1617	1707	1822	1919	2007	2059
Lancaster .... 151 d.	...	...	...	...	...	2217	2310s	2322	...	...	...	...	...	...	...	...	...	...	...	1839	...	...	2117
Preston .... 151 a.	...	...	...	...	...	2237	0001	2342	...	...	...	...	...	...	...	...	...	...	...	1858	...	...	2137
Bolton .... a.	...	...	...	...	...	...	...	...	...	...	...	...	...	...	...	...	...	...	...	1935	...	...	...
Manchester Piccadilly .... 151 a.	...	...	...	...	...	...	...	...	...	...	...	...	...	...	...	...	...	...	...	1956	...	...	...
Manchester Airport ✈ .... 151 a.	...	...	...	...	...	...	...	...	...	...	...	...	...	...	...	...	...	...	...	2017	...	...	...

a – Until July 12 and from Sep. 6.
b – July 19 - Aug. 30.
c – June 21 - Sep. 6.
d – Until June 14 and from Sep. 13.
e – June 22 - Sep. 7.
f – Until June 15 and from Sep. 14.
g – Until June 15.
h – From Sep. 14.
j – Until Sep. 7.
s – Calls to set down only.

△ – Subject to alteration July 19 - Aug. 31.

NT 2nd class BARROW - WHITEHAVEN - CARLISLE 159

km		Ⓐ	Ⓐ	Ⓐ	Ⓐ	Ⓐ	Ⓐ	Ⓐ	Ⓐ	Ⓐ	Ⓐ	Ⓐ		Ⓐ	Ⓐ	Ⓐ	Ⓐ	Ⓐ	Ⓐ	Ⓐ	Ⓐ		⑥
	Lancaster **151** .... d.	...	...	0541	...	...	*0736*	*0848*	1024	1123	*1220*	*1334*	...	1533	*1602*	*1645*	...	*1823*	...	*2017*	...	...	...
0	**Barrow in Furness** .... d.	...	0557	0650	0758	...	0908	1010	1131	1231	1331	1452	...	1640	1728	1805	...	1935	...	2130	...	...	...
26	Millom .... d.	...	0626	0719	0826	...	0936	1038	1158	1259	1359	1520	...	1708	1758	1835	...	2005	...	2200	...	...	...
47	Ravenglass for Eskdale .. 🚂 d.	...	0644	0737	0843	...	0953	1055	1215	1316	1416	1537	...	1725	1815	...	...	...	...	...	...	...	...
56	Sellafield .... d.	...	0658	0751	0856	...	1007	1108	1228	1328	1428	1551	...	1740	1827	...	...	...	...	...	...	...	...
74	**Whitehaven** .... d.	0620	0724	0812	...	0903	1025	1128	1251	1348	1449	1612	...	1800	1855	...	1934	...	2030	...	2151	...	0620
85	Workington .... d.	0638	0742	0831	...	0921	1043	1146	1309	1406	1507	1629	...	1818	1912	...	1952	...	2048	...	2211	...	0638
92	Maryport .... d.	0646	0750	0839	...	0929	1052	1154	1317	1414	1515	1637	...	1826	1920	...	2000	...	2056	...	...	...	0646
119	Wigton .... d.	0707	0812	0900	...	0950	1114	1216	1339	1435	1537	1659	...	1847	1942	...	2021	...	2117	...	...	...	0707
138	**Carlisle** .... a.	0729	0834	0922	...	1012	1135	1236	1401	1458	1559	1721	...	1910	2004	...	2043	...	2139	...	...	...	0729

	⑥	⑥	⑥	⑥	⑥	⑥		⑥	⑥	⑥	⑥	⑥	⑥	⑥	⑥	⑥	⑥	⑥	⑥		⑦	⑦	⑦	⑦
Lancaster **151** .... d.	...	...	...	...	*0736*	0902	...	*1001*	...	1128	*1233*	1332	*1423*	*1602*	1700	...	*1801*	...	2023	...	...	...	...	...
Barrow in Furness .... d.	0609	0655	0758	...	0908	1010	...	1122	...	1233	1350	1452	1533	1726	1810	...	1935	...	2130	...	...	...	...	...
Millom .... d.	0635	0724	0826	...	0936	1038	...	1149	...	1301	1418	1520	1601	1754	1840	...	2005	...	2159	...	...	...	...	...
Ravenglass for Eskdale . 🚂 d.	0651	0742	0843	...	0953	1055	...	1206	...	1318	1435	1537	1618	1811	...	...	...	...	...	...	...	...	...	...
Sellafield .... d.	0705	0756	0856	...	1007	1108	...	1218	...	1330	1447	1551	1630	1822	...	...	...	...	...	...	...	...	...	...
Whitehaven .... d.	0724	0816	...	0915	1025	1129	...	1239	1254	1350	1507	1611	1656	1843	...	1934	...	2030	...	...	1233	1433	1633	1933
Workington .... d.	0742	0834	...	0933	1043	1146	...	...	1312	1408	1525	1629	1714	1901	...	1952	...	2048	...	...	1251	1451	1651	1951
Maryport .... d.	0750	0842	...	0941	1051	1154	...	...	1320	1416	1533	1637	1722	1909	...	2000	...	2056	...	...	1259	1459	1659	1959
Wigton .... d.	0812	0904	...	1002	1113	1216	...	...	1341	1437	1555	1659	1844	1930	...	2021	...	2117	...	...	1318	1518	1718	2018
Carlisle .... a.	0834	0926	...	1024	1136	1238	...	...	1404	1500	1617	1721	1806	1953	...	2044	...	2140	...	...	1341	1543	1743	2043

	Ⓐ	Ⓐ	Ⓐ		Ⓐ	Ⓐ	Ⓐ	Ⓐ	Ⓐ	Ⓐ	Ⓐ	Ⓐ	Ⓐ	Ⓐ	Ⓐ	Ⓐ	Ⓐ	Ⓐ	Ⓐ	Ⓐ	Ⓐ		⑥
Carlisle .... d.	...	...	...	...	0744	...	0838	0938	1040	1150	1247	1420	1512	1631	1727	1814	...	1915	2037	...	2200	...	...
Wigton .... d.	...	...	...	...	0802	...	0856	0956	1058	1208	1305	1438	1530	1649	1744	1832	...	1933	2055	...	2218	...	...
Maryport .... d.	...	0559	...	...	0823	...	0917	1017	1119	1229	1326	1459	1551	1710	1805	1853	...	1954	2116	...	2239	...	...
Workington .... d.	...	0609	...	...	0834	...	0928	1028	1130	1240	1337	1510	1603	1721	1816	1904	...	2005	2127	...	2250	...	...
Whitehaven .... d.	...	0628	0722	...	0854	...	0948	1048	1151	1300	1357	1530	1622	1741	1836	1924	...	2025	2147	...	2310	...	...
Sellafield .... d.	...	0651	0740	...	...	0901	1006	1108	1209	1318	1415	1555	1643	1804	1856	...	...	...	...	...	...	...	...
Ravenglass for Eskdale . 🚂 d.	...	0701	0751	...	...	0911	1016	1118	1219	1328	1425	1605	1654	1814	1906	...	...	...	...	...	...	...	...
Millom .... d.	0609	0720	0810	...	...	0930	1035	1136	1238	1347	1444	1626	1714	1835	1925	...	2012	...	...	2208	...	...	0609
Barrow in Furness .... a.	0642	0754	0843	...	...	1001	1109	1208	1311	1420	1517	1700	1748	1910	1959	...	2045	...	...	2241	...	...	0641
Lancaster **151** .... a.	*0748*	0905	*0947*	...	...	*1118*	*1217*	1315	*1433*	*1532*	1622	*1819*	1906	...	*2114*	...	*2245*	...	...	...	...	...	*0833*

	⑥	⑥	⑥	⑥	⑥	⑥	⑥	⑥	⑥	⑥	⑥	⑥	⑥	⑥	⑥	⑥	⑥	⑥	⑥		⑦	⑦	⑦	⑦
Carlisle .... d.	...	0744	...	0838	0938	1043	1138	...	1247	1420	1525	1636	1740	1814	1900	...	2015	...	2145	...	1410	1710	1910	2110
Wigton .... d.	...	0802	...	0856	0956	1101	1156	...	1305	1438	1543	1654	1758	1832	1918	...	2032	...	2203	...	1427	1727	1927	2127
Maryport .... d.	0613	0823	...	0917	1017	1122	1217	...	1326	1459	1604	1715	1819	1853	1939	...	2052	...	2224	...	1447	1747	1947	2147
Workington .... d.	0624	0834	...	0928	1028	1133	1228	...	1337	1510	1616	1726	1830	1904	1950	...	2104	...	2235	...	1459	1759	1959	2159
Whitehaven .... d.	0644	0854	...	0948	1048	1153	1248	1254	1357	1530	1636	1746	1850	1924	2010	...	2125	...	2255	...	1520	1820	2020	2220
Sellafield .... d.	0707	...	0905	1006	1108	1211	...	1318	1415	1550	1654	1809	1911	...	...	...	...	...	...	...	...	...	...	...
Ravenglass for Eskdale . 🚂 d.	0714	...	0915	1016	1118	1221	...	1324	1425	1600	1704	1816	1921	...	...	...	...	...	...	...	...	...	...	...
Millom .... d.	0733	...	0934	1034	1136	1240	...	1344	1444	1619	1723	1835	1939	...	...	2012	...	2208	...	...	...	...	...	...
Barrow in Furness .... a.	0805	...	1005	1108	1208	1314	...	1416	1517	1653	1755	1909	2012	...	...	2045	...	2241	...	...	...	...	...	...
Lancaster **151** .... a.	0912	...	1112	*1219*	1315	*1433*	...	1532	*1617*	*1817*	1905	*2017*	...	...	...	*2245*	...	...	...	...	...	...	...	...

🚂 – Ravenglass and Eskdale Railway. ✆ 01229 717171. www.ravenglass-railway.co.uk

160 HOLYHEAD - CHESTER - MANCHESTER

2nd class AW, VT

Service on ⑦ valid until September 7 (subject to alteration June 22 - July 27).

km			Ⓐ	Ⓐ	Ⓐ	Ⓐ	Ⓐ	Ⓐ	Ⓐ	Ⓐ	Ⓐ	Ⓐ	Ⓐ	Ⓐ	Ⓐ	Ⓐ	Ⓐ	Ⓐ	Ⓐ	Ⓐ	Ⓐ	Ⓐ	Ⓐ	Ⓐ	Ⓐ
					C	A		B	C	A		C	A		B	C		C	A		B		C		B
0	**Holyhead** d.	Ⓐ	...	...	0425	0448	...	0514	0533	0551	...	0628	0655	...	0715	...	...	0805	0855	...	0923	...	1040	...	1127
40	Bangor d.		...	...	0457	0514	...	0543	0601	0618	...	0706	0722	...	0802	...	...	0902	0922	...	1002	...	1107	...	1200
	Llandudno ‡ d.		...	...	|	|	...	|	|	|	0634	|	|	0745	|	0830	...	|	|	0945	|	1044	|	1144	|
64	Llandudno Junction ‡ d.		0438	...	0515	0532	0546	0607	0619	0636	0644	0724	0740	0754	0825	0839	0854	0925	0940	0954	1025	1053	1125	1153	1223
71	Colwyn Bay d.		0444	...	0521	0538	0552	0613	0627	0642	0650	0730	0747	0800	0831	0845	0900	0931	0947	1000	1031	1059	1131	1159	1229
88	Rhyl d.		0457	...	0531	0549	0602	0623	0638	0653	0703	0740	0758	0813	0841	0856	0913	0941	0958	1013	1041	1112	1141	1212	1240
94	Prestatyn d.		0502	...	0537	|	0608	0629	|	0658	0708	0746	0804	0819	0847	|	0919	0947	1004	1019	1047	1118	1147	1218	1245
116	Flint d.		0516	...	0550	|	0621	0642	0655	0712	0721	0759	0817	0832	0900	|	0932	1000	1017	1032	1100	1131	1200	1231	1259
136	**Chester** a.		0533	...	0605	0617	0638	0659	0710	0726	0738	0814	0831	0850	0914	0923	0950	1015	1031	1050	1115	1149	1216	1249	1313
136	**Chester 150** ♥ d.		0537	0538	...	0626	0640	*0712*	...	0735	0740	...	0835	0852	...	...	0952	...	1035	1052	...	1150	...	1250	...
170	**Crewe 150** ♥ a.		0558	|	...	0647	|	|	...	0754	|	...	0854	|	...	...	|	...	1054	|	...	|	...	|	...
165	Warrington Bank Quay d.		...	0606	...	...	0709	*0739*	...	...	0808	...	...	0919	...	...	1019	...	...	1119	...	1219	...	1319	...
201	**Manchester** Piccadilly a.		...	0643	...	...	0750	*0818*	...	...	0850	...	...	0956	...	...	1056	...	...	1156	...	1256	...	1356	...

	Ⓐ	Ⓐ	Ⓐ	Ⓐ	Ⓐ	Ⓐ	Ⓐ	Ⓐ	Ⓐ	Ⓐ	Ⓐ	Ⓐ	Ⓐ	Ⓐ	Ⓐ	Ⓐ	Ⓐ	Ⓐ	Ⓐ	Ⓐ	Ⓐ	Ⓐ	Ⓐ	Ⓐ	Ⓐ
	A		C		B	A			C		B		C		D					B	B				
Holyhead d.	...	...	1232	...	1328	1358	...	...	1434	...	1544	...	1650	...	1730	...	...	1823	...	1921	...	...	2037	...	...
Bangor d.	1224	...	1307	1331	1407	1425	...	...	1504	...	1623	...	1718	...	1809	...	...	1902	...	2000	2020	...	2106	...	...
Llandudno ‡ d.	|	1244	|	|	|	|	1440	1508	|	1616	|	1705	|	...	|	...	1844	|	1942	|	|	2043	|	2145	...
Llandudno Junction ‡ d.	1242	1253	1325	1354	1425	1443	1449	1517	1527	1625	1646	1715	1737	...	1832	1839	1853	1926	1951	2023	2038	2052	2129	2155	...
Colwyn Bay d.	1248	1259	1331	1400	1431	1450	1455	1523	1533	1631	|	1721	1743	...	|	1845	1859	1932	1957	2029	2044	2058	2135	2201	...
Rhyl d.	1259	1312	1341	1413	1441	1500	1508	1536	1544	1644	|	1733	1753	...	|	1855	1912	1942	2010	2039	2055	2111	2148	2216	...
Prestatyn d.	1305	1318	1347	1418	1447	|	1514	1542	1549	1649	|	1739	1759	...	|	1901	1918	1948	2016	2045	2101	2117	2153	2222	...
Flint d.	1318	1331	1400	1432	1500	|	1527	1555	1603	1703	|	1752	1812	...	|	1914	1931	2001	2029	2058	2114	2130	2207	2237	...
Chester a.	1332	1349	1415	1450	1515	1527	1544	1613	1617	1720	1726	1811	1826	...	1911	1930	1949	2016	2047	2115	2128	2147	2223	2255	...
Chester 150 ♥ d.	1335	1350	...	1452	...	1535	1546	1622	...	1722	...	1816	...	1849	...	...	1950	2018	2050	...	2135	2152	2226	2301	2322
Crewe 150 ♥ a.	1354	|	...	|	...	1554	|	|	...	|	...	|	...	|	...	...	|	2041	|	...	2154	|	2250	2326	|
Warrington Bank Quay d.	...	1419	...	1519	...	...	1619	1651	...	1749	...	1846	...	1919	...	...	2019	...	2120	...	...	2219	...	...	2349
Manchester Piccadilly a.	...	1456	...	1556	...	...	1656	1731	...	1827	...	1930	...	1952	...	...	2052	...	2156	...	...	2257	...	...	0028

		⑥	⑥	⑥	⑥	⑥	⑥	⑥	⑥	⑥	⑥	⑥	⑥	⑥	⑥	⑥	⑥	⑥	⑥	⑥	⑥	⑥	⑥	⑥	⑥
				a	Cb			B		C	A		B	A		C	A		B		C		B		C
Holyhead d.	⑥	...	...	0425	0425	...	...	0522	...	0635	0652	...	0715	0755	...	0820	0855	...	0923	...	1033	...	1123	...	1238
Bangor d.		...	...	0457	0457	...	...	0601	...	0707	0720	...	0802	0822	...	0902	0922	...	1002	...	1105	...	1202	...	1307
Llandudno ‡ d.		...	...	|	|	...	...	|	0634	|	|	0745	|	|	0845	|	|	0945	|	1044	|	1144	|	1244	|
Llandudno Junction ‡ d.		0438	...	0515	0515	0537	...	0624	0644	0725	0738	0754	0825	0840	0854	0925	0940	0954	1025	1053	1125	1153	1225	1253	1325
Colwyn Bay d.		0444	...	0521	05212	0543	...	0630	0650	0731	0744	0800	0831	0847	0900	0931	0947	1000	1031	1059	1131	1159	1231	1259	1331
Rhyl d.		0457	...	0531	0531	0556	...	0640	0703	0741	0755	0813	0841	0858	0913	0941	0958	1013	1041	1112	1141	1212	1241	1312	1341
Prestatyn d.		0502	...	0537	0537	0601	...	0646	0708	0747	0801	0819	0847	0904	0919	0947	1003	1019	1047	1118	1147	1218	1247	1318	1347
Flint d.		0516	...	0550	0550	0615	...	0659	0721	0800	0815	0832	0900	0917	0932	1000	|	1032	1100	1131	1200	1231	1300	1331	1400
Chester a.		0533	...	0604	0604	0633	...	0715	0738	0816	0828	0850	0915	0931	0950	1016	1028	1050	1116	1149	1216	1249	1315	1349	1414
Chester 150 ♥ d.		0537	0538	0613	*0613*	0635	0712	...	0740	...	0835	0852	...	0935	0952	...	1035	1052	...	1150	...	1250	...	1350	...
Crewe 150 ♥ a.		0558	|	...	|	0659	|	...	|	...	0854	|	...	0954	|	...	1054	|	...	|	...	|	...	|	...
Warrington Bank Quay d.		...	0606	0640	*0640*	...	0739	...	0808	...	...	0919	...	...	1019	...	...	1119	...	1219	...	1319	...	1419	...
Manchester Piccadilly a.		...	0643	0718	*0718*	...	0818	...	0845	...	...	0951	...	...	1051	...	...	1151	...	1251	...	1351	...	1456	...

	⑥	⑥	⑥	⑥	⑥	⑥	⑥	⑥	⑥	⑥	⑥	⑥	⑥	⑥	⑥	⑥	⑥	⑥	⑥	⑥		⑦	⑦	⑦	⑦
		B	A		C		B		C		D				B										
Holyhead d.	...	1328	1358	...	1423	...	1523	...	1650	...	1730	...	1823	...	1921	...	2037	...	...	...	⑦	...	0716	0750	0845
Bangor d.	1331	1407	1425	...	1453	...	1602	...	1718	...	1809	...	1902	...	2000	...	2106	...	...	...		...	0743	0828	0913
Llandudno ‡ d.	|	|	|	1442	|	1544	|	1644	|	1744	|	1844	|	1942	|	2043	|	2145	...	...		...	|	|	|
Llandudno Junction ‡ d.	1355	1425	1443	1451	1516	1553	1625	1653	1736	1753	1832	1853	1926	1951	2023	2052	2129	2155	...	...		...	0800	0851	0935
Colwyn Bay d.	1401	1431	1450	1457	1522	1559	1631	1659	1742	1759	1838	1859	1932	1957	2029	2058	2135	2201	...	...		...	0807	0857	0941
Rhyl d.	1414	1441	1500	1510	1533	1612	1641	1712	1752	1812	1848	1912	1942	2010	2039	2111	2148	2216	...	...		...	0820	0908	0954
Prestatyn d.	1419	1447	|	1516	1538	1618	1647	1718	1758	1818	1854	1918	1948	2016	2045	2117	2154	2222	...	...		...	0825	|	0959
Flint d.	1433	1500	|	1529	1552	1631	1700	1731	1811	1831	1907	1931	2001	2029	2058	2130	2207	2237	...	...		...	0839	|	1013
Chester a.	1450	1517	1527	1546	1605	1649	1715	1749	1825	1849	1924	1949	2016	2047	2115	2148	2223	2255	...	...		...	0856	0939	1030
Chester 150 ♥ d.	1452	...	1535	1548	...	1650	...	1750	...	1850	...	1950	2018	2050	...	*2153*	2226	2301	2322	...		0841	0857	0942	1039
Crewe 150 ♥ a.	|	...	1554	|	...	|	...	|	...	|	...	|	2041	|	...	|	2250	2326	|	...		|	0922	|	1103
Warrington Bank Quay d.	1519	...	...	1619	...	1719	...	1819	...	1919	...	2019	...	2120	...	*2220*	...	...	2350	...		0910	...	1012	...
Manchester Piccadilly a.	1551	...	...	1656	...	1756	...	1856	...	1952	...	2057	...	2156	...	*2254*	...	...	0027	...		0947	...	1049	...

	⑦	⑦	⑦	⑦	⑦	⑦	⑦	⑦	⑦	⑦	⑦	⑦		⑦	⑦	⑦	⑦	⑦	⑦	⑦	⑦	⑦	⑦	⑦	⑦
			C	A		A		A		A					C				B						
Holyhead d.	...	...	1020	1055	...	1150	...	1250	...	1355	...	1430	...	1540	1625	...	1730	...	1825	...	1915	...	...	2035	2140
Bangor d.	...	...	1059	1122	...	1217	...	1318	...	1422	...	1508	...	1608	1704	...	1759	...	1904	...	1954	...	...	2114	2209
Llandudno ‡ d.	...	...	|	|	...	|	...	|	...	|	...	|	...	|	|	...	|	...	|	...	|	...	...	|	|
Llandudno Junction ‡ d.	...	...	1122	1140	...	1235	...	1336	...	1440	...	1526	...	1635	1725	...	1824	...	1924	...	2015	...	...	2137	2227
Colwyn Bay d.	...	...	1128	1146	...	1242	...	1342	...	1446	...	1532	...	1641	1731	...	1830	...	1930	...	2021	...	...	2143	2233
Rhyl d.	...	...	1141	1157	...	1253	...	1353	...	1457	...	1545	...	1654	1744	...	1843	...	1943	...	2027	...	...	2156	2243
Prestatyn d.	...	...	1146	1203	...	1359	...	1359	...	1503	...	1551	...	1659	1749	...	1848	...	1948	...	2040	...	...	2201	2249
Flint d.	...	...	1200	1216	...	|	...	1413	...	|	...	1604	...	1713	1803	...	1902	...	2002	...	2046	...	...	2215	2302
Chester a.	...	...	1218	1230	...	1324	...	1426	...	1531	...	1621	...	1734	1821	...	1921	...	2019	...	2100	...	...	2232	2316
Chester 150 ♥ d.	1036	1136	...	1233	1236	1330	1336	1433	1436	1533	1536	1636	...	1736	...	1836	1922	1936	2027	2036	2121	2143	2206	2235	...
Crewe 150 ♥ a.	|	|	...	1253	|	1350	|	1453	|	1552	|	|	...	|	...	|	1947	|	2048	|	2231	|	|	2259	...
Warrington Bank Quay d.	1103	1203	...	...	1303	...	1403	...	1503	...	1603	1703	...	1803	...	1903	...	2003	...	2103	...	2211	2233	...	...
Manchester Piccadilly a.	1141	1240	...	...	1340	...	1441	...	1540	...	1640	1740	...	1840	...	1940	...	2040	...	2140	...	2248	2311	...	...

LLANDUDNO - BLAENAU FFESTINIOG - PORTHMADOG - CAERNARFON

km		⚒	⚒	🚂 X△	🚂 X△		Ⓐ	⑥	⑦	🚂 X△		🚂 Z△	🚂 X△	🚂 Z△	⚒	⑦	🚂 X△	🚂 Z△		🚂 Z△	⑦	⚒	⑥	Ⓐ	
0	**Llandudno** d.	...	...	...	...	...	1008	1022	1022	...	...	...	...	...	1308	1330	...	...	...	...	...	1620	1903	1903	...
5	**Llandudno** Junction d.	0535	0739	...	...	...	1028	1030	1032	...	...	...	...	...	1330	1340	...	...	...	...	1615	1633	1918	1920	...
18	Llanrwst d.	0553	0802	...	...	...	1050	1052	1054	...	...	...	...	...	1352	1402	...	...	...	...	1637	1655	1942	1942	...
24	Betws y Coed d.	0559	0808	...	...	...	1056	1058	1100	...	...	...	...	...	1358	1408	...	...	...	...	1643	1701	1948	1948	...
44	**Blaenau Ffestiniog** d.	0629	0842	...	...	...	1130	1136	1132	...	...	1145	...	1330	1432	1440	...	1505	...	1715	1712	1735	2020	2020	...
63	Minffordd d.	...	...	...	...	...	...	...	...	...	...	1240	...	1440	...	...	...	1600	...	1810	...	...	...	...	...
66	**Porthmadog** Harbour d.	...	...	0940	1045	...	...	...	...	1315	...	1255	1405	1455	...	...	1600	1615	...	1825	...	...	...	...	...
79	Beddgelert d.	...	...	1030	1125	...	...	...	...	1355	...	...	1454	...	...	...	1640	...	...	...	...	...	...	...	...
86	Rhyd Ddu d.	...	...	1055	1155	...	...	...	...	1425	...	...	1515	...	...	...	1705	...	...	...	...	...	...	...	...
94	Waunfawr d.	...	...	1125	1220	...	...	...	...	1455	...	...	1540	...	...	...	1735	...	...	...	...	...	...	...	...
105	**Caernarfon** a.	...	...	1205	1305	...	...	...	...	1535	...	...	1620	...	...	...	1810	...	...	...	...	...	...	...	...

A – To / from London Euston (Table **150**).
B – To / from Birmingham New Street (Table **145** or **150**).
C – To / from Cardiff Central (Table **149**).
D – To / from Shrewsbury (Table **145**).
W – To/from Wolverhampton (Table **145**).
X – Until Nov. 1. A different service operates on ②③④ in June and July (also July 14, 21, 25, 28), Aug. 1 - 31, Sep. 2 - 4, 9 - 11, 16 - 18. No service on ⑦ in June, Oct. 3, 6, 10, 13, 17, 20, 24.
Y – ②③④ in June and July (also July 21, 25, 28), Aug. 1 - 31, Sep. 2 - 4, 9 - 11, 16 - 18. No service on ⑦ in June, Oct. 3, 6, 10, 13, 17, 20, 24.
Z – Until Oct. 30. A reduced service operates on ①⑤ in June, Sep. 19, 22, 26, 29, Oct. 3, 5, 6, 8, 10, 12, 13, 15, 17, 19, 20, 22, 24, 31, Nov. 1, 2, Dec. 26 - 31.

a – Until Sep. 6.
b – From Sep. 13.
***** – Connection by 🚌.
‡ – For full service Llandudno - Llandudno Junction and v.v. see next page.
♥ – For full service Chester - Crewe and v.v. see next page.

△ – Operator: Ffestiniog Railway and Welsh Highland Railways. www.festrail.co.uk
Ffestiniog Railway ✆ 01766 516024. Welsh Highland Railway ✆ 01286 677018

AW, VT 2nd class

MANCHESTER - CHESTER - HOLYHEAD 160

Service on ⑦ valid until September 7 (subject to alteration June 22 - July 27).

		① B	②–⑤ B	Ⓐ B	Ⓐ	Ⓐ	Ⓐ	Ⓐ C	Ⓐ	Ⓐ B	Ⓐ	Ⓐ	Ⓐ A	Ⓐ C	Ⓐ	Ⓐ A	Ⓐ B	Ⓐ	Ⓐ C	Ⓐ	Ⓐ B	Ⓐ	Ⓐ C	Ⓐ	Ⓐ B
Manchester Piccadilly d.	Ⓐ	...	...	...	0548	...	0650	...	0750	...	0850	0850	...	...	0950	...	...	1050	...	1150	...	1250	...	1350	...
Warrington Bank Quay d.		...	...	...	0621	...	0723	...	0824	...	0926	0926	...	...	1026	...	...	1126	...	1226	...	1326	...	1426	...
Crewe 150 ♥ d.		0001	0010	0623	│	0654	│	...	│	...	│	│	0953	...	│	1049	...	│	...	│	...	│	...	│	...
Chester 150 ♥ a.		0022	0032	0643	0649	0717	0750	...	0853	...	0953	0953	1013	...	1053	1113	...	1153	...	1253	...	1353	...	1453	...
Chester d.		0038	0040	0644	0655	0719	0755	0822	0855	0923	0958	1002	1016	1024	1055	1116	1122	1155	1223	1255	1324	1355	1423	1455	1522
Flint d.		0051	0053	0657	0708	0734	0810	0838	0908	0938	│	1018	1029	1039	1110	│	1138	1210	1236	1310	1337	1410	1436	1510	1537
Prestatyn d.		0104	0106	0710	0721	0747	0823	0851	0921	0951	│	1031	1042	1052	1123	│	1151	1223	1249	1323	1350	1423	1449	1523	1550
Rhyl d.		0110	0112	0716	0727	0753	0829	0857	0927	0957	│	1037	1048	1058	1129	1143	1157	1229	1255	1329	1356	1429	1455	1529	1556
Colwyn Bay d.		0121	0123	0727	0738	0807	0843	0911	0938	1011	│	1048	1059	1109	1143	1154	1208	1243	1306	1343	1407	1443	1506	1543	1607
Llandudno Junction ‡ d.		0128	0129	0733	0744	0816	0851	0918	0944	1018	1036	1055	1106	1115	1150	1201	1214	1250	1312	1350	1413	1450	1512	1550	1616
Llandudno ‡ a.		│	│	│	0801	│	...	0926	│	1030	│	1106	│	│	1206	│	│	│	│	1406	│	1506	│	1606	│
Bangor d.		0144	0146	0750	...	0838	...	...	1008	...	1053	...	1127	1140	...	1217	1232	1315	1330	...	1437	...	1531	...	1640
Holyhead ▽ a.		0220	0215	0823	...	0922	...	...	1036	...	1122	...	...	1223	...	1250	1313	...	1413	...	1508	...	1615	...	1712

	Ⓐ	Ⓐ C	Ⓐ	Ⓐ B	Ⓐ	Ⓐ A	Ⓐ C	Ⓐ	Ⓐ	Ⓐ A	Ⓐ B	Ⓐ C	Ⓐ A	Ⓐ D	Ⓐ	Ⓐ A	Ⓐ	Ⓐ C	Ⓐ	Ⓐ	Ⓐ			⑥ B	⑥ B
Manchester Piccadilly d.	1450	...	1550	...	1650	...	...	1719	1750	...	...	*1850*	...	...	1950	...	*2032*	...	2132	2212	2314	...	⑥	...	...
Warrington Bank Quay d.	1526	...	1626	...	1726	...	...	1752	1826	...	...	*1926*	...	...	2026	...	*2124*	...	2224	2256	2348	...		...	...
Crewe 150 ♥ d.	│	...	│	...	│	1749	...	│	│	1857	...	│	1956	...	│	2049	│	...	│	│	│	...		0010	0623
Chester 150 ♥ a.	1553	...	1654	...	1753	1808	...	1822	1853	1916	...	*1953*	2015	...	2053	2113	*2155*	...	2251	2325	0015	...		0032	0643
Chester d.	1555	1625	1655	1727	1755	1810	1824	▬	1855	1923	1932	2006	2026	2034	...	2117	2204	2256	...	...	...	...		0040	0644
Flint d.	1610	1638	1710	1742	1810	1823	1837	...	1910	1936	1947	2018	│	2049	...	2130	2219	2311	...	...	...	...		0053	0657
Prestatyn d.	1623	1651	1723	1755	1823	1836	1850	...	1923	1949	2000	│	│	2102	...	2143	2232	2324	...	...	...	...		0106	0710
Rhyl d.	1629	1657	1729	1801	1829	1842	1856	Ⓐ	1929	1955	2006	2035	2053	2108	...	2150	2238	2330	...	...	...	...		0112	0716
Colwyn Bay d.	1643	1708	1743	1815	1843	1853	1907		1943	2006	2020	2047	2104	2122	...	2201	2252	2344	...	...	...	...		0123	0727
Llandudno Junction ‡ d.	1650	1713	1750	1824	1851	1900	1913	1928	1950	2013	2030	2054	2110	2129	...	2207	2259	2352	...	...	...	...		0129	0733
Llandudno ‡ a.	1705	│	1806	│	1906	│	│	1938	│	│	2043	│	│	│	...	│	│	│	...	...	...	...		│	│
Bangor d.	...	1737	...	1845	...	1921	1933	...	2013	2029	...	2111	2127	2152	...	2224	2322	0014	...	...	...	...		0146	0750
Holyhead ▽ a.	...	1819	...	1916	...	...	2018	...	2045	2059	...	2145	2159	2235	...	2256	0005	0048	...	...	...	...		0215	0823

	⑥	⑥	⑥	⑥ C	⑥	⑥ B	⑥	⑥ C	⑥	⑥ A	⑥ B	⑥	⑥ C	⑥	⑥ B	⑥	⑥ C	⑥	⑥ B	⑥	⑥ A	⑥ C	⑥	⑥ B	⑥
Manchester Piccadilly d.	0533	...	0650	...	0750	...	0850	...	0950	...	...	1050	...	1150	...	1250	...	1350	...	1450	...	...	1550	...	1650
Warrington Bank Quay d.	0621	...	0723	...	0824	...	0926	...	1026	...	...	1126	...	1226	...	1326	...	1426	...	1527	...	...	1626	...	1726
Crewe 150 ♥ d.	│	0703	│	...	│	...	│	...	│	1049	...	│	...	│	...	│	...	│	...	│	1549	...	│	...	│
Chester 150 ♥ a.	0649	0723	0750	...	0853	...	0953	...	1053	1113	...	1153	...	1253	...	1353	...	1453	...	1554	1610	...	1653	...	1753
Chester d.	0655	0725	0755	0822	0855	0924	0955	1023	1055	1116	1124	1155	1223	1255	1322	1355	1423	1455	1522	1556	1612	1624	1655	1724	1755
Flint d.	0710	0739	0810	0836	0910	0937	1010	1036	1110	│	1139	1210	1236	1310	1336	1410	1436	1510	1537	1611	1625	1639	1710	1739	1810
Prestatyn d.	0723	0752	0823	0849	0923	0950	1023	1049	1123	│	1152	1223	1250	1323	1349	1423	1450	1523	1550	1624	1638	1652	1723	1752	1823
Rhyl d.	0729	0758	0829	0855	0929	0956	1029	1055	1129	1143	1158	1229	1257	1329	1355	1429	1457	1529	1556	1630	1645	1658	1729	1758	1829
Colwyn Bay d.	0743	0809	0843	0906	0943	1007	1043	1106	1143	1154	1209	1243	1309	1343	1406	1443	1509	1543	1607	1644	1656	1709	1743	1812	1843
Llandudno Junction ‡ d.	0750	0815	0850	0912	0950	1013	1050	1112	1150	1201	1215	1250	1315	1350	1412	1450	1515	1550	1614	1651	1702	1714	1750	1819	1850
Llandudno ‡ a.	0806	│	0906	│	1006	│	1106	│	1206	│	│	│	│	1406	│	1506	│	1606	│	1707	│	│	1806	│	1906
Bangor d.	...	0838	...	0936	...	1031	...	1136	...	1217	1233	1315	1333	...	1436	...	1532	...	1637	...	1719	1738	...	1843	...
Holyhead ▽ a.	...	0921	...	1014	...	1105	...	1209	...	1250	1312	...	1413	...	1508	...	1613	...	1711	...	1751	1820	...	1913	...

	⑥ A	⑥ C	⑥	⑥ A	⑥ B	⑥ C	⑥	⑥	⑥ C	⑥	⑥	⑥			⑦	⑦	⑦ 🚌	⑦	⑦	⑦ A	⑦	⑦	⑦	⑦	⑦
Manchester Piccadilly d.	...	...	1750	...	...	*1850*	1950	...	*2032*	2150	2226	2314	...	⑦	...	...	0728	...	0956	...	1052	...	1156	...	1256
Warrington Bank Quay d.	...	...	1826	...	...	*1926*	2030	...	*2127*	2224	2256	2348	...		...	...	0838	...	1027	...	1126	...	1226	...	1327
Crewe 150 ♥ d.	1749	...	│	1852	...	│	│	2100	│	│	│	│	...		...	0827	│	0925	│	1042	│	1127	│	1227	│
Chester 150 ♥ a.	1809	...	1853	1912	...	*1954*	2057	2121	*2157*	2253	2325	0015	...		...	0849	0938	0947	1059	1102	1154	1150	1255	1252	1356
Chester d.	1816	1824	1855	1918	1932	2032	...	2126	2236	...	...	...	...		0620	0902	...	0948	...	1107	...	1203	...	1302	...
Flint d.	1829	1839	1910	1931	1947	2047	...	2141	2251	...	...	...	...		0633	0915	...	1003	...	│	...	1218	...	1317	...
Prestatyn d.	1842	1852	1923	1945	2000	2100	...	2154	2305	...	...	...	...		0647	0928	...	1017	...	1130	...	1231	...	1330	...
Rhyl d.	1849	1858	1929	1951	2006	2106	...	2200	2311	...	...	...	...		0653	0934	...	1023	...	1137	...	1237	...	1336	...
Colwyn Bay d.	1900	1909	1943	2002	2020	2119	...	2214	2325	...	...	...	...		0703	0945	...	1037	...	1148	...	1248	...	1350	...
Llandudno Junction ‡ d.	1906	1915	1950	2009	2027	2126	...	2221	2338	...	...	...	...		0710	0954	...	1043	...	1154	...	1254	...	1357	...
Llandudno ‡ a.	│	│	2006	│	│	│	...	│	│	...	...	...	...		│	│	...	│	...	│	...	│	...	│	...
Bangor d.	1923	1933	...	2025	2048	2143	...	2245	*0013**	...	...	...	...		0726	1012	...	1106	...	1211	...	1311	...	1419	...
Holyhead ▽ a.	1955	2018	...	2058	2131	2225	...	2318	*0048**	...	...	...	...		0800	1048	...	1149	...	1243	...	1342	...	1453	...

	⑦	⑦	⑦	⑦	⑦	⑦ C	⑦	⑦	⑦	⑦ C	⑦		⑦	⑦ A	⑦ B	⑦	⑦ A	⑦	⑦ A	⑦	⑦	⑦	⑦	⑦	⑦
Manchester Piccadilly d.	...	1356	...	1456	...	...	1556	...	1656	...	...	...	1756	...	...	1856	...	1956	...	2056	...	2156	...	2256	2325
Warrington Bank Quay d.	...	1427	...	1528	...	...	1627	...	1727	...	...	...	1827	...	...	1928	...	2030	...	2126	...	2226	...	2327	2354
Crewe 150 ♥ d.	1327	│	1427	│	1527	...	│	1627	│	...	1827	...	│	1856	...	│	1952	│	2055	│	2127	│	2229	│	│
Chester 150 ♥ a.	1351	1455	1451	1556	1549	...	1655	1649	1755	...	1849	...	1855	1913	...	1956	2013	2057	2113	2155	2150	2254	2252	2354	0022
Chester d.	1402	...	1502	...	1602	1636	...	1702	...	1829	1852	...	...	1922	1938	...	2018	...	2117	...	2200	...	2300	...	...
Flint d.	1417	...	1517	...	1617	1651	...	1717	...	1844	1907	...	...	1935	1953	...	2031	...	2130	...	2215	...	2315	...	...
Prestatyn d.	1430	...	1530	...	1630	1704	...	1730	...	1857	1921	...	...	1948	2006	...	2044	...	2143	...	2228	...	2328	...	...
Rhyl d.	1436	...	1536	...	1636	1710	...	1736	...	1903	1927	...	...	1955	2012	...	2051	...	2150	...	2234	...	2334	...	...
Colwyn Bay d.	1450	...	1550	...	1650	1724	...	1750	...	1917	1941	...	...	2006	2026	...	2102	...	2201	...	2248	...	2345	...	...
Llandudno Junction ‡ d.	1457	...	1557	...	1657	1731	...	1757	...	1924	1947	...	...	2012	2033	...	2108	...	2207	...	2255	...	2351	...	...
Llandudno ‡ a.	│	...	│	...	│	│	...	│	...	│	│	...	...	│	│	...	│	...	│	...	│	...	│	...	...
Bangor d.	1514	...	1619	...	1714	1754	...	1819	...	1948	2009	...	...	2029	2055	...	2125	...	2224	...	2312	...	0014	...	...
Holyhead ▽ a.	1555	...	1653	...	1757	1837	...	1903	...	2018	2044	...	...	2059	2130	...	2154	...	2256	...	2359	...	0049	...	...

CAERNARFON - PORTHMADOG - BLAENAU FFESTINIOG - LLANDUDNO

	Ⓐ	⑥	Ⓐ	⑥	🚂 Z△	⑦	⚒	🚂 Z△	🚂 XY△		🚂 Z△	⑥	Ⓐ	⑦	🚂 X△	🚂 Z△	🚂 X△	⑦	⚒	🚂 X△	⚒				
Caernarfon d.	...	...	...	...	...	...	...	...	1000	...	...	...	...	...	1320	...	1415	...	...	1610	...	...	...	...	...
Waunfawr d.	...	...	...	...	...	...	...	...	1025	...	...	...	...	...	1350	...	1445	...	...	1640	...	...	...	...	...
Rhyd Ddu d.	...	...	...	...	...	...	...	...	1055	...	...	...	...	...	1425	...	1515	...	...	1705	...	...	...	...	...
Beddgelert d.	...	...	...	...	...	...	...	...	1125	...	...	...	...	...	1455	...	1540	...	...	1735	...	...	...	...	...
Porthmadog Harbour d.	...	...	...	...	1010	...	...	1135	1210	...	1335	...	...	...	1540	1550	1630	...	...	1825	...	...	...	...	...
Minffordd d.	...	...	...	...	1020	...	...	1145	...	...	1345	...	...	...	...	1600	...	...	...	...	...	...	...	...	...
Blaenau Ffestiniog d.	0630	0630	0846	0846	1125	1145	1146	1250	...	...	1445	1457	1457	1503	...	1700	...	1730	1737	...	2023	...	...	...	...
Betws y Coed d.	0656	0656	0913	0913	...	1211	1213	...	...	...	...	1524	1524	1529	...	...	...	1757	1804	...	2050	...	...	...	...
Llanrwst d.	0702	0702	0919	0919	...	1217	1219	...	...	...	...	1530	1530	1535	...	...	...	1803	1810	...	2056	...	...	...	...
Llandudno Junction a.	0726	0731	0948	0944	...	1240	1244	...	...	...	...	1559	1557	1559	...	...	...	1829	1835	...	2121	...	...	...	...
Llandudno a.	...	...	1001	1013	...	1255	1303	...	...	...	...	1613	1617	...	...	...	...	1844	1854	...	2146	...	...	...	...

♥ – All trains Chester - Crewe. Journey time ± 23 minutes:
⚒: 0422, 0455, 0537, 0551, 0626Ⓐ, 0635⑥, 0643Ⓐ, 0717⑥, 0735Ⓐ, 0755, 0835, 0855 and then at 35 and 55 minutes past each hour until 1735, 1755, 1855, 1935, 1955, 2018, 2035⑥, 2055, 2135Ⓐ, 2226, 2301.
⑦: 0756, 0827, 0857, 0927, 0957, 1039, 1057, 1128, 1157, 1221, 1257, 1330, 1357, 1433, 1457, 1533, 1557, 1627, 1657, 1735, 1759, 1835, 1859, 1922, 1935, 1957, 2027, 2037, 2057, 2127, 2157, 2235, 2300.

‡ – All trains Llandudno Junction - Llandudno. Journey time ± 10 minutes:
613⚒, 0651⚒, 0731⚒, 0744Ⓐ, 0750⑥, 0817Ⓐ, 0828⑥, 0850⑥, 0918Ⓐ, 0928⑥, 0950⑥, 953Ⓐ, 1000⑦, 1003⑥, 1018Ⓐ, 1028⑥, 1050⑥⑦, 1055Ⓐ, 1125⚒, 1150⚒, 1200⑦, 228⚒, 1242⑦, 1253⚒, 1258⑦, 1339⑦, 1350⚒, 1402⑦, 1428⚒, 1450⚒, 1500⑦, 530⑥⑦, 1550⚒, 1603, 1626⑥, 1639⑦, 1650⚒, 1705⑦, 1728⑥, 1740⑦, 1750⚒, 326⚒, 1831⑦, 1841⚒, 1850⚒, 1928⚒, 1950⑥, 2030⚒, 2132⚒.

♥ – All trains Crewe - Chester. Journey time ± 23 minutes:
⚒: 0001①, 0010②–⑥, 0623, 0654Ⓐ, 0703⑥, 0723, 0823, 0849Ⓐ, 0923, 0949, 1023, 1049 and then at 23 and 49 minutes past each hour until 1823, 1845Ⓐ, 1852⑥, 1857Ⓐ, 1923, 1949⑥, 1956Ⓐ, 2023, 2042Ⓐ, 2049Ⓐ, 2100, 2136, 2149Ⓐ, 2223, 2321⑥, 2327Ⓐ, 2357⑥.
⑦: 0827, 0925, 0957, 1042, 1057, 1127, 1155, 1227, 1257, 1327, 1357, 1427, 1457, 1527, 1557, 1627, 1652, 1727, 1752, 1827, 1856, 1924, 1952, 2027, 2055, 2127, 2157, 2229,

‡ – All trains Llandudno - Llandudno Junction. Journey time ± 10 minutes:
0634⚒, 0708⚒, 0745⚒, 0802Ⓐ, 0808⑥, 0830Ⓐ, 0845⑥, 0908⑥, 0945⚒, 1008⚒, 1022⑥⑦, 1044⚒, 1107⑥⑦, 1112Ⓐ, 1140⑦, 1144⚒, 1208⚒, 1218⑦, 1244⚒, 1308⚒, 1319⑦, 1330⑦, 1350⑦, 1408⚒, 1420⑦, 1440Ⓐ, 1442⑥, 1508⚒, 1511⑦, 1544⑥⑦, 1608⑥, 1616Ⓑ, 1620⚒, 1644⑥, 1652⑦, 1705Ⓐ, 1708⑥, 1720⑦, 1744⑥, 1805⑦, 1808⚒, 1844⚒, 1855⑦, 1903⚒, 1913⚒, 1942⚒, 2008⑥, 2043⚒, 2145⚒.

161 Sleeper trains LONDON - SCOTLAND — SR

All trains in this table convey 🛏 1, 2 cl., (2) (reservation compulsory) and 🍸.

km		⑦	Ⓐ	⑦	Ⓐ					
0	**London** Euston **150** d.	2057	2116	2327	2350	...	...	...	...	...
28	Watford Junction **150** d.	2117**u**	2133**u**	2347**u**	0010**u**	...	...	...	...	...
254	Crewe **150 151** d.	2334**u**	2353**u**	|	|	...	...	...	...	...
336	Preston **151** d.	0033**u**	0052**u**	|	|	...	...	...	...	...
481	Carlisle **151** a.	|	|	0510**s**	0510**s**	...	...	...	...	...
625	Motherwell a.	|	|	0654**s**	0654**s**	...	...	...	...	...
646	**Glasgow** Central **151** ◧ a.	|	|	0718	0718	...	...	...	...	...
646	**Edinburgh 151** ◧ a.	|	|	0722	0722	...	...	...	...	...
	Dundee **224** a.	0608**s**	0608**s**	...	...	...	...	...	...	...
	Aberdeen **224** ◧ a.	0734	0734	...	...	...	...	...	...	...
	Perth **221** a.	0539**s**	0539**s**	...	...	...	...	...	...	...
	Inverness **221** a.	0836	0836	...	...	...	...	...	...	...
	Fort William **218** a.	0955	0955	...	...	...	...	...	...	...

	⑦	Ⓐ	Ⓐ	⑦					
Fort William **218** d.	...	...	1950	1900	...	...	...	...	...
Inverness **221** d.	...	...	2044	2026	...	...	...	...	...
Perth **221** d.	...	...	2321**u**	2306**u**	...	...	...	...	...
Aberdeen **224** d.	...	...	2143	2143	...	...	...	...	...
Dundee **224** d.	...	...	2306**u**	2306**u**	...	...	...	...	...
Edinburgh 151 d.	2315	2340	|	|	...	...	...	...	...
Glasgow Central **151** d.	2315	2340	|	|	...	...	...	...	...
Motherwell d.	2330**u**	0001**u**	|	|	...	...	...	...	...
Carlisle **151** d.	0112**u**	0144**u**	|	|	...	...	...	...	...
Preston **151** a.	|	|	0436**s**	0445**s**	...	...	...	...	...
Crewe **150 151** a.	|	|	0532**s**	0536**s**	...	...	...	...	...
Watford Junction **150** a.	0623**s**	0623**s**	|	|	...	...	...	...	...
London Euston **150** ◧ a.	0648	0648	0747	0747	...	...	...	...	...

s – Calls to set down only.
u – Calls to pick up only.
◧ – Sleeping-car passengers may occupy their cabins until 0800 following arrival at these stations.

162 BLACKPOOL - LIVERPOOL — Service valid until October 5 — 2nd class — NT

km			⚒	⚒	⚒	⚒	⚒	and at	⚒	⚒	⚒	⚒	⑤⑥	①–④			⑦	⑦	⑦	and at	⑦	⑦	⑦
0	**Blackpool** North **156** d.	⚒	0703	...	0903**t**	1003	1103	the same	1803	1903	2003	2114	2216	2216	...	⑦	...	0900	1000	the same	2100	2200	2300
28	**Preston** **156** d.		0730	0854	0930	1030	1130	minutes	1830	1930	2030	2140	2245	2245	...		...	0925	1025	minutes	2125	2225	2325
52	Wigan North Western d.		0750	0915	0950	1050	1150	past each	1850	1950	2050	2203	2305	*2315**	...		0847	0947	1047	past each	2147	*2258**	*2358**
66	St Helens Central d.		0807	0930	1006	1106	1206	hour until	1906	2006	2106	2221	2323	*2355**	...		0903	1004	1104	hour until	2204	*2338**	*0038**
85	**Liverpool** Lime St a.		0836	0958	1031	1127	1229	★	1927	2029	2129	2253	2354	*0109**	...		0935	1035	1135	★	2235	*0044**	*0144**

		⚒	⚒	⚒	⚒	and at	⚒	⚒	⚒	⚒	⚒	⚒	⑤⑥	①–④			⑦	⑦	⑦	and at	⑦	⑦	⑦
Liverpool Lime Street d.	⚒	0657	0757	0828	0928	the same	1628	1716	1800	1928	2028	2147	2302	2302*	...	⑦	0847	0947	1047	the same	2047	2147	2247*
St Helens Central d.		0717	0815	0949	0949	minutes	1649	1744	1829	1949	2049	2216	2331	0016*	...		0913	1014	1114	minutes	2114	2214	2353*
Wigan North Western d.		0731	0831	1003	1003	past each	1703	1803	1851	2003	2103	2238	2348	0056*	...		0930	1030	1130	past each	2130	2230	0033*
Preston **156** a.		0756	0857	1026	1026	hour until	1726	1830	1915	2026	2129	2302	0013	0153*	...		0953	1053	1153	hour until	2153	2253	0122*
Blackpool North **156** a.		0820**t**	0932**t**	1055**a**	1055	★	1755	1859	1942	2055	2158	2329	...	...	...		1020	1122	1222	★	2222	2222	0217*

a – Ⓐ only.
t – ⑥ only.
* – By 🚌.
★ – Timings may vary by up to 3 minutes.

163 MANCHESTER and LIVERPOOL local services — 2nd class — ME, NT

MANCHESTER - CLITHEROE — Journey time: ± 77 – 85 minutes — *57 km* — NT

From Manchester Victoria: *Service until October 5.*
Trains call at Bolton ± 20 and Blackburn ± 50 minutes later.
⚒: 0555, 0700, 0903, 1003, 1103, 1203, 1303, 1403, 1503, 1603, 1635, 1703, 1803, 1903, 2003, 2103, 2203.
⑦: 0803 and hourly until 2103.

From Clitheroe: *Service until October 5.*
Trains call at Blackburn ± 21 and Bolton ± 50 minutes later.
⚒: 0643Ⓐ, 0705, 0741Ⓐ, 0744⑥, 0826, 0944, 1044, 1144, 1244, 1344, 1444, 1528, 1644, 1744, 1804, 1844, 1944, 2042, 2144, 2244.
⑦: 0944 and hourly until 2244.

MANCHESTER - BUXTON — Journey time: ± 60 – 70 minutes — *41 km* — NT

From Manchester Piccadilly: *Service until October 5.*
Trains call at Stockport ± 11 and New Mills Newtown ± 31 minutes later.
⚒: 0649 and hourly until 1549, 1621, 1649, 1721, 1749, 1821Ⓐ, 1849, 1949, 2049, 2149Ⓐ, 2154⑥, 2310.
⑦: 0855, 0951, 1049 and hourly until 2249.

From Buxton: *Service until October 5.*
Trains call at New Mills Newtown ± 21 and at Stockport ± 46 minutes later.
⚒: 0602, 0623, 0653Ⓐ, 0724, 0749Ⓐ, 0804⑥, 0827 and hourly until 1627, 1702Ⓐ, 1729, 1802Ⓐ, 1829, 1929, 2029, 2129, 2256.
⑦: 0823, 0921, 1029, 1127 and hourly until 2227.

MANCHESTER - NORTHWICH - CHESTER — Journey time: ± 90 – 95 minutes — *73 km* — NT

From Manchester Piccadilly: *Service until October 5.*
Trains call at Stockport ± 13, Altrincham ± 28, and Northwich ± 55 minutes later.
⚒: 0618, 0717 and hourly (except 1709Ⓐ) until 2017, 2117⑥, 2122Ⓐ, 2217, 2317.
⑦: 0922, 1122, 1322, 1522, 1722, 1922, 2122.

From Chester: *Service until October 5.*
Trains call at Northwich ± 30, Altrincham ± 55, and Stockport ± 74 minutes later.
⚒: 0602, 0659, 0759 and hourly until 1659, 1804, 1904, 2004, 2133, 2248.
⑦: 0903, 1104, 1304, 1504, 1704, 1904, 2104.

MANCHESTER - ST HELENS - LIVERPOOL — Journey time: ± 63 minutes — *51 km* — NT

From Manchester Victoria:
Trains call at St Helens Junction ± 30 minutes later.
⚒: 0539, 0602, 0702, 0738, 0802, 0838, 0902 and hourly until 1702, 1738, 1802, 1902, 2002, 2109, 2209**z**, 2309**z**
⑦: 0859**p**, 1001**p** and hourly (note **p** applies to all trains) until 2101**p**.

From Liverpool Lime Street:
Trains call at St Helens Junction ± 28 minutes later.
⚒: 0520, 0620, 0720, 0742, 0820 and hourly until 1720, 1737, 1820, 1920, 2020, 2120, 2206①–④, 2220⑤⑥, 2319⑤⑥, 2319①–④**z**
⑦: 0815**p** and hourly (note **p** applies to all trains) until 2115, 2205.

MANCHESTER - WIGAN - SOUTHPORT — Journey time: ± 80 minutes — *62 km* — NT

From Manchester Piccadilly: *Service until October 5 (subject to alteration July 19 - Aug. 31).*
Trains call at Bolton ± 20 and Wigan Wallgate ± 39 minutes later.
⚒: 0641**v**, 0703**v**, 0738Ⓐ**v**, 0822 and hourly until 1822, 1920, 2020, 2120, 2236.
⑦: 0835, 0935, 1029, 1133, 1235 and hourly until 2035.

From Southport: *Service until October 5 (subject to alteration July 19 - Aug. 31).*
Trains call at Wigan Wallgate ± 30 and Bolton ± 48 minutes later.
⚒: 0622, 0719, 0823, 0924 and hourly until 1624, 1733, 1816, 1921, 2021, 2218.
⑦: 0910, 1005 and hourly until 2205.

MANCHESTER AIRPORT - CREWE — Journey time: ± 33 minutes — *37 km* — N

From Manchester Airport:
⚒: 0547, 0711 and hourly until 1611 1712, 1811. Additional later services (and all day on ⑦) available by changing at Wilmslow.

From Crewe:
⚒: 0634, 0730⑥, 0831, 0933 and hourly until 1833. Additional later services (and all da on ⑦) available by changing at Wilmslow.

LIVERPOOL - BIRKENHEAD - CHESTER — Journey time: ± 42 minutes — *29 km* — M

From Liverpool Lime Street:
Trains call at Liverpool Central ± 2 minutes and Birkenhead Central ± 9 minutes later.
⚒: 0538, 0608, 0643, 0713, 0743, 0755Ⓐ, 0813, 0820Ⓐ, 0843, 0858⑥, 0913, 0928, 0943, 0958 and every 15 minutes until 1858, 1913 and every 30 minutes until 2343.
⑦: 0813, 0843 and every 30 minutes until 2313, 2343.

From Chester:
Trains call at Birkenhead Central ± 33 minutes and Liverpool Central ± 44* minutes later
⚒: 0555, 0630, 0700, 0722Ⓐ, 0730⑥, 0737Ⓐ, 0752Ⓐ, 0800⑥, 0807Ⓐ, 0815⑥, 083 0845 and every 15 minutes until 1830, 1900 and every 30 minutes until 2300.
⑦: 0800, 0830 and every 30 minutes until 2300.

LIVERPOOL - SOUTHPORT — Journey time: ± 44 minutes — *30 km* — M

From Liverpool Central: *Service on ⚒ valid until October 4. Servce on ⑦ until September 28.*
⚒: 0608, 0623, 0638, 0653, 0708 and every 15 minutes until 2308, 2323, 2338.
⑦: 0808, 0823, 0853 and every 30 minutes until 2253, 2338.

From Southport: *Service on ⚒ valid until October 4. Servce on ⑦ until September 28.*
⚒: 0538, 0553, 0608, 0623, 0643, 0658, 0713, 0728, 0738Ⓐ, 0743⑥, 0748Ⓐ, 0758, 0803Ⓐ, 0813 and every 15 minutes until 2258, 2316.
⑦: 0758, 0828, 0858, 0928, 0958 and every 30 minutes until 2258, 2316.

p – Starts/terminates at Manchester **Piccadilly**, not Victoria.
v – Starts/terminates at Manchester **Victoria**, not Piccadilly.
z – By 🚌 on ①–④. Journey time 2½ hours.
* – Trains FROM Chester call at Liverpool Lime Street, then Liverpool Central.

EM Most trains 🍸 LONDON - LEICESTER - NOTTINGHAM, DERBY and SHEFFIELD 170

Service on ⑦ valid June 22 - September 7 (see note ▽). Other services: London St Pancras - Bedford Table 103; Derby - Sheffield Table 127.

km			②–⑤	⑥	Ⓐ	⑥	Ⓐ	⑥	⚒	Ⓐ	⑥	⚒	Ⓐ	⑥	⚒	Ⓐ	⚒	⚒	⚒	⚒	⚒	⚒	Ⓐ E	⚒	⚒	⚒
0	**London** St Pancras ... d.	⚒	0015	0015	0545	0545	0632	0637	...	0652	0652	0655	0724	...	0728	...	0757	0800	0813	0826	0829	0856	...	0859	0915	0926
47	Luton ✈ Parkway ...... d.		0043	0043	|	|	|	|	...	0713	0713	|	|	...	0749	...	|	|	|	|	0848	|	...	|	|	|
49	Luton ...... d.		0047	0047	0612	0612	0654	0659	...	|	|	0718	|	...	|	...	|	0822	|	|	|	|	...	0921	|	|
80	Bedford ...... d.		0111	0111	0627	0627	0709	|	...	|	|	0733	|	...	0803	...	|	0837	|	|	0903	|	...	0936	|	|
105	Wellingborough ...... d.		0131	0131	0639	0639	0721	|	...	|	|	0745	|	...	0815	...	|	0849	|	|	0916	|	...	0948	|	|
116	Kettering ...... d.		0143	0143	0647	0647	0729	0727	0735	|	|	0755	|	...	0822	0832	|	0900	|	|	0923	|	...	0958	|	|
128	**Corby** ...... a.		|	|	|	|	|	|	0747	|	|	|	|	...	|	0841	|	0910	|	|	|	|	0926	1010	|	|
133	Market Harborough .... d.		0155	0155	0657	0657	0739	0737	...	|	|	0805	0816	...	0832	...	|	...	0910	|	0932	|	|	...	1010	|
159	**Leicester** ...... d.		0210	0210	0712	0712	0752	0752	...	0758	0800	0823	0830	0829	0847	...	0900	...	0926	0930	0947	1000	|	...	1026	1029
180	Loughborough ...... d.		—	—	0722	0723	0802	0802	...	0808	0810	0833	0840	0839	0857	...	|	...	|	0939	0957	|	|	...	|	1038
191	E. Midlands Parkway . a.		...	...	0728	|	|	0809	...	0816	|	0842	0847	0846	|	...	|	...	0941	0948	|	|	1028	...	1041	1047
204	**Nottingham** ...... a.		⚒	⚒	|	|	|	|	...	0831	0830	0855	|	|	0917	...	|	...	0954	|	1018	|	|	...	1055	|
207	**Derby** ...... a.		0627	0721	0745	0742	0817	0821	...	...	...	...	0904	0903	...	...	0923	...	...	1004	...	1024	1045	...	...	1104
246	Chesterfield ...... a.		0645	0742	0809	0809	0837	0841	...	...	...	...	0925	0927	...	...	0943	...	...	1025	...	1043	...	...	...	1133
265	**Sheffield** ...... a.		0713	0800	0826	0826	0855	0856	...	...	...	...	0941	0942	...	...	0958	...	...	1041	...	1101	...	...	...	1148

	⚒	⚒	⚒	⚒	⚒	⚒	⚒	⚒	⚒	⚒	⚒	⚒	⚒	⚒	⚒	⚒	⚒	⚒	⚒	⚒	⚒	⚒	⚒	⚒	⚒	⚒
London St Pancras ... d.	0929	0957	1000	1015	1026	1029	1058	1100	1115	1126	1129	1158	1200	1215	1226	1229	1257	1300	1315	1326	1329	1358	1400	1415	1426	1429
Luton ✈ Parkway ...... d.	0948	|	|	|	|	1048	|	|	|	|	1148	|	|	|	|	1248	|	|	|	|	1350	|	|	|	|	1448
Luton ...... d.	|	|	1022	|	|	|	|	1123	|	|	|	|	1223	|	|	|	|	1323	|	|	|	|	1423	|	|	|
Bedford ...... d.	1003	|	1037	|	|	1103	|	1137	|	|	1203	|	1237	|	|	1303	|	1337	|	|	1403	|	1437	|	|	1503
Wellingborough ...... d.	1016	|	1049	|	|	1116	|	1149	|	|	1216	|	1249	|	|	1316	|	1349	|	|	1416	|	1449	|	|	1516
Kettering ...... d.	1022	|	1100	|	|	1122	|	1200	|	|	1222	|	1300	|	|	1322	|	1400	|	|	1422	|	1500	|	|	1522
Corby ...... a.	|	|	1110	|	|	|	|	1210	|	|	|	|	1310	|	|	|	|	1410	|	|	|	|	1510	|	|	|
Market Harborough .... d.	1032	|	...	1110	|	1132	|	...	1210	|	1232	|	...	1310	|	1332	|	...	1410	|	1432	|	...	1510	|	1532
Leicester ...... d.	1047	1100	...	1126	1129	1147	1200	...	1226	1229	1247	1300	...	1326	1329	1347	1400	...	1426	1429	1447	1500	...	1526	1529	1547
Loughborough ...... d.	1057	|	...	|	1138	1157	|	...	|	1238	1257	|	...	|	1338	1357	|	...	|	1438	1457	|	...	|	1538	1557
E. Midlands Parkway . a.	|	|	...	1141	1147	|	|	...	1241	1247	|	|	...	1341	1347	|	|	...	1441	1447	|	|	...	1541	1547	|
Nottingham ...... a.	1118	|	...	1155	|	1218	|	...	1255	|	1318	|	...	1355	|	1418	|	...	1455	|	1518	|	...	1555	|	1618
Derby ...... a.	...	1123	...	...	1204	...	1223	...	...	1304	...	1323	...	...	1404	...	1424	...	...	1504	...	1523	...	...	1604	...
Chesterfield ...... a.	...	1143	...	...	1227	...	1243	...	...	1333	...	1343	...	...	1427	...	1444	...	...	1527	...	1543	...	...	1627	...
Sheffield ...... a.	...	1158	...	...	1241	...	1259	...	...	1348	...	1401	...	...	1441	...	1459	...	...	1541	...	1559	...	...	1642	...

	⚒	⚒	⚒	⑥	Ⓐ	⚒	⚒	⚒	⚒	⚒	⑥	Ⓐ	⚒	⑥	Ⓐ	Ⓐ	⑥	Ⓐ	⑥	⑥ B	Ⓐ	⚒	Ⓐ	⑥	Ⓐ C	⑥
London St Pancras ... d.	1458	1500	1515	1526	1526	1529	1558	1600	1615	1626	1629	1629	1657	1700	1700	1700	1715	1715	1726	1729	1730	1757	1745	1800	1800	1826
Luton ✈ Parkway ...... d.	|	|	|	|	|	1548	|	|	|	|	1650	1648	|	|	|	|	|	|	|	1750	|	|	1808	|	|	|
Luton ...... d.	|	1523	|	|	|	|	|	1622	|	|	|	1653	|	1723	|	|	|	1740	|	|	|	|	|	1823	1823	|
Bedford ...... d.	|	1537	|	|	|	1603	|	1637	|	|	1704	1706	|	1738	1735	1735	|	|	|	1804	1802	|	|	1837	1838	|
Wellingborough ...... d.	|	1549	|	|	|	1616	|	1649	|	|	1716	1719	|	1750	1751	1751	|	|	|	1816	1815	|	1832	1849	1851	|
Kettering ...... d.	|	1600	|	|	|	1622	|	1700	|	|	1723	1725	|	1800	1806	1814	|	|	|	1823	1821	|	1844	1900	1906	|
Corby ...... a.	|	1610	|	|	|	|	|	1710	|	|	|	|	|	1810	1815	|	|	|	|	|	|	|	|	1910	1915	|
Market Harborough .... d.	|	...	1610	|	|	1632	|	...	1710	|	1733	1735	|	...	...	|	1810	1816	|	1833	1831	|	1856	...	...	|
Leicester ...... d.	1600	...	1626	1630	1629	1647	1700	...	1726	1729	1747	1751	1800	...	...	1837	1826	1832	1829	1847	1847	1900	1914	...	...	1929
Loughborough ...... d.	|	...	|	1640	1638	1657	|	...	|	1738	1758	1801	|	...	...	1847	|	|	1840	1858	1856	|	1926	...	...	1939
E. Midlands Parkway . a.	|	...	1641	1647	1646	|	|	...	1741	1746	|	|	|	...	...	1854	1841	1848	1847	|	1904	|	1933	...	...	1948
Nottingham ...... a.	|	...	1655	|	|	1718	|	...	1755	|	1817	1821	|	...	...	|	1854	1908	|	1917	1920	|	1947	...	...	|
Derby ...... a.	1623	...	...	1703	1704	...	1723	...	...	1804	...	...	1823	...	...	1913	...	...	1903	...	...	1923	2031	...	...	2004
Chesterfield ...... a.	1643	...	...	1727	1733	...	1743	...	...	1825	...	...	1843	...	...	1934	...	...	1925	...	...	1943	...	...	...	2026
Sheffield ...... a.	1659	...	...	1741	1748	...	1800	...	...	1841	...	...	1859	...	...	1952	...	...	1941	...	...	1959	...	...	...	2041

	Ⓐ	⑥	Ⓐ	⑥	Ⓐ B	⑥	Ⓐ	⑥	Ⓐ	⚒	⑥	Ⓐ	⑥	Ⓐ	⑥	Ⓐ	Ⓐ	⑥	⚒	⚒	Ⓐ	⑥	⑥	Ⓐ	Ⓐ	⑥
London St Pancras ... d.	1825	1815	1815	1829	1830	1858	1857	1900	1900	1915	1926	1928	1929	1955	1957	1932	2000	2002	2015	2026	2029	2030	2056	2055	2101	2100
Luton ✈ Parkway ...... d.	|	|	|	1850	1850	|	|	|	|	|	|	|	1950	|	|	1955	|	|	|	|	2048	2051	|	|	|	|
Luton ...... d.	1850	|	|	|	|	|	|	1923	1923	|	|	|	|	|	|	|	2022	2025	|	|	|	|	|	|	2123	2123
Bedford ...... d.	|	|	|	1904	1906	|	|	1937	1939	|	|	|	2004	|	|	2009	2037	2039	|	|	2103	2105	|	|	2138	2138
Wellingborough ...... d.	|	|	1900	1916	1919	|	|	1950	1953	|	|	|	2016	|	|	2022	2050	2051	|	|	2116	2117	|	|	2150	2151
Kettering ...... d.	|	|	1908	1923	1926	|	|	2000	2004	|	|	2015	2023	|	|	|	2101	2102	|	|	2122	2124	|	|	2157	2200
Corby ...... a.	|	|	|	|	|	|	|	2010	2014	|	|	|	|	|	|	|	2111	2112	|	|	|	|	|	|	|	2212
Market Harborough .... d.	1925	1910	|	1933	|	|	1949	...	...	2010	|	2025	2033	|	|	2038	...	...	2109	|	2132	2134	|	|	2207	|
Leicester ...... d.	1941	1926	1932	1947	1952	2001	2002	...	...	2025	2033	2041	2047	2102	2105	2053	...	...	2122	2129	2147	2148	2201	2201	2222	2228
Loughborough ...... d.	1952	|	1943	1958	|	|	2013	...	...	|	2043	2051	2058	|	|	2103	...	...	|	2138	2157	2159	|	|	2232	2239
E. Midlands Parkway . a.	|	1942	1950	|	2006	|	2020	...	...	2041	2049	2057	|	|	|	|	...	...	2137	2146	|	2206	|	|	2238	|
Nottingham ...... a.	|	1955	2008	2017	2023	|	|	...	...	2054	|	|	2117	|	|	2128	...	...	2150	|	2218	2220	|	|	|	|
Derby ...... a.	2015	|	|	...	...	2023	2034	...	...	...	2112	2115	...	2129	2131	|	...	...	...	2204	...	...	2224	2222	2253	2259
Chesterfield ...... a.	2038	2052	2109	...	...	2043	2053	...	...	...	...	...	...	2152	2158	2221	...	...	...	...	...	...	2247	2243	...	...
Sheffield ...... a.	2054	2105	2125	...	...	2059	2108	...	...	...	...	...	...	2208	2216	2236	...	...	...	...	...	...	2301	2257	...	...

	⑥	Ⓐ	⚒	⑥	Ⓐ	Ⓐ	⑥	⑥	Ⓐ	⑥	Ⓐ	Ⓐ			⑦	⑦	⑦	⑦	⑦	⑦	⑦	⑦	⑦	⑦	⑦	⑦
London St Pancras ... d.	...	...	2125	2130	2128	2200	2200	...	...	2226	2225	2315	...	⑦	...	0900	0930	1000	1030	1100	1130	1210	1230	1310	1330	1410
Luton ✈ Parkway ...... d.	...	...	|	2151	2149	|	|	...	...	2247	2248	|	...		...	0928	|	1029	|	1129	1159	1231	1253	1331	1352	1431
Luton ...... d.	...	...	|	|	|	2224	2224	...	...	|	|	2346	...		...	|	0959	|	1102	1133	1203	1234	1257	1334	1357	|
Bedford ...... d.	...	...	|	2206	2204	2239	2240	...	...	2303	2303	0012	...	✥	...	0950	1019	1054	1123	1154	1225	1254	1317	1354	1417	1454
Wellingborough ...... d.	...	...	|	2218	2216	2252	2253	...	...	2315	2317	0024	...		...	1003	1031	1108	1134	1207	1236	1307	1331	1407	1431	1407
Kettering ...... d.	2206	2211	|	2225	2223	2300	2301	2306	2311	2322	2326	0042	...		...	1010	1038	1116	1141	1215	1243	1315	1340	1415	1439	1514
Corby ...... a.	2221	2226	|	|	|	|	|	2321	2326	|	|	|	...		...	|	|	|	|	|	|	|	|	|	|	|
Market Harborough .... d.	...	...	2218	2235	2233	2311	2312	...	...	2332	2337	0052	...		...	1020	1049	1127	1151	1225	1253	1325	1351	1425	1451	1525
Leicester ...... d.	...	...	2233	2250	2248	2327	2328	...	...	2347	2353	0107	...		1020	1036	1105	1145	1209	1241	1311	1341	1409	1441	1508	1541
Loughborough ...... d.	...	...	2243	2259	2258	2338	2339	...	...	2356	0004	0117	...		1030	1046	1115	1156	1219	1251	1321	1351	1420	1451	1519	1551
E. Midlands Parkway . a.	...	...	2249	2312	2309	2351	2352	...	...	0008	0016	0128	...		1036	1052	1122	1204	1225	1258	1327	1358	1427	1458	1527	1605
Nottingham ...... a.	...	...	2303	|	|	0009	0010	...	...	|	|	0145	...		|	1108	|	1216	|	1312	|	1414	|	1514	|	1614
Derby ...... a.	...	...	...	2331	2330	...	...	...	...	0027	0034	0210	...		1054	...	1139	...	1242	...	1343	...	1445	...	1549	...
Chesterfield ...... a.	...	...	...	...	...	...	...	...	...	...	0055	...	...		1113	...	1208	...	1311	...	1410	...	1512	...	1610	...
Sheffield ...... a.	...	...	...	...	...	...	...	...	...	...	0112	...	...		1128	...	1223	...	1328	...	1425	...	1529	...	1629	...

	⑦	⑦	⑦	⑦	⑦	⑦	⑦	⑦	⑦	⑦	⑦	⑦	⑦	⑦	⑦	⑦	⑦	⑦	⑦	⑦	⑦	⑦	⑦	⑦	⑦	⑦
London St Pancras ... d.	1440	1510	1535	1610	1635	1640	1705	1710	1735	1740	1805	1810	1835	1840	1903	1910	1935	1940	2000	2010	2035	2040	2110	2130	2230	2300
Luton ✈ Parkway ...... d.	|	1533	|	1631	|	|	|	1731	|	|	|	1831	|	|	|	1931	|	|	|	2031	|	|	2131	|	2251	2330
Luton ...... d.	1504	|	1559	|	|	1702	|	|	|	1802	|	|	|	1902	|	|	|	2002	|	|	|	2104	|	2152	|	|
Bedford ...... d.	1524	1554	1618	1654	|	1724	|	1755	|	1827	|	1855	|	1924	|	1957	|	2024	|	2055	|	2125	2151	2216	2313	2354
Wellingborough ...... d.	1538	1608	1631	1607	|	1737	|	1807	|	1839	|	1808	|	1936	|	2008	|	2036	|	2105	|	2138	2204	2228	2326	0007
Kettering ...... d.	1547	1616	1640	1715	|	1744	|	1815	|	1847	|	1916	|	1944	|	2015	|	2044	|	2114	|	2147	2212	2236	2333	0015
Corby ...... a.	|	|	|	|	|	|	|	|	|	|	|	|	|	|	|	|	|	|	|	|	|	|	|	|	|	|
Market Harborough .... d.	1558	1627	1651	1725	|	1754	|	1824	|	1857	|	1926	|	1954	|	2025	|	2054	|	2124	|	2158	2222	2246	2343	0025
Leicester ...... d.	1617	1644	1709	1743	1752	1810	1824	1841	1853	1912	1924	1941	1953	2009	2025	2042	2047	2109	2124	2139	2153	2216	2238	2301	0004	0048
Loughborough ...... d.	1628	1656	1720	1743	|	1820	|	1851	|	1922	|	1951	|	2019	|	2052	|	2119	2135	2149	2203	|	2252	2311	0014	0058
E. Midlands Parkway . a.	1636	1704	1727	1759	1808	1827	1836	1857	1905	1929	1937	1958	2008	2026	2042	2058	2103	2126	2142	2156	2209	2231	2303	2323	0025	0109
Nottingham ...... a.	|	1716	|	1815	|	|	1848	1914	|	|	1949	2014	|	|	2054	2112	|	|	2154	2209	|	|	2316	|	0042	|
Derby ...... a.	1653	...	1745	...	1823	1842	...	...	1917	1945	...	...	2024	2042	...	...	2115	2141	...	...	2222	2245	...	2341	...	0126
Chesterfield ...... a.	1714	...	1808	...	1844	...	...	...	1938	...	...	...	2043	...	...	...	2134	...	...	...	...	2308	...	0022	...	...
Sheffield ...... a.	1730	...	1824	...	1902	...	...	...	1953	...	...	...	2102	...	...	...	2151	...	...	...	...	2332	...	0015	...	...

– To/from Lincoln (Table **187**).
– To/from Melton Mowbray (sub-table on page 144).
– To/from London St. Pancras (Table **170**).
– 🚌12 Derby - Corby - London St Pancras and v.v.

f – Arrives at Kettering 9 minutes after Corby.

▽ – For ⑦ service until June 15 please contact National Rail (see details on page 97).
✥ – For Kettering - Corby service on ⑦ see next page.

170 SHEFFIELD, DERBY and NOTTINGHAM - LEICESTER - LONDON

Most trains 🍸 EM

Service on ⑦ valid June 22 - September 7 (see note ▽). Other services: London St Pancras - Bedford Table 103; Derby - Sheffield Table 127.

		⚒	Ⓐ	Ⓐ	⑥	⑥	Ⓐ	Ⓐ C	⑥	Ⓐ	⑥	Ⓐ	Ⓐ	⑥	⑥	Ⓐ	Ⓐ	⑥	⑥	Ⓐ	Ⓐ	Ⓐ	⑥	Ⓐ	⑥	⚒
Sheffield d.	⚒	...	...	...	...	0529	...	...	...	0530	...	...	...	...	0629	...	0629	...	...	...	...	0649	...	...	...	0729
Chesterfield d.		...	...	...	...	0541	...	...	...	0542	...	...	...	...	0641	...	0640	...	...	...	...	0701	...	...	...	0741
Derby d.		...	0500	0519	0520	0601	...	...	...	0604	...	...	...	...	0702	...	0705	...	0720	...	...	0722	...	...	...	0801
Nottingham d.		...	|	|	|	|	0532	...	0606	|	0632	...	0630	...	|	0652	|	0706	|	0710	...	|	0730	0755	...	|
E. Midlands Parkway d.		...	0511	|	0535	|	0543	...	|	0617	0643	...	0642	...	|	0704	|	|	0734	0725	...	0733	0741	0804	...	|
Loughborough d.		...	0518	|	0542	|	0552	...	0622	0626	|	...	|	...	|	|	0722	0722	0742	|	...	0741	|	|	...	|
Leicester d.		0445	0529	0543	0553	0624	0604	...	0633	0639	0700	...	0659	...	0725	0719	0736	0733	0753	0742	...	0756	0758	0818	...	0825
Market Harborough d.		|	0543	0558	0607	|	0620	...	0647	0654	0715	...	0713	...	|	0733	|	0747	|	0757	...	|	0813	|	...	|
Corby d.		|	|	|	|	|	|	0635	|	|	|	0708	|	0711	|	|	|	|	|	|	0802	|	|	|	0816	|
Kettering d.		0505	0554	0608	0617	|	0631	0645	0656	0706	|	0717	0724	0720	|	0743	0759	0756	|	0809	0811	0817	|	|	0826	|
Wellingborough d.		0517	0602	0616	0624	|	0640	0654	0704	0714	|	...	0732	...	|	0751	0807	0804	|	|	...	0825	|	|	0832	|
Bedford d.		0537	|	0630	0640	|	|	0709	0718	|	|	...	|	...	|	|	|	0817	|	0829	...	|	|	|	0847	|
Luton d.		|	0625	|	0654	|	|	0724	|	|	|	...	0757	...	|	0815	|	|	|	|	...	|	|	|	0902	|
Luton ✈ Parkway d.		0556	|	|	|	|	0705	|	0733	0741	|	...	|	...	|	|	|	0832	|	|	...	|	|	|	|	|
London St Pancras a.		0620	0649	0708	0719	0729	0731	0748	0757	0807	0814	...	0823	...	0831	0842	0856	0856	0900	0906	...	0910	0913	0926	0926	0933

	Ⓐ	⚒B	⑥	Ⓐ	⚒	⚒	⚒	⚒	⚒	Ⓐ	⑥	⚒	⚒	⚒	⚒	⚒	⚒	⚒	⚒	⚒	⚒	⚒	⚒	⚒	⚒	⚒
Sheffield d.	...	...	...	0746	0737	...	0829	...	0849	...	0834	...	0929	...	0948	...	...	1029	...	1049	...	...	1129	...	1149	...
Chesterfield d.	...	...	...	0759	0750	...	0841	...	0901	...	0847	...	0941	...	0959	...	...	1041	...	1101	...	...	1141	...	1201	...
Derby d.	0736	...	0820	0819	|	...	0901	...	0921	...	|	...	1001	...	1021	...	...	1101	...	1121	...	...	1201	...	1221	...
Nottingham d.	|	0805	|	|	0832	...	|	0905	|	0932	0932	...	|	1005	|	1032	...	|	1105	|	1132	...	|	1205	|	1232
E. Midlands Parkway d.	|	|	0835	0835	0842	...	|	|	0935	0942	0942	...	|	|	1035	1042	...	|	|	1135	1142	...	|	|	1235	1242
Loughborough d.	0754	0821	0842	0843	0859	...	|	0921	0942	|	|	...	|	1021	1042	|	...	|	1121	1142	|	...	|	1221	1242	|
Leicester d.	0805	0832	0853	0854	0913	...	0924	0932	0951	0959	0959	...	1024	1032	1051	1059	...	1124	1132	1151	1159	...	1224	1232	1251	1259
Market Harborough d.	0819	0846	|	|	|	...	|	0946	|	1013	1013	...	|	1046	|	1113	...	|	1146	|	1213	...	|	1245	|	1313
Corby d.	|	|	|	|	|	0916	|	|	|	|	|	1016	|	|	|	|	1116	|	|	|	|	1216	|	|	|	|
Kettering d.	0829	0855	|	|	|	0926	|	0955	|	|	|	1026	|	1055	|	|	1126	|	1155	|	|	1226	|	1254	|	|
Wellingborough d.	0842	0903	|	|	|	0933	|	1003	|	|	|	1032	|	1101	|	|	1133	|	1203	|	|	1233	|	1303	|	|
Bedford d.	0905	0914	|	|	|	0947	|	1016	|	|	|	1047	|	1116	|	|	1147	|	1216	|	|	1247	|	1316	|	|
Luton d.	0919	|	|	|	|	1001	|	|	|	|	|	1102	|	|	|	|	1202	|	|	|	|	1302	|	|	|	|
Luton ✈ Parkway d.	|	0928	|	|	|	|	|	1031	|	|	|	|	|	1131	|	|	|	|	1231	|	|	|	|	1331	|	|
London St Pancras a.	0945	0956	0959	1006	1017	1026	1030	1056	1100	1114	1115	1126	1130	1156	1201	1214	1226	1230	1256	1300	1314	1326	1330	1356	1400	1414

	⚒	⚒	⚒	⚒	⚒	⚒	⚒	⚒	⚒	⚒	⚒	⚒	⚒	⚒	⚒	⚒	⚒	⚒	⑥	Ⓐ	⑥	Ⓐ	⚒	⑥	Ⓐ	⚒
Sheffield d.	...	1229	...	1249	...	...	1329	...	1349	...	...	1429	...	1449	...	...	1529	...	1549	1549	...	...	...	1629	1629	...
Chesterfield d.	...	1241	...	1301	...	...	1341	...	1401	...	...	1441	...	1501	...	...	1541	...	1601	1601	...	...	...	1641	1641	...
Derby d.	...	1301	...	1321	...	...	1401	...	1421	...	...	1501	...	1521	...	...	1601	...	1621	1621	...	...	...	1701	1701	...
Nottingham d.	...	|	1305	|	1332	...	|	1405	|	1432	...	|	1505	|	1532	...	|	1605	|	|	1630	1630	...	|	|	1705
E. Midlands Parkway d.	...	|	|	1335	1342	...	|	|	1435	1442	...	|	|	1535	1542	...	|	|	1635	1635	1642	1640	...	|	|	|
Loughborough d.	...	|	1321	1342	|	...	|	1421	1442	|	...	|	1521	1542	|	...	|	1621	1643	1642	|	|	...	|	|	1721
Leicester d.	...	1324	1332	1351	1359	...	1424	1432	1451	1459	...	1524	1531	1551	1559	...	1624	1632	1654	1651	1659	1656	...	1726	1724	1732
Market Harborough d.	...	|	1346	|	1413	...	|	1446	|	1513	...	|	1546	|	1613	...	|	1646	|	|	1714	1710	...	|	|	1746
Corby d.	1316	|	|	|	|	1416	|	|	|	|	1516	|	|	|	|	1616	|	|	|	|	|	|	1716	|	|	|
Kettering d.	1326	|	1355	|	|	1426	|	1455	|	|	1526	|	1555	|	|	1626	|	1655	|	1714	|	|	1726	|	|	1755
Wellingborough d.	1333	|	1403	|	|	1433	|	1503	|	|	1533	|	1603	|	|	1633	|	1703	|	|	|	|	1733	|	|	1803
Bedford d.	1347	|	1416	|	|	1447	|	1516	|	|	1547	|	1616	|	|	1647	|	1716	|	|	|	|	1747	|	|	1816
Luton d.	1402	|	|	|	|	1502	|	|	|	|	1602	|	|	|	|	1702	|	|	|	|	|	1749	1802	|	1811	|
Luton ✈ Parkway d.	|	|	1431	|	|	|	|	1531	|	|	|	|	1631	|	|	|	|	1731	|	|	|	|	|	|	|	1831
London St Pancras a.	1426	1430	1456	1459	1514	1526	1530	1556	1559	1614	1626	1631	1656	1700	1715	1726	1730	1756	1800	1809	1814	1815	1826	1832	1835	1856

	⑥	Ⓐ	⚒	Ⓐ E	⑥	⚒	⚒	Ⓐ	⑥	⚒	Ⓐ	⑥	⚒	⚒	⚒	⚒	⑥	Ⓐ	⚒	⑥	Ⓐ	⑥	Ⓐ	Ⓐ	⑥	⑥
Sheffield d.	1649	1649	...	...	...	1729	...	1738	1749	...	...	...	1829	...	1847	...	...	...	1929	...	...	...	...	...	2029	...
Chesterfield d.	1701	1701	...	...	...	1741	...	1756	1801	...	...	...	1841	...	1859	...	...	...	1941	...	...	...	...	...	2040	...
Derby d.	1721	1721	...	1636	...	1801	...	1821	1820	...	...	...	1901	...	1921	...	...	...	2001	...	...	...	...	...	2100	...
Nottingham d.	|	|	1732	|	...	|	1805	|	|	1832	...	...	|	1905	|	1932	...	...	|	2005	2002	...	...	2102	|	...
E. Midlands Parkway d.	1735	1735	1743	1647	...	|	|	1835	1835	1842	...	...	|	|	1935	1942	...	...	|	2017	2015	...	...	2114	2113	...
Loughborough d.	1743	1742	|	|	...	|	1821	1842	1843	|	...	...	|	1921	1942	|	...	...	|	2025	2023	...	...	2122	2121	...
Leicester d.	1754	1751	1759	|	...	1826	1832	1853	1854	1859	...	...	1924	1932	1952	1959	...	...	2024	2036	2034	...	...	2133	2131	...
Market Harborough d.	|	|	1813	|	...	|	1846	|	|	1913	...	...	|	1946	|	2013	...	...	|	2049	2047	...	...	2147	...	...
Corby d.	|	|	|	1751	1816	|	|	|	|	|	1856	1916	|	|	|	|	1950	1953	|	|	|	2043	2051	|	...	2143
Kettering d.	|	1814	|	1818f	1826	|	1855	|	|	|	1926f	1926	|	1955	|	|	2026f	2026f	|	2058	2056	2126f	2118f	2157	...	2152
Wellingborough d.	|	|	|	1828	1833	|	1903	|	|	|	1934	1933	|	2003	|	|	2033	2034	|	2107	2105	2133	2127	2204	...	...
Bedford d.	|	|	|	1848	1847	|	1916	|	|	|	1948	1947	|	2016	|	|	2047	2048	|	2120	2118	2147	2142	2219	...	...
Luton d.	|	|	|	1902	1902	|	|	|	|	|	2003	2002	|	|	|	|	2102	2103	|	|	|	2202	2159	2236	...	...
Luton ✈ Parkway d.	|	|	|	|	|	|	1931	|	|	|	|	|	|	2031	|	|	|	|	|	2136	2134	|	|	2239	...	...
London St Pancras a.	1900	1903	1915	1926	1926	1933	1958	2002	2000	2016	2026	2026	2032	2056	2103	2116	2126	2126	2133	2159	2157	2226	2224	2306	...	...

	Ⓐ	⑥	⑥	Ⓐ	⚒	Ⓐ	⑥	Ⓐ			⑦	⑦	⑦	⑦	⑦	⑦	⑦	⑦	⑦	⑦	⑦	⑦	⑦	⑦	⑦	⑦
Sheffield d.	2048	...	...	...	...	2201	2320	2321	...	⑦	...	...	...	...	0818	...	0925	...	1025	1029	1145	...	1249	...	1343	...
Chesterfield d.	2102	...	...	...	...	2213	2332	2345	...		...	...	...	...	0831	...	0938	...	1037	1042	1157	...	1302	...	1356	...
Derby d.	2121	...	...	...	...	2234	0006	0005	...		0651	...	0755	...	0851	...	0959	...	1057	|	1221	...	1322	...	1419	...
Nottingham d.	|	2105	2131	2131	...	...	...	...	...	✣	|	0730	|	0823	|	0921	|	1031	|	1135	|	1250	|	1350	|	1452
E. Midlands Parkway d.	2133	2119	|	|	...	...	...	...	...		0703	0740	0806	0836	0905	0932	1013	1045	1111	1147	1234	1304	1336	1404	1433	1504
Loughborough d.	2140	2127	2146	2146	...	...	...	...	...		|	|	0814	0844	0912	0941	1021	1054	1119	1156	1242	1313	1343	1413	1441	1512
Leicester d.	2153	2138	2158	2158	...	...	...	...	...		0721	0756	0826	0856	0924	0955	1033	1108	1130	1210	1256	1327	1355	1426	1454	1524
Market Harborough d.	|	2151	2212	2212	...	...	...	...	...		0739	0812	0842	0912	0940	1012	1046	1122	1143	1224	1310	1341	1408	1440	1507	1537
Corby d.	|	|	|	|	2243	...	...	...	...		|	|	|	|	|	|	|	|	|	|	|	|	|	|	|	|
Kettering d.	|	2200	2222	2223	2252	...	...	...	...		0750	0822	0852	0922	0950	1023	1056	1133	1153	1235	1321	1352	1418	1451	1517	1547
Wellingborough d.	|	2208	2230	2230	...	...	...	...	...		0802	0833	0903	0933	1002	1031	1103	1141	1201	1243	1329	1400	1426	1459	1524	1554
Bedford d.	|	2222	2244	2245	...	...	...	...	...		0815	0845	0915	0945	1015	1045	1116	1156	1213	1257	1343	1424	1439	1513	1539	1608
Luton d.	|	2236	2302	2302	...	...	...	...	...		0834	|	0935	|	1035	|	1136	|	1234	|	1404	|	1458	|	1558	|
Luton ✈ Parkway d.	|	2240	|	|	...	...	...	...	...		|	0906	|	1006	|	1106	|	1214	|	1317	|	1442	|	1533	|	162
London St Pancras a.	2300	2315	2336	2338	...	...	...	...	...		0915	0945	1015	1048	1117	1148	1214	1241	1258	1344	1430	1509	1522	1600	1622	165

	⑦	⑦	⑦	⑦	⑦		⑦	⑦	⑦		⑦	⑦	⑦		⑦	⑦		⑦	⑦	⑦		⑦	⑦	⑦	⑦	⑦
Sheffield d.	1449	...	...	1529	1550	...	...	...	...	...	1649	...	...	...	...	1750	...	...	...	1848	...	...	1928	2026	...	223
Chesterfield d.	1501	...	...	1542	1602	...	...	...	...	...	1700	...	...	...	...	1803	...	...	...	1900	...	...	1941	2039	...	224
Derby d.	1522	...	...	1602	1626	...	...	...	1655	...	1721	...	...	...	1807	1826	...	...	...	1921	...	...	2003	2101	...	232
Nottingham d.	|	1541	1552	|	|	...	1645	1650	|	...	|	1737	1751	...	|	|	...	1845	1851	|	...	1943	|	|	2119	...
E. Midlands Parkway d.	1536	1551	1605	1616	1637	...	1655	1703	1709	...	1734	1747	1803	...	1821	1837	...	1855	1904	1935	...	1956	2018	2113	2131	...
Loughborough d.	1543	|	1612	1625	|	...	|	1711	1717	...	|	|	1811	...	1828	|	...	1902	1911	1942	...	2003	2027	|	2139	...
Leicester d.	1555	1610	1624	1639	1655	...	1710	1724	1729	...	1753	1806	1824	...	1840	1854	...	1914	1924	1954	...	2015	2040	2132	2154	...
Market Harborough d.	|	|	1637	1653	|	...	|	1737	1742	...	|	|	1837	...	1853	|	...	1927	1937	2007	...	2028	2054	2146	2208	...
Corby d.	|	|	|	|	|	...	|	|	|	...	|	|	|	...	|	|	...	|	|	|	...	|	|	|	|	...
Kettering d.	|	|	1647	1702	|	...	|	1747	1752	...	|	|	1847	...	1905	|	...	1937	1947	2015	...	2038	2105	2157	2218	...
Wellingborough d.	|	|	1655	1712	|	...	|	1754	1759	...	|	|	1854	...	1913	|	...	1945	1954	2024	...	2045	2113	2205	2225	...
Bedford d.	|	|	1708	1730	|	...	|	1807	1814	...	|	|	1908	...	1927	|	...	1958	2008	2039	...	2105	2128	2221	2238	...
Luton d.	1645	|	|	1754	|	...	|	|	1832	...	|	|	|	...	1947	|	...	2017	|	|	...	2125	2147	2237	2255	...
Luton ✈ Parkway d.	|	|	1728	|	|	...	|	1827	|	...	|	|	1927	...	|	|	...	|	2027	2057	...	|	|	|	|	...
London St Pancras a.	1713	1724	1751	1819	1806	...	1823	1850	1856	...	1913	1923	1951	...	2012	2004	...	2042	2051	2122	...	2149	2215	2303	2325	...

✣ – **Kettering - Corby** and v.v. trains on ⑦. Journey time 10 (20 by 🚌) minutes.
Kettering → Corby (June 22 - September 7)
0955, 1055, 1155, 1255, 1355, 1455, 1555, 1650, 1750, 1855, 1950, 2050, 2155.
Corby → Kettering (June 22 - September 7)
0930, 1025, 1125, 1220, 1330, 1425, 1525, 1625, 1720, 1820, 1920, 2020, 2125.

For other notes see previous page.

CORBY - MELTON MOWBRAY - DERBY

km		Ⓐ	Ⓐ D	
0	**Corby** d.	0926	1915	...
23	Oakham d.	0947	1936	...
43	**Melton Mowbray** d.	1000	1948	...
81	East Mids Parkway d.	1028	...	...
97	**Derby** a.	1045	...	...

	Ⓐ D	Ⓐ E	
Derby d.	...	1636	...
East Mids Parkway d.	...	1648	...
Melton Mowbray d.	0600	1714	...
Oakham d.	0612	1727	...
Corby a.	0635	1751	...

NT 2nd class NOTTINGHAM - SHEFFIELD - HUDDERSFIELD and LEEDS 171

NOTTINGHAM - SHEFFIELD - LEEDS

km			Ⓐ	⚒	Ⓐ	⚒	Ⓐ	⚒	Ⓐ	⑥	⚒	⚒	⚒	⚒		⚒	⚒	⚒	Ⓐ	⑥	⚒	⚒	⚒	⑥	⑥
0	**Nottingham** 206 d.	⚒	...	...	...	...	0621	...	0712	0712	...	0817	...	0917	and	...	1717	...	1817	1817	...	1917	...	...	2043
18	Langley Mill d.		...	...	...	...	0640	...	0731	0731	...	0836	...	0936	at	...	1736	...	1836	1836	...	1936	...	...	2108
29	Alfreton 206 d.		...	...	...	...	0648	...	0739	0739	...	0844	...	0944	the	...	1744	...	1844	1844	...	1944	...	...	2116
45	Chesterfield 170 206 d.		...	...	0626	...	0658	...	0749	0749	...	0855	...	0953	same	...	1755	...	1855	1855	...	1955	...	...	2126
64	**Sheffield** 170 206 a.		...	...	0646	...	0716	...	0804	0811	...	0915	...	1015	minutes	...	1815	...	1915	1915	...	2015	...	...	2143
64	**Sheffield** 192 193 d.		0550	0606	0649	0706	0717	0751	0818	0819	0851	0918	0950	1018	past	1750	1818	1850	1922	1916	1951	2018	2106	2224	...
70	Meadowhall 192 193 d.		0556	0612	0655	0712	0723	0757	0825	0825	0857	0924	0956	1024	each	1756	1824	1856	1928	1922	1957	2024	2112	2230	...
90	Barnsley d.		0610	0633	0712	0733	0742	0812	0842	0842	0912	0942	1012	1042	hour	1813	1842	1914	1942	1942	2012	2042	2133	|	...
107	Wakefield Kirkgate d.		0627	0649	0728	0749	0758	0827	0858	0858	0927	0958	1027	1058	until	1828	1858	1929	1957	1959	2028	2058	2152	|	...
130	**Leeds** 127 a.		0650	0728	0751	0825	0819	0849	0918	0920	0949	1018	1049	1118	◇	1851	1925	1952	2018	2020	2049	2118	2229	2338	...

	Ⓐ	①-④	⑥	Ⓐ			⑦	⑦	⑦	⑦	⑦	⑦	⑦	⑦	⑦		⑦	⑦	⑦	⑦	⑦	⑦	⑦	⑦	⑦
Nottingham 206 d.	2047	...	2117	2114	...	⑦	...	...	...	1012	1117	1217	1317	1417	1512	...	1617	1717	1817	1917	1943	...	2015	...	2133
Langley Mill d.	|	...	2136	2141	...		...	...	...	1036	1136	1236	1336	1436	1534	...	1636	1736	1836	1936	|	...	2034	...	2157
Alfreton 206 d.	|	...	2144	2149	...		...	...	...	1044	1144	1244	1344	1444	1544	...	1644	1744	1844	1944	2004	...	2042	...	2205
Chesterfield 170 206 d.	2131	...	2155	2201	...		...	...	...	1055	1155	1254	1354	1454	1554	...	1654	1754	1854	1954	2014	...	2052	...	2216
Sheffield 170 206 a.	2158	...	2214	2219	...		...	...	...	1114	1215	1315	1415	1515	1615	...	1715	1815	1915	2015	2031	...	2117	...	2236
Sheffield 192 193 d.	...	2206	...	...	...		0839	1017	1039	1117	1216	1317	1417	1517	1617	...	1717	1817	1916	2017	...	2039	...	2136	2239
Meadowhall 192 193 d.	...	2212	...	...	...		0845	1023	1045	1123	1223	1323	1423	1523	1623	...	1723	1823	1923	2023	...	2045	...	2142	2245
Barnsley d.	...	2233	...	...	...		0910	1037	1110	1137	1237	1337	1437	1537	1637	...	1737	1837	1937	2037	...	2110	...	|	2310
Wakefield Kirkgate 127 180 d.	...	2254	...	...	...		0929	1055	1129	1153	1255	1353	1453	1553	1653	...	1753	1853	1953	2053	...	2129	...	|	2327
Leeds 127 180 a.	...	2330	...	...	...		1004	1116	1205	1218	1318	1418	1517	1618	1717	...	1817	1918	2018	2117	...	2204	...	2250	0005

		Ⓐ	⑥	Ⓐ	Ⓐ	Ⓐ	⑥	Ⓐ	⑥	⚒	⚒	⚒	⚒	⚒	⚒		⚒	⚒	⚒	⑥	Ⓐ	⚒	⚒	⚒
Leeds 127 180 d.	⚒	...	...	...	...	...	...	0605	0638	0705	0740	0805	0840	0905	0940	and	1705	1740	1805	1840	1840	1905	1945	2030
Wakefield Kirkgate 127 180 d.		...	...	...	...	0604	...	0621	0708	0725	0756	0823	0856	0923	0956	at	1723	1756	1823	1856	1858	1924	2001	2046
Barnsley d.		...	...	0523	...	0621	0622	0638	0726	0742	0814	0840	0914	0940	1014	the	1740	1814	1840	1914	1919	1941	2019	2103
Meadowhall 192 193 d.		...	...	0543	...	0642	0642	0652	0750	0756	0829	0853	0930	0954	1030	same	1753	1828	1854	1932	1936	1954	2037	2121
Sheffield 192 193 a.		...	...	0554	...	0655	0651	0700	0758	0805	0839	0902	0937	1002	1037	minutes	1803	1838	1903	1940	1943	2004	2044	2130
Sheffield 170 206 d.		0505	0554	...	0603	...	0703	0703	...	0808	...	0905	...	1005	...	past	1804	...	1905	...	...	2005	...	...
Chesterfield 170 206 d.		0520	0620	...	0619	...	0719	0720	...	0824	...	0921	...	1021	...	each	1820	...	1921	...	...	2021	...	...
Alfreton 206 d.		|	0630	...	0630	...	0729	0731	...	0834	...	0931	...	1031	...	hour	1831	...	1932	...	...	2031	...	...
Langley Mill d.		|	0638	...	0637	...	0737	0739	...	0842	...	0939	...	1039	...	until	1838	...	1939	...	...	2039	...	...
Nottingham 206 a.		0611	0702	...	0701	...	0800	0801	...	0902	...	1000	...	1100	...	◇	1902	...	2000	...	...	2100	...	...

	⚒	⚒	Ⓐ	⑥			⑦	⑦	⑦	⑦		⑦	⑦	⑦	⑦		⑦	⑦	⑦	⑦		⑦	⑦	⑦	⑦
Leeds 127 180 d.	2037	2137	2237	2244	...	⑦	...	0834	0905	1002	...	1105	1205	1305	1405	...	1505	1604	1705	1803	...	1904	2022	2145	2217
Wakefield Kirkgate 127 180 d.	2107	2207	2310	|	...		...	0903	0921	1018	...	1121	1221	1321	1421	...	1521	1622	1721	1821	...	1921	2051	|	2246
Barnsley d.	2124	2228	2331	|	...		...	0924	0941	1038	...	1141	1241	1341	1441	...	1541	1642	1741	1842	...	1940	2112	|	2312
Meadowhall 192 193 d.	2148	2248	2351	2345	...		...	0944	0957	1051	...	1154	1252	1354	1457	...	1557	1657	1758	1857	...	1954	2133	2246	2332
Sheffield 127 192 193 a.	2157	2258	0002	2358	...		...	0954	1004	1102	...	1203	1304	1405	1506	...	1606	1705	1805	1905	...	2004	2143	2256	2343
Sheffield 127 170 206 d.	...	...	...	...	...		0905	...	1007	1103	...	1206	1306	1407	1507	...	1607	1707	1807	1907	...	2007	...	...	...
Chesterfield 127 170 206 d.	...	...	...	...	...		0921	...	1023	1120	...	1223	1323	1423	1523	...	1623	1723	1823	1923	...	2023	...	...	...
Alfreton 206 d.	...	...	...	...	...		0932	...	1033	1130	...	1233	1333	1433	1533	...	1633	1733	1833	1933	...	2033	...	...	...
Langley Mill d.	...	...	...	...	...		0942	...	1041	1138	...	1241	1341	1441	1541	...	1641	1741	1841	1941	...	2041	...	...	...
Nottingham 170 206 a.	...	...	...	...	...		1000	...	1101	1158	...	1301	1401	1501	1601	...	1701	1801	1901	2001	...	2101	...	...	...

SHEFFIELD - HUDDERSFIELD *'The Penistone Line'*

Service valid until October 5

km			Ⓐ	⚒	⚒	⚒		⚒	⚒	⑥	Ⓐ	⚒	⚒	⚒	⚒			⑦	⑦	⑦	⑦	⑦	⑦	⑦	⑦
0	**Sheffield** d.	⚒	0536	0636	0736	0836	and at	1636	1736	1836	1836	1936	2042	2141	2241	...	⑦	0939	1149	1235	1339	1539	1654	1739	1939
6	Meadowhall d.		0542	0642	0842	0842	the same	1642	1742	1842	1842	1942	2048	2147	2247	...		0945	1155	1241	1345	1543	1700	1746	1945
26	Barnsley d.		0601	0701	0801	0901	minutes	1703	1803	1903	1905	2008	2108	2208	2308	...		1006	1216	1306	1406	1604	1715	1810	2006
38	Penistone d.		0618	0718	0818	0918	past each	1720	1820	1920	1922	2025	2125	2225	2325	...		1023	1233	1323	1423	1621	1732	1827	2023
59	**Huddersfield** a.		0650	0749	0849	0949	hour until ◇	1750	1855	1951	1953	2057	2157	2257	2359	...		1054	1304	1353	1453	1653	1804	1858	2053

		⚒	⚒	⚒	⚒		⚒	Ⓐ	⑥	Ⓐ	⚒	⚒	⚒	⚒			⑦	⑦	⑦	⑦	⑦	⑦	⑦	⑦
Huddersfield d.	⚒	0610	0710	0810	0913	and at	1713	1751	1813	1818	1918	2018	2118	2218	...	⑦	0919	1015	1129	1319	1415	1519	1719	1919
Penistone d.		0642	0742	0842	0944	the same	1744	1831	1844	1849	1949	2052	2149	2249	...		0950	1046	1200	1350	1446	1550	1754	1950
Barnsley d.		0658	0758	0858	1001	minutes	1801	1848	1901	1906	2007	2112	2206	2306	...		1012	1103	1217	1412	1503	1612	1812	2012
Meadowhall 192 193 a.		0720	0820	0920	1020	past each	1821	1906	1920	1924	2027	2130	2225	2326	...		1032	1120	1234	1432	1520	1632	1833	2034
Sheffield 192 193 a.		0729	0829	0928	1030	hour until ◇	1832	1918	1930	1934	2036	2141	2236	2336	...		1044	1128	1247	1443	1528	1644	1844	2043

◇ – Timings may vary by up to 5 minutes.

EM 2nd class NOTTINGHAM - WORKSOP and MATLOCK 172

NOTTINGHAM - WORKSOP *'The Robin Hood Line'*

km			⚒	⚒	⑥	Ⓐ	⚒	⚒		⚒	⚒	⚒	⚒	⑥	Ⓐ	⚒			⑦	⑦	⑦	⑦	⑦	⑦	⑦	⑦
0	**Nottingham** d.	⚒	0540	0605	0659	0701	0827	0926	and	1727	1755	1855	1955	2052	2056	2202	...	⑦	0807	0942	1126	1328	1525	1653	1829	2025
28	Mansfield d.		0613	0638	0740	0740	0900	0957	hourly	1803	1835	1929	2035	2131	2135	2242	...		0840	1016	1200	1401	1558	1726	1902	2058
50	**Worksop** a.		0649	0719	0814	0818	0933	1033	until	1837	1908	2003	2109	2202	2208	2314	...		...	...	...	...	...	...	...	...

		⚒	⚒	⚒	⚒	⚒		⚒	⚒	⚒	⚒	⚒	⚒	⑥	Ⓐ			⑦	⑦	⑦	⑦	⑦	⑦	⑦	⑦
Worksop d.	⚒	0550	0656	0738	0838	0938	and	1642	1746	1841	1922	2015	2119	2219	2223	...	⑦	...	...	...	...	...	...	...	...
Mansfield d.		0621	0729	0810	0910	1010	hourly	1714	1818	1913	1953	2048	2152	2250	2255	...		0855	1033	1215	1415	1612	1739	1921	2110
Nottingham a.		0656	0805	0845	0944	1044	until	1746	1853	1948	2030	2125	2225	2324	2328	...		0931	1107	1249	1450	1646	1813	1955	2144

NOTTINGHAM - DERBY - MATLOCK

km			⚒	Ⓐ	⑥	⑥	Ⓐ	⑥	Ⓐ	⚒		⚒	⑥	Ⓐ	Ⓐ	⑥			⑦	⑦	⑦	⑦	⑦	⑦	⑦
0	**Nottingham** 121 d.	⚒	...	0617	0620	0719	0720	0820	0822	0920		1920	2019	2021	*2120*	*2139*	...	⑦	0926	1127	1323	1528	1722	1922	2122
26	**Derby** 121 a.		...	0650	0652	0749	0750	0850	0853	0950	and	1950	2049	2050	*2151*	*2207*	...		0954	1155	1351	1558	1752	1950	2151
26	**Derby** d.		0540	0652	0654	0752	0752	0852	0855	0952	hourly	1952	2052	2052	2213	2216	...		0956	1156	1356	1558	1756	1952	2153
34	Duffield ◧ d.		0547	0659	0701	0759	0759	0859	0902	0959	until	1959	2059	2059	2220	2223	...		1003	1204	1403	1605	1803	1959	2200
46	Whatstandwell ◧ d.		0602	0714	0716	0814	0814	0914	0917	1014		2014	2114	2114	2235	2239	...		1018	1219	1418	1620	1818	2014	2215
50	Cromford d.		0608	0720	0722	0820	0820	0920	0923	1020	★	2020	2120	2120	2241	2245	...		1024	1224	1424	1626	1824	2020	2221
52	Matlock Bath ◧ d.		0610	0722	0724	0822	0822	0922	0925	1022		2022	2122	2122	2243	2247	...		1026	1227	1426	1628	1826	2022	2223
53	**Matlock** ◧ a.		0614	0726	0728	0826	0826	0926	0929	1026		2026	2126	2126	2247	2250	...		1030	1230	1430	1634	1830	2026	2231

		⚒		⚒	⑥	Ⓐ		⑥	Ⓐ	⚒		⚒		⚒			⑦	⑦	⑦	⑦		⑦	⑦	⑦
Matlock ◧ d.	⚒	0619	...	0736	0836	0836		1936	1936	2036	...	2140	...	2254	...	⑦	1038	1238	1441	1638	...	1838	2038	2244
Matlock Bath ◧ d.		0621	...	0738	0838	0838		1938	1938	2038	...	2142	...	2256	...		1040	1240	1443	1640	...	1840	2040	2246
Cromford d.		0624	...	0741	0842	0841	and	1941	1941	2041	...	2145	...	2259	...		1043	1243	1446	1643	...	1843	2043	2249
Whatstandwell ◧ d.		0629	...	0746	0846	0846	hourly	1946	1946	2046	...	2150	...	2304	...		1048	1248	1451	1648	...	1848	2048	2254
Duffield ◧ d.		0645	...	0803	0903	0903	until	2003	2003	2103	...	2207	...	2321	...		1105	1305	1507	1705	...	1905	2105	2311
Derby a.		0654	...	0811	0911	0911		2011	2011	2111	...	2215	...	2329	...		1112	1312	1515	1712	...	1912	2112	2318
Derby 121 d.		*0709*	...	0813	0913	0916	★	2013	2016	2113	...	*2258*	...	2331	...		1114	1314	1516	1714	...	1914	2114	...
Nottingham 121 a.		*0738*	...	0846	0941	0946		2042	2043	2141	...	*2328*	...	0001	...		1141	1341	1543	1744	...	1944	2141	...

★ – Timings may vary by up to 5 minutes. On Ⓐ trains departing Matlock 0936 - 1536 arrive Nottingham at xx41.

◧ – Visitor attractions near these stations:
Duffield: Ecclesbourne Valley Railway (shares National Rail station). ✆ 01629 823076.
Whatstandwell: National Tramway Museum (1.6 km walk). ✆ 01773 854321.
Matlock Bath: Heights of Abraham (short walk to cable car). ✆ 01629 582365.
Matlock: Peak Rail (shares National Rail station). ✆ 01629 580381.

173 LEEDS - SETTLE - CARLISLE 2nd class NT

km		Ⓐ	⑥	⚒	⑦		⑦ a	⚒	⚒	⑦		⑥	Ⓐ	⑦		⚒	⑦	⑥	Ⓐ		⚒	Ⓐ A	⑥ A	⑦ A
	London Kings Cross **180** ....d.	...	...	...	...	...	...	...	...	...	...	...	...	...	...	...	...	...	...	...	...	1803	1835	1835a
0	**Leeds** **176** d.	0529	0619	0849	0900	...	...	0947	1049	1120	...	1249	1249	1355	...	1449	1745	1750	1806	...	1919	2034	2055	2101
27	Keighley **176** d.	0556	0642	0912	0930	...	...	1012	1112	1142	...	1312	1312	1418	...	1512	1802	1814	1829	...	1942	2057s	2113s	2119s
42	Skipton **176** d.	0615	0656	0926	0948	...	...	1026	1126	1155	...	1326	1326	1433	...	1526	1822	1835	1846	...	2000	2115	2127	2140
58	Hellifield d.	0626	0708	0940	1002	...	1015	|	1137	|	...	1340	1340	1447	...	1537	1833	1849	1900	...	2015	...	...	...
66	**Settle** d.	0636	0715	0950	1010	...	1035	1044	1146	1214	...	1348	1348	1456	...	1545	1841	1857	1908	...	2023	...	...	...
76	Horton in Ribblesdale d.	|	0724	0958	1019	...	1044	|	1154	|	...	1357	1357	1505	...	1553	1850	1906	1917	...	2032	...	...	...
84	Ribblehead d.	0651	0732	1006	1027	...	1052	|	1202	|	...	1405	1405	1513	...	1601	1858	1914	1925	...	2042	...	...	...
99	Garsdale d.	0706	0747	1021	1043	...	1107	|	1217	|	...	1420	1420	1528	...	1616	1913	1929	1940	...	...	...	...	...
115	Kirkby Stephen d.	0718	0759	1034	1056	...	1120	1122	1230	1251	...	1432	1432	1541	...	1629	1926	1941	1952	...	...	...	...	...
132	Appleby d.	0732	0812	1047	1109	...	1134	1136	1243	1305	...	1445	1445	1554	...	1641	1939	1954	2005	...	...	...	...	...
166	Armathwaite d.	0759	0839	1115	1137	...	1202	|	1311	|	...	1512	1512	1622	...	1709	2007	2021	2032	...	...	...	...	...
182	**Carlisle** a.	0817	0858	1134	1155	...	1217	1217	1329	1347	...	1527	1532	1639	...	1728	2024	2041	2052	...	...	...	...	...

	⑥ A	Ⓐ A	⑥	Ⓐ	⑥	Ⓐ	⑦	⑥	⑥	Ⓐ	⑦	Ⓐ	⑥	Ⓐ	⑦	⑥	⚒	⑦	⑦ a	⑥	Ⓐ	Ⓐ	⑥
Carlisle d.	...	...	...	0550	0752	0853	0925	0926	1151	1155	1259	1404	1426	1505	1520	1549	1618	1700	1757	1807	1814	...	...
Armathwaite d.	...	...	...	0604	0806	0907	0939	0940	1205	1209	1313	1418	1440	|	|	|	1632	1714	1811	1821	1828	...	...
Appleby d.	...	...	...	0632	0834	0935	1007	1008	1233	1237	1341	1447	1509	1542	1557	1626	1701	1743	1840	1849	1856	...	...
Kirkby Stephen d.	...	...	...	0646	0847	0948	1021	1021	1246	1250	1355	1500	1522	1555	1610	1639	1714	1757	1854	1902	1909	...	...
Garsdale d.	...	...	...	0659	0900	1002	1034	1035	1259	1303	1408	1513	1535	|	|	|	1727	1810	1907	1915	1922	...	...
Ribblehead d.	...	...	0716	0716	0915	1017	1049	1049	1314	1318	1423	1529	1549	|	|	|	1742	1825	1922	1930	1937	2100	2100
Horton in Ribblesdale d.	...	...	0722	0722	0921	1024	1056	1056	1320	1324	1430	1536	1556	|	|	|	1748	1832	1929	1936	1943	2106	2106
Settle d.	...	...	0730	0730	0929	1032	1104	1104	1328	1332	1438	1544	1604	1635	1646	1716	1757	1841	1937	1944	1951	2114	2114
Hellifield d.	...	...	0739	0739	0937	1039	1113	1111	1337	1341	1447	1552	1611	|	|	|	1806	1849	1946	1952	1959	2123	2123
Skipton **176** d.	0655	0655	0757	0757	0956	1058	1130	1128	1356	1358	1506	1613	1628	1657	1709	1741	1827	1905	...	2007	2015	2148	2138
Keighley **176** d.	0709u	0708u	0809	0809	1008	1108	1140	1138	1408	1409	1516	1623	1639	1708	1719	1751	1838	1915	...	2017	2025	2202	*2200*
Leeds **176** a.	0733	0731	0837	0837	1034	1136	1206	1207	1437	1437	1544	1653	1707	1740	1746	1817	1907	1942	...	2046	2050	2233	*2231*
London Kings Cross **180** a.	0951	1000	...	...	...	...	...	...	...	...	...	...	...	...	...	...	...	...	...	...	...	...	...

A – 12 and 🍷 London Kings Cross - Skipton and v.v. (Table **180**).
a – Until Sep. 7.
s – Calls to set down only.
u – Calls to pick up only.

174 LEEDS - LANCASTER - HEYSHAM 2nd class NT

km	km		Ⓐ	⑥	⑥		Ⓐ	⑦ a	⑦ b		Ⓐ	⑥	⑦		Ⓐ	⑥	⑦		⑥	Ⓐ	⑦			
0	0	**Leeds** **176** d.	...	0554	0819	...	0817	0840	0840	...	1019	1019	1057	...	1314	1353	1457	...	1639	1639	1721	...	...	...
27	27	Keighley **176** d.	...	0621	0843	...	0841	0907	0907	...	1042	1042	11120	...	1339	1416	1520	...	1710	1706	1746	...	...	...
42	42	Skipton **176** d.	0541	0638	0900	...	0855	0926	0926	...	1100	1100	1135	...	1401	1434	1536	...	1724	1725	1801	...	...	...
58	58	Hellifield d.	0556	0652	0914	...	0910	0940	0940	...	1114	1114	1149	...	1415	1448	1550	...	1739	1739	1816	...	...	...
66	66	Giggleswick d.	0607	0703	0925	...	0920	0952	0952	...	1124	1125	1159	...	1425	1459	1600	...	1749	1750	1826	...	...	...
103	103	Carnforth a.	0642	0738	1000	...	0956	1028	1028	...	1200	1200	1234	...	1501	1534	1636	...	1826	1825	1901	...	...	...
113		**Lancaster** a.	0652	0750	1013	...	1026	*1105**	1038	...	1211	1211	1246	...	1515	1545	1646	...	1838	1839	1913	...	...	...
120	112	Morecambe a.	*0736*	*0838*	1031	...	1031	*1130**	1055	...	1243	1236	1316	...	1535	1602	1714	...	1858	1901	1935	...	...	...
127	119	**Heysham Port** a.	...	...	...	...	...	...	*1227c*	...	1301	1254	*1354c*	...	...	...	...	...	...	...	...	...	...	...

		Ⓐ	⑥	⑥		Ⓐ	⑦	⑥		Ⓐ	⑦	Ⓐ		⑥	⑦	Ⓐ		⑥		⑦			
Heysham Port d.	...	...	...	...	...	...	...	1315	...	1317	*1405c*	...	...	...	...	...	...	...	...	...	...	...	...
Morecambe d.	...	*0607*	*0736*	1034	...	1034	1222	1331	...	1333	1446d	1619d	...	1616	1741	1908	...	1909	...	1947	...	...	...
Lancaster d.	...	0708	0823	1049	...	1049	1248	1348	...	1348	1432d	1604d	...	1640	1802	1924	...	1924	...	2002	...	...	...
Carnforth d.	...	0718	0833	1107	...	1107	1258	1358	...	1358	1500	1632	...	1650	1812	1934	...	1934	...	2012	...	...	...
Giggleswick d.	...	0752	0907	1142	...	1142	1332	1433	...	1433	1535	1708	...	1725	1847	2009	...	2009	...	2047	...	...	...
Hellifield d.	...	0803	0919	1153	...	1153	1344	1444	...	1444	1549	1720	...	1736	1858	2020	...	2020	...	2058	...	...	...
Skipton **176** d.	...	0826	0941	1213	...	1212	1403	1510	...	1510	1608	1740	...	1756	1918	2042	...	2038	...	2116	...	...	...
Keighley **176** d.	...	0837	0952	1223	...	1223	1413	1520	...	1520	1618	1750	...	1808	1928	2052	...	2048	...	2126	...	...	...
Leeds **176** a.	...	0906	1022	1248	...	1254	1441	1547	...	1547	1647	1815	...	1836	1956	2117	...	2116	...	2154	...	...	...

a – Until June 15.
b – From June 22.
c – Until Sep. 7.
d – Calls at Lancaster, then Morecambe.
* – Connection by 🚐.

175 LEEDS - HARROGATE - YORK 2nd class NT

km			⚒	Ⓐ	⑥	⑥	Ⓐ	⑥	Ⓐ	⑥	Ⓐ	⚒	⚒		⚒	⚒	Ⓐ	⑥	⚒	⚒	⚒	Ⓐ	⚒
0	**Leeds** **127 188** d.	⚒	0609	0629	0636	0713	0713	0743	0745	0754	0759	0829	0859	and at	1529	1559	1629	1629	1659	1713	1729	1744	1759
29	**Harrogate** d.		0645	0705	0712	0749	0749	0819	0821	0830	0834	0905	0935	the same	1605	1635	1706	1705	1735	1749	1805	1820	1835
36	Knaresborough d.		0655	0716	0721	0758	0759	0836	0830	0840	0845	0915	0945	minutes past each	1614	1645	1715	1714	1745	1801	1814	1829	1845
62	**York** **127 188** a.		0725	0745	0747	0826	0832	0900	0858	...	...	0945	...	hour until	1645	...	1750	1748	...	...	1847	1903	...

	⚒	Ⓐ	⚒		⚒	⑥	Ⓐ			⑦	⑦	⑦	⑦	⑦	⑦	⑦		⑦	⑦	⑦		⑦	⑦	
Leeds **127 188** d.	1829	1859	1929	...	2029	2120	2129	...	⑦	0954	1054	1154	1254	1358	1454	1554	...	1654	1754	1854	...	1954	2119	...
Harrogate d.	1905	1935	2005	...	2105	2156	2205	...		1048	1130	1233	1333	1433	1533	1634	...	1733	1833	1933	...	2033	2156	...
Knaresborough d.	1914	1945	2014	...	2114	2206	2216	...		1055	1139	1242	1327	1443	1542	1642	...	1742	1842	1942	...	2042	2206	...
York **127 188** a.	1945	...	2045	...	2144	...	...	...		1125	1208	1311	1413	1513	1610	1712	...	1810	1913	2013	...	2111	...	...

		⑥	Ⓐ	⑥	Ⓐ	Ⓐ	⑥	Ⓐ	⚒	⑥	Ⓐ	⚒	⚒	⚒	⚒		⚒	⚒	⚒	⚒	⚒	⑥	Ⓐ
York **127 188** d.	⚒	...	...	0653	0650	...	...	...	0757	...	...	0845	0911	...	1011	and at	...	1611	...	1704	1728	...	...
Knaresborough d.		0647	0700	0721	0721	0742	0751	0757	0821	0851	0855	0909	0935	1005	1035	the same minutes	1605	1635	1705	1734	1755	1805	1809
Harrogate d.		0656	0711	0731	0740	0751	0800	0806	0830	0900	0904	0918	0944	1014	1044	past each	1614	1644	1714	1743	1805	1818	1825
Leeds **127 188** a.		0734	0749	0808	0816	0832	0838	0840	0908	0937	0937	0957	1022	1052	1122	hour until	1652	1723	1755	1821	1842	1855	1901

	⚒	Ⓐ	⚒	⚒	⚒	⑥	Ⓐ			⑦	⑦	⑦		⑦	⑦	⑦		⑦	⑦	⑦		⑦	⑦	
York **127 188** d.	1811	...	1913	2011	2113	2157	2211	...	⑦	1114	1217	1320	...	1418	1517	1617	...	1718	1817	1917	...	2017	2127	...
Knaresborough d.	1835	1905	1937	2035	2137	2221	2236	...		1142	1242	1344	...	1442	1542	1641	...	1743	1842	1942	...	2042	2151	...
Harrogate d.	1844	1914	1946	2044	2146	2237	2247	...		1153	1253	1353	...	1452	1553	1651	...	1753	1853	1952	...	2053	2202	...
Leeds **127 188** a.	1925	1952	2025	2123	2224	2314	2324	...		1230	1330	1430	...	1529	1630	1728	...	1830	1930	2029	...	2130	2239	...

Additional trains	⚒A	⑦A	⑦	Ⓐ	⑥	⑥	⑦	Ⓐ	
Leeds d.	1959	2034	2226	2238	2233	2321	2323	2329	...
Harrogate d.	2025	2100	2303	2316	2310	2358	2359	0006	...

Additional trains	⚒	Ⓐ	ⒶA	⑥A	Ⓐ	⑦	⑦	⑦A	⑦
Harrogate d.	0605	0628	0734	0813	0814	0953	1053	1707	2312
Leeds a.	0645	0705	0806	0845	0852	1030	1130	1733	2350

A – 12 and 🍷 Harrogate - Leeds - London Kings Cross and v.v. (Table **180**).

176 WEST YORKSHIRE LOCAL SERVICES 2nd class NT

BRADFORD FORSTER SQUARE - SKIPTON

Journey: ± 38 minutes *30 km*

From Bradford Forster Square: Trains call at **Keighley** ± 21 minutes later.

Ⓐ: 0604, 0640, 0715, 0741, 0809, 0841, 0911 and every 30 minutes until 1611, 1638, 1711, 1738, 1816, 1841, 1907, 1936, 2007, 2105, 2205, 2309.

⑥: 0610, 0711, 0811, 0841 and every 30 minutes until 1611, 1640, 1711, 1741, 1811, 1841, 1907, 1936, 2007, 2105, 2201, 2306.

⑦: 1048, 1248, 1448, 1648, 1848, 2048, 2248.

From Skipton: Trains call at **Keighley** ± 13 minutes later.

Ⓐ: 0601, 0627, 0701, 0727, 0803, 0831, 0901 and every 30 minutes until 1431, 1500, 1531, 1601, 1635, 1701, 1726, 1801, 1833, 1859, 1931, 1954, 2054, 2156.

⑥: 0601, 0706, 0729, 0803, 0831, 0901 and every 30 minutes until 1431, 1500, 1531, 1601, 1633, 1701, 1729, 1801, 1831, 1859, 1931, 1954, 2054, 2154.

⑦: 0936, 1136, 1336, 1536, 1736, 1936, 2139.

Table continues on next page ▶ ▶ ▶

NT 2nd class — WEST YORKSHIRE local services — 176

LEEDS - DONCASTER

Stopping trains. For faster trains see Table 180. Journey: ± 50 minutes *48 km*

From Leeds:

Ⓐ: 0620, 0721, 0821, 0921, 1021, 1121, 1221, 1321, 1421, 1521, 1621, 1657, 1721, 1821, 1921, 2021, 2121, 2240.

⑥: 0621, 0721, 0821, 0921, 1021, 1121, 1221, 1321, 1421, 1521, 1621, 1721, 1821, 1921, 2021, 2121, 2216.

⑦: 1021, 1221, 1421, 1621, 1821, 2021, 2120.

From Doncaster:

Ⓐ: 0626, 0708, 0726, 0756, 0826, 0926, 1026, 1126, 1226, 1326, 1426, 1526, 1626, 1726, 1826, 1922, 2026, 2127, 2226.

⑥: 0626, 0726, 0826, 0926, 1026, 1126, 1226, 1326, 1426, 1526, 1626, 1726, 1826, 1922, 2026, 2122, 2226.

⑦: 0912, 1112, 1312, 1512, 1712, 1927, 2152.

LEEDS - SKIPTON

See also Tables 173/174 Journey: ± 45 minutes *42 km*

From Leeds: Trains call at **Keighley** ± 24 minutes later.

Ⓐ: 0616, 0656, 0725, 0751, 0826, 0856, 0926, 0956 and every 30 minutes until 1625, 1656, 1726, 1741, 1756, 1826, 1856, 1926, 1956, 2026, 2056, 2126, 2156, 2226, 2256, 2318.

⑥: 0656, 0756, 0826, 0856, 0926, 0956 and every 30 minutes until 1626, 1656, 1726, 1756, 1826, 1856, 1926, 1956, 2026, 2056, 2126, 2203, 2226, 2256, 2318.

⑦: 0840, 0900, 1016, 1126, 1216 and hourly until 2116, 2216, 2320.

From Skipton: Trains call at **Keighley** ± 13 minutes later.

Ⓐ: 0547, 0614, 0640, 0707, 0719, 0734, 0745, 0813, 0840, 0916, 0946 and every 30 minutes until 1617, 1647, 1718, 1747, 1815, 1846, 1917, 1946, 2022, 2046, 2116, 2217.

⑥: 0547, 0645, 0745, 0817, 0846, 0916, 0946, and every 30 minutes until 1617, 1647, 1718, 1747, 1817, 1846, 1917, 1946, 2016, 2046, 2116, 2146, 2217.

⑦: 0834, 0914, 1014 and hourly until 1814, 1923, 2014, 2116, 2214, 2314.

LEEDS - BRADFORD FORSTER SQUARE

For Leeds - Bradford Interchange see Tables 190/191 Journey: ± 21 minutes *22 km*

From Leeds:

Ⓐ: 0649, 0739, 0810, 0840, 0910, 0940, 1010, 1040, 1110, 1140, 1210, 1237, 1310, 1340, 1410, 1440, 1510, 1540, 1610, 1635, 1710, 1736, 1810, 1837, 1910, 2101.

⑥: 0710, 0810, 0840, 0910, 0940, 1010, 1040, 1110, 1140, 1210, 1240, 1310, 1340, 1410, 1440, 1510, 1540, 1610, 1635, 1710, 1740, 1810, 1840, 1910, 2158.

⑦: 0834, 0941 and hourly until 2241.

From Bradford Forster Square:

Ⓐ: 0559, 0630, 0655, 0759, 0825, 0901, 0931, 1001, 1031, 1101, 1131, 1201, 1231, 1301, 1331, 1401, 1431, 1501, 1531, 1601, 1631, 1701, 1731, 1801, 1827, 1901, 1931.

⑥: 0601, 0701, 0733, 0759, 0831, 0901, 0931, 1001, 1031, 1101, 1131, 1201, 1231, 1301, 1331, 1401, 1431, 1501, 1531, 1601, 1631, 1701, 1731, 1801, 1831, 1901, 1931.

⑦: 0912 and hourly until 2212, 2306.

LEEDS - ILKLEY

Journey: ± 30 minutes *26 km*

From Bradford Forster Square:

Ⓐ: 0602, 0634, 0702, 0729, 0735, 0802, 0835, 0902, 0932 and every 30 minutes until 1602, 1632, 1702, 1716, 1734, 1747, 1802, 1832, 1902, 1933, 2003, 2106, 2206, 2315.

⑥: 0602, 0702, 0802, 0832, 0902, 0932 and every 30 minutes until 1902, 1933, 2003, 2106, 2206, 2315.

⑦: 0912 and hourly until 2212, 2316.

From Ilkley:

Ⓐ: 0602, 0634, 0710, 0737, 0757, 0815, 0840, 0910, 0940 and every 30 minutes until 1510, 1540, 1612, 1640, 1714, 1742, 1804, 1812, 1840, 1910, 1941, 2029, 2121, 2221, 2321.

⑥: 0610, 0710, 0810, 0840, 0910, 0940 and every 30 minutes until 1910, 1941, 2021, 2121, 2221, 2321.

⑦: 0921 and hourly until 2321.

HUDDERSFIELD - WAKEFIELD WESTGATE

Journey: ± 33 minutes *25 km*

From Huddersfield:

Ⓐ: 0531, 0631, 0735, 0831, 0931, 1031, 1131, 1231, 1331, 1431, 1531, 1631, 1731, 1831, 1931, 2031, 2135.

⑥: 0640, 0735, 0831, 0931, 1031, 1131, 1231, 1331, 1431, 1531, 1631, 1731, 1831, 1931, 2031, 2135.

From Wakefield Westgate:

Ⓐ: 0643, 0744, 0844, 0944, 1044, 1144, 1244, 1344, 1444, 1544, 1644, 1744, 1844, 1948, 2050, 2144, 2248.

⑥: 0730, 0844, 0944, 1044, 1144, 1244, 1344, 1444, 1544, 1644, 1744, 1844, 1948, 2050, 2144, 2244.

BRADFORD FORSTER SQUARE - ILKLEY

Journey: ± 31 minutes *22 km*

From Bradford Forster Square:

Ⓐ: 0615, 0644, 0711, 0745, 0816, 0846, 0916, 0946 and every 30 minutes until 1616, 1644, 1717, 1746, 1811, 1846, 1941, 2038, 2138, 2238, 2320.

⑥: 0615, 0715, 0816, 0846, 0916, 0946 and every 30 minutes until 1616, 1644, 1716, 1746, 1816, 1846, 1941, 2038, 2138, 2238, 2320.

⑦: 1038, 1238, 1438, 1638, 1838, 2038, 2238.

From Ilkley:

Ⓐ: 0617, 0650, 0722, 0748, 0824, 0854, 0921, 0951 and every 30 minutes until 1821, 1851, 1921, 2005, 2040, 2140, 2240.

⑥: 0619, 0722, 0821, 0851, 0921, 0951 and every 30 minutes until 1821, 1851, 1921, 2005, 2040, 2140, 2240.

⑦: 0953, 1153, 1353, 1553, 1753, 1953, 2153.

NT 2nd class — Service until October 5 — HULL - BRIDLINGTON - SCARBOROUGH — 177

km		⚒	⚒	⚒	⚒		⚒	⚒	⑥		Ⓐ	⚒	Ⓐ	⑥		⑦	⑦	⑦	⑦		⑦	⑦	⑦
0	**Hull** △ d.	0653	0814	0947	1114	...	1314	1444	1614	...	1618	1738	1915	1922	...	0925	1025	1205	1405	...	1605	1800	1900
13	Beverley △ d.	0706	0827	1000	1128	...	1328	1457	1627	...	1631	1751	1928	1935	...	0938	1038	1218	1418	...	1618	1813	1913
31	Driffield △ d.	0723	0842	1015	1140	...	1340	1512	1641	...	1645	1808	1942	1949	...	0955	1053	1233	1433	...	1633	1825	1928
50	**Bridlington** △ a.	0739	0857	1031	1155	...	1355	1527	1656	...	1700	1824	1958	2005	...	1011	1108	1248	1448	...	1650	1839	1945
50	**Bridlington** d.	0741	0900	1037	1205	...	1405	1534	1703	...	1703	1834	2003	2018	...	1013	1111	1254	1454	...	1654	1843	...
71	Filey d.	0803	0922	1059	1227	...	1427	1556	1724	...	1724	1856	2025	2040	...	1035	1133	1316	1516	...	1716	1905	...
87	**Scarborough** a.	0822	0941	1117	1244	...	1445	1613	1743	...	1743	1913	2044	2059	...	1054	1151	1334	1535	...	1735	1925	...

		⚒	⚒	⚒	⚒		⚒	⚒	⚒		Ⓐ	⑥	⑥	Ⓐ		⑦	⑦	⑦		⑦	⑦	⑦	⑦
Scarborough d.	...	0650	0902	1000	1128	...	1328	1457	1623	...	1757	1757	1940	2003	...	...	1112	1206	...	1406	1606	1806	1937
Filey d.	...	0704	0916	1014	1142	...	1342	1511	1637	...	1811	1811	1954	2017	...	...	1126	1220	...	1420	1620	1820	1951
Bridlington a.	...	0726	0938	1036	1204	...	1404	1533	1659	...	1833	1833	2016	2042	...	...	1148	1242	...	1442	1642	1842	2013
Bridlington △ d.	...	0730	0941	1041	1209	...	1411	1536	1704	...	1841	1841	2023	2044	...	0951	1151	1245	...	1445	1645	1856	2016
Driffield △ d.	...	0746	0956	1056	1222	...	1424	1551	1717	...	1856	1856	2038	2100	...	1006	1206	1258	...	1458	1658	1911	2029
Beverley △ d.	...	0805	1011	1111	1236	...	1436	1606	1730	...	1911	1911	2053	2114	...	1021	1221	1311	...	1511	1711	1928	2041
Hull △ a.	...	0822	1027	1127	1254	...	1454	1623	1749	...	1927	1930	2111	2130	...	1037	1238	1327	...	1527	1728	1945	2057

△ – All trains Hull - Bridlington and v.v.:

From Hull on ⚒ at 0556, 0623, 0653, 0714, 0752, 0814, 0917, 0947, 1014, 1044, 1114, 1144, 1214, 1244, 1314, 1344, 1414, 1444, 1514, 1544, 1614⑥, 1618Ⓐ, 1644, 1714, 1738, 1814, 1915Ⓐ, 1922⑥, 2014, 2148; on ⑦ at 0900, 0925, 1025, 1125, 1205, 1255, 1405, 1502, 1605, 1655, 1715, 1800, 1900.

From Bridlington on ⚒ at 0644, 0714, 0730, 0808, 0905, 0941, 1011, 1041, 1111, 1141, 1209, 1241, 1311, 1341, 1411, 1441, 1511, 1536, 1609, 1641, 1704, 1736, 1815, 1841, 1910, 2023⑥, 2044Ⓐ, 2128, 2242; on ⑦ at 0951, 1151, 1245, 1345, 1445, 1545, 1645, 1720, 1746, 1816, 1856, 1956, 2016.

NT 2nd class — Subject to alteration July 28 - September 7 — HULL - YORK — 178

km		⚒	⑦	⚒	⚒	⑥	⑦	⚒		⑥	Ⓐ	⑦	⑥	⑦		Ⓐ	⚒	⑦	⚒	⑥		Ⓐ	⑥	⚒	⑦	⑦	⑥
0	**Hull** .... 181 189 d.	0707	0854	0902	1012	1107	1146	1204	...	1308	1315	1317	1415	1418	...	1422	1503	1606	1610	1711	...	1717	1725	1918	1925	2030	2102
50	Selby .. 181 189 d.	0748	0928	0939	1049	1141	1220	1239	...	1349	1358	1351	1449	1452	...	1458	1537	1640	1649	1800	...	1804	1759	1954	2000	2104	2136
84	**York** a.	0822	0952	1011	1120	1205	1253	1304	...	1422	1427	1417	1522	1525	...	1528	1606	1706	1715	1824	...	1827	1825	2024	2025	2128	2158

	Ⓐ	⑥	⚒	⑥	Ⓐ	⑦	⑥	⚒	⑦	⚒	⚒	⑦	⑥	⑦	Ⓐ	⑦	⑥	Ⓐ	⑦	⚒	⑥	Ⓐ	⑦	⑥	⑦	⑥	Ⓐ
York d.	0730	0740	0843	0951	1019	1040	1047	1145	1205	1247	1344	1354	1447	1452	1502	1606	1606	1611	1714	1725	1809	1840	1916	1950	2150	2212	2229
Selby .. 181 189 d.	0750	0800	0907	1010	1039	1059	1106	1204	1224	1306	1408	1423	1506	1511	1521	1634	1632	1637	1733	1751	1838	1912	1935	2009	2212	2231	2248
Hull .... 181 189 a.	0846	0856	0948	1052	1123	1141	1153	1251	1306	1351	1451	1504	1551	1552	1602	1715	1722	1728	1814	1834	1927	1959	2016	2048	2252	2316	2334

a – 3 - 6 minutes later on ⑥.

NT 2nd class — LINCOLN - SHEFFIELD — 179

km		⚒	⚒	⚒	Ⓐ	⚒		⚒	⚒	⚒	⚒	⚒	⚒	⚒	⚒	⚒		⑦	⑦	⑦	⑦	⑦	⑦
0	**Lincoln** d.	...	...	0700	...	0825	and at	1625	1722	...	1824	1943	2027	2127	...	...	...	...	1515	1715	1915	2110	...
26	Gainsborough Lea Rd d.	...	...	0722	...	0848	the same	1648	1744	...	1846	2005	2049	2149	...	...	...	...	1537	1737	1937	2132	...
40	Retford (Low Level) d.	...	0703	0740	...	0902	minutes	1702	1758	1814	1904	2018	2103	2203	2245	...	...	1450	1551	1751	1951	2146	2224
52	Worksop d.	0630	0716	0751	0814	0914	past each	1714	1810	1825	1916	2031	2115	2215	2258	2328	...	1501	1603	1803	2003	2158	2235
78	**Sheffield** a.	0702	0748	0824	0848	0949	hour until	1749	1835	1858	1954	2105	2146	2250	2333	0004	...	1533	1636	1835	2035	2229	2307

	⚒	⚒	⚒	⚒	Ⓐ	⚒		⚒	⚒	⚒	⚒	⚒	⚒	⚒	⚒		⑦	⑦	⑦	⑦	⑦	⑦
Sheffield d.	0539	0546	0643	0730	0744	0844	and at	1644	1723	1744	1845	1948	2045	2144	2244	...	1342	1355	1543	1743	1932	2106
Worksop a.	0601	0615	0714	0759	0810	0913	the same	1713	1753	1816	1915	2017	2124	2213	2322	...	1402	1423	1611	1811	2000	2136
Retford (Low Level) a.	0610	0638	0724	0809	...	0923	minutes	1723	1806	1826	1925	2027	...	2228	...	...	1412	1437	1621	1821	2010	2148
Gainsborough Lea Rd a.	0625	...	0738	0824	...	0938	past each	1738	...	1840	1939	2041	...	...	...	...	1426	...	1635	1835	2024	...
Lincoln a.	0653	...	0806	0852	...	1006	hour until	1806	...	1907	2006	2110	...	...	...	...	1454	...	1702	1903	2050	...

180 LONDON - LEEDS, YORK, NEWCASTLE and EDINBURGH

Most services convey 🍷 GR

Service on ⑦ valid until September 7. For additional services see Tables **127**, **181**, **182**, **183**, **184** and **188**.

km				Ⓐ	Ⓐ	Ⓐ	Ⓐ	Ⓐ	Ⓐ	Ⓐ	Ⓐ	Ⓐ	Ⓐ	Ⓐ	Ⓐ	Ⓐ	Ⓐ	Ⓐ	Ⓐ	Ⓐ	Ⓐ	Ⓐ	Ⓐ	Ⓐ	Ⓐ	Ⓐ
						A																A			
0	**London** Kings Cross	d.	Ⓐ	0550	...	...	0615	0630	0700	0705	0708	0730	0735	0800	0803	0830	0835	0900	0903	0908	0930	0935	1000	1003	1008	1030
44	Stevenage	d.		0612	...	...	0635	0640	|	|	0728	|	0755	|	|	|	0855	|	|	0929	|	0955	|	|	1029	|
123	Peterborough	d.		0643	...	...	0706	0721	0746	0752	0759	0816	|	|	0850	0916	|	0946	0952	1000	1016	|	|	1051	1100	1116
170	Grantham	d.		0703	...	...	0726	0740	|	|	0819	|	0840	|	|	|	0940	|	|	1021	|	1040	|	|	1121	|
193	Newark North Gate	d.		0715	...	...	0738	|	|	|	0831	0844	|	|	|	0944	|	|	|	1033	1044	|	|	|	1135	1144
223	Retford	d.		0730	...	...	0754	|	|	|	0846	|	|	|	|	|	|	|	|	1049	|	|	|	|	...	|
251	Doncaster	d.		0745	0615	...	0810	0813	|	0842	0901	0910	0914	|	0941	1010	1014	|	1043	1105	1110	1114	|	1142	...	1210
283	Wakefield Westgate	a.		0802	|	...	|	0831	|	0900	|	|	0931	|	0959	|	1031	|	1100	|	|	1131	|	1200	...	|
299	**Leeds**	a.		0818	|	0710	|	0848	|	0917	|	|	0948	|	1016	|	1048	|	1116	|	|	1148	|	1216	...	|
303	**York**	d.		▬	0639	0737	0835	...	0855	...	0925	0937	...	0953	...	1035	...	1054	...	1130	1136	...	1154	...	...	1235
351	Northallerton	d.		...	|	|	0853	...	|	...	...	|	...	|	...	1054	...	|	...	...	|	...	|	...	...	1254
374	Darlington	d.		Ⓐ	0707	0805	0908	...	0923	...	...	1006	...	1021	...	1108	...	1122	...	...	1207	...	1222	...	...	1308
409	Durham	d.			0723	0822	0924	...	|	...	...	1022	...	|	...	1124	...	|	...	...	1224	...	|	...	...	1324
432	**Newcastle**	d.		0625	0743	0842	0942	...	0954	...	...	1042	...	1054	...	1142	...	1153	...	...	1245	...	1253	...	...	1342
488	Alnmouth	a.		0654	0808	|	...	...	|	...	...	1107	...	|	...	...	...	|	...	...	1310	...	|	...	...	...
540	Berwick upon Tweed	a.		0717	0832	0931	...	...	1038	...	...	|	...	1138	...	...	...	1237	...	...	|	...	1337	...	...	...
632	**Edinburgh** Waverley	a.		0806	0921	1020	...	...	1122	...	...	1211	...	1222	...	...	...	1322	...	...	1415	...	1420	...	...	...

		Ⓐ	Ⓐ	Ⓐ	Ⓐ	Ⓐ	Ⓐ	Ⓐ	Ⓐ	Ⓐ	Ⓐ	Ⓐ	Ⓐ	Ⓐ	Ⓐ	Ⓐ	Ⓐ	Ⓐ	Ⓐ	Ⓐ	Ⓐ	Ⓐ	Ⓐ	Ⓐ	Ⓐ	Ⓐ
								B										A								C
London Kings Cross	d.	1035	1100	1105	1108	1130	1135	1200	1205	1208	1230	1235	1300	1305	1308	1330	1335	1400	1405	1408	1430	1435	1500	1505	1508	1530
Stevenage	d.	1055	|	|	1129	|	1155	|	|	1229	|	1255	|	|	1329	|	1355	|	|	1428	|	1455	|	|	1529	|
Peterborough	d.	|	|	1152	1159	1216	|	|	1251	1300	1316	|	1346	1352	1400	1416	|	|	1451	1500	1516	|	|	1551	1600	1616
Grantham	d.	1140	|	|	1219	|	1240	|	|	1322	|	1340	|	|	1421	|	1440	|	|	1520	|	1540	|	|	1621	|
Newark North Gate	d.	|	|	|	1231	1244	|	|	|	1336	1344	|	|	|	1434	1444	|	|	|	1534	1544	|	|	|	1633	1645
Retford	d.	|	|	|	1246	|	|	|	|	...	|	|	|	|	1449	|	|	|	|	...	|	|	|	|	1649	|
Doncaster	d.	1214	|	1242	1305	1310	1315	|	1342	...	1410	1414	|	1442	1504	1510	1514	|	1542	...	1610	1614	|	1641	1705	1710
Wakefield Westgate	a.	1231	|	1300	|	|	1332	|	1359	...	|	1431	|	1459	|	|	1531	|	1559	...	|	1631	|	1659	|	|
Leeds	a.	1248	|	1316	|	|	1348	|	1416	...	|	1448	|	1516	|	|	1548	|	1616	...	|	1648	|	1716	|	|
York	d.	...	1253	...	1329	1336	...	1355	...	...	1435	...	1454	...	1530	1535	...	1554	...	...	1635	...	1654	...	1729	1736
Northallerton	d.	...	|	...	...	|	...	|	...	...	1454	...	|	...	...	1554	...	|	...	...	1654	...	|	...	...	1751
Darlington	d.	...	1321	...	...	1407	...	1423	...	...	1508	...	1522	...	...	1608	...	1622	...	...	1708	...	1722	...	...	1809
Durham	d.	...	|	...	...	1423	...	|	...	...	1524	...	|	...	...	1624	...	|	...	...	1724	...	|	...	...	1825
Newcastle	d.	...	1352	...	...	1444	...	1454	...	...	1542	...	1553	...	...	1642	...	1653	...	...	1742	...	1753	...	...	1844
Alnmouth	a.	...	|	...	...	1509	...	|	...	...	...	...	|	...	...	...	...	|	...	...	...	...	|	...	...	1909
Berwick upon Tweed	a.	...	1436	...	...	|	...	1539	...	...	...	...	1637	...	...	...	...	1737	...	...	...	...	1835	...	...	|
Edinburgh Waverley	a.	...	1521	...	...	1613	...	1622	...	...	...	...	1722	...	...	...	...	1823	...	...	...	...	1922	...	...	2013

		Ⓐ	Ⓐ	Ⓐ	Ⓐ	Ⓐ	Ⓐ	Ⓐ	Ⓐ	Ⓐ	Ⓐ	Ⓐ	Ⓐ	Ⓐ	Ⓐ	Ⓐ	Ⓐ	Ⓐ	Ⓐ	Ⓐ	Ⓐ	Ⓐ	Ⓐ	Ⓐ	Ⓐ	Ⓐ
			A							D ♧		E			F			G			H					
London Kings Cross	d.	1535	1600	1606	1609	1630	1633	1700	1703	1719	1730	1733	1749	1800	1803	1819	1830	1833	1900	1903	1906	1930	1933	2000	2005	2035
Stevenage	d.	1555	|	|	1630	|	1653	|	|	|	|	1755	|	|	|	|	|	1853	|	|	1928	|	1953	|	|	2055
Peterborough	d.	|	|	1653	1701	1716	|	|	1751	1807	1817	|	1837	|	1851	1908	1918	|	|	1952	2000	2016	|	|	2051	2126
Grantham	d.	1641	|	|	1722	|	1740	|	|	1828	|	1842	1906	|	|	1928	|	1943	|	|	2021	|	2040	|	|	2146
Newark North Gate	d.	|	|	|	1736	1744	|	|	|	1840	1845	|	|	|	1922	|	1946	|	|	|	2036	2044	|	|	2120	2159
Retford	d.	|	|	|	...	|	1802	|	|	|	|	|	1928	|	|	|	|	2005	|	|	...	|	|	|	|	|
Doncaster	d.	1714	|	1745	...	1810	1818	|	1841	1908	|	1915	1944	|	1950	|	2012	2021	|	2041	...	2110	2114	|	2145	2223
Wakefield Westgate	a.	1731	|	1805	...	|	1835	|	1859	...	|	1933	2002	|	2007	|	|	2038	|	2100	...	|	2131	|	2207	2240
Leeds	a.	1748	|	1821	...	|	1851	|	1917	...	|	1948	2020	|	2021	|	|	2053	|	2118	...	|	2149	|	2223	2258
York	d.	...	1754	...	...	1837	...	1854	...	...	1929	...	...	1951	...	2020	2036	...	2053	...	...	2134	...	2153	...	...
Northallerton	d.	...	|	...	...	1856	...	|	...	...	|	...	...	|	...	2038	|	...	|	...	...	2152	...	|	...	...
Darlington	d.	...	1823	...	...	1910	...	1922	...	...	1957	...	...	2019	...	2053	2105	...	2121	...	...	2207	...	2221	...	...
Durham	d.	...	|	...	...	1926	...	|	...	...	2013	...	...	|	...	2109	2121	...	|	...	...	2223	...	2237	...	...
Newcastle	d.	...	1854	...	...	1945	...	1954	...	...	2031	...	...	2052	...	2127	2141	...	2156	...	...	2242f	...	2256	...	...
Alnmouth	a.	...	|	...	...	|	...	|	...	...	...	...	...	|	...	...	2210	...	|	...	...	2311f	...	...	...	...
Berwick upon Tweed	a.	...	1938	...	...	|	...	2038	...	...	...	...	...	2136	...	...	|	...	2238	...	...	2336f	...	...	...	...
Edinburgh Waverley	a.	...	2022	...	...	2114	...	2122	...	...	...	...	...	2229	...	...	2317	...	2330	...	...	0028f	...	...	...	...

		Ⓐ	Ⓐ	Ⓐ	Ⓐ			⑥	⑥	⑥	⑥	⑥	⑥	⑥	⑥	⑥	⑥	⑥	⑥	⑥	⑥	⑥	⑥	⑥	⑥	⑥
										A											A					
London Kings Cross	d.	2100	2135	2200	2330	...	⑥	...	...	...	0615	0700	0703	0730	0800	0803	0830	0900	0903	0930	1000	1003	1030	1100	1103	1130
Stevenage	d.	2121	2156	|	|	...		...	...	...	0635	0720	0725	|	|	|	|	|	0923	|	|	|	|	|	1123	|
Peterborough	d.	2152	2227	2247	0017s	...		...	...	...	0706	|	0755	0816	|	0849	0916	|	0954	1016	|	1051	1116	|	1154	1216
Grantham	d.	|	2249	2308	0045s	...		...	...	...	0726	|	0814	|	|	0909	|	|	1015	|	|	1110	|	|	1214	|
Newark North Gate	d.	2220	2301	2320	0057s	...		...	...	...	0738	|	0826	|	|	0921	0944	|	1027	|	|	1123	1144	|	1226	|
Retford	d.	|	2317	|	|	...		...	...	...	0754	|	|	0855	|	|	|	|	|	1054	|	|	|	|	|	1254
Doncaster	d.	2246	2333	2351	0124s	...		...	0610	...	0810	|	0851	0912	|	0951	1010	|	1051	1110	|	1151	1210	|	1251	1311
Wakefield Westgate	a.	|	2353	|	|	...		...	|	...	|	|	0907	|	|	1008	|	|	1107	|	|	1207	|	|	1307	|
Leeds	a.	|	0010	|	0236	...		...	|	0710	|	|	0924	|	|	1024	|	|	1125	|	|	1224	|	|	1325	|
York	d.	2312	...	0042	...	...		...	0634	0737	0835	0855	...	0937	0953	...	1035	1053	...	1136	1154	...	1235	1253	...	1336
Northallerton	d.	2342	...	0110s	...	...		...	0652	|	0853	|	...	|	|	...	1054	|	...	|	|	...	1254	|	...	|
Darlington	d.	2357	...	0124s	...	...		...	0707	0806	0908	0923	...	1005	1021	...	1108	1121	...	1205	1223	...	1308	1321	...	1405
Durham	d.	0013	...	0143s	...	...		...	0723	0822	0924	|	...	1021	|	...	1124	|	...	1221	|	...	1324	|	...	1421
Newcastle	d.	0043	...	0216	...	...		0630	0743	0842	0945	0955	...	1040	1055	...	1145	1155	...	1241	1255	...	1345	1355	...	1440
Alnmouth	a.	...	...	...	...	...		0657	0808	|	|	|	...	1105	|	...	|	|	...	1306	|	...	|	|	...	1505
Berwick upon Tweed	a.	...	...	...	...	...		0721	0832	0931	|	1039	...	|	1139	...	|	1239	...	|	1339	...	|	1439	...	|
Edinburgh Waverley	a.	...	...	...	...	...		0815	0920	1024	1110	1128	...	1212	1228	...	1310	1328	...	1413	1424	...	1510	1528	...	1610

		⑥	⑥	⑥	⑥	⑥	⑥	⑥	⑥	⑥	⑥	⑥	⑥	⑥	⑥	⑥	⑥	⑥	⑥	⑥	⑥	⑥	⑥	⑥	⑥	⑥
			B						A											D ♧		E			H	
London Kings Cross	d.	1135	1200	1203	1230	1300	1303	1330	1400	1403	1430	1500	1503	1530	1600	1603	1630	1700	1703	1710	1730	1735	1800	1803	1808	1830
Stevenage	d.	|	|	|	|	|	1323	|	|	|	|	|	1524	|	|	|	|	|	1724	|	|	|	|	|	1829	|
Peterborough	d.	1223	|	1252	1316	|	1354	1416	|	1450	1516	|	1554	1616	|	1650	1716	|	1754	1800	1817	1823	|	1849	1900	1916
Grantham	d.	|	|	1315	|	1401	1414	|	|	1509	|	|	1614	|	|	1712	|	|	1814	1821	|	|	|	|	1921	|
Newark North Gate	d.	|	|	1327	1344	|	1426	|	|	1523	1544	|	1626	|	|	1725	1744	|	1826	|	1846	|	|	1917	1934	1944
Retford	d.	|	|	|	|	|	|	1455	|	|	|	|	|	1654	|	|	|	|	|	|	|	|	|	1933	...	|
Doncaster	d.	1314	|	1354	1410	|	1451	1512	|	1551	1610	|	1651	1710	|	1751	1810	|	1851	1854	1911	1915	|	1949	...	2010
Wakefield Westgate	a.	1331	|	1411	|	|	1507	|	|	1607	|	|	1707	|	|	1808	|	|	1908	...	|	1932	|	2006	...	|
Leeds	a.	1348	|	1429	|	|	1525	|	|	1624	|	|	1725	|	|	1825	|	|	1924	...	|	1948	|	2022	...	|
York	d.	...	1354	...	1435	1453	...	1536	1553	...	1635	1654	...	1735	1752	...	1837	1854	...	...	1936	...	1954	...	...	2035
Northallerton	d.	...	|	...	1454	|	...	|	|	...	1654	|	...	|	|	...	1856	|	...	...	|	...	|	...	...	2054
Darlington	d.	...	1423	...	1508	1521	...	1605	1621	...	1708	1723	...	1803	1821	...	1910	1924	...	...	2004	...	2022	...	...	2108
Durham	d.	...	|	...	1524	|	...	1621	|	...	1724	|	...	1819	|	...	1926	|	...	...	2021	...	|	...	...	2124
Newcastle	d.	...	1455	...	1545	1555	...	1640	1655	...	1745	1755	...	1840	1854	...	1945	1955	...	...	2040	...	2055	...	...	2142
Alnmouth	a.	...	|	...	|	|	...	1705	|	...	|	|	...	1905	|	...	|	|	...	...	...	...	2124	...	...	...
Berwick upon Tweed	a.	...	1539	...	|	1639	...	|	1739	...	|	1839	...	|	1938	...	|	2039	...	...	...	...	2149	...	...	...
Edinburgh Waverley	a.	...	1624	...	1712	1729	...	1809	1826	...	1911	1928	...	2011	2024	...	2114	2124	...	...	...	...	2237	...	...	...

A – To/from Aberdeen (Table **224**).
B – To/from Inverness (Table **221**).
C – To/from Glasgow Central (Table **220**).
D – To/from Hull (Table **181**).
E – To/from Harrogate (Table **175**).
F – To/from Skipton (Table **173**).
G – To/from Bradford Forster Square (Table **182**).
H – To/from Lincoln (Table **186**).
f – ⑤ only.
s – Calls to set down only.
u – Calls to pick up only.
♧ – Hull services are subject to alteration July 27 - Sep. 7.

GR Most services convey 🍷 LONDON - LEEDS, YORK, NEWCASTLE and EDINBURGH 180

Service on ⑦ valid until September 7. For additional services see Tables **127**, **181**, **182**, **183**, **184**, and **188**.

	⑥ F	⑥	⑥ G	⑥	⑥	⑥	⑥			⑦	⑦	⑦	⑦	⑦	⑦	⑦ A	⑦	⑦	⑦	⑦	⑦	⑦	⑦	⑦ B	⑦
London Kings Cross d.	1835	1900	1930	2000	2030	2100	2200	...	⑦	...	...	...	0900	0903	0930	1000	1003	1020	1030	1100	1103	1120	1130	1200	1203
Stevenage d.	|	|	1950	|	|	|	|	...		...	...	...	|	0923	|	|	|	|	|	|	1123	|	|	|	|
Peterborough d.	1923	|	2021	2048	2116	2147	2247	...		...	...	...	|	0954	1016	|	1050	1110	1116	|	1154	1209	1216	|	1250
Grantham d.	|	|	2041	|	2136	|	2307	...		...	...	...	|	1014	|	|	1110	|	|	|	1214	|	|	|	1310
Newark North Gate d.	|	|	2053	2116	2148	|	2319	...		...	...	...	|	1026	|	|	1122	|	1144	|	1226	|	|	|	1322
Retford d.	|	|	|	|	2203	|	2334	...		...	...	...	|	|	1055	|	|	|	|	|	|	|	1255	|	|
Doncaster d.	2013	|	2118	2141	2219	|	2349	...		...	...	0937	|	1051	1111	|	1147	1159	1210	|	1251	|	1311	|	1347
Wakefield Westgate a.	2032	|	2134	|	2235	|	0005	...		...	...	|	|	1108	|	|	1204	|	|	|	1308	|	|	|	1404
Leeds a.	2047	|	2150	|	2252	|	0023	...		...	0830	|	|	1126	|	|	1221	|	|	|	1325	|	|	|	1421
York d.	...	2053	...	2206	...	2254	...	...		...	0900	1001	1049	...	1135	1152	...	1223	1235	1251	...	1317	1335	1352	...
Northallerton d.	...	|	...	|	...	2312	...	...		...	0918	|	|	...	|	|	...	|	1253	|	...	1336	|	|	...
Darlington d.	...	2121	...	2235	...	2327	...	...		...	0935	1029	1117	...	1203	1221	...	1251	1308	1319	...	1351	1403	1421	...
Durham d.	...	|	...	2251	...	2343	...	...		...	0951	1045	|	...	1219	|	...	|	1324	|	...	1407	1419	|	...
Newcastle d.	...	2151	...	2309	...	0001	...	...		0915	1012	1104	1148	...	1244	1253	...	1322	1343	1350	...	1426	1443	1453	...
Alnmouth a.	...	...	...	...	...	...	...	...		|	1042	|	|	...	1309	|	...	...	|	|	...	|	1508	|	...
Berwick upon Tweed a.	...	...	...	...	...	...	...	...		0959	1107	1148	1232	...	|	1337	...	...	|	1434	...	|	|	1537	...
Edinburgh Waverley a.	...	...	...	...	...	...	...	...		1045	1158	1232	1316	...	1418	1421	...	...	1508	1518	...	1558	1616	1621	...

	⑦	⑦	⑦	⑦	⑦	⑦ A	⑦	⑦	⑦	⑦	⑦	⑦	⑦	⑦ C	⑦	⑦	⑦	⑦ D♧	⑦	⑦	⑦	⑦ E	⑦	⑦ F	⑦
London Kings Cross d.	1220	1230	1300	1303	1330	1400	1403	1430	1500	1503	1530	1600	1605	1630	1635	1700	1705	1720	1730	1735	1800	1805	1830	1835	1900
Stevenage d.	|	|	|	1323	|	|	|	|	|	1523	|	|	|	|	1655	|	|	|	|	1755	|	|	|	1855	|
Peterborough d.	1309	1316	|	1354	1416	|	1452	1517	|	1554	1617	|	1653	1716	|	|	1751	|	1817	|	|	1853	1917	|	|
Grantham d.	|	|	|	1414	|	|	1512	|	|	1614	1638	|	1713	|	1740	|	|	1826	1837	1842	|	|	|	1941	|
Newark North Gate d.	|	1344	|	1426	|	|	1524	1546	|	1626	|	|	1725	1744	|	|	1819	1838	|	|	|	1922	1945	|	|
Retford d.	|	|	|	|	1455	|	|	|	|	1642	|	|	|	|	1803	|	|	|	|	|	|	|	|	2004	|
Doncaster d.	1358	1410	|	1451	1511	|	1550	1612	|	1658	1712	|	1751	1810	1820	|	1844	1905	1912	1915	|	1950	2010	2020	|
Wakefield Westgate a.	|	|	|	1508	|	|	1607	|	|	1715	|	|	1810	|	1838	|	1901	...	|	1932	|	2007	|	2037	|
Leeds a.	|	|	|	1525	|	|	1625	|	|	1732	|	|	1828	|	1856	|	1918	...	|	1951	|	2023	|	2052	|
York d.	1423	1435	1453	...	1535	1552	...	1636	1654	...	1736	1749	...	1835	...	1849	...	...	1938	...	1950	...	2036	...	2052
Northallerton d.	|	1453	|	...	|	|	...	1655	|	...	|	|	...	1853	...	|	...	...	|	...	|	...	2055	...	|
Darlington d.	1451	1508	1521	...	1603	1622	...	1710	1723	...	1805	1817	...	1908	...	1917	...	...	2006	...	2018	...	2109	...	2121
Durham d.	1507	1524	|	...	1619	|	...	1727	|	...	1821	|	...	1924	...	|	...	...	2022	...	|	...	2125	...	|
Newcastle d.	1525	1544	1552	...	1638	1653	...	1747	1754	...	1841	1852	...	1943	...	1952	...	...	2041	...	2059	...	2143	...	2152
Alnmouth a.	...	|	|	...	1703	|	...	|	|	...	1906	|	...	|	...	|	...	...	2110	...	|	...	...	...	2223
Berwick upon Tweed a.	...	|	1636	...	|	1737	...	|	1838	...	|	1936	...	|	...	2036	...	...	|	...	2143	...	...	...	2248
Edinburgh Waverley a.	...	1709	1720	...	1809	1821	...	1913	1922	...	2013	2020	...	2114	...	2120	...	...	2218	...	2228	...	...	...	2339

	⑦	⑦ H	⑦	⑦	⑦	⑦	⑦	⑦	⑦	⑦	⑦
London Kings Cross d.	1905	1908	1930	1935	2000	2005	2035	2100	2135	2200	2235
Stevenage d.	|	1929	|	1955	|	|	2055	|	2156	|	|
Peterborough d.	1951	2001	2018	2026	2046	2051	2126	2146	2227	2247	2323s
Grantham d.	|	2022	|	2046	|	|	2146	|	2248	|	2344s
Newark North Gate d.	2019	2036	2047	|	|	|	2158	|	2301	|	2355s
Retford d.	|	...	|	|	|	2130	|	|	2317	|	|
Doncaster d.	2045	...	2115	2119	|	2145	2224	|	2337	2343	0024s
Wakefield Westgate a.	2102	...	|	2136	|	2202	2240	|	2357	|	|
Leeds a.	2118	...	|	2152	|	2219	2257	|	0013	|	0130
York d.	...	...	2140	...	2157	...	...	2304	...	0035	...
Northallerton d.	...	...	|	...	|	...	...	2327	...	0106s	...
Darlington d.	...	...	2219	...	2239	...	...	2353	...	0120s	...
Durham d.	...	...	2235	...	2255	...	...	0009	...	0138s	...
Newcastle d.	...	...	2308	...	2327	...	...	0041	...	0210	...
Alnmouth a.	...	...	...	...	...	...	...	...	...	...	...
Berwick upon Tweed a.	...	...	...	...	...	...	...	...	...	...	...
Edinburgh Waverley a.	...	...	...	...	...	...	...	...	...	...	...

		Ⓐ	Ⓐ	Ⓐ	Ⓐ	Ⓐ	Ⓐ	Ⓐ	Ⓐ G
Edinburgh Waverley d.	Ⓐ	...	...	...	...	...	...	...	...
Berwick upon Tweed d.		...	...	...	...	...	...	...	...
Alnmouth d.		...	...	...	...	...	...	...	...
Newcastle d.		...	...	...	0445	...	0525	...	...
Durham d.		...	...	...	0500	...	0539	...	...
Darlington d.		...	...	...	0518	...	0558	...	...
Northallerton d.		...	...	...	0529	...	0609	...	...
York d.		...	...	...	0600	...	0631	...	...
Leeds d.		...	0505	0530	|	0605	|	0640	0700
Wakefield Westgate d.		...	0517	0543	|	0618	|	0652	0713
Doncaster d.		...	0536	0603	0623	0636	0654	0712	|
Retford d.		...	0551	|	|	0651	|	|	|
Newark North Gate d.		0535	0606	0628	0647	0707	|	0737	|
Grantham d.		0547	0618	0640	0700	0720	0726	|	|
Peterborough d.		0610	0639	0700	0721	0741	0750	|	|
Stevenage a.		|	|	|	|	|	|	|	|
London Kings Cross a.		0700	0731	0752	0812	0834	0843	0850	0859

	Ⓐ	Ⓐ H	Ⓐ	Ⓐ	Ⓐ	Ⓐ D	Ⓐ F	Ⓐ	Ⓐ E	Ⓐ	Ⓐ	Ⓐ	Ⓐ	Ⓐ	Ⓐ	Ⓐ	Ⓐ	Ⓐ	Ⓐ C	Ⓐ	Ⓐ	Ⓐ	Ⓐ	Ⓐ	Ⓐ
Edinburgh Waverley d.	...	...	...	...	0540	...	...	...	...	0548	0626	...	...	0655	0730	...	...	...	0800	0830	...	...	...	...	0930
Berwick upon Tweed d.	...	...	...	...	|	...	...	0600	...	0634	0709	...	...	|	0811	...	...	...	|	0912	...	...	...	...	1011
Alnmouth d.	...	...	...	...	|	...	...	0621	...	0655	|	...	...	|	|	...	...	...	0900	|	...	...	...	...	|
Newcastle d.	0556	...	...	0630	0704	...	...	0655	...	0729	0757	...	...	0825	0859	...	...	...	0930	1000	...	...	...	1025	1059
Durham d.	0610	...	...	0643	|	...	...	0708	...	0742	|	...	...	0838	|	...	...	...	0943	|	...	...	...	1038	|
Darlington d.	0629	...	...	0702	|	...	...	0731	...	0801	0827	...	...	0857	0926	...	...	...	1001	1029	...	...	...	1057	1126
Northallerton d.	|	...	...	0714	|	...	...	|	...	|	|	...	...	0908	|	...	...	...	|	|	...	...	...	1108	|
York d.	0659	...	...	0737	|	...	...	0802	...	0831	0856	...	...	0930	0956	...	1001	...	1031	1059	...	...	...	1130	1156
Leeds d.	|	...	0715	|	|	...	0740	|	0817	|	|	0845	0916	|	|	0945	|	1015	|	|	1045	...	1115	|	|
Wakefield Westgate d.	|	...	0727	|	|	...	0752	|	0829	|	|	0857	0928	|	|	0957	|	1028	|	|	1058	...	1128	|	|
Doncaster d.	|	...	0746	|	|	0758	0811	|	0847	0855	|	0917	0947	0954	|	1017	1025	1046	1056	|	1117	...	1146	1154	|
Retford d.	|	...	|	|	|	|	|	0836	|	|	|	|	|	|	|	|	1039	|	|	|	|	...	|	|	|
Newark North Gate d.	|	0756	|	|	|	0823	0838	|	|	0918	|	|	|	1018	|	|	1054	|	1119	|	|	1154	|	1217	|
Grantham d.	|	|	0818	|	|	0836	|	|	0920	|	|	|	1018	|	|	|	1106	1118	|	|	|	1206	1218	|	|
Peterborough d.	0812	0827	|	0843	|	0902	0907	|	|	0950	|	1009	|	1051	|	1108	1128	|	1152	|	1209	1228	|	1250	|
Stevenage a.	|	0856	0902	|	|	|	|	|	1007	|	|	|	1101	|	|	|	1156	1201	|	|	|	1257	1302	|	|
London Kings Cross a.	0907	0927	0929	0937	0940	0954	1000	1004	1035	1042	1052	1100	1128	1142	1151	1159	1223	1228	1243	1251	1300	1325	1328	1342	1348

	Ⓐ	Ⓐ	Ⓐ	Ⓐ	Ⓐ A	Ⓐ	Ⓐ	Ⓐ	Ⓐ	Ⓐ B	Ⓐ	Ⓐ	Ⓐ	Ⓐ	Ⓐ A	Ⓐ	Ⓐ	Ⓐ	Ⓐ	Ⓐ	Ⓐ	Ⓐ	Ⓐ	Ⓐ	Ⓐ
Edinburgh Waverley d.	...	...	...	1000	1030	...	...	...	...	1130	...	...	...	1200	1230	...	...	...	...	1330	...	...	...	1400	1430
Berwick upon Tweed d.	...	...	...	|	1112	...	...	...	...	|	...	...	...	|	1312	...	...	...	...	1411	...	...	...	|	1512
Alnmouth d.	...	...	...	1100	|	...	...	...	...	|	...	...	...	1300	|	...	...	...	...	|	...	...	...	1500	|
Newcastle d.	...	...	...	1130	1200	...	...	...	1225	1257	...	...	...	1330	1400	...	...	...	1425	1459	...	...	...	1530	1559
Durham d.	...	...	...	1143	|	...	...	...	1238	|	...	...	...	1343	|	...	...	...	1438	|	...	...	...	1544	|
Darlington d.	...	...	...	1201	1229	...	...	...	1257	1326	...	...	...	1401	1429	...	...	...	1457	1526	...	...	...	1603	1628
Northallerton d.	...	...	...	|	|	...	...	...	1308	|	...	...	...	|	|	...	...	...	1508	|	...	...	...	|	|
York d.	...	1201	...	1231	1259	...	...	...	1330	1356	...	1401	...	1431	1459	...	...	...	1530	1556	...	1601	...	1633	1657
Leeds d.	1145	|	1215	|	|	1245	...	1315	|	|	1345	|	1415	|	|	1445	...	1515	|	|	1545	|	1615	|	|
Wakefield Westgate d.	1157	|	1228	|	|	1258	...	1328	|	|	1358	|	1428	|	|	1458	...	1528	|	|	1558	|	1628	|	|
Doncaster d.	1217	1225	1246	1255	|	1317	...	1346	1354	|	1417	1425	1446	1455	|	1517	...	1546	1554	|	1616	1624	1646	1656	|
Retford d.	|	1239	|	|	|	|	...	|	|	|	|	1441	|	|	|	|	...	|	|	|	|	1640	|	|	|
Newark North Gate d.	|	1254	|	1318	|	|	1354	|	1417	|	|	1456	|	1518	|	|	1552	|	1620	|	|	1655	|	1720	|
Grantham d.	|	1306	1318	|	|	|	1406	1418	|	|	|	1508	1517	|	|	|	1604	1618	|	|	|	1707	1718	|	|
Peterborough d.	1307	1328	|	1350	|	1409	1427	|	1452	|	1509	1529	|	1550	|	1608	1625	|	1650	|	1709	1729	|	1751	|
Stevenage a.	|	1357	1401	|	|	|	1456	1501	|	|	|	1557	1601	|	|	|	1655	1702	|	|	|	1758	1803	|	|
London Kings Cross a.	1358	1425	1428	1442	1452	1501	1524	1527	1544	1551	1601	1624	1627	1643	1651	1659	1722	1728	1742	1753	1800	1826	1829	1842	1851

For footnotes see page 148.

First Excel service X1 🚌 PETERBOROUGH - KINGS LYNN 🚌 180a

From Peterborough railway station: Journey 75 minutes. Buses call at **Wisbech** bus station ± 39 minutes later.

Ⓐ: 0704, 0734, 0809 and every 30 minutes until 1309, 1349, 1419, 1449, 1520 and every 30 minutes until 1720, 1755, 1823, 1853, 1923, 2023, 2118, 2318.

⑥: 0739, 0809 and every 30 minutes until 1309, 1349, 1419, 1449, 1520 and every 30 minutes until 1720, 1755, 1823, 1853, 1923, 2023, 2118, 2318.

⑦: 0908, 1008 and hourly until 2108, 2313.

180 EDINBURGH - NEWCASTLE - YORK and LEEDS - LONDON

Most services convey 🍸 GR

Service on ⑦ valid until September 7. For additional services see Tables 127, 181, 182, 183, 184, and 188.

	Ⓐ	Ⓐ	Ⓐ	Ⓐ	Ⓐ	Ⓐ	Ⓐ	Ⓐ	Ⓐ	Ⓐ	Ⓐ	Ⓐ	Ⓐ	Ⓐ	Ⓐ	Ⓐ	Ⓐ	Ⓐ	Ⓐ			⑥	⑥	⑥	⑥
															A				A						
Edinburgh Waverley d.	...	...	...	...	1530	...	...	...	...	1630	...	...	1700	...	1731	...	1830	...	2100	...	⑥	...	...	...	...
Berwick upon Tweed d.	...	...	...	...	1611	...	...	...	...	1712	...	...	|	...	1818	...	1917	...	2148	...		...	...	...	...
Alnmouth d.	...	...	...	...	|	...	...	...	...	|	...	...	1800	...	|	...	1940	...	2211	...		...	...	...	...
Newcastle d.	...	...	...	1625	1659	...	...	...	1725	1759	...	...	1830	...	1906	...	2016	2115	2246	...		...	0445	...	0600
Durham d.	...	...	...	1638	|	...	...	...	1738	|	...	...	1843	...	|	...	2029	2128	2300	...		...	0500	...	0613
Darlington d.	...	...	...	1657	1726	...	...	...	1757	1828	...	...	1901	...	1935	...	2048	2147	2322	...		...	0518	...	0632
Northallerton d.	...	...	...	1708	|	...	...	...	1808	|	...	...	|	...	|	...	|	2158	2348s	...		...	0529	...	|
York d.	...	...	...	1731	1756	...	1801	...	1830	1857	...	...	1931	...	2005	...	2117	2220	0018	...		...	0601	...	0701
Leeds d.	1645	...	1715	|	|	1745	|	1815	|	|	1845	1916	|	1945	|	2045	|	|	0047	...		0505	|	0605	|
Wakefield Westgate d.	1658	...	1728	|	|	1758	|	1828	|	|	1857	1928	|	1958	|	2058	|	|	...	...		0517	|	0618	|
Doncaster d.	1717	...	1746	1755	|	1817	1825	1846	1855	|	1915	1946	1955	2017	2028	2117	2140	2243	...	...		0536	0624	0636	0725
Retford d.	|	...	1800	|	|	|	1841	|	|	|	|	|	|	|	|	2133	|	|	...	...		0550	|	0650	|
Newark North Gate d.	|	1754	|	1818	|	|	1855	|	1918	|	|	|	2018	|	|	|	2204	2307	...	...		0605	|	0705	|
Grantham d.	|	1806	1823	|	|	|	1907	1918	|	|	|	2018	|	|	|	2156	2216	2319	...	...		0617	|	0717	|
Peterborough d.	1808	1827	|	1848	|	1909	1929	|	1951	|	2008	|	2049	2105	2117	2217	2237	2346	...	...		0639	0713	0738	0815
Stevenage a.	|	1856	1906	|	|	|	1958	2003	2019	2025	|	2102	2117	|	2148	2245	2307	0026s	...	...		0709	|	0807	|
London Kings Cross a.	1900	1924	1933	1942	1951	2001	2025	2028	2046	2053	2101	2127	2143	2156	2215	2312	2337	0102	...	...		0734	0804	0836	0908

	⑥	⑥	⑥	⑥	⑥	⑥	⑥	⑥	⑥	⑥	⑥	⑥	⑥	⑥	⑥	⑥	⑥	⑥	⑥	⑥	⑥	⑥	⑥	⑥	⑥
		D		F		G				H	E				C							A			B
Edinburgh Waverley d.	...	...	...	...	...	...	...	...	0620	...	...	0655	0730	...	0800	0830	...	0900	0930	...	1000	1030	...	1100	1130
Berwick upon Tweed d.	...	...	...	...	...	...	...	...	0706	...	...	|	0813	...	|	0913	...	|	1013	...	|	1113	...	|	1213
Alnmouth d.	...	...	...	...	...	...	...	...	0727	...	...	|	|	...	0900	|	...	|	|	...	1100	|	...	|	|
Newcastle d.	...	...	0630	...	0655	...	0722	...	0801	...	...	0825	0900	...	0930	1000	...	1026	1100	...	1130	1200	...	1226	1301
Durham d.	...	...	0643	...	0708	...	0736	...	|	...	...	0838	|	...	0943	|	...	1039	|	...	1143	|	...	1239	|
Darlington d.	...	...	0702	...	0727	...	0754	...	0829	...	...	0857	0929	...	1001	1029	...	1057	1129	...	1201	1229	...	1257	1329
Northallerton d.	...	...	0713	...	|	...	0808	...	|	...	...	0908	|	...	|	|	...	1109	|	...	|	|	...	1309	|
York d.	...	...	0735	...	0757	...	0830	...	0859	...	...	0930	0959	...	1031	1059	...	1131	1159	...	1231	1259	...	1331	1400
Leeds d.	0705	...	|	0738	|	0805	|	0840	|	...	0905	|	|	1005	|	|	1105	|	|	1205	|	|	1305	|	|
Wakefield Westgate d.	0717	...	|	|	|	0818	|	0853	|	...	0918	|	|	1018	|	|	1118	|	|	1218	|	|	1318	|	|
Doncaster d.	0736	0745	0758	0811	0820	0837	0855	0913	|	...	0936	0953	|	1037	1055	|	1136	1155	|	1236	1255	|	1336	1355	|
Retford d.	|	|	|	|	|	0854	|	|	|	...	|	1007	|	|	|	|	|	1209	|	|	|	|	|	1409	|
Newark North Gate d.	0800	|	0822	|	|	0909	0919	|	|	0953	1000	|	|	1101	1118	|	1159	|	|	1302	1318	|	1400	|	|
Grantham d.	0812	0818	|	0843	|	|	0931	|	|	1005	1013	1030	|	1115	|	|	1211	|	|	1314	|	|	1412	|	|
Peterborough d.	0833	0840	0852	|	|	0938	0953	1002	1007	1029	1037	1052	|	1137	1152	|	1234	1251	|	1336	1350	|	1433	1451	|
Stevenage a.	0901	|	|	|	|	|	|	|	|	1100	1107	|	|	|	|	|	1302	|	|	|	|	|	1501	|	|
London Kings Cross a.	0928	0935	0945	0951	0954	1030	1045	1053	1058	1126	1136	1143	1153	1228	1243	1252	1329	1342	1352	1427	1441	1452	1529	1542	1555

	⑥	⑥	⑥	⑥	⑥	⑥	⑥	⑥	⑥	⑥	⑥	⑥	⑥	⑥	⑥	⑥	⑥	⑥	⑥	⑥	⑥	⑥			⑦
				A															A						
Edinburgh Waverley d.	...	1200	...	1230	...	1300	1330	...	1400	1430	...	1500	1530	...	1600	1630	...	1700	1730	...	1830	1900	...	⑦	...
Berwick upon Tweed d.	...	|	...	1313	...	|	1412	...	|	1512	...	|	1612	...	|	1712	...	|	1816	...	1911	1945	...		...
Alnmouth d.	...	1300	...	|	...	|	|	...	1500	|	...	|	|	...	|	|	...	1800	|	...	|	2008	...		...
Newcastle d.	...	1330	...	1400	...	1426	1459	...	1530	1559	...	1626	1659	...	1726	1759	...	1830	1904	...	1958	2043	...		...
Durham d.	...	1343	...	|	...	1439	|	...	1544	|	...	1639	|	...	1739	|	...	1843	|	...	...	2056	...		...
Darlington d.	...	1401	...	1429	...	1457	1529	...	1603	1628	...	1657	1728	...	1757	1828	...	1902	1933	...	...	2115	...		...
Northallerton d.	...	|	...	|	...	1509	|	...	|	|	...	1709	|	...	1809	|	...	|	|	...	...	2128	...		...
York d.	...	1431	...	1459	...	1531	1558	...	1633	1657	...	1731	1758	...	1831	1857	...	1931	2003	...	...	2150	...		0800
Leeds d.	1405	|	1440	|	1505	|	|	1605	|	|	1705	|	|	1805	|	|	1905	|	|	2005	...	|	...		|
Wakefield Westgate d.	1418	|	1453	|	1518	|	|	1618	|	|	1718	|	|	1818	|	|	1919	|	|	2018	...	|	...		|
Doncaster d.	1436	1455	1512	|	1536	1555	|	1636	1656	|	1736	1755	|	1839	1855	|	1937	1955	2026	2036	...	2215	...		0823
Retford d.	|	|	|	|	|	1609	|	|	|	|	|	1809	|	|	|	|	|	|	|	2050	...	...	...		|
Newark North Gate d.	1504	1518	|	|	1600	|	|	1659	1720	|	1759	|	|	1903	1918	|	2001	|	|	2105	...	...	...		|
Grantham d.	1516	|	|	|	1612	|	|	1711	|	|	1811	|	|	1916	|	|	2013	2027	2058	|	...	...	...		|
Peterborough d.	1537	1551	1601	|	1634	1651	|	1733	1751	|	1833	1851	|	1937	1951	|	2034	2051	2120	2134	...	...	...		0911
Stevenage a.	|	|	|	|	1703	|	|	|	|	|	1901	|	|	|	2019	|	2102	|	2149	|	...	...	...		0939
London Kings Cross a.	1628	1643	1653	1656	1731	1744	1751	1825	1842	1852	1928	1942	1952	2028	2046	2051	2129	2142	2218	2225	...	...	...		1007

	⑦	⑦	⑦	⑦	⑦	⑦	⑦	⑦	⑦	⑦	⑦	⑦	⑦	⑦	⑦	⑦	⑦	⑦	⑦	⑦	⑦	⑦	⑦	⑦	⑦
																					A				B
Edinburgh Waverley d.	...	...	...	...	...	...	...	...	0900	0930	...	1000	1030	...	1100	1130	...	...	1200	1220	1230	...	...	1300	1330
Berwick upon Tweed d.	...	...	...	...	...	...	...	...	|	1013	...	|	1112	...	|	1213	...	...	|	|	1313	...	...	|	1413
Alnmouth d.	...	...	...	...	...	...	...	...	|	|	...	1100	|	...	|	|	...	...	1300	|	|	...	...	|	|
Newcastle d.	...	0755	...	0855	...	0925	1000	...	1029	1100	...	1130	1159	...	1226	1300	...	1315	1330	1351	1400	...	1415	1427	1500
Durham d.	...	0809	...	0908	...	0938	|	...	1042	|	...	1143	|	...	1239	|	...	1329	1343	1404	|	...	1429	1441	|
Darlington d.	...	0827	...	0928	...	0957	1028	...	1101	1130	...	1202	1227	...	1258	1330	...	1349	1401	|	1430	...	1449	1459	1530
Northallerton d.	...	|	...	|	...	1008	|	...	1112	|	...	|	|	...	1310	|	...	1401	|	|	|	...	1500	|	|
York d.	...	0858	...	0958	...	1031	1058	...	1134	1159	...	1232	1259	...	1332	1359	...	1423	1431	1449	1459	...	1523	1530	1559
Leeds d.	0805	|	0905	|	1005	|	|	1105	|	|	1205	|	|	1305	|	|	1405	|	|	|	|	1505	|	|	|
Wakefield Westgate d.	0817	|	0918	|	1017	|	|	1117	|	|	1217	|	|	1318	|	|	1418	|	|	|	|	1518	|	|	|
Doncaster d.	0836	|	0937	|	1035	1055	|	1135	1157	|	1235	1255	|	1336	1355	|	1436	1447	1455	|	|	1537	1546	1553	|
Retford d.	0850	|	|	|	1050	|	|	|	1211	|	|	|	|	|	1409	|	|	|	|	|	|	|	|	1608	|
Newark North Gate d.	0905	|	1000	|	1106	1119	|	1159	|	|	1258	1319	|	1400	|	|	1459	|	1519	|	|	1600	1609	|	|
Grantham d.	0917	|	1012	|	1118	|	|	1212	|	|	1310	|	|	1412	|	|	1511	|	|	1540	|	1612	|	|	|
Peterborough d.	0941	1005	1034	1104	1140	1151	1204	1234	1251	|	1332	1351	|	1433	1451	|	1533	1540	1551	|	|	1634	1642	1651	|
Stevenage a.	|	|	1104	|	|	|	|	1306	|	|	|	|	|	1503	|	|	|	|	|	|	|	1704	|	|	|
London Kings Cross a.	1033	1057	1132	1155	1233	1242	1255	1333	1342	1352	1423	1442	1450	1532	1542	1552	1624	1632	1642	1646	1652	1732	1735	1743	1752

	⑦	⑦	⑦	⑦	⑦	⑦	⑦	⑦	⑦	⑦	⑦	⑦		⑦	⑦	⑦	⑦	⑦	⑦	⑦	⑦	⑦	⑦	⑦	⑦
			A						E					A											
Edinburgh Waverley d.	...	1400	1430	...	...	...	1500	1530	...	...	1600	1620	...	1630	...	...	1700	1730	...	1800	...	1830	1900	2000	2100
Berwick upon Tweed d.	...	|	1513	...	...	...	|	1612	...	...	|	|	...	1713	...	...	|	1816	...	|	...	1912	1946	2047	2147
Alnmouth d.	...	1501	|	...	...	...	|	|	...	...	1700	|	...	|	...	...	|	|	...	1900	...	|	|	2110	2210
Newcastle d.	...	1531	1600	...	1615	...	1627	1659	...	...	1730	1749	...	1800	...	...	1829	1903	...	1930	...	2001	2033	2145	2239
Durham d.	...	1544	|	...	1629	...	1640	|	...	...	1743	|	...	|	...	...	1842	|	...	1944	...	|	2046	2159	...
Darlington d.	...	1603	1630	...	1649	...	1659	1728	...	...	1801	1817	...	1830	...	...	1901	1932	...	2003	...	2029	2105	2219	...
Northallerton d.	...	|	|	...	1700	...	|	|	...	...	|	|	...	|	...	...	1912	|	...	|	...	|	|	2232	...
York d.	...	1633	1659	...	1722	...	1730	1759	...	...	1831	1848	...	1859	...	...	1933	2001	...	2032	...	2059	2135	2306	...
Leeds d.	1616	|	|	1645	|	1716	|	|	1745	1816	|	|	...	|	1845	1916	|	|	1945	|	2045	|	|	2336	...
Wakefield Westgate d.	1628	|	|	1658	|	1729	|	|	1758	1828	|	|	...	|	1858	1928	|	|	1958	|	2058	|	|	...	...
Doncaster d.	1647	1656	|	1718	|	1747	1756	|	1819	1846	1855	|	...	|	1919	1946	1957	|	2020	2055	2116	2125	2158	...	...
Retford d.	|	|	|	|	|	1801	|	|	|	|	|	|	...	|	|	2000	|	|	|	|	2130	|	|	...	...
Newark North Gate d.	|	1719	|	1746	1803	|	|	|	1844	|	1918	|	...	|	1946	|	2021	|	2046	2119	|	2149	2221	...	...
Grantham d.	1718	|	|	|	|	1824	1830	|	|	1917	|	1943	...	|	|	2023	|	2050	|	|	2153	2201	2233	...	...
Peterborough d.	|	1751	|	1815	1832	|	1852	|	1914	|	1951	|	...	|	2016	|	2051	2110	2115	2151	2214	2223	2255	...	...
Stevenage a.	1803	|	|	|	|	1909	|	|	|	2002	|	|	...	|	|	2108	|	|	|	|	2244	2253	2333s	...	...
London Kings Cross a.	1834	1842	1853	1908	1923	1934	1943	1950	2009	2027	2042	2048	...	2054	2109	2133	2142	2201	2207	2242	2310	2318	2359	...	...

For footnotes see page 148.

180a KINGS LYNN - PETERBOROUGH

First Excel service X1

From Kings Lynn bus station: Journey 80 minutes. Buses call at **Wisbech** bus station ± 32 minutes later.

Ⓐ: 0537, 0607, 0637, 0707, 0737, 0810 and every 30 minutes until 1140, 1220 and every 30 minutes until 1750, 1901, 1953, 2153.

⑥: 0607, 0637, 0707, 0737, 0810 and every 30 minutes until 1140, 1220 and every 30 minutes until 1750, 1901, 1953, 2153.

⑦: 0744, 0844 and hourly until 1955, 2153.

HT All trains 🍸 LONDON - HULL 181

Subject to alteration July 26 - September 7 (trains will not call at Selby; 🚐 replacement service will be provided).

km		Ⓐ	Ⓐ	⑥	⑦		Ⓐ	⑥	⑦	Ⓐ		⑥	⑦	Ⓐ	⑥ △	Ⓐ △	⑦ △	⑥	⑦	Ⓐ		⑥	⑦	Ⓐ
0	**London** Kings Cross ...... 180 d.	0722	0948	0948	1048	...	1148	1148	1248	1348	...	1448	1447	1548	1710	1719	1720	1748	1743	1850	...	1948	1950	2030
170	Grantham .... 180 d.	0827	1048	1048	1148	...	1248	1248	1348	1449	...	1548	1547	1649	1821	1828	1826	1849	1847	1951	...	2051	2051	2132
223	Retford .... 180 d.	0850	1109	1110	1209	...	1311	1310	1409	1511	...	1609	1608	1710	|	|	|	1911	1908	2012	...	2114	2112	2152
251	Doncaster .... 180 d.	0906	1125	1125	1229	...	1325	1325	1429	1525	...	1626	1630	1725	1854	1908	1905	1926	1930	2033	...	2129	2126	2208
280	Selby .... a.	0922	1140	1140	1244	...	1340	1340	1444	1540	...	1644	1646	1740	1909	1925	1921	1941	1946	2049	...	2144	2142	2223
330	**Hull** .... a.	1003	1221	1219	1325	...	1422	1422	1526	1618	...	1725	1727	1818	1953	2004	2002	2021	2026	2129	...	2225	2223	2306
		Ⓐ	⑥ △	Ⓐ △	Ⓐ		⑥	⑦	Ⓐ	⑥		⑦	Ⓐ	⑥	⑦		Ⓐ	⑥	⑦	Ⓐ		⑥	⑦	Ⓐ
	Hull .... d.	0625	0650	0700	0825	...	0825	0905	1030	1030	...	1120	1230	1330	1435	...	1510	1530	1634	1710	...	1830	1847	1910
	Selby .... d.	0700	0725	0736	0903	...	0905	0940	1106	1106	...	1155	1306	1406	1510	...	1547	1605	1708	1745	...	1905	1921	1945
	Doncaster .... 180 d.	0721	0745	0758	0925	...	0924	1000	1126	1126	...	1222	1325	1426	1529	...	1605	1624	1730	1803	...	1928	1939	2003
	Retford .... 180 d.	0741	|	|	0939	...	0938	1014	1140	1140	...	1236	1339	1440	1544	...	1619	1638	1744	1817	...	1942	1954	2017
	Grantham .... 180 d.	0803	0818	0836	1001	...	1000	1035	1201	1201	...	1256	1401	1502	1606	...	1640	1700	1806	1839	...	2005	2015	2038
	London Kings Cross .... 180 a.	0918	0935	0954	1114	...	1109	1142	1309	1309	...	1407	1510	1610	1715	...	1747	1809	1914	1947	...	2113	2121	2146

s – Calls to set down only. **u** – Calls to pick up only. △ – Operated by GR (Table **180**).

GC All trains 🍸 LONDON - BRADFORD 182

km			Ⓐ	Ⓐ	Ⓐ	Ⓐ △	Ⓐ				⑥	⑥	⑥	⑥	⑥ △				⑦	⑦	⑦	⑦		
0	**London** Kings Cross ...... 180 d.	Ⓐ	1048	1448	1603	1833	1952	...	...	⑥	1048	1548	1636	1923	1930	...	...	⑦	1150	1550	1845	1923	...	...
251	Doncaster .... 180 d.		1224	1624	1738	2021	2123	...	...		1220	1721	1820	2052	2118	...	...		1322	1722	2028	2059	...	...
278	Pontefract Monkhill .... a.		1249	1648	|	|	|	...	...		|	|	|	2116	|	...	...		|	|	|	|	...	...
292	Wakefield Kirkgate .... a.		1307	1705	1809	2038e	2146	...	...		1243	1745	1845	2134	2134e	...	...		1346	1746	2058	2121	...	...
	Mirfield .... a.		1319	1718	1821	|	2200	...	...		1256	1757	1859	2146	|	...	...		1400	1800	2114	2136	...	...
313	Brighouse .... a.		1329	1729	1829	|	2209	...	...		1305	1806	1909	2156	|	...	...		1409	1809	2123	2144	...	...
322	Halifax .... 190 a.		1340	1740	1841	|	2222	...	...		1316	1817	1925	2207	|	...	...		1420	1820	2135	2155	...	...
335	**Bradford** Interchange ..... 190 a.		1353	1753	1854	2123f	2236	...	...		1332	1832	1941	2220	2220f	...	...		1433	1833	2148	2208	...	...
			Ⓐ △	Ⓐ	Ⓐ	Ⓐ	Ⓐ				⑥	⑥ △	⑥	⑥	⑥				⑦	⑦	⑦	⑦		
	Bradford Interchange .... 190 d.	Ⓐ	0630f	0655	0752	1020	1420	...	...	⑥	0655	0733f	0852	1021	1521	...	...	⑦	0758	1207	1507	1600	...	...
	Halifax .... 190 d.		|	0708	0804	1034	1434	...	...		0708	|	0905	1034	1536	...	...		0810	1219	1522	1613	...	...
	Brighouse .... d.		|	0719	0815	1048	1448	...	...		0719	|	0915	1048	1549	...	...		0821	1230	1536	1623	...	...
	Mirfield .... d.		|	0727	0823	1057	1457	...	...		0727	|	0923	1057	1557	...	...	♡	0829	1238	1544	1631	...	...
	Wakefield Kirkgate .... d.		0713e	0743	0855	1112	1514	...	...		0744	0818e	0940	1111	1614	...	...		0846	1255	1602	1648	...	...
	Pontefract Monkhill .... d.		|	0801	|	1136	1534	...	...		0801	|	0957	1130	1634	...	...		|	|	|	|	...	...
	Doncaster .... 180 d.		|	0830	0932	1206	1621	...	...		0832	0837	1024	1208	1711	...	...		0911	1320	1627	1713	...	...
	London Kings Cross .... 180 a.		0859	1014	1115	1343	1810	...	...		1007	1030	1156	1346	1843	...	...		1040	1452	1757	1843	...	...

e – Wakefield Westgate. **s** – Calls to set down only. △ – Operated by GR (Table **180**).
f – Bradford Forster Square. **u** – Calls to pick up only. ♡ – Service on ⑦ valid until September 7.

GC All trains 🍸 LONDON - YORK - SUNDERLAND 183

km			Ⓐ	Ⓐ	Ⓐ	Ⓐ	Ⓐ				⑥	⑥	⑥	⑥	⑥				⑦	⑦	⑦	⑦		
0	**London** Kings Cross ...... 180 d.	Ⓐ	0751	1121	1253	1650	1918	...	...	⑥	0811	1120	1320	1648	1911	...	...	⑦	0948	1348	1647	1822	...	...
303	**York** .... 180 d.		0958	1322	1451	1842	2119	...	...		1019	1319	1519	1842	2101	...	...		1139	1539	1842	2014	...	...
339	Thirsk .... d.		1015	1338	1514	1858	2136	...	...		1036	1336	1536	1858	2118	...	...		1155	1556	1900	2030	...	...
351	Northallerton .... 180 d.		1024	1347	1524	1907	2146	...	...		1045	1346	1546	1907	2127	...	...	♡	1204	1606	1911	2040	...	...
375	Eaglescliffe .... a.		1043	1406	1549	1926	2205	...	...		1105	1405	1605	1926	2146	...	...		1223	1626	1930	2059	...	...
399	Hartlepool .... a.		1110	1425	1609	1944	2225	...	...		1124	1424	1624	1954	2210	...	...		1242	1651	1949	2125	...	...
428	**Sunderland** .... a.		1138	1451	1639	2021	2251	...	...		1150	1450	1650	2021	2236	...	...		1308	1721	2020	2151	...	...
			Ⓐ	Ⓐ	Ⓐ	Ⓐ	Ⓐ				⑥	⑥	⑥	⑥	⑥				⑦	⑦	⑦	⑦		
	Sunderland .... d.	Ⓐ	0645	0842	1228	1518	1731	...	...	⑥	0643	0830	1218	1529	1729	...	...	⑦	0918	1212	1412	1812	...	...
	Hartlepool .... d.		0710	0909	1252	1550	1757	...	...		0710	0856	1245	1553	1754	...	...		0943	1236	1440	1840	...	...
	Eaglescliffe .... d.		0732	0929	1312	1611	1821	...	...		0730	0918	1305	1612	1814	...	...		1004	1304	1504	1904	...	...
	Northallerton .... 180 d.		0753	0947	1331	1631	1842	...	...		0752	0943	1327	1631	1832	...	...	♡	1024	1324	1524	1924	...	...
	Thirsk .... d.		0801	0959	1344	1643	1851	...	...		0801	0952	1336	1643	1843	...	...		1033	1333	1533	1933	...	...
	York .... 180 d.		0820	1027	1406	1702	1911	...	...		0819	1012	1356	1702	1902	...	...		1052	1352	1552	1952	...	...
	London Kings Cross .... 180 a.		1021	1230	1611	1906	2105	...	...		1015	1207	1548	1853	2056	...	...		1243	1544	1745	2144	...	...

s – Calls to set down only. **u** – Calls to pick up only. ♡ – Service on ⑦ valid until September 7.

FC LONDON - PETERBOROUGH 184

km			Ⓐ	Ⓐ	Ⓐ	Ⓐ	Ⓐ	Ⓐ	Ⓐ	Ⓐ	Ⓐ		Ⓐ	Ⓐ	Ⓐ	Ⓐ	Ⓐ	Ⓐ	Ⓐ	Ⓐ	Ⓐ	Ⓐ	Ⓐ
0	**London** Kings Cross ...... 180 d.	Ⓐ	0035	0135	0523	0623	0635	0723	0735	0823	0835	and at	1523	1535	1623	1640	1650	1710	1713	1740	1743	1810	1813
4	Finsbury Park .... d.		0040	0140	0528	0628	0640	0728	0740	0828	0841	the same	1528	1540	1628	|	1655	|	1719	|	1749	|	1819
44	Stevenage .... 180 d.		0112	0220	0600	0647	0713	0747	0813	0846	0913	minutes	1547	1613	1650	|	1717	|	1740	|	1808	|	1839
95	Huntingdon .... d.		0150s	0258s	0638	0722	0749	0822	0849	0921	0949	past each hour until	1622	1649	1731	1726	1754	1759	1818	1829	1846	1859	1917
123	**Peterborough** .... 180 a.		0212	0317	0655	0738	0806	0838	0907	0939	1006	▽	1638	1705	...	1742	1812	1819	1838	1853	1903	1921	1939

	Ⓐ	Ⓐ	Ⓐ	Ⓐ	Ⓐ	Ⓐ	Ⓐ	Ⓐ	Ⓐ	Ⓐ	Ⓐ	Ⓐ	Ⓐ			⑥	⑥	⑥		⑥	⑥	⑥	⑥	⑥
London Kings Cross ...... 180 d.	1840	1843	1910	1923	1953	2010	2023	2110	2123	2210	2223	2301	2323	...	⑥	0001	0035	0135	...	0523	0623	0635	0723	0735
Finsbury Park .... d.	|	1849	|	1928	1958	|	2028	|	2128	|	2228	|	2328	...		|	0040	0140	...	0528	0628	0640	0728	0740
Stevenage .... 180 d.	|	1909	|	1948	2018	|	2048	|	2148	|	2247	|	2347	...		0021	0112	0220	...	0600	0647	0713	0747	0813
Huntingdon .... d.	1927	1947	2001	2023	2056	2052	2124	2154	2224	2254	2323	2345	0023	...		0055s	0150s	0258s	...	0638	0722	0749	0822	0849
Peterborough .... 180 a.	1943	2003	2020	2041	2114	2111	2142	2210	2241	2310	2344	0012	0044	...		0111	0212	0317	...	0655	0738	0805	0838	0906

	⑥	⑥		⑥	⑥	⑥	⑥	⑥	⑥	⑥	⑥	⑥	⑥	⑥	⑥	⑥		⑥	⑥	⑥	⑥	⑥	⑥
London Kings Cross ...... 180 d.	0823	0835	and at	1623	1635	1640	1723	1735	1740	1823	1835	1840	1923	1935	2023	2035	...	2123	2135	2223	2253	2323	2353
Finsbury Park .... d.	0828	0840	the same	1628	1640	|	1728	1740	|	1828	1840	|	1928	1940	2028	2040	...	2128	2140	2228	2258	2328	2358
Stevenage .... 180 d.	0847	0913	minutes	1647	1713	|	1747	1813	|	1847	1912	|	1947	2013	2047	2113	...	2147	2213	2247	2317	2347	0025
Huntingdon .... d.	0922	0949	past each hour until	1722	1749	1726	1822	1849	1826	1922	1948	1926	2023	2049	2122	2149	...	2222	2249	2322	2352	0022	0104s
Peterborough .... 180 a.	0938	1006	▽	1740	1806	1743	1838	1906	1842	1938	2005	1942	2040	2106	2138	2205	...	2238	2306	2338	0013	0043	0125

		⑦	⑦	⑦	⑦	⑦	⑦	⑦	⑦	⑦	⑦		⑦	⑦	⑦	⑦	⑦	⑦	⑦	⑦	⑦	⑦	⑦	⑦
London Kings Cross ...... 180 d.	⑦	0023	0053	0705	0823	0923	1023	1123	1223	1323	1423	...	1523	1623	1710	1723	1735	1810	1823	1923	2023	2123	2223	2323
Finsbury Park .... d.		0028	0058	0710	0828	0928	1028	1128	1228	1328	1428	...	1528	1628	|	1728	1740	|	1828	1928	2028	2128	2228	2328
Stevenage .... 180 d.		0055	0130	0750	0847	0947	1047	1147	1247	1347	1447	...	1547	1647	|	1747	1812	|	1847	1947	2047	2147	2247	2347
Huntingdon .... d.	♡	0133s	0208s	0828	0922	1022	1122	1222	1322	1422	1522	...	1622	1722	1754	1822	1848	1855	1922	2022	2122	2222	2322	0022
Peterborough .... 180 a.		0155	0230	0844	0939	1039	1139	1238	1339	1439	1539	...	1640	1739	1812	1839	1905	1912	1939	2040	2139	2239	2343	0043

For return service and footnotes see next page ▷ ▷ ▷

184 PETERBOROUGH - LONDON FC

Ⓐ	Ⓐ	Ⓐ	Ⓐ	Ⓐ	Ⓐ	Ⓐ	Ⓐ	Ⓐ	Ⓐ	Ⓐ	Ⓐ	Ⓐ	Ⓐ	Ⓐ	Ⓐ	Ⓐ	Ⓐ	Ⓐ	Ⓐ	Ⓐ		Ⓐ
Peterborough 180 d.	0325	0410	0510	0540	0550	0615	0632	0655	0715	0706	0726	0732	0746	0816	0846	0919	0930	0946	1016	1046	and at	1616
Huntingdon d.	0340	0425	0525	0555	0604	0630	0646	0710	0733	0724	0740	0750	0802	0831	0901	0934	0945	1001	1034	1100	the same	1635
Stevenage 180 d.	0415	0504	0604	0625	0641	0659	0724	0736	0759	0802	|	0828	0832	0907	0937	1003	1021	1036	1110	1136	minutes past each	1712
Finsbury Park d.	0452s	0542	0624	0646	0706	|	0744	|	|	0821	|	0848	|	0928	0959	|	|	1056	1142	1156	hour until	1742
London Kings Cross 180 a.	0502	0552	0630	0653	0714	0722	0750	0800	0823	0829	0829	0855	0857	0934	1005	1027	1047	1103	1149	1201	▽	1750

	Ⓐ	Ⓐ	Ⓐ	Ⓐ	Ⓐ	Ⓐ	Ⓐ	Ⓐ	Ⓐ	Ⓐ	Ⓐ	Ⓐ	Ⓐ		⑥	⑥	⑥	⑥	⑥	⑥	⑥	⑥	⑥	⑥
Peterborough 180 d.	1646	1721	...	1755	1821	1846	1916	1946	2016	2043	2127	2146	2227	...		0325	0410	0516	0546	0616	0646	0716	0746	0809
Huntingdon d.	1700	1742	1804	1815	1841	1900	1935	2000	2034	2100	2141	2200	2241	...		0340	0425	0534	0600	0634	0700	0734	0800	0824
Stevenage 180 d.	1736	1819	1835	1850	1917	1936	2011	2036	2110	2136	2216	2236	2319	...		0415	0504	0610	0636	0710	0736	0810	0836	|
Finsbury Park d.	1756	1850	1856	1910	1949	1956	2042	2056	2142	2156	2246	2256	2349	...		0452s	0542	0642	0655	0742	0755	0842	0855	|
London Kings Cross 180 a.	1803	1856	1901	1916	1956	2003	2049	2102	2150	2201	2252	2302	2356	...		0500	0549	0649	0702	0749	0802	0849	0902	0912

	⑥	⑥	⑥	⑥	⑥	⑥	⑥	⑥		⑥	⑥	⑥	⑥	⑥	⑥	⑥	⑥	⑥	⑥	⑥	⑥	⑥	⑥
Peterborough 180 d.	0818	0846	0909	...	0946	1011	1016	1046	and at	1616	1646	1716	1746	1816	1846	1916	1946	2016	2046	2116	2146	2216	2246
Huntingdon d.	0834	0900	0924	0934	1000	1027	1034	1100	the same	1634	1700	1734	1800	1834	1900	1934	2000	2034	2100	2134	2200	2234	2300
Stevenage 180 d.	0910	0936	|	1010	1036	|	1110	1136	minutes past each	1710	1736	1810	1836	1910	1936	2010	2036	2110	2136	2210	2236	2310	2336
Finsbury Park d.	0942	0955	|	1042	1055	|	1142	1155	hour until	1742	1755	1842	1855	1942	1955	2042	2055	2142	2155	2242	2255	2342	2359s
London Kings Cross 180 a.	0951	1002	1012	1049	1102	1116	1149	1202	▽	1749	1802	1849	1902	1949	2002	2049	2102	2149	2202	2249	2302	2349	0009

⑦	⑦	⑦	⑦	⑦	⑦	⑦		⑦	⑦	⑦	⑦	⑦	⑦	⑦	⑦	⑦		⑦	⑦	⑦	⑦	⑦	⑦
Peterborough 180 d.	0546	0646	0746	0846	0915	0946	...	1015	1046	1115	1146	1246	1346	1446	1546	1646	...	1746	1846	1946	2046	2146	2301
Huntingdon d.	0601	0700	0800	0900	0930	1000	...	1030	1100	1130	1200	1300	1400	1500	1600	1700	...	1800	1900	2000	2100	2200	2315
Stevenage 180 d.	0640	0738	0835	0935	|	1035	...	|	1135	|	1235	1335	1435	1535	1636	1735	...	1836	1935	2035	2135	2235	2351
Finsbury Park d.	0713	0801	0855	0955	|	1055	...	|	1155	|	1255	1355	1455	1555	1655	1755	...	1855	1955	2055	2157	2255	0017s
London Kings Cross 180 a.	0723	0809	0901	1001	1016	1101	...	1116	1201	1216	1301	1401	1501	1601	1701	1801	...	1901	2001	2101	2202	2301	0026

s – Stops to set down only.

▽ – Timings may vary by up to 3 minutes.

♡ – Service on ⑦ valid until September 7.

185 PETERBOROUGH - LINCOLN - DONCASTER 2nd class EM

km		⚒	⚒	ⒶD	⚒	⚒	⚒	⑥	Ⓐ	Ⓐ	⚒E	⚒	Ⓐ	⚒	⚒	⑥	ⒶD	⑥	Ⓐ	⚒D	⚒	Ⓐ	⑥	⚒
0	**Peterborough** d.	...	...	...	0630	0730	0833	0932	0935	1040	1149	1241	1340	1510	1625	...	...	1730	1732	...	1836	...	...	2030
27	Spalding d.	...	...	...	0656	0756	0857	0957	0957	1102	1211	1303	1402	1532	1648	...	...	1756	1758	...	1902	...	...	2056
57	Sleaford d.	0650	0743	0840	...	...	0925	1025	1025	1131	1242	1332	1431	1614	1719	1754	1756	...	...	1900	...	2005	2010	...
91	**Lincoln** d.	0726	0815	0915	...	...	0959	1059	1059	1205	1315	1405	1505	1647	1751	1827	1831	...	...	1932	...	2039	2040	...

	⚒	⚒	⚒	⚒	Ⓐ	⚒	⚒	Ⓐ	⑥	Ⓐ	⑥	Ⓐ	Ⓐ	⚒	⚒	⑥	Ⓐ	⚒	⚒	⑥	Ⓐ	⚒	⚒
Lincoln d.	...	...	0705	0800	0910	1015	1110	1210	1330	1330	1441	1441	1512	1601	...	1715	1718	1810	...	1905	1910	...	2048
Sleaford d.	...	...	0737	0834	0942	1050	1142	1242	1403	1403	1516	1516	1544	1634	...	1747	1751	1842	...	1937	1942	...	2121
Spalding d.	0700	0800	...	0901	1007	1117	1207	1307	1428	1429	1541	1546	...	1659	1802	...	...	...	1956	...	...	2059	...
Peterborough a.	0725	0825	...	0927	1031	1143	1233	1332	1453	1455	1607	1612	...	1725	1828	...	...	...	2021	...	...	2125	...

km		ⒶS	⑥	⚒	ⒶP	⑥	⑥	ⒶS	⚒S	
0	**Lincoln** d.	0915	0915	1154	1315	1410	1510	1831	1932	...
26	Gainsborough Lea Road d.	0937	0937	1217	1337	1432	1532	1857	1953	...
60	**Doncaster** a.	1003	1011	1247	1406	1501	1601	1925	2023	...

	⚒	Ⓐ	⑥	Ⓐ	⑥	⑥	Ⓐ	⚒	
Doncaster d.	1024	1301	1305	1427	1507	1627	1934	2033	...
Gainsborough Lea Road d.	1052	1331	1331	1454	1533	1656	2000	2100	...
Lincoln a.	1117	1355	1355	1522	1557	1720	2025	2126	...

D – To/from Doncaster (lower part of table).
E – To/from Doncaster on Ⓐ (lower part of table).
P – To/from Peterborough (Main part of table).
S – To/from Sleaford (Main part of table).

186 GRIMSBY - LINCOLN - NOTTINGHAM 2nd class EM

km		⚒	Ⓐ	⚒A	ⒶB	Ⓐ	⑥	⑥		Ⓐ	⚒	⑥	Ⓐ	⑥	⑥B	Ⓐ		Ⓐ	⑥	⚒	⑦	⚒	⚒	⚒
0	**Grimsby** Town d.	...	0556	...	...	...	...	0650	...	0703	...	...	...	...	...	...	...	0920	0920	...	...	...	...	1128
47	Market Rasen d.	...	0632	...	...	...	...	0726	...	0739	...	...	...	...	...	...	...	0955	0955	...	...	...	...	1203
71	**Lincoln** a.	...	0651	...	...	...	...	0744	...	0757	...	...	...	...	...	...	...	1014	1014	...	...	...	...	1222
71	**Lincoln** d.	0526	0653	0704	0720	0726	0726	0746	...	0759	0835	0901	0910	0919	0930	0932	...	1015	1015	1036	1105	1135	1141	1223
97	Newark North Gate d.	0559	0722	|	0749	|	|	0812	...	0825	|	0925	0935	|	0953	|	...	1042	1044	|	1130	1201	|	1252
98	Newark Castle d.	0610	...	0729	...	0757	0755	...	...	...	0904	...	...	0948	...	0956	...	...	...	1105	...	...	1204	...
126	**Nottingham** a.	0648	...	0757	...	0832	0834	...	...	...	0932	...	...	1027	...	1035	...	...	...	1132	...	...	1232	...

	⚒	⑦	⚒	Ⓐ	⑥	⚒	⑦a		⑦b	⑥	Ⓐ	⑦a	Ⓐ	⚒	Ⓐ		⑥	⑦a	⑦	⚒	⑦	Ⓐ	⚒
Grimsby Town d.	...	...	...	...	...	1349	1403	...	...	...	...	...	...	...	1545	...	1600	...	...	...	...	...	...
Market Rasen d.	...	...	...	...	...	1425	1437	...	...	...	...	...	...	...	1619	...	1633	...	...	...	...	...	...
Lincoln a.	...	...	...	...	...	1444	1456	...	...	...	...	...	...	...	1638	...	1652	...	...	...	...	...	...
Lincoln d.	1230	1300	1340	1433	1435	1446	1500	...	1500	1527	1530	1545	1545	1634	1644	...	1654	1656	1725	1726	1805	1818	1834
Newark North Gate d.	|	1325	|	|	|	1511	1532	...	1532	|	|	1609	1611	|	1712	...	1722	|	1749	|	|	1846	|
Newark Castle d.	1257	...	1405	1459	1501	...	1542	...	1542	1558	1558	...	...	1703	...	...	...	1724	...	1755	1834	...	1902
Nottingham a.	1333	...	1432	1529	1532	...	1611	...	1609	1632	1632	...	...	1732	...	...	...	1753	...	1831	1911	...	1931

	⑦	⑦a	⚒		⑥	⑦	Ⓐ		⑥	⑥	⑦		⑦a	⑦b	Ⓐ		⑦	Ⓐ	Ⓐ				
Grimsby Town d.	...	1818	1828	...	...	...	...	...	1945	...	...	...	2022	...	...	...	...	2123	...	...	...	...	...
Market Rasen d.	...	1859	1902	...	...	...	...	...	2018	...	...	...	2057	...	...	...	...	2157	...	...	...	...	...
Lincoln a.	...	1918	1921	...	...	...	...	...	2037	...	...	...	2115	...	...	...	...	2216	...	...	...	...	...
Lincoln d.	1903	1922	1924	...	1935	2005	2035	...	...	2045	2100	...	2126	2126	2142	...	2210	...	2227	...	...	...	...
Newark North Gate d.	|	1946	1953	...	|	|	|	...	...	|	2131	...	2155	2155	|	...	|	...	|	...	...	...	...
Newark Castle d.	1933	...	...	...	2003	2035	2059	...	...	2110	2140	...	...	...	2207	...	2239	...	2256	...	...	...	...
Nottingham a.	2005	...	...	...	2034	2103	2129	...	...	2139	2209	...	...	...	2232	...	2316	...	2331	...	...	...	...

	⑥	Ⓐ	⚒	Ⓐ	⑥	Ⓐ	⑥	⑥	Ⓐ	Ⓐ	⑥	⑥	⚒	Ⓐ	Ⓐ	⑥	⚒	⑦a	⑦b	Ⓐ	⑥	⚒	⑥
Nottingham d.	...	...	0555	0655	0656	...	...	...	...	0806	0807	...	0920	...	...	...	1029	...	...	1117	1117	...	1227
Newark Castle d.	...	...	0630	0728	0729	...	...	...	...	0840	0842	...	0950	...	...	...	1058	...	...	1152	1155	...	1251
Newark North Gate d.	...	...	|	|	|	0740	...	0820	0831	|	|	0935	|	0957	1050	1052	|	1135	1135	|	|	1206	|
Lincoln a.	...	...	0705	0757	0759	0810	...	0855	0902	0908	0910	0959	1016	1023	1114	1120	1134	1200	1202	1221	1226	1236	1320
Lincoln d.	0538	0557	...	...	...	0815	0815	...	...	...	...	1006	...	1025	...	...	...	1202	...	...	...	1237	...
Market Rasen d.	0554	0613	...	...	...	0832	0832	...	...	...	...	1023	...	1042	...	...	...	1218	...	...	...	1254	...
Grimsby Town a.	0636	0655	...	...	...	0913	0913	...	...	...	...	1102	...	1122	...	...	...	1253	...	...	...	1336	...

	Ⓐ	⚒	⑦	⚒	Ⓐ	⑥	Ⓐ	⑥	⚒	⑥	Ⓐ	⑦a	⑦a	⚒	Ⓐ	⑥	⑦	Ⓐ	⑦b	⑦a	⑥	Ⓐ	⑦
Nottingham d.	1229	...	...	1316	...	...	1429	1429	...	1522	1529	1529	...	1615	...	...	1633	...	...	...	1715	1718	1726
Newark Castle d.	1254	...	...	1351	...	...	1454	1456	...	1550	1554	1559	...	1651	...	...	1659	...	...	...	1749	1753	1800
Newark North Gate d.	|	1302	1335	|	...	...	|	|	1528	|	|	|	1645	|	1645	...	|	1728	1756	1756	|	|	|
Lincoln a.	1321	1330	1402	1424	...	...	1519	1524	1556	1623	1627	1626	1716	1718	1713	...	1731	1800	1820	1820	1824	1828	1833
Lincoln d.	...	...	...	...	1437	1452	...	...	...	...	...	1627	...	...	1722	1722	...	...	...	1822	...	...	...
Market Rasen d.	...	...	...	...	1453	1507	...	...	...	...	...	1643	...	...	1738	1738	...	...	...	1838	...	...	...
Grimsby Town a.	...	...	...	...	1534	1548	...	...	...	...	...	1718	...	...	1815	1818	...	...	...	1913	...	...	...

	Ⓐ	⑥	Ⓐ	⑦		⑥B	Ⓐ	⑦a	Ⓐ		⑥A	⑦	⑥	ⒷB		ⒶA	⑥	⑦	⑦		⑥	Ⓐ	⑦
Nottingham d.	1750	1815	1818	1836	...	...	...	...	1920	...	1929	1935	...	...	...	2030	2030	2039	...	...	2126	2226	2228
Newark Castle d.	1818	1853	1854	1859	...	...	...	...	1955	...	1953	1958	...	...	...	2054	2056	2103	...	...	2157	2257	2303
Newark North Gate d.	|	|	|	1923	...	1934	1935	1953	|	...	|	|	2032	2036	...	|	|	|	2210	...	2209	2309	2317
Lincoln a.	1851	1927	1926	1954	...	2001	2001	2019	2019	...	2026	2030	2056	2102	...	2122	2125	2135	2237	...	2240	2340	2348
Lincoln d.	...	...	...	...	...	...	2002	...	...	...	...	...	2058	...	...	...	...	...	...	...	...	...	...
Market Rasen d.	...	...	...	...	...	...	2019	...	...	...	...	...	2115	...	...	...	...	...	...	...	...	...	...
Grimsby Town a.	...	...	...	...	...	...	2104	...	...	...	...	...	...	...	...	...	...	...	...	...	...	...	...

A – To/from London St Pancras (Table **170**).
B – To/from London Kings Cross (Table **180**).
a – Until Sep. 7.
b – From Sep. 14.

TP THE NORTH EAST and YORKSHIRE - MANCHESTER and LIVERPOOL 188

Due to engineering work services to Hull are subject to alteration July 26 - September 7.
Additional overnight services operate York - Manchester Airport and v.v. Please contact operator for details.

km				Ⓐ	⚒	⚒	⚒	⚒	⚒	⑥	Ⓐ	⚒	⚒	⚒	⚒	⚒	⚒	⚒	⚒	⚒	Ⓐ	⑥	⚒	⚒	⚒	⚒	⚒
0	**Newcastle**	d.	⚒	...	...	...	...	...	...	...	...	...	...	0603	...	...	...	...	0706	...	...	...	...	...	0806	...	...
23	Durham	d.		...	...	...	...	...	...	...	...	...	...	0621	...	...	...	...	0719	...	...	...	...	...	0822	...	...
34	**Middlesbrough**	d.		...	...	...	...	...	...	...	...	0555	...	|	...	0631	...	...	|	0715	...	...	...	...	|	0828	...
58	Darlington	d.		...	...	...	...	...	...	...	...	|	...	0638	...	|	...	...	0736	|	...	...	...	...	0839	|	...
81	Northallerton	d.		...	...	...	...	...	...	...	...	0623	...	0649	...	0659	...	...	|	0743	...	...	...	...	0850	0856	...
93	Thirsk	d.		...	...	...	...	...	...	...	...	0631	...	|	...	0710	...	...	|	0755	...	...	...	...	|	0904	...
**	**Scarborough**	d.		...	...	...	...	...	...	...	...	|	...	|	0630	|	0700	...	|	|	0738	0748	...	...	|	|	0850
**	Malton	d.		...	...	...	...	...	...	...	...	|	...	|	0653	|	0723	...	|	|	0801	0811	...	...	|	|	0913
129	**York**	a.		...	...	...	...	...	...	...	...	0649	...	0712	0718	0728	0747	...	0810	0813	0826	0836	...	...	0915	0921	0938
129	**York**	d.		...	0521	...	0555	0616	...	0640	0645	0652	...	0715	0724	0737	0750	...	0815	0824	0840	0840	0853	...	0915	0924	0941
**	**Hull**	d.		...	|	...	|	|	0549	|	|	|	0637	|	|	|	|	0735	|	|	|	|	|	0839	|	|	|
**	Selby	d.		...	|	...	|	|	0624	|	|	|	0709	|	|	|	|	0808	|	|	|	|	|	0910	|	|	|
170	**Leeds**	a.		...	0547	...	0618	0640	0648	0704	0708	0717	0733	0741	0750	0804	0820	0832	0840	0851	0904	0904	0916	0934	0939	0949	1004
170	**Leeds**	d.		...	0550	...	0620	0644	0653	0710	0710	0720	0735	0744	0753	0809	0824	0835	0844	0854	0909	0909	0920	0935	0944	0953	1009
185	Dewsbury	d.		...	0601	...	0631	|	|	0721	0721	|	0746	|	|	0820	|	0846	|	|	0920	0920	|	0946	|	|	1020
198	Huddersfield	d.		...	0611	...	0640	0702	0711	0731	0731	0739	0756	0802	0811	0830	0842	0856	0902	0912	0930	0930	0940	0956	1002	1011	1030
227	Stalybridge	d.		...	0630	...	0659	|	|	0750	0750	0759	0817	|	|	0850	|	0915	|	|	0950	0950	|	1015	|	|	1050
	Manchester Victoria	d.		...	|	...	|	0735	|	|	|	|	|	0835	|	|	|	|	0935	|	|	|	|	|	1035	|	|
239	**Manchester** Piccadilly	a.		0607	0646	0707	0714	|	0743	0805	0805	0816	0833	|	0843	0905	0913	0931	|	0943	1005	1005	1013	1031	|	1042	1105
255	**Manchester** Airport ✈	a.		|	0710	|	0742	|	0810	|	|	0839	...	|	0910	|	0939	...	|	1010	|	|	1039	...	|	1110	|
265	Warrington Central	a.		0628	...	0728	...	|	...	0830	0830	...	...	|	...	0930	...	...	|	...	1030	1030	...	...	|	...	1130
286	**Liverpool** South Parkway	a.		|	...	|	...	|	...	0847	0847	...	...	|	...	0947	...	...	|	...	1047	1047	...	...	|	...	1147
295	**Liverpool** Lime Street	a.		0652	...	0752	...	0808	...	0859	0859	...	...	0908	...	0959	...	...	1008	...	1059	1059	...	...	1108	...	1159

		⚒	⚒	⚒	⚒	⚒	⚒	⚒	⚒	⚒	⚒	⚒	⚒	⚒	⚒	⚒	⚒	⚒	⚒	⚒	⚒	⚒	⚒	⚒	⚒	⚒	⑥
Newcastle	d.	...	...	0910	...	...	...	...	1005	...	...	...	...	1110	...	...	...	...	1206	...	...	...	...	1310	...	...	...
Durham	d.	...	...	0923	...	...	...	...	1021	...	...	...	...	1123	...	...	...	...	1222	...	...	...	...	1323	...	...	...
Middlesbrough	d.	...	...	|	0925	...	...	...	|	1028	...	...	...	|	1128	...	...	...	|	1228	...	...	...	|	1328	...	...
Darlington	d.	...	...	0940	|	...	...	...	1039	|	...	...	...	1140	|	...	...	...	1239	|	...	...	...	1340	|	...	...
Northallerton	d.	...	...	0951	0956	...	...	...	1050	1056	...	...	...	1151	1156	...	...	...	1250	1256	...	...	...	1351	1356	...	...
Thirsk	d.	...	...	|	1004	...	...	...	|	1104	...	...	...	|	1204	...	...	...	|	1304	...	...	...	|	1404	...	...
Scarborough	d.	...	...	|	|	0950	...	...	|	|	1050	...	...	|	|	1150	...	...	|	|	1250	...	...	|	|	1350	...
Malton	d.	...	...	|	|	1013	...	...	|	|	1113	...	...	|	|	1213	...	...	|	|	1313	...	...	|	|	1413	...
York	a.	...	...	1014	1021	1038	...	...	1113	1121	1138	...	...	1214	1221	1238	...	...	1313	1321	1338	...	...	1414	1421	1438	...
York	d.	0953	...	1016	1024	1041	1053	...	1115	1124	1141	1153	...	1216	1224	1241	1253	...	1315	1324	1341	1353	...	1416	1424	1441	1453
Hull	d.	|	0939	|	|	|	|	1039	|	|	|	|	1139	|	|	|	|	1239	|	|	|	|	1339	|	|	|	|
Selby	d.	|	1010	|	|	|	|	1110	|	|	|	|	1210	|	|	|	|	1310	|	|	|	|	1410	|	|	|	|
Leeds	a.	1016	1034	1039	1049	1104	1116	1134	1138	1150	1204	1216	1234	1239	1249	1304	1318	1334	1339	1349	1404	1416	1434	1440	1449	1504	1516
Leeds	d.	1020	1035	1044	1053	1109	1120	1135	1144	1153	1209	1220	1235	1244	1253	1309	1320	1335	1344	1351	1409	1420	1435	1444	1453	1509	1517
Dewsbury	d.	|	1046	|	|	1120	|	1146	|	|	1220	|	1246	|	|	1320	|	1346	|	|	1420	|	1446	|	|	1520	
Huddersfield	d.	1040	1056	1102	1111	1130	1140	1156	1202	1211	1230	1240	1256	1302	1311	1330	1340	1356	1402	1409	1430	1440	1456	1502	1511	1530	1535
Stalybridge	d.	|	1115	|	|	1150	|	1215	|	|	1250	|	1315	|	|	1350	|	1415	|	|	1450	|	1515	|	|	1550	|
Manchester Victoria	d.	|	|	1135	|	|	|	|	1235	|	|	|		1335	|	|	|		1435	|	|	|	|	1535	|	|	|
Manchester Piccadilly	a.	1113	1131	|	1142	1205	1213	1231	|	1242	1305	1313	1331	|	1342	1405	1413	1431	|	1442	1505	1513	1531	|	1542	1605	1613
Manchester Airport ✈	a.	1139	...	|	1210	|	1239	...	|	1310	|	1339	...	|	1410	|	1439	...	|	1510	|	1539	...	|	1610	|	1639
Warrington Central	a.	...	...	|	...	1230	...	...	|	...	1330	...	...	|	...	1430	...	...	|	...	1530	...	...	|	...	1630	...
Liverpool South Parkway	a.	...	...	|	...	1247	...	...	|	...	1347	...	...	|	...	1447	...	...	|	...	1547	...	...	|	...	1647	...
Liverpool Lime Street	a.	...	...	1208	...	1259	...	...	1308	...	1359	...	...	1408	...	1459	...	...	1508	...	1559	...	...	1608	...	1659	...

		Ⓐ	⚒	⚒	⚒	⚒	⑥	Ⓐ	⚒	⚒	⚒	⚒	⚒	⚒	⚒	⚒	⚒	⚒	⚒	Ⓐ	⑥	Ⓐ	⑥	⚒	⚒	⚒	⚒
Newcastle	d.	...	...	1406	...	...	...	...	...	1508	...	...	...	...	1606	...	...	...	...	1703	1706	...	...	...	...	1804	...
Durham	d.	...	...	1422	...	...	...	...	...	1523	...	...	...	...	1622	...	...	...	...	1719	1722	...	...	...	...	1822	...
Middlesbrough	d.	...	...	|	1428	...	...	...	...	|	1528	...	...	...	|	1626	...	...	...	|	|	1726	1726	...	...	|	...
Darlington	d.	...	...	1439	|	...	...	...	...	1540	|	...	...	...	1639	|	...	...	...	1736	1739	|	|	...	...	1839	...
Northallerton	d.	...	...	1450	1456	...	...	...	...	1551	1556	...	...	...	1650	1654	...	...	...	1747	1751	1754	1756	...	...	1850	...
Thirsk	d.	...	...	|	1504	...	...	...	...	|	1604	...	...	...	|	1702	...	...	...	|	|	1802	1804	...	...	|	...
Scarborough	d.	...	...	|	|	1450	...	...	...	|	|	1550	...	...	|	|	1650	...	...	|	|	|	|	1750	1807a	|	...
Malton	d.	...	...	|	|	1513	...	...	...	|	|	1613	...	...	|	|	1713	...	...	|	|	|	|	1813	|	|	...
York	a.	...	...	1513	1521	1538	...	...	...	1614	1621	1638	...	...	1713	1720	1738	...	...	1810	1815	1820	1822	1838	1851a	1913	...
York	d.	1453	...	1515	1524	1541	1553	1553	...	1616	1624	1641	1653	...	1715	1722	1741	1753	...	1816	1816	1822	1824	1841	1853	1915	...
Hull	d.	|	1439	|	|	|	|	|	1539	|	|	|	|	1639	|	|	|	|	1739	|	|	|	|	|	|	|	1849
Selby	d.	|	1510	|	|	|	|	|	1610	|	|	|	|	1710	|	|	|	|	1810	|	|	|	|	|	|	|	1920
Leeds	a.	1516	1534	1540	1549	1607	1616	1616	1634	1639	1649	1706	1716	1734	1738	1749	1805	1816	1834	1839	1839	1847	1849	1905	1916	1938	1943
Leeds	d.	1520	1535	1544	1553	1609	1620	1620	1636	1644	1653	1709	1720	1736	1744	1753	1809	1820	1835	1844	1844	1853	1853	1909	1920	1941	...
Dewsbury	d.	|	1546	|	|	1620	|	|	1647	|	|	1720	1731	1748	|	|	1820	|	1846	|	|	|	|	1920	|	1952	...
Huddersfield	d.	1540	1556	1602	1611	1630	1640	1640	1656	1702	1711	1730	1740	1757	1802	1811	1830	1840	1856	1902	1902	1911	1911	1930	1940	2002	...
Stalybridge	d.	|	1615	|	|	1650	|	|	1715	|	|	1750	|	1817	|	|	1850	|	1915	|	|	|	|	1950	|	|	...
Manchester Victoria	d.	|	|	1635	|	|	|	|	|	1735	|	|	|	|	1835	|	|	|	|	1935	1935	|	|	|	|	2035	...
Manchester Piccadilly	a.	1613	1631	|	1643	1705	1713	1716	1731	|	1746	1805	1816	1834	|	1842	1905	1914	1931	|	|	1944	1944	2005	2013	|	...
Manchester Airport ✈	a.	1641	...	|	1712	|	1739	...	...	|	1810	|	1839	...	|	1916	|	...	...	|	|	2015	2015	|	...	|	...
Warrington Central	a.	...	...	|	...	1730	...	...	...	|	...	1830	...	...	|	...	1930	...	...	|	|	...	...	2030	...	|	...
Liverpool South Parkway	a.	...	...	|	...	1747	...	...	...	|	...	1847	...	...	|	...	1947	...	...	|	|	...	...	2047	...	|	...
Liverpool Lime Street	a.	...	...	1708	...	1759	...	...	...	1808	...	1859	...	...	1908	...	1959	...	...	2008	2008	...	...	2059	...	2108	...

		⚒	⚒	⚒	⚒	⚒	⚒	⚒	Ⓐ	Ⓐ	⑥	Ⓐ	⑥	⚒	⚒	⚒	⚒	⑥ b	⑥ c	Ⓐ			⑦	⑦	⑦	⑦	⑦
Newcastle	d.	...	...	1910	...	...	...	...	...	2027	...	...	...	...	...	...	...	2155	2155	2155	...	⑦	...	...	...	...	...
Durham	d.	...	...	1923	...	...	...	...	...	2045	...	...	...	...	...	...	...	2210	2210	2210	...		...	...	...	...	...
Middlesbrough	d.	1828	...	|	...	1930	...	...	...	|	...	2052	2052	...	...	...	2150	|	|	|	...		...	...	...	...	...
Darlington	d.	|	...	1940	...	|	...	...	...	2102	...	|	|	...	...	...	2219	2227	2227	2227	...		...	...	...	...	...
Northallerton	d.	1856	...	1951	...	1958	...	...	...	2113	...	2120	2120	...	...	...	2230	2238	2238	2238	...		...	...	...	...	...
Thirsk	d.	1904	...	|	...	2006	...	...	...	|	...	2128	2128	...	...	...	2238	|	|	|	...		...	...	...	...	...
Scarborough	d.	|	1850	|	...	|	1950	...	2045	|	2050	|	|	...	...	2207	|	|	|	|	...		...	...	...	...	...
Malton	d.	|	1913	|	...	|	2013	...	2109	|	2113	|	|	...	...	2230	|	|	|	|	...		...	...	...	...	...
York	a.	1921	1938	2014	...	2025	2038	...	2133	2136	2138	2146	2152	...	...	2255	2258	2302	2302	2302	...		...	...	...	...	...
York	d.	1924	1941	2016	...	...	2041	2116	...	2141	2141	2148	...	...	2230	...	...	2306	2306	2306	...		0612	0712	...	0809	0850
Hull	d.	|	|	|	1959	...	|	|	...	|	|	|	...	2138	|	...	...	|	|	|	...		|	|	...	|	|
Selby	d.	|	|	|	2030	...	|	|	...	|	|	|	...	2212	|	...	...	|	|	|	...		|	|	...	|	|
Leeds	a.	1951	2004	2039	2059	...	2104	2139	...	2205	2205	2212	...	2239	2305	...	...	2332	2332	2332	...		0638	0738	...	0835	0913
Leeds	d.	1953	2009	2041	...	...	2109	2141	...	2209	2209	...	...	2241	2309	...	...	2335	2335	2335	...		0640	0740	...	0840	0915
Dewsbury	d.	|	2020	2052	...	...	2120	2152	...	2220	2220	...	...	2252	2320	...	...	2346	2346	2346	...		0651	0751	...	0851	0926
Huddersfield	d.	2011	2030	2102	...	...	2130	2202	...	2230	2230	...	...	2302	230	...	...	2355	2355	2355	...		0701	0801	...	0901	0936
Stalybridge	d.	|	2050	|	...	...	2150	|	...	2250	2250	...	...	|	|	...	...	|	|	|	...		0719	0819	...	0919	0954
Manchester Victoria	d.	|	|	|	...	...	|	|	...	|	|	...	...	|	|	...	...	|	|	|	...		|	|	...	|	|
Manchester Piccadilly	a.	2045	2105	2133	...	...	2205	2233	...	2305	2305	...	...	2336	0033	...	...	0027	0033	0041	...		0734	0834	0912	0934	1010
Manchester Airport ✈	a.	2113	|	2155	...	...	|	2255	...	|	|	...	...	...	...	...	...	0047	*0110**	0056	...		0754	0854	|	0954	|
Warrington Central	a.	...	2130	...	...	...	2230	...	...	2330	2330	...	...	...	...	...	...	...	...	...	...		...	...	0933	...	1033
Liverpool South Parkway	a.	...	2147	...	...	...	2245	...	...	2345	2345	...	...	...	...	...	...	...	...	...	...		...	...	0948	...	1048
Liverpool Lime Street	a.	...	2159	...	...	...	2256	...	...	2358	2358	...	...	...	...	...	...	...	...	...	...		...	...	1000	...	1100

a – ⑥ June 21 - Sep. 6.
b – Until Oct. 18.
c – From Oct. 25.
d – Not Aug. 3 - Sep. 7.

e – Until Oct. 19.
f – From Oct. 26.
g – From Sep. 14.
h – Until Sep. 7.

j – Aug. 3 - Sep. 7.
k – Depart 0810 from Oct. 26 (by 🚌).
s – Calls to set down only.
* – Connection by 🚌.

** – Distances: York (*0 km*) - Malton (*33 km*) - Scarborough (*67 km*).
Leeds (*0 km*) - Selby (*34 km*) - Leeds (*83 km*).

188 THE NORTH EAST and YORKSHIRE - MANCHESTER and LIVERPOOL TP

Due to engineering work services to Hull are subject to alteration July 26 - September 7.
Additional overnight services operate York - Manchester Airport and v.v. Please contact operator for details.

	⑦	⑦	⑦	⑦	⑦	⑦	⑦	⑦	⑦	⑦	⑦	⑦	⑦	⑦	⑦	⑦	⑦	⑦	⑦	⑦	⑦	⑦	⑦	⑦	⑦	⑦
Newcastle d.	0800	...	...	...	...	0906	...	...	1004	...	...	...	1110	...	...	...	1206	...	...	...	1310	...	...	...	1405	...
Durham d.	0813	...	...	...	...	0919	...	...	1020	...	...	...	1123	...	...	...	1222	...	...	...	1323	...	...	...	1421	...
Middlesbrough d.	|	...	...	...	...	|	...	...	|	1028	...	...	|	...	...	...	|	1228	...	...	|	...	...	...	|	1424
Darlington d.	0831	...	...	...	...	0936	...	...	1039	|	...	...	1140	...	...	...	1240	|	...	...	1340	...	...	...	1438	|
Northallerton d.	0842	...	...	...	...	0947	...	...	1050	1056	...	...	1151	...	...	...	1251	1256	...	...	1351	...	...	...	|	1452
Thirsk d.	0850	...	...	...	...	|	...	...	|	1104	...	...	|	...	...	...	|	1304	...	...	|	...	...	...	|	1500
Scarborough d.	|	...	...	0853	...	|	...	0953c	|	|	1053	...	|	...	1153	...	|	|	1253	...	|	...	1353	...	|	|
Malton d.	|	...	...	0916	...	|	...	1016c	|	|	1116	...	|	...	1216	...	|	|	1316	...	|	...	1416	...	|	|
York a.	0909	...	...	0941	...	1010	...	1041c	1113	1122	1141	...	1214	...	1241	...	1314	1322	1341	...	1414	...	1441	...	1511	1523
York d.	0911	...	0928	0945	...	1012	1028	1045	1115	1124	1145	...	1216	1224	1245	...	1315	1324	1345	...	1416	1424	1445	...	1515	1524
Hull d.	|	0835	|	|	0934d	|	|	|	|	|	|	1137d	|	|	|	1237d	|	|	|	1339d	|	|	|	1429d	|	|
Selby d.	|	0911	|	|	1006	|	|	|	|	|	|	1208	|	|	|	1308	|	|	|	1410	|	|	|	1500	|	|
Leeds a.	0934	0938	0953	1008	1032	1036	1051	1108	1138	1147	1208	1234	1239	1247	1308	1334	1339	1347	1408	1433	1439	1447	1508	1534	1538	1548
Leeds d.	0944	...	0953	1010	1035	1044	1053	1110	1144	1153	1210	1235	1244	1253	1310	1335	1344	1353	1410	1435	1444	1453	1510	1535	1544	1553
Dewsbury d.	|	...	|	1021	1046	|	|	1121	|	|	1221	1246	|	|	1321	1346	|	|	1421	1446	|	|	1521	1546	|	|
Huddersfield d.	1002	...	1011	1030	1056	1102	1111	1130	1202	1211	1230	1256	1302	1311	1330	1356	1402	1411	1430	1456	1502	1511	1530	1556	1602	1611
Stalybridge d.	|	...	|	1050	|	|	|	1150	|	|	1250	|	|	|	1350	|	|	|	1450	|	|	|	1550	|	|	|
Manchester Victoria d.	1035	...	|	|	|	1135	|	|	1235	|	|	|	1335	|	|	|	1435	|	|	|	1535	|	|	|	1635	|
Manchester Piccadilly a.	|	...	1044	1105	1131	|	1142	1205	|	1242	1305	1331	|	1342	1405	1431	|	1442	1505	1531	|	1542	1605	1631	|	1643
Manchester Airport ✈ a.	|	...	1110	|	...	|	1208	|	|	1311	|	...	|	1405	|	...	|	1513	|	...	|	1605	|	...	|	1710
Warrington Central a.	|	...	...	1130	...	|	...	1230	|	...	1330	...	|	...	1430	...	|	...	1530	...	|	...	1630	...	|	...
Liverpool South Parkway a.	|	...	...	1147	...	|	...	1247	|	...	1347	...	|	...	1447	...	|	...	1547	...	|	...	1647	...	|	...
Liverpool Lime Street a.	1108	...	...	1159	...	1208	...	1259	1308	...	1359	...	1408	...	1459	...	1508	...	1559	...	1608	...	1659	...	1708	...

	⑦	⑦	⑦	⑦	⑦	⑦	⑦	⑦	⑦	⑦	⑦	⑦	⑦		⑦	⑦	⑦	⑦	⑦	⑦	⑦	⑦	⑦	⑦	⑦	⑦
Newcastle d.	...	...	1510	...	...	...	1604	...	...	...	1710	...	...	...	1804	...	...	...	1910	...	2010	...	...	...	...	2200
Durham d.	...	...	1523	...	...	...	1620	...	...	...	1723	...	...	...	1822	...	...	...	1923	...	2023	...	...	...	...	2214
Middlesbrough d.	...	...	|	...	...	...	|	1624	...	...	|	...	...	...	|	...	1819	...	|	...	|	...	2041	...	2208	|
Darlington d.	...	...	1540	...	...	...	1638	|	...	...	1740	...	...	...	1840	...	|	...	1940	...	2040	...	|	...	|	2231
Northallerton d.	...	...	1551	...	...	...	|	1652	...	...	1751	...	...	...	|	...	1847	...	1951	...	2051	...	2109	...	2237	2243
Thirsk d.	...	...	|	...	...	...	|	1700	...	...	|	...	...	...	|	...	1858	...	|	...	|	...	2117	...	2245	|
Scarborough d.	1453	...	|	...	1553	...	|	|	1653	...	|	...	1753	...	|	...	|	1853	|	1953	|	...	|	2138	|	|
Malton d.	1516	...	|	...	1616	...	|	|	1716	...	|	...	1816	...	|	...	|	1916	|	2016	|	...	|	2201	|	|
York a.	1541	...	1614	...	1641	...	1711	1723	1741	...	1814	...	1841	...	1913	...	1919	1941	2014	2041	2114	...	2142	2226	2309	2315
York d.	1545	...	1616	1624	1645	...	1715	1724	1745	...	1816	1824	1845	...	1915	...	1924	1945	2016	2045	2116	...	2145	2228	...	2317
Hull d.	|	1539d	|	|	|	1643d	|	|	|	1739d	|	|	|	...	|	1842d	|	|	|	|	|	2049d	|	|	...	|
Selby d.	|	1610	|	|	|	1714	|	|	|	1810	|	|	|	...	|	1915	|	|	|	|	|	2120	|	|	...	|
Leeds a.	1608	1634	1639	1647	1708	1738	1741	1748	1808	1834	1839	1847	1908	...	1938	1942	1947	2008	2039	2108	2139	2147	2208	2251	...	2342
Leeds d.	1610	1635	1644	1653	1710	1738	1744	1753	1810	1835	1844	1853	1910	...	1941	...	1953	2010	2041	2110	2141	...	2210	2253	...	2344
Dewsbury d.	1621	1646	|	|	1721	|	|	|	1821	1846	|	|	1921	...	1952	...	|	2021	2052	2121	2152	...	2221	2304	...	2355
Huddersfield d.	1630	1656	1702	1711	1730	1756	1802	1811	1830	1856	1902	1911	1930	...	2002	...	2011	2030	2102	2130	2202	...	2230	2313	...	0004
Stalybridge d.	1650	|	|	|	1750	|	|	|	1850	|	|	|	1950	...	|	...	|	2050	|	2150	|	...	2250	2332	...	|
Manchester Victoria d.	|	|	1735	|	|	|	1835	|	|	|	1935	|	|	...	2035	...	|	|	|	|	|	...	|	|	...	|
Manchester Piccadilly a.	1705	1729	|	1746	1805	1829	|	1842	1905	1931	|	1944	2005	...	|	...	2045	2105	2135	2205	2233	...	2305	2349	...	0036
Manchester Airport ✈ a.	|	...	|	1805	|	...	|	1910	|	...	|	2005	|	...	|	...	2110	|	...	|	2255	...	|	...	...	0056
Warrington Central a.	1730	...	|	...	1830	...	|	...	1930	...	|	...	2030	...	|	...	...	2130	...	2230	...	...	2330	...	...	...
Liverpool South Parkway a.	1747	...	|	...	1847	...	|	...	1947	...	|	...	2047	...	|	...	...	2147	...	2245	...	...	2345	...	...	...
Liverpool Lime Street a.	1758	...	1808	...	1859	...	1908	...	1959	...	2008	...	2059	...	2108	...	...	2159	...	2256	...	...	2359	...	...	...

		⚒	⚒	⚒	⚒	⚒	⚒	⚒	⚒	⚒	⚒	⚒	⚒	⚒	⚒	⚒	⚒	⚒	⚒	⚒	⚒	⚒	⚒	⚒	⚒	⚒
Liverpool Lime Street d.	⚒	...	...	...	...	...	...	...	0612	...	0622	...	...	0712	...	0715	...	...	0812	...	0822	...	...	0912	...	0922
Liverpool South Parkway d.		...	...	...	...	...	...	...	|	...	0632	...	...	|	...	0725	...	...	|	...	0832	...	...	|	...	0932
Warrington Central d.		...	...	...	...	...	...	...	|	...	0645	...	...	|	...	0741	...	...	|	...	0845	...	...	|	...	0945
Manchester Airport d.		...	0425	...	0530	...	...	...	|	0634	|	0706	...	|	0732	|	0806	...	|	0833	|	0906	...	|	0933	|
Manchester Piccadilly d.		...	0440	...	0547	...	0615	0626	|	0657	0711	0726	0740	|	0757	0810	0826	0841	|	0856	0911	0926	0941	|	0957	1011
Manchester Victoria d.		...	|	...	|	...	|	|	0646	|	|	|	|	0752	|	|	|	|	0852	|	|	|	|	0952	|	|
Stalybridge d.		...	|	...	0600	...	0627	|	0658	|	0725	|	0753	|	|	0825	|	0854	|	|	0925	|	0954	|	|	1025
Huddersfield d.		...	0540	...	0618	...	0646	0656	0717	0727	0746	0755	0813	0821	0827	0846	0855	0913	0921	0927	0946	0955	1013	1021	1027	1046
Dewsbury d.		...	|	...	0627	...	0655	0705	0726	|	0755	0804	0823	|	|	0855	|	0923	|	|	0955	|	1023	|	|	1055
Leeds a.		...	0559	...	0640	...	0708	0718	0739	0746	0809	0817	0836	0841	0846	0909	0915	0936	0940	0946	1008	1015	1036	1040	1046	1108
Leeds d.		...	0601	...	0643	...	0714	0722	0743	0749	0812	0820	0838	0843	0849	0912	0917	0938	0943	0949	1012	1017	1038	1043	1049	1112
Selby d.		...	|	...	|	...	|	0741	|	|	|	|	0858	|	|	|	|	0957	|	|	|	|	1057	|	|	|
Hull a.		...	|	...	|	...	|	0818	|	|	|	|	0931	|	|	|	|	1032	|	|	|	|	1132	|	|	|
York a.		...	0624	...	0706	...	0736	...	0806	0812	0837	0842	...	0906	0912	0936	0940	...	1006	1012	1036	1040	...	1106	1112	1136
York d.		0600	0626	0640	0708	0718	0740	...	0808	0815	0840	...	...	0908	0915	0940	...	...	1008	1015	1040	...	...	1108	1115	1140
Malton d.		|	|	0704	|	|	0804	...	|	|	0904	...	...	|	|	1004	...	...	|	|	1104	...	...	|	|	1204
Scarborough a.		|	|	0729	|	|	0829	...	|	|	0930	...	...	|	|	1029	...	...	|	|	1129	...	...	|	|	1229
Thirsk d.		0616	|	...	0725	0734	...	...	|	0831	...	...	...	|	0931	...	...	...	|	1031	...	...	...	|	1131	...
Northallerton d.		0624	0647	...	0733	0743	...	...	0829	0840	...	...	...	0929	0940	...	...	...	1029	1040	...	...	...	1129	1140	...
Darlington d.		0640	0659	...	0745	|	...	...	0841	|	...	...	...	0941	|	...	...	...	1041	|	...	...	...	1141	|	...
Middlesbrough a.		0707	|	...	|	0817	...	...	|	0912	...	...	...	|	1012	...	...	...	|	1112	...	...	...	|	1212	...
Durham d.		...	0715	...	0801	...	...	...	0857	...	...	...	...	0957	...	...	...	...	1057	...	...	...	...	1157	...	...
Newcastle a.		...	0734	...	0819	...	...	...	0914	...	...	...	...	1015	...	...	...	...	1114	...	...	...	...	1215	...	...

	⚒	⚒	⚒	⚒	⚒	⚒	⚒	⚒	⚒	⚒	⚒	⚒	⚒	⚒	⚒	⚒	⚒	⚒	⚒	⚒	⚒	⚒	⚒	⚒	⚒	⚒
Liverpool Lime Street d.	...	...	1012	...	1022	...	...	1112	...	1122	...	...	1212	...	1222	...	...	1312	...	1322	...	...	1412	...	1422	...
Liverpool South Parkway d.	...	...	|	...	1032	...	...	|	...	1132	...	...	|	...	1232	...	...	|	...	1332	...	...	|	...	1432	...
Warrington Central d.	...	...	|	...	1045	...	...	|	...	1145	...	...	|	...	1245	...	...	|	...	1345	...	...	|	...	1445	...
Manchester Airport d.	1006	...	|	1033	|	1106	...	|	1133	|	1206	...	|	1233	|	1306	...	|	1333	|	1406	...	|	1433	|	1506
Manchester Piccadilly d.	1026	1041	|	1057	1111	1126	1141	|	1157	1211	1226	1241	|	1257	1311	1326	1341	|	1357	1411	1426	1441	|	1457	1511	1526
Manchester Victoria d.	|	|	1052	|	|	|	|	1152	|	|	|	|	1252	|	|	|	|	1352	|	|	|	|	1452	|	|	|
Stalybridge d.	|	1054	|	|	1125	|	1154	|	|	1225	|	1254	|	|	1325	|	1354	|	|	1425	|	1454	|	|	1525	|
Huddersfield d.	1055	1113	1121	1127	1146	1155	1213	1221	1227	1246	1255	1313	1321	1327	1346	1355	1413	1421	1427	1446	1455	1513	1521	1527	1546	1555
Dewsbury d.	|	1123	|	|	1155	|	1223	|	|	1255	|	1323	|	|	1355	|	1423	|	|	1455	|	1523	|	|	1555	|
Leeds a.	1115	1136	1140	1146	1208	1215	1236	1240	1246	1308	1315	1336	1340	1346	1408	1415	1436	1440	1446	1508	1515	1536	1540	1546	1608	1615
Leeds d.	1117	1138	1143	1149	1212	1217	1238	1243	1249	1312	1317	1338	1343	1349	1412	1417	1438	1443	1449	1512	1517	1538	1543	1549	1612	1617
Selby d.	|	1157	|	|	|	|	1257	|	|	|	|	1357	|	|	|	|	1457	|	|	|	|	1557	|	|	|	|
Hull a.	|	1232	|	|	|	|	1332	|	|	|	|	1432	|	|	|	|	1532	|	|	|	|	1632	|	|	|	|
York a.	1140	...	1206	1212	1236	1240	...	1306	1312	1336	1340	...	1406	1412	1436	1440	...	1506	1512	1536	1540	...	1606	1612	1636	1640
York d.	...	...	1208	1215	1240	...	...	1308	1315	1340	...	...	1408	1415	1440	...	...	1508	1515	1540	...	...	1608	1615	1640	...
Malton d.	...	...	|	|	1304	...	...	|	|	1404	...	...	|	|	1504	...	...	|	|	1604	...	...	|	|	1704	...
Scarborough a.	...	...	|	|	1329	...	...	|	|	1429	...	...	|	|	1529	...	...	|	|	1629	...	...	|	|	1729	...
Thirsk d.	...	...	|	1231	...	...	...	|	1331	...	...	...	|	1431	...	...	...	|	1531	...	...	...	|	1631	...	...
Northallerton d.	...	...	1229	1240	...	...	...	1329	1340	...	...	...	1429	1440	...	...	...	1529	1540	...	...	...	1629	1640	...	...
Darlington d.	...	...	1241	|	...	...	...	1341	|	...	...	...	1441	|	...	...	...	1541	|	...	...	...	1641	|	...	...
Middlesbrough a.	...	...	|	1312	...	...	...	|	1412	...	...	...	|	1512	...	...	...	|	1612	...	...	...	|	1712	...	...
Durham d.	...	...	1257	...	...	...	...	1357	...	...	...	...	1457	...	...	...	...	1557	...	...	...	...	1657	...	...	...
Newcastle a.	...	...	1315	...	...	...	...	1415	...	...	...	...	1512	...	...	...	...	1615	...	...	...	...	1712	...	...	...

For footnotes see page 153.

Tables 190 and 192 are temporarily relocated to page 337

TP LIVERPOOL and MANCHESTER - YORKSHIRE and THE NORTH EAST 188

Due to engineering work services to Hull are subject to alteration July 26 - September 7.
Additional overnight services operate York - Manchester Airport and v.v. Please contact operator for details.

	⚒	⚒	⚒	⚒	⚒	⚒	⚒	⚒	⚒	Ⓐ	⑥	⚒	⚒	⚒	⚒	⑥	Ⓐ	⚒	⚒	⚒	⚒	Ⓐ	⚒	⚒	⑥	⚒
Liverpool Lime Street d.	...	1512	...	1522	...	...	1612	...	1622	...	...	...	1710	...	1722	...	...	...	1812	...	1822	...	...	1912	...	1922
Liverpool South Parkway d.	...	|	...	1532	...	...	|	...	1632	...	...	...	|	...	1732	...	...	...	|	...	1832	...	...	|	...	1932
Warrington Central d.	...	|	...	1545	...	...	|	...	1645	...	...	...	|	...	1745	...	...	...	|	...	1845	...	...	|	...	1945
Manchester Airport d.	...	|	1533	|	1606	...	|	1633	|	1703	1706	...	|	1735	|	1806	...	...	|	1835	|	...	1920	|	...	|
Manchester Piccadilly d.	1541	|	1557	1611	1626	1641	|	1656	1711	1725	1725	1741	|	1754	1811	1826	1826	1841	|	1857	1911	1926	1940	|	...	2011
Manchester Victoria d.	|	1552	|	|	|	⚒	1652	|	|	|	|	|	1752	|	|	|	|	|	1852	|	|	|	|	1952	...	|
Stalybridge d.	1554	|	|	1625	|	1653	|	|	1725	1738	1738	1755	|	|	1825	|	|	1854	|	|	1925	|	|	|	...	2025
Huddersfield d.	1613	1621	1627	1646	1655	1713	1721	1727	1746	1757	1757	1816	1821	1827	1846	1855	1855	1914	1921	1927	1946	1956	2009	2021	...	2046
Dewsbury d.	1623	|	|	1655	|	1723	|	|	1755	|	|	1825	|	|	1855	|	|	1924	|	|	1956	|	|	|	...	2055
Leeds a.	1636	1640	1646	1708	1715	1737	1742	1746	1808	1816	1816	1838	1842	1846	1908	1915	1915	1937	1942	1946	2009	2016	2030	2042	...	2108
Leeds d.	1638	1643	1649	1712	1717	1740	1744	1749	1812	1818	1818	1840	1845	1849	1912	1917	1917	1939	1943	1949	2012	2022	2033	2043	2105	2112
Selby d.	1657	|	|	|	|	1801	|	|	|	|	|	1903	|	|	|	|	|	2000	|	|	|	2044	|	|	2127	|
Hull a.	1732	|	|	|	|	1838	|	|	|	|	|	1938	|	|	|	|	|	2038	|	|	|	2118	|	|	2205	|
York a.	...	1706	1712	1736	1743	...	1807	1814	1836	1844	1844	...	1908	1913	1936	1941	1941	...	2007	2012	2035	...	2058	2107	...	2137
York d.	...	1708	1715	1740	...	...	1809	1815	1840	...	...	...	1910	1916	1940	...	...	...	2008	2016	2040	...	...	2108	...	...
Malton d.	...	|	|	1804	...	...	|	|	1904	...	...	...	|	|	2004	...	...	...	|	|	2104	...	...	|	...	...
Scarborough a.	...	|	|	1829	...	...	|	|	1929	...	...	...	|	|	2029	...	...	...	|	|	2129	...	...	|	...	...
Thirsk d.	...	|	1731	...	...	...	|	1831	...	...	...	...	|	1933	...	...	...	...	|	2035	...	...	...	2126	...	...
Northallerton d.	...	1729	1740	...	...	...	1830	1840	...	...	...	...	1931	1941	...	...	...	...	2029	2043	...	...	...	2134	...	...
Darlington d.	...	1741	|	...	...	...	1842	|	...	...	...	...	1943	|	...	...	...	...	2041	|	...	...	...	2146	...	...
Middlesbrough a.	...	|	1812	...	...	...	|	1912	...	...	...	...	|	2014	...	...	...	...	|	2115	...	...	...	|	...	...
Durham d.	...	1757	...	...	...	...	1858	...	...	...	...	...	2001	...	...	...	...	...	2057	...	...	...	...	2202	...	...
Newcastle a.	...	1815	...	...	...	...	1914	...	...	...	...	...	2020	...	...	...	...	...	2113	...	...	...	...	2219	...	...

	Ⓐ	Ⓐ	⑥	Ⓐ	⑥	Ⓐ	⚒	⚒	⚒	⚒	⑥ b	⑥ c	Ⓐ	⑥ b	Ⓐ	⑥ c 🚌		⑦	⑦ e	⑦	⑦ h	⑦	⑦	⑦ j	⑦ h	⑦ g
Liverpool Lime Street d.	...	...	...	2022	2022	...	...	...	2130	...	2230	2230	2230	...	...	...	...		...	...	...	...	...	...	...	...
Liverpool South Parkway d.	...	...	...	2032	2032	...	...	...	2140	...	2240	2240	2240	...	...	...	...		...	...	...	...	...	...	...	...
Warrington Central d.	...	...	...	2045	2045	...	...	...	2153	...	2253	2253	2253	...	...	...	...		...	...	...	...	...	...	...	...
Manchester Airport d.	...	2020	2020	|	|	...	...	2120	|	2223	|	|	|	2320	2320	2325	...		0630	...	...	0730e	0803h	...	...	0830k
Manchester Piccadilly d.	...	2042	2042	2111	2111	...	...	2142	2219	2242	2321	2321	2321	2335	2335	2350	...		0647	...	...	0747e	0821h	...	...	0847
Manchester Victoria d.	...	|	|	|	|	...	...	|	|	|	|	|	|	2352	2352	|	...		|	...	...	|	|	...	...	|
Stalybridge d.	...	|	|	2125	2125	...	...	|	2232	2254	2334	2334	2334	|	|	|	...		0700	...	...	0800e	0833h	...	...	0900
Huddersfield d.	...	2112	2112	2146	2146	...	...	2211	2250	2313	2352	2352	2352	0021	0022	0050	...		0718	...	...	0818e	0852h	...	...	0918
Dewsbury d.	...	|	|	2155	2155	...	...	|	2259	2322	|	0024*	|	0030	0030s	|	...		0727	...	...	0827e	0901h	...	...	0927
Leeds a.	...	2131	2131	2208	2208	...	...	2230	2312	2335	0011	0050*	0031	0043	0044	0125	...		0740	...	...	0840e	0914h	...	...	0940
Leeds d.	2121	2133	2133	2211	2211	...	2221	2233	2316	2337	0015	...	0034	0045	0047	0125	...		0743	...	...	0843	0915	...	0943	0943
Selby d.	2144	|	|	|	|	...	2242	|	|	|	|	...	|	|	|	|	...		|	...	...	|	|	0938	|	|
Hull a.	2222	|	|	|	|	...	2317	|	|	|	|	...	|	|	|	|	...		|	...	...	|	|	1001	|	|
York a.	...	2157	2158	2234	2236	...	...	2258	2342	0003	0043	...	0115	0113	0129	0215	...		0811	...	...	0906	0938	...	1006	1006
York d.	...	2200	2212	2235	...	2242	...	...	...	...	...	...	...	...	...	...	...		...	0847	0855	0908	0942	...	1008	1008
Malton d.	...	2224	2236	|	...	2306	...	...	...	...	...	...	...	...	...	...	...		...	|	0921	|	1006	...	|	|
Scarborough a.	...	2249	2301	|	...	2331	...	...	...	...	...	...	...	...	...	...	...		...	|	0942	|	1031	...	|	|
Thirsk d.	...	...	...	2258	...	...	...	...	...	...	...	...	...	...	...	...	...		...	0903	...	|	...	...	|	|
Northallerton d.	...	...	...	2306	...	...	...	...	...	...	...	...	...	...	...	...	...		...	0911	...	0929	...	...	1029	1029
Darlington d.	...	...	...	2318	...	...	...	...	...	...	...	...	...	...	...	...	...		...	0925	...	0941	...	...	1041	1041
Middlesbrough a.	...	...	...	|	...	...	...	...	...	...	...	...	...	...	...	...	...		...	0952	...	|	...	...	|	|
Durham d.	...	...	...	2334	...	...	...	...	...	...	...	...	...	...	...	...	...		...	...	...	0957	...	...	1057	1057
Newcastle a.	...	...	...	0008	...	...	...	...	...	...	...	...	...	...	...	...	...		...	...	...	1015	...	...	1114	1114

	⑦	⑦	⑦ g	⑦ h	⑦	⑦ h	⑦ g	⑦	⑦	⑦	⑦	⑦	⑦	⑦	⑦	⑦	⑦	⑦	⑦	⑦	⑦	⑦	⑦	⑦	⑦	⑦
Liverpool Lime Street d.	...	0822	...	...	0912	...	...	0922	1003	...	1022	...	1112	...	1122	1212	...	1222	...	1312	...	1322	...	1412	...	1422
Liverpool South Parkway d.	...	0832	...	...	|	...	...	0932	|	...	1032	...	|	...	1132	|	...	1232	...	|	...	1332	...	|	...	1432
Warrington Central d.	...	0844	...	...	|	...	...	0944	|	...	1044	...	|	...	1145	|	...	1245	...	|	...	1345	...	|	...	1445
Manchester Airport d.	...	|	...	...	|	0933	0933	|	|	1033	|	...	|	1133	|	|	1233	|	...	|	1333	|	...	|	1433	|
Manchester Piccadilly d.	...	0910	0928	0943	|	0957	1003	1011	|	1057	1110	1143	|	1157	1211	|	1257	1311	1343	|	1357	1411	1443	|	1457	1511
Manchester Victoria d.	...	|	|	|	0952	|	|	|	1037	|	|	|	1152	|	|	1252	|	|	|	1352	|	|	|	1452	|	|
Stalybridge d.	...	0925	|	|	|	|	|	1025	|	|	1125	|	|	|	1225	|	|	1325	|	|	|	1425	|	|	|	1525
Huddersfield d.	...	0946	1005	1013	1021	1027	1032	1046	1112	1127	1146	1213	1221	1227	1246	1321	1327	1346	1413	1421	1427	1446	1513	1521	1527	1546
Dewsbury d.	...	0955	1015	1023	|	|	|	1055	|	|	1155	1223	|	|	1255	|	|	1355	1423	|	|	1455	1523	|	|	1555
Leeds a.	...	1008	1028	1036	1040	1046	1051	1109	1131	1146	1209	1236	1240	1246	1309	1340	1346	1409	1436	1440	1446	1509	1536	1540	1546	1609
Leeds d.	0952	1012	1038	1038	1043	1049	1053	1112	1138	1149	1212	1238	1243	1248	1312	1343	1349	1412	1438	1443	1449	1512	1538	1543	1549	1612
Selby d.	1013	|	1105	1105	|	|	|	|	|	|	|	1300	|	|	|	|	|	|	1457	|	|	|	1600	|	|	|
Hull a.	1047d	|	1140	1140d	|	|	|	|	|	|	|	1339d	|	|	|	|	|	|	1532d	|	|	|	1634d	|	|	|
York a.	...	1036	...	...	1106	1112	1116	1139	1201	1212	1235	...	1306	1311	1335	1406	1412	1439	...	1506	1511	1539	...	1606	1612	1637
York d.	...	1042	...	...	1108	1117	1117	1142	1203	...	1242	...	1308	1314	1342	1410	...	1442	...	1508	1514	1542	...	1608	...	1642
Malton d.	...	1106	...	...	|	|	|	1206	|	...	1306	...	|	|	1406	|	...	1506	...	|	|	1606	...	|	...	1706
Scarborough a.	...	1131	...	...	|	|	|	1231	|	...	1331	...	|	|	1431	|	...	1531	...	|	|	1631	...	|	...	1731
Thirsk d.	...	...	...	...	|	1134	1134	...	|	...	...	...	|	1334	...	|	...	...	...	|	1531	...	...	|	...	...
Northallerton d.	...	...	...	...	1129	1142	1142	...	1224	...	...	...	1329	1342	...	1431	...	...	...	1529	1540	...	...	1629	...	...
Darlington d.	...	...	...	...	1141	|	|	...	1236	...	...	...	1341	|	...	1443	...	...	...	1541	|	...	...	1641	...	...
Middlesbrough a.	...	...	...	...	|	1214	1214	...	|	...	...	...	|	1413	...	|	...	...	...	|	1612	...	...	|	...	...
Durham d.	...	...	...	...	1157	...	...	...	1252	...	...	...	1357	...	...	1500	...	...	...	1557	...	...	...	1657	...	...
Newcastle a.	...	...	...	...	1215	...	...	...	1307	...	...	...	1416	...	...	1516	...	...	...	1615	...	...	...	1714	...	...

	⑦	⑦	⑦	⑦	⑦	⑦	⑦	⑦	⑦	⑦	⑦	⑦	⑦	⑦	⑦	⑦	⑦	⑦	⑦	⑦	⑦	⑦	⑦	⑦	⑦	⑦
Liverpool Lime Street d.	...	1512	...	1522	...	1612	...	1622	...	1712	...	1722	1812	...	1822	...	...	1912	1922	...	2012	2022	...	...	2152	...
Liverpool South Parkway d.	...	|	...	1532	...	|	...	1632	...	|	...	1732	|	...	1832	...	...	|	1932	...	|	2032	...	...	2202	...
Warrington Central d.	...	|	...	1545	...	|	...	1645	...	|	...	1745	|	...	1845	...	...	|	1945	...	|	2045	...	...	2215	...
Manchester Airport d.	...	|	1533	|	...	|	1633	|	...	|	1735	|	|	1833	|	...	1920	|	|	2020	|	|	...	2120	|	2320
Manchester Piccadilly d.	1543	|	1557	1611	1643	|	1648	1711	1743	|	1757	1811	|	1857	1911	...	1942	|	2011	2043	|	2111	...	2142	2242	2337
Manchester Victoria d.	|	1552	|	|	|	1652	1657	|	|	1752	|	|	1852	|	|	...	|	1952	|	|	2052	|	...	|	|	2352
Stalybridge d.	|	|	|	1625	|	|	|	1725	|	|	|	1825	|	|	1925	...	|	|	2025	|	|	2125	...	|	2255	|
Huddersfield d.	1613	1621	1630	1646	1713	1721	1727	1746	1813	1821	1827	1846	1921	1927	1946	...	2011	2021	2046	2113	2121	2146	...	2211	2313	0021
Dewsbury d.	1623	|	|	1655	1723	|	|	1755	1823	|	|	1855	|	|	1955	...	|	|	2055	|	|	2155	...	2220	2322	0030
Leeds a.	1636	1640	1649	1709	1736	1740	1746	1809	1836	1840	1846	1908	1940	1946	2008	...	2030	2040	2108	2133	2140	2208	...	2233	2335	0043
Leeds d.	1638	1643	1650	1712	1738	1743	1749	1812	1838	1843	1849	1912	1943	1949	2012	2018	2033	2043	2112	2138	2143	2211	2221	2236	2341	0045
Selby d.	1657	|	|	|	1800	|	|	|	1900	|	|	|	|	|	|	2049	|	|	|	2200	|	|	2242	|	|	|
Hull a.	1732d	|	|	|	1834d	|	|	|	1934d	|	|	|	|	|	|	2125d	|	|	|	2234d	|	|	2317d	|	|	|
York a.	...	1706	1713	1737	...	1806	1812	1835	...	1906	1912	1936	2006	2012	2035	...	2056	2106	2137	...	2206	2234	...	2302	0022	0113
York d.	...	1708	1715	1742	...	1808	...	1842	...	1908	1915	1942	2008	...	2042	...	2100	2108	...	...	2208	2235	...	...	...	...
Malton d.	...	|	|	1806	...	|	...	1906	...	|	|	2006	|	...	2106	...	|	|	...	...	2232	|	...	...	...	...
Scarborough a.	...	|	|	1831	...	|	...	1931	...	|	|	2031	|	...	2131	...	|	|	...	...	2257	|	...	...	...	...
Thirsk d.	...	|	1731	...	...	|	...	...	...	|	1933	...	|	...	...	...	2116	|	...	...	...	2258	...	...	...	...
Northallerton d.	...	1729	1740	...	...	1829	...	...	...	1929	1944	...	2029	...	...	...	2124	2129	...	...	...	2306	...	...	...	...
Darlington d.	...	1741	|	...	...	1841	...	...	...	1941	|	...	2041	...	...	...	|	2141	...	...	...	2318	...	...	...	...
Middlesbrough a.	...	|	1812	...	...	|	...	...	...	|	2016	...	|	...	...	...	2158	|	...	...	...	|	...	...	...	...
Durham d.	...	1757	...	...	...	1857	...	...	...	1957	...	...	2057	...	...	...	...	2157	...	...	...	2334	...	...	...	...
Newcastle a.	...	1815	...	...	...	1914	...	...	...	2014	...	...	2114	...	...	...	...	2214	...	...	...	0008	...	...	...	...

For footnotes see page 153.

Tables 190 and 192 are temporarily relocated to page 337

193 CLEETHORPES - DONCASTER - SHEFFIELD - MANCHESTER TP

km			①	②–⑥	⚒	⚒	⚒	⚒	⚒		⚒	⚒	⚒	⚒	⚒	⚒		⚒	⚒	⚒	⚒	⚒	⚒	⚒
0	**Cleethorpes** d.	⚒	...	...	...	...	0504	...	0620	...	0726	0826	0926	1026	1126	1226	...	1326	1426	1526	1626	1726	1826	1926
5	Grimsby Town d.		...	...	...	...	0512	...	0628	...	0734	0834	0934	1034	1134	1234	...	1334	1434	1534	1634	1734	1834	1934
48	Scunthorpe d.		...	...	...	...	0546	...	0703	...	0808	0908	1008	1108	1208	1308	...	1408	1508	1608	1708	1808	1908	2008
85	**Doncaster** a.		...	...	...	...	0623	...	0733	...	0838	0938	1038	1138	1238	1338	...	1438	1538	1638	1738	1838	1938	2040
85	**Doncaster** 192 d.		...	...	...	0539	0625	...	0735	...	0842	0942	1042	1142	1242	1342	...	1442	1542	1642	1742	1842	1942	2042
109	Meadowhall 192 d.		...	...	...	0600	0646	...	0753	...	0901	1001	1101	1201	1301	1401	...	1501	1601	1701	1801	1901	2001	2109
115	**Sheffield** 192 a.		...	...	...	0608	0656	...	0800	...	0908	1008	1108	1208	1308	1408	...	1508	1608	1708	1808	1908	2008	2119
115	**Sheffield** 206 d.		0325	0325	0511	0611	...	0708	0804	...	0911	1011	1111	1211	1311	1411	...	1511	1611	1711	1811	1911	2011	...
175	Stockport 206 a.		|	|	|	0653	...	0753	0853	...	0953	1053	1153	1253	1353	1453	...	1553	1653	1753	1853	1953	2053	...
184	**Manchester** Piccadilly 206 a.		0420	0452	0603	0702	...	0802	0902	...	1002	1102	1202	1302	1402	1502	...	1602	1702	1802	1902	2002	2102	...
200	**Manchester** Airport a.		0440	0512	0628	0729	...	0826	0933	...	1033	1133	1226	1333	1433	1533	...	1633	1733	1826	1933	2039	2136	...

		⑦	⑦		⑦	⑦		⑦	⑦		⑦	⑦		⑦	⑦		⑦	⑦		⑦	⑦		⑦
Cleethorpes d.	⑦	...	...	...	...	0926	...	1026	1126	...	...	1326	...	1426	1526	...	1626	1726	...	1826	1926	...	2026
Grimsby Town d.		...	...	...	...	0934	...	1034	1134	...	...	1334	...	1434	1534	...	1634	1734	...	1834	1934	...	2034
Scunthorpe d.		...	...	...	...	1008	...	1108	1208	...	...	1408	...	1508	1608	...	1708	1808	...	1908	2008	...	2108
Doncaster a.		...	...	...	...	1040	...	1139	1240	...	...	1438	...	1538	1638	...	1738	1838	...	1938	2040	...	2141
Doncaster 192 d.		...	...	...	...	1042	...	1142	1242	...	1342	1442	...	1542	1642	...	1742	1842	...	1942	2042	...	2142
Meadowhall 192 d.		...	...	...	...	1101	...	1201	1300	...	1401	1501	...	1601	1701	...	1801	1901	...	2001	2101	...	2206
Sheffield 192 a.		...	...	...	...	1108	...	1207	1307	...	1409	1508	...	1608	1708	...	1808	1908	...	2008	2108	...	2215
Sheffield 206 d.		0751	0911	...	1011	1111	...	1210	1310	...	1411	1511	...	1611	1711	...	1811	1911	...	2011	2111	...	...
Stockport 206 a.		0831	0953	...	|	1153	...	1252	1353	...	1453	1553	...	1653	1753	...	1853	1953	...	2053	2153	...	...
Manchester Piccadilly 206 a.		0841	1004	...	1104	1204	...	1304	1404	...	1504	1604	...	1704	1804	...	1904	2004	...	2104	2204	...	...
Manchester Airport a.		0910	1029	...	1130	1229	...	1329	1429	...	1529	1629	...	1729	1829	...	1929	2029	...	2129	2229	...	...

		⚒	⑥	Ⓐ	⚒	⚒	⚒	⚒	⚒	⚒	⚒	⚒	⚒	⑥	Ⓐ	⚒	⚒	Ⓐ	⑥	⚒	Ⓐ	⑥	Ⓐ
Manchester Airport d.	⚒	0550	...	...	0655	0753	0855	0955	1055	1155	1255	1355	1455	1555	1555	1655	1755	1855	1855	1955	...	...	2047
Manchester Piccadilly 206 d.		0613	...	...	0720	0820	0920	1020	1120	1220	1320	1420	1520	1620	1620	1720	1820	1918	1918	2020	...	...	2120
Stockport 206 d.		0622	...	...	0728	0828	0928	1028	1128	1228	1328	1428	1528	1628	1628	1728	1828	1926	1926	2028	...	...	2128
Sheffield 206 a.		0702	...	...	0810	0908	1008	1108	1208	1308	1408	1508	1608	1708	1708	1810	1911	2008	2008	2112	...	...	2209
Sheffield 192 d.		...	0709	0712	0812	0910	1010	1110	1210	1310	1410	1510	1610	1710	1710	1811	1912	2010	2026	...	2134	2151	2210
Meadowhall 192 d.		...	0715	0718	0818	0916	1016	1116	1216	1316	1416	1516	1616	1716	1716	1817	1918	2016	2032	...	2140	2158	2216
Doncaster 192 a.		...	0739	0737	0837	0935	1035	1135	1235	1335	1435	1535	1635	1735	1737	1845	1941	2045	2100	...	2202	2220	2243
Doncaster d.		...	0743	0739	0839	0937	1037	1137	1237	1337	1437	1537	1637	1743	1747	1847	1949	2046	2107	...	2205	2225	2245
Scunthorpe d.		...	0810	0805	0905	1003	1103	1203	1303	1403	1503	1603	1703	1809	1813	1914	2015	2112	2133	...	2231	2259	2319
Grimsby Town d.		...	0848	0846	0939	1039	1137	1239	1337	1439	1537	1639	1737	1845	1849	1948	2048	2148	2209	...	2309	2335	2355
Cleethorpes a.		...	0857	0855	0951	1051	1149	1251	1349	1451	1549	1651	1750	1857	1901	2000	2101	2200	2221	...	2320	2347	0009

	⚒	Ⓐ			⑦	⑦	⑦		⑦	⑦	⑦	⑦		⑦	⑦	⑦		⑦	⑦	⑦		⑦	⑦
Manchester Airport d.	2147	2330	...	⑦	0841b	1044	1155	...	1255	1355	1455	1555	...	1655	1755	1855	...	1955	2055	...	...	2155	2255
Manchester Piccadilly 206 d.	2222	2352	...		0858	1118	1218	...	1320	1420	1502	1620	...	1720	1820	1920	...	2018	2120	...	...	2215	2315
Stockport 206 d.	|	|	...		0907	1127	1228	...	1328	1428	1528	1628	...	1728	1828	1928	...	2027	2128	...	...	2223	2323
Sheffield 206 a.	2314	0124	...		0946	1207	1308	...	1408	1508	1609	1708	...	1808	1908	2008	...	2108	2212	...	...	2305	0005
Sheffield 192 d.	...	...	...		0952	1210	1310	...	1410	1510	1610	1710	...	1810	1910	2010	...	2110	...	2230	...	...	...
Meadowhall 192 d.	...	...	...		0958	1216	1316	...	1416	1516	1616	1716	...	1816	1916	2016	...	2116	...	2237	...	...	...
Doncaster 192 a.	...	...	...		1028	1235	1335	...	1435	1535	1635	1735	...	1835	1935	2035	...	2135	...	2256	...	...	...
Doncaster d.	...	...	...		1029	1237	...	...	1437	1537	1637	1737	...	1837	1937	2037	...	2137	...	2258	...	...	...
Scunthorpe d.	...	...	...		1056	1303	...	...	1503	1603	1703	1803	...	1903	2003	2103	...	2203	...	2324	...	...	...
Grimsby Town d.	...	...	...		1133	1337	...	...	1538	1639	1737	1839	...	1937	2037	2139	...	2239	...	2358	...	...	...
Cleethorpes a.	...	...	...		1143	1349	...	...	1549	1651	1749	1851	...	1949	2049	2151	...	2251	...	0010	...	...	...

km	NT 2nd class only		⚒	⚒	⑥	⚒	⚒	⚒	⚒	⚒	⚒	⚒	⚒	⚒	⑥	Ⓐ			⑦	⑦	⑦	⑦	⑦		⑦	⑦
0	**Sheffield** ⊙ d.	⚒	0620	0712	0814	0914	1014	1214	1414	1614	1714	1814	1914	2035	2224	2247	...	⑦	0920	1114	1313	1514	1714	...	1915	2217
16	Grindleford d.		0635	0729	0828	0928	1028	1228	1428	1628	1728	1828	1928	2050	2238	2304	...		0934	1129	1328	1529	1729	...	1929	2232
18	Hathersage d.		0639	0732	0832	0932	1032	1232	1432	1632	1732	1832	1932	2053	2241	2308	...		0938	1132	1331	1532	1732	...	1932	2235
24	Hope d.		0647	0739	0839	0939	1039	1239	1439	1639	1739	1837	1939	2101	2248	2315	...		0945	1139	1338	1539	1739	...	1939	2242
32	Edale d.		0655	0747	0847	0947	1047	1247	1447	1647	1747	1845	1947	2109	2256	2322	...		0952	1147	1346	1547	1747	...	1947	2250
41	Chinley d.		0703	0756	0855	0955	1055	1255	1455	1655	1755	1853	1955	2117	2304	2330	...		1000	1155	1354	1555	1755	...	1955	2258
67	**Manchester** P'dilly ⊙ a.		0734	0835	0934	1034	1133	1334	1534	1734	1835	1934	2034	2205	2339	0001	...		1037	1233	1434	1633	1832	...	2032	2329

NT 2nd class only		⚒	⑥	Ⓐ	⑥	⚒	⚒	⚒	⚒	⚒	⚒	⑥	Ⓐ	⚒	⚒	⚒			⑦	⑦	⑦	⑦	⑦	⑦	⑦	⑦
Manchester P'dilly ⊙ d.	⚒	0546	0635	0708	0749	0849	1049	1249	1449	1549	1649	1749	1750	1849	2046	2228	...	⑦	0745	0922	1140	1340	1540	1740	1940	2211
Chinley d.		0614	0714	0748	0823	0923	1123	1323	1523	1623	1723	1825	1823	1923	2120	2253	...		0823	0959	1217	1417	1617	1817	2017	2243
Edale d.		0623	0723	0758	0832	0932	1132	1332	1532	1632	1732	1834	1832	1932	2129	2301	...		0832	1008	1226	1426	1626	1826	2026	2251
Hope d.		0629	0729	0804	0838	0938	1138	1338	1538	1638	1738	1840	1838	1937	2135	2307	...		0838	1014	1232	1432	1632	1832	2032	2257
Hathersage d.		0636	0736	0811	0845	0945	1145	1345	1545	1645	1745	1847	1845	1945	2141	2315	...		0845	1020	1239	1439	1639	1839	2039	2303
Grindleford d.		0640	0740	0815	0849	0949	1149	1349	1549	1649	1749	1851	1849	1949	2145	2319	...		0848	1024	1243	1443	1643	1843	2043	2307
Sheffield ⊙ a.		0657	0757	0832	0906	1006	1207	1406	1606	1706	1808	1908	1907	2006	2206	2335	...		0906	1044	1300	1459	1701	1901	2101	2324

a – Until Sep. 7.
b – Depart 0820 from Oct. 26 (by 🚌).

⊙ – Additional trains from Sheffield at 1020⑦a, 1114⑥, 1215⑦a, 1314⑥, 1514⑥, 1615⑦a; from Manchester at 0824⑦a, 0949⑥, 1040⑦a, 1149⑥, 1349⑥, 1440⑦a, 1645⑦a.

194 SKEGNESS - NOTTINGHAM 2nd class EM

km			Ⓐ	Ⓐ	Ⓐ	Ⓐ	Ⓐ	Ⓐ	Ⓐ	Ⓐ	Ⓐ	Ⓐ	Ⓐ	Ⓐ	Ⓐ	Ⓐ	Ⓐ	Ⓐ			⑥	⑥	⑥	⑥	⑥	⑥
0	**Skegness** d.	Ⓐ	...	0709	0810	0906	1015	1115	1215	1315	1415	1509	1611	1730	1814	1914	2015	2102	...	⑥	...	0709	0815	0915	1015	1115
38	Boston d.		0613	0746	0845	0941	1050	1150	1250	1350	1450	1544	1648	1805	1849	1949	2050	2137	...		0613	0746	0850	0950	1050	1150
66	Sleaford d.		0635	0811	0907	1003	1112	1212	1312	1413	1512	1610	1713	1827	1913	2013	2118	2200	...		0635	0811	0912	1014	1112	1212
89	Grantham a.		0704	0842	0935	1031	1141	1241	1341	1442	1541	1641	1742	|	1941	2040	2145	|	...		0707	0842	0941	1043	1141	1241
89	Grantham 206 d.		0710	0845	0941	1036	1145	1245	1346	1445	1545	1645	1745	|	1945	2044	2149	|	...		0710	0845	0945	1046	1145	1245
126	**Nottingham** 206 a.		0753	0920	1020	1117	1222	1323	1422	1523	1622	1717	1822	1922	2025	2120	2226	2253	...		0752	0920	1022	1123	1122	1323

	⑥	⑥	⑥	⑥	⑥	⑥	⑥	⑥	⑥	⑥			⑦a	⑦a	⑦a	⑦b	⑦a	⑦	⑦a		⑦b	⑦a	⑦	⑦	⑦a	⑦b
Skegness d.	1215	1315	1415	1509	1611	1730	1814	1919	2015	2102	...	⑦	...	1014	1115	...	1227	1410	1504	...	1617	1622	1807	1915	2043	...
Boston d.	1250	1350	1450	1544	1648	1805	1849	1954	2050	2137	...		0906	1049	1149	1213	1302	1445	1540	...	1652	1657	1842	1950	2118	...
Sleaford d.	1312	1413	1512	1610	1713	1827	1913	2018	2112	2200	...		0928	1111	1211	1235	1324	1507	1603	...	1714	1719	1904	2012	2142	2142
Grantham a.	1341	1442	1541	1641	1742	|	1941	2045	2143	|	...		0957	1140	1240	1304	|	1535	1632	...	1743	|	1933	2041	2210	2210
Grantham 206 d.	1346	1445	1545	1645	1745	|	1945	2048	2147	|	...		1001	1146	1244	...	|	1540	1636	...	1747	|	1937	2045	2213	2213
Nottingham 206 a.	1422	1523	1622	1720	1822	1923	2024	2125	2225	2254	...		1037	1228	1320	...	1416	1617	1713	...	1822	1811	2012	2120	2249	2249

		Ⓐ	Ⓐ	Ⓐ	Ⓐ	Ⓐ	Ⓐ	Ⓐ	Ⓐ	Ⓐ	Ⓐ	Ⓐ	Ⓐ	Ⓐ	Ⓐ	Ⓐ	Ⓐ	Ⓐ			⑥	⑥	⑥	⑥	⑥	⑥
Nottingham 206 d.	Ⓐ	0510	0550	0641	0734	0850	0955	1045	1145	1245	1345	1445	1545	1645	1744	1844	...	2051	...	⑥	0510	0550	0641	0728	0845	0955
Grantham 206 a.		0549	0627	0718	0812	0931	|	1123	1219	1323	1423	1522	1625	1728	1825	1923	...	2132	...		0549	0627	0718	0807	0926	|
Grantham d.		▬	0631	0724	0816	0937	|	1127	1225	1327	1427	1526	1629	1732	1829	1926	...	2138	...		▬	0631	0724	0816	0930	|
Sleaford d.		Ⓐ	0657	0751	0845	1004	1044	1153	1250	1355	1452	1552	1655	1801	1855	1955	2120	2203	...		⑥	0657	0751	0845	0956	1044
Boston d.		0625	0724	0818	0912	1028	1111	1219	1315	1421	1517	1620	1721	1826	1921	2019	2153	2229	...		0625	0724	0818	0911	1022	1111
Skegness a.		0703	0805	0856	0949	1105	1150	1258	1354	1500	1556	1659	1800	1905	2000	2057	...	...	...		0701	0805	0856	0948	1100	1150

	⑥	⑥	⑥	⑥	⑥	⑥	⑥	⑥	⑥	⑥	⑥			⑦a	⑦a	⑦a	⑦a	⑦	⑦b	⑦a	⑦	⑦	⑦a	⑦b	⑦a	⑦b
Nottingham 206 d.	1045	1145	1245	1345	1445	1545	1645	1744	1845	...	2051	...	⑦	...	0900	0941	1109	1155	...	1403	1456	1623	1817	1831	1948	1948
Grantham 206 a.	1123	1219	1325	1423	1522	1625	1728	1825	1923	...	2131	...		...	|	1015	1144	1229	...	1437	1531	1703	1851	1908	2022	2022
Grantham d.	1127	1225	1329	1427	1526	1629	1732	1829	1926	...	2136	...		...	|	1020	1150	1233	1350	1441	1536	1707	1855	1913	2027	2027
Sleaford d.	1153	1250	1355	1452	1552	1655	1801	1855	1955	2121	2201	...		...	0949	1046	1215	1259	1416	1509	1604	1736	1921	1941	2052	2055
Boston d.	1219	1315	1421	1517	1620	1721	1826	1921	2019	2153	2229	...		0931	1016	1111	1241	1324	1445	1539	1631	1802	1950	2010	2120	...
Skegness a.	1258	1354	1500	1556	1659	1800	1905	2000	2057	...	...	...		1007	1055	1150	1320	1400	1524	1618	1710	1838	2026	...	...	...

a – Until Sep. 7.
b – From Sep. 14.

FC — LONDON - KINGS LYNN — 196

Service on ⑦ valid until September 7.

km			Ⓐ	Ⓐ	Ⓐ	Ⓐ	Ⓐ	Ⓐ	Ⓐ	Ⓐ	Ⓐ	Ⓐ	Ⓐ	Ⓐ	Ⓐ	Ⓐ	Ⓐ	Ⓐ	Ⓐ	Ⓐ	Ⓐ	Ⓐ	Ⓐ	Ⓐ
0	**London** Kings Cross ...... **197** d.	Ⓐ	...	0544	0645	0714	0744	0844	0944	1044	1144	1244	1344	1444	1544	1558**p**	1644	1707**p**	1744	1814	1807**p**	1844	1907**p**	1944
93	Cambridge .... **197** d.		0617	0652	0733	0806	0838	0935	1035	1135	1235	1335	1435	1535	1635	1722	1740	1817	1839	1910	1919	1939	2014	2040
117	Ely .... d.		0633	0708	0749	0822	0854	0951	1051	1151	1251	1351	1451	1551	1651	1739	1756	1833	1855	1924	1935	1955	2030	2056
142	Downham Market .... d.		0653	0725	0807	0838	0911	1007	1107	1207	1307	1407	1507	1607	1709	...	1813	1850	1912	1939	1952	2012	2047	2112
160	**Kings Lynn** .... a.		0708	0741	0822	0852	0926	1022	1122	1222	1322	1422	1522	1622	1724	...	1827	1908	1927	1952	2010	2027	2105	2127

	Ⓐ	Ⓐ	Ⓐ	Ⓐ	Ⓐ	Ⓐ	Ⓐ			⑥	⑥	⑥	⑥	⑥	⑥	⑥	⑥	⑥	⑥	⑥	⑥	⑥	⑥	⑥
London Kings Cross ...... **197** d.	2014	2044	2114	2144	2214	2244	2314	...	⑥	...	0644	0744	0844	0944	1044	1144	1244	1344	1444	1544	1644	1744	1814	1844
Cambridge .... **197** d.	2110	2140	2208	2238	2308	2338	0010	...		0635	0735	0835	0935	1035	1135	1235	1335	1435	1535	1635	1735	1835	1904	1935
Ely .... d.	2126	2156	2224	2255	2324	2355	0026	...		0651	0751	0851	0951	1051	1151	1251	1351	1451	1551	1651	1751	1851	1919	1951
Downham Market .... d.	2142	2212	2240	...	2340	...	0042	...		0707	0807	0907	1007	1107	1207	1307	1407	1507	1607	1707	1807	1907	1935	2007
Kings Lynn .... a.	2157	2227	2255	...	2355	...	0057	...		0722	0822	0922	1022	1122	1222	1322	1422	1522	1622	1722	1822	1922	1952	2022

	⑥	⑥	⑥	⑥			⑦	⑦	⑦	⑦	⑦	⑦		⑦	⑦	⑦	⑦	⑦		⑦	⑦	⑦	⑦	⑦
London Kings Cross ...... **197** d.	1944	2044	2214	2314	...	⑦	0753	0915	1015	1115	1215	1315	...	1415	1515	1615	1715	1815	...	1915	2015	2115	2215	2315
Cambridge .... **197** d.	2035	2140	2310	0010	...		0906	1006	1106	1206	1306	1406	...	1506	1606	1706	1806	1906	...	2007	2106	2206	2306	0008
Ely .... d.	2051	2156	2326	0026	...		0922	1022	1122	1222	1322	1422	...	1522	1622	1722	1822	1922	...	2023	2122	2222	2322	0024
Downham Market .... d.	2107	2212	2342	0042	...		0938	1038	1138	1238	1338	1438	...	1538	1638	1738	1838	1938	...	2039	2138	2238	2338	0041
Kings Lynn .... a.	2122	2227	2357	0057	...		0953	1053	1153	1253	1353	1453	...	1553	1653	1753	1853	1953	...	2053	2153	2253	2353	0056

		Ⓐ	Ⓐ	Ⓐ	Ⓐ	Ⓐ	Ⓐ	Ⓐ	Ⓐ	Ⓐ	Ⓐ	Ⓐ	Ⓐ	Ⓐ	Ⓐ	Ⓐ	Ⓐ	Ⓐ	Ⓐ		Ⓐ	Ⓐ	Ⓐ	Ⓐ
Kings Lynn .... d.	Ⓐ	0455	0519	0552	0610	0617	0652	0714	0725	...	0755	0828	0858	...	0955	1055	1155	1255	1355	...	1455	1555	1637	1737
Downham Market .... d.		0508	0533	0605	0621	0631	0705	0728	0737	...	0808	0841	0911	...	1008	1108	1208	1308	1408	...	1508	1608	1650	1750
Ely .... d.		0525	0552	0622	0647	0650	0722	0748	0756	0802	0826	0858	0928	1011	1025	1125	1225	1325	1425	...	1525	1625	1708	1808
Cambridge .... **197** a.		0543	0610	0639	0705	0708	0739	0804	0812	0820	0845	0915	0945	1027	1043	1143	1243	1343	1443	...	1543	1643	1724	1824
London Kings Cross ...... **197** a.		0638	0725**p**	0737	0807	0825**p**	0838	0910	0910	0950**p**	0944	1013	1043	1132	1135	1238	1335	1436	1535	...	1635	1736	1734	1936

	Ⓐ	Ⓐ	Ⓐ	Ⓐ	Ⓐ			⑥	⑥	⑥	⑥	⑥	⑥	⑥	⑥	⑥	⑥	⑥		⑥	⑥	⑥	⑥	⑥
Kings Lynn .... d.	1837	1937	2037	2137	2228	...	⑥	...	0555	0655	0755	0855	0930	0955	1055	1155	1255	1355	...	1455	1555	1655	1755	1835
Downham Market .... d.	1850	1950	2050	2150	2241	...		...	0608	0708	0808	0908	0942	1008	1108	1208	1308	1408	...	1508	1608	1708	1808	1848
Ely .... d.	1908	2008	2108	2208	2258	...		0526	0625	0725	0825	0925	0959	1025	1125	1225	1325	1425	...	1525	1625	1725	1825	1906
Cambridge .... **197** a.	1924	2026	2126	2224	2314	...		0542	0643	0743	0843	0943	1014	1043	1143	1243	1343	1443	...	1543	1643	1743	1843	1922
London Kings Cross ...... **197** a.	2034	2132	2232	2332	0040	...		0639	0736	0836	0936	1035	1105	1137	1235	1335	1435	1535	...	1635	1736	1835	1935	2032

	⑥	⑥	⑥	⑥			⑦	⑦	⑦	⑦	⑦	⑦		⑦	⑦	⑦	⑦	⑦		⑦	⑦	⑦	⑦	⑦
Kings Lynn .... d.	1935	2035	2135	2311	...	⑦	0828	0928	1028	1128	1228	1328	...	1428	1528	1628	1728	1758	...	1828	1928	2028	2128	2228
Downham Market .... d.	1948	2048	2148	2324	...		0841	0941	1041	1141	1241	1341	...	1441	1541	1641	1741	1809	...	1841	1941	2041	2141	2241
Ely .... d.	2006	2106	2206	2343	...		0858	0958	1058	1158	1258	1358	...	1458	1558	1658	1758	1826	...	1858	1958	2058	2158	2258
Cambridge .... **197** a.	2022	2122	2222	2359	...		0915	1015	1115	1215	1315	1415	...	1515	1615	1715	1815	1843	...	1915	2015	2115	2215	2315
London Kings Cross ...... **197** a.	2132	2232	2332	...	...		1009	1108	1208	1308	1408	1508	...	1608	1708	1809	1910	1937	...	2012	2111	2209	2311	0040

p – London **Liverpool Street**.

FC — LONDON KINGS CROSS - CAMBRIDGE — 197

Service on ⑦ valid until September 7.

km			②–⑤	①	Ⓐ	Ⓐ	Ⓐ	Ⓐ	Ⓐ	Ⓐ	and at the same	Ⓐ	Ⓐ	Ⓐ	Ⓐ	Ⓐ	Ⓐ	Ⓐ	Ⓐ	Ⓐ	Ⓐ	Ⓐ	Ⓐ	Ⓐ
0	**London** Kings Cross . d.	Ⓐ	0004	0004	0544	0645	0714	0744	0814	0844	minutes past each	1514	1544	1553	1614	1644	1714	1744	1814	1844	1914	1944	2014	2044
93	**Cambridge** .... a.		0125	0129	0650	0731	0805	0834	0904	0930	hour until ☆	1603	1630	1655	1704	1735	1805	1834	1909	1934	2005	2035	2105	2135

	Ⓐ	Ⓐ	Ⓐ	Ⓐ	Ⓐ			⑥	⑥	⑥	⑥	⑥	⑥	and at the same	⑥	⑥	⑥	⑥	⑥	⑥	⑥	⑥	⑥	⑥
London Kings Cross . d.	2114	2144	2214	2244	2314	...	⑥	0004	0031	0545	0644	0744	0814	minutes past each	1744	1814	1844	1914	1944	2044	2053	2105	2153	2214
Cambridge .... a.	2205	2235	2305	2335	0005	...		0123	0127	0655	0730	0830	0903	hour until ☆	1830	1904	1930	2003	2030	2135	2155	2229	2255	2305

	⑥			⑦	⑦	⑦	⑦	⑦	⑦	⑦	⑦	⑦	⑦	and at the same	⑦	⑦	⑦	⑦		⑦	⑦	⑦	⑦	⑦
London Kings Cross . d.	2314	...	⑦	0015	0638	0753	0853	0915	0953	1015	1053	1115	1153	minutes past each	1915	1953	2015	2053	...	2115	2153	2215	2253	2315
Cambridge .... a.	0005	...		0122	0748	0855	0955	1002	1055	1101	1155	1201	1255	hour until ☆	2002	2055	2101	2155	...	2201	2255	2301	2355	0007

		Ⓐ	Ⓐ	Ⓐ	Ⓐ	Ⓐ	Ⓐ	Ⓐ	Ⓐ	Ⓐ	Ⓐ	Ⓐ	Ⓐ	Ⓐ	Ⓐ	and at the same	Ⓐ	Ⓐ	Ⓐ	Ⓐ	Ⓐ	Ⓐ	Ⓐ	Ⓐ
Cambridge .... d.	Ⓐ	0545	0615	0645	0715	0745	0815	0850	0920	0927	0950	1015	1045	1115	1145	minutes past each	1815	1845	1915	1945	2015	2045	2115	2145
London Kings Cross . a.		0638	0716	0737	0807	0838	0910	0944	1013	1032	1043	1105	1135	1205	1238	hour until ☆	1909	1938	2006	2037	2107	2136	2206	2235

	Ⓐ	Ⓐ			⑥	⑥	⑥	⑥	⑥	⑥	⑥	⑥	and at the same	⑥	⑥	⑥	⑥	⑥	⑥	⑥	⑥	⑥	⑥	⑥
Cambridge .... d.	2230	2315	...	⑥	0545	0645	0715	0745	0815	0845	0915	0945	minutes past each	1715	1745	1815	1845	1915	1945	2015	2045	2145	2155	2230
London Kings Cross . a.	2332	0040	...		0639	0736	0805	0836	0904	0936	1004	1035	hour until ☆	1805	1835	1904	1935	2004	2034	2104	2134	2234	2319	2332

	⑥			⑦	⑦	⑦	⑦	⑦	⑦	⑦	⑦	⑦	⑦	and at the same	⑦	⑦	⑦	⑦		⑦	⑦	⑦	⑦	⑦
Cambridge .... d.	2315	...	⑦	0628	0728	0755	0828	0920	0928	1020	1028	1120	1128	minutes past each	1920	1928	2020	2028	...	2120	2128	2220	2228	2315
London Kings Cross . a.	0042	...		0748	0829	0919	0929	1009	1029	1108	1130	1208	1229	hour until ☆	2012	2031	2111	2129	...	2209	2229	2311	2329	0040

☆ – Timings may vary by up to 3 minutes.

CC, LE — LONDON - SOUTHEND and CAMBRIDGE — 199

Typical off-peak journey time in hours and minutes
READ DOWN ↓ READ UP ↑

Journey times may be extended during peak hours on Ⓐ (0600 - 0900 and 1600 - 1900) and also at weekends.
The longest journey time by any train is noted in the table heading.

LONDON FENCHURCH STREET - SOUTHEND CENTRAL — Longest journey: 1 hour 08 minutes — CC

km	A				A
0	0h00	↓	d.**London** F Street....a.	↑	1h04
8	0h08	↓	d.West Ham..........d.	↑	0h56
12	0h14	↓	d.Barking..........d.	↑	0h50
39	0h34	↓	d.Basildon..........d.	↑	0h29
56	0h53	↓	a.**Southend** Central..d.	↑	0h10
63	1h03		a.Shoeburyness........d.		0h00

From London Fenchurch Street: 0510⚒/0640⑦ and at least every 30 minutes (every 10 - 20 minutes 0840⚒ - 2010⚒) until 2340.

From Southend Central*: 0429⚒/0544⑦ and at least every 30 minutes (every 15 minutes 0914⚒ - 2014⚒) until 2244, 2314⚒.

A – During peak hours on Ⓐ (0600 - 0900 and 1600 - 1900) trains may not make all stops.
* – Trains depart Shoeburyness 10 minutes before Southend Central.

LONDON LIVERPOOL STREET - SOUTHEND VICTORIA — Longest journey: 1 hour 14 minutes — LE

km					
0	0h00	↓	d.**London** L Street....a.	↑	0h58
6	0h07	↓	d.Stratford..........d.	↑	0h49
32	0h26	↓	d.Shenfield..........d.	↑	0h35
53	0h43	↓	d.Rayleigh..........d.	↑	0h16
64	0h54	↓	a.**Southend** Airport...d.	↑	0h05
66	1h01		a.**Southend** Victoria .d.		0h00

From London Liverpool Street: 0528⚒/0814⑦ and at least every 30 minutes (every 20 minutes 0635⚒ - 2213⚒) until 2344.

From Southend Victoria: 0400⚒/0749⑦ and at least every 30 minutes (every 20 minutes 0630⚒ - 2130⚒) until 2249⑦/2300⚒.

LONDON LIVERPOOL STREET - CAMBRIDGE — Longest journey: 1 hour 39 minutes — LE

km					
0	0h00	↓	d.**London** L Street....a.	↑	1h23
10	0h12	↓	d.Tottenham Hale.....d.	↑	1h09
36	0h32	↓	d.Harlow Town..........d.	↑	0h48
48	0h46	↓	d.Bishops Stortford....d.	↑	0h37
67	1h02	↓	d.Audley End..........d.	↑	0h19
89	1h23		a.**Cambridge**..........d.		0h00

From London Liverpool Street: on Ⓐ at 0528, 0558 and every 30 minutes until 1528 then 1558, 1628, 1643, 1713, 1743, 1813, 1843, 1911, 1928, 1958, 2028 and every 30 minutes until 2258 then 2328, 2358⑤; on ⑥ at 0521, 0558, 0628, 0658 and every 30 minutes until 2328 then 2358; on ⑦ at 0743, 0828, 0928 and hourly until 2228.

From Cambridge: on Ⓐ at 0448, 0520, 0548, 0551 and every 30 minutes until 0821 then 0848, 0918, 1004, 1021 and at 04 and 21 minutes past each hour until 1521 then 1551 and every 30 minutes until 1921, 2004, 2021, 2104, 2121, 2204, 2221, 2251; on ⑥ at 0425, 0521, 0604, 0621 and at 04 and 21 minutes past each hour until 2221 then 2251; on ⑦ at 0732 and hourly until 2232.

200 LONDON - HARWICH, IPSWICH and NORWICH

🍸 conveyed by most Norwich trains — LE

For Rail - Sea - Rail services London - Amsterdam and v.v. via Harwich and Hoek van Holland see Table 15a.

km			Ⓐ	Ⓐ	Ⓐ	Ⓐ	Ⓐ C	Ⓐ	Ⓐ	Ⓐ	Ⓐ	Ⓐ	Ⓐ	Ⓐ	Ⓐ		Ⓐ	Ⓐ	Ⓐ	Ⓐ	Ⓐ	Ⓐ	Ⓐ A	Ⓐ
0	**London** Liverpool Street d.	Ⓐ	...	0600	...	0625	...	0638	0700	0730	0755	...	0830	0900	...	and	1530	1600	...	*1602*	1630	*1632*	1700	1702
48	Chelmsford d.		...	0630	...	0658	...	0710	|	0803	|	...	0903	|	...	at	1600	|	...	*1634*	|	*1704*	|	1736
84	Colchester d.		0610	0650	...	0723	...	0743	0751	0823	0847	...	0923	0947	...	the	1621	1647	...	*1704*	1717	*1727*	|	1801
97	Manningtree d.		0618	0658	0724	0731	...	0751	0759	0831	0855	0900	0931	0955	1000	same	1629	1655	1700	1724	|	1757	|	1809
112	**Harwich** International d.		0635	|	0741	|	0750	0810	|	|	|	0917	|	|	1017	minutes	|	|	1717	1741	|	1815	|	|
115	**Harwich** Town a.		0640	|	0746	|	|	0815	|	|	|	0922	|	|	1022	past	|	|	1722	1746	|	1822	|	|
111	**Ipswich** 205 d.		...	0711	...	0744	0820	...	0812	0844	0908	...	0944	1008	...	each	1641	1708	...	...	1736	...	1800	1825
130	Stowmarket 205 d.		...	0722	...	0755	0835	...	0823	0855	|	...	0955	|	...	hour	1652	1719	...	...	1747	...	|	1836
153	Diss d.		...	0735	...	0808	...	...	0836	0908	0929	...	1008	1029	...	until	1705	1732	...	...	1800	...	1821	1848
185	**Norwich** a.		...	0754	...	0827	...	...	0855	0927	0948	...	1027	1050	...		1724	1753	...	...	1822	...	1842	1909

	Ⓐ	Ⓐ	Ⓐ	Ⓐ	Ⓐ	Ⓐ	Ⓐ	Ⓐ	Ⓐ	Ⓐ	Ⓐ	Ⓐ	Ⓐ	Ⓐ	Ⓐ	Ⓐ	Ⓐ	Ⓐ	Ⓐ	Ⓐ	Ⓐ	Ⓐ	Ⓐ	Ⓐ	Ⓐ
London Liverpool Street d.	1730	...	1750	...	1810	1830	...	1820	1900	...	1930	1932	...	2000	...	2030	...	2100	...	2102	2130	...	2230	...	2330
Chelmsford d.	|	...	|	...	|	|	...	1857	|	...	|	2002	...	|	...	2103	...	|	...	2134	2203	...	2303	...	0003
Colchester d.	|	...	1843	...	1902	1923	...	1930	1947	...	2020	2025	...	2047	...	2123	...	2147	...	2204	2223	...	2323	...	0023
Manningtree d.	1827	1835	1852	1900	1911	1932	1938	1940	1955	2000	2028	2034	2038	2055	2100	2132	...	2156	2200	2212	2232	2300	2332	2336	0032
Harwich International d.	|	1852	|	1917	|	|	1955	2001	|	2017	|	2054	2055	|	2117	|	2138	|	2217	2228	|	2317	|	2353	|
Harwich Town a.	|	1857	|	1922	|	|	2000	...	|	2022	|	...	2100	|	2122	|	|	|	2222	...	|	2322	|	2358	|
Ipswich 205 d.	1839	...	1904	...	1923	1944	...	...	2008	...	2041	...	...	2108	...	2145	2204	2209	...	...	2245	...	2345	...	0045
Stowmarket 205 d.	1850	...	1916	...	1934	1955	...	...	2019	...	2052	...	...	2119	...	2156	...	2220	...	...	2256	...	2356	...	0056
Diss d.	1903	...	1929	...	1947	2008	...	...	2032	...	2105	...	...	2132	...	2209	...	2233	...	...	2309	...	0009	...	0109
Norwich a.	1925	...	1950	...	2009	2030	...	...	2051	...	2124	...	...	2151	...	2229	...	2253	...	...	2329	...	0029	...	0143

		⑥	⑥	⑥	⑥	⑥ C	⑥	⑥	⑥	⑥	⑥	⑥		⑥	⑥	⑥	⑥	⑥	⑥	⑥	⑥	⑥	⑥	⑥
London Liverpool Street d.	⑥	...	0534	...	0630	...	0638	0700	...	0730	0800	...	and	1930	1932	2000	...	2030	...	2100	...	2102	2130	...
Chelmsford d.		...	0610	...	0703	...	0712	|	...	0803	|	...	at	2003	2007	|	...	2103	...	|	...	2134	2203	...
Colchester d.		0552	0640	...	0723	...	0740	0747	...	0823	0847	...	the	2023	2032	2047	...	2123	...	2147	..	2204	2223	...
Manningtree d.		0600	0648	0700	0731	...	0748	0755	0800	0831	0855	0900	same	2031	2040	2055	2100	2132	...	2155	2200	2212	2232	2300
Harwich International d.		0617	|	0717	|	0750	0809	|	0817	|	|	0917	minutes	|	2056	|	2117	|	2138	|	2217	2228	|	2317
Harwich Town a.		0622	|	0722	|	|	...	|	0822	|	|	0922	past	|	...	|	2122	|	|	|	2222	...	|	2322
Ipswich 205 d.		...	0700	...	0744	0820	...	0808	...	0844	0908	...	each	2044	...	2108	...	2145	2203	2208	...	...	2245	...
Stowmarket 205 d.		...	*0721*	...	0755	0835	...	|	...	0855	|	...	hour	2055	...	|	...	2156	...	...	...	...	2256	...
Diss d.		...	*0734*	...	0808	...	...	0829	...	0908	0929	...	until	2108	...	2129	...	2209	...	...	...	...	2309	...
Norwich a.		...	*0753*	...	0827	...	...	0850	...	0927	0950	...		2127	...	2150	...	2229	...	...	...	...	2329	...

	⑥	⑥	⑥			⑦ C	⑦	⑦	⑦	⑦	⑦		⑦	⑦	⑦	⑦	⑦	⑦	⑦	⑦	⑦	⑦	⑦	⑦
London Liverpool Street d.	2230	...	2330	...	⑦	...	0755	...	0830	0902	...	and	1930	2002	...	...	2030	2102	...	2130	2202	2230	2302	2330
Chelmsford d.	2303	...	|	...		...	0834	0840	|	0943	...	at	|	2043	...	...	|	2143	...	|	2243	|	2343	|
Colchester d.	2323	...	0026	...		...	0857	0914	0925	1013	...	the	2025	2113	...	...	2125	2213	...	2225	2313	2325	0013	0025
Manningtree d.	2332	2336	0035	...		...	0905	0922	0933	1021	1026	same	2033	2121	...	2126	2134	2221	2226	2234	2321	2334	0021	0034
Harwich International d.	|	2353	|	...		0830	0925	|	|	|	1043	minutes	|	|	2110	2143	|	|	2243	|	|	|	|	|
Harwich Town a.	|	2358	|	...		|	*0948*	|	|	|	1048	past	|	|	|	2148	|	|	2248	|	|	|	|	|
Ipswich 205 d.	2345	...	0048	...		0902	...	0935	0946	1033	...	each	2046	2133	2137	...	2147	2233	...	2247	2333	2347	0039	0047
Stowmarket 205 d.	2356	...	0100	...		0918	...	...	0957	...	...	hour	2057	...	...	...	2158	...	...	2258	...	2358	...	0058
Diss d.	0009	...	0113	...		...	...	...	1010	...	...	until	2110	...	...	...	2211	...	...	2311	...	0011	...	0111
Norwich a.	0035	...	0138	...		...	...	...	1031	...	...		2131	...	...	...	2231	...	...	2331	...	0031	...	0136

		Ⓐ	Ⓐ	Ⓐ	Ⓐ	Ⓐ	Ⓐ	Ⓐ	Ⓐ	Ⓐ	Ⓐ	Ⓐ	Ⓐ A	Ⓐ	Ⓐ	Ⓐ	Ⓐ	Ⓐ	Ⓐ	Ⓐ		Ⓐ	Ⓐ	Ⓐ
Norwich d.	Ⓐ	...	0455	0525	...	0555	...	...	0622	0645	...	0703	0740	...	...	0800	0830	...	0900	0930	and	...	1600	...
Diss d.		...	0514	0544	...	0614	...	...	0640	0704	...	0721	0758	...	...	0817	0847	...	0917	0947	at	...	1617	...
Stowmarket 205 d.		...	0527	0557	...	0627	...	...	0652	0717	...	0734	|	...	...	0829	0909	...	0929	|	the	...	1629	...
Ipswich 205 d.		...	0542	0612	...	0642	...	0659	0707	0732	...	0749	0820	...	...	0843	0919	...	0943	1009	same	...	1643	...
Harwich Town d.		0524	|	|	0624	|	0652	|	|	|	0716	|	|	0758	0828	|	|	0928	|	|	minutes	1628	|	1653
Harwich International d.		0529	|	|	0629	|	0657	0728	|	|	0721	|	|	0803	0833	|	|	0933	|	|	past	1633	|	1658
Manningtree d.		0546	0553	0623	0646	0653	0714	...	0718	0743	0738	0759	|	0820	0850	0853	0930	0950	0953	1019	each	1650	1653	1715
Colchester d.		...	0605	0635	...	0705	...	...	0730	|	0754	0810	|	0837	...	0903	|	...	1003	1030	hour	...	1703	...
Chelmsford d.		...	|	|	...	|	...	...	|	|	0819	|	|	0859	...	0921	|	...	1021	|	until	...	1721	...
London Liverpool St. a.		...	0654	0727	...	0758	...	...	0823	0842	0858	0904	0924	0936	...	0956	1019	...	1055	1119		...	1758	...

	Ⓐ	Ⓐ	Ⓐ	Ⓐ	Ⓐ	Ⓐ	Ⓐ	Ⓐ	Ⓐ	Ⓐ	Ⓐ	Ⓐ	Ⓐ	Ⓐ C	Ⓐ	Ⓐ	Ⓐ	Ⓐ	Ⓐ	Ⓐ	Ⓐ		⑥	⑥	⑥
Norwich d.	1630	...	1700	1730	...	1800	1830	...	1900	1930	...	2000	...	...	2030	...	2100	...	2200	...	...	⑥	0500	0530	...
Diss d.	1647	...	1717	1747	...	1817	1847	...	1917	1947	...	2017	...	...	2047	...	2117	...	2217	...	...		0517	0547	...
Stowmarket 205 d.	|	...	1729	1759	...	1829	|	...	1929	|	...	2029	...	2045	|	...	2129	...	2229	...	...		0529	|	...
Ipswich 205 d.	1709	...	1743	1813	...	1843	1909	...	1943	2009	...	2043	...	2104	2109	...	2143	...	2243	...	...		0543	0609	...
Harwich Town d.	|	1728	|	|	1826	|	|	1928	|	|	2028	|	...	|	|	2128	|	2228	|	2328	...		|	|	0628
Harwich International d.	|	1733	|	|	1831	|	|	1933	|	|	2033	|	2045	2130	|	2133	|	2233	|	2333	...		|	|	0633
Manningtree d.	1719	1750	1753	|	1848	1853	1919	1950	1953	2019	2050	2053	2058	...	2119	2150	2153	2250	2253	2350	...		0553	0619	0650
Colchester d.	1730	...	1803	1830	...	1903	1930	...	2003	2030	...	2103	2112	...	2130	...	2203	...	2303	2359	...		0603	0630	...
Chelmsford d.	|	...	1821	|	...	1921	|	...	2021	|	...	2121	2140	...	|	...	2221	...	2325	...	...		0621	|	...
London Liverpool St. a.	1819	...	1855	1917	...	1955	2019	...	2055	2119	...	2155	2214	...	2219	...	2255	...	0004	...	...		0655	0719	...

	⑥	⑥	⑥	⑥	⑥	⑥	⑥	⑥	⑥	⑥		⑥	⑥	⑥	⑥	⑥	⑥	⑥	⑥	⑥	⑥ C	⑥	⑥	⑥
Norwich d.	0600	...	0630	...	...	0700	0730	...	0800	0830	and	1730	...	1800	1830	...	1900	...	2000	...	...	...	2100	...
Diss d.	0617	...	0647	...	...	0717	0747	...	0817	0847	at	1747	...	1817	1847	...	1917	...	2017	...	...	...	2117	...
Stowmarket 205 d.	0629	...	|	...	...	0729	|	...	0829	|	the	1759	...	1829	|	...	1929	...	2029	...	2045	...	2129	...
Ipswich 205 d.	0643	0659	0709	...	...	0743	0809	...	0843	0909	same	1813	...	1843	1909	...	1943	...	2043	...	2101	...	2143	...
Harwich Town d.	|	|	|	...	0728	|	|	0828	|	|	minutes	|	1828	|	|	1928	|	2028	|	...	|	2128	|	2228
Harwich International d.	|	0728	|	0720	0733	|	|	0833	|	|	past	|	1833	|	|	1933	|	2033	|	2045	2130	2133	|	2233
Manningtree d.	0653	...	0719	0733	0750	0753	0819	0850	0853	0919	each	|	1850	1853	1919	1950	1953	2050	2053	2058	...	2150	2153	2250
Colchester d.	0703	...	0730	0743	...	0803	0830	...	0903	0930	hour	1830	...	1903	1930	...	2003	...	2103	2112	...	...	2203	...
Chelmsford d.	0721	...	|	0809	...	0821	|	...	0921	|	until	|	...	1921	|	...	2021	...	2121	2140	...	...	2221	...
London Liverpool St. a.	0755	...	0819	0845	...	0855	0919	...	0955	1019		1919	...	1955	2019	...	2055	...	2155	2214	...	...	2301	...

	⑥			⑦	⑦	⑦	⑦	⑦	⑦	⑦	⑦	⑦	⑦		⑦	⑦ C	⑦	⑦	⑦	⑦	⑦	⑦	⑦	⑦
Norwich d.	2200	...	⑦	...	0700	...	...	0800	...	...	0900	...	...	and	...	...	2000	...	...	2100	...	...	2200	...
Diss d.	2217	...		...	0717	...	...	0817	...	...	0917	...	...	at	...	...	2017	...	...	2117	...	...	2217	...
Stowmarket 205 d.	2229	...		...	0729	...	...	0829	...	...	0929	...	...	the	...	2018	2029	...	...	2129	...	...	2229	...
Ipswich 205 d.	2243	...		...	0743	0751	0809	0843	...	0909	0943	...	1009	same	...	2036	2043	...	2109	2143	...	2209	2243	...
Harwich Town d.	|	...		...	|	|	|	|	0853	|	|	0953	|	minutes	...	|	|	2053	|	|	2153	|	|	2253
Harwich International d.	|	...		0720	|	0819	|	|	0858	|	|	0958	|	past	2035	2105	|	2058	|	|	2158	|	|	2258
Manningtree d.	2253	...		0733	0753	...	0819	0853	0915	0919	0953	1015	1019	each	2048	...	2053	2115	2119	2153	2215	2219	2253	2315
Colchester d.	2303	...		0742	0803	...	0830	0903	...	0930	1003	...	1030	hour	2057	...	2103	...	2130	2203	...	2230	2303	2324
Chelmsford d.	2325	...		0804	|	...	0858	|	...	0958	|	...	1058	until	2115	...	|	...	2158	|	...	2258	2325	...
London Liverpool St. a.	0010	...		0859	0904	...	0944	1003	...	1044	1103	...	1144		2202	...	2204	...	2240	2303	...	2340	0007	...

A – THE EAST ANGLIAN - 🍽 London Liverpool Street - Norwich and v.v.
C – To/from Cambridge (Table **204**).

s – Stops to set down only.
u – Stops to pick up only.

LE 2nd class IPSWICH - LOWESTOFT 201

km		Ⓐ 2	Ⓐ 2	⑥ 2	Ⓐ 2	⑥ 2	⚒	and at	⚒	Ⓐ 2	⑥ 2	⚒	Ⓐ 2	⑥ 2	⚒	⚒ 2	⚒	⚒		⑦		⑦
0	**Ipswich** d.	0620	...	0717	0735	0817	0917	the same	1517	1554	1617	1717	1813	1817	1917	2017	2117	2217	...	1002	and	2202
17	Woodbridge d.	0637	...	0732	0753	0832	0932	minutes	1532	1618	1632	1732	1830	1832	1932	2032	2132	2232	...	1019	every	2219
36	Saxmundham d.	0658	0744	0754	0815	0854	0954	past each	1554	1640	1654	1754	1851	1854	1954	2054	2154	2254	...	1040	**2** hours	2240
65	Beccles d.	...	0816	0825	0846	0925	1025	hour until	1625	1719	1725	1825	1925	1925	2025	2125	2225	2325	...	1112	until	2312
79	**Lowestoft** a.	...	0833	0843	0906	0943	1043	☆	1643	1736	1751	1843	1943	1943	2043	2143	2243	2343	...	1130		2330

	Ⓐ	⑥	Ⓐ	Ⓐ	⑥	Ⓐ 2	⑥ 2	⚒	and at	⚒	⑥ 2	Ⓐ 2	Ⓐ	⑥	⚒ 2	⚒	⚒ 2	⚒ 2		⑦		⑦
Lowestoft d.	0525	0607	0614	0641	0707	0727	0807	0907	the same	1507	1607	1607	1702	1707	1807	1907	2007	2107	...	0805	and	2005
Beccles d.	0541	0625	0630	0657	0725	0743	0825	0925	minutes	1525	1625	1625	1725	1725	1825	1925	2025	2125	...	0821	every	2021
Saxmundham d.	0613	0657	0703	0729	0757	0817	0857	0957	past each	1557	1657	1707	1757	1757	1857	1957	2057	2157	...	0853	**2** hours	2053
Woodbridge d.	0635	0718	0725	0751	0818	0839	0918	1018	hour until	1618	1718	1728	1818	1818	1918	2018	2118	2218	...	0914	until	2114
Ipswich a.	0653	0736	0744	0809	0836	0857	0936	1036	☆	1636	1736	1746	1836	1836	1936	2037	2136	2236	...	0932		2132

LE 2nd class NORWICH and IPSWICH local services 203

NORWICH - GREAT YARMOUTH
Journey time ± 32 minutes *30 km (33 km via Reedham)*

From Norwich: Trains noted 'r' call at **Reedham** 18 - 21 minutes later.

Ⓐ: 0506, 0613, 0652, 0736**r**, 0809, 0836, 0936, 1036, 1136**r**, 1236, 1336, 1440, 1536, 1640, 1706, 1736, 1806, 1840, 1933, 2040, 2140, 2300.

⑥: 0530**r**, 0636, 0706, 0736**r**, 0836, 0809, 0936, 1036, 1136**r**, 1236, 1336, 1436, 1536, 1640, 1706, 1736, 1806, 1840, 1933, 2040, 2140, 2300.

⑦: 0736**r**, 0845, 0936**r**, 1045, 1136**r**, 1245, 1336**r**, 1445, 1536**r**, 1645, 1736**r**, 1845, 1936**r**, 2045, 2136**r**, 2236.

From Great Yarmouth: Trains noted 'r' call at **Reedham** 12 - 14 minutes later.

Ⓐ: 0545, 0624, 0658, 0732, 0817, 0845, 0917, 1017, 1117, 1217, 1317, 1417, 1517**r**, 1617, 1717, 1747**r**, 1817, 1847**r**, 1917, 2017, 2117, 2217, 2334**r**.

⑥: 0615, 0717, 0745, 0817, 0847, 0917, 1017, 1117, 1217, 1317, 1417, 1512**r**, 1617, 1717, 1747**r**, 1817, 1847**r**, 1917, 2017, 2117, 2217, 2334**r**.

⑦: 0820**r**, 0922, 1018**r**, 1122, 1218**r**, 1322, 1420**r**, 1522, 1618**r**, 1722, 1818**r**, 1922, 2020**r**, 2122, 2220**r**, 2320**r**.

NORWICH - LOWESTOFT
Journey time ± 38 minutes *38 km*

From Norwich: Trains noted 'r' call at **Reedham** 18 - 21 minutes later.

Ⓐ: 0536**r**, 0627**r**, 0645**r**, 0755**r**, 0855, 1005**r**, 1058, 1205**r**, 1258, 1405**r**, 1455**r**, 1550**r**, 1658**r**, 1750**r**, 1900**r**, 2005**r**, 2105**r**, 2205**r**, 2240**r**.

⑥: 0540**r**, 0650**r**, 0750**r**, 0855, 1005**r**, 1058, 1205**r**, 1258, 1405**r**, 1458**r**, 1550**r**, 1658**r**, 1750**r**, 1905**r**, 2005**r**, 2105**r**, 2205**r***, 2240**r**.

⑦: 0725, 0857**r**, 1057**r**, 1257**r**, 1457**r**, 1657**r**, 1857**r**, 2057**r**.

From Lowestoft: Trains noted 'r' call at **Reedham** 18 - 21 minutes later.

Ⓐ: 0542**r**, 0635**r**, 0735**r**, 0747**r**, 0850**r**, 0948**r**, 1057, 1148**r**, 1257, 1348**r**, 1457, 1548**r**, 1648**r**, 1748**r**, 1848**r**, 1955**r**, 2057, 2148**r**, 2248**r**, 2330**r**.

⑥: 0638**r**, 0740**r**, 0848**r**, 0948**r**, 1057, 1148**r**, 1257, 1348**r**, 1457, 1548**r**, 1648**r**, 1748**r**, 1848**r**, 1955**r**, 2057, 2148**r**, 2248**r**, 2330**r**.

⑦: 0950**r**, 1150**r**, 1350**r**, 1550**r**, 1750**r**, 1950**r**, 2150**r**, 2335**r**.

NORWICH - SHERINGHAM (🚂)
Journey time ± 57 minutes *49 km*

From Norwich:
Trains call at **Hoveton and Wroxham** 🚂 ± 15 minutes, and **Cromer** ± 45 minutes later.

⚒: 0510Ⓐ, 0520⑥, 0540Ⓐ, 0545⑥, 0715, 0821, 0945, 1045, 1145, 1245, 1345, 1445, 1545, 1645, 1745, 1855, 1955, 2115, 2245.

⑦: 0836, 0945**a**, 1036, 1145**a**, 1236, 1345**a**, 1436, 1545**a**, 1636, 1745**a**, 1836, 1945**a**, 2036.

From Sheringham:
Trains call at **Cromer** ± 11 minutes, and **Hoveton and Wroxham** 🚂 ± 39 minutes later.

⚒: 0621⑥, 0631Ⓐ, 0715, 0822, 0946, 1046, 1146, 1246, 1346, 1446, 1546, 1649, 1749, 1853, 1956, 2110, 2217, 2347 (also 0553Ⓐ from Cromer).

⑦: 0942, 1042**a**, 1142, 1242**a**, 1342, 1442**a**, 1542, 1642**a**, 1742, 1842**a**, 1942, 2042**a**, 2142.

IPSWICH - FELIXSTOWE
Journey time ± 25 minutes *25 km*

From Ipswich:

Ⓐ: 0504, 0604, 0714, 0825, 0857, 0958 and hourly until 2058 then 2228.

⑥: 0558, 0658, 0758, 0858, 0958, 1058 and hourly until 2058 then 2228.

⑦: 0955**a**, 1055 and hourly until 1955.

From Felixstowe:

Ⓐ: 0534, 0636, 0747, 0854, 0928 and hourly until 2128 then 2301.

⑥: 0628, 0728, 0828, 0928, 1028 and hourly until 2128 then 2258.

⑦: 1025**a**, 1125 and hourly until 2025.

a – Until Sep. 7.

🚂 – Heritage and Tourist railways:

NORTH NORFOLK RAILWAY: Sheringham - Holt and v.v. *8 km*. ✆ 01263 820800. www.nnrailway.co.uk
BURE VALLEY STEAM RAILWAY: Wroxham - Aylsham and v.v. ✆ 01253 833858. www.bvrw.co.uk

LE IPSWICH - CAMBRIDGE and PETERBOROUGH 205

km		⚒ 2	⚒	⚒	Ⓐ	⑥	⑥	Ⓐ	⚒ H	⚒	⚒	⚒	⚒	⚒	⚒	⚒	⚒	⚒	⚒	⚒	⚒	⚒	Ⓐ
0	**Ipswich** 200 d.	0510	0600	0616	0654	0720	0800	0803	0820	0920	0958	1020	1120	1158	1220	1320	1358	1420	1520	1558	1620	1720	1749
19	Stowmarket 200 d.	0526	0612	0631	0709	0735	0812	0815	0835	0935	1011	1035	1135	1211	1235	1335	1411	1435	1535	1611	1635	1735	1804
42	Bury St Edmunds d.	0549	0629	0654	0733	0757	0829	0831	0857	0957	1029	1057	1157	1229	1257	1357	1429	1457	1557	1629	1657	1757	1825
65	Newmarket d.	0609	|	0714	0752	0817	|	|	0916	1017	|	1116	1217	|	1316	1417	|	1516	1617	|	1717	1817	|
88	**Cambridge** 208 a.	0633	|	0739	0819	0839	|	|	0939	1039	|	1139	1239	|	1339	1439	|	1539	1639	|	1739	1839	|
82	Ely 208 d.	...	0656	...	...	...	0858	0858	...	...	1058	...	...	1258	...	...	1458	...	...	1658	...	...	1858
108	March 208 d.	...	0715	...	...	...	0917	0917	...	...	1117	...	...	1317	...	...	1517	...	...	1717	...	...	1917
132	**Peterborough** 208 a.	...	0737	...	...	...	0939	0939	...	...	1139	...	...	1339	...	...	1539	...	...	1739	...	...	1939

	⑥	⚒	Ⓐ	⑥	⚒	⚒	⚒ 2	⚒ 2		⑦	⑦ a	⑦ H	⑦	⑦	⑦	⑦	⑦	⑦	⑦	⑦	⑦	⑦	⑦ 2
Ipswich 200 d.	1758	1817	1913	1920	1958	2020	2117	2219	...	0732	0755	0902	0955	1102	1155	1302	1355	1502	1555	1702	1755	1902	2102
Stowmarket 200 d.	1811	1832	1928	1935	2011	2035	2133	2235	...	0748	0807	0918	1007	1118	1207	1318	1407	1518	1607	1718	1807	1918	2118
Bury St Edmunds d.	1829	1857	1957	1957	2029	2057	2156	2257	...	0811	0824	0941	1024	1141	1224	1341	1424	1541	1624	1741	1824	1941	2141
Newmarket d.	|	1916	2017	2017	|	2116	2217	...	...	0831	|	1001	|	1201	|	1401	|	1601	|	1801	|	2001	2201
Cambridge 208 a.	|	1939	2039	2039	|	2139	2240	...	...	0857	|	1025	|	1225	|	1425	|	1625	|	1825	|	2024	2224
Ely 208 d.	1858	...	...	...	2058	...	...	...	...	...	0852	...	1052	...	1252	...	1452	...	1652	...	1852	...	...
March 208 d.	1917	...	...	...	2117	...	...	...	...	...	0909	...	1109	...	1309	...	1509	...	1709	...	1909	...	...
Peterborough 208 a.	1939	...	...	...	2139	...	...	...	...	...	0931	...	1131	...	1331	...	1531	...	1731	...	1931	...	...

	Ⓐ	⚒ 2	⚒ 2	⚒	⚒		⚒	⚒	⚒	⚒	⚒		⚒	⚒	⚒	⚒		⚒	⚒	⚒		⚒	⚒
Peterborough 208 d.	...	...	...	...	0750	...	...	...	0950	...	...	...	1150	...	...	1350	...	...	...	1550	...	...	...
March 208 d.	...	...	...	...	0809	...	...	...	1009	...	...	...	1209	...	...	1409	...	...	...	1609	...	...	...
Ely 208 d.	...	...	...	...	0832	...	...	...	1032	...	...	...	1232	...	...	1432	...	...	...	1632	...	...	...
Cambridge 208 d.	...	...	0642	0744	|	...	0844	0944	|	1044	1144	...	|	1244	1344	|	...	1444	1544	|	...	1644	1744
Newmarket d.	...	...	0702	0805	|	...	0904	1005	|	1104	1205	...	|	1304	1405	|	...	1504	1605	|	...	1705	1805
Bury St Edmunds d.	0531	0621	0723	0824	0858	...	0924	1024	1058	1124	1224	...	1258	1324	1424	1458	...	1524	1624	1658	...	1725	1825
Stowmarket 200 d.	0552	0642	0745	0845	0914	...	0945	1045	1114	1145	1245	...	1314	1345	1445	1514	...	1545	1645	1714	...	1745	1845
Ipswich 200 a.	0607	0702	0802	0902	0928	...	1002	1102	1128	1202	1302	...	1328	1402	1502	1528	...	1602	1702	1728	...	1804	1902

	⚒	⚒	⚒ H	⚒	⚒	⚒	⚒	⚒ 2		⑦ 2	Ⓐ a	⑦	⑦	⑦	⑦	⑦	⑦	⑦	⑦	⑦ H	⑦	⑦	⑦ 2
Peterborough 208 d.	1750	...	...	1950	...	...	2145	...	...	...	0950	...	1150	...	1350	...	1547	...	1745	...	1947	...	...
March 208 d.	1809	...	...	2009	...	...	2204	...	...	...	1009	...	1209	...	1409	...	1606	...	1804	...	2006	...	...
Ely 208 d.	1832	...	...	2032	...	...	2226	...	...	...	1032	...	1232	...	1432	...	1629	...	1829	...	2029	...	...
Cambridge 208 d.	|	1844	1944	|	2044	2144	|	2244	...	0912	|	1112	|	1312	|	1512	|	1712	|	1912	|	2112	2250
Newmarket d.	|	1904	2005	|	2104	2205	|	2306	...	0934	|	1134	|	1334	|	1534	|	1734	|	1934	|	2134	2312
Bury St Edmunds d.	1858	1924	2024	2058	2124	2224	2252	2327	...	0955	1058	1155	1258	1355	1458	1555	1655	1755	1855	1955	2055	2155	2333
Stowmarket 200 d.	1914	1945	2045	2114	2145	2245	2308	2348	...	1018	1114	1218	1314	1418	1514	1618	1711	1818	1911	2018	2111	2218	2355
Ipswich 200 a.	1928	2004	2100	2128	2202	2302	2322	0005	...	1036	1128	1236	1328	1436	1528	1636	1725	1836	1925	2036	2125	2236	0011

H – To / from Harwich International (Table **200**).

a – Until Sep. 7.

206 NORWICH - NOTTINGHAM - SHEFFIELD - MANCHESTER - LIVERPOOL
2nd class EM

km		⑥	Ⓐ	Ⓐ	⑥	Ⓐ	⑥	Ⓐ	⑥	Ⓐ	⑥	⑦	Ⓐ	⑥	⑦	⑦	⑥	Ⓐ	⑦	⑦	⑥	Ⓐ	⑦	Ⓐ	⑥	⑦
																			a	b						
0	**Norwich** 207 d.	...	...	...	...	...	...	0550	0550	0651	0653	...	0757	0757	...	...	0857	0857	0939	...	0957	0957	1047	1057	1057	...
49	Thetford 207 d.	...	...	...	...	...	...	0623	0623	0719	0722	...	0824	0824	...	...	0924	0924	1006	...	1024	1024	1114	1124	1124	...
86	Ely 207 d.	...	...	...	...	...	...	0651	0648	0744	0748	...	0848	0848	...	...	0946	0946	1038	...	1048	1053	1139	1148	1148	...
135	**Peterborough** 180 d.	...	...	...	...	...	...	0727	0727	0826	0828	...	0927	0925	...	...	1022	1028	1111	...	1123	1128	1216	1226	1225	...
181	Grantham 180 d.	...	...	...	...	...	...	0758	0758	0855	0859	...	0958	0953	...	...	1054	1100	1156	...	1156	1200	1251	1259	1258	...
218	**Nottingham** a.	...	...	...	...	...	...	0840	0839	0926	0935	...	1035	1036	...	...	1135	1134	1230	...	1236	1235	1329	1336	1336	...
218	**Nottingham** 171 d.	0520	0521	0639	0640	0747	0747	0847	0848	0947	0947	0947	1047	1047	1048	1144	1147	1147	1240	1240	1247	1247	1342	1347	1347	1447
247	Alfreton 171 d.	|	|	0700	0701	0808	0809	0908	0910	1008	1010	1005	1108	1110	1109	1205	1210	1208	1304	1304	1310	1308	1406	1408	1410	1511
264	Chesterfield 171 d.	0549	0549	0710	0711	0820	0820	0920	0921	1020	1020	1018	1120	1120	1119	1215	1221	1220	1317	1317	1321	1320	1416	1420	1420	1521
283	**Sheffield** 171 a.	0615	0615	0728	0728	0837	0837	0937	0938	1037	1037	1037	1137	1137	1135	1232	1237	1237	1333	1333	1337	1339	1434	1437	1437	1539
283	**Sheffield** 193 d.	0620	0620	0732	0732	0841	0841	0941	0941	1041	1041	1041	1141	1141	1139	1237	1240	1240	1338	1338	1341	1343	1437	1440	1441	1543
343	Stockport 193 a.	0722	0722	0824	0824	0925	0925	1025	1025	1125	1125	1125	1224	1224	1225	1325	1325	1325	1425	1425	1425	1425	1525	1525	1525	1625
352	**Manchester** Piccadilly 193 a.	0734	0734	0836	0836	0936	0936	1036	1036	1136	1136	1137	1236	1236	1237	1337	1336	1336	1437	1437	1436	1436	1537	1536	1536	1637
378	Warrington Central 188 a.	0753	0753	0857	0857	0957	0957	1057	1057	1157	1157	1158	1257	1257	1258	1358	1357	1357	1458	1458	1457	1457	1558	1557	1557	1658
399	**Liverpool** SP ▷ 188 a.	0818	0818	0915	0915	1015	1015	1115	1115	1215	1215	1216	1315	1315	1316	1416	1415	1415	1516	1516	1515	1515	1616	1615	1615	1716
408	**Liverpool** Lime Street 188 a.	0831	0833	0932	0931	1031	1031	1131	1131	1231	1231	1230	1331	1331	1330	1430	1431	1431	1530	1530	1531	1531	1630	1631	1631	1730

	Ⓐ	⑥	Ⓐ	⑥	⑦	⑦	Ⓐ	⑥	⑦	⑥	Ⓐ	Ⓐ	⑥	⑦	⑥	⑦	Ⓐ	⑥	Ⓐ	⑦	⑦	⑥	Ⓐ	⑥	Ⓐ	⑦
																									A	
Norwich 207 d.	1157	1157	1257	1257	...	1353	1357	1357	1453	1457	1457	1548	1552	1554	1654	1654	1657	1750	1754	1754	1856	1857	1857	...	...	2052
Thetford 207 d.	1224	1224	1324	1324	...	1420	1424	1424	1520	1524	1524	1623	1623	1621	1724	1721	1727	1823	1827	1821	1923	1924	1924	...	...	2119
Ely 207 d.	1248	1248	1348	1348	...	1445	1448	1448	1546	1547	1547	1647	1647	|	1747	1748	1752	1848	1852	1848	1948	1948	1952	...	...	2144
Peterborough 180 d.	1327	1328	1426	1426	1434	1523	1528	1524	1624	1627	1627	1724	1725	1723	1826	1826	1826	1930	1926	1926	2030	2026	2027	2127	2131	2223
Grantham 180 d.	1358	1358	1458	1458	1509	1555	1601	1557	1656	1656	1658	1757	1759	1755	1858	1858	1857	2003	1959	1957	2102	2058	2059	2202	|	2255
Nottingham a.	1435	1436	1532	1536	1539	1624	1635	1636	1725	1736	1735	1833	1833	1827	1934	1933	1934	2037	2031	2031	2134	2132	2133	2232	2154	2328
Nottingham 171 d.	1447	1447	1547	1547	1547	1642	1647	1644	1741	1744	1745	1847	1847	1840	1939	1943	1941	...	...	...	...	...	...	...	...	...
Alfreton 171 d.	1508	1510	1608	1610	1608	1709	1708	1705	1805	1807	1808	1908	1910	1904	2000	2004	2002	...	...	...	...	...	...	...	...	...
Chesterfield 171 d.	1521	1520	1621	1620	1618	1719	1718	1715	1815	1818	1820	1921	1921	1915	2010	2014	2013	...	...	...	...	...	...	...	...	...
Sheffield 171 a.	1537	1537	1637	1637	1634	1739	1736	1734	1832	1833	1836	1937	1937	1931	2028	2031	2027	...	...	...	...	...	...	...	...	...
Sheffield 193 d.	1541	1541	1641	1641	1639	1744	1741	1738	1836	1838	1842	1940	1940	1935	2032	2035	2031	...	...	...	...	...	...	...	...	...
Stockport 193 a.	1625	1625	1725	1725	1728	1825	1825	1825	1925	1925	1925	2025	2025	2025	2120	2124	2120	...	...	...	...	...	...	...	...	...
Manchester Piccadilly 193 a.	1636	1636	1736	1736	1737	1837	1836	1836	1937	1936	1936	2036	2036	2038	2132	2136	2132	...	...	...	...	...	...	...	...	...
Warrington Central 188 a.	1657	1657	1802	1802	1758	1858	1857	1857	1958	1957	1957	2057	2057	...	...	...	...	...	...	...	...	...	...	...	...	...
Liverpool SP ▷ 188 a.	1715	1715	1821	1821	1816	1916	1918	1918	2016	2015	2016	2119	2119	...	...	...	...	...	...	...	...	...	...	...	...	...
Liverpool Lime Street 188 a.	1731	1731	1835	1835	1830	1930	1934	1935	2030	2030	2035	2136	2132	...	...	...	...	...	...	...	...	...	...	...	...	...

	Ⓐ	⑥	⚒	⑥	Ⓐ	⑥	Ⓐ	Ⓐ	⑥	⑦	⑥	Ⓐ	⑥	Ⓐ	⑦	Ⓐ	⑥	⑦	Ⓐ	⑥	⑦	Ⓐ	⑥	⑦	Ⓐ	⑥
	A	A	A							a					a											
Liverpool Lime Street 187 d.	...	...	...	...	...	...	...	0647	0649	...	0742	0742	0852	0852	...	0952	0952	...	1052	1052	...	1152	1152	...	1252	1252
Liverpool SP ▷ 188 d.	...	...	...	...	...	...	...	0657	0659	...	0752	0753	0903	0903	...	1003	1003	...	1103	1103	...	1203	1203	...	1303	1303
Warrington 188 d.	...	...	...	...	...	...	...	0715	0715	...	0813	0813	0919	0919	...	1019	1019	...	1119	1119	...	1219	1219	...	1319	1319
Manchester Piccadilly 193 d.	...	...	...	...	...	...	...	0742	0742	...	0843	0843	0943	0943	...	1043	1043	...	1143	1143	...	1243	1243	1244	1343	1343
Stockport 193 d.	...	...	...	...	...	...	...	0754	0754	...	0854	0854	0954	0954	...	1054	1054	...	1154	1154	...	1254	1254	1255	1354	1354
Sheffield 193 d.	...	...	...	...	...	...	...	0834	0834	...	0934	0934	1034	1034	...	1133	1133	...	1234	1234	...	1335	1334	1337	1434	1434
Sheffield 171 d.	...	...	...	...	...	...	...	0838	0838	...	0937	0936	1038	1038	1049	1137	1137	...	1236	1237	1241	1338	1337	1348	1436	1437
Chesterfield 171 d.	...	...	...	...	...	...	...	0853	0853	...	0952	0952	1053	1052	1104	1152	1152	...	1252	1252	1256	1354	1352	1402	1452	1452
Alfreton 171 d.	...	...	...	...	...	...	...	0903	0903	...	1002	1002	1103	1103	1114	1202	1202	...	1302	1302	1307	1405	1402	1412	1459	1504
Nottingham 171 a.	...	...	...	...	...	...	...	0926	0927	...	1027	1027	1127	1127	1139	1227	1228	...	1327	1327	1328	1427	1427	1433	1525	1527
Nottingham d.	0456	0506	0610	0745	0752	0834	0835	0934	0934	0952	1034	1034	1134	1134	1150	1234	1234	1237	1334	1334	1347	1434	1434	1445	1534	1534
Grantham 180 d.	|	|	|	0820	0828	0910	0909	1011	1009	1029	1110	1110	1207	1211	1223	1309	1308	1314	1410	1407	1422	1511	1510	1520	1610	1607
Peterborough 180 d.	0627	0627	0735	0859	0859	0943	0940	1045	1040	1109	1141	1141	1240	1242	1256	1341	1340	1343	1441	1443	1459	1540	1541	1558	1641	1639
Ely 207 d.	0701	0701	0811	0941	0942	1016	1013	1118	1113	1143	1213	1213	1313	1314	1331	1413	1413	1416	1513	1518	1531	1613	1613	1631	1713	1713
Thetford 207 a.	0728	0730	0836	1006	1006	1043	1037	1143	1137	1213	1238	1238	1337	1339	1355	1438	1437	1443	1538	1542	1555	1637	1638	1655	1738	1737
Norwich 207 a.	0813	0813	0913	1043	1044	1115	1112	1215	1213	1253	1313	1313	1413	1413	1428	1511	1513	1521	1613	1615	1635	1713	1713	1726	1813	1813

	⑦	Ⓐ	⑥	⑦	Ⓐ	⑥	⑦	Ⓐ	⑥	⑦	Ⓐ	⑥	⑦	Ⓐ	⑥	⑦	Ⓐ	⑥	⑦	Ⓐ	⑥	⑦	⑥	⑦	⑥	Ⓐ
Liverpool Lime Street 187 d.	1252	1352	1352	1352	1452	1452	1452	1552	1552	1552	1652	1652	1652	1752	1752	1752	1852	1852	1852	1952	1952	1952	2052	2121	2137	2137
Liverpool SP ▷ 188 d.	1303	1403	1403	1403	1503	1503	1503	1603	1603	1603	1703	1703	1703	1803	1803	1803	1903	1903	1903	2003	2003	2003	2103	2131	2147	2147
Warrington 188 d.	1319	1419	1419	1419	1519	1519	1519	1619	1619	1619	1719	1719	1719	1819	1819	1819	1919	1919	1919	2019	2019	2019	2119	2147	2203	2203
Manchester Piccadilly 193 d.	1344	1443	1443	1444	1543	1543	1544	1643	1643	1644	1743	1743	1744	1843	1843	1844	1943	1943	1944	2043	2043	2044	2143	2211	2228	2228
Stockport 193 d.	1354	1454	1454	1454	1554	1554	1554	1654	1654	1654	1754	1754	1754	1854	1854	1854	1954	1954	1954	2054	2054	2054	2152	2228	2238	2238
Sheffield 193 d.	1437	1534	1534	1535	1634	1634	1637	1739	1737	1734	1847	1836	1836	1933	1933	1935	2035	2036	2035	2134	2134	2134	2231	2324	2235	2235
Sheffield 171 d.	1441	1538	1538	1539	1638	1638	1643	1745	1741	1740	1851	1850	1839	1937	1937	1940	2041	2039	2040	2139	2138	2140	2235	2327	2238	2337
Chesterfield 171 d.	1457	1552	1553	1553	1653	1653	1657	1801	1759	1754	1906	1904	1854	1951	1952	1954	2056	2054	2054	2155	2154	2156	2251	2342	2253	0002
Alfreton 171 d.	1508	1602	1603	1603	1704	1704	1707	1811	1809	1805	1916	1915	1905	2003	2003	2005	2108	2105	2105	2205	2204	2214	2302	2352	|	|
Nottingham 171 a.	1532	1626	1628	1628	1727	1727	1730	1831	1831	1828	1941	1939	1933	2029	2031	2030	2133	2133	2133	2235	2233	2236	2332	0021	0030	0039
Nottingham d.	1550	1635	1634	1645	1734	1734	1736	1837	1837	1846	...	...	...	2034	2034	2045	...	...	...	...	...	...	...	...	...	...
Grantham 180 d.	1622	1712	1706	1721	1811	1815	1817	1907	1908	1928	...	...	...	2110	2107	2120	...	...	...	...	...	...	...	...	...	...
Peterborough 180 d.	1659	1742	1740	1757	1845	1844	1849	1940	1941	1959	...	...	...	2138	2140	2153	...	...	...	...	...	...	...	...	...	...
Ely 207 d.	1732	1814	1813	1832	1919	1919	1922	2013	2014	2032	...	...	...	2213	2213	2226	...	...	...	...	...	...	...	...	...	...
Thetford 207 a.	1756	1839	1837	1856	1950	1943	1949	2036	2038	2056	...	...	...	2237	2237	2250	...	...	...	...	...	...	...	...	...	...
Norwich 207 a.	1830	1915	1913	1929	2022	2016	2026	2113	2113	2137	...	...	...	2318	2319	2324	...	...	...	...	...	...	...	...	...	...

A – Via Melton Mowbray (Table **208**). **a** – Until Sep. 7. ▷ – Liverpool South Parkway.

207 CAMBRIDGE - NORWICH
LE

km		⚒	Ⓐ	⑥	⑥	Ⓐ	⚒	⚒		⚒	⚒	⑥	Ⓐ	⑥	Ⓐ	⑥	Ⓐ	⑥	Ⓐ		⑦	⑦	⑦	⑦
0	**Cambridge** d.	⚒	0605	0607	0700	0704	0812	0912	and at the same minutes past each hour until △	1712	1812	1912	1925	2012	2020	2112	2115	2230	2255	...	⑦	0852	1052	115[illegible]
24	Ely 206 d.		0620	0622	0716	0719	0828	0927		1728	1828	1928	1940	2028	2037	2128	2130	2245	2310	...		0907	1107	120[illegible]
63	Thetford 206 d.		0644	0647	0743	0747	0853	0951		1753	1853	1953	2004	2053	2101	2153	2155	2309	2334	...		0934	1134	123[illegible]
94	Wymondham d.		0711	0714	0813	0816	0915	1015		1815	1915	2015	2027	2115	2124	2215	2217	2332	2357	...		0956	1156	125[illegible]
110	**Norwich** 206 a.		0727	0728	0830	0830	0930	1030		1830	1930	2030	2041	2130	2138	2232	2232	2346	0011	...		1013	1213	131[illegible]

	⑦	⑦	⑦	⑦	⑦	⑦	⑦	⑦	⑦
Cambridge d.	1252	1352	1452	1552	1652	1752	1852	1952	2152
Ely 206 d.	1307	1407	1507	1607	1707	1807	1907	2007	2207
Thetford 206 d.	1334	1431	1531	1634	1731	1831	1931	2031	2231
Wymondham d.	1356	1454	1554	1656	1754	1854	1954	2054	2254
Norwich 206 a.	1413	1513	1613	1713	1813	1910	2013	2110	2313

	⚒	Ⓐ	⑥	Ⓐ	⑥	Ⓐ	⑥	⚒	
Norwich 206 d.	⚒	0533	0537	0633	0640	0737	0740	0840	and at the same minutes past each hour until △
Wymondham d.		0545	0549	0645	0652	0749	0752	0852	
Thetford 206 d.		0606	0610	0706	0713	0810	0813	0913	
Ely 206 a.		0631	0635	0731	0738	0837	0838	0938	
Cambridge a.		0652	0656	0753	0759	0859	0859	0959	

	⚒	⑥	Ⓐ	⚒	⚒	⚒	⚒	⑥	Ⓐ	Ⓐ	⑥		⑦	⑦	⑦	⑦	⑦	⑦	⑦	⑦	⑦	⑦	⑦	⑦	⑦
Norwich 206 d.	1440	1535	1540	1638	1735	1838	1940	2040	2115	2240	2240	...	⑦	0903	1003	1103	1203	1303	1403	1503	1603	1703	1803	2003	220[illegible]
Wymondham d.	1452	1547	1552	1650	1747	1850	1952	2052	2127	2252	2252	...		0915	1015	1115	1215	1315	1415	1515	1615	1715	1815	2015	221[illegible]
Thetford 206 d.	1513	1613	1613	1713	1813	1911	2013	2113	2148	2313	2313	...		0936	1036	1136	1236	1336	1436	1536	1636	1736	1836	2036	223[illegible]
Ely 206 a.	1538	1638	1638	1738	1839	1938	2039	2138	2216	2338	2338	...		1003	1101	1203	1301	1401	1501	1603	1701	1801	1901	2101	230[illegible]
Cambridge a.	1559	1659	1659	1759	1859	1959	2059	2159	2235	2359	2359	...		1022	1123	1222	1322	1422	1522	1622	1722	1822	1922	2122	232[illegible]

△ – Timings may vary by up to 2 minutes.

XC STANSTED AIRPORT - CAMBRIDGE - PETERBOROUGH - LEICESTER - BIRMINGHAM 208

km		Ⓐ	Ⓐ	Ⓐ	Ⓐ	Ⓐ	Ⓐ	Ⓐ	Ⓐ	Ⓐ	Ⓐ	Ⓐ	Ⓐ	Ⓐ	Ⓐ	Ⓐ	Ⓐ	Ⓐ		⑥	⑥	⑥	⑥	⑥
0	**Stansted Airport** d.	...	0516	0612	0721	0821	0921	1027	1127	1227	1327	1427	1527	1627	1727	1821	1921	2021	...	...	0525	0627	0727	0827
40	**Cambridge** d.	0515	0555	0655	0801	0901	1001	1101	1201	1301	1401	1501	1601	1701	1801	1901	2001	2101	...	0515	0555	0657	0801	0901
64	Ely 205 d.	0530	0610	0712	0815	0915	1015	1115	1215	1315	1415	1515	1615	1715	1815	1915	2015	2115	...	0530	0610	0712	0815	0915
89	March 205 d.	0546	0628	0729	0832	0932	1032	1132	1232	1332	1432	1532	1632	1732	1834	1932	2032	2132	...	0546	0628	0729	0832	0932
113	**Peterborough** 205 d.	0610	0652	0752	0852	0952	1052	1152	1252	1352	1452	1552	1652	1752	1852	1952	2052	2152	...	0610	0652	0751	0852	0952
131	Stamford d.	0623	0705	0805	0905	1005	1105	1205	1305	1405	1505	1605	1705	1805	1905	2005	2105	2205	...	0623	0705	0805	0905	1005
154	Oakham d.	0637	0719	0819	0919	1019	1119	1219	1319	1419	1519	1619	1719	1819	1919	2019	2119	2219	...	0637	0719	0819	0919	1019
174	Melton Mowbray d.	0648	0730	0830	0930	1030	1130	1230	1330	1430	1530	1630	1730	1830	1930	2030	2130	2230	...	0648	0730	0830	0930	1030
197	**Leicester** d.	0710	0751	0848	0948	1048	1148	1248	1348	1448	1548	1648	1748	1848	1948	2048	2148	2248	...	0710	0748	0848	0948	1048
227	Nuneaton a.	0728	0816	0907	1006	1106	1206	1306	1406	1506	1606	1708	1814	1906	2006	2107	2206	2306	...	0728	0807	0907	1006	1106
244	Coleshill Parkway a.	0744	0832	0925	1025	1125	1225	1325	1425	1525	1624	1724	1832	1925	2025	2125	2225	2325	...	0747	0823	0925	1024	1124
259	**Birmingham** New St. a.	0758	0845	0938	1038	1138	1238	1338	1438	1538	1638	1738	1846	1938	2038	2138	2238	2338	...	0803	0838	0938	1038	1138

	⑥	⑥	⑥	⑥		⑥	⑥	⑥	⑥	⑥	⑥	⑥		⑦	⑦	⑦		⑦	⑦	⑦	⑦		⑦	⑦	⑦
Stansted Airport d.	0927	1027	1127	1227	...	1327	1427	1527	1627	1727	1827	1927	...	1025	1125	1225	...	1325	1425	1525	1625	...	1725	1825	1925
Cambridge d.	1001	1101	1201	1301	...	1401	1501	1601	1701	1801	1901	2001	...	1100	1200	1300	...	1400	1500	1600	1700	...	1800	1900	2000
Ely 205 d.	1015	1115	1215	1315	...	1415	1515	1615	1715	1815	1915	2015	...	1115	1215	1315	...	1415	1515	1615	1715	...	1815	1915	2015
March 205 d.	1032	1132	1232	1332	...	1432	1532	1632	1732	1834	1932	2032	...	1132	1232	1332	...	1432	1532	1632	1732	...	1832	1932	2032
Peterborough 205 d.	1052	1152	1252	1352	...	1452	1552	1652	1752	1852	1952	2052	...	1153	1253	1353	...	1453	1553	1653	1753	...	1853	1953	2053
Stamford d.	1105	1205	1305	1405	...	1505	1605	1705	1805	1905	2005	2105	...	1206	1306	1406	...	1506	1606	1706	1806	...	1906	2006	2106
Oakham d.	1119	1219	1319	1419	...	1519	1619	1719	1819	1919	2019	2119	...	1220	1320	1420	...	1520	1620	1720	1820	...	1920	2020	2120
Melton Mowbray d.	1130	1230	1330	1430	...	1530	1630	1730	1830	1930	2030	2130	...	1232	1332	1432	...	1532	1632	1731	1832	...	1932	2032	2132
Leicester d.	1148	1248	1348	1448	...	1548	1648	1748	1848	1948	2048	2148	...	1250	1350	1450	...	1550	1650	1750	1850	...	1950	2050	2150
Nuneaton a.	1206	1306	1406	1506	...	1606	1706	1807	1906	2007	2107	2206	...	1309	1409	1509	...	1609	1709	1809	1909	...	2009	2108	2209
Coleshill Parkway a.	1224	1324	1424	1524	...	1624	1724	1824	1924	2024	2124	2224	...	1325	1424	1524	...	1624	1724	1825	1924	...	2025	2125	2225
Birmingham New St a.	1238	1338	1438	1538	...	1638	1738	1838	1938	2038	2138	2238	...	1338	1438	1538	...	1638	1738	1839	1938	...	2038	2138	2238

	ⒶA	Ⓐ	ⒶA	Ⓐ	Ⓐ	Ⓐ	Ⓐ	Ⓐ	Ⓐ	Ⓐ	Ⓐ	Ⓐ	Ⓐ	Ⓐ	Ⓐ	Ⓐ	Ⓐ	Ⓐ	Ⓐ		⑥A	⑥	⑥A	⑥
Birmingham New St. d.	...	0522	...	0622	0722	0822	0922	1022	1122	1222	1322	1422	1522	1622	1652	1722	1822	1922	2022	...	...	0522	...	0622
Coleshill Parkway △ d.	...	0536	...	0636	0735	0836	0936	1036	1136	1236	1336	1436	1536	1636	1706	1736	1836	1936	2036	...	...	0536	...	0636
Nuneaton d.	...	0552	...	0652	0751	0852	0952	1052	1152	1252	1352	1452	1552	1652	1720	1752	1852	1952	2052	...	...	0552	...	0652
Leicester d.	...	0615	...	0718	0818	0918	1018	1118	1218	1318	1418	1518	1618	1718	1755	1818	1918	2018	2118	...	...	0615	...	0718
Melton Mowbray d.	0536	0632	0653	0735	0835	0935	1035	1135	1235	1335	1435	1535	1635	1735	1813	1835	1935	2035	2135	...	0538	0632	0653	0735
Oakham d.	0548	0643	0705	0746	0846	0946	1046	1146	1246	1346	1446	1546	1646	1746	1825	1846	1946	2046	2146	...	0550	0644	0705	0746
Stamford d.	0603	0657	0719	0800	0900	1000	1100	1200	1300	1400	1500	1600	1700	1800	1839	1900	2000	2100	2200	...	0605	0658	0719	0800
Peterborough 205 d.	0627	0712	0735	0818	0918	1018	1118	1218	1318	1418	1518	1618	1718	1818	1859	1918	2018	2118	2218	...	0627	0712	0735	0818
March 205 d.	0642	0730	0750	0833	0933	1033	1133	1233	1333	1433	1533	1633	1737	1833	1914	1933	2033	2133	2233	...	0642	0730	0750	0833
Ely 205 d.	0701	0751	0811	0852	0951	1052	1152	1252	1352	1452	1552	1652	1758	1852	1933	1952	2052	2152	2254	...	0701	0752	0811	0852
Cambridge a.	...	0807	...	0908	1010	1108	1208	1308	1408	1508	1608	1708	1816	1908	1952	2008	2108	2208	2310	...	...	0808	...	0908
Stansted Airport a.	...	0839	...	0940	1040	1140	1240	1340	1440	1540	1640	1740	1854	1940	...	2040	2140	2252	...	...	...	0839	...	0940

	⑥	⑥	⑥	⑥	⑥	⑥	⑥	⑥	⑥	⑥	⑥	⑥	⑥	⑥		⑦	⑦	⑦	⑦	⑦	⑦	⑦	⑦	⑦	⑦
Birmingham New St. d.	0722	0822	0922	1022	1122	1222	1322	1422	1522	1622	1722	1822	1922	2022	...	1122	1222	1322	1422	1522	1622	1722	1822	1922	2022
Coleshill Parkway △ d.	0736	0836	0936	1036	1136	1236	1336	1436	1536	1636	1736	1836	1936	2036	...	1136	1236	1336	1436	1536	1636	1736	1836	1936	2036
Nuneaton d.	0752	0852	0952	1052	1152	1252	1352	1452	1552	1652	1752	1852	1952	2052	...	1152	1252	1352	1452	1552	1652	1752	1852	1952	2052
Leicester d.	0818	0918	1018	1118	1218	1318	1418	1518	1618	1718	1818	1918	2018	2118	...	1219	1319	1419	1519	1619	1716	1819	1919	2019	2116
Melton Mowbray d.	0835	0935	1035	1135	1235	1335	1435	1535	1635	1735	1835	1935	2035	2135	...	1236	1336	1436	1536	1636	1736	1836	1936	2036	2136
Oakham d.	0846	0946	1046	1146	1246	1346	1446	1546	1646	1746	1846	1946	2046	2146	...	1247	1347	1447	1547	1647	1748	1848	1948	2048	2147
Stamford d.	0900	1000	1100	1200	1300	1400	1500	1600	1700	1800	1900	2000	2100	2200	...	1301	1401	1501	1601	1701	1801	1902	2001	2101	2201
Peterborough 205 d.	0918	1018	1118	1218	1318	1418	1518	1618	1718	1818	1918	2018	2118	2214	...	1318	1418	1518	1618	1718	1818	1918	2018	2118	2216
March 205 a.	0933	1033	1133	1233	1333	1433	1533	1633	1737	1833	1932	2032	2133	2229	...	1334	1434	1533	1633	1733	1833	1932	2032	2133	2231
Ely 205 a.	0952	1051	1151	1252	1352	1452	1552	1652	1800	1852	1952	2052	2152	2247	...	1351	1452	1552	1652	1752	1852	1951	2050	2152	2251
Cambridge a.	1008	1108	1208	1308	1408	1508	1608	1708	1816	1908	2008	2108	2208	2303	...	1408	1508	1608	1708	1808	1908	2007	2107	2207	2306
Stansted Airport a.	1040	1140	1240	1340	1440	1540	1640	1740	1853	1940	2040	2140	2240	...	...	1444	1545	1645	1745	1845	1945	2045	2145	2245	...

A – 🚌 Nottingham - Norwich and v.v. (Table **206**).

△ – 🚌 connections available to the National Exhibition Centre (NEC) and Birmingham International Airport.

☛ Full service **Leicester - Birmingham New Street**:

⚒: 0549⑥, 0617Ⓐ, 0643Ⓐ, 0649⑥, 0710, 0724Ⓐ, 0748⑥, 0751Ⓐ, 0816, 0848 then at 18 and 48 minutes past each hour until 2116, 2148, 2216⑥, 2227Ⓐ, 2248Ⓐ.

⑦: 1119, 1219, 1250 and at 19 and 50 minutes past each hour until 2019, 2050, 2150, 2219.

☛ Full service **Birmingham New Street - Leicester**:

⚒: 0522, 0552, 0622, 0652, 0722, 0752, 0822, 0852 and every 30 minutes until 1522, 1552, 1609Ⓐ, 1622, 1652, 1709Ⓐ, 1722, 1752, 1822, 1852, 1922, 1952, 2022, 2052, 2222.

⑦: 0952, 1052, 1122, 1152 and every 30 minutes until 1922, 2022, 2052, 2152.

NT 2nd class MIDDLESBROUGH - NEWCASTLE 210

km		⚒	Ⓐ	⑥	⚒	⚒	⚒		⚒	⚒	⚒	⚒	⚒	⑥	Ⓐ		⑦	⑦	⑦	⑦	⑦	⑦
0	**Middlesbrough** d.	...	0650	0655	0732	0832	0932	and at	1532	1632	1743	1832	1942	2046	2101	...	0931	1131	1331	1531	1745	1933
9	Stockton d.	...	0701	0703	0743	0843	0943	the same	1543	1643	1754	1843	1953	2057	2112	...	0942	1142	1342	1542	1756	1944
28	Hartlepool d.	0703	0720	0725	0802	0901	1001	minutes past each	1602	1702	1813	1902	2012	2116	2131	...	1001	1201	1401	1601	1815	2003
57	Sunderland d.	0730	0755	0755	0830	0930	1030	hour until	1630	1730	1842	1929	2038	2143	2158	...	1028	1228	1428	1628	1843	2029
77	**Newcastle** a.	0751	0816	0816	0852	0951	1051	❖	1651	1751	1906	1955	2104	2204	2219	...	1048	1248	1448	1648	1905	2050

	Ⓐ	⑥	⚒	⚒		⚒	⚒	⚒	⚒	⚒	Ⓐ	⑥	Ⓐ	⑥		⑦	⑦	⑦	⑦	⑦	⑦
Newcastle d.	0600	0600	0700	0730	and at	1630	1653	1730	1830	1930	2030	2033	2118	2130	...	0945	1200	1400	1600	1800	2000
Sunderland d.	0620	0628	0719	0750	the same	1650	1715	1750	1850	1950	2050	2053	2138	2151	...	1006	1221	1422	1621	1821	2021
Hartlepool d.	0646	0653	0749	0815	minutes past each	1715	1739	1818	1915	2017	2115	2122	2203	2215	...	1031	1245	1445	1645	1845	2045
Stockton d.	...	...	0804	0833	hour until	1733	1756	1837	1933	2035	2133	2140	2221	2234	...	1049	1304	1504	1704	1904	2104
Middlesbrough a.	...	...	0823	0848	❖	1748	1816	1850	1948	2049	2148	2155	2236	2248	...	1106	1318	1518	1716	1916	2120

❖ – Timings may vary by ± 5 minutes.

NT 2nd class MIDDLESBROUGH - WHITBY 211

km		⚒	⑦A	⚒	⑦A	⑦A	⚒	⑦A	⚒	
0	**Middlesbrough** d.	0704	0845	1028	1107	1343	1404	1623	1740	...
46	Grosmont 🚂 d.	0817	0953	1136	1215	1455	1515	1734	1849	...
56	**Whitby** 🚂 a.	0838	1017	1159	1236	1515	1535	1755	1911	...

	⚒	⑦A	⚒	⑦A	⑦A	⚒	⑦A	⚒	
Whitby 🚂 d.	0850	1025	1218	1246	1525	1600	1805	1919	...
Grosmont 🚂 d.	0907	1042	1235	1303	1542	1617	1822	1936	...
Middlesbrough a.	1017	1207	1346	1416	1653	1731	1932	2047	...

A – Until Nov. 2.

🚂 – The North Yorkshire Moors Railway (✆ 01751 472508. www.nymr.co.uk) operates services Pickering - Grosmont - Whitby and v.v.

NT 2nd class BISHOP AUCKLAND - DARLINGTON - MIDDLESBROUGH - SALTBURN 212

km		⚒	⚒	⚒	⚒	⚒	⚒	⚒	⚒	Ⓐ	⑥	⚒		⑦A	⑦		⑦	⑦	⑦		⑦A	⑦
0	**Bishop Auckland** d.	0717	0821	0926	1125	1325	1525	1623	1805	1902	1916	2110	...	0847	1007	...	1207	1507	1707	...	1807	1907
4	Shildon d.	0722	0826	0931	1130	1330	1530	1628	1810	1907	1921	2115	...	0852	1012	...	1212	1512	1712	...	1812	1912
19	**Darlington** a.	0743	0847	0953	1151	1351	1551	1650	1831	1928	1942	2136	...	0913	1033	...	1233	1533	1733	...	1833	1933
19	**Darlington** ▶ d.	0744	0859	0953	1153	1353	1553	1653	1833	1930	1955	2138	...	0915	1035	...	1235	1535	1735	...	1835	1936
43	**Middlesbrough** ▶ d.	0811	0925	1020	1220	1420	1620	1720	1859	1957	2023	2205	...	0943	1101	...	1301	1601	1801	...	1901	2003
55	Redcar Central ▶ d.	...	0937	1032	1232	1432	1632	1732	1910	2009	...	2217	...	0955	1113	...	1313	1613	1813	...	1913	2015
63	**Saltburn** ▶ a.	...	0955	1051	1249	1450	1649	1750	1926	2025	...	2234	...	1010	1129	...	1329	1629	1829	...	1929	2031

For return service and footnotes see next page ▷ ▷ ▷

212 SALTBURN - MIDDLESBROUGH - DARLINGTON - BISHOP AUCKLAND — 2nd class NT

		⚒	⚒	⑥	Ⓐ	⚒	⚒	⚒	⚒	⚒	⚒	⚒	⚒	⚒			⑦A	⑦	⑦	⑦		⑦	⑦A	⑦
Saltburn ▷ d.	⚒	...	...	0621	0628	...	0754	0957	1157	1357	1457	1630	1730	1930	...	⑦	...	...	1036	1336	...	1536	1636	1736
Redcar Central ▷ d.		...	...	0634	0641	...	0807	1010	1210	1410	1510	1643	1743	1943	...		...	...	1049	1349	...	1549	1649	1749
Middlesbrough ▷ d.		0545	...	0646	0654	...	0820	1022	1221	1421	1521	1657	1755	1955	...		...	0850	1102	1402	...	1602	1702	1802
Darlington ▷ a.		0614	...	0719	0724	...	0850	1052	1252	1452	1552	1726	1825	2026	...		...	0919	1131	1431	...	1631	1732	1831
Darlington d.		...	0648	...	...	0748	0852	1054	1254	1454	1553	1728	1832	2032	...		0817	0929	1132	1432	...	1632	1734	1834
Shildon d.		...	0707	...	...	0807	0911	1113	1313	1513	1612	1747	1851	2051	...		0836	0948	1151	1451	...	1651	1753	1853
Bishop Auckland a.		...	0715	...	...	0815	0918	1120	1320	1520	1620	1754	1856	2058	...		0844	0953	1157	1459	...	1657	1759	1859

▶ – All trains Darlington - Middlesbrough - Redcar - Saltburn:

⚒: 0628, 0658, 0725Ⓐ, 0730⑥, 0823⑥, 0830Ⓐ, 0859, 0930, 0953, 1030, 1053, 1130, 1153, 1230, 1253, 1330, 1353, 1430, 1453, 1530, 1553, 1630, 1653, 1730, 1753Ⓐ, 1800⑥, 1833, 1930, 2030, 2138.

⑦: 0835, 0915**A**, 0933, 1035, 1135, 1235, 1335, 1434, 1535, 1633, 1735, 1835, 1936, 2035, 2145.

▷ – All trains Saltburn - Redcar - Middlesbrough - Darlington:

⚒: 0621⑥, 0628Ⓐ, 0710, 0725, 0754, 0830, 0930, 0957, 1030, 1057, 1130, 1157, 1230, 1257, 1330, 1357, 1430, 1457, 1530, 1555, 1630, 1655, 1730, 1757, 1830, 1857, 1930, 2030Ⓐ, 2034⑥, 2130, 2239.

⑦: 0936, 1036, 1146, 1236, 1336, 1436, 1536, 1636, 1736, 1836, 1936, 2042, 2136, 2243.

A – Until Nov. 2.

☛ – For return service see previous page.

213 NEWCASTLE - CARLISLE — 2nd class NT

Service until October 5.

km			Ⓐ	Ⓐ	Ⓐ	Ⓐ	Ⓐ	Ⓐ	Ⓐ	Ⓐ	Ⓐ	Ⓐ	Ⓐ	Ⓐ	Ⓐ	Ⓐ	Ⓐ			⑥	⑥	⑥	⑥	⑥	⑥
0	**Newcastle** d.	Ⓐ	0646	0824	0924	1022	1122	1222	1323	1424	1524	1622	1716	1754	1824	1925	2118	...	⑥	0630	0824	0924	1022	1122	1223
6	MetroCentre d.		0654	0832	0932	1032	1132	1232	1333	1432	1532	1632	1724	1802	1833	1934	2126	...		0638	0832	0932	1033	1132	1232
36	Hexham d.		0717	0858	0955	1055	1155	1255	1357	1455	1556	1703	1750	1833	1906	2005	2157	...		0709	0859	0955	1055	1155	1255
62	Haltwhistle d.		0740	0921	1014	1118	1214	1318	1416	1518	1618	1726	1813	1855	1925	2028	2220	...		0732	0922	1013	1118	1214	1318
99	**Carlisle** a.		0813	0957	1046	1157	1247	1354	1450	1557	1651	1800	1850	1932	1957	2103	2256	...		0807	0957	1046	1157	1247	1357
	Glasgow Central **214** a.		1037	...	...	...	...	...	1737	...	...	...	2139	...	...	...	...	...		1037	...	...	...	...	...

	⑥	⑥	⑥	⑥		⑥	⑥	⑥	⑥	⑥			⑦	⑦	⑦	⑦		⑦	⑦	⑦	⑦	⑦		⑦	⑦
Newcastle d.	1322	1424	1524	1622	...	1716	1754	1824	1925	2118	...	⑦	0910	1010	1110	1210	...	1310	1410	1510	1610	1710	...	1810	2015
MetroCentre d.	1332	1432	1532	1632	...	1724	1802	1833	1934	2126	...		0918	1018	1118	1218	...	1318	1418	1518	1618	1718	...	1818	2024
Hexham d.	1357	1455	1555	1703	...	1752	1833	1906	2005	2157	...		0949	1051	1149	1251	...	1349	1451	1549	1651	1749	...	1851	2057
Haltwhistle d.	1417	1518	1616	1726	...	1813	1856	1925	2028	2220	...		1011	1114	1208	1314	...	1408	1510	1611	1710	1808	...	1914	2120
Carlisle a.	1450	1555	1651	1800	...	1850	1932	1957	2103	2256	...		1045	1149	1240	1349	...	1440	1542	1647	1742	1840	...	1949	2155
Glasgow Central **214** a.	1737	...	...	...	...	2139	...	...	...	...	...		...	...	...	...	...	...	...	...	...	...	...	...	...

		Ⓐ	Ⓐ	Ⓐ	Ⓐ	Ⓐ	Ⓐ	Ⓐ	Ⓐ	Ⓐ	Ⓐ	Ⓐ	Ⓐ	Ⓐ	Ⓐ	Ⓐ			⑥	⑥	⑥	⑥	⑥	⑥	⑥
Glasgow Central **214** d.	Ⓐ	...	...	...	0708	...	...	...	...	1212	...	...	...	1612	...	...	...	⑥	...	...	...	0708	...	...	...
Carlisle d.		0628	0718	0828	0939	1028	1135	1228	1332	1436	1528	1628	1728	1837	1941	2128	...		0625	0718	0828	0939	1028	1135	1228
Haltwhistle d.		0700	0750	0900	1007	1100	1203	1300	1404	1505	1556	1700	1801	1909	2010	2200	...		0657	0750	0900	1007	1100	1203	1300
Hexham d.		0722	0812	0922	1026	1122	1222	1322	1426	1523	1615	1722	1823	1931	2028	2222	...		0719	0813	0922	1026	1122	1222	1322
MetroCentre d.		0753	0845	0946	1050	1146	1246	1346	1450	1547	1638	1746	1854	2002	2059	2253	...		0750	0846	0946	1050	1146	1246	1346
Newcastle a.		0807	0858	0959	1103	1159	1259	1359	1503	1600	1648	1759	1907	2015	2112	2306	...		0807	0900	0959	1103	1159	1259	1359

	⑥	⑥	⑥	⑥		⑥	⑥	⑥	⑥			⑦	⑦	⑦		⑦	⑦	⑦		⑦	⑦	⑦		⑦	⑦
Glasgow Central **214** d.	...	1212	...	...	...	...	1612	...	...	...	⑦	...	...	...	...	...	...	...	...	...	...	...	...	...	...
Carlisle d.	1332	1436	1528	1628	...	1728	1840	1941	2128	...		0902	1004	1108	...	1204	1308	1410	...	1505	1610	1708	...	1804	2015
Haltwhistle d.	1404	1505	1556	1700	...	1801	1912	2010	2200	...		0934	1036	1136	...	1236	1336	1438	...	1537	1638	1736	...	1836	2043
Hexham d.	1426	1523	1615	1722	...	1823	1934	2028	2222	...		0956	1058	1156	...	1258	1356	1458	...	1559	1658	1756	...	1858	2102
MetroCentre d.	1450	1547	1639	1746	...	1854	2005	2100	2253	...		1029	1129	1230	...	1330	1430	1530	...	1633	1730	1830	...	1930	2135
Newcastle a.	1503	1600	1651	1759	...	1907	2018	2113	2305	...		1041	1141	1241	...	1341	1441	1541	...	1644	1741	1841	...	1941	2148

214 CARLISLE - DUMFRIES - GLASGOW — 2nd class SR

km		⚒	⚒	⚒	⑥	Ⓐ	⑥	⚒	⑥	⚒	⑦	⑥		⚒	⑦	⚒	⑥	Ⓐ	⚒	⑦	⚒		⑥	⚒	⑦	⚒
	Newcastle **213** d.	...	...	...	0630	0646	...	...	...	...	...	...	...	1323	...	...	...	...	...	...	1716	...	...	...	...	...
0	**Carlisle** d.	...	0523	0608	0815	0815	0955	1115	1220	1312	1312	1422	...	1512	1512	1617	1712	1716	1757	1912	1917	...	2022	2112	2122	2310
16	Gretna Green d.	...	0534	0619	0826	0826	1006	1126	1231	1323	1323	1433	...	1523	1523	1628	1723	1727	1808	1923	1928	...	2033	2123	2133	2321
28	Annan d.	...	0543	0627	0834	0834	1014	1134	1240	1331	1331	1441	...	1531	1531	1636	1731	1735	1816	1931	1937	...	2041	2131	2141	2329
53	**Dumfries** d.	0546	0600	0646	0853	0853	1032	1153	1257	1348	1350	1459	...	1550	1549	1654	1749	1753	1833	1950	1955	...	2059	2150	2159	2347
124	Auchinleck d.	0634	...	0734	0941	0941	...	1241	...	1438	1438	...	...	1638	...	...	...	...	1923	2038	2044	...	...	2238	...	...
146	**Kilmarnock** ▽ d.	0652	...	0755	0957	0957	...	1257	...	1457	1457	...	...	1657	...	...	...	...	1957a	2057	2100	...	...	2257	...	...
185	**Glasgow Central** ▽ a.	0731	...	0837	1037	1037	...	1335	...	1534	1536	...	...	1737	...	...	...	...	2037	2135	2139	...	...	2336	...	...

	⚒	⚒	⑥	Ⓐ	⚒	⚒	⑥	⚒	⑦	⑥	⚒	⚒	⑦	⑥	⑦	⚒	⚒	⑥	⑦	⚒	⚒	⑥	Ⓐ	⑥⑦	Ⓐ
Glasgow Central ▽ d.	...	...	...	...	0708	0837	...	1012	...	...	1212	1312	...	...	1512	...	1612	...	...	1742	1912	...	2112	2212	2312
Kilmarnock ▽ d.	...	...	...	...	0750	0918	...	1051	...	...	1250	1350	...	...	1553	...	1651	...	...	1826	1951	...	2153	2249	2359
Auchinleck d.	...	...	...	...	0807	0935	...	1108	...	...	1307	1407	...	...	1610	...	1708	...	...	1842	2008	...	2210	2306	0022
Dumfries d.	0458	0617	0743	0745	0858	1025	1102	1158	1300	1310	1357	1457	1501	1602	1700	1707	1758	1841	1901	1933	2100	2213	2300	2356	0115
Annan d.	0513	0632	0758	0800	0913	1040	1117	1213	1315	1325	1413	1512	1516	1617	1715	1722	1813	1856	1916	1948	2115	2228	2315	0011	...
Gretna Green d.	0522	0641	0807	0809	0922	1049	1126	1222	1324	1334	1421	1521	1525	1626	1724	1731	1822	1905	1925	1957	2124	2237	2324	0020	...
Carlisle a.	0535	0654	0820	0822	0937	1104	1139	1235	1337	1352	1435	1534	1542	1639	1737	1744	1835	1918	1938	2011	2143	2250	2337	0034	...
Newcastle **213** a.	...	0858	...	0959	1103	...	...	...	...	...	1600	...	...	...	...	...	2018	...	...	...	...	...	...	...	...

a – Arrive 1940.

▽ – Frequent additional services are available (half-hourly on ⚒, hourly on ⑦).

215 GLASGOW and KILMARNOCK - STRANRAER — 2nd class SR

For ⛴ Cairnryan - Belfast and v.v. see Table 2002.

km		⚒	⚒	⚒	⚒		⚒	⚒	⚒	⑦	⚒	⚒		⚒	⑦	⚒	⚒	⑦		⚒	⚒	⑥	Ⓐ
0	**Glasgow Central** **216** d.	...	...	...	...	...	0938	...	1150	1155	...	...	...	1512	1522	...	1712	1754	...	...	...	...	221
12	Paisley Gilmour St **216** d.	...	...	...	...	...	0950	...	1202	1206	...	...	...	|	1533	...	|	1805	...	...	...	...	|
43	Kilwinning **216** d.	...	...	...	...	...	1014	...	1221	1223	...	...	...	|	1550	...	|	1822	...	...	...	...	|
	Kilmarnock a.	...	...	...	...	...	|	...	|	|	...	...	...	1551	|	...	1751	|	...	...	...	...	225
	Kilmarnock d.	...	...	...	0837	...	|	1104	|	|	1304	1404	...	1603	|	1704	1803	|	...	1905	2110	2306	230
56	Troon **216** d.	...	...	...	0849	...	|	1116	|	|	1316	1416	...	1616	|	1718	1817	|	...	1917	2121	2318	231
61	Prestwick Airport ✈ **216** d.	...	...	...	0854	...	|	1123	|	|	1321	1421	...	1622	|	1722	1821	|	...	1922	2126	2323	232
67	**Ayr** **216** a.	...	...	...	0903	...	1037	1128	1241	1241	1329	1430	...	1630	1608	1732	1830	1840	...	1931	2134	2330	233
	Ayr d.	0528	0635	0837	0905	...	1039	1129	1242	1242	1334	1431	...	1631	1614	1732	1831	1842	...	1932	2135	2331	233
101	Girvan d.	0555	0702	0903	0932	...	1104	1157	1308	1308	1410	1458	...	1659	1640	1758	1858	1908	...	2003	2202	2357	235
121	Barrhill d.	...	...	0922	...	...	1124	...	1327	1327	...	...	...	...	1659	1818	...	1927	...	2023	...	0016	001
163	**Stranraer** a.	...	...	0958	...	...	1200	...	1404	1404	...	...	...	...	1735	1854	...	2004	...	2059	...	0052	005

km		⚒	⚒	⚒	⚒		⑥	Ⓐ	⑦	⚒	⚒	⚒		Ⓐ	⑦	⚒	⚒	⚒		⚒	⑦	⚒	⚒
0	**Stranraer** d.	...	...	0701	...	...	1010	1010	1040	...	1250	...	...	...	1440	1443	...	...	...	1908	1940	2113	...
42	Barrhill d.	...	...	0735	...	...	1044	1044	1114	...	1330	...	...	...	1514	1517	...	...	...	1943	2019	2148	...
61	Girvan d.	0600	0707	0753	0944	...	1106	1106	1132	1243	1348	1433	...	1503	1532	1535	1733	1910	...	2001	2037	2206	222
96	**Ayr** a.	0628	0735	0821	1012	...	1135	1139	1201	1319	1416	1510	...	1531	1601	1604	1809	1938	...	2030	2106	2234	225
96	**Ayr** **216** d.	...	0736	...	1013	...	1135	1140	1201	1320	1417	1518	...	1532	1601	1605	1815	1939	...	2030	2106	2235	...
102	Prestwick Airport ✈ **216** d.	...	|	...	1021	...	1143	1147	|	1327	|	1525	...	|	|	1613	1822	1946	...	|	|	|	...
106	Troon **216** d.	...	0747	...	1026	...	1148	1152	|	1332	|	1530	...	|	|	1618	1829	1952	...	|	|	2245	...
120	**Kilmarnock 214** a.	...	0807	...	1041	...	1204	1208	|	1348	|	1548	...	|	|	1634	1846	2007	...	|	|	|	...
	Kilmarnock 214 d.	...	...	...	...	...	...	...	|	...	|	1557	...	|	|	...	...	...	...	|	|	|	...
	Kilwinning **216** d.	...	...	...	...	...	...	...	1216	...	1437	|	...	1553	1616	...	...	...	...	2058	2121	2255	...
	Paisley Gilmour St **216** a.	...	...	...	...	...	...	...	1236	...	1459	|	...	1622	1636	...	...	...	...	2120	2141	2314	...
	Glasgow Central **216** a.	...	...	...	...	...	...	...	1249	...	1512	1633	...	1636	1650	...	...	...	...	2132	2154	2325	...

🚌 connections to / from Cairnryan are operated by Scottish Citylink www.citylink.co.uk

SR GLASGOW - AYR, ARDROSSAN and LARGS 216

Typical off-peak journey time in hours and minutes
READ DOWN ↓ READ UP ↑

Journey times may be extended during peak hours on Ⓐ (0600 - 0900 and 1600 - 1900) and also at weekends.
The longest journey time by any train is noted in the table heading.

GLASCOW CENTRAL - AYR — Longest journey: 1 hour 04 minutes SR

km	△ (down)		Station			△ (up)
0	0h00	↓	Glasgow Central	d.	↑	0h49
43	0h25		Kilwinning	d.		0h22
48	0h29	↓	Irvine	d.	↑	0h18
56	0h37		Troon	d.		0h11
61	0h41	↓	Prestwick Airport ✈	d.	↑	0h07
67	0h52		Ayr	a.		0h00

From Glasgow Central: On ⚒ at 0015②–⑥, 0600, 0630, 0700, 0730, 0745, 0800, 0838, 0900, 0930, 1000, 1030 and every 30 minutes until 1500, 1530, 1600, 1604⑥, 1627, 1700, 1728Ⓐ, 1730⑥, 1800 and every 30 minutes until 2330; On ⑦ at 0900 and every 30 minutes until 1900, 2000, 2100, 2200, 2300.

From Ayr: On ⚒ at 0513, 0540, 0602, 0620Ⓐ, 0633, 0650, 0705, 0719, 0740, 0805, 0828, 0850, 0923, 0950 and at the same minutes past each hour until 1325, 1350, 1425, 1450, 1524, 1548, 1623, 1654, 1723, 1753, 1825, 1850, 1915 and every 30 minutes until 2215, 2300; On ⑦ at 0845 and every 30 minutes until 1945, 2045, 2145, 2300.

△ – Trains at 0015⚒ - 0838⚒ and 1900⚒ - 2330⚒ and all day on ⑦ call additionally at Paisley Gilmour Street.

GLASGOW CENTRAL - ARDROSSAN - LARGS — Longest journey: 1 hour 10 minutes SR

km	Down		Station			Up
0	0h00	↓	Glasgow Central	d.	↑	0h59
12	0h10		Paisley Gilmour St	d.		0h46
43	0h19	↓	Kilwinning	d.	↑	0h25
50	0h28		Ardrossan Sth Beach	d.		0h17
54	0h49	↓	Fairlie	d.	↑	0h05
69	0h56		Largs	a.		0h00

From Glasgow Central: On ⚒ at 0615, 0715, 0848 and hourly until 1448, 1545⑥, 1548Ⓐ, 1630, 1714⑥, 1722Ⓐ, 1749, 1848, 1945, 2045, 2145, 2245, 2315①–④, 2345⑤; On ⑦ at 0940 and hourly until 2140, 2242.

From Largs: On ⚒ at 0641, 0722Ⓐ, 0742, 0833Ⓐ, 0853⑥, 0953 and hourly until 1553, 1648, 1733, 1852, 1952, 2052, 2152, 2252; On ⑦ at 0854 and hourly until 2154, 2300.

SR 2nd class Most services 🍸 GLASGOW - OBAN, FORT WILLIAM and MALLAIG 218

km																										
				⚒	Ⓐ	⑥	⚒ A	Ba	⚒	⚒	⑦ G	⑦ D	⑦ G	⚒	Ⓐ Ca		⑦ G	⑦ G	⚒	⚒	Ⓐ	⚒	⑦	⑦	⚒	⚒
	Edinburgh 220	d.	...	...	...	...	0450	...	0715	0715	...	0810	0830	0930	...	...	1100	1100	1115	1115	...	1530	1700	1700	1715	1715
0	Glasgow Queen St	d.	...	...	0520	0530	|	...	0821	0821	...	0845	0956	1037	...	...	1220	1220	1221	1221	...	1637	1820	1820	1821	1821
10	Westerton	d.	...	...	0533	0543	0556	...	|	|	...	|	|	|	...	...	|	|	|	|	...	|	|	|	|	|
16	Dalmuir	d.	...	...	0839	...	0603	...	0841	0841	...	0927u	1016	1056	...	...	1234	1234	1242	1242	...	1654	1834	1834	1842	1842
26	Dumbarton Central	d.	...	...	0548	...	0614	...	0851	0851	...	|	1025	1105	...	...	1245	1245	1251	1251	...	1705	1844	1844	1851	1851
40	Helensburgh Upper	d.	...	...	0603	...	0631	...	0906	0906	...	0952	1040	1128	...	...	1306	1306	1306	1306	...	1722	1905	1905	1906	1906
51	Garelochhead	d.	...	...	0614	...	0644	...	0917	0917	...	1003	1051	1140	...	...	1317	1317	1319	1319	...	1734	1916	1916	1917	1917
68	Arrochar & Tarbet	d.	...	...	0634	...	0708	...	0936	0936	...	1023	1111	1201	...	...	1337	1337	1340	1340	...	1758	1936	1936	1936	1936
81	Ardlui	d.	...	...	0652	...	0723x	...	0950	0950	...	1037	1127	1214	...	...	1353	1353	1356	1356	...	1812	1952	1952	1952	1952
95	Crianlarich	a.	...	...	0708	...	0744	...	1008	1008	...	1053	1144	1230	...	...	1409	1409	1412	1412	...	1828	2008	2008	2008	2008
95	Crianlarich	d.	...	...	0718	...	0746	...	1015	1021	...	1056	1146	1233	...	...	1415	1421	1418	1424	...	1831	2014	2020	2014	2020
	Dalmally	d.	...	...	0749	...	|	...	1042	|	...	1122	1214	1259	...	...	1442	|	1444	|	1705	1857	2040	|	2040	|
	Taynuilt	d.	...	...	0811	...	|	...	1103	|	...	1142	1240	1320	...	...	1503	|	1505	|	1724	1920	2100	|	2100	|
162	Oban	a.	...	...	0835	...	|	...	1127	|	...	1206	1304	1343	...	...	1527	|	1528	|	1747	1943	2124	|	2124	|
115	Bridge of Orchy	d.	...	...	...	...	0816	...	...	1048	...	...	...	...	...	...	...	1446	...	1449	...	...	...	2045	...	2045
140	Rannoch	d.	...	...	...	...	0846	...	...	1109	...	...	...	...	...	...	...	1509	...	1512	...	...	...	2108	...	2108
177	Roy Bridge	d.	...	...	...	...	0931x	...	...	1148	...	...	...	...	...	...	...	1548	...	1551	...	...	...	2146	...	2146
183	Spean Bridge	d.	...	...	...	...	0939	...	...	1155	...	...	...	...	...	...	...	1556	...	1558	...	...	...	2153	...	2153
197	Fort William	a.	...	...	...	...	0955	...	...	1208	...	...	...	...	...	...	...	1609	...	1611	...	...	...	2206	...	2206
197	Fort William	d.	...	0830	...	...	...	1015	...	1212	1212	...	...	...	1430	...	...	1619	...	1619	...	...	...	2214	...	2214
223	Glenfinnan	d.	...	0905	...	...	...	1122	...	1246	1246	...	...	...	1520	...	...	1655	...	1655	...	...	...	2247	...	2247
251	Arisaig	d.	...	0938	...	...	...	|	...	1319	1319	...	...	...	|	...	...	1727	...	1727	...	...	...	2320	...	2320
259	Morar	d.	...	0946	...	...	...	|	...	1327	1327	...	...	...	|	...	...	1736	...	1736	...	...	...	2328	...	2328
264	Mallaig	a.	...	0953	...	...	...	1225	...	1334	1334	...	...	...	1629	...	...	1743	...	1743	...	...	...	2335	...	2335

		Ⓐ	⑥	Ⓐ	⑥	Ⓐ	⚒	⚒	⑦ G	⑦ G	Ⓐ	Ba	⑦ G	⑥	⑦ D	⚒	⚒	⑦	⑦	⑦ A	⑦	H	Ⓐ A	②–⑥	Ⓐ Ca
lallaig	d.	...	...	0603	0603	...	...	1010	...	1010	...	1410	...	...	...	1605	...	1605	...	...	...	1815	...	...	1840
lorar	d.	...	...	0609	0609	...	...	1017	...	1017	...	|	...	...	...	1612	...	1612	...	...	...	1822	...	...	|
risaig	d.	...	...	0619	0619	...	...	1026	...	1026	...	|	...	...	...	1621	...	1621	...	...	...	1831	...	...	|
lenfinnan	d.	...	...	0651	0651	...	...	1059	...	1059	...	|	...	...	...	1654	...	1654	...	...	...	1904	...	...	|
ort William	a.	...	...	0725	0725	...	...	1132	...	1132	...	1600	...	...	...	1728	...	1728	...	...	...	1937	...	...	2024
ort William	d.	...	...	0742	0742	...	...	1140	...	1140	...	...	...	...	...	1737	...	1737	...	1900	...	...	1950	...	...
pean Bridge	d.	...	...	0755	0755	...	...	1156	...	1156	...	...	...	...	...	1751	...	1751	...	1920	...	...	2010	...	...
oy Bridge	d.	...	...	0802	0802	...	...	1202	...	1202	...	...	...	...	...	1757	...	1757	...	1927x	...	...	2017x	...	...
annoch	d.	...	...	0845	0845	...	...	1242	...	1242	...	...	...	...	...	1837	...	1837	...	2015	...	...	2106	...	...
idge of Orchy	d.	...	...	0905	0905	...	...	1303	...	1303	...	...	...	...	...	1858	...	1857	...	2048	...	...	2134	...	...
Oban	d.	0521	0811	|	|	0857	1211	|	1211	|	1441	...	1611	1611	1711	|	1811	|	1811	|	...	...	|	...	...
Taynuilt	d.	0544	0835	|	|	0920	1235	|	1237	|	1506	...	1635	1634	1735	|	1835	|	1835	|	...	...	|	...	...
Dalmally	d.	0603	0856	|	|	0940	1301	|	1258	|	1526	...	1656	1654	1756	|	1858	|	1856	|	...	...	|	...	...
rianlarich	a.	0631	0924	0929	0932	1008	1333	1327	1328	1332	1554	...	1725	1722	1825	1922	1929	1927	1926	2118	...	...	2204	...	...
rianlarich	d.	0632	0938	0933	0938	1014	1339	1339	1338	1338	1556	...	1731	1725	1826	1935	1935	1933	1933	2119	...	...	2205	...	...
rdlui	d.	0650	0956	0951	0956	1029	1355	1355	1354	1354	1611	...	1748	1743	1841	1951	1951	1951	1951	2140x	...	...	2226x	...	...
rochar & Tarbet	d.	0708	1010	1005	1010	1043	1410	1410	1408	1408	1627	...	1802	1757	1855	2006	2006	2006	2006	2158	...	...	2244	...	...
arelochhead	d.	0728	1032	1030	1032	1104	1431	1431	1428	1428	1649	...	1823	1819	1817	2026	2026	2026	2026	2224	...	...	2310	...	...
elensburgh Upper	d.	0740	1044	1044	1044	1116	1443	1443	1440	1440	1700	...	1834	1831	1929	2038	2038	2038	2038	2238	...	...	2324	...	...
umbarton Central	a.	0755	1059	1059	1059	1129	1458	1458	1453	1453	1713	...	1847	1844	|	2051	2051	2053	2053	2252	...	...	2338	...	...
almuir	a.	|	1110	1110	1110	1138	1507	1507	1505	1505	1722	...	1856	1853	1955s	2100	2100	2104	2104	2304	...	...	2350	...	...
esterton	a.	|	|	|	|	|	|	|	|	|	|	...	|	|	|	|	|	|	|	2314	2328	...	2358	0006	...
lasgow Queen St.	a.	0837	1130	1130	1130	1200	1530	1530	1528	1528	1748	...	1915	1919	2045	2118	2118	2120	2120	|	2349	...	|	0020	...
Edinburgh 220	a.	0951	1235	1235	1235	1307	1636	1636	1652	1652	1849	...	2021	2021	2109	2222	2222	2223	2223	0022	...	...	0107	...	...

– Ⓡ. (12) (limited accommodation), 🛏 1,2 cl. and 🍸 London Euston - Fort William and v.v. (Table 161).
– THE JACOBITE – 🚂. Ⓡ May 18 - Oct. 24 (also ⑥⑦ June 21 - Sept. 21).
– THE JACOBITE – 🚂. Ⓡ Ⓐ June 2 - Aug. 29.
– ⑦ Jun. 22 - Aug 24.

G – ⑦ May. 18 - Oct. 26.
H – Daily May. 18 - Oct. 26; ⚒ Oct. 27 - Dec 13.

a – National Rail tickets not valid. To book ✆ 0845 128 4681 www.westcoastrailways.co.uk

d – Change at Dalmuir.
s – Calls to set down only.
u – Calls to pick up only.
x – Calls on request.

SCOTTISH ISLAND FERRIES 219

ledonian MacBrayne Ltd operates numerous ferry services linking the Western Isles of Scotland to the mainland and to each other. Principal routes – some of which are seasonal – are listed low (see also the map on page 98). Service frequencies, sailing-times and reservations: ✆ +44 (0)800 066 5000; fax +44 (0)1475 635 235; www.calmac.co.uk

drossan – Brodick (Arran)
aonaig – Lochranza (Arran)
nnacraig – Port Askaig (Islay)
nnacraig – Port Ellen (Islay)
Kilchoan – Tobermory (Mull)
Leverburgh (Harris) – Berneray (North Uist)
Mallaig – Armadale (Skye)
Mallaig – Eigg, Muck, Rum and Canna
Oban – Castlebay (Barra) and Lochboisdale (South Uist)
Oban – Coll and Tiree
Oban – Colonsay, Port Askaig (Islay) and Kennacraig
Oban – Craignure (Mull)
Uig (Skye) – Lochmaddy (North Uist)
Uig (Skye) – Tarbert (Harris)
Ullapool – Stornaway (Lewis)
Wemyss Bay – Rothesay (Bute)

220 EDINBURGH - GLASGOW — EC, SR, XC

EDINBURGH - MOTHERWELL - GLASGOW CENTRAL

km		⚒	⚒	⚒2	⑥A	ⒶA	⚒2	⚒A	⚒2	⑦Ac	⑦A	⚒A	⚒2	⑦A	⚒A	⚒2	A	⚒2	⚒2	⚒A	⑦A	ⒶB	⑦A	⑥A	ⒶA	⑦B
0	**Edinburgh** Waverley d.	0624	0726	0754	0911	0911	1016	1111	1151	1217	1310	1312	1351	1510	1511	1548	1711	1742	1826	1911	1918	2017	2112	2113	2114	2122
71	Motherwell d.	0704	0810	0900	0953	1001	1132	1152	1258	1256	1350	1352	1452	1553	1552	1641	1752	1831	1933	1952	1959	2103	2153	2156	2159	2205
92	**Glasgow** Central a.	0722	0832	0924	1015	1027	1155	1211	1326	1314	1409	1412	1514	1613	1612	1703**b**	1811	1856	1954	2015**a**	2021	2125	2214	2221	2228	2226

	⚒A	⚒B	⚒2	⚒A	⚒A	Ⓐ2	⑥	⑦A	⚒A	⚒2	⑦A	⚒A	⚒2	⑦A	⑦A	⚒A	⚒2	⚒A	⑦A	⑦A	⚒A	⚒2	⑦	⑥	Ⓐ
Glasgow Central d.	0601	0650	0705	0750	0900	0932	0948	1055	1100	1148	1151	1300	1348	1349	1455	1500	1550	1652	1655	1857	1900	1950	2058	2105	2105
Motherwell d.	0617	0706	0720	0805	0915	0959	1006	1110	1114	1209	1208	1314	1416	1404	1511	1514	1607	1706	1711	1911	1914	2006	2118	|	2123
Edinburgh Waverley a.	0702	0752	0828	0856	1004	1053	1119	1156	1157	1305	1254	1356	1525	1447	1556	1601	1710	1757	1756	1955	1957	2058	2208	2159	2223

EDINBURGH - FALKIRK - GLASGOW QUEEN STREET

Journey time: ± 51 minutes *76 km*

From **Edinburgh Waverley**: Trains call at **Falkirk High** ± 27 minutes later.

⚒: 0555, 0630, 0645Ⓐ, 0700, 0715, 0730, 0745 and every 15 minutes until 1930, 2000 and every 30 minutes until 2330.

⑦: 0800, 0830 and every 30 minutes until 2100, 2130, 2200, 2230, 2300, 2330.

From **Glasgow Queen Street**: Trains call at **Falkirk High** ± 21 minutes later.

⚒: 0600, 0630, 0645Ⓐ, 0700, 0715, 0730, 0745 and every 15 minutes until 1930, 2000 and every 30 minutes until 2330.

⑦: 0750, 0830 and every 30 minutes until 2130, 2200, 2230, 2300, 2330.

EDINBURGH - AIRDRIE - GLASGOW QUEEN STREET

Journey time: ± 64 (* 75) minutes *71 km*

From **Edinburgh Waverley**: Trains call at **Airdrie** ± 43 minutes later.

⚒: 0621*, 0648*, 0721*, 0748*, 0821*, 0840, 0908, 0937 and every 30 minutes until 1738, 1805, 1837, 1921*, 1951*, 2021*, 2051*, 2121*, 2151*, 2221*, 2251*.

⑦: 0838*, 0906*, 0938*, 1006*, 1040*, 1110* and every 30 minutes (* applies to all trains) until 1840*, 1940*, 2040*, 2140*, 2240*.

From **Glasgow Queen Street**: Trains call at **Airdrie** ± 19 minutes later.

⚒: 0558*, 0629*, 0654, 0724, 0754 and every 30 minutes until 1822, 1900*, 1930*, 2000*, 2030*, 2100*, 2130*, 2200*, 2230*.

⑦: 0810*, 0845*, 0915*, 0945*, 1015*, 1045* and every 30 minutes (* applies to all trains until 1845*, 1945*, 2045*, 2145*.

A – To/from destinations on Tables **115** and **127**.
B – To/from London Kings Cross (Table **180**).
a – 2009 on ⑥.
b – 1723 on ⑥.
c – Additional trip 1023 on ⑦.

221 EDINBURGH and GLASGOW - INVERNESS — Most trains 🍸 SR

km		⚒A	⚒	⚒	⑦	⚒		⚒	⑦	⚒	⚒	⑦		⑦	⚒	⑦	⚒a	⑦a		⚒	⑦	⑦	⚒	⚒
	London Kings Cross **180** d.	2057**d**	...			...	...	...	...	...	...		...	...	...	...	1200	1145	...	...	...	...	...	...
0	**Edinburgh** Waverley **224** d.	|	...	0834	0933	...	...	1035	...	...	1335	1356	...	...	...	1550	1633	1632	...	1741	1750	...	...	1944
42	Kirkcaldy **224** d.	|	...	0907	1009	...	...	1110**u**	...	...	1410**u**	1430	...	...	...	1623	|	|	...	1815	1823	...	...	2017
54	Markinch **224** d.	|	...	0916	1018	...	...	1119	...	...	1419	|	...	...	...	1632	|	|	...	1825	1832	...	...	2026
	Glasgow Queen St **224** d.	|	0710	|	|	1010	...	|	1110	1209	|	|	...	1438	1508	|	|	|	...	|	|	1810	1811	|
	Stirling **224** d.	0455	0736	|	|	1037	...	|	1140	1236	|	|	...	1507	1536	|	1723	1720	...	|	|	1840	1842	|
91	**Perth** **224** d.	0539	0810	0947	1051	1116	...	1153	1216	1313	1451	1511	...	1546	1617	1705	1802	1801	...	1858	1904	1917	1921	2101
116	Dunkeld & Birnam d.	0600	0830	|	1108	1136	...	|	1234	1329	1508	1529	...	|	1634	1722	|	|	...	1918	...	1933	1938	2118
137	Pitlochry d.	0616	0843	1019	1121	1149	...	1222	1247	1342	1521	1542	...	1613	1647	1735	1831	1832	...	1931	...	1946	1951	2133
148	Blair Atholl d.	0628	0852	1028	1130	|	...	1232	|	1352	1530	1551	...	|	1656	|	|	|	...	|	...	1956	2001	2142
186	Dalwhinnie d.	0700	0917	1054	1154	|	...	1259	|	|	1555	1622	...	|	|	|	|	|	...	|	...	2019	2024	2207
202	Newtonmore d.	0712	0927	|	1204	|	...	1309	|	|	|	1632	...	|	1728	|	|	|	...	|	...	2030	2034	2217
207	Kingussie d.	0719	0936	1107	1209	1234	...	1315	1334	1428	1608	1637	...	1656	1733	1818	1916	1916	...	2014	...	2035	2039	2222
226	Aviemore d.	0743	0950	1122	1220	1245	...	1332	1346	1439	1619	1649	...	1710	1744	1829	1929	1930	...	2026	...	2046	2051	2234
282	**Inverness** a.	0836	1027	1157	1257	1328	...	1410	1427	1523	1654	1727	...	1745	1821	1905	2006	2008	...	2101	...	2124	2126	2310

km		⚒2	⚒	⚒b	⚒	⑦b		⚒	⚒	⑦	⑦	⚒	⑦	⚒	⑦	⚒	⑦	⚒		⚒	⑦	⚒	⑦B	ⒶB
0	**Inverness** d.	...	0650	0755	0845	0940	...	0941	1045	1050	1245	1253	1330	1447	1522	1551	1624	1730	...	1846	1851	2015	2026	2044
56	Aviemore d.	...	0725	0830	0924	1019	...	1026	1123	1125	1323	1332	1406	1523	1557	1635	1710	1814	...	1928	1930	2106	2115	2131
75	Kingussie d.	...	0737	0843	0936	1032	...	1038	1136	1137	1335	1345	1418	1535	1609	1647	1722	1826	...	1940	1942	2118	2129	2144
80	Newtonmore d.	...	|	|	0940	1037	...	|	|	|	1340	1349	|	|	|	1651	|	|	...	1945	1946	2122	2135	2150
96	Dalwhinnie d.	...	|	|	|	|	...	1052	|	1151	|	|	|	1549	|	|	|	|	...	1957	1958	2134	2150	2204
134	Blair Atholl d.	0712	|	|	|	1109	...	1113	|	|	1411	1420	|	|	|	1722	1754	|	...	2018	2019	2155	2215	2230
145	Pitlochry d.	0726	0817	0924	1019	1123	...	1123	1224	1219	1421	1431	1458	1619	1649	1732	1804	1905	...	2028	2029	2205	2229	2243
166	Dunkeld & Birnam d.	0739	0830	|	|	1137	...	1136	1237	1234	1434	1443	|	1634	1701	1744	1818	1918	...	2041	2041	2216	2243	2258
191	**Perth** **224** d.	0802	0850	0957	1053	1159	...	1202	1302	1254	1454	1502	1529	1654	1722	1806	1839	1939	...	2102	2106	2236	2306	232
244	Stirling **224** a.	|	|	1029	1127	1234	...	|	|	|	1524	|	|	1728	|	|	1908	2013	...	|	|	2309	2351	0006
291	**Glasgow** Queen St **224** a.	|	|	|	1213	|	...	|	|	|	1558	|	|	1809	|	|	1941	2045	...	|	|	2343	|	|
	Markinch **224** a.	0831	|	|	...	|	...	1230	1330	1321	...	1531	1557	...	1750	1835	...	...	...	2131	2133	...	|	|
	Kirkcaldy **224** a.	0840	0924	|	...	|	...	1240	1340	1331	...	1540	1607	...	1759	1844	...	...	...	2142	2142	...	|	|
	Edinburgh Waverley **224** a.	0922	1004	1117	...	1320	...	1323	1424	1409	...	1622	1644	...	1836	1921	...	...	...	2219	2219	...	|	|
	London Kings Cross **180** a.	...	...	1554	...	1808	...	...	...	...	...	...	...	...	...	...	...	...	...	...	...	...	0747**e**	0747

A – Ⓡ. 🛏 1,2 class and (2). Train stops to set down only.
B – Ⓡ. 🛏 1,2 class and (2). Train stops to pick up only.
a – Via Falkirk Grahamston (d. 1704).
b – Via Falkirk Grahamston (d. 1046⚒/1249⑦).
d – London Euston (departs on ⑦–⑤, see Table **161**).
e – London Euston (see Table **161**).
s – Calls to set down only.
u – Stops to pick up only.

222 EDINBURGH and GLASGOW - STIRLING — SR

Edinburgh Waverley - Stirling: *75 km*

⚒: 0518, 0633, 0703, 0733, 0803, 0833, 0903, 0933 and every 30 minutes until 1604, 1636, 1703, 1733, 1803, 1833, 1903, 1933, 2033, 2133, 2233, 2303, 2333.

⑦: 0934, 1035, 1106, 1135, 1206. 1235, 1306, 1335, 1406, 1436, 1506, 1535, 1606, 1635, 1706, 1735, 1806, 1835, 1935, 2035, 2135, 2235.

Stirling - Edinburgh Waverley: Journey time: ± 50 minut

⚒: 0530, 0636, 0717, 0731Ⓐ, 0749Ⓐ, 0807, 0837, 0909, 0937, 1007, 1037 and every 3 minutes until 1737, 1807, 1837, 1907, 1937, 2007, 2037, 2107, 2207, 2317.

⑦: 0905, 0951, 1110, 1148, 1210, 1247, 1310, 1346, 1410, 1446, 1510, 1547, 1610, 164 1710, 1810, 1917, 2010, 2110, 2210.

☛ All trains (except the 0731Ⓐ from Stirling) call at **Falkirk Grahamston**: *41 km* (± 30 minutes) from Edinburgh; *34 km* (± 20 minutes) from Stirling.

Glasgow Queen St - Stirling: *47 km*

⚒: 0614, 0648, 0718, 0749, 0818, 0848 and every 30 minutes until 1818, 1848, 1918, 1948, 2018, 2048, 2118, 2148, 2218, 2248, 2318, 2348.

⑦: 0937, 1015, 1045, 1110, 1115, 1145, 1215, 1315, 1345, 1415, 1440, 1515, 1545, 1615, 1715, 1745, 1810, 1815, 1915, 1945, 2015, 2115, 2145, 2215, 2345.

Stirling - Glasgow Queen St: Journey time: ± 35 minut

⚒: 0554, 0623, 0655, 0723, 0739, 0753, 0811, 0823, 0853 and every 30 minutes until 1723, 1751, 1819, 1853, 1923, 1953, 2021, 2053, 2123, 2153, 2223, 2253.

⑦: 0925, 0939, 1025, 1125, 1143, 1225, 1325, 1338, 1425, 1438, 1524, 1528, 1542, 162 1640, 1725, 1738, 1825, 1837, 1909, 1925, 1958, 2025, 2125, 2144.

224 EDINBURGH and GLASGOW - DUNDEE - ABERDEEN — Most services 🍸 GR, SR, XC

km		⚒	⚒ Y	⚒	⚒	⚒	⚒ 2	⚒ 2	⚒	⚒	⚒ 2	⚒	⑦	⚒	⚒	⚒	⑦	Ⓐ	⑥	⑦	⑥	Ⓐ	⑦	⚒ 2	⚒
0	**Edinburgh** Waverley ... **221** d.	...	0440	...	0530	...	0633	0700	0728	...	0733	0800	0804	0828	...	0900	0910	0928	0928	0915	...	...	...	0935	10
42	Kirkcaldy **221** d.	...	0518	...	0603	...	0706	0736	0803	...	0809	0834	0840	|	...	0934	0950	|	|	1003	...	...	...	1010	103
54	Markinch **221** d.	...	|	...	0612	...	0715	0747	|	...	0819	0843	|	|	...	0943	|	|	|	1012	...	...	...	1019	104
82	Leuchars △ d.	...	0546	...	0633	...	|	0808	0826	...	|	0906	0906	0925	...	1003	1014	|	1025	1034	...	...	...	|	110
	Glasgow Queen St .. **221** d.	...	|	...	|	0556	|	|	|	0742	|	|	|	|	0841	|	|	|	|	|	0941	0941	0937	|	|
	Stirling **221** d.	...	|	...	|	0625	|	|	|	0809**u**	|	|	|	|	0908	|	|	|	|	|	1008	1008	1010	|	|
	Perth **221** d.	...	|	0600	|	0700	0746	|	|	0842	0854	|	|	|	0942	|	|	|	|	|	1040	1040	1047	1052	|
95	**Dundee** d.	0539	0608	0625	0652	0723	0812	0824	0842	0904	...	0922	0920	0939	1005	1019	1029	1034	1039	1048	1102	1102	1111	...	11
123	Arbroath d.	0609	0631	0647	0712	0742	...	...	0859	0923	...	...	0936	0958	1021	...	1046	1051	1056	1104	1124	1124	1133	...	...
145	Montrose d.	0625	0648	0702	0726	0757	...	...	0913	0938	...	...	0950	|	1040	...	1102	1105	1110	1120	1138	1143	1148	...	...
184	Stonehaven d.	0650	0713	0725	0751	0821	...	...	0935	|	...	...	1010	1034	1102	...	1125	1126	1131	1142	1203	1212	1213	...	...
210	**Aberdeen** a.	0714	0734	0747	0814	0847	...	...	0954	1017	...	...	1029	1054	1124	...	1147	1146	1151	1205	1223	1235	1237	...	...

Y – Ⓡ. 🛏 1,2 class and (2) London Euston - Aberdeen. Departs London previous day. Train stops to set down only.
Z – Ⓡ. 🛏 1,2 class and (2) Aberdeen - London Euston. Train stops to pick up only.
a – Ⓐ only.
b – ⑥ only.
d – On ⑥ also calls at Stirling (d. 1710).
e – Additional trips ⚒ 2148, 2319. ⑦ 1750, 1855
f – Additional trips Ⓐ 0615, ⚒ 2243 ⑦ 0936, 1254, 1529, 1722. 2106.
g – To/from destinations on Table **180**.
k – Additional trips ⑦ 1245, 1449, 1645.
p – Additional trips ⑦ 1030, 1229, 1431, 1628.
s – Stops to set down only.
u – Stops to pick up only.
x – To/from destinations on Table **127**.
△ – Frequent 🚌 connections available to/fr **St Andrews**. Journey 10 minutes. Operator: Stagecoach (routes **94**, **96**, 9

GR, SR, XC Most services 🍸

EDINBURGH and GLASGOW - DUNDEE - ABERDEEN 224

	⚒ g	⚒	⚒	⑦	⚒ 2	⚒	⑦ 2	⚒	⚒ 2	⑦ k	⚒	⚒	⚒	⚒ 2	⑦	⚒	⚒	⑦ 2	⚒	⑦	⚒	⚒	⚒ g	⑦ g	⚒
Edinburgh Waverley .... **221** d.	1028	...	1035	1050	1100	1128	1134	...	1135	...	1200	1228	...	1235	1240	1300	1328	1331	...	...	1335	1400	1428	1433	...
Kirkcaldy .... **221** d.	1105	...	1110u	1123	1134	|	1208	...	1210	...	1234	|	...	1310	1313	1334	|	1408	...	...	1410u	1434	1505	1511	...
Markinch .... **221** d.	|	...	1119	|	1143	|	1218	...	1219	...	1243	|	...	1319	|	1343	|	1418	...	...	1419	1443	|	|	...
Leuchars .... △ d.	1130	...	|	1147	1203	1226	1239	...	|	...	1303	1323	...	|	1337	1403	1423	1439	...	...	|	1503	1530	1536	...
Glasgow Queen St ... **221** d.	|	1041	|	*1045*	|	|	|	1141	|	1145	|	|	1241	|	|	|	|	|	1341	1345	|	|	|	|	1441
Stirling .... **221** d.	|	1109	|	*1111*	|	|	|	1207	|	1211	|	|	1307	|	|	|	|	|	1408	1413	|	|	|	|	1507
Perth .... **221** d.	|	1139	1153	*1142*	|	|	|	1237	1252	1246	|	|	1339	1352	|	|	|	|	1438	1450	1450	|	|	|	1540
Dundee .... d.	1144	1202	...	1208	1219	1240	1255	1300	...	1310	1319	1339	1402	...	1351	1419	1437	1455	1502	1513	...	1519	1548	1550	1602
Arbroath .... d.	1202	1218	...	1224	...	1256	...	1319	...	1326	...	1355	1418	...	1407	...	1454	...	1524	1532	...	...	1605	1608	1621
Montrose .... d.	1218	1233	...	1239	...	|	...	1333	...	1341	...	1410	1433	...	1421	...	|	...	1541	1548	...	...	1621	1624	1636
Stonehaven .... d.	1241	|	...	1300	...	1330	...	|	...	1402	...	1431	1454	...	1445	...	1527	...	|	1610	...	...	1644	1647	|
Aberdeen .... a.	1303	1313	...	1320	...	1350	...	1416	...	1422	...	1450	1514	...	1505	...	1547	...	1626	1633	...	...	1706	1709	1715

	⚒ 2	⚒	⚒	⑦ 2	⚒	⑦	⚒ 2	⚒ 2	⑦	⚒	⚒	⚒	⚒ 2	⚒ 2	⑦	⑦ 2	⚒	⚒	⑦	⚒	⑦	Ⓐ 2	⑥ x	Ⓐ x	⑦ x
Edinburgh Waverley .... **221** d.	1435	1500	1528	1534	...	...	1535	1600	1605	1628	...	...	1633	1700	1705	1734	1736	...	...	1741	1750	1800	1811	1810	1813
Kirkcaldy .... **221** d.	1510	1534	|	1608	...	...	1612	1633	1639	|	...	...	1709	1739	1739	1808	|	...	...	1815	1823	1840	1844	1847	1845
Markinch .... **221** d.	1519	1543	|	1618	...	...	1621	1642	1648	|	...	...	1718	1748	|	1818	|	...	...	1825	1832	1850	1853	1857	1854
Leuchars .... △ d.	|	1603	1625	1639	...	...	|	1703	1708	1726	...	...	|	1811	1804	1839	1834	...	...	|	|	1911	1914	1923	1915
Glasgow Queen St ... **221** d.	|	|	|	|	1541	1545	|	|	|	|	1611	1641	|	|	|	|	|	1741	1745	|	|	|	|	|	|
Stirling .... **221** d.	|	|	|	|	|	1612	|	|	|	|	1639	1711b	|	|	|	|	|	1816	1813	|	|	|	|	|	|
Perth .... **221** d.	1553	|	|	|	1637	1647	1653	|	|	|	1719	1740	1752	|	|	|	|	1855	1845	1857	1904	|	|	|	|
Dundee .... d.	...	1621	1639	1655	1700	1710	...	1719	1722	1740	1746	1803	...	1827	1818	1855	1849	1918	1909	...	...	1927	1930	1936	1931
Arbroath .... d.	...	...	1655	...	1719	1726	...	...	1743	1756	1810	1822	...	...	1835	...	1905	1936	1928	...	...	...	1949	1952	1947
Montrose .... d.	...	...	1709	...	1733	1741	...	...	1759	1811	...	|	...	...	1850	...	1922	1951	1944	...	...	...	2003	2006	2001
Stonehaven .... d.	...	...	1733	...	1755	1805	...	...	1821	1835	...	1855	...	...	1912	...	1944	2015	2009	...	...	...	2024	2027	2023
Aberdeen .... a.	...	...	1753	...	1815	1825	...	...	1842	1857	...	1915	...	...	1935	...	2007	2036	2029	...	...	...	2042	2048	2042

	⚒ g	⑦ g	⚒	⚒ 2	⚒ 2	⑦ 2	⚒	⚒	⑦	⚒	⚒ 2	⚒ x	Ⓐ g	⚒	⚒ 2	⑦	⚒	⚒	⚒	⑦	⚒ 2	⑦ 2	⚒ 2 e	⚒ 2	⚒ 2
Edinburgh Waverley .... **221** d.	1833	1836	...	1840	1900	1915	1928	...	...	1944	2000	2014	2032	...	2044	2100	2108	2140	...	...	2208	2225	2239	...	2308
Kirkcaldy .... **221** d.	1913	1913	...	1919	1934	2000	|	...	...	2017	2045	2052b	2111	...	2117	2135	2154	2212	...	...	2254	2310	2324	...	2354
Markinch .... **221** d.	|	|	...	1929	1943	2009	|	...	...	2026	2054	2102	|	...	2126	2144	2203	|	...	...	2303	2319	2333	...	0003
Leuchars .... △ d.	1938	1937	...	|	2003	2030	2029	...	...	|	2115	2126	2137	...	|	2205	2224	2235	...	...	2328	2340	|	...	0024
Glasgow Queen St ...... **221** d.	|	|	1841	|	|	|	|	1941	1945	|	|	|	|	2041	|	|	|	|	2141	2145	|	|	|	2248	|
Stirling .... **221** d.	|	|	1907	|	|	|	|	2007	2012	|	|	|	|	2107	|	|	|	|	2207	2212	|	|	|	2333	|
Perth .... **221** d.	|	|	1942	2001	|	|	|	2038	2047	2058	|	|	|	2143	2200	|	|	|	2241	2247	|	|	0005	0009	|
Dundee .... d.	1955	1952	2005	...	2019	2046	2043	2100	2110	...	2131	2142	2152	2209	...	2221	2240	2250	2303	2310	2344	2356	...	0036a	0040
Arbroath .... d.	2012	2009	2026	...	...	...	2059	2117	2126	...	...	...	2209	2227	...	2240	...	2306	2327	2329	...	...	...	...	...
Montrose .... d.	2028	2025	2041	...	...	...	2114	2131	2141	...	...	...	2225	2241	...	2255	...	2320	2341	2344	...	...	...	...	...
Stonehaven .... d.	2051	2048	|	...	...	...	2135	2155	2205	...	...	...	2248	2302	...	2316	...	2341	0005	0005	...	...	...	...	...
Aberdeen .... a.	2113	2110	2122	...	...	...	2153	2215	2225	...	...	...	2310	2322	...	2339	...	0004	0025	0025	...	...	...	...	...

km		Ⓐ 2 f	⚒ 2	⑥ 2	⚒ 2	⚒ 2	⚒ x	⚒ 2	⚒	⚒	⚒ 2	⚒	⑦ 2	⚒ 2	⚒	⚒	⚒ 2	⚒	⑦ 2	⑦	⚒	⚒ g	⚒ x	⑦ 2	⚒
0	**Aberdeen** .... d.	...	...	...	...	...	...	...	0526	0546	...	...	...	...	0633	0703	...	...	...	...	0740	0752	0820	...	...
26	Stonehaven .... d.	...	...	...	...	...	...	...	0545	0602	...	...	...	...	0652	0720	...	...	...	...	0756	0810	0838	...	...
65	Montrose .... d.	...	...	...	...	...	...	...	0610	0624	...	...	...	...	0713	0744	...	...	...	...	0817	0833	0859	...	...
87	Arbroath .... d.	...	...	...	...	...	...	...	0625	0638	...	...	...	...	0727	0758	...	...	...	...	0831	0849	0915	...	...
115	**Dundee** .... d.	...	...	...	0553	0605	0632	...	0650	0658	0709	0736	0724	...	0752	0822	0829	...	...	0845	0854	0907	0932	0924	0941
149	**Perth** .... **221** d.	0513	0518	0537	0619	|	|	0655	0715	|	|	|	|	0802	0813	|	|	0850	0845	0906	0915	|	|	|	|
202	Stirling .... **221** a.	|	0553	|	0654	|	|	|	0752	|	|	|	|	|	0843	|	|	|	|	0938	0943	|	|	|	|
249	**Glasgow** Queen St .. **221** a.	|	0634	|	0734	|	|	|	0834	|	|	|	|	|	0916	|	|	|	|	1014	1014	|	|	|	|
	Leuchars .... △ d.	|	...	|	...	0618	0646	|	...	0712	0723	0749	0737	|	...	|	0842	|	|	...	...	0921	0947	0937	0954
	Markinch .... **221** a.	0543	...	0606	...	0640	0710	0738	...	|	0747	0809	0759	0831	...	|	0904	|	0915	...	...	|	1008	0959	1016
	Kirkcaldy .... **221** a.	0553	...	0616	...	0649	0720	0747	...	0740	0756	0818	0807	0840	...	|	0913	0924	0924	...	...	0943	1016	1008	1025
	Edinburgh Waverley ... **221** a.	0646	...	0706	...	0740	0804	0824	...	0821	0846	0901	0901	0922	...	0932	0959	1004	1017	...	...	1025	1058	1103	1111

	⚒ 2	⚒	⚒	⚒	⚒ 2	⑦	⚒	⑦ g	⚒ g	⑦ 2	⚒	⚒	⚒	⚒	⑦ x	⚒ 2	⚒	⑦	⚒	⑦ g	⚒	⑦ 2	⚒	⚒ 2	⚒
Aberdeen .... d.	...	0842	0907	...	...	0924	0935	0947	0952	...	...	...	1038	1103	1108	...	...	1129	1142	1147	1206	...	...	...	1240
Stonehaven .... d.	...	|	|	...	...	0941	0953	1005	1010	...	...	...	|	1120	1125	...	...	1145	|	1205	1224	...	...	...	1256
Montrose .... d.	...	0918	0946	...	...	1005	1015	1028	1033	...	...	...	1114	1144	1146	...	...	1208	1217	1228	|	...	...	...	1320
Arbroath .... d.	...	0932	1000	...	...	1020	1029	1044	1049	...	...	...	1128	1158	1202	...	...	1222	1231	1244	1259	...	...	...	1334
Dundee .... d.	...	0952	1017	1034	...	1046	1052	1103	1108	1120	1134	...	1149	1215	1221	1234	...	1243	1252	1302	1315	1320	1334	...	1354
Perth .... **221** d.	1002	1014	|	|	1102	1108	1114	|	|	|	|	1202	1211	|	|	|	1302	1305	1314	|	|	|	|	1402	1415
Stirling .... **221** a.	|	1043	|	|	|	1142	1143	|	|	|	|	|	1241	|	|	|	|	1337	1343	|	|	|	|	|	1443
Glasgow Queen St ... **221** a.	|	1115	|	|	|	1214	1216	|	|	|	|	|	1315	|	|	|	|	1411	1416	|	|	|	|	|	1516
Leuchars .... △ d.	|	...	1028	1047	|	...	...	1117	1123	1133	1147	|	...	1228	1234	1247	|	...	...	1317	1328	1333	1347	|	...
Markinch .... **221** a.	1031	...	|	1108	1130	...	...	|	|	1155	1208	1230	...	|	1255	1308	1330	...	...	|	|	1355	1408	1431	...
Kirkcaldy .... **221** a.	1040	...	|	1118	1140	...	...	1139	1145	1204	1218	1240	...	|	1303	1318	1340	...	...	1339	|	1404	1417	1440	...
Edinburgh Waverley .... **221** a.	1125	...	1132	1200	1222	...	...	1220	1226	1242	1257	1323	...	1332	1342	1357	1424	...	...	1423	1429	1445	1454	1522	...

	⑦	⚒	⚒	⚒	⑦	⚒	⑦ g	⚒	⑦ 2	⚒	⚒ 2	⚒	⚒ g	⑦	⚒ 2	⚒ 2	⑦	⚒	⚒	⑦ 2	⚒ 2	⚒	⚒	⚒	⑦
Aberdeen .... d.	1247	1309	...	...	1331	1338	1347	1404	...	...	...	1439	1452	1511	...	...	1528	1533	1602	...	...	...	1637	1709	1710
Stonehaven .... d.	1306	1325	...	...	1348	1356	1405	1420	...	...	...	|	1510	1530	...	...	1544	1549	1619	...	...	...	1655	|	1726
Montrose .... d.	1331	1347	...	...	1409	1418	1428	|	...	...	...	1515	1533	1551	...	...	1609	1610	|	...	...	...	1717	1749	1748
Arbroath .... d.	1345	1401	...	...	1424	1432	1444	1457	...	...	...	1529	1549	1605	...	...	1623	1624	1655	...	...	...	1731	1803	1801
Dundee .... d.	1407	1417	1434	...	1445	1454	1502	1516	1515	1534	...	1551	1607	1624	1649	...	1643	1646	1716	1720	1726	...	1750	1821	1818
Perth .... **221** d.	|	|	|	1502	1508	1516	|	|	|	|	1600	1613	|	|	|	1702	1705	1711	|	|	|	1806	1814	|	|
Stirling .... **221** a.	|	|	|	|	1542	1543	|	|	|	|	|	1641s	|	|	|	|	1737	1743	|	|	|	|	1843	|	|
Glasgow Queen St ... **221** a.	|	|	|	|	1614	1615	|	|	|	|	|	1718	|	|	|	|	1812	1815	|	|	|	|	1916	|	|
Leuchars .... △ d.	1420	1428	1447	|	...	...	1516	1528	1528	1547	|	...	1622	1637	1702	|	...	...	1729	1733	1739	|	...	1834	1831
Markinch .... **221** a.	|	|	1508	1531	...	...	|	|	1550	1610	1629	...	|	|	1723	1731	...	...	|	1755	1803	1835	...	|	|
Kirkcaldy .... **221** a.	1445	|	1517	1540	...	...	1538	|	1559	1619	1638	...	1644	1702	1732	1748	...	...	|	1804	1812	1844	...	|	1856
Edinburgh Waverley .... **221** a.	1523	1534	1558	1622	...	...	1622	1629	1638	1659	1720	...	1726	1740	1823	1826	...	...	1832	1844	1849	1921	...	1934	1935

	⚒ 2	⚒ 2	⚒	⑦	⚒ g	⑦ 2	⚒ 2	⚒	⚒	⑦	⚒ 2	⚒	⑦	⚒	⑦	⚒	⚒	⚒	⑥ x	⑦	Ⓐ x	Ⓑ Z	⑦–④	⑥	⑤
Aberdeen .... d.	...	...	1736	1747	1818	...	...	1830	1909	1907	...	...	1936	1947	2007	2009	2042	2105	2117	2128	2131	2143	2227	2227	2323
Stonehaven .... d.	...	...	1752	1804	1836	...	...	1849	1926	1924	...	...	1952	2005	2026	2025	2058	2121	2135	2145	2149	2201	2246	2246	2342
Montrose .... d.	...	...	1817	1828	1859	...	...	1912	1950	1945	...	...	2014	2027	2050	2046	2120	2145	2156	2206	2210	2226	2310	2310	0006
Arbroath .... d.	1819	...	1831	1843	1915	...	...	1926	2004	1959	...	...	2028	2041	2104	2100	2134	2159	2212	2222	2226	2244	2324	2324	0020
Dundee .... d.	1843	...	1854	1903	1932	1916	...	1949	2020	2022	2043	...	2050	2100	2121	2119	2154	2216	2230	2239	2243	2306	2349	2348	0045
Perth .... **221** d.	|	1911	1916	1926	|	|	2002	2011	|	|	|	2102	2111	2121	|	|	2216	|	|	|	|	|	0013	...	0109
Stirling .... **221** a.	|	|	1943	1958	|	|	|	2041	|	|	|	|	2143	2149	|	|	2247	|	|	|	|	|	...	...	...
Glasgow Queen St ... **221** a.	|	|	2015	2032	|	|	|	2114	|	|	|	|	2218	2221	|	|	2319	|	|	|	|	|	...	...	...
Leuchars .... △ d.	1856	|	...	...	1946	1929	|	...	2032	2035	2056	|	...	...	2134	2132	...	2229	2243	2252	2256	2325	...	...	...
Markinch .... **221** a.	1917	1944	...	...	|	1951	2030	...	|	|	2117	2131	...	...	2157	2154	...	2251	2303	2313	2317	|	...	...	...
Kirkcaldy .... **221** a.	1926	1953	...	...	2009	2000	2040	...	|	2101	2126	2142	...	...	2206	2203	...	2300	2312	2321	2325	2355	...	...	...
Edinburgh Waverley .... **221** a.	2009	2031	...	...	2050	2053	2120	...	2131	2138	2217	2219	...	...	2243	2252	...	2349	2355	2358	0005	0037	...	...	...

footnotes see previous page

225 INVERNESS - ELGIN - ABERDEEN

🍷 on most trains SR

km			⚒	⚒	⚒	⚒	⚒	⚒	⚒	⚒	Ⓐ	⚒	⚒	⚒	⚒	⚒	⚒		⑦	⑦	⑦	⑦	⑦	⑦	⑦
0	**Inverness** d.	⚒	0453	0554	...	0709	0900	1057	1246	1427	...	...	1529	1715	1813	2001	2133	⑦	0959	1233	1529	1713	1800	2103	2142
24	Nairn d.		0508	0609	...	0725	0916	1114	1301	1442	...	...	1546	1731	1828	2017	2148		1014	1248	1544	1729	1815	2118	2157
40	Forres d.		0519	0620	...	0736	0927	1125	1312	1453	...	...	1557	1742	1839	2028	2158		1025	1259	1555	1740	1826	2129	2208
59	**Elgin** d.		0533	0634	...	0750	0949	1141	1330	1509	...	...	1611	1759	1856	2044	2213		1039	1313	1609	1754	1841	2143	2223
89	Keith d.		0554	0655	...	0811	1009	1202	1349	1530	...	...	1632	1820	1918	...	2234		1100	1334	1631	1815	...	2205	...
109	Huntly d.		0609	0711	...	0838	1023	1216	1403	1545	...	...	1651	1844	1938	...	2251		1120	1352	1646	1835	...	2221	...
130	Insch d.		0625	0727	...	0857	1048	1235	1419	1603	...	...	1706	1859	1954	...	2306		1136	1408	1702	1851	...	2237	...
147	**Inverurie** d.		0639	0743	...	0910	1100	1247	1431	1617	...	...	1718	1912	2006	...	2319		1148	1420	1714	1903	...	2249	...
164	Dyce ✈ d.		0650	0759	0908	0923	1113	1302	1443	1630	1639	1705	1734	1927	2022	...	2332		1201	1435	1728	1917	...	2301	...
174	**Aberdeen** a.		0702	0810	0919	0934	1125	1313	1454	1642	1650	1716	1745	1938	2034	...	2343		1212	1446	1739	1928	...	2313	...

		⚒	⚒	⚒	⚒	⚒	⚒	⚒	⚒	⚒	⚒	⚒	⚒	⚒	⚒	⚒			⑦	⑦		⑦	⑦		⑦
Aberdeen d.	⚒	...	...	0614	0715	0819	0852	1013	1200	1338	1527	1652	1721	1820	2012	2156	...	⑦	1000	1300	...	1522	1801	...	2127
Dyce ✈ d.		...	...	0623	0727	0830	0900	1022	1209	1347	1537	1700	1732	1831	2021	2205	...		1009	1309	...	1531	1811	...	2136
Inverurie d.		...	...	0639	0742	0843	...	1034	1221	1359	1549	...	1747	1843	2033	2217	...		1021	1321	...	1543	1823	...	2148
Insch d.		...	...	0651	0754	0856	...	1047	1234	1412	1602	...	1759	1856	2045	2229	...		1034	1334	...	1556	1836	...	2201
Huntly d.		...	...	0712	0811	0912	...	1103	1250	1428	1618	...	1816	1912	2105	2249	...		1050	1351	...	1612	1858	...	2222
Keith d.		...	...	0726	0825	0926	...	1118	1305	1443	1637	...	1830	1926	2119	2304	...		1108	1406	...	1634	1913	...	2236
Elgin d.		0658	0723	0752	0846	0948	...	1140	1329	1508	1659	...	1855	1948	2140	2325	...		1129	1427	...	1655	1935	...	2257
Forres d.		0711	0743	0805	0901	1002	...	1153	1342	1522	1715	...	1909	2001	2204	2338	...		1142	1440	...	1709	1949	...	2311
Nairn d.		0727	0754	0816	0917	1013	...	1204	1353	1545	1732	...	1920	2018	2215	2349	...		1153	1451	...	1730	2000	...	2322
Inverness a.		0745	0812	0836	0935	1031	...	1222	1413	1603	1748	...	1939	2036	2233	0007	...		1211	1509	...	1749	2018	...	2340

Other trains **Inverurie - Aberdeen**: On ⚒ at 0713, 0816, 0845Ⓐ, 1038, 1133, 1333, 1524, 1638⑥, 1647Ⓐ, 1751, 1842, 1945, 2124; On ⑦ at 1102, 1255, 1458, 1620, 1730, 2122.
Other trains **Aberdeen - Inverurie**: On ⚒ at 0748, 0958, 1103, 1250, 1457, 1552, 1652Ⓐ, 1754, 1912, 2055, 2250; On ⑦ at 1035, 1225, 1426, 1550, 1648, 2035.

226 NORTH HIGHLAND BRANCHES

2nd class SR

INVERNESS - THURSO and WICK

🍷 on most Wick trains

km		⚒	⚒	⚒	⚒		
0	**Inverness** ‡ d.	0704	1037	1400	1713	1754	2108
16	Beauly ‡ d.	0718	1051	1414	1727	1808	2122
21	Muir of Ord ‡ d.	0727	1057	1420	1734	1814	2128
30	Dingwall ‡ d.	0743	1109	1433	1748	1827	2141
51	Invergordon ‡ d.	0801	1125	1450	1804	1844	2158
71	Tain ‡ d.	0818	1145	1507	1821	1902	2215
93	Ardgay ‡ d.	0833	1200	1523	1838	1917	...
108	Lairg d.	0852	1217	1541	...	1937	...
136	Golspie d.	0917	1243	1606	...	2003	...
146	Brora d.	0930	1254	1617	...	2013	...
163	Helmsdale d.	0946	1309	1632	...	2029	...
237	Georgemas Jcn a.	1050	1411	1735	...	2130	...
248	**Thurso** a.	1102	1423	1747	...	2142	...
248	**Thurso** d.	1102	1423	1747	...	2142	...
237	Georgemas Jcn d.	1114	1435	1759	...	2154	...
260	**Wick** a.	1132	1452	1816	...	2211	...

	⚒	⚒	⚒	⑦	⚒	⚒
Wick d.	...	0620	0812	1151	1235	1600
Georgemas Jcn d.	...	0637	0829	1208	1252	1617
Thurso a.	...	0646	0838	1217	1301	1626
Thurso d.	...	0649	0839	1218	1302	1627
Georgemas Jcn d.	...	0701	0851	1230	1314	1639
Helmsdale d.	...	0801	0948	1331	1415	1740
Brora d.	...	0816	1003	1346	1430	1755
Golspie d.	...	0826	1012	1356	1440	1804
Lairg d.	0633	0853	1038	1422	1506	1830
Ardgay ‡ d.	0649	0911	1053	1437	1524	1846
Tain ‡ d.	0704	0926	1109	1453	1539	1901
Invergordon ‡ d.	0722	0944	1126	1510	1556	1919
Dingwall ‡ d.	0742	1003	1147	1529	1615	1939
Muir of Ord ‡ d.	0755	1014	1158	1542	1629	1951
Beauly ‡ d.	0801	1020	|	1548	1633	1956
Inverness ‡ a.	0815	1035	1215	1604	1648	2010

‡ – Additional trains operate Inverness - Invergordon (- Tain - Ardgay) and v.v.:
From Inverness: 1000†T, 1302†T, 1442⚒N, 1523†N, 2330⑤⑥T.
From Invergordon: 0655⚒A, 1129†T, 1429†T, 1539⚒, 1620†N, 1958⚒A, 2237T.

A – From/to Ardgay.
N – From/to Invergordon.
T – From/to Tain.
X – From Sept.28 ⚒ only.
Y – Until Sept 28 only.

INVERNESS - KYLE OF LOCHALSH

km		⚒	⚒	⑦	⚒	⚒	X
0	**Inverness** d.	0858	1058	1100	1217	1333	175
16	Beauly d.	0912	1112	1114	1231	1347	180
21	Muir of Ord d.	0918	1118	1120	1237	1353	18
30	Dingwall d.	0932	1131	1133	1249	1405	183
49	Garve d.	0954	1152	1154	...	1426	185
75	Achnasheen d.	1019	1219	1221	...	1451	19
104	Strathcarron d.	1047	1246	1248	...	1519	194
116	Stromeferry d.	1104	1304	1306	...	1536	200
124	Plockton d.	1116	1316	1318	...	1548	20
133	**Kyle of Lochalsh** a.	1128	1328	1330	...	1600	202

	⚒	⚒	⑦ Y	⚒	⚒	⑦	⚒
Kyle of Lochalsh d.	0620	...	1018	1205	1437	1520	17
Plockton d.	0632	...	1030	1216	1449	1532	17
Stromeferry d.	0643	...	1041	1228	1500	1543	17
Strathcarron d.	0701	...	1058	1245	1518	1601	17
Achnasheen d.	0728	...	1126	1315	1547	1628	18
Garve d.	0753	...	1151	1341	1613	1654	18
Dingwall d.	0816	1254	1216	1405	1634	1716	19
Muir of Ord d.	0830	1307	1227	1421	1648	1729	19
Beauly d.	0836	1313	1233	1426	1653	1735	19
Inverness a.	0850	1327	1249	1440	1709	1749	19

227 🚌 INVERNESS - ULLAPOOL - STORNOWAY

Until October

	C	A	C	B	⑥⑦	C			
Inverness 🚌 d.	0710	0810	1410	1500	1540	2055	...	...	...
Ullapool 🚌 a.	0830	0930	1530	1620	1700	2215	...	...	...
Ullapool ⛴ d.	0945	1045	1715	1815	1815	0000	...	...	...
Stornoway ⛴ a.	1230	1330	2000	2100	2100	0245	...	...	...

	B	A	B	A	⑦	B			
Stornoway ⛴ d.	0600	0700	1330	1430	1430	2045	...	...	...
Ullapool ⛴ a.	0845	0945	1615	1715	1715	2330	...	...	...
Ullapool 🚌 d.	0850	0950	1620	1720	1720	2335	...	...	...
Inverness 🚌 a.	1010	1110	1740	1840	1840	0055	...	...	...

A – ①–⑥ May 19 - June 22; ①②④⑥ June 23 - Sep. 7; ①–⑥ from Sep. 8.
B – ①–⑤ May 19 - June 22; ①②④ June 23 - Sep. 7; ①–⑤ from Sep. 8.
C – ③⑤ June 23 - Sep. 7.

☛ Latest passenger check-in for ⛴ is 30 minutes before departure.
Operators: 🚌 Scottish Citylink (service **961**). www.citylink.co.uk. ✆ (0) 871 266 3333.
⛴ Caledonian MacBrayne. www.calmac.co.uk. ✆ (0)800 066 5000.

228 🚌 INVERNESS - FORT WILLIAM - OBAN

Until October

Service number	19	19	919	919	919	919	919	19	19
	①–⑤	⑥	①–⑥					①–⑥	①–⑥
Inverness bus station d.	0633	0640	0845	1030	1245	1445	1645	1830	2015
Fort Augustus d.	0734	0741	0948	1105	1348	1548	1748	1931	2116
Fort William bus station a.	0844	0844	1045	1226	1445	1645	1845	2020	2205
Service number			918		918		918		
			①–⑥		①–⑥		①–⑥		
Fort William bus station d.	...	...	1100	...	1500	...	1900	...	...
Ballachulish tourist office d.	...	...	1127	...	1527	...	1927	...	...
Oban Station Road a.	...	...	1227	...	1627	...	2027	...	...

Service number	19	19	919	918	919	919	19	918	19
	①–⑤	⑥		①–⑥		①–⑥	①–⑥	①–⑥	①–
Oban Station Road d.	...	...	...	0840	...	1240	...	1640	...
Ballachulish tourist office d.	...	...	...	0939	...	1339	...	1739	...
Fort William bus station a.	...	...	...	1008	...	1408	...	1808	...
Service number				919		919		919	
Fort William bus station d.	0720	0730	0845	1030	1215	1415	1740	1815	204
Fort Augustus d.	0809	0819	0938	1123	1308	1508	1843	1903	212
Inverness bus station a.	0920	0920	1041	1226	1411	1611	1944	2001	22

Operator: Scottish Citylink. www.citylink.co.uk. ✆ (0) 871 266 3333.

229 ISLE OF MAN RAILWAYS

2013 service ✆ +44 (0)1624 66336

km	*Manx Electric Railway*	A	A	A	A					
0	**Douglas** Derby Castle ‡ d.	0940	1110	1240	1440	...	...	...	...	...
4	Groudle d.	0952	1122	1252	1452	...	...	...	...	...
11	Laxey d.	1010	1140	1310	1510	...	...	...	...	...
29	**Ramsey** a.	1055	1225	1355	1555	...	...	...	...	...

	A	A	A	A	A	A	A	A	A
Ramsey d.	1010	1110	1140	1240	1340	1440	1510	1610	16
Laxey d.	1055	1155	1225	1325	1425	1525	1555	1655	17
Groudle d.	1113	1213	1243	1343	1443	1543	1613	1713	17
Douglas Derby Castle ‡ a.	1125	1225	1255	1355	1455	1555	1625	1725	17

km	*Snaefell Mountain Railway*	B	B	B	B	B	B	B		
0	**Laxey** d.	1015	1115	1215	1315	1400	1455	1545	...	...
8	**Summit** a.	1045	1145	1245	1345	1430	1525	1615	...	...

	B	B	B	B	B	B	B		
Summit d.	1110	1215	1315	1415	1500	1555	1645	...	...
Laxey a.	1140	1245	1345	1445	1530	1625	1715	...	...

km	*Isle of Man Steam Railway*	C	C	C	C					
0	**Douglas** Railway Station ‡ d.	0950	1150	1350	1550	...	...	...	...	...
9	Santon d.	1011	1211	1411	1611	...	...	...	...	...
16	Castletown d.	1027	1227	1427	1627	...	...	...	...	...
25	**Port Erin** a.	1050	1250	1450	1650	...	...	...	...	...

	C	C	C	C				
Port Erin d.	0950	1150	1350	1550	...	...	...	...
Castletown d.	1012	1212	1412	1612	...	...	...	...
Santon d.	1032	1232	1432	1632	...	...	...	...
Douglas Railway Station ‡ a.	1050	1250	1450	1650	...	...	...	...

A – Apr. 4 - Nov. 2 (not Apr. 9, 10, Oct. 6, 10, 13, 17, 20, 24). Minimum service shown. Additional services operate on most dates.
B – Apr. 11 - Nov. 2 (not Oct. 6, 10, 13, 17, 20, 24). Minimum service shown. Additional services operate on most dates in June - September.
C – ⑤⑥⑦ Mar. 7 - 30 (also Mar. 17, 24, 31); Apr. 1 - Nov. 5 (not Apr. 2, 3, 9, 10, 30, May 1, 7, 8, 14, 15, Sep. 9, 10, 16, 17, 23, 24, 30, Oct. 1, 7 - 9, 14 - 16, 21 - 23). Enhanced services w different timetables operate on ④–⑦ in July and August and on certain other dates.
‡ – 🚌 services **23**, **24**, **25**, **26** connect Derby Castle and the Steam Railway Station.

IRELAND

SEE MAP PAGE 98

Operators: Iarnród Éireann (**IÉ**), www.irishrail.ie Northern Ireland Railways (**NIR**), www.translink.co.uk Bus Éireann, www.buseireann.ie Ulsterbus, www.translink.co.uk and Dublin Area Rapid Transit (**DART**), www.irishrail.ie Most cross-border services are jointly operated.

Timings: Rail: **NIR** services are valid until further notice. **IÉ** services are valid until further notice.
DART services are valid until further notice.
Bus: **Ulsterbus** services are valid until further notice. **Bus Éireann** services are valid until further notice.

Rail services: Except for *Enterprise* cross-border expresses (for details, see Table **230** below), **all trains** convey *Standard* (2nd) class seating. Most express trains in the Republic of Ireland, as noted in the tables, also have first class accommodation.
On public holiday dates in the **Republic of Ireland**, DART trains run as on Sundays; outer-suburban services to or from Drogheda and Dundalk do not run. Other services may be amended, though most main-line trains run normally. All services are subject to alteration during the Christmas, New Year and Easter holiday periods.

Bus services: **Bus Éireann** and **Ulsterbus**: services are shown in detail where there is no comparable rail service; only basic information is given for other routes. Buses do not always call at the rail station, but usually stop nearby. Where possible the stop details are given in the station bank or as a footnote. On longer routes, a change of bus may be required – please check with the driver. At holiday times bus travellers should consult detailed leaflets or seek further information from the operator. **Bus Éireann**: ✆ +353 1 836 6111 (Dublin) or + 353 21 450 8188 (Cork); **Ulsterbus**: ✆ + 028 9033 3000 (Translink, Belfast). **Dublin Busáras** (bus station) is a 5 minute walk from Dublin Connolly station.

The Dublin Tram service (Luas) connects Dublin Connolly and Heuston stations at frequent intervals. Journey time is 14 minutes, depending on traffic conditions.
See Dublin City Plan on page 29.

NIR, IÉ — BELFAST - DUNDALK - DUBLIN — 230

Enterprise express trains (*E*) convey Standard (2nd) class and Premium (1st) class seating, 🍸 (Café Bar and trolley service) and ✕ (at-seat meal service in Premium)

km		Ⓐ	Ⓐ	⑥	Ⓐ	⚒	⚒ *E*	⑥	⚒	⚒ *E*	⚒	⚒	⚒	⚒ *E*	⚒	⚒	⚒ *E*	⚒	⚒ *E*	⚒	⑤	⑥	Ⓐ	⚒ *E*	⚒	⑥	Ⓐ
0	**Belfast** Central § d.	...	...	...	...	...	0650	...	0750x	0800	...	...	1010t	1035	...	1210t	1235	1340t	1405	...	...	1540t	1601t	1605	...	1659	1709
13	Lisburn § d.	...	...	...	...	...	|	...	0801	|	...	...	1032	1047	...	1232	1247	1402	1418	...	...	1602	1612	1618	...	1732	1732
42	Portadown § d.	...	...	...	*0615*	...	0721	...	0826	0831	...	...	1058	1108	...	1258	1308	1428	1441	...	...	1628	1638	1641	...	1800	1805
71	Newry d.	...	...	...	0645	...	0742	...	▬	0852	...	...	...	1130	...	...	1330	▬	1502	...	...	▬	▬	1702	...	1824	1829
95	**Dundalk** d.	0545	0630	0705	0710	...	0800	0815	Ⓐ	0910	0955	1045	...	1148	1240	...	1348	⚒	1520	...	1605	⚒	⚒	1720	...	...	...
131	Drogheda d.	0609	0654	0729	0736	0800	0822	0839	0835	|	1019	1109	...	1208	1305	...	1410	1417	1541	1605	1630	1700	1730	1741	1800	...	...
148	Balbriggan d.	0623	0711	0746	0754	0815	|	0854	0851	|	1034	1123	...	|	1320	...	|	1433	|	1621	|	1716	|	|	1815	...	...
154	Skerries d.	0629	0718	0752	0800	0821	|	0900	0857	|	1040	1129	...	|	1326	...	|	1439	|	1627	|	1722	|	|	1821	...	...
168	Malahide d.	|	0735	0809	|	0837	|	0915	0912	|	1057	1144	...	|	1341	...	|	1454	|	1642	|	1737	|	|	1838	...	...
183	**Dublin** Connolly a.	0659	0758	0830	0835	0858	0904	0931	0930	1000	1115	1200	...	1244	1400	...	1444	1515	1617	1704	1714	1758	1813	1815	1857	...	...

	Ⓐ	⚒ *E*	⚒	⚒ *E*	⚒	⑦	⑦ *E*	⑦ *E*	⑦ *E*	⑦ *E*	⑦ *E*
elfast Central § d.	1801t	1805	1940t	2005	...	...	1000	1300	1500	1600	1900
sburn § d.	1812	1818	2002	2018	...	...	1013	*1302*	*1502*	*1602*	*1902*
ortadown § d.	1838	1841	2028	2041	...	...	1040	1332	1532	1632	1932
ewry d.	▬	1902	▬	2102	...	...	1101	1354	1554	1654	1954
undalk d.	⚒	1920	⚒	2120	...	0920	1121	1415	1615	1715	2015
rogheda d.	1850	1941	2005	2142	2205	0945	1142	1436	1636	1736	2036
albriggan d.	1905	|	2021	|	2220	1000	|	|	|	|	|
kerries d.	1911	|	2027	|	2226	1006	|	|	|	|	|
alahide d.	1926	|	2042	|	2241	1021	|	|	|	|	|
ublin Connolly a.	1945	2015	2100	2218	2301	1041	1213	1513	1715	1815	2105

	Ⓐ	⑥	Ⓐ	⚒ *E*	⚒ y	⚒ *E*	⚒	⚒	⚒ *E*	⚒	⚒	⚒ *E*
Dublin Connolly d.	...	...	0715	0735	0847	0935	1006	1035	1100	1104	1236	1320
Malahide d.	...	...	0730	|	0907	|	1025	1053	|	1126	1252	|
Skerries d.	...	...	0744	|	0922	|	1040	1108	|	1140	1307	|
Balbriggan d.	...	...	0750	|	0927	|	1045	1113	|	1146	1312	|
Drogheda d.	...	...	0804	0808	0945	1006	1103	1130	1136	1203	1329	1350
Dundalk d.	...	...	...	0830	1010	1030	▬	...	1158	1227	▬	1415
Newry d.	0655	0720	...	0848	...	1048	⚒	...	1216	...	⚒	1435
Portadown § d.	0720	0745	...	0909	...	1109	1115	...	1237	...	1245	1456
Lisburn § a.	0745	0808	...	*0938*	...	1133	1138	...	|	...	1308	1520
Belfast Central § a.	0806	0840	...	0945	...	1147	1159t	...	1315	...	1329t	1535

	⚒	⚒ *E*	⚒	⚒	⚒ *E*	⚒	⚒	Ⓐ	Ⓐ	⑥	⚒	⚒	⚒ *E*	⚒	⚒	⚒ *E*	⚒	⚒	Ⓐ	⚒	⑦ *E*	⑦ *E*	⑦ *E*	⑦ *E*	⑦ *E*	⑦	
ublin Connolly d.	1336	1520	1550	1621	1650	1651	...	...	1721	1721	1802	1840	1900	1920	2020	2050	...	2137	2237	2337	1000	1300	1600	1800	1900	2122	...
alahide d.	1354	|	1609	1639	|	1712	...	...	|	1742	1821	|	|	1939	2038	|	...	2155	2255	2356	|	|	|	|	|	2140	...
erries d.	1408	|	1623	1654	|	1726	...	...	1751	1757	1836	1906	|	1953	2053	|	...	2209	2309	0010	|	|	|	|	|	2155	...
lbriggan d.	1414	|	1629	1659	|	1732	...	...	1756	1802	1847	1912	|	1959	2058	|	...	2215	2315	0016	|	|	|	|	|	2200	...
ogheda d.	1431	1550g	1648	1716	|	1749	...	...	1813	1819	1904	1927	1932	2016	2115	2120	...	2231	2332	0032	1030	1330	1630	1830	1930	2220	...
ndalk d.	...	1612g	▬	▬	1743	▬	...	...	1837	1845	1928f	...	1955	▬	...	2142	...	2256e	2356	*0059*	1052	1352	1652	1852	1952	2243	...
wry d.	...	1630g	Ⓐ	⑥	1802	⚒	1850	1950	...	...	...	...	2013	⚒	...	2200	...	...	...	...	1110	1410	1710	1910	2010	...	...
rtadown § d.	...	1651g	1705	1715	1824	1845	1915	2015	...	...	...	...	2034	2045	...	2221	2225	...	...	...	1132	1432	1732	1932	2032	...	...
sburn § a.	...	|	1730	1738	1850	1908	1938	2038	...	...	...	...	2058	2108	...	|	2248	...	...	...	1202	*1508*	*1808*	*2008*	*2108*	...	...
lfast Central § a.	...	1729j	1739t	1759t	1905	1929t	2010	2110	...	...	...	...	2115	2129t	...	2255	2309t	...	...	...	1216	1507	1807	2007	2107	...	...

- – 1000 on ⑥.
- – ⑤ only.
- – Not ⑥.

g – 3-6 minutes later on ⑥.
j – 1735 on ⑥.
t – Belfast **Great Victoria Street**.

x – Belfast **Great Victoria Street**. On ⑥ depart 0740.

y – From Rosslare Europort on Ⓐ; from Gorey on ⑥; see table **237**.

§ – Other local trains run Belfast - Lisburn - Portadown and v.v.

IR — BELFAST - LONDONDERRY and PORTRUSH — 231

m			Ⓐ	⚒	⚒		⚒	⚒	⚒	⚒			Ⓐ	Ⓐ			⑦	⑦	⑦	⑦	⑦	⑦	⑦		
	Belfast GVSt. ★ d.	...	0605	0710	0810	and at the	1910	2010	2110	2240	...		...	...	...	...	0920	1120	1320	1520	1720	1920	2120	...	...
0	**Belfast** Central d.	...	0615	0720	0820	same	1920	2020	2120	2250	...		1646	1746	...	...	0930	1130	1330	1530	1730	1930	2130	...	...
33	Antrim d.	...	0643	0747	0847	minutes	1947	2047	2147	2317	...	addi-	1714	1814	...	...	0957	1157	1357	1557	1757	1957	2157	...	...
52	Ballymena d.	...	0657	0803	0903	past each	2003	2103	2203	2330	...	tional	1728	1828	...	...	1011	1211	1411	1611	1811	2011	2211	...	...
7	**Coleraine** d.	...	0743	0843	0943	hour	2043	2143	2243	0005	...	trains	1810	1910	...	...	1052	1252	1452	1652	1852	2052	2247	...	...
7	Portrush a.	...	|	|	0955	until	|	2155	|	...	...	→	...	...	...	...	|	|	|	|	|	|	...	...	...
51	**Londonderry** a.	...	0825	0925	...		2125	...	2325	...	...		...	...	...	...	1134	1334	1534	1734	1934	2134	...	...	...

	Ⓐ	Ⓐ	⑥	Ⓐ	⑥	Ⓐ	Ⓐ	⑥	⚒	⚒		⚒	⚒	⚒	Ⓐ			⑦	⑦	⑦	⑦	⑦	⑦	⑦	
ndonderry d.	...	...	...	0605	0635	...	0713	0733	...	0933	and at the	...	1933	...	2133	...	...	...	0942	1142	1342	1542	1742	1942	...
ortrush d.	...	0605	0610	|	|	0705	|	|	0905	|	same	1905	|	2105	|	...	...	...	|	|	|	|	|	|	...
eraine d.	0550	0620	0623	0652	0721	0719	0819	0819	0919	1019	minutes	1919	2019	2119	2219	...	...	0828	1028	1228	1428	1628	1828	2028	...
lymena d.	0626	0700	0700	0730	0800	0800	0900	0900	1000	1100	past each	2000	2100	2200	2300	...	...	0904	1104	1304	1504	1704	1904	2104	...
rim d.	0644	0714	0714	0747	0814	0814	0914	0914	1014	1114	hour	2014	2114	2214	2316	...	...	0918	1118	1318	1518	1718	1918	2118	...
fast Central a.	0712	0739	0739	0816	0839	0839	0939	0939	1039	1139	until	2039	2139	2239	2341	...	...	0943	1143	1343	1543	1743	1943	2143	...
fast GVSt. ★ a.	0722	0750	0750	0825	0850	0851	0950	0950	1050	1150		2050	2150	2250	...	...	...	0953	1153	1353	1553	1753	1953	2153	...

m		Ⓐ	⑥	⚒	⚒	⚒	⚒	and at the same	⚒	⚒			⑦	⑦	⑦	⑦	⑦	⑦	⑦					
0	Coleraine d.	0550	0555	0645	0745	0845	0943	minutes past	2143	2245	...	...	0950	1055	1255	1455	1655	1855	2055	...	...	...	...	...
0	Portrush a.	0600	0605	0657	0757	0857	0955	each hour	2155	2257	...	...	1002	1107	1307	1507	1707	1907	2107	...	...	...	...	...

	Ⓐ	⑥	⑥	Ⓐ	⚒	⚒	and at the same	⚒	⚒	Ⓐ	⑥	Ⓐ	⑥			⑦	⑦	⑦	⑦	⑦	⑦	⑦		
trush d.	0605	0610	0703	0705	0803	0905	minutes past	2003	2105	2203	2223	2303	2305	...	...	1010	1210	1410	1610	1810	2010	2110	...	...
eraine a.	0616	0621	0715	0716	0815	0916	each hour	2015	2116	2214	2235	2315	2317	...	...	1022	1222	1422	1622	1822	2022	2122	...	...

- Belfast GVSt. (Belfast Great Victoria St.) is the nearest station to Belfast City Centre and the Europa Buscentre is adjacent.

terbus 212 express 🚌 service, Belfast - Londonderry. Journey time: 1 hour 40 minutes.
0630, 0745, 0830, 0900, 0930 and every 30 mins. until 1430, 1500, 1520, 1540, 1600, 1620, 1640, 1700, 1720, 1740, 1800, 1830, 1900, 1930, 2030, 2130, 2300.
0645, 0930, 1030, 1130, 1230, 1330, 1400 and every 30 mins. to 1800, 1830 then 1930, 2030, 2130, 2300.
0830, 1000, 1130, 1330, 1430, 1600, 1730, 1930, 2030, 2130, 2215.

Ulsterbus 212 express 🚌 service, Londonderry - Belfast. Journey time: 1 hour 45 minutes.
Ⓐ: 0520, 0540, 0600, 0620, 0640, 0700, 0720, 0740, 0800, 0830 and every 30 minutes until 1630, 1700 then 1800, 1930, 2100.
⑥: 0700, 0800, 0830, 0900, 0930, 1000, 1030, 1100, 1130, 1200, 1230, 1300, 1400, 1500, 1600, 1700, 1800, 1930, 2100.
⑦: 0800, 0900, 1030, 1200, 1330, 1500, 1600, 1700, 1800, 1900.

232 BELFAST - ENNISKILLEN and ARMAGH
Ulsterbus 251, 261

From Belfast ★ to Enniskillen (Bus Stn) (journey time 2 hours 15 mins)

Ⓐ: 0805, 0905 and hourly until 1905, 2005.
⑥: 1005, 1205, 1405, 1505, 1605, 1805, 2005.
⑦: 1605, 2005.

From Enniskillen (Bus Stn) to Belfast ★

Ⓐ: 0725, 0825, and hourly until 1625, 1725, 1825 ◧.
⑥: 0725, 0925, 1125, 1225, 1325, 1525, 1725.
⑦: 1225, 1525, 1725.

From Belfast ★ to Armagh (Bus Stn) (journey time 1 hour 25 mins)

Ⓐ: 0800, 0945, 1045, 1145, 1245, 1345, 1445, 1645, 1715, 1745, 1845, 1945, 2115.
⑥: 1045, 1245, 1445, 1745, 1845, 2005.
⑦: 1335, 1735, 2015, 2200.

From Armagh (Bus Stn) to Belfast ★

Ⓐ: 0630, 0715, 0805, 0905, 1005, 1105, 1205, 1305, 1505, 1605, 1705, 1805.
⑥: 0730, 0905, 1105, 1305, 1605, 1705.
⑦: 1210, 1410, 1610, 1830, 2015.

Buses call at Portadown (Market Street) 40 - 75 minutes from Belfast and Portadown (Northern Bank 20–30 minutes from Armagh (Bus Stn).

◧ – Change at Dungannon; arrive Europa Buscentre 2140.
★ – Europa Buscentre / Great Victoria St. Rail Station.

233 BELFAST - LARNE and BANGOR
NIR

From Belfast Central – Ⓐ: 0550, 0655, 0745 **H**, 0855 **H**, and hourly until 1355 **H**, 1455, 1523 **H**, 1555 **H**, 1644, 1714 **H**, 1744, 1825, 1925 **H**, 2025 **H**, 2125 **H**, 2225 **H**, 2325 **H**.
⑥: 0725 **H**, 0825 **H**, and hourly until 2225 **H**, 2325 **H**. ⑦: 0955 **H**, 1155 **H**, 1355 **H**, 1555 **H**, 1755 **H**, 1955 **H**, 2155 **H**.

From Larne Town – Ⓐ: 0558 **S**, 0628 **S**, 0653, 0735 **S**, 0800, 0858 **S**, 0958 **S** and hourly until 1458 **S**, 1553, 1625 **S**, 1706 **S**, 1736, 1828, 1928 **S**, 2028 **S**, 2128 **S**, 2228 **S**.
⑥: 0600 **S**, 0628 **S**, 0728 **S**, 0828 **S** and hourly until 2028 **S**, 2128 **S**, 2228 **S**. ⑦: 0858 **S**, 1058 **S**, 1258 **S**, 1458 **S**, 1658 **S**, 1858 **S**, 2058 **S**.

Trains call at: Carrickfergus 27 - 29 minutes from Belfast and 28 - 31 minutes from Larne and Whitehead 38 - 40 minutes from Belfast, 18 - 21 minutes from Larne.

Trains marked **H** arrive Larne **Harbour** 4 minutes after Larne **Town**. Trains marked **S** depart Larne **Harbour** 3 minutes before Larne **Town**. Journey time Belfast Central - Larne Harbour 57 - 65 min

A frequent train service operates between Belfast Central and Bangor. Journey time 30–31 minutes. 20 km. Approximate timings from Belfast ①–⑥: 2 per hour at xx12 and xx42 minutes past eac hour, ⑦: xx42. Approximate timings from Bangor ①–⑥: 2 per hour at xx27 and xx57 minutes past each hour, ⑦: xx57.

234 DUBLIN - LONDONDERRY
Bus Éireann 33 / Ulsterbus 274

Dublin Busáras	d.	0600	...	1000	...	1330	...	1730	1800	...	2200
Dublin Airport ✈ △	d.	0620	...	1020	...	1350	...	1750	1820	...	2220
Monaghan	d.	0750	...	1200	...	1530	...	1930	1950	...	2340
Omagh ▽	a.	0840	...	1250	...	1620	...	2020	2040	...	0030
Strabane ▽	a.	0905	...	1320	...	1650	...	2050	2105	...	0055
Londonderry	a.	0930	...	1350	...	1720	...	2120	2130	...	0120

Londonderry	d.	0430	...	0730	...	1030	1230	...	1630	...	230
Strabane △	d.	0455	...	0755	...	1055	1255	...	1655	...	232
Omagh △	d.	0530	...	0830	...	1120	1330	...	1730	...	235
Monaghan	d.	0630	...	0930	...	1210	1430	...	1830	...	004
Dublin Airport ✈ ▽	a.	0800	...	1100	...	1340	1600	...	2000	...	021
Dublin Busáras	a.	0820	...	1120	...	1400	1620	...	2020	...	023

△ – Buses call here to pick up only. ▽ – Buses call here to set down only. ☛ The calling point in each town is the bus station unless otherwise indicated

234a DUBLIN - DONEGAL
Bus Éireann 30

Dublin Busáras	d.	0730	0930	1130	1330	1530	1730	1930	2200	2400	...
Dublin Airport ✈ △	d.	0750	0950	1150	1350	1550	1750	1950	2220	0020	...
Virginia	d.	0855	1055	1255	1455	1655	1855	2055	2325	0125	...
Cavan	d.	0925	1125	1325	1525	1725	1925	2125	2350	0150	...
Enniskillen	d.	1015	1215	1415	1615	1815	2015	2215	0040	0240	...
Ballyshannon	d.	1100	1300	1500	1700	1900	2100	2300	0125	0325	...
Donegal ⊡	a.	1120	1320	1520	1720	1920	2120	2320	0145	0345	...

Donegal ⊡	d.	0100	0500	0700	0900	1100	1300	1500	1700	1900	...
Ballyshannon	d.	0120	0520	0720	0920	1120	1320	1520	1720	1920	...
Enniskillen	d.	0205	0605	0805	1005	1205	1405	1605	1805	2005	...
Cavan	d.	0255	0655	0900	1100	1300	1500	1705	1900	2055	...
Virginia	d.	0320	0725	0925	1125	1325	1525	1730	1925	2125	...
Dublin Airport ✈ ▽	a.	0445	0830	1030	1230	1430	1630	1835	2030	2230	...
Dublin Busáras	a.	0505	0850	1050	1250	1450	1650	1855	2050	2250	...

● – Dublin **Busáras**. △ – Buses call here to pick up only. ▽ – Buses call here to set down only. ⊡ – Donegal **Abbey Hotel**.

235 LONDONDERRY - GALWAY and GALWAY - CORK
Bus Éireann 51, 64

		⚒	⚒		⚒						⑤⑦
Londonderry	d.	...	...	0715	...	0915	1115	...	1530	1830	...
Letterkenny	d.	...	...	0750	...	0950	1150	...	1605	1905	...
Donegal (Abbey Hotel)	d.	...	0640	0835	...	1035	1235	...	1650	1955	...
Ballyshannon	d.	...	0700	0855	...	1055	1255	...	1710	2015	...
Sligo	d.	0600	0800	0945	1000	1200	1400	1600	1815	2100	2105
Ireland West Airport Knock	d.	|	0855	...	1055	1250	1450	1655	|	...	|
Knock	d.	0705	0915	...	1115	1310	1510	1715	1920	...	2203
Claremorris (Dalton St.)	d.	|	|	...	1122	|	1517	1722	|	...	|
Galway (Bus Station) ✣	a.	0835	1045	...	1245	1445	1645	1845	2040	...	2335

Galway (Bus Station) ✣	d.	...	...	0705	0805		1705	1805	1905	2005
Ennis	d.	...	...	0820	0920		1820	1920	2020	2120
Shannon Airport ✈	d.	...	...	0850	0950	and	1850	1950	2050	2150
Limerick (Colbert Rail Station)	a.	...	...	0920	1020	hourly	1920	2020	2120	2220
Limerick (Colbert Rail Station)	d.	0725	0835	0935	1035	until	1935	2035	...	...
Mallow (Town Park)	d.	0830	0940	1040	1140		2040	2140	...	...
Cork	a.	0915	1025	1125	1225		2125	2225	...	...

Cork	d.	...	...	0725	0825		1725	1825	1925	205
Mallow (Town Park)	d.	...	...	0800	0900		1800	1900	2000	213
Limerick (Colbert Rail Station)	a.	...	...	0910	1010	and	1910	2010	2110	224
Limerick (Colbert Rail Station)	d.	0725	0825	0925	1025	hourly	1925	2025	...	...
Shannon Airport ✈	d.	0755	0855	0955	1055	until	1955	2055	...	...
Ennis	d.	0825	0925	1025	1125		2025	2125	...	...
Galway (Bus Station) ✣	a.	0945	1045	1145	1245		2145	2245	...	...

		⚒	⚒		⚒						⑤
Galway (Bus Station) ✣	d.	0600	...	0845	1030	...	1200	1410	1600	1810	..
Claremorris (Dalton St.)	d.	0655	...	|	1138	...	1308	|	|	1918	..
Knock	d.	0705	...	1005	1150	...	1320	1530	1720	1930	..
Ireland West Airport Knock	d.	0725	...	1025	1210	...	1340	1550	1745	|	..
Sligo	d.	0830	0855	1145	1315	1330	1500	1710	1905	2045	21
Ballyshannon	d.	...	0945	1225	...	1410	1540	1750	1945	...	21
Donegal (Abbey Hotel)	d.	...	1015	1250	...	1435	1605	1815	2005	...	22
Letterkenny	d.	...	1110	1340	...	1520	1650	1855	2050	...	22
Londonderry	a.	...	1145	1415	...	1555	1725	1930	2125	...	23

✣ – Change buses at Galway. Minimum connection time 45 minutes. ☛ The calling point in each town is the bus station unless otherwise indicated.

236 DUBLIN - SLIGO

km			⚒ 🍷		⚒ 🍷	⚒ 🍷	⚒ 🍷	⚒ 🍷	⚒ 🍷	Ⓐ	Ⓐ	⚒ 🍷	
0	**Dublin** Connolly	d.	0800	...	1105	1305	1505	1600	1705	1715	1805	1905	...
26	Maynooth	d.	0830	...	1136	1335	1535	1629	1734	1758	1835	1937	...
83	Mullingar	d.	0910	...	1216	1416	1615	1715	1815	1844	1919	2023	...
125	**Longford**	d.	0942	...	1247	1445	1646	1745	1846	1916	1950	2052	...
143	Dromod	d.	1000	...	1259	1457	1658	1759	1901	...	...	2104	...
159	Carrick on Shannon	d.	1016	...	1314	1513	1713	1815	1918	...	...	2121	...
173	Boyle	d.	1028	...	1334	1534	1727	1834	1931	...	...	2133	...
219	**Sligo**	a.	1109	...	1410	1610	1806	1909	2006	...	...	2209	...

		⑦ 🍷		⑦ 🍷		⑦ 🍷	⑦ 🍷	⑦ 🍷		⑦ 🍷		
Dublin Connolly	d.	0905	...	1305	...	1505	1600	1705	...	1905	...	..
Maynooth	d.	0932	...	1333	...	1534	1629	1733	...	1933	...	..
Mullingar	d.	1013	...	1413	...	1614	1714	1819	...	2016	...	..
Longford	d.	1043	...	1443	...	1644	1750	1849	...	2045	...	..
Dromod	d.	1056	...	1456	...	1656	1802	1904	...	2057	...	..
Carrick on Shannon	d.	1113	...	1512	...	1712	1817	1920	...	2114	...	..
Boyle	d.	1134	...	1534	...	1729	1836	1933	...	2127	...	..
Sligo	a.	1210	...	1610	...	1808	1910	2008	...	2204	...	..

		Ⓐ	Ⓐ	Ⓐ 🍷	⚒ 🍷	⚒ 🍷	⚒ 🍷	⚒ 🍷	⚒ 🍷	⚒ 🍷			
Sligo	d.	...	...	0545	0700	0900	1100	1300	1500	1800	...	...	...
Boyle	d.	...	...	0617	0733	0933	1136	1333	1533	1834	...	...	...
Carrick on Shannon	d.	...	...	0628	0745	0945	1148	1346	1546	1846	...	...	...
Dromod	d.	...	...	0643	0800	1001	1202	1401	1601	1900	...	...	...
Longford	d.	0540	0615	0657	0815	1016	1217	1416	1616	1919	...	...	...
Mullingar	d.	0614	0649	0726	0845	1047	1253	1453	1652	1959	...	...	...
Maynooth	d.	0657	0730	0810	0933	1128	1334	1534	1733	2040	...	...	...
Dublin Connolly	a.	0736	0818	0847	1000	1158	1404	1604	1803	2108	...	...	...

		⑦ 🍷		⑦ 🍷		⑦ 🍷		⑦ 🍷		⑦ 🍷		⑦ 🍷
Sligo	d.	0900	...	1100	...	1300	...	1500	...	1630	...	18
Boyle	d.	0933	...	1133	...	1333	...	1533	...	1704	...	18
Carrick on Shannon	d.	0945	...	1145	...	1345	...	1545	...	1717	...	18
Dromod	d.	1000	...	1200	...	1400	...	1600	...	1732	...	19
Longford	d.	1015	...	1215	...	1415	...	1615	...	1748	...	19
Mullingar	d.	1051	...	1246	...	1452	...	1652	...	1819	...	19
Maynooth	d.	1131	...	1327	...	1533	...	1733	...	1900	...	20
Dublin Connolly	a.	1203	...	1355	...	1606	...	1800	...	1932	...	21

236a BALLYBROPHY - ROSCREA - LIMERICK

km			Ⓐ	⚒ 🍷	⚒		⚒h ◇✗	⚒	⑦ ◇🍷	⑦		
0	**Dublin** Heuston	d.	...	0900	...	...	1800	...	1825	...	...	...
107	Ballybrophy	d.	...	0958	1005	...	1854	1900	1933	1940	...	...
123	Roscrea	d.	...	...	1025	...	...	1921	|	2001	...	...
154	Nenagh	d.	0745	...	1105	...	...	2002	|	2040	...	...
199	**Limerick Colbert**	a.	0845	...	1204	...	...	2100	2042	2139	...	...

		⚒	⚒h ◇✗		⚒	⚒h ◇✗	⑦	⑦ 🍷			
Limerick Colbert	d.	0630	0740	...	1655	...	1725	1820	...	...	...
Nenagh	d.	0739	|	...	1750	...	1822	|	...	...	...
Roscrea	d.	0817	|	...	1828	...	1901	|	...	...	...
Ballybrophy	d.	0841	0845	...	1851	1855	1924	1927	...	...	...
Dublin Heuston	a.	...	0955	...	...	2000	...	2042	...	...	...

h – ✗ on Ⓐ, 🍷 on
◇ – Also conveys 1st class.

IÉ DUBLIN - ROSSLARE 237

km		⚒		⚒ 🍷	Ⓐ	Ⓐ	⚒ § 🍷		⑦	⑦ 🍷	⑦ § 🍷	
0	**Dublin Connolly** ▲ d.	0940	...	1336	1637	1736	1838	...	1025	1345	1830	...
11	Dún Laoghaire ▲ d.	0958	...	1355	1658	1758	1857	...	1041	1402	1847	...
21	Bray ▲ d.	1017	...	1417	1717	1817	1917	...	1101	1423	1904	...
47	Wicklow d.	1040	...	1441	1742	1844	1942	...	1126	1446	1929	...
80	Arklow d.	1108	...	1510	1811	1916	2010	...	1154	1514	1957	...
97	Gorey d.	1121	...	1522	1824	1930	2023	...	1206	1527	2010	...
126	Enniscorthy d.	1142	...	1541	1844	1951	2042	...	1225	1546	2029	...
150	**Wexford** d.	1202	...	1604	1905	2012	2104	...	1248	1608	2051	...
160	Rosslare Strand d.	1219	...	1621	1919	...	2121	...	1304	1625	2108	...
166	**Rosslare** Europort a.	1226	...	1626	1925	...	2128	...	1310	1632	2115	...

	Ⓐ	Ⓐ y	⑥ y	⚒ 🍷		⚒ 🍷		⚒		⑦ 🍷	⑦ 🍷	⑦	
Rosslare Europort d.	...	0535	...	0720	...	1255	...	1755	...	0940	1420	1740	...
Rosslare Strand d.	...	0540	...	0724	...	1301	...	1801	...	0944	1426	1745	...
Wexford d.	...	0559	...	0743	...	1320	...	1820	...	1003	1445	1805	...
Enniscorthy d.	...	0623	...	0804	...	1341	...	1844	...	1024	1506	1827	...
Gorey d.	0555	0645	0645	0824	...	1401	...	1903	...	1044	1528	1847	...
Arklow d.	0608	0700	0700	0837	...	1413	...	1915	...	1057	1540	1900	...
Wicklow d.	0638	0733	0733	0904	...	1441	...	1942	...	1124	1608	1928	...
Bray ▲ d.	0704	0802	0802	0932	...	1503	...	2004	...	1147	1631	1953	...
Dún Laoghaire ▲ d.	0722	0820	0820	0950	...	1521	...	2022	...	1206	1648	2011	...
Dublin Connolly ▲ a.	0746	0846	0847	1015	...	1545	...	2044	...	1230	1710	2035	...

y – To Dundalk; see table **230**. § – Does not connect with Ferry: Rosslare - Fishguard. ▲ – Additional surburban trains (*DART*) run Howth - Dublin Connolly - Dún Laoghaire - Bray. Trains run every 10 - 15 minutes on ⚒, every 20 - 30 minutes on ⑦.

IÉ / Bus Éireann 370 LIMERICK - WATERFORD 239

km		⚒	⚒			⚒	⚒			
0	**Limerick Colbert** d.	0845	...	...	...	1745	...	...	...	...
35	**Limerick Junction** d.	0921	0945	...	...	1811	1840	...	...	...
40	Tipperary d.	...	0957	...	...	...	1852	...	...	...
62	Cahir d.	...	1020	...	...	...	1915	...	...	...
79	Clonmel d.	...	1037	...	...	...	1932	...	...	...
101	Carrick on Suir d.	...	1101	...	...	...	1956	...	...	...
124	**Waterford** a.	...	1126	...	...	...	2020	...	...	...

	⚒	⚒				⚒	⚒		
Waterford d.	0720	...	...	...	...	1625	...	...	...
Carrick on Suir d.	0745	...	...	...	...	1650	...	...	...
Clonmel d.	0808	...	...	...	...	1713	...	...	...
Cahir d.	0825	...	...	...	...	1730	...	...	...
Tipperary d.	0847	...	...	...	...	1751	...	...	...
Limerick Junction a.	0900	0940	...	...	...	1805	1834	...	...
Limerick Colbert a.	...	1014	...	...	...	...	1859	...	...

IÉ DUBLIN - GALWAY, BALLINA and WESTPORT 240

km		⚒	⚒ 🍷	⚒ 🍷	⚒ 🍷	⚒ 🍷	⚒ 🍷	⚒ ◇🍷	⚒ 🍷	⚒ 🍷	⚒h ◇✕	⚒	⚒ ◇🍷	⚒ ◇🍷	⚒ ◇🍷	⚒ 🍷
0	**Dublin Heuston 245** d.	...	0735	...	0925	1125	1245	1325	1445	1535	1630	1710	1730	1815	1830	1935
48	Kildare 245 d.	...	0801	...	|	|	|	|	|	|	1659	1739	|	|	|	|
67	Portarlington 245 d.	...	0814	...	1002	1201	1322	1402	1522	1611	|	1756	1811	|	1910	2011
93	Tullamore d.	...	0830	...	1018	1218	1338	1417	1540	1629	1726	1813	1829	1904	|	2030
129	**Athlone** d.	0730	0905	0908	1045	1242	1403	1448	1604	1658	1750	1845	1857	1925	1945	2053
152	Ballinasloe d.	0743	0919	|	1058	1257	|	1501	|	1711	1806	...	1913	|	2000	2108
187	Athenry 242 d.	0814	0946	|	1117	1318	|	1522	|	1733	1827	...	1932	|	2022	2129
208	**Galway 242** a.	0830	1005	|	1140	1340	|	1540	|	1755	1845	...	1950	|	2040	2150
160	Roscommon d.	...	...	0931	▬	...	1429	▬	1628	▬	...	...	...	1954	▬	...
186	Castlerea d.	...	...	0946	...	...	1448	...	1647	...	...	...	...	2013	...	...
204	Ballyhaunis d.	...	...	1003	...	...	1502	...	1701	...	...	...	...	2026	...	...
222	Claremorris d.	...	...	1017	⚒	...	1516	⚒	1715	⚒	...	...	...	2040	⚒	...
240	Manulla Junction § d.	...	...	1031	1033	...	1529	1532	1728	1730	...	...	...	2053	2057	...
273	**Ballina** a.	...	...	|	1101	...	|	1600	|	1758	...	...	...	|	2125	
246	Castlebar d.	...	...	1037	...	...	1536	...	1735	...	...	...	...	2100	...	...
264	**Westport** a.	...	...	1055	...	...	1555	...	1755	...	...	...	...	2120	...	...

km		⑦ 🍷	⑦	⑦ 🍷	⑦ ◇🍷	⑦ 🍷	⑦ 🍷	⑦ 🍷	⑦ ◇🍷	⑦ ◇🍷	⑦
0	**Dublin Heuston 245** d.	0800	...	1135	1335	1430	1535	1635	1830	1845	2030
48	Kildare 245 d.	0827	...	1203	1405	|	|	|	1902	1916	|
67	Portarlington 245 d.	0840	...	1216	1419	1506	|	1714	1915	1929	2109
93	Tullamore d.	0856	...	1238	1440	1530	1632	1732	1933	1953	2125
129	**Athlone** d.	0920	0940	1304	1507	1600	1658	1803	2000	2019	2151
152	Ballinasloe d.	0936	|	1319	|	1615	|	1817	|	2033	2206
187	Athenry 242 d.	0959	|	1343	|	1639	|	1843	|	2054	2226
208	**Galway 242** a.	1017	|	1400	|	1707	|	1904	|	2112	2245
160	Roscommon d.	...	1002	▬	1530	▬	1729	▬	2023	▬	...
186	Castlerea d.	...	1021	...	1550	...	1748	...	2043	...	...
204	Ballyhaunis d.	...	1034	...	1604	...	1802	...	2057	...	...
222	Claremorris d.	...	1048	⑦	1620	⑦	1822	⑦	2111	⑦	...
240	Manulla Junction § d.	...	1102	1105	1633	1637	1835	1837	2124	2128	...
273	**Ballina** a.	...	|	1133	|	1705	|	1905	|	2156	...
246	Castlebar d.	...	1109	...	1641	...	1843	...	2132	...	...
264	**Westport** a.	...	1130	...	1700	...	1900	...	2150	...	...

	Ⓐ	Ⓐ	Ⓐ 🍷	⚒ 🍷	⚒	⚒ ◇🍷	⚒	⚒ 🍷	⚒ 🍷	⚒	⚒ 🍷	⚒ 🍷	⚒	⚒ 🍷	⚒ ◇🍷	Ⓐ
Westport d.	...	...	0515	...	...	0715	...	0945	...	...	1310	...	...	1815	...	...
Castlebar d.	...	...	0527	...	...	0728	...	0957	...	...	1323	...	...	1827	...	...
Ballina d.	...	...	|	...	0705	|	0935	|	...	1300	|	...	1805	|	...	...
Manulla Junction § d.	...	...	|	...	0733	0736	1003	1005	...	1328	1330	...	1833	1835	...	...
Claremorris d.	...	...	0545	...	▬	0750	▬	1020	...	▬	1344	...	▬	1849	...	...
Ballyhaunis d.	...	...	0558	...	...	0804	...	1033	...	...	1357	...	...	1902	...	...
Castlerea d.	...	...	0611	...	⚒h	0818	⚒	1046	...	⚒	1410	...	⚒	1915	...	...
Roscommon d.	...	...	0629	...	◇✕	0838	🍷	1105	...	🍷	1432	...	◇🍷	1934	...	...
Galway 242 d.	...	0530	|	0630	0730	|	0930	|	1130	1330	|	1530	1720	|	1915	2215
Athenry 242 d.	...	0545	|	0644	0745	|	0944	|	1145	1347	|	1550	1736	|	1931	2230
Ballinasloe d.	...	0607	|	|	0805	|	1007	|	1205	1409	|	1615	1807	|	2001	2252
Athlone d.	0520	0625	0655j	0720	0823	0903	1023	1132	1222	1426	1458	1632	1823	2000	2019	2309
Tullamore d.	0543	0649	0717j	0742	0846	0929	1052	1157	1251	1450	1523	1705	1847	2029	2047	...
Portarlington 245 d.	0601	0707	0735j	|	0904	0947	1109	1222	1309	1509	1547	1731	1909	2049	2105	...
Kildare 245 d.	0615	0718	0750j	|	|	|	|	|	|	|	|	|	|	|	|	...
Dublin Heuston 245 a.	0700	0757	0824j	0840	0945	1030	1150	1305	1350	1550	1630	1810	1950	2130	2145	...

	⑦	⑦ 🍷	⑦ 🍷	⑦	⑦ ◇🍷	⑦	⑦ 🍷	⑦ 🍷	⑦	⑦ 🍷
Westport d.	...	0750	...	...	1315	...	1545	...	...	1745
Castlebar d.	...	0803	...	...	1328	...	1558	...	...	1758
Ballina d.	0740	|	...	1305	|	1535	|	...	1735	|
Manulla Junction § d.	0808	0811	...	1333	1336	1603	1606	...	1803	1806
Claremorris d.	▬	0825	...	▬	1350	▬	1620	...	▬	1820
Ballyhaunis d.	...	0839	...	...	1404	...	1634	...	...	1834
Castlerea d.	⑦	0853	...	⑦	1418	⑦	1648	...	⑦	1848
Roscommon d.	🍷	0913	...	🍷	1438	◇🍷	1708	...	🍷	1908
Galway 242 d.	0805	|	1100	1300	|	1505	|	1700	1800	|
Athenry 242 d.	0820	|	1117	1315	|	1520	|	1716	1815	|
Ballinasloe d.	0844	|	1139	1339	|	1542	|	1740	1840	|
Athlone d.	0902	0938	1157	1357	1505	1600	1740	1802	1900	1934
Tullamore d.	0931	1002	1220	1423	1531	1631	1807	1827	1931	2010
Portarlington 245 d.	0949	1020	1238	1441	1549	1653	1826	1845	1950	2028
Kildare 245 d.	1002	|	1253	|	|	1707	1839	1859	|	|
Dublin Heuston 245 a.	1034	1105	1325	1525	1630	1740	1910	1935	2030	2110

• – An additional journey runs on ⑦: Galway depart 1925, Athenry 1940, Ballinasloe 2000, arrive Athlone 2018. h – ✕ on Ⓐ, 🍷 on ⑥. j – Also runs on ⑥. ◇ – Also conveys [1st class coach]. § – Passenger transfer point only.

IÉ DUBLIN - KILKENNY - WATERFORD 241

km		⚒ 🍷	⚒ ◇🍷	⚒ 🍷	⚒ 🍷	⚒ 🍷	⚒ 🍷	⚒ ◇🍷	Ⓐ		⑦ 🍷	⑦ 🍷	⑦ ◇🍷	⑦ 🍷
0	**Dublin H** ◧ .. △ d.	0725	1015	1315	1510	1640	1735	1835	2015	...	0910	1410	1745	1840
48	Kildare △ d.	0753	1042	|	1539	1717	1806	1905	2101	...	0940	1439	1814	1908
72	Athy d.	0813	1059	1358	1556	1735	1825	1923	2116	...	0957	1458	1832	1927
90	Carlow d.	0827	1111	1412	1607	1747	1837	1938	2128	...	1011	1510	1844	1939
06	Muine Bheag d.	0843	1122	1424	1619	1758	1848	1949	...	...	1025	1521	1858	1951
30	**Kilkenny** a.	0901	1140	1441	1636	1817	1906	2008	...	...	1043	1541	1917	2009
	Kilkenny d.	0905	1145	1446	1640	1821	1910	2013	...	...	1047	1546	1921	2013
47	Thomastown d.	0916	1155	1456	1651	1831	1921	2023	...	...	1058	1556	1932	2024
79	**Waterford** a.	0940	1220	1525	1715	1900	1946	2048	...	...	1120	1620	1956	2050

	Ⓐ	⚒ ◇🍷	⚒ 🍷	⚒ 🍷	⚒ 🍷	⚒ 🍷	⚒ ◇🍷	⚒ 🍷	Ⓐ		⑦ ◇🍷	⑦ 🍷	⑦ 🍷	⑦ 🍷
Waterford d.	...	0605	0710	0750	1100	1305	1450	1825	...	...	0905	1240	1510	1805
Thomastown d.	...	0624	|	0809	1119	1324	1511	1846	...	...	0924	1259	1529	1824
Kilkenny a.	...	0639	|	0824	1134	1339	1525	1900	...	...	0939	1314	1545	1839
Kilkenny d.	...	0642	|	0828	1141	1343	1530	1902	...	...	0943	1318	1549	1843
Muine Bheag d.	...	0656	|	0846	1155	1357	1545	1921	...	...	0957	1331	1603	1857
Carlow d.	0630	0708	0759	0858	1207	1411	1609	1935	2135	...	1010	1343	1614	1908
Athy d.	0641	0719	0812	0910	1219	1423	1621	1949	2145	...	1024	1355	1626	1926
Kildare △ d.	0658	0737	|	0928	1237	1441	1635	2009	2200	...	1042	1416	1644	1945
Dublin H ◧ .. △ a.	0740	0811	0900	1000	1310	1515	1706	2040	2245	...	1116	1450	1720	2020

– Also conveys [1st class coach]. ◧ – Full name is **Dublin Heuston**. △ – For additional trains Dublin - Kildare and v.v, see Tables **240**, **245**.

IÉ LIMERICK JUNCTION - LIMERICK - GALWAY 242

km		⚒	⚒		⚒	⚒	⚒		⑦	⑦	⑦	⑦
0	**Limerick Jct** 243 d.	...	0838	...	1340	...	...	...	...	1140	...	...
35	**Limerick** ¶ 245 d.	0555	0920	...	1420	1800	1945	...	0900	1220	1555	1815
74	Ennis 245 d.	0649x	0958	...	1458	1900	2025	...	0940	1304	1635	1857
03	Gort d.	0712	1020	...	1520	1925	2047	...	1002	1326	1701	1924
32	Athenry 240 d.	0747	1055	...	1553	1957	2118	...	1033	1357	1732	1955
52	**Galway** 240 a.	0805	1113	...	1610	2016	2139	...	1052	1415	1750	2015

	⚒	⚒		⚒	⚒	⚒	⚒	⑦	⑦	⑦	⑦
Galway 240 d.	0620	1030	...	1345	1745	1835	...	0830	1155	1610	1830
Athenry 240 d.	0639	1048	...	1406	1811	1859	...	0850	1215	1633	1851
Gort d.	0716	1118	...	1432	1836	1924	...	0916	1241	1701	1921
Ennis 245 d.	0745	1141	...	1500	1859	1946	2110	0938	1303	1723	1943
Limerick ¶ 245 a.	0825	1220	...	1539	1937	...	2149	1019	1342	1803	2021
Limerick Jct 243 a.	...	...	...	1611	2008	...	...	...	1415	...	...

– Arrive 0634. ¶ – Limerick Colbert.

IÉ LIMERICK JUNCTION - LIMERICK 243

Shuttle service connecting with main-line trains. *35 km.* Journey time : 25 - 40 minutes. For through services to or from Dublin Heuston see Table **245**.

om Limerick Junction ⚒: 0807, 0838, 0940, 1040, 1140, 1240, 1340, 1440, 1540, 1621, 1740, 1813, 1834, 1938, 2044, 2238.
⑦: 1013, 1140, 1335, 1419, 1540, 1618, 1742, 1818, 1942, 2050.

om Limerick Colbert ⚒: 0540, 0625, 0725, 0855, 0945, 1045, 1145, 1245, 1345, 1445, 1545, 1645, 1745, 1850, 1940, 2045.
⑦: 0940, 1045, 1245, 1350, 1445, 1545, 1645, 1745, 1845, 1945.

245 DUBLIN - LIMERICK, TRALEE and CORK IÉ

km		⚒h ◇✕	⚒	⚒ 🍷	⚒	⚒ 🍷	⚒	⚒ ◇🍷	⚒	⚒ ◇🍷	⚒	⚒h ◇✕	⚒	⚒h ◇✕	⚒	⚒ ◇🍷	⚒	⚒ ◇🍷	⚒ 🍷	⚒	⚒h ◇✕	⚒	⚒h ◇✕	⚒h ◇✕	⚒
0	**Dublin Heuston** .. **240** d.	0700	...	0800	...	0900	...	1000	...	1100	...	1200	...	1300	...	1400	...	1500	1525	...	1600	...	1625	1700	...
48	Kildare .... **240** d.	|	...	|	...	|	...	|	...	|	...	|	...	|	...	|	...	|	1552	...	|	...	|	|	...
67	Portarlington ...... **240** d.	|	...	|	...	|	...	|	...	|	...	|	...	|	...	|	...	|	1605	...	|	...	1703	|	...
82	Portlaoise .... d.	0742	...	|	...	0943	...	1042	...	1142	...	1242	...	1342	...	1442	...	|	1615	...	|	...	1713	|	...
107	Ballybrophy .... d.	|	...	|	...	0958	...	|	...	|	...	|	...	|	...	1458	...	|	1631	...	|	...	1729	|	...
127	Templemore .... d.	|	...	0902	...	|	...	|	...	1206	...	|	...	|	...	|	...	|	1643	...	|	...	1740	|	...
139	Thurles .... d.	0813	...	0912	...	1015	...	1113	...	1215	...	1313	...	1413	...	1516	...	1609	1653	...	1709	...	1749	|	...
172	**Limerick Junction** .. § d.	0834x	0838	0933x	0940	1036x	1040	1134x	1140	1236x	1240	1334x	1340	1434x	1440	1537x	1540	|	|	...	1730x	1740	1810	1827	1834
208	**Limerick** ¶ ..... § **242** a.	|	0907	|	1014	|	1113	|	1216	|	1313	|	1414	|	1513	|	1613	|	1740	1800	|	1813	1840	|	1859
**	Ennis .... **242** a.	|	0957	|	...	|	...	|	1309	|	...	|	1457	|	...	|	1709	|	...	1837	|	...	...	|	...
208	Charleville .... d.	|	...	|	...	1057	...	|	...	1257	...	|	...	|	...	|	...	1645	...	...	|	...	...	|	...
232	**Mallow** .... **246** d.	0907	...	1007	...	1113	...	1207	...	1313	...	1407	...	1507	...	1611	...	1700	...	...	1803	...	...	1900	...
	Tralee **246** .... a.	|	...	|	...	|	...	|	...	|	...	|	...	|	...	|	...	|	...	...	|	...	...	|	...
266	**Cork** .... **246** a.	0935	...	1035	...	1145	...	1235	...	1345	...	1435	...	1535	...	1640	...	1730	...	...	1830	...	...	1930	...

	⚒h ◇✕	⚒	⚒ ◇🍷	⚒h ◇✕	⚒	⚒ ◇🍷	⚒	⚒ ◇	⚒	⑦ ◇🍷	⑦	⑦	⑦ ◇🍷	⑦	⑦ ◇🍷	⑦ ◇🍷	⑦	⑦ ◇🍷	⑦ 🍷	⑦ ◇🍷	⑦ ◇🍷	⑦ 🍷	⑦ ◇🍷	⑦ ◇🍷	⑦ ◇🍷
Dublin Heuston ... **240** d.	1705	...	1725	1800	...	1900	...	2100	...	0830	...	...	1000	...	1125	1200	...	1300	1325	1400	1500	1525	1600	1700	1800
Kildare .... **240** d.	|	...	1752	|	...	|	...	|	...	|	...	...	|	...	1151	|	...	|	1351	|	|	1551	|	|	|
Portarlington ...... **240** d.	|	...	1805	|	...	|	...	|	...	|	...	...	|	...	1204	|	...	|	1404	|	|	1604	|	|	|
Portlaoise .... d.	|	...	1815	|	...	1944	...	2142	...	0912	...	...	1042	...	1214	|	...	|	1414	|	|	1614	|	|	|
Ballybrophy .... d.	1800	...	1831	1854	...	1959	...	|	...	|	...	...	|	...	1230	|	...	|	1430	|	|	1630	|	|	|
Templemore .... d.	1812	...	1843	|	...	2010	...	|	...	|	...	...	|	...	1244	|	...	|	1443	|	|	1643	|	|	|
Thurles .... d.	1821	...	1853	1912	...	2019	...	2213	...	0944	...	...	1112	...	1254	1308	...	1408	1453	1508	1608	1653	1708	1808	1908
Limerick Junction ... § d.	|	...	|	1933x	1938	2040x	2044	2234x	2238	1008x	1013	...	1137x	1140	|	1333x	1335	|	|	1531x	|	|	1731x	|	1931x
Limerick ¶ ..... § **242** a.	|	...	1940	|	2009	|	2115	|	2303	|	1038	...	|	1205	1340	|	1400	|	1540	*1613*	|	1741	*1813*	|	*2013*
Ennis .... **242** a.	|	...	*2023*	|	2104	|	...	|	...	|	1129	...	|	1257	...	|	*1449*	|	*1635*	|	|	...	*1857*z	|	|
Charleville .... d.	1857	...	...	|	...	2101	...	|	...	1028	...	...	|	...	...	|	...	1445	...	|	|	...	1751	|	|
Mallow .... **246** d.	1914	1930	...	2007	...	2116	...	2307	...	1044	...	1050	1210	...	...	1406	...	1502	...	1605	1702	...	1808	1902	2005
Tralee **246** .... a.	2051	|	...	|	...	|	...	|	...	1220	...	|	|	...	...	|	...	|	...	|	|	...	|	|	|
Cork .... **246** a.	...	1955	...	2035	...	2145	...	2335	...	...	...	1112	1235	...	...	1430	...	1530	...	1630	1730	...	1835	1930	2030

	⑦ 🍷	⑦	⑦ ◇🍷	⑦ ◇🍷	⑦	⑦ ◇🍷	⑦ ◇	⑦ 🍷
Dublin Heuston .. **240** d.	1825	...	1900	1905	...	1925	2100	2110
Kildare .... **240** d.	1854	...	|	|	...	1958	|	2139
Portarlington ...... **240** d.	1907	...	|	1942	...	2011	2135	2152
Portlaoise .... d.	1918	...	|	|	...	2022	|	2203
Ballybrophy .... d.	1933	...	|	|	...	2037	|	|
Templemore .... d.	1946	...	|	|	...	2051	|	|
Thurles .... d.	1955	...	2008	2021	...	2101	2212	2235
Limerick Junction .. § d.	|	...	|	2047x	2050	|	2235x	|
Limerick ¶ .... § **242** a.	2042	2050	|	|	2115	2147	|	2320
Ennis .... **242** a.	...	2129	|	|	▬	...	|	...
Charleville .... d.	...	...	|	2104	⑦	...	|	...
Mallow .... **246** d.	...	...	2102	2121	2130	...	2308	...
Tralee **246** .... a.	...	...	|	2255	|	...	|	...
Cork .... **246** a.	...	...	2130	...	2155	...	2335	...

	⚒	⚒	⚒h ◇✕	⚒ 🍷	⚒	⚒h ◇✕	⚒	⚒h ◇✕	⚒	⚒h ◇✕	⚒	⚒
Cork .... **246** d.	...	...	0600	...	...	0700	...	...	0800	...	...	...
Tralee **246** .... d.	...	...	|	...	...	|	...	...	|	0700	...	...
Mallow .... **246** d.	...	...	0622	...	...	0721	...	...	0825	0834	...	...
Charleville .... d.	...	...	0636	...	...	|	...	...	...	0850	...	...
Ennis .... **242** d.	...	...	|	...	...	|	0650	...	...	|	0745	...
Limerick Colbert .. § **242** d.	0540	0625	|	0640	0725	|	0730	0740	...	|	0825	0855
Limerick Junction .... § d.	0607	0651	0657	|	0753	0756	...	|	...	0913	...	0923
Thurles .... d.	0639	...	|	0725	...	0816	...	0826	...	|	...	0943
Templemore .... d.	0638	...	|	0733	...	|	...	0834	...	|	...	|
Ballybrophy .... d.	0650	...	|	0744	...	|	...	0845	...	|	...	|
Portlaoise .... d.	0704	...	|	0759	...	|	...	0900	...	|	...	|
Portarlington .... **240** d.	0715	...	|	0811	...	|	...	|	...	|	...	|
Kildare .... **240** d.	0730	...	|	0823	...	|	...	|	...	|	...	|
Dublin Heuston .... **240** a.	0805	...	0830	0855	...	0930	...	0955	...	1045	...	1059

	⚒	⚒ ◇🍷	⚒	⚒ ◇🍷	⚒	⚒ 🍷	⚒	⚒ 🍷	⚒	⚒h ◇✕	⚒	⚒	⚒ ◇🍷	⚒	⚒ ◇🍷	⚒	⚒h ◇✕	⚒	⚒h ◇✕	⚒	⚒	⚒ ◇🍷	⚒	Ⓐ ◇🍷	⚒ ◇🍷
Cork .... **246** d.	...	0920	...	1020	...	1120	...	1230	...	1320	...	...	1420	...	1520	...	1620	...	1720	...	...	1820	...	1920	2020
Tralee **246** .... d.	...	|	...	|	...	|	...	|	...	|	...	...	|	...	|	...	|	...	|	...	...	|	...	|	|
Mallow .... **246** d.	...	0941	...	1041	...	1141	...	1241	...	1341	...	...	1441	...	1541	...	1641	...	1741	...	...	1841	...	1941	2041
Charleville .... d.	...	|	...	1058	...	|	...	|	...	|	...	...	1458	...	|	...	1658	...	|	...	...	1858	...	|	|
Ennis .... **242** d.	...	|	1000	|	...	|	*1141*	|	...	|	1325	...	|	1500	|	...	|	...	|	1720	...	|	1859	|	|
Limerick ¶ ..... § **242** d.	0945	|	1045	|	1145	|	1245	|	1345	|	1404	1445	|	1545	|	1645	|	1745	|	1759	1850	|	1940	|	*2045*
Limerick Junction ... § d.	1012	1016	1111	1119	1211	1216	1311	1316	1411	1416	...	1511	1519	1611	1616	1711	1719	1811	1817	...	1916	1919	2008	2015	2116
Thurles .... d.	...	1036	...	|	...	1236	...	|	...	1436	...	...	1539	...	1636	...	1739	...	1836	...	...	1939	...	2035	2136
Templemore .... d.	...	|	...	1144	...	|	...	1341	...	|	...	...	|	...	|	...	1748	...	|	...	...	1949	...	|	|
Ballybrophy .... d.	...	|	...	|	...	1255	...	|	...	|	...	...	|	...	|	...	|	...	1855	...	...	|	...	|	|
Portlaoise .... d.	...	1105	...	|	...	1308	...	1405	...	1505	...	...	|	...	1705	...	1811	...	1908	...	...	2012	...	2105	2205
Portarlington ...... **240** d.	...	|	...	|	...	|	...	|	...	|	...	...	|	...	|	...	|	...	|	...	...	|	...	|	|
Kildare .... **240** d.	...	|	...	|	...	|	...	|	...	|	...	...	|	...	|	...	|	...	|	...	...	|	...	|	|
Dublin Heuston ... **240** a.	...	1155	...	1255	...	1400	...	1455	...	1555	...	...	1655	...	1755	...	1905	...	2000	...	...	2105	...	2155	2255

	⑦ ◇🍷	⑦ ◇🍷	⑦	⑦ ◇🍷	⑦ ◇🍷	⑦ ◇🍷	⑦ ◇🍷	⑦	⑦ ◇🍷	⑦	⑦ ◇🍷	⑦ ◇🍷	⑦ ◇🍷	⑦	⑦ ◇🍷	⑦ ◇🍷	⑦ ◇🍷	⑦	⑦ ◇🍷	⑦ ◇🍷	⑦	⑦ ◇🍷	⑦ ◇🍷	⑦	⑦ ◇🍷
Cork .... **246** d.	...	0820	...	...	1020	...	1220	...	1320	...	...	1420	...	...	1520	...	1620	...	1720	...	...	1820	...	...	192
Tralee **246** .... d.	...	|	...	...	|	...	|	1150	|	...	...	|	1340	...	|	...	|	...	|	...	...	|	1750	...	|
Mallow .... **246** d.	...	0842	...	...	1041	...	1242	1316	1342	...	...	1441	1514	...	1541	...	1641	...	1741	...	...	1842	1922	...	194
Charleville .... d.	...	0858	...	...	1057	...	1258	1331	|	...	...	1457	1530	...	|	...	1657	...	|	...	...	1858	|	...	|
Ennis .... **242** d.	*0740*	|	0938	...	|	*1135*	|	|	|	1303	...	|	|	...	|	*1515*	|	...	|	*1723*	...	|	|	1900	|
Limerick ¶ .... § **242** d.	0825	|	1019	1025	*1045*	1225	*1245*	|	|	1342	1420	|	|	1545	|	1620	|	1745	|	1820	1845	|	|	1945	|
Limerick Junction ... § d.	|	0917	...	|	1116	|	1317	1352	1415	...	|	|	|	1611	1614	|	|	1811	1814	|	1912	1917	1957	2011	201
Thurles .... d.	0909	|	...	1110	1136	1309	1337	1413	1435	...	1505	1533	1609	...	1634	1704	1733	...	1834	1904	...	1937	2018	...	203
Templemore .... d.	0918	|	...	1120	|	1318	|	|	|	...	1514	|	|	...	|	1713	|	...	|	1913	...	|	|	...	|
Ballybrophy .... d.	0930	|	...	1132	|	1330	|	|	|	...	1528	|	|	...	|	1727	|	...	|	1927	...	|	|	...	|
Portlaoise .... d.	0944	|	...	1146	|	1344	|	|	|	...	1544	|	|	...	|	1742	|	...	|	1942	...	|	|	...	|
Portarlington ...... **240** d.	0955	|	...	1157	|	1355	|	|	|	...	1555	|	1648	...	|	1753	|	...	|	1955	...	|	|	...	|
Kildare .... **240** d.	1009	|	...	1211	|	1409	|	|	|	...	1608	|	|	...	|	1807	|	...	|	2009	...	|	|	...	|
Dublin Heuston ... **240** a.	1040	1050	...	1243	1255	1441	1455	1535	1550	...	1640	1650	1730	...	1750	1840	1850	...	1950	2042	...	2055	2138	...	215

h – ✕ on Ⓐ, 🍷 on ⑥. x – Arr 1 - 2 mins. earlier. z – Change at Limerick C. ◇ – Also conveys [1st class]. § – Also Table **243**. ** – Limerick - Ennis: *39 km*. ¶ – Limerick Colbert

246 (DUBLIN -) CORK - MALLOW - TRALEE IÉ

km		⚒	⚒	⚒	⚒	⚒	⚒	⚒h ◇✕	⚒		⑦	⑦ ◇🍷	⑦	⑦	⑦	⑦	⑦ ◇🍷
0	**Cork** .... **245** d.	0645	0855	*1020*	*1220*	*1420*	*1655*	*1845*	2055	...	0855	*1020*	1210	1435	*1620*	1845	*2050*
	Dublin **245** ..... d.	|	*0700*	*0900*	*1100*	*1300*	*1500*	1705	*1900*	...	|	0830	*1000*	*1300*	*1500*	*1700*	1905
34	**Mallow** .... **245** d.	0725	0923	1120	1320	1518	1725	1914	2124	...	0925	1044	1244	1517	1725	1925	2121
66	Millstreet .... d.	0747	0945	1142	1342	1540	1747	1941	2146	...	0947	1110	1310	1542	1748	1948	2145
100	Killarney .... d.	0817	1015	1215	1415	1615	1816	2015	2214	...	1014	1140	1340	1622	1825	2026	2218
134	**Tralee** .... a.	0852	1050	1250	1450	1650	1851	2051	2249	...	1049	1220	1415	1700	1859	2102	2255

	①	②–⑤	⚒h ◇✕	⚒	⚒	⚒	⚒	⚒	⚒		⑦	⑦	⑦ ◇🍷	⑦	⑦	⑦ ◇🍷	⑦
Tralee .... d.	0455	0555	0700	0905	1105	1305	1505	1705	1905	...	0710	1150	1340	1510	1710	1750	1915
Killarney .... d.	0525	0625	0734	0936	1136	1336	1536	1736	1936	...	0741	1222	1421	1541	1744	1826	1946
Millstreet .... d.	0549	0649	0806	1002	1202	1402	1602	1806	2002	...	0807	1249	1448	1607	1810	1854	2012
Mallow .... **245** d.	0729x	0729z	0834	1032	1232	1432	1632	1843	2037	...	0843	1316	1514	1635	1844	1922	2045
Dublin **245** .... a.	*0830*	*0930*	1045	*1255*	*1455*	*1655*	*1905*	*2100*	*2255*	...	*1050*	1535	1730	*1850*	*2055*	2138	|
Cork .... **245** a.	0750	0750	*0915*	*1145*	*1345*	*1535*	*1730*	1905	2058	...	0905	*1430*	*1630*	*1730*	1909	*2030*	2107

h – ✕ on Ⓐ, 🍷 on ⑥. x – Arrive 0614. z – Arrive 0714. ◇ – Also conveys [1st class].

CORK - MIDLETON Journey time: 24 minutes *19 km*

⚒ 0615, 0645 Ⓐ, 0715, 0745 Ⓐ, 0815, 0845 Ⓐ, 0915, 1015, then hourly until 1715, 1745,Ⓐ, 1815, 1915, 2015, 2115, 2215.

† 0815, 0915, 1115, 1215, 1415, 1615, 1715, 1815, 2015.

MIDLETON - CORK

⚒ 0615, 0645, 0715 Ⓐ, 0745, 0815 Ⓐ, 0845, 0915 Ⓐ, 0945, 1045 then hourly until 1745, 1815 Ⓐ, 1845, 1945, 2045, 2145, 2245.

† 0845, 0945, 1145, 1245, 1445, 1645, 1745, 1845, 2045.

CORK - COBH Journey time: 24 minutes *19 km*

⚒ 0530 Ⓐ, 0600 ⑥, 0630 Ⓐ, 0700, 0730, 0800, 0830 Ⓐ, 090 1000, then hourly until 1600, 1630, 1700, 1730, 1800, 183 1900 Ⓐ, 2000, 2100, 2230.

† 0800, 0900, 1100, 1200, 1300, 1430, 1600, 1700, 1800, 194 2100, 2200.

COBH - CORK

⚒ 0600 Ⓐ, 0630 ⑥, 0700 Ⓐ, 0730, 0800 Ⓐ, 0830, 0900 Ⓐ, 093 1030, then hourly until 1630, 1700, 1730, 1800, 1830, 190 1930 Ⓐ, 2030, 2130, 2300.

† 0830, 0930, 1130, 1230, 1330, 1500, 1630, 1730, 1830, 203 2130, 2230.

FRANCE

SEE MAP PAGES 172/3

Operator: Société Nationale des Chemins de Fer Français (SNCF), unless otherwise shown.

Services: Most trains convey first and second classes of accommodation; many purely local services are second class only (it is not possible to show classes in the tables). *TGV* (*train à grande vitesse*) trains have a bar car in the centre of the train selling drinks and light refreshments. Selected *TGV* trains have an at-seat meal service in first class. On some *Intercité* services refreshments are available from a trolley wheeled through the train. Certain other long-distance trains also have refreshments available (sometimes seasonal or on certain days of the week), but it is not possible to identify these in the tables as this information is no longer supplied. Regional and local trains (outside Paris) are classified *TER* (*Train Express Regional*). Domestic night trains have sleeping accommodation which consists of modern four-berth couchettes (first class) or six-berth couchettes (second class). Women-only compartments are available on request. There are no sleeping cars on domestic trains in France. Note that all luggage placed on luggage racks must be labelled.

Timings: Valid **June 15 - December 13, 2014**. Amended services operate on and around public holidays; whilst we try to show holiday variations, passengers are advised to confirm train times locally before travelling during these periods. Public holidays in 2014 are Jan. 1, Easter Monday (Apr. 21), May 1, 8, Ascension Day (May 29), Whit Monday (June 9), July 14, Aug. 15, Nov. 1, 11, Dec. 25. **Engineering work** can often affect schedules; major changes are shown in the tables where possible but other changes may occur at short notice.

Tickets: **Seat reservations** are **compulsory** for travel by all *TGV* and night trains (also *Intercité* shown with Ⓡ), and are also available for a small fee on many other long distance trains. Advance reservations are recommended for travel to ski resorts during the winter sports season. **Supplements** (which include the cost of seat reservation) are payable for travel in *TGV*, certain *Intercité* and night trains. All rail tickets (except passes) must be date-stamped before boarding the train using the self-service validating machines (composteurs) at the platform entrances. Note that where two *TGV* units are coupled together, they will often carry different train numbers for reservation purposes.

Note: The *TGV* services **Lille Europe - Charles de Gaulle ✈ - Marne-la-Vallée - Lyon / Bordeaux / Rennes / Nantes** are shown in the International section (Table **11**).

PARIS - LILLE - TOURCOING — 250

TGV Nord high-speed trains

For slower trains via Douai see Table **256**. For **Charles de Gaulle ✈ - Lille** see Table **11**. Certain trains continue to Dunkerque, Calais or Boulogne - see Table **265**.

km		TGV 7205	TGV 7007	TGV 7511*	TGV 7015	TGV 7021	TGV 7223	TGV 7029		TGV 7033	TGV 7535*	TGV 7043	TGV 7045		TGV 7049	TGV 7053	TGV 7559*	TGV 7061	TGV 7265*		TGV 7067	TGV 7269*	TGV 7271	
		Ⓐ	Ⓐ			①–⑥	①–⑥	⑦					Ⓐ			⑤		Ⓐ			Ⓐ		Ⓐ	
			L		J	b	b	e					R			J		J			Q			
0	**Paris Nord** d.	0646	0716	0746	0816	0846	0946	0946	...	1046	1146	1246	1316	...	1446	1516	1546	1616	1646	...	1716	1746	1816	...
227	**Lille Europe** a.	0745	|	0845	|	|	1045	|	...	|	1245	|	|	...	|	|	1645	|	1745	...	|	1845	|	...
227	**Lille Flandres** 415 a.	...	0818	...	0918	0948	...	1048	...	1148	...	1348	1418	...	1548	1618	...	1718	...	...	1818	...	1918	...
237	Roubaix ◇ 415 a.	...	...	...	...	...	...	...	...	...	...	...	...	...	...	...	...	...	...	...	...	...	1941	...
240	**Tourcoing** 415 a.	...	...	...	...	...	...	...	...	...	...	...	...	...	...	...	...	...	...	...	...	...	1946	...

	TGV 7073	TGV 7277	TGV 7281	TGV 7083		TGV 7089	TGV 7091	TGV 7093	TGV 7097	
	⑤		Ⓑ	①–⑥		⑤⑦	①–⑥	⑤⑦		
	J		h	b		w	b	v	r	
Paris Nord d.	1833	1846	1916	1946	...	2016	2052	2146	2221	...
Lille Europe a.	|	1945	|	|	...	|	⊡	|	⊡	...
Lille Flandres 415 a.	1935	...	2018	2048	...	2118	2210	2248	2339	...
Roubaix ◇ 415 a.	...	...	2041	...	...	...	...	...	...	...
Tourcoing 415 a.	...	...	2046	...	...	...	...	...	...	...

	TGV 7000	TGV 7206	TGV 7008	TGV 7216	TGV 7020		TGV 7229	TGV 7530	TGV 7030
	Ⓐ	①–⑥	Ⓐ	Ⓐ	Ⓐ		①–⑥	Ⓐ	Ⓒ
		b◧	J				b		J
Tourcoing 415 d.	...	0612	...	...	...	...	...	...	...
Roubaix ◇ 415 d.	...	0617	...	...	...	...	...	...	...
Lille Flandres 415 d.	0551	0641	0701	...	0741	...	...	...	...
Lille Europe d.	⊡	|	|	0713	|	...	0813	0842	0842
Paris Nord a.	0708	0744	0802	0814	0844	...	0914	0944	0944

	TGV 7536*	TGV 7040	TGV 7546*	TGV 7248	TGV 7550	TGV 7254	TGV 7058	TGV 7066	TGV 7070		TGV 7572*	TGV 7074	TGV 7076	TGV 7082	TGV 7288*	TGV 7290		TGV 7292*	TGV 7094	TGV 7294		TGV 7096	TGV 7298	
						①–⑥			⑤			Ⓐ		Ⓐ		Ⓐ		Ⓒ	⑤	⑦		①–⑥	⑦	
				d		b			J			P		R					J	e			e	
Tourcoing 415 d.	...	...	...	1110	...	...	...	...	...	...	...	...	...	...	...	...	...	...	...	2012	...	...	...	...
Roubaix ◇ 415 d.	...	...	...	1115	...	...	...	...	...	...	...	...	...	...	...	...	...	...	...	2017	...	...	...	...
Lille Flandres 415 d.	...	1011	...	1141	...	...	1511	1611	1641	...	...	1741	1811	1841	...	...	...	...	2041	2041	...	2120	...	...
Lille Europe d.	0913	|	1113	|	1313	1413	|	|	|	...	1713	|	|	|	1913	1940	...	2013	|	|	...	⊡	2213	...
Paris Nord a.	1014	1114	1214	1244	1414	1514	1614	1714	1744	...	1814	1844	1914	1944	2014	2041	...	2114	2144	2144	...	2238	2314	...

– To July 5 / from Aug. 25.
– To July 10 / from Aug. 25.
– Ⓐ to July 4 / from Aug. 25 (also July 11, 18, 25, Aug. 1, 8, 14, 22).
– Ⓐ to July 28 / from Aug. 25 (also Aug. 1, 8, 14, 22).
– Ⓐ to July 25 / from Aug. 25 (also Aug. 1, 8, 14, 22).
– Not June 9, July 14, Nov. 11.

d – Daily to July 27 / from Aug. 25 (also Aug. 1, 8, 14, 22).
e – Also June 9, July 14, Nov. 11.
h – Also Nov. 1.
r – Depart 2208 Oct. 5, 12, 2218 Oct. 10, 11. Arrive Lille Europe June 2 - 6.
v – Also June 9, July 14, Aug. 14, Nov. 11; not Aug. 15.
w – Also June 9, July 14, Nov. 11; not Aug. 1, 8, 15, 22.

TGV – Ⓡ, supplement payable.
⊡ – Via Arras (Table **256**).
◇ – Also calls at Croix Wasquehal.
◧ – Timings may vary on Oct. 4, 11.

* – Train numbers vary as follows:
7265 is numbered **7065** on ⑦, **7565** on ⑥.
7269 is numbered **7571** on ⑥.
7288 is numbered **7586** on ⑦, **7588** on ⑥.
7292 is numbered **7592** on ⑥.
7511 is numbered **7515** on Ⓒ.
7535 is numbered **7035** on ⑦.
7536 is numbered **7036** on ⑦.
7546 is numbered **7046** on Ⓒ.
7559 is numbered **7059** on ⑥.
7572 is numbered **7072** on ⑦.

PARIS - SOISSONS - LAON — 251

km		Ⓐ	⑥	⑥	Ⓐ‡	†	⑥	Ⓐ	Ⓒ	Ⓐ	Ⓐ	Ⓒ	Ⓐ	⚒n	Ⓐ	⑥	†r	Ⓐ	Ⓐ	Ⓒ	Ⓐ		Ⓐ	
0	**Paris Nord** d.	0603	0618	0701	0705	0813	0813	0831	0946	0955	1158	1326	1326	1446	1530	1627	1631	1631	1751	1746	1851	2008	2116	...
61	Crépy-en-Valois d.	0657	0658	0741	0741	0857	0907	0909	1025	1033	1234	1400	1403	1535	1609	1707	1716	1706	1833	1823	1926	2042	2153	...
105	Soissons d.	0727	0727	0811	0811	0930	0938	0944	1053	1101	1303	1430	1437	1606	1641	1734	1743	1740	1908	1856	2001	2113	2221	...
140	**Laon** a.	0751	0752	0835	0835	0953	1001	1012	1117	1125	1327	1454	1505	1632	1706	1756	1806	1807	1935	1924	2028	2137	2245	...

	Ⓐ	Ⓐ	⑥	Ⓐ	†	⚒	†	Ⓐ	⑥r	Ⓐ	Ⓒ	Ⓒ	Ⓐ	Ⓐ	Ⓒ	Ⓐ	Ⓐ	Ⓒ	Ⓐs	Ⓐ	Ⓐ	†	†r	⚒
Laon d.	0510	0530	0633	0635	0708	0754	0843	0943	0942	1126	1126	1230	1245	1411	1602	1624	1711	1741	1811	1910	2020	2030	2115	2119
Soissons d.	0536	0559	0702	0706	0733	0822	0909	1008	1008	1155	1152	1256	1312	1437	1629	1654	1736	1806	1834	1937	2045	2055	2138	2144
Crépy-en-Valois d.	0604	0630	0734	0740	0802	0852	0937	1037	1037	1226	1220	1324	1339	1506	1657	1726	1805	1837	1904	2007	2114	2126	2205	2213
Paris Nord a.	0640	0710	0812	0826	0850	0927	1017	1112	1113	1300	1300	1412	1417	1542	1742	1810	1840	1912	1939	2042	2158	2200	2257	2257

– To July 12 / from Aug. 25.
– To July 12 / from Aug. 30.

s – On Ⓐ July 28 - Aug. 22 Laon d. 1837, Paris a. 2016.
‡ – Starts from Crépy-en-Valois July 28 - Aug. 22.

Timings may vary by up to 20 minutes July 27 - Aug. 24. On Nov. 1 service is as on ⑦.

AMIENS - TERGNIER - LAON - REIMS — 252

km		Ⓐ	⑥	F§	Ⓐ§	⑥	†		Ⓐ§	Ⓑ‡	⑥	F	Ⓐ§	†	⚒	Ⓐ		⑥	Ⓐn	Ⓑ	⚒	⑤	†n	†	
0	**Amiens** d.	0618	0618	0718	0818	0900	0900	...	...	1218	1319	1459	...	1600	1618	1718	...	1800	1800	1818	1918	1918	...	2100	...
59	Ham (Somme) d.	0706	0706	0806	0904	0944	0944	...	...	1307	1407	1545	...	1644	1706	1806	...	1845	1845	1906	2006	2006	...	2145	...
80	Tergnier a.	0725	0725	0825	0925	0958	0958	...	...	1325	1425	1558	...	1658	1725	1825	...	1857	1858	1925	2025	2025	...	2158	...
80	Tergnier d.	0735	0735	0835	0935	1000	0959	...	1235	1335	1435	1559§	1659	1659	1735	1835	...	1858	1859	1937	...	2035	2035	2159	...
108	**Laon** a.	0801	0802	0902	1001	1020	1020	...	1301	1401	1501	1619§	1720	1720	1801	1901	...	1919	1922	2002	...	2102	2102	2220	...

	Ⓐn	E	Ⓐ	⚒		⚒	†		†	Ⓐ§	F§	⑥		Ⓐ	⚒	†	Ⓐ	Ⓐ	Ⓐn	Ⓐ		Ⓒ	Ⓐn	⑤n	
Laon d.	...	0558	0641	0658	...	0741	0840	...	1159	1159	1258	1312	...	1558§	1658§	1701	1738	1758	1841	1858	...	1942	1958	1958	...
Tergnier a.	...	0624	0702	0724	...	0802	0902	...	1225	1225	1325	1333	...	1625	1725	1727	1800	1825	1902	1925	...	2003	2025	2025	...
Tergnier d.	0603	0634	0703	0734	...	0803	0903	...	1235	1235	1335	1334	...	1635	1735	1735	1801	1835	1903	1935	...	2004	...	2035	...
Ham (Somme) d.	0617	0655	0716	0755	...	0817	0916	...	1255	1255	1355	1347	...	1657	1755	1755	1817	1855	1917	1955	...	2017	...	2055	...
Amiens a.	0700	0742	0802	0842	...	0900	1002	...	1342	1342	1442	1431	...	1750	1842	1842	1900	1942	2000	2043	...	2101	...	2142	...

LAON - REIMS

Timings may vary from Sept. 29

km		⚒	Ⓐ	Ⓐ§	⑥	†	⚒§	Ⓐ§	Ⓐr	r	⑥s	Ⓐ	†n
0	Laon d.	0636	0745	1010	1027	1202	1314	1702	1730	1827	1940	2010	2010
52	Reims a.	0725	0827	1045	1103	1249	1403	1740	1812	1914	2013	2045	2045

	D	Ⓐ§	G	†	Ⓐ§	⑥	Ⓐ§	⚒	†	Ⓐr	Ⓐ	
Reims d.	0643	0717	0735	1102	1119	1222	1227	1515	1700	1705	1737	1846
Laon a.	0732	0755	0811	1150	1154	1305	1314	1551	1736	1749	1824	1933

– ⚒ to July 5; Ⓐ July 7 - Aug. 29; ⚒ from Sept. 1.
– ⚒ to July 12; Ⓐ July 15 - Aug. 22; ⚒ from Aug. 25.
– Ⓐ to July 11 / from Aug. 25.

G – Ⓒ July 6 - Aug. 31.
n – To July 11 / from Aug. 25.
r – Subject to alteration from Nov. 3.

s – To July 5 / from Sept. 6.
§ – Subject to alteration on Ⓐ from Sept. 15 with 🚌 substitution.
‡ – Subject to alteration.

🚌 AMIENS - TGV HAUTE-PICARDIE — 253

SNCF 🚌 service

TGV departures and arrivals at TGV Haute-Picardie (Table **11**) have 🚌 connections from / to Amiens and St Quentin. Departs 50 - 60 mins before the train; journey 40 minutes, Ⓡ.

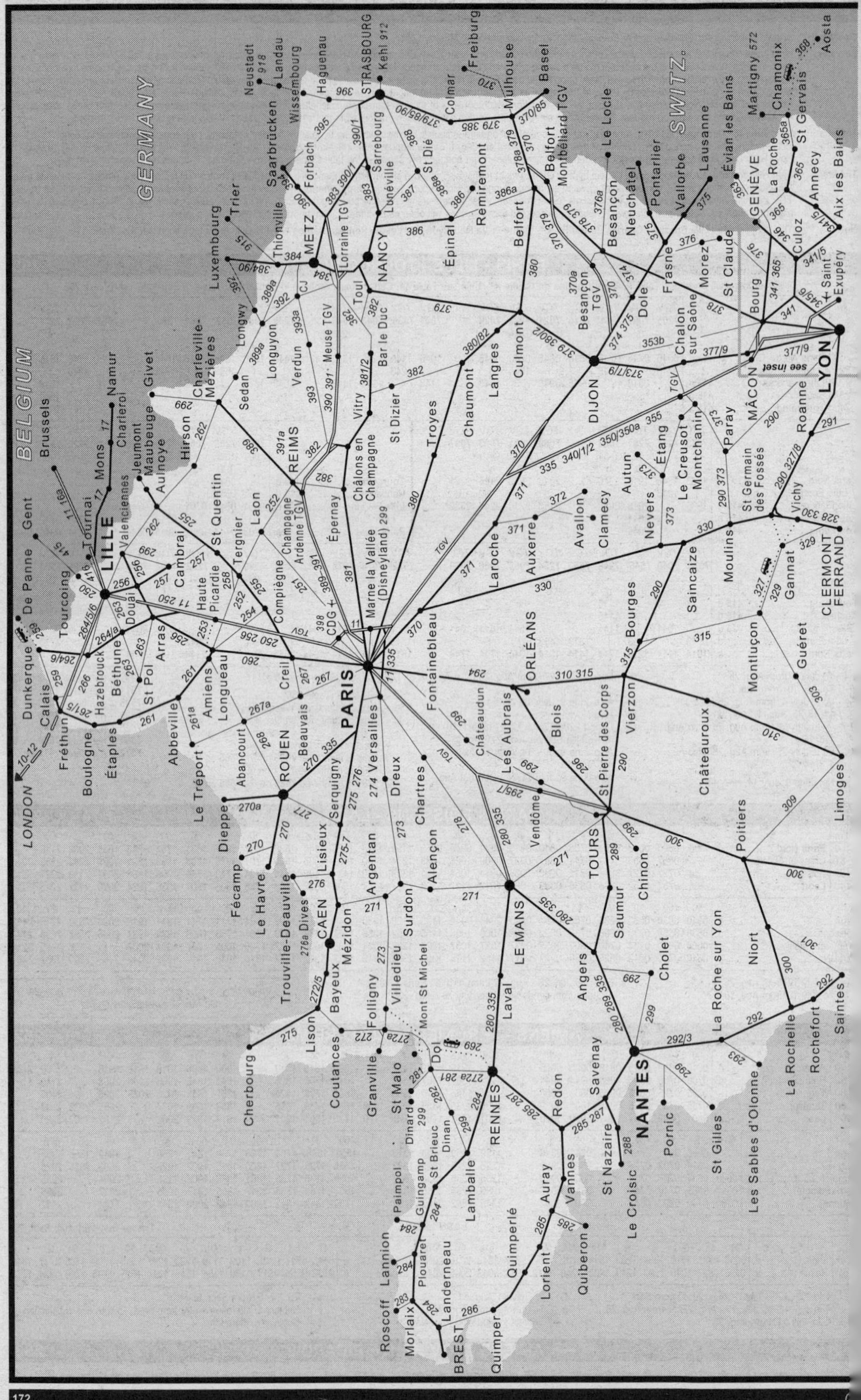
GERMANY
BELGIUM
SWITZ.
LONDON
PARIS
LILLE
ROUEN
CAEN
RENNES
LE MANS
NANTES
TOURS
ORLÉANS
DIJON
LYON
REIMS
METZ
NANCY
STRASBOURG
MÂCON
GENÈVE
CLERMONT FERRAND
Brussels
Gent
Namur
Charleroi
Mons
Tournai
Tourcoing
De Panne
Dunkerque
Calais
Fréthun
Boulogne
Étaples
Hazebrouck
Béthune
St Pol
Arras
Douai
Valenciennes
Cambrai
St Quentin
Jeumont
Maubeuge
Aulnoye
Hirson
Givet
Charleville-Mézières
Sedan
Longwy
Luxembourg
Trier
Thionville
Saarbrücken
Forbach
Neustadt
Landau
Wissembourg
Haguenau
Kehl
Sarrebourg
Lunéville
St Dié
Épinal
Remiremont
Colmar
Freiburg
Mulhouse
Basel
Belfort
Montbéliard TGV
Le Locle
Besançon
Besançon TGV
Neuchâtel
Pontarlier
Vallorbe
Lausanne
Frasne
Morez
St Claude
Évian les Bains
Martigny
Chamonix
St Gervais
Aosta
La Roche
Annecy
Aix les Bains
Culoz
Bourg
Saint Exupéry
Longuyon
Verdun
Meuse TGV
Lorraine TGV
Toul
Bar le Duc
Vitry
St Dizier
Châlons en Champagne
Champagne Ardenne TGV
Épernay
Laon
Tergnier
Compiègne
Haute Picardie
Amiens
Longueau
Abbeville
Le Tréport
Abancourt
Beauvais
Creil
CDG
Marne la Vallée (Disneyland)
Troyes
Chaumont
Langres
Culmont
Dole
Chalon sur Saône
Le Creusot Montchanin
Étang
Autun
Paray
Roanne
Vichy
St Germain des Fossés
Moulins
Nevers
Saincaize
Clamecy
Avallon
Auxerre
Laroche
Fontainebleau
Versailles
Dreux
Chartres
Serquigny
Lisieux
Dieppe
Fécamp
Le Havre
Trouville-Deauville
Dives
Mézidon
Argentan
Surdon
Alençon
Bayeux
Lison
Cherbourg
Coutances
Folligny
Villedieu
Mont St Michel
Granville
Dol
St Malo
Dinard
Dinan
St Brieuc
Lamballe
Guingamp
Paimpol
Lannion
Plouaret
Morlaix
Roscoff
Landerneau
BREST
Quimper
Quimperlé
Lorient
Auray
Quiberon
Vannes
Redon
Savenay
St Nazaire
Le Croisic
Pornic
St Gilles
Les Sables d'Olonne
La Roche sur Yon
La Rochelle
Rochefort
Saintes
Niort
Poitiers
Limoges
Châteauroux
Vierzon
Bourges
Montluçon
Guéret
Gannat
St Pierre des Corps
Chinon
Saumur
Angers
Cholet
Laval
Vendôme
Blois
Les Aubrais
Châteaudun
see inset

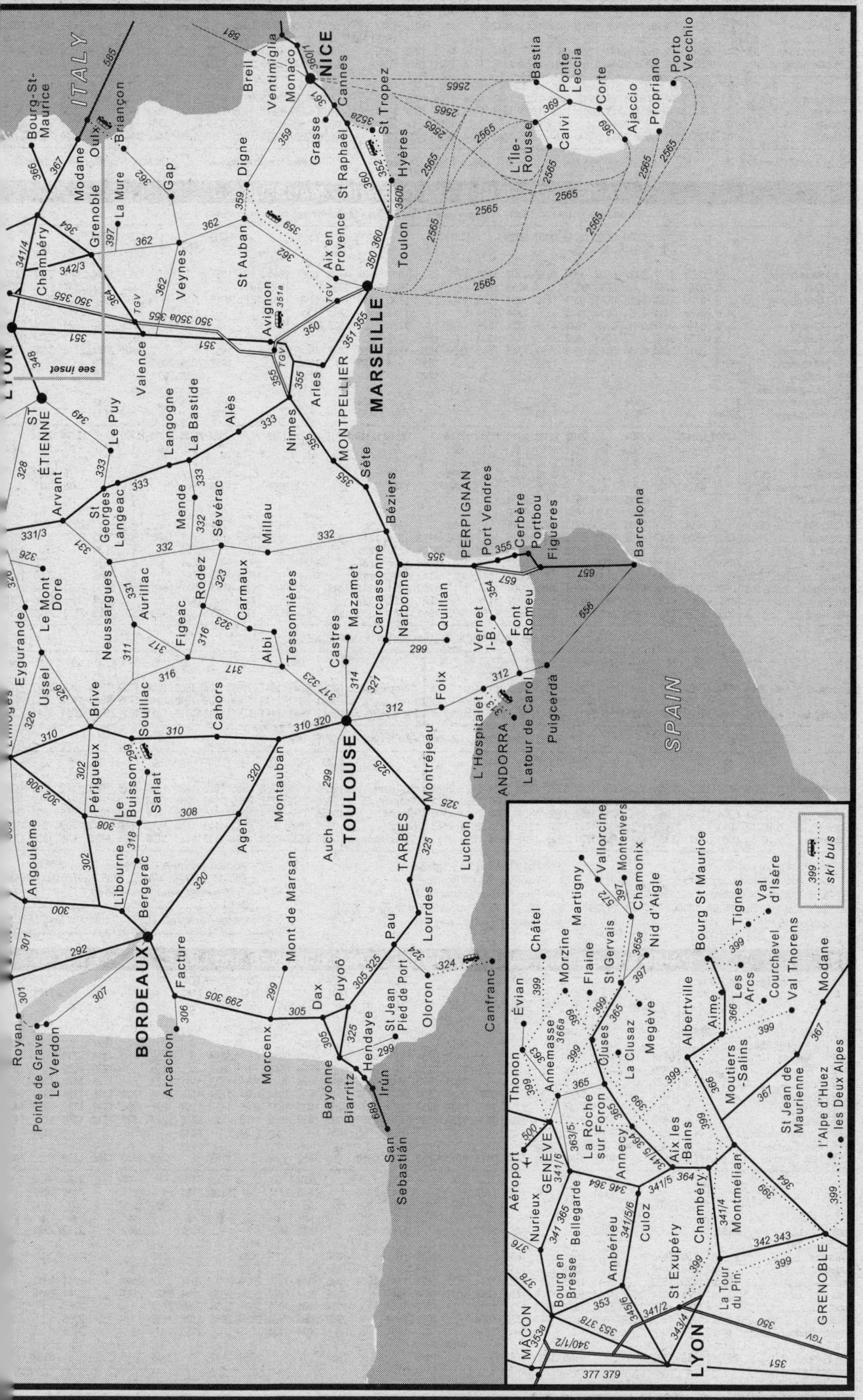
ITALY
SPAIN
ANDORRA
see inset
Bourg-St-Maurice
Modane
Oulx
Briançon
Grenoble
La Mure
Gap
Chambéry
LYON
ST ÉTIENNE
Valence
Le Puy
Arvant
St Georges Langeac
Langogne
La Bastide
Alès
Mende
Sévérac
Millau
Nîmes
Arles
Avignon
Veynes
St Auban
Digne
Aix en Provence
MARSEILLE
Toulon
Hyères
St Raphaël
St Tropez
Grasse
Cannes
NICE
Monaco
Ventimiglia
Breil
Bastia
Ponte-Leccia
Corte
Calvi
L'Île-Rousse
Ajaccio
Propriano
Porto Vecchio
MONTPELLIER
Sète
Béziers
Narbonne
Carcassonne
Quillan
PERPIGNAN
Port Vendres
Cerbère
Portbou
Figueres
Barcelona
Vernet I-B.
Font Romeu
Latour de Carol
Puigcerdà
L'Hospitalet
Foix
TOULOUSE
Castres
Mazamet
Albi
Tessonnières
Carmaux
Rodez
Figeac
Aurillac
Neussargues
Le Mont Dore
Eygurande
Ussel
Limoges
Brive
Souillac
Cahors
Montauban
Sarlat
Le Buisson
Périgueux
Angoulême
Libourne
Bergerac
Agen
BORDEAUX
Royan
Pointe de Grave
Le Verdon
Facture
Arcachon
Morcenx
Mont de Marsan
Dax
Puyoô
Bayonne
Biarritz
Hendaye
Irún
San Sebastián
St Jean Pied de Port
Pau
Oloron
Canfranc
Lourdes
TARBES
Montréjeau
Luchon
Auch
TGV
MÂCON
Bourg en Bresse
Ambérieu
St Exupéry
LYON
La Tour du Pin
GRENOBLE
Chambéry
Montmélian
Aix les Bains
Culoz
Bellegarde
Nurieux
Aéroport
GENÈVE
Annemasse
Thonon
Évian
Châtel
Morzine
La Roche sur Foron
Annecy
Cluses
La Clusaz
Flaine
St Gervais
Megève
Martigny
Vallorcine
Montenvers
Chamonix
Nid d'Aigle
Albertville
Moutiers-Salins
Aime
Bourg St Maurice
Les Arcs
Tignes
Val d'Isère
Courchevel
Val Thorens
St Jean de Maurienne
Modane
l'Alpe d'Huez
les Deux Alpes
399 ski bus

254 AMIENS - COMPIÈGNE

km			Ⓐ	Ⓐ	Ⓐ	Ⓐ	Ⓐ J	Ⓐ	Ⓐ J	Ⓐ	Ⓐ	Ⓐ	Ⓐ J	Ⓐ		⑥	⑥	†	Ⓒ n	⑥	†	⑥ J	† J	Ⓒ	Ⓒ u	Ⓒ	Ⓒ
0	**Amiens** d.	Ⓐ	0552	0622	0741	0908	1052	1222	1445	1642	1701	1745	1819	1943	Ⓒ	0541	0706	0745	0926	1122	1130	1245	1330	1604	1721	1854*	2003
5	Longueau d.		|	0628	0748	|	|	1228	|	|	1707	1751	|	1949		0547	|	|	0932	|	|	1251	1336	|	1727	|	2009
36	Montdidier d.		0624	0702	0825	0943	1123	1301	1515	1712	1740	1823	1903	2023		0620	0737	0815	1007	1152	1200	1324	1409	1634	1800	1924	2042
76	**Compiègne** a.		0653	0737	0904	1014	1151	1337	1543	1738	1818	1901	1936	2052		0656	0811	0846	1042	1223	1231	1401	1445	1710	1839	1956	2118

		Ⓐ	Ⓐ J	Ⓐ	Ⓐ	Ⓐ	Ⓐ	Ⓐ	Ⓐ J	Ⓐ	Ⓐ J	Ⓐ	Ⓐ	Ⓐ		⑥	⑥	†	Ⓒ	⑥ J	†	⑥	†	Ⓒ J	Ⓒ	Ⓒ u	Ⓒ
Compiègne d.	Ⓐ	0548	0629	0708	0750	0835	0913	1053	1222	1445	1642	1748	1835	1910	Ⓒ	0541	0708	0745	0930	1122	1130	1245	1330	1600	1725	1850*	2003
Montdidier d.		0626	0701	0749	0824	0913	0942	1122	1300	1514	1713	1825	1904	1950		0619	0739	0817	1006	1154	1202	1323	1408	1633	1802	1923	2041
Longueau a.		0701	|	0824	|	0944	|	|	1335	|	|	1857	|	2024		0650	|	|	1037	|	|	1354	1438	|	1832	|	2111
Amiens a.		0708	0735	0833	0852	0951	1014	1152	1342	1543	1744	1905	1937	2031		0658	0807	0850	1045	1223	1231	1402	1446	1702	1839	1952	2118

J – To July 12/from Aug. 25. n – Not on ⑥ July 19 - Aug. 23. u – Not on † July 13 - Aug. 24. * – 3 mins later from July 5. *On Nov. 1. service will be as on ⑦.*

255 PARIS - COMPIÈGNE - ST QUENTIN - MAUBEUGE

For additional local trains Paris - Compiègne and Compiègne - St Quentin see below main table

km				12301	12303	12305	12307	12309		12311			12313		2315			12319			12321	12323			
		Ⓐ	†	Ⓐ	⚒	Ⓑ			Ⓐ	Ⓐ	Ⓐ			Ⓐ		Ⓑ	Ⓐ		Ⓐ	†	Ⓐ		Ⓑ	Ⓐ	
						h	c					n			d				J						
0	**Paris** Nord d.	0631	0707	0737	0807	0907	1037	1207	1407	1437	...	1607	1637	1704	1737	1804	1819	1837	...	...	1907	1937	2007	2107	2237
51	Creil d.	0701	0734	|	0835	0937	|	1235	1435	|	...	1635	|	1735	|	1835	1851	|	...	...	1935	|	2034	2140	2305
84	**Compiègne** d.	0725	0758	0818	0901	1001	1118	1301	1501	1518	...	1700	1718	1801	1818	1901	1913	1918	...	...	2002	2018	2101	2201	2331
108	Noyon d.	0738	0812	|	0914	1014	|	1314	1514	|	...	1713	|	1814	|	1914	...	|	...	...	2015	|	2114	2214	2344
124	Chauny d.	0748	0824	|	0924	1024	|	1324	1525	|	...	1724	|	1825	|	1924	...	|	...	...	2025	|	2124	2224	2355
131	Tergnier d.	0756	0832	|	0932	1032	|	1332	1533	|	1638	1732	|	1833	|	1932	...	|	...	...	2032	|	2131	2232	0002
154	**St Quentin** a.	0810	0846	0850	0946	1046	1150	1346	1546	1550	1656	1746	1750	1846	1850	1946	...	1950	...	...	2046	2050	2146	2246	0016
154	**St Quentin** 257 d.	...	...	0852	...	...	1152	...	...	...	1657	...	1752	...	1852	...	...	1952	2005	2005	...	2052	...	...	...
181	Busigny 257 d.	...	...	|	...	...	|	...	...	...	1720	...	|	...	1909	...	...	|	2027	2027	...	|	...	...	...
207	*Cambrai* 257 a.	...	...	|	...	...	|	...	...	...	...	...	|	...	1933	...	...	|	...	...	...	|	...	...	...
217	Aulnoye Aymeries 262 d.	...	...	0924	...	...	1224	...	...	...	...	...	1824	...	...	...	...	2024	...	...	...	2124	...	...	...
229	**Maubeuge** 262 a.	...	...	0933	...	...	1233	...	...	...	...	...	1833	...	...	...	...	2033	...	...	...	2133	...	...	...

	12300	12302		2304		2306	12308	2310	12312	12314		12316	12316	12318	12320	12322		12324	12326	12328	12330		12334	12332	
	⚒ ‡	Ⓐ		Ⓐ b	Ⓑ v	⑥ bt	⚒	† b	⚒ ‡	Ⓒ	Ⓐ	Ⓐ c	Ⓒ	Ⓐ	†		Ⓐ	†	⚒	Ⓐ	†	⚒	†	Ⓐ	†
Maubeuge 262 d.	...	0525	...	...	...	...	0725	...	...	1025	...	1133	...	...	...	1525	...	1625	...	...	1722	...	1925	1933	...
Aulnoye Aymeries 262 d.	...	0536	...	...	...	...	0736	...	...	1036	...	1144	...	...	...	1536	...	1636	...	...	1734	...	1936	1947	...
Cambrai 257 d.	...	|	...	0623	...	0634	|	0734	...	|	...	|	...	...	...	|	...	|	...	...	|	...	|	|	...
Busigny 257 d.	...	|	...	0651	...	0700	|	0800	...	|	...	|	...	...	...	|	...	|	...	...	|	...	|	|	...
St Quentin 257 a.	...	0604	...	0705	...	0713	0804	0814	...	1104	...	1212	...	...	...	1604	...	1704	...	...	1807	...	2004	2014	...
St Quentin d.	0513	0606	0613	0707	0707	0715	0806	0815	1013	1106	1113	1214	1213	1406	1513	1606	1613	1706	1713	1806	1809	1913	2006	2016	2035
Tergnier d.	0529	|	0628	|	0722	0730	|	0830	1028	|	1129	1230	1230	|	1530	|	1629	|	1730	|	|	1930	|	2031	2049
Chauny d.	0536	|	0634	|	0729	0737	|	0837	1035	|	1135	1237	1237	|	1536	|	1635	|	1736	|	|	1936	|	2038	2055
Noyon d.	0547	|	0644	0730	0740	0747	|	0847	1047	|	1146	1247	1247	|	1548	|	1645	|	1747	|	|	1946	|	2050	2106
Compiègne d.	0601	0643	0658	0744	0754	0801	0843	0901	1101	1143	1200	1301	1301	1443	1601	1643	1659	1743	1801	1843	1844	2000	2043	2104	2119
Creil d.	0627	|	0727	|	0817	0827	|	0927	1127	|	1227	1327	1327	|	1627	|	1726	|	1827	|	|	2027	|	2126	2140
Paris Nord a.	0653	0726	0753	0829	0850	0853	0923	0953	1153	1223	1253	1353	1353	1523	1653	1723	1753	1823	1853	1923	1923	2053	2123	2153	221

ADDITIONAL LOCAL TRAINS PARIS - COMPIÈGNE

	⚒		Ⓐ	⚒	Ⓐ	⚒	Ⓐ		⚒	n	†	⑥
Paris Nord d.	0649	0849	1049	1249	1449	1649	1719	1749	1849	1949	2049	2149
Creil d.	0721	0920	1121	1321	1521	1721	1751	1821	1921	2022	2122	2221
Compiègne a.	0756	0956	1156	1356	1557	1756	1813	1856	1959	2056	2156	2256

▽		Ⓐ	†	⑥		⑥	Ⓑ		Ⓑ	Ⓐ	Ⓐ	⑥
Compiègne d.	0805	0847	1047	1105	1204	1502	1604	1702	1804	1907	2047	210
Creil d.	0841	0912	1110	1141	1239	1540	1640	1739	1840	1939	2112	213
Paris Nord a.	0911	0941	1141	1211	1311	1611	1711	1811	1911	2011	2141	220

ADDITIONAL LOCAL TRAINS COMPIÈGNE - ST QUENTIN

	⚒	⚒	Ⓐ	⑥	†	⑥	Ⓐ	Ⓐ	⑥	Ⓐ J	w	
Compiègne d.	0625	0825	1222	1225	1325	1349	1622	1722	1725	1825	1925	2025
Noyon d.	0650	0850	1245	1250	1349	1412	1644	1745	1750	1850	1950	2051
Chauny d.	0704	0904	1255	1304	1401	1425	1654	1755	1804	1904	2004	2106
Tergnier d.	0713	0913	1301	1313	1412	1435	1701	1807	1813	1913	2013	2113
St Quentin a.	0733	0933	1321	1333	1433	1453	1721	1824	1833	1933	2033	2133

	⚒	⑥	Ⓐ	†	Ⓐ	⑥	Ⓐ	†	Ⓑ J	†	Ⓐ	u
St Quentin d.	0626	0726	0738	0935	1026	1326	1338	1426	1626	1726	1738	182
Tergnier d.	0646	0746	0757	0956	1047	1346	1358	1446	1647	1746	1757	184
Chauny d.	0655	0755	0804	1002	1055	1355	1404	1455	1655	1755	1803	185
Noyon d.	0709	0809	0814	1013	1109	1409	1415	1509	1709	1809	1812	190
Compiègne a.	0735	0835	0838	1034	1135	1435	1438	1535	1735	1835	1834	193

J – To July 11/from Aug. 25.
b – Starts from St Quentin July 15 - Aug. 24.
c – Not St Quentin - Maubeuge or v.v. May 5 - June 6.
d – Terminates at St Quentin July 14 - Aug. 24, Nov. 24 - 29.
h – Not Aug. 15.
n – Not on ⑥ July 19 - Aug. 23.
t – Also Aug. 15; not Nov. 1.
u – Runs 12 minutes later on Ⓐ.
v – On Ⓐ runs 6-7 minutes later (Paris a. 0853).
w – Not on † July 13 - Aug. 24.
▽ – Additional journeys Compiègne - Paris: 0505 Ⓐ, 0605 ⚒, 0647 Ⓐ, 0701 Ⓐ, 0705 ⑥, 0726 Ⓐ, 1940 Ⓐ
‡ – Train number shown applies on Ⓐ.

Timings may vary Sept. 15 - Oct. 10 and Nov. 4 - 21

256 PARIS and AMIENS - ARRAS - DOUAI - VALENCIENNES and LILLE

km ★	*Paris - Lille: see* **250**		◇			◇					*TGV* 7105		*TGV* 7107			*TGV* 7111		*TGV* 7113					*TGV* 7121	
		Ⓐ	Ⓐ	Ⓐ	⚒	Ⓐ	Ⓐ J	†	Ⓐ	⑥	Ⓐ	Ⓐ	⑥ t	⑥	†	Ⓒ	⑥	Ⓐ	Ⓑ	⑥	Ⓐ ⊗	Ⓒ	C	†
0	**Paris** Nord 265 d.	...	...	...	...	...	...	...	...	...	0752	...	0852	...	...	0952	...	1052	...	...	...	...	1252	...
	Rouen 268 d.	...	...	...	...	...	...	...	0617	...	|	...	|	0817	...	|	...	|	...	...	1117	...	|	..
131	**Amiens** d.	0538	...	...	0638	...	...	...	0738	0738	|	0838	|	0938	0938	|	1038	|	1138	...	1238	1238	|	..
162	Albert d.	0559	...	...	0659	...	...	...	0759	0759	|	0858	|	0959	0959	|	1059	|	1159	...	1259	1259	|	...
199	Arras 265 a.	0622	...	...	0723	...	...	...	0823	0823	0841	0923	0941	1023	1023	1041	1123	1141	1223	...	1323	1323	1341	..
199	Arras d.	0624	0647	...	0724	0747	...	*0757*	0825	0824	0844	0924	0944	1024	1024	1044	1124	1144	1224	1239	1325	1324	1344	140
224	Douai a.	0637	|	...	0737	|	...	*0826*	0837	0837	0859	0937	0959	1037	1037	1059	1137	1159	1237	1305	1337	1337	1359	142
224	Douai 257 ▶ d.	0639	|	0708	0739	|	0808	0834	0839	0839	0908	0939	1008	1039	1039	1108	1139	1208	1239	1307	1339	1339	1408	142
260	Valenciennes ▶ a.	|	|	|	|	|	|	|	|	|	0934	|	1034	|	|	1134	|	1234	|	|	|	|	1434	|
257	**Lille** Europe a.	|	0708	|	|	0808	|	|	|	|	...	|	...	|	|	...	|	...	|	|	|	|	...	|
257	**Lille** Flandres 257 a.	0658	...	0729	0758	...	0830	0913	0858	0858	...	0958	...	1058	1058	...	1158	...	1258	1330	1358	1358	...	145

				TGV 7131				*TGV* 7137	◇		*TGV* 7141	*TGV* 7343		*TGV* 7145	*TGV* 7145		*TGV* 5266	*TGV* 7151		*TGV* 7091		*TGV* 7159	*TGV* 7097	
	⑥	Ⓐ	Ⓒ d		Ⓐ	†		Ⓐ	Ⓐ	Ⓑ	Ⓑ h	Ⓐ	Ⓐ	Ⓑ J	⑥ t		♥	G	Ⓐ	①–⑥ b		⑦ e	z	
Paris Nord 265 d.	...	...	...	1452	...	...	...	1652	...	...	1752	1822	...	1852	1852	...	...	1952	...	2052	...	2152	2221	...
Rouen 268 d.	...	...	...	|	...	...	...	|	...	...	|	|	...	|	|	1815	...	|	...	|	...	|	|	..
Amiens d.	1338	1438	...	|	1538	...	1638	|	...	1738	|	|	1838	|	|	1938	...	|	2038	|	...	|	|	..
Albert d.	1359	1459	...	|	1601	...	1659	|	...	1759	|	|	1859	|	|	1959	...	|	2058	|	...	|	|	..
Arras 265 a.	1423	1523	...	1541	1623	...	1723	1741	...	1823	1841	1911	1923	1941	1941	2023	...	2041	2122	2141	...	2241	2312	..
Arras d.	1424	1524	1523	1544	1624	1714	1724	1744	1817	1824	1844	...	1924	1944	1944	2024	2036	2044	2123	2147	...	2244	2318	..
Douai a.	1437	1537	1537	1559	1637	1733	1737	1759	|	1837	1859	...	1937	1959	1959	2037	2050	2059	2137	|	...	2259	|	..
Douai 257 ▶ d.	1439	1539	1539	1608	1639	1743	1739	1808	|	1839	1908	...	1939	2008	2008	2039	2053	2108	2139	|	...	2308	|	..
Valenciennes ▶ a.	|	|	|	1634	|	|	|	1834	|	|	1934	...	|	2034	2034	|	|	2134	|	|	...	2334	|	..
Lille Europe a.	|	|	|	...	|	|	|	...	1838	|	...	...	|	...	...	|	|	...	|	|	...	...	|	..
Lille Flandres 257 a.	1458	1558	1559	...	1658	1825	1758	...	...	1858	...	...	1958	...	...	2058	2112	...	2158	2210	...	...	2339	..

LILLE and VALENCIENNES - DOUAI - ARRAS - AMIENS and PARIS — 256

Lille - Paris: see **250**	*TGV* **7000** Ⓐ	*TGV* **7100** Ⓐ	Ⓐ	⑥	*TGV* **7102** Ⓐ	*TGV* **5110** ♥	⚒	Ⓐ J	*TGV* **7106** B	⑥	Ⓑ	*TGV* **7108** ⑦ e	Ⓐ J	⑥	Ⓐ	Ⓒ	*TGV* **7118** Ⓒ	Ⓐ	*TGV* **5226** ♥	⚒	†	*TGV* **7124** ①–⑥ b		*TGV* **7136** D	*TGV* **5222** ♥
Lille Flandres .... **257** d.	0551	...	0602	0602	...	0654	0702	0731	...	0802	0802	...	0902	0902	1002	1002	...	1102	1106	1202	1202	...	1302	...	1445
Lille Europe ....d.	|	...	|	|	...	|	|	|	...	|	|	...	|	|	|	|	...	|	|	|	|	...	|	...	|
Valenciennes .... ▶ d.	|	0548	|	|	0617	|	|	|	0717	|	|	0817	|	|	|	|	1017	|	|	|	|	1217	|	1417	|
Douai .... **257** ▶ a.	|	0614	0621	0621	0641	0713	0721	0753	0741	0821	0821	0841	0921	0921	1026	1021	1041	1121	1126	1221	1221	1241	1321	1441	1505
Douai ....d.	|	0626	0623	0623	0651	0716	0724	...	0751	0823	0823	0851	0923	0923	1028	1023	1051	1123	1129	1223	1223	1251	1323	1451	1508
Arras ....a.	0614	0644	0636	0635	0706	0729	0735	...	0807	0835	0835	0907	0936	0937	1042	1036	1106	1135	1144	1235	1236	1307	1335	1506	1523
Arras .... **265** d.	0617	0647	0637	0637	0717	...	0737	...	0817	0837	0837	0917	...	...	...	1038	1117	1137	...	1237	...	1317	1337	1517	...
Albert ....d.	|	|	0658	0701	|	...	0802	...	|	0901	0901	|	...	...	...	1101	|	1201	...	1301	...	|	1401	|	...
Amiens ....a.	|	|	0717	0721	|	...	0821	...	|	0921	0921	|	...	...	...	1121	|	1221	...	1321	...	|	1421	|	...
Rouen **268** ....a.	|	|	0832	...	|	...	...	...	|	1044	...	|	...	...	...	...	|	1346	...	...	...	|	...	|	...
Paris Nord .... **265** a.	0708	0738	...	...	0808	...	...	...	0908	...	...	1008	...	...	...	...	1208	...	...	...	...	1408	...	1608	...

		Ⓐ	*TGV* **7142** Ⓑ h	*TGV* **7342** ⑥ t	Ⓐ	⑥	◇ Ⓐ	*TGV* **7148** Ⓑ h	*TGV* **7348** ⑥ t	Ⓐ	Ⓐ	Ⓒ	◇ Ⓐ	Ⓐ	*TGV* **7154** ⑦ e	*TGV* **7154** ①–⑥ b	*TGV* **9846** ♥	†	Ⓐ	Ⓑ	⑥	*TGV* **7096** ①–⑥	*TGV* **7160** ⑦ e	Ⓐ	
Lille Flandres .... **257** d.	1602	1630	...	...	1702	1702	...	...	...	1731	1802	1802	...	1902	...	...	...	1935	2002	2102	2106	2120	...	2208	...
Lille Europe ....d.	|	|	...	...	|	|	1721	...	...	|	|	|	1851	|	...	...	2002	|	|	|	|	|	...	|	...
Valenciennes .... ▶ d.	|	|	1617	...	|	|	|	1717	...	|	|	|	|	|	1917	1920	|	|	|	|	|	|	2117	|	...
Douai .... **257** ▶ a.	1621	1650	1642	...	1721	1721	|	1741	...	1753	1821	1821	|	1921	1941	1946	|	2018	2021	2121	2136	|	2141	2243	...
Douai ....d.	1623	1658	1652	...	1723	1723	|	1751	...	...	1823	1823	|	1923	1951	1958	|	2023	2023	2123	2138	|	2151	2245	...
Arras ....a.	1635	1713	1706	...	1735	1736	1743	1807	...	...	1835	1835	1912	1935	2006	2014	2025	2037	2035	2138	2152	2142	2207	2259	...
Arras .... **265** d.	1637	...	1717	1717	1737	...	...	1817	1817	...	1837	1837	...	1937	2017	2017	...	...	2037	...	...	2147	2217	...	...
Albert ....d.	1702	...	|	|	1802	...	...	|	|	...	1859	1901	...	2003	|	|	...	...	2103	...	...	|	|	...	...
Amiens ....a.	1721	...	|	|	1821	...	...	|	|	...	1921	1921	...	2021	|	|	...	...	2121	...	...	|	|	...	...
Rouen **268** ....a.	...	...	|	|	1946	...	...	|	|	...	...	2046	...	...	|	|	...	...	...	...	...	|	|	...	...
Paris Nord .... **265** a.	...	...	1808	1808	...	...	...	1908	1908	...	...	...	...	...	2108	2108	...	...	...	...	...	2238	2308	...	...

– ①–⑥ to July 5; ① July 7 - Aug. 18 (also July 15; not July 14); ①–⑥ from Aug. 25.
– ⑥ (also ⑤ to July 4 / from Aug. 29), also Aug. 15.
– ⑥⑦ (also ⑤ to July 4 / from Aug. 29), also July 14.
– Daily to July 6; Ⓒ July 12 - Aug. 24; daily from Aug. 25.
– To July 4 / from Aug. 25.
– Not June 9, July 14, Nov. 11.

d – Not June 29, July 13, 27.
e – Also June 9, July 14, Nov. 11.
h – Not Aug. 15.
t – Also Aug. 15.
z – Depart 2208 Oct. 5, 12, 2218 Oct. 10, 11. Arrive Lille Europe June 2-6.
TGV – Ⓡ, supplement payable.

⊗ – Subject to alteration Oct. 6-10, Nov. 3-21.
◇ – TER à Grande Vitesse (via high-speed line). Supplement *Grande Vitesse* is payable (€3 per day).
♥ – For origin / destination see Table **11**.
★ – Paris - Arras via high-speed line is *179 km*.
▶ – Additional local trains runs Douai - Valenciennes (journey 30-40 mins).

LILLE - DOUAI - CAMBRAI - ST QUENTIN — 257

km		Ⓐ b	Ⓐ P	⑥ Pt	⑥	Ⓐ	† P	Ⓐ	⑥	⚒	Ⓐ	†	⑥	†	Ⓐ J	Ⓐ	⑥	Ⓐ	†	⑥	Ⓐ	⑥	⑥	Ⓐ	⚒
0	Lille Flandres ...... **256** d.	...	...	...	*0602*	0606	...	0706	0736	0806	*0902*r	0906	1006	1110	1136	1206	1206	1236	*1302*	*1302*	1332	1406	1506	1536	1606
34	Douai .... **256** a.	...	...	...	*0621*	0638	...	0738	0808	0838	*0921*r	0938	1038	1142	1208	1238	1238	1308	*1321*	*1321*	1405	1438	1538	1608	1638
34	Douai ....d.	...	...	...	0635	0640	...	0740	0811	0840	0940	0940	1040	1144	1211	1240	1240	1311	1331	1340	...	1440	1540	1611	1640
66	**Cambrai** Ville ....a.	...	...	...	0713	0713	...	0813	0844	0913	1013	1013	1113	1213	1244	1313	1313	1344	1401	1413	...	1513	1613	1643	1713
66	**Cambrai** Ville ....d.	0515	0623	0634	0714	0714	0734	0814	...	0914	...	1014	1114	...	1247	1314	1314	...	1402	...	...	1514	...	...	1714
82	Caudry ....d.	0528	0638	0648	0727	0727	0748	0827	...	0927	...	1027	1127	...	1300	1327	1327	...	1416	...	...	1527	...	...	1727
92	Busigny .... **255** d.	0539	0651	0700	0736	0737	0800	0837	...	0937	...	1036	1137	...	1310	1337	1338	...	1425	...	...	1537	...	...	1737
119	**St Quentin** .... **255** a.	0559	0705	0713	0757	0757	0814	0857	...	0957	...	1057	1157	...	...	1358	1358	...	...	...	...	1557	...	...	1757
	Paris Nord **255** ....a.	...	0829	0853	...	...	0953	...	...	...	...	...	...	...	...	...	...	...	...	...	...	...	...	...	...

	Ⓐ J	Ⓐ	†	Ⓐ	Ⓑ	⑥	Ⓐ	Ⓐ	⑥	Ⓐ d	⚒	†
…le Flandres .... **256** d.	1636	1706	1706	1736	1806	*1802*	1836	1906	1935	2006	2035	2135
…uai .... **256** a.	1708	1738	1738	1808	1838	*1821*	1908	1938	2017	2038	2118	2217
…uai ....d.	1711	1740	1740	1811	1840	1840	1911	1940	2019	2040	...	...
…mbrai Ville ....a.	1743	1813	1813	1843	1913	1913	1944	2013	2053	2113	...	...
…mbrai Ville ....d.	...	1814	1814	...	1914	1914	...	2014	2054	2114	...	...
…udry ....d.	...	1827	1827	...	1928	1927	...	2028	2109	2127	...	...
…signy .... **255** d.	...	1838	1837	...	1937	1937	...	2037	2119	2137	...	...
…Quentin .... **255** a.	...	1857	1857	...	1957	1957	...	2057	...	2157	...	...
…Paris Nord **255** ....a.	...	...	...	...	...	...	...	...	...	...	...	...

	Ⓐ	Ⓐ b	⑥	Ⓐ	⚒ k	Ⓐ	Ⓐ	⑥
Paris Nord **255** ....d.	...	...	...	...	...	...	...	...
St Quentin .... **255** d.	...	0505	...	...	0603	...	0705	...
Busigny .... **255** d.	...	0524	...	...	0623	...	0724	0725
Caudry ....d.	...	0533	...	...	0634	...	0732	0735
Cambrai Ville ....a.	...	0547	...	...	0646	...	0747	0747
Cambrai Ville ....d.	0506	0548	...	0617	0648	0717	0748	0748
Douai ....a.	0537	0620	...	0649	0720	0749	0820	0820
Douai .... **256** d.	*0542*	0622	0643	0652	0722	0752	0822	0822
Lille Flandres .... **256** a.	*0621*	0655	0725	0725	0755	0825	0855	0855

	Ⓐ	⚒	†	Ⓐ	⑥	Ⓐ	Ⓐ	†	⑥	Ⓐ	⑥	†	Ⓐ J	Ⓐ	⑥	Ⓒ	Ⓐ	†		P	Ⓐ	⑥	†	⑥	◇
…Paris Nord **255** ....d.	...	...	...	...	...	...	...	...	...	...	...	...	...	...	...	...	...	...	...	1737	...	...	...	...	...
…Quentin .... **255** d.	...	0805	...	0905	1005	...	1205	1205	1205	...	1406	...	...	1605	1605	...	...	1703	1805	1852	1906	...	1905	2005	2105
…signy .... **255** d.	...	0824	...	0924	1025	...	1225	1223	1225	1338	1425	1434	...	1624	1625	...	...	1723	1824	1909	1925	...	1925	2025	2126
…udry ....d.	...	0833	...	0933	1034	...	1234	1232	1235	1349	1435	1443	...	1634	1634	...	...	1734	1833	1919	1936	...	1934	2034	2137
…mbrai Ville ....a.	...	0847	...	0947	1047	...	1247	1245	1247	1407	1447	1455	...	1647	1647	...	...	1747	1847	1933	1948	...	1947	2048	2149
…mbrai Ville ....d.	0818	0848	0848	...	1048	1148	1248	1246	1248	1417	1448	1456	1548	1648	1648	1717	1748	1748	1848	...	1949	1948	1948	...	...
…uai ....a.	0849	0920	0920	...	1120	1220	1320	1319	1320	1449	1520	1529	1619	1720	1720	1749	1820	1820	1920	...	2020	2020	2020	...	...
…uai .... **256** d.	...	0922	0922	...	1122	1222	1322	1322	*1339*	*1539*	1522	*1539*	*1639*	1722	*1739*	1752	1822	1822	1923	...	2022	2022	*2039*	...	...
…e Flandres .... **256** a.	...	0955	0955	...	1155	1255	1355	1355	*1358*	*1558*	1555	*1559*	*1658*	1755	*1758*	1831	1855	1855	1955	...	2055	2055	*2058*	...	...

– To July 4 / from Aug. 25.
– For train numbers see Table **255**.
– Not June 16 - Sept. 19 Cambrai - St Quentin or v.v.
– Not June 1 - Oct. 10 Cambrai - St Quentin.

k – Not June 1 - Aug. 24 St Quentin - Cambrai.
r – To July 4 / from Aug. 25.
t – Also Aug. 15; not Nov. 1.
◇ – Subject to alteration.

Engineering work July 5 - Aug. 24
There will be no rail service Cambrai - St Quentin or v.v.
Services are subject to alteration Nov. 22-30.

AMIENS - ST QUENTIN — 258

…m		Ⓐ	Ⓐ J	⑥	†	⚒ b		Ⓐ	Ⓐ		Ⓐ
0	**Amiens** ....d.	0642	0742	0742	1042	1242	...	1642	1742	1842	1942
…59	Ham (Somme) ....d.	0717	0817	0817	1116	1317	...	1717	1817	1917	2017
…76	**St Quentin** ....a.	0737	0838	0838	1137	1337	...	1737	1837	1937	2037

	Ⓐ	⚒	Ⓐ b	†	⚒ J §		Ⓐ	⚒	†	
St Quentin ....d.	0622	0722	0822	0922	1222	...	1722	1822	2022	...
Ham (Somme) ....d.	0644	0744	0844	0944	1244	...	1744	1844	2045	...
Amiens ....a.	0721	0818	0918	1018	1318	...	1818	1918	2121	...

– To July 12 / from Aug. 25.
b – Subject to alteration Oct. 27-31.
§ – Subject to alteration Oct. 27-31, Nov. 17 - Dec. 5.

🚌 CALAIS - DUNKERQUE - DE PANNE — 259

🚌 TER/BCD	⚒	Ⓐ‡	Ⓐ	⑥‡	Ⓐ‡	Ⓐ	⚒‡	Ⓐ‡	⚒	Ⓐ‡	⑥‡	Ⓐ‡	Ⓐ‡	Ⓐ‡	Ⓐ	Ⓐ‡	Ⓐ‡	Ⓐ‡
…ulogne Ville ....d.	...	0620	...	...	...	...	...	...	...	...	...	...	...	...	...	...	...	...
…ais Ville △ ....d.	0530	0700	0705	0720	0730	0725	0820	0850	1220	1235	1255	1320	1630	1700	1716	1800	1830	1930
…nkerque △ ....a.	0708	0740	0742	0755	0820	0830	0855	0927	1345	1310	1330	1405	1705	1735	1854	1835	1905	2005
…nkerque Pôle Marine ... a.	...	0745	...	0800	0825	...	0900	0932	...	1315	1335	1410	1710	1740	...	1840	1910	2010

🚌 TER/BCD	⚒	Ⓐ‡	Ⓐ‡	⑥‡	Ⓐ	Ⓐ‡	Ⓐ‡	⚒	⑥	Ⓐ‡	⑥‡	Ⓐ‡	Ⓐ‡	Ⓐ	Ⓐ‡	Ⓐ	Ⓐ‡	
…nkerque Pôle Marine ... d.	...	0640	0700	0714	...	0804	0840	...	...	1320	1335	1644	1734	...	1839	...	1940	...
…nkerque △ ....d.	0620	0644	0704	0718	0730	0807	0843	1211	1320	1324	1338	1648	1738	1740	1842	1855	1943	...
…ais Ville △ ....a.	0737	0728	0750	0800	0823	0845	0920	1343	1421	1405	1415	1730	1820	1918	1920	2000	2020	...
…logne Ville ....a.	...	...	...	...	...	0925	...	...	...	...	1450	...	...	...	...	...	...	...

DUNKERQUE - DE PANNE (Summer)
Ⓒ May - Sept. (daily July / Aug).
Subject to confirmation
Operator DK'BUS. Journey 40 minutes. Connects at De Panne Esplanade with coastal tram (Table **406**). Through fares.
From Dunkerque Gare 0930, 1030, 1530, 1630, 1730, 1830. From De Panne Esplanade 1030, 1130, 1630, 1730, 1830, 1930.

DUNKERQUE - ADINKERKE (DE PANNE STATION) Operator DK'BUS Marine (route 2). Journey 40-50 minutes. Connects at De Panne station with coastal tram service (Table **406**).
…m Dunkerque Gare: ⚒: 0604, 0705, 0804, 0906, 1005, 1106, 1159 and approx hourly until 2008. †: 0758, 0857, 0953, 1053, 1153, 1257, 1354, 1453, 1553, 1653, 1753, 1852, 1952.
…m Adinkerke (De Panne station): ⚒ : 0715 and hourly to 2015, 2111. †: 0915 and hourly to 2015, 2112.

Operated by Ligne BCD (rail tickets valid). No service on †.
△ – Adjacent to rail station.
Rail service Calais - Dunkerque is currently suspended.

260 PARIS - AMIENS

km		12001	2003	2003		12005	12007	2007		2009			12011			2013		12015			2017			12019	
		Ⓐ	Ⓐ	⑥	⑥	Ⓐ	⚒	†			⚒	†	⚒	†	⑥			Ⓐ	Ⓑ	⑥		Ⓒ	Ⓐ	Ⓑh	Ⓐ
0	**Paris** Nord d.	0628	0658	0658	0710	0728	0828	0828	0910	1004	1110	1110	1228	1228	1307	1404	...	1604	1610	1628	1701	1710	1728	1801	1807
51	Creil d.	0656	0729	0729	0744	0756	0856	0856	0943	|	1143	1143	1256	1256	1345	|	...	|	1643	1656	|	1743	1756	|	1843
66	Clermont-de-l'Oise d.	0707	|	|	0800	0807	0907	0907	0959	|	1159	1159	|	1307	1400	|	...	|	1659	1706	|	1759	1807	|	1859
81	St Just en Chaussée d.	0718	|	|	0814	0818	0918	0918	1013	|	1212	1212	|	1318	1413	|	...	|	1712	1718	|	1813	1817	|	1913
126	Longueau d.	0741	0805	0805	0845	0841	0941	0941	1044	1105	...	1244	1332	1342	1441	1505	...	1705	...	1743	1805	1844	1841	1905	1951
131	**Amiens** a.	0747	0810	0810	0850	0847	0947	0947	1049	1110	...	1249	1338	1347	1446	1510	...	1710	...	1749	1810	1849	1847	1910	1957
	Boulogne **261** a.	...	0946	0958	...	...	...	1136	...	1254	...	...	...	...	...	1646	...	...	...	...	1958	...	...	...	...

		2021		12023		12025	12027			
	⚒		†	Ⓐ	⑥	Ⓐ			Ⓐ	†
Paris Nord d.	1828	1904	1910	1928	1928	2004	2028	2128	2228	2228
Creil d.	1856	|	1943	|	1956	|	2056	2204	2300	2301
Clermont-de-l'Oise d.	1907	|	1959	2007	2008	|	2107	2220	2312	2312
St Just en Chaussée d.	1917	|	2011	2018	2018	|	2118	2229	2323	2323
Longueau d.	1941	2005	2043	2041	2042	2105	2141	2258	2347	2349
Amiens a.	1947	2010	2049	2047	2047	2110	2147	2303	2353	2355
Boulogne **261** a.	...	2158	...	...	...	2258z	...	...	...	...

		12002			12004		2006	12008	
	⚒	Ⓐ	⚒	†	Ⓐ	⑥	†	⑥t	
Boulogne **261** d.	...	...	...	...	...	...	0501	...	...
Amiens d.	0509	0548	0600	0610	0614	0614	0650	0650	0714
Longueau d.	0516	0556	0607	0617	0621	0621	0657	0657	0721
St Just en Chaussée d.	0547	|	0648	0648	0645	0645	|	|	0744
Clermont-de-l'Oise d.	0600	|	0701	0701	0656	0656	|	|	0756
Creil d.	0617	|	0718	0718	|	0707	|	|	0807
Paris Nord a.	0650	0656	0750	0750	0732	0732	0756	0756	0832

	12010	12012	2014			12016		2018		12020		2022			2024	12026	2028	12030	2032	2032		12034	2036		
	Ⓐ	Ⓐ		Ⓐ	Ⓒ	⚒	Ⓐ		Ⓐ	⚒	Ⓑ	⚒	Ⓐ	Ⓒ			†	Ⓐ	Ⓒ	Ⓐ	Ⓒ	Ⓐ	†	†	Ⓐ
Boulogne **261** d.	...	...	0704	...	...	...	...	1012	...	...	...	1412	...	...	1512	...	1604	...	1704	1712	...	...	1904	...	...
Amiens d.	0750	0814	0850	...	0909	1014	1114	1150	...	1323	1514	1550	...	1609	1650	1714	1750	1814	1850	1850	1913	2014	2050	2114	2208
Longueau d.	0757	0821	0857	...	0916	1021	1121	1157	...	1330	1521	1557	...	1616	1657	1721	1757	1821	1857	1857	1920	2021	2057	2121	2215
St Just en Chaussée d.	|	0845	|	0947	0947	1045	1144	|	1247	|	1544	|	1647	1647	|	1745	|	1845	|	|	1943	2045	|	2145	2238
Clermont-de-l'Oise d.	|	0856	|	1001	1001	1056	1156	|	1301	|	1556	|	1701	1701	|	1756	|	1856	|	|	1954	2056	|	2156	2249
Creil d.	|	0907	|	1017	1018	1107	1207	|	1317	1407	1607	|	1717	1718	|	1807	|	1907	|	|	2005	2107	|	2207	2301
Paris Nord a.	0856	0932	0956	1050	1050	1132	1232	1256	1350	1432	1632	1656	1750	1750	1756	1832	1856	1932	1956	1956	2032	2132	2156	2232	2332

h – Not Aug. 15.
t – Also Aug. 15.
z – For days of running see Table **261**.

On Nov. 1 service is as on ⑦

261 AMIENS - BOULOGNE - CALAIS

For *TGV* service Paris - Étaples / Boulogne / Calais see Table **265**. Faster services Paris - Calais are available by changing at Lille (Tables **250** / **266**) or Hazebrouck (Tables **264** / **266**).

km												2003	2003			2007						2009			
		Ⓐ	⚒	Ⓐ	Ⓐ	⚒	Ⓐ	†	⚒	⚒	Ⓐz	Ⓐ	⑥	†	⑥	†	Ⓐ	†	⑥	⚒	†		⚒	†	Ⓒ
	Paris Nord **260** d.	...	...	...	...	...	...	...	...	...	...	0658	0658	...	...	0828	...	...	...	...	...	1004	...	...	...
0	**Amiens** d.	...	...	...	...	...	0624	...	0724	...	...	0823	0823	...	0923	1000	...	1019	...	...	...	1123	...	...	...
45	Abbeville d.	...	...	...	...	...	0659	...	0759	...	...	0851	0851	...	0955	1028	...	1053	...	...	...	1149	...	...	...
58	Noyelles sur Mer d.	...	...	...	...	...	0707	...	0807	...	...	|	0903	...	1004	1040	...	1102	...	...	...	1200	...	...	...
85	Rang du Fliers ⊙ d.	...	0552a	...	...	...	0724	...	0824	...	...	0915	0926	...	1023	1104	⊖	1121	⊖	...	...	1221	...	△	...
96	Étaples-Le Touquet § d.	...	0600a	0630	...	0700	0732	...	0832	...	...	0926	0938	...	1031	1116	1121	1129	1131	1201t	...	1233	1251a	1349	...
123	**Boulogne** Ville § a.	...	0626a	0647	...	0726	0758	...	0847	...	...	0946	0958	...	1046	1136	1146	1144	1156	1227t	...	1254	1309a	1408	...
123	**Boulogne** Ville d.	0547	0627	0648	0711	0727	0803	0811	0849	0911	0947	...	...	1045	1048	...	1148	1146	1207	1227	1247	...	1311	1410	144
130	Wimille-Wimereux d.	0555	0635	0656	0719	0735	0812	0819	0856	0919	0955	...	...	1053	1056	...	1156	1155	1214	1235	1255	...	1319	|	145
140	Marquise-Rinxent d.	0603	0642	0703	0727	0743	0820	0827	0904	0928	1003	...	...	1102	1103	...	1203	1203	1222	1243	1303	...	1327	1421	150
157	Calais Fréthun **265** d.	0615	0700	0714	0739	0801	0831	0839	0915	0939	1015	...	...	1114	1114	...	1214	1215	1240	1302	1314	...	1339	1433	151
165	**Calais** Ville **265** a.	0622	0711	0722	0748	0810	0840	0848	0922	0948	1022	...	...	1121	1121	...	1221	1222	1248	1310	1321	...	1348	1440	152

		▷			2013													2017						2021	202
	⑥	⚒	Ⓐ	†		⑥	⑥	Ⓐ	Ⓐ	†	Ⓐ	Ⓐ	⑥u	Ⓐ	†	⚒	Ⓐ		⑥	Ⓐ	Ⓐ	†	†		G
Paris Nord **260** d.	...	...	...	...	1404	...	...	...	...	...	...	...	...	...	...	...	...	1701	...	...	...	...	...	1904	200
Amiens d.	...	1424	...	...	1523	...	...	...	...	...	1624	...	...	...	...	1724	...	1823	...	...	1924	1924	...	2023	212
Abbeville d.	...	1459	...	...	1551	...	...	...	...	...	1659	...	...	...	...	1758	...	1852	...	...	1959	1957	...	2052	215
Noyelles sur Mer d.	...	1507	...	...	|	...	...	...	...	...	1707	...	...	...	...	1808	...	1904	...	...	2007	2006	...	2105	220
Rang du Fliers ⊙ d.	...	1523	...	...	1615	...	...	1643	...	...	1724	1728r	...	⊖	1821	1827	⊖	1927	...	⊖	2024	2025	⊖	2128	222
Étaples-Le Touquet § d.	1451	1530	...	...	1626	1630	...	1651	1701	...	1732	1736r	...	1824	1829	1836	1922	1938	...	2024	2031	2033	2036	2139	223
Boulogne Ville § a.	1509	...	...	...	1646	1650	...	1709	1726	...	1746	1758	...	1839	1846	1857	1946	1958	...	2040	...	2047	2054	2158	225
Boulogne Ville d.	1511	...	1611	1647	...	1652	1708	1711	1727	1744	1748	1809	1811	1840	1848	1859	1948	...	2011	2043	...	2049	2056	...	...
Wimille-Wimereux d.	1519	...	1619	1655	...	1659	1716	1719	1735	1751	1756	1818	1819	1848	1856	1907	1956	...	2019	2051	...	2057	2107	...	...
Marquise-Rinxent d.	1527	...	1627	1703	...	1707	1724	1727	1743	1758	1804	1827	1827	1856	1903	1915	2004	...	2027	2058	...	2104	2114	...	...
Calais Fréthun **265** d.	1539	...	1638	1714	...	1717	1735	1739	1802	1809	1815	1840	1839	1914	1914	1929	2015	...	2039	2110	...	2114	2126	...	...
Calais Ville **265** a.	1548	...	1648	1721	...	1724	1741	1748	1810	1818	1822	1849	1848	1922	1921	1937	2022	...	2048	2118	...	2121	2134	...	...

	2006			2014											2018									2022	
	Ⓐ	Ⓐ	⚒		Ⓐ	⑥	Ⓐ	Ⓐ	Ⓐ	Ⓐ	⑥	†	⑥	Ⓐ		Ⓐ	Ⓐ	Ⓒ	⑥	⚒	Ⓐ	⑥	Ⓒ	⚒	⚒
Calais Ville **265** d.	...	0525	0612	...	0648	0647	0712	0738	0748	0806	0812	0839	0912	0929	...	...	1012	1112	...	1148	1216	1239	1312	...	13
Calais Fréthun **265** d.	...	0533	0622	...	0659	0657	0724	0746	0758	0815	0821	0847	0922	0940	...	...	1024	1121	...	1157	1225	1246	1321	...	13
Marquise-Rinxent d.	...	0545	0634	...	0717	0715	0736	0757	0816	0826	0832	0857	0933	0951	...	...	1036	1133	...	1216	1244	1257	1332	...	13
Wimille-Wimereux d.	...	0553	0641	...	0725	0723	0743	0805	0823	0834	0839	0905	0940	0958	...	...	1043	1140	...	1224	1252	1305	1340	...	14
Boulogne Ville a.	...	0600	0648	...	0732	0731	0750	0812	0832	0840	0846	0912	0948	1005	...	...	1051	1148	...	1231	1259	1311	1348	...	14
Boulogne Ville § d.	0501	0602	...	0704	0733	...	0752	0814	...	0841	0910	0913	...	1006	1012	...	...	...	1220	1233	1300	1312	...	1412	...
Étaples-Le Touquet § d.	0522	0618	...	0724	0759	...	0809	0829	...	0859	0929	0928	...	1022	1033	...	...	...	1238	1259	1315	1328	...	1433	...
Rang du Fliers ⊙ d.	0533	0626	...	0734	...	...	...	0837	...	⊖	0938	0937	...	1031	1043	...	...	...	1245	⊖	1323	1336	...	1443	...
Noyelles sur Mer d.	0555	0646	...	0757	...	...	...	0855	...	...	0955	0955	...	1049	|	←	...	...	...	...	...	1353	...	|	...
Abbeville d.	0608	0657	...	0809	...	...	...	0904	...	...	1005	1004	...	1058	1109	1121	...	...	...	...	...	1403	...	1509	...
Amiens a.	0636	0736	...	0836	...	...	...	0936	...	...	1037	1036	...	→	1136	1205	...	...	...	...	...	1437	...	1536	...
Paris Nord **260** a.	0756	...	...	0956	...	...	...	...	...	...	...	...	...	...	1256	...	...	...	...	...	...	...	...	1656	...

	2024			2028					2032	2032							2036							
	†	Ⓐ	⑥	†	⚒z	†	Ⓐ	⑥	Ⓒ	Ⓐ	Ⓐ	Ⓐ	†	⚒	Ⓐ	Ⓒ	†	Ⓐ	Ⓐ		†	⑥	Ⓐ	Ⓒ
Calais Ville **265** d.	...	1439	1512	...	1538	1610	1612	1612	...	...	1648	1712	1712	1738	1748	1807	...	1831	1928	...	2008	2012	2042	2212
Calais Fréthun **265** d.	...	1447	1521	...	1546	1619	1624	1622	...	...	1657	1721	1720	1746	1758	1817	...	1841	1939	...	2017	2021	2049	2221
Marquise-Rinxent d.	...	1458	1532	...	1557	1631	1634	1633	...	...	1717	1733	1731	1757	1818	1830	...	1852	1951	...	2028	2033	2100	2233
Wimille-Wimereux d.	...	1506	1540	...	1605	1638	1641	1641	...	...	1725	1740	1739	1805	1825	1839	...	1900	1959	...	2036	2041	2108	2240
Boulogne Ville a.	...	1514	1548	...	1612	1645	1651	1649	...	...	1732	1748	1746	1812	1832	1847	...	1907	2006	...	2044	2048	2114	2248
Boulogne Ville § d.	1512	...	...	1604	1614	1646	1652	...	1704	1712	1733	...	1747	1813	1833	...	1904	1908	...	...	...	...	2115	...
Étaples-Le Touquet § d.	1533	...	...	1624	1629	1704	1709	...	1724	1733	1758	...	1802	1830	1859	...	1926	1926	...	...	...	...	2131	...
Rang du Fliers ⊙ d.	1543	...	...	1634	1638	△	1717	...	1734	1743	⊖	...	⊖	1839	...	...	1935	...	...	...	...	...	2138	...
Noyelles sur Mer d.	|	...	...	1657	1656	...	...	...	1757	|	...	...	...	1856	...	...	1956	...	...	...	...	...	...	...
Abbeville d.	1609	...	...	1709	1706	...	...	...	1809	1809	...	...	...	1905	...	...	2009	...	...	...	...	...	...	...
Amiens a.	1636	...	...	1736	1736	...	...	...	1836	1836	...	...	...	1936	...	...	2036	...	...	...	...	...	...	...
Paris Nord **260** a.	1756	...	...	1856	...	...	...	...	1956	1956	...	...	...	...	...	...	2156	...	...	...	...	...	...	...

ALSO:	⚒	⚒◇	⚒◇‡	†	Ⓐ	⚒	Ⓐ		⚒	Ⓑ	‡
Amiens d.	0654	0721	0821	0854	0924	1054	1224	1254	1554	1654	1854
Abbeville a.	0738	0806	0906	0937	0958	1137	1258	1337	1639	1739	1937

	⑥	⚒b	Ⓐ	†		Ⓐ	⚒	Ⓐ	Ⓑ‡	⑥‡	
Abbeville d.	0604	0642	0745	0923	1221	1308	1621	1721	1821	2002	21
Amiens a.	0637	0725	0818	1008	1306	1342	1706	1806	1906	2037	21

G – ⑤ June 20 - Sept. 12 (also June 6, Aug. 14, Oct. 31, Nov. 7).
a – Ⓐ only.
b – Not on ⑥ July 20 - Aug. 23.
r – To July 4 / from Aug. 25.
t – ⑥ only.
u – Additional train runs on ⑥ July 5 - Aug. 23 non-stop Boulogne (d. 1756) - Calais (a. 1831) - Lille (Table **266**).

z – Runs up to 7 mins earlier Calais - Boulogne or v. v. June 10 - 28 and from Nov. 12.
△ – To / from Lille via Bethune and St Pol (Table **263**).
▷ – Terminates at Abbeville on Ⓐ Sept. 22 - Oct. 10.
◇ – From Le Tréport (Table **261a**).
⊖ – To / from Arras (Table **263**).
⊙ – Rang du Fliers-Verton-Berck.

§ – See also Table **263**.
‡ – Not July 13 - Aug. 24.

Amiens - Calais and v.v.: timings may vary by up to 4 minutes June 10 - 28 and from Nov. 11. On Nov. 1 service is as on ⑦.

ABBEVILLE - LE TRÉPORT 261a

km																
		🚌	🚌 ⚒	⑦L	🚌 †	⑦L	⑥K	🚌 †	🚌	🚌 ⚒	🚌 Ⓐ	⑥	Ⓑ	🚌 ⑥	⚒b	🚌 ⑤
	Laon 252 d.	...	...	...	...	0821	0826	...	...	...	...	...	...	...	...	...
	Amiens 261 d.	...	...	0847	...	|	0941	...	...	...	...	...	...	...	...	...
0	Abbeville d.	0641	0900	0917	0947	1002	1009	1102	1157	1347	1557	1600	1745	1807	1856	2057
37	Le Tréport a.	0745	1007	0950	1053	1036	1042	1207	1303	1453	1703	1646	1836	1910	1943	2201

	⚒	⚒J	🚌 Ⓐ	🚌	🚌 Ⓐz	🚌 ⑥	🚌 †	🚌 Ⓐ	🚌 ⑥	🚌 Ⓑ	🚌 ⑥		⑥K	⑦L	⑦L	
Le Tréport d.	0628	0738	0752	0953	1152	1205	1555	1607	1657	1707	1752	...	1805	1841	1927	...
Abbeville a.	0718	0818	0854	1059	1258	1309	1659	1711	1759	1811	1854	...	1838	1914	2000	...
Amiens 261 a.	0806	0906	...	...	...	...	...	...	...	...	...	...	1904	|	2029	...
Laon 252 a.	...	...	...	...	...	...	...	...	...	...	...	...	2030	2110	...	...

J – To July 12/from Aug. 25.
K – ⑥ July 5 - Aug. 30.
L – ⑦ July 6 - Aug. 31 (also July 14, Aug. 15).
b – By 🚌 (arrive 2016) on Ⓐ July 15 - Aug. 22.
z – On ③ Le Tréport d. 1205, Abbeville a. 1309.

On Nov. 1 service is as on ⑦.

LILLE - VALENCIENNES - MAUBEUGE and CHARLEVILLE MÉZIÈRES 262

km																											
		⑥	⚒ w	Ⓐ	Ⓐ J	Ⓐ	⑥	Ⓐ	Ⓐ J	⑥	⑥	Ⓐ ⊕	Ⓐ ⊕‡	⑥	Ⓐ ⊕‡	Ⓐ ⊕‡	Ⓒ	† ev	⑥ w	† e	†	Ⓐ ⊕‡	⑥	Ⓐ ⊕§	Ⓐ ⊕‡	⑥	⑥
0	Lille Flandres ▷ d.	0535	0535	...	0535	0635	0635	0705	0735	0735	...	0805	0835	0835	0905	0935	0935	...	...	1135	...	1201	1201	1235	...	1235	1305
48	Valenciennes ▷ d.	0621	0619	...	0619	0719	0721	0750	0820	0821	...	0850	0920	0921	0950	1020	1021	...	...	1221	...	1231	1232	1321	...	1321	1349
82	Aulnoye Aymeries a.	0649	0649	...	0649	0749	0750	0816	0849	0849	...	0916	0949	0949	1016	1049	1049	...	...	1249	...	1253	1253	1349	...	1349	1415
82	Aulnoye Aymeries d.	0652	0701	...	0710	0801	0801	0818	0901	0852	0901	0918	1001	0952	1018	1101	1052	1101	1101	1301	1258	1255	1255	1355	1401	1401	1417
94	**Maubeuge** a.	0702	|	...	0724	|	|	0830	|	0904	|	0929	|	1004	1030	|	1105	|	|	|	1310	1304	1303	1405	|	|	1430
104	Jeumont a.	0710	|	...	0735	|	|	0839	|	0912	|	0939	|	1012	1039	|	1112	|	|	|	1320	...	1312	1413	|	|	1442
94	Avesnes d.	...	0717	...	...	0817	0817	...	0918	...	0917	...	1013	...	...	1113	...	1111	1117	1312	...	...	...	...	1412	1411	...
123	Hirson a.	...	0746	0753	...	0846	0844	...	0946	...	0945	...	1038	...	...	1138	...	1134	1145	1336	...	...	...	...	1438	1434	...
184	**Charleville-Mézières** a.	...	...	0833	...	...	0925	...	...	...	...	...	...	...	...	1222*	...	1215	...	...	...	...	...	...	...	1524	...

	Ⓐ ⊕§	†	† e	Ⓐ ⊕‡	⚒	⚒	Ⓐ	Ⓐ	Ⓒ	Ⓐ	Ⓐ	† v	⑥	Ⓐ	Ⓐ	Ⓐ J	Ⓐ		Ⓒ v	†	Ⓐ	⑥	Ⓐ	Ⓐ	△	E	Ⓐ △
Lille Flandres ▷ d.	1335	1335	...	...	1435	...	1535	1605	1635	1701	1635	...	...	1731	1801	1831	...	1835	...	...	1901	...	1935	...	2035	...	2135
Valenciennes ▷ d.	1421	1418	...	...	1521	...	1619	1650	1721	1731	1720	...	...	1802	1831	1902	...	1920	...	...	1931	...	2021	...	2121	...	2221
Aulnoye Aymeries a.	1449	1447	...	...	1549	...	1649	1716	1749	1753	1749	...	...	|	1853	|	...	1949	...	...	1953	...	2049	...	2149	...	2249
Aulnoye Aymeries d.	1455	1452	1452	1501	1555	1601	1701	1718	1752	1755	1801	1801	1801	|	1855	|	...	2001	...	1958	1955	2017	2055	2101	2155	2201	2254
Maubeuge a.	1505	1504	|	|	1605	|	|	1731	1803	1803	|	|	|	|	1903	|	...	|	...	2012	2003	2028	2105	|	2205	|	2304
Jeumont a.	1513	1512	|	|	1612	|	|	1744	1812	1812	|	|	|	|	1912	|	...	|	...	2024	2012	2042	2113	|	2213	|	2312
Avesnes d.	...	...	1503	1512	...	1612	1713	...	...	...	1813	1811	1817	1827	...	1929	...	2012	...	...	...	...	...	2113	...	2212	...
Hirson a.	...	...	1527	1538	...	1645	1738	...	...	...	1838	1834	1844	1846	...	1950	1955	2038	2041	...	...	...	...	2138	...	2238	...
Charleville-Mézières a.	...	...	...	...	...	...	...	...	...	...	...	1915	...	1924	...	...	2033	...	2119	...	...	...	...	...	...	...	...

	Ⓐ	Ⓐ J	Ⓐ J	⚒	Ⓐ	⚒	Ⓐ		Ⓐ	⚒	⚒	Ⓐ	Ⓒ w	Ⓑ	⑥	Ⓐ	Ⓐ ⊕‡	Ⓐ ⊕‡	⑥	† Je	Ⓒ	Ⓐ ⊕‡	Ⓐ ⊕§	⑥ w	⑥	Ⓐ ⊕§	Ⓐ ⊕‡
Charleville-Mézières d.	...	...	...	...	...	...	0624	...	...	...	...	...	...	...	...	...	...	...	0939	...	...	1043*	...	...	...	...	...
Hirson d.	...	...	0613	...	...	0616	0713	...	...	0716	...	0816	0827	...	...	0925	...	...	1027	1101	...	1127	...	1200	...	...	1216
Avesnes d.	...	...	0634	...	...	0644	0735	...	...	0744	...	0844	0851	...	...	0951	...	...	1050	1125	...	1151	...	1225	...	...	1243
Jeumont d.	0520	0549	|	0615	0648	|	|	0715	0749	|	0820	|	|	0849	0922	|	0948	1049	|	|	1122	|	1149	|	1218	...	|
Maubeuge d.	0529	0558	|	0629	0656	|	|	0730	0758	|	0829	|	|	0857	0930	|	0956	1057	|	|	1130	|	1157	|	1231	1235	|
Aulnoye Aymeries a.	0541	0606	|	0641	0704	0659	|	0741	0806	0800	0841	0900	0900	0907	0942	1000	1008	1107	1059	1135	1142	1200	1207	1235	1242	1252	1258
Aulnoye Aymeries d.	0543	0608	|	0643	0706	0709	|	0743	0808	0811	0843	...	...	0911	0944	...	1011	1111	1113	...	1144	...	1211	...	1244	...	1311
Valenciennes ▷ d.	0612	0631	0700	0711	0728	0740	0800	0811	0831	0841	0911	...	...	0941	1013	...	1041	1141	1143	...	1210	...	1241	...	1313	...	1341
Lille Flandres ▷ a.	0655	0659	0729	0755	0759	0825	0829	0855	0859	0925	0955	...	...	1025	1055	...	1125	1225	1225	...	1252	...	1325	...	1355	...	1425

	⑥	⑦	† ev	†	Ⓐ J⊕‡	Ⓐ ⊕‡	⚒ ⊕		Ⓐ	Ⓐ	Ⓐ	† v	⑥	Ⓒ	Ⓐ	Ⓐ	Ⓐ	†	†	Ⓐ	Ⓐ	†	† v	⑥	⑥	Ⓐ z	Ⓐ △
Charleville-Mézières d.	1140	...	1320	...	...	...	...	...	...	...	...	1627	...	...	...	...	...	...	...	1841	...	...	1940	...	1937	2055	...
Hirson d.	1227	1227	1358	...	1425	...	1525	...	...	1616	...	1718	1726	...	1715	1815	...	1901	...	1925	...	...	2027	...	2127	2131	...
Avesnes d.	1250	1250	1425	...	1451	...	1551	...	...	1644	...	1744	1749	...	1745	1845	...	1926	...	1951	...	...	2050	...	2150	2156	...
Jeumont d.	|	|	|	1418	|	...	|	1549	1620	|	1715	|	|	1748	|	|	1849	|	1917	|	1949	2048	|	2141	|	|	2148
Maubeuge d.	|	|	|	1429	|	...	|	1557	1629	|	1733	|	|	1756	|	|	1857	|	1930	|	1957	2056	|	2149	|	|	2156
Aulnoye Aymeries a.	1259	1259	1435	1442	1500	...	1600	1607	1641	1700	1741	1759	1759	1807	1800	1900	1907	1935	1946	2000	2007	2107	2059	2159	2159	2205	2207
Aulnoye Aymeries d.	1313	1313	...	1444	...	1511	...	1611	1643	1711	1743	...	...	1809	1811	...	1910	...	1948	...	2010	...	2113	...	2213	...	2213
Valenciennes ▷ d.	1342	1343	...	1513	...	1541	...	1641	1711	1741	1811	...	...	1843	1841	...	1941	...	2013	...	2041	...	2142	...	2243	...	2243
Lille Flandres ▷ a.	1425	1425	...	1555	...	1625	...	1725	1755	1825	1855	...	...	1925	1925	...	2025	...	2055	...	2125	...	2225	...	2325	...	2325

ADDITIONAL TRAINS LILLE - VALENCIENNES

	Ⓐ J	Ⓐ	Ⓐ	Ⓐ	Ⓒ	Ⓐ	Ⓐ	†	Ⓐ	⑥	Ⓐ J		Ⓐ	Ⓐ	†	⑥	Ⓐ		Ⓐ J	Ⓒ	Ⓐ	Ⓒ	Ⓐ		
Lille Flandres d.	0513	0813	0913	1013	1035	1113	1213	1235	1313	1335	1413	...	1613	1713	1735	1740	1813	...	1913	1935	2013	2135	2235	...	...
Valenciennes a.	0555	0855	0953	1055	1125	1201	1255	1325	1355	1417	1455	...	1655	1755	1819	1830	1855	...	1955	2025	2055	2225	2323	...	...

	⑥	Ⓐ	Ⓐ J	Ⓐ	Ⓐ J	Ⓐ		Ⓐ	†	Ⓐ	⑥	Ⓐ J		⑥	Ⓐ	†	Ⓐ	Ⓒ	Ⓐ J		Ⓐ	Ⓐ	⑥		
Valenciennes d.	0435	0440	0604	0705	0805	0905	...	1105	1137	1205	1230	1305	...	1531	1605	1606	1705	1728	1805	...	1904	2005	2006	...	...
Lille Flandres a.	0526	0527	0647	0747	0847	0947	...	1147	1227	1247	1321	1347	...	1621	1647	1656	1747	1821	1847	...	1947	2047	2057	...	...

E – Ⓒ (daily to July 6/from Aug. 23).
J – To July 4/from Aug. 25.
e – Not June 9.
v – On June 8 subject to alteration Hirson - Charleville and v.v.
w – Will not run on ⑥ July 5 - Aug. 23.

z – Subject to alteration Nov. 17-21.
▷ – For additional trains see panel below main table.
△ – Subject to alteration on Ⓐ Nov. 17-28.
⊕ – Subject to alteration east of Valenciennes on Ⓐ May 5 - June 27.

‡ – Subject to alteration from Oct. 27.
§ – Subject to alteration Sept. 29 - Dec. 5.
* – Subject to alteration Sept. 8-19.

On Nov. 1 service is as on ⑦.

BOULOGNE - ST POL - ARRAS / BÉTHUNE 263

km																									
		Ⓐ	Ⓐ	⚒	⚒	⚒	⚒	Ⓐ	† J	†	⚒	Ⓐ J	⚒	†	Ⓐ	†	Ⓐ	†	⑥	Ⓒ	Ⓐ	⑥	†	Ⓒ	Ⓐ
	Calais Ville 261 d.	...	...	...	...	...	...	0806	...	...	...	...	1148	...	...	...	...	1610	...	...	1648	...	1712	...	1831
0	**Boulogne** Ville 261 d.	0404	...	0512	...	0632	...	0841	0903	...	...	...	1233	1343	...	1505	1533	1646	1632	...	1733	1732	1747	...	1908
27	Étaples Le Touquet 261 d.	0426	...	0537	...	0659	...	0901	0933	...	...	...	1301	1403	...	1523	1601	1706	1703	...	1800	1759	1804	...	1927
39	Montreuil d.	0438	...	0549	...	0710	...	0914	0945	...	...	...	1312	1414	...	1535	1613	1718	1715	...	1812	1812	1816	...	1938
60	Hesdin d.	0503	...	0619	...	0740	...	0941	1010	...	...	...	1341	1439	...	1600	1642	1744	1740	...	1842	1845	1845	...	...
88	St Pol sur Ternoise d.	0529	0541	0701	0715	0810	0815	1012	1035	1043	1115	1215	1412	1504	1515	1627	1712	1815	1814	1830	1914	1915	1912	1927	...
127	**Arras** a.	0606	|	0740	|	0847	|	1048	1108	|	|	|	1448	1531	|	1658	1752	|	|	1908	1952	1946	1938	|	...
120	Béthune ▷ d.	...	0620	...	0750	...	0850	...	...	1118	1150	1250	...	...	1550	...	...	1848	1848	...	...	...	...	1956	...
162	Lille Flandres ▷ a.	...	0658	...	0825x	...	0925	...	...	1158	1225	1325	...	...	1625	...	...	1925	1925	...	...	...	...	2034	...

	⚒	⚒	Ⓐ	Ⓐ	Ⓒ	⑥	†	†	⑥	Ⓐ	⑥	Ⓐ	Ⓐ	Ⓐ	Ⓐ	Ⓐ	Ⓒ J	Ⓐ	Ⓐ	⑥ J	†	Ⓒ	Ⓐ	Ⓐ	⑥ J
Lille Flandres ▷ d.	...	...	0835	...	0902	...	...	1135	...	1235	1235	...	1535	...	1635	...	...	1735	...	...	...	1802	1835	...	1913
Béthune ▷ d.	...	...	0912	...	0946	...	...	1212	...	1312	1312	...	1612	...	1712	...	...	1812	...	...	...	1847	1912	...	1958
Arras d.	...	0617a	|	0928	|	0948	0955	|	1228	|	|	1328	|	1628	|	1728	1742r	|	1828	1828	1828	|	|	1928	1953
St Pol sur Ternoise d.	0546	0706	0945	1014	1018	1026	1037	1246	1308	1345	1414*	1414	1645	1714	1745	1810	1815	1845	1916	1917	1916	1919	1945	2010	2031
Hesdin d.	0617	0738	...	1042	...	1053	1104	1313	1344	...	1443	1444	...	1744	...	1844	1843	...	1947	1949	1954	...	...	2036	2056
Montreuil d.	0646	0805	...	1109	...	1119	1129	1339	1410	...	1508	1509	...	1813	...	1910	1908	...	2012	2015	2019	...	...	2101	2120
Étaples Le Touquet 261 d.	0700	0817	...	1121	...	1131	1146	1349	1422	...	1520	1519	...	1824	...	1922	1920	...	2024	2026	2036	...	...	2112	2136
Boulogne Ville 261 a.	0726	0843	...	1146	...	1156	1213	1408	1441	...	1539	...	...	1839	...	1946	1948	...	2040	2042	2054	...	...	2133	2155
Calais Ville 261 a.	0810	...	...	1221	...	1248	...	1440	...	...	...	...	...	1922	...	2022	...	...	2118	...	2134	...	...	...	...

J – To July 4/from Aug. 25.
a – Ⓐ only.
r – 1748 on †.

x – 0830 on ⑥ July 5 - Aug. 23.
▷ – Additional trains run Béthune - Lille and v.v.
* – Arrive 1344.

Subject to alteration Oct. 28-30, Nov. 4-6. On Nov. 1 service is as on ⑦.
Timings may vary by 2-3 minutes June 10-28 and from Nov. 12.

264 PARIS and LILLE - DUNKERQUE *High-speed trains*

VIA LILLE For local trains Lille Flandres - Dunkerque see Table 266

km		◇	TGV 7205	TGV 7511	◇	◇		◇	◇	TGV 7269	TGV 7269	TGV 7571
		Ⓐ	Ⓐ	Ⓐ	†	⚒		Ⓐ	Ⓐ	⑦	Ⓐ	⑥
										e		t
	Paris Nord **250** .. d.	...	0646	0746	...	...	...	...	...	1746	1746	1746
0	**Lille** Europe .... d.	0712	0750	0850	1150	1250	...	1650	1750	1849	1851	1849
76	**Dunkerque** .... a.	0744	0823	0923	1223	1323	...	1723	1823	1923	1923	1923

	TGV 7214	◇	TGV 7530	◇	TGV 7552		◇	TGV 7288	TGV 7588	TGV 7298
	Ⓐ	Ⓐ	Ⓐ	†	①-⑥		Ⓐ	Ⓑ	⑥	⑦
					b				t	e
Dunkerque .... d.	0632	0724	0759	1035	1232	...	1634	1832	1832	2132
Lille Europe .... d.	0703	0754	0832	1106	1306	...	1707	1905	1905	2205
Paris Nord **250** . a.	0814	...	0944	...	1414	...	...	2014	2014	2314

VIA BÉTHUNE For local trains Arras - Béthune - Hazebrouck see Table 264a

km		TGV 7305	TGV 7307	TGV 7311	TGV 7321	TGV 7331	TGV 7335	TGV 7337	TGV 7339	TGV 7343	TGV 7345	TGV 7351	TGV 7357
		Ⓐ	⑥	©	①-⑥		⑤	©	①-④	Ⓐ	Ⓑ		⑤
			t		b	D	f		m		h	E	f△
0	**Paris Nord** ...... **256** d.	0752	0852	0952	1252	1452	1622	1652	1722	1822	1852	1952	2152
199	Arras .... **256** d.	0850	0950	1050	1350	1548	1714	1748	1814	1914	1950	2050	2248
219	Lens .... d.	0905	1005	1105	1405	1603	1729	1803	1829	1929	2005	2105	2303
238	Béthune .... d.	0918	1018	1118	1418	1618	1745	1818	1845	1945	2018	2118	2318
272	Hazebrouck .... a.	0938	1038	1138	1438	1638	1805	1838	1905	2009	2038	2138	2338
312	**Dunkerque** .... a.	1004	1104	1204	1504	1704	1832	1904	1932	...	2104	2204	0004

	TGV 7302	TGV 7304	TGV 7308	TGV 7318	TGV 7336	TGV 7342	TGV 7348	TGV 7354	TGV 7356
	Ⓐ	Ⓐ	⑥					⑦	⑤⑦
			t					e	v
Dunkerque .... d.	0556	...	0756	0956	1356	1556	1656	...	1956
Hazebrouck .... d.	0620	0640	0820	1020	1420	1620	1720	1920	2020
Béthune .... d.	0643	0713	0843	1043	1443	1643	1743	1943	2043
Lens .... d.	0656	0727	0857	1057	1457	1657	1757	1957	2057
Arras .... **256** d.	0717	0747	0917	1117	1517	1717	1817	2017	2117
Paris Nord ..... **256** a.	0808	0838	1008	1208	1608	1808	1908	2108	2208

D – Daily to July 6; ⑤⑥⑦ July 11 - Aug. 24 (also July 14); daily from Aug. 25.
E – ⑥⑦ (also ⑤ to July 4 / from Aug. 29), also Aug. 15.
b – Not June 9, July 14, Nov. 11.
e – Also June 9, July 14, Nov. 11.
f – Also Aug. 14; not Aug. 15.
h – Not Aug. 15.
m – Not holidays or Aug. 14.
t – Also Aug. 15.
v – Also June 9, July 14, Aug. 14, Nov. 11; not Aug. 15.
TGV – Ⓡ, supplement payable.
◇ – TER à Grande Vitesse (TER GV) via high-speed line (1, 2 class). Supplement *Grande Vitesse* payable (€3, valid all day). Reservation not necessary.
△ – On Oct. 31, Nov. 7 will not call at Lens or Béthune.

Departures from Dunqerque (via Béthune) may be 3 minutes earlier on Ⓐ Oct. 7 - 24.
On © Oct. 11 - Nov. 2 Paris - Dunkerque and v.v. trains which normally run via Béthune will run non-stop Arras - Dunkerque and v.v. in altered timings.

264a ARRAS - BÉTHUNE - HAZEBROUCK *Local Trains*

For *TGV* trains see Table **264**

km		Ⓐ	⑥	Ⓐ	Ⓐ	⚒	Ⓐ	⚒	†	Ⓐ	⚒	©	Ⓐ	Ⓐ	⑥	⑥	Ⓐ	Ⓐ	†	Ⓐ	⚒	†	Ⓐ	Ⓐ	①-④
										J			J												J•
0	**Arras** .... d.	0556	0623	0622	0657	0723	0804	0823	0856	0904	0923	1056	1204	1223	1225	1256	1257	1323	1356	1456	1604	1556	1623	1651	1714
20	Lens .... d.	0613	0642	0646	0713	0742	0818	0842	0913	0917	0942	1113	1218	1246	1244	1313	1313	1342	1413	1513	1618	1613	1642	1706	1728
39	Béthune .... d.	0631	0703	0705	0733	0801	0835	0901	0931	0934	1000	1131	1235	1305	1303	1331	1335	1401	1431	1531	1636	1631	1701	1728	1743
51	Lillers .... d.	0641	0716	0718	0746	0810	0844	0910	0940	0943	1009	1140	1246	1315	1315	1340	1347	1410	1440	1540	1645	1640	1710	1740	|
73	**Hazebrouck** .... a.	0700	0736	0741	0807	0826	0900	0926	0956	1000	1026	1156	1302	1336	1334	1356	1406	1426	1456	1556	1702	1656	1726	1759	1803
	Dunkerque **266** ...... a.	...	...	...	...	...	...	0959r	...	...	...	...	...	...	...	...	...	...	...	...	...	...	...	...	1828

	Ⓐ	Ⓐ	©	⑤	Ⓐ	Ⓐ	Ⓐ	Ⓐ	©	©	©	Ⓐ
				J			J					z
Arras .... d.	1723	1757	1756	1814	1823	1904	1923	1956	1956	2056	2156	2204
Lens .... d.	1746	1813	1813	1828	1846	1918	1941	2010	2013	2113	2213	2218
Béthune .... d.	1805	1831	1831	1842	1907	1936	2000	2029	2031	2131	2231	2237
Lillers .... d.	1816	1840	1840	1851	1918	1944	2009	2039	2040	2140	2240	2246
Hazebrouck .... a.	1836	1859	1856	1904	1937	2000	2026	2056	2056	2156	2256	2302
Dunkerque **266** ...... a.	...	...	...	1929	...	...	...	...	...	...	...	...

	Ⓐ	Ⓐ	⑥	Ⓐ	⑥	Ⓐ	Ⓐ	⑥	Ⓐ
							J	v	
Dunkerque **266** ..... d.	...	...	...	...	...	...	0637	0630	...
Hazebrouck .... d.	0504	0552	0605	0623	0634	0653	0701	0704	0734
Lillers .... d.	0521	0614	0622	0643	0650	0723	0717	0721	0751
Béthune .... d.	0531	0629	0631	0656	0700	0737	0727	0731	0801
Lens .... d.	0549	0648	0649	0715	0722	0756	0745	0749	0821
Arras .... a.	0607	0703	0703	0737	0739	0811	0757	0803	0838

	⚒	Ⓐ	⑥	†	Ⓐ	⑥	Ⓐ	⑥	Ⓐ	Ⓑ	⑥	Ⓐ	Ⓐ		Ⓐ	Ⓐ	©	Ⓐ	Ⓐ	©	Ⓐ	©	Ⓐ	Ⓐ	
			v										J					J							
Dunkerque **266** ...... d.	...	...	0856	...	...	...	...	...	...	...	...	...	...	...	...	...	...	...	...	...	...	...	...	...	...
Hazebrouck .... d.	0834	0934	0934	1004	1034	1134	1201	1234	1252	1434	1434	1501	1604	1634	1652	1723	1734	1804	1823	1834	1901	1934	2001	2104	...
Lillers .... d.	0850	0951	0950	1021	1051	1150	1218	1253	1312	1451	1450	1518	1621	1650	1714	1744	1751	1821	1846	1850	1918	1950	2017	2121	...
Béthune .... d.	0900	1001	1000	1031	1101	1200	1228	1304	1326	1501	1500	1528	1631	1701	1728	1757	1801	1831	1859	1901	1928	2001	2027	2131	...
Lens .... d.	0922	1022	1022	1049	1122	1222	1246	1324	1348	1522	1521	1545	1649	1722	1749	1817	1822	1849	1918	1922	1945	2022	2044	2149	...
Arras .... a.	0939	1039	1039	1103	1139	1239	1300	1339	1403	1539	1539	1600	1703	1739*	1803	1839	1839	1903	1937	1939	1956	2039	2056	2203	...

J – To July 4 / from Aug. 25.
r – ⑥ July 5 - Aug. 23.
v – Not Oct. 11, 18, 25, Nov. 1.
z – Subject to alteration Sept. 15 - 18, Oct. 2, 6 - 9.
• – Not holidays.
* – 1745 on Ⓐ from Aug. 25.

On Nov. 1 service is as on ⑦.

265 (PARIS) - LILLE - CALAIS / BOULOGNE *High-speed trains*

For Paris - Boulogne via Amiens see Table **260**. For local trains Lille - Calais see Table **266**. For local trains Calais - Boulogne - Rang du Fliers see Table **261**.

km		TGV 7505		TGV 7513	TGV 7515	🚌		TGV 7223	TGV 7535		TGV 7559	🚌		TGV 7265	TGV 7565		TGV 7569	TGV 7569		TGV 7277	TGV 7277	🚌		◇	🚌
		Ⓐ	Ⓐ	Ⓐ	©	†	⚒	①-⑥	①-⑥	⚒	Ⓑ	†	Ⓐ	Ⓐ	⑥	⚒	Ⓐ	⑦			⑦	Ⓑ	⑥	†	†
						r		b	b		h	r			t			e	◐		e	r‡			r
	Paris Nord **250** .... d.	0646	...	0746	0746	...	...	0946	1146	...	1546	...	...	1646	1646	...	1746	1746	...	1846	1846	...	...	...	...
0	**Lille** Europe .... d.	0754	...	0854	0854	...	...	1054	1254	...	1654	...	...	1754	1754	...	1855	1853	...	1954	1954	...	...	2054	...
99	Calais Fréthun ..... **261** a.	0826	0831	0923	0923	0930	0939	1122	1323	1339	1723	1730	1739	1823	1823	1839	1923	1921	1929	2023	2023	2030	2039	2123	2130
107	**Calais** Ville ...... **261** a.	|	0840	|	|	0945	0948	1131	|	1348	|	1745	1748	|	|	1849	|	|	1937	|	|	2045	2048	|	2145
133	**Boulogne** Ville .... a.	0855	...	0953	0953	...	...	...	1353	...	1753	...	...	1853	1853	...	1953	1953	...	2053	2053	...	...	2153	...
160	Étaples-Le Touquet ..... a.	...	...	...	1012	...	...	...	1412	...	...	...	...	1912	...	...	2012	...	...	...	2113	...	...	...	...
171	Rang du Fliers ⊙ ...... a.	...	...	...	1023	...	...	...	1423	...	...	...	...	1923	...	...	2023	...	...	...	2125	...	...	...	...

	TGV 7216	🚌		TGV 7229		🚌	TGV 7537	TGV 7537		TGV 7546	🚌		TGV 7551	TGV 7551	TGV 7254		TGV 7573		TGV 7586		TGV 7290	🚌	TGV 7292	TGV 7592	◇
	Ⓐ	⑥	Ⓐ	①-⑥	Ⓐ	⑥	Ⓐ	⑥	Ⓐ	Ⓐ	©	Ⓐ		©	①-⑥	⚒	①-⑥	©	⑦	Ⓐ	Ⓐ	©	⑦	⑥	†
		r		b		r		t			r				b		b		e			r	e	t	
Rang du Fliers ⊙ .... d.	...	...	...	0630	...	...	0714	...	...	...	...	...	...	1130	...	...	1530	...	...	...	...	...	1841	...	...
Étaples-Le Touquet ...... d.	...	...	...	0642	...	...	0725	...	...	...	...	...	...	1142	...	...	1542	...	...	...	...	...	1853	...	...
Boulogne Ville .... d.	...	...	...	0703	...	...	0745	0745	...	1003	...	...	1203	1203	...	...	1603	...	1803	...	1827	...	1914	1914	2017
Calais Ville .... **261** d.	0617	0710	0712	|	0748	0752	|	|	1012	|	1210	1216	|	|	1325	1612	|	1807	|	1831	|	1915	|	|	|
Calais Fréthun ...... **261** d.	0629	0725	0724	0731	0758	0807	0815	0815	1024	1032	1225	1225	1232	1232	1336	1624	1631	1817	1831	1841	1900	1930	1942	1942	2047
Lille Europe .... a.	0658	...	...	0801	...	...	0845	0845	...	1101	...	...	1301	1301	1406	...	1701	...	1901	...	1930	...	2010	2010	2115
Paris Nord **250** .... a.	0814	...	...	0914	...	...	1014	1014	...	1214	...	...	1414	1414	1514	...	1814	...	2014	...	2041	...	2114	2114	...

b – Not June 9, July 14, Nov. 11.
e – Also June 9, July 14, Nov. 11.
h – Not Aug. 15.
r – By 🚌 Calais Fréthun - Calais Ville and v.v. Rail tickets valid. Operated by Ligne BCD.
t – Also Aug. 14.
TGV – Ⓡ, supplement payable.
◐ – By 🚌 (see note r) on †, arrive Calais Ville 1945.
⊙ – Rang du Fliers - Verton - Berck.
◇ – TER à Grande Vitesse (TER GV) via high-speed line (1, 2 class). Supplement *Grande Vitesse* payable (€3, valid all day). Reservation not necessary.
‡ – Runs 5 minutes later on Ⓐ.

June 10 - 28 and from Nov. 12:
Departures from Rang du Fliers, Étaples and Boulogne towards Lille and Paris may be up to 5 minutes earlier.

ALTERNATIVE ROUTES PARIS - CALAIS
Via Lille (Tables **250** and **266**)
Via Hazebrouck (Tables **264** and **266**)
Via Amiens, Boulogne (Tables **260** and **261**)

LILLE - DUNKERQUE and CALAIS — 266

Local trains

For trains via high-speed line see Table **264** Lille - Dunkerque and Table **265** Lille - Calais

km		Ⓐ	Ⓐ	Ⓐ b	⑥ z	Ⓐ	⑥ Jz	Ⓐ	Ⓐ	⑥ d	Ⓐ	Ⓐ J	⑥ z	⚒ d	Ⓐ	Ⓐ	Ⓒ d	Ⓐ	† z	Ⓐ	Ⓐ	Ⓒ d	Ⓒ Lz	Ⓐ	Ⓐ	Ⓒ d	Ⓒ d
0	**Lille** Flandres d.	...	...	...	...	0615	...	0635	0645	0645	0700	0715	...	0735	...	0800	0815	0835	...	0845	0900	0935	...	1000	1015	1015	1135
22	Armentières d.	...	...	...	...	|	...	0649	0703	0659	0713	|	...	0751	...	0813	0829	0849	...	0902	0913	0950	...	1013	|	1029	1150
47	Hazebrouck d.	0543	0619	0633	0635	0648	0648	0713	0722	0719	0735	0748	0748	0813	0819	0835	0848	0913	0915	0918	0935	1013	1019	1035	1048	1048	1213
87	**Dunkerque** a.	|	0653	|	|	0719	0720	|	0755	0753	|	0819	0822	|	0853	|	0920	|	|	0953	|	|	1055	|	1119	1119	|
68	St Omer d.	0557	...	0650	0654	...	...	0726	...	...	0753	...	...	0826	...	0853	...	0926	0929	...	0953	1026	...	1053	...	...	1225
109	**Calais** Ville a.	0625	...	0725	0726	...	...	0756	...	...	0826	...	...	0856	...	0926	...	0956	0958	...	1026	1056	...	1126	...	...	1256

	Ⓒ z	Ⓐ	Ⓐ	⑥ d	Ⓐ J	Ⓐ	⚒ d	⚒ z	Ⓐ	⑥ z	† d	⑥ d	Ⓐ	⑥ z	Ⓐ	Ⓐ	Ⓒ d	† z	d	Ⓐ	Ⓐ	Ⓐ J	d	† z	Ⓐ	⑥ z	Ⓐ
Lille Flandres d.	...	1200	1215	1215	1219	1235	1245	...	1315	...	1315	1335	1345	...	1400	...	1435	...	1545	1600	1615	1619	1633	...	1645	...	1700
Armentières d.	...	1213	|	1229	1234	1249	1259	...	|	...	1329	1350	1402	...	1413	...	1450	...	1559	1613	|	1634	1649	...	1702	...	1713
Hazebrouck d.	1217	1235	1248	1248	1253	1313	1319	1333	1348	1348	1348	1413	1418	1419	1435	1448	1513	1519	1618	1635	1648	1653	1713	1719	1719	1719	1735
Dunkerque a.	1253	|	1319	1319	|	|	1353	|	1419	1420	1420	|	1453	1455	|	1520	|	1545	1653	|	1719	|	|	1743	1752	1753	|
St Omer d.	...	1253	...	...	1306	1326	...	1352	...	...	...	1426	...	...	1453	...	1526	...	...	1653	...	1705	1726	...	...	...	1753
Calais Ville a.	...	1326	...	...	...	1356	...	1426	...	...	...	1456	...	...	1526	...	1556	...	...	1726	...	...	1756	...	...	...	1826

	Ⓐ	Ⓒ d	Ⓐ	①–④ Ju	Ⓐ	Ⓐ	Ⓐ	Ⓐ J	Ⓐ	d	Ⓐ	Ⓐ	Ⓐ	† d	⑥ d	Ⓐ	Ⓐ	Ⓐ	d	† z	⑥ z	† d	Ⓐ	⑥ d	Ⓐ	† d	Ⓐ J⊖
Lille Flandres d.	1715	1715	1719	...	1735	1745	1800	1815	1819	1835	1845	1900	...	1915	1915	1919	1935	2015	2035	...	...	2115	2115	2115	2215	2300	2312
Armentières d.	|	1731	1734	...	1749	1802	1813	|	1834	1849	1902	1913	...	1931	1932	1934	1950	|	2049	...	...	2129	2129	2129	2229	2314	2326
Hazebrouck d.	1748	1748	1753	1806	1813	1818	1835	1848	1853	1913	1918	1935	1948	1949	1951	1953	2018	2048	2113	2119	2119	2148	2148	2148	2248	2335	2349
Dunkerque a.	1819	1820	|	1828	|	1853	|	1919	|	|	1953	|	2020	2021	2023	|	2053	2119	|	2143	2153	2211	2220	2219	2321	|	...
St Omer d.	...	...	1806	...	1826	...	1853	...	1906	1925	...	1953	...	...	...	2006	...	...	2126	...	...	...	...	...	...	2347	...
Calais Ville a.	...	...	...	...	1856	...	1926	...	...	1956	...	2026	...	...	...	...	...	...	2156	...	...	...	...	...	...	0014	...

	Ⓐ	Ⓐ	Ⓐ	Ⓐ J	Ⓐ	⑥ d	Ⓐ	Ⓐ	⑥ d	Ⓐ	⑥ uz	Ⓐ Ju	Ⓐ	Ⓐ	Ⓐ	⑥ d	Ⓐ	⑥ d	Ⓐ	Ⓐ	Ⓐ	⑥ Jz	Ⓐ	⑥ d	Ⓐ	Ⓒ	Ⓐ
Calais Ville d.	...	0454	...	...	...	...	0534	...	...	0606	...	...	...	...	0634	0635	...	...	0706	...	...	...	0734	0735	...	...	0833
St Omer d.	...	0524	...	0554	...	...	0607	...	...	0635	...	...	0654	...	0708	0704	...	...	0735	0754	...	...	0808	0808	...	...	0908
Dunkerque d.	...	|	0508	|	0540	0539	|	0608	0608	|	0630	0637	|	0640	|	|	0708	0708	|	|	0740	0739	|	|	0808	0839	|
Hazebrouck d.	0448	0536	0543	0608	0613	0613	0626	0643	0644	0649	0702	0659	0708	0713	0726	0727	0743	0744	0749	0808	0813	0811	0826	0827	0843	0913	0926
Armentières d.	0512	...	0600	0627	|	0630	0646	0657	0701	0711	...	...	0726	|	0745	0746	0757	0800	0811	0825	|	...	0845	0844	0857	0930	0945
Lille Flandres a.	0525	...	0614	0640	0644	0644	0659	0714	0714	0725	...	...	0740	0744	0759	0759	0814	0814	0825	0840	0844	...	0859	0859	0914	0944	0959

	⑥ uz	Ⓐ	†	d	Ⓐ J	⑥ d	† d	Ⓐ	Ⓐ	Ⓐ	Ⓒ d		Ⓐ	⑥ d	Ⓐ J	Ⓐ J	Ⓐ	Ⓐ	⑥ d	Ⓐ	⑥ d	†		z	Ⓒ d	⑥ d	Ⓐ
Calais Ville d.	...	...	...	0906	...	...	...	1034	...	1106	1135	...	...	...	1206	...	...	1234	1235	...	...	...	...	...	1335	...	1434
St Omer d.	...	...	...	0935	...	...	...	1108	...	1135	1204	...	...	...	1235	1254	...	1308	1306	...	...	...	...	...	1405	...	1508
Dunkerque d.	0856	0908	0908	|	1040	1039	1039	|	1108	|	|	...	1208	1208	...	|	1240	|	|	1308	1308	1308	...	1339	|	1439	|
Hazebrouck d.	0932	0943	0942	0949	1113	1110	1110	1126	1143	1149	1227	...	1243	1244	...	1308	1313	1325	1327	1343	1342	1342	...	1411	1427	1513	1526
Armentières d.	...	0957	...	1011	|	1127	1128	1145	1157	1211	1246	...	1257	1306	...	1325	|	...	1346	1357	1400	1359	...	...	1446	1530	1546
Lille Flandres a.	...	1014	...	1025	1144	1144	1144	1159	1214	1225	1259	...	1314	1325	...	1340	1344	...	1359	1414	1414	1414	...	...	1459	1544	1559

	Ⓐ	z	Ⓐ	Ⓒ d	Ⓐ	Ⓐ J	Ⓒ d	Ⓐ	Ⓐ	Ⓐ	Ⓐ	† z	⑥ z	Ⓐ	Ⓒ d	Ⓐ	Ⓒ d	Ⓒ z	Ⓐ	Ⓒ d‡	Ⓒ d	Ⓐ	Ⓐ	Ⓒ d	Ⓐ	Ⓐ	Ⓒ d
Calais Ville d.	...	...	1534	1535	...	...	...	1634	...	1706	...	...	...	1734	1735	...	...	...	1834	1835	...	...	1906	1935	...	2034	...
St Omer d.	...	...	1607	1604	...	...	...	1708	...	1735	...	...	...	1809	1805	...	...	...	1911	1904	...	...	1935	2004	...	2111	...
Dunkerque d.	1508	1539	|	|	1608	1640	1639	|	1708	|	1740	1738	1739	|	|	1808	1808	1849	|	|	1908	1908	|	|	2008	|	2108
Hazebrouck d.	1543	1611	1626	1627	1643	1713	1711	1727	1743	1748	1813	1811	1811	1826	1827	1843	1844	1921	1926	1927	1939	1942	1949	2027	2043	2126	2137
Armentières d.	1557	...	1645	1646	1657	|	1728	1745	1757	1810	|	...	...	1845	1846	1857	1900	...	1946	1946	1957	...	2011	2046	2100	2145	2156
Lille Flandres a.	1614	...	1659	1659	1714	1744	1744	1759	1814	1825	1844	...	...	1859	1859	1914	1914	...	1959	1959	2014	...	2025	2059	2114	2159	2214

J – To July 4/from Aug. 25.
L – Not on ⑥ July 5 - Aug. 23.
b – From Bethune, depart 0602.
d – Subject to alteration June 7,8, 14-22, Oct. 11 - Nov. 2.
u – To/from Arras (Table **264a**).
z – Subject to alteration on Ⓒ Oct. 11 - Nov. 2.
⊖ – Subject to alteration.
‡ – On ⑥ July 5 - Aug. 23 from Boulogne (Calais d. 1841).

PARIS - BEAUVAIS — 267

km		Ⓐ r	⑥ t	Ⓐ r	Ⓐ u	⑥ t	† z	Ⓐ r	Ⓒ	Ⓐ	d		⚒ J		⑥ t	Ⓐ r	Ⓐ r	Ⓒ J	Ⓐ r	⑦ L	Ⓐ r	⑥ t	Ⓐ r	Ⓐ r	Ⓒ
0	**Paris** Nord d.	0605	0631	0635	0735	0801	0801	0850	0901	1001	1101	1201	1301	1401	1601	1605	1635	1701	1705	1731	1735	1801	1805	1835	1901
80	**Beauvais** a.	0722	0741	0750	0850	0919	0920	1005	1018	1118	1218	1318	1418	1519	1719	1720	1747	1818	1822	1848	1847	1919	1920	1947	2019

	Ⓐ r	Ⓐ J	⚒	Ⓑ	Ⓒ
Paris Nord d.	1905	1931	2001	2101	2201
Beauvais a.	2020	2049	2119	2218	2319

	Ⓐ	⑥ t	Ⓐ	Ⓐ	⑥ t	† s	Ⓐ	Ⓐ	Ⓒ d	Ⓐ	⚒	†	Ⓐ J	Ⓒ	⚒	
Beauvais d.	0513	0537	0540	0613	0627	0627	0640	0713	0737	0740	0837	0937	1037	1037	1137	1237
Paris Nord a.	0625	0657	0655	0725	0742	0743	0755	0823	0857	0855	0957	1057	1157	1157	1257	1357

	⚒ b		⑥ t	Ⓐ J	Ⓐ	Ⓒ	Ⓐ	Ⓐ	Ⓒ b	Ⓐ	⑥ t	† z	Ⓐ	Ⓒ	†	
Beauvais d.	1337	1437	1637	1640	1710	1737	1740	1808	1837	1840	1937	1939	2010	2037	2137	...
Paris Nord a.	1457	1557	1757	1753v	1823*	1857	1853*	1923*	1957	1953*	2057	2057	2127	2157	2257	...

Most trains call at Persan-Beaumont (30 mins from Paris).
CREIL - BEAUVAIS: 14 journeys on Ⓐ, 7 on ⑥, 4 on †.

J – To July 14/from Aug. 25.
L – ⑦ July 20 - Aug. 24 (also Aug. 15).
b – Not on ⑥ July 19 - Aug. 23.
d – Not on ⑦ July 13 - Aug. 24.
r – Depart Paris 4 mins earlier Ⓐ July 21 - Aug. 29.
s – Runs 9 mins earlier July 20 - Aug. 24.
t – Not Nov. 1.
u – On Ⓐ July 21 - Aug. 29 d. 0716, a. 0837.
v – 1813 on Aug. 25-29.
z – To/from Le Tréport (Table **267a**).
* – 20 mins later July 21 - Aug. 29.

BEAUVAIS - LE TRÉPORT — 267a

km		Ⓐ Ju	Ⓐ u	† L	† M	⑥ t	⚒ u	Ⓐ	†	Ⓐ u	⑥ t	⑤–⑦ u‡
	Paris Nord **267** d.	...	...	0801	0801	...	...	...	...	...	...	...
0	**Beauvais** d.	...	0738	0926	0926	0924	1234	1800	1823	...	1853	2025
	Rouen ⊖ **268** d.	...	|	|	|	|	|	|	|	...	|	|
49	Abancourt **268** d.	0642	0834	1021	1017	1021	1334	1855	1916	1933	1949	2121
103	Eu d.	0726	0919	1107	|	1106	1420	...	2001	2017	2035	2207
106	**Le Tréport** a.	0730	0924	1111	1058	1111	1424	...	2005	2021	2039	2211

	Ⓐ u	⑥ t	†	⑥ t	⚒ u	†	⚒	† L	† M	† M
Le Tréport d.	0545	0650	0740	0857	1205	1245	1726	1757	1757	2028
Eu d.	0550	|	|	0901	1210	1250	1731	1802	|	2033
Abancourt **268** d.	0634	0735	0822	0944	1302	1334	1824	1846	1843	2121
Rouen ⊖ **268** a.	|	|	|	|	|	|	|	|	|	|
Beauvais a.	0730	0830	0919	1049	1358	1430	1925	1939	1938	2158
Paris Nord **267** a.	...	...	...	...	...	...	...	2057	2057	2301

J – To July 11/from Aug. 25.
L – † to June 29/from Sept. 7.
M – † July 6 - Aug. 31.
t – Not Nov. 1.
u – Subject to alteration on Ⓐ Nov. 17-28.
⊖ – Rouen Rive-Droite.
‡ – Also holidays.

AMIENS - ROUEN — 268

km		① g	Ⓐ	⑥ t	†	Ⓐ	Ⓐ	⑥ t	†	⑤ v	①–④ n	Ⓑ h	⑥ J	⑥ S	† S	Ⓐ	Ⓐ	Ⓒ
	Lille Flandres **256** d.	...	0602	0802	...	...	1102	...	...	...	...	...	...	...	...	1702	...	1802
0	**Amiens** d.	0557	0719	0927	0927	1027	1227	1244	1421	1657	1657	1727	1733	1755	...	1827	1857	1927
31	Poix de Picardie d.	0616	0737	0944	0944	1044	1244	1305	1439	1719	1720	1745	1755	1817	...	1844	1920	1944
52	Abancourt d.	0628	0749	0956	0956	1056	1256	1320	1451	1733	1735	1758	1809	1831	1850	1856	1936	1956
73	Serqueux d.	0644	0803	1010	1014	1110	1310	1336	1510	1749	1753	1814	1826	1848	1905	1912	1953	2010
121	**Rouen** Rive-Droite a.	0725	0832	1044	1045	1146	1346	1422	1546	1822	...	1846	1907	1929	1936	1946	...	2046

	Ⓐ	Ⓐ	Ⓐ		⑥ t	⑥ S	†		Ⓐ	⚒		Ⓐ			Ⓐ		⑤ f	†
ouen Rive-Droite d.	...	0617	0717	...	0817	0912	0915	...	1117	1217	...	1617	...	1815	1835	...	1917	1917
erqueux d.	0609	0647	0747	...	0847	0943	0948	...	1149	1249	...	1649	...	1847	1916	...	1949	1949
bancourt d.	0626	0703	0803	...	0904	0959	1003	...	1202	1303	...	1703	...	1900	1932	...	2003	2003
oix de Picardie d.	0641	0715	0815	...	0917	...	1015	...	1215	1315	...	1715	...	1913	...	...	2015	2015
miens a.	0703	0732	0832	...	0934	...	1032	...	1232	1332	...	1732	...	1931	...	...	2032	2032
Lille Flandres **256** a.	...	0858	...	...	1058	...	...	...	1358	...	...	...	...	2058	...	...	...	...

J – ⑥ to June 28/from Sept. 6 (not Nov. 1).
S – July 5 - Aug. 31.
f – Also Aug. 14.
g – Also June 10, July 15, Nov. 12; not June 9, July 14.
h – Also Nov. 1.
n – Not holidays.
t – Not Nov. 1.
v – Not Aug. 15.

269 🚌 RENNES / DOL - MONT ST MICHEL

By 🚌 Keolis Emeraude

km	🚌	W	S	Ⓐ	Ⓒ					
0	**Rennes** Gare Routière ⊡ d.	0940	0945	...	...	...	1135	1250	1645	...
	Dol (Gare SNCF) d.	|	|	1040	1115	...	|	|	|	...
68	**Mont St Michel** a.	1055	1100	1110	1145	...	1250	1405	1800	...

🚌	Ⓐ	Ⓒ			S	W		⑦S	
Mont St Michel d.	0900	0925	1125	1425	1605	1610	1720	1835	...
Dol (Gare SNCF) a.	|	|	|	|	1640	1640	|	1905	...
Rennes Gare Routière ⊡ a.	1015	1040	1240	1540	...	...	1840	...	...

S – July 6 - Aug. 24. **W** – Not July 6 - Aug. 24. ⊡ – Adjacent to rail station. Operator: Keolis Emeraude, St Malo. ✆ 02 99 19 70 70. www.keolis-emeraude.com

Connections (not guaranteed) at Rennes or Dol with *TGV* services to / from Paris. Combined rail / bus tickets available from rail stations. Rail passes not valid.

270 PARIS - ROUEN - LE HAVRE

km								3101		13101		3103	3103	13103	3105	13105	3191	3107	3193				13107	3109	3113
		⚒	⚒	Ⓐ	Ⓐ	⚒	Ⓐ	Ⓐ	⑥	Ⓐ	⑦	⑥	Ⓐ			①–⑥	⑦	Ⓐ	⑥	⑥	†	⚒		⚒	⑥
							K	J	q		e	t				b	e		t	u					t
0	**Paris** St Lazare § d.	...	...	...	...	0611	...	0653	...	0720	...	0750	0753	0820	0850	1020	1036	1050	1050	...	...	...	1220	1250	1350
57	Mantes la Jolie § d.	...	...	0627	...	0644	...	|	0731	0752	...	|	|	0852	|	1052	1108	|	|	...	...	...	1252	|	|
79	Vernon (Eure) d.	...	...	0649	...	0710	...	|	0749	0811	...	|	|	0911	|	1111	1127	|	|	...	...	...	1311	|	|
111	Val de Reuil d.	...	...	0709	...	0731	...	|	0810	0830	...	|	|	0930	|	1130	1148	|	|	...	...	...	1330	|	|
126	Oissel d.	...	...	0720	...	0741	...	|	0822	0840	...	|	|	0940	|	1140	1205	|	|	...	...	...	1340	|	|
140	**Rouen** Rive-Droite a.	...	...	0730	...	0750	...	0812	0837	0851	...	0912	0912	0951	1012	1151	1218	1212	1203	...	...	...	1351	1405	1512
140	**Rouen** Rive-Droite d.	0630	0700	...	0735	...	0804	0815	...	...	0904	0915	0915	...	1015	...	...	1215	...	1209	1230	1250	...	1408	1515
178	Yvetot d.	0655	0733	...	0807	...	0827	0838	...	...	0927	0938	0938	...	1038	...	...	1238	...	1232	1253	1323	...	1432	1538
203	Bréauté-Beuzeville ▲ d.	0713	0751	...	0823	...	0840	0852	...	...	0940	0952	0952	...	1052	...	...	1252	...	1245	1306	1340	...	1447	1552
228	**Le Havre** a.	0733	0813	...	0839	...	0855	0906	...	...	0955	1006	1006	...	1106	...	...	1306	...	1259	1320	1402	...	1501	1606

	3111	13109	3115	3117		3119	13111		3121		3123	13113	13115	3125		13117	3127	3129	13119			3131		13121	13123
	⑤				⑥	⑥	Ⓑ	†	Ⓐ	Ⓐ		Ⓒ	Ⓐ		Ⓐ	Ⓒ	①–④	⑤	Ⓐ	⑥	†	Ⓐ	Ⓐ	⑦	Ⓐ
	R			L	u	t	h				L						m	J		u				e	
Paris St Lazare § d.	1350	1420	1450	1550	...	1620	1620	...	1650	1653	1725	1720	1730	1750	1753	1820	1825	1825	1830	...	...	1850	1853	1920	1930
Mantes la Jolie § d.	|	1452	|	|	...	1652	1652	...	|	1725	|	1752	|	|	1825	1852	|	|	|	...	...	|	1925	1952	|
Vernon (Eure) d.	|	1511	|	|	...	1711	1711	...	|	1747	|	1811	1819	|	1850	1911	|	|	1919	...	...	1940	1950	2011	2019
Val de Reuil d.	|	1530	|	|	...	1731	1730	...	|	1809	|	1830	1837	|	1910	1930	|	|	1937	...	...	|	2010	2030	2037
Oissel d.	|	1540	|	|	...	1741	1740	...	|	1819	|	1840	1847	|	1919	1940	|	|	1947	...	...	|	2020	2040	2047
Rouen Rive-Droite a.	1512	1551	1612	1712	...	1751	1751	...	1812	...	1837	1851	1858	1912	...	1951	1940	1937	1956	...	...	2012	2029	2051	2056
Rouen Rive-Droite d.	...	...	1615	1715	1704	1754	...	1804	1815	...	1840	...	...	1915	...	...	...	1940	...	2004	2006	2015	...	...	...
Yvetot d.	...	...	1638	1738	1727	1817	...	1829	1837	...	1903	...	...	1938	...	...	...	2003	...	2031	2032	2038	...	...	...
Bréauté-Beuzeville ▲ d.	...	...	1652	1752	1740	1831	...	1842	1851	...	1917	...	...	1952	...	...	...	2017	...	2045	2047	2052	...	...	...
Le Havre a.	...	...	1706	1806	1755	1845	...	1856	1905	...	1932	...	...	2006	...	...	...	2032	...	2100	2102	2106	...	...	...

	3133	5376	13125	3135	3137	3139	3137	13127	3141	13129	3141	13131
		TGV	Ⓐ	⑥	①–④	⑤	⑦	⑤	⑤	①–④	⑦	⑥
	C	♥	J	t	m	f	d	f	◇	H	◇	◇
Paris St Lazare § d.	1950	...	2020	2020	2050	2050	2120	2120	2205	2319	2350	2350
Mantes la Jolie § d.	|	2031	2052	2052	|	2124	2152	2152	2237	2357	0022	0022
Vernon (Eure) d.	|	|	2111	2111	|	2138	2211	2211	2256	0016	0041	0041
Val de Reuil d.	|	|	2130	2131	|	2159	2231	2230	2315	0037	0102	0100
Oissel d.	|	|	2140	2141	|	2208	2241	2242	2326	0046	0112	0110
Rouen Rive-Droite a.	2112	2120	2151	2151	2212	2217	2251	2251	2334	0055	0121	0121
Rouen Rive-Droite d.	2115	2124	...	2154	2215	2220	2254	...	2337	...	0124	...
Yvetot d.	2138	|	...	2217	2237	2242	2317	...	0002	...	0147	...
Bréauté-Beuzeville ▲ d.	2152	|	...	2231	2252	2256	2331	...	0016	...	0201	...
Le Havre a.	2206	2211	...	2245	2306	2311	2345	...	0030	...	0215	...

		13100	13102	3100		13104	13106	3104
	Ⓐ	Ⓐ	⑥	Ⓐ	Ⓐ	Ⓐ	Ⓐ	⑥
			t			J		t
Le Havre d.	...	...	...	0527	...	...	...	0612
Bréauté-Beuzeville ▲ d.	...	...	...	0543	...	...	...	0628
Yvetot d.	...	...	...	0559	...	...	...	0644
Rouen Rive-Droite a.	...	...	...	0621	...	...	...	0706
Rouen Rive-Droite d.	0527	0551	0607	0624	...	0636	0657	0709
Oissel d.	0536	0601	0617	|	0640	|	0707	0718
Val de Reuil d.	0546	0611	0628	|	0649	0657	0718	0728
Vernon (Eure) d.	0607	0633	0649	|	0709	0718	0739	0749
Mantes la Jolie § a.	0631	0656	0706	|	0731	|	0756	0806
Paris St Lazare § a.	0708	0735	0740	0738	0808	0815	0835	0840

	13108	3102			3106	13110		5316		3108	13112		13114	3110		3112	13116	3114	13118	3116			3118	13120	3120
	⑦	Ⓐ	Ⓐ	⑥	Ⓐ	①–⑥	Ⓐ	*TGV*			①–⑥	Ⓐ	Ⓑ	⑥		⚒	⑥	⑦		⚒	Ⓐ	⑥	Ⓐ		
	e	J				b		♥			J b		h	t			t	•			K	u	J		
Le Havre d.	...	0628	...	0640	0658	...	0725	0750	...	0758	...	0903	...	0911	...	0958	...	1058	...	1158	1232	1237	1258	...	1358
Bréauté-Beuzeville ▲ d.	...	0645	...	0704	0714	...	0740	|	...	0814	...	0917	...	0927	...	1014	...	1114	...	1214	1256	1301	1314	...	1414
Yvetot d.	...	0659	...	0723	0730	...	0756	|	...	0830	...	0933	...	0943	...	1030	...	1130	...	1230	1319	1319	1330	...	1430
Rouen Rive-Droite a.	...	0721	...	0756	0752	...	0824	0840	...	0852	...	0957	...	1005	...	1052	...	1152	...	1252	1352	1352	1352	...	1452
Rouen Rive-Droite d.	0707	0724	0712	...	0755	0807	...	0845	...	0855	0907	...	1007	1008	...	1055	1107	1155	1207	1255	...	...	1355	1407	1455
Oissel d.	0717	|	0739	...	|	0817	...	|	...	|	0917	...	1017	1017	...	|	1117	|	1217	|	...	...	|	1417	|
Val de Reuil d.	0728	|	0748	...	|	0828	...	|	...	|	0928	...	1028	1028	...	|	1128	|	1228	|	...	...	|	1428	|
Vernon (Eure) d.	0749	|	0809	...	|	0849	...	|	...	|	0949	...	1049	1049	...	|	1149	|	1249	|	...	...	|	1449	|
Mantes la Jolie § a.	0806	|	0831	...	|	0906	...	0930	...	|	1006	...	1106	1106	...	|	1206	|	1306	|	...	...	|	1506	|
Paris St Lazare § a.	0840	0838	0908	...	0915	0940	...	...	...	1010	1040	...	1140	1140	...	1210	1240	1310	1340	1410	...	...	1510	1540	1610

	3122	3138		13122	3124	3190		13124	3192	3126	3128		13126		3130		13128	3194	3132	3134		13130		3136	
	⑤		Ⓐ	⑦	Ⓐ	⑦		Ⓐ	⑥	⑦		Ⓐ	⑦	⑥		⑥	Ⓐ	⑦		Ⓑ	⑥	⑦		⑦	
	f	Y		d		d			t	e			d	q	M	u		e		v	u	e			
Le Havre d.	...	1458	...	...	1558	...	...	...	...	1611	1658	...	...	...	1756	1803	...	...	1911	1958	2000	...	...	2110	...
Bréauté-Beuzeville ▲ d.	...	1513	...	...	1614	...	...	...	...	1627	1714	...	...	...	1812	1817	...	...	1927	2014	2015	...	...	2126	...
Yvetot d.	...	1527	...	...	1630	...	...	...	...	1643	1730	...	...	...	1828	1833	...	...	1943	2030	2031	...	...	2142	...
Rouen Rive-Droite a.	...	1550	...	...	1652	...	...	...	...	1705	1752	...	...	...	1850	1857	...	...	2005	2052	2053	...	...	2204	...
Rouen Rive-Droite d.	1556	1553	1607	1607	1655	1655	...	1707	1708	1708	1755	1807	1807	1823	1853	...	1912	1955	2008	2055	...	2107	...	2207	...
Oissel d.	|	|	1619	1617	|	|	...	1717	1718	1717	|	1817	1817	1838	|	...	|	|	2017	|	...	2117	...	2217	...
Val de Reuil d.	|	|	1628	1628	|	|	...	1728	1728	1728	|	1826	1828	1850	|	...	1929	|	2028	|	...	2128	...	2228	...
Vernon (Eure) d.	|	|	1649	1649	|	|	...	1749	1749	1749	|	1847	1849	1911	|	...	1949	|	2049	|	...	2149	...	2249	...
Mantes la Jolie § a.	|	|	1706	1706	|	|	...	1806	1806	1806	|	1906	1906	1929	|	...	2006	|	2106	|	...	2206	...	2306	...
Paris St Lazare § a.	1710	1712	1740	1740	1812	1810	...	1840	1840	1840	1910	1940	1940	...	2010	...	2040	2110	2140	2210	...	2240	...	2340	...

C – Will not run on ⑥ July 5 - Aug. 23.
H – ①–④ Oct. 13 - 20 only.
J – To July 4 / from Aug. 25.
K – July 7 - Aug. 22.
L – Ⓐ to July 4; ⑤ July 11 - Aug. 8 (also Aug. 14); Ⓐ from Aug. 22.
M – Ⓑ to July 6; ⑤⑦ July 11 - Aug. 22 (also July 14, Aug. 14; not July 13, Aug. 15); Ⓑ from Aug. 25 (also Nov. 11; not Nov. 9).
R – ⑤ (not July 11 - Aug. 22, Nov. 7).
Y – June 9, July 14, Aug. 15, 24, 31, Nov. 11 only.
b – Not June 9, July 14, Nov. 11.
d – Also June 9, July 14, Nov. 11; not July 13, Nov. 9.
e – Also June 9, July 14, Nov. 11.
f – Also Aug. 14; not Aug. 15.
h – Not Aug. 15.
m – Not holidays.
q – Not Nov. 1, 8.
t – Also Aug. 15.
u – Not Sept. 27, Nov. 1, Dec. 6.
v – Not July 13, Aug. 15, Oct. 12, 19, Nov. 9.
TGV – Ⓡ, supplement payable, 🍸.
♥ – To/from Lyon and Marseille (Table **335**).
▲ – Trains run 6 - 8 times per day from either Le Havre or Bréauté-Beuzeville to Fécamp.
◇ – Subject to alteration.
§ – Frequent suburban trains run Paris - Mantes-la-Jolie.
• – Also Nov. 11. Subject to alteration June 29, July 20.

Timings may vary by a few minutes (particularly until June 16 and on Ⓐ Sept. 8 - Oct. 3 when Paris departures may be 2 - 6 minutes earlier).

Trains are subject to cancellation or considerable alteration ⑥⑦ June 29 - July 13 (also July 14, 20), ⑥⑦ Sept. 20 - Oct. 19, Nov. 8, 9, Dec. 6, 7.

270a ROUEN - DIEPPE

km		⚒	Ⓐ	Ⓐ	†	⚒		Ⓐ	⑥t	†	⑥t	Ⓐ	†S	⑥t	⑥t	Ⓐ	Ⓐ	Ⓐ		Ⓐ	⑥S	Ⓐ	Ⓒ	Ⓐ	Ⓐ	
0	**Rouen** Rive-Droite d.	0638	0711	0725	0841	0901	1000	1201	1215	1225	1242	1341	1341	1401	1501	1601	1625	1701	1725	1801	1801	1825	1901	1925	2000	2129
63	**Dieppe** a.	0743	0758	0841	0940	0950r	1051	1251	1300	1310	1344	1439	1441	1447	1546	1650	1732	1747	1832	1850	1847	1927	1950r	2013	2050	2214

	Ⓐ	⚒	Ⓐ	Ⓐ	Ⓒ	Ⓐ	Ⓐ	⑥t		⚒	Ⓐ	⑥t	†	Ⓐ	†	Ⓐ	⑥t	†S	Ⓐ	†	⑥t	Ⓐ	Ⓐ	⚒	†	†S
Dieppe d.	0532	0616	0658	0713	0751	0758	0811	0814	0956	1155	1312	1313	1318	1358	1556	1558	1609	1700	1701	1746	1801	1801	1859	1946	2013	2101
Rouen Rive-Droite a.	0615	0715	0745	0817	0835	0845	0919	0919	1045	1245	1418	1419	1424	1445	1642	1645	1655	1746	1807	1833	1906	1913	1949	2044	2113	2146

S – June 7 - Sept. 14. **r** – On ⑥ arrive 5 minutes earlier. **t** – Not Nov. 1.

CAEN - ALENÇON - LE MANS - TOURS — 271

km		⚒	Ⓐ	Ⓐ	Ⓐ	†	⚒	△	⑥	Ⓐ	⊕				Ⓑ h	†	⚒	①–④ m	⑤ f	†	⑥ u	Ⓐ	⑥ u	Ⓐ	Ⓐ	†
0	**Caen** 275/7 d.	...	0538z	...	0558	...	0729	0905	1028	1037	...	1246	...	...	1650	...	...	1745	1745	1745	...	1817	1830	...	2000	2135
23	Mézidon 275/7 d.	...	0552z	...	0614	...	0743	0922	1043	1052	...	1302	...	...	1706	...	...	1801	1802	1802	...	1832	1844	...	2014	2150
67	Argentan 273 d.	...	0616	...	0642	...	0808	0947	1107	1114	...	1326	...	...	1732	...	...	1833	1837	1835	...	1859	1910	...	2040	2213
82	Surdon 273 d.	...	|	...	0653	...	0817	|	1118	1124	...	1336	...	...	|	...	...	1842	1848	1848	...	1909	1919	...	2049	|
91	Sées d.	...	0630	...	0701	...	0824	|	1125	1131	...	1344	...	...	1747	...	...	1849	1855	1855	...	1916	1926	...	2056	2227
111	Alençon d.	...	0643	...	0715	0829	0837	1013	1139	1144	...	1357	...	1624r	1759	...	...	1903	1908	1909	1915	1929	1939	...	2108	2240
166	**Le Mans** a.	...	0729	...	0805	0859	0909	1041	1217	1221	...	1427	...	1712	1831	...	...	...	...	1944	1946	1959	2008	...	...	2310
166	**Le Mans** d.	0625	...	0739	...	...	...	1043	...	...	1240	1438	1638	...	1838	1903	1907	...	...	1947	...	...	...	2017	...	...
215	Château du Loir d.	0656	...	0810	...	...	...	1113	...	...	1311	1506	1712	...	1909	1954	1953	...	...	2018	...	...	...	2102	...	...
262	St Pierre des Corps a.	|	...	|	...	...	...	1141	...	...	|	1534	|	...	|	|	|	...	...	|	...	...	...	|	...	...
265	**Tours** a.	0738	...	0838	...	...	...	1153	...	...	1339	1545	1742	...	1938	2029	*2050*s	...	...	2048	...	...	...	2139	...	...

	Ⓐ	⑥ u	Ⓐ	Ⓐ	⚒	† d	⚒	†	⑥ u	Ⓐ	⚒ ⊕	⑥ t	Ⓐ ⊗	Ⓐ	⑤ f		⑥ u	①–④ m	⑤ f	Ⓐ	Ⓑ h	†	⑤ f	†	①–④ m	⑤⑦ v
Tours d.	...	...	*0527*z	0635	0749	0905	0907	1021	...	...	1159	1225	1422	...	1519	1654	...	...	...	1729	1821	...	...	1907	...	2121
St Pierre des Corps d.	...	...	|	|	|	0920	0922	|	...	...	|	|	|	...	|	|	...	...	...	|	|	...	...	1922	...	|
Château du Loir d.	...	...	*0556*z	0709	0821	0949	0951	1050	...	...	1229	1307	1453	...	1550	1724	...	...	...	1812	1852	...	...	1952	...	2153
Le Mans a.	...	...	*0643*z	0758	0853	1020	1024	1121	...	...	1259	1357	1523	...	1618	1751	...	...	...	1857	1921	...	...	2021	...	2221
Le Mans d.	0623z	0657	0659	*0856*	...	1034	1036	*1240*	1240	1240	...	...	1530	...	1623	1754	1858	1900	1900	*1930*	...	1958	2003	2025	2029	...
Alençon d.	0657	0748	0749	*0945*	...	1104	1107	*1329*	1328	1332	...	...	1606	1722	1722	1830	1928	1930	1936	*2019*	...	2027	2033	2056	2107	...
Sées d.	0709	0801	0802	...	...	1116	1119	...	1340	1345	...	...	1618	1734	1734	1842	1940	1942	1950	...	...	2039	2045	2108	2120	...
Surdon 273 d.	0715	0808	0809	...	...	1124	1126	...	1347	1352	...	...	|	1741	1742	1850	1948	1949	1958	...	...	2045	2052	|	2127	...
Argentan 273 d.	0725	0818	0819	...	...	1134	1136	...	1356	1402	...	...	1632	1751	1751	1901	1958	1958	2014	...	...	2055	2102	2122	2137	...
Mézidon 275/7 d.	0751	0846	0847	...	...	1158	1159	...	1422	1430	...	...	1655	1820	1820	1924	2025	2029	2049	...	...	2121	2128	|	...	...
Caen 275/7 a.	0805	0900	0902	...	...	1212	1213	...	1437	1444	...	...	1710	1834	1834	1939	2040	2043	2104	...	...	2135	2142	2157	...	...

d – Not Nov. 16.
f – Also Aug. 14; not Aug. 15.
h – Also Nov. 1.
m – Not holidays or Aug. 14.
r – 1628 on †, 1641 on ⑥.
s – ⑥ only (by 🚌).

t – Not Nov. 1.
u – Not Nov. 1, 15.
v – Also holidays and Aug. 14.
z – ① (also June 10, July 15, Nov. 12; not June 9, July 14, Nov. 10).
⊕ – Subject to alteration on Ⓐ July 15 - 18, Aug. 18 - Oct. 3, Nov. 10 - Dec. 5.

⊗ – Subject to alteration on July 15, 16.
△ – On Ⓐ Oct. 27 - Nov. 11 calls at Tours before St Pierre des Corps.

Subject to alteration on Nov. 15, 16

CAEN - COUTANCES - GRANVILLE / RENNES — 272

km		① Jy	Ⓐ	⑥	Ⓐ	Ⓐ	Ⓐ	B	🚌 K	J	Ⓐ K	Ⓒ K	Ⓐ		Ⓐ		🚌	† K	⑥ K	⚒	🚌 ⑥	🚌 Ⓐ	⑤ f	A	⑥ K
0	**Caen** 275 d.	0545	0613	0708	0709	0830	0910	0911	...	1110	1110	1120	1211	1238	1336	1413	...	1517	1520	1606	...	...	1711	1729	1736
30	Bayeux 275 d.	0601	0636	0725	0725	0851	0927	0927	...	1127	1127	1138	1229	1300	1357	1429	...	1540	1543	1628	...	...	1727	1745	1752
57	Lison 275 d.	0618	0657	0743	0742	0910	0945	0943	...	1145	1144	1156	1248	1319	1417	1445	...	1601	1604	1648	...	...	1744	1802	1808
75	St Lô d.	0633	0709	0756	0801	0924	0958	0956	...	1156	1156	1208	1302	1335	1435	1500	...	1614	1617	1701	1707	1732	1758	1816	1821
105	**Coutances** a.	0654	0731	0819	0822	...	1020	1018	1025	1220	1220	1230	1325	*1419*c	...	1521	1528	1638	1641	...	1744	1802	1820	1837	1843
143	Granville a.	*0744*r	*0816**	*0856**	|	...	...	|	1058	*1259*c	...	1258	*1405**	*1452*c	...	|	1601	1715	1713	...	...	...	*1900**	*1917**	*1922**
252	*Rennes 272a* a.	0850	...	...	1003	...	...	1202	...	...	...	...	...	...	...	1706	...	...	...	...	...	...	2005	2032	2025

	Ⓐ	🚌 ⑤ J	⑤ f	①–④ m	⑥ J△	Ⓐ	⑤ f	N	†	🚌 Ⓐ ◧
Caen 275 d.	1735	...	1805	1808	1808	1842	1908	1910	1919	...
Bayeux 275 d.	1755	...	1827	1831	1830	1904	1930	1932	1941	...
Lison 275 d.	1812	...	1848	1850	1851	1923	1949	1953	2001	2041
St Lô d.	1830	1838	1903	1903	1903	1941	2002	2006	2015	2101
Coutances a.	...	1915	1927	1930	1929	...	2024	2028	2035	2131
Granville a.	...	1948	...	...	...	...	*2104**	...	*2115**	...
Rennes 272a a.	...	...	...	...	...	...	2208	...	2215	...

	⚒	🚌 Ⓐ	🚌 ⑥	⚒	Ⓒ 🚌	Ⓒ K	Ⓐ J	Ⓐ	Ⓒ J	B	Ⓐ
Rennes 272a d.	...	...	...	...	...	...	0547	...	...	0825	0906
Granville d.	...	0547	0600	...	...	0751	*0649*n	...	*0745**	*0936**	*1017**
Coutances d.	0608	0620	0633	...	0709	0818	0739	0825	0828	1019	1102
St Lô d.	0632	0657	0710	0720	0746	0841	0801	0849	0852	1041	1125
Lison 275 d.	0649	0717	...	0737	0806	0858	0814	0906	0909	1056	1139
Bayeux 275 d.	0708	...	...	0755	...	0916	0829	0923	0926	1110	1153
Caen 275 a.	0731	...	...	0819	...	0933	0847	0941	0943	1129	1211

	Ⓐ	⚒	🚌 ⑤ f	Ⓐ	Ⓐ	† J	† K		D	F	E	† K	⑤ f	①–④ m	⑤ J	† J	⑥ J△	①–④ m		⑥ K	† K	⑤ f	†	⑥ K	⑦ Je
Rennes 272a d.	...	...	...	...	...	1240	...	...	1455	...	...	...	...	...	1628	1648	1648	1654	...	...	...	1824	1845	1859	2043
Granville d.	...	*1152**	1248	...	...	*1345*n	...	...	*1601**	...	*1636*s	*1650**	*1651**	*1710**	|	*1755**	*1755**	*1801**	...	1916	1925	*1943**	*1952**	*2005**	*2144*n
Coutances d.	...	1236	1321	1331	...	1436	1435	*1541*a	1639	*1643**	1719	1734	1735	*1744**	1830	1838	1839	1844	...	1943	1952	2026	2036	2048	2234
St Lô d.	1227	1301	...	1354	1500	1500	1500	1628	1700	1727	1742	1758	1758	1831	1902	1859	1904	1905	...	2006	2022	2048	2058	2110	2256
Lison 275 d.	1244	1314	...	1408	1513	1514	1513	1642	1714	1740	1756	1811	1811	1844	1916	1913	1917	1919	...	2020	2038	2101	2112	2123	2310
Bayeux 275 d.	1301	1329	...	1425	1529	1529	1530	1700	1730	1800	1811	1829	1827	1901	1930	1927	1931	1933	...	2038	2056	2115	2126	2140	2324
Caen 275 a.	1326	1349	...	1443	1546	1546	1548	1722	1749	1822	1830	1846	1846	1926	1948	1945	1950	1951	...	2055	2113	2133	2144	2156	2342

OR NOTES SEE FOOT OF PAGE

🚌 services are subject to confirmation from July 6.

COUTANCES / GRANVILLE - DOL - ST MALO / RENNES — 272a

km		🚌 Ⓐ J	① Jy	🚌 Ⓐ	Ⓐ	🚌 ⑥	B	Ⓐ K	Ⓒ K		🚌 J		K	🚌 ⑤ f	⑤ f			A	⑥ K		🚌 ⑤ f	⑤ f	🚌 †	†	
0	*Caen 272* d.	...	0545	...	0709	...	0911	...	...	...	...	1413	...	...	1711	...	...	1729	1736	...	...	1908	...	1919	...
105	**Coutances** d.	...	0657	...	0823	...	1021	...	...	...	...	1522	...	...	1822	...	...	1845	1844	...	...	2026	...	2037	...
•	Granville 273 d.	0649	|	0814	|	1011	|	1047	1111	...	1513	|	1723	1812	|	...	1847	|	|	...	2018	|	2028	|	...
132	Folligny 273 d.	0709	0721	0834	0843	1031	1041	1058	1123	...	1533	1543	1735	1832	1842	...	1857	1906	1904	...	2038	2048	2048	2057	...
151	Avranches d.	...	0739	...	0857	...	1055	1113	1137	...	...	1557	1749	...	1856	...	...	1922	1919	...	...	2103	...	2111	...
173	Pontorson ⊡ d.	...	0758	...	0914	...	1114	1130	1154	...	...	1614	1806	...	1913	...	...	1942	1936	...	...	2120	...	2128	...
194	Dol 281 a.	...	0816	...	0931	...	1130	1146	1211	...	...	1630	1822	...	1929	...	...	1959	1952	...	...	2136	...	2144	...
	St Malo 281 a.	...	|	...	|	...	|	1209	1234	...	...	|	1845	...	|	...	...	|	|	...	...	|	...	|	...
252	**Rennes** 281 a.	...	0850	...	1003	...	1202	...	...	...	...	1706	...	...	2005	...	...	2032	2025	...	...	2208	...	2215	...

	Ⓐ J	B	🚌 ⑥	Ⓐ	🚌 Ⓐ	Ⓐ K	Ⓒ K	† J	D	🚌 ⑤ J	⑤ J	🚌 ⑤ J	† J	⑥ J△	🚌 Ⓒ J	①–④ m	🚌 ①–④ J	Ⓒ K	Ⓐ K	⑤ f	🚌 ⑤ J	†	🚌 † J	⑥ K	⑦ Je
Rennes 281 d.	0547	0825	...	0906	...	...	...	1240	1455	...	1628	...	1648	1648	...	1654	...	...	...	1824	...	1845	...	1859	2043
St Malo 281 d.	|	|	...	|	...	1057	1120	|	|	...	|	...	|	|	...	|	...	1735	1749	|	...	|	...	|	|
Dol 281 d.	0621	0857	...	0938	...	1121	1143	1313	1526	...	1658	...	1719	1719	...	1726	...	1758	1812	1858	...	1916	...	1930	2116
Pontorson ⊡ d.	0644	0920	...	1001	...	1143	1205	1337	1543	...	1722	...	1741	1741	...	1749	...	1820	1834	1921	...	1939	...	1953	2139
Avranches d.	0706	0943	...	1024	...	1205	1227	1400	1605	...	1745	...	1803	1803	...	1810	...	1842	1857	1942	...	2002	...	2015	2201
Folligny 273 d.	0719	0957	1002	1040	1045	1219	1241	1415	1618	1628	1800	1806	1817	1816	1821	1824	1829	1856	1911	1957	2002	2016	2021	2028	2214
Granville 273 a.	|	|	1022	|	1105	1230	1252	|	|	1648	|	1826	|	|	1841	|	1849	1907	1926	|	2022	|	2041	|	|
Coutances a.	0738	1018	...	1100	...	...	...	1434	1638	...	1820	...	1836	1836	...	1843	...	...	...	2017	...	2034	...	2047	2233
Caen 272 a.	0847	1129	...	1211	...	...	...	1546	1749	...	1948	...	1945	1950	...	1951	...	...	...	2133	...	2144	...	2156	2342

OTES FOR TABLES 272 AND 272a

– ①–④ (also ⑥⑦ to July 5 / from Aug. 30), not Aug. 14.
– ⑥ (also ⑦ July 6 - Aug. 24), also July 14, Aug. 15; not Nov. 1.
– ⑤ (daily July 6 - Aug. 24).
– ①②③④⑥ (also ⑦ to June 29 / from Aug. 31), not July 14, Aug. 14.
– Ⓐ to July 4; ①–④ m July 7 - Aug. 22, Ⓐ from Aug. 25.
– To July 4 / from Aug. 25.
– July 6 - Aug. 24.
– ①②③④⑥ (not holidays or Aug. 14).

a – Ⓐ only. By 🚌.
c – Ⓒ only. By 🚌.
e – Also June 9, Nov. 11; not June 8, Nov. 9
f – Also Aug. 14; not Aug. 15.
m – Not holidays or Aug. 14.
n – By 🚌 from Granville (change to train at Folligny, Table **272a**).
r – By 🚌 Folligny (Table **272a**) - Granville.
s – ①②③④⑦ (also holidays). By 🚌.
y – Also June 10, Nov. 12; not June 9, Nov. 10.

◧ – Additional 🚌 run at 2142 ⑤–⑦, 2329 Ⓐ.
⊡ – Pontorson-Mont St Michel (10 km from Mont St Michel).
△ – Not Nov. 1.
• – Granville - Folligny is *15 km*.
* – By 🚌.

Timings may vary by up to 5 minutes.
🚌 services are subject to confirmation from July 6.

273 PARIS - DREUX - GRANVILLE

TEMPORARILY RELOCATED TO PAGE 225

274 ° PARIS - VERSAILLES

RER (express Métro) Line C: **Paris Austerlitz** - St Michel Notre Dame - **Versailles Rive Gauche** (for Château). Every 15 - 30 minutes. Journey 40 minutes.
Alternative service: RER Line C: Paris Austerlitz - St Michel Notre Dame - Versailles Chantiers. Journey 39 minutes.
SNCF suburban services: Paris St Lazare - Versailles Rive Droite (journey 28 - 35 minutes); Paris Montparnasse - Versailles Chantiers (journey 12 - 28 minutes). See also Table **278**.

275 PARIS - CAEN - CHERBOURG

For other trains Paris - Lisieux (- Trouville-Deauville) see Table **276**

km		3325								3331	3301			3333		3327		3335		3303	3337		3305		3341	
		①	⚒	Ⓐ	Ⓐ	⚒	Ⓐ	⚒	⚒	Ⓐ	Ⓐ	Ⓐ		⑥	⑥		Ⓐ	Ⓐ	Ⓐ	Ⓒ	Ⓒ	Ⓒ	Ⓐ	Ⓐ	Ⓒ	Ⓒ
		g	⊖				J	⊡						t	d	T										
0	**Paris** St Lazare ▷ d.	0026	...	...	...	...	...	...	...	0643	0705	...	...	0743	...	0813	...	0843	...	0908	0943	...	1008	...	1143	...
57	Mantes la Jolie ▷ d.	|	...	...	...	...	...	...	...	|	|	...	...	|	...	|	...	|	...	|	|	...	|	...	|	...
108	Evreux ▷ d.	0132	...	...	...	...	0609	...	...	0742	|	...	...	0842	...	|	...	0942	...	|	1042	...	|	...	1242	...
160	Bernay d.	0211	...	...	...	...	0647	...	...	0809	|	...	...	0909	...	|	...	1009	...	|	1109	...	|	...	1309	...
191	Lisieux **277** d.	0240	...	0609	...	0644	0703	...	0744	0827	|	...	0844	0927	...	|	0944	1027	...	|	1127	...	|	...	1327	...
216	Mézidon **271 277** d.	|	...	0624	...	0659	0716	...	0759	|	|	...	0859	|	...	|	0959	|	...	|	|	...	|	...	|	...
239	**Caen** **271 277** a.	0317	...	0644	...	0719	0735	...	0819	0852	0857	...	0919	0952	...	1006	1019	1052	...	1059	1152	...	1159	...	1352	...
239	**Caen** **272** d.	0320	0551	...	0658	...	...	0800	...	...	0900	0910	...	...	1000	1009	...	...	1100	1102	...	1200	1202	1300	...	1400
269	Bayeux **272** d.	0350	0607	...	0714	...	...	0816	...	...	|	0927	...	...	1016	1026	...	...	1116	1118	...	1216	1218	1316	...	1416
296	Lison **272** d.	0411	0624	...	0730	...	...	0832	...	...	|	0944	...	...	1031	1044	...	...	1133	1137	...	1231	1237	1331	...	1431
314	Carentan d.	0425	0634	...	0740	...	...	0842	...	...	0938	...	...	...	1041	1057	...	...	1144	1149	...	1242	1249	1341	...	1441
343	Valognes d.	0445	0649	...	0755	...	...	0857	...	...	0953	...	...	...	1057	1113	...	...	1159	1205	...	1257	1305	1357	...	1457
371	**Cherbourg** a.	0501	0704	...	0810	...	...	0912	...	...	1008	...	...	...	1112	1130	...	...	1214	1220	...	1312	1320	1412	...	1512

	3307	3309		3343		3345	3347	3311			3313		3361	3349	3315		3351	3317		3353	3319	3321	3355	3323	3357	3359
	Ⓐ	⑥	Ⓐ	Ⓐ	Ⓐ	⑤	Ⓒ	Ⓐ	Ⓐ	Ⓐ	Ⓒ		⑤	Ⓐ	Ⓐ	Ⓐ		Ⓐ	Ⓒ	Ⓐ	⑤	Ⓒ		Ⓑ	⑥	⑤
		t				x							B								f			h	t	v
Paris St Lazare ▷ d.	1208	1308	...	1343	...	1408	1443	1508	...	...	1608	...	1604	1643	1707	...	1743	1805	...	1843	1902	1908	1958	2043	2043	2143
Mantes la Jolie ▷ d.	|	|	...	|	...	|	|	|	...	...	|	...	|	|	|	...	|	|	...	|	|	|	2038	|	|	|
Evreux ▷ d.	|	|	...	1442	...	1508	1542	|	...	...	|	...	|	1742	|	...	1842	|	...	1942	|	|	2105	2141	2142	2242
Bernay d.	|	|	...	1509	...	1535	1609	|	...	...	|	...	1724	1809	|	...	1909	|	...	2009	|	|	2132	2208	2209	2309
Lisieux **277** d.	|	|	1444	1527	...	1553	1627	|	1644	1725	|	1749	1742	1827	|	1844	1927	|	...	2027	|	|	2151	2225	2227	2327
Mézidon **271 277** d.	|	|	1459	|	...	|	|	|	1659	1739	|	1804	|	|	|	1859	|	|	...	|	|	|	|	|	|	|
Caen **271 277** a.	1359	1459	1519	1552	...	1619	1652	1659	1719	1757	1759	1823	1808	1852	1859	1919	1952	1959	...	2052	2057	2059	2216	2247	2254	2352
Caen **272** d.	1402	1502	...	...	1600	...	...	1701	...	1800	1802	1826	...	...	1902	...	...	2002	2000	...	2100	2102	...	2250	...	...
Bayeux **272** d.	1418	1518	...	...	1616	...	...	1717	...	1816	1818	1842	...	...	1918	...	...	2018	2016	...	2118	2118	...	2307	...	...
Lison **272** d.	1437	1537	...	...	1631	...	...	1734	...	1832	1837	1858	...	...	1937	...	...	2037	2031	...	2137	2137	...	2325	...	...
Carentan d.	1449	1549	...	...	1641	...	...	1746	...	1842	1849	1908	...	...	1949	...	...	2049	2041	...	2149	2149	...	2337	...	...
Valognes d.	1505	1605	...	...	1657	...	...	1802	...	1857	1905	1923	...	...	2005	...	...	2105	2057	...	2205	2205	...	2352	...	...
Cherbourg a.	1520	1620	...	...	1712	...	...	1817	...	1912	1920	1938	...	...	2020	...	...	2120	2112	...	2220	2220	...	0008	...	...

	3330	3332		3300	3364	3334				3302			3338			3340	3304	3304			3306	3342			3344	3324
	Ⓐ	①–⑥	Ⓐ	Ⓐ	①		⚒	Ⓐ	Ⓒ		Ⓐ	Ⓒ		⚒		⑤	⑥	①–④		†	⑤	Ⓒ	Ⓐ	⚒	Ⓐ	
		b			E					§						f		m			f		q			S
Cherbourg d.	...	...	...	0545	0619	...	0630	0717	...	0735	...	...	...	0939	...	...	1036	1036	...	1137	1153	...	...	1244	...	1252
Valognes d.	...	...	...	0603	0637	...	0645	0733	...	0752	...	...	...	0955	...	...	1053	1053	...	1153	1211	...	...	1300	...	1310
Carentan d.	...	...	...	0614	0652	...	0700	0748	...	0807	...	...	...	1010	...	...	1109	1109	...	1208	1226	...	...	1315	...	1326
Lison **272** d.	...	...	...	0626	0704	...	0711	0759	...	0820	0906	0909	...	1021	...	...	1120	1120	...	1219	|	...	...	1325	...	1338
Bayeux **272** d.	...	...	...	0648	0720	...	0729	0815	...	0839	0923	0924	...	1037	...	...	1139	1139	...	1235	|	...	...	1342	...	1357
Caen **272** a.	...	...	...	0703	0735	...	0750	0831	...	0854	0941	0943	...	1052	...	...	1154	1154	...	1251	1307	...	...	1358	...	1412
Caen **271 277** d.	0509	0609	0634	0706	0738	0744	0752	0834	0834	0857	...	...	1009	...	1108	1151	1157	1157	...	...	1310	1309	1308	...	1409	1415
Mézidon **271 277** d.	|	|	0654	|	|	|	0811	0854	0854	|	...	...	|	...	1128	|	|	|	...	...	|	|	1328	...	|	|
Lisieux **277** d.	0536	0636	0708	|	|	0811	0825	0908	0908	|	...	...	1036	...	1142	|	|	|	...	...	1336	1336	1342	...	1436	1442
Bernay d.	0554	0654	...	|	|	0829	...	...	...	|	...	...	1054	...	...	|	|	|	...	...	1354	1354	...	...	1454	1500
Evreux ▷ d.	0621	0721	...	|	|	0856	...	...	...	|	...	...	1121	...	...	|	|	|	...	...	1421	1421	...	...	1521	1527
Mantes la Jolie ▷ a.	|	|	...	|	|	0922	...	...	...	|	...	...	|	...	...	|	|	|	...	...	|	|	...	...	|	|
Paris St Lazare ▷ a.	0718	0820	...	0858	0935	0958	...	...	...	1048	...	...	1217	...	...	1345	1347	1347	...	...	1518	1518	...	...	1618	1624

	3308	3326		3346			3368	3348			3312	3310			3314		3316	3350			3318		3352	3320		3322
			Ⓐ	Ⓒ	Ⓐ		⑦		Ⓐ	⚒	⑦	Ⓐ	Ⓐ	Ⓐ	Ⓐ	†	⑥	⑦	⑥	Ⓐ	⑦		⑦	Ⓐ	Ⓐ	⑦
		R					D				e		J				t	e	d		e		e			k
Cherbourg d.	1336	1355	...	...	...	1537	...	...	...	1619	1636	1654	...	...	1736	1739	1750	...	1819	1819	1835	...	...	1903	1947	2005
Valognes d.	1353	1413	...	...	...	1553	...	...	...	1634	1653	|	...	...	1753	1755	1808	...	1834	1835	1852	...	...	1920	2003	2023
Carentan d.	1409	1430	...	...	...	1608	...	...	...	1649	1708	|	...	...	1809	1810	1823	...	1850	1850	1908	...	...	1935	2018	2038
Lison **272** d.	1420	1442	1514	...	...	1619	...	...	...	1659	1721	|	...	...	1820	1821	1835	...	1901	1901	1920	...	...	1946	2029	2050
Bayeux **272** d.	1439	1500	1529	...	...	1635	...	...	...	1716	1739	|	...	...	1839	1835	1853	...	1915	1917	1938	...	...	2006	2043	2108
Caen **272** a.	1454	1516	1546	...	...	1651	...	...	...	1731	1755	1754	...	...	1854	1852	1908	...	1932	1932	1954	...	...	2022	2101	2124
Caen **271 277** d.	1457	1519	1548	1609	1634	...	1657	1709	1722	1734	1757	1757	1823	1834	1857	...	1911	1909	...	1934	1957	...	2009	2024	...	2127
Mézidon **271 277** d.	|	|	1603	|	1654	...	|	|	1742	1754	|	|	1842	1854	|	...	|	|	...	1954	|	...	|	|	...	|
Lisieux **277** d.	|	|	1617	1636	1708	...	|	1736	1757	1808	|	|	1855	1908	|	...	1936	1936	...	2008	|	...	2036	2048	...	|
Bernay d.	|	|	...	1654	...	...	|	1754	...	...	|	|	1911	...	|	...	1953	1954	...	...	|	...	2054	|	...	|
Evreux ▷ d.	|	|	...	1721	...	...	|	1821	...	...	|	|	1948	...	|	...	2020	2021	...	...	|	...	2121	|	...	|
Mantes la Jolie ▷ a.	|	|	...	|	...	...	|	|	...	...	|	|	...	...	|	...	|	|	...	...	|	...	|	|	...	|
Paris St Lazare ▷ a.	1648	1717	...	1818	...	...	1854	1918	...	...	1947	1947	...	...	2047	...	2118	2118	...	...	2147	...	2218	2218	...	2318

LOCAL TRAINS PARIS - EVREUX - SERQUIGNY △

	Ⓐ	Ⓐ	Ⓐ	Ⓐ	Ⓐ	Ⓐ	Ⓐ	Ⓐ	
Paris St Lazare d.	0905	1110	1308	1608	1710	1810	1907	2011	...
Mantes la Jolie d.	0941	1144	1344	1644	1747	1847	1947	2047	...
Evreux a.	1017	1220	1418	1715	1819	1919	2019	2119	...
Serquigny a.	...	1253	...	1755	1856	1956	...	...	...

	Ⓐ	Ⓐ	Ⓐ		Ⓐ	Ⓐ		Ⓐ	Ⓐ
Serquigny d.	...	0605	0705	...	...	1305	...	...	1805
Evreux d.	0539	0640	0740	...	1139	1340	...	1741	1840
Mantes la Jolie a.	0616	0716	0816	...	1213	1413	...	1813	1912
Paris St Lazare a.	0652	0758	0858	...	1248	1450	...	1853	...

B – ⑤ from Sept. 5.
D – ⑦ from Sept. 7 (not Oct. 12, 19, Nov. 9).
E – ① from Sept. 1 (also Nov. 12; not Nov. 10).
J – To July 4 / from Aug. 25.
R – June 9, Nov. 11 only.
S – ⑦ June 29 - Aug. 31 (also June 9, Aug. 15, Nov. 2, 11; not July 13).
T – ⑥ June 28 - Aug. 30 (also Aug. 15, Nov. 8; not July 5, 12).

b – Not June 9, July 5, 12, 14, Sept. 20, Oct. 4, 11, 18, Nov. 11.
d – Not Nov. 1.
e – Also June 9, July 14, Nov. 11; not July 13.
f – Also Aug. 14; not Aug. 15.
g – Also June 10, July 15, Nov. 12; not June 9, July 14, Nov. 10.
h – Not July 13, Aug. 15.
k – Also June 9, July 14, Nov. 11.
m – Not holidays or Aug. 14 (runs Aug. 15).
q – Runs 26 minutes later on ③ during school term; runs 8 minutes later certain dates.

t – Also Aug. 15.
v – Not Aug. 15.
x – Also June 7, 14, 21, Aug. 14.

▷ – For additional trains see panel below main table (also Table **276**).
△ – Frequent suburban trains run Paris - Mantes-la-Jolie. Additional local trains run Mantes la Jolie - Evreux and Evreux - Serquigny.
⊡ – Runs 14 minutes later on ②–⑤.
⊖ – Runs 5 - 6 minutes later from Aug. 9.
§ – Subject to alteration on May 25.

Timings may vary by a few minutes.
Departures from Paris may be 2 - 3 minutes later on certain dates.
Numbered trains are subject to alteration on July 5, 6, 12 - 14, Oct. 4, 5, 11, 12, 18, 19.

PARIS - LISIEUX - TROUVILLE DEAUVILLE 276

km				3371		3373		3375	3377		3379		3395	3381			3383		3385			3387	3389	3391	3393
		⚒	Ⓑ	Ⓐ	⑥	Ⓒ	Ⓐ	Ⓐ	⑥	⚒	Ⓐ	Ⓒ		⑥	⑥	Ⓐ	⑤	①–④	⑤			⑤	⑦	⑥	Ⓐ
			h		t			S	F				Z	T			f	m	S f	B	c	S f	S u	P	
0	**Paris** St Lazare ..... ▷ d.	...	...	0745	...	0845	...	0944	1010	...	1145	...	1212	1345	...	...	1545	...	1633	...	...	1810	1820	1845	1910
108	Evreux ..... ▷ d.	...	...	0842	...	0942	...	|	1108	...	1242	...	|	1442	...	...	1642	...	|	...	...	|	1919	1942	2007
160	Bernay ..... ▷ d.	...	...	0909	...	1009	...	|	1135	...	1309	...	|	1509	...	...	1709	...	|	...	...	|	1946	2009	2037
191	**Lisieux** ..... ▷ d.	0735	0835	0927	0935	1027	1035	|	1153	1235	1327	1335	|	1527	1535	1633	1727	1735	1817	1835	1935	1952	2005	2027	2057
209	Pont l'Évêque ..... d.	0748	0848	0939	0948	1039	1048	|	1205	1248	1339	1348	|	1539	1548	1648	1739	1748	1828	1848	1946	2004	2018	2039	2108
221	**Trouville-Deauville** ..... a.	0757	0857	0948	0957	1048	1057	1131	1215	1257	1348	1357	1408	1548	1557	1658	1748	1757	1838	1857	1955	2013	2027	2048	2117

		3370				3372					3374	3376	3390		3378			3380	3392	3382	3384			3386	3388
	⚒	Ⓐ	†				⑥	Ⓐ	⑤–⑦	Ⓐ		Ⓐ			⑦		Ⓐ	Ⓒ		⑦	Ⓐ	†	Ⓐ	⑥	⑦
				B		D	t⊡		w		E	S	Y		d		b		Y	V		△		S u	R
Trouville-Deauville ..... d.	0700	0711	0737	0804	1004	1112	1153	1204	1302	1404	1412	1415	1550	1604	1638	1702	1804	1811	1844	1853	1911	2004	2016	2031	2058
Pont l'Évêque ..... d.	0709	0721	0746	0813	1013	1122	1206	1213	1312	1413	1422	1425	|	1613	1650	1712	1813	1821	|	|	1921	2013	2025	|	2108
Lisieux ..... ▷ d.	0722	0734	0759	0826	1026	1134	1219	1226	1326	1426	1434	1440	|	1626	1704	1726	1826	1834	|	|	1934	2028	2038	|	2120
Bernay ..... ▷ d.	...	0754	...	...	...	1154	...	...	...	...	1454	1501	|	...	1723	...	...	1854	|	|	1954	...	...	|	2139
Evreux ..... ▷ d.	...	0821	...	...	...	1221	...	...	...	...	1521	1528	|	...	1750	...	...	1921	|	|	2021	...	...	|	2207
Paris St Lazare ..... ▷ a.	...	0918	...	...	...	1316r	...	...	...	...	1616r	1628	1756	...	1846	...	...	2016	2041	2046	2116	...	...	2226	2303

B – Ⓐ (also ⑥ July 12 - Aug. 23).
D – Ⓐ (also ⑥ June 28 - Aug. 30). Depart 1108 on Ⓐ June 30 - Aug. 29.
E – ⒸJune 28 - Aug. 31 (also Nov. 2, 11).
F – ⑥ to Sept. 20 (also ⑦ June 29 - Aug. 31), also Aug. 15, Oct. 25, Nov. 1; not July 5, 6, 12, 13.
P – ⑥ July 19 - Aug. 30 (also June 28, Aug. 15).
R – ⑦ to Sept. 28 (also June 9; not July 6, 13, Sept. 21).
S – June 29 - Aug. 31.
T – ⑥ to Sept. 13 (also Aug. 15, Sept. 27, Nov. 2, 11; not July 5, 12).
V – ⑦ June 1 - Sept. 28 (also June 9, July 14; not July 13).
Y – Nov. 11 only.
Z – Aug. 15, Nov. 1, 8 only.
b – Not on ⑤ July 4 - Aug. 29; not July 14, Aug. 14.
c – Not on ⑤ July 11 - Aug. 8; not July 14, Aug. 22.
d – Also June 9, July 14, Nov. 11; not July 13.
f – Also Aug. 14; not Aug. 15.
h – Not Aug. 15.
m – Not holidays.
r – Arrive 14 minutes later on July 5, 12.
t – Also Aug. 15.
u – Also July 14; not July 13.
w – Also June 9, July 14, Aug. 14, Nov. 11.
▷ – For other trains see Table 275.
△ – On Aug. 15 depart 2001.
⊡ – Runs 7 - 11 minutes later from Nov. 8.

Departures from Paris may be 2 - 3 minutes earlier on Ⓐ June 2 - 16 and Ⓐ Sept. 8 - Oct. 3.

TROUVILLE DEAUVILLE - DIVES CABOURG 276a

24 km Journey 30 minutes

From Trouville Deauville: 0834 Ⓐ **K**, 0957 Ⓐ **K**, 1104 Ⓒ, 1141 Ⓐ **K**, 1225 **Q**, 1359 ①–④ **F**, 1406 ⑥⑦ **b**, 1409 ⑤ **P**, 1418 **Y**, 1559 ⑥ **L**, 1609 Ⓐ **K**, 1645 ⑦ **d**, 1750 ①–④ **F**, 1756 ⑤ **P**, 1900 ⑦ **M**, 2005 ①–④ **F**, 2005 ⑥ **N**, 2021 ⑤ **P**, 2038 ⑦ **M**, 2111 ⑥ **N**, 2126 Ⓐ⑤ **E**, 2126 ①–④ **F**, 2133 ⑤ **P**.

From Dives Cabourg: 0620 ① **B**, 0620 Ⓐ **K**, 0913 Ⓐ **K**, 1023 Ⓒ **K**, 1034 Ⓐ **K**, 1140 **S**, 1222 ⑥ **R**, 1322 **D**, 1522 Ⓐ **K**, 1522 ⑥ **H**, 1558 ⑦ **e**, 1710 Ⓐ **K**, 1731 Ⓒ, 1832 Ⓐ **K**, 1951 ⑦ **M**, 2041 ①–④ **F**, 2057 ⑤ **P**.

B – ① to June 23 / from Sept. 1 (also June 10, Nov. 12; not June 9, Nov. 10).
D – ⑥ Apr. 5 - Nov. 1 (daily June 29 - Aug. 31).
E – To June 27 / from Sept. 4.
F – ①–④ June 30 - Aug. 28 (not July 14, Aug. 14).
H – ⑥ Mar. 29 - Sept. 27 (also Aug. 15, Nov. 1, 2).
K – June 28 - Aug. 31.
L – ⑥ Mar. 29 - Sept. 27 (also Aug. 15, Nov. 2, 11).
M – ⑦ June 29 - Aug. 31 (also July 14).
N – ⑥ June 28 - Aug. 30 (also Aug. 15).
P – ⑤ July 4 - Aug. 29 (also Aug. 14; not Aug. 15).
Q – ⑥ Apr. 5 - Nov. 1 (also ⑦ June 29 - Aug. 31), also Aug. 15.
R – ⑥ from Nov. 8.
S – Ⓒ Apr. 5 - Nov. 2; ⑦ from Nov. 9 (also Nov. 11).
Y – Aug. 15, Nov. 1, 8 only.
b – Also June 9, July 14, Nov. 11; not Nov. 1, 8.
d – Also June 9, July 14, Nov. 1; not Nov. 2.
e – Also June 9, July 14; not Nov. 2.

ROUEN - LISIEUX - CAEN 277

km		Ⓐ	⑥	Ⓐ	Ⓐ	Ⓐ	†	⑥	†	①	②–⑤	Ⓐ	Ⓐ	⑥	⑤	⑤	†		Ⓐ	⑥	⚒	†	Ⓐ	†
					E	F				F u	F ‡	M	L		f	v								
0	**Rouen** Rive Droite ..... d.	0602	0702	0702	...	1002	1002	1002	1202	1202	1202	...	...	1302	1502n	1602	1602	...	1702	1702	1802	1802	1902	1902
23	Elbeuf-St Aubin ..... d.	0620	0720	0722	1019	1020	1020	1020	1220	1220	1218	1220	...	1320	1520	1620	1620	...	1718	1720	1818	1820	1920	1920
73	Serquigny ..... d.	0649	|	|	|	|	|	1049	1249	1249	1251	1249	1327	1349	|	1649	1649	...	1745	1745	1854	1854	|	|
83	Bernay ..... ▷ d.	0657	0751	0756	1053	1051	1054	1058	1256	1258	1300	1257	1335	1358	1552	1656	1658	...	1754	1753	1901	1901	1952	1954
114	Lisieux ..... ▷ d.	0713	0808	0812	1109	1108	1110	1115	1313	1315	1320	1314	1351	1414	1609	1713	1715	...	1811	1810	1918	1918	2009	2010
139	Mézidon 271 ..... ▷ d.	0728	0824	0826	1123	1123	1124	1129	1328	1329	1337	1329	1406	1428	1623	1728	1728	...	1825	1825	1932	1932	2023	2023
162	**Caen 271** ..... ▷ a.	0742	0837	0839	1137	1137	1137	1142	1342	1342	1353	1342	1420	1442	1637	1742	1742	...	1839	1839	1946	1946	2037	2037

	Ⓐ		⑥	Ⓐ	Ⓐ	Ⓐ	Ⓒ		①–④	⑤	Ⓒ		Ⓐ	Ⓒ	Ⓐ	†	⑥		Ⓐ		⑤	†	⑥	
					E	F			F §	F											f		S	
Caen 271 ..... ▷ d.	0552	...	0718	0720	1020	1020	1020	...	1205	1218	1218	...	1715	1723	1809	1818	1818	...	1916	...	2011	2029	2021	...
Mézidon 271 ..... ▷ d.	0606	...	0732	0734	1034	1034	1034	...	1221	1232	1232	...	1729	1737	1823	1832	1832	...	1930	...	2025	2043	2035	...
Lisieux ..... ▷ d.	0620	...	0746	0748	1048	1048	1048	...	1238	1246	1245	...	1743	1750	1838	1845	1846	...	1943	...	2039	2057	2049	...
Bernay ..... ▷ d.	0637	...	0803	0805	1105	1105	1105	...	1259	1303	1302	...	1800	1807	1856	1902	1903	...	2000	...	2056	2114	2106	...
Serquigny ..... d.	0644	...	0810	0812	|	|	|	...	1307	1310	1310	...	|	|	1903	1910	1910	...	|	...	|	|	|	...
Elbeuf-St Aubin ..... d.	0719	...	0840	0840	1137	1138	1138	...	1339	1339	1339	...	1831	1840	1932	1939	1939	...	2033	...	2136	2146	2138	...
Rouen Rive Droite ..... a.	0739	...	0900	0900	...	1156	1156	...	1400	1400	1400	...	1851	1857	1951	2000	2000	...	2051	...	2156	2204	2157	...

– June 30 - Aug. 14.
– To June 27 / from Aug. 18.
– June 30, July 1 only.
– Ⓐ July 2 - Aug. 14.
S – ⑥ Apr. 12 - Sept. 20.
f – Also Aug. 14; not Aug. 15.
n – Not July 4 - Aug. 15.
u – Also June 10; not June 9.
v – Not June 8, July 4 - Aug. 15, Nov. 10.
▷ – See also Table 275.
§ – Not holidays or Nov. 10.
‡ – Not holidays.

Subject to alteration on June 28, 29. On Nov. 1 service is as on ⑦.

PARIS - CHARTRES - LE MANS 278

For *TGV* trains Paris - Le Mans via the high-speed line see Table **280**

km		Ⓐ	Ⓐ	⚒	⚒	Ⓐ										Ⓐ	Ⓐ	Ⓐ	†	⑥	Ⓑ	Ⓐ	Ⓐ	Ⓐ	Ⓑ
0	**Paris** Montparnasse .. 274 d.	0533	...	0609	0639	0740	0809	0906	1009	1106	1209	1306	1409	1506	1609	1624	1639	1706v	1706	1706	1709	1724	1739	1754	1806
17	Versailles Chantiers .. 274 d.	0546	...	0625	0654	0754	0825	0922	1025	1122	1225	1322	1425	1522	1625	1640	1655	1722*	1722	1722	1725	1739	1755	1809	1822*
48	Rambouillet ..... d.	0602	...	0645	0713	0813	0845	0943	1045	1143	1245	1342	1445	1542	1645	1700	1715	|	|	1743	1745	1800	1815	1830	|
88	**Chartres** ..... d.	0640	0648	0725	0743	0851	0925	1009	1125	1209	1325	1410	1525	1609	1726	1731	1755	1809	1809	1813	1825	1831	1855	1859	1909
149	Nogent le Rotrou ..... d.	...	0736	...	0820	...	...	1047	...	1247	...	1446	...	1647	*1824*	1824	...	1847	1847	1853	...	1924	...	...	1947
211	**Le Mans** ..... a.	...	0824	...	0856	...	...	1124	...	1324	...	1524r	...	1724		...	...	1924	1924	1935	...	...	...	...	2024

		Ⓐ	Ⓐ				Ⓑ		Ⓐ	①⑦
Paris Montparnasse ..... 274 d.	1809	1824	1854	1906	1939	2009	2106	2209	2302	0020
Versailles Chantiers ..... 274 d.	1825	1840	1909	1922	1955	2025	2122	2225	2321	0036
Rambouillet ..... d.	1846	1900	1930	1943	2015	2045	2142	2245	2344	0104
Chartres ..... d.	1926	1931	1959	2010	2055	2125	2209	2325	0022	0141
Nogent le Rotrou ..... d.	...	2024	...	2047	...	...	2247	...	...	...
Le Mans ..... a.	...	...	...	2128	...	...	2324	...	...	...

	Ⓐ	Ⓐ	⑥	Ⓐ	⚒	Ⓐ		Ⓐ	⚒
Le Mans ..... d.	...	0336	...	...	...	...	...	0534	...
Nogent le Rotrou ..... d.	...	0414	...	...	...	0530	...	0614	...
Chartres ..... d.	0404	0452	0451	0534	0604	0627	0632	0652	0702
Rambouillet ..... d.	0446	0520	0520	0616	0646	0701	0714	|	0744
Versailles Chantiers .... 274 d.	0508	0541	0541	0638	0708	0723	0738	0741*	0808
Paris Montparnasse .... 274 a.	0520	0553	0553	0650	0720	0735	0750	0753	0820

	Ⓐ	Ⓐ		Ⓐ	⚒	Ⓐ	Ⓐ	Ⓒ				Ⓐ	Ⓒ						Ⓐ				Ⓑ	†
Le Mans ..... d.	0552	...	...	0632	...	...	0736	0736s	...	0936	...	1128	1136	...	1336r	...	1536	...	...	1736	...	1936	...	2136
Nogent le Rotrou ..... d.	0624	0630	*0630s*	0709	...	0733	0814	0811	...	1014	...	1213	1214	...	1414	...	1614	...	...	1813	...	2014	...	2214
Chartres ..... d.	0722	0727	0734	0757	0802	0827	0852	0850	0934	1052	1134	1252	1251	1334	1452	1534	1652	1734	1802	1851	1934	2052	2134	2252
Rambouillet ..... d.	|	0801	0816	0831	0846	0901	0919	0919	1016	1119	1216	1319	1320	1416	1519	1616	1719	1816	|	1920	2016	2119	2214	2319
Versailles Chantiers ..... 274 d.	0811*	0823	0838	0853	0908	0923	0941	0940	1038	1141	1238	1341	1341	1438	1541	1638	1741	1838	|	1941	2038	2141	2234	2341
Paris Montparnasse ..... 274 a.	0824	0835	0850	0905	0920	0935	0953	0953	1050	1153	1250	1353	1353	1450	1553	1650	1753	1850	1920	1953	2050	2153	2246	2353

– ⚒ only.
– ⑥ only.
v – Departs from Montparnasse Vaugirard platforms.
* – Will not convey passengers travelling Paris - Versailles or v.v.

Timings may vary by a few minutes

For service July 6 - Aug. 24 see page 558

280 PARIS - LE MANS - RENNES and NANTES

TGV Atlantique

Valid until July 5

TGV trains convey 🍸. Many trains continue to destinations in Tables **281**, **284**, **285**, **288** and **293**. For other trains Massy - Nantes via St Pierre des Corps see Table **335**.

km		Ⓐ	⑥	Ⓐ	⑥	Ⓐ	Ⓐ	TGV 8801 ①–⑤	TGV 8903 ①–⑤	TGV 8603 Ⓐ	TGV 8603 ⑥ A	Ⓐ	TGV 8805 ①–⑥ A	TGV 8081 Ⓐ	TGV 8711 Ⓒ	TGV 8909	TGV 8611 g	TGV 8813	TGV 8715	TGV 5486 ☆	TGV 5471 g☆		TGV 5214
	Lille Europe **11** d.	...	...	...	...	...	...	...	...	...	...	...	...	...	...	...	...	...	...	...	...	...	0836
	Charles de Gaulle ✈ d.	...	...	...	...	...	...	...	...	...	...	...	...	...	...	...	...	...	...	...	...	...	0949
	Marne la Vallée § d.	...	...	...	...	...	...	...	...	...	...	...	...	...	...	...	...	...	...	0932	0932	...	1003
0	**Paris** Montparnasse d.	...	...	...	...	...	...	0623	0653	0704	0708	...	0723	0736	0808	0853	0908	0953	1008	|	|	...	|
14	Massy TGV d.	...	...	...	...	...	...	|	0705	|	|	...	0739	0748	|	|	|	|	|	1008	1008	...	1038
202	**Le Mans** d.	0612	0612	0630	0637	0650	0703	0720	|	|	|	0824	0831	|	0906	|	|	1051	|	1101	1108	1105	1130
292	Laval d.	|	|	0736	0733	|	0753	|	|	0839	|	|	|	|	0949	|	|	|	|	|	1149	|	|
327	Vitré d.	|	|	0759	0757	|	0822	|	|	|	|	|	|	|	|	|	|	|	|	|	|	|	|
365	**Rennes** a.	|	|	0819	0816	|	0850	|	|	0919	0919	|	|	0954	1027	|	1114	|	1215	|	1228	|	|
251	Sablé a.	0634	0639	...	...	0712	...	|	|	...	...	0846	0853	...	...	|	...	|	...	|	...	1126	|
299	Angers St Laud **289** a.	0657	0701	...	...	0736	...	0759	|	...	...	0909	0916	...	...	1027	...	1130	...	1140	...	1149	1210
387	**Nantes 289** a.	0748	0751	...	...	0820	...	0848	0907	...	...	0950	1003	...	...	1106	...	1210	...	1218	...	1231	1256

	TGV 5211	⑦ A	TGV 8815 ①–⑤	TGV 8617 g	TGV 8817	TGV 8717	TGV 8819	TGV 8621 ⑤ G	TGV 5227 m	TGV 5225	TGV 8821	TGV 8623 ①–④ d	TGV 8629 ⑤⑥† n	⑤	⑤	TGV 8821 Ⓐ	TGV 8839 ⑦	TGV 8729 G	TGV 5232 p	TGV 5209 ⑦–④ F	TGV 8829	TGV 8033 ⑤⑦ em	①–⑥
Lille Europe **11** d.	0836	...	...	...	...	...	...	...	1106z	1106z	...	...	...	...	...	...	...	...	1352	1352	...	...	...
Charles de Gaulle ✈ d.	0949	...	...	...	...	...	...	...	1249	1249	...	...	...	...	...	...	...	...	1449	1449	...	...	...
Marne la Vallée § d.	1003	...	...	...	...	...	...	...	1303	1303	...	...	...	...	...	...	...	...	1503	1503	...	...	...
Paris Montparnasse d.	|	...	1053	1108	1153	1208	1223	1307	|	|	1353	1408	1408	...	...	1453	1453	1508	|	|	1553	1608	...
Massy TGV d.	1038	...	|	|	|	|	|	|	1338	1342	|	|	|	...	...	|	|	|	1538	1538	|	|	...
Le Mans d.	1134	1138	|	1206	|	1306	|	1406	1431	1440	1450	|	|	1535	1531	|	1551	|	1634	1630	|	|	1702
Laval d.	|	1229	|	1246	|	|	|	|	|	|	|	|	1542	|	1622	|	|	|	|	|	|	|	|
Vitré d.	|	1254	|	1307	|	|	|	|	|	|	|	|	|	|	1639	|	|	|	|	|	|	|	|
Rennes a.	1250	1327	|	1330	|	1422	|	1522	1549	|	|	1616	1622	|	1657	|	|	1715	1749	|	|	1813	|
Sablé a.	...	...	|	...	|	...	1337	...	...	|	|	...	...	1556	...	|	|	...	...	|	|	...	1725
Angers St Laud **289** a.	...	...	|	...	1325	...	1401	...	...	1520	1530	...	...	1618	...	1626	1630	...	...	1709	1726	...	1748
Nantes 289 a.	...	...	1259	...	1411	...	1440	...	...	1559	1609	...	...	1659	...	1707	1759	...	...	1752	1811	...	1829

	TGV 8831 ⑤ G	TGV 8737 Ⓐ	†	Ⓐ	TGV 8833 Ⓐ	TGV 8747 Ⓐ	TGV 8745 Ⓒ j	TGV 8937 ⑦–④ F	①–④	⑤	TGV 8645 ①–④ d	TGV 8691 ⑤ G	TGV 8939 Ⓐ	TGV 8841	TGV 8659 q	TGV 5488 ①–⑤ ☆	TGV 8943 ⑤⑥ H	TGV 8095 Ⓐ	TGV 8845 Ⓐ	TGV 8979	TGV 8665 r	①–④	†
Lille Europe **11** d.	...	...	...	...	...	...	...	...	...	...	...	...	...	...	...	...	...	...	...	...	...	...	...
Charles de Gaulle ✈ d.	...	...	...	...	...	...	...	...	...	...	...	...	...	...	...	...	...	...	...	...	...	...	...
Marne la Vallée § d.	...	...	...	...	...	...	...	...	...	...	...	...	...	...	...	1732	...	...	...	...	...	...	...
Paris Montparnasse d.	1623	1641	...	...	1653	1708	1708	1723	...	...	1741	1741	1749	1753	1808	|	1823	1841	1849	1853	1908	...	...
Massy TGV d.	|	|	...	...	|	|	|	|	...	...	|	|	|	|	|	1807	|	|	|	|	|	...	...
Le Mans d.	|	1738	1742	1742	1750	|	1806	|	1821	1823	|	1838	|	1851	|	1900	|	|	|	1951	2006	2016	2016
Laval d.	|	1820	|	1833	|	|	1849	|	|	|	1915	1922	|	|	|	|	|	2014	|	|	|	|	|
Vitré d.	|	|	|	1850	|	|	|	|	|	|	|	|	|	|	|	|	|	2035	|	|	|	|	|
Rennes a.	|	1900	|	1912	|	1916	1927	|	|	|	1955	1959	|	|	2017	|	|	2057	|	|	2122	|	|
Sablé a.	|	...	1804	...	|	...	...	|	1843	1845	...	...	|	|	...	|	|	...	|	2012	...	2037	2037
Angers St Laud **289** a.	1757	...	1828	...	1830	...	...	|	1907	1909	...	...	|	1930	...	1941	|	...	|	2035	...	2100	2100
Nantes 289 a.	1837	...	1910	...	1916	...	...	1928	1949	1952	...	...	1958	2010	...	2026	2032	...	2054	2118	...	2141	2141

	⑤	TGV 8761	TGV 5231	TGV 5237 p	TGV 8849 ⑦ J	TGV 8949 ⑤ G		TGV 8851 ①–④ L	TGV 5488 ⑦ ☆	TGV 8071 ⑤⑥† G△	TGV 8777 ⑤ k	TGV 8853 Ⓒ	TGV 8077 ①–④ d	TGV 8679 ⑤ G	TGV 8075 ⑦ Zm		TGV 8855 ①–④ K	TGV 8855 ①–④ L	TGV 5234 ⑤	TGV 8857 ⑤⑦	TGV 8079 ⑦ v	TGV 8779 ⑤ G	
Lille Europe **11** d.	...	...	1752	1752	...	...	...	...	...	...	...	...	...	...	...	...	...	...	1952	...	...	...	...
Charles de Gaulle ✈ d.	...	...	1848	1848	...	...	...	...	...	...	...	...	...	...	...	...	...	...	2049	...	...	...	...
Marne la Vallée § d.	...	...	1901	1901	...	...	...	...	1932	...	...	...	...	...	...	...	...	...	2103	...	...	...	...
Paris Montparnasse d.	...	1941	|	|	1953	1953	...	1953	|	2008	2024	2053	2108	2108	2108	...	2123	2123	|	2153	2208	2208	...
Massy TGV d.	...	|	1938	1938	|	|	...	|	2008	|	|	|	|	|	|	...	|	|	2138	|	|	|	...
Le Mans d.	2020	|	2031	2038	|	|	...	2051	2100	2105	2120	|	|	|	2205	...	2220	2220	2231	2250	|	2306	...
Laval d.	|	|	|	2119	|	|	...	|	|	2148	|	|	2241	|	2247	...	|	|	|	|	2341	2349	...
Vitré d.	|	|	|	|	|	|	...	|	|	|	|	|	|	2302	2309	...	|	|	|	|	|	|	...
Rennes a.	|	2147	|	2158	|	|	...	|	|	2227	2236	|	2322	2322	2332	...	|	|	|	|	0022	0027	...
Sablé a.	2041	...	|	...	|	|	...	|	|	...	...	|	...	...	...	...	|	|	|	|	...	...	...
Angers St Laud **289** a.	2104	...	2110	...	|	2128	...	2130	2140	...	...	2225	...	...	...	...	2300	2300	2311	2330	...	...	...
Nantes 289 a.	2144	...	2149	...	2205	2207	...	2210	2219	...	...	2304	...	...	...	...	...	2339	2357	0009	...	...	...

	TGV 8800 ① M	TGV 8802 Ⓐ	TGV 8052 Ⓐ	TGV 8690 Ⓐ	TGV 8804 Ⓐ	TGV 5254 ①–⑥ A	TGV 5252 ⚒ J	TGV 8908 ②–⑤ P	TGV 8810 ⑥ Q	TGV 8706 ①–⑥ A	①–⑤		①–⑤	TGV 8908 Ⓐ	TGV 8970 Ⓐ	①–⑤	TGV 8610 ①–⑥ w	TGV 8816 T	TGV 8712 Ⓐ	TGV 5478 ①–⑥ A☆	TGV 8818 Ⓐ	TGV 8082 ① A	TGV 8618 ⑥ Q
Nantes 289 d.	0500	0525	...	...	0600	...	0605	0630	0630	...	0629	...	0634	0630	0700	0735	...	0730	...	0735	0800	...	...
Angers St Laud **289** d.	0542	0605	...	...	0640	...	0643	|	0708	...	0713	...	0740	|	|	0818	...	0809	...	0814	0839	...	...
Sablé d.	|	0630	...	...	|	...	|	|	|	...	0740	...	0812	|	|	0844	...	|	...	|	|	...	...
Rennes d.	|	|	0530	0603	|	0607	|	|	|	0633	|	0705	|	|	|	|	0703	|	0733	|	|	0803	0903
Vitré d.	|	|	0553	|	|	|	|	|	|	|	|	0725	|	|	|	|	|	|	|	|	|	|	|
Laval d.	|	|	0613	|	|	|	|	|	|	0710	|	0746	|	|	|	|	|	|	|	|	|	0841	|
Le Mans d.	0625	0653	0658	|	|	0722	0733	|	0750	|	0804	0837	0843	|	|	0909	0818	|	0849	0857	|	0923	|
Massy TGV a.	|	|	|	|	|	0821	0821	|	|	|	...	...	...	|	|	...	|	|	|	0945	|	|	|
Paris Montparnasse a.	0720	0749	0759	0812	0816	|	|	0837	0845	0853	...	...	...	0837	0909	...	0917	0944	0948	|	1014	1023	1117
Marne la Vallée § a.	...	...	...	...	...	0857	0857	...	...	...	...	...	...	...	...	...	...	...	...	1027	...	...	...
Charles de Gaulle ✈ a.	...	...	...	...	...	0911	0911	...	...	...	...	...	...	...	...	...	...	...	...	...	...	...	...
Lille Europe **11** a.	...	...	...	...	...	1017	1017	...	...	...	...	...	...	...	...	...	...	...	...	...	...	...	...

	TGV 8820 Ⓐ	TGV 8618 Ⓐ	TGV 8824	TGV 5272	TGV 5270	TGV 8620 Ⓐ	TGV 8926 Ⓐ	TGV 8622 Ⓒ	TGV 5256 ⑦	TGV 8928 Ⓒ	†	①–⑥	TGV 8974 ⑥ Q	TGV 8084 ①–④ d	TGV 8084 ⑤ G	TGV 8084 Ⓒ j	TGV 8832 Ⓐ	TGV 8730 j	TGV 8834	TGV 5280 x	TGV 5278	TGV 5460 p☆	TGV 5480 ⑤–⑦ ☆
Nantes 289 d.	0900	...	1000	...	1005	...	1105	...	...	1131	1137	1204	1200	...	...	...	1300	...	1400	...	1404	...	1433
Angers St Laud **289** d.	0940	...	1038	...	1043	...	1144	...	...	1209	1219	1246	1239	...	...	...	1340	...	1438	...	1443	...	1511
Sablé d.	|	...	|	...	|	...	|	...	...	|	1245	1308	|	...	...	...	|	...	|	...	|	...	|
Rennes d.	|	0903	|	1004	|	1033	|	1103	1114	|	|	|	|	1233	1233	1303	|	1403	|	1408	|	1433	|
Vitré d.	|	|	|	|	|	|	|	|	|	|	|	|	|	|	|	|	|	|	|	|	|	|	|
Laval d.	|	|	|	1042	|	1111	|	1140	|	|	|	|	|	1311	1311	1341	|	|	|	|	|	1511	|
Le Mans d.	|	1019	|	1126	1133	1154	|	1224	1229	|	1310	1336	1323	1354	1354	|	1423	|	1522	1522	1533	1555	1602
Massy TGV a.	|	|	|	1222	1222	|	|	|	1322	|	...	...	|	|	|	|	|	|	|	1622	1622	1652	1652
Paris Montparnasse a.	1117	1121	1214	|	|	1253	1320	1323	|	1344	...	...	1420	1453	1504	1523	1518	1611	1619	|	|	|	|
Marne la Vallée § a.	...	...	...	1256	1256	...	...	...	1357	...	...	...	...	...	...	...	...	...	...	1657	1657	1727	1727
Charles de Gaulle ✈ a.	...	...	...	1311	1311	...	...	...	1411	...	...	...	...	...	...	...	...	...	...	1711	1711	...	...
Lille Europe **11** a.	...	...	...	1407	1407	...	...	...	1507	...	...	...	...	...	...	...	...	...	...	1807	1807	...	...

A – Not June 9.
B – Not May 1, 8.
C – Not May 8.
F – Not May 1, 7, 8, 28, 29.
G – Also May 7, 28.
H – Also May 1, 7, 8, 28, 29.
J – Not May 8, 29.
L – May 12 - July 3 (also May 5,6. Not May 28, 29, June 9).
M – Not June 9. Also June 10.
P – Not May 1, 8, 29, June 10.
Q – Also May 1, 8, 29.
T – Not June 22.

NOTES CONTINUED ON NEXT PAGE →

NANTES and RENNES - LE MANS - PARIS 280

	TGV 8938	TGV 8068			TGV 8847	TGV 8646		TGV 8752	TGV 8944			TGV 8978	TGV 8088	TGV 8088	TGV 8660	TGV 5290	TGV 5288	TGV 8946		TGV 8848	TGV 8762	TGV 8762	TGV 8668
	Ⓑ	Ⓑ	Ⓑ	⑥	①–④		Ⓐ			†	①–⑤	Ⓐ	Ⓐ	Ⓒ	Ⓑ			①–⑥	⑤	Ⓑ	Ⓐ	Ⓒ	
	V	s			U			p						p	s			V		V		p	p
Nantes 289 d.	1500	...	1515	1530	1600	...	...	...	1700	1714	1732	1730	...	...	...	...	1755	1800	1837	1830	...	...	...
Angers St Laud **289** d.	|	...	1557	1612	1639	...	...	...	1739	1757	1822	|	...	...	...	...	1834	1840	1921	|	...	...	...
Sablé d.	|	...	1621	1641	|	...	...	...	|	1823	1847	|	...	...	...	...	|	1904	1947	|	...	...	...
Rennes d.	|	1503	|	|	|	1603	1631	1703	|	|	|	|	1733	1733	1803	1807	|	|	|	|	1833	1833	1903
Vitré d.	|	|	|	|	|	|	1654	|	|	|	|	|	|	|	|	|	|	|	|	|	1855	1854	|
Laval d.	|	|	|	|	|	1640	1715	|	|	|	|	|	1811	1812	|	|	|	|	|	|	|	|	|
Le Mans d.	|	1619	1648	1714	|	1723	1806	|	1823	1848	1912	|	1953	|	|	1925	1933	|	2012	|	|	1954	|
Massy TGV a.	|	|	...	...	|	|	...	|	|	...	...	|	|	|	|	2021	2021	|	...	|	|	|	|
Paris Montparnasse a.	1711	1719	...	...	1814	1822	...	1911	1920	...	...	1937	1953	1953	2011	|	|	2019	...	2037	2049	2054	2111
Marne la Vallée § a.	...	...	...	...	...	...	...	...	...	...	...	...	...	...	...	2056	2056	...	...	...	...	...	...
Charles de Gaulle ✈ a.	...	...	...	...	...	...	...	...	...	...	...	...	...	...	...	2111	2111	...	...	...	...	...	...
Lille Europe **11** a.	...	...	...	...	...	...	...	...	...	...	...	...	...	...	...	2251	2251	...	...	...	...	...	...

	TGV 8850			TGV 8982	TGV 8774		TGV 8952	TGV 8780			TGV 8854		TGV 8688	TGV 8682		TGV 8856	TGV 8076		TGV 8958	TGV 8798		TGV 8960	TGV 8796
	Ⓑ	①–⑤		⑦	⑦		⑤⑥†			†	①–④		⑦	Ⓑ		⑤⑦	⑤		⑦	⑤		⑦	⑦
	V			Z	Z		G	p			d		Zm	V		e	G		Z	Z		Z	Zm
Nantes 289 d.	1900	1906	...	1930	...	...	2000	...	...	2008	2030	...	...	...	...	2100	...	...	2200	...	...	2225	...
Angers St Laud **289** d.	1940	1949	...	|	...	...	2040	...	...	2051	2109	...	...	...	...	2139	...	...	|	...	...	2304	...
Sablé d.	|	2016	...	|	...	...	|	...	...	2116	|	...	...	...	...	|	...	...	|	...	...	|	...
Rennes d.	|	|	...	|	1933	...	|	2003	...	|	|	...	2033	2103	...	|	2133	...	|	2203	...	|	2233
Vitré d.	|	|	...	|	|	...	|	|	...	|	|	...	2055	|	...	|	|	...	|	|	...	|	|
Laval d.	|	|	...	|	|	...	|	2040	...	|	|	...	|	|	...	|	2211	...	|	|	...	|	2313
Le Mans d.	2022	2042	...	|	2049	...	|	|	...	2141	|	...	|	|	...	2222	2254	...	|	|	...	|	|
Massy TGV a.	|	...	...	|	|	...	|	|	...	...	|	...	|	|	...	|	|	...	|	|	...	|	|
Paris Montparnasse a.	2119	...	...	2141	2150	...	2215	2219	...	...	2244	...	2254	2311	...	2319	2353	...	0007	0011	...	0039	0053
Marne la Vallée § a.	...	...	...	...	...	...	...	...	...	...	...	...	...	...	...	...	...	...	...	...	...	...	...
Charles de Gaulle ✈ a.	...	...	...	...	...	...	...	...	...	...	...	...	...	...	...	...	...	...	...	...	...	...	...
Lille Europe **11** a.	...	...	...	...	...	...	...	...	...	...	...	...	...	...	...	...	...	...	...	...	...	...	...

NOTES - CONTINUED FROM PREVIOUS PAGE

U – Not May 1, 7, 8, 28, 28, June 9.
V – Not May 1, 8, 29.
Z – Also June 9.
d – Not May 1, 7, 8, 28, 29, June 9.
e – Also May 7, 28, June 9.
g – Not May 25, June 8, 9.
j – Not May 24, June 8, 9.
k – Also May 7, 8, 28.
m – Not June 8.
n – Also May 7, 28. Not May 24, June 7, 8.
p – Not May 24, June 7, 8.
q – Not May 24, 30, 31, June 7, 8.
r – Not May 24, 31, June 7, 8.
s – Not May 1, 8, 29, June 8.
t – Not May 24, June 7, 8.
v – Also June 9. Not June 8.
w – Not May 31, June 9.
x – Not May 24, June 7, 8, 9.
z – Lille **Flandres**.

TGV – Ⓡ, supplement payable, 🍸.

☆ – From/to Strasbourg (Table **391**).

§ – Marne la Vallée-Chessy (station for Disneyland Paris).

△ – On May 24 and June 7, 8 does not call at Laval and arrives Rennes 2348.

RENNES - ST MALO 281

Valid until July 5

km	*TGV trains,* Ⓡ	TGV 8081	TGV 8091	TGV 8083	TGV 8085	TGV 5227	TGV 8089	TGV 8095	TGV 8099	TGV 8097
		Ⓐ	Ⓒ	Ⓐ	Ⓒ	⑤⑦	Ⓒ	Ⓐ	⑦	⑤
			d			v			e	f
	Paris Montparnasse **280** d.	0736	0808	1008	1008	...	1508	1841	1908	2024
	Lille Flandres **11** d.	|	|	|	|	1106	|	|	|	|
0	**Rennes 272** d.	0959	1034	1222	1222	1549	1722	2100	2132	2243
58	Dol **272** d.	1029	1106	|	1253	|	|	2128	|	2311
81	**St Malo** a.	1046	1121	1305	1310	1635	1806	2147	2212	2330

TGV trains, Ⓡ	TGV 8080	TGV 8082	TGV 8084	TGV 8084	TGV 8084	TGV 8088	TGV 5290	TGV 8092	
	①–⑥	①	①–④	⑤	Ⓒ		⑤⑦	Ⓒ	
	h	h	n	f	g	j	v	j	
St Malo d.	0604	0711	1140	1140	1210	1640	1710	1910	...
Dol **272** d.	0620	0726	|	|	|	1656	|	1926	...
Rennes 272 a.	0653	0758	1228	1258	1258	1728	1802	1958	...
Lille Flandres **11** a.	|	|	|	|	|	|	2251	|	...
Paris Montparnasse **280** a.	0917	1023	1453	1504	1523	1953	...	2219	...

	⚒	⚒	⑥⑦ b	Ⓐ	Ⓒ	Ⓐ	⑥	A	⚒	⑤ f	Ⓒ	Ⓐ	Ⓐ	Ⓐ	⑦	Ⓐ	⑥⑦	Ⓐ	Ⓐ	⑤	⑥	⑦	①–④	⑤ f	† c	Ⓐ
Rennes 272 d.	0630	0730	0930	0940	1130	1245	1300	1343	1440	1535	1635	1635	1700	1730	1733	1800	1830	1835	1910	1928	1940	1945	2005	2028	2030	2208
Dol **272** d.	0709	0808	1006	1018	1208	1325	1343	1417	1516	1611	1710	1715	1738	1808	1811	1844	1905	1910	1947	2009	2016	2023	2024	2106	2105	2246
St Malo a.	0730	0828	1022	1032	1222	1343	1402	1435	1530	1625	1724	1734	1752	1828	1825	1903	1928	1925	2002	2023	2030	2037	2057	2120	2119	2300

	Ⓐ	Ⓐ	⚒	Ⓐ		⑥	Ⓐ	⑥⑦	⑥	③	†	⚒		Ⓐ	†	⑤ f	Ⓒ	Ⓐ	Ⓐ	†	⑥	Ⓐ	†	Ⓐ		⑦ c
St Malo d.	0550	0620	0650	0720	0750	0850	0927	0950	1050	1220	1250	1244	1450	1548	1550	1650	1720	1720	1745	1747	1815	1820	1830	1850	1955	2050
Dol **272** d.	0604	0638	0703	0738	0805	0903	0941	1004	1109	1239	1304	1303	1505	1602	1604	1704	1734	1739	1804	1806	1834	1835	1844	1906	2009	2104
Rennes 272 a.	0641	0719	0744	0819	0845	0941	1019	1043	1148	1320	1341	1349	1537	1636	1642	1736	1808	1820	1849	1850	1913	1916	1916	1945	2043	2137

A – Departs Rennes 1352 on Ⓒ from May 29 (Dol d. 1429, St Malo a. 1442).
b – Also May 8, 29, June 9.
c – Not June 8.
d – Not May 25, June 8, 9.
e – Also June 9.
f – Also May 7, 28.
g – Not May 24, June 8, 9.
h – Not June 9.
j – Not June 7, 8.
n – Not May 1, 7, 8, 28, 29, June 9.
v – Also May 7, 28, June 9. Not June 8.

DOL - DINAN 282

Valid until July 5

km		Ⓐ	⑥	Ⓐ	Ⓒ	⑥	Ⓐ	† b	† c	⑥	Ⓒ	Ⓐ	Ⓐ	†	† d	Ⓐ	⑤⑥ a
0	**Dol** d.	0702	0818	1037	1115	1305	1423	1425	1434	1521	1725	1730	1849	1920	2110	2136	2251
28	**Dinan** a.	0725	0841	1100	1138	1328	1446	1448	1457	1552	1756	1759	1919	1943	2133	2159	2314

		Ⓐ	⚒		⑥	Ⓐ		Ⓒ	⑥		⚒	Ⓐ	†		⑥	Ⓐ	† d
Dinan d.	...	0630	0732	...	0927	1230	...	1230	1435	...	1621	1806	1810	...	1851	1936	2034
Dol a.	...	0657	0800	...	0957	1258	...	1258	1458	...	1650	1829	1833	...	1918	2004	2057

a – Also May 7, 28.
b – Until May 25.
c – From June 1 (also May 29, June 9).
d – Not June 8.

MORLAIX - ROSCOFF 283

Valid until July 5

orlaix - St Pol de Leon (*21* km) - **Roscoff** (*28* km). Journey 30 minutes (38 mins by 🚌). 🚌 journeys serve Roscoff port at sailing times.

rom **Morlaix**: 0805🚌Ⓐ, 0840🚌⚒a, 1030⚒b, 1106Ⓐc, 1106⑥j, 1115🚌⚒b, 1151†, 1309⚒, 1525🚌⑥k, 1526†, 1625🚌①–④e, 1715🚌⑤f, 1805🚌①–④g, 1820🚌Ⓒk, 005🚌⑤f, 2005🚌†m, 2010🚌⑦n, 2110🚌①–④h, 2140🚌⑤f.

rom **Roscoff**: 0635🚌Ⓐb, 0640🚌Ⓐc, 0755🚌Ⓐb, 0800🚌Ⓐc, 0820🚌⑥d, 0830🚌⑥a, 1125🚌†m, 1130🚌⑦p, 1133⑥d, 1139Ⓐ, 1139⑥a, 1320🚌Ⓐb, 1320🚌⑥d, 1328†m, 330🚌Ⓐa, 1330🚌⑥a, 1339†q, 1429⑥d, 1435⑥a, 1530Ⓐ, 1625🚌⑥d, 1630🚌⑥a, 1705†m, 1708†q, 1710🚌①–④b, 1715🚌①–④g, 1830🚌Ⓐb, 1835🚌Ⓐc, 1925🚌†m, 935🚌†p, 2045🚌⑤f.

a – Until May 24.
b – From May 26.
c – Until May 23.
d – From May 31.
e – Schooldays only.
f – Also May 7, 28.
g – Until May 22 (not May 7, 28).
h – Not May 7, 28.
j – Until May 24.
k – Also May 8, 29.
m – From June 1 (also June 9).
n – Not June 29.
p – Until May 25 (not May 8).
q – Until May 25.

For service July 6 - Aug. 24 see page 560

284 RENNES - ST BRIEUC - MORLAIX - BREST

Valid until July 5

km	*TGV* trains convey 🍷	Ⓐ	Ⓐ	Ⓐ	Ⓐ	⑥	Ⓐ	⑥	Ⓐ	Ⓐ	⑥ T	*TGV* **8603** Ⓐ	Ⓐ	⚒ ▽	†	† Y	Ⓐ	⑥	*TGV* **8611**	⚒	Ⓑ V	⑥	③ W	⑥		*TGV* **8617** ⚒ A
	Paris ⊡ **280** d.	...	...	...	...	...	...	...	...	...	...	0704	...	...	...	...	...	...	0908	...	...	...	...	...	...	1108
0	**Rennes** d.	...	...	...	0612	...	0620	0640	0700	0720	0830	0922	...	...	0957	...	1040	1042	1117	...	...	...	...	1238	1344	1333
80	Lamballe **299** d.	...	...	...	0651	...	0723	0745	|	0809	0906	0959	...	...	1034	...	1119	1119	|	...	...	...	...	1314	1442	|
101	**St Brieuc 299** d.	...	...	...	0704	0708	0737	0800	0747	0823	0919	1012	...	...	1048	...	1131	1132	1204	...	...	1223	1235	1327	1500	1421
132	Guingamp d.	...	...	...	0721	0726	...	...	|	...	0938	1033	...	1046	1105	...	...	1150	1225	...	1234	1243	1301	1346	...	1442
158	Plouaret-Trégor d.	...	...	...	0736	0741	...	...	|	...	0953	|	...	1101	1121	1134	...	1205	|	...	1250	1301	1320	1401	...	1457
175	Lannion a.	...	0556	...	*0822*z	|	...	...	|	...	|	|	...	1120	|	1153	...	*1235*z	|	...	1307	1320	1338	|	...	|
189	Morlaix d.	0614	0637	0725	0800	0803	...	...	0830	...	1012	1101	1112	...	1140	...	...	1223	1253	1305	...	...	...	1420	...	1513
215	Landivisiau d.	0628	0657	0741	0815	0820	...	...	|	...	1027	|	1128	...	1155	...	...	1238	|	1328	...	...	...	1435	...	|
230	Landerneau **286** d.	0638	0709	0751	0828	0834	...	...	|	...	1037	|	1138	...	1205	...	...	1248	|	1341	...	...	...	1445	...	1536
248	**Brest 286** a.	0653	0724	0809	0840	0846	...	...	0902	...	1049	1134	1150	...	1217	...	...	1301	1327	1359	...	...	...	1457	...	1550

	TGV **8617** ⑦ B	V	*TGV* **8627** ①-④ C	⑤ D	Ⓒ	Ⓐ	⑥	①-④ Q	*TGV* **8621** ⑤ D	Ⓐ	† U	⑤ D	*TGV* **8623** ①-④ C	⑤ D	*TGV* **8623** Ⓒ	Ⓐ	Ⓒ	†	⑥	①-④ Q	⑤ D	①-④ Q	⑤ D	†	Ⓒ	Ⓐ
Paris ⊡ **280** d.	1108	...	1208	...	...	...	...	...	1307	...	...	...	1408	...	1408	...	...	...	...	...	...	...	...	...	...	...
Rennes d.	1333	...	1429	1435	1435	...	...	...	1525	...	...	1600	1619	1623	1625	...	...	...	...	...	1650	1710	1720	1729	1737	1744
Lamballe **299** d.	1410	...	|	1512	1513	...	...	...	1601	...	...	1638	|	1707	1701	...	...	...	...	...	1728	1806	1806	1808	1838	1821
St Brieuc 299 d.	1425	...	1515	1525	1526	...	...	...	1616	...	...	1651	1708	1719	1715	...	...	...	1730	1733	1741	1820	1819	1821	1852	1834
Guingamp d.	1446	...	1536	1542	1543	...	...	...	1638	...	...	1709	1729	...	1736	...	...	...	1752	1800	1759	...	...	1837	...	1851
Plouaret-Trégor d.	1501	1508	|	1556	1557	...	1603	1634	|	...	1700	1722	|	...	1751	...	...	1755	1811	1818	1813	...	...	1851	...	1905
Lannion a.	|	1526	|	*1636*z	|	...	1622	1653	|	...	1720	*1746*z	|	...	|	...	...	1817	1830	1837	*1853*z	...	...	*1913*z	...	|
Morlaix d.	1517	...	1603	1614	1615	1630	...	...	1706	1720	...	1741	1757	...	1807	1809	1817	...	...	...	1831	...	...	1908	...	1923
Landivisiau d.	|	...	|	|	1631	1646	...	...	|	1744	...	1757	|	...	|	1828	1837	...	...	...	1847	...	...	1924	...	1940
Landerneau **286** d.	1541	...	|	1638	1641	1656	...	...	|	1756	...	1807	|	...	|	1838	1847	...	...	...	1857	...	...	1934	...	1950
Brest 286 a.	1555	...	1638	1650	1654	1708	...	...	1740	1814	...	1819	1830	...	1842	1853	1905	...	...	...	1910	...	...	1946	...	2002

	⑤ D	*TGV* **8633** ⑤⑦ E	①-④ Q	①-④ Q	†	†	⑥	Ⓐ	*TGV* **8647** ⑤ D	*TGV* **8643** ①-④ C	⑤	Ⓐ	Ⓐ		†	*TGV* **8645** ①-④ C	*TGV* **8649** ⑤ D	*TGV* **8655** ①-④ C	*TGV* **8657** ⑤-⑦ F	Ⓐ	†	*TGV* **8663** ⑤ G	*TGV* **8665** ⑥-④ H	Ⓒ	*TGV* **8667** ⑤ D	*TGV* **8679** ⑥ J
Paris ⊡ **280** d.	...	1608	...	...	...	...	...	...	1712	1708	...	...	...	...	...	1741	1741	1808	1808	...	...	1908	1908	...	1908	2108
Rennes d.	...	1818	1826	...	1838	...	1845	1847	|	1925	1927	...	1935	...	1940	1958	2009	2020	2020	2033	...	2125	2125	...	2130	2325
Lamballe **299** d.	...	|	1902	...	1937	...	1922	1942	|	|	2005	...	2025	...	2016	2035	2047	|	|	2124	...	|	2203	...	2211	|
St Brieuc 299 d.	...	1905	1914	1922	1947	...	1935	1953	2006	2012	2018	...	2036	...	2029	2051	2100	2108	2109	2135	...	2212	2218	...	2225	0012
Guingamp d.	...	1926	1931	1943	...	...	1951	...	|	2032	2036	...	...	...	2046	...	2120	|	2131	...	2143	2233	2238	...	...	0033
Plouaret-Trégor d.	1933	|	|	1959	...	2001	2006	...	|	|	2051	2056	...	...	2100	...	2135	|	|	...	2200	2248	2254	2303	...	|
Lannion a.	1952	|	|	2017	...	2020	*2032*z	...	|	|	|	2121	...	...	*2125*z	...	2152	|	|	...	2219	|	|	2322	...	|
Morlaix d.	...	1953	2001	...	...	...	2023	...	|	2059	2110	...	...	...	2119	...	...	|	2158	...	...	2304	2309	...	...	0059
Landivisiau d.	...	|	|	...	...	...	2040	...	|	|	|	...	...	...	2135	...	...	|	|	...	...	|	|	...	...	|
Landerneau **286** d.	...	2017	|	...	...	...	2050	...	|	|	2133	...	...	...	2145	...	...	|	|	...	...	2328	2333	...	...	|
Brest 286 a	...	2031	2034	...	...	...	2102	...	2121	2132	2149	...	...	...	2157	...	...	2219	2231	...	...	2342	2347	...	...	0133

	TGV **8690** Ⓐ	*TGV* **8612** ⑥ K	*TGV* **8610** Ⓐ	Ⓐ	⑥	Ⓐ	Ⓐ	Ⓐ	⚒ T	*TGV* **8618** ⑥ K	*TGV* **8618** Ⓐ	Ⓐ	Ⓐ	Ⓐ Z	Ⓐ b	*TGV* **8620** Ⓐ	⑥	†	⑥	*TGV* **8622** ⑥ K	*TGV* **8624** ⑦	⑥	†	⚒	Ⓐ V	Ⓐ
Brest 286 d.	...	0445	0448	0525	...	0537	...	0629	...	0645	0645	0702	0749	...	...	0817	0810	...	...	0843	0847	1022	1031	...	...	1122
Landerneau **286** d.	...	|	|	0536	...	|	...	0641	...	0658	0658	0720	0801	...	...	|	0827	...	...	|	|	1034	1042	...	...	1135
Landivisiau d.	...	|	|	0546	...	|	...	0651	...	|	|	0732	0811	...	...	|	0839	...	...	|	|	|	1052	...	...	1145
Morlaix d.	...	0518	0522	0605	...	0608	...	0713	...	0721	0721	0755	0827	...	...	0849	0905	...	...	0915	0919	1057	1107	...	...	1212
Lannion d.	...	|	*0501*y	—	...	*0556*z	...	—	0651	|	|	—	...	0826	0834	|	—	0856	0903	|	|	|	|	...	1203	...
Plouaret-Trégor d.	...	|	*0517*y	Ⓐ	...	0625	...	†	0708	|	|	Ⓐ	...	0844	0852	|	Ⓒ	0914	0925	0934	|	|	1125	...	1221	...
Guingamp d.	...	0548	0551		...	0639	0702		0731	0751	0751		...	0858	0908	0920		0928	...	0950	0950	1126	1139	...	...	...
St Brieuc 299 d.	0507	0606	0609	0614	0633	0657	0725	0733	0751	0810	0810	0901	...	...	...	0938	0926	...	...	1008	1008	1144	1156	1234	...	...
Lamballe **299** d.	0520	0619	|	0625	0644	0708	0740	0745	...	|	|	0916	...	...	...	|	0941	...	...	|	|	1157	1208	1248	...	...
Rennes a.	0557	0657	0657	0723	0745	0753	0840	0850	...	0858	0858	1013	...	...	...	1024	1048	...	...	1054	1054	1236	1250	1345	...	...
Paris ⊡ **280** a.	0812	0917	0917	...	...	...	...	...	...	1117	1121	...	...	...	...	1253	...	...	...	1323	1323	...	...	...	...	...

	⑥	⑦	*TGV* **8634** Ⓑ L	⑤ D	Ⓐ	⑥	Ⓒ	†	*TGV* **8646**	⑥ d	Ⓒ	Ⓐ	①-④	⑤ c	⑦ Y	*TGV* **8660** Ⓑ M	† U	①-④	⑤ D	⑤ D	⑥	①-④ Q	⑤ D	*TGV* **8672** ⑥ N	*TGV* **8670** ⑦ B	*TGV* **8668** Ⓐ
Brest 286 d.	1130	...	1145	1204	1230	1230	...	1308	1340	...	1429	1427	1515	...	...	1539	1600	...	...	...	...	...	1630	1646	1653	1700
Landerneau **286** d.	1142	...	|	1215	1247	1247	...	1325	|	...	1440	1438	1527	...	...	|	1611	...	...	...	...	...	1641	|	|	|
Landivisiau d.	1152	...	|	1225	1300	1300	...	1338	|	...	1450	1448	1537	...	...	|	1621	...	...	...	...	...	1651	|	|	|
Morlaix d.	1209	...	1218	1241	1323	1323	...	1401	1415	...	1507	1504	1603	...	...	1611	1637	...	...	...	...	...	1707	1719	|	|
Lannion d.	*1152*z	1206	|	|	...	...	1353	...	|	1432	|	|	—	1553	1559	|	*1628*z	...	...	1657	1657	1701	|	|	|	|
Plouaret-Trégor d.	1226	1230	1237	1258	...	...	1412	...	|	1450	1525	1521	†	1611	1622	1631	1655	...	...	1715	1715	1720	1724	|	|	|
Guingamp d.	1241	...	1252	1313	...	...	1428	...	1445	...	1539	1535		...	...	1646	1709	...	...	...	1730	1735	1738	1749	1752	|
St Brieuc 299 d.	1258	...	1310	1330	...	...	1453	...	1505	...	1555	1553	1606	...	...	1706	1726	1726	1725	...	...	1755	1756	1807	1812	1813
Lamballe **299** d.	1310	...	|	1342	...	...	...	...	1519	...	1607	1604	1620	...	...	1719	1738	1739	1739	...	...	...	1808	1821	|	|
Rennes a.	1353	...	1358	1421	...	...	...	...	1557	...	1650	1653	1720	...	...	1757	1817	1817	1836	...	...	...	1853	1858	1857	1858
Paris ⊡ **280** a.	...	...	1611	...	...	...	...	...	1822	...	...	...	...	...	...	2011	...	...	...	...	...	...	...	2111	2111	2111

	†	①-④ Q	Ⓐ	*TGV* **8676** ⑦ B	Ⓐ	⑥	⑤ D	†	Ⓐ	†	Ⓐ Q	*TGV* **8688** ⑦ P	†	⑤⑥ D	①-④ Q	⑤ S	⑤ R	⑥	*TGV* **8696** ⑦ B	*TGV* **8682** Ⓐ	†	Ⓐ	⑤ D	*TGV* **8686** ⑦ B	† U	†
Brest 286 d.	...	...	1704	1712	1717	...	...	1729	1734	...	1800	1813	...	...	...	1829	1834	1834	...	1848	1902	1933	...	1948	2102	...
Landerneau **286** d.	...	...	1718	|	1732	...	...	1740	1745	...	1817	|	...	...	...	1840	1845	1845	...	|	1913	1950	...	2001	2113	...
Landivisiau d.	...	...	1727	|	1745	...	...	1750	1755	...	1829	|	...	...	...	1850	1855	1855	...	|	1923	2003	...	|	|	...
Morlaix d.	...	...	1742	1746	1800	...	...	1806	1810	...	1853	1847	...	...	...	1905	1910	1910	...	1922	1939	2018	...	2025	2135	...
Lannion d.	1726	1734	...	|	—	...	1755	|	|	1819	|	|	...	1858	1902	|	|	|	1918	|	|	...	2026	|	*2129*z	2226
Plouaret-Trégor d.	1745	1753	...	|	Ⓐ	...	1814	1823	1828	1837	1912	|	...	1917	1920	1923	1928	1928	|	|	1955	...	2045	|	2153	2245
Guingamp d.	1800	1808	...	1815		...	1828	1838	1842	1855	...	1917	...	...	1935	1937	1942	1942	1948	1952	2010	...	...	|	2207	...
St Brieuc 299 d.	...	1827	...	1833	1834	1825	1849	1855	1859	1917	...	1938	1945	...	...	1954	1959	1959	2006	2011	2027	...	...	2108	2225	...
Lamballe **299** d.	...	...	...	1846	1847	1839	...	1907	1911	...	...	|	2001	...	...	2006	2012	2012	2019	|	2039	...	...	|	2237	...
Rennes a.	...	...	...	1924	1940	1942	...	1945	1953	...	...	2028	2053	...	...	2047	2050	2050	2058	2058	2115	...	...	2155	2316	...
Paris ⊡ **280** a.	...	...	...	2150	...	...	...	...	...	...	...	2254	...	...	...	...	...	...	2311	2311	...	...	...	0011	...	...

A – Not June 9.
B – Also June 9.
C – Not May 1, 7, 8, 28, 29, June 9.
D – Also May 7, 28.
E – Also May 7, 28, June 9. Not June 8.
F – Also May 7, 28. Not May 24, 30, 31, June 7, 8.
G – Also May 7, 28. Not May 30.
H – Not May 7. 24, 28, 31, June 7, 8.
J – Also May 1, 8, 29.
K – Also May 1, 8, 29. Not May 31.
L – Not May 1, 8, 29, June 8, 9.
M – Not May 1, 8, 29, June 8.
N – Also May 1, 8, 29. Not May 24, June 7.
P – Also June 9. Not June 8.
Q – Not May 7, 28.
R – Until May 23 (also May 7).
S – From May 30.
T – Not June 21.
U – Not June 8.
V – Until May 30 and from June 16.
W – Not June 4, 11.
X – Also May 8, 29. Not June 7, 21.
Y – Not May 8, 29.
Z – From May 26.
b – Until May 23.
c – June 1 - 29.
d – Also May 8, 29.
y – Connection from / to Guingamp.
z – Connection from / to Plouaret-Trégor.

▽ – Also May 8, 29. Not June 7, 21. Not Ⓐ June 2 - 13.

TGV – Ⓡ, supplement payable, 🍷.

⊡ – Paris Montparnasse.

GUINGAMP - PONTRIEUX - PAIMPOL
Trains operate 4 - 5 times per day. *47 km*. Journey 45 minutes.

For service July 6 - Aug. 24 see page 561

RENNES and NANTES - QUIMPER 285

Valid until July 5

km		Ⓐ	Ⓐ	Ⓐ	Ⓐ	⑥	Ⓐ	TGV 8705 Ⓐ A	†	⑥	⑥	Ⓒ	TGV 8711 Ⓒ	Ⓐ d	Ⓐ	⑥	TGV 8715 B	TGV 8715 Ⓒ C	⑥ U	Ⓐ	TGV 8717 D		13895	TGV 8723 ⑤ E
0	*Paris* ⊡ **280** d.	...	...	...	...	...	...	0704	...	...	...	...	0808	...	...	...	1008	1008	...	...	1208	...	...	1348
365	**Rennes 287** d.	...	0626	...	0644	0654	0723	0926	0930	...	0930	...	1031	...	1040	1127	1218	1218	...	1343	1425	1433	...	|
	Nantes ◧ d.	0612	|	0651	|	|	|	|	|	0920	|	1007	|	1029	|	|	|	|	1227	|	|	|	1520	|
	Savenay ◧ d.	0636	|	0715	|	|	|	|	|	|	|	1029	|	1051	|	|	|	|	1249	|	|	|	|	|
437	Redon **287** ◧ d.	0712	0712	0743	0737	0735	0759	|	1005	1012	1012	1055	1107	1127	1127	1202	1253	1300	1316	1419	|	1518	1602	|
492	Vannes d.	0741	0741	...	0808	0804	0825	1024	1030	1037	1037	...	1133	1157	1157	1232	1319	1327	1345	1445	1522	...	1633	1650
511	Auray d.	0753	0753	...	0818	0817	|	1037	1043	1049	1049	...	1147	1209	1209	1245	1332	1342	1357	1458	1535	...	1646	1703
545	Lorient d.	0814	0814	...	0843	0836	0851	1056	1102	1109	1109	...	1206	1230	1230	1306	1351	1402	1418	1516	1555	...	1708	1722
565	Quimperlé d.	0825	0825	...	...	0848	|	|	1114	1121	1121	...	|	1242	1242	1318	1406	1416	1429	...	|	...	1721	|
612	**Quimper** a.	0853	0853	...	...	0915	0926	1133	1142	1147	1147	...	1244	1309	1309	1346	1437	1449	1457	...	1632	...	1750	1800

	⑤ H	⑤	⑦ J	①-④ c	①-④ c	⑤ H	⑥ ⊖	† ⊖	⑤ H	TGV 8729 ⑥-④ F	†	⑤ H	⑤ H	Ⓑ	⑥	⑥	⑤ H	Ⓐ	†	† j	TGV 8737 ①-④ G	TGV 8739 ⑤ H	TGV 8745 ⑦ J	TGV 8747 Ⓐ K
Paris ⊡ **280** d.	...	...	...	...	...	...	...	...	...	1508	...	...	...	...	...	...	...	...	...	...	1641	1641	1708	1708
Rennes 287 d.	1610	...	...	...	1635	1638	...	...	1654	1718	...	1728	...	1756	1756	...	...	...	1826	...	1903	1903	1930	1919
Nantes ◧ d.	|	1619	1620	1620	|	|	1641	1659	|	|	1723	|	1724	|	|	1741	1809	1821	|	...	|	|	|	|
Savenay ◧ d.	|	1640	1642	1642	|	|	|	|	|	|	1745	|	1746	|	|	1803	|	1843	|	...	|	|	|	|
Redon **287** ◧ d.	1649	1707	1710	1720	1720	1714	1725	1742	1733	|	1810	1804	1821	1836	1842	1842	1853	1913	1920	1927	1940	1940	|	|
Vannes d.	1720	...	...	1745	1745	1739	1751	1810	1800	1818	...	1830	...	1907	1913	1913	1922	...	...	1958	2008	2008	2026	2016
Auray d.	1732	...	...	1758	1758	...	|	|	1813	1832	...	...	...	1920	1925	1925	1934	...	...	2010	...	2022	2040	2030
Lorient d.	1753	...	...	1817	1817	...	1818	1837	1834	1852	...	...	...	1941	1946	1946	1954	...	...	2032	...	2041	2058	2050
Quimperlé d.	1805	...	...	|	|	...	|	|	1846	|	...	...	...	1953	1957	1957	2006	...	...	2044	...	|	|	2104
Quimper a.	1832	...	...	1852	1852	...	1852	1911	1914	1930	...	...	...	2020	2025	2025	2033	...	...	2110	...	2119	2135	2136

	TGV 8473 ⑥ L	3854 ♠		†	TGV 8759 ①-④ M		†	①-④ c		TGV 8757 ⑤ H	⑦ J		3856 ⑤⑦ ♠	①-④ e		⑥ f	TGV 8761 ⑤⑥† N		TGV 5237 ①-④ q♥	TGV 5237 ⑤⑦ P♥		TGV 8777 ⑤	TGV 8779 ⑤ R	
Paris ⊡ **280** d.	1708	...	...	...	1808	...	...	...	...	1858	...	...	...	...	...	...	1941	...	...	...	...	2024	2208	...
Rennes 287 d.	1930	...	...	...	2024	...	2032	2029	...	|	...	...	...	...	...	...	2150	...	2203	2203	...	2239	0030	...
Nantes ◧ d.	|	1905	...	1940	|	...	|	|	...	|	2043	...	2105	2126	...	2126	|	...	|	|	...	|	|	...
Savenay ◧ d.	|	1929	...	2002	|	...	|	|	...	|	2104	...	2129	2147	...	2147	|	...	|	|	...	|	|	...
Redon **287** ◧ d.	2005	2014	...	2030	|	...	2108	2117	...	|	2131	...	2204	2215	...	2215	2232	...	2238	2238	...	2321	|	...
Vannes d.	2030	2045	...	...	2121	...	2134	2146	...	2200	...	...	...	...	...	...	2300	...	2304	2304	...	2348	0129	...
Auray d.	2043	2059	...	...	|	...	2147	...	...	2214	...	...	...	...	...	...	2314	...	2318	2318	...	0003	0142	...
Lorient d.	2101	2120	...	...	2148	...	2205	...	...	2234	...	...	...	...	...	...	2334	...	2336	2336	...	0023	0202	...
Quimperlé d.	2115	|	...	...	|	...	2217	...	...	|	...	...	...	...	...	...	2348	...	...	2349	...	|	...	...
Quimper a.	2146	2206	...	...	2226	...	2245	...	...	2312	...	...	...	...	...	...	0021	...	...	0020	...	0102	...	...

	TGV 8704 ① S	TGV 8706 ⑥ T	Ⓐ	Ⓐ	TGV 8712 Ⓐ	Ⓐ	⑥ U	Ⓐ	Ⓐ	3830 ♠	⑦ J	TGV 8718 ⑥ U	TGV 8718 Ⓐ	⑥	Ⓐ b	Ⓐ	TGV 5272 ②-⑤ V♥	TGV 5272 ①⑥ r♥	Ⓐ	TGV 8720 Ⓐ	TGV 8724 Ⓒ W	† ⊖	⑦ J	⑥ ⊖
Quimper d.	0417	...	...	0518	0522	...	...	0604	...	0608	...	0633	0633	0703	...	0713	...	0739	0738	0809	0839	0917	...	0941
Quimperlé d.	|	...	...	0545	|	...	...	|	...	|	...	0704	0704	0729	...	0739	...	0810	0808	0839	0909	|	...	|
Lorient d.	0453	0458	...	0557	0559	...	...	0638	...	0647	...	0719	0719	0742	...	0752	0823	0823	0823	0854	0924	0953	...	1017
Auray d.	0512	|	...	0621	|	...	...	0658	...	0712	...	0739	0739	0803	...	0813	0842	0842	0915	0914	0944	|	...	|
Vannes d.	0526	0525	...	0635	0628	0649	...	0712	...	0728	...	0754	0754	0816	...	0832	0856	0856	...	0928	0958	1022	...	1046
Redon **287** d.	0551	0551	0648	0711	|	0725	0741	0745	0750	0758	0811	0819	0819	0847	0851	0907	0923	0923	...	|	|	1053	1101	1117
Savenay ◧ d.	|	|	0724	|	|	|	0810	|	0818	|	|	|	|	|	0922	|	|	|	...	|	|	|	|	|
Nantes ◧ a.	|	|	0745	|	|	|	0831	|	0840	0853	|	|	|	|	0945	|	|	|	...	|	|	1136	|	1158
Rennes 287 ◧ a.	0628	0628	...	0753	0728	0821	...	0825	...	...	0852	0855	0855	0923	...	0942	0959	0959	...	1028	1058	...	1151	...
Paris ⊡ **280** a.	0853	0853	...	...	0948	...	...	...	...	...	...	1117	1121	...	...	...	...	...	...	1253	1323	...	...	...

	13894	Ⓒ	TGV 8730 X	①-④	⑤	①-④ c	⑤ H	Ⓒ	Ⓒ	TGV 8752 D	⑦	Ⓐ	Ⓐ	†	⑤	①-④	†	†	Ⓐ	TGV 8762 Ⓐ	TGV 8762 Ⓒ Y	†	①-④	Ⓐ
Quimper d.	0859	1027	1142	1218	1225	...	1317	1317	...	1433	...	1504	...	...	1538	...	1539	1539	...	1617	1617	1618	...	...
Quimperlé d.	1028	1054	|	1245	1252	...	1344	1344	...	1503	...	1534	...	...	1606	...	1606	1606	...	|	|	1646	...	...
Lorient d.	1041	1107	1220	1259	1305	...	1357	1357	...	1521	...	1547	...	...	1625	1626	1620	1620	...	1657	1655	1659	1716	...
Auray d.	1106	1128	1239	1320	1324	...	1414	1421	...	1540	...	1611	...	...	1649	1649	1644	1644	...	1716	1715	1723	1743	...
Vannes d.	1120	1142	1254	1334	1341	...	1428	1435	...	1554	...	1624	...	1638	1702	1702	1659	1659	...	1730	1730	1736	1755	...
Redon **287** d.	1154	1212	1320	1413	1413	1423	1503	1512	1523	1623	1653	1656	1703	1712	1736	1737	1736	1740	1743	|	|	1810	1830	1841
Savenay ◧ d.	1224	|	|	|	|	1449	1526	|	1547	|	1725	1722	|	|	|	...	|	1806	1810	|	|	|	...	1908
Nantes ◧ a.	1250	|	|	|	|	1511	1550	|	1611	|	1750	1745	|	|	|	...	|	1827	1833	|	|	|	...	1931
Rennes 287 ◧ a.	...	1250	1355	1453	1453	...	...	1547	...	1658	...	...	1805	1753	1812	...	1811	...	...	1828	1828	1853	...	...
Paris ⊡ **280** a.	...	...	1611	...	...	...	...	...	...	1911	...	...	...	...	...	...	...	...	...	2049	2054	...	...	...

	①-④	⑦ J	⑤ H	TGV 8774 ⑦ J	⑥	⑥	TGV 8776 ⑦ J	TGV 8780 Ⓐ	Ⓐ	† J	⑤	†	①-④	TGV 8794 ⑦ J	①-④ c	⑤ H	TGV 8790 ⑤	†	†	TGV 8978 ⑦ J	①-⑤	TGV 8796 ⑦ J	①-⑤	†
Quimper d.	1704	...	...	1715	...	1724	1746	1746	...	1750	1757	...	1824	1834	...	...	1845	1910	...	1947	1957	...	...	2027
Quimperlé d.	|	...	...	|	...	1751	|	|	...	1817	1825	...	1852	1905	...	...	|	1937	...	|	2024	...	...	2055
Lorient d.	1741	...	1742	1751	...	1804	1822	1824	...	1831	1836	...	1904	1919	...	...	1922	1950	...	2025	2036	2057	...	2109
Auray d.	|	...	1809	1811	...	1825	1842	1845	...	1852	1859	...	1923	1939	...	...	1942	2014	...	2044	2059	2118	...	2131
Vannes d.	1813	...	1821	1825	...	1838	1857	1859	...	1906	1911	...	1935	1952	...	...	1957	2029	...	2058	2111	2131	...	2145
Redon **287** d.	1847	1857	1857	1851	1901	1913	|	|	1926	1938	1940	1945	2013	2019	2024	2036	|	2105	2113	|	2144	|	2229	2217
Savenay ◧ d.	|	1926	...	|	1928	|	|	|	1954	|	|	2014	|	|	2048	2102	|	|	2140	|	2211	|	|	|
Nantes ◧ a.	|	1948	...	|	1950	|	|	|	2015	|	|	2034	|	|	2110	2125	|	|	2204	|	2233	|	|	|
Rennes 287 ◧ a.	1920	...	...	1928	...	1953	|	1958	...	2012	2015	...	2053	2055	...	...	2055	2139	...	2158	...	2228	2311	2251
Paris ⊡ **280** a.	...	...	...	2150	...	...	2208	2219	...	...	...	...	...	2311	...	...	2311	...	...	0011	...	0053	...	...

– Not Ⓐ June 2 - 13.
– From May 5 (not May 25, June 8, 9).
– Ⓒ until May 14.
– Until June 30.
– Until June 21 (also May 7, 28).
– Not May 7, 24.
– Not May 7, 8, 28, 29, June 9.
– Also May 7, 28.
– Also June 9.
– Until June 30.
– Also May 8, 29. Not May 24, June 7.
– Until June 30 (not May 7, 8, 28, June 9).
– Also May 7, 28. Not May 24, June 7, 8.
– Also May 7, 28, June 9. Not June 8.

R – Also May 7, 28.
S – Also June 10. Not Apr. 21, June 9.
T – Also May 8, 9, 29, 30.
U – Also May 8, 29.
V – Not May 8, 29, June 10, June 17 - 20.
W – Until June 29.
X – Not June 16 - 20.
Y – Not May 24, June 7, 8.

b – Not May 31 - June 9.
c – Not May 7, 28.
d – Until May 30 and from June 23.
e – Also May 9, 30. Not 7, 28..
f – Also May 8, 29, June 9.

j – Not June 8.
q – Not May 7, 8, 28, 29, June 9.
r – Also May 8, 29 June 10. Not June 9, 16.

TGV –Ⓡ, supplement payable, 🍸.

⊡ – Paris Montparnasse.
◧ – See also **287** Nantes - Redon, **287/8** Nantes - Savenay.
♥ – From / to Lille Europe (Table **11**).
♠ – From / to Bordeaux (Table **292**).
⊖ – To / from Brest (Table **286**).

AURAY - QUIBERON: runs in Summer only

 For service July 6 - Aug. 24 see page 562

286 BREST - QUIMPER — Valid May 5 - July 5

km		Ⓐ	⑥	Ⓐ	†	⑥	Ⓐ	⑥	†	Ⓐ	Ⓒ	⑤ f	Ⓒ	Ⓐ	Ⓐ	†	⑥	⑤ f	† g
0	**Brest 284** d.	0553	0707	0716	0810	0833	0842	0920	1011	1159	1159	1545	1631	1712	1835	1851	1945	2012	2017
18	Landerneau **284** d.	0606	0720	0728	|	|	0854	0931	1025	1211	1211	1557	1643	1725	1853	1903	2000	2027	2032
72	Châteaulin d.	0644	0800	0806	|	|	0929	1010	1101	1247	1247	1634	1721	1803	1926	1939	2036	2104	2109
102	**Quimper** a.	0708	0823	0830	0915	0939	0953	1033	1124	1310	1309	1659	1744	1826	1951	2002	2059	2127	2132

		Ⓐ	⑥	Ⓐ	†	⑥		Ⓐ	Ⓐ	Ⓒ	⑤ g	Ⓐ	Ⓒ		⑥	Ⓐ	†	⑤ f	† g
Quimper d.	...	0618	0734	0739	0922	0944	...	0959	1453	1453	1608	1737	1757	...	1855	1900	1913	2038	2043
Châteaulin d.	...	0646	0802	0808	0946	1012	...	1023	1517	1517	1636	1805	1821	...	|	1928	1941	2106	2111
Landerneau **284** d.	...	0725	0840	0842	1021	1048	...	1100	1552	1552	1714	1843	1859	...	|	2002	2015	2143	2149
Brest 284 a.	...	0738	0853	0856	1034	1100	...	1112	1605	1605	1727	1857	1912	...	2003	2015	2027	2155	2203

CAT 🚌 *31*, journey approx 90 minutes.
From Brest : 0700Ⓐ, 0810†, 0833⑥, 1000Ⓐ, 1440⚒, 1610⑤, 1800Ⓐ.
0710Ⓐ, 1135⑤, 1245†, 1255⚒, 1640⚒, 1730Ⓐ, 1740†, 1808①⑤.

f – Also May 7, 28.
g – Not June 8.

287 RENNES - REDON - NANTES — Valid May 5 - July 5

km		Ⓐ	⑥ f	Ⓐ	Ⓐ d	Ⓐ a	†	⑥	Ⓐ e	Ⓒ	**8711** A☆	Ⓐ	①–④ c	⑤ b	⑤	Ⓒ	⑤ b	Ⓑ	①–⑤	⑥	Ⓑ	†	Ⓐ	Ⓐ	†
0	**Rennes** § d.	0710	...	...	...	0854	...	...	...	1000	1031	1210	...	1415	...	...	1535	...	1641	1700	...	1729	1745	...	...
72	Redon § a.	|	...	...	...	|	...	...	...	|	1113	|	...	|	...	...	|	...	|	|	...	|	|	...	...
72	Redon ◇ d.	|	0741	0750	0851	|	1050	1112	1200	|	...	|	1423	|	1503	1523	|	1653	|	|	1740	|	|	1841	1857
106	Savenay ◇ d.	|	0810	0818	0922	|	|	|	1227	|	...	|	1449	|	1526	1547	|	1722	|	|	1806	|	|	1908	1926
145	**Nantes** ◇ a.	0826	0831	0840	0945	1009	1136	1158	1250	1115	...	1324	1511	1529	1550	1611	1650	1750	1806	1815	1833	1845	1900	1931	1948

	⑥	Ⓐ	†	**8737** Ⓐ☆	⑥	①–④	†	①–④ c	⑤ b	⑤ b
Rennes § d.	1815	1831	1858	1903	1920	1927	1948	...	...	...
Redon § a.	1855	1917	1937	1945	|	|	|	...	...	...
Redon ◇ d.	1901	1926	1945	...	|	|	|	2022	2036	2144
Savenay ◇ d.	1928	1954	2014	...	|	|	|	2048	2102	2211
Nantes ◇ a.	1950	2015	2034	...	2035	2044	2105	2110	2125	2233

	Ⓐ	Ⓐ	Ⓐ	Ⓐ	⑥ f	Ⓐ g	Ⓒ	⑥ f	Ⓐ	Ⓐ
Nantes ◇ d.	0612	0651	0724	0730	0756	0917	1007	1227	1229	1253
Savenay ◇ d.	0636	0715	|	0752	|	0940	1029	1249	|	1315
Redon ◇ a.	0701	0743	|	0836	|	1007	1055	1314	|	1343
Redon § d.	...	0753	|	...	|	1013	1101	...	|	...
Rennes § a.	...	0838	0842	...	0914	1050	1151	...	1357	...

	⑥ f	⑥	Ⓐ	⑥	**8752** ☆	Ⓐ	Ⓑ b	⑥	①–④ c	†	Ⓐ b	⑥	Ⓑ	⑥	**8774** B☆	Ⓐ	Ⓐ		**8794** B☆	†	Ⓐ	⑤ b	⑦	①–④ h	⑦ C
Nantes ◇ d.	1256	1312	1440	1503	...	1600	1619	1641	1648	1723	1724	1741	1758	1803	...	1821	1905	1925	...	1940	1950	2025	2043	2126	2105
Savenay ◇ d.	|	1336	|	|	...	|	1640	|	|	1745	1746	1803	|	|	...	1843	1929	|	...	2002	2018	2047	2104	2147	2129
Redon ◇ a.	|	1403	|	|	...	|	1710	1723	|	1810	1821	1831	|	|	...	1912	2000	|	...	2030	2045	2112	2131	2215	2204
Redon § d.	|	...	|	|	1616	|	...	...	|	...	...	...	|	|	1846	...	...	|	2012	...	...	2119	...	2229	2233
Rennes § a.	1410	...	1559	1617	1658	1717	...	...	1805	...	...	...	1913	1917	1928	...	...	2044	2055	...	...	2154	...	2306	2311

A – ⑥⑦.
B – ⑦.
C – From Bordeaux (*IC* **3856**)
a – Until May 30 and from June 16.
b – Also May 7, 28.
c – Not May 7, 28.
d – Not May 31 - June 9.
e – Not June 16 - 21.
f – Also May 8, 29.
g – Not June 9 - 20.
h – Also May 9, 30. Not May 7, 28.
k – Not Apr. 19, 26, May 3.
☆ – *TGV* train, [R]. Supplement payable.
◇ – For other trains Redon - Nantes see Table **285**, for Savenay - Nantes see Tables **285** and **288**.
§ – For other trains see Table **285**.

288 NANTES - ST NAZAIRE - LE CROISIC

Valid until July 5

km	*TGV* trains convey 🍷	①–⑤	①–⑤	①–⑥	*TGV* **8903** ①–⑤	Ⓒ ▷	①–⑤	*TGV* **8911**	△	①–⑤	⑥	Ⓒ	①–⑤	⑤	*TGV* **8919** ⑥ e	①–⑤		⑥	⑤	*TGV* **8921** ⑦–④ g	①–⑤	*TGV* **8925** ⑥ f	①–⑤	⑥	†	①–⑤
	Paris ⊡ **280** d.	...	...	...	0653	...	...	0853	...	...	...	...	...	...	1053	...	...	...	...	1353	...	1453	...	...	...	...
0	**Nantes 285/7** d.	0656	0753	0800	0911	0943	1008	1110	1156	1200	1234	1223	1229	1234	1303	1312	...	1531	1604	1613	1643	1709	1719	1729	1805	1805
39	Savenay **285/7** d.	0720	0820	0834	|	1005	1029	|	1226	1231	1308	1244	1250	1309	|	1347	...	1606	1636	|	1704	|	1741	1753	1831	|
64	**St Nazaire** d.	0739	0835	0859	0945	1020	1045	1147	1249	1246	1331	1301	1307	1332	1336	1403	...	1626	1650	1646	1728	1741	1757	1808	1847	1847
79	Pornichet d.	0753	...	0910	...	1031	1058	|	1259	...	...	1312	1318	1343	1351	...	...	1636	1700	|	1741	|	1809	1819	1858	1858
83	La Baule Escoublac d.	0800	...	0915	...	1039	1104	1159	1308	...	...	1321	1326	1349	1405	...	...	1643	1707	1705	1748	1757	1817	1826	1907	1907
90	**Le Croisic** a.	0815	...	0926	...	1050	1117	1211	1318	...	...	1333	1338	1359	1415	...	...	1659	1717	1717	1802	1809	1832	1839	1920	1920

	①–④ a	⑤ b	⑥	† r	①–④ a	*TGV* **8953** ⑦–④ f	*TGV* **8951** ⑤ g	⑤⑥ b	⑤ b	①–④ a	*TGV* **8961** ①–④ h	*TGV* **8961** ⑤ g	*TGV* **8965** k	† r	①–④ a	*TGV* **5230** ⑤⑦ ♥m	*TGV* **8979** ⑤ g	①–④ a	⑤ b	† r	*TGV* **8987** ⑤ n		† r	①–④ c	⑤⑥ b	*TGV* **8995** ⑤ n
Paris ⊡ **280** d.	...	...	...	...	...	1723	1723	...	...	...	1749	1749	1823	...	...	...	1953	...	...	...	2053	...	...	...	...	2153
Nantes 285/7 d.	1841	1841	1841	1900	1909	1933	1932	1946	1955	1959	2006	2006	2036	2034	2131	2153	2211	2222	2222	2222	2308	...	2325	2325	2325	0013
Savenay **285/7** d.	1915	1916	1917	1923	1943	|	|	|	2026	2024	|	|	|	2059	2158	|	|	2249	2249	2249	|	...	2346	2353	2354	|
St Nazaire d.	1929	1929	1940	1937	2019	2008	2006	2021	2045	2037	2042	2048	2109	2120	2212	2226	2245	2302	2303	2302	2342	...	0002	0006	0008	0046
Pornichet d.	1940	...	1950	1948	2031	...	2019	2035	2057	...	|	|	|	2132	2222	2239	2258	...	2314	...	|	...	0013	...	0019	|
La Baule Escoublac d.	1950	...	1958	1955	2040	...	2025	2043	2103	...	2058	2112	2124	2140	2227	2247	2304	...	2321	...	2358	...	0020	...	0026	0102
Le Croisic a.	2004	...	2011	2008	2052	...	2042	2056	2115	...	2110	2126	2137	2152	2238	2303	2320	...	2333	...	0010	...	0033	...	0037	0114

	①	*TGV* **8906** ① s	*TGV* **8904** ②–⑤ t	①–⑤	⑥	①–⑤	①–⑤	⑥	①–⑤	Ⓒ	①–⑤	Ⓒ ▷	①–⑤	△	*TGV* **5270** z ♥		*TGV* **8926** Ⓐ	*TGV* **8928** Ⓒ	①–⑤		①–⑤	*TGV* **8932** ⑦ q		①–⑤	*TGV* **8942** Ⓑ u	⑤
Le Croisic d.	0435	...	...	...	0547	0610	...	...	0634	0710	0730	0806	0829	0853	0850	...	0958	1025	1036	...	...	1147	1219	...	...	1430
La Baule Escoublac d.	0448	...	...	...	0557	0624	...	...	0646	0722	0744	0820	0842	0907	0903	...	1010	1037	1048	...	...	1201	1231	...	...	1440
Pornichet d.	0455	...	...	...	0602	0632	...	...	0653	0730	0751	0825	0847	0913	0911	...	|	|	1056	...	...	1207	1238	...	...	1447
St Nazaire d.	0505	0547	0551	0557	0613	0644	0647	0649	0705	0741	0807	0837	0859	0925	0924	...	1026	1053	1107	...	1207	1221	1248	1352	1419	1458
Savenay **285/7** d.	0520	0603	|	0616	0627	0659	0705	0709	0729	0755	0825	0851	0913	0940	|	...	|	|	1122	...	1221	|	1311	1408	|	1513
Nantes 285/7 a.	0544	0625	0625	0649	0648	0720	0738	0743	0750	0820	0848	0913	0934	1005	1000	...	1100	1126	1143	...	1243	1255	1345	1439	1455	1544
Paris ⊡ **280** a.	...	0837	0837	...	...	...	...	...	...	...	...	...	...	...	...	...	1320	1344	...	...	...	1519	...	...	1711	...

	①–④ a	*TGV* **8942** ⑤–⑦ g	①–⑤	†	*TGV* **8944** ①–④ v	①–⑤	⑥	①–⑤	†	①–⑤	⑤	*TGV* **8950** w	①–④ a	①–⑤	*TGV* **8980** Ⓒ	①–⑤	†	⑥	①–④ a	⑤	†		*TGV* **8958** ⑦ q	①–⑤	*TGV* **8960** ⑦ yq	⑤
Le Croisic d.	...	1451	1520	1520	1553	...	1628	...	1652	...	...	1746	...	1815	1855	...	1903	1903	1933	1939	2020	...	2053	...	2112	...
La Baule Escoublac d.	...	1502	1536	1536	1604	...	1644	...	1706	...	...	1801	...	1827	1906	...	1919	1919	1947	1951	2032	...	2104	...	2126	...
Pornichet d.	...	|	1542	1542	|	...	1651	...	1713	...	...	1808	...	1834	|	...	1926	1925	1952	1956	2038	...	|	...	2133	...
St Nazaire d.	1458	1518	1552	1552	1621	1631	1701	1701	1725	1736	1800	1821	1829	1846	1922	1926	1939	1939	2002	2008	2050	...	2121	2116	2146	2214
Savenay **285/7** d.	1513	|	1609	1609	|	1648	1714	1726	1742	1752	1815	|	1848	1915	|	1940	|	|	|	2024	2110	...	|	2134	|	2232
Nantes 285/7 a.	1545	1555	1630	1630	1655	1711	1741	1758	1813	1814	1847	1855	1917	1945	1955	2005	2015	2015	2035	2045	2136	...	2155	2201	2220	2252
Paris ⊡ **280** a.	...	1814	...	...	1920	...	...	...	...	...	...	2119	...	...	2237x	...	...	...	...	...	...	...	0007	...	0039	...

a – Not Apr. 30, May 7, 28.
b – Also Apr. 30, May 7.
c – From Apr. 7 (not Apr. 30, May 7).
d – ①–④ only.
e – Also May 1, 8, 29.
f – Not Apr. 30, May 1, 7, 8, 28, 29.
g – Also Apr. 30, May 7, 28.
h – Not Apr. 21, 30, May 1, 7, 8, 28, 29, June 9.
j – Until Mar. 28.
k – ⑥ until Mar. 22; ⑤⑥ from Mar. 29 (also Apr. 30, May 1, 7, 8, 28, 29).
m – Also Apr. 21, 30, May 7, 28, June 9.
n – From May 2 (also May 7, 28).
p – Also Apr. 7, May 1, 8, 29, June 2, 10, 16, 23, 30.
q – Also Apr. 21, June 9.
r – Not May 1, 8, 29.
s – Also Apr. 2, June 10. not Apr. 21, June 9.
t – Not Apr. 22, May 1, 8, 29, June 10.
u – Not May 1, 8, 29.
v – ①–⑤ until Mar. 30; ①–④ from Mar. 31 (not Apr. 21, 30, May 1, 7, 8, 28, 29, June 9).
w – ⑤⑦ until Mar. 30; Ⓑ from Mar. 31 (not May 1, 8, 29).
x – Arrive 2215 from Apr. 5.
y – From Apr. 6.
z – ①⑥ until Apr. 12; ⑥ apr. 19 - May 31 (also May 1, 8, 29); ①⑥ from June 2 (also June 10, not June 9).

TGV – [R], supplement payable, 🍷.

⊡ – Paris Montparnasse.
♥ – To / from Lille Europe (Table **11**).
△ – June 22 only.
▷ – Not June 22.

NANTES - ANGERS - TOURS 289

For other *TGV* trains Nantes - Angers - Lyon (via Massy) see Table **335**

km	For notes see Table **290**	*TGV*	*TGV*	*TGV*								*TGV*		*TGV*											
		5302	**5304**	**5304**		**4402**						**5322**	**4406**	**5328**											
		②–④	①	①	Ⓐ	⑥	Ⓐ	©	Ⓐ	Ⓐ		♠	⑦	Ⓐ	⑤	①–④	©	Ⓐ	①–④	⑤	⑦	⑦	⑥	©	†
		A	**C**	**D**		**G**		**g**	**T**		**p**	**M**	**H**		**k**	**m**	**p**		**z**	**k**	**S**	**F**	**E**	**F**	**n**
0	**Nantes 280** d.	0456	0449	0453	...	0622	0713	0916	...	1118	...	1252	1344	1451	...	1615	...	1639	1816	1818	1845	1910	2018	2025	2214
88	Angers St Laud **280** d.	0536	0532	0533	0630	0704	0800	1000	1053	1201	1253	1333	1429	1530	1551	1700	1735	1750	1900	1900	1932	1951	2100	2114	2257
132	Saumur d.	|	0558	0558	0704	0727	0822	1023	1126	1222	1327	|	1452	1558	1625	1722	1808	1815	1924	1924	1955	2012	2122	2138	2319
196	St Pierre des Corps a.	0628	0628	0628	|	|	0851	1054	|	1255	|	1428	|	1628	|	1755	|	|	1955	1955	|	|	2151	2216	|
199	**Tours** a.	|	|	|	0745	0800	|	|	1228	|	1419	|	1524	|	1718	1811	1848	1854	|	|	2038	2053	|	|	2351
202	St Pierre des Corps a.	|	|	|	...	0824	|	|	...	|	...	|	1549	|	...	...	...	...	|	|	...	...	|	|	...
	Orléans **296** a.	◐	◐	◐	...	|	1005	1157	...	1408	...	◐	|	◐	...	...	...	...	2057	2057	...	...	2257	2318	...
	Lyon Part Dieu **290** a.	0928	0944	0944	...	1340	...	...	...	...	...	1730	2106	1930	...	...	...	...	...	...	...	...	...	...	...

For notes see Table **290**					*TGV*						*TGV*										*TGV*		**4506**
					5352						**5368**										**5380**		**4507**
	Ⓐ	Ⓐ	©	©	Ⓐ	Ⓐ	①–⑥	©			♠	⑤⑥	①–④	Ⓐ	†	Ⓐ		†	⑤		♣		⑤–⑦
			B	**F**			**q**	**p**			**N**	**h**	**m**		**n**			**n**	**k**		**P**		**w**
Lyon Part Dieu **290** d.	...	...	...	...	0630	...	...	...	...	...	1430	...	...	...	...	...	...	...	...	...	1830	...	1533
Orléans **296** d.	...	0704	0704	0704	◐	1127	...	...	...	...	◐	1706	1706	...	...	...	...	1804	...	...	◐	...	|
St Pierre des Corps d.	...	|	|	|	|	|	...	...	...	...	|	|	|	...	...	...	...	|	...	...	|	...	2110
Tours d.	0714	|	|	|	|	|	1245	1512	1612	...	|	|	|	1739	1842	1842	...	|	2112	...	|	...	2140
St Pierre des Corps d.	|	0804	0804	0804	0932	1240	|	|	|	...	1732	1806	1806	|	|	|	...	1906	|	...	2132	...	|
Saumur d.	0753	0837	0837	0842	|	1317	1338	1552	1653	...	|	1837	1837	1843	1923	1939	...	1939	2153	...	2207	...	2216
Angers St Laud **280** d.	0819	0900	0900	0908	1025	1338	1424	1615	1717	...	1825	1900	1901	1914	1948	2016	...	2002	2218	...	2233	...	2239
Nantes 280 a.	0901	0942	0940	0951	1102	1419	...	1655	1802	...	1903	1942	1942	...	...	...	...	2042	...	...	2315	...	2320

Additional services operate Saumur - Tours and v.v.

FOR NOTES SEE BELOW

TOURS - BOURGES - NEVERS - MOULINS - LYON 290

Local service liable to alteration around public holidays. For faster *TGV* trains Nantes / Tours - Massy - Lyon and v.v. see Table **335**

km							**4402**	**4412**	**4412**			**16842**	**16840**			**4406**	**4416**							
		Ⓐ	Ⓐ		Ⓐ	⚒	⑥	Ⓐ	Ⓐ						Ⓐ	⑦	①–⑥	Ⓐ	⑥	Ⓑ	Ⓑ		⚒	†
		Zw		**Zy**			**G**	**J**	**K**			**J**	**Q**			**H**	**L**			**n**	**n**		**s**	**x**
	Nantes **289** d.	...	...	...	...	...	0622	...	...	...	...	...	...	...	...	1344	...	...	...	...	...	...	...	...
0	**Tours** d.	...	...	...	0558	0658	0819	0819	0819	0958	...	1157	1157	1358	...	1544	1544	...	1658	1658	1758	1900	2045	2045
3	St Pierre des Corps d.	...	...	...	0605	0705	0826	0826	0826	1005	...	1204	1204	1405	...	1551	1551	...	1705	1705	1805	1907	2052	2052
	Orléans **315** d.	...	0608	...	|	|	|	|	|	|	...	|	|	|	1615	|	|	1715	|	|	|	|	|	|
113	Vierzon **315** d.	...	0658	...	0725	0828	0927	0927	0927	1128	...	1322	1322	1528	1707	1652	1652	1805	1828	1828	1928	2028	2218	2220
145	**Bourges** **315** d.	...	0730	...	0745	0847	0948	0948	0948	1150	...	1341	1341	1547	1730	1715	1715	1830	1847	1847	1951	2047	...	2239
203	Saincaize a.	...	|	...	...	|	|	1019	|	...	...	1415	|	|	|	|	|	|	|	|	|	|	...	...
214	**Nevers** a.	...	0821	...	...	0925	1024	|	1024	...	...	|	1417	1625	1821	1751	1751	1920	1925	1925	2038	2124	...	...
214	**Nevers** d.	0530	...	0830	...	0928	1037	|	1037	...	...	|	1424	...	...	1804	1804	...	...	1926	...	...	...	...
	Dijon **373** a.	|	...	|	...	1150	|	|	|	...	...	|	|	...	...	|	|	...	...	2148	...	...	...	...
203	Saincaize d.	0538	...	0838	...	...	1046	1044	1046	...	...	1425	|	...	...	1814	1814	...	...	...	...	...	...	...
252	**Moulins-sur-Allier** d.	0604	...	0904	...	...	1116	1114	1116	...	...	1456	1456	...	...	1843	1843	...	...	...	...	...	...	...
	Digoin d.	0647	...	0945	...	...	|	|	|	...	...	1539	1539	...	...	|	|	...	...	...	...	...	...	...
	Paray le Monial d.	0702	...	0957	...	...	|	|	|	...	...	1550	1550	...	...	|	|	...	...	...	...	...	...	...
293	St Germain des Fossés **328** d.	|	...	|	...	...	1141	1141	1141	...	...	|	|	...	...	1908	1908	...	...	...	...	...	...	...
360	Roanne **328** d.	|	...	|	...	...	1229	1229	1229	...	...	|	|	...	...	1956	1956	...	...	...	...	...	...	...
457	**Lyon** Part Dieu **328** a.	|	...	1157	...	...	1340	1340	1340	...	...	1748	1748	...	...	2106	2106	...	...	...	...	...	...	...
461	**Lyon** Perrache **328** a.	0904	...	1205	...	...	...	...	...	...	...	1801	1801	...	...	...	...	...	...	...	...	...	...	...

									4504	**4504**	**4504**		**16850**	**16848**						**4506**	**4516**			
	Ⓐ	Ⓐ	Ⓐ	Ⓐ	©	Ⓐ	⚒	⚒	Ⓐ	Ⓐ	⑥	⑤				Ⓐ	Ⓐ	Ⓑ	Ⓐ			†	©	Ⓐ
									K	**J§**	**f**	**k**	**J**	**R**				**n**		**K**	**J**	**n**	**Zv**	**Zw**
Lyon Perrache **328** d.	...	...	...	...	...	...	...	...	...	...	...	...	1145	1145	...	...	...	...	...	...	...	...	1743	1747
Lyon Part Dieu **328** d.	...	...	...	...	...	...	...	...	0854	0854	0854	...	1158	1158	...	...	...	...	...	1533	1533	...	1756	1800
Roanne **328** d.	...	...	...	...	...	...	...	...	1012	1012	1012	...	|	|	...	...	...	...	...	1647	1647	...	|	|
St Germain des Fossés .. **328** d.	...	...	...	...	...	...	...	...	1058	1058	1058	...	|	|	...	...	...	...	...	1735	1735	...	|	|
Paray le Monial d.	...	...	...	...	...	...	...	...	|	|	|	...	1400	1400	...	...	...	...	...	|	|	...	2000	2013
Digoin d.	...	...	...	...	...	...	...	...	|	|	|	...	1410	1410	...	...	...	...	...	|	|	...	2010	2022
Moulins-sur-Allier d.	...	...	...	...	...	...	...	...	1137	1137	1137	...	1455	1455	...	...	...	...	...	1802	1802	...	2059	2105
Saincaize a.	...	...	...	...	...	...	...	...	1206	1205	1205	...	1525	|	...	...	...	...	...	1833	1831	...	2130	2135
Dijon **373** d.	...	...	...	...	...	...	0712	...	|	|	|	...	|	|	...	...	...	1609	...	|	|	...	|	|
Nevers a.	...	...	...	...	...	...	0929	...	1215	|	1215	...	|	1528	...	...	...	1830	...	1845	|	...	2137	2143
Nevers d.	...	0535	0635	0639	0735	0739	0935	...	1228	|	1228	...	|	1535	1635	1639	1739	1835	1839	1904	|	1935	...	...
Saincaize d.	...	|	|	|	|	|	|	...	|	1235	|	...	1535	|	|	|	|	|	|	|	1911	|	...	...
Bourges **315** d.	...	0614	0714	0733	0814	0833	1014	1214	1308	1308	1308	1514	1614	1614	1714	1733	1833	1914	1933	1944	1944	2014	...	...
Vierzon **315** d.	0534	0634	0734	0755	0834	0854	1034	1234	1330	1330	1330	1534	1634	1634	1734	1755	1857	1934	1955	2006	2006	2034	...	...
Orléans **315** a.	|	|	|	0845	|	0945	|	|	|	|	|	|	|	|	|	1845	1945	|	2045	|	|	|	...	...
St Pierre des Corps d.	0700	0755	0857	...	0957	...	1157	1357	1433	1433	1438	1658	1757	1757	1858	...	...	2057	...	2110	2110	2157	...	...
Tours a.	0705	0802	0902	...	1002	...	1204	1402	1438	1438	1443	1703	1802	1802	1903	...	...	2102	...	2115	2115	2202	...	...
Nantes **289** a.	...	...	...	...	...	...	...	...	...	...	...	...	...	...	...	...	...	...	...	2320r	2320r	...	...	...

NOTES FOR TABLES 289 AND 290

A – ②③④ until July 3 and from Aug. 27 (not Nov. 10).
B – Until July 5 and from Aug. 30 (not June 22, Sept. 20, Oct. 11, 12, 19).
C – ① until June 30 and from Aug. 25.
D – ① from Sept. 29 (also Nov. 12; not Nov. 10).
E – Until July 5 and from Aug. 30 (also Nov. 11; not Sept. 20, Oct. 11, 18).
– July 6 - Aug. 24.
G – ⑥ (also Aug. 15; not June 14, Aug. 16, Sept. 20, Oct. 11, Nov. 8).
H – ⑦ (also June 9, July 14, Nov. 11; not June 8, 15, July 13).
– June 10 - 18.
K – From June 19 (not Nov. 10).
– ①–⑥ from June 19 (not July 14, Nov. 11).
M – Not ⑥ Sept. 13 - Oct. 18.

N – Not Sept. 20, 27, 28, Oct. 11, Nov. 22, Dec. 13.
P – Not ⑥ Sept. 13 - Oct. 11.
Q – Daily June 19 - 22; ⑥⑦ July 5 - 13; daily July 14 - 20, Aug. 23 - Oct. 5; ⑥⑦ Oct. 11 - 26; daily Nov. 15 - Dec. 13 (also Nov. 2).
R – June 19 - July 6, July 12 - 27, Aug. 22 - Oct. 5, Oct. 11 - 19, Oct. 25 - Dec. 13 (not Nov. 8 - 10).
S – Aug. 31 - Dec. 7.
T – Until Aug. 29.
Z – Not July 28 - Aug. 22.

f – Also Aug. 15; not Nov. 8.
g – Not June 22, Sept. 20, Oct. 9, 11, 19, Nov. 22.
h – Also Aug. 14, Nov. 10; not Sept. 20, Oct. 11, 18, Nov. 22, Dec. 13.
k – Also Aug. 14; not Aug 15.
m – Not July 14, Aug. 14, Nov. 10.
n – Not Aug. 15.

p – Not Sept. 20, Oct. 11, 18, Nov. 22, Dec. 13.
q – Not July 14, Sept. 20, Oct. 11, Nov. 11, 22, Dec. 13.
r – ⑤⑥⑦ only.
s – Also Aug. 15, Nov. 1.
t – Also Aug. 15.
v – Not Nov. 8, 9.
w – Not Nov. 10.
x – Not Aug. 15, Nov. 1.
y – Not Nov. 8 - 11.
z – Not July 14, Aug. 14, Nov. 11.
§ – Runs up to 17 minutes later Bourges - Tours on July 15 - 17, July 21 - Aug. 8, Aug. 20 - 29.
♠ – To / from Marseille (Table **335** / **350**).
♣ – From Montpellier, depart 1628 (Table **355**).
◐ – Via Massy.

ROANNE - ST ÉTIENNE 291

km		Ⓐ	Ⓐ	⚒	Ⓐ	⚒		Ⓐ		Ⓐ				Ⓐ	Ⓐ		Ⓑn			Ⓐ				†p
0	**Roanne** d.	0524	0554	0624	0652	0724	...	0824	0854	0954	1054	...	1224	1354	1454	...	1554	1654	...	1724	1822	1924	...	2054
80	**St Étienne** Châteaucreux a.	0637	0707	0737	0807	0837	...	0937	1007	1107	1207	...	1337	1507	1607	...	1707	1807	...	1837	1936	2037	...	2207

	Ⓐ	⚒	⚒			Ⓐ	⚒		Ⓐ				Ⓐ			Ⓐ	⚒				Ⓐ		p	
St Étienne Châteaucreux d.	0553	0623	0723	...	0823	0853	0953	...	1153	1223	...	1453	1553	1653	...	1723	1753	...	1823	...	1853	1953	2053	...
Roanne a.	0706	0736	0836	...	0936	1006	1107	...	1306	1336	...	1606	1706	1806	...	1836	1906	...	1936	...	2006	2106	2206	...

– Not Aug. 15.
p – Not Oct. 5.

292 NANTES - LA ROCHELLE - BORDEAUX

km		Ⓐ	Ⓐ	13899 ⚒ x	Ⓐ ◇		Ⓐ	3830 K	3830 L	⚒	3835	Ⓐ	⑤ h	D◇	3833 ⑦ L	3833 ⑤ j			3837	⑤⑥ s	①–④ e	3839 ⑤† z	①–④	⑤† g
	Quimper **285** d.	...	...	...	...	...	...	0613	0620	...	...	...	...	...	...	...	...	...	...	...	...	...	...	...
0	**Nantes** ▷ d.	...	...	...	...	...	...	0900	0907	...	1305	...	...	...	1505	1505	...	...	1701	...	...	1905	1935	...
77	La Roche sur Yon ▷ d.	...	...	...	...	...	...	0948	0954	...	1348	...	...	...	1548	1551	...	...	1746	...	...	1951	2030	...
113	Luçon d.	...	...	...	...	...	...	1020	1021	...	1416	...	...	...	1616	1619	...	...	1818	...	...	2018	2054	...
	La Rochelle Porte Dauphine d.	...	...	...	...	...	...	|	|	...	|	...	...	...	|	|	...	1803	|	2019	2028	|	|	...
180	**La Rochelle** d.	...	...	0556	0635	0818	0947	1102	1102	1146	1458	...	1634	1640	1658	1702	1741	1810	1901	2026	2036	2100	2138	2143
209	Rochefort d.	...	...	0624	0656	0839	1009	1122	1122	1207	1516	...	1655	1701	1719	1733	1806	1841	1922	2055	2107	2120	...	2212
253	Saintes d.	0520	0609	0701	0731	0910	1039	1152	1152	1238	1548	1731	1728	1735	1749	1804	1845	1917	1952	...	2134	2150	...	2239
376	**Bordeaux** St Jean a.	0708	0743	0839	...	1037	...	1307	1307	1408	1707	1908	...	...	1907	1924	2014	...	2107	...	...	2307	...	...
	Toulouse **320** a.	...	...	...	...	...	...	...	...	...	...	...	...	...	...	...	...	...	2344	...	...	...	...	...

	Ⓐ	Ⓐ	⑥ t	Ⓐ	Ⓐ	Ⓐ ◇	Ⓐ f	Ⓒ p	3840 ①⑥ A	3842	⚒ y	3850 ⑤† B	⑤ Eg	3854	◇	3856 R	Ⓐ			3858 ⑤⑦ k	3888 ①–④ m	13898 ⑤⑦ n	⑤ g	C
Toulouse **320** d.	...	...	...	...	...	...	...	...	...	0813	...	...	...	...	...	...	...	...	...	...	...	...	...	...
Bordeaux St Jean d.	...	...	...	...	...	...	0753	0823	0854	1054	1253	1254	1353	1454	...	1654	1710	1745	...	1854	1854	1954	2053	2053
Saintes d.	0532	...	0614	0623	0704	0742	0925	0950	1014	1214	1423	1416	1521	1613	1739	1816	1859	1924	...	2012	2031	2127	2220	2219
Rochefort d.	0600	...	0651	0659	0739	0817	0953	1021	1044	1244	1452	1444	1552	1642	1812	1845	...	...	...	2041	2102	2157	2251	...
La Rochelle d.	0629	0642	0720	0730	0800	0839	1014	1043	1107	1307	1514	1506	1614	1702	1834	1905	...	...	...	2105	2123	2220	2314	...
La Rochelle Porte Dauphine a.	0635	|	0726	0736	...	...	...	...	|	|	...	|	...	|	...	|	...	...	...	|	...	...	...	...
Luçon d.	...	0722	...	...	...	...	...	...	1145	1345	...	1543	...	1742	...	1948	...	...	...	2142	...	...	...	...
La Roche sur Yon ▷ d.	...	0752	...	...	...	...	...	...	1212	1412	...	1612	...	1808	...	2014	...	...	...	2209	...	...	...	...
Nantes ▷ a.	...	0846	...	...	...	...	...	...	1257	1457	...	1655	...	1855	...	2100	...	...	...	2255	...	...	...	...
Quimper **285** a.	...	...	...	...	...	...	...	...	...	...	...	...	...	2202	...	...	...	...	...	...	...	...	...	...

ADDITIONAL TRAINS LA ROCHELLE - ROCHEFORT

	Ⓐ	⑥ t	Ⓐ	⚒ tx			Ⓐ	Ⓒ N	Ⓐ	Ⓐ
La Rochelle Pte Dauphine d.	0650	0732	0742	0850	1220	1415	1600	1659	1709	1829
La Rochelle d.	0657	0739	0749	0857	1227	1422	1607	1706	1716	1836
Rochefort d.	0725	0807	0817	0925	1305	1450	1642	1734	1744	1904

	Ⓐ	⚒ tx		Ⓐ M		Ⓐ			Ⓐ	
Rochefort d.	0757	0845	...	1045	1330	1610	1710	...	1749	1930
La Rochelle d.	0827	0915	...	1115	1400	1640	1740	...	1819	2000
La Rochelle Pte D'phine a.	0832	0920	...	1120	1405	1645	1745	...	1824	2005

A – ①⑥ July 5 - Aug. 30 (also July 15, Aug. 15).
B – ⑤† July 6 - Aug. 24 (also Aug. 14).
C – ①②③④⑦ (also Aug. 15, Nov. 1; not Aug. 14).
D – Ⓐ (also Aug. 15; not ⑤ July 4 - Aug. 29, Aug. 14).
E – July 11 - Aug. 22.
K – Until July 5.
L – From July 6.
M – Not ① July 7 - Aug. 25; July 15.
N – Not † July 6 - Aug. 24.
e – Not July 14, Aug. 14.
f – Also ⑥ July 5 - Aug. 23.
g – Also Aug. 14; not Aug. 15.
h – July 4 - Aug. 29 (also Aug. 14; not Aug. 15).
j – July 4 - Aug. 29 (also Aug. 14, 31).
k – Also July 14, Aug. 14, Nov. 11; not July 13, Aug. 15, Nov. 9.
m – Not July 14, Nov. 11.
n – Also July 14, Aug. 14; not July 13, Aug. 15.
p – Not July 14, Aug. 15.
r – Depart 0613 until July 5.
s – Also Aug. 14.
t – Also Aug. 15.
x – Also Nov. 1.
y – Not Aug. 14.
z – Not July 13, Aug. 15, Nov. 1, 9.
◇ – To/from Angoulême (Table **301**).
▷ – See also Table **293**.

293 NANTES - LES SABLES D'OLONNE

Subject to alteration from Sept. 20

km		Ⓐ	Ⓐ	Ⓐ	⑥ t	Ⓐ J	⑥ J	Ⓐ J	† Jq	⑥ J	Ⓐ B	⑦ B	⑥ B		*TGV* 8973 ⚒ CE	*TGV* 8971 B	⑥ Bt	Ⓑ B	Ⓐ J	Ⓒ J	⑤ Bk	⑥ Bt	Ⓑ Bu	Ⓐ J	*TGV* 8975 D
	Paris ⊡ **280** d.	...	...	...	...	...	...	...	...	...	...	...	...	...	...	...	...	...	...	...	...	...	...	...	1220
0	**Nantes** ▷ d.	0620	...	0705	0706	0752	0805	0848	0848	0848	0922	0942	0946	...	1118	1118	1151	1154	1233	1232	1233	1316	1324	1424	1452
77	La Roche sur Yon ▷ a.	0712	...	0804	0804	0858	0909	0934	0936	0934	1006	1030	1030	...	1201	1202	1238	1238	1324	1320	1325	1405	1412	1508	1532
77	La Roche sur Yon d.	...	0736	0830	0830	...	...	...	0938	0935	1007	1031	1032	...	1204	1205	1239	1239	1332	1322	1328	1410	1414	1510	1535
114	**Les Sables d'Olonne** a.	...	0808	0859	0901	...	...	...	1005	1003	1034	1110	1110	...	1230	1231	1306	1305	1359	1349	1357	1440	1447	1540	1600

	①–⑥ Bw	⑦ Bz	Ⓐ J	Ⓐ B	Ⓐ J	Ⓐ J	Ⓐ B	Ht	Ⓐ J	Ⓐ B	Ⓐ B	⑥ J	①–④ Bx	①–④ J	⑤ k	⑥ Bt	①–④ J	⑤⑦ Jy	*TGV* 8979* F	①–④ x	† qu	⑤ k	⑤ Jk	⑦	
Paris ⊡ **280** d.	...	...	...	...	...	...	...	...	...	...	...	...	...	...	...	...	...	...	1853	...	...	...	...	...	...
Nantes ▷ d.	1623	1626	1634	1641	1713	1735	1735	1737	1816	1816	1823	1926	1943	2010	2010	2020	2048	2043	2130	2140	2147	2217	2214	2230	...
La Roche sur Yon ▷ a.	1707	1722	1720	1738	1812	1829	1830	1836	1906	1905	1926	2017	2033	2100	2101	2110	2135	2128	2212	2230	2236	2306	2306	2316	...
La Roche sur Yon d.	1710	1724	1722	1800	1814	1847	1844	1839	1909	1918	...	2030	...	...	...	...	...	2130	2215	...	2248	2308	2308	...	...
Les Sables d'Olonne a.	1740	1754	1751	1840	1846	1916	1918	1909	1936	1945	...	2057	...	...	...	...	...	2158	2240	...	2315	2334	2332	...	...

	Ⓐ	N	⑥ t	*TGV* 8990 Ⓐ J	*TGV* 8970 Ⓐ A	②–⑤ Bv	Ⓐ B	Ⓐ J	Ⓐ	Ⓐ B	Ⓒ	Ⓐ	⚒ J	Ⓐ	⑥ B	⑥ Bt	*TGV* 8974 ⑥	*TGV* 8972 Ⓑ Bn	⑥ J	Ⓐ J	⚒ J	B	Ⓐ J	⑤ Bk	Ⓒ J
Les Sables d'Olonne d.	...	0523	...	0538	0543	0551	0622	0629	0659	...	0724	0735	...	0919	0935	0957	1042	1042	1123	1129	1156	1157	1408	1416	1423
La Roche sur Yon a.	...	0549	...	0603	0608	0618	0648	0653	0725	...	0750	0806	...	0945	1003	1024	1107	1107	1147	1154	1232	1234	1434	1443	1450
La Roche sur Yon ▷ d.	0509	0551	0602	0605	0610	0620	0650	0655	0727	0753	0752	*0818*	0845	0946	1005	1026	1109	1109	1149	1156	1234	1236	1436	1445	...
Nantes ▷ a.	0601	0641	0648	0645	0651	0720	0745	0746	0820	0846	0841	*0910*	0936	1036	1055	1116	1150	1150	1240	1240	1330	1335	1521	1525	...
Paris ⊡ **280** a.	...	...	...	0912	0912	...	...	...	...	...	...	...	...	...	...	...	1421	1421	...	...	...	...	...	...	...

	Ⓑ Bu	Ⓐ J	⑦ Jp	*TGV* 8976 ⑦ Cy	*TGV* 8998 Ⓐ L	*TGV* 8978* G	Ⓐ B	*TGV* 8980 ⑥ J		Ⓐ J	† Jq	† Jq	⑦ By	Ⓐ B	⑥ Bt	Ⓐ J	*TGV* 8982 K	⑥ J	Ⓐ J	⑦ Bz	Ⓐ B	B	Ⓐ B	⑦ Bq	
Les Sables d'Olonne d.	1457	1509	...	1543	1604	1610	1632	1643	...	1635	1641	1641	1651	1711	1711	1721	1810	1810	1815	1840	1848	1925	1952	2024	...
La Roche sur Yon a.	1523	1537	...	1606	1629	1634	1656	1706	...	1701	1707	1707	1717	1739	1739	1752	1835	1836	1843	1904	1915	1951	2019	2053	...
La Roche sur Yon ▷ d.	1525	1538	1634	1608	1631	1636	1658	1709	...	1703	1709	1709	1718	1741	1741	1756	1838	1838	1845	1906	1917	1953	...	*2122*	...
Nantes ▷ a.	1610	1622	1724	1651	1712	1720	1753	1751	...	1759	1808	1808	1808	1833	1839	1846	1921	1938	1942	1950	2008	2042	...	*2208*	...
Paris ⊡ **280** a.	...	...	...	1928	1940	1939	...	2025	...	...	...	...	...	...	...	...	2147	...	...	...	...	...	...	...	...

A – Sept. 29 - Dec. 12.
B – July 6 - Aug. 24.
C – Not July 6 - Aug. 24.
D – July 21 - Aug. 24.
E – Daily from Sept. 29.
F – Not June 23 - July 18.
G – Daily July 6 - Aug. 24; Ⓐ Sept. 29 - Dec. 12.
H – Ⓒ until July 5; ⑥ July 12 - Aug. 30; Ⓒ Aug. 31 - Dec. 7.
J – To July 5/from Aug. 25.
K – ⑦ until June 29; daily July 6 - Aug. 24; ⑦ Aug. 31 - Sept. 28; daily Oct. 5 - 26; † Nov. 2 - Dec. 13.
L – Ⓐ until July 4 and Aug. 25 - Sept. 19.
M – Until June 29 and Aug. 31 - Sept. 28.
N – ① July 7 - Aug. 18; Ⓐ Sept. 29 - Dec. 12 (also July 15; not July 14).
k – Also Aug. 14; not Aug. 15.
n – Not Aug. 15.
p – Not Nov. 11.
q – Not Nov. 1.
t – Also Aug. 15.
u – Not Aug. 15.
v – Not July 15.
w – Not July 14.
x – Not Aug. 14.
y – Also Nov. 11.
z – Also July 14.
TGV – Ⓡ, supplement payable, 🍷.
⊡ – Paris Montparnasse.
▷ – For additional trains see Table **292**.

* – **The train number shown is altered as below:**
8978 runs as **8996** from Oct. 27.
8979 runs as **8977** on ⑤.

294 PARIS - LES AUBRAIS - ORLÉANS

TEMPORARILY RELOCATED TO PAGE 238

PARIS - TOURS 295

TGV trains via high-speed line. For other trains see Table 296. For Lille - Tours see Table 297

km	TGV trains convey 🍷	TGV	TGV	TGV	TGV	TGV	TGV	TGV	TGV	TGV	TGV	TGV	TGV	TGV	TGV	TGV	TGV	TGV	TGV	TGV	TGV	TGV	TGV	TGV	TGV
		8403	**8301**	**8341**	**8407***	**8411**	**8303**	**8413**	**8415**	**8433**	**8321**	**8323**	**8437**	**8325**	**8327**	**8331**	**8445**	**8333**	**8481**	**8335**	**8353**	**8457**	**8337**	**8357**	**8355**
			①–⑥						①–④		⑤	Ⓐ		Ⓐ		Ⓐ	Ⓒ	①–⑥	①–④	⑦	①–④	⑦	⑤	⑦	⑤
		h	a	h				E	b		e							a	b	m	X	d	n	m	
0	**Paris** Montparnasse ... d.	0641	0716	0746	0843	1046	1216	1243	1404	1446	1516	1616	1646	1732	1816	1834	1846	1916	1946	2016	2036	2046	2116	2122	2201
14	Massy-TGV ... d.	0653	|	|	|	|	|	|	|	|	|	|	|	1744	|	|	|	|	|	|	|	|	|	|	|
162	Vendôme-Villiers TGV. d.	|	0802	|	|	|	1302	|	|	|	1601	1702	|	1824	1902c	1925	|	2002	|	2102	2121	|	2202	|	|
221	St Pierre des Corps ... a.	0745	0821	0846	0945	1145	1321	1345	1459	1545	1620	1721	1746	1845	1921	1946	1946	2021	2046	2121	2145	2146	2221	2220	2300
221	St Pierre des Corps ... d.	0817	0824	0900	1004	1207	1324	1407	...	1607	1623	1724	1819	1852	1924	...	2005	2024	...	2124	...	...	2224	...	...
224	**Tours** ... a.	0822	0829	0905	1009	1212	1329	1412	...	1612	1628	1729	1824	1857	1929	...	2010	2029	...	2129	...	...	2229	...	...

	TGV	TGV	TGV	TGV	TGV	TGV	TGV	TGV	TGV	TGV	TGV	TGV	TGV	TGV	TGV	TGV	TGV	TGV	TGV	TGV	TGV	TGV	TGV	TGV	TGV
	8340	**8300**	**8302**	**8302**	**8342**	**8342**	**8306**	**8402**	**8308**	**8410**	**8310**	**8310**	**8430**	**8432**	**8320**	**8322**	**8436**	**8324**	**8326**	**8350**	**8328**	**8350**	**8330**	**8444**	**8448**
	①	①–⑤	①–④	⑤⑥				⑦	①–⑥		Ⓒ	Ⓐ			⑤⑦			Ⓐ	⑤⑦				⑦		⑦
	f	k	a	g	C	A	A	hm	a	h			y		j				j	X	B	S	m		
Tours ... d.	...	0608	0648	0648	...	...	0731	0734	0759	0939	1131	1201	1347	1532	1631	1731	1739	1831	1931	...	2032	...	2131	...	2303
St Pierre des Corps ... a.	...	0616	0653	0653	...	...	0736	0739	0804	0944	1136	1206	1352	1537	1636	1736	1744	1836	1936	...	2037	...	2136	...	2308
St Pierre des Corps ... d.	0600	0616	0656	0656	0719	0719	0739	0815	0815	1015	1139	1209	1415	1615	1639	1739	1815	1839	1939	2014	2040	2101	2139	2215	2315
Vendôme-Villiers TGV .. d.	|	0638	0718	0718	|	0741	|	|	0838	|	1201	1231	|	|	1701	1801	|	1901	2001	|	2101	|	2201	|	|
Massy-TGV ... a.	|	|	|	0800	|	|	|	|	|	|	|	|	|	|	|	|	|	|	|	|	|	|	|	|	|
Paris Montparnasse ... a.	0702	0729	0808	0812	0825	0828	0845	0916	0924	1120	1248	1318	1516	1718	1748	1848	1919	1948	2048	2118	2148	2201	2248	2318r	0019

A – Ⓐ until July 21 and from Aug. 22 (also July 25, Aug. 1, 8).
B – ⑤ until July 4 and from Aug. 29.
C – Ⓒ until July 13; ①②③④⑥⑦ July 14 - Aug. 21; Ⓒ Aug. 23 - Dec. 13.
D – ①–④ until July 3; Ⓒ July 6 - Aug. 24; ①–④ Aug. 25 - Dec. 11 (also Oct. 17, 24; not July 20).
E – ⑤ (also ⑥ July 12 - Aug. 23).
S – July 6 - Aug. 24.
X – Not July 6 - Aug. 24.

a – Not July 14, Nov. 11.
b – Not Aug. 14.
c – Ⓒ only.
d – Also July 14, 18, Aug. 14, 22, Sept. 26, Oct. 24, 31.
e – Also Aug. 14; not Aug. 15.
f – Also July 15, Nov. 12; not July 14, Nov. 10.
g – Not ⑤ Sept. 26 - Oct. 24, Nov. 1.
h – Not July 20.
j – Also July 14, Aug. 14, Nov. 11; not Aug. 15.

k – Also Nov. 11; not July 14.
m – Also July 14, Nov. 11.
n – Also Aug. 14; not Aug. 15, Nov. 28, Dec. 5.
r – Arrive 2330 on some dates.
t – Also Aug. 15.
y – Runs 8 minutes later ⑥⑦ Oct. 27 - Nov. 7.

TGV –🅁, supplement payable, 🍷.

ORLÉANS - BLOIS - TOURS 296

Valid from July 1

For fast TGV services Paris - Tours and v.v. see Table 295. Certain trains continue to / from Le Croisic (Table 288)

km																								
		Ⓐ	⚒	Ⓒ	Ⓐ		Ⓐ	⚒		Ⓐ	Ⓑ			Ⓒ	Ⓒ	Ⓐ		Ⓐ	⑥	Ⓒ		Ⓐ	⚒	⑥
	Paris Austerlitz **294** ... d.	...	...	...	...	...	...	...	...	...	0735	...	...	...	1038	...	...	...	...	...	...	...	...	1238
0	**Orléans** ... d.	...	0642	0704	0704	...	0710	0742	...	0802	|	0842	...	1042	|	1127	...	1135	1226	1242	...	1245	...	|
2	Les Aubrais-Orléans ... d.	...	|	|	|	...	|	|	...	|	0837	|	...	|	1137	|	...	|	|	|	...	|	...	1337
30	Beaugency ... d.	...	0700	0720	0720	...	0732	0800	...	0831	|	0900	...	1100	|	1144	...	1153	1254	1300	...	1304	...	|
61	Blois ... d.	0634	0719	0736	0736	...	0752	0819	...	0858	0903	0919	...	1119	1203	1204	...	1214	1313	1319	...	1325	1332	1403
93	Amboise ... d.	0656	0738	0750	0750	...	0812	0838	...	...	0919	0938	...	1138	1219	1221	...	1233	...	1338	...	1347	1355	1419
115	St Pierre des Corps ... a.	0712	0750	0802	0802	...	0826	0850	...	...	0933	0950	...	1150	1231	1238	...	1248	...	1350	...	1402	1415	1431
118	**Tours** ... a.	0719	0757	|	|	...	0833	0857	...	...	0941	0957	...	1157	1238	|	...	1255	...	1357	...	1409	1422	1438
	Nantes **289** ... a.	...	...	0940	0951	...	...	...	...	...	...	...	...	...	...	1419	...	...	...	...	...	...	...	...

	Ⓐ ▽		Ⓐ			⚒	Ⓐ	Ⓐ		†	Ⓑ	⚒		Ⓐ		Ⓒ ▽	Ⓐ	Ⓐ				Ⓑ	⑤⑥† ▽	
Paris Austerlitz **294** ... d.	1259	...	...	...	...	...	...	...	...	...	...	...	1738	...	...	...	...	1838	...	...	...	...	2308	...
Orléans ... ▷ d.	|	1442	1542	1642	...	1706	1709	1742	...	1804	...	1810	|	1842	...	1847	1910	|	...	1942	2042	2142	|	...
Les Aubrais-Orléans ... ▷ d.	1400	|	|	|	...	|	|	|	...	|	...	|	1837	|	...	|	|	1937	...	|	|	|	0007	...
Beaugency ... d.	|	1500	1600	1700	...	1721	1738	1801	...	1821	...	1839	|	1900	...	1905	1938	|	...	2000	2100	2200	|	...
Blois ... d.	1427	1519	1619	1719	...	1738	1756	1821	...	1838	1844	1857	1903	1919	...	1925	1957	2003	...	2019	2119	2219	0033	...
Amboise ... d.	1443	1538	1638	1738	...	1752	...	1839	...	1852	1909	...	1919	1938	...	1944	...	2019	...	2038	2138	2238	0049	...
St Pierre des Corps ... a.	1454	1550	1650	1750	...	1804	...	1853	...	1904	1926	...	1931	1950	...	1956	...	2031	...	2050	2150	2250	0101	...
Tours ... a.	1501	1557	1657	1757	...	|	...	1900	...	|	1933	...	1938	2004	...	2004	...	2038	...	2057	2157	2257	0108	...
Nantes **289** ... a.	...	...	...	...	...	1942	...	...	...	2042	...	...	...	...	...	...	...	...	...	...	...	...	...	...

	Ⓐ	Ⓐ	⚒	⚒	Ⓐ	Ⓐ	Ⓐ	⚒	Ⓐ	Ⓒ	Ⓐ		Ⓒ	Ⓒ	Ⓐ		Ⓒ	Ⓒ ▽	Ⓐ	⑥	⑥		Ⓐ	Ⓐ
Nantes **289** ... d.	...	...	...	...	...	...	...	...	...	...	0713	...	...	...	...	...	0916	...	...	...	...	...	1118	...
Tours ... d.	0503	...	0603	0619	...	0628	0702	...	0750	0803	|	...	0919	1003	1003	...	|	1119	1119	1203	...	...	|	1239
St Pierre des Corps ... d.	0510	...	0610	0626	...	0635	0709	...	0756	0810	0857	...	0926	1010	1010	...	1056	1126	1126	1210	...	...	1257	1246
Amboise ... d.	0521	...	0621	0639	...	0649	0721	...	0807	0822	0908	...	0939	1021	1021	...	1109	1139	1140	1221	...	...	1308	1257
Blois ... d.	0541	0602	0641	0657	0702	0713	0741	0805	0827	0841	0926	...	0957	1041	1044	...	1126	1157	1214	1241	1255	...	1328	1336
Beaugency ... d.	0559	0620	0659	|	0721	...	0759	0824	0846	0859	0945	...	|	1059	1103	...	1141	|	|	1259	1319	...	1346	1358
Les Aubrais-Orléans ... a.	|	|	|	0723	|	...	|	|	|	|	|	...	1023	|	|	...	|	1223	1249	|	|	...	|	|
Orléans ... a.	0618	0650	0718	|	0750	...	0818	0851	0904	0918	1005	...	|	1118	1124	...	1157	|	|	1318	1350	...	1408	1420
Paris Austerlitz **294** ... a.	...	...	...	0822	...	...	...	...	...	...	...	...	1122	...	...	...	...	1322	1346	...	...	...	...	...

		⑤†	Ⓐ	⚒		Ⓐ	†	Ⓐ	Ⓑ			⚒	⚒			Ⓐ	⑥–④	⑤	Ⓐ		Ⓑ	⑥†	Ⓐ	
Nantes **289** ... d.	...	...	...	...	...	...	...	...	...	...	...	...	...	...	...	...	...	...	1816	...	...	2018	...	...
Tours ... d.	1403	1503	1519	1602	...	...	1619	1627	1703	...	1719	...	1727	1803	...	1827	1903	1910	|	...	2103	|	2203	...
St Pierre des Corps ... d.	1410	1510	1526	1609	...	...	1626	1634	1710	...	1726	...	1734	1810	...	1834	1910	1917	1957	...	2110	2156	2210	...
Amboise ... d.	1421	1521	1539	1620	...	...	1639	1651	1721	...	1739	...	1751	1821	...	1852	1922	1928	2009	...	2121	2208	2221	...
Blois ... d.	1441	1541	1557	1641	...	1655	1657	1713	1741	...	1757	1802	1813	1841	...	1913	1941	1948	2026	...	2141	2226	2241	...
Beaugency ... d.	1459	1559	|	1659	...	1721	|	...	1759	...	|	1828	...	1859	...	...	2000	2007	2042	...	2159	2241	2259	...
Les Aubrais-Orléans ... a.	|	|	1623	|	...	|	1723	...	|	...	1824	|	...	|	...	...	|	|	|	...	|	|	|	...
Orléans ... a.	1518	1618	|	1718	...	1750	|	...	1818	...	|	1857	...	1918	...	...	2019	2025	2057	...	2218	2257	2318	...
Paris Austerlitz **294** ... a.	...	...	1722	...	...	...	1822	...	...	...	1922	...	...	...	...	...	...	...	...	...	...	...	...	...

▽ – Subject to alteration.

Subject to alteration on and around public holidays

LILLE - CHARLES DE GAULLE ✈ - TOURS 297

Trains continue to / from Bordeaux (Table **300**). Connections St Pierre des Corps - Tours are by local train.

TGV trains convey 🍷	TGV		TGV		TGV		TGV		
	5200		**5218**		**5222**		**5240**		
Lille Europe **11** ... d.	0717	...	1308f	...	1445f	...	1709f	...	...
Charles de Gaulle ✈ ... d.	0819	...	1407	...	1621	...	1808	...	...
Marne la Vallée - Chessy ... d.	0833	...	1433	...	1634	...	1833	...	...
Massy-TGV ... d.	0908	...	1508	...	1708	...	1908	...	...
St Pierre des Corps ... a.	0959	...	1559	...	1759	...	2000	...	...
St Pierre des Corps ... d.	1024	...	1620	...	1819	...	2027	...	...
Tours ... a.	1029	...	1625	...	1824	...	2035	...	...

	TGV		TGV	TGV		TGV		TGV	
	5260		**5264**	**5264**		**5266**		**5284**	
			Ⓐ	Ⓒ					
Tours ... d.	0939	...	1147	1147	...	1739	...	1927	...
St Pierre des Corps ... a.	0944	...	1152	1152	...	1744	...	1932	...
St Pierre des Corps ... d.	1001	...	1201	1201	...	1801	...	2001	...
Massy-TGV ... a.	1052	...	1252	1252	...	1852	...	2052	...
Marne la Vallée - Chessy ... a.	1127	...	|	1327	...	1927	...	2127	...
Charles de Gaulle ✈ ... a.	1145	...	1332	1341	...	1941	...	2141	...
Lille Europe **11** ... a.	1257f	...	1428	1437	...	2112f	...	2244	...

f – Lille **Flandres**.

299 OTHER LOCAL SERVICES

ANGERS - CHOLET *60 km*

Angers depart: 0645Ⓐ, 0714⑥, 0721Ⓐ, 0745⚒, 0843⚒, 0938⚒, 1155, 1250Ⓐ, 1303⑥, 1336†, 1553Ⓐ, 1638⑥, 1721Ⓐ, 1741Ⓐ, 1843⚒, 1938Ⓑ, 2043, 2147⑤†, 2248⑤†.

Cholet depart: 0615Ⓐ, 0635Ⓐ, 0656Ⓐ, 0716⑥, 0738Ⓐ, 0832†, 0843⚒, 0945Ⓐ, 1103⑥, 1243⚒, 1352, 1649Ⓑ, 1733, 1838Ⓑ, 1939⑤⑥, 1953Ⓑ, 2147†.

Journey 45 - 50 minutes (90 minutes by 🚌). *Timings may vary by a few minutes from July 6*

BAYONNE - ST JEAN PIED DE PORT *Valid until Sept. 29 50 km*

	①C	A		E			E		G	
Bayonne d.	0714	0745	...	1107	...	1455	1806	...	2110	...
St Jean Pied de Port a.	0832	0904	...	1225	...	1614	1931	...	2228	...

	①C	B							F	
St Jean Pied de Port d.	0530	0550	...	0925	...	1331	1625	...	1937	...
Bayonne a.	0656	0716	...	1043	...	1449	1744	...	2055	...

BORDEAUX - MONT DE MARSAN *Valid until Sept. 14 147 km*

	⚒	Ⓐ			⚒			⚒	†e	Ⓑ	
Bordeaux 305 d.	...	0623	0858	1058	1258	1559	1730	...	...	2158	...
Morcenx 305 d.	0654	0734	1001	1201	1401	1706	1834	1955	2006	2301	...
Mont de Marsan a.	0724	0800	1025	1225	1425	1730	1859	2026	2036	2325	...

	Ⓐ	⚒	⚒		⚒			e	Ⓐ	†	†e
Mont de Marsan d.	0535	0603	0733	1040	1233	1433	1640	1801	1832	1933	2041
Morcenx 305 d.	0601	0633	0758	1105	1258	1458	1705	1830	1904	1958	2112
Bordeaux 305 a.	0702	...	0902	1205	1401	1601	1805	...	2005	2101	...

CARCASSONNE - LIMOUX - QUILLAN *Valid until July 5*

		🚌 ⚒	⚒	🚌 †	⚒n	⚒	🚌	⚒	⚒	🚌 †	⚒
0	Carcassonne d.	0709	0720	0940	1036	1237	1337	1600	1736	1847	1908
26	Limoux a.	0738	0752	1018	1109	1310	1410	1633	1808	1925	1940
54	Quillan a.	0818	...	1058	*1158*r	1346	1450	*1722*r	...	2005	2016

	⚒	⚒	🚌 †	⚒n	🚌 †	⚒	⚒	🚌 †	⚒	🚌 ⚒	🚌 †
Quillan d.	0604	...	0805	*1028*r	1103	1356	*1553*r	1619	...	1817	2005
Limoux d.	0638	0804	0845	1118	1145	1431	1645	1703	1818	1900	2045
Carcassonne a.	0713	0837	0918	1151	1223	1505	1718	1740	1851	1937	2118

CHARLEVILLE MÉZIÈRES - GIVET Journey 60 - 80 minutes *64 km*

To July 5 / from Aug. 31:
Charleville Mézières depart: 0557⚒p, 0643⚒p, 0743Ⓐ, 0955⚒p, 1049, 1220⚒, 1259⑥, 1336, 1455, 1615, 1635Ⓐ, 1730⚒, 1812Ⓐ, 1842Ⓐ, 1915⚒, 1938Ⓑ, 2055, 2025Ⓐ.
Givet depart: 0433⚒p, 0540⚒p, 0600⚒p, 0618Ⓐ, 0636Ⓒ, 0643Ⓐ, 0722Ⓐ, 0736⑥, 0821Ⓐ, 1012, 1209⑥, 1226⚒, 1401⚒, 1433Ⓑ, 1547Ⓑ, 1714⚒, 1742, 1812Ⓐ, 1907Ⓑ.

July 6 - Aug. 30:
Charleville Mézières depart: 0438Ⓐ, 0643⚒, 0739Ⓐ, 0955⑥, 1049⑦, 1227⑥, 1331Ⓒ, 1615, 1730⑦, 1837Ⓐ, 1934, 2055.
Givet depart: 0554⚒, 0639, 1008Ⓒ, 1201⑥, 1350⑥, 1444⑦, 1546Ⓐ, 1739, 1856Ⓑ.

DINARD - ST MALO

🚌 : 7 - 10 times per day (3 - 5 on †), journey 24 minutes. Operator: TIV. *11 km*

⛴ : *Le Bus de Mer* passenger ferry operates 12 - 17 times daily from April to September. Journey time 10 minutes. Operator: Compagnie Corsaire.

LILLE - LENS *Valid until July 4 39 km*

Lille Flandres depart: Ⓐ : 0615, 0642, 0715, 0719, 0818, 0918, 1218, 1242, 1318, 1542, 1618, 1642, 1656, 1715, 1719, 1742, 1815, 1819, 1842, 1915, 1919, 2018, 2118; ⑥ : 0645, 0742, 0918, 1019, 1119, 1218, 1318, 1519, 1618, 1719, 1819, 1919, 2019; †: 1019, 1119, 1318, 1519, 1618, 1719, 1819, 1919, 2019.

Lens depart: Ⓐ : 0454, 0554, 0640, 0654, 0710, 0736, 0740, 0754, 0810, 0836, 0854, 1110, 1210, 1254, 1547, 1639, 1708, 1736, 1754, 1854, 2010; ⑥ : 0454, 0554, 0654, 0740, 0754, 0840, 0954, 1054, 1154, 1254, 1354, 1454, 1554, 1654, 1754, 1854, 1954; †: 0838, 1054, 1254, 1454, 1654, 1754, 1854, 1954.

Journey 40 - 47 minutes.

NANTES - CHOLET Journey 45 - 68 minutes *65 km*

Nantes depart: 0630Ⓐ, 0805Ⓐ🚌, 0915①🚌, 0930Ⓒ🚌, 1100⑥🚌, 1236Ⓒ, 1317Ⓐ, 1320Ⓐ🚌, 1350⑤†🚌c, 1635⚒🚌, 1705Ⓐ, 1730Ⓐ🚌, 1735Ⓒ🚌, 1800Ⓐ🚌, 1846, 1920⑤🚌, 2010†🚌.

Cholet depart: 0605⑥, 0608Ⓐ, 0743Ⓐ, 0805⑥🚌, 1019🚌, 1222†, 1240⚒🚌, 1540⑤🚌, 1605†🚌c, 1640Ⓐ, 1820Ⓐ, 1900†🚌, 2005🚌, 2043†d.

NANTES - PORNIC Journey 70 - 75 minutes *60 km*

To July 5 / from Aug. 25:
Nantes depart: Ⓐ : 1437, 1623, 1747, 1839.
⑥ : 1227, 1717. † : 0952, 1128, 1940.
Pornic depart: Ⓐ : 0612, 0708, 1114, 1429, 1743.
⑥ : 1005, 1420, 1841. † : 0831, 1429, 1738.

July 6 - Aug. 24:
Nantes depart: Ⓐ : 0915, 1127, 1424, 1619, 1747, 1825, 1955⑤, 2126①–④.
⑥ : 1226, 1430, 1717. † : 0952, 1128, 1418, 2142.
Pornic depart: Ⓐ : 0612, 0708, 1119, 1325, 1548, 1737, 1944.
⑥ : 0731, 1342, 1604, 1845. † : 0831, 1119, 1533, 1820, 2036.

NANTES - ST GILLES CROIX DE VIE Journey 70 - 80 minutes *87 km*

To July 5 / from Aug. 25:
Nantes depart: Ⓐ : 0708, 1226, 1322, 1726, 1810, 2001, 2029.
⑥ : 1015, 1242, 1429. ⑦ : 1017, 2020.
St Gilles depart: Ⓐ : 0441①, 0717, 0921, 1157, 1549, 1629, 1812.
⑥ : 0705, 0814, 1214, 1647. ⑦ : 0950.

July 6 - Aug. 24:
Nantes depart: Ⓐ : 0708, 1020, 1309, 1511, 1726, 1838, 2046①–④, 2134⑤, 2222⑤.
⑥ : 1017, 1125, 1324, 1725, 1840. ⑦ : 1017, 1243, 1620, 1827, 2020.
St Gilles depart: Ⓐ : 0445①, 0528, 0615, 0911, 0939, 1211, 1312, 1553, 1811.
⑥ : 0706, 0815, 1208, 1303, 1654, 1806. ⑦ : 0717, 0950, 1221, 1555, 1704, 2029.

Trains call at Challans approx 1 hour after leaving Nantes.

PARIS - CHÂTEAUDUN - VENDÔME - TOURS *Valid from July 1*

		Ⓐ	⚒		Ⓐ	⚒▽		Ⓐ	⑦	Ⓐ		⑦
0	Paris Austerlitz d.	...	...	0811	1011	...	1356	1611	...	1811	1911	2111
134	Châteaudun d.	...	0634	0946	1146	1204	1521	1748	1834	1947	2048	2233
178	Vendôme d.	0620	0714	...	...	1243	1600	...	1914	...	2127	...
248	Tours a.	0724	0824	...	...	1354	...	...	2024	...	...	...

	Ⓐ	⚒		⚒▽	Ⓐ		⑤⑦	Ⓑ	⑤	⑦	⚒	
Tours d.	...	...	...	1236	...	...	1536	...	1736	...	1838	2036
Vendôme d.	0535	...	...	1350	...	1620	1701	...	1846	1915	1948	2144
Châteaudun d.	0616	0717	1208	1428	1603	1700	1740	1802	1926	1955	2028	...
Paris Austerlitz a.	0749	0849	1334	...	1745	1830	...	1930	...	2130	...	...

PARIS - DISNEYLAND (Marne la Vallée - Chessy) *32 km*

Trains run approximately every 15 minutes 0500 - 2400 on RER Line A:
Paris Châtelet les Halles - Paris Gare de Lyon - Marne la Vallée Chessy (for Disneyland).
Operator: RATP. For *TGV* services serving Marne la Vallée see Tables **11** and **391**.

Journey 39 minutes.

ROYAN - POINTE DE GRAVE ⛴ Valid Mar. 2014 - Mar. 2015

Mar. 21 - June 26 and **Sept. 2 - 28**:
From Royan: 0750, 0930, 1100, 1230, 1400, 1545, 1715, 1900, 2030.
From Pointe de Grave (Le Verdon): 0715, 0855, 1025, 1155, 1325, 1510, 1640, 1825, 1955.

June 27 - Sept. 1: approx every 50 minutes 0715 - 2115 (0630 - 2030 from Pointe de Grave).

Sept. 29 - Mar. 15 ✾:
From Royan: 0745Ⓐ, 0830Ⓒ, 1000Ⓐ, 1015Ⓒ, 1200, 1500, 1715, 1915.
From Pointe de Grave: 0715Ⓐ, 0800Ⓒ, 0930Ⓐ, 0945Ⓒ, 1130, 1430, 1645, 1845.

Sailing time approx 20 minutes. ✆ 05 56 73 37 73. www.transgironde.fr

ST BRIEUC - DINAN *Valid until July 5*

km		Ⓐ	⑥	†	⚒	⑥	Ⓐ	†	①–④ f	⑤ g
0	St Brieuc **284** d.	0646	0717	1237	1318	1713	1718	1715	1842	1848
21	Lamballe **284** d.	0707	0735	1254	1334	1730	1734	1731	1858	1904
62	Dinan a.	0743	0809	1329	1410	1805	1809	1808	1934	1940

	Ⓐ	⑥	Ⓐ	Ⓐ	Ⓒ	Ⓐ	①–④ f	⑥	⑤ g	†
Dinan d.	0623	0657	0749	1102	1141	1610	1816	1820	1824	1920
Lamballe **284** a.	0702	0730	0821	1133	1211	1645	1851	1855	1859	1955
St Brieuc **284** a.	0719	0747	0835	1150	1231	1701	1908	1912	1916	2012

SOUILLAC - SARLAT 🚌 *Valid until Aug. 31 30 km*

Souillac (rail station) depart: 0910⑥, 1500, 1836†, 2235⑤.

Sarlat (rail station) depart: 1142, 1720†.

Service by 🚌 (Trans Périgord Ligne 06). Journey 41 minutes.
Other journeys run at school times.

TOULOUSE - AUCH *Valid until July 5 88 km*

Toulouse Matabiau depart: 0624Ⓐ, 0724, 1224, 1424Ⓐ, 1624Ⓐ, 1724, 1824, 2024.
Auch depart: 0707, 0807Ⓐ, 0907, 1107, 1407, 1707, 1807, 1907.

Journey 90 minutes.

TOURS - CHINON *49 km*

Tours depart: 0640⚒🚌, 0742Ⓐ, 0820⑦🚌, 0915⚒, 1220⑦🚌, 1236⚒, 1515, 1641Ⓐ 1732Ⓐ, 1805⚒🚌, 1851, 2014Ⓑ.

Chinon depart: 0622Ⓐ, 0652⚒, 0749Ⓐ, 0839Ⓐ, 0935⚒🚌, 1003†🚌, 1138⚒, 1352, 1604⑦🚌, 1609Ⓐ, 1738⚒, 1829Ⓑ, 2022⑦, 2022⚒🚌.

Journey 45 - 50 minutes (70 - 80 minutes by 🚌).

VALENCIENNES - CAMBRAI *40 km*

Valenciennes depart: Ⓐ: 0606, 0629, 0737, 0956, 1206, 1306, 1705, 1732, 1806, 1906
⑥: 0630, 0800, 1230, 1300. †: 1729, 2025.

Cambrai depart: Ⓐ: 0613, 0650, 0714, 0745, 1052, 1214, 1311, 1714, 1814, 1914.
⑥: 0646, 0746, 0950, 1217, 1350. †: 1745, 1922.

Service is subject to confirmation. Journey 40 - 50 minutes.

A – ②–⑦ (daily July 7 - Aug. 31).
B – ②–⑥ (daily July 6 - Aug. 25).
C – Until June 30 and Sept. 1 - 29.
E – ⚒ (daily July 6 - Aug. 24).
F – † (daily July 7 - Aug. 23).
G – ⑤† (daily July 6 - Aug. 24).

e – Not July 13.
f – Not May 7, 28.
g – Also May 7, 28.
n – Not Oct. 16.
p – Also Nov. 1.
r – By 🚌.
x – Change at Ste Pazanne.

▽ – Subject to alteration.

✾ – On Oct. 17 - Nov. 2 the 1715 sailing from Royar is replaced by sailings at 1615 and 1745; the 1645 sailing from Pointe de Grave is replaced by sailings at 1545 and 1715.

PARIS - POITIERS - LA ROCHELLE and BORDEAUX 300

Certain *TGV* services continue to Toulouse (Table **320**), Hendaye, Irún or Tarbes (Table **305**) or Arcachon (Table **306**).

km	*TGV* trains convey 🍸				*TGV* 8401		*TGV* 8501	*TGV* 8403	*TGV* 8371	*TGV* 8531	*TGV* 8341		*TGV* 8473*	*TGV* 8407*	*TGV* 5200		*TGV* 8503		*TGV* 8373	*TGV* 8533	*TGV* 8411	*TGV* 5202	*TGV* 5450	*TGV* 5202	*TGV* 5450
		Ⓐ	Ⓐ	⚒ c	①–⑥ z	⚒ b	①–⑥ b	a	n	①–⑥ b	a	⑦ d	a		a	Ⓒ e		j	n			Ⓒ ‡	Ⓒ	Ⓐ ‡	Ⓐ
	Lille Europe **11** d.	...	...	...	...	...	...	...	...	...	...	...	...	...	0717§	...	...	...	...	...	...	0921	...	0921	...
	Strasbourg **391** d.	...	...	...	...	...	...	...	...	...	...	...	...	...	|	...	...	...	...	...	...	|	0746	|	0746
	Charles de Gaulle ✈ d.	...	...	...	...	...	...	...	...	...	...	...	...	...	0819	...	...	...	...	...	...	1016	|	1016	|
	Marne la Vallee - Chessy d.	...	...	...	...	...	...	...	...	...	...	...	...	...	0833	...	...	...	...	...	...	1033	1033	1033	1033
0	**Paris** Montparnasse **295** d.	...	...	...	0600	...	0628	0641	0712	0728	0746	...	0828	0843	|	...	0928	...	1012	1025	1046	|	|	|	|
14	Massy TGV **295** d.	...	...	...	|	...	|	0653	|	|	|	...	|	|	0908	...	|	...	|	|	|	1108	1108	1108	1108
162	Vendôme-Villiers TGV d.	...	...	...	|	...	|	|	|	|	|	...	|	|	|	...	|	...	|	|	|	|	|	|	|
	Tours d.	...	...	0615	|	...	|	*0734*	|	|	|	...	|	*0939*	|	...	|	...	|	|	|	*1147*	*1147*	*1147*	*1147*
221	St Pierre des Corps **295** d.	...	...	|	|	...	|	0749	|	|	0849	...	|	0949	0959	...	|	...	|	|	1145	1202	1202	1202	1202
289	Châtellerault d.	...	...	0710	|	...	|	0818	|	|	0918	...	|	|	|	...	|	...	|	|	|	|	|	|	|
311	Futuroscope ⊖ d.	...	...	|	|	...	|	|	|	|	0934	...	|	|	|	...	|	...	|	|	|	1238	1238	|	|
321	**Poitiers** a.	...	...	0726	0741	...	|	0833	0851	|	0942	...	|	1033	1041	...	|	...	1151	|	1233	|	|	1241	1241
321	**Poitiers** ▷ d.	0603	0654	...	0744	0754	|	0836	0854	|	...	0954	|	1036	1044	1054	|	1109	1154	|	1236	|	|	1244	1244
401	Niort d.	0703	0750	...	|	0844	|	|	0945	|	...	1044	|	|	|	1144	|	1159	1245	|	|	|	|	|	|
468	**La Rochelle** a.	0749	0835	...	|	0930	|	|	1030	|	...	1130	|	|	|	1230	|	1244	1330	|	|	|	|	|	|
434	Angoulême ▷ d.	...	...	...	0835	...	|	0927	...	|	...	...	|	1127	1135	...	|	...	...	|	1327	1335	1335	1335	1335
533	Libourne **302** ▷ d.	...	...	...	|	...	|	1008	...	|	...	...	|	1208	|	...	|	...	...	|	1408	|	|	|	|
570	**Bordeaux** St Jean **302** ▷ a.	...	...	...	0937	...	0942	1032	...	1042	...	...	1142	1232	1237	...	1242	...	...	1342	1432	1437	1437	1437	1437

	TGV 8577*			*TGV* 8375	*TGV* 8505	*TGV* 8413	*TGV* 8381		*TGV* 8415	*TGV* 8417	*TGV* 8541*		*TGV* 8433	*TGV* 5218	*TGV* 5452	*TGV* 8383			*TGV* 8511	*TGV* 8435	*TGV* 8385			*TGV* 8437	*TGV* 5222
	S v	⚒ b				C	⑤⑦ t w		①–④ m	⑤–⑦ w	x	Ⓐ			‡			Ⓐ		Ⓐ	⑤⑦ q		Ⓐ		
Lille Europe **11** d.	...	...	...	...	...	...	...	...	...	...	...	...	...	1308f	...	...	...	...	...	...	...	...	...	...	1445f
Strasbourg **391** d.	...	...	...	...	...	...	...	...	...	...	...	...	...	|	1201	...	...	...	...	...	...	...	...	...	|
Charles de Gaulle ✈ d.	...	...	...	...	...	...	...	...	...	...	...	...	...	1407	|	...	...	...	...	...	...	...	...	...	1621
Marne la Vallee - Chessy d.	...	...	...	...	...	...	...	...	...	...	...	...	...	1433	1433	...	...	...	...	...	...	...	...	...	1634
Paris Montparnasse **295** d.	1128	...	...	1212	1225	1246	1312	...	1404	1404	1428	...	1446	|	|	1512	...	...	1525	1604	1612	...	...	1646	|
Massy TGV **295** d.	|	...	...	|	|	|	|	...	|	|	|	...	|	1508	1508	|	...	...	|	|	|	...	...	|	1708
Vendôme-Villiers TGV d.	|	...	...	|	|	|	|	...	|	|	|	...	|	|	|	|	...	...	|	|	|	...	...	|	|
Tours d.	|	...	1228	|	|	*1327*	|	...	*1448*	|	|	...	*1532*	*1532*	*1532*	|	...	1628	|	|	|	...	1726	*1739*	*1745*
St Pierre des Corps **295** d.	|	...	|	|	|	1349	|	...	1502y	|	|	...	1549	1559	1559	|	...	|	|	|	|	...	|	1749	1802
Châtellerault d.	|	...	1312	|	|	|	|	...	|	|	|	...	1618	|	|	|	...	1716	|	|	|	...	1812	|	|
Futuroscope ⊖ d.	|	...	|	|	|	|	|	...	|	|	|	...	|	|	|	|	...	|	|	|	|	...	|	|	|
Poitiers a.	|	...	1340	1351	|	1433	1451	...	|	1541	|	...	|	1641	1641	1651	...	1733	|	1741	1751	...	1829	1833	1841
Poitiers ▷ d.	|	1255	...	1354	|	1436	1454	...	|	1544	|	1628	|	1644	1644	1654	1728	...	|	1744	1754	1828	...	1836	1844
Niort d.	|	1350	...	1442	|	|	1545	...	|	|	|	1720	|	|	|	1742	1831	...	|	|	1843	1927	...	|	|
La Rochelle a.	|	1436	...	1526	|	|	1626	...	|	|	|	1806	|	|	|	1826	1918	...	|	|	1926	2013	...	|	|
Angoulême ▷ d.	|	...	...	...	|	1527	...	...	1635	1635	|	...	1727	1735	1735	...	...	...	|	1835	...	...	...	1929	1935
Libourne **302** ▷ d.	|	...	...	...	|	1608	...	...	|	|	|	...	1808	|	|	...	...	...	|	|	...	...	...	2009	|
Bordeaux St Jean **302** ▷ a.	1442	...	...	...	1542	1632	...	...	1737	1737	1742	...	1832	1837	1837	...	...	...	1842	1937	...	...	...	2032	2037

	TGV 8387	*TGV* 8593			*TGV* 8351	*TGV* 8441*	*TGV* 8391	*TGV* 8513	*TGV* 8445	*TGV* 8445	*TGV* 5240	*TGV* 5454	*TGV* 8393	*TGV* 8449*		*TGV* 8481		*TGV* 8453	*TGV* 8397		*TGV* 8455	*TGV* 8353	*TGV* 8457	*TGV* 8355	
	V		Ⓐ		Ⓐ		Ⓐ		Ⓐ	Ⓒ		‡	①–⑥ b	①–⑤ t	⑦ d	①–④ m	Y	⑤ v	⑤ v	⑤ v	F	①–④ H	G	⑤ L	
Lille Europe **11** d.	...	...	...	...	...	...	...	...	...	...	1709f	...	...	...	...	...	...	...	...	...	...	...	...	...	...
Strasbourg **391** d.	...	...	...	...	...	...	...	...	...	...	|	1601	...	...	...	...	...	...	...	...	...	...	...	...	...
Charles de Gaulle ✈ d.	...	...	...	...	...	...	...	...	...	...	1808	|	...	...	...	...	...	...	...	...	...	...	...	...	...
Marne la Vallee - Chessy d.	...	...	...	...	...	...	...	...	...	...	1833	1833	...	...	...	...	...	...	...	...	...	...	...	...	...
Paris Montparnasse **295** d.	1712	1724	...	...	1732	1804	1812	1825	1834	1846	|	|	1912	1926	...	1946	...	2004	2012	...	2028	2036	2046	2201	...
Massy TGV **295** d.	|	|	...	...	1744	|	|	|	|	|	1908	1908	|	|	...	|	...	|	|	...	|	|	|	|	...
Vendôme-Villiers TGV d.	|	|	...	...	|	|	|	|	|	|	|	|	|	|	...	|	...	|	|	...	|	|	|	|	...
Tours d.	|	|	...	1828	|	|	|	|	*1927*	*1927*	*1935*	*1935*	|	|	2028	|	...	|	|	...	|	*2111*	*2135*	*2253*	...
St Pierre des Corps **295** d.	|	|	...	|	1845	|	|	|	1947	1949	2003	2003	|	|	|	2049	...	|	|	...	|	2149	2149	2303	...
Châtellerault d.	|	|	...	1912	1918	|	|	|	2018	2018	|	|	|	|	2112	2118	...	|	|	...	|	|	2218	|	...
Futuroscope ⊖ d.	|	|	...	|	|	1939	|	|	|	|	|	|	|	|	|	|	...	|	|	...	|	|	|	|	...
Poitiers a.	1851	|	...	1931	1935	|	1951	|	|	|	2041	2041	2051	|	2131	2133	...	2141	2151	...	|	2230	|	2341	...
Poitiers ▷ d.	1854	|	1936	...	...	|	1954	|	|	|	2044	2044	2054	|	...	2136	2154	2144	2154	2211	|	...	|	...	...
Niort d.	1942	|	2027	...	...	|	2045	|	|	|	|	|	2142	|	...	|	2244	|	2245	2301	|	...	|	...	...
La Rochelle a.	2026	|	...	...	...	|	2130	|	|	|	|	|	2226	|	...	|	2330	|	2330	2347	|	...	|	...	...
Angoulême ▷ d.	...	|	...	...	...	2035	...	|	2127	2127	2135	2135	...	|	...	2224	...	2235	...	...	|	...	2327	...	...
Libourne **302** ▷ d.	...	|	...	...	...	|	...	|	2208	2208	|	|	...	|	...	...	...	|	...	...	|	...	0008	...	...
Bordeaux St Jean **302** ▷ a.	...	2042	...	...	...	2137	...	2142	2232	2232	2237	2237	...	2242	...	...	...	2342	...	...	2352	...	0037	...	...

LOCAL TRAINS ANGOULÊME - BORDEAUX

	Ⓐ	⚒	⚒ r	†		⚒	†	⚒	Ⓐ	†
Angoulême d.	0601	...	0707	1004	...	...	...	1803	1901	2001
Coutras **302** d.	0653	0733	0756	1053	...	1237	1425	1853	1948	2053
Libourne **302** d.	0707	0746	0810	1107	...	1250	1440	1907	2000	2107
Bordeaux St Jean **302** a.	0733	0823	0835	1133	...	1331	1520	1933	...	2133

	Ⓐ	Ⓐ	†	†	⚒	Ⓐ	Ⓒ	†			p
Bordeaux St Jean **302** d.	0627	0637	0827	0928	1137	1337	1437	1628	1727	1837	2037
Libourne **302** d.	0654	0713	0853	1005	1218	1417	1518	1709	1753	1918	2118
Coutras **302** d.	0708	0725	0906	1020	1232	1431	1531	1722	1807	1931	2131
Angoulême a.	0800	...	0956	...	...	1520	...	...	1856	...	...

– ①–④ until July 3; Ⓒ July 6 - Aug. 24; ①–④ Aug. 25 - Dec. 11 (also Oct. 17, 24).
– ⑤ (also ⑥ July 12 - Aug. 23, Aug. 14; not Oct. 31, Nov. 7).
– ⑦ July 6 - Aug. 24; ⑤⑦ Aug. 29 - Dec. 12 (also July 14, Nov. 11; not Sept. 19, Oct. 3).
– ⑤⑦ (also July 13, 14, Aug. 14, Oct. 31, Nov. 11; not July 4, 11, 25, Aug. 1, 8, 15, 29, Sept. 5, 12, 19, Oct. 3, 10, 17).
– Not July 6 - Aug. 24.
– Ⓒ June 22 - July 5; Ⓐ July 21 - Aug. 21; Ⓒ Aug. 30 - Oct. 26; ⑤⑥⑦ Oct. 31 - Dec. 12 (also Nov. 1, 11).
– Until Nov. 7 (also Aug. 14). Runs 35 minutes later throughout on Sept. 26, Oct. 10, 17, 24, Nov. 7.
– ⑤ (also Ⓒ July 6 - Aug. 24, Aug. 14; not Aug. 15).
– Daily **except** ⑤ (not July 14, Aug. 14, 15, Nov. 1, 11).
– ①②③④⑦ (not Aug. 14).

– Not July 20.
– Not July 14, Nov. 11.
– Also Aug. 15, Nov. 1.
– Also July 14, Nov. 11.
– Not July 5, 12, Aug. 2.
– Lille **Flandres**.
– Also July 14, Aug. 15, Nov. 11.
– Not July 14, Aug. 15, Nov. 11.
– July 5, 12, Aug. 2 only.
– Not July 14, Aug. 14, 15.
– Not July 20.
– Not July 13, Nov. 1.

q – Also July 14, Nov. 11; not Aug. 15, Nov. 10.
r – Not July 14, Aug. 15, Nov. 1, 11.
s – Not Aug. 14.
t – Not Aug. 15.
v – Also Aug. 14; not Aug. 15.
w – Also July 14, Aug. 14, Nov. 11.
x – Not Oct. 25, Nov. 8.
y – Depart 1511 from Sept. 15.
z – Not July 14.

TGV – Ⓡ, supplement payable, 🍸.
⊖ – Not for journeys to/from Poitiers or Châtellerault.
▷ – For local trains Angoulême - Bordeaux see below main table. For local trains Poitiers - Angoulême see panel on next page.
‡ – Days and dates of running to be confirmed.
§ – Depart 0703 on Oct. 4, 11, 12; 0715 on Oct. 5.

*** – Train numbers vary as follows:**
8407 runs as **8471** on certain dates.
8441 runs as **8479** on ⑤.
8449 runs as **8515** on ⑤.
8541 runs as **8591** on certain dates.
8573 runs as **8461** Sept. 15 - Nov. 21.
8577 runs as **8535** on Ⓒ.

300 BORDEAUX and LA ROCHELLE - POITIERS - PARIS

Certain *TGV* services start from Toulouse (Table **320**), Hendaye or Tarbes (Table **305**) or Arcachon (Table **306**).

TGV trains convey 🍸	*TGV* 8340 ① m	*TGV* 8342	Ⓐ	*TGV* 8400 Ⓐ	*TGV* 8370 ⑥ a	*TGV* 8370 Ⓐ	*TGV* 8402 ⑦ e	*TGV* 8402 ①–⑥ b	⚒ b		*TGV* 8404* ①–⑤ x	*TGV* 8406 ①–⑥ b	Ⓐ	*TGV* 8372 Ⓑ K	*TGV* 5440 ‡	*TGV* 5260 z	Ⓐ	*TGV* 8410	*TGV* 8500 ①–⑥ b			*TGV* 8412 Ⓐ	*TGV* 8530 p	*TGV* 8374 z
Bordeaux St Jean **302** ▷ d.	...	...	...	0510	...	...	0528	0528	...	...	0618	0623	...	...	0723	0723	...	0728	0818	...	...	0823	0918	...
Libourne **302** ▷ d.	...	...	...	|	...	...	0554	0554	...	...	|	0645r	...	...	|	|	...	0754	|	...	...	|	|	...
Angoulême ▷ d.	...	...	...	0613	...	...	0636	0636	...	...	|	0728	...	...	0826	0826	...	0836	|	...	...	0928	|	...
La Rochelle d.	...	...	...	|	0530	0535	|	|	...	...	|	|	0643	0735	|	|	0744	|	|	...	0830	|	|	0930
Niort d.	...	...	...	|	0617	0622	|	|	...	...	|	|	0731	0821	|	|	0830	|	|	...	0916	|	|	1017
Poitiers ▷ a.	...	...	...	|	0705	0711	|	|	...	...	|	0816	0825	0905	0913	0913	0919	|	|	...	1004	1016	|	1105
Poitiers d.	0515	0623	0630	|	0708	0714	|	|	0730	...	|	0819	...	0908	0916	0916	...	|	|	...	...	1019	|	1108
Futuroscope ⊖ d.	|	|	|	|	|	|	|	|	|	...	|	|	...	|	|	|	...	|	|	...	...	|	|	|
Châtellerault d.	|	0642	0647	|	|	|	0739	0742	0747	...	|	|	...	|	|	|	...	0942	|	...	...	|	|	|
St Pierre-des-Corps **295** a.	0556	0710	|	|	|	|	0810	0810	|	...	|	|	...	|	0958	0958	...	1011	|	...	...	|	|	|
Tours a.	*0608*	*0723*	0735	|	|	|	*0822*	*0822*	0832	...	|	|	...	|	*1009*	*1009*	...	*1029*	|	...	...	|	|	|
Vendôme-Villiers TGV d.	|	|	...	|	|	|	|	...	...	...	|	|	...	|	|	|	...	|	|	...	...	|	|	|
Massy TGV **295** a.	|	|	...	|	|	|	|	...	...	...	|	|	...	|	1052	1052	...	|	|	...	...	|	|	|
Paris Montparnasse **295** a.	0702	0828	...	0833	0853	0906	0916	...	...	...	0937	1001	...	1052	|	|	...	1120	1152	...	...	1201	1237	1252
Marne la Vallee - Chessy a.	...	...	...	...	...	...	...	...	...	...	...	...	...	...	1127	1127	...	...	...	...	...	...	...	...
Charles de Gaulle ✈ a.	...	...	...	...	...	...	...	...	...	...	...	...	...	...	|	1145	...	...	...	...	...	...	...	...
Strasbourg **391** a.	...	...	...	...	...	...	...	...	...	...	...	...	...	...	1359	|	...	...	...	...	...	...	...	...
Lille Europe **11** a.	...	...	...	...	...	...	...	...	...	...	...	...	...	...	...	1257f	...	...	...	...	...	...	...	...

	TGV 5264 Ⓐ M	*TGV* 5264 Ⓐ L	*TGV* 5264 Ⓒ z	*TGV* 8510	*TGV* 8380	*TGV* 5442 Ⓐ M	*TGV* 5442 Ⓐ L	*TGV* 5442 Ⓒ	*TGV* 5277 ①–⑥ ‡	*TGV* 8430 D	*TGV* 8430 E		*TGV* 8540 n	*TGV* 8581	*TGV* 8432	*TGV* 8382	*TGV* 8434	*TGV* 8542 J	*TGV* 5266	*TGV* 5445 ①–⑤ ‡	*TGV* 8436	† e	⚒ b	*TGV* 8384
Bordeaux St Jean **302** ▷ d.	0923	0923	0923	1118	...	1123	1123	1123	1123	1128	1128	...	1218	1318	1328	...	1423	1518	1523	1523	1528	...	...	...
Libourne **302** ▷ d.	|	|	|	|	...	|	|	|	|	1154	1154	...	|	|	1354	...	|	|	|	|	1554	...	...	...
Angoulême ▷ d.	1026	1026	1026	|	...	1226	1226	1226	1226	1236	1236	...	|	|	1436	...	1528	|	1626	1626	1636	...	...	...
La Rochelle d.	|	|	|	|	1135	|	|	|	|	|	|	...	|	|	|	1430	|	|	|	|	|	...	...	1630
Niort d.	|	|	|	|	1221	|	|	|	|	|	|	...	|	|	|	1518	|	|	|	|	|	...	...	1716
Poitiers ▷ a.	1113	1113	1113	|	1305	1313	1313	1313	1313	|	|	...	|	|	1523	1606	|	|	1712	1712	1722	...	...	1805
Poitiers d.	1116	1116	1116	|	1308	1316	1316	1316	1316	|	|	1334	|	|	1526	1609	|	|	1715	1715	1725	1730	1735	1808
Futuroscope ⊖ d.	|	|	|	|	|	|	|	|	|	1331	1331	|	|	|	|	|	|	|	1725	1725	|	|	|	|
Châtellerault d.	|	|	|	|	|	|	|	|	|	|	|	1355	|	|	|	|	1635	|	|	|	1742	1747	1752	|
St Pierre-des-Corps **295** a.	1158	|	1158	|	|	1358	|	1358	1358	1411	1420t	|	|	|	1611	|	|	|	1758	1758	1812	|	|	|
Tours a.	*1212*	|	*1212*	|	|	*1415*	|	*1412*	*1412*	|	1406	1458	|	|	*1625*	|	|	|	*1824*	*1824*	*1824*	1846	1846	|
Vendôme-Villiers TGV d.	|	|	|	|	|	|	|	|	|	|	|	...	|	|	|	|	|	|	|	|	|	...	...	|
Massy TGV **295** a.	1253	1252	1253	|	|	1453	1453	1453	1453	|	|	...	|	|	|	|	|	|	1854	1854	|	...	...	|
Paris Montparnasse **295** a.	|	|	|	1445	1449	|	|	|	|	1516	1524	...	1537	1637	1718	1752	1758	1836	|	|	1919	...	...	1952
Marne la Vallee - Chessy a.	|	|	1327	...	...	1527	1527	1527	1527	...	...	...	...	...	...	...	...	...	1929	1929	...	...	...	...
Charles de Gaulle ✈ a.	1333	1332	1341	...	...	|	|	|	1545	...	...	...	...	...	...	...	...	...	1942	|	...	...	...	...
Strasbourg **391** a.	|	|	|	...	...	1802	1802	1802	|	...	...	...	...	...	...	...	...	...	|	2207	...	...	...	...
Lille Europe **11** a.	1428	1428	1437	...	...	...	...	...	1638	...	...	...	...	...	...	...	...	...	2112f	...	...	...	...	...

	TGV 8440*	Ⓑ v	*TGV* 8583	*TGV* 8386 ⑤ k	*TGV* 5284 Ⓐ	*TGV* 5284 Ⓒ	*TGV* 8350 H	⑥ a	Ⓑ v	*TGV* 8350 G	*TGV* 8516 q	Ⓐ	*TGV* 8442*	*TGV* 8585 s	*TGV* 8390		*TGV* 8444*	*TGV* 8518*	*TGV* 8392 ⑤⑦ v	*TGV* 8448 ⑤ t	*TGV* 8448 ⑦ w	*TGV* 8548 ⑦ y	*TGV* 8394 ⑦ e	
Bordeaux St Jean **302** ▷ d.	1623	...	1718	...	1723	1723	...	...	...	...	1818	...	1823	1918	...	...	1928	2018	...	2028	2028	2118	...	...
Libourne **302** ▷ d.	|	...	|	...	|	|	...	...	...	...	|	...	|	|	...	...	1954	|	...	2054	2054	|	...	...
Angoulême ▷ d.	1728	...	|	...	1826	1826	...	...	...	...	|	...	1928	|	...	...	2037	|	...	2136	2136	|	...	...
La Rochelle d.	|	1647	|	1735	|	|	...	1745	1745	...	|	1828	|	|	1935	1943	|	|	2035	|	|	|	2135	...
Niort d.	|	1733	|	1817	|	|	...	1831	1831	...	|	1915	|	|	2022	2030	|	|	2118	|	|	|	2221	...
Poitiers ▷ a.	1816	1832	|	1906	1913	|	...	1928	1928	...	|	2005	2016	|	2105	2117	2123	|	2205	2227	2227	|	2305	...
Poitiers d.	1819	...	|	1909	1916	|	1919	1938	1938	1952	|	...	2019	|	2108	...	2126	|	2208	2230	2230	|	2308	...
Futuroscope ⊖ d.	|	...	|	|	|	1922	1929	|	|	2007	|	...	|	|	|	...	|	|	|	|	|	|	|	...
Châtellerault d.	|	...	|	|	|	|	1943	2009	2016	2025	|	...	|	|	|	...	|	|	|	|	|	|	|	...
St Pierre-des-Corps **295** a.	|	...	|	|	1958	1958	2011	...	|	2057	|	...	|	|	|	...	2211	|	|	|	2311	|	|	...
Tours a.	|	...	|	|	*2010*	*2010*	*2032*	...	2050	|	|	...	|	|	|	...	|	|	|	|	|	|	|	...
Vendôme-Villiers TGV d.	|	...	|	|	|	|	|	...	...	|	|	...	|	|	|	...	|	|	|	|	|	|	|	...
Massy TGV **295** a.	|	...	|	|	2054	2054	|	...	...	|	|	...	|	|	|	...	|	|	|	|	|	|	|	...
Paris Montparnasse **295** a.	2001	...	2034	2052	|	|	2119	...	...	2201	2136	...	2200	2236	2255	...	2330	2339	2353	0015	0019	0033	0053	...
Marne la Vallee - Chessy a.	...	...	...	...	2128	2128	...	...	...	...	...	...	...	...	...	...	...	...	...	...	...	...	...	...
Charles de Gaulle ✈ a.	...	...	...	...	2142	2142	...	...	...	...	...	...	...	...	...	...	...	...	...	...	...	...	...	...
Strasbourg **391** a.	...	...	...	...	|	|	...	...	...	...	...	...	...	...	...	...	...	...	...	...	...	...	...	...
Lille Europe **11** a.	...	...	...	...	2246	2244	...	...	...	...	...	...	...	...	...	...	...	...	...	...	...	...	...	...

LOCAL TRAINS POITIERS - ANGOULÊME

	Ⓐ			⚒ c	Ⓐ	Ⓑ v		Ⓐ	
Poitiers d.	0612	0750	...	1304	1608	1720	1808	1926	...
Ruffec d.	0651	0835	...	1353	1653	1803	1854	2004	...
Angoulême a.	0717	0901	...	1418	1718	1828	1917	2029	...

	Ⓐ	⚒ c	Ⓐ	† e		⑦ b		Ⓑ v	Ⓐ	
Angoulême d.	0625	0731	0843	0943	...	1243	...	1643	1743	1843
Ruffec d.	0657	0756	0909	1009	...	1309	...	1709	1809	1909
Poitiers a.	0744	0839	0952	1048	...	1352	...	1748	1848	1948

A – ②–⑤ (also ① July 7 - Aug. 18; not July 14, Aug. 15, Nov. 11, 12).
D – Daily until Oct. 26 and Nov. 8 - Dec. 13 (also Nov. 1, 2).
E – Ⓑ Oct. 27 - Nov. 7.
G – July 6 - Aug. 24.
H – Not July 6 - Aug. 24.
J – Daily until Oct. 26; Ⓒ Nov. 1-30; daily Dec. 1-13 (not Nov. 8, 9).
K – Daily July 6 - Aug. 24.
L – Oct. 27 - Nov. 7.
M – Not Oct. 27 - Nov. 7.

a – Also Aug. 15.
b – Not July 14, Nov. 11.
c – Also Aug. 15, Nov. 1.
e – Also July 14, Nov. 11.
f – Lille **Flandres**.
h – Also July 14, Nov. 11; not July 20.
k – Also Aug. 14; not Aug. 15.
m – Also July 15, Nov. 12; not July 14, Nov. 10.
n – Not Oct. 25, 26, Nov. 8, 9, 10.
p – Not July 20, Nov. 8, 9, 10.
q – Not Sept. 6, 20, 27.

r – ②–⑤ only.
s – Not July 19.
t – Via Tours.
v – Not Aug. 15.
w – Also July 14, Aug. 14, Nov. 11.
x – Not Aug. 15, Nov. 10, 11.
y – Also July 14, Nov. 11; not Aug. 10, Nov. 9.
z – Not July 20.

TGV – Ⓡ, supplement payable, 🍸.
▷ – For local trains Bordeaux - Angoulême see panel on previous page. For local trains Angoulême - Poitiers see below main table.
⊖ – Not for journeys to/from Poitiers or Châtellerault.
‡ – Days and dates of running to be confirmed.

* – **Train numbers vary as follows :**
8404 runs as **8470** on ①.
8440 runs as **8476** on Ⓒ (daily July 5 - Aug. 24).
8442 runs as **8478** on Ⓒ (daily July 5 - Aug. 24).
8444 runs as **8472** on ⑦.
8518 runs as **8546** on certain dates.

ANGOULÊME - SAINTES - ROYAN 301

km			Ⓐ	Ⓐ	Ⓐ	Ⓐ	Ⓐ	⑥	⑦					⚒	Ⓐ						Ⓐ	⚒	⚒	Ⓑ	Ⓐ
		E		◇			X	L	Sh	S	H	S		Sz	Y	T	J			◇		w	n	z	
	Paris Austerlitz ◐ d.	...	...	...	...	...	...	...	...	...	...	...	...	...	...	...	...	...	...	...	...	...	...	...	...
0	**Angoulême** d.	...	...	0641	...	0733	...	...	...	0940	0940	...	...	1139	1233	...	1400	...	...	1640	...	...	1740	...	1841
49	Cognac d.	...	...	0719	...	0813	...	...	...	1017	1017	...	...	1224	1314	...	1438	...	...	1720	...	...	1822	...	1922
•77	Niort d.	0551	...	|	0636	|	0739	...	...	|	|	1013	...	|	|	1259	|	...	1512	|	...	1728	|	1820	|
75	**Saintes** a.	0646	...	0740	0751	0832	0837	...	...	1036	1036	1108	...	1242	1333	1357	1457	...	1607	1738	...	1830	1840	1925	1941
75	**Saintes** d.	...	0736	...	0800	...	...	0930	0954	...	1101	1110	...	1248	...	1359	1505	...	1616	...	1751	...	1846	...	1949
111	**Royan** a.	...	0805	...	0829	...	...	0959	1023	...	1130	1139	...	1317	...	1428	1534	...	1645	...	1822	...	1915	...	2018

	†	⑥	⑤	Ⓑ			⑤†	⑤⑦	⑤	
	x	y	k	z		G	p	m	k	
Paris Austerlitz ◐ d.	...	...	...	...	...	...	...	...	...	...
Angoulême d.	1844	1955	1955	2039	...	2140	2140	...	2240	...
Cognac d.	1922	2033	2039	2120	...	2220	2220	...	2319	...
Niort d.	|	|	|	|	...	|	|	2200	|	...
Saintes a.	1941	2053	2058	2139	...	2239	2239	2255	2338	...
Saintes d.	2017	2100	2105	2146	...	2300	...	2258	2346	...
Royan a.	2046	2129	2134	2215	...	2330	...	2327	0015	...

	Ⓐ	Ⓐ	Ⓐ		⚒	⑥		Ⓐ	Ⓐ	Ⓐ
					y	y			◇	
Royan d.	...	...	0603	...	0627	...	...	0658	...	0811
Saintes a.	...	...	0632	...	0656	...	...	0727	...	0842
Saintes d.	0606	0618	0638	...	0709	0715	...	...	0733	...
Niort a.	0715	|	|	...	0814	|	...	...	|	...
Cognac d.	...	0636	0657	...	...	0734	...	...	0751	...
Angoulême a.	...	0720	0740	...	...	0810	...	...	0828	...
Paris Austerlitz ◐ a.	...	...	...	...	...	...	...	...	...	...

	Ⓒ	Ⓐ								①–④		Ⓐ		†				Ⓐ	⑤	⑦	⑤	†		⑥	⑤†
		t		Z	R	F		V	Q	X	W		D◇	x					k	j	k	x	P	M	Sk
Royan d.	0831	0840	1029	...	1327	1432	...	1538	1538	...	...	1657	...	1659	...	1805	...	1858	...	1918	...	1943	2030	2213	2224
Saintes a.	0900	0909	1058	...	1356	1501	...	1607	1607	...	...	1726	...	1728	...	1834	...	1929	...	1947	...	2012	2059	2242	2253
Saintes d.	0911	0911	1108	1254	1402	1508	...	1616	1618	1616	1618	...	1739	1739	...	1841	1841	1935	2016	2016	2019	2019	...	...	...
Niort a.	1005	1005	|	|	1456	|	...	1708	|	1708	|	...	|	|	...	1954	|	|	2108	2108	|	|	...	...	...
Cognac d.	...	...	1126	1313	...	1527	...	...	1636	...	1636	...	1800	1800	...	...	1900	1953	...	...	2038	2038	...	...	...
Angoulême a.	...	...	1206	1350	...	1603	...	...	1717	...	1717	...	1836	1836	...	...	1940	2030	...	...	2120	2120	...	...	...
Paris Austerlitz ◐ a.	...	...	...	...	...	...	...	...	...	...	...	...	...	...	...	...	...	...	...	...	...	...	...	...	...

D – Ⓐ (also Aug. 15; not ⑤ July 4 - Aug. 29, Aug. 14).
E – ① until June 30 and from Aug. 25 (also Nov. 12).
F – Ⓑ until July 4; daily July 6 - Aug. 24; Ⓑ Aug. 25 - Oct. 5; ⑦ Oct. 12 - Nov. 2; Ⓑ Nov. 9 - Dec. 12 (not June 23 - 27).
G – ①②③④⑦ until July 31 and Aug. 25 - Oct. 30 (not July 13, 14).
H – Daily until July 5, Aug. 25 - Oct. 19, Nov. 8 - Dec. 13 (also Oct. 25, 26, Nov. 1, 2).
J – Daily until Oct. 3; ⑥⑦ Oct. 4 - 26; daily Nov. 8 - Dec. 13 (also Nov. 1, 2).
L – July 12 - Aug. 23 (also Aug. 15).
M – July 12 - Aug. 23 (not July 19).
P – ①②③④ July 7 - Aug. 21 (not July 14, Aug. 14).
Q – ①②③④ (not July 7 - Aug. 21).
R – Ⓐ until July 4; ⚒ July 7 - Aug. 23; Ⓐ Aug. 25 - Dec. 12 (also Aug. 15; not June 23 - 27, Sept. 15 - 19, Sept. 29 - Nov. 7, Nov. 24 - 28).

S – July 6 - Aug. 24.
T – Daily until Sept. 28; ⑥⑦ Oct. 4 - 26; daily Oct. 27 - Dec. 13 (not Sept. 15 - 19, Nov. 24 - 28).
V – ⑤⑦ (daily July 6 - Aug. 24, also Nov. 11; not June 27, Oct. 31, Nov. 7).
W – ⑤⑦ (daily July 6 - Aug. 24, also Nov. 11).
X – Not July 5 - Aug. 24.
Y – Not July 5 - Aug. 24, Oct. 4 - Nov. 9.
Z – ⚒ until Oct. 4; ⑥ Oct. 11 - Nov. 8; ⚒ Nov. 10 - Dec. 13 (also Aug. 15).
h – Also July 14.
j – Also July 14, Nov. 11.
k – Also Aug. 14; not Aug. 15.
m – Also July 14, Aug. 14, Nov. 11.

n – Also Aug. 15, Nov. 1.
p – Not Aug. 15, Nov. 1, 10.
t – Not June 23 - 27.
w – Not July 14, Nov. 11.
x – Not Aug. 15, Nov. 1.
y – Also Aug. 15.
z – Not Aug. 15.
◇ – To / from La Rochelle (Table **292**).
◐ – See Table **300** for *TGV* connections at Niort or Angoulême.
• – Distance from Saintes.

BORDEAUX - PÉRIGUEUX - BRIVE and LIMOGES 302

km					4490			4492		4480															
		Ⓐ	Ⓒ	⚒		①–④	Ⓐ	⑥	†		⚒	Ⓐ	Ⓑ		Ⓐ	⚒	Ⓑ	Ⓐ	Ⓐ	Ⓐ	†	Ⓐ		⑤†	†
			p		A	M		h			j		V		T		m							q	n
0	**Bordeaux** St Jean 300 d.	0558	...	0658	0732	0732	0827	0833	1029	1058	1232	1358	...	1558	1632	1658	1732	1758	1832	...	1832	1932	2032	...	2158
37	Libourne 300 d.	0623	...	0723	0758	0758	0854	|	1054	1124	1258	1423	...	1623	1656	1724	1759	1824	1858	...	1858	1959	2059	...	2224
53	Coutras 300 d.	0635	...	0735	0810	0810	0906	|	1106	1138	1310	1435	...	1635	1711	1735	1811	1835	1910	...	1910	2011	2111	...	2235
93	Mussidan d.	0703	...	0804	0835	0836	0932	|	1132	1208	1336	1503	...	1703	1737	1803	1837	1903	1936	...	1936	2040	2137	...	2304
129	Périgueux a.	0727	...	0833	0857	0857	0953	0958	1153	1234	1357	1527	...	1727	1758	1827	1857	1927	1957	...	1957	2101	2158	...	2328
129	Périgueux ▷ d.	0737	0737	...	0859	...	...	1000	...	1240	1402	...	1550	...	...	1837	...	...	...	2004	2004	...	...	2212	...
203	**Brive la Gaillarde** ▷ a.	|	|	...	0951	...	...	1045	...	|	|	...	|	...	...	|	...	...	...	|	|	...	...	|	...
	Clermont Ferrand **326** a.	|	|	...	1349z	...	...	1457z	...	|	|	...	|	...	...	|	...	...	...	|	|	...	...	|	...
166	Thiviers d.	0802	0802	...	...	...	...	...	...	1304	1422	...	1610	...	...	1913	...	...	...	2024	2024	...	...	2233	...
228	**Limoges** ▷ a.	0843	0843	...	...	...	...	...	...	1343x	1459	...	1655	...	...	1958	...	...	...	2110	2110	...	...	2314	...

																					4581	4591			
	Ⓐ	⚒	Ⓐ	Ⓐ	Ⓐ	†	⚒	⚒	⚒	†		Ⓑ			Ⓐ	Ⓑ	Ⓐ	Ⓑ	⑥				Ⓐ	†	
									R	p		mp				m	T	m			j	E	T	n	
Limoges ▷ d.	...	...	...	0603	0722	...	...	...	1103	1103	...	1232	...	...	1520	...	...	1715	...	...	1803	...	...	...	...
Thiviers d.	...	...	...	0649	0801	...	...	...	1147	1147	...	1325	...	...	1611	...	...	1800	...	...	1844	...	...	...	...
Clermont Ferrand **326** d.	...	...	...	|	|	...	...	...	|	|	...	|	...	...	|	...	...	|	...	...	|	1432z	...	...	...
Brive la Gaillarde ▷ d.	...	...	...	|	|	...	...	...	|	|	...	|	1305	...	|	...	...	|	...	...	|	1829	...	2027	...
Périgueux ▷ a.	...	...	...	0718	0821	...	...	...	1210	1210	...	1353	1358	...	1639	...	...	1822	...	...	1908	1927	...	2122	...
Périgueux d.	0558	0633	0702	0733	...	0834	0854	1003	1230	...	...	...	1406	1603	...	1703	1804	1829	1828	...	1921	1933	2006	2127	...
Mussidan d.	0619	0657	0723	0757	...	0858	0918	1024	1255	...	...	...	1428	1624	...	1724	1825	1858	1857	...	1942	1956	2027	2148	...
Coutras 300 d.	0649	0726	0750	0826	...	0928	0948	1050	1324	...	...	...	1455	1650	...	1750	1850	1927	1926	...	2018	|	2053	2215	...
Libourne 300 d.	0700	0737	0801	0837	...	0940	0959	1101	1335	...	...	...	1506	1701	...	1801	1901	1937	1937	...	2032	2040	2106	2227	...
Bordeaux St Jean 300 a.	0728	0803	0827	0903	...	1004	1026	1128	1403	...	...	...	1532	1728	...	1828	1928	2003	2003	...	2100	2111	2130	2255	...

ADDITIONAL TRAINS PÉRIGUEUX - BRIVE

	Ⓐ	⚒	①–④	Ⓒ	Ⓐ	†	⑥	⑤†	⑥	Ⓐ	Ⓑ
		c	N	S	w		n	f	n		m
Périgueux d.	0623	0738	0903	1051	1250	1355	1455	1639	1745	1809	2003
Brive la Gaillarde a.	0726	0837	0956	1151	1347	1448	1548	1735	1850	1912	2056

	Ⓐ	⑥	Ⓐ	Ⓐ	†	Ⓐ		⑤	
		n		w			P	k	
Brive la Gaillarde d.	0614	0708	0737	1122	1505	1705	1805	2010	...
Périgueux a.	0718	0800	0830	1215	1558	1758	1905	2111	...

ADDITIONAL TRAINS PÉRIGUEUX - LIMOGES

	Ⓐ	Ⓐ		⚒		Ⓑ	†			†	
				R		V			j		
Périgueux d.	0448	0616	...	0840	...	1313	1402	...	1733	1837	...
Thiviers d.	0509	0648	...	0901	...	1342	1422	...	1801	1913	...
Limoges a.	0553	0737	...	0946	...	1431	1459	...	1858	1958	...

	⑥	⑥	Ⓒ	⚒	Ⓐ	Ⓑ	Ⓑ	⑥	Ⓑ
		n	j	jm				j	
Limoges d.	0603	1208	1432	1734	1842	2011	2103	2203	2303
Thiviers d.	0649	1305	1520	1825	1935	2102	2147	2247	2347
Périgueux a.	0718	1331	1548	1852	2001	2122	2207	2307	0007

A – ⑤ until July 4; Ⓐ July 7 - Aug. 28; ⑤ Sept. 5 - Oct. 24; Ⓐ Oct. 27 - 31; ⑤ Nov. 14 - Dec. 12.
E – ⑤⑦ until July 6; Ⓑ July 7 - Aug. 31; ⑤⑦ Sept. 5 - Oct. 26; daily Oct. 27 - Nov. 2; ⑤⑦ Nov. 7 - Dec. 12.
M – Not July 7 - Aug. 28, Oct. 27 - Nov. 6.
N – Not July 7 - Aug. 28, Oct. 13 - Nov. 6.
– ①②③④⑥ until July 5, Aug. 30 - Oct. 25, Nov. 8 - Dec. 11 (also Nov. 10; not Nov. 11).

R – Not Nov. 17 - 28, Nov. 30 - Dec. 5.
S – Daily July 6 - Aug. 24.
T – Not July 6 - Aug. 24.
V – Not Nov. 17 - 21, 24 - 28.
c – On ⑥ d. 0748, a. 0841.
f – Also Aug. 14, Oct. 31; not Nov. 10.
h – Also Aug. 15; not Aug. 16.

j – Not Sept. 20, 27.
k – Also Aug. 14; not Aug. 15.
m – Also Nov. 1.
n – Not Nov. 1.
p – Not Sept. 21, 28.
q – Also Aug. 14; not Nov. 1.
w – Not Oct. 13 - Nov. 6.
x – Arrive 1406 on ①–⑤ Nov. 17 - 28.

z – Until July 4.
▷ – See below main table for additional trains Périgueux - Brive and Périgueux - Limoges.

LIMOGES - MONTLUÇON 303

km		Ⓐ	⚒m	G		H	🚌 Ⓐ§	Ⓑ	Ⓑ	
0	**Limoges** d.	0711	0811	1211	...	1611	...	1711	1811	1911
78	Guéret d.	0820	0921	1321	...	1720	1730	1820	1920	2020
156	**Montluçon** d.	...	1022	1422	...	...	1839	...	...	...

	Ⓐ	⚒m	🚌 ⚒§	⚒m	F			H	Ⓑ	
Montluçon d.	...	...	0718	...	1137	...	1637	...	...	...
Guéret d.	0620	0739	0829	0839	1239	...	1739	1839	1939	...
Limoges a.	0725	0849	...	0949	1349	...	1849	1949	2049	...

– ⑥ until Oct. 25; ①②③④⑥ Oct. 27 - Dec. 13 (also Nov. 1).
– Ⓒ until Oct. 26; ①②③④⑥⑦ Oct. 27 - Dec. 13.
H – ⚒ until July 5; Ⓐ July 7 - Aug. 29; ⚒ Sept. 1 - Dec. 13 (also Nov. 1).
m – Also Nov. 1.
§ – Subject to confirmation.

305 BORDEAUX - TARBES, HENDAYE and IRÚN

For night train Paris - Tarbes - Hendaye - Irún see top of next page.

km	All *TGV* convey 🍸												TGV 8571		TGV 8531		TGV 8573			TGV 8533	TGV 8578		TGV 8577	TGV 8535
		Ⓐ	Ⓐ	Ⓐ	⚒	Ⓐ	Ⓐ			⚒	⑥	†	①–⑥	⑦				⚒	Ⓐ		Ⓐ		⑤	Ⓒ
		t	t	t		y	y			v	S	Q	k		A		F	c	K	b	G		f	S
	Paris Montparnasse **300** d.	...	...	...	...	...	...	...	...	...	...	...	...	...	0728	...	0828	...	...	1025	...	...	1128	1128
0	**Bordeaux** St Jean d.	...	...	...	...	...	0646	0746	...	...	0936	0947	0951	...	1051	...	1151	...	1247	1351	...	...	1447	1447
109	Morcenx d.	...	...	...	...	...	0747	0843	...	...	1031	1045	|	...	|	...	|	...	1345	|	...	...	|	|
148	Dax a.	...	...	...	...	...	0806	0903	...	...	1050	1105	1100	...	1200	...	1300	...	1405	1500	...	...	1600	1600
148	Dax d.	0602	0642	0712	0742	0811	0815	0908	0911	1012	1052	1107	1107	1111	1205	...	1309	1312	1410	1505	1508	...	1603	1603
179	Puyoô **325** d.	|	|	|	|	0829	|	|	0929	|	|	|	|	1129	|	...	|	|	|	|	|	...	|	|
193	Orthez **325** d.	|	|	|	|	0840	|	|	0940	|	|	|	|	1140	|	...	1340	|	|	|	1544	...	|	|
233	Pau **325** d.	|	|	|	|	0904	|	|	1006	|	|	|	1206	1208	|	...	1406	|	|	|	1613	...	1655	|
272	Lourdes **325** d.	|	|	|	|	...	|	|	...	|	|	|	1235	1236	|	...	1440	|	|	|	1647	...	1730	|
293	**Tarbes 325** a.	|	|	|	|	...	|	|	...	|	|	|	1252	1251	|	...	1455	|	|	|	1704	...	1746	|
199	**Bayonne 325** d.	0648	0729	0759	0829	...	0846	0939	...	1101	1123	1159	...	...	1238	...	...	1359	1440	1535	...	...	...	1635
209	Biarritz **325** d.	0657	0738	0808	0838	...	0855	0949	...	1110	1132	1209	...	...	1251	...	...	1408	1449	1546	...	...	...	1648
222	St Jean de Luz **325** d.	0709	0751	0821	0851	...	0908	1002	...	1122	1144	1223	...	...	1305	...	...	1421	1502	1602	...	...	...	1702
235	Hendaye **325** a.	0720	0804	0834	0904	...	0921	1014	...	1134	1156	1235	...	...	1315	...	...	1434	1515	1611	...	...	...	1711
237	**Irún 325** a.	...	...	...	...	...	...	...	...	...	...	...	...	...	1324	...	...	...	...	...	...	...	...	...

					TGV 8537						TGV 8541	TGV 8591								TGV 8593	TGV 8543		TGV 8545
	①–④		Ⓐ	Ⓐ			Ⓐ	Ⓐ			Ⓐ		⑦–④		⑥	⚒	†	†					Ⓑ	⑤
	o	J	K	ty		c	t	y			t	B			j	K	y	s	L			D		f
Paris Montparnasse **300** d.	...	...	...	...	...	...	...	...	...	...	...	1428	1428	...	...	...	...	...	...	...	1728	...	...	...
Bordeaux St Jean d.	1446	1451	...	...	...	1551	...	...	...	1646	...	1751	1751	...	...	1846	1846	...	...	...	2051	...	...	2251
Morcenx d.	1542	1547	...	...	...	|	...	...	...	1747	...	|	|	...	...	1951	1951	...	...	...	|	...	...	|
Dax a.	1602	1606	...	...	...	1700	...	...	...	1806	...	1900	1900	...	...	2010	2010	...	...	...	2200	...	...	2358
Dax d.	1607	1608	1611	1642	...	1705	1712	1742	1811	1815	1842	1905	1909y	...	1912	2015	2019	2015	2019	...	2209	2205	2212	0003
Puyoô **325** d.	|	|	1629	|	...	|	|	|	1829	|	|	|	|	...	|	|	2037	|	2037	...	|	|	|	|
Orthez **325** d.	|	|	1639	|	...	|	|	|	1839	|	|	|	1938y	...	|	|	2048	|	2047	...	2239	|	|	|
Pau **325** d.	|	|	1704	|	...	|	|	|	1904	|	|	|	2004y	...	|	|	2116	|	2116	...	2303r	|	|	|
Lourdes **325** d.	|	|	...	|	...	|	|	|	...	|	|	|	2042y	...	|	|	2143	|	2144	...	2329r	|	|	|
Tarbes 325 a.	|	|	...	|	...	|	|	|	...	|	|	|	2056y	...	|	|	2158	|	2202	...	2345r	|	|	|
Bayonne 325 d.	1640	1640	...	1729	...	1735	1759	1828	...	1846	1929	1935	...	...	1959	2046	...	2046	...	...	...	2235	2258	0035
Biarritz 325 d.	1649	1653	...	1738	...	1746	1808	...	...	1857	1938	1948	...	...	2008	2056	...	2056	...	...	...	2248	...	0048
St Jean de Luz **325** d.	1702	1707	...	1751	...	1802	1821	...	...	1910	1951	2002	...	...	2021	2109	...	2109	...	...	...	2302	...	0100
Hendaye **325** a.	1715	1719	...	1804	...	1811	1834	...	...	1922	2004	2011	...	...	2034	2121	...	2121	...	...	...	2311	...	0111
Irún 325 a.	...	...	...	...	...	1820	...	...	...	...	...	...	...	...	...	...	...	...	...	...	...	...	...	...

						TGV 8561	TGV 8530											TGV 8540		TGV 8581			TGV 8542	
	⚒	①	Ⓐ	Ⓐ	Ⓐ	①–⑥			Ⓐ	⑥	Ⓐ	Ⓐ	Ⓐ	Ⓒ	Ⓐ	Ⓐ	Ⓐ		⑥		Ⓐ			Ⓐ
	H	L		t	y	h	a		t	w	t	P	y	m		t	ty	d	S	m	S	c	C	
Hendaye 325 d.	0505	...	...	0600	...	...	0645	...	0650	...	0729	...	0756	...	...	0844	0922	0945	1042	...	1145	1226	1245	...
St Jean de Luz **325** d.	0519	...	...	0613	...	...	0659	...	0705	...	0742	...	0809	...	...	0857	0935	0959	1055	...	1158	1239	1259	...
Biarritz **325** d.	0532	...	...	0627	...	...	0713	...	0719	...	0755	...	0822	...	...	0910	0949	1013	1108	...	1211	1252	1313	...
Bayonne 325 d.	0543	...	...	0637	0702	...	0725	...	0732	0732	0804	...	0831	...	...	0921	0958	1025	1118	...	1221	1303	1325	...
Tarbes 325 d.	|	0430	...	|	|	0610	|	...	|	|	|	0708	...	0807	...	|	|	|	|	1016	|	|	|	...
Lourdes **325** d.	|	0446	...	|	|	0627	|	...	|	|	|	0723	...	0823	...	|	|	|	|	1039	|	|	|	...
Pau **325** d.	|	0515	0626	|	|	0659	|	...	|	|	|	0752	...	0853	0853	|	|	|	|	1106	|	|	|	1351
Orthez **325** d.	|	0541	0650	|	|	0725	|	...	|	|	|	0818	...	0918	0918	|	|	|	|	1131	|	|	|	1416
Puyoô **325** d.	|	0552	0700	|	|	|	|	...	|	|	|	0829	...	0929	0929	|	|	|	|	|	|	|	|	1427
Dax a.	0616	0610	0718	0723	0748	0751	0755	...	0818	0818	0848	0852	...	0948	0948	0953	1044	1055	1147	1156	1250	1348	1355	1446
Dax d.	0620	...	...	0727	...	...	0800	...	...	...	...	0857	...	0950	...	0958	...	1100	1150	1200	1253	...	1400	...
Morcenx d.	0640	...	...	0748	...	...	|	...	...	...	...	0918	...	1010	...	1018	...	|	1209	|	1314	...	|	...
Bordeaux St Jean a.	0745	...	...	0845	...	...	0909	...	...	...	...	1015	...	1108	...	1115	...	1209	1303	1309	1413	...	1509	...
Paris Montparnasse **300** a.	...	...	...	...	...	...	1237	...	...	...	...	...	...	...	...	...	...	1537	...	1637	...	...	1836	...

			TGV 8583	TGV 8544			TGV 8585						TGV 8546				TGV 8587	TGV 8548						
	Ⓐ	⑤†		Ⓑ	†	Ⓑ		Ⓐ	Ⓐ	Ⓑ	⑤†	①–④		Ⓐ	⚒		⑦	⑦	⚒		†	†	⚒	
	K	x	n	e		K	p	t			M	z	E				q	g				N	S	
Hendaye 325 d.	1343	...	...	1445	...	1545	...	1626	...	...	1722	1722	1745	...	...	...	...	1845	1844	...	...	1942	2030	...
St Jean de Luz **325** d.	1356	...	...	1459	...	1558	...	1639	...	...	1735	1735	1759	...	...	...	...	1859	1857	...	...	1956	2043	...
Biarritz **325** d.	1409	...	...	1513	...	1611	...	1652	...	...	1748	1748	1813	...	...	...	...	1913	1911	...	...	2009	2055	...
Bayonne 325 d.	1418	1502	...	1525	...	1620	...	1700	1732	...	1758	1757	1825	1832	...	...	...	1925	1920	...	...	2019	2104	...
Tarbes 325 d.	|	|	1411	|	1507	|	1608	...	|	...	|	...	|	|	...	...	1815	|	|	...	...	|	|	...
Lourdes **325** d.	|	|	1437	|	1523	|	1632	...	|	...	|	...	|	|	...	...	1840	|	|	...	...	|	|	...
Pau **325** d.	|	|	1504	|	1553	|	1700	...	|	1713	|	...	|	|	1856	...	1907	|	|	...	1953	|	|	...
Orthez **325** d.	|	|	|	|	1618	|	1725	...	|	1744	|	...	|	|	1921	...	|	|	|	...	2019	|	|	...
Puyoô **325** d.	|	|	|	|	1629	|	|	...	|	1758	|	...	|	|	1931	...	|	|	|	...	2030	|	|	...
Dax a.	1450	1548	1551	1555	1648	1652	1751	...	1818	1820	1830	...	1855	1918	1948	...	1951	1955	1952	...	2048	2052	2149	...
Dax d.	1455	...	1600	...	...	1657	1800	...	...	...	1835	...	1900	...	...	...	...	2000	1957	...	...	2055	...	...
Morcenx d.	1515	...	|	...	...	1717	|	...	...	...	1854	...	|	...	...	...	...	|	2016	...	...	2117	...	...
Bordeaux St Jean a.	1610	...	1709	...	...	1813	1909	...	...	...	2000	...	2009	...	...	...	...	2109	2117	...	...	2213	...	...
Paris Montparnasse **300** a.	...	...	2036	...	...	...	2236	...	...	...	...	...	2337	...	...	...	...	0037	...	...	...	...	...	...

A – ①–⑥ until Sept. 12; ⑥ Sept. 13 - Nov. 22; ①–⑥ Nov. 29 - Dec. 13 (also Oct. 6 - 10; not July 14, Oct. 25, Nov. 8).
B – ⑤⑥ until July 5; daily July 6 - Aug. 24; ⑤⑥ Aug. 29 - Dec. 13 (not Oct. 25, Nov. 8).
C – Daily June 30 - Sept. 14, Oct. 4 - 12; Ⓒ Oct. 18 - Nov. 30; daily Dec. 1 - 13 (also Sept. 21, 27, 28; not Oct. 25, Nov. 8, 9).
D – Ⓑ until July 6; daily July 7 - Aug. 29; Ⓑ Aug. 31 - Sept. 26; ⑤ Oct. 3 - Nov. 28; Ⓑ Nov. 30 - Dec. 12 (also Nov. 11).
E – ⑥⑦ until June 29; daily July 5 - Aug. 24; ⑥⑦ Aug. 30 - Nov. 2, Nov. 22 - Dec. 13 (also Nov. 11, 15, 16; not July 19, Oct. 25).
F – Daily until Sept. 14; Ⓒ Sept. 20 - Nov. 23; daily Nov. 24 - Dec. 13 (also Oct. 6 - 10; not July 20).
G – Sept. 15 - Oct. 3, Oct. 13 - Nov. 21.
H – Not Oct. 25, Nov. 10.
J – ⑤⑦ July 4 - Aug. 24; ⑤ Aug. 29 - Dec. 12 (also July 14, Aug. 14).
K – Daily July 6 - Aug. 24.
L – Also July 15, Nov. 12; not July 14, Nov. 10.
M – Also Aug. 14; not Nov. 9.
N – Not Nov. 9.
P – Not Nov. 10, 12.
Q – Runs 8 minutes later throughout on holidays.
S – July 6 - Aug. 25.

a – Not July 20, Oct. 25, 26, Nov. 8, 9, 10.
b – Not July 20, Oct. 25, Nov. 8, 9, 10.
c – Not Oct. 25, Nov. 8, 9, 10.
d – Not Oct. 25, 26, Nov. 8, 9, 10.
e – Not Aug. 15, Nov. 10.
f – Also Aug. 14; not Aug. 15.
g – Also July 14, Nov. 11; not Nov. 9.
h – Not July 14, Nov. 8, 9, 10.
j – Not Nov. 1, 8.
k – Not July 14, Nov. 11.
m – Not Nov. 8 - 11.
n – Not Nov. 3 - 14, 17 - 21.
o – Not July 14, Aug. 14, Oct. 30, Nov. 11.
p – Not July 19, Nov. 8 - 11.
q – Also July 14; not Nov. 9.
r – 13 - 14 minutes later on Ⓒ.
s – Not Oct. 5.
t – Not Nov. 10.
v – Not Nov. 8, 10.
w – Not Nov. 1.
x – Also Aug. 14; not Nov. 10.
y – Not July 6 - Aug. 24.
z – Not July 14, Aug. 14, Nov. 10.

TGV – 🅁, supplement payable, 🍸.

NIGHT TRAINS PARIS / GENÈVE - HENDAYE - IRÚN — 305 (contd)

NIGHT TRAIN **PARIS - IRÚN**

🛏 1, 2 cl. and (2) (reclining). *Timings and dates may vary.*

See below for dates	4053 🅁 ◇	*See below for dates*	4052 🅁 ⊡
Paris Austerlitz .... d.	2152	*Irún* .... d.	...
Les Aubrais-Orléans .... d.	2252	**Hendaye** .... d.	1924
Tarbes .... a.	0542	St Jean de Luz .... d.	1936
Lourdes .... a.	0605	Biarritz .... d.	1951
Pau .... a.	0635	**Bayonne** .... d.	2001
Orthez .... a.	0700	Dax .... d.	2058
Dax .... a.	0730	Orthez .... d.	2128
Bayonne .... a.	0834	Pau .... d.	2154
Biarritz .... a.	0846	Lourdes .... d.	2225
St Jean de Luz .... a.	0859	**Tarbes** .... d.	2243
Hendaye .... a.	0911	Les Aubrais-Orléans .... a.	0608
Irún .... a.	0922	**Paris** Austerlitz .... a.	0720

From Paris: ①⑤⑦ (daily July 4 - Sept. 1; also Nov. 11; not Oct. 24).

From Hendaye: ①⑤⑦ (daily July 4 - Sept. 1, Oct. 24 - Nov. 7).

◇ – Variations: Until June 30 Paris d. 2139; departures on ① Sept. 8 - Oct. 20 run Tarbes - Irún up to 1 hour later.

⊡ – Variations: June 9, 16 departures arrive Les Aubrais 0638, Paris 0753; June 15, 22 departures run earlier Hendaye - Pau (Hendaye d. 1907, Paris a. 0743); July 27 departure runs later (Hendaye d. 1951, Paris a. 0728).

NIGHT TRAIN **GENÈVE - IRÚN**

🛏 1, 2 cl. and (2) (reclining)

Genève .... d.	...	Irún .... d.	...
Lyon Part Dieu .... d.	...	**Hendaye** .... d.	...
Valence Ville .... d.	...	Biarritz .... d.	...
Toulouse Matabiau .... a.	...	**Bayonne** .... d.	...
Tarbes .... a.	...	Dax .... d.	...
Lourdes .... a.	...	Pau .... d.	...
Pau .... a.	...	Lourdes .... d.	...
Dax .... a.	...	**Tarbes** .... d.	...
Bayonne .... a.	...	**Toulouse** Matabiau .... d.	...
Biarritz .... a.	...	Valence Ville .... a.	...
Hendaye .... a.	...	**Lyon** Part Dieu .... a.	...
Irún .... a.	...	**Genève** .... a.	...

SERVICE WITHDRAWN

BORDEAUX - ARCACHON — 306

TGV Trains

km	*TGV services,* 🅁	*TGV* 8471 A			*TGV* 8473 Ⓒ s	*TGV* 8477 Ⓒ H		*TGV* 8479 ⑤ f		
	Paris Montparnasse **300** .... d.	0843	...	...	1025	...	...	1804	...	...
0	**Bordeaux** St Jean .... d.	1235	...	...	1355	1457	...	2142	...	...
40	Facture Biganos .... d.	1300	...	...	1419	1525	...	2207	...	...
56	La Teste .... a.	|	...	...	|	|	...	2219	...	...
59	**Arcachon** .... a.	1314	...	...	1443	1543	...	2224	...	...

TGV services, 🅁	*TGV* 8470 ① g		*TGV* 8476 Ⓒ s		*TGV* 8478 Ⓒ s		*TGV* 8472 ⑦ z		
Arcachon .... d.	0534	...	1536	...	1719	...	1843	...	...
La Teste .... d.	|	...	|	...	|	...	1849	...	...
Facture Biganos .... d.	0550	...	1553	...	1738	...	1901	...	...
Bordeaux St Jean .... a.	0613	...	1615	...	1800	...	1923	...	...
Paris Montparnasse **300** . a.	0937	...	2001	...	2159	...	2318	...	...

Local services *(subject to alteration from Sept. 14)*

	Ⓐ△		Ⓐy	⚒	Ⓒ	Ⓐ			Ⓐy				Ⓐ		Ⓐy	Ⓐ		Ⓐ		Ⓐy				⑤†s	⑤f
Bordeaux St Jean .... d.	0705	0805	0835	0905	1005	1105	1239	1305	1335	1405	1505	1605	1635	1705	1719	1735	1805	1835	1905	1935	2005	2105	2205	2305	2355
Facture Biganos .... d.	0735	0835	0905	0935	1035	1135	1309	1335	1405	1435	1535	1635	1705	1735	1750	1805	1835	1905	1935	2005	2035	2135	2235	2335	0025
Arcachon .... ⊖ a.	0756	0856	0926	0956	1056	1156	1331	1356	1426	1456	1556	1656	1726	1756	1812	1826	1856	1926	1956	2026	2056	2156	2256	2356	0047

	⚒	Ⓐy	⚒	Ⓐ	⚒s	Ⓐ						Ⓐ		Ⓒ			Ⓐy		Ⓐ		Ⓐy		⚒s	†	H
Arcachon .... ⊖ d.	0545	0621	0631	0645	0703	0733	0803	0903	1003	1103	1203	1233	1303	1403	1503	1603	1633	1703	1733	1803	1833	1903	2003	2103	2203
Facture Biganos .... d.	0608	0646	0655	0708	0725	0755	0825	0925	1025	1125	1225	1255	1325	1425	1525	1625	1655	1725	1755	1825	1855	1925	2025	2125	2225
Bordeaux St Jean .... a.	0640	0715	0725	0740	0755	0825	0855	0955	1055	1155	1255	1325	1355	1455	1555	1655	1725	1755	1825	1855	1925	1955	2055	2155	2255

A – ⑤⑥⑦ until July 6; Ⓐ July 7 - Aug. 21; Ⓒ Aug. 30 - Oct. 26; ⑤⑥† Oct. 31 - Dec. 13 (also Sept. 5, 12, Nov. 10; not Sept. 14).

H – July 6 - Aug. 24.

f – Also Aug. 14; not Aug. 15.

g – Also Nov. 12; not July 7 - Aug. 18, Nov. 10.

s – Daily July 6 - Aug. 24.

y – Not July 7 - Aug. 22.

z – Also July 14, Nov. 11.

TGV – 🅁, supplement, 🍸.

⊖ – Trains also call at La Teste, 4 - 5 mins from Arcachon.

△ – Additional journeys run from Bordeaux at 0635 Ⓐ, 0735 Ⓐ y.

BORDEAUX - LE VERDON - POINTE DE GRAVE — 307

Valid to July 5 / from August 25

km		Ⓐ△	Ⓐ	Ⓒ	⚒	Ⓐ			Ⓐ		Ⓑ	
0	**Bordeaux** St Jean ..... d.	0711	0811	0911	1111	1211	1311	1611	1711	1811	1941	...
19	Blanquefort .... d.	0748	0847	0947	1147	1247	1347	1647	1747	1847	2015	...
35	Margaux .... d.	0809	0909	1009	1209	1309	1409	1709	1809	1909	2035	...
57	Pauillac .... d.	0830	0930	1030	1230	1330	1430	1730	1830	1930	2055	...
76	Lesparre .... d.	0845	0944	1045	1244	1344	1445	1744	1845	1945	2110r	...
102	Soulac sur Mer .... d.	0905	...	1105	...	...	1505	...	1905	2005	...	...
109	**Le Verdon** .... a.	0912	...	1112	...	...	1512	...	1912	2012	...	...
112	Pointe de Grave .... ▷ a.	...	...	...	...	...	...	...	...	...	...	...

	Ⓐ▽	Ⓐ		⑥	Ⓐ		Ⓐ		Ⓐ	
Pointe de Grave ... ▷ d.	...	...	...	...	...	...	...	...	...	...
Le Verdon .... d.	0547	0625	0747c	0947	...	1147	...	1552c	1647	1747c
Soulac sur Mer .... d.	0554	0632	0754c	0954	...	1154	...	1559c	1654	1754c
Lesparre .... d.	0614	0651	0814	1014	1114	1214	1414	1620	1714	1814
Pauillac .... d.	0629	0706	0829	1029	1129	1229	1429	1635	1729	1829
Margaux .... d.	0648	0729	0853	1053	1153	1253	1453	1655	1753	1853
Blanquefort .... d.	0709	0747	0914	1114	1214	1314	1514	1714	1814	1914
Bordeaux St Jean .... a.	0749	0819	0949	1149	1249	1349	1549	1749	1849	1949

July 6 - August 24

km		Ⓐ						Ⓐ		Ⓐ	
0	**Bordeaux** St Jean ⊖ d.	0711	0911	1111c	...	1311c	1611	1711	1811	1941	...
19	Blanquefort .... d.	0748	0947	1147	...	1347	1647	1747	1847	2015	...
35	Margaux .... d.	0809	1009	1209	...	1409	1709	1809	1909	2035	...
57	Pauillac .... d.	0830	1030	1230	...	1430	1730	1830	1930	2055	...
76	Lesparre .... d.	0845	1045	1245	...	1445	1745	1844	1945	2111	...
102	Soulac sur Mer .... d.	0905	1105	1305	...	1505	1805	...	2005	2130	...
109	**Le Verdon** .... a.	0912	1112	1313	...	1513	1813	...	2012	2138	...
112	Pointe de Grave ..... ▷ a.	0917	1117	1317	...	1517	1817	...	...	...	...

	Ⓐ	⚒	Ⓐ							
Pointe de Grave ..... ▷ d.	...	...	...	...	0942	1142	1342	...	1642	1842
Le Verdon .... d.	...	...	0625	0747	0947	1147	1347	...	1647	1847
Soulac sur Mer .... d.	...	...	0632	0754	0954	1154	1354	...	1654	1854
Lesparre .... d.	0549	0614	0651	0814	1014	1214	1414	...	1714	1914
Pauillac .... d.	0604	0629	0706	0829	1029	1229	1429	...	1729	1929
Margaux .... d.	0623	0648	0729	0853	1053	1253	1453	...	1753	1953
Blanquefort .... d.	0643	0709	0747	0914	1114	1314	1514	...	1814	2014
Bordeaux St Jean ⊖ .a.	0719	0749	0819	0949	1149	1349	1549	...	1849	2049

– Ⓒ only.

– ⑤† only.

△ – Additional journey runs at 0641 Ⓐ to Lesparre.

▽ – Additional journeys run at 0529 Ⓐ from Pauillac (Bordeaux a. 0649) and 0549 Ⓐ from Lesparre (Bordeaux a. 0719).

▷ – For ferry schedule Pointe de Grave - Royan see Table **299**.

308 PÉRIGUEUX - LE BUISSON - AGEN

Subject to alteration from September 15

km		① T	Ⓐ	Ⓒ	Ⓐ	Ⓒ G		Ⓐ	⚒	Ⓐ	E	⑤† f
0	**Périgueux** d.	0506	...	...	0759	0948	1226	1434	1731	1830	1913	1913
40	Les Eyzies d.	0536	...	...	0828	1017	1258	1523	1809	1905	1948	1949
57	Le Buisson d.	0552	...	...	0847	1034	1313	1540	1831	1920	2003	2006
108	M'pron Libos ‡ d.	0639	0730	0929	0931	1121	1358	1624	1914	...	...	2055
152	**Agen** a.	0719	0813	1002	1005	1200	1431	1704	1947	...	...	2130

	⚒ ⊖	†	Ⓐ		Ⓑ	†	⑥	Ⓐ		Ⓑ g	⑤ T
Agen d.	...	...	0727	1119	1434	...	1628	1730	1836	2000	2051
M'pron Libos ‡ d.	...	...	0802	1154	1507	...	1704	1809	1915	2039	2126
Le Buisson d.	0720	0846	0848	1240	1551	1732	1751	...	2007	...	2210
Les Eyzies d.	0735	0902	0903	1257	1607	1747	1810	...	2023	...	2226
Périgueux a.	0810	0936	0938	1328	1635	1822	1840	...	2052	...	2254

E – ①②③④⑥ (not July 14, Aug. 14).
G – Daily July 6 - Aug. 24.
T – Not July 6 - Aug. 24.
f – Also Aug. 14.
g – Not July 13.
⊖ – Runs 7 minutes later throughout on ⑥.
‡ – Monsempron Libos.

309 LIMOGES - ANGOULÊME and POITIERS

km		J	Ⓐ		⑥		†q	⚒		p		⑤†r
0	**Limoges** d.	0532	0553	...	0822	...	1220	1233	...	1725	...	1837
122	**Angoulême** a.	0732	0808	...	1008	...	1415	1426	...	1922	...	2037

	⚒n	M	G	③		†p	H	Ⓐ	Ⓒp	⑤k	†S
Angoulême d.	0555	0752	1204	1230	...	1454	1707	1820	1900	1948	2205
Limoges a.	0750	0938	1352	1424	...	1643	1855	2019	2102	2142	2347

km		Ⓐ			Ⓐ	Ⓐ			Ⓐ	†p	⑤k	
0	**Limoges** d.	0610	0810	1210	1302	1410	1610	1808	2010	2030	2230	...
139	**Poitiers** a.	0756	0956	1356	1505	1556	1756	1956	2156	2212	0012	...

	⚒n		⚒	Ⓐ	Ⓑ		Ⓐ		⚒n	†p	⑤k
Poitiers d.	0559	0804	1204	1251	1404	1604	1650	1804	2004	2148	2225
Limoges a.	0753	0951	1351	1457	1551	1751	1857	1953	2151	2337	0011

G – ①②④⑤⑥ (not holidays).
H – Ⓑ (Ⓐ only July 7 - Aug. 29).
J – ①⑤ (not July 6 - Aug. 31).
M – Ⓐ (① only July 21 - Aug. 25; not July 14).
S – July 6 - Aug. 31.
k – Also Aug. 14; not Aug. 15.
n – Also Nov. 1.
p – Not Nov. 1.
q – Not Nov. 1, 2.
r – Also Aug. 14; not Nov. 1.

310 PARIS - LIMOGES - TOULOUSE

Valid until August 24

For faster TGV services Paris - Agen - Toulouse and v.v. see Table 320. Additional relief trains run on peak dates.

km		⚒	Ⓐ	Ⓐ	⚒	⚒	Ⓐ	★ 3601 Ⓐ	⚒ f	★ 3611 ⚒	★ 3613 ⑦ x	Ⓐ	★ 3621	⚒	★ 3701 D ☆	★ 3631 C	★ 3703 ⑥⑦ ☆v	Ⓒ	★ 3635 ⑤⑦ ⊡z	⑤ t	★ 3637 ⑤–⑦ x	⚒ w	★ 3643	Ⓐ
	Lille Europe d.	...	...	...	...	...	...	...	...	...	...	...	...	...	...	...	...	...	...	...	...	...	...	...
0	**Paris** Austerlitz **294 315** d.	...	...	...	...	...	...	0637	...	0749	0739	...	0837	...	0920	0942j	1005	...	1140	...	1236	...	1339	...
	Orléans 315 d.	...	...	...	...	...	0650	|	0750	|	|	...	|	...	|	|	|	1050	|	...	|	1302	|	...
119	Les Aubrais-Orléans **294 315** d.	...	...	...	...	...	|	|	|	0847	0847	...	|	...	1031	1038	1113	|	|	...	|	|	1447	...
200	Vierzon **315** d.	...	...	...	...	0649	0749	0809	0849	|	|	...	1009	...	|	|	|	1154	1318	...	|	1412	|	...
236	Issoudun d.	...	...	...	...	0714	0814	0828	0912	|	|	...	|	...	|	|	|	1217	|	...	1428	1433	|	...
263	Châteauroux d.	...	...	...	...	0732	0832	0845	0932	0948	0948	...	1039	...	1137	|	1223	1235	1348	...	1445	1450	1548	...
294	Argenton sur Creuse d.	...	...	...	...	0749	0849	|	0949	|	|	...	1056	...	|	|	|	1251	|	...	|	...	|	...
341	La Souterraine d.	...	...	...	...	0818	▬	0923	...	|	|	...	1121	...	|	|	|	...	|	...	1523	...	|	...
400	**Limoges** a.	...	...	...	...	0854	Ⓒ	0954	...	1054	1054	...	1154	...	1249	1254	1353	...	1454	...	1554	...	1654	...
400	**Limoges** d.	...	...	...	0733	...	0907	0957	...	1057	1057	...	1154	1228	1253	1257	1357	...	1457	...	▬	...	1657	1707
459	Uzerche d.	...	...	...	0823	...	0956	|	...	1134	1134	...	1233	1317	|	|	|	...	1534	...	...	...	|	1756
499	**Brive la Gaillarde** a.	...	...	...	0852	...	1024	1100	...	1159	1159	...	1300	1345	1354	1358	1456	...	1600	...	N	...	1757	1824
499	**Brive la Gaillarde** d.	...	0601	0704	▬	...	...	...	...	1202	1202	1308	...	...	1404	1401	1459	...	...	1705	1732	...	1800	...
536	Souillac d.	...	0627	0728	...	...	...	...	...	|	1227	1332	...	...	|	1427	|	...	...	1729	1756	...	1825	...
559	Gourdon d.	...	0642	0743	⚒	...	...	...	...	|	1243	1347	...	...	|	1443	|	...	...	1744	1811	...	1841	...
600	Cahors d.	0609	0711	0809	0900	...	...	...	...	1305	1311	1413	...	...	1518	1511	1601	...	...	1811	1838	...	1909	...
639	Caussade d.	0636	0738	0836	0927	...	...	...	...	|	1337	1438	...	...	|	1537	|	...	...	1838	1907	...	1936	...
662	Montauban **320** d.	0654	0756	0854	0945	...	...	...	...	1346	1353	1455	...	...	1602	1554	1641	...	...	1856	1928	...	1953	...
713	**Toulouse** Matabiau **320** a.	0735	0835	0935	1024	...	...	...	...	1414	1422	1540	...	...	1630	1622	1707	...	...	1935	2012	...	2022	...
	Portbou **355** a.	...	...	...	...	...	...	...	...	...	...	...	...	...	...	...	...	...	...	...	...	...	...	...

	Ⓐ	Ⓑ	Ⓐ	★ 3651 Ⓐ	Ⓐ	Ⓐ	Ⓒ	Ⓒ	★ 3655 Ⓐ	Ⓐ	★ 3661 ⑤⑦ q	★ 3669 ①–④ m	Ⓐ	★ 3665 ⑥ v	★ 3665 ⑦	Ⓐ	★ 3667	★ 3663 ⑤ t	★ 3681	TGV 5248 B		3731 ♦ 🅁	3751 ♦ P🅁	3753 ♦ Q🅁
Lille Europe d.	...	...	...	...	...	...	...	...	...	...	...	...	...	...	...	...	...	...	...	1802	...	...	...	...
Paris Austerlitz **294 315** d.	...	...	...	1540	...	...	...	...	1652r	...	1738	1738	...	1812k	1804	...	1838	1849	1936	|	...	2152	2239	2239
Orléans 315 d.	...	...	...	|	...	...	...	1650	|	...	|	|	...	|	|	1850	|	|	|	|	...	|	|	|
Les Aubrais-Orléans **294 315** d.	...	...	...	|	...	...	...	|	|	...	|	|	...	|	|	|	|	2015	|	2042	...	2259	2355	2355
Vierzon **315** d.	...	...	1644	1718	...	1733	...	1749	|	1822	|	1918	1933	1937	1937	1948	2009	2056	2109	2116	...	2344	|	|
Issoudun d.	...	...	1705	|	...	1754	...	1812	|	1843	|	|	1954	|	|	2012	2028	|	|	|	...	|	|	|
Châteauroux d.	1639	...	1724	1748	...	1809	1809	1831	1846	1912	1948	1948	2009	2008	2008	2030	2045	2127	2139	2149	...	|	|	|
Argenton sur Creuse d.	1655	...	1750	|	...	1825	1825	1857	|	1930	|	|	2025	2025	2025	...	|	2145	2156	|	...	|	|	|
La Souterraine d.	1722	...	...	|	...	1854	1854	1926	1923	1959	|	|	2053	2051	2051	...	2123	2211	2223	2229	...	|	|	|
Limoges a.	1755	...	...	1854	...	1939	1939	▬	1954	...	2054	2054	2139	2124	2124	...	2157	2246	2254	2257	...	0118	|	|
Limoges d.	...	1807	...	1857	1907	...	...	...	...	...	2057	2057	...	2127	2127	...	...	2249	2257	2300	...	0121	|	|
Uzerche d.	...	1856	...	1934	1958	...	...	...	...	...	2134	2134	...	2204	2204	...	...	2326	|	|	...	|	|	|
Brive la Gaillarde a.	...	1924	...	2000	2027	...	...	†	...	...	2159	2159	...	2229	2229	...	...	2351	2357	2400	...	|	|	|
Brive la Gaillarde d.	...	...	...	...	...	...	...	2016	...	...	2202	2202	...	2232	2232	...	...	2354	...	...	...	|	|	|
Souillac d.	...	...	...	...	...	...	...	2040	...	...	2228	2228	...	2257	2257	...	...	0020	...	...	...	|	|	0422
Gourdon d.	...	...	...	...	...	...	...	2056	...	...	2244	2244	...	2313	2313	...	...	0036	...	...	...	|	|	0440
Cahors d.	...	...	...	...	...	...	...	2122	...	...	2311	2314	...	2341	2339	...	...	0104	...	...	...	|	0510	0510
Caussade d.	...	...	...	...	...	...	...	2149	...	...	...	...	...	|	...	...	...	|	...	...	...	|	|	0544
Montauban **320** d.	...	...	...	...	...	...	...	2207	...	...	...	...	...	|	...	...	...	|	...	...	...	|	0608	0608
Toulouse Matabiau **320** a.	...	...	...	...	...	...	...	2235	...	...	...	...	...	0046	...	...	...	0206	...	...	...	|	0645	0645
Portbou **355** a.	...	...	...	...	...	...	...	...	...	...	...	...	...	...	...	...	...	...	...	...	...	0822	...	...

	★ 3600 Ⓐ	Ⓐ	★ 3604 Ⓐ	★ 3602 Ⓒ	⚒	★ 3606 Ⓐ	⚒	⚒	TGV 5296 A	⚒ f		Ⓐ	★ 3610 ⚒	★ 3612 ⑦ x	Ⓐ	★ 3620 ⚒	②–⑤ n	① h	Ⓒ		★ 3700 H ☆	★ 3630	★ 3634 ⑤⑥ y	★ 3632 ⑦ x
Cerbère **355** d.	...	...	...	...	...	...	...	...	...	...	...	...	...	...	...	...	...	...	...	...	...	0725	...	...
Toulouse Matabiau **320** d.	...	...	...	...	...	...	...	...	...	...	...	...	...	...	0622	0646	0725	0725	...	...	1042	1047	...	...
Montauban **320** d.	...	...	...	...	...	...	...	...	...	...	...	...	...	...	0703	0714	0806	0806	...	...	1110	1114	...	...
Caussade d.	...	...	...	...	...	...	...	...	...	...	...	...	...	...	0719	|	0823	0823	...	...	|	1131	...	...
Cahors d.	...	...	...	...	...	...	...	...	...	...	...	...	0644	...	0747	0756	0849	0850	...	...	1153	1159	...	...
Gourdon d.	...	...	...	...	...	...	...	...	...	...	...	...	0711	...	0813	|	▬	0919	...	...	|	1226	...	...
Souillac d.	...	...	...	...	...	...	...	...	...	...	...	...	0728	...	0829	|	...	0935	...	...	|	1243	...	...
Brive la Gaillarde a.	...	...	...	...	...	...	...	...	...	...	...	...	0757	...	0853	0857	...	1001	...	...	1304	1308	...	...
Brive la Gaillarde d.	...	...	0459	0500	...	...	0604	...	0704	...	...	0733	0800	0800	▬	0900	...	...	...	1247	1315	1311	...	1357
Uzerche d.	...	...	0525	0525	...	...	0633	...	|	...	...	0802	0825	0825	...	|	...	...	...	1317	|	|	...	142
Limoges a.	...	...	0603	0603	...	...	0721	...	0803	...	...	0850	0903	0903	...	1003	...	...	...	1407	1415	1411	...	150
Limoges d.	0502	...	0606	0606	...	0706	...	0723	0806	...	0823	...	0906	0906	...	1006	...	...	1223	...	1418	1414	1506	150
La Souterraine d.	0537	...	|	0637	0607	0738	...	0808	0837	...	0908	...	|	|	...	1037	⑥	...	1308	...	|	|	1537	153
Argenton sur Creuse d.	|	...	|	|	0636	|	...	0836	|	0910	0936	...	|	|	Ⓐ	1101	f	...	1336	...	|	|	|	|
Châteauroux d.	0614	0629	0711	0714	0718e	0817	...	0853	0914	0929	0951	...	1011	1011	1110	1119	1229	...	1351	...	1525	|	1614	161
Issoudun d.	0630	0647	|	0730	0736	|	...	0907	|	0947	...	...	|	|	1127	|	1247	...	...	...	|	|	1630	163
Vierzon **315** d.	0651	0713	0742	0751	0800	0851	...	0927	0951	1013	...	...	|	|	1206	|	1313	...	...	...	|	|	1651	165
Les Aubrais-Orléans **294 315** a.	|	|	|	|	|	|	...	...	1026	|	...	...	1112	1111	|	1221	|	...	...	...	1634	1621	|	|
Orléans 315 a.	|	0810	|	|	0854	|	...	...	|	1110	...	...	|	|	1257	|	1410	...	...	...	|	|	|	|
Paris Austerlitz **294 315** a.	0818	...	0922	0918	...	1021	...	...	|	...	...	...	1218	1218	...	1322	...	...	...	...	1739	1721	1820	182
Lille Europe a.	...	...	...	...	...	...	...	...	1305	...	...	...	...	...	...	...	...	...	...	...	...	...	...	...

TOULOUSE - LIMOGES - PARIS — 310

Valid until August 24

	★				★	★		★		★				★			★						♦	♦	♦
Train number		3640			3652	3660		3664		3672				3680			3690						3750	3752	3730
	Ⓑ p		Ⓒ	⑤ p	⑦ x	①–⑥ w	⚒	⑦ x	Ⓐ	⑦ x	M	Ⓑ	Ⓐ	Ⓑ p	⑤ y		Ⓑ	Ⓑ	Ⓑ	Ⓐ	Ⓒ	Ⓐ	P🅁	Q🅁	🅁
Cerbère **355** d.	...	...	...	...	...	...	...	...	...	...	...	...	...	...	...	...	...	...	...	...	...	...	...	...	2016
Toulouse Matabiau **320** d.	...	...	1225	1337	1338	...	...	...	...	1438	1448	...	...	...	1544	...	1638	1724	...	1825	1925	1925	2234	2230	0050
Montauban **320** d.	...	...	1306	1406	1406	...	...	...	...	1506	1533	...	...	...	1627	...	1706	1805	...	1905	1956	2006	2304	2300	|
Caussade d.	...	...	1324	1421	1422	...	...	...	...	1522	1550	...	...	...	1642	...	1722	1821	...	1921	2011	2024	|	2317	|
Cahors d.	...	...	1350	1446	1449	...	...	...	...	1549	1616	...	...	...	1720	...	1749	1848	...	1948	2036	2051	2349	2345	|
Gourdon d.	...	...	▬	1512	1516	...	...	...	...	1616	1643	...	...	...	1749	...	1817	1915	...	2015	2102	...	|	0013	|
Souillac d.	...	...	...	1528	1533	...	...	...	...	1633	1659	...	...	...	1805	...	1835	1931	...	2031	2117	...	|	0030	|
Brive la Gaillarde a.	...	...	...	1551	1557	...	...	...	...	1657	1722	...	...	...	1830	...	1900	1955	...	2055	2141	...	|	|	|
Brive la Gaillarde d.	...	1500	...	▬	1600	1603	...	...	1650	1700	...	...	1736	1800	...	1836	1903	...	2006	...	...	...	|	|	|
Uzerche d.	...	1526	...	...	|	|	...	...	1718	|	...	...	1805	1825	...	1905	|	...	2035	...	...	...	|	|	|
Limoges a.	...	1603	...	...	1703	1703	...	...	1755	1803	...	...	1854	1903	...	1954	2003	...	2124	...	...	...	|	|	|
Limoges d.	...	1606	...	1623	1706	1706	1723	1736	...	1806	...	1823	▬	1906	...	...	2006	...	...	...	...	...	|	|	|
La Souterraine d.	...	|	...	1708	|	1738	1808	1807	...	|	...	1908	Ⓐ	1937	...	...	|	...	...	...	...	...	|	|	|
Argenton sur Creuse d.	1610	|	...	1736	|	1801	1836	1831	...	|	...	1936	1910	|	...	...	|	...	...	...	...	...	|	|	|
Châteauroux d.	1629	1711	1729	1753	1812	1820	1853	1849	...	1911	...	1951	1929	2014	...	...	2111	...	...	...	...	...	|	|	|
Issoudun d.	1647	|	1747	1807**b**	|	|	1907	1906	...	|	...	...	1947	2030	...	...	|	...	...	...	...	...	|	|	|
Vierzon **315** d.	1713	|	1813	1827**b**	|	1852	1927	1928	...	|	...	...	2013	2051	...	...	2147	...	...	...	...	...	|	|	0530
Les Aubrais-Orléans **294 315** a.	|	|	|	...	1911	|	...	|	...	2011	...	...	|	|	...	...	2223	...	...	...	...	...	0535	0535	0620
Orléans 315 a.	1810	|	1910	...	|	|	...	|	...	|	...	...	2110	|	...	...	|	...	...	...	...	...	|	|	|
Paris Austerlitz **294 315** a.	...	1919	...	...	2018	2021	...	2059	...	2119	...	...	...	2221	...	...	2321	...	...	...	...	...	0655	0652	0726
Lille Europe a.	...	...	...	...	...	...	...	...	...	...	...	...	...	...	...	...	...	...	...	...	...	...	...	...	...

♦ – **NOTES** (LISTED BY TRAIN NUMBER):

3730 – 🛏 1,2 cl., 💺 (reclining) Cerbère - Paris and Latour de Carol (**3970**) - Toulouse - Paris. Train number is **3732** July 4 - Aug. 31 (Cerbère d. 1919 on ①–④ June 24 - July 1, July 7 - 10, 17; 1940 on other dates).

3731 – 🛏 1,2 cl., 💺 (reclining) Paris - Portbou; 🛏 1,2 cl., 💺 (reclining) Paris - Latour de Carol (train **3971**). Train number is **3733** July 4 - Aug. 31.

3750-3 – 🛏 1,2 cl. and 💺 (reclining) Paris - Toulouse and v.v. Conveys (to / from Brive) portions Paris - Rodez / Albi and v.v.on dates in Table **316**.

A – ①⑤⑥⑦ (also July 15, Aug. 14). Also calls at Marne la Vallée (a. 1152) and Charles de Gaulle ✈ (a. 1207).
B – ④⑤⑥⑦ (also July 14, Aug. 13). Also calls at Charles de Gaulle ✈ (d. 1859) and Marne la Vallée (d. 1918). Runs up to 15 minutes later La Souterraine - Brive on June 26, 27, July 17, 24, 31.
C – To Cerbère (Table **355**).
D – ①⑤ (not July 14, Aug. 15).
H – ①⑤⑥⑦ only.
M – ①②③④⑥ (not July 14).
N – ①②③④⑦ (also Aug. 15; not Aug. 14).
P – ①–④ (not July 14).
Q – ⑤⑥⑦ (also July 14).

b – Ⓑ only.
e – Arrive 0700.
f – Also Aug. 15.
h – Also days after holidays.
j – Depart 0925 until June 30.
k – Depart 1753 until June 28.
m – Not July 14, Aug. 14.
n – Not days after holidays.
p – Not Aug. 15.
q – Also July 14, Aug. 14; not Aug. 15.
r – Depart up to 30 minutes earlier until June 30.
t – Also Aug. 14; not Aug. 15.
v – Also July 14, Aug. 15.
w – Not July 14.
x – Also July 14.
y – Also Aug. 14.
z – Also July 14; not Aug. 15.

TGV – 🅁, supplement payable, 🍸.

§ – Subject to retiming on some dates (Paris a. 1737).
⊡ – On July 11, 18, 25 Paris d. 1200 and runs 8 - 10 minutes later throughout.
★ – *Intercités* service, 🅁.
☆ – Also conveys couchettes and reclining seats for daytime use (also vending machines).

BRIVE - AURILLAC — 311

Subject to alteration from September 6

km		Ⓐ	⑥ r			† t	⚒		Ⓑ m	⑥ r
0	**Brive la Gaillarde 316** d.	1133	1212	1405	...	1803	1803	...	2217	2244
27	St Denis-près-Martel **316** d.	1158	1241	1428	...	1830	1830	...	2241	2307
102	**Aurillac** a.	1320	1358	1547	...	1946	1950	...	2358	0024

	Ⓐ	⚒	Ⓒ	Ⓐ		† p	⑤ S	q	
Aurillac d.	0520	0701	1058	1113	...	1502	1602	1714	...
St Denis-près-Martel **316** d.	0642	0818	1215	1231	...	1620	1719	1829	...
Brive la Gaillarde 316 a.	0707	0843	1239	1255	...	1644	1743	1851	...

S – Daily July 6 - Aug. 24.
m – Also Nov. 1.
p – Not July 13, Nov. 1.
q – Not Aug. 15.
r – Not Nov. 1.
t – Not July 13, Nov. 1.

TOULOUSE - LATOUR DE CAROL — 312

Subject to alteration from October 13

km		3971 ◇🅁 P		Ⓐ							
	Paris Austerlitz **310** d.	2152	...	...	...	...	...	...	...	...	...
0	**Toulouse** Matabiau d.	0458	0645	0745	0845	1045	1445	1645	1745	1845	1945
65	Pamiers d.	0549	0750	0850	0950	1150	1550	1750	1850	1950	2050
83	Foix a.	0600	0803	0904	1003	1202	1602	1802	1904	2002	2104
83	Foix d.	0602	0805	0906	1005	1205	1605	1805	1906	2005	2106
123	Ax les Thermes d.	0650	0848	0943	1048	1248	1648	1848	1943	2048	2143
144	L'Hospitalet ⊖ a.	0721	0920	...	1120	1320	1720	1920	...	2120	...
163	**Latour de Carol** a.	0751	0952	...	1152	1352	1752	1952	...	2152	...

	Ⓐ									3970 ◇🅁 P
Latour de Carol d.	0521	0721	0921**c**	...	1321	...	...	1721	1921	2020
L'Hospitalet ⊖ d.	0552	0752	0952**c**	...	1352	...	...	1752	1952	2050
Ax les Thermes d.	0620	0820	1020	1123	1420	1523	1723	1820	2020	2121
Foix a.	0704	0904	1104	1203	1504	1603	1803	1904	2104	2211
Foix d.	0705	0905	1105	1204	1505	1604	1804	1905	2105	2213
Pamiers d.	0721	0921	1121	1221	1521	1621	1821	1921	2121	2230
Toulouse Matabiau a.	0819	1019	1219	1319	1619	1718	1918	2018	2221	2316
Paris Austerlitz **310** a.	...	...	...	...	...	...	...	...	...	0726

P – Ⓑ until June 27; daily from June 29; not Sept. 20, Dec. 9, 10, 11 (from Paris and Latour de Carol).
c – Ⓒ only.
⊖ – Full name: Andorre-L'Hospitalet. For 🚌 connections to / from Andorra see Table **313**.
◇ – 🛏 1, 2 cl. and 💺 (reclining).

ANDORRA 🚌 — 313

Subject to alteration

🚌		☆			⊖			
Andorre-L'Hospitalet (Gare) d.	0810	0935	1945	...	and	...	...	...
Pas de la Casa d.	0840	1001	2000	0845	hourly	2045	...	...
Soldeu ⊙ d.	0900	...	2025	0855	until	2055	...	...
Andorra la Vella a.	0920	...	2105	0940	...	2140	...	...

🚌		☆			⊖			
Andorra la Vella d.	0545	...	1700	0745	and	1945	...	...
Soldeu ⊙ d.	0610	...	1735	0825	hourly	2025	...	...
Pas de la Casa d.	0640	1245	1815	0840	until	2040	...	...
Andorre-L'Hospitalet (Gare) a.	0710	1310	1930	...	...	...	...	...

⊙ – Also calls at Canillo, Encamp and Escaldes.
⊖ – Additional journeys operated by Cooperativa Interurbana (service L4) run from Andorra hourly 0720 - 1920, from Pas de la Casa hourly 0820 - 2020.
☆ – Operated by SNCF. Terminates on French side of the border, 100 metre walk from central bus stop in Pas de la Casa.
Operator: La Hispano Andorrana, Av. Santa Coloma, entre 85 - 87, Andorra la Vella, ✆ + 376 821 372. www.andorrabus.com. Subject to cancellation when mountain passes are closed by snow.
Additional service: approx hourly (5 per day on ⑦) Escaldes - Andorra la Vella - Sant Julià de Lòria - Seu d'Urgell (Spain).

TOULOUSE - CASTRES - MAZAMET — 314

Subject to alteration from September 29

km		Ⓐ	Ⓐ	⚒n	†p			Ⓐ	Ⓐ	Ⓐ			
0	**Toulouse** ◇ d.	0543	0643	0743	0843	1143	1343	1543	1643	1723	1743	1843	2043
86	Castres a.	0659	0759	0859	0959	1259	1459	1659	1759	1841	1859	1959	2159
105	**Mazamet** a.	0716	0816	0916	1016	1316	1516	1716	1816	1858	1916	2016	2218

	Ⓐ	Ⓐ	Ⓐ		Ⓐ	Ⓑ	⚒	⚒			Ⓐ	
Mazamet d.	0526	0546	0626	0726	0826	1026	1226	1426	...	1726	1819	1926
Castres d.	0551	0612	0654	0754	0854	1054	1254	1454	...	1754	1854	1954
Toulouse ◇ d.	0702	0726	0802	0902	1002	1202	1402	1602	...	1903	2002	2102

n – Also Nov. 1.
p – Not Nov. 1.
◇ – Toulouse Matabiau.

315 PARIS - VIERZON - BOURGES - MONTLUÇON

There are currently no trains Bourges / Vierzon - Montluçon and v.v. 1200 ① - 1200 ⑤ until July 4. Most services operate at weekends except on special holiday dates.
Times should be confirmed locally no longer than a few days before travelling.

km				3903				3909						3913	3915							3917	3921	
		Ⓐ ⊖	⚒ t	⚒	⚒				Ⓐ	Ⓐ ⊖	Ⓐ	Ⓐ ⊖	⚒	G	⑤ k			①–④ r	†	Ⓐ	Ⓑ		⑤† q	⑤† p
0	**Paris** Austerlitz ... 310 d.	...	...	0705	...	...	...	1229	...	...	...	...	...	1708	1708	...	...	...	...	...	...	1908	2108	...
	Orléans ... 310 d.	0608	0715	|	...	0913	...	|	1451	1615	...	1715	1750	|	|	...	1815	...	...	1915	1950	|	|	...
119	Les Aubrais-Orléans ... 310 d.	|	|	0808	...	|	...	1325	|	|	...	|	|	1808	1808	...	|	...	...	|	|	2008	2208	...
178	Salbris ... d.	0645	0750	0835	...	0950	...	|	1530	1654	...	1753	1829	1835	1835	...	1853	...	...	1952	2029	2035	2235	...
200	Vierzon ... 310 ▷ d.	0658	0804	0852	0902	1004	1017	1403	1545	1707	...	1805	1844	1852	1852	...	1907	1924	...	2006	2044	2052	2252	2300
232	**Bourges** ... ▷ a.	0726	0825	0911	|	1025	|	1421	...	1726	...	1826	...	1911	1911	...	1927	|	...	2026	...	2111	2311	|
	Bourges ... d.	...	...	...	|	...	|	1438	...	...	1729	...	...	...	1928	...	...	|	1929	...	...	2131	...	|
•291	St Amand-Montrond-Orval ... d.	...	...	...	0956	...	1109	1525	...	...	1822	...	...	...	2020	...	...	2020	2020	...	...	2218	...	2353
•341	**Montluçon** ... a.	...	...	...	1031	...	1143	1600	...	...	1904	...	...	...	2056	...	...	2054	2103	...	...	2254	...	0026

					3904						3908			3916	3914			3920		3918				3924
	Ⓐ	Ⓐ	Ⓐ	⚒	⚒ §	Ⓐ	⑥	⚒t ⊖	Ⓐ	Ⓐ ⊖			⚒	⑦	⚒	Ⓐ	Ⓐ ⊖	†	⊖	⚒	Ⓐ	Ⓐ ⊖	Ⓐ r	⑦
Montluçon ... d.	...	...	...	0535	...	...	0613	...	0653	...	0844	...	1035	...	...	...	...	1651	...	1706	1735	...	1911	1906
St Amand-Montrond-Orval ... d.	...	...	...	0609	...	0627	0650	...	0735	...	0920	...	1108	...	...	...	...	1727	...	1742	1835	...	1945	1942
Bourges ... a.	...	...	...	|	...	0713	|	...	|	...	1011	...	|	...	...	...	...	1811	...	1828	1921	...	|	2030
Bourges ... ▷ d.	...	...	0633	|	0649	...	|	0733	|	0833	1029	...	|	1349	1547	1633	1733	1828	1833	1845	...	1933	|	2049
Vierzon ... 310 ▷ d.	0555	0613	0655	0702	0709	...	0742	0755	0837	0854	1049	...	1159	1409	1607	1656	1755	1848	1857	1909	...	1955	2038	2108
Salbris ... d.	0609	0629	0709	...	0725	...	...	0809	...	0909	|	...	...	1425	1623	1708	1809	|	1910	1925	...	2007	...	2122
Les Aubrais-Orléans ... 310 a.	|	|	|	...	0752	...	...	|	...	|	1121	...	...	1452	1650	|	|	1921	|	1952	...	|	...	2147
Orléans ... 310 a.	0645	0710	0745	...	|	...	...	0845	...	0945	|	...	...	|	|	1745	1845	|	1945	|	...	2045	...	|
Paris Austerlitz ... 310 a.	...	...	...	...	0853	...	...	...	...	...	1218	...	...	1552	1752	...	...	2018	...	2052	...	...	...	2245

LOCAL TRAINS VIERZON - BOURGES (see also Table **290**) *Subject to alteration 0900 - 1600.*

	Ⓐ	⑥h	Ⓐ	⚒t		Ⓐ		Ⓐ		
Vierzon ... d.	0618	0657	0740	0840	1440	1540	1640	1744	1840	1940
Bourges ... a.	0646	0726	0808	0907	1508	1608	1708	1810	1907	2008

	Ⓐ		Ⓐ		⚒			Ⓐ		
Bourges ... d.	0653	0752	0852	...	1252	...	1652	1750	1853	...
Vierzon ... a.	0720	0820	0920	...	1321	...	1720	1818	1920	...

G – ①②③④⑦ (not Aug. 14).
h – Also Aug. 15.
k – Also Aug. 14; not Aug. 15.
p – Not Nov. 1.
q – Also Aug. 14; not July 13, Aug. 15.
r – Not July 14, Nov. 11.
t – Also Aug. 15, Nov. 1.
§ – Runs 20 minutes earlier Bourges - Les Aubrais-Orléans until June 23.
⊖ – To / from Nevers (Table **290**).
▷ – For additional trains see below main table.
• – Via Bourges (Montluçon is *327* km direct).

316 BRIVE - FIGEAC - RODEZ

km		3751								
		A ◇🅁	⚒ n		Ⓐ		Ⓐ		R	⑦ T
	Paris Austerlitz **310** ... d.	2239	...	...	...	...	...	...	...	...
0	**Brive la Gaillarde** ... 311 d.	0342	0607	0735	1123	1328	1615	1822	2211	2211
27	St Denis-près-Martel ... 311 d.	0406	0633	0758	1149	1353	1649	1900	2234	2234
45	Rocamadour-Padirac ... d.	0423	0648	0815	1208	1409	1704	1917	2250	2250
53	Gramat ... d.	0431	0655	0823	1215	1417	1711	1927	2259	2259
88	Figeac ... 317 d.	0505	0723	0853	1242	1445	1740	1959	2329	2329
94	Capdenac ... 317 d.	0514	0733	0900	1251	1453	1748	2007	2341	2351
109	Viviez-Decazeville ... d.	0530	0748	0915	1306	1507	1802	2022	2355	0005
161	**Rodez** ... 323 a.	0622	0836	1000	1353	1552	1852	2107	0042	0052
227	Carmaux ... 323 a.	0744j	...	...	...	...	...	...	...	...
244	**Albi** ... 323 a.	0805j	...	...	...	...	...	...	...	...

									3754
	⚒ n	⑦ q	Ⓐ						B ◇🅁
Albi ... 323 d.	...	...	...	...	...	...	...	...	2051k
Carmaux ... 323 d.	...	...	...	...	...	...	...	...	2111k
Rodez ... 323 d.	0630	0828	1022	1219	1420	1630	1800	...	2245
Viviez-Decazeville ... d.	0717	0916	1108	1307	1508	1717	1847	...	2333
Capdenac ... 317 d.	0732	0930	1124	1323	1524	1733	1918	...	2350
Figeac ... 317 d.	0739	0938	1131	1332	1533	1741	1925	...	2359
Gramat ... d.	0807	1007	1159	1400	1604	1811	1955	...	0031
Rocamadour-Padirac ... d.	0814	1014	1209	1410	1611	1818	2002	...	0040
St Denis-près-Martel ... 311 d.	0830	1029	1224	1429	1627	1835	2017	...	0056
Brive la Gaillarde ... 311 a.	0853	1052	1245	1452	1650	1857	2043	...	0119
Paris Austerlitz **310** ... a.	...	...	...	...	...	...	...	...	0655

A – Runs Paris - Rodez daily except Dec. 24, 31; Paris - Albi on ⑤ from Oct. 3. Train **3751/3753/3755/3757**.
B – Runs Rodez - Paris daily except Dec. 24, 31; Albi - Paris on ⑦ from Oct. 5. Train **3756/3754/3750/3752**.
R – Ⓑ until Sept. 28; Ⓐ from Sept. 29 (not Nov. 11).
T – From Oct. 5 (also Nov. 11).
j – From Oct. 4.
k – From Oct. 5.
n – Also Nov. 1.
q – Not Nov. 1.
◇ – 🛏 1, 2 cl. and (2) (reclining).

317 AURILLAC - FIGEAC - TOULOUSE

km		Ⓐ			Ⓐ				⑤ v	
	Clermont Ferrand **331** ... d.	...	...	...	...	1034	...	...	...	...
0	**Aurillac** ... d.	...	0646d	0854d	...	1255	1653	1840	2107	...
65	Figeac ... 316 d.	0606	0806	1006	1206	1405	1806	2000	2223	...
71	Capdenac ... 316 d.	0614	0814	1014	1214	1415	1814	...	...	...
100	Villefranche de Rouergue ... d.	0641	0844	1042	1242	1442	1842	...	...	...
117	Najac ... d.	0656	0859	1056	1256	1457	1857	...	...	...
170	Gaillac ... 323 d.	0744	0948	1142	1341	1543	1943	...	...	...
224	**Toulouse** Matabiau ... 323 a.	0824	1024	1224	1420	1624	2024	...	...	...

	⚒	① q	Ⓐ	W		Y		Ⓐ	
Toulouse Matabiau ... 323 d.	...	0533	...	0653	0859	1303	1704	1809	1900
Gaillac ... 323 d.	...	0611	...	0734	0938	1340	1742	1848	1942
Najac ... d.	...	0657	...	0829	1026	1426	1826	1933	2030
Villefranche de Rouergue ... d.	...	0712	...	0843	1043	1443	1843	1948	2045
Capdenac ... 316 d.	0548	0741	0822	0912	1112	1513	1910	2014	2114
Figeac ... 316 d.	0559	0749	0830	0919	1119	1521	1917	2022	2121
Aurillac ... a.	0729	...	0949	...	1231d	1631	2028f	2133	2231c
Clermont Ferrand **331** ... a.	...	...	...	...	...	1905	...	...	...

W – ②③④⑤ (not July 15).
Y – Not Ⓐ Nov. 3 - 21.
c – Ⓒ only.
d – ⚒ only.
f – ⑤ (also Aug. 14; not Aug. 15).
q – Also July 15, Nov. 12.
v – Also Aug. 14; not Aug. 15.

318 BORDEAUX - LIBOURNE - BERGERAC - SARLAT

km		① y	Ⓐ	⚒			Ⓐ z	Ⓒ		⚒ J	Ⓐ K	R			Ⓐ		Ⓐ P	Ⓐ Q		Ⓐ	H	⑤ k		Ⓑ
0	**Bordeaux** St Jean ... ▷ d.	...	0605	0705	0805	...	...	1005	...	1205	1305	1405	...	1605	1705	...	...	...	1805	1905	2005	2005	...	2205
37	Libourne ... ▷ d.	...	0635	0735	0835	...	1035	1035	...	1236	1335	1435	...	1635	1735	...	1757	1811	1835	1935	2035	2035	...	2235
77	Ste Foy la Grande ... d.	...	0710	0812	0908	...	1109	1109	...	1309	1412	1511	...	1708	1809	...	1835	1851	1909	2009	2109	2109	...	2310
99	**Bergerac** ... a.	...	0729	0832	0929	...	1129	1129	...	1328	1431	1530	...	1729	1828	...	1857	1911	1928	2028	2128	2128	...	2328
99	**Bergerac** ... d.	0548	0733	...	0932	...	1133	1133	...	...	...	1533	...	1731	...	...	...	...	1931	...	...	2131	...	...
135	Le Buisson ... d.	0627	0821	...	1020	...	1219	1219	...	...	...	1619	...	1821	...	...	...	...	2018	...	...	2205	...	...
168	**Sarlat** ... a.	0658	0851	...	1049	...	1248	1248	...	...	...	1648	...	1851	...	...	...	...	2047	...	...	2235	...	...

	Ⓐ y	Ⓐ	⚒	Ⓐ M	Ⓐ L	Ⓐ	†	⚒		z	Ⓐ K		z		Ⓐ z	Ⓒ r			Ⓑ n			Ⓐ	⑤† t	
Sarlat ... d.	...	...	...	...	...	0606	...	0708	...	0908	...	...	1105	...	...	1327	...	1505z	...	...	1705	...	1908	...
Le Buisson ... d.	...	...	...	...	...	0641	...	0738	...	0939	...	...	1137	...	...	1357	...	1535z	...	...	1737	...	1937	...
Bergerac ... a.	...	...	...	...	...	0728	...	0828	...	1029	...	...	1227	...	...	1430	...	1629z	...	...	1829	...	2028	...
Bergerac ... d.	0539	0614	0630	0648	0704	0732	0832	0835	...	1032	1132	...	1230	...	1434	1434	...	1632	1730	...	1832	1932	2032	...
Ste Foy la Grande ... d.	0556	0632	0650	0710	0725	0753	0852	0852	...	1051	1151	...	1250	...	1454	1454	...	1651	1750	...	1851	1951	2051	...
Libourne ... ▷ a.	0627	0710	0727	0749	0805	0827	0927	0927	...	1127	1227	...	1327	...	1526	1527	...	1727	1827	...	1927	2027	2127	...
Bordeaux St Jean ... ▷ a.	0655	0737	0755	...	...	0855	0955	0955	...	1155	1255	...	1355	...	...	1555	...	1755	1855	...	1955	2055	2155	...

H – Daily **except** ⑤ (also Aug. 15; not Aug. 14).
J – Until Aug. 30 and from Sept. 20 (also Sept. 6, 13).
K – Until July 4, Aug. 25 - 29, Sept. 22 - Dec. 12.
L – Until July 4, Aug. 25 - Sept. 11, Sept. 22 - Dec. 12.
M – Sept. 12 - 19.
N – Not Sept. 1 - 19.
P – Not Sept. 11 - 19.
Q – Sept. 11 - 18.
R – Not Sept. 1 - 21.
k – Also Aug. 14; not Aug. 15.
n – Also Nov. 1.
r – Not Nov. 1.
t – Daily July 6 - Aug. 24; also Aug. 14.
y – Not July 6 - Aug. 24.
z – Not Sept. 1 - 19.
▷ – See also Tables **300** and **302**.

Valid until October 28 — BORDEAUX - TOULOUSE — 320

km		4655 4654 ★ q	⑥	Ⓐ	*TGV* 6859 e	4657 4656 ★	*TGV* 8501 ①–⑥ j		4659 4658 ★ z	*TGV* 8503 k	4663 4662 ★ y		4665 4664 ★ w	*TGV* 8505		4667 4666 ★ F	Ⓐ	4669 4668 ★ x		*TGV* 8511		3837 v	*TGV* 8513		*TGV* 8515 ⑤ a
	Paris M'parnasse **300** d.	...	...	...	...	...	0628	...	...	0928	...	...	...	1225	...	...	...	...	...	1525	...	...	1825	...	1926
	Nantes **292** d.	...	...	...	...	...	|	...	...	|	...	...	...	|	...	...	...	...	...	|	...	1701	|	...	|
0	**Bordeaux** St Jean d.	0731	...	0636	0838	0935	0947	...	1047	1247	1331	...	1445	1547	...	1644	...	1730	...	1847	...	2131	2147	...	2247
79	Marmande d.	|	...	0740	|	|	|	...	|	|	1410	...	|	|	...	|	...	1809	...	|	...	2211	|	...	|
136	Agen d.	0840	0821	0821	0943	1042	1053	...	|	1353	1440	...	|	1653	1714	|	1822	1840	...	1952	2023	2241	2253	...	2353
206	Montauban d.	0918	0911	0911	1021	1120	1130	...	|	1430h	|	...	|	1729h	1811	|	1911	1918	...	2031	2114	2318	2330s	...	0028
257	**Toulouse** Matabiau a.	0944	0940	0940	1046	1146	1157	...	1249	1458h	1544	...	1646	1757h	1840	1846	1940	1944	...	2057	2143	2344	2358s	...	0053
	Narbonne **321** a.	1101	...	...	1201	1301	...	...	|	...	1701	...	|	...	...	|	...	2101	...	...	...	...	...	...	...
	Montpellier **355** a.	1203	...	...	1259	1403	...	...	1503	...	1803	...	1903	...	...	2049	...	2203	...	...	...	...	...	...	...
	Marseille **355** a.	1343	...	...	...	1542	...	...	1642	...	1943	...	2042	...	...	2224	...	2342	...	...	...	...	...	...	...
	Nice **360** a.	...	...	...	...	...	...	...	1937	...	...	...	2341	...	...	...	...	...	...	...	...	...	...	...	...

	Ⓐ	*TGV* 8500 ①–⑥ j	3842 u	*TGV* 8510			*TGV* 8512 ⑦ m	4754 4755 ★	*TGV* 8514		4756 4757 ★ t		*TGV* 8516	4760 4761 ★ d	Ⓑ	⑥ h		*TGV* 8518	4762 4763 ★ x	Ⓐ	4764 4765 ★ z		*TGV* 6811 r	4768 4769 ★ x	
Nice **360** d.	...	...	...	...	...	...	...	...	...	...	...	...	...	1023	...	...	...	...	...	...	1221	...	...	...	...
Marseille **355** d.	...	...	...	...	...	...	...	0818	...	...	1013	...	...	1322	...	...	...	...	1417	...	1522	...	...	1718	...
Montpellier **355** d.	...	...	...	...	...	...	...	0957	...	...	1148	...	...	1457	...	...	...	...	1557	...	1657	...	1757	1857	...
Narbonne **321** d.	...	...	...	...	...	...	...	1058	...	...	1251	...	...	|	...	...	...	...	1658	...	|	...	1858	|	...
Toulouse Matabiau d.	...	0605	0813	0904g	...	...	1104	1218	1304g	...	1416	...	1604h	1711	1717	1717	...	1804h	1817	1821	1913	1921	2016	2112	...
Montauban d.	...	0633	0841	0932g	...	...	1132	|	1332g	...	1443	...	1632h	|	1748	1748	...	1832h	1844	1852	|	1952	2046	|	...
Agen d.	0632	0711	0917	1010	...	1045	1210	1319	1410	1441	1520	...	1710	|	1841	1836	...	1910	1921	1940	|	2040	2123	|	...
Marmande d.	0709	|	0947	|	...	1119	|	1350	|	1518	1550	...	|	|	1918	...	...	|	1952	...	|	...	|	|	...
Bordeaux St Jean a.	0758	0813	1025	1113	...	1208	1313	1429	1513	1609	1629	...	1813	1913	2008	...	...	2013	2030	...	2114	...	2226	2313	...
Nantes **292** a.	...	|	1457	|	...	...	...	...	...	...	...	...	|	...	...	...	...	...	...	...	...	...	...	...	...
Paris M'parnasse **300** a.	...	1152	...	1445	...	...	...	...	...	...	...	...	2136	...	...	...	...	...	...	...	...	...	...	...	...

FOR NOTES SEE TABLE 321 BELOW

Local trains Bordeaux - Agen (journey approx 90 mins):
From Bordeaux 0552①**o**, 0631⑥, 0710Ⓐ, 1052, 1252Ⓐ, 1253⑥, 1452, 1652Ⓑ, 1754**l**, 1852Ⓐ, 1855Ⓒ, 2052Ⓑ.
From Agen 0447⚒, 0533Ⓐ, 0610⑥, 0745Ⓐ, 0845†, 1241⑥, 1245Ⓐ, 1640Ⓑ, 1735Ⓑ, 1841⑥, 1945†.

Valid until October 28 — TOULOUSE - CARCASSONNE - NARBONNE — 321

Other night trains: Hendaye / Bordeaux - Marseille - Nice see Table **355**; Hendaye - Genève see Table **305**

km		3731 Ⓡ ♦Q	Ⓐ	*TGV* 6863 ♦f	Ⓐ	⚒		4655 4654 ★ q	Ⓐ	*TGV* 6859 e		4657 4656 ★	4659 4658 ★ z	Ⓒ	*TGV* 6861 ①–⑥ r	4663 4662 ★ y	Ⓐ	3631 ★ S	4665 4664 ★ w		*TGV* 6857 r	Ⓐ	4667 4666 ★ F	Ⓐ	4669 4668 ★ x
	Paris Austerlitz **310** d.	2152	...	...	...	...	...	...	...	...	...	...	...	...	...	...	...	0942b	...	...	...	...	...	...	...
	Bordeaux **320** d.	|	...	...	...	...	...	0731	...	0838	...	0935	1047	...	...	1331	...	|	1445	...	...	...	1644	...	1730
0	**Toulouse** Matabiau d.	|	...	0550	0605	0713	0811	0949	1012	1050	...	1151	1254	1315	1450	1549	1555	1626	1651	1655	1750	1755	1851	1855	1949
55	Castelnaudary d.	0512	...	|	0656	0750	0907	|	1102	|	...	|	|	1406	|	|	1637	1655	|	1734	|	1836	|	1938	|
91	**Carcassonne** d.	0533	0647	|	0719	0814	0929	1033	1124	1134	...	1234	|	1428	1534	1633	1700	1715	|	1757	1834	1858	|	2000	2033
128	Lézignan d.	0554	0707	|	0738	0833	0948	|	1143	|	...	|	|	1445	|	|	1719	|	|	1816	|	1916	|	2019	|
150	**Narbonne** a.	0609	0718	0658	0751	0847	1001	1101	1157	1201	...	1301	|	1457	1601	1701	1732	1747	|	1828	1901	1929	|	2032	2101
	Montpellier **355** a.	|	...	0758	...	...	...	1203	...	1259	...	1403	1503	...	1658	1803	...	|	1903	...	1958	...	2049	...	2203
	Marseille **355** a.	|	...	|	...	...	...	1343	...	|	...	1542	1642	...	|	1943	...	|	2042	...	|	...	2224	...	2342
	Nice **360** a.	|	...	|	...	...	...	...	...	|	...	...	1937	...	|	...	...	|	2341	...	|	...	...	...	...
	Lyon Part Dieu **350** a.	|	...	0955	...	...	...	...	...	1452	...	...	...	...	1850	...	...	|	...	...	2157	...	...	...	...
	Perpignan **355** a.	0722	...	...	...	...	...	...	...	...	...	...	...	...	...	...	...	1849	...	...	...	...	...	...	...
	Cerbère **355** a.	0812	...	...	...	...	...	...	...	...	...	...	...	...	...	...	...	1937	...	...	...	...	...	...	...
	Portbou **355** a.	0822	...	...	...	...	...	...	...	...	...	...	...	...	...	...	...	...	...	...	...	...	...	...	...

	Ⓐ	Ⓐ	⚒	3630 ★ S	*TGV* 6809 ⚒	4754 4755 ★			4756 4757 ★ t	*TGV* 6813 p	4760 4761 ★ d		Ⓐ	4762 4763 ★ x	Ⓐ	4764 4765 ★ z			*TGV* 6811 r	4768 4769 ★ x	*TGV* 6817 n	4766 4767 ★ E	3730 Ⓡ ♦C	3732 Ⓡ ♦R	3730 Ⓡ ♦P
Cerbère **355** d.	...	...	...	0725	...	...	...	...	...	...	...	...	...	...	...	...	...	...	...	...	...	...	1919	1940	2016
Perpignan **355** d.	...	...	...	0816	...	...	...	...	...	...	...	...	...	...	...	...	...	...	...	...	...	...	2009	2053	2107
Lyon Part Dieu **350** d.	...	...	...	|	0705	...	...	...	...	1110	...	...	...	...	...	...	...	...	1609	...	1808	...	|	|	|
Nice **360** d.	...	...	...	|	|	...	...	...	...	|	1023	...	...	...	...	1221	...	...	|	...	|	...	|	|	|
Marseille **355** d.	...	...	...	|	|	0818	...	...	1013	|	1322	...	...	1417	...	1522	...	...	|	1718	|	1918	|	|	|
Montpellier **355** d.	...	...	...	|	0858	0957	...	...	1148	1257	1457	...	...	1557	...	1657	...	...	1757	1857	2001	2057	|	|	|
Narbonne d.	0632	0657	0732	0920	0958	1058	...	1232	1251	1358	|	1558	1632	1658	1732	|	...	1805	1858	|	2059	2158	2127	2207	2207
Lézignan d.	0645	0710	0745	|	|	|	...	1245	|	|	|	1611	1645	|	1745	|	...	1818	|	|	|	|	2143	2222	2222
Carcassonne d.	0704	0729	0804	0951	1029	1129	...	1304	1323	1429	|	1629	1709	1729	1804	|	...	1839	1928	|	2130	2230	2204	2243	2243
Castelnaudary d.	0725	0751	0825	1011	|	|	...	1325	|	|	|	1650	1729	|	1825	|	...	1900	|	|	|	|	2242	2304	2304
Toulouse Matabiau a.	0804	0840	0904	1042	1111	1213	...	1404	1412	1512	1706	1738	1808	1812	1904	1908	...	1949	2012	2107	2220	2318	2323	2332	2332
Bordeaux **320** a.	...	...	...	|	...	1429	...	...	1629	...	1913	...	...	2030	...	2114	...	...	2226	2313	...	...	|	|	|
Paris Austerlitz **310** a.	...	...	...	1721c	...	...	...	...	...	...	...	...	...	...	...	...	...	...	...	...	...	...	0722	0722	0726

ADDITIONAL LOCAL TRAINS

	Ⓐ		Ⓐ	Ⓒ	Ⓐ	Ⓐ	Ⓐ	Ⓐ	Ⓒ	Ⓐ	
Toulouse Mat. d.	...	0655	...	...	1214	...	1715	...	1811	1815	1953
Castelnaudary d.	0555	0739	...	...	1304	...	1805	...	1903	1905	2051
Carcassonne d.	0617	0805	1013	1113	1327	1723	1828	1832	1925	1928	2115
Lézignan d.	0635	...	1034	1132	1347	1742	...	1845	1943	...	...
Narbonne a.	0647	...	1047	1145	1400	1755	...	1904	1955	...	...

	Ⓐ		Ⓐ	Ⓐ	Ⓒ				Ⓐ			
Narbonne d.	...	...	0805	0905	1002	...	...	...	1457	...	1705	...
Lézignan d.	...	...	0818	0919	1016	...	...	...	1510	...	1719	...
Carcassonne d.	0600	0627	0838	0940	1035	...	1204	...	1529	...	1740	...
Castelnaudary d.	0623	0650	...	...	...	...	1227	...	1550	...	...	...
Toulouse Mat. a.	0704	0740	...	...	...	...	1308	...	1640	...	...	...

♦ – **NOTES FOR TABLES 320/1** (LISTED BY TRAIN NUMBER):

730 – 🛏 1,2 cl. and (2) (reclining) Cerbère - Paris. Train number is **3732** July 4 - Aug. 31.
731 – 🛏 1,2 cl. and (2) (reclining) Paris - Portbou. Train number is **3733** July 4 - Aug. 31.
863 – (12) 🍸 Toulouse - Montpellier - Lyon - Dijon.

– ①–④ June 24 - July 1, July 7 - 10, 17.
– ⑤† (not July 13, Aug. 15, Sept. 19, 21, Nov. 1).
– ⑤⑦ (also July 14, Aug. 14; not July 13, Aug. 15, Sept. 19, 21).
– ①②③④⑦ until June 22; ①–⑤ June 24 - July 3; daily Sept. 1 - Oct. 28 (also June 29; not July 13, 14, Aug. 14, Sept. 6, 20, 27).
– Not June 21. 28, Sept. 6, 19, 20, 26, 27, Oct. 10, 17, 24.
– ⑤–⑦ July 4 - 13; daily July 25 - Aug. 31.
– Daily until Aug. 24; ①–⑤ Aug. 25 - Sept. 4; daily from Sept. 5 (also Aug. 30, 31; not Sept. 6, 7, 20, 21, 27, 28).
– Also Aug. 14; not Aug. 15.
– Depart 0925 until June 30.
– Arrive 1737 on ①–⑤ Aug. 25 - Sept. 4 (1806 on Aug. 29).
– Not Sept. 6, 7, 19, 20, 21. Starts at Nice on ⑥⑦ (also ① June 30 - Aug. 31, Sept. 22).
– Not Sept. 20, 27, 28, Oct. 4. Runs only Narbonne - Lyon Sept. 15 - 26.
– Not Sept. 13, 20, 27, Oct. 4. Runs only Toulouse - Montpellier on ⑦ Sept. 14 - 28.
– Not Sept. 7, 21, 28.
– Not Sept. 6, 20, 27.

j – Not July 14.
k – Not July 20.
l – Not July 13.
m – Also July 14.
n – Not Sept. 27.
o – Also July 15; not July 14.
p – Also Sept. 20; not Sept. 14 - 28, Oct. 5.
q – Not Sept. 15 - 26.
r – Not Sept. 13, 20, 27, Oct. 4.
s – Not June 28, 29.
t – Not Sept. 15 - 26.
u – Not June 22, 23, 29, 30.
v – Not June 21, 22, 28, 29.
w – Not Sept. 6, 20.
x – Not Sept. 19 - 21.
y – Not Sept. 19 - 21, Oct. 27, 28.
z – Not Sept. 6, 19 - 21.

TGV – Ⓡ, supplement payable, 🍸.
★ – *Intercités* service, Ⓡ.

323 TOULOUSE - ALBI - RODEZ - MILLAU — Valid until October 26

km		Ⓐ			y		Ⓐ					Ⓐ	Ⓐ		Ⓐ		Ⓐ		Ⓐ	†		P🅁	⚒	
0	**Toulouse** Matabiau 317 d.	0604	0729	0911	1012	1118	1216	...	1306	1410	...	1635	1712	1737	1750	...	1812	1836	1913	1912	...	...	1930	2115
54	Gaillac 317 d.	0646	0811	1002	1052	1159	1302	...	1359	1454	...	1728	1758	1820	1839	...	1904	1921	2001	2001	...	...	2015	2200
75	**Albi Ville** d.	0702	0824	1023	1108	1218	1325	...	1421	1510	...	1748	1817	1837	1904	...	1923	1935	2024	2025	...	2051	2034	2222
92	Carmaux d.	0720	0840	1038	1124	1234	1350	...	1436	1531	...	1806	...	1854	1920	...	...	1953	...	2042	...	2111	2050	2239
158	**Rodez** a.	0823s	0943s	...	1217s	1338s	...	...	...	1634s	...	...	...	1957s	...	...	...	2052s	...	2147s	...	2217	2149s	...

	Ⓐ	⚒	Ⓐ		Ⓐ		P🅁	⚒	†				Ⓐ		Ⓐ			Ⓐ	Ⓒ	Ⓐ	Ⓑ	⑥		
Rodez d.	...	...	...	...	0618s	...	0648	0738s	...	0831s	1026s	...	1225s	...	...	1429s	...	1636s	1636s	1725s	1847s	1847s	2102s	...
Carmaux d.	0521	0553	0619	0645	0721	...	0746	0841	0841	0928	1125	1144	1324	...	1453	1530	1646	1738	1738	1827	1952	1952	2204	...
Albi Ville d.	0538	0610	0636	0703	0740	...	0805	0858	0858	0946	1143	1200	1341	...	1511	1547	1704	1759	1801	1846	2009	2009	2221	...
Gaillac 317 d.	0557	0631	0657	0721	0755	...	...	0911	0911	1001	1200	1221	1358	...	1533	1600	1727	1821	1821	1904	2027	2027	2235	...
Toulouse Matabiau 317 a.	0648	0717	0746	0812	0835	...	...	0953	0953	1042	1239	1309	1440	...	1617	1640	1818	1910	1910	1945	2107	2110	2315	...

km		Ⓐk	⑥		Ⓑ		⑤	X	†m	
0	**Rodez** d.	0619	0635	...	1356	...	1905	1916	2043	...
44	Sévérac-le-Château 332 d.	0702	0718	...	1440	...	1948	1959	2128	...
74	**Millau 332** a.	0734	0750	...	1513	...	2020	2031	2202	...

	①n	Ⓑj		Ⓒ	⑤q	⑥	W		Z	⑤q
Millau 332 d.	0455	0910	...	1528	1625	1715	1753	...	2046	2107
Sévérac-le-Château 332 d.	0525	0940	...	1558	1655	1758	1823	...	2116	2137
Rodez d.	0608	1023	...	1641	1738	1830	1906	...	2159	2220

P – 🛏 1, 2 cl. and 💺 (reclining) Paris - Rodez - Albi and v.v. For days of running see Table **316**.
W – ①-④ (also July 13; not July 14, Aug. 14).
X – ①-④ (not July 14).
Z – ①-④ (not July 14, Aug. 14).
j – Not July 14, Aug. 15, Oct. 6-16.
k – Not Oct. 6-9, 13-16.
m – Not Aug. 15.
n – Not July 14.
q – Also July 13, Aug. 14; not Aug. 15.
s – From Sept. 29.
y – ①⑤ (not July 14, Aug. 15).

324 PAU - OLORON - CANFRANC — Valid until October 26

36 km	Ⓐ			Ⓐ	Ⓒ	Ⓐ			G	H	⑤y
Pau d.	0730	0910	1225	1402	1407	1531	...	1710	1838	1855	2025	2146
Oloron-Ste-Marie a.	0808	0948	1303	1440	1445	1609	...	1748	1916	1933	2103	2224

	⑥	†	Ⓐ			Ⓐ	Ⓒ	Ⓐ			G	H
Oloron-Ste-Marie d.	0722	0800	0816	1003	...	1308	1319	1447	1614	1753	1933	1938
Pau a.	0800	0838	0854	1041	...	1346	1357	1525	1652	1831	2011	2016

🚌 OLORON - CANFRANC (rail tickets valid). Canfranc buses continue to/from Somport, 11 mins beyond Canfranc. *Subject to alteration.*

54 km	Ⓐ					Ⓑ	G	H	
Oloron-Ste-Marie d.	0820	0955	...	1450	...	1810	1925	1940	...
Bedous (Gare) d.	0853	1028	...	1523	...	1843	1958	2013	...
Urdos (Douane) 🛃 d.	0915	1050	...	1545	...	1905	2020	2035	...
Canfranc (Gare) 670 a.	0933	1108	...	1603	...	...	...	...	...

	Ⓐ	Ⓐ	Ⓒ	Ⓐ		†	G	H	
Canfranc (Gare) 670 d.	...	1141	1151	1316	...	1626	1806	1811	...
Urdos (Douane) 🛃 d.	0650	1158	1208	1333	...	1643	1823	1828	...
Bedous (Gare) d.	0713	1221	1231	1356	...	1706	1846	1851	...
Oloron-Ste-Marie a.	0749	1257	1307	1432	...	1742	1922	1927	...

G – ①②③④⑥ (not July 14, Aug. 14).
H – ⑤† (also Aug. 14).
y – Also Aug. 14; not Aug. 15.

325 TOULOUSE - TARBES - PAU - BAYONNE - HENDAYE — Valid until October 26

km									14141	14143	14145								14151				14155			
		Ⓐ	Ⓐ	⑥	Ⓐ	Ⓐ	Ⓐ		⚒	▽	▽	⑥	Ⓐ	†	⑤	①-④	Ⓐ	⑤		⑤†	Ⓐ	Ⓒ		⑤†		
				r		N	X		r	r	r				k	t		X	v	p	j	n	w	Q		
0	**Toulouse** Matabiau d.	...	...	...	0559	...	...	0731	0832	1009	1222	1238	1241	1241	1440	1440	...	1555	1620	...	1731	1731	1838	...	1939	2041
91	St Gaudens d.	...	...	...	0731	...	...	0838	|	1109	|	1359	1407	1415	1600	1601	...	1701	1724	...	1841	1851	|	...	2102	2201
104	Montréjeau d.	...	...	...	0740	...	...	0847	0941	|	1329	1411	1417	1426	1611	1612	...	1710	|	...	1850	1901	|	...	2113	2210
121	Lannemezan d.	...	...	...	0753	...	...	0900	|	|	|	1422	1429	1437	1623	1623	...	1723	|	...	1904	1915	1954	...	2127	2224
158	**Tarbes** 305 d.	...	0629	0651	0822	...	...	0933	1024	1155	1403	1449	1456	1505	1647	1648	...	1753	1806	...	1933	1944	2020	...	2156	2253
179	Lourdes 305 d.	...	0646	0707	0838	...	...	...	1056	1214	1418	...	...	...	1704	1706	...	...	1821	...	1950	2003	2038	...	2214z	2309
218	**Pau** 305 d.	0614	0720	0741	0907	0937	0955	...	1128	1242	1449	...	...	...	...	1735	1737	...	1847	1937	...	2031	2106	2237	2242z	...
258	Orthez 305 d.	0638	0745	0805	...	1002	1020	...	|	1307	1513	...	...	...	...	...	1802	...	1912	2002	...	...	2130	2302	...	...
272	Puyoô 305 d.	0649	0756	0816	...	1013	1031	...	|	|	|	...	...	...	...	...	1813	...	|	2013	...	...	|	2313	...	...
	Dax 305 d.	|	|	|	...	|	1048	...	|	|	|	...	...	...	...	...	|	...	|	|	...	...	|	|	...	...
323	**Bayonne** § 305 a.	0738	0837	0858	...	1058	...	...	1236	1350	1556	...	...	...	...	...	1855	...	1956	2058	...	...	2213	2355	...	...
323	**Bayonne** § 305 d.	...	...	...	...	...	...	...	...	1428	...	...	...	...	...	...	...	...	2028	...	...	...	...	...	...	...
333	Biarritz § 305 d.	...	...	...	...	...	...	...	...	1439	...	...	...	...	...	...	...	...	2039	...	...	...	...	...	...	...
346	St Jean de Luz 305 d.	...	...	...	...	...	...	...	...	1452	...	...	...	...	...	...	...	...	2052	...	...	...	...	...	...	...
359	Hendaye 305 a.	...	...	...	...	...	...	...	...	1501	...	...	...	...	...	...	...	...	2102	...	...	...	...	...	...	...
361	**Irún** 305 a.	...	...	...	...	...	...	...	...	...	...	...	...	...	...	...	...	...	...	...	...	...	...	...	...	...

										14140			14142			14144				14148				14150	
	Ⓒ	Ⓐ	⑥	Ⓑ	⚒	Ⓐ	Ⓐ	⚒	Ⓐ	Ⓐ			▽	⑦	Ⓐ	▽			Ⓐ	†	⑤	Ⓑ			†
							X	R					q		▽	r			▽	r	k			r	
Hendaye 305 d.	...	...	...	...	...	...	...	...	...	0656	...	...	...	...	...	...	...	...	...	1400	...	...	...	1656	...
St Jean de Luz 305 d.	...	...	...	...	...	...	...	...	...	0711	...	...	...	...	...	...	...	...	...	1412	...	...	...	1708	...
Biarritz § 305 d.	...	...	...	...	...	...	...	...	...	0724	...	...	...	...	...	...	...	...	...	1425	...	...	...	1721	...
Bayonne § 305 a.	...	...	...	...	...	...	...	...	...	0733	...	...	...	...	...	...	...	...	...	1434	...	...	...	1731	...
Bayonne § 305 d.	...	...	...	...	...	0609	...	0705	...	0805	...	...	1003	...	...	1146	...	...	1410	1504	...	1723	...	1803	2003
Dax 305 d.	...	...	...	...	...	|	0650	|	0811	|	...	...	|	1111	1210	|	...	...	|	|	...	|	1811	|	|
Puyoô 305 d.	...	...	...	...	...	0646	0708	0746	0829	|	...	...	|	1129	1228	|	...	...	1448	|	...	1806	1829	|	2046
Orthez 305 d.	...	...	...	...	...	0657	0719	0756	0840	|	...	...	1053	1140	1238	|	...	...	1459	1607	...	1816	1839	1852	2057
Pau 305 d.	...	...	...	...	0703h	0727	0745	0823	0904	0913	0936	...	1117	1208	1303	1312	...	1533f	1525	1632	1736	1847	1904	1916	2130
Lourdes 305 d.	0500	0512	0600	0611	0732	0802	...	...	...	0942	1005	...	1144	1236	...	1342	...	1601f	...	1659	1805	1922	...	1944	2205
Tarbes 305 d.	0518	0528	0618	0629	0808	0819	...	...	...	0958	1022	...	1204	1251	...	1359	1507	1623	...	1733	1824	1938	...	2003	2221
Lannemezan d.	0549	0600	0650	0700	0839	...	...	...	...	|	1052	...	|	...	...	1427	1539	1653	...	|	1855	...	...	2031	...
Montréjeau d.	0600	0611	0701	0711	0851	...	...	...	...	|	1105	...	1242	...	...	|	1550	1705	...	|	1907	...	...	|	...
St Gaudens d.	0610	0620	0711	0722	0900	...	...	...	...	1042	1115	...	|	...	...	|	1600	1715	...	1824	1916	...	...	|	...
Toulouse Matabiau a.	0729	0732	0829	0832	1024	...	...	...	...	1138	1229	...	1342	...	...	1539	1721	1829	...	1927	2025	...	...	2144	...

TOULOUSE - LUCHON *For connections Toulouse - Montréjeau see also main table.* 🚌 service is subject to alteration.

	3991	🚌	🚌		🚌		🚌	🚌			🚌	🚌
	🅁H	⚒	⚒				†	⚒	Ⓐ		Ⓒ	
Paris Aust. **310** d.	2152	...	...	...	...	...	...	...	...	...	...	...
Toulouse Mat. d.	0532	...	...	0739	...	...	...	...	1640	1700	...	...
St Gaudens d.	0641	...	...	0904	...	...	...	...	1756	1828	...	...
Montréjeau d.	0710	0718	0805	0932	1100	...	1345	1625	1805	1836	1848	2106
Luchon ◐ a.	0807	0813	0853	1026	1150	...	1433	1713	...	...	1936	2151

	🚌	🚌	🚌		🚌		🚌	🚌		🚌	🚌	3990
	⚒	⚒			†		⚒	⚒		Ⓐ	⑥	🅁Y
Luchon d.	0620	0823	0936	1037a	1227	...	1450	1606	1732c	1755	1815	2121
Montréjeau d.	0711	0915	1024	1143	1315	...	1535	1656	1839	1850	1900	2237
St Gaudens d.	...	...	...	1154	...	...	...	...	1849	...	...	2248
Toulouse Mat. a.	...	...	...	1325	...	...	...	...	2000	...	...	2357
Paris Aust. **310** a.	...	...	...	...	...	...	...	...	...	...	...	0726

H – From Paris on ⑤ (daily July 4 - Aug. 30): 🛏 1, 2 cl. Paris - Luchon.
N – Daily July 6 - Aug. 24.
Q – Daily July 6 - Aug. 24, also Aug. 14; not July 13, Oct. 19, 26.
S – July 6 - Aug. 24.
X – Not July 6 - Aug. 24.
Y – ⑦ (daily July 5 - Aug. 31), also Nov. 11; not Nov. 9: 🛏 1, 2 cl. Luchon - Paris.

a – Ⓐ only.
c – Ⓒ only.
f – ⑤ only.
h – ① (also July 15; not July 14).
j – Also Aug. 15.
k – Also Aug. 14; not Aug. 15.

n – Not Aug. 15.
p – Also Aug. 14; not Oct. 19, 26.
q – Not Oct. 25, 26.
r – Not Oct. 25.
t – Not July 14, Aug. 14.
v – Not Sept. 28 - Oct. 2, Oct. 5-9, 12-16, 19-23, 25, 26.
w – Not Oct. 19-21, 25, 26.
z – ④⑤⑥⑦ only.

◐ – Luchon - Montréjeau is 35 km.
▽ – Subject to alteration until June 22.
§ – 🚌 services available to/from Biarritz town.

BRIVE - USSEL - CLERMONT FERRAND 326

SERVICE FROM JULY 6

km	km		🚌			🚌	🚌		4490	🚌	4492	🚌	🚌	🚌	🚌			🚌	🚌		🚌	🚌		🚌	🚌	
				⚒	⚒	†				Ⓑ	⑥	⑥	Ⓐ		Ⓒ			⑤⑦		Ⓑ	⑤	⑤		†	Ⓑ	⑦
					q	v		⊕	G	h	k	k		R	v	⊗	◇	b	L		f	f		v	q	w
		Bordeaux **302** d.	...	...	...	...	...	...	0732	...	0833	...	...	...	...	...	...	...	...	...	...	...	...	...	...	...
0		**Brive la Gaillarde** ▷ d.	0619	...	0749	...	...	0905	0953	...	1047	...	1050	...	...	...	1333	...	...	1713	...	...	1830	...	...	1913
26		Tulle ▷ d.	0652	...	0817	...	...	0931	1032	...	1124	...	1130	...	...	...	1406	...	...	1750	...	...	1901	...	...	1945
79		Meymac d.	0756	...	▬	...	...	▬	1135	...	1233	...	1238	...	...	...	1510	...	...	1854	...	...	2007	...	...	2050
92		**Ussel** a.	0808	...		...	...	...	1147	...	1247	...	1302	...	...	...	1522	...	...	1906	...	...	2019	...	...	2102
92		**Ussel** d.	▬	0818	🚌	1008	...	🚌	...	1207	...	1255	...	...	1510	...	...	...	...	...	...	...	1915	...	...	2026	...
110		Eygurande-Merlines d.	⚒	0838	⚒	1028	...	A	...	1227	...	1315	...	...	1530	...	...	...	...	...	...	...	1935	...	...	2046	...
	0	**Le Mont Dore** d.	0559	|	0843	|	1046	1221	...	|	...	|	...	1508	|	1541	...	*1730*	1745	...	1930	|	...	2041	|	...
	5	La Bourboule d.	0606	|	0851	|	1054	1229	...	|	...	|	...	1516	|	1549	...	*1738*	1753	...	1938	|	...	2049	|	...
132	13	Laqueuille d.	0617	0858	0903	1048	1106	1242	...	1247	...	1335	...	1529	1550	1600	...	1755	1805	...	1950	1955	...	2101	2106	...
197		**Clermont Ferrand** a.	0732	...	1003	...	1230	...	...	1347	...	1435	...	...	...	1716	...	1909	1910	...	...	2055	...	...	2206	...

		🚌		🚌	🚌			🚌	🚌		🚌		🚌	🚌		4591	🚌	🚌		🚌	🚌		🚌	🚌	🚌	🚌
	⚒	Ⓐ	Ⓐ			Ⓑ	⑥		Ⓒ		Ⓐ	⑤⑦			①–④		⚒	⚒	Ⓑ	⑥		Ⓑ	Ⓐ	⑤	⑤	†
	q					h▽	p	A	v	⊗		s	N	R	t	E	q			n				f	f	v
Clermont Ferrand d.	...	...	...	1010	...	...	...	...	*1246*	1308	...	...	1434	...	...	...	1605	...	1742	1745	1803	...	1948	...	*2119*	*2145*
Laqueuille d.	...	...	...	1110	1115	...	...	1252	1351	1427	1436	...	1534	1539	...	...	1705	1710	1856	1904	1903	...	2048	2053	2214	2240
La Bourboule a.	...	...	...	|	1127	...	...	1303	|	1437	|	...	|	1552	...	...	|	1724	1907	1916	|	...	2100	|	2226	2252
Le Mont Dore a.	...	...	...	|	1133	...	...	1312	|	1445	|	...	|	1559	...	...	|	1731	1914	1924	|	...	2108	|	2234	2300
Eygurande-Merlines d.	...	...	...	1130	...	...	...	...	1411	...	1456	...	1554	...	...	...	1725	...	...	...	1923	...	...	2111	...	...
Ussel a.	...	...	...	1150	...	...	...	...	1431	...	1516	...	1614	...	...	...	1745	...	...	...	1943	...	...	2131	...	...
Ussel d.	0536	0618	...	...	...	1205	1219	...	...	...	...	1538	...	...	1626	1633	...	...	...	...	...	1953	...	...	...	...
Meymac d.	0549	|	...	...	...	1218	1232	...	...	...	...	1551	...	...	1639	1648	...	...	...	...	...	2006	...	...	...	...
Tulle ▷ d.	0656	0738	0743	...	...	1328	1338	...	...	...	...	1708r	...	...	1745	1804	...	...	...	...	...	2115	...	...	...	...
Brive la Gaillarde ▷ a.	0725	...	0809	...	...	1353	1403	...	...	...	...	1733	...	...	1810	1827	...	...	...	...	...	2140	...	...	...	...
Bordeaux **302** a.	...	...	...	...	...	...	...	...	...	...	...	...	...	...	...	2111	...	...	...	...	...	...	...	...	...	...

LIMOGES - USSEL

km			⑥	Ⓑ	⑥	Ⓑ			①–④		⑤⑦	
		M	p	c	p	h⊖			m		s	
0	**Limoges** d.	0556	1013	1010	1302	1319	...	1802	1936	...	2109	...
98	Meymac d.	0731	1142	1150	1435	1452	...	1937	2108	...	2237	...
111	**Ussel** a.	0743	1154	1202	1447	1505	...	1950	2120	...	2249	...

	⚒			⑥	Ⓑ	⑥	①–④	⑦	⑤	
	q	M		p d	h⊖		m⊠	w	f	d
Ussel d.	0633	0814	...	1200	1220	1336	1354	1553	1604	1755
Meymac d.	0646	0827	...	1213	1233	1349	1407	1606	1617	1808
Limoges a.	0817	0958	...	1347	1402	1520	1536	1735	1748	1947

A – Ⓐ July 7 - Aug. 29; ⑤ from Sept. 5 (also Oct. 20–23, 27–30).
E – Ⓑ July 6 - Aug. 31 (not July 13, Aug. 15); ⑤⑦ from Sept. 5 (also Oct. 27–30).
G – Ⓐ July 7 - Aug. 29; ⑤ from Sept. 5 (also Oct. 27–30).
L – ①②③④⑥ (not July 14, Aug. 14, Nov. 1, 11).
M – Ⓐ July 7 - Aug. 29; ① from Sept. 1 (also Nov. 12).
N – Ⓑ July 6 - Aug. 31; ⑤⑦ from Sept. 5 (also Oct. 20–23, 27–30).
R – Ⓑ July 6 - Aug. 31 (not July 13); ⑤⑦ from Sept. 5 (also Oct. 20–23, 27–30).

b – Also July 14, Aug. 14, Nov. 11; not July 13.
c – Not Aug. 15, Sept. 7, 19, 21, 28.
d – Not Sept. 6, 20, 27.
f – Also Aug. 14; not Aug. 15.
h – Not Aug. 15.
k – Also Aug. 15; not Aug. 16.
m – Not July 14, Aug. 14, Nov. 11.
n – Not Nov. 1.
p – Also Aug. 15.
q – Also Nov. 1.
r – Arrives 1654.
s – Also July 14, Aug. 14, Nov. 11.
t – Not July 7 - Aug. 28, Oct. 20–30, Nov. 11.
v – Not July 13, Nov. 1.
w – Also July 14, Aug. 15, Nov. 11.

◇ – Runs 10 minutes later on ⑥ (also Aug. 15). Subject to alteration on ①–⑤ Sept. 22 - Oct. 3.
▽ – Subject to alteration on ①–⑤ Sept. 15 - Oct. 3.
⊗ – Subject to alteration on ①–④ Sept. 1–18. Subject to alteration Laqueuille - Le Mont Dore and v.v. on ①–⑤ Oct. 6–24.
⊖ – Subject to alteration on ①–⑤ Sept. 8–19.
⊕ – Subject to alteration on ①–④ Sept. 22 - Oct. 2.
⊠ – Subject to alteration Sept. 8–18.
▷ – Additional local trains run Brive - Tulle and v.v.

MONTLUÇON - LYON 327

Certain timings between Vichy and Lyon are subject to alteration on ①–⑤ Sept. 15 - Oct. 3 (see Table **328**). For other rail journeys via Riom - Châtel-Guyon see Tables **328** and **329**.

km		🚌		🚌		🚌		🚌		🚌	
		①g	⚒	⚒		Ⓐm	Ⓐ	⑥		Ⓑ	Ⓑ
0	**Montluçon** 329 d.	0503	...	0721	...	1001	...	1600	...	1615	...
68	Gannat 329 d.	0621	...	0841	...	|	...	|	...	|	...
91	**St Germain des Fossés** d.	|	...	|	...	1125	1141	|	...	|	...
	Vichy **330** d.	0646	0659	0910	0929	...	|	|	...	|	...
158	Roanne 328 d.	...	0749	...	1017	...	1229	1830	1845	1845	1917
255	**Lyon** Part Dieu 328 a.	...	0856	...	1120	...	1340	...	|	...	2020
259	**Lyon** Perrache 328 a.	...	0917	...	1131	...	...	...	2020	...	2031

		🚌		🚌		🚌		🚌		🚌
	⚒	Ⓐ				⑤⑦				⑤⑦
Lyon Perrache 328 d.	...	...	1000	...	1629	v	1729	...	2029	v
Lyon Part Dieu 328 d.	0854	...	1012	...	1640	...	1740	...	2040	...
Roanne 328 d.	1012	...	1130	1230	1745	...	1847	...	2145	...
Vichy **330** d.	|	...	...	|	1832	1845	1932	1955	2232	2245
St Germain des Fossés d.	1055	1136	...	|	...	|	...	|	...	|
Gannat 329 d.	...	|	...	|	...	|	...	2025	...	2315
Montluçon 329 a.	...	1302	...	1500	...	2012	...	2143	...	0034

g – Also July 15, Nov. 12; not July 14.
m – 10–11 minutes earlier until July 4.
v – Also July 14, Aug. 14, Nov. 11; not July 13.

CLERMONT FERRAND - LYON 328

Subject to alteration Nov. 8–11

km		⚒				Ⓑ		Ⓑ	⚒		†
		q	✣			q			A		v
0	**Clermont Ferrand** ▷ d.	0626	0857	1157	1357	1457	1657	1757	1812	...	1957r
14	Riom - Châtel-Guyon ▷ d.	0635	0906	1206	1406	1506	1706	1806	1821	...	2006r
55	Vichy **330** d.	0659	0929	1230‡	1428‡	1530	1729	1830	1844	...	2028
65	St Germain des Fossés d.	|	|	|	|	|	|	|	1852	1908	|
132	Roanne **290** ▶ d.	0749	1017	1317	1516	1617	1817	1917	...	1956	2114
229	**Lyon** Part Dieu **290** ▶ a.	0856	1120	1420	1620	1720	1920	2020	...	2106	2218
233	**Lyon** Perrache **290** a.	0917	1131	1431	1631	1733	1931	2031	...	...	2228

	⚒	⚒	⚒						
	q			⊠					
Lyon Perrache **290** d.	0629	...	...	1129	1429	1629	1729	1829	2029
Lyon Part Dieu **290** ▶ d.	0640	0854	...	1140	1440	1640	1740	1840	2040
Roanne **290** ▶ d.	0748	1012	...	1244	1549	1745	1847	1944	2145
St Germain des Fossés d.	|	1055	1140	|	|	|	|	|	|
Vichy **330** d.	0833	...	1149	1332b	1634	1833	1933	2030	2233
Riom - Châtel-Guyon ▷ d.	0855	...	1211	1353f	1657	1855	1955	2051	2255
Clermont Ferrand ▷ a.	0904	...	1223	1405f	1707	1905	2004	2103	2304

CLERMONT FERRAND - ST ÉTIENNE *Subject to alteration July 22 - Aug. 29*

km		⚒⊖	Ⓐ⊕	⊖⊕	⊖⊕		Ⓐ	†d	⚒m	Ⓐ
0	**Clermont Ferrand** d.	0712	0913	1119	1323	1622	1721	1807	1840	1933
46	Thiers d.	0813	0958	1151	1412	1712	1804	1841	1933	2027
112	Montbrison d.	0921	...	1300	1523	1821	...	1949	2041	...
145	**St Étienne** Châteaucreux a.	0951	...	1330	1556	1859	...	2020	2120	...

	⚒	⚒	⊕	Ⓐ⊕	⊖⊕	†	Ⓐ	⚒	†
St Étienne Châteaucreux d.	...	0630	0848	...	1230	1534	...	1743	1918
Montbrison d.	...	0703	0923	...	1302	1602	...	1823	1951
Thiers d.	0704	0811	1040	1206	1410	1710	1742	1931	2059
Clermont Ferrand a.	0752	0908	1110	1250	1450	1801	1833	2020	2134

A – To July 5 / from Aug. 25.
– Not Oct. 13–17, 27–31.
– Also July 14, Nov. 11.
– Not Oct. 5.
– July 7–11, Oct. 24 Riom d. 1409, Clermont a. 1418.

h – Not Aug. 15.
m – Not Aug. 30, Oct. 4.
p – To Lyon Perrache.
q – Also Nov. 1.
r – 2 minutes earlier on Sept. 21, 28, Oct. 5.
v – Not July 13, Nov. 1.

‡ – Not July 7–11, Oct. 6–10, 20–24.
⊕ – Subject to alteration on Ⓐ Oct. 27 - Nov. 14.
⊖ – Subject to alteration on ①–⑤ Sept. 15 - Oct. 10.
✣ – Subject to alteration on ①–⑤ Sept. 15 - Oct. 3.
⊠ – Subject to alteration June 30 - July 4, Sept. 1–4, 6, 8–11, ①–⑥ Sept. 13 - Oct. 3, Oct. 10.
▷ – See also Tables **329** and **330**.

▶ – Other trains Roanne - Lyon Part Dieu (journey time 77–95 minutes):
From Roanne at 0503 Ⓐ, 0603, 0630 Ⓐ, 0710 ⚒, 0718 ⑦ **c**, 0730 ⚒, 0830 ⚒, 0930, 1130, 1245 **p**, 1445 Ⓐ **p**, 1645 ⚒ **p**, 1745 Ⓑ **h p**, 1845 **p**. **From Lyon Part Dieu** at 0612 ⚒, 0712, 0812 ⚒, 1012, 1212, 1412 Ⓐ, 1512 ⚒, 1612, 1712 ⚒, 1812, 1912 Ⓐ, 2012 Ⓑ, 2112.

MONTLUÇON - CLERMONT FERRAND 329

km		⑥	Ⓐ	Ⓐ		Ⓐ			Ⓑ		⑦
		k				v⊗	z	d	n q		e
0	**Montluçon 327** d.	...	0601	0700	0828	1036	1221	...	1703	1833	1928
14	Commentry d.	...	0613	0711	0840	1047	1235	...	1716	1846	1940
68	Gannat **327** d.	0705	0706	0803	0926	1132	1327	1625	1804	1938	2033
96	Riom - Châtel-Guyon ▷ d.	0729	0729	0825	0942	1152	1346	1651	1829	2002	2050
110	**Clermont Ferrand** ▷ a.	0741	0741	0836	0952	1201	1355	1703	1838	2011	2100

	Ⓐ	Ⓐ		⚒		Ⓑ	Ⓐ	⚒	Ⓐ	Ⓑ
				v	d	q				q
Clermont Ferrand ▷ d.	0605	0636	0748	1218	1401	1648	1715	1745	1816	1901
Riom - Châtel-Guyon ▷ d.	0615	0645	0801	1230	1413	1702	1727	1757	1830	1913
Gannat **327** d.	0631	0707	0821	1249	1437	1727	1750	1823	1853	1940
Commentry d.	0721	0811	0909	1344	...	1818n	...	1915	...	2031
Montluçon 327 a.	0733	0823	0919	1355	...	1828n	...	1925	...	2041

– Not July 7–11, ①–⑤ Sept. 15 - Oct. 10, Oct. 20–24.
– Also July 14, Aug. 15, Nov. 11; not July 13.
– Not Nov. 1.

n – Not Sept. 15 - Oct. 5.
q – Also Nov. 1.
v – Not ①–⑤ Sept. 15 - Oct. 3.
z – Not ①–⑤ Sept. 15 - Nov. 7.

⊗ – Runs 8–10 minutes **earlier** July 7–11, Oct. 6–10, 20–24.
▷ – See also Tables **328** and **330**.

Timings may vary by 1–2 minutes Sept. 15 - Oct. 5

330 PARIS - NEVERS - CLERMONT FERRAND

km																									
							5951		5955				5959	5963			5967		5971	5973		5977	5979	5983	5981
							🅁★		🅁★				🅁★	🅁★			🅁★		🅁★	🅁★		🅁★	🅁★	🅁★	🅁★
		⚒	⚒	Ⓐ	⚒	Ⓑ	①–⑥	⚒		⚒	⚒	Ⓐ				Ⓐ	⑤	Ⓐ		Ⓐ	Ⓑ	Ⓐ			⑤
			J			s	b				⊙	⊙			D		f			J	s	J	L	A	f
0	**Paris** Bercy ⊠	▶ d.	...	...	...	...	...	0700	...	0858	...	...	...	1300	1400	...	...	1500	...	1600	1700	...	1800	1800	1900	1900
254	**Nevers**	▶ d.	...	...	...	0700	...	0859	...	1059	...	...	...	1459	1559	...	...	1659	...	1759	1859	...	|	1959	2059	2059
314	Moulins sur Allier	d.	0612	0642	0711	0742	0812	0928	...	1128	1212	1312p	1412	1528	1626	1642	1713	1728	1740	1828	1928	1937	|	2028	2128	2128
355	St Germain des Fossés	▷ d.	0637	0708	0737	0809	0838	|	1140	|	1238	1339	1438	|	|	1708	1739	|	1807	|	|	2002	|	|	|	2149
365	Vichy	▷ d.	0646	0717	0746	0817	0847	0955	1149	1155	1246x	1347	1447	1555	1655	1717	1748	1755	1815	1858	1955	2011	|	2055	2155	2159
406	Riom - Châtel-Guyon	▷ d.	0708	0738	0809	0839	0910	1019	1211	1219	1308	1409	1510	1624	1726	1740	1811	1819	1837	1926	2019	2033	|	2119	2219	2223
420	**Clermont Ferrand**	▷ a.	0717	0747	0817	0847	0918	1028	1223	1228	1318	1421	1518	1635	1738	1750	1822	1828	1846	1939	2028	2042	2104	2128	2228	2231

		5948	5950	5954		5958			5962		5966			5970	5974		5978			5982			5986		5990	
		🅁★	🅁★	🅁★		🅁★			🅁★		🅁★			🅁★	🅁★		🅁★			🅁★			🅁★		🅁★	
		①	②–⑤	Ⓐ	Ⓐ	⑥	Ⓐ	⚒		⑥	①–⑥	⚒	⚒		⑦	Ⓐ		Ⓐ	Ⓐ	Ⓑ		⚒	⑦			
		g	w	J			J			k	b		⊕	⊗	e					h	z	J	e¶		¶	
Clermont Ferrand	▷ d.	0528	0532	0602r	0612	0632	0710	0743	0832	0842	1032	1042	1242	1332	1432	1542	1624	1642	1710	1727	1742	1812	1832	1842	1929	2029
Riom - Châtel-Guyon	▷ d.	0539	0542	|	0621	0642	0719	0752	0842	0851	1042	1051	1251	1342	1442	1551	1636	1651	1719	1738	1751	1821	1842	1851	1939	2039
Vichy	▷ d.	0601	0605	|	0644	0705	0741	0814	0905	0914	1105	1114	1314	1405	1505	1614	1701	1714	1742	1805	1814	1844	1905	1914	2002	2100
St Germain des Fossés	▷ d.	0611	|	|	0652	|	0750	0822	|	0922	|	1122	1322	|	|	1622	|	1722	1750	|	1822	1853	|	1922	|	2109
Moulins sur Allier	d.	0632	0631	|	0719	0731	0818	0846	0931	0948	1131	1148	1348	1431	1531	1648	1731	1750	1815	1831	1849	1918	1931	1950	2028	2133
Nevers	▶ d.	0701	0701	|	0754	0801	...	0918	1001	...	1201	...	...	1501	1601	...	1801	...	...	1901	...	...	2001	...	2101	...
Paris Bercy ⊠	▶ a.	0857	0857	0901	...	0957	...	...	1157	...	1357	...	...	1657	1757	...	1957	...	...	2057	...	...	2157	...	2257‡	...

STOPPING TRAINS PARIS - NEVERS (SEE NOTE ⊠)

km												
			5901	5905		5909		5911	5915	5917	5919	5921
			Ⓐ			①–⑥		Ⓐ	Ⓐ	Ⓒ	Ⓐ	⑦
				⊕	⊙	b						e
0	**Paris** Bercy d.	...	0715	0915	...	1415	...	1704	1804	1804	1904	2004
119	Montargis d.	...	0814	1014	...	1514	...	1812	1912	1912	2012	2112
155	Gien d.	...	0836	1036	...	1536	...	1835	1935	1934	2034	2135
196	Cosne d.	0732	0859	1059	1236	1600	1745	1859	1959	1958	2058	2159
228	La Charité d.	0757	0920	1119	1301	1620	1810	1916	2016	2017	2118	2216
254	**Nevers** d.	0825	0943	1140	1325	1641	1834	1938	2038	2038	2138	2238

	5900	5904	5906	5908			5910	5912	5914		5916	
	Ⓐ	Ⓐ	⑥	Ⓐ	Ⓐ	⑥		Ⓐ	⑦	⚒		
			t					⊗	e	s		
Nevers d.	0455	0555	0624	0724	0835	0935	1019	1424	1624	1635	1824	2135
La Charité d.	0518	0618	0645	0745	0859	0955	1041	1445	1647	1659	1845	2159
Cosne d.	0534	0634	0705	0805	0923	1017	1102	1505	1703	1723	1905	2223
Gien d.	0558	0658	0728	0828	...	...	1128	1528	1727	...	1928	...
Montargis d.	0622	0722	0751	0851	...	...	1152	1551	1751	...	1951	...
Paris Bercy a.	0732	0832	0849j	0949	...	...	1251	1649	1849	...	2049	...

A – ①②③④⑥⑦ (also Aug. 15; not Aug. 14).
D – ⑥⑦ (daily to July 6 / from Aug. 23).
J – To July 5 and from Aug. 25.
L – ⑦ (Ⓑ July 6 - Aug. 24; not Aug. 15).

b – Not July 14, Nov. 11.
e – Also July 14, Nov. 11.
f – Also Aug. 14; not Aug. 15.
g – Also July 15, Nov. 12; not June 14, Nov. 10.
h – Not Aug. 15.
j – 0913 on Aug. 15, Oct. 11, Nov. 15.
k – Not Nov. 1.
p – 1306 July 7 – 1, Oct. 6 – 10, 20 – 24.

r – 0559 Sept. 15 - Oct. 3.
s – Also Nov. 1.
t – Also Aug. 15.
w – Not July 15, Aug. 15, Nov. 11, 12.
x – Not June 30 - July 4, Oct. 13 – 17, 27 – 31.
y – Not July 28 - Aug. 22.
z – Not July 28 - Aug. 21.

★ – *INTERCITÉS*. 🅁.
▶ – For additional trains see below main table.
▷ – See also Tables **328** and **329**.
⊗ – Subject to alteration July 7 – 11, Oct. 6 – 10, 20 – 24.
¶ – Subject to alteration on Dec. 7.

⊙ – Subject to alteration June 30 - July 4, Oct. 13 – 17, 27 – 31.
⊕ – Subject to alteration on ①–⑤ June 30 - July 11 and ①–⑤ Oct. 6 – 31.
‡ – Arrives Paris Gare de Lyon on ①–⑤ June 16 – 27 (see also note ⊠). Arrives up to 26 minutes later on certain dates.
⊠ – Services run from / to Paris Gare de Lyon (not Bercy) on Aug. 9, 10, Sept. 6, 20, 21, 27, 28.

Timings between Paris and Nevers may vary on June 15, Aug. 9, 10, Sept. 6, 13, 20, 21, 27, 28, Oct. 4, 5, 11, 12 (see also note ⊠ above).

Nov. 8 – 11 all services (Paris -) Moulins - Clermont Ferrand and v.v. are subject to alteration. On Nov. 12, 13, 14 timings Moulins - Clermont Ferrand and v.v. may vary by up to 14 minutes.

331 CLERMONT FERRAND - NEUSSARGUES - AURILLAC

km													
		⚒			⑤		Ⓐ	⑦	①–⑥	⑦	Ⓐ	⑤	⑦
			T✤	B◇	f R			v	◧	v		f	v
0	**Clermont Ferrand**	§ d.	0559	1034	1303	...	1648	1748	1755	1841	1957	2004	2123	2138
36	Issoire	§ d.	0627	1102	1330	...	1718	1816	1824	1909	2025	2032	2151	2206
61	Arvant	§ d.	0646	1121	1350	...	1737	1838	1845	1929	2045	2053	2211	2226
85	Massiac-Blesle	d.	0707	1142	1411	...	1757	1901	1906	1949	2106	2113	2232	2247
111	**Neussargues**	a.	0728	1201	1430	...	1817	1922	1925	2009	2126	2133	2251	2306
111	**Neussargues**	d.	0730	1202	*1437*	1616	1818	1926	1926	2012	2127	2134	2252	2307
120	Murat (Cantal)	d.	0740	1211	*1446*	1625	1827	1935	1936	2021	2136	2143	2301	2316
131	Le Lioran	d.	0751	1223	*1457*	1639	1839	1951	1947	2032	2149	2154	2313	2328
168	**Aurillac**	a.	0823	1252	*1527*	1711	1908	2020	2019	2102	2220	2224	2343	2358

		⚒	Ⓐ					Ⓐ	Ⓐ	⑦
			⊡	◇	◇	B◇	T			v
Aurillac	d.	0554	0755	1027	1328	...	1643	1744	1918	1952
Le Lioran	d.	0625	0826	1100	1401	...	1715	1815	1949	2022
Murat (Cantal)	d.	0637	0838	1111	1412	...	1727	1829	2001	2034
Neussargues	a.	0645	0847	1119	1420	...	1734	1838	2009	2043
Neussargues	d.	0646	0848	1120	...	1435	1735	1839	2010	2044
Massiac-Blesle	d.	0708	0909	1143	...	1456	1758	1900	2031	2107
Arvant	§ d.	0728	0932	1204	...	1518	1818	1921	2051	2128
Issoire	§ d.	0748	0953	1223	...	1537	1836	1940	2110	2146
Clermont Ferrand	§ a.	0820	1020	1253	...	1602	1905	2008	2137	2214

B – To / from Béziers (Table **332**).
R – To Brive (Table **311**).
T – To / from Toulouse (Table **317**).

f – Also Aug. 14; not Aug. 15.
v – Also July 14, Aug. 15, Nov. 11; not July 13.

⊡ – Subject to alteration Sept. 22 - Oct. 10.
◇ – Subject to alteration on ①–⑤ Sept. 8 – 26.
✤ – Subject to alteration on ①–⑤ Sept. 8 - Oct. 10.

◧ – Runs 10 – 15 minutes later on July 14, Aug. 15, Nov. 11.
§ – See also Table **333**.

332 (CLERMONT FERRAND) - NEUSSARGUES - MILLAU - BÉZIERS

km												
			🚌			🚌		🚌				
			⚒	⚒	⚒	⚒	⚒	⚒			⑤	†
							□			◇	d	
0	**Clermont Ferrand**	▷ d.	...	...	...	...	...	...	...	1303	...	...
111	**Neussargues**	▷ d.	...	...	...	...	...	...	...	1436	...	...
130	St Flour ⊖	d.	...	...	...	...	...	...	...	1459	...	...
168	St Chély d'Apcher	d.	...	...	...	...	1131	...	...	1539	1630	...
201	Marvejols	d.	...	...	...	...	1206	...	...	1615	1707	...
243	Sévérac le Château	d.	...	...	...	...	1300	...	...	1702	1756	...
273	Millau	⊙ d.	...	0600	...	...	1330	...	...	1738	1826	2052
352	Bédarieux	△ d.	0619	0717	0844	1315	1445	1625	1734	1854	1940	2211
394	**Béziers**	△ a.	0714	0750	0918	1400	1518	1710	1808	1928	2014	2244

						🚌	🚌				
		⚒	⚒		⑤	⚒	⚒			⑤	⑦
		□		◇	d				A	d	z▽
Béziers	△ d.	0642	0800	0937	...	1215	1530	1644	1818	1856	1856
Bédarieux	△ d.	0718	0834	1010	...	1300	1615	1719	1856	1943	1940
Millau	⊙ d.	0840	...	1127	1410	...	...	...	2013	2100	2053
Sévérac le Château	d.	0908	...	1159	1438	...	...	...	...	...	2129
Marvejols	d.	0955	...	1248	1524	...	...	...	...	...	2218
St Chély d'Apcher	d.	1029	...	1325	1603	...	...	...	...	...	2251
St Flour ⊖	d.	...	...	1405	...	...	...	...	...	...	...
Neussargues	▷ a.	...	...	1425	...	...	...	...	...	...	...
Clermont Ferrand	▷ a.	...	...	1602	...	...	...	...	...	...	...

km												
			🚌	🚌	🚌		🚌	🚌	🚌	🚌	🚌	🚌
			Ⓐt¶	✤	⚒	⑤d			⑤f	Ⓑ	⑤⑥e	Ⓑs
	Clermont Ferrand	▷ d.	*0647*r	*1034*r	1050	...	1645	*1648*r	*1648*r	*1748*q	1955	2125
	Massiac-Blesle	▷ d.	0758	1155	|	...	|	1804	1804	1910	|	|
	St Flour ⊖	d.	0824	1219	|	...	|	1829	1829	1935	|	2235
	St Chély d'Apcher	d.	...	...	1220	...	1820	...	1856	...	2130	2303
0	Marvejols	● d.	...	...	1300	1720	1900	...	1934	...	2210	2340
35	**Mende**	● a.	...	...	1340	1807	1945	...	|	...	2255	0023
	Millau	a.	...	...	...	...	...	...	2101	...	...	...

		🚌	🚌	🚌	🚌	🚌	🚌	🚌		🚌	🚌
		⚒	⚒	⊠		†	h	⚒	⑤d	Ⓐ	†
Millau	d.	...	...	...	...	...	...	...	...	...	...
Mende	● d.	...	0645	...	0950	1445	...	1545	1615	...	1730
Marvejols	● d.	...	0730	...	1045	1540	...	1635	1702	...	1820
St Chély d'Apcher	d.	...	0806	...	1132	1623	...	1710	...	...	1858
St Flour ⊖	d.	0632	0835	1108	|	1650	1723	1745	...	1825	1930
Massiac-Blesle	▷ a.	0657	|	1132	|	|	1747	|	...	1850	|
Clermont Ferrand	▷ a.	*0820*r	1000	*1253*r	1310	1810	*1905*r	1910	...	*2008*r	2050

A – ①②③④⑥⑦ (also Oct. 24, 31; runs daily July 5 - Sept. 4).
B – ②–⑤ (not July 15, Aug. 15, Nov. 11, 12).
D – ①–④ to July 3; ⚒ July 7 - Aug. 30; ①–④ from Sept. 1 (not Nov. 11).
G – July 7 - Aug. 30.

d – Not July 11 - Aug. 29, Oct. 24, 31.
e – ⑤⑥ (also Aug. 14; not Aug. 15, Nov. 1). Runs 5 minutes later on ⑥.
f – Also Aug. 14; not Aug. 15.
h – Not July 11, 18, 25, Aug. 1, 8, 14, 22.
q – Not July 13. Connection by train (departs *1755* on †).
r – Connection by train.
s – Also Nov. 1. Runs 15 minutes later on † to June 29 / from Aug. 24. Runs 25 minutes later July 6 - Aug. 22.
t – Change from train to bus at Arvant (d. 0741).
v – Also Nov. 11; not July 6 - Aug. 31, Oct. 19, 26, Nov. 9.
z – Not July 6 - Aug. 31, Oct. 19, 26.

⊖ – St Flour - Chaudes Aigues.
▷ – See Table **331**.
▽ – From Montpellier (d. 1802).

¶ – Connecting train subject to alteration Oct. 6 – 17.
⊠ – Connecting train subject to alteration on ①–⑤ Sept. 8 – 26.
✤ – Connecting train subject to alteration on ①–⑤ Sept. 8 - Oct. 10.

◇ – Subject to alteration on ①–⑤ Sept. 8 – 26 Clermont Ferrand - Neussargues and v.v. A change of train at Neussargues may be required.
□ – Subject to alteration Béziers - Marvejols and v.v. on ①–④ Oct. 6 – 30. Subject to alteration Marvejols - St Chély and v.v. on ①–④ Sept. 22 - Oct. 30.
● – Other rail services Marvejols - Mende and v.v.: **From Marvejols** at 0700 **B**, 0755 ⑥ **G**, 1351 ⚒ **G** and 2228 ⑦ **v**. **From Mende** at 1113 ⚒ **G**, 1730 **D** and 2125 ⑦ **v**.
△ – Additional 🚌 journeys Bédarieux - Béziers and v.v.: **From Bédarieux** at 0715 †, 1221 † and 1610 †. **From Béziers** at 1049 †, 1445 †, 1730 ⚒ and 2045 ⑤ **f**.
⊙ – Additional SNCF 🚌 service Millau - Montpellier (journey 85 - 125 minutes): **From Millau** at 0700 ⚒, 0730 †, 1000, 1510 and 1716. **From Montpellier** 0955, 1205, 1800 ⚒ and 2210.

☛ Bus services in this table are operated on behalf of SNCF. Rail tickets valid. Serves railway stations.

CLERMONT FERRAND - LE PUY EN VELAY and NIMES 333

Services St Georges d'Aurac - Le Puy en Velay and v.v. are subject to alteration June 28 - Aug. 2.

km		Ⓐ	⑥ p	Ⓐ	🚌 Ⓐ A	⚒ C	Ⓐ ⊗	🚌 Ⓐ	⑦ r	⑥ k	🚌 ⑥ k	🚌	☆	⊡	🚌		🚌	⑤⑦ y	◧		🚌	⚒	Ⓐ	Ⓐ	🚌 ⑤ w	⑦ e
0	**Clermont Ferrand** ▷ d.	...	...	0545	...	...	0647	...	...	0728	...	...	...	0949	...	1249	...	...	...	1640	...	1757	1852	2004	...	2110
36	Issoire ▷ d.	...	...	0613	...	...	0715	...	...	0757	...	...	...	1018	...	1318	...	...	...	1709	...	1825	1920	2032	...	2138
61	Arvant ▷ d.	...	...	0632	...	...	0737	...	...	0817	...	...	...	1037	...	1339	...	...	...	1727	...	1845	1939	2050	2055	2158
71	Brioude d.	...	...	0643	...	...	0746	...	...	0826	...	...	...	1049	...	1349	1355	...	...	1737	...	1854	1948	...	2110	2208
95	St Georges d'Aurac d.	...	...	0710	...	...	0806	...	...	0844	...	...	...	1112	...	|	|	...	...	1758	1802	1917	2011	...	|	2231
103	Langeac d.	...	...	|	...	...	0814	0818	...	0852	0858	...	...	|	...	1415	|	...	...	1806	|	|	|	...	2148	|
147	**Le Puy en Velay** a.	...	...	0757	...	...	|	0904	...	|	0944	...	...	1200	...	|	1503	...	...	|	1854	2004	2059	...	2234	2319
170	Langogne d.	...	...	...	...	...	0943	...	...	1025	...	1232	...	...	...	1542	...	...	...	1940	...	...	...	...	...	...
∆47	**Mende** d.	0450	...	...	0840	0846	|	...	0846	|	...	|	1147	...	1443	|	...	1650	1832	|	...	...	...	...	...	...
188	La Bastide-St Laurent d.	0605	0701	...	0950	0955	1003	...	1003	1045	...	1257	1307	...	1553	1605	...	1805	1942	2010	...	...	...	...	...	...
241	Grand Combe la Pise d.	0709	0808	...	...	...	1101	...	1101	1143	...	...	1407f	...	...	1708	...	1911	...	2109	...	...	...	...	...	...
254	Alès a.	0724	0824	...	...	...	1116	...	1116	1158	...	...	1422f	...	...	1723	...	1925	...	2124	...	...	...	...	...	...
254	Alès ▶ d.	0726	0826	...	...	...	1118t	...	1118	1211	...	...	1427	...	...	1725	...	1926	...	2126	...	...	...	...	...	...
303	**Nimes 355** ▶ a.	0758	0858	...	...	...	1150t	...	1150	1243	...	...	1458	...	...	1759	...	1958	...	2158	...	...	...	...	...	...

	① g	②–⑤ d	⚒ ⊡	① m	🚌 ⑦ e		🚌 B	⚒ C	⚒	⊖	🚌			🚌		🚌	🚌 Ⓑ	Ⓐ	⑦ e	Ⓑ	🚌 ⑤ w	◇	🚌		⑤ v	🚌 ⑤ v
Nimes 355 ▶ d.	...	...	...	0715	...	0814	...	...	...	1218	...	...	...	...	1411	...	...	...	...	1700	...	1818b	...	...	2118	...
Alès ▶ a.	...	...	...	0750	...	0845	...	...	...	1250	...	...	...	...	1441	...	...	...	...	1737	...	1852b	...	...	2150	...
Alès d.	...	...	...	0751	...	0846	...	...	...	1252	...	...	...	...	1443	...	...	...	...	1752	...	1854	...	...	2156	...
Grand Combe la Pise d.	...	...	...	0809	...	0901	...	...	...	1307	...	...	...	...	1459	...	...	...	...	1807	...	1910	...	...	2211	...
La Bastide-St Laurent d.	...	...	...	0913	...	1002j	1001	1006	...	1416	1417	...	...	...	1603	1610	...	...	...	1913	...	2014j	2013	...	2313	2321
Mende a.	...	...	...	|	...	|	1111	1111	...	1525	|	...	...	...	|	1720	...	...	...	|	...	2122	|	...	...	|
Langogne d.	...	...	...	0932	...	1026	...	...	...	...	1442	...	...	...	1622	...	...	...	...	1936	...	...	2038	...	...	2346
Le Puy en Velay d.	0526z	0616	0806	...	1110	|	...	...	1210	...	...	...	1606	1654	|	...	1910	...	1954	|	2026	...	...	...	...	...
Langeac d.	|	|	|	...	|	1155	...	...	|	...	...	...	|	|	1747	...	|	...	|	2104	2112	...	...	...	...	...
St Georges d'Aurac d.	0616z	0706	0856	...	|	1204	...	...	1259	...	...	...	1656	1747	1800	...	|	...	2043	2112	|	...	...	...	...	...
Brioude d.	0641	0726	0916	...	1213	1223	...	...	1319	...	...	...	1716	...	1821	...	2018	...	2103	2130	2150	...	...	...	...	...
Arvant ▷ d.	0649	0738	0924	...	...	1233	...	...	1331	...	...	...	1726	...	1831	...	2034	2051	2113	2139	2201	...	...	...	...	...
Issoire ▷ d.	0710	0758	0945	...	...	1251	...	...	1351	...	...	...	1747	...	1851	...	...	2110	2133	2159	...	...	...	...	...	...
Clermont Ferrand ▷ a.	0742	0827	1015	...	...	1319	...	...	1419	...	...	...	1817	...	1916	...	...	2137	2200	2229	...	...	...	...	...	...

A – To July 4 and from Sept. 1.
B – † (daily to July 6 and from Aug. 31).
C – July 7 - Aug. 30 only.

b – 7 minutes earlier on ⑤ (also ⑥⑦ July 12 - Aug. 31).
d – Not July 15, Aug. 15, Nov. 11, 12.
e – Also July 14, Aug. 15, Nov. 11; not July 13.
f – 3 minutes earlier on ⑤ (not Aug. 15).
g – Also July 15, Nov. 12; not July 14.
j – Arrives 6 minutes earlier.
k – Not Nov. 1.
m – Also Nov. 12; not July 7 - Sept. 1, Oct. 20, 27, Nov. 10.
p – Not July 12 - Aug. 30, Oct. 25, Nov. 1.
r – Also July 14, Aug. 15.
t – 3 minutes later July 7 - Aug. 29. Subject to alteration Oct. 20–31.
v – Not July 11 - Aug. 29, Oct. 24, 31.
w – Also Aug. 14; not Aug. 15.
y – Also July 14, Nov. 1, 11; not July 11, 18, 25, Aug. 1, 8, 22, 29, Oct. 24, 31.
z – Not July 7–28.

☆ – Subject to alteration on ①–④ Sept. 22 - Oct. 2.
⊖ – Subject to alteration on ①–④ Sept. 22 - Oct. 16.
⊡ – Subject to alteration on ①–⑤ Sept. 22 - Oct. 10.
¶ – Subject to alteration on ①–⑤ Oct. 20–31.

⊗ – Subject to alteration Oct. 6–17.
◇ – From Narbonne and Montpellier on Ⓐ (Table **355**).
◧ – By 🚌 on ①②③④⑥⑦ (daily July 5 - Aug. 4, Oct. 18 - Nov. 6).
∆ – Distance from La Bastide.
▷ – See also Table **331**.
▶ – Other trains Alès - Nimes (journey time 32–41 minutes): **From Alès** at 0600 Ⓐ, 0628 Ⓐ, 0656, 0756 ⚒, 0826, 0926 Ⓐ ¶, 1226 Ⓐ, 1256, 1526, 1642 Ⓐ, 1823 Ⓐ, 1926. **From Nimes** at 0618 Ⓐ, 0654 Ⓐ, 0715 ⚒, 0745 Ⓐ, 0918 Ⓐ ¶, 1018 Ⓐ ¶, 1118 ¶, 1318 Ⓐ, 1518 Ⓐ, 1618, 1733 ⚒, 1918 Ⓐ, 2118.

TGV services LYON - MASSY - LE MANS - RENNES and NANTES 335

For slower services via Bourges see Table **290**. For Lille - Massy - Rennes / Nantes see Table **11**. For Strasbourg - Massy - Rennes / Nantes see Table **391**.

	TGV **5352** Ⓐ B	*TGV* **5352** ①-⑤ E		*TGV* **5350**	*TGV* **5365** ⑥ t		*TGV* **5368**	*TGV* **5372** ⊗	*TGV* **5371** y	*TGV* **5380**	*TGV* **5387**	*TGV* **5394** ⑥ G	*TGV* **5393** ⑥ G	
Marseille **350** d.	...	...	...	0846	0846	...	1242	1444	1444	...	...	...	...	...
Avignon TGV **350** d.	...	...	...	0916	0916	...	1320	1521	1521	...	...	...	...	...
Montpellier **355** d.	...	...	...	|	|	...	|	|	|	1628	1628	...	...	...
Valence TGV **355** d.	...	...	...	0949	0949	...	|	|	|	1747	1747	...	...	...
Bourg St Maurice **366** d.	...	...	...	|	|	...	|	|	|	|	|	1624	1624	...
yon Perrache d.	0616	0616	...	|	|	...	|	|	|	|	|	|	|	...
yon Part Dieu d.	0630	0630	...	1030	1030	...	1430	1630	1630	1830	1830	|	|	...
lassy TGV d.	0838	0838	...	1238*	1238*	...	1638	1838*	1838	2038	2048*	2154	2154	...
St Pierre des Corps a.	0929	|	...	|	|	...	1729t	|	|	2129f	|	|	|	...
Futuroscope **300** a.	|	|	...	|	|	...	|	|	|	|	|	|	|	...
Poitiers 300 a.	|	|	...	|	|	...	|	|	|	|	|	|	|	...
e Mans **280** a.	|	0930	...	1328	1328	...	|	1928	1928	|	2136	2241	2241	...
Rennes 280 a.	|	|	...	1446k	|	...	|	|	2101	|	2255‡	|	0003	...
aumur a.	|	|	...	...	|	...	|	|	...	2204f	...	|	...	...
ngers St Laud **280** a.	1022	1022	...	...	1415	...	1822	2010	...	2230	...	2327	...	...
lantes 280 a.	1102	1102	...	...	1454	...	1903	2048	...	2308	...	0012	...	...

	TGV **5302** ②–④ u	*TGV* **5304** ① g	*TGV* **5308** ⑥ H	*TGV* **5310** ⑥ H	*TGV* **5314** c	*TGV* **5312** ☒	*TGV* **5318** c	*TGV* **5326** ✥	*TGV* **5322** ⊙	*TGV* **5328** Ⓐ	*TGV* **5346**	*TGV* **5342** ⑤⑦ z	*TGV* **5344** ⑤⑦ z	
lantes 280 d.	0456	0453b	0619	...	...	0705e	...	0908j	1252	1454r	...	1905r	...	...
ngers St Laud **280** d.	0536	0533b	0716	...	...	0743e	...	0946j	1333	1534r	...	1944r	...	...
aumur d.	|	0558	|	...	...	|	...	|	|	1558	...	|	...	...
Rennes 280 d.	|	|	|	0639	0707h	|	0908h	|	|	|	1607x	|	1907v	...
e Mans **280** d.	|	|	0804	0804	0833	0833	1033	1033	|	|	1732	2033	2033	...
Poitiers 300 d.	|	|	|	|	|	|	|	|	|	|	|	|	|	...
Futuroscope **300** a.	|	|	|	|	|	|	|	|	|	|	|	|	|	...
St Pierre des Corps d.	0631	0631	|	|	|	|	|	|	1431	1631	|	|	|	...
lassy TGV d.	0725	0725	0855	0855	0925	0925	1126	1126	1524	1725	1825	2124	2124	...
yon Part Dieu a.	0928	0944	|	|	1130	1130	1330	1330	1730	1930	2030	2330	2330	...
yon Perrache a.	0941	1004	|	|	|	|	|	|	|	1943	|	2343p	2343p	...
Bourg St Maurice **366** a.	...	...	1424	1424	|	|	|	|	|	...	|	...	...	...
Valence TGV **355** a.	...	...	...	...	|	|	1411	1411	1811	...	2110	...	...	...
Montpellier **355** a.	...	...	...	...	|	|	1530	1530	|	...	|	...	...	...
Avignon TGV **350** a.	...	...	...	...	1238	1238	...	...	1845	...	2145	...	...	...
Marseille **350** a.	...	...	...	...	1316	1316	...	...	1918	...	2216	...	...	...

LYON - ROUEN	*TGV* **5376** ♥	
Marseille **350** d.	1544	...
Avignon TGV **350** d.	1614	...
Valence TGV **355** d.	1649	...
yon Part Dieu d.	1730	...
lassy-Palaiseau a.	1937	...
ersailles Chantiers a.	1955	...
lantes la Jolie a.	2028	...
ouen Rive Droite a.	2120	...
Le Havre **270** a.	2211	...

ROUEN - LYON	*TGV* **5316** Ⓐ	*TGV* **5316** ♣
Le Havre **270** d.	0750	0750
Rouen Rive Droite d.	0845	0845
Mantes la Jolie d.	0933	0933
Versailles Chantiers d.	1006	1006
Massy-Palaiseau d.	1024	1024
Lyon Part Dieu a.	1226	1226
Valence TGV **355** a.	1310	|
Avignon TGV **350** a.	1344	1338
Marseille **350** a.	1416	1416

Services in this table are subject to alteration on ⑥⑦ Sept. 13 - Oct. 19

B – To Aug. 29 / from Nov. 10 (also Oct. 20–24).
E – Sept. 1 - Oct. 17 and Oct. 27 - Nov. 7.
G – ⑥ until Mar. 15.
H – ⑥ until Mar. 22.

b – Until Aug. 25 Nantes d. 0449, Angers d. 0532.
c – Not July 13, Sept. 6, 7.
e – Until July 5 (also Aug. 25 - Sept. 26) departs Nantes 0658, Angers 0736.
f – Not Oct. 11.
g – Also Nov. 12; not July 7 - Aug. 18, Nov. 10.
h – 6–7 minutes earlier until July 5.
j – Departs up to 5 minutes earlier until June 29 (also Aug. 25 - Sept. 28; see note ✥ for service on June 22).
k – Not July 13, Sept. 6, 13. Arrives 1450 on ⑥ (also Aug. 15).
p – ⑦ from July 6 (also July 14, Aug. 8, 14, 22, 29, Sept. 5, 12, 19, 26, Nov. 11).
r – 3–5 minutes earlier until July 4 and Aug. 25 - Sept. 26.
t – Not Sept. 20, Oct. 11, Nov. 22.
u – Also Nov. 10; not July 8 - Aug. 26, Nov. 11, 12.
v – Not July 13. 1901 until July 4.
x – Not July 13, Sept. 6. 1601 until July 5.
y – Not July 13, Sept. 6, 13.
z – Also July 14, Aug. 14, Nov. 11; not Aug. 15.

TGV – Ⓡ, supplement payable, 🍷.

* – 1–2 minutes earlier June 23 - July 20.
‡ – On July 12, 13, Sept. 6 service is diverted, arriving Rennes 80–85 minutes later.
⊙ – Subject to alteration on Nov. 22, Dec. 13.
⊗ – On Dec. 6 does not call at Le Mans, arrives Angers 2029, Nantes 2110.
☒ – On June 22 departs Nantes 0540 and does not call at Angers. Subject to alteration on Dec. 7.
✥ – On June 22, Dec. 12 departs Nantes up to 90 minutes **earlier** and does not call at Angers.
♥ – Subject to alteration on July 19. Terminates at Versailles on June 28. Terminates at Mantes la Jolie on Nov. 8, 9. Terminates at Rouen on Dec. 6.
♣ – ⑥⑦ only. Subject to alteration on July 19, Sept. 6, 7. Starts from Versailles on June 29. Starts from Mantes la Jolie on July 6, 13, 20, Nov. 8, 9. Starts from Rouen on Sept. 27, 28, Dec. 7.

FRANCE

340 PARIS - LYON *TGV Sud-Est*

For Charles de Gaulle ✈ - Marne la Vallée - Lyon see Table **11**. For Paris - Lyon St Exupéry ✈ see Table **342**. Trains not serving Lyon Perrache continue to/from other destinations.

km	*TGV* trains convey 🍸	*TGV* 6601	*TGV* 6641	*TGV* 6681	*TGV* 6603	*TGV* 6643	*TGV* 6605	*TGV* 6605	*TGV* 6605	*TGV* 6607	*TGV* 6609	*TGV* 6611	*TGV* 6613	*TGV* 6685	*TGV* 6615	*TGV* 6617	*TGV* 6657	*TGV* 6619	*TGV* 6621	*TGV* 6659	*TGV* 6687	*TGV* 6623	*TGV* 6663	*TGV* 6627
		Ⓐ	Ⓐ	①–⑥	①–⑥	Ⓐ	①–⑤		⑥								⑤			Ⓐ				
			J	b	b	J	Y	B									J			J			R	
0	**Paris** Gare de Lyon ▷ d.	0550	0628	0658	0658	0728	0753	0753	0753	0858	0958	1058	1153	1258	1258	1353	1428	1457	1553	1628	1657	1657	1728	1753
303	Le Creusot TGV d.	0717	|	|	|	|	0914z	0913	0917	|	|	|	1313	|	|	1514	|	|	1714	|	|	|	|	1914
363	Mâcon Loché TGV ▷ a.	|	|	|	|	|	|	0933	0935	|	|	|	|	|	|	|	|	1631	|	|	|	|	|	|
427	**Lyon** Part-Dieu a.	0756	0826	0856	0856	0924	0957	0959	1001	1056	1156	1256	1356	1456	1456	1556	1624	1657	1756	1824	1856	1856	1926	1956
431	**Lyon** Perrache a.	0809	0839	...	0909	0937	1010	1011	1013	1109	1209	1309	1409	...	1509	1609	1637	1714	1809	1837	...	1909	1938	2009

	TGV 6665	*TGV* 6689	*TGV* 6629	*TGV* 6669	*TGV* 6631	*TGV* 6671	*TGV* 6633	*TGV* 6635	
						⑦	Ⓑ	⑤⑦	
	M			S		e	h	d⊖	
Paris Gare de Lyon ▷ d.	1828	1856	1856	1928	1953	2028	2058	2157	...
Le Creusot TGV d.	|	|	|	|	2112	|	|	|	...
Mâcon Loché TGV ▷ a.	|	|	|	|	2133	|	|	|	...
Lyon Part-Dieu a.	2024	2056	2056	2124	2200	2224	2256	2356	...
Lyon Perrache a.	2037	...	2109	2137	2213	2237	2309v	0009	...

	TGV 6640	*TGV* 6602	*TGV* 6642	*TGV* 6644	*TGV* 6604	*TGV* 6690	*TGV* 6648	*TGV* 6608	*TGV* 6608	*TGV* 6610
	①	Ⓐ	P	N	①–⑥	①–⑥	T			
	g				b	b		Ⓐ	Ⓒ	
Lyon Perrache d.	0521	0551	0621	0639	0647	...	0721	0751	0751	0851
Lyon Part-Dieu d.	0534	0604	0634	0652	0705	0705	0734	0804	0804	0904
Mâcon Loché TGV ▷ d.	0601	0632	|	|	|	|	|	|	0833	|
Le Creusot TGV d.	0622	0652	|	|	|	|	|	0846	0855	|
Paris Gare de Lyon ▷ a.	0743	0813	0832	0849	0902	0902	0934	1007	1015	1102

	TGV 6612	*TGV* 6612	*TGV* 6692	*TGV* 6614	*TGV* 6616	*TGV* 6694	*TGV* 6618	*TGV* 6620	*TGV* 6622	*TGV* 6624	*TGV* 6624	*TGV* 6664	*TGV* 6626	*TGV* 6668	*TGV* 6628	*TGV* 6638	*TGV* 6696	*TGV* 6630	*TGV* 6632	*TGV* 6674	*TGV* 6634	*TGV* 6672	*TGV* 6676	*TGV* 6678
											②–⑤	Ⓑ				Ⓑ				⑦	Ⓑ	⑤	⑦	⑦
	C	Q								L	J	J		R		J				e	h	f	e	
Lyon Perrache d.	0951	0951	...	1046	1121	...	1247	1351	1451	1551	1551	1621	1651	1721	1751	1821	...	1847	1951	2021	2051	2151	2151	2221
Lyon Part-Dieu d.	1004	1004	1105	1105	1134	1305	1305	1404	1504	1604	1604	1634	1704	1734	1804	1834	1904	1904	2004	2034	2104	2204	2204	2234
Mâcon Loché TGV ▷ d.	|	1031	|	|	|	|	|	|	|	|	1631	|	|	|	|	|	|	|	|	|	|	|	2230	|
Le Creusot TGV d.	1048	1053	|	|	|	|	|	1446	|	1646r	1653	|	|	|	1847t	|	|	|	2046	|	|	2246	2251	|
Paris Gare de Lyon ▷ a.	1207	1212	1302	1302	1332	1502	1502	1607	1702	1807	1815	1832	1902	1932	2007	2032	2102	2101	2207	2232	2302	0008	0011	0032

B – ⑦ to Sept. 7; Ⓑ from Sept. 14.
C – ⑥⑦ (daily July 5 - Oct. 5).
J – To July 4 / from Aug. 25.
L – ①⑥⑦ (daily July 5 - Aug. 25).
M – Ⓑ to July 4; ⑤ July 11 - Aug. 8 (also Aug. 14, 22); Ⓑ from Aug. 25.
N – ①–④ to July 3 / from Aug. 25 (not Nov. 11).
P – ①–⑤ to July 7; ① July 21 - Aug. 18; Ⓐ from Aug. 20.
Q – ①–⑤ June 16 - July 4; ①–⑤ from Oct. 6.
R – ①–⑤ to July 4; ⑤ July 11 - Aug. 8 (also Aug. 14); Ⓐ from Aug. 22.
S – Ⓑ to July 6; ⑤⑦ July 11 - Aug. 17 (also July 14, Aug. 14); Ⓑ from Aug. 22.

T – Daily to July 6; Ⓒ July 12 - Aug. 17; daily from Aug. 23.
Y – ①–⑤ to Sept. 12.

b – Not July 14, Nov. 11.
d – Also July 14, Aug. 14, Nov. 11; not Aug. 15.
e – Also July 14, Nov. 11.
f – Also Aug. 14; not July 4, Aug. 1. Runs 4 minutes earlier on Aug. 22.
g – Also Nov. 12; not July 7 - Aug. 18, Nov. 10.

h – Not Aug. 15.
r – 1649 until Aug. 19.
t – 1845 on June 15, 20.
v – ⑦ to July 27; Ⓑ Aug. 3 - Sept. 28 (not Aug. 15); ⑦ from Oct. 5 (also Nov. 10).
z – Not Aug. 19 – 29.

TGV –Ⓡ, supplement payable, 🍸.

⊖ – Terminates at Lyon Part Dieu on ⑤.
▷ – For other trains Paris - Mâcon Loché TGV and v.v. see Tables **341** and **342**.

341 PARIS - GENÈVE, CHAMBÉRY and ANNECY *TGV trains*

For the night trains Paris Austerlitz - Aix les Bains - Chambéry - Bourg St Maurice / Modane see Tables **365** and **366** (Paris - Annecy see Table **365**). SEE NOTE ⊠.

km	All trains convey 🍸	*TGV* 9767	*TGV* 9239	*TGV* 6931	*TGV* 9761	*TGV* 9241	*TGV* 9771	*TGV* 9763	*TGV* 6935	*TGV* 9765	*TGV* 6503	*TGV* 6937	*TGV* 6503	*TGV* 9245	*TGV* 6939	*TGV* 9769	*TGV* 9779	*TGV* 9773	*TGV* 6941	*TGV* 9249	*TGV* 9775	*TGV* 9777	*TGV* 6511
		Ⓐ	A	D	Ⓐ	G	Y	Ⓒ	⑦	①–⑥	⑦		⑥				ⒷY					Ⓑ	⑤
		♥	M			M		⊗	L	b⊕	Q			M		W	h	⊕		M	⊕	⊕	f
0	**Paris** Gare de Lyon **340** d.	0611	0641	0641	0707	0749	0802	0811	0845	0911	0911	0949	1011	1041	1041	1111	1157	1211	1245	1441	1511	1611	1615
363	Mâcon Loché TGV **340** d.	|	|	|	|	0926	|	|	|	|	|	1126q	|	|	|	|	|	|	|	|	|	|	|
406	Bourg-en-Bresse **365** d.	|	|	|	0859	|	|	1005	|	|	1107	1149	1204	|	|	1303j	|	1405	|	|	|	1805	|
	Lyon St Exupéry TGV ✈ **342** d.	|	0836	0836	|	0949	|	|	|	|	|	|	|	1235	1235	|	|	|	|	1635	|	|	|
439	Nurieux Brion a.	|	|	|	|	|	|	|	|	|	|	|	|	|	|	|	|	|	|	|	|	|	|
470	Bellegarde ⊠ **346** a.	0857	|	|	0947	|	|	1058	|	1148	1159	|	1259	|	|	1348	|	1500	|	|	1748	1858	1909
503	**Genève** ⊠ **346** a.	0927	|	|	1016	|	1230	1127	|	1216	⊖	|	⊖	|	|	1416	1630	1527	|	|	1816	1927	⊖
•532	Chambéry a.	...	0935	0935	...	1046	...	...	1135	...	...	|	...	1336	1336	...	...	...	1535	1735	...	...	...
•532	Chambéry **345 364** d.	...	...	0948	...	...	...	...	1147	...	...	|	...	...	1347	...	...	...	1547	...	...	...	...
•546	Aix les Bains **345 364** a.	...	...	0958	...	...	...	...	1158	...	...	1251	...	...	1358	...	...	...	1559	...	...	...	...
•585	**Annecy** **345 364** a.	...	...	1030	...	...	...	...	1230	...	...	1330	...	...	1430	...	...	...	1630	...	...	...	...

	TGV 6947	*TGV* 6949	*TGV* 9783	*TGV* 9781	*TGV* 6951	*TGV* 9785	*TGV* 6953	*TGV* 9789
		Ⓑ	Y				⑤	⑤
		h			J	◇	v	⊕
Paris Gare de Lyon **340** d.	1645	1748	1757	1811	1843	1911	1947	2011
Mâcon Loché TGV **340** d.	|	1926	|	|	|	|	2128	|
Bourg-en-Bresse **365** d.	|	1949	|	2006j	|	2105	2151	2204
Lyon St Exupéry TGV ✈ **342** d.	|	|	|	|	|	|	|	|
Nurieux Brion a.	|	|	|	2032	|	|	|	|
Bellegarde ⊠ **346** a.	|	|	|	2059	|	2150	|	2250
Genève ⊠ **346** a.	|	|	2218	2127	|	2219	|	2319
Chambéry a.	1935	|	...	...	2135	...	2310	...
Chambéry **345 364** d.	1947	|	...	...	2147	...	|	...
Aix les Bains **345 364** a.	1958	2051	...	...	2158	...	2255z	...
Annecy **345 364** a.	2030	2130	...	...	2229	...	...	...

	TGV 6960	*TGV* 9760	*TGV* 9782	*TGV* 9764	*TGV* 6962	*TGV* 9766	*TGV* 9768	*TGV* 6964	*TGV* 9240
	①–⑥	①–⑥	Y	①–⑥		⑦			
	b	a		b⊗		e⊗	⊕	E	M
Annecy **345 364** d.	0531	...	...	...	0730‡	...	...	0931	...
Aix les Bains **345 364** d.	0601	...	...	...	0801‡	...	...	1000	...
Chambéry **345 364** a.	0612	...	...	...	0812‡	...	...	1011	...
Chambéry d.	0625	...	...	...	0825	...	...	1022*	1022
Genève ⊠ **346** d.	|	0612	0738	0742	|	0829	0942	|	|
Bellegarde ⊠ **346** d.	|	0643	|	0808	|	0900	1010	|	|
Nurieux Brion d.	|	0708	|	|	|	0927	|	|	|
Lyon St Exupéry TGV ✈ **342** a.	|	|	|	|	|	|	|	1126	1126
Bourg-en-Bresse **365** d.	|	0736	|	0858	|	0957	|	|	|
Mâcon Loché TGV **340** d.	|	|	|	|	|	|	|	|	|
Paris Gare de Lyon **340** a.	0915	0927	1204	1049	1115	1149	1249	1323	1323

	TGV 9770		*TGV* 9244	*TGV* 6972		*TGV* 9772	*TGV* 9774	*TGV* 6508		*TGV* 6976	*TGV* 9786	*TGV* 9778	*TGV* 6504		*TGV* 9788	*TGV* 9776		*TGV* 6980	*TGV* 6504	*TGV* 9780	*TGV* 6984	*TGV* 9784	*TGV* 9248
	Ⓐ					Ⓒ	Ⓐ	⑦			ⒷY		⑦		Y	⑦		Ⓑ	⑥	Ⓑ	Ⓑ		
			M			⊕	⊕	e			h					e⊕			R	⊕	h	⊕	M
Annecy **345 364** d.	...	...	...	1231	...	...	...	...	...	1531	...	...	...	...	...	...	...	1731	...	...	1831	...	...
Aix les Bains **345 364** d.	...	...	1311x	1311	...	...	...	...	...	1601	...	...	...	...	...	...	...	1801	...	...	1908	...	...
Chambéry **345 364** a.	...	...	|	|	...	...	...	...	...	1613	...	...	...	...	...	...	...	1813	...	...	|	...	...
Chambéry d.	...	...	1252	|	...	...	...	...	...	1625p	...	...	...	...	...	...	...	1824r	...	...	|	...	2024
Genève ⊠ **346** d.	1142	...	|	|	...	1342	1429	⊖	...	|	1541	1629	⊖	...	1738c	1742	...	|	⊖	1829	|	1942	|
Bellegarde ⊠ **346** d.	1210	...	|	|	...	1410	1501	1502	...	|	|	1700	1655t	...	|	1810	...	|	1911	1910	|	2010	|
Nurieux Brion d.	|	...	|	|	...	|	|	|	...	|	|	|	|	...	|	|	...	|	|	|	|	|	|
Lyon St Exupéry TGV ✈ **342** a.	|	...	|	|	...	|	|	|	...	|	|	|	|	...	|	|	...	|	|	|	|	|	2125
Bourg-en-Bresse **365** d.	|	...	1413	1413	...	|	1557	1557	...	|	|	1756	1813	...	|	|	...	|	2000	|	2013	|	|
Mâcon Loché TGV **340** d.	|	...	1434	1434	...	|	|	|	...	|	|	|	1834	...	|	|	...	|	|	|	2034	|	|
Paris Gare de Lyon **340** a.	1449	...	1611	1611	...	1649	1749	1749	...	1918	2010k	1949	2011	...	2202	2049	...	2115	2149	2149	2211	2249	2319

A – ⑥⑦ (daily from Sept. 13).
D – ①–⑥ to July 11; Ⓐ July 15 - Aug. 22; ①–⑥ from Aug. 25 (not Nov. 11).
E – Daily to July 5; ②–⑤ July 8 - Aug. 22; daily from Aug. 25.
G – ①–⑤ to Sept. 12.
J – To July 5 / from Aug. 25.
L – ⑦ July 6 - Aug. 24 (also July 14).
M – 🚌12 Paris - Modane - Torino - Milano and v.v. (Table 44). Special 'global' fares payable.
Q – July 6 - Aug. 24.
R – ⑥ July 12 - Aug. 16 (also Aug. 15).
W – ⑦ (also Nov. 11; daily July 13 - Aug. 19).
Y – July 15 - Aug. 24 only. Runs via Vallorbe.

a – Also ⑦ July 20 - Aug. 17; not July 14, Nov. 11.
b – Not July 14, Nov. 11.
c – 1741 on ⑥⑦ (also Aug. 1).
e – Also July 14, Nov. 11.
f – Also Aug. 14; not Aug. 15, 22.
h – Not Aug. 15.
j – July 15 - Aug. 19 only.
k – 2032 on ⑦ July 20 - Aug. 17.
p – 1617 on July 19, 26.
q – 1123 Aug. 19 – 30.
r – 1826 until Sept. 29.
t – 1704 until Aug. 17.
v – Also Aug. 14.

x – Calls after Chambéry.
z – Calls before Chambéry.

TGV –Ⓡ, supplement payable, 🍸.

♥ – From Aug. 25.
‡ – Until Sept. 29.
* – 1024 on ⑥⑦ (daily from Sept. 13).
⊖ – To / from Évian les Bains (Table **363**).
• – Via St Exupéry TGV (Paris - Aix via Bourg is *511* km).
⊗ – Does not run July 15 - Aug. 29.
⊕ – Does not run July 15 - Aug. 24.
◇ – Does not run July 14 - Aug. 24.

⊠ – Alterations to services to / from Bellegarde and Genève **until Sept. 22**: July 15 - Aug. 2 services may be cancelled (as indicated) or do not run between Bellegarde and Genève. Most services via Bellegarde are suspended Aug. 20 – 24 (also certain services on the morning of Aug. 25). Timings of services to / from Genève may vary by a few minutes un July 14, also Aug. 25 - Sept. 22 (please che your reservation for confirmed timings).

Services via Chambéry are subject to alteration or cancellation on July 20, 27, Dec. 6, 7.

PARIS - LYON ST EXUPÉRY ✈ - GRENOBLE 342

Shows complete service Paris - Lyon St Exupéry ✈ and v.v. Journeys not serving Grenoble continue to destinations in other tables

km	All trains convey 🍸	TGV 6901 ①–④ m	TGV 9239 E⊖	TGV 6905 ①–⑥ ⊡	TGV 9241 ①–⑤ G		TGV 6911		TGV 9245 ⊖	TGV 6193 H		TGV 6917 v		TGV 9249 ⊖	TGV 6919		TGV 6921 J	TGV 6195 ⊗	TGV 6923 Ⓑ		TGV 6925 A	TGV 6927		TGV 6929 ⑤⑦ w
0	**Paris** Gare de Lyon .... **341** d.	0637	0641	0737	0749	...	0937	...	1041	1119	...	1241	...	1441	1537	...	1641	1719	1737	...	1839	1937	...	2041
363	Mâcon Loché TGV .... **341** d.	|	|	|	0926	...	|	...	|	1256	...	|	...	|	|	...	|	1856	|	...	|	|	...	|
441	Lyon St Exupéry ✈ .... a.	|	0834	0930	0947	...	1130	...	1233	1320	...	|	...	1633	1730	...	|	1919	1930	...	2029	2130	...	|
441	Lyon St Exupéry ✈ .... d.	|	...	0933	...	...	1133	...	...	...	...	|	...	...	1733	...	|	...	1933	...	2032	2133	...	|
553	**Grenoble** .... a.	0938	...	1040	...	...	1240	...	...	...	...	1537	...	...	1840	...	1937	...	2040	...	2137	2240	...	2337

	TGV 6900 ①–④ m	TGV 6192 Ⓐ	TGV 6902 Ⓐ		TGV 6904 ①–⑥ b	TGV 6906 D		TGV 6194 L	TGV 6194 H	TGV 6908	TGV 9240 ⊖		TGV 6910		TGV 6920 Ⓑ J		TGV 6922	TGV 6198 △		TGV 6924		TGV 9248 ◇		TGV 6928 ⑦ e
Grenoble .... d.	0520	...	0623	...	0720	0823	...	...	...	1023	...	...	1320	...	1520	...	1720	...	...	1920	...	...	...	2120
Lyon St Exupéry ✈ .... a.	0625	...	|	...	0825	|	...	...	...	|	...	...	1428	...	1626	...	1827	...	...	2026	...	...	...	2226
Lyon St Exupéry ✈ .... d.	0628	0641	|	...	0828	|	...	0935	1041	|	1131	...	1439	...	1629	...	1830	1841	...	2029	...	2128	...	2229
Mâcon Loché TGV .... **341** d.	|	0704	|	...	|	|	...	|	1105	|	|	...	|	...	|	...	|	1904	...	|	...	|	...	|
Paris Gare de Lyon .... **341** a.	0823	0841	0919	...	1023	1119	...	1130	1241	1319	1323	...	1637	...	1823	...	2024	2041	...	2223	...	2319	...	0023

A – ①–⑤ to July 4; ⑤ July 11 - Aug. 15 (also Aug. 14); Ⓐ from Aug. 22.
D – ①–⑥ to July 5; ⑥ July 12 - Aug. 9 (also Aug. 15); ①–⑥ from Aug. 23 (not Nov. 11).
E – ⑥⑦ to Sept. 7; daily from Sept. 13.
G – ①–⑤ to Sept. 12.
H – ⑥⑦ to June 29; daily July 5 - Oct. 5; ⑥⑦ from Oct. 18.
J – To July 5 and from Aug. 25.

L – ①–⑤ to July 4 / from Oct. 6 (not Nov. 10, 11).

b – Not July 14, Nov. 11.
e – Also July 14, Nov. 11.
m – Not July 7 - Aug. 21, Nov. 11.
v – Not Aug. 15, Nov. 11.
w – Also July 14, Aug. 14, Nov. 11; not Aug. 15.

TGV – Ⓡ, supplement payable, 🍸.

⊡ – Subject to alteration Sept. 1 – 10.
⊗ – Subject to alteration on Oct. 11, 12.
△ – Not Nov. 9. Subject to alteration on Oct. 11, 12.
⊖ – Subject to alteration July 20, 27, Dec. 6, 7.
◇ – Subject to alteration July 20,27.

LYON - GRENOBLE 343

km		⚒	Ⓐ		Ⓐ		Ⓐ	Ⓐ	Ⓒ	Ⓐ				Ⓐ	Ⓒ	Ⓐ		Ⓐ		Ⓐ		Ⓐ		Ⓐ	
0	**Lyon** Part-Dieu .... **344** d.	0608	0644	0714	0744	0814	0844	0914	0914	0944	1014	1114	1214	1314	1314	1344	1414	1444	1514	1544	1614	1644	1714	1744	1814
41	Bourgoin-Jallieu ... **344** d.	0637	0713	0741	0812	0838	0915	0939	0941	1013	1038	1141	1241	1339	1342	1413	1438	1513	1540	1613	1643	1713	1740	1813	1838
56	La Tour du Pin ..... **344** d.	0648	0724	0752	0823	|	0924	0950	0951	1024	|	1152	|	1351	1352	1424	|	1524	1550	1624	|	1724	1751	1824	|
104	Voiron .... d.	0717	0753	0822	0854	0918	0955	1020	1020	1054	1118	1221	1318	1420	1421	1454	1518	1554	1619	1654	1719	1753	1820	1854	|
129	**Grenoble** .... a.	0733	0810	0837	0913	0933	1013	1036	1036	1110	1133	1236	1334	1436	1436	1510	1533	1610	1637	1710	1734	1810	1837	1910	1933

	Ⓐ	Ⓐ	Ⓒ	Ⓐ			B	⑥n 🚌	🚌	
Lyon Part-Dieu ..... **344** d.	1844	1914	1914	1944	2014	2114	2206	2206*	2314*	...
Bourgoin-Jallieu .... **344** d.	1913	1939	1941	2013	2039	2142	2235	2257	0005	...
La Tour du Pin ...... **344** d.	1924	1950	1952	2024	|	2152	2246	|	|	...
Voiron .... d.	1953	2020	2021	2053	2118	2221	2317	|	|	...
Grenoble .... a.	2010	2036	2036	2110	2133	2236	2333	0005	0110	...

	⚒	Ⓐ		Ⓐ		Ⓐ		Ⓒ	Ⓐ	Ⓐ
Grenoble .... d.	0524	0550	0627	0649	0724	0750	...	0827	0827	0850
Voiron .... d.	0541	0607	0644	0706	0741	0807	...	0844	0844	0907
La Tour du Pin .... **344** d.	0611	0637	0713	0737	0809	0837	...	|	|	0937
Bourgoin-Jallieu .... **344** d.	0622	0648	0724	0748	0819	0848	...	0921	0922	0948
Lyon Part-Dieu .... **344** a.	0646	0716	0750	0816	0846	0916	...	0946	0946	1016

	Ⓒ	Ⓐ	Ⓐ				Ⓐ		Ⓐ	Ⓒ	Ⓐ		Ⓐ	Ⓐ	Ⓒ	Ⓐ		Ⓐ		Ⓐ		🚌		Ⓑ	⑥n 🚌
Grenoble .... d.	0924	0924	0950	1027	1124	1227	1250	1324	1427	1427	1450	1524	1550	1627	1627	1647	1723	1747	1824	1850	1924	1947	2025	2124	2123
Voiron .... d.	0941	0941	1007	1044	1141	1244	1307	1341	1444	1444	1507	1541	1607	1644	1644	1706	1741	1806	1841	1907	1941	|	2042	2141	2153
La Tour du Pin ...... **344** d.	1009	1011	1037	|	1209	|	1337	1411	|	|	1537	1611	1637	|	|	1737	1811	1837	|	1937	2011	|	2112	2211	2233
Bourgoin-Jallieu .... **344** d.	1019	1022	1048	1122	1219	1322	1348	1422	1522	1522	1548	1622	1648	1722	1722	1748	1822	1848	1919	1948	2022	|	2123	2222	2248
Lyon Part-Dieu ..... **344** a.	1046	1046	1116	1146	1246	1346	1416	1446	1546	1550	1616	1646	1716	1746	1750	1816	1846	1916	1946	2016	2046	2116*	2150	2248	2335*

B – Ⓑ to Aug. 31; ⑤⑦ from Sept. 5 (also Oct. 13 – 16, Nov. 11; not Sept. 14, 21, 28, Oct. 5).

n – Not Nov. 1. * – Bus station on eastern side of station (Rue de la Villette).

Subject to alteration on ⑥⑦ Sept. 13 - Oct. 5.
Timings may vary by up to 5 minutes Sept. 15 - Oct. 28.

LYON - CHAMBÉRY 344

Certain journeys continue to / from Moutiers Salins or Bourg St Maurice (Table **366**) or Modane (Table **367**). **Subject to alteration on July 20, 27, Sept. 27, Dec. 6, 7.**

km		⚒	⚒		‡		Ⓑ	⑥		Ⓐ	Ⓒ ◇		‡	n⊡	⚒ ¶	¶	Ⓐ	¶	¶	¶	¶	Ⓐ		¶
0	**Lyon** Part Dieu .... **343** d.	0640	0732	...	0840	...	0926r	0940	...	1032t	1040	...	1140	1240	1340	1440	1540	1640	1740	1840	1940	2040	...	2140
41	Bourgoin-Jallieu .... **343** d.	0705	|	...	0905	...	|	|	...	|	1105	...	|	1305	|	1505	|	1705	|	1905	|	2105	...	|
56	La Tour du Pin .... **343** d.	0716	0809	...	0916	...	|	|	...	a	1115	...	|	1316	|	1516	|	1716	|	1916	|	2115	...	|
106	**Chambéry** .... a.	0758	0858	...	0958	...	1053	1058	...	1158	1158	...	1258	1358	1459	1558	1658	1758	1859	1958	2058	2158	...	2258

	⚒	⚒	◇	‡	Ⓐ		Ⓒ n‡	⚒ ¶	§	¶	¶	¶	¶	Ⓑ e	Ⓑ e	¶	¶							
Chambéry .... d.	0602	0702	0802	0902	0956v	...	1102	1202	1302	1402z	1502	1602	1702	1802	1902	2002	2102	...	...	...	...	...	...	...
La Tour du Pin .... **343** d.	0643	|	0844	|	1045	...	|	1245	|	1445	|	1646	|	1844	|	2045	|	...	...	...	...	...	...	...
Bourgoin-Jallieu .... **343** d.	0656	|	0856	|	1056	...	|	1256	|	1456	|	1657	|	1856	|	2056	|	...	...	...	...	...	...	...
Lyon Part Dieu .... **343** a.	0720	0820	0920	1020	1120	...	1220	1320	1420	1520	1620	1720	1820	1920	2020	2120	2220	...	...	...	...	...	...	...

a – Via Aix les Bains (Table **345**).
e – Also Nov. 1.
n – Not Nov. 1.
r – 0934 from Aug. 31.
t – 1034 from Sept. 1.

v – 1002 from Sept. 15.
z – 1401 from Sept. 30.

‡ – Subject to alteration on Sept. 14, 21, 28, Oct. 5.
¶ – Subject to alteration on Sept. 13, 20, Oct. 4.

§ – Subject to alteration on Sept. 13, 20, 28, Oct. 4.
◇ – Subject to alteration on Sept. 14, 21, Oct. 5.
⊡ – On Sept. 13, 20, Oct. 4 does not call at Bourgoin or La Tour du Pin.

Timings may vary by up to 3 minutes Sept. 14 - Oct. 28

LYON - AIX LES BAINS - ANNECY 345

SERVICE UNTIL AUGUST 29. For fast trains Lyon - Chambéry see Table **344**

km		Ⓐ	⚒△	Ⓐ	⑥	🚌 †	Ⓐ	⑥	Ⓐ	Ⓒ	🚌 Ⓐ	Ⓐ	Ⓐ△	Ⓐ	Ⓒ	Ⓐ	Ⓒ	Ⓐ△			Ⓐ	d△	ⒶJ	Ⓒ	Ⓐ	⑥⑦
0	**Lyon** Part Dieu ¶ **346** d.	...	...	0640	0701	0708	0732	0800	0840	1000	1008	1032	...	1140	1200	1340	1400	...	1600	1656	1800	...	1840	1900	2040	2100
50	Ambérieu .... **346** d.	0613	0713	|	0734	|	|	0834	|	1034	|	|	1213	|	1234	|	1434	1613	1634	1736	1834	1914	|	1934	|	2134
102	Culoz .... **346** d.	0651	0751	c	0808	|	c	|	c	|	|	|	1251	c	|	c	|	1651	|	|	|	1951	c	|	c	2205
124	Aix les Bains ...... **364** d.	0712	0812	0832	0832	0835	0925	0925	1025	1125	|	1148	1312	1325	1325	1525	1525	1712	1728	1825	1925	2012	2026	2026	2228	2228
138	**Chambéry** ...... **364** a.	0726	0825	|	|	|	|	|	|	|	|	1158	1325	|	|	|	|	1725	|	|	|	2025	|	|	|	|
163	**Annecy** .... **364** a.	...	...	0901	0901	0910	1007	1007	1107	1207	1159	...	...	1407	1407	1607	1607	...	1808	1907	2000	...	2106	2106	2300	2300

	Ⓐ△	Ⓐ	⚒	Ⓐ△		🚌 Ⓐ	⑥	🚌 †	Ⓐ	Ⓒ	🚌 Ⓐ	⚒△	🚌 Ⓐ	Ⓒ	Ⓐ	Ⓒ	Ⓐ	Ⓒ	Ⓐ	d	Ⓐ	Ⓐ△	Ⓒ	Ⓐ	🚌 Ⓐ	⑦⊙
Annecy .... **364** d.	...	0600	0653	...	0753	0900	0953	1000	1053	1153	1200	...	1300	1353	1353	1553	1553	1653	1653	...	1753	...	1853	1853	2000	2053
Chambéry .... **364** d.	0537	|	|	0737	|	|	|	|	|	|	|	1237	|	|	|	|	|	|	|	1734	|	1834	|	|	|	|
Aix les Bains .... **364** d.	0551	0642	0739	0751	0838	|	1042	1030	1133	1242	|	1251	|	1442	1437	1642	1642	1742	1729	1751	1842	1851	1942	1942	|	2144
Culoz .... **346** d.	0610	|	|	0810	|	|	|	|	c	|	|	1310	|	|	c	|	c	1759	c	1810	c	1910	|	c	|	|
Ambérieu .... **346** d.	0647	0728	0825	0847	0928	|	1127	|	|	1328	|	1347	|	1527	|	1728	|	1829	|	1847	|	1947	2028	|	|	2228
Lyon Part Dieu ¶ .**346** a.	...	0800	0905	...	1003	1052	1204	1210	1320	1400	1352	...	1452	1604	1620	1800	1820	1904	1920	...	2020	...	2105	2120	2152	2300

J – From July 15.
c – Via Chambéry.
d – Not July 20, 27.

△ – Subject to alteration on Ⓐ July 15 - Aug. 22.
⊙ – ⑦ (also July 14; not July 13). On July 14 departs Aix les Bains 2137, arrives Lyon 2314 (not calling at Ambérieu).

¶ – 🚌 services depart / arrive at bus station on eastern side of station (Rue de la Villette).

☛ Other non-stop journeys Lyon - Annecy by 🚌 on Ⓐ (journey time: 1 hr 51 m). From Lyon Part Dieu ¶ at 0608, 1308 and 1508.

346 LYON - BELLEGARDE - GENÈVE

SERVICE UNTIL AUGUST 29. Most services via Bellegarde are suspended Aug. 20 – 24 (also certain services on the morning of Aug. 25). Timings are subject to alteration Aug. 25 – 29.
WARNING! All journeys to / from Genève are subject to alteration July 15 - Aug. 24. During this period a replacement bus service operates Bellegarde - Genève (please confirm timings locally).

km																										
		⚒ △	⚒ n	🚌 △	❖	△	🚌 ❖	△	🚌 ❖	△	n	*TGV* 9750 N	△	🚌 ❖	*TGV* 9748 M	Ⓑ △	①–⑤ n¶	n	△	🚌 Ⓒ ❖	①–⑤ n	*TGV* 9754 P	† △	R △	⑤f △	🚌 ❖
0	**Lyon Perrache** .... d.	0625	...	...	...	1025	...	1224	...	1423	...	...	...	...	...	...	...	...	...	...	...	...	...	2019	...	...
4	**Lyon Part Dieu** . 345 d.	0636	...	0838	...	1038	...	1238	...	1438	...	1534	1638	...	1734	1738	...	...	1834	...	...	1929	2030	2030	2034	...
54	Ambérieu .... 345 d.	0710	...	0910	...	1111	...	1310	...	1512	...	|	1710	...	|	1812	...	...	|	...	...	|	2102	2103	2106	...
106	Culoz .... 345 d.	0743	...	0943	...	1144	...	1346	...	1544	...	|	1747	...	|	1844	...	...	1944	...	...	|	2141	2142	2141	...
139	Bellegarde 341 364 ◐ d.	0809	0836	1008	...	1211	...	1408	...	1609	1638	1654s	1809	...	1853s	1909	1918	1951	2009	...	2016	2046s	2209	2209	2209	...
	St Julien en G. ⊡.. a.	0833	|	1031	1045	1231	1240	1430	1440	1629	|	|	1829	1840	|	1930	|	|	2031	2040	|	|	2231	2231	2230	2240
172	**Genève** ... 341 364 ◐ a.	...	0916	...	1115	...	1310	...	1510	...	1716	1724	...	1910	1924	...	1957	2027	...	2110	2057	2116	...	...	...	2310

	①–⑤ n	⚒	①–⑥ n	⚒ △	🚌 † ❖	⚒ n	△	*TGV* 9752 M	🚌 ❖	△	🚌 ❖	△	*TGV* 9756 N	🚌 ❖	△	*TGV* 9744 P	n	△	🚌 Ⓒ ❖	①–⑤ n	△		⑦e △	①–⑤ n	△❖	①–⑤ n
Genève .... 341 364 ◐ d.	0502	...	0558	...	0645	0659	...	0842	0830	...	1045	...	1242	1235	...	1442	1459	...	1635	1702	...	...	...	1902	...	2016
St Julien en G. ⊡... d.	|	...	|	0630	0715	|	0730	|	0915	0932k	1120	1130	|	1315	1330	|	|	1530	1715	|	1730	...	1830	|	1930	|
Bellegarde 341 364 ◐ d.	0537	0552	0633	0657	...	0725	0756	0920u	...	0957k	...	1152	1311u	...	1351	1511u	1525	1554	...	1737	1752	...	1855	1937	1952	2051
Culoz .... 345 d.	...	0616	...	0719	...	...	0818	|	...	1022k	...	1214	|	...	1418	|	...	1623	...	...	1816	...	1925	...	2019	...
Ambérieu .... 345 d.	...	0654	...	0756	...	...	0855	|	...	1056	...	1250	|	...	1451	|	...	1656	...	...	1853	...	2002	...	2055	...
Lyon Part Dieu ... 345 a.	...	0728	...	0832	...	...	0931	1037	...	1126	...	1322	1432	...	1521	1633	...	1725	...	...	1922	...	2028	...	2126	...
Lyon Perrache .... a.	...	...	...	...	...	...	0945	...	...	1139	...	1333	...	...	...	...	...	...	...	...	...	...	...	...	2141	...

M – Until July 14. (12) Genève - Lyon - Marseille and v.v. (Table **350**).
N – (12) Genève - Marseille - Nice and v.v. (Table **350**).
P – (12) Genève - Montpellier and v.v. (Table **355**).
R – ①②③④⑥ (not July 14, Nov. 1, 11).
e – Also July 14; not July 13.
f – Not Aug. 15.

k – Aug. 25 – 29 St Julien d. 0930, Bellegarde d. 0952, Culoz d. 1020.
n – Not July 15 - Aug. 24.
s – Arrival time. Calls to set down only.
u – Calls to pick up only.
TGV – Ⓡ, supplement payable, 🍷.
⊡ – St Julien en Genevois.

❖ – Subject to confirmation.
¶ – On ⑤ Bellegarde d. 1924, Genève a. 2001.
◐ – Additional journeys (not July 15 - Aug. 24): **From Bellegarde** at 0556 ①–⑤, 0657 ⑥, 0729 ①–⑤, 1251 ①–⑤, 1719 ①–⑤, 1800 ①–⑤ and 2125 ①–⑤. **From Genève** at 1202 ①–⑤, 1602 ①–⑤ and 1802 ①–⑤. A replacement 🚌 service operates July 15 - Aug. 24.
△ – To / from Évian les Bains (Table **363**) and / or St Gervais (Table **365**).

348 LYON - ST ÉTIENNE

TGV trains (Paris) - Lyon - St Étienne

		TGV 6681 ①–⑥ b		*TGV* 6685		*TGV* 6687		*TGV* 6689	
Paris Gare de Lyon **340** ...... d.	...	0658	...	1258	...	1657	...	1856	...
Lyon Part-Dieu .... d.	...	0905	...	1505	...	1905	...	2105	...
St Étienne Châteaucreux .... a.	...	0950	...	1550	...	1950	...	2150	...

		TGV 6691 ①–⑥ b		*TGV* 6693		*TGV* 6695		*TGV* 6697	
St Étienne Châteaucreux .... d.	...	0613	...	1013	...	1212	...	1813	...
Lyon Part-Dieu .... a.	...	0659	...	1058	...	1259	...	1859	...
Paris Gare de Lyon **340** .... a.	...	0902	...	1302	...	1502	...	2102	...

Local Trains Lyon - St Étienne (see shaded boxes below)

km																									
		⚒	⚒ w	⑥ k	Ⓐ	Ⓐ'		Ⓐ		Ⓒ	Ⓐ	Ⓐ	Ⓐ		①–⑥ v	Ⓐ		⊗	Ⓐ		①–⑥ v	Ⓐ			Ⓐ
0	**Lyon** Part-Dieu .... d.	...	0624	...	...	0654	0705	...	0724	...	...	0754	...	0824	...	0854	0924	...	0954	1024	...	1054	1124	...	1154
	Lyon Perrache .... d.	0540	|	0631	0640	|	|	0710	|	0731	0740	|	0810	|	0831	|	|	0931	|	|	1031	|	|	1131	|
22	Givors Ville .... d.	0558	0642	0658	0658	0712	|	0728	0742	0758	0758	0812	0828	0842	0858	0912	0942	0958	1012	1042	1058	1112	1142	1158	1212
47	St Chamond .... d.	0617	0701	0717	0717	0731	|	0747	0801	0817	0817	0831	0847	0901	0917	0931	1001	1016	1031	1101	1117	1131	1201	1216	1231
59	**St Étienne** ⊙ .... a.	0626	0710	0726	0726	0740	0753	0756	0810	0826	0826	0840	0856	0910	0926	0940	1010	1026	1040	1110	1126	1140	1210	1226	1240

			①–⑥ v	Ⓐ			Ⓐ		①–⑥ v	Ⓐ			Ⓐ	Ⓐ		⑥	Ⓐ	Ⓐ	⚒	Ⓐ		Ⓒ	Ⓐ	Ⓐ	Ⓐ
Lyon Part-Dieu .... d.	1206	1224	...	1254	1324	...	1354	1424	...	1454	1524	...	1554	...	1624	...	...	1654	1702	...	1724	...	...	1754	...	1824
Lyon Perrache .... d.	|	|	1231	|	|	1331	|	|	1431	|	|	1531	|	1601	|	1631	1640	|	|	1710	|	1731	1740	|	1810	|
Givors Ville .... d.	|	1242	1258	1312	1342	1358	1412	1442	1458	1512	1542	1558	1612	1628	1642	1658	1658	1712	|	1728	1742	1758	1758	1812	1828	1842
St Chamond .... d.	|	1301	1317	1331	1401	1417	1431	1501	1517	1531	1601	1619	1631	1646	1701	1717	1725	1731	|	1747	1801	1817	1817	1831	1847	1901
St Étienne ⊙ .... a.	1247	1310	1326	1340	1410	1426	1440	1510	1526	1540	1610	1628	1640	1656	1710	1726	1738	1742	1746	1756	1810	1826	1826	1840	1856	1910

	⑥	Ⓐ	Ⓐ	Ⓐ		Ⓐ		①–⑥ v	Ⓑ h⊠	⊠¶	Ⓑh ⊠‡
Lyon Part-Dieu .... d.	...	...	1854	...	1924	...	1954	2024	...	2124	2224	2324
Lyon Perrache .... d.	1831	1840	|	1910	|	1931	|	|	2031	|	|	|
Givors Ville .... d.	1858	1858	1912	1928	1942	1958	2012	2042	2058	2142	2244	2344
St Chamond .... d.	1917	1917	1931	1947	2001	2017	2031	2101	2117	2201	2302	0002
St Étienne ⊙ .... a.	1926	1926	1940	1956	2010	2026	2040	2110	2126	2210	2311	0011

	Ⓐ	Ⓐ ◇	⚒	Ⓐ	Ⓐ	Ⓐ		Ⓐ	⑥ k	Ⓐ
St Étienne ⊙ .... d.	0520	0534	0550	0604	0620	0634	0650	0704	0704	0713
St Chamond .... d.	0530	0543	0559	0613	0630	0643	0659	0713	0713	|
Givors Ville .... d.	0548	0602	0618	0632	0648	0702	0718	0732	0732	|
Lyon Perrache .... a.	|	0627	|	0657	|	0720	|	0750	0757	|
Lyon Part-Dieu ...... a.	0606	...	0636	...	0706	...	0736	...	...	0754

	Ⓐ	Ⓐ			⚒	Ⓐ	Ⓐ		①–⑥ v	Ⓐ			Ⓐ		①–⑥ v	Ⓐ			Ⓐ		①–⑥ v	Ⓐ				Ⓐ
St Étienne ⊙ .... d.	0720	0734	0750	0804	0813	0820	0834	0850	0904	0920	0950	1004	1020	1050	1104	1120	1150	1204	1220	1250	1304	1320	1350	1404	1413	1420
St Chamond .... d.	0730	0743	0759	0813	|	0829	0844	0859	0913	0930	0959	1013	1030	1059	1113	1130	1159	1213	1230	1259	1313	1330	1359	1413	|	1430
Givors Ville .... d.	0748	0802	0818	0832	|	0848	0902	0918	0932	0948	1018	1032	1048	1118	1132	1148	1218	1232	1248	1318	1332	1348	1418	1432	|	1448
Lyon Perrache .... a.	|	0820	|	0850r	|	|	0927	|	0957	|	|	1057	|	|	1157	|	|	1257	|	|	1357	|	|	1457	|	|
Lyon Part-Dieu .... a.	0806	...	0836	...	0854	0906	...	0936	...	1006	1036	...	1106	1136	...	1206	1236	...	1306	1336	...	1406	1436	...	1454	1508

		①–⑥ v	Ⓐ			Ⓐ	Ⓐ		Ⓐ	⑥	Ⓐ	Ⓐ		Ⓐ	Ⓒ	Ⓐ	Ⓐ		Ⓐ	⑥	Ⓑ q	Ⓐ			Ⓑ	⊠‡
St Étienne ⊙ .... d.	1450	1504	1520	1550	1604	1620	1634	1650	1704	1704	1720	1734	1750	1804	1804	1820	1834	1850	1904	1904	1913	1920	2004	2020	2120	2250
St Chamond .... d.	1459	1513	1530	1600	1613	1630	1643	1700	1713	1713	1730	1743	1800	1813	1813	1830	1843	1900	1913	1913	|	1930	2013	2030	2129	2259
Givors Ville .... d.	1518	1532	1548	1618	1632	1648	1702	1718	1732	1732	1748	1802	1818	1832	1832	1848	1902	1918	1932	1932	|	1948	2032	2048	2148	2318
Lyon Perrache .... a.	|	1557	|	|	1657	|	1720	|	1750	1757	|	1820	|	1850	1857	|	1920	|	1950	1957	|	|	2057	|	|	|
Lyon Part-Dieu .... a.	1536	...	1606	1636	...	1706	...	1736	...	...	1806	...	1836	...	...	1906	...	1936	...	...	2004z	2006	...	2106	2206	2336

b – Not July 14, Nov. 11.
h – Not Aug. 15.
k – Not Nov. 1.
q – Also Nov. 1.
r – 0857 on Ⓒ.

v – Not July 14, Aug. 15, Nov. 11.
w – Not Sept. 23, Oct. 7.
z – 1954 from Aug. 31.
TGV – Ⓡ, supplement payable, 🍷.
⊙ – St Étienne Châteaucreux.

⊗ – Subject to alteration on ①–⑤ Sept. 15 - Oct. 10.
◇ – Subject to alteration Sept. 29 - Oct. 10.
⊠ – Subject to alteration on Ⓐ until Aug. 29.
¶ – By 🚌 on Sept. 28, Oct. 5.
‡ – By 🚌 on Sept. 28, Oct. 5, 19, Nov. 16.

Timings may vary by up to 4 minutes until Aug. 30.

Subject to alteration on June 15, Aug. 13 – 17, Nov. 16, 22, 23, 29, 30.

349 ST ÉTIENNE - LE PUY

SERVICE UNTIL AUGUST 30

km																								
		Ⓐ 🚌		🚌			🚌		†	† 🚌	⑥ 🚌	Ⓐ	Ⓐ 🚌	Ⓐ	Ⓐ 🚌	†	⚒	Ⓐ 🚌	Ⓒ 🚌	Ⓐ	Ⓐ 🚌		🚌	⑤⑦j 🚌
	Lyon Part Dieu **348** .... d.	...	...	...	...	1206	...	...	...	...	...	...	...	...	...	...	1702	...	...	1740p	...	1931p	...	...
0	**St Étienne** Châteaucreux ..... d.	0508	...	1002	...	1252	...	...	1553	...	1600	1615	...	1719	...	1748	1750	...	...	1830	...	2031	...	2200
15	Firminy .... d.	0533	...	1027	...	1309	1319	...	1609	1618	1625	1637	1647	1744	1754	1805	1805	1817	1816	1851	1901	2051	2101	2225
88	**Le Puy en Velay** .... a.	0737	...	1229	...	...	1521	...	...	1815	1822	...	1844	...	1859	...	...	1922	2013	...	2058	...	2258	0023

	Ⓐ 🚌	Ⓐ 🚌	Ⓐ	⚒ 🚌	⚒	Ⓐ 🚌	Ⓐ		🚌		🚌			⑤⑦j 🚌	†	Ⓐ	Ⓐ 🚌	Ⓐ	† 🚌	Ⓑ	🚌		⑦e 🚌	†
Le Puy en Velay .... d.	0408	0553	...	0640	...	0645	...	...	0953	...	1145	...	...	1608	...	...	1611	...	1611	...	1724	...	1840	...
Firminy .... d.	0538	0658	0708	0745	0755	0847	0857	...	1128	1138	1344	1354	...	1713	1723	1738	1808	1818	1808	1854	1928	1938	2042	2052
St Étienne Châteaucreux ...... a.	0603	...	0729	...	0810	...	0913	...	...	1159	...	1410	...	...	1739	1759	...	1839	1833	1911	...	1959	...	2107
Lyon Part Dieu **348** .... a.	...	...	0820p	...	0858	...	...	...	...	1257p	...	1454	...	...	...	1850p	...	...	...	2004	...	2057p	...	...

e – Also July 14, Aug. 15; not July 13.
j – Also July 14, Aug. 14; not July 13, Aug. 15.

p – Lyon **Perrache**.

Subject to alteration on June 15, Aug. 13 – 17.

For *TGV* trains Paris - Valence Ville - Avignon Centre see Table **351**. Certain Paris - Toulon trains continue to Hyères (Table **350b**).

Services to Toulon and Nice are subject to alteration / cancellation on Sept. 6, 7, Nov. 8, 9, 10. Services via Lyon Part Dieu are subject to alteration on ⑥⑦ Sept. 13 - Oct. 19.

km	All *TGV* trains are 🅁	*TGV* 6807 ① g		*TGV* 6805 ①–⑤ A	*TGV* 6805 ⑥⑦ x	*TGV* 6101 Ⓐ	*TGV* 6801	*TGV* 6171 K	*TGV* 6103 n	*TGV* 6103 D	*TGV* 6835 ①–⑤ J	*TGV* 5102	*TGV* 6161		*TGV* 6833 ⑥⑦ m	*TGV* 6105 L	*TGV* 6173	*TGV* 9810	*TGV* 5110	*TGV* 6107	*TGV* 9752 C	*TGV* 6820	*TGV* 6842 B
	Brussels Midi **11** d.	...	...	...	...	...	...	...	...	...	...	...	...	...	...	...	...	0710	...	...	...	...	...
	Lille Europe **11** d.	...	...	...	...	...	...	...	...	...	...	0537t	...	...	...	...	...	|	0654f	...	...	...	...
	Charles de Gaulle ✈ **11** d.	...	...	...	...	...	...	...	...	...	...	0658	...	...	...	...	...	0831	0831	...	...	...	...
	Marne la Vallée-Chessy § **11** d.	...	...	...	...	...	...	...	...	...	...	0711	...	...	...	...	...	0843	0843	...	...	...	...
0	**Paris** Gare de Lyon ▶ d.	...	...	...	...	0619	...	0649	0711	0719	...	|	0745	...	...	0837	0849	|	|	0907	...	...	...
	Strasbourg **379** d.	...	...	...	...	|	...	|	|	|	0535v	|	|	...	0617k	|	|	|	|	|	...	...	...
	Metz **379** d.	...	...	...	...	|	...	|	|	|	|	|	|	...	|	|	|	|	|	|	...	0606r	...
	Dijon **379** d.	...	...	...	...	|	0608	|	|	|	|	|	|	...	|	|	|	|	|	|	...	0922	0922
	Genève **346** d.	...	...	...	...	|	|	|	|	|	|	|	|	...	|	|	|	|	|	|	0842	|	|
•	**Lyon** Part Dieu ▶ d.	0048p	...	0636	0702j	|	0807	|	|	|	0858	0906	|	...	1006	|	|	1036	1036	|	1050	1106	1106
	Lyon St Exupéry ✈ ▶ d.	|	...	|	|	|	|	|	|	|	|	|	|	...	|	|	|	|	|	|	|	|	|
527	Valence TGV ▶ d.	|	...	0713	|	|	0844	|	|	|	|	|	|	...	|	|	|	1113	1113	|	|	|	|
657	**Avignon** TGV d.	|	...	0748	0814	0901	|	0931	0950	0959	|	1011	|	...	1111	1119	1130	1147	1147	1154	1202	1211	1211
731	Aix en Provence TGV d.	|	...	0811	0836	0924	0937	|	1012	1021	1024	1034	1047	...	1135	1142	|	|	|	1217	1225	|	|
750	**Marseille** St Charles a.	|	...	0823	0850	0935	0950	|	1024	1034	1036	1046	|	...	1148	1154	|	1216	1216	1228	1236	1247	1247
750	**Marseille** St Charles **360** d.	|	...	0831	0858	...	...	|	...	...	...	...	|	...	...	...	|	...	...	...	...	1300	...
817	**Toulon** **360** a.	0547	...	0918	0942	...	...	1039	...	...	...	...	1140	...	...	...	|	...	...	...	...	1344	...
885	Les Arcs-Draguignan **360** a.	0621	...	0952	1017	...	...	|	...	...	...	...	|	...	...	...	1312	...	...	...	...	|	...
911	St Raphaël-Valescure **360** a.	0636	...	1008	1033	...	...	1128	...	...	...	...	1228	...	...	...	1328	...	...	...	...	1435	...
944	**Cannes** **360** a.	0700	...	1032	1058	...	...	1154	...	...	...	...	1254	...	...	...	1354	...	...	...	...	1504	...
955	Antibes **360** a.	0713	...	1043	1108	...	...	1206	...	...	...	...	1306	...	...	...	1406	...	...	...	...	1514	...
975	**Nice** **360** a.	0735	...	1103	1129	...	...	1226	...	...	...	...	1326	...	...	...	1426	...	...	...	...	1535	...

	TGV 5312 N	*TGV* 9801	*TGV* 6109	*TGV* 6175	*TGV* 5316 Ⓐ H	*TGV* 5316 ⑥⑦ ♥H	*TGV* 6111		*TGV* 6189 K	*TGV* 9826	*TGV* 5164	*TGV* 6113	*TGV* 6177		*TGV* 9756		*TGV* 6837	*TGV* 6115 w	*TGV* 9828	*TGV* 6145	*TGV* 6179 G	*TGV* 9828	*TGV* 6117
Brussels Midi **11** d.	...	0817	...	...	...	...	...	...	...	1031	...	...	...	...	...	...	...	...	1217	...	...	...	...
Lille Europe **11** d.	...	0902	...	...	...	...	...	...	...	|	1043	...	...	...	...	...	...	...	1303	...	...	...	...
Charles de Gaulle ✈ **11** d.	...	0958	...	...	...	...	...	...	...	1158	1158	...	...	...	...	...	...	...	1358	...	...	...	...
Marne la Vallée-Chessy § **11** d.	...	1011	...	...	...	...	...	...	...	1211	1211	...	...	...	...	...	...	...	1411	...	...	...	...
Paris Gare de Lyon ▶ d.	...	|	1037	1049	...	...	1107	...	1141	|	|	1237	1249	...	...	...	...	1419	|	1437	1449	...	1507
Strasbourg **379** d.	...	|	|	|	...	...	|	...	|	|	|	|	|	...	...	...	1105	|	|	|	|	...	|
Metz **379** d.	...	|	|	|	...	...	|	...	|	|	|	|	|	...	...	...	|	|	|	|	|	...	|
Dijon **379** d.	...	|	|	|	...	...	|	...	|	|	|	|	|	...	...	...	|	|	|	|	|	...	|
Genève **346** d.	...	|	|	|	...	...	|	...	|	|	|	|	|	...	1242b	...	|	|	|	|	|	...	|
Lyon Part Dieu ▶ d.	1136	1210	|	|	1236	1236	|	...	|	1406	1406	|	|	...	1436	...	1536	|	1606	|	|	...	|
Lyon St Exupéry ✈ ▶ d.	|	|	|	|	|	|	|	...	|	|	|	|	|	...	|	...	|	|	|	|	|	...	|
Valence TGV ▶ d.	|	|	|	|	1313	|	|	...	|	1443	1443	|	|	...	1513	...	1614	|	|	|	|	...	|
Avignon TGV d.	1241	1313	1320	1330	1347	1341	1352	...	1427	|	|	|	1530	...	1548	...	1649	|	1710	1719	1729	...	1749
Aix en Provence TGV d.	1304	1336	1344	|	|	1404	1414	...	|	1534	1534	1542	|	...	|	...	|	|	1734	1742	|	...	1813
Marseille St Charles a.	1316	1349	1358	|	1416	1416	1426	...	|	1546	1546	1554	|	...	1619	...	1716	1724	1746	1754	|	←	1824
Marseille St Charles **360** d.	...	1404	...	|	...	...	...	...	|	...	...	...	|	...	1631	...	...	...	1801	...	|	1801	...
Toulon **360** a.	...	1502	...	1439	...	...	...	...	|	...	...	...	1639	...	1716	...	...	...	→	...	1839	1844	...
Les Arcs-Draguignan **360** a.	...	...	...	1516	...	...	...	...	1612	...	...	...	|	...	|	...	...	...	...	...	|	1921	...
St Raphaël-Valescure **360** a.	...	...	...	|	...	...	...	...	1628	...	...	...	1728	...	1806	...	...	...	...	...	1928	1937	...
Cannes **360** a.	...	...	...	1554	...	...	...	...	1654	...	...	...	1754	...	1832	...	...	...	...	...	1954	2002	...
Antibes **360** a.	...	...	...	1606	...	...	...	...	1706	...	...	...	1805	...	1843	...	...	...	...	...	2005	2013	...
Nice **360** a.	...	...	...	1626	...	...	...	...	1733	...	...	...	1826	...	1905	...	...	...	...	...	2029	2033	...

	TGV 5322 ⊙N	*TGV* 6119 Ⓑ	*TGV* 6815	*TGV* 6121 Ⓑ d	*TGV* 6181	*TGV* 6815	*TGV* 6123	*TGV* 5134	*TGV* 6183	*TGV* 6183 ⑤–⑦ z		*TGV* 6127	*TGV* 9580 ♣	*TGV* 6187 ⑤ w	*TGV* 5346 R	*TGV* 6129	*TGV* 6822 e	*TGV* 6827		*TGV* 5124	*TGV* 6131		*TGV* 6137 ⑤⑦
Brussels Midi **11** d.	...	...	...	...	...	...	...	...	...	...	...	...	...	...	...	...	...	...	...	...	...	...	...
Lille Europe **11** d.	...	...	...	...	...	...	...	1554	...	...	...	...	...	...	...	...	...	...	...	1826	...	...	...
Charles de Gaulle ✈ **11** d.	...	...	...	...	...	...	...	1658	...	...	...	...	...	...	...	...	...	...	...	1928	...	...	...
Marne la Vallée-Chessy § **11** d.	...	...	...	...	...	...	...	1711	...	...	...	...	...	...	...	...	...	...	...	1941	...	...	...
Paris Gare de Lyon ▶ d.	...	1619	...	1637	1649	...	1707	|	1745	1745	...	1819	...	1847	...	1907	...	...	...	|	2019	...	2107
Strasbourg **379** d.	...	|	...	|	|	...	|	|	|	|	...	|	1615	|	...	|	...	1703	...	|	|	...	|
Metz **379** d.	...	|	...	|	|	...	|	|	|	|	...	|	|	|	...	|	1601	|	...	|	|	...	|
Dijon **379** d.	...	|	1621y	|	|	...	|	|	|	|	...	|	|	|	...	|	1920	1920	...	|	|	...	|
Genève **346** d.	...	|	|	|	|	...	|	|	|	|	...	|	|	|	...	|	|	|	...	|	|	...	|
Lyon Part Dieu ▶ d.	1736	|	1806	|	|	...	|	1906	|	|	...	|	2006	|	2036	|	2104	2104	...	2136	|	...	|
Lyon St Exupéry ✈ ▶ d.	|	|	|	|	|	...	|	|	|	|	...	|	|	|	|	|	|	|	...	|	|	...	|
Valence TGV ▶ d.	1814	|	|	1852	|	...	|	|	|	|	...	|	|	|	2113	|	2143	2143	...	|	|	...	|
Avignon TGV d.	1848	|	1911	|	1931	...	1949	2011	|	|	...	2101	2111	2131	2148	2154	2217	2217	...	2241	2302	...	2354
Aix en Provence TGV d.	|	|	1935	1942	|	...	2013	2034	2045	2045	...	|	2134	|	|	2217	|	|	...	2304	2325	...	0017
Marseille St Charles a.	1918	1924	1947	1954	|	←	2024	2046	|	|	...	2129	2146	|	2216	2229	2247	2247	...	2316	2337	...	0029
Marseille St Charles **360** d.	...	...	2001	...	|	2001	...	...	|	|	...	...	...	|	...	2236	...	...	...	...	...	...	...
Toulon **360** a.	...	...	→	...	2039	2045	...	...	2139	2139	...	...	...	2240	...	2323	...	...	...	...	...	...	...
Les Arcs-Draguignan **360** a.	...	...	...	...	2115	2119	...	...	...	|	...	...	...	|	...	...	...	...	...	...	...	...	...
St Raphaël-Valescure **360** a.	...	...	...	...	|	2137	...	...	...	2228	...	...	...	2328	...	...	...	...	...	...	...	...	...
Cannes **360** a.	...	...	...	...	2154	2201	...	...	...	2254	...	...	...	2354	...	...	...	...	...	...	...	...	...
Antibes **360** a.	...	...	...	...	2206	2213	...	...	...	2305	...	...	...	0005	...	...	...	...	...	...	...	...	...
Nice **360** a.	...	...	...	...	2226	2233	...	...	...	2326	...	...	...	0026	...	...	...	...	...	...	...	...	...

– ①–⑤ (also Sept. 6, 7, Nov. 8, 9). Terminates at Marseille June 16–27, Sept. 1–12, 15–19, Oct. 13–31, Nov. 8–10. Departs Lyon 0634 Sept. 22 - Oct. 10.
– From Basel (Table **379**).
– Until July 14.
– June 16–20 only.
– Daily to Sept. 14; ⑤⑥ from Sept. 19.
– 🚃12 Le Havre - Rouen - Lyon - Marseille (Table **335**).
– ①–⑤ to July 4 / from Aug. 25 (not Sept. 1).
– July 6 - Aug. 24.
– Daily to Aug. 30; ①–⑥ from Sept. 1.
– From Nantes via Massy TGV (Table **335**).
– From Rennes via Massy TGV (Table **335**).

– 1130 July 15 - Aug. 24 (by 🚌 Genève - Bellegarde July 15 - Aug. 19 / Genève - Ambérieu Aug. 20–24).
– Ⓑ (daily July 6 - Aug. 29).
– Not Aug. 15, 16, Oct. 12, 19, 26, Nov. 2, 9.
Lille **Flandres**.
– Also July 15; not July 14, Aug. 18, Sept. 29, Oct. 6, 20, Nov. 10.
0700 on Sept. 20, Oct. 4, 11, 12, 18, 19, 25, 26.
– 0609 on June 15; 0616 Sept. 13 - Oct. 26.
– ⑥⑦ (daily July 5 - Aug. 24; not June 21–29, Sept. 14).
– Not June 16–20.

p – Lyon **Perrache**.
r – Not Aug. 15, 16, 17.
t – 0528 on Oct. 4, 5, 6, 11, 12, 13.
v – 0519 until June 20; 4–5 minutes earlier from Sept. 2 - Nov. 28.
w – Not Aug. 15.
x – Not Sept. 27, 28. Arrivals Toulon - Antibes are 3–5 minutes later from Nov. 15.
y – 1619 Nov. 8–29.
z – Also July 14, Aug. 14, Nov. 11.

TGV – 🅁, supplement payable, 🍸.

♣ – From Frankfurt (Main), Table **47**.
♥ – Subject to alteration on July 19, Sept. 6, 7.
⊙ – Subject to alteration on Nov. 22, Dec. 13.
▶ – For Paris to Lyon see Table **340** (for Paris to St Exupéry ✈ see Table **342**).
For additional trains from Paris and Lyon to Valence TGV see Table **355**.
For Lyon to Valence Ville see Table **351**.
• – Distance Lyon Part Dieu - Valence TGV = *104 km*.
§ – Station for Disneyland Paris.

Additional low-cost 'Ouigo' TGV trains run from Marne la Vallée-Chessy – see Table ***350a***

Timings may vary by 1–2 minutes on certain dates (please check your reservation)

350 NICE - TOULON - MARSEILLE - AVIGNON - LYON / PARIS *TGV Méditerranée*

For *TGV* trains Avignon Centre - Valence Ville - Paris see Table **351**. Certain Toulon - Paris trains start from Hyères (Table **350b**).

Services from Nice and Toulon are subject to alteration / cancellation on Sept. 6, 7, Nov. 8, 9, 10. Services via Lyon Part Dieu are subject to alteration on ⑥⑦ Sept. 13 - Oct. 19.

All *TGV* trains are [R]	*TGV* 6102	*TGV* 6150	*TGV* 6136	*TGV* 6136	*TGV* 6866	*TGV* 9854		*TGV* 5144*	*TGV* 6106	*TGV* 6106	*TGV* 9582	*TGV* 9582	*TGV* 6108	*TGV* 5350	*TGV* 9860	*TGV* 6112		*TGV* 6852	*TGV* 6172	*TGV* 6852	*TGV* 6114	*TGV* 6116	*TGV* 6116
	①–⑤	Ⓐ	S	⑦						⑥	J	U	①–⑥										© D
				e	v					t	♣	♣	p	R				w		w			
Nice 360 d.	...	...	...	...	...	...	...	...	...	...	...	...	...	...	...	...	...	0725	0734	...	...	...	...
Antibes 360 d.	...	...	...	...	...	...	...	...	...	...	...	...	...	...	...	...	...	0744	0754	...	...	...	...
Cannes 360 d.	...	...	...	...	...	...	...	...	...	...	...	...	...	...	...	...	...	0755	0805	...	...	...	...
St Raphaël-Valescure 360 d.	...	...	...	...	...	...	...	...	...	...	...	...	...	...	...	...	...	0820	|	...	...	...	...
Les Arcs-Draguignan 360 d.	...	...	...	...	...	...	...	...	...	...	...	...	...	...	...	...	...	|	0844	...	...	...	...
Toulon 360 d.	...	0504	...	0513c	...	...	...	...	...	0640	...	...	0740	...	0813	...	...	0914	0921	...	...	...	1037
Marseille St Charles 360 a.	...	|	...	0559	...	...	...	...	...	0729	...	...	0829	...	0901	...	...	0958	|	←	...	...	1120
Marseille St Charles d.	0536	|	0606	0606	0614	0644	...	0714	0736	0736	0759	0814	0836	0846	0912	0936	...	1008	|	1008	1036	1131	1131
Aix en Provence TGV d.	0551	0600	0621	0621	0629	|	...	0730	0751	0751	0813	0829	|	|	0926	0951	...	→	1015	1025	|	1151	1151
Avignon TGV d.	0614	0623	0643	0643	|	0716	...	|	0814	0814	0839	0851	|	0916	0948	1014	...	...	|	|	|	1214	1214
Valence TGV ▶ d.	|	0657	|	|	0720	0749	...	|	|	|	|	|	|	0949	|	|	...	...	|	1118	|	|	|
Lyon St Exupéry ✈ ▶ d.	|	|	|	|	|	|	...	|	|	|	|	|	|	|	|	|	...	...	|	|	|	|	|
Lyon Part Dieu ▶ a.	|	|	|	|	0756	0824	...	0850	|	|	0950	0954	|	1025	1050	|	...	...	|	1154	|	|	|
Genève **346** a.	|	|	|	|	|	|	...	|	|	|	|	|	|	...	|	|	...	...	|	...	|	|	|
Dijon **379** a.	|	|	|	|	0943	|	...	|	|	|	|	|	|	...	|	|	...	...	|	...	|	|	|
Metz **379** a.	|	|	|	|	1253y	|	...	|	|	|	|	|	|	...	|	|	...	...	|	...	|	|	|
Strasbourg **379** a.	|	|	|	|	...	|	...	|	|	|	1343	1343	|	...	|	|	...	...	|	...	|	|	|
Paris Gare de Lyon ▶ a.	0853	0911	0923	0923	...	|	...	|	1053	1053	...	...	1141	...	|	1253	...	...	1310	...	1341	1453	1453
Marne la Vallée-Chessy § **11** a.	...	...	...	...	...	1018	...	1048	...	...	...	...	...	...	1248	...	...	...	...	...	...	...	...
Charles de Gaulle ✈ **11** a.	...	...	...	...	...	1032	...	1102	...	...	...	...	...	...	1302	...	...	...	...	...	...	...	...
Lille Europe **11** a.	...	...	...	...	...	1138	...	1157	...	...	...	...	...	...	|	...	...	...	...	...	...	...	...
Brussels Midi **11** a.	...	...	...	...	...	1226	...	...	...	...	...	...	...	...	1420	...	...	...	...	...	...	...	...

	TGV 9866	*TGV* 6174	*TGV* 9866	*TGV* 9866	*TGV* 5368	*TGV* 6874	*TGV* 6188	*TGV* 6118	*TGV* 9750	*TGV* 6176	*TGV* 5192	*TGV* 6872	*TGV* 6120	*TGV* 5372	*TGV* 6864	*TGV* 6885	*TGV* 6170	*TGV* 6864	*TGV* 6885	*TGV* 6122	*TGV* 5376	*TGV* 9748	*TGV* 6178
													②–④										
	M	M	M		N		K		△			❖	A	N	E	E B	L	F	F B		♥ H	C	G
Nice 360 d.	0927	0934	...	...	...	...	1034	...	1057	1132	...	...	...	...	1204	...	1234	1232	...	...	...	...	1334
Antibes 360 d.	0946	0954	...	...	...	...	1054	...	1116	1151	...	...	...	...	1230	...	1255	1253	...	...	...	...	1354
Cannes 360 d.	0958	1006	...	...	...	...	1106	...	1127	1203	...	...	...	...	1245	...	1306	1304	...	...	...	...	1406
St Raphaël-Valescure 360 d.	1023	1031	...	...	...	...	1131	...	1153	1229	...	...	...	...	1315	...	1331	1330	...	...	...	...	1431
Les Arcs-Draguignan 360 d.	1039	|	...	...	...	...	|	...	|	|	...	...	...	...	|	...	|	|	...	...	...	...	1447
Toulon 360 d.	1115	1121	...	...	...	...	1219	...	1246	1319	...	...	...	...	1408	...	1419	1419	...	...	...	...	|
Marseille St Charles 360 a.	1159	|	←	...	...	...	|	...	1331	|	...	...	...	...	1505j	...	|	1505	...	...	...	...	|
Marseille St Charles d.	1214	|	1214	1214	1242	1242	|	1336	1345	|	1414	1414	1436	1444	1514	1514	|	1519	1519	1536	1544	1544	|
Aix en Provence TGV d.	→	|	|	|	1257	1257	|	1351	1400	1415	1429	1429	|	1459	1529	1529	|	|	|	|	|	|	|
Avignon TGV d.	...	1231	1245	1245	1320	1320	1331	1414	1422	|	1451	1451	|	1521	1552	1552	1533	1552	1552	1608	1614	1614	1632
Valence TGV ▶ d.	...	|	1320	1320	|	|	|	|	|	|	|	|	|	|	|	|	|	|	|	|	1649	1649	|
Lyon St Exupéry ✈ ▶ d.	...	|	|	|	|	|	|	|	|	|	|	|	|	|	|	|	|	|	|	|	|	|	|
Lyon Part Dieu ▶ a.	...	|	1354	1354	1424	1424	|	|	1524	|	1554	1554	|	1624	1700	1700	|	1700	1700	|	1724	1724	|
Genève **346** a.	...	|	|	|	...	|	|	|	1716b	|	|	|	|	...	|	|	|	|	|	|	...	1924	|
Dijon **379** a.	...	|	|	|	...	|	|	|	...	|	|	1738	|	...	1838	1838	|	1838	1838	|	...	...	|
Metz **379** a.	...	|	|	|	...	|	|	|	...	|	|	|	|	...	2211r	...	|	2153‡	...	|	...	...	|
Strasbourg **379** a.	...	|	|	|	...	1858	|	|	...	|	|	1944	|	...	...	...	|	...	...	|	...	...	|
Paris Gare de Lyon ▶ a.	...	1511	|	|	...	...	1615	1653	...	1711	|	...	1741	...	...	...	1818	...	...	1853	...	...	1911
Marne la Vallée-Chessy § **11** a.	...	...	1550	1550	...	...	...	...	...	...	1749	...	...	...	...	...	...	...	...	...	...	...	...
Charles de Gaulle ✈ **11** a.	...	...	1603	1603	...	...	...	...	...	...	1801	...	...	...	...	...	...	...	...	...	...	...	...
Lille Europe **11** a.	...	...	1657	1657	...	...	...	...	...	...	1944f	...	...	...	...	...	...	...	...	...	...	...	...
Brussels Midi **11** a.	...	...	1743	1743	...	...	...	...	...	...	...	...	...	...	...	...	...	...	...	...	...	...	...

	TGV 6124	*TGV* 6126	*TGV* 6156	*TGV* 5182	*TGV* 6128	*TGV* 6184	*TGV* 6130	*TGV* 5180*	*TGV* 6870	*TGV* 6138		*TGV* 6168	*TGV* 5194	*TGV* 6132	*TGV* 6850	*TGV* 6876	*TGV* 6180	*TGV* 6134	*TGV* 6876	*TGV* 6140		*TGV* 6186	*TGV* 6144
										Ⓑ		•	⑦		⑤⑦					⑤⑦		⑦	⑦
		Y								d			T					Z					
Nice 360 d.	...	...	...	...	...	1534	...	...	...	...	...	1634	...	...	...	1727	1734	...	...	...	...	1831	...
Antibes 360 d.	...	...	...	...	...	1554	...	...	...	...	...	1654	...	...	...	1746	1754	...	...	...	...	1854	...
Cannes 360 d.	...	...	...	...	...	1606	...	...	...	...	...	1706	...	...	...	1756	1806	...	...	...	...	1906	...
St Raphaël-Valescure 360 d.	...	...	...	...	...	1632	...	...	...	...	...	1731	...	...	...	1821	|	...	...	...	...	1931	...
Les Arcs-Draguignan 360 d.	...	...	...	...	...	|	...	...	...	...	...	1747	...	...	...	1838	1844	...	...	...	...	|	...
Toulon 360 d.	...	...	1618	...	...	1721	...	...	...	...	...	|	...	...	...	1915	1920	...	...	...	...	2020	...
Marseille St Charles 360 a.	...	...	|	...	...	|	...	...	...	...	...	|	...	...	...	1959	|	...	←	...	...	|	...
Marseille St Charles d.	1606	1636	|	1714	1736	|	1806	1814	1823	1836	...	|	1914	1936	1943	2014	|	2006	2014	2030	...	|	214
Aix en Provence TGV d.	1621	|	1715	1729	1751	|	1821	1829	1838	|	...	|	1931	1951	1959	→	|	2020	2029	|	...	2115	215
Avignon TGV d.	1644	|	|	1751	1814	1833	|	1851	|	|	...	1931	1953	2013	|	...	2031	|	2053	2101	...	|	221
Valence TGV ▶ d.	|	|	|	|	|	|	1910	|	|	|	...	|	|	|	2051	...	|	2110	|	|	...	|	|
Lyon St Exupéry ✈ ▶ d.	|	|	|	|	|	|	|	|	|	|	...	|	|	|	|	...	|	|	|	|	...	|	|
Lyon Part Dieu ▶ a.	|	|	|	1854	|	|	|	1956	2000	|	...	|	2054	|	2128	...	|	|	2158h	|	...	|	|
Genève **346** a.	|	|	|	|	|	|	|	|	|	|	...	|	|	|	...	...	|	|	|	|	...	|	|
Dijon **379** a.	|	|	|	|	|	|	|	|	|	|	...	|	|	|	...	...	|	|	2344x	|	...	|	|
Metz **379** a.	|	|	|	|	|	|	|	|	|	|	...	|	|	|	...	...	|	|	...	|	...	|	|
Strasbourg **379** a.	|	|	|	|	|	|	|	|	2326q	|	...	|	|	|	...	...	|	|	...	|	...	|	|
Paris Gare de Lyon ▶ a.	1923	1941	2015	|	2053	2111	2123	|	...	2141	...	2215	|	2253	...	...	2315	2323	...	2341	...	0015	005
Marne la Vallée-Chessy § **11** a.	...	...	...	2048	...	...	...	2148	...	...	...	...	2249	...	...	...	...	...	...	...	...	...	...
Charles de Gaulle ✈ **11** a.	...	...	...	2101	...	...	...	2202	...	...	...	...	2303	...	...	...	...	...	...	...	...	...	...
Lille Europe **11** a.	...	...	...	2157g	...	...	...	2304k	...	...	...	...	0004n	...	...	...	...	...	...	...	...	...	...
Brussels Midi **11** a.	...	...	...	...	...	...	...	...	...	...	...	...	...	...	...	...	...	...	...	...	...	...	...

A – ②–④ (also Nov. 10; not July 15, Aug. 14, Nov. 11, 12).
B – To Basel (Table **379**).
C – Until July 14.
D – © (daily July 5 - Aug. 24).
E – Daily to Sept. 5 (not June 15, 21, 22); ①–⑤ Sept. 8–19, Oct. 13–31. Subject to alteration on Aug. 2, 3, 9, 10, 15, 16.
F – ⑥⑦ to June 22; daily from Sept. 13 (not Sept. 15–19, Oct. 13–17, 20–24, 27–31). Subject to alteration on Sept. 13, 29.
G – Daily to Sept. 14; ⑥⑦ from Sept. 20 (also Nov. 11).
H – (12) Marseille - Lyon - Rouen - Le Havre (Table **335**).
J – Until June 20.
K – July 6 - Aug. 24.
L – ①–⑤ June 16–27; daily July 6 - Aug. 24; ①–⑤ Sept. 1–19; ①–⑤ Oct. 13–31.
M – ⑥⑦ to June 22; daily June 28 - Aug. 31, Sept. 20 - Oct. 12 and from Nov. 1 (also Sept. 13, 14, Oct. 18, 19, 25, 26).
N – To Nantes via Massy TGV (Table **335**).
R – To Rennes via Massy TGV (Table **335**).
S – ①②③④⑦ (not Aug. 14).
T – ⑦ to Aug. 24 (also July 14).
U – From June 21.
Y – ①⑤⑦ (not Aug. 15, Nov. 10).
Z – Daily to July 6; ⑤⑦ July 11 - Aug. 22; daily from Aug. 24.

b – 1816 July 15 - Aug. 24 (by 🚌 Bellegarde - Genève July 15 - Aug. 19 / Ambérieu - Genève Aug. 20–24).
c – 0516 from Nov. 16.
d – Ⓑ (daily July 6 - Aug. 29).
e – Also July 14.
f – Lille **Flandres**.
g – On ①–⑤ June 23 - July 4 diverted to Lille Flandres (a. 2200).
h – 2201 Sept. 13 - Oct. 28.
j – 1455 to June 27 and from Sept. 1.
k – On ①–⑤ June 23 - Aug. 1 and ①–⑤ Oct. 6–17 diverted to Lille Flandres (a. 2307).
n – July 13–28 diverted to Lille Flandres (a. 0008).
p – Not July 14.
q – Arrives 2332 until June 20. Subject to alteration Lyon - Strasbourg on Aug. 23, 24, 30, 31, Sept. 6, 7, Nov. 22–25.
r – Not Aug. 14. Arrives 2153 from Sept. 1.
t – Also Aug. 15.
v – Not Aug. 15, 16, 17, Oct. 12, 19, 26, Nov. 2, 9.
w – Not Sept. 27, 28.
x – Subject to alteration Lyon - Dijon from Sept. 1.
y – 1305 until Aug. 3.

TGV – [R], supplement payable, 🍷.
♣ – To Frankfurt (Main), Table **47**.
△ – Certain departure times are 1–3 minutes earlier July 15 - Aug. 24.
❖ – Subject to alteration Sept. 13 - Oct. 31.
♥ – Subject to alteration on July 19.
‡ – 2209 until June 22.
▶ – For Lyon - Paris see Table **340** (for St Exupéry ✈ Paris see Table **342**). For other trains Valence TGV Lyon and Paris see Table **355**. For Valence Ville - Lyon see Table **351**.
§ – Station for Disneyland Paris.
• – **5144** is combined with **9862** Lyon - Lille. **5180** is combined with **5186** Lyon - Lille.

Additional low-cost 'Ouigo' TGV trains run to Marne la Vallée-Chessy – see Table ***350a***.

Timings between Nice / Marseille and Lyon may vary by a few minutes until Mar. 14

MARNE LA VALLÉE - MARSEILLE and MONTPELLIER — 350a

Ouigo low-cost TGV

Low-cost *TGV* services branded **Ouigo**, internet booking only through www.ouigo.com, special conditions apply. For normal *TGV* services see Tables **350** and **355**.

	TGV 6299 B	*TGV* 6250 ⑤–⑦	*TGV* 6252 ①	*TGV* 6254 ②–④	*TGV* 6256 ②–④	*TGV* 6258 A	*TGV* 6260 ⑥	*TGV* 6262 ⑤⑦	*TGV* 6264 ①	*TGV* 6266 ②–④	*TGV* 6268 ②–④	*TGV* 6270 ①	*TGV* 6272 ⑤⑦	*TGV* 6274 ⑥
Marne la Vallée § d.	...	0948	1020	1100	1222	1222	1744	1748	1909	1926	2018	2044	2052	2052
Lyon Part Dieu a.	...	|	|	|	|	|	|	|	2100	|	2208	|	|	2242
Lyon Perrache d.	0603	|	|	|	|	|	|	|	...	|	...	|	|	...
Lyon St Exupéry ✈ d.	|	1139	1212	1251	1411	1411	1933	1941	...	2114	...	2230	2241	...
Valence TGV d.	|	|	|	1321	|	|	|	2007	...	|	...	2256	2307	...
Avignon TGV d.	0708	1233	1305	|	1504	|	|	|	...	|	...	|	|	...
Aix en Provence TGV d.	0731	|	|	|	|	|	2041	|	...	2225	...	2349	0001	...
Marseille St Charles a.	0743	1302	1335	|	1534	|	2054	|	...	2237	...	0001	0013	...
Nimes a.	...	...	...	1406	...	1515	...	2053	...	...	...	...	...	...
Montpellier a.	...	...	...	1434	...	1549	...	2120	...	...	...	...	...	...

	TGV 6276 ⑤⑥ c	*TGV* 6278 ⑦	*TGV* 6280 ①	*TGV* 6282 ②–④	*TGV* 6284 ①–⑥	*TGV* 6296 ⑦	*TGV* 6286 ⑤⑦	*TGV* 6286 ⑥	*TGV* 6288 ①	*TGV* 6290 ②–④	*TGV* 6292 ②–④	*TGV* 6294 A	*TGV* 6298 ⑥
Montpellier d.	...	...	...	...	...	...	...	...	...	1524	...	1635	...
Nimes d.	...	...	...	...	...	...	...	...	...	1552	...	1703	...
Marseille St Charles d.	0610	...	0624	...	0825	0836	1354	1356	1455	|	1628	|	2144
Aix en Provence TGV d.	|	...	|	...	0840	|	1409	|	|	|	|	|	|
Avignon TGV d.	0640	...	0656	...	|	0906	|	|	1527	|	1658	|	|
Valence TGV d.	|	...	|	...	|	|	|	|	|	1643	|	1753	|
Lyon St Exupéry ✈ d.	|	...	0749	...	0956	1000	1522	1522	1619h	1713	1752	1823	|
Lyon Perrache d.	|	0713	|	0835	|	|	|	|	|	|	|	|	2312
Marne la Vallée § a.	0917	0911	0935	1034	1144	1146	1709	1709	1805	1859	1938	2013	...

A – ①⑤⑥⑦.
B – ①⑤⑥⑦ (not Sept. 14, 21, 27, 28, Oct. 5).
c – Not Aug. 16.
h – Not July 7 - Aug. 18.

§ – Marne la Vallée - Chessy (station for Disneyland Paris). Journey from central Paris is approximately 40 minutes on RER Line A.

***Ouigo** services: internet booking only; special conditions apply. Timings may vary by a few minutes on certain dates (please check when booking).*

TOULON - HYÈRES — 350b

SUBJECT TO ALTERATION FROM SEPT. 1

km						*TGV* 6155				*TGV* 6159 E	
	Paris ◇ **350** d.	...	...	...	...	1049	...	...	...	1649	...
	Marseille **350 360** d.	...	...	...	...	|	...	...	...	|	...
0	**Toulon** d.	0622	0722	0822	1222	1447	1722	1822	1922	2051	...
20	**Hyères** a.	0643	0743	0843	1243	1502	1743	1843	1943	2106	...

	Ⓐ			*TGV* 6116 D	⊗	f	*TGV* 6156		
Hyères d.	0611	0700	0800	1010	1030	1325	1550	1754	1910
Toulon a.	0631	0721	0821	1027	1051	1346	1606	1815	1932
Marseille **350 360** a.	0735	0825	0925	1120	1155	1450	|	1925	...
Paris ◇ **350** a.	...	...	...	1453	...	...	2015	...	...

D – Ⓒ (daily July 5 - Aug. 24).
E – ⑤⑦ (daily July 6 - Aug. 24).
f – Runs 5 minutes later on June 15, 21, 22.
TGV – Ⓡ, supplement payable, 🍸.
⊗ – Subject to alteration on ①–⑤ to June 27.
◇ – Paris Gare de Lyon.

351 LYON - VALENCE - AVIGNON - MARSEILLE

km	All *TGV* trains are Ⓡ						17705			TGV 6191	17709		17713		TGV 6193	17717		17721				TGV 6193	17725	17725
		⚒	⚒	⚒		⚒				①–⑥		⚒								⚒	Ⓐ		⑤†	
										⊡		⊗	⊗	⊗	B	⊗						D	c	c
	Paris Gare de Lyon ▲ d.	...	...	...	...	...	...	...	...	0737	...	...	...	...	1119	...	...	...	...	...	...	1541	...	...
	Lyon St Exupéry TGV ✈ d.	...	...	...	...	...	...	...	...	0940	...	...	...	...	1325	...	...	...	...	...	...	|	...	...
0	**Lyon** Perrache ▷ d.	...	...	0540	...	...	...	...	...	|	...	...	...	...	|	...	...	...	...	...	...	|	...	...
0	**Lyon** Part-Dieu ▷ d.	...	...	|	...	0620	0720	0820	...	|	0920	1020	1120	1220	|	1320	1420	1520	...	1620	...	|	1720	1720
32	Vienne ▷ d.	...	...	0603	...	0640	0740	0840	...	|	0940	1040	1140	1240	|	1340	1440	1540	...	1640	...	|	1740	1740
87	Tain-Hermitage-Tournon ▷ d.	...	...	0641	...	0720	0815	0920	...	|	1015	1119	1215	1319	|	1415	1520	1615	...	1719	...	|	1815	1815
105	**Valence** Ville ▷ a.	...	...	0652	...	0731	0826	0931	...	1009	1026	1130	1226	1330	1356	1426	1531	1626	...	1730	...	1806	1826	1826
105	**Valence** Ville d.	0553	0634	...	0704	...	0829	...	0934	1012	1029	1133	1229	1333	1359	1429	...	1629	1704	1733	1804	1809	1829	1829
150	Montélimar d.	0617	0702	...	0732	...	0851	...	1002	1036	1051	1202	1251	1402	1423	1451	...	1651	1732	1802	1832	1846	1852	1852
202	Orange d.	0650	0737	...	0807	...	0927	...	1037	1102	1127	1237	1327	1437	|	1526	...	1727	1807	1837	1907	|	1927	1927
230	**Avignon** Centre a.	0713	0759	...	0829	...	0941	...	1059	1115	1141	1259	1341	1459	1503	1541	...	1741	1829	1859	1929	1947	1941	1941
230	**Avignon** Centre ▷ d.	0716	...	...	...	...	0944	...	...	...	1144	...	1344	...	1506	1544	...	1744	...	...	...	1950	1944	...
265	Arles 355 ▷ d.	0735	...	...	...	...	1003	...	...	...	1203	...	1403	...	1525	1603	...	1803	...	...	...	2009	2003	...
299	Miramas ▷ d.	0758	...	...	...	...	1021	...	...	...	1221	...	1421	...	1544	1621	...	1821	...	...	...	2029	2021	...
328	Vitrolles (for ✈) ⊖ 355 ▷ d.	0816	...	...	...	...	1039	...	...	...	1239	...	1439	...	...	1639	...	1839	...	...	...	...	|	...
351	**Marseille** St Charles 355 ▷ a.	0838	...	...	...	...	1054	...	...	...	1254	...	1454	...	...	1654	...	1854	...	...	...	...	2054	...

			TGV 6195	17729		TGV 6197		
				b		v		
Paris Gare de Lyon ▲ d.	...	...	1719	...	...	1937	...	...
Lyon St Exupéry TGV ✈ d.	...	...	1925	...	...	2137	...	...
Lyon Perrache ▷ d.	1740	...	|	...	...	|	...	...
Lyon Part-Dieu ▷ d.	|	1820	|	1920	2020	|	2120	...
Vienne ▷ d.	1803	1840	|	1940	2040	|	2140	...
Tain-Hermitage-Tournon ▷ d.	1841	1919	|	2015	2120	|	2220	...
Valence Ville ▷ a.	1852	1930	1956	2026	2131	2207	2231	...
Valence Ville d.	1904	1933	1959	2029	...	2210	...	...
Montélimar d.	1932	2002	2022	2051	...	2232	...	...
Orange d.	2007	2037	2049	2127	...	|	...	...
Avignon Centre a.	2029	2059	2103	2141	...	2308	...	...
Avignon Centre ▷ d.	...	...	2106	2144	...	...	...	...
Arles 355 ▷ d.	...	...	2125	2203	...	...	...	...
Miramas ▷ d.	...	...	2144	2221	...	...	...	...
Vitrolles (for ✈) ⊖ 355 ▷ d.	...	...	...	2239	...	...	...	...
Marseille St Charles 355 ▷ a.	...	...	...	2254	...	...	...	...

		TGV 6192		17702	17702					TGV 6194
	Ⓐ	Ⓐ	⚒	①⑥	⚒	Ⓐ		⚒		
				k	z					E
Marseille St Charles 355 ▷ d.	...	...	...	0506	...	...	...	...	...	...
Vitrolles (for ✈) ⊖ 355 ▷ d.	...	...	...	|	...	...	...	...	...	...
Miramas ▷ d.	...	...	...	0539	...	...	...	...	...	0655
Arles 355 ▷ d.	...	...	...	0556	...	...	...	...	...	0718
Avignon Centre ▷ a.	...	...	...	0615	...	...	...	...	...	0737
Avignon Centre d.	...	0501	0531	0618	0618	0631	0631	0701	0731	0740
Orange d.	...	|	0553	0634	0634	0654	0654	0724	0754	0802
Montélimar d.	0528	0539	0628	0710	0710	0729	0729	0800	0830	0834
Valence Ville a.	0556	0601	0656	0731	0731	0756	0756	0826	0856	0900
Valence Ville ▷ d.	0608	0604	0708	0734	0734	0808	...	0829	...	0902
Tain-Hermitage-Tournon ▷ d.	0619	|	0719	0745	0745	0819	...	0839	...	|
Vienne ▷ d.	0658	|	0758	0819	0819	0858	...	0919	...	|
Lyon Part-Dieu ▷ a.	|	|	|	0840	0840	|	...	0940	...	|
Lyon Perrache ▷ a.	0720	|	0820	...	...	0920	...	...	...	|
Lyon St Exupéry TGV ✈ a.	...	0636	...	...	...	...	...	...	...	0933
Paris Gare de Lyon ▲ a.	...	0841	...	...	...	...	...	...	...	1130

	17706	TGV 6194	17704		17714	TGV 6196			17716		17718	TGV 6198	TGV 6198					17724						
												⑦	①–⑥			Ⓐ	†			⚒		⑤†	†	①–④
	⊗	B	⊗	G	⊗	w	⚒					t	d											m
Marseille St Charles 355 ▷ d.	0706	...	0906	...	1106	...	...	...	1306	...	1506	...	...	...	...	...	...	1706	...	...	...	1906	...	1918
Vitrolles (for ✈) ⊖ 355 ▷ d.	0721	...	0921	...	1121	...	...	...	1321	...	1521	...	...	...	...	...	...	1721	...	...	...	1921	...	1937
Miramas ▷ d.	0740	0815	0939	...	1139	...	...	...	1339	...	1539	1616	1618	...	...	...	...	1739	...	...	...	1939	...	1958
Arles 355 ▷ d.	0757	0835	0957	...	1157	...	...	...	1357	...	1557	1636	1638	...	...	...	...	1757	...	...	...	1957	...	2020
Avignon Centre ▷ a.	0815	0852	1015	...	1215	...	...	...	1415	...	1615	1652	1654	...	...	...	...	1815	...	...	...	2015	...	2037
Avignon Centre d.	0818	0857	1018	1201	1218	1257	...	1301	1418	...	1618	1657	1657	...	1701	1731	...	1818	1901	1931	1931	2018	...	2040
Orange d.	0834	0913	1034	1224	1234	|	...	1323	1434	...	1634	1713	1713	...	1724	1754	...	1834	1924	1954	1954	2035	...	2056
Montélimar d.	0910	0940	1109	1259	1310	1338	...	1359	1510	...	1710	1741	1740	1728r	1800	1830	1852y	1910	1959	2030	2030	2109	...	2129
Valence Ville a.	0931	1001	1131	1326	1331	1359	...	1426	1531	...	1731	1801	1801	1756r	1826	1856	1916y	1931	2026	2056	2056	2132	...	2151
Valence Ville ▷ d.	0934	1004	1134	...	1334	1402	1429	...	1534	...	1734	1804	1804	1808	1829	...	1921	1934	2029	2108	...	...	2140	...
Tain-Hermitage-Tournon ▷ d.	0945	|	1145	...	1345	|	1439	...	1545	...	1745	|	|	1819	1839	...	1933	1945	2039	2119	...	...	2150	...
Vienne ▷ d.	1019	|	1219	...	1419	|	1519	...	1619	...	1819	|	|	1858	1919	...	2008	2019	2119	2158	...	...	2230	...
Lyon Part-Dieu ▷ a.	1040	|	1240	...	1440	|	1540	...	1640	...	1840	|	|	|	1940	...	2030	2040	2140	|	...	...	2250	...
Lyon Perrache ▷ a.	...	|	...	...	...	|	...	...	...	...	...	|	|	1920	...	...	...	...	...	2220	...	...	...	...
Lyon St Exupéry TGV ✈ a.	...	1036	...	...	...	1432	...	...	...	...	...	1836	1836	...	...	...	...	...	...	...	...	...	...	...
Paris Gare de Lyon ▲ a.	...	1241	...	...	...	1637	...	...	...	...	...	2041	2041	...	...	...	...	...	...	...	...	...	...	...

ADDITIONAL TRAINS LYON - VALENCE

	Ⓐ	Ⓐ	N	Ⓐ		Ⓐ	Ⓐ	Ⓑ	Ⓐ	
Lyon Perrache d.	0640	0740	1340	1540	1640	1710	1810	1840	1912	1940
Lyon Part Dieu d.	|	|	|	|	|	|	|	|	|	|
Vienne d.	0703	0803	1403	1603	1703	1733	1833	1903	1933	2003
Tain-Hermitage-Tournon d.	0741	0841	1441	1641	1741	1811	1911	1941	2011	2041
Valence Ville a.	0752	0852	1452	1652	1752	1822	1922	1952	2022	2052

	Ⓐ	⚒	†	⚒	Ⓐ T	L	Ⓑ q	P	Ⓑ q	Ⓑ
Valence Ville d.	0538	0638	0708	0738	1029	1229	1508	1608	1708	1908
Tain-Hermitage-Tournon d.	0549	0649	0719	0749	1039	1239	1519	1619	1719	1919
Vienne d.	0628	0728	0758	0828	1119	1319	1558	1658	1758	1958
Lyon Part Dieu a.	|	|	|	|	1140	1340	|	|	|	|
Lyon Perrache a.	0649	0750	0820	0850	...	...	1620	1720	1820	2020

ADDITIONAL TRAINS AVIGNON - MARSEILLE (SEE NOTE ❖)

	⚒	Ⓐ h		⚒	Ⓐ		⚒ n	Ⓐ	Ⓐ			H	Ⓐ J	Ⓐ		Ⓐ	Ⓐ		Ⓐ			Ⓐ	Ⓐ	s	
Avignon Centre d.	0545	0546	0616	0623	0644	0646	0723	0744	0816	1016	1216	1223	1234	1416	1423	1516	1616	1623	1716	1723	1816	1823	1916	1923	2016
Arles 355 d.	0605	|	0636	|	0703	|	|	0805	0837	1037	1237	|	1305	1437	|	1537	1637	|	1737	|	1837	|	1937	|	2037
Cavaillon d.	|	0619	|	0657	|	0719	0757	|	|	|	|	1257	|	|	1457	|	|	1657	|	1757	|	1857	|	1956	|
Salon de Provence d.	|	0635	|	0718	|	0735	0818	|	|	|	|	1319	|	|	1518	|	|	1719	|	1819	|	1919	|	2018	|
Miramas d.	0627	0645	0658	0731	0724	0745	0831	0824	0859	1059	1259	1331	1328	1459	1530	1559	1659	1731	1759	1832	1859	1931	1957	2028	2059
Vitrolles (for ✈) ⊖ 355 d.	0648	0708	0719	0753	|	0808	0853	|	0921	1121	1321	1353	1348	1521	1552	1621	1721	1753	...	1854	1920	1953	...	...	2121
Marseille St Charles 355 a.	0705	0732	0748	0812	0754	0832	0912	0854	0950	1150	1350	1412	1412	1550	1611	1650	1750	1812	...	1914	1950	2012	...	...	2142

	Ⓐ	Ⓐ g					Ⓐ	⚒		H	Ⓐ ⊠				Ⓐ	Ⓐ			Ⓐ	A		Ⓐ	s	Ⓐ	
Marseille St Charles 355 d.	...	...	0610	...	0648	0718	...	0725	0808	0850	1010	...	1210j	1248	1410	...	1548	...	1648	1748	...	1810	1848	1948	2048
Vitrolles (for ✈) ⊖ 355 d.	...	...	0640	...	0707	0736	...	0749	0840	0909	1040	...	1239	1307	1440	...	1607	...	1707	1809	...	1826	1907	2007	2104
Miramas d.	0629	0631	0703	0706	0730	0756	0803	0815	0903	0933	1103	...	1303	1331	1503	1632	1631	...	1731	1832	...	1845	1931	2031	2128
Salon de Provence d.	|	0640	|	0715	0739	|	|	0824	|	0942	|	...	|	1340	|	|	1640	...	1741	1841	...	|	1940	2040	|
Cavaillon d.	|	0701	|	0731	0801	|	|	0839	|	1003	|	...	|	1401	|	|	1701	...	1803	1902	...	|	2001	2101	|
Arles 355 d.	0651	|	0725	|	|	0816	0827	|	0925	|	1125	...	1325	|	1525	1655	|	...	|	|	...	1908	|	|	2149
Avignon Centre a.	0710	0734	0744	0804	0834	...	0845	0912	0944	1036	1144	...	1344	1434	1544	1713	1734	...	1834	1935	...	1927	2034	2134	2205

A – Daily to Nov. 7; ①–⑤ from Nov. 12.
B – ⑥⑦ to June 29; daily July 5 - Oct. 5; ⑥⑦ from Oct. 18.
D – ①–⑤ to July 4 / from Oct. 6.
E – ①–⑤ to July 4 / from Oct. 6 (not Nov. 10, 11).
G – Ⓒ (daily July 5 - Oct. 5).
H – Ⓒ (daily to July 6 and from Oct. 4).
J – July 7 - Oct. 3.
L – Daily to Oct. 5 (not June 16–20); Ⓒ Oct. 11 - Nov. 30; daily from Dec. 6.
N – ①–⑥ June 21 - Oct. 4 (not July 14); ⑥ Oct. 11 - Nov. 29; ①–⑥ from Dec. 6.
P – ①–⑥ (not July 14, Nov. 11).
T – June 23 - Oct. 3 and from Dec. 8.

b – Not July 5, Oct. 27–31.
c – Not Nov. 1.
d – Not July 11, 18, 25, Aug. 1, 8, 15, 22.
g – Not June 16, 23, 30, Oct. 27, Nov. 3, 10, 17, 24, Dec. 1, 8.
h – Not Nov. 10, 17, 24, Dec. 1, 8. On June 16, 23, 30, Oct. 27, Nov. 3 service is diverted, not calling at Salon or Cavaillon.
j – 1220 on ①–⑤ Sept. 15–26.
k – Also July 15, Nov. 12; not July 14, Sept. 20, Nov. 1.
m – Not July 14, Nov. 11.
n – Not Nov. 22.
q – Also Nov. 1.
r – ⑦ to June 29 and from Aug. 31 (not Oct. 19, 26).
s – Not Nov. 15, 16, 22, 23, 29, 30, Dec. 6, 7.
t – Also ⑤ July 11 - Aug. 22; not Nov. 9.
v – Not July 5, Oct. 10, 18.
w – Not June 16–20.
y – ⑦ to June 29 and from Aug. 31.
z – Not Sept. 16–20.
TGV – Ⓡ, supplement payable, 🍸.
⊡ – Subject to alteration Sept. 1–10.

▲ – For *TGV* services via high-speed line see Table **340** Paris - Lyon, Table **350** Paris - Avignon - Marseille, Table **355** Paris - Montpellier.
▷ – For additional trains Lyon - Valence Ville and Avignon - Marseille see below main table.
⊖ – Full station name is Vitrolles Aéroport Marseille-Provence. A shuttle bus runs to the airport terminal (journey 5 minutes) connecting with trains.
⊗ – Subject to alteration on Ⓐ to July 4 / from Sept. 6 (diversions between Lyon and Avignon with extended journey times, earlier departures and later arrivals).
⊠ – Runs 23–32 minutes later Sept. 15–26.
❖ – Timings via Salon may vary by up to 3 minutes Nov. 3–22 (services via Cavaillon do not run Nov. 8–11).

WARNING! All services running between Valence and Avignon are subject to alteration on Oct. 11, 12

AVIGNON CENTRE - AVIGNON TGV — 351a

Journey time: 5–6 minutes

From **Avignon Centre** at 0558 Ⓐ, 0628, 0658, 0737 Ⓐ **d**, 0758, 0828, 0836 **n**, 0858, 0919 ⚒ **n**, 0928, 0958, 1058, 1116, 1135, 1157, 1228, 1258, 1328, 1336, 1358, 1437 **n**, 1458, 1527, 1619 Ⓐ **n**, 1627, 1658 Ⓒ, 1721, 1737 **n**, 1758, 1828, 1836 Ⓐ **n**, 1937 **A**, 2037 **e**, 2137 Ⓐ **n**, 2150 Ⓒ and 2228.

From **Avignon TGV** at 0627 Ⓐ, 0657, 0727 Ⓐ, 0757, 0827, 0857, 0913, 0927, 0936 ⚒ **n**, 0957, 1027, 1127, 1144, 1213 **n**, 1227, 1257, 1327, 1357, 1413 **n**, 1427, 1526, 1557, 1613 **n**, 1657, 1713 **n**, 1736 Ⓐ **n**, 1757, 1813 Ⓐ **n**, 1836 **e**, 1857, 1913 **e**, 1957, 2122, 2205 and 2309.

A – Daily to Nov. 7; ①–⑤ from Nov. 12.
d – Not Nov. 3, 10, 17, 24, Dec. 1, 8.
e – Not Nov. 8–11, 15, 16, 22, 23, 29, 30, Dec. 6, 7.
n – Not Nov. 8–11.

🚌 TOULON - ST TROPEZ — 352

🚌 routes 7801/2

🚌 **Toulon** Gare Routière (adjacent to railway station) → Hyères → Le Lavandou → **St Tropez** Gare Routière. *84 km.* Journey 2 hrs 5 mins - 2 hrs 40 mins.

From Toulon: 0550 ⚒, 0620 ⚒ **d**, 0650 ⚒, 0720 ⚒ **d**, 0810, 0900 ⚒ **d**, 1030 ⚒, 1210 **d**, 1300, 1415, 1530 ⚒ **d**, 1645, 1745, 1815 **d** and 2100.

From St Tropez at 0600 ⚒ **d**, 0640 ⚒, 0845, 1010, 1110 ⚒ **d**, 1150, 1230 ⚒ **d**, 1350, 1600, 1630 **d**, 1700, 1730 ⚒ **d**, 1830 ⚒ **d** and 1930.

d – Direct (not via Le Lavandou), journey 1 hr 45 mins.

Operator: Groupement SUMA, 13340 Rognac ✆ (in France) 0 810 006 177 www.varlib.fr SERVICE JULY 5 - AUG. 31, 2014.

🚌 ST RAPHAEL - ST TROPEZ — 352a

🚌 route 7601

🚌 **St Raphael** Gare Routière (adjacent to railway station) → St Aygulf → Ste Maxime → Grimaud → Port Grimaud (certain journeys) → **St Tropez** Gare Routière. *35 km.* Journey approx 1 hr 30 mins.

From St Raphael: 0600, 0750, 0915, 1100, 1300, 1340, 1500, 1615, 1745, 1915, 2040.
From St Tropez: 0600, 0730, 0925, 1100, 1230, 1330, 1515, 1630, 1730, 1900, 2100.

Operator: Groupement SUMA, 13340 Rognac ✆ (in France) 0 810 006 177 www.varlib.fr Subject to alteration from July 5, 2014.

LYON - BOURG EN BRESSE — 353

For additional trains Lyon - Bourg en Bresse (- Besançon) see Table **378**

km		ⒶL ⊖	Ⓐ	ⒶL	⚒	Ⓐ	①–⑥ b	Ⓐ		ⒶL	Ⓐ	①–⑥ b	Ⓐ	ⒶL ⊖		Ⓐ	①–⑥ b	ⒶL ⊖	Ⓐ	ⒶL ⊖		Ⓐ	①–⑥ b	⑦	①–⑥ b	
0	**Lyon** Perrache ... d.	...	0609	...	0709	0809	1009	1109	1209	...	1309	1409	1509	...	1609	1657	1709	...	1757	...	1808	1857	1909	1955	2009	2109z
5	**Lyon** Part Dieu ... d.	...	0620	...	0720	0820	1020	1120	1220	...	1320	1420	1520	...	1620	1708	1720	...	1808	...	1820	1908	1920	2008	2020	2120z
∆	Ambérieu ... d.	0652	|	0811	|	|	|	|	|	1311	|	|	|	1705	|	|	|	1805	|	1905	|	|	|	2044	|	|
65	**Bourg en Bresse** ... a.	0715	0729	0835	0829	0929	1129	1229	1329	1335	1429	1529	1629	1727	1729	1757	1829	1828	1857	1927	1929	1957	2029	2102	2129	2230

	⚒	Ⓐ	⚒	Ⓐ	⚒ c	ⒶL ⊖f		Ⓐ	①–⑥ b	Ⓐ c	Ⓒ		Ⓐ	ⒶL	①–⑥ b	Ⓐ		ⒶL	①–⑥ b	ⒶL ⊖f		Ⓐ	ⒶL ⊖f		ⒶL ⊖f	Ⓑ h
Bourg en Bresse ... d.	0531	0601	0631	0703	0723	0727	0731	0803	0831	0844	0844	1031	1131	1225	1231	1331	1431	1625	1631	1727	1731	1831	1833	1931	1935	2031
Ambérieu ... a.	|	|	|	|	0747	0753	|	|	|	0901	0901	|	|	1251	|	|	|	1651	|	1751	|	|	1857	|	1959	|
Lyon Part Dieu ... a.	0640	0710	0740	0752	0826k	...	0840	0905	0940	0936t	0935r	1140	1240	...	1340	1440	1540	...	1740	...	1840	1940	...	2040	...	2140
Lyon Perrache ... a.	0653	0721	0753	0805	0845	...	0855	...	0953	0949t	...	1153	1253	...	1353	1455	1553	...	1753	...	1853	1953	...	2053	...	2153

L – To July 11 and from Aug. 25.
b – Not July 14, Nov. 11.
c – Not Aug. 20–25.
f – 2–6 minutes later June 30 - July 11.
h – Not Aug. 15.
k – 0822 from Aug. 30.
r – 0926 from Aug. 30.
t – From Sept. 1 arrives Lyon Part Dieu 0926, Lyon Perrache 0945.
z – On ⑤† departs Lyon Perrache 2113, Lyon Part Dieu 2125.
⊖ – To/from Mâcon Ville (Table **353a**).
∆ – Ambérieu - Bourg en Bresse: *31* km.

MÂCON - BOURG EN BRESSE — 353a

		ⒶL	🚌 Ⓒ	ⒶL	🚌	ⒶL	🚌	ⒶL	ⒶL	ⒶL	🚌 Ⓒ
0	Mâcon Ville ... d.	0657	0727	0757	0927	1305	1457	1657	1803	1905	2057
37	Bourg en Bresse ... a.	0725f	0829	0827	1029	1334f	1559	1725f	1831f	1933f	2130
	Ambérieu **353** ... a.	0753f	...	...	...	...	...	1751f	1857f	1959f	...

	ⒶL	🚌	ⒶL	🚌	ⒶL	🚌 Ⓒ	ⒶL	ⒶL	ⒶL	🚌 Ⓒ
Ambérieu **353** ... d.	0652	...	...	...	...	...	1705	1805	1905	...
Bourg en Bresse ... d.	0716	0934	1228	1340	1620	1634	1728	1829	1928	1934
Mâcon Ville ... a.	0741	1037	1258	1443	1651	1737	1757	1859	1957	2037

Additional journeys by 🚌: from Mâcon Ville at 1057 Ⓐ, 1657 Ⓒ, 1757 Ⓒ and 1957 Ⓐ; from Bourg en Bresse at 0634 Ⓐ, 0734, 1034 Ⓐ and 1805 Ⓐ.

L – To July 11 and from Aug. 25.
f – 2–6 minutes later June 30 - July 11.
☛ Journeys by 🚌 are subject to confirmation.

DIJON - BOURG EN BRESSE — 353b

km		Ⓐ		Ⓒ		c		Ⓐ		
0	**Dijon** ... d.	0633	...	0833	...	1233	...	1729j	1843	...
30	St Jean de Losne ... d.	0705	...	0905	...	1305	...	1805	1915	...
86	Louhans ... d.	0744	...	0944	...	1344	...	1844	1957	...
140	**Bourg en Bresse** ... a.	0816	...	1016	...	1417	...	1916	2030	...

	Ⓐ			⚒d				⑦w	
Bourg en Bresse ... d.	0530	0632	...	1142	...	1737	...	1840	...
Louhans ... d.	0602	0705	...	1215	...	1813	...	1912	...
St Jean de Losne ... d.	0637	0745	...	1254	...	1847	...	1947	...
Dijon ... a.	0703	0815	...	1325	...	1914	...	2014	...

c – Not July 7–11, 15–18, Sept. 15–19, Oct. 13–17, 20–24, Nov. 10, 12–14, 17–21, 24–28.
d – Not ①–⑤ June 23 - July 18, Sept. 15–19, Oct. 13–17, 20–24, Nov. 10–14, 17–21, 24–28.
j – 1733 to Sept. 1 and from Nov. 3.
w – Also July 14, Aug. 15, Nov. 11.

PERPIGNAN - VILLEFRANCHE - LATOUR DE CAROL — 354

km		⚒ H	J		N	H	Ⓐ H	Ⓐ N		Ⓑ q	M
0	**Perpignan** ... d.	0626	0726	0826	1226	1246	1446	1646	1746	1846	1946
40	Prades-Molitg les Bains ... d.	0711	0811	0911	1309	1331	1531	1731	1831	1931	2031
46	**Villefranche** ⊡ ... a.	0719	0819	0919	1317	1339	1539	1739	1839	1939	2039

	⚒		K	H	Ⓐ H	N	L		Ⓑ H
Villefranche ⊡ ... d.	0625	0725	0825	1245	1445	1525	1745	1845	1945
Prades-Molitg les Bains. d.	0633	0733	0833	1253	1453	1533	1753	1853	1953
Perpignan ... a.	0713	0813	0913	1333	1533	1613	1833	1933	2033

VILLEFRANCHE - LATOUR DE CAROL *Petit Train Jaune* Narrow gauge, 2nd class. In summer most trains include open sightseeing carriages. **SERVICE MAY 29 - SEPT. 28.**

km		B	B		F	G	B	B	
0	**Villefranche-Vernet les Bains** ... d.	0855	0958	...	1315	1329	1527	1735	...
28	Mont Louis la Cabanasse ... d.	1025	1130	...	1446	1451	1655	1859	...
35	Font Romeu-Odeillo-Via ... d.	1046	1157	...	1506	1511	1714	1926	...
56	Bourg Madame ... d.	...	1255	...	...	...	...	2022	...
63	**Latour de Carol** ... a.	...	1311	...	...	...	...	2038	...

	B		B		B		B	B
Latour de Carol ... d.	0828	...	...	...	...	...	1456	...
Bourg Madame ... d.	0848	...	...	...	...	...	1517	...
Font Romeu-Odeillo-Via ... d.	1000	...	1106	...	1526	...	1631	1736
Mont Louis la Cabanasse ... d.	1032	...	1136	...	1556	...	1701	1804
Villefranche-Vernet les Bains .. a.	1149	...	1255	...	1715	...	1820	1920

B – May 29 - Sept. 28.
F – May 29 - July 5.
G – July 6 - Sept. 28.
H – Until July 5.
J – Daily to July 5; ⚒ from July 7.
K – Daily to July 4; Ⓐ from July 7.
L – Daily to July 11; Ⓑ from July 13 (also Nov. 1).
M – Ⓑ to June 27; daily from June 29.
N – From July 6.
q – Also Nov. 1.
⊡ – Villefranche-Vernet les Bains.

355 PARIS - MONTPELLIER - PERPIGNAN - PORTBOU

km		Ⓐ	3733 Q [R]	3731 P [R]	Ⓐ c	⚒ c	⚒ c	Ⓐ	4250 4251 R [R]	Ⓐ c	Ⓐ	⚒	Ⓐ	† m	© m	Ⓐ	Ⓐ ☆	Ⓐ	TGV 9730 ■	© T	¶	TGV 6809 ①–⑥ s		TGV 9741 ⊕ ♠
	Brussels Midi **11** d.	...	...	...	...	...	...	...	...	...	...	...	...	...	...	...	...	...	...	...	...	...	...	...
	Lille Europe **11** d.	...	...	...	...	...	...	...	...	...	...	...	...	...	...	...	...	...	...	...	...	...	...	...
	Charles de Gaulle ✈ **11** d.	...	...	...	...	...	...	...	...	...	...	...	...	...	...	...	...	...	...	...	...	...	...	...
	Marne la Vallée § **11** d.	...	...	...	...	...	...	...	...	...	...	...	...	...	...	...	...	...	...	...	...	...	...	...
0	**Paris** Gare de Lyon ▶ d.	...	2157a	2157a	...	...	...	...	...	...	...	...	...	...	...	...	...	...	...	...	...	...	...	...
	Dijon **379** d.	...	│	│	...	...	...	...	...	...	...	...	...	...	...	...	...	...	...	...	...	...	...	...
	Genève **346** d.	...	│	│	...	...	...	...	...	...	...	...	...	...	...	...	...	...	...	...	...	...	...	...
	Lyon Part Dieu ▶ d.	...	│	│	...	...	...	...	...	...	...	...	...	...	...	...	...	...	...	...	...	0706	...	0736
527	Valence TGV ▶ d.	...	│	│	...	...	...	...	...	...	...	...	...	...	...	...	...	...	...	...	...	0743	...	0814
	Nice **360** d.	...	│	│	...	...	...	...	...	...	...	...	...	...	...	...	...	...	...	...	...	│	...	│
▵128	**Marseille** St Charles d.	...	│	│	...	...	...	...	...	...	...	...	...	...	...	0600	...	...	0710	...	...	│	0718	│
▵105	Vitrolles Aéroport Marseille ‡ d.	...	│	│	...	...	...	...	...	...	...	...	...	...	...	0616	...	...	│	...	...	│	0736	│
▵42	Arles d.	...	│	│	...	...	...	...	...	...	...	...	...	...	...	0657	...	...	│	...	...	│	0817	│
▵49	**Avignon** Centre d.	...	◐	◐	...	...	...	...	...	...	...	0609r	0638	...	...	│	...	0709	0746v	...	0734	│	│	│
▵28	Tarascon-sur-Rhône d.	...	│	│	...	...	...	...	...	...	...	0623r	0654	...	...	0707	...	0723	│	...	0749	│	0826	│
686	**Nimes** d.	...	│	│	0507	...	0543	...	0609	0613	0643	0646	0713	0713	...	0721	0743	0746	0809	...	0813	0831	0843	0905
712	Lunel d.	...	│	│	0525	...	0559	...	│	0631	0659	0706	0731	0731	...	...	0759	0806	│	...	0831	│	0859	│
736	**Montpellier** a.	...	│	│	0540	...	0613	...	0634	0646	0713	0729	0746	0746	...	...	0814	0829	0834	...	0846	0854	0914	0930
736	**Montpellier** d.	...	│	│	0550	...	0616	...	0638	0650	0716	...	0750	0750	0750	...	0820	...	0837	...	0850	0858	0920r	0935
756	Frontignan d.	...	│	│	0604	...	0633	...	│	0704	0733	...	0804	0804	0804	...	0834	...	│	...	0904	│	0934r	│
763	Sète d.	...	│	│	0611	...	0640	...	0658	0711	0740	...	0811	0811	0811	...	0841	...	│	...	0911	0917	0942r	│
786	Agde d.	...	│	│	0624	...	0656	...	0713	0724	0756	...	0824	0824	0824	...	0859	...	│	...	0924	│	0959r	│
807	Béziers d.	...	│	│	0637	...	0711	...	0727	0737	0811	...	0837	0837	0837	...	0913	...	0919	...	0937	0943	1012r	│
833	**Narbonne** a.	...	0609	0609	0650	...	0729	...	0741	0750	0830	...	0850	0850	0850	...	0927	...	│	...	0950	0955	1025r	1031
833	**Narbonne** d.	...	0635	0643	0655	0655	0732	0734	0745	0755	...	...	0855	0855	0855	...	...	...	│	0948	0955	0958	...	1034
	Carcassonne **321** a.	...	│	│	│	│	0802	│	│	│	...	...	│	│	│	...	...	...	│	│	│	1026	...	│
	Toulouse **321** a.	...	│	│	│	│	0904	│	│	│	...	...	│	│	│	...	...	...	│	│	│	1111	...	│
	Bordeaux **320** a.	...	│	│	│	│	...	│	│	│	...	...	│	│	│	...	...	...	│	│	│	...	...	│
854	Port la Nouvelle d.	...	0650	│	0709	0709	...	0747	│	0809	...	...	0909	0909	0909	...	...	...	│	1001	1009	...	...	│
896	**Perpignan** a.	...	0722	0720	0740	0740	...	0815	0819	0840	...	...	0940	0940	0940	...	...	...	1003	1027	1040	...	...	1107
896	**Perpignan** d.	0620	0726	0724	0745	0745	...	...	0823	0845	...	...	...	0945	0945	...	...	...	...	1030	1045	...	...	...
918	Argelès sur Mer d.	0635	0746	0745	0802	0802	...	...	0843	0902	...	...	...	1002	1002	...	...	...	...	1045	1102	...	...	...
923	Collioure d.	0640	0753	0752	0807	0807	...	...	0850	0907	...	...	...	1007	1007	...	...	...	...	1050	1107	...	...	...
926	Port Vendres d.	0644	0758	0758	0811	0811	...	...	0855	0911	...	...	...	1011	1011	...	...	...	...	1054	1111	...	...	...
931	Banyuls sur Mer d.	0649	0805	0805	0816	0816	...	...	0902	0916	...	...	...	1016	1016	...	...	...	...	1059	1116	...	...	...
938	Cerbère **657** a.	0654	0812	0812	0822	0822	...	...	0908	0922	...	...	...	1022	1022	...	...	...	...	1105	1122	...	...	...
940	**Portbou** **657** a.	...	0822	0822	...	...	...	...	0917	...	...	...	...	...	...	...	...	...	...	...	1128	...	...	...

	TGV 6201 ①–⑤ d	Ⓐ	4754 4755 ★	TGV 9711 ♠	◇	TGV 5104 ●	TGV 6205 E	TGV 6205 ①–⑥ b	4756 4757 ★ n	Ⓐ		© E	TGV 6207 G	TGV 6207 ⑥ K		⚒	TGV 6813 ⊗	Ⓐ J	Ⓐ	TGV 9713 ♥	⊖	TGV 9812 ●		⑤ f
Brussels Midi **11** d.	...	...	...	...	...	...	...	...	...	...	...	...	...	...	...	...	...	...	...	...	...	0817	...	...
Lille Europe **11** d.	...	...	...	...	...	0537e	...	...	...	...	...	...	...	...	...	...	...	...	...	...	...	0902	...	...
Charles de Gaulle ✈ **11** d.	...	...	...	...	...	0658	...	...	...	...	...	...	...	...	...	...	...	...	...	...	...	0958	...	...
Marne la Vallée § **11** d.	...	...	...	...	...	0711	...	...	...	...	...	...	...	...	...	...	...	...	...	...	...	1011	...	...
Paris Gare de Lyon ▶ d.	0607	...	...	0715	...	│	0807	0807	...	...	...	...	0915	0915	...	...	...	...	...	1007	...	│	...	...
Dijon **379** d.	│	...	...	│	...	│	│	│	...	...	...	...	│	│	...	...	...	...	...	│	...	│	...	...
Genève **346** d.	│	...	...	│	...	│	│	│	...	...	...	...	│	│	...	...	...	...	...	│	...	│	...	...
Lyon Part Dieu ▶ d.	│	...	...	│	...	0910	│	│	...	...	...	...	│	│	...	...	1110	...	...	│	...	1206	...	...
Valence TGV ▶ d.	0822	...	...	│	...	0948	1022	1022	...	...	...	...	│	│	...	...	│	...	...	1221	...	│	...	...
Nice **360** d.	│	...	...	│	...	│	│	│	...	...	...	...	│	│	...	...	│	...	...	│	...	│	...	...
Marseille St Charles d.	│	...	0818	│	...	│	│	│	1013	...	...	...	│	│	...	...	│	...	...	│	1154	│	...	...
Vitrolles Aéroport Marseille ‡ d.	│	...	│	│	...	│	│	│	│	...	...	...	│	│	...	...	│	...	...	│	1209	│	...	...
Arles d.	│	...	0902	│	...	│	│	│	│	...	...	...	│	│	...	...	│	...	...	│	1244	│	...	...
Avignon Centre d.	│	0840	│	│	0940	│	│	│	│	...	...	...	│	│	1139	1139	│	...	1210	│	│	│	1340	1340
Tarascon-sur-Rhône d.	│	0854	│	│	0954	│	│	│	│	...	...	...	│	│	1153	1153	│	...	1224	│	1254	│	1354	1354
Nimes d.	0909	0913	0928	1009	1013	1039	1109	1109	1120	...	...	...	1209	1209	1213	1213	1228	...	1247	1309	1313	1319	1413	1413
Lunel d.	│	0931	│	│	1031	│	│	│	│	...	...	...	│	│	1231	1231	│	...	1309	│	1331	│	1431	1431
Montpellier a.	0934	0946	0953	1034	1046	1104	1134	1134	1144	...	...	...	1234	1234	1246	1246	1253	...	1329	1334	1346	1350	1446	1446
Montpellier d.	...	0950	0957	1037	1050	...	1139	1141	1148	1152	...	1205	...	1241	1250	1250	1257	1305	...	1337	1350	▬	1450	1450
Frontignan d.	...	1004	│	│	1104	...	│	│	│	1206	...	1220	...	│	1304	1304	│	1322	...	│	1404	...	1504	1504
Sète d.	...	1011	1017	│	1111	...	1159	1201	1208	1213	...	1228	...	1301	1311	1311	1317	1330	...	│	1411	...	1511	1511
Agde d.	...	1024	│	│	1124	...	1215	1217	│	1227	...	1245	...	1317	1324	1324	│	1345	...	│	1424	...	1524	1524
Béziers d.	...	1037	1041	│	1137	...	1229	1229	1235	1239	...	1300	...	1331	1337	1337	1342	1400	...	1418	1437	...	1537	1537
Narbonne a.	...	1050	1055	1132	1150	...	1243	...	1248	1252	...	1315	...	1344	1350	1350	1355	1418	...	1432	1450	...	1550	1550
Narbonne d.	...	1055	1058	1135	1155	...	1246	...	1251	1255	1255	...	...	1347	1355	1355	1358	...	...	1435	1455	...	1555	1555
Carcassonne **321** a.	...	│	1127	│	│	...	│	...	1321	│	│	...	...	│	│	│	1427	...	...	│	│	...	│	│
Toulouse **321** a.	...	│	1213	│	│	...	│	...	1412	│	│	...	...	│	│	│	1512	...	...	│	│	...	│	│
Bordeaux **320** a.	...	│	1429q	│	│	...	│	...	1629	│	│	...	...	│	│	│	...	...	...	│	│	...	│	│
Port la Nouvelle d.	...	1109	...	│	1209	...	│	...	...	1309	1309	...	...	│	1409	1409	...	...	...	│	1509	Ⓐ	1609	1609
Perpignan a.	...	1140	...	1208	1240	...	1326	...	...	1340	1340	...	...	1420	1440	1440	...	...	...	1508	1540	⊡	1640	1640
Perpignan d.	...	...	...	...	1245	...	...	...	...	...	...	...	...	...	...	1445	...	...	...	...	...	1545	...	1645
Argelès sur Mer d.	...	...	...	...	1302	...	...	...	...	...	...	...	...	...	...	1502	...	...	...	...	...	1602	...	1702
Collioure d.	...	...	...	...	1307	...	...	...	...	...	...	...	...	...	...	1507	...	...	...	...	...	1607	...	1707
Port Vendres d.	...	...	...	...	1311	...	...	...	...	...	...	...	...	...	...	1511	...	...	...	...	...	1611	...	1711
Banyuls sur Mer d.	...	...	...	...	1316	...	...	...	...	...	...	...	...	...	...	1516	...	...	...	...	...	1616	...	1716
Cerbère **657** a.	...	...	...	...	1322	...	...	...	...	...	...	...	...	...	...	1522	...	...	...	...	...	1622	...	1722
Portbou **657** a.	...	...	...	...	1328	...	...	...	...	...	...	...	...	...	...	1528	...	...	...	...	...	...	...	...

E – July 5 - Aug. 24.
G – Daily to Aug. 24 (not July 14); ⑥ from Aug. 30.
J – To July 4 and from Aug. 25.
K – ⑥ July 5 - Aug. 23 (also Aug. 15).
P – Not June 21, 28, July 4 - Aug. 31, Sept. 6, 20, 27. 🛏 1,2 cl. and [2] (reclining) Paris Austerlitz - Toulouse - Narbonne - Portbou. Departs Paris 2152 until June 30; 2154 on ⑤ Sept. 19 - Oct. 24; 2135 on Oct. 31.
Q – July 4 - Aug. 31. 🛏 1,2 cl. and [2] (reclining) Paris Austerlitz - Toulouse - Narbonne - Portbou.
R – For days of running see Table **379**. 🛏 1,2 cl. and [2] (reclining) Luxembourg - Metz - Portbou; 🛏 1,2 cl., [2] (reclining) Strasbourg - Portbou. Timings may vary.
T – © June 28 - Aug. 31. From Toulouse (Table **321**).

a – Paris **Austerlitz**.
b – Not July 5 - Aug. 23, Nov. 11.
c – Not Oct. 20.
d – Also ⑥ July 5 - Aug. 23; not July 14, Nov. 11.
e – 0528 on Oct. 4, 6, 11, 12, 13.
f – Also Aug. 14; not Aug. 15.
m – Not Dec. 7.
n – Not Sept. 15–26.
q – Not ①–⑤ Oct. 27 - Nov. 14.
r – Ⓐ only.
s – Not July 14, Aug. 15, Nov. 11.
v – Avignon **TGV**. Also calls at Aix en Provence TGV (d. 0724).

TGV – [R], supplement payable, 🍸.

⊗ – Subject to alteration on Sept. 14–19, 21–28, Oct. 5.
● – Subject to alteration on Sept. 14, 21, 27, 28, Oct. 5.
⊕ – Subject to alteration on Sept. 14, 21, 28, Oct. 5.
◇ – Subject to alteration Perpignan - Portbou from Dec. 1.
¶ – Not Dec. 7. Subject to alteration Perpignan - Portbou on ①–⑤ from Dec. 1.
☆ – Also runs on ⑥ (not Nov. 1) Nimes - Montpellier.
★ – *INTERCITÉS*. [R].
▶ – For additional trains from Paris and Lyon to Valence TGV see Table **350**. For Lyon to Valence Ville see Table **351**.
♠ – To Barcelona (Tables **13**/**49**).
♥ – To Barcelona from July 6 (Table **13**). Train number **6233** until July 5.
■ – [12] Marseille - Barcelona - Madrid (Table **49**).
⊡ – Runs 4 minutes later July 7 - Aug. 22.
⊖ – Runs 3–10 minutes later Frontignan - Perpignan on Ⓐ July 7 - Aug. 22.

◐ – Via Limoges and Toulouse (Table **310**).
▵ – Distance from Nimes. Marseille to Nimes via Avignon TGV is *135 km*.
§ – Marne la Vallée - Chessy (station for Disneyland Paris).
‡ – Vitrolles Aéroport Marseille-Provence. A shuttle bus runs to the airport terminal (journey time 5 minutes). For additional trains see Table **351**.

Certain departure times from Avignon, Marseille, Vitrolles, Arles and Tarascon may be up to 6 minutes later to July 14 and from Oct. 11.

Services Lyon / Avignon / Marseille - Montpellier - Narbonne - Perpignan / Toulouse are subject to alteration or cancellation Sept. 19 – 21.

Toulouse / Bordeaux arrivals may be up to 21 minutes later from Oct. 29

*Additional low-cost 'Ouigo' TGV trains run from Marne la Vallée-Chessy in the eastern suburbs of Paris. See Table **350a**.*

PARIS - MONTPELLIER - PERPIGNAN - PORTBOU 355

	4760 4761 ★ h	TGV 6839 ♣	TGV 5318 5326 △	TGV 6211	Ⓐ p	4762 4763 ★	Ⓐ	Ⓐ m	TGV 9743 ⑦ D♠	TGV 9743 ①–⑥ D♠		4764 4765 ★ c	3631 ★ L	Ⓐ	Ⓐ	TGV 9715 ♠	Ⓑ	TGV 6811 ⊖	⑦ e	Ⓐ J	Ⓐ J	Ⓒ k	Ⓐ	TGV 9744 b
Brussels Midi **11** d.	...	...	...	...	...	...	...	...	...	...	...	...	...	...	...	...	...	...	...	...	...	...	...	...
Lille Europe **11** d.	...	...	...	...	...	...	...	...	...	...	...	...	...	...	...	...	...	...	...	...	...	...	...	...
Charles de Gaulle ✈ **11** d.	...	...	...	...	...	...	...	...	...	...	...	...	...	...	...	...	...	...	...	...	...	...	...	...
Marne la Vallée § **11** d.	...	...	...	...	...	...	...	...	...	...	...	...	...	...	...	...	...	...	...	...	...	...	...	...
Paris Gare de Lyon ▶ d.	...	...	...	1207	...	...	...	...	...	...	...	...	0942a	...	...	1407	...	...	...	...	...	...	...	...
Dijon **379** d.	...	1122	...	|	...	...	...	...	...	...	...	...	|	...	...	|	...	...	...	...	...	...	...	...
Genève **346** d.	...	|	...	|	...	...	...	...	...	...	...	...	|	...	...	|	...	...	...	...	...	...	...	1442
Lyon Part Dieu ▶ d.	...	1310	1336	|	...	...	...	...	1430	1430	...	...	|	...	...	|	...	1610	...	...	...	...	...	1636
Valence TGV ▶ d.	...	1348	1414	1422	...	...	...	...	|	|	...	...	|	...	...	1621	...	|	...	...	...	...	...	|
Nice **360** d.	1023y	|	|	|	...	...	...	...	|	|	...	1221	|	...	...	|	...	|	...	...	...	...	...	|
Marseille St Charles d.	1322	|	|	|	...	1417	...	...	|	|	...	1522	|	...	...	|	...	|	...	...	1614	1614	...	|
Vitrolles Aéroport Marseille ‡ d.	|	|	|	|	...	|	...	...	|	|	...	|	|	...	...	|	...	|	...	...	1631	1631	...	|
Arles d.	|	|	|	|	...	1459	...	...	|	|	...	|	|	...	...	|	...	|	...	...	1712	1712	...	|
Avignon Centre d.	|	|	|	|	...	|	...	...	|	|	1537	|	◐	...	...	|	1638r	|	...	...	|	|	1710	|
Tarascon-sur-Rhône d.	|	|	|	|	...	|	...	...	|	|	1550	|	|	...	...	|	1654r	|	...	...	1721	1721	1725	|
Nimes d.	|	1433	1505	1509	1513	1528	...	1543	1548	1549	1613	|	|	...	1643	1709	1713	1728	...	...	1743	1743	1747	1759
Lunel d.	|	|	|	|	1531	|	...	1559	|	|	1631	|	|	...	1702	|	1731	|	...	...	1759	1759	1812	|
Montpellier a.	1453	1457	1530	1534	1546	1553	...	1614	1618	1623	1646	1653	|	...	1716	1734	1746	1753	...	...	1814	1811	1824	1828
Montpellier d.	1457	▬	...	1541	1550	1557	...	1620	1625	1628	1650	1657	|	1705	1720	1737	1750	1757	1802	1805	1820	1814	...	...
Frontignan d.	|	...	...	|	1604	|	...	1634	|	|	1704	|	|	1722	1734	|	1804	|	1817	1822	1834	1834	...	...
Sète d.	|	...	...	1601	1611	1617	...	1641	|	|	1711	|	|	1730	1741	|	1811	|	1824	1830	1841	1841	...	...
Agde d.	|	...	...	1618	1624	|	...	1659	|	|	1724	|	|	1745	1759	|	1824	|	1837	1845	1859	1858	...	...
Béziers d.	|	...	...	1630	1637	1641	...	1713	1718	1719	1737	|	|	1800	1813	|	1837	1842	1848	1900	1913	1913	...	...
Narbonne a.	|	...	...	...	1650	1655	...	1727	|	|	1750	|	1747	1818	1827	1832	1850	1855	...	1918	1927	1929	...	...
Narbonne d.	|	...	...	...	1655	1658	1719	1732	|	|	1755	|	1814	1819	...	1835	1855	1858	...	...	...	...	...	...
Carcassonne **321** a.	|	...	...	...	|	1727	|	1802	|	|	|	|	|	|	...	|	|	1926	...	...	...	...	...	...
Toulouse **321** a.	1706	...	...	...	|	1812	|	1904	|	|	|	1908	|	|	...	|	|	2012	...	...	...	...	...	...
Bordeaux **320** a.	1913	...	...	...	|	2030	|	...	|	|	|	2114	|	|	...	|	|	2226	...	...	...	...	...	...
Port la Nouvelle d.	...	...	...	...	1709	...	1732	...	|	|	1809	...	|	1832	...	|	1909	...	...	...	...	...	...	...
Perpignan a.	...	...	...	...	1740	...	1802	...	1807	1807	1840	...	1849	1902	...	1908	1940	...	...	...	...	...	...	...
Perpignan d.	...	1711	...	...	1745	...	...	...	...	...	1845	...	1852	...	...	...	1945	...	...	...	...	...	...	...
Argelès sur Mer d.	...	1727	...	...	1802	...	...	...	...	...	1902	...	1911	...	...	...	2002	...	...	...	...	...	...	...
Collioure d.	...	1732	...	...	1807	...	...	...	...	...	1907	...	1918	...	...	...	2007	...	...	...	...	...	...	...
Port Vendres d.	...	1736	...	...	1811	...	...	...	...	...	1911	...	1924	...	...	...	2011	...	...	...	...	...	...	...
Banyuls sur Mer d.	...	1740	...	...	1816	...	...	...	...	...	1916	...	1930	...	...	...	2016	...	...	...	...	...	...	...
Cerbère **657** a.	...	1746	...	...	1822	...	...	...	...	...	1922	...	1937	...	...	...	2022	...	...	...	...	...	...	...
Portbou **657** a.	...	1751	...	...	...	...	...	...	...	...	1928	...	...	...	...	...	...	...	...	...	...	...	...	...

		4768 4769 ★	TGV 6841 S	Ⓐ	Ⓐ	TGV 9717 ♠		Ⓐ	TGV 6817 g		TGV 9732 D ♠	TGV 6215 A	Ⓑ d	4766 4767 ⑤⑦ t★	TGV 5119	TGV 6217	TGV 9836 ⊖ x	TGV 9836 ⑤⑦ u	TGV 6219 B	TGV 6219 ⑤ f	n	TGV 6221 n	TGV 6225 ⑤⑦ w	TGV 5137 ⑦j
Brussels Midi **11** d.	...	...	...	...	...	...	...	...	...	...	...	...	...	...	...	...	1617	1617	...	...	...	...	...	...
Lille Europe **11** d.	...	...	...	...	...	...	...	...	...	...	...	...	...	...	1554	...	1703	1703	...	...	...	...	...	2002
Charles de Gaulle ✈ **11** d.	...	...	...	...	...	...	...	...	...	...	...	...	...	...	1658	...	1758	1758	...	...	...	...	...	2116
Marne la Vallée § **11** d.	...	...	...	...	...	...	...	...	...	...	...	...	...	...	1711	...	1811	1811	...	...	...	...	...	2130
Paris Gare de Lyon ▶ d.	...	...	...	...	...	1607	...	...	...	...	...	1715	...	...	|	1807	|	|	1915	1915	...	2007	2111	|
Dijon **379** d.	...	...	...	...	...	|	...	...	...	...	...	|	...	...	|	|	|	|	|	|	...	|	|	|
Genève **346** d.	...	...	...	...	...	|	...	...	...	...	...	|	...	...	|	|	|	|	|	|	...	|	|	|
Lyon Part Dieu ▶ d.	...	...	1706	...	...	|	...	...	1810	...	...	|	...	...	1910	|	2010	2010	|	|	...	|	|	2333
Valence TGV ▶ d.	...	...	1746	...	...	1821	...	...	1846	...	...	|	...	...	1947	2022	2048	2048	|	|	...	2222	2327	0011
Nice **360** d.	...	...	|	...	...	|	...	...	|	...	...	|	...	...	|	|	|	|	|	|	...	|	|	|
Marseille St Charles d.	...	1718	|	...	1722	|	...	...	|	1817	1910	|	...	1918	|	|	|	|	|	|	...	|	|	|
Vitrolles Aéroport Marseille ‡ d.	...	|	|	...	1747	|	...	...	|	1835	|	|	...	|	|	|	|	|	|	|	...	|	|	|
Arles d.	...	|	|	...	1831	|	...	...	|	1917	|	|	...	2000	|	|	|	|	|	|	...	|	|	|
Avignon Centre d.	1740	|	|	1810	|	|	1840	1840	|	|	1946v	|	1940	|	|	|	|	|	|	|	2140r	|	|	|
Tarascon-sur-Rhône d.	1754	|	|	1824	1840	|	1854	1854	|	1926	|	|	1954	|	|	|	|	|	|	|	|	|	|	|
Nimes d.	1813	|	1832	1847	1854	1909	1913	1913	1934	1943	2005	2009	2013	2028	2032	2109	2133	2133	2209	2209	2213	2309	0017	0059
Lunel d.	1832	|	|	1914	...	|	1931	1931	|	1958	|	|	2031	|	|	|	|	|	|	|	2231	|	|	|
Montpellier a.	1846	1853	1858	1926	...	1934	1946	1946	1958	2010	2030	2034	2046	2053	2058	2134	2158	2158	2234	2234	2246	2334	0052	0122
Montpellier d.	1850	1857	...	1929	...	1941	1950	1950	2001	2014	2037	...	2050	2057	...	2141	...	2202	2241	2241	2250	...	...	...
Frontignan d.	1904	|	...	1948	...	|	2004	2004	|	2027	|	...	2104	|	...	|	...	|	|	|	2304	...	...	...
Sète d.	1911	|	...	1954	...	2001	2011	2011	|	2035	|	...	2111	2116	...	2201	...	2222	2301	2301	2311	...	...	...
Agde d.	1924	|	...	2009	...	2017	2024	2024	|	2050	|	...	2124	|	...	2217	...	2239	2317	2317	2325	...	...	...
Béziers d.	1937	|	...	2025	...	2031	2037	2037	2043	2103	2118	...	2137	2142	...	2232	...	2254	2329	2331	2341	...	...	...
Narbonne a.	1950	|	...	2040	...	2044	2050	2050	2056	2116	|	...	2150	2155	...	2245	...	2307z	...	2349	2358	...	...	...
Narbonne d.	1955	|	...	...	...	2047	...	2055	2059	...	|	...	2155	2158	...	2248	...	2310z	...	2352	...	...	...	...
Carcassonne **321** a.	|	|	...	...	...	|	...	|	2127	...	|	...	|	2228	...	|	...	|	...	|	...	...	...	...
Toulouse **321** a.	|	2107	...	...	...	|	...	|	2220	...	|	...	|	2318	...	|	...	|	...	|	...	...	...	...
Bordeaux **320** a.	|	2313	...	...	...	|	...	|	...	...	|	...	|	...	...	|	...	|	...	|	...	...	...	...
Port la Nouvelle d.	2009	...	...	...	...	|	...	2109	...	...	|	...	2209	...	...	|	...	|	...	|	...	...	...	...
Perpignan a.	2040	...	...	...	...	2120	...	2138	...	...	2210	...	2240	...	...	2322	...	2342z	...	0055	...	...	...	...
Perpignan d.	...	...	...	...	...	...	...	2141	...	...	...	...	...	...	...	...	...	...	...	...	...	...	...	...
Argelès sur Mer d.	...	...	...	...	...	...	...	2158	...	...	...	...	...	...	...	...	...	...	...	...	...	...	...	...
Collioure d.	...	...	...	...	...	...	...	2203	...	...	...	...	...	...	...	...	...	...	...	...	...	...	...	...
Port Vendres d.	...	...	...	...	...	...	...	2207	...	...	...	...	...	...	...	...	...	...	...	...	...	...	...	...
Banyuls sur Mer d.	...	...	...	...	...	...	...	2212	...	...	...	...	...	...	...	...	...	...	...	...	...	...	...	...
Cerbère **657** a.	...	...	...	...	...	...	...	2218	...	...	...	...	...	...	...	...	...	...	...	...	...	...	...	...
Portbou **657** a.	...	...	...	...	...	...	...	...	...	...	...	...	...	...	...	...	...	...	...	...	...	...	...	...

A – Ⓐ (daily July 6 - Aug. 29).
B – Ⓑ (daily July 6 - Aug. 29).
D – Runs from a date to be announced.
– To July 4 and from Aug. 25.
– 🚃12 Paris Austerlitz - Toulouse - Cerbère. Subject to alteration on June 15, Sept. 6, 7, 20, 21, 27, 28, Nov. 3–6, 10, 12, 13. Runs 56–63 minutes later Narbonne - Cerbère Oct. 27–31 (also Nov. 7, 14).
– From Strasbourg (Table **379**). Subject to alteration on Sept. 13, 20, 27, Oct. 4, 11, 18.
– Paris **Austerlitz**. Departs 0925 until June 30.
– Not Aug. 20–24. Departs Genève 1330 July 15 - Aug. 19 (by 🚌 Genève - Bellegarde).
– Not Sept. 6, 19, 20, 21, Nov. 8, 9, 10.
– Ⓑ (also Nov. 1). Runs daily Avignon - Nimes and Narbonne - Perpignan.
– Also Nov. 1, 11; not July 6 - Aug. 31, Oct. 19, 26. To St Chély d'Apcher (Table **332**).
– Also Aug. 14; not Aug. 15.
– Not Sept. 27. Departs Lyon 1808 Sept. 14 - Oct. 28 (1810 on Sept. 20, Oct. 4).
– Not Sept. 6, 7, 19, 20, 21, Nov. 8, 9.
– Also July 14, Nov. 11; not Sept. 7, Oct. 19.
– Runs daily July 5 - Aug. 24.

m – Not Oct. 31.
n – Not Oct. 18, 19, Dec. 6.
p – Runs daily Montpellier - Narbonne June 30 - Aug. 29.
r – Ⓐ only.
t – Also July 14, Aug. 14, Nov. 11; not July 13, Aug. 15, Sept. 19, 21. On Aug. 14 departs Marseille 1914, Arles 1959.
u – Also July 14, Aug. 14, Nov. 11; not Aug. 15.
v – Avignon **TGV**. Also calls at Aix en Provence TGV (d. 1924).
w – Also July 14, Nov. 11; not Aug. 15, Oct. 19.
x – Not Aug. 15.
y – ①⑥⑦ to Aug. 31 (also Sept. 13, 14, 22; not June 16, 23); daily Sept. 27 - Oct. 12; ⑥⑦ Oct. 18–26; daily from Nov. 1 (not Nov. 8, 9, 10).
z – On ⑤ (also Aug. 14) Narbonne a. 2309, d. 2315, Perpignan a. 2356.

TGV – Ⓡ, supplement payable, 🍷.

⊖ – Subject to alteration on Sept. 13, 20, 27, Oct. 4.
▶ – For Paris to Lyon see Table **340**. For additional trains from Paris and Lyon to Valence TGV see Table **350**. For Lyon to Valence Ville see Table **351**.
♠ – To Barcelona (Tables **13**/**49**).

♣ – 🚃12 Strasbourg - Montpellier; 🚃12 (**6824**) Metz - Montpellier (see Table **379**). Lyon d. 1307 Sept. 15 - Oct. 28. Dijon d. 1120 or 1121 Sept. 9 - Nov. 29. Subject to alteration on Sept. 14, 20, 27, 28, Oct. 4, 12, 19.
★ – *INTERCITÉS*. Ⓡ.
◐ – Via Limoges and Toulouse (Table **310**).
△ – From Nantes and Rennes (Table **335**). Subject to alteration on Sept. 13, 20, 27, 28, Oct. 4.
§ – Marne la Vallée - Chessy (station for Disneyland Paris).
‡ – Vitrolles Aéroport Marseille-Provence. A shuttle bus runs to the airport terminal (journey time 5 minutes). For additional trains see Table **351**.

Certain departures times from Avignon, Marseille, Vitrolles, Arles and Tarascon may be up to 6 minutes later to July 14 and from Oct. 11.

Services Lyon / Avignon / Marseille - Montpellier - Narbonne - Perpignan / Toulouse are subject to alteration or cancellation Sept. 19–21.

Toulouse / Bordeaux arrivals may be up to 21 minutes later from Oct. 29.

355 CERBÈRE - PERPIGNAN - MONTPELLIER - PARIS

	TGV 6202 Ⓐ J	TGV 6202 Ⓐ	Ⓐ c	Ⓐ	TGV 6230 ①–⑥ b	d	Ⓐ	TGV 9862 ②–⑤ f	TGV 9862 ① g	TGV 9862 ⑥ w	TGV 9862 ⑥⑦ y	Ⓐ	TGV 6204 T	TGV 6204 e	Ⓐ K	Ⓐ J	⑥ m	⚒	Ⓐ J	©	TGV 6863 ⊗	©	Ⓐ ⊠	Ⓐ
Cerbère 657 d.	...	...	...	...	...	...	...	...	...	...	...	...	...	...	...	...	...	...	...	...	...	...	0540	...
Banyuls sur Mer 657 d.	...	...	...	...	...	...	...	...	...	...	...	...	...	...	...	...	...	...	...	...	...	...	0547	...
Port Vendres d.	...	...	...	...	...	...	...	...	...	...	...	...	...	...	...	...	...	...	...	...	...	...	0552	...
Collioure d.	...	...	...	...	...	...	...	...	...	...	...	...	...	...	...	...	...	...	...	...	...	...	0556	...
Argelès sur Mer d.	...	...	...	...	...	...	...	...	...	...	...	...	...	...	...	...	...	...	...	...	...	...	0601	...
Perpignan a.	...	...	...	...	...	...	...	...	...	...	...	...	...	...	...	...	...	...	...	...	...	...	0617	...
Perpignan d.	...	...	...	...	...	...	...	...	0518	0520	...	...	0537	...	0538	0544	...	...	...	0558	...	...	0622	...
Port la Nouvelle d.	...	...	...	...	...	...	...	...	|	|	...	...	|	...	0608	0614	...	...	...	0629	...	...	0654	...
Bordeaux **320** d.	...	...	...	...	...	...	...	...	|	|	...	...	|	...	|	|	...	...	...	|	...	...	|	...
Toulouse **321** d.	...	...	...	...	...	...	...	...	|	|	...	...	|	...	|	|	...	...	...	|	0550	...	|	...
Carcassonne **321** d.	...	...	...	...	...	...	...	...	|	|	...	...	|	...	|	|	...	...	...	|	|	...	|	0647
Narbonne a.	...	...	...	...	...	...	...	...	0551	0553	...	...	0611	...	0621	0627	...	...	...	0643	0658	...	0706	0718
Narbonne d.	...	...	0428	...	...	0531	...	...	0554	0556	...	0601	0614	...	0625	0631	0631	...	0641	0645	0701	...	0709	0721
Béziers d.	0417	...	0447	...	...	0547	...	...	0612	0614	...	0616	0631	...	0642	0647	0647	...	0700	0705	0718	...	0725	0741
Agde d.	0434	...	0502	...	...	0600	...	...	0626	0629	...	0630	0644	...	0655	0700	0700	...	0714	0720	|	←	0736	0755
Sète d.	0454	...	0518	...	...	0615	...	...	0643	0646	...	0646	0659	...	0712	0715	0715	...	0730	0735	0741	0745	0750	0811
Frontignan d.	|	...	0525	...	...	0621	...	...	|	|	...	0652	|	...	0718	0721	0721	...	0736	→	|	0750	0757	0817
Montpellier a.	0517	...	0537	...	...	0634	...	...	0659	0701	...	0710	0717	...	0734	0734	0734	...	0754	...	0758	0810	0810	0835
Montpellier d.	0524	0524	0539	...	0624	0639	0642	0702	0703	0705	0705	0713	0724	0734	0739	0739	...	0742	...	...	0802	0813	0813	0839
Lunel d.	|	|	0553	...	|	0653	0656	|	|	|	|	0729	|	|	0753	0753	...	0756	...	...	|	0829	0829	0853
Nimes d.	0552	0552	0611	0648	0652	0711	0723	0729	0728	0729	0729	0749	0753	0753	0808	0808	...	0823	...	...	0829	0849	0849	0908
Tarascon-sur-Rhône d.	|	|	0631	0709	|	0733	0743	|	|	|	|	0806	|	|	...	...	...	0843	...	...	|	0906	0906	...
Avignon Centre a.	|	|	|	0720	|	|	0755	|	|	|	|	0820	|	|	...	...	...	0855	...	...	|	0920	0920	...
Arles d.	|	|	0644	...	|	0743	...	|	|	|	|	...	|	|	...	...	...	...	...	...	|	...	...	...
Vitrolles Aéroport Marseille ‡ d.	|	|	0729	...	|	0825	...	|	|	|	|	...	|	|	...	...	...	...	...	...	|	...	...	...
Marseille St Charles a.	|	|	0747	...	|	0842	...	|	|	|	|	...	|	|	...	...	...	...	...	...	|	...	...	...
Nice **360** a.	|	|	...	...	|	...	...	|	|	|	|	...	|	|	...	...	...	...	...	...	|	...	...	...
Valence TGV d.	|	|	...	...	0741	...	...	0820	0820	0820	0820	...	|	|	...	...	...	...	...	...	0915	...	...	...
Lyon Part Dieu a.	|	|	...	...	|	...	...	0854	0854	0854	0854	...	|	|	...	...	...	...	...	...	0949	...	...	...
Genève **346** a.	|	|	...	...	|	...	...	|	|	|	|	...	|	|	...	...	...	...	...	...	|	...	...	...
Dijon **379** a.	|	|	...	...	|	...	...	|	|	|	|	...	|	|	...	...	...	...	...	...	1133	...	...	...
Paris Gare de Lyon a.	0845	0845	...	...	0953	...	...	|	|	|	|	...	1045	1045	...	...	...	...	...	...	...	...	...	...
Marne la Vallée § **11** a.	...	...	...	...	...	...	...	1048	1048	1048	1048	...	...	...	...	...	...	...	...	...	...	...	...	...
Charles de Gaulle + **11** a.	...	...	...	...	...	...	...	1102	1102	1102	1102	...	...	...	...	...	...	...	...	...	...	...	...	...
Lille Europe **11** a.	...	...	...	...	...	...	...	1157	1157	1157	1157	...	...	...	...	...	...	...	...	...	...	...	...	...
Brussels Midi **11** a.	...	...	...	...	...	...	...	1251	1251	1243	1243	...	...	...	...	...	...	...	...	...	...	...	...	...

	TGV 5166 ⊕	Ⓐ		TGV 9700 ♥	Ⓐ	3630 ★ L	TGV 6878 M S	TGV 6878 N S	Ⓐ		TGV 6208	TGV 9734 H ⊕♠	4655 4654 ★ n	⊡	TGV 9702 ♠	Ⓐ	TGV 6859 ⊙	Ⓐ ⊡	Ⓐ	TGV 6210 G	TGV 9722 H ♠	Ⓐ	4657 4656 ★	© K
Cerbère 657 d.	...	...	0635	...	0705	0725	...	...	0740	...	...	...	...	0935	...	...	...	1035	...	...	...	...	...	...
Banyuls sur Mer 657 d.	...	...	0642	...	0712	0734	...	...	0747	...	...	...	...	0942	...	...	...	1042	...	...	...	...	...	...
Port Vendres d.	...	...	0647	...	0717	0741	...	...	0752	...	...	...	...	0947	...	...	...	1047	...	...	...	...	...	...
Collioure d.	...	...	0651	...	0721	0746	...	...	0755	...	...	...	...	0951	...	...	...	1051	...	...	...	...	...	...
Argelès sur Mer d.	...	...	0657	...	0727	0754	...	...	0801	...	...	...	...	0957	...	...	...	1057	...	...	...	...	...	...
Perpignan a.	...	...	0713	...	0743	0812	...	...	0817	...	...	...	...	1013	...	...	...	1113	...	...	...	...	...	...
Perpignan d.	...	0640	0718	0737	0748	0816	...	...	0822	0822	...	0846	...	1018	1051	...	...	...	1118	...	1152	...	...	...
Port la Nouvelle d.	...	0710	0749	|	0818	|	...	...	0853	0853	...	|	...	1049	|	...	...	...	1149	...	|	...	...	...
Bordeaux **320** d.	...	|	|	|	|	|	...	...	|	|	...	|	0731	|	|	...	0838	...	|	...	|	...	0935	...
Toulouse **321** d.	...	|	|	|	|	|	...	...	|	|	...	|	0949	|	|	...	1050	...	|	...	|	...	1151	...
Carcassonne **321** d.	...	|	|	|	|	|	...	...	|	|	...	|	1033	|	|	...	1134	...	|	...	|	...	1234	...
Narbonne a.	...	0724	0802	0811	0830	0854	...	...	0905	0905	...	0921	1101	1102	1125	...	1201	...	1202	...	|	...	1301	...
Narbonne d.	...	...	0809	0814	0832	0920z	...	...	0909	0909	...	0924	1104	1109	1128	...	1204	...	1209	...	|	1241	1304	1309
Béziers d.	...	...	0825	0831	0847	|	...	...	0925	0925	...	|	1120	1125	|	...	1220	...	1225	1230j	1242	1300	1321	1325
Agde d.	...	...	0836	0846	0900	|	...	...	0936	0936	...	|	|	1136	|	...	|	...	1236	1244j	|	1314	|	1336
Sète d.	...	...	0850	0902	0915	|	...	...	0950	0950	...	|	1144	1150	|	...	|	...	1250	1259j	|	1330	1344	1350
Frontignan d.	...	...	0857	|	0921	|	...	...	0957	0957	...	|	|	1157	|	...	|	...	1257	|	|	1336	|	1357
Montpellier a.	...	...	0910	0920	0934	|	...	...	1010	1010	...	1027	1203	1210	1218	...	1259	...	1310	1316j	1321	1354	1403	1410
Montpellier d.	0853	...	0913	0924	...	|	0950	1002	1013	1013	1024	1031	1207	1213	1225	1237	1302	...	1313	1324	1329	...	1407	...
Lunel d.	|	...	0929	|	...	|	|	|	1029	1029	|	|	|	1229	|	1300	|	...	1329	|	|	...	|	...
Nimes d.	0924	...	0949	0952	...	|	1017	1029	1049	1049	1052	1058	1234	1249	1252	1323	1329	...	1349	1352	1356	...	1434	...
Tarascon-sur-Rhône d.	|	...	1006	|	...	◐	|	|	1106	1106	|	|	|	1306	|	1343	|	...	1406	|	|	...	|	...
Avignon Centre a.	|	...	|	|	...	|	|	|	1120	1120	|	|	|	1320	|	1355	|	...	1420	|	1412v	...	|	...
Arles d.	|	...	1016	|	...	|	|	|	...	...	|	|	1259	...	|	...	|	...	...	|	|	...	1459	...
Vitrolles Aéroport Marseille ‡ d.	|	...	1050	|	...	|	|	|	...	...	|	|	|	...	|	...	|	...	...	|	|	...	|	...
Marseille St Charles a.	|	...	1105	|	...	|	|	|	...	...	|	|	1343	...	|	...	|	...	...	|	1450	...	1542	...
Nice **360** a.	|	...	...	|	...	|	|	|	...	...	|	|	...	...	|	...	|	...	...	|	...	...	...	...
Valence TGV d.	1019	...	...	|	...	|	|	|	...	...	1139	1145	...	...	1341	...	1416	...	...	|	...	...	...	...
Lyon Part Dieu a.	1054	...	...	|	...	|	1140	1150	...	...	|	1224	...	...	|	...	1451	...	...	|	...	...	...	...
Genève **346** a.	|	...	...	|	...	|	...	...	...	...	|	...	...	...	|	...	...	...	...	|	...	...	...	...
Dijon **379** a.	|	...	...	|	...	|	...	...	...	...	|	...	...	...	|	...	...	...	...	|	...	...	...	...
Paris Gare de Lyon a.	|	...	...	1245	...	1718a	...	...	...	...	1353	...	...	...	1553	...	...	...	...	1645	...	...	...	...
Marne la Vallée § **11** a.	1248	...	...	...	...	...	...	...	...	...	...	...	...	...	...	...	...	...	...	...	...	...	...	...
Charles de Gaulle + **11** a.	1302	...	...	...	...	...	...	...	...	...	...	...	...	...	...	...	...	...	...	...	...	...	...	...
Lille Europe **11** a.	1424	...	...	...	...	...	...	...	...	...	...	...	...	...	...	...	...	...	...	...	...	...	...	...
Brussels Midi **11** a.	...	...	...	...	....	...	...	...	...	...	...	...	...	...	...	...	...	...	...	...	...	...	...	...

G – Daily to Aug. 24 (not July 14); ⑦ from Aug. 31.
H – Runs from a date to be announced.
J – To July 4 and from Aug. 25.
K – July 5 - Aug. 24.
L – (12) Cerbère - Toulouse - Paris Austerlitz. Subject to alteration on Sept. 6, 7, 20, 21, 27, 28.
M – Until June 20.
N – From June 21 (not Sept. 13, 14, 20, 27, Oct. 4, 12, 19).
S – To Strasbourg (Table **379**).
T – Daily to July 5; ⑥ July 12 - Aug. 23; daily from Aug. 25 (not Dec. 7).

a – Paris **Austerlitz**. 1721 until June 30; 1737 on ①–④ Aug. 25 - Sept. 4; 1806 on Aug. 29; 1730 on Ⓐ Oct. 27 - Nov. 25.
b – Not July 14, Nov. 11.
c – Not Oct. 20.
d – Not Oct. 19, Dec. 7.
e – Not Dec. 7.
f – Also Nov. 10; Not July 15, Aug. 15, Nov. 12.
g – Also July 15, Nov. 12; not July 14, Nov. 10.
j – ①–⑥ July 7 - Aug. 23 (not July 14).
m – Not Nov. 1.
n – Not Sept. 15 - 26.
p – 1128 on ⑦.
v – Avignon **TGV**. Also calls at Aix en Provence TGV (a. 1435).
w – Also Aug. 15; not Sept. 20, 27.
y – Also July 14, Aug. 15; not Sept. 14, 21, 27, 28, Oct. 5.
z – 0916 from Oct. 27.

TGV – Ⓡ, supplement payable.

⊕ – Subject to alteration on Sept. 14, 21, 27, 28, Oct. 5.
⊗ – Not July 14, Aug. 15, Nov. 11, Dec. 7. Subject to alteration on Sept. 13, 14, 20, 21, 27, 28, Oct. 4, 5. Timings at Valence, Lyon and Dijon may vary by a few minutes on certain dates.
⊙ – Subject to alteration on Sept. 20, 27, 28, Oct. 4. Does not run Bordeaux - Narbonne on ①–⑤ Sept. 15 - 26
⊡ – Subject to alteration Cerbère - Perpignan from Dec. 1.
⊠ – Not ②–⑤ Oct. 17 - Nov. 7, Nov. 20, 21, 25, 28. Does not run Cerbère - Perpignan on Sept. 18.
♠ – From Barcelona (Tables **13**/**49**).
♥ – From Barcelona from July 6 (Table **13**). Train number **6206** until July 5.
◐ – Via Toulouse and Limoges (Table **310**).
★ – *INTERCITÉS*. Ⓡ.
‡ – Vitrolles Aéroport Marseille-Provence. A shuttle bus runs to the airport terminal (journey time 5 minutes). For additional trains see Table **351**.
§ – Marne la Vallée - Chessy (station for Disneyland Paris).

Services Perpignan / Toulouse - Narbonne - Montpellier - Avignon / Marseille / Lyon are subject to alteration or cancellation Sept. 19 - 21.

Certain departures from Bordeaux, Toulouse and Carcassonne may be up to 22 minutes earlier from Oct. 29.

CERBÈRE - PERPIGNAN - MONTPELLIER - PARIS

		TGV 6212	TGV 9868	4659 4658		TGV 6882		TGV 9704	TGV 5380				TGV 6861		TGV 6218	TGV 6218	TGV 9754			TGV 5186	4663 4662			TGV 6220
	Ⓐ		◇	★ c		L		♠	△	ⒶD		Ⓐ	①–⑥ ◇		B	A	x◇	Ⓐ ☆	⚒	◇	★		Ⓒ	
Cerbère ... 657 d.	...	...	...	...	1235	...	...	...	...	...	...	...	...	1435	...	...	...	...	...	...	...	...	1535	...
Banyuls sur Mer ... 657 d.	...	...	...	...	1242	...	...	...	...	...	...	...	...	1442	...	...	...	...	...	...	...	...	1542	...
Port Vendres ... d.	...	...	...	...	1247	...	...	...	...	...	...	...	...	1447	...	...	...	...	...	...	...	...	1547	...
Collioure ... d.	...	...	...	...	1251	...	...	...	...	...	...	...	...	1451	...	...	...	...	...	...	...	...	1551	...
Argelès sur Mer ... d.	...	...	...	...	1257	...	...	...	...	...	...	...	...	1457	...	...	...	...	...	...	...	...	1557	...
Perpignan ... a.	...	...	...	...	1313	...	...	...	...	...	...	...	...	1513	...	...	...	...	...	...	...	...	1613	...
Perpignan ... d.	1218	1237**h**	...	...	1318	...	1418	1450	...	...	...	...	...	1518	...	1537	...	...	...	...	...	1618	1618	...
Port la Nouvelle ... d.	1249	|	...	...	1349	...	1449	|	...	...	...	...	...	1549	...	|	...	...	...	...	...	1649	1649	...
Bordeaux **320** ... d.	|	|	...	1047	|	...	|	|	...	...	...	...	...	|	...	|	...	...	...	...	1331**q**	|	|	...
Toulouse **321** ... d.	|	|	...	1254	|	...	|	|	...	...	...	...	1450	|	...	|	...	...	...	...	1549	|	|	...
Carcassonne **321** ... d.	|	|	...	|	|	...	|	|	...	...	...	...	1534	|	...	|	...	...	...	...	1633	|	|	...
Narbonne ... a.	1302	1311**h**	...	|	1406	...	1502	1524	...	...	...	...	1601	1604	...	1614	...	...	...	...	1701	1702	1702	...
Narbonne ... d.	...	1314**h**	...	|	1409	...	1509	1527	...	1531	...	...	1604	1609	...	1617	...	1631	...	...	1704	1709	1709	...
Béziers ... d.	...	1330	...	|	1425	...	1525	|	...	1547	...	...	1620	1625	...	1634	...	1647	...	...	1720	1725	1725	1730
Agde ... d.	...	1344	...	|	1436	...	1536	|	...	1600	...	...	|	1636	...	1648	...	1700	...	...	|	1736	1736	1744
Sète ... d.	...	1359	...	|	1450	...	1550	|	...	1615	...	...	|	1650	...	1702	...	1715	...	...	1744	1750	1750	1758
Frontignan ... d.	...	|	...	|	1457	...	1557	|	...	1621	...	...	|	1657	...	|	...	1721	...	...	|	1757	1757	|
Montpellier ... a.	...	1417	...	1503	1510	...	1610	1617	...	1634	...	...	1658	1710	...	1717	...	1735	...	...	1803	1810	1810	1817
Montpellier ... d.	...	1424	1502	1507	1513	1600	1613	1624	1628	1639	1639	1643	1702	1713	1724	1724	1728	1739	1743	1802	1807	1813	1813	1824
Lunel ... d.	...	|	|	|	1529	|	1629	|	|	1653	1653	1706	|	1729	|	|	|	1753	1803	|	|	1829	1829	|
Nimes ... d.	...	1452	1529	|	1549	1627	1649	1652	1656	1711	1711	1723	1729	1749	1752	1752	1756	1808	1823	1829	1835	1849	1849	1852
Tarascon-sur-Rhône ... d.	...	|	|	|	1606	|	1706	|	|	1732	1732	1743	|	1806	|	|	|	...	1843	|	|	1906	1906	|
Avignon Centre ... a.	...	|	|	|	1620	|	1720	|	|	|	|	1755	|	1820	|	|	|	...	1855	|	|	1920	1920	|
Arles ... d.	...	|	|	|	...	|	...	|	|	1742	1742	...	|	...	|	|	|	...	...	|	1900	...	...	|
Vitrolles Aéroport Marseille ‡ d.	...	|	|	|	...	|	...	|	|	1823	1823	...	|	...	|	|	|	...	...	|	|	...	...	|
Marseille St Charles ... a.	...	|	|	1642	...	|	...	|	|	1840	1840	...	|	...	|	|	|	...	...	|	1943	...	...	|
Nice **360** ... a.	...	|	|	1937	...	|	...	|	|	...	...	...	|	...	|	|	|	...	...	|	...	...	...	|
Valence TGV ... d.	...	1539	1616	...	...	1718	...	1741	1747	...	...	...	|	...	|	|	1847	...	...	1916	...	...	...	1941
Lyon Part Dieu ... a.	...	|	1650	...	...	1754	...	|	1824	...	...	...	1850	...	|	|	1924	...	...	1950	...	...	...	|
Genève **346** ... a.	...	|	|	...	...	|	...	|	...	...	...	...	...	...	|	|	2116**b**	...	...	|	...	...	...	|
Dijon **379** ... a.	...	|	|	...	...	1938	...	|	...	...	...	...	...	...	|	|	...	...	...	|	...	...	...	|
Paris Gare de Lyon ... a.	...	1753	|	...	...	...	...	1953	...	...	...	...	...	...	2045	2045	...	...	...	|	...	...	...	2153
Marne la Vallée § **11** ... a.	...	...	1849	...	...	...	...	...	...	...	...	...	...	...	...	...	...	...	...	2148	...	...	...	...
Charles de Gaulle ✈ **11** ... a.	...	...	1903	...	...	...	...	...	...	...	...	...	...	...	...	...	...	...	...	2202	...	...	...	...
Lille Europe **11** ... a.	...	...	1957	...	...	...	...	...	...	...	...	...	...	...	...	...	...	...	...	2304**z**	...	...	...	...
Brussels Midi **11** ... a.	...	...	2043	...	...	...	...	...	...	...	...	...	...	...	...	...	...	...	...	...	...	...	...	...

		4665 4664		TGV 9706				TGV 6857		TGV 6224	TGV 6224	TGV 9738	4667 4666				TGV 6228	TGV 9724	4669 4668			3732	3730	4350 4351
		★ w		♠	Ⓒ	Ⓐ	Ⓒ T	◇	Ⓑ	⑤⑦ f	⑦ e	◇ ♠	⑤⑦ t★	Ⓐ	①–④ m		⑦ e	■	★	n		Q Ⓡ	P Ⓡ	R Ⓡ
Cerbère ... 657 d.	...	...	1635	...	...	...	1730	...	1735	...	...	...	...	1835	1835	...	...	...	...	1935	...	1940	2016	2022
Banyuls sur Mer ... 657 d.	...	...	1642	...	...	...	1737	...	1742	...	...	...	...	1842	1842	...	...	...	...	1942	...	1949	2025	2031
Port Vendres ... d.	...	...	1647	...	...	...	1742	...	1747	...	...	...	...	1847	1847	...	...	...	...	1947	...	1956	2032	2038
Collioure ... d.	...	...	1651	...	...	...	1745	...	1751	...	...	...	...	1851	1851	...	...	...	...	1951	...	2001	2037	2043
Argelès sur Mer ... d.	...	...	1657	...	...	...	1750	...	1757	...	...	...	...	1857	1857	...	...	...	...	1957	...	2008	2045	2051
Perpignan ... a.	...	...	1713	...	...	...	1806	...	1813	...	...	...	...	1913	1913	...	...	...	...	2013	...	2026	2103	2110
Perpignan ... d.	...	...	1722	1751	...	...	1810	...	1820	...	1837	1851	...	...	1918	1918	...	1952	...	2018	...	2053	2107	2114
Port la Nouvelle ... d.	...	...	1752	|	...	...	1839	...	1851	...	|	|	...	...	1949	1949	...	|	...	2049	...	2127	|	|
Bordeaux **320** ... d.	...	1445	|	|	...	...	|	...	|	...	|	|	1644	...	|	|	...	|	1730	|	...	|	|	|
Toulouse **321** ... d.	...	1651	|	|	1655	1655	|	1750	|	...	|	|	1851	...	|	|	...	|	1949	|	...	|	|	|
Carcassonne **321** ... d.	...	|	|	|	1757	1757	|	1834	|	...	|	|	|	...	|	|	...	|	2033	|	...	|	|	|
Narbonne ... a.	...	|	1806	1824	1828	1828	1851	1901	1904	...	1911	1924	|	...	2004	2004	...	|	2101	2106	...	2141	2141	2150
Narbonne ... d.	1721	|	1809	1827	1831	1831	...	1904	1909	...	1914	1927	|	...	2009	2009	...	|	2104	2109	...	2207	2207	2154
Béziers ... d.	1741	|	1825	1844	1849	1849	...	1919	1925	...	1931	|	|	...	2025	2025	...	2042	2120	2125	...	|	|	2210
Agde ... d.	1756	|	1836	|	1901	1901	...	|	1936	...	1944	|	|	...	2036	2036	...	|	|	2136	...	|	|	2224
Sète ... d.	1813	|	1850	|	1915	1915	...	1942	1950	...	1959	|	|	...	2050	2050	...	|	2144	2150	...	|	|	2239
Frontignan ... d.	1819	|	1857	|	1921	1921	...	|	1957	...	|	|	|	...	2057	2057	...	|	|	2157	...	|	|	|
Montpellier ... a.	1836	1903	1910	1921	1934	1934	...	1958	2010	...	2017	2021	2049	...	2110	2110	...	2121	2203	2210	...	|	|	2257
Montpellier ... d.	1839	1907	1913	1924	1939	1943	...	2002	2013	2024	2024	2028	2053	...	2113	2113	2124	2128	2207	2213	...	|	|	2300
Lunel ... d.	1853	|	1929	|	1953	2006	...	|	2029	|	|	|	|	...	2129	2129	|	|	|	2229	...	|	|	|
Nimes ... d.	1911	|	1949	1952	2008	2024	...	2029	2046	2052	2052	2059	|	...	2146	2146	2152	2156	2234	2246	...	|	|	2325
Tarascon-sur-Rhône ... d.	1932	|	2006	|	...	2043	...	|	...	|	|	|	|	...	...	...	|	|	|	...	...	◐	◐	...
Avignon Centre ... a.	|	|	2020	|	...	2055	...	|	...	|	|	|	|	...	...	...	|	2220**v**	|	...	...	|	|	...
Arles ... d.	1943	|	...	|	...	...	...	|	...	|	|	|	|	...	...	...	|	|	2259	...	...	|	|	...
Vitrolles Aéroport Marseille ‡ d.	2022	|	...	|	...	...	...	|	...	|	|	|	|	...	...	...	|	|	|	...	...	|	|	...
Marseille St Charles ... a.	2038	2042	...	|	...	...	...	|	...	|	|	|	2224	...	...	...	|	2258	2342	...	...	|	|	...
Nice **360** ... a.	...	2341**y**	...	|	...	...	...	|	...	|	|	|	...	...	...	...	|	...	...	...	...	|	|	...
Valence TGV ... d.	...	...	...	|	...	...	...	2118	...	2140	2140	2146	...	...	...	...	2241	...	...	...	...	|	|	...
Lyon Part Dieu ... a.	...	...	...	|	...	...	...	2154	...	|	|	2224	...	...	...	...	|	...	...	...	...	|	|	...
Genève **346** ... a.	...	...	...	|	...	...	...	...	...	|	|	...	...	...	...	...	|	...	...	...	...	|	|	...
Dijon **379** ... a.	...	...	...	|	...	...	...	...	...	|	|	...	...	...	...	...	|	...	...	...	...	|	|	...
Paris Gare de Lyon ... a.	...	...	...	2245	...	...	...	...	...	2353	2353	...	...	...	...	...	0053	...	...	...	...	0722**a**	0722**a**	...
Marne la Vallée § **11** ... a.	...	...	...	...	...	...	...	...	...	...	...	...	...	...	...	...	...	...	...	...	...	...	...	...
Charles de Gaulle ✈ **11** ... a.	...	...	...	...	...	...	...	...	...	...	...	...	...	...	...	...	...	...	...	...	...	...	...	...
Lille Europe **11** ... a.	...	...	...	...	...	...	...	...	...	...	...	...	...	...	...	...	...	...	...	...	...	...	...	...
Brussels Midi **11** ... a.	...	...	...	...	...	...	...	...	...	...	...	...	...	...	...	...	...	...	...	...	...	...	...	...

– ①⑦ July 9 - Aug. 24 (also Aug. 14, 15, 16).
– Ⓑ to July 7; ①⑥ July 13 - Aug. 4; daily Aug. 8 – 19 (also Aug. 24, 25); Ⓑ from Aug. 31.
– Ⓐ (daily June 30 - Aug. 29).
– Not ⑥ Sept. 13 - Oct. 18. (12) Montpellier - Dijon - Strasbourg; conveys on dates in Table **379** (12) (**6868**) Montpellier - Dijon - Metz.
– Not June 21, 23, 28, July 4 - Aug. 31, Sept. 6, 20, 27. 🛏 1, 2 cl. and (2) (reclining) Cerbère - Narbonne - Toulouse - Paris Austerlitz. Runs 40 – 58 minutes earlier Cerbère - Narbonne on June 24, 25, 26, 30, July 1. Subject to alteration on Ⓐ from Nov. 3.
– July 4 - Aug. 31. 🛏 1, 2 cl. and (2) (reclining) Cerbère - Narbonne - Toulouse - Paris Austerlitz. Runs 21 - 44 minutes earlier Cerbère - Narbonne on July 7, 8, 9, 10, 17.
– For days of running see Table **379**. 🛏 1, 2 cl. and (2) (reclining) Cerbère - Metz - Luxembourg; 🛏 1, 2 cl. and (2) (reclining) Cerbère - Strasbourg. Timings may vary.
– Ⓒ June 28 - Aug. 31. To Toulouse (Table **321**).

– Paris **Austerlitz**.
– 2216 July 15 - Aug. 19 (by 🚌 Bellegarde - Genève).
– Not Sept. 6, 19, 20, 21, Nov. 8, 9, 10. Starts from Toulouse on Ⓐ from Oct. 29.
– Also July 14, Nov. 11.
– Also July 14, Aug. 14, Nov. 11; not Aug. 15.
– July 6 - Aug. 24 only.
– Not July 14, Nov. 11.
– Not Oct. 18.
– Not ①–⑤ Oct. 27 - Nov. 14.
– Also July 14, Aug. 14, Nov. 11; not July 13, Aug. 15, Sept. 19, 21.
– Avignon **TGV**. Also calls at Aix en Provence TGV (a. 2244).
– Not Nov. 10. Starts from Toulouse on ①–⑤ Oct. 29 - Nov. 14 (also on Sept. 6, 20).

x – Not Aug. 20 – 24.
y – ⑤–⑦ (also July 14, Nov. 11; not June 15, 22, Aug. 31, Sept. 6, Nov. 8, 9).
z – On ①–⑤ June 23 - Aug. 1 and ①–⑤ Oct. 6 – 17 diverted to Lille Flandres (a. 2307).

TGV – Ⓡ, supplement payable.

◇ – Subject to alteration on Sept. 13, 20, 27, Oct. 4.
♠ – From Barcelona (Tables **13/49**).
■ – (12) Madrid - Barcelona - Marseille (Table **49**).
◐ – Via Toulouse and Limoges (Table **310**).
★ – *INTERCITÉS*. Ⓡ.
△ – To Nantes and Rennes (Table **335**). Subject to alteration on Sept. 13, 20, 27, Oct. 4.
☆ – To Mende (Table **333**).
‡ – Vitrolles Aéroport Marseille-Provence. A shuttle bus runs to the airport terminal (journey time 5 minutes). For additional trains see Table **351**.
§ – Marne la Vallée - Chessy (station for Disneyland Paris).

Services Perpignan / Toulouse - Narbonne - Montpellier - Avignon / Marseille / Lyon are subject to alteration or cancellation Sept. 19 – 21.

Certain departures from Bordeaux, Toulouse and Carcassonne may be up to 22 minutes earlier from Oct. 29.

Additional low-cost 'Ouigo' TGV trains run to Marne la Vallée-Chessy in the eastern suburbs of Paris. See Table ***350a****.*

359 NICE - ANNOT - DIGNE

2nd class only

km	CP ▲						CP ▲	⚒	†				
0	**Nice** (Gare CP) d.	0655	0925	1305	1715	1813	**Digne** d.	...	...	0715	1045	1425	1735
	Plan du Var d.	0741	0957	1341	1757	1854	St. André les Alpes d.	...	...	0812	1143	1524	1830
41	Villars sur Var d.	0801	1017	1401	1818	1915	Thorame Haute d.	...	...	0824	1156	1536	1842
58	Puget Théniers d.	0821	1038	1421	1839	1937	Annot d.	0540	0715	0850	1219	1600	1910
64	Entrevaux d.	0830	1046	1429	1847	1945	Entrevaux d.	0558	0733	0908	1238	1619	1929
78	Annot d.	0851	1106	1449	1908	2001	Puget Théniers d.	0606	0741	0916	1246	1627	1938
96	Thorame Haute d.	0915	1130	1512	1932	...	Villars sur Var d.	0627	0802	0937	1306	1648	1957
106	St André les Alpes d.	0927	1144	1523	1945	...	Plan du Var d.	0649	0823	0958	1328	1710	2018
150	**Digne** a.	1020	1239	1620	2041	...	**Nice** (Gare CP) a.	0731	0900	1030	1400	1745	2057

🚂 *TRAIN DES PIGNES* steam train, 2014

⑦ May 11 - Oct. 26

Puget Théniers 1055 → Annot 1205

Annot 1500 → Puget Théniers 1540

Also calls at Entrevaux

www.gecp.asso.fr

🚌 ★	🚌 v	🚌	🚌	🚌
Digne △ d.	0750	1100	1340	1640
Digne (Gare) d.	0755	1110	1350	1655
Manosque-Gréoux d.	0850	1210	1450	1805
Aix en Provence TGV a.	0950	1315	1555	1905
Aéroport Marseille ✈ a.	1010	1330	1610	1925

🚌 ★	🚌 ⚒	🚌	🚌	🚌 z
Aéroport Marseille ✈ d.	0925	1225	1455	1800
Aix en Provence TGV d.	0955	1255	1525	1830
Manosque-Gréoux a.	1100	1355	1625	1930
Digne (Gare) a.	1150	1450	1720	2020
Digne △ a.	1155	1455	1725	2025

🚌 ☆	🚌 u	🚌 u	🚌 ⑤⑦r	🚌 ⑥
Digne △ d.	0910	1145	1735	2010
Digne (Gare) d.	0915	1150	1740	2013
St Auban casino a.	0950	|	|	|
Sisteron (Gare) a.	1010	1237	1827	2055
Veynes (Gare) a.	...	1335	1925	2150

🚌 ☆	🚌	🚌 u	🚌 ⑦	🚌 ⑤r
Veynes (Gare) d.	0645	1435	2012	2035
Sisteron (Gare) d.	0743	1533	2103	2128
St Auban casino d.	|	|	|	|
Digne (Gare) a.	0825	1615	2145	2210
Digne △ a.	0830	1620	2150	2215

r – Not Aug. 15.
u – Not May 1.
v – Additional journey: 0515 ⚒.
z – Additional journey: 2040 (2105 from Aix TGV).

△ – Gare Routière (bus station).
▲ – Narrow gauge railway, operated by Chemins de Fer de Provence (CP).
☆ – LER route 33, operated by Autocars Payan or SCAL. SNCF rail tickets valid. For rail connections see **362**.

★ – LER (Lignes Express Régionales) Route 26, operated by Autocars Payan. Combined tickets 🚌 + TGV available.

360 MARSEILLE - TOULON - NICE - VENTIMIGLIA

Subject to alteration / cancellation on Sept. 6, 7, Nov. 8, 9, 10. Services via Lyon Part Dieu are subject to alteration on ⑥⑦ Sept. 13 - Oct. 5.

km	All *TGV* trains are [R]	*TGV* 6807 ① g	17471 Ⓐ	5773 [R] B	Ⓐ	17473 Ⓐ	4283 4282 [R] W	4249 4283 [R] W		17475 x		*TGV* 6805 ①–⑤ E	*TGV* 6805 ⑥⑦ c	*TGV* 6171 K	*TGV* 6161		*TGV* 6173		17483	*TGV* 6820		*TGV* 6175	17487
	Brussels Midi **11** d.	...	...	...	...	...	...	...	...	...	...	...	...	...	...	...	...	...	...	...	...	...	...
	Lille Europe **11** d.	...	...	...	...	...	...	...	...	...	...	...	...	...	...	...	...	...	...	...	...	...	...
	Paris Gare de Lyon **350** ▶ d.	...	...	2123a	...	...	...	...	...	...	...	...	...	0649	0745	...	0849	...	...	...	...	1049	...
	Strasbourg **379** d.	...	...	|	...	...	2014	...	...	...	...	...	...	|	|	...	|	...	...	...	...	|	...
	Metz **379** d.	...	...	|	...	...	|	2040	...	...	...	...	...	|	|	...	|	...	...	0606r	...	|	...
	Dijon **379** d.	...	...	|	...	...	|	|	...	...	...	...	...	|	|	...	|	...	...	0922	...	|	...
	Genève **346** d.	...	...	|	...	...	|	|	...	...	...	...	...	|	|	...	|	...	...	|	...	|	...
	Lyon Part-Dieu **350** d.	0048p	...	|	...	...	|	|	...	...	...	0636	0702j	|	|	...	|	...	...	1106	...	|	...
	Bordeaux **320** d.	|	...	|	...	...	|	|	...	...	...	|	|	|	|	...	|	...	...	|	...	|	...
	Toulouse **321** d.	|	...	|	...	...	|	|	...	...	...	|	|	|	|	...	|	...	...	|	...	|	...
	Montpellier **355** d.	|	...	|	...	...	|	|	...	...	...	|	|	|	|	...	|	...	...	|	...	|	...
0	**Marseille** St Charles **350** ▶ d.	|	0531	|	...	0631	0658	0658	...	0731	...	0831	0858	|	|	...	|	...	1231n	1300	...	|	1431
67	**Toulon** **350** ▶ a.	0547	0616	0645	...	0716	0745	0745	...	0816	...	0918	0942	1039	1140	...	|	...	1316n	1344	...	1439	1516
67	**Toulon** d.	0550	0618	0647	0651	0718	0746	0746	0751	0818	...	0921	0945	1043	1143	...	|	1251	1319	1347	...	1443	1518
100	Carnoules d.	|	0636	|	0722	0736	|	|	0822	0836	...	|	|	|	|	...	|	1321	1336	|	...	|	1536
135	Les Arcs-Draguignan ▷ d.	0623	0655	0722	0749	0755k	0823	0823	0849	0855	...	0955	1019	|	|	...	1315	1349	1356	|	...	1519	1555
158	Fréjus ▷ d.	|	|	0738	...	|	|	|	...	|	...	|	|	|	|	...	|	...	|	|	...	|	|
162	St Raphaël-Valescure ▷ d.	0639	0712	0743	...	0809	0840	0840	...	0909	...	1011	1036	1132	1232	...	1332	...	1411	1438	...	|	1610
195	**Cannes** ▷ d.	0703	0738	0808	...	0838	0907	0907	...	0937	...	1035	1101	1158	1258	...	1358	...	1437	1507	...	1558	1637
206	Antibes ▷ d.	0716	0749	0821	...	0849	0919	0919	...	0948	...	1046	1111	1209	1309	...	1409	...	1448	1517	...	1609	1649
229	**Nice** Ville ▷ a.	0735	0806	0846	...	0906	0941	0941	...	1005	...	1103	1129	1226	1326	...	1426	...	1506	1535	...	1626	1706
229	**Nice** Ville ▷ d.	...	...	...	...	...	...	...	...	...	...	...	...	...	...	...	...	...	...	...	...	...	...
245	Monaco-Monte Carlo ▷ a.	...	...	...	...	...	...	...	...	...	...	...	...	...	...	...	...	...	...	...	...	...	...
252	Menton ▷ a.	...	...	...	...	...	...	...	...	...	...	...	...	...	...	...	...	...	...	...	...	...	...
262	**Ventimiglia** ▷ a.	...	...	...	...	...	...	...	...	...	...	...	...	...	...	...	...	...	...	...	...	...	...

	TGV 6189 K		*TGV* 6177	*TGV* 6177 A	Ⓐ	*TGV* 9756	4659 4658 ★ z		17491 Ⓐ	*TGV* 6179 G	*TGV* 9828		17495			*TGV* 6181	*TGV* 6815	17499 ⑤–⑦ w	①–④ m	*TGV* 6183 ⑤–⑦ y	4665 4664 ⑤–⑦ d★		*TGV* 6187 ⑤ f
Brussels Midi **11** d.	...	...	...	...	...	...	...	...	...	...	1217	...	...	...	...	...	...	...	...	...	...	...	...
Lille Europe **11** d.	...	...	...	...	...	...	...	...	...	...	1303	...	...	...	...	...	...	...	...	...	...	...	...
Paris Gare de Lyon **350** ▶ d.	1141	...	1249	1249	...	...	...	...	...	1449	|	...	...	...	...	1649	...	...	...	1745	...	...	1847
Strasbourg **379** d.	|	...	|	|	...	...	...	...	...	|	|	...	...	...	...	|	...	...	...	|	...	...	|
Metz **379** d.	|	...	|	|	...	...	...	...	...	|	|	...	...	...	...	|	...	...	...	|	...	...	|
Dijon **379** d.	|	...	|	|	...	...	...	...	...	|	|	...	...	...	...	|	1621v	...	...	|	...	...	|
Genève **346** d.	|	...	|	|	...	1242b	...	...	...	|	|	...	...	...	...	|	|	...	...	|	...	...	|
Lyon Part-Dieu **350** d.	|	...	|	|	...	1436	...	...	...	|	1606	...	...	...	...	|	1806	...	...	|	...	...	|
Bordeaux **320** d.	|	...	|	|	...	|	1047e	...	...	|	|	...	...	...	...	|	|	...	...	|	1445e	...	|
Toulouse **321** d.	|	...	|	|	...	|	1254e	...	...	|	|	...	...	...	...	|	|	...	...	|	1651e	...	|
Montpellier **355** d.	|	...	|	|	...	|	1507	...	...	|	|	...	...	...	...	|	|	...	...	|	1907	...	|
Marseille St Charles **350** ▶ d.	|	...	|	|	...	1631	1659	...	1730	|	1801	...	1831	...	...	|	2001	2031	2031	|	2059	...	|
Toulon **350** ▶ a.	|	...	1639	1639	...	1716	1744	...	1816	1839	1844	...	1916	...	...	2039	2045	2116	2118	2139	2146	...	224
Toulon d.	|	1551	1643	1643	1651	1717	1746	1751	1818	1843	1847	1851	1918	1954	...	2043	2047	2118	2121	2143	2149	...	224
Carnoules d.	|	1621	|	|	1722	|	|	1821	1835	|	|	1921	1935	2025	...	|	|	2135	2139	|	|	...	|
Les Arcs-Draguignan ▷ d.	1615	1649	|	|	1749	|	1823	1849	1856	|	1924	1949	1954	2052	...	2118	2122	2155	2157	|	2224	...	|
Fréjus ▷ d.	|	...	|	|	...	|	|	...	|	|	|	...	|	...	...	|	|	|	...	|	|	...	|
St Raphaël-Valescure ▷ d.	1632	...	1732	1732	...	1809	1840	...	1911	1932	1940	...	2010	...	...	|	2140	2211	...	2232	2240	...	233
Cannes ▷ d.	1658	...	1758	1758	...	1835	1907	...	1937	1958	2005	...	2037	...	...	2157	2205	2237	...	2258	2307	...	235
Antibes ▷ d.	1709	...	1808	1808	...	1846	1918	...	1948	2008	2016	...	2049	...	...	2209	2216	2247	...	2308	2319	...	000
Nice Ville ▷ a.	1733	...	1826	1826	...	1905	1937	...	2005	2029	2033	...	2107	...	...	2226	2233	2305	...	2326	2341	...	002
Nice Ville ▷ d.	...	...	...	1836	...	...	...	...	...	...	...	...	...	...	...	...	...	...	...	...	...	...	...
Monaco-Monte Carlo ▷ a.	...	...	...	1852	...	...	...	...	...	...	...	...	...	...	...	...	...	...	...	...	...	...	...
Menton ▷ a.	...	...	...	1905	...	...	...	...	...	...	...	...	...	...	...	...	...	...	...	...	...	...	...
Ventimiglia ▷ a.	...	...	...	1924	...	...	...	...	...	...	...	...	...	...	...	...	...	...	...	...	...	...	...

A – Until Oct. 4.
B – TRAIN BLEU – 🛏 1, 2 cl., (2) (reclining) Paris Austerlitz - Nice. Days of running are subject to confirmation and timings may vary. Train number **5763** certain dates.
E – ①-⑤ from June 30 (not Sept. 1 – 19, Oct. 13 – 31). Departs Lyon 0634 Sept. 22 - Oct. 10.
G – Daily to Sept. 14; ⑤⑥ from Sept. 19.
K – July 6 - Aug. 24.
W – 🛏 1, 2 cl., (2) (reclining) Luxembourg - Metz - Nice; 🛏 1, 2 cl., (2) (reclining) Strasbourg - Nice. For days of running see Table **379**. Timings may vary.

a – Paris **Austerlitz**. Departs 2104 on Sept. 28.
b – 1130 July 15 - Aug. 24 (by 🚌 Genève - Bellegarde July 15 - Aug. 19 / Genève - Ambérieu Aug. 20 – 24).
c – Not Sept. 27, 28. Timings Toulon - Antibes are 3 – 5 minutes later from Nov. 15.
d – ⑤-⑦ (also July 14, Nov. 11; not June 15, 22, Aug. 31). Starts from Toulouse on ⑤ Oct. 31 - Nov. 14 (also on Sept. 20). From Nov. 11 Toulon a. 2143, d. 2146, Les Arcs d. 2223.
e – 6 – 7 minutes earlier from Oct. 29.
f – Not Aug. 15.
g – ① (also July 15; not July 14, Aug. 18, Sept. 29, Oct. 6, 20, Nov. 10). On June 23, Nov. 3, 17 Toulon a. 0544, d. 0547, Les Arcs d. 0621, St Raphaël d. 0638.
j – 0700 on Sept. 20, Oct. 4, 11, 12, 18, 19, 25, 26.
k – Until Nov. 7.
m – ①-④ (not July 14, Nov. 11). Runs 4 – 5 minutes **earlier** Toulon - Les Arcs from Nov. 12.

n – Not June 16 – 20, 23 – 27, Sept. 1 – 5, 8 – 12, 15 – 19, Oct. 13 – 17, 20 – 24, 27 – 31.
p – Lyon **Perrache**.
r – Not Aug. 15, 16, 17.
v – 1619 Nov. 8 – 29.
w – Also July 14, Nov. 11.
x – Not Sept. 6, 7, 8, Nov. 8 – 11.
y – Also July 14, Aug. 14, Nov. 11.
z – Not Sept. 19, 20, 21. Starts from Toulouse on Ⓐ from Oct. 29.

TGV – [R], supplement payable, 🍸.

▷ – For local trains Les Arcs - Cannes - Nice - Ventimiglia see Table 36
▶ – For complete *TGV* service Paris - Marseille - Toulon see Table **350**. For local trains Marseille - Toulon see separate panel on next page.
★ – *INTERCITÉS*. [R].

Timings of local trains may vary by a few minutes from Nov. 11

VENTIMIGLIA - NICE - TOULON - MARSEILLE 360

Subject to alteration / cancellation on Sept. 6, 7 Nov. 8, 9, 10. Services via Lyon Part Dieu are subject to alteration on ⑥⑦ Sept. 13 - Oct. 5.

All *TGV* trains are Ⓡ	⚒		17470 Ⓐ q	Ⓐ	17474		*TGV* 6852 w	*TGV* 6172		17478 y	*TGV* 9866 M	*TGV* 6174 Q	*TGV* 6174 M	4760 4761 ★ ♠	*TGV* 6188 K	*TGV* 9750 △		*TGV* 6176 D	*TGV* 6176	*TGV* 6864 E	4764 4765 ★ z	*TGV* 6864 F	*TGV* 6170 L
Ventimiglia ▷ d.	...	...	...	...	...	...	...	...	...	...	...	0839	...	...	...	...	...	1039	...	...	...	...	1139p
Menton ▷ d.	...	...	...	...	...	...	...	...	...	...	...	0854	...	...	...	...	...	1053	...	...	...	...	1154p
Monaco-Monte Carlo ▷ d.	...	...	...	...	...	...	...	...	...	...	...	0907	...	...	...	...	...	1106	...	...	...	...	1207p
Nice Ville ▷ a.	...	...	...	...	...	...	...	...	...	...	...	0924	...	...	...	...	...	1122	...	...	...	...	1224p
Nice Ville ▷ d.	...	...	0555	...	0654	...	0725	0734	...	0855	0927	0934	0934	1023	1034	1057	...	1132	1132	1204	1221	1232	1234
Antibes ▷ d.	...	...	0614	...	0713	...	0744	0754	...	0914	0946	0954	0954	1043	1054	1116	...	1151	1151	1230	1241	1253	1255
Cannes ▷ d.	...	...	0625	...	0726	...	0755	0805	...	0927	0958	1006	1006	1055	1106	1127	...	1203	1203	1245	1254	1304	1306
St Raphaël-Valescure ▷ d.	...	...	0651	...	0750	...	0820	|	...	0951	1023	1031	1031	1120	1131	1153	...	1229	1229	1315	1319	1330	1331
Fréjus ▷ d.	...	...	0655	...	|	...	|	|	...	|	|	|	|	|	|	|	...	|	|	|	|	|	|
Les Arcs-Draguignan ▷ d.	0559	0636	0709	0712	0806	0810	|	0844	...	1005	1039	|	|	1137	|	|	1210	|	|	|	1335	|	|
Carnoules d.	0626	0704	|	0740	0825	0836	|	|	...	1023	|	|	|	|	|	|	1238	|	|	|	|	|	|
Toulon a.	0656	0735	0743	0810	0843	0907	0911	0917	...	1041	1113	1117	1117	1211	1216	1243	1309	1315	1315	1405	1410	1417	1416
Toulon 350 ▶ d.	0658	...	0746	...	0846	...	0914	0921	...	1044n	1115	1121	1121	1214	1219	1246	...	1319	1319	1408	1413	1419	1419
Marseille St Charles 350 ▶ a.	0800	...	0835	...	0931	...	0958	|	...	1129n	1159	|	|	1259	|	1331	...	|	|	1505j	1459	1505	|
Montpellier **355** a.	...	...	...	...	...	...	|	|	...	...	|	|	|	1453	|	|	...	|	|	|	1653	|	|
Toulouse **321** a.	...	...	...	...	...	...	|	|	...	...	|	|	|	1706e	|	|	...	|	|	|	1908e	|	|
Bordeaux **320** a.	...	...	...	...	...	...	|	|	...	...	|	|	|	1913e	|	|	...	|	|	|	2114e	|	|
Lyon Part-Dieu **350** a.	...	...	...	...	...	...	1154	|	...	...	1354	|	|	...	|	1524	...	|	|	1700	...	1700	|
Genève **346** a.	...	...	...	...	...	...	...	|	...	...	|	|	|	...	|	1716b	...	|	|	|	...	|	|
Dijon **379** a.	...	...	...	...	...	...	...	|	...	...	|	|	|	...	|	...	...	|	|	1838	...	1841	|
Metz **379** a.	...	...	...	...	...	...	...	|	...	...	|	|	|	...	|	...	...	|	|	2211r	...	2153	|
Strasbourg **379** a.	...	...	...	...	...	...	...	|	...	...	|	|	|	...	|	...	...	|	|	...	...	...	|
Paris Gare de Lyon **350** ▶ a.	...	...	...	...	...	...	...	1310	...	...	|	1511	1511	...	1615	...	...	1711	1711	...	...	...	1818
Lille Europe **11** a.	...	...	...	...	...	...	...	...	...	...	1657	...	...	...	...	...	...	...	...	...	...	...	...
Brussels Midi **11** a.	...	...	...	...	...	...	...	...	...	...	1743	...	...	...	...	...	...	...	...	...	...	...	...

	17482 Ⓐ	Ⓑ		*TGV* 6178 G	17486		*TGV* 6184		Ⓐ	*TGV* 6168	17490		*TGV* 6876	*TGV* 6180	17494 Ⓑ		*TGV* 6186 ⑦	17498		4382 4383 Ⓡ W	4382 4348 Ⓡ W		5774 Ⓡ B
Ventimiglia ▷ d.	...	...	...	...	...	...	...	...	...	...	...	...	...	...	...	...	...	...	...	...	...	...	...
Menton ▷ d.	...	...	...	...	...	...	...	...	...	...	...	...	...	...	...	...	...	...	...	...	...	...	...
Monaco-Monte Carlo ▷ d.	...	...	...	...	...	...	...	...	...	...	...	...	...	...	...	...	...	...	...	...	...	...	...
Nice Ville ▷ a.	...	...	...	...	...	...	...	...	...	...	...	...	...	...	...	...	...	...	...	...	...	...	...
Nice Ville ▷ d.	1255	...	...	1334	1355	...	1534	...	...	1634	1655	...	1727	1734	1755	...	1831	1855	...	1903	1903	...	2000
Antibes ▷ d.	1315	...	...	1354	1414	...	1554	...	...	1654	1715	...	1746	1754	1814	...	1854	1914	...	1923	1923	...	2019
Cannes ▷ d.	1327	...	...	1406	1426	...	1606	...	...	1706	1726	...	1756	1806	1825	...	1906	1926	...	1935	1935	...	2031
St Raphaël-Valescure ▷ d.	1351	...	...	1431	1450	...	1632	...	...	1731	1751	...	1821	|	1850	...	1931	1953	...	2001	2001	...	2055
Fréjus ▷ d.	|	...	...	|	|	...	|	...	...	|	|	...	|	|	|	...	|	1957	...	|	|	...	2059
Les Arcs-Draguignan ▷ d.	1406	1410	...	1447	1505	...	|	...	1710	1747	1807	1811	1838	1844	1906	...	|	2011	...	2019	2019	...	2116
Carnoules d.	|	1438	...	|	1524	...	|	...	1738	|	|	1838	|	|	1925	...	|	2030	...	|	|	...	|
Toulon a.	1440	1509	...	|	1542	...	1717	...	1809	|	1840	1909	1912	1917	1943	...	2017	2048	...	2054	2054	...	2151
Toulon 350 ▶ d.	1443	...	...	|	1545	...	1721	...	...	|	1843	...	1915	1920	1946	...	2020	2050	...	2058	2058	...	2153
Marseille St Charles 350 ▶ a.	1529	...	...	|	1631	...	|	...	...	|	1929	...	1959	|	2031	...	|	2136	...	2141	2141	...	|
Montpellier **355** a.	...	...	...	|	...	...	|	...	...	|	...	...	|	|	...	...	|	...	...	|	|	...	|
Toulouse **321** a.	...	...	...	|	...	...	|	...	...	|	...	...	|	|	...	...	|	...	...	|	|	...	|
Bordeaux **320** a.	...	...	...	|	...	...	|	...	...	|	...	...	|	|	...	...	|	...	...	|	|	...	|
Lyon Part-Dieu **350** a.	...	...	...	|	...	...	|	...	...	|	...	...	2158	|	...	...	|	...	...	|	|	...	|
Genève **346** a.	...	...	...	|	...	...	|	...	...	|	...	...	|	|	...	...	|	...	...	|	|	...	|
Dijon **379** a.	...	...	...	|	...	...	|	...	...	|	...	...	2344x	|	...	...	|	...	...	|	|	...	|
Metz **379** a.	...	...	...	|	...	...	|	...	...	|	...	...	...	|	...	...	|	...	...	|	0824	...	|
Strasbourg **379** a.	...	...	...	|	...	...	|	...	...	|	...	...	...	|	...	...	|	...	...	0858	...	...	|
Paris Gare de Lyon **350** ▶ a.	...	...	...	1911	...	...	2111	...	...	2215	...	...	...	2315	...	...	0015	...	...	...	...	...	0738a
Lille Europe **11** a.	...	...	...	...	...	...	...	...	...	...	...	...	...	...	...	...	...	...	...	...	...	...	...
Brussels Midi **11** a.	...	...	...	...	...	...	...	...	...	...	...	...	...	...	...	...	...	...	...	...	...	...	...

LOCAL TRAINS MARSEILLE - TOULON (SEE NOTE ⊠)

km		⚒	⊕	⚒		Ⓐ⊡	⊡	⊡		⚒					Ⓐ				Ⓐ			Ⓐ				C	t
0	**Marseille** d.	0605	0635	0704	0735	0805	0835	0935	1105	1135	1235	1335	1435	1505	1535	1605	1635	1705	1735	1805	1835	1905	1934	2005	2035	2105	2243
27	Cassis • d.	0629	0701	0730	0800	0830	0900	1000	1131	1201	1300	1400	1500	1530	1600	1630	1700	1730	1800	1831	1900	1931	2000	2032	2100	2131	2308
37	La Ciotat d.	0636	0708	0737	0807	0837	0907	1008	1138	1208	1307	1407	1507	1537	1607	1637	1707	1737	1807	1838	1907	1938	2007	2039	2107	2138	2315
51	Bandol d.	0647	0719	0748	0819	0848	0919	1018	1149	1219	1318	1419	1518	1548	1618	1648	1718	1749	1818	1850	1918	1949	2018	2050	2118	2150	2327
67	**Toulon** a.	0705	0738	0807	0837	0907	0937	1035	1207	1237	1337	1435	1536	1607	1635	1707	1737	1806	1835	1908	1935	2008	2035	2109	2135	2209	2345

	Ⓐ	⊕	⊕	⚒	Ⓐ¶	Ⓐ	⊕¶		¶		⊡¶	Ⓐ⊡	◇		⊙¶	Ⓐ			Ⓐ		Ⓐ		¶			
Toulon d.	0509	0522	0603	0622	0633	0649	0723	0751	0823	0925	1054	1151	1222	1321	1354	1422	1523	1548	1621	1651	1724	1751	1822	1923	2023	2121
Bandol d.	0519	0537	0619	0638	0650	0705	0739	0807	0839	0940	1110	1207	1237	1337	1409	1437	1539	1604	1637	1707	1740	1807	1838	1939	2039	2137
La Ciotat d.	0531	0549	0631	0650	0702	0717	0752	0819	0852	0952	1122	1219	1249	1349	1422	1449	1551	1616	1649	1719	1752	1819	1851	1951	2051	2149
Cassis • d.	|	0556	0638	0657	0710	0724	0759	0826	0900	0959	1130	1226	1256	1356	1429	1456	1558	1623	1656	1726	1759	1826	1859	1958	2058	2156
Marseille a.	0604	0625	0709	0725	0735	0755	0825	0855	0925	1028	1155	1255	1325	1425	1455	1525	1627	1655	1725	1755	1828	1855	1925	2027	2127	2225

B – TRAIN BLEU – 🛏 1, 2 cl., (2) (reclining) Nice - Paris Austerlitz. Days of running are subject to confirmation and timings may vary. Runs with train number **5776** or **5778** on certain dates.
C – ⑥⑦ to July 6; daily from July 12.
D – ⑥⑦ June 15–29.
E – Daily to Sept. 5 (not June 15, 21, 22); ①–⑤ Sept. 8–19; ①–⑤ Oct. 13–31. Subject to alteration on Aug. 2, 3, 9, 10, 15, 16.
F – ⑥⑦ to June 22; daily from Sept. 13 (not Sept. 15–19, Oct. 13–17, 20–24, 27–31). Subject to alteration on Sept. 13, 29. Arrives Metz 2209 until June 22.
G – Daily to Sept. 14; ⑥⑦ from Sept. 20 (also Nov. 11).
K – July 6 - Aug. 24.
L – ①–⑤ June 16–27; daily July 6 - Aug. 24; ①–⑤ Sept. 1–19; ①–⑤ Oct. 13–31.
M – ⑥⑦ to June 22; daily June 28 - Aug. 31, Sept. 20 - Oct. 12 and from Nov. 1 (also Sept. 13, 14, Oct. 18, 19, 25, 26).
Q – Daily June 30 - Aug. 24; ①–⑤ Sept. 22 - Oct. 3.
W – 🛏 1, 2 cl., (2) (reclining) Nice - Metz - Luxembourg; 🛏 1, 2 cl., (2) (reclining) Nice - Strasbourg. For days of running see Table **379**. Timings may vary.

a – Paris **Austerlitz**.
b – 1816 July 15 - Aug. 24 (by 🚌 Bellegarde - Genève July 15 - Aug. 19 / Ambérieu - Genève Aug. 20–24).
e – 3–11 minutes later from Oct. 29.
j – 1455 to June 27 and from Sept. 1.
n – Not June 16–20, 23–27, Sept. 1–5, 8–12, 15–19, Oct. 13–17, 20–24, 27–31.
p – ①–⑤ June 16–27; ①–⑤ Sept. 1–19.
q – Also calls at La Ciotat (d. 0804).
r – Not Aug. 14. Arrives 2153 from Sept. 1.
t – Not June 16–20.

w – Not Sept. 27, 28.
x – Subject to alteration Lyon - Dijon from Sept. 1.
y – Not June 17, Sept. 2.
z – Not Sept. 19, 20, 21. Runs 3 minutes later Nice - Toulon from Nov. 11.

TGV – Ⓡ, supplement payable, 🍸.

♠ – ①⑥⑦ to Aug. 31 (also Sept. 13, 14, 22; not June 16, 23); daily Sept. 27 - Oct. 12; ⑥⑦ Oct. 18–26; daily from Nov. 1 (not Nov. 8, 9, 10).
△ – Certain departure times are 1–3 minutes earlier July 15 - Aug. 24.
⊕ – Subject to alteration Nov. 8–11.
⊡ – Subject to alteration on ①–⑤ June 16–27, ①–⑤ Sept. 1–19, ①–⑤ Oct. 13–31.
⊙ – Subject to alteration on ①–⑤ June 16–27, ①–⑤ Sept. 1–19, ①–⑤ Oct. 13–31. Runs 5–6 minutes earlier June 28 - Aug. 31.
⊠ – Subject to alteration Nov. 8–10. Timings may vary by a few minutes from Nov. 11.
◇ – Runs 28–31 minutes later on ①–⑤ June 16–27, ①–⑤ Sept. 1–19, ①–⑤ Oct. 13–31.
¶ – From Hyères (Table 352).
▷ – For local trains Les Arcs - Cannes - Nice - Ventimiglia see Table **361**.
▶ – For complete *TGV* service Paris - Marseille - Toulon see Table **350**. For local trains Marseille - Toulon see separate panel above.
★ – *INTERCITÉS*. Ⓡ.
• – Cassis station is located 4 km from Cassis town.

Timings of local trains may vary by a few minutes from Nov. 11

For TGV / Intercités / night trains over this route see Table 360

361 LES ARCS - ST RAPHAEL - CANNES - NICE - MONACO - VENTIMIGLIA *Local trains*

Subject to alteration Sept. 6, 7, 11 – 14, 20, 21 and from Oct. 6

km		①–⑤	①–⑤		①–⑤		①–⑤		①–⑤	⑥⑦	①–⑤		①–⑤	Ⓐ	①–⑥		①–⑥	①–⑥	①–⑥	①–⑤		①–⑤	Ⓐ			
		p												◇									◇		L	
0	**Les Arcs-Draguignan** .. d.	...	...	...	...	...	0536	...	0555	0558	...	...	0628	0655	...	...	0700	...	...	...	0729	...	0755	...	...	...
23	Fréjus d.	...	...	...	...	...	0549	...	0611	0614	...	...	0642	|	...	...	0714	...	...	...	0744	...	|	...	...	...
27	St Raphaël-Valescure d.	...	...	...	...	...	0554	...	0617	0618	...	...	0646	0712	...	...	0719	...	...	...	0748	...	0809	...	...	...
31	Boulouris sur Mer d.	...	...	...	...	...	0558	...	0621	0623	...	...	0651	|	...	...	0724	...	...	...	0753	...	|	...	...	...
**	Grasse d.	...	...	...	...	...	|	...	|	|	...	0630a	|	|	...	0708	|	...	0738	0738	|	...	|	...	...	0847
60	**Cannes** d.	...	0517	...	0541	0611	0624	0641	0650	0651	...	0710	0725	0738	...	0741	0751	...	0813	0813	0827	...	0838	0841	...	0912
69	Juan les Pins d.	...	0526	...	0551	0622	0635	0650	0700	0701	...	0720	0733	|	...	0751	0801	...	0823	0823	0835	...	|	0851	...	0922
71	Antibes d.	...	0529	...	0554	0626	0638	0653	0703	0704	...	0723	0737	0749	...	0754	0805	...	0826	0826	0839	...	0849	0854	0910	0925
80	Cagnes sur Mer d.	...	0538	...	0606	0636	0650	0705	0711	0711	...	0735	0744	|	...	0807	0813	...	0838	0838	0847	...	|	0907	0922	0937
94	**Nice** Ville a.	...	0552	...	0622	0652	0704	0722	0727	0727	...	0751	0758	0806	...	0822	0827	...	0854	0854	0858	...	0906	0922	0936	0953
94	**Nice** Ville d.	0525	0555	0625	0625	0655	0707	0725	...	...	0743	0754	...	...	0812	0825	...	0843	...	0857	...	0907	...	0925	0945	0956
99	Villefranche sur Mer d.	0532	0602	0633	0633	0702	0715	0732	...	...	0750	0801	...	...	0820	0833	...	0850	...	0905	...	0915	...	0933	0953	1003
101	Beaulieu sur Mer d.	0535	0606	0636	0636	0705	0718	0735	...	...	0753	0804	...	...	0823	0836	...	0853	...	0908	...	0918	...	0936	0956	1006
104	Eze d.	0539	0609	0640	0640	0709	|	0739	...	...	|	0808	...	...	|	0840	...	|	...	0912	...	|	...	0940	|	1010
110	**Monaco-Monte Carlo** d.	0548	0619	0649	0649	0719	0728	0749	...	...	0803	0818	...	...	0833	0849	...	0903	...	0921	...	0928	...	0949	1005	1020
114	Cap Martin-Roquebrune d.	0554	0624	0654	0654	0724	|	0754	...	...	|	0823	...	...	|	0855	...	|	...	0926	...	|	...	0954	|	1025
117	Menton d.	0600	0631	0701	0701	0730	0738	0800	...	...	0813	0828	...	...	0843	0901	...	0913	...	0933	...	0937	...	1001	1015	1031
127	**Ventimiglia** a.	0613	0643	0714	0714	0743	...	0813	...	...	...	...	...	...	...	0913	...	...	...	0945	...	...	...	1013	...	1043

					①–⑤						⑥⑦			①–⑤							①–⑤			①–⑤		
		b ◇														◇									◇	
Les Arcs-Draguignan d.	0828	0855	...	...	...	...	1028	...	...	...	...	...	1228	...	...	1356	...	...	...	...	...	...	1528	...	1555	...
Fréjus d.	0842	|	...	...	...	...	1042	...	...	...	...	...	1242	...	...	|	...	...	...	...	...	...	1542	...	|	...
St Raphaël-Valescure d.	0847	0909	...	...	...	...	1047	...	...	...	...	...	1247	...	...	1411	...	...	...	...	...	...	1547	...	1610	...
Boulouris sur Mer d.	0851	|	...	...	...	...	1051	...	...	...	...	...	1251	...	...	|	...	...	...	...	...	...	1551	...	|	...
Grasse d.	|	|	...	0938	...	1038	|	...	...	...	...	1238	|	...	1338	|	...	1438	...	...	...	1538	|	...	|	...
Cannes d.	0926	0937	0942	1010	1040	1110	1126	1141	...	...	1241	1310	1326	1340	1410	1437	1441	1511	...	1540	...	1611	1626	...	1637	1641
Juan les Pins d.	0934	|	0952	1020	1050	1120	1134	1151	...	...	1251	1320	1334	1350	1420	|	1451	1521	...	1550	...	1621	1634	...	|	1651
Antibes d.	0938	0948	0955	1023	1053	1123	1138	1154	...	...	1254	1323	1338	1353	1423	1448	1454	1524	...	1553	1615	1624	1638	...	1649	1654
Cagnes sur Mer d.	0945	|	1006	1035	1106	1135	1144	1206	...	...	1306	1335	1344	1406	1435	|	1506	1536	...	1606	1627	1636	1644	...	|	1705
Nice Ville a.	0958	1005	1022	1052	1122	1152	1158	1222	...	...	1323	1352	1358	1422	1452	1506	1522	1552	...	1622	1642	1653	1658	...	1706	1722
Nice Ville d.	...	...	1025	1054	1125	...	...	1225	1255	1326	1326	1355	...	1425	1455	...	1525	1555	1607	1625	1645	1656	...	1707	...	1725
Villefranche sur Mer d.	...	...	1032	1101	1133	...	...	1233	1302	1333	1333	1402	...	1433	1502	...	1533	1602	1615	1632	1653	1703	...	1715	...	1732
Beaulieu sur Mer d.	...	...	1036	1104	1136	...	...	1236	1305	1336	1336	1405	...	1436	1505	...	1536	1605	1618	1635	1656	1706	...	1718	...	1735
Eze d.	...	...	1040	1108	1140	...	...	1240	1309	1340	1340	1409	...	1440	1509	...	1540	1609	|	1639	|	1710	...	|	...	1739
Monaco-Monte Carlo d.	...	...	1049	1117	1149	...	...	1249	1318	1350	1350	1419	...	1449	1519	...	1549	1619	1628	1648	1705	1720	...	1728	...	1748
Cap Martin-Roquebrune d.	...	...	1055	1122	1154	...	...	1255	1324	1355	1355	1424	...	1454	1524	...	1554	1624	|	1654	|	1725	...	|	...	1754
Menton d.	...	...	1101	1129	1201	...	...	1301	1330	1401	1401	1430	...	1501	1530	...	1601	1630	1637	1700	1715	1731	...	1737	...	1800
Ventimiglia a.	...	...	1113	1143	1213	...	...	1313	1343	1414	1414	1443	...	1513	1543	...	1613	1643	...	1713	...	1744	...	...	...	1813

			①–⑥	①–⑤		①–⑤			①–⑤				Ⓐ							①–④	⑤–⑦		⑤–⑦	⑤–⑦	⑥	⑥⑦
	t												◇			◇		♥	⊙	m	v		w ◇	z		
Les Arcs-Draguignan d.	...	...	1628	...	...	...	...	1728	...	...	...	1828	1856	...	...	1954	...	...	...	...	...	...	2155	...	...	...
Fréjus d.	...	...	1642	...	...	...	...	1741	...	...	...	1842	|	...	...	|	...	...	...	...	...	...	|	...	...	...
St Raphaël-Valescure d.	...	...	1647	...	...	...	...	1746	...	...	...	1847	1911	...	...	2010	...	...	...	...	...	...	2211	...	...	...
Boulouris sur Mer d.	...	...	1651	...	...	...	...	1750	...	...	...	1851	|	...	...	|	...	...	...	...	...	...	|	...	...	...
Grasse d.	...	1638	|	...	...	...	1738	|	...	...	1838	|	|	...	1938	|	...	2038	...	2138	2138	...	|	...	...	2238
Cannes d.	...	1710	1726	...	1740	...	1810	1825	...	1840	1911	1926	1937	1942	2010	2037	2041	2110	2140	2209	2210	...	2237	2242	2242	2310
Juan les Pins d.	...	1720	1734	...	1750	...	1820	1832	...	1850	1921	1933	|	1951	2020	|	2051	2120	2150	...	2221	...	|	2252	2252	2320
Antibes d.	...	1723	1738	...	1753	...	1823	1835	...	1853	1924	1936	1948	1954	2023	2049	2054	2123	2153	...	2225	...	2247	2255	2255	2323
Cagnes sur Mer d.	...	1736	1744	...	1806	...	1835	1842	...	1906	1936	1943	|	2007	2035	|	2106	2135	2206	...	2236	...	|	2306	2306	2335
Nice Ville a.	...	1752	1758	...	1822	...	1852	1858	...	1922	1952	1958	2005	2023	2052	2107	2122	2152	2222	...	2252	...	2305	2323	2323	2352
Nice Ville d.	1740	1755	...	1813	1825	1843	1855	...	1907	1925	1955	...	...	2026	2055	...	2125	2155	2225	...	2255	...	...	...	2326	2355
Villefranche sur Mer d.	1748	1802	...	1821	1832	1850	1902	...	1915	1932	2002	...	...	2033	2102	...	2132	2202	2232	...	2302	...	...	...	2333	0002
Beaulieu sur Mer d.	1751	1805	...	1824	1835	1853	1905	...	1918	1935	2005	...	...	2036	2105	...	2135	2205	2235	...	2305	...	...	...	2336	0005
Eze d.	|	1809	...	|	1839	|	1909	...	|	1939	2009	...	...	2040	2109	...	2139	2209	2239	...	2309	...	...	...	2340	0009
Monaco-Monte Carlo d.	1802	1819	...	1833	1848	1903	1919	...	1927	1948	2019	...	...	2049	2119	...	2148	2219	2249	...	2319	...	...	...	2349	0019
Cap Martin-Roquebrune d.	|	1824	...	|	1854	|	1924	...	|	1954	2024	...	...	2054	2124	...	2154	2224	2254	...	2324	...	...	...	2355	0024
Menton d.	1813	1830	...	1843	1900	1913	1930	...	1937	2000	2030	...	...	2101	2130	...	2200	2230	2300	...	2330	...	...	...	0001	0030
Ventimiglia a.	...	1843	...	...	1913	...	1943	...	...	2013	2043	...	...	2113	2143	...	2213	2243	2313	...	2343	...	...	...	0013	0043

	①–⑤	Ⓑ	⑥	Ⓐ	①–⑤	①–⑥									①–⑤			①–⑤		①–⑥		①–⑥			①–⑤	⑥⑦
				◇	n			◇									y ◇									
Ventimiglia d.	...	...	...	...	0527	...	0550	...	...	0617	0650	...	...	0720	...	0750	...	...	0817	...	0850	...	...	0917	0949	0950
Menton d.	...	...	...	...	0538	...	0602	...	...	0629	0702	...	...	0732	0746	0802	...	0823	0829	0846	0902	0923	...	0930	1001	1002
Cap Martin-Roquebrune d.	...	...	...	...	|	...	0609	...	...	0636	0709	...	...	0739	|	0809	...	|	0836	|	0909	|	...	0936	1008	1009
Monaco-Monte Carlo d.	...	...	...	...	0547	...	0615	...	...	0642	0715	...	...	0745	0757	0814	...	0834	0842	0857	0915	0934	...	0942	1013	1014
Eze d.	...	...	...	...	|	...	0623	...	...	0650	0723	...	...	0753	|	0823	...	|	0850	|	0923	|	...	0951	1022	1023
Beaulieu sur Mer d.	...	...	...	...	0556	...	0627	...	...	0654	0727	...	...	0757	0806	0826	...	0843	0854	0906	0927	0943	...	0954	1025	1026
Villefranche sur Mer d.	...	...	...	...	0559	...	0630	...	...	0657	0731	...	...	0800	0809	0830	...	0846	0857	0909	0930	0946	...	0958	1029	1030
Nice Ville a.	...	...	...	...	0606	...	0637	...	...	0704	0737	...	...	0807	0816	0836	...	0853	0904	0915	0937	0953	...	1004	1035	1036
Nice Ville d.	...	0538	0555	0555	0609	0609	0639	0654	0701	0706	0740	0801	...	0810	0819	0838	0855	...	0906	0918	0940	...	1001	1006	1037	1038
Cagnes sur Mer d.	...	0554	|	|	0626	0626	0656	|	0714	0723	0757	0814	...	0827	0833	0855	|	...	0923	0932	0957	...	1014	1023	1054	1055
Antibes d.	...	0607	0612	0614	0638	0638	0708	0713	0723	0735	0810	0823	...	0839	0845	0907	0914	...	0936	0944	1009	...	1023	1035	1107	1108
Juan les Pins d.	...	0610	|	|	0641	0641	0711	|	0726	0739	0813	0826	←	0842	...	0910	|	...	0939	...	1012	...	1026	1038	1110	1111
Cannes d.	0551	0621	0621	0625	0656	0656	0719	0726	0735	0815j	0821	0834	0838	0851	...	0920	0927	...	0947	...	1023	...	1035	1046	1118	1121
Grasse a.	0623	0646	0646	|	0723	0723	...	|	|	0838	→	|	0903	...	...	0953	|	...	...	...	1053	...	|	...	...	1153
Boulouris sur Mer d.	...	...	...	|	...	...	...	|	0810	...	...	0909	...	...	...	...	|	...	...	...	...	...	1110	...	...	...
St Raphaël-Valescure d.	...	...	...	0651	...	...	...	0750	0815	...	...	0914	...	...	...	...	0951	...	...	...	...	...	1115	...	...	...
Fréjus d.	...	...	...	0655	...	...	...	|	0818	...	...	0918	...	...	...	...	|	...	...	...	...	...	1119	...	...	...
Les Arcs-Draguignan a.	...	...	...	0707	...	...	...	0805	0832	...	...	0932	...	...	...	...	1004	...	...	...	...	...	1132	...	...	...

	①–⑤			①–⑤		Ⓐ		①–⑤			⑥⑦			⑥⑦							①–⑥				Ⓑ	①–⑤
			⊡			◇				◇										◇					◇	
Ventimiglia d.	1018	1050	...	...	1150	...	...	1220	1250	...	1320	1320	1350	1350	1420	1450	...	1520	1550	...	...	1618	...	1650	...	...
Menton d.	1031	1102	...	...	1202	...	...	1232	1302	...	1332	1332	1402	1402	1432	1502	...	1532	1602	...	...	1630	1646	1702	...	1723
Cap Martin-Roquebrune d.	1037	1109	...	...	1209	...	...	1239	1309	...	1339	1339	1409	1409	1439	1509	...	1539	1609	...	...	1637	|	1709	...	|
Monaco-Monte Carlo d.	1043	1115	...	...	1215	...	...	1245	1315	...	1345	1345	1415	1415	1445	1515	...	1545	1615	...	...	1643	1657	1715	...	1734
Eze d.	1052	1123	...	...	1223	...	...	1253	1323	...	1353	1353	1423	1423	1453	1523	...	1553	1623	...	...	1651	|	1723	...	|
Beaulieu sur Mer d.	1055	1127	...	...	1227	...	...	1257	1327	...	1357	1357	1427	1427	1457	1527	...	1557	1627	...	...	1655	1706	1727	...	1743
Villefranche sur Mer d.	1059	1130	...	...	1230	...	...	1300	1330	...	1400	1400	1431	1431	1500	1530	...	1600	1630	...	...	1658	1709	1730	...	1746
Nice Ville a.	1105	1137	...	...	1237	...	...	1307	1337	...	1407	1407	1437	1437	1507	1537	...	1607	1637	...	...	1705	1716	1737	...	1753
Nice Ville d.	1108	1139	1154	1209	1239	1255	1301	1310	1339	1355	1410	...	...	1439	1510	1539	1601	1610	1639	1655	1701	1707	...	1739	1755	...
Cagnes sur Mer d.	1125	1155	1207	1224	1255	|	1314	1327	1355	|	1427	...	...	1456	1527	1555	1616	1627	1656	|	1714	1724	...	1755	|	...
Antibes d.	1137	1209	1215	1235	1309	1315	1323	1339	1409	1414	1439	...	...	1509	1539	1609	1623	1639	1708	1715	1723	1737	...	1807	1814	...
Juan les Pins d.	1140	1212	1218	1238	1312	|	1326	1342	1412	|	1442	...	...	1512	1542	1612	1626	1642	1711	|	1726	1740	...	1810	|	...
Cannes d.	1149	1222	1227	1246	1322	1327	1335	1351	1422	1426	1451	...	...	1522	1551	1622	1635	1651	1721	1726	1735	1748	...	1820	1825	...
Grasse a.	...	1253	|	...	1353	|	|	...	1453	|	...	...	...	1553	...	1653	|	...	1753	|	|	...	...	1853	|	...
Boulouris sur Mer d.	...	...	1301	...	...	|	1409	...	...	|	...	...	...	...	...	...	1710	...	...	|	1809	...	...	...	|	...
St Raphaël-Valescure d.	...	...	1307	...	...	1351	1415	...	...	1450	...	...	...	...	...	...	1715	...	...	1751	1815	...	...	...	1850	...
Fréjus d.	...	...	1311	...	...	|	1419	...	...	|	...	...	...	...	...	...	1719	...	...	|	1819	...	...	...	|	...
Les Arcs-Draguignan a.	...	...	1323	...	...	1404	1432	...	...	1503	...	...	...	...	...	...	1732	...	...	1805	1832	...	...	...	1904	...

FOR NOTES SEE NEXT PAGE

Ⓐ – Mondays to Fridays, except holidays Ⓑ – Daily except Saturdays Ⓒ – Saturdays, Sundays and holidays

Local trains VENTIMIGLIA - MONACO - NICE - CANNES - ST RAPHAEL - LES ARCS 361

Subject to alteration Sept. 6, 7, 11–14, 20, 21 and from Oct. 6

			①-⑤					①-⑤			①-⑤				①-④	⑤-⑦		⑤-⑦	⑥⑦	①-⑤	⑥⑦	⑥⑦	⑤-⑦	⑥⑦
					◇								D	E						G			H	H
Ventimiglia .... d.	...	1720	...	1750	...	...	1820	...	1850	1920	...	1950	2020	2020	2048	2050	2120	2120	2150	2150	2220	2250r	2320	2320
Menton .... d.	...	1732	1746	1802	...	1822	1832	1852	1902	1932	1946	2002	2032	2032	2101	2102	2132	2132	2202	2202	2232	2302r	2332	2332
Cap Martin-Roquebrune .... d.	...	1739	|	1809	...	|	1839	|	1909	1939	|	2009	2039	2039	2107	2109	2139	2139	2209	2209	2239	2309r	2339	2339
Monaco-Monte Carlo .... d.	...	1745	1757	1815	...	1833	1845	1903	1915	1945	1958	2015	2045	2045	2113	2114	2145	2145	2214	2215	2244	2315r	2345	2345
Eze .... d.	...	1753	|	1823	...	|	1853	|	1923	1953	|	2023	2053	2053	2122	2123	2153	2153	2223	2223	2253	2323r	2353	2353
Beaulieu sur Mer .... d.	...	1757	1806	1827	...	1842	1857	1912	1927	1957	2007	2027	2057	2057	2125	2126	2157	2157	2226	2227	2256	2327r	2357	2357
Villefranche sur Mer .... d.	...	1800	1809	1830	...	1845	1900	1915	1930	2000	2010	2030	2100	2100	2129	2130	2200	2200	2230	2230	2300	2330r	0000	0000
Nice Ville .... a.	...	1807	1816	1837	...	1852	1907	1922	1937	2007	2017	2037	2107	2107	2135	2136	2207	2207	2236	2237	2306	2337r	0007	0007
Nice Ville .... d.	1801	1809	...	1839	1855	...	1910	1925	1939	2010	...	2039	2110	2110	2138	2138	...	2210	2238	...	2308	2340	...	0010
Cagnes sur Mer .... d.	1814	1826	...	1856	|	...	1927	1940	1956	2027	...	2055	2127	2127	2155	2155	...	2227	2255	...	2325	2357	...	0027
Antibes .... d.	1823	1839	...	1908	1914	...	1939	1951	2008	2039	...	2109	2139	2139	2207	2208	...	2239	2308	...	2338	0009	...	0039
Juan les Pins .... d.	1826	1842	...	1911	|	...	1942	...	2011	2042	...	2112	2142	2142	2210	2211	...	2242	2311	...	2341	0013	...	0042
Cannes .... d.	1835	1850	...	1921	1926	...	1951	...	2022	2053	...	2122	2151	2153	2219	2221	...	2251	2321	...	2349	0022	...	0051
Grasse .... a.	|	...	...	1953	|	...	...	...	2053	|	...	2153	...	|	...	2253	...	...	2353	...	...	...	...	...
Boulouris sur Mer .... d.	1909	...	...	...	|	...	...	...	...	2126	...	...	...	2227	...	...	...	...	...	...	...	...	...	...
St Raphaël-Valescure .... d.	1915	...	...	...	1953	...	...	...	...	2131	...	...	...	2231	...	...	...	...	...	...	...	...	...	...
Fréjus .... d.	1919	...	...	...	1957	...	...	...	...	2135	...	...	...	2235	...	...	...	...	...	...	...	...	...	...
Les Arcs-Draguignan .... a.	1932	...	...	...	2009	...	...	...	...	2147	...	...	...	2247	...	...	...	...	...	...	...	...	...	...

D – To July 5 and from Aug. 25.
E – ⑤-⑦ July 6 - Aug. 24 (also July 14).
G – From June 23.
H – July 6 - Aug. 23 (does not run July 27).
L – July 6 - Aug. 24.

a – ①-⑤ only.

b – Not Sept. 6–8.
j – Arrives 0748.
m – Not July 14, Nov. 11.
n – Not June 17–20.
p – Not Sept. 2–5.
r – From July 13.
t – Not Oct. 4, 5.

v – Also July 14; not Sept. 5.
w – Also July 14, Nov. 11.
y – Not June 17, Sept. 2.
z – Not Sept. 5.

◇ – To/from Marseille (Table **360**).
⊙ – Does not run Nice - Ventimiglia Sept. 1–6.

♥ – Does not run Nice - Ventimiglia on July 14, Aug. 15.
⊡ – Runs 7–8 minutes later from Sept. 20 (also on June 15, 21, 22, Sept. 13, 14; not ①-⑤ Oct. 13–31).

** – Grasse - Cannes = *17 km.*

BRIANÇON - GRENOBLE, LYON and MARSEILLE 362

km	SEE NOTE ⊠																							
		⚒	②-⑤	①	①	Ⓐ			⚒	Ⓐ	Ⓐ		Ⓐ		🚌 ⚒		Ⓒ	Ⓐ	Ⓒ	Ⓐ		Ⓒ	🚌 Ⓐ	5820 Ⓡ
			e	h	g		A	B		XG				▲			△	△				v		D‡
0	**Briançon** .... d.	...	...	0451	...	...	0535	0535	...	0613	0646	0757	...	0943	1115	1242	1437	1505	1544	1644	1752	1752	1820	2029
13	L'Argentière les Écrins .... d.	...	...	0504	...	...	0548	0547	...	0625	0658	0812	...	0957	1135	1257	1449	1518	1556	1700	1807	1807	1840	2045
28	Montdauphin-Guillestre .... d.	...	...	0516	...	...	0600	0558	...	0636	0712	0825	...	1008	1150	1313	1501	1530	1609	1714	1823	1823	1855	2059
45	Embrun .... d.	...	...	0530	...	...	0614	0613	...	0652	0732	0841	...	1023	1225	1329	1515	1544	1625	1730	1837	1837	1920	2119
82	**Gap** .... a.	...	...	0601	...	...	0645	0650	...	0724	0803	0913	...	1056	1310	1358	1549	1623	1657	1802	1910	1910	1955	2153
82	**Gap** .... d.	0522	...	0602	...	...	0651	0655	...	0727	...	0920	...	1059	...	1401	1601	1628	1701	1805	...	1913	...	2156
109	Veynes-Dévoluy .... a.	0541	...	0621	...	...	0714	0714	...	0748	...	0942	...	1118	...	1428	1631	1647	1723	1827	...	1933	...	2225
109	Veynes-Dévoluy .... d.	0544	0621	0622	0628	...	0727	0727	0743	...	...	0945	...	1121	...	1431	1640	1650	1726	1830	...	1936	...	2228
172	Die .... d.	|	0713	0714	|	...	0819	0826	|	...	...	|	...	1216	...	|	1749j	1749	|	|	...	|	...	2328
209	Crest .... d.	|	0748	0748	|	...	0854	0900	|	...	...	|	...	1259	...	|	1825	1825	|	|	...	|	...	0004
244	**Valence** Ville **364** .... a.	|	0813	0813	|	...	0919	0924	|	...	...	|	...	1323	...	|	1851	1851	|	|	...	|	...	|
	Valence TGV .... a.	|	0830	0830	|	...	0931	0939	|	...	...	|	...	1337	...	|	1901	1901	|	|	...	|	...	|
	Paris Austerlitz .... a.	|	...	...	|	...	...	...	|	...	...	|	...	...	...	|	...	...	|	|	...	|	...	0738t
159	Sisteron .... d.	0623	...	...	0707	...	...	...	0830	...	...	1029	...	...	...	1513	...	...	1809	1915	...	2017	...	...
176	Château Arnoux - St Auban .... d.	0636	...	...	0720	...	...	...	0843	...	...	1042	...	...	...	1528	...	...	1825	1939	...	2035	...	...
209	Manosque-Gréoux .... d.	0703	...	...	0746	0746	...	...	0906	...	...	1107	1304	...	...	1556	...	...	1855	2005	...	2102	...	...
278	Aix en Provence .... ▷ d.	0750	...	...	0830	0830	...	...	0950	...	...	1150	1350	...	...	1650	...	...	1950	2051	...	2150	...	...
315	**Marseille** St Charles .... ▷ a.	0821	...	...	0912	0912	...	...	1021	...	...	1221	1421	...	...	1721	...	...	2023	2121	...	2221	...	...

SEE NOTE ⊠																								
	Ⓐ	5809 Ⓡ		⑥	Ⓐ		Ⓐ	⚒		Ⓒ	Ⓐ	⊡			⑤	①-④	①-④	†	⑤	Ⓑ	⑤	Ⓑ	⑤†	🚌 ①-④
		D§		k								G			f	m	m		f			w		m
Marseille St Charles .... ▷ d.	...	...	...	0635	...	0835	0935	...	1235	...	...	...	...	1635	...	...	1735	1735	1735	1835	1835	...	...	...
Aix en Provence .... ▷ d.	...	...	...	0712	...	0911	1012	...	1311	...	...	...	...	1711	...	...	1811	1812	1812	1911	1911	...	...	...
Manosque-Gréoux .... d.	...	...	...	0753	...	0953	1053	...	1358	...	...	...	...	1800	...	...	1854	1903	1853	2008j	2008j	...	...	...
Château Arnoux - St Auban .... d.	...	...	...	0816	...	1016	...	...	1427	...	...	...	...	1824	...	...	...	1929	1935j	2034	2034	...	...	...
Sisteron .... d.	...	...	...	0831	...	1030	...	...	1441	...	...	...	...	1839	...	...	...	1943	1952	2047	2047	...	...	...
Paris Austerlitz .... d.	...	2123r	...	|	...	|	...	...	|	...	...	...	...	|	...	...	...	|	|	|	|	...	...	...
Valence TGV .... d.	...	|	...	|	...	|	...	1021	|	1428	...	...	1632	|	1826	1826	...	|	|	|	|	1959	1959	...
Valence Ville **364** .... d.	...	|	...	|	...	|	...	1032	|	1437	...	...	1643	|	1836	1837	...	|	|	|	|	2019	2019	...
Crest .... d.	...	0442	...	|	...	|	...	1058	|	1502	...	...	1712	|	1901	1904	...	|	|	|	|	2048	2048	...
Die .... d.	...	0517	...	|	...	|	...	1136	|	1539	...	...	1747	|	1934	1938	...	|	|	|	|	2126	2126	...
Veynes-Dévoluy .... a.	...	0620	...	0911	...	1113	...	1232	1523	1632	...	...	1842	1934	2025	2030	...	2028	2035	2125	2125	2223	2223	...
Veynes-Dévoluy .... d.	...	0623	...	0914	...	1119	...	1235	1526	1635	...	1802	1848	1949	2026	...	...	2029	2040	2128	2128	2231	2231	...
Gap .... a.	...	0649	...	0942	...	1147	...	1254	1547	1655	...	1826	1908	2008	2045	...	...	2049	2100	2150	2150	2250	2250	...
Gap .... d.	0617	0654	...	0945	1029	1150	...	1257	1551	1658	1734	1834	1911	2011	2046	...	...	...	...	...	2154	...	2253	2255
Embrun .... d.	0653	0734	...	1022	1104	1221	...	1330	1626	1732	1808	1915	1946	2043	2121	...	...	...	...	...	2226	...	2326	2335
Montdauphin-Guillestre .... d.	0710	0754	...	1037	1118	1239	...	1345	1644	1750	1824	1930	2001	2058	2136	...	...	...	...	...	2241	...	2341	2355
L'Argentière les Écrins .... d.	0721	0811	...	1049	1129	1256	...	1357	1658	1805	1836	1940	2013	2109	2146	...	...	...	...	...	2252	...	2351	0015
Briançon .... a.	0735	0830	...	1103	1142	1309	...	1410	1711	1818	1849	1954	2026	2123	2159	...	...	...	...	...	2305	...	0004	0035

GAP - GRENOBLE *Subject to alteration until June 27 and Sept. 22 - Oct. 10*

km		⚒	Ⓐ X		N					
	Briançon (see above) .... ⊠ d.	...	0613	...	...	...	...	...	...	...
0	**Gap** .... ⊠ d.	...	0727	0727	1127	1330	...	1726	1929	...
27	Veynes-Dévoluy .... d.	0550	0751	0751	1149	1352	...	1748	1951	...
117	St Georges de Commiers .... d.	0718	0918	0918	1318	1520	...	1918	2120	...
136	**Grenoble** .... a.	0743	0943	0943	1343	1543	...	1943	2143	...

	L					⊡		⑥	F 🚌
Grenoble .... d.	0809	1009	1209	1409	1609	1609	1809	1809	2010
St Georges de Commiers .... d.	0832	1032	1232	1435	1630	1630	1832	1832	|
Veynes-Dévoluy .... d.	1003	1202	1405	1606	1802	1802	2001	2004	2200
Gap .... ⊠ a.	1025	1221	1425	1627	1826	1826	...	2023	2225
Briançon (see above) .. ⊠ a.	...	...	...	...	...	1954	...	...	...

LOCAL TRAINS MARSEILLE - AIX EN PROVENCE Journey time: 35–45 minutes

From Marseille at 0005 ♥, 0505 Ⓐ, 0605, 0635 Ⓐ, 0705 ⚒, 0735 Ⓐ, 0745, 0805 Ⓐ, 0845, 0905, 1105, 1205, 1305, 1335 Ⓐ, 1345, 1405, 1435 Ⓐ, 1505, 1535 Ⓐ, 1605, 1645 Ⓐ, 1710, 1745, 1805 Ⓐ, 1850 Ⓑ **w**, 1905, 1935 Ⓐ, 1945 Ⓐ, 2005, 2105, 2205 and 2305 ¶.

From Aix en Provence at 0510 Ⓐ, 0550 Ⓐ, 0610, 0630 ⚒, 0650 Ⓐ, 0710 Ⓐ, 0730, 0810 Ⓐ, 0850, 0910, 1110, 1210, 1230, 1250 Ⓐ, 1310, 1410, 1450 Ⓐ, 1510, 1550 Ⓐ, 1610, 1630 Ⓐ, 1710, 1730, 1750 Ⓐ, 1810, 1830 Ⓐ, 1850, 1910, 1930 Ⓐ, 2010, 2110 Ⓑ **w**, 2210 and 2310 ¶.

A – ⑥⑦ to June 29; daily July 5 - Sept. 21 (not Aug. 19, Sept. 9); Ⓒ from Nov. 1.
B – Runs on Aug. 19 and Sept. 9 only.
D – Conveys 🛏 1, 2 cl. and (2) (reclining).
F – ⑤ (not Aug. 15).
G – To / from Grenoble (see panel below main table).
– Daily June 28 - Sept. 20; ⚒ from Oct. 11.
N – Daily June 28 - Aug. 30; ⚒ Sept. 1–20 and from Oct. 11.
X – June 30 - Sept. 19 and from Nov. 3.

– Also July 7, 21, 28, Aug. 4, 11, 18; not Aug. 15, Nov. 11.
– Not Aug. 15.
– Also July 15, Nov. 12; not July 14.
– Not July 7 - Aug. 18.
– Arrives 13–17 minutes earlier.
– Not Nov. 1.
m – Not July 14, Nov. 11.
– 2150 on certain dates.

t – Arrival time may vary.
v – Not Sept. 28.
w – Also Nov. 1.

⊡ – ①②③④⑦ June 29 - Sept. 21 and from Nov. 2.
▲ – Not Nov. 21. Subject to alteration Sept. 15 - Oct. 31. Subject to alteration Crest - Valence on ①-⑤ June 16 - July 4 and Ⓐ Nov. 3–28.
△ – Subject to alteration Sept. 15 - Oct. 31.
◇ – Gare SNCF (rail station).
‡ – Train number **5818** on † (daily July 4 - Aug. 31). Train number **5828** on June 15. Subject to alteration Sept. 15 - Oct. 31 (also Sept. 8–12).
§ – Train number **5803** on † (daily July 3 - Aug. 31). Subject to alteration Sept. 15 - Oct. 30.
♥ – Not Nov. 8. Subject to alteration on ②-⑥ Nov. 18–29.
¶ – Subject to alteration on ①-⑤ Nov. 17–28.

⊠ – Services Briançon - Gap - Veynes - Valence and v.v. are subject to alteration Sept. 22 - Oct. 31.

🚌 BRIANÇON - OULX *Valid until Aug. 31, 2014*

Ⓡ			①-⑤			
Briançon ◇ .... d.	0700	0935	1200	1415	1635	1815
Oulx ◇ .... a.	0800	1035	1300	1505	1730	1905

Ⓡ		⑥⑦	①-⑤			
Oulx ◇ .... d.	0845	1140	1310	1600	1725	1945
Briançon ◇ .... a.	0945	1240	1400	1700	1815	2040

Operator: 05 voyageurs ✆ +33 (0)4 92 502 505
www.05voyageurs.com
Reservation compulsory at least 36 hours in advance.

363 BELLEGARDE - ANNEMASSE - ÉVIAN LES BAINS

Trains from Lyon / Bellegarde may divide at Belllegarde and / or Annemasse - take care to travel in the correct portion. For connections Paris - Bellegarde and v.v. see Table **341**.

SUBJECT TO ALTERATION FROM AUGUST 30. Services via Bellegarde may be suspended or diverted/retimed Aug. 20 – 24 (also certain services on the morning of Aug. 25).

km		①–⑤	Ⓐ	Ⓐ	⑥		①–⑤ n	n	P	*TGV* **6503** ⑦ Q	*TGV* **6503** ⑥	n	P		n	①–⑤	①–⑤		①–⑤	Ⓑ	*TGV* **6511** ⑤ f		⑤ v	⑤ d	w
	Paris Gare de Lyon **341** d.	...	...	...	...	...	...	...	...	0911	1011	...	...	...	...	...	...	...	...	...	1615	...	...	...	...
	Lyon Part-Dieu **346** d.	...	...	0636	0636	0838	...	1038	1038	|	|	1238	1238	1438	1438	...	...	1638	...	1738	|	1834	...	2034	2030
0	**Bellegarde** **365** d.	...	0704t	0809	0809	1008	...	1211	1211	1207	1312	1408	1409	1609	1609	...	...	1809	...	1909	1916	2009	...	2209	2209
38	Annemasse **365** a.	...	0744t	0846	0845	1044	...	1244	1244	1247	1355	1445	1444	1644	1644	...	...	1844	...	1944	2002	2044	...	2244	2244
38	Annemasse d.	0715	0749	0853	0855	1053	1220	1252	*1254**	1307	1411	1452	*1454**	...	1652	1751	1820	1852	1920	1953	2011	2052	2127	2253	2252
68	Thonon les Bains d.	0744	0825	0929	0928	1131	1249	1331	*1344**	1340	1437	1531	*1544**	...	1726	1831	1851	1931	1951	2029	2053	2131	2153	2322	2331
77	**Évian les Bains** a.	0752	...	0938	0938	1138	1256	1338	*1404**	1347	1444	1538	*1604**	...	1733	1838	1859	1938	1959	2036	2101	2138	2202	2330	2338

	⚒	⚒		①–⑤	①–⑤	①–⑤	Ⓒ	Ⓐ		P	n	①–⑤ n	*TGV* **6508** ⑦ e	P	n	*TGV* **6504** ⑦	*TGV* **6504** ⑥ R	P	n	①–⑤ n	⑦ z	⑦ s g	①–⑤		Ⓑ
Évian-les-Bains d.	0502	0521	0625	0703	0715	0800	0821	...	1025	*1150**	1221	1302	1322	*1350**	1421	1522	1737	*1557**	1621	1656	1715	1741	1802	1821	2044
Thonon-les-Bains d.	0511	0532	0636	0712	0724	0808	0832	0832	1035	*1210**	1229	1310	1336	*1410**	1432	1534	1748	*1617**	1632	1705	1725	1751	1810	1832	2055
Annemasse a.	0542	0606	0706	0743	0804	0836	0909	0909	1106	*1307**	1306	1339	1400	*1507**	1507	1603	|	*1707**	1706	1736	1806	1816	1839	1907	2124
Annemasse **365** d.	0547	0617	0717	...	...	...	0919	0919**k**	1117	1317	1317	...	1415	1517	1517	1618	|	1717	1717	...	1817	...	...	1917	2131
Bellegarde **365** a.	0624	0650	0754	...	...	...	0955	0955**k**	1150	1349	1349	...	1454	1550	1550	1701	1908	1750	1750	...	1850	...	...	1950	2210
Lyon Part-Dieu **346** a.	...	0832	0931	...	...	...	1126	1126	1322	1521	1521	...	|	1725	1725	|	|	1922	1922	...	2028	...	...	2126**x**	...
Paris Gare de Lyon **341** a.	...	...	...	...	...	...	...	...	...	...	...	...	1749	...	...	2011	2149**j**	...	...	...	...	...	...	...	...

P – July 7 – 11, 21 – 25; Ⓐ Aug. 11 – 29; Ⓐ Oct. 27 - Nov. 14. Subject to confirmation.
Q – July 6 - Aug. 24.
R – ⑥ July 12 - Aug. 23 (also Aug. 15)

d – Not Aug. 15.
e – Also July 14, Nov. 11.
f – Also Aug. 14; not Aug. 15, 22.

g – To Annecy, Chambéry, Grenoble (Tables **365** and **364**).
j – 2228 on July 12.
k – Aug. 25 – 29 departs Annemasse 0917, arrives Bellegarde 0950.
n – Not July 7 – 11, 21 – 25, Aug. 11 – 14, 18 – 22, 25 – 29, Oct. 27 – 31, Nov. 3 – 7, Nov. 10, 12, 13, 14.
s – Not July 13 – 27.
t – Not June 23 - July 11. Departs Bellegarde 0709 from Aug. 25.
v – From Valence, Grenoble, Chambéry, Annecy (Tables **364** and **365**).

w – ①②③④⑥⑦ (also Aug. 15).
x – Subject to confirmation until Aug. 24.
z – Also July 14; not July 13.

TGV – ®, supplement payable, 🍷.

* – By 🚌.

364 GENÈVE and ANNECY - CHAMBÉRY - GRENOBLE - VALENCE

Rail services do not run Bellegarde - Genève and v.v. July 15 - Aug. 19. All services via Bellegarde are subject to alteration / cancellation Aug. 20 – 24.

km		Ⓐ	⚒	Ⓐ	⚒			⚒	⚒ r⊖	⊗			Ⓒ	Ⓐ	⑥	⊗	⊗	⊗	Ⓒ							
0	**Genève** ⊠ **341 346** d.	...	...	...	...	...	...	...	0659	...	...	...	...	...	...	0959	...	...	...	1159	...	...	...	1459	...	...
33	Bellegarde **341 346** d.	...	...	...	...	...	...	...	0727	...	...	...	...	...	...	1027	...	...	...	1227	...	...	...	1527	...	...
66	Culoz **346** d.	...	...	...	...	...	...	...	|	...	...	...	...	...	...	|	...	...	...	|	...	...	...	|	...	...
	Annecy **341 345** d.	...	...	...	0544	...	...	0637	|	0746	...	0839	0839	0939	0953	|	1039	...	1139	|	1245	1337	1444	|	...	1537
88	Aix les Bains **341 345** d.	...	...	...	0626	...	...	0726	0806	0826	...	0926	0926	1026	1035	1106	1126	...	1226	1306	1326	1426	1526	1606	...	1626
102	**Chambéry** **341 345** a.	...	...	...	0636	...	...	0737	0817	0837	...	0937	0937	1037	...	1117	1137	...	1237	1317	1337	1437	1537	1617	...	1637
102	**Chambéry** ▷ d.	...	0539	*0557*	0638	...	0657	0739	0820	0839	0857	...	0939	...	...	1120	1139	1239	1239	1320	1339	1439	1539	1620	1624	1639
116	Montmélian ▷ d.	...	0550	*0609*	0650	...	0709	0750	|	0850	0909	...	0950	...	...	|	1150	1251	1251	|	1350	1450	1550	|	1635	1650
165	**Grenoble** ▷ a.	...	0627	*0657*	0727	...	0757	0827	0906	0927	0957	...	1027	...	...	1206	1227	1327	1327	1406	1427	1527	1627	1706	1721	1727
165	**Grenoble** d.	0602	0630	0709	0730	0730	...	0830	...	0930	...	...	1030	...	...	1209	1230	1330	1330	...	1430	1530	1630	1709	...	1730
242	Romans-Bourg de Péage d.	0701	0728	0759	0828	0828	...	0928	...	1028	...	...	1128	...	...	1259	1328	1428	1428	...	1527	1629	1727	1759	...	1828
249	Valence TGV ⊙ a.	0708	0735	0804	0834	0834	...	0934	...	1034	...	...	1134	...	...	1304	1334	1435	1435	...	1534	1636	1734	1804	...	1834
259	**Valence** Ville ⊙ a.	0718	0744	0814	0844	0844	...	0944	...	1044	...	...	1144	...	...	1314	1344	1444	1444	...	1544	1646	1744	1814	...	1844

	Ⓑ		D		⚒	⚒A		B	①–⑥	⑦ ◧
Genève ⊠ **341 346** d.	...	...	1642	...	...	1757	...	1842	...	...
Bellegarde **341 346** d.	...	...	1709	...	...	1827	...	1909	...	...
Culoz **346** d.	...	...	1744	...	...	1853	...	1944	...	...
Annecy **341 345** d.	1644	...	|	1739	...	|	1839	|	1936	1937
Aix les Bains **341 345** d.	1720	...	1806	1826	...	1910	1926	2005	2026	2025
Chambéry **341 345** a.	1731	...	1817	1837	...	1920	1937	2017	2037	2035
Chambéry ▷ d.	1739	1757	1820	1839	...	1921	1939	2020	2039	2043
Montmélian ▷ d.	1750	1809	|	1850	...	|	1950	|	2050	2056
Grenoble ▷ a.	1827	1857	1906	1927	...	2002	2027	2106	2127	2132
Grenoble d.	1830	...	1909f	1930	1942	...	2030	...	...	...
Romans-Bourg de Péage d.	1927	...	1959f	2028	2103	...	2127	...	...	...
Valence TGV ⊙ a.	1934	...	2004f	2034	2110	...	2134	...	...	...
Valence Ville ⊙ a.	1944	...	2014f	2044	2120	...	2144	...	...	...

	Ⓐ ⊡	⚒	⚒ ◇	Ⓐ	Ⓐ	⚒ ◇	⚒	⚒	⚒ ◇	Ⓐ ◇	◇
Valence Ville ⊙ d.	...	...	...	...	...	...	0524	...	...	0615	...
Valence TGV ⊙ d.	...	...	...	...	...	...	0534	...	...	0626	...
Romans-Bourg de Péage d.	...	...	...	...	...	...	0543	...	←	0634	...
Grenoble a.	...	...	...	...	...	...	0647	...	0647	0730	...
Grenoble ▷ d.	0507	...	0539	...	0634	0639	→	0654	0703	0734	0734
Montmélian ▷ d.	0544	...	0626	...	0710	0726	...	|	0753	0810	0810
Chambéry ▷ a.	0554	...	0635	...	0720	0735	...	0739	0803	0820	0820
Chambéry **341 345** d.	0557	0622	...	0648	0723	...	...	0743	...	0823	0823
Aix les Bains **341 345** d.	0610	0636	...	0659	0736	...	...	0757	...	0840	0840
Annecy **341 345** a.	|	0715	...	0744	0815	...	...	|	...	0915	0915
Culoz **346** d.	0633	...	...	...	...	...	...	|	...	...	...
Bellegarde **341 346** a.	0658	...	...	...	...	...	...	0832	...	...	...
Genève ⊠ **341 346** a.	0736	...	...	...	...	...	...	0900	...	...	...

		⚒	Ⓐ	† ◇		Ⓐ				⊗	⊗	⊗	⊗	⊗			e	◐			Ⓐ		Ⓑ t		Ⓒ v	Ⓑ
Valence Ville ⊙ d.	0646	...	0715	...	0815	0915	1015	...	...	1215	1315	1346	1415	1515	1615	1645	...	1715	1746	1815	...	1915	2015	2115	2115	2215
Valence TGV ⊙ d.	0656	...	0726	...	0826	0926	1026	...	...	1226	1326	1356	1426	1526	1626	1656	...	1726	1756	1826	...	1926	2026	2126	2126	2226
Romans-Bourg de Péage d.	0704	...	0735	...	0834	0935	1035	...	...	1235	1335	1403	1434	1534	1634	1704	...	1735	1804	1834	...	1934	2034	2134	2134	2235
Grenoble a.	0751	...	0830	...	0930	1030	1130	...	...	1330	1430	1451	1530	1630	1730	1751	...	1830	1851	1930	...	2030	2130	2230	2230	2330
Grenoble ▷ d.	0754	...	▬	0839	0934	...	1134	1154	1234	1334	1434	1454	1534	1634	1734	1754	1803	1834	*1903*	1934	2003	2034	2134	...	2234	...
Montmélian ▷ d.	|	...	...	0926	1010	...	1210	|	1310	1410	1510	|	1610	1710	1810	|	1853	1911	*1953*	2010	2053	2110	2210	...	2310	...
Chambéry ▷ a.	0839	...	Ⓑ	0935	1020	...	1220	1239	1320	1420	1520	1539	1620	1720	1820	1839	1903	1920	*2003*	2020	2103	2120	2220	...	2320	...
Chambéry **341 345** d.	0843	...	0923	...	1023	...	1223	1243	1323	1423	1523	1543	1623	1723	1823	1843	...	1923	...	2023	...	2123	2223	...	...	...
Aix les Bains **341 345** d.	0857	0925	0936	...	1036	...	1236	1257	1336	1436	1536	1557	1636	1736	1836	1857	...	1936	...	2037	...	2136	2236	...	...	...
Annecy **341 345** a.	|	1007	1015	...	1115	...	1315	|	1415	1515	1615	|	1715	1815	1915	|	...	2015	...	2122	...	2215	2315**z**	...	...	...
Culoz **346** d.	|	...	...	...	...	...	...	|	...	...	...	|	...	...	...	|	...	...	...	...	...	...	...	...	...	...
Bellegarde **341 346** a.	0932	...	...	...	...	...	...	1332	...	...	...	1632	...	...	...	1932	...	...	...	...	...	...	...	...	...	...
Genève ⊠ **341 346** a.	1000	...	...	...	...	...	...	1400	...	...	...	1700	...	...	...	2015	...	...	...	...	...	...	...	...	...	...

ADDITIONAL JOURNEYS CHAMBÉRY - GRENOBLE

	⚒	⚒	Ⓐ	Ⓐ	⚒	Ⓐ	Ⓐ		Ⓐ	⚒	⚒	Ⓐ	⚒
Chambéry d.	0624	0724	0757	0824	1224	1257	1324	1424	1657	1724	1824	1857	1924
Montmélian d.	0635	0735	0809	0835	1235	1309	1335	1435	1709	1735	1835	1909	1935
Grenoble a.	0721	0821	0857	0921	1321	1357	1421	1521	1757	1821	1921	1957	2021

	Ⓐ◇		Ⓐ	Ⓐ		Ⓐ	⚒	Ⓐ	Ⓐ		Ⓐ	Ⓐ
Grenoble d.	0739	1003	1139	1203	1303	1403	1539	1603	1639	1703	1739	1839
Montmélian d.	0825	1053	1226	1253	1353	1453	1626	1653	1726	1753	1826	1926
Chambéry a.	0835	1103	1235	1303	1403	1503	1635	1703	1735	1803	1835	1935

A – Until July 12.
B – July 15 - Aug. 19; daily from Sept. 22. Does not run Genève - Bellegarde July 15 - Aug. 19.
D – Ⓐ to July 11; ⑤ July 18 - Aug. 15; Ⓐ from Aug. 25.

e – Not July 12, 19, 26, Aug. 2, 9, 16, 23.
f – ⑤ only.
r – Not July 12.
t – Not July 20, 27, Aug. 10, 17, Oct. 12.
v – Not June 15, 22, 29, July 19, 26, Aug. 2, 10, Sept. 14, 21, Oct. 12, 25, Dec. 7.

z – Not ①–④ Sept. 15 - Oct. 2.

◧ – From Évian les Bains (Table **363**).
◐ – Extended to Évian les Bains (Table **363**) on ⑤.
⊖ – Runs 3 – 5 minutes later Aix-les-Bains - Grenoble on ⑥ to July 5 / from Aug. 30. July 15 - Aug. 19 starts from Bellegarde (d. 0733), then Aix les Bains d. 0820, Chambéry a. 0831, d. 0844, Grenoble a. 0931.
⊗ – Subject to alteration Grenoble - Valence and v.v. on Ⓐ Nov. 10 – 28 (also June 16 – 20).
⊡ – Subject to alteration July 7 – 11.

◇ – Timings Grenoble - Chambéry may vary by 1 – 2 minutes July 1 - Aug. 14.
⊙ – Additional 🚌 runs 2 – 3 times per hour.
▷ – For additonal trains see panel below main table.
⊠ – Genève timings are subject to alteration (please confirm locally). July 15 - Aug. 19 services do not run between Bellegarde and Genève (a replacement 🚌 operates during this period).

Services are subject to alteration on July 20, 27

GENÈVE AÉROPORT ✈ - CHAMBÉRY - GRENOBLE 364a

Daily 🚌 service operated by Aerocar, www.aerocar.fr. Journey 1 hr to Chambéry (Gare Routière), 2 hrs 15 m to Grenoble (Gare Routière). Rail tickets not valid. Reduced service on May 1.

Genève Aéroport (Secteur International): depart 1115, 1315, 1530, 1800, 2030.

Grenoble: depart 0600, 0830, 1115, 1330, 1530 (from Chambéry 55–60 minutes later).

PARIS / ANNECY - LA ROCHE SUR FORON - ST GERVAIS 365

Trains from Lyon / Bellegarde may convey portions for Genève and/or Évian les Bains. For connections Genève Eaux-Vives - Annemasse / La Roche sur Foron see Table **366a**.

SUBJECT TO ALTERATION FROM AUGUST 30. SEE ALSO NOTE ⊠.

km	*TGV* trains convey 🍸			5705 5594					*TGV* 6467	*TGV* 9761				*TGV* 9765			*TGV* 6473	*TGV* 9769				*TGV* 9773		
		①–⑥		B	Ⓐ		⚒	Ⓒ	⑥	Ⓐ		Ⓐ		①–⑥			⑥			Ⓐ				
				®◇	◧				M		⊡	⊡★		b⊕	⊡	★	L	W				⊕		
0	**Paris Gare de Lyon** 341 d.	...	...	2312a	...	...	...	...	0707	0707	...	...	...	0911	...	...	1011	1111	...	...	...	1211	...	...
406	Bourg en Bresse 341 d.	...	...	|	...	...	...	...	|	0859	...	...	...	|	...	...	1204	1303j	...	...	...	1405	...	...
	Lyon Perrache 346 d.	...	...	|	...	...	0625	...	|	|	...	...	...	|	1025	...	|	|	1224	...	...	|	1423	...
	Lyon Part-Dieu 346 d.	...	...	|	...	...	0636	...	|	|	0838	...	...	|	1038	...	|	|	1238	...	...	|	1438	...
470	Bellegarde 341 a.	...	...	△	...	...	0807	...	0946	0947	1006	...	...	1148	1208	...	1259	1348	1408	...	...	1500	1608	...
470	Bellegarde ⊖ d.	...	...	|	...	...	0809	...	0952	...	1008	...	...	...	1211	...	1312	...	1408	...	...	...	1609	...
508	Annemasse ⊖ a.	...	...	|	...	...	0846	...	1025	...	1044	...	...	...	1244	...	1355	...	1445	...	...	...	1644	...
508	Annemasse ▷ d.	0650	...	|	...	...	0850	...	1034	...	1050	...	...	...	1250	...	1407	...	1450	...	...	...	1650	...
•	**Annecy** ▷ d.	|	...	0659	0732	...	|	0932	|	...	|	1132	...	...	|	1332	|	...	|	1532	...	...	|	1732
525	La Roche sur Foron ▷ a.	0707	...	0738	0807	...	0907	1007	|	...	1107	1207	...	...	1307	1407	|	...	1507	1607	...	...	1707	1807
525	La Roche sur Foron d.	0712	...	0758	0812	...	0912	1012	|	...	1112	1212	...	...	1312	1412	|	...	1512	1612	...	...	1712	1812
547	Cluses (Haute-Savoie) d.	0737	...	0824	0837	...	0937	1037	1124	...	1137	1237	...	...	1337	1437	1457	...	1537	1637	...	...	1737	1837
566	Sallanches Megève d.	0750	...	0839	0850	...	0951	1050	1139	...	1150	1250	...	...	1350	1450	1518	...	1550	1650	...	...	1750	1850
572	**St Gervais** a.	0756	...	0845	0856	...	0956	1056	1145	...	1156	1256	...	...	1356	1456	1524	...	1556	1656	...	...	1756	1856

	TGV 9775		*TGV* 9777		*TGV* 6511			*TGV* 9785		
			Ⓑ	Ⓑ	⑤f				⑤	
	⊕		⊕					⊙	v	
Paris Gare de Lyon 341 d.	1511	...	1611	...	1615	...	...	1911	...	...
Bourg en Bresse 341 d.	|	...	1805	...	|	...	...	2105	...	...
Lyon Perrache 346 d.	|	...	|	...	|	...	...	|	...	...
Lyon Part-Dieu 346 d.	|	1638	|	1738	|	1834	...	|	2034	...
Bellegarde 341 a.	1748	1808	1858	1907	1909	2007	...	2150	2206	...
Bellegarde ⊖ d.	...	1809	...	1909	1916	2009	...	...	2209	...
Annemasse ⊖ a.	...	1844	...	1944	2002	2044	...	...	2244	...
Annemasse ▷ d.	...	1850	...	1950	...	2050	...	...	2250	...
Annecy ▷ d.	...	|	...	|	...	|	...	...	|	...
La Roche sur Foron ▷ a.	...	1907	...	2009	...	2107	...	...	2307	...
La Roche sur Foron d.	...	1912	...	2012	...	2112	...	...	2312	...
Cluses (Haute-Savoie) d.	...	1937	...	2036	...	2137	...	...	2337	...
Sallanches Megève d.	...	1950	...	2050	...	2150	...	...	2350	...
St Gervais a.	...	1956	...	2056	...	2156	...	...	2356	...

				TGV 9764			*TGV* 9768		
	⚒			①–⑥					Ⓐ
				b⊗			⊕		◧★
St Gervais d.	0504	...	0604	...	0703	0804	...	...	0904
Sallanches Megève d.	0509	...	0609	...	0708	0809	...	...	0910
Cluses (Haute-Savoie) d.	0523	...	0623	...	0722	0823	...	...	0923
La Roche sur Foron a.	0546	...	0647	...	0746	0846	...	...	0947
La Roche sur Foron ▷ d.	0552	...	0653	...	0751	0853	...	...	0952
Annecy ▷ a.	|	...	|	...	0829	|	...	...	1029
Annemasse ▷ a.	0610	...	0710	...	...	0910	...	...	...
Annemasse ⊖ d.	0617	...	0717	...	...	0919k	...	...	...
Bellegarde ⊖ a.	0650	...	0754	...	...	0955k	...	...	...
Bellegarde 341 d.	0657	...	0756	0808	...	0957k	1010	...	...
Lyon Part-Dieu 346 a.	0832	...	0931	|	...	1126	|	...	...
Lyon Perrache 346 a.	...	...	0945	|	...	1139	|	...	...
Bourg en Bresse 341 d.	...	...	...	0858	...	...	|	...	...
Paris Gare de Lyon 341 a.	...	...	...	1049	...	...	1249	...	...

		TGV 9770			*TGV* 9772	*TGV* 6482				*TGV* 9778		*TGV* 9776				*TGV* 9780	*TGV* 6486		*TGV* 9784			5598 5708		5596 5706
		Ⓐ	Ⓒ		Ⓒ	⑥	Ⓐ					⑦		Ⓐ	⑦	Ⓑ	⑥				Ⓑ	C	Ⓑ	D
	⊡			⊡	⊕	dM	⊡★					e⊕			h	⊕	dL		⊕			®◇		®◇
St Gervais d.	1004	...	1104	1204	...	1244	1304	1404	1504	...	1604	...	...	1704	1704	...	1709	1804	...	...	1904	1913	2004	2026
Sallanches Megève d.	1009	...	1109	1209	...	1252	1309	1409	1509	...	1609	...	...	1709	1710	...	1717	1810	...	...	1909	1923	2009	2036
Cluses (Haute-Savoie) d.	1023	...	1123	1223	...	1308	1323	1423	1523	...	1623	...	...	1723	1723	...	1738	1823	...	...	1923	1944	2023	2057
La Roche sur Foron a.	1047	...	1147	1247	...	|	1348	1447	1548	...	1647	...	...	1748	1747	...	|	1847	...	...	1948	2004	2047	2132
La Roche sur Foron ▷ d.	1053	...	1152	1253	...	|	1353	1453	1553	...	1653	...	...	1753	1753	...	|	1853	...	...	1953	2025	2053	2152
Annecy ▷ a.	|	...	1229	|	...	|	1429	|	1629	...	|	...	...	1829	|	...	|	|	...	...	2029	2102	|	2222
Annemasse ▷ a.	1110	...	...	1310	...	1349	...	1510	...	...	1710	...	...	...	1810	...	|	1910	...	...	...	|	2110	|
Annemasse ⊖ d.	1117	...	...	1317	...	1410	...	1517	...	...	1717	...	...	...	1817	...	|	1917	...	...	...	|	2131	|
Bellegarde ⊖ a.	1150	...	...	1349	...	1454	...	1550	...	...	1750	...	...	...	1850	...	1908	1950	...	...	...	|	2210	|
Bellegarde 341 d.	1152	1210	...	1351	1410	1502	...	1554	...	1700	1752	1810	...	...	1855	1910	1911	1952x	2010	...	...	▽	...	▽
Lyon Part-Dieu 346 a.	1322	|	...	1521	|	|	...	1725	...	|	1922	|	...	...	2028	|	|	2126x	|	...	...	|	...	|
Lyon Perrache 346 a.	1333	|	...	...	|	|	...	...	...	|	...	|	...	...	...	|	|	2141x	|	...	...	|	...	|
Bourg en Bresse 341 d.	...	|	...	...	|	1557	...	...	...	1756	...	|	...	...	...	|	2000	...	|	...	...	|	...	|
Paris Gare de Lyon 341 a.	...	1449	...	...	1649	1749	...	...	...	1949	...	2049	...	...	...	2149	2149t	...	2249	...	...	0618a	...	0618a

ANNECY - ANNEMASSE Direct services

	⚒	Ⓐ	⚒		⚒		Ⓑ	Ⓐ	⑤	
		★	★♥		★				A	
Annecy d.	0632	0932	1032	...	1432	...	1832	1932	2032	...
La Roche sur Foron a.	0706	1007	1106	...	1506	...	1906	2006	2106	...
La Roche sur Foron d.	0710	...	1110	...	1510	...	1910	2010	2109	...
Annemasse a.	0726	...	1126	...	1525	...	1926	2026	2125	...

	Ⓐ	⚒		Ⓐ	⚒		Ⓑ	⑦z	Ⓑ
				★	★⊡			A	
Annemasse d.	0633	0830	...	...	1233	...	1633	1825	2033
La Roche sur Foron a.	0649	0846	...	...	1249	...	1649	1843	2049
La Roche sur Foron d.	0652	0851	...	1208	1252	...	1652	1853	2052
Annecy a.	0729	0929	...	1240	1329	...	1729	1929	2129

– 🚌12 Grenoble - Chambéry - Annecy - Évian and v.v. See also Tables **363** and **364**.
– ⑤–⑦ (daily July 4 - Aug. 31; also Nov. 11). Subject to alteration on July 19, 26. Departs Paris 2255 on July 4. Departs Paris 2142 on Oct. 5.
– ⑥⑦. Subject to alteration July 20, 27.
– ⑤ (①–⑤ July 4 - Aug. 29; also Nov. 11).
– ⑥ July 12 - Aug. 16.
– ⑥ July 12 - Aug. 23.
– ⑦ (also Nov. 11; daily July 13 - Aug. 19).

– Paris **Austerlitz**.
– Not July 14, Nov. 11.
– Also Aug. 15.
– Also July 14, Nov. 11.

f – Also Aug. 14; not Aug. 15, 22.
h – Also July 14; not July 13.
j – July 15 - Aug. 19 only.
k – Aug. 25–29 Annemasse d. 0917, Bellegarde a. 0950, d. 0952.
t – 2228 on July 12.
v – Not Aug. 15.
x – Subject to confirmation until Aug. 24.
z – Not July 13–27.

TGV – ®, supplement payable, 🍸.

⊗ – Does not run July 15 - Aug. 29.
⊕ – Does not run July 15 - Aug. 24.
⊙ – Does not run July 14 - Aug. 24.
◇ – 🛏 1,2 cl. and 🚌2 (reclining).
◧ – Subject to alteration on Oct. 6, 13, 20.

⊡ – Subject to alteration on ①–⑤ Sept. 15 - Oct. 3 Annemasse - La Roche sur Foron - St Gervais and v.v.
★ – Subject to alteration on ①–⑤ Oct. 6–24 Annecy - La Roche sur Foron and v.v.
♥ – Subject to alteration on ①–⑤ Sept. 15 - Oct. 24 La Roche sur Foron - Annemasse.
▷ – For additional trains Annemasse - La Roche sur Foron - Annecy see panel below main table.
△ – Via Aix les Bains (a. 0553).
▽ – Via Aix les Bains (d. 2203 ⑥⑦, 2304 **D**).
⊖ – For additional trains Bellegarde - Annemasse see Table **363**.
• – Annecy to La Roche sur Foron is 39 km.
⊠ – Alterations to services to / from Bellegarde **until Sept. 22**: July 15 - Aug. 29 many *TGV* services are cancelled (as indicated). All services via Bellegarde are subject to alteration / cancellation Aug. 20–24 (also certain services on the morning of Aug. 25). Timings of *TGV* services may vary by a few minutes until July 14, also Aug. 25 - Sept. 22 (please check your reservation for confirmed timings).

ST GERVAIS - CHAMONIX 365a

km											
0	**St Gervais** d.	0706	0806	0906	1006	1206	1306	1406	1606	then	2106
9	Les Houches d.	0733	0833	0933	1033	1233	1333	1433	1633	hourly	2133
20	**Chamonix** a.	0750	0850	0950	1050	1250	1350	1450	1650	until	2150

				Ⓒ						
Chamonix d.	0714	0814	0914	1014	1214	1314	1414	1614	then	2014
Les Houches d.	0732	0832	0932	1032	1232	1332	1432	1632	hourly	2032
St Gervais a.	0757	0857	0957	1057	1257	1357	1457	1657	until	2057

any journeys continue to / from Le Châtelard or Martigny (Table **572**)

FRANCE

366 (PARIS) - CHAMBÉRY - ALBERTVILLE - BOURG ST MAURICE

For Paris - Chambéry see Table **341**. Subject to alteration on July 20, 27, Dec. 6, 7. Timings may vary by 1–2 minutes July 1 - Aug. 7.

km	*TGV* trains convey 🍷																							
										TGV 6429														5705
		🚌 Ⓐ	Ⓐ ✣	🚌 Ⓐ	🚌 Ⓐ	✣⊠	🚌 Ⓐ	Ⓐ ✣⊠	⑥ §	⑥ D	🚌 Ⓐ	Ⓐ ✣⊠	Ⓒ ‡		Ⓐ	🚌 Ⓐ	⚒		Ⓐ	⚒ ¶		🚌 ⚒		[R] ◇ ♠
0	**Paris Gare de Lyon** ...... 341 d.	...	...	...	...	...	...	...	...	0844	...	...	...	...	...	...	...	...	...	...	...	...	...	2312a
	Lyon Part Dieu **344** ......d.	...	...	...	...	...	...	...	0940r	|	...	1140e	1140	...	...	...	...	...	...	1740	...	...	...	|
	Aix les Bains ......d.	...	...	...	...	...	...	...	|	|	...	|	|	...	...	...	...	...	...	|	...	...	...	|
532	**Chambéry** ...... **367** d.	0601	0711	...	0811	0911	0950	1111	1110	1149	1230	1311	1306	...	1511	...	1611	1711	1811	1911	2011	2117	...	0528
545	Montmélian ...... **367** d.	0619	0721	...	0830	0921	|	1121	1121	|	|	1321	1316	...	1521	...	1621	1721	1821	1922	2021	2135	...	|
557	St Pierre d'Albigny ...... **367** d.	0637	0730	...	0845	0930	|	1130	1129	|	|	1330	1325	...	1530	...	1630	1730	1830	1930	2030q	2150	...	|
580	Albertville ......a.	0715	0751	...	0910	0951	1040	1153	1152	1225	1320	1352	1347	...	1551	...	1651	1752	1851	1953	2051	2215	...	0602
580	Albertville ......d.	0715	0801	...	0910	1001	1040	1202	1202	1235	1320	1401	1400	...	1601	...	1701	1801	1859	2003	2101	2215	...	0630
608	**Moûtiers-Salins** ......d.	0743	0824	0855	0940	1026	1110	1226	1226	1303	1350	1425	1428	...	1624	1635	1723	1826	1924	2026	2123	2250	...	0702
623	Aime la Plagne ......d.	0758	...	0910	...	1040	|	1240	1240	1322	|	1439	1443	...	...	1650	1740	1840	1941	2043	2140	|	...	0722
630	Landry ......d.	0808	...	0920	...	1048	|	1248	1247	1331	|	1447	1451	...	...	1700	1748	1847	1949	2051	2148	|	...	0732
637	**Bourg St Maurice** ......a.	0820	...	0932	...	1055	1140	1255	1255	1338	1420	1455	1458	...	...	1715	1755	1855	19560	2058	2155	2330	...	0740

																	TGV 6436						5708	5706
	🚌 Ⓐ	⚒	Ⓐ	⑥ L	Ⓑ ✣	🚌 †	🚌 Ⓐ	Ⓐ ✣	🚌 Ⓐ	✣⊠		⚒ ✣⊠		⊠	🚌 Ⓐ	Ⓐ	⑥ D	†	⚒	🚌 Ⓐ	†	⚒	[R] ◇ ♥	[R] ◇ ♣
Bourg St Maurice ......d.	...	0505	0608	0705	0705	0710	0805	...	0905	1105	...	1305	...	1505	1548	...	1607	1704	1705	1800	1905	1905	2024	2108
Landry ......d.	...	0513	0616	0713	0713	0717	0817	...	0912	1113	...	1313	...	1513	1555	...	1617	1713	1713	1807	1913	1913	2034	2118
Aime la Plagne ......d.	...	0521	0624	0721	0721	0726	0826	...	0921	1121	...	1321	...	1521	1604	...	1628	1721	1721	1816	1921	1921	2046	2128
Moûtiers-Salins ......d.	0436	0536	0638	0736	0736	0755	0845	0855	0945	1138	...	1338	...	1538	1628	1638	1655	1739	1738	1840	1939	1938	2104	2151
Albertville ......a.	0511	0559	0659	0759	0759	0840	...	0916	1020	1159	...	1359	...	1559	...	1659	1720	1759	1759	1915	1959	1959	2132	2212
Albertville ......d.	0511	0608	0708	0808	0808	0840	...	0925	1020	1208	...	1408	...	1608	...	1708	1732	1808	1811	1915	2008	2008	2152	2232
St Pierre d'Albigny ...... **367** d.	0531	0631	0731	0831	0831	0908	...	0950	1050	1236	...	1431	...	1631	...	1731	|	1831	1834	1945	2031	2031	|	|
Montmélian ...... **367** d.	0546	0640	0741	0840	0840	0923	...	1000	1105	1245	...	1440	...	1640	...	1740	|	1840	1843	2000	2040	2040	|	|
Chambéry ...... **367** a.	0612	0649	0751	0849	0849	0950	...	1009	1124	1253	...	1449	...	1649	...	1749	1810	1849	1852	2026	2049	2049	2227	2310
Aix les Bains ......a.	0631	|	...	|	...	...	...	...	...	...	...	...	...	...	...	...	|	|	...	...	|	...	|	|
Lyon Part Dieu **344** ......a.	...	0820	...	1020	...	...	...	...	...	...	...	...	...	...	...	...	|	2020	...	...	2220	...	|	|
Paris Gare de Lyon ...... **341** a.	...	...	...	...	...	...	...	...	...	...	...	...	...	...	...	...	2127	...	...	...	...	...	0618a	0618a

D – ⑥ July 12 - Aug. 23.
L – To Sept. 20.

a – Paris **Austerlitz**.
e – Change trains at Chambéry until Aug. 29.
q – ①–④ (not July 14, Nov. 11).
r – 0939 Sept. 20 - Oct. 25.

TGV – [R], supplement payable, 🍷.

◇ – 🛏 1, 2 cl., (2) (reclining).
§ – Subject to alteration on Sept. 27.
‡ – Subject to alteration on Sept. 14, 21, 27, 28, Oct. 5.
¶ – Subject to alteration on Sept. 13, 20, 27, Oct. 4.
⊠ – Subject to alteration on ①–⑤ Oct. 13–31.

✣ – Subject to alteration Albertville - Moutiers - Bourg St Maurice and v.v. on Ⓐ June 30 - Aug. 1.
♠ – ⑤–⑦ (daily July 4 - Aug. 31; also Nov. 11). Subject to alteration on July 19, 26. Departs Paris 2255 on July 4. Departs Paris 2142 on Oct. 5.
♣ – ⑤ (①–⑤ July 4 - Aug. 29; also Nov. 11).
♥ – ⑥⑦. Subject to alteration July 20, 27.

366a 🚌 GENÈVE - ANNEMASSE

🚌 **TPG route 61 Genève Cornavin railway station - Annemasse rail station** **Journey time: 34–43 minutes** *TER tickets valid between Genève Rieu and Annemasse*

From Genève Cornavin Ⓐ: 0650 and every 15 minutes until 1920 then 1936, 1951, 2008, 2025, 2051, 2121, 2151, 2221.
⑥: 0636 and every 30 minutes until 2136. ⑦ and holidays: 0843 and every 30 minutes until 2143.

From Annemasse Ⓐ: 0620 and every 15 minutes until 1535 then 1549, 1603, 1618, 1633, 1648, 1703, 1718, 1732, 1747, 1802, 1817, 1833, 1850, 1907, 1925, 1944, 2007, 2035, 2105, 2135
⑥: 0551 and every 30 minutes until 2051. ⑦ and holidays: 0757 and every 30 minutes until 2057.

🚌 GENÈVE EAUX VIVES - ANNEMASSE - ANNECY

SNCF 🚌 service	🚌	🚌 ⚒	🚌	🚌	🚌	🚌	🚌 Ⓒ	🚌	🚌 Ⓐ	🚌	🚌
Genève Eaux-Vives .... d.	0648	0848	1045	1048	1248	1448	1648	1725	1800	1910	2115
Annemasse ...... ▷ a.	0708	0908	|	1108	1308	1508	1708	|	|	|	2135
La Roche sur Foron ▷ a.	0741	0941	1120	1141	1341	1541	1741	1800	1845	1955	2200
Annecy ...... ▷ a.	...	...	1155	...	...	...	...	1835	...	...	2235

	🚌 ⚒	🚌	🚌 Ⓐ	🚌 Ⓒ	🚌	🚌	🚌	🚌	🚌 ⚒	🚌	🚌
Annecy ...... ▷ d.	0615	0700	...	...	...	...	...	...	1625	...	...
La Roche sur Foron ▷ d.	0650	0735	0812	0812	1012	1212	1412	1612	1700	1812	2012
Annemasse ...... ▷ d.	|	|	|	0847	1042	1242	1442	1647	|	1847	2042
Genève Eaux-Vives .... a.	0740	0825	0858	0912	1102	1302	1502	1702	1750	1912	2112

▷ – See also Table **365**.

367 CHAMBÉRY - MODANE

Subject to alteration on July 20, 27, Dec. 6, 7. Timings may vary by up to 3 minutes July 1 - Aug. 7.

km																									
					TGV 9239					*TGV* 9241			*TGV* 9245			*TGV* 6407			*TGV* 9249						
		⚒	Ⓐ		A M	C	Ⓐ F	🚌 Ⓐ F	🚌 Ⓐ	①–⑤ F M	Ⓐ	Ⓒ ‡	M	Ⓒ n §	Ⓐ	⑥ D	Ⓐ	⚒	M			⑤	⑦	Ⓑ	🚌 ⑥ n
	Paris Gare de Lyon **341** ...d.	...	...	...	0641	...	...	...	...	0749	...	...	1041	...	...	1149	...	...	1441	...	...	...	...	...	...
	Lyon St Exupéry ✈ **342** ...d.	...	...	...	0836	...	...	...	...	0949	...	...	1235	...	...	|	...	...	1635	...	...	...	...	...	...
	Lyon Part Dieu **344** ......d.	...	...	...	|	...	...	...	...	|	...	1040	|	1240r	...	|	...	...	|	...	...	...	...	...	...
0	**Chambéry** ...... **366** d.	0646	0746	...	0944	0957	0957	...	1046	1050	1216	1216	1342	1415	1416	1528	1616	1716	1742	1816	1916	2016	2016	2116	2116
14	Montmélian ...... **366** d.	0656	0756	...	|	1006	1006	...	|	|	1226	1226	|	1425	1426	|	1626	1726	|	1826	1926	2026	2026	2126	2135
26	St Pierre d'Albigny ...... **366** d.	0705	0805	...	|	1014	1014	...	|	|	1235	1235	|	1435	1434	|	1635	1735	|	1835	1935	|	2035	2135	2150
61	St Avre la Chambre ......d.	0732	0832	...	|	1043	1043	...	1207	|	1302	1305	|	1505	1503	1612	1702	1803	|	1903	2002	2102	2103	2202	2230
71	St Jean de Maurienne ⊖ ....d.	0741	0841	...	|	1052	1050	1100	1222	|	1311	1314	|	1514	1514	1624	1711	1811	1824	1911	2011	2110	2111	2211	2245
83	St Michel-Valloire ......d.	0750	0850	...	|	1103	...	1120	1242	|	1323	1323	|	1523	1525	1636	1720	1820	|	1920	2020	2120	2120	2220	2305
99	**Modane** ......a.	0806	0906	...	1049	1117	...	1140	1300	1150	1336	1337	1450	1536	1538	1650	1736	1836	1845	1936	2036	2136	2136	2236	2320

							TGV 9240				*TGV* 9244									*TGV* 6414				*TGV* 9248	
	⚒	Ⓐ	⑥ L	🚌 †	⚒	🚌 Ⓐ	M	C	🚌 Ⓐ F	Ⓐ F	M			🚌 Ⓐ			⚒	†	Ⓐ	⑥ D		⚒	†	M	Ⓑ
Modane ......d.	0524	0624	0624	0640	0717	0812	0913	1019	1053	...	1149	1228	...	1340	1450	...	1624	1624	1724	1733	...	1824	1824	1918	1939
St Michel-Valloire ......d.	0538	0638	0637	0655	0731	0832	|	1039	1110	...	|	1242	...	1400	1503	...	1637	1640	1738	1751	...	1838	1840	|	195[illegible]
St Jean de Maurienne ⊖ ......d.	0549	0649	0648	0710	0749	0847	0935	1051	1126	1136	|	1252	...	1415	1519	...	1647	1651	1748	1804	...	1848	1851	|	200[illegible]
St Avre la Chambre ......d.	0557	0657	0657	0720	0757	0857	|	1104	...	1144	|	1303	...	1425	1527	...	1655	1701	1756	1816	...	1856	1901	|	201[illegible]
St Pierre d'Albigny ...... **366** d.	0626	0726	0727	0800	0826	|	|	1131	...	1212	|	1330	...	1510	1557	...	1723	1723	1826	|	...	1923	1927	|	204[illegible]
Montmélian ...... **366** d.	0635	0735	0736	0815	0835	|	|	1139	...	1220	|	1339	...	1525	1614	...	1735	1736	1835	|	...	1935	1936	|	205[illegible]
Chambéry ...... **366** a.	0644	0744	0745	0835	0844	1005	1016	1150	...	1229	1248	1348	...	1545	1624	...	1743	1745	1843	1856	...	1943	1945	2017	205[illegible]
Lyon Part Dieu **344** ......a.	...	...	0920	...	...	...	|	...	...	...	|	...	...	...	...	...	...	1920	...	|	...	...	2120	|	...
Lyon St Exupéry ✈ **342** ...a.	...	...	...	...	...	...	1126	...	...	...	|	...	...	...	...	...	...	...	...	|	...	...	...	2125	...
Paris Gare de Lyon **341** ...a.	...	...	...	...	...	...	1323	...	...	...	1611	...	...	...	...	...	...	...	...	2211	...	...	...	2319	...

A – ⑥⑦ (daily from Sept. 13).
C – Ⓒ (daily from Sept. 13).
D – ⑥ July 12 - Aug. 23.
F – To Sept. 12.
L – To Sept. 20.
M – (12) and 🍷 Paris - Torino - Milano and v.v. (Table **44**). [R], special 'global' fares payable.

n – Not Nov. 1.
r – 1239 on ⑥ Sept. 13 - Oct. 25.

TGV – [R], supplement payable, 🍷.

‡ – Subject to alteration on Sept. 14, 21, 27, Oct. 5.
§ – Subject to alteration on Sept. 27.
⊖ – 🚌 calls at Arvan not rail station.

SAT / SAVDA — 🚌 CHAMONIX - MONT BLANC TUNNEL - COURMAYEUR — 368

By 🚌, journey 45 minutes. Reservation compulsory by 1700 on previous day through SAT, Chamonix station ✆ +33 (0) 450 530 115 or SAVDA, Aosta bus station ✆ +39 0165 367 032.

Dec. 21 - Apr. 13: From Chamonix (rail station) 0830, 0930, 1100, 1500, 1615, 1730. From Courmayeur 0815, 0945, 1200, 1400, 1615, 1730.

Apr. 14 - June 27: From Chamonix (rail station) 0830, 1145⚒, 1445⚒, 1830. From Courmayeur 0945, 1045⚒, 1600⚒, 1700. On May 1 service is as on ⑦.

June 28 - Aug. 31: From Chamonix (rail station) 0830, 1030, 1145, 1430, 1630, 1800. From Courmayeur 0900, 1100, 1200, 1400, 1600, 1800.

SAVDA — 🚌 COURMAYEUR - PRÉ ST DIDER - AOSTA

Courmayeur △ d.	0645	0735	0835	0935	and	1935	2035	2135	...	...
Pré St Didier 586 d.	0655	0745	0845	0945	hourly	1945	2045	2145	...	...
Aosta ⊡ 586 a.	0745	0835	0935	1035	until	2035	2135	2235	...	...

Aosta ⊡ 586 d.	0645	0745	0845	0945	1045	1145	1245	1335	1445	and	2145
Pré St Didier 586 d.	0735	0835	0935	1035	1135	1235	1335	1425	1535	hourly	2235
Courmayeur △ a.	0745	0845	0945	1045	1145	1245	1345	1437	1545	until	2245

△ – P. le Monte Bianco.

⊡ – Autostazione (bus station).

Narrow gauge. 2nd class. — CORSICAN RAILWAYS — 369

June 30 - September 7

km																									
		⚒	⚒							⚒	⚒		⚒	⚒				⚒			Ⓐ	⑥	Ⓑh	Ⓐ	⑥
0	**Bastia** d.	0610	0719	...	0752	0828	...	0911	0940	1025	...	1210	1344	1450	1508	...	...	1612	1644	...	1725	1811	1811	1915	1918
10	Biguglia d.	0625	0734	...	0807	0843	...	0926	0955	1040	...	1225	1359	1505	1523	...	...	1627	1659	...	1740	1827	1827	1930	1933
22	Casamozza d.	0638	0748	...	0822	0856	...	0942	1009	1053	...	1238	1412	1518	1538	...	...	1640	1714	...	1753	1840	1841	1943	1946
47	Ponte Leccia a.	—	—	...	0901	...	...	1019	1046	—	...	—	...	—	1613	...	...	—	1753	...	...	...	1918	...	...
47	Ponte Leccia d.	...	...	...	0903	...	...	1025	1048	...	...	...	...	...	1615	...	...	...	1758	1806	...	...	1920	...	...
98	Ile Rousse ▶ d.	...	...	0900	|	...	1100	1144	|	...	...	1330	...	...	|	1630	1830	...	|	1924	...	...	|	...	...
120	**Calvi** ▶ a.	...	...	0945	|	...	1145	1220	|	...	...	1415	...	...	|	1715	1915	...	|	2000	...	...	|	...	...
74	Corté d.	...	...	...	0943	...	...	...	1127	...	1332	...	...	...	1654	—	...	...	1840	...	...	...	1954	...	...
90	Vivario d.	...	...	...	1015	...	...	...	1159	...	1404	...	...	...	1726	...	...	...	1912	...	...	...	...	...	...
107	Vizzavona d.	Ⓐ	Ⓐ	...	1037	...	...	...	1220	⚒	1423	...	...	⚒	1748	⚒	...	Ⓐ	1931	...	...	...	...	...	...
145	Mezzana d.	0700	0759	...	1126	...	...	...	1308	1335	1512	...	...	1742	1836	1900	...	1946	2018	...	...	...	...	...	...
158	**Ajaccio** a.	0716	0815	...	1142	...	...	...	1324	1351	1528	...	...	1758	1852	1916	...	2002	2034	...	...	...	...	...	...

	⚒	⚒r	⚒			Ⓐ	Ⓐ		⚒				⚒	⚒	⚒				Ⓐ	⑥		⚒	⚒	⚒	Ⓐ
Ajaccio d.	...	...	...	...	...	0639	0721	0741	...	0921	...	...	...	1107	1215	...	...	1453	...	...	1636	...	1715	1815	1925
Mezzana d.	...	...	...	...	...	0655	0737	0759	...	0939	...	...	...	1126	1231	...	...	1512	...	...	1653	...	1731	1831	1941
Vizzavona d.	...	...	...	...	...	—	—	0851	...	1037	...	...	...	1220	—	...	...	1604	...	...	1747	...	—	...	...
Vivario d.	...	...	...	...	...	...	...	0907	...	1053	...	...	...	1236	...	...	...	1620	...	...	1803	...	...	...	...
Corté d.	...	0622	...	...	...	...	...	0942	...	1127	...	...	...	1305	...	...	...	1654	...	...	1840	...	...	...	...
Calvi d.	...	|	...	...	0700	0800	1000	|	...	|	1230	...	...	—	...	1430	1520	|	...	...	|	...	1730	...	...
Ile Rousse d.	...	|	...	...	0738	0845	1045	|	...	|	1315	...	...	...	...	1515	1603	|	...	...	|	...	1815	...	...
Ponte Leccia a.	...	0656	...	...	0855	...	...	1016	...	1201	...	...	...	...	...	...	1720	1728	...	...	1914	...	...	...	...
Ponte Leccia d.	...	0658	...	...	0900	...	...	1023	...	1203	...	...	...	⚒	⚒	...	...	1730	...	...	1919	...	...	...	...
Casamozza d.	0645	0736	0753	0901	0941	...	...	1103	1120	1241	...	1310	1417	1538	1645	...	...	1813	1842	1845	1957	2008	...	...	...
Biguglia d.	0658	0751	0807	0914	0955	...	...	1117	1133	1255	...	1323	1430	1551	1659	...	...	1827	1855	1858	2010	2021	...	...	...
Bastia a.	0713	0812	0823	0930	1009	...	...	1131	1148	1309	...	1338	1445	1606	1714	...	...	1841	1910	1913	2024	2036	...	...	...

– Not July 13, Aug. 15.
– Not Aug. 16.

Operator: Chemins de fer Corse (CFC) - operation is contracted to SNCF.
For Calvi - Ajaccio journeys change at Ponte Leccia (use both directions of table).

PARIS - DREUX - GRANVILLE — 273

Temporarily relocated from page 181

km			3411		3413		16511			3421		3431	3435			3441	3443		3445			3451	3453		
		E	Ⓐ		Ⓒ		⑦e	Ⓐ					⑤f	⑥t		Ⓐ	Ⓒ		⑤f	Ⓐ		Ⓐ	Ⓒ		
0	**Paris Montparnasse** ⊖ d.	...	0738	...	0850	...	0927	0927	...	1055	...	1355	1528	1527	...	1643	1655	...	1713	1813	...	1943	1955	...	...
17	Versailles Chantiers ▲ d.	...	|	...	0902	...	|	|	...	|	...	|	|	|	...	|	|	...	|	1828	...	|	2007	...	...
82	**Dreux** ▶ d.	0456	0824	...	0938	...	1014	1014	...	|	...	1443	|	1614	...	|	|	...	|	1914	...	2044	2044	...	...
118	Verneuil sur Avre d.	0528	0844	...	0957	...	1045	1036	...	1157	...	1503	|	1643	...	1759	1759	...	|	1938	...	2103	2103	...	...
142	L'Aigle d.	0547	0857	...	1011	...	1103	1050	...	1210	...	1516	1639	1702	...	1813	1813	...	1840	1952	...	2116	2116	...	...
183	Surdon 271 d.	0616	0917	...	1031	...	1133	1118	...	|	...	1536	|	1727	...	1833	1833	...	1900	2018	...	2137	2137	...	...
198	Argentan 271 d.	0627	0928	...	1041	...	1143	1128	...	1239	...	1547	1708	1737	...	1844	1844	...	1911	2028	...	2147	2147	...	...
226	Briouze d.	0649	0943	...	1057	...	1200	...	...	|	...	1602	|	...	...	|	|	...	1927	...	...	2203	2203	...	...
243	Flers d.	0701	0954	...	1107	...	1211	...	...	1302	...	1613	1732	...	...	1906	1906	...	1939	...	...	2213	2213	...	...
272	Vire d.	0719	1011	...	1123	...	1228	...	...	1318	...	1629	1748	...	...	1922	1922	...	1956	...	...	2229	2229	...	...
298	Villedieu les Poêles d.	0738	1026	...	1138	...	1243	...	...	1333	...	1645	1802	...	...	1937	1937	...	2011	...	...	2244	2244	...	...
313	Folligny 272 d.	0750	1036	...	1148	...	1255	...	...	|	...	|	|	...	...	|	|	...	2021	...	...	|	|	...	...
328	**Granville** 272 a.	0801	1045	...	1158	...	1305	...	...	1350	...	1702	1820	...	...	1954	1954	...	2031	...	...	2301	2301	...	...

	16510					3410	3410	3412		3420			3430		3432		3440			3444		13272	3450	3454	
	①g	Ⓐ	⑥	†		⑥v	Ⓐ	†			⑥t		⚒	Ⓐ	†			⑤f	H	†		†		†	
Granville 272 d.	0445	...	...	...	...	0600	0600	0700	...	0905	...	...	1200	...	1359	...	1509	1654	1705	1707	...	...	1847	1957	...
Folligny 272 d.	|	...	...	...	...	|	|	|	...	|	...	...	|	...	|	...	|	1706	1717	|	...	...	1858	2008	...
Villedieu les Poêles d.	0504	...	...	...	...	0618	0618	0718	...	0923	...	...	1218	...	1418	...	1527	1718	1728	1726	...	...	1907	2020	...
Vire d.	0519	...	...	...	...	0633	0633	0733	...	0938	...	...	1233	...	1433	...	1542	1739	1747	1741	...	...	1922	2035	...
Flers d.	0537	...	...	...	...	0650	0650	0750	...	0955	...	...	1250	...	1450	...	1559	1758	1806	1758	...	...	1939	2052	...
Briouze d.	0549	...	...	...	...	0701	0701	0801	...	|	...	...	1301	...	1501	...	|	1810	1819	1809	...	...	1951	2103	...
Argentan 271 d.	0606	0606	0606	0632	...	0717	0717	0817	...	1019	1156	...	1317	1402	1517	...	1623	1831	1840	1825	...	1926	2009	2119	...
Surdon 271 d.	0616	0616	0616	0643	...	0726	0726	0826	...	1028	1207	...	1327	1413	1526	...	|	...	...	|	...	1936	2019	|	...
L'Aigle d.	0642	0642	0642	0711	...	0747	0747	0847	...	1049	1232	...	1347	1442	1547	...	1650	...	...	1852	...	2004	2041	2146	...
Verneuil sur Avre d.	0656	0656	0656	0725	...	0800	0800	0900	...	1102	1250	...	1400	1456	1600	...	1703	...	...	|	...	2019	2055	2159	...
Dreux ▶ d.	0720	0720	0720	0749	...	0820	0820	0920	...	|	1320	...	1420	1520	|	...	|	...	...	|	...	2043	2116	2219	...
Versailles Chantiers ▲ a.	0803	0803	|	|	...	|	|	|	...	|	|	...	|	|	|	...	|	...	...	|	...	2119	|	.2254	...
Paris Montparnasse ⊖ a.	0816	0816	0805	0835	...	0905	0916	1005	...	1205	1405	...	1505	1605	1705	...	1805	...	...	2005	...	2131	2205	2307	...

– Ⓐ to July 4; ①⑤ July 7 - Aug. 22 (also Aug. 14; not Aug. 15); Ⓐ from Aug. 25.
– ①-④ to July 7 (also July 15; not June 9); ① July 21 - Aug. 18; ①-④ from Aug. 25 (not Nov. 11).

– Also June 9, July 14, Nov. 11; not June 8.
Also Aug. 14; not Aug. 15.
– Also June 10, July 15, Nov. 12; not June 9, July 14, Nov. 10.
– Not Nov. 1.

▲ – Local travel to / from Paris not permitted on some trains (see Table **274** for local services).
▶ – Suburban trains run Paris - Versailles - Dreux approx hourly.
⊖ – Most trains use **Vaugirard** platforms (5 - 10 mins walk from Montparnasse main concourse).

370 PARIS - DIJON - BESANÇON - MULHOUSE - BASEL *TGV Rhin-Rhône*

For *TGV* trains Lyon - Dijon - Mulhouse - Strasbourg see Table **379**. Local services: Tables **371** Paris - Dijon, **374** Dijon - Besançon, **378** Besançon - Belfort, **370b** Belfort - Mulhouse.

Timings may vary by up to 8 minutes Sept. 2 - Nov. 1 (please check your reservation for confirmed timings). Services are subject to alteration / cancellation on ⑥⑦ Oct. 4 – 19.

km		*TGV* 6701	*TGV* 6743	*TGV* 9203	*TGV* 9261	*TGV* 6747	*TGV* 9211	*TGV* 6703	*TGV* 9269	*TGV* 9213	*TGV* 9271	*TGV* 9215	*TGV* 6755	*TGV* 6741	*TGV* 9273	*TGV* 9219	*TGV* 6759	*TGV* 9589	*TGV* 9277	*TGV* 9223	*TGV* 6757	*TGV* 6707	*TGV* 5130	*TGV* 6709	*TGV* 6753
		Ⓐ	Ⓐ	①–⑥		Ⓒ					⑦		Ⓐ	⑤				Ⓑ							⑤⑦
				p						◧	e			J						B	E	⊙	♥⊙	G⊙	w
	Lille Europe **11** d.	...	...	...	...	...	...	...	...	...	...	...	...	...	...	...	...	...	...	...	...	...	1900f	...	...
0	**Paris** Gare de Lyon d.	0623	0653	0719	0802	0853	1023	1123	1157	1223	1357	1423	1453	1523	1557	1623	1653	1723t	1757	1823	1852	1923	|	2023	2053
212	Montbard d.	|	0800	|	|	1000	|	|	|	|	|	|	1600	|	|	|	1759	|	|	|	2000	|	2109	|	2159
287	**Dijon** a.	0758	0834	0853	0934	1034	1158	1258	1334	1358	1534	|	1634	1658	1734	|	1834	1858	1934	1958	2034	2058	2143	2158	2234
287	**Dijon** d.	0801	0837	0856	0937	1037	1201	1301	1337	1401	1537	|	1637	...	1737	|	1837	1901	1937	2001	2037	2101	2146	2201	2237
333	Dole a.	|	|	|	0959	|	|	|	1359	|	1559	|	|	...	1759	|	|	|	1958	|	2100	|	|	|	2300
364	**Besançon TGV** ⊖ d.	0831	0908	|	▽	1108	|	1332	▽	|	▽	|	1708	...	▽	|	1910	1930	▽	|	|	2130	2218	2230	|
377	Besançon Viotte a.	|	0920	|	...	1120	|	|	...	|	...	|	1720	...	...	|	1920	|	...	|	2129	|	|	|	2328
446	Belfort Montbéliard TGV d.	0856	...	0941	...	...	|	1357	...	|	...	1643	...	...	...	1842	...	1954	...	|	...	2156	2241	2256	...
491	Mulhouse **385** d.	0919	...	1006	...	...	1306	1419	...	1506	...	1707	...	...	...	1907	...	2021	...	2106	...	2219	2303	2319	...
	Freiburg (Brsg) Hbf a.	...	...	|	...	...	|	...	...	|	...	|	...	...	...	|	...	2111	...	|	...	...	...	...	...
525	**Basel** **385** a.	...	...	1026	...	...	1326	...	...	1526	...	1726	...	...	...	1926	...	...	...	2126	...	...	...	...	...
	Zürich HB **510** a.	...	...	1126	...	...	1426	...	...	1626	...	1835	...	...	...	2026	...	...	...	2226	...	...	...	...	...

	TGV 6750	*TGV* 6700	*TGV* 5152	*TGV* 6745	*TGV* 9260	*TGV* 9588	*TGV* 9206	*TGV* 9264	*TGV* 6704	*TGV* 9210	*TGV* 6749	*TGV* 9218	*TGV* 9268	*TGV* 9222	*TGV* 6706	*TGV* 6706	*TGV* 6740	*TGV* 9226	*TGV* 9270	*TGV* 6708	*TGV* 6765	*TGV* 6765	*TGV* 9230	*TGV* 9272	*TGV* 6767
	Ⓐ	①–⑥				①–⑥					①–⑥					⑦	⑦	Ⓑ				⑦			⑦
		p	♠					◇		B	p⊗				H	D	J	z	V		A	e			e
Zürich HB **510** d.	...	...	...	...	...	...	0734	...	...	0934	...	1134	...	1334	...	...	...	1534	...	...	...	...	1727	...	...
Basel **385** d.	...	...	...	...	...	...	0834	...	...	1034	...	1234	...	1434	...	...	...	1634	...	...	...	...	1834	...	...
Freiburg (Brsg) Hbf d.	...	...	...	...	...	0657	|	...	...	|	...	|	...	|	...	...	...	|	...	...	...	...	|	...	...
Mulhouse **385** d.	...	0540	0551	...	...	0743	0856	...	0940	1056	...	1256	...	1456	1537	1542	...	1656	...	1740	...	...	1859	...	...
Belfort Montbéliard TGV d.	...	0605	0617	...	...	0808	0921	...	1005	|	...	1321	...	|	1603	1607	...	|	...	1805	...	...	1922	...	...
Besançon Viotte d.	0533	|	|	0636	...	|	|	...	|	|	1234	|	...	|	|	|	...	|	...	|	1836	1827	|	...	2047
Besançon TGV ⊖ d.	|	0630	0642	0649	▽	0830	|	▽	1030	|	1248	|	▽	|	1628	1632	...	|	▽	1830	1849	1841	|	▽	2101
Dole d.	0600	|	|	|	0800	|	|	1000	|	|	|	|	1400	|	|	|	...	|	1800	|	|	|	|	2001	|
Dijon a.	0622	0658	0710	0718	0822	0858	|	1022	1058	1159	1316	|	1422	1600	1656	1700	...	1759	1822	1858	1918	1910	|	2023	2129
Dijon d.	0625	0701	0713	0725	0825	0901	|	1025	1101	1202	1323	|	1425	1603	1659	1703	1725	1802	1825	1901	1925	1925	|	2025	2132
Montbard d.	0701	|	0748	0801	|	|	|	|	|	|	1403	|	|	|	1735	|	1802	|	|	|	|	2003	|	|	|
Paris Gare de Lyon a.	0807	0837	|	0907	1002	1037	1137	1202	1237	1337	1506	1537	1602	1737	1837	1837	1907	1937	2003	2037	2107	2106	2137	2202	2307
Lille Europe **11** a.	...	...	0957	...	...	...	...	...	...	...	...	...	...	...	...	...	...	...	...	...	...	...	...	...	...

LOCAL TRAINS MULHOUSE - FREIBURG

km										
		①–⑤			①–⑤			①–⑤	⑥⑦	
			n	n	n⊡					
0	**Mulhouse** d.	0630	0831	1026	1253	1434	1753	1923	1927	...
19	Neuenburg 🚌 d.	0658	0851	1045	1313	1503	1814	1943	1947	...
22	Müllheim (Baden) a.	0702	0856	1050	1318	1508	1819	1948	1952	...
22	Müllheim (Baden) **912** d.	*0706*	*0906*	*1055*	*1323*	1510	*1823*	*1955*g	1952	...
51	**Freiburg** (Brsg) Hbf **912** a.	*0736*	*0934*	*1123*	*1344*	1529	*1844*	*2021*g	2011	...

	①–⑤			①–⑤				①–⑤	⑥⑦
		n	n	n					
Freiburg (Brsg) Hbf **912** d.	*0628*k	*0915*	*1115*	*1315*	...	1645	*1815**	*1935*	2027
Müllheim (Baden) **912** a.	*0654*	*0934*	*1134*	*1336*	...	1704	*1834**	*2003*	2045
Müllheim (Baden) d.	0707	0945	1140	1340	...	1705	1839	2009	2050
Neuenburg 🚌 d.	0712	0950	1145	1345	...	1710	1844	2014	2055
Mulhouse a.	0730	1011	1205	1406	...	1730	1904	2040	2115

- **A** – ①–⑤ to July 4; ⑤ July 11 - Aug. 15; Ⓐ from Aug. 22.
- **B** – Conveys [12] (**9214/9225**) Bern - Basel - Paris and v.v.
- **D** – ⑦ to June 29 / from Nov. 2 (also Aug. 31, Nov. 11).
- **E** – Ⓑ to July 4; Ⓐ July 7 - Aug. 22; Ⓑ from Aug. 25.
- **G** – Ⓑ to July 6; ⑤⑦ July 11 - Aug. 17 (also July 14, Aug. 14); Ⓑ from Aug. 22.
- **H** – ①–⑤ to June 27; Ⓑ June 30 - Aug. 29 (not Aug. 15); Ⓐ from Sept. 1.
- **J** – To July 4 and from Aug. 29.
- **V** – ⑤⑦ to July 11; daily July 13 - Aug. 24 (not Aug. 15); ⑤⑦ from Aug. 29 (also Nov. 1, 11; not Aug. 31). 7 – 9 minutes later on Ⓑ July 15 - Aug. 24 (arrives Paris 2032 on ⑦ July 20 - Aug. 17).
- **e** – Also July 14, Nov. 11.
- **f** – Lille **Flandres**.
- **g** – On June 19, Oct. 3, Nov. 1 Müllheim d. 2023, Freiburg a. 2044.
- **k** – 0627 July 31 - Sept. 12.
- **n** – Not Oct. 13 – 17.
- **p** – Not July 14, Nov. 11.
- **t** – Departs 1711 Sept. 2 - Oct. 31.
- **w** – Also July 14, Aug. 14, Nov. 11; not Aug. 15.
- **z** – Not Aug. 15.
- *TGV* – [R], supplement payable, 🍸.
- * – 5 minutes earlier on ⑥⑦ Aug. 2 - Sept. 14.
- ⊙ – Not Nov. 24, 25.
- ▽ – To / from Lausanne (Table **375**).
- ⊖ – Besançon Franche-Comté TGV.
- ♥ – Via Charles de Gaulle ✈ (d. 1958) and Marne la Vallée-Chessy (d. 2011).
- ♠ – Via Marne la Vallée-Chessy (a. 0849) and Charles de Gaulle ✈ (a. 0903).
- ◧ – Subject to alteration on Dec. 6, 7.
- ⊗ – Subject to alteration Sept. 8 – 11. May run up to 36 minutes later Dijon - Paris on Ⓐ.
- ⊡ – Departure times are up to 4 minutes earlier July 31 - Sept. 12.
- ◇ – Runs up to 6 minutes later July 15 - Aug. 24.

370a BESANÇON VIOTTE - BESANÇON FRANCHE-COMTÉ TGV *SERVICE FROM JUNE 21*

km																										
		D	E	D	E		D §	E §					D	E	D	E	D	E	Ⓑ			ⒷE	ⒷD	Ⓐ	E	D
0	Besançon Viotte d.	0600	0605	0735	0736	0805	1005	1007	...	1142	1308	1334	1431	1434	1600	1605	1735	1737	1805	1854	2037	2101	2109	2135	2205	2209
13	Besançon TGV ⊖ a.	0615	0620	0748	0749	0821	1018	1020	...	1155	1322	1354	1444	1447	1613	1618	1748	1750	1820	1909	2050	2116	2123	2154	2220	2223

	Ⓒ⊡	Ⓐ⊕	E	D		D	E		r §			D	E	N	⑦Q	Ⓑ		D	E	ⒷE	ⒷD	ⒶE	ⒶD	⑥	ⒷE	ⒷD
Besançon TGV ⊖ d.	0650	0706	0808	0819	0838	1032	1040	1212	1340	1411	1504	1635	1640	1820	1825	1851	1940	2110	2117	2137	2143	2207	2210	2225	2237	224
Besançon Viotte a.	0703	0719	0826	0834	0853	1046	1055	1227	1355	1426	1517	1650	1655	1833	1842	1908	1955	2129	2132	2156	2157	2226	2228	2242	2252	225

- **D** – Sept. 2 - Oct. 31.
- **E** – June 21 - Sept. 1 and from Nov. 1.
- **N** – ①–⑥ from June 23 (not July 14, Nov. 11).
- **Q** – ⑦ (also July 14, Nov. 11). 5 – 9 minutes later Sept. 7 - Oct. 26.
- **r** – Not ①–⑤ Oct. 27 - Nov. 7.
- ⊕ – Runs 4 minutes **earlier** Sept. 2 - Oct. 31.
- ⊡ – Runs 6 minutes **earlier** Sept. 6 - Oct. 26.
- § – To / from Le Locle (Table **376a**)
- ⊖ – Besançon Franche-Comté TGV

371 PARIS - SENS - AUXERRE and DIJON

For *TGV* services Paris - Dijon see Table **370**. Certain Paris - Auxerre trains continue to / from destinations in Table **372**.

km																										
		Ⓐ	⚒w	Ⓐ	Ⓐ		⚒w	Ⓐ	Ⓒ		Ⓒ⊙		Ⓑ◇	⚒w	Ⓐ	Ⓑ			Ⓑ	Ⓐ	Ⓒ	Ⓐ	Ⓒ	Ⓑ		
0	**Paris** Bercy ▲ ▷ d.	...	...	0613	...	0738	0838	0923	0938	1038	...	1238	...	1338	1438	...	1538	1631r	...	1731	1738	1831	1838	...	1931r	203
113	Sens ▷ d.	...	0617	0719	...	0834	0934	1034	1034	1134	...	1334	...	1434	1534	...	1634	1734	...	1834	1834	1934	1934	...	2034	213
147	Joigny ▷ d.	...	0647	0748	...	0850	0950	1050	1050	1150	...	1350	...	1450	1550	...	1650	1750	...	1850	1850	1950	1950	...	2050	215
	Auxerre d.	0536	|	|	...	|	|	|	|	|	1136	|	1336	|	|	1536e	|	|	1736	|	|	|	|	1939e	|	|
156	Laroche Migennes ▷ a.	0553	0655	0755	...	0858	0956	1058	1058	1156	1153	1356	1353	1458	1556	1553e	1658	1756	1753	1858	1858	1956	1956	1953e	2058	215
156	Laroche Migennes ▷ d.	0601	0701	0759	0801	0901	0959	1101	1101	1158	1201	1405b	1402	1501	1559	1601	1701	1805	1802	1901	1901	*2004*	1959h	2001	2101	215
175	**Auxerre** ▷ a.	|	|	0814	|	|	1013	|	|	1213	|	1419b	|	|	1614	|	|	1819	|	|	|	*2019*	2014h	|	|	221
197	Tonnerre d.	0627	0727	...	0827	0927	...	1124	1127	...	1227	...	1427	1527	...	1627	1727	...	1827	1927	1927	...	...	2027	2127	...
243	Montbard d.	0653	0753	...	0853	0953	...	1149	1153	...	1253	...	1452	1553	...	1653	1753	...	1853	1953	1953	...	...	2053	2153	...
315	**Dijon** a.	0730	0830	...	0930	1034	...	1236	1230	...	1336	...	1534	1630	...	1734	1830	...	1930	2030	2030	...	...	2130	2230	...
	Lyon Part Dieu **377** a.	...	1044	...	...	1244	...	1444	1444	...	...	...	...	1844	...	...	2044	...	...	2244t	2244e	...	...	...	...	...

	Ⓐ	Ⓐ	⑥	⑥	Ⓐ	Ⓑ		⚒w	⚒w ⊙	⚒w			⊙		Ⓒ	Ⓐ			Ⓑ				Ⓐ	⑦e		Ⓑ⊗
Lyon Part Dieu **377** d.	...	...	...	...	...	...	...	0516y	...	...	0716	...	...	...	1116	1116	...	1316	...	...	1516	...	...	...	1716	...
Dijon d.	...	...	...	0529	0529	0629	...	0729	0829	...	0929	...	1207k	...	1329	1331	...	1529	1629	...	1729	1829	...	...	1929	202
Montbard d.	...	...	...	0607	0607	0706	...	0807	0906	...	1007	...	1306	...	1407	1418	...	1607	1706	...	1807	1906j	...	...	2007	212
Tonnerre d.	...	...	...	0633	0633	0731	...	0833	0931	...	1033	...	1331	...	1433	1439	...	1633	1731	...	1833	1931	...	...	2033	214
Auxerre ▷ d.	0446	*0536*	0546	|	|	|	0739	|	|	0946	|	1146	|	1346	|	|	1546c	|	|	1746	|	|	*1936*	1946	|	|
Laroche Migennes ▷ a.	0500	*0553*	0600	0656	0656	0757	0753	0856	0957	1000	1056	1200	1357	1400	1456	1500	1600c	1656	1757	1800	1856	1958	*1953*	2000	2056	221
Laroche Migennes ▷ d.	0502	0559	0602	0701	0701	0806	0802	0901	1006	1002	1101	1202	...	1402	1501	1501	1602	1701	...	1802	1901	2009z	2004	2004	2101	222
Auxerre a.	|	|	|	|	|	0822	|	|	1022	|	|	|	...	|	|	|	|	|	...	|	|	2026z	|	|	|	223
Joigny ▷ d.	0509	0609	0609	0709	0709	...	0809	0909	...	1010	1109	1209	...	1409	1509	1509	1610	1709	...	1809	1909	...	2013	2013	2109	...
Sens ▷ d.	0527	0627	0627	0726	0726	...	0827	0926	...	1027	1126	1227	...	1427	1526	1526	1627	1726	...	1827	1926	...	2040	2040	2126	...
Paris Bercy ▲ ▷ a.	0628	0728	0722	0822	0828	...	0922	1022	...	1136	1222	1322	...	1522	1622	1622	1722	1822	...	1922	2022	...	2148	2148	2222	...

CONTINUED ON NEXT PAGE

☛ *WARNING! Services from / to Paris are subject to alteration on various dates (see shaded box in the notes for Table 371 on the next page*

PARIS - SENS - AUXERRE and DIJON — 371 (contd.)

LOCAL TRAINS PARIS - LAROCHE MIGENNES   For faster trains see the main part of Table **371** on the previous page.

km							⑦e	⚒w¶				Ⓐ	Ⓒ	Ⓐ	Ⓐ	Ⓒ	Ⓐ	Ⓐ	Ⓒ	Ⓐ	Ⓐ		Ⓒ		m	
0	**Paris** Gare de Lyon .. d.	0649	0749	0849	1049	1149	1249	1249	1349	1449	1549	1619	1649	1700	1719	1749	1800	1819	1849	1900	1919	1949	2049	2149	2238*	2249
45	Melun d.	0715	0815	0915	1115	1215	1315	1315	1415	1515	1615	1645	1715	|	1745	1815	|	1845	1915	|	1945	2015	2115	2215	|	2315
60	Fontainebleau-Avon .. d.	0728	0827	0928	1128	1227	1328	1328	1427	1528	1627	1658	1728	|	1758	1828	|	1858	1928	|	1957	2028	2128	2229	|	2327
79	Montereau d.	0750	0845	0950	1150	1245	1350	1350	1445	1550	1645	1720	1750	1750	1820	1850	1850	1920	1950	1950	2015	2050	2150	2245	|	2345
113	Sens a.	0818	...	1018	1218	...	1418	1418	...	1618	...	1747	1818	1817	1847	1918	1917	1947	2018	2017	...	2118	2217	...	2347	...
113	Sens d.	0837	...	1037	1220	...	1420	1437	...	1637	...	1749	1837	1819	1849	1937	1919	1949	2037	2019	...	2137	2219	...	2349	...
147	Joigny d.	0905	...	1106	1248	...	1448	1506	...	1705	...	1818	1906	1848	1918	2006	1948	2017	2106	2048	...	2206	2248	...	0018	...
156	**Laroche Migennes** ... a.	0913	...	1113	1255	...	1455	1513	...	1713	...	1825	1913	1855	1925	2013	1955	2025	2113	2055	...	2213	2255	...	0025	...

		Ⓐ	⑥	Ⓐ	Ⓐ	Ⓒ	Ⓐ	⑥	†	Ⓐ	Ⓐ		✣		Ⓒ	Ⓐ✣			⑦e	⚒		⑦e	Ⓐ	Ⓒ		
Laroche Migennes ... d.	0404	0504	0504	0534	0604	0604	0634	0647	...	0704	...	0747	1006	...	1205	1207	...	1406	1447	...	1546	1647	1747	1806	...	...
Joigny d.	0411	0511	0511	0541	0611	0611	0641	0654	...	0711	...	0754	1013	...	1212	1214	...	1413	1454	...	1555	1654	1754	1813	...	...
Sens a.	0438	0538	0538	0608	0638	0638	0708	0722	...	0738	...	0822	1038	...	1239	1238	...	1438	1521	...	1622	1722	1822	1838	...	...
Sens d.	0440	0540	0540	0610	0640	0640	0710	0740	...	0740	...	0840	1040	...	1241	1240	...	1440	1540	...	1640	1740	1840	1840	...	...
Montereau d.	0512	0610	0612	0642	0710	0712	0742	0812	0812	0810	0819	0912	1112	1212	1312	1312	1412	1512	1612	1612	1712	1812	1912	1912	2012	2112
Fontainebleau-Avon ... d.	0530	|	0630	0700	|	0730	0800	0830	0830	|	0836	0930	1130	1230	1330	1330	1430	1530	1630	1630	1730	1830	1930	1930	2030	2130
Melun d.	0543	|	0643	0713	|	0743	0813	0843	0843	|	0849	0943	1143	1243	1343	1343	1443	1543	1643	1643	1743	1843	1943	1943	2043	2143
Paris Gare de Lyon ... a.	0611	0700	0711	0741	0800	0811	0841	0911	0911	0907	0917	1011	1211	1311	1411	1411	1511	1611	1711	1715	1813	1911	2011	2013	2111	2211

ADDITIONAL LOCAL TRAINS LAROCHE MIGENNES - AUXERRE

	⑥		Ⓐ	⚒w	Ⓒ	Ⓐ					Ⓐ	
Laroche Migennes ..... d.	0031	...	0628	0705	0905	0905	1105	1505	1705	1905	2004	2105
Auxerre a.	0044	...	0651	0723	0918	0923	1123	1523	1723	1923	2019	2123

	⚒w					Ⓐ			Ⓐ	
Auxerre d.	0637	0837	1037	...	1437	1540	1637	1837	1936	2037
Laroche Migennes .. a.	0655	0855	1055	...	1455	1556	1655	1855	1953	2055

b – 5–6 minutes earlier on ⑥.
c – Ⓒ only.
e – ⑦ (also July 14, Aug. 15, Nov. 11).
– 3 minutes later on ⑦e.
– 1903 on June 15, 20.
– 1229 on Ⓒ.
m – Not Nov. 16.
– 7 minutes later on Ⓒ.

t – Change trains at Dijon on ⑤ (also Aug. 14).
w – Also Nov. 1.
y – ① (also Nov. 12; not July 14).
z – ⑥ only.
¶ – Subject to alteration on July 7–10, 17, 18.

* – 2234 on ①–⑤ Oct. 13 - Dec. 5 (also June 16–20, Nov. 2, 9).
⊠ – 10–14 minutes **earlier** Dijon - Laroche Sept. 2 - Oct. 31.
▲ – Services run from / to Paris Gare de Lyon (not Bercy) on Aug. 9, 10, Sept. 6, 20, 21, 27, 28.
✣ – Subject to alteration on Ⓐ June 23 - July 25.
⊙ – Subject to alteration on Oct. 4, 5, 11, 12, 18, 19, Dec. 6, 7.
◇ – Subject to alteration on Oct. 19, Dec. 7.
▷ – For other stopping services Paris Gare de Lyon - Laroche Migennes - Auxerre see top of next page.

WARNING! Services from / to Paris are subject to alteration or cancellation on various dates including June 15, Aug. 9, 10, Sept. 6, 7, 13, ⑥⑦ Sept. 20 - Oct. 19, Nov. 29, 30, Dec. 6, 7. Alterations may apply on certain other dates, particularly for off-peak journeys, so please confirm timings locally before travelling.

AUXERRE - CLAMECY / AVALLON — 372

km		Ⓐ	Ⓐ	Ⓒ	Ⓒ	Ⓐ⊗	Ⓐ	⑥	⑥		⑥	Ⓑ	⑥	⑦e	Ⓐ	⑦e	Ⓐ	Ⓐ	⑥	⑥	Ⓐ	Ⓐ	⑦e	⑦e
	Paris Bercy **371** d.	...	0613	*0738*	*0738*	0838	1038	1038	1038	...	1238	1238	...	...	1438	...	1631	1631	*1738*	...	*1831*	*1831*	1838	1838
	Laroche Migennes **371** d.	0628	0759	0905	0905	0959	1158	1159	1159	...	1359	1405	1407	...	1559	*1705*	1805	1805	1905	...	2004	2004	2002	2002
0	**Auxerre** d.	0653	0815	0921	0921	1018	1218	1218	1237	...	1415	1421	1430	1444	1615	1757	1826	1826	1925	...	2021	2021	2019	2019
17	Cravant-Bazarnes d.	0719	0838	0945	0948	1043	1241	1235	1304	...	1431	1444	1455	1500	1639	1821	1849	1852	1949	1953	2044	2047	2043	2047
53	Clamecy a.	|	0912	|	1022	|	1316	|	1340	...	|	|	1533	1537	1715	|	|	1928	2024	|	|	2123	|	2123
86	Corbigny a.	|	...	|	1104	|	...	|	...	...	|	|	...	1617	...	|	|	2008	...	|	|	...	|	...
41	Sermizelles-Vézelay § d.	0746	...	1013	...	1111	...	1259	...	...	1501	1513	...	...	...	1854	1917	...	...	2021	2113	...	2111	...
55	**Avallon** a.	0758	...	1026	...	1123	...	1311	...	...	1514	1525	...	...	...	1906	1929	...	...	2034	2125	...	2124	...

	Ⓐ	Ⓐ	⚒w	⚒w	Ⓐ⊗		Ⓒ	Ⓐ⊡	Ⓒ		⑥	Ⓐ	⑥	Ⓐ		⑤f	⑦e	⑦e	①–④m	Ⓐ	⑥	⑥	⑦e	⑦e
Avallon d.	0527	...	0628	...	0839	...	...	...	1046	...	...	1231	1242	...	...	1631	...	1636	1639	...	1725	...	...	1836
Sermizelles-Vézelay § d.	0541	...	0642	...	0853	...	...	...	1100	...	...	1245	1301	...	...	1645	...	1650	1653	...	1739	...	...	1850
Corbigny d.	|	...	|	0551	|	...	...	...	|	...	1142	|	|	...	...	|	...	|	|	...	|	...	1756	|
Clamecy d.	|	0528	|	0631	|	...	1026	1045	|	...	1222	|	|	1435	...	|	1635	|	|	1727	|	1735	1837	|
Cravant-Bazarnes d.	0615	0615	0717	0717	0924	...	1104	1125	1131	...	1306	1315	1331	1515	...	1715	1724	1724	1724	1806	1807	1815	1925	1925
Auxerre a.	0635	0635	0737	0737	0944	...	1126	1144	1144	...	1325	1339	1344	1538	...	1739	1744	1744	1744	1824	...	1835	1944	1944
Laroche Migennes **371** a.	0655	0655	0753	0753	1000	...	...	1200	1200	...	...	1400	1400	1556	...	1800	1800	1800	1800	1855	...	1855	2000	2000
Paris Bercy **371** a.	*0828*	*0828*	0922	0922	1136	...	...	1322	1322	...	...	1522	1522	*1722*	...	1922	1922	1922	1922	*2022*	...	*2022*	2148	2148

– Also July 14, Aug. 15, Nov. 11.
– Also Aug. 14; not Aug. 15.
– Not July 14, Aug. 14, Nov. 11.

w – Also Nov. 1.
§ – Station is 9 km from Vézelay.

⊗ – Subject to alteration Sept. 29 - Oct. 17.
⊡ – Subject to alteration Oct. 6–24.

WARNING! Services from / to Paris are subject to alteration on various dates (see shaded panel under Table 371).

DIJON - MONTCHANIN - ÉTANG - AUTUN / NEVERS — 373

km		Ⓐ	Ⓐ	⚒w	Ⓑ	⚒w	⊗	⚒w	Ⓑf	⚒w	Ⓐ	⑦e	
0	**Dijon** **377** d.	...	0612	0712	0812	1012	1212	1412	1609	1712	1810	1812	1912
37	Beaune **377** d.	...	0634	0734	0834	1034	1234	1434	1634h	1734	1834	1834	1934
81	**Montchanin** d.	...	0659	0800	0859	1103	1259	1459	1700	1759	1859	1859	1959
89	Le Creusot d.	△	0706	0806	0906	1110	1306	1506	1707	1806	1906	1906	2006
111	Étang d.	0606	0721	0821	0921	1125	1321	1521	1721	1821	1925	1921	2021
126	**Autun** a.	|	|	|	|	|	|	|	|	|	1943	|	|
179	Decize d.	0647	0804	0904	1004	1207	1404	1604	1805	1904	...	2004	2104
216	**Nevers** a.	0719	0829	0929	1029	1232	1429	1629	1830	1929	...	2029	2129
	Vierzon **290** a.	...	...	1032j	...	...	...	...	1932v	...	...	...	...
	Tours **290** a.	...	...	1202j	...	...	...	...	2102v	...	...	...	...

	①g	②–⑤m	⚒w	Ⓑ	⚒w	⑦e		Ⓐ◇		Ⓑ	⑥	Ⓐ	Ⓑ
Tours **290** d.	...	...	...	...	0658v	...	...	...	...	...	...	...	1658v
Vierzon **290** d.	...	...	...	...	0828v	...	...	...	...	...	...	...	1828v
Nevers d.	0530	...	0630	0730	0928	0930	1130	1330	1530	1730	1830	1846	1926
Decize d.	0557	...	0657	0757	0954	0957	1157	1357	1557	1757	1857	1918	1953
Autun d.	*0611*	0611	|	|	|	|	|	|	|	|	|	|	|
Étang d.	0640	0640	0740	0840	1038	1040	1240	1440	1640	1840	1940	2000	2036
Le Creusot d.	0655	0655	0754	0855	1054	1055	1255	1455	1655	1855	1955	▽	2052
Montchanin d.	0703	0703	0803	0903	1101	1103	1303	1503	1703	1903	2003	...	2102
Beaune **377** d.	0728	0728	0828	0928	1128	1128	1328	1528	1728	1928	2027	...	2128
Dijon **377** a.	0749	0749	0850	0949	1150	1149	1351	1550	1750	1950	2049	...	2148

CONNECTIONS CHALON - MONTCHANIN

km		Ⓐ	⚒w	w⊗	Ⓑ	⚒w	Ⓑ	
0	**Chalon sur Saône** d.	...	0710	1410	1610	1710	1810	1910
15	Chagny d.	0622	0722	1422	1622	1722	1822	1922
44	**Montchanin** d.	0649	0749	1449	1649	1749	1849	1949

	Ⓐ	⚒w	Ⓐ	◧	Ⓐ	Ⓑ	Ⓑ	⑥
Montchanin ★ d.	0711	0811	0911	1111	1511	1711	1911	2011
Chagny ★ d.	0737	0837	0937	1137	1537	1737	1937	2037
Chalon sur Saône ★ a.	0749	0849	0949	1149	1549	1749	1949	2049

CONNECTIONS ÉTANG - AUTUN ⊡

	Ⓐ	⚒w	⊠	🚌 ⚒w	⑥	Ⓑ	🚌 ⚒w	Ⓑ	Ⓐ	🚌 ⚒w	†
Étang d.	0725	0825	1325	1525	1645	1725	1825	1845	2003	2041	2045
Autun a.	0743	0843	1343	1546	1703	1743	1846	1903	2021	2102	2103

	Ⓐ	⚒w	🚌 ⚒w	⚒w	⚒w	🚌 ⚒w		Ⓑ	🚌 ⑥	🚌 Ⓐ	†
Autun d.	0546	0632	0709	0757	1217	1249	1617	1817	1909	1949	1958
Étang a.	0604	0650	0730	0815	1235	1310	1635	1835	1930	2010	2016

CONNECTIONS MONTCHANIN - PARAY LE MONIAL - MOULINS SUR ALLIER

km		Ⓐ	⑥	⚒b		⚒w	Ⓑ	⚒w	Ⓑ	
0	**Montchanin** d.	0708	0808	1108	1308	1508	1708	1808	1908	2008
15	Montceau les Mines d.	0722	0822	1121	1321	1520	1721	1821	1921	2021
50	Paray le Monial **290** d.	0751	0851	1201	1351	1545	1751	1851	1951	2051
61	Digoin **290** d.	...	...	1210	...	...	...	...	...	...
117	**Moulins sur Allier** **290** a.	...	...	1256	...	...	...	...	...	...
	Clermont Ferrand **330** a.	...	...	1421x	...	...	...	...	...	...

	Ⓐ	⚒w			⚒w		Ⓑ	⑥	Ⓑz
Clermont Ferrand **330** d.	...	...	...	...	...	...	...	...	1742
Moulins sur Allier **290** d.	...	...	...	...	...	...	...	...	1903
Digoin **290** d.	...	...	...	...	...	...	...	...	1948
Paray le Monial **290** d.	0609	0709	1009	...	1409	1609	1809	1909	2009
Montceau les Mines d.	0639	0739	1039	...	1439	1639	1839	1939	2039
Montchanin d.	0652	0752	1052	...	1452	1652	1852	1952	2052

– Also Nov. 1; not July 28 - Aug. 22.
– Also July 14, Aug. 15, Nov. 11.
Not Aug. 15.
– Also July 15, Nov. 12; not July 14.
– ①②③④⑦ (not Aug. 14).
Not June 16–20, Sept. 22, Sept. 29 - Oct. 3, Oct. 27–31, Nov. 1, 3–7, Dec. 1–5.
– Not July 15, Aug. 15, Nov. 11, 12.

v – Not June 15–18.
w – ⚒ (also Nov. 1).
x – Not June 30 - July 4, Oct. 13–17, 27–31.
z – Not July 28 - Aug. 21.

△ – From Autun, depart 0546.
▽ – To Autun, arrive 2021.
⊗ – Subject to alteration on ①–⑤ Nov. 24 - Dec. 5.

◧ – Subject to alteration on ①–④ Nov. 10–20.
◇ – Subject to alteration Nov. 10–21.
⊠ – By 🚌 on ⑦e (arrives Autun 1346).
★ – Additional journeys Montchanin - Chagny - Chalon: From Montchanin at 0651⑥ and 1811⑥.
⊡ – Additional 🚌 journeys: From Étang at 0745⚒w, 1445Ⓐ and 1925⑦e. From Autun at 1209⑦e, 1506Ⓐ, 1749⚒w and 1849⑦e.

374 DIJON - DOLE - BESANÇON *Local Services*

For *TGV* services see Table **370** (Paris - Dijon - Besançon - Basel) and Table **379** (Strasbourg - Besançon - Dijon).

SERVICE JUNE 21 - SEPT. 1 AND FROM NOV. 1. See page 238 for service Sept. 2 - Oct. 31.

km		Ⓐ◇		Ⓑ	Ⓐ		⚒			Ⓐ		Ⓐ	Ⓐ	Ⓐ	D											
0	**Dijon** 375 d.	0509	0613	0641	0709	0713	0741	0809	1009	1109	1213	1241	1341	1509	1609	1613	1646	1713	1741	1813	1841	1913	2009	2109	2209
32	Auxonne d.	0529	0640	0701	0729	0740	0801	0829	1029	1129	1240	1301	1401	1529	1631	1640	1706	1743	1804	1841	1906	1941	2029	2129	2229
46	Dole 375 d.	0539	0650	0710	0739	0750	0810	0839	1039	1138	1250	1310	1410	1539	1641	1650	1717	1753	1817	1851	1917	1951	2039	2139	2239
91	**Besançon** Viotte a.	0605	0724	0737	0805	0824	0837	0905	1105	1205	1326	1337	1437	1605	1713	1724	1742	1828	1847	1927	1943	2026	2105	2205	2305
	Belfort 378 a.	...	0856	...	...	...	...	...	...	...	...	...	...	...	...	1856	...	1956	...	...	...	...	...	...	...

	Ⓐ		⚒		⚒			Ⓐ				Ⓐ			Ⓐ	Ⓒ		Ⓐ	E	†				†	⚒
Belfort 378 d.	...	...	...	...	...	0604	...	...	...	...	...	...	...	...	...	...	...	...	...	...	1704	...	...	...	...
Besançon Viotte d.	0514	0556	0607	0625	0713	0733	0754	0856	0956	1233	1356	1456	1556	1633	1656	1723	1733	1756	1823	1826	1833	1933	2023	2121	2123
Dole 375 d.	0542	0622	0633	0701	0750	0811	0822	0922	1021	1311	1422	1522	1622	1710	1722	1748	1811	1822	1852	1853	1911	2011	2050	2150	2150
Auxonne d.	0551	0631	0642	0710	0759	0820	0831	0931	1031	1320	1431	1531	1631	1719	1731	1757	1820	1831	1904	1903	1920	2020	2059	2159	2159
Dijon 375 a.	0610	0651	0706	0738	0818	0847	0851	0951	1051	1347	1451	1551	1651	1747	1751	1818	1847	1851	1926	1926	1947	2047	2118	2218	2218

D – ⑤–⑦ (also July 14, Aug. 14, Nov. 10, 11).
E – ⚒ to July 5; ⑥ July 12 - Aug. 30 (also Sept. 1); ⚒ from Nov. 3.
◇ – Runs 4–6 minutes earlier Nov. 12–21.

375 (PARIS) - DIJON - LAUSANNE and NEUCHÂTEL

See Table **40** for Paris - Bern (via Basel). Timings of *TGV* services may vary by up to 8 minutes Sept. 2 - Nov. 1. *TGV* services are subject to alteration/cancellation on ⑥⑦ Oct. 4–19.

km					*TGV* 9261						*TGV* 9269			*TGV* 9271				*TGV* 9273			*TGV* 9277		
		⚒ m	Ⓐ n			p		⚒ p	† v			p		⑦ e	D	Ⓐ q			q t			g	⑤⑦ z
0	*Paris Gare de Lyon* 370 d.	...	...	...	0802	...	...	...	...	...	1157	...	...	1357	...	...	...	1557	...	...	1757	...	...
287	**Dijon** 374 d.	...	...	...	0937	...	...	...	...	...	1337	...	...	1537	...	...	...	1737	...	...	1937	...	...
333	Dole 374 376 d.	0614	...	...	1003	...	...	1118	1118	...	1402	...	...	1603	...	...	...	1802	1814	...	2000	...	2014
365	Mouchard 376 d.	0647	...	...	|	...	...	1142	1142	...	|	...	...	|	...	...	...	|	1844	...	|	...	2037
389	Andelot 376 d.	0706	...	...	|	...	...	1203	1205	...	|	...	...	|	...	...	...	|	1905	...	|	...	...
410	Frasne d.	0721	0817	...	1046	1055	...	1217	1219	...	1446	1455	...	1646	1719	1802	...	1846	1920	...	2044	2052	...
426	Pontarlier 🏛 a.	0737	0833	...	|	1106	...	1233	1235	...	|	1506	...	|	1729	1818	...	|	1936	...	|	2103	...
490	**Neuchâtel 511** a.	...	...	...	|	1152	...	...	...	...	|	1556	...	|	...	...	...	|	...	...	|	2152	...
434	Vallorbe 🏛 a.	...	...	...	1059	...	...	...	...	...	1459	...	...	1659	...	...	...	1859	...	...	2059	...	...
480	**Lausanne** a.	...	...	...	1137	...	...	...	...	...	1537	...	...	1737	...	...	...	1937	...	...	2137	...	...

			TGV 9260				*TGV* 9264	*TGV* 9264					*TGV* 9268		*TGV* 9270	*TGV* 9270					*TGV* 9272		
	Ⓐ n			Ⓐ n		f	r	A		⚒ k	† s				E	B		Ⓐ q	q t	q			⑤⑦ z
Lausanne d.	...	...	0624	...	...	...	0824	0824	...	...	...	...	1224	...	1624	1624	...	...	...	...	1824	...	...
Vallorbe 🏛 d.	...	...	0659	...	...	...	0859	0907	...	...	...	...	1300	...	1701	1707	...	...	...	...	1901	...	...
Neuchâtel 511 d.	...	...	|	...	...	0810	|	|	...	...	...	1211	|	...	|	|	...	...	...	1804	|	...	...
Pontarlier 🏛 d.	0555	...	|	0742	...	0855	|	|	...	1128	...	1254	|	...	|	|	...	1742	1828	1849	|	...	...
Frasne d.	0612	...	0714	0758	...	0907	0917	0923	...	1145	...	1307	1316	...	1716	1722	...	1758	1845	1900	1917	...	...
Andelot 376 d.	0625	...	|	...	...	...	|	|	...	1204	1204	...	|	...	|	|	...	...	1903	...	|	...	...
Mouchard 376 d.	0648	...	|	...	...	...	|	|	...	1221	1221	...	|	...	|	|	...	...	1919	...	|	...	212
Dole 374 376 d.	0710	...	0800	...	...	...	1000	1006	...	1245	1245	...	1400	...	1800	1807	...	...	1942	...	2001	...	214
Dijon 374 a.	...	...	0822	...	...	...	1022	1027	...	...	...	...	1422	...	1822	1831	...	...	...	...	2023	...	...
Paris Gare de Lyon 370 a.	...	...	1002	...	...	...	1202	1204	...	...	...	...	1602	...	2003	2010	...	...	...	...	2202	...	...

A – July 15 - Aug. 24.
B – Ⓑ July 15 - Aug. 24 (not Aug. 15). Arrives Paris 2032 on ⑦ July 20 - Aug. 17.
D – ①–⑤ (not July 14, Aug. 1, Sept. 8–25, Oct. 20–23, 27–30, Nov. 11).
E – ⑤⑦ to July 13 (also July 14); ⑥ July 19 - Aug. 23; ⑤⑦ from Aug. 29 (also Nov. 1, 11; not Aug. 31).
e – Also July 14, Nov. 11.
f – Not ①–⑤ Sept. 5–26.
g – Not Sept. 5, 8–25.
k – Not ①–⑤ Sept. 8–26.
m – Not Sept. 8–27.
n – Not Sept. 9–26.
p – Not Sept. 8–26.
q – Not Sept. 8–25.
r – Not July 15 - Aug. 24.
s – Not Oct. 12, 19.
t – Not Oct. 11, 18.
v – Not Sept. 14, 21, Oct. 12, 19.
z – Also July 14, Aug. 14, Nov. 10, 11; not July 13.

TGV – *TGV Lyria*, 🅁, supplement payable, 🍸. Special 'global' fares including the reservation fee are payable for international journeys.

376 DOLE / BESANÇON - MOREZ - ST CLAUDE

km		Ⓐ		s	s		⑤ f	Ⓐ L	q	⑤⑦ z	🚌 ⊖	🚌 ⑤⑦ v
0	**Dole** 375 d.	...	0614r	...	1014	...	...	...	1814	...	...	...
	Besançon 378 d.	0603	|	1004	|	...	1640	1751	|	...	...	...
32	Mouchard 375 378 d.	0641	0647r	1034	1039	...	1712	1822	1844	...	...	2042
56	Andelot 375 d.	...	0709	...	1101	1207	1736	...	1902	1907	1907	|
70	Champagnole d.	...	0738	...	1118	1221	1749	...	...	1922	1926	2123
105	Morez d.	...	0829	...	1212	1313	1845	...	...	2014	2021	2213
128	**St Claude** a.	...	0900	...	1240	1340y	1915	...	...	2040	2101	2257

	① g	⊡	Ⓐ		s	⑤	①–④ m	t	c	⑤† d	Ⓑ
St Claude d.	0444	0620	...	0954	...	1510k	1551	...	1725	1725	...
Morez d.	0515	0651	...	1029	...	1545	1626	...	1801	1801	...
Champagnole d.	0602	0737	...	1147j	...	1631	1712	...	1847	1847	...
Andelot 375 d.	0619	0759	...	1158	...	1647	|	...	1858	1909	...
Mouchard 375 378 a.	0637	0817	0841	1220x	1225	1705	1754*	1802	1918q	1925	192
Besançon 378 a.	...	|	0909	|	1255	1738	|	1842	|	1956	195
Dole 375 a.	...	0845	...	1245x	...	...	1845*	...	1942q	...	...

ST CLAUDE - OYONNAX - BOURG EN BRESSE

km		⚒n	⚒n	🚌 †	🚌 ⚒	🚌 ⚒	ⒶP	🚌 Ⓒ	🚌	🚌 Ⓐ	†u	🚌
0	**St Claude** d.	0547	0702	0807	0810	1025	1247	1345	1610	1710	1745	1825
32	Oyonnax d.	0624	0739	0852	0855	1110	1324	1430	1655	1755	1825	1910
45	Brion Montréal § d.	0640	0755	0912	0920	1135	1340	1455	1720	1820	1840	1933
48	Nurieux Brion ◧ d.	0643	0759	0917	0927	|	1344	|	1727	1827	1844	|
81	**Bourg en Bresse** a.	0721	0832	1010	1020	1220	1422	1545	1820	1920	1921	2020
	Lyon P. Dieu 353 a.	...	0936e	...	...	...	...	...	...	...	...	...

	🚌 Ⓐ	🚌 ⚒		🚌 Ⓒ	ⒶP	🚌	🚌 ⚒	🚌	ⒷQ	R	🚌
Lyon P. Dieu 353 d.	...	...	...	...	...	...	...	...	...	...	...
Bourg en Bresse d.	0620	0740	...	1030	1038	1240	1340	1605	1720	1823	194
Nurieux Brion ◧ d.	0711	|	...	|	1120	1336	|	|	1759	1903	203
Brion Montréal § d.	0718	0825	...	1113	1124	1343	1425	1650	1803	1906	|
Oyonnax a.	0743	0850	...	1138	1138	1413	1450	1715	1818	1921	20
St Claude a.	0828	0935	...	1223	1216	1448	1535	1800	1900	1959	21

L – To July 4 and from Sept. 1.
P – Ⓐ from June 30 (not Aug. 20–25).
Q – Ⓑ from June 29 (not Aug. 15, 20, 21, 22, 25).
R – Daily from June 28 (not Aug. 20–25).

c – Not Oct. 20 - Nov. 2.
d – Also Aug. 14, Nov. 10.
e – Ⓐ until Aug. 29.
f – Not Aug. 15.
g – Also July 15, Nov. 12; not July 14.
j – Arrives 1115.
k – Not Oct. 10, 17.
m – Not July 7 - Aug. 28, Oct. 6–30, Nov. 11.
n – Not Aug. 20–25.
q – Not Sept. 8–25, Oct. 11, 18.
r – ⚒ (not Sept. 8–27).
s – Not Oct. 12, 19.
t – Not Oct. 11, 18.
u – Not June 15, 22, Aug. 24.
v – Also July 14, Aug. 14, Nov. 1, 10, 11.
x – Not ①–⑤ Sept. 8–26, Oct. 12, 19.
y – Not ①–⑤ Oct. 6–17.
z – Also July 14, Aug. 14, Nov. 10, 11; not July 13.
⊡ – ①–⑤ to July 5; ⑥ July 12 - Aug. 2… ⚒ from Aug. 30 (not Oct. 18–31).
⊖ – ①②③④⑥ (not July 14, Aug. 14, Nov. 1, 10, 11).
* – Connection by 🚌 Champagnole - Mouchard - Dole.
◧ – For *TGV* connection Paris - Nurieu… Brion and v.v. see Table **341**.
§ – Brion Montréal la Cluse.

376a BESANÇON - LE LOCLE - LA CHAUX DE FONDS

km		A	A		⚒		⊗	Ⓐ		
0	Besançon TGV ⊖ 370a d.	...	...	...	...	...	1340	...	...	...
13	**Besançon** Viotte d.	...	...	...	0700	0858	1400	1721	1933	...
80	Morteau d.	0516	0621	0725	0826	1029	1525	1856	2100	...
93	Le Locle △ d.	0534	0639	0745	...	1050	1548	...	2118	...
101	**La Chaux de Fonds** △ a.	0543	0648	0754	...	1057	1555	...	2125	...

	A		A		⚒⊗		A	C	Ⓐ	
La Chaux de Fonds △ d.	0551	...	0656	0810	...	1608	1703	1708	...	21
Le Locle △ d.	0559	...	|	0818	...	1618	1713	1718	...	21
Morteau d.	0616	0637	0720	0835	1237	1634	1735	1735	1937	22
Besançon Viotte a.	...	0759	...	0959	1359	1759	1900	1900	2103	..
Besançon TGV ⊖ 370a a.	...	...	...	1020	...	...	...	...	...	..

A – ①–⑤ (not Aug. 1).
C – ⑥⑦ (also Aug. 1).
△ – See also Table **512**.
⊖ – Full name: Besançon Franche-Comté TGV.
⊗ – Not ①–⑤ Oct. 27 - Nov. 7.

Local Services DIJON - CHALON SUR SAÔNE - LYON 377

For *TGV* services Dijon - Lyon and Paris - Dijon - Chalon sur Saône see Table **379**.

km		Ⓐ		Ⓐ	s	Ⓐ		Ⓐ	Ⓐ	Ⓒ	Ⓐ		Ⓐ	⚒w		Ⓐ	Ⓑ	⑥	Ⓐ	⑥	⑦m	Ⓐ	⑦m	⚒w	‡⊗
	Paris Bercy **371** ▲ d.	...	...	...	...	...	0738	...	0923	0938	...	...	...	1338	...	...	1538	1538	...	...	...	1731v	1738	...	...
0	**Dijon** 373 d.	0540	0640	0740	0840j	0940	1040	1140	1240	1240	1340	1440	1540	1640	1640	1740	1840	1844	1940	1950	2020	2040	2040	2050	2212
37	Beaune 373 d.	0600	0700	0800	0900	1000	1100	1200	1300	1300	1400	1500	1600	1700	1700	1800	1900	1904	2000	2020	2050	2100	2100	2120	2240
52	Chagny d.	0612	0712	0812	0912	1012	1112	1212	1312	1312	1412	1512	1612	1712	1712	1812	1912	1915	2012	2033	2103	2112	2112	2133	2251
67	**Chalon sur Saône** d.	0623	0723	0823	0923	1023	1123	1223	1323	1323	1423	1523	1623	1723	1723	1823	1923	1925	2023	2043	2112	2123	2123	2143	2305
125	Mâcon Ville d.	0656	0756	0856	0956	1056	1156	1256	1356	1356	1456	1556	1656	1756	1756	1856	1956	1958	2056	...	...	2156	2156	...	...
163	Villefranche sur Saône ⊖ d.	0721	0821	0921	1021	1121	1221	1321	1421	1421	1521	1621	1721	1821	1821	1921	2020	2022	2121	...	...	2221	2221	...	...
197	**Lyon** Part Dieu a.	0744	0844	0944	1044	1144	1244	1344	1444	1444	1544	1644	1744	1844	1844	1944	2044	2044	2144	...	...	2244	2244	...	...
201	**Lyon** Perrache a.	...	...	...	...	...	...	...	...	...	...	...	...	...	...	...	2057	2057	...	...	...	...	2257	...	...

	Ⓐ	Ⓒ	Ⓐ	⑥	①g	Ⓐ	Ⓐ			Ⓐ			Ⓐ	Ⓐ	Ⓒ	Ⓐ		Ⓐ		Ⓐ		Ⓐ		Ⓐ	
Lyon Perrache d.	...	...	...	...	0504	...	0604	...	...	...	0900a	...	...	...	...	...	...	...	...	...	...	...	...	...	2104
Lyon Part Dieu d.	...	...	...	...	0516	...	0616	0716	...	0816	0916	...	1016	1116	1116	1216	1316	1416	1516	1616	1716	1816	1916	2016	2116
Villefranche sur Saône ⊖ d.	...	...	...	...	0541	...	0641	0740	...	0841	0941	...	1041	1141	1141	1241	1341	1441	1541	1641	1741	1841	1941	2041	2139
Mâcon Ville d.	...	...	...	0601	0605	0605	0705	0805	...	0905	1005	...	1105	1205	1205	1305	1405	1505	1605	1705	1805	1905	2005	2105	2202
Chalon sur Saône d.	0554	0606	0617	0634	0638	0638	0738	0838	0917	0938	1038	1117	1138	1237	1238	1338	1438	1538	1638	1737	1838	1937	2038	2138	...
Chagny d.	0604	0617	0627	0645	0649	0649	0749	0849	0927	0949	1049	1127	1149	1246	1249	1349	1449	1549	1649	1747	1849	1947	2049	2149‡	...
Beaune 373 d.	0614	0629	0639	0656	0700	0700	0800	0900	0939	1000	1100	1139	1200	1257	1300	1400	1500	1600	1700	1758	1900	1958	2100	2200‡	...
Dijon 373 a.	0641	0702	0711	0715	0719	0719	0820	0919	1010	1021	1121	1210	1221	1315	1319	1421	1519	1621	1719	1819	1919	2020	2121	2222‡	...
Paris Bercy **371** ▲ a.	...	...	...	1022	1022	1022	...	1222	...	...	...	...	...	1622	1622	...	1822	...	2022	...	2222	...	...	...	...

ADDITIONAL LOCAL TRAINS DIJON - CHALON SUR SAÔNE

	⚒w	⚒w		Ⓐ		Ⓐ		Ⓐ	Ⓐ		
Dijon d.	0646	0725	0825z	1050	1221	1450	1625	1650	1725z	1750	1825
Beaune d.	0716	0754	0853	1120	1251	1520	1653	1720	1753	1820	1853
Chagny d.	0729	0804	0903	1133	1303	1533	1703	1733	1803	1833	1903
Chalon sur Saône d.	0743	0818	0918	1143	1318	1543	1718	1743	1818	1843	1918

	⚒w	Ⓐ	Ⓐ		⚒w	Ⓐ			Ⓐ	Ⓑ	
Chalon sur Saône d.	0717	0742	0817	1242	1416	1617	1642	1717	1742	1814	1918
Chagny d.	0727	0757	0827	1255	1426	1627	1657	1727	1757	1828	1933
Beaune d.	0739	0806	0839	1305	1438	1639	1706	1739	1806	1840	1944
Dijon a.	0811	0838	0910	1334y	1510	1713	1735	1811	1834	1912	2010

LOCAL TRAINS MÂCON - LYON ◇

	Ⓐ	⚒	Ⓐ	⚒	Ⓐ	Ⓐ		⑦e	Ⓐ	
Mâcon Ville d.	0602	0635	0724	0735	0825	0835	1235	1657	1735	1835
Villefranche sur Saône ⊖ d.	0636	0706	0749	0806	0850	0906	1306	1720	1806	1906
Lyon Part Dieu a.	0701	|	0814	|	0914	|	|	1744	|	|
Lyon Perrache a.	...	0735	0826	0835t	0926	0936	1335	...	1835	1935

	Ⓐ		Ⓐ	Ⓐ	Ⓐ	⚒	Ⓐ	Ⓐ		Ⓐ
Lyon Perrache d.	0725	0825	1325	1625	1633	1725	1733	1825	1925	2204
Lyon Part Dieu d.	|	|	|	|	1646	|	1746	|	|	2216
Villefranche sur Saône ⊖ d.	0755	0855	1355	1655	1710	1756	1810	1855	2000	2239
Mâcon Ville a.	0825	0925	1425	1725	1733	1826	1833	1925	2030	2302

– Ⓐ only.
– Also July 14, Nov. 11.
– Also Nov. 12; not July 14.
– 0838 on ⑦ Sept. 21 - Nov. 23 (also Nov. 11).
– Also July 14, Aug. 15, Nov. 11.
– From Sens on ⚒ (Table **371**).
– 0843 on ⑥.
– Change trains at Dijon on ⑤ (also Aug. 14).
– Also Nov. 1.

y – 1338 until June 20 (also Sept. 13, 14, 20, 27, Oct. 4, 12, 19, Nov. 1–29).
z – 2 minutes earlier Sept. 9 - Nov. 29.
▲ – Services run from / to Paris Gare de Lyon (not Bercy) on Aug. 9, 10, Sept. 6, 20, 21, 27, 28.
‡ – Subject to alteration on ①–⑤ Sept. 4 - Oct. 10 and ①–⑤ Oct. 27 - Nov. 28.
⊗ – Subject to alteration on Sept. 6, 7, Nov. 29. Timings may vary by up to 5 minutes Sept. 13 - Nov. 23.

◇ – Certain trains continue beyond Lyon to / from Valence.
⊖ – Villefranche is also served by 🚌 service to Mâcon Loché TGV station, connecting with *TGV* trains to / from Paris (Tables **340/1**).

WARNING! Services from / to Paris are subject to alteration or cancellation on various dates including June 15, Aug. 9, 10, Sept. 6, 7, 13, ⑥⑦ Sept. 20 - Oct. 19, Nov. 29, 30, Dec. 6, 7. Other services in this table are subject to alteration on Sept. 13, 14.

Local Services LYON - LONS-LE-SAUNIER - BESANÇON - BELFORT 378

For *TGV* services Lyon - Besançon Franche-Comté TGV - Belfort Montbéliard TGV - (Strasbourg) via high-speed line see Table **379**. Subject to alteration on Oct. 11, 12, 18, 19.

km		†	⚒	⚒	Ⓐ	Ⓐ	Ⓐ	⊡	Ⓐ	Ⓒ¶		⊙	⚒	*TGV* **6874** S⊖	Ⓐ	Ⓒ	Ⓐ		Ⓐ	Ⓒ	Ⓑ	Ⓐ	Ⓒ	⑤†
0	**Lyon** Perrache 353 d.	...	...	...	...	...	...	0717	...	...	...	...	...	...	...	...	...	...	1617	1617	1715k	1817	1813k	2113
5	**Lyon** Part-Dieu 353 d.	...	...	...	...	...	...	0728k	0941a	0941	...	...	...	1434	...	...	...	...	1628k	1628k	1728k	1829k	1826k	2125
	Ambérieu 353 d.	...	...	...	...	...	...	|	|	|	...	...	...	|	...	...	...	...	|	|	1757	1859	1859	|
65	Bourg-en-Bresse 353 d.	...	...	...	...	...	0717	0816	1020	1020	...	...	...	1516f	...	...	...	...	1719	1721	1816	1919	1919	2232
29	**Lons-le-Saunier** d.	...	0544	0613	0643p	...	0801	0901	1101	1101	...	1213	1501	1559f	1607	1607	1701	1713	1801	1801	1858	2001	2001	2312
78	Mouchard d.	...	0628	0702	0721p	0802	0841	0937	1138	1138	...	1302	1539	|	1641	1645	1737	1802	1841	1841	...	2041	2041	...
18	**Besançon** Viotte a.	...	0710	0742	0751p	0846	0909	1009	1209	1209	...	1342	1609	1654§	1709	1717	1809	1842	1909	1909	...	2109	2109	...
18	**Besançon** Viotte ▷ d.	0711	0712	...	0811	...	...	1011	1211j	...	1232	...	...	1657§	1711	...	1811p	...	1911	...	...	...	2115	...
97	Montbéliard ▷ d.	0808	0808	...	0908	...	...	1110	1309j	...	1342	...	...	|	1808	...	1908p	...	2008	...	...	...	2213	...
15	**Belfort** ▷ a.	0824	0824	...	0924	...	...	1124	1324j	...	1356	...	...	1726z	1824	...	1924p	...	2024	...	...	...	2228	...

	⚒	Ⓐ	Ⓐ‡		Ⓐ	⚒w	⑦m		⚒		*TGV* **6837** S⊕					Ⓐ	⑦m	Ⓐ		Ⓐ	⚒	Ⓐ		
Belfort ▷ d.	...	...	0459	...	0636p	0736	...	...	0936	...	1226z	1204	...	1336	1536	1536	1536	1636	...	1732	...	...	1838	1936
Montbéliard ▷ d.	...	...	0516	...	0653p	0751	...	...	0953	...	|	1218	...	1352	1553	1553	1553	1653	...	1748	...	...	1853	1952
Besançon Viotte ▷ a.	...	...	0615	...	0749p	0849	...	...	1049	...	1254§	1328	...	1449	1649	1649	1649	1749	...	1849	...	...	1950	2049
Besançon Viotte d.	...	0603	...	0651	0751	0851	0851	1004	1052	1218	1257§	...	1351	1451	1651	1651	1651	1751p	1817	1851	1851	1918	1952	...
Mouchard d.	...	0642	...	0720	0822	0922	0922	1034	1122	1303	|	...	1423	1522	1722	1722	1722	1823p	1900	1922	1922	1957	2023	...
Lons-le-Saunier d.	0600	0730	...	0758	0900	1001	1001	...	1200	1344	1401f	...	1500	1602	1800	1802	1802	1900p	1944	2000	2000	...	2102	...
Bourg-en-Bresse 353 d.	0642	...	...	0844	...	1045	1045	...	...	...	1438f	...	...	1646	...	1844	1845	...	...	...	...	...	2146	...
Ambérieu 353 d.	|	...	...	0903h	...	|	|	...	...	...	|	...	...	|	...	...	|	...	...	...	...	...	|	...
Lyon Part-Dieu 353 a.	0736	...	...	0926h	...	1136r	1137r	...	...	...	1527	...	...	1744r	...	...	1931	...	...	...	...	...	2236c	...
Lyon Perrache 353 a.	0747	...	...	0945a	...	1147r	1145r	...	...	...	...	...	...	1757r	...	...	1946	...	...	...	...	...	2249c	...

	Ⓐp	Ⓐ	Ⓑ		Ⓐ					Ⓐ
Dijon **374** ⊠ d.	...	...	...	0604t	...	...	...	1613	1713	...
Besançon Viotte d.	0530	0611	0632	0732	1311	1511	1632	1732	1832	2011
Montbéliard d.	0640	0712	0741	0842	1408	1608	1741	1842	1942	2109
Belfort a.	0655	0727	0756	0856	1424	1624	1756	1856	1956	2124

		Ⓐ	Ⓐ	Ⓐ		Ⓐ					⚒
Belfort d.	0604	0704	0804	0836	0936	1136	1304	1704	1819	2036	2136
Montbéliard d.	0618	0718	0817	0853	0953	1153	1318	1718	1833	2053	2151
Besançon Viotte a.	0728	0828	...	0949	1049	1249	1428	1828	1943	2149	...
Dijon **374** ⊠ a.	0847	...	...	...	...	...	...	1952	...	...	...

12 Strasbourg - Lyon - Marseille and v.v. (Table **379**).

Ⓐ from Sept. 1.
⑥⑦ to Aug. 24 (also July 4, Aug. 1); daily from Aug. 30. Arrives 8 minutes earlier from Aug. 30.
Not Ⓐ Nov. 10–28. Departs Bourg 1441 from Aug. 30.
Ⓒ (daily from Aug. 30).

j – 4 minutes later on ① (also July 15, Nov. 12).
k – 2–8 minutes later from Aug. 30.
m – Also July 14, Aug. 15, Nov. 11.
p – To July 4 / from Sept. 1.
r – 6–19 minutes earlier from Aug. 30.
t – 0613 to Sept. 1 / from Nov. 1.
w – Also Nov. 1.
z – Belfort Montbéliard TGV station (see Table **379**).

¶ – Runs 7–19 minutes later until Aug. 23.
‡ – Runs 5 minutes earlier until June 20. Runs 5 minutes later June 23 - Sept. 1.
⊠ – Dijon timings may vary until June 20.
⊡ – Does not run Lyon - Bourg-en-Bresse on ②–⑥ to Aug. 30 (not July 5, Aug. 2).
⊙ – Not ① July 7 - Aug. 25, July 15, Aug. 16, Nov. 2. On ③ (not Nov. 12) Lons le Saunier d. 1220, Mouchard d. 1304, Besançon a. 1346.

⊕ – Subject to alteration on Sept. 13, 20, 27. Oct. 4, 12, 19. Bourg d. 1441 from Aug. 30.
⊖ – Subject to alteration on Sept. 13, 20, 27, 28, Oct. 4, 11, 18. Bourg d. 1522 until Aug. 29.
§ – On Ⓐ Nov. 10–28 calls at Besançon TGV.
▷ – For additional trains Besançon - Belfort and v.v. see below main table.

Timings Besançon - Belfort and v.v. may vary by up to 7 minutes Nov. 11–22

Local services BELFORT - MULHOUSE 378a

km		Ⓐ		Ⓐn§	⚒	Ⓐ	Ⓒ	Ⓐn	n	Ⓐ	Ⓐ	Ⓒ	Ⓐ	n	Ⓐn	Ⓐ	n	Ⓐ	†	Ⓐ	⚒n	†	Ⓐ	⚒n	†	Ⓐnv
0	**Belfort** d.	0529	0558	0631	0700	0732	0737	0806	1004	1106	1206	1210	1303	1404	1506	1606	1706	1733	1754	1806	1842	1855	1906	2006	2042	2106
3	Altkirch d.	0550	0618	0652	0721	0752	0758	0827	1025	1126	1227	1234	1327	1425	1526	1626	1727	1757	1820	1827	1906	1921	1927	2026	2106	2127
9	**Mulhouse** a.	0609	0636	0710	0740	0810	0815	0839	1039	1139	1239	1246	1339	1439	1539	1639	1739	1809	1839	1839	1917	1939	1939	2040	2119	2140

	Ⓐ		Ⓐn	Ⓐ◧			Ⓐn		Ⓐn	Ⓒ	Ⓐ		Ⓐn	Ⓐ	†	⚒n	Ⓐ	n	Ⓐ	Ⓐ	⚒n	†	Ⓐ	n		Ⓐnv
Mulhouse d.	0620	0650	0723	0800	0822	...	0919	...	1023	1123	1223	1315	1423	1523	1559	1619	1719	1750	1823	1903	1923	1928	2021	2053	...	2153
Altkirch d.	0632	0702	0735	0816	0834	...	0932	...	1035	1135	1235	1334	1435	1535	1618	1638	1739	1808	1838	1922	1935	1947	2039	2107	...	2207
Belfort a.	0653	0726	0757	0839	0855	...	0954	...	1056	1156	1256	1355	1456	1556	1639	1659	1800	1829	1859	1943	1956	2011	2100	2128	...	2227

Not Ⓐ July 15 - Aug. 22.
v – Not Nov. 24, 25.
◧ – 4 minutes earlier Sept. 2 - Oct. 31.
§ – 7–8 minutes earlier July 7–11.

379 STRASBOURG / METZ - DIJON - LYON - (NICE / MONTPELLIER) *TGV services*

Timings may vary by up to 8 minutes Sept. 2 - Nov. 29 (please check your reservation for confirmed timings). Services are subject to alteration / cancellation on ⑥⑦ Sept. 13 - Oct. 19.

km	*TGV* trains convey 🍸	*TGV* 6801	*TGV* 6835	*TGV* 6833	*TGV* 6781	*TGV* 6820	*TGV* 6842		*TGV* 6824	*TGV* 6839		*TGV* 6837		*TGV* 6841	*TGV* 6815			*TGV* 9580	*TGV* 6783	*TGV* 6822	*TGV* 6827		*TGV* 6849
			①-⑤ J	⑥⑦ m	Ⓐ L	⊡			d									F	Ⓑ z	b			g
0	**Strasbourg** 385 d.	...	0535	0617	...	...	...	...	...	0917	...	1105	...	1308	...	...	...	1615	...	...	1703	...	1939
65	Colmar 385 d.	...	0601	|	...	...	...	...	...	|	...	1133	...	|	...	...	...	|	...	...	1731	...	|
	Basel 385 d.	...	|	|	...	...	0729	...	...	|	...	|	...	|	...	...	...	|	...	...	|	...	|
106	**Mulhouse** 370 d.	...	|	0707	...	...	0756	...	...	1006	...	1201	...	1407	...	...	...	1708	...	...	1809	...	|
151	Belfort Montbéliard TGV 370 d.	...	|	0734	...	...	0819	...	...	|	...	1226	...	1432	...	...	...	1735	...	...	|	...	2041
233	**Besançon TGV** ⊖ 370 d.	...	0659	0759	...	...	0848	...	...	|	...	1257v	...	1456	...	...	...	1800	...	...	|	...	2107
	Metz d.	...	|	|	...	0606	|	...	0810	|	...	|	...	|	...	...	...	|	...	1601	|	...	|
	Nancy d.	...	|	|	...	0647	|	...	0851	|	...	|	...	|	...	...	...	|	...	1643	|	...	|
	Toul d.	...	|	|	...	0709	|	...	|	|	...	|	...	|	...	...	...	|	...	|	|	...	|
	Neufchâteau d.	...	|	|	...	|	|	...	0934	|	...	|	...	|	...	...	...	|	...	1726	|	...	|
	Culmont Chalindrey d.	...	|	|	...	|	|	...	|	|	...	|	...	|	...	...	...	|	...	1819	|	...	|
	Paris Gare de Lyon **370** d.	...	|	|	0653	|	|	...	|	|	...	⊙	...	|	...	...	...	|	1653	|	|	...	|
310	**Dijon** 370 a.	...	|	|	0834	0907	0915	...	1107	1112	...	|	...	|	...	...	...	|	1834	1907	1912	...	|
310	**Dijon** 377 d.	0608	|	|	0846	0922	0922	...	1122	1122	...	|	...	|	1621	...	1750	|	1846	1920	1920	...	|
347	Beaune 377 d.	|	|	|	0908	|	|	...	|	|	...	|	...	|	|	...	1820	|	1908	|	|	...	|
377	**Chalon sur Saône** 377 d.	0647	|	0856	0926	|	|	...	1158	1158	...	|	...	|	1655	...	1843	1858	1926	|	|	...	|
435	Mâcon Ville 377 d.	|	|	|	...	1022	1022	...	|	|	...	|	...	1621	|	...	...	|	...	2018	2018	...	|
507	**Lyon** Part Dieu 377 a.	0755	0852	0956	...	1057	1057	...	1256	1256	...	1527	...	1656	1756	...	...	1956	...	2056	2056	...	2252
	Lyon Perrache a.	|	|	|	...	|	|	...	|	|	...	|	...	|	|	...	...	|	...	|	|	...	...
	Valence TGV **350** a.	0841	|	|	...	|	|	...	1345	1345	...	1611	...	1743	|	...	...	|	...	2140	2140	...	...
	Avignon TGV **350** a.	|	|	1108	...	1209	1209	...	|	|	...	1646	...	|	1908	...	...	2108	...	2214	2214	...	...
	Aix en Provence TGV **350** a.	0934	1021	1132	...	|	|	...	|	|	...	|	...	|	1932	...	...	2131	...	|	|	...	...
	Marseille **350** a.	0950	1036	1148	...	1247	1247	...	|	|	...	1716	...	|	1947	...	...	2146	...	2247	2247	...	...
	Toulon **350** a.	...	...	...	...	1344j	...	...	|	|	...	...	...	|	2045n	...	...	...	...	...	...	...	...
	Nice **360** a.	...	...	...	...	1535j	...	...	|	|	...	...	...	|	2233n	...	...	...	...	...	...	...	...
	Nimes **355** a.	...	...	...	...	...	...	...	1430	1430	...	...	...	1829	...	...	...	...	...	...	...	...	...
	Montpellier **355** a.	...	...	...	...	...	...	...	1457	1457	...	...	...	1858	...	...	...	...	...	...	...	...	...

km		*TGV* 6780	*TGV* 6888	*TGV* 6880		*TGV* 6866	*TGV* 9582	*TGV* 6863	*TGV* 6863	*TGV* 6782	*TGV* 6878		*TGV* 6874	*TGV* 6872	*TGV* 6885	*TGV* 6864	*TGV* 6885	*TGV* 6864	*TGV* 6784	*TGV* 6882	*TGV* 6868	*TGV* 6870	*TGV* 6876
		①-⑤	Ⓐ M	C		⊗	F	①-⑥ w T	⑦ s T	Ⓐ M				▲	E	E ◇	D	D	⑦ e	♥	♠	●	♣
	Montpellier **355** d.	...	...	...	...	...	...	0802	0802	...	1002	...	...	...	...	...	...	...	...	1600	1600	...	...
	Nimes **355** d.	...	...	...	...	...	...	0829	0829	...	1029	...	...	...	...	...	...	...	...	1627	1627	...	...
	Nice **360** d.	...	...	...	...	...	...	|	|	...	|	...	...	...	...	1204	...	1232j	...	|	|	...	1727
	Toulon **350** d.	...	...	...	...	...	...	|	|	...	|	...	...	...	...	1408	...	1419j	...	|	|	...	1915
	Marseille **350** d.	...	...	...	...	0614	0814	|	|	...	|	...	1242	1414	1514	1514	1519	1519	...	|	|	1823	201
	Aix en Provence TGV **350** d.	...	...	...	...	0629	0829	|	|	...	|	...	1257	1429	1529	1529	|	|	...	|	|	1838	202
	Avignon TGV **350** d.	...	...	...	...	|	0851	|	|	...	|	...	1320	1451	1552	1552	1552	1552	...	|	|	|	205
	Valence TGV **350** d.	...	...	...	...	0720	|	0915	0917	...	|	...	|	|	|	|	|	|	...	1718	1718	|	|
	Lyon Perrache d.	...	...	...	...	|	|	|	|	...	|	...	|	|	|	|	|	|	...	|	|	|	|
0	**Lyon** Part Dieu 377 d.	...	0608y	0600	...	0804	1004	0954	0958	...	1204	...	1434	1604	1704	1704	1704	1704	...	1804	1804	2008	221
72	Mâcon Ville 377 d.	...	|	0637	...	|	|	|	|	...	|	...	|	1641	1741	1741	1741	1741	...	|	|	|	224
130	**Chalon sur Saône** 377 d.	0635	|	0706	...	0906	1107	|	|	1233	1306	...	|	|	|	|	|	|	1835	1907	1907	|	231
160	Beaune 377 d.	0653	|	|	...	|	|	|	|	1252	|	...	|	|	|	|	|	|	1854	|	|	|	|
197	**Dijon** 377 a.	0714	|	0739	...	0943	|	1133	1132	1311	|	...	|	1738	1838	1838	1838	1838	1915	1938	1938	|	234
197	**Dijon** 370 d.	0725	|	0752	...	0952	|	...	...	1323*	|	...	|	1747	1852	1856	1852	1856	1925	1947	1951	|	...
	Paris Gare de Lyon **370** a.	0907	|	|	...	|	|	...	...	1506*	|	...	⊙	|	|	|	|	|	2106	|	|	|	...
274	Culmont Chalindrey d.	...	|	|	...	1045	|	...	...	...	|	...	|	|	|	|	|	|	...	|	|	|	...
348	Neufchâteau d.	...	|	|	...	|	|	...	...	...	|	...	|	|	|	|	|	|	...	|	2119	|	...
392	Toul d.	...	|	|	...	|	|	...	...	...	|	...	|	|	|	2053	|	2053	...	|	|	|	...
425	**Nancy** a.	...	|	|	...	1211k	|	...	...	...	|	...	|	|	|	2112f	|	2112f	...	|	2206	|	...
482	**Metz** a.	...	|	|	...	1253k	|	...	...	...	|	...	|	|	|	2153f	|	2153f	...	|	2246	|	...
	Besançon TGV ⊖ 370 d.	...	0801	0823	...	...	1205	...	...	...	1404	...	1657v	|	1921	...	1921	...	...	|	...	2200	...
	Belfort Montbéliard TGV 370 d.	...	0825	0849	...	...	1230	...	...	...	1429	...	1729	|	1948	...	1948	...	...	|	...	|	...
	Mulhouse 370 d.	...	|	0919	...	...	1255	...	...	...	1455	...	1803	1857	2016	...	2016	...	...	2100	...	|	...
	Basel 385 a.	...	|	|	...	...	|	...	...	...	|	...	|	|	2037	...	2037	...	...	|	...	|	...
	Colmar 385 d.	...	|	0942	...	...	|	...	...	...	|	...	1833	|	...	...	...	...	...	2122	...	2300	...
	Strasbourg 385 a.	...	0925	1010	...	...	1343	...	...	...	1543	...	1858	1944	...	...	...	...	...	2148	...	2326	...

NIGHT TRAINS

STRASBOURG - NICE / PORT BOU 🛏 1, 2 cl., 🚃2 (reclining)

	4283 4282 Ⓡ ⊠	4283 4250 Ⓡ ⊠
Strasbourg d.	2014	2014
Sélestat d.	2038	2038
Colmar d.	2053	2053
Mulhouse d.	2126	2126
Belfort d.	2213	2213
Culmont Chalindrey d.	0015	|
Avignon Centre a.	0523	|
Arles a.	0545	|
Marseille St Charles a.	0632	|
Toulon a.	0745	|
Cannes **360** a.	0905	|
Nice **360** a.	0941	|
Nimes a.	...	0606
Montpellier a.	...	0634
Béziers **355** a.	...	0725
Narbonne **355** a.	...	0741
Perpignan **355** a.	...	0819
Cerbère **355** a.	...	0908
Portbou **355** a.	...	0917

	4382 4383 Ⓡ ⊠	4350 4382 Ⓡ ⊠
Port Bou **355** d.	...	...
Cerbère **355** d.	...	2022
Perpignan **355** d.	...	2114
Narbonne **355** d.	...	2154
Béziers **355** d.	...	2210
Montpellier d.	...	2300
Nimes d.	...	2328
Nice **360** d.	1903	|
Cannes **360** d.	1935	|
Toulon d.	2058	|
Marseille St Charles d.	2202	|
Arles d.	2247	|
Avignon Centre d.	2308	|
Culmont Chalindrey a.	0432	|
Belfort a.	0643	|
Mulhouse a.	0731	0731
Colmar a.	0809	0809
Sélestat a.	0830	0830
Strasbourg a.	0858	0858

LUXEMBOURG - NICE / PORT BOU 🛏 1, 2 cl., 🚃2 (reclining)

	4251 4283 Ⓡ ⊠	4251 4250 Ⓡ ⊠
Luxembourg d.	1928	1928
Thionville d.	2008	2008
Metz d.	2040	2040
Nancy d.	2133	2133
Toul d.	2156	2156
Neufchâteau d.	2223	2223
Culmont Chalindrey d.	0015	|
Avignon Centre a.	0523	|
Arles a.	0545	|
Marseille St Charles a.	0632	|
Toulon a.	0745	|
Cannes **360** a.	0905	|
Nice **360** a.	0941	|
Nimes a.	...	0606
Montpellier a.	...	0634
Narbonne **355** a.	...	0741
Perpignan **355** a.	...	0819
Cerbère **355** a.	...	0908
Portbou **355** a.	...	0917

	4382 4351 Ⓡ ⊠	435 435 Ⓡ ⊠
Port Bou **355** d.	...	...
Cerbère **355** d.	...	202
Perpignan **355** d.	...	211
Narbonne **355** d.	...	215
Montpellier d.	...	230
Nimes d.	...	232
Nice **360** d.	1903	|
Cannes **360** d.	1935	|
Toulon d.	2058	|
Marseille St Charles d.	2202	|
Arles d.	2247	|
Avignon Centre d.	2308	|
Culmont Chalindrey a.	0432	|
Neufchâteau a.	0643	064
Toul a.	0709	070
Nancy a.	0731	073
Metz a.	0824	082
Thionville a.	0851	085
Luxembourg a.	0935	093

C – Ⓒ (daily July 5 - Aug. 24). Subject to alteration Sept. 6 - Oct. 26.
D – ⑥⑦ to June 22; daily from Sept. 13 (not Sept. 15–19, Oct. 13–17, 20–24, 27–31). Subject to alteration on Sept. 13, 29.
E – Daily to Sept. 5 (not June 15, 21, 22); ①-⑤ Sept. 8–19, Oct. 13–31. Subject to alteration on Aug. 2, 3, 9, 10.
F – 🚃12 Frankfurt - Strasbourg - Marseille and v.v. (Table **47**).
J – ①-⑤ to July 4 / from Aug. 25 (not Sept. 1).
L – Ⓐ to July 4 / from Aug. 22.
M – Ⓐ to July 4 / from Aug. 25.
T – From Toulouse (Table **321**).

b – Not Aug. 15, 16, Oct. 12, 19, 26, Nov. 2, 9.
d – Not Aug. 15, 16, 17, Oct. 12, 19, 26, Nov. 2, 9.
e – Also July 14, Nov. 11; not July 13.
f – 9–18 minutes later until Aug. 31.
g – Not Aug. 24, Sept. 1, 7, 13, 21, Oct. 11, 18.
j – Not Sept. 6, Nov. 8, 9, 10.
k – 10–12 minutes later until Aug. 3.
m – ⑥⑦ (daily July 5 - Aug. 24; not June 21–29, Sept. 14).
n – Not Sept. 6, Nov. 9.
r – Not Sept. 6, Nov. 9, 10.
s – Not Dec. 7.
v – Besançon **Viotte** (calls at Besançon TGV station on Ⓐ Nov. 10–28).
w – Not July 14, Aug. 15, Nov. 11.
y – 0602 Nov. 3–28.
z – Not Aug. 15.

TGV – Ⓡ, supplement payable, 🍸.

* – May run up to 36 minutes later Dijon - Paris.
⊗ – Does not run Dijon - Metz on Aug. 15, 16, 17, Oct. 12, 19, 26, Nov. 2
◇ – Does not run Dijon - Metz on Aug. 14, 15, 16.
⊡ – Does not run Metz - Dijon on Aug. 15, 16, 17.
♥ – Does not run Mulhouse - Strasbourg on Aug. 23, 24, 30, 31, Sept. 6 20, 21, Oct. 19, Nov. 23.
♠ – Subject to alteration July 14–18, 21–25, Aug. 14, 15, 16, 23, 30, Sept. 13, 20.
● – Subject to alteration on Aug. 23, 24, 30, 31, Sept. 6, 7, Nov. 22–2
♣ – Subject to alteration from Sept. 1.
▲ – Subject to alteration Sept. 13 - Oct. 31.
⊠ – Days of running are subject to confirmation. Timings may vary.
⊙ – Via Lons le Saunier and Bourg en Bresse (Table **378**).
⊖ – Full name: Besançon Franche-Comté TGV.

PARIS - TROYES - BELFORT 380

For *TGV* trains Paris - Belfort Montbéliard TGV via high-speed line see Table **370**. **SUBJECT TO ALTERATION UNTIL JULY 5.**

km		1539		11641	11643	1643	1643	1647	1645		11649	1741	1741	11743	1745	1749	1747	1747	11749	11841	1843	11847	11941		11943
		Ⓐ	Ⓐ	⚒	Ⓐ	⑥ k	⑦ d	Ⓐ ❖	⑥ k		⊡	n	C n		Ⓑ f	†	⚒	⑥ k	Ⓐ			Ⓑ r	◧		⑦ w
0	**Paris** Est d.	...	...	0642	0742	0742	0742	0843	0912	...	1212	1312	1312	1412	1512	1642	1642	1642	1712	1812	1842	1942	2042	...	2212
110	Nogent sur Seine d.	...	0651	0741	|	|	0841	|	1011	...	1311	|	|	1511	|	|	1742	1742	1818	1912	|	2041	2141	...	2311
129	Romilly sur Seine d.	...	0703	0754	|	|	0855	|	1025	...	1325	|	|	1525	|	|	1756	1756	1833	1925	|	2055	2154	...	2325
166	**Troyes** d.	0527	0724	0816	0905	0907	0918	1015	1046	...	1346	1436	1438	1546	1639	1808	1818	1818	1855	1947	2009	2117	2216	...	2347
221	Bar sur Aube d.	0554	0757	0852	...	|	|	|	|	...	1418	...	|	1618	|	1843	1853	1853	...	2022	|	...	2248	...	...
262	Chaumont 382 d.	0616	0818	0917	...	0957	1006	1105	1134	...	1440	...	1530	1640	1730	1908	1918	1918	...	2048	2100	...	2310	...	...
296	Langres 382 d.	0637	...	0937	...	|	|	|	|	...	1500	...	|	1700	|	1930	1939	1939	...	2108	|	...	2330	...	...
307	Culmont Chalindrey 382 d.	0647	...	0945	...	|	|	|	|	...	1508	...	|	1708	1757	1943	1949	1950	...	2118	|	...	2339	...	...
	Dijon 382 a.	0745	...	...	...	|	|	|	|	...	...	...	|	...	|	|	...	|	...	...	|	...	...	...	...
380	Vesoul d.	...	...	...	...	1103	1109	1215	1235	...	...	...	1633	...	1836	2023	...	2030	...	...	2203	...	...	...	...
410	Lure 386a d.	...	...	...	...	1123	1130	1236	...	...	...	...	1653	...	1856	2042	...	2050	...	...	2223	...	...	...	...
442	**Belfort** 386a a.	...	...	...	...	1144	1152	1305	...	...	...	...	1714	...	1917	2103	...	2111	...	...	2244	...	...	...	...

	11640	11642	11644		1942	1646	11742	11942	1742	1742	11944		11746	1840	1543	11842	1842	1844	11946	1848	11948	1946	1944	1545	1545
	⚒	Ⓐ	Ⓐ	Ⓐ	⑥ k	Ⓐ	†	⚒	C e	e	⊠			Ⓒ f	⊖	Ⓐ	⑥	† f	⊗	Ⓑ f		⑦ s	⚒ ◧	①–④ m	⑤ t
Belfort ▲ 386a d.	...	...	...	...	0459	0512	...	...	0820	...	...	...	...	1320	...	...	...	1442	...	1648	...	1757	1806	...	...
Lure ▲ 386a d.	...	...	...	...	0521	0533	...	...	0842	...	...	...	...	1341	...	...	...	1504	...	1709	...	1821	1828	...	...
Vesoul ▲ d.	...	...	...	...	0541	0552	...	...	0902	...	...	...	...	1400	...	...	1521	1524	...	1729	...	1839	1847	...	...
Dijon 382 d.	...	...	...	...	|	|	...	...	|	...	...	...	...	|	1405‡	...	|	|	1551‡	|	...	|	|	1904	1905
Culmont Chalindrey 382 d.	...	...	0525	0610	0619	|	0644e	0817	|	...	1047	...	...	|	1453	...	|	|	1644	|	1817	1916	1928	1954	1959
Langres 382 d.	...	...	0536	0619	0629	|	0654e	0826	|	...	1056	...	...	|	1503	...	|	|	1653	|	1826	1926	|	2005	2010
Chaumont 382 d.	...	...	0559	0640	0650	0657	0716	0847	1002	...	1116	...	...	1503	1524	...	1625	1625	1715	1833	1847	1948	1956	2023	2031
Bar sur Aube d.	...	...	0620	0702	0712	|	0739	0909	|	...	1138	...	...	|	1545	...	|	|	1738	|	1909	2009	|	...	2054
Troyes d.	0512	0602	0655	0732	0745	0742	0814	0945	1050	1050	1212	...	1412	1550	1616	1712	1712	1712	1812	1920	1942	2042	2042	...	2126
Romilly sur Seine d.	0534	0624	0716	...	0805	0803	0836	1005	|	|	1233	...	1434	|	...	1733	1733	1733	1833	|	2003	2103	|	...	...
Nogent sur Seine d.	0548	0638	0730	...	0818	0817	0850	1017	|	|	1247	...	1448	|	...	1747	1747	1747	1847	|	2017	2117	|	...	...
Paris Est a.	0646	0746	0831	...	0916	0916	0947	1116	1216	1216	1346	...	1546	1716	...	1846	1846	1846	1946	2046	2116	2216	2216	...	...

C – ⑥⑦ to July 27; daily from Aug. 2 (not Oct. 20–24).
d – Also Nov. 1, 11.
e – Not Oct. 12.
f – Not Aug. 15.
k – Not Nov. 1.
m – Not July 14, Aug. 14, Nov. 10, 11.
n – Not July 13, Sept. 30, Oct. 1, 2.
r – Not July 13, Aug. 15.
s – Also July 14, Aug. 15, Nov. 11; not July 13.
t – Also Aug. 14, Nov. 10; not Aug. 15.
w – Also July 14, Nov. 1, 11; not July 13.
◧ – Not Sept. 29 - Oct. 3.
❖ – Subject to confirmation.
⊗ – Subject to alteration on Aug. 16, 17.
⊖ – Subject to alteration Aug. 14–19, Sept. 30 - Oct. 2, Nov. 10, 11.
▲ – Departures may be up to 5 minutes earlier until Aug. 3.
⊡ – Not Oct. 13–17. On ①–⑤ Sept. 15 - Oct. 10 does not run Chaumont - Culmont. Oct. 20–24 does not run Troyes - Culmont.
‡ – ⑥⑦ (daily June 15–22, July 5–27, Aug. 30 - Sept. 14, Oct. 11 - Nov. 2 and from Dec. 6).
⊠ – Does not run Culmont - Troyes on ①–⑤ Sept. 29 - Oct. 24.

PARIS - CHÂLONS EN CHAMPAGNE - BAR LE DUC 381

km										*TGV* 2777							*TGV* 2785			*TGV* 2787				
		Ⓐ ◇	Ⓐ ◇	Ⓐ ◇	Ⓒ ⊕	Ⓐ ◇	⑥ ⊕	† k⊕	◇⊕	⊠	◇	Ⓐ ◇	⊕	Ⓐ ⊕		⊕	Ⓐ		Ⓐ ⊕	⑦ e	Ⓒ	Ⓐ h⊕	⑤h f⊕	†
0	**Paris** Est d.	0636	0736	0836	0836	1036	1036	1036	1236	1358	...	1436	1636	1736	...	1836	1928	...	1936	2028	2036	2136	2136	2236
95	Château Thierry d.	0724	0824	0924	0924	1124	1124	1124	1324	|	...	1524	1724	1831	...	1931	|	...	2031	|	2124	2224	2224	2324
142	Épernay d.	0752	0852	0948	0952	1151	1151	1152	1352	|	...	1552	1752	1859	...	1959	|	...	2059	|	2152	2252	2252	2350
	Champagne-Ardenne TGV . d.	|	|	|	|	|	|	|	|	1441	...	|	|	|	...	|	2012	...	|	2111	|	|	|	|
*172	**Châlons en Champagne** ▷ d.	0810	0910	1008	1010	1210	1210	1208	1410	1505	...	1610	1810	1914	1920	2016	2038	2041	2116	2134	2208	2308	2310	0008
205	Vitry le François ▷ d.	0828	0928	...	1028	1228	1228	...	1428	1523	1530	1628	1828	...	1939	2034	2058	2102	2133f	2154	...	...	2328	...
234	**St Dizier** ▷ a.	0846	*0954*	...	*1054*	*1251*	1246	...	1446	|	1550	1646	|	...	1957	2052	|	2120	2152f	|	...	...	|	...
255	**Bar le Duc** ▷ a.	...	0953	...	1052	1252	...	...	...	1547	...	...	1852	...	...	...	2122	...	...	2219	...	...	2352	...

					TGV 2778															*TGV* 2784				
	Ⓐ	⚒	⑥	Ⓐ	①–⑥ b	Ⓐ	②–⑤ c	A	† k	⑥	⑥	Ⓐ ◇	† k	Ⓐ ◇	◇	Ⓐ ◇	◇	Ⓑ			Ⓐ ◇	† k	①–④ m	
Bar le Duc ▷ d.	...	...	...	...	0613	...	...	...	...	...	0933	...	...	...	1133	1333	...	...	...	1713	...	...	...	1937
St Dizier ▷ d.	...	...	0556	0601	|	0636	...	0737	0930	0933	|	0937	...	1122	|	|	1537	...	1650	|	1737	1837	1936	|
Vitry le François ▷ d.	...	...	0617	0622	0639	0658	...	0758	0950	0952	0958	0958	...	1142	1158	1358	1558	...	1713	1739	1758	1858	1956	2003
Châlons en Champagne ▷ d.	0516	0613	0635	0645	0657	0716	0815	0816	1007	...	1016	1016	1016	...	1216	1416	1616	1716y	1735	1757	1816	1916	...	2021
Champagne-Ardenne TGV . d.	|	|	...	...	0721	|	|	|	...	...	|	|	|	...	|	|	|	|	...	1820	|	|	...	|
Épernay d.	0535	0633	...	...	|	0732	0833	0833	...	...	1037	1037	1037	...	1233	1433	1632	1733	...	|	1832	1932	...	2037
Château Thierry d.	0601	0701	...	...	|	0801	0901	0901	...	...	1101	1101	1101	...	1301	1501	1701	1801	...	|	1901	2001	...	2101
Paris Est a.	0653	0753	...	...	0801	0853	0953	0953	...	...	1153	1153	1153	...	1353	1553	1753	1853	...	1901	1953	2053	...	2154

A – ①⑥⑦ (also July 15, Aug. 15, Nov. 11, 12; not June 16, 23, 30).
b – Not July 14, Aug. 16, Nov. 10, 11.
c – Not July 15, Aug. 15, Nov. 11, 12. Starts from Épernay until July 4.
e – Also July 14, Nov. 11; not July 13, Nov. 9.
f – ⑤ (also Aug. 14; not Aug. 15).
h – Not July 7–18.
k – Not Nov. 1.
m – Not July 14, Aug. 14, Nov. 11.
y – Not Aug. 4–8, 11–14, 18–22, Sept. 8–10.
TGV – Ⓡ, supplement payable, 🍷.
◇ – Subject to alteration on Ⓐ.
⊕ – Until July 15 timings at Châlons / Vitry / Bar le Duc / St Dizier are up to 15 minutes later.
⊠ – Subject to alteration on Ⓐ Aug. 28 - Sept. 5 and on Ⓐ from Oct. 27.
▷ – For other trains see Table **382**.
* – *188 km via high-speed line.*

Subject to alteration on Oct. 10, 11, 12, Nov. 8, 9.

REIMS - CHÂLONS EN CHAMPAGNE - METZ / NANCY / DIJON 382

km	SEE NOTE ⊠	⑥	Ⓐ	⑥ k	Ⓐ			⚒ ◇	A		† k
0	**Reims** d.	...	0619	0751	...	...	...		1647	...	...
31	Épernay d.	0612	0644	0816	...	...	...	1611	1712	...	1822
61	**Châlons en Champ.** 381 d.	0629	0704	0834	...	...	...	1636	1729	...	1842
94	Vitry le François 381 d.	0646	0723	0851	...	...	...	1654	1747	...	1858
143	Bar le Duc 381 d.	0714	0754	0916	1002	1223	1610	1720	1817	1911	1922
243	**Metz** (*see below*) a.	|	|	|	|	|	|	1815	|	|	2024
183	Commercy d.	0734	0818	0937	1025	1244	1633	...	1838	1934	...
209	Toul d.	0749	0834	0952	1046	1300	1654	...	1855	1952	...
242	**Nancy** a.	0811	0855	1011	1108	1318	1715	...	1923	2009	...

SEE NOTE ⊠			◇				Ⓑ	Ⓐ	⑤ ◐	†
Nancy d.	0701	1011	1332	1612	1711	1802	1802	2032	2032	2032
Toul d.	0719	1033	1352	1633	1731	1823	1823	2052	2052	2053
Commercy d.	0734	1053	1412	1646	1750	1837	1837	2107	2107	2107
Metz (*see below*) d.	|	|	|	|	|	|	|	|	|	|
Bar le Duc 381 d.	0756	1115	1436	1707	1813	1857	1859	2127	2129	2129
Vitry le François 381 d.	0823	...	1502	...	...	...	1926	...	2152	2153
Châlons en Champ. 381 d.	0841	...	1519	...	...	...	1944	...	2210	2209
Épernay d.	0906	...	1535	...	...	...	2014	...	2227	...
Reims a.	0925	...	...	...	...	...	2039	...	...	...

km		⑥	Ⓑ ⊗	◇	⑤ D	Ⓐ	† k	⑥	Ⓐ		
0	**Reims** d.	0727	0732	1311	1509	1640	1733	1733	1749	1824	2002
58	**Châlons en Champ.** 381 d.	0805	0814	1355	1544	1721	1814	1817	1826	1920	2041
91	Vitry le François 381 d.	0825	0833	1415	1602	1744	1833	1837t	1847	1939	2102
120	St Dizier 381 d.	0844	0854	1436	1622	1805	1854	1856t	1906	1957	2122
193	Chaumont 380 d.	0928	0937	1519	1712	1852	1938	...	...	...	2206
227	Langres 380 d.	0949	0958	1541	1733	1915	1959	...	...	...	2228
238	Culmont Chalindrey 380 d.	0959	1009	1551	1744	1924	2009	...	...	...	2236
315	**Dijon** 380 a.	1046	1102	1641	1839	...	2102	...	...	...	...

	⑥	Ⓐ	⚒ t	Ⓐ ●	Ⓒ	⊖	⑤⑦ r			Ⓑ
Dijon 380 d.	...	...	...	...	...	1405‡	...	...	...	1802
Culmont Chalindrey 380 d.	...	...	0533	0658	...	1453	...	...	...	1850
Langres 380 d.	...	...	0544	0707	...	1503	...	...	...	1900
Chaumont 380 d.	...	...	0606	0728	1130	1522	1528	...	1734	1921
St Dizier 381 d.	0556	0601	0654	0818	1214	...	1615	1650	1843	2006
Vitry le François 381 d.	0617	0622	0717	0838	1235	...	1635	1713	1903	2026
Châlons en Champ. 381 d.	0637	0648	0740	0900	1255	...	1656	1737	1927	2048
Reims a.	0721	0731	0820	0936	1330	...	1732	1815	2004	2133

	⚒	† §	E	⑤ f
Bar le Duc d.	0719	0748	1227v	1918
Metz a.	0817	0850	1325	2011

	§	E	
Metz d.	0830	1332	1828
Bar le Duc a.	0923	1427	1921

– Until Aug. 3.
– ⑤ to Oct. 24 (also Aug. 14; not Aug. 15, 29, Sept. 5).
– ①⑤ (not July 7 - Aug. 29, Oct. 20 - Nov. 14).
– ⑤ (also Aug. 14; not Aug. 15). Departs Bar le Duc 1908 Aug. 8 - Sept. 26.
– Not Nov. 1.
– Also July 14, Aug. 14, Nov. 11.
– 10 minutes later until July 12.
– 1218 Sept. 1–29.
● – Runs up to 7 minutes earlier until July 4.
⊗ – On ①–⑤ Sept. 29 - Nov. 7 does not run Reims - Chaumont.
◇ – Subject to alteration on Ⓐ.
¶ – Runs Chaumont - St Dizier only on Oct. 31 - Dec. 5 (also Aug. 22).
‡ – ⑥⑦ (daily June 15–22, July 5–27, Aug. 30 - Sept. 14, Oct. 11 - Nov. 2 and from Dec. 6).
⊖ – Subject to alteration Aug. 14–19, Sept. 30 - Oct. 2, Nov. 10, 11.
§ – Not Oct. 12, 19, 26, Nov. 2, 9.
◐ – Not July 11, 18, Aug. 15.
⊠ – Until Aug. 3 services are subject to alteration / cancellation (timings may vary by up to 25 minutes). Please check locally. Subject to alteration Nov. 8–11.

Subject to alteration on Aug. 15, 16, 17, Oct. 11, 12

383 METZ and NANCY - STRASBOURG

km		Ⓐ	299 ①–⑥	Ⓐ	⑥ k	Ⓐ	Ⓑ q	Ⓐ	Ⓐ	Ⓒ a m	⑥ k	† z	91 m B	Ⓐ	Ⓒ m	⑥ k	Ⓐ	Ⓑ q	⑥ k	295 Ⓐ	†	Ⓐ	97 B	⚒	†	Ⓐ
	Luxembourg **384** d.	...	0542	...	...	...	...	...	...	...	...	...	1100	...	...	...	...	...	...	1430	...	...	1615	...	...	...
0	**Metz** d.	...	0637h	...	...	0747h	...	0833h	...	0936	...	...	1144v	...	1225	...	1255	...	...	1515	...	...	1657c	...	1741h	1742
Δ	**Nancy** 387 d.	0615	│	0715	0715	│	0815	│	0915	│	1015	1115	│	1215	│	1315	│	1415	1515	│	1614	1615	│	1715	│	│
	Lunéville 387 d.	0633	│	0732	0733	│	0833	│	0933	│	1032	1133	│	1233	│	1333	│	1433	1533	│	1632	1633	│	1732	│	│
88	Sarrebourg d.	0656	│	0758	0759	│	0856	0929	0957	1031f	1058	1156	│	1258	1328	1355	1357	1456	1556	│	1656	1656	│	1758	│	│
91	Réding d.	0700	0724	│	│	0832	│	│	│	│	│	│	│	│	1332	1400	1401	│	│	1602	│	│	│	│	1827	1828
114	Saverne d.	0715	0742	0814	0815	0847	0912	0947	1014	1048f	1115	1212	│	1316	1348	1414	1417	1512	1612	1617	1712	1713	│	1814	1844	1844
159	**Strasbourg** a.	0742	0809	0839	0839	0909	0939	1009	1039	1111f	1139	1239	1305	1339	1411	1439e	1439	1539	1639	1639	1739	1739	1814	1839	1909	1909
	Mulhouse **385** a.	0844	...	0944	...	...	...	...	1144	...	...	...	1413	...	...	...	...	...	...	1744	...	...	1914	...	...	...
	Basel **385** a.	0909	...	1009	...	...	...	...	1209	...	...	...	1438	...	...	...	...	...	...	1809	...	...	1942	...	...	...

	†	Ⓐ	Ⓐ	Ⓐ	⑥ k	Ⓐ	Ⓒ	† ♣	†	2583 Ⓑ ¶♥	
Luxembourg **384** d.	...	...	...	...	...	...	...	...	...	...	...
Metz d.	...	...	1825	...	...	1930	1930	...	2032	...	...
Nancy 387 d.	1815	1815	│	1915	1915	│	│	2015	│	2052	...
Lunéville 387 d.	1833	1833	│	1933	1933	│	│	2033	│	2113	...
Sarrebourg d.	1856	1857	1929	1956	1956	2027	2027	2056	│	2139	...
Réding d.	│	1901	│	│	│	│	2031	│	2115	│	...
Saverne d.	1912	1916	1946	2013	2013	2046	2046	2112	2131	2156	...
Strasbourg a.	1939	1939	2009	2039	2039	2109	2110	2139	2155	2219	...
Mulhouse **385** a.	...	...	...	2145	...	...	...	...	...	...	...
Basel **385** a.	...	...	...	2209	...	...	...	...	...	...	...

	Ⓐ	2584 ①–⑥ b♥	Ⓐ	Ⓐ	⑥	Ⓐ	Ⓐ	⑥ k	† m	296 Ⓐ
Basel **385** d.	...	...	...	...	...	...	...	...	...	...
Mulhouse **385** d.	...	...	...	...	...	...	...	...	...	0616
Strasbourg d.	...	0546	0602j	0620	...	0650	0720	0720	0750	0750
Saverne d.	...	0609	0623	0645	...	0713	0744	0744	0813	0813
Réding d.	...	│	0639	│	...	│	0758	│	0827	0827
Sarrebourg d.	...	0627	0653	0703	0728	0737	0802	0808	│	│
Lunéville 387 d.	0550	0651	│	0726	0756	│	0831	│	│	│
Nancy 387 a.	0624	0710	│	0743	0825	│	0850	│	│	│
Metz a.	...	...	0744	...	...	0832	...	0902	0924	0912
Luxembourg **384** a.	...	...	...	...	...	...	...	...	...	0958

	Ⓐ	Ⓒ	m	Ⓐ	Ⓒ	Ⓐ		Ⓒ m p	Ⓐ	90 m B	⑥ k	Ⓐ	Ⓑ q	Ⓑ q	Ⓐ	⑥ k	96 B	Ⓐ	†	Ⓐ	⑥ k	294 †	Ⓐ	†	⑥ k	298 Ⓐ
Basel **385** d.	...	...	...	...	...	...	...	...	...	1316	...	...	...	...	...	...	1618	...	...	...	...	...	1751	...	...	...
Mulhouse **385** d.	...	...	...	...	...	...	...	...	...	1341	...	...	...	...	...	...	1646	...	...	...	...	...	1816	...	...	...
Strasbourg d.	0820j	0820	0950	1020	1020	1150	1220	1250	1420j	1450	1520	1550	1620	1650j	1720	1720	1750	1820j	1820	1850	1850	1850	1920j	1950	1950	1950
Saverne d.	0844	0846	1013	1042	1046	1215	1243	1314	1444	│	1546	1614	1643	1712	1742	1746	1813	1843	1845	1914	1915	1916	1943	2013	2015	2016
Réding d.	│	0900	│	│	│	1231	│	1331	│	│	1600	1630	│	1729	│	│	│	1857	│	│	│	1930	1957	│	│	2030
Sarrebourg d.	0901	0904	1037	1058	1101	1241	1301	1341	1500	│	1604	1641	1700	1740	1759	1801	│	1902	1901	1940	1939	│	2002	2030	2030	│
Lunéville 387 d.	0924	0926	│	1124	1125	│	1325	│	1524	│	1626	│	1725	│	1825	1825	│	1924	1926	│	│	│	2025	2053	2055	│
Nancy 387 a.	0943	0945	│	1143	1143	│	1344	│	1543	│	1644	│	1743	│	1843	1844	│	1943	1944	│	│	│	2043	2110	2113	│
Metz a.	...	...	1130	...	...	1337	...	1440	...	1607	...	1737	...	1833	...	...	1908	...	...	2033	2032	2017	...	...	...	2116
Luxembourg **384** a.	...	...	...	...	...	...	...	...	...	1649	...	...	...	...	...	...	1949	...	...	...	...	2117	...	...	...	2200

B – [12] Basel - Brussels and v.v. (Table **43**).
a – Not Aug. 24.
b – Not July 14, Nov. 11.
c – 1656 July 8 - Aug. 21.
e – 1444 July 12 - Aug. 23.
f – 2–5 minutes later July 12 - Aug. 17.
h – 2–3 minutes earlier July 8 - Aug. 21.

j – Departs up to 5 minutes earlier on Ⓐ July 7 - Aug. 22.
k – Not Nov. 1.
m – Not Oct. 12, 19, 26, Nov. 2, 9.
p – Not Nov. 1, 11.
q – Also Nov. 1.
v – 1142 on ①–⑤ Aug. 5–21.

z – Runs 9–11 minutes **earlier** on July 14, Aug. 15, Nov. 1, 11.
♥ – *TGV* train, Ⓡ, 🍷. To/from Paris (Table **390**).
¶ – Not Aug. 15. Subject to alteration Sept. 29 - Oct. 3, Oct. 13–17. Arrives Strasbourg 2224 on Ⓐ June 16 - July 18.

♣ – Runs 4–5 minutes later on July 14, Aug. 15, Nov. 1, 11.
Δ – Nancy - Sarrebourg: *80* km.

Timings Metz - Strasbourg and v.v. may vary by up to 4 minutes July 8 - Aug. 4.

384 LUXEMBOURG - METZ - NANCY

For *TGV* trains Luxembourg - Metz - Paris see Table **390**. For long distance trains to Lyon and southern France see Table **379**. Timings may vary by up to 4 minutes Sept. 9 - Oct. 6.

km		Ⓐ	⚒	H	⑦ t r	299 E S	⚒	⑦ y	A	⑥ k	⚒	H w	A	H	A	⑦ y	⑥ k	A	Ⓐ		A		C	Ⓐ	A	C
0	**Luxembourg** d.	...	...	0502	0526	0542	...	...	0614	...	...	0655	0715	0731	0740	...	...	0755	...	0829	0859	...	0940	...	1030	...
34	Thionville d.	...	...	0530	0556	0603	...	...	0642	0642	...	0725	0735	0756	0806	0806	0808	0824	...	0857	0926	...	1006	1010	1057	...
46	Hagondange d.	...	...	0541	0608	│	...	...	0652	0652	...	0733	0744	0805	0819	0817	0818	0832	...	0908	0937	...	1015	1019	1108	...
64	**Metz** a.	...	...	0556	0624	0621	...	...	0706	0706	...	0745	0755	0818	0833	0835	0836	0845	...	0919	0958	...	1026	1031	1122	...
64	**Metz** d.	0551	0555	...	0627	...	0638	0659	0710	0710	0729	...	0758	0824	...	0838	...	...	0901	0924	...	...	1029	1035	1124	1124
93	Pont-à-Mousson d.	0617	0627	...	0646	...	0700	0728	0728	0727	0749	...	0820	0844	...	0906	...	...	0919	0944	...	...	1051	1058	1144	1145
121	**Nancy** a.	0633	0700	...	0706	...	0717	0759	0744	0744	0808	...	0838	0904	...	0936	...	...	0936	1000	...	...	1109	1116	1201	1204

	91 B	Ⓐ		H	Ⓐ		A		D		295 Ⓐ b		Ⓐ d	A	97 B	Ⓐ	A	⑦ y	⑥ k	A	Ⓐ	†	⚒	Ⓐ	A	
Luxembourg d.	1100	...	1130	1159	...	1230	1255	1328	1328	1406	1430	1531	...	1555	1615	...	1630	1635	1640	1655	...	1730	1730	...	1755	1831
Thionville d.	1121	...	1157	1225	...	1254	1318	1351	1351	1434	1452	1559	...	1619	1636	...	1658	1703	1703	1724	...	1759	1759	...	1823	1900
Hagondange d.	│	...	1206	1234	...	1305	1330	1400	1400	1445	│	1608	...	1628	│	...	1709	1714	1714	1734	...	1807	1808	...	1834	1909
Metz a.	1141	...	1220	1246	...	1319	1347	1416	1416	1504	1512	1620	...	1639	1655	...	1727	1726	1726	1746	...	1821	1821	...	1854	1921
Metz d.	...	1157	1222	...	1301	1321	...	...	1421	1524	...	1624	1633	...	...	1700	1730	1729	1729	...	1800	1823	1824	1843	1900	1924
Pont-à-Mousson d.	...	1216	1246	...	1323	1342	...	...	1445z	1544	...	1644	│	...	...	1718	1754	1754	1754	...	1818	1846	1846	1901	1921	1944
Nancy a.	...	1231	1302	...	1339	1358	...	...	1501z	1602	...	1701	1709	...	...	1737	1814	1813	1813	...	1835	1905	1905	1919	1939	2000

	H	Ⓐ			A x	A	⑦ y	⚒	†	A	H v	🚌	⑦ e
Luxembourg d.	1840	...	1939	...	2015	2059	2115	...	...	2145	2215	...	2235
Thionville d.	1907	...	2003	...	2040	2124	2137	2142‡	...	2210	2241	...	2255
Hagondange d.	1919	...	2012	...	2050	2133	2148	2153	...	2222	2250	...	2305
Metz a.	1933	...	2023	...	2108	2145	2207	2211	...	2237	2302	...	2317
Metz d.	...	1953	2025	2116	2116	...	...	2214	2224	...	...	2314	...
Pont-à-Mousson d.	...	2014	2046	2145	2145	...	...	2233	2245	...	...	2359	...
Nancy a.	...	2030	2102	2215	2215	...	...	2251	2301	...	...	0051	...

	H	A	A	H	L	H	⑥ k	A	⑥ h r
Nancy d.	...	...	...	...	0540	0621	...	0640	0644
Pont-à-Mousson d.	...	...	...	...	0604	0638	...	0701	0704
Metz a.	...	...	...	...	0632	0657	...	0730	0731
Metz d.	...	0531	0554	0623	0635	0700	0719	0737	0743
Hagondange d.	...	0543	0610	0641	0650	0712	0738	0750	0754
Thionville d.	0533	0553	0619	0653	0700	0727	0751	0759	0804
Luxembourg a.	0600	0620	0647	0719	0729	0751	0817	0829	0832

	⚒	Ⓐ r	H	A	⑦ y	Ⓐ	Ⓐ		296 Ⓐ S	Ⓐ d	Ⓒ	Ⓐ	A m	C			Ⓐ		A		Ⓐ	C		90 B	A	Ⓐ
Nancy d.	0657	0704	0721	...	0721	0755	...	0821	...	0855	0917	0953	...	1021	1122	...	1149	1223	1254	1321	1418	1418	1521	...	...	1552
Pont-à-Mousson d.	0714	│	0741	...	0751	0812	...	0837	...	0915	0934	1011	...	1039	1140	...	1206	1242	1310	1338	1435	1436	1539	...	...	1609
Metz a.	0737	0742	0800	...	0821	0832	...	0856	...	0933	0953	1032	...	1057	1159	...	1223	1259	1328	1357	1454	1455	1558	...	...	1626
Metz d.	...	0746	0802	0818	...	...	0841	0900	0915	...	...	...	1052	1100	1201	1218	...	1301	1330	1400	1500	1458	1601	1609	1624	...
Hagondange d.	...	0800	0815	0836	...	...	0852	0912	│	...	...	...	1113	1113	1214	1234	...	1314	1345	1413	1514	1510	1612	│	1640	...
Thionville d.	...	0810	0825	0849	...	...	0900	0923	0935	...	...	...	1127	1126	1224	1248	...	1324	1358	1424	1532j	1532j	1623	1629	1654	...
Luxembourg a.	...	...	0851	0914	...	...	...	0945	0958	...	...	...	1159	1147	1245	1315	...	1346	1421	1445	1551	1551	1646	1649	1717	...

	A		Ⓐ	Ⓐ	A		Ⓑ	A	⚒	† g	96 B	Ⓐ	A	Ⓒ r	Ⓐ		294 † S	Ⓐ	⑥ r	† r	298 Ⓐ S	Ⓐ	Ⓐ	Ⓐ	¶	🚌
Nancy d.	...	1621	...	1650	...	1721	1744	...	1819	1821	...	1853	...	1921	1921	...	...	2021	2021	2021	...	...	2053	2200	...	2255
Pont-à-Mousson d.	...	1638	...	1708	...	1738	1805	...	1838	1838	...	1911	...	1938	1938	...	...	2038	2038	2037	...	...	2126	2217	...	2346
Metz a.	...	1657	...	1728	...	1757	1828	...	1857	1857	...	1933	...	1957	1957	...	...	2057	2057	2058	...	...	2200	2238	...	0040
Metz d.	1645	1700	1718	...	1739	1759	...	1838	1900	1900	1910	...	1942	1959	2000	2020	2033	2100	2100	2100	2118	2128	2222	...	2321	...
Hagondange d.	1659	1713	1732	...	1750	1813	...	1850	1914	1913	│	...	1954	2011	2014	2038	│	2112	2114	2113	│	2146	2235	...	2341	...
Thionville d.	1711	1732j	1743	...	1800	1832j	...	1905	1934j	1934j	1929	...	2007	2032j	2032j	2048	2055	2132j	2127	2132j	2139	2156	2242	...	2354	...
Luxembourg a.	1732	1759	...	...	1829	1859	...	1930	1959	1959	1949	...	2035	2053	2053	...	2117	2153	2147	2153	2200	...	...	...	0019	...

A – ①–⑤ (not Aug. 15).
B – [12] Basel - Brussels and v.v. (Table **43**).
C – ⑥⑦ (also Aug. 15).
D – ⑤–⑦ (also July 14; not July 11, Sept. 5).
E – ①–⑥.
H – ①–⑥ (not Aug. 15, Nov. 1).
L – ①–⑤ (not ②–⑤ July 15 - Aug. 1, Aug. 15).
S – To/from Strasbourg (Table **383**).

b – To Strasbourg and Basel (Table **383**).
d – To/from St Dié (Table **387**).
e – Also Aug. 15, Nov. 1; not Aug. 10, 17, Sept. 7, 14.
g – From Sept. 7.
h – Not Aug. 16, Nov. 1.
j – Arrives 11–13 minutes earlier.
k – Not Nov. 1.

m – Not July 21 - Aug. 29.
r – To/from Remiremont (Table **386**).
t – Also Aug. 15.
v – Not Aug. 9, 16, Sept. 6, 13.
w – Not June 23.
x – Not July 18.
y – Also Aug. 15, Nov. 1.
z – 7–8 minutes later July 4 - Aug. 31.

¶ – Not July 28 - Aug. 1, Aug. 9, 10, 16, 1 Sept. 6, 7, 13, 14, 22–26, Sept. 29 - Oct. 3, Nov. 12–14, 17–21.
‡ – 2141 on July 12, Oct. 31.

Subject to alteration until approximately 1700 on Oct. 12, 19, 26, Nov. 2, 9.

Local Services

STRASBOURG - MULHOUSE - BASEL 385

For *TGV* trains Paris - Strasbourg - Colmar see Table **390**. For *TGV* trains Paris - Dijon - Mulhouse - Basel see Table **370**.

km		Ⓐ	Ⓐ	⑥ k	Ⓐ	①–⑥	Ⓑ q	⑥ k	Ⓐ	Ⓐ ◇	Ⓒ	Ⓐ		◇	Ⓐ	Ⓒ		Ⓒ	Ⓐ ◇	Ⓐ	Ⓒ		91 nB	Ⓐ	Ⓒ	⑥⑦
	Luxembourg 384 d.	...	...	...	...	...	...	...	...	...	...	...	...	...	...	...	...	...	...	...	...	...	1100	...	...	...
	Metz 383 d.	...	...	...	...	...	...	...	...	...	...	...	...	...	...	...	...	...	...	...	...	...	1144c	...	...	...
0	**Strasbourg** ◧ d.	...	0518	0551	0621	...	0651	0651	0721	0751	0751	0821	...	0851	0951	0951	...	1051	1051	1151	1151	...	1311	1351	1351	...
43	Sélestat ◧ d.	...	0538	0616	0640	...	0710	0711	0740	0812	0816	0840	...	0910	1010	1016	...	1110	1111	1210	1216	...	1339	1410	1416	...
65	Colmar ◧ d.	...	0550	0628	0653	...	0723	0723	0753	0824	0828	0853	...	0923	1023	1028	...	1123	1123	1223	1228	...	1352	1423	1428	...
106	**Mulhouse** ▷ d.	0546	0616	0654	0716	0719	0746	0746	0816	0846	0855	0916	0919	0946	1046	1055	1119	1146	1146	1246	1255	1319	1415	1446	1455	1519
140	**Basel** ▷ a.	0611	0639	...	0739	0750	0809	0820	0839	0909	...	0939	0950	1009	1109	...	1150	1209	1209	1309	...	1350	1438	1509	...	1550

		†	Ⓐ	⑥ k	Ⓑ q		Ⓒ	295 Ⓐ	Ⓐ	Ⓑ q	⑥ k	97 B	Ⓑ q	⑥ k	Ⓐ	Ⓐ	†	Ⓑ q	⑥ k	Ⓒ z	Ⓐ ◇	Ⓐ	† z	y	† z	Ⓐ ⊡
Luxembourg 384 d.	...	...	...	...	...	...	...	1430	...	...	...	1615	...	...	...	...	...	...	...	...	...	...	...	...	...	...
Metz 383 d.	...	...	...	...	...	...	...	1515	...	...	...	1657b	...	...	...	...	...	...	...	...	...	...	...	...	...	...
Strasbourg ◧ d.	1451	1551	1551	1551	1621	...	1651	1651	1721	1751	1751	1820	1851	1851	1921	...	1921	1951	1951	2051	2051	2122	2122	2221	2251	2321
Sélestat ◧ d.	1510	1610	1610	1616	1640	...	1710	1712	1740	1810	1816	1841	1910	1916	1940	...	1940	2010	2016	2110	2112	2147	2149	2246	2310	2346
Colmar ◧ d.	1523	1621	1623	1627	1653	...	1723	1723	1753	1823	1828	1853	1923	1927	1953	...	1953	2023	2028	2123	2125	2159	2202	2259	2323	0000
Mulhouse ▷ d.	1546	1646	1646	1653	1716	1719	1746	1746	1816	1846	1855	1916	1946	1955	2014	2019	2025j	2046	2055	2146	2147	2221	2225	2320e	2344	0020
Basel ▷ a.	1609	1709	1709	...	1739	1750	1809	1809	1839	1909	...	1942	2009	...	...	2050	2048	2109	...	2209	2209	...	...	...	...	...

	Ⓐ	⑥ k	Ⓐ	Ⓐ	296 Ⓐ		①–⑥	Ⓐ	Ⓒ	Ⓐ	Ⓐ	†	⚒ ‡		Ⓐ	Ⓐ	⑥ d	⑦	Ⓐ	Ⓒ	Ⓐ		Ⓒ	Ⓐ		90 nB
Basel ▷ d.	...	...	0521	0537	...	0622	0639	0651	...	0721	0751	0821	0821	0839	0851	...	...	...	0921	1021	1021	1039	...	1121	1221	1316
Mulhouse ▷ d.	0501r	0533	0545	0600	0616	0646	0710	0716	0730	0746	0816	0846	0848	0910	0916	0923	0932	0935	0946	1046	1046	1110	1135	1146	1246	1341
Colmar ◧ d.	0521	0559	0604	0629	0644	0707	...	0737	0757	0807	0837	0907	0908	...	0936	0958	0957	1002	1006	1107	1109	...	1202	1207	1307	1403
Sélestat ◧ d.	0534	0611	0616	0642	0656	0719	...	0749	0809	0819	0849	0919	0920	...	0947	|	1010	1014	1017	1119	1121	...	1214	1219	1319	1416
Strasbourg ◧ a.	0600	0637	0636	0709	0724	0739	...	0809	0835	0839	0909	0939	0939	...	1007	1034	1037	1039	1037	1139	1141	...	1239	1239	1339	1437
Metz 383 a.	...	...	...	...	0914	...	...	...	...	...	...	...	...	...	...	...	...	...	...	...	...	...	...	...	...	1607
Luxembourg 384 a.	...	...	...	...	0958	...	...	...	...	...	...	...	...	...	...	...	...	...	...	...	...	...	...	...	...	1649

	Ⓒ ⊗	Ⓐ	⑥⑦	Ⓒ	Ⓐ	Ⓐ	96 B		Ⓑ q	⑥ k	Ⓑ q	Ⓑ q◇			⑥ k	Ⓑ q	①–⑤	Ⓑ q	⑥ k	⑤ f	Ⓐ	† z	⑥ p	①–⑤	Ⓐ	† z
Basel ▷ d.	...	1421	1439	...	1521	1551	1618	1639	1651	...	1721	1751	1821	1839	...	1921	1939	...	1951	2021	2039	2121	...	2239	...	...
Mulhouse ▷ d.	1434	1446	1510	1532	1546	1616	1646	1710	1716	1735	1746	1816	1846	1910	1935	1946	2010	2016	2016	2046	2116	2146	2316	2310	2330	2338
Colmar ◧ d.	1501	1507	...	1558	1606	1637	1707	...	1737	1802	1807	1837	1907	...	2002	2007	...	2037	2037	2107	2136	2207	2344	...	2358	0006
Sélestat ◧ d.	1513	1519	...	1610	1617	1649	1719	...	1749	1814	1819	1849	1919	...	2014	2019	...	2049	2049	2119	2148	2219	2358	...	0013	0020
Strasbourg ◧ a.	1539	1539	...	1636	1637	1709	1740	...	1809	1839	1839	1909	1939	...	2039	2039	...	2110	2110	2139	2214	2239	0026	...	0040	0048
Metz 383 a.	...	...	...	...	...	...	1908	...	...	...	...	...	...	...	...	...	...	...	...	...	...	...	...	...	...	...
Luxembourg 384 a.	...	...	...	...	...	...	1949	...	...	...	...	...	...	...	...	...	...	...	...	...	...	...	...	...	...	...

B – 🚃12 Basel - Brussels and v.v. (Table **43**).
– To July 11 and from Aug. 25.
– 1656 July 8 - Aug. 21.
– 1142 on ①-⑤ Aug. 5-21.
– Also July 14, Aug. 15, Nov. 11.
– Not July 6-10, 13, 15, 16, 17.
– Not Aug. 15.
– Arrives 2014.
– Not Nov. 1.

n – Not Oct. 12, 19, 26, Nov. 2, 9.
p – Not Aug. 23, 30, Sept. 6, 20, Nov. 1, 22.
q – Also Nov. 1.
r – Not July 7 – 11, 16, 17, 18.
y – Not Aug. 23, 24, 30, 31, Sept. 6, 7, 20, 21, Oct. 19, Nov. 22, 23.
z – Not Aug. 24, 31, Sept.7, 21, Oct. 19, Nov. 23.

◧ – For *TGV* trains see Table **390**.
◇ – To/from Nancy (Table **383**).
⊗ – Runs 9 minutes **earlier** on Aug. 15, Nov. 11.

‡ – Runs 3 minutes later Mulhouse - Strasbourg on Ⓐ Sept. 2 - Oct. 31.
⊡ – On July 7 – 10, 15, 16, 17 runs Strasbourg - Colmar only.

▷ – **Additional local trains** Mulhouse - Basel and v.v. (journey 31 minutes):
From Mulhouse at 0449①–⑤**L**, 0549①–⑥, 0619, 0649①–⑤**L**, 0749Ⓑ, 0819①–⑤**L**, 1219①–⑤**L**, 1419①–⑤**L**, 1419⑥, 1549①–⑤, 1619①–⑥, 1649①–⑤**L**, 1749①–⑤, 1819①–⑤**L**, 1819⑥, 1849①–⑤, 1919, 1949①–⑤**L**.
From Basel at 0609①–⑤**L**, 0709, 0739①–⑤**L**, 0809①–⑥, 1139①–⑤**L**, 1239, 1339①–⑤**L**, 1539①–⑥, 1609①–⑤**L**, 1709①–⑤, 1739①–⑤**L**, 1739⑥, 1809①–⑤, 1909①–⑤**L**, 2039⑥⑦, 2139①–⑤**L**.

NANCY - ÉPINAL - REMIREMONT 386

Services between Épinal and Remiremont are subject to alteration on Ⓐ July 7 - Aug. 29

km		Ⓐ z◇	Ⓐ d	⚒	⚒	† yL	⚒		⚒ ❖	❖	†	⚒ ❖	❖	⚒ ❖	⚒	2571 ♥		Ⓐ	Ⓐ		Ⓐ	Ⓐ	Ⓑ	⑥	Ⓐ ◇	⚒
	Paris Est 390 d.	...	...	...	...	...	...	...	...	...	...	...	...	...	...	1213	...	...	...	...	...	...	...	...	...	...
0	**Nancy** d.	0604	...	0620	0705	0708	0720	...	0820	0901	1006	1124	1206	1223	1303	1347	1406	1506	...	1606	1620	1703	1720	1720	1750	1806
74	Épinal a.	0707	...	0721	0759	0758	0818	...	0914	0952	1100	1215	1300	1331	1400	1428	1459	1559	...	1659	1720	1759	1820	1827	1844	1859
74	Épinal d.	...	0720	...	0801	0800	...	...	0916	1002	1102	1229	1302	...	...	1431	1501	...	1616	1701	...	1801	...	...	...	1901
100	**Remiremont** a.	...	0750	...	0825	0825	...	...	0940	1028	1125	1254	1333	...	...	1452	1525	...	1645	1724	...	1830	...	...	...	1926

	Ⓐ	Ⓒ	Ⓐ	2573 Ⓒ ♥	2573 Ⓐ ♥	Ⓐ		P	⑤⑦ u	
Paris Est 390 d.	...	...	...	1813	1813	...	...	...	...	...
Nancy d.	1820	1905	1920	1947	1952	2016	2122	2215	2258	...
Épinal a.	1920	1959	2015	2028	2032	2110	2214	2313	2354	...
Épinal d.	...	2001	2016	2031	2035q	...	2216	...	...	...
Remiremont a.	...	2028	2040	2052	2056q	...	2240	...	...	...

	Ⓐ d	⑥ vL	Ⓐ M	2574 Ⓐ ♥	Ⓐ	⑥ k		⚒	⚒	⚒ w	⑦ t	2576 Ⓒ ♥
Remiremont d.	...	0513	0535	0600r	...	...	0629	0700	...	0830	0840	0906
Épinal a.	...	0537	0559	0620r	...	...	0657	0728	...	0854	0904	0925
Épinal d.	0505	0539	0601	0623	0628	0630	0659	0738	0800	0856	0906	0928
Nancy a.	0558	0642	0659	0705	0732	0739	0755	0838	0856	0950	0958	1011
Paris Est 390 a.	...	...	...	0846	...	...	...	...	...	...	...	1146

	Ⓐ ❖	❖	⚒ ❖	⚒ ❖	❖	Ⓐ ❖		⚒	2578 A ♥	Ⓐ	⚒	†	Ⓐ	Ⓒ	2580 ⑦ e♥	Ⓐ	⑥ kL	† L	Ⓐ	Ⓐ	⑥ kL	† L	⚒	①–④ m	⑤ R◇	⑦ Q◇
Remiremont d.	...	1040	...	...	1218	1413	...	1536	1604	...	...	1630	1649	...	1726	1730	1730	1742	...	1837	1835	1842	1934	...	...	...
Épinal a.	...	1104	...	...	1251	1438	...	1600	1625	...	...	1657	1717	...	1746	1758	1758	1810	...	1902	1900	1904	1958	...	...	...
Épinal d.	1000	1105	1200	1238	1253	...	1500	1602	1627	1637	1656	1659	1719	1725	1749	1800	1800	1812	1841	1904	1901	1906	2000	2138	2138	2138
Nancy a.	1054	1200	1253	1339	1350	...	1559	1654	1709	1739	1753	1753	1830	1824	1831	1853	1857	1906	1939	1957	1957	2001	2057	2230	2234	2234
Paris Est 390 a.	...	...	...	...	...	...	...	...	1846	...	...	...	...	...	2016	...	...	...	...	...	...	...	...	...	...	...

– ①–⑥ to July 5; ⑤⑥ July 11 - Aug. 23; ①–⑥ from Aug. 29 (not Nov. 11).
– To/from Luxembourg (Table **384**).
– To Metz and Thionville (Table **384**).
– ①②③④⑥ to July 5; ⑥ July 12 - Aug. 23; ①②③④⑥ from Aug. 30 (not Oct. 27 - Nov. 6, Nov. 11).

Q – ⑦ from Aug. 31 (also Nov. 11).
R – From Aug. 29.

d – Not ②–⑤ July 8 - Aug. 29.
e – Also July 14, Nov. 11.
k – Not Nov. 1.
m – Not July 14, Nov. 11.

q – Not July 7 - Aug. 28.
r – Ⓐ to July 7; ① July 21 - Aug. 25; Ⓐ from Sept. 1.
t – Also July 14, Aug. 15, Nov. 11.
u – Also Nov. 1, 11; not ⑤ July 11 - Aug. 29, Oct. 31, Nov. 7.
v – Not July 12 - Aug. 30, Nov. 1.

w – Also Nov. 1.
y – Not Oct. 12 - Nov. 9.
z – Not ① June 16 - Aug. 25.

❖ – Subject to alteration on ①–⑤ Oct. 27 - Nov. 7.
♥ – *TGV* train, 🅁, 🍸, supplement payable.
◇ – To/from Belfort on dates in Table **386a**.

ÉPINAL - BELFORT 386a

SERVICE FROM AUG. 30 (please check locally for service until Aug. 29).

km		R	① g	Ⓑ		Ⓑ s		⑤		
0	*Nancy 386* d.	...	0604	...	...	...	...	1750	...	...
74	**Épinal** d.	0627	0712	0957	...	1435	...	1849	1849	...
32	Luxeuil les Bains d.	0712	0800	1042	...	1520	...	1939	1939	...
50	Lure 380 d.	0726	0813	1056	...	1534	...	1953	1953	...
82	**Belfort** 380 a.	0758	0834	1128	...	1558h	...	2025	2025	...

	Ⓐ		b		Ⓑ		⑦ c	⑤	P
Belfort 380 d.	0601	...	1101	...	1704	...	2001	2007	2035
Lure 380 d.	0632	...	1132	...	1735	...	2032	2038	2107
Luxeuil les Bains d.	0646	...	1146	...	1748	...	2045	2051	2120
Épinal a.	0733	...	1233	...	1836	...	2133	2136	2206
Nancy 386 a.	...	...	...	...	...	...	2234	2234	...

– ①②③④⑥ (not Nov. 1, 10, 11).
– ②–⑥ (not Nov. 1, 11, 12).

b – Not Dec. 13.
c – Also Nov. 11.

g – Also Nov. 12.
h – Not ①–⑤ Sept. 15 - Oct. 24, Nov. 10 – 14, 17 – 21.

s – Not ①–⑤ Oct. 13 – 24.

387 NANCY - LUNÉVILLE - ST DIÉ

km											2591									2593					2595	
		⚒	⚒	Ⓐ		Ⓒ	Ⓐ		Ⓐ		⑦	⚒	†	Ⓐ	Ⓐ	Ⓒ		⚒	†	Ⓐ	Ⓒ	Ⓐ	Ⓐ	†	⑦	⚒
											e♥				m					♥					e♥	
	Paris Est **390** d.	...	...	...	...	...	...	...	...	...	1413	...	...	...	...	...	...	...	...	1813	...	...	...	...	2013	...
0	**Nancy** **383** d.	0550	0628	0800	0905	1035	1201	1230	1257	1400	1554	1600	1625	1659	1726	1735	1756	1857	1857	1947	1956	1958	2126	2130	2154	2232
33	Lunéville **383** d.	0615	0655	0825	0928	1109	1222	1248	1322	1422	1614	1619	1647	1722	1747	1755	1821	1918	1921	|	2021	2039	2146	2205	|	2305
84	**St Dié** a.	0712	0804	0914	1010	...	1318	1345	1402	1509	1644	1715	1739	1820	1848	1900	1914	2013	2014	2035	2102	2123	2224	...	2242	...

						2596	2596														2598				
	⚒	Ⓐ		Ⓐ	⑥	†	⑥	Ⓐ	Ⓐ	⑥		Ⓒ		Ⓐ		Ⓐ	⚒	†	⚒	†	⚒	⑦		†	Ⓐ	
					n		k♥	♥	m	n												e♥				
St Dié d.	0521	0611	...	0637	0638	0644	0716	0720	0729	0730	0855	1050	...	1202	1214	1448	...	1545	1558	1615	1640	1742	1757	...	1853	1944
Lunéville **383** d.	0610	0655	0658	0738	0739	0736	|	|	0818	0817	0948	1129	1151	1242	1309	1541	1551	1633	1641	1714	1742	1814	1843	1918	1950	2042
Nancy **383** a.	0632	0714	0727	0759	0759	0800	0804	0810	0842	0842	1006	1152	1224	1303	1330	1607	1624	1655	1702	1734	1800	1835	1901	1957	2014	2101
Paris Est **390** a.	...	...	...	...	...	...	0946	0945	...	...	...	...	...	...	...	...	...	...	...	...	...	2016	...	...	...	...

e – Also July 14, Nov. 11.
k – Also Aug. 15; not Aug. 16.
m – From / to Metz (Table **384**).
n – Not Nov. 1.
w – Also July 14, Nov. 11; not July 13.
♥ – *TGV* train, 🅁, 🍸, supplement payable.

388 STRASBOURG - ST DIÉ

km		Ⓐ❖	Ⓐ	⑥n	†	Ⓐ	Ⓐ	⑥n	†	Ⓐ	
0	**Strasbourg** d.	0520	0655	0855	0955	0955	1205	1255	1355	1555	1755
9	Entzheim Aéroport ✈ ‡ d.	0528	0705	0904	1006	1003	1213	1304	1406	1604	1805
19	Molsheim d.	0541	0714	0912	1016	1012	1221	1313	1417	1615	1813
87	**St Dié** a.	*0727*r	0840	1033	1124	1132	1351	1437	1529	1736	1929

	Ⓐ❖	Ⓑp	⑥n	⚒	Ⓐ	⑥n	†	†	Ⓐ	⑥n	†
St Dié d.	0734	0857t	0909	1212j	1538	1610	1653	1755	1802	1832	1956
Molsheim d.	0846	1010t	1023	1335	1704	1724	1806	1920	1916	1957	2106
Entzheim Aéroport ✈ ‡ d.	0854	1018t	1030	1342	1712	1732	1815	1929	1924	2005	2115
Strasbourg a.	0901	1026	1040	1351	1721	1740	1826	1939	1932	2015	2126

j – 1216 on ⑥.
n – Not Nov. 1.
p – Also Nov. 1.
r – Change trains at Rothau (a. 0610, d. 0639).
t – On † departs St Dié 0856, Molsheim 1006, Entzheim 1015.
‡ – Trains run between Strasbourg and Entzheim Aéroport approx. 3 per hour on Ⓐ, 2 per hour on ⑥, 1 per hour on †.
❖ – Subject to alteration June 23 - Aug. 22.

Services are subject to alteration June 23 - Aug. 1 (also on ①–⑤ Oct. 6 – 17)

388a ST DIÉ - ÉPINAL

km		⚒	Ⓐ	⑥n	Ⓐ❖	†	†	Ⓐ	Ⓐ	⑥n	Ⓐ	†
0	**St Dié** d.	0600	0738	1038	1216	1333	1612	1645	1825	1905	1942	1954
60	**Épinal** a.	0705	0844	1145	1326	1438	1716	1750	1932	2010	2049	2100

	Ⓐ	⚒	†	⚒❖	†	Ⓐ	⑥	Ⓐ	†	⚒
Épinal d.	0558	0738	1025	1220	1452	1644	1710	1825	1834	2042
St Dié a.	0708	0846	1130	1325	1557	1752	1815	1934	1939	2151

n – Not Nov. 1.
❖ – Subject to alteration on Ⓐ Oct. 6 - Dec. 5.
☛ All services are subject to alteration July 6 - Aug. 29.

389 PARIS - REIMS - CHARLEVILLE MÉZIÈRES - SEDAN

SERVICE FROM JULY 7

km					TGV 2709		TGV 2713	TGV 2715				TGV 2733			TGV 2777			TGV 2743					TGV 2747		TGV 2751	TGV 2753
		Ⓐ	⚒	Ⓐ	①–⑥		①–⑥	⑦	①⑤	⑥			⚒	†		Ⓐ	⚒			⚒	⑦	Ⓐ	Ⓑ	Ⓑ	N	⑤
					b		b	e	Q		◇			q					♥	s	m		h	q		f
0	**Paris** Est d.	...	...	...	0758	...	1028	1028	...	...	...	1258	...	...	1358	...	...	1528	...	...	...	...	1728	...	1828	1828
	Épernay d.	...	0632a	...	|		|	|	...	...	...	|	1328n	...	|	...	...	|	...	1639	...	1715	|	...	|	|
136	Champ. Ardenne TGV § d.	...	|	...	|	0933	|	|	...	...	...	|	|	...	1438	1448	...	|	1632	|	...	|	|	...	|	|
147	**Reims** § a.	...	0703a	...	0844	0940	1116	1116	...	...	...	1344	1352n	...	...	1455	...	1616	1639	1711	...	1750	1816	...	1916	1916
147	**Reims** d.	0632	0706	0740	0848	0943	...	1120	1130	1130	1232	...	1354	1354	...	1500	1622	...	1651	1718	1729	1752	...	1828	1921	1921
186	Rethel d.	0655	0728	0804	0912	1005	...	1143	1153	1153	1255	...	1417	1417	...	1522	1645	...	1716	1743	1750	1818	...	1852	1943	1943
235	**Charleville-Mézières** a.	0728	0758	0836	0939	1034	...	1209	1220	1220	1326	...	1444	1444	...	1549	1713	...	1745	1816	1819	1844	...	1924	2010	2010
255	**Sedan** a.	0752	0820	0903a	1002	1058g	...	...	...	1255	1350c	...	1511g	1511	...	1615	1736	...	1814	1845	1838	...	...	1950	2033	...

		TGV 2785			TGV 2757		TGV 2787		TGV 2759		TGV 2765
		Ⓐ		①–④	⑤⑦	⑤⑦	⑦	⑤⑦	P	M	⑤⑦
				¶	r	r	d	r			r
Paris Est d.	...	1928	...	...	1958	...	2028	...	2058	...	2128
Épernay d.	1903	|	...	...	|	...	|	...	|	...	|
Champ. Ardenne TGV § d.	|	2009	2019	2019	|	...	2108	2113	|	...	|
Reims § a.	1938	...	2028	2028	2044	...	...	2121	2144	...	2216
Reims d.	1947	...	...	2037	...	2054	...	2124	...	2154	2220
Rethel d.	2013	...	...	2102	...	2118	...	2148	...	2220	2242
Charleville-Mézières a.	2039	...	...	2129	...	2144	...	2214	...	2247	2310
Sedan a.	2103	...	...	...	...	2205k	...	2236	...	2310	2333

	TGV 2706		TGV 2778			TGV 2712	TGV 2714			TGV 272
	Ⓐ	①–⑥	①–⑥	Ⓐ	⑥	①–⑥	Ⓐ	Ⓐ		Ⓒ
			t		z	b				
Sedan d.	...	0529	...	0602	0606	...	0658	0702	0734	0758
Charleville-Mézières d.	*0541*	0600	...	0624	0629	...	0720	0736	0802	0820
Rethel d.	*0608*	0630	...	0657	0703	...	0749	0808	0832	084
Reims a.	*0632*	0653	...	0721	0729	...	0810	0831	0856	091
Reims § d.	0643	0655t	...	0730	...	0743	0815	...	0900	091
Champ. Ardenne TGV § d.	|	0705t	0721	|	...	|	|	...	0912	|
Épernay a.	|	...	|	0807	...	|	|	...	...	|
Paris Est a.	0731	...	0801	...	...	0831	0901	...	...	100

			TGV 2722	TGV 2724			TGV 2738				TGV 2752	TGV 2754		TGV 2784			TGV 2756	TGV 2760	TGV 2762					TGV 2764		TG 276
	⚒	⑦	①–⑥	⑦		Ⓑ	Ⓑ		⑦	Ⓐ	①–⑥	⑦	⚒		⑦	Ⓐ	⑤⑦	P	⑤		†	⑥	Ⓐ	⑦		⑦
		e	b	e	q◇	◇	h		m		b	e	s		m		r		f			w		e		e
Sedan d.	0851	1021	1022	...	1116g	1211g	...	1450•	1547	1547•	...	...	1633	...	1702	1702k	...	...	...	1801	1848	1848	1852	...	2013	205
Charleville-Mézières d.	0910	1045	1045	...	1138	1240	...	1511	1608	1608	...	1619	1700	...	1722	1722	...	...	...	1834	1907	1907	1910	...	2038	212
Rethel d.	0941	1112	1114	...	1205	1314	...	1542	1637	1642	...	1648	1730	...	1756	1757	...	...	...	1907	1937	1937	1938	...	2106	214
Reims a.	1002	1132	1138	...	1228	1340	...	1605	1700	1705	...	1710	1751	...	1820	1824	...	...	...	1929	1957	1957	1959	...	2127	221
Reims § d.	1004‡	...	1143	1143	1237v	...	1415	...	1727	1735	1715	1715	1753	...	...	1828	1843	1915	1944	1932	1959	1959k	2000k	2015	...	221
Champ. Ardenne TGV § d.	|	...	|	|	|	...	|	...	1741	1744	|	|	1805	1820	...	|	|	|	|	1944	|	|	|	|	...	|
Épernay a.	1030‡	...	|	|	1313v	...	|	...	...	...	|	|	...	|	...	1910	|	|	|	...	2032	2032k	2031k	|	...	|
Paris Est a.	...	...	1231	1231	...	...	1501	...	...	...	1801	1801	...	1901	...	...	1931	2001	2031	...	...	...	...	2101	...	230

M – ①②③④⑥ (also Aug. 15; not July 5, 14, Aug. 14, Nov. 11).
N – ①②③④⑥⑦ (also Aug. 15; not Aug. 14).
P – ①②③④⑥ (also Aug. 15; not July 14, Aug. 14, Nov. 11).
Q – ①⑤ (not July 14). Subject to alteration from Oct. 13.

a – Ⓐ (not July 7 - Aug. 29).
b – Not July 14, Nov. 11.
c – ⑥⑦ (also July 14, Aug. 15).
d – Also July 14, Nov. 11; not July 13, Nov. 9.
e – Also July 14, Nov. 11.
f – Also Aug. 14; not Aug. 15.
g – Not Sept. 15 – 19.
h – Not Aug. 15.
j – Ⓑ until Oct. 12; † from Oct. 19.
k – From Aug. 25.
m – Also July 14, Aug. 15, Nov. 11.
n – Not ①–⑤ Sept. 22 - Oct. 24.
q – Not Nov. 11.
r – Also July 14, Aug. 14, Nov. 11; not Aug. 15.
s – Also Nov. 1.
t – Not July 14, Aug. 16, Oct. 11, Nov. 10, 11.
v – Ⓒ (also Sept. 15 – 19).
w – Not Nov. 1.
z – Also Aug. 15.
TGV – 🅁, supplement payable, 🍸.
‡ – Not ①–⑤ Oct. 7 – 24.
• – Not Sept. 15, 16.
¶ – Not July 14, Aug. 14, Nov. 11.
◇ – Subject to alteration on Ⓐ from Oct. 13.
⊖ – Subject to alteration on Ⓐ from Oct. 27.
⊠ – Subject to alteration July 28 - Aug. 1, Sept. 15 – 19, Sept. 29 - Oct. 3, Oct. 6 – 10 and ①–⑤ from Oct. 27.
☆ – 2 Longwy - Metz and v.v. (see bo directions of Table).
⊗ – Runs 26 – 52 minutes later on ⑤ fro July 11 (not calling at Hayange).
♥ – Runs 2 – 4 minutes earlier Reims - Sedan on ⑤ from July 11 (not Aug. 1
§ – For full service see Table **391a**.

389a CHARLEVILLE MÉZIÈRES - LONGWY and METZ

SERVICE FROM JULY

km		⚒	Ⓐ	⚒	†	⚒	⚒	⚒	⑦	
		☆			q	g⊠	☆	⊗	m	
	Reims **389** d.	...	0632	0706	1354	1354	...	1622	1729	1947
0	**Charleville-Mézières** **389** d.	...	0733	0806	1449	1449	...	1718	1824	2044
20	Sedan **389** a.	...	0752	0820	1511	1511	...	1736	1838	2103
20	Sedan d.	...	0754	0821	1512	1512	...	1737	1839	2104
69	Montmédy d.	...	0825	0852	1543	1543	...	1808	1910	2134
91	Longuyon **392** d.	0633	0847	0906	1601	1602	1811	1822	1924	2153
107	**Longwy** **392** a.	|	0859	|	1614	1614	1823	|	|	2204
	Hayange d.	0703	...	0936	...	...	...	1851	1955	...
170	**Metz** a.	0733	...	1002	...	...	...	1915	2019	...

	Ⓐ	⚒	Ⓒ	⚒	Ⓑ⊖		Ⓒ	Ⓐ	⚒	
		☆			gs				☆	
Metz d.	...	...	...	0704	...	...	...	...	1714	183
Hayange d.	...	...	...	0732	...	...	...	...	1740	185
Longwy **392** d.	0548	0619	0645	|	1012	...	1745	1751	|	|
Longuyon **392** d.	0605	0632	0703	0801	1031	...	1802	1808	1810	19
Montmédy d.	0619	...	0717	0819	1044	...	1816	1822	...	19
Sedan a.	0649	...	0748	0850	1114	...	1847	1851	...	20
Sedan **389** d.	0702	...	0804	0851	1116	...	1848	1852	...	20
Charleville-Mézières **389** a.	0731	...	0819	0905	1133	...	1902	1906	...	20
Reims **389** a.	0831	...	...	1002	1228j	...	1957	1959	...	21

FOR NOTES SEE TABLE 389 ABOVE

☛ Subject to alteration on Nov. 9.

TGV EST EUROPÉEN 390

PARIS - STRASBOURG - COLMAR

For additional connections Strasbourg - Colmar see Table **385**

km	*TGV* trains convey 🍷	*TGV* 2403 ①–④ z	*TGV* 2363 ①–⑥ b	*TGV* 9571	*TGV* 2407	*TGV* 2365	*TGV* 9573	*TGV* 2369 ①–⑥ b	*TGV* 2433	*TGV* 2373 ⑦ e	*TGV* 9575 ⊙	*TGV* 2443	*TGV* 9577 Ⓑ c	*TGV* 2457 m	*TGV* 2377	*TGV* 2583 Ⓑ f ¶◇	*TGV* 2465 ⊗	*TGV* 2471 ⑤⑦ u
0	**Paris** Est ... d.	0625	0655	0725	0825	1055	1125	1255	1355	1455	1525	1655	1725	1755	1855	1913	2025	2155p
405	Saverne ... a.	|	|	|	|	|	|	|	1553	|	|	|	|	|	|	2153	|	|
450	**Strasbourg** ... a.	0844	0914	0942	1043	1314	1342	1514	1618	1714	1742	1914	1942	2014	2114	2219	2244	0014
450	**Strasbourg** ... 385 d.	...	0920	0947	...	1320	1347	1520	...	1720	1747	...	1947	...	2119x	...	...	...
	Stuttgart Hbf **931** ... a.	...	|	1104	...	|	1504‡	|	...	|	1904	...	2105‡	...	|	...	...	...
493	Sélestat ... 385 a.	...	|	...	...	|	...	|	...	|	...	...	...	...	2136x	...	...	...
515	**Colmar** ... 385 a.	...	0945	...	...	1346	...	1545	...	1745	...	...	...	...	2150x	...	...	...

	TGV 2400 ① G	*TGV* 2584 ①–⑥ b◇	*TGV* 2404 ①–⑤ n	*TGV* 2350 ①–⑥ b	*TGV* 2410 Ⓑ j	*TGV* 9578 ①–⑥	*TGV* 2420 ①–⑥ b	*TGV* 2354 ⑦ e	*TGV* 9576 ⊙	*TGV* 2356 ①–⑥ b	*TGV* 2424 ☆	*TGV* 9574	*TGV* 2358	*TGV* 2440 Ⓑ j⊖	*TGV* 2360 ①–⑥ b	*TGV* 2448 ⑦ e	*TGV* 2450 ⑦ w	*TGV* 2450 ⑤ f	*TGV* 2452 Ⓑ h	*TGV* 9572 ⑥⑦	*TGV* 2454 Ⓐ	*TGV* 2362 ⑦ e	*TGV* 9570 ①–⑤	*TGV* 2460 ⑥⑦	*TGV* 2470 ⑤ J	*TGV* 2474 ⑦ s
Colmar ... 385 d.	...	...	...	0608	...	...	...	0808	...	1011	...	...	1414	...	1614	...	...	...	...	...	...	1814	...	...	...	...
Sélestat ... 385 d.	...	...	...	0622	...	...	...	0821	...	|	...	...	|	...	|	...	...	...	...	...	...	|	...	...	...	...
Stuttgart Hbf **931** ... d.	...	...	...	|	...	0655*	...	|	0855	|	...	1255*	|	...	|	...	...	...	...	1655*	...	|	1855*	...	...	...
Strasbourg ... 385 a.	...	...	...	0640	...	0811	...	0840	1011	1040	...	1411	1440	...	1640	...	...	...	...	1811	...	1842	2011	...	...	...
Strasbourg ... d.	0541	0546	0616	0646	0716	0816	0846	0846	1016	1046	1142	1416	1446	1546	1646	1646	1712	1716	1746	1816	1846	1846	2016	2016	2046	2146
Saverne ... d.	|	0609	|	|	|	|	|	|	|	|	1208	|	|	|	|	|	1737	|	|	|	|	|	|	|	|	|
Paris Est ... a.	0805	0846	0835	0905	0935	1035	1105	1105	1235	1305	1406	1635	1705	1805	1905	1905	1935	1935	2005	2035	2105	2105	2235	2235	2305	0005

PARIS - METZ - LUXEMBOURG

km	*TGV* trains convey 🍷	*TGV* 2601 ① G	*TGV* 2803 ①–⑥ b	*TGV* 2809 △	*TGV* 2615 △	*TGV* 2827 △	*TGV* 2621 ①–④ q	*TGV* 2821 ⑤–⑦ t	*TGV* 2831 Ⓑ j	*TGV* 2633	*TGV* 2835	*TGV* 2839 Ⓑ f	*TGV* 2843 ⑦ e	*TGV* 2643 ①–⑥ b	*TGV* 2647 ⑤⑦ r
0	**Paris** Est ... 381 d.	0640	0740	0840	1040	1340	1540	1540	1640	1740	1840	1940	2040	2040	2140
136	Champagne-Ardenne TGV ... 381 d.	|	|	0923	|	|	|	|	|	|	|	|	|	|	|
236	Meuse TGV ... a.	|	|	|	|	|	|	|	|	1839	|	|	|	|	|
315	**Metz** ... a.	0804	0904	1011	1204	1504	1704	1704	1805	1911	2004	2104	2204	2204	2304
315	**Metz** ... 384 d.	...	0908	1015	...	1508	...	1708	1809	...	2008	2108	2208	...	...
345	Thionville ... 384 a.	...	0925	1033	...	1525	...	1725	1825	...	2025	2125	2225	...	...
379	**Luxembourg** ... 384 a.	...	0948	1059	...	1548	...	1748	1848	...	2048	2148	2248	...	...

	TGV 2650 ① g	*TGV* 2650 ②–⑤ o	*TGV* 2853 Ⓐ	*TGV* 2855 ①–⑥ b	*TGV* 2654 ⑦ e△	*TGV* 2660 ②–⑤ o	*TGV* 2861 A △	*TGV* 2865 △	*TGV* 2869 △	*TGV* 2672 v△	*TGV* 2881	*TGV* 2684 ⑤⑦ §	*TGV* 2877 ⑤⑦ f t	*TGV* 2676 E	*TGV* 2682 ⑦ e	*TGV* 2891 Ⓐ	*TGV* 2893 ⑦ w
Luxembourg ... 384 d.	...	...	0611	0640	...	...	0811	1011	1310	...	1611	...	1811	...	...	1930	2004
Thionville ... 384 d.	...	...	0633	0702	...	...	0833	1033	1331	...	1632	...	1833	...	...	1955	2025
Metz ... 384 a.	...	...	0651	0720	...	...	0851	1051	1351	...	1651	...	1851	...	...	2013	2043
Metz ... d.	0615	0630	0656	0725	0725	0856	0856	1056	1356	1556	1656	1756	1856	1856	1956	2018	2048
Meuse TGV ... d.	0650	0704	|	|	|	|	|	|	|	|	|	|	|	|	|	|	|
Champagne-Ardenne TGV ... 381 a.	|	|	|	|	|	|	|	|	|	|	|	|	|	|	|	2105	2136
Paris Est ... 381 a.	0750	0805	0820	0850	0850	1020	1020	1220	1520	1720	1820	1920	2020	2020	2120	2150	2220

PARIS - NANCY

Certain trains continue beyond Nancy to Épinal and Remiremont (Table **386**) or to Lunéville and St Dié (Table **387**). Train **2583/4** continues to / from Strasbourg.

km	*TGV* trains convey 🍷	*TGV* 2501 ①–⑥ d	*TGV* 2503	*TGV* 2505 ②–⑦ ◐	*TGV* 2505 ① g	*TGV* 2571	*TGV* 2509 Ⓐ	*TGV* 2591 ⑦ e	*TGV* 2515	*TGV* 2517 Ⓐ	*TGV* 2573	*TGV* 2583 Ⓑ f	*TGV* 2519 ①–⑥ b	*TGV* 2595 ⑦ w	*TGV* 2521 ⑤⑦ k
0	**Paris** Est ... 381 d.	0713	0813	1013	1113	1213	1413	1413	1543	1713	1813	1913	2013	2013	2113
136	Champagne-Ardenne TGV ... 381 d.	0756	|	|	|	|	|	|	1627	|	|	|	|	|	|
236	Meuse TGV ... d.	|	0915	|	|	|	1515	1515	|	|	|	|	2115	2115	|
330	**Nancy** ... a.	0851	0950	1143	1243	1343	1550	1550	1721	1843	1943	2043	2150	2150	2245

	TGV 2531 Ⓐ a	*TGV* 2584 ①–⑥ b	*TGV* 2596 ⑥ ◧	*TGV* 2533 ⑦ e	*TGV* 2596 Ⓐ	*TGV* 2535 Ⓐ	*TGV* 2576 Ⓒ	*TGV* 2537	*TGV* 2539 Ⓐ	*TGV* 2541 Ⓒ	*TGV* 2543 Ⓐ	*TGV* 2545 ⑦ e	*TGV* 2578 ①–⑥ b	*TGV* 2547 ①–⑥ d	*TGV* 2598 ⑦ e	*TGV* 2549 ⑤⑥ y	*TGV* 2551 Ⓑ f	*TGV* 2553 ⑦ w
Nancy ... d.	0617	0716	0810	0810	0817	0940	1017	1210	1340	1510	1617	1717	1717	1810	1841	1917	2017	2117
Meuse TGV ... d.	|	|	0846	0846	|	|	|	1246	|	|	|	|	|	1846	1916	|	|	|
Champagne-Ardenne TGV ... 381 d.	|	|	|	|	|	1037	|	|	1436	1606	|	|	|	|	|	|	|	|
Paris Est ... 381 a.	0746	0846	0946	0946	0945	1116	1146	1346	1516	1646	1746	1846	1846	1946	2016	2046	2146	2246

PARIS - SAARBRÜCKEN

🅁 on cross-border journeys and journeys within France. *ICE* trains convey ✕, *TGV* trains convey 🍷.

km		*ICE* 9551 ①–⑥	*TGV* 9553 ⑦	*TGV* 9553 ①–⑥	*ICE* 9555 Ⓑ	*TGV* 9565 ⑥	*TGV* 9557 Ⓑ	*ICE* 9559
0	**Paris** Est ... d.	0706	0906	0910	1310	1310	1710	1906
372	Forbach 🏛 ... a.	0846	1045	|	|	|	|	2046
383	**Saarbrücken** Hbf ... a.	0856	1055	1055	1456	1456	1856	2056
	Frankfurt (Main) Hbf **919** .. a.	1058	1258	1258	1658	1658	2058	2258

	ICE 9558 ①–⑤	*TGV* 9568 ⑥	*TGV* 9556 ①–⑤	*ICE* 9566 ⑥	*TGV* 9556 ⑦	*ICE* 9554	*TGV* 9552	*ICE* 9550 Ⓑ
Frankfurt (Main) Hbf **919** ... d.	0600	0654	0857	0901	0857	1301	1658	1901
Saarbrücken Hbf ... d.	0800	0903	1102	1102	1102	1502	1903	2102
Forbach 🏛 ... d.	0810	0914	|	|	1112	|	1913	|
Paris Est ... a.	0950	1054	1250	1250	1251	1650	2054	2250

– ①⑥⑦ (also July 15, Aug. 15, Nov. 11, 12; not Nov. 10).
– ①②③④⑥ (also Aug. 15; not July 14, Aug. 14, Nov. 11).
– ① to June 30 / from Aug. 25 (also Nov. 12; not Nov. 10).
– To July 4 and from Aug. 29.

– Not ③④⑤ July 9 - Aug. 22.
– Not July 14, Nov. 11.
– Also June 21, Aug. 16, Sept. 27, Oct. 4.
– Not July 14, Aug. 15, 16, Nov. 11.
– Also July 14, Nov. 11.
– Not Aug. 15.
– Also July 15, Nov. 12; not July 14, Nov. 10.
– Not Aug. 13, 15.
Not July 13, Aug. 15.
– Also July 14, Aug. 14, Nov. 11; not July 13, Aug. 15.
– Not July 13, Aug. 13, 15, 16.
– Not July 14, Aug. 14, 15, Nov. 11.
– Also Nov. 10; not July 15, Aug. 15, Nov. 11, 12.

p – 2125 on ⑤ July 11 - Aug. 22 (also Aug. 14).
q – Not July 14, Aug. 14, Nov. 11.
r – Also Aug. 14, Nov. 11; not July 13, Aug. 15.
s – Also Nov. 11.
t – Also July 14, Aug. 14, Nov. 11.
u – Also Aug. 14, Nov. 11; not Aug. 15, Oct. 3, 10, 17.
v – Not July 13, Aug. 15, 16.
w – Also July 14, Nov. 11; not July 13.
x – Not Aug. 23, 24, 30, 31, Sept. 6, 7, 20, 21, Oct. 19, Nov. 23.
y – Also Aug. 14.
z – Not July 14, Aug. 13, 14, Nov. 11.

TGV – 🅁, supplement payable, 🍷.

§ – Also July 14, Aug. 14, Nov. 11; not July 13, Aug. 15.
◐ – Also July 14, Nov. 10; not July 15, Nov. 12.
◧ – Also Aug. 15; not Aug. 16.
△ – Not ⑦ Oct. 12 - Nov. 9.

⊗ – Not Sept. 29 - Oct. 3, Oct. 13–17. Arrives Strasbourg 2305 on Aug. 2.
⊙ – To / from München (Table **32**).
◇ – Via Nancy, calling also at Sarrebourg (Table **383**).
☆ – On ⑦ (also July 14, Nov. 11) Strasbourg d. 1146, not calling at Saverne.
⊖ – On ①–③ July 7 - Aug. 20 (not July 14, Aug. 13) departs Strasbourg 1601, arrives Paris 1834.
* – 15 minutes earlier July 31 - Sept. 14.
‡ – 13–14 minutes later July 31 - Sept. 14.
¶ – Subject to alteration Sept. 29 - Oct. 3, Oct. 13–17. Arrives Strasbourg 2224 on Ⓐ June 16 - July 18.

Timings of services to / from Strasbourg may vary by up to 10 minutes July 8 - Aug. 4 (earlier departures possible)

391 STRASBOURG - NORTHERN and WESTERN FRANCE

	TGV 5420	TGV 5153	TGV 5486	TGV 5471	TGV 5450	TGV 5450	TGV 5422	TGV 5452	TGV 5424	TGV 5488	TGV 5454	TGV 5488	TGV 5426	TGV 5284
			A	z	Ⓐ	Ⓒ		‡		D	B ‡	C	Ⓑ	◇
Strasbourg d.	0611	...	0701	0701	0746	0746	0946	1201	1216	1501	1601	1701	1901	...
Lorraine TGV d.	0725	...	0813	0813	0858	0858	1100	1314	1333	1615	1714	1815	2013	...
Meuse TGV d.	|	...	|	|	0924	0924	|	|	|	|	|	|	|	...
Champagne-Ardenne TGV d.	0814	...	0900	0900	0950	0950	1144	1354	1412	1700	1754	1900	2100	...
Marne la Vallée - Chessy § a.	|	...	0929	0929	1023	1023	|	1426	|	1728	1825	1928	|	...
Massy TGV a.	|	...	1005	1005	1105	1105	|	1505	|	1804	1905	2005	|	...
Paris Charles de Gaulle ✈ a.	0844	0908	|	|	|	|	1215	|	1449	|	|	|	2132	2146
TGV Haute Picardie a.	...	|	|	|	|	|	...	|	|	|	|	|	...	2212
Arras a.	...	|	|	|	|	|	...	|	|	|	|	|	...	|
Lille Europe a.	...	0957	|	|	|	|	...	|	1558	|	|	|	...	2244g
Le Mans a.	...	...	1058	1058	|	|	...	|	...	1854	|	2057	...	...
Angers a.	...	...	1140	|	|	|	...	|	...	1941	|	2140	...	...
Nantes a.	...	...	1218	|	|	|	...	|	...	2019	|	2219	...	...
Laval a.	...	...	...	1149j	|	|	...	|	...	...	|	...	...	...
Rennes a.	...	...	...	1228j	|	|	...	|	...	...	|	...	...	...
St Pierre des Corps a.	...	...	...	...	1159	1159	...	1559	...	...	2000	...	...	...
Futuroscope a.	...	...	...	...	|	1235	...	|	...	...	|	...	...	...
Poitiers a.	...	...	...	...	1241	|	...	1641	...	...	2041	...	...	...
Angoulême a.	...	...	...	...	1332	1332	...	1732	...	...	2132	...	...	...
Bordeaux St Jean a.	...	...	...	...	1437	1437	...	1837	...	...	2237	...	...	...

	TGV 5104	TGV 5400	TGV 5202	TGV 5402	TGV 5478	TGV 5440	TGV 5164	TGV 5406	TGV 5442	TGV 5480	TGV 5460	TGV 5416	TGV 5445	
	d ◇	①–⑥	◇		E	H ⊖	◇			L	z		m ⊖	
Bordeaux St Jean d.	...	...	...	...	...	0723	...	...	1123	...	...	...	1523	...
Angoulême d.	...	...	...	...	...	0826	...	...	1226	...	...	...	1626	...
Poitiers d.	...	...	...	...	...	0916	...	...	1316	...	...	...	1715	...
Futuroscope d.	...	...	...	...	...	|	...	...	|	...	...	...	1725	...
St Pierre des Corps d.	...	...	...	...	...	1001	...	...	1401h	...	...	...	1801	...
Rennes d.	...	...	...	...	...	|	...	...	|	...	1433t	...	|	...
Laval d.	...	...	...	...	...	|	...	...	|	...	1511t	...	|	...
Nantes d.	...	...	...	...	0735k	|	...	...	|	1433r	|	...	|	...
Angers d.	...	...	...	...	0814k	|	...	...	|	1511r	|	...	|	...
Le Mans d.	...	...	...	...	0857	|	...	...	|	1602r	1602v	...	|	...
Lille Europe d.	0557	...	0921	...	|	|	1043	...	|	|	|	1724f	|	...
Arras d.	|	...	|	...	|	|	|	...	|	|	|	|	|	...
TGV Haute Picardie d.	|	...	|	...	|	|	1115	...	|	|	|	1754	|	...
Paris Charles de Gaulle ✈ d.	0653	0744	1011	1026	|	|	1144	1252	|	|	|	1828	|	...
Massy TGV d.	...	|	...	|	0955	1055	...	|	1455	1656	1656	|	1855	...
Marne la Vallée - Chessy § d.	...	|	...	|	1031	1131	...	|	1531	1731	1731	|	1935	...
Champagne-Ardenne TGV a.	...	0814	...	1055	1100	1159	...	1323	1559	1759	1759	1859	2002	...
Meuse TGV a.	...	|	...	|	|	|	...	|	|	|	|	|	2029	...
Lorraine TGV a.	...	0859	...	1138	1145	1246	...	1403	1646	1846	1846	1944	2050	...
Strasbourg a.	...	1014	...	1253	1259	1359	...	1520	1800	1959	1959	2059	2203	...

A – Daily to Aug. 25; ①⑤⑥⑦ from Aug. 29 (also Nov. 11, 12; not Oct. 19, Nov. 10, Dec. 7).
B – Daily to July 6; ④–⑦ July 10 - Aug. 17 (also July 14, Aug. 13); daily from Aug. 21.
C – ⑦ to July 6; Ⓒ July 12 - Aug. 24; ⑦ from Aug. 31 (also Nov. 11).
D – ①–⑤ to June 4; ④⑤ July 10 - Aug. 14; ①–⑤ from Aug. 21 (not Nov. 11).
E – ①–⑥ to July 5; ①⑤⑥⑦ July 6 - Aug. 24 (also July 15, Aug. 14); ①–⑥ from Aug. 25 (not Nov. 11).
H – Daily to July 7; ①⑤⑥⑦ July 11 - Aug. 18 (also July 15, Aug. 14); daily from Aug. 22.
L – Daily to Aug. 25; ①⑤⑥⑦ from Aug. 29 (also Nov. 11, 12; not Oct. 18, Nov. 10, Dec. 6).

d – Not Sept. 27, 28, Oct. 4, 5, 6, 11, 12, 13, 19, 26.
f – Lille **Flandres**.
g – Arrives Lille Flandres on ①–⑤ June 23 - July 4 and ①–⑤ Oct. 6–17.
h – Not ①–⑤ Oct. 27 - Nov. 7.
j – 3 minutes later until July 5.
k – Until July 5 and Aug. 25 - Sept. 27 departs Nantes 0731, Angers 0809.
m – Not Sept. 29 - Oct. 3, Oct. 13–17. On Aug. 2 does not call at Lorraine and arrives Strasbourg 2224.
r – Until July 5 and Aug. 25 - Sept. 28 departs Nantes 1428, Angers 1506. Until June 29 departs Le Mans 1600.
t – Until July 5 departs Rennes 1427, Laval 1507.
v – 1600 on ②–④ from Aug. 26 (also Oct. 18, Nov. 10, Dec. 6; not Nov. 11, 12).
z – Not July 13, Sept. 6, 13.

TGV – 🅁, supplement payable, 🍷.

◇ – To/from destinations in Table **11**.
⊖ – Trains **5440** and **5445** are attached to Bordeaux - Lille trains **5260** and **5266** between Bordeaux and Marne la Vallée (Table **11**).
‡ – Between Marne la Vallée and Bordeaux trains **5452** and **5454** are attached to Lille - Bordeaux trains **5218** and **5240** (Table **11**).
§ – Station for Disneyland Paris.

Timings Strasbourg - Champagne-Ardenne and v.v. may vary by up to 5 minutes July 8 - Aug. 4

CONNECTING 🚌 SERVICES
Bus services connect with the trains in Table **391** on the following routes (for further details ✆ 03 87 78 67 09):
Nancy - Lorraine TGV (journey 35 minutes)
Metz - Lorraine TGV (journey 25 minutes)
Verdun - Meuse TGV (journey 25 minutes)

391a REIMS - CHAMPAGNE ARDENNE TGV

Certain trains continue to/from destinations in Tables **382** and **389**

	P	Ⓐ	Ⓒ				Ⓐ			H	⚒w				F	⑦s	⑥	Ⓐ⊖	⚒w	⑦s			Ⓑ	⑦e
Châlons en Champagne **382** d.	...	0648	...	...	...	...	...	...	...	...	...	...	...	...	...	...	...	...	...	...	...	...	...	...
Reims d.	0655	0736	0738	0837	0900	0922	1013	1032	1127	1148	1301	1322	1349	1547	1635	1727	1732	1735	1753	1757	1837	1932	2037	2115
Champagne-Ardenne TGV a.	0705	0746	0746	0845	0912	0930	1021	1040	1135	1156	1309	1330	1357	1555	1643	1741	1741	1744	1805	1805	1845	1944	2045	2124

		Ⓑ	⑥			Ⓐ			◧		⚒w		z				J						Ⓑt	⑦e
Champagne-Ardenne TGV d.	0820	0904	0905	0933	1001	1043	1112	1158	1212	...	1333	1410	1424	1448	...	1632	1709	...	1813	1904	...	2019	2113	2150
Reims a.	0828	0911	0913	0940	1008	1051	1120	1205	1219	...	1341	1417	1432	1456	...	1639	1717	...	1823	1912	...	2028	2121	2159
Châlons en Champagne **382** a.	...	0956	...	...	...	...	...	...	1326n	...	...	1455r	...	...	...	...	...	...	1915	...	...	...	...	...

F – ④⑤ (also ⑥ July 12 - Aug. 23; not Aug. 15).
H – Daily to July 7; ①⑤⑥⑦ July 11 - Aug. 18 (also July 15, Aug. 14); daily from Aug. 22.
J – ④⑤ (also ⑥ July 12 - Aug. 30).
P – ①–⑥ (not July 14, Nov. 11).
e – Also July 14, Nov. 11.
n – Not July 21–25, July 28 - Aug. 1, Nov. 24–28, Dec. 1–5, 8–12.
r – ⚒ only.
s – Also July 14, Aug. 15, Nov. 11.
t – Not Aug. 15.
w – Also Nov. 1.
z – Not July 15, Nov. 12.
◧ – Subject to alteration on Aug. 26, 27.
⊖ – Runs 3 minutes earlier June 16–20, Sept. 15, 16.

392 LONGWY - NANCY / LUXEMBOURG

Longwy - Nancy

km		Ⓐ	⚒	Ⓐ	⑥ k	Ⓐ ▲	†	⑥ k	†	Ⓐ	†
0	**Longwy** 389a d.	0531	0640	0838	1210	1218	1241	1657	1730	1828	1938
16	Longuyon 389a d.	0545	0654	0852	1224	1232	1254	1710	1743	1841	1951
57	Conflans-Jarny d.	0615	0724	0922	1254	1302	1326	1740	1813	1912	2021
100	Pont-à-Mousson d.	0652	0754	0951	1323	1332	1353	1808	1843	1940	2049
128	**Nancy** a.	0709	0811r	1007	1340	1348	1410	1826	1902	1957	2107

	Ⓐ	Ⓐ ▲	⑥ k	†	⑥ k	Ⓐ ▲	†	Ⓐ	Ⓐ	⑥ k	†	† v
Nancy d.	0604	0900	0907	1006	1254	1402	1707	1734	1836	1908	1936	225
Pont-à-Mousson d.	0622	0919	0925	1023	1311	1422	1724	1753	1856	1926	1955	231
Conflans-Jarny d.	0652	0948	0955	1052	1348	1455	1754	1826	1925	1955	2025	233
Longuyon 389a d.	0722	1020	1023	1121	1419	1525	1826	1856	1953	2025	2054	001
Longwy 389a a.	0734	1032	1036	1133	1432	1537	1838	1908	2005	2038	2106	002

Longwy - Luxembourg

km		①–⑤ n	①–⑤ n	①–⑥ pt	①–⑤ n	①–⑥ p	①–⑤ n	①–⑤ n	①–⑤ b	①–⑤ n	①–⑥ ps
0	**Longwy** d.	0617	0647	0714	0747	0817	0847	0917	1317	*1651*	1843
8	Rodange 🏛 d.	0626	0655	0726	0756	0826	0856	0926	1326	1709	1852
27	**Luxembourg** a.	0649	0719	0749	0819	0849	0919	0949	1349	1738	1912

	①–⑥ p	⑥ k	①–⑤ n		①–⑤ b	①–⑤ n	①–⑤ n	①–⑤ n	①–⑤ n	①–⑥ p	①–⑤ n	①– n
Luxembourg d.	0613	0713	0743	...	1213	1613	1643	1713	1743	1813	1843	191
Rodange 🏛 d.	0639	0739	0809	...	1239	1639	1709	1739	1809	1839	1909	193
Longwy a.	0646	0746	0816	...	1246	1646	1716	1746	1816	1846	1916	194

b – Not July 28 - Aug. 1, Aug. 15, Sept. 29 - Oct. 10, Nov. 17–21.
f – Not Aug. 15.
k – Not Nov. 1.
n – Not June 23, Aug. 15.
p – Not June 23, Aug. 15, Nov. 1.
r – 0815 on ⑥.
s – On ⑥ Longwy d. 1907, Rodange d. 1915, Luxembourg a. 2010.
t – On ⑥ Longwy d. 0728, Rodange d. 0736, Luxembourg a. 0825.
v – Not July 14.
¶ – Departs 0448 until July 4.
§ – Departs 1815 until July 4.
▲ – Subject to alteration (may be operated by 🚌 with extended journey time).

LONGWY - METZ Rail service: from Longwy at 0619 ⚒; from Metz at 1714 ⚒ (Table **389a**).
🚌 service (journey 55 mins):
From Longwy at 0501 Ⓐ¶, 0735, 0945 ⚒, 1135 Ⓐ, 1140 ⑥ 1515 ⑤**f**, 1645 Ⓐ, 1839 †, 1908 Ⓐ, 1920 ⑥**k**.
From Metz at 0620 Ⓐ, 0919 Ⓐ, 0920 ⑥**k**, 1026 †, 1220 ⚒, 1520 ⑤**f**, 1615 Ⓐ, 1805 ⑥**k**, 1820 Ⓐ§, 2020 Ⓒ, 2119

393 🚌 CHÂLONS EN CHAMPAGNE - VERDUN

SERVICE FROM JULY

km		Ⓐ 🚌	Ⓒ 🚌	Ⓐ 🚌	🚌		Ⓐ 🚌		🚌	
0	**Châlons en Champagne** d.	0820	1020	1220	1420	...	1820	...	2050	...
62	Ste Menehould Médiathèque d.	0923	1123	1323	1523	...	1923	...	2153	...
107	**Verdun** a.	1008	1208	1408	1608	...	2008	...	2238	...

	Ⓐ 🚌	Ⓒ 🚌		Ⓐ 🚌	🚌		Ⓐ 🚌		🚌
Verdun d.	0543	0612	...	1017	1212	...	1517	...	181
Ste Menehould Médiathèque d.	0628	0657	...	1102	1257	...	1602	...	190
Châlons en Champagne a.	0730	0800	...	1205	1400	...	1705	...	200

VERDUN - METZ 393a

km		ⒶJ	Ⓐ	⚒n	● J	🚌 Ⓐ	⑤J	J	⊗ ⒶJ	†	⑤f
0	**Verdun** d.	...	0638	...	1047	1203	1552	...	1812	1925	2218
40	Conflans-Jarny d.	0618	0718	0735	1125	1256	1629	1725	1851	2004	2254
66	Hagondange d.	|	|	0813	1158k	|	1706	1804	1925	|	|
84	**Metz** a.	0653	0753	0827	1214	1335	1719	1817	1938	2037	2331

	🚌 Ⓐ¶	⚒J	⊖ ⒶJ	⑥J	🚌 Ⓐ	⊗ Ⓐ	†	⚒	ⒶJ	⑥r	🚌 Ⓐ
Metz d.	0705	0727	1231	1251	1420	1629	1656t	1743	1820	1831	1851
Hagondange d.	|	0743	1246	1305	|	|	1713t	1758	|	1849	|
Conflans-Jarny d.	0749	0816	1325	1346	1504	1703	1758	1831	1855	1929	1935
Verdun a.	0835	...	1359	1420	1550	1738	1833	...	1929	2004	2021

J – To July 5 and from Aug. 25.
f – ⑤ to Nov. 28 (also Aug. 14). Runs 7–13 minutes later until Aug. 1.
k – 1201 on certain dates.
n – Not ⑥ July 12 - Aug. 23.
r – Not Nov. 1.
t – From Oct. 5 departs Metz 1704, Hagondange 1718.
¶ – On ① Metz d. 0620, Conflans-Jarny d. 0702, Verdun a. 0748.
⊖ – Subject to alteration on June 18, Oct. 6 - Nov. 6, Nov. 17, 24.
⊗ – Subject to alteration on ①–④ Oct. 27 - Nov. 6.
● – Subject to alteration on ①–⑤ Oct. 6 - Nov. 7 (also on June 18, Sept. 21, Nov. 1, 2, 16, 17).

METZ - FORBACH - SAARBRÜCKEN 394

km		Ⓐ	Ⓐ	⑥ h	⚒	Ⓐ	† w	⑥ h	Ⓐ ❖	⑥ h	† w	⚒ ⊡	⚒ ⊖	† f	⑤ ⊡	♠ ⊖		Ⓐ		①–④ z	Ⓐ	†	⑥ h	Ⓐ	s	Ⓑ c	† d
0	**Metz** d.	0555	0642	0642	0741	0839	0840	0848	0930	1044	1044	1218	1242	1341	1345	1348	1549	1645	1747	1816	1834	1842	1921	1924	2019	2214	2339
50	St Avold d.	0633	0718	0722	0813	0911	0919	0926	1004	1115	1122	1256	1313	1422	1417	1421	1620	1719	1818	1853	1915	1926	2008	2003	2050	2246*	0013
70	Forbach a.	0650	0734	0738	0826	0925	0932	0940	1019	1129	1139	1313	1328	1435	1431	1435	1634	1732	1832	1909	1928	1941	2025	2020	2104	2300*	0027
70	Forbach d.	0655	*0743*	0743	*0832*	*0938*	*0938*	0945	*1025*	*1140*	1143	*1321*v	*1340*a	1437	*1437*	1437	*1645*	*1737*	*1842*	1918	*1938*	*1953*	2031	2024	*2117*r	*2314*z	0029
81	**Saarbrücken** a.	0704	*0752*	0752	*0841*	*0947*	*0947*	0954	*1034*	*1149*	1152	*1330*v	*1349*a	1446	*1446*	1446	*1654*	*1746*	*1851*	1927	*1947*	*2002*	2040	2033	*2126*r	*2323*z	0038

	⑥ y	Ⓐ ⊗	⚒	⚒	Ⓐ	© x	Ⓐ	Ⓐ	† x	⚒	Ⓐ ❖	⚒ ❖	⚒ ■	†	⊕	Ⓐ	†	⑥ h	Ⓑ q	Ⓐ	⚒	Ⓑ	†	⑥ h	⑤ f	①–④ z	Ⓐ
Saarbrücken d.	0420	*0420*	*0553*a	*0631*	*0651*	0731	*0731*	*0831*	*0917*	*0924*	*1131*	*1153*h	1233	1233	*1431*	*1631*	1631	1633	...	1731	*1753*h	*1829*	*1912*	1931	*1931*	1934	2240
Forbach a.	0429	*0429*	*0602*a	*0640*	*0700*	0740	*0740*	*0840*	*0926*	*0933*	*1140*	*1202*h	1242	1242	*1440*	*1640*	1640	1642	...	1740	*1802*h	*1838*	*1921*	1941	*1940*	1944	2249
Forbach d.	0449	0451	0610	0647	0707	0745	0750	0845	0931	0939	1145	1207	1248	1244	1445	1645	1645	1645	1707	1747	1807	1847	1925	1946	1950	1949	...
St Avold d.	0505	0508	0625	0702	0723	0759	0805	0859	0948	0952	1200	1223	1305	1258	1458	1659	1659	1659	1725	1803	1822	1902	1938	2001	2004	2003	...
Metz a.	0550	0550	0704	0737	0800	0832	0837	0932	1033	1024	1238	1301	1338	1339	1530	1731	1731	1738	1804t	1838	1859	1936	2010	2035	2036	2036	...

– Ⓐ only.
– Change at Béning.
– Also Nov. 1; not June 22, 29.
– Not June 22, 29, Nov. 1.
– Not Aug. 15.
– ⑥ (not Nov. 1).
– Also Nov. 1.
– ⚒ only.
– Not June 21.
– 1810 on †.
– Not ⑤.
– Not Aug. 24.
– Not Aug. 24, 31.

y – Not Aug. 23 - Sept. 6, Sept. 20 - Oct. 11, Nov. 22, Dec. 13.
z – ①–④ (not July 14, Nov. 11).
* – On † St Avold d. 2252, Forbach a. 2305.
♠ – ①②③④⑥ (not July 14, Nov. 1, 11).
⊗ – Subject to alteration on ①–④ Aug. 19 - Sept. 5, ①–④ Sept. 16 - Oct. 10, Nov. 18–21, Dec. 9–12.
❖ – Subject to alteration Sept. 29 - Oct. 3, Nov. 12–14.
⊡ – Subject to alteration Sept. 22–26, Nov. 3–7.
⊖ – Subject to alteration Sept. 22–26, Sept. 29 - Oct. 3, Nov. 3–7, 12–14.
⊕ – Subject to alteration Sept. 22–26, Sept. 29 - Oct. 3, Nov. 3–7, 10–14.
■ – Subject to alteration Sept. 22–25, Sept. 29 - Oct. 3, Nov. 3–6, 12–14. Aug. 5 - Sept. 20 and Oct. 4–10 Forbach d. 1247, St Avold d. 1302, Metz a. 1340.

☒ – Subject to alteration on ①–⑤ June 16–27 and ①–⑤ Sept. 22 - Oct. 10.
¶ – Runs to July 5 and from Aug. 25 only.

METZ - SARREGUEMINES
Journey times: Through journeys 60–70 minutes.
Journeys with a change of trains 70–90 minutes.
From Metz at 0839 Ⓐ b ¶, 0840 † w b ¶, 1210 Ⓐ ☒, 1250 ⑥ h, 1549 † b ¶, 1717 Ⓐ, 1817 ⑥ h and 1921 Ⓑ.
From Sarreguemines at 0612 ⚒, 0725 Ⓐ, 0814 Ⓐ b ¶, 0914 ⑥ h b ¶, 1210 † b ¶, 1417 ⚒ ☒, 1705 †, 1901 † b ¶ and 1914 Ⓐ b ¶.

Services are subject to alteration until approximately 1630 on ⑦ Oct. 12 - Nov. 9

STRASBOURG - SAARBRÜCKEN 395

km		Ⓐ J	Ⓐ	⑥ k	Ⓐ		Ⓐ J❖	©		B ❖	⑥ k	Ⓐ ❖		Ⓐ ❖	†	D	Ⓐ	⑥ k	Ⓐ	Ⓐ	†	⑥ k	Ⓐ	†
0	**Strasbourg** d.	0556b	0633	0733	0757	...	0933	0933	...	1133	1233	1233	...	1433	1433	1533	1633	1733	1733	1833	1833	1933	2003	2010
71	Diemeringen d.	0647	0725	0824	0851	...	1025	1025	...	1225	1325	1325	...	1525	1525	1625	1734	1825	1837	1927	1925	2025	2055	2110
97	Sarreguemines a.	0708	0746	0846	0912	...	1046	1046	...	1246	1346	1346	...	1546	1546	1646	1800	1846	1903	1949	1946	2046	2116	2135
97	Sarreguemines 🚋 ▲ d.	0711	...	0855	0927	...	...	1055	...	1256	...	1355	...	...	1555	1655	...	...	...	...	1955	2055	2122	...
115	**Saarbrücken Hbf** ▲ a.	0729	...	0915	0947	...	...	1115	...	1315	...	1415	...	...	1614	1715	...	...	...	...	2016	2115	2142	...

	Ⓐ	Ⓐ J	⑥ k	Ⓐ	Ⓐ	⑥ k	†	D ❖		©	Ⓐ ❖	⑥ k	Ⓐ ❖	†	⑥ k	Ⓐ J❖	Ⓐ J	†	Ⓐ	†	Ⓐ	⑥ k	†	Ⓐ
Saarbrücken Hbf ▲ d.	0442	...	...	...	...	...	0653	0745	...	0945	...	1145	1145	1241	...	1327	...	1615	1615	1715	...	1745	...	1815
Sarreguemines 🚋 ▲ a.	0459	...	...	...	...	...	0713	0805	...	1005	...	1205	1205	1301	...	1354	...	1635	1635	1735	...	1805	...	1835
Sarreguemines d.	0503	0535	0610	0608	0702	0710	0714	0810	...	1010	1010	1210	1212	1310	1410	1410	1540	1640	1640h	1740	1740	1810	1828	1840
Diemeringen d.	0526	0559	0631	0633	0727	0731	0734	0831	...	1031	1031	1231	1233	1331	1430	1431	1601	1701	1702h	1801	1802	1831	1852	1901
Strasbourg a.	0625	0700	0723	0735	0828	0823	0829	0925	...	1123	1125	1323	1325	1423	1524	1527	1655	1753	1755	1853	1859	1923	1951	1955

SAARBAHN LIGHT RAIL SERVICE **S1 SARREGUEMINES - SAARBRÜCKEN** ⊖

	⚒	Ⓐ	⚒	Ⓐ				
Sarreguimes (Bahnhof) d.	0516	0546	0616	0646	0716	hourly ◐	2316	0016
Saarbrücken Hbf a.	0545	0615	0645	0715	0745	until	2345	0045

	⚒	Ⓐ	⚒	Ⓐ	⚒	Ⓐ			
Saarbrücken Hbf d.	0440	0510	0540	0610	0640	0710	0740	hourly ◧	2340
Sarreguimes (Bahnhof) a.	0510	0540	0610	0640	0710	0740	0810	until	0010

– Ⓑ to July 14; ⑦ July 20 - Aug. 17; Ⓑ from Aug. 24 (also Nov. 1).
– ①–⑥ to July 12; ⑥ July 19 - Aug. 16; ⚒ from Aug. 23.
– To July 11 and from Aug. 24.
– 0552 July 7–11.
– 4–5 minutes earlier July 7 - Aug. 22.
– Not Nov. 1.

❖ – Subject to alteration on ①–⑤ Oct. 13–31.
◐ – Every 30 minutes 0716 - 0916 and 1216 - 2116 on Ⓐ, 0816 - 1816 on ⑥, 1216 - 1816 on †.
◧ – Every 30 minutes 0740 - 0840 and 1140 - 2040 on Ⓐ, 0740 - 1740 on ⑥, 1140 - 1740 on †.
▲ – For additional light rail service Sarreguemines - Sarrbrücken see below main table.
⊖ – Operated by Saarbahn (www.saarbahn.de). In Saarbrücken also serves city centre and continues beyond main station to / from destinations in the northern suburbs.

STRASBOURG - WISSEMBOURG 396

To July 6 and from Aug. 24

km		⚒	Ⓐ	⑥k	Ⓐ‡	†	⑥k	Ⓐ‡	†	⑥k	Ⓐ‡	Ⓐ‡	⑥k	†	⑥k	Ⓐ	⑥k	©	Ⓐ	Ⓐ	Ⓐ	†	Ⓐ	⑥k	†
0	**Strasbourg** d.	0608	0729	0754	0808	0854	0854	1038*	1154*	1206*	1229*	1338	1354	1454	1554	1638	1654	1724	1729*	1805	1834	1854	1930	1954	1954
34	Haguenau d.	0644	0800	0827	0844	0927	0927	1113	1226	1237	1253	1420	1425	1526	1626	1715	1727	1755r	1753	1831	1900	1926	1953	2026	2027
66	**Wissembourg** § a.	0722	0830	0853	0918	1001	1009	1148	1253	1315	1330	1447	1453	1553	1653	1744	1758	1824	1830	1858	1941	1953	2023	2100	2109

	Ⓐ	⑥k	Ⓐ	Ⓐ	⑥k	†	Ⓐ◇	⑥k	Ⓐ¶	©	†	Ⓐ¶	⑥k	©	Ⓐ¶	Ⓐ¶	⑥k	†	⑥k	Ⓐ	†	⑥k	Ⓐ	Ⓐ	†
Wissembourg § d.	0606	0643	0643	0730	0746	0836	0841	0930	0941	1041	1141	1216	1241	1341	1350	1538	1541	1641	1730	1753	1830	1857	1904	*1954*	2036
Haguenau d.	0644	0724	0724	0800	0814	0909	0918	1008	1019	1107	1208	1249	1308	1408	1419	1606	1608	1708	1758	1832	1908	1935	1935	2029	2103
Strasbourg a.	0721	0749	0752	0824	0838	0938	0954	1038	1054	1138	1238	1324	1338	1438	1454	1630	1638	1738	1828	1858	1938	2010	2009	2104	2138

July 7 - Aug. 23

km		Ⓐ	⑥	Ⓐ	⑥	†	⑥		Ⓐ	†	⑥	Ⓐ		⑥	†	⑥	⑥	⑥	†	Ⓐ	Ⓐ	†	Ⓐ	⑥	†
0	**Strasbourg** d.	0601	0603	0729	0754	0854	0854	...	1038	1150	1206	1224	...	1354	1456	1554	1654	1726	1726	1729	1826	1854	1926	1954	1954
34	Haguenau d.	0644	0644	0800	0827	0927	0927	...	1113	1226	1237	1302	...	1425	1527	1626	1727	1757	1758	1808	1905	1926	2001	2026	2027
66	**Wissembourg** § a.	0720	0722	0830	0853	1001	1009	...	1148	1253	1315	1341	...	1453	1554	1653	1758	1824	1824	1843	1944	1953	2031	2100	2109

	Ⓐ	⑥	Ⓐ	Ⓐ	⑥	Ⓐ	†	⑥	†	⑥	†	Ⓐ	⑥	†	⑥	Ⓐ		⑥	†	⑥	†	⑥	Ⓐ		†
Wissembourg § d.	0606	0643	0641	0727	0746	0841	0847	0930	1041	1049	1121	1216	1241	1341	1343	1349	...	1544	1650	1730	1830	1902	1906	...	2036
Haguenau d.	0644	0724	0723	0759	0814	0918	0921	1008	1108	1115	1151	1249	1308	1407	1410	1420	...	1611	1717	1756	1906	1945	1947	...	2103
Strasbourg a.	0722	0750	0756	0824	0842	0954	0951	1038	1140	1146	1223	1324	1338	1438	1440	1456	...	1644	1750	1828	1937	2022	2024	...	2138

Not Nov. 1.
1757 on ⑥ (not Nov. 1).
* – 1–2 minutes earlier until July 5.
◇ – Runs 2 minutes later until July 4.
§ – For connections see Table **918**.
‡ – Oct. 27 - Nov. 7 by 🚌 Haguenau - Wissembourg (arrives Wissembourg up to 30 minutes later).
¶ – Oct. 27 - Nov. 7 by 🚌 Wissembourg - Haguenau (departs Wissembourg up to 37 minutes earlier).
☛ Additional services run Strasbourg - Haguenau (1–2 trains per hour).

397 PRIVATE TOURIST RAILWAYS

MER DE GLACE - TRAIN DE MONTENVERS

✆ 04.50.53.22.75. www.compagniedumontblanc.fr

From Chamonix (200 metres from SNCF station) to Montenvers 'Mer de Glace' (altitude 1913 metres). Journey 20 minutes. Valid Dec. 2013 - Dec. 2014. No service Sept. 29 - Oct. 17, 2014. A cable car takes visitors to the ice grotto inside the glacier (provisionally closed May 11–28 and Sept. 28 - Dec. 20).

Dec. 21 - Mar. 7: from Chamonix 1000 - 1600, returning until 1630. Runs every 20–30 mins.
Mar. 8 - Apr. 30: from Chamonix 1000 - 1630, returning until 1700. Runs every 20–30 mins.
May 1 - July 4: from Chamonix 0830 - 1630 △, returning until 1700. Runs every 20–30 mins.
July 5 - Aug. 31: from Chamonix 0800 - 1800, returning until 1830. Runs every 20–30 mins.
Sept. 1–14: from Chamonix 0830 - 1700 △, returning until 1730. Runs every 20–30 mins.
Sept. 15 – 28: from Chamonix 0830 - 1630 △, returning until 1700. Runs every 20–30 mins.
Oct. 18 - Nov. 2: from Chamonix 1000 - 1600, returning until 1630. Runs every 30–60 mins.
Nov. 3 - Dec. 19: 1000, 1200, 1400, 1500, 1600, returning 1130, 1330, 1430, 1530, 1630.

△ – Departure at 0900 runs if sufficient demand.

PANORAMIQUE DES DÔMES

Electric rack railway from the foot to the summit of Le puy de Dôme. Journey: 15 minutes. 2014 service (no service Apr. 7–11 and Oct. 13–17) www.panoramiquedesdomes.fr

To Mar. 31 and from Sept. 29 (also Apr. 30): Departures every 40 minutes 1000 - 1800, returning from the summit 1020 - 1820. **Apr. 1 - June 30 and Sept. 1–28** (not Apr. 30): Departures every 40 minutes 0900 - 1900, returning 0920 - 1920. **July 1 - Aug. 31**: Departures every 20 minutes 0900 - 2300, returning 0920 - 2320.

TRAMWAY DU MONT BLANC

The highest rack railway in France. www.compagniedumontblanc.fr

✆ 04.50.53.22.75.

Winter season: Dec. 14, 2013 - Apr. 6, 2014

Runs from St Gervais Le Fayet (opposite SNCF station) to Bellevue (altitude 1794 metres). Journey 60 minutes.

Mondays to Fridays (not school holidays):
Depart St Gervais: 0900, 1100, 1310, 1430 (also 1000 if sufficient demand, returning 1100).
Depart Bellevue: 1000, 1200, 1430, 1630 (to Feb. 14), 1700 (from Feb. 15).

Saturdays and Sundays (also school holidays):
Depart St Gervais: 0900, 1000, 1100, 1310, 1410, 1510.
Depart Bellevue: 1000, 1100, 1200, 1410, 1510, 1630 (to Feb. 14), 1700 (from Feb. 15).

Summer season: June 14 - Sept. 14, 2014

From St Gervais Le Fayet (opposite SNCF station) to Nid d'Aigle (altitude 2372 metres). Journey 70 minutes.

June 14 - July 11 and Aug. 25 - Sept. 14:
Depart St Gervais Le Fayet: 0800, 0940, 1040, 1210, 1340, 1410, 1510.
Depart Nid d'Aigle: 0920, 1050, 1220, 1350, 1520, 1600, 1650.

July 12 - Aug. 24:
Depart St Gervais Le Fayet: 0720, 0830, 0930, 1000, 1110, 1220, 1330, 1400, 1520, 1630, 1740.
Depart Nid d'Aigle: 0835, 0940, 1050, 1125, 1230, 1340, 1455, 1610, 1640, 1750, 1900.

398 PARIS - PARIS AÉROPORTS

See page 31 for plan of central Paris

CHARLES DE GAULLE - PARIS

VAL shuttle train: air terminals - RER/TGV station.

Roissyrail (RER line B): Aéroport Charles de Gaulle 2 TGV - Paris Châtelet les Halles. Frequent service 0450 - 2400.

Journey time from Charles de Gaulle:

Gare du Nord	35 minutes
Châtelet les Halles ★	38 minutes
St Michel Notre Dame	40 minutes
Antony (for Orly, see middle panel)	58 minutes

★ Cross-platform interchange with *RER* for Gare de Lyon.

ORLY - PARIS (*VAL + RER B*)

VAL light rail: Orly Sud - Orly Ouest - Antony (7 minutes). Frequent service ①–⑤: 0600 - 2230; ⑦: 0700 - 2300. Cross platform interchange with RER line B (below).

RER line B: Antony - Paris. Frequent service 0510 - 0010.

Journey time from Antony:

St Michel Notre Dame	20 minutes
Châtelet les Halles ☆	25 minutes
Gare du Nord	29 minutes

☆ Interchange with *RER* for Gare de Lyon.

ORLY - PARIS (*Orlyrail*)

🚌: Orly (Ouest and Sud) - Pont de Rungis Aéroport d'Or station. Frequent shuttle service.

RER line C: Pont de Rungis Aéroport d'Orly - Paris. Ever 15 minutes approx. 0500 - 2330 (0530 - 2400 from Paris).

Journey time from Pont de Rungis Aéroport d'Orly:

Paris Austerlitz	24 minutes
St Michel Notre Dame	27 minutes
Musée d'Orsay	31 minutes
Champ de Mars Tour Eiffel	39 minutes

399 SAVOIE SKI BUSES

See winter editions

294 PARIS - LES AUBRAIS - ORLÉANS

Valid from July

km		Ⓐ	Ⓑ	⚒		Ⓒ				⑤		⚒	Ⓑ		Ⓐ		Ⓐ	⑤ d				Ⓐ	⑤⑦ ◇	Ⓒ	①–(
0	**Paris** Austerlitz .... ▷ d.	0627	0738	0827	0927	1038	1127	1259	1327	1427	1527	1627	1727	1738	1757	1827	1838	1857	1908	1927	...	2027	2108	2127	230
119	Les Aubrais-Orléans . ▷ a.	0724	0834	0925	1025	1134	1225	1357	1425	1525	1625	1725	1825	1834	1855	1925	1934	1956	2005	2025	...	2125	2205	2225	000
121	**Orléans** .... a.	0732	...	0932	1032	...	1232	...	1432	1532	1632	1732	1832	...	1902	1932	...	2004	...	2032	...	2132	...	2232	001

	⚒	Ⓐ	Ⓐ	Ⓐ		⚒		Ⓒ	⚒	Ⓒ	Ⓐ	⚒		Ⓐ ...	⑤	†	⚒			⚒	†	⚒	† ◇	†	
Orléans .... d.	0458	0558	0628	0658	0728	0828	0928	...	1132	...	...	1328	1528	...	1628	...	1728	...	1928	...	2028	2128	...	2228	...
Les Aubrais-Orléans .. ▷ d.	0505	0605	0635	0705	0735	0835	0935	1026	1138	1226	1249	1335	1535	1626	1635	1726	1735	1827	1935	1955	2035	2135	2150	2235	...
Paris Austerlitz .... ▷ a.	0603	0703	0734	0807	0834	0933	1033	1122	1236	1322	1346	1433	1633	1722	1733	1822	1833	1922	2033	2052	2133	2233	2245	2333	...

LOCAL TRAINS

km		Ⓐ	⚒	†	⚒	Ⓐ		Ⓐ		
0	**Paris** Austerlitz .... § d.	0553	0653	1023	1223	1623	1723	1823	1936	...
56	Étampes .... § d.	0625	0725	1056	1255	1655	1755	1855	2009	...
88	Toury .... d.	0652	0752	1123	1325	1718	1821	1924	2034	...
119	Les Aubrais-Orléans .... a.	0721	0821	1157	1354	1750	1845	1955	2058	...
121	**Orléans** .... a.	0727	0827	1202	1400	1754	1854	1959	2104	...

	Ⓐ	⑥	Ⓐ	†	⑥	Ⓐ	Ⓐ		Ⓐ
Orléans .... d.	0624	0731	0754	1014	1235	1248	1724	1824	193
Les Aubrais-Orléans .... d.	0629	0737	0800	1019	1241	1254	1729	1830	194
Toury .... d.	0702	0811	0828	1048	1308	1311	1800	1858	20
Étampes .... § d.	0732	0840	0849	1117	1334	1339	1832	1931	204
Paris Austerlitz .... § a.	0807	0915	0920	1149	1407	1415	1903	2002	21

d – From Aug. 29.

▷ – For *Intercités* trains (Ⓡ) Paris - Les Aubrais-Orléans and v.v. see Table **310**; for other trains see Table **296** and **315**.

§ – Suburban trains run Paris Austerlitz - Étampes and v.v. approximately every 30 minutes (journey 55 minutes).

◇ – For days of running see Table **315**.

374 DIJON - DOLE - BESANÇON

Local Service

SERVICE SEPT. 2 - OCT. 31 (see page 228 for service to Sept. 1/from Nov. 1). For *TGV* services see Table **370** (Paris - Dijon - Besançon - Basel)/Table **379** (Strasbourg - Besançon - Dijc

km		Ⓐ	n	Ⓑn	Ⓐ	n	⚒	n	n	Ⓐ	n	Ⓐ	Ⓐ	Ⓐ	D	r	r	r	r	r	r	r	r	r	r
0	**Dijon** .... **375** d.	0505	0604	0637	0704	0713	0737	0809	1009	1104	1213	1241	1342j	1505	1600	1613	1629	1713	1741	1813	1841	1913	2005	2109	22
32	Auxonne .... d.	0525	0634	0658	0725	0740	0758	0831	1031	1125	1240	1304	1404j	1525	1623	1643	1651	1745	1804	1843	1906	1943	2028	2131	22
46	Dole .... **375** d.	0539	0650	0710	0739	0752	0810	0847	1043	1138	1255	1317	1415	1540	1636	1654	1704	1757	1817	1854	1917	1955	2039	2143	22
91	**Besançon** Viotte .... a.	0605	0724	0737	0805	0826	0837	0912	1109	1205	1331	1350	1441	1605	1704	1728	1732	1832	1847	1931	1943	2031	2106	2208	23
	Belfort **378** .... a.	...	0856	...	...	...	...	...	...	...	...	...	...	...	...	1856	...	1958	...	...	...	...	...	...	..

	Ⓐ	n	⚒	n	⚒	n	n	Ⓐ	n	n	r	Ⓐ	r	r	Ⓐ	Ⓒr	r	Ⓐ	⚒r	†	r	r	r	†	⚒
Belfort **378** .... d.	...	...	...	...	...	0604	...	...	...	...	...	...	...	...	...	...	...	...	...	...	1704	...	...	...	.
Besançon Viotte .... d.	0511	0554	0559	0620	0713	0729	0746	0856	0952	1228	1347	1448	1551	1628	1647	1713	1729	1747	1823	1826	1833	1932	2017	2116	21
Dole .... **375** d.	0536	0618	0629	0655	0745	0806	0817	0924	1017	1306	1417	1519	1617	1705	1717	1743	1805	1817	1852	1853	1911	2008	2043	2144	21
Auxonne .... d.	0545	0629	0638	0708	0753	0815	0826	0933	1026	1315	1426	1527	1626	1714	1726	1752	1814	1826	1903	1905	1920	2016	2053	2153	21
Dijon .... **375** a.	0610	0653	0708	0738	0818	0847	0851	1000	1051	1347	1451	1551	1651	1747	1751	1818	1847	1851	1927	1936	1952	2047	2118	2218	22

D – ⑤–⑦ (not Oct. 11, 18). j – Departs Dijon 1341, Auxonne 1403 on Sept. 2, 3, 4, 5, 8. n – Not Oct. 12, 19. r – Not Oct. 11, 18.

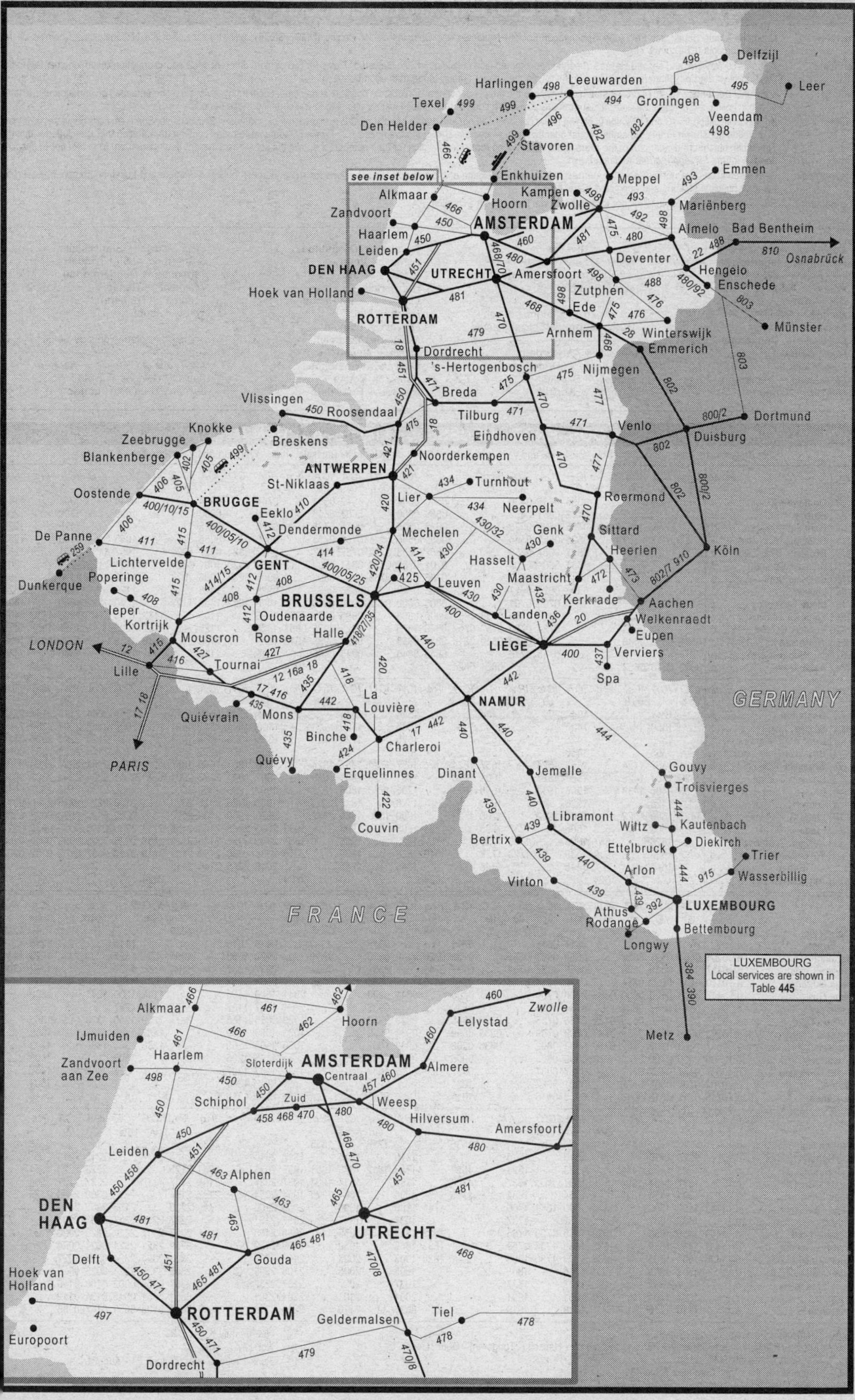
Delfzijl
Harlingen
Leeuwarden
Leer
Texel
Groningen
Veendam
Den Helder
Stavoren
Enkhuizen
Emmen
Alkmaar
Kampen
Hoorn
Zwolle
Meppel
Mariënberg
Zandvoort
AMSTERDAM
Haarlem
Almelo
Bad Bentheim
Leiden
Deventer
Osnabrück
DEN HAAG
UTRECHT
Amersfoort
Hengelo
Enschede
Hoek van Holland
Zutphen
Ede
ROTTERDAM
Arnhem
Winterswijk
Münster
Emmerich
Dordrecht
's-Hertogenbosch
Nijmegen
Breda
Vlissingen
Roosendaal
Tilburg
Dortmund
Knokke
Venlo
Duisburg
Zeebrugge
Breskens
Eindhoven
Blankenberge
Noorderkempen
ANTWERPEN
Oostende
Turnhout
St-Niklaas
BRUGGE
Lier
Roermond
Neerpelt
Eeklo
Genk
De Panne
Dendermonde
Mechelen
Sittard
Lichtervelde
Heerlen
Köln
GENT
Hasselt
Dunkerque
Poperinge
Maastricht
Leuven
Ieper
BRUSSELS
Kerkrade
Aachen
Oudenaarde
Landen
Kortrijk
Welkenraedt
Ronse
Halle
Eupen
LONDON
Mouscron
LIÈGE
Verviers
Lille
Tournai
Spa
NAMUR
GERMANY
Quiévrain
La Louvière
Mons
Binche
Charleroi
PARIS
Quévy
Erquelinnes
Dinant
Jemelle
Gouvy
Troisvierges
Couvin
Libramont
Wiltz
Kautenbach
Bertrix
Diekirch
Ettelbruck
Trier
Arlon
Wasserbillig
Virton
FRANCE
Athus
Rodange
LUXEMBOURG
Bettembourg
Longwy
Metz
see inset below
LUXEMBOURG
Local services are shown in Table 445
Alkmaar
Hoorn
Zwolle
Lelystad
IJmuiden
Haarlem
Zandvoort aan Zee
Sloterdijk
AMSTERDAM
Centraal
Almere
Zuid
Schiphol
Weesp
Hilversum
Amersfoort
Leiden
Alphen
DEN HAAG
UTRECHT
Delft
Gouda
Hoek van Holland
ROTTERDAM
Tiel
Europoort
Geldermalsen
Dordrecht

BELGIUM and LUXEMBOURG

Operator: Nationale Maatschappij der Belgische Spoorwegen/Société Nationale des Chemins de fer Belges (NMBS/SNCB): www.b-rail.be; Société Nationale des Chemins de fer Luxembourgeois (CFL): www.cfl.lu.

Services: All trains convey first and second classes of seating accommodation unless otherwise indicated. Trains for two or more different destinations are often linked together for part of their journeys, and passengers should be careful to join the correct portion of the train upon boarding.

Timings: Valid until **December 13, 2014** unless stated otherwise in the table, but minor alterations are possible at any time. Local train services may be amended on and around the dates of public holidays (see page 2), and passengers are advised to confirm train times locally if planning to travel during these periods.

Route: Route identification for *IC* and *IR* trains is shown in the column heading, and details of each routing is shown in table footnotes as applicable. Some services originate / terminate at a station not shown in this Timetable, consequently these places are shown in parenthesis [...]. Similarly, some routes may continue to a station that is included within the Timetable, but that particular part of the route is not shown. If no route identification (or train number) is shown the service is a local or peak-hour train. *Note that not all services operate for the full length of the routing shown.*

Reservations: Seat reservations are not available for journeys wholly within Belgium or Luxembourg. Reservations for some journeys *between* Belgium and Luxembourg can, however, be made at principal stations and appointed travel agents.

Supplements: Supplements are not payable except for **International** journeys on *EC* trains.

Dutch-language forms of some **French-language** Belgian names

Aarlen = **Arlon**
Aat = **Ath**
Bergen = **Mons**
Doornik = **Tournai**
Duinkerke = **Dunkerque** (France)
Hoei = **Huy**
Luik = **Liège**
Moeskroen = **Mouscron**
Namen = **Namur**
Nijvel = **Nivelles**
Rijsel = **Lille** (France)
's Gravenbrakel = **Braine le Comte**
Wezet = **Visé**

French-language forms of some **Dutch-language** Belgian names

Anvers = **Antwerpen**
Audenarde = **Oudenaarde**
Bruges = **Brugge**
Courtrai = **Kortrijk**
Dixmude = **Diksmuide**
Furnes = **Veurne**
Gand = **Gent**
Hal = **Halle**
La Panne = **De Panne**
Lierre = **Lier**
Louvain = **Leuven**
Malines = **Mechelen**
Menin = **Menen**
Ostende = **Oostende**
Renaix = **Ronse**
Roulers = **Roeselare**
Saint Nicolas = **Sint Niklaas**
Saint Trond = **Sint Truiden**
Termonde = **Dendermonde**
Tirlemont = **Tienen**
Tongres = **Tongeren**
Ypres = **Ieper**

Some other places outside Belgium

Aken / Aix la Chapelle = **Aachen**
Keulen / Cologne = **Köln**
Londen / Londres = **London**

400 OOSTENDE - BRUSSELS - LIÈGE - AACHEN

For *Thalys* trains Paris - Brussels - Köln / Oostende and v.v. – see Tables 16/21; for *ICE* trains Brussels - Köln - Frankfurt and v.v. – see Tables 20/21

km	Route	IRq †	IRq ⑥	IRq Ⓐ		ICE Ⓐ	ICA Ⓐ	ICA Ⓒ	IRq Ⓒ	IRq Ⓐ	ICA Ⓐ	ICA Ⓒ	ICO Ⓐh	ICA Ⓐ	ICA Ⓒ	IRq	ICA	ICO Ⓐh	ICA	ICO Ⓐh	IRq	ICA	ICO Ⓐh	ICA	IRq	ICA
0	**Oostende** d.	...	...	...	...	0356	0435	0436	...	...	0540	0544	...	0642	0644	...	0744	...	0844	...	...	0944	...	1044	...	1144
22	Brugge d.	...	...	...	...	0412	0451	0452	...	...	0557	0600	...	0658	0658	...	0800	...	0900	...	...	1000	...	1100	...	1200
62	Gent Sint-Pieters d.	...	...	...	...	0455	0525	0525	...	...	0625	0625	...	0725	0725	...	0825	...	0925	...	...	1025	...	1125	...	1225
114	**Brussels** Midi / Zuid a.	...	...	...	...	0525	0555	0555	...	...	0655	0655	...	0755	0755	...	0855	...	0955	...	...	1055	...	1155	...	1255
114	**Brussels** Midi / Zuid d.	...	...	...	...	0527	0557	0558	...	...	0657	0658	0724	0757	0757	...	0857	0924	0957	1024	...	1057	1124	1157	...	1257
116	Brussels Central d.	...	...	...	...	0531	0601	0602	...	...	0701	0702	0728	0801	0802	...	0901	0928	1001	1028	...	1101	1128	1201	...	1301
118	Brussels Nord d.	...	...	...	...	0545	0606	0607	...	...	0706	0707	0733	0806	0807	...	0906	0933	1006	1033	...	1106	1133	1206	...	1306
148	Leuven d.	...	...	...	...	0602	0625	0627	...	...	0726	0727	|	0826	0827	...	0926	|	1026	|	...	1126	|	1226	...	1326
218	**Liège** Guillemins a.	...	...	...	...	...	0700	0701	...	...	0800	0800	0822	0900	0900	...	1000	1022	1100	1122	...	1200	1222	1300	...	1400
218	**Liège** Guillemins d.	...	...	0553	...	...	0705	0705	0733	0733	0805	0805	...	0905	0905	0933	1005	...	1105	...	1133	1205	...	1305	1333	1405
242	Verviers Central d.	...	...	0624	...	...	0724	0725	0757	0757	0825	0825	...	0925	0925	0957	1025	...	1125	...	1157	1225	...	1325	1357	1425
255	Welkenraedt d.	0554	0559	0638	...	...	0738	0738	0810	0810	0838	0838	...	0938	0938	1010	1038	...	1138	...	1210	1238	...	1338	1410	1438
261	**Eupen** a.	|	|	|	...	...	0745	0745	|	|	0845	0845	...	0945	0945	|	1045	...	1145	...	|	1245	...	1345	|	1445
274	**Aachen** Hbf a.	0609	0616	0652	...	...	...	...	0824	0824	...	...	...	...	...	1024	...	...	...	...	1224	...	...	...	1424	...

km	Route	ICO Ⓐh	ICA	ICO Ⓐh	IRq	ICA	ICO Ⓐ	IRq Ⓐ	ICA	ICO Ⓐ	IRq	ICA	ICO Ⓐ	ICA	ICO Ⓐh	IRq	ICA Ⓒ	ICA Ⓐ	ICA Ⓒ	ICA Ⓐ	IRq	ICA	ICA	ICA Ⓐ	ICA Ⓒ	ICA
(via	**Oostende** d.	...	1244	...	...	1344	...	...	1444	...	...	1544	...	1644	...	...	1744j	1745	1844j	1845	...	1944	2044	2145	2144	2250
hsl)	Brugge d.	...	1300	...	...	1400	...	...	1500	...	...	1600	...	1700	...	...	1800j	1801	1900j	1901	...	2000	2100	2201	2200	2305
	Gent Sint-Pieters d.	...	1325	...	...	1425	...	...	1525	...	...	1625	...	1725	...	...	1825j	1825	1925j	1925	...	2025	2125	2225	2225	2329
	Brussels Midi / Zuid a.	...	1355	...	...	1455	...	...	1555	...	...	1655	...	1755	...	...	1855j	1855	1955j	1955	...	2055	2155	2255	2255	0004
0	**Brussels** Midi / Zuid d.	1324	1357	1424	...	1457	1524	...	1557	1624	...	1657	1724	1757	1824	...	1858	1857	1958	1957	...	2057	2157	2257	2258	0006
	Brussels Central d.	1328	1401	1428	...	1501	1528	...	1601	1628	...	1701	1728	1801	1828	...	1902	1901	2002	2001	...	2101	2201	2301	2302	0010
4	Brussels Nord d.	1333	1406	1433	...	1506	1533	...	1606	1633	...	1706	1733	1806	1833	...	1907	1906	2007	2006	...	2106	2206	2306	2307	0015
	Leuven d.	|	1426	|	...	1526	|	...	1626	|	...	1726	|	1826	|	...	1927	1926	2027	2026	...	2126	2226	2326	2330	0033
107	**Liège** Guillemins a.	1422	1500	1522	...	1600	1622	...	1700	1722	...	1800	1826	1900	1922	...	2000	2000	2100	2100	...	2200	2302	0023	0023	0125
107	**Liège** Guillemins d.	...	1505	...	1533	1605	...	1632	1705	...	1733	1805	...	1905	...	1933	2005	2005	2105	2105	2133	2205	2305	0025	0025	0127
	Verviers Central d.	...	1525	...	1557	1625	...	1706	1725	...	1757	1825	...	1925	...	1957	2025	2025	2125	2125	2157	2225	2325	0050	0050	0150
	Welkenraedt d.	...	1538	...	1610	1638	...	1723	1738	...	1810	1838	...	1938	...	2010	2038	2038	2139	2139	2210	2237	2337	0102	0102	0202
	Eupen a.	...	1545	...	|	1645	...	|	1745	...	|	1845	...	1945	...	|	2045	2045	2146	2146	|	...	...	...	...	...
157	**Aachen** Hbf a.	...	...	...	1624	...	...	1738	...	...	1824	...	...	...	...	2024	...	...	...	...	2224	...	...	...	...	...

Route	ICA Ⓐ	ICA Ⓒ	ICA Ⓐ	ICA Ⓒ	ICO Ⓐ	ICA Ⓐ	ICA Ⓒ	IRq Ⓒ	ICO Ⓐ	ICA	IRq Ⓐ	ICO Ⓐ	ICA		IRq	ICO Ⓐh	ICA	ICA		IRq	ICO Ⓐh	ICA	ICO Ⓐh		ICA	IRq
Aachen Hbf d.	...	...	...	...	...	...	...	0635	...	...	0658	...	...	...	0835	...	...	...	...	1035	...	...	...	...	...	1235
Eupen d.	...	...	...	...	...	0614	0615	|	...	0715	|	...	0815	...	|	...	0915	1015	...	|	...	1115	...	...	1215	|
Welkenraedt d.	0404	0404	0521	0522	...	0622	0623	0651	...	0723	0726	...	0823	...	0851	...	0923	1023	...	1051	...	1123	...	...	1223	1251
Verviers Central d.	0417	0417	0535	0536	...	0636	0637	0704	...	0737	0741	...	0837	...	0904	...	0937	1037	...	1104	...	1137	...	...	1237	1304
Liège Guillemins a.	0440	0440	0552	0554	...	0652	0654	0725	...	0754	0810	...	0854	...	0925	...	0954	1054	...	1125	...	1154	...	...	1254	1325
Liège Guillemins d.	0443	0443	0600	0600	0639	0700	0700	...	0741	0800	...	0841	0900	...	...	0941	1000	1100	...	...	1141	1200	1241	...	1300	...
Leuven d.	0537	0537	0637	0637	|	0734	0737	...	|	0837	...	|	0937	...	...	|	1037	1137	...	...	|	1237	|	...	1337	...
Brussels Nord d.	0556	0556	0656	0655	0729	0756	0755	...	0829	0855	...	0929	0955	...	...	1029	1055	1155	...	...	1229	1255	1329	...	1355	...
Brussels Central d.	0600	0600	0700	0659	0733	0800	0759	...	0833	0859	...	0933	0959	...	...	1033	1059	1159	...	...	1233	1259	1333	...	1359	...
Brussels Midi / Zuid a.	0603	0603	0703	0702	0736	0803	0802	...	0836	0903	...	0936	1003	...	...	1036	1103	1203	...	...	1236	1303	1336	...	1403	...
Brussels Midi / Zuid d.	0605	0605	0705	0705	...	0805	0805	...	...	0905	...	...	1005	...	...	...	1105	1205	...	...	...	1305	...	...	1405	...
Gent Sint-Pieters d.	0637	0637	0737	0737	...	0837	0837	...	...	0937	...	...	1037	...	...	...	1137	1237	...	...	...	1337	...	...	1437	...
Brugge d.	0701	0702	0801	0802	...	0901	0902	...	...	1001	...	...	1101f	...	...	...	1201f	1301	...	...	...	1401	...	...	1501	...
Oostende a.	0715	0716	0815	0816	...	0915	0916	...	...	1016	...	...	1116f	...	...	...	1216f	1316	...	...	...	1416	...	...	1516	...

Route	ICO Ⓐh	ICA	ICA	IRq	ICO Ⓐh	ICA	ICO Ⓐh	ICA		IRq	ICO Ⓐh	ICA	IRq Ⓐ	ICA	IRq	ICA	ICA		IRq	ICA	ICE Ⓐ	ICE Ⓒ	ICA Ⓒ	ICA Ⓐ	IRq	
Aachen Hbf d.	...	...	...	1435	...	...	...	...	...	1635	...	...	1756	...	1835	...	...	...	2035	...	...	...	...	...	2235	...
Eupen d.	...	1315	1415	|	...	1515	...	1615	...	|	...	1715	|	1815	|	1915	2015	...	|	2115	...	...	2215	2215	|	...
Welkenraedt d.	...	1323	1423	1451	...	1523	...	1623	...	1651	...	1723	1812	1823	1851	1923	2023	...	2051	2123	...	...	2223	2223	2251	...
Verviers Central d.	...	1337	1437	1504	...	1537	...	1637	...	1704	...	1737	...	1837	1904	1937	2037	...	2104	2137	...	...	2237	2237	2304	...
Liège Guillemins a.	...	1354	1454	1525	...	1554	...	1654	...	1725	...	1754	...	1854	1925	1954	2054	...	2125	2154	...	...	2300	2300	2325	...
Liège Guillemins d.	1341	1400	1500	...	1541	1600	1641	1700	...	...	1741	1800	...	1900	...	2000	2100	...	...	2200	...	2153	2309	2309	...	...
Leuven d.	|	1437	1537	...	|	1637	|	1737	...	...	|	1837	...	1937	...	2037	2137	...	...	2237	2258	2257	0003	0003	...	...
Brussels Nord d.	1429	1455	1555	...	1629	1655	1729	1755	...	...	1829	1855	...	1955	...	2055	2155	...	...	2255	2317	2317	0020	0020	...	...
Brussels Central d.	1433	1459	1559	...	1633	1659	1733	1759	...	...	1833	1859	...	1959	...	2059	2159	...	...	2259	2321	2321	0024	0024	...	...
Brussels Midi / Zuid a.	1436	1503	1603	...	1636	1703	1736	1803	...	...	1836	1903	...	2003	...	2103	2203	...	...	2303	2324	2324	0027	0027	...	...
Brussels Midi / Zuid d.	...	1505	1605	...	...	1705	...	1805	...	...	...	1905	...	2005	...	2105	2205	...	...	2305	2337	2326	0029	0029	...	...
Gent Sint-Pieters d.	...	1537	1637	...	...	1737	...	1837	...	...	...	1937	...	2037	...	2137	2237	...	...	2337	0009	0002	0108	0116	...	...
Brugge d.	...	1601	1701	...	...	1801	...	1901	...	...	...	2001	...	2101	...	2201	2301	...	...	0001	0051	0045	0134	0142	...	...
Oostende a.	...	1616	1716	...	...	1816	...	1916	...	...	...	2016	...	2116	...	2216	2316	...	...	0015	0105	0059	0147	0155	...	...

ICA – Oostende - Brussels - Liège - Eupen.
ICE – Knokke / Blankenberge / (Oostende) - Brussels - Leuven - Hasselt [- Tongeren] - Genk / Liège. See also Tables **405**/**430**.
ICO – Brussels - Liège - Visé. See also Table **436**.
IRq – Liège - Verviers - Aachen.

f – Not Ⓐ July 7 - Aug. 22.
h – Not July 7 - Aug. 22.
j – Runs 1 minute later Ⓒ June 21 - Aug. 31.

BRUGGE - ZEEBRUGGE 402

km				Ⓐ	Ⓐ		Ⓐ	▲	Ⓐ		Ⓐt			Ⓒ	Ⓒt		Ⓒ	Ⓒt		Ⓒ	Ⓒt	
0	Brugge	d.	Ⓐ	0604	0704	...	0804	and	2004	...	2110	...	Ⓒ	0704	0806	...	0904	1006	and in	1904	2006	...
15	Zeebrugge Dorp	a.		0624n	0724n	...	0826n	hourly	2024n	...	|	...		|	|	...	|	|	the same	|	|	...
15	Zeebrugge Strand	a.		0625t	0727t	...	0828t	until	2027t	...	2127	...		0725	0827	...	0927	1027	pattern until	1927	2027	...

			Ⓐ	Ⓐ	Ⓐ		Ⓐ	▲	Ⓐ		Ⓐt			Ⓒ	Ⓒt		Ⓒ	Ⓒt		Ⓒ	Ⓒt
ʼeebrugge Strand	d.	Ⓐ	0633t	0733t	0833t	...	0933t	and	2033t	...	2133	...	Ⓒ	0733	0833	...	0933	1033	and in	1933	2033
ʼeebrugge Dorp	d.		0635n	0735n	0835n	...	0935n	hourly	2035n	...	|	...		|	|	...	|	|	the same	|	|
Brugge	a.		0656	0756	0856	...	0956	until	2056	...	2154	...		0754	0854	...	0956	1054	pattern until	1956	2054

ı – Not June 21 - Aug. 31.
– June 21 - Aug. 31.

▲ – Times may vary by ± 3 minutes on some journeys.

KNOKKE and BLANKENBERGE - BRUSSELS 405

km	Route			ICE ⒶO	ICK Ⓐ	ICE Ⓐ	ICK Ⓐ	ICE Ⓐ	ICE Ⓐ	ICK Ⓐ	ICE Ⓐ	ICE Ⓐ	▲	ICK Ⓐ	ICE Ⓐ	ICE Ⓐ		ICK Ⓐ	ICE Ⓐ	ICE Ⓐ	ICK Ⓐ	ICE Ⓐ	ICE Ⓐ	ICE Ⓐ	ICE Ⓐ
0	**Knokke**	d.	Ⓐ	...	...	...	...	...	0604	...	...	0704	and	...	...	2004	...	...	...	2104	...	...	2205	...	2305
	Blankenberge	d.		...	...	...	...	0608	|	...	0710	|	at the	...	2010	|	...	...	2110	|	...	2206	|	2310	|
22	**Brugge**	a.		...	...	...	...	0622	0627	...	0724	0727	same	...	2024	2027	...	...	2124	2127	...	2220	2227	2324	2328
22	**Brugge**	d.		0410	...	0536	...	0636	0636	...	0736	0736	minutes	...	2036	2036	...	...	2136	2136	...	2236	2236	...	...
62	Gent Sint-Pieters	d.		0455	0503	0604	0612	0704	0704	0713	0804	0804	past	2013	2104	2104	...	2113	2204	2204	2213	2300	2258	...	...
96	Denderleeuw	d.		|	0546	|	0645	|	|	0747	|	|	each	2047	|	|	...	2147	|	|	2247	|	|	...	...
119	**Brussels** Midi / Zuid	a.		0525	0606	0634	0704	0734	0734	0806	0834	0834	hour	2106	2134	2134	...	2206	2234	2234	2306	2330	2330	...	...
121	Brussels Central	a.		0530	0611	0639	0711	0739	0739	0811	0839	0839	until	2111	2139	2139	...	2214	2239	2239	...	...	...	...	...
123	Brussels Nord	a.		0534	0615	0643	0715	0743	0743	0815	0843	0843		2115	2143	2143	...	2218	2243	2243	...	...	...	...	...

km	Route			ICE Ⓒ	IRi Ⓒ	ICE Ⓒ	IRi Ⓒ		ICE Ⓒ	ICE Ⓒ	IRi Ⓒ	▲	ICE Ⓒ	ICE Ⓒ	IRi Ⓒ		ICE Ⓒ	ICE Ⓒ	IRi Ⓒ		ICE Ⓒ	ICE Ⓒ		ICE Ⓒ	ICE Ⓒ
	Knokke	d.	Ⓒ	...	...	...	...	...	...	0704	...	and	...	2000	...	...	...	2104	...	...	...	2205	...	...	2305h
0	Blankenberge	d.		...	...	...	...	...	0710	|	...	at the	2010	|	...	...	2110	|	...	...	2210	|	...	2310	|
15	**Brugge**	a.		...	...	...	...	...	0724	0727	...	same	2024	2027	...	...	2124	2127	...	...	2224	2228	...	2324	2328h
15	**Brugge**	d.		0526	...	0636	...	...	0736	0736	...	minutes	2036	2036	...	...	2136	2136	...	...	2236	2236	...	...	2336h
55	Gent Sint-Pieters	d.		0604	0612	0704	0712	...	0804	0804	0812	past	2104	2104	2112	...	2204	2204	2212	...	2304	2304	...	...	0004h
	Denderleeuw	d.		|	0646	|	0746	...	|	|	0846	each	|	|	2146	...	|	|	2246	...	|	|	...	...	|
107	**Brussels** Midi / Zuid	a.		0634	0705	0734	0805	...	0834	0834	0905	hour	2134	2134	2205	...	2234	2234	2305	...	2334	2334	...	...	0034h
109	Brussels Central	a.		0639	0710	0739	0810	...	0839	0839	0910	until	2139	2139	2210	...	2239	2239	2310	...	...	...	...	...	0039h
111	Brussels Nord	a.		0643	0714	0743	0814	...	0843	0843	0914		2143	2143	2214	...	2243	2243	2314	...	...	...	...	...	0043h

Route			ICE Ⓐ	ICE Ⓐ	ICE Ⓐ	ICE Ⓐ		ICK Ⓐ	ICE Ⓐ	ICE Ⓐ	▲	ICK Ⓐ	ICE Ⓐ	ICE Ⓐ		ICK Ⓐ	ICE Ⓐ	ICE Ⓐ		ICK Ⓐ	ICE Ⓐ		ICK Ⓐ	ICE ⒶO	
ussels Nord	d.	Ⓐ	...	...	...	...	...	0545	0617	0617	and	1945	2017	2017	...	2045	2117	2117	...	2145	2217	...	2245	2317	...
ussels Central	d.		...	...	...	...	...	0549	0621	0621	at the	1949	2021	2021	...	2049	2121	2121	...	2149	2221	...	2249	2321	...
ussels Midi / Zuid	d.		...	...	...	...	...	0555	0626	0626	same	1955	2026	2026	...	2055	2126	2126	...	2155	2226	...	2255	2337	...
Denderleeuw	d.		...	...	...	...	...	0616	|	|	minutes	2016	|	|	...	2116	|	|	...	2216	|	...	2316	|	...
ent Sint-Pieters	d.		...	...	...	...	...	0647	0701	0701	past	2047	2101	2101	...	2147	2201	2201	...	2247	2301	...	2347	0009	...
ugge	a.		...	...	...	...	...	...	0724	0724	each	...	2124	2124	...	...	2224	2224	...	...	2324	...	...	0049	...
ugge	d.		0532	0536	0632	0636	...	...	0732	0736	hour	...	2132	2136	...	...	2232	2236	...	...	...	...	...	...	...
Blankenberge	a.		|	0550	|	0650	...	...	|	0750	until	...	|	2150	...	...	|	2250	...	...	...	...	...	...	...
ıokke	a.		0554	...	0654	...	...	...	0754	...		...	2154	...	...	...	2254	...	...	...	...	...	...	...	...

Route			ICE Ⓒ	ICE Ⓒ	IRi Ⓒ	ICE Ⓒ	ICE Ⓒ	IRi Ⓒ	ICE Ⓒ	ICE Ⓒ	IRi Ⓒ	▲	ICE Ⓒ	ICE Ⓒ	IRi Ⓒ		ICE Ⓒ	ICE Ⓒ	IRi Ⓒ		ICE Ⓒ	IRi Ⓒ	ICE ⒸO	
ussels Nord	d.	Ⓒ	...	...	0545	...	...	0645	0717	0717	0745	and	2017	2017	2045	...	2117	2117	2145	...	2217	2245	2317	...
ussels Central	d.		...	...	0549	...	...	0649	0721	0721	0749	at the	2021	2021	2049	...	2121	2121	2149	...	2221	2249	2321	...
ussels Midi / Zuid	d.		...	...	0555	0626	0626	0655	0726	0726	0755	same	2026	2026	2055	...	2126	2126	2155	...	2226	2255	2326	...
Denderleeuw	d.		...	...	0616	|	|	0716	|	|	0816	minutes	|	|	2116	...	|	|	2216	...	|	2316	|	...
ent Sint-Pieters	d.		...	...	0649	0659	0659	0749	0759	0759	0849	past	2059	2059	2149	...	2159	2159	2249	...	2259	2349	0002	...
ugge	a.		...	...	...	0724	0724	...	0824	0824	...	each	2124	2124	...	...	2224	2224	...	...	2324	...	0043	...
ugge	d.		0632	0636	...	0732	0736	...	0832	0836	...	hour	2132	2136	...	...	2235	2236	...	...	...	...	...	...
Blankenberge	a.		|	0650	...	|	0750	...	|	0850	...	until	|	2150	...	...	|	2250	...	...	...	...	...	...
okke	a.		0654	...	...	0754	...	...	0854	...	...		2154	...	...	...	2257	...	...	...	...	...	...	...

E – Knokke / Blankenberge / (Oostende) - Brussels - Leuven - Hasselt [- Tongeren] - Genk / Liège. See also Tables **400/430**.
K – Gent - Brussels - Leuven - Hasselt - Genk. See also Table **430**.
– De Panne - Gent - Brussels - Brussels Airport - Mechelen. See also Tables **411/425**.

O – From / to Oostende.
h – June 21 - Oct. 31 only.
▲ – Times may vary by ± 3 minutes on some journeys.

e Lijn ✆ 059 56 53 53

KNOKKE - OOSTENDE - DE PANNE 406

Belgian Coastal Tramway

m **Knokke** (railway station):
ɔrinciple services operate daily 0630 – 2030, with enhanced frequency as follows:
vember - Easter: every 20 minutes 1008 – 1748.
ster - June: every 15 minutes 0858 – 1728.
y and August: every 10 minutes 0803 – 1833.
ɔtember and October: every 15 minutes 0858 – 1728.
ıct times are subject to minor variation.

From **De Panne** (railway station):
In principle services operate daily 0600 – 2000, with enhanced frequency as follows:
November - Easter: every 20 minutes 0849 – 1729.
Easter - June: every 15 minutes 0854 – 1739.
July and August: every 10 minutes 0829 – 1929.
September and October: every 15 minutes 0854 – 1739.
Exact times are subject to minor variation.

ɔkke → Heist + *0h06* → Zeebrugge + *0h11* → Blankenberge + *0h23* → **Oostende** + *1h00* → Middelkerke + *1h25* → Nieuwpoort + *1h49* → Koksijde + *2h02* → **De Panne** + *2h21*
Panne → Koksijde + *0h19* → Nieuwpoort + *0h32* → Middelkerke + *0h56* → **Oostende** + *1h19* → Blankenberge + *1h57* → Zeebrugge + *2h05* → Heist + *2h14* → **Knokke** + *2h21*

ınections into NMBS / SNCB rail services are available at Knokke (Table **405**), Zeebrugge (Table **402**), Blankenberge (Table **405**), Oostende (Tables **400/10/15**) and De Panne (Table **411**). De Panne railway station is situated in Adinkerke.

POPERINGE - KORTRIJK - BRUSSELS 408

Route		ICL Ⓐ	ICL Ⓒ	ICL Ⓐ	ICL Ⓒ	ICL Ⓐ	ICL Ⓒ	ICL Ⓐx	ICL Ⓒ		ICL Ⓒ	ICL Ⓐ	ICL Ⓒ
Poperinge	‡ d.	0430	...	*0527*	0531	0624	0631	0730	0731	✣	2031	2130	2131
Ieper	‡ d.	0438	...	*0535*	0539	0633	0639	0738	0739		2039	2138	2139
Menen	‡ d.	0456	...	*0554*	0558	0654	0658	0756	0758	▲	2058	2156	2158
Kortrijk	‡ a.	0508	...	*0607*	0609	0709	0709	0808	0809	and	2109	2208	2209
Kortrijk	d.	0514	0515	0614	0615	0712	0715	0814	0815	hourly	2115	2214	...
Oudenaarde	d.	0532	0532	0632	0632	0731	0732	0832	0832	until	2132	2231	...
Zottegem	d.	0544	0546	0645	0646	0744	0746	0845	0846		2146	2245	...
Denderleeuw	d.	0602	0606	0702	0706	0802	0806	0902	0906		2206	2306	...
Brussels Midi/Zuid	a.	0619	0624	0719	0724	0819	0824	0919	0924		2224	2323	...
Brussels Central	a.	0624	...	0724	0734	0824	0834	0924	0934		2234	2328	...
Brussels Nord	a.	0628	...	0728	0738	0828	0838	0928	0938		2238	2332	...

Route		ICL Ⓐ	ICL Ⓒ	ICL Ⓐ	ICL Ⓒ	ICL Ⓐy		ICL Ⓒ	ICL Ⓐ	ICL Ⓒ	ICL Ⓐ
Brussels Nord	d.	0528	...	0632	0722	0732	♠	2122	2132	2222	2232
Brussels Central	d.	0532	...	0636	0726	0736		2126	2136	2226	2236
Brussels Midi / Zuid	d.	0536	0636	0641	0736	0741	▲	2136	2141	2236	2241
Denderleeuw	d.	0553	0654	0700	0754	0800	and	2154	2200	2254	2259
Zottegem	d.	0611	0715	0716	0815	0816	hourly	2215	2216	2315	2322
Oudenaarde	d.	0626	0729	0728	0829	0828	until	2229	2228	2329	2336
Kortrijk	a.	0644	0745	0745	0845	0845		2245	2245	2345	2352
Kortrijk	‡ d.	0646	0751	0750	0851	0850		2251	2250	...	...
Menen	‡ d.	0701	0805	0803	0905	0903		2305	2303	...	...
Ieper	‡ d.	0716	0822	0821	0922	0921		2322	2321	...	...
Poperinge	‡ a.	0723	0829	0828	0929	0928		2329	2328	...	...

– Poperinge - Kortrijk - Brussels [- Dendermonde - Sint-Niklaas].

A change of train is necessary at Kortrijk on the 1230, 1430 departures from Poperinge.
A change of train is necessary at Kortrijk on the 0732 and 1032 departures from Brussels.

Times may vary by ± 3 minutes on some journeys.

‡ – Additional trains **Kortrijk - Poperinge and v.v.**: From Kortrijk: 0651Ⓒ; from Poperinge: 2013Ⓐ, 2131Ⓒ.
✣ – Variations Ⓐ: Poperinge d. 1819/1919; Ieper d. 1833/1933, Menen d. 1854/1954, then as pattern to Brussels Nord. Additional service Ⓐ d. 2013 change at Kortrijk d. 2114 arr. Brussells Nord 2228.
♠ – Variations Ⓐ: Brussels Nord 1632/1732 as pattern to Kortrijk then Menen d. 1805/1905 d. Ieper d. 1827/1927, Poperingea.1835/1935.

410 OOSTENDE - GENT - ANTWERPEN

km	Route		ICC Ⓐ	ICC Ⓐ	ICG Ⓐ		ICC Ⓐ	ICG Ⓐ		ICC Ⓐ	ICG Ⓐ	▲	ICC Ⓐ	ICG Ⓐ		ICC Ⓐ	ICG Ⓐ		ICC Ⓐ			ICC Ⓒ	ICG Ⓒ
0	**Oostende** d.	Ⓐ	...	...	0601	...	...	0701	...	...	0801	and at	...	2101	...	...	2201	...	...	...	Ⓒ	...	0540
22	Brugge d.		...	...	0617	...	...	0717	...	...	0817	the same	...	2117	...	...	2218	...	...	...		...	0606
62	**Gent** Sint-Pieters d.		0505	0616	0646	...	0716	0746	...	0816	0846	minutes	2116	2146	...	2216	2246	...	2316	...		0616	0632
89	Lokeren d.		0528	0639	0708	...	0739	0808	...	0839	0908	past	2139	2208	...	2239	2308	...	2339	...		0639	0654
102	Sint-Niklaas d.		0538	0650	0718	...	0750	0818	...	0850	0918	each	2150	2218	...	2249	2318	...	2350	...		0649	0704
125	Antwerpen Berchem a.		0553	0705	0737	...	0805	0837	...	0905	0937	hour	2205	2237	...	2304	2337	...	0005	...		0706	0719
127	**Antwerpen Centraal** a.		0558	0710	0742	...	0810	0842	...	0910	0942	until	2210	2242	...	2309	2342	...	0010	...		0711	0725

Route	ICC Ⓒ	ICG Ⓒ	▲	ICC Ⓒ	ICG Ⓒ		ICC Ⓒ		
Oostende d.	...	0650	and at	...	2150	...	...	...	...
Brugge d.	...	0706	the same	...	2206	...	...	...	...
Gent Sint-Pieters d.	0716	0732	minutes	2216	2232	...	2316	...	...
Lokeren d.	0739	0754	past	2239	2254	...	2339	...	...
Sint-Niklaas d.	0749	0804	each	2249	2304	...	2349	...	...
Antwerpen Berchem a.	0806	0819	hour	2306	2319	...	0006	...	...
Antwerpen Centraal a.	0811	0825	until	2311	2325	...	0011	...	...

Route		ICC Ⓐ	ICG Ⓐ	ICC Ⓐ	ICG Ⓐ		ICC Ⓐ	ICG Ⓐ	ICC Ⓐ	ICG Ⓐ
Antwerpen Centraal d.	Ⓐ	0450	0505	0549	0607	...	0650	0718	0750	0818
Antwerpen Berchem d.		0455	0510	0554	0612	...	0655	0723	0755	0823
Sint-Niklaas d.		0512	0531	0611	0636	...	0712	0744	0812	0844
Lokeren d.		0521	0540	0620	0646	...	0724	0753	0822	0853
Gent Sint-Pieters d.		0544	0601	0644	0707	...	0744	0814	0844	0914
Brugge a.		...	0632	...	0736	...	...	0843	...	0943
Oostende a.		...	0647	...	0752	...	...	0859	...	0959

Route	ICC Ⓐ	ICG Ⓐ	▲	ICC Ⓐ	ICG Ⓐ		ICC Ⓐ	ICC Ⓐ			ICG Ⓒ	ICC Ⓒ	ICG Ⓒ		ICC Ⓒ	ICG Ⓒ	▲	ICC Ⓒ	ICG Ⓒ		ICC Ⓒ	ICC Ⓒ
Antwerpen Centraal d.	0850	0918	and at	2050	2118	...	2203	2303	...	Ⓒ	0525	0549	0635	...	0649	0735	and at	2049	2135	...	2200	2300
Antwerpen Berchem d.	0855	0923	the same	2055	2123	...	2208	2308	...		0531	0554	0641	...	0654	0741	the same	2054	2141	...	2205	2305
Sint-Niklaas d.	0912	0944	minutes	2112	2144	...	2224	2324	...		0548	0613	0658	...	0713	0758	minutes	2113	2158	...	2224	2324
Lokeren d.	0922	0953	past	2122	2153	...	2233	2333	...		0557	0622	0707	...	0722	0807	past	2122	2207	...	2233	2333
Gent Sint-Pieters a.	0944	1014	each	2144	2214	...	2255	2355	...		0618	0644	0728	...	0744	0828	each	2144	2228	...	2255	2355
Brugge a.	...	1043	hour	...	2243	...	...	...	...		0654	...	0754	...	...	0854	hour	...	2254	...	...	...
Oostende a.	...	1059	until	...	2259	...	...	...	...		0710	...	0810	...	...	0910	until	...	2310	...	...	...

ICC – Lille - Mouscron - Kortrijk (- Oostende) - Gent - Antwerpen. See also Table **415**.
ICG – Oostende - Gent - Antwerpen.

▲ – Times may vary by ± 3 minutes on some journeys.

411 DE PANNE - GENT

km	Route		IRi Ⓐ	IRi Ⓐ	IRi Ⓐ		IRi Ⓐ	▲	IRi Ⓐ		IRi Ⓐ	IRi Ⓐ	IRi Ⓐ	IRi Ⓐ	IRi Ⓐ	IRi Ⓐ			IRi Ⓒ		IRi Ⓒ	
0	**De Panne** § d.	Ⓐ	0455	0554	0655	...	0755	and at	1455	...	1555	1655	1755	1855	1955	2055	...	Ⓒ	0655	and at	2055	...
5	Veurne d.		0503	0602	0703	...	0803	the same	1503	...	1603	1703	1803	1903	2003	2103	...		0703	the same	2103	...
20	Diksmuide d.		0515	0613	0715	...	0815	minutes	1515	...	1615	1715	1815	1915	2015	2115	...		0715	minutes	2115	...
39	Lichtervelde d.		0533	0631	0731	...	0833	past each	1533	...	1633	1733	1833	1933	2033	2133	...		0733	past each	2133	...
56	Tielt d.		0544	0642	0742	...	0844	hour	1544	...	1644	1744	1844	1944	2044	2144	...		0744	hour	2144	...
86	**Gent** Sint-Pieters a.		0610	0706	0806	...	0909	until	1609	...	1709	1809	1909	2009	2109	2209	...		0809	until	2209	...

Route		IRi Ⓐ	IRi Ⓐ	IRi Ⓐ		IRi Ⓐ	▲	IRi Ⓐ		IRi Ⓐ	IRi Ⓐ	IRi Ⓐ	IRi Ⓐ	IRi Ⓐ	IRi Ⓐ			IRi Ⓒ		IRi Ⓒ	
Gent Sint-Pieters d.	Ⓐ	0551	0651	0751	...	0851	and at	1551	...	1651	1751	1851	1951	2051	2151	...	Ⓒ	0651	and at	2051	...
Tielt d.		0617	0717	0817	...	0917	the same	1617	...	1717	1817	1917	2017	2117	2216	...		0717	the same	2117	...
Lichtervelde d.		0636	0736	0836	...	0936	minutes	1636	...	1736	1836	1936	2036	2131	2231	...		0736	minutes	2136	...
Diksmuide d.		0651	0751	0851	...	0951	past each	1651	...	1751	1851	1951	2051	2146	2245	...		0751	past each	2151	...
Veurne d.		0703	0803	0903	...	1003	hour	1703	...	1803	1903	2003	2103	2157	2256	...		0803	hour	2203	...
De Panne § a.		0709	0809	0909	...	1009	until	1709	...	1810	1910	2009	2109	2203	2303	...		0809	until	2209	...

IRi – De Panne - Gent - Brussels - Brussels Airport - Mechelen. See also Tables **405/425**.

▲ – Times may vary by ± 3 minutes on some journeys.

§ – Connection available into the **Belgian Coastal Tramway**. See Table **406** for details. De Panne railway station is situated in Adinkerke.

412 RONSE - GENT - EEKLO

km			Ⓐ	Ⓐ	Ⓐ	Ⓐ	Ⓐ	Ⓐ	Ⓐ	Ⓐ	Ⓐ	Ⓐ	Ⓐ	Ⓐ	Ⓐ	Ⓐ	Ⓐ	Ⓐ	Ⓐ	Ⓐ		Ⓒ	Ⓒ	Ⓒ	Ⓒ	Ⓒ	Ⓒ	Ⓒ	Ⓒ
0	**Ronse** d.	Ⓐ	0510	0610	0710	0816	0910	1010	1110	1210	1310	1410	1510	1610	1710	1810	1914	2010	2110	2202	Ⓒ	0709	0909	1109	1309	1512	1712	1912	21
14	Oudenaarde a.		0520	0620	0720	0826	0920	1020	1120	1220	1320	1420	1520	1620	1720	1820	1924	2020	2120	2212		0719	0919	1119	1319	1522	1722	1922	21
14	Oudenaarde d.		0523	0629	0730	0832	0932	1032	1132	1232	1332	1432	1532	1632	1732	1832	1932	2032	2132	2220		0721	0921	1121	1321	1532	1732	1932	21
39	**Gent** St-Pieters a.		0549	0656	0757	0859	0959	1059	1159	1259	1359	1459	1559	1659	1759	1859	1959	2059	2159	2247		0748	0948	1148	1384	1559	1759	1959	21

km			Ⓐ	Ⓐ	Ⓐ	Ⓐ	Ⓐ		Ⓐ		Ⓐ		Ⓐ	Ⓐ	Ⓐ		Ⓐ	Ⓐ			Ⓒ	Ⓒ	Ⓒ	Ⓒ	Ⓒ	Ⓒ	Ⓒ	Ⓒ
0	**Gent** St-Pieters d.	Ⓐ	0635	0711	0801	0841	0941	...	1041	and	1741	...	1759	1841	1941	...	2041	2141	...	Ⓒ	0612	0812	1012	1212	1412	1612	1812	20
7	Gent Dampoort d.		0645	0722	0810	0851	0951	...	1051	hourly	1751	...	1809	1851	1951	...	2051	2151	...		0622	0822	1022	1222	1422	1622	1822	20
27	**Eeklo** a.		0710	0747	0835	0917	1017	...	1117	until	1817	...	1834	1917	2017	...	2117	2217	...		0647	0847	1047	1247	1447	1647	1847	20

		Ⓐ	Ⓐ	Ⓐ	Ⓐ		Ⓐ		Ⓐ		Ⓐ	Ⓐ	Ⓐ	Ⓐ	Ⓐ	Ⓐ	Ⓐ			Ⓒ	Ⓒ	Ⓒ	Ⓒ	Ⓒ	Ⓒ	Ⓒ	Ⓒ	
Eeklo d.	Ⓐ	0543	0620	0712	0755	...	0843	and	1443	...	1543	1625	1743	1843	1943	2043	2143	...	Ⓒ	0713	0913	1113	1313	1513	1713	1913	2113	...
Gent Dampoort d.		0610	0647	0739	0822	...	0910	hourly	1510	...	1610	1652	1810	1910	2010	2110	2210	...		0739	0939	1139	1339	1539	1739	1939	2139	...
Gent St-Pieters a.		0619	0656	0748	0831	...	0919	until	1519	...	1620	1701	1819	1919	2019	2119	2219	...		0748	0948	1148	1348	1548	1748	1948	2148	...

		Ⓐ	Ⓐ	Ⓐ	Ⓐ	Ⓐ	Ⓐ	Ⓐ	Ⓐ	Ⓐ	Ⓐ	Ⓐ	Ⓐ	Ⓐ	Ⓐ	Ⓐ	Ⓐ	Ⓐ			Ⓒ	Ⓒ	Ⓒ	Ⓒ	Ⓒ	Ⓒ	Ⓒ	Ⓒ	
Gent St-Pieters d.	Ⓐ	0555	0701	0801	0901	1001	1101	1201	1301	1401	1501	1601	1701	1801	1901	2001	2101	2212	...	Ⓒ	0801	1001	1201	1401	1612	1812	2012	2212	...
Oudenaarde a.		0625	0729	0828	0928	1028	1128	1228	1328	1428	1528	1629	1728	1828	1928	2028	2128	2240	...		0827	1029	1229	1429	1640	1840	2040	2240	...
Oudenaarde d.		0635	0734	0840	0940	1040	1140	1240	1340	1440	1540	1634	1740	1840	1940	2040	2140	...	...		0838	1038	1238	1438	1645	1845	2045	...	...
Ronse a.		0645	0744	0850	0950	1050	1150	1250	1350	1450	1550	1644	1750	1850	1950	2050	2150	...	...		0848	1048	1248	1448	1655	1855	2055	...	...

Additional services operate Ronse - Gent and v.v. at peak times.

414 KORTRIJK - GENT - MECHELEN - LEUVEN

km	Route	IRf Ⓐ	IRf Ⓐ	IRf Ⓒ	IRf Ⓐ	IRf Ⓒ	IRf Ⓐ	IRf Ⓒ	IRf Ⓐ		IRf Ⓐ	IRf Ⓒ	IRf Ⓐ	IRf Ⓒ	IRf Ⓐ
0	**Kortrijk** d.	0413	0511	0518	0617	0618	0715	0718	0817		2117	2118	2217	2218	2318
42	**Gent** St-Pieters a.	0447	0546	0552	0651	0652	0752	0752	0851	and	2151	2152	2251	2252	2354
42	**Gent** St-Pieters d.	0452	0548	0605	0653	0705	0755	0805	0853	hourly	2153	2205	2257	2305	...
72	Dendermonde d.	0519	0616	0630	0719	0730	0819	0830	0919	until	2219	2230	2322	2329	...
99	**Mechelen** a.	0538	0638	0655	0738	0755	0838	0855	0938		2238	2255	...	...	...

Route	IRf Ⓐ	IRf Ⓒ	IRf Ⓒ	IRf Ⓐ	IRf Ⓒ	IRf Ⓐ		IRf Ⓒ	I
Mechelen d.	...	...	...	0622	0705	0722		2205	22
Dendermonde d.	0541	...	0631	0643	0731	0743	and	2231	22
Gent St-Pieters a.	0604	...	0655	0706	0755	0806	hourly	2255	2
Gent St-Pieters d.	0606	0608	0708	0708	0808	0808	until	2308	2
Kortrijk a.	0640	0642	0742	0742	0842	0842		2342	2

km	Route	IRf Ⓐ	IRa Ⓐ	IRf Ⓐ	IRa Ⓒ		IRa Ⓐ	IRf Ⓐ	IRa Ⓒ		IRa Ⓐ	IRf Ⓐ	IRa Ⓒ	IRa Ⓐ	IRf Ⓐ	IRa Ⓒ	IRa Ⓐ	IRf Ⓐ		IRa Ⓒ	IRa Ⓐ	IRf Ⓐ		IRa Ⓒ	IRa Ⓐ	IRf Ⓐ	IRa Ⓒ	I
0	Mechelen d.	0542	0622	0642	0656	...	0722	0742	0756	and hourly	1522	1542	1556	1622	1649	1656	1722	1749	...	1756	1822	1842	and hourly	2156	2222	2242	2256	2
24	Leuven a.	0615	0647	0715	0722	...	0747	0815	0822	until	1547	1615	1622	1647	1720	1722	1747	1820	...	1822	1847	1915	until	2222	2247	2315	2322	2

Route	IRa Ⓐ	IRf Ⓐ		IRa Ⓐ	IRf Ⓐ	IRa Ⓒ		IRa Ⓐ	IRa Ⓒ	IRf Ⓐ		IRa Ⓐ	IRa Ⓒ	IRf Ⓐ		IRa Ⓐ	IRa Ⓒ	IRf Ⓐ		IRa Ⓐ	IRa Ⓒ	IRf Ⓐ		IRa Ⓐ	IRa Ⓒ	IRf Ⓐ	
Leuven d.	0513	0545	...	0613	0643	0638	...	0713	0738	0743	...	0813	0838	0845	and hourly	2013	2038	2045	...	2113	2138	2145	...	2213	2238	2245	...
Mechelen a.	0538	0618	...	0638	0713	0704	...	0738	0804	0813	...	0838	0904	0918	until	2038	2104	2118	...	2138	2204	2218	...	2238	2304	2318	...

IRa – Leuven - Mechelen [- Sint-Niklaas].
IRf – Kortrijk - Gent - Mechelen - Leuven.

LILLE - KORTRIJK - OOSTENDE and GENT 415

Lille - Mouscron and v.v. subject to alteration on French and Belgian public holidays

km	Route	ICC Ⓐ	ICC	ICC Ⓐ	ICC Ⓒ	ICC Ⓐ	ICC Ⓒ	ICC Ⓐ	ICC Ⓐ	ICC ⑥	ICC †	ICC	ICC	ICC ⚒		ICC	ICC	ICC	ICC	ICC	ICC	ICC	ICC	ICC	ICC	ICC Ⓒ	ICC Ⓐ
0	**Lille** Flandres § d.	...	...	...	...	...	...	...	0708	0707	...	...	...	0808	...	0908	...	...	1008	1108	...	1207	...	1308	...	1403	1408
10	Roubaix § d.	...	...	...	...	...	...	...	0718	0719	...	...	...	0820	...	|	...	...	1018	1118d	...	1218	...	|	...	1418	1418
12	Tourcoing 🏛 § d.	...	...	...	...	...	...	...	0722	0723	...	...	...	0822	...	|	...	...	1022	1122d	...	1222	...	|	...	1422	1423
18	Mouscron d.	...	...	...	...	0631	0631	...	0731	0731	0731	...	...	0831	...	0931	...	...	1031	1131	...	1231	...	1331	...	1431	1431
30	**Kortrijk** ⊖ a.	...	...	...	...	0639	0639	...	0739	0739	0739	...	...	0839	...	0939	...	...	1039	1139	...	1239	...	1339	...	1439	1439
30	**Kortrijk** ⊖ d.	0446	0546	0552	0607	0648	0646	0648	0748	0748	0748	0748	0848	0848	...	0948	0948	1048	1048	1148	1148	1248	1248	1348	1348	1448	1448
	Brugge ◇ a.	0532	|	0632	0651	|	|	0727	|	|	|	0829	0927	|	...	1027	|	1127	|	|	1227	|	1327	1427	|	|	|
	Oostende ◇ a.	0548	|	0650	0748	|	|	0743	|	|	|	0843	0943	|	...	1043	|	1143	|	|	1243	|	1343	1443	|	|	|
72	**Gent** Sint-Pieters a.	...	0614	...	...	0714	0714	...	0814	0814	0814	...	...	0914	...	...	1014	...	1114	1214	...	1314	...	...	1414	1514	1514

Route	ICC		ICC Ⓒ	ICC Ⓐ	ICC	ICC ⑥	ICC Ⓑ	ICC	ICC Ⓒ	ICC Ⓐ	ICC	ICC †	ICC Ⓐ	ICC ⑥	ICC Ⓒ		ICC Ⓐ	ICC	ICC	ICC ⚒	ICC †	ICC	ICC Ⓐ	ICC Ⓒ	ICC	ICC Ⓒ	ICC Ⓐ
Lille Flandres § d.	...	...	1508	...	...	1603	1608	...	1708	1708	...	1803	1808	1807	...	...	...	1908	...	2008	2008	...	2108	2107	...	2208	2208
Roubaix § d.	...	...	|	...	...	1617	1618	...	1718	1718	...	1818	1818	1819	...	...	...	1918	...	2018	|	...	2118	2118	...	2218	2218
Tourcoing 🏛 § d.	...	...	|	...	...	1622	1622	...	1722	1723	...	1822	1822	1824	...	...	...	1922	...	2022	|	...	2122	2122	...	2222	2222
Mouscron d.	...	...	1531	1533	...	1631	1631	...	1731	1731	...	1831	1831	1831	...	...	...	1931	...	2031	2031	...	2131	2131	...	2231	2231
Kortrijk ⊖ a.	...	...	1539	1541	...	1639	1639	...	1739	1739	...	1839	1839	1839	...	...	...	1939	...	2039	2039	...	2139	2139	...	2241	2241
Kortrijk ⊖ d.	1448	...	1548	1548	1548	1648	1648	1648	1748	1751	1748	1848	1846	1848	1848	...	1851	1948	1948	2048	2048	2048	2148	2148	2148	2243	2248
Brugge ◇ a.	1527	...	|	|	1627	|	|	1727	1827	1830	|	|	|	|	1927	...	1930	|	2027	|	|	2127	2227	2232	|	|	|
Oostende ◇ a.	1543	...	|	|	1643	|	|	1743	1843	1847	|	|	|	|	1944	...	1947	|	2043	|	|	2143	2243	2252	|	|	|
Gent Sint-Pieters a.	...	...	1614	1614	...	1714	1714	...	...	...	1814	1914	1912	1914	...	...	...	2014	...	2114	2114	...	...	...	2214	2314	2314

km	Route	ICC Ⓐ	ICC ⑥	ICC Ⓐ	ICC Ⓐ	ICC †	ICC ⑥	ICC Ⓐ	ICC	ICC	ICC	ICC Ⓐ	ICC Ⓒ	ICC	ICC Ⓐ	ICC Ⓒ	ICC	ICC	ICC	ICC	ICC	ICC Ⓐ	ICC Ⓒ	ICC	ICC	ICC	ICC
	Gent Sint-Pieters d.	...	*0538*	0546	...	0646	0646	0646	0746	...	...	0846	0846	...	0946	0946	...	1046	1146	...	...	1246	*1246*	...	1346	...	1446
0	**Oostende** ◇ d.	0512	|	|	0605	|	|	|	|	0710	0810	|	|	0910	|	|	1010	|	|	1110	1210	|	|	1310	|	1410	|
22	Brugge ◇ d.	0531	|	|	0625	|	|	|	|	0731	0831	|	|	0931	|	|	1031	|	|	1131	1231	|	|	1331	|	1431	|
75	**Kortrijk** ⊖ a.	0611	*0612*	0612	0705	0712	0712	0712	0812	0812	0912	0912	0912	1012	1012	1012	1112	1112	1212	1212	1312	1314	*1312*	1412	1412	1512	1512
	Kortrijk ⊖ d.	...	0620	0620	...	0720	0720	0720	...	0820	...	0920	0920	...	1019	1020	...	1120	...	1220	...	1320	1320	...	1420	...	1520
	Mouscron d.	...	0630	0630	...	0728	0730	0730	...	0828	...	0930	0930	...	1027	1030	...	1130	...	1230	...	1330	1330	...	1430	...	1530
	Tourcoing 🏛 § a.	...	|	|	...	...	0734	0735	...	0835	...	0935	0935	...	...	|	...	|	...	1235	...	|	1335	...	|	...	1535
	Roubaix § a.	...	|	|	...	...	0739	0740	...	0840	...	0940	0938	...	...	|	...	|	...	1239	...	|	1339	...	|	...	1540
	Lille Flandres § a.	...	0650	0650	...	...	0754	0750	...	0850	...	0950	0950	...	...	1050	...	1150	...	1250	...	1350	1350	...	1450	...	1550

Route	ICC	ICC Ⓐ	ICC Ⓒ	ICC		ICC Ⓐ	ICC Ⓒ	ICC	ICC Ⓐ	ICC Ⓐ	ICC Ⓒ	ICC	ICC	ICC	ICC Ⓐ	ICC Ⓒ		ICC Ⓐ	ICC Ⓒ	ICC	ICC Ⓐ	ICC Ⓒ	ICC	ICC Ⓐ	ICC Ⓒ	ICC	ICC
Gent Sint-Pieters d.	1546	...	...	...	...	1646	1646	...	1746	...	1746	...	1846	1946	...	...	...	...	...	2046	...	...	2146	...	...	2257	2357
Oostende ◇ d.	|	1510	1511	1610	...	|	|	1710	|	...	|	1810	|	|	1910	1911	...	2010	2011	|	2110	2111	|	2210	2210	|	|
Brugge ◇ d.	|	1531	1532	1631	...	|	|	1731	|	...	|	1831	|	|	1931	1932	...	2031	2032	|	2131	2132	|	2231	2231	|	|
Kortrijk ⊖ a.	1614	1612	1612	1712	...	1714	1712	1812	1814	...	1812	1912	1912	2012	2011	2012	...	2111	2112	2112	2211	2212	2212	2315	2320	2323	0032
Kortrijk ⊖ d.	...	1620	1620	...	...	1720	1720	...	...	1820	1820	...	1920	...	2020	2020	...	...	...	2120	...	...	2219	...	...	...	...
Mouscron d.	...	1630	1630	...	...	1730	1730	...	...	1830	1830	...	1930	...	2030	2030	...	...	...	2130	...	...	2227	...	...	...	...
Tourcoing 🏛 § a.	...	1635	1634	...	...	1735	1735	...	...	1835	1835	...	1935	...	|	|	...	...	...	|	...	...	...	...	...	...	...
Roubaix § a.	...	1640	1639	...	...	1740	1740	...	...	1840	1840	...	1940	...	|	|	...	...	...	|	...	...	...	...	...	...	...
Lille Flandres § a.	...	1650	1654	...	...	1750	1750	...	...	1850	1850	...	1950	...	2050	2050	...	...	...	2150	...	...	...	...	...	...	...

ICC – Lille - Mouscron - Kortrijk (- Oostende) - Gent - Antwerpen. See also Table **410**.

d – ⚒ only.

⊖ – Connections may be available to service(s) in previous column(s).

§ – Frequent services Lille Flandres - Lille Europe - Roubaix and Tourcoing are operated by the Lille *VAL* métro (Line 2) or by tram. For *TGV* trains see Table **250**.

◇ – For additional services between Oostende and Brugge see Tables **400**/**410**.

LILLE - TOURNAI - MONS 416

Subject to alteration on Belgian and French holidays

km	Route		ICD Ⓐ	ICD Ⓐ	ICD Ⓐ	ICD Ⓐ	ICD Ⓐ	ICD Ⓐ	ICD Ⓐ	ICD Ⓐ	ICD Ⓐ	ICD Ⓐ		ICD Ⓐ	ICD Ⓐ	ICD Ⓐ	ICD Ⓐ	ICD Ⓐ	ICD Ⓐ	ICD Ⓐ	ICD Ⓐ	ICD Ⓐ	ICD Ⓐ		ICD Ⓐ	ICD Ⓐ	
0	**Lille** Flandres d.	Ⓐ	...	0609	...	0709	0736	0809	0909	1025	...	1209	...	1325	...	1509	1609	1709	1736	1809	1920	...	2025	...	...	2215	...
25	Tournai 🏛 § a.		...	0644	...	0744	0803	0844	0944	1044	...	1244	...	1344	...	1544	1644	1744	1802	1844	1944	...	2044	...	...	2242	...
25	Tournai d.		0553	...	0657	0757	...	0857	0957	1057	1157	1257	...	1357	1457	1557	1657	1757	...	1857	...	1957	2057	...	2157	...	...
73	**Mons** a.		0624	...	0724	0824	...	0924	1024	1124	1224	1324	...	1424	1524	1624	1724	1824	...	1924	...	2024	2124	...	2224	...	...

Route		ICD Ⓒ	ICD Ⓒ	ICD Ⓒ	ICD Ⓒ	ICD Ⓒ	ICD Ⓒ	ICD ⑥	ICD †	ICD ⑥	ICD †	ICD ⑥	ICD †	ICD Ⓒ	ICD Ⓒ	ICD ⑥	ICD †	ICD ⑥	ICD †	ICD Ⓒ	ICD Ⓒ	ICD †	ICD ⑥	ICD †	ICD ⑥	ICD Ⓒ
Lille Flandres d.	Ⓒ	...	...	0739j	0839r	0948	1055	1149	1154	1239	1254	1349	1354	1454	1554	1647	1654	1739	1747	1847	1947	2047	2051	2154	...	2224
Tournai 🏛 § a.		...	...	0814	0914	1014	1114	1214	1214	1314	1314	1414	1414	1514	1614	1714	1714	1814	1814	1914	2014	2114	2114	2214	...	2242
Tournai d.		0626	0726	0826	0926	1026	1126	1226	1226	1326	1326	1426	1426	1526	1626	1726	1726	1826	1826	1926	2026	2126	2126	2235	2235	...
Saint-Ghislain d.		0655	0755	0855	0955	1055	1155	1255	1255	1355	1355	1455	1455	1555	1655	1755	1755	1855	1855	1955	2055	2155	2155	2303	2303	...
Mons a.		0706	0806	0906	1006	1106	1206	1306	1306	1406	1406	1506	1506	1606	1706	1806	1806	1906	1906	2006	2106	2206	2206	2315	2315	...

Route		ICD Ⓐ	ICD Ⓐ	ICD Ⓐ	ICD Ⓐ	ICD Ⓐ	ICD Ⓐ	ICD Ⓐ	ICD Ⓐ	ICD Ⓐ	ICD Ⓐ	ICD Ⓐ	ICD Ⓐ	ICD Ⓐ	ICD Ⓐ	ICD Ⓐ	ICD Ⓐ	ICD Ⓐ	ICD Ⓐ	ICD Ⓐ	ICD Ⓐ	ICD Ⓐ	ICD Ⓐ	ICD Ⓐ	ICD Ⓐ	ICD Ⓐ
Mons d.	Ⓐ	...	0629	0629	0734	...	0734	0835	0935	...	1035	1135	1235	1335	1435	1535	...	1635	1735	...	1835	1935	...	2035	2135	2235
Tournai a.		...	0656	0656	0803	...	0803	0903	1003	...	1103	1203	1303	1403	1503	1603	...	1703	1802	...	1903	2002	...	2103	2202	2319
Tournai 🏛 § d.		0616	*0658*	0716	...	0811	0816	0916	...	1016	1116	1216	1316	...	1516	1616	1653	1716	...	1815	1916	...	2015	2116	...	...
Lille Flandres a.		0651	*0724*	0751	...	0835	0851	0935	...	1035	1135	1251	1351	...	1551	1651	1723	1751	...	1851	1951	...	2035	2144	...	...

Route		ICD †	ICD ⑥	ICD Ⓒ	ICD Ⓒ	ICD ⑥	ICD †		ICD Ⓒ	ICD †	ICD ⑥	ICD †	ICD ⑥	ICD Ⓒ		ICD †	ICD ⑥	ICD Ⓒ	ICD Ⓒ	ICD Ⓒ	ICD Ⓒ	ICD Ⓒ	ICD Ⓒ		ICD Ⓒ	ICD Ⓒ
Mons d.	Ⓒ	0653	0653	0753	0853	0953	0953	...	1053	1153	1153	1253	1253	1353	...	1453	1453	1553	1653	1753	1853	1953	2053	...	2153	2253
Saint-Ghislain d.		0706	0706	0806	0906	1006	1006	...	1106	1206	1206	1306	1306	1406	...	1506	1506	1606	1706	1806	1906	2006	2106	...	2206	2306
Tournai a.		0734	0734	0834	0934	1034	1034	...	1134	1234	1234	1334	1334	1434	...	1534	1534	1634	1734	1834	1934	2034	2134	...	2234	2334
Tournai 🏛 § d.		0746	0746	0846	0946	1046	1046	...	1146	1246	1246	1346	1346	1446	...	1546	1546	1646	1746	1846	1946	2046	2146	...	...	...
Lille Flandres a.		0806	0819	0914	1006	1106	1114	...	1206	1306	1314	1406	1414	1506	...	1606	1616	1714	1814	1906	2016	2106	2206	...	...	...

ICD – Lille - Tournai - Mons - Charleroi - Namur - Liège [- Herstal]. See also Table **442**.

g – ⑥ only.
j – Depart 0755 on †.
r – Depart 0847 on †.

§ – Ticket point is Blandain.

BINCHE - LA LOUVIÈRE - BRUSSELS 418

km	Route	IRI Ⓐ		IRI Ⓒ	IRI Ⓐ		IRI Ⓐ	IRI Ⓒ	IRI Ⓐ	IRI Ⓒ
0	**Binche** d.	0516	...	0547	0616		2016	2047	2116	2147
9	La Louvière Sud d.	0528	...	0558	0628	and at	2028	2058	2228	2158
12	**La Louvière** Centre d.	0534	...	0604	0634	the same	2034	2104	2134	2204
31	Braine-le-Comte d.	0555	...	0623	0655	minutes	2055	2123	2155	2223
47	Halle d.	0609	...	|	0709	past each	2109	|	2209	|
60	**Brussels** Midi / Zuid a.	0619	...	0645	0719	hour	2119	2145	2219	2245
62	Brussels Central a.	0624	...	0650	0724	until	2124	2150	2224	2250
64	**Brussels** Nord a.	0628	...	0654	0728		2128	2154	2228	2254

Route	IRI Ⓐ	IRI Ⓒ	IRI Ⓐ	IRI Ⓒ		IRI Ⓐ	IRI Ⓒ		IRI Ⓐ
Brussels Nord d.	0532	0606	0632	0706		2132	2206	...	2232
Brussels Central d.	0536	0610	0636	0710	and at	2136	2210	...	2236
Brussels Midi / Zuid d.	0541	0615	0641	0715	the same	2141	2215	...	2241
Halle d.	0552	|	0652	|	minutes	2152	|	...	2252
Braine-le-Comte d.	0607	0639	0707	0739	past each	2207	2239	...	2307
La Louvière Centre d.	0628	0658	0728	0758	hour	2228	2258	...	2340
La Louvière Sud a.	0632	0702	0732	0802	until	2232	2302	...	2344
Binche a.	0644	0713	0744	0813		2244	2313	...	2356

IRI – Binche - Brussels [- Louvain-la-Neuve Université].

420 CHARLEROI - BRUSSELS - ANTWERPEN

Thalys services (Paris -) Brussels – Antwerpen – Amsterdam and v.v, also international services Brussels – Antwerpen – Roosendaal – Den Haag and v.v , see Table 18.

km	Route	Ⓐ	Ⓐ	IRd Ⓐ	ICI Ⓐ	IRn Ⓐ	ICN Ⓐ	IRd Ⓐ	ICI Ⓐ	IRn Ⓐ	ICN Ⓐ	IRd Ⓐ	ICI Ⓐ	IRn Ⓐ			ICN Ⓐ	IRd Ⓐ	ICI Ⓐ	IRn Ⓐ	ICN Ⓐ	IRd Ⓐ	ICI Ⓐ	IRn Ⓐ	ICN Ⓐ	IRd Ⓐ
0	**Charleroi** Sud d.		...	...	0436	...	0537	...	0605	...	0635	...	0708	...	...	▲	1637	...	1708	...	1737	...	1808	...	1837	...
26	Nivelles d.		...	...	0507	...	0601	...	0627	...	0659	...	0729	...	...	and at	1701	...	1729	...	1801	...	1829	...	1901	...
55	**Brussels** Midi / Zuid d.		0448	0533	0556	0605	0628	0632	0656	0704	0728	0732	0756	0804	...	the same	1728	1732	1756	1805	1828	1832	1856	1905	1927	1931
57	**Brussels** Central d.		0452	0537	0600	0609	0632	0636	0700	0708	0732	0736	0800	0808	...	minutes	1732	1736	1800	1809	1832	1836	1900	1909	1931	1935
59	**Brussels** Nord d.		0457	0542	0605	0614	0637	0642	0705	0713	0737	0742	0805	0813	...	past each	1737	1742	1805	1814	1837	1842	1905	1914	1936	1941
79	Mechelen d.		0527	0600	0623	0632	0653	0700	0723	0732	0753	0800	0823	0832	...	hour	1753	1800	1823	1832	1853	1900	1923	1932	1953	1959
101	Antwerpen Berchem a.		0545	0619	0637	0649	0707	0719	0737	0749	0807	0819	0837	0849	...	until	1807	1819	1837	1849	1907	1919	1937	1949	2007	2029
103	**Antwerpen** Centraal a.		0551	0624	0643	0655	0713	0724	0743	0755	0813	0824	0843	0855	...		1813	1824	1843	1855	1913	1925	1943	1955	2013	2035

Route	ICI Ⓐ	IRn Ⓐ	ICN Ⓐ	IRd Ⓐ	ICI Ⓐ	ICN Ⓐ	IRd Ⓐ	ICI Ⓐ	ICN Ⓐ	IRd Ⓐ	ICI Ⓐ	ICN Ⓐ	IRd Ⓐ	Ⓒ	IRn Ⓒ	ICI Ⓒ	IRn Ⓒ	ICI Ⓒ		IRn Ⓒ	ICI Ⓒ	IRn Ⓒ	ICI Ⓒ	IRn Ⓒ	ICI Ⓒ
Charleroi Sud d.	1908	...	1937	...	2008	2037	...	2108	2137	...	2208	2237	...		...	0540	...	0640	▲	...	2040	...	2140	...	2240
Nivelles d.	1929	...	2001	...	2029	2101	...	2129	2201	...	2229	2301	...		...	0603	...	0703	and at	...	2103	...	2203	...	2303
Brussels Midi / Zuid d.	1956	2005	2027	2031	2056	2127	2131	2156	2227	2231	2256	2327	2331		0601	0632	0701	0732	the same	2101	2132	2201	2232	2301	2332
Brussels Central d.	2000	2009	2031	2035	2100	2131	2135	2200	2231	2235	2300	2331	2335		0605	0636	0705	0736	minutes	2105	2136	2205	2236	2305	2336
Brussels Nord d.	2005	2014	2036	2041	2105	2136	2141	2205	2236	2241	2305	2335	2344		0610	0641	0710	0741	past each	2110	2141	2210	2241	2310	2341
Mechelen d.	2023	2032	2053	2059	2123	2153	2159	2223	2253	2259	2323	...	0008		0628	0703	0728	0803	hour	2128	2203	2228	2303	2328	0003
Antwerpen Berchem a.	2037	2049	2107	2129	2137	2207	2229	2237	2307	2329	2337	...	0036		0647	0717	0747	0817	until	2147	2217	2247	2317	2347	0018
Antwerpen Centraal a.	2043	2055	2113	2135	2143	2213	2235	2243	2313	2335	2343	...	0041		0652	0722	0752	0822		2152	2222	2252	2322	2352	0022

Route	Ⓐ	Ⓐ	ICN Ⓐ	ICI Ⓐ	IRd Ⓐ	ICN Ⓐ	IRn Ⓐ	ICI Ⓐ	IRd Ⓐ	ICN Ⓐ	IRn Ⓐ	ICI Ⓐ	IRd Ⓐ	ICN Ⓐ	IRn Ⓐ	ICI Ⓐ	IRd Ⓐ	ICN Ⓐ		IRn Ⓐ	ICI Ⓐ	IRd Ⓐ	ICN Ⓐ	IRn Ⓐ	ICI Ⓐ
Antwerpen Centraal d.		0418	...	0517	0536	0547	0604	0617	0636	0647	0705	0717	0736	0747	0805	0817	0836	0847	▲	1805	1817	1836	1847	1905	1917
Antwerpen Berchem d.		0424	...	0523	0541	0553	0610	0623	0641	0653	0711	0723	0741	0753	0811	0823	0841	0853	and at	1811	1823	1841	1853	1911	1923
Mechelen d.		0455	...	0540	0602	0609	0630	0640	0702	0709	0730	0740	0802	0809	0830	0840	0902	0990	the same	1830	1840	1902	1909	1930	1940
Brussels Nord d.		0520	0525	0557	0620	0625	0646	0657	0720	0725	0747	0759	0820	0825	0847	0857	0920	0925	minutes	1846	1857	1920	1925	1946	1957
Brussels Central d.		0524	0529	0601	0625	0629	0651	0701	0725	0729	0752	0803	0825	0829	0852	0901	0925	0929	past each	1851	1901	1924	1929	1951	2001
Brussels Midi / Zuid d.		0527	0534	0606	0628	0634	0656	0706	0728	0734	0756	0808	0828	0834	0856	0906	0928	0934	hour	1855	1906	1927	1934	1955	2006
Nivelles d.		...	0600	0632	...	0700	...	0732	...	0800	...	0833	...	0900	...	0932	...	1000	until	...	1932	...	2000	...	2032
Charleroi Sud a.		...	0623	0652	...	0723	...	0752	...	0823	...	0853	...	0923	...	0952	...	1023		...	1952	...	2023	...	2052

Route	IRd Ⓐ	ICN Ⓐ	IRn Ⓐ	ICI Ⓐ	IRd Ⓐ	ICN Ⓐ	ICI Ⓐ	IRd Ⓐ	ICN Ⓐ	ICI Ⓐ	IRd Ⓐ	ICI Ⓐ	IRd Ⓐ	IRd Ⓐ	Ⓒ	ICI Ⓒ	ICI Ⓒ	IRn Ⓒ	ICI Ⓒ	IRn Ⓒ	ICI Ⓒ	IRn Ⓒ		ICI Ⓒ	IRn Ⓒ
Antwerpen Centraal d.	1925	1947	2005	2017	2025	2047	2117	2125	2147	2217	2225	2317	2325	0025		...	0538	0608	0638	0703	0738	0808	▲	2238	2308
Antwerpen Berchem d.	1931	1953	2011	2023	2031	2053	2123	2131	2153	2223	2231	2323	2331	0031		...	0543	0613	0643	0708	0743	0713	and at	2243	2313
Mechelen d.	2003	2009	2030	2040	2103	2109	2140	2203	2209	2240	2303	2340	0003	0103		...	0600	0634	0700	0728	0800	0834	the same	2300	2334
Brussels Nord d.	2021	2026	2046	2057	2121	2126	2157	2221	2226	2257	2335	2357	0025	0127		0519	0621	0652	0721	0746	0821	0852	minutes	2321	2352
Brussels Central d.	2025	2030	2051	2101	2125	2130	2201	2225	2230	2301	2339	0001	0029	0131		0523	0625	0655	0725	0749	0825	0855	past each	2325	2355
Brussels Midi / Zuid d.	2028	2035	2055	2106	2128	2135	2206	2228	2235	2306	2342	0006	0032	0134		0528	0630	0659	0730	0754	0830	0849	hour	2330	2359
Nivelles d.	...	2100	...	2132	...	2200	2232	...	2300	2332	...	0046	...	...		0558	0658	...	0758	...	0858	...	until	2358	...
Charleroi Sud a.	...	2123	...	2152	...	2223	2252	...	2323	2352	...	0114	...	...		0620	0720	...	0820	...	0920	...		0020	...

ICI – Charleroi - Brussels - Antwerpen.
ICN – Charleroi - Brussels - Antwerpen - Essen.
IRd – Antwerpen - Brussels - Ath [- Grammont] - Tournai - Mouscron - Kortrijk. See also Table **427**.
IRn – Brussels - Antwerpen.

▲ – Times may vary by ± 3 minutes on some journeys.
Other variations: *IRn* departures on Ⓐ at 10xx, 11xx, 12xx, 13xx, 14xx, 20xx do not run July 8 - Aug. 23.

421 ANTWERPEN - NOORDERKEMPEN and ROOSENDAAL

km	km	Route	Ⓐ	ICN Ⓐ	IRs Ⓐ		Ⓐ	ICN Ⓐ	IRs Ⓐ	Ⓐ	ICN Ⓐ	IRs Ⓐ			Ⓐ	ICN Ⓐ	IRs Ⓐ		Ⓐ	ICN Ⓐ	IRs Ⓐ	Ⓐ	ICN Ⓐ
0	0	**Antwerpen** Centraal d.		0616	0639	...	0649	0720	0739	0749	0816	0839	...	▲ and at	1749	1816	1839	...	1849	1916	1939	1949	2016
	24	Noorderkempen a.		|	0656	...	|	|	0756	|	|	0856	...	the same	|	|	1856	...	|	|	1956	|	|
15		Kapellen d.		0630	...	...	0708	0741	...	0808	0830	...	...	minutes past each	1808	1830	...	...	1908	1930	...	2008	2030
33		Essen 🏛 a.		0648	...	...	0728	0756	...	0828	0848	...	...	hour	1828	1848	...	...	1928	1948	...	2028	2048
41		**Roosendaal** a.		...	...	...	0736	...	...	0836	...	...	...	until	1836	...	...	...	1936	...	...	2038	...

Route	IRs Ⓐ		Ⓐ	ICN Ⓐ	Ⓐ	ICN Ⓐ	Ⓐ	ICN Ⓐ	Ⓐ		Ⓒ	Ⓒ		Ⓒ	Ⓒ	IRs Ⓒ			IRs Ⓒ	Ⓒ		Ⓒ	Ⓒ	
Antwerpen Centraal d.	2039	...	2049	2116	2149	2216	2249	2316	2350	...		0620	...	0720	0820	0835	...	▲ and at	2035	2120	...	2220	2320	...
Noorderkempen a.	2056	...	|	|	|	|	|	|	|	...		|	...	|	|	0852	...	the same minutes	2052	|	...	|	|	...
Kapellen d.	...	...	2108	2130	2208	2230	2308	2330	0008	...		0639	...	0739	0839	...	...	past each	...	2139	...	2239	2339	...
Essen 🏛 a.	...	...	2128	2148	2228	2248	2328	2348	0030	...		0659	...	0759	0859	...	...	hour	...	2159	...	2590	2359	...
Roosendaal a.	...	...	2136	...	2236	...	2339	...	...	...		0707	...	0807	0907	...	...	until	...	2207	...	...	...	...

Route	Ⓐ	ICN Ⓐ	Ⓐ	IRs Ⓐ	ICN Ⓐ	Ⓐ	IRs Ⓐ	ICN Ⓐ	Ⓐ	IRs Ⓐ	ICN Ⓐ	Ⓐ		IRs Ⓐ		ICN Ⓐ	Ⓐ		IRs Ⓐ	ICN Ⓐ	Ⓐ	IRs Ⓐ	ICN Ⓐ
Roosendaal d.		...	...	...	...	...	...	...	0724	...	...	0824	...	...	▲ and at	...	1824	...	...	...	1924	...	...
Essen 🏛 d.		0505	0530	...	0612	0630	...	0712	0732	...	0812	0832	...	...	the same	1812	1832	...	...	1912	1932	...	2012
Kapellen d.		0526	0551	...	0631	0651	...	0731	0752	...	0831	0850	...	...	minutes past each	1831	1852	...	...	1931	1952	...	2031
Noorderkempen d.		|	|	0605	|	|	0711	|	|	0805	|	|	...	0905	hour	|	|	...	1905	|	|	2005	|
Antwerpen Centraal a.		0544	0611	0621	0644	0711	0727	0744	0811	0821	0844	0911	...	0921	until	1844	1911	...	1921	1944	2011	2021	2044

Route	Ⓐ		ICN	Ⓐ	Ⓐ				Ⓒ	Ⓒ		IRs Ⓒ	Ⓒ			IRs Ⓒ	Ⓒ			Ⓒ	Ⓒ			
Roosendaal d.	2024	...	...	2124	2224	...	...		...	0653	...	...	0753	...	▲ and at	...	1953	...	...	2053	2153	...	...	...
Essen 🏛 d.	2032	...	2112	2132	2232	...	...		0601	0701	...	...	0801	...	the same	...	2001	...	...	2101	2201	...	...	...
Kapellen d.	2052	...	2131	2152	2252	...	...		0621	0721	...	...	0821	...	minutes past each	...	2021	...	...	2121	2221	...	...	...
Noorderkempen d.	|	...	|	|	|	...	...		|	|	...	0805	|	...	hour	2005	|	...	...	|	|	...	...	...
Antwerpen Centraal a.	2111	...	2144	2211	2311	...	...		0640	0740	...	0821	0840	...	until	2021	2040	...	...	2140	2240	...	...	...

ICN – Charleroi - Brussels - Antwerpen - Essen.
IRs – Antwerpen - Noorderkempen.

g – ⑥ only.

▲ – Times may vary by ± 2 minutes on some journeys.
Other variations: no service from Antwerpen at 1035Ⓒ, 1139Ⓐ, 1339Ⓐ, 1535Ⓒ; from Noorderkempen at 1005Ⓒ, 1105Ⓐ, 1305Ⓐ, 1505Ⓒ.

422 CHARLEROI - COUVIN

km	Route	IRr Ⓐ	IRr Ⓐ	Ⓒ	IRr Ⓐ	IRr Ⓐ	Ⓒ	Ⓐ	IRr Ⓐ	Ⓒ	Ⓐ	IRr Ⓐ	IRr Ⓐ	Ⓒ	Ⓐ	IRr Ⓐ	Ⓒ	IRr Ⓐ	IRr Ⓐ	Ⓒ	IRr Ⓐ	IRr Ⓐ	IRr Ⓐ	Ⓒ	Ⓐ	IRr Ⓐ	Ⓒ	Ⓐ
0	**Charleroi** Sud d.	0618	0713	0754	0814	0909	0954	1010	1114	1154	1230	1311	1405	1402	1507	1541	1554	1613	1718	1754	1819	1918	1952	1954	2010	2107	2230	223
18	Berzée d.	0634	0729	0815	0830	0924	1015	1032	1130	1215	1252	1328	1421	1423	1529	1557	1615	1629	1733	1815	1835	1934	2008	2015	2032	2123	2251	225
22	Walcourt d.	0639	0735	0822	0835	0929	1022	1038	1135	1222	1259	1333	1426	1430	1535	1603	1622	1635	1739	1822	1840	1945	2013	2022	2038	2128	2258	230
35	Philippeville d.	0652	0750	0837	0847	0941	1037	1052	1147	1237	1313	1346	1438	1445	1550	1615	1637	1650	1751	1837	1852	1957	2025	2037	2053	2141	2313	231
48	Mariembourg ▲ d.	0708	0802	0847	0858	0952	1047	1103	1158	1248	1324	1357	1449	1454	1600	1625	1647	1700	1802	1847	1903	2007	2035	2047	2103	2151	2323	232
53	**Couvin** a.	0714	0808	0853	0904	0958	1053	1109	1204	1254	1330	1403	1455	1502	1606	1631	1653	1706	1808	1853	1909	2013	2041	2053	2109	2157	2329	233

Route		IRr Ⓐ	Ⓒ	IRr Ⓐ	IRr Ⓐ	Ⓒ	IRr Ⓐ	IRr Ⓐ	Ⓒ	Ⓐ	IRr Ⓐ	Ⓒ	IRr Ⓐ	Ⓐ	IRr Ⓐ	Ⓒ	IRr Ⓐ	Ⓐ	IRr Ⓐ	Ⓒ	IRr Ⓐ	IRr Ⓐ	Ⓒ	IRr Ⓐ	IRr Ⓐ	Ⓒ	Ⓐ	Ⓒ
Couvin d.	...	0448	0507	0553	0635	0707	0733	0830	0907	0923	1033	1107	1150	1223	1245	1259	1349	1419	1501	1507	1532	1709	1706	1809	1911	1907	2056	205
Mariembourg ▲ d.	...	0455	0514	0600	0642	0714	0740	0837	0914	0930	1041	1114	1158	1231	1302	1306	1357	1427	1508	1514	1539	1716	1714	1817	1918	1914	2103	210
Philippeville d.	...	0506	0525	0612	0653	0725	0751	0848	0925	0942	1053	1125	1209	1243	1314	1317	1408	1439	1519	1525	1551	1727	1725	1828	1930	1925	2114	211
Walcourt d.	...	0518	0539	0626	0705	0739	0806	0901	0939	0956	1105	1139	1222	1258	1326	1331	1420	1453	1531	1539	1603	1739	1739	1840	1942	1939	2128	213
Berzée d.	...	0525	0546	0630	0709	0746	0811	0905	0946	1001	1109	1146	1226	1303	1330	1338	1424	1500	1535	1546	1607	1743	1746	1845	1946	1946	2133	213
Charleroi Sud a.	...	0540	0606	0645	0725	0806	0828	0922	1006	1023	1126	1206	1242	1324	1345	1358	1441	1522	1551	1606	1624	1803	1806	1904	2002	2006	2155	215

IRr – Charleroi - Couvin.

▲ – Service available on certain dates Mariembourg - Treignes and v.v. Some trains operated by steam locomotive.
Operator: Chemin de Fer à Vapeur des 3 Vallées (CFV3V), Chaussée de Givet 49-51, 5660 Mariembourg. ✆ / fax +32 60 312 44

CHARLEROI - ERQUELINNES — 424

29 km Journey time: ±40 minutes

From **Charleroi** Sud:
Ⓐ: 0621, 0721, and hourly until 2021, 2113.
Ⓒ: 0648, 0848 and every two hours until 2048.

From **Erquelinnes**:
Ⓐ: 0510, 0605 and hourly until 2005.
Ⓒ: 0732, 0932 and every two hours until 2132.

All services call at Thuin (*14 km*, 17 minutes from Charleroi).

Jeumont (France) is approximately *2 km* from Erquelinnes (see Table **262**).

BRUSSELS NATIONAAL AIRPORT ✈ — 425

From BRUSSELS MIDI / ZUID: Journey time: ± 21 minutes

Ⓐ: 0448, 0500, 0515, 0530, 0548, 0600, 0612, 0630, 0648, 0659, 0730, 0748, 0759, 0830, 0848, 0859, 0915, 0930, 0948, 1000, 1015, 1030, 1048 and at the same minutes past each hour until 1548, then 1600, 1630, 1648, 1700, 1730, 1748, 1800, 1815, 1830, 1848 and at the same minutes past each hour until 2248, then 2300, 2315.
Ⓒ: 0450, 0509, 0518, 0530, 0550, 0610, 0618, 0630, 0650 and at the same minutes past each hour until 2250, then 2310, 2318.

All services call at Brussels Central (± 4 minutes later) and Brussels Nord (± 9 minutes later).

From ANTWERPEN CENTRAAL: Journey time: ± 34 Ⓐ, 45 Ⓒ minutes

Ⓐ: 0440, 0509, 0542, 0609, 0642, 0709, 0742 and at the same minutes past each hour until 2242, 2309.
Ⓒ: 0542, 0642, 0742 and hourly until 2142.

From GENT ST PIETERS: Journey time: ± 54 §, 90 ‡ minutes

Ⓐ: 0421 ‡, 0520 ‡ 0616 §, and at the same minutes past each hour until 2116 §, 2120 ‡, 2216 §.
Ⓒ: 0528 ‡, 0628 ‡ and hourly until 2128 ‡.

From LEUVEN: Journey time: ± 14 minutes

Ⓐ: 0529, 0607, 0629, 0707, 0729 and at the same minutes past each hour until 2207, 2229, 2307, 2329.
Ⓒ: 0507, 0607 and hourly until 2307.

From MECHELEN: Journey time: ± 11 minutes

Ⓐ: 0504, 0535, 0606 and at the same minutes past each hour until 2235, 2306, 2335.
Ⓒ: 0545, 0615, 0645, 0715, 0745, 0815 and at the same minutes past each hour until 2145, 2215 then 2245, 2345.

From MONS: Journey time: ± 70 minutes

Ⓐ: 0507, 0607, 0707, 0806, 0907, 1007 and hourly until 2207.
Ⓒ: 0521, 0621, 0721 and hourly until 2221.

To BRUSSELS MIDI / ZUID: Journey time: ± 21 minutes

Ⓐ: 0524, 0536, 0551, 0609, 0624, 0636, 0651, 0709, 0736, 0751, 0809, 0836, 0851, 0909, 0924, 0936, 0951 and at the same minutes past each hour until 1536, then 1551, 1609, 1636, 1646, 1709, 1736, 1751, 1809, 1824, 1836, 1851 and at the same minutes past each hour until 2351, then 0024.
Ⓒ: 0522, 0530, 0550, 0607, 0622, 0630, 0650, 0707, 0722, 0730, 0750 and at the same minutes past each hour until 2350.

Services also call at Brussels Nord (journey time ± 12 minutes) and Brussels Central (journey time ± 17 minutes).

To ANTWERPEN CENTRAAL: Journey time: ± 34 Ⓐ, 45 Ⓒ minutes

Ⓐ: 0440, 0509, 0542 and at the same minutes past each hour until 2209, 2242, 2309.
Ⓒ: 0735, 0835 and hourly until 2035, 2137, 2235.

To GENT ST PIETERS: Journey time: ± 54 §, 90 ‡ minutes

Ⓐ: 0551 §, 0609 ‡, 0651 § and at the same minutes past each hour until 2051 §, 2109 ‡, 2209 ‡, 2309 ‡.
Ⓒ: 0607 ‡, 0707 ‡ and hourly until 2207 ‡.

To LEUVEN: Journey time: ± 14 minutes

Ⓐ: 0516, 0539, 0618, 0639 and at the same minutes past each hour until 1739; then 1821, 1839, 1918, 2018, 2039, 2118, 2139, 2218, 2239, 2318, 2339.
Ⓒ: 0539, 0640 and hourly until 2240, 2340.

To MECHELEN: Journey time: ± 11 minutes

Ⓐ: 0514, 0544, 0614, 0644 and at the same minutes past each hour until 2214; then 2244, 2314, 2344.
Ⓒ: 0604, 0704, 0735 and at the same minutes past each hour until 2004, 2035: then 2104, 2137, 2204, 2235, 2304.

To MONS: Journey time: ± 70 minutes

Ⓐ: 0536, 0636 and hourly until 2136.
Ⓒ: 0530, 0630 and hourly until 2230.

CQ – Antwerpen Centraal - Mechelen - Brussels Airport - Leuven [- Landen].
Rh – Gent - Denderleeuw - Brussels - Brussels Airport.
Ri – De Panne - Gent - Brussels - Brussels Airport - Mechelen. See also Tables **405/411**.
IRj – Quévy - Mons - Brussels - Brussels Airport. See also Table **435**.
IRo – Brussels - Brussels Airport - Leuven.
IRp – Brussels - Brussels Airport.

MOUSCRON - TOURNAI - BRUSSELS — 427

km	Route		IRd Ⓐ	ICH Ⓐ	IRd Ⓐ	ICH Ⓐ	IRd Ⓐ	ICH Ⓐ	IRd Ⓐ	ICH Ⓐ		IRd Ⓐ	ICH Ⓐ	IRd Ⓐ	ICH Ⓐ	IRd Ⓐ	ICH Ⓐ	
0	**Mouscron** d.	Ⓐ	...	0436	...	0531	0558	0636	0702	0736	▲	2002	2036	...	2136	...	2236	...
20	**Tournai** a.		...	0451	...	0546	0613	0651	0719	0751	and at	2019	2051	...	2151	...	2251	...
20	**Tournai** d.		0421	0453	0521	0552	0621	0653	0721	0753	the same	2021	2053	...	2153	...	2253	...
38	Leuze d.		0434	0506	0534	0606	0634	0706	0734	0806	minutes	2034	2106	...	2206	...	2306	...
50	Ath d.		0449	0517	0549	0616	0649	0717	0749	0817	past each	2049	2117	2149	2217	2249	2317	...
101	**Brussels** Midi / Zuid a.		0530	0553	0630	0653	0730	0752	0830	0851	hour	2129	2153	2229	2253	2327	2352	...
103	Brussels Central a.		0536	0558	0635	0658	0735	0757	0835	0857	until	2134	2158	2234	2258	2334	2357	...
105	**Brussels** Nord a.		0540	0602	0640	0702	0740	0801	0840	0901		2139	2202	2239	2302	2338	0001	...

Route		ICH Ⓒ	ICH Ⓒ		ICH Ⓒ	ICH ⑥
Mouscron d.	Ⓒ	0524	0607	▲	1407	1507
Tournai a.		0538	0621	and at	1421	1521
Tournai d.		0540	0640	the same	1440	1540
Leuze d.		0552	0652	minutes	1452	1552
Ath d.		0603	0703	past each	1503	1603
Brussels Midi / Zuid a.		0639	0739	hour	1539	1639
Brussels Central a.		0644	0744	until	1544	1644
Brussels Nord a.		0648	0748		1548	1648

Route	ICH †	ICH ⑥		ICH †	ICH ⑥	ICH †	ICH Ⓒ
ouscron d.	1524	1607	▲	2024	2107	2124	2215
ournai a.	1533	1621	and at	2038	2121	2138	2229
ournai d.	1540	1640	the same	2040	2140	2140	2240
euze d.	1552	1652	minutes	2052	2152	2152	2252
h d.	1603	1709	past each	2103	2203	2203	2303
ussels Midi / Zuid a.	1639	1739	hour	2139	2239	2239	2339
ussels Central a.	1644	1744	until	2144	2244	2244	2344
ussels Nord a.	1648	1748		2148	2248	2248	2348

Route		IRd Ⓐ	ICH Ⓐ	IRd Ⓐ	ICH Ⓐ	IRd Ⓐ		ICH Ⓐ	IRd Ⓐ	ICH Ⓐ	IRd Ⓐ
Brussels Nord d.	Ⓐ	...	0452	0520	0558	0620	▲	1758	1820	1858	1920
Brussels Central d.		...	0456	0524	0602	0625	and at	1802	1825	1902	1924
Brussels Midi / Zuid d.		...	0501	0530	0607	0630	the same	1807	1830	1907	1930
Ath d.		...	0543	0618	0644	0718	minutes	1844	1918	1944	2018
Leuze d.		...	0552	0627	0654	0727	past each	1854	1927	1954	2027
Tournai a.		...	0604	0639	0706	0739	hour	1906	1939	2006	2039
Tournai d.		0541	0608	0641	0708	0741	until	1908	1941	2008	...
Mouscron a.		0557	0623	0657	0723	0757		1923	1957	2023	...

Route	ICH Ⓐ	IRd Ⓐ	ICH Ⓐ	IRd Ⓐ	ICH Ⓐ	IRd Ⓐ	ICH Ⓐ	IRd Ⓐ	
ussels Nord d.	1958	2021	2058	2121	2205	2221	2258	2335	...
ussels Central d.	2002	2025	2102	2125	2209	2225	2302	2339	...
ussels Midi / Zuid d.	2007	2030	2107	2130	2214	2230	2307	2346	...
h d.	2044	2111	2144	2211	2249	2311	2344	0024	...
uze d.	2054	...	2154	...	2259	...	2354	...	...
ournai a.	2106	...	2206	...	2311	...	0006	...	...
ournai d.	2108	...	2208	...	2325	...	...	...	...
ouscron a.	2123	...	2223	...	2340	...	...	...	...

	ICH Ⓒ		ICH Ⓒ	ICH †	ICH ⑥	ICH †		ICH ⑥	ICH †	ICH ⑥	ICH Ⓒ	ICH Ⓒ	ICH Ⓒ	ICH Ⓒ
Ⓒ	0612	▲	1312	1412	1412	1512	▲	1812	1912	1912	2012	2112	2212	2326
	0616	and at	1316	1416	1416	1516	and at	1816	1916	1916	2016	2116	2216	2330
	0621	the same	1321	1421	1421	1521	the same	1821	1921	1921	2021	2121	2221	2334
	0659	minutes	1359	1459	1459	1559	minutes	1859	1959	1959	2059	2159	2259	0012
	0708	past each	1408	1508	1508	1608	past each	1908	2008	2008	2108	2208	2308	0021
	0720	hour	1420	1520	1520	1620	hour	1920	2020	2020	2120	2220	2320	0034
	0739	until	1439	1522	1539	1622	until	1939	1622	2039	2139	2239	2339	...
	0753		1453	1536	1553	1636		1953	2036	2053	2153	2253	2353	...

H – Mouscron - Tournai - Brussels [- Schaerbeek].
d – Antwerpen - Brussels - Ath [- Grammont] - Tournai - Mouscron - Kortrijk. See also Table **421**.

▲ – Times may vary by ± 4 minutes on some journeys.

430 BRUSSELS - HASSELT, GENK and LIÈGE

km	Route		ICK Ⓐ	ICK Ⓐ	ICF Ⓐ	ICE Ⓐ	ICK Ⓐ	ICF Ⓐ	ICE Ⓐ		ICK Ⓐ	ICF Ⓐ	ICE Ⓐ		ICK Ⓐ	ICF Ⓐ	ICE Ⓐ	ICK Ⓐ	ICF Ⓐ	ICE Ⓐ			ICE Ⓒ	ICE Ⓒ	ICE Ⓒ	ICE Ⓒ
0	**Brussels** Midi / Zuid d.	Ⓐ	...	0508	0531	0527	0608	0631	0636	...	0708	0731	0736	✣	2108	2131	2136	2211	2231	2236	...	Ⓒ	0636	0636	0736	0736
2	Brussels Central d.		...	0512	0535	0531	0612	0635	0640	...	0712	0735	0740	▲	2112	2135	2140	2215	2235	2240	...		0640	0640	0740	0740
4	Brussels Nord d.		...	0517	0540	0545	0617	0640	0645	...	0717	0740	0745	and	2117	2140	2145	2222	2240	2245	...		0645	0645	0745	0745
33	Leuven a.		...	0536	0557	0602	0636	0657	0702	...	0736	0757	0802	at the	2136	2157	2202	2239	2257	2302	...		0703	0703	0803	0803
33	Leuven d.		...	0538	0559	0612	0638	0659	0712	...	0738	0759	0812	same	2138	2159	2212	2241	2259	2312	...		0705	0705	0805	0805
64	Landen a.		...	0559	0622	|	0659	0722	|	...	0759	0822	|	minutes	2159	2222	|	2311	2322	|	...		0726	0726	0826	0826
64	Landen d.		...	0601	0624	|	0701	0724	|	...	0801	0824	|	past	2201	2224	|	2313	2323	|	...		0734	0738	0834	0838
	Aarschot d.		...	|	|	0624	|	|	0727	...	|	|	0824	each	|	|	2224	|	|	2327	...		|	|	|	|
	Diest d.		...	|	|	0635	|	|	0745	...	|	|	0835	hour	|	|	2235	|	|	2345	...		|	|	|	|
75	Sint-Truiden d.		...	0610	|	|	0710	|	|	...	0810	|	|	until	2210	|	|	2322	|	|	...		0744	|	0844	|
92	Hasselt d.		0527	0627	|	0650	0727	|	0803	...	0827	|	0850		2227	|	2250	2339	|	0003	...		0803	|	0903	|
108	**Genk** a.		0545	0645	|	...	0745	|	...	...	0845	|	...		2245	|	...	2356	|	...	...		0819	|	0919	|
	Liège Guillemins a.		...	...	0652	...	...	0755	...	...	...	0855	...		...	2254	...	...	2354	...	...		...	0807	...	0907

Route	ICE Ⓒ	ICE Ⓒ		ICE Ⓒ	ICE Ⓒ
Brussels Midi / Zuid d.	0836	0836		2236	2236
Brussels Central d.	0840	0840	▲	2240	2240
Brussels Nord d.	0845	0845	and	2245	2245
Leuven a.	0903	0903	at the	2303	2303
Leuven d.	0905	0905	same	2305	2305
Landen a.	0926	0926	minutes	2326	2326
Landen d.	0934	0938	past	2334	2338
Aarschot d.	|	|	each	|	|
Diest d.	|	|	hour	|	|
Sint-Truiden d.	0944	|	until	2344	|
Hasselt d.	1003	|		0003	|
Genk a.	1019	|		0019	|
Liège Guillemins a.	...	1007		...	0007

Route		ICK Ⓐ	ICE Ⓐ	ICF Ⓐ	ICK Ⓐ	ICE Ⓐ	ICF Ⓐ	ICK Ⓐ	ICE Ⓐ	ICF Ⓐ	ICK Ⓐ		ICE Ⓐ	ICF Ⓐ	ICK Ⓐ
Liège Guillemins d.	Ⓐ	...	...	0508	...	...	0608	...	...	0705	...	...	...	0808	...
Genk d.		...	...	|	0515	...	|	0610	...	|	0707	...	...	|	0815
Hasselt d.		0426	0457	|	0534	0557	|	0629	0657	|	0726	...	0810	|	0834
Sint-Truiden d.		0442	|	|	0549	|	|	0646	|	|	0744	...	|	|	0849
Diest d.		|	0516	|	|	0614	|	|	0714	|	|	...	0825	|	|
Aarschot d.		|	0535	|	|	0635	|	|	0735	|	|	...	0837	|	|
Landen a.		0451	|	0538	0558	|	0638	0656	|	0737	0755	...	|	0838	0858
Landen d.		0454	|	0539	0600	|	0639	0658	|	0739	0758	...	|	0839	0900
Leuven a.		0522	0548	0601	0622	0648	0701	0722	0748	0801	0822	...	0848	0901	0922
Leuven d.		0524	0558	0604	0624	0658	0704	0724	0758	0804	0824	...	0858	0903	0924
Brussels Nord a.		0543	0615	0620	0643	0715	0720	0742	0815	0820	0842	...	0915	0920	0941
Brussels Central a.		0548	0620	0625	0648	0720	0725	0747	0820	0825	0847	...	0920	0925	0946
Brussels Midi / Zuid a.		0552	0624	0629	0652	0724	0729	0751	0824	0829	0851	...	0924	0929	0950

km	Route		ICE Ⓐ	ICF Ⓐ	ICK Ⓐ		ICE Ⓐ	ICF Ⓐ	ICK Ⓐ	ICE Ⓐ	ICF Ⓐ	ICK Ⓐ	Ⓐ			ICE Ⓒ	ICE Ⓒ		ICE Ⓒ	ICE Ⓒ		ICE Ⓒ	ICE Ⓒ	ICE Ⓒ	ICE Ⓒ
	Liège Guillemins d.		...	2008	...	...	...	2108	...	...	2208	...	...	...	Ⓒ	0553	...	▲	1953	...	...	2053	...	2153	...
	Genk d.	▲	...	|	2015	...	...	|	2115	...	|	2215	...	...		|	0541	and	|	1941	...	|	2041	|	2141
0	Hasselt d.	and	2010	|	2034	...	2110	|	2134	2210	|	2233	2239	...		|	0601	at the	|	2001	...	|	2101	|	2201
	Sint-Truiden d.	at the	|	|	2049	...	|	|	2149	|	|	...	|	...		|	0617	same	|	2017	...	|	2117	|	2217
21	Diest d.	same	2025	|	|	...	2125	|	|	2225	|	...	2255	...		|	|	minutes	|	|	...	|	|	|	|
39	Aarschot d.	minutes	2037	|	|	...	2137	|	|	2237	|	...	2314	...		|	|	past	|	|	...	|	|	|	|
	Landen a.	past	|	2038	2058	...	|	2138	2158	|	2238	...	|	...		0622	0626	each	2022	2026	...	2122	2126	2222	2226
	Landen d.	each	|	2039	2100	...	|	2139	2200	|	2239	...	|	...		0634	0634	hour	2034	2034	...	2134	2134	2234	2234
55	Leuven a.	hour	2048	2101	2122	...	2148	2201	2222	2248	2301	...	2326	...		0655	0655	until	2055	2055	...	2155	2155	2255	2255
55	Leuven d.	until	2058	2103	2124	...	2158	2203	2224	2258	2303	...	...	...		0657	0657		2057	2057	...	2157	2157	2257	2257
84	Brussels Nord a.		2115	2120	2143	...	2215	2220	2243	2315	2320	...	...	...		0714	0714		2114	2114	...	2214	2214	2314	2314
86	Brussels Central a.		2120	2125	2148	...	2220	2225	2248	2321	2325	...	...	...		0720	0720		2120	2120	...	2220	2220	2320	2321
88	**Brussels** Midi / Zuid a.		2124	2129	2152	...	2224	2229	2252	2324	2329	...	...	...		0724	0724		2124	2124	...	2224	2224	2324	2324

ICE – Knokke / Blankenberge - Gent - Brussels - Leuven - Hasselt [- Tongeren] - Genk / Liège. See also Tables **400/405**.
ICF – Quiévrain - Mons - Brussels - Liège. See also Table **435**.
ICK – Gent - Brussels - Leuven - Hasselt - Genk. See also Table **405**.

✣ – Variations: Brussels Midi d. 1636; as pattern to Leuven, then Aarschot d. 1727, Diest d. 1745, Hasselt a. 1803.
▲ – Times may vary by ± 3 minutes on some journeys.

432 ANTWERPEN - HASSELT - LIÈGE

km	Route		IRc Ⓐ	IRc Ⓐ	IRc Ⓐ		IRc Ⓐ	IRc Ⓐ	IRc Ⓐ	IRc Ⓐ			IRc Ⓒ	IRc Ⓒ	IRc Ⓒ		IRc Ⓒ		IRc Ⓒ	IRc Ⓒ	IRc Ⓒ	IRc Ⓒ
0	**Antwerpen** Centraal d.	Ⓐ	...	0530	0630		1930	2030	2130	2230	...	Ⓒ	...	...	0642		1842	...	1942	2042	2142	2242
2	Antwerpen Berchem d.		...	0535	0635	and	1935	2035	2135	2235	...		...	...	0647	and	1847	...	1947	2047	2147	2247
14	Lier d.		...	0545	0645		1945	2045	2145	2245	...		...	...	0657		1857	...	1957	2057	2157	2257
41	Aarschot d.		...	0612	0712	hourly	2012	2112	2212	2312	...		...	...	0723	hourly	1923	...	2023	2123	2223	2323
59	Diest d.		...	0624	0724		2024	2124	2224	2324	...		...	...	0735		1935	...	2035	2135	2241	2337
80	**Hasselt** a.		...	0638	0738	until	2038	2138	2238	2338	...		...	...	0750	until	1950	...	2050	2150	2258	2350
80	**Hasselt** d.		0544	0645	0744		2044	2144	...	...	...		0556	0656	0756		1956	...	2056	2204	2304	...
107	Tongeren d.		0607	0707	0807		2107	2206	...	...	...		0618	0718	0818		2018	...	2118	2227	2327	...
135	**Liège** Guillemins a.		0644	0744	0844		2144	...	...	...	...		0652	0752	0852		2052	...	2152	...	...	...

Route		IRc Ⓐ	IRc Ⓐ	IRc Ⓐ	IRc Ⓐ		IRc Ⓐ		IRc Ⓐ			IRc Ⓒ	IRc Ⓒ		IRc Ⓒ		IRc Ⓒ		IRc Ⓒ		
Liège Guillemins d.	Ⓐ	...	...	0616	0716	...	0816		2116	...	Ⓒ	...	0608	...	0708		2008	...	2108	...	...
Tongeren d.		...	0550	0654	0754	...	0854	and	2154	...		...	0644	...	0744	and	2044	...	2146	...	...
Hasselt a.		...	0613	0716	0816	...	0916		2216	...		...	0705	...	0805		2105	...	2208	...	...
Hasselt d.		0522	0622	0722	0822	...	0922	hourly	2222	...		0610	0710	...	0810	hourly	2110	...	2210	...	...
Diest d.		0537	0636	0737	0837	...	0937		2237	...		0624	0724	...	0824		2124	...	2224	...	...
Aarschot d.		0554	0654	0754	0854	...	0954	until	2254	...		0642	0742	...	0842	until	2142	...	2242	...	...
Lier d.		0615	0715	0815	0915	...	1015		2315	...		0704	0804	...	0904		2204	...	2304	...	...
Antwerpen Berchem a.		0625	0725	0825	0925	...	1025		2325	...		0713	0813	...	0913		2213	...	2313	...	...
Antwerpen Centraal a.		0630	0730	0830	0930	...	1030		2330	...		0718	0818	...	0918		2218	...	2318	...	...

IRc – Antwerpen - Liège.

434 ANTWERPEN and BRUSSELS - LIER - TURNHOUT and NEERPELT

km	Route		ICR Ⓐ	IRe Ⓐ	IRg Ⓐ	▲	IRg Ⓐ	ICR Ⓐ	IRe Ⓐ	Ⓐ	ICR Ⓐ	IRe Ⓐ	ICR Ⓐ	IRe Ⓐ			IRe Ⓒ	IRe Ⓒ	IRg Ⓒ	▲	IRe Ⓒ	IRg Ⓒ	IRe Ⓒ	IRg Ⓒ	
0	**Antwerpen** Centraal d.	Ⓐ	...	0610	0647	and	2047	...	2110	2151	...	2237	...	2336	...	Ⓒ	0618	0718	0726	and	2218	2226	2318	2328	...
2	Antwerpen Berchem d.		...	0616	0652	at	2052	...	2116	2157	...	2242	...	2342	...		0624	0724	0731	at	2224	2231	2324	2333	...
	Brussels Midi / Zuid d.		0538	|	|	the	|	2038	|	|	2138	|	2238	|	...		|	|	|	the	|	|	|	|	...
	Mechelen d.		0605	|	|	same	|	2105	|	|	2205	|	2305	|	...		|	|	|	same	|	|	|	|	...
14	Lier d.		0623	0627	0706	minutes	2106	2123	2127	2210	2223	2255	2323	2355	...		0634	0734	0741	minutes	2234	2241	2338	2343	...
34	Herentals d.		0639	0642	0722	past	2123	2139	2142	...	2239	2318	2339	0019	...		0648	0748	0802	past	2248	2302	2358	0005	...
	Turnhout a.		0654	|	0739	each	2139	2154	|	...	2254	|	2354	|	...		|	|	0817	each	|	2317	|	0020	...
46	Geel d.		...	0654	...	hour	...	...	2154	...	...	2332	...	0032	...		0659	0759	...	hour	2259	...	0011	...	...
55	Mol d.		...	0706	...	until	...	...	2206	...	...	2342	...	0040	...		0708	0808	...	until	2308	...	0019	...	...
79	**Neerpelt** a.		...	0725	...		...	...	2225	...	...	0001	...	...	...		0726	0826	...		2326	...	...	...	...

km	Route		IRe Ⓐ	ICR Ⓐ	IRe Ⓐ	ICR Ⓐ	IRg Ⓐ	▲	IRg Ⓐ	IRe Ⓐ	ICR Ⓐ	IRe Ⓐ	ICR Ⓐ	IRe Ⓐ			IRe Ⓒ	IRe Ⓒ	IRg Ⓒ	IRe Ⓒ	IRg Ⓒ	▲	IRe Ⓒ	IRg Ⓒ	IRe Ⓒ
	Neerpelt d.	Ⓐ	0435	...	0532	...	...	and	...	2035	...	2135	...	...	...	Ⓒ	...	0534	...	0634	...	and	2034	...	213
	Mol d.		0459	...	0558	...	...	at	...	2059	...	2159	...	...	...		0449	0554	...	0654	...	at	2054	...	215
	Geel d.		0507	...	0606	...	...	the	...	2107	...	2207	...	...	...		0456	0601	...	0701	...	the	2101	...	220
0	Turnhout d.		|	0459	|	0605	0621	same	2022	|	2105	|	2205	←	...		|	|	0643	|	0743	same	|	2143	|
18	Herentals d.		0520	0523	0620	0623	0639	minutes	2039	2120	2123	2218	2223	2228	...		0507	0613	0700	0713	0800	minutes	2113	2200	221
38	Lier d.		0535	0539	0635	0639	0656	past	2056	2135	2139	→	2239	2251	...		0522	0627	0720	0727	0820	past	2127	2220	222
55	Mechelen a.		|	0555	|	0655	|	each	|	|	2155	...	2255	|	...		|	|	|	|	|	each	|	|	|
79	**Brussels** Midi / Zuid a.		|	0622	|	0723	|	hour	|	|	2222	...	2322	|	...		|	|	|	|	|	hour	|	|	|
	Antwerpen Berchem a.		0544	...	0644	...	0708	until	2108	2144	...	...	...	2306	...		0531	0636	0729	0736	0829	until	2136	2229	223
	Antwerpen Centraal a.		0549	...	0650	...	0713		2113	2150	...	...	...	2312	...		0537	0642	0734	0742	0834		2142	2234	224

ICR – Brussels - Turnhout.
IRe – Antwerpen - Mol [- Hasselt] - Neerpelt.
IRg – Antwerpen - Turnhout.
▲ – Times may vary by ± 5 minutes on some journeys.

BRUSSELS - MONS - QUÉVY and QUIÉVRAIN — 435

km	Route		IRj	ICF	IRj	ICF	IRj	ICF	IRj	ICF	IRj		ICF	IRj	ICF	IRj	ICF	IRj	ICF	IRj	ICF	IRj	ICF	IRj
			Ⓐ	Ⓐ	Ⓐ	Ⓐ	Ⓐ	Ⓐ	Ⓐ	Ⓐ	Ⓐ		Ⓐ	Ⓐ	Ⓐ	Ⓐ	Ⓐ	Ⓐ	Ⓐ	Ⓐ	Ⓐ	Ⓐ	Ⓐ	Ⓐ
0	**Brussels** Nord d.	Ⓐ	0453	0515	0553	0622	0653	0722	0754	0822	0853		1322	1353	1422	1453	1522	1552	1623	1652	1722	1752	1822	1853
2	Brussels Central d.		0457	0519	0557	0626	0657	0726	0758	0826	0857	▲	1326	1357	1426	1457	1526	1558	1627	1658	1726	1758	1826	1857
4	**Brussels** Midi / Zuid d.		0504	0524	0604	0633	0704	0733	0804	0833	0904	and at	1333	1404	1433	1504	1533	1604	1633	1704	1733	1804	1833	1904
33	Braine-le-Comte d.		0529	0543	0629	0655	0729	0755	0829	0855	0929	the same	1355	1429	1455	1529	1555	1629	1655	1729	1755	1829	1855	1929
39	Soignies d.		0535	0549	0635	0701	0735	0801	0835	0901	0935	minutes	1401	1435	1501	1535	1601	1635	1701	1735	1801	1835	1901	1935
64	**Mons** a.		0552	0604	0652	0716	0752	0816	0852	0916	0952	past each	1416	1452	1516	1552	1616	1652	1716	1752	1816	1852	1915	1952
64	**Mons** d.		0554	0606	0654	0718	0754	0818	0854	0918	0954	hour	1418	1454	1518	1612	1618	1654	1718	1754	1818	1859	1918	1959
	Quévy a.		0612	|	0712	|	0812	|	0912	|	1012	until	|	1512	|	1630	|	1712	|	1812	|	1917	|	2017
74	Saint-Ghislain d.		...	0620	...	0733	...	0832	...	0932	...		1432	...	1534	...	1634	...	1734	...	1834	...	1932	...
84	**Quiévrain** a.		...	0635	...	0749	...	*0856*	...	*0956*	...		*1456*	...	1550	...	1650	...	1750	...	1850	...	*1956*	...

Route	ICF	IRj	ICF	IRj		ICF	IRj	ICF	ICF			IRj		IRj		IRj		IRj	IRj	IRj	IRj	IRj	IRj	IRj
	Ⓐ	Ⓐ	Ⓐ	Ⓐ		Ⓐ	Ⓐ	Ⓐ	Ⓐ			Ⓒ		Ⓒ		Ⓒ		Ⓒ	Ⓒ	Ⓒ	Ⓒ	Ⓒ	Ⓒ	Ⓒ
Brussels Nord d.	1922	1953	2022	2053	...	2122	2153	2222	2322	...	Ⓒ	0544	...	0644	▲	1544	...	1644	1744	1844	1944	2044	2144	2244
Brussels Central d.	1926	1957	2026	2057	...	2126	2157	2226	2326	...		0548	...	0648		1548	...	1648	1748	1848	1948	2048	2148	2248
Brussels Midi / Zuid d.	1933	2004	2033	2104	...	2133	2204	2235	2335	...		0554	...	0654	and at	1554	...	1654	1754	1854	1954	2054	2154	2254
Braine-le-Comte d.	1955	2029	2055	2129	...	2155	2229	2255	2358	...		0615	...	0715	the same	1615	...	1715	1815	1915	2015	2115	2215	2315
Soignies d.	2001	2035	2101	2135	...	2201	2235	2301	0004	...		0621	...	0721	minutes	1621	...	1721	1821	1921	2021	2121	2221	2321
Mons a.	2016	2052	2116	2152	...	2216	2253	2316	0022	...		0639	...	0739	past each	1639	...	1739	1839	1939	2039	2139	2239	2339
Mons d.	2018	2054	2118	2154	...	2218	...	2318	0023	...		0641	...	0741	hour	1641	...	1741	1841	1941	2041	2141	2241	2341
Quévy a.	|	2112	|	2212	...	|	...	|	|	...		|	...	|	until	|	...	|	|	|	|	|	|	|
Saint-Ghislain d.	2034	...	2134	...	...	2232	...	2332	0037	...		0654	...	0754		1654	...	1754	1854	1954	2054	2154	2254	2354
Quiévrain a.	2050	...	2150	...	...	...	...	...	...	...		*0724*	...	*0824*		*1724*	...	*1824*	*1924*	*2024*	*2124*	...	...	...

km	Route		ICF	IRj	ICF	IRj	ICF	IRj	ICF	IRj	ICF	IRj	ICF	IRj	ICF	IRj		ICF	IRj	ICF	IRj		ICF
			Ⓐ	Ⓐ	Ⓐ	Ⓐ	Ⓐ	Ⓐ	Ⓐ	Ⓐ	Ⓐ	Ⓐ	Ⓐ	Ⓐ	Ⓐ	Ⓐ		Ⓐ	Ⓐ	Ⓐ	Ⓐ		Ⓐ
	Quiévrain d.	Ⓐ	...	...	0510	...	0603	...	0709	...	0807	...	*0904*	...	*1004*	...		*1504*	...	1610	...		1910
	Saint-Ghislain d.		0423	...	0527	...	0627	...	0727	...	0827	...	0927	...	1027	...	▲	1527	...	1627	...	▲	1927
0	Quévy d.		|	0446	|	0546	|	0646	|	0744	|	0846	|	0946	|	1046	and at	|	1546	|	1646	and at	|
15	**Mons** a.		0435	0502	0541	0602	0641	0702	0741	0800	0841	0902	0941	1002	1041	1102	the same	1541	1602	1641	1702	the same	1941
	Mons d.		0436	0507	0543	0607	0643	0707	0743	0806	0843	0907	0943	1007	1043	1107	minutes	1543	1607	1643	1707	minutes	1943
	Soignies d.		0500	0526	0600	0626	0700	0726	0800	0826	0900	0926	1000	1026	1100	1126	past each	1600	1626	1700	1726	past each	2000
	Braine-le-Comte d.		0507	0532	0607	0633	0707	0733	0807	0832	0907	0932	1007	1032	1107	1132	hour	1607	1632	1707	1732	hour	2007
	Brussels Midi / Zuid a.		0525	0555	0625	0656	0727	0755	0827	0856	0927	0957	1028	1057	1127	1157	until	1627	1655	1727	1757	until	2027
	Brussels Central a.		0534	0603	0634	0702	0734	0802	0834	0902	0934	1003	1034	1103	1134	1203		1634	1701	1734	1803		2034
	Brussels Nord a.		0538	0607	0638	0707	0738	0807	0836	0908	0938	1007	1038	1107	1138	1207		1638	1705	1738	1807		2038

Route	IRj	ICF	IRj	ICF	IRj		ICF			IRj	IRj	IRj	IRj	IRj	IRj	IRj		IRj		IRj		IRj	IRj	
	Ⓐ	Ⓐ	Ⓐ	Ⓐ	Ⓐ		Ⓐ			Ⓒ	Ⓒ	Ⓒ	Ⓒ	Ⓒ	Ⓒ	Ⓒ		Ⓒ		Ⓒ		Ⓒ		
Quiévrain d.	...	*2004*	...	2110	...	...	2210	...	Ⓒ	...	...	...	*0736*	*0836*	*0936*	*1036*	...	*1136*		*1936*	...	*2036*	*2136*	...
Saint-Ghislain d.	...	2027	...	2127	...	...	2227	...		0506	0606	0706	0806	0906	1006	1106	...	1206	▲	2006	...	2106	2206	...
Quévy d.	1946	|	2046	|	2146	...	|	...		|	|	|	|	|	|	|	...	|	and at	|	...	|	|	...
Mons a.	2002	2041	2102	2141	2202	...	2241	...		0519	0619	0719	0819	0919	1019	1119	...	1219	the same	2019	...	2119	2219	...
Mons d.	2007	2043	2107	2143	2207	...	2243	...		0521	0621	0721	0821	0921	1021	1121	...	1221	minutes	2021	...	2121	2221	...
Soignies d.	2026	2100	2126	2200	2226	...	2300	...		0540	0640	0740	0841	0940	1040	1141	...	1240	past each	2040	...	2140	2240	...
Braine-le-Comte d.	2031	2107	2132	2207	2232	...	2307	...		0546	0646	0746	0846	0946	1046	1146	...	1246	hour	2046	...	2146	2246	...
Brussels Midi / Zuid a.	2057	2127	2157	2227	2257	...	2330	...		0606	0706	0806	0906	1006	1106	1206	...	1306	until	2106	...	2206	2306	...
Brussels Central a.	2103	2134	2203	2234	2303	...	2335	...		0613	0713	0813	0913	1013	1113	1213	...	1313		2113	...	2213	2313	...
Brussels Nord a.	2107	2138	2207	2238	2307	...	2339	...		0617	0717	0817	0917	1017	1117	1217	...	1317		2117	...	2217	2317	...

ICF – Quiévrain - Mons - Brussels - Liège. See also Table **430**.
IRj – Quévy / Quiévrain - Mons - Brussels - Brussels Airport. See also Table **425**.

▲ – Times may vary by ± 3 minutes on some journeys.

LIÈGE - MAASTRICHT — 436

km	Route					ICO			ICO		ICO			ICO			ICO		ICO		ICO		ICO			ICO			
			Ⓐ	Ⓐ	Ⓐ	Ⓐh	Ⓐ	Ⓐ	Ⓐh	Ⓐ	Ⓐh		Ⓐ	Ⓐh	Ⓐ	Ⓐ	Ⓐh	Ⓐ	Ⓐh	Ⓐ	Ⓐ	Ⓐ	Ⓐ	Ⓐ	Ⓐ	Ⓐh	Ⓐ	Ⓐ	Ⓐ
0	**Liège** Guillemins d.	Ⓐ	0610	0708	0810	0825	0910	1010	1025	1110	1125	...	1210	1225	1310	1410	1425	1510	1525	1610	1625	1710	1725	1810	1910	1925	2010	2110	2210
19	Visé d.		0628	0729	0828	0843	0928	1028	1043	1128	1143	...	1228	1243	1328	1428	1443	1528	1543	1628	1643	1728	1743	1828	1928	1943	2028	2128	2228
32	**Maastricht** a.		0643	0744	0843	...	0943	1043	...	1143	...	...	1243	...	1343	1443	...	1543	...	1643	...	1743	...	1843	1943	...	2043	2143	2243

Route											
		⑥		Ⓒ		Ⓒ		Ⓒ	Ⓒ	Ⓒ		
Liège Guillemins d.	Ⓒ	0617	...	0717	and	1917	...	2017	2117	2217	...	...
Visé d.		0634	...	0735	hourly	1935	...	2035	2135	2235	...	...
Maastricht a.		0650	...	0750	until	1950	...	2050	2150	2250	...	...

Route			ICO		ICO		ICO			ICO		ICO
		Ⓐ	Ⓐ	Ⓐ	Ⓐ	Ⓐ	Ⓐh	Ⓐ	Ⓐ	Ⓐh	Ⓐ	Ⓐh
Maastricht d.	Ⓐ	0619	...	0719	...	0819	...	0919	1019	...	1119	...
Visé d.		0635	0717	0735	0822	0835	0922	0935	1035	1122	1135	1222
Liège Guillemins a.		0651	0735	0751	0839	0851	0939	0951	1051	1139	1151	1239

Route			ICO			ICO		ICO		ICO																		
		Ⓐ	Ⓐh	Ⓐ	Ⓐ	Ⓐh	Ⓐ	Ⓐh	Ⓐ	Ⓐh	Ⓐ	Ⓐ	Ⓐ	Ⓐ	Ⓐ	Ⓐ	Ⓐ			⑥	⑥	†	Ⓒ		Ⓒ	Ⓒ	Ⓒ	Ⓒ
Maastricht d.	Ⓐ	1219	...	1319	1419	...	1519	...	1619	...	1719	1819	1919	2019	2119	2219	2319	...	Ⓒ	...	0711	...	0811	and	2011	2111	2211	2311
Visé d.		1235	1322	1335	1435	1522	1535	1622	1635	1722	1735	1835	1935	2035	2135	2235	2335	...		0625	0725	0725	0825	hourly	2025	2125	2225	2325
Liège Guillemins a.		1251	1339	1351	1451	1539	1551	1639	1651	1739	1751	1851	1951	2051	2151	2251	2351	...		0643	0743	0743	0843	until	2043	2143	2243	2343

ICO – Brussels - Liège - Visé. See also Table **400**.

h – Not July 7 - Aug. 22.

VERVIERS - SPA — 437

16 km Journey time: 24 minutes

From **Verviers** Central:

Ⓐ: 0546 and hourly until 2146.
Ⓒ: 0646 and hourly until 2146.

From **Spa**:

Ⓐ: 0550, 0634, 0650, 0734, 0750 and hourly until 2150.
Ⓒ: 0650 and hourly until 2150.

All trains continue beyond Spa to Spa-Géronstère (*1 km* from Spa).

ARDENNES LOCAL SERVICES — 439

Additional services operate on Ⓐ at peak times

km																										
		Ⓐ		Ⓐ	Ⓐ		Ⓐ											Ⓐ			Ⓐ	Ⓒ	Ⓐ			Ⓐ
0	**Libramont 440** d.	...	...	0547	...	0650	...	0755	0853	0955	1053	1155	1253	1355	1453	1555	1652	1655	1755	1853	1953	1955	...	2054	2155	2255
12	Bertrix a.	...	...	0555	...	0658	...	0804	0901	1004	1101	1204	1301	1404	1501	1604	1701	1704	1804	1901	2002	2004	...	2102	2204	2304
12	Bertrix d.	...	0505	...	...	0707	0703	0805	0907	1005	1107	1205	1307	1405	1507	1605	1707	1705	1805	1907	2005	2005	2007	...	2205	...
	Dinant 440 a.	...	0606	...	...	0808	|	|	1008	|	1208	|	1408	|	1608	|	1808	|	|	2008	|	|	2108	...	|	...
57	Virton a.	...	...	...	...	...	0734	0835	...	1035	...	1235	...	1435	...	1635	...	1735	1835	...	2035	2035	...	...	2235	...
57	Virton d.	0538	...	...	0651	...	0736	0838a	...	1038a	...	1238a	...	1438a	...	1638a	...	1738	1838a	...	2038	...	...	...	...	...
85	Athus a.	0558	...	...	0711	...	0755	0858a	...	1058a	...	1258a	...	1458a	...	1658a	...	1758	1858a	...	2058	...	...	...	...	...
85	Athus **445** d.	0602	...	...	0718	...	0802	0902a	...	1102a	...	1302a	...	1502a	...	1702a	...	1802	1902a	...	2102	...	...	...	...	...
100	**Arlon 440** a.	0616	...	...	0731	...	0816	0916a	...	1116a	...	1316a	...	1516a	...	1715a	...	1816	1916a	...	2116	...	...	...	...	...

km																										
		Ⓐ				Ⓐ	Ⓒ	Ⓐ						Ⓐ	Ⓒ			Ⓐ			Ⓐ				Ⓐ	Ⓐ
	Arlon 440 d.	...	...	...	...	0644	...	0744	...	0944a	...	1144a	...	1344	...	...	1545a	1618	...	1744a	1844	...	1944a	...	2042	...
	Athus **445** a.	...	...	...	...	0658	...	0758	...	0958a	...	1158a	...	1358	...	...	1558a	1632	...	1758a	1858	...	1958a	...	2058	...
	Athus d.	...	...	...	...	0702	...	0802	...	1002a	...	1202a	...	1402	...	...	1602a	1636	...	1802a	1902	...	2002a	...	2106	...
	Virton a.	...	...	...	...	0722	...	0822	...	1022a	...	1222a	...	1422	...	...	1622a	1656	...	1822a	1922	...	2022a	...	2126	...
	Virton d.	...	...	0625	...	0724	0825	0825	...	1025	...	1225	...	1425	1428	...	1625	...	...	1825	...	...	2025	...	2129	...
0	**Dinant 440** d.	...	...	|	0644	|	|	|	0852	|	1052	|	1252	|	|	1452	|	...	1652	|	...	1853	|	2052	|	2152
72	Bertrix a.	...	...	0654	0748	0755	0854	0854	0953	1054	1153	1254	1353	1454	1457	1553	1654	...	1753	1854	...	1954	2054	2153	2159	2253
	Bertrix d.	0455	0556	0655	0753	0756	0855	0858	0959	1055	1159	1255	1359	1455	1458	1600	1655	...	1759	1855	...	1959	2055	...	2200	...
	Libramont 440 a.	0504	0605	0704	0801	0805	0904	0907	1007	1104	1207	1304	1407	1504	1507	1608	1704	...	1807	1904	...	2007	2104	...	2209	...

– Ⓐ only.

440 BRUSSELS - NAMUR - DINANT and LUXEMBOURG

km	Route				ICJ	ICJ	ICM			ICJ	ICJ	ICM		ICJ	ICJ	ICM	EC 91	ICJ	ICM	ICM	ICJ	ICM	ICJ	ICM	ICJ	ICM
		Ⓐ	Ⓐ	Ⓐ	Ⓒ	Ⓐ		Ⓐ	Ⓒ	Ⓐ	Ⓒ		Ⓐh	Ⓐ	Ⓒ		♦			Ⓐ						
0	**Brussels** Midi / Zuid .. d.	...	...	...	...	...	...	...	...	0533	...	0603	0609	0633	0633	0703	0733	0733	0803	...	0833	0903	0933	1003	1033	1103
2	Brussels Central .... d.	...	...	...	...	...	...	...	...	0537	...	0607	0613	0637	0637	0707	0737	0737	0807	...	0837	0907	0937	1007	1037	1107
4	**Brussels** Nord .... d.	...	...	...	...	...	...	...	...	0542	...	0612	0618	0642	0642	0712	0742	0742	0812	...	0842	0912	0942	1012	1042	1112
10	Brussels Luxembourg d.	...	...	...	...	...	...	...	...	0554	...	0624	0631	0654	0654	0724	0754	0754	0824	...	0854	0924	0954	1024	1054	1124
33	Ottignies .... d.	...	...	...	...	...	...	...	...	0615	...	0645	|	0715	0715	0745	0815	0815	0845	...	0915	0945	1015	1045	1115	1145
48	Gembloux .... d.	...	...	...	...	...	...	...	...	0627	...	0657	|	0727	0727	0757	0827	0827	0857	...	0927	0957	1027	1057	1127	1157
65	**Namur** .... a.	...	...	...	...	...	...	...	...	0639	...	0709	0712	0739	0739	0809	0839	0839	0909	...	0939	1009	1039	1109	1139	1209
65	**Namur** .... d.	...	...	...	...	0530	0609	...	...	0640	...	0711v	0714	0741	0741	0811v	0841	0841	0911c	0917	0941	1011v	1043	1111v	1141	1211v
	Dinant .... a.	...	...	...	...	|	0639	...	...	|	...	0739v	|	|	|	0839v	|	|	0939c	0946	|	1039v	|	1139v	|	1239v
94	Ciney .... d.	...	...	...	...	0555	...	0608	...	0703	...	▬	|	0803	0803	...	0903	0903	...	...	1003	...	1105	...	1203	...
117	Marloie .... d.	...	...	...	...	0610	...	0632	...	0718	...	...	|	0818	0818	...	0918	0918	...	...	1018	...	1120	...	1218	...
123	Jemelle .... d.	...	...	0550	...	0616	...	0639	0645	0723	...	...	|	0823	0823	...	0924	0924	...	...	1023	...	1125	...	1223	...
155	Libramont .... d.	...	...	0622	...	0644	...	0712	0713	0745	...	Ⓐ	0813	0845	0845	...	0945	0945	...	...	1045	...	1147	...	1245	...
201	Arlon .... d.	0539	0638	0704	0722	0722	...	0752	0752	0822	0822	0843	0843	0922	0922	...	1018	1018	...	...	1122	...	1222	...	1322	...
229	**Luxembourg** .... a.	0604	0703	0726	0740	0740	...	0818z	...	0840	0840	0901	0901	0940	0940	...	1036	1036	...	...	1140	...	1240	...	1340	...

km	Route	ICJ	ICJ	ICM	ICJ	ICM	EC 97	ICJ	ICM		ICJ	ICM	ICJ	ICJ	ICM	ICJ	ICJ	ICM	ICJ	ICJ	ICM		ICJ	ICM	ICJ	ICM
		Ⓒ	Ⓐ				♦			Ⓐh			Ⓒ	Ⓐ		Ⓒ	Ⓐ		Ⓒ	Ⓐ		Ⓐ				
	Brussels Midi / Zuid .. d.	1133	1133	1203	1233	1303	1309	1333	1403	1409	1433	1503	1533	1533	1603	1633	1633	1703	1733	1733	1803	1809	1833	1903	1933	2003
	Brussels Central .... d.	1137	1137	1207	1237	1307	1313	1337	1407	1413	1437	1507	1537	1537	1607	1637	1637	1707	1737	1737	1807	1813	1837	1907	1937	2007
	Brussels Nord .... d.	1142	1142	1212	1242	1312	1318	1342	1412	1418	1442	1512	1542	1542	1612	1642	1642	1712	1742	1742	1812	1818	1842	1912	1942	2012
	Brussels Luxembourg d.	1154	1154	1224	1254	1324	1329	1354	1424	1431	1454	1524	1554	1554	1624	1654	1654	1724	1754	1754	1824	1831	1854	1924	1954	2024
	Ottignies .... d.	1215	1215	1245	1315	1345	|	1415	1445	|	1515	1545	1615	1615	1645	1715	1715	1745	1815	1815	1845	|	1915	1945	2015	2045
	Gembloux .... d.	1227	1227	1257	1327	1357	|	1427	1457	|	1527	1557	1627	1627	1657	1726	1727	1757	1827	1827	1857	|	1927	1957	2027	2057
	Namur .... a.	1239	1239	1309	1339	1409	1414	1439	1509	1514	1539	1609	1639	1640	1709	1737	1740	1809	1838	1840	1909	1914	1939	2009	2039	2109
0	**Namur** .... d.	1241	1241	1311v	1341	1411v	1416	1441	1511v	1516	1541	1611v	1642	1642	1711r	1739	1742	1811v	1840	1842	1911v	1916	1943	2011v	2041	2111v
27	**Dinant** .... a.	|	|	1339v	|	1439v	|	|	1539v	|	|	1639v	|	|	1739r	|	|	1839r	|	|	1939v	|	|	2039v	|	2139v
	Ciney .... d.	1303	1303	...	1403	...	|	1503	▬	|	1603	...	1704	1704	...	1803	1804	...	1902	1906	...	|	2005	...	2103	...
	Marloie .... d.	1318	1318	...	1418	...	|	1518	...	|	1618	...	1718	1719	...	1818	1819	...	1917	1921	...	|	2020	...	2118	...
	Jemelle .... d.	1323	1323	...	1423	...	|	1523	...	|	1623	...	1724	1726	...	1824	1826	...	1922	1927	...	1953	2025	...	2123	...
	Libramont .... d.	1345	1345	...	1445	...	1513	1545	Ⓐ	1613	1645	...	1747	1748	...	1848	1847	...	1943	1948	...	2013	2047	...	2145	...
	Arlon .... d.	1422	1422	...	1522	...	1542	1622	1646	1646	1722	...	1825	1825	...	1925	1925	...	2025	2025	...	2045	2122	...	2222	...
	Luxembourg .... a.	1440	1445	...	1540	...	1600	1640	1704	1704	1740	...	1843	1843	...	1943	1943	...	2043	2043	...	21036	2140	...	2240	...

Route	ICJ	ICM	ICJ			ICM	ICM	ICJ	ICJ	ICJ
						Ⓐ	Ⓒ	Ⓐ	Ⓒ	Ⓒ
Brussels Midi / Zuid ... d.	2033	2103	2133	...	...	2203	2203	2233	2233	2333
Brussels Central .... d.	2037	2107	2137	...	...	2207	2207	2237	2237	2337
Brussels Nord .... d.	2042	2112	2142	...	...	2212	2212	2242	2242	2342
Brussels Luxembourg d.	2054	2124	2154	...	...	2224	2223	2254	2254	2355
Ottignies .... d.	2115	2145	2215	...	...	2245	2243	2315	2315	0023
Gembloux .... d.	2127	2157	2227	...	...	2257	2257	2327	2327	0035
Namur .... a.	2139	2209	2239	...	...	2309	2309	2339	2339	0046
Namur .... d.	2141	2211v	2241	...	...	2317	...	2341	...	...
Dinant .... a.	|	2239v	|	...	...	2346	...	|	...	...
Ciney .... d.	2203	...	2303	...	...	...	...	0003	...	...
Marloie .... d.	2218	...	2318	...	...	...	...	0018	...	...
Jemelle .... d.	2223	...	2323	...	...	...	...	0022	...	...
Libramont .... d.	2245	...	2345	...	...	...	...	...	...	...
Arlon .... d.	2325	...	0017	...	...	...	...	...	...	...
Luxembourg .... a.	2343	...	...	...	...	...	...	...	...	...

Route		ICJ	ICJ	ICM	ICM	ICJ	ICJ	ICM	ICJ	ICJ	ICM	ICJ
	Ⓐ	Ⓒ	Ⓐ	Ⓐ	Ⓒ	Ⓐ	Ⓒ		Ⓐ	Ⓒ		Ⓐ
Luxembourg .... d.	...	...	...	...	...	...	...	...	0517	...	...	0617
Arlon .... d.	...	...	...	...	...	0438	...	...	0540	0543	...	0640
Libramont .... d.	...	...	...	...	...	0514	...	...	0614	0616	...	0714
Jemelle .... d.	...	...	0435	...	...	0535	...	...	0635	0637	...	0735
Marloie .... d.	...	...	0442	...	...	0542	...	...	0642	0644	...	0742
Ciney .... d.	...	...	0458	...	...	0557	...	...	0656	0659	...	0758
Dinant .... d.	...	...	|	0513	...	|	...	0611x	|	|	0711x	|
Namur .... a.	...	...	0519	0542	...	0618	...	0641x	0716	0719	0741x	0818
Namur .... d.	0411	0436	0521	0551	0551	0620	0621	0651	0720	0721	0751	0820
Gembloux .... d.	0433	0449	0535	0605	0605	0634	0636	0705	0734	0735	0805	0834
Ottignies .... d.	0452	0501	0547	0617	0618	0647	0649	0718	0747	0748	0818	0847
Brussels Luxembourg . a.	0527	0526	0606	0635	0636	0706	0706	0736	0806	0806	0836	0906
Brussels Nord .... a.	0537	0537	0618	0648	0648	0718	0718	0748	0818	0818	0848	0918
Brussels Central ..... a.	0541	0542	0623	0653	0653	0723	0723	0753	0823	0823	0853	0923
Brussels Midi / Zuid .. a.	0545	0546	0627	0657	0657	0727	0727	0757	0827	0827	0857	0927

Route	ICJ		ICM	ICJ	ICM	ICJ		ICM	ICJ	ICM	ICJ	ICM		ICJ	ICM	ICJ	ICM	ICJ	ICM	ICM	ICM	ICJ	ICM	ICJ	ICJ	ICM
	Ⓒ	Ⓐ					Ⓐh												Ⓐ	Ⓐ	Ⓒ			Ⓒ	Ⓐ	
Luxembourg .... d.	0620	0650	...	0720	...	0820	0854	...	0920	...	1020	...	...	1120	...	1220	...	1323	...	...	...	1420	...	1520	1520	...
Arlon .... d.	0640	0714	...	0743	...	0843	0915	...	0943	...	1043	...	...	1143	...	1243	...	1343	...	...	...	1443	...	1544	1543	...
Libramont .... d.	0714	0743	...	0815	...	0915	0943	...	1015	...	1115	...	...	1215	...	1313	...	1413	...	...	...	1515	...	1615	1615	...
Jemelle .... d.	0735	0804	...	0836	...	0936	|	...	1036	...	1136	...	...	1236	...	1334	...	1434	...	...	...	1536	...	1636	1636	...
Marloie .... d.	0742	|	...	0843	...	0943	|	...	1043	...	1143	...	...	1243	...	1340	...	1440	...	...	...	1543	...	1643	1642	...
Ciney .... d.	0758	|	...	0859	...	0959	|	...	1059	...	1159	...	...	1259	...	1354	...	1454	...	...	...	1557	...	1658	1658	...
Dinant .... d.	|	|	0813x	|	0913x	|	|	1013x	|	1113x	|	1213x	...	|	1313x	|	1413x	|	1512	...	1520	|	1613x	|	|	1713x
Namur .... a.	0818	0841	0842x	0919	0942x	1019	1042	1042x	1119	1142x	1219	1242x	...	1319	1342x	1416	1442x	1516	1543	...	1549	1618	1642x	1718	1718	1742x
Namur .... d.	0820	0843	0851	0921	0951	1021	1044	1051	1121	1151	1221	1251	...	1321	1351	1421	1451	1521	...	1551	1551	1621	1651	1721	1721	1751
Gembloux .... d.	0834	|	0905	0935	1005	1035	|	1105	1135	1205	1235	1305	...	1335	1405	1435	1505	1535	...	1604	1605	1635	1705	1735	1735	1805
Ottignies .... d.	0847	|	0917	0947	1017	1047	|	1117	1147	1217	1247	1317	...	1347	1417	1447	1517	1547	...	1617	1618	1647	1717	1747	1747	1817
Brussels Luxembourg a.	0906	0924	0936	1006	1036	1106	1124	1136	1206	1236	1306	1336	...	1406	1436	1506	1536	1606	...	1636	1636	1706	1736	1806	1806	1836
Brussels Nord .... a.	0918	0936	0948	1018	1048	1118	1136	1148	1218	1248	1318	1348	...	1418	1448	1518	1548	1618	...	1648	1648	1718	1748	1818	1818	1848
Brussels Central .... a.	0923	0941	0953	1023	1053	1123	1141	1153	1223	1253	1323	1353	...	1423	1453	1523	1553	1623	...	1653	1653	1723	1753	1823	1823	1853
Brussels Midi / Zuid ... a.	0927	0945	0957	1027	1057	1127	1145	1157	1227	1257	1327	1357	...	1427	1457	1527	1557	1627	...	1657	1657	1727	1757	1827	1827	1857

Route	ICJ	ICJ	EC 90		ICM	ICJ	ICJ		ICM		ICJ	ICM	ICJ	EC 96	ICM	ICJ		ICM	ICM	ICJ	ICJ					
	Ⓒ	Ⓐ	♦			Ⓒ	Ⓐ	Ⓐh						♦				Ⓐ	Ⓒ	Ⓒ	Ⓐ				Ⓐ	
Luxembourg .... d.	1620	1620	1700	...	...	1717	1717	1755	...	...	1820	...	1920	2000	...	2020	...	...	...	2120	2120	...	...	...	2350	...
Arlon .... d.	1640	1643	1720	...	...	1740	1740	1817	...	...	1843	...	1943	2020	...	2043	...	...	...	2143	2143	...	...	...	0015	...
Libramont .... d.	1714	1717	1748	...	...	1815	1812	1848	...	...	1915	...	2015	|	...	2115	...	...	...	2217	2215	...	...	...	...	...
Jemelle .... d.	1735	1737	|	...	...	1836	1833	|	...	...	1936	...	2036	|	...	2136	...	...	...	2237	2236	...	...	...	...	...
Marloie .... d.	1742	1743	|	...	...	1843	1840	|	...	...	1943	...	2043	|	...	2144	...	...	...	...	2243	...	...	...	...	...
Ciney .... d.	1759	1757	|	...	...	1859	1854	|	...	...	1959	...	2059	|	...	2159	...	...	...	...	2259	...	...	...	...	...
Dinant .... d.	|	|	|	...	1813x	|	|	|	1913x	...	|	2013x	|	|	2113x	|	...	2213	2220	...	|	...	...	...	...	...
Namur .... a.	1820	1818	1842	...	1842x	1919	1916	1944	1942x	...	2019	2042x	2119	2141	2142x	2219	...	2242	2249	...	2319	...	...	...	...	...
Namur .... d.	1822	1821	1844	...	1851	1921	1921	1946	1951	...	2021	2051	2121	2148	2151	2221	...	...	...	...	...	...	...	...	...	...
Gembloux .... d.	1834	1835	|	...	1905	1935	1935	|	2005	...	2035	2105	2135	|	2205	2235	...	...	...	...	...	...	...	...	...	...
Ottignies .... d.	1847	1847	|	...	1917	1947	1947	|	2017	...	2047	2117	2147	|	2217	2247	...	...	...	...	...	...	...	...	...	...
Brussels Luxembourg a.	1906	1906	1926	...	1936	2006	2006	2028	2036	...	2106	2136	2206	2229	2236	2306	...	...	...	...	...	...	...	...	...	...
Brussels Nord .... a.	1918	1918	1941	...	1948	2018	2018	2042	2048	...	2118	2148	2218	2241	2248	2318	...	...	...	...	...	...	...	...	...	...
Brussels Central .... a.	1923	1923	1947	...	1953	2023	2023	2047	2053	...	2123	2153	2223	2247	2253	2323	...	...	...	...	...	...	...	...	...	...
Brussels Midi / Zuid ... a.	1927	1927	1951	...	1957	2027	2027	2051	2057	...	2127	2157	2227	2251	2257	2327	...	...	...	...	...	...	...	...	...	...

♦ – **NOTES** (LISTED BY TRAIN NUMBERS)

ICJ – Brussels - Namur - Luxembourg.
ICM – Brussels - Namur - Dinant. Also Brussels - Namur - Liège [- Liers] – see also Table **442**.

90 – VAUBAN – (12) Zürich - Basel - Luxembourg - Brussels.
91 – VAUBAN – (12) Brussels - Luxembourg - Basel.
96 – IRIS – (12) Chur - Zürich - Basel - Luxembourg - Brussels.
97 – IRIS – (12) Brussels - Luxembourg - Basel.

c – Ⓒ only.
e – † only.
h – Not July 7 - Aug. 22.
r – 8–10 minutes later on Ⓐ.
v – 5–7 minutes later on Ⓐ.
x – 7–10 minutes later on Ⓒ.
z – Not June 23; Also July 21, Nov. 11.

LIÈGE - NAMUR - CHARLEROI - MONS 442

For *Thalys* trains Liège - Paris and v.v. – see Table 17

km	Route		IRk Ⓐ	IRk Ⓐ	ICD Ⓐ	ICM Ⓐ	IRk Ⓐ	ICD Ⓐ	ICM Ⓐ	IRk Ⓐ	ICD Ⓐ	ICM Ⓐ	IRk Ⓐ	ICD Ⓐ		IRk Ⓐ	ICM Ⓐ	ICD Ⓐ		IRk Ⓐ	ICM Ⓐ	ICD Ⓐ	ICM Ⓐ	IRk Ⓐ	ICD Ⓐ
0	**Liège** Guillemins d.	Ⓐ	...	...	...	0459	...	0544	0557	...	0647	0657	...	0746	...	...	0759	0847	▲	...	1359	1447	1459	...	1547
29	Huy d.		...	...	...	0521	...	0604	0619	...	0706	0719	...	0806	...	...	0821	0906	and at	...	1421	1506	1521	...	1606
40	Andenne d.		...	...	...	0532	...	|	0631	...	|	0731	...	|	...	...	0832	|	the same	...	1432	|	1532	...	|
59	**Namur** d.		...	0449	...	0546	0549	0629	0645	0649	0729	0745	0749	0829	...	0841	0846	0929	minutes	1441	1446	1529	1546	1549	1629
76	Jemeppe-sur-Sambre d.		...	0506	...	...	0606	|	...	0706	|	...	0806	|	...	0906	...	|	past each	1506	...	|	...	1606	|
81	Tamines d.		...	0513	...	...	0613	0650	...	0713	0750	...	0813	0850	...	0913	...	0950	hour until	1513	...	1550	...	1613	1650
96	**Charleroi** Sud d.		0419	0528	0554	...	0628	0702	...	0728	0802	...	0828	0902	...	0928	...	1002		1528	...	1602	...	1628	1702
117	La Louvière Sud d.		0438	0547	0613	...	0647	0719	...	0747	0819	...	0847	0919	...	0947	...	1019		1547	...	1619	...	1647	1719
137	**Mons** a.		0501	0601	0628	...	0701	0732	...	0801	0832	...	0901	0933	...	1001	...	1033		1601	...	1633	...	1701	1733

Route	ICM Ⓐ	IRk Ⓐ	ICD Ⓐ		ICM Ⓐ	IRk Ⓐ	ICD Ⓐ	ICM Ⓐ	ICD Ⓐ	ICD Ⓐ			ICD Ⓒ	ICD Ⓒ	ICD Ⓒ	ICD Ⓒ	ICD Ⓒ		ICD Ⓒ		ICD Ⓒ		ICD Ⓒ	ICD Ⓒ
iège Guillemins d.	1559	...	1647	▲	1959	...	2047	2059	2147	2247	...	Ⓒ	...	...	0649	0749	0849	...	0949		2049	...	2149	2249
luy d.	1621	...	1706	and at	2021	...	2106	2121	2206	2308	...		...	...	0711	0810	0910	...	1010	and at	2110	...	2212	2310
ndenne d.	1632	...	|	the same	2032	...	|	2132	|	2320	...		...	...	0722	0822	0922	...	1022	the same	2122	...	2223	2322
amur d.	1646	1649	1729	minutes	2046	2049	2129	2146	2229	2336	...		...	0638	0738	0838	0938	...	1038	minutes	2138	...	2238	2336
emeppe-sur-Sambre. d.	...	1706	|	past each	...	2106	|	...	|	2352	...		...	0656	0756	0854	0956	...	1056	past each	2156	...	2256	...
amines d.	...	1713	1750	hour until	...	2113	2150	...	2250	2359	...		...	0704	0804	0902	1004	...	1104	hour until	2204	...	2304	...
harleroi Sud d.	...	1728	1802		...	2128	2202	...	2302	0011	...		0619	0719	0819	0919	1019	...	1119		2219	...	2317	...
a Louvière Sud d.	...	1747	1819		...	2147	2219	...	2319	...	...		0637	0737	0837	0937	1037	...	1137		2237	...	...	...
lons a.	...	1801	1833		...	2201	2233	...	2334	...	...		0651	0751	0851	0951	1051	...	1151		2251	...	...	...

Route		ICM Ⓐ	IRk Ⓐ	ICD Ⓐ	ICM Ⓐ	IRk Ⓐ	ICD Ⓐ	ICM Ⓐ	IRk Ⓐ	ICD Ⓐ		ICM Ⓐ	IRk Ⓐ	ICD Ⓐ		ICM Ⓐ	IRk Ⓐ	ICD Ⓐ		IRk Ⓐ	ICM Ⓐ	ICD Ⓐ	IRk Ⓐ	ICM Ⓐ	ICD Ⓐ
lons d.	Ⓐ	...	0458	...	...	0558	0626	...	0658	0726	...	...	0758	0826	▲	...	1358	1426	...	1458	...	1526	1558	...	1626
a Louvière Sud d.		...	0514	...	...	0614	0643	...	0714	0743	...	...	0814	0843	and at	...	1414	1443	...	1514	...	1543	1614	...	1643
harleroi Sud d.		...	0534	0600	...	0640	0700	...	0734	0800	...	...	0834	0900	the same	...	1434	1500	...	1534	...	1600	1634	...	1700
amines d.		...	0548	0611	...	0654	0711	...	0748	0811	...	...	0848	0911	minutes	...	1448	1511	...	1548	...	1611	1648	...	1711
emeppe-sur-Sambre. d.		...	0555	|	...	0702	|	...	0755	|	...	...	0855	|	past each	...	1455	|	...	1555	...	|	1655	...	|
amur d.		0614	0614	0633	0714	0717	0733	0814	0811	0833	...	0914	0919	0933	hour until	1514	1519	1533	...	1611	1614	1633	1711	1715	1733
ndenne d.		0628	...	|	0728	...	|	0828	...	|	...	0928	...	|		1528	...	|	...	...	1628	|	...	1728	|
uy d.		0640	...	0655	0740	...	0755	0840	...	0855	...	0940	...	0955		1540	...	1555	...	...	1640	1655	...	1740	1755
ège Guillemins a.		0700	...	0713	0800	...	0813	0900	...	0913	...	1000	...	1013		1600	...	1613	...	...	1700	1713	...	1800	1813

Route	IRk Ⓐ	ICM Ⓐ	ICD Ⓐ		IRk Ⓐ	ICM Ⓐ	ICD Ⓐ	ICM Ⓐ	ICD Ⓐ	ICM Ⓐ	IRk Ⓐ	ICD Ⓐ				ICD Ⓒ	ICD Ⓒ	ICD Ⓒ	ICD Ⓒ	ICD Ⓒ		ICD Ⓒ	ICD Ⓒ	ICD Ⓒ
ons d.	1658	...	1726	▲	1958	...	2026	...	2126	...	2158	2226	...	...	Ⓒ	...	0608	0708	0808	0908		2008	2108	2208
a Louvière Sud d.	1714	...	1743	and at	2014	...	2043	...	2143	...	2214	2243	...	...		...	0624	0724	0824	0924	and at	2024	2124	2224
harleroi Sud d.	1734	...	1800	the same	2034	...	2100	...	2200	...	2234	2300	...	...		...	0643	0743	0843	0943	the same	2043	2143	2243
amines d.	1748	...	1811	minutes	2048	...	2111	...	2211	...	2248	2315	...	...		...	0657	0757	0857	0957	minutes	2057	2157	2257
emeppe-sur-Sambre. d.	1755	...	|	past each	2055	...	|	...	|	...	2255	2322	...	...		...	0705	0805	0905	1005	past each	2105	2205	2305
amur d.	1811	1815	1833	hour until	2111	2114	2133	2214	2233	2314	2311	2340	...	...		0624	0724	0824	0924	1024	hour until	2124	2224	2322
ndenne d.	...	1828	|		...	2128	|	2228	|	2328	...	2354	...	...		0639	0739	0839	0939	1039		2138	2238	...
uy d.	...	1840	1855		...	2140	2155	2240	2255	2340	...	0006	...	...		0651	0751	0851	0951	1051		2149	2249	...
ège Guillemins a.	...	1900	1913		...	2200	2213	2300	2313	2400	...	0026	...	...		0711	0811	0911	1011	1111		2211	2311	...

D – Lille - Tournai - Mons - Charleroi - Namur - Liège [- Herstal]. See also Table **416**.
M – Brussels - Namur - Liège [- Liers]. See also Table **440**.
k – [Jambes -] Namur - Charleroi - Mons [- Tournai].

▲ – Times may vary by ± 3 minutes on some journeys.

LIÈGE - LUXEMBOURG 444

km	Route	IRm	IRm	IRm	IRm	IRm	IRm	IRm	IRm Ⓐ	IRm	IRm	IRm
0	**Liège** Guillemins d.	0718	0918	1118	1318	1518	1618	1718	1750	1918	2118	2318
23	Rivage d.	0740	0940	1140	1340	1540	1641	1740	1819	1940	2140	2343
31	Aywaille d.	0749	0949	1149	1349	1549	1650	1749	1827	1949	2149	2353
58	Trois-Ponts d.	0812	1012	1212	1412	1612	1719	1812	1850	2012	2212	0016
70	Vielsalm d.	0824	1024	1224	1424	1624	1730	1824	1902	2024	2224	0028
81	**Gouvy** d.	0836	1036	1236	1436	1636	1740	1836	1912	2035	2236	0038
91	Troisvierges **445** d.	0845	1045	1245	1445	1645	...	1845	...	2045	2245	...
99	Clervaux **445** d.	0853	1053	1253	1453	1653	...	1853	...	2053	2253	...
14	Kautenbach **445** d.	0908	1108	1308	1508	1708	...	1908	...	2108	2308	...
29	Ettelbruck **445** d.	0920	1121	1321	1521	1721	...	1921	...	2121	2321	...
41	Mersch **445** d.	0930	1131	1331	1531	1731	...	1931	...	2132	2332	...
60	**Luxembourg 445** a.	0945	1144	1344	1544	1744	...	1944	...	2144	2344	...

Route	IRm Ⓐ	IRm Ⓒ	IRm Ⓐ	IRm	IRm	IRm	IRm	IRm	IRm	IRm	IRm
Luxembourg 445 d.	...	...	...	0715	0915	1115	1315	1515	1715	1915	2115
Mersch **445** d.	...	...	...	0729	0929	1129	1329	1529	1729	1929	2129
Ettelbruck **445** d.	...	...	...	0741	0941	1141	1341	1541	1741	1941	2141
Kautenbach **445** d.	...	...	...	0753	0953	1153	1353	1553	1753	1953	2153
Clervaux **445** d.	...	...	...	0809	1009	1209	1409	1609	1809	2009	2209
Troisvierges **445** d.	...	...	...	0816	1016	1216	1416	1616	1816	2016	2216
Gouvy d.	0621	0625	0702	0826	1026	1226	1426	1626	1826	2026	2226
Vielsalm d.	0632	0636	0713	0836	1036	1236	1436	1636	1837	2036	2236
Trois-Ponts d.	0644	0648	0725	0848	1048	1248	1448	1648	1850	2048	2248
Aywaille d.	0706	0710	0749	0910	1110	1310	1510	1710	1911	2110	2310
Rivage d.	0716	0720	0759	0920	1120	1320	1520	1720	1921	2120	2320
Liège Guillemins a.	0735	0742	0821	0942	1142	1342	1542	1742	1942	2142	2342

m – [Liers -] Liège - Gouvy - Luxembourg.

Additional journeys on Ⓐ:
Liège - Gouvy and v.v.: 1830 from Liège; 0507 from Gouvy.
Gouvy - Luxembourg and v.v.: 0539, 0639 from Gouvy, 1615, 1815 from Luxembourg.

LUXEMBOURG – summary of services 445

In principle, services shown below operate at the same minutes past each hour between 0800 and 2000, but variations are possible.
Only principal stations are listed, and additional services are available at peak times.

embourg (xx15) → Mersch (xx29) → Ettelbruck (xx41) → Kautenbach (xx53) → rvaux (xx09) → Troisvierges (xx16).

embourg (xx20, also xx50⚒) → Bettembourg (xx32, also xx02⚒) → Noertzange (xx36, xx06⚒) → Esch-sur-Alzette (xx45, also xx15⚒) → Pétange (xx10, also xx40⚒) → ange (xx15, also xx45⚒).

embourg (xx50, also xx20⚒) → Mersch (xx11, also xx41⚒) → Ettelbruck (xx28, also 6⚒) → Kautenbach (xx42) → Wiltz (xx57).

embourg (xx48) → Wasserbillig (xx32).

embourg (xx47) → Kleinbettingen (xx06).

embourg (xx45⚒) → Ettelbruck (xx10⚒, also xx35⚒, xx43†) → Diekirch (xx15⚒, also 0⚒, xx48†).

embourg (xx52, also xx22⚒) → Pétange (xx15, also xx45⚒) → Rodange (xx22, also 2⚒) → Athus (xx26, also xx56⚒).

embourg (xx04, xx34) → Dudelange-Centre (xx12, xx42) → Volmerange-les-Mines 8⚒, xx48⚒).

Troisvierges (xx44) → Clervaux (xx53) → Kautenbach (xx08) → Ettelbruck (xx21) → Mersch (xx31) → **Luxembourg** (xx44).

Rodange (xx45, also xx15⚒) → Pétange (xx52, also xx22⚒) → Esch-sur-Alzette (xx17, also xx47⚒) → Noertzange (xx24, also xx54⚒) → Bettembourg (xx30, also xx00⚒) → **Luxembourg** (xx40, also xx10⚒).

Wiltz (xx05) → Kautenbach (xx18) → Ettelbruck (xx35, also xx05⚒) → Mersch (xx49, also xx19⚒) → **Luxembourg** (xx10, also xx40⚒).

Wasserbillig (xx26) → **Luxembourg** (xx07).

Kleinbettingen (xx15) → **Luxembourg** (xx33).

Diekirch (xx45⚒, also xx12†, xx20⚒) → Ettelbruck (xx51⚒, also xx17†, xx25⚒) → **Luxembourg** (xx14⚒).

Athus (xx34, also xx04⚒) → Rodange (xx39, also xx09⚒) → Pétange (xx44, also xx14⚒) → **Luxembourg** (xx08, xx38⚒).

Volmerange-les-Mines (xx12⚒, xx42⚒) → Dudelange-Centre (xx18, xx48) → Bettembourg (xx26, xx56).

NETHERLANDS

SEE MAP PAGE 239

Operator: NS – Nederlandse Spoorwegen (unless otherwise indicated) www.ns.nl

Services: Trains convey first- and second-class seated accommodation, unless otherwise indicated in the tables. Some trains consist of portions for two or more destinations, and passengers should be careful to join the correct part of the train. The destination of each train portion is normally indicated beside the entrance doors. Train numbers of internal services are no announced or displayed on stations and are therefore not indicated in these tables. Sleeping cars (🛏) and couchettes (▬) are conveyed on international night trains only.

Timings: Valid **until December 13**, 2014.

Holidays: Unless otherwise indicated, services marked ⚒ do not run on ⑦ or on Apr. 21;
those marked Ⓐ do not run on ⑥⑦ or on Apr. 21, May 29, June 9;
those marked † run on ⑦ and on Apr. 21;
those marked © run on ⑥⑦ and on Apr. 21, May 29, June 9.
No trains, other than international services, will run between ± 2000 hours on Dec. 31 and ± 0200 on Jan. 1.

Tickets: There are ticket offices at all main stations. In addition, tickets to all destinations within the Netherlands are available from the ticket machines situated on every station. Tickets nc bearing a pre-printed date must be date-stamped in the validating machines at platform entrances. Access to station platforms is strictly limited to persons in possession of a vali travel ticket, and high penalty fares are therefore charged for tickets bought from the conductor on board trains.

Reservations: Seat reservations are available only on international trains to, from, or via France and Germany.

450 AMSTERDAM - DEN HAAG - ROTTERDAM - ROOSENDAAL - VLISSINGEN

km		C	A	◧	C	C◧	Ⓐ	⚒	⚒	Ⓐ	Ⓐ	⚒	Ⓐ	⚒	⚒◧		Ⓑh	Ⓐ		◧	Ⓐ		◧	Ⓐ	
0	**Amsterdam** Centraal ..... ★ d.	0027	0027	0028	0057	0058	...	0527	0528	0557	0558	...	0612	0627	0628	...	0642	0642	0657	0658	0712	0727	0728	0742	0757
5	Amsterdam Sloterdijk ..... ★ d.	0033	0033	0035	0103	0105	...	0533	0535	0603	0605	...	0618	0633	0635	...	0648	0648	0703	0705	0718	0733	0735	0748	0803
17	**Schiphol** ✈ ..... ★ d.	|	|	0046	|	0116	...	|	0546	|	0616	...	|	|	0646	...	|	|	|	0716	|	|	0746	|	|
	Haarlem ..... d.	0044	0044	|	0114	|	...	0544	|	0614	|	...	0629	0644	|	...	0659	0659	0714	|	0729	0744	|	0759	0814
44	Leiden Centraal ..... a.	0103	0103	0103	0133	0133	...	0603	0603	0633	0633	...	0649	0703	0703	...	0719	0719	0733	0733	0749	0803	0803	0819	0833
44	Leiden Centraal ..... d.	0105	0107	0105	0135	0137	...	0605	0605	0635	0635	...	0650	0705	0705	...	0720	0720	0735	0735	0750	0805	0805	0820	0835
	Den Haag Centraal .. **471** a.	0117	|	|	0147	|	...	0617	|	0647	|	...	|	0717	|	...	|	|	0747	|	|	0717	|	|	0847
60	**Den Haag** HS ..... **18 471** d.	...	0121	0118	...	0149	...	▬	0619	...	0649	...	0704	...	0719	...	0734	0734	...	0749	0804	...	0819	0834	...
68	Delft ..... **471** d.	...	...	...	...	...	...	...	0625	...	0655	...	0710	...	0725	...	0740	0740	...	0755	0810	...	0825	0840	...
78	Schiedam Centrum ..... d.	...	...	...	...	...	...	Ⓐ	0633	...	0703	...	0718	...	0733	...	0748	0748	...	0803	0818	...	0833	0848	...
82	**Rotterdam** Centraal **18 471** d.	...	...	...	...	...	...	0611	0641	...	0711	0711	0725	...	0741	0741	0753	0755	...	0811	0825	...	0841	0855	...
102	Dordrecht ..... **18 471** d.	...	...	...	...	...	...	0627	0657	...	0727	0727	0741	...	0757	0757	...	0811	...	0827	0841	...	0857	0911	...
140	**Roosendaal** ..... **18** d.	...	...	...	...	...	0622	0652	0722	...	0752	0752	...	...	0822	0822	...	...	...	0852	...	...	0922	...	...
153	Bergen op Zoom ..... d.	...	...	...	...	...	0631	0701	0731	...	0801	0801	...	...	0831	0831	...	...	...	0901	...	...	0931	...	...
190	Goes ..... d.	...	...	...	...	...	0702	0732	0802	...	0832	0832	...	...	0902	0902	...	...	...	0932	...	...	1002	...	...
209	Middelburg ..... d.	...	...	...	...	...	0716	0746	0816	...	0846	0846	...	...	0916	0916	...	...	...	0946	...	...	1016	...	...
215	**Vlissingen** ..... a.	...	...	...	...	...	0724	0754	0824	...	0854	0854	...	...	0924	0924	...	...	...	0954	...	...	1024	...	...

	◧	⚒		◧	⚒		◧	⚒		◧	⚒		◧	⚒		◧	⚒		◧			◧		
Amsterdam Centraal ..... ★ d.	0758	0812	0827	0828	0842	0857	0858	0912	0927	0928	0942	0957	0958	1012	1027	1028	1042	1057	1058	1112	1127	1128	1142	and at the same minutes past each hour until
Amsterdam Sloterdijk ..... ★ d.	0805	0818	0833	0835	0848	0903	0905	0918	0933	0935	0948	1003	1005	1018	1033	1035	1048	1103	1105	1118	1133	1135	1148	
Schiphol ✈ ..... ★ d.	0816	|	|	0846	|	|	0916	|	|	0946	|	|	1016	|	|	1046	|	|	1116	|	|	1146	|	
Haarlem ..... d.	|	0829	0844	|	0859	0914	|	0929	0944	|	0959	1014	|	1029	1044	|	1059	1114	|	1129	1144	|	1159	
Leiden Centraal ..... a.	0833	0849	0903	0903	0919	0933	0933	0949	1003	1003	1019	1033	1033	1049	1103	1103	1119	1133	1133	1149	1203	1203	1219	
Leiden Centraal ..... d.	0835	0850	0905	0905	0920	0935	0935	0950	1005	1005	1020	1035	1035	1050	1105	1105	1120	1135	1135	1150	1205	1205	1220	
Den Haag Centraal ..... **471** a.	|	|	0917	|	|	0947	|	|	1017	|	|	1047	|	|	1117	|	|	1147	|	|	1217	|	|	
Den Haag HS ..... **18 471** d.	0849	0904	...	0919	0934	...	0949	1004	...	1019	1034	...	1049	1104	...	1119	1134	...	1149	1204	...	1219	1234	
Delft ..... **471** d.	0855	0910	...	0925	0940	...	0955	1010	...	1025	1040	...	1055	1110	...	1125	1140	...	1155	1210	...	1225	1240	
Schiedam Centrum ..... d.	0903	0918	...	0933	0948	...	1003	1018	...	1033	1048	...	1103	1118	...	1133	1148	...	1203	1218	...	1233	1248	
Rotterdam Centraal **18 471** d.	0911	0925	...	0941	0955	...	1011	1025	...	1041	1055	...	1111	1125	...	1141	1155	...	1211	1225	...	1241	1255	
Dordrecht ..... **18 471** d.	0927	0941	...	0957	1011	...	1027	1041	...	1057	1111	...	1127	1141	...	1157	1211	...	1227	1241	...	1257	1311	
Roosendaal ..... **18** d.	0952	...	...	1022	...	...	1052	...	...	1122	...	...	1152	...	...	1222	...	...	1252	...	...	1322	...	
Bergen op Zoom ..... d.	1001	...	...	1031	...	...	1101	...	...	1131	...	...	1201	...	...	1231	...	...	1301	...	...	1331	...	
Goes ..... d.	1032	...	...	1102	...	...	1132	...	...	1202	...	...	1232	...	...	1302	...	...	1332	...	...	1402	...	
Middelburg ..... d.	1046	...	...	1116	...	...	1146	...	...	1216	...	...	1246	...	...	1316	...	...	1346	...	...	1416	...	
Vlissingen ..... a.	1054	...	...	1124	...	...	1154	...	...	1224	...	...	1254	...	...	1324	...	...	1354	...	...	1424	...	

		◧			◧			◧			◧			◧			◧			◧		◧			◧
Amsterdam Centraal ..... ★ d.	1957	1958	2012	2027	2028	2042	2057	2058	2112	2127	2128	2142	2157	2158	2212	2227	2229	...	2257	2258	2327	2328	...	2357	235
Amsterdam Sloterdijk ..... ★ d.	2003	2005	2018	2033	2035	2048	2103	2105	2118	2133	2135	2148	2203	2205	2218	2233	2235	...	2303	2305	2333	2335	...	0003	000
Schiphol ✈ ..... ★ d.	|	2016	|	|	2046	|	|	2116	|	|	2146	|	|	2216	|	|	2246	...	|	2316	|	2346	...	|	00
Haarlem ..... d.	2014	|	2029	2044	|	2059	2114	|	2129	2144	|	2159	2214	|	2229	2244	|	...	2314	|	2344	|	...	0014	|
Leiden Centraal ..... a.	2033	2033	2049	2103	2103	2119	2133	2133	2149	2203	2203	2219	2233	2233	2249	2303	2303	...	2333	2333	0003	0003	...	0033	00
Leiden Centraal ..... d.	2035	2035	2050	2105	2105	2120	2135	2135	2150	2205	2205	2220	2235	2235	2250	2305	2305	...	2335	2335	0005	0005	...	0035	00
Den Haag Centraal ..... **471** a.	2047	|	|	2117	|	|	2147	|	|	2217	|	|	2247	|	|	2317	|	...	2347	|	0017	|	...	0047	|
Den Haag HS ..... **18 471** d.	...	2049	2104	...	2119	2134	...	2149	2204	...	2219	2234	...	2249	2304	...	2319	...	...	2349	...	0019	...	...	00
Delft ..... **471** d.	...	2055	2110	...	2125	2140	...	2155	2210	...	2225	2240	...	2255	2310	...	2325	...	...	2355	...	0025	...	...	00
Schiedam Centrum ..... d.	...	2103	2118	...	2133	2148	...	2203	2218	...	2233	2248	...	2303	2318	...	2333	...	...	0003	...	0033	...	...	01
Rotterdam Centraal **18 471** d.	...	2111	2125	...	2141	2155	...	2211	2225	...	2241	2255	...	2311	2325	...	2341	...	...	0011	...	0041	...	...	01
Dordrecht ..... **18 471** d.	...	2127	2141	...	2157	2211	...	2227	2241	...	2257	2311	...	2327	2341	...	2357	...	...	0026	...	0056	...	...	...
Roosendaal ..... **18** d.	...	2152	...	...	2222	...	...	2252	...	...	2322	...	...	2352	...	...	0019	...	...	...	...	0126	...	...	...
Bergen op Zoom ..... d.	...	2201	...	...	2231	...	...	2301	...	...	2331	...	...	0001	...	...	...	...	...	...	...	...	...	...	...
Goes ..... d.	...	2232	...	...	2302	...	...	2332	...	...	0002	...	...	0032	...	...	...	...	...	...	...	...	...	...	...
Middelburg ..... d.	...	2246	...	...	2316	...	...	2346	...	...	0016	...	...	0046	...	...	...	...	...	...	...	...	...	...	...
Vlissingen ..... a.	...	2254	...	...	2324	...	...	2354	...	...	0024	...	...	0054	...	...	...	...	...	...	...	...	...	...	...

A – ①–⑤ (not May 30, June 10).
C – ⑥⑦ (also May 30, June 10).
h – Not May 29, June 9.

◧ – From Lelystad, Leeuwarden or Groningen (Table **460**).
★ – **Additional trains** Amsterdam Centraal - Schiphol ✈ at 0013, 0513 ⚒, 0543 ⚒, 0613, 0643 and at 13 and 43 minutes past each hour until 2313, 2343.

☛ For NIGHT NETWORK **Amsterdam** – **Schiphol/Haarlem** – **Den Haag** – **Rotterdam**, see Table **454**.
For INTERNATIONAL SERVICES **Den Haag** – **Rotterdam** – **Roosendaal** – **Antwerpen** - **Brussels**, see Table **18**.

451 AMSTERDAM - ROTTERDAM - BREDA

Intercity direct services via the high-speed line. Supplement payable (except for local journeys Amsterdam - Schiphol and Rotterdam - Breda).

km		910 D	912 D	1014 Ⓐ	914	916	918	920	922	924	926	928	930	932	934	936	938	940	942	944	946	948	950	952	9
0	**Amsterdam** Centraal ..... d.	0555	0625	0640	0655	0725	0755	0825	0855	0925	0955	1025	1055	1125	1155	1225	1255	1325	1355	1425	1455	1525	1555	1625	16
17	**Schiphol** ✈ ..... d.	0609	0639	0654	0709	0739	0809	0839	0909	0939	1009	1039	1109	1139	1209	1239	1309	1339	1409	1439	1509	1539	1609	1639	17
70	**Rotterdam** Centraal ..... a.	0637	0706	0721	0736	0806	0836	0906	0936	1006	1036	1106	1136	1206	1236	1306	1336	1406	1436	1506	1536	1606	1636	1706	17
70	**Rotterdam** Centraal ..... d.	0639	0709	...	0739	0809	0839	0909	0939	1009	1039	1109	1139	1209	1239	1309	1339	1409	1439	1509	1539	1609	1639	1709	17
117	**Breda** ..... a.	0703	0733	...	0803	0833	0903	0933	1003	1033	1103	1133	1203	1233	1303	1333	1403	1433	1503	1533	1603	1633	1703	1733	18

	1056 Ⓐ	956	958	960	962	964	966		970		974		978
Amsterdam Centraal ..... d.	1710	1725	1755	1825	1855	1925	1955	...	2055	...	2155	...	2255
Schiphol ✈ ..... d.	1724	1739	1809	1839	1909	1939	2009	...	2109	...	2209	...	2309
Rotterdam Centraal ..... a.	1751	1806	1836	1906	1936	2006	2036	...	2136	...	2236	...	2336
Rotterdam Centraal ..... d.	...	1809	1839	1909	1939	2009	2039	...	2139	...	2239	...	2339
Breda ..... a.	...	1833	1903	1933	2003	2033	2103	...	2203	...	2303	...	0003

D – ①–⑥ (not Apr. 21, May 29, June 9).

For explanation of standard symbols, see page 4

VLISSINGEN - ROOSENDAAL - ROTTERDAM - DEN HAAG - AMSTERDAM 450

km		Ⓐ◧	Ⓐ		⚒◧	⚒	Ⓐ		Ⓐ◧	⑥k◧	⚒	Ⓐ	Ⓐ◧	Ⓒ◧		Ⓐ	Ⓐ◧	⚒◧	◧		Ⓐ	⚒◧	◧		⚒
	Vlissingen d.	...	...	...	...	...	...	...	...	...	...	...	...	...	...	...	0536	...	...	...	...	0606	...	...	...
	Middelburg d.	...	...	...	...	...	...	...	...	...	...	...	...	...	...	...	0543	...	...	...	...	0613	...	...	...
	Goes d.	...	...	...	...	...	...	...	...	...	...	...	...	...	...	...	0558	...	...	...	...	0628	...	...	...
	Bergen op Zoom d.	...	...	...	...	...	...	...	0527	...	...	...	0557	...	...	...	0627	...	...	...	...	0657	...	...	...
	Roosendaal 18 d.	...	...	...	...	...	...	...	0541	...	...	...	0611	...	...	...	0640	0640	...	...	...	0710	...	...	...
	Dordrecht 18 471 d.	...	...	...	...	...	0550	...	0605	0605	...	0620	0635	0635	...	0650	0705	0705	0705	...	0720	0735	0735	...	0750
	Rotterdam Centraal 18 471 d.	0522	...	...	0552	...	0607	...	0622	0622	...	0637	0652	0652	...	0707	0722	0722	0722	...	0737	0752	0752	...	0807
	Schiedam Centrum d.	0527	...	...	0557	...	0612	...	0627	0627	...	0642	0657	0657	...	0712	0727	0727	0727	...	0742	0757	0757	...	0812
	Delft 471 d.	0535	...	...	0605	...	0620	...	0635	0635	...	0650	0705	0705	...	0720	0735	0735	0735	...	0750	0805	0805	...	0820
	Den Haag HS 18 471 d.	0543	...	...	0613	...	0628	...	0643	0643	...	0658	0713	0713	...	0728	0743	0743	0743	...	0758	0813	0813	...	0828
0	**Den Haag** Centraal 471 d.	|	0544	...	|	0614	|	...	|	|	0644	|	|	|	0714	|	|	|	|	0744	|	|	|	0814	|
15	Leiden Centraal a.	0555	0555	...	0625	0625	0640	...	0655	0655	0655	0710	0725	0725	0725	0740	0755	0755	0755	0755	0810	0825	0825	0825	0840
15	Leiden Centraal d.	0557	0557	...	0627	0627	0642	...	0657	0657	0657	0712	0727	0727	0727	0742	0757	0757	0757	0757	0812	0827	0827	0827	0842
43	**Haarlem** d.	|	0617	...	|	0647	0702	...	|	|	0717	0732	|	|	0747	0802	|	|	|	0817	0832	|	|	0847	0902
	Schiphol ✈ ★ d.	0614	|	...	0644	|	|	...	0713	0714	|	|	0743	0744	|	|	0814	0814	0814	|	|	0844	0844	|	|
57	Amsterdam Sloterdijk ★ a.	0625	0625	...	0655	0655	0710	...	0725	0725	0725	0740	0755	0755	0755	0810	0825	0825	0825	0825	0840	0855	0855	0855	0910
62	**Amsterdam** Centraal ★ a.	0631	0632	...	0701	0702	0717	...	0731	0731	0732	0747	0801	0801	0802	0817	0831	0831	0831	0832	0847	0901	0901	0902	0917

	⚒◧	◧		⚒	◧		⚒	◧		⚒	◧		⚒	◧		⚒		◧			◧			
Vlissingen d.	0636	...	...	...	0706	...	...	0736	...	...	0806	...	...	0836	...	...	...	0906	...	...	0936	...	...	and at the same minutes past each hour until
Middelburg d.	0643	...	...	...	0713	...	...	0743	...	...	0813	...	...	0843	...	...	...	0913	...	...	0943	...	...	
Goes d.	0658	...	...	...	0728	...	...	0758	...	...	0828	...	...	0858	...	...	...	0928	...	...	0958	...	...	
Bergen op Zoom d.	0727	...	...	...	0757	...	...	0827	...	...	0857	...	...	0927	...	...	...	0957	...	...	1027	...	...	
Roosendaal 18 d.	0740	...	...	...	0810	...	...	0840	...	...	0910	...	...	0940	...	...	...	1010	...	...	1040	...	...	
Dordrecht 18 471 d.	0805	0805	...	0820	0835	...	0850	0905	...	0920	0935	...	0950	1005	...	1020	...	1035	...	1050	1105	...	1120	
Rotterdam Centraal 18 471 d.	0822	0822	...	0837	0852	...	0907	0922	...	0937	0952	...	1007	1022	...	1037	...	1052	...	1107	1122	...	1137	
Schiedam Centrum d.	0827	0827	...	0842	0857	...	0912	0927	...	0942	0957	...	1012	1027	...	1042	...	1057	...	1112	1127	...	1142	
Delft 471 d.	0835	0835	...	0850	0905	...	0920	0935	...	0950	1005	...	1020	1035	...	1050	...	1105	...	1120	1135	...	1150	
Den Haag HS 18 471 d.	0843	0843	...	0858	0913	...	0928	0943	...	0958	1013	...	1028	1043	...	1058	...	1113	...	1128	1143	...	1158	
Den Haag Centraal 471 d.	|	|	0844	|	|	0914	|	|	0944	|	|	1014	|	|	1044	|	...	|	1114	|	|	1144	|	
Leiden Centraal a.	0855	0855	0855	0910	0925	0925	0940	0955	0955	1010	1025	1025	1040	1055	1055	1110	...	1125	1125	1140	1155	1155	1210	
Leiden Centraal d.	0857	0857	0857	0912	0927	0927	0942	0957	0957	1012	1027	1027	1042	1057	1057	1112	...	1127	1127	1142	1157	1157	1212	
Haarlem d.	|	|	0917	0932	|	0947	1002	|	1017	1032	|	1047	1102	|	1117	1132	...	|	1147	1202	|	1217	1232	
Schiphol ✈ ★ d.	0914	0914	|	|	0944	|	|	1014	|	|	1044	|	|	1114	|	|	...	1144	|	|	1214	|	|	
Amsterdam Sloterdijk ★ a.	0925	0925	0925	0940	0955	0955	1010	1025	1025	1040	1055	1055	1110	1125	1125	1140	...	1155	1155	1210	1225	1225	1240	
Amsterdam Centraal ★ a.	0931	0931	0932	0947	1001	1002	1017	1031	1032	1047	1101	1102	1117	1131	1132	1147	...	1201	1202	1217	1231	1232	1247	

	◧			◧			◧			◧												E	G		
Vlissingen d.	1906	...	...	1936	...	...	2006	...	...	2036	...	...	2106	...	...	2136	...	...	2206	...	...	2236	2236	...	2306
Middelburg d.	1913	...	...	1943	...	...	2013	...	...	2043	...	...	2113	...	...	2143	...	...	2213	...	...	2243	2243	...	2313
Goes d.	1928	...	...	1958	...	...	2028	...	...	2058	...	...	2128	...	...	2158	...	...	2228	...	...	2258	2258	...	2328
Bergen op Zoom d.	1957	...	...	2027	...	...	2057	...	...	2127	...	...	2157	...	...	2227	...	...	2257	...	...	2327	2327	...	2357
Roosendaal 18 d.	2010	...	...	2040	...	...	2110	...	...	2140	...	...	2210	...	...	2240	...	...	2310	...	...	2340	2340	...	0007
Dordrecht 18 471 d.	2035	...	2050	2105	...	2120	2135	...	2150	2205	...	...	2235	...	...	2305	...	...	2335	...	...	0005	0005	...	...
Rotterdam Centraal 18 471 d.	2052	...	2107	2122	...	2137	2152	...	2207	2222	...	...	2252	...	...	2322	...	...	2352	...	...	0022	0022	...	...
Schiedam Centrum d.	2057	...	2112	2127	...	2142	2157	...	2212	2227	...	...	2257	...	...	2327	...	...	2357	...	...	0027	0027	...	...
Delft 471 d.	2105	...	2120	2135	...	2150	2205	...	2220	2235	...	...	2305	...	...	2335	...	...	0005	...	...	0035	0035	...	...
Den Haag HS 18 471 d.	2113	...	2128	2143	...	2158	2213	...	2228	2243	...	...	2313	...	...	2343	...	...	0013	...	...	0043	0043	...	...
Den Haag Centraal 471 d.	|	2114	|	|	2144	|	|	2214	|	|	2244	...	|	2314	...	|	2344	...	|	0014	...	|	|	...	...
Leiden Centraal a.	2125	2125	2140	2155	2155	2210	2225	2225	2240	2255	2255	...	2325	2325	...	2355	2355	...	0025	0025	...	0055	0055	...	...
Leiden Centraal d.	2127	2127	2142	2157	2157	2212	2227	2227	2242	2257	2257	...	2327	2327	...	2357	2357	...	0027	0027	...	0057	0057	...	...
Haarlem d.	|	2147	2202	|	2217	2232	|	2247	2302	|	2317	...	|	2347	...	|	0017	...	|	0047	...	|	|	...	...
Schiphol ✈ ★ d.	2144	|	|	2214	|	|	2244	|	|	2314	|	...	2344	|	...	0014	|	...	0044	|	...	|	0114	...	...
Amsterdam Sloterdijk ★ a.	2155	2155	2210	2225	2225	2240	2255	2255	2310	2325	2325	...	2355	2355	...	0025	0025	...	0055	0055	...	0123	0123	...	...
Amsterdam Centraal ★ a.	2201	2202	2217	2231	2232	2247	2301	2302	2317	2331	2332	...	0001	0002	...	0031	0032	...	0101	0104	...	0128	0128	...	...

E – ①②⑦ (not June 9).
G – ③–⑥ (also June 9).
k – Also May 29, June 9.

◧ – To Lelystad, Leeuwarden or Groningen (Table **460**).
★ – **Additional trains** Schiphol ✈ - Amsterdam Centraal at 0028, 0528 Ⓒ, 0542 Ⓐ, 0603 ⚒, 0604 †, 0628, 0658 and at 28 and 58 minutes past each hour until 2328, 2358.

☛ For NIGHT NETWORK **Rotterdam** – **Den Haag** – **Haarlem/Schiphol** – **Amsterdam**, see Table **454**.
For INTERNATIONAL SERVICES **Brussels** – **Antwerpen** – **Roosendaal** – **Rotterdam** - **Den Haag**, see Table **18**.

BREDA - ROTTERDAM - AMSTERDAM 451

Intercity direct services via the high-speed line. Supplement payable (except for local journeys Breda - Rotterdam and Schiphol - Amsterdam).

	905 D	**907** D	**909**	**1011** Ⓐ	**911**	**913**	**915**	**917**	**919**	**921**	**923**	**925**	**927**	**929**	**931**	**933**	**935**	**937**	**939**	**941**	**943**	**945**	**947**	**949**	**951**
Breda d.	0627	0657	0727	...	0757	0827	0857	0927	0957	1027	1057	1127	1157	1227	1257	1327	1357	1427	1457	1527	1557	1627	1657	1727	1757
Rotterdam Centraal a.	0652	0722	0752	...	0822	0852	0922	0952	1022	1052	1122	1152	1222	1252	1322	1352	1422	1452	1522	1552	1622	1652	1722	1752	1822
Rotterdam Centraal d.	0654	0724	0754	0808	0824	0854	0924	0954	1024	1054	1124	1154	1224	1254	1324	1354	1424	1454	1524	1554	1624	1654	1724	1754	1824
Schiphol ✈ a.	0720	0750	0820	0834	0850	0920	0950	1020	1050	1120	1150	1220	1250	1320	1350	1420	1450	1520	1550	1620	1650	1720	1750	1820	1850
Amsterdam Centraal a.	0736	0806	0836	0849	0906	0936	1006	1036	1106	1136	1206	1236	1306	1336	1406	1436	1506	1536	1606	1636	1706	1736	1806	1836	1906

	1053 Ⓐ	**953**	**955**	**957**	**959**	**961**	**963**	**965**		**969**	
Breda d.	...	1827	1857	1927	1957	2027	2057	2127	...	2227	...
Rotterdam Centraal a.	...	1852	1922	1952	2022	2052	2122	2152	...	2252	...
Rotterdam Centraal d.	1838	1854	1924	1954	2024	2054	2124	2154	...	2254	...
Schiphol ✈ a.	1904	1920	1950	2020	2050	2120	2150	2220	...	2320	...
Amsterdam Centraal a.	1920	1936	2006	2036	2106	2136	2206	2236	...	2336	...

D – ①–⑥ (not Apr. 21, May 29, June 9).

UTRECHT - AMSTERDAM - ROTTERDAM - EINDHOVEN Night Network 454

	⑥⑦		⑥⑦		①–③	⑥⑦	④⑤		①–③	⑥⑦	④⑤		①–③	⑥⑦	④⑤		①–③	⑥⑦	④⑤		④–⑥	①–③		†
Utrecht Centraal d.	...	...	...	...	...	...	...	...	0058	0058	0058	...	0207	0207	0207	...	0307	0307	0307	...	0407	0407	...	0507
Amsterdam Centraal d.	...	...	...	...	0045	0046	0045	...	0145	0145	0145	...	0245	0245	0245	...	0345	0345	0345	...	0445	0445	...	0545
Schiphol ✈ d.	...	...	...	...	0103	0103	0103	...	|	0203	0203	...	|	0303	0303	...	|	0403	0403	...	0503	|	...	0602
Leiden Centraal d.	...	...	...	...	0123	0123	0123	...	0223	0223	0223	...	0323	0323	0323	...	0423	0423	0423	...	0523	0523	...	0623
Den Haag HS d.	...	...	...	...	0138	0138	0144	...	0238	0238	0244	...	0338	0338	0344	...	0438	0438	0444	...	0538	0538	...	0638
Delft d.	...	...	...	...	0146	0146	|	...	0246	0246	|	...	0346	0346	|	...	0446	0446	|	...	0546	0546	...	0646
Rotterdam Centraal d.	0002	...	0102	...	0157	0202	0226	...	0259	0302	0326	...	0359	0402	0426	...	0457	0459	0526	...	0559	0559	...	0659
Dordrecht d.	0017	...	0117	...	...	0217	...	...	...	0317	...	...	...	0417	...	...	...	...	...	...	...	...	...	...
Breda d.	0035	...	0135	...	...	0235	...	...	...	0335	...	...	...	0435	...	...	...	...	...	...	...	...	...	...
Tilburg d.	0055	...	0155	...	...	0255	...	...	...	0355	...	...	...	0455	...	...	...	...	...	...	...	...	...	...
Eindhoven a.	0118	...	0218	...	...	0318	...	...	...	0418	...	...	...	0518	...	...	...	...	...	...	...	...	...	...

		①–③		④⑤	⑥⑦	①–③		④⑤	⑥⑦	①–③		④⑤	⑥⑦	①–③		④⑤	⑥⑦	①–③		④⑤	⑥⑦	①–③		†
Eindhoven d.	...	...	...	...	...	...	...	...	0030	...	...	...	0130	...	...	...	0230	...	...	...	0330	...	...	...
Tilburg d.	...	...	...	...	...	...	...	...	0102	...	...	...	0202	...	...	...	0302	...	...	...	0402	...	...	...
Breda d.	...	...	...	...	...	...	...	...	0119	...	...	...	0219	...	...	...	0319	...	...	...	0419	...	...	...
Dordrecht d.	...	0005	...	...	...	...	...	...	0141	...	...	...	0241	...	...	...	0341	...	...	...	0441	...	...	...
Rotterdam Centraal d.	...	0022	...	0032	0102	0102	...	0132	0202	0202	...	0232	0302	0302	...	0332	0402	0402	...	0432	0502	0502	...	0602
Delft d.	...	0035	...	|	0114	0114	...	|	0214	0214	...	|	0314	0314	...	|	0414	0414	...	|	0514	0514	...	0614
Den Haag HS d.	...	0043	...	0123	0123	0123	...	0224	0223	0223	...	0324	0323	0323	...	0424	0423	0423	...	0524	0523	0523	...	0623
Leiden Centraal d.	...	0057	...	0138	0138	0142	...	0238	0238	0239	...	0338	0338	0338	...	0438	0438	0438	...	0538	0538	0538	...	0640
Schiphol ✈ d.	...	|	...	0200	0200	|	...	0300	0300	|	...	0400	0400	|	...	0500	0500	|	...	0600	0600	0600	...	0703
Amsterdam Centraal a.	0117	0128	...	0214	0214	0215	...	0314	0314	0315	...	0414	0414	0414	...	0514	0514	0514	...	0615	0615	0615	...	0718
Utrecht Centraal a.	0151	...	...	0255	0251	0251	...	0355	0351	0351	...	0455	0451	0451	...	0555	0551	0551	...	...	0649	...	...	0751

457 ALMERE - UTRECHT

km		Ⓐ	Ⓐ	Ⓐ		Ⓐ			⚒			⚒						
0	**Almere** Buiten d.	0603	0633	0702	0732	0802	0832	...	0902	0932	and at the same	2002	2032	...	2132	2232	2332	...
6	**Almere** Centrum d.	0610	0640	0709	0739	0809	0839	...	0909	0939	minutes past	2009	2039	...	2139	2239	2339	...
26	Naarden-Bussum d.	0627	0657	0727	0757	0827	0857	...	0927	0957	each hour until	2027	2057	...	2157	2257	2357	...
32	Hilversum d.	0633	0703	0733	0803	0833	0903	...	0933	1003		2033	2103	...	2203	2303	0003	...
49	**Utrecht** Centraal a.	0650	0720	0750	0820	0850	0920	...	0950	1020		2050	2120	...	2220	2320	0020	...

	B	⑥⑦c			Ⓐ	⚒	Ⓐ		⚒			⚒						
Utrecht Centraal d.	0011	0041	...	...	0611	0641	0711	...	0741	0811	and at the same	1841	1911	...	2011	2111	2211	2311
Hilversum d.	0028	0058	...	...	0628	0658	0728	...	0758	0828	minutes past	1858	1928	...	2028	2128	2228	2328
Naarden-Bussum d.	0034	0103	...	...	0633	0703	0733	...	0803	0833	each hour until	1903	1933	...	2033	2133	2233	2333
Almere Centrum d.	0051	0121	...	...	0651	0721	0751	...	0821	0851		1921	1951	...	2051	2151	2251	2351
Almere Buiten a.	0057	0127	...	...	0657	0727	0757	...	0827	0857		1927	1957	...	2057	2157	2257	2357

B – ②③⑥⑦ (also May 30; not Apr. 22).

c – Also May 30, June 10.

460 DEN HAAG - SCHIPHOL - AMSTERDAM - ALMERE - ZWOLLE

km		Ⓐ	Ⓐ	⑥k	Ⓐ	Ⓐ R	⚒	†	Ⓐ R	⑥k R	Ⓐ	†	Ⓐ B	⑥k D	Ⓐ	⚒ B	† D	⚒	⚒ V	† D	⚒	⚒ V	† D	⚒
0	**Den Haag** Centraal 450 d.	...	...	...	...	...	...	...	...	...	...	...	...	...	0704	...	...	0734a	...	...	0804	...	...	0834
	Den Haag HS 450 d.	...	...	...	...	0543	...	...	0613	0613	...	...	0643	0643	|	0713	0713	|	0743	0743	|	0813	0813	|
15	Leiden Centraal 450 d.	...	...	...	...	0557	...	...	0627	0627	...	...	0657	0657	0717	0727	0727	0747a	0757	0757	0817	0827	0827	0847
42	**Schiphol** ✈ 450 d.	...	...	...	...	0614	...	...	0644	0644	0703	...	0713	0714	0733	0743	0744	0803	0814	0814	0833	0844	0844	0903
51	**Amsterdam** Zuid d.	...	...	...	...	|	...	...	|	|	0712	...	|	|	0742	|	|	0812	|	|	0842	|	|	0912
56	Duivendrecht d.	...	...	...	...	|	...	...	|	|	0717	...	|	|	0747	|	|	0817	|	|	0847	|	|	0917
	Amsterdam Sloterdijk 450 d.	...	...	...	...	0625	...	...	0655	0655	|	...	0725	0725	|	0755	0755	|	0825	0825	|	0855	0855	|
	Amsterdam Centraal 450 d.	...	...	...	0607	0637	0637	...	0707	0707	|	0737	0737	0737	|	0807	0807	|	0837	0837	|	0907	0907	|
80	**Almere** Centrum d.	...	...	...	0630	0700	0700	...	0730	0730	0734	0758	0800	0800	0804	0830	0830	0834	0900	0900	0904	0930	0930	0934
104	**Lelystad** Centrum d.	0543	0613	0643	0649	0719	0719	0743	0745	0749	0749	0813	0815	0819	0819	0845	0849	0849	0915	0919	0919	0945	0949	0949
154	**Zwolle** a.	0615	0645	0715	0715	0745	0745	0815	...	0815	0815	0845	...	0845	0845	...	0915	0915	...	0945	0945	...	1015	1015
	Leeuwarden **482** a.	|	0756	|	|	0856	0856	|	...	|	|	0956	...	0956	0956	...	|	|	...	1056	1056	...	|	|
	Groningen **482** a.	0724	...	0824	0814	...	...	0914	...	0914	0914	...	...	...	...	...	1014	1014	...	...	...	...	1114	1114

	⚒ V	† D	⚒	⚒ V	† V	⚒	V		V			V		V		V		V		V ◇	V	V	⑤⑥k V
Den Haag Centraal 450 d.	...	...	0904	...	...	0934	...	1004	...	1034		...	2004	...	2034	...	2104	...	2134	...	...	...	...
Den Haag HS 450 d.	0843	0843	|	0913	0913	|	0943	|	1013	|	and at	1943	|	2013	|	2043	|	2113	|	2143	2213	2243	2243
Leiden Centraal 450 d.	0857	0857	0917	0927	0927	0947	0957	1017	1027	1047		1957	2017	2027	2047	2057	2117	2127	2147	2157	2227	2257	2257
Schiphol ✈ 450 d.	0914	0914	0933	0944	0944	1003	1014	1033	1044	1103	the same	2014	2033	2044	2103	2114	2133	2144	2203	2214	2244	2314	2314
Amsterdam Zuid d.	|	|	0942	|	|	1012	|	1042	|	1112		|	2042	|	2112	|	2142	|	2212	|	|	|	|
Duivendrecht d.	|	|	0947	|	|	1017	|	1047	|	1117	minutes	|	2047	|	2117	|	2147	|	2217	|	|	|	|
Amsterdam Sloterdijk 450 d.	0925	0925	|	0955	0955	|	1025	|	1055	|		2025	|	2055	|	2125	|	2155	|	2225	2255	2325	2325
Amsterdam Centraal 450 d.	0937	0937	|	1007	1007	|	1037	|	1107	|	past each	2037	|	2107	|	2137	|	2207	|	2237	2307	2337	2337
Almere Centrum d.	1000	1000	1004	1030	1030	1034	1100	1104	1130	1134		2100	2104	2130	2134	2200	2204	2230	2234	2300	2330	0000	0000
Lelystad Centrum d.	1015	1019	1019	1045	1049	1049	1115	1119	1145	1149	hour until	2115	2119	2145	2149	2215	2219	2245	2249	2319	2349	0019	0019
Zwolle a.	...	1045	1045	...	1115	1115	...	1145	...	1215		...	2145	...	2215	...	2245	...	2315	2345	0015	0045	0045
Leeuwarden **482** a.	...	1156	1156	...	|	|	...	1256	...	|		...	2256	...	|	...	2356	...	|	0056	|	...	|
Groningen **482** a.	...	...	...	...	1214	1214	...	...	...	1314		...	...	...	2314	...	...	...	0025	...	0123n	...	0156

	Ⓐ V		Ⓐ	Ⓐ V		Ⓐ	Ⓐ V	Ⓐ	⑥k V	⚒ V	Ⓐ	⚒	⚒ V	⑥k	Ⓐ	† V	V	⚒	† V	V		†	⚒	V
Groningen **482** d.	...	...	...	...	...	...	...	0532r	0546	...	...	...	...	0635	0646	0646	...	...	...	...	...	0735	0746	...
Leeuwarden **482** d.	...	...	...	...	...	0504	...	|	|	...	0604	...	...	|	|	|	...	0704	0704	...	...	|	|	...
Zwolle d.	...	...	0545	...	...	0615	...	0645	0645	...	0715	0715	...	0745	0745	0745	...	0815	0815	...	...	0845	0845	...
Lelystad Centrum d.	0544	...	0611	0614	...	0641	0644	0711	0714	0714	0741	0741	0744	0811	0811	0814	0814	0841	0844	0844	...	0911	0911	0914
Almere Centrum d.	0601	...	0627	0631	...	0657	0701	0726	0731	0731	0757	0757	0801	0826	0827	0831	0831	0857	0901	0901	...	0926	0927	0931
Amsterdam Centraal 450 a.	0623	...	|	0653	...	|	0723	|	0753	0753	|	|	0823	|	|	0853	0853	|	0923	0923	...	|	|	0953
Amsterdam Sloterdijk 450 a.	0635	...	|	0705	...	|	0735	|	0805	0805	|	|	0835	|	|	0905	0905	|	0935	0935	...	|	|	1005
Duivendrecht d.	|	...	0644	|	...	0714	|	0744	|	|	0814	0814	|	0844	0844	|	|	0914	|	|	...	0944	0944	|
Amsterdam Zuid d.	|	...	0650	|	...	0720	|	0750	|	|	0820	0820	|	0850	0850	|	|	0920	|	|	...	0950	0950	|
Schiphol ✈ 450 a.	0645	...	0656	0715	...	0726	0745	0756	0815	0815	0826	0826	0845	0856	0856	0915	0915	0926	0945	0945	...	0956	0956	1015
Leiden Centraal 450 a.	0703	...	0714	0733	...	0744	0803	0814	0833	0833	0844	0844	0903	0914	0914	0933	0933	0944	1003	1003	...	1014	1014	1033
Den Haag HS 450 a.	0717	...	|	0747	...	|	0817	|	0847	0847	|	|	0917	|	|	0947	0947	|	1017	1017	...	|	|	1047
Den Haag Centraal 450 a.	...	...	0726	...	...	0756	...	0826	...	...	0856	0856	...	0926	0926	...	...	0956	...	...	...	1026	1026	...

		V		V			V		V		V		V		S	D	S	R			⑤⑥k		⑤⑥k
Groningen **482** d.	...	...	0846	...		...	...	1846	...	...	...	1946	...	...	...	2046	...	2146	...	2246	2246	...	2326
Leeuwarden **482** d.	0804	...	|	...	and at	1804	...	|	...	1904	...	|	...	2004	...	|	2104	|	2204	|	|	...	|
Zwolle d.	0915	...	0945	...		1915	...	1945	...	2015	...	2045	...	2115	...	2145	2215	2245	2315	2345	2345	...	0035
Lelystad Centrum d.	0941	0944	1011	1014	the same	1941	1944	2011	2014	2041	2044	2111	2114	2141	2144	2214	2244	2314	2344	0014	0014	...	0106
Almere Centrum d.	0957	1001	1027	1031		1957	2001	2027	2031	2057	2101	2127	2131	2157	2201	2231	2301	2331	0001	0031	0031	...	0122
Amsterdam Centraal 450 a.	|	1023	|	1053	minutes	|	2023	|	2053	|	2123	|	2153	|	2223	2253	2323	2354	0024	0053	0053	...	0142
Amsterdam Sloterdijk 450 a.	|	1035	|	1105		|	2035	|	2105	|	2135	|	2205	|	2235	2305	2335	0005	0035	...	0105	...	...
Duivendrecht d.	1014	|	1044	|	past each	2014	|	2044	|	2114	|	2144	|	2214	|	|	|	|	|	...	|	...	...
Amsterdam Zuid d.	1020	|	1050	|		2020	|	2050	|	2120	|	2150	|	2220	|	|	|	|	|	...	|	...	...
Schiphol ✈ 450 a.	1026	1045	1056	1115	hour until	2026	2045	2056	2115	2126	2145	2156	2215	2226	2245	2315	2345	0015	0045	...	0115	...	...
Leiden Centraal 450 a.	1044	1103	1114	1133		2044	2103	2114	2133	2144	2203	2214	2233	2244	2303	2333	0003	0033	0103	...	0133	...	...
Den Haag HS 450 a.	|	1117	|	1147		|	2117	|	2147	|	2217	|	2247	|	2317	2347	0017	0047	0118	...	0149	...	...
Den Haag Centraal 450 a.	1056	...	1126	...		2056	...	2126	...	2156	...	2226	...	2256	...	...	...	...	...	...	...	...	...

Other stopping trains **Amsterdam - Zwolle**

km		G	⑥⑦c			Ⓐ	Ⓐ	Ⓐ	⑥k	Ⓐ	⚒	⚒	†		⚒	†								
0	**Amsterdam** Centraal d.	0010	0040	...	...	...	...	0540	...	0610	...	0640	...	0710	0710	0737	0740	0810	0840	and every	2210	2240	2310	2340
14	Weesp d.	0029	0059	...	...	...	...	0559	...	0629	...	0659	...	0729	0729	|	0759	0829	0859	30 minutes	2229	2259	2329	2359
30	**Almere** Centrum d.	0043	0113	...	...	...	...	0613	...	0643	...	0713	...	0743	0743	0758	0813	0843	0913	until	2243	2313	2343	0013
36	Almere Buiten d.	0049	0119	...	...	...	...	0619	...	0649	...	0719	...	0749	0749	|	0819	0849	0919		2249	2319	2349	0019
54	**Lelystad** Centrum d.	0102	0132	...	...	0543	0613	0634	0643	0704	0704	0734	0743	0802	0804	0813	0834	0904	0934		2304	2334	0004	0032
75	Dronten d.	...	...	...	...	0555	0625	0646	0655	0716	0716	0746	0755	...	0816	0825	0846	0916	0946		2316	2346	0016	...
88	Kampen Zuid d.	...	...	...	...	0604	0634	0654	0704	0724	0724	0754	0804	...	0824	0834	0854	0924	0954		2324	2354	0024	...
104	**Zwolle** a.	...	...	...	...	0615	0645	0705	0715	0735	0735	0805	0815	...	0835	0845	0905	0935	1005		2335	0005	0035	...

	⑥⑦c				Ⓐ		Ⓐ		Ⓐ		Ⓐ		⚒		⚒									
Zwolle d.	0035	...	...	...	...	...	0525	...	0555	...	0625	...	0655	...	0725	...	0755	0825	and every	2155	2225	2255	2325	2355
Kampen Zuid d.	0044	...	...	...	...	...	0535	...	0605	...	0635	...	0705	...	0735	...	0805	0835	30 minutes	2205	2235	2305	2335	0005
Dronten d.	0053	...	...	...	...	...	0543	...	0613	...	0643	...	0713	...	0743	...	0813	0843	until	2213	2243	2313	2343	0013
Lelystad Centrum d.	0106	...	...	0448	0504	0527	0557	0557	0627	0627	0657	0657	0727	0727	0757	0757	0827	0857		2227	2257	2327	2357	0025
Almere Buiten d.	|	...	...	0501	0517	0540	0610	0610	0640	0640	0710	0710	0740	0740	0810	0810	0840	0910		2240	2310	2340	0010	...
Almere Centrum d.	0122	...	...	0507	0524	0547	0617	0617	0647	0647	0717	0717	0747	0747	0817	0817	0847	0917		2247	2317	2347	0017	...
Weesp a.	|	...	...	0521	0538	0601	0631	0631	0701	0701	0731	0731	0801	0801	0831	0831	0901	0931		2301	2331	0001	0031	...
Amsterdam Centrum a.	0142	...	...	*0540*	0558	0620	0650	0650	0720	0720	0750	0750	0820	0820	0850	0850	0920	0950		2320	2350	0021	0050	...

B – From Bergen op Zoom (Table **450**).
D – From / to Dordrecht (Table **450**).
G – ②③⑥⑦ (also May 30; not Apr. 22).
R – From / to Rotterdam (Table **450**).
S – To Roosendaal (Table **450**).
V – From / to Vlissingen (Table **450**).

a – Ⓐ only.
c – Also May 30, June 10.
k – Also May 29, June 9.
n – 0129 on the mornings of ④⑤ (not May 30).
r – 0536 on ①④⑤.

◇ – Change trains at Lelystad Centrum on ③.

HAARLEM - ALKMAAR - HOORN 461

km		④–⑦	H 🚌		Ⓐ	Ⓐ	⚒	⚒		⚒														
0	**Haarlem** d.	0054	0100	...	...	...	0642a	0712a	0742v	0812	0842	0912		1912	1942	1954	2024	2054	2124	2154	2224	2254	2324	2354
11	Beverwijk d.	0110	0136	...	...	...	0652a	0722a	0752v	0822	0852	0922	and every	1922	1952	2010	2040	2110	2140	2210	2240	2310	2340	0010
22	Castricum 466 d.	0124	0208	...	...	...	0703a	0733a	0803v	0833	0903	0933		1933	2003	2024	2053	2124	2153	2224	2253	2324	2353	0024
34	**Alkmaar** 466 a.	0136	0233	...	...	...	0714a	0744a	0814v	0844	0914	0944	30 minutes	1944	2014	2036	2104	2136	2204	2236	2304	2336	0004	0036
34	**Alkmaar** 466 d.	...	...	...	0615	0645	0715	0745	0815	0845	0915	0945		1945	2015	...	2115	...	2215	...	2315	...	0015	...
40	Heerhugowaard 466 d.	...	...	...	0623	0653	0723	0753	0823	0853	0923	0953	until	1953	2023	...	2123	...	2223	...	2323	...	0023	...
57	**Hoorn** a.	...	...	...	0639	0709	0739	0809	0839	0909	0939	1009		2009	2039	...	2139	...	2239	...	2339	...	0039	...

	Ⓐ	Ⓐ	⚒	⚒																				J	⑤⑥k
Hoorn d.	0550	0620	0650	0720	0750	0820v	0850	0920v	0950	1020		1820	1850	1920	1950	...	2050	...	2150	...	2250	...	2350	2350
Heerhugowaard 466 d.	0606	0636	0706	0736	0806	0836v	0906	0936v	1006	1036		1836	1906	1936	2006	...	2106	...	2206	...	2306	...	0006	0006
Alkmaar 466 a.	0615	0645	0715	0745	0815	0845v	0915	0945v	1015	1045	and every	1845	1915	1944	2014	...	2114	...	2214	...	2314	...	0014	0014
Alkmaar 466 d.	0616	0646	0716	0746	0816	0846	0916	0946	1016	1046	30 minutes	1846	1916	1954	2023	2053	2123	2153	2223	2253	2324	2354	0024	0036
Castricum 466 d.	0626	0656	0726	0756	0826	0856	0926	0956	1026	1056	until	1856	1926	2005	2034	2104	2134	2204	2234	2304	2335	0005	0035	0047
Beverwijk d.	0638	0708	0738	0808	0838	0908	0938	1008	1038	1108		1908	1938	2017	2047	2117	2147	2217	2247	2317	2347	0017	0047	0100
Haarlem a.	0648	0719	0749	0819	0849	0919	0949	1019	1049	1119		1919	1949	2035	2105	2135	2205	2235	2305	2335	0005	0035	0105	0117

H – ①–③.
J – ①②③④⑦ (not May 29, June 9).
a – Ⓐ only.
k – Also May 29, June 9.
v – ⚒ only.

SCHIPHOL and AMSTERDAM - ENKHUIZEN 462

km			⑥⑦c	⑥⑦c		Ⓐ	Ⓐ	Ⓐ	Ⓐ	Ⓒ	Ⓐ	Ⓐ	⑥k	Ⓐ										
0	**Amsterdam** Centraal 466 d.	0009	0039	0150	...	...	0600	0630	...	0700	0709	...	0730	0739	...	0809	...	0839	and at	...	2309	...	2339	...
	Schiphol ✈ d.	|	|	|	...	0610	|	|	0640	|	|	0710	|	|	0740	|	0810	|	the same	2240	|	2310	|	2340
5	Amsterdam Sloterdijk 466 d.	0014	0044	0156	...	0621	0606	0636	0651	0706	0715	0721	0737	0745	0751	0815	0821	0845	minutes	2251	2315	2321	2345	2351
12	Zaandam 466 d.	0024	0054	0204	...	0627	0614	0644	0657	0714	|	0727	0744	|	0757	|	0827	|	past each	2257	|	2327	|	2357
44	**Hoorn** d.	0052	0121	0231	...	0654	0642	0712	0724	0742	0742	0754	0812	0812	0824	0842	0854	0912	hour until	2324	2342	2354	0012	0024
62	**Enkhuizen** a.	0120c	0145	...	...	...	0708	0739	...	0808	0808	...	0838	0837	...	0907	...	0937		...	0007	...	0037	...

	Ⓐ	⚒	⚒	Ⓐ	Ⓐ	Ⓐ	⚒	Ⓐ	Ⓐ	⚒	⚒	⚒	⚒											
Enkhuizen d.	0443	...	...	...	0524	...	0554	...	0624	...	...	0654	...	0724	...	0754	...	and at	2224	...	2254	...	2324	2354
Hoorn d.	0506	0506	...	0536	0550	0606	0620	0636	0650	0650	0706	0720	0736	0750	0806	0820	0836	the same	2250	2306	2320	2336	2350	0020
Zaandam 466 d.	0534	0534	0534	0602	|	0632	|	0702	|	|	0732	|	0802	|	0832	|	0902	minutes	|	2332	|	0002	0017	0047
Amsterdam Sloterdijk 466 a.	0540	0540	0540	0608	0614	0638	0644	0708	0714	0714	0738	0744	0808	0814	0838	0844	0908	past each	2314	2338	2344	0008	0024	0054
Schiphol ✈ a.	0551	0551	|	0620	|	0650	|	0720	|	|	0750	|	0820	|	0850	|	0920	hour until	|	2350	|	0020	|	|
Amsterdam Centraal 466 a.	...	...	0546	...	0623	...	0653	...	0723	0723	...	0753	...	0823	...	0853	...		2323	...	2353	...	0031	0101

c – ⑥⑦ (also May 29, June 9).
k – Also May 29, June 9.

LEIDEN - ALPHEN - UTRECHT and GOUDA 463

km		Ⓐ	⚒	⚒							
0	**Leiden** Centraal d.	0552	0622	0652	0722	0752	and every	2322	2352	0022	...
15	Alphen a/d Rijn d.	0607	0637	0707	0737	0807	30 minutes	2337	0007	0037	...
34	Woerden d.	0624	0654	0724	0754	0824	until	2354	0024	0054	...
50	**Utrecht** Centraal a.	0634	0704	0734	0804	0834		0004	0034	0104	...

	Ⓐ	⚒	⚒						
Utrecht Centraal d.	0555	0625	0655	0725	0755	and every	2325	2355	0025
Woerden d.	0606	0636	0706	0736	0806	30 minutes	2336	0006	0036
Alphen a/d Rijn d.	0623	0653	0723	0753	0823	until	2353	0023	0053
Leiden Centraal a.	0637	0707	0737	0807	0837		0007	0037	0107

km		Ⓐ	Ⓐ	Ⓐ	⑥k	Ⓐ	Ⓒ	Ⓐ	Ⓒ	Ⓐ	Ⓒ	Ⓐ	Ⓒ						Ⓒ	Ⓐ	Ⓒ	Ⓐ	
0	**Leiden** Centraal d.	0608	0638	0708	...	0738	...	0808	...	0838	...	0908	...	...	...	and every	...	...	...	1508	...	1538	and at the same
15	Alphen a/d Rijn ★ d.	0623	0653	0723	0738	0753	0808	0823	0838	0853	0908	0923	0938	1008	1038	30 minutes	1408	1438	1508	1523	1538	1553	minutes past
32	**Gouda** ★ a.	0643	0713	0743	0758	0813	0828	0843	0858	0913	0928	0943	0958	1028	1058	until	1428	1458	1528	1543	1558	1613	each hour until

	Ⓒ	Ⓐ	Ⓒ	Ⓐ	Ⓒ					
Leiden Centraal d.	...	1838	...	1908	...	...	...	and every	...	...
Alphen a/d Rijn d.	1838	1853	1908	1923	1938	2008	2038	30 minutes	0008	0038
Gouda a.	1858	1913	1928	1943	1958	2028	2058	until	0028	0058

	Ⓐ	Ⓐ	⑥k	Ⓐ	⑥k	Ⓐ	Ⓒ	Ⓐ	Ⓒ	Ⓐ	Ⓒ
Gouda d.	0617	0647	0702	0717	0732	0747	0802	0817	0832	0847	0902
Alphen a/d Rijn a.	0636	0706	0721	0736	0751	0806	0821	0836	0851	0906	0921
Leiden Centraal a.	0651	0721	...	0751	...	0821	...	0851	...	0921	...

	Ⓐ	Ⓒ						Ⓒ	Ⓐ	Ⓒ	Ⓐ		Ⓒ	Ⓐ	Ⓒ	Ⓐ	Ⓒ					
Gouda d.	0917	0932	1002	1032	and every	1402	1432	1502	1517	1532	1547	and at the same	1832	1847	1902	1917	1932	2002	2032	and every	0002	0032
Alphen a/d Rijn d.	0936	0951	1021	1051	30 minutes	1421	1451	1521	1536	1551	1606	minutes past	1851	1906	1921	1936	1951	2021	2051	30 minutes	0021	0051
Leiden Centraal a.	0951	...	...	...	until	...	...	...	1551	...	1621	each hour until	...	1921	...	1951	...	...	...	until	...	...

k – Also May 29, June 9.
★ – **Additional trains** Alphen - Gouda at 0553 Ⓐ and 0708 ⑥ **k**.

AMSTERDAM - GOUDA - ROTTERDAM 465

For fast trains **Amsterdam** - **Rotterdam**, see Table **450**. For other trains **Gouda** - **Rotterdam**, see Table **481**.

km		Ⓐ	⑥k	⚒	⚒					
0	**Amsterdam** Centraal d.	0617	0618	0647	0717	0747	0817		2317	2347
6	Amsterdam Amstel d.	0625	0627	0655	0725	0755	0825	and every	2325	2355
9	Duivendrecht d.	0629	0630	0659	0729	0759	0829		2329	2359
27	Breukelen d.	0649	0649	0719	0749	0819	0849	30 minutes	2349	0019
40	Woerden d.	0658	0658	0728	0758	0828	0858		2358	0028
56	**Gouda** d.	0712	0712	0742	0812	0842	0912	until	0012	0042
70	Rotterdam Alexander d.	0724	0724	0754	0824	0854	0924		0024	0054
80	**Rotterdam** Centraal a.	0734	0734	0804	0834	0904	0934		0034	0104

	Ⓐ	Ⓐ	⚒	⚒					
Rotterdam Centraal d.	0525	0555	0625	0655	0725	0755		2255	2325
Rotterdam Alexander d.	0535	0605	0635	0705	0735	0805	and every	2304	2335
Gouda d.	0549	0619	0649	0719	0749	0819		2319	2349
Woerden d.	0602	0632	0702	0732	0802	0832	30 minutes	2331	0002
Breukelen d.	0611	0641	0711	0741	0811	0841		2341	0011
Duivendrecht d.	0629	0659	0729	0759	0829	0859	until	2359	0029
Amsterdam Amstel d.	0633	0703	0733	0803	0833	0903		0003	0033
Amsterdam Centraal a.	0642	0712	0742	0812	0842	0912		0011	0042

k – Also May 29, June 9.

AMSTERDAM - ALKMAAR - DEN HELDER 466

km				Ⓐ	Ⓐ	⚒	Ⓐ	⑥k	Ⓐ	Ⓒ					†	⚒								
	Nijmegen 468 d.	...	...	...	...	...	...	...	...	...	0535a	0612v	0642v	0712	0735	0742	0812	0842	0912		2042	2112	2142	2212
	Arnhem 468 d.	...	...	...	...	...	...	...	...	...	0601a	0631v	0701v	0731	0801	0801	0833j	0901	0931		2101	2131	2201	2233
	Utrecht Centraal 468 d.	...	...	...	...	...	...	...	...	...	0640v	0710	0740	0810	0840	0840	0910	0940	1010	and every	2140	2210	2240	2310
0	**Amsterdam** Centraal 459 d.	0017	...	0527f	...	...	0612	0617	0642	0647	0712	0742	0812	0842	0912	0912	0942	1012	1042		2212	2242	2312	2342
5	Amsterdam Sloterdijk 459 d.	0022	...	0532f	...	...	0618	0622	0648	0652	0718	0748	0818	0848	0918	0918	0948	1018	1048	30 minutes	2218	2248	2318	2348
12	Zaandam 459 d.	0029	...	0539f	...	...	0624	0629	0654	0659	0724	0754	0824	0854	0924	0924	0954	1024	1054		2224	2254	2324	2354
29	Castricum 461 d.	0049	...	0602	...	...	0637	0651	0707	0726	0737	0807	0837	0907	0937	0937	1007	1037	1107	until	2237	2307	2337	0007
41	**Alkmaar** 461 d.	0101	...	0612	0620	0650	0650	0701	0720	0736	0750	0820	0850	0920	0950	0950	1020	1050	1120		2250	2320	2350	0020
48	Heerhugowaard 461 d.	0109	...	...	0628	0658	0659	...	0728	...	0758	0828	0858	0928	0958	0958	1028	1058	1128		2258	2328	2358	0028
83	**Den Helder** a.	0135z	...	...	0656	0726	0726	...	0756	...	0826	0856	0926	0956	1026	1026	1056	1126	1156		2326	2356	0031	0056

	⚒	Ⓐ	Ⓐ	Ⓐ	Ⓒ	⚒	†	⚒	†	⚒		†	⚒	†	⚒									
en Helder d.	...	0504	0534	0604	...	0634	0704	0704	0734	0734		1734	1734	1804	1804	1834	1904	1934	2004	2034	2104	2134	2204	2304
eerhugowaard 461 d.	...	0530	0600	0630	...	0700	0729	0730	0759	0800		1759	1800	1829	1830	1859	1929	1959	2029	2059	2129	2159	2229	2329
lkmaar 461 d.	0503	0542	0612	0642	0650g	0712	0741	0742	0811	0812	and every	1811	1812	1841	1842	1911	1941	2011	2041	2111	2141	2211	2241	2341
astricum 461 d.	0512	0550	0620	0650	0701g	0720	0751	0750	0821	0820		1821	1820	1851	1850	1921	1951	2021	2051	2121	2151	2221	2251	2351
aandam 459 d.	0534	0605	0635	0705	0730	0735	0805	0805	0835	0835	30 minutes	1835	1835	1905	1905	1935	2005	2035	2105	2135	2205	2235	2305	0005
msterdam Sloterdijk 459 d.	0540	0612	0642	0712	0738	0742	0812	0812	0842	0842		1842	1842	1912	1912	1942	2012	2042	2112	2142	2212	2242	2312	0012
msterdam Centraal 459 a.	0546	0618	0648	0718	0744	0748	0818	0818	0848	0848	until	1848	1850	1918	1918	1948	2018	2048	2118	2148	2218	2248	2318	0018
Utrecht Centraal 468 a.	...	0651	0721	0751	...	0821	0851	0851	0921	0921		1921	1921	1951	1951	2021	2051	2121	2151	2221	2251	2321	2351	0051
Arnhem 468 a.	...	0729	0759	0829	...	0859	0929	0929	0959	0959		1959	1959	2029	2029	2059	2129	2159	2229	2259	2329	2359	0029	0129n
Nijmegen 468 a.	...	0747	0817	0847	...	0917	0947	0947	1017	1017		2017	2017	2047	2047	2117	2147	2217	2247	2317	2347	0022	0050	0150p

– Ⓐ only.
– 3 minutes later on ④⑤.
– 4 minutes later on †.
j – 0831 on †.
k – Also May 29, June 9.
n – 0132 on ① (also Apr. 22).
p – 0153 on ① (also Apr. 22). *0210* on ④⑤ (by 🚌 from Arnhem).
v – ⚒ only.
z – *0221* on the mornings of ②③ (by 🚌 from Heerhugowaard).

468 AMSTERDAM and SCHIPHOL ✈ - ARNHEM - NIJMEGEN

km		A	①m	④⑤			Ⓐ	Ⓐ	Ⓐ	Ⓐ	Ⓐ	⚒	Ⓐ	⚒	⚒	Ⓐ	⚒	†	⚒		⚒		⚒		⚒
0	**Amsterdam** Centraal ... 470 d.	0022	0022	...	...	...	...	...	0529	...	...	...	0622	...	0652	...	0722	...	...	0752	...	0822	...	0852	...
6	Amsterdam Amstel .... 470 d.	0030	0030	...	...	...	...	...	0538	...	...	...	0630	...	0700	...	0730	...	...	0800	...	0830	...	0900	...
	Schiphol ✈ .... 470 d.	|	|	...	...	...	...	...	|	...	...	...	|	...	|	0700	|	...	0730	|	0800	|	0830	|	0900
	Amsterdam Zuid ...... 470 d.	|	|	...	...	...	...	...	|	...	...	...	|	...	|	0709	|	...	0739	|	0809	|	0839	|	0909
39	**Utrecht** Centraal .... 470 a.	0051	0051	...	...	...	...	...	0612	...	...	...	0651	...	0721	0732	0751	...	0802	0821	0832	0851	0902	0921	0932
39	**Utrecht** Centraal .... d.	0053	0053	...	...	...	0553	0608	...	0623	0638	0653	0653	0708	0723	0738	0753	0753	0808	0823	0838	0853	0908	0923	0938
79	Ede-Wageningen .... d.	0118	0118	...	...	...	0617	0632	...	0647	0702	0717	0717	0732	0747	0802	0817	0819	0831	0847	0902	0917	0932	0947	1002
96	**Arnhem** .... a.	0129	0132	🚌	...	...	0629	0644	...	0659	0714	0729	0729	0744	0759	0814	0829	0829	0844	0859	0914	0929	0944	0959	1014
96	**Arnhem** .... 475 d.	0134t	0137	0139	...	...	0634	0649	...	0704	0719	0734	0734	0749a	0804	0819	0834	0834	0849a	0904	0919	0934	0949	1004	1019
114	**Nijmegen** .... 475 a.	0150t	0153	0210	...	...	0647	0702	...	0717	0732	0747	0747	0802a	0817	0832	0847	0847	0902a	0917	0932	0947	1005	1017	1032

		⚒		⚒		⚒		⚒														Ⓑn	⑥k		
Amsterdam Centraal .... 470 d.	0922	...	0952	...	1022	...	1052	...	1122	...	1152	...		2022	...	2052	...	2122	2152	2222	2252	2252	2322	2352
Amsterdam Amstel .... 470 d.	0930	...	1000	...	1030	...	1100	...	1130	...	1200	...	and at	2030	...	2100	...	2130	2200	2230	2300	2300	2330	0000
Schiphol ✈ .... 470 d.	|	0930	|	1000	|	1030	|	1100	|	1130	|	1200	the same	|	2030	|	2100	|	|	|	|	|	|	|
Amsterdam Zuid ...... 470 d.	|	0939	|	1009	|	1039	|	1109	|	1139	|	1209		|	2039	|	2109	|	|	|	|	|	|	|
Utrecht Centraal .... 470 a.	0951	1002	1021	1032	1051	1102	1121	1132	1151	1202	1221	1232	minutes	2051	2102	2121	2132	2151	2221	2251	2321	2321	2351	0021
Utrecht Centraal .... d.	0953	1008	1023	1038	1053	1108	1123	1138	1153	1208	1223	1238	past each	2053	2108	2123	2138	2153	2223	2253	2323	2323	2353	...
Ede-Wageningen .... d.	1017	1031	1047	1102	1117	1132	1147	1202	1217	1232	1247	1302	hour until	2117	2132	2147	2202	2219	2249	2319	2349	2349	0019	...
Arnhem .... a.	1029	1044	1059	1114	1129	1144	1159	1214	1229	1244	1259	1314		2129	2144	2159	2214	2229	2259	2329	2359	2359	0029	...
Arnhem .... 475 d.	1034	1049	1104	1119	1134	1149	1204	1219	1234	1249	1304	1319		2134	2149	2204	2219	2234	2304	2334	0004	0007	0034	...
Nijmegen .... 475 a.	1047	1105	1117	1135	1147	1202	1217	1232	1247	1302	1317	1332		2147	2202	2217	2232	2247	2317	2347	0020	0022	0050	...

km		Ⓐ	Ⓐ	⚒	Ⓐ	Ⓐ		⚒	⚒		⚒	⚒		⚒	†	⚒	⚒	†	⚒	⚒		⚒		⚒	
	Nijmegen .... 475 d.	...	...	...	0535	...	...	0612	0627a	...	0642	0657a	0712	0727a	0735	0742	0757a	0812	0812	0827a	0842	0857a	0912	0927	0942
	Arnhem .... 475 a.	...	...	...	0554	...	...	0626	0640a	...	0656	0710a	0726	0740a	0754	0756	0810a	0826	0826	0840a	0856	0910a	0926	0940	0956
	Arnhem .... d.	...	0546	...	0601	0616	...	0631	0646	...	0701	0716	0731	0746	0801	0801	0816	0831	0833	0846	0901	0916	0931	0946	1001
	Ede-Wageningen .... d.	...	0556	...	0611	0626	...	0641	0656	...	0711	0726	0741	0756	0811	0811	0826	0841	0843	0856	0911	0926	0941	0956	1011
	Utrecht Centraal .... a.	...	0622	...	0637	0652	...	0707	0722	...	0737	0752	0808	0822	0838	0837	0852	0908	0907	0922	0938	0952	1008	1022	1038
0	**Utrecht** Centraal .... 470 d.	0558	0628	0640	0640	0658	0710	0710	0728	0740	0740	0758	0810	0828	0840	0840	0858	0910	0910	0928	0940	0958	1010	1028	1040
36	**Amsterdam** Zuid ...... 470 a.	0622	0652	|	|	0722	|	|	0752	|	|	0822	|	0852	|	|	0922	|	|	0952	|	1022	|	1052	|
45	**Schiphol** ✈ .... 470 a.	0629	0659	|	|	0729	|	|	0759	|	|	0829	|	0859	|	|	0929	|	|	0959	|	1029	|	1059	|
	Amsterdam Amstel .... 470 a.	...	...	0658	0658	...	0728	0728	...	0758	0758	...	0828	...	0858	0858	...	0928	0928	...	0958	...	1028	...	1058
	Amsterdam Centraal ... 470 a.	...	...	0707	0707	...	0737	0737	...	0807	0807	...	0837	...	0907	0907	...	0937	0937	...	1007	...	1037	...	1107

	⚒		⚒						❖															
Nijmegen .... 475 d.	0957	1012	1027	1042	1057	1112	1126	1142		1857	1912	1927	1942	1956	2012	2026	2042	2112	2142	2212	2242	2312	...	2342
Arnhem .... 475 a.	1010	1026	1040	1056	1110	1126	1140	1156	and at	1910	1926	1940	1956	2010	2026	2040	2056	2126	2156	2226	2256	2326	...	2356
Arnhem .... d.	1016	1033	1046	1101	1116	1131	1146	1201	the same	1916	1933	1946	2001	2016	2031	2046	2101	2131	2201	2233	2301	2331	...	0001
Ede-Wageningen .... d.	1026	1043	1056	1111	1126	1141	1156	1211		1926	1943	1956	2011	2026	2041	2056	2111	2141	2211	2243	2311	2341	...	0011
Utrecht Centraal .... a.	1052	1108	1122	1138	1152	1207	1222	1237	minutes	1952	2007	2022	2037	2052	2107	2122	2138	2208	2238	2308	2338	0008	...	0038
Utrecht Centraal .... 470 d.	1058	1110	1128	1140	1158	1210	1228	1240	past each	1958	2010	2028	2040	...	2110	...	2140	2210	2240	2310	2340	...	0025	...
Amsterdam Zuid .... 470 a.	1122	|	1152	|	1222	|	1252	|	hour until	2022	|	2052	|	...	|	...	|	|	|	|	|	...	|	...
Schiphol ✈ .... 470 a.	1129	|	1159	|	1229	|	1259	|		2029	|	2059	|	...	|	...	|	|	|	|	|	...	|	...
Amsterdam Amstel .... 470 a.	...	1128	...	1158	...	1228	...	1258		...	2028	...	2058	...	2128	...	2158	2228	2258	2328	2358	...	0045	...
Amsterdam Centraal .... 470 a.	...	1137	...	1207	...	1237	...	1307		...	2037	...	2107	...	2137	...	2207	2237	2307	2337	0007	...	0054	...

A – ②–⑦ (not Apr. 22).

a – Ⓐ only.

k – Also May 29, June 9.
m – Also Apr. 22.
n – Not May 29, June 9.

t – ②③⑥⑦ (not Apr. 22).

❖ – Timings may vary by 1–2 minutes.

☛ Many trains from / to Amsterdam Centraal start from / continue to Den Helder (see Table **466**). For INTERNATIONAL TRAINS **Amsterdam – Arnhem – Köln**, see Table **28**.

470 AMSTERDAM and SCHIPHOL ✈ - EINDHOVEN - SITTARD - MAASTRICHT and HEERLEN

km		Ⓐ	Ⓐ	⚒	Ⓐ		Ⓐ	⚒	Ⓐ		⚒		⚒								B	①②j			
0	**Amsterdam** Centraal . 468 d.	...	...	...	...	...	0607	...	0637	...	0707	...	0737	...	0807	0837		2107	2137	2207	2237	2237	2307	2337	2352
6	Amsterdam Amstel ..... 468 d.	...	...	...	...	...	0615	...	0645	...	0715	...	0745	...	0815	0845	and at	2115	2145	2215	2245	2245	2315	2345	0000
39	**Utrecht** Centraal .... 468 a.	...	...	...	...	...	0636	...	0706	...	0736	...	0806	...	0836	0906		2136	2206	2236	2306	2306	2336	0006	0021
39	**Utrecht** Centraal .... d.	...	...	...	...	...	0638	...	0708	...	0738	...	0808	0808	0838	0908	the same	2138	2208	2238	2308	2308	2338	0008	*0026*
87	's-Hertogenbosch .... d.	...	*0541*	...	*0611*	...	0709	...	0739	...	0809	...	0839	0839	0909	0939	minutes	2209	2239	2309	2339	2339	0009	0039	*0108*
119	**Eindhoven** .... a.	...	*0611*	...	*0641*	...	0727	...	0757	...	0827	...	0857	0857	0927	0957		2227	2257	2327	2357	2357	0028	0101	...
119	**Eindhoven** .... d.	...	0632	...	0702	...	0732	0732	0802	0802	0832	0832	0902	0902	0932	1002	past each	2232	2302	2332	0002	0002	...	...	...
148	Weert .... d.	...	0649	...	0719	...	0749	0749	0819	0819	0849	0849	0919	0919	0949	1019	hour until	2249	2319	2349	0019	0020	...	...	...
172	Roermond .... d.	...	0703	0707	0733	0737	0803	0803	0833	0833	0903	0903	0933	0933	1003	1033		2303	2333	0003	0033	0037	...	...	...
196	Sittard .... a.	...	0718	0726	0748	0756	0818	0818	0848	0848	0918	0918	0948	0948	1018	1048		2318	2348	0018	0048	0052	...	...	...
196	Sittard .... d.	0634	0722	0734	0751	0804	0821	0821	0851	0851	0921	0921	0951	0951	1021	1051		2321	2351	0021	0051	0053	...	...	...
218	**Maastricht** .... a.	0654	0736	0754	0806	0824	0836	0836	0906	0906	0936	0936	1006	1006	1036	1106		2336	0006	0036	0106	0107	...	...	...

	Ⓐ	Ⓐ	Ⓐ	⚒	Ⓐ	⚒	⚒		⚒															B	①②
Maastricht .... d.	...	...	0528	...	0558	...	0628	...	0657	...	0728	0758		1928	1958	2028	2058	2128	2158	2228	2258	...	...	2358	2358
Sittard .... a.	...	...	0543	...	0613	...	0643	...	0713	...	0743	0813	and at	1943	2013	2043	2113	2143	2213	2243	2313	...	...	0013	0013
Sittard .... d.	...	...	0544	...	0614	...	0644	...	0714	...	0744	0814		1944	2014	2044	2114	2144	2214	2244	2314	...	...	0014	0014
Roermond .... d.	...	...	0559	...	0629	...	0659	...	0729	...	0759	0829	the same	1959	2029	2059	2129	2159	2229	2259	2329	...	...	0029	0029
Weert .... d.	...	...	0612	...	0642	...	0712	...	0742	...	0812	0842		2012	2042	2112	2142	2212	2242	2312	2342	...	...	0042	0045
Eindhoven .... a.	...	...	0629	...	0659	...	0729	...	0759	...	0829	0859	minutes	2029	2059	2129	2159	2229	2259	2329	2359	...	...	0059	0103
Eindhoven .... d.	0532	0602	0632	...	0702	0702	0732	0732	0802	0802	0832	0902	past each	2032	2102	2132	2202	2232	2302	2332	...	0020	...	...	...
's-Hertogenbosch .... d.	0553	0623	0653	...	0723	0723	0753	0753	0823	0823	0853	0923	hour until	2053	2123	2153	2223	2253	2323	2353	...	0049	...	...	...
Utrecht Centraal .... a.	0622	0652	0722	...	0752	0752	0822	0822	0852	0852	0922	0952		2122	2152	2222	2251	2322	2352	0022	...	...	...	...	...
Utrecht Centraal .... 468 d.	0625	0655	0725	0725	0755	0755	0825	0825	0855	0855	0925	0955		2125	2155	2225	2255	2325	2356	0025	...	...	...	...	...
Amsterdam Amstel .... 468 a.	0643	0713	0743	0743	0813	0813	0843	0843	0913	0913	0943	1013		2143	2213	2243	2315	2345	0015	0045	...	...	...	...	...
Amsterdam Centraal ... 468 a.	0652	0722	0752	0752	0822	0822	0852	0852	0922	0922	0952	1022		2152	2222	2252	2323	2354	0024	0054	...	...	...	...	...

SCHIPHOL ✈ - EINDHOVEN - SITTARD - HEERLEN

km		Ⓐ	Ⓐ	Ⓐ	Ⓐ	⚒	Ⓐ	⚒																	
0	**Schiphol** ✈ .... 468 d.	...	...	...	0617	...	0647	0647	0717	0747		1717	1747	1817	1847	1917	1947	2017	2047	2117	2147	2217	2247	2317	2347
9	**Amsterdam** Zuid .... 468 d.	...	...	...	0625	...	0655	0655	0725	0755	and at	1725	1755	1825	1855	1925	1955	2025	2055	2125	2155	2225	2255	2325	2355
45	**Utrecht** Centraal .... 468 a.	...	...	...	0647	...	0717	0717	0747	0817	the same	1747	1817	1847	1917	1947	2017	2047	2117	2147	2217	2247	2317	2347	0017
45	**Utrecht** Centraal .... ¶ d.	...	...	...	0653	...	0723	▬	0753	0823		1753	1823	1853	1923	1953	2023	...	...	...	...	...	...	...	...
93	's-Hertogenbosch .... ¶ d.	...	...	*0641*	0725	...	0755	...	0825	0855	minutes	1825	1855	1925	1955	2025	2055	...	...	...	...	...	...	...	...
125	**Eindhoven** .... ¶ d.	...	...	0716	0746	0746	0816	0816	0846	0916	past each	1846	1916	1944	2014	2044	2114	...	...	...	...	...	...	...	...
154	Weert .... ¶ d.	...	...	0733	0803	0803	0833	0833	0903	0933	hour until	1903	1933	▬	▬	▬	▬	...	...	...	...	...	...	...	...
178	Roermond .... ¶ d.	...	*0707*	0747	0817	0817	0847	0847	0917	0947		1917	1947	...	...	...	...	...	...	...	...	...	...	...	...
202	Sittard .... ★ ¶ d.	0649	0736	0806	0836	0836	0906	0906	0936	1006		1936	2006	2106	2206	2306	0006	...	...	...	...	...	...	...	...
221	**Heerlen** .... ★ a.	0711	0751	0821	0851	0851	0921	0921	0951	1021		1951	2021	2121	2221	2321	0021	...	...	...	...	...	...	...	...

	Ⓐ	Ⓐ	Ⓐ	Ⓐ	⚒	⑥k	⚒		⚒		†														
Heerlen .... ★ d.	...	...	0544	0614	...	0625	0644	...	0714	...	0725	0744	...	0814	0844		1814	1844	...	1925	2025	2125	2225	...	...
Sittard .... ★ ¶ d.	...	...	0600	0630	...	0640	0700	...	0730	...	0740	0800	...	0830	0900	and at	1830	1900	...	1940	2040	2140	2240	...	...
Roermon .... ¶ d.	...	...	0615	0645	...	...	0715	...	0745	...	...	0815	...	0845	0915	the same	1845	1915	...	▬	▬	▬	▬	...	...
Weert .... ¶ d.	...	...	0628	0658	...	...	0728	...	0758	...	...	0828	...	0858	0928		1858	1928	...	...	...	...	...	...	...
Eindhoven .... ¶ d.	...	0618	0648	0718	0718	...	0748	0748	0818	0818	...	0848	...	0918	0948	minutes	1918	1948	...	...	...	...	...	...	...
's-Hertogenbosch .... ¶ d.	0608	0638	0708	0738	0738	...	0808	0808	0838	0838	...	0908	...	0938	1008	past each	1938	2008	...	...	...	...	...	...	...
Utrecht Centraal .... ¶ a.	0637	0707	0737	0807	0807	...	0837	0837	0907	0907	...	0937	...	1007	1037	hour until	2007	2037	...	...	...	...	...	...	...
Utrecht Centraal .... 468 d.	0643	0713	0743	0813	0813	...	0843	0843	0913	0913	...	0943	...	1013	1043		2013	2043	...	2113	2143	2213	2243	2313	234
Amsterdam Zuid .... 468 a.	0705	0735	0805	0835	0835	...	0905	0905	0935	0935	...	1005	...	1035	1105		2035	2105	...	2135	2205	2235	2305	2335	000
Schiphol ✈ .... 468 a.	0712	0742	0812	0842	0842	...	0912	0912	0942	0942	...	1012	...	1042	1112		2042	2112	...	2142	2212	2242	2312	2342	001

B – ③–⑦ (also Apr. 21, June 9).
j – Not Apr. 21, June 9.
k – Also May 29, June 9.

¶ – See also Amsterdam - Maastricht panel above.
★ – Other trains **Sittard - Heerlen** and v.v. (journey: 22 minutes).
From Sittard at 0719 and hourly until 2319.
From Heerlen at 0647 and hourly until 2347.

DEN HAAG - EINDHOVEN - VENLO 471

km		Ⓐ	Ⓐ	Ⓐ		Ⓐ	Ⓐ	Ⓐ	⚒	⚒	⚒												
0	**Den Haag** Centraal 450 d.	...	...	...	...	0513	...	0553	...	0623	0653	...	...	0723	0753	and every 30 minutes until	2123	2153	...	2223	...	...	2253
2	**Den Haag** HS 450 d.	...	...	...	...	0519	...	0558	...	0628	0658	...	...	0728	0758		2128	2158	...	2228	...	...	2258
10	Delft 450 d.	...	...	...	...	0529	...	0605	...	0635	0705	...	...	0735	0805		2135	2205	...	2235	...	...	2305
24	**Rotterdam** Centraal 450 451 d.	...	...	...	...	0543	0548	0618	0618	0648	0718	...	...	0748	0818		2148	2218	...	2248	...	...	2318
44	Dordrecht 450 d.	...	...	...	...	...	0602	0632	0632	0702	0732	...	...	0802	0832		2202	2232	...	2302	...	...	2332
74	Breda 450 451 475 d.	0540	...	...	...	...	0621	0651	0651	0721	0751	...	...	0821	0851		2221	2251	...	2321	...	...	2351
95	Tilburg 475 d.	0553	0558	...	...	...	0636	0706	0706	0736	0806	...	...	0836	0906		2236	2306	...	2336	...	...	0006
132	**Eindhoven** a.	...	0628	...	...	...	0700	0730	0730	0800	0830	...	...	0900	0930		2300	2330	...	2400	...	...	0031
132	**Eindhoven** d.	...	...	0634	...	...	0704	0734	0734	0804	0834	0834	...	0904	0934		2304	2334	...	...	0016	...	0032
145	Helmond d.	...	...	0643	...	...	0713	0743	0743	0813	0843	0843	...	0913	0943		2313	2343	...	...	0029	...	0041
183	**Venlo** a.	...	...	0711	...	...	0743	0813	0813	0843	0913	0913	...	0943	1013		2343	0013	...	...	...	...	0109

	Ⓐ	Ⓐ	Ⓐ	Ⓐ	⚒	†	⚒										
Venlo d.	...	...	0550	0620	...	...	0650	0720	0750	0820	0850	and every 30 minutes until	2120	2150	2220	2250	2320
Helmond d.	...	...	0620	0650	...	...	0720	0750	0820	0850	0920		2150	2220	2250	2320	2350
Eindhoven a.	...	...	0629	0659	...	...	0729	0759	0829	0859	0929		2159	2229	2259	2329	2359
Eindhoven d.	0533	0603	0633	0703	0703	0732	0733	0803	0833t	0903	0933		2203	2233	2303	2333	▬
Tilburg 475 d.	0555	0625	0655	0725	0725	0755	0755	0825	0855	0925	0955		2225	2255	2325	2355	...
Breda 450 451 475 d.	0609	0639	0709	0739	0739	0809	0809	0839	0909	0939	1009		2239	2309	2339	0009	...
Dordrecht 450 d.	0628	0658	0728	0758	0758	0828	0828	0858	0928	0958	1028		2258	2328	2358	0028	...
Rotterdam Centraal 450 451 a.	0642	0712	0742	0812	0812	0841	0842	0912	0942	1012	1042		2312	2342	0012	0042	0047
Delft 450 a.	0655	0725	0755	0825	0825	0855	0855	0925	0955	1025	1055		2325	2355	0025	...	0101
Den Haag HS 450 a.	0702	0732	0802	0832	0832	0902	0902	0932	1002	1032	1102		2332	0002	0032	...	0112
Den Haag Centraal 450 a.	0707	0737	0807	0837	0837	0907	0907	0937	1007	1037	1107		2337	0007	0037	...	0118y

t – 0832 on ⑥ (also May 29, June 9).
y – ③④⑥⑦ (also May 30, June 10).

☛ For NIGHT NETWORK **Amsterdam – Den Haag – Rotterdam – Eindhoven**, see Table **454**.

Operated by **Veolia** (NS tickets valid) MAASTRICHT - HEERLEN - KERKRADE and AACHEN 472

km		Ⓐ	Ⓐ	⚒	⚒									Ⓐn		Ⓐn	⚒		⚒	z	⊡	z
0	**Maastricht** d.	0511e	0541	0611	0641	0711	0741	and every 30 minutes until	2311	2341	0011	0041	A	0702	and every 30 minutes until	0932	1002	and every 30 minutes until	1232	1302	and every 30 minutes until	2232
11	Valkenburg d.	0524e	0554	0624	0654	0724	0754		2324	2354	0024	0054	L	0713		0943	1013		1243	1313		2243
24	**Heerlen** d.	0543	0613	0643	0713	0743	0813		2343	0013	0041	0111	S	0724		0954	1024		1254	1324		2254
33	**Kerkrade Centrum** a.	0556	0626	0656	0726	0756	0826		2356	0026	...	...	O	...		...	...		...	...		...

	Ⓐ	Ⓐ		⚒	⚒									Ⓐn		Ⓐn	⚒		⚒	z	⊡	z
Kerkrade Centrum d.	...	...	0559	...	0629	0659v	0729	0759	and every 30 minutes until	2329	2359	0029	A	...	and every 30 minutes until	...	...	and every 30 minutes until	...	...	and every 30 minutes until	...
Heerlen d.	0514	0544	0614	0614	0644	0714	0744	0814		2344	0014	0044	L	0630		0900	0930		1200	1230		2200
Valkenburg d.	0530	0600	0630	0630	0700	0730	0800	0830		0000	0030	0059	S	0641		0911	0941		1211	1241		2211
Maastricht a.	0545	0615	0645	0645	0715	0745	0815	0845		0015	0045	0112	O	0652		0922	0952		1222	1252		2222

e – 2 minutes later on ①④⑤.
n – Not Mar. 3, 4.
v – ⚒ only.
z – Not Apr. 20.

HEERLEN - AACHEN 473

km		A	E							
0	**Heerlen** d.	0528	0628	...	0728	and hourly until	2228	...	...	...
10	Herzogenrath ⊞ 802 a.	0543	0643	...	0743		2243	...	...	...
24	**Aachen** Hbf 802 a.	0601	0701	...	0801		2301	...	...	...

	A	E						
Aachen Hbf 802 d.	0632	0732	...	0832	and hourly until	2132	...	2302
Herzogenrath ⊞ 802 d.	0650	0750	...	0850		2150	...	2320
Heerlen a.	0705	0805	...	0905		2205	...	2336

A – ①–⑤ (not Apr. 18, 21, May 1, 29, June 9, 19, Oct. 3).
E – ①–⑥ (not Apr. 18, 21, May 1, 29, June 9, 19, Oct. 3, Nov. 1).

ROOSENDAAL - 's-HERTOGENBOSCH - NIJMEGEN - ARNHEM - ZWOLLE 475

km		Ⓐ	Ⓐ	Ⓐ	Ⓐ	⚒	Ⓐ	⚒	†	⑥k	Ⓐ	†	⚒												
0	**Roosendaal** d.	...	...	...	...	...	0520	...	...	...	0550	...	0620	0650b	0720	0750	0820	0850	and every 30 minutes until	2120	2150	2220	...	2250	2320
23	Breda 472 d.	...	...	...	...	...	0540	...	...	...	0610	...	0640	0710b	0740	0810	0840	0910		2140	2210	2240	...	2310	2340
44	Tilburg 472 d.	...	...	...	...	...	0554	...	...	...	0624	...	0654	0724	0754	0824	0854	0924		2154	2224	2254	...	2324	2354
67	**'s-Hertogenbosch** d.	...	...	0526	...	...	0611	...	...	...	0641	...	0711	0741	0811	0841	0911	0941		2211	2241	2311	...	2341	0010
86	Oss d.	...	...	0544	...	...	0626	...	...	...	0656	...	0726	0756	0826	0856	0926	0956		2226	2256	2326	...	2356	...
110	**Nijmegen** a.	...	...	0606	...	...	0644	...	...	...	0714	...	0744	0814	0844	0914	0944	1014		2244	2314	2344	...	0014	...
110	**Nijmegen** 468 d.	...	*0535*	*0612*	0618	...	0648	0648	...	*0712*	0718	*0735*	0748	0818	0848	0918	0948	1018		2248	2318	2348	0003	0018	...
129	**Arnhem** 468 a.	...	*0554*	*0626*	0638	...	0708	0708	...	*0726*	0738	*0754*	0808	0838	0908	0938	1008	1038		2308	2338	0008	0021	0038	...
129	**Arnhem** d.	...	0602	...	0640	...	0710	0710	0729	0740	0740	0810	0810	0840	0910	0940	1010	1040		2310	2340	...	0024	...	...
145	Dieren d.	...	0622	...	0651	...	0721	0721	0748	0752	0752	0821	0821	0851	0921	0952	1021	1051		2321	2351	...	0042	...	...
159	Zutphen d.	0604	0634	...	0704	0704	0734	0734	0804	0804	0804	0834	0834	0904	0934	1004	1034	1104		2334	0004	...	0054	...	...
174	Deventer d.	0617	0647	...	0717	0717	0747	0747	0817	0817	0817	0847	0847	0917	0947	1017	1047	1117		2347	0017	...	...	...	...
204	**Zwolle** a.	0641	0711	...	0741	0741	0811	0811	0841	0841	0841	0911	0911	0941	1011	1041	1111	1141		0011	0041	...	...	...	...

	Ⓐ	Ⓐ	Ⓐ	Ⓐ	⚒	Ⓐ	⚒		⚒		⚒		⚒									Ⓑn	⑥k		
Zwolle d.	...	...	...	...	...	...	...	...	0619a	...	0649a	...	0719	...	0749	0819	and every 30 minutes until	2119	2149	2219	2249	...	...	2319	2349
Deventer d.	...	...	...	...	...	...	...	...	0645a	...	0715a	...	0745	...	0815	0845		2145	2215	2245	2315	...	...	2345	0015
Zutphen d.	...	...	...	0548	...	0606	...	...	0658	...	0728	...	0758	0758	0828	0858		2158	2228	2258	2328	...	...	2358	0028
Dieren d.	...	...	...	0600	...	0617	...	...	0708	...	0738	...	0808	0808	0838	0908		2208	2238	2308	2338	...	...	0008	0038
Arnhem a.	...	...	...	0620	...	0636	...	...	0721	...	0751	...	0821	0821	0851	0921		2221	2250	2321	2351	...	...	0021	0051
Arnhem 468 d.	...	...	0552	0622	...	▬	0652	...	0722	...	0752	0752	0822	0822	0852	0922		2222	2252	2322	2352	*0004*	*0007*	*0034*	...
Nijmegen 468 a.	...	...	0612	0642	...	...	0712	...	0742	...	0812	0812	0842	0842	0912	0942		2242	2312	2342	0012	*0020*	*0022*	*0050*	...
Nijmegen d.	...	...	0618	0648	...	...	0718	...	0748	...	0818	0818	0848	0848	0918	0948		2248	2318	2348	...	0023	0025	...	...
Oss d.	...	...	0636	0706	...	...	0736	...	0806	...	0836	0836	0906	0906	0936	1006		2306	2336	0006	...	0045	0045	...	...
's-Hertogenbosch d.	...	0620	0650	0720	0720	...	0750	0750	0820	0820	0850	0850	0920	0920	0950	1020		2320	2350	0020	...	0103	0104	...	...
Tilburg 472 d.	*0555*	0636	0706	0736	0736	...	0806	0806	0836	0836	0906	0906	0936	0936	1006	1036		2336	0006	0036	...	...	...	...	...
Breda 472 d.	0621	0651	0721	0751	0751	0751	0821	0821	0851	0851	0921	0921	0951	0951	1021	1051		2351	0021	0057p	...	...	...	...	...
Roosendaal a.	0639	0709	0739	0809	0809	0809	0839	0839	0909	0909	0939	0939	1009	1009	1039	1109		0009	0039	0115p	...	...	...	...	...

a – Ⓐ only.
b – On † Roosendaal d. 0644, Breda d. 0703.
k – Also May 29, June 9.
n – Not May 29, June 9.
p – 6 minutes earlier on the mornings of ① (also Apr. 22).

Operated by **Arriva** (NS tickets valid) 2nd class only ARNHEM and ZUTPHEN - WINTERSWIJK 476

Arnhem - Winterswijk

km		S		Ⓐ	Ⓐ	Ⓐ	Ⓒ	Ⓐ	Ⓐ	Ⓒ	Ⓐ															
0	**Arnhem** d.	0003	...	0559	0630	0730	0733	0800	0830	0833	0900	0933	1033	1130	1233	1330	1433	1530	1633	1730	1833	1930	2033	2133	2233	2333
14	Zevenaar d.	0018	...	0614	0645	0745	0748	0815	0845	0848	0916	0948	1048	1148	1248	1348	1448	1548	1648	1748	1848	1948	2048	2148	2248	2348
30	Doetinchem d.	0037	...	0634	0704	0804	0807	0834	0904	0907	0937	1007	1107	1207	1307	1407	1507	1607	1707	1807	1907	2007	2107	2207	2307	0007
64	**Winterswijk** a.	0110	...	0707	0737	0837	0840	0910	0940	0940	1010	1040	1140	1240	1340	1440	1540	1640	1740	1840	1940	2040	2140	2240	2340	0040

	⑦w		Ⓐ	Ⓐ	Ⓐ	Ⓒ	Ⓐ	Ⓐ	Ⓒ	Ⓐ															Ⓐ
Winterswijk d.	0020	...	0518	0547	0647	0650	0717	0747	0750	0817	0850	0950	1050	1150	1250	1350	1450	1550	1650	1750	1850	1950	2050	2150	2250	2320
Doetinchem d.	0053	...	0549	0619	0720	0723	0750	0820	0823	0850	0923	1023	1123	1223	1323	1423	1523	1623	1723	1823	1923	2023	2123	2223	2323	2353
Zevenaar d.	0112	...	0607	0639	0739	0742	0809	0839	0842	0909	0942	1042	1142	1242	1342	1442	1542	1642	1742	1842	1942	2042	2142	2242	2342	0012
Arnhem a.	0127	...	0623	0654	0754	0757	0824	0854	0857	0924	0957	1057	1157	1257	1357	1457	1557	1657	1757	1857	1957	2057	2157	2257	2357	0027

Zutphen - Winterswijk

km		S		Ⓐ	Ⓐ	⑥k	Ⓐ	Ⓒ				
0	**Zutphen** d.	0006	...	0632	0702	0706	0802	0806	0906	and hourly until	2306	...
22	Ruurlo d.	0022	...	0648	0718	0722	0818	0822	0922		2322	...
43	**Winterswijk** a.	0040	...	0706	0736	0740	0836	0840	0940		2340	...

	Ⓐ	Ⓐ	⑥k	Ⓐ	Ⓐ	Ⓒ				⚒
Winterswijk d.	0616	0646	0650	0716	0746	0750	0850	and hourly until	2250	2350
Ruurlo d.	0634	0704	0708	0734	0804	0808	0908		2308	0008
Zutphen a.	0650	0720	0724	0750	0820	0824	0924		2324	0024

S – ②–⑦ (not Apr. 22).
k – Also May 29, June 9.
w – Also May 30, June 10.

477 NIJMEGEN - VENLO - ROERMOND

Operated by **Veolia** (NS tickets valid)

km		Ⓐh	Ⓐh	⚒d	⚒d						
0	**Nijmegen** d.	0538	0608	0638	0708	0738	0808	and every 30 minutes until	2238	2308	2338
24	Boxmeer d.	0600	0630	0700	0730	0800	0830		2300	2330	0000
39	Venray d.	0615	0645	0715	0745	0815	0845		2315	2345	0015
61	**Venlo** d.	0634	0704	0734	0804	0834	0904		2334	0004	0035
84	**Roermond** a.	0657	0727	0757	0827	0857	0927		2357	0027	...

	⚒	⚒								
Roermond d.	...	0606a	0636a	0706v	0736v	0806	0836	and every 30 minutes until	2236	2306
Venlo d.	0600	0630	0700	0730	0800	0830	0900		2300	2330
Venray d.	0617	0647	0717	0747	0817	0847	0917		2317	2347
Boxmeer d.	0630	0700	0730	0800	0830	0900	0930		2330	0000
Nijmegen a.	0652	0722	0752	0822	0852	0922	0952		2352	0022

Additional journeys: **Venlo** → **Roermond** at 0534 Ⓐ, 0604 Ⓐ; **Nijmegen** → **Venlo** at 0008; **Venlo** → **Nijmegen** at 0530 Ⓐ; **Roermond** → **Venlo** at 2336, 0006, 0036.

a – Ⓐ only. **d** – Runs daily Venlo - Roermond. **h** – Also runs on ⑥ Venlo - Roermond. **v** – ⚒ only.

478 ARNHEM - TIEL - GELDERMALSEN - UTRECHT and 's-HERTOGENBOSCH

km		Ⓐ	Ⓐ	Ⓐ	Ⓐ	Ⓐ	⚒	⚒	⚒	⚒													
0	**Tiel** d.	...	0551	...	0621	...	0651	...	0721	...	0751	...	0821	...	and at the same minutes past each hour until	1951	...	2021	...	...	2051	...	2121
	's-Hertogenbosch d.	0532	|	0602	|	0632	|	0702	|	0732	|	0802	|	0832		|	2002	|	2032	...	|	2102	|
12	Geldermalsen a.	0548	0603	0618	0633	0648	0703	0718	0733	0748	0803	0818	0833	0848		2003	2018	2033	2048	...	2103	2119	2133
38	**Utrecht** Centraal a.	0618	0631	0648	0701	0718	0731	0748	0801	0818	0831	0848	0901	0918		2031	2048	2101	2118	...	2131	2148	2201

Tiel d.	...	2151	...	2221	2251	...	2321	2351	...	0021	...
's-Hertogenbosch d.	2132	|	2202	|	|	2302	|	|	0002	|	...
Geldermalsen a.	2149	2203	2219	2233	2303	2319	2333	0003	0019	0033	...
Utrecht Centraal a.	2218	2231	2248	2301	2331	2348	0001	0031	0048	0101	...

km		Ⓐ	Ⓐ	Ⓐ		Ⓐ	Ⓐ	⚒	⚒
0	**Utrecht** Centraal d.	0525	0541	0555	...	0611	0625	0641	0655
26	Geldermalsen d.	0553	0610	0623	...	0640	0653	0710	0723
48	**'s-Hertogenbosch** a.	|	0625	|	...	0655	|	0725	|
	Tiel a.	0605	...	0635	...	...	0705	...	0735

Utrecht Centraal d.	0711	0725	0741	0755	and at the same minutes past each hour until	1911	1925	1941	1955	2011	2025	2041	2055	2111	2125	2141	2155	2225	2241	2255	2325	2341	2355
Geldermalsen d.	0740	0753	0810	0823		1940	1953	2010	2023	2040	2053	2110	2123	2140	2153	2210	2223	2253	2310	2323	2353	0010	0023
's-Hertogenbosch a.	0755	|	0825	|		1955	|	2025	|	2055	|	2125	|	2155	|	2225	|	|	2325	|	|	0025	|
Tiel a.	...	0805	...	0835		...	2005	...	2035	...	2105	...	2135	...	2205	...	2235	2305	...	2335	0005	...	0035

ARNHEM - TIEL and v.v. Operated by ***Arriva*** (NS tickets valid). 2nd class only. *44 km.* Journey time: 36 – 40 minutes.

From Arnhem at 0029 ⑦, 0629 Ⓐ, 0659 Ⓐ, 0729 Ⓐ, 0759 Ⓐ, 0829 ⚒, 0929 and hourly until 1529; then 1559 Ⓐ, 1629, 1659 Ⓐ, 1729, 1759 Ⓐ, 1829, 1929, 2029, 2129, 2229 and 2329.

From Tiel at 0616 Ⓐ, 0646 Ⓐ, 0716 Ⓐ, 07146 ⚒, 0816 Ⓐ, 0846, 0939 Ⓐ, 0946 Ⓒ, 1046, 1146, 1246, 1346, 1446, 1539 †, 1546 ⚒, 1616 Ⓐ, 1646, 1716 Ⓐ, 1746, 1816 Ⓐ, 1846, 1937 Ⓐ, 1946 Ⓒ, 2046, 2146, 2246 and 2346 ⑥.

479 DORDRECHT - GELDERMALSEN

Operated by **Arriva** (NS tickets valid); 2nd class only

km		Ⓐ	⚒	⚒							
0	**Dordrecht** d.	0441	0508	0538	0608	0638	0708	and every 30 minutes until	2338	0008	0038
10	Sliedrecht d.	0453	0520	0550	0620	0650	0720		2350	0020	0050
24	Gorinchem d.	0509	0539	0609	0639	0709	0739		0009	0039	0105
49	**Geldermalsen** a.	0534	0604	0633	0704	0733	0803		0033	0104	...

	Ⓐ	⚒	⚒							
Geldermalsen d.	0539	0609	0639	0709	0739	and every 30 minutes until	2339	0009	0039	0109
Gorinchem d.	0606	0636	0706	0736	0806		0006	0036	0105	0135
Sliedrecht d.	0621	0651	0721	0751	0821		0021	0051	0120	0150
Dordrecht a.	0633	0703	0733	0803	0833		0033	0103	0131	0201

480 AMSTERDAM and SCHIPHOL ✈ - AMERSFOORT - DEVENTER - ENSCHEDE

SCHIPHOL ✈ - AMSTERDAM CENTRAAL - AMERSFOORT

km		Ⓐ	Ⓐ	Ⓐ	⚒		⚒	Ⓐ	†	⚒	⚒												③–⑥	B
0	**Schiphol** ✈ d.	...	...	...	0603	...	0628	...	0658	0658	...	0728	...	0758	...	0828	and at the same minutes past each hour until	...	2228	...	2258	2328	2358	2358
17	**Amsterdam** Centraal d.	0601	0552	0631	0622	0701	0652	0731	0722	0722	0801	0752	0831	0822	0901	0852		2301	2252	2331	2322	2352	0022	0022
31	Weesp d.	|	0614	|	0644	|	0714	|	0738	0744	|	0814	|	0844	|	0914		|	2314	|	2344	0014	0044	0039
40	Naarden-Bussum d.	|	0621	|	0651	|	0721	|	0745	0751	|	0821	|	0851	|	0921		|	2321	|	2351	0021	0051	*0110**
46	Hilversum d.	0622	0631	0652	0701	0722	0731	0752	0754	0801	0822	0831	0852	0901	0922	0931		2322	2331	2352	0001	0031	0101	*0127**
53	Baarn d.	|	0636	|	0706	|	0736	|	0800	0806	|	0836	|	0906	|	0936		|	2336	|	0006	0037	0106	*0141**
62	**Amersfoort** a.	0635	0644	0705	0715	0735	0745	0805	0808	0815	0835	0845	0905	0915	0935	0945		2335	2345	0005	0015	0045	0115	*0201**

		⊙	Ⓐ	Ⓐ	Ⓐ		Ⓐ		⚒		⚒		⚒										⑤⑥r	
Amersfoort d.	0015	0451	0545	0615	0626	0645	0656	0715	0726	0745	0756	0815	0826	0845	0856	0915	0926	and at the same minutes past each hour until	2245	2256	2315	2326	2345	2356
Baarn d.	0022	0458	0552	0622	|	0652	|	0722	|	0752	|	0822	|	0852	|	0922	|		2252	|	2322	|	2352	|
Hilversum d.	0031	0505	0601	0631	0638	0701	0708	0731	0738	0801	0808	0831	0838	0901	0908	0931	0938		2301	2308	2331	2338	0001	0008
Naarden-Bussum d.	0040	0514	0610	0640	|	0710	|	0740	|	0810	|	0840	|	0910	|	0940	|		2310	|	2340	|	0010	|
Weesp a.	0047	0521	0617	0647	|	0717	|	0747	|	0817	|	0847	|	0917	|	0947	|		2317	|	2347	|	0017	|
Amsterdam Centraal a.	0108	0540	0639	0708	0700	0738	0730	0808	0800	0838	0830	0909	0900	0938	0930	1009	1000		2338	2330	0008	2400	0038	0030
Schiphol ✈ a.	...	0603v	0703	0733	...	0803	...	0833	...	0903	...	0933	...	1003	...	1033	...		0003	...	0033	...	...	...

SCHIPHOL ✈ - AMSTERDAM ZUID - AMERSFOORT - ENSCHEDE

km		Ⓐ	Ⓐ	⚒H	⚒	⚒	H			H			H				H			H			H	
0	**Schiphol** ✈ d.	0537	0607	...	0637	0707	...	0737	0807	...	0837	0907	...	0937	and at the same minutes past each hour until	2107	...	2137	2207	...	2237	2307	...	2337
9	Amsterdam Zuid d.	0545	0615	...	0645	0715	...	0745	0815	...	0845	0915	...	0945		2115	...	2145	2215	...	2245	2315	...	2345
14	Duivendrecht d.	0551	0621	...	0651	0721	...	0751	0821	...	0851	0921	...	0951		2121	...	2151	2221	...	2251	2321	...	2351
37	Hilversum d.	0608	0638	...	0708	0738	...	0808	0838	...	0908	0938	...	1008		2138	...	2208	2238	...	2308	2338	...	0008
53	**Amersfoort** d.	0623	0651	0653	0723	0751	0753	0823	0851	0853	0923	0951	0953	1023		2151	2153	2223	2251	2253	2323	2351	2353	0021
96	Apeldoorn d.	0648	...	0718	0748	...	0818	0848	...	0918	0948	...	1018	1048		...	2218	2248	...	2318	2348	...	0018	...
111	**Deventer** d.	0700	...	0730	0800	...	0830	0900	...	0930	1000	...	1030	1100		...	2230	2300	...	2330	0000	...	0030	...
149	Almelo 492 d.	0726	...	0756	0826	...	0856	0926	...	0956	1027	...	1056	1126		...	2256	2326	...	2356	0026	...	0056	...
164	**Hengelo** 492 d.	0738	...	0808	0838	...	0908	0938	...	1008	1038	...	1108	1138		...	2308	2338	...	0008	0038	...	0108	...
172	**Enschede** 492 a.	0745	...	0815	0845	...	0915	0945	...	1015	1045	...	1115	1145		...	2315	2345	...	0015	0045	...	0115	...

	ⒶH	Ⓐ	Ⓐ	ⒶH	⚒H	Ⓐ	⚒	⚒H	H	⚒	⚒		H				H			H			U	
Enschede 492 d.	0445	...	0516	0545	...	...	0616	0645	...	...	0716	...	0745	...	0816	and at the same minutes past each hour until	2045	...	2116	2145	...	2216	2245	...
Hengelo 492 d.	0454	...	0524	0554	...	...	0624	0654	...	...	0724	...	0754	...	0824		2054	...	2124	2154	...	2224	2254	...
Almelo 492 d.	0506	...	0536	0606	...	...	0636	0706	...	...	0736	...	0806	...	0836		2106	...	2136	2206	...	2236	2306	...
Deventer d.	0532	...	0602	0632	0632	...	0702	0732	0732	...	0802	0802	0832	...	0902		2132	...	2202	2232	...	2302	2332	...
Apeldoorn d.	0543	...	0613	0643	0643	...	0713	0743	0743	...	0813	0813	0843	...	0913		2143	...	2213	2243	...	2313	2343	...
Amersfoort d.	0607	0610	0640	0707	0707	0710	0740	0807	0807	0810	0840	0840	0907	0910	0940		2207	2210	2240	2307	2310	2340	0007	0010
Hilversum d.	...	0623	0653	...	...	0723	0753	...	...	0823	0853	0853	...	0923	0953		...	2223	2253	...	2323	2353	...	0023
Duivendrecht d.	...	0640	0710	...	...	0740	0810	...	...	0840	0910	0910	...	0940	1010		...	2240	2310	...	2340	0010	...	0040
Amsterdam Zuid d.	...	0646	0716	...	...	0746	0816	...	...	0846	0916	0916	...	0946	1016		...	2246	2316	...	2346	0016	...	0046
Schiphol ✈ a.	...	0653	0723	...	...	0753	0823	...	...	0853	0923	0922	...	0953	1023		...	2253	2323	...	2353	0023	...	0053

Through trains AMSTERDAM CENTRAAL - DEVENTER - HENGELO

	♥	Ⓐ	Ⓐ		♥	♥	♥	♥		Ⓐ	Ⓐ	♥	Ⓐ	Ⓐ	♥
Amsterdam Centraal d.	0701	0731	0801	...	0901	1101	1301	1501	...	1601	1631	1701	1731	1801	1901
Hilversum d.	0722	0752	0822	...	0922	1122	1322	1522	...	1622	1652	1722	1752	1822	1922
Amersfoort d.	0737	0807	0837	...	0937	1137	1337	1537	...	1637	1707	1737	1807	1837	1937
Apeldoorn a.	0801	0832	0902	...	1001	1201	1401	1601	...	1702	1732	1801	1832	1902	2001
Deventer a.	0815	0843	0913	...	1015	1215	1415	1615	...	1713	1743	1815	1843	1913	2015
Almelo a.	0843	...	...	...	1043	1243	1443	1643	...	...	...	1843	...	...	2043
Hengelo a.	0856	...	...	...	1056	1256	1456	1656	...	...	...	1856	...	...	2056

	Ⓐ	Ⓐ	Ⓐ	Ⓐ	⚒	Ⓐ	♥	♥	♥	♥	Ⓐ	♥	Ⓐ	♥	♥
Hengelo d.	...	...	...	...	...	...	0903	1103	1303	1503	...	1703	...	1903	2103
Almelo d.	...	...	...	...	...	...	0916	1116	1316	1516	...	1716	...	1916	2116
Deventer d.	0649	0719	0749	0819	0849	0919	0943	1143	1343	1543	1719	1743	1819	1943	2143
Apeldoorn d.	0700	0730	0800	0830	0900	0930	1000	1200	1400	1600	1730	1800	1830	2000	2200
Amersfoort a.	0724	0754	0824	0854	0924	0954	1024	1224	1424	1624	1754	1824	1855	2024	2224
Hilversum a.	0737	0807	0837	0907	0937	1007	1038	1238	1438	1638	1807	1838	1908	2038	2238
Amsterdam Centraal a.	0800	0830	0900	0930	1000	1030	1100	1300	1500	1700	1830	1900	1930	2100	2300

B – ①②⑦.
H – From / to Den Haag (Table **481**).
U – 🚌 Enschede - Utrecht (- Den Haag ⑤⑥). See Table **481**.

r – Also May 29, June 9.
v – ⚒ only.

* – By 🚌 Weesp - Amersfoort.
⊙ – Runs 4 – 6 minutes **earlier** Amersfoort - Weesp on †.
♥ – *IC* service to / from Germany via Bad Bentheim. Conveys ✕. See Table **22** for further details.

ROTTERDAM and DEN HAAG - UTRECHT - ZWOLLE 481

km			Ⓐ	Ⓐ	⚒	Ⓐ	Ⓐ	⚒	Ⓐ	Ⓐ	⚒	⚒	⚒	⚒▷	⑥k	Ⓐ	⚒	⚒		⚒▷	⑥k	Ⓐ	⚒		⚒▷	
0	**Rotterdam** Centraal	d.	...	...	...	...	0605	...	0620	...	...	...	0635	0650	...	...	...	0705	...	0720	...	...	...	0735	0750	...
10	Rotterdam Alexander	d.	...	...	...	...	0613	...	0628	...	...	...	0643	0658	...	...	...	0713	...	0728	...	...	...	0743	0758	...
	Den Haag Centraal	d.	...	0554	...	0609	|	...	|	0624	...	0639	|	|	0653	0654	0709	|	...	|	0723	0724	0739	|	|	0754*
24	Gouda	d.	...	0612	...	0627	0624	...	0639	0642	...	0657	0654	0709	0713	0712	0727	0724	...	0739	0743	0742	0757	0754	0809	0812
56	**Utrecht** Centraal	a.	...	0631	...	0647	0643	...	0658	0701	...	0717	0713	0728a	0731	0731	0747	0743	...	0758a	0801	0801	0817	0813	0828a	0831
56	**Utrecht** Centraal	d.	0620	0635	0635	...	0650	0650	...	0705	0705	...	0720	...	0735	0735	...	0750	...	...	0805	0805	...	0820	...	0835
77	**Amersfoort**	a.	0634	0651	0651	...	0704	0704	...	0721	0721	...	0734	...	0751	0751	...	0804	...	...	0821	0821	...	0834	...	0851
77	**Amersfoort**	d.	0637	0653	0653	...	0707	0707	...	...	...	...	0737	...	0753	0753	...	0807	0807	...	...	...	...	0837	...	0853
	Deventer 480	a.	|	0728	0728	...	|	|	...	...	...	...	|	...	0828	0828	...	|	|	...	...	...	...	|	...	0928
	Enschede 480	a.	|	0815	0815	...	|	|	...	...	...	...	|	...	0915	0915	...	|	|	...	...	...	...	|	...	1015
144	**Zwolle**	a.	0712	...	...	...	0742	0742	...	...	...	...	0813	...	...	...	...	0842	0842	...	...	...	...	0912	...	...
	Leeuwarden 482	a.	0828	...	...	...	|	|	...	...	...	...	0917	...	...	...	...	|	|	...	...	...	...	1017	...	...
	Groningen 482	a.	...	...	...	...	0844	0844	...	...	...	...	...	...	...	...	...	0944	0944	...	...	...	...	...	...	...

		⚒		⚒▷		⚒		⚒▷			⚒		⚒▷		⚒		⚒▷		⚒		⚒▷		⚒		⚒▷	
Rotterdam Centraal	d.	...	0805	0820	...	...	0835	0850	...	...	...	0905	0920	...	...	0935	0950	...	...	1005	1020	...	...	1035	1050	...
Rotterdam Alexander	d.	...	0813	0828	...	...	0843	0858	...	...	...	0913	0928	...	...	0943	0958	...	...	1013	1028	...	...	1043	1058	...
Den Haag Centraal	d.	0809	|	|	0824*	0839	|	|	0854*	...	0909	|	|	0924*	0939	|	|	0954*	1009	|	|	1024*	1039	|	|	1054*
Gouda	d.	0827	0824	0839	0842	0857	0854	0909	0912	...	0927	0924	0939	0942	0957	0954	1009	1012	1027	1024	1039	1042	1057	1054	1109	1112
Utrecht Centraal	a.	0847	0843	0858a	0901	0917	0913	0928a	0931	...	0947	0943	0958a	1001	1017	1013	1028a	1031	1047	1043	1058a	1101	1117	1113	1128a	1131
Utrecht Centraal	d.	...	0850	...	0905	...	0920	...	0935	...	...	0950	...	1005	...	1020	...	1035	...	1050	...	1105	...	1120	...	1135
Amersfoort	a.	...	0904	...	0921	...	0934	...	0951	...	...	1004	...	1021	...	1034	...	1051	...	1104	...	1121	...	1134	...	1151
Amersfoort	d.	...	0907	...	...	...	0937	...	0953	...	...	1007	...	...	...	1037	...	1053	...	1107	...	...	...	1137	...	1153
Deventer 480	a.	...	|	...	...	...	|	...	1028	...	...	|	...	...	...	|	...	1128	...	|	...	...	...	|	...	1228
Enschede 480	a.	...	|	...	...	...	|	...	1115	...	...	|	...	...	...	|	...	1215	...	|	...	...	...	|	...	1315
Zwolle	a.	...	0942	...	...	...	1012	...	...	...	...	1042	...	...	...	1112	...	...	...	1142	...	...	...	1212	...	...
Leeuwarden 482	a.	...	|	...	...	...	1117	...	...	...	...	|	...	...	...	1217	...	...	...	|	...	...	...	1317	...	...
Groningen 482	a.	...	1044	...	...	...	...	...	...	...	...	1144	...	...	...	...	...	...	...	1244	...	...	...	...	...	...

				▶				▶		and at the same minutes past each hour until			▶				▶								
Rotterdam Centraal	d.	...	1105	1120	...	...	1135	1150	...		...	2005	2020	...	...	2035	2050	...	2105	...	2135	...	2205	...	2235
Rotterdam Alexander	d.	...	1113	1128	...	...	1143	1158	...		...	2013	2028	...	...	2043	2058	...	2113	...	2143	...	2213	...	2243
Den Haag Centraal	d.	1109	|	|	1124*	1139	|	|	1154*		2009	|	|	2024*	2039	|	|	2054*	|	2124	|	2154*	|	2224	|
Gouda	d.	1127	1124	1139	1142	1157	1154	1209	1212		2027	2024	2039	2042	2057	2054	2109	2112	2124	2142	2154	2212	2224	2242	2254
Utrecht Centraal	a.	1147	1143	1158a	1201	1217	1213	1228a	1231		2047	2043	2058a	2101	2117	2113	2128a	2131	2143	2201	2213	2231	2243	2301	2313
Utrecht Centraal	d.	...	1150	...	1205	...	1220	...	1235		...	2050	...	2105	...	2120	...	2135	2150	2205	2220	2235	2250	2305	2320
Amersfoort	a.	...	1204	...	1221	...	1234	...	1251		...	2104	...	2121	...	2134	...	2151	2204	2221	2234	2251	2304	2321	2334
Amersfoort	d.	...	1207	...	...	...	1237	...	1253		...	2107	...	...	...	2137	...	2153	2207	...	2237	2253	2307	...	2337
Deventer 480	a.	...	|	...	...	...	|	...	1328		...	|	...	...	...	|	...	2228	|	...	|	2328	|	...	|
Enschede 480	a.	...	|	...	...	...	|	...	1415		...	|	...	...	...	|	...	2315	|	...	|	0015	|	...	|
Zwolle	a.	...	1242	...	...	...	1312	...	...		...	2142	...	...	...	2212	...	...	2242	...	2312	...	2342	...	0012
Leeuwarden 482	a.	...	|	...	...	...	1417	...	...		...	|	...	...	...	2318	...	...	|	...	0018	...	|	...	...
Groningen 482	a.	...	1344	...	...	...	...	...	...		...	2244	...	...	...	...	...	...	2344	...	...	...	0044	...	...

			†	⚒				
Rotterdam Centraal	d.	...	2305	2305	...	2335	...	...
Rotterdam Alexander	d.	...	2313	2313	...	2343	...	...
Den Haag Centraal	d.	2254*	|	|	2324	|	2354	...
Gouda	d.	2312	2324	2324	2342	2354	0012	...
Utrecht Centraal	a.	2331	2343	2343	0001	0013	0031	...
Utrecht Centraal	d.	2335	2350	2350	0005	0020	0035	...
Amersfoort	a.	2351	0004	0004	0021	0034	0051	...
Amersfoort	d.	2353	0007	0007	...	...	...	...
Deventer 480	a.	0028	|	|	...	...	...	...
Enschede 480	a.	0115	|	|	...	...	...	...
Zwolle	a.	...	0042	0048	...	...	...	...
Leeuwarden 482	a.	...	...	|	...	...	...	...
Groningen 482	a.	...	...	0157r	...	...	...	...

km			Ⓐ	Ⓐ	Ⓐ	Ⓐ	Ⓐ	Ⓐ	Ⓐ	Ⓐ	⚒	⚒⊙	⚒	Ⓐ
	Groningen 482	d.	...	...	...	...	...	...	...	...	...	...	...	0505j
	Leeuwarden 482	d.	...	...	...	...	...	...	...	...	...	...	...	|
	Zwolle	d.	...	...	...	...	...	...	0548	...	...	...	...	0618
	Enschede 480	d.	...	...	...	...	0445	...	|	...	...	...	...	|
	Deventer 480	d.	...	...	...	...	0532	...	|	...	...	...	...	|
	Amersfoort	a.	...	...	...	...	0607	...	0622	...	...	...	...	0652
	Amersfoort	d.	...	...	...	...	0610	...	0626	...	0640a	...	...	0656
	Utrecht Centraal	a.	...	...	...	...	0625	...	0641	...	0655a	...	...	0711
0	**Utrecht** Centraal	d.	0559	0602	0614	0617	0629	0632	0647	0644	0659	0702a	0717	0717
32	Gouda	d.	0619	0622	0634	0637	0649	0652	0707	0704	0719	0722	0737	0737
60	**Den Haag** Centraal	a.	0638	|	0652	|	0707	|	|	0722	0738	|	|	|
	Rotterdam Alexander	d.	...	0631	...	0646	...	0701	0716	...	...	0731	0746	0746
	Rotterdam Centraal	a.	...	0640	...	0655	...	0710	0725	...	...	0740	0755	0755

		⚒	⚒	⚒⊙	⚒	⚒	⚒	⚒⊙		⚒	⚒		⚒⊙		⚒		⚒⊙	Ⓒ	Ⓐ	⚒		⚒⊙	†	⚒	⚒	
Groningen 482	d.	...	...	...	...	...	...	...	...	0605	...	...	...	...	...	...	...	0705	0716	...	...	...	...	...	...	...
Leeuwarden 482	d.	...	...	...	0544a	...	...	...	...	|	...	...	...	0644h	...	...	...	|	|	...	...	...	0735	0744	...	...
Zwolle	d.	...	...	...	0648	...	...	...	...	0718	...	...	...	0748	...	...	...	0818	0818	...	...	...	0848	0848	...	...
Enschede 480	d.	...	0545a	...	|	...	...	...	...	|	...	0645v	...	|	...	...	...	|	|	...	0745	...	|	|	...	...
Deventer 480	d.	...	0632	...	|	...	...	...	...	|	...	0732	...	|	...	...	...	|	|	...	0832	...	|	|	...	...
Amersfoort	a.	...	0707	...	0722	...	...	...	...	0752	...	0807	...	0822	...	...	...	0852	0852	...	0907	...	0922	0922	...	...
Amersfoort	d.	...	0710	...	0726	...	0740	...	...	0756	...	0810	...	0826	...	0840	...	0856	0856	...	0910	...	0926	0926	...	0940
Utrecht Centraal	a.	...	0725	...	0741	...	0755	...	...	0811	...	0825	...	0841	...	0855	...	0911	0911	...	0925	...	0941	0941	...	0955
Utrecht Centraal	d.	0714	0729	0732a	0747	0744	0759	0802a	0817	0817	0814	0829	0832a	0847	0844	0859	0902a	0917	0917	0914	0929	0932a	0947	0947	0944	0959
Gouda	d.	0734	0749	0752	0807	0804	0819	0822	0837	0837	0834	0849	0852	0907	0904	0919	0922	0937	0937	0934	0949	0952	1007	1007	1004	1019
Den Haag Centraal	a.	0752	0807	|	|	0822	0838	|	|	|	0852	0907	|	|	0922	0938	|	|	|	0952	1008	|	|	|	1022	1038
Rotterdam Alexander	d.	...	...	0801	0816	...	...	0831	0846	0846	...	...	0901	0916	...	...	0931	0946	0946	...	...	1001	1016	1016	...	...
Rotterdam Centraal	a.	...	...	0810	0825	...	...	0840	0855	0855	...	...	0910	0925	...	...	0940	0955	0955	...	...	1010	1025	1025	...	...

		⚒⊙		⚒		⚒⊙		⚒		⚒⊙		⚒		⚒⊙				⊖				⊖	and at the same minutes past each hour until		
Groningen 482	d.	...	0816	...	...	...	...	...	...	...	0916	...	...	...	...	...	...	...	1016	...	...	...		...	...
Leeuwarden 482	d.	...	|	...	...	...	0844	...	...	...	|	...	...	...	0944	...	...	...	|	...	...	...		1744	...
Zwolle	d.	...	0918	...	...	...	0948	...	...	...	1018	...	...	...	1048	...	...	...	1118	...	...	...		1848	...
Enschede 480	d.	...	|	...	0845	...	|	...	...	...	|	...	0945	...	|	...	...	...	|	...	1045	...		|	...
Deventer 480	d.	...	|	...	0932	...	|	...	...	...	|	...	1032	...	|	...	...	...	|	...	1132	...		|	...
Amersfoort	a.	...	0952	...	1007	...	1022	...	...	...	1052	...	1107	...	1122	...	...	...	1152	...	1207	...		1922	...
Amersfoort	d.	...	0956	...	1010	...	1026	...	1040	...	1056	...	1110	...	1126	...	1140	...	1156	...	1210	...		1926	...
Utrecht Centraal	a.	...	1011	...	1025	...	1041	...	1055	...	1111	...	1125	...	1141	...	1155	...	1211	...	1225	...		1941	...
Utrecht Centraal	d.	1002a	1017	1014	1029	1032a	1047	1044	1059	1102a	1117	1114	1129	1132a	1147	1144	1159	1202a	1217	1214	1229	1232a		1947	1944
Gouda	d.	1022	1037	1034	1049	1052	1107	1104	1119	1122	1137	1134	1149	1152	1207	1204	1219	1222	1237	1234	1249	1252		2007	2004
Den Haag Centraal	a.	|	|	1052	1108	|	|	1122	1138	|	|	1152	1208	|	|	1222	1238	|	|	1252	1308	|		|	2022
Rotterdam Alexander	d.	1031	1046	...	...	1101	1116	...	...	1131	1146	...	...	1201	1216	...	...	1231	1246	...	...	1301		2016	...
Rotterdam Centraal	a.	1040	1055	...	...	1110	1125	...	...	1140	1155	...	...	1210	1225	...	...	1240	1255	...	...	1310		2025	...

			⊖				⊖																		⑤⑥k	
Groningen 482	d.	...	...	1806z	...	...	...	...	...	...	1916	...	...	...	2016	...	...	...	2116	...	...	...	2216	...	...	...
Leeuwarden 482	d.	...	...	|	...	...	...	1844	...	...	|	...	1944	...	|	...	2044	...	|	...	2144	...	|	...	...	2235
Zwolle	d.	...	...	1918	...	...	...	1948	...	...	2018	...	2048	...	2118	...	2148	...	2218	...	2248	...	2318	...	...	2348
Enschede 480	d.	...	...	|	...	1845	...	|	...	...	|	1945	|	...	|	2045	|	...	|	2145	|	...	|	2245	2245	|
Deventer 480	d.	...	...	|	...	1932	...	|	...	...	|	2032	|	...	|	2132	|	...	|	2232	|	...	|	2332	2332	|
Amersfoort	a.	...	...	1952	...	2007	...	2022	...	...	2052	2107	2122	...	2152	2207	2222	...	2252	2307	2322	...	2352	0007	0007	0022
Amersfoort	d.	1940	...	1956	...	2010	...	2026	...	2040	2056	2110	2126	2140	2156	2210	2226	2240	2256	2310	2326	2340	2356	0010	0010	0026
Utrecht Centraal	a.	1955	...	2011	...	2025	...	2041	...	2055	2111	2125	2141	2155	2211	2225	2241	2255	2311	2325	2341	2355	0011	0025	0025	0041
Utrecht Centraal	d.	1959	2002a	2017	2014	2029	2032a	2047	2044	2059	2117	2129	2147	2159	2217	2229	2247	2259	2317	2329	2347	2359	0017	...	0029	...
Gouda	d.	2019	2022	2037	2034	2049	2052	2107	2104	2119	2137	2149	2207	2219	2237	2249	2307	2319	2337	2350	0007	0020	0037	...	0050	...
Den Haag Centraal	a.	2038	|	|	2052	2108	|	|	2122	2138	|	2208	|	2238	|	2308	|	2338	|	0008	|	0038	|	...	0108	...
Rotterdam Alexander	d.	...	2031	2046	...	...	2101	2116	...	...	2146	...	2216	...	2246	...	2316	...	2346	...	0016	...	0046	...	...	...
Rotterdam Centraal	a.	...	2040	2055	...	...	2110	2125	...	...	2155	...	2225	...	2255	...	2325	...	2355	...	0025	...	0055	...	...	...

– Ⓐ only.
– ⚒ only. 0635 on ⑥ (also May 29, June 9).
– 0502 on ②③.
– Also May 29, June 9.
– 0200 on the mornings of ④⑤ (not May 30).
– ⚒ only.
– 1816 on Ⓒ.

* – Departs Den Haag 1 minute **earlier** on Ⓒ.
▷ – On ⑥ (also May 29, June 9) attached to train in following column at Gouda.
⊙ – On ⑥ (also May 29, June 9) detached from train in the preceding column at Gouda.
▶ – On Ⓒ attached to train in following column at Gouda.
⊖ – On Ⓒ detached from train in the preceding column at Gouda.

482 ZWOLLE - GRONINGEN and LEEUWARDEN

km		Ⓐ	Ⓐ	ⒶL	Ⓐ	Ⓐ	⑥k	Ⓐ	⚒L	Ⓐ	⑥kL	Ⓐ	⚒	Ⓐ		Ⓐ			⑥k	Ⓐ	†L			
	Rotterdam Centraal **481** . d.	...	...	...	...	...	...	...	...	...	...	...	...	...	0605a	0522	...	...	0552	...	...	0635v	...	0705v
	Utrecht Centraal **481** d.	...	...	...	...	...	...	...	...	...	...	...	0620a	...	0650v	|	...	...	|	...	...	0720v	...	0750v
	Amersfoort **481** d.	...	...	...	...	...	...	...	...	...	...	...	0637a	...	0707v	|	...	...	|	...	...	0737v	...	0807
	Den Haag Centraal **460** d.	...	...	...	...	...	...	...	...	...	...	...	|	...	|	0543h	...	...	0613h	...	...	|	...	|
	Schiphol ✈ **460** d.	...	...	...	...	...	...	...	...	...	...	...	|	...	|	0614	...	...	0644	0703	...	|	...	|
	Amsterdam Zuid **460** d.	...	...	...	...	...	...	...	...	...	...	...	|	...	|	|	...	...	|	0712	...	|	...	|
	Amsterdam Centraal **460** d.	...	...	...	...	...	...	...	...	...	...	0607	|	...	|	0637	0637v	...	0707	|	...	|	...	|
	Zwolle **460 481** a.	...	...	...	...	...	...	...	...	...	...	0715	0712a	...	0742v	0745	0745v	...	0815	0815	...	0812v	...	0842
0	**Zwolle** d.	0545	0553	0616	0623	0626	0645	0647	0653	0656	0716	0717	0723	0726	0747	0753	0753	0756	0817	0817	0817	0823	0826	0847
27	Meppel d.	0602	0609	0631	0638	0642	0701	|	0709	0713	0731	|	0738	0742	|	0809	0809	0813	|	|	|	|	0842	|
	Steenwijk d.	|	0618	|	0647	|	|	|	0718	|	|	|	0747	|	|	0818	0818	|	|	|	|	0847	|	|
	Heerenveen d.	|	0634	|	0704	|	|	|	0734	|	|	|	0803	|	|	0834	0834	|	|	|	|	0900	|	|
	Leeuwarden a.	|	0656	|	0726	|	|	|	0756	|	|	|	0828	|	|	0856	0856	|	|	|	|	0917	|	|
47	Hoogeveen d.	0614	...	0643	...	0654	0713	|	...	0724	0743	|	...	0754	|	...	...	0824	|	|	|	...	0854	|
77	Assen d.	0633	...	0702	...	0714	0732	0727	...	0744	0802	0757	...	0814	0827	...	...	0844	0857	0857	0857	...	0914	0927
104	**Groningen** a.	0653	...	0724	...	0734	0751	0744	...	0804	0824	0814	...	0834	0844	...	...	0904	0914	0914	0914	...	0934	0944

	⑥k	©	Ⓐ	⚒	†	⚒				†	⚒	⚒	†	⚒				†	⚒	⚒	†	⚒		
Rotterdam Centraal **481** .. d.	0622	...	...	...	0652	...	0735	...	0805	0722	...	...	0752	...	0835	...	0905	0822	...	...	0852	...	0935	...
Utrecht Centraal **481** d.	|	...	...	...	|	...	0820	...	0850	|	...	...	|	...	0920	...	0950	|	...	...	|	...	1020	...
Amersfoort **481** d.	|	...	...	...	|	...	0837	...	0907	|	...	...	|	...	0937	...	1007	|	...	...	|	...	1037	...
Den Haag Centraal **460** d.	0643h	...	0704	...	0713h	0734a	|	...	|	0743h	0804	...	0813h	0834	|	...	|	0843h	0904	...	0913h	0934	|	...
Schiphol ✈ **460** d.	0714	...	0733	...	0744	0803	|	...	|	0814	0833	...	0844	0903	|	...	|	0914	0933	...	0944	1003	|	...
Amsterdam Zuid **460** d.	|	...	0742	...	|	0812	|	...	|	|	0842	...	|	0912	|	...	|	|	0942	...	|	1012	|	...
Amsterdam Centraal **460** d.	0737	0737	|	...	0807	|	|	...	|	0837	|	...	0907	|	|	...	|	0937	|	...	1007	|	|	...
Zwolle **460 481** a.	0845	0845	0845	...	0915	0915	0912	...	0942	0945	0945	...	1015	1015	1012	...	1042	1045	1045	...	1115	1115	1112	...
Zwolle d.	0853	0853	0853	0856	0917	0917	0923	0926	0947	0953	0953	0956	1017	1017	1023	1026	1047	1053	1053	1056	1117	1117	1123	1126
Meppel d.	0909	0909	0909	0913	|	|	|	0942	|	1009	1009	1013	|	|	|	1042	|	1109	1109	1113	|	|	|	1142
Steenwijk d.	0918	0918	0918	|	|	|	0947	|	|	1018	1018	|	|	|	1047	|	|	1118	1118	|	|	|	1147	|
Heerenveen d.	0934	0934	0934	|	|	|	1000	|	|	1034	1034	|	|	|	1100	|	|	1134	1134	|	|	|	1200	|
Leeuwarden a.	0956	0956	0956	|	|	|	1017	|	|	1056	1056	|	|	|	1117	|	|	1156	1156	|	|	|	1217	|
Hoogeveen d.	...	...	...	0924	|	|	...	0954	|	...	...	1024	|	|	...	1054	|	...	...	1124	|	|	...	1154
Assen d.	...	...	...	0944	0957	0957	...	1014	1027	...	...	1044	1057	1057	...	1114	1127	...	...	1244	1157	1157	...	1214
Groningen a.	...	...	...	1004	1014	1014	...	1034	1044	...	...	1104	1114	1114	...	1134	1144	...	...	1204	1214	1214	...	1234

			⚒◐				and at the same minutes past each hour until											⊡	③L		⚒	⑤⑥k
Rotterdam Centraal **481** .. d.	1005	...	...	...	1035	...		2005	...	...	...	2035	...	2105	...	...	2135	2205	2122	...	2152	2305	2222
Utrecht Centraal **481** d.	1050	...	...	...	1120	...		2050	...	...	...	2120	...	2150	...	...	2220	2250	|	...	|	2350	|
Amersfoort **481** d.	1107	...	...	...	1137	...		2107	...	...	...	2137	...	2207	...	...	2237	2307	|	...	|	0007	|
Den Haag Centraal **460** d.	|	1004	...	1034	|	...		|	2004	...	2034	|	...	|	2104	2134	|	|	2143h	...	2213h	|	2243h
Schiphol ✈ **460** d.	|	1033	...	1103	|	...		|	2033	...	2103	|	...	|	2133	2203	|	|	2214	...	2244	|	2314
Amsterdam Zuid **460** d.	|	1042	...	1112	|	...		|	2042	...	2112	|	...	|	2142	2212	|	|	|	...	|	|	|
Amsterdam Centraal **460** d.	|	|	...	|	|	...		|	|	...	|	|	...	|	|	|	|	|	2237	...	2307	|	2337
Zwolle **460 481** a.	1142	1145	...	1215	1212	...		2142	2145	...	2215	2212	...	2242	2245	2315	2312	2342	2345	...	0015	0048	0045
Zwolle d.	1147	1153	1156	1217	1223	1226		2147	2153	2156	2217	2223	2226	2247	2253	2317	2323	2347	2353	2353	0017	0050	0053
Meppel d.	|	1209	1213	|	|	1242		|	2209	2213	|	2238	2242	|	2309	2332	2338	|	0009	0009	0032	0105	0109
Steenwijk d.	|	1218	|	|	1247	|		|	2218	|	|	2247	|	|	2318	|	2347	|	0018	0018	|	|	0118
Heerenveen d.	|	1234	|	|	1300	|		|	2234	|	|	2300	|	|	2334	|	0000	|	0034	0034	|	|	0134
Leeuwarden a.	|	1256	|	|	1317	|		|	2256	|	|	2318	|	|	2356	|	0018	|	0056	0056	|	|	0156
Hoogeveen d.	|	...	1224	|	...	1254		|	...	2224	|	...	2254	|	...	2344	...	|	...	...	0044	0116‡	...
Assen d.	1227	...	1244	1257	...	1314		2227	...	2244	2257	...	2314	2327	...	0003	...	0027	...	...	0102‡	0134‡	...
Groningen a.	1244	...	1304	1314	...	1334		2244	...	2304	2314	...	2334	2344	...	0025	...	0044	...	...	0123‡	0157‡	...

km		Ⓐ	Ⓐ	Ⓐ	Ⓐ	⑥k	Ⓐ	⚒	Ⓐ	⑥k	Ⓐ	⑥k	Ⓐ	†	Ⓐ	⚒	†	©	Ⓐ	⚒	†	⚒	†	⚒
	Groningen d.	...	0505t	...	0536t	0546	...	0605	0623	...	...	0635	0646	0646	0653	...	...	0705	0716	0723	...	...	0735	0746
	Assen d.	...	0525t	...	0557t	0602	...	0625	0644	...	...	0657	0702	0702	0714	...	...	0725	0732	0744	...	...	0757	0802
	Hoogeveen d.	...	0544	...	0615	|	...	0644	0703	...	...	0715	|	|	0733	...	...	0744	|	0803	...	...	0815	|
0	**Leeuwarden** d.	0504	|	0544	|	|	0604	|	|	0635	0644	|	|	|	|	0704	0704	|	|	|	0735	0744	|	|
29	Heerenveen d.	0526	|	0601	|	|	0626	|	|	0657	0701	|	|	|	|	0726	0726	|	|	|	0757	0801	|	|
53	Steenwijk d.	0541	|	0614	|	|	0641	|	|	0711	0714	|	|	|	|	0741	0741	|	|	|	0811	0814	|	|
67	Meppel d.	0552	0556	0622	0627	|	0652	0656	0716	0720	0722	0727	|	|	0746	0752	0752	0756	|	0816	0820	|	0827	|
94	**Zwolle** a.	0608	0613	0638	0643	0643	0708	0713	0733	0738	0738	0743	0743	0743	0803	0808	0808	0813	0813	0833	0838	0838	0843	0843
	Zwolle **460 481** d.	0615	0618	0648	0645	0645	0715	0718	...	0748	0748	0745	0745	0745	...	0815	0815	0818	0818	...	0848	0848	0845	0845
	Amsterdam Centraal **460** a.	|	|	|	|	0753	|	|	...	|	|	|	|	0853	...	|	0923	|	|	...	|	|	|	|
	Amsterdam Zuid **460** a.	0719	|	|	0749	|	0819	|	...	|	|	0849	0849	|	...	0919	|	|	|	...	|	|	0949	0949
	Schiphol ✈ **460** a.	0726	|	|	0756	0815	0826	|	...	|	|	0856	0856	0915	...	0926	0945	|	|	...	|	|	0956	0956
	Den Haag Centraal **460** a.	0756	|	|	0826	0847h	0856	|	...	|	|	0926	0926	0947h	...	0956	1017h	|	|	...	|	|	1026	1026
	Amersfoort **481** a.	...	0652	0722	...	|	...	0752	...	0822	0822	...	...	|	...	...	|	0852	0852	...	0922	0922	...	...
	Utrecht Centraal **481** a.	...	0711	0741	...	|	...	0811	...	0841	0841	...	...	|	...	...	|	0911	0911	...	0941	0941	...	...
	Rotterdam Centraal **481** . a.	...	0755	0825	...	0908	...	0855	...	0925	0925	...	...	1008	...	...	1038	0955	0955	...	1025	1025	...	...

	⚒◧						and at the same minutes past each hour until							Ⓐ	©								
Groningen d.	0753	...	0816	0823	...	0846		1716	1723	...	1746	1753	...	1806	1816	1823	...	1846	1853	...	1916	1923	...
Assen d.	0814	...	0832	0844	...	0902		1732	1744	...	1802	1814	...	1826	1832	1844	...	1902	1914	...	1932	1944	...
Hoogeveen d.	0833	...	|	0903	...	|		|	1803	...	|	1833	...	1846	|	1903	...	|	1933	...	|	2003	...
Leeuwarden d.	|	0804	|	|	0844	|		|	|	1744	|	|	1804	|	|	|	1844	|	|	1904	|	|	1944
Heerenveen d.	|	0826	|	|	0901	|		|	|	1801	|	|	1826	|	|	|	1901	|	|	1926	|	|	2001
Steenwijk d.	|	0841	|	|	0914	|		|	|	1814	|	|	1841	|	|	|	1914	|	|	1941	|	|	2014
Meppel d.	0846	0852	|	0916	|	|		|	1816	|	|	1846	1852	1858	|	1916	|	|	1946	1952	|	2016	|
Zwolle a.	0903	0908	0913	0933	0938	0943		1813	1833	1838	1843	1903	1908	1913	1913	1934	1938	1943	2003	2008	2013	2033	2038
Zwolle **460 481** d.	...	0915	0918	...	0948	0945		1818	...	1848	1845	...	1915	1918	1918	...	1948	1945	...	2015	2018	...	2048
Amsterdam Centraal **460** a.	...	|	|	...	|	|		|	...	|	|	...	|	|	|	...	|	|	...	|	|	...	|
Amsterdam Zuid **460** a.	...	1019	|	...	|	1049		|	...	|	1949	...	2019	|	|	...	|	2049	...	2119	|	...	|
Schiphol ✈ **460** a.	...	1026	|	...	|	1056		|	...	|	1956	...	2026	|	|	...	|	2056	...	2126	|	...	|
Den Haag Centraal **460** a.	...	1056	|	...	|	1126		|	...	|	2026	...	2056	|	|	...	|	2126	...	2156	|	...	|
Amersfoort **481** a.	...	...	0952	...	1022	...		1852	...	1922	...	...	...	1952	1952	...	2022	...	...	...	2052	...	2122
Utrecht Centraal **481** a.	...	...	1011	...	1041	...		1911	...	1941	...	...	...	2011	2011	...	2041	...	...	...	2111	...	2141
Rotterdam Centraal **481** .. a.	...	...	1055	...	1125	...		1955	...	2025	...	...	...	2055	2055	...	2125	...	...	...	2155	...	2225

																				⑤⑥k	⑤⑥k	D	⑤⑥k	D
Groningen d.	1946	1953	...	2016	2023	...	2046	2053	...	2116	2123	...	2146	2153	...	2216	2223	...	2246	2246	...	2323	2326	...
Assen d.	2002	2014	...	2032	2044	...	2102	2114	...	2132	2144	...	2202	2214	...	2232	2244	...	2302	2302	...	2344	2347	...
Hoogeveen d.	|	2033	...	|	2103	...	|	2133	...	|	2203	...	|	2233	...	|	2303	...	|	|	...	0003	0006	...
Leeuwarden d.	|	|	2004	|	|	2044	|	|	2104	|	|	2144	|	|	2204	|	|	2235	|	|	2328	|	|	2330
Heerenveen d.	|	|	2026	|	|	2101	|	|	2126	|	|	2201	|	|	2226	|	|	2257	|	|	2350	|	|	2354
Steenwijk d.	|	|	2041	|	|	2114	|	|	2141	|	|	2214	|	|	2241	|	|	2311	|	|	0004	|	|	001[illegible]
Meppel d.	|	2046	2052	|	2116	|	|	2146	2152	|	2216	|	|	2246	2252	|	2316	2322	|	|	0013	0016	0018	002[illegible]
Zwolle a.	2043	2103	2108	2113	2133	2138	2143	2203	2208	2213	2233	2238	2243	2303	2308	2313	2333	2338	2343	2343	0030	0033	0034	003[illegible]
Zwolle **460 481** d.	2045	...	2115	2118	...	2148	2145	...	2215	2218	...	2248	2245	...	2315	2318	...	2348	2345	2345	...	...	0035	...
Amsterdam Centraal **460** a.	|	...	|	|	...	|	2253	...	2323	|	...	|	2354	...	0024	|	...	|	0053	0053	...	...	0142	...
Amsterdam Zuid **460** a.	2149	...	2219	|	...	|	|	...	|	|	...	|	|	...	|	|	...	|	...	|	...	...	...	...
Schiphol ✈ **460** a.	2156	...	2226	|	...	|	2315	...	2345	|	...	|	0015	...	0045	|	...	|	...	0115	...	...	...	...
Den Haag Centraal **460** a.	2226	...	2256	|	...	|	2347h	...	0017h	|	...	|	0047h	...	0118h	|	...	|	...	0149h	...	...	...	...
Amersfoort **481** a.	...	...	...	2152	...	2222	|	...	|	2252	...	2322	|	...	...	2352	...	0022	...	...	...	...	...	...
Utrecht Centraal **481** a.	...	...	...	2211	...	2241	|	...	|	2311	...	2341	|	...	...	0011	...	0041	...	...	...	...	...	...
Rotterdam Centraal **481** .. a.	...	...	...	2255	...	2325	0008	...	0038	2355	...	0025	0109	...	...	0055	...	...	...	...	...	...	...	...

D – ①②③④⑦ (not May 29, June 9).
L – From Lelystad (Table **460**).
a – Ⓐ only.

h – Den Haag **HS**.
k – Also May 29, June 9.
t – Departs up to 4 minutes **earlier** on ②③.
v – ⚒ only.

⊡ – Daily except ③.
‡ – 2–6 minutes later on the mornings of ④⑤ (not May 30).
◐ – The services from Zwolle at 1556, 1656, 1756, 1856, 1956 and 2056 run daily.
◧ – The services from Groningen at 1453, 1553 and 1653 run daily.

For traffic arrangements on Dutch holiday dates, see page 250

Operated by Syntus (NS tickets valid) 2nd class only — OLDENZAAL - HENGELO - ZUTPHEN — 488

km					Ⓐ	Ⓐ	⚒	⚒				⚒				⚒				Ⓐ					
0	**Oldenzaal** d.	0003	0033	...	0603	0633	0703	0733	...	...	0803	0833	0833	and at the same minutes past each hour until	2003	2033	2033	...	2103	2133	2133	2203	2233	2303	2333
11	**Hengelo** a.	0013	0043	...	0613	0643	0713	0743	...	...	0813	0843	0843		2013	2043	2043	...	2113	2143	2143	2213	2243	2313	2343
11	**Hengelo** d.	0016	0046	...	0616	0646	0716	0746	...	...	0816	0846	...		2016	2046	...	...	2116	2146	...	2216	...	2316	...
26	Goor d.	0031	0100	...	0631	0701	0731	0801	0801	...	0831	0901	...		2031	2101	...	...	2131	2201	...	2231	...	2331	...
39	Lochem d.	0039	...	...	0639	0709	0739	0809	0809	...	0839	0909	...		2039	2109	...	...	2139	2209	...	2239	...	2339	...
56	**Zutphen** a.	0053	...	...	0653	0723	0753	0823	0823	...	0853	0923	...		2053	2123	...	...	2153	2223	...	2253	...	2353	...

			Ⓐ	Ⓐ	Ⓐ	⚒	Ⓐ	⚒	⚒			⚒				⚒			Ⓐ					
Zutphen d.	0006	...	...	...	0606	...	0636	...	0706	...	0736	0806	...	and at the same minutes past each hour until	1936	2006	...	2036	2106	...	2136	...	2236	...	2336
Lochem d.	0021	...	...	...	0621	...	0651	...	0721	...	0751	0821	...		1951	2021	...	2051	2121	...	2151	...	2251	...	2351
Goor d.	0029	...	0530	0600	0630	0630	0700	0700	0730	0730	0800	0830	...		2000	2030	...	2100	2130	...	2200	...	2300	...	0000
Hengelo a.	...	...	0544	0614	0644	0644	0714	0714	0744	0744	0814	0844	...		2014	2044	...	2114	2144	...	2214	...	2314	...	0014
Hengelo d.	...	...	0548	0618	0648	0648	0718	0718	0748	0748	0818	0848	0848		2018	2048	2048	2118	2148	2148	2218	2248	2318	2348	0018
Oldenzaal a.	...	...	0558	0628	0658	0658	0728	0728	0758	0758	0828	0858	0858		2028	2058	2058	2128	2158	2158	2228	2258	2328	2358	0028

ZWOLLE - ENSCHEDE — 492

km		Ⓐ	Ⓐ	⚒	⚒						
0	**Zwolle** d.	0549	0619	0649	0719	0749	0819	and every 30 minutes until	2249	2319	2349
18	Raalte d.	0605	0635	0705	0735	0805	0835		2305	2335	0005
32	Nijverdal d.	0616	0646	0716	0746	0816	0846		2316	2346	0016
44	Almelo 480 a.	0631	0701	0731	0801	0831	0901		2331	0001	0031
59	Hengelo 480 a.	0645	0715	0745	0815	0845	0915		2345	0015	0045
67	**Enschede** 480 a.	0657	0727	0757	0827	0857	0927		2357	0027	0057

	Ⓐ	Ⓐ	Ⓐ	⚒	⚒					
Enschede 480 d.	*0445*	*0516*	0604	0634	0704	0734	0804	and every 30 minutes until	2234	2304
Hengelo 480 d.	0516	0546	0616	0646	0716	0746	0816		2246	2316
Almelo 480 d.	0531	0601	0631	0701	0731	0801	0831		2301	2331
Nijverdal d.	0545	0615	0645	0715	0745	0815	0845		2315	2345
Raalte d.	0554	0624	0654	0724	0754	0824	0854		2324	2354
Zwolle a.	0611	0641	0711	0741	0811	0841	0911		2341	0011

Operated by Arriva (NS tickets valid) — ZWOLLE - EMMEN — 493

km		Ⓐ	⚒	Ⓐ						⚒	⚒
0	**Zwolle** d.	0620	0650	0720	0750	0820	and at the same minutes past each hour until	2220	2250	2320	2350
23	Ommen d.	0638	0708	0738	0808	0838		2238	2308	2338	0008
34	Mariënberg d.	0645	0715	0745	0815	0845		2245	2315	2345	0015
55	Coevorden d.	0700	0734	0800	0834	0900		2300	2334	0000	0036
75	**Emmen** a.	0715	0753	0815	0853	0915		2315	2353	0015	0053

	Ⓐ	Ⓐ	⚒	⚒						⚒	⚒
Emmen d.	0538	0615	0638	0715	0738	0815	and at the same minutes past each hour until	2215	2238	2315	2338
Coevorden d.	0559	0631	0659	0731	0759	0831		2231	2259	2331	2359
Mariënberg d.	0616	0646	0716	0746	0816	0846		2246	2316	2346	0016
Ommen d.	0623	0653	0723	0753	0823	0853		2253	2323	2353	0023
Zwolle a.	0640	0710	0740	0810	0840	0910		2310	2340	0010	0040

n – Not Apr. 22.
w – Also May 30, June 10.

☛ Other journeys Zwolle - Emmen and v.v.: **From Zwolle** at 0020 ②–⑦ n, 0056 ⑦ w and 0550 Ⓐ. **From Emmen** at 0020 ②–⑦ n and 0512 Ⓐ.

Operated by Arriva (NS tickets valid) — LEEUWARDEN - GRONINGEN — 494

km				Ⓐ	Ⓐ	⑥k	Ⓐ	⚒	Ⓐ	Ⓐ	⚒		Ⓐ	⚒		⚒	⚒		⚒	⚒			⚒	✣
0	**Leeuwarden** d.	0024	...	0551	0618	0621	0643	0651	0721	0743	0751	0821	0843	0851	0921	0943	0951	1021	1043	1051	1121	1143	1151	and at the same minutes past each hour until
25	Buitenpost d.	0047	...	0616	0646	0646	0659	0716	0746	0759	0816	0846	0859	0916	0946	0959	1016	1046	1059	1116	1146	1159	1216	
54	**Groningen** a.	0109	...	0640	0709	0710	0718	0740	0810	0818	0840	0910	0918	0940	1010	1018	1040	1110	1118	1140	1210	1218	1240	

			⚒						†		
Leeuwarden d.	1821	1843	1851	1921	1943	2021	2043	2121	2143	2221	2324
Buitenpost d.	1846	1859	1916	1946	1959	2046	2059	2146	2159	2246	2348
Groningen a.	1910	1918	1939	2010	2018	2110	2118	2209	2218	2310	0009

			Ⓐ	⚒	Ⓐ	⚒	Ⓐ	Ⓐ	⚒	⚒	Ⓐ
Groningen d.	0027	...	0548	0621	0641	0651	0721	0741	0751	0821	0841
Buitenpost d.	0051	...	0612	0645	0659	0715	0745	0759	0815	0845	0859
Leeuwarden a.	0114	...	0637	0710	0716	0740	0812	0816	0840	0910	0916

		⚒	⚒		⚒	⚒		†	⚒		⚒		†	⚒	⚒		†	⚒	⚒					
Groningen d.	0851	0921	0941	0951	1021	1041	1051	1121	1121	and at the same minutes past each hour until	1841	1851	1921	1921	1941	1951	2021	2021	2041	2051	2127	2227	...	2327
Buitenpost d.	0915	0945	0959	1015	1045	1059	1115	1139	1145		1859	1915	1939	1945	1959	2015	2039	2045	2059	2115	2151	2251	...	2351
Leeuwarden a.	0940	1010	1016	1040	1110	1116	1140	1159	1210		1916	1940	1959	2010	2016	2040	2059	2110	2116	2140	2216	2316	...	0016

k – Also May 29, June 9.
✣ – On Ⓐ Leeuwarden d. 1550/1650 (not 1551/1651)

Operated by Arriva ★ — GRONINGEN - NIEUWESCHANS - LEER — 495

km				A	Ⓐ	⑥k	Ⓐ	⑥k	Ⓐ	Ⓐ	Ⓒ	⑦w	E	⚒		⚒		E	⚒		⚒		E	⚒
0	**Groningen** 498 d.	0020	...	0506	0516	0546	0549	0613	0619	0650	0652	0722	0722	0752	0822	0852	0922	0922	0952	1022	1052	1122	1122	1152
15	Hoogezand-Sappemeer 498 d.	0035	...	0521	0531	0601	0604	0628	0634	0706	0707	0737	0737	0807	0837	0907	0937	0937	1007	1037	1107	1137	1137	1207
34	Winschoten d.	0053	...	0541	0550	0620	0623	0648	0658	0729	0731	0757	0801	0831	0901	0926	0956	1001	1026	1101	1126	1156	1201	1226
46	Nieuweschans 🏛 d.	0103	...	0552	...	...	...	0658	0707	0740	0740k	0811	0811	0840	0911	...	...	1011	...	1111	...	...	1211	...
72	**Leer** (Ostfriesl) a.	...	...	0615	...	...	...	0721h	...	...	...	0834	0834	...	0934	...	...	1034h	...	1134	...	...	1234h	...

		⚒		E	⚒		⚒		E	⚒		⚒		E	⚒		⚒		E			⚒		
Groningen 498 d.	1222	1252	1322	1322	1352	1422	1452	1522	1522	1552	1622	1652	1722	1722	1752	1822	1852	1922	1922	2022	2122	2122	2222	2322
Hoogezand-Sappemeer 498 d.	1237	1307	1337	1337	1407	1437	1507	1537	1537	1607	1637	1707	1737	1737	1807	1837	1907	1937	1937	2037	2137	2137	2237	2337
Winschoten d.	1301	1326	1356	1401	1426	1501	1526	1556	1601	1626	1701	1726	1756	1801	1826	1901	1926	1956	2001	2101	2156	2201	2301	2355
Nieuweschans 🏛 d.	1311	...	...	1411	...	1511	...	...	1611	...	1711	...	...	1811	...	1911	...	...	2011	2111	...	2210	2310	0005
Leer (Ostfriesl) a.	1334	...	...	1434h	...	1534	...	...	1634h	...	1734	...	...	1834h	...	1934	...	...	2034h	2134	...	...	...	...

					Ⓐ	⑥k	Ⓐ	A	Ⓐ	Ⓒ	Ⓐ	⑥k		⚒		⚒		⚒		⚒	E		⚒	
Leer (Ostfriesl) d.	...	...	...	...	...	...	...	0621	...	...	...	0726h	...	...	...	...	0926	...	1026	...	1126h	...	...	1226
Nieuweschans 🏛 d.	0010	0108	...	...	...	...	...	0644	0715	0719k	0749	0749	0819c	0849	...	...	0949	...	1049	...	1149	...	...	1249
Winschoten d.	0019	0117	...	...	0555	0625	0628	0656	0726	0731	0800	0801	0831	0901	0901	0931	1001	1031	1101	1131	1201	1201	1231	1301
Hoogezand-Sappemeer 498 d.	0038	0136	...	...	0614	0647	0647	0715	0745	0750	0819	0820	0850	0920	0920	0950	1020	1050	1120	1150	1220	1220	1250	1320
Groningen a.	0055	0154	...	...	0631	0704	0703	0733	0803	0807	0837	0837	0907	0937	0937	1007	1037	1107	1137	1207	1237	1237	1307	1337

	⚒	E		⚒		⚒	E		⚒		⚒	E		⚒		⚒	E			E		⚒		
Leer (Ostfriesl) d.	...	1326h	...	...	1426	...	1526h	...	...	1626	...	1726h	...	...	1826	...	1926h	...	2026	2126h	...	...	2226	...
Nieuweschans 🏛 d.	...	1349	...	...	1449	...	1549	...	...	1649	...	1749	...	...	1849	...	1949	...	2049	2149	...	2219	2249	2319
Winschoten d.	1331	1401	1401	1431	1501	1531	1601	1601	1631	1701	1731	1801	1801	1831	1901	1931	2001	2001	2101	2201	2201	2231	2301	2331
Hoogezand-Sappemeer 498 d.	1350	1420	1420	1450	1520	1550	1620	1620	1650	1720	1750	1820	1820	1850	1920	1950	2020	2020	2120	2220	2220	2250	2320	2350
Groningen a.	1407	1437	1437	1507	1537	1607	1637	1637	1707	1737	1807	1837	1837	1907	1937	2007	2037	2037	2137	2237	2237	2307	2337	0007

A – ①–⑤ (not Apr. 21, May 29, June 9).
E – ①–⑥ (not Apr. 21).
c – Ⓒ only.
h – Not June 9.
k – ⑥ (also May 29, June 9).
w – Also Apr. 21.
★ – NS tickets are valid Groningen - Nieuweschans and v.v.

Operated by Arriva (NS tickets valid); 2nd class only — LEEUWARDEN - STAVOREN — 496

km		Ⓐ	Ⓐ	Ⓐ	⑥k	Ⓐ	Ⓐ	⑥k		Ⓐ	⑥k	†	Ⓐ	Ⓐ	⑥k	Ⓐ	Ⓒ	Ⓐ	Ⓐ	⑥k		Ⓐ	⚒	
0	**Leeuwarden** d.	0531	0543	0600	0610	0621	0641	0643	...	0701	0703	0713	0721	0741	0743	0801	0803	0821	0841	0843	0903	0923	0943	and at the same minutes past each hour until
22	Sneek a.	0550	0602	0619	0629	0640	0700	0702	...	0720	0722	0732	0740	0800	0802	0820	0822	0840	0902	0902	0922	0942	1002	
22	Sneek d.	0551	...	0622	0632	0653	...	...	...	0724	0730	...	...	...	...	0828	0830	...	...	...	0930	...	...	
51	**Stavoren** a.	0618	...	0649	0659	0720	...	...	...	0751	0757	...	...	...	...	0855	0857	...	...	...	0957	...	...	

		Ⓐ	⚒		Ⓐ				⑤⑥k		
Leeuwarden d.	1803	1823	1843	1903	1923	2003	2103	2223	2223	2323	...
Sneek a.	1822	1842	1902	1922	1942	2022	2122	2242	2242	2342	...
Sneek d.	1830	...	...	1930	...	2030	2130	...	2243	...	...
Stavoren a.	1857	...	...	1957	...	2057	2157	...	2310	...	...

	Ⓐ	Ⓐ	Ⓐ	Ⓐ	⑥k	Ⓐ	†	⑥k	Ⓐ	Ⓐ	⑥k
Stavoren d.	...	...	0623	...	...	0654	...	0704	0725	...	...
Sneek a.	...	...	0650	...	...	0721	...	0730	0752	...	...
Sneek d.	0614	0635	0655	0715	0717	0735	0737	0737	0755	0815	0817
Leeuwarden a.	0636	0656	0716	0736	0738	0756	0758	0758	0816	0836	0838

	Ⓐ	⑥k		Ⓐ	⚒		Ⓐ		⚒		Ⓐ	⚒		Ⓐ								⑤⑥k			
Stavoren d.	0801	0804	...	...	...	0904	...	and at the same minutes past each hour until	...	1804	...	...	1904	...	2004	...	2104	...	2204	...	...	2321	...	...	...
Sneek a.	0827	0830	...	...	...	0930	...		...	1830	...	...	1930	...	2030	...	2130	...	2230	...	...	2346	...	...	...
Sneek d.	0834	0837	0837	0857	0917	0937	0957		1817	1837	1857	1917	1937	1957	2037	...	2137	...	2237	...	2347	2347	...	...	...
Leeuwarden a.	0856	0858	0858	0918	0938	0958	1018		1838	1858	1918	1938	1958	2018	2058	...	2158	...	2258	...	0008	0008	...	...	...

– Also May 29, June 9.

497 ROTTERDAM - HOEK VAN HOLLAND

km						Ⓐ	⚒	Ⓐ	⚒	Ⓐ		Ⓐ		Ⓐ									
0	**Rotterdam** Centraal	d.	0002	...	...	0532	0602	0617	0632	0647	0702	0717	0732	0747	...	0802	0832	and every 30	2302	2332	...	...	...
4	Schiedam Centrum	d.	0007	...	...	0537	0607	0622	0637	0652	0707	0722	0737	0752	...	0807	0837	minutes until	2307	2337	...	...	...
10	Vlaardingen Centrum	d.	0014	...	...	0544	0614	0629	0644	0659	0714	0729	0744	0759	...	0814	0844		2314	2344	...	...	...
27	**Hoek van Holland** Haven	a.	0032	...	...	0602	0632	0647	0702	0717	0732	0747	0802	0817	...	0832	0902		2332	0002	...	...	...

					Ⓐ	Ⓐ	Ⓐ	⚒	Ⓐ	⚒	Ⓐ		Ⓐ										
Hoek van Holland Haven	d.	0026	...	...	0556	0626	0641	0656	0711	0726	0741	0756	0811	...	0826	0856	and every 30	2326	2356	...	...	...	...
Vlaardingen Centrum	d.	0043	...	...	0613	0643	0658	0713	0728	0743	0758	0813	0828	...	0843	0913	minutes until	2343	0013	...	...	...	...
Schiedam Centrum	a.	0051	...	...	0621	0651	0706	0721	0736	0751	0806	0821	0836	...	0851	0921		2351	0021	...	...	...	...
Rotterdam Centraal	a.	0057	...	...	0627	0657	0712	0727	0742	0757	0812	0827	0842	...	0857	0927		2357	0027	...	...	...	...

498 OTHER BRANCH LINES

ALMELO – MARIËNBERG Operated by **Arriva** (NS tickets valid) *19 km* Journey time: 22–23 minutes

From Almelo:
0618 Ⓐ, 0648 Ⓐ, 0718 Ⓐ, 0748 ⚒, 0818 Ⓐ, 0848, 0948, 1048, 1148, 1248, 1318 ⚒, 1348, 1418 ⚒, 1448, 1518 ⚒, 1548, 1618 ⚒, 1648, 1718 ⚒, 1748, 1818 ⚒, 1848, 1948, 2048, 2148, 2248, 2355 ② and 2357 ①③④⑤⑥⑦.

From Mariënberg:
0553 Ⓐ, 0623 Ⓐ, 0653 Ⓐ, 0723 ⚒, 0753 Ⓐ, 0823, 0853 Ⓐ, 0923, 1023, 1123, 1223, 1323, 1353 ⚒, 1423, 1453 ⚒, 1523, 1553 ⚒, 1623, 1653 ⚒, 1723, 1753 ⚒, 1823, 1923, 2023, 2123, 2223 and 2323.

AMERSFOORT – EDE-WAGENINGEN Operated by **Connexxion** (NS tickets valid) *34 km* Journey time: 37–38 minutes.

From Amersfoort:
0011 **H**, 0041 ⑦ **c**, 0111 ⑦ **c**, 0511 Ⓐ, 0541 **P**, 0611 **P**, 0641 **P**, 0711, 0741, 0811, 0841 and every 30 minutes until 2341.
All trains call at Barneveld Centrum (17 minutes from Amersfoort)

From Ede-Wageningen:
0025, 0055 **H**, 0125 ⑦ **c**, 0155 ⑦ **c**, 0555 Ⓐ, 0625 **P**, 0655 **P**, 0725 **P**, 0755, 0825, 0855 and every 30 minutes until 2355.
All trains call at Barneveld Centrum (20 minutes from Ede-Wageningen)

APELDOORN – ZUTPHEN Operated by **Arriva** (NS tickets valid) *18 km* Journey time: 18–20 minutes

From Apeldoorn:
0007, 0637 Ⓐ, 0707 Ⓐ, 0737 Ⓐ, 0807 ⚒, 0837, 0907 and every 30 minutes until 2337.

From Zutphen:
0606 Ⓐ, 0636 Ⓐ, 0706 Ⓐ, 0736 ⚒, 0806, 0836 and every 30 minutes until 2336.

GRONINGEN – DELFZIJL Operated by **Arriva** (NS tickets valid) *38 km* Journey time: 37–39 minutes

From Groningen:
0018, 0514 Ⓐ, 0544 Ⓐ, 0548 ⑥ **k**, 0613 Ⓐ, 0618 Ⓒ, 0644 Ⓐ, 0648 **S**, 0714 Ⓐ, 0718 Ⓒ, 0744 Ⓐ, 0748 ⑥ **k**, 0818, 0848 ⚒ and at 18 and 48 ⚒ minutes past each hour until 1718, 1748 ⚒; then 1818, 1848 Ⓐ, 1918, 2018, 2048 ④ **d**, 2118, 2218 and 2318.

From Delfzijl:
0000, 0100, 0526 ① **m**, 0556 Ⓐ, 0626 Ⓐ, 0630 ⑥ **k**, 0656 Ⓐ, 0700 Ⓒ, 0726 Ⓐ, 0730 **S**, 0756 Ⓐ, 0800 Ⓒ, 0830 ⚒, 0900, 0930 ⚒ and at 00 and 30 ⚒ minutes past each hour until 1800, 1830 ⚒; then 1900, 1930 Ⓐ, 2000, 2100, 2200 and 2300.

GRONINGEN – VEENDAM 🚂 Operated by **Arriva** (NS tickets valid) *29 km* Journey time: 30–31 minutes

From Groningen:
0008, 0456 Ⓐ, 0535 Ⓐ, 0606 Ⓐ, 0608 ⑥ **k**, 0636 Ⓐ, 0708, 0738 ⚒ and at 08 and 38 ⚒ minutes past each hour until 1808, 1838 ⚒; then 1908, 2008, 2108, 2208 and 2308.
All trains call at Hoogezand-Sappemeer (15 minutes from Groningen)

From Veendam:
0048, 0531 Ⓐ, 0615 Ⓐ, 0646 ⚒, 0716 Ⓐ, 0746 Ⓐ, 0748 Ⓒ, 0818 ⚒, 0848 and at 18 ⚒ and 48 minutes past each hour until 1918 ⚒, 1948; then 2048, 2148, 2248 and 2348.
All trains call at Hoogezand-Sappemeer (15 minutes from Veendam)

HAARLEM – ZANDVOORT aan Zee *8 km* Journey time: 10–11 minutes

From Haarlem:
0009, 0039, 0548 Ⓐ, 0618 ⚒, 0649 ⚒, 0709, 0739 and every 30 minutes until 2339.

From Zandvoort:
0000 ①②④⑤⑥⑦, 0009 ③, 0030, 0054, 0609 Ⓐ, 0639 ⚒, 0709 ⚒, 0739, 0809, 0839 and every 30 minutes until 2339.

LEEUWARDEN – HARLINGEN Haven ¶ Operated by **Arriva** (NS tickets valid) *26 km* Journey time: 25–26 minutes 2nd class only

From Leeuwarden:
0538 Ⓐ, 0621 ⑥ **k**, 0638 Ⓐ, 0703 Ⓐ, 0721 ⑥ **k**, 0738 Ⓐ, 0746 Ⓒ, 0803 Ⓐ, 0821 Ⓒ, 0838 Ⓐ, 0846 Ⓒ, 0921, 0946 ⚒, 1021, 1046 ⚒, 1121, 1146 ⚒, 1221, 1246, 1321, 1346, 1421, 1446, 1521, 1546 ⚒, 1621, 1646 ⚒, 1721, 1746, 1821, 1846, 1921, 1946, 2021, 2121, 2221 and 2325.

From Harlingen Haven:
0607 Ⓐ, 0632 Ⓐ, 0650 ⑥ **k**, 0707 Ⓐ, 0732 Ⓐ, 0750 ⑥ **k**, 0807 Ⓐ, 0815 Ⓒ, 0832 Ⓐ, 0850 Ⓒ, 0915, 0950 ⚒, 1015, 1050 ⚒, 1115, 1150 ⚒, 1215, 1250, 1315, 1350, 1415, 1450, 1515, 1550 ⚒, 1615, 1650 ⚒, 1715, 1750, 1815, 1850, 1915, 1950, 2015, 2050, 2150, 2250 and 2354.

ZWOLLE – KAMPEN *13 km* Journey time: 10 minutes

From Zwolle:
0549 Ⓐ, 0619 Ⓐ, 0649 ⚒, 0719 ⚒, 0749 and at 19 ⚒ and 49 minutes past each hour until 1319 ⚒, 1349; then 1419, 1449 and every 30 minutes until 2349.

From Kampen:
0003, 0603 Ⓐ, 0633 Ⓐ, 0703 ⚒, 0733 ⚒, 0803, 0833 ⚒ and at 03 and 33 ⚒ minutes past each hour until 1303, 1333 ⚒; then 1403, 1433 and every 30 minutes until 2333.

H – ④–⑦ (not May 31).
P – ①–⑥ (not Apr. 21, May 29, June 9).
S – ⑥ to Apr. 26; ⑥⑦ May 3 - Sept. 28 (also May 29, June 9); ⑥ from Oct. 4.

c – Also May 30, June 10.
d – Not May 29.
k – Also May 29, June 9.
m – Not Apr. 21, June 9.

¶ – For ⛴ to / from Terschelling and Vlieland. All trains also call at Harlingen (station for the town centre), 3 minutes from Harlingen Haven.
🚂 – Station for *Museumspoorlijn S.T.A.R.* Steam trains operate to / from Stadskanaal on ⑦ May - September (and selected other dates). www.stadskanaalrail.nl

499 OTHER 🚌 and ⛴ LINES

ALKMAAR – LEEUWARDEN 🚌 *Arriva Qliner* route **350** Journey time: 1 hr 56 m - 2 hrs 8 m

From Alkmaar rail station:
On Ⓐ at 0523, 0618, 0718, 0818, 0918, 1023, 1123, 1223, 1323, 1423, 1518, 1613, 1713, 1823, 1923, 2023 and 2123.
On ⑥ at 0640 and hourly until 2140.
On ✝ at 0840 and hourly until 2240.

From Leeuwarden bus station:
On Ⓐ at 0602 and hourly until 2202.
On ⑥ at 0719 and hourly until 2219.
On ✝ at 0819 and hourly until 2219.

DEN HELDER – TEXEL ⛴ *TESO*: ✆ +31 (0)222 36 96 00 Journey time: 20 minutes

🚌 route **33**: Den Helder rail station (departs 18 minutes before ships sail) to Havenhoofd.
From Den Helder Havenhoofd: 0630 ⚒, 0730 ⚒ **d**, 0830 and hourly until 2130.

From Texel ('t Horntje ferryport): 0600 ⚒, 0700 ⚒ **d**, 0800 and hourly until 2100.
🚌 route **33**: Den Helder Havenhoofd to rail station (journey: 7 minutes).

ENKHUIZEN – STAVOREN ⛴ *Rederij V & O* ▲: ✆ +31 (0) 228 32 66 67 Journey time: ± 90 minutes

From Enkuizen Spoorhaven: 0830 **A**, 1230 **B**, 1530 **C**, 1630 **B**.

From Stavoren: 1010 **A**, 1410 **B**, 1710 **C**, 1810 **B**.

VLISSINGEN – BRESKENS ⛴ *Veolia Transport Fast Ferries* ▲ Journey time: 20 minutes
0805, 0905 and hourly until 2105; *also* 0605 Ⓐ, 0705 Ⓐ, 0735 Ⓐ and 2205 Ⓐ.
Additional sailings operate Apr. 21 - Sept. 14 and Oct. 13–17.

BRESKENS ferryport – **BRUGGE** rail station 🚌 *Veolia* route **42** Journey time: 80 minutes
0632 Ⓐ, 0732 ⚒, 0832 ⚒, 0932, 1032 and hourly until 2032.

BRUGGE rail station – **BRESKENS** ferryport 🚌 *Veolia* route **42** Journey time: 80 minutes
0705 ⚒, 0805 ⚒, 0905, 1005 and hourly until 2005; then 2105 ⚒.

BRESKENS – VLISSINGEN ⛴ *Veolia Transport Fast Ferries* ▲ Journey time: 20 minutes
0835, 0935 and hourly until 2135; *also* 0635 Ⓐ, 0655 Ⓐ, 0735 Ⓐ, 0805 Ⓐ, 1705 Ⓐ, 1805 Ⓐ and 2235 Ⓐ. Additional sailings operate Apr. 21 - Sept. 14 and Oct. 13–17.

A – Daily Apr. 19 - Sept. 29 (not Apr. 21, 26, 28); ⑥⑦ Oct. 4–19 (also Oct. 14–17).
B – Daily May 1 - Sept. 29.
C – Daily Apr. 19–30 (not Apr. 21, 26, 28); ⑥⑦ Oct. 4–19 (also Oct. 14–17).

d – Runs daily Mar. 31 - Oct. 4.

▲ – Conveys foot passengers, cycles and mopeds only.

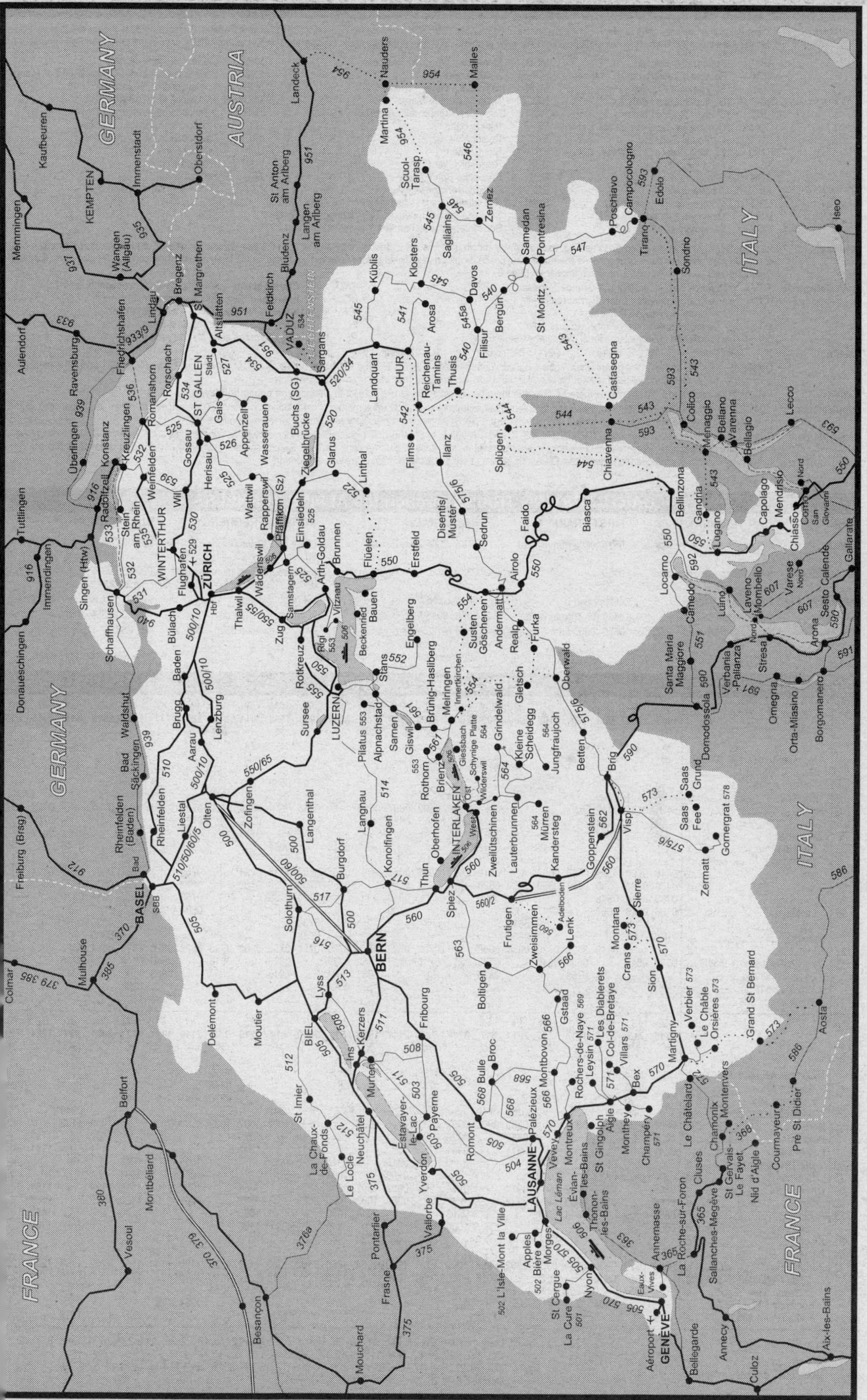
GERMANY
AUSTRIA
ITALY
FRANCE
LIECHTENSTEIN
BASEL
ZÜRICH
BERN
LUZERN
LAUSANNE
GENÈVE
CHUR
ST GALLEN
WINTERTHUR
INTERLAKEN
BIEL
Lac Léman
Schaffhausen
Konstanz
Olten
Aarau
Solothurn
Fribourg
Neuchâtel
Yverdon
Montreux
Vevey
Sion
Brig
Visp
Zermatt
Spiez
Thun
Brienz
Andermatt
Göschenen
Airolo
Bellinzona
Lugano
Locarno
Chiasso
Domodossola
St Moritz
Davos
Klosters
Landquart
Sargans
Buchs (SG)
Bregenz
Lindau
Friedrichshafen
Mulhouse
Belfort
Besançon
Vallorbe
Pontarlier
Chamonix
Martigny
Tirano
Milano

SWITZERLAND

Operators: There are numerous operators of which Schweizerische Bundesbahnen (SBB)/Chemins de fer Fédéraux (CFF)/Ferrovie Federali Svizzere (FFS) is the principal: www.sbb.ch. Bus services are provided by PostAuto/Autopostale (PA): www.postauto.ch. Table headings show the operators' initials; abbreviations used in the European Rail Timetable are:

AB	Appenzeller Bahnen	MOB	Montreux - Oberland Bernois	SMC	Sierre - Montana - Crans
BLM	Bergbahn Lauterbrunnen - Mürren	MThB	Mittelthurgau Bahn	SNCF	Société Nationale des Chemins de Fer Francais
BLS	BLS Lötschbergbahn	MVR	Montreux - Vevey Riviera	SOB	Schweizerische Südostbahn
BOB	Berner Oberland Bahnen	NStCM	Nyon-St Cergue-Morez	THURBO	an alliance of MThB and SBB
BRB	Brienz - Rothorn Bahn	PA	PostAuto / Autopostale / AutoDaPosta	TMR	Transports de Martigny et Régions
CGN	Compagnie Générale de Navigation	PB	Pilatus Bahn	TPC	Transports Publics du Chablais
CP	CarPostal Suisse	RA	RegionAlps	TPF	Transports Publics Fribourgeois
FART	Ferrovie Autolinee Regionali Ticinesi	RB	Rigi Bahnen	URh	Untersee und Rhein
FS	Ferrovie dello Stato	RBS	Regionalverkehr Bern - Solothurn	WAB	Wengernalpbahn
GGB	Gornergrat Bahn	RhB	Rhätische Bahn	ZB	Zentralbahn
JB	Jungfraubahn	RM	Regionalverkehr Mittelland	ZSG	Zürich Schifffahrtsgesellschaft
MBC	Morges - Bière - Cossonay	SBB	Schweizerische Bundesbahnen		
MIB	Meiringen - Innertkirchen Bahn	SBS	Schweizerische Bodensee-Schifffahrtsgesellschaft		
MGB	Matterhorn Gotthard Bahn	SGV	Schifffahrtsgesellschaft des Vierwaldstättersees		

Services: All trains convey first and second class seating, **except** where shown otherwise in footnotes or by a '1' or '2' in the train column, or where the footnote shows sleeping and/or couchette cars only. For most local services you **must** be in possession of a valid ticket before boarding your train. Some international trains convey sleeping cars (🛏) and/or couchette cars (▬), descriptions of which appear on page 8.

Train Categories:

TGV	French high-speed **Train à Grande Vitesse**;	*CNL*	**City Night Line** quality international overnight hotel train;
ICE	German high-speed **InterCity Express** train;	*IC*	**InterCity** quality internal express train;
RJ	Austrian high-speed **Railjet** train;	*ICN*	**InterCity Neigezug** high-speed tilting train;
EC	**EuroCity** quality international express train;	*IR*	**InterRegio** fast inter-regional trains;
EN	**EuroNight** quality international overnight express train;	*RE*	**RegioExpress** semi-fast regional trains.

Catering: ✕ – Restaurant; (✕) – Bistro; (🍸) – Bar coach; 🍸 – Minibar.
Details of catering is shown in the tables where known, but as a general guide *ICE*, *RJ*, *EC* and *ICN* trains convey ✕ or (✕), *IC* services convey ✕ or (🍸), and *TGV* and *IR* trains convey (🍸) or 🍸. Catering facilities may not be open for the whole journey and may vary from that shown.

Timings: Valid until **December 13, 2014** unless otherwise stated in the table. Local services are subject to alteration on **public holidays**.

Supplements: *TGV*, *ICE* and *RJ* high-speed trains may be used for internal Swiss journeys without supplement. For international journeys *TGV* services are priced as 'global' fare, and *EC* trains serving Italy are subject to the payment of a supplement; both types require compulsory reservation for international travel.

Reservations: Seat reservations may be made on all *TGV*, *ICE*, *RJ*, *EC*, *IC* and *ICN* trains. In *EN* and *CNL* night services seat reservations (where seats are conveyed) are compulsory (with a supplement also payable). Reservation is recommended for travel in first class panorama cars. Fares in Switzerland are calculated according to distance and many Swiss railways use artificially inflated tariff-kilometres. Distances shown in tables below, however, are actual kilometres.

CAR-CARRYING TRAINS through the ALPINE TUNNELS

TUNNEL	CAR TERMINALS	FIRST TRAIN*	LAST TRAIN*	NORMAL FREQUENCY	INFORMATION ✆
FURKA:	Oberwald - Realp	0535 (0605 from Realp)	2135 (2205 from Realp)	every 60 minutes (every 30 minutes on ①⑤⑥⑦).	027 927 76 66, 027 927 76 76
LÖTSCHBERG:	Kandersteg - Goppenstein	0550	2350 (2320 from Goppenstein)	every 30 minutes, more frequent 0805–2120 on ⑤⑥⑦ and mid-June – mid-Oct.	0900 55 33 33
OBERALP:	Andermatt - Sedrun	unspecified	unspecified	every 60 minutes	027 927 77 07, 027 927 77 40
SIMPLON:	Brig - Iselle (Italy)	0445 (0521 from Iselle)	2336 (0018 from Iselle)	9–10 services per day	0900 300 300
VEREINA:	Selfranga (Klosters) - Sagliains	0520 (0550 from Sagliains)	2050 (2120 from Sagliains) Dec. 15 - Apr. 30, Dec. 1-13, services continue for a further 2 hours	every 30 minutes 0620–1920	081 288 37 37

* – Not necessarily daily.

500 BERN and BIEL - ZÜRICH SBB

km		*IR* 1903 y	*IR* 1903 z	*IR* 2005	*IC* 707 ✕	*IR* 2107	*IR* 1909	*ICN* 509	*IR* 2009 Ⓐ	*IC* 809 ✕	*RE* 3209	*IC* 709 (✕) F	*IR* 2109	*IR* 1911	*ICN* 1511 ✕	*IR* 2011	*IC* 811 ✕	*RE* 3211	*IC* 711 ✕	*IR* 2111	*IR* 1915	*ICN* 515	*IR* 2015	*IC* 815 ✕
	Genève Aéroport ✈ **505** d.	...	...	...	...	...	...	...	...	...	...	...	...	...	...	...	...	...	...	...	...	...	...	...
	Genève **505** d.	...	...	...	...	...	...	...	...	...	...	...	...	...	...	...	...	...	0545	...	...	0614	...	...
	Lausanne **505** d.	...	...	...	...	...	...	...	...	...	...	...	...	...	0539	...	...	...	0620	...	...	|	...	...
	Brig **560** d.	...	...	...	...	...	...	...	...	...	...	...	...	...	|	...	0547	...	|	...	...	|	...	0649
0	**Bern** d.	0421	0421	0440	0530r	...	...	...	0539	0602	0607	0632	...	0636	|	0639	0702	0707	0732	...	0736	|	0739	0802
23	Burgdorf d.	|	|	0454	|	...	...	...	0552	|	0620	|	...	|	|	0652	|	0720	|	...	|	|	0752	|
47	Langenthal d.	|	|	0513	|	...	...	...	0611	|	0641	|	...	|	|	0711	|	0741	|	...	|	|	0811	|
	Biel / Bienne d.	|	|	|	|	0515	...	0543	|	|	|	|	0613	|	0644	|	|	|	|	0715	|	0746	|	|
	Solothurn d.	|	|	|	|	0533	...	0601	|	|	|	|	0632	|	0702	|	|	|	|	0733	|	0801	|	|
67	**Olten** a.	0446	0500	0525	0555	0557	...	0618	0623	0628	0654	|	0657	0702	0718	0724	|	0754	|	0757	0802	0818	0824	|
67	**Olten** d.	0448	0501	0535	0557	0559	0603	0620	...	0631	▬	|	0659	0703	0720	0729	|	▬	|	0759	0803	0820	0829	|
80	Aarau d.	0458	0510	0545	|	|	0614	0630	...	|	0653	|	|	0714	0730	|	|	0753	|	|	0814	0830	|	|
90	Lenzburg d.	0506	0518	0554	|	|	|	|	...	|	0700	|	|	|	|	|	|	0800	|	|	|	|	|	|
	Brugg d.	|	|	|	|	|	0630	|	...	|	|	|	|	0730	|	|	|	|	|	|	0830	|	|	|
	Baden a.	|	|	|	|	|	0638	|	...	|	|	|	|	0738	|	|	|	|	|	|	0838	|	|	|
122	**Zürich** HB a.	|	|	0619	0628	0630	0654	0656	...	0702	0722	0728	0730	0754	0756	0802	0758	0822	0828	0830	0854	0856	0902	0858
	Zürich Flughafen ✈ **530/5** a.	0530	0542	...	0650	0646	...	0720	...	0716	...	0750	0746	...	0820	...	0816	...	0850	0846	...	0920	...	0916
	St Gallen **530** a.	...	...	...	0753	|	...	0815	...	|	...	0853	|	...	0915	...	|	...	0953	|	...	1015	...	|
	Konstanz **535** a.	...	...	...	...	0754	...	...	...	|	...	...	0854	...	...	...	|	...	...	0954	...	...	...	|
	Romanshorn **535** a.	...	...	...	...	...	...	...	...	0817	...	...	...	...	...	...	0918	...	...	...	...	...	...	1018

km		*RE* 3215	*IC* 715 (✕)	*IR* 2115	*IR* 1917	*ICN* 1517 ✕	*IR* 2017	*IC* 817 (✕)	*RE* 3217	*IC* 717 ✕	*IR* 2117	*IR* 1919	*ICN* 519	*IR* 2019	*IC* 819 ✕	*RE* 3219	*IC* 719 ✕	*IR* 2119	*IR* 1921	*ICN* 1521 ✕	*IR* 2021	*IC* 821 (✕)	*RE* 3221	*IC* 721 ✕
	Genève Aéroport ✈ **505** d.	...	0636	...	...	...	...	...	...	0736j	...	...	0805j	...	...	...	0836j	...	...	...	...	...	...	0936
	Genève **505** d.	...	0645	...	...	...	...	...	...	0745	...	...	0814	...	...	...	0845	...	...	...	...	...	...	0945
	Lausanne **505** d.	...	0720	...	...	0745	...	...	...	0820	...	...	|	...	...	...	0920	...	...	0945	...	...	...	1020
	Brig **560** d.	...	|	...	...	|	...	0749	...	|	...	...	|	...	0849	...	|	...	...	|	...	0949	...	|
	Bern d.	0807	0832	...	0836	|	0839	0902	0907	0932	...	0936	|	0939	1002	1007	1032	...	1036	|	1039	1102	1107	113
	Burgdorf d.	0820	|	...	|	|	0852	|	0920	|	...	|	|	0952	|	1020	|	...	|	|	1052	|	1120	|
	Langenthal d.	0841	|	...	|	|	0911	|	0941	|	...	|	|	1011	|	1041	|	...	|	|	1111	|	1141	|
0	**Biel / Bienne** d.	|	|	0815	|	0846	|	|	|	|	0915	|	0946	|	|	|	|	1015	|	1046	|	|	|	|
25	Solothurn d.	|	|	0833	|	0901	|	|	|	|	0933	|	1001	|	|	|	|	1033	|	1101	|	|	|	|
60	**Olten** a.	0854	|	0857	0902	0918	0924	|	0954	|	0957	1002	1018	1024	|	1054	|	1057	1102	1118	1124	|	1154	|
60	**Olten** d.	▬	|	0859	0903	0920	0929	|	▬	|	0959	1003	1020	1029	|	▬	|	1059	1103	1120	1129	|	▬	|
73	Aarau d.	0853	|	|	0914	0930	|	|	0953	|	|	1014	1030	|	|	1053	|	|	1114	1130	|	|	1153	|
	Lenzburg d.	0900	|	|	|	|	|	|	1000	|	|	|	|	|	|	1100	|	|	|	|	|	|	1200	|
91	Brugg d.	|	|	|	0930	|	|	|	|	|	|	1030	|	|	|	|	|	|	1130	|	|	|	|	|
100	Baden a.	|	|	|	0938	|	|	|	|	|	|	1038	|	|	|	|	|	|	1138	|	|	|	|	|
122	**Zürich** HB a.	0922	0928	0930	0954	0956	1002	0958	1022	1028	1030	1054	1056	1102	1058	1122	1128	1130	1154	1156	1202	1158	1222	122
	Zürich Flughafen ✈ **530/5** a.	...	0950	0946	...	1020	...	1016	...	1050	1046	...	1120	...	1116	...	1150	1146	...	1220	...	1216	...	125
	St Gallen **530** a.	...	1053	|	...	1115	...	|	...	1153	|	...	1215	...	|	...	1253	|	...	1315	...	|	...	135
	Konstanz **535** a.	...	...	1054	...	...	...	|	...	...	1154	...	...	...	|	...	...	1254	...	...	...	|	...	...
	Romanshorn **535** a.	...	...	...	...	...	...	1118	...	...	...	...	...	...	1218	...	...	...	...	...	...	1318	...	...

F – From Fribourg.
j – Dec. 15 - July 14.
r – Depart 0513 on dates in note **z**.
y – Daily (not Jan. 26, 27, Feb. 17, 23-28, Mar. 3-6, 31, May 12-15, 17-22, 26, June 2, Aug. 11, Sept. 8, 29, 30, Oct. 1, 2, 6-9, 26, 27, Nov. 1-3, 8-10, 17, Dec. 1, 8).
z – Jan. 26, 27, Feb. 17, 23-28, Mar. 3-6, 31, May 12-15, 17-22, 26, June 2, Aug. 11, Sept. 8, 29, 30, Oct. 1, 2, 6-9, 26, 27, Nov. 1-3, 8-10, 17, Dec. 1, 8.

SBB BERN and BIEL - ZÜRICH 500

	IR 2121	IR 1923	ICN 523 ✕	IR 2023		IC 823 ✕	RE 3223	IC 723 ✕	IR 2123	IR 1925	ICN 1525 ✕	IR 2025		IC 825 (✕)	RE 3225	IC 725 ✕	IR 2125	IR 1927	ICN 527	IR 2027		IC 827 ✕	RE 3227	IC 727 ✕
Genève Aéroport ✈ 505 d.	...	...	1009	...	...	...	...	1036j	...	...	...	...	...	...	...	1136j	...	...	1209	...	...	...	...	1236j
Genève 505 d.	...	...	1018	...	...	...	...	1045	...	...	...	...	...	...	...	1145	...	...	1218	...	...	...	...	1245
Lausanne 505 d.	...	...	|	...	...	...	...	1120	...	...	1145	...	...	...	...	1220	...	...	|	...	...	...	...	1320
Brig 560 d.	...	...	|	...	...	1049	...	|	...	...	|	...	...	1149	...	|	...	...	|	...	...	1249	...	|
Bern d.	...	1136	|	1139	...	1202	1207	1232	...	1236	|	1239	...	1302	1307	1332	...	1336	|	1339	...	1402	1407	1432
Burgdorf d.	...	|	|	1152	...	|	1220	|	...	|	|	1252	...	|	1320	|	...	|	|	1352	...	|	1420	|
Langenthal d.	...	|	|	1211	...	|	1241	|	...	|	|	1311	...	|	1341	|	...	|	|	1411	...	|	1441	|
Biel / Bienne d.	1115	|	1146	|	...	|	|	|	1215	|	1246	|	...	|	|	|	1315	|	1346	|	...	|	|	|
Solothurn d.	1133	|	1201	|	...	|	|	|	1233	|	1301	|	...	|	|	|	1333	|	1401	|	...	|	|	|
Olten a.	1157	1202	1218	1224	...	|	1254	|	1257	1302	1318	1324	...	|	1354	|	1357	1402	1418	1424	...	|	1454	|
Olten d.	1159	1203	1220	1229	...	|	—	|	1259	1303	1320	1329	...	|	—	|	1359	1403	1420	1429	...	|	—	|
Aarau d.	|	1214	1230	|	...	|	1253	|	|	1314	1330	|	...	|	1353	|	|	1414	1430	|	...	|	1453	|
Lenzburg d.	|	|	|	|	...	|	1300	|	|	|	|	|	...	|	1400	|	|	|	|	|	...	|	1500	|
Brugg d.	|	1230	|	|	...	|	|	|	|	1330	|	|	...	|	|	|	|	1430	|	|	...	|	|	|
Baden a.	|	1238	|	|	...	|	|	|	|	1338	|	|	...	|	|	|	|	1438	|	|	...	|	|	|
Zürich HB a.	1230	1254	1256	1303	...	1258	1322	1328	1330	1354	1356	1402	...	1358	1422	1428	1430	1454	1456	1502	...	1458	1522	1528
Zürich Flughafen ✈ 530/5 a.	1246	...	1320	...	...	1316	...	1350	1346	...	1420	...	...	1416	...	1450	1446	...	1520	...	...	1516	...	1550
St Gallen 530 a.	|	...	1415	...	...	|	...	1453	|	...	1515	...	...	|	...	1553	|	...	1615	...	...	|	...	1653
Konstanz 535 a.	1354	...	...	...	...	|	...	...	1454	...	...	...	...	|	...	...	1554	...	...	...	...	|	...	...
Romanshorn 535 a.	...	...	...	...	...	1418	...	...	...	...	...	...	...	1518	...	...	...	...	...	...	...	1618	...	...

	IR 2127	IR 1929	ICN 1529 ✕	IR 2029	IC 829 ✕	RE 3229	IC 729 (✕)	IR 2129	IR 1931	ICN 531 ✕	IR 2031		IC 831 ✕	RE 3231	IC 731 ✕	IR 2131	IR 1935	ICN 1535 ✕	IR 2035		IC 835 (✕)	RE 3235	IC 735 (✕)	IR 2135
Genève Aéroport ✈ 505 d.	...	...	...	...	...	...	1336j	...	...	1409	...	...	...	...	1436j	...	...	...	...	...	...	...	1536j	...
Genève 505 d.	...	...	...	...	...	...	1345	...	...	1418	...	...	...	...	1445	...	...	...	...	...	...	...	1545	...
Lausanne 505 d.	...	...	1345	...	...	...	1420	...	...	|	...	...	...	...	1520	...	...	1545	...	...	...	...	1620	...
Brig 560 d.	...	...	|	...	1349	...	|	...	...	|	...	...	1449	...	|	...	...	|	...	...	1549	...	|	...
Bern d.	...	1436	|	1439	1502	1507	1532	...	1536	|	1539	...	1602	1607	1632	...	1636	|	1639	...	1702	1707	1732	...
Burgdorf d.	...	|	|	1452	|	1520	|	...	|	|	1552	...	|	1620	|	...	|	|	1652	...	|	1720	|	...
Langenthal d.	...	|	|	1511	|	1541	|	...	|	|	1611	...	|	1641	|	...	|	|	1711	...	|	1741	|	...
Biel / Bienne d.	1415	|	1446	|	|	|	|	1515	|	1546	|	...	|	|	|	1615	|	1646	|	...	|	|	|	1715
Solothurn d.	1433	|	1501	|	|	|	|	1533	|	1601	|	...	|	|	|	1633	|	1701	|	...	|	|	|	1733
Olten a.	1457	1502	1518	1524	|	1554	|	1557	1602	1618	1624	...	|	1654	|	1657	1702	1718	1724	...	|	1754	|	1757
Olten d.	1459	1503	1520	1529	|	—	|	1559	1603	1620	1629	...	|	—	|	1659	1703	1720	1729	...	|	—	|	1759
Aarau d.	|	1514	1530	|	|	1553	|	|	1614	1630	|	...	|	1653	|	|	1714	1730	|	...	|	1753	|	|
Lenzburg d.	|	|	|	|	|	1600	|	|	|	|	|	...	|	1700	|	|	|	|	|	...	|	1800	|	|
Brugg d.	|	1530	|	|	|	|	|	|	1630	|	|	...	|	|	|	|	1730	|	|	...	|	|	|	|
Baden a.	|	1538	|	|	|	|	|	|	1638	|	|	...	|	|	|	|	1738	|	|	...	|	|	|	|
Zürich HB a.	1530	1554	1556	1602	1558	1622	1628	1630	1654	1656	1702	...	1658	1722	1728	1730	1754	1756	1802	...	1758	1822	1828	1830
Zürich Flughafen ✈ 530/5 a.	1546	...	1620	...	1616	...	1650	1646	...	1720	...	...	1716	...	1750	1746	...	1820	...	...	1816	...	1850	1846
St Gallen 530 a.	|	...	1715	...	|	...	1753	|	...	1815	...	...	|	...	1853	|	...	1915	...	...	|	...	1953	|
Konstanz 535 a.	1654	...	...	...	|	...	...	1754	...	...	...	...	|	...	...	1854	...	...	...	...	|	...	...	1954
Romanshorn 535 a.	...	...	...	...	1718	...	...	...	...	...	...	...	1818	...	...	...	...	...	...	...	1918	...	...	...

	IR 1937	ICN 537	IR 2037	IC 837 ✕	RE 3237		IC 737 ✕	IR 2137	IR 1939	ICN 1539 ✕	IR 2039	IC 839 (✕)	RE 3239	IC 739 ✕	IR 2139	IR 1941	ICN 541 ✕		IR 2041	IC 841 ✕	RE 3241	IC 741 ✕	IR 2141	IR 1943
Genève Aéroport ✈ 505 d.	...	1609	...	...	...	...	1636j	...	...	...	...	...	...	1736j	...	...	1809	...	...	...	...	1836j	...	...
Genève 505 d.	...	1618	...	...	...	...	1645	...	...	...	...	...	...	1745	...	...	1818	...	...	...	...	1845	...	...
Lausanne 505 d.	...	|	...	...	...	...	1720	...	...	1745	...	...	...	1820	...	...	|	...	...	...	...	1920	...	...
Brig 560 d.	...	|	...	1649	...	...	|	...	...	|	...	1749	...	|	...	...	|	...	...	1849	...	|	...	...
Bern d.	1736	|	1739	1802	1807	...	1832	...	1836	|	1839	1902	1907	1932	...	1936	|	...	1939	2002	2007	2032	...	2036
Burgdorf d.	|	|	1752	|	1820	...	|	...	|	|	1852	|	1920	|	...	|	|	...	1952	|	2020	|	...	|
Langenthal d.	|	|	1811	|	1841	...	|	...	|	|	1911	|	1941	|	...	|	|	...	2011	|	2041	|	...	|
Biel / Bienne d.	|	1746	|	|	|	...	|	1815	|	1846	|	|	|	|	1915	|	1946	...	|	|	|	|	2015	|
Solothurn d.	|	1801	|	|	|	...	|	1833	|	1901	|	|	|	|	1933	|	2001	...	|	|	|	|	2033	|
Olten a.	1802	1818	1824	|	1854	...	|	1857	1902	1918	1924	|	1954	|	1957	2002	2018	...	2024	|	2054	|	2057	2102
Olten d.	1803	1820	1829	|	—	...	|	1859	1903	1920	1929	|	—	|	1959	2003	2020	...	2029	|	—	|	2059	2103
Aarau d.	1814	1830	|	|	1853	...	|	|	1914	1930	|	|	1953	|	|	2014	2030	...	|	|	2053	|	|	2114
Lenzburg d.	|	|	|	|	1900	...	|	|	|	|	|	|	2000	|	|	|	|	...	|	|	2100	|	|	|
Brugg d.	1830	|	|	|	|	...	|	|	1930	|	|	|	|	|	|	2030	|	...	|	|	|	|	|	2130
Baden a.	1838	|	|	|	|	...	|	|	1938	|	|	|	|	|	|	2038	|	...	|	|	|	|	|	2138
Zürich HB a.	1854	1856	1902	1858	1922	...	1928	1930	1954	1956	2002	1958	2022	2028	2030	2054	2056	...	2102	2058	2122	2128	2130	2154
Zürich Flughafen ✈ 530/5 a.	...	1920	...	1916	...	...	1950	1946	...	2020	...	2016	...	2050	2046	...	2120	...	...	2116	...	2150	...	...
St Gallen 530 a.	...	2015	...	|	...	...	2053	|	...	2115	...	|	...	2153	|	...	2215	...	...	|	...	2253	...	...
Konstanz 535 a.	...	...	...	|	...	...	...	2054	...	...	...	|	...	...	2154	...	...	...	...	|	...	...	...	...
Romanshorn 535 a.	...	...	...	2018	...	...	...	...	...	...	...	2118	...	...	...	...	...	...	...	2218	...	...	...	...

	ICN 1543 ✕	IR 2043	IC 843 (✕)	RE 3243	IR 2143	IC 743 ✕	IR 1945		ICN 545 ✕	IR 2045	IC 845	RE 3245	IC 745 ✕	IR 1947		IC 847	ICN 1547	RE 3647	RE 3247	IC 747	IC 849	ICN 1549	RE 3249	IC 803 m
Genève Aéroport ✈ 505 d.	...	...	...	...	...	1936j	...	...	2009	...	...	...	2036j	...	...	...	...	...	...	2136j	...	...	...	...
Genève 505 d.	...	...	...	...	...	1945	...	...	2018	...	...	...	2045	...	...	...	...	...	...	2145	...	...	...	...
Lausanne 505 d.	1945	...	...	...	...	2020	...	...	|	...	...	...	2120	...	...	...	2145	...	...	2220	...	...	...	2345
Brig 560 d.	|	...	1949	...	...	|	...	...	|	...	...	...	|	...	...	...	|	...	...	|	...	...	...	|
Bern d.	|	2039	2102	2107	...	2132	...	...	|	2137	2202	2207	2232	...	...	2302	|	...	2307	2332	0002	...	0007	0102
Burgdorf d.	|	2052	|	2120	...	|	...	...	|	2152	|	2222	|	...	...	|	|	...	2322	|	|	...	0022	|
Langenthal d.	|	2111	|	2141	...	|	...	...	|	2211	|	2242	|	...	...	|	|	...	2342	|	|	...	0042	|
Biel / Bienne d.	2046	|	|	|	2115	|	...	...	2146	|	|	|	|	...	...	|	2246	...	|	|	|	2346	|	|
Solothurn d.	2101	|	|	|	2133	|	...	...	2203	|	|	|	|	...	...	|	2305	...	|	|	|	0005	|	|
Olten a.	2118	2124	|	2154	2157	2158	...	...	2219	2224	2228	2254	2258	...	...	2328	2330	...	2354	2358	0028	0030	0056	0128
Olten d.	2120	...	|	—	...	2200	2203	...	2220	...	2230	—	2300	2303	...	2330	2335	2340	—	0000	0033	0035	...	0133
Aarau d.	2130	...	|	2153	...	|	2214	...	2230	...	|	2253	|	2314	...	|	2345	2349	2353	0009	|	0045	...	0143
Lenzburg d.	|	...	|	2200	...	|	|	...	|	...	|	2300	|	|	...	|	|	|	0000	|	|	0052	...	|
Brugg d.	|	...	|	|	...	|	2230	...	|	...	|	|	|	2330	...	|	|	0003	|	|	|	|	...	|
Baden a.	|	...	|	|	...	|	2238	...	|	...	|	|	|	2338	...	|	|	0013	|	|	|	|	...	|
Zürich HB a.	2156	...	2158	2222	...	2231	2254	...	2256	...	2301	2322	2331	2354	...	0001	0010	0042	0022	0033	0104	0112	...	0207
Zürich Flughafen ✈ 530/5 a.	2220	...	2216	...	...	...	...	...	2320	...	2316	...	...	...	...	...	0027	...	...	...	...	...	...	...
St Gallen 530 a.	2315	...	|	...	...	...	...	...	0018	...	|	...	...	...	...	...	0125	...	...	...	...	...	...	...
Konstanz 535 a.	...	...	|	...	...	...	...	...	...	...	|	...	...	...	...	...	...	...	...	...	...	...	...	...
Romanshorn 535 a.	...	...	2318	...	...	...	...	...	...	...	0018	...	...	...	...	...	...	...	...	...	...	...	...	...

j – Dec. 15 - July 14.

m – ⑤⑥ (not Apr. 18).

500 ZÜRICH - BIEL and BERN SBB

	RE 3206 Ⓐ	IR 2006	IC 706	IR 2106	RE 3208	IR 2008	IC 808 ✕	ICN 508	IR 1908	IR 2108	IC 708 ✕	RE 3708	IC 1008 🍷 Ⓐ		IR 2010	IC 810 (✕)	ICN 1510 ✕	IR 1910	IR 2110	IC 710 ✕	RE 3710	IC 1012 🍷 Ⓐ	IR 2012	IC 812 ✕
Romanshorn **535** d.	...	...	...	...	...	...	...	...	...	...	...	...	...	...	...	0538	...	...	...	...	...	...	...	0638
Konstanz **535** d.	...	...	...	...	...	...	...	...	...	...	...	...	...	...	...	|	...	...	0603	...	...	...	...	|
St Gallen **530** d.	...	...	...	...	...	...	...	...	...	...	0511	...	...	...	...	|	0544	...	|	0611	...	...	...	|
Zürich Flughafen ✈ **530/5** d.	...	...	...	...	...	...	...	...	...	...	0613	...	...	...	...	0640	0643	...	0710	0713	...	...	...	0743
Zürich HB d.	...	...	0521	...	...	0557	0602	0604	0606	0630	0632	0638	0649	...	0657	0702	0704	0706	0730	0732	0738	0749	0757	0802
Baden d.	...	...	|	...	...	|	|	|	0622	|	|	|	|	...	|	|	|	0722	|	|	|	|	|	|
Brugg d.	...	...	|	...	...	|	|	|	0632	|	|	|	|	...	|	|	|	0732	|	|	|	|	|	|
Lenzburg d.	...	...	0541	...	...	|	|	|	|	|	|	0658	|	...	|	|	|	|	|	|	0758	|	|	|
Aarau d.	...	...	0549	...	...	|	|	0629	0647	|	|	0705	|	...	|	|	0729	0747	|	|	0805	|	|	|
Olten a.	...	...	0558	...	...	0628	|	0638	0656	0700	|	▬	|	...	0728	|	0738	0756	0800	|	▬	|	0828	|
Olten d.	0506	0536	0603	0603	0606	0636	|	0640	0658	0703	|	0706	|	...	0736	|	0740	0758	0803	|	0806	|	0836	|
Solothurn d.	|	|	|	0628	|	|	|	0659	|	0728	|	|	|	...	|	|	0759	|	0828	|	|	|	|	|
Biel / Bienne a.	|	|	|	0645	|	|	|	0713	|	0745	|	|	|	...	|	|	0813	|	0845	|	|	|	|	|
Langenthal d.	0518	0549	|	...	0618	0649	|	|	|	...	|	0718	|	...	0749	|	|	|	...	|	0818	|	0849	|
Burgdorf d.	0538	0607	|	...	0638	0707	|	|	|	...	|	0738	|	...	0807	|	|	|	...	|	0838	|	0907	|
Bern a.	0553	0621	0628	...	0653	0721	0658	|	0725	...	0728	0753	0749	...	0821	0758	|	0825	...	0828	0853	0849	0921	0858
Brig **560** a.	...	...	|	...	...	...	0811	|	...	...	|	...	...	...	...	0911	|	...	...	|	...	...	...	1011
Lausanne **505** a.	...	...	0740	...	...	...	...	|	...	...	0840	...	...	...	...	...	0915	...	...	0940	...	...	...	...
Genève **505** a.	...	...	0815	...	...	...	...	0842	...	...	0915	...	...	...	...	...	...	...	...	1015	...	...	...	...
Genève Aéroport ✈ **505** a.	...	...	0824j	...	...	...	...	0851	...	...	0924j	...	...	...	...	...	...	...	...	1024j	...	...	...	...

	ICN 512	IR 1912	IR 2112	IC 712 ✕	RE 3712	IR 2016	IC 816 (✕)	ICN 1514 ✕	IR 1916		IR 2116	IC 716 ✕	RE 3716	IR 2018	IC 818 ✕	ICN 518	IR 1918		IR 2118	IC 718 (✕)	RE 3718	IR 2020	IC 820 ✕	ICN 1520 ✕
Romanshorn **535** d.	...	...	...	...	...	...	0741	...	...	...	...	...	...	...	0841	...	...	...	...	...	...	...	0941	...
Konstanz **535** d.	...	...	0703	...	...	...	|	...	...	...	0803	...	...	...	|	...	...	...	0903	...	...	...	|	...
St Gallen **530** d.	0642	...	|	0711	...	...	|	0748	...	...	|	0811	...	...	|	0848	...	...	|	0911	...	...	|	0948
Zürich Flughafen ✈ **530/5** d.	0739	...	0810	0813	...	...	0840	0843	...	...	0910	0913	...	...	0940	0943	...	...	1010	1013	...	...	1040	1043
Zürich HB d.	0804	0806	0830	0832	0838	0857	0902	0904	0906	...	0930	0932	0938	0957	1002	1004	1006	...	1030	1032	1038	1057	1102	1104
Baden d.	|	0822	|	|	|	|	|	|	0922	...	|	|	|	|	|	|	1022	...	|	|	|	|	|	|
Brugg d.	|	0832	|	|	|	|	|	|	0932	...	|	|	|	|	|	|	1032	...	|	|	|	|	|	|
Lenzburg d.	|	|	|	|	0858	|	|	|	|	...	|	|	0958	|	|	|	|	...	|	|	1058	|	|	|
Aarau d.	0829	0847	|	|	0905	|	|	0929	0947	...	|	|	1005	|	|	1029	1047	...	|	|	1105	|	|	1129
Olten a.	0838	0856	0900	|	▬	0928	|	0938	0956	...	1000	|	▬	1028	|	1038	1056	...	1100	|	▬	1128	|	1138
Olten d.	0840	0858	0903	|	0906	0936	|	0940	0958	...	1003	|	1006	1036	|	1040	1058	...	1103	|	1106	1136	|	1140
Solothurn d.	0859	|	0928	|	|	|	|	0959	|	...	1028	|	|	|	|	1059	|	...	1128	|	|	|	|	1159
Biel / Bienne a.	0913	|	0945	|	|	|	|	1013	|	...	1045	|	|	|	|	1113	|	...	1145	|	|	|	|	1213
Langenthal d.	|	|	...	|	0918	0949	|	|	|	...	...	|	1018	1049	|	|	|	...	...	|	1118	1149	|	|
Burgdorf d.	|	|	...	|	0938	1007	|	|	|	...	...	|	1038	1107	|	|	|	...	...	|	1138	1207	|	|
Bern a.	|	0925	...	0928	0953	1021	0958	|	1025	...	...	1028	1053	1121	1058	|	1125	...	...	1128	1153	1221	1158	|
Brig **560** a.	|	...	...	|	...	...	1111	|	...	...	...	|	...	...	1211	|	...	...	...	|	...	...	1311	|
Lausanne **505** a.	|	...	...	1040	...	...	...	1115	...	...	...	1140	...	...	...	|	...	...	...	1240	...	...	...	1315
Genève **505** a.	1042	...	...	1115	...	...	...	...	...	...	...	1215	...	...	...	1242	...	...	...	1315	...	...	...	...
Genève Aéroport ✈ **505** a.	1051	...	...	1124j	...	...	...	...	...	...	...	1224j	...	...	...	1251	...	...	...	1324j	...	...	...	...

	IR 1920	IR 2120	IC 720 ✕	RE 3720	IR 2022	IC 822 ✕	ICN 522 ✕	IR 1922		IR 2122	IC 722 (✕)	RE 3722	IR 2024	IC 824 (✕)	ICN 1524 ✕	IR 1924	IR 2124	IC 724 ✕	RE 3724	IR 2026	IC 826 ✕	ICN 526 ✕	IR 1926	IR 2126
Romanshorn **535** d.	...	...	...	...	...	1041	...	...	...	...	...	...	...	1141	...	...	...	...	...	...	1241	...	...	...
Konstanz **535** d.	...	1003	...	...	...	|	...	...	...	1103	...	...	...	|	...	...	1203	...	...	...	|	...	...	1303
St Gallen **530** d.	...	|	1011	...	...	|	1048	...	...	|	1111	...	...	|	1148	...	|	1211	...	...	|	1248	...	|
Zürich Flughafen ✈ **530/5** d.	...	1110	1113	...	...	1140	1143	...	...	1210	1213	...	...	1240	1243	...	1310	1313	...	...	1340	1343	...	1410
Zürich HB d.	1106	1130	1132	1138	1157	1202	1204	1206	...	1230	1232	1238	1257	1302	1304	1306	1330	1332	1338	1357	1402	1404	1406	1430
Baden d.	1122	|	|	|	|	|	|	1222	...	|	|	|	|	|	|	1322	|	|	|	|	|	|	1422	|
Brugg d.	1132	|	|	|	|	|	|	1232	...	|	|	|	|	|	|	1332	|	|	|	|	|	|	1432	|
Lenzburg d.	|	|	|	1158	|	|	|	|	...	|	|	1258	|	|	|	|	|	|	1358	|	|	|	|	|
Aarau d.	1147	|	|	1205	|	|	1229	1247	...	|	|	1305	|	|	1329	1347	|	|	1405	|	|	1429	1447	|
Olten a.	1156	1200	|	▬	1228	|	1238	1256	...	1300	|	▬	1328	|	1338	1356	1400	|	▬	1428	|	1438	1456	1500
Olten d.	1158	1203	|	1206	1236	|	1240	1258	...	1303	|	1306	1336	|	1340	1358	1403	|	1406	1436	|	1440	1458	1503
Solothurn d.	|	1228	|	|	|	|	1259	|	...	1328	|	|	|	|	1359	|	1428	|	|	|	|	1459	|	1528
Biel / Bienne a.	|	1245	|	|	|	|	1313	|	...	1345	|	|	|	|	1413	|	1445	|	|	|	|	1513	|	1545
Langenthal d.	|	...	|	1218	1249	|	|	|	...	...	|	1318	1349	|	|	|	...	|	1418	1449	|	|	|	...
Burgdorf d.	|	...	|	1238	1307	|	|	|	...	...	|	1338	1407	|	|	|	...	|	1438	1507	|	|	|	...
Bern a.	1225	...	1228	1253	1321	1258	|	1325	...	...	1328	1353	1421	1358	|	1425	...	1428	1453	1521	1458	|	1525	...
Brig **560** a.	...	...	|	...	...	1411	|	...	...	...	|	...	...	1511	|	...	...	|	...	...	1611	|	...	...
Lausanne **505** a.	...	...	1340	...	...	...	|	...	...	...	1440	...	...	...	1515	...	...	1540	...	...	...	|	...	...
Genève **505** a.	...	...	1415	...	...	...	1442	...	...	...	1515	...	...	...	...	...	...	1615	...	...	...	1642	...	...
Genève Aéroport ✈ **505** a.	...	...	1424j	...	...	...	1451	...	...	...	1524j	...	...	...	...	...	...	1624j	...	...	...	1651	...	...

	IC 726 ✕	RE 3726	IR 2028	IC 828 (✕)	ICN 1528 ✕	IR 1928	IR 2128	IC 728 ✕	RE 3728	IR 2030	IC 830 ✕	ICN 530	IR 1930		IR 2130	IC 730 ✕	RE 3730	IR 2032	IC 832 (✕)	ICN 1532 ✕	IR 1932	IR 2132	IC 732 ✕	RE 3732
Romanshorn **535** d.	...	...	...	1341	...	...	...	...	...	...	1441	...	...	...	...	...	...	...	1541	...	...	...	...	...
Konstanz **535** d.	...	...	...	|	...	...	1403	...	...	...	|	...	...	...	1503	...	...	...	|	...	...	1603	...	...
St Gallen **530** d.	1311	...	...	|	1348	...	|	1411	...	...	|	1448	...	...	|	1511	...	...	|	1548	...	|	1611	...
Zürich Flughafen ✈ **530/5** d.	1413	...	...	1440	1443	...	1510	1513	...	...	1540	1543	...	...	1610	1613	...	...	1640	1643	...	1710	1713	...
Zürich HB d.	1432	1438	1457	1502	1504	1506	1530	1532	1538	1557	1602	1604	1606	...	1630	1632	1638	1657	1702	1704	1706	1730	1732	1738
Baden d.	|	|	|	|	|	1522	|	|	|	|	|	|	1622	...	|	|	|	|	|	|	1722	|	|	|
Brugg d.	|	|	|	|	|	1532	|	|	|	|	|	|	1632	...	|	|	|	|	|	|	1732	|	|	|
Lenzburg d.	|	1458	|	|	|	|	|	|	1558	|	|	|	|	...	|	|	1658	|	|	|	|	|	|	1758
Aarau d.	|	1505	|	|	1529	1547	|	|	1605	|	|	1629	1647	...	|	|	1705	|	|	1729	1747	|	|	1805
Olten a.	|	▬	1528	|	1538	1556	1600	|	▬	1628	|	1638	1656	...	1700	|	▬	1728	|	1738	1756	1800	|	▬
Olten d.	|	1506	1536	|	1540	1558	1603	|	1606	1636	|	1640	1658	...	1703	|	1706	1736	|	1740	1758	1803	|	1806
Solothurn d.	|	|	|	|	1559	|	1628	|	|	|	|	1659	|	...	1728	|	|	|	|	1759	|	1828	|	|
Biel / Bienne a.	|	|	|	|	1613	|	1645	|	|	|	|	1713	|	...	1745	|	|	|	|	1813	|	1845	|	|
Langenthal d.	|	1518	1549	|	|	|	...	|	1618	1649	|	|	|	...	...	|	1718	1749	|	|	|	...	|	1818
Burgdorf d.	|	1538	1607	|	|	|	...	|	1638	1707	|	|	|	...	...	|	1738	1807	|	|	|	...	|	1838
Bern a.	1528	1553	1621	1558	|	1625	...	1628	1653	1721	1658	|	1725	...	...	1728	1753	1821	1758	|	1825	...	1828	1853
Brig **560** a.	|	...	...	1711	|	...	...	|	...	...	1811	|	...	...	...	|	...	...	1911	|	...	...	|	...
Lausanne **505** a.	1640	...	...	...	1715	...	...	1740	...	...	...	|	...	...	...	1840	...	...	...	1915	...	...	1940	...
Genève **505** a.	1715	...	...	...	...	...	...	1815	...	...	...	1842	...	...	...	1915	...	...	...	...	...	...	2015	...
Genève Aéroport ✈ **505** a.	1724j	...	...	...	...	...	...	1824j	...	...	...	1851	...	...	...	1924j	...	...	...	...	...	...	2024j	...

j – Dec. 15 - July 14.

SBB — ZÜRICH - BIEL and BERN — 500

km (via hsl)		IR 2036	IC 836 ✕	ICN 536	IR 1936	IR 2136	IC 736 ✕	RE 3736	IR 2038	IC 838 ✕	ICN 1538 ✕	IR 1938		IR 2138	IC 738 (✕)	RE 3738	IR 2040	IC 840 ✕	ICN 540 ✕	IR 1940	IR 2140	IC 740 ✕	RE 3740	IR 2042
	Romanshorn **535** d.	...	1641	...	...	...	...	...	...	1741	...	...	...	...	...	...	...	1841	...	...	...	...	...	...
	Konstanz **535** d.	...	|	...	...	1703	...	...	...	|	...	...	...	1803	...	...	...	|	...	...	1903	...	...	...
	St Gallen **530** d.	...	|	1648	...	|	1711	...	...	|	1748	...	...	|	1811	...	...	|	1848	...	|	1911	...	...
	Zürich Flughafen + **530/5** d.	...	1740	1743	...	1810	1813	...	...	1840	1843	...	...	1910	1913	...	...	1940	1943	...	2010	2013	...	...
	Zürich HB d.	1757	1802	1804	1806	1830	1832	1838	1857	1902	1904	1906	...	1930	1932	1938	1957	2002	2004	2006	2030	2032	2038	2057
	Baden d.	|	|	|	1822	|	|	|	|	|	|	1922	...	|	|	|	|	|	|	2022	|	|	|	|
	Brugg d.	|	|	|	1832	|	|	|	|	|	|	1932	...	|	|	|	|	|	|	2032	|	|	|	|
	Lenzburg d.	|	|	|	|	|	|	1858	|	|	|	|	...	|	|	1958	|	|	|	|	|	|	2058	|
	Aarau d.	|	|	1829	1847	|	|	1905	|	|	1929	1947	...	|	|	2005	|	|	2029	2047	|	|	2105	|
	Olten a.	1828	|	1838	1856	1900	|	—	1928	|	1938	1956	...	2000	|	—	2028	|	2038	2056	2100	|	—	2128
0	**Olten** d.	1836	|	1840	1858	1903	|	1906	1936	|	1940	1958	...	2003	|	2006	2036	|	2040	2058	2103	|	2106	2137
	Solothurn d.	|	|	1859	|	1928	|	|	|	|	1959	|	...	2028	|	|	|	|	2059	|	2128	|	|	|
	Biel/Bienne a.	|	|	1913	|	1945	|	|	|	|	2013	|	...	2045	|	|	|	|	2113	|	2145	|	|	|
	Langenthal d.	1849	|	|	|	...	|	1918	1949	|	|	|	...	...	|	2018	2049	|	|	|	...	|	2118	2149
	Burgdorf d.	1907	|	|	|	...	|	1938	2007	|	|	|	...	...	|	2038	2107	|	|	|	...	|	2138	2209
62	**Bern** a.	1921	1858	|	1925	...	1928	1953	2021	1958	|	2025	...	...	2028	2053	2121	2058	|	2125	...	2128	2153	2223
	Brig **560** a.	...	2011	|	...	...	|	...	...	2111	|	...	...	...	|	...	...	...	|	...	...	|	...	...
	Lausanne **505** a.	...	...	|	...	...	2040	...	...	...	2115	...	...	...	2140	...	...	...	|	...	...	2240	...	...
	Genève **505** a.	...	...	2046	...	...	2115	...	...	...	...	...	...	...	2215	...	...	...	2246	...	...	2327	...	...
	Genève Aéroport + **505** a.	...	...	2055j	...	...	2124j	...	...	...	...	...	...	...	2224j	...	...	...	...	...	...	2338j	...	...

km (via hsl)		IC 842 (✕)	ICN 1542 ✕	IR 1942	IR 2142	IC 742 (✕) F	RE 3742	IC 844 ✕	IR 2044	ICN 1544 ✕	IR 1944	IC 744 ✕	RE 3744	IC 846	IR 2046	ICN 1546	IR 1946	IC 746	RE 3746	IC 800	IR 1948	IR 2002 n	IC 802 n	
	Romanshorn **535** d.	1941	...	...	...	...	...	2041	...	...	...	...	...	2141	...	...	...	...	...	...	...	...	...	...
	Konstanz **535** d.	|	...	...	2003	...	...	|	...	...	...	...	...	|	...	...	...	...	...	...	...	...	...	...
	St Gallen **530** d.	|	1948	...	|	2011	...	|	...	2048	...	2111	...	|	...	2148	...	...	...	...	...	...	...	...
	Zürich Flughafen + **530/5** d.	2040	2043	...	2110	2113	...	2140	...	2143	...	2213	...	2240	...	2243	...	...	...	...	...	...	...	...
	Zürich HB d.	2102	2104	2106	2130	2132	2138	2202	...	2204	2206	2232	2238	2302	...	2304	2306	2332	2338	0002	0006	...	0102	...
	Baden d.	|	|	2122	|	|	|	|	...	|	2222	|	|	|	...	|	2322	|	|	|	0022	...	|	...
	Brugg d.	|	|	2132	|	|	|	|	...	|	2232	|	|	|	...	|	2332	|	|	|	0030	...	|	...
	Lenzburg d.	|	|	|	|	|	2158	|	...	|	|	|	2258	|	...	|	|	|	2358	|	...	...	|	...
	Aarau d.	|	2129	2147	|	|	2205	|	...	2229	2247	|	2305	|	...	2329	2347	|	0005	|	...	...	|	...
	Olten a.	|	2138	2155	2200	|	...	2232	...	2238	2256	2301	...	2332	...	2338	2356	0001	...	0031	...	...	0131	...
0	**Olten** d.	|	2140	...	2203	|	...	2235	2237	2240	...	2304	...	2335	2337	2340	...	0004	...	0035	...	0037	0135	...
	Solothurn d.	|	2159	...	2228	|	...	|	|	2258	...	|	...	|	|	0005	...	|	...	|	...	|	|	...
58	**Biel/Bienne** a.	|	2213	...	2245	|	...	|	|	2314	...	|	...	|	|	0022	...	|	...	|	...	|	|	...
	Langenthal d.	|	|	...	...	|	...	|	2249	|	...	|	...	|	2349	|	...	|	...	|	...	0049	|	...
	Burgdorf d.	|	|	...	...	|	...	|	2309	|	...	|	...	|	0009	|	...	|	...	|	...	0109	|	...
	Bern a.	2158	|	...	...	2228	...	2302	2324	|	...	2331	...	0002	0023	|	...	0031	...	0102	...	0123	0202	...
	Brig **560** a.	...	|	...	...	...	...	...	...	|	...	...	...	...	...	|	...	...	...	...	...	...	...	...
	Lausanne **505** a.	...	2315	...	...	...	...	...	...	0015	...	...	...	...	...	0124q	...	...	...	...	...	...	...	...
	Genève **505** a.	...	...	...	...	...	...	...	...	...	...	...	...	...	...	...	...	...	...	...	...	...	...	...
	Genève Aéroport + **505** a.	...	...	...	...	...	...	...	...	...	...	...	...	...	...	...	...	...	...	...	...	...	...	...

F – To Fribourg. **j** – Dec. 15 - July 14. **n** – ⑥⑦ (not Apr. 19). **q** – ⑥⑦ (not Apr. 19, Aug. 2).

NStCM. Narrow gauge. 2nd class only — NYON - ST CERGUE - LA CURE — 501

km		j	⚒	j		j		j							j			j							k
0	**Nyon** d.	0522	0552g	0622	0652	0722	0752	0822	0852	0952	1052	...	1152	1222	and at the same minutes past each hour until	1852	1922	...	1952	2052	2152	2322	...	0057
19	St Cergue d.	0601	0631	0701	0731	0759	0831	0859	0931	1031	1131	...	1231	1259		1931	1959	...	2031	2130	2226	2356	...	0131
27	La Cure a.	0614	0644	0714	0744	...	0844	...	0944	1044	1144	...	1244	...		1944	...	...	2044	...	...	...	...	...

	j		j	⚒	j		j						j			j			j			j			
La Cure d.	...	...	0616	0646	0716	0748	...	0848	0948	1048	1148	1248	...	1348	1448	...	and at the same minutes past each hour until	1748	...	1848	1948	...	2048	...	...
St Cergue d.	0533	0604	0633	0704	0733	0804	0833	0904	1004	1104	1204	1304	1333	1404	1504	1533		1804	1833	1904	2004	2033	2104	2233	0004
Nyon a.	0608	0638	0708	0738	0808	0838	0908	0938	1038	1138	1238	1338	1408	1438	1538	1608		1838	1908	1938	2038	2108	2138	2308	0038

g – ⑥ (also Sept. 22). **j** – Ⓐ (not Sept. 22). **k** – ⑥⑦ (not Apr. 19).

MBC. Narrow gauge. 2nd class only — MORGES - BIÈRE and L'ISLE MONT LA VILLE — 502

Subject to 🚌 replacement August 8 - 17

km		⚒		⚒		⚒		⚒			⚒		⚒		⚒			⚒		⚒					⑥⑦ supplement
0	**Morges** d.	0615	0704	0744	0846	0946	1046	1136	...	1222	1304	1404	1504	1604	1646	1734	...	1808	1904	1946	2034	2204	2336	...	0116
12	Apples a.	0632	0721	0801	0903	1003	1103	1153	...	1239	1321	1421	1521	1621	1703	1751	...	1825	1921	2003	2051	2221	2353	...	0133
19	**Bière** a.	0643	0732	0812	0914	1014	1114	1204	...	1250	1332	1432	1532	1632	1714	1802	...	1836	1932	2014	2102	2232	0004	...	0144

	⚒		⚒	Ⓐ		⚒		⚒		⚒		⚒		⚒		⚒			⚒					⑥⑦
Bière d.	0542	0623	0654	0712	0752	0854	0954	1054	1144	1212	1312	1354	1454	1612	1654	1724	...	1816	1854	1954	2124	2254	...	0024
Apples d.	0552	0633	0704	0722	0802	0904	1004	1104	1154	1222	1322	1404	1504	1622	1704	1734	...	1826	1904	2004	2134	2304	...	0034
Morges a.	0612	0653	0724	0742	0822	0924	1024	1124	1214	1242	1342	1424	1524	1642	1724	1754	...	1846	1924	2024	2154	2324	...	0054

km			⚒									Ⓐ			⚒			⚒			⑤⑥	⑥⑦		⑥⑦ supplement	
0	Apples d.	0559	0633	0722	...	0904	1104	1240	...	1422	1622	1704	...	1752	1826	1922	...	2004	2052	...	2222	2354	...	0134	...
11	L'Isle Mont la Ville d.	0613	0647	0736	...	0918	1118	1254	...	1436	1636	1718	...	1806	1840	1936	...	2018	2106	...	2236	0008	...	0148	...

		⚒											Ⓐ			⚒			⚒			⑤⑥		⑥⑦
L'Isle Mont la Ville d.	0616	0648	...	0745	0947	...	1137	1305	...	1447	1647	...	1735	1809	...	1847	1947	...	2035	2117	...	2247	...	0017
Apples a.	0631	0703	...	0800	1002	...	1152	1320	...	1502	1702	...	1750	1824	...	1902	2002	...	2050	2132	...	2302	...	0032

supplement – Supplement payable.

SBB — YVERDON - FRIBOURG — 503

km		Ⓐ		Ⓐ						K
0	**Yverdon** d.	0521	0602	0621	0702	and hourly until	2102	2202	2302	0048
18	Estavayer-le-Lac d.	0539	0618	0639	0718		2118	2218	2318	0104
28	Payerne d.	0553	0629	0653	0730		2130	2230	2328	0114
50	**Fribourg** a.	0621	0658	0721	0758		2158	2258	...	...

							G	†	H
Fribourg d.	...	0601a	0701	0803	and hourly until	2203	2303	...	2338
Payerne d.	0531	0631	0731	0831		2231	2331	2331	0010
Estavayer-le-Lac d.	0540	0640	0740	0840		2240	2340j	2340	0019
Yverdon a.	0557	0657	0757	0857		2257	2357j	2357	0036

– ①②③④⑦ (also Apr. 18, Aug. 1).
– ⑤⑥ (not Apr. 18, Aug. 1).
K – ⑥⑦ (also Apr. 18, 21, May 29, June 9, Aug. 1).
a – Ⓐ only.
j – Not Apr. 21, May 29, June 9.

SBB — LAUSANNE - PALÉZIEUX - PAYERNE — 504

km						▲				⑥⑦
0	**Lausanne 505** d.	0524	0624	0724	0824	and hourly until	2124	...	2324	0247
21	Palézieux **505** d.	0541	0641	0741	0841		2141	...	2348	0309
38	Moudon d.	0600	0700	0800	0900		2200	...	0007	...
58	Payerne **511** a.	0621	0722	0821	0919		2219	...	0026	...

						▲			
Payerne **511** d.	0539	0639	0738	...	0839	and hourly until	2239	...	...
Moudon d.	0559	0659	0759	...	0859		2259	...	...
Palézieux **505** d.	0618	0718	0818	...	0918		2318	...	...
Lausanne 505 a.	0636	0736	0836	...	0936		2336	...	...

▲ – Times may vary by ± 3 minutes on some journeys.

505 GENÈVE - LAUSANNE - BIEL, BASEL and BERN

SBB

km		ICN 509	ICN 1609	IR 2509	IC 709	ICN 1511	IR 2511	ICN 611	RE 2705	IC 711	RE 2605	IR 2515	ICN 515	ICN 1615	IC 715	RE 2607	IR 2517	ICN 617	ICN 1517	IC 717	RE 2609	IR 2519	ICN 519	ICN 1619	IC 719	RE 2611
				m	(✕)	✕				✕				✕	✕			✕	✕	✕					✕	
0	Genève A ✈ 570 d.	...	...	...	...	...	...	...	0507	...	...	...	...	...	0636	...	0702j	0705j	...	0736j	...	0802j	0805j	...	0836j	...
6	**Genève 570** d.	...	...	...	...	...	...	...	0521	0545	0551	0611	0614	...	0645	0651	0711	0714	...	0745	0751	0811	0814	...	0845	0851
27	Nyon **570** d.	...	...	...	...	...	...	...	0537	|	0607	|	0627	...	|	0707	|	0727	...	|	0807	|	0827	...	|	0907
53	Morges **570** d.	...	...	...	...	...	...	...	0558	|	0628	|	0641	...	|	0728	|	0741	...	|	0828	|	0841	...	|	0928
66	**Lausanne 570** a.	...	...	...	...	...	...	...	0609	0618	0639	0645	|	...	0718	0739	0746	|	...	0818	0839	0846	|	...	0918	0939
	Lausanne 504 d.	...	...	0445	...	0539	0545	...	...	0620	0641	0647	|	0645	0720	0742	0750	|	0745	0820	0842	0850	|	0845	0920	0942
	Yverdon d.	...	...	|	...	0604	|	...	...	|	|	|	0704	0707	|	|	|	0804	0807	|	|	|	0904	0907	|	|
	Neuchâtel d.	...	...	|	...	0624	|	...	...	|	|	|	0724	0727	|	|	|	0824	0827	|	|	|	0924	0927	|	|
	Biel / Bienne a.	...	...	|	...	0641	|	...	...	|	|	|	0741	0743k	|	|	|	0841	0843k	|	|	|	0941	0943k	|	|
	Biel / Bienne d.	0543	0549	|	...	0644	|	0649	...	|	|	|	0746	0749	|	|	|	0849	0846	|	|	|	0946	0949	|	|
	Moutier d.	|	0608	|	...	|	|	0708	...	|	|	|	|	0808	|	|	|	0908	|	|	|	|	|	1008	|	|
	Delémont d.	|	0623	|	...	|	|	0723	...	|	|	|	|	0823	|	|	|	0923	|	|	|	|	|	1023	|	|
	Basel a.	|	0653	|	...	|	|	0753	...	|	|	|	|	0853	|	|	|	0953	|	|	|	|	|	1053	|	|
87	Palézieux **504** d.	|	...	0501	...	|	0601	...	...	|	0658	0703	|	...	|	0758	|	...	|	|	0858	|	|	...	|	0958
106	Romont **568** d.	|	...	0516	...	|	0616	...	...	|	0713	|	|	...	|	0813	|	...	|	|	0913	|	|	...	|	1013
132	Fribourg **508 568** d.	|	...	0534	0604	|	0634	...	...	0704	...	0734	|	...	0804	...	0834	...	|	0904	...	0934	|	...	1004	...
163	**Bern** a.	|	...	0556	0626	|	0656	...	...	0726	...	0756	|	...	0826	...	0856	...	|	0926	...	0956	|	...	1026	...
	Olten **500** a.	0618	...	|	|	0718	|	...	...	|	...	|	0818	...	|	...	|	...	0918	|	...	|	1018	...	|	...
	Luzern **565** a.	|	...	0700	|	|	0800	...	...	|	...	0900	|	...	|	...	1000	...	|	|	...	1100	|	...	|	...
	Zürich HB **500** a.	0656	...	...	0728	0756	...	...	...	0828	...	...	0856	...	0928	...	...	...	0956	1028	...	...	1056	...	1128	...
	Zürich Flug ✈ **530** a.	0720	...	...	0750	0820	...	...	...	0850	...	...	0920	...	0950	...	...	...	1020	1050	...	...	1120	...	1150	...
	St Gallen **530** a.	0815	...	...	0853	0915	...	...	...	0953	...	...	1015	...	1053	...	...	...	1115	1153	...	...	1215	...	1253	...

km		IR 2521	ICN 621	ICN 1521	IC 721	RE 2613	IR 2523	ICN 523	ICN 1623		IC 723	RE 2615	IR 2525	ICN 625	ICN 1525	IC 725	RE 2617	IR 2527	ICN 527	ICN 1627	IC 727	RE 2619	IR 2529	ICN 629	ICN 1529	IC 729
			✕	✕	✕			✕	✕		✕			✕	✕	✕				✕	✕			✕	✕	✕
	Genève A ✈ 570 d.	0906j	0909	...	0936j	...	1006j	1009	...	...	1036j	...	1106j	1109	...	1136j	...	1206j	1209	...	1236j	...	1306j	1309	...	1336j
	Genève 570 d.	0915	0918	...	0945	0951	1015	1018	...	...	1045	1051	1115	1118	...	1145	1151	1215	1218	...	1245	1251	1315	1318	...	1345
	Nyon **570** d.	|	|	...	|	1007	|	|	...	...	|	1107	|	|	...	|	1207	|	|	...	|	1307	|	|	...	|
	Morges **570** d.	|	|	...	|	1028	|	|	...	...	|	1128	|	|	...	|	1228	|	|	...	|	1328	|	|	...	|
	Lausanne 570 a.	0948	|	...	1018	1039	1048	|	...	...	1118	1139	1148	|	...	1218	1239	1248	|	...	1318	1339	1348	|	...	1418
0	**Lausanne 504** d.	0950	|	0945	1020	1042	1050	|	1045	...	1120	1142	1150	|	1145	1220	1242	1250	|	1245	1320	1342	1350	|	1345	1420
39	Yverdon d.	|	1004	1007	|	|	|	1104	1107	...	|	|	|	1204	1207	|	|	|	1304	1307	|	|	|	1404	1407	|
75	Neuchâtel d.	|	1024	1027	|	|	|	1124	1127	...	|	|	|	1224	1227	|	|	|	1324	1327	|	|	|	1424	1427	|
105	**Biel / Bienne** a.	|	1041	1043k	|	|	|	1141	1143k	...	|	|	|	1241	1243k	|	|	|	1341	1343k	|	|	|	1441	1443k	|
105	**Biel / Bienne** d.	|	1049	1046	|	|	|	1146	1149	...	|	|	|	1249	1246	|	|	|	1346	1349	|	|	|	1449	1446	|
129	Moutier d.	|	1108	|	|	|	|	|	1208	...	|	|	|	1308	|	|	|	|	|	1408	|	|	|	1508	|	|
140	Delémont d.	|	1123	|	|	|	|	|	1223	...	|	|	|	1323	|	|	|	|	|	1423	|	|	|	1523	|	|
179	**Basel** a.	|	1153	|	|	|	|	|	1253	...	|	|	|	1353	|	|	|	|	|	1453	|	|	|	1553	|	|
	Palézieux **504** d.	|	...	|	|	1058	|	|	...	...	|	1158	|	...	|	|	1258	|	|	...	|	1358	|	...	|	|
	Romont **568** d.	|	...	|	|	1113	|	|	...	...	|	1213	|	...	|	|	1313	|	|	...	|	1413	|	...	|	|
	Fribourg **508 568** d.	1034	...	|	1104	...	1134	|	...	...	1204	...	1234	...	|	1304	...	1334	|	...	1404	...	1434	...	|	1504
	Bern a.	1056	...	|	1126	...	1156	|	...	...	1226	...	1256	...	|	1326	...	1356	|	...	1426	...	1456	...	|	1526
	Olten **500** a.	|	...	1118	|	...	|	1218	...	...	|	...	|	...	1318	|	...	|	1418	...	|	...	|	...	1518	|
	Luzern **565** a.	1200	...	|	|	...	1300	|	...	...	|	...	1400	...	|	|	...	1500	|	...	|	...	1600	...	|	|
	Zürich HB **500** a.	...	...	1156	1228	...	...	1256	...	...	1328	...	...	...	1356	1428	...	...	1456	...	1528	...	...	...	1556	1628
	Zürich Flug ✈ **530** a.	...	...	1220	1250	...	...	1320	...	...	1350	...	...	...	1420	1450	...	...	1520	...	1550	...	...	...	1620	1650
	St Gallen **530** a.	...	...	1315	1353	...	...	1415	...	...	1453	...	...	...	1515	1553	...	...	1615	...	1653	...	...	...	1715	1753

km		RE 2621	IR 2531	ICN 531	ICN 1631	IC 731	RE 2623	IR 2535	ICN 635	ICN 1535	IC 735	RE 2625	IR 2537	ICN 537	ICN 1637		IC 737	RE 2629	IR 2539	ICN 639	ICN 1539	IC 739	RE 2631	IR 2541	ICN 541	ICN 1641
				✕	✕	✕				✕	✕				✕		✕				✕	✕				✕
	Genève A ✈ 570 d.	...	1406j	1409	...	1436j	...	1506j	1509	...	1536j	...	1606j	1609	...	...	1636j	...	1706j	1709	...	1736j	...	1806j	1809	...
	Genève 570 d.	1351	1415	1418	...	1445	1451	1515	1518	...	1545	1551	1615	1618	...	...	1645	1651	1715	1718	...	1745	1751	1815	1818	...
	Nyon **570** d.	1407	|	|	...	|	1507	|	|	...	|	1607	|	|	...	...	|	1707	|	|	...	|	1807	|	|	...
0	Morges **570** d.	1428	|	|	...	|	1528	|	|	...	|	1628	|	|	...	...	|	1728	|	|	...	|	1828	|	|	...
	Lausanne 570 a.	1439	1448	|	...	1518	1539	1548	|	...	1618	1639	1648	|	...	...	1718	1739	1748	|	...	1818	1839	1848	|	...
	Lausanne 504 d.	1442	1450	|	1445	1520	1542	1550	|	1545	1620	1642	1650	|	1645	...	1720	1742	1750	|	1745	1820	1842	1850	|	1845
39	Yverdon d.	|	|	1504	1507	|	|	|	1604	1607	|	|	|	1704	1707	...	|	|	|	1804	1807	|	|	|	1904	1907
	Neuchâtel d.	|	|	1524	1527	|	|	|	1624	1627	|	|	|	1724	1727	...	|	|	|	1824	1827	|	|	|	1924	1927
	Biel / Bienne a.	|	|	1541	1543k	|	|	|	1641	1643k	|	|	|	1741	1743k	...	|	|	|	1841	1843k	|	|	|	1941	1943k
	Biel / Bienne d.	|	|	1546	1549	|	|	|	1649	1646	|	|	|	1746	1749	...	|	|	|	1849	1846	|	|	|	1946	1949
	Moutier d.	|	|	|	1608	|	|	|	1708	|	|	|	|	|	1808	...	|	|	|	1908	|	|	|	|	|	2008
	Delémont d.	|	|	|	1623	|	|	|	1723	|	|	|	|	|	1823	...	|	|	|	1923	|	|	|	|	|	2023
	Basel a.	|	|	|	1653	|	|	|	1753	|	|	|	|	|	1853	...	|	|	|	1953	|	|	|	|	|	2053
	Palézieux **504** d.	1458	|	|	...	|	1558	|	...	|	|	1658	|	|	...	...	|	1758	|	...	|	|	1858	|	|	...
	Romont **568** d.	1513	|	|	...	|	1613	|	...	|	|	1713	|	|	...	...	|	1813	|	...	|	|	1913	|	|	...
	Fribourg **508 568** d.	...	1534	|	...	1604	...	1634	...	|	1704	...	1734	|	...	...	1804	...	1834	...	|	1904	...	1934	|	...
	Bern a.	...	1556	|	...	1626	...	1656	...	|	1726	...	1756	|	...	...	1826	...	1856	...	|	1926	...	1956	|	...
	Olten **500** a.	...	|	1618	...	|	...	|	...	1718	|	...	|	1818	...	...	|	...	|	...	1918	|	...	|	2018	...
	Luzern **565** a.	...	1700	|	...	|	...	1800	...	|	|	...	1900	|	...	...	|	...	2000	...	|	|	...	2100	|	...
	Zürich HB **500** a.	...	...	1656	...	1728	...	...	...	1756	1828	...	...	1856	...	...	1928	...	...	...	1956	2028	...	...	2056	...
	Zürich Flug ✈ **530** a.	...	...	1720	...	1750	...	...	...	1820	1850	...	...	1920	...	...	1950	...	...	...	2020	2050	...	...	2120	...
	St Gallen **530** a.	...	...	1815	...	1853	...	...	...	1915	1953	...	...	2015	...	...	2053	...	...	...	2115	2153	...	...	2215	...

	IC 741	RE 2635	IR 2543	ICN 643	ICN 1543	IC 743	RE 2637	IR 2545	ICN 545	ICN 1645	IC 745	RE 2639	IR 2547	ICN 647	ICN 1547	IC 747	IR 2641	IR 2549	ICN 1647	IR 2501	ICN 1649		RE 2699	RE 2647	IR 2503	
	✕				✕	✕ §			✕	✕	✕ §					✕ §							y		w	
Genève A ✈ 570 d.	1836j	...	1906j	1909	...	1936j	...	2006j	2009	...	2036j	...	...	2105j	...	2136j	...	2153	...	...	...	...	...	0028j	...	...
Genève 570 d.	1845	1851	1915	1918	...	1945	1951	2015	2018	...	2045	2051	...	2114	...	2145	2151	2203	...	...	...	...	...	0037	...	...
Nyon **570** d.	|	1907	|	|	...	|	2007	|	|	...	|	2107	...	2127	...	|	2207	2217	...	...	...	...	...	0053	...	...
Morges **570** d.	|	1928	|	|	...	|	2028	|	|	...	|	2128	...	2141	...	|	2228	2232	...	...	...	...	...	0114	...	...
Lausanne 570 a.	1918	1939	1948	|	...	2018	2039	2048	|	...	2118	2138	...	|	...	2218	2239	2242	...	...	...	...	...	0125	...	...
Lausanne 504 d.	1920	1942	1950	|	1945	2020	2042	2050	|	2045	2120	...	2145	|	2145	2220	...	2245	2245	2345	2345	...	...	...	0130	...
Yverdon d.	|	|	|	2004	2007	|	|	|	2104	2107	|	...	|	2204	2207	|	...	|	2307	|	0007	...	...	...	|	...
Neuchâtel d.	|	|	|	2024	2027	|	|	|	2124	2127	|	...	|	2224	2227	|	...	|	2327	|	0027	...	...	...	|	...
Biel / Bienne a.	|	|	|	2041	2043k	|	|	|	2141	2143k	|	...	|	2241	2243k	|	...	|	2343	|	0043	...	...	...	|	...
Biel / Bienne d.	|	|	|	2049	2046	|	|	|	2146	2149	|	...	|	2249	2246	|	...	|	2349	|	...	...	0049	...	|	...
Moutier d.	|	|	|	2108	|	|	|	|	|	2208	|	...	|	2308	|	|	...	|	0008	|	...	...	0108	...	|	...
Delémont d.	|	|	|	2123	|	|	|	|	|	2223	|	...	|	2323	|	|	...	|	0018	|	...	...	0118	...	|	...
Basel a.	|	|	|	2153	|	|	|	|	|	2253	|	...	|	2353	|	|	...	|	...	|	...	...	...	...	|	...
Palézieux **504** d.	|	1958	|	...	|	|	2058	|	|	...	|	...	2201	...	|	|	...	2301	...	0001	...	...	...	...	0146	...
Romont **568** d.	|	2013	|	...	|	|	2113	|	|	...	|	...	2216	...	|	|	...	2316	...	0016	...	...	...	...	0201	...
Fribourg **508 568** d.	2004	...	2034	...	|	2104	...	2134	|	...	2204	...	2234	...	|	2304	...	2334	...	0034	...	...	...	...	0218	...
Bern a.	2026	...	2056	...	|	2126	...	2156	|	...	2226	...	2256	...	|	2326	...	2356	...	0059	...	...	...	...	...	...
Olten **500** a.	|	...	|	...	2118	2158	...	|	2219	...	2258	...	|	...	2330	2358	...	...	...	...	...	...	...	...	...	...
Luzern **565** a.	|	...	2200	...	|	|	...	2300	|	...	|	...	2400	...	|	|	...	...	...	...	...	...	...	...	...	...
Zürich HB **500** a.	2128	...	...	...	2156	2231	...	...	2256	...	2331	...	...	...	0010	0033	...	...	...	...	...	...	...	...	...	...
Zürich Flug ✈ **530** a.	2150	...	...	...	2220	...	...	...	2320	...	...	...	...	...	0027	...	...	...	...	...	...	...	...	...	...	...
St Gallen **530** a.	2253	...	...	...	2315	...	...	...	0018	...	...	...	...	...	0125	...	...	...	...	...	...	...	...	...	...	...

j – Dec. 15 - July 14.
k – Connects with train in previous column(s).
m – ① (also Apr. 22, June 10; not Apr. 21, June 9).
w – ⑥⑦ (also Apr. 21, June 9, Aug. 1).
y – ⑥⑦ (also Apr. 18, 21, May 29, June 9, Aug. 1).
§ – Train number prefixed by "**10**" Jan. 6 - Mar. 13.

SBB BERN, BASEL and BIEL - LAUSANNE - GENÈVE 505

	RE 2602	RE 2604	ICN 1604	ICN 504	IR 2504	RE 2606	IC 704	ICN 1506	ICN 606	IR 2506	RE 2610	IC 706	ICN 1608	ICN 508	IR 2508	RE 2614	IC 708	ICN 1510	ICN 610	IR 2510	RE 2616	IC 710	ICN 1612	ICN 512	IR 2512
							✗	✗				✗	✗				✗	✗				✗	✗		
St Gallen **530** d.	...	...	...	...	...	...	...	...	...	...	...	...	...	...	...	...	0511	0544	...	...	...	0611	...	0642	...
Zürich Flughafen + **530** d.	...	...	...	...	...	...	...	...	...	...	...	...	...	...	...	...	0613	0643	...	...	...	0713	...	0739	...
Zürich HB **500** d.	...	...	...	...	...	...	...	...	...	...	...	0521	...	0604	...	...	0632	0704	...	...	...	0732	...	0804	...
Luzern **565** d.	...	...	...	...	...	...	...	...	...	...	...	|	...	|	0600	...	|	|	...	0700	...	|	...	|	0800
Olten **500** d.	...	...	...	...	...	...	...	...	...	...	...	0603	...	0640	|	...	|	0740	...	|	...	|	...	0840	|
Bern d.	...	...	...	...	0459	...	0534	...	...	0604	...	0634	...	|	0704	...	0734	|	...	0804	...	0834	...	|	0904
Fribourg **508 568** d.	...	...	...	...	0521	...	0556	...	...	0626	...	0656	...	|	0726	...	0756	|	...	0826	...	0856	...	|	0926
Romont **568** d.	...	...	...	...	0539	...	|	...	...	|	0647	|	...	|	|	0747	|	|	...	|	0847	|	...	|	|
Palézieux **504** d.	...	...	...	...	0554	...	|	...	...	|	0702	|	...	|	|	0802	|	|	...	|	0902	|	...	|	|
Basel d.	...	...	...	...	|	...	|	...	...	|	|	|	0603	|	|	|	|	|	0703	|	|	|	0803	|	|
Delémont d.	...	...	...	...	|	...	|	...	0542	|	|	|	0642	|	|	|	|	|	0742	|	|	|	0842	|	|
Moutier d.	...	...	...	...	|	...	|	...	0552	|	|	|	0652	|	|	|	|	|	0752	|	|	|	0852	|	|
Biel / Bienne a.	...	...	...	...	|	...	|	...	0610k	|	|	|	0710	0713k	|	|	|	0813	0810k	|	|	|	0910	0913k	|
Biel / Bienne d.	...	...	0513	0516	|	...	|	0613	0616	|	|	|	0716	0719	|	|	|	0816	0819	|	|	|	0916	0919	|
Neuchâtel d.	...	...	0531	0534	|	...	|	0631	0634	|	|	|	0734	0737	|	|	|	0834	0837	|	|	|	0934	0937	|
Yverdon d.	...	...	0550	0553	|	...	|	0650	0653	|	|	|	0753	0756	|	|	|	0853	0856	|	|	|	0953	0956	|
Lausanne 504 a.	...	...	0615	|	0610	...	0640	0715	|	0710	0718	0740	0815	|	0810	0818	0840	0915	|	0910	0918	0940	1015	|	1010
Lausanne 570 d.	0421	0506	...	|	0612	0621	0642	...	|	0712	0721	0742	...	|	0812	0821	0842	...	|	0912	0921	0942	...	|	1012
Morges **570** d.	0433	0518	...	0616	|	0632	|	...	0716	|	0732	|	...	|	|	0832	|	...	|	|	0932	|	...	|	|
Nyon **570** d.	0456	0541	...	0630	|	0653	|	...	0730	|	0753	|	...	|	|	0853	|	...	|	|	0953	|	...	|	|
Genève 570 a.	0512	0557	...	0643	0646	0709	0715	...	0743	0746	0809	0815	...	0842	0845	0909	0915	...	0942	0945	1009	1015	...	1042	1045
Genève Aéroport + **570** a.	0521	0607	...	0652t	0655t	...	0724t	...	0752t	0755t	...	0824t	...	0851	0854t	...	0924t	...	0951	0954t	...	1024t	...	1051	1054t

	RE 2618	IC 712	ICN 1514	ICN 614	IR 2516	RE 2620	IC 716	ICN 1618	ICN 518	IR 2518	RE 2622	IC 718	ICN 1520	ICN 620	IR 2520	RE 2624	IC 720	ICN 1622	ICN 522	IR 2522	RE 2626	IC 722	ICN 1524	ICN 624	IR 2524
		✗	✗	✗			✗	✗				✗	✗	✗			✗	✗	✗			✗	✗	✗	
St Gallen **530** d.	...	0711	0748	...	...	...	0811	...	0848	...	...	0911	0948	...	...	...	1011	...	1048	...	...	1111	1148	...	...
Zürich Flughafen + **530** d.	...	0813	0843	...	...	...	0913	...	0943	...	...	1013	1043	...	...	...	1113	...	1143	...	...	1213	1243	...	...
Zürich HB **500** d.	...	0832	0904	...	...	...	0932	...	1004	...	...	1032	1104	...	...	...	1132	...	1204	...	...	1232	1304	...	...
Luzern **565** d.	...	|	|	...	0900	...	|	...	|	1000	...	|	|	...	1100	...	|	...	|	1200	...	|	|	...	1300
Olten **500** d.	...	|	0940	...	|	...	|	...	1040	|	...	|	1140	...	|	...	|	...	1240	|	...	|	1340	...	|
Bern d.	...	0934	|	...	1004	...	1034	...	|	1104	...	1134	|	...	1204	...	1234	...	|	1304	...	1334	|	...	1404
Fribourg **508 568** d.	...	0956	|	...	1026	...	1056	...	|	1126	...	1156	|	...	1226	...	1256	...	|	1326	...	1356	|	...	1426
Romont **568** d.	0947	|	|	...	|	1047	|	...	|	|	1147	|	|	...	|	1247	|	...	|	|	1347	|	|	...	|
Palézieux **504** d.	1002	|	|	...	|	1102	|	...	|	|	1202	|	|	...	|	1302	|	...	|	|	1402	|	|	...	|
Basel d.	|	|	|	0903	|	|	|	1003	|	|	|	|	|	1103	|	|	|	1203	|	|	|	|	|	1303	|
Delémont d.	|	|	|	0942	|	|	|	1042	|	|	|	|	|	1142	|	|	|	1242	|	|	|	|	|	1342	|
Moutier d.	|	|	|	0952	|	|	|	1052	|	|	|	|	|	1152	|	|	|	1252	|	|	|	|	|	1352	|
Biel / Bienne a.	|	|	1013	1010k	|	|	|	1110	1113k	|	|	|	1213	1210k	|	|	|	1310	1313k	|	|	|	1413	1410k	|
Biel / Bienne d.	|	|	1016	1019	|	|	|	1116	1119	|	|	|	1216	1219	|	|	|	1316	1319	|	|	|	1416	1419	|
Neuchâtel d.	|	|	1034	1037	|	|	|	1134	1137	|	|	|	1234	1237	|	|	|	1334	1337	|	|	|	1434	1437	|
Yverdon d.	|	|	1053	1056	|	|	|	1153	1156	|	|	|	1253	1256	|	|	|	1353	1356	|	|	|	1453	1456	|
Lausanne 504 a.	1018	1040	1115	|	1110	1118	1140	1215	|	1210	1218	1240	1315	|	1310	1318	1340	1415	|	1410	1418	1440	1515	|	1510
Lausanne 570 d.	1021	1042	...	|	1112	1121	1142	...	|	1212	1221	1242	...	|	1312	1321	1342	...	|	1412	1421	1442	...	|	1512
Morges **570** d.	1032	|	...	|	|	1132	|	...	|	|	1232	|	...	|	|	1332	|	...	|	|	1432	|	...	|	|
Nyon **570** d.	1053	|	...	|	|	1153	|	...	|	|	1253	|	...	|	|	1353	|	...	|	|	1453	|	...	|	|
Genève 570 a.	1109	1115	...	1142	1145	1209	1215	...	1242	1245	1309	1315	...	1342	1345	1409	1415	...	1442	1445	1509	1515	...	1542	1545
Genève Aéroport + **570** a.	...	1124t	...	1151	1154t	...	1224t	...	1251	1254t	...	1324t	...	1351	1354t	...	1424t	...	1451	1454t	...	1524t	...	1551	1554t

	RE 2628	IC 724	ICN 1626	ICN 526	IR 2526	RE 2630	IC 726	ICN 1528	ICN 628	IR 2528	RE 2632	IC 728	ICN 1630	ICN 530	IR 2530	RE 2634	IC 730	ICN 1532	ICN 632	IR 2532	RE 2636	IC 732	ICN 1636	ICN 536	IR 2536
		✗	✗	✗			✗	✗				✗	✗				✗	✗	✗			✗	✗		
St Gallen **530** d.	...	1211	...	1248	...	...	1311	1348	...	...	...	1411	...	1448	...	...	1511	1548	...	...	...	1611	...	1648	...
Zürich Flughafen + **530** d.	...	1313	...	1343	...	...	1413	1443	...	...	...	1513	...	1543	...	...	1613	1643	...	...	...	1713	...	1743	...
Zürich HB **500** d.	...	1332	...	1404	...	...	1432	1504	...	...	...	1532	...	1604	...	...	1632	1704	...	...	...	1732	...	1804	...
Luzern **565** d.	...	|	...	|	1400	...	|	|	...	1500	...	|	...	|	1600	...	|	|	...	1700	...	|	...	|	1800
Olten **500** d.	...	|	...	1440	|	...	|	1540	...	|	...	|	...	1640	|	...	|	1740	...	|	...	|	...	1840	|
Bern d.	...	1434	...	|	1504	...	1534	|	...	1604	...	1634	...	|	1704	...	1734	|	...	1804	...	1834	...	|	1904
Fribourg **508 568** d.	...	1456	...	|	1526	...	1556	|	...	1626	...	1656	...	|	1726	...	1756	|	...	1826	...	1856	...	|	1926
Romont **568** d.	1447	|	...	|	|	1547	|	|	...	|	1647	|	...	|	|	1747	|	|	...	|	1847	|	...	|	|
Palézieux **504** d.	1502	|	...	|	|	1602	|	|	...	|	1702	|	...	|	|	1802	|	|	...	|	1902	|	...	|	|
Basel d.	|	|	1403	|	|	|	|	|	1503	|	|	|	1603	|	|	|	|	|	1703	|	|	|	1803	|	|
Delémont d.	|	|	1442	|	|	|	|	|	1542	|	|	|	1642	|	|	|	|	|	1742	|	|	|	1842	|	|
Moutier d.	|	|	1452	|	|	|	|	|	1552	|	|	|	1652	|	|	|	|	|	1752	|	|	|	1852	|	|
Biel / Bienne a.	|	|	1510	1513k	|	|	|	1613	1610k	|	|	|	1710	1713k	|	|	|	1813	1810k	|	|	|	1910	1913k	|
Biel / Bienne d.	|	|	1516	1519	|	|	|	1616	1619	|	|	|	1716	1719	|	|	|	1816	1819	|	|	|	1916	1919	|
Neuchâtel d.	|	|	1534	1537	|	|	|	1634	1637	|	|	|	1734	1737	|	|	|	1834	1837	|	|	|	1934	1937	|
Yverdon d.	|	|	1553	1556	|	|	|	1653	1656	|	|	|	1753	1756	|	|	|	1853	1856	|	|	|	1953	1956	|
Lausanne 504 a.	1518	1540	1615	|	1610	1618	1640	1715	|	1710	1718	1740	1815	|	1810	1818	1840	1915	|	1910	1918	1940	2015	|	2010
Lausanne 570 d.	1521	1542	...	|	1612	1621	1642	...	|	1712	1721	1742	...	|	1812	1821	1842	...	|	1915	1921	1942	...	|	2015
Morges **570** d.	1532	|	...	|	|	1632	|	...	|	|	1732	|	...	|	|	1832	|	...	1919	|	1932	|	...	2019	|
Nyon **570** d.	1553	|	...	|	|	1653	|	...	|	|	1753	|	...	|	|	1853	|	...	1933	|	1953	|	...	2033	|
Genève 570 a.	1609	1615	...	1642	1645	1709	1715	...	1742	1745	1809	1815	...	1842	1845	1909	1915	...	1946	1949	2009	2015	...	2046	2049
Genève Aéroport + **570** a.	...	1624t	...	1651	1654t	...	1724t	...	1751	1754t	...	1824t	...	1851	1854t	...	1924t	...	1955t	1958t	...	2024t	...	2055t	2058t

	RE 2638	IC 736	ICN 1538	ICN 638	IR 2538	RE 2640	IC 738	ICN 1640	ICN 540	IR 2540	IC 740	ICN 642	ICN 1542	IR 2542	IR 1444	IC 742	ICN 1644	ICN 1544	IR 2548	IR 1446	ICN 646		IR 2502	ICN 1546	RE 2600
		✗	✗				✗	✗			✗	✗	✗			✗		✗					j		y
St Gallen **530** d.	...	1711	1748	...	...	...	1811	...	1848	...	1911	...	1948	...	...	2011	...	2048	...	...	...	...	...	2148	...
Zürich Flughafen + **530** d.	...	1813	1843	...	...	...	1913	...	1943	...	2013	...	2043	...	...	2113	...	2143	...	...	...	...	...	2243	...
Zürich HB **500** d.	...	1832	1904	...	...	...	1932	...	2004	...	2032	...	2104	...	...	2132	...	2204	...	...	...	...	...	2304	...
Luzern **565** d.	...	|	|	...	1900	...	|	...	|	2000	|	...	|	2100	...	|	...	|	...	...	...	...	...	|	...
Olten **500** d.	...	|	1940	...	|	...	|	...	2040	|	|	...	2140	|	...	|	...	2240	...	...	...	...	...	2340	...
Bern d.	...	1934	|	...	2004	...	2034	...	|	2104	2134	...	|	2204	...	2234	...	|	2308	...	...	...	0008	|	...
Fribourg **508 568** d.	...	1956	|	...	2026	...	2056	...	|	2126	2156	...	|	2226	...	2255	...	|	2330	...	...	...	0032	|	...
Romont **568** d.	1947	|	|	...	|	2047	|	...	|	2144	|	...	|	2244	...	...	...	|	2348	...	...	...	0050	|	...
Palézieux **504** d.	2002	|	|	...	|	2102	|	...	|	2159	|	...	|	2259	...	...	...	|	0003	...	...	...	0105	|	...
Basel d.	|	|	|	1903	|	|	|	2003	|	|	|	2103	|	|	...	...	2203	|	|	...	2303	...	|	|	...
Delémont d.	|	|	|	1942	|	|	|	2042	|	|	|	2142	|	|	...	...	2242	|	|	...	2337	...	|	|	...
Moutier d.	|	|	|	1952	|	|	|	2052	|	|	|	2152	|	|	...	...	2252	|	|	...	...	...	|	|	...
Biel / Bienne a.	|	|	2013	2010k	|	|	|	2110	2113k	|	|	2210	2213k	|	...	...	2310	2314	|	...	...	...	|	0022	...
Biel / Bienne d.	|	|	2016	2019	|	|	|	2116	2119	|	|	2219r	2216	|	...	...	...	2316	|	...	...	...	|	0025x	...
Neuchâtel d.	|	|	2034	2037	|	|	|	2134	2137	|	|	2237r	2234	|	...	...	...	2334	|	...	...	...	|	0043x	...
Yverdon d.	|	|	2053	2056	|	|	|	2153	2156	|	|	2256r	2253	|	...	...	...	2353	|	...	...	...	|	0102x	...
Lausanne 504 a.	2018	2040	2115	|	2110	2118	2140	2215	|	2215	2240	|	2315	2315	...	...	...	0015	0019	...	...	...	0121	0124x	...
Lausanne 570 d.	2021	2042	...	|	...	2121	2142	...	|	2221	2248	|	...	...	2321	...	...	...	...	0023	...	...	...	...	0133
Morges **570** d.	2032	|	...	2119	...	2132	|	...	2219	2233	2257	2319r	...	...	2333	...	...	...	...	0035	...	...	...	...	0144
Nyon **570** d.	2053	|	...	2133	...	2153	|	...	2233	2251	2313	2333r	...	...	2351	...	...	...	...	0053	...	...	...	...	0205
Genève 570 a.	2109	2115	...	2146	...	2209	2215	...	2246	2305	2327	2346r	...	...	0005	...	...	...	...	0107	...	...	...	...	0223
Genève Aéroport + **570** a.	...	2124t	...	2155t	...	...	2224t	...	...	2314t	2338t	...	...	...	0014t	...	...	...	...	...	...	...	...	...	...

– ①⑥⑦ (also Apr. 22, June 10, Aug. 1).
– Connects with train in previous column(s).
r – † only.
t – Dec. 15 - July 14.
x – ⑥⑦ (not Apr. 19, Aug. 2).
y – ⑥⑦ (also Apr. 18, 21, May 29, June 9, Aug. 1).

✗ – Restaurant (✗) – Bistro (🍸) – Bar coach 🍸 – Minibar

506 SWISS LAKES

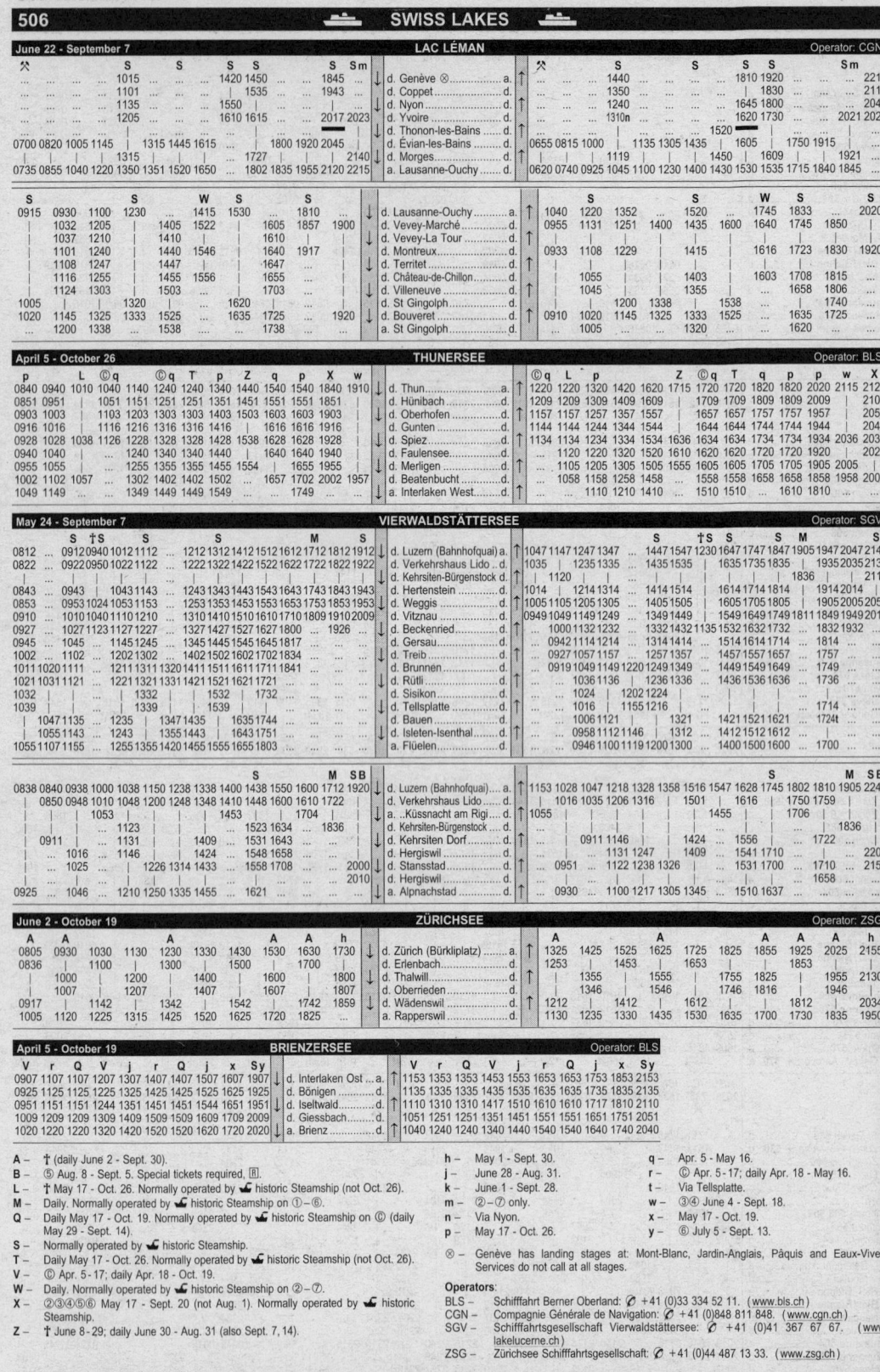

June 22 - September 7 — LAC LÉMAN — Operator: CGN

	⚒				S		S		S	S			S	Sm
d. Genève ⊗	...	...	...	...	1015	...	...	...	1420	1450	...	...	1845	...
d. Coppet	...	...	...	...	1101	...	...	...	|	1535	...	...	1943	...
d. Nyon	...	...	...	...	1135	...	...	...	1550	|	...	...	|	...
d. Yvoire	...	...	...	...	1205	...	...	...	1610	1615	...	...	2017	2023
d. Thonon-les-Bains	...	...	...	...	|	...	...	...	...	|	...	...	▬	|
d. Évian-les-Bains	0700	0820	1005	1145	|	1315	1445	1615	...	|	1800	1920	2045	|
d. Morges	|	|	|	|	1315	|	|	|	...	1727	|	|	|	2140
a. Lausanne-Ouchy	0735	0855	1040	1220	1350	1351	1520	1650	...	1802	1835	1955	2120	2215

	⚒			S			S		S	S			Sm	
Genève ⊗ a.	...	...	...	1440	...	...	...	...	1810	1920	...	...	...	2210
Coppet d.	...	...	...	1350	...	...	...	...	|	1830	...	...	...	2114
Nyon d.	...	...	...	1240	...	...	...	...	1645	1800	...	...	...	2048
Yvoire d.	...	...	...	1310n	...	...	...	...	1620	1730	...	...	2021	2025
Thonon-les-Bains d.	...	...	...	|	...	...	...	1520	▬	|	...	...	|	...
Évian-les-Bains d.	0655	0815	1000	|	1135	1305	1435	|	1605	|	1750	1915	|	...
Morges d.	|	|	|	1119	|	|	|	1450	|	1609	|	|	1921	...
Lausanne-Ouchy d.	0620	0740	0925	1045	1100	1230	1400	1430	1530	1535	1715	1840	1845	...

	S			S		W	S		S	
d. Lausanne-Ouchy	0915	0930	1100	1230	...	1415	1530	...	1810	...
d. Vevey-Marché	|	1032	1205	|	1405	1522	|	1605	1857	1900
d. Vevey-La Tour	|	1037	1210	|	1410	|	|	1610	|	|
d. Montreux	|	1101	1240	|	1440	1546	|	1640	1917	|
d. Territet	|	1108	1247	|	1447	|	|	1647	...	|
d. Château-de-Chillon	|	1116	1255	|	1455	1556	|	1655	...	|
d. Villeneuve	|	1124	1303	|	1503	...	|	1703	...	|
d. St Gingolph	1005	|	|	1320	|	...	1620	|	...	|
d. Bouveret	1020	1145	1325	1333	1525	...	1635	1725	...	1920
a. St Gingolph	...	1200	1338	...	1538	....	...	1738	...	...

		S			S		W	S		S
Lausanne-Ouchy a.	1040	1220	1352	...	1520	...	1745	1833	...	2020
Vevey-Marché d.	0955	1131	1251	1400	1435	1600	1640	1745	1850	|
Vevey-La Tour d.	|	|	|	|	|	|	|	|	|	|
Montreux d.	0933	1108	1229	|	1415	|	1616	1723	1830	1920
Territet d.	|	|	|	|	|	|	|	|	|	...
Château-de-Chillon d.	|	1055	|	|	1403	|	1603	1708	1815	...
Villeneuve d.	|	1045	|	|	1355	|	...	1658	1806	...
St Gingolph d.	|	|	1200	1338	|	1538	...	|	1740	...
Bouveret d.	0910	1020	1145	1325	1333	1525	...	1635	1725	...
St Gingolph d.	...	1005	...	...	1320	...	...	1620	...	...

April 5 - October 26 — THUNERSEE — Operator: BLS

	p		L	©q		©q	T	p	Z	q	p	X	w
d. Thun	0840	0940	1010	1040	1140	1240	1240	1340	1440	1540	1540	1840	1910
d. Hünibach	0851	0951	|	1051	1151	1251	1251	1351	1451	1551	1551	1851	|
d. Oberhofen	0903	1003	|	1103	1203	1303	1303	1403	1503	1603	1603	1903	|
d. Gunten	0916	1016	|	1116	1216	1316	1316	1416	|	1616	1616	1916	|
d. Spiez	0928	1028	1038	1126	1228	1328	1328	1428	1538	1628	1628	1928	|
d. Faulensee	0940	1040	|	...	1240	1340	1340	1440	|	1640	1640	1940	|
d. Merligen	0955	1055	|	...	1255	1355	1355	1455	1554	|	1655	1955	|
d. Beatenbucht	1002	1102	1057	...	1302	1402	1402	1502	...	1657	1702	2002	1957
a. Interlaken West	1049	1149	...	...	1349	1449	1449	1549	...	...	1749	...	...

	©q	L	p			Z	©q	T	q	p	p	w	X
Thun a.	1220	1220	1320	1420	1620	1715	1720	1720	1820	1820	2020	2115	2120
Hünibach d.	1209	1209	1309	1409	1609	|	1709	1709	1809	1809	2009	|	2109
Oberhofen d.	1157	1157	1257	1357	1557	|	1657	1657	1757	1757	1957	|	2057
Gunten d.	1144	1144	1244	1344	1544	|	1644	1644	1744	1744	1944	|	2044
Spiez d.	1134	1134	1234	1334	1534	1636	1634	1634	1734	1734	1934	2036	2034
Faulensee d.	...	1120	1220	1320	1520	1610	1620	1620	1720	1720	1920	|	2020
Merligen d.	...	1105	1205	1305	1505	1555	1605	1605	1705	1705	1905	2005	|
Beatenbucht d.	...	1058	1158	1258	1458	...	1558	1558	1658	1658	1858	1958	2003
Interlaken West d.	...	...	1110	1210	1410	...	1510	1510	...	1610	1810	...	...

May 24 - September 7 — VIERWALDSTÄTTERSEE — Operator: SGV

			S	†S		S			S				M		S
d. Luzern (Bahnhofquai)	0812	...	0912	0940	1012	1112	...	1212	1312	1412	1512	1612	1712	1812	1912
d. Verkehrshaus Lido	0822	...	0922	0950	1022	1122	...	1222	1322	1422	1522	1622	1722	1822	1922
d. Kehrsiten-Bürgenstock	|	...	|	|	|	|	...	|	|	|	|	|	|	|	|
d. Hertenstein	0843	...	0943	|	1043	1143	...	1243	1343	1443	1543	1643	1743	1843	1943
d. Weggis	0853	...	0953	1024	1053	1153	...	1253	1353	1453	1553	1653	1753	1853	1953
d. Vitznau	0910	...	1010	1040	1110	1210	...	1310	1410	1510	1610	1710	1809	1910	2009
d. Beckenried	0927	...	1027	1123	1127	1227	...	1327	1427	1527	1627	1800	...	1926	...
d. Gersau	0945	...	1045	...	1145	1245	...	1345	1445	1545	1645	1817	...	...	...
d. Treib	1002	...	1102	...	1202	1302	...	1402	1502	1602	1702	1834	...	...	...
d. Brunnen	1011	1020	1111	...	1211	1311	1320	1411	1511	1611	1711	1841	...	...	...
d. Rütli	1021	1031	1121	...	1221	1321	1331	1421	1521	1621	1721	...	...	...	...
d. Sisikon	1032	|	|	...	|	1332	|	|	1532	|	1732	...	...	...	...
d. Tellsplatte	1039	|	|	...	|	1339	|	|	1539	|	|	...	...	...	...
d. Bauen	|	1047	1135	...	1235	|	1347	1435	|	1635	1744	...	...	...	...
d. Isleten-Isenthal	|	1055	1143	...	1243	|	1355	1443	|	1643	1751	...	...	...	...
a. Flüelen	1055	1107	1155	...	1255	1355	1420	1455	1555	1655	1803	...	...	...	...

						S		†S	S		S	M			S
Luzern (Bahnhofquai) a.	1047	1147	1247	1347	...	1447	1547	1230	1647	1747	1847	1905	1947	2047	2147
Verkehrshaus Lido d.	1035	|	1235	1335	...	1435	1535	|	1635	1735	1835	|	1935	2035	2137
Kehrsiten-Bürgenstock d.	|	1120	|	|	...	|	|	|	|	|	|	1836	|	|	2114
Hertenstein d.	1014	|	1214	1314	...	1414	1514	|	1614	1714	1814	|	1914	2014	|
Weggis d.	1005	1105	1205	1305	...	1405	1505	|	1605	1705	1805	|	1905	2005	2059
Vitznau d.	0949	1049	1149	1249	...	1349	1449	|	1549	1649	1749	1811	1849	1949	2010
Beckenried d.	...	1000	1132	1232	...	1332	1432	1135	1532	1632	1732	...	1832	1932	...
Gersau d.	...	0942	1114	1214	...	1314	1414	...	1514	1614	1714	...	1814	...	...
Treib d.	...	0927	1057	1157	...	1257	1357	...	1457	1557	1657	...	1757	...	...
Brunnen d.	...	0919	1049	1149	1220	1249	1349	...	1449	1549	1649	...	1749	...	...
Rütli d.	...	...	1036	1136	|	1236	1336	...	1436	1536	1636	...	1736	...	...
Sisikon d.	...	...	1024	|	1202	1224	|	...	|	|	|	...	|	...	...
Tellsplatte d.	...	...	1016	|	1155	1216	|	...	|	|	|	...	1714	...	...
Bauen d.	...	...	1006	1121	|	|	1321	...	1421	1521	1621	...	1724t	...	...
Isleten-Isenthal d.	...	...	0958	1112	1146	|	1312	...	1412	1512	1612	...	|	...	...
Flüelen d.	...	...	0946	1100	1119	1200	1300	...	1400	1500	1600	...	1700	...	...

										S			M	SB
d. Luzern (Bahnhofquai)	0838	0840	0938	1000	1038	1150	1238	1338	1400	1438	1550	1600	1712	1920
d. Verkehrshaus Lido	|	0850	0948	1010	1048	1200	1248	1348	1410	1448	1600	1610	1722	|
a. ..Küssnacht am Rigi	|	|	|	1053	|	|	|	|	1453	|	|	1704	|	|
d. Kehrsiten-Bürgenstock	|	|	|	...	1123	|	|	|	...	1523	1634	...	1836	|
d. Kehrsiten Dorf	|	0911	|	...	1131	|	|	1409	...	1531	1643	...	...	|
d. Hergiswil	|	...	1016	...	1146	|	|	1424	...	1548	1658	...	...	|
d. Stansstad	|	...	1025	...	|	1226	1314	1433	...	1558	1708	...	...	2000
d. Hergiswil	|	...	|	...	|	|	|	|	...	|	...	...	...	2010
a. Alpnachstad	0925	...	1046	...	1210	1250	1335	1455	...	1621	...	...	...	...

										S			M	SB
Luzern (Bahnhofquai) a.	1153	1028	1047	1218	1328	1358	1516	1547	1628	1745	1802	1810	1905	2247
Verkehrshaus Lido d.	|	1016	1035	1206	1316	|	1501	|	1616	|	1750	1759	|	|
..Küssnacht am Rigi d.	1055	|	|	|	|	|	|	1455	|	|	1706	|	|	|
Kehrsiten-Bürgenstock d.	...	|	|	|	|	|	|	...	|	|	...	|	1836	|
Kehrsiten Dorf d.	...	|	0911	1146	|	|	1424	...	1556	|	...	1722	...	|
Hergiswil d.	...	|	...	1131	1247	|	1409	...	1541	1710	...	|	...	2205
Stansstad d.	...	0951	...	1122	1238	1326	|	...	1531	1700	...	1710	...	2155
Hergiswil d.	...	|	...	|	|	|	|	...	|	|	...	1658	...	...
Alpnachstad d.	...	0930	...	1100	1217	1305	1345	...	1510	1637	...	...	...	...

June 2 - October 19 — ZÜRICHSEE — Operator: ZSG

	A	A			A			A	A	h
d. Zürich (Bürkliplatz)	0805	0930	1030	1130	1230	1330	1430	1530	1630	1730
d. Erlenbach	0836	|	1100	|	1300	|	1500	|	1700	|
d. Thalwil	|	1000	|	1200	|	1400	|	1600	|	1800
d. Oberrieden	|	1007	|	1207	|	1407	|	1607	|	1807
d. Wädenswil	0917	|	1142	|	1342	|	1542	|	1742	1859
a. Rapperswil	1005	1120	1225	1315	1425	1520	1625	1720	1825	...

	A			A			A	A	A	h
Zürich (Bürkliplatz) a.	1325	1425	1525	1625	1725	1825	1855	1925	2025	2155
Erlenbach d.	1253	|	1453	|	1653	|	|	1853	|	|
Thalwil d.	|	1355	|	1555	|	1755	1825	|	1955	2130
Oberrieden d.	|	1346	|	1546	|	1746	1816	|	1946	|
Wädenswil d.	1212	|	1412	|	1612	|	|	1812	|	2034
Rapperswil d.	1130	1235	1330	1435	1530	1635	1700	1730	1835	1950

April 5 - October 19 — BRIENZERSEE — Operator: BLS

	V	r	Q	V	j	r	Q	j	x	Sy
d. Interlaken Ost	0907	1107	1107	1207	1307	1407	1407	1507	1607	1907
d. Bönigen	0925	1125	1125	1225	1325	1425	1425	1525	1625	1925
d. Iseltwald	0951	1151	1151	1244	1351	1451	1451	1544	1651	1951
d. Giessbach	1009	1209	1209	1309	1409	1509	1509	1609	1709	2009
a. Brienz	1020	1220	1220	1320	1420	1520	1520	1620	1720	2020

	V	r	Q	V	j	r	Q	j	x	Sy
Interlaken Ost a.	1153	1353	1353	1453	1553	1653	1653	1753	1853	2153
Bönigen d.	1135	1335	1335	1435	1535	1635	1635	1735	1835	2135
Iseltwald d.	1110	1310	1310	1417	1510	1610	1610	1717	1810	2110
Giessbach d.	1051	1251	1251	1351	1451	1551	1551	1651	1751	2051
Brienz d.	1040	1240	1240	1340	1440	1540	1540	1640	1740	2040

A – † (daily June 2 - Sept. 30).
B – ⑤ Aug. 8 - Sept. 5. Special tickets required, Ⓡ.
L – † May 17 - Oct. 26. Normally operated by historic Steamship (not Oct. 26).
M – Daily. Normally operated by historic Steamship on ①–⑥.
Q – Daily May 17 - Oct. 19. Normally operated by historic Steamship on © (daily May 29 - Sept. 14).
S – Normally operated by historic Steamship.
T – Daily May 17 - Oct. 26. Normally operated by historic Steamship (not Oct. 26).
V – © Apr. 5 - 17; daily Apr. 18 - Oct. 19.
W – Daily. Normally operated by historic Steamship on ②–⑦.
X – ②③④⑤⑥ May 17 - Sept. 20 (not Aug. 1). Normally operated by historic Steamship.
Z – † June 8 - 29; daily June 30 - Aug. 31 (also Sept. 7, 14).

h – May 1 - Sept. 30.
j – June 28 - Aug. 31.
k – June 1 - Sept. 28.
m – ②–⑦ only.
n – Via Nyon.
p – May 17 - Oct. 26.

q – Apr. 5 - May 16.
r – © Apr. 5 - 17; daily Apr. 18 - May 16.
t – Via Tellsplatte.
w – ③④ June 4 - Sept. 18.
x – May 17 - Oct. 19.
y – ⑥ July 5 - Sept. 13.

⊗ – Genève has landing stages at: Mont-Blanc, Jardin-Anglais, Pâquis and Eaux-Vives. Services do not call at all stages.

Operators:
BLS – Schifffahrt Berner Oberland: ✆ +41 (0)33 334 52 11. (www.bls.ch)
CGN – Compagnie Générale de Navigation: ✆ +41 (0)848 811 848. (www.cgn.ch)
SGV – Schifffahrtsgesellschaft Vierwaldstättersee: ✆ +41 (0)41 367 67 67. (www.lakelucerne.ch)
ZSG – Zürichsee Schifffahrtsgesellschaft: ✆ +41 (0)44 487 13 33. (www.zsg.ch)

508 FRIBOURG - MURTEN - INS

TPF

Temporarily relocated to page 270

SBB BASEL - ZÜRICH 510

Night trains (after 2000) subject to alteration June 1-6, Aug. 17-22, Nov. 2-7 owing to engineering work between Basel and Brugg

Via Lenzburg

km		IC 553	IR 1809	ICE 759	IC 559	IR 1811	IC 761	IC 561	IR 1815	ICE 3	IC 563	IR 1817		IC 767	IC 565	IR 1819	ICE 5	TGV 9203	IC 567	IR 1821	IC 771	IC 571	IR 1823	IC 773	IC 573
				✕	🍷		✕	(✕)		♦	(✕)			✕	✕		F	♦	y✕		🍷	(✕)		🍷	✕
0	**Basel** SBB d.	0533	0547	0607	0633	0647	0707	0733	0747	0807	0833	0847	...	0907	0933	0947	1007	1033	1033	1047	1107	1133	1147	1207	1233
14	Liestal d.	|	0557	|	|	0657	|	|	0757	|	|	0857	...	|	|	0957	|	|	|	1057	|	|	1157	|	|
50	Aarau d.	|	0623	|	|	0723	|	|	0823	|	|	0923	...	|	|	1023	|	|	|	1123	|	|	1223	|	|
59	Lenzburg d.	|	0630	|	|	0730	|	|	0830	|	|	0930	...	|	|	1030	|	|	|	1130	|	|	1230	|	|
91	**Zürich** HB a.	0626	0652	0700	0726	0752	0800	0826	0852	0900	0926	0952	...	1000	1026	1052	1100	1126	1126	1152	1200	1226	1252	1300	1326
	Chur **520** a.	...	...	...	0852	...	...	0952	...	...	1052	...	...	...	1152	...	...	...	...	...	...	1352	...	...	1452

	IR 1825	IC 775	TGV 9211	IR 1827	EC 7	EC 207	IR 1829	ICE 73	TGV 9213	IR 1831	EC 9	IC 581	IR 1835	ICE 75	IC 585	TGV 9215	IR 1837		IC 787	IC 587	IR 1839	ICE 77	TGV 9219	IR 1841	IC 791
		🍷	Z		♦			K	Z		♦	(✕)		H	✕	Z			✕	✕		K	Z		(✕)
Basel SBB d.	1247	1307	1333	1347	1407	1433	1447	1507	1533	1547	1607	1633	1647	1707	1733	1736	1747	...	1807	1833	1847	1907	1933	1947	2007
Liestal d.	1257	|	|	1357	|	|	1457	|	|	1557	|	|	1657	|	|	|	1757	...	|	|	1857	|	|	1957	|
Aarau d.	1323	|	|	1423	|	|	1523	|	|	1623	|	|	1723	|	|	|	1823	...	|	|	1923	|	|	2023	|
Lenzburg d.	1330	|	|	1430	|	|	1530	|	|	1630	|	|	1730	|	|	|	1830	...	|	|	1930	|	|	2030	|
Zürich HB a.	1352	1400	1426	1452	1500	1526	1552	1600	1626	1652	1700	1726	1752	1800	1826	1835	1852	...	1900	1926	1952	2000	2026	2052	2100
Chur **520** a.	...	...	...	...	...	1652	...	...	...	...	...	1852	...	...	1952	...	...	...	...	2052	...	...	...	...	...

	IC 591	IR 1843	IC 793	ICE 79	TGV 9223	IR 1845	IC 795	IR 1847	IC 797	
			p	Hq	Z					
Basel SBB d.	2033	2047	2107	2107	2133	2147	2207	2247	2307	...
Liestal d.	|	2057	|	|	|	2157	|	2257	|	...
Aarau d.	|	2123	|	|	|	2223	|	2323	|	...
Lenzburg d.	|	2130	|	|	|	2230	|	2330	|	...
Zürich HB a.	2126	2152	2200	2200	2226	2252	2300	2352	2400	...
Chur **520** a.	...	...	...	...	...	...	...	...	...	...

	IR 1806	IC 758	ICE 78	IR 1808	IC 558	IC 760	IR 1810	TGV 9206	ICE 76	IR 1812
		p	♦		🍷	(✕)		Z	K	
Chur **520** d.	...	...	...	...	0506d	...	...	...	...	...
Zürich HB d.	0508	0600	0600	0608	0634	0700	0708	0734	0800	0808
Lenzburg d.	0528	|	|	0628	|	|	0728	|	|	0828
Aarau d.	0536	|	|	0636	|	|	0736	|	|	0836
Liestal d.	0601	|	|	0701	|	|	0801	|	|	0901
Basel SBB a.	0612	0653	0653	0712	0727	0753	0812	0827	0853	0912

	IC 562	IC 768	IR 1816	TGV 9210	ICE 74	IR 1818	IC 568	EC 8	IR 1820	TGV 9218	ICE 72	IR 1822	EC 206	EC 6	IR 1824	TGV 9222	IC 774	IR 1826	IC 576	IC 766	IR 1828	TGV 9226	IC 580	IC 780	IR 1830
	✕			Z	K		(✕)	♦		Z	H			♦		Z	🍷		(✕)	🍷		♦	🍷	🍷	
Chur **520** d.	0708	...	...	...	...	...	0908	...	...	...	...	...	1108	...	...	...	...	...	1308	...	...	...	...	...	...
Zürich HB d.	0834	0900	0908	0934	1000	1008	1034	1100	1108	1134	1200	1208	1234	1300	1308	1334	1400	1408	1434	1500	1508	1534	1534	1600	1608
Lenzburg d.	|	|	0928	|	|	1028	|	|	1128	|	|	1228	|	|	1328	|	|	1428	|	|	1528	|	|	|	1628
Aarau d.	|	|	0936	|	|	1036	|	|	1136	|	|	1236	|	|	1336	|	|	1436	|	|	1536	|	|	|	1636
Liestal d.	|	|	1001	|	|	1101	|	|	1201	|	|	1301	|	|	1401	|	|	1501	|	|	1601	|	|	|	1701
Basel SBB a.	0927	0953	1012	1027	1053	1112	1127	1153	1212	1227	1253	1312	1327	1353	1412	1427	1453	1512	1527	1553	1612	1627	1627	1653	1712

	IC 582	ICE 1172	ICE 292	ICE 272	IR 1832	TGV 9230	IC 582	IC 786	IR 1836	IC 586	ICE 4	IR 1838	IC 588	IC 788	IR 1840	IC 590	ICE 790	IR 1842	IC 594	IC 794	IR 1844	IC 798	IR 1846	IR 1802	IR 1804
	✕	♦	♦	♦		Z	✕	✕		(✕)	F		(✕)	✕		(✕)	✕								m
Chur **520** d.	...	...	...	...	...	...	1608	...	...	1708	...	...	1808	...	...	1908	...	...	...	...	...	...	...	...	...
Zürich HB d.	1634	1700	1700	1700	1708	1727	1734	1800	1808	1834	1900	1908	1934	2000	2008	2034	2100	2108	2134	2200	2208	2300	2308	0008	0108
Lenzburg d.	|	|	|	|	1728	|	|	|	1828	|	|	1928	|	|	2028	|	|	2128	|	|	2228	|	2328	0028	0128
Aarau d.	|	|	|	|	1736	|	|	|	1836	|	|	1936	|	|	2036	|	|	2136	|	|	2236	|	2336	0036	0136
Liestal d.	|	|	|	|	1801	|	|	|	1901	|	|	2001	|	|	2101	|	|	2201	|	|	2301	|	0001	0101	0201
Basel SBB a.	1727	1753	1753	1753	1812	1823	1827	1853	1912	1927	1953	2012	2027	2053	2112	2127	2153	2212	2227	2253	2312	0001	0012	0112	0212

Via Baden

km		IR 2057	IR 1953	IR 2059	IR 1955	IR 1957 Ⓐ	IR 2061		IR 1961	IR 2065	IR 1963	IR 2067	IR 1967	IR 2069		IR 1969	IR 2071	IR 1971	IR 2073	IR 1973	IR 2075		IR 1975	IR 2077
0	**Basel** SBB d.	0440	0513	0540	0613	0630	0640	...	0713	0740	0813	0840	0913	0940	...	1013	1040	1113	1140	1213	1240	...	1313	1340
17	Rheinfelden d.	0451	0525	0551	0625	0642	0651	...	0725	0751	0825	0851	0925	0951	...	1025	1051	1125	1151	1225	1251	...	1325	1351
57	Brugg d.	0520	0600	0620	0700	0715	0720	...	0800	0820	0900	0920	1000	1020	...	1100	1120	1200	1220	1300	1320	...	1400	1420
66	Baden d.	0529	0608	0629	0708	0724	0729	...	0808	0829	0908	0929	1008	1029	...	1108	1129	1208	1229	1308	1329	...	1408	1429
88	**Zürich** HB a.	|	0624	|	0724	0740	|	...	0824	|	0924	|	1024	|	...	1124	|	1224	|	1324	|	...	1424	|
	Zürich Flughafen ✈ **530/5** a.	0556	...	0656	...	...	0756	...	...	0856	...	0956	...	1056	...	...	1156	...	1256	...	1356	...	...	1456

	IR 1977	IR 2079	IR 1979	IR 2081		IR 1981	IR 2085	IR 1985		IR 2087	IR 1987	IR 2089		IR 1989	IR 2091	IR 1991		IR 1993	IR 1995	IR 1997		IR 1999	
Basel SBB d.	1413	1440	1513	1540	...	1613	1640	1713	...	1740	1813	1840	...	1913	1940	2013	...	2113	2213	2313	...	0013	...
Rheinfelden d.	1425	1451	1525	1551	...	1625	1651	1725	...	1751	1825	1851	...	1925	1951	2025	...	2125	2225	2325	...	0025	...
Brugg d.	1500	1520	1600	1620	...	1700	1720	1800	...	1820	1900	1920	...	2000	2020	2100	...	2200	2300	0000	...	0100	...
Baden d.	1508	1529	1608	1629	...	1708	1729	1808	...	1829	1908	1929	...	2008	2029	2108	...	2208	2308	0008	...	0108	...
Zürich HB a.	1524	|	1624	|	...	1724	|	1824	...	|	1924	|	...	2024	|	2124	...	2224	2324	0024	...	0124	...
Zürich Flughafen ✈ **530/5** a.	...	1556	...	1656	...	...	1756	...	...	1856	...	1956	...	...	2056	...	...	...	...	...	...	...	...

	IR 1956	IR 2058	IR 1958		IR 2060	IR 1960	IR 2062		IR 1962	IR 2066	IR 1966		IR 2068	IR 1968	IR 2070		IR 1970	IR 2072	IR 1972		IR 2074	IR 1974	IR 2076
Zürich Flughafen ✈ **530/5** d.	...	0604	...	...	0704	...	0804	...	...	0904	...	...	1004	...	1104	...	...	1204	...	...	1304	...	1404
Zürich HB d.	0536	|	0636	...	|	0736	|	...	0836	|	0936	...	|	1036	|	...	1136	|	1236	...	|	1336	|
Baden d.	0552	0633	0652	...	0733	0752	0833	...	0852	0933	0952	...	1033	1052	1133	...	1152	1233	1252	...	1333	1352	1433
Brugg d.	0601	0642	0702	...	0742	0802	0842	...	0902	0942	1002	...	1042	1102	1142	...	1202	1242	1302	...	1342	1402	1442
Rheinfelden d.	0635	0717	0734	...	0810	0834	0910	...	0934	1010	1034	...	1110	1134	1210	...	1234	1310	1334	...	1410	1434	1510
Basel SBB a.	0651	0734	0747	...	0824	0847	0924	...	0947	1024	1047	...	1124	1147	1224	...	1247	1324	1347	...	1424	1447	1524

	IR 1976	IR 2078	IR 1978	IR 2080		IR 1980	IR 2082	IR 1982	IR 2086		IR 1984	IR 2088	IR 1988		IR 2090	IR 1990	IR 2092		IR 1992	IR 1994		IR 1996	
Zürich Flughafen ✈ **530/5** d.	...	1504	...	1604	...	...	1704	...	1804	...	...	1904	...	...	2004	...	2104	...	...	...	...	...	...
Zürich HB d.	1436	|	1536	|	...	1636	|	1736	|	...	1836	|	1936	...	|	2036	|	...	2136	2236	...	2336	...
Baden d.	1452	1533	1552	1633	...	1652	1733	1752	1833	...	1852	1933	1952	...	2033	2052	2133	...	2152	2252	...	2352	...
Brugg d.	1502	1542	1602	1642	...	1702	1742	1802	1842	...	1902	1942	2002	...	2042	2102	2142	...	2202	2302	...	0002	...
Rheinfelden d.	1534	1610	1634	1710	...	1734	1810	1834	1910	...	1934	2010	2034	...	2110	2134	2210	...	2234	2334	...	0034	...
Basel SBB a.	1547	1624	1647	1724	...	1747	1824	1847	1924	...	1947	2024	2047	...	2124	2147	2224	...	2247	2347	...	0047	...

– **NOTES** (LISTED BY TRAIN NUMBER)

– [12] and ✕ (①–⑤ **h**, Karlsruhe -) Basel - Zürich.
– [12] and ✕ Zürich - Basel - Dortmund (- Hamburg ⑧ **z**).
– [12] and ✕ (①–⑥ **e**, Hamburg -) Dortmund - Basel - Zürich.
– [12] and ✕ Zürich - Dortmund - Hamburg (- Kiel ⑦ **w**, train number **2**).
– [12] and ✕ Hamburg - Basel - Zürich.
– June 15 - Dec. 13: [12] and ✕ Zürich - Basel - Hamburg.
2 – Ⓐ Dec. 16 - July 30; ①–⑤ July 31 - Dec. 12 (not May 1, Oct. 3): [12] and ✕ Zürich - Basel - Hamburg.
2 – ⑦ (also Apr. 21, June 9; not Apr. 20, June 8): [12] and ✕ Zürich - Basel - Berlin Ost.
72 – ⑥ (also Apr. 18, 20, May 1, 29, June 8, Oct. 3): [12] and ✕ Zürich - Basel - Hamburg.
03 – ①–⑥ (not Apr. 21, June 9, July 14, Nov. 11): [12] and (🍷) Paris Lyon - Basel - Zürich.
26 – ⑧ Dec. 15 - Apr. 30; ①②③⑤⑦ May 2-14; ⑧ May 15 - Dec. 12 (not May 29, Aug. 15): [12] and (🍷) Zürich - Basel - Paris Lyon.

F – [12] and ✕ Frankfurt (Main) - Basel - Zürich and v.v.
H – [12] and ✕ Zürich - Basel - Hamburg and v.v.
K – [12] and ✕ Zürich - Basel - Hamburg - Kiel and v.v.
Z – [12] and (🍷) Paris Lyon - Basel - Zürich and v.v.

d – ⚒ only.
e – Not Apr. 21, June 9.
h – Not Apr. 21, June 9, Oct. 3.
m – ⑥⑦ (not Apr. 19).
p – Dec. 15 - June 14.
q – June 15 - Dec. 13.
w – Also Apr. 21, June 9; not Apr. 20, June 8.
y – ⑦ (also Apr. 21, June 9, July 14, Nov. 11).
z – Not Apr. 20, June 8.

508 FRIBOURG - MURTEN - INS — TPF

Temporarily relocated from page 268

km		⚒	⚒	†	▲		▲			⑤⑥
0	Fribourg **505** d.	0502	0532	0602	0632	and at the	2132	...	2232	2332
22	Murten d.	0530	0600	0630	0700	same minutes	2200	...	2300	0000
32	Ins **511** a.	0540	0610	0640	0710	past each	2210	...	2310	0010
45	Neuchâtel **511** a.	...	0624	...	0724	hour until	2224	...	...	...

	⚒		▲		▲				⑥⑦
Neuchâtel **511** d.	...	0636d	0736	and at the	2136		2236	...	...
Ins **511** d.	0547	0648	0748	same minutes	2148	...	2248	2325	0028
Murten d.	0601	0701	0801	past each	2201	...	2301	2336	0039
Fribourg **505** a.	0628	0728	0828	hour until	2228	...	2328	0003	0106

d – ⚒ only.

▲ – Departures from Fribourg at 1032, 1132; from Neuchâtel at 0936, 1036 do not operate Fribourg - Murten and v.v. on Oct. 5.

511 BERN - PAYERNE and NEUCHÂTEL — BLS

km		Ⓐ	⚒																								n				m
0	**Bern** d.	0553	...	0653	...	...	0753	0808	...	...	and at	1953	2008	...	...	2034	2108	...	...	2134	2208	...	...	2234	2308	...	2334	0010	...	...
22	Kerzers ▲ d.	0610	0634	0710	0734	...	0810	0831	0834	...	the same	2010	2031	2034	...	2101	2131	2134	...	2201	2231	2234	...	2301	2331	2334	0001	0038	0040	...
	Murten d.	|	0643	|	0743	0803	|	|	0843	0903	minutes	|	|	2043	2103	|	|	2143	2203	|	|	2243	2303	|	|	2343	|	|	0049	0052
	Avenches d.	|	0649	|	...	0811	|	|	...	0911	past each	|	|	...	2111	|	|	...	2211	|	|	...	2311	|	|	2350	|	|	...	0100
	Payerne **504** a.	|	0657	|	...	0823	|	|	...	0923	hour	|	|	...	2123	|	|	...	2223	|	|	...	2323	|	|	0002	|	|	...	0112
30	Ins **508** d.	0617	...	0717	...	...	0817	0838	...	...	until	2017	2038	...	...	2107	2138	...	...	2207	2238	...	...	2313	2338	...	0013	0045	...	...
43	**Neuchâtel 508** a.	0627	...	0727	...	...	0827	0857	...	...		2027	2057	...	...	*2124*	2157	...	...	*2224*	2257	...	...	2326	2357	...	0026	0100	...	...

km																														
	Neuchâtel 508 d.	0633	...	0733	...	0801	0833	...	...	0901	0933	and at	...	...	1901	1933	...	...	2001	...	...	2101	...	...	2201	...	...	2336	...	0009
	Ins **508** d.	0643	...	0743	...	0817	0843	...	...	0917	0943	the same	...	...	1917	1943	...	...	2017	...	...	2117	...	...	2217	...	...	2352	...	0025
0	Payerne **504** d.	- |	0634	|	0736	|	|	0834	...	|	|	minutes	1834	...	|	|	1936	...	|	2036	...	|	2136	...	|	2236	...	|	0006	|
11	Avenches d.	|	0648	|	0748	|	|	0848	...	|	|	past each	1848	...	|	|	1948	...	|	2048	...	|	2148	...	|	2248	...	|	0017	|
18	Murten d.	|	0656	|	0756	|	|	0856	0917	|	|	hour	1856	1917	|	|	1956	2017	|	2056	2117	|	2156	2217	|	2256	2317	|	0025	|
26	Kerzers ▲ d.	0649	*0726*	0749	*0826*	0830	0849	...	0926	0930	0949	until	...	1926	1930	1949	...	2026	2030	...	2126	2130	...	2226	2230	...	2326	0000	0034	0038
	Bern a.	0707	...	0807	...	0852	0907	...	...	0952	1007		...	...	1952	2007	...	...	2052	...	...	2152	...	...	2252	...	...	0026	...	0103

m – ⑥⑦ (also Apr. 18, 21, May 29, June 9, Aug. 1).
n – ①②③④⑦ (also Apr. 18, Aug. 1).

▲ – **Rail service KERZERS - LYSS and v.v.**: *17 km*, journey 20 minutes.
From **Kerzers**: 0607 and hourly until 2307. From **Lyss**: 0535 and hourly until 2335, then 0009.

512 BIEL and NEUCHÂTEL - LA CHAUX DE FONDS - LE LOCLE — SBB

km		Ⓐ						▲				Ⓒ	Ⓐ															
0	**Biel / Bienne** d.	...	0614	...	0717	...	0749	and at	1517	...	1549	...	...	1717	...	1817	...	1917	...	...	2017	2117	...	2217	...	2323	...	2354
28	St Imier d.	...	0641	...	0744	...	0830	the same	1544	...	1630	...	...	1744	...	1844	...	1944	...	...	2047	2151	...	2251	...	2357	...	0028
	Neuchâtel d.	0528	|	0632	|	0732	|	minutes	|	1532	|	1632	...	|	1732	|	1832	|	1932	2032	|	|	2137	|	2237	|	2337	|
44	La Chaux de Fonds d.	0602	0655	0703	0758	0801	0847	past each	1558	1601	1647	1701	1703	1758	1801	1858	1901	1958	2001	2101	2109	2209	2213	2309	2313	0014	0017	0045
52	**Le Locle** a.	0610	...	0711	...	0809	...	hour until	...	1607	...	1707	1712	...	1809	...	1909	...	2009	2109	...	...	2221	...	2321	...	0025	...

km									⊡			▲	⊡															
0	**Le Locle** d.	0543	...	0648	...	0754	...	0832	0850	...	...	and at	1750	...	...	1850	...	...	1950	...	2032	...	2132	...	2232	...	2332	...
8	La Chaux de Fonds d.	0557	0559	0702	0702	0802	0802	0842	0902	0902	0913	the same	1802	1802	1813	1902	1902	1913	2002	2002	2042	2053	2142	2153	2242	2253	2342	2355
37	**Neuchâtel** a.	0625	|	0729	|	0829	|	0919	0929	|	|	minutes	1829	|	|	1929	|	|	2029	|	2119	|	2219	|	2319	|	0019	|
	St Imier d.	...	0612	...	0715	...	0815	...	...	0915	0929	past each	...	1815	1829	...	1915	1929	...	2015	...	2109	...	2209	...	2309	...	0012
	Biel / Bienne a.	...	0639	...	0742	...	0842	...	...	0942	1010	hour until	...	1842	1910	...	1942	2010	...	2042	...	2142	...	2242	...	2342	...	0045

⊡ – 10xx and 15xx departures from Le Locle depart at 1041 and 1540.
▲ – Times may vary by ± 3 minutes on some journeys.

Additional services operate.

513 BERN - BIEL — SBB

km		Ⓐ						and at the																	y
0	**Bern** d.	0500	0530	0600	0613	0630	0643	same minutes	2000	2013	2030	2043	...	2100	2113	2130	2200	2213	2230	2300	2313	2330	0013	0015	011
23	Lyss d.	0523	0553	0623	0630	0653	0700	past each	2023	2030	2053	2100	...	2123	2130	2153	2223	2230	2253	2323	2330	2353	0030	0038	0134
34	**Biel / Bienne** a.	0536	0606	0636	0638	0706	0708	hour until	2036	2038	2106	2108	...	2136	2138	2206	2236	2238	2306	2336	2338	0006	0038	0051	014

							and at the																	y
Biel / Bienne d.	0518	...	0552	0554	0622	0624	same minutes	1952	1954	2022	2024	...	2052	2054	2122	2124	2154	2222	2224	2254	2322	2324	2354	0026
Lyss d.	0530	...	0601	0607	0631	0637	past each	2001	2007	2031	2037	...	2101	2107	2131	2137	2207	2231	2237	2307	2331	2337	0007	0035
Bern a.	0553	...	0617	0630	0647	0700	hour until	2017	2030	2047	2100	...	2117	2130	2147	2200	2230	2247	2300	2330	2347	2400	0030	005

y – ⑥⑦ (not Apr. 19).

514 BERN - LUZERN via Langnau — BLS

For faster services Bern - (Olten -) Luzern see Tables 505 / 565

km												
0	**Bern** d.	0536a	0612	0636	0712	and at	2136	2212	2236	2312	2342	0012
21	Konolfingen d.	0552a	0634	0652	0734	the same	2152	2234	2252	2334	2356	0034
38	Langnau d.	0605	0652	0705	0752	minutes	2205	2252	2305	2352	0008	0052
75	Wolhusen d.	0645	...	0745	...	past each	2245	...	2345	...	...	...
96	**Luzern** a.	0703	...	0803	...	hour until	2303	...	0010	...	...	...

Luzern d.	0557	...	and at	2057	...	2157	...	2216	...	2316	001
Wolhusen d.	0615	...	the same	2115	...	2215	...	2240	...	2344	004
Langnau d.	0653	0707	minutes	2153	2207	2253	2307	...	0008	0022	011
Konolfingen d.	0707	0726	past each	2207	2226	2307	2326	...	0026	...	...
Bern a.	0726	0748	hour until	2226	2248	2326	2348	...	0048	...	...

a – Ⓐ only.

Additional services operate.

516 BERN - SOLOTHURN — Narrow gauge. RBS

km		⚒	⚒				and at the same																	
0	**Bern** RBS d.	0513	0550	...	0605	0635	minutes past	1905	1935	...	2005	...	2035	2105	2141	...	2211	2241	2311	2341	...	0011	...
34	Solothurn a.	0556	0627	...	0642	0712	each hour until	1942	2012	...	2042	...	2112	2142	2224	...	2254	2324	2354	0024	...	0054	...

						and at the same																	🚌
Solothurn d.	0519	0549	...	0619	0649	minutes past	1919	1949	...	2019	...	2049	2119	...	2135	2208	...	2238	2308	...	2338	...	001
Bern RBS a.	0556	0626	...	0656	0726	each hour until	1956	2026	...	2056	...	2126	2156	...	2220	2250	...	2320	2350	...	0020	...	010

y – ⑥⑦ only.

BLS — SOLOTHURN - BURGDORF - THUN — 517

km																											
0	**Solothurn** d.	0601	0701	...	0801	0901	...	1001	1101	...	1201	1301	...	1401	1501	...	1601	1701	...	1801	...	1901	...	...	...	...	...
5	Biberist Ost d.	0606	0706	...	0806	0906	...	1006	1106	...	1206	1306	...	1406	1506	...	1606	1706	...	1806	...	1906	...	...	...	...	...
21	**Burgdorf** a.	0627	0727	...	0827	0927	...	1027	1127	...	1227	1327	...	1427	1527	...	1627	1727	...	1827	...	1927	...	...	...	...	...
21	**Burgdorf** d.	0630	0730	*0747*	0830	0930	*0947*	1030	1130	*1147*	1230	1330	*1347*	1430	1530	*1547*	1630	1730	*1747*	1830	*1847*	1930	*1947*	*2047*	*2147*	*2247*	*2347*
28	Hasle-Rüegsau d.	0639	0739	0801**d**	0839	0939	1001**d**	1039	1139	1201	1239	1339	1401	1439	1539	1601	1639	1739	1801	1839	1901	1939	2001	2101	2201	2301	0001
46	Konolfingen a.	0700	0800	0822**d**	0900	1000	1022**d**	1100	1200	1222	1300	1400	1422	1500	1600	1622	1700	1800	1822	1900	1922	2000	2022	2122	2222	2322	0022
46	Konolfingen d.	0701	0801	0835	0901	1001	1035	1101	1201	1235	1301	1401	1435	1501	1601	1635	1701	1801	1835	1901	1935	2001	2035	2135	2235	2335	0035
61	**Thun** a.	0719	0819	0856	0919	1019	1056	1119	1219	1256	1319	1419	1456	1519	1619	1656	1719	1819	1856	1919	1956	2019	2056	2156	2255	2355	0055

	Ⓐ																										
Thun d.	0532	0639	0739	0839	0903	0939	1039	1103	1139	1239	1303	1339	1439	1503	1539	1639	1703	1739	1803	1839	1903	1939	2009	2109	2209	2309	0009
Konolfingen a.	0553	0658	0758	0858	0924	0958	1058	1124	1158	1258	1324	1358	1458	1524	1558	1658	1724	1758	1824	1858	1924	1958	2030	2130	2230	2330	0030
Konolfingen d.	0600	0700	0800	0900	0935**d**	1000	1100	1135	1200	1300	1335	1400	1500	1535	1600	1700	1735	1800	1835	1900	1935	2000	2035	2135	2235	2335	0035
Hasle-Rüegsau d.	0620	0720	0820	0920	0957**d**	1020	1120	1157	1220	1320	1357	1420	1520	1557	1620	1720	1757	1820	1857	1920	1957	2020	2057	2157	2257	2357	0057
Burgdorf a.	0629	0729	0829	0929	*1012*	1029	1129	*1212*	1229	1329	*1412*	1429	1529	*1612*	1629	1729	*1812*	1829	*1912*	1929	*2012*	2029	*2112*	*2212*	*2312*	*0012*	0106
Burgdorf d.	0632	0732	0832	0932	...	1032	1132	...	1232	1332	...	1432	1532	...	1632	1732	...	1832	...	1932	...	...	...	...	...	...	...
Biberist Ost d.	0650	0750	0850	0950	...	1050	1150	...	1250	1350	...	1450	1550	...	1650	1750	...	1850	...	1950	...	...	...	...	...	...	...
Solothurn a.	0657	0757	0857	0957	...	1057	1157	...	1257	1357	...	1457	1557	...	1657	1757	...	1857	...	1957	...	...	...	...	...	...	...

d – ⚒ only.
h – Change at Hasle-Rüegsau.

Additional services operate:
Solothurn - Burgdorf: 0436Ⓐ, 0518⚒, 0536Ⓐ, 0636Ⓐ, 0736Ⓐ, 1636Ⓐ, 1736Ⓐ, 1836Ⓐ, 2017, 2117, 2217, 2317, 0017⑦.
Burgdorf - Thun: 0451⚒, 0517Ⓐ, 0547⚒**h**, 0647⚒**h**, 0847⚒**h**, 1047**h**, 1247**h**, 1447**h**, 1647**h**.
Thun - Burgdorf: 0503⚒**h**, 0603⚒**h**, 0703Ⓐ, 0703⑥**h**, 0803⚒**h**, 1003⚒**h**, 1203**h**, 1403**h**, 1603**h**.
Burgdorf - Solothurn: 0502Ⓐ, 0532, 0555Ⓐ, 0632Ⓒ, 0655Ⓐ, 1555Ⓐ, 1655Ⓐ, 1755Ⓐ, 1855Ⓐ, 2015, 2115, 2215, 2315.

SBB Valid June 15 - Dec. 13 — ZÜRICH - SARGANS - CHUR — 520

km		RE 1757	IC 555	RJ 161 ✕ W	IC 10759 🍸	RE 1761	IC 559 (✕)	IC 10761 🍸	RE 1763	IC 561 (✕)	EC 163 ✕ ♦	RE 1765	IC 563 (✕)		IC 10765 🍸	RE 1767	IC 565 ✕	RJ 165 ✕ B	RE 1769	IC 569 (✕)	IC 10769 🍸	RE 1771	IC 571 (✕)	RJ 167 ✕ W	RE 1773	IC 573 ✕
	Basel SBB 510 d.	...	...	...	...	...	0633	...	...	0733	...	...	0833	...	...	...	0933	...	...	...	...	...	1133	...	...	1233
0	**Zürich** HB d.	0612	0637	0640	0707	0712	0737	0807	0812	0837	0840	0912	0937	...	1007	1012	1037	1040	1112	1137	1207	1212	1237	1240	1312	1337
12	Thalwil d.	0621	|	|	|	0721	|	|	0821	|	|	0921	|	...	|	1021	|	|	1121	|	|	1221	|	|	1321	|
24	Wädenswil d.	0632	|	|	|	0732	|	|	0832	|	|	0932	|	...	|	1032	|	|	1132	|	|	1232	|	|	1332	|
33	Pfäffikon d.	0641	|	|	|	0741	|	|	0841	|	|	0941	|	...	|	1041	|	|	1141	|	|	1241	|	|	1341	|
57	Ziegelbrücke d.	0659	|	|	|	0759	|	|	0859	|	|	0959	|	...	|	1059	|	|	1159	|	|	1259	|	|	1359	|
90	**Sargans 534** d.	0723	0733	0737	0803	0823	0833	0903	0923	0933	0937	1023	1033	...	1103	1123	1133	1137	1223	1233	1303	1323	1333	1337	1423	1433
106	Buchs 534 a.	|	|	0748	|	|	|	|	|	|	0948	|	|	...	|	|	|	1148	|	|	|	|	|	1348	|	|
103	Landquart d.	0734	0743	...	0813	0834	0843	0913	0934	0943	...	1034	1043	...	1113	1134	1143	...	1234	1243	1313	1334	1343	...	1434	1443
116	**Chur** a.	0743	0752	...	0822	0843	0852	0922	0943	0952	...	1043	1052	...	1122	1143	1152	...	1243	1252	1322	1343	1352	...	1443	1452
	St Moritz 540 a.	...	*0958*	...	...	...	*1058*	...	...	*1158*	...	...	*1258*	...	...	...	*1358*	...	...	*1458*	...	...	*1558*	...	...	*1658*

	IC 10773 🍸	RE 1775	IC 575 ✕	RJ 169 ✕ W	RE 1777	EC 207 (✕)	IC 10777 🍸	RE 1779	IC 579 (✕)	RJ 363 ✕ W	RE 1783	IC 581 (✕)	IC 10785 🍸	RE 1785	IC 585 ✕	RJ 365 ✕ N	RE 1787	IC 587 ✕	RE 1789	IC 589	EN 465 ♦	RE 1791	IC 595	RE 1793	EN 467 ♦	RE 1795
Basel SBB 510 d.	...	...	...	...	...	1433	...	...	...	...	...	1633	...	...	1733	...	...	1833	...	...	*1933*	...	...	...	*2133*	...
Zürich HB d.	1407	1412	1437	1440	1512	1537	1607	1612	1637	1640	1712	1737	1807	1812	1837	1840	1912	1937	2012	2037	2040	2112	2137	2212	2240	2312
Thalwil d.	|	1421	|	|	1521	|	|	1621	|	|	1721	|	|	1821	|	|	1921	|	2021	|	|	2121	|	2221	|	2321
Wädenswil d.	|	1432	|	|	1532	|	|	1632	|	|	1732	|	|	1832	|	|	1932	|	2032	|	|	2132	|	2232	|	2332
Pfäffikon d.	|	1441	|	|	1541	|	|	1641	|	|	1741	|	|	1841	|	|	1941	|	2041	|	|	2141	|	2241	|	2341
Ziegelbrücke d.	|	1459	|	|	1559	|	|	1659	|	|	1759	|	|	1859	|	|	1959	|	2059	|	|	2159	|	2259	|	2359
Sargans 534 d.	1503	1523	1533	1537	1623	1633	1703	1723	1733	1737	1823	1833	1903	1923	1933	1937	2023	2033	2123	2133	2137**u**	2223	2233	2323	2337	0029
Buchs 534 a.	|	|	|	1548	|	|	|	|	|	1748	|	|	|	|	|	1948	|	|	|	|	2208**u**	|	|	|	2348	|
Landquart d.	1513	1534	1543	...	1634	1643	1713	1734	1743	...	1834	1843	1913	1934	1943	...	2034	2043	2134	2143	...	2234	2243	2334	...	0040
Chur a.	1522	1543	1552	...	1643	1652	1722	1743	1752	...	1843	1852	1922	1943	1952	...	2043	2052	2143	2152	...	2243	2252	2343	...	0049
St Moritz 540 a.	...	...	*1758*	...	...	*1858*	...	...	*1958*	...	...	*2058*	...	...	*2157*	...	...	*2258*	...	...	...	...	...	...	...	...

	IC 558 ⚒	RE 1760	EN 466 ♦	IC 560 🍸	RE 1762	IC 562 ✕	RE 1764	EN 464 ♦	IC 566	RE 1766	IC 10766 🍸	IC 568 (✕)	RE 1768		RJ 362 ✕ N	IC 570 (✕)	RE 1770	IC 10770 🍸	EC 206 (✕)	RE 1772	RJ 364 ✕ W§	IC 574 ✕	RE 1774	IC 10774 🍸	IC 576 (✕)	RE 1776
St Moritz 540 d.	...	...	...	...	...	...	...	...	*0542f*	...	...	*0702*	...	...	...	*0802*	...	...	*0902*	...	...	*1002*	...	...	*1102*	...
Chur d.	0508	0516	...	0608	0616	0708	0716	...	0808	0816	0838	0908	0916	...	...	1008	1016	1038	1108	1116	...	1208	1216	1238	1308	1316
Landquart d.	0518	0525	...	0618	0625	0718	0725	...	0818	0825	0848	0918	0925	...	...	1018	1025	1048	1118	1125	...	1218	1225	1248	1318	1325
Buchs 534 d.	|	|	0601**s**	|	|	|	|	0753**s**	|	|	|	|	|	...	1012	|	|	|	|	|	1212	|	|	|	|	|
Sargans 534 d.	0528	0537	|	0628	0637	0728	0737	0823**s**	0828	0837	0858	0928	0937	...	1025	1028	1037	1058	1128	1137	1225	1228	1237	1258	1328	1337
Ziegelbrücke d.	0547	0600	|	|	0700	|	0800	|	|	0900	|	|	1000	...	|	|	1100	|	|	1200	|	|	1300	|	|	1400
Pfäffikon d.	|	0619	|	|	0719	|	0819	|	|	0919	|	|	1019	...	|	|	1119	|	|	1219	|	|	1319	|	|	1419
Wädenswil d.	|	0629	|	|	0729	|	0829	|	|	0929	|	|	1029	...	|	|	1129	|	|	1229	|	|	1329	|	|	1429
Thalwil d.	|	0639	|	|	0739	|	0839	|	|	0939	|	|	1039	...	|	|	1139	|	|	1239	|	|	1339	|	|	1439
Zürich HB a.	0623	0648	0720	0723	0748	0823	0848	0920	0923	0948	0953	1023	1048	...	1120	1123	1148	1153	1223	1248	1320	1323	1348	1353	1423	1448
Basel SBB 510 a.	0727	...	...	...	...	0927	...	...	...	...	...	1127	...	...	...	...	...	...	1327	...	...	...	...	...	1527	...

	RJ 160 ✕ W	IC 578 (✕)	RE 1778	IC 10778 🍸	IC 582 ✕	RE 1780	RJ 162 ✕ B	IC 584 ✕	RE 1782	IC 10782 🍸	IC 586 (✕)	RE 1784	EC 164 ✕ ♦	IC 588 (✕)	RE 1786	IC 10786 🍸	IC 590 (✕)	RE 1788	RJ 166 ✕ W	IC 592	RE 1790	IC 596 †	RE 1792	RJ 168 ✕ W	RE 1794	
St Moritz 540 d.	...	*1202*	...	...	*1302*	...	...	*1402*	...	...	*1502*	...	...	*1602*	...	...	*1702*	...	...	*1802*	...	*1902*	...	...	*2002*	...
Chur d.	...	1408	1416	1438	1508	1516	...	1608	1616	1638	1708	1716	...	1808	1816	1838	1908	1916	...	2008	2016	2108	2114	...	2214	...
Landquart d.	...	1418	1425	1448	1518	1525	...	1618	1625	1648	1718	1725	...	1818	1825	1848	1918	1925	...	2018	2025	2118	2124	...	2224	...
Buchs 534 d.	1412	|	|	|	|	|	1612	|	|	|	|	|	1812	|	|	|	|	|	2012	|	|	|	|	2212	|	...
Sargans 534 d.	1425	1428	1437	1458	1528	1537	1625	1628	1637	1658	1728	1737	1825	1828	1837	1858	1928	1937	2025	2028	2037	2128	2137	2225	2237	...
Ziegelbrücke d.	|	|	1500	|	|	1600	|	|	1700	|	|	1800	|	|	1900	|	|	2000	|	|	2100	|	2200	|	2300	...
Pfäffikon d.	|	|	1519	|	|	1619	|	|	1719	|	|	1819	|	|	1919	|	|	2019	|	|	2119	|	2219	|	2319	...
Wädenswil d.	|	|	1529	|	|	1629	|	|	1729	|	|	1829	|	|	1929	|	|	2029	|	|	2129	|	2229	|	2329	...
Thalwil d.	|	|	1539	|	|	1639	|	|	1739	|	|	1839	|	|	1939	|	|	2039	|	|	2139	|	2239	|	2339	...
Zürich HB a.	1520	1523	1548	1553	1623	1648	1720	1723	1748	1753	1823	1848	1920	1923	1948	1953	2023	2048	2120	2123	2148	2223	2248	2320	2348	...
Basel SBB 510 a.	...	...	...	...	1727	...	...	1827	...	...	1927	...	...	2027	...	...	2127	...	...	...	...	...	...	...	...	...

Additional services SARGANS - BUCHS and v.v.

Sargans d.	0500	0535	0600	0635	and at the same minutes past each hour until	2300	2335	...	0000
Buchs a.	0512	0544	0612	0644		2312	2344	...	0012

Buchs d.	0615	0648	0715	0748	and at the same minutes past each hour until	2315	2348	0015	0048
Sargans a.	0625	0659	0725	0759		2325	2359	0025	0059

♦ – **NOTES** (LISTED BY TRAIN NUMBER)

163/4 – TRANSALPIN – 🚃1,2 and ✕ Zürich - Graz and v.v.
164/5 – ZÜRICHSEE – 🛏 1, 2 cl., ▬ 2 cl. and 🚃2 Graz - Innsbruck - Feldkirch - Zürich and v.v.; 🛏 1, 2 cl. and ▬ 2 cl. Zagreb (**414/5**) - Schwarzach-St Veit - Zürich and v.v.; 🚃2 Beograd (**414/5**) - Zagreb - Zürich and v.v. Train numbers **1364/5** Sept. 1 - 27 (from Zürich and Graz).
466/7 – WIENER WALZER – 🛏 1, 2 cl., ▬ 2 cl. and 🚃2 Budapest - Wien - Zürich and v.v.

B – 🚃1,2 and ✕ Budapest - Wien - Zürich and v.v.
N – 🚃1,2 and ✕ Innsbruck - Zürich and v.v.
W – 🚃1,2 and ✕ Wien - Zürich and v.v.

f – 0605 on †.
s – Stops to set down only.
u – Stops to pick up only.
§ – To Salzburg on †.

✕ – Restaurant (✕) – Bistro (🍸) – Bar coach 🍸 – Minibar

522 ZIEGELBRÜCKE - LINTHAL — Valid June 15 - Dec. 13 — SBB

km											
	Zürich HB d.	...	...	...	0643		1743	...		...	...
0	Ziegelbrücke d.	0430	0530	0630	0730	and	1830	1904	and	2304	0004
11	Glarus d.	0444	0544	0644	0744	hourly	1844	1919	hourly	2319	0019
16	Schwanden d.	0500	0600	0700	0800	until	1900	1929	until	2329	0026
27	Linthal ▲ a.	0517	0617	0717	0817		1917	1946		2346	...

	Ⓐ									
Linthal ▲ d.	0443	0543		1843	...	1946	2011		2311	0011
Schwanden d.	0508	0608	and	1908	...	2008	2033	and	2333	0033
Glarus d.	0517	0617	hourly	1917	...	2017	2043	hourly	2343	0043
Ziegelbrücke a.	0530	0630	until	1930	...	2030	2056	until	2356	0056
Zürich HB a.	0617	0717		2017	...	...	...		...	...

d – ⚒ only.
q – Also Aug. 15.

▲ – 🚌 service **Linthal** - **Flüelen** Bahnhof (Table **550**) and v.v. operates **June 21 - September 21, 2014** over the Klausenpass. 🅁. Journey time: ± 2 hours 45 minutes. **NO WINTER SERVICE**.

From **Linthal**: 0825Ⓒ **q**, 0925, 1025, 1525, 1725Ⓒ **q**. From **Flüelen**: 0600Ⓒ **q**, 0730, 0930, 1500Ⓒ **q**, 1530.

Operator: PostAuto Zentralschweiz, Luzern. ✆ (Luzern) 058 448 06 22, fax: 058 667 34 33.

525 ARTH GOLDAU - ST GALLEN - ROMANSHORN — Valid June 15 - Dec. 13 — SBB, SOB*

km			2407			2411			2413			2415			2441			2443			2445			
			S			S			S			S			S			S			S			
	Luzern **550** d.	...	...	...	...	...	...	...	...	...	...	0740	...		1940	...	...	...	...	...	...	...	...	...
0	**Arth Goldau** d.	...	...	...	*0519*	...	...	*0619*	...	...	...	0814	...		2014	...	2113	...	...	2213	...	...	2313	...
20	Biberbrugg ◐ ● d.	...	...	...	0550	...	...	0653	...	...	...	0837	...		2037	...	2137	...	...	2237	...	...	2337	...
26	Samstagern ◐ ● d.	...	...	...	0601	...	...	0701	...	...	...	│	...	and at	│	...	2145	...	...	2245	...	...	2345	...
34	Pfäffikon ● d.	...	...	...	0617	...	...	0717	...	...	...	0854	...	the same	2054	...	2157	...	...	2257	...	...	2357	...
38	Rapperswil ● a.	...	...	...	0622	...	...	0722	...	...	...	0859	...	minutes	2059	...	2202	...	...	2302	...	...	0001	...
38	Rapperswil d.	...	0603	...	...	0703	...	...	0803	...	...	0903	...	past each	2103	...	...	2203	...	...	2303	...	...	...
66	Wattwil d.	0559	0628	0629	...	0728	0729	...	0828	0829	...	0928	0929	hour	2128	2129	...	2228	...	...	2328	...	...	...
89	Herisau d.	0624	0647	0654	...	0747	0754	...	0847	0854	...	0947	0954	until	2147	2154	...	2249	...	...	2349	...	...	...
97	**St Gallen** a.	0633	0655	0703	...	0755	0803	...	0855	0903	...	0955	1003		2155	2203	...	2257	...	...	2357	...	...	...
97	**St Gallen 532** d.	*0636*	...	0704	...	...	0804	...	...	0904	...	...	1004		...	2204	...	...	2304	...	...	0004	...	...
119	**Romanshorn 532** a.	*0700*	...	0730	...	...	0830	...	...	0930	...	...	1030		...	2230	...	...	2330	...	...	0030	...	...

		2404				2406				2408			2432			2434		2436			2438		2440
		S	Ⓒ	Ⓐ		S				S			S			S		S			S		S
Romanshorn 532 d.	...	...	...	...	0530	...	...	...	0630	...		1830	...	...	1930	...	2030	...	...	2130	...	2230	...
St Gallen 532 a.	...	...	...	...	0555	...	...	...	0655	...		1855	...	...	1955	...	2055	...	...	2155	...	2255	...
St Gallen d.	...	...	...	...	0557	0605	...	...	0657	0705		1857	1905	...	1957	2005	2057	2105	...	...	2205	...	2305
Herisau d.	...	0513	...	...	0606	0613	...	...	0706	0713	and at	1906	1913	...	2006	2013	2106	2113	...	...	2213	...	2313
Wattwil d.	...	0533	...	...	0630	0633	...	...	0730	0733	the same	1930	1933	...	2030	2033	2130	2133	...	...	2233	...	2333
Rapperswil a.	...	0557	...	...	...	0657	...	...	...	0757	minutes	...	1957	...	...	2057	...	2157	...	...	2257	...	2357
Rapperswil ● d.	0544	...	0636	0636	...	...	0659	...	...	0759	past each	...	1959	...	...	*2057*	...	*2157*	...	...	*2257*	...	*0003*
Pfäffikon ● d.	0549	...	0642	0642	...	...	0704	...	...	0805	hour	...	2005	...	...	*2102*	...	*2202*	...	...	*2302*	...	*0007*
Samstagern ◐ ● d.	0559	...	0654	0658	...	...	0714	...	...	│	until	...	│	...	...	*2113*	...	*2213*	...	...	*2313*	...	*0019*
Biberbrugg ◐ ● d.	0616	...	0702	0705	...	...	0721	...	...	0821		...	2021	...	...	*2121*	...	*2221*	...	...	*2321*	...	...
Arth Goldau a.	0641	...	...	...	...	...	0746	...	...	0846		...	2046	...	...	*2146*	...	*2246*	...	...	*2346*	...	...
Luzern **550** a.	...	...	...	...	...	...	...	...	...	0920		...	2120	...	...	...	...	...	...	...	...	...	...

km		Ⓐ			and at					
0	**Wädenswil** d.	0541	0609	0634	the same	2209	2234	2309	2334	0009
6	Samstagern ● d.	0549	0617	0642	minutes	2217	2242	2317	2342	0021
11	Biberbrugg ● d.	0558	0625	0651	past each	2225	2251	2325	2351	0028
17	**Einsiedeln** ● a.	0605	0632	0658	hour until	2232	2258	2332	2358	0035

	Ⓐ			and at					Z
Einsiedeln ● d.	0454	0525	0558	the same	2225	2258	2325	...	0000
Biberbrugg ● d.	0501	0532	0607	minutes	2232	2307	2332	...	0007
Samstagern ● d.	0510	0541	0617	past each	2241	2317	2341	...	0017
Wädenswil a.	0518	0549	0625	hour until	2249	2325	2349	...	0025

S – VORALPEN EXPRESS – 🚃 Luzern / Arth Goldau / Rapperswil - St Gallen and v.v. Also conveys (🍸) on most services.
Z – Night of ⑤/⑥ and ⑥/⑦ (also July 31 / Aug. 1).

◐ – For service to Einsiedeln – see panel.
● – Additional services run Einsiedeln - Biberbrugg - Samstagern - Pfäffikon - Rapperswil and v.v.
* – Operated by SOB, except Rapperswil - Wattwil (SBB).

526 GOSSAU - APPENZELL - WASSERAUEN — Narrow gauge. AB

km		⚒																								
0	**Gossau** d.	0547	0647	0747	0852	0952	1052	1122	1152	1222	1252	1322	1422	1522	1552	1622	1722	1752	...	1852	1952	2052	...	2152	2252	2352
5	Herisau a.	0554	0654	0754	0859	0959	1059	1129	1159	1229	1259	1329	1429	1529	1559	1629	1729	1759	...	1859	1959	2059	...	2159	2259	2359
5	Herisau d.	0555a	0700	0800	0900	1000	1100	1130	1200	1230	1300	1330	1430	1530	1600	1630	1730	1800	...	1900	2000	2100	...	2200	2300	0000
15	Urnäsch d.	0610a	0715	0815	0915	1015	1115	1145	1215	1245	1315	1345	1445	1545	1615	1645	1745	1815	...	1915	2015	2115	...	2215	2315	0015
26	**Appenzell** d.	0631a	0731	0831	0931	1031	1131	1201	1231	1301	1330	1401	1501	1601	1631	1701	1803	1831	...	1930	2030	2130	...	2230	2330	0030
32	**Wasserauen** a.	0642a	0742	0842	0942	1042	1142	1212	1242	1312	...	1412	1512	1612	1642	1712	1814	1842	...	*1942*y	*2042*y	*2142*y	...	...	...	...

																						🚌 j		
Wasserauen d.	...	...	0648a	0748	0848	0948	1048	1148	1218	1248	1318	...	1418	1518	1618	1648	1718	1818	1848	...	*1942*y	*2042*y	2142	...	...
Appenzell d.	0605a	0630	0700a	0800	0900	1000	1100	1200	1230	1300	1330	1400	1430	1530	1630	1700	1730	1830	1900	1930	2000	2100	2153	2200	2300
Urnäsch d.	0620a	0645	0715a	0815	0915	1015	1115	1215	1245	1315	1345	1415	1445	1545	1645	1715	1745	1845	1915	1945	2015	2115	...	2215	2315
Herisau a.	0634a	0700	0730a	0830	0930	1030	1130	1230	1300	1330	1400	1430	1500	1600	1700	1730	1800	1900	1930	2000	2030	2130	...	2230	2330
Herisau d.	0636	0701	0731	0831	0931	1031	1131	1231	1301	1331	1401	1431	1501	1601	1701	1731	1801	1901	1931	2001	2031	2131	...	2231	2331
Gossau a.	0641	0707	0737	0837	0937	1037	1137	1237	1307	1337	1407	1437	1507	1607	1707	1737	1807	1907	1937	2007	2037	2137	...	2237	2337

a – Ⓐ only. j – May 11 - Nov. 2. y – Connection by 🚌. Additional services operate May 11 - Nov. 2.

527 ST GALLEN - APPENZELL — Narrow gauge rack railway. AB

km		⚒	⚒	Ⓐ			⚒			and				q							Ⓐ			🚌	🚌	🚌 z
0	**St Gallen** d.	0608	0638a	0708	0738d	0808	0838	0908	0938	every	1608	1638	1708	1722	1738	1808	1838	1908	1938	2008	2108	2138	...	2230	2330	0030
7	Teufen d.	0624	0654a	0724	0754d	0824	0854	0924	0954	30	1624	1654	1724	1738	1754	1824	1854	1924	1954	2024	2124	2154	...	2242	2342	0042
14	Gais ▲ d.	0640	0710	0740	0810	0840	0910	0940	1010	minutes	1640	1710	1740	1750	1810	1840	1910	1940	2010	2040	2140	2210	...	2252	2352	0052
20	**Appenzell** a.	0651	0721	0751	0821	0851	0921	0951	1021	until	1651	1721	1751j	1759	1821	1851	1921	1951	2021	2051	2151	2221	...	2302	0002	0102

	⚒	Ⓐ	⚒	Ⓐ		⚒				and				Ⓒ	Ⓐ						Ⓐ		🚌	🚌	🚌	🚌 k
Appenzell d.	0515	0608	0638	0701	0708c	0738	0808	0838	0908	every	1538	1608	1638	1708	1708	1738	1808	1838	1908	1938	2008	2038	2108	2155	2249	2349
Gais ▲ d.	0527	0620	0650	0711	0720	0750	0820	0850	0920	30	1550	1620	1650	1720	1725	1750	1820	1850	1920	1950	2020	2050	2117	2204	2258	2358
Teufen d.	0540	0633	0703	0724	0733	0803	0833	0903	0933	minutes	1603	1633	1703	1733	1738	1803	1833	1903	1933	2003	2033	2103	2127	2215	2308	0008
St Gallen a.	0558	0651	0721	0739	0751	0821	0851	0921	0951	until	1621	1651	1721	1751	1756	1821	1851	1921	1951	2021	2051	2121	2140	2228	2321	0021

a – Ⓐ only.
c – Ⓒ only.
d – ⚒ only.
j – Ⓒ Jan. 4 - July 6; daily July 7 - Aug. 10; Ⓒ Aug. 16 - Dec. 13.
k – ⑤⑥ (also Apr. 17, 20, 30, May 28, 29, June 8, July 31).
q – Ⓐ Jan. 3 - July 4, Aug. 11 - Dec. 12.
z – ⑥⑦ (also Apr. 18, 21, May 1, 29, 30, June 9, Aug. 1).

▲ – Rail service **Gais - Altstätten Stadt** and v.v. *8 km*. Journey time: 19 - 22 minutes. **Operator**: AB.
From **Gais**: 0621Ⓐ, 0721 and hourly until 1821, then 1921🚌, 2021🚌.
From **Altstätten Stadt**: 0648Ⓐ, 0748 and hourly until 1848, then 1948🚌, 2048🚌.
·A bus connects Altstätten Stadt with Altstätten SBB station (Table **534**). Journey time: 6 minutes.

529 ZÜRICH - ZÜRICH FLUGHAFEN ✈ — Valid June 15 - Dec. 13 — SBB

Additional services are available at peak times. Journey time: 9 - 13 minutes

From **Zürich** HB:
0502, 0521, 0539, 0547, 0601, 0607, 0609, 0614, 0617, 0637, 0639, 0644, 0647, 0707, 0709, 0714, 0717, 0737, 0739, 0744, 0747, 0801, 0807, 0809, 0814, 0817, 0837, 0839, 0844, 0847, and at xx01, xx07, xx09, xx14, xx17, xx37, xx39, xx44, xx47 minutes past each hour until 2047, then 2107, 2109, 2114, 2117, 2139, 2144, 2147, 2207, 2209, 2214, 2217, 2239, 2247, 2307, 2309, 2314, 2317, 0008⑥⑦, 0017.

From **Zürich** Flughafen:
0502, 0540, 0602, 0606, 0613, 0632, 0636, 0640, 0643, 0702, 0706, 0710, 0713, 0732, 0736, 0739, 0743, 0802, 0806, 0810, 0813, 0832, 0836, 0840, 0843, 0847, 0902, 0906, 0910, 0913, 0932, 0936, 0940, 0943, 0947, and at xx02, xx06, xx10, xx13, xx32, xx36, xx40, xx43, xx47 minutes past each hour until 2047, then 2102, 2106, 2110, 2113, 2132, 2136, 2140, 2143, 2202, 2213, 2232, 2236, 2240, 2243, 2302, 2332, 2336, 2340, 2343, 0002, 0041.

SBB ZÜRICH - ST GALLEN 530

km		IC 705	ICN 507	IC 707		ICN 509	EC 191	IC 709	ICN 1511	IC 711		ICN 515	EC 193	IC 715	ICN 1517	IC 717	ICN 519	IC 719		ICN 1521	IC 721	ICN 523	EC 195	IC 723
		✕		✕			✕	(✕)	✕	✕			✕	(✕)	✕	✕		✕		✕	✕	✕	✕	✕
							M	F					M										M	
	Genève Aéroport ✈ **505** d.	...	...	...	...	...	...	...	...	...	...	...	...	0636	...	0736j	0805j	0836j	...	...	0936j	1009	...	1036j
	Genève **505** d.	...	...	...	...	...	...	...	...	0545	...	0614	...	0645	...	0745	0814	0845	...	...	0945	1018	...	1045
	Lausanne **505** d.	...	...	...	...	...	...	...	0539	0620	...	|	...	0720	0745	0820	|	0920	...	0945	1020	|	...	1120
	Biel **500** d.	...	...	...	...	0543	...	...	0644	|	...	0746	...	|	0846	|	0946	|	...	1046	|	1146	...	|
	Bern **500** d.	...	...	0530z	...	|	...	0632	|	0732	...	|	...	0832	|	0932	|	1032	...	|	1132	|	...	1232
0	**Zürich HB 535** d.	0539	0609	0639	...	0709	0716	0739	0809	0839	...	0909	0916	0939	1009	1039	1109	1139	...	1209	1239	1309	1316	1339
10	**Zürich Flughafen** ✈ **535** d.	0552	0622	0652	...	0722	0728u	0752	0822	0852	...	0922	0928u	0952	1022	1052	1122	1152	...	1222	1252	1322	1328u	1352
30	Winterthur **535** d.	0607	0637	0707	...	0737	0742	0807	0837	0907	...	0937	0942	1007	1037	1107	1137	1207	...	1237	1307	1337	1342	1407
57	Wil **539** d.	0625	0654	0725	...	0754	|	0825	0854	0925	...	0954	|	1025	1054	1125	1154	1225	...	1254	1325	1354	|	1425
78	Gossau d.	0645	0707	0745	...	0807	|	0845	0907	0945	...	1007	|	1045	1107	1145	1207	1245	...	1307	1345	1407	|	1445
87	**St Gallen** a.	0653	0715	0753	...	0815	0818	0853	0915	0953	...	1015	1018	1053	1115	1153	1215	1253	...	1315	1353	1415	1418	1453

	ICN 1525	IC 725	ICN 527		IC 727	ICN 1529	IC 729	ICN 531	IR 3831	IC 731	ICN 1535	EC 197	IC 735	ICN 537	IC 737	ICN 1539	IC 739		ICN 541	IC 741	ICN 1543	IR 3849	ICN 545	ICN 1547
	✕	✕			✕	✕	(✕)	✕		✕	✕	✕	(✕)		✕	✕	✕							
									Ⓐ			M												
Genève Aéroport ✈ **505** d.	...	1136j	1209	...	1236j	...	1336j	1409	...	1436j	...	...	1536j	1609	1636j	...	1736j	...	1809	1836j	...	...	2009	...
Genève **505** d.	...	1145	1218	...	1245	...	1345	1418	...	1445	...	...	1545	1618	1645	...	1745	...	1818	1845	...	...	2018	...
Lausanne **505** d.	1145	1220	|	...	1320	1345	1420	|	...	1520	1545	...	1620	|	1720	1745	1820	...	|	1920	1945	...	|	2145
Biel **500** d.	1246	|	1346	...	|	1446	|	1546	...	|	1646	...	|	1746	|	1846	|	...	1946	|	2046	...	2146	2246
Bern **500** d.	|	1332	|	...	1432	|	1532	|	...	1632	|	...	1732	|	1832	|	1932	...	|	2032	|	...	|	|
Zürich HB 535 d.	1409	1439	1509	...	1539	1609	1639	1709	1733	1739	1809	1816	1839	1909	1939	2009	2039	...	2109	2139	2209	2239	2309	0017
Zürich Flughafen ✈ **535** d.	1422	1452	1522	...	1552	1622	1652	1722	1745	1752	1822	1828u	1852	1922	1952	2022	2052	...	2122	2152	2222	2252	2322	0029
Winterthur **535** d.	1437	1507	1537	...	1607	1637	1707	1737	1801	1807	1837	1842u	1907	1937	2007	2037	2107	...	2137	2207	2237	2307	2337	0044
Wil **539** d.	1454	1525	1554	...	1625	1654	1725	1754	|	1825	1854	|	1925	1954	2025	2054	2125	...	2154	2225	2254	2325	2354	0100
Gossau d.	1507	1545	1607	...	1645	1707	1745	1807	|	1845	1907	|	1945	2007	2045	2107	2145	...	2207	2245	2307	2345	0011	0118
St Gallen a.	1515	1553	1615	...	1653	1715	1753	1815	1839	1853	1915	1919u	1953	2015	2053	2115	2153	...	2215	2253	2315	2353	0018	0125

		IC 708	ICN 1510	IC 710	ICN 512	IR 3810	IC 712	ICN 1514	IC 716	ICN 518	IC 718	ICN 1520		IC 720	EC 196	ICN 522	IC 722	ICN 1524		IC 724	ICN 526	IC 726	ICN 1528	IC 728
			✕	✕			✕	✕	✕		(✕)	✕		✕	✕	✕	(✕)	✕		✕	✕	✕	✕	✕
						R									M									
St Gallen d.	0432	0511	0544	0611	0642	0644	0711	0748	0811	0848	0911	0948	...	1011	1042	1048	1111	1148	...	1211	1248	1311	1348	1411
Gossau d.	0439	0519	0551	0619	0649	0652	0719	0756	0819	0856	0919	0956	...	1019	|	1056	1119	1156	...	1219	1256	1319	1356	1419
Wil **539** d.	0456	0539	0610	0639	0706	0711	0739	0810	0839	0910	0939	1010	...	1039	|	1110	1139	1210	...	1239	1310	1339	1410	1439
Winterthur **535** d.	0516	0558	0628	0658	0725	0733	0758	0828	0858	0928	0958	1028	...	1058	1119	1128	1158	1228	...	1258	1328	1358	1428	1458
Zürich Flughafen ✈ **535** a.	0529	0611	0641	0711	0737	|	0811	0841	0911	0941	1011	1041	...	1111	1132s	1141	1211	1241	...	1311	1341	1411	1441	1511
Zürich HB 535 a.	...	0623	0653	0723	0751	0759	0823	0853	0923	0953	1023	1053	...	1123	1144	1153	1223	1253	...	1323	1353	1423	1453	1523
Bern **500** a.	...	0728	|	0828	|	...	0928	|	1028	|	1128	|	...	1228	...	|	1328	|	...	1428	|	1528	|	1628
Biel **500** a.	...	|	0813	|	0913	...	|	1013	|	1113	|	1213	...	|	...	1313	|	1413	...	|	1513	|	1613	|
Lausanne **505** a.	...	0840	0915	0940	|	...	1040	1115	1140	|	1240	1315	...	1340	...	|	1440	1515	...	1540	|	1640	1715	1740
Genève **505** a.	...	0915	...	1015	1042	...	1115	...	1215	1242	1315	...	...	1415	...	1442	1515	...	...	1615	1642	1715	...	1815
Genève Aéroport ✈ **505** a.	...	0924j	...	1024j	1051	...	1124j	...	1224j	1251	1324j	...	...	1424j	...	1451	1524j	...	...	1624j	1651	1724j	...	1824j

	ICN 530	IC 730	EC 194	ICN 1532	IC 732	ICN 536	IC 736		ICN 1538	IC 738		ICN 540	IC 740	EC 192	ICN 1542	IC 742	ICN 1544	IC 744		EC 190	ICN 1546	ICN 548	ICN 500	
	✕	✕	✕	✕	✕		✕		✕	(✕)		✕	✕	✕	✕	(✕)	✕	✕		✕				
			M											M		F				M				
St Gallen d.	1448	1511	1542	1548	1611	1648	1711	...	1748	1811	...	1848	1911	1942	1948	2011	2048	2111	...	2142	2148	2248	2348	...
Gossau d.	1456	1519	|	1556	1619	1656	1719	...	1756	1819	...	1856	1919	|	1956	2019	2056	2119	...	|	2156	2256	2356	...
Wil **539** d.	1510	1539	|	1610	1639	1710	1739	...	1810	1839	...	1910	1939	|	2010	2039	2110	2139	...	|	2210	2310	0010	...
Winterthur **535** d.	1528	1558	1619	1628	1658	1728	1758	...	1828	1858	...	1928	1958	2019	2028	2058	2128	2158	...	2219	2228	2328	0028	...
Zürich Flughafen ✈ **535** a.	1541	1611	1632s	1641	1711	1741	1811	...	1841	1911	...	1941	2011	2032s	2041	2111	2141	2211	...	2232s	2241	2341	0041	...
Zürich HB 535 a.	1553	1623	1644	1653	1723	1753	1823	...	1853	1923	...	1953	2023	2044	2053	2123	2153	2223	...	2244	2253	2353	0053	...
Bern **500** a.	|	1728	...	|	1828	|	1928	...	|	2028	...	|	2128	...	|	2228	|	2331	...	...	|	|	|	...
Biel **500** a.	1713	|	...	1813	|	1913	|	...	2013	|	...	2113	|	...	2213	...	2314	...	...	...	0022	...	...	...
Lausanne **505** a.	|	1840	...	1915	1940	|	2040	...	2115	2140	...	|	2240	...	2315	...	0015	...	...	...	0124y	...	...	...
Genève **505** a.	1842	1915	...	...	2015	2046	2115	...	...	2215	...	2246	2327	...	...	...	...	...	...	...	...	...	...	...
Genève Aéroport ✈ **505** a.	1851	1924j	...	...	2024j	2055j	2124j	...	...	2224j	...	...	2338j	...	...	...	...	...	...	...	...	...	...	...

F – From/to Fribourg.
M – 🚂12 Zürich - München and v.v.
R – Ⓐ: 🚂12 Rorschach - Zürich.

j – Dec. 15 - July 14.
s – Stops to set down only.
u – Stops to pick up only.

y – ⑥⑦ (not Apr. 19, Aug. 2).
z – Depart 0513 on Jan. 26, 27, Feb. 17, 23-28, Mar. 3-6, 31, May 12-15, 17-22, 26, June 2, Aug. 11, Sept. 8, 29, 30, Oct. 1, 2, 6-9, 26, 27, Nov. 1-3, 8-10, 17, Dec. 1, 8.

SBB Valid June 15 - Dec. 13 WINTERTHUR - SCHAFFHAUSEN 531

km																								
0	Winterthur d.	0542	0606	0619	0642	and at the same	1806	1819	1842	1906	1919	1942	2006	2019	2042	...	2106	2119	2142	2208	2242	2308	2342	...	0012
30	Schaffhausen a.	0614	0638	0646	0714	minutes past each hour until	1838	1846	1914	1938	1946	2014	2038	2046	2114	...	2138	2146	2214	2238	2314	2338	0014	...	0041

						Ⓐ		Ⓐ			Ⓐ													
chaffhausen d.	0514	0521	0546	0614	0621	0631	0646	0701	0714	0721	0731	0746	0814	0821	0846	and at the same	2014	2021	2046	2121	2146	2221	2246	2321	2346
interthur a.	0542	0554	0619	0642	0654	0659	0719	0729	0742	0754	0759	0819	0842	0854	0919	minutes past each hour until	2042	2054	2119	2154	2219	2254	2319	2354	0023

SBB, THURBO* SCHAFFHAUSEN - ROMANSHORN - RORSCHACH 532

km																								
0	**Schaffhausen 939/40** d.	...	...	...	...	0503	...	0531	...	0601	...		2031	...	2101	...	...	2131	2201	...	2231	2301	2331	0005
20	Stein am Rhein d.	...	...	...	...	0527	...	0557	...	0627	...		2057	...	2127	...	...	2157	2227	...	2257	2327	2357	0027
46	**Kreuzlingen** d.	0500	...	0530	...	0600	...	0630	...	0700	...	and at	2130	...	2200	...	...	2230	2300	...	2330	0000	0026	0056
47	Kreuzlingen Hafen d.	0502	...	0532	...	0602	...	0632	...	0702	...	the same	2132	...	2202	...	...	2232	2302	...	2332	0002	...	...
65	**Romanshorn** a.	0525	...	0555	...	0625	...	0655	...	0725	...	minutes	2155	...	2225	...	...	2255	2325	...	2355	0025	...	...
65	**Romanshorn** d.	0530	0532	0600	0601	0630	0632	0700	0701	0730	0732	past each	2200	2201	2230	2232	...	*2301*	2330	2332	*0001*	*0032*	...	...
	St Gallen **525** a.	0555	|	0624	|	0655	|	0724	|	0755	|	hour	2224	|	2255	|	...	|	2355	|	|	|	...	...
73	Arbon a.	...	0540	...	0610	...	0640	...	0710	...	0740	until	...	2210	...	2240	...	*2310*	...	2340	*0010*	*0040*	...	...
79	Rorschach Hafen a.	...	0548	...	0618	...	0648	...	0718	...	0748		...	2218	...	2248	...	*2318*	...	2348	*0018*	*0048*	...	...
80	**Rorschach** a.	...	0551	...	0621	...	0651	...	0721	...	0751		...	2221	...	2251	...	*2321*	...	2351	*0021*	*0051*	...	...

orschach d.	...	...	...	...	0609	...	0639	...		2109	...	2139	...	...	2209	...	2239	...	2309	...	2339	...	0009	...
orschach Hafen d.	...	...	...	...	0610	...	0640	...		2110	...	2140	...	...	2210	...	2240	...	2310	...	2340	...	0010	...
rbon d.	...	...	...	...	0619	...	0649	...	and at	2119	...	2149	...	...	2219	...	2249	...	2319	...	2349	...	0019	...
St Gallen **525** d.	...	...	...	...	|	0604	|	0636	the same	|	2104	|	2136	...	|	2204	|	2236	|	2304	|	...	|	0004
omanshorn a.	...	...	...	...	0628	0630	0658	0700	minutes	2128	2130	2158	2200	...	2228	2230	2258	2300	2328	2330	2358	...	0028	0030
omanshorn d.	...	0502	0532	0602	...	0632	...	0702	past each	...	2132	...	2202	...	...	2232	...	2302	...	2332	...	0002	...	0032
euzlingen Hafen d.	...	0523	0553	0623	...	0653	...	0723	hour	...	2153	...	2223	...	...	2253	...	2323	...	2353	...	0023	...	0053
euzlingen d.	0501	0531	0601	0631	...	0701	...	0731	until	...	2201	...	2231	...	...	2301	...	2331	...	0001	...	0026	...	0056
ein am Rhein d.	0530	0600	0630	0700	...	0730	...	0800		...	2230	...	2300	...	...	2330	...	0003	...	0030	...	...	...	...
chaffhausen 939/40 a.	0556	0626	0656	0726	...	0756	...	0826		...	2256	...	2326	...	...	2356	...	0030	...	0054	...	...	...	...

* – SBB operate Romanshorn - Rorschach; THURBO operate Schaffhausen - Romanshorn.

533 SCHAFFHAUSEN - KREUZLINGEN

Valid April 5 - Oct. 19, 2014 (no winter service) URh

	✕A		✕C		✕A		✕A		
Schaffhausen d.	0910	...	1110	...	1318	...	1518	...	...
Stein am Rhein d.	1115	...	1315	...	1523	...	1723	...	...
Kreuzlingen Hafen a.	1355	...	1555	...	1805	...	2005y	...	...

	✕A		✕B		✕A		✕D		
Kreuzlingen Hafen d.	0900	...	1100	...	1427	...	1627	...	...
Stein am Rhein d.	1130	...	1330	...	1657	...	1857	...	...
Schaffhausen a.	1245	...	1445	...	1815	...	2015y	...	...

A – Ⓒ Apr. 5 - 13; daily Apr. 18 - Oct. 5.
B – Ⓒ Apr. 5 - 13; daily Apr. 18 - Oct. 19.
C – † Apr. 6 - June 22; daily June 28 - Sept. 14, Oct. 5 - 19 (also June 19, Sept. 21, 28, Oct. 3).
D – † Apr. 6 - June 22; daily June 28 - Sept. 14 (also June 19, Sept. 21, 28, Oct. 3, 5).
y – Not Aug. 9.

534 ST GALLEN - BUCHS - CHUR

SBB

km		RE 3803 R	RE 3805 R	RE 3807 R	EC 191 M	RE 3809 R	RE 3811 R	EC 193 M	RE 3813 R	RE 3815 R	RE 3817 R	RE 3819 R	EC 195 M	RE 3821 R	RE 3823 R	RE 3825 R	RE 3827 R	RE 3829 R	EC 197 M	RE 3833 R	RE 3835 R	IC 589				RE 1795
	Wil 530 d.	...	0602	0702	...	0802	0902		1002	1102	1202	1302	...	1402	1502	1602	1702	1802	...	1902	2002	...	...	...	...	...
0	**St Gallen** d.	0526	0626	0726	0819	0826	0926	1019	1026	1126	1226	1326	1419	1426	1526	1626	1726	1826	1919	1926	2026	...	2126	2226	2326	...
16	Rorschach d.	0540	0640	0740	|	0840	0940	|	1040	1140	1240	1340	|	1440	1540	1640	1740	1840	|	1940	2040	...	2140	2240	2340	...
27	**St Margrethen** d.	0547	0647	0747	0840	0847	0947	1040	1047	1147	1247	1347	1440	1447	1547	1647	1747	1847	1940	1947	2047	...	2147	2247	2347	...
39	Altstätten 527 d.	0600	0700	0800	...	0900	1000	...	1100	1200	1300	1400	...	1500	1600	1700	1800	1900	...	2000	2100	...	2200	2300	0000	...
65	**Buchs 520** ⊖ d.	0615	0715	0815	...	0915	1015	...	1115	1215	1315	1415	...	1515	1615	1715	1815	1915	...	2015	2115	...	2215	2315	0015	...
81	Sargans **520** ⊖ d.	0627	0727	0827	...	0927	1027	...	1127	1227	1327	1427	...	1527	1627	1727	1827	1927	...	2027	2125	2133	2225	2325	0025	0029
93	Landquart **520** d.	0640	0739	0839	...	0939	1039	...	1139	1239	1339	1439	...	1539	1639	1739	1839	1939	...	2039	...	2143	...	...	...	0040
107	**Chur 520** a.	0649	0748	0848	...	0948	1048	...	1148	1248	1348	1448	...	1548	1648	1748	1848	1948	...	2048	...	2152	...	...	...	0049

	RE 3808 R	RE 3812 R	RE 3814 R	RE 3816 R	RE 3818 R	EC 196 M	RE 3820 R	RE 3822 R	RE 3824 R	RE 3826 R	RE 3828 R	EC 194 M	RE 3830 R	RE 3832 R	RE 3834 R	RE 3836 R	EC 192 M	RE 3838 R	RE 3840 R	EC 190 M	RE 1792		RE 1794			
Chur 520 d.	...	0612	0712	0812	0912	...	1012	1112	1212	1312	1412	...	1512	1612	1712	1812	...	1912	2012	...	2114	...	2214	...	2300	*2300*
Landquart **520** d.	...	0622	0722	0822	0922	...	1022	1122	1222	1322	1422	...	1522	1622	1722	1822	...	1922	2022	...	2124	...	2224	...	2309	*2309*
Sargans **520** ⊖ d.	0535	0635	0735	0835	0935	...	1035	1135	1235	1335	1435	...	1535	1635	1735	1835	...	1935	2035	...	2131	2135	2231	2235	2320	2335
Buchs 520 ⊖ d.	0545	0645	0745	0845	0945	...	1045	1145	1245	1345	1445	...	1545	1645	1745	1845	...	1945	2045	...	...	2145	...	2245	...	2345
Altstätten **527** d.	0601	0701	0801	0901	1001	...	1101	1201	1301	1401	1501	...	1601	1701	1801	1901	...	2001	2101	...	...	2201	...	2301	...	0001
St Margrethen d.	0612	0712	0812	0912	1012	1020	1112	1212	1312	1412	1512	1520	1612	1712	1812	1912	1920	2012	2112	2120	...	2212	...	2312	...	0012
Rorschach d.	0620	0720	0820	0920	1020	|	1120	1220	1320	1420	1520	|	1620	1720	1820	1920	|	2020	2120	|	...	2220	...	2320	...	0020
St Gallen a.	0634	0734	0834	0934	1034	1041	1134	1234	1334	1434	1534	1541	1634	1734	1834	1934	1941	2034	2134	2141	...	2234	...	2334	...	0034
Wil 530 a.	0658	0758	0858	0958	1058	...	1158	1258	1358	1458	1558	...	1658	1758	1858	1958	...	2058	2158	...	...	...	...	...	...	...

⊖ – 🚌 services to **VADUZ (LIECHTENSTEIN)**

[line 11]	Ⓐ	Ⓐ	Ⓐ	⚒		Ⓐ					and at the										⚒	⑥
Feldkirch (Bahnhof) d.	...	...	...	...	...	0625	0655	...	0725	0755	same minutes	1825	1855	...	1925	1955	2055	2155	...	2255	2325	2355
Schaan (Bahnhof) d.	0520	0532	0602	0632	...	0702	0732	...	0802	0832	past each	1902	1932	...	2002	2032	2132	2232	...	2332	0002	0032
Vaduz Post d.	0527	0543	0613	0643	...	0713	0743	...	0813	0843	hour until	1913	1943	...	2010	2043	2143	2243	...	2340	0010	0040
Sargans (Bahnhof) a.	0558	0615	0645	0715	...	0745	0815	...	0845a	0915		1945a	2015	...	...	2115	2215	2315d	...	...	...	...

[line 11]	Ⓐ								and at the								⑥			
Sargans (Bahnhof) d.	...	0544a	0614a	...	0644	...	0714a	0744	same minutes	1914a	1944	...	2044	2144	...	2244	...	2344	...	...	...
Vaduz Post d.	0548	0618	0648	...	0718	...	0748	0818	past each	1948	2018	...	2118	2218	...	2318	...	0018	...	...	...
Schaan (Bahnhof) d.	0600	0630	0700	...	0730	...	0800	0830	hour until	2000	2030	...	2130	2230	...	2328	...	0028	...	...	...
Feldkirch (Bahnhof) a.	0636	0706	0736	...	0806	...	0836	0906		2036	2106	...	2206	2306	...	...	...	...	...	...	...

🚌 [line 12] **Buchs** (Bahnhof) - **Vaduz** (Post) and v.v. Journey time: ± 15 minutes. Service shown operates on Ⓐ only. Services also operate between Buchs and Schaan (every 20 minutes on Ⓐ, every 30 minutes on Ⓒ). Operator: LIEmobil, Postplatz 7, FL-9494 Schaan. ✆ +423 237 94 94, fax +423 237 94 99, (www.liemobil.li).

From **Buchs**: 0648, 0703, 0718, 0733, 0748, 0803, 1618, 1633, 1648, 1703, 1718, 1733, 1748. From **Vaduz**: 0652, 0707, 0722, 0737, 0752, 1622, 1637, 1652, 1707, 1722, 1737, 1752.

M – (12) and ✕ Zürich - München and v.v.
R – RHEINTAL EXPRESS.
a – Ⓐ only.
d – ⚒ only.

535 ZÜRICH - KONSTANZ and ROMANSHORN

Valid June 15 - Dec. 13 SBB

km		IC 807 (✕)	IR 2107	IC 809 ✕	IR 2109	IC 811 ✕	IR 2111	IC 815 ✕	IR 2115	IC 817 (✕)	IR 2117	IC 819 ✕	IR 2119	IC 821 (✕)	IR 2121	IC 823 ✕	IR 2123	IC 825 (✕)	IR 2125	IC 827 ✕	IR 2127	IC 829 ✕	IR 2129	IC 831 ✕	IR 2131
	Brig 560 d.	...	...	...	...	0547	...	0649	...	0749	...	0849	...	0949	...	1049	...	1149	...	1249	...	1349	...	1449	...
	Bern 500 d.	...	...	0602	...	0702	...	0802	...	0902	...	1002	...	1102	...	1202	...	1302	...	1402	...	1502	...	1602	...
	Biel 500 d.	...	0515	|	0613	|	0715	|	0815	|	0915	|	1015	|	1115	|	1215	|	1315	|	1415	|	1515	|	1615
0	**Zürich HB 530** d.	0607	0637	0707	0737	0807	0837	0907	0937	1007	1037	1107	1137	1207	1237	1307	1337	1407	1437	1507	1537	1607	1637	1707	1737
10	**Zürich Flug** ✈ **530** d.	0618	0648	0718	0748	0818	0848	0918	0948	1018	1048	1118	1148	1218	1248	1318	1348	1418	1448	1518	1548	1618	1648	1718	1748
30	Winterthur **530** d.	0635	0705	0735	0805	0835	0905	0935	1005	1035	1105	1135	1205	1235	1305	1335	1405	1435	1505	1535	1605	1635	1705	1735	1805
46	Frauenfeld d.	0647	0717	0747	0817	0847	0917	0947	1017	1047	1117	1147	1217	1247	1317	1347	1417	1447	1517	1547	1617	1647	1717	1747	1817
64	Weinfelden **539** ▲ d.	0700	0730	0800	0830	0900	0930	1000	1030	1100	1130	1200	1230	1300	1330	1400	1430	1500	1530	1600	1630	1700	1730	1800	1830
	Kreuzlingen ▲ a.	|	0750	|	0850	|	0950	|	1050	|	1150	|	1250	|	1350	|	1450	|	1550	|	1650	|	1750	|	1850
	Konstanz ▲ a.	|	0754	|	0854	|	0954	|	1054	|	1154	|	1254	|	1354	|	1454	|	1554	|	1654	|	1754	|	1854
86	**Romanshorn** a.	0718	...	0817	...	0918	...	1018	...	1118	...	1218	...	1318	...	1418	...	1518	...	1618	...	1718	...	1818	...

	IC 835 (✕)	IR 2135	IC 837 ✕	IR 2137	IC 839 (✕)	IR 2139	IC 841 ✕	IC 843	IC 845	IC 801 ⑥⑦
Brig 560 d.	1549	...	1649	...	1749	...	1849	1949	...	...
Bern 500 d.	1702	...	1802	...	1902	...	2002	2102	2202	...
Biel 500 d.	|	1715	|	1815	|	1915	|	|	|	...
Zürich HB 530 d.	1807	1837	1907	1937	2007	2037	2107	2207	2307	0008
Zürich Flug ✈ **530** d.	1818	1848	1918	1948	2018	2048	2118	2218	2318	0018
Winterthur **530** d.	1835	1905	1935	2005	2035	2105	2135	2235	2335	0035
Frauenfeld d.	1847	1917	1947	2017	2047	2117	2147	2247	2347	0046
Weinfelden **539** ▲ d.	1900	1930	2000	2030	2100	2130	2200	2300	0000	0058
Kreuzlingen ▲ a.	|	1950	|	2050	|	2150	|	|	|	|
Konstanz ▲ a.	|	1954	|	2054	|	2154	|	|	|	|
Romanshorn a.	1918	...	2018	...	2118	...	2218	2318	0018	0115

	IC 810 (✕)	IR 2110	IC 812 ✕	IR 2112	IC 816 (✕)	IR 2116	IC 818 ✕	IR 2118	IC 820 ✕	IR 2120
Romanshorn d.	0538	...	0638	...	0741	...	0841	...	0941	...
Konstanz ▲ d.	|	0603	|	0703	|	0803	|	0903	|	1003
Kreuzlingen ▲ d.	|	0607	|	0707	|	0807	|	0907	|	1007
Weinfelden **539** ▲ d.	0559	0629	0659	0729	0759	0829	0859	0929	0959	1029
Frauenfeld d.	0612	0642	0712	0742	0812	0842	0912	0942	1012	1042
Winterthur **530** d.	0625	0655	0728	0755	0825	0855	0925	0955	1025	1055
Zürich Flughafen ✈ **530** a.	0638	0708	0741	0808	0838	0908	0938	1008	1038	1108
Zürich HB 530 a.	0651	0721	0753	0821	0851	0921	0951	1021	1051	1121
Biel 500 d.	|	0845	|	0945	|	1045	|	1145	|	1245
Bern 500 a.	0758	...	0858	...	0958	...	1058	...	1158	...
Brig 560 a.	0911	...	1011	...	1111	...	1211	...	1311	...

km		IC 822 ✕	IR 2122	IC 824 (✕)	IR 2124	IC 826 ✕	IR 2126	IC 828 (✕)	IR 2128	IC 830 ✕	IR 2130	IC 832 (✕)	IR 2132	IC 836 ✕	IR 2136	IC 838 ✕	IR 2138	IC 840 ✕	IR 2140	IC 842 (✕)	IR 2142	IC 844 ✕	IC 846	IC 848	
	Romanshorn d.	1041	...	1141	...	1241	...	1341	...	1441	...	1541	...	1641	...	1741	...	1841	...	1941	...	2041	2141	2238	233[illegible]
0	**Konstanz** ▲ d.	|	1103	|	1203	|	1303	|	1403	|	1503	|	1603	|	1703	|	1803	|	1903	|	2003	|	|	|	|
1	Kreuzlingen ▲ d.	|	1107	|	1207	|	1307	|	1407	|	1507	|	1607	|	1707	|	1807	|	1907	|	2007	|	|	|	|
24	Weinfelden **539** ▲ d.	1059	1129	1159	1229	1259	1329	1359	1429	1459	1529	1559	1629	1659	1729	1759	1829	1859	1929	1959	2029	2059	2159	2259	235[illegible]
	Frauenfeld d.	1112	1142	1212	1242	1312	1342	1412	1442	1512	1542	1612	1642	1712	1742	1812	1842	1912	1942	2012	2042	2112	2212	2312	001[illegible]
	Winterthur **530** d.	1125	1155	1225	1255	1325	1355	1425	1455	1525	1555	1625	1655	1725	1755	1825	1855	1925	1955	2025	2055	2125	2225	2325	002[illegible]
	Zürich Flug ✈ **530** a.	1138	1208	1238	1308	1338	1408	1438	1508	1538	1608	1638	1708	1738	1808	1838	1908	1938	2008	2038	2108	2138	2238	2338	...
	Zürich HB 530 a.	1151	1221	1251	1321	1351	1421	1451	1521	1551	1621	1651	1721	1751	1821	1851	1921	1951	2021	2051	2121	2151	2251	2351	...
	Biel 500 a.	|	1345	|	1445	|	1545	|	1645	|	1745	|	1845	|	1945	|	2045	|	2145	|	2245	|	|	...	...
	Bern 500 a.	1258	...	1358	...	1458	...	1558	...	1658	...	1758	...	1858	...	1958	...	2058	...	2158	...	2302	0002	...	...
	Brig 560 a.	1411	...	1511	...	1611	...	1711	...	1811	...	1911	...	2011	...	2111	...	...	...	...	...	...	...	...	...

▲ – Additional services operate **Weinfelden - Konstanz and v.v.** journey time: 30 – 36 minutes. A change of trains may be necessary at Kreuzlingen.
From **Weinfelden**: 0530Ⓐ, 0602, 0630Ⓐ, 0702, 0735Ⓐ, 0802, 0902, 1002, 1102, 1202, 1302, 1402, 1502, 160[illegible] 1635Ⓐ, 1702, 1735Ⓐ, 1802, 1835Ⓐ, 1902, 1935Ⓐ, 2002, 2102, 2202, 2302, 0002.
From **Konstanz**: 0521, 0542Ⓐ, 0621, 0642Ⓐ, 0721, 0748Ⓐ, 0821, 0921, 1021, 1121, 1221, 1321, 1421, 152[illegible] 1548Ⓐ, 1621, 1648Ⓐ, 1721, 1748Ⓐ, 1821, 1848Ⓐ, 1921, 2021, 2121, 2221, 2321.

SBS ⛴ ROMANSHORN - FRIEDRICHSHAFEN car ferry service 536

Journey time: 41 minutes. ✕ available 0836 - 2036 from Romanshorn; 0841 - 2041 from Friedrichshafen. 🍸 on other sailings. Operator: SBS ✆ 071 466 78 88

From **Romanshorn**: 0936 and hourly until 1636.
From **Friedrichshafen**: 0941 and hourly until 1641.

Services shown operate daily. Additional hourly service available on certain dates from 0536 - 0836 and 1736 - 2036 from Romanshorn; 0541 - 0841 and 1741 - 2041 from Friedrichshafen.

THURBO WEINFELDEN - WIL 539

km		Ⓐ		Ⓐ		Ⓐ		Ⓐ		and	
0	Weinfelden **535** d.	0502	0532	0602	0632	0702	0732	0802	0832	hourly	2332
19	Wil **530** a.	0529	0555	0629	0655	0729	0755	0829	0855	until	2355

	Ⓐ		Ⓐ		Ⓐ		Ⓐ		and		
Wil **530** d.	0531	0601	0631	0701	0731	0801	0831	0901	hourly	2301	0001
Weinfelden **535** a.	0557	0625	0657	0725	0757	0825	0857	0925	until	2325	0025

Additional services operate on Ⓐ:
Weinfelden depart 1602, 1702, 1802, 1902; Wil depart 1631, 1731, 1831, 1931.

RhB. Narrow gauge CHUR - ST MORITZ 540

For *Glacier Express* services see Table **575**

km		2⚒	⚒		△	961 ♦🅁✓	1323 ♦	951 ♦🅁✓	953 ♦🅁✓	△	955 ♦🅁✓	△	△	△	△	△	△	△	△	△	△	△		K
0	**Chur 575** d.	0503	...	0658	0758	...	...	0832	0858	0858	0931	0958	1058	1158	1258	1358	1458	1558	1658	1758	1858	1958	2056	...
10	Reichenau-Tamins **575** d.	0514	...	0709	0808	...	...	|	0908u	0908	|	1008	1108	1208	1308	1408	1508	1608	1708	1808	1908	2008	2107	...
27	Thusis d.	0539	...	0730	0830	...	...	|	0930u	0930	|	1030	1130	1230	1330	1430	1530	1630	1730	1830	1930	2030	2133	...
41	Tiefencastel d.	0556	...	0747	0847	...	...	0916u	0947u	0947	1016u	1047	1147	1247	1347	1447	1547	1647	1747	1847	1947	2047	2150	...
	Davos Platz d.	|	...	|	|	0814	...	|	|	|	|	|	|	|	|	|	|	|	|	|	|	|	|	...
51	**Filisur 545a** d.	0612	...	0802	0902	|	...	0933u	1002u	1002	1033u	1102	1202	1302	1402	1502	1602	1702	1802	1902	2002	2102	2205	...
59	Bergün / Bravuogn d.	0630	...	0814	0914	|	...	0947u	1014u	1014	1047	1114	1214	1314	1414	1514	1614	1714	1814	1914	2014	2114	2217	...
72	Preda d.	0645x	...	0830	0930	|	...	...	|	1030	|	1130	1230	1330	1430	1530	1630	1730	1830	1930	2030	2130	2234	...
84	**Samedan** a.	0700	...	0846	0946	|	...	...	|	1046	|	1146	1246	1346	1446	1546	1646	1746	1847	1947	2047	2145	2249	...
84	**Samedan 546** d.	...	0712	0850	0948	0916u	1010	...	1049u	1048	|	1148	1248	1348	1448	1548	1648	1748	1848	1948	2048	2150	2251	2337
89	Pontresina **546/7** a.	...	|	|	|	|	|	...	1056	|	1121	|	|	|	|	|	|	|	|	|	|	|	|	|
87	Celerina **546/7** d.	...	0715	0853	0951	|	1013	...	...	1051	...	1151	1251	1351	1451	1551	1651	1751	1851	1951	2051	2153	2254	2340
89	**St Moritz 546/7** a.	...	0719	0857	0958	0924u	1019	...	...	1058	...	1158	1258	1358	1458	1558	1658	1758	1858	1958	2058	2157	2258	2344

	Ⓐ	K⚒	⚒	†	△	△	△	△	△	△	△	△	△	△	950 ♦🅁✓	952 ♦🅁✓	1358 ♦	960 ♦🅁✓	954 ♦🅁✓	△	△	△		
St Moritz 546/7 d.	...	0501	0542	0605	0702	0802	0902	1002	1102	1202	1302	1402	1502	1602	...	...	1637	1639	...	1702	1802	1902	2002	2102
Celerina **546/7** d.	...	0504	0545	0608	0705	0805	0905	1005	1105	1205	1305	1405	1505	1605	...	...	1640	|	...	1705	1805	1905	2005	2105
Pontresina **546/7** d.	...	|	|	|	|	|	|	|	|	|	|	|	|	|	...	1619s	|	|	1702s	|	|	|	|	|
Samedan 546 a.	...	0508	0549	0611	0709	0809	0909	1009	1109	1209	1309	1409	1509	1609	...	|	1645	|	1708s	1709	1809	1909	2009	2109
Samedan d.	0512	...	0550	0612	0717	0817	0917	1017	1117	1217	1317	1417	1517	1617	1627s	|	...	|	|	1717	1817	1917	2017	...
Preda d.	|	...	0603	|	0730	0830	0930	1030	1130	1230	1330	1430	1530	1630	|	|	...	|	|	1730	1830	1930	2031	...
Bergün / Bravuogn d.	0538	...	0619	0638	0747	0847	0947	1047	1147	1247	1347	1447	1547	1647	1658s	1658s	...	|	1747s	1747	1847	1948	2048	...
Filisur 545a d.	0550	...	0634	0650	0801	0901	1001	1101	1201	1301	1401	1501	1601	1701	1717s	1717s	...	|	1800s	1801	1901	2001	2101	...
Davos Platz a.	|	...	|	|	|	|	|	|	|	|	|	|	|	|	|	|	...	1808	|	|	|	|	|	...
Tiefencastel d.	0610	...	0653	0710	0815	0915	1015	1115	1215	1315	1415	1515	1615	1715	1732s	1732s	...	...	1815s	1815	1915	2015	2115	...
Thusis d.	0627	...	0711	0727	0833	0933	1033	1133	1233	1333	1433	1533	1633	1733	1750s	1750s	...	...	1831s	1833	1933	2033	2133	...
Reichenau-Tamins **575** d.	0648	...	|	0748	0853	0953	1053	1153	1253	1353	1453	1553	1653	1753	|	|	...	...	1852s	1853	1953	2053	2155	...
Chur 575 a.	0658	...	0744	0758	0903	1003	1103	1203	1303	1403	1503	1603	1703	1803	1827	1827	...	...	1903	1903	2003	2103	2209	...

♦ – **NOTES** (LISTED BY TRAIN NUMBER)

950/1 – BERNINA EXPRESS – May 10 - Oct. 26: 🚃 [panorama car] and 🍸 Tirano - Chur and v.v.
952/5 – BERNINA EXPRESS – © Jan. 11 - May 4, Nov. 1 - Dec. 13: 🚃 [panorama car] and 🍸 Chur - Pontresina - Tirano and v.v.
953/4 – BERNINA EXPRESS – Ⓐ Jan. 6 - May 9, Oct. 27 - Dec. 12: 🚃 [panorama car] and 🍸 Chur - Pontresina - Tirano and v.v.
960/1 – BERNINA EXPRESS – May 10 - Oct. 26: 🚃 [panorama car] and 🍸 Tirano - St Moritz - Davos and v.v.
1323 – ENGADIN STAR – May 10 - Dec. 13: 🚃 Landquart - Klosters - St Moritz.
1358 – ENGADIN STAR – 🚃 St Moritz - Klosters - Landquart.

K – 🚃 St Moritz - Klosters and v.v.
s – Stops to set down only.
u – Stops to pick up only.
x – Stops only on request.
△ – Conveys 🚃 [panorama car] Dec. 15 - Mar. 30, 🅁, ✓.
✓ – Supplement payable.
Catering (✕ and / or 🍸) available on most services.

RhB. Narrow gauge CHUR - AROSA 541

km		⚒											q
0	**Chur** d.	0516	0622	0808	0908	...	1008	and	1908	2006	2106	2300
18	Langwies d.	0556	0706	0849	0949	...	1049	hourly	1949	2044	2143	2340x
26	Arosa a.	0613	0723	0909	1009	...	1109	until	2009	2103	2206	2358

	⚒	Ⓐ	©							t	
Arosa d.	0552	0625	0651	0748	...	0848	and	1948	2108	0003	...
Langwies d.	0609	0641	0707	0804	...	0904	hourly	2004	2123	0018x	...
Chur a.	0652	0723	0750	0852	...	0952	until	2052	2207	0059	...

q – Daily Dec. 15 - Apr. 21; ⑤⑥⑦ Apr. 25 - Nov. 23; daily Nov. 24 - Dec. 13 (also May 29, June 9).
t – Daily Dec. 15 - Apr. 22; ①⑥⑦ Apr. 26 - Nov. 24; daily Nov. 25 - Dec. 13 (also May 30, June 10).
x – Stops only on request.

PA 🚌 CHUR - FLIMS 542

🚌 **Chur** (Postautostation) - **Flims** Dorf (Post), ± 35 minutes, and **Flims** Waldhaus (Caumasee), ± 40 minutes.

From **Chur**:
0603⚒, 0638Ⓐ, 0658, 0758 and hourly until 1758, then 1828Ⓐ, 1858, 1928Ⓐ, 2000, 2100, 2200, 2300.

From **Flims** Waldhaus (± 5 minutes from Flims Dorf):
0516⚒, 0613, 0700Ⓐ, 0714, 0814, 0914 and hourly until 1914, then 2013, 2113, 2213, 2313.

Additional services available

PA, RhB* 🚌 ST MORITZ and TIRANO - CHIAVENNA - LUGANO 543

					P🅁	B🅁				
St Moritz, Bahnhof § d.	0725	0908	1108	1208	1220	...	1308	1508	1708	1908
Silvaplana, Post § d.	0737	0921	1121	1221	1232u	...	1321	1521	1721	1921
Sils / Segl Maria, Posta § d.	0744	0929	1129	1229	1239u	...	1329	1529	1729	1929
Maloja, Posta § d.	0756	0944	1144	1244	1250u	...	1344	1554	1744	1941
Castasegna 🏛 § d.	0835	1028	1228	1328	1327u	...	1428	1638	1828	2020
Tirano, Stazione d.	|	|	|	|	|	1420	|	|	|	|
Chiavenna, Stazione § d.	0858	1051	1251	1351	1410	|	1451	1701	1851	2043
Menaggio d.	...	...	...	...	1505x	|	...	...	...	...
Lugano, Stazione ◐ a.	...	...	...	...	1620s	1730	...	...	...	...
Lugano, Autosilo Balestra a.	...	...	...	...	1630	...	...	...	...	...

					B🅁	Q🅁				
Lugano, Autosilo Balestra d.	...	...	...	...	...	1135	...	...	...	...
Lugano, Stazione ◐ d.	...	...	...	...	1000	1155u	...	...	...	...
Menaggio d.	...	...	...	...	|	1245x	...	...	...	...
Chiavenna, Stazione § d.	0708	0908	1108	1308	|	1410	1408	1508	1708	1915
Tirano, Stazione d.	|	|	|	|	1300	|	|	|	|	|
Castasegna 🏛 § d.	0728	0928	1128	1328	...	1426s	1428	1528	1728	1933
Maloja, Posta § d.	0814	1014	1214	1414	...	1500s	1514	1614	1814	2014
Sils / Segl Maria, Posta § d.	0827	1027	1227	1427	...	1511s	1527	1627	1827	2027
Silvaplana, Post § d.	0836	1036	1236	1436	...	1519s	1536	1636	1836	2036
St Moritz, Bahnhof § a.	0851	1051	1251	1451	...	1535	1551	1651	1851	2051

B – Bernina Express service. Runs Mar. 29 - Oct. 26.
P – Palm Express service. Runs ⑤⑥⑦ (daily June 13 - Oct. 19).
Q – Palm Express service. Runs ①⑥⑦ (daily June 14 - Oct. 20).
s – Stops to set down only.
u – Stops to pick up only.
x – Calls only if advance reservation is made.

§ – Additional services operate June 14 - Oct. 19 St Moritz - Chiavenna and v.v.
◐ – 🏛 is at Gandria.
* – Operators:
Tirano - Lugano: RhB, Reservation: ✆ (081) 288 65 65;
St Moritz - Chiavenna - Lugano: PA, Reservation: ✆ St Moritz (058) 448 35 35; fax (058) 667 49 81.

544 🚌 CHUR - BELLINZONA and CHIAVENNA — PA

km			Py	Bj	Bh	B		Py	B	Bh		B	Bh		B	B		B	Py	Bh		B		[R]⊬g	[R]⊬g
0	Chur Postautostation 540 d.	...	...	0808	0813	0913	...	...	1008	1113	...	1208	1313	...	1408	1513	...	1608	...	1713	...	1808	...	...	...
40	Thusis Bahnhof 540 ⊡ d.	0735	...	0835	0840	0940	0935	...	1035	1140	1135	1235	1340	1335	1435	1540	1535	1635	...	1740	1735	1835	1935	2250	2359
64	Splügen Post d.	0809	0820	0904	0904	1004	1009	1020	1104	1204	1209	1304	1404	1409	1504	1604	1609	1704	1715	1804	1809	1904	2009	2330	0040
	San Bernardino Posta a.	0829	|	0923	0923	1023	1029	|	1123	1223	1229	1323	1423	1429	1523	1623	1629	1723	|	1823	1829	1923	2029	...	...
	Chiavenna Stazione ◐ a.	|	1015	|	|	|	|	1215	|	|	|	|	|	|	|	|	|	|	1910	|	|	|	|	...	...
179	Bellinzona Stazione a.	*0950*	...	1020	1013	1113	*1150*	...	1220	1313	*1350*	1420	1513	*1550*	1620	1713	*1750*	1820	...	1913	*1950*	2020	*2150*	...	...

	Ⓐ		Py		B	B		Bh	B		Bh	B		B	Py	B		Bh	Py	B		B	[R]⊬g	[R]⊬n
Bellinzona Stazione d.	...	*0707*	...	*0807*	0845	0940	*1007*	1045	1140	*1207*	1245	1340	*1407*	1445	...	1540	*1607*	1645	...	1740	*1807*	1845	...	...
Chiavenna Stazione ◐ d.	...	|	0750	|	|	|	|	|	|	|	|	|	|	|	1440	|	|	|	1640	|	|	|	...	...
San Bernardino Posta d.	0600	0823	|	0923	0935	1031	1123	1135	1231	1323	1335	1431	1523	1535	|	1631	1723	1735	|	1831	1923	1935r	...	...
Splügen Post d.	0622	0845	0940	0945	0953	1051	1145	1153	1251	1345	1353	1451	1545	1553	1630	1651	1745	1753	1830	1851	1945	1953r	2351	0056
Thusis Bahnhof 540 ⊙ d.	0705	0925	...	1025	1020	1125	1225	1220	1325	1425	1420	1525	1625	1620	...	1725	1825	1820	...	1925	2025	2020r	0018	0123
Chur Postautostation 540 a.	...	...	...	...	1045	1150	...	1245	1350	...	1445	1550	...	1645	...	1750	...	1845	...	1950	...	2045r	...	...

B – San Bernardino Route Express. [R].
P – Splügen Pass service. Supplement payable.
g – ⑤⑥ (also Apr. 17, May 28, July 31; not Apr. 18, Aug. 1).
h – June 7 - Oct. 19.
j – Dec. 15 - June 6, Oct. 20 - Dec. 13.
n – ⑥⑦ (also Apr. 18, May 29, Aug. 1; not Apr. 19, Aug. 2).
r – 5 minutes later on †.
y – June 7 - Oct. 12.
⊙ – Stops to set down only.
⊡ – Stops to pick up only.
◐ – 🏨 is at Splügen Pass.
⊬ – Supplement payable.

Reservations: ✆ Chur (058) 386 31 66; Thusis (058) 453 24 07.

545 CHUR - LANDQUART - KLOSTERS - DAVOS / SCUOL TARASP — Narrow gauge. RhB

km		Ⓐ	⚒	Ⓐ				2w		1323 ♦			2w		L		A							
	Chur 520/534 d.	...	...	*0550*	...	...	0721	...	0753	...	...	0821	...	0853	...	...	0921	...	1021			1721	...	1821
	Landquart 520/534 a.	...	...	*0609*	...	...	0740k	...	0809	...	...	0840k	...	0909	...	...	0940k	...	1040k	and at		1740k	...	1840k
0	Landquart d.	0450	0533	0620	0647	0747	0749	0753	...	0820	0847	0849	0853	...	0920	0947	0949	1047	1049	the same	1747	1749	1847	1849
21	Küblis d.	0509x	0606	0645	0712	0810	0814	0823	...	0847	0910	0914	0923	...	0947	1010	1014	1110	1114	minutes	1810	1814	1910	1914
30	Klosters Dorf d.	0520x	0619	0657	0724	|	0829	0845	...	|	|	0929	0945	...	|	|	1029	|	1129	past each	|	1829	|	1929
32	Klosters 🚗 d.	0528	0626	0703	0734	0829	0834	0852	...	0902	0929	0934	0952	...	1002	1029	1034	1129	1134	hour	1829	1834	1929	1934
	Sagliains 546 🚗 § a.	|	|	|	0754	|	0853	|	...	...	|	0953	|	...	...	|	1053	|	1153	until	|	1853	|	1953
	Ardez a.	|	|	|	0808	|	0903	|	...	...	|	1003	|	...	...	|	1103	|	1203		|	1903	|	2003
	Scuol-Tarasp 546 a.	|	|	|	0818	|	0915	|	...	...	|	1015	|	...	...	|	1115	|	1215		|	1915	|	2015
47	Davos Dorf d.	0549	0652	0724	...	0850	...	0917	...	...	0950	...	1017	...	...	1050	...	1150	...		1850	...	1950	...
50	Davos Platz 545a a.	0556	0656	0731	...	0856	...	0925	...	...	0956	...	1025	...	...	1056	...	1156	...		1856	...	1956	...

	h								🚌 z	🚌 y⊡
Chur 520/534 d.	...	*1921*	1953	...	2053	...	2153	...	...	...
Landquart 520/534 a.	...	*1940*	2010	...	2110	...	2210	...	...	...
Landquart d.	1920	1947	—	2047	—	2147	—	2247	2343	0043
Küblis d.	1947	2013	...	2113	...	2213	...	2313	0012	0112
Klosters Dorf d.	|	2025	...	2125	...	2225	...	2325	0027	0127
Klosters 🚗 d.	2002	2030	2034	2130	2134	2230	2232	2330	0031	0133
Sagliains 546 🚗 § a.	|	|	2054	|	2154	|	2249	|	...	|
Ardez a.	|	|	2108	|	2208	|	...	|	...	|
Scuol-Tarasp 546 a.	|	|	2118	|	2218	|	...	|	...	|
Davos Dorf d.	2023	2051	...	2151	...	2251	...	2351	...	0153
Davos Platz 545a a.	2029	2057	...	2157	...	2257	...	2357	...	0200

	⚒		Ⓐ		h					Lh
Davos Platz 545a d.	0500	0600	0628	0700	0724	...	0802	...	0902	...
Davos Dorf d.	0503	0603	0631	0703	0728	...	0806	...	0906	...
Scuol-Tarasp 546 d.	|	|	|	|	|	0740	|	0840	|	...
Ardez d.	|	|	|	|	|	0747	|	0847	|	...
Sagliains 546 🚗 § d.	|	|	|	|	|	0803	|	0903	|	...
Klosters 🚗 d.	0527	0627	0656	0727	0754	0825	0833	0925	0933	0948
Klosters Dorf d.	0529	0629	0659	0729	|	0828	|	0928	|	|
Küblis d.	0544	0644	0714	0744	0813	0844	0849	0944	0949	1014
Landquart a.	0613	0713	0737	0813	0836	0910	0913k	1010	1013k	1036
Landquart 520/534 d.	*0618*	*0717*	*0748*	*0817*	...	0917	...	1017	...	...
Chur 520/534 a.	*0639*	*0737*	*0806*	*0837*	...	0937	...	1037	...	...

km						Lh						1358 ♦											🚌	z
	Davos Platz 545a d.	...	1002	...	1102	...	...	1202		...	1702	...	...	1802	...	1902	...	2002	...	2102	2150	...	...	...
	Davos Dorf d.	...	1006	...	1106	...	...	1206	and at	...	1706	...	...	1806	...	1906	...	2005	...	2105	2154	...	...	...
0	Scuol-Tarasp 546 d.	0940	|	1040	|	...	1140	|	the same	1640	|	...	1740	|	1840	|	1940	|	2040	|	|	2140	...	2234
	Ardez d.	0947	|	1047	|	...	1147	|	minutes	1647	|	...	1747	|	1847	|	1947	|	2047	|	|	2147	...	2242
17	Sagliains 546 🚗 § d.	1003	|	1103	|	...	1203	|	past each	1703	|	...	1803	|	1903	|	2003	|	2103	|	|	2203	...	2302
39	Klosters 🚗 d.	1025	1033	1125	1133	1148	1225	1233	hour	1725	1733	1755	1825	1833	1925	1933	2023	2029	2121	2129	2217	2222	...	2321
	Klosters Dorf d.	1028	|	1128	|	|	1228	|	until	1728	|	|	1828	|	1928	|	—	2032	—	2132	—	2224	...	...
	Küblis d.	1044	1049	1144	1149	1214	1244	1249		1744	1749	1814	1844	1849	1944	1949	...	2046	...	2146	...	2239	...	...
	Landquart a.	1110	1113k	1210	1213k	1236	1310	1313k		1810	1813k	1836	1910	1913k	2010	2013k	🚌	2113	🚌	2213	🚌	2305	...	...
	Landquart 520/534 d.	1117	...	1217	...	...	1317	...		1817	...	...	1917	...	2017j	...	2045	...	2145	...	2245	...	2342	
	Chur 520/534 a.	1137	...	1237	...	...	1337	...		1837	...	...	1937	...	2037j	...	2109	...	2209	...	2309	...	0014	...

♦ – NOTES (LISTED BY TRAIN NUMBER)
1323 – ENGADIN STAR – May 10 - Dec. 13: [12] Landquart - St Moritz.
1358 – ENGADIN STAR – [12] St Moritz - Landquart.

A – AQUALINO – [12] Disentis/Mustér - Scuol-Tarasp.
L – [12] Landquart - St Moritz and v.v.
h – June 15 - Dec. 13.
j – Connection on Ⓐ.
k – Connects with train in previous column.
w – Dec. 21 - Mar. 8.
x – Stops only on request.
y – ⑥⑦ (also Apr. 18, May 29, Aug. 1; not Apr. 19).
z – ⑤⑥ (also Apr. 17, May 28, July 31; not Apr. 18).
⊡ – Special fares apply.
§ – Sagliains station can only be used for changing trains.
🚗 – Car-carrying shuttle available (see page 262).

545a DAVOS - FILISUR — Narrow gauge. RhB

For *Glacier Express* services see Table 575

km		⚒							
0	Davos Platz 545 d.	0605	0731	0831	0931	and hourly until	1931	2031	...
16	Filisur 540 a.	0630	0756	0856	0956		1956	2056	...

	⚒							
Filisur 540 d.	0635	0804	and hourly until	1904	2004	2104	...	...
Davos Platz 545 a.	0700	0829		1929	2029	2129	...	...

546 PONTRESINA / ST MORITZ - SCUOL TARASP — Narrow gauge. RhB

km		⚒ S	⚒	⚒	⚒	⚒	†	† P			⚒						1350 L					1358 ♦		
0	St Moritz 540/7 d.	0501	...	0542	...	0602	0605	...	...	0702	0724	...	0802		...	1402	1437	...	1502	...	1602	1637	...	1702
	Pontresina 540/7 d.	|	0538	|	...	|	|	0603	0702	|	|	0802	|	and at	1402	|	|	1502	|	1602	|	|	1702	|
5	Samedan 540 a.	0508	0544	0549	...	0608	0611	0610	0708	0709k	0730	0808	0809k	the same	1408	1409k	1445	1508	1509k	1608	1609k	1645	1708	1709k
5	Samedan d.	0509	...	...	0600	0609	...	0614	0714	...	0731	0814	...	minutes	1414	...	1446	1514	...	1614	...	1646	1714	...
15	Zuoz d.	0523	...	...	0613	0622	...	0627	0727	...	0745	0827	...	past each	1427	...	1459	1527	...	1627	...	1659	1727	...
32	Zernez ⊖ d.	0543	...	...	0643	...	...	0647	0747	...	...	0849	...	hour	1449	...	1519	1549	...	1649	...	1719	1749	...
38	Susch d.	0549	...	...	0649	...	...	0653	0753	...	...	0855	...	until	1455	...	...	1555	...	1655	...	...	1755	...
40	Sagliains 545 § a.	0553	...	...	0653	...	...	0657	0757	...	...	0900	...		1500	...	...	1600	...	1700	...	...	1800	...
57	Scuol-Tarasp 545 a.	...	...	...	0716	...	...	...	...	...	...	0923	...		1523	...	...	1623	...	1723	...	...	1823	...

♦ – NOTES (LISTED BY TRAIN NUMBER)
1358 – ENGADIN STAR – [12] St Moritz - Landquart (a. 1836).

L – [12] St Moritz - Landquart (a. 1636).
P – [12] Pontresina - Klosters (a. 0722).
S – [12] St Moritz - Klosters (a. 0623).
k – Connects with train in previous column.
§ – Sagliains station can only be used for changing trains.
⊖ – For 🚌 service **Zernez - Malles and v.v.** – see next page.

PONTRESINA / ST MORITZ - SCUOL TARASP 546

Narrow gauge. RhB

St Moritz 540/7 d.	...	1802	...	1902	...	2002	...	2102	...
Pontresina 540/7 d.	1802	|	1902	|	2002	|	2102	|	2202j
Samedan **540** a.	1808	1809k	1908	1909k	2008	2009k	2108	2109k	2208j
Samedan d.	1814	...	1914	...	2014	▬	2114	▬	2214
Zuoz d.	1827	...	1927	...	2027	...	2127	...	2227
Zernez ⊖ d.	1849	...	1949	...	2047	...	2147	...	2247
Susch d.	1855	...	1955	...	2053	...	2153	...	2253
Sagliains **545** § a.	1900	...	2000	...	2057	2059	2157	2159	2259
Scuol-Tarasp 545 a.	1923	...	2023	...	...	2118	...	2218	2319

	⚒	⚒	S	⚒	⚒		⚒					1323 ♦	
Scuol-Tarasp 545 d.	...	0527	...	...	0607	0640	...	0740	...	...	0834	...	0934
Sagliains **545** § d.	...	0546	...	...	|	0703	...	0800	0803	...	0856	...	0956
Susch d.	...	0549	0553	...	0627	0705	...	▬	0805	...	0858	...	0958
Zernez ⊖ d.	...	...	0602	...	0638	0713	...	...	0813	...	0908	0933	1008
Zuoz d.	...	...	0622	0633	0657	0734	0757	...	0834	...	0927	0956	1027
Samedan a.	...	...	0633	0646	0711	0746	0811	...	0846k	...	0942k	1009	1042
Samedan **540** d.	0525	...	0635	0649	0712	0748	0812r	0850	0851	0948	0949	1010	1049y
Pontresina 540/7 a.	0531	...	|	0656	|	0755	|	|	0857	|	0956	|	1056y
St Moritz 540/7 a.	...	...	0642	...	0719	...	0819r	0857	...	0958	...	1019	...

		L					Q					M												q	K
Scuol-Tarasp 545 d.	...	...	1034	...	1134	...	...	1234	...	1334	...	...	1434	...		1834	...	1934	...	*2040*	...	*2140*	...	2234	...
Sagliains **545** § d.	...	...	1056	...	1156	...	...	1256	...	1356	...	...	1456	...	and at	1856	...	1956	...	2103	...	2203	...	2253	2254
Susch d.	...	...	1058	...	1158	...	...	1258	...	1358	...	...	1458	...	the same	1858	...	1958	...	2105	...	2205	...	...	2256
Zernez ⊖ d.	...	1033	1108	...	1208	...	1233	1308	...	1408	...	1448	1508	...	minutes	1908	...	2008	...	2113	...	2213	...	...	2304
Zuoz d.	...	1056	1127	...	1227	...	1259	1327	...	1427	...	1506	1527	...	past each	1927	...	2027	...	2134	...	2234	...	...	2323
Samedan a.	...	1109	1142	...	1242	...	1311	1342	...	1442	...	1521	1542	...	hour	1942	...	2042	...	2146	...	2246	...	...	2336
Samedan **540** d.	1048	1110	1149	1148	1249	1248	1312	1349	1348	1449	1448	1522	1549	1548	until	1949	2048	*2051*	2048	2151	2150	2251	2251	...	2337
Pontresina 540/7 a.	|	|	1156	|	1256	|	|	1356	|	1456	|	|	1556	|		1956	|	*2057*	|	2157	|	2257	|	...	|
St Moritz 540/7 a.	1058	1119	...	1158	...	1258	1320	...	1358	...	1458	1530	...	1558		...	2058	...	2058	...	2157	...	2258	...	2344

♦ – **NOTES** (LISTED BY TRAIN NUMBER)

1323 – ENGADIN STAR – May 10 - Dec. 13: [12] Landquart (d. 0820) - St Moritz.

K – [12] Klosters (d. 2232) - St Moritz.
L – [12] Landquart (d. 0920) - St Moritz.
M – ⑥ Dec. 21 - June 14; daily June 15 - Dec. 13: [12] Landquart (d. 1320) - St Moritz.
Q – [12] Landquart (d. 1120) - St Moritz.
S – Ⓐ Landquart (d. 0456) - St Moritz.

h – May 10 - Oct. 19.
j – Connection on ⑥.
k – Connects with train in previous column.
q – ⑤⑥ (also Apr. 17, May 28, July 31; not Apr. 18).
r – ⚒ Dec. 16 - June 14; daily June 15 - Dec. 13.
y – By connecting train on Ⓐ Jan. 6 - May 9, Oct. 27 - Dec. 12.

§ – Sagliains station can only be used for changing trains.

⊖ – 🚌 service **Zernez - Malles and v.v.** (journey ±1 h 35 minutes):
From **Zernez**: 0715, 0815 **h**, 0915, 1015 **h**, 1032, 1115, 1215 **h**, 1315, 1415 **h**, 1515, 1615, 1715.
From **Malles / Mals** bahnhof: 0610 **h**, 0657⚒, 0803, 0903, 1003 **h**, 1103, 1203 **h**, 1303, 1403 **h**, 1503, 1545 **h**, 1603, 1703, 1803 **h**, 1903.
Operator: AutoDaPosta (PA), Agentura Scuol, CH-7550 Scuol. ✆ +41 (0)58 453 28 28, fax +41 (0)58 667 63 94.

ST MORITZ - TIRANO 547

Narrow gauge. RhB

km		🚌						961 ♦R⁄	🚌 w		951 ♦R⁄			953 ♦R⁄	955 ♦R⁄	973 ♦R⁄	🚌 w						975 ♦R⁄		
0	**St Moritz** d.	...	...	...	...	0745	0845	0929	...	0945	...	1045	...	...	...	1122	...	1145	1245	1345	1445	...	1522	1545	1645
2	Celerina Staz ⊡ d.	...	...	...	...	0748	0848	|	...	0948	...	1048	...	...	...	|	...	1148	1248	1348	1448	...	|	1548	1648
6	**Pontresina** a.	...	...	...	...	0755	0855	|	...	0955	...	1055	...	...	...	|	...	1155	1255	1355	1455	...	|	1555	1655
6	**Pontresina 540** d.	...	...	...	0704d	0809	0904	0952u	...	1009	...	1104	...	1103	1121	1131u	...	1209	1304	1409	1504	...	1531u	1609	1704
12	Morteratsch ⊡ d.	...	...	...	0713d	0818	0913	|	...	1018	...	1113	...	|	|	|	...	1218	1313	1418	1513	...	1542u	1618	1713
17	Bernina Diavolezza ⊡ d.	...	...	...	0723d	0828	0923	|	...	1028	...	1123	...	|	|	|	...	1228	1323	1428	1523	...	|	1628	1723
18	Bernina Lagalb ⊡ d.	...	...	...	0725d	0830	0925	|	...	1030	...	1125	...	|	|	|	...	1230	1325	1430	1525	...	|	1630	1725
22	Ospizio Bernina d.	...	...	...	0734d	0839	0934	1019s	...	1039	...	1134	...	1135s	1146s	|	...	1239	1334	1439	1534	...	1559	1639	1734
27	Alp Grüm d.	...	...	...	0746d	0853	0946	1033s	...	1053	1101s	1146	...	1145s	1156s	1209s	...	1253	1346	1453	1546	...	1614	1653	1746
44	**Poschiavo** a.	...	...	...	0827d	0933	1027	1113s	...	1133	1159s	1227	...	1227s	1250s	1250s	...	1333	1427	1533	1627	...	1650s	1733	1827
44	**Poschiavo** d.	0610	0626	0736	0829	0938	1029	|	1135	1138v	|	1229	...	|	|	|	1335	1338v	1429	1538	1629	...	|	1738	1829
48	Le Prese d.	0616	0634x	0744x	0837	0946	1037	1127s	1140	1146v	1208s	1237	...	1237s	1258s	1258s	1340	1346v	1437	1546	1637	...	1658s	1746	1837
51	Miralago ⊡ d.	0620	0639	0749	0843	0952	1043	|	1143	1152v	|	1243	...	|	|	|	1343	1352v	1443	1552	1643	...	|	1752	1843
54	Brusio ⊡ d.	0624	0647	0757	0851	1000	1051	|	1147	1200v	|	1251	...	|	|	|	1347	1400v	1451	1600	1651	...	|	1800	1851
58	Campocologno 🏛 d.	0629	0657	0807	0903	1012	1103	|	1152	1212v	|	1303	...	|	|	|	1352	1412v	1503	1612	1703	...	|	1812	1903
61	**Tirano** a.	0638	0712	0823	0912	1021	1112	1202	1158	1221v	1236	1312	...	1312	1326	1326	1358	1421v	1512	1621	1712	...	1727	1821	1912

		🚌 R			🚌 R	Ⓐ		🚌 h	🚌 R	
St Moritz d.	1745	...	...	1845	...	1945	2020	...	...	...
Celerina Staz ⊡ d.	1748	...	...	1848	...	1948	2023	...	...	...
Pontresina a.	1755	...	...	1855	...	1955	2030	m	...	...
Pontresina 540 d.	1809	...	...	1904	...	2009	...	2057	...	...
Morteratsch ⊡ d.	1818	...	...	1913	...	2017	...	|	...	...
Bernina Diavolezza ⊡ d.	1828	...	...	1921	...	2024	...	|	...	...
Bernina Lagalb ⊡ d.	1830	...	...	1924	...	2026	...	|	...	...
Ospizio Bernina d.	1839x	...	...	1933x	...	2033x	...	|	...	...
Alp Grüm d.	1849x	...	...	1942x	...	2041x	...	|	...	...
Poschiavo a.	1935	...	...	2029	...	2134	...	2135	...	...
Poschiavo d.	...	1937	...	...	2032	...	...	...	2137	...
Le Prese d.	...	1943s	...	...	2038s	...	...	...	2143s	...
Miralago ⊡ d.	...	1947s	...	...	2042s	...	...	...	2147s	...
Brusio ⊡ d.	...	1951s	...	...	2046s	...	...	...	2151s	...
Campocologno 🏛 d.	...	1955s	...	...	2050s	...	...	...	2155s	...
Tirano a.	...	2005	...	...	2100	...	...	...	2205	...

	⚒	†	🚌							976 ♦R⁄
Tirano d.	...	...	0655	...	0740	...	0850	0940	...	1003
Campocologno 🏛 d.	...	...	0702	...	0752	...	0901	0952	...	|
Brusio ⊡ d.	...	...	0706	...	0759	...	0909	0959	...	|
Miralago ⊡ d.	...	...	0711	...	0805	...	0916	1005	...	|
Le Prese d.	...	...	0714	...	0810	...	0922	1010	...	1030u
Poschiavo a.	...	...	0730	...	0822	...	0931	1022	...	|
Poschiavo d.	0628	...	...	0733	0824	...	0933	1024	...	1044u
Alp Grüm d.	0705x	...	...	0815	0904	...	1015	1104	...	1122s
Ospizio Bernina d.	0714x	...	...	0824	0912	...	1024	1112	...	1131s
Bernina Lagalb ⊡ d.	0722	...	...	0832	0920	...	1032	1120	...	|
Bernina Diavolezza ⊡ d.	0724	...	...	0834	0922	...	1034	1122	...	|
Morteratsch ⊡ d.	0734	...	...	0844	0931	...	1044	1131	...	|
Pontresina 540 a.	0750	...	...	0858	0950	...	1058	1150	...	1205s
Pontresina d.	0757	0757	...	0901	0957	...	1101	1157	...	|
Celerina Staz ⊡ d.	0802	0802	...	0906	1002	...	1106	1202	...	|
St Moritz a.	0809	0809	...	0912	1009	...	1112	1209	...	1217

				🚌 w			🚌 w		952 ♦R⁄	950 ♦R⁄	960 ♦R⁄	954 ♦R⁄		p	q		978 ♦R⁄					🚌 h			
Tirano d.	1050	...	1127v	1200	1250	1340v	1400	...	1404	1404	1422	1433	...	1433	1450	...	1514	...	1540	1650	1740	...	1855	1940	...
Campocologno 🏛 d.	1101	...	1136v	1206	1301	1352v	1406	...	|	|	|	|	...	1442	1501	...	|	...	1552	1701	1752	...	1903	1952	...
Brusio ⊡ d.	1109	...	1143v	1210	1309	1359v	1410	...	|	|	|	|	...	1449	1509	...	|	...	1559	1709	1800	...	1911	2000	...
Miralago ⊡ d.	1116	...	1149v	1214	1316	1405v	1414	...	|	|	|	|	...	1455	1516	...	|	...	1605	1716	1807	...	1918	2007	...
Le Prese d.	1122	...	1154v	1217	1322	1410v	1417	...	1432u	1432u	1449u	1500u	...	1500	1522	...	1538u	...	1610	1721x	1812x	...	1923x	2012x	...
Poschiavo a.	1131	...	1215v	1222k	1331	1422v	1422k	...	|	|	|	|	...	1512	1531	...	|	...	1622	1732	1823	...	1934	2023	...
Poschiavo d.	1133	...	1224	...	1333	1424	...	...	1444u	1444u	1507u	1513u	...	1513	1533	...	1558u	...	1624	1734	1825	1905	...	...	...
Alp Grüm d.	1215	...	1304	...	1415	1504	...	...	1527u	1527u	1545u	1558u	...	1558	1615	...	|	...	1704	1811x	1902x	|	...	...	...
Ospizio Bernina d.	1224	...	1312	...	1424	1512	...	...	|	...	1600u	1607u	...	1607	1624	...	1652u	...	1712	1820x	1911x	|	...	...	...
Bernina Lagalb ⊡ d.	1232	...	1320	...	1432	1520	...	...	|	...	|	|	...	1615	1632	...	|	...	1720	1828	1919	|	...	...	...
Bernina Diavolezza ⊡ d.	1234	...	1322	...	1434	1522	...	...	|	...	|	|	...	1617	1634	...	|	...	1722	1830	1921	|	...	...	...
Morteratsch ⊡ d.	1244	...	1331	...	1444	1531	...	...	|	...	|	|	...	1626	1644	...	|	...	1731	1840	1931	|	...	...	...
Pontresina 540 a.	1258	...	1350	...	1458	1550	...	...	1616	...	1626s	1644	...	1644	1658	...	1720s	...	1750	1857	1950	2000	...	...	...
Pontresina d.	1301	...	1357	...	1501	1557	...	...	...	...	|	...	...	1657	1701	...	|	...	1757	1901	1957	n	...	...	...
Celerina Staz ⊡ d.	1306	...	1402	...	1506	1602	...	...	...	...	|	...	...	1702	1706	...	|	...	1802	1906	2002	...	...	...	...
St Moritz a.	1312	...	1409	...	1512	1609	...	...	...	...	1637	...	...	1708	1712	...	1730	...	1809	1912	2009	...	...	...	...

– **NOTES** (LISTED BY TRAIN NUMBER)

50/1 – BERNINA EXPRESS – May 10 - Oct. 26: [12] [panorama car] and 🍸 Chur - Tirano and v.v.
52/5 – BERNINA EXPRESS – Ⓒ Jan. 11 - May 4; Ⓒ Nov. 1 - Dec. 13: [12] [panorama car] and 🍸 Chur - Pontresina - Tirano and v.v.
53/4 – BERNINA EXPRESS – Ⓐ Jan. 6 - May 9, Oct. 27 - Dec. 12: [12] [panorama car] and 🍸 Chur - Pontresina - Tirano and v.v.
60/1 – BERNINA EXPRESS – May 10 - Oct. 26: [12] [panorama car] and 🍸 Tirano - St Moritz - Davos and v.v.
73/6 – BERNINA EXPRESS – May 10 - Oct. 26: [12] [panorama car] and 🍸 Tirano - St Moritz and v.v.
75/8 – BERNINA EXPRESS – May 10 - Oct. 26: [12] [panorama car] and 🍸 Tirano - St Moritz and v.v.

d – ⚒ only.
h – ⑤⑥⑦ (also Apr. 17, 21, May 28, 29, June 9).
k – Connects with train in previous column.
m – From Samedan (d. 2050).
n – To Samedan (a. 2008).
p – Ⓐ Jan. 6 - May 9, Oct. 27 - Dec. 12.
q – Ⓒ Jan. 11 - May 11; daily May 12 - Oct. 26; Ⓒ Nov. 1 - Dec. 13.
s – Stops to set down only.
u – Stops to pick up only.
v – May 10 - Oct. 26.
w – Dec. 15 - May 9, Oct. 27 - Dec. 13.
x – Stops only on request.

⊡ – Request stop.
⁄ – Supplement payable.

550 LUZERN and ZÜRICH - LOCARNO, CHIASSO and MILANO

Valid June 15 - Dec. 13 SBB, FS

	RE	RE		ICN	IR		ICN	IR		EC		ICN	IR		EC	IR	ICN	IR	EC		ICN	IR		ICN	IR	EC
	25259	25261		657	2257		861	2159	2415	313		863	2163	2417	253	2263	863	2165	315	2419	667	2267	2421	869	2169	317
				✕	△		✕		(🍷) S	✕ ◧		✕	△	(🍷) S	🍷 ◧	⑥y	✕	△	✕ ◧	(🍷) S	✕	△	(🍷) S	✕	△	🍷 ◧
Basel SBB **565** d.	...	...	...	0504	...	...	...	0604	...	...	...	...	0704	...	...	...	...	0804	...	...	0904	...	...	...	1004	...
Olten **565** d.	...	...	...	0530	...	...	...	0630	...	...	...	...	0730	...	...	...	...	0830	...	...	0930	...	...	...	1030	...
Luzern 565 d.	...	...	...	0618	...	...	...	0718	0740	...	...	...	0818	0840	0847	...	...	0918	...	0940	1018	...	1040	...	1118	...
Küssnacht am Rigi d.	...	...	...	|	...	...	...	|	0758	...	...	...	|	0858	|	...	...	|	...	0958	|	...	1058	...	|	...
Zürich HB d.	...	...	...	|	0609	...	0709	|	|	0732	...	0809	|	|	|	0832	0909	|	0932	|	|	1009	|	1109	|	1132
Zug d.	...	...	...	|	0631	...	0731	|	|	0800	...	0831	|	|	|	0900	0931	|	1000	|	|	1031	|	1131	|	1200
Arth-Goldau a.	...	...	...	0644	0646k	...	0746	0744k	0811	0814	...	0846	0844k	0911	0914	0914	0946	0944k	1014	1011k	1044	1046k	1111	1146	1144k	1214
Arth-Goldau d.	...	...	...	0650	0653	...	0750	0753	...	0817	...	0850	0853	▬	0916	0919	0950	0953	1017	▬	1050	1053	▬	1150	1153	1217
Schwyz d.	...	...	...	|	0701	...	|	0801	...	|	...	|	0901	...	|	|	|	1001	|	...	|	1101	...	|	1201	|
Brunnen d.	...	...	...	|	0705	...	|	0805	...	|	...	|	0905	...	|	|	|	1005	|	...	|	1105	...	|	1205	|
Flüelen d.	...	...	...	|	0715	...	|	0815	...	|	...	|	0915	...	|	|	|	1015	|	...	|	1115	...	|	1215	|
Erstfeld d.	...	...	...	|	0724	...	|	0824	...	|	...	|	0924	...	|	|	|	1024	|	...	|	1124	...	|	1224	|
Göschenen d.	...	...	...	|	0750	...	|	0850	...	|	...	|	0950	...	|	1007	|	1050	|	...	|	1150	...	|	1250	|
Airolo d.	...	0614	...	|	0801	...	|	0901	...	|	...	|	1001	...	|	1018	|	1101	|	...	|	1201	...	|	1301	|
Faido d.	...	0633	...	|	0819	...	|	0919	...	|	...	|	1019	...	|	|	|	1119	|	...	|	1219	...	|	1319	|
Biasca d.	0556j	0656	...	|	0840	...	|	0940	...	|	...	|	1040	...	|	1055	|	1140	|	...	|	1240	...	|	1340	|
Bellinzona a.	0610j	0710	...	0823	0853	...	0923	0953	...	0957	...	1023	1053	...	1057k	1108	1123	1153	1157	...	1223	1253	...	1323	1353	1357
Bellinzona ▲ d.	0614	0714	0803	0825	0854	0903	0925	0954	...	0959	1003	1025	1054	1103	1059	1110	1125	1154	1159	1203	1225	1254	1303	1325	1354	1359
Locarno 551 ▲ a.	|	|	|	|	0913	|	|	1013	...	|	|	|	1113	|	|	|	|	1213	|	|	|	1313	|	|	1413	|
Lugano a.	0642	0742	0833	0847	...	0933	0947	...	...	1024	1033	1047	...	1133	1124	1136	1147	...	1224	1233	1247	...	1333	1347	...	1424
Lugano d.	0643	0743	0834	▬	...	0934	...	...	...	1026	1034	...	...	1134	1126	1140	...	...	1226	1234	...	...	1334	...	...	1426
Capolago-Riva San Vitale d.	|	|	0848	...	...	0948	...	...	...	|	1048	...	...	1148	|	|	...	...	|	1248	...	...	1348	...	...	|
Mendrisio d.	0658	0758	0854	...	...	0954	...	...	...	|	1054	...	...	1154	|	1157	...	...	|	1254	...	...	1354	...	...	|
Chiasso a.	0705	0805	0902	...	...	1002	...	...	...	1048	1102	...	...	1202	1148	1205	...	...	1248	1302	...	...	1402	...	...	1448
Chiasso 🏛 § d.	0708	0808	...	0908	...	...	...	...	...	1052	...	...	...	...	1211	...	...	...	1252	...	...	...	...	...	...	1452
Como San Giovanni § a.	0712	0812	...	0912	...	...	...	...	...	1056	...	...	...	...	1215	...	...	...	|	...	...	...	...	...	...	1456
Milano Centrale § a.	0750	0850	...	0950	...	...	...	...	...	1135	...	...	...	...	1250	...	...	...	1335	...	...	...	...	...	...	1535

		ICN	IR		ICN	IR	EC		ICN	IR		ICN	IR	EC		ICN	IR	RE		ICN	IR	EC		ICN	IR	
	2423	671	2271	2425	873	2173	319	2427	675	2275	2429	877	2177	321	2433	679	2279	10679	2435	881	2181	323	2437	683	2283	2439
	(🍷) S	✕	△	(🍷) S	✕	△	✕ ◧	(🍷) S	✕		(🍷) S	✕	△	✕ ◧	(🍷) S	✕	△	j	(🍷) S	✕	△	✕ ◧	(🍷) S	✕	△	(🍷) S
Basel SBB **565** d.	...	1104	...	...	...	1204	...	...	1304	...	...	...	1404	...	...	1504	...	...	...	...	1604	...	...	1704	...	...
Olten **565** d.	...	1130	...	...	...	1230	...	...	1330	...	...	...	1430	...	...	1530	...	...	...	...	1630	...	...	1730	...	...
Luzern 565 d.	1140	1218	...	1240	...	1318	...	1340	1418	...	1440	...	1518	...	1540	1618	...	...	1640	...	1718	...	1740	1818	...	1840
Küssnacht am Rigi d.	1158	|	...	1258	...	|	...	1358	|	...	1458	...	|	...	1558	|	...	...	1658	...	|	...	1758	|	...	1858
Zürich HB d.	|	|	1209	|	1309	|	1332	|	|	1409	|	1509	|	1532	|	|	1609	...	|	1709	|	1732	|	|	1809	|
Zug d.	|	|	1231	|	1331	|	1400	|	|	1431	|	1531	|	1600	|	|	1631	...	|	1731	|	1800	|	|	1831	|
Arth-Goldau a.	1211k	1244	1246k	1311	1346	1344k	1414	1411k	1444	1446k	1511	1546	1544k	1614	1611k	1644	1646k	...	1711	1746	1744k	1814	1811k	1844	1846k	1911
Arth-Goldau d.	▬	1250	1253	▬	1350	1353	1417	▬	1450	1453	▬	1550	1553	1617	▬	1650	1653	...	▬	1750	1753	1817	▬	1850	1853	▬
Schwyz d.	...	|	1301	...	|	1401	|	...	|	1501	...	|	1601	|	...	|	1701	...	...	|	1801	|	...	|	1901	...
Brunnen d.	...	|	1305	...	|	1405	|	...	|	1505	...	|	1605	|	...	|	1705	...	...	|	1805	|	...	|	1905	...
Flüelen d.	...	|	1315	...	|	1415	|	...	|	1515	...	|	1615	|	...	|	1715	...	...	|	1815	|	...	|	1915	...
Erstfeld d.	...	|	1324	...	|	1424	|	...	|	1524	...	|	1624	|	...	|	1724	...	...	|	1824	|	...	|	1924	...
Göschenen d.	...	|	1350	...	|	1450	|	...	|	1550	...	|	1650	|	...	|	1750	...	...	|	1850	|	...	|	1950	...
Airolo d.	...	|	1401	...	|	1501	|	...	|	1601	...	|	1701	|	...	|	1801	...	...	|	1901	|	...	|	2001	...
Faido d.	...	|	1419	...	|	1519	|	...	|	1619	...	|	1719	|	...	|	1819	...	...	|	1919	|	...	|	2019	...
Biasca d.	...	|	1440	...	|	1540	|	...	|	1640	...	|	1740	|	...	|	1840	...	...	|	1940	|	...	|	2040	2105
Bellinzona a.	...	1423	1453	...	1523	1553	1557	...	1623	1653	...	1723	1753	1757	...	1823	1853	...	...	1923	1953	1957	...	2023	2053	2119
Bellinzona ▲ d.	1403	1425	1454	1503	1525	1554	1559	1603	1625	1654	1703	1725	1754	1759	1803	1825	1854	...	1903	1925	1954	1959	2003	2025	2058	2133
Locarno 551 ▲ a.	|	|	1513	|	|	1613	|	|	|	1713	|	|	1813	|	|	|	1913	...	|	|	2013	|	|	|	|	|
Lugano a.	1433	1447	...	1533	1547	...	1624	1633	1647	...	1733	1747	...	1824	1833	1847	...	...	1933	1947	...	2024	2033	2047	2128	2203
Lugano d.	1434	...	...	1534	...	...	1626	1634	▬	...	1734	...	...	1826	1834	▬	...	1854	1934	...	...	2026	2034	...	2130	2204
Capolago-Riva San Vitale d.	1448	...	...	1548	...	...	|	1648	...	...	1748	...	...	|	1848	...	...	|	1948	...	...	|	2048	...	2145	2218
Mendrisio d.	1454	...	...	1554	...	...	|	1654	...	...	1754	...	...	|	1854	...	...	1910	1954	...	...	|	2054	...	2153	2224
Chiasso a.	1502	...	...	1602	...	...	1648	1702	...	...	1802	...	...	1848	1902	...	...	1917	2002	...	...	2048	2102	...	2202	2232
Chiasso 🏛 § d.	...	...	...	...	...	...	1652	...	1708	...	...	...	...	1852	...	1908	...	...	...	...	...	2052	...	...	...	...
Como San Giovanni § a.	...	...	...	...	...	...	|	...	1712	...	...	...	...	|	...	1912	...	...	...	...	...	2056	...	...	...	...
Milano Centrale § a.	...	...	...	...	...	...	1735	...	1750	...	...	...	...	1935	...	1950	...	...	...	...	...	2135	...	...	...	...

	ICN	IR	EC		ICN	IR	ICN	IR	IR	IR	RE
	885	2185	325	2441	689	2289	889	2191	2195	2293	2295
	✕	△	✕ ◧	(🍷) S	✕	△				△	
Basel SBB **565** d.	...	1804	...	...	1904	...	...	2004	...	...	...
Olten **565** d.	...	1830	...	...	1930	...	...	2030	...	...	...
Luzern 565 d.	...	1918	...	1940	2018	...	...	2118	2218	...	...
Küssnacht am Rigi d.	...	|	...	1958	|	...	...	|	|	...	...
Zürich HB d.	1909	|	1932	|	|	2009	2109	|	|	2209	2309
Zug d.	1931	|	2000	|	|	2031	2131	|	|	2231	2331
Arth-Goldau a.	1946	1944k	2014	2011k	2044	2046k	2146	2144k	2244	2246	2346
Arth-Goldau d.	1950	1953	2017	▬	2050	2053	2150	2154	...	2254	*2355*
Schwyz d.	|	2001	|	...	|	2101	|	2202	...	|	*0003*
Brunnen d.	|	2005	|	...	|	2105	|	2206	...	|	*0006*
Flüelen d.	|	2015	|	...	|	2115	|	2216	...	|	*0016*
Erstfeld d.	|	2024	|	...	|	2124	|	2226	...	2317	*0025*
Göschenen d.	|	2050	|	...	|	2150	|	...	...	2342	...
Airolo d.	|	2101	|	...	|	2201	|	...	...	2352	...
Faido d.	|	2119	|	...	|	2219	|	...	...	0010	...
Biasca d.	|	2140	|	...	|	2240	|	...	...	0031	...
Bellinzona a.	2123k	2153	2157	...	2223	2253	2323	...	...	0042	...
Bellinzona ▲ d.	2125	...	2159	2203	2225	2258	2325	...	...	0043	...
Locarno 551 ▲ a.	|	...	|	|	|	|	|	...	...	|	...
Lugano a.	2147	...	2224	2233	2247	2328	2347	...	...	0114	...
Lugano d.	...	...	2226	2234	2248	2330	2348	...	...	0116	...
Capolago-Riva San Vitale d.	...	...	|	2248	|	2345	|	...	...	0131	...
Mendrisio d.	...	...	|	2254	2304	2353	0005	...	...	0139	...
Chiasso a.	...	...	2248	2302	2312	0002	0012	...	...	0148	...
Chiasso 🏛 § d.	...	...	2252	...	...	...	...	...	...	...	...
Como San Giovanni § a.	...	...	2256	...	...	...	...	...	...	...	...
Milano Centrale § a.	...	...	2335	...	...	...	...	...	...	...	...

	IR	ICN	IR	ICN		IR	ICN		IR	ICN
	2164	854	2166	856		2264	668		2170	870
		✕	△	✕		△	✕		△	✕
Milano Centrale § d.	...	...	...	...	...	...	...	...	...	...
Como San Giovanni § d.	...	...	...	...	...	...	...	...	...	...
Chiasso 🏛 § a.	...	...	...	...	...	...	...	...	...	...
Chiasso d.	...	0444	...	0546	0558	0611	0641	0658	0711	0745
Mendrisio d.	...	0452	...	0554	0606	0620	0650	0706	0720	0752
Capolago-Riva San Vitale d.	...	|	...	|	0610	|	|	0710	|	|
Lugano a.	...	0508	...	0610	0626	0635	0705	0726	0735	0807
Lugano d.	...	0510	...	0612	0627	0637	0712	0727	0737	0812
Locarno 551 ▲ d.	...	|	...	|	|	|	|	|	|	|
Bellinzona ▲ a.	...	0532	...	0634	0657	0704	0734	0757	0804	0834
Bellinzona d.	...	0534	0606	0636	▬	0706	0736	▬	0806	0836
Biasca d.	...	|	0618	|	...	0718	|	...	0818	|
Faido d.	...	|	0640	|	...	0740	|	...	0840	|
Airolo d.	...	|	0658	|	...	0758	|	...	0858	|
Göschenen d.	...	|	0708	|	...	0808	|	...	0908	|
Erstfeld d.	0627	|	0734	|	...	0834	|	...	0934	|
Flüelen d.	0636	0653	0742	|	...	0842	|	...	0942	|
Brunnen d.	0650	|	0754	|	**2408**	0854	|	**2410**	0954	|
Schwyz d.	0655	|	0758	|	(🍷)	0858	|	(🍷)	0958	|
Arth-Goldau a.	0706	0709k	0806	0809k	S	0906	0909k	S	1006	1009k
Arth-Goldau d.	0714	0713	0814	0813	0848	0913	0914	0948	1014	1013
Zug d.	|	0729	|	0829	|	0929	|	|	|	1029
Zürich HB a.	|	0751	|	0851	|	0951	|	|	|	1051
Küssnacht am Rigi d.	|	...	|	...	0900	...	|	1000	|	...
Luzern 565 a.	0741	...	0841	...	0920	...	0941	1020	1041	...
Olten **565** a.	0827	...	0927	...	...	...	1027	...	1127	...
Basel SBB **565** a.	0855	...	0955	...	...	...	1055	...	1155	...

S – VORALPEN EXPRESS – 12 Luzern - Arth Goldau - Rapperswil - St Gallen and v.v.

j – ①–⑤ (not June 19, Aug. 1, 15, Dec. 8).
k – Connects with train in previous column(s).
y – June 21 - Oct. 25.

△ – Panorama car.
◧ – Supplement payable in Italy and for international journeys.

▲ – For additional services Locarno - Bellinzona and v.v. – see panel on page 279.
§ – For additional services Chiasso - Como San Giovanni - Milano Port Garibaldi and v.v. – see panel on page 279.

FS, SBB — MILANO, CHIASSO and LOCARNO - ZÜRICH and LUZERN — Valid June 15 - Dec. 13 — 550

km				ICN		EC	IR	ICN		IR	ICN		EC	IR	ICN		IR	ICN		EC	IR	ICN		IR	ICN	
				672		312	2176	874		2272	676		314	2178	878		2276	680		316	2182	882		2280	684	
				✕		✕	△	✕			✕		✕	△	✕		△	✕		✕	△	✕		△	✕	
						◧							◧							◧						
0	**Milano** Centrale § d.	...	0810	...	...	0825	...	...	...	...	...	...	1025	...	...	...	...	...	...	1225	...	...	...	...	...	...
47	Como San Giovanni § d.	...	0847	...	...	0903	...	...	...	...	...	...	1103	...	...	...	...	...	...	|	...	...	...	...	...	...
51	**Chiasso** 🏛 § a.	...	0852	...	...	0908	...	...	...	...	...	...	1108	...	...	...	...	...	...	1308	...	...	...	...	...	...
51	**Chiasso** d.	0758	▬	...	0858	0912	...	...	0958	...	...	1058	1112	...	...	1158	...	...	1258	1312	...	...	1358	...	...	1458
58	Mendrisio d.	0806	...	...	0906	|	...	...	1006	...	...	1106	|	...	...	1206	...	...	1306	|	...	...	1406	...	...	1506
63	Capolago-Riva San Vitale d.	0810	*IR*	...	0910	|	...	...	1010	...	...	1110	|	...	...	1210	...	...	1310	|	...	...	1410	...	...	1510
77	**Lugano** a.	0826	**2268**	...	0926	0932	...	...	1026	...	...	1126	1132	...	...	1226	...	...	1326	1332	...	...	1426	...	...	1526
77	**Lugano** d.	0827	△	0912	0927	0934	...	1012	1027	...	1112	1127	1134	...	1212	1227	...	1312	1327	1334	...	1412	1427	...	1512	1527
	Locarno 551 ▲ d.	|	0847	|	|	|	0947	|	|	1047	|	|	|	1147	|	|	1247	|	|	|	1347	|	|	1447	|	|
106	Bellinzona ▲ a.	0857	0904	0934	0957	0959	1004	1034	1057	1104	1134	1157	1159	1204	1234	1257	1304	1334	1357	1359	1404	1434	1457	1504	1534	1557
106	Bellinzona d.	▬	0906	0936	▬	1001	1006	1036	▬	1106	1136	▬	1201	1206	1236	▬	1306	1336	▬	1401	1406	1436	▬	1506	1536	▬
125	Biasca d.	...	0918	|	...	|	1018	|	...	1118	|	...	|	1218	|	...	1318	|	...	|	1418	|	...	1518	|	...
151	Faido d.	...	0940	|	...	|	1040	|	...	1140	|	...	|	1240	|	...	1340	|	...	|	1440	|	...	1540	|	...
171	Airolo d.	...	0958	|	...	|	1058	|	...	1158	|	...	|	1258	|	...	1358	|	...	|	1458	|	...	1558	|	...
187	Göschenen d.	...	1008	|	...	|	1108	|	...	1208	|	...	|	1308	|	...	1408	|	...	|	1508	|	...	1608	|	...
216	Erstfeld d.	...	1034	|	...	|	1134	|	...	1234	|	...	|	1334	|	...	1434	|	...	|	1534	|	...	1634	|	...
225	Flüelen d.	...	1042	|	...	|	1142	|	...	1242	|	...	|	1342	|	...	1442	|	...	|	1542	|	...	1642	|	...
237	Brunnen d.	**2412**	1054	|	**2414**	|	1154	|	**2416**	1254	|	**2418**	|	1354	|	**2420**	1454	|	**2422**	|	1554	|	**2424**	1654	|	**2426**
240	Schwyz d.	(🍷)	1058	|	(🍷)	|	1158	|	(🍷)	1258	|	(🍷)	|	1358	|	(🍷)	1458	|	(🍷)	|	1558	|	(🍷)	1658	|	(🍷)
248	**Arth-Goldau** a.	**S**	1106	1109**k**	**S**	1143**k**	1206	1209**k**	**S**	1306	1309**k**	**S**	1343**k**	1406	1409**k**	**S**	1506	1509**k**	**S**	1543**k**	1606	1609**k**	**S**	1706	1709**k**	**S**
248	**Arth-Goldau** d.	1048	1113	1114	1148	1145	1214	1213	1248	1313	1314	1348	1345	1414	1413	1448	1513	1514	1548	1545	1614	1613	1648	1713	1714	1748
264	Zug d.	|	1129	|	|	1201	|	1229	|	1329	|	|	1401	|	1429	|	1529	|	|	1601	|	1629	|	1729	|	|
293	**Zürich** HB a.	|	1151	|	|	1228	|	1251	|	1351	|	|	1428	|	1451	|	1551	|	|	1628	|	1651	|	1751	|	|
*	Küssnacht am Rigi d.	1100	...	|	1200	...	|	...	1300	...	|	1400	...	|	...	1500	...	|	1600	...	|	...	1700	...	|	1800
*	**Luzern 565** a.	1120	...	1141	1220	...	1241	...	1320	...	1341	1420	...	1441	...	1520	...	1541	1620	...	1641	...	1720	...	1741	1820
	Olten **565** a.	...	...	1227	...	...	1327	...	...	...	1427	...	...	1527	...	...	...	1627	...	...	1727	...	...	...	1827	...
	Basel SBB **565** a.	...	...	1255	...	...	1355	...	...	...	1455	...	...	1555	...	...	...	1655	...	...	1755	...	...	...	1855	...

	EC	IR	ICN		EC	IR		RE		EC	IR		RE		IR			EC	IR	ICN		IR	ICN		EC	
	318	2184	886		258	2284		25274		320	2188		25276		2288			322	2192	894		2292	696		324	
	✕	△	✕		🍷	△				🍷					△			✕	△	✕		△			✕	
	◧				◧			j		◧			j					◧							◧	
Milano Centrale § d.	1425	...	...	...	1510	...	1610	1610	...	1625	...	1710	...	...	...	1810	...	1825	...	...	...	...	...	...	2025	...
Como San Giovanni § d.	|	...	...	...	1544	...	1647	1647	...	|	...	1747	...	...	...	1847	...	|	...	...	...	...	...	...	2103	...
Chiasso 🏛 § a.	1508	...	...	...	1549	...	1652	1652	...	1708	...	1752	...	...	...	1852	...	1908	...	...	...	...	...	...	2108	...
Chiasso d.	1512	...	...	1558	1612	...	▬	1655	1658	1712	...	▬	1755	1758	...	▬	1858	1912	...	...	1958	...	...	2058	2112	2158
Mendrisio d.	|	...	...	1606	|	...	*ICN*	1702	1706	|	...	*ICN*	1802	1806	...	*ICN*	1906	|	...	...	2006	...	...	2106	|	2206
Capolago-Riva San Vitale d.	|	...	...	1610	|	...	**688**	|	1710	|	...	**890**	|	1810	...	**692**	1910	|	...	...	2010	...	...	2110	|	2210
Lugano a.	1532	...	...	1626	1632	...	✕	1717	1726	1732	...	✕	1817	1826	...	✕	1926	1932	...	...	2026	...	...	2126	2132	2226
Lugano d.	1534	...	1612	1627	1634	...	1712	1717	1727	1734	...	1812	1817	1827	...	1912	1927	1934	...	2012	2027	...	2112	2127	2134	2227
Locarno 551 ▲ d.	|	1547	|	|	|	1647	|	|	|	|	1747	|	|	|	1847	|	|	|	1947	|	|	2047	|	|	|	|
Bellinzona ▲ a.	1559	1604	1634	1657	1659	1704	1734	1746	1757	1759	1804	1834	1846	1857	1904	1934	1957	1959	2004	2034	2057	2104	2134	2157	2159	2257
Bellinzona d.	1601	1606	1636	▬	1701	1706	1736	...	▬	1801	1806	1836	...	▬	1906	1936	...	2001	2006	2036	...	2106	2136	...	2201	2306
Biasca d.	|	1618	|	...	|	1718	|	...	...	|	1818	|	...	...	1918	|	...	|	2018	|	...	2118	|	...	|	2318
Faido d.	|	1640	|	...	|	1740	|	...	...	|	1840	|	...	...	1940	|	...	|	2040	|	...	2140	|	...	|	2340
Airolo d.	|	1658	|	...	|	1758	|	...	...	|	1858	|	...	...	1958	|	...	|	2058	|	...	2158	|	...	|	2358
Göschenen d.	|	1708	|	...	|	1808	|	...	...	|	1908	|	...	...	2008	|	...	|	2108	|	...	2208	|	...	|	...
Erstfeld d.	|	1734	|	...	|	1834	|	...	...	|	1934	|	...	...	2034	|	...	|	2134	|	...	2234	|	...	|	...
Flüelen d.	|	1742	|	...	|	1842	|	...	...	|	1942	|	...	...	2042	|	...	|	2142	|	...	2242	|	...	|	...
Brunnen d.	|	1754	|	**2428**	|	1854	|	...	**2430**	|	1954	|	...	**2432**	2054	|	...	|	2154	|	...	2254	|	...	|	...
Schwyz d.	|	1758	|	(🍷)	|	1858	|	...	(🍷)	|	1958	|	...	(🍷)	2058	|	...	|	2158	|	...	2258	|	...	|	...
Arth-Goldau a.	1743**k**	1806	1809**k**	**S**	1843**k**	1906	1909**k**	...	**S**	1943**k**	2006	2009**k**	...	**S**	2106	2109**k**	...	2143	2206	2209**k**	...	2306	2309**k**	...	2343	...
Arth-Goldau d.	1745	1814	1813	1848	1845	1913	1914	...	1948	1945	2014	2013	...	2048	2113	2114	...	2145	2214	2213	...	2313	2314	...	2345	...
Zug d.	1801	|	1829	|	|	1929	|	...	|	2001	|	2029	...	|	2129	|	...	2201	|	2229	...	2329	|	...	0001	...
Zürich HB a.	1828	|	1851	|	|	1951	|	...	|	2028	|	2051	...	|	2151	|	...	2228	|	2251	...	2351	|	...	0028	...
Küssnacht am Rigi d.	...	|	...	1900	|	...	|	...	2000	...	|	...	...	2100	...	|	...	...	|	...	...	...	|	...	...	...
Luzern 565 a.	...	1841	...	1920	1913	...	1941	...	2020	...	2041	...	...	2120	...	2141	...	...	2241	...	...	...	2341	...	...	...
Olten **565** a.	...	1927	...	...	...	...	2027	...	...	...	2127	...	...	...	...	2227	...	...	2327	...	...	...	...	...	...	...
Basel SBB **565** a.	...	1955	...	...	...	...	2055	...	...	...	2155	...	...	...	...	2259	...	...	2359	...	...	...	...	...	...	...

▲ – Additional services **BELLINZONA - LOCARNO and v.v.**:

km																			
				and at the same					n			n				and at the same			
0	Bellinzona d.	0500	0530	minutes past	1600	1630	...	1700	1715	1730	1800	1815	1830	...	1900 1930	minutes past	2300 2330	...	0000 0049 ... ...
21	Locarno a.	0526	0556	each hour until	1626	1656	...	1726	1744	1756	1826	1844	1856	...	1926 1956	each hour until	2326 2356	...	0026 0113 ... ...

					and at the same					n			n			and at the same				
Locarno d.	0534	...	0604	0634	minutes past	1604	1634	...	1704	1717	1734	1804	1817	1834	...	1904 1934	minutes past	2304 2334	...	0016 0046 0119
Bellinzona a.	0601	...	0631	0701	each hour until	1631	1701	...	1731	1744	1801	1831	1844	1901	...	1931 2001	each hour until	2331 0001	...	0040 0111 0143

– Additional services **MILANO PORTA GARIBALDI - COMO SAN GIOVANNI - CHIASSO and v.v.** (2nd class only): Operator: Trenord

Milano Porta Garibaldi d.	0539	0639	0739	0839	and at	2039	2139	2239
Monza d.	0555	0655	0755	0855	the same	2055	2155	2255
Como San Giovanni d.	0639	0739	0839	0939	minutes past	2139	2239	2339
Chiasso a.	0644	0744	0844	0944	each hour until	2144	2244	2344

Chiasso d.	0516	0616	0716	and at	1916	2016	2116	2216
Como San Giovanni d.	0522	0622	0722	the same	1922	2022	2122	2222
Monza d.	0604	0704	0804	minutes past	2004	2104	2204	2304
Milano Porta Garibaldi a.	0621	0721	0821	each hour until	2021	2121	2221	2321

– **NOTES** (LISTED BY TRAIN NUMBER)

– VORALPEN EXPRESS – (12) St Gallen - Rapperswil - Arth Goldau - Luzern.

– ①–⑤ (not June 19, Aug. 1, 15, Dec. 8).

– Connects with train in previous column(s).

– Ⓐ Dec. 16 - June 27; ①–⑤ Sept. 1 - Dec. 5; ②–⑤ Dec. 9-12 (also Apr. 18; not Mar. 19, May 1, June 19).

△ – Panorama car.

◧ – Supplement payable in Italy and for international journeys.

▲ – For additional services Locarno - Bellinzona and v.v. – see panel above.

§ – For additional services Chiasso - Como San Giovanni - Milano Porta Garibaldi and v.v. – see panel above.

* – Other distances: Arth-Goldau *0*, Küssnacht am Rigi *12 km*, Luzern *28 km*.

FART — LOCARNO - DOMODOSSOLA — 551

km				C	V	C	V	V		V	C	C
				🍷	🍷	🍷	🍷	🍷	🍷	🍷q		
0	**Locarno 550** d.	0647	0749	0849	1049	1149	1249	1449	1549	1649	1748	1848
20	Camedo 🏛 d.	0724	0824	0924	1124**u**	1224	1324**u**	1524**u**	1624	1724**u**	1824	1924
26	Re d.	0740	0840**x**	0940**x**	1140**x**	1240**x**	1340**x**	1540**x**	1640	1740**x**	1840**x**	1940
34	S M Maggiore § d.	0753	0853**x**	0953**x**	1153**x**	1253**x**	1353**x**	1553**x**	1653	1753**x**	1853**x**	1953
53	**Domodossola 590** a.	0836	0936	1036	1236	1336	1436	1636	1736	1836	1936	2036

			C	V	V		V	Y	C	C	C
		🍷q	🍷	🍷	🍷		🍷	🍷	🍷		
Domodossola 590 d.	0530**a**	0825	0925	1025	1125	1240	1325	1525	1625	1725	2025
S. M. Maggiore § d.	0612**a**	0910**x**	1010**x**	1110**x**	1210**x**	1324	1410**x**	1610**x**	1710**x**	1810	2109
Re d.	0625	0922**x**	1022**x**	1122**x**	1222**x**	1339	1422**x**	1622**x**	1722**x**	1822	2122
Camedo 🏛 d.	0639	0940	1040	1140	1240	1355	1440	1640	1740	1840	2138
Locarno 550 a.	0720	1019	1119	1219	1319	1432	1519	1719	1819	1919	2215

– CENTOVALLI EXPRESS.

– TRENO PANORAMICO VIGEZZO VISION – Conveys panorama car (supplement payable).

– Daily. Apr. 6 - Oct. 12 runs as TRENO PANORAMICO VIGEZZO VISION – Conveys panorama car (supplement payable).

a – ①–⑤ only.

q – Apr. 6 - Oct. 12.

u – Stops to pick up only.

x – Stops only on request.

§ – Full name is Santa Maria Maggiore.

552 LUZERN - STANS - ENGELBERG

Narrow gauge rack railway. ZB

km		E		E				E			E		🚌			🚌			🚌			🚌		T	T
0	**Luzern 561** d.	0505	0527	0610	0627	0657	and at	1910	1927	1957	2010	2027	...	2057	2127	...	2157	2227	...	2257	2327	...		0836	0936
9	Hergiswil **561** d.	0517	0541	|	0641	0711	the same	|	1941	2011	|	2041	...	2111	2141	...	2211	2241	...	2311	2341	...	EXTRA	0847	0947
11	Stansstad d.	0521	0544	|	0644	0714	minutes	|	1944	2014	|	2044	...	2114	2144	...	2214	2244	...	2314	2344	...	SERVICES	0851	0951
15	Stans d.	0525	0548	0624	0648	0719	past each	1924	1948	2019	2024	2048	...	2119	2148	...	2219	2248	...	2319	2348	...	▶▶▶	0856	0956
19	Dallenwil d.	0530	0553	0629	0653	...	hour until	1929	1953	...	2029	2053	2055	...	2153	2155	...	2253	2255	...	2353	2355		|	|
34	**Engelberg** a.	0554	...	0653	...	...		1953	...	...	2053	...	2116	...	...	2216	...	...	2316	...	...	0016		0931	1031

				E				E			E		🚌			🚌			🚌			🚌		T	T
	Engelberg d.	...	*0535*y	0601	...	...	and at	2001	...	...	2101	...	2130	...	...	2230	...	...	2330	...	...	0018		1631	1731
	Dallenwil d.	0504	0604	0629	...	0704	the same	2029	...	2104	2129	...	2153	2204	...	2253	2304	...	2353	0004	...	0038	EXTRA	|	|
	Stans d.	0510	0610	0635	0640	0710	minutes	2035	2040	2110	2135	2140	...	2210	2240	...	2310	2340	...	0010	0040	0046	SERVICES	1704	1804
	Stansstad d.	0514	0614	|	0644	0714	past each	|	2044	2114	|	2144	...	2214	2244	...	2314	2344	...	0014	0044	...	▶▶▶	1708	1808
	Hergiswil **561** d.	0518	0618	|	0648	0718	hour until	|	2048	2118	|	2148	...	2218	2248	...	2318	2348	...	0018	0048	...		1712	1812
	Luzern 561 a.	0531	0632	0649	0702	0732		2049	2102	2132	2149	2202	...	2232	2302	...	2332	0002	...	0032	0102	...		1724	1824

E – LUZERN - ENGELBERG EXPRESS. Conveys panorama car.
T – ⑥⑦ Jan. 11 - Mar. 30; Ⓒ July 5 - Oct. 12.
y – Connection by 🚌.

553 MOUNTAIN RAILWAYS IN CENTRAL SWITZERLAND

2nd class only. RB

km			p			and		p	q	
0	Arth-Goldau d.	0800	0910	...	1010	hourly	1610	1710	1810	...
9	Rigi Kulm a.	0845	0947	...	1047	until	1647	1747	1847	...

		p			and		p	q	
Rigi Kulm d.	0900	1004	...	1104	hourly	1704	1804	1904	...
Arth-Goldau a.	0948	1048	...	1148	until	1748	1848	1948	...

December 15 - April 17 and October 20 - December 13

km					and					
0	Rigi Kulm d.	1000	...	1100	hourly	1600	...	1700	...	...
7	Vitznau a.	1040	...	1140	until	1640	...	1740	...	...

				and					n
Vitznau d.	0915	...	1015	hourly	1515	...	1615	...	1742
Rigi Kulm a.	0945	...	1045	until	1545	...	1645	...	1812

April 18 - May 23 and September 8 - October 19

				and					
Rigi Kulm d.	1000	...	1100	hourly	1900	...	2000	...	...
Vitznau a.	1040	...	1140	until	1940	...	2040	...	...

				and					
Vitznau d.	0915	...	1015	hourly	1815	...	1915	...	...
Rigi Kulm a.	0945	...	1045	until	1845	...	1945	...	...

May 24 - September 7

		†	⚒				🚂		and		
Rigi Kulm d.	1000	1050	1100	1200	1300	1400	1401	1500	hourly	2000	2240
Vitznau a.	1040	1140	1140	1240	1340	1440	1455	1540	until	2040	2320

			†	🚂⚡			and				
Vitznau d.	0915	1015	1050	1051	...	1115	hourly	1915	...	2205	...
Rigi Kulm a.	0945	1045	1120	1213	...	1145	until	1945	...	2235	...

ALPNACHSTAD - PILATUS KULM. Narrow gauge rack railway. *5 km*. Journey time: 30 minutes uphill, 40 minutes downhill. **Operator**: PB, ✆ 041 329 11 11.
Services run daily **early May - November 16** (weather permitting). **No winter service** (December - April).
From **Alpnachstad**: 0810**j**, 0850, 0935, 1015, 1055, 1135, 1220, 1300, 1345, 1425, 1505, 1550, 1630**j**, 1710**j**, 1750**k**.
From **Pilatus Kulm**: 0845**j**, 0930, 1010, 1050, 1130, 1215, 1255, 1340, 1420, 1500, 1545, 1625, 1705**j**, 1745**j**, 1845**k**.

BRIENZ - BRIENZER ROTHORN. Narrow gauge rack railway. *8 km*. Most services operated by steam train. Journey time: 55–60 minutes uphill, 60–70 minutes downhill.
Operator: BRB, ✆ 033 952 22 22. Service valid **June 7 - October 26**, and is subject to weather conditions on the mountain and demand. Extra trains may run at busy times. **No winter service**.
From **Brienz**: 0730**h**, 0836, 0940, 1000③, 1045, 1145, 1258, 1358, 1458, 1636.
From **Brienzer Rothorn**: 0830**h**, 0938, 1115, 1220, 1328, 1428, 1528, 1628, 1740.

h – ⑦ Sept. 7 - 28.
j – Until Oct. 25.
k – June 22 - Aug. 23.
n – Daily Dec. 21 - Mar. 9; ⑥⑦ Mar. 15 - Apr. 13; daily Oct. 20 - Dec. 13.
p – Daily Dec. 21 - Mar. 9; Ⓒ Mar. 15 - Apr. 13; daily Apr. 18 - Oct. 26; ⑥⑦ Nov. 1 - Dec. 7.
q – ⑤⑥⑦ May 2 - June 29; daily June 30 - Aug. 31; ⑤⑥⑦ Sept. 5 - Oct. 26 (also May 29, June 9, 19).
🚂 – † July 6 - Aug. 31. Reservations: ✆ 041 399 87 87.
⚡ – Supplement payable (CHF 20).

554 🚌 MEIRINGEN - ANDERMATT

Service June 21 - October 12 (no winter service) PA

	🅁⚡	🅁⚡	🅁⚡	🅁⚡	🅁⚡	🅁⚡		🅁⚡	🅁⚡	🅁⚡	🅁⚡
Meiringen Bahnhof d.	...	0850	0925	...	...	1050	...	1325	1330	1520	...
Steingletscher, Susten d.	...	0944	|	1000	...	|	...	|	1430	|	...
Susten Passhöhe d.	...	...	|	1010	...	|	...	|	1440	|	...
Göschenen Bahnhof d.	...	...	|	1049	...	|	...	|	1519	|	...
Grimsel Passhöhe d.	...	...	1100	|	...	1204	...	1439	|	1634	...
Gletsch Post d.	...	...	1110	|	...	1215	...	1450	|	1645	...
Oberwald Bahnhof a.	...	...	1125	|	...	1230	...	1505	|	1700	...
Oberwald Bahnhof d.	0945	...	...	|	1220	...	...	...	|	...	1704
Gletsch Post d.	0957	...	...	|	1233	...	...	...	|	...	1720
Furka Passhöhe d.	1023	...	...	|	1407	...	...	...	|	...	1743
Realp Post d.	...	...	...	|	1433	...	...	...	|	...	1809
Andermatt Bahnhof a.	...	...	...	1104	1441	...	...	...	1534	...	1817

	🅁⚡	🅁⚡	🅁⚡	🅁⚡	🅁⚡	🅁⚡		🅁⚡	🅁⚡	🅁⚡	🅁⚡
Andermatt Bahnhof d.	...	...	0830	...	...	...	...	...	1539	1559	...
Realp Post d.	...	...	0842	...	...	...	...	...	1551	|	...
Furka Passhöhe d.	...	...	0906	...	1024	...	...	...	1615	|	...
Gletsch Post d.	...	...	1005	...	1054	...	...	...	1645	|	...
Oberwald Bahnhof a.	...	...	1020	...	1109	...	...	...	1700	|	...
Oberwald Bahnhof d.	...	...	...	1030	...	1250	...	1530	...	|	1704
Gletsch Post d.	...	...	...	1046	...	1302	...	1542	...	|	1716
Grimsel Passhöhe d.	...	...	...	1125	...	1330	...	1610	...	|	1736
Göschenen Bahnhof d.	0910	...	...	|	...	|	...	|	...	1615	|
Susten Passhöhe d.	0945	...	...	|	...	|	...	|	...	1650	|
Steingletscher, Susten d.	0950	1000	...	|	...	|	...	|	...	1720	|
Meiringen Bahnhof a.	...	1050	...	1225	...	1434	...	1714	...	1810	1835

⚡ – Supplement payable.

555 ZÜRICH FLUGHAFEN ✈ - ZÜRICH - LUZERN

SBB

km																Ⓐ			Ⓐ					Ⓐy			
0	**Zürich** Flughafen ✈ **530/5** d.	...	...	...	...	...	...	...	0847	...	and at	1547	...	...	...	1647	...	...	1747	...	...	...	1847	...	1947
10	**Zürich** HB **530/5** d.	0535	0604	0635	0704	0735	0804	0835	0904	0935	the same	1604	1635	...	1641	1704	1735	1741	1804	1835	...	1841	1904	1935	2004
22	Thalwil d.	0545	0614	0645	0714	0745	0814	0845	0914	0945	minutes	1614	1645	...	|	1714	1745	|	1814	1845	...	|	1914	1945	2014
39	Zug d.	0602	0629	0702	0729	0802	0829	0902	0929	1002	past each	1629	1702	...	1712	1729	1802	1812	1829	1902	...	1912	1929	2002	2029
49	Rotkreuz d.	0610	|	0710	|	0810	|	0910	|	1010	hour	|	1710	...	1721	|	1810	1821	|	1910	...	1921	|	2010	|
67	**Luzern** a.	0625	0649	0725	0749	0825	0849	0925	0949	1025	until	1649	1725	...	1739	1749	1825	1839	1849	1925	...	1939	1949	2025	2049

									x	x	x
Zürich Flughafen ✈ **530/5** d.	...	2047	...	...	...	...	...	...	...	...	...
Zürich HB **530/5** d.	2035	2104	2135	2204	2235	2304	2335	0008	0135	0235	0335
Thalwil d.	2045	2114	2145	2214	2245	2314	2345	0017	|	|	|
Zug d.	2102	2129	2202	2229	2302	2329	0002	0035	0155	0255	0355
Rotkreuz d.	2110	|	2210	|	2310	|	0010	0046	0202	0302	0402
Luzern a.	2125	2149	2225	2249	2325	2349	0025	0107	0225	0325	0425

				Ⓐ				Ⓐ	
Luzern d.	0455	0528	0610	0620	0635	...	0710	0720	0735
Rotkreuz d.	0513	0548	|	0636	0648	...	|	0736	0748
Zug d.	0526	0558	0631	0647	0658	...	0731	0747	0758
Thalwil d.	0542	0616	0646	|	0716	...	0746	|	0816
Zürich HB **530/5** a.	0555	0625	0656	0719	0725	...	0756	0819	0825
Zürich Flughafen ✈ **530/5** a.	0613	...	...	...	...	...	0813	...	...

																							x	x	x
Luzern d.	0810	0835	and at	1510	1535	...	1610	1635	1710	1735	1810	1835	1910	1935	2010	2035	2110	2135	2210	2235	2310	2335	0035	0135	0235
Rotkreuz d.	|	0848	the same	|	1548	...	|	1648	|	1748	|	1848	|	1948	|	2048	|	2148	|	2248	|	2348	0048	0146	024
Zug d.	0831	0858	minutes	1531	1558	...	1631	1658	1731	1758	1831	1858	1931	1958	2031	2058	2131	2158	2231	2258	2331	2358	0058	0153	025
Thalwil d.	0846	0916	past each	1546	1616	...	1646	1716	1746	1816	1846	1916	1946	2016	2046	2116	2146	2216	2246	2316	2346	0016	0116	0211j	031
Zürich HB **530/5** a.	0856	0925	hour	1556	1625	...	1656	1725	1756	1825	1856	1925	1956	2025	2056	2125	2156	2225	2256	2325	2356	0025	0125	0225	032
Zürich Flughafen ✈ **530/5** a.	0913	...	until	1613	...	...	1713	...	1813	...	1913	...	2013	...	...	...	...	...	...	...	...	...	...	...	...

j – June 15 - Dec. 13 (also Aug. 1).
x – ⑥⑦ (also Apr. 18, 21, May 29, 30, June 9, Aug. 1).
y – Dec. 16 - June 13.

SBB — BASEL - BERN - INTERLAKEN and BRIG — 560

km		IC 955	IC 806	ICE 1055	IC 957	IC 808	EC 51	IC 959	IC 810	ICE 1061	IC 961	IC 812	IC 1063	ICE 271	IC 816	IC 1067	IC 967	IC 818	IC 1069	IC 969	IC 820	IC 1071	ICE 275	IC 822	EC 57	IC 973	IC 824	IC 1075	ICE 277
		✕	(✕)		(✕)	✕	✕	(✕)	(✕)	✕	✕	✕	(✕)	✕	(✕)	(✕)	✕	✕	✕	(✕)	✕	✕	✕	✕	✕	(✕)	(✕)	✕	✕
							◧							◆									◆		◧				Bn
	Romanshorn **535** ... d.	...	...	...	...	...	...	...	0538	...	...	0638	...	...	0741	...	...	0841	...	...	0941	...	...	1041	...	...	1141	...	...
	Zürich Flug ✈ **535**. d.	...	...	...	...	...	...	...	0640	...	...	0743	...	...	0840	...	...	0940	...	...	1040	...	...	1140	...	...	1240	...	...
	Zürich HB **500** .... d.	...	...	...	...	0602	...	...	0702	...	...	0802	...	...	0902	...	...	1002	...	...	1102	...	...	1202	...	...	1302	...	...
0	**Basel** SBB .... d.	...	...	0524	0559	|	0631	0659	|	0731	0759	|	0831	0859	|	0931	0959	|	1031	1059	|	1131	1159	|	1231	1259	|	1331	1359
14	Liestal .... d.	...	...	0534	0609	|	|	0709	|	|	0809	|	|	0909	|	|	1009	|	|	1109	|	|	1209	|	|	1309	|	|	1409
39	Olten .... d.	...	...	0559	0629	|	0659	0729	|	0759	0829	|	0859	0929	|	0959	1029	|	1059	1129	|	1159	1229	|	1259	1329	|	1359	1429
101	**Bern** .... a.	...	...	0627	0656	0658k	0727	0756	0758k	0827	0856	0858k	0927	0956	0958k	1027	1056	1058k	1127	1156	1158k	1227	1256	1258k	1327	1356	1358k	1427	1456
101	**Bern** .... d.	0604	0607	0634	0704	0707	0734	0804	0807	0834	0904	0907	0934	1004	1007	1034	1104	1107	1134	1204	1207	1234	1304	1307	1334	1404	1407	1434	1504
132	Thun .... d.	0622	0625	0654	0722	0725	0754	0822	0825	0854	0922	0925	0954	1022	1025	1054	1122	1125	1154	1222	1225	1254	1322	1325	1354	1422	1425	1454	1522
142	**Spiez** .... a.	0631	0634	0702	0731	0734	0802	0831	0834	0902	0931	0934	1002	1031	1034	1102	1131	1134	1202	1231	1234	1302	1331	1334	1402	1431	1434	1502	1531
142	**Spiez** .... ▲ d.	0633	0636	0703	0733	0736	0805	0833	0836	0903	0933	0936	1005	1033	1036	1103	1133	1136	1205	1233	1236	1303	1333	1336	1405	1433	1436	1503	1533
	Interlaken West.. ▲ d.	0652	|	0723	0752	|	|	0852	|	0923	0952	|	|	1053	|	1123	1153	|	|	1252	|	1323	1353	|	|	1453	|	1523	1553
	Interlaken Ost... ▲ a.	0657	|	0728	0757	|	|	0857	|	0928	0957	|	|	1057	|	1128	1157	|	|	1257	|	1328	1357	|	|	1457	|	1528	1557
197	Visp .... d.	...	0703	...	...	0803	0832	...	0903	...	...:	1003	1032	...	1103	...	...	1203	1232	...	1303	...	...	1403	1432	...	1503	...	...
206	**Brig** .... a.	...	0711	...	...	0811	0840	...	0911	...	...	1011	1040	...	1111	...	...	1211	1240	...	1311	...	...	1411	1440	...	1511	...	...
	Milano C **590** .... a.	...	...	...	...	...	1035	...	...	...	...	...	...	...	...	...	...	...	...	...	...	...	...	...	1635	...	...	...	...

	IC 826	IC 1077	IC 977	IC 828	IC 1079	IC 979	IC 830	IC 1081	IC 981	IC 832	EC 59	ICE 371	IC 836	IC 1085	ICE 341	IC 838	IC 1087	ICE 373	IC 1089	IC 1091	IC 991	IC 1093	TGV 9225	IC 993	IC 1095	IC 1097	IC 1099	IC 951	IC 953
	✕	(✕)	✕	(✕)	(✕)	(✕)	✕	(✕)	✕	(✕)	✕	✕	✕	(✕)	✕	✕	✕	✕	✕				(🍷)						
											◧	B						B	①–⑥	⑦					①–⑥	⑦			L
Romanshorn **535** ....d.	1241	...	...	1341	...	...	1441	...	...	1541	...	...	1641	...	...	1741	...	...	...	...	...	...	...	...	...	...	...	...	...
Zürich Flug ✈ **535**..d.	1340	...	...	1440	...	...	1540	...	...	1640	...	...	1740	...	...	1840	...	...	...	...	...	...	...	...	...	...	...	...	...
Zürich HB **500** ....d.	1402	...	...	1502	...	...	1602	...	...	1702	...	...	1802	...	...	1902	...	...	...	...	...	...	...	...	...	...	...	...	...
Basel SBB ....d.	|	1431	1459	|	1531	1559	|	1631	1659	|	1731	1759	|	1831	1859	|	1931	1959	2031	2031	2059	2131	2136	...	...	...	2231	...	...
Liestal ....d.	|	|	1509	|	|	1609	|	|	1709	|	|	1809	|	|	1909	|	|	2009	|	|	2109	|	|	...	...	...	|	...	...
Olten ....d.	|	1459	1529	|	1559	1629	|	1659	1729	|	1759	1829	|	1859	1929	|	1959	2029	2059	2059	2129	2200	2202	...	...	...	2300	...	...
Bern ....a.	1458k	1527	1556	1558k	1627	1656	1658k	1727	1756	1758k	1827	1856	1858k	1927	1956	1958k	2027	2056	2127	2127	2156	2227	2250	...	...	...	2327	...	...
Bern ....d.	1507	1534	1604	1607	1634	1704	1707	1734	1804	1807	1834	1904	1907	1934	2004	2007	2034	2107	2134	2134	2207	...	2302	2308	2234	2234	2339	0008	0108
Thun ....d.	1525	1554	1622	1625	1654	1722	1725	1754	1822	1825	1854	1922	1925	1954	2022	2025	2054	2125	2154	2154	2225	...	|	2326	2254	2254	2358	0028	0133
Spiez ....a.	1534	1602	1631	1634	1702	1731	1734	1802	1831	1834	1902	1931	1934	2002	2031	2034	2102	2134	2202	2202	2234	...	|	2335	2302	2302	0007	0038	0143
Spiez .... ▲ d.	1536	1605	1633	1636	1703	1733	1736	1805	1833	1836	1905	1933	1936	2003	2033	2036	2105	2135	2205	2205	2235	...	|	2336	2305	2305	...	0038	0143
Interlaken West.. ▲ d.	|	|	1652	|	1723	1753	|	|	1852	|	|	1952	|	2023	2049	|	|	2152	|	|	2252	...	2349	2356	|	|	...	0053	0200
Interlaken Ost... ▲ a.	|	|	1657	|	1728	1757	|	|	1857	|	|	1957	|	2028	2054	|	|	2157	|	|	2257	...	2353	0001	f	f	...	0059	0205
Visp ....d.	1603	1632	...	1703	...	...	1803	1832	...	1903	1932	...	2003	...	...	2103	2132	...	2232	|	...	...	...	...	2335	|	...	...	...
Brig ....a.	1611	1640	...	1711	...	...	1811	1840	...	1911	1940	...	2011	...	...	2111	2140	...	2240	2301	...	...	...	...	2343	0010	...	...	...
Milano C **590** ....a.	...	...	...	...	...	...	...	...	...	...	2135	...	...	...	...	...	...	...	...	...	...	...	...	...	...	...	...	...	...

km		IC 952	IC 809	IC 1058	ICE 372	IC 811	IC 1060	IC 956	IC 815	IC 1064	ICE 370	IC 817	IC 1066	IC 962	IC 819	EC 50	ICE 278	IC 821	IC 1070	IC 968	IC 823	IC 1072	ICE 276	IC 825	IC 1074	IC 974	IC 827	EC 52	IC 978
			✕		✕	✕	(✕)	(✕)	✕	✕	✕	(✕)	(✕)	✕	✕	✕	✕	(✕)	(✕)	✕	✕	(✕)	✕	(✕)	✕	(✕)	✕	✕	(✕)
					By						B					◧	B						Bp					◧	
	Milano C **590** .... d.	...	...	...	...	...	...	...	...	...	...	...	...	...	...	0725	...	...	...	...	...	...	...	...	...	...	...	1125	...
	Brig .... d.	...	...	...	...	0547	...	...	0649	0720	...	0749	...	...	0849	0920	...	0949	...	...	1049	1120	...	1149	...	...	1249	1320	...
	Visp .... d.	...	...	...	...	0554	...	...	0657	0728	...	0757	...	...	0857	0928	...	0957	...	...	1057	1128	...	1157	...	...	1257	1328	...
0	**Interlaken** Ost... ▲ d.	...	...	0521	0600	f	0627	0700	|	|	0800	|	0830	0900	|	|	1000	|	1030	1100	|	|	1200	|	1230	1300	|	|	1400
2	Interlaken West.. ▲ d.	...	...	0526	0605	|	0632	0705	|	|	0805	|	0835	0905	|	|	1005	|	1035	1105	|	|	1205	|	1235	1305	|	|	1405
18	**Spiez** .... ▲ a.	...	...	0548	0621	0624	0652	0721	0724	0753	0821	0824	0852	0921	0924	0953	1021	1024	1052	1121	1124	1153	1221	1224	1252	1321	1324	1353	1421
	Spiez .... d.	0520	...	0550	0622	0625	0654	0722	0725	0754	0822	0825	0854	0922	0925	0954	1022	1025	1054	1122	1125	1154	1222	1225	1254	1322	1325	1354	1422
	Thun .... d.	0530	...	0601	0632	0636	0704	0732	0736	0804	0832	0836	0904	0932	0936	1004	1032	1036	1104	1132	1136	1204	1232	1236	1304	1332	1336	1404	1432
	Bern .... a.	0552	...	0623	0652	0654k	0723	0752	0754k	0823	0852	0854k	0923	0952	0954k	1023	1052	1054k	1123	1152	1154k	1223	1252	1254k	1323	1352	1354k	1423	1452
	Bern .... d.	0604	0602	0634	0704	0702	0734	0804	0802	0834	0904	0902	0934	1004	1002	1034	1104	1102	1134	1204	1202	1234	1304	1302	1334	1404	1402	1434	1504
	Olten .... d.	0632	0631	0705	0732	|	0805	0832	|	0905	0932	|	1005	1032	|	1105	1132	|	1205	1232	|	1305	1332	|	1405	1432	|	1505	1532
	Liestal .... d.	0648	|	|	0748	|	|	0848	|	|	0948	|	|	1048	|	|	1148	|	|	1248	|	|	1348	|	|	1448	|	|	1548
	Basel SBB .... a.	0659	|	0729	0759	|	0829	0859	|	0929	0959	|	1029	1059	|	1129	1159	|	1229	1259	|	1329	1359	|	1429	1459	|	1529	1559
	Zürich HB **500** .... a.	...	0702	...	...	0758	...	...	0858	...	...	0958	...	...	1058	...	...	1158	...	...	1258	...	...	1358	...	...	1458	...	...
	Zürich Flug ✈ **535**. a.	...	0716	...	...	0816	...	...	0916	...	...	1016	...	...	1116	...	...	1216	...	...	1316	...	...	1416	...	...	1516	...	...
	Romanshorn **535** ... a.	...	0817	...	...	0918	...	...	1018	...	...	1118	...	...	1218	...	...	1318	...	...	1418	...	...	1518	...	...	1618	...	...

	IC 829	IC 1078	ICE 376	IC 831	IC 1080	IC 982	IC 835	ICE 332	IC 986	IC 837	IC 1086	IC 988	IC 839	IC 1088	IC 990	IC 841	IC 1090	IC 992	IC 843	EC 56	ICE 336	IC 1092	ICE 338	ICE 342	IC 1094	ICE 344	IC 998	IC 1096	IC 1098
	✕	✕	✕	✕	✕	(✕)	(✕)	✕	✕	✕	(✕)	✕	(✕)	(✕)	(✕)	✕	(✕)	✕	(✕)	✕	✕		✕						
			◆																	◧					①–⑥			⑦	v
Milano C **590** ....d.	...	...	...	...	...	...	...	...	...	...	...	...	...	...	...	...	...	...	...	1825	...	...	...	...	...	...	...	...	...
Brig ....d.	1349	...	...	1449	1520	...	1549	...	...	1649	1720	...	1749	...	...	1849	1920	...	1949	2020	...	2120	...	...	2220	...	...	2226	...
Visp ....d.	1357	...	...	1457	1528	...	1557	...	...	1657	1728	...	1757	...	...	1857	1928	...	1957	2028	...	2128	...	...	2228	...	...	|	...
Interlaken Ost... ▲ d.	|	1430	1500	|	|	1600	|	1630	1700	|	|	1800	|	1830	1900	|	|	2000	|	|	2100	|	...	2200	|	...	2300	|	2333
Interlaken West.. ▲ d.	|	1435	1505	|	|	1605	|	1635	1705	|	|	1805	|	1835	1905	|	|	2005	|	|	2105	|	...	2205	|	...	2305	|	2338
Spiez .... ▲ a.	1424	1452	1521	1524	1553	1621	1624	1652	1721	1724	1753	1821	1824	1852	1921	1924	1953	2021	2024	2053	2121	2153	...	2221	2253	...	2321	2322	2356
Spiez ....d.	1425	1454	1522	1525	1554	1622	1625	1654	1722	1725	1754	1822	1825	1854	1922	1925	1954	2022	2025	2054	2122	2154	...	2222	2254	...	2322	2325	2357
Thun ....d.	1436	1504	1532	1536	1604	1632	1636	1704	1732	1736	1804	1832	1836	1904	1932	1936	2004	2032	2036	2104	2132	2204	...	2232	2304	...	2332	2336	0007
Bern ....a.	1454k	1523	1552	1554k	1623	1652	1654k	1723	1752	1754k	1823	1852	1854k	1923	1952	1954k	2023	2052	2054k	2123	2152	2223	...	2252	2323	...	2352	2354	0025
Bern ....d.	1502	1534	1604	1602	1634	1704	1702	1734	1804	1802	1834	1904	1902	1934	2004	2002	2034	2104	2102	2134	*2202*	...	2234	...	...	2334	...	...	...
Olten ....d.	|	1605	1632	|	1705	1732	|	1805	1832	|	1905	1932	|	2005	2032	|	2105	2132	|	2205	*2230*	...	2306	...	...	0006	...	...	...
Liestal ....d.	|	|	1648	|	|	1748	|	|	1848	|	|	1948	|	|	2048	|	|	2148	|	|	|	...	|	...	...	0022	...	...	...
Basel SBB ....a.	|	1629	1659	|	1729	1759	|	1829	1859	|	1929	1959	|	2029	2059	|	2129	2159	|	2229	|	...	2330	...	...	0033	...	...	...
Zürich HB **500** ....a.	1558	...	...	1658	...	...	1758	...	...	1858	...	...	1958	...	...	2058	...	...	2158	...	*2301*	...	...	...	...	...	...	...	...
Zürich Flug ✈ **535**..a.	1616	...	...	1716	...	...	1816	...	...	1916	...	...	2016	...	...	2116	...	...	2216	...	*2316*	...	...	...	...	...	...	...	...
Romanshorn **535** ....a.	1718	...	...	1818	...	...	1918	...	...	2018	...	...	2118	...	...	2218	...	...	2318	...	*0018*	...	...	...	...	...	...	...	...

◆ – **NOTES** (LISTED BY TRAIN NUMBER)

71 – [12] and ✕ (Hamburg ① **g** - Frankfurt ①–⑥ **h** -) Basel - Interlaken.
75 – [12] and ✕ (Berlin ①–⑤ **h** -) Frankfurt - Basel - Interlaken.
76 – [12] and ✕ Interlaken - Basel - Frankfurt (- Hamburg ⑤⑦ **z**).

– [12] and ✕ Interlaken - Basel - Berlin and v.v.
– MOONLINER – ⑥⑦ (not Apr. 19).
– [12] and (🍷) Paris Lyon - Interlaken and v.v.

– Via Frutigen.
– Also Apr. 22, June 10; not Apr. 21, June 9.
– Not Apr. 21, June 9, Oct. 3.
– Connects with train in previous column.
– Runs as train **297** on † Dec. 15 - July 27; ⑦ Aug. 3 - Dec. 7 (not Apr. 18, May 29).

p – Runs as train **296** on ⑥ (also Apr. 20, June 8).
v – ⑤⑥ (not Apr. 18).
y – Runs as train **392** on ⑤–⑦ (also Apr. 17, 21, 30, May 28, June 9, Oct. 2; not Apr. 18, May 2, 30, Oct. 3).
z – Also Apr. 17, 21, 30, May 28, June 9, Oct. 2; not Apr. 18, 20, May 2, 30, June 8, Oct. 3.
◧ – Supplement payable for journeys from / to Italy.

▲ – Additional connections available **Spiez - Interlaken and v.v.**:
From **Spiez**: 0805, 1005, 1205, 1405, 1605, 1805, 1905.
From **Interlaken** Ost: 0729, 0929, 1129, 1329, 1529, 1729, 1929.

561 LUZERN - INTERLAKEN

ZB. Narrow gauge rack railway

km			Ⓐ	Ⓐ			L			L				L			L			L			L		
0	**Luzern 552**	d.	...	...	...	0542	0605	0612	0642	0705	0712	0742		1705	1712	1742	1805	1812	1842	1905	1912	1942	2005	2012	2042
9	Hergiswil **552**	d.	...	...	...	0554	|	0624	0654	|	0724	0754		|	1724	1754	|	1824	1854	|	1924	1954	|	2024	2054
13	Alpnachstad	d.	...	...	...	0559	|	0629	0659	|	0729	0759		|	1729	1759	|	1829	1859	|	1929	1959	|	2029	2059
15	Alpnach Dorf	d.	...	...	...	0601	|	0631	0701	|	0731	0801	and at	|	1733	1801	|	1831	1901	|	1931	2001	|	2031	2101
21	Sarnen	d.	...	...	...	0609	0624	0641	0709	0724	0741	0809	the same	1724	1741	1809	1824	1841	1909	1924	1941	2009	2024	2041	2109
23	Sachseln	d.	...	...	...	0613	0628	0645	0713	0728	0745	0813	minutes	1728	1745	1813	1828	1845	1913	1928	1945	2013	2028	2045	2113
29	Giswil	d.	...	...	...	0621	0638	0654	0721	0738	0754	0821	past each	1738	1754	1821	1838	1854	1921	1938	1954	2021	2038	2054	2121
36	Lungern	d.	...	...	...	▬	0652	...	▬	0752	...	▬	hour	1752	...	▬	1852	...	...	1952	▬	...	2052	▬	...
40	Brünig Hasliberg	d.	...	...	...	...	0704	...	...	0804	...	...	until	1804	...	...	1904	...	...	2004	...	...	2104	...	...
45	**Meiringen ●**	a.	...	...	...	...	0717	...	...	0817	...	...		1817	...	...	1917	...	...	2017	...	...	2117	...	...
45	**Meiringen ●**	d.	0515	0545	0614	0651	0722	...	0751	0822	...	0851		1822	...	1851	1922	...	...	...	2020	...	...	2120	...
58	**Brienz**	d.	0527	0558	0628	0702	0733	...	0802	0835	...	0902		1835	...	1902	1935	...	...	...	2033	...	...	2132	...
65	Oberried	d.	0537	0608	0639	0712	0744	...	0812	|	...	0912		|	...	1912	1944	...	...	...	2043	...	...	2142	...
74	**Interlaken** Ost	a.	0550	0621	0651	0724	0754	...	0824	0855	...	0924		1855	...	1924	1955	...	...	...	2055	...	...	2155	...

		L								
Luzern 552	d.	2105	2112	2142	2212	2242	2312	2342	0012	0042
Hergiswil **552**	d.	|	2124	2154	2224	2254	2324	2354	0024	0054
Alpnachstad	d.	|	2129	2159	2229	2259	2329	2359	0029	0059
Alpnach Dorf	d.	|	2131	2201	2231	2301	2331	0001	0031	0101
Sarnen	d.	2124	2141	2209	2241	2309	2341	0009	0041	0109
Sachseln	d.	2128	2145	2213	2245	2313	2345	0013	0045	0113
Giswil	d.	2138	2154	2221	2254	2321	2354	0021	0054	0121
Lungern	d.	2152	▬	...	▬	...	...	...	...	...
Brünig Hasliberg	d.	2204	...	...	...	...	...	...	...	...
Meiringen ●	a.	2217	...	...	y	...	...	...	...	...
Meiringen ●	d.	...	2220	...	2320	...	...	...	...	...
Brienz	d.	...	2232	...	2332	...	...	...	...	...
Oberried	d.	...	2242	...	2342	...	...	...	...	...
Interlaken Ost	a.	...	2255	...	2355	...	...	...	...	...

					L		Ⓐ		L	Ⓐ	
Interlaken Ost	d.	...	...	...	...	...	0554	...	...	0627	...
Oberried	d.	...	...	...	...	...	0608	...	...	0639	...
Brienz	d.	...	...	...	...	...	0618	...	...	0650	...
Meiringen ●	a.	...	...	...	...	...	0631	...	...	0703	...
Meiringen ●	d.	...	...	...	0541	...	...	...	0641	▬	...
Brünig Hasliberg	d.	...	...	...	0553	...	...	...	0653	...	...
Lungern	d.	...	...	...	0605	...	...	...	0705	...	...
Giswil	d.	0505	0537	0605	0622	0637	...	0705	0722	0737	0805
Sachseln	d.	0513	0545	0613	0629	0645	...	0713	0729	0745	0813
Sarnen	d.	0517	0549	0617	0635	0649	...	0717	0735	0749	0817
Alpnach Dorf	d.	0524	0554	0624	|	0654	...	0724	|	0754	0824
Alpnachstad	d.	0529	0559	0629	|	0659	...	0729	|	0759	0829
Hergiswil **552**	d.	0534	0604	0634	|	0704	...	0734	|	0804	0834
Luzern 552	a.	0547	0617	0647	0655	0717	...	0747	0755	0817	0847

		L			L				L				L			L							z	
Interlaken Ost	d.	0704	...	0733	0804	...	0833		1804	...	1833	...	1904	...	1933	2004	...	2106	...	2206	...	2306	0006	...
Oberried	d.	0714	...	0744	|	...	0844		|	...	1844	...	|	...	1946	2015	...	2118	...	2218	...	2318	0017	...
Brienz	d.	0725	...	0754	0825	...	0854		1825	...	1854	...	1925	...	1957	2025	...	2130	...	2230	...	2330	0027	...
Meiringen ●	a.	0736	...	0807	0836	...	0907	and at	1836	...	1907	...	1936	...	2009	2036	...	2142	...	2242	...	2342	0039	...
Meiringen ●	d.	0741	...	▬	0841	...	▬	the same	1841	...	▬	...	1941	...	▬	2041	...	▬	...	▬	...	▬	...	...
Brünig Hasliberg	d.	0753	...	...	0853	...	...	minutes	1853	...	...	...	1953	...	...	2053	...	...	...	...	...	...	...	...
Lungern	d.	0805	...	...	0905	...	...	past each	1905	...	...	...	2005	...	...	2105	...	...	...	...	...	...	...	...
Giswil	d.	0822	0837	0905	0922	0937	1005	hour	1922	1937	2005	...	2022	2037	2105	2122	2137	2205	2237	2305	2337	0005	...	...
Sachseln	d.	0829	0845	0913	0929	0945	1013	until	1929	1945	2013	...	2029	2045	2113	2129	2145	2213	2245	2313	2345	0013	...	...
Sarnen	d.	0835	0849	0917	0935	0949	1017		1935	1949	2017	...	2035	2049	2117	2135	2149	2217	2249	2317	2349	0017	...	...
Alpnach Dorf	d.	|	0854	0924	|	0954	1024		|	1954	2024	...	|	2054	2124	|	2154	2224	2254	2324	2354	0024	...	...
Alpnachstad	d.	|	0859	0929	|	0959	1029		|	1959	2029	...	|	2059	2129	|	2159	2229	2259	2329	2359	0029	...	...
Hergiswil **552**	d.	|	0904	0934	|	1004	1034		|	2004	2034	...	|	2104	2134	|	2204	2234	2304	2334	0004	0034	...	...
Luzern 552	a.	0855	0917	0947	0955	1017	1047		1955	2017	2047	...	2055	2117	2147	2155	2217	2247	2317	2347	0017	0047	...	...

L – LUZERN - INTERLAKEN EXPRESS. Conveys [panorama car] (reservation recommended). Also conveys (✕) on most services.

n – ✕ Dec. 16 - May 17; daily May 18 - Aug. 30; ①-⑥ Sept. 1 - Dec. 13.

q – ⓒ May 17 - Aug. 24.

y – ⑤⑥ (not Apr. 18, Aug. 1).

z – ⑥⑦ (not Apr. 19, Aug. 2).

● – Rail service **Meiringen** - **Innertkirchen** and v.v. Narrow gauge. 2nd class only. *5 km*. Journey time: 11 minutes. **Operator**: MIB.

From **Meiringen**: 0612Ⓐ, 0635Ⓐ, 0655, 0715, 0745, 0815✕, 0845, 0945, 1045, 1115, 1145, 1215**n** 1245, 1315, 1345, 1415**q**, 1445, 1515**q**, 1545, 1615, 1645, 1715Ⓐ, 1745, 1815Ⓐ, 1845, 1945 2045, 2145, 2245**y**.

From **Innertkirchen**: 0600Ⓐ, 0624Ⓐ, 0645, 0705, 0731, 0801, 0831✕, 0901, 1001, 1101, 1131, 1201 1231**n**, 1301, 1331, 1401, 1431**q**, 1501, 1531**q**, 1601, 1631, 1701, 1731Ⓐ, 1801, 1831Ⓐ, 1901 2001, 2101, 2201**y**.

562 SPIEZ - BRIG (via Lötschberg pass)

BLS

km				T																	*IC* 1095 ①-⑥	*IC* 1097 ⑦		
	Bern	d.	...	...	0739	0839	0939	1039	1139	...	1239	1339	1439	1539	1639	1739	1839	1939	...	...	...	2234	2234	...	...
0	**Spiez**	d.	0612	0712	0812	0912	1012	1112	1212	...	1312	1412	1512	1612	1712	1812	1912	2012	...	2112	2212	2305	2305	...	0012
14	Frutigen ●	d.	0625	0725	0825	0925	1025	1125	1225	...	1325	1425	1525	1625	1725	1825	1925	2025	...	2125	2225	2317	2317	...	0025
31	Kandersteg 🚗	d.	0642	0742	0842	0942	1042	1142	1242	...	1342	1442	1542	1642	1742	1842	1942	2042	...	2142	2242	|	2334	...	0042
48	Goppenstein 🚗	d.	0657	0757	0857	0957	1057	1157	1257	...	1357	1457	1557	1657	1757	1857	1957	2057	...	2157	2257	|	2347	...	0053
74	**Brig**	a.	0724	0824	0924	1024	1124	1224	1324	...	1424	1524	1624	1724	1824	1924	2024	2124	...	2224	2324	2343	0010	...	0120

			IC 811 R																						
Brig	d.	0516	0547		0636	0736	0836	...	0936	1036	1136	...	1236	1336	1436	1536	1636	1736	...	1836	1936	2036	...	2207	...
Goppenstein 🚗	d.	0542	|	...	0701	0801	0901	...	1001	1101	1201	...	1301	1401	1501	1601	1701	1801	...	1901	2001	2101	...	2232	...
Kandersteg 🚗	d.	0554	|	←	0713	0813	0913	...	1013	1113	1213	...	1313	1413	1513	1613	1713	1813	...	1913	2013	2113	...	2243	...
Frutigen ●	d.	0609	0613	0630	0730	0830	0930	...	1030	1130	1230	...	1330	1430	1530	1630	1730	1830	...	1930	2030	2130	...	2301	...
Spiez	a.	→	0624	0644	0744	0844	0944	...	1044	1144	1244	...	1344	1444	1544	1644	1744	1844	...	1944	2044	2144	...	2314	...
Bern	a.	...	0654	0720	0820	0920	1020	...	1120	1220	1320	...	1420	1520	1620	1720	1820	1920	...	...	...	...	...	...	...

♦ – **NOTES** (LISTED BY TRAIN NUMBER)

R – [panorama car] and ✕ Brig - Romanshorn.

T – From Thun.

🚗 – Car-carrying shuttle available (see page 262).

● – 🚌 **SERVICE FRUTIGEN - ADELBODEN and v.v.**: 20 km, journey ±30 minutes.

From **Frutigen**: 0615Ⓐ, 0631, 0700Ⓐ, 0731, 0800, 0831, 0900ⓒ, 0931, 1000ⓒ, 1031, 1131 and hourly until 1631, then 1700, 1731, 1800, 1831, 1900Ⓐ, 1931, 2031, 2131, 2231, 2331.

From **Adelboden** (Post): 0535Ⓐ, 0550, 0622Ⓐ, 0650, 0730, 0750, 0830ⓒ, 0850, 0930ⓒ, 0950, 1050 and hourly until 1550, then 1630, 1650, 1730, 1750, 1830Ⓐ, 1850, 1950, 2050, 2150, 2225.

Operator: AFA, 3715 Adelboden. ✆ +41 (0)33 673 74 74, fax +41 (0)33 673 74 70.

BLS SPIEZ - ZWEISIMMEN 563

km									©								Ⓐ	©			Ⓐ	©		Ⓐ	Ⓐ
	Interlaken Ost **560** ... d.	...	...	...	...	...	...	...	0908	...	...	...	...	...	...	1308	...	...	...	...	1508	1508	...	...	...
0	**Spiez 560** d.	0606	0712	0736	0818	0846	0912	...	0936	1018	1112	1136	1218	1312	...	1336	1418	1512	1512	...	1536	1536	1618	1641	1712
11	Erlenbach im Simmental . d.	0624	0729	0750	0833	|	0929	...	0950	1033	1129	1150	1233	1329	...	1350	1433	1529	1529	...	1550	1550	1633	1655	1729
26	Boltigen d.	0642	0746	0810	0850	0911	0946	...	1010	1050	1146	1210	1250	1346	...	1410	1450	1546	1546	...	1608	1610	1650	1711	1746
35	**Zweisimmen** a.	0653	0757	0819	0859	0920	0957	...	1019	1059	1157	1219	1259	1357	...	1419	1459	1556	1557	...	1616	1619	1659	1720	1756

	©	Ⓐ	©		Ⓐ					
Interlaken Ost **560** ... d.	...	1708	1708	...	...	...	...	...	...	...
Spiez 560 d.	1712	1736	1736	1818	1841	1912	2012	2107	2207	2339
Erlenbach im Simmental .. d.	1729	1750	1750	1833	1855	1929	2029	2121	2221	2353
Boltigen d.	1746	1808	1810	1850	1911	1946	2046	2140	2240	0011
Zweisimmen a.	1757	1816	1819	1859	1920	1957	2057	2150	2250	0022

	Ⓐ		Ⓐ		Ⓐ					
Zweisimmen d.	0539	0557	0633	0701	0738	...	0801	0903	0938	1001
Boltigen d.	0547	0606	0642	0710	0746	...	0810	0910	0946	1010
Erlenbach im Simmental .... d.	0604	0625	0657	0729	0803	...	0832	0930	1003	1032
Spiez 560 a.	0619	0640	0712	0747	0818	...	0847	0947	1018	1047
Interlaken Ost **560** a.	...	...	...	...	...	...	...	...	...	...

											Ⓐ	©	©			Ⓐ	©								
Zweisimmen d.	1103	1138	1201	1303	1338	...	1401	1503	1538	...	1600	1601	1629	1703	1738	1800	1801	...	1903	2001	2106	...	2206	2306	...
Boltigen d.	1110	1146	1210	1310	1346	...	1410	1510	1546	...	1608	1610	1636	1710	1746	1808	1810	...	1910	2010	2115	...	2215	2315	...
Erlenbach im Simmental .. d.	1130	1203	1232	1330	1403	...	1432	1530	1603	...	1626	1632	1655	1730	1803	1826	1832	...	1929	2030	2134	...	2234	2334	...
Spiez 560 a.	1147	1218	1247	1347	1418	...	1447	1547	1618	...	1641	1647	1710	1747	1818	1841	1847	...	1945	2045	2149	...	2249	2350	...
Interlaken Ost **560** ... a.	...	1249	...	...	1449	...	...	...	1649	...	...	...	...	...	1849	...	...	...	...	...	...	...	...	...	...

Narrow gauge rack railway. BOB, WAB, JB INTERLAKEN - KLEINE SCHEIDEGG - JUNGFRAUJOCH 564

km						m	v			m	m			m	m			m	m			m	m			m	
0	**Interlaken** Ost d.	0635	0635	0705	0705	0735	0735	0805	0805	0835	0835	0905	0905	0935	0935	1005	1005	1035	1035	1105	1105	1135	1135	1205	1205	1235	1305
3	Wilderswil ▲ d.	0640	0640	0710	0710	0740	0740	0810	0810	0840	0840	0910	0910	0940	0940	1010	1010	1040	1040	1110	1110	1140	1140	1210	1210	1240	1310
8	Zweilütschinen d.	0646	0647	0716	0717	0746	0747	0816	0817	0846	0847	0916	0917	0946	0947	1016	1017	1046	1047	1116	1117	1146	1147	1216	1217	1246	1316
12	**Lauterbrunnen** ● a.	0655	|	0725	|	0755	|	0825	|	0855	|	0925	|	0955	|	1025	|	1055	|	1125	|	1155	|	1225	|	1255	1325
	change trains		|		|		|		|		|		|		|		|		|		|		|		|		
12	**Lauterbrunnen** d.	0707	|	0737	|	0807	|	0837	|	0907	|	0937	|	1007	|	1037	|	1107	|	1137	|	1207	|	1237	|	1307	1337
16	Wengen a.	0721	|	0751	|	0821	|	0851	|	0921	|	0951	|	1021	|	1051	|	1121	|	1151	|	1221	|	1251	|	1321	1351
16	Wengen d.	0724	|	0754	|	0824r	|	0854	|	0924r	|	0954	|	1024r	|	1054	|	1124r	|	1154	|	1224r	|	1254	|	1324r	1354
19	Grindelwald a.	|	0709	|	0739	|	0809	|	0839	|	0909	|	0939	|	1009	|	1039	|	1109	|	1139	|	1209	|	1239	|	|
	change trains	|		|		|	r	|		|	r	|		|	r	|		|	r	|		|	r	|		|	|
19	Grindelwald d.	|	0717	|	0747	|	0817	|	0847	|	0917	|	0947	|	1017	|	1047	|	1117	|	1147	|	1217	|	1247	|	|
20	Grindelwald Grund . d.	|	0725	|	0755	|	0825	|	0855	|	0925	|	0955	|	1025	|	1055	|	1125	|	1155	|	1225	|	1255	|	|
23*	**Kleine Scheidegg** a.	0750	0749	0820	0819	0850r	0849	0920	0919	0950r	0949	1020	1019	1050r	1049	1120	1119	1150r	1149	1220	1219	1250r	1249	1320	1319	1350r	1420

				m			m	m			m	m			v			⚒	⚒								
Interlaken Ost d.	1305	1405	1405	1435	1505	1505	1535	1535	1605	1605	1635	1635	1705	1705	1735	1805	1805	1835	1835	1905	1905	2002	2005	2102	2105	2202	2205
Wilderswil ▲ d.	1310	1410	1410	1440	1510	1510	1540	1540	1610	1610	1640	1640	1710	1710	1740	1810	1810	1840	1840	1910	1910	2007	2010	2107	2110	2207	2210
Zweilütschinen d.	1317	1416	1417	1447	1516	1517	1546	1547	1616	1617	1646	1647	1716	1717	1746	1816	1817	1846	1847	1916	1917	2013	2016	2113	2116	2213	2216
Lauterbrunnen ● a.	|	1425	|	|	1525	|	1555	|	1625	|	1655	|	1725	|	1755	1825	|	1855	|	1925	|	2022	|	2122	|	2222	|
change trains	|		|	|		|		|		|		|		|			|		|		|		|		|		|
Lauterbrunnen d.	|	1437	|	|	1537	|	1607	|	1637	|	1707	|	1737	|	1807	1837	|	1907	|	1937	|	2030	|	2130	|	2230	|
Wengen a.	|	1451	|	|	1551	|	1621	|	1651	|	1721	|	1751	|	1821	1851	|	1921	|	1951	|	2044	|	2144	|	2244	|
Wengen d.	|	1454	|	|	1554	|	1624r	|	1654	|	...	|	1754r	|	...	...	|	...	|	...	|	...	|	...	|	...	|
Grindelwald a.	1339	|	1439	1509	|	1539	|	1609	|	1639	...	1709	|	1739	...	...	1839	...	1909	...	1939	...	2035	...	2135	...	2235
change trains		|		r	|		|	r	|			r	|	r					r								
Grindelwald d.	1347	|	1447	1517	|	1547	|	1617	|	1647	...	1717	|	1747	...	...	1847	...	1917	...	...	...	...	...	...	...	...
Grindelwald Grund.. d.	1355	|	1455	1525	|	1555	|	1625	|	1655	...	1722	|	1755	...	...	1852	...	1922	...	...	...	...	...	...	...	...
Kleine Scheidegg a.	1419	1520	1519	1549	1620	1619	1650r	1649	1720	1719	...	...	1820r	1819	...	...	...	...	...	...	...	...	...	...	...	...	...

												r						r				r				r	
Kleine Scheidegg d.	...	...	...	...	...	...	...	...	...	...	...	...	0801t	0803t	0831	0833	0901r	0903	0931	0933	1001r	1003	1031	1033	1101r	1103	1131
Grindelwald Grund.. d.	...	...	...	...	...	...	...	0708	...	0738	...	0808	|	0838	|	0908	|	0938	|	1008	|	1038	|	1108	|	1138	|
Grindelwald a.	...	...	...	...	...	...	...	0712	...	0742	...	0812	|	0842	|	0912	|	0942	|	1012	|	1042	|	1112	|	1142	|
change trains			⚒							v			|	m	|		|	m	|		|	m	|		|	m	|
Grindelwald d.	0519	...	0547	...	0619	...	...	0719	...	0749	...	0819	|	0849	|	0919	|	0949	|	1019	|	1049	|	1119	|	1149	|
Wengen a.	|	...	|	...	|	...	...	|	...	|	...	|	0830t	|	0900	|	0930r	|	1000	|	1030r	|	1100	|	1130r	|	1200
Wengen d.	|	0512	|	0605	|	0642	0703	|	0733	|	0803	|	0833	|	0903	|	0933	|	1003	|	1033	|	1103	|	1133	|	1203
Lauterbrunnen a.	|	0529	|	0622	|	0659	0721	|	0751	|	0821	|	0851	|	0921	|	0951	|	1021	|	1051	|	1121	|	1151	|	1221
change trains	|		|		|	v		|	m	|		|	m	|		|	m	|		|	m	|		|	m	|	
Lauterbrunnen ● d.	|	0533	|	0633	|	0703	0733	|	0803	|	0833	|	0903	|	0933	|	1003	|	1033	|	1103	|	1133	|	1203	|	1233
Zweilütschinen d.	0537	0543	0611	0643	0643	0713	0743	0743	0813	0813	0843	0843	0913	0913	0943	0943	1013	1013	1043	1043	1113	1113	1143	1143	1213	1213	1243
Wilderswil ▲ d.	0543	0549	0617	0649	0649	0719	0749	0749	0819	0819	0849	0849	0919	0919	0949	0949	1019	1019	1049	1049	1119	1119	1149	1149	1219	1219	1249
Interlaken Ost a.	0550	0554	0622	0654	0654	0724	0754	0754	0824	0824	0854	0854	0924	0924	0954	0954	1024	1024	1054	1054	1124	1124	1154	1154	1224	1224	1254

							r				r				r				r			r					
Kleine Scheidegg d.	1133	1231	1233	1331	1333	1401r	1403	1431	1433	1501r	1503	1531	1533	1601r	1603	1631	1633	1701r	1703	1731	1733	1833	1831r	...	...	...	...
Grindelwald Grund.. d.	1208	|	1308	|	1408	|	1438	|	1508	|	1538	|	1608	|	1638	|	1708	|	1738	|	1808	1908	|	...	...	...	...
Grindelwald a.	1212	|	1312	|	1412	|	1442	|	1512	|	1542	|	1612	|	1642	|	1712	|	1742	|	1812	1912	|	...	...	...	...
change trains		|		|		|	m	|		|	m	|		|	m	|		|	v	|			|				
Grindelwald d.	1219	|	1319	|	1419	|	1449	|	1519	|	1549	|	1619	|	1649	|	1719	|	1749	|	1819	1919	|	2019	...	2119	...
Wengen a.	|	1300	|	1400	|	1430r	|	1500	|	1530r	|	1600	|	1630r	|	1700	|	1730r	|	1800	|	|	1900r	|	...	|	...
Wengen d.	|	1303	|	1403	|	1433	|	1503	|	1533	|	1603	|	1633	|	1703	|	1733	|	1803	|	|	1903	|	2003	|	2103
Lauterbrunnen a.	|	1321	|	1421	|	1451	|	1521	|	1551	|	1621	|	1651	|	1721	|	1751	|	1821	|	|	1921	|	2021	|	2120
change trains	|		|		|	m	|		|	m	|		|	m	|		|	v	|		|	|		|		|	
Lauterbrunnen ● d.	|	1333	|	1433	|	1503	|	1533	|	1603	|	1633	|	1703	|	1733	|	1803	|	1833	|	|	1933	|	2033	|	2133
Zweilütschinen d.	1243	1343	1343	1443	1443	1513	1513	1543	1543	1613	1613	1643	1643	1713	1713	1743	1743	1813	1813	1843	1843	1940	1944	2040	2044	2140	2144
Wilderswil ▲ d.	1249	1349	1349	1449	1449	1519	1519	1549	1549	1619	1619	1649	1649	1719v	1719v	1749	1749	1819	1819	1849	1849	1946	1950	2046	2050	2146	2150
Interlaken Ost a.	1254	1354	1354	1454	1454	1524	1524	1554	1554	1624	1624	1654	1654	1724v	1724v	1754	1754	1824	1824	1854	1854	1950	1954	2050	2054	2150	2154

At times of heavy snowfall (November 1 - April 30) the Eigergletscher - Jungfraujoch service is subject to cancellation

km					t		t			t			t		t			t			t		t	
0	**Kleine Scheidegg** d.	0800	0830	...	0900	0930	1000	...	1030	1100	1130	...	1200	1230	1300	...	1330	1400	1430	...	1500	1530	1630	...
2	Eigergletscher d.	0810	0840	...	0910	0940	1010	...	1040	1110	1140	...	1210	1240	1310	...	1340	1410	1440	...	1510	1540	1640	...
9	**Jungfraujoch** a.	0852	0922	...	0952	1022	1052	...	1122	1152	1222	...	1252	1322	1352	...	1422	1452	1522	...	1552	1622	1716	...

	t		t			t			t		t			t			t		t			t	
Jungfraujoch d.	0900	0930	1000	...	1030	1100	1130	...	1200	1230	1300	...	1330	1400	1430	...	1500	1530	1600	...	1640	1745	...
Eigergletscher d.	0940	1010	1040	...	1110	1140	1210	...	1240	1310	1340	...	1410	1440	1510	...	1540	1610	1640	...	1710	1810	...
Kleine Scheidegg a.	0950	1020	1050	...	1120	1150	1220	...	1250	1320	1350	...	1420	1450	1520	...	1550	1620	1650	...	1720	1820	...

m – Daily Dec. 21 - Mar. 30; © Apr. 5 - 27; daily Apr. 28 - Oct. 26.
n – Dec. 21 - Apr. 6, May 24 - Oct. 19.
r – Dec. 21 - Oct. 26.
t – Mar. 29 - Oct. 26.
v – Daily Dec. 16 - Nov. 1; ①–⑥ Nov. 3 - Dec. 13.

* – Via Wengen (*28 km* via Grindelwald).

● – Cableway operates **Lauterbrunnen** - **Grütschalp**, and narrow gauge railway **Grütschalp** - **Mürren**, *total: 5 km*. **Operator**: BLM. Journey time: 20 minutes allowing for the connection.
From **Lauterbrunnen**: 0610, 0631, 0701, 0731, 0801 and every 30 minutes♦ until 1831, then 1931, 2031 **n**.
From **Mürren**: 0606, 0636, 0706 and every 30 minutes♦ until 1906, then 2006.
♦ – Additional services available Dec. 21 - Apr. 6, May 24 - Oct. 19.

▲ – Narrow gauge rack railway operates **May 29 - Oct. 26 Wilderswil** - **Schynige Platte**. *7 km*. Journey time: 52 minutes. **Operator**: BOB. Service may be reduced In bad weather.
From **Wilderswil**: 0725, 0805, 0845, 0925, 1005, 1045, 1125, 1205, 1245, 1325, 1405, 1445, 1525, 1605, 1645.
From **Schynige Platte**: 0821, 0901, 0941, 1021, 1101, 1141, 1221, 1301, 1341, 1421, 1501, 1541, 1621, 1701, 1753.

565 BASEL, OLTEN and BERN - LUZERN SBB

km		ICN 657	IR 2451	RE 3557	IR 2509	IR 2159	IR 2453	RE 3559	IR 2511	IR 2163	IR 2455	RE 3561	IR 2515	IR 2165	IR 2457	RE 3565		IR 2517	ICN 667	IR 2459	RE 3567	IR 2519	IR 2169	IR 2461	RE 3569	IR 2521	ICN 671
		G	Ⓐ			L				△ L				△ L					✕ G				△ L				✕ G
	Genève Aéroport ✈ **505** d.	...	...	...	...	...	...	...	...	...	...	...	...	...	...	...	...	0702j	...	...	...	0802j	...	...	...	0906j	...
	Genève **505** d.	...	...	...	...	...	...	...	...	...	...	...	0611	...	...	...	...	0711	...	...	...	0811	...	...	...	0915	...
	Lausanne **505** d.	...	...	...	0445z	...	...	...	0545	...	...	...	0647	...	...	...	...	0750	...	...	...	0850	...	...	...	0950	...
0	**Basel** SBB d.	0504	...	...	|	0604	0617	...	|	0704	0717	...	|	0804	0817	...	...	|	0904	0917	...	|	1004	1017	...	|	1104
14	Liestal d.	|	...	...	|	|	0627	...	|	|	0727	...	|	|	0827	...	...	|	|	0927	...	|	|	1027	...	|	|
21	Sissach d.	|	...	...	|	|	0633	...	|	|	0733	...	|	|	0833	...	...	|	|	0933	...	|	|	1033	...	|	|
39	**Olten** a.	0528	...	...	|	0628	0647	...	|	0728	0747	...	|	0828	0847	...	...	|	0928	0947	...	|	1028	1047	...	|	1128
39	**Olten** d.	0530	0549	0606	|	0630	0649	0706	|	0730	0749	0806	|	0830	0849	0906	...	|	0930	0949	1006	|	1030	1049	1106	|	1130
	Bern d.	|	|	|	0600	|	|	|	0700	|	|	|	0800	|	|	|	...	0900	|	|	|	1000	|	|	|	1100	|
47	Zofingen d.	|	0558	0613	0628	|	0658	0713	0728	|	0758	0813	0828	|	0858	0913	...	0928	|	0958	1013	1029	|	1058	1113	1128	|
69	Sursee d.	|	0611	0632	0641	|	0711	0732	0741	|	0811	0832	0841	|	0911	0932	...	0941	|	1011	1032	1041	|	1111	1132	1141	|
95	**Luzern** a.	0605	0630	0655	0700	0705	0730	0755	0800	0805	0830	0855	0900	0905	0930	0955	...	1000	1005	1030	1055	1100	1105	1130	1155	1200	1205

	IR 2463	RE 3571	IR 2523	IR 2173	IR 2465	RE 3573	IR 2525	ICN 675	IR 2467	RE 3575	IR 2527		IR 2177	IR 2469	RE 3577	IR 2529	ICN 679	IR 2471	RE 3579	IR 2531	IR 2181	IR 2473	RE 3581	IR 2535	ICN 683	IR 2475	RE 3585
				△ L				✕ G					△ L				✕ G				△ L				✕ G		
Genève Aéroport ✈ **505** d.	...	...	1006j	...	...	...	1106j	...	...	...	1206j	...	...	...	...	1306j	...	...	...	1406j	...	...	...	1506j	...	...	...
Genève **505** d.	...	...	1015	...	...	...	1115	...	...	...	1215	...	...	...	...	1315	...	...	...	1415	...	...	...	1515	...	...	...
Lausanne **505** d.	...	...	1050	...	...	...	1150	...	...	...	1250	...	...	...	...	1350	...	...	...	1450	...	...	...	1550	...	...	...
Basel SBB d.	1117	...	|	1204	1217	...	|	1304	1317	...	|	...	1404	1417	...	|	1504	1517	...	|	1604	1617	...	|	1704	1717	...
Liestal d.	1127	...	|	|	1227	...	|	|	1327	...	|	...	|	1427	...	|	|	1527	...	|	|	1627	...	|	|	1727	...
Sissach d.	1133	...	|	|	1233	...	|	|	1333	...	|	...	|	1433	...	|	|	1533	...	|	|	1633	...	|	|	1733	...
Olten a.	1147	...	|	1228	1247	...	|	1328	1347	...	|	...	1428	1447	...	|	1528	1547	...	|	1628	1647	...	|	1728	1747	...
Olten d.	1149	1206	|	1230	1249	1306	|	1330	1349	1406	|	...	1430	1449	1506	|	1530	1549	1606	|	1630	1649	1706	|	1730	1749	1806
Bern d.	|	|	1200	|	|	|	1300	|	|	|	1400	...	|	|	|	1500	|	|	|	1600	|	|	|	1700	|	|	|
Zofingen d.	1158	1213	1228	|	1258	1313	1328	|	1358	1413	1428	...	|	1458	1513	1528	|	1558	1613	1628	|	1658	1713	1728	|	1758	1813
Sursee d.	1211	1232	1241	|	1311	1332	1341	|	1411	1432	1441	...	|	1511	1532	1541	|	1611	1632	1641	|	1711	1732	1741	|	1811	1832
Luzern a.	1230	1255	1300	1305	1330	1355	1400	1405	1430	1455	1500	...	1505	1530	1555	1600	1605	1630	1655	1700	1705	1730	1755	1800	1805	1830	1855

	IR 2537	IR 2185	IR 2477	RE 3587	IR 2539	ICN 689	IR 2479	RE 3589	IR 2541	IR 2191	IR 2481	RE 3591	IR 2543	IR 2193	IR 2483	RE 3593	IR 2545	IR 2197	IR 2485	RE 3595	IR 2547	IR 2199	IR 2487	RE 3597		IR 2151	IR 2153
		△ B				✕ C				E																	q
Genève Aéroport ✈ **505** d.	1606j	...	...	...	1706j	...	...	...	1806j	...	...	...	1906j	...	...	...	2006j	...	...	...	...	...	...	...	...	...	...
Genève **505** d.	1615	...	...	...	1715	...	...	...	1815	...	...	...	1915	...	...	...	2015	...	...	...	...	...	...	...	...	...	...
Lausanne **505** d.	1650	...	...	...	1750	...	...	...	1850	...	...	...	1950	...	...	...	2050	...	...	...	2145	...	...	...	...	...	...
Basel SBB d.	|	1804	1817	...	|	1904	1917	...	|	2004	2017	...	|	2104	2117	...	|	2202	2217	...	|	2302	2317	...	...	0000	0101
Liestal d.	|	|	1827	...	|	|	1927	...	|	|	2027	...	|	|	2127	...	|	2211	2227	...	|	2311	2327	...	...	0009	0110
Sissach d.	|	|	1833	...	|	|	1933	...	|	|	2033	...	|	|	2133	...	|	|	2233	...	|	|	2333	...	...	|	0116
Olten a.	|	1828	1847	...	|	1928	1947	...	|	2028	2047	...	|	2128	2147	...	|	2228	2247	...	|	2328	2347	...	...	0026	0128
Olten d.	|	1830	1849	1906	|	1930	1949	2006	|	2030	2049	2106	|	2130	2149	2206	|	2230	2249	2306	|	2330	...	0006	...	0033	0136
Bern d.	1800	|	|	|	1900	|	|	|	2000	|	|	|	2100	|	|	|	2200	|	|	|	2300	|	...	|	...	|	|
Zofingen d.	1828	|	1858	1913	1928	|	1958	2013	2028	|	2058	2113	2128	|	2158	2213	2228	|	2256	2313	2328	|	...	0013	...	0040	0143
Sursee d.	1841	|	1911	1932	1941	|	2011	2032	2041	|	2111	2132	2141	|	2211	2232	2241	|	...	2332	2341	|	...	0034	...	0054	0157
Luzern a.	1900	1905	1930	1955	2000	2005	2030	2055	2100	2105	2130	2155	2200	2205	2230	2255	2300	2305	...	2355	2400	0005	...	0056	...	0114	0215

km (via hsl)		RE 3556	IR 2452	IR 2160	IR 2508	RE 3558	IR 2454	IR 2162	IR 2510	RE 3560	IR 2456	IR 2164	IR 2512	RE 3562	IR 2458	IR 2166	IR 2516	RE 3566	IR 2460	ICN 668		IR 2518	RE 3568	IR 2462	IR 2170	IR 2520	RE 3570
							△					E				△ B				✕ C					△ C		
	Luzern d.	0456	0530a	0554	0600	0605	0630	0654	0700	0705	0730	0754	0800	0805	0830	0854	0900	0905	0930	0954	...	1000	1005	1030	1054	1100	1105
	Sursee d.	0521	0548a	|	0618	0626	0648	|	0718	0726	0748	|	0818	0826	0848	|	0918	0926	0948	|	...	1018	1026	1048	|	1118	1126
0	Zofingen d.	0543	0602a	|	0632	0643	0702	|	0732	0743	0802	|	0832	0843	0902	|	0932	0943	1002	|	...	1032	1043	1102	|	1132	1143
63	**Bern** a.	|	|	|	0700	|	|	|	0800	|	|	|	0900	|	|	|	1000	|	|	|	...	1100	|	|	|	1200	|
	Olten a.	0552	0610a	0627	|	0652	0710	0727	|	0752	0810	0827	|	0852	0910	0927	|	0952	1010	1027	...	|	1052	1110	1127	|	1152
	Olten d.	...	0612	0630	|	...	0712	0730	|	...	0812	0830	|	...	0912	0930	|	...	1012	1030	...	|	...	1112	1130	|	...
	Sissach d.	...	0627	|	|	...	0727	|	|	...	0827	|	|	...	0927	|	|	...	1027	|	...	|	...	1127	|	|	...
	Liestal d.	...	0633	|	|	...	0733	|	|	...	0833	|	|	...	0933	|	|	...	1033	|	...	|	...	1133	|	|	...
	Basel SBB a.	...	0644	0655	|	...	0744	0755	|	...	0844	0855	|	...	0944	0955	|	...	1044	1055	...	|	...	1144	1155	|	...
	Lausanne **505** a.	...	...	...	0810	...	...	...	0910	...	...	...	1010	...	...	...	1110	...	...	...	...	1210	...	...	...	1310	...
	Genève **505** a.	...	...	...	0845	...	...	...	0945	...	...	...	1045	...	...	...	1145	...	...	...	...	1245	...	...	...	1345	...
	Genève Aéroport ✈ **505** a.	...	...	...	0854j	...	...	...	0954j	...	...	...	1054j	...	...	...	1154j	...	...	...	...	1254j	...	...	...	1354j	...

	IR 2464	ICN 672	IR 2522	RE 3572	IR 2466	IR 2174		IR 2524	RE 3574	IR 2468	ICN 676	IR 2526	RE 3576	IR 2470	IR 2178		IR 2528	RE 3578	IR 2472	ICN 680	IR 2530	RE 3580	IR 2474	IR 2182	IR 2532	RE 3582	IR 2476
		✕ G				△ L					✕ G				△ L					✕ G				△ L			
Luzern d.	1130	1154	1200	1205	1230	1254	...	1300	1305	1330	1354	1400	1405	1430	1454	...	1500	1505	1530	1554	1600	1605	1630	1654	1700	1705	1730
Sursee d.	1148	|	1218	1226	1248	|	...	1318	1326	1348	|	1418	1426	1448	|	...	1518	1526	1548	|	1618	1626	1648	|	1718	1726	1748
Zofingen d.	1202	|	1232	1243	1302	|	...	1332	1343	1402	|	1432	1443	1502	|	...	1532	1543	1602	|	1632	1643	1702	|	1732	1743	1802
Bern a.	|	|	1300	|	|	|	...	1400	|	|	|	1500	|	|	|	...	1600	|	|	|	1700	|	|	|	1800	|	|
Olten a.	1210	1227	|	1252	1310	1327	...	|	1352	1410	1427	|	1452	1510	1527	...	|	1552	1610	1627	|	1652	1710	1727	|	1752	1810
Olten d.	1212	1230	|	...	1312	1330	...	|	...	1412	1430	|	...	1512	1530	...	|	...	1612	1630	|	...	1712	1730	|	...	1812
Sissach d.	1227	|	|	...	1327	|	...	|	...	1427	|	|	...	1527	|	...	|	...	1627	|	|	...	1727	|	|	...	1827
Liestal d.	1233	|	|	...	1333	|	...	|	...	1433	|	|	...	1533	|	...	|	...	1633	|	|	...	1733	|	|	...	1833
Basel SBB a.	1244	1255	|	...	1344	1355	...	|	...	1444	1455	|	...	1544	1555	...	|	...	1644	1655	|	...	1744	1755	|	...	1844
Lausanne **505** a.	...	...	1410	...	...	...	...	1510	...	...	...	1610	...	...	...	...	1710	...	...	...	1810	...	...	...	1910	...	...
Genève **505** a.	...	...	1445	...	...	...	...	1545	...	...	...	1645	...	...	...	...	1745	...	...	...	1845	...	...	...	1949	...	...
Genève Aéroport ✈ **505** a.	...	...	1454j	...	...	...	...	1554j	...	...	...	1654j	...	...	...	...	1754j	...	...	...	1854j	...	...	...	1958j	...	...

	ICN 684	IR 2536	RE 3586	IR 2478	IR 2186	IR 2538	RE 3588	IR 2480	ICN 688	IR 2540	RE 3590	IR 2482	IR 2188	IR 2542	RE 3592	IR 2484	ICN 692	IR 2544	RE 3594	IR 2486	IR 2192	IR 2546	RE 3596	ICN 696	RE 3598	IR 2150	
	✕ G				△ L				✕ G				L				✕ G				△ L			G		q	
Luzern d.	1754	1800	1805	1830	1854	1900	1905	1930	1954	2000	2005	2030	2054	2100	2105	2130	2154	2200	2205	...	2254	2300	2305	2354	0005	0049	...
Sursee d.	|	1818	1826	1848	|	1918	1926	1948	|	2018	2026	2048	|	2118	2126	2148	|	2218	2226	...	|	2318	2326	|	0026	0108	...
Zofingen d.	|	1832	1843	1902	|	1932	1943	2002	|	2032	2043	2102	|	2132	2143	2202	|	2232	2243	2302	|	2332	2343	|	0043	0121	...
Bern a.	|	1900	|	|	|	2000	|	|	|	2100	|	|	|	2200	|	|	|	2300	|	|	|	2400	|	|	|	|	...
Olten a.	1827	|	1852	1910	1927	|	1952	2010	2027	|	2052	2110	2127	|	2152	2210	2227	...	2252	2310	2327	...	2352	0027	0052	0128	...
Olten d.	1830	|	...	1912	1930	|	...	2012	2030	|	...	2112	2130	|	...	2212	2233	...	...	2312	2333	...	...	0035	...	0136	...
Sissach d.	|	|	...	1927	|	|	...	2027	|	|	...	2127	|	|	...	2227	|	...	...	2327	|	...	...	|	...	|	...
Liestal d.	|	|	...	1933	|	|	...	2033	|	|	...	2133	|	|	...	2233	2250	...	...	2333	2349	...	...	0052	...	0153	...
Basel SBB a.	1855	|	...	1944	1955	|	...	2044	2055	|	...	2144	2155	|	...	2244	2259	...	...	2344	2359	...	...	0102	...	0202	...
Lausanne **505** a.	...	2010	...	...	...	2110	...	...	...	2215	...	...	...	2315	...	...	...	...	...	...	...	...	...	...	...	...	...
Genève **505** a.	...	2049	...	...	...	...	...	...	...	2305	...	...	...	...	...	...	...	...	...	...	...	...	...	...	...	...	...
Genève Aéroport ✈ **505** a.	...	2058j	...	...	...	...	...	...	...	2314j	...	...	...	...	...	...	...	...	...	...	...	...	...	...	...	...	...

B – 🚃12 Basel - Bellinzona and v.v.
C – 🚃12 Basel - Chiasso and v.v.
E – 🚃12 Basel - Erstfeld and v.v.
G – 🚃12 Basel - Lugano and v.v.
L – 🚃12 Basel - Locarno and v.v.

a – Ⓐ only.
j – Dec. 15 - July 14.
q – ⑥⑦ (not Apr. 19).
z – ① (also Apr. 22, June 10; not Apr. 21, June 9).

△ – Panorama car.

Narrow gauge. MOB — LENK - ZWEISIMMEN - MONTREUX — 566

km																											
		Ⓐ		Ⓐ				Ⓒ												Ⓐ		Ⓐ					⑤⑥
0	**Lenk** d.	0611	0634	0703	0737	0837	0937	1003	1037	1103	1137	1237	1303	1337	1437	1537	1603	1637	1737	1803	1842	1903	1937	2037	2132	2232	2326
13	**Zweisimmen** a.	0629	0652	0721	0755	0855	0955	1021	1055	1121	1155	1255	1321	1355	1455	1555	1621	1655	1755	1821	1900	1921	1955	2055	2150	2250	2344

km																										
						2111			3115	2217	2119				3123			2127	2229		2131					
									🍸	🍸	🍸				🍸			🍸	🍸							
						G			G	C	G★				G			C	G	Ⓐ	G★		Ⓒ	Ⓐ		
0	**Zweisimmen** d.	0411	0517	0613	0700	0825	0905	1005	1025	1105	1225	...	1305	1405	1425	1505	...	1625	1705	1724	1825	...	1905	1926	2005	2102	2155
9	Saanenmöser d.	0426	0531	0628	0714	0839	0919	1019	1039	1119	1239	...	1319	1419	1439	1519	...	1639	1719	1738	1839	...	1919	1941	2019	2116	2208
11	Schönried d.	0431	0536	0633	0719	0843	0924	1024	1043	1124	1243	...	1324	1424	1443	1524	...	1643	1724	1743	1843	...	1924	1946	2024	2121	2213
16	**Gstaad** d.	0440	0545	0642	0730	0853	0937	1034	1053	1137	1253	...	1337	1434	1453	1537	...	1653	1737	1752	1853	...	1937	1956	2037	2130	2232
19	Saanen d.	0444	0549	0647	0735	0858	0942	1038	1058	1142	1258	...	1342	1438	1458	1542	...	1658	1742	1756	1858	...	1942	2000	2042	2135	2236
23	Rougemont d.	0450	0555	0653	0741	0903	0948	1044	1103	1148	1303	...	1348	1444	1503	1548	...	1703	1748	...	1903	...	1948	2006	2048	2141	2241
29	Châteaux d'Oex d.	0503	0607	0704	0806	0913	1006	...	1113	1206	1313	...	1406	...	1513	1606	...	1713	1806	...	1913	...	2006	2016	2101	2152	2251
40	**Montbovon** d.	0522	0623	0723	0826	0928	1026	...	1128	1226	1328	...	1426	...	1528	1626	...	1728	1826	...	1928	...	2026	2030	2116	2208	...
51	Les Avants § d.	0543	0644	0744	0847	0948	1047	...	1148	1247	1348	...	1447	...	1548	1647	...	1748	1847	...	1948	...	2051	2051	2135	2228	...
55	Chamby ⊙ § d.	0555	0651	0751	0855	0955	1055	...	1155	1255	1355	...	1455	...	1555	1655	...	1755	1855	...	1959	...	2058	2058	2142	2235	...
58	Chernex § d.	0600	0658	0758	0904	1004	1104	...	1204	1304	1404	...	1504	...	1604	1704	...	1804	1904	...	2004	...	2103	2103	2147	2241	...
62	**Montreux** § a.	0610	0707	0807	0913	1013	1113	...	1213	1313	1413	...	1513	...	1613	1713	...	1813	1913	...	2013	...	2111	2111	2158	2249	...

						2112		2216	2118	3118			2124			3126		2228	2128			2234					
								🍸	(🍸)	🍸			🍸			🍸		🍸	🍸								
	Ⓐ	Ⓐ	Ⓒ			G		C	Ⓡ T	G★			G			C		G	G★		Ⓐ	G					
Montreux § d.	...	...	...	0537	0637	0744	...	0844	0857	0944	...	1044	1144	...	1244	1344	...	1444	1544	1644	...	1744	...	1844	1944	2111	2211
Chernex § d.	...	...	...	0548	0648	0753	...	0853	|	0953	...	1053	1153	...	1253	1353	...	1453	1553	1653	...	1753	...	1853	1953	2121	2221
Chamby ⊙ § d.	...	...	...	0556	0653	0800	...	0858	|	1000	...	1058	1200	...	1258	1400	...	1458	1600	1658	...	1758	...	1858	1958	2126	2226
Les Avants § d.	...	...	...	0604	0701	0807	...	0907	|	1007	...	1107	1207	...	1307	1407	...	1507	1607	1707	...	1807	...	1907	2007	2134	2239
Montbovon d.	...	0521	0521	0622	0722	0828	...	0927	0946	1028	...	1127	1228	...	1327	1428	...	1527	1628	1727	...	1827	...	1927	2029	2154	2259
Châteaux d'Oex d.	...	0539	0550	0639	0737	0843	...	0944	...	1043	...	1144	1243	...	1344	1443	...	1544	1643	1744	...	1844	...	1944	2045	2213	2315
Rougemont d.	...	0554	0603	0651	0750	0853	...	0959	...	1053	1112	1159	1253	...	1359	1453	1512	1559	1653	1759	...	1903	...	2005	2057	2224	2327
Saanen d.	0500	0559	0620	0657	0756	0859	...	1005	...	1059	1118	1205	1259	...	1405	1459	1518	1605	1659	1805	1821	1908	...	2010	2103	2229	2333
Gstaad d.	0505	0604	0625	0703	0803	0905	...	1011	...	1105	1124	1211	1305	...	1411	1505	1524	1611	1705	1811	1827	1915	...	2015	2110	2233	2339
Schönried d.	0513	0612	0634	0711	0812	0914	...	1020	...	1114	1133	1220	1314	...	1420	1514	1533	1620	1714	1820	1836	1924	...	2024	2121	2241	2347
Saanenmöser d.	0518	0616	0639	0715	0817	0918	...	1025	...	1118	1138	1225	1318	...	1425	1518	1538	1625	1718	1825	1841	1929	...	2029	2126	2246	2351
Zweisimmen a.	0535	0629	0653	0729	0834	0932	...	1043	...	1132	1153	1243	1332	...	1443	1532	1553	1643	1732	1843	1854	1944	...	2044	2142	2300	0005

	Ⓐ	Ⓐ		Ⓐ				Ⓒ												Ⓐ		Ⓐ					⑤⑥
Zweisimmen d.	0511	0550	0611	0634	0703	0803	0903	0937	1003	1037	1103	1137	1203	1303	1403	1503	1537	1603	1703	1737	1803	1824	1903	2003	2103	2155	2306
Lenk a.	0529	0608	0629	0652	0721	0821	0921	0956	1021	1056	1121	1156	1221	1321	1421	1521	1556	1621	1721	1756	1821	1842	1921	2021	2121	2213	2324

§ – ADDITIONAL SERVICES LES AVANTS - MONTREUX and v.v. (2nd class only):

	Ⓐ	Ⓐ	Ⓐ		Ⓐ		Ⓐ	Ⓐ			
Les Avants d.	0620	0718	0813	...	1319	...	1713	1813	...	2320	...
Chamby ⊙ d.	0629	0725	0820	...	1326	...	1720	1820	...	2327	...
Chernex d.	0634	0731	0832	...	1332	...	1732	1832	...	2332	...
Montreux a.	0645	0741	0841	...	1341	...	1741	1841	...	2342	...

	Ⓐ	Ⓐ	Ⓐ		Ⓐ	Ⓐ	Ⓐ	Ⓐ			
Montreux d.	0549	0615	0715	...	1215	1615	1715	1815	2150	2250	2345
Chernex d.	0558	0624	0730	...	1224	1624	1724	1824	2159	2259	2355
Chamby ⊙ d.	0603	0629	0735	...	1229	1629	1729	1829	2204	2304	0000s
Les Avants a.	0610	0636	0742	...	1236	1636	1736	1836	2211	2311	0007

C – GOLDEN PASS CLASSIC – [12] and (✕).
G – GOLDEN PASS PANORAMIC – conveys [12] [panorama car].
T – TRAIN DU CHOCOLAT – ①③④ May 1 - June 30; daily July 1 - Aug. 31; ①③④ Sept. 1 - Oct. 30. Conveys [1] only.

s – Stops to set down only.

★ – Also conveys VIP accommodation. Ⓡ
⊙ – Chamby is a request stop.

Narrow gauge. 2nd class only. TPF — MONTBOVON - BULLE - PALÉZIEUX and BROC — 568

km																								
		⚒		Ⓐ		⚒	†		Ⓐ	Ⓐ	Ⓒ													
0	**Montbovon** d.	...	...	0540	...	0640	...	...	0723	...	0740	...	...	0840	...		1840	...	1940	...	2040	...	...
13	Gruyères d.	...	...	0558	...	0658	...	...	0745	...	0758	...	...	0858	...	and at	1858	...	1958	...	2058	...	...
17	**Bulle** ▲ a.	...	...	0608	...	0708	...	...	0753	...	0808	...	...	0908	...	the same	1908	...	2008	...	2108	...	...
17	**Bulle** d.	0513	0554	0612	0613	0712	0712	0733	...	0812	0812	0833	...	0912	0933	minutes	1912	1933	...	2033	...	2118	...
	Châtel-St Denis d.	0539	0629	|	0643	|	|	0759	...	|	|	0859	...	|	0959	past each	|	1959	...	2059	...	2145	...
	Palézieux a.	0550	0640	|	0655	|	|	0810	...	|	|	0910	...	|	1010	hour until	|	2010	...	2110	...	2155	...
22	**Broc**-Fabrique a.	...	...	0624	...	0724	0724	...	...	0824	0824	...	...	0924	...		1924	...	...	...	...	...	...

km																								
		Ⓐ	⚒	⚒	Ⓐ																			
	Broc-Fabrique d.	...	...	...	0636	...	...	0736	...	...	0836	...	...	0936		...	1936	...	...	...	...	...	...
0	**Palézieux** d.	...	...	0605	|	...	0646	|	...	0746	|	...	0846	|	and at	1846	|	...	1946	2046	2115	2205	...
7	Châtel-St Denis d.	...	...	0618	|	...	0700	|	...	0800	|	...	0900	|	the same	1900	|	...	2000	2100	2128	2218	...
27	**Bulle** a.	...	...	0644	0648	...	0727	0748	...	0827	0848	...	0927	0948	minutes	1927	1948	...	2027	2127	2153	2243	...
	Bulle ▲ d.	0450	0552	...	...	0652	...	...	0753	...	0852	...	...	0952	past each	...	1952	...	...	...	...	...	...
	Gruyères d.	0457	0559	...	...	0659	...	...	0800	...	0859	...	...	0959	hour until	...	1959	...	...	...	...	...	...
	Montbovon a.	0518	0620	...	...	0720	...	...	0821	...	0920	...	...	1020		...	2020	...	...	...	...	...	...

▲ – **BULLE - ROMONT - FRIBOURG and v.v.:** Operator: TPF

km										
0	Bulle d.	0552	0620	0652	and at the same minutes	2020	2052	2120	2220y	2320y
18	Romont d.	0611	0639	0711	past each	2039	2111	2139	2239	2339
44	Fribourg a.	0629	0656	0729	hour until	2056	2129	2156	2256	2356

Fribourg d.	0604	0631	and at the same minutes	2004	2031	2104	2204	2304	...
Romont d.	0623	0649	past each	2023	2049	2123	2223	2323	...
Bulle a.	0642	0708	hour until	2042	2108	2142	2242y	2342y	...

– 🚌 connection ①–⑤ May 1 - July 31.

Narrow gauge rack railway. 2nd class only. MVR — MONTREUX - CAUX - ROCHERS DE NAYE — 569

Caux - Rochers de Naye and v.v.: no service during bad weather

km																										
0	**Montreux** d.	0547	0644	0744	...	0847	0947	1047	...	1147	1247	1347	...	1447	1547	...	1647	1747	...	1847	1944	2044	...	2144	2244
3	Glion ▲ d.	0558	0655	0755	...	0900	1000	1100	...	1200	1300	1400	...	1500	1600	...	1700	1800	...	1900	1955	2055	...	2155	2255
5	Caux a.	0607	0704	0804	...	0911	1011	1111	...	1211	1311	1411	...	1511	1611	...	1711	1811	...	1911	2004	2104	...	2204	2304
10	**Rochers de Naye** a.	...	...	...	...	0941z	1041z	1141z	...	1241z	1341z	1441z	...	1541z	1641z	...	1741t	1841r	...	...	...	...	...	...	...

ochers de Naye d.	...	...	...	...	...	0946z	...	1046z	1146z	1246z	...	1346z	1446z	...	1546z	1646z	...	1746t	1846r	...	...	...	...	...	...
aux d.	0612	0712	...	0812	0916	1016	...	1116	1216	1316	...	1416	1516	...	1616	1716	...	1816	1916	...	2016	2116	2216	...	...
lion ▲ d.	0625	0725	...	0825	0929	1029	...	1129	1229	1329	...	1429	1529	...	1629	1729	...	1829	1929	...	2029	2129	2229	...	...
ontreux a.	0637	0737	...	0837	0941	1041	...	1141	1241	1341	...	1441	1541	...	1641	1741	...	1841	1941	...	2041	2141	2241	...	...

– June 21 - Aug. 24.
– May 24 - Sept. 28.
– Dec. 15 - Apr. 21, May 3 - Dec. 13.

▲ – Funicular railway operates **Glion** - **Territet** and v.v. (no service Aug. 18-22): From **Glion** and **Territet**: 0515, 0530, 0545, 0600 and every 15 minutes until 2115, then 2145, 2215, 2245, 2315, 2350, 0020, 0050, 0130⑥⑦.
Operator: MVR, ✆ 021 989 81 90.

570 GENÈVE - LAUSANNE - SION - BRIG SBB

For *TGV Lyria* services Paris - Lausanne - Montreux - Brig and v.v. – see Table 42

km		*IR* 1703	*IR* 1403	*EC* 35 ✕ ◧	*IR* 1705	*IR* 1405	*IR* 1707	*IR* 1407		*EC* 37 ✕ ◧V	*IR* 1709	*IR* 1409	*IR* 1711	*IR* 1411	*IR* 1713	*IR* 1413	*IR* 1715	*IR* 1415		*IR* 1717	*IR* 1417	*IR* 1719	*IR* 1419	*EC* 39 ✕ ◧	*IR* 1721	*IR* 1421
0	Genève Aéroport + 505 d.	...	...	...	...	0553	0623	0653	...	...	0723	0753	0823	0853	0923	0953	1023	1053	...	1123	1153	1223	1253	...	1323	1353
6	**Genève 505** d.	...	0456	0542	0533	0603	0633	0703	...	0742	0733	0803	0833	0903	0933	1003	1033	1103	...	1133	1203	1233	1303	1342	1333	1403
27	Nyon **505** d.	...	0510	|	0547	0617	0647	0717	...	|	0747	0817	0847	0917	0947	1017	1047	1117	...	1147	1217	1247	1317	|	1347	1417
53	Morges **505** d.	...	0528	|	0602	0632	0702	0732	...	|	0802	0832	0902	0932	1002	1032	1102	1132	...	1202	1232	1302	1332	|	1402	1432
66	**Lausanne 505** a.	...	0540	0615	0612k	0642	0712	0742	...	0815	0812k	0842	0912	0942	1012	1042	1112	1142	...	1212	1242	1312	1342	1415	1412k	1442
66	**Lausanne** ▲ d.	...	0546	0617	0620	0646	0720	0746	...	0818	0821	0846	0920	0946	1020	1046	1120	1146	...	1220	1246	1320	1346	1418	1421	1446
84	Vevey ▲ d.	...	0600	|	0634	0700	0734	0800	...	|	0835	0900	0934	1000	1034	1100	1134	1200	...	1234	1300	1334	1400	|	1435	1500
92	**Montreux** ▲ d.	...	0606	0635	0640	0706	0740	0806	...	0836	0841	0906	0940	1006	1040	1106	1140	1206	...	1240	1306	1340	1406	1436	1441	1506
105	Aigle d.	...	0617	|	0651	0717	0751	0817	...	|	0852	0917	0951	1017	1051	1117	1151	1217	...	1251	1317	1351	1417	|	1452	1517
114	Bex d.	...	0624	|	|	0724	|	0824	...	|	|	0924	|	1024	|	1124	|	1224	...	|	1324	|	1424	|	|	1524
118	St Maurice d.	...	0630	|	|	0730	|	0830	...	|	|	0930	|	1030	|	1130	|	1230	...	|	1330	|	1430	|	|	1530
133	Martigny d.	0608	0641	|	0710	0741	0810	0841	...	|	0913	0941	1010	1041	1112	1141	1210	1241	...	1310	1341	1410	1441	|	1513	1541
158	**Sion** d.	0624	0656	0713	0725	0756	0825	0856	...	0913	0928	0956	1025	1056	1128	1156	1225	1256	...	1325	1356	1425	1456	1513	1528	1556
174	Sierre d.	0634	0706	|	0735	0806	0835	0906	...	|	0938	1006	1035	1106	1138	1206	1235	1306	...	1335	1406	1435	1506	|	1538	1606
184	Leuk d.	0642	0714	|	0743	0814	0843	0914	...	|	|	1014	1043	1114	|	1214	1243	1314	...	1343	1414	1443	1514	|	|	1614
203	Visp d.	0655	0725	|	0755	0825	0855	0925	...	|	0955	1025	1055	1125	1155	1225	1255	1325	...	1355	1425	1455	1525	|	1555	1625
212	**Brig** a.	0702	0732	0740	0802	0832	0902	0932	...	0940	1002	1032	1102	1132	1202	1232	1302	1332	...	1402	1432	1502	1532	1540	1602	1632
	Milano Centrale **590** a.	...	...	0935	...	...	...	...	...	1135	...	...	...	...	...	...	...	...	...	...	...	...	...	1735	...	...

	IR 1723	*IR* 1423	*IR* 1725	*IR* 1425	*IR* 1727 Ⓐ	*IR* 1729	*IR* 1427	*IR* 1429 Ⓐ	*IR* 1731 Ⓐ	*IR* 1733	*IR* 1431	*EC* 41 ✕ ◧	*IR* 1735	*IR* 1435		*IR* 1737	*IR* 1437	*IR* 1739	*IR* 1439	*IR* 1741	*IR* 1441	*IR* 1743	*IR* 1443	*IR* 1745	*IR* 1445	*RE* 4051 q
Genève Aéroport + 505 d.	1423	1453	1523	1553	...	1623	1653	...	...	1723	1753	...	1823	1853	...	1923	1953	2023	2052	2123	...	2223	2247	...	2350j	...
Genève 505 d.	1433	1503	1533	1603	1642	1633	1703	1712	1742	1733	1803	1842	1833	1903	...	1933	2003	2033	2101	2133	...	2233	2256	...	2359	...
Nyon **505** d.	1447	1517	1547	1617	|	1647	1717	|	|	1747	1817	|	1847	1917	...	1947	2017	2047	2115	2147	...	2247	2310	...	0013	...
Morges **505** d.	1502	1532	1602	1632	|	1702	1732	|	|	1802	1832	|	1902	1932	...	2002	2032	2102	2130	2202	...	2302	2328	...	0031	...
Lausanne 505 a.	1512	1542	1612	1642	1715	1712	1742	1745	1815	1812	1842	1915	1912k	1942	...	2012	2042	2112	2140	2212	...	2312	2340	...	0043	...
Lausanne ▲ d.	1520	1546	1620	1646	1718	1720	1746	1751	1818	1820	1846	1918	1921	1946	...	2020	2046	2120	2146	2220	2246	2320	...	0024	...	0130
Vevey ▲ d.	1534	1600	1634	1700	|	1734	1800	1805	|	1834	1900	|	1935	2000	...	2034	2100	2134	2200	2234	2300	2334	...	0038	...	0144
Montreux ▲ d.	1540	1606	1640	1706	1736	1740	1806	1811	1836	1840	1906	1936	1941	2006	...	2040	2106	2140	2206	2240	2306	2340	...	0044	...	0150
Aigle d.	1551	1617	1651	1717	1747	1751	1817	1822	1847	1851	1917	|	1952	2017	...	2051	2117	2151	2217	2251	2317	2351	...	0055	...	0203
Bex d.	|	1624	|	1724	|	|	1824	1836	|	|	1924	|	|	2024	...	|	2124	|	2224	|	2324	|	...	0102	...	0210
St Maurice d.	|	1630	|	1730	|	|	1830	1841	|	|	1930	|	|	2030	...	|	2130	|	2230	|	2330	|	...	0108	...	0215
Martigny d.	1610	1641	1710	1741	1807	1810	1841	...	1907	1910	1941	|	2013	2041	...	2110	2141	2212	2240	2310	2341	0010	...	0119	...	...
Sion d.	1625	1656	1725	1756	1823	1825	1856	...	1923	1925	1956	2013	2028	2056	...	2125	2156	2228	...	2325	2354	0025	...	0133	...	...
Sierre d.	1635	1706	1735	1806	1833	1835c	1906	...	1933	1935c	2006	|	2038	2106	...	2135	2206	2238	...	2335	...	0035	...	...	...	...
Leuk d.	1643	1714	1743	1814	1842	1843c	1914	...	1942	1943c	2014	|	|	2114	...	2143	2214	|	...	2343	...	0043	...	...	...	...
Visp d.	1655	1725	1755	1825	1855	1855c	1925	...	1955	1955c	2025	|	2055	2125	...	2155	2225	2255	...	2355	...	0055	...	...	...	...
Brig a.	1702	1732	1802	1832	1902	1902c	1932	...	2002	2002c	2032	2040	2102	2132	...	2202	2232	2302	...	0002	...	0102	...	...	...	...
Milano Centrale **590** a.	...	...	...	...	...	...	...	...	...	...	...	2235	...	...	...	...	...	...	...	...	...	...	...	...	...	...

	RE 2702	*IR* 1704	*IR* 1406	*IR* 1708	*IR* 1408 Ⓐ	*IR* 1410	*IR* 1712	*IR* 1710 Ⓐ	*IR* 1412 Ⓐ	*IR* 1414	*IR* 1714	*IR* 1416	*IR* 1716	*IR* 1418	*IR* 1718	*IR* 1420	*IR* 1720	*EC* 32 ✕ ◧		*IR* 1422	*IR* 1722	*IR* 1424	*IR* 1724	*IR* 1426	*IR* 1726	*IR* 1428
Milano Centrale **590** d.	...	...	...	...	...	...	...	...	...	...	...	...	...	...	...	...	...	0825	...	...	...	...	...	...	...	...
Brig d.	...	...	0428	...	...	0528	0558c	0601	...	0628	0658	0728	0758	0828	0858	0928	0958	1020	...	1028	1058	1128	1158	1228	1258	1328
Visp d.	...	...	0436	...	...	0536	0606c	0609	...	0636	0706	0736	0806	0836	0906	0936	1006	|	...	1036	1106	1136	1206	1236	1306	1336
Leuk d.	...	...	0447	...	...	0547	0616c	0621	...	0647	0716	0747	|	0847	0916	0947	|	|	...	1047	1116	1147	1216	1247	1316	1347
Sierre d.	...	...	0455	...	...	0555	0623c	0630	...	0655	0723	0755	0821	0855	0923	0955	1021	|	...	1055	1123	1155	1223	1255	1323	1355
Sion d.	...	0425	0506	0532	...	0606	0635	0642	...	0706	0735	0806	0832	0906	0935	1006	1032	1048	...	1106	1135	1206	1235	1306	1335	1406
Martigny d.	...	0439	0519	0546	...	0619	0648	0657	...	0719	0748	0819	0846	0919	0948	1019	1046	|	...	1119	1148	1219	1248	1319	1348	1419
St Maurice d.	...	0450	0529	0556	0617	0629	|	|	...	0729	|	0829	|	0929	|	1029	|	|	...	1129	|	1229	|	1329	|	1429
Bex d.	...	0455	0535	0601	0629	0635	|	|	0729	0735	|	0835	|	0935	|	1035	|	|	...	1135	|	1235	|	1335	|	1435
Aigle d.	...	0502	0542	0608	0637	0642	0709	0715	0737	0742	0809	0842	0907	0942	1009	1042	1107	|	...	1142	1209	1242	1309	1342	1409	1442
Montreux ▲ d.	...	0513	0553	0619	0648	0653	0719	0725	0748	0753	0819	0853	0918	0953	1019	1053	1118	1125	...	1153	1219	1253	1319	1353	1419	1453
Vevey ▲ d.	...	0520	0600	0626	0655	0700	0726	|	0755	0800	0826	0900	0925	1000	1026	1100	1125	|	...	1200	1226	1300	1326	1400	1426	1500
Lausanne ▲ a.	...	0534	0614	0640	0709	0714	0740	0743	0809	0814	0840	0914	0939	1014	1040	1114	1139	1142k	...	1214	1240	1314	1340	1414	1440	1514
Lausanne 505 d.	0451	0536	0618	0648	0715	0718	0748	0745	0815	0818	0848	0918	0948	1018	1048	1118	1148	1145	...	1218	1248	1318	1348	1418	1448	1518
Morges **505** d.	0502	0545	0627	0657	|	0727	0757	|	|	0827	0857	0927	0957	1027	1057	1127	1157	|	...	1227	1257	1327	1357	1427	1457	1527
Nyon **505** d.	0523	0601	0643	0713	|	0743	0813	|	|	0843	0913	0943	1013	1043	1113	1143	1213	|	...	1243	1313	1343	1413	1443	1513	1543
Genève 505 a.	0539	0615	0657	0727	0749	0757	0827	0818	0849	0857	0927	0957	1027	1057	1127	1157	1227	1218	...	1257	1327	1357	1427	1457	1527	1557
Genève Aéroport + 505 a.	0548	0624	0707	0737	0758j	0807	0837	0829j	0858j	0907	0937	1007	1037	1107	1137	1207	1237	...	...	1307	1337	1407	1437	1507	1537	1607

	IR 1728	*EC* 34 ✕ ◧	*IR* 1430	*IR* 1730	*IR* 1432	*IR* 1732	*IR* 1434	*IR* 1734 Ⓐ	*IR* 1734 Ⓒ	*IR* 1436	*IR* 1736 Ⓐ	*IR* 1736 Ⓒ	*IR* 1438	*IR* 1738	*EC* 36 ✕ ◧	*IR* 1440	*IR* 1740	*IR* 1442	*IR* 1742	*EC* 42 ✕ ◧V	*RE* 2742	*IR* 1444	*RE* 4092 p	*RE* 2744	*IR* 1446	*RE* 4050 q
Milano Centrale **590** d.	...	1225	...	...	...	...	...	...	...	...	...	...	...	...	1725	...	...	...	...	1925	...	...	...	...	...	...
Brig d.	1358	1420	1428	1458	1528	1558	1628	1658	1658	1728	1758	1758	1828	1858	1923	1928	1958	2028	2058	2123	...	2128	...	...	2228	...
Visp d.	1406	|	1436	1506	1536	1606	1636	1706	1706	1736	1806	1806	1836	1906	|	1936	2006	2036	2106	|	...	2136	...	...	2236	...
Leuk d.	|	|	1447	1516	1547	1616	1647	|	1716	1747	|	1816	1847	|	|	1947	2016	2047	|	|	...	2147	...	...	2247	...
Sierre d.	1421	|	1455	1523	1555	1623	1655	1721	1723	1755	1821	1823	1855	1921	|	1955	2023	2055	2121	|	...	2155	...	...	2255	...
Sion d.	1432	1448	1506	1535	1606	1635	1706	1732	1735	1806	1832	1835	1906	1932	1950	2006	2035	2106	2132	2150	...	2206	...	...	2306	...
Martigny d.	1446	|	1519	1548	1619	1648	1719	1746	1748	1819	1846	1848	1919	1946	|	2019	2048	2119	2146	|	...	2219	...	...	2319	...
St Maurice d.	|	|	1529	|	1629	|	1729	|	|	1829	|	|	1929	|	|	2029	|	2129	|	|	...	2229	2252	...	2329	0035
Bex d.	|	|	1535	|	1635	|	1735	|	|	1835	|	|	1935	|	|	2035	|	2135	|	|	...	2235	2301	...	2335	0040
Aigle d.	1507	|	1542	1609	1642	1709	1742	1807	1809	1842	1907	1909	1942	2007	|	2042	2109	2142	2207	|	...	2242	2308	...	2342	0046
Montreux ▲ d.	1518	1525	1553	1619	1653	1719	1753	1818	1819	1853	1918	1919	1953	2018	2025	2053	2119	2153	2218	2225	...	2253	2319	...	2353	005
Vevey ▲ d.	1525	|	1600	1626	1700	1726	1800	1825	1826	1900	1925	1926	2000	2025	|	2100	2126	2200	2225	|	2235	2300	2326	2335	0000	010
Lausanne ▲ a.	1539	1542k	1614	1640	1714	1740	1814	1839	1840	1914	1939	1940	2014	2039	2042k	2114	2140	2214	2239	2242	2249	2314	2340	2349	0014	012
Lausanne 505 d.	1548	1545	1618	1648	1718	1748	1818	1848	1848	1918	1948	1948	2018	2048	2045	2118	2148	*2221*	...	2245	2251	2321	...	2351	0023	...
Morges **505** d.	1557	|	1627	1657	1727	1757	1827	1857	1857	1927	1957	1957	2027	2057	|	2127	2157	*2233*	...	|	2302	2333	...	0002	0035	...
Nyon **505** d.	1613	|	1643	1713	1743	1813	1843	1913	1913	1943	2013	2013	2043	2113	|	2143	2213	*2251*	...	|	2323	2351	...	0023	0053	...
Genève 505 a.	1627	1618	1657	1727	1757	1827	1857	1927	1927	1957	2027	2027	2057	2127	2118	2157	2227	*2305*	...	2318	2339	0005	...	0039	0107	...
Genève Aéroport + 505 a.	1640	...	1707	1740	1807	1837	1907	1937	1937	2007	2037	2037	2107	2137	...	2207	2237	*2314*j	...	...	2348j	0014r	...	0048n	...	...

▲ – Local services **Lausanne** - **Montreux** - **Villeneuve and v.v.**

	★		★			★		★	★	★	★
Lausanne d.	0600	0635	0700	0735	and at	2000	2035	2100	2200	2300	0006
Vevey d.	0622	0652	0722	0752	the same	2022	2052	2122	2222	2322	0028
Montreux d.	0631	0701	0731	0801	minutes	2031	2101	2131	2231	2331	0037
Territet d.	0632	|	0732	|	past each	2032	|	2132	2232	2332	0038
Veytaux-Chillon d.	0634	|	0734	|	hour until	2034	|	2134	2234	2334	0040
Villeneuve a.	0638	0706	0738	0806		2038	2106	2138	2238	2338	0044

	★	★			★		★	★	★	
Villeneuve d.	0524	0624	0653	and at	2024	2053	2124	2224	2324	235
Veytaux-Chillon d.	0526	0626	|	the same	2026	|	2126	2226	2326	|
Territet d.	0527	0628	|	minutes past	2028	|	2128	2228	2328	|
Montreux d.	0530	0630	0657	each	2030	2057	2130	2230	2330	235
Vevey d.	0540	0640	0707	hour until	2040	2107	2140	2240	2340	000
Lausanne a.	0602	0702	0724		2102	2124	2202	2302	0002	002

♦ – **NOTES** (LISTED BY TRAIN NUMBER)

V – (12) and ✕ Genève - Milano - Venezia and v.v.

c – Ⓒ only.
j – Dec. 15 - July 14.
k – Connects with train in previous column.
n – ⑥⑦ Dec. 21 - July 13 (also Apr. 18, 21, May 29, June 9).
p – ⑤⑥ (also Apr. 17, 20, May 28, June 8, July 31).
q – ⑥⑦ (also Apr. 18, 21, May 29, June 9, Aug. 1).
r – Dec. 16 - July 15.

◧ – Supplement payable for journeys from / to Italy.
★ – Service also calls at all intermediate stations.

2nd class only — Local services from VEVEY, AIGLE and BEX — 571

VEVEY - BLONAY: Narrow gauge. *6 km*. Journey time: 14–16 minutes. **Operator**: MVR.

From **Vevey**: 0604⚒, 0624Ⓐ, 0646, 0704⚒, 0724Ⓐ, 0746, 0804⚒, 0824Ⓐ, 0846, 0904⚒, 0938, 1004⚒, 1038, 1113⚒, 1138, 1204⚒, 1238, 1304⚒, 1338, 1404⚒, 1438, 1504⚒, 1538, 1604⚒, 1628Ⓐ, 1642, 1704⚒, 1728Ⓐ, 1742, 1804⚒, 1828Ⓐ, 1842, 1904Ⓐ, 1942, 2004Ⓐ, 2042, 2142, 2242, 2342, 0042⑥⑦.

From **Blonay**: 0540⚒, 0606, 0626Ⓐ, 0640⚒, 0706, 0726Ⓐ, 0740⚒, 0806, 0826Ⓐ, 0840⚒, 0906, 0940⚒, 1006, 1040⚒, 1115, 1140⚒, 1206, 1240⚒, 1306, 1340⚒, 1406, 1440⚒, 1506, 1540⚒, 1606, 1622Ⓐ, 1644⚒, 1706, 1722Ⓐ, 1744⚒, 1806, 1822Ⓐ, 1844Ⓐ, 1906, 1936Ⓐ, 2006, 2103, 2203, 2303, 0003⑥⑦.

AIGLE - LEYSIN: Narrow gauge rack railway. *6 km*. Journey time: 29–39 minutes. **Operator**: TPC.

From **Aigle**: 0550Ⓐ, 0612Ⓐ, 0620Ⓒ, 0720, 0756, 0856 and hourly until 2256.

From **Leysin** Grand Hotel: 0525, 0624Ⓐ, 0642Ⓐ, 0655Ⓒ, 0753 and hourly until 2253, then 2327.

AIGLE - LES DIABLERETS: Narrow gauge. *23 km*. Journey time: 45–55 minutes. **Operator**: TPC.

From **Aigle**: 0620, 0720, 0820, 0920, 1054, 1140Ⓐ, 1155Ⓒ, 1240Ⓐ, 1255Ⓒ, 1354, 1456, 1602, 1659, 1803, 1855, 2054, 2154.

From **Les Diablerets**: 0613, 0713, 0811, 0913, 1047, 1150, 1248, 1332Ⓐ, 1347Ⓒ, 1506, 1547, 1706, 1748, 1904, 2047, 2147.

AIGLE - CHAMPÉRY: Narrow gauge rack railway. 2nd class only. **Operator**: TPC. Additional services operate Aigle - Monthey Ville and v.v.

km																											
		⚒			⚒				⚒		⚒		⚒					⚒								⑥y	
0	**Aigle** d.	0518	0619	0720	0807	0822	0922	1022	1055	1124	1155	1224	1255	1322	1422	1522	1624	1655	1724	1824	1855	1955	2055	2153	2255	...	2355
11	Monthey Ville d.	0547	0645	0748	0826	0848	0948	1048	1114	1153	1214	1258	1314	1348	1448	1548	1648	1714	1748	1848	1921	2021	2114	2213	2314	2330	0014
23	**Champéry** a.	0620	0720	0821	...	0921	1021	1130	...	1226	...	1331	...	1421	1521	1628	1721	...	1821	1921	1954	2054	...	2245	...	0003	...

		Ⓐ		⚒					⚒		⚒		⚒						⚒							z	⑦w
Champéry d.	...	...	0600	0631a	0700d	0734	0834	0934	...	1034	...	1139	...	1254	1334	1434	1534	1634	...	1734	1834	1934	2034	2134	...	2246	0004
Monthey Ville d.	0540	0611	0641	0712	0742	0814	0914	1014	1029	1116	1131	1216	1231	1342	1414	1514	1616	1716	1731	1816	1916	2016	2116	2216	2317	2321	0039
Aigle a.	0600	0631	0703	0732	0802	0834	0934	1034	1049	1136	1151	1236	1251	1402	1434	1534	1636	1736	1751	1836	1936	2036	2136	2236	2337	2337	...

BEX - VILLARS-SUR-OLLON: *12 km*. Journey time: 40–46 minutes. All trains call at Bex (Place du Marché), and Bévieux (*3 km* and 4 minutes from Bex). **Operator**: TPC.

From **Bex**: 0633, 0739, 0839, 0939, 1039, 1149, 1239, 1339, 1439, 1549, 1639, 1739, 1839, 1939, 2139.

From **Villars**: 0539, 0644, 0733, 0833, 0933, 1033, 1143, 1233, 1333, 1433, 1543, 1633, 1733, 1833, 1933, 2046.

VILLARS-SUR-OLLON - COL-DE-BRETAYE: *5 km*. Journey time: 18–20 minutes. **Operator**: TPC.

From **Villars**:
Dec. 15-20, Apr. 22 - June 13, Sept. 22 - Dec. 13: 0935, 1135**j**, 1235, 1335**j**, 1535, 1635**j**.
Dec. 21 - Apr. 21: 0800, 0830, 0900, 0930 and every 30 minutes until 1730.
June 14 - Sept. 21: 0835, 0935 and hourly until 1735.

From **Col-de-Bretaye**:
Dec. 15-20, Apr. 22 - June 13, Sept. 22 - Dec. 13: 1000, 1200**j**, 1300, 1400**j**, 1600, 1700**j**.
Dec. 21 - Apr. 21: 0825, 0855, 0925, 0955 and every 30 minutes until 1725, then 1805.
June 14 - Sept. 21: 0900, 1000 and hourly until 1800.

a – Ⓐ only.
d – ⚒ only.
j – Dec. 15-20, May 17 - June 13, Sept. 22 - Oct. 26 (also Dec. 13).
w – Also Aug. 2.
y – Also Aug. 1.
z – Change at Monthey En Place for connection to Aigle.

2nd class only. SNCF, TMR — MARTIGNY - CHAMONIX — Valid March 31 - May 11 — 572

Narrow gauge rack railway. **Vallorcine - Argentière and v.v. currently operated by 🚌**

km																									
				Ⓐ	Ⓒ																			♣	♣y
0	**Martigny** d.	...	0550	...	...	...	0643	0743	0843	0943	1043	1143	1243	1343	...	1443	1543	1643	1743	1843	1943	2043	2143	2243	2343
7	Salvan d.	...	0604	...	...	...	0657	0757	0857	0957	1057	1157	1257	1357	...	1457	1557	1657	1757	1857	1957	2057	2157	2257	2357
9	Les Marécottes d.	...	0611	...	...	...	0704	0804	0904	1004	1104	1204	1304	1404	...	1504	1604	1704	1804	1904	2004	2104	2204	2304	0004
14	Finhaut d.	...	0623	...	...	...	0716	0816	0916	1016	1116	1216	1316	1416	...	1516	1616	1716	1816	1916	2016	2116	2216	2316s	0016s
18	Le Châtelard Frontière 🏛 a.	...	0632	...	...	...	0725	0825	0925	1025	1125	1225	1325	1425	...	1525	1625	1725	1825	1925	2025	2125	2225	2325	0025
18	Le Châtelard Frontière 🏛 d.	...	...	...	...	...	...	0826	0926	...	...	1226	...	...	...	1526	1626	1726	1826	...	...	...	...	...	...
21	**Vallorcine** a.	...	...	...	...	...	...	0832	0932	...	...	1232	...	...	...	1532	1632	1732	1832	...	...	...	...	...	...
21	**Vallorcine** 🚌 d.	*0625*	...	*0656*	*0725*	*0814*	...	*0914*	*1014*	...	...	*1314*	...	...	...	*1614*	*1714*	*1814*	*1914*	...	...	...	...	...	...
28	Argentière Haute Savoie 🚌 a.	*0643*	...	*0714*	*0743*	*0833*	...	*0933*	*1033*	...	...	*1333*	...	...	...	*1633*	*1733*	*1833*	*1933*	...	...	...	...	...	...
28	Argentière Haute Savoie d.	0653	...	0724	0753	0853	...	0953	1053	...	...	1353	...	...	...	1653	1753	1853	1953	...	...	...	...	...	...
32	Les Tines d.	0703	...	0734	0803	0903	...	1003	1103	...	...	1403	...	...	...	1703	1803	1903	2003	...	...	...	...	...	...
36	**Chamonix** a.	0710	...	0742	0810	0910	...	1010	1110	...	...	1410	...	...	...	1710	1810	1910	2010	...	...	...	...	...	...
	St Gervais **365a** a.	0757	...	0857	0857	0957	...	1057	...	...	...	1457	...	...	...	1757	1857	1957	2057	...	...	...	...	...	...

	Ⓐ		Ⓐ																					♣
St Gervais **365a** d.	...	...	...	...	...	0706	0806	0906	...	...	...	1206	...	1406	...	...	1606	1706	1806	1906	...	...	...	...
hamonix d.	...	...	0620	...	...	0754	0854	0954	...	...	...	1254	...	1454	...	...	1654	1754	1854	1954	...	...	...	...
es Tines d.	...	...	0628	...	...	0804	0904	1004	...	...	...	1304	...	1504	...	...	1704	1804	1904	2004	...	...	...	...
rgentière Haute Savoie a.	...	...	0637	...	...	0813	0913	1013	...	...	...	1313	...	1513	...	...	1713	1813	1913	2013	...	...	...	...
rgentière Haute Savoie 🚌 d.	...	...	*0651*	...	...	*0818*	*0918*	*1018*	...	...	...	*1318*	...	*1518*	...	...	*1718*	*1818*	*1918*	*2018*	...	...	...	...
allorcine 🚌 a.	...	...	*0709*	...	...	*0836*	*0936*	*1036*	...	...	...	*1336*	...	*1536*	...	...	*1736*	*1836*	*1936*	*2036*	...	...	...	...
allorcine d.	...	...	...	...	...	0843	0943	1043	...	...	...	1343	...	1543	...	...	1743	1843	1943	...	...	...	...	...
e Châtelard Frontière 🏛 a.	...	...	...	...	...	0849	0949	1049	...	...	...	1349	...	1549	...	...	1749	1849	1949	...	...	...	...	...
e Châtelard Frontière 🏛 d.	0516	0642	...	0750	...	0850	0950	1050	1150	1250	...	1350	1450	1550	1650	...	1750	1850	1950	...	2050	2150	2231	2329
inhaut d.	0525	0651	...	0759	...	0859	0959	1059	1159	1259	...	1359	1459	1559	1659	...	1759	1859	1959	...	2059	2159	2240	2338
es Marécottes d.	0538	0704	...	0812	...	0912	1012	1112	1212	1312	...	1412	1512	1612	1712	...	1812	1912	2012	...	2112	2212	2253	2351
alvan d.	0542	0708	...	0816	...	0916	1016	1116	1216	1316	...	1416	1516	1616	1716	...	1816	1916	2016	...	2116	2216	2257	2355
artigny a.	0602	0727	...	0835	...	0935	1035	1135	1235	1335	...	1435	1535	1635	1735	...	1835	1935	2035	...	2135	2235	2316	0018

– Stops to set down only.
y – ⑤⑥ only.
♣ – Runs only by prior reservation ✆ 027 764 12 71.

SION VALLEY RESORTS — 573

ARTIGNY - ORSIÈRES▲ and LE CHÂBLE: *19 km*. Journey time: 26 minutes to both resorts. ▲ – A change of train is necessary at Sembrancher. **Operator**: RA.

rom **Martigny**: 0613Ⓐ **L**, 0813, 0915, 1013, 1115, 1213, 1313, 1413, 1515, 1613Ⓒ, 1645, 1721, 1813, 1913, 2015, 2123, 2323⑤⑥.

From **Orsières and Le Châble**: 0539Ⓐ, 0646, 0809, 0911, 1009, 1111, 1209, 1309, 1409, 1511, 1609, 1641Ⓒ, 1717, 1809, 1909, 2047, 2241⑤⑥.

E CHÂBLE - VERBIER: 🚌 service. Journey time: ± 25 minutes. **Operator**: PA.

rom **Le Châble** Gare: 0645⚒, 0715†, 0800⚒, 0850, 0955, 1050⚒**r**, 1050†, 1135⚒**t**, 1205⚒**r**, 1255, 1355, 1610, 1715, 1806, 1900, 1955, 2050, 2151**p**, 0005**v**.

rom **Verbier** Post: 0615⚒, 0720⚒, 0740†, 0840⚒, 0925, 1025, 1130⚒**r**, 1230, 1330, 1525, 1640, 1740, 1835, 1930, 2020, 2115, 2216**p**, 0030**v**.

ARTIGNY - AOSTA: 🚌 service via Grand St Bernard tunnel. Service runs daily throughout the year (**not Dec. 25**). Journey time: ± 1 hour 45 minutes. **Operator**: TMR/SAVDA.

rom **Martigny** Gare: 0825, 1830. From **Aosta** Stazione: 1100, 1600.

ION - CRANS-SUR-SIERRE: 🚌 service. Journey time: ± 45 minutes. **Operator**: PA.

rom **Sion** Gare: 0645⚒, 0745, 0840⚒, 1000, 1045⚒, 1150, 1230⚒ 1345, 1510Ⓒ, 1540Ⓐ**z**, 1650⚒, 1700†, 1800, 1910.

From **Crans-sur-Sierre** Post: 0645, 0740⚒, 0835, 0930⚒, 1050, 1135⚒, 1245, 1335⚒, 1545, 1635, 1805, 1905.

ERRE - CRANS-SUR-SIERRE - MONTANA: 🚌 service. Principal stop in **Crans-sur-Sierre** is Hotel Scandia (± 40 minutes from Sierre, ± 8 minutes from Montana. **Operator**: SMC.

rom **Sierre** Gare: 0743, 0848, 0945⚒**z**, 1045⚒**z**, 1138, 1201⚒**z**, 1230⚒**z**, 1340, 1440⚒**z**, 1542, 1650Ⓐ**z**, 1711, 1750, 1845⚒**z**, 1940, 2045, 2200.

From **Montana** Gare: 0602⚒**z**, 0622Ⓐ**z**, 0632, 0738†**x**, 0838⚒**z**, 1003, 1039⚒**z**, 1133⚒**z**, 1227, 1334⚒**z**, 1436, 1601, 1603Ⓐ**z**, 1636, 1733⚒**z**, 1816, 1907, 2045.

RIG - SAAS-FEE: 🚌 service. Journey time: 50–70 minutes. All services call at **Visp** (Bahnhof Süd) ± 20 minutes from Brig, and **Saas Grund** (Post) ± 12 minutes from Saas Fee.

rom **Brig** (Bahnhof): 0420, 0545, 0615, 0645 and every 30 minutes until 1045, then 1115, 1140, 1215, 1250, 1315, 1345 and every 30 minutes until 1845, then 1945, 2045, 2215.

From **Saas-Fee**: 0531, 0601, 0630, 0700, 0730, 0752, 0822, 0852, 0922, 0952 and every 30 minutes until 1852, then 1930, 2030.

perator: PA. Seat reservation **compulsory** from Saas Fee to Brig. Reserve seats at least two hours before departure: ✆ 058 454 26 16.

– Destination Orsières; change trains at Sembrancher for Le Châble.
– Dec. 21 - Apr. 27.
– ①②④⑤⑥ Dec. 16 - June 17; ⚒ June 20 - Aug. 14; ①②④⑤⑥ Aug. 16 - Dec. 13 (also Mar. 5, Apr. 23; not Apr. 21, May 29, June 9, Nov. 1, Dec. 8).
t – ③ Dec. 18 - June 18, Aug. 20 - Dec. 10 (not Mar. 5, 19, Apr. 23, Oct. 29).
v – ① Dec. 23 - Apr. 28 (also Mar. 20, Apr. 22).
x – Also Mar. 19, June 19, Aug. 15, Nov. 1, Dec. 8; not Apr. 18.
z – Also Apr. 18; not Mar. 19, June 19, Aug. 15, Nov. 1, Dec. 8.

575 GLACIER EXPRESS — MGB, RhB*

Glacier Express through services (compulsory reservation). **No service Oct. 27 - Dec. 13, 2014.** For local services see Table **576**. Narrow gauge railway (part rack).

km		WINTER SERVICE ▶▶▶	902 ⊡ 🍴		SUMMER SERVICE ▶▶▶	906 ☆ V 2	900 ★ T 🍴	902 ★ 🍴	904 ★ S 🍴
0	**Zermatt** d.		0852	...		...	0752	0852	0952
21	St Niklaus △ d.		|	...		...	|	|	1033
36	Visp △ d.		|	...		...	|	|	|
45	**Brig** △ d.		1018	...		...	0918	1018	1118
62	Fiesch △ d.		1048	...		...	0948	1048	1148
86	Oberwald △ d.	**Dec. 15**	1121	...	**May 10**	...	1021	1121	|
113	**Andermatt** a.	**to**	1148	...	**to**	...	1048	1148	1248
113	**Andermatt** d.	**May 9**	1154	...	**Oct. 26**	...	1054	1154	1254
142	**Disentis / Mustér** a.		1255	...		...	1155	1255	1355
142	**Disentis / Mustér** d.		1327	...		0844	1227	1327	1427
201	**Chur** ▽ a.		1434	...		1001	1334	1434	1534
228	Thusis ▽ a.		1528	...		1130	1428	1528	1628
242	Tiefencastel ▽ a.		1547	...		1147	1447	1547	1647
252	**Filisur 545a** ▽ a.		1601	...		1201	1501	1601	1701
	Davos Platz **545a** a.		|	...		|	|	|	|
285	**Samedan 546** ▽ a.		1646	...		1246	1546	1646	1746
288	Celerina **546/7** ▽ a.		1653	...		1253	1553	1653	1753
290	**St Moritz 546/7** a.		1658	...		1258	1558	1658	1758

	WINTER SERVICE ▶▶▶	903 ⊡ 🍴		SUMMER SERVICE ▶▶▶	901 ★ S 🍴	903 ★ 🍴	905 ★ T 🍴	907 ☆ V 2
St Moritz 546/7 d.		0902	...		0802	0902	1002	1402
Celerina **546/7** △ d.		0905	...		0805	0905	1005	1405
Samedan 546 △ d.		0917	...		0827	0917	1017	1417
Davos Platz **545a** d.		|-	...		|	|	|	|
Filisur 545a △ d.		1001	...		0901	1001	1101	1501
Tiefencastel △ d.	**Dec. 15**	1015	...	**May 10**	0915	1015	1115	1515
Thusis △ d.	**to**	1033	...	**to**	0933	1033	1133	1533
Chur △ d.	**May 9**	1127	...	**Oct. 26**	1027	1127	1227	1656
Disentis / Mustér a.		1227	...		1127	1227	1327	1811
Disentis / Mustér d.		1237	...		1137	1237	1337	...
Andermatt a.		1350	...		1250	1350	1450	...
Andermatt d.		1354	...		1308	1408	1508	...
Oberwald ▽ a.		1418	...		|	1437	1537	...
Fiesch ▽ a.		1510	...		1410	1510	1610	...
Brig ▽ a.		1540	...		1440	1540	1640	...
Visp ▽ a.		1602	...		1502	1602	1702	...
St Niklaus ▽ a.		|	...		1527	|	|	...
Zermatt a.		1700	...		1600	1700	1800	...

All Glacier Express trains convey 🚃 [panorama cars]. Reservations can be made at any Swiss station. Reservations for 🍴 are obligatory in advance through Railgourmino swissAlps AG, ✆ Chur (081) 300 15 15 until Apr. 30. From May 1 contact RhB, ✆ 081 288 65 65. Meals are served between 1100 and 1330 at your seat. Further information: www.glacierexpress.ch

S – June 14 - Sept. 21.
T – May 10 - Oct. 12.
V – May 31 - Sept. 21.

△ – Calls to pick up only.
▽ – Calls to set down only.

☆ – Ⓡ (reservation fee including supplement: 12 CHF).
⊡ – Ⓡ (reservation fee including supplement: 13 CHF).
★ – Ⓡ (reservation fee including supplement: 33 CHF).

* – For operators see foot of page.

576 *Local Services* ZERMATT - BRIG - ANDERMATT (- GÖSCHENEN) - DISENTIS - CHUR — MGB, RhB*

Narrow gauge railway (part rack). For *Glacier Express* through services see Table **575**

ZERMATT - BRIG

km										
0	**Zermatt** d.	0539	0613	0739		1839	1913	2013	2113	2213
8	Täsch ◧ d.	0550	0624	0750	and	1850	1924	2024	2124	2224
21	St Niklaus d.	0614	0652	0814	every	1914	1952	2052	2152	2249
29	Stalden-Saas d.	0637	0712	0837	hour	1937	2012	2112	2212	2309
36	Visp a.	0647	0723	0847	until	1947	2023	2123	2223	2319
36	Visp d.	0652	0725	0852	△	1952	2025	2125	2225	2321
45	**Brig** a.	0703	0736	0903		2003	2035	2135	2235	2330

					Ⓐ				①–⑥	⑦
Brig d.	0510	0552		1552	1626	1652		2052	2225	2308
Visp a.	0520	0603	and	1603	1636	1703	and	2103	2236	2318
Visp d.	0529	0610	every	1610	1643	1710	every	2110	2240	2323
Stalden-Saas d.	0539	0620	hour	1620	1654	1720	hour	2120	2250	2333
St Niklaus d.	0555	0637	until	1637	1714	1737	until	2137	2310	2350
Täsch ⊡ d.	0621	0701	▽	1701	1737	1801	▽	2201	2333	0013
Zermatt a.	0633	0713		1713	1752	1813		2213	2344	0025

VISP - BRIG - ANDERMATT

km									①–⑥	⑦
	Visp d.	...	0708	0808		1908	2008	2108	2236	2255
0	**Brig** d.	0623	0723	0823	and	1923	2023	2123	2250	2312
7	Mörel d.	0633	0733	0833	every	1933	2033	2133	2300	2320
10	Betten d.	0639	0739	0839	hour	1939	2039	2139	2306	2326
17	Fiesch d.	0656	0756	0856	until	1956	2056	2156	2322	2343
41	Oberwald 🚗 d.	0744	0844	0944		2044	2144j	*2237*z	...	...
59	Realp ▲ 🚗 § d.	0805	0905	1005		2105	2205t	...	...	...
68	**Andermatt** a.	0820	0920	1020		2120	2220t	...	...	...

							t			①–⑥	⑦
Andermatt d.	...	...	0737	0837		1837	1909	1937	2037	...	...
Realp ▲ 🚗 § d.	...	...	0750	0850	and	1850	1922	1950	2050	...	...
Oberwald 🚗 d.	*0612*z	0712	0812	0912	every	1912	1946	2012	2112	*2250*z	*2250*z
Fiesch d.	0656	0756	0856	0956	hour	1956	2027	2056	2156	2326	2346
Betten d.	0715	0815	0915	1015	until	2015	2048	2115	2215	2344	0004
Mörel d.	0722	0822	0922	1022		2022	2054	2122	2222	2351	0011
Brig a.	0733	0833	0933	1033		2033	2104	2133	2233	0001	0021
Visp a.	0750	0850	0950	1050		2050	...	2150	...	...	...

ANDERMATT - GÖSCHENEN

km												
0	**Andermatt** d.	0638	0725	0748	0828	0848	and hourly until	1828	1848	1948	2048	2128
4	**Göschenen** a.	0652	0739	0803	0842	0903		1842	1903	2003	2103	2142

Göschenen d.	0712	0753	0812	0853	and hourly until	1812	1853	1912	2012	2112	2153
Andermatt a.	0722	0803	0822	0903		1822	1903	1922	2022	2122	2203

ANDERMATT - DISENTIS

km		🚌Ⓐ	🚌		w◇		w◇		w◇			w◇				w◇								🚌	🚌v	🚌v
0	**Andermatt** 🚗 d.	...	...	0727	0755	0827	0855	0927	0955	...	1027	1055	1127	1227	1327	1355	...	1427	1527	1627	1727	1827	...	...	...	...
10	Oberalppass d.	...	...	0750	0814	0850	0914	0950	1014	...	1050	1114	1150	1250	1350	1414	...	1450	1550	1650	1750	1850	...	...	...	...
19	Sedrun 🚗 d.	0615	0705	0816	...	0916	...	1016	...	...	1116	...	1216	1316	1416	...	...	1516	1616	1716	1816	1916	...	2001	2101	2201
29	**Disentis / Mustér** a.	0638	0725	0836	...	0936	...	1036	...	...	1136	...	1236	1336	1436	...	...	1536	1636	1736	1836	1936	...	2021	2121	2221

	🚌	n	r												w◇					🚌	🚌		🚌v	🚌v	🚌q
Disentis / Mustér d.	0640	0708	0714	0814	0914	...	1014	1114	1214	...	1314	1414	1514	...	...	1614	1714	1814	...	1919	2022	...	2122	2222	0015
Sedrun 🚗 d.	0650	0731	0731	0831	0931	...	1031	1131	1231	...	1331	1431	1531	...	...	1631	1731	1831	...	1936	2038	...	2138	2238	0031
Oberalppass d.	...	0753	0753	0853	0953	...	1053	1153	1253	...	1353	1453	1553	...	1620	1653	1753	1853	...	...	...	...	...	...	...
Andermatt 🚗 a.	...	0822	0822	0922	1022	...	1122	1222	1322	...	1422	1522	1622	...	1653	1722	1822	1922	...	...	...	...	...	...	...

DISENTIS - CHUR

km			⚒								
0	**Disentis / Mustér** d.	0544	0615	0644	0744	and	1744	1844	1944	2044	...
12	Trun d.	0600	0629	0700	0800	every	1800	1900	2000	2100	...
30	Ilanz d.	0624	0653	0724	0824	hour	1824	1924	2024	2124	...
49	Reichenau-Tamins d.	0650	0716x	0750	0849	until	1849	1949	2049	2150	...
59	**Chur** a.	0703	0732	0803	0901		1901	2001	2101	2203	...

	⚒									
Chur d.	0611	0656	0756	0856	and	1856	1956	2059	2259	...
Reichenau-Tamins d.	0625	0705	0805	0905	every	1905	2005	2113	2311	...
Ilanz d.	0653	0733	0833	0933	hour	1933	2033	2140	2333	...
Trun d.	0714	0754	0854	0954	until	1954	2054	2158	2351	...
Disentis / Mustér a.	0731	0811	0911	1011		2011	2111	2217	0009	...

j – Arrive 2137.
n – Dec. 15 - May 9, Oct. 27 - Dec. 13.
q – ⑥⑦ Dec. 15 - Mar. 30.
r – May 10 - Oct. 26.
t – ⑤ Dec. 20 - Mar. 21, May 16 - Oct. 24.
v – Dec. 15 - Apr. 21.
w – Dec. 21 - Mar. 23.

x – Stops only on request.
z – Connection by 🚌.
◧ – Calls to pick up only.
⊡ – Calls to set down only.
◇ – Subject to favourable weather conditions.
§ – Realp is a request stop.

△ – Additional services Zermatt - Visp: 1113, 1213, 1613, 1713, 1813.
▽ – Additional services Visp - Zermatt: 0843, 1043, 1243, 1843.
▲ – 🚂 service (summer only, not daily) runs Realp - Furka - Gletsch - Oberwald and v.v. Operator: Dampfbahn Furka-Bergstrecke ✆ 0848 000 144.
🚗 – Car-carrying shuttle available (see page 262).
* – For operators see foot of page.

578 ZERMATT - GORNERGRAT — Narrow gauge rack railway. GGB

Journey 33 minutes uphill, 44 minutes downhill, *9 km. Services are liable to be suspended in bad weather*

Dec. 15 - Apr. 27, June 7 - Oct. 19, Nov. 29 - Dec. 13:
From Zermatt: 0700, 0800, 0824, 0848, 0912**x***, 0936**x***, 1000**x***, 1024**x***, 1048**x***, 1112**x***, 1136, 1200, 1224, 1248, 1312, 1336, 1400, 1424, 1448, 1512, 1536, 1600, 1624, 1712, 1800**m**, 1924**p**.
From Gornergrat: 0735, 0843, 0907, 0931, 0955, 1019, 1043, 1107, 1131, 1155, 1219, 1243, 1307, 1331, 1355, 1419, 1443, 1507, 1531, 1555, 1619, 1643, 1707, 1755, 1857**m**, 2007**p**.

Apr. 28 - June 6, Oct. 20 - Nov. 28:
From Zermatt: 0700**r**, 0824, 0936**q**, 1024, 1136, 1224, 1336, 1424, 1536**q**, 1624, 1712**q**, 1800**q**.
From Gornergrat: 0735**r**, 0931, 1019**q**, 1131, 1219, 1331, 1419, 1531, 1619**q**, 1707, 1755**q**, 1857**q**.

m – Dec. 15 - Apr. 27, June 7 - Oct. 19.
p – Dec. 15 - Apr. 21, June 20 - Sept. 21.
q – Apr. 28 - June 6, Oct. 20 - Nov. 2.
r – Daily Apr. 28 - June 6, Oct. 20 - Nov. 2; ①–⑤ Nov. 3-28.
x – Not Apr. 22-27.
* – Duplicated by non-stop journeys Dec. 22 - Apr.
(journey 29 minutes).

* – Operators: MGB, Zermatt - Andermatt / Göschenen - Disentis; RhB, Disentis - Chur.

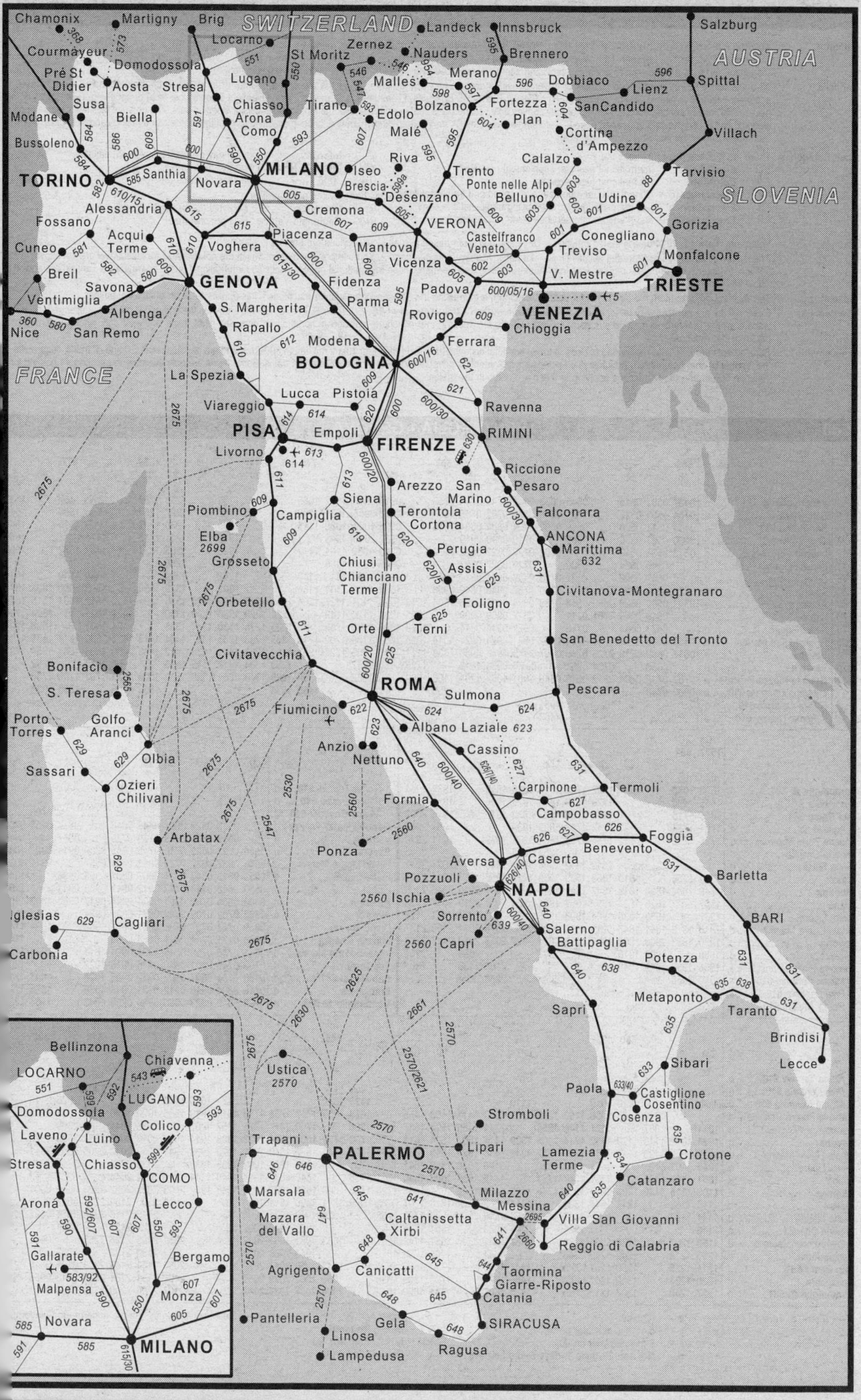
SWITZERLAND
AUSTRIA
SLOVENIA
FRANCE
Chamonix
Martigny
Brig
Locarno
Landeck
Innsbruck
Salzburg
Courmayeur
Domodossola
Zernez
Nauders
Brennero
Pré St Didier
Aosta
Stresa
Lugano
St Moritz
Malles
Merano
Dobbiaco
Lienz
Spittal
Susa
Biella
Chiasso
Arona
Como
Tirano
Edolo
Bolzano
Fortezza
SanCandido
Modane
Bussoleno
Malé
Plan
Cortina d'Ampezzo
Villach
Riva
Calalzo
TORINO
Santhia
Novara
MILANO
Iseo
Brescia
Desenzano
Trento
Ponte nelle Alpi
Belluno
Tarvisio
Udine
Alessandria
Cremona
Fossano
Acqui Terme
Piacenza
VERONA
Castelfranco Veneto
Conegliano
Gorizia
Cuneo
Voghera
Mantova
Vicenza
Treviso
Monfalcone
Breil
Savona
GENOVA
Fidenza
Padova
V. Mestre
TRIESTE
Ventimiglia
Albenga
Parma
VENEZIA
Nice
San Remo
S. Margherita
Rapallo
Rovigo
Chioggia
Modena
Ferrara
BOLOGNA
La Spezia
Viareggio
Lucca
Pistoia
Ravenna
PISA
Empoli
FIRENZE
RIMINI
Livorno
Riccione
Pesaro
Arezzo
San Marino
Siena
Piombino
Campiglia
Terontola Cortona
Falconara
Elba
ANCONA
Marittima
Grosseto
Perugia
Chiusi Chianciano Terme
Assisi
Civitanova-Montegranaro
Orbetello
Foligno
Orte
Terni
San Benedetto del Tronto
Civitavecchia
Bonifacio
S. Teresa
ROMA
Sulmona
Pescara
Fiumicino
Porto Torres
Golfo Aranci
Albano Laziale
Anzio
Nettuno
Cassino
Olbia
Sassari
Ozieri Chilivani
Carpinone
Termoli
Formia
Campobasso
Arbatax
Foggia
Benevento
Ponza
Aversa
Caserta
Pozzuoli
NAPOLI
Barletta
Ischia
Iglesias
Cagliari
Sorrento
Salerno
Battipaglia
BARI
Carbonia
Capri
Potenza
Metaponto
Taranto
Sapri
Brindisi
Lecce
Sibari
Ustica
Paola
Castiglione Cosentino
Cosenza
Stromboli
Trapani
PALERMO
Lipari
Lamezia Terme
Crotone
Marsala
Milazzo
Messina
Catanzaro
Mazara del Vallo
Caltanissetta Xirbi
Villa San Giovanni
Reggio di Calabria
Agrigento
Canicatti
Taormina
Giarre-Riposto
Catania
Pantelleria
Gela
SIRACUSA
Linosa
Ragusa
Lampedusa
Bellinzona
Chiavenna
LOCARNO
LUGANO
Domodossola
Colico
Laveno
Luino
Stresa
Chiasso
COMO
Arona
Lecco
Gallarate
Bergamo
Malpensa
Monza
Novara
MILANO

ITALY

Operator: Services are operated by Trenitalia, a division of Ferrovie dello Stato Italiane S.p.a. (FS), unless otherwise noted: www.trenitalia.com.
Trenord is a joint venture between Trenitalia and Ferrovie Nord Milano (LeNord) that operates local services, mainly in the Lombardia region: www.trenord.it. Nuovo Trasporto Viaggiatori (NTV) is an open-access operator providing alternative services over the high-speed network: www.italotreno.it.

Services: All trains convey First and Second classes of travel unless otherwise shown by a figure "2" at the top of the column, or in a note in the Table heading. Four classes of accommodation is available on Frecciarossa (*FR*) services: Executive, Business, Premium and Standard class. Overnight sleeping car (🛏) or couchette (▬) trains do not necessarily convey seating accommodation or may convey only second class seats - refer to individual footnotes. Excelsior sleeping cars offer en-suite facilities. Descriptions of sleeping and couchette cars appear on page 8. Refreshment services (✕ or 🍸) where known, may only be available for part of the journey, and may be added to or taken away from trains during the currency of the timetable.

Train Categories: There are 8 categories of express train:

EC	**EuroCity**	international express; supplement payable.
EN	**EuroNight**	international night express.
FA	**Frecciargento**	tilting trains used on both high-speed and traditional lines.
FB	**Frecciabianca**	fast premium fare services using traditional lines.
FR	**Frecciarossa**	fast premium fare services using high-speed lines.
IC	**InterCity**	internal day express; supplement payable.
ICN	**InterCity Notte**	internal night express.
ITA	**.italo**	high-speed service (operated by NTV).

Other services are classified:

R	**Regionale**	Regional (local) train.
RV	**Regionale Veloce**	Fast regional train.

Timings: Valid from **June 15, 2014** unless stated otherwise. Days and dates of running and all local services are subject to alteration.
Trains may be cancelled or altered at holiday times – for public holiday dates see page 2. Some international trains which are not available for local travel are not shown in this section; these include some sleeper services from Austria, France and Germany – see International pages. Trains and international buses operating via Tarvisio are shown in Table **88**.

Tickets: Tickets must be date-stamped by the holder before boarding the train using the self-service validating machines – this applies to all tickets except passes.

Reservations: Reservations are **compulsory** for all journeys by services for which a **train category** (*EC, EN, FA, FB, FR, IC, ICN*) is shown in the timing column and passengers boarding without a prior reservation may be surcharged. Reservations for sleeping and couchette car accommodation on domestic night trains are valid only when presented with personal identification.

Supplements Supplements are calculated according to class of travel and total distance travelled (minimum 10km, maximum 3000km), and are payable on all *EC* and *IC* trains, regardless of the number of changes of train. A higher fare (including supplement) is payable for travel by *FA, FB* and *FR* trains. Some trains are only available to passengers holding long distance tickets and the restrictions applying to these are noted in the tables.

580 VENTIMIGLIA - GENOVA

km		*IC* 655 ⚒	⚒			Ⓐ	*IC* 505	2	Ⓒ	Ⓐ 2	*IC* 663	⚒ 2	⚒ 2	2	Ⓐ 2	*IC* 745	Ⓒ	Ⓐ	2	⚒ 2	† 2	*IC* 1539 †		2	*IC* 677	Ⓒ	p T2
0	**Ventimiglia** 🏛 **581** d.	0437	0502	0515	...	0545	0633	0646	0748	0748	0858	...	0910	0948j	1022	1059	...	...	1150	...	1218	1250	...	1357x	1459	...	1533
5	Bordighera d.	0444	0509	0522	...	|	0640	0655	0755	0755	0905	...	0918	0955j	1031	1106	...	...	1157	...	1227	1257	...	1404x	1506	...	1540
16	**San Remo 581** d.	0454	0517	0530	...	0559	0650	0704	0804	0804	0915	...	0926	1003j	1039	1115	...	...	1205	...	1235	1307	...	1412x	1515	...	1549
24	Taggia-Arma d.	0500	0523	0536	...	0605	|	0710	0810	0810	|	...	0932	1010j	1045	|	...	...	1211	...	1241	1313	...	1414	|	...	1554
39	Imperia Porto Maurizio d.	0513	0535	0548	...	|	0707	0722	0822	0822	0932	...	0943	1032	1101	1132	...	...	1225	...	1253	1331	...	1432	1532	...	1606
41	Imperia Oneglia d.	|	0540	0554	...	0620	|	0729	0827	0827	|	...	0948	1035	1106	|	...	...	1234	...	1258	|	...	1437	|	...	|
46	Diano Marina d.	|	0547	0602	...	0627	0715	0736	0834	0834	0940	...	0955	1042	1113	1140	...	...	1242	...	1305	|	...	1444	1540	...	1614
61	Alassio d.	0533	0600	0621	...	0650	0730	0757	0849	0849	0956	...	1012	1056	1131	1156	...	...	1302	...	1329	1355	...	1503	1556	1608	1642
67	**Albenga** d.	0541	0606	0628	0650	0658	0738	0804	0855	0855	1004	1013	1020	1104	1137	1204	1210	1210	1309	1324	1336	1404	1410	1512	1604	1615	1649
76	Loano d.	|	0619	0649	0701	0711	|	0817	0909	0909	|	1023	1035	1120	1149	|	1220	1220	1320	1339	1350	|	1420	1521	|	1624	1700
79	Pietra Ligure d.	|	0623	0654	|	0715	|	0822	0914	0914	|	1028	1046	1130	1153	|	1225	1225	1330	1347	1355	|	1424	1531	|	1628	1704
85	Finale Ligure Marina d.	0559	0630	0701	0710	0724	0752	0831	0921	0921	1018	1035	1053	1138	1202	1218	1233	1233	1338	1357	1404	1418	1431	1539	1618	1635	1711
108	**Savona** d.	0617	0650	0719	0726	0745	0807	0900k	0941	0958	1033	1111	1110	1203	1225	1233	1251	1255	1403	1430	1422	1433	1450	1603	1633	1654	1727
120	Varazze d.	|	0658	|	0734	0757	|	0913k	0956	1013	|	1125	...	1217	...	|	1259	1304	1417	1445	1435	|	1459	1617	|	1702	...
151	**Genova** Piazza Principe § a.	0702	0738	0804	0812	0840	0848	1001	1052	1101	1106	1209	...	1302	...	1306	1329	1346	1501	1539	1539	1504	1532	1707	1706	1730	...
	Milano Centrale **610** a.	0900	0940	...	...	...	|	...	...	...	1250	...	...	...	...	1450	1535	...	...	...	...	1650	1735	...	1855	1935	...
	Pisa Centrale **610** a.	...	...	...	...	...	1056	...	...	...	...	...	...	...	...	...	...	...	...	...	...	...	...	...	...	...	...
	Roma Termini **610** a.	...	...	...	...	...	1403	...	...	...	...	...	...	...	...	...	...	...	...	...	...	...	...	...	...	...	...

	IC 1537 Ⓒ	*IC* 681 Ⓐ	Ⓐ	Ⓒ	† T2	⚒ T2	†p 2	⚒ 2	*IC* 747		T2	2
Ventimiglia 🏛 **581** d.	1638	1658	...	...	1722	1722	1816	1816	1859	...	1932	1951
Bordighera d.	1645	1705	...	...	1729	1729	1824	1825	1906	...	1939	1958
San Remo 581 d.	1655	1715	...	...	1738	1738	1833	1833	1915	...	1948	2007
Taggia-Arma d.	1701	1721	...	...	1743	1743	1839	1839	|	...	1954	2014
Imperia Porto Maurizio d.	1720	1735	...	...	1755	1755	1851	1851	1932	...	2011	2030
Imperia Oneglia d.	|	|	...	...	|	|	1855	1856	|	...	|	2035
Diano Marina d.	|	|	...	...	1812	1812	1904	1904	1940	...	2023	2041
Alassio d.	1741	1756	...	1810	1839	1839	1933	1933	1956	...	2041	2101
Albenga d.	1749	1804	1810	1818	1847	1847	1940	1941	2004	2010	2048	2109
Loano d.	1757	|	1825	1827	1857	1857	1951	1954	|	2019	2057	2123
Pietra Ligure d.	1807	|	1833	1835	1904	1908	1955	1958	|	2024	2101	2128
Finale Ligure Marina d.	1815	1818	1841	1843	1911	1915	2002	2005	2018	2031	2109	2137
Savona d.	1830	1833	1900	1902	1927	1927	2021	2022	2033	2050	2127	2203
Varazze d.	1838	|	1908	1910	...	...	2028	...	|	2058	...	2217
Genova Piazza Principe § a.	1906	1906	1949	1949	...	...	|	...	2106	2136	...	2301
Milano Centrale **610** a.	2050	2050	...	...	...	...	2255v	...	2250	2335n	...	...
Pisa Centrale **610** a.	...	...	...	...	...	...	...	...	...	...	...	...
Roma Termini **610** a.	...	...	...	...	...	...	...	...	...	...	...	...

	Ⓐ 2	⑥ 2	Ⓐ 2	2	⚒ 2	† 2	T2	⚒ 2	*IC* 654	Ⓑ 2
Roma Termini **610** d.	...	...	...	...	...	...	...	...	...	...
Pisa Centrale **610** d.	...	...	...	...	...	...	...	...	...	...
Milano Centrale **610** d.	...	...	...	...	...	...	...	...	0705	...
Genova Piazza Principe § d.	...	0522	0522	0607	0646	0646	...	0814	0855	090
Varazze d.	...	0605	0605	0653	0729	0729	...	0857	|	094
Savona d.	0525	0622	0622	0710	0745	0745	0839	0914	0929	100
Finale Ligure Marina d.	0543	0637	0637	0729	0801	0801	0857	0930	0941	103
Pietra Ligure d.	0553	0643	0643	0737	0807	0807	0903	0936	|	104
Loano d.	0559	0648	0648	0742	0812	0812	0908	0941	|	105
Albenga d.	0609	0655	0702	0805	0824	0824	0917	0950	1003	110
Alassio d.	0622	0702	0709	0812	0831	0831	0934	...	1011	111
Diano Marina d.	0639	0724	0737	0835	0851	0851	1004	...	1024	114
Imperia Oneglia d.	0646	0731	0744	0841	0858	0858	|	...	|	114
Imperia Porto Maurizio d.	0651	0736	0750	0845	0904	0904	1011	...	1033	115
Taggia-Arma d.	0702	0748	0801	0856	0916	0916	1022	...	|	120
San Remo 581 d.	0708	0754	0807	0902	0922	0925	1028	...	1047	121
Bordighera d.	0718	0804	0816	0912	0931	0938	1038	...	1056	122
Ventimiglia 🏛 **581** a.	0728	0810	0823	0920	0939	0950	1045	...	1104	123

	†p 2	p T2		*IC* 660 Ⓐ	*IC* 1536 Ⓒ	2		*IC* 742	2		Ⓐ 2	Ⓒ 2	Ⓐ T2		*IC* 744	⚒	Ⓑ	⑥	Ⓐ	Ⓒ	*IC* 676	Ⓐ 2	Ⓒ 2	*IC* 518		*IC* 690	
Roma Termini **610** d.	...	...	...	...	...	...	...	...	...	...	...	...	...	...	...	...	...	...	...	...	...	...	...	1557	...	...	...
Pisa Centrale **610** d.	...	...	...	...	...	...	...	...	...	...	...	...	...	...	...	...	...	...	...	...	...	...	...	1902	...	...	...
Milano Centrale **610** d.	0805v	...	...	0910	0910	...	...	1110	...	...	...	...	...	1425	1510	...	...	...	...	1625	1705	...	...	|	2025	2110	...
Genova Piazza Principe § d.	|	...	1016	1055	1055	1100	1215	1255	1300	1411	1453	1453	...	1626	1655	1717	1738	1738	1814	1830	1855	1900	1900	2122	2231	2255	...
Varazze d.	1011	...	1057	|	1121	1144	1256	|	1344	1455	1522	1537	...	1656	|	1756	1817	1825	1857	1902	|	1938	1944	|	2309	|	...
Savona d.	1024	1039	1110	1129	1132	1214	1306	1329	1414	1507	1534	1613	1639	1706	1729	1807	1829	1838	1908	1914	1929	2012	2007	2157	2333	2329	...
Finale Ligure Marina d.	1039	1056	1123	1141	1144	1236	1322	1341	1434	1524	1552	1635	1654	1723	1741	1827	1846	1900	1929	1933	1941	2032	2032	2209	2351	2341	...
Pietra Ligure d.	1045	1102	1131	|	1151	1242	1329	|	1440	1530	1558	1641	1705	1731	|	1834	1852	1909	1935	1939	|	2038	2038	|	2357	|	...
Loano d.	1051	1107	1136	|	1157	1247	1334	|	1445	1536	1603	1646	1711	1736	|	1840	1857	1914	1940	1944	|	2044	2044	|	0002	|	...
Albenga d.	1103	1115	1146	1203	1207	1254	1345	1403	1454	1546	1611	1653	1728	1748	1803	1853	1907	1925	1948	1952	2003	2052	2052	2223	0010	0001	...
Alassio d.	1110	1132	...	1211	1215	1301	...	1411	1502	1555c	1618	1703	1735y	1755c	1811	1900	1914	1934	...	...	2011	2100	2100	2231	0017	0009	...
Diano Marina d.	1141	1157	...	|	|	1317	...	1424	1516	...	1639	1728	1758	...	1824	1916	1941	2000	...	...	|	2115	2115	2244	0034	0022	...
Imperia Oneglia d.	1148	|	...	|	|	1325	...	|	1523	...	1651	1736	|	...	|	1923	1949	2007	...	...	|	2121	2121	|	0041	|	...
Imperia Porto Maurizio d.	1153	1207	...	1230	1236	1330	...	1433	1531	...	1657	1741	1807	...	1833	1931	1953	2012	...	...	2031	2125	2125	2253	|	0031	..
Taggia-Arma d.	1205	1218	...	1242	1248	1343	...	|	1544	...	1708	1753	1819	...	|	1943	2005	2023	...	...	2042	2136	2136	|	0057	|	..
San Remo 581 d.	1211	1225	...	1250	1257	1350x	...	1447	1550	...	1714	1800	1826	...	1847	1950	2011	2029	...	...	2050	2141	2141	2309	0103	0048	..
Bordighera d.	1220	1234	...	1300	1307	1400x	...	1456	1600	...	1723	1809	1836	...	1856	2000	2020	2039	...	...	2100	2151	2151	2319	0113	0058	..
Ventimiglia 🏛 **581** a.	1227	1240	...	1307	1315	1410x	...	1504	1607	...	1731	1820	1842	...	1904	2007	2027	2049	...	...	2107	2200	2200	2326	0120	0105	..

T – From/to Torino.
c – Ⓒ only.
j – 5–6 minutes later on ⚒.
k – 8 minutes later on Ⓐ.
n – Not Apr. 20, June 1, days before holidays.
p – From Apr. 20.
v – Milano **Rogoredo**.
x – Not Ⓒ from Apr. 20.
y – Depart 1742 on Ⓒ.
§ – Local services may use the underground platforms

VENTIMIGLIA and NICE - CUNEO 581

2nd class only

km																									
			d	ew		z		fx		y			z		z		• f	d	z			ew		y	z
	Ventimiglia	d.	...	...	...	...	...	...	...	...	1030	...	...	...	...	...	...	...	...	...	1840	...	...	...	...
0	**Nice** Ville	d.	...	0613	...	0736	...	0823	...	0913	|	...	1213	...	1501	...	1634	...	1721	...	|	1808	...	1856	1945
34	Sospel	d.	...	0722	...	0828	...	0914	...	1001	|	...	1306	...	1552	...	1726	...	1816	...	|	1906	...	1946	2037
43	Breil sur Roya	a.	...	0734	...	0840	...	0927	...	1013	1103	...	1318	...	1604	...	1738	...	1828	...	1912	1918	...	1959	2049
	Breil sur Roya	d.	...	...	...	...	...	...	...	1017	1104	...	1320	...	...	...	...	...	...	...	1913	...	...	...	...
	Tende	d.	...	...	...	...	...	...	...	1114	1155	...	1417	...	...	...	...	...	...	...	2004	...	...	...	...
	Limone 🏔	d.	0635	...	0735	...	0935	...	1135	...	1227	1335	...	1535	...	1735	...	1835	...	1935	2035	...	2135	...	...
	Cuneo	a.	0711	...	0811	...	1011	...	1211	...	1303	1411	...	1611	...	1811	...	1911	...	2011	2118	...	2211	...	...
	Fossano **582**	a.	...	...	0835	...	1035	...	1235	...	...	1435	...	1635	...	1835	...	...	...	2035	...	...	2235	...	...

km																									
			fq	ep		fq	d	t			z		z		fq			z		z		z	d	z	
	Fossano **582**	d.	...	...	...	...	...	...	...	...	...	0925	...	1125	...	1325	...	...	1525	...	1725	...	...	...	1925
0	**Cuneo**	d.	...	...	0551	...	0651	...	0751	0851	...	0951	...	1151	...	1351	1413	...	1551	...	1751	...	1851	...	1951
29	Limone 🏔	d.	...	...	0625	...	0725	...	0827	0925	...	1025	...	1225	...	1425	1449	...	1625	...	1825	...	1925	...	2025
47	Tende	d.	...	...	...	...	...	...	0856	...	...	...	1157	...	...	...	1517	1548	...	...	...	...	...	...	...
75	Breil sur Roya	a.	...	...	...	...	...	...	0947	...	...	...	1250	...	...	...	1606	1641	...	...	...	...	...	...	...
75	Breil sur Roya	d.	0545	0612	...	0709	...	0750	0948	...	1040	...	1253	...	1539	...	1607	1650	...	1739	...	1829	...	2000	...
	Sospel	d.	0558	0625	...	0722	...	0803	|	...	1052	...	1306	...	1552	...	|	1702	...	1751	...	1841	...	2012	...
*	**Nice** Ville	a.	0650	0716	...	0813	...	0900	|	...	1143	...	1356	...	1646	...	|	1755	...	1844	...	1931	...	2102	...
96	**Ventimiglia**	a.	...	...	...	...	...	...	1020	...	...	...	...	...	...	...	1639	...	...	...	...	...	...	...	...

d – ①–⑥ (not Italian public holidays).
e – ①–⑤ (not French public holidays).
f – ①–⑥ (not French public holidays).
p – Not Apr. 19 - May 2.
q – Not Apr. 20 - May 2.
t – Not Apr. 21 - May 3.
w – Not Apr. 19 - May 4.
y – Not Apr. 21 - May 2.
z – Not Apr. 22 - May 2.
• – Subject to alteration during periods of planned engineering work.

TORINO - CUNEO and SAVONA 582

Most trains 2nd class only

km																										
					†q	†q	V			†qL		⚒	†q		Vq	p										
0	**Torino** Porta Nuova	d.	0525	...	0555	0610	0625	...	...	0655	0725	...	0750	...	0825	0825	...	0925	...	1025	...	...	1125	...	1225	...
52	Savigliano	d.	0603	...	0635	0654	0703	...	...	0735	0803	...	0837	...	0903	0903	...	1003	...	1103	...	...	1203	...	1303	...
64	Fossano	d.	0612	0622	0643	0703	0713	0725	...	0743	0812	0822	0847	...	0913	0913	0925	1012	1022	1113	1125	...	1212	1222	1313	1325
90	**Cuneo**	a.	0636	|	|	|	|	0749	...	|	0836	|	|	...	|	|	0949	1036	|	|	1149	...	1236	|	|	1349
83	Mondovi	d.	...	0640	0659	0715	0728	...	...	0759	...	0840	0902	...	0928	0928	...	...	1040	1128	...	...	...	1240	1328	...
103	Ceva	d.	...	0700	0716	0729	0743	...	...	0817	...	0900	0921	...	0943	0943	...	...	1100	1143	...	...	...	1300	1342	...
153	**Savona**	a.	...	0752d	0803	0818	0836	...	...	0912	...	...	1007	...	1036	1036	...	...	...	1236	...	...	...	...	1436	...

				V										Ⓐ						⚒				
Torino Porta Nuova	d.	1325	...	1425	...	...	1525	...	1625	...	...	1725	...	1750	1825	...	...	1855	1925	1955	2025	...	2125	2325	...
Savigliano	d.	1403	...	1503	...	...	1603	...	1703	...	...	1803	...	1829	1903	...	...	1931	2003	2032	2103	...	2203	0014	...
Fossano	d.	1412	1422	1513	1525	...	1612	1622	1713	1725	...	1812	1822	1837	1913	1925	...	1941	2012	2041	2113	2125	2212	0022	...
Cuneo	a.	1436	|	|	1549	...	1636	|	|	1749	...	1836	|	1901	|	1949	...	|	2036	|	|	2149	2236	0046	...
Mondovi	d.	...	1440	1528	...	...	...	1640	1728	...	...	...	1840	...	1928	...	...	1956	...	2100	2128	...	...	...	...
Ceva	d.	...	1500	1543	...	...	...	1700	1743	...	...	...	1900	...	1943	...	...	2018	...	2120	2143	...	...	...	...
Savona	a.	...	...	1636	...	...	...	...	1836	...	...	...	...	...	2036	...	...	2112	...	...	2236	...	...	...	...

		Ⓐ					⚒	⚒			⚒								⚒					
Savona	d.	...	...	...	...	0530	...	...	...	...	...	...	0730	...	0808d	...	...	0930	...	...	...	...	1130	...	...
Ceva	d.	...	...	0520	...	0618	...	0650	0700	...	...	...	0818	...	0900	...	...	1018	1100	...	...	...	1218	1300	...
Mondovi	d.	...	...	0540	...	0633	...	0706	0720	...	...	...	0833	...	0920	...	...	1033	1120	...	...	...	1233	1320	...
Cuneo	d.	0424	0524	|	0612	|	0654	|	|	0724	0751	0812	|	...	|	0924	1012	|	|	1124	...	1212	|	|	1324
Fossano	d.	0448	0547	0558	0635	0647	0718	0723	0738	0747	0811	0835	0847	...	0938	0947	1035	1047	1138	1147	...	1235	1247	1338	1346
Savigliano	d.	0456	0556	...	...	0656	0726	0733	...	0756	0821	...	0856	...	...	0956	...	1056	...	1156	...	...	1256	...	1354
Torino Porta Nuova	a.	0535	0635	...	...	0735	0805	0815	...	0835	0905	...	0935	...	...	1035	...	1135	...	1235	...	...	1335	...	1435

										†q		p	Vq	†q			†q		V			†qL		V	
Savona	d.	...	1328	...	...	...	1530	...	...	1645	...	1730	1730	1749	...	...	1845	...	1930	...	...	2029	...	2130	...
Ceva	d.	...	1418	1500	...	...	1618	1700	...	1736	...	1818	1818	1838	1900	...	1938	...	2018	2100	...	2115	...	2218	...
Mondovi	d.	...	1433	1520	...	...	1633	1720	...	1750	...	1833	1833	1853	1920	...	1953	...	2033	2120	...	2133	...	2233	...
Cuneo	d.	1412	|	|	1524	1612	|	|	1724	|	1812	|	|	|	|	1924	|	2012	|	|	2124	|	2212	|	...
Fossano	d.	1435	1447	1538	1547	1635	1647	1738	1747	1802	1835	1847	1847	1907	1938	1947	2011	2035	2047	2138	2147	2155	2235	2247	...
Savigliano	d.	...	1456	...	1556	...	1656	...	1756	1810	...	1856	1856	1915	...	1956	2020	...	2056	...	2156	2205	...	2256	...
Torino Porta Nuova	a.	...	1535	...	1635	...	1735	...	1835	1850	...	1935	1935	1955	...	2035	2110	...	2135	...	2235	2250	...	2335	...

– [2] Torino - Ventimiglia - Imperia and v.v.
– From/to Ventimiglia.
d – ⚒ only.
p – Until Apr. 19.
q – From Apr. 20.

MILANO MALPENSA AEROPORTO ✈ 583

LeNord

								x		and at	x				x										
Milano Centrale	d.	0525	0625	0725	0825	0925	...	0955	1025	the same	1455	1525	...	1625	1655	...	1725	1825	...	1925	2025	...	2125	2225	...
Milano Porta Garibaldi	d.	0535	0635	0735	0835	0935	...	1005	1035	minutes	1505	1535	...	1635	1705	...	1735	1835	...	1935	2035	...	2135	2235	...
Milano Bovisa	d.	0542	0642	0742	0842	0942	...	1012	1042	past each	1512	1542	...	1642	1712	...	1742	1842	...	1942	2042	...	2142	2242	...
Malpensa Aeroporto ✈	a.	0617	0717	0817	0917	1017	...	1041	1117	hour until	1541	1617	...	1717	1741	...	1817	1917	...	2017	2117	...	2217	2317	...

						x		x		x				x	and at		x					and at		
Malpensa Aeroporto ✈	d.	0543	0643	0743	0843	0919	0943	1019	1043	1119	1143	...	1243	1319	the same	1543	1619	...	1643	...	1743	the same	2243	...
Milano Bovisa	a.	0618	0718	0818	0918	0948	1018	1048	1118	1146	1218	...	1318	1348	minutes	1618	1648	...	1718	...	1818	minutes	2318	...
Milano Porta Garibaldi	a.	0625	0725	0825	0925	0955	1025	1055	1125	1153	1225	...	1325	1355	past each	1625	1655	...	1725	...	1825	past each	2325	...
Milano Centrale	a.	0635	0735	0835	0935	1005	1035	1105	1135	1203	1235	...	1335	1405	hour until	1635	1705	...	1737	...	1835	hour until	2335	...

All services below operate as *Malpensa Express*. Special fare payable.

Milano Cadorna	d.	0428	0458	0528	0558	0628	0658	0728	0758	0828	0858	0928	0958	1028	1058	1128	1158	1228	1258	1328	1358	1428	1458	1528	1558	1628	1658	...
Milano Bovisa	d.	0433	0503	|	0603	|	0703	|	0803	0833	|	|	1003	|	|	|	|	|	1303	1333	1403	|	|	|	|	|	|	...
Malpensa Aeroporto ✈	a.	0504	0534	0557	0634	0657	0734	0757	0834	0904	0927	0957	1034	1057	1127	1157	1227	1257	1334	1404	1434	1457	1527	1557	1627	1657	1727	...

Milano Cadorna	d.	1728	1758	and each	2228	2258	...	2328	...	...	...
Milano Bovisa	d.	1733	1803	hour	2233	2303	...	2333	...	...	...
Malpensa Aeroporto ✈	a.	1804	1834	until	2304	2334	...	0004	...	...	...

Malpensa Aeroporto ✈	d.	0526	0556	0626	0656	0726	0756	0826	0903	0933	and each
Milano Bovisa	a.	0556	0626	0656	0726	0756	0826	0856	|	|	hour
Milano Cadorna	a.	0602	0632	0702	0732	0802	0832	0902	0932	1002	until

Malpensa Aeroporto ✈	d.	1203	1233	...	1303	1326	1403	1426	1503	1533	1603	1633	1703	1726	1803	1826	1903	1926	2003	2033	2103	2126	2156	2226	2256	2326	2356	0026
Milano Bovisa	a.	|	|	...	|	1356	|	1456	|	|	|	|	|	1756	|	1856	|	1956	|	|	|	2156	2226	2256	2326	2356	0026	0056
Milano Cadorna	a.	1232	1302	...	1332	1402	1432	1502	1532	1602	1632	1702	1732	1802	1832	1902	1932	2002	2032	2102	2132	2202	2232	2302	2332	0002	0032	0102

– *Malpensa Express*. Special fare payable.

Operator: Ferrovie Nord Milano (LeNord), Piazzale Cadorna 14, 20123 Milano. ✆ + 39 02 85 111, fax: + 39 02 85 11 708, www.trenord.it

584 TORINO - OULX - BARDONECCHIA

2nd class only

km																									
		⚒	⚒	†	⚒	⚒		⚒	†	⚒	⚒		⚒	†	⚒	⚒		⚒	†	⚒	⚒		⚒	†	⚒
0	**Torino** Porta Nuova d.	0445	0520	0545	0545	0620	0645	0720	0745	0745	0820	0845	0920	0945	0945	1020	1045	1120	1145	1145	1220	1245	1320	1345	1345
46	Bussoleno d.	0542	0604	0631	0642	0704	0742	0804	0831	0842	0904	0942	1004	1031	1042	1104	1142	1204	1231	1242	1304	1342	1404	1431	1442
	Susa a.	0551	|	|	0651	|	0751	|	|	0851	|	0951	|	|	1051	|	1151	|	|	1251	|	1351	|	|	1451
76	Oulx-Claviere-Sestriere ▲ d.	...	0632	0700	...	0732	...	0831	0900	...	0932	...	1032	1100	...	1132	...	1232	1300	...	1332	...	1432	1500	...
87	Bardonecchia d.	...	0644	0712	...	0744	...	0842	0912	...	0944	...	1044	1112	...	1144	...	1244	1312	...	1344	...	1444	1512	...

km																									
		⚒		⚒	†	⚒	⚒		⚒	†	⚒	⚒		⚒	†	⚒	⚒			⚒	†	⚒	⚒		
	Torino Porta Nuova d.	1420	1445	1520	1545	1545	1620	1645	1718	1745	1745	1820	1845	1920	1945	1945	2020	2045	...	2120	2145	2145	2220	2245	...
0	Bussoleno d.	1504	1542	1604	1631	1642	1704	1742	1802	1831	1842	1904	1942	2004	2031	2042	2104	2142	...	2204	2231	2242	2304	2340	...
8	Susa a.	|	1551	|	|	1651	|	1751	|	|	1851	|	1951	|	|	2051	|	2151	...	|	|	2251	|	...	...
	Oulx-Claviere-Sestriere ▲ d.	1532	...	1632	1700	...	1732	...	1830	1900	...	1932	...	2032	2100	...	2132	...	...	2232	2300	...	2332	...	...
	Bardonecchia d.	1544	...	1644	1712	...	1744	...	1842	1912	...	1944	...	2044	2112	...	2144	...	...	2244	2312	...	2344	...	...

	⚒	†	⚒	†	⚒	⚒	⚒	⚒	†	⚒		⚒	⚒	†		⚒		⚒	⚒	†	⚒		⚒	⚒	†
Bardonecchia d.	...	...	...	0510	0516	...	0616	...	0648	0716	...	0816	...	0848	...	0916	...	1016	...	1048	1118	...	1218	...	1248
Oulx-Claviere-Sestriere ▲ d.	...	...	...	0523	0529	...	0629	...	0701	0729	...	0829	...	0901	...	0929	...	1029	...	1101	1131	...	1231	...	1301
Susa d.	...	...	0509	|	|	0609	|	0709	|	|	0809	|	0909	|	...	|	1009	|	1109	|	|	1209	|	1309	|
Bussoleno d.	0419	0450	0519	0552	0558	0619	0658	0719	0730	0758	0819	0858	0919	0930	...	0958	1019	1058	1119	1130	1158	1219	1258	1319	1330
Torino Porta Nuova a.	0515	0545	0615	0645	0640	0715	0740	0815	0815	0840	0915	0940	1015	1015	...	1040	1115	1140	1215	1215	1240	1315	1340	1415	1415

	⚒		⚒	⚒	†	⚒		⚒	⚒	†	⚒			⚒	⚒	†	⚒		⚒	⚒	†	⚒		⚒	
Bardonecchia d.	1316	...	1416	...	1448	1518	...	1616	...	1648	1716	...	...	1816	...	1848	1918	...	2016	...	2048	2116	...	2216	...
Oulx-Claviere-Sestriere ▲ d.	1329	...	1429	...	1501	1531	...	1629	...	1701	1729	...	...	1829	...	1901	1931	...	2029	...	2101	2129	...	2229	...
Susa d.	|	1409	|	1509	|	|	1609	|	1709	|	|	...	1809	|	1909	|	|	2009	|	2109	|	|	2209	|	...
Bussoleno d.	1358	1419	1458	1519	1530	1558	1619	1658	1719	1730	1758	...	1819	1858	1919	1930	1958	2019	2058	2119	2130	2158	2219	2258	...
Torino Porta Nuova a.	1440	1515	1540	1615	1615	1640	1715	1740	1815	1815	1840	...	1915	1940	2015	2015	2040	2115	2140	2215	2215	2240	2317	2340	...

▲ – Station for the resorts of Cesana, Claviere and Sestriere.

585 TORINO - MILANO

For high-speed services – see Table 600. For France-Italy *TGV* service – see Table 44

km																								
			FB 9707 T		*FB* 9709 🍸		*FB* 9713 🍸					*FB* 9723 🍸			*FB* 9727 🍸		*ICN* 795 ♦		*FB* 9733 🍸		*FB* 9737 T			
0	**Torino** Porta Nuova **586** d.	0454	0535	0554	0610	0649	0710	...	0754	0854	1054	1110	1154	1254	1310	...	1335	1354	1410	1449	1510	...	1554	1654
6	**Torino** Porta Susa **586** d.	0506	0544u	0606	0619u	0701	0719u	...	0806	0906	1106	1119u	1206	1306	1319u	...	1348u	1406	1419u	1501	1519u	...	1606	1706
29	Chivasso **586** d.	0520	|	0620	|	0715	|	...	0820	0920	1120	|	1220	1320	|	...	|	1420	|	1515	|	...	1620	1720
60	Santhià d.	0537	|	0637	|	0732	|	...	0837	0937	1137	|	1237	1337	|	...	|	1437	|	1532	|	...	1637	1737
79	Vercelli d.	0549	0624	0649	0659	0744	0759	...	0849	0949	1149	1159	1249	1349	1359	...	1429	1449	1459	1544	1559	...	1649	1749
101	Novara d.	0605	0638	0705	0713	0801	0813	...	0905	1005	1204	1213	1305	1405	1412	...	1444	1505	1513	1601	1613	...	1705	1805
153	**Milano** Centrale **605** a.	0646	0716	0746	0750	0841	0845	...	0946	1046	1246	1254	1346	1446	1450	...	1542g	1546	1550	1641	1645	...	1746	1846
	Venezia SL **605** a.	...	0958v	...	1040	...	1140	...	...	...	...	1540	...	...	1740	...	...	...	1840	...	1928v	...	...	...

	FB 9745 🍸			*FB* 9753 🍸			*ICN* 1911 ♦	2	
Torino Porta Nuova **586** d.	1710	1754	1854	1910	1954	2054	2125	2154	2254
Torino Porta Susa **586** d.	1719u	1806	1906	1919u	2006	2106	2140u	2206	2306
Chivasso **586** d.	|	1820	1920	|	2020	2120	|	2220	2320
Santhià d.	|	1837	1937	|	2037	2137	|	2237	2337
Vercelli d.	1759	1849	1949	1959	2049	2149	2222	2249	2349
Novara d.	1813	1905	2005	2013	2105	2205	2238	2305	0005
Milano Centrale **605** a.	1854	1946	2046	2054	2146	2246	2315g	2346	0046
Venezia SL **605** a.	2140	...	...	2340	...	...	...	...	...

			ICN 1910 ♦			*FB* 9702 🍸		*FB* 9710 T	
Venezia SL **605** d.	...	...	...	...	...	0620	...	0832v	...
Milano Centrale d.	0518	0618	0713g	0718	0818	0910	0918	1110	1118
Novara d.	0559	0659	0750	0759	0859	0948	0959	1148	1159
Vercelli d.	0614	0714	0806	0814	0914	1006	1014	1206	1214
Santhià d.	0625	0725	0829	0825	0925	|	1025	|	1225
Chivasso **586** d.	0644	0744	|	0844	0944	|	1044	|	1244
Torino Porta Susa **586** a.	0658	0758	0910s	0858	0958	1040s	1058	1240s	1258
Torino Porta Nuova **586** a.	0710	0810	0920	0910	1010	1050	1110	1250	1310

	FB 9712 🍸			*FB* 9716 T			*ICN* 794 ♦		*FB* 9726 🍸		*FB* 9728 🍸			*FB* 9732 🍸			*FB* 9740 🍸		*FB* 9746 🍸			⚒	2 ①	
Venezia SL **605** d.	0850	...	...	1132v	...	...	...	...	1320	...	1420	...	...	1520	...	...	1720	...	1820	...	...	...	...	...
Milano Centrale d.	1140	1218	1318	1410	...	1418	1443g	1518	1610	1618	1710	...	1718	1810	1818	1915	2006	2018	2110	2115	2218	2318	0018	...
Novara d.	1218	1259	1359	1448	...	1459	1519	1559	1648	1659	1748	...	1759	1848	1859	1957	2048	2059	2148	2157	2259	2359	0059	...
Vercelli d.	1231	1314	1414	1506	...	1514	1535	1614	1706	1714	1806	...	1814	1906	1914	2011	2106	2114	2206	2212	2314	0014	0116	...
Santhià d.	|	1325	1425	|	...	1525	|	1625	|	1725	|	...	1825	|	1925	2022	|	2125	|	2223	2325	0025	0127	...
Chivasso **586** d.	|	1344	1444	|	...	1544	|	1644	|	1744	|	...	1844	|	1944	2041	|	2144	|	2241	2344	0044	0148	...
Torino Porta Susa **586** a.	1310s	1358	1458	1540s	...	1558	1632s	1658	1740s	1758	1840s	...	1858	1940s	1958	2053	2140s	2158	2240s	2255	2358	0100	0206	...
Torino Porta Nuova **586** a.	1320	1410	1510	1550	...	1610	1645	1710	1750	1810	1850	...	1910	1950	2010	2105	2150	2210	2250	2307	0010	0110	...	...

♦ – **NOTES** (LISTED BY TRAIN NUMBER)

794 – 🛏 1, 2 cl., 🛌 2 cl. (4 berth) and (2) Reggio di Calabria - Milano - Torino.
795 – 🛏 1, 2 cl., 🛌 2 cl. (4 berth) and (2) Torino - Milano - Reggio di Calabria.
1910 – 🛌 2 cl. (4 berth) and (2) Salerno - Napoli - Milano - Torino.
1911 – 🛌 2 cl. (4 berth) and (2) Torino - Milano - Napoli - Salerno.

T – (12) and 🍸 Torino - Milano - Venezia Mestre - Trieste and v.v.

g – Milano **Porta Garibaldi**.
v – Venezia **Mestre**.

586 TORINO - AOSTA - PRÉ SAINT DIDIER

Most trains 2nd class only

km																										
							†	⚒	†	⚒	⚒		⚒	†	⚒			⚒				⚒		†	⚒	
0	**Torino** Porta Nuova **585** d.	...	0528	...	0728	0828	0928	1128	1128	...	1228	1328	1428	1428	...	...	1628	...	1728	...	1828	...	1928	2028	...	222
6	**Torino** Porta Susa **585** d.	...	0537	...	0737	0837	0937	1137	1137	...	1237	1337	1437	1437	...	...	1637	...	1737	...	1837	...	1937	2037	...	223
29	Chivasso **585** d.	*0523*	0602	...	0802	0902	1002	1202	1202	*1223*	1302	1402	1502	1502	1523	...	1702	...	1802	*1823*	1902	...	2002	2102	*2123*	230
62	Ivrea a.	*0605*	0636	...	0829	0929	1029	1229	1229	*1305*	1329	1429	1529	1529	1605	...	1729	...	1829	*1905*	1929	...	2029	2129	*2205*	232
62	Ivrea d.	0614	...	0645	*0835*	*0935*	*1036*	*1235*	*1245*	1310	*1339*	*1445*	*1535*	*1545*	...	1641	*1745*	1758	*1845*	1910	*1945*	1958	*2045*	*2136*	2210	*233*
79	Pont Saint Martin d.	0627	...	0658	*0847*	*0947*	*1048*	*1247*	*1258*	1330	*1352*	*1458*	*1548*	*1558*	...	1654	*1758*	1827	*1858*	1927	*1958*	2027	*2058*	*2148*	2227	*234*
91	Verrès d.	0642	...	0713	*0858*	*0957*	*1104*	*1258*	*1313*	1344	*1413*	*1513*	*1558*	*1613*	...	1713	*1813*	1842	*1913*	1942	*2013*	2042	*2113*	*2158*	2242	*235*
104	Chatillon-Saint Vincent d.	0701	...	0724	*0910*	*1008*	*1115*	*1309*	*1324*	1400	*1424*	*1524*	*1609*	*1624*	...	1724	*1824*	1901	*1924*	2001	*2024*	2101	*2124*	*2210*	2301	*001*
129	**Aosta** a.	0721	...	0751	*0931*	*1029*	*1136*	*1331*	*1351*	1421	*1451*	*1551*	*1633*	*1651*	...	1751	*1851*	1921	*1951*	2021	*2051*	2121	*2151*	*2232*	2321	*003*

		⚒						⚒	†		⚒			⚒		⚒	⚒				⚒				
Aosta d.	0516	0538	0626	...	0726	0826	1032	1132	1138	1226	...	1338	1426	1501	1526	1626	1638	1703	1726	1826	1857	1926	2026	2126	...
Chatillon-Saint Vincent d.	0537	0601	0647	...	0747	0847	1053	1153	1201	1247	...	1359	1447	1524	1547	1647	1659	1724	1747	1847	1924	1947	2047	2147	...
Verrès d.	0548	0613	0658	...	0758	0858	1104	1204	1214	1258	...	1413	1458	1534	1558	1658	1713	1735	1758	1858	1942	1958	2058	2158	...
Pont Saint Martin d.	0559	0627	0711	...	0811	0911	1114	1218	1230	1311	...	1427	1511	1548	1611	1711	1728	1759	1811	1911	1958	2011	2111	2211	...
Ivrea a.	0612	0642	0724	...	0824	0924	1126	1233	1242	1324	...	1442	1524	1606	1624	1726	1742	1814	1824	1924	2012	2024	2124	2224	...
Ivrea d.	*0620*	*0648*	*0729*	0748	*0831*	*0931*	*1131*	*1248*	*1248*	*1331*	1431	*1448*	*1531*	...	*1631*	*1731*	*1748*	...	*1831*	*1931*	...	*2031*	*2131*	...	*223*
Chivasso **585** a.	*0653*	*0735*	*0753*	0835	*0853*	*0953*	*1153*	*1335*	*1335*	*1353*	1453	*1535*	*1553*	...	*1653*	*1753*	*1835*	...	*1853*	*1953*	...	*2053*	*2153*	...	*225*
Torino Porta Susa **585** a.	*0722*	...	*0820*	0858	*0922*	*1022*	*1222*	...	...	*1422*	1522	...	*1622*	...	*1722*	*1822*	...	...	*1922*	*2022*	...	*2122*	*2222*	...	*235*
Torino Porta Nuova **585** a.	*0732*	...	*0830*	0910	*0932*	*1032*	*1232*	...	...	*1432*	1532	...	*1632*	...	*1732*	*1832*	...	...	*1932*	*2032*	...	*2132*	*2232*	...	*001*

km																									
		⚒	⚒	†	⚒	†	⚒	†	⚒	†		†	⚒	†	⚒	†	⚒	†	⚒	†	⚒	†	⚒	†	
0	Aosta d.	0541	0629	0633	0730	0755	0833	0940	1034	1042	...	1203	1226	1318	1336	1420	1441	1522	1603	1638	1726	1735	1826	1848	1956	...
32	Pré Saint Didier ▲ a.	0622	0723	0720	0825	0841	0927	1026	1124	1132	...	1253	1316	1408	1431	1510	1536	1612	1654	1724	1816	1825	1920	1938	2046	...

	⚒	⚒	†	⚒	†	⚒	†	⚒	†	†	⚒	†	⚒	†	⚒	†	⚒	†	⚒	†	⚒	†	⚒	†
Pré Saint Didier ▲ d.	0631	0732	0747	0835	0932	1030	1040	1132	1202	1316	1338	1418	1443	1520	1559	1630	1722	1734	1828	1846	1952	1954	2054	2058
Aosta a.	0720	0821	0836	0924	1021	1123	1126	1221	1247	1401	1428	1503	1533	1605	1653	1719	1815	1819	1918	1931	2045	2040	2143	2143

▲ – A connecting 🚌 service is available Pré Saint Didier - Courmayeur and v.v. (see Table 36

BRIG - STRESA - MILANO 590

km									EC 35		EC 51		EC 37			EC 57			EC 39				EC 59		EC 41	
			2 ♠	2	2		♠	⚒	†	🍷 ◧	2 ♠	🍷 ◧	2	🍷 ◧V	2 ♠		🍷 ◧	♠	2 ⚒	🍷 ◧	2 ♠	2	2 ♠	🍷 ◧		🍷 ◧	2
	Genève 570	d.	...	...	...	...	...	...	...	0542	...	...	...	0742	...	...	...	...	...	1342	...	...	...	...	...	1842	...
	Lausanne 570	d.	...	...	...	...	...	...	...	0617	...	...	...	0818	...	...	...	...	...	1418	...	...	...	...	...	1918	...
	Basel 560	d.	...	...	...	...	...	...	...	|	...	0631	...	|	...	...	1231	...	...	|	...	...	...	1731	...	|	...
	Bern 560	d.	...	...	...	...	...	...	...	|	...	0734	...	|	...	...	1334	...	...	|	...	...	...	1834	...	|	...
0	**Brig** 🏛	d.	...	...	...	...	...	...	...	0744	...	0844	...	0944	...	...	1444	...	...	1544	...	...	...	1944	...	2044	...
42	**Domodossola** 🏛 §	a.	...	...	...	...	...	...	...	0812	...	0912	...	1012	...	...	1512	...	...	1612	...	...	...	2012	...	2112	...
42	**Domodossola 551**	d.	0458	0510	0550	0606	0657	0722	0750	0817	0828	0917	0948	1017	1254	1402	1517	1525	1549	1617	1658	1810	1855	2017	1945	2117	2155
72	Verbània-Pallanza	d.	0518	0531	0612	0627	0718	0743	0817	|	0848	|	1014	|	1316	1433	|	1545	1617	|	1718	1836	1914	|	2015	|	2223
77	Baveno	d.	|	0535	|	0632	|	|	0822	|	|	|	1019	|	|	1438	|	|	1622	|	|	1841	|	|	2020	|	2228
81	Stresa	d.	0525	0539	0619	0637	0725	0751	0827	0839	0855	0939	1024	|	1323	1443	1539	1552	1626	1639	1725	1845	1921	|	2025	2139	2232
98	Arona	d.	0537	0557	0632	0658	0738	0804	0851	|	0907	|	1050	|	1336	1502	|	1604	1652	|	1738	1903	1935	|	2050	|	2251
124	Gallarate ▲	d.	0558	0626	0652	0732	0759	0828	0925	|	0931	|	1118	1104	1358	1532	|	1625	1725	|	1758	1933	1958	2104	2123	|	2321
150	Rho	d.	|	|	|	0801	|	0849	0944	|	|	|	1143	|	|	1559	|	|	1746	|	|	2001	|	|	2144	|	2345
165	**Milano** Porta Garibaldi	a.	|	0655	0728	0816	0839	0902	1000	|	|	|	1200	|	|	1613	|	|	1805	|	|	2013	|	|	2159	|	2357
167	**Milano** Centrale	a.	0640	...	...	...	...	...	...	0935	1010	1035	...	1135	1432	...	1635	1700	...	1735	1837	...	2035	2135	...	2235	...

				EC 50		EC 32		EC 52		EC 34							EC 36			EC 56			EC 42				
			2	🍷 ◧	2 ♠	🍷 ◧		🍷 ◧		🍷 ◧		2 ♠	2	2 ♠	2		🍷 ◧	2	♠	🍷 ◧			🍷 ◧V	2	2	2 ♠	
Milano Centrale	d.	...	...	0725	0805	0825	...	1125	...	1225	...	1323	...	1523	...	...	1725	...	1730	1825	...	...	1925	1920	...	2123	...
Milano Porta Garibaldi	d.	0455	0612	|	|	|	0900	|	...	|	1250	|	1447	|	1600	...	|	1649	|	|	1800	1840	|	|	2047	|	...
Rho	d.	0511	0627	|	|	|	0912	|	...	|	1303	|	1500	|	|	...	|	1701	|	|	|	|	|	|	2100	|	...
Gallarate ▲	d.	0540	0651	0756	0840	|	0931	|	...	|	1327	1401	1527	1600	1635	...	|	1727	1802	|	1831	1915	1958	2003	2128	2201	...
Arona	d.	0607	0720	|	0859	|	0959	|	...	|	1348	1421	1555	1621	1703	...	|	1755	1824	|	1911	1937	|	2023	2157	2222	...
Stresa	d.	0627	0739	|	0912	0921	1018	1221	...	1321	1408	1434	1613	1634	1724	...	1821	1824	1837	1921	1929	1957	|	2034	2216	2235	...
Baveno	d.	0632	0743	|	|	|	1023	|	...	|	1412	|	1617	|	1728	...	|	1829	|	|	1933	2001	|	|	2220	|	...
Verbània-Pallanza	d.	0637	0749	|	0919	|	1029	|	...	|	1417	1442	1622	1642	1734	...	|	1834	1845	|	1939	2006	|	2042	2225	2242	...
Domodossola 551	a.	0708	0817	0843	0938	0943	1104	1243	...	1343	1441	1505	1643	1705	1805	...	1843	1901	1905	1943	2003	2033	2043	2102	2253	2305	...
Domodossola 🏛 §	d.	...	...	0848	...	0948	...	1248	...	1348	...	...	...	...	...	...	1848	...	...	1948	...	...	2048	...	...	...	...
Brig 🏛	a.	...	...	0916	...	1016	...	1316	...	1416	...	...	...	...	...	...	1916	...	...	2016	...	...	2116	...	...	...	...
Bern 560	a.	...	...	1023	...	|	...	1423	...	|	...	...	...	...	...	...	|	...	...	2123	...	...	|	...	...	...	...
Basel 560	a.	...	...	1129	...	|	...	1529	...	|	...	...	...	...	...	...	|	...	...	2229	...	...	|	...	...	...	...
Lausanne 570	a.	...	...	...	...	1142	...	...	...	1542	...	...	...	...	...	...	2042	...	...	...	...	...	2242	...	...	...	...
Genève 570	a.	...	...	...	...	1218	...	...	...	1618	...	...	...	...	...	...	2118	...	...	...	...	...	2318	...	...	...	...

Local service BRIG - DOMODOSSOLA and v.v. (2nd class only):

km			Ⓐ	⑥y			Ⓒ		⑥		Ⓐ		
0	**Brig**	d.	0600	0840	0948	1044	1144	1244	1344	1644	1744	1844	0013
23	Iselle di Trasquera §	d.	0617	|	|	|	1203	|	|	|	1804	1904	0033
42	**Domodossola**	a.	0635	0907	1017	1112	1222	1312	1412	1712	1822	1922	0054

			Ⓐ	⚒			⑥	⑥				†
Domodossola	d.	0354	0505	0615	0655	1048	1148	1307	1448	1648	1748	1941
Iselle di Trasquera §	d.	0417	0529	0636	0715	|	|	1327	|	|	|	|
Brig	a.	0432	0543	0650	0732	1116	1216	1340	1516	1716	1816	2011

– (12) and 🍷 Genève - Milano - Venezia Santa Lucia and v.v.

– Schooldays only.

– Also Apr. 17, 18, May 29, 30.

– 🅁 inclusive of supplement.

– Operator: Trenord.

– Ticket point is **Iselle**.

▲ – 🚌 service **Gallarate - Milano Malpensa Aeroporto and v.v.**: *Subject to alteration*
From **Gallarate**: 0555Ⓐ, 0631⚒, 0723, 0800⚒, 0825, 0900Ⓐ, 0930, 0955Ⓐ, 1100, 1205⚒, 1240**s**, 1355, 1435Ⓐ, 1605, 1705, 1810, 1920Ⓐ, 2015Ⓐ.
From **Malpensa** ✈ Terminal 1: 0534Ⓐ, 0605⚒, 0645, 0715⚒, 0756, 0829Ⓐ, 0900, 0930Ⓐ, 1030, 1130⚒, 1215⚒**s**, 1250⚒**s**, 1313**s**, 1353Ⓐ**s**, 1530, 1628, 1738, 1845Ⓐ, 1950Ⓐ.
Journey time 25 minutes. Operator: S.A.C.O. ✆ 0331 25 84 11.

nd class only — DOMODOSSOLA and ARONA - NOVARA 591

km			⚒		Ⓐ	⚒				⚒	Ⓒ		Ⓒ				⚒		Ⓒ		Ⓐ				Ⓒ	Ⓐ	
0	**Domodossola**	d.	0522	...	0618	0622	...	...	0653	0758	...	...	...	...	...	1250	1331	...	...	1557	...	...	1747	...	1902	1902	...
38	Omegna	d.	0618	...	|	0657	...	...	0750	0848	...	...	...	...	...	1342	1430	...	...	1646	...	...	1842	...	1943	1945	...
44	Pettenasco	d.	0625	...	|	0704	...	...	0758	0855	...	...	...	...	...	1349	|	...	...	1652	...	...	1849	...	1950	1951	...
47	Orta-Miasino	d.	0630	...	|	0709	...	...	0803	0900	...	...	...	...	...	1358	1444	...	...	1657	...	...	1855	...	1959	1959	...
60	Borgomanero	d.	0642	...	|	0721	...	...	0818	0912	...	...	...	...	...	1414	1458	...	...	1713	1812	...	1908	...	2017	2017	...
	Arona	d.	|	0637	0704	|	...	0756	|	|	1002	...	1205	...	1400	|	|	...	1636	|	|	1845	|	...	|	|	...
	Oleggio	d.	|	0659	0721	|	...	0818	|	|	1022	...	1228	...	1424	|	|	...	1658	|	|	1911	|	...	|	|	...
90	**Novara**	a.	0714	0721	0734	0751	...	0836	0852	0940	1040	...	1246	...	1441	1451	1525	...	1716	1753	1842	1931	1941	...	2046	2046	...

km			⚒	⚒				Ⓒ	Ⓒ				⚒			Ⓐ		Ⓐ			Ⓐ		Ⓐ				
0	**Novara**	d.	0538	0553	0639	...	0656	0913	1002	...	1223	1254	1350	...	1414	1421	1519	1632	1732	1740	1822	...	1832	...	1920	1926	...
7	Oleggio	d.	|	0610	|	...	0722	0928	1023	...	|	1311	|	...	1441	|	|	|	|	1759	|	...	1846	...	|	1941	...
37	**Arona**	a.	|	0636	|	...	0742	0952	1047	...	|	1334	|	...	1504	|	|	|	|	1823	|	...	1906	...	|	2004	...
	Borgomanero	d.	0608	...	0722	...	...	...	...	...	1252	...	1430	...	...	1454	1556	1701	1810	...	1912	...	|	...	2003	...	...
	Orta-Miasino	d.	0631	...	0736	...	...	...	...	...	1306	...	1443	...	...	...	1612	1713	1826	...	1932	...	|	...	2017	...	...
	Pettenasco	d.	0636	...	0741	...	...	...	...	...	1311	...	1448	...	...	...	1616	1718	1832	...	1937	...	|	...	2021	...	...
	Omegna	d.	0658	...	0749	...	...	...	...	...	1318	...	1459	...	...	...	1623	1725	1841	...	1944	...	|	...	2027	...	...
93	**Domodossola**	a.	0744	...	0850	...	...	...	...	...	1409	...	1548	...	...	...	1716	1803	1936	...	2018	...	2007	...	2117	...	...

nd class only

Local services NOVARA - ALESSANDRIA and v.v.

km				⚒		⚒				⚒	⚒	†	†
0	Novara ▲	d.	0608	0708	0808	0908	...	1423	...	1608	1708	1908	2027
7	Alessandria ▲	a.	0715	0815	0915	1015	...	1532	...	1715	1815	2015	2134

		♠†			⚒				♠⚒		⚒
Alessandria ▲	d.	0645	...	1245	1345	...	1645	1745	1845	1945	2045
Novara ▲	a.	0753	...	1352	1452	...	1752	1852	1957	2052	2152

– Operator: Trenord.

▲ – Additional journeys available by changing trains at Mortara (25 km from Novara).

perator: Trenord — BELLINZONA - LUINO - MILANO MALPENSA ✈ 592

km											
0	**Bellinzona 550**	d.	0554	0755	...	...	...	...	...	...	...
9	Cadenazzo	d.	0608	0808	...	1208	1408	1608	1808	2008	...
7	Pino-Tronzano 🏛	d.	0630	0830	...	1230	1430	1630	1830	2030	...
0	**Luino 608**	d.	0649	0852	...	1252	1452	1652	1852	2052	...
5	Laveno Mombello	d.	0710	0908	...	1308	1508	1708	1908	2108	...
6	Gallarate	d.	0747	0947	...	1347	1547	1747	1947	2147	...
1	**Milano** Malpensa Aeroporto ✈	a.	0811	1011	...	1411	1610	1810	2011	2211	...

Milano Malpensa Aeroporto ✈	d.	0550	0750	...	1150	1350	1550	1750	1950	...
Gallarate	d.	0612	0813	...	1213	1413	1613	1813	2013	...
Laveno Mombello	d.	0647	0845	...	1245	1445	1645	1845	2045	...
Luino 608	d.	0710	0915	...	1315	1515	1715	1915	2115	...
Pino-Tronzano 🏛	d.	0720	0930	...	1330	1530	1730	1930	2130	...
Cadenazzo	d.	0743	0953	...	1353	1553	1753	1953	2154	...
Bellinzona 550	a.	0752	...	...	...	...	...	...	2203	...

593 MILANO - COLICO - TIRANO

Operator: Trenord

km																									
		2				2																2	🚌	2	2
				†C		†		†		⚒							⚒	⚒							
0	**Milano** Centrale ▷ d.	...	0620	0622p	...	0720	0820	0920	1020	1120	1220	...	1420	...	1620	1720	1750	1820	1920	...	2020	2120	...	2250	2352
12	Monza ▷ d.	...	0632	0641	...	0732	0834	0932	1032	1132	1232	...	1432	...	1632	1732	1804	1832	1932	...	2032	2132	...	2306	0011
50	Lecco ▷ d.	...	0702	0718	...	0802	0902	1002	1102	1201	1302	...	1502	...	1702	1802	1836	1902	2002	...	2102	2202	...	2350	0055
72	Varenna-Esino d.	...	0724	0753	...	0824	0924	1024	1124	...	1324	...	1524	...	1724	1824	...	|	2024	...	2124	2236	...	...	...
75	Bellano-Tartavalle Terme d.	...	0729	0802	...	0829	0929	1029	1129	...	1329	...	1529	...	1729	1829	...	1929	2029	...	2129	2241	...	...	...
89	**Colico** ▲ a.	...	0747	0823	...	0847	0947	1047	1147	...	1347	...	1547	...	1747	1847	...	1947	2047	...	2147	2300	2305	...	...
130	Sondrio a.	0535	0821	...	...	0920	1021	1121	1221	...	1421	...	1621	...	1821	1921	...	2021	2121	..	2221	...	2347	...	...
156	**Tirano** ♣ a.	0607	0850	...	...	0950	1050	1207	1250	...	1450	...	1650	...	1850	...	...	2050	2150	...	...	...	...	...	...

	2	2		2																		2	2	2	2
				⚒		⚒	†	⚒							⚒	†		†C		†		†	⚒		
Tirano ♣ d.	...	...	0610	...	0710	...	0907	0910	...	1110	...	1310	...	1510	...	1550	1710	...	...	1810	1910	1950	...	...	2123
Sondrio d.	...	0532	0638	...	0738	...	0938	0938	...	1138	...	1338	...	1538	...	1638	1738	...	...	1839	1938	2038	...	2123	2200
Colico ▲ d.	0505	0604	0716	...	0816	...	1016	1016	...	1216	...	1416	...	1616	...	1716	1816	1837	...	1916	2016	2116	2116	2200	...
Bellano-Tartavalle Terme d.	0521	0618	0732	...	0832	...	1032	1032	...	1232	...	1432	...	1632	...	1732	1832	1901	...	1932	2032	2132	2132	2214	...
Varenna-Esino d.	0526	0623	0737	...	0837	...	1037	1037	...	1237	...	1437	...	1637	...	1737	1837	1906	...	1937	2037	2137	2137	2220	...
Lecco ▽ d.	0549	0652	0759	0828	0901	0959	1101	1101	...	1301	...	1501	...	1701	1733	1801	1901	1946	...	2001	2101	2201	2201	2243	...
Monza ▽ a.	0622	0726	0826	0857	0926	1026	1126	1126	...	1326	...	1526	...	1726	1757	1826	1926	2015	...	2026	2126	2226	2226	2315	...
Milano Centrale ▽ a.	0640	0738	0838	0912	0940	1040	1140	1140	...	1340	...	1540	...	1740	1818	1840	1940	2044p	...	2040	2140	2240	2240	2330	...

▲ – **COLICO - CHIAVENNA and v.v.:** 2nd class only

km																									
				⚒		†C	⚒			⚒			⚒			⚒			⚒		⚒			⚒	
0	Colico d.	0550	0707	0810	...	0824	0846	...	1002	1046	...	1202	1246	...	1404	1446	1602	...	1646	1802	1852	...	2002	2112	...
27	Chiavenna a.	0618	0737	0834	...	0848	0917	...	1032	1117	...	1232	1317	...	1434	1517	1632	...	1717	1832	1922	...	2032	2142	...

		⚒	⚒		⚒	†		⚒		⚒			⚒			⚒		⚒		†C			⚒		
Chiavenna d.	0626	0702	0745	...	0843	0850	...	0928	1043	1128	...	1243	1326	1443	...	1528	1643	1728	...	1802	...	1845	1930	...	2040
Colico a.	0656	0735	0808	...	0916	0920	...	0958	1116	1158	...	1316	1356	1516	...	1558	1716	1758	...	1834	...	1919	2000	...	2110

C – †: (2) Milano - Colico - Chiavenna and v.v.
k – ①–⑤ schooldays only.
p – Milano **Porta Garibaldi**.

▷ – Local trains run Milano Porta Garibaldi - Lecco hourly 0652 - 2152.
▽ – Local trains run Lecco - Milano Porta Garibaldi hourly 0607 - 2207.

♣ – 🚌 **TIRANO - EDOLO and v.v.** subject to alteration

		⚒			k			⚒					
Tirano Stazione d.	0840	1040	1245	1435	1635	1700	**Edolo** d.	0615	0915	1115	1515	1715	...
Aprica S Pietro a.	0920	1120	1350	1515	1720	1745	Aprica S Pietro d.	0650	0940	1140	1540	1740	...
Edolo a.	0945	1145	1420	1540	1745	1810	**Tirano** Stazione a.	0730	1020	1220	1620	1820	...

♣ – For 🚌 service Tirano - Edolo and v.v. – see panel.
Operator: Automobilistica Perego (AP): ✆ (0342) 701 200; fax (0342) 704 400.

595 INNSBRUCK - BOLZANO / BOZEN - VERONA - BOLOGNA

km																											
		FA		*FA*			*FA*											*EC*	*EC*					*FA*		*EC*	
		9461		**9463**			**9465**											**1289**	**81**					**9477**		**85**	
		🍷		🍷	2	2	🍷	2	2	2	2	2	2	2	2	2	2	✕	✕		2	2		🍷	2	✕	2
				♦	⚒	⚒		⚒M		M	Ⓐ	M	Ⓐ	Ⓒ	ⒸM	Ⓒ	M	♠e	♠g			M			M	♠	⚒
	München Hbf **951** d.	...	...	...	...	...	...	...	...	...	...	...	...	...	...	...	...	0738	0738	...	...	...	...	...	...	0938	...
0	**Innsbruck** Hbf ▲ d.	...	...	...	...	...	...	...	...	...	...	...	...	...	...	...	...	0927	0927	...	...	...	...	...	...	1127	...
37	**Brennero / Brenner** 🏛 ▲ a.	...	...	...	...	...	...	...	...	...	...	...	...	...	...	...	...	1002	1002	...	...	...	...	...	...	1202	...
37	**Brennero / Brenner** 🏛 d.	...	...	...	...	...	...	0535	0608	0638	...	0738	0808	...	0838	...	0938	1010	1014	...	...	1038	...	...	1138	1214	...
60	Vipiteno / Sterzing d.	...	...	...	...	...	...	0554	0627	0657	...	0757	0827	...	0857	...	0957	|	|	...	...	1057	...	...	1157	|	...
78	Fortezza / Franzensfeste d.	...	...	...	0540	...	...	0612	0645	0715	0745	0815	0845	...	0915	...	1015	1042	1046	...	...	1115	...	...	1215	1246	...
89	Bressanone / Brixen d.	...	...	...	0550	...	...	0622	0655	0725	0755	0825	0855	...	0925	...	1025	1051	1056	...	...	1125	...	...	1225	1256	...
99	Chiusa / Klausen d.	...	...	...	0558	...	...	0630	0703	0733	0804	0833	0903	...	0933	...	1033	|	|	...	...	1133	...	...	1233	|	...
127	**Bolzano / Bozen** a.	...	...	...	0621	...	...	0655	0729	0759	0829	0859	0929	...	0959	...	1059	1117	1127	...	...	1159	...	...	1259	1327	...
					|				|	2	|	2⑥	Ⓒ				2	|	|						2⚒	|	
127	**Bolzano / Bozen** d.	...	0500	...	0625	0636	0700	...	0731	0736	0831	0831	...	0936	...	1031	...	1119	1131	...	1136	...	1231	1300	1236	1331	133
143	Ora / Auer d.	...	0512	...	0638	0655	|	...	0743	0755	0843	0843	...	0955	...	1043	...	|	|	...	1155	...	1243	|	1255	|	135
165	Mezzocorona d.	...	0526	...	0654	0716	|	...	0756	0816	0856	0856	...	1016	...	1056	...	|	|	...	1216	...	1256	|	1316	|	141
182	**Trento** ♣ d.	...	0540	...	0711	0738	0732	...	0810	0833	0908	0908	...	1033	...	1108	...	1152	1204	...	1233	...	1310	1332	1333	1404	143
206	Rovereto d.	...	0554	...	0724	0752	0747	...	0825	0847	0924	0924	...	1047	...	1124	...	|	1219	...	1247	...	1325	1347	1347	1419	144
274	**Verona** Porta Nuova **605** a.	...	0645	...	0816	0851	0840	...	0914	0951	1016	1016	...	1151	...	1216	...	1239	1256	...	1351	...	1414	1440	1451	1458	155
274	**Verona** Porta Nuova d.	0650	0701	0750	...	...	0850	...	...	...	...	...	1026	...	...	...	1226	1241	1313	1326	...	...	1426	1450	...	1515	...
388	**Bologna** Centrale a.	0740	0825	0840	...	...	0940	...	...	...	...	...	1150	...	...	...	1351	|	1407	1451	...	...	1554	1540	...	1620	...
	Milano Centrale **615** a.	|	...	|	...	...	|	...	...	...	...	...	...	...	...	...	...	|	...	...	...	...	...	|	...	...	...
	Venezia S L **605** a.	|	...	|	...	...	|	...	...	...	...	...	...	...	...	...	...	1356	...	...	...	...	...	|	...	...	...
	Firenze SMN **620** a.	0820c	...	0920c	...	...	1020c	...	...	...	...	...	...	...	...	...	...	...	...	...	...	...	...	1620c	...	...	...
	Roma Termini **620** a.	0940	...	1040	...	...	1140	...	...	...	...	...	...	...	...	...	...	...	...	...	...	...	...	1740	...	...	...

				FA	*EC*		*FA*				*FA*		*EC*						*EC*				*ICN*			*EN*	*E*
				9481	**87**		**9483**				**9485**		**89**						**83**				**763**			**485**	**48**
	2		2	🍷	✕	2	🍷	2	2	2	🍷	2	✕	2	2		2	2	✕	2	2	2		2	2		48
	M		M		♠	⚒	♦	M		Ⓐ		M	♠		M		Ⓐ	M	♠	M		M	♦			♦	D
München Hbf **951** d.	...	...	...	...	1138	...	...	...	...	...	...	...	1338	...	...	...	...	...	1538	...	...	...	...	...	...	2108	21
Innsbruck Hbf ▲ d.	...	...	...	...	1327	...	...	...	...	...	...	...	1527	...	...	...	...	...	1727	...	...	...	...	...	...	2305	23
Brennero / Brenner 🏛 ▲ a.	...	...	...	...	1402	...	...	...	...	...	...	...	1602	...	...	...	...	...	1802	...	...	...	...	...	...	|	|
Brennero / Brenner 🏛 d.	1238	1308	1338	...	1414	...	...	1438	1508	...	...	1538	1614	...	1638	1708	...	1738	1814	1838	1908	1938	...	...	2138	|	|
Vipiteno / Sterzing d.	1257	1327	1357	...	|	...	...	1457	1527	...	...	1557	|	...	1657	1727	...	1757	|	1857	1927	1957	...	...	2157	|	|
Fortezza / Franzensfeste d.	1315	1345	1415	...	1446	...	...	1515	1545	...	...	1615	1646	...	1715	1745	...	1815	1846	1915	1945	2015	...	...	2215	0029	00
Bressanone / Brixen d.	1325	1355	1425	...	1456	...	...	1525	1555	...	...	1625	1656	...	1725	1755	...	1825	1856	1925	1955	2025	...	...	2225	0038	00
Chiusa / Klausen d.	1333	1403	1433	...	|	...	...	1533	1603	...	...	1633	|	...	1733	1803	...	1833	|	1933	2003	2033	...	...	2233	|	
Bolzano / Bozen a.	1359	1429	1459	...	1527	...	...	1559	1629	...	...	1659	1727	...	1759	1829	...	1859	1927	1959	2029	2059	...	...	2259	0107	01
		|	2Ⓐ		|	...		2	|			2Ⓐ	|		2Ⓐ	|			|	2	|	2Ⓐ			|	|	
Bolzano / Bozen d.	...	1431	1436	1500	1531	...	...	1536	1631	1636	1700	1706	1731	1736	1806	1831	1836	...	1931	1936	2031	2036	2130	2136	2301	0109	01
Ora / Auer d.	...	1443	1455	|	|	...	...	1555	1643	1655	|	1722	|	1755	1822	1843	1855	...	|	1955	2043	2055	2144	2155	2317	|	
Mezzocorona d.	...	1456	1516	|	|	...	...	1616	1656	1716	|	1742	|	1816	1842	1856	1916	...	|	2016	2056	2116	2200	2216	2337	|	
Trento ♣ d.	...	1510	1538	1532	1604	...	...	1633	1710	1738	1732	1755	1804	1833	1855	1910	1933	...	2004	2033	2110	2133	2216	2231	2348	0142	01
Rovereto d.	...	1525	1552	1547	1619	...	...	1647	1725	1752	1747	1810	1819	1847	1910	1925	1947	...	2019	2047	2125	2147	2232	...	...	|	
Verona Porta Nuova **605** a.	...	1614	1654	1640	1657	...	...	1751	1814	1854	1840	...	1858	1951	...	2014	2051	...	2056	2151	2217	2251	2316	...	...	0237	02
Verona Porta Nuova d.	...	1626	...	1650	1659	1708	1750	...	1826	...	1850	...	...	...	...	2104	...	...	...	...	...	...	2336	...	...	0305	07
Bologna Centrale a.	...	1754	...	1740	|	1854	1840	...	1954	...	1940	...	...	...	...	2225	...	...	...	...	...	...	0101	...	...	0420	
Milano Centrale **615** a.	...	...	...	|	|	...	|	...	...	...	|	...	...	...	...	...	...	...	...	...	...	...	|	...	...	|	09
Venezia S.L. **605** a.	...	...	...	|	1810	...	|	...	...	...	|	...	...	...	...	...	...	...	...	...	...	...	|	...	...	|	
Firenze SMN **620** a.	...	...	...	1820c	...	...	1920c	...	...	...	2020c	...	...	...	...	...	...	...	...	...	...	...	0257c	...	...	0615	
Roma Termini **620** a.	...	...	...	1940	...	...	2040	...	...	...	2140	...	...	...	...	...	...	...	...	...	...	...	0600	...	...	0922	

♦ – NOTES (LISTED BY TRAIN NUMBER)

485 – LUPUS – 🛏 1, 2 cl. (Excelsior), 🛏 1, 2 cl., ▬ 2 cl. and (2) München - Bologna (**235**) - Roma. Supplement payable.
763 – ▬ 2 cl. (4 berth) and (2) Bolzano - Roma.
9463 – (12) and 🍷 Brescia - Verona - Roma.
9483 – (12) and 🍷 Brescia - Verona - Roma.

D – APUS – 🛏 1, 2 cl. (Excelsior), 🛏 1, 2 cl. and ▬ 2 cl. München (**485**) - Verona (**480**) - Milano. Supplement payable.

M – To Merano. See Table **597**.
c – Firenze **Campo di Marte**.
e – ⑥⑦ Mar. 29 - Nov. 2.
g – ①–⑤ Mar. 31 - Oct. 31; daily Nov. 3 - Dec. 13.

♠ – Also available to passengers without reservation. Operator within Italy: LeNor
▲ – For additional trains Innsbruck - Brenne Brenner – see page 295. Austrian holi dates apply Innsbruck - Brennero / Bren
♣ – For Trento - Malé - Marilleva and v.v. – page 295.

BOLOGNA - VERONA - BOLZANO / BOZEN - INNSBRUCK 595

	2 ⚒	2 ⚒	2 †	2 ⚒	*ICN* **764** ♦	2 ⚒	2 ⚒		2	2 Ⓐ		2 Ⓐ	*EC* **88** ✕ ♠	*FA* **9460** 🍷	2 Ⓒ	2	2 †	*EC* **80** ✕ ♠	*FA* **9462** 🍷	2 ⚒		*FA* **9464** 🍷 ♦	2 ⚒	*EC* **84** ✕ ♠	*FA* **9466** 🍷	2	
Roma Termini **620** d.	...	...	...	...	2300	...	...	...	...	...	...	...	...	0630	...	...	...	...	0815	...	...	0915	...	...	1015	...	...
Firenze SMN **620** d.	...	...	...	...	0215c	...	...	...	...	...	...	...	...	0750c	...	...	...	...	0935c	...	...	1035c	...	...	1135c	...	...
Venezia S L **605** d.	...	...	...	...	|	...	...	...	...	...	...	...	...	|	...	...	...	...	|	...	...	|	...	...	|	...	...
Milano Centrale **615** d.	...	...	...	...	|	...	...	...	...	...	...	...	...	|	...	...	...	...	|	...	...	|	...	...	|	...	...
Bologna Centrale d.	...	...	...	...	0400	...	...	...	0613	...	0710	...	...	0830	...	0810	...	...	1015	...	1010f	1115	...	1152	1215	...	1210
Verona Porta Nuova **605** a.	...	...	...	...	0530	...	...	...	0754	...	0838	...	...	0920	...	0940	...	...	1105	...	1138f	1205	...	1247	1305	...	1338
Verona Porta Nuova d.	...	...	...	0525	0552	0609	0709	0748	▬	0809	...	0846	0904	0930	0909	▬	0946	1102	1115	1109	1150	▬	1209	1304	1315	1309	1350
Rovereto d.	...	...	...	0613	0657	0714	0814	0837	...	0914	...	0934	0943	1009	1014	...	1034	1143	1157	1209	1239	...	1314	1343	1357	1409	1439
Trento ♣ d.	...	0605	...	0630	0714	0732	0832	0853	...	0932	...	0949	0959	1025	1032	...	1049	1159	1214	1232	1254	...	1332	1359	1414	1432	1454
Mezzocorona d.	...	0617	...	0644	0727	0746	0846	0905	...	0946	...	1000	|	|	1046	...	1100	|	|	1246	1305	...	1346	|	|	1446	1505
Ora / Auer d.	...	0636	...	0706	0745	0806	0906	0919	...	1006	...	1013	|	|	1106	...	1113	|	|	1306	1319	...	1406	|	|	1506	1519
Bolzano / Bozen a.	...	0652	...	0722	0805	0822	0922	0930	...	1022	...	1038	1031	1103	1122	...	1128	1231	1248	1322	1330	...	1422	1431	1448	1522	1530
		2 ⚒ M		2 M		2 M		|	2 M				|			2 Ⓒ M	2 M	|		▬ 2 M	|	2 M		|	2 M		|
Bolzano / Bozen d.	0601	0701	0701	0801	...	0901	...	0932	1001	...	...	...	1034	...	...	1101	1201	1234	...	1301	1332	1401	...	1434	1501	...	1532
Chiusa / Klausen d.	0626	0726	0726	0826	...	0926	...	0955	1026	...	...	...	|	...	...	1126	1226	|	...	1326	1355	1426	...	|	1526	...	1555
Bressanone / Brixen d.	0635	0735	0735	0835	...	0935	...	1004	1035	...	...	...	1104	...	...	1135	1235	1304	...	1335	1404	1435	...	1504	1535	...	1604
Fortezza / Franzensfeste d.	0645	0745	0745	0845	...	0945	...	1015	1045	...	...	...	1115	...	...	1145	1245	1315	...	1345	1415	1445	...	1515	1545	...	1615
Vipiteno / Sterzing d.	0703	0803	0803	0903	...	1003	...	1033	1103	...	...	...	|	...	...	1203	1303	|	...	1403	1433	1503	...	|	1603	...	1633
Brennero / Brenner 🏛 a.	0722	0822	0822	0922	...	1022	...	1052	1122	...	...	...	1148	...	...	1222	1322	1348	...	1422	1452	1522	...	1548	1622	...	1652
Brennero / Brenner 🏛 ▲ d.	...	...	...	...	...	...	...	...	...	...	...	...	1200	...	...	...	...	1400	...	...	...	...	...	1600	...	...	...
Innsbruck Hbf ▲ a.	...	...	...	...	...	...	...	...	...	...	...	...	1232	...	...	...	...	1432	...	...	...	...	...	1632	...	...	...
München Hbf **951** a.	...	...	...	...	...	...	...	...	...	...	...	...	1421	...	...	...	...	1624	...	...	...	...	...	1821	...	...	...

	2 M	2 Ⓐ	*EC* **86** ✕ ♠	2 Ⓐ	2		2 Ⓐ	2 Ⓐ	*EC* **188** ✕ ♠ g	*EC* **1288** ✕ ♠ e	2 M	2		2 M	2 Ⓐ	2	*FA* **9478** 🍷		*FA* **9480** 🍷	2 Ⓑ	2 ⚒	*FA* **9482** 🍷 ♦			2	*EN* **484** ♦	*EN* **481** **484** D
Roma Termini **620** d.	...	...	...	...	...	...	...	...	...	...	...	...	...	...	...	...	1615	...	1715	...	...	1815	...	...	...	1904	...
Firenze SMN **620** d.	...	...	...	...	...	...	...	...	...	...	...	...	...	...	...	...	1735c	...	1835c	...	...	1935c	...	...	...	2211	...
Venezia S L **605** d.	...	...	1335	...	...	...	...	...	...	1550	...	...	...	...	...	...	|	...	|	...	...	|	...	...	...	|	...
Milano Centrale **615** d.	...	...	|	...	...	...	...	...	...	|	...	...	...	...	...	...	|	...	|	...	...	|	...	...	...	|	2135
Bologna Centrale d.	...	...	|	...	...	1410	...	...	1552	|	...	...	1610	...	...	...	1815	1810	1915	...	...	2015	2010	2110	...	2315	|
Verona Porta Nuova **605** a.	...	...	1455	...	...	1538	...	...	1645	1659	...	...	1738	...	...	...	1905	1938	2005	...	...	2105	2138	2238	...	0020	2308
Verona Porta Nuova d.	...	1409	1502	...	1509	1550	...	1609	1702	1702	...	1709	1750	...	1809	1909	1915	1950	...	2009a	2109	...	2150	...	2249	0101	0101
Rovereto d.	...	1514	1543	1550	1614	1639	1650	1714	1743	1743	...	1814	1839	...	1914	2009	1957	2039	...	2114a	2214	...	2239	...	2336	|	|
Trento ♣ d.	...	1532	1559	1605	1632	1654	1705	1732	1759	1759	...	1832	1854	...	1932	2032	2014	2054	...	2132	2232	...	2254	...	2351	0156	0156
Mezzocorona d.	...	1546	|	1616	1646	1705	1716	1746	|	|	...	1846	1905	...	1946	2046	|	2105	...	2146	2246	...	2305	...	...	|	|
Ora / Auer d.	...	1606	|	1636	1706	1719	1736	1806	|	|	...	1906	1919	...	2006	2106	|	2119	...	2205	2306	...	2319	...	...	|	|
Bolzano / Bozen a.	...	1622	1631	1652	1722	1730	1752	1822	1831	1831	...	1922	1930	...	2022	2122	2048	2130	...	2222	2322	...	2331	...	...	0228	0228
			|	2 M		|	2 M	|	|	|			|					|		2						|	|
Bolzano / Bozen d.	1601	...	1634	1701	...	1732	1801	1824	1834	1834	1901	...	1932	2001	...	...	...	2132	...	2232	...	...	...	...	...	0230	0230
Chiusa / Klausen d.	1626	...	|	1723	...	1755	1826	1847	|	|	1926	...	1955	2026	...	...	...	2155	...	2256	...	...	...	...	...	|	|
Bressanone / Brixen d.	1635	...	1704	1731	...	1804	1835	1856	1904	1904	1935	...	2004	2035	...	...	...	2204	...	2305	...	...	...	...	...	|	|
Fortezza / Franzensfeste d.	1645	...	1715	1745	...	1815	1845	1905	1915	1915	1945	...	2015	2045	...	...	...	2215	...	2314	...	...	...	...	...	|	|
Vipiteno / Sterzing d.	1703	...	|	1803	...	1833	1903	1923	|	|	2003	...	2033	2103	...	...	...	2233	...	...	...	...	...	...	...	|	|
Brennero / Brenner 🏛 a.	1722	...	1748	1822	...	1852	1922	1944	1948	1948	2022	...	2052	2122	...	...	...	2252	...	...	...	...	...	...	...	|	|
Brennero / Brenner 🏛 ▲ d.	...	...	1800	...	...	...	...	...	2000	2000	...	...	...	...	...	...	...	...	...	...	...	...	...	...	...	|	|
Innsbruck Hbf ▲ a.	...	...	1832	...	...	...	...	...	2032	2032	...	...	...	...	...	...	...	...	...	...	...	...	...	...	...	0431	0431
München Hbf **951** a.	...	...	2021	...	...	...	...	...	2221	2221	...	...	...	...	...	...	...	...	...	...	...	...	...	...	...	0630	0630

▲ – **INNSBRUCK - BRENNERO / BRENNER and v.v. stopping services**: 2nd class only

km		⚒																							
0	**Innsbruck** Hbf d.	0522	0552	0652	...	0752	0852	0952	...	1052	1152	...	1252	1352	1452	...	1552	1652	1752	...	1852	1952	...	2222	2355	...
18	Matrei d.	0540	0610	0710	...	0810	0910	1010	...	1111	1210	...	1310	1411	1510	...	1610	1710	1811	...	1910	2010	...	2240	0013	...
23	Steinach in Tirol d.	0545	0615	0715	...	0815	0915	1015	...	1116	1215	...	1315	1416	1515	...	1615	1715	1816	...	1915	2015	...	2245	0018	...
37	**Brennero / Brenner** 🏛 a.	0602	0632	0732	...	0832	0932	1032	...	1132	1232	...	1332	1432	1532	...	1632	1732	1832	...	1932	2032	...	2302	0035	...

		⚒			⚒																			
rennero / Brenner 🏛 d.	0528	0558	0628	...	0658	0728	0828	...	0928	1028	1128	...	1228	1328	...	1428	1528	...	1628	1728	...	1828	1928	...	2128	2304
teinach in Tirol d.	0547	0617	0647	...	0717	0746	0846	...	0947	1047	1147	...	1247	1347	...	1447	1547	...	1647	1747	...	1847	1947	...	2147	2323
latrei d.	0551	0621	0651	...	0721	0750	0850	...	0951	1051	1151	...	1251	1351	...	1451	1551	...	1651	1751	...	1851	1951	...	2151	2327
nnsbruck Hbf a.	0608	0638	0708	...	0739	0808	0908	...	1008	1108	1208	...	1308	1408	...	1508	1608	...	1708	1808	...	1908	2008	...	2208	2344

♦ – **NOTES** (LISTED BY TRAIN NUMBER)

64 – 2 cl. (4 berth) and (2) Roma - Bolzano.
84 – LUPUS – 1, 2 cl. (Excelsior), 1, 2 cl., 2 cl. and (2) Roma (**234**) - Bologna - München. Supplement payable.
464 – (12) and 🍷 Roma - Verona - Brescia.
482 – (12) and 🍷 Roma - Verona - Brescia.

– APUS – 1, 2 cl. (Excelsior), 1, 2 cl. and 2 cl. Milano (**481**) - Verona (**484**) - München. Supplement payable.
– From Merano. See Table **597**.
– Ⓐ only.
– Firenze **Campo di Marte**.
– ⑥⑦ Mar. 29 - Nov. 2.
– Ⓒ only.
– ①–⑤ Mar. 31 - Oct. 31; daily Nov. 3 - Dec. 13.
– June 28 - Aug. 31.

– Also available to passengers without reservation. Operator within Italy: LeNord.
– For additional trains Brennero / Brenner - Innsbruck – see panel above. Austrian holiday dates apply Brennero / Brenner - Innsbruck.
– For Trento - Malé - Marilleva and v.v. – see panel.

♣ – **TRENTO - MALÉ and v.v.**: **Valid June 28 - Sept. 9, 2014**
56 *km*, journey time 70–90 minutes
From **Trento**: 0614⚒, 0713⚒, 0830, 0924⚒, 1020, 1106⚒, 1202, 1236⚒, 1329, 1402⚒, 1420†, 1511, 1625, 1714⚒, 1723, 1838, 1928.
From **Malé**: 0535⚒, 0610†, 0634⚒, 0651⚒, 0739⚒, 0848, 0948⚒, 1055, 1150, 1244, 1352, 1444, 1545, 1651, 1749, 1906, 2024.

MALÉ - MARILLEVA and v.v.: **Valid June 28 - Sept. 9, 2014**
11 *km*, journey time 11–14 minutes
From **Malé**: 0600⚒, 0654⚒, 0747, 0844, 1004, 1054, 1153, 1238⚒**m**, 1336, 1426⚒**m**, 1500, 1557⚒**m**, 1646, 1730⚒**m**, 1755, 1827⚒, 1904⚒**m**.
From **Marilleva**: 0618⚒, 0724⚒, 0830, 0932, 1030, 1134, 1217, 1307⚒**m**, 1427, 1458⚒**m**, 1530, 1627⚒**m**, 1730, 1754⚒**m**, 1824⚒, 1849, 2004.

Operator: Trentino Transporti Esercizio S.p.a, Via Innsbruck 65, 38121 Trento; ✆ +39 0 461 821000, fax +39 0 461 031407.

596 FORTEZZA / FRANZENSFESTE - S. CANDIDO / INNICHEN - LIENZ
2nd class only

km																										
			§	§		§	§		§		§	§		§	§		§	§		§	◧		§		§
		⚒	Ⓐ							Ⓐ						Ⓒ									
0	**Fortezza / Franzensfeste** d.	...	0547	0650	...	0750	0850	...	0950	...	1050	1150	...	1250	1350	...	1450	1550	...	1650	1750	...	1850	1950	2050
33	Brunico / Bruneck d.	...	0630	0730	...	0830	0930	...	1030	...	1130	1230	...	1330	1430	...	1530	1630	...	1730	1830	...	1930	2030	2130
61	Dobbiaco / Toblach d.	...	0706	0806	...	0906	1006	...	1106	...	1206	1306	...	1406	1506	...	1606	1706	...	1806	1906	...	2006	2106	2206
65	**S. Candido / Innichen** a.	...	0710	0810	...	0910	1010	...	1110	...	1210	1310	...	1410	1510	...	1610	1710	...	1810	1910	...	2010	2110	2210
65	**S. Candido / Innichen** ▦ d.	0640	...	...	0852	...	...	1037	...	1137	...	...	1313	...	...	1513	...	...	1717	...	...	1913	...	...	...
78	Sillian ▦ d.	0654	...	...	0906	...	...	1052	...	1151	...	...	1326	...	...	1526	...	...	1736	...	...	1926	...	...	...
108	**Lienz 971** a.	0725	...	...	0937	...	...	1123	...	1223	...	...	1356	...	...	1556	...	...	1811	...	...	1958	...	...	...

		◧	§		§	§		§		§		§		§	§		§		§	§	§		§	§	
	⚒								Ⓐ							Ⓒ									
Lienz 971 d.	0527	...	...	0800	...	...	0940	...	1036	...	1202	...	...	...	...	1421	...	1604	...	...	...	1819	...	...	...
Sillian d.	0600	...	...	0832	...	...	1012	...	1110	...	1233	...	...	...	...	1453	...	1635	...	...	...	1851	...	...	...
S. Candido / Innichen ▦ a.	0614	...	...	0846	...	...	1025	...	1123	...	1247	...	...	...	...	1507	...	1647	...	...	...	1905	...	...	...
S. Candido / Innichen ▦ d.	...	0650	0750	...	0850	0950	...	1050	...	1150	...	1250	...	1350	1450	...	1550	...	1650	1750	1850	...	1950	2050	...
Dobbiaco / Toblach d.	...	0655	0755	...	0855	0955	...	1055	...	1155	...	1255	...	1355	1455	...	1555	...	1655	1755	1855	...	1955	2055	...
Brunico / Bruneck d.	...	0731	0831	...	0931	1031	...	1131	...	1231	...	1331	...	1431	1531	...	1631	...	1731	1831	1931	...	2031	2131	...
Fortezza / Franzensfeste a.	...	0810	0910	...	1010	1110	...	1210	...	1310	...	1410	...	1510	1610	...	1710	...	1810	1910	2010	...	2110	2210	...

§ – Operated by *SAD* (for contact details see Table **598**).
◧ – Operated by *SAD* on Ⓒ (for contact details see Table **598**).

597 BOLZANO / BOZEN - MERANO / MERAN
2nd class only

km																											
					⚒§	Ⓒ	⚒§		⚒§		⚒§		⚒§			⚒		⚒§		⚒		⚒§		⚒			Ⓐ
	Brennero **595** d.	0535**d**	0638	0738	...	0838	...	0938	...	1038	...	1138	...	1238	1338	...	1438	...	1538	...	1638	...	1738	...	1838	1938	...
0	**Bolzano / Bozen** d.	0657	0801	0901	0935	1001	1035	1101	1135	1201	1235	1301	1335	1401	1501	1535	1601	1635	1701	1735	1801	1835	1901	1935	2001	2101	2203
32	Merano / Meran a.	0742	0844	0944	1014	1044	1114	1144	1214	1244	1314	1344	1414	1444	1544	1614	1644	1714	1744	1814	1844	1914	1944	2014	2044	2144	2247

	⚒			⚒§		⚒§	Ⓒ	⚒§		⚒§		⚒§		⚒§			Ⓐ§		⚒		⚒§		⚒			⚒	†§
Merano / Meran d.	0602	0714	0816	0846	0916	0946	1016	1046	1116	1146	1216	1246	1316	1346	1416	1516	1546	1616	1646	1716	1746	1816	1846	1916	2016	2146	2146
Bolzano / Bozen a.	0648	0759	0859	0926	0959	1026	1059	1126	1159	1226	1259	1326	1359	1426	1459	1559	1626	1659	1726	1759	1826	1859	1926	1959	2059	2227	2227
Brennero **595** a.	0822	0922	1022	...	1122	...	1222	...	1322	...	1422	...	1522	...	1622	1722	...	1822	...	1922	...	2022	...	2122	...	...	...

d – ⚒ only.

§ – Operated by SAD (for contact details see Table **598**).

Additional journeys operate on ⚒.

598 MERANO / MERAN - MALLES / MALS
2nd class only SAD

km																										
		⚒			w			w			w			w			w			w						
0	Merano / Meran d.	0538	0638	0716	0746	0816	0916	0946	1016	1116	1146	1216	1316	1346	1416	1516	1546	1616	1716	1746	1816	1916	1946	2046	2146	2250
60	Malles / Mals **546 / 954** a.	0654	0754	0838	0855	0938	1038	1055	1138	1238	1255	1338	1438	1455	1538	1638	1655	1738	1838	1855	1938	2038	2055	2155	2255	2358

	⚒			w			w			w			w			w			w			w				
Malles / Mals **546 / 954** d.	0520	0542	0616	0703	0720	0820	0903	0920	1020	1103	1120	1220	1303	1320	1420	1503	1520	1620	1703	1720	1820	1903	1920	2020	2120	...
Merano / Meran a.	0630	0654	0732	0813	0843	0943	1013	1043	1143	1213	1243	1343	1413	1443	1543	1613	1643	1743	1813	1843	1943	2013	2039	2139	2239	...

w – ⚒ until Mar. 15; daily from Mar. 17.

Trains call at Silandro / Schlanders 46–54 minutes after leaving Merano, 24–28 minutes after leaving Malles.

Ferrovia della Val Venosta Operator: Servizi Autobus Dolomiti (SAD), Via Conciapelli 60, I-39100 Bolzano. ✆ +39 0471 97 12 59, fax +39 0471 97 00 42.

599 ITALIAN LAKES (LAGO MAGGIORE, GARDA, COMO)

Lago Maggiore: ⛴ services link Arona, Stresa, Baveno, Laveno, Luino and Locarno throughout the year on an irregular schedule.
Operator: Navigazione sul Lago Maggiore, P. le Baracca 1, 28041 Arona, Italy. ✆ +39 (0)322 233 200, fax: +39 (0)322 249 530. www.navigazionelaghi.it

Lago di Garda: ⛴ services link Desenzano, Peschiera, Garda, Salo, Gardone and Riva, (April to September only), on an irregular schedule.
Operator: Navigazione sul Lago di Garda, Piazza Matteotti 1, 25015 Desenzano del Garda, Italy. ✆ +39 (0)30 914 9511, fax: +39 (0)30 914 9520. www.navigazionelaghi.it

Lago di Como: ⛴ services link Como, Bellagio, Menaggio, Varenna, Bellano and Colico (April to September only) on an irregular schedule.
Operator: Navigazione Lago di Como, Via Per Cernobbio 18, 22100 Como, Italy. ✆ +39 (0)31 579 211, fax: +39 (0)31 570 080. www.navigazionelaghi.it

Hydrofoil service **June 1 - October 5, 2014**:

	⚒		†	⚒	⚒	†	⚒	†	⚒	⚒	
Como d.	0733	0900	1110	1225	1330	1400	1420	1615	1710	1810	1920
Tremezzo d.	0819**r**	0939	1153	1302	1419	1445	1457	1652	1746	1857	1957
Bellagio d.	0813**r**	0946	1200	1309	1439**r**	1452	1504	1658	1752	1904	2003
Menaggio d.	0807	0954	1208	1314	1430	1500	1509	1704	1758	1919	2009
Bellano d.	...	1004	1218	...	1455	1516	...	1713	1807	...	2021
Colico a.	...	1037	1251	...	1528	1549	...	1740	...	...	2044

	⚒	⚒	†	⚒		⚒	†	⚒		†	⚒
Colico d.	0606	...	0707	...	1037	...	1356	...	1604	1741	...
Bellano d.	0630	...	0738	...	1119	...	1424	...	1644	1806	1808
Menaggio d.	0641	0703	0748	0808	1129	1316	1435	1511	1654	1814	1833
Bellagio d.	0647	0712	0757	0814	1138	1330	1442	1525	1704	1820	1839
Tremezzo d.	0653	0718	0803	0820	1144	1336	1448	1531	1710	1826	1845
Como a.	0730	0805	0850	0857	1226	1412	1525	1607	1800	1905	1916

r – Via Menaggio.

599a LAKE GARDA 🚌 services
Valid from June 9, 2014

Desenzano FS → Salo +*0h33* → Gardone +*0h38* → Maderno +*0h46* → Toscolano +*0h49* → Gargnano +*1h00* → Limone +*1h32* → **Riva** +*1h50*.
Route LN027. From Desenzano: 0600, 0810, 1135, 1330, 1620, 1830.

Verona P N → **Peschiera** FS +*0h51* → Lazise +*1h13* → Bardolino +*1h25* → **Garda** +*1h35*.
Route 164. From Verona: 0540, 0740, 0840 and hourly until 2040.

Verona P N → Lazise +*0h46* → Bardolino +*0h58* → **Garda** +*1h08*.
Route 162. From Verona: 0638, 1008, 1408, 1608, 2008.

Garda → Torri del Benaco +*0h14* → Porto Brenzone +*0h34* → Malcesine +*0h46* → Torbole +*1h04* → **Riva** +*1h14*
Route 184. From Garda: 0615, 0715, 0815 and hourly until 2015.

Services from Verona Porta Nuova bus station, and Peschiera and Desenzano railway stations (Table **605**).

Operator: Azienda Transporti Verona s.r.l., Lungadige Galtarossa 5, 37133 Verona. ✆ 045 8057811, fax 045 8057800.

Riva → Limone +*0h18* → Gargnano +*0h50* → Toscolano +*1h01* → Maderno +*1h04* → Gardone +*1h12* → Salo +*1h17* → **Desenzano** FS +*1h50*.
Route LN027. From Riva: 0540, 0810, 0910, 1245, 1510, 1710.

Garda → Bardolino +*0h10* → Lazise +*0h22* → **Peschiera** FS +*0h44* → **Verona P N** +*1h32*.
Route 164. From Garda: 0653, 0753, 0853 and hourly until 1853, then 2153.

Garda → Bardolino +*0h10* → Lazise +*0h22* → **Verona P N** +*1h09*.
Route 162. From Garda: 0736, 1046, 1246, 1646, 1846, 2046.

Riva → Torbole +*0h10* → Malcesine +*0h31* → Porto Brenzone +*0h43* → Torri del Benaco +*1h03* → **Garda** +*1h14*.
Route 184. From Riva: 0539, 0639, 0739 and hourly until 1939.

Additional local services run serving the lakeside resorts.

Other operators: Brescia Transporti ✆ 030 44061, fax 030 3754505; Trentino Transporti ✆ 0461 821000, fax 0461 031407.

HIGH-SPEED SERVICES – southbound 600

Operator: Trenitalia

Trenitalia high-speed services

All trains 🄁 and 🍸

km	km		FR 9601	FR 9501 ⚒ A	FR 9603 Ⓐ	FA 9401	FA 9403 ⚒	FR 9503 9505 ⚒	FA 9461	FR 9607	FR 9507 M	FR 9509	FR 9609 Ⓑy	FR 9561 Ⓐ	FA 9463 B	FR 9611 Ⓐ	FA 9407	FR 9593 Nq	FR 9513	FR 9563 9565 ⚒	FA 9465 Y	FR 9615	FA 9411 T	FA 9413 U	FR 9517
	0	**Venezia** Santa Lucia ♣ d.	...	...	...	...	0615	...	...	...	...	...	...	...	...	...	0725	...	...	...	...	...	...	...	...
	9	**Venezia** Mestre ♣ d.	...	...	...	0537	0627	...	...	...	...	...	...	...	...	...	0737	...	...	...	...	...	0837	0847	...
	37	Padova d.	...	...	...	0553	0642	...	...	...	...	...	...	...	...	...	0753	...	...	...	...	...	0853	0903	...
0		**Torino** Porta Nuova d.	...	...	...	|	|	...	...	0550	...	...	...	0615	...	...	|	...	...	0715	...	0750	|	|	0802
6		**Torino** Porta Susa d.	...	...	...	|	|	...	...	0600	...	...	...	0625	...	...	|	...	...	0725	...	0800	|	|	0814
		Verona Porta Nuova d.	...	...	...	|	|	...	0650	|	...	...	...	|	0750	...	|	...	...	|	0850	|	|	|	|
148		**Milano** Centrale a.	...	...	...	|	|	...	|	0650	...	...	...	0709**g**	|	...	|	...	...	0809**g**	|	0850	|	|	0902
148		**Milano** Centrale d.	...	...	0608	|	|	0623	|	0700	0550	0715	0725	0712**g**	|	0800	|	0750	0815	0812**g**	|	0900	|	|	0915
158		**Milano** Rogoredo d.	...	...	|	|	|	|	|	0709	|	|	|	0734	|	|	|	|	|	0832	|	|	|	|	|
299		Reggio Emilia AV d.	...	...	0656	|	|	0711	|	|	|	|	|	0813	|	|	|	0834	|	0911	|	|	|	|	|
363	160	**Bologna** Centrale d.	...	0600	|	0653	|	0735	0743	|	0755	0820	0830	0835	0843	|	0853	0855	0920	0935	0943	|	0953	1003	1020
455	—	**Firenze** SMN a.	...	0641	|	0730	|	0810	0820**c**	|	0830	0855	|	0910	0920**c**	|	0930	...	0955	1010	1020**c**	|	1030	1040	1055
455	0	**Firenze** SMN d.	...	0650	|	0738	|	0819	0822**c**	|	0839	0904	|	0919	0922**c**	|	0938	...	1004	1019	1022**c**	|	1038	1048	1104
	257	**Roma** Tiburtina a.	...	0824	|	0858	0923	0939	|	0949	0958	1024	|	1039	|	|	1058	...	1124	1139	|	|	1158	1208	1224
716	261	**Roma** Termini a.	...	0835	0910	0910	0935	0950	0940	0959	1010	1035	1024	1050	1040	1055	1110	...	1135	|	1140	1155	1210	1220	1235
716		**Roma** Termini d.	0735	0845	0920	...	...	1000	...	1010	...	1045	1035	...	...	...	...	...	1145	|	...	...	...	...	1245
938		**Napoli** Centrale a.	0845	0955	1028	...	...	1110	...	1120	...	1155	1145	...	...	...	...	...	1255	1250	...	...	...	...	1355
988		Salerno a.	...	...	...	...	...	1159	...	...	...	...	...	...	...	...	...	...	...	1342	...	...	...	...	...

	FR 9567 ⚒	FR 9619	FA 9415	FR 9521 9523	FR 9623 Ⓐ	FA 9419	FR 9525	FR 9627 Ⓐ	FA 9423	FR 9529	FR 9631 Ⓐ	FA 9427	FR 9533	FR 9635 Ⓑy	FA 9431	FR 9583 ⑤	FR 9537	FR 9639	FR 9569 9571 Ⓑy	FA 9477 Y	FA 9435	FA 9437	FR 9541 9543	FR 9573	FR 9643 Ⓑy
Venezia Santa Lucia ♣ d.	...	...	0925	...	...	1025	...	...	1125	...	...	1225	...	...	1325	...	...	...	...	...	1425	1435	...	...	...
Venezia Mestre ♣ d.	...	...	0937	...	...	1037	...	...	1137	...	...	1237	...	...	1337	...	...	...	...	...	1437	1447	...	...	...
Padova d.	...	...	0953	...	...	1053	...	...	1153	...	...	1253	...	...	1353	...	...	...	...	...	1453	1503	...	...	...
Torino Porta Nuova d.	0815	...	|	...	0950	|	...	...	|	...	1150	|	...	...	|	...	...	...	1315	...	|	|	...	1415	...
Torino Porta Susa d.	0825	...	|	...	1000	|	...	...	|	...	1200	|	...	...	|	...	...	...	1325	...	|	|	...	1425	...
Verona Porta Nuova d.	|	...	|	...	|	|	...	...	|	...	|	|	...	...	|	...	...	...	|	1450	|	|	...	|	...
Milano Centrale a.	0909**g**	...	|	...	1050	|	...	...	|	...	1250	|	...	...	|	...	...	...	1409**g**	|	|	|	...	1509**g**	...
Milano Centrale d.	0912**g**	1000	|	1015	1100	|	1115	1200	|	1215	1300	|	1315	1400	|	1405	1415	1500	1412**g**	|	|	|	1515	1512**g**	1600
Milano Rogoredo d.	0932	|	|	|	|	|	|	|	|	|	|	|	|	|	|	|	|	|	1432	|	|	|	|	1532	|
Reggio Emilia AV d.	1011	|	|	|	|	|	|	|	|	|	|	|	|	|	|	|	|	|	1511	|	|	|	|	1611	|
Bologna Centrale d.	1035	|	1053	1120	|	1153	1220	|	1253	1320	|	1353	1420	|	1453	1508	1520	|	1535	1543	1553	1603	1620	1635	|
Firenze SMN a.	1110	|	1130	1155	|	1230	1255	|	1330	1355	|	1430	1455	|	1530	1545	1555	|	1610	1620**c**	1630	1640	1655	1710	|
Firenze SMN d.	1119	|	1138	1204	|	1238	1304	|	1338	1404	|	1438	1504	|	1538	1554	1604	|	1619	1622**c**	1638	1648	1704	1719	|
Roma Tiburtina a.	1239	|	1258	1324	|	1358	1424	|	1458	1524	|	1558	1624	|	1658	1714	1724	|	1739	|	1758	1808	1824	1839	|
Roma Termini a.	1250	1255	1310	1335	1355	1410	1435	1455	1510	1535	1555	1610	1635	1655	1710	1725	1735	1755	|	1740	1810	1820	1835	1850	1855
Roma Termini d.	...	1305	...	1345	...	1425	1445	...	...	1545	...	...	1645	1705	...	...	1745	...	|	...	...	...	1845	...	...
Napoli Centrale a.	...	1415	...	1455	...	1535	1555	...	...	1655	...	...	1755	1815	...	...	1855	...	1850	...	...	...	1955	...	...
Salerno a.	...	...	...	1542	...	...	...	...	...	...	...	...	...	...	...	...	...	...	1942	...	...	...	2044	...	...

	FA 9439 9441	FR 9585 ⑤	FR 9545	FR 9645 Ⓑy	FA 9481 Y	FR 9647	FA 9443	FA 9445	FR 9549 9551	FR 9575	FA 9483 B	FR 9591 N	FR 9651 Ⓑy	FA 9447	FR 9553	FR 9653 Ⓑy	FA 9485 Y	FR 9555 Ⓑy	FR 9655	FA 9451	FR 9587 ⑤	FR 9557	FA 9455	FR 9559 Ⓑy	FR 9663 ⑦
Venezia Santa Lucia ♣ d.	1525	...	...	...	...	...	1625	1635	...	...	...	...	...	1725	...	...	...	...	...	1825	...	...	1925	...	...
Venezia Mestre ♣ d.	1537	...	...	...	...	...	1637	1647	...	...	...	...	...	1737	...	...	...	...	...	1837	...	...	1937	...	...
Padova d.	1553	...	...	...	...	...	1653	1703	...	...	...	...	...	1753	...	...	...	...	...	1853	...	...	1953	...	...
Torino Porta Nuova d.	|	...	...	...	...	1550	|	|	...	1615	...	...	...	|	...	...	...	...	1750	|	...	1802	|	1902	1950
Torino Porta Susa d.	|	...	...	...	...	1600	|	|	...	1625	...	...	...	|	...	...	...	...	1800	|	...	1814	|	1914	2000
Verona Porta Nuova d.	|	...	...	...	1650	|	|	|	...	|	1750	...	...	|	...	...	1850	...	|	|	...	|	|	|	|
Milano Centrale a.	|	...	...	...	|	1650	|	|	...	1709**g**	|	...	...	|	...	...	|	...	1850	|	...	1902	|	2002	2050
Milano Centrale d.	|	1605	1615	1625	|	1700	|	|	1715	1712**g**	|	1743	1800	|	1815	1825	|	1835	1900	|	1905	1915	|	2015	2100
Milano Rogoredo d.	|	|	|	|	|	1709	|	|	|	1732	|	|	|	|	|	|	|	|	|	|	|	|	|	|	|
Reggio Emilia AV d.	|	|	|	|	|	|	|	|	|	1811	|	1834	|	|	|	|	|	1923	|	|	|	|	|	|	|
Bologna Centrale d.	1653	1708	1720	1730	1743	|	1753	1803	1820	1835	1843	1855	|	1853	1920	1930	1943	1948	|	1953	2008	2020	2053	2120	|
Firenze SMN a.	1730	1745	1755	|	1820**c**	|	1830	1840	1855	1910	1920**c**	...	|	1930	1955	|	2020**c**	2023	|	2030	2045	2055	2130	2155	|
Firenze SMN d.	1738	1754	1804	|	1822**c**	|	1838	1848	1904	1919	1922**c**	...	|	1938	2004	|	2022**c**	...	|	2038	2054	2104	2138	2204	|
Roma Tiburtina a.	1858	|	1924	|	|	1949	1958	2008	2024	2039	|	...	|	2058	2124	|	|	...	|	2158	2214	2224	2258	2324	|
Roma Termini a.	1910	1920	1935	1924	1940	1959	2010	2020	2035	2050	2040	...	2055	2110	2135	2124	2140	...	2155	2210	2225	2235	2310	2335	2355
Roma Termini d.	1923	1930	1945	1940	...	...	...	...	2045	...	...	...	2105	...	2145	2135	...	...	...	...	...	...	...	...	...
Napoli Centrale a.	2035	2040	2055	2050	...	...	...	...	2155	...	...	...	2215	...	2255	2245	...	...	...	...	...	...	...	...	...
Salerno a.	2124	...	...	...	...	...	...	...	2244	...	...	...	...	...	...	...	...	...	...	...	...	...	...	...	...

– Via Arezzo – see Table **620**.
– From Brescia – see Table **605**.
– Via Modena – see Table **615**.
– To Ancona – see Table **630**.

T – From Trieste – see Table **601**.
U – From Udine – see Table **601**.
Y – From Bolzano – see Table **595**.

c – Firenze **Campo di Marte**.
g – Milano **Porta Garibaldi**.
q – June 15 - Sept. 13.
y – Not days before holidays.

♣ – Local journeys are not permitted Venezia Santa Lucia - Mestre and v.v.

Operator: Nuovo Trasporto Viaggiatori (NTV)

Italo high-speed services

Club, Prima and Smart class

All trains 🄁

Subject to alteration from June 15. *Trenitalia* tickets and passes not valid

www.italotreno.it

	ITA 9903 9905	ITA 9907	ITA 9971 9973	ITA 9981	ITA 9911	ITA 9993	ITA 9915 9917	ITA 9919	ITA 9983	ITA 9923 9925	ITA 9927 h	ITA 9931 9933	ITA 9985	ITA 9995	ITA 9935 h	ITA 9975 Ⓑk	ITA 9939 9941	ITA 9943	ITA 9987 9989	ITA 9947	ITA 9951 9953	ITA 9977 Ⓑk	ITA 9997	ITA 9991	ITA 9959 n	ITA 9963 Ⓑp
Torino Porta Susa d.	...	...	0615	...	...	...	0747	0847	...	...	...	1147**j**	...	1232	...	1315	...	...	...	...	1640	...	...	...	...	1947
Milano Porta Garibaldi d.	...	0627	0703	...	0734	0748	0834	0934	...	1034	1134	1234	...	1319	1334	1403	1427	1534	...	1634	1727	1803	1834	...	1934	2034
Milano Rogoredo d.	...	0647	0723	...	0754	0814	0854	0954	...	1054	1154	1254	...	1339	1354	1423	1447	1554	...	1654	1747	1823	1854	...	1954	2054**r**
Reggio Emilia ⊖ d.	...	0726	|	...	|	0851	|	|	...	|	|	|	...	1414	|	|	1526	|	...	|	1826	|	1931	...	|	|
Venezia Santa Lucia d.	...	|	|	0625	|	|	|	|	0955	|	|	|	1255	|	|	|	|	|	1555	|	|	|	|	1855	|	|
Venezia Mestre d.	...	|	|	0637	|	|	|	|	1007	|	|	|	1307	|	|	|	|	|	1607	|	|	|	|	1907	|	|
Padova d.	...	|	|	0653	|	|	|	|	1023	|	|	|	1323	|	|	|	|	|	1623	|	|	|	|	1923	|	|
Bologna Centrale d.	...	0750	|	0803	0850	0919	0950	1050	1123	1150	1250	1350	1423	1447	1450	|	1550	1650	1723	1750	1850	|	2002	2023	2050	2147**r**
Rimini d.	...	|	|	|	|	1016		|	|	|	|	|	|	1542	|	|	|	|	|	|	|	|	2057	|	|	...
Pesaro d.	...	|	|	|	|	1035		|	|	|	|	|	|	1602	|	|	|	|	|	|	|	|	2117	|	|	...
Ancona a.	...	|	|	|	|	1106		|	|	|	|	|	|	1634	|	|	|	|	|	|	|	|	2147	|	|	...
Firenze SMN a.	...	0825	|	0840	0925	...	1025	1125	1200	1225	1325	1425	1500	...	1525	|	1625	1725	1800	1825	1925	|	...	2100	2125	...
Firenze SMN d.	0733	0833	|	0848	0933	...	1033	1133	1208	1233	1333	1433	1508	...	1533	|	1633	1733	1808	1833	1933	|	...	2108	2133	...
Roma Tiburtina a.	0853	0953	1003	1008	1053	...	1153	1253	1328	1353	1453	1553	1628	...	1653	1703	1753	1853	1930	1953	2053	2103	...	2228	2253	...
Roma Tiburtina d.	0856	0956	1006	1011	1056	...	1156	1256	1337	1356	1456	1556	1637	...	1656	1706	1756	1856	1937	1956	2056	2106	...	2237	2256	...
Roma Ostiense a.	|	|	|	1025	1109	...	|	1309	1350	|	1509	|	1650	...	1709	1720	|	|	|	|	|	2120	...	2250	2309	...
Napoli Centrale a.	1005	1105	1115	...	...	...	1305	...	...	1505	...	1705	...	...	...	...	1905	2005	2045	2105	2205	...	...	...	...	...
Napoli Centrale d.	1017	...	1127	...	...	...	1320	...	...	1520	...	1720	...	...	...	...	1917	...	2100	...	2217	...	...	...	...	...
Salerno a.	1054	...	1204	...	...	...	1404	...	...	1604	...	1804	...	...	...	...	1954	...	2137	...	2254	...	...	...	...	...

– ①⑤⑥⑦ (not Apr. 20, 21).
⑧ (not Apr. 20, 21, May 1).

k – Not Apr. 20, 21, May 1.
n – Not Apr. 19, 20, 30.

p – Not Apr. 20.
r – ①②③④⑦ only.

⊖ – Reggio Emilia Mediopadana.

600 HIGH-SPEED SERVICES – northbound

Trenitalia high-speed services

All trains 🅁 and 🍸 — Operator: Trenitalia

km		FR 9596 ⚒	FR 9500 ⚒	FR 9602 Ⓐ	FR 9502 ⚒	FR 9592 N	FR 9504 ⚒	FA 9460 Y	FA 9402	FR 9606	FR 9566 Ⓑy	FR 9608 Ⓐ	FR 9508	FA 9406	FR 9610 Ⓐ	FA 9462 Y	FR 9512 9514	FA 9408	FA 9410 9412	FR 9614	FA 9464 B	FR 9568 9570 ⚒	FR 9518	FA 9414	FR 9618
	Salerno d.	...	...	...	...	...	...	...	...	...	...	...	...	...	...	...	0612	...	0636	...	...	0714	...	...	...
	Napoli Centrale d.	...	...	...	...	...	...	...	...	...	...	0610	...	...	0640	...	0700	...	0730	0740	...	0805	0800	...	0840
	Roma Termini a.	...	...	...	...	...	...	...	...	...	...	0720	...	...	0750	...	0810	...	0840	0850	...	|	0907	...	0947
	Roma Termini d.	...	...	0600	...	...	0620	0630	0650	0700	0705	0730	0720	0750	0800	0815	0820	0835	0850	0900	0915	|	0920	0950	1000
	Roma Tiburtina d.	...	...	|	...	...	0629	|	0700	0707	0715	|	0729	0800	|	|	0829	0845	0900	|	|	0915	0929	1000	|
	Firenze SMN a.	...	...	|	...	...	0751	0748c	0822	|	0836	|	0851	0922	|	0933c	0951	1007	1022	|	1033c	1036	1051	1122	|
	Firenze SMN d.	...	0653	|	0730	...	0800	0750c	0830	|	0845	|	0900	0930	|	0935c	1000	1015	1030	|	1035c	1045	1100	1130	|
0	**Bologna** Centrale d.	...	0731	|	0808	0810	0838	0830	0910	|	0923	0928	0938	1010	|	1015	1038	1055	1110	|	1115	1123	1138	1210	|
	Reggio Emilia AV d.	...	0752	|	|	0837	|	|	|	|	0944	|	|	|	|	|	|	|	|	|	|	1144	|	|	|
	Milano Rogoredo a.	...	|	|	|	|	|	|	|	0947	1025	|	|	|	|	|	|	|	|	|	|	1225	|	|	|
	Milano Centrale a.	...	0840	0855	0910	0920	0940	|	|	0959	1043g	1029	1040	|	1055	|	1140	|	|	1155	|	1243g	1240	|	1255
	Milano Centrale d.	0800	...	0905	...	...	...	|	|	...	1045g	...	...	|	1105	|	...	|	|	...	|	1245g	...	|	...
114	**Verona** Porta Nuova a.	|	...	|	...	...	...	0920	|	...	|	...	...	|	|	1105	...	|	|	...	1205	|	...	|	...
	Torino Porta Susa a.	0848	...	0952	...	...	...	...	|	...	1130	...	...	|	1152	...	...	|	|	...	...	1330	...	|	...
	Torino Porta Nuova a.	0900	...	1005	...	...	...	...	|	...	1145	...	...	|	1205	...	...	|	|	...	...	1345	...	|	...
	Padova d.	...	...	...	...	...	...	...	1009	...	...	...	...	1109	...	...	...	1154	1209	...	...	...	...	1309	...
	Venezia Mestre ♣ a.	...	...	...	...	...	...	...	1023	...	...	...	...	1123	...	...	...	1208	1223	...	...	...	...	1323	...
	Venezia Santa Lucia ♣ a.	...	...	...	...	...	...	...	1035	...	...	...	...	1135	...	...	...	1220	1235	...	...	...	...	1335	...

	FA 9466 Y	FR 9572 ⚒	FR 9520	FA 9416	FA 9418	FR 9622 Ⓐ	FR 9524 9526	FA 9422	FR 9626 Ⓐ	FR 9528	FA 9426	FR 9630	FR 9532	FA 9430	FR 9634 Ⓑy	FR 9536	FR 9584 ⑤	FA 9434	FR 9638	FR 9574 9576 Ⓑy	FR 9540	FA 9438	FR 9642 Ⓑy	FR 9578	FA 9478 Y
Salerno d.	...	...	...	...	...	...	0912	...	...	...	...	...	...	...	...	...	...	...	...	1314	...	...	...	...	...
Napoli Centrale d.	...	...	0900	...	...	0940	1000	...	...	1100	...	...	1200	...	...	1300	...	...	...	1405	1400	...	1440	...	...
Roma Termini a.	...	...	1010	...	...	1050	1110	...	...	1210	...	...	1310	...	...	1410	...	...	...	|	1510	...	1550	...	...
Roma Termini d.	1015	1005	1020	1035	1050	1100	1120	1150	1200	1220	1250	1300a	1320	1350	1400	1420	1431	1450	1500	|	1520	1550	1600	1605	1615
Roma Tiburtina d.	|	1015	1029	1045	1100	|	1129	1200	|	1229	1300	|	1329	1400	|	1429	1439	1500	|	1515	1529	1600	|	1615	|
Firenze SMN a.	1133c	1136	1151	1207	1222	|	1251	1322	|	1351	1422	|	1451	1522	|	1551	1601	1622	|	1636	1651	1722	|	1736	1733c
Firenze SMN d.	1135c	1145	1200	1215	1230	|	1300	1330	|	1400	1430	|	1500	1530	|	1600	1610	1630	|	1645	1700	1730	|	1745	1735c
Bologna Centrale d.	1215	1223	1238	1255	1310	|	1338	1410	|	1438	1510	|	1538	1610	|	1638	1650	1710	|	1723	1738	1810	|	1823	1815
Reggio Emilia AV d.	|	1244	|	|	|	|	|	|	|	|	|	|	|	|	|	|	|	|	|	1744	|	|	|	1844	|
Milano Rogoredo a.	|	1325	|	|	|	|	|	|	|	|	|	|	|	|	|	|	|	|	|	1825	|	|	|	1925	|
Milano Centrale a.	|	1343g	1340	|	|	1355	1440	|	1455	1540	|	1555a	1640	|	1655	1740	1750	|	1755	1843g	1840	|	1855	1943g	|
Milano Centrale d.	|	1345g	...	|	|	1405	...	|	...	...	|	1605	...	|	1705	...	...	|	1805	1845g	...	|	...	1945g	|
Verona Porta Nuova a.	1305	|	...	|	|	|	...	|	...	...	|	|	...	|	|	...	...	|	|	|	...	|	...	|	1905
Torino Porta Susa a.	...	1430	...	|	|	1452	...	|	...	...	|	1652	...	|	1752	...	...	|	1852	1930	...	|	...	2030	...
Torino Porta Nuova a.	...	1445	...	|	|	1505	...	|	...	...	|	1705	...	|	1805	...	...	|	1905	1945	...	|	...	2045	...
Padova d.	...	...	...	1354	1409	...	...	1509	...	...	1609	...	...	1709	...	...	...	1809	...	...	...	1909	...	...	...
Venezia Mestre ♣ a.	...	...	...	1408	1423	...	...	1523	...	...	1623	...	...	1723	...	...	...	1823	...	...	...	1923	...	...	...
Venezia Santa Lucia ♣ a.	...	...	...	1420	1435	...	...	1535	...	...	1635	...	...	1735	...	...	...	1835	...	...	...	1935	...	...	...

	FR 9544	FR 9644 Ⓑy	FA 9440 T	FA 9442 U	FR 9646	FA 9480	FR 9548 9550	FR 9594 Nq	FA 9444 Ⓑy	FA 9446	FR 9650 Ⓑy	FR 9580	FA 9482 B	FR 9552	FR 9652 Ⓑy	FR 9588 ⑤	FR 9586 ⑦	FA 9450	FR 9654	FR 9556 9558	FR 9560 M	FA 9454	FR 9562 Ⓑy	FR 9564 Ⓑy	FR 9662 ⑦
Salerno d.	...	...	...	...	...	...	1512	...	...	...	...	...	...	...	...	...	...	...	...	1712	...	...	...	...	...
Napoli Centrale d.	1500	1510	...	...	...	...	1600	...	...	1630	1640	...	...	1700	1710	...	1715	...	...	1800	...	...	1900	1930	1940
Roma Termini a.	1610	1620	...	...	...	...	1710	...	...	1740	1750	...	...	1810	1820	...	1825	...	...	1910	...	...	2010	2040	2050
Roma Termini d.	1620	1630	1635	1650	1700	1715	1720	...	1725	1750	1800	1805	1815	1820	1830	1827	1835	1850	1900	1920	1935	1950	2020	2050	2100
Roma Tiburtina d.	1629	|	1645	1700	1707	|	1729	...	1735	1800	|	1815	|	1829	|	1838	|	1900	|	1929	1945	2000	2029	2100	|
Firenze SMN a.	1751	|	1807	1822	|	1833c	1851	...	|	1922	|	1936	1933c	1951	|	2001	2001	2022	|	2051	2106	2122	2151	2222	|
Firenze SMN d.	1800	|	1815	1830	|	1835c	1900	...	|	1930	|	1945	1935c	2000	|	2010	2010	2030	|	2100	2115	2130	2200	...	|
Bologna Centrale d.	1838	1828	1855	1910	|	1915	1938	1940	|	2010	|	2023	2015	2038	2028	2050	2050	2110	|	2138	2153	2210	2238	...	|
Reggio Emilia AV d.	|	|	|	|	|	|	|	2006	|	|	|	2044	|	|	|	|	|	|	2118	|	|	|	|	...	|
Milano Rogoredo a.	|	|	|	|	1949	|	|	|	|	|	|	2124	|	|	|	|	|	|	|	|	|	|	|	...	|
Milano Centrale a.	1940	1929	|	|	1959	|	2040	2050	|	|	2055	2143g	|	2140	2129	2150	2150	|	2202	2240	2350	|	2340	...	2355
Milano Centrale d.	...	...	|	|	2010	|	...	...	|	|	...	2145g	|	...	...	...	...	|	2212	...	...	|	...	...	...
Verona Porta Nuova a.	...	...	|	|	|	2005	...	...	|	|	...	|	2105	...	...	...	...	|	|	...	...	|	...	...	...
Torino Porta Susa a.	...	...	|	|	2059	...	...	...	|	|	...	2230	...	...	...	...	...	|	2302	...	...	|	...	...	...
Torino Porta Nuova a.	...	...	|	|	2110	...	...	...	|	|	...	2245	...	...	...	...	...	|	2312	...	...	|	...	...	...
Padova d.	...	...	1954	2009	...	...	...	...	2019	2109	...	...	...	...	...	...	...	2209	...	...	...	2309	...	...	...
Venezia Mestre ♣ a.	...	...	2008	2021	...	...	...	...	2032	2123	...	...	...	...	...	...	...	2223	...	...	...	2323	...	...	...
Venezia Santa Lucia ♣ a.	...	...	...	...	...	...	...	...	2044	2135	...	...	...	...	...	...	...	2235	...	...	...	2335	...	...	...

B – To Brescia – see Table 605.
M – Via Modena – see Table 615.
N – From Ancona – see Table 630.
T – From Trieste – see Table 601.
U – To Udine – see Table 601.
Y – To Bolzano – see Table 595.
a – Ⓐ only.
c – Firenze **Campo di Marte**.
g – Milano **Porta Garibaldi**.
q – June 15 - Sept. 13.
y – Not days before holidays.
♣ – Local journeys are not permitted Venezia Santa Lucia - Mestre and v.

Italo high-speed services

Club, Prima and Smart class — Operator: Nuovo Trasporto Viaggiatori (NTV)

All trains 🅁 — **Subject to alteration from June 15.** *Trenitalia* tickets and passes not valid — www.italotreno.i

	ITA 9906 Ⓐq	ITA 9972 Ⓑk	ITA 9992	ITA 9910 k	ITA 9980	ITA 9914	ITA 9918 9920	ITA 9982 9984	ITA 9922	ITA 9926	ITA 9994	ITA 9930 9932	ITA 9934 h	ITA 9986	ITA 9938	ITA 9974 9976	ITA 9942 h	ITA 9946 9948	ITA 9988	ITA 9950	ITA 9954 9956	ITA 9996	ITA 9978 Ⓑk	ITA 9990	ITA 9962 9964	ITA 996 996
Salerno d.	...	...	...	...	...	...	0657	0720	...	...	...	0957	...	...	...	1252	...	1357	...	...	1557	...	...	...	1757	185
Napoli Centrale a.	...	...	...	...	...	...	0733	0759	...	...	...	1033	...	...	...	1328	...	1433	...	...	1633	...	...	...	1833	193
Napoli Centrale d.	...	...	...	...	...	0645	0745	0815	...	0945	...	1045	...	...	1245	1340	...	1445	...	...	1645	...	...	...	1845	194
Roma Ostiense d.	...	0626	...	0640	0710	|	|	|	0940	|	...	|	1240	1310	|	|	1440	|	1610	1640	|	...	1826	1840	|	|
Roma Tiburtina a.	...	0640	...	0653	0723	0753	0853	0923	0953	1053	...	1153	1253	1323	1353	1448	1453	1553	1623	1653	1753	...	1840	1853	1953	205
Roma Tiburtina d.	...	0650	...	0655	0725	0755	0855	0925	0955	1055	...	1155	1255	1325	1355	1450	1455	1555	1625	1655	1755	...	1850	1855	1955	205
Firenze SMN a.	...	|	...	0817	0847	0917	1017	1047	1117	1217	...	1317	1417	1447	1517	|	1617	1717	1747	1817	1917	...	|	2017	2117	221
Firenze SMN d.	...	|	...	0825	0855	0925	1025	1055	1125	1225	...	1325	1425	1455	1525	|	1625	1725	1755	1825	1925	...	|	2025	2125	...
Ancona d.	...	|	0645	|	|	|	|	|	|	|	1150	|	|	|	|	|	|	|	|	|	|	1813	|	|	|	...
Pesaro d.	...	|	0725	|	|	|	|	|	|	|	1225	|	|	|	|	|	|	|	|	|	|	1844	|	|	|	...
Rimini d.	...	|	0745	|	|	|	|	|	|	|	1245	|	|	|	|	|	|	|	|	|	|	1903	|	|	|	...
Bologna Centrale d.	0744	|	0845	0903	0935	1003	1103	1135	1203	1303	1345	1403	1503	1535	1603	|	1703	1803	1835	1903	2003	2005	|	2105	2203	...
Padova a.	|	|	|	|	1034	|	|	1232	|	|	|	|	|	1632	|	|	|	|	1932	|	|	|	|	2202	|	...
Venezia Mestre a.	|	|	|	|	1048	|	|	1248	|	|	|	|	|	1648	|	|	|	|	1948	|	|	|	|	2218	|	...
Venezia Santa Lucia a.	|	|	|	|	1100	|	|	1300	|	|	|	|	|	1700	|	|	|	|	2000	|	|	|	|	2230	|	...
Reggio Emilia ⊖ d.	0809	|	0909	|	...	1024	|	...	|	1324	1409	|	|	...	|	|	|	|	...	|	2022	2029	|	...	|	...
Milano Rogoredo a.	0850	0930	0952	0956	...	1103	1156	...	1256	1403	1448	1456	1556	...	1656	1730	1756	1856	...	1956	2103	2109	2130	...	2256	...
Milano Porta Garibaldi a.	0910	0954	1012	1018	...	1125	1218	...	1318	1425	1512	1518	1618	...	1718	1754	1818	1918	...	2018	2125	2132	2154	...	2318	...
Torino Porta Susa a.	...	1044	1105	...	...	1212j	...	...	...	...	...	1605	...	...	...	1844	...	2005	...	2105	...	...	2244	...	...	...

h – ①⑤⑥⑦ (not Apr. 20, 21).
j – ⑧ (not Apr. 20, 21, May 1).
k – Not Apr. 20, 21, May 1.
q – Not Apr. 21.
⊖ – Reggio Emilia Mediopadana.

VENEZIA - UDINE - TRIESTE 601

Venezia - Trieste direct services

km		2 ⚒	2 ⚒	IC 735				FB 9707 T						IC 589 ♦				FB 9737 T		FA 9449 ♦	FB 9741 M	IC 593 ♦	FB 9747 M	
	Roma Termini **616** d.	...	...	...	...	...	...	...	...	...	...	...	...	1030	...	...	...	...	...	1635	...	1540	...	...
0	**Venezia** Santa Lucia **605** d.	...	...	...	0641	0741	0941	...	1041	1241	1341	1441	1541	|	1641	1741	1841	...	1941	|	...	|	...	2241
9	**Venezia** Mestre **605** d.	...	...	0550	0653	0753	0953	1020	1053	1253	1353	1453	1553	1646	1653	1753	1853	1949	1953	2021	2046	2138	2155	2253
42	S. Dona di Piave-Jesolo ◧ d.	...	...	0616	0716	0816	1016	1046	1116	1316	1416	1516	1616	1709	1716	1816	1916	|	2016	|	|	2159	|	2316
69	Portogruaro-Caorle d.	0531	0613	0635	0737	0837	1037	1104	1137	1337	1437	1537	1637	1730	1737	1837	1937	2029	2037	|	2129	2216	|	2337
83	Latisana-Lignano-Bibione d.	0542	0624	0648	0748	0848	1048	1114	1148	1348	1448	1548	1648	1740	1748	1848	1948	|	2048	|	|	2226	|	2348
101	S. Giorgio di Nogaro d.	0555	0637	0701	0801	0901	1101	|	1201	1401	1501	1601	1701	|	1801	1901	2001	|	2101	|	|	|	|	0001
112	Cervignano-Aquileia-Grado d.	0604	0646	0710	0810	0910	1110	1131	1210	1410	1509	1610	1710	1800	1810	1910	2010	|	2110	|	|	2246	|	0010
129	Monfalcone d.	0617	0659	0723	0823	0923	1123	1145	1223	1423	1523	1623	1723	1816	1823	1923	2023	2059	2123	|	2159	2301	|	0023
157	**Trieste** Centrale ⊗ a.	0640	0722	0746	0846	0946	1146	1208	1246	1446	1546	1646	1746	1839	1846	1946	2046	2122	2151	2146	2222	2331	2319	0046

	2 ⚒			FB 9790 M	FB 9710 T	FA 9404 ♦		IC 584 ♦			FB 9716 T		IC 594 ♦					FB 9748 M					IC 734	
Trieste Centrale ⊗ d.	...	0515	0610	0616	0638	0645	0715	0721	0815	0915	0938	1215	1301	1315	1415	1515	1615	1701	1715	1815	1915	2115	2206	...
Monfalcone d.	...	0539	0638	|	0703	|	0739	0746	0839	0939	1003	1239	1326	1339	1439	1539	1639	1726	1739	1839	1939	2139	2230	...
Cervignano-Aquileia-Grado d.	...	0551	0651	|	|	|	0751	0758	0851	0951	|	1251	1336	1351	1451	1551	1651	1736	1751	1851	1951	2151	2242	...
S. Giorgio di Nogaro d.	...	0559	0659	|	|	|	0759	|	0859	0959	|	1259	|	1359	1459	1559	1659	|	1759	1859	1959	2159	2251	...
Latisana-Lignano-Bibione d.	...	0613	0713	|	|	|	0813	0821	0913	1013	|	1313	1351	1413	1513	1613	1713	1750	1813	1913	2013	2213	2304	...
Portogruaro-Caorle d.	0538	0624	0724	|	0733	|	0824	0832	0924	1024	1033	1324	1401	1424	1524	1624	1724	1800	1824	1924	2024	2223	2315	...
S. Dona di Piave-Jesolo ◧ d.	0601	0642	0742	|	|	|	0842	0850	0942	1042	|	1342	1419	1442	1542	1642	1742	1816	1842	1942	2042	...	2337	...
Venezia Mestre **605** a.	0636	0708	0808	0740	0814	0824	0908	0912	1008	1108	1114	1408	1452	1508	1608	1708	1808	1842	1908	2008	2108	...	0005	...
Venezia Santa Lucia **605** a.	0650	0720	0820	...	...	|	0920	|	1020	1120	...	1424	|	1520	1620	1720	1820	...	1920	2020	2120	...	...	...
Roma Termini **616** a.	...	...	...	...	...	1210	...	1520	...	...	...	...	2042	...	...	...	...	...	...	...	...	...	...	...

Venezia - Trieste via Udine

km		EN 234 ♦	Ⓐ	2 Ⓐ	ICN 774 ♦	2 Ⓐ	2 ⚒	⚒	2 †	2 †	2 ⚒	2 ⚒	†	FB 9720 ♦	2 Ⓐm	2 †	2 Ⓒp		2 ⚒	2 Ⓒ		2 ⚒	2 ⚒	⚒	2 †
0	**Venezia** Santa Lucia d.	...	0504	0515	0536	0604	0615	0704	...	0715	0715	0804	0804	...	0904	...	0915	1004	...	1115	1204	...	1215	1304	...
9	**Venezia** Mestre d.	0130	0516	0529	|	0616	0629	0716	...	0729	0729	0816	0816	0913	0916	...	0929	1016	...	1129	1216	...	1229	1316	...
30	Treviso Centrale d.	|	0536	0554	0614	0636	0654	0736	...	0754	0754	0836	0836	0930	0936	...	0954	1036	...	1154	1236	...	1254	1336	...
57	Conegliano **603** d.	|	0555	0622	0637	0655	0722	0755	...	0822	0822	0855	0855	0948	0955	...	1022	1055	...	1222	1255	...	1322	1355	...
74	Sacile d.	|	0608	0638	0656	0708	0738	0808	...	0838	0838	0908	0908	|	1008	...	1038	1108	...	1238	1308	...	1338	1408	...
87	Pordenone d.	|	0619	0652	0706	0719	0752	0819	...	0852	0852	0919	0919	1007	1019	...	1052	1119	...	1252	1319	...	1352	1419	...
136	**Udine** a.	0244	0653	0730	0740	0753	0830	0853	...	0930	0930	0953	0953	1035	1053	...	1130	1153	...	1330	1353	...	1430	1453	...
136	**Udine** d.	...	0656	0742	0755	...	...	0856	0912	...	0933	...	0956	...	...	1112	...	1156	1238	...	1356	1418	...	...	1512
169	Gorizia Centrale d.	...	0720	0812	0828	...	...	0920	0942	...	1003	...	1020	...	...	1142	...	1220	|	...	1420	1448	...	...	1542
192	Monfalcone d.	...	0741	0835	0855	...	...	0941	1005	...	1026	...	1041	...	...	1205	...	1241	1316	...	1441	1511	...	...	1605
219	**Trieste** Centrale ⊗ a.	...	0804	0904	0920	...	...	1004	1034	...	1055	...	1104	...	...	1234	...	1304	1340	...	1504	1540	...	...	1634

	2		Ⓐm	2 Ⓐ	2 †	2		2 ⚒	2 Ⓐ	Ⓐ	2 †	2		2 Ⓐ	Ⓐ	†	2 ⚒	2		FA 9442 ♦	FB 9744 ♦	EN 236 ♦	2		
Venezia Santa Lucia d.	1315	1404	1504	...	...	1515	1604	...	1615	1704	...	1715	1804	1815	1904	1904	...	1915	2004	...	...	2057	2115	2204	2304
Venezia Mestre d.	1329	1416	1516	...	...	1529	1616	...	1629	1716	...	1729	1816	1829	1916	1916	...	1929	2016	2040	...	2109	2129	2216	2316
Treviso Centrale d.	1354	1436	1536	...	...	1554	1636	...	1654	1736	...	1754	1836	1854	1936	1936	...	1954	2036	2056	2129	2136	2154	2236	2336
Conegliano **603** d.	1422	1455	1555	...	...	1622	1655	...	1722	1755	...	1822	1855	1922	1955	1955	...	2022	2055	2115	2145	2156	2222	2255	2355
Sacile d.	1438	1508	1608	...	...	1638	1708	...	1738	1808	...	1838	1908	1938	2008	2008	...	2038	2108	|	2156	|	2238	2308	0008
Pordenone d.	1452	1519	1619	...	...	1652	1719	...	1752	1819	...	1852	1919	1952	2019	2019	...	2052	2119	2136	2205	2217	2252	2319	0019
Udine a.	1530	1553	1653	...	...	1730	1753	...	1830	1853	...	1930	1953	2030	2053	2053	...	2130	2153	2205	2230	2245	2330	2353	0053
Udine d.	...	1556	1656	1708	1712	...	1756	1812	...	1856	1912	...	1956	...	...	2112	2112	...	2156	...	...	...	...	2356	...
Gorizia Centrale d.	...	1620	1720	|	1742	...	1820	1842	...	1919	1938	...	2020	...	...	2142	2142	...	2220	...	...	...	...	0026	...
Monfalcone d.	...	1641	1741	1747	1805	...	1841	1905	...	1941	1959	...	2041	...	...	2205	2205	...	2241	...	...	...	...	0049	...
Trieste Centrale ⊗ a.	...	1704	1804	1810	1834	...	1904	1934	...	2004	2022	...	2104	...	...	2234	2234	...	2304	...	...	...	...	0118	...

	EN 235 ♦	Ⓐ	FB 9705 ♦		EN 237 ♦		FA 9413 ♦	⚒	2 ⚒	2 ⚒		2 †	2 ⚒		2 †	Ⓐm	2 Ⓐm		2	Ⓐ	2 †	⑥	FB 9729 ♦	2 ⚒	2 ⚒
Trieste Centrale ⊗ d.	...	...	...	...	...	...	...	0526	0556	0620	0656	0726	0726	0856	0926	...	...	1056	...	1126	1126	...	...	...	1226
Monfalcone d.	...	...	...	...	...	...	...	0556	0626	0644	0720	0756	0756	0920	0956	...	...	1120	...	1156	1156	...	...	...	1256
Gorizia Centrale d.	...	...	...	...	...	...	...	0618	0648	|	0741	0818	0818	0941	1018	...	...	1141	...	1218	1218	...	...	...	1318
Udine a.	...	...	...	...	...	...	...	0648	0718	0722	0804	0848	0848	1004	1048	...	...	1204	...	1248	1248	...	...	...	1348
Udine d.	0137	0507	0550	0607	0625	0631	0655	0700	0731	...	0807	0907	...	1007	...	1107	1131	1207	1231	1307	...	1307	1325	1331	...
Pordenone d.	|	0542	0619	0642	0700	0710	0729	0740	0810	...	0842	0942	...	1042	...	1142	1210	1242	1310	1342	...	1342	1354	1410	...
Sacile d.	|	0552	0632	0652	|	0724	|	0752	0824	...	0852	0952	...	1052	...	1152	1224	1252	1324	1352	...	1352	|	1424	...
Conegliano **603** d.	|	0605	0649	0705	0724	0740	0755	0805	0840	...	0905	1005	...	1105	...	1205	1240	1305	1340	1405	...	1405	1413	1440	...
Treviso Centrale d.	0235	0625	0710	0725	0748	0807	0816	0825	0907	...	0925	1025	...	1125	...	1225	1307	1325	1407	1425	...	1425	1432	1507	...
Venezia Mestre a.	0256	0644	...	0744	0812	0832	0837	0844	0932	...	0944	1044	...	1144	...	1244	1332	1344	1432	1444	...	1444	1449	1532	...
Venezia Santa Lucia a.	...	0656	...	0756	0824	0846	...	0900	0946	...	0956	1056	...	1156	...	1256	1346	1356	1446	1456	...	1456	...	1546	...

		2	Ⓐ	2 Ⓒ	2 Ⓐm	2 ⚒		2	2 Ⓒ	Ⓐm	2 Ⓐ	2 Ⓐ		2	2 Ⓒ	Ⓐm	†	2 Ⓑ	2 Ⓐ				ICN 771 ♦		2
Trieste Centrale ⊗ d.	1256	...	1326	1326	...	1426	1456	...	1526	...	...	1626	1656	...	1726	1756	...	...	1850	1856	1926	2026	2040	...	2218
Monfalcone d.	1320	...	1356	1356	...	1456	1520	...	1556	...	...	1656	1720	...	1756	1820	...	...	1914	1920	1956	2056	2106	...	2248
Gorizia Centrale d.	1341	...	1418	1418	...	1518	1541	...	1618	...	...	1718	1741	...	1818	1841	...	...	|	1941	2018	2118	2131	...	2310
Udine a.	1404	...	1448	1448	...	1548	1604	...	1648	...	...	1748	1804	...	1848	1904	...	...	1952	2004	2048	2148	2156	←	2340
Udine d.	1407	1431	1507	...	1531	...	1607	1631	...	1707	1731	...	1807	1831	...	1907	1907	1931	...	2007	...	→	2158	2207	...
Pordenone d.	1442	1510	1542	...	1610	...	1642	1710	...	1742	1810	...	1842	1910	...	1942	1942	2010	...	2042	...	...	2233	2242	...
Sacile d.	1452	1524	1552	...	1624	...	1652	1724	...	1752	1824	...	1852	1924	...	1952	1952	2024	...	2052	...	...	2243	2252	...
Conegliano **603** d.	1505	1540	1605	...	1640	...	1705	1740	...	1805	1840	...	1905	1940	...	2005	2005	2040	...	2105	...	...	2255	2305	...
Treviso Centrale d.	1525	1607	1625	...	1707	...	1725	1807	...	1825	1907	...	1925	2007	...	2025	2025	2107	...	2125	...	...	2314	2325	...
Venezia Mestre a.	1544	1632	1644	...	1732	...	1744	1832	...	1844	1932	...	1944	2032	...	2044	2044	2132	...	2144	...	...	|	2344	...
Venezia Santa Lucia a.	1556	1646	1656	...	1746	...	1756	1846	...	1856	1946	...	1956	2046	...	2056	2056	2146	...	2156	...	...	2348	2356	...

– **NOTES** (LISTED BY TRAIN NUMBER)

4/5 – 🛏 1,2 cl. (Excelsior), 🛏 1,2 cl., ▬ 2 cl. and [2] Roma - Venezia Mestre - Villach - Wien and v.v.; 🛏 1,2 cl., ▬ 2 cl. and [2] Milano (**480/1**) - Venezia Mestre - Wien and v.v.

6 – 🛏 1,2 cl., ▬ 2 cl. and [2] Venezia - Udine - Villach (**498**) - Salzburg (**945**) - Wien; 🛏 1,2 cl. (Excelsior), 🛏 1,2 cl., ▬ 2 cl. and [2] Venezia - Villach (**498**) - Salzburg (**462**) - München.

7 – 🛏 1,2 cl., ▬ 2 cl. and [2] Wien (**944**) - Salzburg (**499**) - Villach - Udine - Venezia; 🛏 1,2 cl. (Excelsior), 🛏 1,2 cl., ▬ 2 cl. and [2] München (**463**) - Salzburg (**499**) - Villach - Venezia.

4 – [12] Trieste - Venezia Mestre (**585**) - Roma.

9 – [12] Roma (**588**) - Venezia Mestre (**589**) - Trieste.

3 – [12] Roma (**592**) - Venezia Mestre - Trieste.

4 – [12] Trieste - Venezia Mestre (**595**) - Roma.

1/4 – ▬ 2 cl. (4 berth) and [2] Trieste (**770/5**) - Udine - Venezia - Roma and v.v.

04 – [12] and 🍸 Trieste - Venezia Mestre (**9411**) - Roma.

9413/42 – [12] and 🍸 Udine - Venezia Mestre - Roma and v.v.

9449 – [12] and 🍸 Roma (**9440**) - Venezia Mestre - Trieste.

9705/44 – [12] and 🍸 Udine - Treviso (**9706/43**) - Vicenza - Milano and v.v.

9720/29 – [12] and 🍸 Udine - Venezia Mestre (**9701/30**) - Milano and v.v.

M – [12] and 🍸 Milano - Trieste and v.v.

T – [12] and 🍸 Torino - Milano - Trieste and v.v.

m – Not Apr. 17 - 21.   **p** – Also Apr. 17, 18.

◧ – A frequent 🚌 service operates 0600 - 1930 to Lido di Jesolo; 1 – 2 per hour, journey time 35 minutes.

⊗ – 🚋 service **Trieste** (Piazza Oberdan) - **Villa Opicina** (Stazione Trenovia) and v.v. *Linea Tranviaria.* Operator: Trieste Trasporti S.p.A.
From **Trieste**: 0711, 0731, 0751 and every 20 minutes until 2011.
From **Villa Opicina**: 0700, 0720, 0740 and every 20 minutes until 2000.
Service currently replaced by 🚌 (times may vary).

602 VICENZA - TREVISO
2nd class only except where shown

km																								
																							FB 9743	
		⚒	⚒	⚒		†	Ⓐy				⚒			⚒		⚒	⚒	⚒					♦	
0	**Vicenza** d.	0614	0714	0814	...	0914	1114	...	1214	...	1314	1414	...	1514	...	1614	1714	1814	...	1914	2014	...	2026	...
24	Cittadella d.	0639	0739	0839	...	0939	1139	...	1239	...	1339	1439	...	1539	...	1639	1739	1839	...	1939	2039	...	2052	...
36	Castelfranco Veneto d.	0655	0755	0855	...	0955	1155	...	1255	...	1355	1455	...	1555	...	1655	1755	1855	...	1955	2055	...	2108	...
60	**Treviso** Centrale a.	0721	0821	0921	...	1021	1221	...	1321	...	1421	1521	...	1621	...	1721	1821	1921	...	2021	2121	...	2127	...

			FB 9706																					
	⚒	⚒		♦			⚒		†	†		⚒			⚒			⚒			⚒			
Treviso Centrale d.	0539	0639	...	0712	...	0739	0839	...	0939	1139	...	1239	1339	...	1439	1539	...	1639	1739	...	1839	...	2039	...
Castelfranco Veneto d.	0607	0707	...	0727	...	0807	0907	...	1007	1207	...	1307	1407	...	1507	1607	...	1707	1807	...	1907	...	2107	...
Cittadella d.	0621	0721	...	0738	...	0821	0921	...	1021	1221	...	1321	1421	...	1521	1621	...	1721	1821	...	1921	...	2121	...
Vicenza a.	0646	0746	...	0803	...	0846	0946	...	1046	1246	...	1346	1446	...	1546	1646	...	1746	1846	...	1946	...	2146	...

♦ – NOTES (LISTED BY TRAIN NUMBER)

9706 – 🚌12 and 🍷 Udine (**9705**) - Treviso - Milano.
9743 – 🚌12 and 🍷 Milano - Treviso (**9744**) - Udine.

y – Not Apr. 17 - 21.

603 CONEGLIANO and PADOVA - BELLUNO and CALALZO
2nd class only

km																										
		⚒	⚒	⚒				⚒	⚒	⚒	†	†	†	†				⚒	⚒	⚒	⚒					
0	**Conegliano 601** d.	0641	...	...	0741	...	...	0841	...	...	0941	...	...	...	1241	...	...	1341	...	...	1441	...	...	1641	...	...
14	Vittorio Veneto d.	0702	...	...	0802	...	...	0902	...	...	1002	...	...	...	1302	...	...	1402	...	...	1502	...	...	1702	...	...
	Padova d.	|	0529	...	|	0629	...	|	0729	...	|	0829	...	0929	|	1129	...	|	1229	...	|	1329	...	|	1529	...
	Castelfranco Veneto d.	|	0558	...	|	0658	...	|	0758	...	|	0858	...	0958	|	1158	...	|	1258	...	|	1358	...	|	1558	...
	Montebelluna d.	|	0615	...	|	0715	...	|	0815	...	|	0915	...	1015	|	1215	...	|	1315	...	|	1415	...	|	1615	...
	Feltre d.	|	0655	...	|	0755	...	|	0855	...	|	0955	...	1055	|	1255	...	|	1355	...	|	1455	...	|	1655	...
	Belluno d.	|	0730	0745	|	0830	0845	|	0930	0945	|	1030	1045	1130	|	1330	1345	|	1430	1445	|	1530	1545	|	1730	1745
41	Ponte nelle Alpi-Polpet a.	0732	...	0753	0832	...	0853	0932	...	0953	1032	...	1053	...	1332	...	1353	1432	...	1453	1532	...	1553	1732	...	1753
41	Ponte nelle Alpi-Polpet § d.	0734	...	0754	0834	...	0854	0934	...	0954	1034	...	1054	...	1334	...	1354	1434	...	1454	1534	...	1554	1734	...	1754
	Belluno § a.	0742	...	|	0842	...	|	0942	...	|	1042	...	|	...	1342	...	|	1442	...	|	1542	...	|	1742	...	|
78	**Calalzo ▲** a.	...	...	0842	...	...	0942	...	...	1042	...	...	1142	...	...	...	1442	...	...	1542	...	...	1642	...	...	1842

	⚒				†	Ⓐ	Ⓑ				
Conegliano 601 d.	1741	1841	...	...	1941	...	...	...	2041	...	...
Vittorio Veneto d.	1802	1902	...	...	2002	...	...	...	2102	...	...
Padova d.	|	|	1729	...	|	1829	...	1929	|	2129	...
Castelfranco Veneto d.	|	|	1758	...	|	1858	...	1958	|	2158	...
Montebelluna d.	|	|	1815	...	|	1915	...	2015	|	2215	...
Feltre d.	|	|	1855	...	|	1955	...	2055	|	2255	...
Belluno d.	|	|	1930	1945	|	2030	2045	2130	|	2330	...
Ponte nelle Alpi-Polpet a.	1832	1932	...	1953	2032	...	2053	...	2132	...	...
Ponte nelle Alpi-Polpet § d.	1834	1934	...	1954	2034	...	2054	...	2134	...	...
Belluno § a.	1842	1942	...	|	2042	...	|	...	|	...	...
Calalzo ▲ a.	...	...	...	2042	...	...	2142	...	2142	...	...

	⚒	⚒	⚒		⚒		⚒				
Calalzo ▲ d.	...	...	...	...	0643	...	...	0743	...	...	0943
Belluno § d.	...	0516	...	0616	|	...	0716	|	...	0816	|
Ponte nelle Alpi-Polpet § a.	...	0524	...	0624	0724	...	0724	0824	...	0824	1024
Ponte nelle Alpi-Polpet d.	...	0533	...	0633	0725	...	0733	0825	...	0833	1025
Belluno d.	0448	|	0548	|	0733	0748	|	0833	0848	|	1033
Feltre d.	0528	|	0628	|	...	0828	|	...	0928	|	...
Montebelluna d.	0611	|	0711	|	...	0911	|	...	1011	|	...
Castelfranco Veneto d.	0632	|	0732	|	...	0932	|	...	1032	|	...
Padova a.	0701	|	0801	|	...	1001	|	...	1101	|	...
Vittorio Veneto d.	...	0601	...	0701	...	...	0801	...	...	0901	...
Conegliano 601 a.	...	0618	...	0718	...	...	0818	...	...	0918	...

km																										
					⚒	⚒	⚒		†		⚒	⚒	Ⓑ	†	†	⑥		⚒	Ⓑ	Ⓑ	†		⚒	†		
0	**Calalzo ▲** d.	...	...	...	1243	...	...	1343	...	...	...	...	1543	...	...	1643	...	...	1743	...	...	1843	...	...	...	1943
	Belluno § d.	...	1016	...	|	...	1316	|	...	1416	...	1516	|	...	1616	|	...	1716	|	...	1816	|	...	...	1916	|
37	Ponte nelle Alpi-Polpet § a.	...	1024	...	1324	...	1324	1424	...	1424	...	1524	1624	...	1624	1724	...	1724	1824	...	1824	1924	...	...	1924	2024
37	Ponte nelle Alpi-Polpet d.	...	1033	...	1325	...	1333	1425	...	1433	...	1533	1625	...	1633	1725	...	1733	1825	...	1833	1925	...	...	1933	2025
44	**Belluno** d.	1048	|	1248	1333	1348	|	1433	1448	|	1548	|	1633	1648	|	1733	1748	|	1833	1848	|	1933	1948	1948	|	2033
75	Feltre d.	1128	|	1328	...	1428	|	...	1528	|	1628	|	...	1728	|	...	1828	|	...	1928	|	...	2028	2028	|	...
110	Montebelluna d.	1211	|	1411	...	1511	|	...	1611	|	1711	|	...	1811	|	...	1911	|	...	2011	|	...	2111	2111	|	...
127	Castelfranco Veneto d.	1232	|	1432	...	1532	|	...	1632	|	1732	|	...	1832	|	...	1932	|	...	2032	|	...	2132	2132	|	...
158	**Padova** a.	1301	|	1501	...	1601	|	...	1701	|	1801	|	...	1901	|	...	2001	|	...	2101	|	...	2201	2210	|	...
	Vittorio Veneto d.	...	1101	...	...	...	1401	...	...	1501	...	1601	...	...	1701	...	...	1801	...	...	1901	...	...	...	2001	...
	Conegliano 601 a.	...	1118	...	...	...	1418	...	...	1518	...	1618	...	...	1718	...	...	1818	...	...	1918	...	...	...	2018	...

§ – See other direction of table for further connections.

▲ – Full name of station is Calalzo-Pieve di Cadore-Cortina.

604 VAL GARDENA / GRÖDNERTAL and CORTINA 🚌 services

Service **445/446**											
	⚒										
S. Candido / Innichen d.	...	0840	...	1040	...	1340	...	1540	...	1740	...
Dobbiaco / Toblach ♣ d.	0710	0850	0910	1050	1110	1350	1410	1550	1610	1750	1810
Cortina a.	0755	...	0955	...	1155	...	1455	...	1655	...	1855

Service **445/446**											
	⚒										
Cortina d.	0805	...	1005	...	1305	...	1505	...	1705	...	190
Dobbiaco / Toblach ♣ d.	0845	0905	1045	1105	1345	1405	1545	1605	1745	1805	194
S. Candido / Innichen a.	...	0915	...	1115	...	1415	...	1615	...	1815	...

♣ – Dobbiaco town. Services also call at Dobbiaco railway station en route between Dobbiaco town and Cortina (5 minutes from town stop).

Service **350**											
	⚒										
Bolzano / Bozen ♦ d.	0644	0826	...	1126	...	...	1526	...	1726	...	1926
Ponte Gardena / Waidbruck d.	0715	0857	1057	1157	1257	1357	1557	1657	1757	1857	1957
Ortisei / St Ulrich ▲ d.	0747	0927	1127	1227	1327	1427	1627	1727	1827	1927	2027
Santa/St Cristina ▲ d.	0800	0940	1140	1240	1340	1440	1640	1740	1840	1940	2040
Selva / Wolkenstein ▲ d.	0809	0949	1149	1249	1349	1449	1649	1749	1849	1949	2049
Plan ▲ a.	0812	0952	1152	1252	1352	1452	1652	1752	1852	1952	2052

Service **350**											
	⚒										
Plan ▲ d.	0604	0704	0834	0904	1034	1304	1334	1504	1704	1734	190
Selva / Wolkenstein ▲ d.	0607	0707	0837	0907	1037	1307	1337	1507	1707	1737	190
Santa/St Cristina ▲ d.	0616	0716	0846	0916	1046	1316	1346	1516	1716	1746	19
Ortisei / St Ulrich ▲ d.	0631	0731	0901	0931	1101	1331	1401	1531	1731	1801	193
Ponte Gardena / Waidbruck d.	0659	0759	0931	0959	1131	1359	1431	1559	1759	1831	200
Bolzano / Bozen ♦ a.	0730j	0830	1002	...	...	1430	...	1630	...	1902	...

♦ – Bolzano / Bozen town. Services also call at railway station (2 minutes from town stop).

▲ – Extra buses run Ortisei/St Ulrich - Plan and v.v. in summer.

j – Terminates at Bolzano railway station (a. 0728) on working days (not schooldays).

Valid until December 13, 2014.
Operator: Servizi Autobus Dolomiti, Via Conciapelli 60, 39100, Bolzano / Bozen. ✆: + 39 0471 450111 Fax: + 39 0471 970042.

🚌 service **30 Cortina - Calalzo**. 35 km. Journey time: 55 minutes.
Valid until September 14, 2014.

From **Cortina Autostazione** (Bus Station):
0535⚒, 0625⚒, 0635†, 0720⚒, 0827⚒, 0830†, 0925⚒, 1115, 1210, 1240, 1315⚒, 1402, 1505, 1615, 1705⚒, 1725†, 1755⚒, 1920⚒, 1940⚒, 2010†, 2140†.

Operator: Dolomitibus, via Col Da Ren 14, 32100, Belluno, Italy.
✆ +39 00 437 217 111, fax +39 00 437 940 522.

From **Calalzo Stazione** (FS rail station):
0625⚒, 0647⚒, 0658, 0730†, 0740⚒, 0820, 0950, 1025⚒, 1100⚒, 1215⚒, 1300, 1400†, 1455, 1520†, 1545⚒, 1620†, 1645⚒, 1750⚒, 1835†, 1905, 2045.

MILANO - VERONA - VENEZIA 605

km					*FA*	*FB*	*FB*		*FB*	*FB*		*FB*	*FB*			*FB*	*FB*	*EC*	*FB*	*EC*		*FB*	*FB*	
					9463	**9701**	**9703**		**9707**	**9709**		**9711**	**9713**			**9715**	**9791**	**1289**	**9717**	**37**		**9721**	**9723**	
		2			🍷	🍷	🍷		🍷	🍷		🍷	🍷			🍷	🍷	✕	🍷	🍷		🍷	🍷	
		Ⓐ			R	♦			♦	T		Ⓐ	T	Ⓐ			Ⓒ	♦		♦			T	Ⓐ
0	**Milano** Centrale d.	...	...	...	...	0635	0705	...	0735	0805	...	0835	0905	...	...	0935	1035	...	1135	1205	...	1235	1305	...
4	**Milano** Lambrate d.	...	...	...	...	|	|	...	|	|	...	|	|	...	...	|	|	...	|	|	...	|	|	...
34	Treviglio d.	...	...	...	...	|	|	...	|	|	...	|	|	...	...	|	|	...	|	|	...	|	|	...
83	Brescia d.	...	...	0628d	0705	0723	0753	...	0823	0853	...	0923	0953	...	...	1023	1123	...	1223	1253	...	1323	1353	...
111	Desenzano-Sirmione **599a** d.	...	...	0651d	|	0737	|	...	|	0907	...	|	1007	...	...	|	|	...	1237	|	...	1337	|	...
125	Peschiera del Garda **599a** § d.	...	...	0700d	|	|	0813	...	0843	|	...	0943	|	...	...	1043	1143	...	|	1313	...	|	1413	...
148	**Verona** Porta Nuova **599a** a.	...	...	0719d	0739	0757	0827	...	0857	0927	...	0957	1027	...	...	1057	1157	...	1257	1327	...	1357	1427	...
148	**Verona** Porta Nuova **595** d.	0521	0621	0721	...	0759	0829	0821	0859	0929	0921	0959	1029	1021	...	1059	1159	1241	1259	1329	1321	1359	1429	1421
200	Vicenza d.	0602	0702	0802	...	0826	0856	0902	0926	0956	1002	1026	1056	1102	...	1126	1226	|	1326	1356	1402	1426	1456	1502
230	Padova **616** d.	0621	0721	0821	...	0844	0914	0921	0944	1014	1021	1044	1114	1121	...	1144	1244	1328	1344	1414	1421	1444	1514	1521
258	**Venezia** Mestre **616** a.	0636	0736	0836	...	0858	0928s	0936	0958	1028s	1036	1058s	1128s	1136	...	1158s	1258s	1344	1358s	1428	1436	1458s	1528s	1536
258	**Venezia** Mestre **616** d.	0638	0738	0838	...	...	|	0938	1020	|	1038	|	|	1138	...	|	|	1346	|	1430	1438	|	|	1538
267	**Venezia** Santa Lucia **616** a.	0648	0748	0848	...	...	0940	0948	|	1040	1048	1110	1140	1148	...	1210	1310	1356	1410	1440	1448	1510	1540	1548
	Trieste Centrale **601** a.	...	...	...	...	...	...	...	1208	...	...	...	...	...	...	...	...	...	...	...	...	...	...	...

	FB		*FB*		*EC*	*FB*		*FA*	*FB*		*FB*		*FB*	*FB*			*FB*	*FB*	*FB*	*FB*	*FB*			*EN*
	9725		**9727**		**87**	**9733**		**9483**	**9735**		**9737**		**9739**	**9741**			**9743**	**9745**	**9747**	**9749**	**9753**			**481**
	🍷		🍷		✕	🍷		🍷	🍷		🍷		🍷	🍷			🍷	🍷	🍷	🍷	🍷			
			T		♦◧	T		R			♦						♦	T			T			♦
Milano Centrale d.	1405	...	1505	...	...	1605	...	...	1635	...	1705	...	1735	1805	...	...	1835	1905	1935	2005	2105	...	...	2135
Milano Lambrate d.	|	...	|	...	...	|	...	...	|	...	|	...	|	|	...	...	|	|	|	|	|	...	...	|
Treviglio d.	|	...	|	...	...	|	...	...	|	...	|	...	|	|	...	...	|	|	|	|	|	...	...	|
Brescia d.	1453	...	1553	...	...	1653	...	1704	1723	...	1753	...	1823	1853	...	...	1923	1953	|	2053	2153	...	...	2225u
Desenzano-Sirmione **599a** d.	1507	...	|	...	...	1707	...	|	1737	...	|	...	1837	1907	...	...	|	2007	|	|	|	...	...	2242u
Peschiera del Garda **599a** § d.	|	...	1613	...	...	|	...	|	|	...	1813	...	|	|	...	...	1943	|	|	2113	2213	...	...	2252u
Verona Porta Nuova **599a** a.	1527	...	1627	...	...	1727	...	1740	1757	...	1827	...	1857	1927	...	...	1957	2027	2049	2127	2227	...	...	2308u
Verona Porta Nuova **595** d.	1529	1521	1629	1621	1659	1729	1721	...	1759	1821	1829	...	1859	1929	1921	...	1959	2029	2051	2129	2229	2221	...	2338u
Vicenza d.	1556	1602	1656	1702	|	1756	1802	...	1826	1902	1856	...	1926	1956	2002	...	2024	2056	|	2156	2256	2302	...	0011u
Padova **616** d.	1614	1621	1714	1721	1743	1814	1821	...	1844	1921	1914	...	1944	2014	2021	...	...	2114	|	2214	2314	2321	...	0033u
Venezia Mestre **616** a.	1628s	1636	1728s	1736	1758	1828s	1836	...	1858s	1936	1928	...	1958s	2028	2036	...	...	2128s	2145	2228s	2328s	2336	...	0053u
Venezia Mestre **616** d.	|	1638	|	1738	1800	|	1838	...	|	1938	1949	...	|	2046	2038	...	...	|	2155	|	|	2338	...	...
Venezia Santa Lucia **616** a.	1640	1648	1740	1748	1810	1840	1848	...	1910	1948	|	...	2010	|	2048	...	...	2140	|	2240	2340	2348	...	...
Trieste Centrale **601** a.	...	...	...	...	...	...	...	...	...	...	2122	...	...	2222	...	...	...	...	2319	...	...	...	...	...

	FB	*EN*		*FB*	*FB*	*FB*		*FB*	*FB*		*FB*	*FB*	*FB*		*FB*	*FA*		*FB*	*FB*		*FB*		*FB*	*EC*
	9700	**480**		**9702**	**9704**	**9706**		**9790**	**9708**		**9710**	**9712**	**9792**		**9714**	**9464**		**9716**	**9718**		**9722**		**9726**	**86**
	🍷			🍷	🍷	🍷		🍷	🍷		🍷	🍷	🍷		🍷	🍷		🍷	🍷		🍷		🍷	✕
		♦		T		♦			Ⓐ		♦	T	Ⓒ			R		♦		Ⓐ			T	♦◧
Trieste Centrale **601** d.	...	...	...	...	...	...	...	0616	...	...	0638	...	...	...	...	...	...	0938	...	...	...	...	...	...
Venezia Santa Lucia **616** d.	0540	...	0610	0620	0650	...	0712	|	0750	0812	|	0850	0950	...	1050	...	1112	|	1150	1212	1250	1312	1320	1335
Venezia Mestre **616** a.	|	...	0620	|	|	...	0722	0740	|	0822	0814	|	|	...	|	...	1122	1114	|	1222	|	1322	|	1345
Venezia Mestre **616** d.	0552u	0530s	0622	0632u	0702u	...	0724	0750	0802u	0824	0832	0902u	1002u	...	1102u	...	1124	1132	1202u	1224	1302u	1324	1332u	1347
Padova **616** d.	0607	0547s	0638	0648	0718	...	0740	|	0818	0840	0848	0918	1018	...	1118	...	1140	1148	1218	1240	1318	1340	1348	1407
Vicenza d.	0623	0609s	0658	0705	0735	0805	0759	|	0835	0859	0905	0935	1035	...	1135	...	1159	1205	1235	1259	1335	1359	1405	|
Verona Porta Nuova **595** a.	0650	0645s	0739	0730	0800	0830	0839	0843	0900	0939	0930	1000	1100	...	1200	...	1239	1230	1300	1339	1400	1439	1430	1455
Verona Porta Nuova **599a** d.	0652	0720s	...	0732	0802	0832	...	0845	0902	...	0932	1002	1102	...	1202	1215	...	1232	1302	...	1402	...	1432	...
Peschiera del Garda **599a** § d.	0707	0741s	...	0747	|	0847	...	|	|	...	0947	|	1117	...	|	|	...	|	1317	...	|	...	1447	...
Desenzano-Sirmione **599a** d.	0716	0759s	...	|	0822	|	...	|	0922	...	|	1022	|	...	1222	|	...	1252	|	...	1422	...	|	...
Brescia d.	0734	0817s	...	0809	0839	0909	...	|	0939	...	1009	1039	1139	...	1239	1250	...	1309	1339	...	1439	...	1509	...
Treviglio d.	|	|	...	|	|	|	...	|	|	...	|	|	|	...	|	...	...	|	|	...	|	...	|	...
Milano Lambrate d.	|	|	...	|	|	|	...	|	|	...	|	|	|	...	|	...	...	|	|	...	|	...	|	...
Milano Centrale a.	0825	0930	...	0855	0925	0955	...	1000	1025	...	1055	1125	1225	...	1325	...	...	1355	1425	...	1525	...	1555	...

		FB	*FB*			*FB*	*EC*		*EC*		*FB*		*FB*	*FB*		*FB*		*FB*		*FB*	*FA*			
		9728	**9730**			**9732**	**1288**		**42**		**9738**		**9740**	**9742**		**9746**		**9748**		**9750**	**9482**			
		🍷	🍷			🍷	✕		🍷		🍷		🍷	🍷		🍷		🍷		🍷	🍷			
	⚒	T	♦			T	♦		♦				T			T					R	Ⓐ		
Trieste Centrale **601** d.	...	...	...	...	...	...	...	...	...	...	...	...	...	...	...	...	...	1701	...	...	...	...	...	...
Venezia Santa Lucia **616** d.	1412	1420	...	1512	...	1520	1550	1612	1620	...	1650	1712	1720	1750	1812	1820	...	|	1912	1950	...	2012	2112	...
Venezia Mestre **616** a.	1422	|	...	1522	...	|	1600	1622	1630	...	|	1722	|	|	1822	|	...	1842	1922	|	...	2022	2122	...
Venezia Mestre **616** d.	1424	1432u	1502	1524	...	1532u	1602	1624	1632	...	1702u	1724	1732u	1802u	1824	1832u	...	1902	1924	2002u	...	2024	2124	...
Padova **616** d.	1440	1448	1518	1540	...	1548	1618	1640	1648	...	1718	1740	1748	1818	1840	1848	...	1918	1940	2018	...	2040	2140	...
Vicenza d.	1459	1505	1535	1559	...	1605	|	1659	1705	...	1735	1759	1805	1835	1859	1905	...	1935	1959	2035	...	2059	2159	...
Verona Porta Nuova **595** a.	1539	1530	1600	1639	...	1630	1659	1739	1730	...	1800	1839	1830	1900	1939	1930	...	2000	2039	2100	...	2139	2239	...
Verona Porta Nuova **599a** d.	...	1532	1602	...	...	1632	...	...	1732	...	1802	...	1832	1902	...	1932	...	2002	...	2102	2115	...	...	...
Peschiera del Garda **599a** § d.	...	|	|	...	...	1647	...	...	1747	...	|	...	1846	1917	...	|	...	2017	...	|	|	...	...	...
Desenzano-Sirmione **599a** d.	...	1552	1622	...	...	|	...	...	|	...	1822	...	|	|	...	1952	...	|	...	2122	|	...	...	...
Brescia d.	...	1609	1639	...	...	1709	...	...	1809	...	1839	...	1909	1939	...	2009	...	2039	...	2139	2155	...	...	...
Treviglio d.	...	|	|	...	...	|	...	...	|	...	|	...	|	|	...	|	...	|	...	|	...	...	...	...
Milano Lambrate d.	...	|	|	...	...	|	...	...	|	...	|	...	|	|	...	|	...	|	...	|	...	...	...	...
Milano Centrale a.	...	1655	1725	...	...	1755	...	...	1855	...	1925	...	1955	2025	...	2055	...	2125	...	2225	...	...	...	...

MILANO - VERONA and v.v. local services :

Operator: Trenord

				Ⓐ		†				Ⓐ						Ⓐ								
Milano Centrale d.	0625	0725	0825	0850	...	0925	1125	1225	...	1325	1425	1525	1625	1725	...	1815	1825	1925	2025	2125	2225	...	0015	...
Milano Lambrate d.	0633	0733	0833	0900	...	0933	1133	1233	...	1333	1433	1533	1633	1733	...	1825	1833	1933	2033	2133	2233	...	0022	...
Treviglio d.	0659	0756	0856	0926	...	0956	1156	1256	...	1356	1456	1556	1656	1756	...	1844	1856	1956	2056	2156	2256	...	0049	...
Brescia d.	0735	0835	0935	1012	...	1035	1233	1335	...	1435	1535	1635	1735	1835	...	1917	1935	2035	2135	2235	2335	...	0135	...
Desenzano-Sirmione **599a** d.	0751	0851	0951	...	...	1051	...	1351	...	1451	1551	1651	1751	1851	...	...	1951	2051	2151	2251	2352	...	...	...
Peschiera del Garda **599a** § d.	0801	0901	1001	...	...	1101	...	1401	...	1501	1601	1701	1801	1901	...	...	2001	2101	2201	2301	0002	...	...	...
Verona Porta Nuova **599a** a.	0820	0920	1020	...	...	1120	...	1420	...	1520	1620	1720	1820	1920	...	...	2020	2120	2220	2320	0020	...	...	...

		⚒		Ⓐ				Ⓐ									†					Ⓐ		
Verona Porta Nuova **599a** d.	0540	...	...	0654	0740	0836	...	...	...	1240	1340	1440	1540	1640	1740	...	1810	1840	1940	2040	...	...	2140	...
Peschiera del Garda **599a** § d.	0557	...	...	0712	0757	0853	...	...	...	1257	1357	1457	1557	1657	1757	...	1827	1857	1957	2057	...	...	2157	...
Desenzano-Sirmione **599a** d.	0607	...	...	0721	0807	0903	...	...	...	1307	1407	1507	1607	1707	1807	...	1837	1907	2007	2107	...	...	2207	...
Brescia d.	0627	0656	0727	0740	0827	0927	...	1027	1247	1327	1427	1527	1627	1727	1827	...	1855	1927	2027	2127	...	2144	2227	...
Treviglio d.	0702	0734	0802	0813	0902	1002	...	1102	1332	1402	1502	1602	1702	1802	1902	...	1932	2002	2102	2202	...	2232	2302	...
Milano Lambrate d.	0728	0753	0828	0837	0928	1028	...	1128	1358	1428	1528	1628	1728	1825	1928	...	1958	2028	2128	2228	...	2302	2328	...
Milano Centrale a.	0736	0800	0835	0845	0935	1035	...	1135	1405	1435	1535	1635	1735	1835	1935	...	2005	2035	2135	2235	...	2310	2335	...

– **NOTES** (LISTED BY TRAIN NUMBER)

– [12] and 🍷 Genève - Milano - Venezia.
R inclusive of supplement.

– [12] and 🍷 Venezia - Milano - Genève.
R inclusive of supplement.

7 – [12] and ✕ Venezia - Verona - München and v.v.
Operator within Italy: LeNord.

– 🛏 1, 2 cl., 🛌 2 cl. and [2] Wien (**235**) - Venezia Mestre - Milano; 🛏 1, 2 cl. (Excelsior), 🛏 1, 2 cl. and 🛌 2 cl. München (**485**) - Verona - Milano.

– 🛏 1, 2 cl., 🛌 2 cl. and [2] Milano - Venezia Mestre (**234**) - Wien; 🛏 1, 2 cl. (Excelsior), 🛏 1, 2 cl. and 🛌 2 cl. Milano - Verona (**484**) - München.

1288/9 – ⑥⑦ Mar. 29 - Nov. 2: [12] and ✕ Venezia - Verona - München and v.v.
9701 – [12] and 🍷 Milano - Venezia Mestre (**9720**) - Udine.
9706 – [12] and 🍷 Udine (**9705**) - Treviso - Milano.
9707 – [12] and 🍷 Torino - Milano - Venezia Mestre - Trieste.
9710 – [12] and 🍷 Trieste - Venezia Mestre - Milano - Torino.
9716 – [12] and 🍷 Trieste - Venezia Mestre - Milano - Torino.
9730 – [12] and 🍷 Udine (**9729**) - Venezia Mestre - Milano.
9737 – [12] and 🍷 Torino - Milano - Venezia Mestre - Trieste.
9743 – [12] and 🍷 Milano - Treviso (**9744**) - Udine.

R – [12] and 🍷 Roma - Brescia and v.v.
T – [12] and 🍷 Torino - Milano - Venezia and v.v.

d – ⚒ only.
s – Stops to set down only.
u – Stops to pick up only.
♠ – Operator: Trenord.
◧ – Also available to passengers without reservation. Operator within Italy: LeNord.
§ – Station for Gardaland Park. Free shuttle bus available.

607 MILANO LOCAL SERVICES

MILANO - BERGAMO: Some services 2nd class only

km								Ⓐ	Ⓒ	Ⓐ	Ⓒ															
0	**Milano** Centrale ◇	d.	0540	0610	0710	0810	0910	1010	1010	1110	1110	...	1210	1310	1410	1510	1610	1710	...	1810	1910	2010	2110	2210	2340	...
56	**Bergamo**	a.	0628	0658	0758	0858	0958	1058	1103	1158	1203	...	1258	1358	1458	1558	1658	1758	...	1858	1958	2058	2158	2258	0050	...

					Ⓐ				Ⓒ	Ⓐ	Ⓒ	Ⓐ														
Bergamo	d.	0502	0602	0702	0732	...	0802	0902	0957	1002	1057	1102	...	1202	1302	1402	1502	1602	1702	...	1802	1902	2002	2102	2202	2302
Milano Centrale ◇	a.	0550	0650	0750	0830	...	0850	0950	1050	1050	1150	1150	...	1250	1350	1450	1550	1650	1750	...	1850	1950	2050	2150	2250	2350

Additional trains run approximately hourly Milano Porta Garibaldi - Bergamo via Monza, journey 64 minutes, *43 km*.

MILANO - COMO LAGO: *46 km* Journey: 52–65 minutes 2nd class only

From **Milano** Cadorna: 0610⚒, 0640, 0710⚒, 0740, 0759Ⓐ, 0840, 0859, 0940, 1040, 1140, 1210⚒, 1240, 1310⚒†q, 1340, 1359†, 1410Ⓐ, 1440, 1510Ⓐ, 1540, 1610Ⓐ, 1640, 1659Ⓐ, 1710⚒, 1740, 1759Ⓐ, 1810, 1840, 1859Ⓐ, 1910⚒, 1940, 2010⚒, 2040, 2110.

From **Como Nord Lago**: 0547⚒, 0617, 0636Ⓐ, 0647⚒, 0717, 0736Ⓐ, 0747⚒, 0817, 0836⚒, 0917, 0936Ⓐ, 1017, 1117, 1217, 1247⚒, 1317, 1347⚒, 1417, 1447Ⓐ, 1517, 1547Ⓐ, 1617, 1647Ⓐ, 1717, 1747, 1817, 1836†, 1847⚒, 1917, 1947, 2017, 2117.

MILANO - VARESE - LAVENO: *72 km* Journey: 87–107 mins 2nd class only

From **Milano** Cadorna: 0606⚒, 0636, 0706Ⓐ, 0749, 0849, 0936, 1036, 1136, 1206⚒, 1249, 1349, 1449Ⓐ, 1536, 1606Ⓐ, 1649, 1719Ⓐ, 1749, 1819Ⓐ, 1849, 1919Ⓐ, 1936Ⓒ, 2019Ⓐ.

From **Laveno-Mombello** FN: 0537Ⓐ, 0607⚒, 0637, 0707⚒, 0737, 0807Ⓐ, 0837, 0937, 1037, 1137, 1237, 1307⚒, 1337, 1437, 1537, 1637, 1737, 1807Ⓐ, 1837, 1937, 2037.

Additional journeys run Milano Cadorna - Varese (journey 63 minutes).

q – Not June 14.

MILANO - LUINO: *91 km* 2nd class only

		⚒				⚒				Ⓐ		⚒	
Milano P Garibaldi	d.	0651	*0732*	*0832*	*1032*	*1232*	*1332*	*1532*	*1732*	1752	*1832*	1852	2232
Gallarate **590**	d.	0728	0813	0913	1213	1313	1413	1613	1813	1826	1913	1926	2259
Laveno-Mombello	d.	0810	0845	0945	1245	1345	1445	1645	1845	1909	1945	2009	2331
Luino 592	a.	0830	0908	1003	1308	1408	1508	1708	1908	1927	2008	2027	2350

		⚒		†					⚒				⚒
Luino 592	d.	0627	0720	0852	1052	1252	1352	1452	1552	1652	1752	1852	1952
Laveno-Mombello	d.	0648	0736	0908	1108	1308	1408	1508	1608	1708	1808	1908	2008
Gallarate **590**	a.	0726	0803	0946	1147	1346	1447	1546	1647	1746	1847	1946	2047
Milano P Garibaldi	a.	0800	0847	*1028*	*1228*	*1428*	*1528*	*1628*	*1728*	*1828*	*1928*	*2028*	*2128*

Additional journeys are available by changing at Gallarate.

MILANO - CREMONA - MANTOVA:

km													
0	**Milano** C	d.	0620	0820	1020	1220	...	1420	1620	1715	1820	1915	2020
60	Codogno	d.	0703	0903	1103	1303	...	1503	1703	1758	1903	1958	2103
88	Cremona	d.	0733	0930	1130	1330	...	1530	1730	1820	1930	2020	2130
151	**Mantova**	a.	0814	1010	1210	1410	...	1610	1810	1912	2019	2110	2210

Mantova	d.	0518	0610	0641	0850	1050	1250	1450	1650	1850	2050	...
Cremona	d.	0617	0658	0733	0930	1130	1330	1530	1730	1930	2130	...
Codogno	a.	0638	0719	0753	0952	1152	1352	1552	1752	1952	2152	...
Milano Centrale	a.	0730	0810	0840	1040	1240	1440	1640	1840	2040	2240	...

BRESCIA - EDOLO: *103 km* Journey: 120–150 minutes approx. 2nd class only

From **Brescia**: 0600⚒, 0707†, 0907, 1107, 1307, 1507, 1707, 1758Ⓐ, 1907.

From **Edolo**: 0554⚒, 0647⚒, 0754, 0954, 1154, 1354, 1554, 1754, 1954†.

For 🚌 Edolo - Tirano see Table **593**.

Minor alterations are possible, especially around holiday dates

Operator: Trenord; ✆ contact centre 800 500 005; www.trenord.it

609 Local services in NORTHERN and CENTRAL ITALY
2nd class only

ALESSANDRIA - ACQUI TERME: *34 km* Journey 28–38 minutes

From **Alessandria**: 0645, 0745, 0940, 1045⚒, 1145, 1345, 1545, 1745, 1945.

From **Acqui Terme**: 0647⚒, 0737, 0942, 1137, 1337, 1437⚒, 1537, 1737, 1937.

BOLOGNA - PORRETTA TERME: *59 km* Journey 60–72 minutes

From **Bologna** Centrale: 0552⚒, 0630⚒, 0704, 0804⚒, 0904, 1004⚒, 1104, 1204, 1304, 1404, 1504, 1604, 1704, 1734, 1804, 1834Ⓐ, 1904, 1934Ⓐ, 2004, 2104, 2204.

From **Porretta Terme**: 0500⚒, 0550, 0608, 0640, 0718, 0750⚒, 0822, 0922⚒, 1022, 1122⚒, 1222, 1322, 1422, 1522, 1622, 1722, 1821, 1921, 2021, 2050Ⓐ, 2122Ⓐ.

CAMPIGLIA - PIOMBINO: *16 km* Journey 22–30 minutes

From **Campiglia Marittima**: 0556⚒, 1008**m**, 1336⚒, 1535, 1647, 1736**n**, 1806, 1839**j**, 2055†**h**.

From **Piombino Marittima**: 0635⚒, 0915, 1053**m**, 1140**k**, 1527⚒, 1608, 1726, 1812Ⓐ, 1812†**f**, 1845.

GENOVA - ACQUI TERME: *58 km* Journey 65–81 minutes

From **Genova** Piazza Principe: 0612, 0714⚒, 0736†, 0905⚒, 0907†, 1021Ⓐ, 1039†, 1206†, 1314⑥, 1318Ⓐ, 1342†, 1418⚒, 1437†, 1548⚒, 1607†, 1712Ⓐ, 1744, 1820Ⓐ, 1914†, 1918⚒, 2043.

From **Acqui Terme**: 0520⚒, 0602†, 0610⚒, 0703⚒, 0736†, 0740⚒, 0854Ⓐ, 0900†, 1034†, 1203†, 1215⚒, 1316⚒, 1334†, 1414⚒, 1552⚒, 1601†, 1744†, 1817⚒, 1916†, 2049.

PORRETTA TERME - PISTOIA: *40 km* Journey 48–55 minutes

From **Porretta Terme**: 0655⚒, 0717, 0926⚒, 1324, 1521, 1824.

From **Pistoia**: 0600, 0825⚒, 1222, 1422, 1721, 1926.

ROVIGO - CHIOGGIA:

km			⚒	⚒	Ⓑ	†	⚒	⚒	†	⚒	Ⓑy	Ⓐg	
0	**Rovigo**	d.	0615	0815	0915	1115	1315	1415	1515	1615	1715	1815	1915
25	Adria	d.	0642	0842	0942	1142	1342	1442	1542	1642	1742	1842	1942
57	**Chioggia**	a.	0725	0925	1025	1225	1425	1525	1625	1725	1825	1925	2025

		⚒g	⚒			⚒	†	⚒	Ⓐ		Ⓐz	⑥
Chioggia	d.	0535	0635	0735	0935	1235	1335	1435	1535	1735	1835	2035
Adria	d.	0614	0714	0814	1014	1314	1414	1514	1614	1814	1914	2114
Rovigo	a.	0645	0745	0845	1045	1345	1445	1545	1645	1845	1945	2145

SANTHIÀ - BIELLA S. PAOLO: *27 km* Journey 20–35 minutes

From **Santhià**: 0640, 0740⚒, 0840, 0940⚒, 1040, 1148⚒, 1240, 1348⚒, 1440, 1548⚒, 1640, 1740⚒, 1840, 1916⚒, 1940⚒, 2040, 2140⚒.

From **Biella S. Paolo**: 0601⚒, 0701⚒, 0712⚒, 0753†, 0801⚒, 0901⚒, 0953†, 1002⚒, 1102⚒, 1141⚒, 1153†, 1301⚒, 1341⚒, 1353†, 1501⚒, 1541⚒, 1553†, 1701⚒, 1753†, 1801⚒, 1833⚒, 1909⚒, 1953†, 2101⚒, 2153†.

SIENA - GROSSETO:

km			⚒	†	†	⚒		⚒	⚒	†	⚒		
0	**Siena**	d.	0628	0753	1020	1243	1345	1447	1552	1645	1743	1845	195
29	Buonconvento	d.	0653	0816	1045	1306	1408	1510	1615	1708	1808	1908	201
102	**Grosseto** 🚌	a.	...	*0945*	*1225*	*1425*	*1540*	*1640*	*1735*	*1840*	*1937*	*2040*	*214*

			†		⚒	⚒	†	⚒	†	⚒	†	⚒
Grosseto 🚌	d.	...	*0945*	*1240*	*1350*	*1430*	*1550*	*1645*	*1740*	*1735*	*1850*	*192*
Buonconvento	d.	0823	1110	1416	1518	1623	1716	1815	1914	1918	2030	203
Siena	a.	0846	1135	1439	1544	1649	1739	1838	1939	1944	2056	205

Buonconvento - Grosseto and v.v. currently operated by 🚌.

TRENTO - BASSANO DEL GRAPPA:

km						⚒		⚒		⚒			
0	**Trento**	d.	0605	and	0905	1005	1105	1205	1305	1405	1505	and	200
31	Levico Terme	d.	0655	hourly	0955	1055	1155	1255	1355	1455	1555	hourly	205
44	Borgo Valsugana Centro	d.	0709	until	1009	1109	1209	1309	1409	1509	1609	until	210
97	Bassano del Grappa	a.	0815		1115	1215	1315	1415	1515	1615	1715		22

					†	⚒		⚒		⚒			
Bassano del Grappa	d.	0725	0825	0925	1025	1125	1325	1425	1525	1625	1725	and	21
Borgo Valsugana Centro	d.	0826	0926	1026	1126	1226	1426	1526	1626	1726	1826	hourly	22
Levico Terme	d.	0844	0944	1044	1144	1244	1444	1544	1644	1744	1844	until	22
Trento	a.	0928	1028	1128	1228	1328	1528	1628	1728	1828	1928		23

VENEZIA - BASSANO DEL GRAPPA:

km				⚒				⚒	⚒			
0	**Venezia** Santa Lucia	d.	0756	0856	0956	1156	1356	1456	1656	1756	1956	20
9	Venezia Mestre	d.	0808	0908	1008	1208	1408	1508	1708	1808	2008	21
45	Castelfranco Veneto	d.	0846	0946	1046	1246	1446	1546	1746	1846	2046	21
64	Bassano del Grappa	a.	0905	1005	1105	1305	1505	1605	1805	1905	2105	22

					⚒		⚒				⚒
Bassano del Grappa	d.	0625	0825	1025	1225	1325	1425	1525	1725	1925	20
Castelfranco Veneto	d.	0646	0846	1046	1246	1346	1446	1546	1746	1946	20
Venezia Mestre	a.	0722	0922	1122	1322	1422	1522	1622	1822	2022	21
Venezia Santa Lucia	a.	0734	0934	1134	1334	1434	1534	1634	1834	2034	21

Additional services operate on ⚒.

VERONA PORTA NUOVA - MANTOVA - MODENA:

km				⚒									
0	**Verona** PN	d.	...	*0630*	*0830*d	0930	...	*1230*d	*1430*d	*1630*d	*1830*d	*2030*d	.
37	Mantova	d.	0629	0731	0931	1016	1131	1331	1531	1731	1931	2131	.
56	Suzzara	d.	0656	0756	0956	...	1156	1356	1556	1756	1956	2159	.
98	**Modena**	a.	0740	0840	1046	...	1242	1440	1642	1842	2042	2242	.

				†	⚒		⚒					
Modena	d.	0707	0907	1107	1209	1307	1409	1507	1707	1907	2007	22
Suzzara	d.	0755	0955	1155	1255	1355	1455	1555	1755	1955	2055	22
Mantova	d.	0815	1015	1215	1315	1415	1515	1615	1815	2015	2115	23
Verona PN	a.	*0915*	...	*1317*	*1417*	*1517*	*1617*	*1717*	*1917*	*2117*	...	

d – ⚒ only.
f – From Apr. 20.
g – Not Apr. 17-21.
h – From May 25.
j – † until May 30; Ⓒ from May 31.
k – † from Apr. 20 (also June 14).
m – Ⓒ until Apr. 13; ⑥ Apr. 19 - May 24.
n – Ⓑ until Apr. 13; Ⓐ from Apr. 14.
y – Until June 8.
z – Until June 6.

◇ – Services from Centrale also call at Lambrate (8 mins from Centrale).
§ – Operated by *FER*. Trenitalia tickets valid. See Table **612** for details.

TORINO and MILANO - GENOVA - PISA 610

km		IC 501	FB 9761			FB 9763		IC 651			IC 503			IC 653	IC 505						IC 1533	IC 657			
			🍷	2	2	🍷	2		2		2					2	2	2	2					2	
		♦		⚒			⚒		✝			⚒		♦	♦			F			♦	♦			
0	**Torino** Porta Nuova **615** d.	...	...	...	...	...	...	...	...	0530	0605	...	0630	...	...	...	...	...	...	...	...	...	0730	...	0820
56	Asti **615** d.	...	...	...	...	...	...	...	...	0607	0641	...	0707	...	...	...	...	...	...	...	...	...	0807	...	0904
91	Alessandria **615** d.	...	...	...	...	...	...	...	...	0631	0702	...	0731	...	...	...	...	...	...	...	...	...	0831	...	0931
112	Novi Ligure d.	...	...	...	...	...	...	...	...	0644	0718	...	0744	...	...	...	...	...	...	...	...	...	0844	...	0944
	Milano Centrale d.	...	...	...	...	...	...	0610	...	|	|	0625	|	0705	...	...	0645	...	0725	...	0810	0810	|	...	|
	Milano Rogoredo d.	...	...	...	...	...	...	|	...	|	|	0639	|	0716	...	...	|	...	0739	...	|	|	|	...	|
	Pavia d.	...	...	...	...	...	...	0635	...	|	|	0659	|	0735	...	...	|	...	0759	...	0835	0835	|	...	|
	Voghera **615** d.	...	...	...	...	...	...	|	...	|	|	0715	|	0751	...	...	|	...	0815	...	0851	0851	|	...	|
	Tortona **615** d.	...	...	...	...	...	...	0659	...	|	|	0727	|	|	...	...	|	...	0827	...	|	|	|	...	|
166	**Genova** Piazza Principe a.	...	...	...	...	...	...	0742	...	0730	0805	0819	0830	0840	...	...	|	...	0914	...	0942	0942	0930	...	1030
166	**Genova** Piazza Principe d.	...	0551	...	0606	0705	0711	0745	...	0732	...	0819	...	...	0851	...	|	...	0917	...	0947	0947	0932	1004	1032
169	**Genova** Brignole d.	...	0600**u**	...	0615	0713**u**	0720	0754	...	0741	...	0829	...	...	0900	...	|	...	0926	...	0958	0958	0938	1013	1038
194	S. Margherita-Portofino d.	...	|	...	0647	|	0759	0816	...	0827	...	...	...	...	|	...	|	...	1003	...	1022	1030	▬	1053	...
196	Rapallo d.	...	|	...	0652	0736	0803	0821	...	0831	...	...	...	...	0922	...	**w**	...	1008	...	1027	1036	...	1059	...
205	Chiavari d.	...	|	...	0701	0745	0811	0830	...	0839	...	...	...	...	0931	...	|	...	1016	...	1036	1045	...	1110	...
212	Sestri Levante d.	0514	|	...	0710	|	0820	0839	...	0851	...	...	...	...	|	...	|	...	1029	...	1044	1053	...	1128	...
235	Levanto d.	0531	|	...	0730	|	0840	0855	...	0919	...	...	...	...	|	...	|	...	1055	...	1059	1112	...	1150	...
240	Monterosso d.	0537	|	...	0735	|	0845	0901	...	0924	...	...	...	...	|	...	|	...	1100	...	1104	1119	2	1156	...
249	Riomaggiore d.	|	|	...	|	|	0856	|	...	0941	...	...	...	...	|	...	|	...	1122	...	|	|	⚒	1217	...
256	**La Spezia** Centrale d.	0552	0651	0657	0750	0820	0908	0919	0913	0949	...	...	...	...	1006	1020	|	...	1132	...	1120	1140	1215	1229	...
272	Sarzana d.	0606	|	0717	...	|	0924	|	0930	...	...	...	...	...	|	1035	1043	1056	...	...	|	|	1228	...	...
282	Carrara-Avenza d.	0615	|	0725	...	|	0931	|	0938	...	...	...	...	...	|	1043	1052	1106	...	...	1137	|	1236	...	...
289	Massa Centro d.	0623	|	0731	...	0841	0937	0942	0944	...	...	...	...	...	1028	1049	1100	1112	...	...	1145	1207	1242	...	...
310	Viareggio d.	0637	|	0751	...	0854	1008	0958	1006	...	...	...	...	...	1041	1109	1124	1132	...	...	1206	1222	1259	...	...
331	**Pisa** Centrale **611** a.	0653	0730	0814	...	0910	1038	1019	1038	...	...	...	...	...	1056	1142	1148	1200	...	...	1221	1245	1322	...	...
	Livorno Centrale **611** a.	0710	0744	...	...	0927	...	1039	...	...	...	...	...	...	1119	...	...	...	...	...	1239	1307	...	...	...
	Roma Termini **611** a.	1018**o**	1003	...	...	1203	...	...	...	...	...	...	...	...	1403	...	...	...	...	...	...	...	...	...	...

	IC 659	IC 1535	FB 9773		IC 741	IC 511		IC 665				FB 9777				IC 669		IC 515		IC 743	FB 9781		IC 673		
			🍷						2			🍷		2	2			2			🍷			2	
	♦	♦			♦	♦								✝	Ⓐ			⚒		♦					©A
Torino Porta Nuova **615** d.	...	...	...	1030	...	1105	1130	...	...	...	1230	...	...	...	...	...	1330	1405	...	...	1520	1530	...	...	...
Asti **615** d.	...	...	...	1107	...	1143	1207	...	...	...	1307	...	...	...	...	...	1407	1443	...	...	1600	1607	...	...	...
Alessandria **615** d.	...	...	...	1131	...	1202	1231	...	...	...	1331	...	...	...	...	...	1431	1502	...	...	1616	1631	...	...	...
Novi Ligure d.	...	...	...	1144	...	|	1244	...	...	...	1344	...	...	...	...	...	1444	1516	...	...	|	1644	...	...	...
Milano Centrale d.	0910	0910	...	|	1110	|	|	1210	...	1225	|	1310	...	...	...	1405	|	|	1425	1510	|	|	1605	...	1625
Milano Rogoredo d.	|	|	...	|	|	|	|	|	...	1239	|	|	...	...	...	1416	|	|	1439	|	|	|	1616	...	1639
Pavia d.	0935	0935	...	|	1135	|	|	1235	...	1258	|	1335	...	...	...	1435	|	|	1459	1535	|	|	1635	...	1659
Voghera **615** d.	|	|	...	|	1151	|	|	|	...	1315	|	|	...	...	...	1451	|	|	1513	1551	|	|	1651	...	1715
Tortona **615** d.	0959	0959	...	|	|	|	|	1259	...	1327	|	|	...	...	...	|	|	|	1524	|	|	|	|	...	1727
Genova Piazza Principe a.	1040	1040	...	1230	1240	1248	1330	1342	...	1415	1430	1440	...	...	...	1542	1530	1553	1614	1640	1701	1730	1744	...	1815
Genova Piazza Principe d.	...	...	1212	1232	...	1251	1332	1347	1411	1415	1432	1452	...	...	...	1547	1532	1556	...	...	1704	1732	1748	1811	...
Genova Brignole d.	...	...	1221**u**	1238	...	1300	1338	1358	1420	1423	1438	1513	...	...	...	1558	1538	1602	...	...	1713	1738	1758	1820	...
S. Margherita-Portofino d.	...	...	|	▬	...	|	▬	1422	1456	...	...	|	...	...	...	|	1624	...	...	...	|	...	1822	1849	...
Rapallo d.	...	...	|	...	...	1322	...	1427	1500	...	...	1537	...	...	...	1628	1628	...	...	...	1737	...	1827	1853	...
Chiavari d.	...	...	|	...	...	1331	...	1436	1508	...	...	1545	...	...	...	1637	1636	...	...	...	1745	...	1836	1902	...
Sestri Levante d.	...	...	|	...	...	1339	...	1444	1518	...	...	|	...	...	...	1645	1655	...	...	...	|	...	1844	1916	...
Levanto d.	...	...	|	...	...	|	...	1459	1538	...	...	|	...	...	...	1700	1724	...	...	...	|	...	1859	1935	...
Monterosso d.	...	...	|	...	...	|	...	1505	1543	...	...	|	...	...	...	1706	1730	...	...	...	|	...	1905	1940	...
Riomaggiore d.	...	...	|	2	...	|	2	|	1552	...	...	|	...	...	...	|	1750	...	...	...	|	...	|	1949	...
La Spezia Centrale d.	...	...	1314	1319	...	1409	1414	1521	1600	...	...	1620	...	1640	1715	1722	1757	...	...	...	1820	...	1922	1957	...
Sarzana d.	...	...	|	1334	...	|	1429	...	...	...	...	|	...	1700	1730	...	...	...	...	...	|	...	|	...	...
Carrara-Avenza d.	...	...	|	1342	...	1426	1439	...	...	...	...	|	...	1708	1738	...	...	...	...	...	|	...	1940	...	...
Massa Centro d.	...	...	1333	1348	...	1433	1445	...	...	...	...	1641	...	1714	1744	...	...	...	...	...	1841	...	1948	...	...
Viareggio d.	...	...	|	1406	...	1446	1502	...	...	...	...	1654	...	1733	1803	...	...	...	...	...	1854	...	2002	...	...
Pisa Centrale **611** a.	...	...	1355	1427	...	1501	1526	...	...	...	...	1710	...	1751	1825	...	...	...	...	...	1910	...	2020	...	...
Livorno Centrale **611** a.	...	...	1409	...	...	1519	...	...	...	...	...	1727	...	...	...	...	...	...	...	...	1927	...	2035	...	...
Roma Termini **611** a.	...	...	1632	...	...	1803	...	...	...	...	...	2003	...	...	...	...	...	...	...	...	2203	...	...	...	...

		IC 675	FB 9787					IC 679		IC 519			IC 685	IC 521			ICN 785	IC 687		IC 689		ICN 799	♠	♠	
	2		🍷	2	2					2				2	2									2	
	Ⓐ	♦												Ⓑp	⑤y		♦		V	♦		♦	⚒		
Torino Porta Nuova **615** d.	...	...	...	...	...	...	1730	...	...	1805	...	1830	...	1840	...	1930	...	...	...	...	2130	2155	...	...	...
Asti **615** d.	...	...	...	...	...	...	1807	...	...	1843	...	1907	...	1921	...	2007	...	...	...	...	2207	2236	...	...	...
Alessandria **615** d.	...	...	...	...	...	...	1831	...	...	1902	...	1931	...	1943	...	2031	...	...	...	...	2231	2259	...	...	...
Novi Ligure d.	...	...	...	...	...	...	1844	...	...	1916	...	1943	...	|	...	2044	...	...	...	...	2244	|	...	...	...
Milano Centrale d.	1625	1705	...	...	...	1705	|	1805	...	|	1825	|	1905	|	1836**g**	|	2005	2010	2025	2110	|	|	2225	2325	...
Milano Rogoredo d.	1639	1715	...	...	...	|	|	1816	...	|	1839	|	1916	|	|	|	|	|	2039	|	|	|	2239	2339	...
Pavia d.	1659	1735	...	...	...	|	|	1835	...	|	1859	|	1935	|	|	|	2032	2038	2059	2135	|	|	2257	2359	...
Voghera **615** d.	1715	1751	...	...	...	|	|	1851	...	|	1915	|	1951	|	|	|	2050	2057	2115	2151	|	|	2320	0023	...
Tortona **615** d.	1727	|	...	...	...	|	|	1902	...	|	1930	|	|	|	|	|	2102	|	2127	|	|	|	...	...	...
Genova Piazza Principe a.	1815	1840	...	...	...	|	1930	1945	...	1953	2020	2030	2042	2035	|	2130	2146	2152	2217	2240	2330	2350	...	...	...
Genova Piazza Principe d.	1815	...	1907	...	...	|	1934	1948	←	1955	2020	2032	2045	2037	|	2132	2149	2158	...	...	2332	2353	...	...	...
Genova Brignole d.	1825	...	1915**u**	...	1920	|	1940	1958	1949	2001	2028	2038	2056	2043	|	2138	2158	2207	...	...	2338	0002	...	...	...
S. Margherita-Portofino d.	...	...	|	...	1956	|	→	2022	2032	...	...	...	|	...	|	...	|	2229	...	...	...	|	...	...	...
Rapallo d.	...	...	|	...	2000	**w**	...	2027	2036	...	...	...	2123	...	**w**	...	|	2234	...	...	...	0028	...	...	...
Chiavari d.	...	...	|	...	2008	|	...	2036	2046	...	...	...	2133	...	|	...	|	2243	...	...	...	0038	...	...	...
Sestri Levante d.	...	...	|	...	2018	|	...	2044	2102	...	...	...	2141	...	|	...	|	2255	...	...	...	|	...	...	...
Levanto d.	...	...	|	...	2038	|	...	2059	2126	...	...	...	|	...	|	...	|	2311	...	...	...	|	...	...	...
Monterosso d.	...	...	|	...	2043	|	...	2105	2132	...	...	...	|	...	|	...	|	2317	...	...	...	|	...	...	...
Riomaggiore d.	...	...	|	...	2052	|	...	|	2153	...	...	...	|	...	|	...	|	|	...	...	...	|	...	...	...
La Spezia Centrale d.	...	...	2007	2018	2100	|	...	2124	2202	...	...	...	2213	...	|	...	2303	2332	...	...	...	0127	...	...	...
Sarzana d.	...	...	|	2033	...	2043	...	|	...	...	...	...	2226	...	2233	...	|	...	...	...	...	|	...	...	...
Carrara-Avenza d.	...	...	|	2041	...	2051	...	|	...	...	...	...	2235	...	2241	...	|	...	...	...	...	|	...	...	...
Massa Centro d.	...	...	2027	2047	...	2057	...	2146	...	...	...	...	2242	...	2249	...	|	...	...	...	...	|	...	...	...
Viareggio d.	...	...	|	2108	...	2118	...	2200	...	...	...	...	2255	...	2306	...	2341	...	...	...	...	|	...	...	...
Pisa Centrale **611** a.	...	...	2049	2127	...	2138	...	2216	...	...	...	...	2311	...	2320	...	2358	...	...	...	...	0216	...	...	...
Livorno Centrale **611** a.	...	...	...	...	...	2155	...	2234	...	...	...	...	2330	...	2338	...	0015	...	...	...	...	0237	...	...	...
Roma Termini **611** a.	...	...	...	...	...	...	...	...	...	...	...	...	...	...	...	...	0313**o**	...	...	...	...	0555**o**	...	...	...

– **NOTES** (LISTED BY TRAIN NUMBER)

01 – ⚒: [12] Sestri Levante - Napoli.
05 – [12] Ventimiglia - Genova - Roma.
11 – [12] Torino - Salerno.
53 – [12] Milano - Genova (**654**) - Ventimiglia.
57 – Ⓐ: [12] Milano - Livorno - Grosseto.
59 – Ⓐ: [12] Milano - Genova (**660**) - Ventimiglia.
75 – [12] Milano - Genova (**676**) - Ventimiglia.
89 – [12] Milano - Genova (**690**) - Ventimiglia.
41 – [12] Milano - Genova (**742**) - Ventimiglia.
43 – [12] Milano - Genova (**744**) - Ventimiglia.

785 – 🛏 1,2 cl. (T2) and ▬ 2 cl. (4 berth) Milano - Genova - Siracusa; 🛏 1,2 cl. (T2) and ▬ 2 cl. (4 berth) Milano - Messina (**781**) - Palermo.
799 – ▬ 2 cl. (4 berth) and [2] Torino - Napoli - Salerno.
1533 – ©: [12] Milano - Livorno - Grosseto.
1535 – ©: [12] Milano - Genova (**1536**) - Ventimiglia.

A – To Albenga.
F – [2] Bergamo - Fidenza - Aulla - Pisa.
V – To Ventimiglia.

g – Milano **Porta Garibaldi**.
o – Roma **Ostiense**.
p – Not days before holidays.
u – Stops to pick up only.
w – Via Fidenza and Aulla.
y – Also Apr. 24; not Apr. 25.
♠ – Operator: Trenord.

610 PISA - GENOVA - MILANO and TORINO

km				ICN 796		IC 652	IC 500	IC 656		IC 502			IC 658		ICN 784		IC 662	IC 504		FB 9760			IC 664	FB 9764	IC 666
							2			2	2	2						2		🍷		2		🍷	
				♦			⚒	♦	V		⚒	⚒			♦								♦		
	Roma Termini **640** d.	...	...	0003o	...	...	...	...	...	...	...	...	...	...	...	...	...	...	...	...	...	...	...	0657	...
	Livorno Centrale d.	...	...	0309	...	...	...	...	...	...	...	...	0526	...	0543	0552	0630	...	...	...	...	...	...	0930	...
	Pisa Centrale d.	...	...	0326	...	...	...	...	...	...	...	...	0544	...	0600	0610	0647	...	...	0825	...	...	...	0947	...
	Viareggio d.	...	...	|	...	...	...	...	...	...	...	...	0600	...	0619	0628	0704	...	...	|	...	...	...	1003	...
	Massa Centro d.	...	...	|	...	...	...	...	...	...	...	...	0614	...	|	0645	0717	...	...	0849	...	...	...	1017	...
	Carrara-Avenza d.	...	...	|	...	...	...	...	...	...	...	...	|	...	|	0651	0724	...	...	|	...	...	...	|	...
	Sarzana d.	...	...	|	...	...	...	...	...	...	...	...	|	...	|	0701	0732	...	...	|	...	...	...	|	...
	La Spezia Centrale d.	...	...	0425	...	0459	...	...	...	...	0538	0625	0638	...	0701	|	0746	...	...	0910	...	...	...	1039	1042
	Riomaggiore d.	...	...	|	...	|	...	...	...	...	0547	|	|	...	|	|	|	...	...	|	...	...	...	|	|
	Monterosso d.	...	...	|	...	0517	...	...	...	...	0602	|	0654	...	|	|	|	...	...	|	...	...	...	|	1058
	Levanto d.	...	...	|	...	0524	...	...	...	...	0607	0642	0701	...	|	|	0803	...	...	|	...	...	...	|	1103
	Sestri Levante d.	...	0432	|	...	0540	...	...	...	...	0634	0659	0716	...	|	|	0819	...	...	|	...	0938	...	|	1118
	Chiavari d.	...	0443	0510	...	0552	...	...	...	...	0644	0708	0724	...	|	|	0827	...	...	|	...	0951	...	1113	1126
	Rapallo d.	...	0451	0520	...	0601	...	...	...	...	0655	|	0733	...	|	w	0836	...	...	|	...	1002	...	1122	1135
	S. Margherita-Portofino d.	...	0455	|	...	0607	...	...	...	...	0659	|	0739	...	|	|	|	...	...	|	...	1006	...	|	|
	Genova Brignole d.	0522	0534	0555	0622	0635	0657	...	...	0750	0756	0745	0809	0822	0830s	|	0904	...	...	1003	1022	1056	...	1150	1210
	Genova Piazza Principe a.	0530	0540	0601	0630	0641	0703	...	...	0756	0802	0751a	0815	0830	0839s	|	0910	...	...	1009	1030	1102	...	1156	1216
0	**Genova** Piazza Principe d.	0530	0543	0606	0630	0644	0708	0721	0753	0808	...	...	0818	0830	0842s	|	0919	0924	0930	...	1030	...	1121	1159	1219
72	Tortona **615** d.	|	0630	|	|	|	|	|	0837	|	...	...	0859	|	0922s	|	|	|	|	...	|	...	|	|	|
89	Voghera **615** d.	|	0641	|	|	0734	|	0808	0848	|	...	...	0911	|	0935s	|	1008	|	|	...	|	...	1208	|	1308
115	Pavia d.	|	0701	|	|	0751	|	0825	0904	|	...	...	0928	|	0958s	|	1025	|	|	...	|	...	1225	|	1325
144	**Milano** Rogoredo a.	|	0719	|	|	0810	|	0846	0921	|	...	...	|	|	|	|	|	|	|	...	|	...	|	|	|
154	**Milano** Centrale a.	|	0735	|	|	0823	|	0900	0940	|	...	...	0955	|	1045	1020	1050	|	|	...	|	...	1250	|	1350
	Novi Ligure d.	0614	...	|	0714	...	0741	...	...	0841	...	...	...	0914	...	...	...	|	1014	...	1114	...	...	|	...
	Alessandria **615** d.	0631	...	0657	0731	...	0757	...	...	0857	...	...	...	0931	...	...	...	1010	1031	...	1131	...	...	1244	...
	Asti **615** d.	0654	...	0723	0754	...	0818	...	...	0918	...	...	...	0954	...	...	...	1029	1054	...	1154	...	...	1302	...
	Torino Porta Nuova **615** a.	0730	...	0810	0830	...	0855	...	...	0955	...	...	...	1030	...	...	...	1110	1130	...	1230	...	...	1340	...

		IC 746					IC 670				IC 510	IC 1540			IC 674		IC 512	FB 9772	IC 678					IC 680	
				2					2	2				2		2	2	🍷							
		♦		Ⓐ	ⒸA						♦	♦	A				⚒		♦			Ⓐ	ⒸA		
Roma Termini **640** d.	...	...	...	...	...	...	...	...	...	...	0957	...	...	...	...	...	...	1157	...	...	...	...	...	...	...
Livorno Centrale d.	...	...	...	...	...	...	1124	...	...	...	1245	...	...	...	1324	1419	...	1430	...	...	...	...	...	...	...
Pisa Centrale d.	...	...	...	...	...	...	1142	...	...	1234	1303	...	...	...	1342	1435	...	1447	...	...	...	...	...	...	...
Viareggio d.	...	...	...	...	...	...	1200	...	...	1254	1318	...	...	...	1402	1454	...	1503	...	...	...	...	...	...	...
Massa Centro d.	...	...	...	...	...	...	1212	...	...	1312	1331	...	...	...	1414	1512	...	1517	...	...	...	...	...	...	...
Carrara-Avenza d.	...	...	...	...	...	...	1219	...	...	1318	1339	...	...	...	|	1517	...	|	...	...	...	...	...	...	...
Sarzana d.	...	...	...	...	...	...	|	...	...	1326	|	...	...	...	|	1531	...	|	...	...	...	...	...	...	...
La Spezia Centrale d.	...	...	...	...	...	1225	1238	...	1254	1341	1400	...	...	1404	1438	1545	...	1539	...	...	1558	...	...	1637	...
Riomaggiore d.	...	...	...	...	...	1233	|	...	1303	...	|	...	...	1413	|	▬	...	|	...	...	1606	...	...	|	...
Monterosso d.	...	...	...	...	...	1242	1254	...	1312	...	|	...	...	1421	1454	...	...	|	...	...	1621	...	...	1654	...
Levanto d.	...	...	...	...	...	1247	1301	...	1317	...	|	...	...	1426	1501	...	...	|	...	...	1626	...	...	1701	...
Sestri Levante d.	...	...	...	...	...	1307	1316	...	1337	...	1430	...	...	1446	1516	...	...	|	...	...	1654	...	...	1716	...
Chiavari d.	...	...	...	...	...	1317	1324	...	1346	...	1439	...	...	1455	1524	...	...	1613	...	...	1703	...	...	1724	...
Rapallo d.	...	...	...	...	...	1325	1333	...	1357	...	1448	...	...	1503	1533	...	...	1622	...	...	1712	...	...	1733	...
S. Margherita-Portofino d.	...	...	...	...	...	1329	1339	←	1401	...	|	...	...	1507	1539	...	...	|	...	...	1716	...	...	1739	←
Genova Brignole d.	1222	...	1322	1333	...	1415	1410	1422	1445	...	1515	...	...	1546	1610	1622	1640	1656	...	1722	1757	...	...	1803	1822
Genova Piazza Principe a.	1230	...	1330	1341	...	→	1416	1428	1451	...	1521	...	...	1552	1616	1630	1646	1702	...	1730	→	...	...	1809	1828
Genova Piazza Principe d.	1230	1321	1330	1341	1343	...	1419	1430	...	...	1524	1519	1544	...	1619	1630	1649	1712	1721	1730	...	1743	1743	1819	1830
Tortona **615** d.	|	|	|	1431	1431	...	|	|	...	...	|	|	1630	...	1700	|	|	|	|	|	...	1830	1830	1900	|
Voghera **615** d.	|	1408	|	1443	1443	...	1508	|	...	...	|	1608	1641	...	|	|	|	|	1810	|	...	1841	1841	|	|
Pavia d.	|	1425	|	1502	1502	...	1525	|	...	...	|	1625	1702	...	1725	|	|	1819	1827	|	...	1902	1902	1925	|
Milano Rogoredo a.	|	|	|	1520	1520	...	|	|	...	...	|	|	1720	...	|	|	|	|	|	|	...	1920	1920	|	|
Milano Centrale a.	|	1450	|	1535	1535	...	1550	|	...	...	|	1650	1735	...	1750	|	|	1850	1855	|	...	1935	1935	1950	|
Novi Ligure d.	1314	...	1414	...	...	...	...	1514	...	...	|	...	...	...	...	1714	1722	...	...	1814	...	...	...	...	1914
Alessandria **615** d.	1331	...	1431	...	...	...	...	1531	...	...	1609	...	...	...	...	1731	1736	...	...	1831	...	...	...	...	1931
Asti **615** d.	1354	...	1454	...	...	...	...	1554	...	...	1632	...	...	...	...	1754	1800	...	...	1854	...	...	...	...	1954
Torino Porta Nuova **615** a.	1430	...	1530	...	...	...	...	1630	...	...	1710	...	...	...	...	1830	1840	...	...	1930	...	...	...	...	2030

		FB 9774		IC 682	IC 1538					IC 1534	IC 684			IC 748	IC 518					FB 9782		FB 9784			IC 522
	2	🍷	2			2	2	2	2				2				A	2	2	🍷	2	🍷	2	2	
	Ⓑ			♦	♦				⑦y	♦	♦	F		♦	♦		Ⓑp								♦
Roma Termini **640** d.	...	1357	...	...	...	...	...	...	...	...	...	...	...	...	1557	...	...	...	...	1657	...	1827	...	...	1941o
Livorno Centrale d.	...	1615	...	...	...	...	...	...	1703	1718	1726	...	...	...	1845	...	...	...	...	1930	...	2047	...	...	2233
Pisa Centrale d.	1538	1629	...	...	...	...	1634	...	1720	1736	1744	1822	1834	...	1902	...	...	...	1909	1947	2042	2101	...	...	2250
Viareggio d.	1558	|	...	...	...	...	1654	...	1736	1753	1802	1840	1854	...	1918	...	...	...	1926	2003	2102	|	...	...	2307
Massa Centro d.	1615	1652	...	...	...	...	1712	...	1753	1813	1816	1858	1912	...	1931	...	...	...	1946	2017	2119	|	...	...	2320
Carrara-Avenza d.	1621	|	...	...	...	...	1718	...	1759	1819	|	1904	1918	...	|	...	...	...	1951	|	2130	|	...	...	2327
Sarzana d.	1628	|	...	...	...	...	1726	...	1807	|	|	1912	1926	...	|	...	...	...	1958	|	2143	|	...	...	2335
La Spezia Centrale d.	1645	1715	1658	...	...	1720	1741	1756	|	1840	1840	▬	1940	...	1958	...	...	2002	|	2039	2158	2142	2153	2310	0002
Riomaggiore d.	...	|	1705	...	...	1729	...	1805	|	|	|	...	...	...	|	...	...	2011	|	|	...	|	2202	2319	|
Monterosso d.	...	|	1713	...	...	1746	...	1815	|	1855	1855	...	...	...	|	...	...	2020	|	|	...	|	2210	2335	0018
Levanto d.	...	|	1718	...	...	1751	...	1820	|	1901	1901	...	...	...	|	...	...	2025	|	|	...	|	2215	2340	0024
Sestri Levante d.	...	|	1739	...	...	1821	...	1841	|	1916	1916	...	...	...	|	...	...	2044	|	|	...	|	2235	0005	0040
Chiavari d.	...	|	1756	...	...	1830	...	1850	|	1924	1924	...	...	...	2033	...	...	2053	|	2113	...	|	2244	0014	...
Rapallo d.	...	|	1804	...	...	1840	...	1900	w	1933	1933	...	...	...	2042	...	...	2103	w	2122	...	|	2252	0024	...
S. Margherita-Portofino d.	...	|	1808	...	...	1844	...	1904	|	1939	1939	...	...	...	|	...	...	2107	|	|	...	|	2256	0029	...
Genova Brignole d.	...	1808s	1852	...	...	1934	...	1943	|	2010	2010	2022	...	...	2113	2122	...	2159	|	2147s	...	2234s	2341	0123	...
Genova Piazza Principe a.	...	1816	1858	...	...	1940	...	1949	|	2016	2016	2030	...	...	2119	2130	...	2205	|	2157	...	2242	2347	...	...
Genova Piazza Principe d.	...	...	...	1921	1921	1943	...	...	|	2019	2019	2030	...	2121	...	2130	2149	...	|	...	...	...	...	...	...
Tortona **615** d.	...	...	...	2000	2000	2033	...	...	|	|	|	|	...	|	...	|	2236	...	|	...	...	...	...	...	...
Voghera **615** d.	...	...	...	|	|	2045	...	...	|	2108	2108	|	...	2208	...	|	2247	...	|	...	...	...	...	...	...
Pavia d.	...	...	...	2025	2025	2102	...	...	|	2125	2125	|	...	2225	...	|	2303	...	|	...	...	...	...	...	...
Milano Rogoredo a.	...	...	...	|	|	2120	...	...	|	|	|	|	...	|	...	|	2320	...	|	...	...	...	...	...	...
Milano Centrale a.	...	...	...	2050	2050	2135	...	...	2148g	2150	2150	|	...	2250	...	|	2335	...	2320	...	...	...	...	...	...
Novi Ligure d.	...	...	...	...	...	...	...	...	...	...	...	2114	...	...	...	2214	...	...	...	...	...	...	...	...	...
Alessandria **615** d.	...	...	...	...	...	...	...	...	...	...	...	2131	...	...	...	2231	...	...	...	...	...	...	...	...	...
Asti **615** d.	...	...	...	...	...	...	...	...	...	...	...	2154	...	...	...	2254	...	...	...	...	...	...	...	...	...
Torino Porta Nuova **615** a.	...	...	...	...	...	...	...	...	...	...	...	2230	...	...	...	2340	...	...	...	...	...	...	...	...	...

♦ – **NOTES** (LISTED BY TRAIN NUMBER)

510 – [12] Salerno - Torino.
518 – [12] Roma - Ventimiglia.
522 – Ⓑ (not days before holidays): [12] Napoli - Sestri Levante.
656 – ⚒: [12] Ventimiglia (**655**) - Genova - Milano.
664 – [12] Ventimiglia (**663**) - Genova - Milano.
678 – [12] Ventimiglia (**677**) - Genova - Milano.
682 – Ⓐ: [12] Ventimiglia (**681**) - Genova - Milano.
684 – Ⓐ: [12] Grosseto - Livorno - Milano.
746 – [12] Ventimiglia (**745**) - Genova - Milano.
748 – [12] Ventimiglia (**747**) - Genova - Milano.

784 – 🛏 1,2 cl. (T2) and ▬ 2 cl. (4 berth) Siracusa - Genova - Milano; 🛏 1,2 cl. (T2) and ▬ 2 cl. (4 berth) Palermo (**782**) - Messina - Milano.
796 – ▬ 2 cl. (4 berth) and [2] Salerno - Napoli - Torino.
1534 – Ⓒ: [12] Grosseto - Livorno - Milano.
1538 – Ⓒ: [12] Ventimiglia (**1537**) - Genova - Milano.
1540 – †: [12] Ventimiglia (**1539**) - Genova - Milano.

A – From Albenga.
F – [2] Pisa - Aulla - Fidenza - Bergamo.
V – From Ventimiglia.

a – Ⓐ only.
g – Milano **Porta Garibaldi**.
o – Roma **Ostiense**.
p – Not Apr. 20, June 1, and days before holidays.
s – Stops to set down only.
w – Via Aulla, Fidenza.
y – Also Apr. 21, June 2; not Apr. 20, June 1.
♠ – Operator: Trenord.

PISA - ROMA 611

km		ICN 785	ICN 799		IC 1571		IC 501	FB 9761		FB 9763	IC 505			IC 1533	IC 657	FB 9773			IC 511			FB 9777		FB 9781		
				2				🍷		🍷			2			🍷		2		2		🍷		🍷	2	2
		◆	◆	⚒	†		◆				◆			Ⓒ	Ⓐ				◆							Ⓑy
	Torino P N **610** d.	...	2155	...	...	...	...	...	...	...	...	...	...	...	...	...	...	...	1105	...	...	...	...	1520	...	...
	Milano Centrale **610** d.	2005	|	...	...	...	...	...	...	...	...	...	...	0810	0810	...	...	...	|	...	...	1310	...	|	...	...
	Genova P P **610** d.	2149	2353	...	...	...	...	0551	...	0705	0851	...	...	0947	0947	1212	...	...	1251	...	...	1452	...	1704	...	...
0	**Pisa** Centrale **610** d.	0001	0221	...	...	0545	0656	0732	0745	0913	1106	1145	1229	1224	1250	1357	1343	1412	1504	...	1545	1713	1745	1913	1945	2150
20	**Livorno** Centrale d.	0015	0240	...	0527	0603	0712	0746	0803	0929	1121	1203	1246	1254	1323	1411	1400	1429	1519	...	1603	1729	1803	1929	2003	2209
43	Rosignano d.	|	|	...	|	0620	|	|	0820	|	|	1220	1307	|	|	|	1416	1450	|	...	1620	|	1820	|	2020	2230
54	Cecina d.	|	|	...	0549	0629	0737	|	0829	|	1143	1229	1317	1318	1348	|	1424	1459	|	...	1629	|	1829	1949	2029	2238
89	Campiglia Marittima d.	|	|	...	0611	0651	0757	|	0851	1003	|	1251	1345	1336	1406	|	1452	1525	1554	...	1651	1803	1851	|	2051	2306
106	Follonica d.	|	|	...	0624	0702	0808	|	0902	|	1205	1302	1354	1346	1418	|	1503	...	1605	...	1702	|	1902	|	2102	2318
148	Grosseto d.	|	0357	0419	0650	0730	0829	0838	0930	1029	1226	1330	1435	1408	1443	1503	1530	...	1625	1629	1730	1829	1930	2029	2130	2343
186	Orbetello-Monte Argentario d.	|	|	0444	0709	0753	0850	|	0953	|	|	1353	...	...	...	|	1553	...	|	1655	1753	|	1953	|	2153	...
225	Tarquinia d.	|	|	0518	|	0829	|	|	1029	|	|	1429	...	...	...	|	1629	...	|	1729	1829	|	2029	|	2229	...
255	**Civitavecchia** d.	|	0500	0532	0750	0844	0935	|	1044	1118	1316	1444	...	...	...	1551	1644	...	1716	1743	1844	1918	2044	2118	2251	...
264	S. Marinella d.	|	|	0539	|	0851	|	|	1051	|	|	1451	...	...	...	|	1651	...	|	1750	1851	|	2051	|	2251	...
286	Ladispoli-Cerveteri d.	|	|	0555	|	0905	|	|	1105	|	|	1505	...	...	...	|	1705	...	|	1805	1905	|	2105	|	2305	...
329	**Roma** Ostiense a.	0313	0555	0633	0834	0936	1018	|	1136	|	1352	1536	...	...	...	|	1736	...	1752	1837	1936	|	2136	|	2336	...
336	**Roma** Termini **640** a.	...	|	0648	0845	0948	|	1003	1148	1203	1403	1548	...	...	...	1632	1748	...	1803	1848	1948	2003	2148	2203	2348	...
	Napoli Centrale **640** a.	...	0817	...	1103	...	1229	...	...	...	...	...	...	...	...	...	...	...	2029	...	...	...	...	...	...	...

	ICN 784					FB 9764	IC 510		FB 9772		FB 9774	IC 1534	IC 684		IC 518		FB 9782	FB 9784		IC 522	IC 1572				ICN 796
		2	2	2	2	🍷			🍷		🍷						🍷	🍷					2	2	
	◆	⚒	†				◆					Ⓒ	Ⓐ		◆					◆	⑥q				◆
Napoli Centrale **640** d.	...	...	...	...	...	...	0731	...	...	...	...	...	...	...	...	...	...	...	...	1731	1731	...	...	...	2142
Roma Termini **640** d.	...	...	...	...	0612	0657	0957	1012	1157	1212	1357	...	...	1412	1557	1612	1657	1827	1812	|	|	2012	2112	2212	|
Roma Ostiense d.	0243	...	...	...	0623	|	1007	1023	|	1223	|	...	...	1423	1607	1623	|	|	1823	1941	1941	2023	2121	2223	0003
Ladispoli-Cerveteri d.	|	...	...	...	0651	|	|	1051	|	1251	|	...	...	1451	|	1651	|	|	1900	|	|	2051	2152	2300	|
S. Marinella d.	|	...	...	...	0706	|	|	1106	|	1306	|	...	...	1506	|	1706	|	|	1915	|	|	2106	2208	2315	|
Civitavecchia d.	|	...	...	...	0715	0741	1047	1115	1241	1315	1439	...	...	1515	1647	1715	1741	1908	1924	2023	2023	2115	2217	2324	0050
Tarquinia d.	|	...	...	...	0729	|	|	1129	|	1328	|	...	...	1528	|	1728	|	|	1937	|	|	2128	2230	2336e	|
Orbetello-Monte Argentario d.	|	0602	...	...	0801	|	|	1202	|	1400	|	...	...	1600	|	1800	|	|	2009	2102	2102	2200	2303	0009e	|
Grosseto d.	0431	0628	0647	0738	0831	0832	1139	1227	1332	1427	1524	1604	1610	1627	1739	1825	1832	1954	2033	2121	2121	2227	2327	0034e	0153
Follonica d.	|	0654	0710	0810	0855	|	1158	1254	|	1453	|	1625	1632	1653	1758	1857	|	|	2057	2141	2141	2253	...	...	|
Campiglia Marittima d.	|	0706	0722	0825	0905	|	1209	1305	1356	1504	|	1636	1643	1704	|	1906	1856	|	2108	2151	2151	2304	...	...	|
Cecina d.	|	0731	0746	0850	0927	0909	|	1327	|	1527	|	1655	1702	1727	1822	1928	|	|	2128	2210	2210	2327	...	...	|
Rosignano d.	|	0739	0754	0900	0936	|	|	1336	|	1536	|	|	|	1736	|	1936	|	|	2136	|	|	2336	...	...	|
Livorno Centrale d.	0540s	0800	0812	0926	0958	0930	1245	1358	1430	1558	1615	1718	1726	1758	1845	1958	1930	2047	2158	2233	2234	2358	...	...	0309
Pisa Centrale **610** a.	0557s	0815	0829	0950	1015	0944	1300	1415	1444	1615	1627	1733	1741	1815	1859	2015	1944	2059	2215	2247	...	0015	...	...	0323
Genova P P **610** a.	0830	...	...	...	...	1156	1521	...	1702	...	1816	2016	2016	...	2119	...	2157	2242	...	...	...	...	...	...	0601
Milano Centrale **610** a.	1045	...	...	...	...	|	|	...	1850	...	...	2150	2150	...	...	...	...	...	...	...	...	...	...	...	|
Torino P N **610** a.	...	...	...	...	...	1340	1710	...	...	...	...	...	...	...	...	...	...	...	...	...	...	...	...	...	0810

◆ – **NOTES** (LISTED BY TRAIN NUMBER)

01 – ⚒: [12] Sestri Levante - Napoli.
05 – [12] Ventimiglia - Genova - Roma.
10 – [12] Salerno - Torino.
11 – [12] Torino - Salerno.
18 – [12] Roma - Genova - Ventimiglia.
22 – Ⓑ (not days before holidays): [12] Napoli - Sestri Levante.
84 – 🛌 1,2 cl. (T2) and 🛏 2 cl. (4 berth) Siracusa - Genova - Milano; 🛌 1,2 cl. (T2) and 🛏 2 cl. (4 berth) Palermo (**782**) - Messina - Milano.
85 – 🛌 1,2 cl. (T2) and 🛏 2 cl. (4 berth) Milano - Genova - Siracusa; 🛌 1,2 cl. (T2) and 🛏 2 cl. (4 berth) Milano - Messina (**781**) - Palermo.

796 – 🛏 2 cl. (4 berth) and [2] Salerno - Napoli - Torino.
799 – 🛏 2 cl. (4 berth) and [2] Torino - Napoli - Salerno.

e – † only.
q – Also days before holidays.
s – Stops to set down only.
y – Not Apr. 20, June 1, and days before holidays.

PARMA and FIDENZA - SARZANA and LA SPEZIA 612

Most services 2nd class only

km																											
		⚒						B		⚒		⚒		⚒		⚒						⚒	⑤w		⚒	⚒	†
	Milano Centrale d.	...	...	...	...	...	0645	...	...	...	...	...	...	...	...	...	...	...	...	...	1705	...	1836g	...	...	...	...
0	**Parma** d.	...	...	0515	0616	0748	|	...	...	...	1252	...	1339	...	1442	...	1539j	1642	...	1744	|	1944	|	2043	2144	2238	2238
*	**Fidenza** d.	...	...	|	|	|	0824	0913	...	...	|	...	|	...	|	...	|	|	...	|	1830	|	2030	|	|	|	|
23	Fornovo d.	...	...	0533	0646	0813	0843	0930	...	...	1322	...	1405	...	1510	...	1612	1713	...	1809	1855	2009	2047	2114	2211	2308	2308
61	Borgo Val di Taro d.	...	0544	0605	0728	0846	0935	0959	...	1325	1359	...	1444	...	1549	...	1644	1749	...	1846	1943	2044	2134	2149	2244	2343	2343
79	Pontremoli d.	0545	0601	0627	0743	0903	0953	1018	1216	1342	1416	1421	1503	1542	1607	1621	1700	1807	1821	1901	2000	2101	2152	2206	2300	2358	2359
00	Aulla Lunigiana d.	0608	0623	0657	0807	0922	1021	1035	1238	1410	...	1443	1522	1610	...	1643	1721	...	1843	1922	2020	2121	2211	2225	...	...	0019
08	S. Stefano di Magra d.	0615	0631	0704	0814	0930	1028	1042	1246	1416	...	1451	1531	1616	...	1651	1729	...	1851	1929	2030	2130	2219	2232	...	...	0026
16	**Sarzana** a.	|	0638	|	|	|	1042	1055	1254	|	...	1459	|	|	...	1659	|	...	1859	|	2042	|	2232	|	...	...	|
	Pisa C **611** a.	|	0736	|	|	|	1148	1200	1345	|	...	1551	|	|	...	1751	|	...	1951	|	2138	|	2320	|	...	...	|
	Livorno **611** a.	|	...	|	|	|	...	...	...	|	...	...	|	|	...	...	|	...	...	|	2155	|	2338	|	...	...	|
20	**La Spezia** Centrale a.	0633	...	0722	0833	0948	...	...	...	1433	...	...	1550	1633	...	...	1746	...	...	1947	...	2148	...	2250	...	...	0042

	⚒				⚒	⚒	Ⓐ	Ⓒ		⚒			⚒		⚒		⚒	⚒	⚒	⑦n		B	⚒				G
Spezia Centrale d.	...	0540	0615	...	0810	0927	1012	1012	1226	...	1327	1419r	...	...	1527	1610	...	...	1729	...	1809	...	1927	...	2012	...	2102
Livorno **611** d.	...	|	|	0552	|	|	|	|	|	...	|	|	...	...	|	|	...	...	|	1703	|	...	|	...	|	...	|
Pisa C **611** a.	...	|	|	0610	|	|	|	|	|	...	|	|	1405	...	|	|	1605	...	|	1720	|	1822	|	1909	|	2006	|
Sarzana d.	...	|	|	0701	|	|	|	|	|	...	|	|	1457	...	|	|	1657	...	|	1807	|	1913	|	1958	|	2058	|
Stefano di Magra d.	...	0551	0631	0711	0829	0945	1030	1030	1242	...	1344	1436	1509	...	1544	1629	1712	...	1747	1815	1828	1925	1943	2009	2029	2109	2118
lla Lunigiana d.	...	0558	0638	0718	0838	0952	1038	1038	1249	...	1351	1443	1516	...	1551	1637	1718	...	1754	1823	1836	1932	1950	2016	2038	2116	2126
ntremoli d.	0551	0627	0657	0740	0858	1015	1058	1058	1308	1351	1413	1500	1539	1551	1612	1656	1739	1748	1816	1846	1858	1952	2015	2035	2057	2139	2148
rgo Val di Taro d.	0609	0642	0713	0800	0914	...	1114	1115	1323	1407	...	1516	...	1608	...	1713	...	1805	...	1901	1914	2008	...	2051	2114	...	2205
rnovo d.	0646	0716	0749	0843	0957	...	...	1149	1405	1446	...	1551	...	1647	...	1746	...	1851	...	1940	1949	2047	...	2140	2150	...	2244
Fidenza a.	|	|	|	0903	|	...	...	|	|	|	...	|	...	|	...	|	...	|	...	2000	|	2103	...	2156	|	...	|
rma a.	0709	0740	0807	|	1016	...	...	1210	1428	1510	...	1615	...	1711	...	1807	...	1915	...	|	2010	...	...	|	2210	...	2310
Milano Centrale a.	...	...	...	1020	...	...	...	...	...	...	...	...	...	...	...	...	...	...	...	2148g	...	...	...	2320	...	...	...

– [2] Bergamo - Pisa and v.v.
– [2] Savona / Genova - La Spezia - Parma.

g – Milano **Porta Garibaldi**.
j – Depart 1546 on †.
n – Also Apr. 21, June 2; not Apr. 20, June 1.
r – Depart 1422 on †.
w – Also Apr. 24; not Apr. 25.

* – Fidenza - Fornovo is *25 km*.

613 FIRENZE - SIENA, PISA, PISA AEROPORTO ✈ and LIVORNO

Most services 2nd class only

Pisa Centrale - Pisa Aeroporto and v.v. is currently closed for construction work (see footnote)

km		⚒		⚒			y		⚒	1237/9 ♦						⚒		⚒	⚒						⚒
0	**Firenze** SMN **614** d.	0430	0535	...	0608	0620	0653	0700	...	0710	0728	...	0753	0810	0828	0910	0928	0953	1010	1028	1053	1100	1110	1128	...
34	Empoli d.	0506	0601	0621	0645	0650	0730	0722	0726	|	0803	0806	0827	0840	0858	0940	0958	1027	1040	1058	1127	|	1140	1158	1208
	Poggibonsi ▲ d.	|	|	0702	|	0729	|	|	0811	|	|	0848	|	0915	|	1015	|	|	1115	|	|	|	1215	|	1249
	Siena 609 619 a.	|	|	0731	|	0752	|	|	0840	|	|	0914	|	0938	|	1038	|	|	1138	|	|	|	1238	|	1314
81	**Pisa** Centrale **614** ¶ d.	0555	0640	...	0732	...	0809	0752	...	0839	0837	...	0903	...	0932	...	1032	1103	...	1132	1203	1153	...	1229	...
	Pisa Aeroporto ✈ ¶ a.	|	|	...	...	...	|	|	...	|	|	...	...	...	|	...	|	...	...	|	...	|	...	|	...
101	**Livorno** Centrale a.	0616	0654	...	...	...	0824	0808	...	0856	0851	...	...	...	0948	...	1048	...	...	1148	...	1208	...	1244	...

km		⚒					⚒	⚒	⚒						⚒			⚒			⑥	Ⓑ	⚒	⚒	⚒
	Firenze SMN **614** d.	1153	1210	1228	...	1253	1300	1310	1328	...	1338	1353	1410	1428	...	1453	1500	1510	1528	...	1546	1553	1610	1628	...
0	Empoli d.	1227	1240	1258	1308	1327	|	1340	1358	1408	1413	1427	1440	1458	1508	1527	|	1540	1558	1608	1626	1627	1640	1658	1708
38	Poggibonsi ▲ d.	|	1315	|	1349	|	|	1415	|	1449	|	|	1514	|	1549	|	|	1615	|	1649	|	|	1715	|	1749
63	**Siena 609 619** a.	|	1338	|	1414	|	|	1438	|	1514	|	|	1537	|	1614	|	|	1638	|	1714	|	|	1738	|	1814
	Pisa Centrale **614** ¶ d.	1304	...	1332	...	1403	1401	...	1432	...	1509	1503	...	1532	...	1603	1553	...	1632	...	1703	1703	...	1732	...
	Pisa Aeroporto ✈ ¶ a.	...	...	|	...	...	|	...	|	...	|	...	...	|	...	...	|	...	|	...	...	...	...	|	...
	Livorno Centrale a.	...	...	1348	...	...	1416	...	1448	...	1526	...	...	1548	...	...	1612	...	1648	...	...	...	...	1748	...

		⚒				Ⓐ							⚒			⚒	⚒			⚒				
Firenze SMN **614** d.	1653	1700	1710	1728	1738	1753	1810	1828	1853	1900	1910	1928	...	1953	2010	2028	...	2038	2053	2110	2128	2157	2307	0040
Empoli d.	1727	|	1740	1758	1813	1827	1840	1858	1927	|	1940	1958	2008	2027	2040	2058	2108	2113	2127	2139	2158	2233	2343	0115
Poggibonsi ▲ d.	|	|	1815	|	|	|	1915	|	|	|	2015	|	2049	|	2115	|	2150	|	|	2216	|	|	|	|
Siena 609 619 a.	|	|	1838	|	|	|	1938	|	|	|	2038	|	2114	|	2140	|	2214	|	|	2242	|	|	|	|
Pisa Centrale **614** ¶ d.	1803	1753	...	1832	1858	1904	...	1932	2003	1949	...	2032	...	2103	...	2128	...	2159	2205	...	2232j	2327	0032	0159
Pisa Aeroporto ✈ ¶ a.	...	|	...	|	|	...	...	|	...	...	...	|	...	...	...	...	...	...	|	...	|	|	|	...
Livorno Centrale a.	...	1808	...	1846	1913	...	...	1948	...	...	...	2048	...	...	...	...	...	...	2224	...	2248j	2344	0047	...

km				⚒		⚒	⚒	†	⚒		⚒	†	⚒			⚒				⚒	†	⚒	†	⚒	⚒
	Livorno Centrale d.	...	0521	...	0612	...	...	...	...	...	0710	...	...	0730	0743	...	0812	...	0852	...	...	0912	0912	...	1012
0	Pisa Aeroporto ✈ ¶ d.	...	|	...	|	...	...	...	...	...	|	...	...	|	|	...	|	...	|	...	...	|	|	...	|
2	**Pisa** Centrale **614** ¶ d.	0415	0539	...	0629	...	...	...	0701	...	0732	0732	...	0754	0801	...	0832	...	0912	...	...	0932	0932	...	1032
	Siena 609 619 d.	|	|	0543	|	0613	0625	0627	|	0636	|	|	0702	|	|	0732	|	0818	|	0847	0847	|	|	0918	|
	Poggibonsi ▲ d.	|	|	0606	|	0648	|	0649	|	0659	|	|	0728	|	|	0805	|	0846	|	0909	0909	|	|	0946	|
	Empoli d.	0453	0618	0645	0659	0723	0709	0723	0744	0750	0804	0804	0820	0832	0847	0852	0904	0921	|	0940	0940	1004	1017	1021	1104
	Firenze SMN **614** a.	0527	0652	0721	0727	0752	0734	0750	0820	0827	0832	0832	0855	0907	0922	...	0932	0950	1000	1005	1010	1032	1046	1050	1132

		⚒		⚒	⚒				⚒							⚒		⚒	⚒			Ⓑ		⚒
Livorno Centrale d.	...	...	1112	...	...	...	1212	...	...	1252	1312	...	...	1343	1412	...	...	1452	1512	...	...	1540	1608	...
Pisa Aeroporto ✈ ¶ d.	...	...	|	...	...	...	|	...	...	|	|	...	...	|	|	...	...	|	|	...	...	|	|	...
Pisa Centrale **614** ¶ d.	1054	1112	1132	...	1154	...	1232	...	1254	1312	1332	...	1354	1401	1432	...	1454	1512	1532	1554	...	1601	1632	...
Siena 609 619 d.	|	|	|	1118	|	1141	|	1218	|	|	|	1318	|	|	|	1418	|	|	|	|	1518	|	|	1618
Poggibonsi ▲ d.	|	|	|	1146	|	1212	|	1246	|	|	|	1346	|	|	|	1446	|	|	|	|	1546	|	|	1646
Empoli d.	1132	|	1204	1221	1232	1252	1304	1321	1332	|	1404	1421	1432	1447	1504	1521	1532	|	1604	1632	1621	1647	1704	1721
Firenze SMN **614** a.	1207	1200	1232	1250	1307	...	1332	1350	1407	1400	1432	1450	1507	1524	1532	1550	1607	1600	1632	1712	1650	1724	1732	1750

					Ⓑ	⑥	Ⓑ					⚒		1236/8 ♦	⚒		Ⓐ			⚒				
Livorno Centrale d.	...	1652	1712	...	...	...	...	1812	...	...	1852	...	...	1920	...	...	...	...	2012	...	...	...	2112	...
Pisa Aeroporto ✈ ¶ d.	...	|	|	...	...	...	...	|	...	...	|	...	...	|	...	...	...	...	|	...	...	...	|	...
Pisa Centrale **614** ¶ d.	1654	1712	1732	...	1754	1754	1801	1832	...	1854	1912	...	1932	1946	...	1954	2001	...	2032	2038	...	2101	2132	...
Siena 609 619 d.	|	|	|	1719	|	|	|	|	1818	|	|	1841	|	|	1918	|	|	1941	|	|	2018	|	|	2120
Poggibonsi ▲ d.	|	|	|	1746	|	|	|	|	1846	|	|	1912	|	|	1946	|	|	2012	|	|	2046	|	|	2147
Empoli d.	1732	1737	1804	1821	1832	1836	1847	1904	1921	1932	|	1952	2004	|	2021	2033	2047	2052	2104	2111	2121	2147	2204	2221
Firenze SMN **614** a.	1807	1801	1832	1850	1907	1915	1922	1932	1950	2007	2000	...	2032	2044	2050	2107	2122	...	2132	2142	2150	2222	2232	2253

♦ – NOTES (LISTED BY TRAIN NUMBER)

1236/8 – ⑥ Apr. 12 - Sept. 27: 🛏 1, 2 cl. (T2), 🛏 2 cl. and 🚃 Livorno - Wien.

1237/9 – ⑤ Apr. 11 - Sept. 26 (from Wien): 🛏 1, 2 cl. (T2), 🛏 2 cl. and 🚃 Wien - Livorno.

j – 5–7 minutes later on ⚒.

y – (daily from Apr. 20).

▲ – Poggibonsi-S. Gimignano.

¶ – Pisa Centrale - Pisa Aeroporto and v.v. has closed for conversio into an automated metro route (due to open December 2015 Currently a shuttle 🚌 service operates every 10 minutes betwee 0600 and 2400. Journey time: ±8 minutes.

Operator: Pisa Mover.

614 FIRENZE - LUCCA - VIAREGGIO and PISA

Most services 2nd class only

km		⚒	⚒	⚒									†	Ⓐ			z			z			⚒		
0	**Firenze** SMN **613** d.	0510	...	...	...	0603	0710	...	0810	...	0910	...	1010	...	...	1210	...	and at	1910	...	2010	...	2110	2210	...
17	Prato Centrale d.	0533	...	...	...	0623	0729	...	0831	...	0931	...	1031	...	...	1231	...	the same	1931	...	2031	...	2131	2231	...
34	Pistoia d.	0551	...	...	...	0640	0745	...	0844	...	0944	...	1044	...	...	1244	...	minutes	1944	...	2044	...	2144	2246	...
47	Montecatini Centro d.	0604	...	...	...	0658	0802	...	0901	...	1001	...	1101	...	...	1301	...	past each	2001	...	2101	...	2200	2301	...
78	Lucca ⊡ d.	0646	0652	0708	0742	0755	0830	0842	0930	0942	1030	1042	1130	1242	1312	1330	1342	hour	2030	2042	2130	2142	2242	2330	...
101	**Viareggio** a.	0707	|	|	|	|	0850	|	0950	|	1053	|	1150	|	|	1350	|	until	2050	|	2150	|	2302	2350	...
	Pisa Centrale **613** ⊡ a.	...	0716	0741	0813	0825	...	0913	...	1013	...	1109	...	1313	1343	...	1413		...	2113	...	2213	...	...	...

km		⚒																					⚒		
0	**Pisa** Centrale **613** ⊡ d.	0613	...	...	0704	0750	...	0850	...	0950	...	...	1250	...	1343	...	1450	...	and at	1950	...	2050	...	2150	...
	Viareggio d.	|	0628	0710	|	|	0810	|	0910	|	1010	1207	|	1310	|	1410	|	1510	the same	|	2010	|	2110	|	221
24	Lucca ⊡ d.	0639	0648	0727	0736	0822	0831	0917	0931	1017	1031	1231	1317	1331	1409	1431	1517	1531	minutes	2017	2031	2117	2131	2217	223
	Montecatini Centro d.	...	0715	0753	...	...	0857	...	0957	...	1057	1257	...	1357	...	1457	...	1557	past each	...	2057	...	2157	...	225
	Pistoia d.	...	0732	0812	...	...	0912	...	1012	...	1112	1312	...	1412	...	1512	...	1612	hour	...	2112	...	2212	...	231
	Prato Centrale d.	...	0747	0827	...	...	0929	...	1030	...	1128	1329	...	1430	...	1529	...	1629	until	...	2129	...	2229	...	232
	Firenze SMN **613** a.	...	0806	0850	...	...	0950	...	1100	...	1150	1350	...	1450	...	1550	...	1650		...	2150	...	2250	...	235

z – 1842 departure from Lucca does not run on †.

⊡ – Additional services operate Lucca - Pisa Centrale and v.v. on ⚒.

MILANO and TORINO - BOLOGNA 615

For high-speed services – see Table 600

km			*FR* 9507 🍷	A	P	*IC* 583 ◆	R	2	*IC* 1589 ◆	*IC* 1591 ◆		*FB* 9803 🍷C			A	A		*FB* 9807 🍷C		*IC* 1545 ◆	A	*FB* 9809 🍷T			*FB* 9811 🍷C	
0	**Milano** Centrale d.	0515	0550	...	0615	0650	...	0645	0710	0710	0715	0735	...	...	...	...	0920	...	...	1000	...	1035	...	1120	1135	...
10	**Milano** Rogoredo d.	0527	|	...	|	0702	...	0659	0722	0722	0727	|	...	...	...	...	0933	...	...	1012	...	|	...	1133	|	...
	Torino P N **610** d.	|	|	...	|	|	...	|	|	|	|	|	...	...	...	...	|	0832	...	|	...	|	...	|	|	...
	Asti **610** d.	|	|	...	|	|	...	|	|	|	|	|	...	...	...	...	|	0908	...	|	...	|	...	|	|	...
	Alessandria **610** d.	|	|	...	|	|	...	|	|	|	|	|	...	...	...	...	|	0924	...	|	...	|	...	|	|	...
	Tortona **610** d.	|	|	...	|	|	...	|	|	|	|	|	...	...	...	...	|	|	...	|	...	|	...	|	|	...
	Voghera **610** d.	|	|	...	|	|	0700	|	|	|	|	|	...	0805	...	...	|	|	...	|	...	|	...	|	|	...
72	Piacenza d.	0609	0634	0652	0715	0745	0752	0759	0810	0810	0815	0820	←	0845	0852	0952	1014	1020	←	1048	1052	1120	...	1215	1220	←
107	Fidenza d.	0632	|	0715	0739	0803	0815	0821	0827	0827	0841	|	0843	...	0915	1015	1041	|	1043	1105	1115	|	...	1241	|	1243
129	Parma d.	0646	0701	0730	0754	0816	0830	...	0840	0840	→	0846	0856	...	0930	1030	→	1046	1056	1121	1130	1146	...	→	1246	1256
157	Reggio Emilia d.	0704	0717	0747	0810	0833	0847	...	0855	0855	...	0900	0914	...	0947	1047	...	1100	1114	1138	1147	1200	...	...	1300	1314
182	Modena d.	0721	0731	0801	0826	0850	0901	...	0924	0924	...	0915	0932	...	1001	1101	...	1115	1132	1153	1201	1215	...	...	1315	1332
219	**Bologna** Centrale **620** a.	0804	0752	0828	0902	0914	0928	...	0954	0954	...	0938	1008	...	1028	1128	...	1138	1208	1219	1228	1238	...	...	1338	1408
	Roma Termini **620** a.	...	1010	...	...	1317t	...	...	1344t	1344t	...	...	...	...	...	...	...	...	...	...	...	...	...	...	...	...

	A	*FB* 9813 🍷C	R		*FB* 9815 🍷C		A	A	*IC* 597 ◆		*FB* 9819 🍷B		*ICN* 795 ◆		A	R			*FB* 9823 🍷E		*IC* 599 ◆		A		*FB* 9825 🍷A	
Milano Centrale d.	...	1235	...	1320	1335	...	...	...	1450	1520	1535	...	1544g	...	...	...	1705	1720	1735	...	1745	...	...	1815	1835	...
Milano Rogoredo d.	...	|	...	1333	|	...	...	...	1501	1533	|	...	|	...	...	...	1717	1733	|	...	1800	...	...	1827	|	...
Torino P N **610** d.	...	|	...	|	|	...	...	...	|	|	|	...	|	...	...	...	|	|	|	...	|	...	...	|	|	...
Asti **610** d.	...	|	...	|	|	...	...	...	|	|	|	...	|	...	...	...	|	|	|	...	|	...	...	|	|	...
Alessandria **610** d.	...	|	...	|	|	...	...	...	|	|	|	...	|	...	...	...	|	|	|	...	|	...	...	|	|	...
Tortona **610** d.	...	|	...	|	|	...	...	...	|	|	|	...	|	...	...	...	|	|	|	...	|	...	...	|	|	...
Voghera **610** d.	...	|	...	|	|	...	...	...	|	|	|	...	|	1607	...	...	|	|	|	...	|	1807	...	|	|	...
Piacenza d.	1252	1320	1346	1414	1420	←	1452	1552	1545	1614	1620	←	1630	1647	1652	1752	1805	1814	1820	←	1845	1847	1852	1909	1922	←
Fidenza d.	1315	|	1415	1441	|	1443	1515	1615	1603	1641	|	1643	|	...	1715	1815	1826	1841	|	1843	1903	...	1915	1931	|	1933
Parma d.	1330	1346	1430	→	1446	1456	1530	1630	1616	→	1646	1656	1705	...	1730	1830	...	→	1846	1856	1916	...	1930	→	1948	1956
Reggio Emilia d.	1347	1400	1447	...	1500	1514	1547	1647	1633	...	1700	1714	1722	...	1747	1847	...	...	1900	1914	1933	...	1947	...	2002	2016
Modena d.	1401	1415	1501	...	1515	1532	1601	1701	1650	...	1715	1732	1741	...	1801	1901	...	...	1915	1932	1950	...	2001	...	2017	2034
Bologna Centrale **620** a.	1428	1438	1528	...	1538	1608	1628	1728	1714	...	1738	1808	|	...	1828	1928	...	...	1938	2008	2014	...	2028	...	2038	2108
Roma Termini **620** a.	...	...	...	...	...	...	...	...	2115t	...	...	...	2313t	...	...	...	...	...	...	...	...	...	...	...	...	...

	R	2 ⑤w		*FB* 9829 🍷A	*ICN* 765 ◆			*ICN* 755 ◆	2		*ICN* 757 ◆	*ICN* 1911 ◆	
Milano Centrale d.	...	1836g	1920	1935	1950	...	...	2050	...	2115	...	2317g	...
Milano Rogoredo d.	...	1903	1933	|	|	...	...	|	...	2127	...	|	...
Torino P N **610** d.	...	|	|	|	|	...	...	|	...	|	2020	|	...
Asti **610** d.	...	|	|	|	|	...	...	|	...	|	2101	|	...
Alessandria **610** d.	...	|	|	|	|	...	...	|	...	|	2122	|	...
Tortona **610** d.	1850	|	|	|	|	...	...	|	...	|	2139	|	...
Voghera **610** d.	1903	|	|	|	|	2007	...	|	...	|	2153	|	...
Piacenza d.	1952	2007	2014	2020	|	2047	2052	2134	2152	2212	2230	0011	...
Fidenza d.	2015	2028	2043	|	|	...	2115	|	2215	2242	|	|	...
Parma d.	2030	...	2056	2046	|	...	2130	2206	2230	2303	|	0101	...
Reggio Emilia d.	2047	...	2114	2100	|	...	2147	2224	2247	...	|	|	...
Modena d.	2101	...	2134	2115	|	...	2201	2240	2301	...	|	|	...
Bologna Centrale **620** a.	2128	...	2214	2138	2155	...	2230	2305	2326	...	2347	0215	...
Roma Termini **620** a.	...	...	...	...	...	...	...	...	...	...	...	0717t	...

	ICN 1580 ◆	*ICN* 1910 ◆	*ICN* 758 ◆					*ICN* 752 ◆
Roma Termini **620** d.	...	2343t	...	...	...	...	...	...
Bologna Centrale **620** d.	0357	0418	0432	0500	...	0528	0552	0620
Modena d.	|	|	|	0524	...	0559	0625	0645
Reggio Emilia d.	|	|	|	0538	...	0613	0642	0702
Parma d.	|	0521	|	0553	0610	0629	0705	0724
Fidenza d.	|	|	|	0607	0624	0641	0726	|
Piacenza d.	0516	0602	|	0638	0648	0708	0754	0816
Voghera **610** d.	0550	|	|	0718	|	|	|	|
Tortona **610** d.	0603	|	|	...	|	|	|	|
Alessandria **610** d.	0624	|	|	...	|	|	|	|
Asti **610** d.	0646	|	|	...	|	|	|	|
Torino P N **610** a.	0740	|	|	...	|	|	|	|
Milano Rogoredo a.	...	|	|	...	0731	0746	0837	|
Milano Centrale a.	...	0711g	0712	...	0745	0800	0850	0930

	FB 9802 🍷A	A	*ICN* 754 ◆			*FB* 9804 🍷A	A	*FB* 9806 🍷E	A		*IC* 580 ◆		A	*FB* 9810 🍷B	A	*ICN* 794 ◆		R		*FB* 9814 🍷C	A			A	*FB* 9818 🍷C	A
Roma Termini **620** d.	...	...	...	...	...	...	...	...	...	...	...	...	...	...	...	0639t	...	...	...	...	...	...	...	...	...	...
Bologna Centrale **620** d.	0705	0728	0734	...	0752	0818	0828	0918	0928	...	0946	0952	1028	1118	1128	1142	1152	1228	...	1318	1328	...	1352	1428	1518	1528
Modena d.	0725	0756	|	...	0825	0840	0856	0941	0956	...	1007	1025	1056	1141	1156	1217	1225	1256	...	1341	1356	...	1425	1456	1541	1556
Reggio Emilia d.	0738	0810	|	...	0842	0853	0910	0954	1010	...	1021	1042	1110	1154	1210	1234	1242	1310	...	1354	1410	...	1442	1510	1554	1610
Parma d.	0753	0825	|	...	0905	0908	0925	1010	1025	...	1036	1105	1125	1210	1225	1256	1305	1325	...	1410	1425	...	1505	1525	1610	1625
Fidenza d.	|	0837	|	0905	0923	|	0937	|	1037	...	1054	1117	1137	|	1237	|	1326	1337	...	|	1437	...	1517	1537	|	1637
Piacenza d.	0824	0905	0911	0930	0950	0937	1005	1041	1105	1115	1119	1149	1205	1241	1305	1328	1353	1405	1423	1441	1505	...	1551	1605	1641	1705
Voghera **610** d.	|	...	0941	|	|	|	...	|	...	1155	|	|	...	|	...	|	|	...	1504	|	...	...	|	...	|	...
Tortona **610** d.	|	...	0953	|	|	|	...	|	...	...	|	|	...	|	...	|	|	...	1516	|	...	...	|	...	|	...
Alessandria **610** d.	|	...	1015	|	|	|	...	|	...	...	|	|	...	|	...	|	|	...	...	|	...	...	|	...	|	...
Asti **610** d.	|	...	1041	|	|	|	...	|	...	...	|	|	...	|	...	|	|	...	...	|	...	...	|	...	|	...
Torino P N **610** a.	|	...	1120	|	|	|	...	|	...	...	|	|	...	|	...	|	|	...	...	|	...	...	|	...	|	...
Milano Rogoredo a.	0904	...	...	1007	1031	1012	...	|	...	...	1204	1231	...	|	...	|	1431	...	...	|	...	...	1631	...	|	...
Milano Centrale a.	0915	...	...	1020	1045	1025	...	1125	...	...	1215	1245	...	1325	...	1441g	1445	...	...	1525	...	...	1645	...	1725	...

km				R	*IC* 590 ◆	*FB* 9822 🍷T	A			*FB* 9824 🍷C	R	*IC* 1546 ◆	2 ⑦v	*FB* 9826 🍷C	A			*IC* 596 ◆	2	P	*FB* 9830 🍷C	A	*IC* 1588 ◆	*IC* 1590 ◆	*FR* 9560 🍷	R
	Roma Termini **620** d.	...	...	...	1241t	...	...	...	...	...	...	...	...	...	...	...	...	1641t	...	...	...	...	1710t	1710t	1935	...
	Bologna Centrale **620** d.	...	1552	1628	1646	1718	1728	...	1752	1818	1828	1840	...	1918	1928	1952	2028	2046	...	2052	2118	2128	2135	2135	2153	2218
	Modena d.	...	1625	1656	1707	1741	1756	...	1825	1841	1856	1910	...	1941	1956	2025	2056	2108	...	2116	2141	2156	2203	2203	2217	2244
	Reggio Emilia d.	...	1642	1710	1721	1754	1810	...	1842	1854	1910	1924	...	1954	2010	2042	2110	2122	...	2132	2154	2210	2217	2217	2231	2258
	Parma d.	...	1703	1725	1736	1810	1825	...	1905	1910	1925	1940	...	2010	2025	2105	2125	2138	...	2149	2210	2225	2235	2235	2247	2325
	Fidenza d.	...	1715	1737	1754	|	1837	...	1923	|	1937	1954	2003	|	2037	2126	2137	2154	2158	2205	|	2237	2249	2249	|	...
0	Piacenza d.	1715	1750	1805	1819	1841	1905	1915	1950	1941	2005	2019	2026	2041	2105	2150	2205	2219	2226	2245	2241	2305	2312	2312	2321	...
58	Voghera **610** d.	1755	|	...	|	|	...	1955	|	|	...	|	|	|	...	|	...	|	|	|	|	...	|	|	|	...
75	Tortona **610** d.	...	|	...	|	|	...	...	|	|	...	|	|	|	...	|	...	|	|	|	|	...	|	|	|	...
97	Alessandria **610** d.	...	|	...	|	|	...	...	|	2045	...	|	|	|	...	|	...	|	|	|	|	...	|	|	|	...
132	Asti **610** d.	...	|	...	|	|	...	...	|	2102	...	|	|	|	...	|	...	|	|	|	|	...	|	|	|	...
188	**Torino** P N **610** a.	...	|	...	|	|	...	...	|	2140	...	|	|	|	...	|	...	|	|	|	|	...	|	|	|	...
	Milano Rogoredo a.	...	1831	...	1904	|	...	...	2031	...	...	2102	2119	|	...	2231	...	2302	2309	2327	|	...	2351	2351	|	...
	Milano Centrale a.	...	1845	...	1915	1925	...	...	2045	...	...	2115	2148g	2125	...	2245	...	2315	2320	2340	2325	...	0005	0005	2350	...

◆ – **NOTES** (LISTED BY TRAIN NUMBER)

80 – [12] Terni - Milano.
83 – [12] Milano - Napoli.
90 – [12] Napoli - Milano.
96 – [12] Napoli - Milano.
97 – [12] Milano - Napoli.
99 – [12] Milano - Terni.
52 – 🛏 1, 2 cl., 🛌 2 cl. (4 berth) and [2] Lecce - Bologna - Milano.
54 – ①–⑥: 🛏 1, 2 cl., 🛌 2 cl. (4 berth) and [2] Lecce - Bologna - Torino.
55 – 🛏 1, 2 cl., 🛌 2 cl. (4 berth) and [2] Milano - Bologna - Lecce.
57 – 🛏 1, 2 cl., 🛌 2 cl. (4 berth) and [2] Torino - Bologna - Lecce.
58 – 🛏 1, 2 cl., 🛌 2 cl. (4 berth) and [2] Lecce - Bologna - Milano.
65 – 🛏 1, 2 cl., 🛌 2 cl. (4 berth) and [2] Milano - Bologna - Lecce.
94 – 🛏 1, 2 cl., 🛌 2 cl. (4 berth) and [2] Reggio di Calabria - Milano - Torino.
95 – 🛏 1, 2 cl., 🛌 2 cl. (4 berth) and [2] Torino - Milano - Reggio di Calabria.

1545 – ⑥: [12] Milano - Lecce.
1546 – ⑦ (also Dec. 8; not Dec. 7): [12] Lecce - Milano.
1580 – ⑦ (also Dec. 8; not Dec. 7): 🛏 1, 2 cl., 🛌 2 cl. (4 berth) and [2] Lecce - Bologna - Torino.
1588 – ⑦ from Sept. 21 (also Dec. 8; not Dec. 7): [12] Reggio di Calabria - Milano.
1589 – ⑥ from Sept. 20: [12] Milano - Reggio di Calabria.
1590 – ⑦ until Sept. 14: [12] Reggio di Calabria - Milano.
1591 – ⑥ to Sept. 13: [12] Milano - Reggio di Calabria.
1910 – 🛌 2 cl. (4 berth) and [2] Salerno - Napoli - Milano - Torino.
1911 – 🛌 2 cl. (4 berth) and [2] Torino - Milano - Napoli - Salerno.

A – From/to Ancona.
B – From/to Bari.
C – From/to Lecce.
E – From/to Pescara.
P – ⑥⑦ (also Apr. 21, 25, June 2; not Apr. 20, 26, June 1): [2] Milano - Pescara and v.v.
R – From/to Rimini.
T – From/to Taranto.

g – Milano **Porta Garibaldi**.
t – Roma **Tiburtina**.
v – Also Apr. 21, June 2; not Apr. 20, June 1.
w – Also Apr. 24; not Apr. 25.

616 VENEZIA - BOLOGNA

For additional high-speed trains Venezia - Padova - Bologna - Roma see Table **600** (only trains calling at Rovigno or Ferrara are included below)

km		*EN*	*EN*			*FB*	*FA*			*FA*	*IC*						*FB*	*IC*	*FA*			*FA*					*ICN*
		235	**1237/9**			**9801**	**9407**			**9411**	**585**						**9817**	**595**	**9439**			**9447**					**771**
		♦	♦	⚒		♦				T	♦						♦	♦	♦								♦
0	**Venezia** Santa Lucia **605** d.	...	...	...	0642	0657	0725	0742	0842	...	...	1042	1142	1242	1342	1442	1457	...	1525	1542	1642	1725	1742	1842	1942	2142	0008
9	**Venezia** Mestre **605** d.	0311	...	0554	0654	0709**u**	0737**u**	0754	0854	0837	0929	1054	1154	1254	1354	1454	1509**u**	1514	1537**u**	1554	1654	1737**u**	1754	1854	1954	2154	0021
37	Padova **605** d.	|	0418	0610	0710	0724	0753	0810	0910	0853	0945	1110	1210	1310	1410	1510	1524	1532	1553	1610	1710	1753	1810	1910	2010	2210	0045
81	Rovigo d.	|	0445	0650	0750	0746	0813	0850	0950	|	1022	1150	1250	1350	1450	1550	1546	1600	1613	1650	1750	|	1850	1950	2050	2248	0119
113	Ferrara d.	0419	0506	0712	0811	0803	|	0911	1011	0925	1042	1211	1311	1411	1511	1611	1603	1621	|	1711	1811	1825	1911	2011	2111	...	0141
160	**Bologna** Centrale a.	0448	0541	0743	0840	0835	0850	0940	1040	0950	1108	1240	1340	1440	1540	1640	1635	1645	1650	1740	1840	1850	1940	2040	2140	...	0212
	Roma Termini **600 620** a.	0922	...	...	...	...	1110	...	...	1210	1520	...	...	...	...	...	...	2042	1910	...	...	2110	...	...	...	...	0635

	ICN					*FA*		*FA*				*FB*		*IC*					*FA*		*IC*	*FB*	*FA*		*EN*	*EN*	
	774					**9406**		**9412**				**9816**		**588**					**9442**		**592**	**9828**	**9450**		**1236/8**	**234**	
	♦	⚒										♦		♦					U		♦	♦			♦	♦	
Roma Termini **600 620** d.	2235	...	...	...	...	0750	...	0850	...	...	...	...	...	1030	...	...	...	...	1650	...	1540	...	1850	...	...	1904	...
Bologna Centrale d.	0318	0620	0720	0820	0920	1010	1020	1110	...	1220	1320	1416	1422	1452	1520	1620	1722	1820	1910	1920	1952	2016	2110	2120	2224	2330	...
Ferrara d.	0349	0651	0751	0851	0951	1032	1051	|	...	1251	1351	1443	1452	1518	1551	1651	1751	1851	|	1951	2018	2043	2132	2151	2256	2356	...
Rovigo d.	0411	0710	0810	0910	1010	|	1110	1146	...	1310	1410	1500	1510	1534	1610	1710	1810	1910	1946	2010	2035	2100	|	2210	2319	|	...
Padova **605** d.	0450	0751	0851	0951	1051	1109	1147	1209	...	1347	1451	1539	1551	1602	1651	1751	1851	2000	2009	2051	2102	2141	2209	2251	2347	0041	...
Venezia Mestre **605** a.	0508	0806	0906	1006	1106	1123**s**	1203	1223**s**	...	1403	1506	1556**s**	1606	1619	1706	1806	1906	2014	2021	2106	2118	2153**s**	2223**s**	2306	...	0102	...
Venezia Santa Lucia **605** a.	0520	0818	0918	1018	1118	1135	1218	1235	...	1418	1518	1609	1618	...	1718	1818	1918	2026	...	2118	...	2205	2235	2318	...	...	...

♦ – **NOTES** (LISTED BY TRAIN NUMBER)

234 – 🛏 1,2 cl. (Excelsior), 🛏 1,2 cl., ▬ 2 cl. and [2] Roma - Venezia Mestre - Villach - Wien.
235 – 🛏 1,2 cl. (Excelsior), 🛏 1,2 cl., ▬ 2 cl. and [2] Wien - Villach - Venezia Mestre - Roma.
585 – [12] Trieste (**584**) - Venezia Mestre - Roma.
588 – [12] Roma - Venezia Mestre (**589**) - Trieste.
592 – [12] Roma - Venezia Mestre (**593**) - Trieste.
595 – [12] Trieste (**594**) - Venezia Mestre - Roma.
771 – ▬ 2 cl. (4 berth) and [2] Trieste (**770**) - Udine - Venezia - Roma.
774 – ▬ 2 cl. (4 berth) and [2] Roma - Venezia - Udine (**775**) - Trieste.
1236/8 – ⑥ Apr. 12 - Sept. 27: 🛏 1,2 cl. (T2), ▬ 2 cl. and [2] Livorno - Wien.
1237/9 – ⑤ Apr. 11 - Sept. 26 (from Wien): 🛏 1,2 cl. (T2), ▬ 2 cl. and [2] Wien - Livorno.

9412 – [12] and 🍷 Salerno - Venezia.
9439 – [12] and 🍷 Venezia - Salerno.
9801 – [12] and 🍷 Venezia - Bologna - Lecce.
9816 – [12] and 🍷 Lecce - Bologna - Venezia.
9817 – [12] and 🍷 Venezia - Bologna - Lecce.
9828 – [12] and 🍷 Lecce - Bologna - Venezia.

T – To / from Trieste (Table **601**).
U – To / from Udine (Table **601**).

s – Stops to set down only.
u – Stops to pick up only.

619 SIENA - CHIUSI-CHIANCIANO TERME *2nd class only*

km		⚒	†	†	⚒	†		⚒	⚒	⚒	†	⚒		†	⚒	⚒		⚒	†	⚒		⚒	†	⚒	
0	Siena **609 613** d.	0554	0600	0802	0804	1002	...	1215	1328	1357	1402	1443	...	1602	1604	1655	...	1743	1802	1815	...	1927	2002	2024	...
89	Chiusi-Chianciano Terme **620** a.	0715	0721	0927	0923	1127	...	1330	1448	1523	1523	1615	...	1727	1719	1820	...	1851	1927	1940	...	2053	2127	2142	...

	⚒	⚒	†		⚒	⚒	†		⚒	†	⚒		†	⚒	⚒	†	⚒		†	⚒	⚒	†	⚒		
Chiusi-Chianciano Terme **620** d.	0430	0600	0627	...	0645	0707	0830	...	0914	1030	1045	...	1230	1348	1510	1630	1706	...	1830	1840	1955	2030	2130	...	...
Siena **609 613** a.	0546	0723	0745	...	0750	0826	0950	...	1035	1150	1157	...	1350	1519	1632	1750	1836	...	1950	2003	2122	2150	2242	...	...

BOLOGNA - FIRENZE (- PERUGIA - FOLIGNO) - ROMA 620

For high-speed services – see Table 600

km		ICN 763 ♦	ICN 771 ♦	ICN 1911 ♦	⚒	IC 581 ⚒	EN 235 ♦	EN 1237/9 ♦	FR 9501 ⚒		2 ⚒			IC 583	IC 1589 ♦	IC 1591 ♦			IC 585 ♦			2			2
	Milano Centrale **615** d.	...	...	2317g	...	...	...	...	...	...	...	...	...	0650	0710	0710	...	...	...	...	...	...	...	...	...
0	**Bologna** Centrale **615** d.	0118	0217	0230	...	...	0515	0546	0600	...	...	...	...	0918	0958	0958	...	...	1118	...	...	...	...	...	...
81	Prato Centrale d.	|	|	|	...	...	|	|	|	...	...	...	...	1008	1044	1044	...	...	1208	...	...	...	...	...	...
97	**Firenze** S M Novella d.	0257c	0326c	0407c	...	...	0615	0655	0641	...	...	...	...	1017r	1052r	1052r	...	...	1217r	...	...	...	...	...	...
97	**Firenze** S M Novella d.	0300c	0329c	0410c	...	0550	0630	...	0650	0640	0734	0802	0909	1020r	1055r	1055r	1109	1209	1220r	...	1309	1409	...	1509	1609
185	Arezzo d.	|	0425	|	...	0630	0710	...	0725	0743	0855	0913	1013	1102	|	|	1213	1313	1302	...	1413	1513	...	1613	1713
203	Castiglion Fiorentino d.	|	|	|	...	|	|	...	|	0755	0907	0924	1024	|	|	|	1224	1324	|	...	1424	1524	...	1624	1724
219	Terontola-Cortona d.	|	0445	|	0609	0650	|	...	|	0808	0921	0941	1038	|	|	|	1238	1341	|	...	1438	1541	...	1638	1741
	Passignano sul Trasimeno d.	|	|	|	|	|	|	...	|	|	|	0952	|	|	|	|	|	1349	|	...	|	1550	...	|	1750
	Perugia 625 d.	|	|	|	|	|	|	...	|	|	|	1025	|	|	|	|	|	1424	|	...	|	1627	...	|	1825
	Assisi **625** d.	|	|	|	|	|	|	...	|	|	|	1045	|	|	|	|	|	1447	|	...	|	1649	...	|	1847
	Foligno **625** a.	|	|	|	|	|	|	...	|	|	|	1104	|	|	|	|	|	1501	|	...	|	1703	...	|	1901
230	Castiglione del Lago d.	|	|	|	0617	|	|	...	|	0815	0930	...	1045	|	|	|	1245	...	|	...	1445	...	...	1645	...
248	Chiusi-Chianciano Terme **619** d.	|	0507	0550	0629	0710	0741	...	|	0831	0943	...	1057	1145	1238	1238	1257	...	1345	...	1457	...	...	1657	...
288	Orvieto d.	0500	|	|	0657	0731	0805	...	|	0859	...	...	1123	1210	|	|	1323	...	1410	...	1523	...	...	1723	...
330	Orte **625** d.	|	|	0644	0731	|	|	...	|	0943	...	...	1200	1245	|	|	1400	...	1445	...	1600	...	...	1800	...
408	**Roma** Tiburtina **625** a.	|	|	0717	0809	|	|	...	0824	1044	...	...	1234	1317	1344	1344	1434	...	|	...	1639	...	...	1833	...
413	**Roma** Termini **625 640** a.	0600	0635	|	0821	0826	0922	...	0835	...	...	...	1246	|	|	|	1446	...	1520	...	1656	...	...	1846	...
	Napoli Centrale **640** a.	...	...	0938	...	...	...	...	0955	...	...	...	...	1529	1609	1609	...	...	...	...	...	...	...	...	...

	IC 595 ♦	2	2	IC 597	ICN 795 ♦				IC 599 ♦	
Milano Centrale **615** d.	...	...	...	1450	1544g	...	...	...	1745	...
Bologna Centrale **615** d.	1648	...	...	1718	|	...	...	...	2018	...
Prato Centrale d.	1732	...	...	1808	1910	...	...	...	2108	...
Firenze S M Novella d.	1740r	...	...	1817r	1929c	...	...	...	2120	...
Firenze S M Novella d.	1743r	1709	1809	1820r	1932c	1909	2009	2109	2142	...
Arezzo d.	1828	1813	1913	1902	|	2013	2113	2213	2224	...
Castiglion Fiorentino d.	|	1824	1924	|	|	2024	2124	2224	|	...
Terontola-Cortona d.	1847	1838	1941	1924	|	2038	2140	2238	2249	...
Passignano sul Trasimeno d.	|	|	1950	|	|	|	2151	|	|	...
Perugia 625 d.	|	|	2024	|	|	|	2221	|	2318	...
Assisi **625** d.	|	|	2051	|	|	|	2241	|	2339	...
Foligno **625** a.	|	|	2106	|	|	|	2257	|	2350	...
Castiglione del Lago d.	|	1845	...	|	|	2045	...	2245	...	...
Chiusi-Chianciano Terme **619** d.	1905	1910	...	1945	|	2101	...	2257	...	...
Orvieto d.	1928	1936	...	2010	|	2127	...	2323	...	...
Orte **625** d.	2000	2014	...	2045	|	2207	...	2358	...	...
Roma Tiburtina **625** a.	|	2045	...	2115	2313	2245	...	0032	...	...
Roma Termini **625 640** a.	2042	2102	...	|	...	2300	...	0045	...	...
Napoli Centrale **640** a.	...	...	...	2330	...	...	...	...	...	...

	⚒	2 ⚒	IC 580 ♦		ICN 794 ♦				
Napoli Centrale **640** d.	...	...	...	...	0420	...	...	...	...
Roma Termini **625 640** d.	...	...	...	0603	|	...	0728	...	0858
Roma Tiburtina **625** d.	...	...	...	0612	0639	...	0737	...	0907
Orte **625** d.	...	...	...	0647	|	...	0811	...	0942
Orvieto d.	...	...	...	0721	|	...	0844	...	1015
Chiusi-Chianciano Terme **619** d.	0543	...	...	0758t	|	...	0909	...	1058t
Castiglione del Lago d.	0556	...	...	0809	|	...	0920	...	1109
Foligno **625** d.	|	0515	0555	|	|	...	|	0912	|
Assisi **625** d.	|	0530	0608	|	|	...	|	0925	|
Perugia 625 d.	|	0600	0635	|	|	...	|	0953	|
Passignano sul Trasimeno d.	|	0636	|	|	|	...	|	1021	|
Terontola-Cortona d.	0604	0656	0710	0819	|	...	0927	1036	1119
Castiglion Fiorentino d.	0617	0709	|	0831	|	...	0940	|	1131
Arezzo d.	0632	0725	0732	0843	|	...	0952	1100	1143
Firenze S M Novella a.	0738	0835	0807	0948	1000c	...	1057	1157	1248
Firenze S M Novella d.	...	...	0819	...	1003c	...	...	...	...
Prato Centrale d.	...	...	0837	...	1030	...	...	...	...
Bologna Centrale **615** a.	...	...	0942	...	1138	...	...	...	...
Milano Centrale **615** a.	...	...	1215	...	1441g	...	...	...	...

km			IC 588 ♦		IC 590					IC 592 ♦		IC 596		IC 1588 ♦	IC 1590 ♦		IC 598 Ⓑ p	EN 1236/8 ♦	EN 234 ♦			ICN 774 ♦	ICN 764 ♦	ICN 1910 ♦	
	Napoli Centrale **640** d.	...	...	...	1031	...	...	...	...	...	...	1431	...	1442	1442	...	...	...	...	...	...	...	...	2132	...
	Roma Termini **625 640** d.	...	1030	...	|	...	1303	...	1458	1540	...	|	...	|	|	1712	1816	...	1904	...	1958	2235	2300	|	...
	Roma Tiburtina **625** d.	...	|	1112	1241	...	1312	...	1507	|	...	1641	...	1710	1710	1722	|	...	|	...	2008	|	|	2343	...
	Orte **625** d.	...	1110	1147	1314	...	1347	...	1542	1617	...	1715	...	|	|	1756	|	...	|	...	2042	|	2341	0018	...
	Orvieto d.	...	1145	1221	1345	...	1421	...	1616	1645	...	1745	...	1811	1811	1829	1920	...	2011	...	2116	|	0013	|	...
	Chiusi-Chianciano Terme **619** d.	...	1210	1258t	1410	...	1458	...	1658t	1710	...	1810	...	1835	1835	1858	1946	...	2044	...	2144	0007	|	|	...
	Castiglione del Lago d.	...	|	1309	|	...	1509	...	1709	|	...	|	...	|	|	1909	|	...	|	...	2155	|	|	|	...
	Foligno **625** d.	1105	|	|	|	1303	|	1503	|	|	1708	|	...	|	|	|	|	...	|	1903	|	|	|	|	...
	Assisi **625** d.	1119	|	|	|	1317	|	1517	|	|	1721	|	...	|	|	|	|	...	|	1917	|	|	|	|	...
0	**Perugia 625** d.	1141	|	|	|	1339	|	1539	|	|	1744	|	...	|	|	|	|	...	|	1941	|	|	|	|	...
31	Passignano sul Trasimeno d.	1209	|	|	|	1408	|	1609	|	|	1811	|	...	|	|	|	|	...	|	2009	|	|	|	|	...
43	Terontola-Cortona d.	1219	|	1319	|	1419	1519	1619	1719	1730	1820	1830	...	1853	1853	1919	2004	...	|	2019	2202	0025	|	|	...
	Castiglion Fiorentino d.	1231	|	1331	|	1431	1531	1631	1731	|	1832	|	...	|	|	1931	|	...	|	2031	2215	|	|	|	...
	Arezzo d.	1243	1255	1343	1455	1443	1543	1643	1743	1755	1843	1855	...	1916	1916	1943	2026	...	2115	2043	2228	0047	|	|	...
	Firenze S M Novella a.	1348	1336r	1448	1536r	1548	1648	1753	1848	1836r	1948	1936r	...	2005r	2005r	2048	2100	...	2156	2148	2328	0144c	0212c	0254c	...
	Firenze S M Novella d.	...	1339r	...	1539r	...	...	...	...	1839r	...	1939r	...	2008r	2008r	...	...	2105	2211	...	...	0147c	0215c	0257c	...
	Prato Centrale d.	...	1352	...	1552	...	...	...	...	1852	...	1952	...	2026	2026	...	...	|	|	...	...	|	|	|	...
	Bologna Centrale **615** a.	...	1443	...	1640	...	...	...	...	1948	...	2038	...	2125	2125	...	...	2217	2302	...	...	0313	0342	0413	...
	Milano Centrale **615** a.	...	...	...	1915	...	...	...	...	...	...	2315	...	0005	0005	...	...	...	...	...	...	...	...	0711g	...

♦ – **NOTES** (LISTED BY TRAIN NUMBER)

234 – 1,2 cl. (Excelsior), 1,2 cl., 2 cl. and (2) Roma - Venezia Mestre - Villach - Wien; 1,2 cl. (Excelsior), 1,2 cl., 2 cl. and (2) Roma - Bologna (**484**) - München.
235 – 1,2 cl. (Excelsior), 1,2 cl., 2 cl. and (2) Wien - Villach - Venezia Mestre - Roma; 1,2 cl. (Excelsior), 1,2 cl., 2 cl. and (2) München (**485**) - Bologna - Roma.
580 – (12) Terni - Milano.
585 – (12) Trieste (**584**) - Venezia Mestre - Roma.
588 – (12) Roma - Venezia Mestre (**589**) - Trieste.
592 – (12) Roma - Venezia Mestre (**593**) - Trieste.
595 – (12) Trieste (**594**) - Venezia Mestre - Roma.
599 – (12) Milano - Terni.
763 – 2 cl. (4 berth) and (2) Bolzano - Roma.
764 – 2 cl. (4 berth) and (2) Roma - Bolzano.
771 – 2 cl. (4 berth) and (2) Trieste (**770**) - Udine - Venezia - Roma.
774 – 2 cl. (4 berth) and (2) Roma - Venezia - Udine (**775**) - Trieste.

794 – 1,2 cl., 2 cl. (4 berth) and (2) Reggio di Calabria - Milano - Torino.
795 – 1,2 cl., 2 cl. (4 berth) and (2) Torino - Milano - Reggio di Calabria.
1236/8 – ⑥ Apr. 12 - Sept. 27: 1,2 cl. (T2), 2 cl. and (2) Livorno - Wien.
1237/9 – ⑤ Apr. 11 - Sept. 26 (from Wien): 1,2 cl. (T2), 2 cl. and (2) Wien - Livorno.
1588 – ⑦ from Sept. 21 (also Dec. 8; not Dec. 7): (12) Reggio di Calabria - Milano.
1589 – ⑥ from Sept. 20: (12) Milano - Reggio di Calabria.
1590 – ⑦ until Sept. 14: (12) Reggio di Calabria - Milano.
1591 – ⑥ until Sept. 13: (12) Milano - Reggio di Calabria.
1910 – 2 cl. (4 berth) and (2) Salerno - Napoli - Milano - Torino.
1911 – 2 cl. (4 berth) and (2) Torino - Milano - Napoli - Salerno.

c – Firenze **Campo di Marte**.
g – Milano **Porta Garibaldi**.
p – Not days before holidays.
r – Firenze **Rifredi**.
t – Arrive 12 – 18 minutes earlier.
z – Not Apr. 26.

FERRARA and BOLOGNA - RAVENNA - RIMINI 621

2nd class only except where shown

For express services Bologna - Faenza - Rimini and v.v. – see Table 630

km		⚒	9851 R	⊙	⊙	⊙	⊙ ⚒		⚒	⊙ ⚒	⚒	⊙ †		⊙ ⚒		⊙ ⚒	⊙ †j	⊙ †k	⊙ †j		⚒	⚒	⊙	
0	**Ferrara** d.	...	...	0516	...	0545	0609	...	...	0713	...	0816	...	0817	...	0922	0939	1004	1033	...	...	...	1215	...
	Bologna Centrale **630** d.	...	...	|	...	|	|	...	0650	|	...	|	0754	|	0906	|	|	|	|	1106	...	1206	|	...
	Imola d.	...	...	|	...	|	|	...	0712	|	...	|	0826	|	0938	|	|	|	|	1136	...	1235	|	...
	Castelbolognese-Riolo Terme d.	...	...	|	...	|	|	...	0719	|	...	|	0832	|	0946	|	|	|	|	1142	...	1242	|	...
	Lugo d.	...	...	|	...	|	|	...	0734	|	...	|	0847	|	1000	|	|	|	|	1200	...	1300	|	...
74	**Ravenna** a.	...	...	0619	...	0702	0724	...	0805	0830	...	0921	0917	0925	1027	1030	1052	1114	1137	1227	...	1327	1329	...
74	**Ravenna** d.	0525	0622	...	0628	...	...	0752	...	...	0835	...	0924	0934	...	...	1053	1116	1147	...	1245	...	...	1336
95	Cervia-Milano Marittima d.	0544	|	...	0650	...	...	0811	...	...	0900	...	0943	0958	...	...	1114	1134	1207	...	1307	...	...	1400
103	Cesenatico d.	0550	|	...	0657	...	...	0817	...	...	0906	...	0949	1005	...	...	1122	1142	1215	...	1313	...	...	1410
124	**Rimini 630** a.	0608	0656	...	0727	...	...	0850	...	...	0932	...	1015	1027	...	...	1155	1216	1255	...	1345	...	...	1447

– *FB* train. (12) and 🍷 Ravenna - Rimini - Roma.

j – From June 8.
k – Until June 2.

⊙ – Operated by *TPER*. Trenitalia tickets valid. See Table **612** for details.

621 FERRARA and BOLOGNA - RAVENNA - RIMINI

2nd class only except where shown

For express services Bologna - Faenza - Rimini and v.v. – see Table 630

		⚒	⊙ ⚒	⊙		⚒	⚒m					⊙ ⚒			⚒	⊙					⊙		⚒	
Ferrara d.	...	...	1309	1423	...	...	...	1615	...	...	...	1701	...	...	...	1814	...	...	...	...	2050	...	...	...
Bologna Centrale **630** d.	1306	...	|	|	1406	1506	...	|	1606	...	...	|	1706	...	1752	|	1806	...	1906	2007	|	...	2106	2206
Imola d.	1336	...	|	|	1436	1536	...	|	1635	...	...	|	1734	...	|	|	1835	...	1935	2034	|	...	2135	2236
Castelbolognese-Riolo Terme d.	1342	...	|	|	1442	1542	...	|	1642	...	...	|	1742	...	1817	|	1842	...	1942	2042	|	...	2142	2242
Lugo d.	1400	...	|	|	1501	1600	...	|	1700	...	...	|	1800	...	1831	|	1900	...	2000	2100	|	...	2200	2256
Ravenna a.	1427	...	1441	1530	1527	1627	...	1723	1727	...	...	1814	1827	...	1851	1926	1927	...	2027	2127	2150	...	2227	2320
Ravenna d.	...	1435	...	...	1532	...	1635	...	...	1735	...	...	...	1835	...	...	1935	...	...	...	...	2155	...	...
Cervia-Milano Marittima d.	...	1502	...	...	1554	...	1654	...	...	1754	...	...	...	1857	...	...	1956	...	...	...	...	2213	...	...
Cesenatico d.	...	1508	...	...	1603	...	1702	...	...	1803	...	...	...	1904	...	...	2006	...	...	...	...	2220	...	...
Rimini 630 a.	...	1535	...	...	1630	...	1730	...	...	1835	...	...	...	1931	...	...	2034	...	...	...	...	2248	...	...

km																								
			Ⓐ	⚒			⊙		⊙ ⚒	⚒	⚒	⊙ ⚒		⊙ †	⊙	⊙	†	⚒	†	†	⊙ ⚒			
	Rimini 630 d.	...	0516	...	...	0614	...	0658	...	0736	...	...	0820	...	0900	...	...	...	1036	...	...	...	1230	...
	Cesenatico d.	...	0537	...	...	0642	...	0724	...	0801	...	...	0852	...	0935	...	...	...	1104	...	...	...	1300	...
	Cervia-Milano Marittima d.	...	0543	...	...	0651	...	0730	...	0812	...	...	0859	...	0942	...	...	...	1113	...	...	...	1306	...
	Ravenna a.	...	0602	...	...	0712	...	0751	...	0827	...	...	0921	...	1003	...	...	...	1140	...	...	...	1325	...
0	**Ravenna** d.	0503	...	0621	0628	...	0726	0755	0753	...	0833	0849	0933	0932	...	1032	1131	1133	...	1143	1227	1233	...	1333
28	Lugo d.	0528	...	|	0657	...	|	0815	|	...	0901	|	1000	|	...	|	1200	1200	...	|	|	1300	...	1400
42	Castelbolognese-Riolo Terme d.	0544	...	|	0714	...	|	|	|	...	0916	|	1016	|	...	|	1214	1216	...	|	|	1316	...	1416
50	Imola d.	0551	...	|	0721	...	|	|	|	...	0923	|	1023	|	...	|	1221	1223	...	|	|	1323	...	1423
84	**Bologna** Centrale **630** a.	0621	...	|	0743	...	|	0854	|	...	0954	|	1053	|	...	|	1251	1254	...	|	|	1354	...	1454
	Ferrara a.	...	...	0734	...	...	0847	...	0914	...	...	1005	...	1053	...	1142	...	...	...	1250	1348	...	...	...

	⊙		⚒	⊙ ⚒		⊙	⚒m	⊙ †j	⚒		⊙	⚒	⊙ ⚒	Ⓑ			⊙	Ⓐ	⑥		†	⚒	**9852** R	⊙
Rimini 630 d.	...	1318	...	...	1418	...	1508	1509	...	...	1632	...	...	1733	...	1837	...	1937	1937	...	2037	2037	2117	...
Cesenatico d.	...	1350	...	...	1451	...	1535	1542	...	...	1701	...	...	1802	...	1905	...	2006	2007	...	2105	2105	|	...
Cervia-Milano Marittima d.	...	1359	...	...	1501	...	1541	1555	...	...	1708	...	...	1808	...	1912	...	2012	2013	...	2113	2121	|	...
Ravenna a.	...	1418	...	...	1523	...	1604	1617	...	...	1733	...	...	1826	...	1931	...	2028	2030	...	2131	2137	2153	...
Ravenna d.	1341	...	1433	1453	1533	1540	...	1620	1633	1733	1735	1809	1824	...	1833	1933	1957	...	...	2033	...	...	...	2200
Lugo d.	|	...	1501	|	1600	|	...	|	1700	1800	|	1831	|	...	1900	2000	|	...	...	2100	...	...	...	|
Castelbolognese-Riolo Terme d.	|	...	1516	|	1616	|	...	|	1716	1816	|	|	|	...	1916	2016	|	...	...	2116	...	...	...	|
Imola d.	|	...	1523	|	1623	|	...	|	1723	1822	|	1846	|	...	1922	2023	|	...	...	2123	...	...	...	|
Bologna Centrale **630** a.	|	...	1554	|	1654	|	...	|	1754	1854	|	1908	|	...	1954	2054	|	...	...	2154	...	...	...	|
Ferrara a.	1501	...	...	1611	...	1653	...	1732	...	...	1849	...	1936	...	...	...	2109	...	...	...	...	...	...	2300

R – *FB* train. 🅁 and 🍷 Roma - Rimini - Ravenna.

j – From June 8.
m – Until May 31.

⊙ – Operated by *TPER*. Trenitalia tickets valid. See Table **612** for details.

622 ROMA AIRPORTS ✈

ROMA FIUMICINO AIRPORT ✈

Leonardo Express rail service Roma Termini - Roma Fiumicino ✈. *31 km* Journey time: 32 minutes. Special fare payable.

From **Roma** Termini: 0550, 0620, 0650, and every 30 minutes until 2250.

From **Roma Fiumicino**: 0638, 0708, 0738, and every 30 minutes until 2338.

Additional rail service (2nd class only) operates from Roma Tiburtina **and** Roma Ostiense - Roma Fiumicino ✈. *39 km* Journey times: Tiburtina - ✈ ± 45 minutes; Ostiense - ✈ ± 30 minutes.

From **Roma** Tiburtina (Ostiense 15 minutes later): ◐
0501, 0546⚒, 0601, 0601⚒, 0616⚒, 0631, 0646⚒, 0701, 0716⚒, 0731, 0746⚒, 0801, 0816⚒, 0831, 0846Ⓐ, 0901, 0916⚒, 0931, 0946⚒, 1001, 1016⚒, 1031, 1046⚒, 1101⚒, 1116Ⓐ, 1131⚒, 1146Ⓐ, 1201Ⓐ, 1216Ⓐ, 1231⚒, 1246⚒, 1301⚒, 1316Ⓐ, 1331, 1346⚒, 1401, 1416⚒, 1431, 1446⚒, 1501, 1516⚒, 1531, 1546⚒, 1601, 1616⚒, 1631, 1646⚒, 1701, 1716⚒, 1731, 1746⚒ then 1801, 1816Ⓐ, 1831, 1846Ⓐ, 1901, 1916Ⓐ, 1931, 2001, 2031, 2101, 2131, 2201.

From **Roma Fiumicino** ✈: ◐
0557, 0627, 0642⚒, 0657, 0712⚒, 0727, 0742⚒, 0757, 0812⚒, 0827⚒, 0842Ⓐ, 0857⚒ 0912Ⓐ, 0927⚒, 0942Ⓐ, 0957⚒, 1012Ⓐ, 1027⚒, 1042Ⓐ, 1057, 1112⚒, 1127, 1142⚒ 1157, 1212⚒, 1227, 1242⚒, 1257, 1312⚒, 1327, 1342⚒, 1357, 1412⚒, 1427, 1442⚒, 1457 1512⚒, 1527, 1542⚒, 1557, 1612⚒, 1627, 1642⚒, 1657, 1712⚒, 1727, 1742⚒, 1757 1812⚒, 1827, 1842⚒, 1857, 1912Ⓐ, 1927, 1942Ⓐ, 1957, 2012Ⓐ, 2027, 2057, 2127, 2212 2227.

ROMA CIAMPINO AIRPORT ✈

Frequent services operate Roma Termini - Ciampino and v.v., journey approximately 15 minutes. There is a 🚌 service between Ciampino station and airport.

◐ – A reduced service operates in July and August.

623 ROMA - ANZIO and ALBANO LAZIALE

ROMA - ANZIO *57 km* Journey time: 56 – 68 minutes. 2nd class only. All services continue to Nettuno (*3 km* and 4 – 6 minutes from Anzio).

From **Roma** Termini:
⚒: 0507, 0607, 0714, 0821, 0942, 1042, 1142, 1242, 1342, 1406Ⓐ, 1442, 1542, 1642, 1742, 1806Ⓐ, 1842, 1906, 1942, 2042, 2136.
†: 0714, 0821, 0942, 1142, 1342, 1442, 1642, 1842, 1942, 2042, 2136.

From **Anzio**:
⚒: 0453, 0559, 0635, 0703, 0736Ⓐ, 0757, 0912, 1014, 1112, 1212, 1312, 1412, 1514, 1612, 1630Ⓐ, 1712, 1812, 1917, 2012, 2202.
†: 0635, 0736, 0912, 1014, 1312, 1514, 1712, 1812, 2012, 2202.

ROMA - ALBANO LAZIALE *29 km* Journey time: 40 – 58 minutes. 2nd class only.

From **Roma** Termini: 0542⚒, 0721, 0821, 0921⚒, 1221, 1321⚒, 1421, 1521⚒, 1621, 1721⚒, 1821, 1921⚒, 2021, 2121⚒.

From **Albano Laziale**: 0629⚒, 0700⚒, 0743⚒, 0838, 1023, 1144⚒, 1343, 1443⚒, 1543 1643⚒, 1743, 1843⚒, 1943, 2043⚒, 2140⚒, 2145†.

All trains call at Marino Laziale and Castel Gandolfo approximately 35 and 40 minutes from Roma, 7 and 15 minutes from Albano Laziale respectively.

624 ROMA - PESCARA

2nd class only

km																									
		⚒	†	⚒	†	⚒	⚒	⚒	†	⚒		⚒	†	⚒	⚒	Ⓑ	†	⚒		†	⚒	⚒	†	⚒	
0	**Roma** Tiburtina § ▲ d.	...	...	...	0742	0742	...	1033	...	1233	...	...	1433	1433	1527	1533	1633	1633	...	1833	1833	1933	1933	1938	2052
40	Tivoli ▲ d.	...	...	...	0833	0832	...	1124	...	1308	...	...	1510	1510	1613	1614	1703	1723	...	1907	1908	2019	2019	2036	213
108	Avezzano d.	0612	0615	0730	0941	0945	...	1256	1300	1409	...	...	1613	1617	1720	1720	1804	1823	...	2019	2013	2127	2130	2155	224
172	Sulmona **627** d.	0747	0747	0844	1049	1049	1230	1410	1410	1540	...	1614	1728	1730	...	...	1920	1922	...	2121	2126	...	...	...	...
226	Chieti a.	0846	0840	0937	1127	1127	1336	1516	1511	1621	...	1707	1814	1826	...	...	2001	2003	...	2209	2209	...	...	...	...
240	**Pescara** Centrale a.	0910	0858	0951	1145	1145	1359	1535	1527	1641	...	1729	1840	1846	...	...	2018	2019	...	2225	2225	...	...	...	...

	⚒		⚒	⚒	†		⚒	†	⚒	⚒	†	⚒	Ⓐ	⚒	⚒	†	Ⓐ	⑥	†	⚒	†	†	⚒		Ⓑ
Pescara Centrale d.	...	...	...	...	...	0615	0704	0921	0921	...	...	...	1146	1334	1406	1406	...	...	1610	1655	...	1815	1815	1911	212
Chieti d.	...	...	...	...	...	0628	0719	0935	0935	...	...	...	1203	1354	1423	1423	...	...	1629	1711	...	1831	1830	1928	214
Sulmona **627** d.	...	...	...	0557	0557	0724	0825	1025	1025	...	...	...	1259	1448	1513	1513	...	...	1727	1800	...	1919	1923	2034	223
Avezzano d.	0508	0530	0629	0654	0656	0814	0920	1121	1121	1259	1307	1425	1430	...	1615	1614	1721	1721	1840	1903	1910	2018	2031	...	...
Tivoli ▲ d.	0614	0640	0736	0759	0759	0921	1022	1225	1230	1417	1416	1555	...	...	1722	1728	1827	1827	...	2020	2018	2131	2137	...	...
Roma Tiburtina § ▲ a.	0700	0731	0830	0845	0845	0959	1059	1259	1259	1459r	1459	1654	...	...	1759	1759	1859	1912	...	2059	2059	2225t	2225t	...	...

r – Arrive 1515 on ⑥.
t – Roma **Termini**.

§ – Roma Tiburtina **Piazzale Est**.

▲ – Additional services operate Roma Tiburtina (Piazzale Est) - Tivoli and v.v., journey 60 – 75 minutes.

ROMA - PERUGIA and ANCONA 625

km		2 Ⓐ	2 ⚒	2 ⚒	*IC* 580 T	2 †	2 ⚒		2 ⚒	⚒		*IC* 534	⚒	2 ⚒			*IC* 540		Ⓐ	*FB* 9852 R	2 ⚒	Ⓑj		⚒	*IC* 546 Ⓑp		
0	**Roma** Termini **620** d.	...	...	...	...	...	...	0545	...	0709	0758	0935	1128	1158	1328	1423	1535	1558	1700	1740	...	1758	1834	1858	1955	2058	2250
5	**Roma** Tiburtina **620** d.	...	...	...	...	...	...	0554	...	0718	0807	|	1137	1207	1337	1432	|	1607	1710	|	....	1807	1842	1907	2005	2109	2259
83	Orte **620** d.	...	...	...	...	...	...	0634	0707	0751	0841	1011	1211	1240	1410	1506	|	1640	|	|	...	1840	1917	1941	2035	2141	2331
112	Terni d.	...	...	...	0505	...	...	0654	0733	0816	0903	1029	1235	1305	1432	1526	1629	1704	1802	1827	...	1905	1943	2006	2054	2204	2354
141	Spoleto d.	...	...	...	0532	...	...	0716	0806	0851	0929	1055	1300	1329	1458	1551	1656	1732	1825	|	...	1929	2008	2029	2121	2226	0024
167	**Foligno** a.	...	...	...	0553	...	...	0740	0830	0907	0951	1113	1319	1350	1515	1607	1715	1752	1844	1900	...	1947	2029	2048	2136	2242	0040
167	**Foligno** d.	...	...	0545	0555	0622	0644	0742	0832a	...	0953	1115	1321	*1416*	1517	1609	1717	1754	...	1902	...	1949	2031	2050	2138	2244	...
	Spello d.	...	...	|	|	|	|	|	0838a	...	0958	|	|	|	|	1614	|	|	...	|	...	1956	|	2056	|	|	...
	Assisi d.	...	...	|	0608	|	|	|	0847a	...	1008	|	|	|	|	1622	|	|	...	|	...	2006	|	2105	2151	|	...
	Perugia Ponte SG ▲ d.	...	...	|	0623	|	|	|	0859a	...	1020	|	|	|	|	1635	|	|	...	|	...	2018	|	2118	2202	|	...
	Perugia 620 a.	...	...	|	0633	|	|	|	0913a	...	1030	|	|	|	|	1651	|	|	...	|	...	2027	|	2128	2213	|	...
224	Fabriano d.	0500	0600	0641	...	0714	0734	0840	...	...	...	1205	1415	*1522*	1616	...	1806	1846	...	1939	1950	...	2122	...	...	2333	...
268	Jesi d.	0539	0641	0733	...	0800	0822	0922	...	...	...	1236	1501	*1605*	1702	...	1836	1922	...	2008	2035	...	2155	...	...	0010	...
286	Falconara Marittima **630** d.	0555	0700	0750	...	0818	0843	0938	...	...	...	1250	1520	*1625*	1720	...	1850	1941	...	2019	2049	...	2209	...	...	0025	...
295	**Ancona 630/2** a.	0603	0711	0801	...	0834	0855	0955	...	...	...	1300	1535	*1638*	1731	...	1859	1951	...	...	2058	...	2220	...	...	0040	...

km		⚒		⚒r	*IC* 531 ⚒	†	*IC* 533	2 Ⓐ	*FB* 9851 R			2 ⚒	Ⓐ	⚒		⚒	*IC* 541	2 ⚒		2 Ⓐ	2	2 Ⓐ			2 ⚒	2	*IC* 599 T
	Ancona 630/2 d.	...	0350	...	...	...	0625	0651	...	0845	...	...	...	1250	1344	...	1530	1557	...	1652	1733	...	1821	1937	2009	2130	...
	Falconara Marittima **630** d.	...	0403	...	...	...	0639	0701	0754	0855	...	...	...	1305	1354	...	1540	1607	...	1705	1745	...	1830	1946	2020	2139	...
	Jesi d.	...	0415	...	...	...	0656	0720	0806	0910	...	...	...	1323	1409	...	1552	1624	...	1722	1801	...	1850	1959	2036	2153	...
	Fabriano d.	...	0451	...	...	...	0732	0808	0840	0948	...	...	...	1412	1451	...	1625	1712	...	1814	1854	...	1939	2035	2117	2235	...
0	**Perugia 620** d.	...	|	0554	0640	0712	|	...	|	|	1103	1225	1348	|	|	1556	|	|	1756	...	...	1942	|	|	...	|	2318
11	Perugia Ponte SG ▲ d.	...	|	0603	0651	0721	|	...	|	|	1112	1234	1357	|	|	1605	|	|	1805	...	...	1951	|	|	...	|	2328
24	Assisi d.	...	|	0616	0703	0732	|	...	|	|	1126	1245	1410	|	|	1619	|	|	1817	...	...	2003	|	|	...	|	2339
35	Spello d.	...	|	0626	|	0741	|	...	|	|	1136	1253	1424	|	|	1627	|	|	1826	...	...	2013	|	|	...	|	|
40	**Foligno** a.	...	0537	0634	0715	0748	0818	...	0916	1039	1146	1301	1434	1513	1548	1638	1711	1814	1834	...	...	2023	2029	2135	...	2334	2350
	Foligno d.	0500	0539	0636	0717	0749	0820	...	0918	1041	1148	...	1436	1515	1550	1640	1713	...	1836	...	...	...	2031	2137	...	...	2354
	Spoleto d.	0515	0558	0653	0733	0809	0836	...	|	1057	1206	...	1455	1532	1606	1656	1731	...	1858	...	...	...	2048	2152	...	...	0011
	Terni d.	0545	0623	0733	0758	0833	0900	...	0951	1123	1235	...	1524	1607	1629	1727	1757	...	1928	...	...	...	2118	2225	...	...	0035
	Orte **620** d.	0606	0651	0801	0816	0854	0918	...	|	1149	1305	...	1547	1632	1657	1749	|	...	1949	...	...	...	2140	2246	...	...	...
	Roma Tiburtina **620** a.	0638	0725	0836	0844	0928	|	...	|	1219	1339	...	1620	...	1728	1818	|	...	2020	...	...	...	2209	2318	...	...	...
	Roma Termini **620** a.	0648	0737	0848	0856	0942	0956	...	1033	1233	1356	...	1633	...	1746	1833	1856	...	2035	...	...	...	2225	2330	...	...	...

R – (12) and 🍷 Ravenna - Rimini - Roma and v.v.
T – (12) Terni - Perugia - Milano and v.v.
a – Ⓐ only.
j – Not Apr. 20, June 1.
p – Not days before holidays.
r – Not Apr. 21, June 2.
▲ – Perugia Ponte San Giovanni.

ROMA - CASERTA - NAPOLI and FOGGIA 626

km		2 ⚒	2 ⚒	2 ⚒	2 ⚒	2 ⚒	2 ⚒	2	*FA* 9351 🍷	*IC* 703 2	2 †	2 ⚒	2 †	2 ⚒	2 ⚒	2	*FA* 9355 🍷	*IC* 705 T	2	2 †	2 ⚒	2 Ⓑ	2 ⚒	*FA* 9357 🍷	2	2	*ICN* 789 ♦
0	**Roma** Termini d.	...	...	...	...	0535	...	0621	0805	0814	1014	1014	...	1235	...	1242	1450	1606	...	1642	1642	1707	1742	1800	1807	1942	2358
138	Cassino d.	0520	0550	...	0717	0736	0820	0831	|	0949	1227	1245	1317	1406	1410	1442	|	|	1805	1840	1902	1843	1940	|	1946	2140	0140
170	Vairano-Caianello d.	0552	0620	0700	0746	...	0851	...	|	1008	...	...	1348	1431	1439	...	|	|	1836	1912	1936	...	...	|	2008	...	|
216	Caserta d.	0636	0702	0746	0830	...	0938	...	0915	1038	...	...	1433	1513	1522	...	1603	1801	1922	2000	2020	...	...	1914	2045	...	0236
	Napoli Centrale a.	0717	0745	0830	0912	...	1017	...	|	|	...	...	1514	|	1602	...	|	|	2000	...	...	...	...	|	...	...	|
279	Benevento d.	...	...	...	...	...	...	...	0952	1125	...	...	...	1615	...	...	1640	1848	...	...	...	...	...	1952	...	...	0324
380	**Foggia 631** a.	...	...	...	...	...	...	...	1056	1250	...	...	...	...	...	...	1741	2018	...	...	...	...	...	2056	...	...	0449
	Bari Centrale **631** a.	...	...	...	...	...	...	...	1208	1420	...	...	...	...	...	...	1848	2143	...	...	...	...	...	2208	...	...	0634
	Lecce **631** a.	...	...	...	...	...	...	...	1332	...	...	...	...	...	...	...	2012	...	...	...	...	...	...	2332	...	...	0818

km		*ICN* 788 ♦	2 ⚒	2 ⚒	2 †	2 ⚒	2	2 ⚒	2 ⚒	2	*FA* 9350 🍷	2	2 ⚒	2 ⚒	2 ⚒	2 ⚒	2 ⚒	*FA* 9354 🍷	2 †	2 †	2 ⚒	2 ⚒	2	*IC* 704 2	2 Ⓐ	*IC* 710 R	*FA* 9358 🍷
	Lecce **631** d.	2230	...	...	...	...	...	...	...	...	0545	...	...	...	...	...	...	1153	...	...	...	...	...	...	...	...	1650
	Bari Centrale **631** d.	0015	...	...	...	...	...	...	...	...	0715	...	...	...	...	...	...	1317	...	...	...	...	...	1605	...	1705	1817
	Foggia 631 d.	0200	...	...	...	...	...	...	...	...	0822	...	...	...	...	...	...	1422	...	...	...	...	...	1738	...	1827	1922
	Benevento d.	0321	...	...	...	...	...	...	0625	...	0925	...	...	...	...	...	...	1525	...	...	...	...	...	1857	...	1948	2031
0	**Napoli** Centrale d.	|	...	...	...	0500	...	...	|	0738	|	...	1138	...	...	1313	...	|	1540	...	1637	1738	...	|	1938	|	|
34	Caserta d.	0411	0420	0500	0512	0542	0610	0645	0728	0817	1011	...	1217	1318	...	1358	1545	1604	1615	...	1714	1817	...	1958	2018	2037	2110
80	Vairano-Caianello d.	|	0505	0547	0557	0626	0646	0727	0803	0902	|	...	1301	1407	...	1447	1629	|	1700	...	1806	1859	...	2025	2103	|	|
112	Cassino d.	|	0538	0621	0627	...	0711	0800	0834	0935	|	1024	1335	1441	1521	...	1702	|	1735	1932	1845	1932	2020	2048	2136	|	|
250	**Roma** Termini a.	0634	...	0820	0834	...	0848	...	1013	...	1120	1220j	...	...	1720	...	...	1720	...	2148	...	...	2241	2220	...	2300	2220

♦ – **NOTES** (LISTED BY TRAIN NUMBER)

788 – ⑦ (also Dec. 8; not Dec. 7): 🛏 2 cl. (4 berth) and (2) Lecce - Roma.
789 – ⑤: 🛏 2 cl. (4 berth) and (2) Roma - Lecce.

R – ⑦ (also Dec. 8; not Dec. 7): (12) Taranto - Roma.
T – ⑤: (12) Roma - Taranto.
j – Arrive 1227 on †.

ROMA and NAPOLI - CAMPOBASSO - TERMOLI 627

Campobasso - Termoli and v.v. currently replaced by 🚌 between Larino and Termoli (37 km) – timings below show total journey time

km			⚒	⚒		†	⚒			⚒	†	⚒			⚒	†	⚒		⚒				⚒	⚒	†
0	**Roma** Termini d.	...	...	...	0615	...	...	0907	...	...	...	...	...	...	...	1435	1435	...	...	...	1735	...	1935	2035	2035
138	Cassino d.	...	...	...	0741	...	...	1032t	...	...	...	...	...	...	...	1557	1600v	...	1705	...	|	...	|	|	|
	Napoli Centrale d.	...	...	...	|	...	...	|	...	...	...	1211	...	1410	...	|	|	...	|	1713	|	1930	|	|	|
	Caserta d.	...	...	...	|	...	0805	|	...	...	...	1246	...	1440	...	|	|	...	|	1746	|	2009	|	|	|
	Vairano-Caianello d.	...	...	...	|	...	0850	|	...	...	...	1321	...	1515	...	|	|	...	|	1821	|	2040	|	|	|
187	Isernia d.	...	...	0646	0826	...	0934	1109	...	...	...	1414	...	1553	...	1641	1643	...	1755	1903	1943	2121	2141	2231	2238
198	Carpinone ♣ d.	...	...	0657	0837	...	|	1120	...	...	...	1427	...	1604	...	1652	1656	...	1807	1914	1955	2132x	|	|	|
246	**Campobasso** ▲ a.	0553	0646	0752	0919	0940	1036	1205	1219	1415	1511	1520	...	1701	1720	1742	1746	...	1902	2004	2043	2218	2230	2322	2332
333	Termoli a.	0736	0838	...	...	1120	...	...	1410	1605	1700	...	...	...	1908	...	...	...	...	...	...	...	...	...	...

km		⚒		⚒	⚒	†				⚒				⚒	⚒	†	†	⚒	⚒	†				⚒	
	Termoli d.	...	...	...	...	...	0645	...	...	...	...	1220	...	1325	...	1425	...	1500	...	1550	...	...	...	1800	...
	Campobasso ▲ d.	0515	0552	0628	0655	0727	0824	0836	...	1225	1316	1403	1420	1506	1534	1603	1630	1643	1704	1733	1800	...	1938	1940	...
	Carpinone ♣ d.	0554	0634	0716	|	0810	...	0924	...	1308	1359	...	1501	...	1624	...	1715	...	1745	...	1846	...	2025	...	...
0	Isernia d.	0606	0645	0727	0745	0823	...	0936	...	1320	1411	...	1514	...	1640	...	1727	...	1758	...	1900	...	2037	...	...
46	Vairano-Caianello d.	0648	|	0815	|	0909	...	|	...	|	1459	...	|	...	1727	...	|	...	|	...	1950	...	|	...	...
92	Caserta a.	0715	|	0849	|	0938	...	|	...	|	1536	...	|	...	1805	...	|	...	|	...	2025	...	|	...	...
126	**Napoli** Centrale a.	0752	|	0926	|	1008	...	|	...	|	1608	...	|	...	...	...	|	...	|	...	2100	...	|	...	...
	Cassino a.	...	0727	...	|	...	...	1015	...	1408	...	...	1552j	...	...	...	1804r	...	1833k	...	...	...	2117	...	...
	Roma Termini a.	...	0853	...	0953	...	...	1140	...	...	...	...	1727	...	...	...	1927	...	1953	...	...	...	2254	...	...

♣ – 🚌 SULMONA - CASTEL DI SANGRO - CARPINONE

	⚒	⚒		⚒	⚒	⚒
ulmona **624** d.	...	...	1110	...	...	1930
astel di Sangro d.	0615	0805	1210	1240	1830	2030
arpinone a.	0718	0908	...	1343	1933	...

	⚒	⚒	⚒	⚒		⚒
Carpinone d.	...	0653	0853	1433	...	2038
Castel di Sangro d.	0610	0758	0958	1538	1710	2143
Sulmona **624** a.	0720	...	...	...	1820	...

▲ – 🚌 **CAMPOBASSO - BENEVENTO and v.v.**: (*67 km*, journey time 70 minutes).
From Campobasso: 0620⚒, 1305⚒, 1415⚒, 1750⚒.
From Benevento: 0640⚒, 0740⚒, 1420⚒, 1740⚒.

- Not Apr. 21, 22, May 1.
- Not Apr. 22.
r – Not Apr. 21.
t – Not Apr. 18, 19.
v – Not Apr. 17 - 19.
x – Stops on request only.

629 SARDINIA

Some trains 2nd class only

km																										
		⚒	⚒		⚒	†	†	†	†	⚒		†	⚒	†	⚒	⚒	⚒	†	⚒	⚒	†	⚒	†	⚒	⚒	
0	**Cagliari** d.	...	...	...	...	...	...	...	...	...	...	0630	0640	...	0702	0830	...	0905	0952	...	1010	1100	1140	1200	...	...
17	Decimomannu d.	...	...	...	...	...	...	...	...	...	...	0644	0654	...	0717	0845	...	0919	1011	...	1029	1119	1155	1215	...	...
95	**Oristano** d.	...	...	...	...	...	...	...	...	...	...	0737	0745	...	0828	0952	...	1037	1114	...	1130	1229	1259	1313	...	...
154	Macomer d.	...	...	...	...	...	...	...	...	...	...	0828	0835	...	▬	▬	...	1143	1208	...	...	...	▬	▬	...	...
214	Ozieri-Chilivani a.	...	...	...	...	...	...	...	...	...	...	0920	0915	...	†	⚒	...	▬	...	...	...	...	...	...	...	...
214	Ozieri-Chilivani d.	...	0631	...	0701	0740	0745	...	0849	0920	...	0926	0918	0924	1028	1042	1044	...	...	...	...	...	...	⚒	1414	1513
	Sassari d.	...	|	0700	0750	0827	|	0832	0928	0958	...	1007	|	|	1108	1122	|	...	...	1315	...	...	...	1419	|	1554
	Porto Torres a.	...	|	0715	0804	...	|	0845	...	...	...	...	|	|	...	...	|	...	...	1330	...	...	...	1434	|	...
	Porto Torres M a.	...	|	0718	0807	...	|	0849	...	...	...	...	|	|	...	...	|	...	...	1333	...	...	⚒	1437	|	...
285	Olbia a.	0645	0736	...	...	...	0851	...	...	...	...	...	1015	1028	...	...	1144	1310	...	...	...	...	1430	...	1521	...
306	Golfo Aranci a.	0708	...	...	...	...	...	...	...	...	...	...	...	...	...	...	...	1335	...	...	...	...	1455	...	...	...

km																										
			⚒	⚒	⚒	⚒	†	⚒		⚒	⚒	†	⚒	†	†	⚒			†	⚒	⚒		Ⓐ			🚌
	Cagliari d.	...	...	1330	1400	...	1445	1500	...	1600	1640	1640	...	...	1655	1700	1740	...	1815	1830	🚌	1930	2018	2037	...	2200
	Decimomannu d.	...	...	1350	1416	...	1459	1515	...	1614	|	|	...	...	1714	1714	1754	...	1829	1844	...	1949	|	2051	...	2219
	Oristano d.	1323	1443	1511	1528	...	1606	1612	...	1703	1736	1738	...	...	1824	1829	1857	...	1939	1957	2005	2055	2120	2158	...	0009
	Macomer d.	1419	1541	...	▬	...	1703	1701	...	...	1821	1823	1830	...	1923	1928	1946	...	...	...	2113	...	...	...	...	...
	Ozieri-Chilivani a.	1505	...	...	...	...	1751	1752	...	...	|	1906	1913	...	...	...	2034	...	...	...	...	...	...	...	...	...
0	Ozieri-Chilivani d.	1516	...	...	...	1701	1800	1800	1805	...	|	1915	1914	1914	...	...	2036	2040	...	...	...	...	...	...	...	...
47	**Sassari** d.	|	...	...	...	|	1843	1842	|	...	1931	2003	|	|	...	...	|	2120	...	...	...	...	...	...	...	...
66	Porto Torres d.	|	...	...	...	|	1859	1856	|	...	...	...	|	|	...	...	|	...	...	...	...	...	...	...	...	...
67	Porto Torres M a.	|	...	...	...	|	1903	1900	|	...	...	...	|	|	...	...	|	...	...	...	...	...	...	...	...	...
	Olbia a.	1619	...	...	1624	1802	...	...	1910	...	...	...	2009	2009	...	...	2133	...	...	...	...	...	...	...	...	...
	Golfo Aranci a.	...	...	...	1649	...	...	...	...	...	...	...	...	...	...	...	...	...	...	...	...	...	...	...	...	...

	⚒	⚒	†	⚒	⚒	⚒	⚒	†	⚒	⚒	⚒	⚒	†	†		†	⚒	†	⚒	⚒	†	†	⚒	⚒	⚒	⚒
Golfo Aranci d.	...	...	...	...	🚌	...	...	...	...	...	...	...	...	...	...	...	0715	...	...	...	...	...	...	...	...	...
Olbia d.	...	...	...	...	...	...	...	...	...	0605	...	...	...	0637	...	...	0738	0745	...	0815	0922	...	0933	...	...	...
Porto Torres M d.	...	...	...	...	...	...	...	...	...	|	...	...	...	|	0730	...	▬	|	...	|	|	0920	|	0939	...	...
Porto Torres d.	...	...	...	...	...	...	...	...	...	|	...	...	...	|	0733	...	...	|	...	|	|	0923	|	0942	...	...
Sassari d.	...	...	...	...	...	...	...	...	0550	|	0645	0645	0655	|	0748	0800	...	|	0833	|	|	0939	|	1000	...	1330
Ozieri-Chilivani a.	...	...	...	...	...	...	...	...	0629	0656	|	0721	0734	0737	...	0841	...	0844	0912	0912	1021	1025	1036	1039	...	1411
Ozieri-Chilivani d.	...	...	...	...	...	...	...	...	...	0659	|	0728	0742	...	...	...	...	0846	...	0917	...	1032	...	1046	...	▬
Macomer d.	...	...	...	...	0540	...	0650	...	...	0744	0758	0809	0829	...	...	...	⚒	0933	...	1002	...	1118	...	1130	1315	†
Oristano d.	0450	0530	0545	0600	0635	0640	0747	0750	...	...	0841	0858	0915	...	...	...	0915	1019	...	1049	...	1203	...	1212	1412	1445
Decimomannu d.	0548	0640	0649	0712	...	|	0841	0849	...	...	|	|	1006	...	...	...	1006	1116	...	1146	...	1307	...	1305	1510	1549
Cagliari a.	0607	0700	0702	0728	...	0744	0856	0902	...	...	0936	0959	1020	...	...	...	1019	1131	...	1159	...	1320	...	1319	1523	1608

	⚒	⚒	†		⚒		†	⚒	⚒	⚒	⚒	⚒		†		†		⚒	⚒	†			†	⚒		
Golfo Aranci d.	...	...	...	1340	...	...	...	...	...	...	1525	...	...	...	1747	...	...	...	...	...	...	...	...	...	...	...
Olbia d.	...	...	...	1404	...	1409	...	...	...	...	1550	1600	1655	...	1811	...	1825	...	...	...	...	...	...	...	1925	...
Porto Torres M d.	1347	...	...	...	...	|	...	...	1530	...	▬	|	|	...	▬	...	|	...	...	...	...	1915	...	...	|	...
Porto Torres d.	1350	...	...	...	...	|	...	...	1533	...	...	|	|	...	...	...	|	...	...	...	...	1918	...	...	|	...
Sassari d.	1405	...	...	...	...	|	1426	...	1548	1615	...	|	|	1719	...	...	|	...	1843	1850	...	1933	1940	1950	|	...
Ozieri-Chilivani a.	...	...	...	...	...	1511	1508	...	...	1653	...	1656	1755	1758	...	...	1934	...	1929	1936	...	...	2023	2029	2032	...
Ozieri-Chilivani d.	...	...	...	...	...	...	1518	...	...	...	†	1658	...	...	...	...	...	...	1939	1942	...	...	...	...	...	...
Macomer d.	...	...	1427	...	...	...	1603	1612	...	...	1725	1739	...	...	⚒	...	...	...	2026	2027	...	...	...	...	...	...
Oristano d.	...	1446	1522	...	1619	...	1650	1710	...	...	1824	1828	...	...	1913	1957	...	2013	2122	2117	...	...	...	...	...	...
Decimomannu d.	...	1559	1636	...	1730	...	1751	1810	...	...	1934	1913	...	...	2028	2111	...	2127	2212	2217	...	...	...	...	...	...
Cagliari a.	...	1617	1658	...	1749	...	1806	1825	...	...	1949	1926	...	...	2042	2132	...	2141	2226	2232	...	...	...	...	...	...

km																										
		⚒	⚒	⚒	Ⓐ					⚒	⚒	Ⓑ	Ⓑ	⚒	⚒	Ⓑ	Ⓑ	⚒	⚒			⚒	⚒	⚒		
0	**Cagliari** d.	0526	0545	...	0615	0645	...	0745	...	0845	...	0945	...	1045	...	1145	...	1245	...	1345	...	1418	1445	...	1545	...
17	Decimomannu d.	0541	0604	...	0635	0705	...	0805	...	0904	...	1005	...	1105	...	1203	...	1304	...	1404	...	1432	1504	...	1604	...
46	Villamassargia a.	0601	0629	0639	0701	0729	0734	0829	0834	0929	0934	1029	1034	1129	1134	1229	1234	1329	1334	1429	1434	1457	1529	1534	1629	1634
	Carbonia Serbariu a.	|	0652	|	|	|	0751	0847	|	|	0951	1047	|	|	1150	1247	|	|	1350	1447	|	|	|	1550	1647	|
55	**Iglesias** a.	0611	...	0648	0712	0739	...	...	0843	0939	...	...	1043	1139	...	...	1243	1339	...	...	1443	1506	1539	...	...	1643

	Ⓑ	Ⓑ			Ⓐ	Ⓐ				🚌
Cagliari d.	1645	...	1745	...	1845	...	1945	...	2045	...
Decimomannu d.	1704	...	1804	...	1904	...	2004	...	2105	...
Villamassargia a.	1729	1734	1829	1834	1929	1934	2029	2034	2129	2135
Carbonia Serbariu a.	|	1750	1847	|	|	1950	2047	|	|	2158
Iglesias a.	1739	...	...	1843	1939	...	...	2043	2138	...

	⚒	⚒	⚒	†	⚒			Ⓐ		
Iglesias d.	0554	...	0626	0630	0654	...	0722	0754	0819	...
Carbonia Serbariu d.	|	0616	|	|	|	0710	|	|	|	0810
Villamassargia d.	0603	0638	0633	0638	0703	0726	0731	0803	0826	0831
Decimomannu d.	0633	0703	...	0703	0734	...	0755	0833	...	0855
Cagliari a.	0652	0724	...	0723	0755	...	0810	0852	...	0915

km																										
		⚒	⚒	Ⓑ	Ⓑ	⚒	⚒	Ⓑ	Ⓑ	⚒	⚒			⚒	⚒	⚒			Ⓑ	Ⓑ			Ⓐ	Ⓐ		
	Iglesias d.	...	0922	1019	...	...	1122	1219	...	...	1322	1419	...	...	1522	1554	1619	...	...	1722	1819	...	...	1922	2019	...
0	**Carbonia** Serbariu d.	0910	|	|	1010	1110	|	|	1210	1310	|	|	1410	1510	|	|	|	1610	1710	|	|	1810	1910	|	|	2010
23	Villamassargia d.	0926	0931	1026	1031	1126	1131	1226	1231	1326	1331	1426	1431	1526	1531	1602	1626	1631	1726	1731	1826	1831	1926	1931	2026	2031
	Decimomannu d.	...	0955	...	1055	...	1156	...	1255	...	1355	...	1454r	...	1555	1631	...	1655	...	1755	...	1855	...	1955	...	2055
	Cagliari a.	...	1015	...	1115	...	1214	...	1315	...	1413	...	1512r	...	1612	1645	...	1716	...	1812	...	1915	...	2013	...	2114

r – 6–7 minutes later on ⚒.

Narrow gauge services on Sardinia are operated by ARST Gestione FdS, Via Zagabria 54, 09129 Cagliari. ✆ +39 070 4098 1, fax +39 070 4098 220, www.arst.sardegna.it.

Regular services operate on the following routes to differing frequencies: Monserrato (Cagliari) - Isili (*74 km*); Macomer - Nuoro (*61 km*); Sassari - Alghero (*30 km*); Sassari - Nulvi (*35 km*); Sassari - Sorso (*11 km*).

Additionally, summer only tourist services operate on the following routes: Sassari - Tempio (*91 km*); Tempio - Palau Marina (*59 km*); Macomer - Bosa Marina (*46 km*); Mandas - Arbatax (*159 km*); Isili - Sorgono (*83 km*).

See www.treninoverde.com.

MILANO - BOLOGNA - RIMINI - ANCONA 630

km		2 ⚒	2 †	2 ⚒	FB 9851 🍷 ◆	2 ⚒	2 ⚒			IC 603	FB 9801 🍷 ◆	FR 9593 q		FB 9803 🍷	P	IC 605 ◆	Ⓒ	Ⓐ	FB 9807 🍷		IC 607	FB 9809 🍷 ◆		IC 1545 ◆	FB 9811 🍷
	Torino Porta Nuova **615** d.	...	...	...	...	...	...	...	...	...	...	...	...	...	...	...	...	...	0832	...	...	...	...	...	...
0	**Milano** Centrale **600/15** d.	...	...	...	...	...	...	...	...	...	...	0750	...	0735	0615	...	...	...	|	...	...	1035	...	1000	1135
219	**Bologna** Centrale d.	...	...	...	...	...	...	0635	0735	0800	0842	0858	0835	0942	0911	1000	1035	1035	1142	1135	1200	1242	1235	1223	1342
254	Imola d.	...	...	...	...	...	...	0701	0801	|	|	|	0901	|	0945	|	1101	1101	|	1201	|	|	1301	|	|
261	Castelbolognese-Riolo Terme d.	...	...	...	...	...	...	0709	0809	|	|	|	0909	|	|	|	1109	1109	|	1209	|	|	1309	|	|
269	Faenza d.	...	...	...	...	...	...	0716	0816	0825	|	|	0916	|	0954	1025	1116	1124	|	1216	1225	|	1316	1256	|
284	Forlì d.	...	...	...	...	...	...	0727	0827	0836	|	0931	0927	|	1003	1036	1127	1142	|	1227	1236	|	1327	1306	|
302	Cesena d.	...	...	...	...	...	...	0742	0842	0848	|	|	0945	|	1014	1048	1142	1205	|	1244	1248	|	1342	1328	|
331	**Rimini 621** ● ⊖ d.	0547	0621	0621	0659	0703	0717	0805	0903	0910	0936	0957	1005	1036	1042	1110	1203	1232	1236	1315	1310	1336	1403	1352	1436
340	Riccione d.	0558	0631	0631	|	0714	0728	0814	0911	0922	|	|	1014	|	1052	1119	1213	1242	|	1325	1319	|	1413	1400	|
349	Cattolica-Gabicce d.	0606	0639	0640	|	0722	0737	0823	0918	|	|	|	1022	|	1100	|	1222	1255	|	1335	|	|	1423	|	|
364	Pesaro d.	0617	0650	0651	0717	0733	0749	0834	0929	0941	0955	1017	1033	1058	1113	1135	1233	1309	1258	1347	1335	1359	1434	1415	1455
376	Fano d.	0625	0658	0659	|	0742	0757	0842	0937	0950	|	|	1041	|	|	1144	1241	1317	|	1355	1344	|	1442	1424	|
398	Senigallia d.	0640	0713	0713	|	0757	0811	0857	0952	1002	|	|	1055	|	1132	1156	1255	1331	|	1410	1356	|	1457	1438	|
415	Falconara Marittima **625** d.	0654	0727	0728	0744	0811	0828	0907	1002	|	|	|	1110	|	|	|	1305	1347	|	1426	|	|	1508	|	|
423	**Ancona 625/32** a.	0707	0738	0741	...	0824	0843	0919	1012	1018	1026	1049	1121	1129	1154	1214	1317	1400	1331	1442	1414	1428	1519	1459	1528
	Pescara Centrale **631** a.	...	...	...	...	...	...	...	...	1151	1137	...	...	1240	1406	1350	...	...	1442	...	1554	1537	...	1655	1640
	Bari Centrale **631** a.	...	...	...	...	...	...	...	...	1500	1432	...	...	1518	...	1700	...	...	1721	...	1905	1820	...	2033	1921
	Lecce **631** a.	...	...	...	...	...	...	...	...	1648	1600	...	...	1643	...	...	...	...	1846	...	...	...	...	2227	2043

	2 ⚒		IC 609	FB 9813 🍷		FB 9815 🍷		IC 611	FB 9817 🍷 ◆		FB 9819 🍷		IC 613		FR 9591 🍷	FB 9823 🍷		FB 9825 🍷		FB 9829 🍷		ICN 765 ◆	ICN 755 ◆	ICN 757 ◆	
Torino Porta Nuova **615** d.	...	...	...	...	...	...	...	...	...	...	...	...	...	...	...	...	...	...	...	...	...	...	...	2020	...
Milano Centrale **600/15** d.	...	...	...	1235	...	1335	...	...	...	...	1535	...	...	...	1743	1735	...	1835	...	1935	...	1950	2050	|	...
Bologna Centrale d.	...	1335	1400	1442	1435	1542	1535	1600	1642	1635	1742	1735	1800	1835	1858	1942	1935	2042	2035	2142	2135	2200	2310	2352	...
Imola d.	...	1401	|	|	1501	|	1601	|	|	1701	|	1801	|	1901	|	|	2001	|	2101	|	2201	|	|	|	...
Castelbolognese-Riolo Terme d.	...	1409	|	|	1512	|	1609	|	|	1709	|	1809	|	1909	|	|	2009	|	2109	|	2209	|	|	|	...
Faenza d.	...	1416	1425	|	1519	|	1616	1625	|	1716	1807	1816	1825	1916	|	2007	2016	2107	2116	|	2216	2234	2337	|	...
Forlì d.	...	1427	1436	|	1530	|	1627	1636	|	1727	1817	1827	1836	1927	1931	2017	2027	2117	2127	|	2227	2246	2348	|	...
Cesena d.	...	1442	1448	|	1545	|	1642	1648	|	1742	1829	1842	1848	1945	|	2029	2042	2129	2142	|	2242	2300	0002	|	...
Rimini 621 ● ⊖ d.	1447	1503	1510	1536	1606	1636	1705	1710	1736	1803	1848	1903	1910	2005	1957	2048	2114	2148	2203	2236	2320	2330	0025	0058	...
Riccione d.	1500	1510	1519	|	1615	|	1717	1719	|	1813	|	1911	1920	2015	|	|	...	|	2213	|	...	|	|	|	...
Cattolica-Gabicce d.	1508	1517	|	|	1624	|	1727	|	|	1821	|	1921	|	2025	|	|	...	|	2222	|	...	|	|	|	...
Pesaro d.	1519	1528	1535	1555	1635	1655	1745	1735	1755	1832	1908	1932	1938	2036	2018	2107	...	2207	2233	2255	...	0000	|	|	...
Fano d.	1527	1536	1544	|	1643	|	...	1744	|	1840	|	1940	1947	2044	|	|	...	|	2241	|	...	|	|	|	...
Senigallia d.	1542	1550	1556	|	1657	|	...	1756	|	1855	|	1953	2002	2059	|	|	...	|	2256	|	...	|	|	|	...
Falconara Marittima **625** d.	1553	1603	|	|	1708	|	...	|	|	1905	|	2009	|	2109	|	|	...	|	2306	|	...	|	|	|	...
Ancona 625/32 a.	1608	1620	1614	1626	1721	1726	...	1814	1826	1919	1941	2028	2019	2119	2049	2138	...	2240	2319	2327	...	0048	0131	0206	...
Pescara Centrale **631** a.	...	...	1750	1737	...	1837	...	1950	1937	...	2055	...	2150	...	...	2256	...	...	...	...	...	0228	0310	0340	...
Bari Centrale **631** a.	...	...	2100	2018	...	2118	...	2300	2218	...	2336	...	...	...	...	...	...	...	...	...	...	0619	0644	0707	...
Lecce **631** a.	...	...	2248	2140	...	2240	...	...	2340	...	...	...	...	...	...	...	...	...	...	...	...	0915	0830	0852	...

	ICN 1580 ◆	ICN 758 ◆	ICN 752 ◆		FB 9802 🍷	ICN 754 ◆		FA 9592 🍷	FB 9804 🍷		FB 9806 🍷		Ⓐ	Ⓒ		IC 604	FB 9810 🍷		IC 606		FB 9814 🍷		FB 9816 🍷 ◆		IC 608
Lecce **631** d.	1835	1815	2120	...	...	2210	...	...	...	...	...	...	...	...	...	...	...	...	...	...	0613	...	0710	...	0625
Bari Centrale **631** d.	2030	2133	2309	...	...	0001	...	...	...	...	...	...	...	...	...	...	0532	...	0600	...	0738	...	0838	...	0807
Pescara Centrale **631** d.	0008	0105	0240	...	...	0323	...	...	...	...	0600	...	...	...	...	0710	0811	...	0905	...	1015	...	1115	...	1105
Ancona 625/32 d.	0139	0231	0406	0435	0500	0510	0533	0610	0620	0635	0716	0743	0825	0840	...	0836	0926	...	1036	1040	1126	1135	1226	1240	1236
Falconara Marittima **625** d.	|	|	|	0444	|	|	0541	|	|	0645	|	0754	0834	0850	...	|	|	...	|	1049	|	1144	|	1250	|
Senigallia d.	|	|	|	0457	|	|	0551	|	|	0657	|	0806	0844	0900	...	0853	|	...	1052	1059	|	1157	|	1300	1252
Fano d.	|	|	|	0512	|	|	0606	|	|	0715	|	0821	0858	0914	...	0907	|	...	1106	1115	|	1215	|	1315	1306
Pesaro d.	|	|	|	0520	0528	0543	0615	0636	0649	0725	0745	0829	0906	0923	...	0917	0955	...	1116	1124	1155	1224	1255	1324	1316
Cattolica-Gabicce d.	|	|	|	0534	|	|	0626	|	|	0736	|	0840	0917	0934	...	|	|	...	|	1136	|	1235	|	1335	|
Riccione d.	|	|	|	0543	|	|	0632	|	|	0747	|	0846	0926	0943	...	0934	|	...	1132	1144	|	1245	|	1344	1332
Rimini 621 ● ⊖ d.	0245	0324	0459	0600	0550	0610	0645	0654	0709	0800	0806	0857	0940	0957	...	0947	1017	1041	1147	1157	1217	1300	1317	1357	1347
Cesena d.	|	|	|	0618	0607	0628	0711	|	0725	0816	0824	0916	1000	1016	...	1007	|	1108	1207	1216	|	1318	|	1416	1407
Forlì d.	|	|	|	0631	0620	0640	0724	0718	0736	0827	0836	0927	1015	1027	...	1019	|	1123	1219	1227	|	1329	|	1427	1419
Faenza d.	|	|	|	0642	0629	0650	0735	|	0746	0838	0846	0937	1032	1037	...	1029	|	1133	1229	1237	|	1339	|	1438	1429
Castelbolognese-Riolo Terme d.	|	|	|	0649	|	|	0743	|	|	0844	|	0944	1044	1044	...	|	|	1140	|	1244	|	1345	|	1444	|
Imola d.	|	|	|	0656	|	|	0756	|	|	0856	|	0956	1056	1056	...	|	|	1146	|	1256	|	1356	|	1456	|
Bologna Centrale a.	0352	0427	0615	0722	0701	0727	0821	0807	0814	0921	0914	1021	1121	1121	...	1100	1114	1221	1300	1321	1314	1421	1412	1521	1500
Milano Centrale **600/15** a.	|	0712	0930	...	0915	|	...	0920	1025	...	1125	...	...	...	...	...	1325	...	...	...	1525	...	...	...	...
Torino Porta Nuova **615** a.	0740	...	...	...	...	1120	...	...	...	...	...	...	...	...	...	...	...	...	...	...	...	...	...	...	...

	FB 9818 🍷	2	2 ⚒	IC 610		FB 9822 🍷 ◆	2	2 ⚒	FB 9824 🍷	IC 1546 ◆	IC 612 ◆		FB 9826 🍷	FR 9594 q	P	FB 9828 🍷 ◆	IC 614		FB 9830 🍷		2 ⚒	FB 9852 🍷 ◆		2	
Lecce **631** d.	0813	...	...	0820	...	...	...	...	1113	1010	...	...	1213	...	...	1313	...	...	1413	...	...	...	...	...	...
Bari Centrale **631** d.	0938	...	...	1004	...	1138	...	...	1238	1148	1204	...	1338	...	...	1438	1404	...	1538	...	...	...	...	...	...
Pescara Centrale **631** d.	1215	...	...	1305	...	1415	...	...	1515	1451	1505	...	1615	...	1550	1715	1705	...	1815	...	...	...	...	...	...
Ancona 625/32 d.	1326	...	1337	1436	1440	1526	...	1549	1626	1617	1636	1640	1726	1742	1755	1826	1836	1840	1926	...	1949	...	2040	2240	...
Falconara Marittima **625** d.	|	...	1348	|	1450	|	...	1601	|	|	|	1649	|	|	1803	|	|	1850	|	...	1959	2029	2050	2249	...
Senigallia d.	|	...	1403	1452	1500	|	...	1616	|	1632	1652	1702	|	|	1816	|	1852	1902	|	...	2014	|	2102	2301	...
Fano d.	|	...	1417	1506	1515	|	...	1630	|	1645	1706	1716	|	|	1829	|	1906	1917	|	...	2028	|	2117	2315	...
Pesaro d.	1355	...	1426	1516	1524	1555	...	1639	1655	1701	1716	1725	1755	1814	1841	1855	1916	1925	1955	...	2036	2053	2126	2323	...
Cattolica-Gabicce d.	|	...	1437	|	1535	|	...	1650	|	|	|	1736	|	|	1901	|	|	1936	|	...	2046	|	2137	2334	...
Riccione d.	|	...	1445	1532	1544	|	...	1659	|	1717	1732	1744	|	|	1912	|	1932	1944	|	...	2056	|	2145	2341	...
Rimini 621 ● ⊖ d.	1419	1444	1458	1547	1557	1618	1644	1711	1722	1727	1747	1757	1819	1837	1927	1917	1947	1957	2023	2050	2108	2115	2157	2355	...
Cesena d.	|	1509	...	1607	1616	|	1709	...	|	1744	1807	1816	|	|	1944	|	2007	2016	|	2111	...	...	2216	...	...
Forlì d.	|	1527	...	1619	1627	|	1727	...	|	1757	1819	1827	|	1902	1956	|	2019	2027	|	2125	...	...	2227	...	...
Faenza d.	|	1537	...	1629	1638	|	1736	...	|	1807	1829	1837	|	|	2007	|	2029	2037	|	2135	...	...	2238	...	...
Castelbolognese-Riolo Terme d.	|	1544	...	|	1644	|	1744	...	|	|	|	1844	|	|	|	|	|	2044	|	2142	...	...	2244	..	...
Imola d.	|	1556	...	|	1656	|	1756	...	|	|	|	1856	|	|	2017	|	|	2056	|	2148	...	...	2256	...	...
Bologna Centrale a.	1514	1621	...	1700	1721	1714	1821	...	1814	1833	1900	1921	1914	1937	2047	2012	2100	2121	2114	2213	...	...	2321	...	...
Milano Centrale **600/15** a.	1725	...	...	...	...	1925	...	...	|	2115	...	...	2125	2050	2340	...	...	...	2325	...	...	...	...	...	...
Torino Porta Nuova **615** a.	...	...	...	...	...	...	...	...	2140	...	...	...	...	...	...	...	...	...	...	...	...	...	...	...	...

– **NOTES** (LISTED BY TRAIN NUMBER)

5 – [12] Bologna - Bari - Taranto.
2 – [12] Taranto - Bari - Bologna.
2 – 🛏 1, 2 cl., ▬ 2 cl. (4 berth) and [2] Lecce - Bologna - Milano.
4 – ①–⑥: 🛏 1, 2 cl., ▬ 2 cl. (4 berth) and [2] Lecce - Bologna - Torino.
5 – 🛏 1, 2 cl., ▬ 2 cl. (4 berth) and [2] Milano - Bologna - Lecce.
7 – 🛏 1, 2 cl., ▬ 2 cl. (4 berth) and [2] Torino - Bologna - Lecce.
3 – 🛏 1, 2 cl., ▬ 2 cl. (4 berth) and [2] Lecce - Bologna - Milano.
5 – 🛏 1, 2 cl., ▬ 2 cl. (4 berth) and [2] Milano - Bologna - Lecce.
45 – ⑥: [12] Milano - Lecce.
46 – ⑦ (also Dec. 8; not Dec. 7): [12] Lecce - Milano.
30 – ⑦ (also Dec. 8; not Dec. 7): 🛏 1, 2 cl., ▬ 2 cl. (4 berth) and [2] Lecce - Bologna - Torino.

9801 – [12] and 🍷 Venezia - Bologna - Lecce.
9809 – [12] and 🍷 Milano - Bari - Taranto.
9816 – [12] and 🍷 Lecce - Bologna - Venezia.
9817 – [12] and 🍷 Venezia - Bologna - Lecce.
9822 – [12] and 🍷 Taranto - Bari - Milano.
9828 – [12] and 🍷 Lecce - Bologna - Venezia.
9851/2 – [12] and 🍷 Ravenna - Rimini - Roma and v.v.

P – ⑥⑦ (also Apr. 21, 25, June 2; not Apr. 20, 26, June 1): [2] Milano - Pescara and v.v.

q – June 15 - Sept. 13.

⊖ – Connections may be available to service(s) in previous column(s).
● – For 🚌 service Rimini - San Marino and v.v. – see page 314.

631 ANCONA - BARI - LECCE

km					*ICN* 765	*ICN* 789	*ICN* 755	*ICN* 757	*ICN* 765						*FA* 9351					*IC* 703	*FB* 9801		*IC* 603	*FB* 9803	
		2 ⚒	2	2 ⚒	♦	♦	♦	♦	♦	2 ⚒	2 ⚒	2		2 ⚒	🍷	2 ⚒	2 ⚒	2 ⚒	2 ⚒	2	🍷 ♦	2		🍷	2 ⚒
	Torino Porta Nuova **615** d.	...	...	...	...	...	...	2020	...	...	...	...	...	...	...	...	...	...	...	...	...	...	...	...	...
	Milano Centrale **615/30** d.	...	...	...	1950	...	2050	|	...	...	...	...	...	...	...	...	...	...	...	...	...	...	...	0735	...
	Bologna Centrale **615/30** d.	...	...	...	2200	...	2310	2352	...	...	...	...	...	...	...	...	...	...	...	...	0842	...	0800	0942	...
0	**Ancona 625/30** d.	...	...	...	0051	...	0134	0209	...	...	...	...	...	...	...	...	...	...	...	...	1029	...	1021	1132	...
43	Civitanova Marche-Montegranaro d.	...	...	...	|	...	|	|	...	...	...	...	...	...	...	...	...	...	...	...	|	...	1042	|	...
85	S. Benedetto del Tronto d.	...	...	...	|	...	|	|	...	...	...	...	...	...	...	...	...	...	...	...	|	...	1111	|	...
146	**Pescara** Centrale a.	...	...	...	0228	...	0310	0340	...	...	...	...	...	...	...	...	...	...	...	...	1137	...	1151	1240	...
146	**Pescara** Centrale d.	...	...	...	0230	...	0312	0342	...	...	...	...	...	...	...	...	...	...	...	...	1140	...	1153	1243	...
236	Termoli d.	...	...	...	|	...	|	|	...	...	...	...	...	...	...	...	...	...	...	...	1228	...	1247	1329	...
	Roma Termini **626** d.	...	...	...	|	2358	|	|	...	...	...	...	...	...	0805	...	...	...	...	0814	|	...	|	|	...
323	**Foggia 626** a.	...	...	...	0444	0449	0515	0535	...	...	...	...	...	...	1056	...	...	...	...	1250	1316	...	1335	1412	...
323	**Foggia** d.	...	...	...	0448	0508	0519	0539	...	0606	0710	...	...	...	1105	...	...	...	...	1305	1319	...	1338	1415	1420
391	Barletta d.	...	...	...	0527	0542	0554	0620	...	0648	0752	...	...	...	1136	...	...	...	...	1337	1348	...	1410	1444	1502
446	**Bari** Centrale a.	...	...	...	0619	0634	0644	0707	←	0741	0843	...	...	...	1208	...	...	...	...	1420	1432	...	1500	1518	1549
446	**Bari** Centrale ▲ d.	0503	0535	0610	0641	0638	0648	0711	0641	0744	0845	0940	...	1200	1212	1224	1257	1320	1415	...	1436	1440	1504	1522	1551
	Gioia del Colle ▲ d.	|	|	|	→	|	|	|	0717	|	|	|	...	|	|	|	|	|	|	...	|	|	|	|	|
	Taranto 638 ▲ a.	|	|	|	...	|	|	|	0755	|	|	|	...	|	|	|	|	|	|	...	|	|	|	|	|
487	Monopoli d.	0537	0609	0638	...	0705	0715	0739	|	0820	0914	1014	...	1224	|	1258	1330	1345	1440	...	|	1514	1530	|	1620
501	Fasano d.	0545	0618	0646	...	0716	0726	0750	|	0829	0922	1022	...	1232	|	1306	1338	|	1449	...	|	1522	1542	|	1629
521	Ostuni d.	0558	0631	0657	...	0730	0740	0804	|	0840	0935	1035	...	|	|	1319	1349	|	1500	...	|	1535	1558	|	1642
557	**Brindisi** ♣ d.	0622	0657	0717	...	0753	0804	0827	0847	0906	1002	1058	...	1303	1311	1342	1410	1425	1523	...	1536	1601	1625	1616	1707
596	**Lecce** a.	0655	0730	0740	...	0818	0830	0852	0915	0934	1033	1130	...	1326	1332	1414	1440	1450	1555	...	1600	1632	1648	1643	1739

			IC 605	*FB* 9807		*FB* 9809	*IC* 607	*FA* 9355	*FB* 9811			*IC* 1545	*FB* 9813	*IC* 1545	*IC* 609	*FB* 9815	*IC* 705	*FA* 9357	*FB* 9817		*IC* 611	*FB* 9819	*IC* 613	*FB* 9823	
	2 ⚒	P	♦	🍷	2	🍷		🍷	🍷	2	2 ⚒	♦	🍷	♦		🍷	⑤	🍷	🍷 ♦	2		🍷		🍷	
Torino Porta Nuova **615** d.	...	...	...	0832	...	...	...	...	...	...	...	...	...	...	...	...	...	...	...	...	...	...	...	...	...
Milano Centrale **615/30** d.	...	0615	...	|	...	1035	...	...	1135	...	...	1000	1235	...	...	1335	...	...	...	...	...	1535	...	1735	...
Bologna Centrale **615/30** d.	...	0911	1000	1142	...	1242	1200	...	1342	...	...	1223	1442	...	1400	1542	...	...	1642	...	1600	1742	1800	1942	...
Ancona 625/30 d.	...	1158	1217	1334	...	1431	1417	...	1531	...	...	1501	1629	...	1617	1729	...	...	1829	...	1817	1944	2022	2141	...
Civitanova Marche-Montegranaro d.	...	1246	1238	|	...	|	1438	...	|	...	...	1528	|	...	1638	|	...	...	|	...	1838	|	2043	|	...
S. Benedetto del Tronto d.	...	1321	1312	|	...	|	1512	...	|	...	...	1558	|	...	1712	|	...	...	|	...	1912	2022	2113	2221	...
Pescara Centrale a.	...	1406	1350	1442	...	1537	1554	...	1640	...	...	1655	1737	...	1750	1837	...	...	1937	...	1950	2055	2150	2256	...
Pescara Centrale d.	...	...	1352	1445	...	1540	1556	...	1643	...	...	1659	1740	...	1752	1840	...	...	1940	...	1952	2057	...	...	...
Termoli d.	...	...	1447	1533	...	1628	1647	...	1731	...	...	1754	1828	...	1856	1928	...	...	2028	...	2056	2146	...	...	...
Roma Termini **626** d.	...	...	|	|	...	|	|	1450	|	...	...	|	|	...	|	|	1606	1800	|	...	|	|	...	...	...
Foggia 626 a.	...	...	1535	1614	...	1711	1735	1741	1814	...	...	1845	1911	...	1943	2011	2018	2056	2111	...	2142	2229	...	...	...
Foggia d.	...	...	1538	1617	...	1714	1738	1750	1817	...	...	1848	1914	...	1946	2014	2036	2105	2114	...	2145	2232	...	...	...
Barletta d.	...	...	1610	1649	...	1743	1813	1820	1846	...	...	1932	1943	←	2016	2044	2109	2136	2144	...	2216	2303	...	...	...
Bari Centrale a.	...	...	1700	1721	...	1820	1905	1848	1921	...	...	2033	2018	2033	2100	2118	2143	2208	2218	...	2300	2336	...	...	...
Bari Centrale ▲ d.	1635	...	1715	1725	1813	1833	...	1852	1925	1937	2027	→	2022	2037	2104	2122	2201	2212	2222	2243	...	...	...	...	...
Gioia del Colle ▲ d.	|	...	1747	|	|	1905	...	|	|	|	|	...	|	|	|	|	2232	|	|	|	...	...	...	...	...
Taranto 638 ▲ a.	|	...	1820	|	|	1939	...	|	|	|	|	...	|	|	|	|	2310	|	|	|	...	...	...	...	...
Monopoli d.	1706	...	...	|	1849	...	...	|	|	2011	2101	...	|	2109	2129	|	...	|	|	2317	...	...	...	...	...
Fasano d.	1715	...	...	|	1857	...	...	|	|	2019	2110	...	|	2119	2140	|	...	|	|	2325	...	...	...	...	...
Ostuni d.	1726	...	...	|	1911	...	...	|	|	2032	2124	...	|	2134	2157	|	...	|	|	2338	...	...	...	...	...
Brindisi ♣ d.	1747	...	...	1819	1934	...	...	1950	2019	2057	2148	...	2116	2158	2225	2216	...	2307	2316	0000	...	...	...	...	...
Lecce a.	1819	...	...	1846	2005	...	...	2012	2043	...	2220	...	2140	2227	2248	2240	...	2332	2340	0031	...	...	...	...	...

	FB 9806	*IC* 604	*FB* 9810	*IC* 606			*FA* 9350		*FB* 9814		*IC* 608	*FB* 9816			*FB* 9818	*IC* 610	*FB* 9822		*IC* 1546	*IC* 612		*FB* 9824		*FA* 9354	*FB* 982
	🍷		🍷		2 ⚒	2	🍷	2 ⚒	🍷			🍷 ♦	2 ⚒	2 ⚒	🍷		🍷	2 ⚒	🍷 ♦		2 ⚒	🍷	P	🍷	🍷
Lecce d.	...	...	...	...	0450	0508	0545	0553	0613	...	0625	0710	0715	0755	0813	0820	...	1005	1010	...	1040	1113	...	1153	121
Brindisi ♣ d.	...	...	...	...	0519	0536	0608	0623	0636	...	0651	0736	0744	0824	0836	0846	...	1036	1034	...	1109	1136	...	1217	123
Ostuni d.	...	...	...	...	0542	0600	|	0646	|	...	0713	|	|	0845	|	0908	...	1057	1055	...	1131	|	...	|	|
Fasano d.	...	...	...	...	0555	0615	|	0703	|	...	0726	|	0815	|	|	0921	...	1109	1108	...	1145	|	...	|	|
Monopoli d.	...	...	...	...	0605	0623	|	0720	|	...	0736	|	0824	0902	|	0931	...	1118	1118	...	1153	|	...	|	|
Taranto 638 ▲ d.	...	...	...	...	|	|	|	|	|	...	|	|	|	|	|	|	1010	|	|	1025	|	|	...	|	|
Gioia del Colle ▲ d.	...	...	...	...	|	|	|	|	|	...	|	|	|	|	|	|	1050	|	|	1102	|	|	...	|	|
Bari Centrale ▲ a.	...	...	...	...	0641	0700	0708	0758	0734	...	0803	0834	0852	0929	0934	1000	1125	1155	1144	1139	1228	1234	...	1313	133
Bari Centrale d.	...	...	0532	0600	0645	...	0715	0800	0738	...	0807	0838	...	...	0938	1004	1138	...	1148	1204	1230	1238	...	1317	133
Barletta d.	...	...	0602	0643	0732	...	0745	0856	0808	...	0850	0908	...	...	1008	1048	1208	...	1230	1248	1320	1308	...	1345	140
Foggia a.	...	...	0632	0712	...	...	0813	0932	0837	...	0919	0937	...	...	1037	1119	1237	...	1258	1319	1406	1337	...	1413	143
Foggia 626 d.	...	...	0635	0715	...	...	0822	...	0840	...	0922	0940	...	...	1040	1122	1240	...	1300	1322	...	1340	...	1422	144
Roma Termini **626** a.	...	...	|	|	...	...	1120	...	|	...	|	|	...	...	|	|	|	...	|	|	...	|	...	1720	|
Termoli d.	...	...	0721	0805	...	...	...	...	0926	...	1011	1026	...	...	1126	1208	1326	...	1401	1411	...	1426	...	...	152
Pescara Centrale a.	...	...	0808	0903	...	...	...	...	1012	...	1103	1112	...	...	1212	1303	1412	...	1449	1503	...	1512	...	...	16
Pescara Centrale d.	0600	0710	0811	0905	...	...	...	...	1015	...	1105	1115	...	...	1215	1305	1415	...	1451	1505	...	1515	1550	...	16
S. Benedetto del Tronto d.	0630	0745	0841	0940	...	...	...	...	|	...	1140	|	...	...	|	1340	|	...	1527	1540	...	|	1631	...	|
Civitanova Marche-Montegranaro d.	|	0810	|	1008	...	...	...	...	|	...	1208	|	...	...	|	1408	|	...	1551	1608	...	|	1658	...	|
Ancona 625/30 a.	0713	0833	0923	1033	...	...	...	...	1123	...	1233	1223	...	...	1323	1433	1523	...	1614	1633	...	1623	1749	...	172
Bologna Centrale **615/30** a.	0914	1100	1114	1300	...	...	...	...	1314	...	1500	1412	...	...	1514	1700	1714	...	1833	1900	...	1814	2047	...	191
Milano Centrale **615/30** a.	1125	...	1325	...	...	...	...	...	1525	...	...	...	...	...	1725	...	1925	...	2115	...	...	|	2340	...	212
Torino Porta Nuova **615** a.	...	...	...	...	...	...	...	...	...	...	...	...	...	...	...	...	...	...	...	...	...	2140	...	...	...

♦ – **NOTES** (LISTED BY TRAIN NUMBER)

605 – [12] Bologna - Bari - Taranto.
755 – 🛏 1, 2 cl., 🛏 2 cl. (4 berth) and [2] Milano - Bologna - Lecce.
757 – 🛏 1, 2 cl., 🛏 2 cl. (4 berth) and [2] Torino - Bologna - Lecce.
765 – 🛏 1, 2 cl., 🛏 2 cl. (4 berth) and [2] Milano - Bologna - Lecce.
789 – ⑤: 🛏 2 cl. (4 berth) and [2] Roma - Lecce.
1545 – ⑥: [12] Milano - Lecce.
1546 – ⑦ (also Dec. 8; not Dec. 7): [12] Lecce - Milano.
9801 – [12] and 🍷 Venezia - Bologna - Lecce.
9816 – [12] and 🍷 Lecce - Bologna - Venezia.
9817 – [12] and 🍷 Venezia - Bologna - Lecce.

n – Also Apr. 24, 30; not Apr. 25, May 2.

P – ⑥⑦ (also Apr. 21, 25, June 2; not Apr. 20, 26, June 1): [2] Milano - Pescara and v.v.

▲ – For additional services Bari - Taranto and v.v. – see page 315.
♣ – For additional services Taranto - Brindisi and v.v. – see panel.
● – For 🚌 service Rimini - San Marino and v.v. – see panel.

♣ – **Local services TARANTO - BRINDISI and v.v.**:
2nd class only, 70 km, journey ± 60 minutes.

From **Taranto**: 0554⚒, 0615⚒, 0900⚒, 1130⚒🚌, 1140†🚌, 1250⚒, 1420⚒, 1540⚒🚌, 1650⚒, 1850⚒, 1930⚒🚌, 2210🚌.

From **Brindisi**: 0430🚌, 0525⚒🚌, 0654⚒, 0749⚒, 0930†🚌, 1050⚒, 1345⚒🚌, 1450⚒, 1650⚒, 1725⚒🚌, 1810⚒, 2000⚒, 2015⚒🚌.

● – 🚌 service **RIMINI - SAN MARINO and v.v.**: **Valid until June 7, 2014**
27 km, journey 50–55 minutes.

From **Rimini** (FS railway station): 0810, 0925, 1040, 1155⚒, 1215†, 1310⚒, 1425, 1540, 1655, 1810, 1925⚒.

From **San Marino** (P. Le Calcigni): 0645⚒, 0800, 0915, 1030, 1145⚒, 1215†, 1300⚒, 1415, 1530, 1645, 1800, 1915⚒.

Operator: BonelliBus s.a.s., Via Murano 47838, Riccione ✆ +39 0541 662 069.

LECCE - BARI - ANCONA 631

		IC 614	*FB* 9828			*FB* 9830	*IC* 704		*IC* 710				*FA* 9358				*ICN* 1580	*ICN* 758			*ICN* 752	*ICN* 754	*ICN* 788	
	2		🍷 ♦	2 ⚒	2	🍷	2	2 ⚒	⑦q	2	2 ⚒	2 ⚒	🍷	2 ⚒		2 ⚒	♦	♦	2		♦	♦	♦	
Lecce d.	1158	...	1313	1320	1338	1413	...	1435	...	1516	1615	1635	1650	1715	...	1832	1835	1815	2008	...	2120	2210	2230	...
Brindisi ♣ d.	1226	...	1336	1345	1407	1436	...	1505	...	1545	1637	1657	1713	1744	...	1854	1904	1847	2038	...	2148	2238	2255	...
Ostuni d.	1247	...	|	1406	1430	|	...	1527	...	1609	1658	|	|	1808	...	1915	1927	|	2102	...	2211	2301	2317	...
Fasano d.	1302	...	|	1417	1444	|	...	1541	...	1623	1710	1727	|	1822	...	1927	1942	|	2116	...	2226	2316	2330	...
Monopoli d.	1319	...	|	1425	1453	|	...	1549	...	1631	1719	1736	|	1830	...	1936	1953	|	2124	...	2237	2327	2340	...
Taranto 638 ▲ d.	|	...	|	|	|	|	...	|	1540	|	|	|	|	|	...	|	|	1949	|	...	|	|	|	...
Gioia del Colle ▲ d.	|	...	|	|	|	|	...	|	1612	|	|	|	|	|	...	|	|	2023	|	...	|	|	|	...
Bari Centrale ▲ a.	1357	...	1434	1502	1530	1534	...	1630	1649	1710	1755	1801	1810	1910	...	2010	2026	2108	2203	...	2305	2357	0010	...
Bari Centrale d.	...	1404	1438	...	...	1538	1605	...	1705	...	...	...	1817	...	...	...	2030	2133	...	...	2309	0001	0015	...
Barletta d.	...	1448	1508	...	...	1608	1648	...	1737	...	...	...	1845	...	...	...	2121	2221	...	...	2357	0034	0103	...
Foggia a.	...	1519	1537	...	...	1637	1722	...	1810	...	...	...	1913	...	...	...	2200	2302	...	...	0037	0111	0145	...
Foggia 626 d.	...	1522	1540	...	...	1640	1738	...	1827	...	...	...	1922	...	...	...	2203	2306	...	...	0041	0115	0200	...
Roma Termini **626** a.	...	|	|	...	...	|	2220	...	2300	...	...	...	2220	...	...	...	|	|	...	...	|	|	0634	...
Termoli d.	...	1608	1626	...	...	1726	...	...	...	...	...	...	...	...	...	...	2304	|	...	...	|	|	...	...
Pescara Centrale a.	...	1703	1712	...	...	1812	...	...	...	...	...	...	...	...	...	...	0005	0103	...	...	0238	0321	...	...
Pescara Centrale d.	...	1705	1715	...	...	1815	...	...	...	...	...	...	...	...	...	...	0008	0105	...	...	0240	0323	...	...
S. Benedetto del Tronto d.	...	1740	|	...	...	|	...	...	...	...	...	...	...	...	...	...	|	|	...	...	|	|	...	...
Civitanova Marche-Montegranaro d.	...	1808	|	...	...	|	...	...	...	...	...	...	...	...	...	...	|	|	...	...	|	|	...	...
Ancona 625/30 a.	...	1833	1823	...	...	1923	...	...	...	...	...	...	...	...	...	...	0135	0227	...	...	0402	0507	...	...
Bologna Centrale **615/30** a.	...	2100	2012	...	...	2114	...	...	...	...	...	...	...	...	...	...	0352	0427	...	...	0615	0727	...	...
Milano Centrale **615/30** a.	...	...	...	...	...	2325	...	...	...	...	...	...	...	...	...	...	|	0712	...	...	0930	|	...	...
Torino Porta Nuova **615** a.	...	...	...	...	...	...	...	...	...	...	...	...	...	...	...	...	0740	...	...	...	...	1120	...	...

▲ – BARI - TARANTO and v.v. local services: 2nd class only

km																									
		⚒	⚒		⚒	†		⚒		⚒	⚒		†	⚒		†	⚒		⚒			⚒			
0	**Bari** d.	0530	0624	...	0710	0813	...	1019	...	1308	1335	...	1443	1455	...	1605	1615	...	1741	1814	...	1928	...	2040	...
54	Gioia del Colle d.	0610	0706	...	0758	0854	...	1102	...	1342	1418	...	1523	1527	...	1645	1656	...	1815	1855	...	2009	...	2123	...
115	**Taranto** a.	0650	0746	...	0840	0937	...	1143	...	1415	1500	...	1604	1608	...	1725	1734	...	1855	1947	...	2049	...	2207	...

	⚒	⚒		⚒	†		⚒	⚒		†		⚒		⚒	⚒		†	⚒				⚒	†	⚒	
Taranto d.	0525	0617	...	0630	0633	...	0717	0814	...	1035	...	1220	...	1345	1428	...	1504	1540	...	1658	...	1910	1910	1958	...
Gioia del Colle d.	0601	0658	...	0713	0713	...	0756	0853	...	1114	...	1301	...	1425	1505	...	1545	1621	...	1736	...	1942	1950	2036	...
Bari a.	0640	0739	...	0755	0755	...	0838	0933	...	1155	...	1351	...	1514	1540	...	1635	1703	...	1811	...	2025	2033	2118	...

♦ – NOTES (LISTED BY TRAIN NUMBER)

752 – 🛏 1, 2 cl., ━ 2 cl. (4 berth) and (2) Lecce - Bologna - Milano.
754 – ①-⑥: 🛏 1, 2 cl., ━ 2 cl. (4 berth) and (2) Lecce - Bologna - Torino.
758 – 🛏 1, 2 cl., ━ 2 cl. (4 berth) and (2) Lecce - Bologna - Milano.
788 – ⑦ (also Dec. 8; not Dec. 7): ━ 2 cl. (4 berth) and (2) Lecce - Roma.
1580 – ⑦ (also Dec. 8; not Dec. 7): 🛏 1, 2 cl., ━ 2 cl. (4 berth) and (2) Lecce - Bologna - Torino.
9828 – (12) and 🍷 Lecce - Bologna - Venezia.

q – Also Dec. 8; not Dec. 7.

▲ – For additional services Bari - Taranto and v.v. – see panel.
♣ – For additional services Brindisi - Taranto and v.v. – see page 314.

ANCONA - ANCONA MARITTIMA 632

2nd class only *2 km* Journey time: 7 – 10 minutes

From **Ancona**: 0606Ⓐ, 0709⚒, 0717Ⓐ, 0743⚒, 0804⚒, 0826⚒, 0845⚒, 0856⚒, 0946⚒, 1200Ⓐ, 1251⚒, 1301⚒, 1341Ⓐ, 1508⚒, 1521Ⓐ, 1602Ⓐ, 1610Ⓐ, 1650Ⓐ, 1701Ⓐ, 1748Ⓐ, 1915⚒, 1928⚒.

From **Ancona Marittima**: 0640Ⓐ, 0730⚒, 0738Ⓐ, 0812⚒, 0835⚒, 0905⚒, 0914⚒, 0927⚒, 1013⚒, 1240Ⓐ, 1310⚒, 1328⚒, 1407Ⓐ, 1540Ⓐ, 1548⚒, 1622Ⓐ, 1709Ⓐ, 1723Ⓐ, 1736Ⓐ, 1812Ⓐ, 1940⚒, 2000⚒.

PAOLA - COSENZA - SIBARI 633

2nd class only

km																												
		⚒		†	⚒	⚒	⚒	⚒	⚒	†	⚒	⚒	©	⚒	†	⚒	⚒			⚒	⚒	⚒		⚒	⚒		⚒	†
	Napoli Centrale **640** d.	...	...	...	...	...	...	...	...	...	...	...	0630	...	...	...	...	...	0830	...	...	...	...	...	...	1232	...	...
0	**Paola 640** d.	0535	...	0640	0701	...	0725	0820	0858	0930	0932	...	1043	...	1135	1200	1235	...	1250	1330	...	1400	1430	1531	1606	1640	...	...
	Cosenza d.	|	0602	|	|	0730	|	|	|	|	|	1025	|	1140	...	...	...	1250	|	|	1403	...	...	...	...	...	1725	1730
21	Castiglione Cosentino a.	0551	0607	0656	0718	0736	0742	0836	0915	0946	0946	1030	1057	1146	1152	1218	1252	1256	1306	1352	1408	1417	1446	1547	1623	1703	1730	1735
21	Castiglione Cosentino d.	0553	0607	0658	0720	0736	0744	0838	0917	0948	0948	1030	1059	1146	1154	1220	1254	1256	1308	1354	1408	1419	1448	1549	1625	1705	1730	1735
26	**Cosenza 640** a.	0600	|	0705	0725	|	0750	0845	0922	0955	0955	|	1105	|	1200	1225	1300	|	1315	1400	|	1425	1455	1555	1630	1710	|	|
	Sibari 635 a.	...	0700	...	...	0832	...	...	...	...	...	1125	...	1238	...	...	...	1350	...	...	1503	...	...	...	...	...	1830	1830

	⚒		⚒	⚒	†		⚒	†	⚒	
Napoli Centrale **640** d.	...	...	...	...	...	...	...	...	...	1910
Paola 640 d.	...	1855	1930	2037	...	2115	2155	2230	2235	2303
Cosenza d.	1816	|	|	|	2115	|	|	|	|	|
Castiglione Cosentino a.	1822	1912	1947	2053	2121	2131	2212	2247	2252	2317
Castiglione Cosentino d.	1822	1914	1949	2055	2121	2133	2214	2249	2254	2319
Cosenza 640 a.	|	1920	1955	2100	|	2140	2220	2255	2300	2325
Sibari 635 a.	1914	...	...	...	2220	...	...	...	...	...

		⚒	⚒	⚒	†	⚒		⚒	⚒	⚒	†
Sibari 635 d.	...	...	...	0545	...	0630	...	...	...	...	0810
Cosenza 640 d.	0545	0625	0635	|	0650	|	0735	0750	0830	0848	|
Castiglione Cosentino a.	0552	0632	0642	0645	0657	0727	0743	0757	0837	0855	0903
Castiglione Cosentino d.	0552	0632	0642	0646	0657	0728	0743	0757	0837	0855	0904
Cosenza a.	|	|	|	0652	|	0733	|	|	|	|	0910
Paola 640 a.	0607	0648	0700	...	0715	...	0801	0815	0855	0918	...
Napoli Centrale **640** a.	1015	...	...	...	...	...	...	...	...	...	...

km																												
		⚒	†	†	⚒	⚒	©		⚒	⚒		⚒	⚒	†	⚒	⚒	†	⚒	†	⚒		⚒	†	⚒	†			⚒
0	**Sibari 635** d.	0835	0910	...	0925	...	...	...	1245	...	...	...	...	...	1508	...	1620	1650	...	...	...	1845	1904	...	...	...	...	...
	Cosenza 640 d.	|	|	1010	|	1120	1225	1300	|	1350	1450	1505	1540	1555	|	1705	|	|	1740	1750	1825	|	|	1950	1955	2045	2125	2205
62	Castiglione Cosentino a.	0928	1002	1017	1020	1127	1231	1307	1340	1357	1457	1512	1548	1602	1604	1712	1712	1743	1747	1757	1832	1940	1956	1957	2001	2054	2132	2213
62	Castiglione Cosentino d.	0930	1004	1017	1022	1127	1231	1307	1341	1357	1457	1512	1548	1602	1605	1712	1713	1745	1747	1757	1832	1941	1959	1957	2001	2054	2132	2213
67	**Cosenza** a.	0935	1010	|	1028	|	|	|	1347	|	|	|	|	|	1612	|	1720	1750	|	|	|	1947	2005	|	|	|	|	|
	Paola 640 a.	...	...	1035	...	1145	1250	1322	...	1420	1512	1530	1605	1620	...	1730	...	...	1805	1815	1850	...	...	2015	2020	2110	2150	2232
	Napoli Centrale **640** a.	...	...	...	...	...	1717	...	...	...	1940	...	...	...	...	...	...	...	...	...	2305	...	...	...	...	...	...	...

CATANZARO LIDO - LAMEZIA TERME 634

2nd class only

km																								
		⚒🚌		⚒		⚒🚌				⚒				⚒		†		⚒		🚌				
0	Catanzaro Lido 635 d.	0510	...	0630	...	0740	...	0830	...	1030	...	1245	...	1440	...	1745	...	1845	...	2243	...	...	...	...
9	Catanzaro d.	0520	...	0638	...	0750	...	0838	...	1038	...	1253	...	1448	...	1753	...	1853	...	2254	...	...	...	...
47	**Lamezia Terme** Centrale **640** a.	0600	...	0720	...	0830	...	0920	...	1120	...	1335	...	1530	...	1835	...	1935	...	2343	...	...	...	...

	🚌		⚒🚌		⚒						⚒		⚒		⚒		†					
Lamezia Terme Centrale **640** d.	0550	...	0715	...	0730	...	0930	...	1340	...	1605	...	1730	...	1905	...	1905	...	...	...	...	...
Catanzaro d.	0636	...	0750	...	0813	...	1013	...	1423	...	1648	...	1813	...	1953	...	1948	...	...	...	...	...
Catanzaro Lido 635 a.	0645	...	0800	...	0820	...	1020	...	1430	...	1655	...	1820	...	2000	...	1955	...	...	...	...	...

635 REGGIO DI CALABRIA - SIBARI - TARANTO
2nd class only

km		🚌 ⚒	⚒	⚒	🚌 ⚒	⚒	Ⓐ	†	⚒	Ⓐ	†	⚒	Ⓐ	🚌 ⚒	⚒	⚒	Ⓐ	†	†	⚒	🚌 ⚒	*IC* **562/3**	Ⓐ	⚒	🚌 ⚒	†
0	**Reggio di Calabria** Centrale **640** d.	...	...	...	...	...	0505	...	0605	...	0627	0805	...	...	...	...	1005	1018	...	...	...	1200	1210	...	...	...
30	Melito di Porto Salvo d.	...	...	...	...	...	0533	...	0640	...	0704	0840	...	...	...	...	1039	1057	...	...	...	1227	1245	...	...	...
96	Locri d.	...	...	...	...	...	0616	...	0740	...	0808	0941	...	...	...	...	1143	1203	...	...	...	1319	1346	...	...	...
101	Siderno d.	...	...	...	...	...	0621	...	0745	...	0814	0947	...	...	...	...	1148	1209	...	...	...	1326	1356	...	...	...
112	Roccella Jonica d.	...	...	...	...	...	0632	...	0807	...	0831	1007	...	...	...	...	1207	1225	...	...	...	1343	1408	...	...	...
160	Soverato d.	...	...	...	...	...	0709	...	0848	...	0923	1048	...	...	...	...	1259	1314	...	...	...	1421	1445	...	...	...
178	Catanzaro Lido a.	...	...	...	...	...	0727	...	0905	...	0940	1105	...	...	...	...	1312	1333	...	...	...	1438	1500	...	...	...
178	Catanzaro Lido **634** d.	...	...	0550	...	0645	0732	0740	...	0923	...	...	1120	...	...	1220	...	...	1357	1405	...	1441	...	1520	...	1630
238	**Crotone** d.	...	...	0641	...	0739	0815	0826	...	1017	...	...	1221	...	...	1316	...	...	1442	1455	...	1538	...	1612	...	1720
325	Rossano d.	...	...	0755	...	0855	...	▬	...	1116	...	...	1334	...	...	1439	...	...	1551	1606	...	1644	...	1732	...	1837
336	Corigliano Calabro d.	...	...	0804	...	0903	...	🚌	...	1124	...	...	1343	...	...	1447	...	...	1600	1616	...	1700	...	1741	...	1846
351	**Sibari 633** a.	...	...	0815	...	0915	...	⚒	...	1135	...	...	1355	...	...	1458	...	...	1610	1630	...	1716	...	1755	...	1857
351	**Sibari** d.	0503	0545	...	...	...	...	1003	...	...	...	...	...	1358	1403	...	...	...	...	...	1648	1719	...	▬	1843	...
366	Trebisacce d.	0517	0602	...	...	...	...	1017	...	...	...	...	...	1412	1415	...	...	...	...	...	1702	1735	...	⚒	1857	...
430	Metaponto **638** d.	0635	0700	...	0944	...	...	1135	...	...	...	...	...	1530	1510	...	...	...	...	...	1820	1832	...	1847	2015	...
473	**Taranto 631/8** a.	0730	...	...	1034	...	...	1245	...	...	...	...	...	1640	...	...	...	...	...	...	1915	1905	...	1922	2110	...

	⚒	⚒	†	⚒	⚒	⚒	†	⚒	†
Reggio di Calabria Centrale **640** d.	1405	...	1528	1605	...	1805	1808	2005	2015
Melito di Porto Salvo d.	1439	...	1607	1639	...	1837	1847	2040	2050
Locri d.	1542	...	1713	1741	...	1940	1948	2137	2147
Siderno d.	1548	...	1719	1747	...	1946	1954	2142	2152
Roccella Jonica d.	1607	...	1734	1807	...	2000	2008	2155	2205
Soverato d.	1647	...	1822	1845	...	2033	...	...	...
Catanzaro Lido a.	1705	...	1840	1900	...	2050	...	...	...
Catanzaro Lido **634** d.	▬	1800	...	...	1930	...	...	...	...
Crotone d.	...	1853	...	...	2019	...	...	...	...
Rossano d.	...	2004	...	...	2134	...	...	...	...
Corigliano Calabro d.	...	2013	...	...	2143	...	...	...	...
Sibari 633 a.	...	2025	...	...	2155	...	...	...	...
Sibari d.	...	...	...	...	...	...	...	...	...
Trebisacce d.	...	...	...	...	...	...	...	...	...
Metaponto **638** d.	2040	...	...	...	...	...	...	...	...
Taranto 631/8 a.	2115	...	...	...	...	...	...	...	...

	⚒	Ⓐ	†	⚒	⚒	†	⚒	🚌 ⚒	⚒
Taranto 631/8 d.	...	...	...	...	...	...	...	0515	0520
Metaponto **638** d.	...	...	...	...	...	...	...	0627	0559
Trebisacce d.	...	...	...	...	...	...	...	0743	...
Sibari 633 a.	...	...	...	...	...	...	...	0757	...
Sibari d.	...	...	...	0602	...	...	0730	...	...
Corigliano Calabro d.	...	...	...	0614	...	...	0742	...	...
Rossano d.	...	...	...	0622	...	...	0756	...	...
Crotone d.	...	...	...	0740	...	...	0914	...	...
Catanzaro Lido a.	...	...	...	0835	...	...	1000	...	...
Catanzaro Lido **634** d.	0605	0805	0805	...	1005	1015	...	...	...
Soverato d.	0619	0818	0822	...	1019	1028	...	...	...
Roccella Jonica d.	0656	0856	0914	...	1056	1103	...	...	...
Siderno d.	0708	0909	0928	...	1109	1115	...	...	...
Locri d.	0713	0914	0934	...	1115	1120	...	...	...
Melito di Porto Salvo d.	0821	1021	1043	...	1222	1222	...	...	...
Reggio di Calabria Centrale **640** a.	0855	1057	1122	...	1257	1252	...	...	...

	†	⚒	⚒	⚒	*IC* **558/9**	†	🚌 ⚒	🚌 ⚒	⚒	⚒		⚒	†	⚒	🚌 ⚒	⚒	⚒	🚌 ⚒	⚒	Ⓐ	†	Ⓐ	⚒	🚌 ⚒	🚌 ⚒
Taranto 631/8 d.	...	...	...	...	0820	...	0835	0900	...	...	0941	...	...	...	1235	...	1420	1425	...	...	...	...	...	1755	1915
Metaponto **638** d.	...	0715	...	...	0856	...	0915	0957	...	...	1013	...	...	...	1313	...	1458	1517	1520	...	...	...	...	1852	2012
Trebisacce d.	...	0815	...	...	0948	...	...	1116	...	...	▬	...	...	...	▬	...	▬	1628	1614	...	...	...	...	2008	2126
Sibari 633 a.	...	0830	...	...	1003	...	...	1135	...	...	...	...	...	...	...	...	...	1643	1628	...	...	...	...	2022	2140
Sibari d.	...	...	0918	...	1006	1030	...	...	1140	...	...	...	...	1400	...	1518	...	...	...	1645	1718	1845	1940	...	...
Corigliano Calabro d.	...	...	0931	...	1022	1044	...	...	1153	...	...	...	...	1412	...	1531	...	...	...	1659	1729	1858	1952	...	...
Rossano d.	...	...	0939	...	1034	1054	...	...	1201	...	...	...	...	1420	...	1539	...	...	...	1708	1737	1907	2005	...	...
Crotone d.	...	...	1052	...	1140	1215	...	...	1315	...	...	...	...	1537	...	1707	...	...	...	1820	1853	2017	2115	...	...
Catanzaro Lido a.	...	...	1142	...	1239	1300	...	...	1400	...	†	...	...	1630	⚒	1755	†	...	...	1911	1940	2105	...	...	...
Catanzaro Lido **634** d.	1135	...	...	1205	1242	...	...	...	...	1405	1405	1605	1640	...	1805	...	1850	...	...	1914	...	2108	...	...	...
Soverato d.	1148	...	...	1219	1258	...	...	...	...	1422	1424	1620	1657	...	1819	...	1911	...	...	1931	...	2121	...	...	...
Roccella Jonica d.	1223	...	...	1256	1341	...	...	...	...	1456	1519	1658	1750	...	1857	...	2015	...	...	2023	...	2200	...	...	...
Siderno d.	1234	...	...	1309	1355	...	...	...	...	1509	1532	1710	1802	...	1909	...	2027	...	...	2033	...	...	...	...	...
Locri d.	1240	...	...	1320	1402	...	...	...	...	1514	1537	1715	1808	...	1914	...	2033	...	...	2039	...	...	...	...	...
Melito di Porto Salvo d.	1342	...	...	1421	1500	...	...	...	...	1621	1651	1821	1917	...	2021	...	2143	...	...	2141	...	...	...	...	...
Reggio di Calabria Centrale **640** a.	1412	...	...	1457	1525	...	...	...	...	1655	1732	1855	2000	...	2055	...	2210	...	...	2215	...	...	...	...	...

638 NAPOLI - POTENZA - TARANTO
2nd class only

km		⚒	*IC* **701**	†	⚒	⚒	⚒	⚒			*IC* **707** §	
	Roma T **640** d.	...	0626	...	...	...	...	...	...	...	1526	...
0	**Napoli** C **640** d.	...	0845	...	...	...	...	...	...	1635	1746	...
26	Pompei d.	...	|	...	...	...	...	...	...	|	|	...
54	Salerno d.	0540	0924	0942	...	1354	1457	...	1624	1718	1824	2016
74	Battipaglia **640** d.	0600	0939	1007	...	1416	1515	...	1644	1735	1840	2033
166	**Potenza** Centrale d.	0743	1059	1151	1429	1556	1710	1715	1829	1922	2004	2207
273	Metaponto **635** d.	...	1218	...	1605	...	...	1847	...	2040	2124	...
317	**Taranto 635** a.	...	1250	...	1644	...	...	1922	...	2115	2156	...

		⚒	*IC* **700** §			*IC* **702**	⚒	⚒		⚒	
Taranto 635 d.	...	0520	0805	0941	...	1400	1420	...	...	...	...
Metaponto **635** d.	...	0600	0839	1015	...	1433	1459	...	...	...	...
Potenza Centrale d.	0700	0735	1000	1153	1405	1558	1639	1746	1856	2050	...
Battipaglia **640** d.	0829	...	1124	1322	1551	1721	...	1947	2049	2227	...
Salerno d.	0845	...	1138	1337	1612	1737	...	2005	2109	2244	...
Pompei a.	...	...	|	|	...	|	...	...	...	...	...
Napoli C **640** a.	...	...	1215	1420	...	1810	...	...	...	...	...
Roma T **640** a.	...	...	1434	...	...	2034	...	...	...	...	...

§ – Also conveys 1st class.

639 NAPOLI - SORRENTO, BAIANO and SARNO
2nd class only Circumvesuviana Ferrovia

Services depart from Napoli Porta Nolana station and call at Napoli Piazza Garibaldi ▲ 2 minutes later.

A reduced service operates in peak summer.

NAPOLI (Porta Nolana) **- SORRENTO and v.v.** Journey: 55 - 68 minutes. *45 km.* All services call at Ercolano, Pompei Villa di Misteri, Castellammare di Stabia, Vico Equense and Meta.

From **Napoli:** 0609, 0640, 0644⚒, 0709, 0739⚒, 0811, 0839, 0909, 0939 and every 30 minutes until 1309, 1341, 1409, 1439, 1511, 1539, 1609, 1639, 1709, 1741, 1809, 1839, 1911, 1939, 2009, 2039, 2109, 2139.

From **Sorrento:** 0601, 0625, 0722, 0738⚒, 0755, 0826, 0852⚒, 0907, 0937, 1037, 1107 and every 30 minutes until 1307, 1325, 1356, 1422, 1455, 1526, 1607, 1637, 1707, 1725, 1756, 1822, 1855, 1926, 2007, 2037, 2107, 2137.

NAPOLI (Porta Nolana) **- BAIANO and v.v.** Journey 60 minutes.

From **Napoli:** 0618, 0648⚒, 0718, 0748, 0818, 0918, 1018, 1118, 1148⚒, 1218, 1318, 1418, 1448⚒, 1518, 1618, 1718, 1748Ⓐ, 1818, 1848, 1918, 1948.

From **Baiano:** 0602, 0632⚒, 0700, 0730, 0802, 0832, 0902, 0932, 1002, 1102, 1202, 1302, 1332⚒, 1402, 1502, 1602, 1632⚒, 1702, 1802, 1902, 1932Ⓐ, 2002.

NAPOLI (Porta Nolana) **- SARNO and v.v.** Journey 65 minutes. All services call at Poggiomarino (49 minutes from Napoli, 12 minutes from Sarno).

From **Napoli:** 0632, 0651 **p**, 0722, 0802, 0902, 1002, 1102, 1132⚒, 1202, 1302, 1402, 1432⚒, 1502, 1602, 1702, 1732Ⓐ, 1802, 1832, 1932, 2002 **p**.

From **Sarno:** 0619, 0649, 0719, 0759, 0819, 0849, 0949, 1049, 1149, 1249, 1335⚒ **p**, 1349, 1449, 1549, 1619⚒, 1649, 1749, 1849, 1919Ⓐ, 1949.

p – From / to Poggiomarino only.

▲ – Adjacent to **Napoli Centrale** main line station - connection is by moving walkway. Operator: Circumvesuviana Ferrovia ✆ +39 081 77 22 444, fax +39 081 77 22 450.

Frequent 🚌 services operate along the Amalfi Coast between Sorrento and Salerno. Up to 2 services on ⚒, less frequent on †. Change of buses at Amalfi is necessary. Operator SITA, Via Campegna 23, 80124 Napoli. ✆ +39 081 610 67 11, fax +39 081 239 5 10.

ROMA - NAPOLI - COSENZA and REGGIO DI CALABRIA 640

For high-speed services – see Table 600

km		2 ⚒	2 †	2	2	2	2	*ICN* 799 ♦	*IC* 701 ♦	*ICN* 1911 ♦	*IC* 723 ♦	*IC* 721 K	2 ⚒	2 ①–⑥	2 †	2 ⚒	2 ⚒	*IC* 1571 ♦	*IC* 551 ⚒q	*IC* 1551 ⚒p	2 ⚒	2 †	*IC* 501 ♦	*FB* 9873 🍷⚒	2
	Torino P N **610** d.	...	...	...	...	...	...	2155	...	2125	...	...	...	...	...	...	...	...	...	...	...	...	...	...	...
	Milano C **615** d.	...	...	...	...	...	...	|	...	2317g	...	...	...	...	...	...	...	...	...	...	...	...	...	...	...
	Venezia S L **616** d.	...	...	...	...	...	...	|	...	|	...	...	...	...	...	...	...	...	...	...	...	...	...	...	...
	Bologna C **620** d.	...	...	...	...	...	...	|	...	0230	...	...	...	...	...	...	...	...	...	...	...	...	...	...	...
0	**Roma** Termini **620** d.	...	...	...	...	0542	...	0558o	0626	0725t	0726	0726	...	0749	...	...	...	0900	0926	0926	...	...	1021o	1056	...
62	Latina d.	...	...	...	...	0618	...	0637	0657	|	0757	0757	...	0824	...	...	...	0931	0957	0957	...	...	1057	|	...
129	Formia-Gaeta d.	...	...	...	...	0707	...	0717	0734	|	0834	0834	...	0900	...	...	...	1008	1034	1034	...	...	1134	|	...
195	Aversa d.	...	...	...	...	0750	...	0757	0809	|	0909	0909	...	0937	...	...	...	1043	1109	1109	...	...	1209	|	...
	Caserta **626** d.	...	...	...	...	|	...	|	|	|	|	|	...	|	...	...	...	|	|	|	...	...	|	|	...
214	**Napoli** Centrale **626** a.	...	...	...	...	0810	...	0817	0829	0938	0929	0929	...	1000	...	...	...	1103	1129	1129	...	...	1229	1241	...
214	**Napoli** Centrale d.	0542	0542	0630	0735	...	0830	0835	0845	0955	0950	0950	...	...	...	...	...	...	1145	1145	...	1140	...	1255	...
240	Pompei d.	0612	0612	0702	0805	...	0900	|	|	|	|	|	...	...	...	...	...	...	|	|	...	1216	...	|	...
268	Salerno d.	0636	0636	0732	0838	...	0931	0912	0924	1032	1029	1029	...	...	...	...	...	...	1222	1222	...	1242	...	1334	...
288	Battipaglia **638** d.	0653	0653	0752	0856	...	0946	...	0937	...	|	|	...	...	...	...	...	...	1237	1237	...	1302	...	|	...
318	Agropoli-Castellabate d.	0715	0715	0814	0923	...	1008	...	...	...	|	|	...	...	...	...	...	...	|	1253	...	1326	...	|	...
349	Ascea d.	0742	0742	0841	0949	...	1036	...	...	...	|	|	...	...	...	...	...	...	|	|	...	1356	...	|	...
395	Sapri d.	0823	0825	0921	1030	...	1114	...	...	...	1136	1136	...	...	...	...	1305	...	1341	1344	1430	1437	...	1440	...
407	Maratea d.	...	0841	0936	...	...	1125	...	...	...	|	|	...	...	...	...	1316	...	1352	1355	1439	1446	...	|	...
455	Belvedere Marittimo d.	...	0918	1009	...	...	1209	...	...	...	|	|	...	...	...	...	1354	...	|	|	1522	1522	...	|	...
489	Paola **633** d.	...	0945	1040	...	...	1250	...	...	...	1228	1228	1235	...	1255	1330	1430	...	1442	1450	1550	1550	...	1526	1530
	Cosenza **633** a.	...	...	1105c	...	...	1315	...	...	...	|	|	|	...	|	|	1455	...	|	|	...	...	...	|	|
546	**Lamezia Terme** Centrale a.	...	...	...	...	...	...	...	...	...	1257	1257	1310	...	1333	1408	...	...	1515	1523	...	...	...	1552	1608
546	**Lamezia Terme** Centrale **634** d.	...	...	...	...	...	...	...	...	...	1300	1300	1312	...	1335	1410	...	...	1518	1526	...	...	...	1555	1610
616	Gioia Tauro d.	...	...	...	...	...	...	...	...	...	|	|	1354	...	1416	1455	...	...	1601	1607	...	...	...	1634	1654
652	Villa S. Giovanni **641** a.	...	...	...	...	...	...	...	...	...	1405	1405	1430	...	1453	1530	...	...	1628	1634	...	...	...	1659	1730
652	Villa S. Giovanni d.	...	...	...	...	...	...	...	...	...	1425	1425	1432	...	1455	1532	...	...	1631	1637	...	...	...	1702	1732
667	**Reggio di Calabria** C **635** a.	...	...	...	...	...	...	...	...	...	|	|	1450	...	1510	1550	...	...	1648	1653	...	...	...	1715	1750
	Siracusa **641** a.	...	...	...	...	...	...	...	...	...	|	1829	...	...	...	...	...	...	...	...	...	...	...	...	...
	Palermo C **641** a.	...	...	...	...	...	...	...	...	...	1900	...	...	...	...	...	...	...	...	...	...	...	...	...	...

	2	2 y	*IC* 727 ♦	*IC* 729 L	2 ⚒		*IC* 1573 †	2 ⚒	*IC* 553	2 Ⓑ	2 ⚒	2	*IC* 583	*FB* 9877 🍷	*IC* 1589 ♦	*IC* 1591 ♦	2 ⑥	*IC* 555	2 ⚒	2 ⚒	2 †	2	2	*IC* 707 ♦
Torino P N **610** d.	...	...	...	...	...	...	...	...	...	...	...	...	...	...	...	...	...	...	...	...	...	...	...	...
Milano C **615** d.	...	...	...	...	...	...	...	...	...	...	...	...	0650	...	0710	0710	...	...	...	...	...	...	...	...
Venezia S L **616** d.	...	...	...	...	...	...	...	...	...	...	...	...	|	...	|	|	...	...	...	...	...	...	...	...
Bologna C **620** d.	...	...	...	...	...	...	...	...	...	...	...	...	0918	...	0958	0958	...	...	...	...	...	...	...	...
Roma Termini **620** d.	...	1036	1126	1126	...	...	1156	...	1226	...	...	1236	1322t	1356	1356t	1356t	1336	1426	...	...	...	1436	...	1526
Latina d.	...	1112	1157	1157	...	...	1227	...	1257	...	...	1312	1357	|	1432	1432	1412	1457	...	...	...	1512	...	1557
Formia-Gaeta d.	...	1207	1234	1234	...	...	1304	...	1334	...	...	1359	1434	|	1515	1515	1518	1534	...	...	...	1602	...	1634
Aversa d.	...	1252	1309	1309	...	...	1339	...	1409	...	...	1445	1509	|	1547	1547	1556	1609	...	...	...	1648	...	1709
Caserta **626** d.	...	|	|	|	...	...	|	...	|	...	...	|	|	|	|	|	|	|	...	...	...	|	...	|
Napoli Centrale **626** a.	...	1312	1329	1329	...	...	1359	...	1429	...	...	1507	1529	1541	1609	1609	1618	1629	...	...	...	1710	...	1729
Napoli Centrale d.	1232	...	1345	1345	...	...	1415	1335	1450	...	1525	...	...	1555	1625	1625	...	1650	...	1715	1730	...	1740	1746
Pompei d.	1302	...	|	|	...	...	|	1407	|	...	1555	...	...	|	|	|	...	|	...	|	|	...	1812	|
Salerno d.	1326	...	1424	1424	...	...	1453	1432	1527	...	1617	...	...	1634	1706	1706	...	1729	...	1755	1811	...	1843	1824
Battipaglia **638** d.	1344	...	|	|	...	...	1508	1446	1540	...	1631	...	...	|	|	|	...	1743	...	1814	1828	...	1858	1838
Agropoli-Castellabate d.	1412	...	|	|	...	...	|	1508	1556	...	1651	...	...	|	|	|	...	1800	...	1835	1849	...	1921	...
Ascea d.	1437	...	|	|	...	...	|	1532	|	...	1718	...	...	|	1758	1757	...	1827	...	1901	1914	...	1955	...
Sapri d.	1515	...	1532	1532	...	...	1610	1615	1640	...	1800	...	...	1740	1834	1832	...	1902	1915	1939	1950	...	2042	...
Maratea d.	1525	...	|	|	...	...	1620	...	|	...	...	...	...	|	|	|	...	|	1925	...	...	...	...	...
Belvedere Marittimo d.	1608	...	|	|	...	...	|	...	|	...	...	...	...	|	|	|	...	|	2002	...	...	...	...	...
Paola **633** d.	1640	...	1622	1622	1635	...	1707	...	1737	1740	...	...	...	1826	1930	1930	...	1958	2037	...	...	...	...	...
Cosenza **633** a.	1710	...	|	|	|	...	|	...	|	|	...	...	...	|	|	|	...	|	2100	...	...	...	...	...
Lamezia Terme Centrale a.	...	...	1651	1651	1710	...	1743	...	1809	1817	...	...	...	1852	2004	2004	...	2030	...	...	...	...	...	...
Lamezia Terme Centrale **634** d.	...	...	1654	1654	1712	...	1746	...	1812	1819	...	...	...	1855	2007	2007	...	2033	...	...	...	...	...	...
Gioia Tauro d.	...	...	|	|	1756	...	1827	...	1853	1902	...	...	...	1934	2049	2145	...	2114	...	...	...	...	...	...
Villa S. Giovanni **641** a.	...	...	1800	1800	1831	...	1854	...	1921	1938	...	...	...	1959	2117	2209	...	2141	...	...	...	...	...	...
Villa S. Giovanni d.	...	...	1820	1820	1833	...	1857	...	1924	1940	...	...	...	2002	2120	2212	...	2144	...	...	...	...	...	...
Reggio di Calabria C **635** a.	...	...	|	|	1850	...	1913	...	1945	2000	...	...	...	2015	2140	2230	...	2203	...	...	...	...	...	...
Siracusa **641** a.	...	...	2245	|	...	...	...	...	...	...	...	...	...	...	...	...	...	...	...	...	...	...	...	...
Palermo C **641** a.	...	...	...	2300	...	...	...	...	...	...	...	...	...	...	...	...	...	...	...	...	...	...	...	...

km		*IC* 561	2	*FA* 9377/9 🍷	*IC* 561	2	*IC* 591	2	*IC* 511	2 ⚒	2 Ⓑ	2	2 ①–⑥	*ICN* 1955 ♦	*ICN* 1957 D	*IC* 597	*ICN* 1959 ♦	*ICN* 1961 C	*ICN* 795 ♦	*ICN* 789 ♦	2 ⚒	2	2 ⚒	*ICN* 785 ♦	*ICN* 781 A
	Torino P N **610** d.	...	...	...	...	...	...	...	1105	...	...	...	...	...	...	...	...	...	1335	...	...	...	...	...	...
	Milano C **615** d.	...	...	...	...	...	...	...	|	...	...	...	...	...	...	1450	...	...	1544g	...	...	...	...	2005	2005
	Venezia S L **616** d.	...	...	...	...	...	...	...	|	...	...	...	...	...	...	|	...	...	|	...	...	...	...	|	|
	Bologna C **620** d.	...	...	...	...	...	...	...	|	...	...	...	...	...	...	1718	...	...	|	...	...	...	...	|	|
0	**Roma** Termini **620** d.	1626	1636	1730	...	...	1726	...	1826	...	1836	1931	2056	2131	2131	2122t	2226	2226	2317t	2358	...	...	...	0316o	0316o
	Latina d.	1657	1717	|	...	...	1757	...	1857	...	1915	2006	2132	2205	2205	2157	2301	2301	|	|	...	...	...	|	|
	Formia-Gaeta d.	1734	1805	|	...	...	1834	...	1934	...	2005	2042	2220	2244	2244	2234	2340	2340	|	|	...	...	...	|	|
	Aversa d.	1809	1848	|	...	...	1909	...	2009	...	2051	|	2302	|	|	2311	|	|	|	|	...	...	...	|	|
216	Caserta **626** d.	|	|	|	←	...	|	...	|	...	|	2141	|	|	|	|	|	|	|	0232	...	...	...	|	|
	Napoli Centrale **626** a.	1829	1910	1843	1829	...	1929	...	2029	...	2113	2219	2324	2337	2337	2330	|	|	|	...	...	...	...	|	|
	Napoli Centrale d.	1850	...	1855	1850	1910	1950	2001	2053	2122	...	...	...	2353	2353	...	|	|	|	...	...	...	...	|	|
	Pompei d.	→	...	|	|	1941	|	2032	|	|	...	...	...	|	|	...	|	|	|	...	...	...	...	|	|
287	Salerno d.	...	...	1928	1923	2006	2027	2102	2130	2203	...	...	...	|	|	...	0124	0124	0221	...	...	...	0551	0556s	0556s
—	Battipaglia **638** d.	...	...	|	1946	2022	...	2120	...	2223	...	...	...	|	|	...	|	|	|	...	...	...	0611	0616s	0616s
	Agropoli-Castellabate d.	...	...	|	|	2042	...	2144	...	2242	...	...	...	|	|	...	|	|	|	...	...	...	0632	0635s	0635s
	Ascea d.	...	...	|	|	2111	...	2210	...	2303	...	...	...	|	|	...	|	|	|	...	...	...	0710	0700s	0700s
	Sapri d.	...	...	|	2048	2148	...	2245	...	2340	...	...	...	|	|	...	|	|	0347	...	...	...	0749	0735s	0735s
	Maratea d.	...	...	|	2059	2157	...	...	...	...	...	...	...	|	|	...	|	|	|	...	...	...	0758	0746s	0746s
	Belvedere Marittimo d.	...	...	|	|	2229	...	...	...	...	...	...	...	|	|	...	|	|	|	...	...	...	0831	|	|
0	Paola **633** d.	...	...	2103	2144	2303	...	...	...	...	...	...	...	0248	0248	...	0341	0341	0444	...	0525	0730	0900	0838s	0838s
26	Cosenza **633** a.	...	...	|	|	2325	...	...	...	...	...	...	...	|	|	...	|	|	|	...	|	|	...	|	|
	Lamezia Terme Centrale a.	...	...	2129	2216	...	...	...	...	...	...	...	...	|	|	...	|	|	0521	...	0603	0808	...	0916s	0916s
	Lamezia Terme Centrale **634** d.	...	...	2132	2219	...	...	...	...	...	...	...	...	|	|	...	|	|	0524	...	0605	0810	...	0919s	0919s
	Gioia Tauro d.	...	...	|	2300	...	...	...	...	...	...	...	...	|	|	...	|	|	0707	...	0647	0855	...	1004s	1004s
	Villa S. Giovanni **641** a.	...	...	2225	2326	...	...	...	...	...	...	...	...	0425	0425	...	0520	0520	0743	...	0720	0930	...	1040s	1040s
	Villa S. Giovanni d.	...	...	2228	2329	...	...	...	...	...	...	...	...	0445	0445	...	0540	0540	0746	...	0722	0932	...	1105s	1105s
	Reggio di Calabria C **635** a.	...	...	2242	2343	...	...	...	...	...	...	...	...	|	|	...	|	|	0805	...	0740	0950	...	|	|
	Siracusa **641** a.	...	...	...	...	...	...	...	...	...	...	...	...	0935	|	...	1025	|	...	...	...	...	...	1548	|
	Palermo C **641** a.	...	...	...	...	...	...	...	...	...	...	...	...	...	1002	...	...	1035	...	...	...	...	...	...	1637

FOR NOTES SEE PAGE 319

640 REGGIO DI CALABRIA and COSENZA - NAPOLI - ROMA

For high-speed services – see Table 600

				IC 582			IC 510	ICN 1960	ICN 1958					IC 590				IC 550		FA 9372/4	IC 550	IC 700			IC 552
	2	2	2		2	2				2	2	2	2		2	2			2	🍷			2	2	
	①–⑥	①–⑥	⑦				♦	♦	W	⚒					⚒	⚒			⚒			♦		①–⑥	
Palermo C **641** d.	...	...	...	...	...	...	...	...	2110	...	...	...	...	...	...	...	...	...	...	...	...	...	...	...	...
Siracusa **641** d.	...	...	...	...	...	...	...	2145	|	...	...	...	...	...	...	...	...	...	...	...	...	...	...	...	...
Reggio di Calabria C **635** d.	...	...	...	...	...	...	...	|	|	...	...	...	...	...	...	0505	...	0610	...	0635	...	...	0705	...	0810
Villa S. Giovanni **641** a.	...	...	...	...	...	...	...	0200	0200	...	...	...	...	...	...	0520	...	0626	...	0648	...	...	0720	...	0825
Villa S. Giovanni d.	...	...	...	...	...	...	...	0230	0230	...	...	...	...	...	...	0522	...	0629	...	0651	...	...	0722	...	0828
Gioia Tauro d.	...	...	...	...	...	...	...	|	|	...	...	...	...	...	...	0558	...	0657	...	|	...	...	0755	...	0858
Lamezia Terme Centrale a.	...	...	...	...	...	...	...	|	|	...	...	...	...	...	...	0640	...	0737	...	0748	...	...	0836	...	0938
Lamezia Terme Centrale **634** d.	...	...	...	...	...	...	...	|	|	...	...	...	...	...	...	0642	...	0740	...	0751	...	...	0838	...	0940
Cosenza **633** d.	...	...	...	...	...	...	...	|	|	...	...	...	0545	...	0625	0740	...	|	0735	|	...	...	|	...	|
Paola **633** d.	...	...	...	...	...	...	...	0431	0431	...	...	...	0610	...	0650	...	...	0813	0801	0823	...	...	0920	...	1017
Belvedere Marittimo d.	...	...	...	...	...	...	...	|	|	...	...	...	0636	...	0723	...	...	|	0841	|	...	...	...	...	|
Maratea d.	...	...	...	...	...	...	...	|	|	...	...	...	0709	...	0807	...	...	0902	0919	|	...	...	...	...	|
Sapri d.	...	...	...	...	...	0430	...	|	|	0550	0615	0640	0721	...	0820	...	...	0912	0930	|	...	...	...	...	1113
Ascea d.	...	...	...	...	...	0508	...	|	|	0632	0654	0715	0759	...	...	...	...	|	...	|	...	...	...	...	|
Agropoli-Castellabate d.	...	...	...	...	...	0536	...	|	|	0656	0719	0737	0838	...	...	...	...	|	...	|	←	...	...	...	1157
Battipaglia **638** d.	...	...	...	...	...	0600	...	|	|	0714	0742	0758	0901	...	...	...	...	1011	...	|	1013	1124	...	...	1222
Salerno d.	...	...	...	0529	...	0618	0630	0646s	0646s	0732	0801	0818	0918	...	...	...	...	→	...	0952	1027	1138	...	...	1237
Pompei d.	...	...	...	|	...	0636	|	|	|	|	0825	|	0940	...	...	...	...	...	...	|	|	|	...	...	|
Napoli Centrale a.	...	...	...	0605	...	0717	0707	0723	0723	0810	0905	0856	1015	...	...	...	...	...	...	1023	1059	1215	...	...	1315
Napoli Centrale **626** d.	0515	0522	0532	0631	0636	...	0731	0739	0739	...	...	...	...	1031	...	...	...	...	...	1035	1131	1231	...	1241	1331
Caserta **626** d.	|	|	|	|	|	...	|	|	|	...	...	...	...	|	...	...	...	...	...	|	|	|	...	|	|
Aversa d.	0532	0547	0550	0648	0654	...	0748	|	|	...	...	...	...	1048	...	...	...	...	...	|	1148	1248	...	1259	1348
Formia-Gaeta d.	0611	0633	0638	0722	0740	...	0822	0833	0833	...	...	...	...	1122	...	...	...	...	...	|	1222	1322	...	1352	1422
Latina d.	0652	0720	0722	0759	0825	...	0859	0912	0912	...	...	...	...	1159	...	...	...	...	...	|	1259	1359	...	1438	1459
Roma Termini **620** a.	0734	0806	0806	0834	0904	...	0934	0951	0951	...	...	...	...	1237	...	...	...	...	...	1150	1334	1434	...	1524	1534
Bologna C **620** a.	...	...	...	...	...	...	|	...	...	...	...	...	...	1640	...	...	...	...	...	...	...	...	...	...	...
Venezia SL **616** a.	...	...	...	...	...	...	|	...	...	...	...	...	...	|	...	...	...	...	...	...	...	...	...	...	...
Milano C **615** a.	...	...	...	...	...	...	|	...	...	...	...	...	...	1915	...	...	...	...	...	...	...	...	...	...	...
Torino PN **610** a.	...	...	...	...	...	...	1710	...	...	...	...	...	...	...	...	...	...	...	...	...	...	...	...	...	...

	FB 9872	IC 596	IC 1590	IC 1588			IC 556			IC 728	IC 722			IC 1572	IC 522		IC 702				FB 9878			IC 724	IC 730
	🍷				2	2		2	2			2	2			2	2	2	2	2	🍷	2			
			♦	♦	y			⚒		♦	N			♦	♦	⚒	♦				Ⓑv	⚒		♦	P
Palermo C **641** d.	...	...	...	...	...	...	...	...	...	0700	...	...	...	...	...	...	...	...	...	...	...	...	...	...	1005
Siracusa **641** d.	...	...	...	...	...	...	...	...	...	|	0733	...	...	...	...	...	...	...	...	...	...	...	...	1025	|
Reggio di Calabria C **635** d.	0840	...	0845	0925	...	...	1005	...	...	|	|	...	...	...	...	1205	...	...	...	1305	1345	1405	...	|	|
Villa S. Giovanni **641** a.	0852	...	0901	0938	...	...	1019	...	...	1125	1125	...	...	...	...	1222	...	...	...	1320	1357	1420	...	1425	1425
Villa S. Giovanni d.	0855	...	0904	0941	...	...	1022	...	...	1155	1155	...	...	...	...	1224	...	...	...	1322	1400	1422	...	1455	1455
Gioia Tauro d.	0926	...	0935	1015	...	...	1053	...	...	|	|	...	...	...	...	1257	...	...	...	1358	1431	1458	...	|	|
Lamezia Terme Centrale a.	1003	...	1103	1058	...	...	1133	...	...	1259	1259	...	...	...	...	1340	...	...	...	1440	1510	1540	...	1601	1601
Lamezia Terme Centrale **634** d.	1006	...	1106	1101	...	...	1136	...	...	1302	1302	...	...	...	...	1342	...	...	...	1442	1513	1542	...	1604	1604
Cosenza **633** d.	|	...	|	|	...	...	|	...	1225c	|	|	...	...	...	...	|	...	...	1450	|	|	1645	...	|	|
Paola **633** d.	1036	...	1141	1141	...	...	1217	...	1253	1336	1336	...	...	...	...	1420	...	...	1515	1520	1541	...	...	1636	1636
Belvedere Marittimo d.	|	...	|	|	...	...	|	...	1325	|	|	...	...	...	...	...	...	...	1545	...	|	...	...	|	|
Maratea d.	|	...	|	|	...	...	|	...	1418	|	|	...	...	...	...	...	...	...	1627	...	|	...	...	|	|
Sapri d.	1123	...	1236	1234	...	1245	1313	1325	1433	1426	1426	...	←	...	...	...	...	...	1639	...	1626	...	...	1725	1725
Ascea d.	|	...	1307	1306	...	1324	1343	1404	1516	|	|	...	1516	...	...	...	...	...	1718	...	|	...	...	|	|
Agropoli-Castellabate d.	|	...	|	|	...	1349	1403	1432	→	|	|	...	1540	...	...	...	...	...	1756	...	|	...	...	|	|
Battipaglia **638** d.	|	...	|	|	...	1417	1421	1458	...	|	|	...	1602	...	...	...	1721	...	1820	...	|	...	...	|	|
Salerno d.	1228	...	1351	1350	...	1446	1438	1518	...	1536	1536	...	1620	...	...	...	1737	...	1846	...	1731	...	...	1836	1836
Pompei d.	|	...	|	|	...	1505	|	1552	...	|	|	...	1641	...	...	...	|	...	1905	...	|	...	...	|	|
Napoli Centrale a.	1300	...	1426	1426	...	1543	1515	1624	...	1613	1613	...	1717	...	...	...	1810	...	1940	...	1805	...	...	1915	1915
Napoli Centrale **626** d.	1319	1431	1442	1442	1448	...	1531	...	...	1631	1631	1648	...	1731	1731	...	1831	1848	...	...	1819	...	...	1931	1931
Caserta **626** d.	|	|	|	|	|	...	|	...	...	|	|	|	...	|	|	...	|	|	...	...	|	...	...	|	|
Aversa d.	|	1448	1500	1500	1507	...	1548	...	...	1648	1648	1707	...	1748	1748	...	1848	1907	...	...	|	...	...	1948	1948
Formia-Gaeta d.	|	1522	1538	1538	1558	...	1622	...	...	1722	1722	1758	...	1822	1822	...	1922	1958	...	...	|	...	...	2022	2022
Latina d.	|	1559	1615	1615	1644	...	1659	...	...	1759	1759	1844	...	1859	1859	...	1959	2044	...	...	|	...	...	2059	2059
Roma Termini **620** a.	1504	1639t	1656t	1656t	1724	...	1734	...	...	1834	1834	1924	...	1939o	1939o	...	2034	2124	...	...	2004	...	...	2134	2134
Bologna C **620** a.	...	2038	2125	2125	...	...	...	...	...	...	...	...	...	...	...	...	...	...	...	...	...	...	...	...	...
Venezia SL **616** a.	...	|	|	|	...	...	...	...	...	...	...	...	...	...	...	...	...	...	...	...	...	...	...	...	...
Milano C **615** a.	...	2315	0005	0005	...	...	...	...	...	...	...	...	...	...	...	...	...	...	...	...	...	...	...	...	...
Torino PN **610** a.	...	...	...	...	...	...	...	...	...	...	...	...	...	...	...	...	...	...	...	...	...	...	...	...	...

		IC 560	IC 1560		ICN 1910				ICN 796							ICN 784	ICN 782				ICN 788	ICN 794	ICN 1956	ICN 1954	
	2			2		2	2	2		2	2	2	2	2				2	2	2					
	⚒	q	r		♦	†	⚒	⚒	♦		Ⓐ		⚒	†		♦	Z		⚒		♦	♦	♦	X	
Palermo C **641** d.	...	...	...	...	...	...	...	...	...	...	...	...	...	...	...	...	1257	...	...	...	...	...	...	1830	...
Siracusa **641** d.	...	...	...	...	...	...	...	...	...	...	...	...	...	...	...	1340	|	...	...	...	...	...	1910	|	...
Reggio di Calabria C **635** d.	...	1505	1505	...	...	...	...	...	...	...	1605	...	1705	1705	...	|	|	1805	1905	...	...	2135	|	|	...
Villa S. Giovanni **641** a.	...	1517	1517	...	...	...	...	...	...	...	1620	...	1720	1720	...	1815	1815	1820	1920	...	...	2152	2335	2335	...
Villa S. Giovanni d.	...	1520	1520	...	...	...	...	...	...	...	1622	...	1722	1722	...	1845	1845	1822	1922	...	...	2155	0005	0005	...
Gioia Tauro d.	...	1555	1554	...	...	...	...	...	...	...	1656	...	1757	1757	...	1920	1920	1858	1957	...	...	2243	|	|	...
Lamezia Terme Centrale a.	...	1633	1632	...	...	...	...	...	...	...	1735	...	1840	1840	...	2008	2008	1940	2040	...	...	0015	|	|	...
Lamezia Terme Centrale **634** d.	...	1636	1635	...	...	...	...	...	...	...	1742	...	1842	1842	...	2011	2011	1942	2042	...	...	0018	|	|	...
Cosenza **633** d.	...	|	|	...	...	...	1635	...	...	...	|	1825	|	1945	...	|	|	2043	|	...	...	|	|	|	...
Paola **633** d.	...	1716	1709	...	...	1710	1709	...	...	...	1820	1853	1920	...	...	2048	2048	...	2120	...	...	0058	0143	0143	...
Belvedere Marittimo d.	...	|	|	...	...	1739	1739	...	...	...	1847	1929	...	...	...	|	|	...	...	...	...	|	|	|	...
Maratea d.	...	1801	1802	...	...	1817	1815	...	...	...	1928	2016	...	...	...	2143	2143	...	...	...	...	|	|	|	...
Sapri d.	1730	1812	1813	...	...	1830	1825	1830	...	1925	1940	2031	...	...	...	2156	2156	...	...	...	...	0159	|	|	...
Ascea d.	1811	|	|	...	...	1908	...	1908	...	2008	...	2117	...	...	...	2228	2228	...	...	...	...	|	|	|	...
Agropoli-Castellabate d.	1834	|	1903	...	...	1932	...	1932	...	2035	...	2144	...	...	...	2254	2254	...	...	...	...	|	|	|	...
Battipaglia **638** d.	1901	1923	1923	...	...	1955	...	1955	...	2102	...	2207	...	...	...	2315	2315	...	...	...	...	|	|	|	...
Salerno d.	1918	1937	1937	...	2038	2017	...	2017	2050	2119	...	2226	...	...	...	2333	2333	...	...	...	...	0325	0411	0411	...
Pompei d.	1941	|	|	...	|	2048	...	2048	|	2141	...	|	...	...	...	|	|	...	...	...	...	|	|	|	...
Napoli Centrale a.	2020	2015	2015	...	2114	2120	...	2120	2127	2227	...	2305	...	...	...	|	|	...	...	...	...	0405	|	|	...
Napoli Centrale **626** d.	...	2031	2031	2048	2132	...	...	...	2142	...	...	...	...	...	...	|	|	...	...	0404	...	0420	|	|	...
Caserta **626** d.	...	|	|	|	|	...	...	...	|	...	...	...	...	...	...	|	|	...	...	|	0411	|	|	|	...
Aversa d.	...	2048	2048	2107	|	...	...	...	2201	...	...	...	...	...	...	|	|	...	...	0427	|	0440	|	|	...
Formia-Gaeta d.	...	2122	2122	2158	|	...	...	...	2239	...	...	...	...	...	...	|	|	...	...	0511	|	0518	0549s	0549s	...
Latina d.	...	2159	2159	2244	|	...	...	...	2319	...	...	...	...	...	...	|	|	...	...	0547	|	0554	0630s	0630s	...
Roma Termini **620** a.	...	2234	2234	2324	2338t	...	...	...	2400o	...	...	...	...	...	...	0240o	0240o	...	...	0627	0634	0631t	0713	0713	...
Bologna C **620** a.	...	...	...	...	|	...	...	...	|	...	...	...	...	...	...	|	|	...	...	...	...	|	...	...	...
Venezia SL **616** a.	...	...	...	...	|	...	...	...	|	...	...	...	...	...	...	|	|	...	...	...	...	|	...	...	...
Milano C **615** a.	...	...	...	...	0711g	...	...	...	|	...	...	...	...	...	...	1045	1045	...	...	...	...	1441g	...	...	...
Torino PN **610** a.	...	...	...	...	0920	...	...	...	0810	...	...	...	...	...	...	...	...	...	...	...	...	1645	...	...	...

FOR NOTES SEE PAGE 319

VILLA SAN GIOVANNI - MESSINA - SIRACUSA and PALERMO 641

km		2 ⚒	2 ⚒	ICN 1957 D	ICN 1955 ♦	2 ⚒	2 †	2 Ⓑ	ICN 1961 C	ICN 1959 ♦	2 ⚒	2 ⚒	2	2 ⚒	2 ⚒	ICN 785 ♦	ICN 781 A	2 ⚒	2 †	2 ⚒	2	2	IC 721 K	IC 723 ♦	2 ⚒	2 ⚒	2 Ⓐ
0	**Villa S. Giovanni 640** ▲ d.	...	...	0445	0445	...	...	...	0540	0540	...	...	...	...	...	1105	1105	...	...	...	...	...	1425	1425	...	...	...
9	**Messina** Centrale ▲ a.	...	...	0610	0610	...	...	...	0710	0710	...	...	...	...	...	1245	1245	...	...	...	...	...	1530	1530	...	...	...
9	**Messina** Centrale d.	0500	0525	0635	0644	0635	0655	0708	0735	0745	0800	0938	1125	1218	1230	1310s	1320	1320	1405	1410	1423	1546	1555	1605	1620	1635	1715
	Taormina-Giardini d.	|	0603	|	0731	0756	0759	|	|	0827	0901	1016	|	1320	|	1349s	|	1412	1508	1503	|	|	1636	|	1711	1753	|
	Giarre-Riposto **644** d.	|	0622	|	0748	0821	0819	|	|	0842	0918	1038	|	1341	|	1404s	|	1430	1534	1529	|	|	1652	|	1728	1810	|
	Catania Centrale a.	|	0647	|	0818	0856	0856	|	|	0908	0945	1108	|	1406	|	1434s	|	1454	1602	1558	|	|	1719	|	1757	1835	|
	Catania Centrale d.	|	0650	|	0822	...	...	|	|	0911	...	...	|	1410	|	1438s	|	...	...	...	|	|	1722	|	1800	...	|
	Augusta d.	|	0753	|	0909	...	...	|	|	1000	...	...	|	1504	|	1524s	|	...	...	...	|	|	1810	|	1857	...	|
	Siracusa 648 a.	|	0815	|	0935	...	...	|	|	1025	...	...	|	1532	|	1548	|	...	...	...	|	|	1829	|	1918	...	|
45	Milazzo d.	0521	...	0657s	...	...	...	0727	0757s	...	...	...	1157	...	1301	...	1342s	...	...	...	1454	1618	...	1627	...	...	1738
174	Cefalù d.	0701	...	0847s	...	...	...	0909	0944s	...	...	...	1402	...	1505	...	1525s	...	...	...	1709	1826	...	1801	...	...	1905
204	Termini Imerese **645/7** d.	0730	...	0932s	...	...	...	0927	1007s	...	...	...	1433	...	1534	...	1606s	...	...	...	1736	1900	...	1826	...	...	1936
241	**Palermo** C **645/7** a.	0800	...	1002	...	...	...	0950	1035	...	...	...	1500	...	1601	...	1637	...	...	...	1800	1930	...	1900	...	...	2000

	2 ⚒	2 †	2 ⚒	2 ⚒	2 †	2	2 ⚒	IC 729 L	IC 727 ♦	2 ⚒
Villa S. Giovanni 640 ▲ d.	...	...	...	...	...	...	...	1820	1820	...
Messina Centrale ▲ a.	...	...	...	...	...	...	...	1930	1930	...
Messina Centrale d.	1725	1720	1750	1840	1840	1910	1920	1955	2005	2145
Taormina-Giardini d.	|	1801	1852	1932	1941	|	2023	|	2046	2228
Giarre-Riposto **644** d.	|	1817	1907	1950	2001	|	2041	|	2102	2241
Catania Centrale a.	|	1839	1932	2011	2034	|	2105	|	2126	2307
Catania Centrale d.	|	1844	...	2013	...	|	...	|	2129	...
Augusta d.	|	1934	...	2059	...	|	...	|	2222	...
Siracusa 648 a.	|	1958	...	2124	...	|	...	|	2245	...
Milazzo d.	1758	...	...	...	...	1932	...	2017	...	...
Cefalù d.	2005	...	...	...	...	2116	...	2206	...	...
Termini Imerese **645/7** d.	2034	...	...	...	...	2138	...	2231	...	...
Palermo C **645/7** a.	2100	...	...	...	...	2205	...	2300	...	...

	2 ⚒	2 ⚒	2	2 ⚒	2 ⚒	IC 722 N	IC 728 ♦	2 †	2	2	2	IC 730 P
Palermo C **645/7** d.	...	...	...	0608	...	...	0700	...	0807	...	0903	1005
Termini Imerese **645/7** d.	...	...	...	0633	...	...	0732	...	0831	...	0931	1031
Cefalù d.	...	...	...	0656	...	...	0758	...	0852	...	1007	1055
Milazzo d.	...	...	...	0840	...	...	0937	...	1036	...	1203	1229
Siracusa 648 d.	...	0513	...	|	0632	0733	|	...	|	0840	|	|
Augusta d.	...	0532	...	|	0700	0754	|	...	|	0904	|	|
Catania Centrale a.	...	0619	...	|	0747	0840	|	...	|	0957	|	|
Catania Centrale d.	0510	0622	0636	|	0749	0843	|	0930	|	1000	|	|
Giarre-Riposto **644** d.	0533	0642	0657	|	0810	0906	|	0952	|	1026	|	|
Taormina-Giardini d.	0549	0701	0716	|	0827	0922	|	1011	|	1044	|	|
Messina Centrale a.	0710	0752	0821	0903	0920	0956	1000	1058	1104	1135	1230	1255
Messina Centrale ▲ d.	...	...	...	...	...	1015	1015	...	...	...	...	1315
Villa S. Giovanni 640 ▲ a.	...	...	...	...	...	1125	1125	...	...	...	...	1425

km		IC 724 ♦	2 ⚒	2 ⚒	2 ⚒	2 †	2 ⚒	ICN 782 Z	ICN 784 ♦	2 ⚒	2 ⚒	2 ⚒	2 ⚒	2	2 Ⓐ	2 ⚒	2 †	2 ⚒	2	2 Ⓐ	2 ⚒	ICN 1956 ♦	ICN 1954 X	2 ⚒	2	ICN 1960 ♦	ICN 1958 W
	Palermo C **645/7** d.	...	...	1108	...	...	...	1257	...	1308	1405	...	...	1508	1608	...	...	...	1708	1805	...	...	1830	...	2008	...	2110
	Termini Imerese **645/7** d.	...	...	1136	...	...	...	1324u	...	1334	1433	...	...	1535	1632	...	...	...	1733	1832	...	...	1902u	...	2032	...	2139u
	Cefalù d.	...	...	1206	...	...	...	1352u	...	1401	1506	...	...	1603	1652	...	...	...	1804	1902	...	...	1926u	...	2055	...	2207u
	Milazzo d.	...	...	1410	...	...	...	1555u	...	1612	1657	...	...	1802	1829	...	...	...	2013	2036	...	...	2125u	...	2236	...	2347u
0	**Siracusa 648** d.	1025	...	|	...	...	...	|	1340	|	|	1426	...	|	|	...	...	1716	|	|	...	1910	|	...	|	2145	|
31	Augusta d.	1046	...	|	...	...	...	|	1400	|	|	1447	...	|	|	...	...	1737	|	|	...	1935	|	...	|	2206	|
87	**Catania** Centrale a.	1134	...	|	...	...	...	|	1450	|	|	1544	...	|	|	...	...	1833	|	|	...	2023	|	...	|	2251	|
87	**Catania** Centrale d.	1137	1224	|	1356	1400	1423	|	1456	|	|	1546	1620	|	|	1744	1810	1836	|	|	1938	2026	|	2046	|	2254	|
117	Giarre-Riposto **644** d.	1203	1254	|	1420	1428	1451	|	1522	|	|	1606	1650	|	|	1812	1836	1901	|	|	2005	2051	|	2114	|	2318	|
135	Taormina-Giardini d.	1220	1319	|	1449	1454	1519	|	1539	|	|	1621	1721	|	|	1835	1904	1919	|	|	2032	2107	|	2135	|	2333	|
182	**Messina** Centrale a.	1300	1435	1445	1535	1556	1612	1620	1625	1644	1720	1738	1803	1830	1852	1945	2000	2008	2051	2101	2131	2150	2155	2230	2300	0015	0020
182	**Messina** Centrale ▲ d.	1315	...	...	...	...	...	1640	1640	...	...	...	...	...	...	...	...	...	...	...	...	2210	2210	...	...	0035	0035
191	**Villa S. Giovanni 640** ▲ a.	1425	...	...	...	...	...	1815	1815	...	...	...	...	...	...	...	...	...	...	...	...	2335	2335	...	...	0200	0200

♦ – **NOTES FOR TABLES 640/641**

501 – ⚒: [12] Sestri Levante - Napoli.
510 – [12] Salerno - Torino.
522 – Ⓑ (not days before holidays): [12] Napoli - Sestri Levante.
700 – [12] Taranto - Roma.
701 – [2] Roma - Taranto.
702 – [2] Taranto - Roma.
707 – [12] Roma - Taranto.
723 – [12] Roma - Palermo; [12] Roma - Messina (**721**) - Siracusa.
724 – [12] Siracusa - Roma; [12] Palermo (**730**) - Messina - Roma.
727 – [12] Roma - Siracusa; [12] Roma - Messina (**729**) - Palermo.
728 – [12] Palermo - Roma; [12] Siracusa (**722**) - Messina - Roma.
784 – 🛏 1,2 cl. (T2) and ▬ 2 cl. (4 berth) Siracusa - Genova - Milano; 🛏 1,2 cl. (T2) and ▬ 2 cl. (4 berth) Palermo (**782**) - Messina - Milano.
785 – 🛏 1,2 cl. (T2) and ▬ 2 cl. (4 berth) Milano - Genova - Siracusa; 🛏 1,2 cl. (T2) and ▬ 2 cl. (4 berth) Milano - Messina (**781**) - Palermo.
788 – ⑦ (also Dec. 8; not Dec. 7): ▬ 2 cl. (4 berth) and [2] Lecce - Roma.
789 – ⑤: ▬ 2 cl. (4 berth) and [2] Roma - Lecce.
794 – 🛏 1,2 cl., ▬ 2 cl. (4 berth) and [2] Reggio di Calabria - Milano - Torino.
795 – 🛏 1,2 cl., ▬ 2 cl. (4 berth) and [2] Torino - Milano - Reggio di Calabria.
796 – ▬ 2 cl. (4 berth) and [2] Salerno - Napoli - Torino.
799 – ▬ 2 cl. (4 berth) and [2] Torino - Napoli - Salerno.
1571 – †: [12] Livorno - Napoli.
1572 – ⑥ (also days before holidays): [12] Napoli - Livorno.
1588 – ⑦ from Sept. 21 (also Dec. 8; not Dec. 7): [12] Reggio di Calabria - Milano.
1589 – ⑥ from Sept. 20: [12] Milano - Reggio di Calabria.
1590 – ⑦ until Sept. 14: [12] Reggio di Calabria - Milano.
1591 – ⑥ until Sept. 13: [12] Milano - Reggio di Calabria.
1910 – ▬ 2 cl. (4 berth) and [2] Salerno - Napoli - Milano - Torino.
1911 – ▬ 2 cl. (4 berth) and [2] Torino - Milano - Napoli - Salerno.

1955 – 🛏 1,2 cl. and ▬ 2 cl. (4 berth) Roma - Siracusa; 🛏 1,2 cl. and ▬ 2 cl. (4 berth) Roma - Messina (**1957**) - Palermo.
1956 – 🛏 1,2 cl. and ▬ 2 cl. (4 berth) Siracusa - Roma; 🛏 1,2 cl. and ▬ 2 cl. (4 berth) Palermo (**1954**) - Messina - Roma.
1959 – 🛏 1,2 cl. and ▬ 2 cl. (4 berth) Roma - Siracusa; 🛏 1,2 cl. and ▬ 2 cl. (4 berth) Roma - Messina (**1961**) - Palermo.
1960 – 🛏 1,2 cl. and ▬ 2 cl. (4 berth) Siracusa - Roma; 🛏 1,2 cl. and ▬ 2 cl. (4 berth) Palermo (**1958**) - Messina - Roma.

A – 🛏 1,2 cl. (T2) and ▬ 2 cl. (4 berth) Milano (**785**) - Genova - Messina - Palermo.
C – 🛏 1,2 cl. and ▬ 2 cl. (4 berth) Roma (**1959**) - Messina - Palermo.
D – 🛏 1,2 cl. and ▬ 2 cl. (4 berth) Roma (**1955**) - Messina - Palermo.
K – [12] Roma (**723**) - Messina - Siracusa.
L – [12] Roma (**727**) - Messina - Palermo.
N – [12] Siracusa - Messina (**728**) - Roma.
P – [12] Palermo - Messina (**724**) - Roma.
W – 🛏 1,2 cl. and ▬ 2 cl. (4 berth) Palermo - Messina (**1960**) - Roma.
X – 🛏 1,2 cl. and ▬ 2 cl. (4 berth) Palermo - Messina (**1956**) - Roma.
Z – 🛏 1,2 cl. (T2) and ▬ 2 cl. (4 berth) Palermo - Messina (**784**) - Genova - Milano.

c – © only.
g – Milano **Porta Garibaldi**.
j – Venezia **Mestre**.
o – Roma **Ostiense**.
p – June 16 - Sept. 13.
q – Sept. 15 - Dec. 13.
r – June 15 - Sept. 14.
s – Stops to set down only.
t – Roma **Tiburtina**.
u – Stops to pick up only.
v – Not days before holidays.
y – Not May 1.

▲ – Through trains are conveyed by ⛴ Villa S. Giovanni - Messina and v.v. See **Table 2695** for other available sailings.

Ferrovia Circumetnea

CATANIA - RANDAZZO - RIPOSTO 644

Winter service valid from September 16, 2013. No service on †

km		⚒	⚒	⚒	⚒	⚒	⚒	⚒	⚒	⚒	⚒	⚒	⚒	⚒	⚒
0	**Catania** ▲ d.	...	0543	0640	0745	...	0931	1108	1211	1330	1505	1619	1821	1919	2005
20	Paternò d.	...	0616	0721	0820	...	1007	1145	1253	1407	1541	1655	1857	1956	2038
36	Adrano N. d.	...	0651	0757	0854	...	1039	1217	1328	1439	1617	1728	1928	2027	...
52	Bronte d.	...	0718	0823	0925	...	1105	1243	1405	1510	1643	1754	1954	...	...
71	Randazzo d.	0632	0749	0854	0956	1110	1136	1315	1435	1541	1715	1825	2025	...	...
109	Giarre **640** a.	0745	0850	...	...	1210	...	1416	...	...	1815	...	...	...	...
111	**Riposto** a.	0749	0854	...	...	1214	...	1420	...	...	1819	...	...	...	...

	⚒	⚒	⚒	⚒	⚒	⚒	⚒	⚒	⚒	⚒	⚒	⚒	⚒	⚒
Riposto d.	...	...	...	*0625*	*0826*	0950	...	...	1231	...	1350	1455	...	...
Giarre **640** d.	...	...	...	*0629*	*0830*	0955	...	...	1236	...	1355	1500	...	...
Randazzo d.	0506	0609	0645	0817	0959	1053	1239	1331	1338	1439	1501	1600	1722	1830
Bronte d.	0537	0641	0721	0849	1029	...	1311	1406	...	1509	...	...	1756	1901
Adrano N. d.	0603	0710	0758	0916	1056	...	1335	1439	...	1534	...	...	1824	1928
Paternò d.	0636	0741	0838	0949	1128	...	1407	1511	...	1603	...	...	1856	1957
Catania ▲ a.	0710	0815	0912	1022	1202	...	1441	1545	...	1635	...	...	1933	2034

▲ – Catania Borgo station. The Metropolitana di Catania operates a metro service Borgo - Porto and v.v. (3.8 km) via Catania Centrale station. Weekdays only, every 15 minutes 0700 – 2045.

645 PALERMO and AGRIGENTO - CATANIA
2nd class only except where shown

km			⚒	⚒	⚒	Ⓐ	⚒p			⚒p	⚒		Ⓐp	⚒	q	†	⚒		⚒	z	t	†	⚒	⚒	
0	**Palermo** Centrale **647**	d.	...	...	...	0638	...	...	...	...	...	...	...	...	...	...	...	...	...	...	...	...	...	...	...
37	Termini Imerese **647**	d.	...	...	...	0705	...	...	...	...	...	...	...	...	...	...	...	...	...	...	...	...	...	...	...
70	Roccapalumba-Alia **647**	d.	...	0617	0651	|	0849	...	...	1249	...	...	1349	...	1449	...	1549	...	1649	...	1849	...	...	1949	...
	Agrigento Centrale **647**	d.	...	|	|	|	|	...	0935	|	1252	...	|	1355	|	...	|	...	|	...	|	1831	1835	|	...
	Aragona-Caldare **647**	d.	...	|	|	|	|	...	1000	|	1311	...	|	1414	|	...	|	...	|	...	|	1849	1901	|	...
	Canicattì **648**	d.	...	|	|	|	|	...	1044	|	1348	...	|	1451	|	...	|	...	|	...	|	1926	1936	|	...
	Caltanissetta Xirbi **648**	a.	...	0707	0742	0821	0947	...	|	1347	|	...	1449	|	1547	...	1641	...	1750	...	1946	|	|	2042	...
	Caltanissetta Centrale **648**	d.	0540	|	0758	|	1003	...	1117	1403	1414	...	1504	1519	1603	1620	1656	...	|	1743	2003	1955	2005	2058	...
127	Caltanissetta Xirbi **648**	d.	0549	0708	...	0822	...	...	1126	...	...	...	...	...	...	1628	...	...	1751	1751	...	...	...	...	...
154	Enna	d.	0620	0734	...	0842	...	...	1159	...	...	...	...	...	...	1702	...	...	1822	1822	...	...	...	...	...
243	**Catania** Centrale ♣	a.	0736	0850	...	0950	...	...	1322	...	...	...	...	...	...	1818	...	...	1950	1950	...	...	...	...	...

km			⚒	⚒	⚒p	⚒	⚒	⚒p	†	⚒	Ⓐp	†q	⚒	⚒	⚒				Ⓐ	t	⚒	⚒	⚒	⚒	†
	Catania Centrale ♣	d.	...	...	...	...	...	...	0933	0933	...	...	...	...	...	...	1416	...	1532	...	...	...	1630	1838	1838
	Enna	d.	...	...	...	...	...	...	1057	1058	...	...	...	...	...	...	1539	...	1642	...	...	...	1756	2001	2009
0	Caltanissetta Xirbi **648**	a.	...	...	...	...	...	...	1127	1127	...	...	...	...	...	...	1607	...	1701	...	...	...	1823	2028	2035
6	Caltanissetta Centrale **648**	d.	0442	0500	0551	0605	0638	0945	1139	1141	1153	1245	1245	1415	1445	...	1615	1625	|	1658	1749	1751	1834	2039	2050
	Caltanissetta Xirbi **648**	d.	0457	0515	0606	|	|	1000	|	...	1208	1300	1300	1430	1500	...	...	|	1702	1714	|	1806	...	...	...
35	Canicattì **648**	d.	|	|	|	0641	0717	|	1216	...	|	|	|	|	|	...	...	1703	|	|	1827	|	...	...	...
65	Aragona-Caldare **647**	d.	|	|	|	0713	0750	|	1248	...	|	|	|	|	|	...	...	1741	|	|	1902	|	...	...	...
78	**Agrigento** Centrale **647**	a.	|	|	|	0732	0810	|	1309	...	|	|	|	|	|	...	...	1802	|	|	1921	|	...	...	...
	Roccapalumba-Alia **647**	d.	0551	0612	0716	...	...	1100	...	...	1311	1401	1411	1540	1611	...	...	...	|	1811	...	1911	...	...	...
	Termini Imerese **647**	d.	...	...	...	...	...	...	...	...	...	...	...	...	...	...	...	...	1816	...	...	...	...	...	...
	Palermo Centrale **647**	a.	...	...	...	...	...	...	...	...	...	...	...	...	...	...	...	...	1837	...	...	...	...	...	...

p – Until June 7.
q – Not Apr. 20.
t – Not June 8.
z – † (daily from June 8; also Apr. 17 - 22).

♣ – 🚌 service **CATANIA - GELA and v.v.**: 137 km, journey ± 3 hours. From **Catania**: 1435⚒, 1920⚒. From **Gela**: 0547⚒, 1240⚒.

646 PALERMO - TRAPANI
2nd class only

km			⚒	⚒	⚒		⚒	†	⚒ 🚌	†	† 🚌	⚒	⚒ 🚌		⚒	⚒	🚌	†	⚒		⚒			🚌	⚒
0	**Palermo** Centrale ▲	d.	...	...	...	...	0637	0739	...	1039	...	1039	...	...	...	...	...	1439	1439	...	...	1809	...	...	1939
32	Piraineto ▲	d.	...	...	...	...	0743	0836	...	1136	...	1139	...	...	...	...	...	1538	1539	...	...	1901	1910	...	2035
73	Castellammare del Golfo	d.	...	...	...	...	0831	0915	...	1215	...	1226	...	...	...	...	...	1621	1620	...	...	...	1955	...	2115
79	Alcamo Diramazione	d.	...	...	...	...	0839	0922	1116	1222	1230	1233	1245	...	...	1534	1626	1630	1628	...	...	...	2005	2010	2122
121	Castelvetrano	d.	0619	0640	0722	0825	0920	0958	|	1259	|	1312	|	...	1400	1613	|	1713	1710	...	1815	...	2041	|	2159
144	Mazara del Vallo	d.	0639	0701	0742	0847	0939	1018	|	...	|	1336	|	...	1420	1631	|	1732	1734	...	1836	...	2106	|	...
165	Marsala	d.	0658	0724	0802	0903	0956	1035	|	...	|	1355	|	...	1441	1649	|	1752	1755	...	1854	...	2123	|	...
196	**Trapani**	a.	0739	0755	0837	0932	1021	1104	1230	...	1343	1425	1352	...	1516	1718	1728	1819	1825	...	1929	...	2154	2112	...

km			⚒	⚒		🚌	⚒	⚒ 🚌	†	† 🚌	⚒		⚒	⚒	⚒	🚌	⚒		🚌		Ⓐ		⚒		
0	**Trapani**	d.	...	0430	0543	0628	0653	0836	0836	0923	0938	...	1200	1240	1342	1403	1435	1601	1622	...	1728	1830	1945	2025	...
	Marsala	d.	...	|	0612	|	0728	|	0910	|	1016	...	1234	1314	1415	|	1507	1627	|	...	1759	1857	2013	2059	...
	Mazara del Vallo	d.	...	|	0636	|	0747	|	0929	|	1031	...	1253	1333	1442	|	1527	1646	|	...	1817	1913	2033	2122	...
	Castelvetrano	d.	0502	|	0701	|	0807	|	0954	|	1052	...	1316	1357	1508	|	1551	1709	|	...	1844	1932	2056	2148	...
47	Alcamo Diramazione	d.	0540	0532	0739	0730k	...	0947	1037	1025k	1134	...	...	1433	...	1448	...	1750	1735k	...	...	2008	...	...	...
53	Castellammare del Golfo	d.	0547	...	0746	...	...	...	1045	...	1141	...	...	...	...	...	...	1757	...	...	...	2018	...	...	...
94	Piraineto ▲	d.	0628	...	0829	...	...	...	1128	...	1227	...	...	...	...	...	...	1840	...	1905	...	2105	...	...	...
126	**Palermo** Centrale ▲	a.	0727	...	0927	...	...	...	1227	...	1327	...	...	...	...	...	...	...	...	1957	...	2200	...	...	...

k – Connects into train in previous column.

▲ – Additional services operate Palermo Centrale - Piraineto and v.v.

647 PALERMO - AGRIGENTO
2nd class only

km			⚒	⚒	h	⚒	Ⓐp			⚒				
0	**Palermo** Centrale **645**	d.	0548	0749	0849	1149	1249	1349	1449	1549	1649	1749	1847	2022
37	Termini Imerese **645**	d.	0617	0814	0914	1214	1314	1415	1515	1614	1714	1814	1915	2048
70	Roccapalumba-Alia **645**	d.	0645	0844	0945	1245	1345	1445	1545	1642	1743	1845	1945	2118
125	Aragona-Caldare **645**	d.	0734	0934	1034	1334	1434	1534	1640	1732	1835j	1935	2046	2209
139	**Agrigento** C **645**	a.	0753	0952	1052	1352	1452	1552	1658	1752	1852j	1952	2104	2230

		⚒	⚒			Ⓐp	h	⚒	⚒	†			
Agrigento C **645**	d.	0510	0614	0814	1014	1214	1314	1414	1514	1620	1710	1814	2014
Aragona-Caldare **645**	d.	0529	0632	0832	1031	1232	1331	1431	1531	1637	1729	1831	2033
Roccapalumba-Alia **645**	d.	0622	0722	0921	1120	1321	1420	1520	1623	1727	1822	1922	2122
Termini Imerese **645**	d.	0658	0753	0953	1153t	1353	1453	1553	1653	1758	1854	1953	2151
Palermo C **645**	a.	0726	0824	1016	1216t	1416	1516	1616	1716	1822	1920	2016	2216

h – Not Apr. 20.
j – 10 – 12 minutes later on †.
p – Until June 7.
t – 5 – 7 minutes later on †.

648 SIRACUSA - CALTANISSETTA
2nd class only

km			⚒	⚒	⚒	⚒	⚒	⚒	⚒	⚒	⚒	⚒	⚒
0	**Siracusa 640**	d.	🚌	...	1010	...	...	1358	1425	...	1735	...	1922
62	Pozzallo	d.	...	...	1111	...	...	1501	1536	...	1841	...	2026
92	Modica	d.	...	0544	1153	...	1352	...	1616	...	1921	1927	2110
112	Ragusa	d.	...	0611	1219	...	1418	...	...	...	...	1953	...
153	Vittoria	d.	...	0650	1301	...	1459	...	...	...	...	2032	...
183	Gela **645**	d.	0620	...	1328	1420	1531	...	...	1729	...	2101	...
218	Licata	d.	0701	...	...	1455	1616	...	...	1805	...	...	...
264	Canicattì **645**	d.	0740	...	...	1544	1708	...	...	1858	...	...	...
293	**Caltanissetta** C **645**	d.	0810	...	...	1617	1740	...	...	1931	...	...	...

		⚒	⚒	⚒	⚒	⚒	⚒	⚒	⚒	⚒	⚒	
Caltanissetta C **645**	d.	...	...	...	...	0543	...	1128	...	1419	...	...
Canicattì **645**	d.	...	...	...	...	0614	...	1202	...	1452	...	...
Licata	d.	...	...	...	...	0659	...	1249	...	1553	...	...
Gela **645**	d.	...	...	...	...	0732	...	1324	1424	1625	1742	...
Vittoria	d.	...	...	0700	...	0805	...	...	1500	...	1813	...
Ragusa	d.	...	...	0750	...	0854	...	...	1552	...	1904	...
Modica	d.	0541	0621	0810	0821	0914	...	...	1613	...	1925	...
Pozzallo	d.	0614	0654	...	0854	...	1516	...	...	...	2000	...
Siracusa 640	a.	0715	0755	...	0955	...	1620	...	...	...	2110	...

MALTA

Frequent bus services throughout Malta and Gozo are operated by Malta Public Transport Services Ltd. Website: www.publictransport.com.mt. Travellers will also find useful information on the unofficial website www.maltabybus.com.

649 PRINCIPAL BUS SERVICES

Routes from Valletta: **1** L'Isla (Senglea), **2** Birgu (Vittoriosa), **3** Birgu, Kalkara, Rinella, **12/13** Sliema, San Giljan (St Julian's), **12** Sliema, St Pauls's Bay, Bugibba, Qawra, **31/45** Mosta, Bugibba, Qawra, **31/35/36** Naxxar, **37** Armier Bay (summer), **41/42** Mosta, Mellieha, Ghadira, Cirkewwa (for Gozo ferry), **44** Ghajn Tuffieha (Golden Bay), **51/52/53** Rabat / Mdina, **51** Imtarfa, **52** Dingli, **61** Zebbug, **62** Siggiewi, **71** Zurrieq (also Blue Grotto and Ghar Lapsi in summer), **72** Qrendi, **81/85/X86** Marsaxlokk, **82** Birzebbuga, **91/92/93** Marsaskala, **94** Xghajra, **X4/X5/X7** Airport.

Routes from Airport: **X1** Mellieha, Cirkewwa (for Gozo ferry), **X2** San Giljan (St Julian's), Sliema, **X3** Rabat / Mdina, Bugibba, **X4/X5/X7** Valletta, **X4** Birzebbuga, **X5** Marsaskala, **X7** Birgu.

Gozo: routes from Rabat (Victoria): **301** Mgarr (for ferry to Cirkewwa), **302** Ramla, **305** Sannat, **306** Xlendi, **307** Xaghra, **308** Ta' Pinu, Ghasri, **309** Zebbug, **310** Marsalforn, **311** Dwejra.

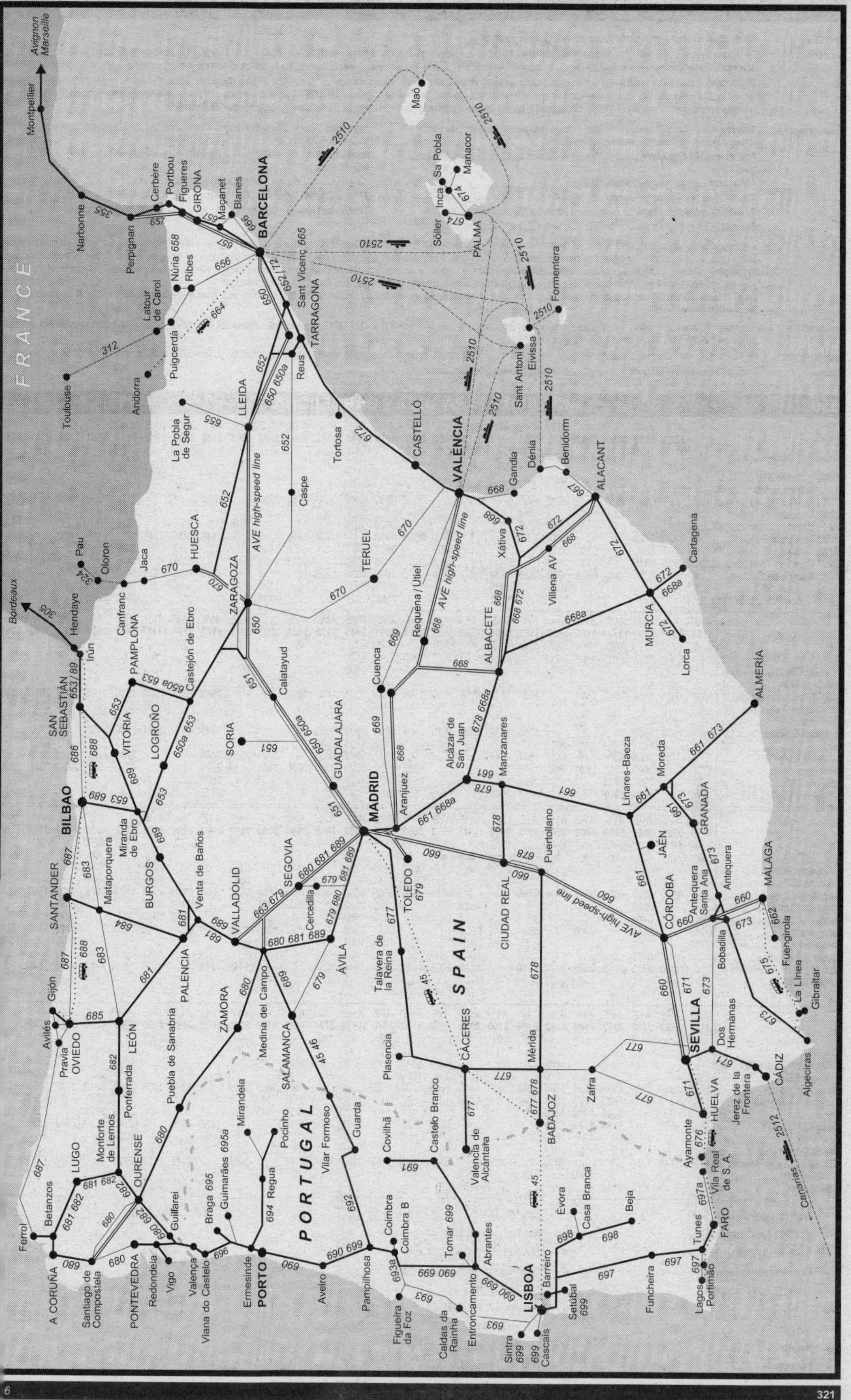
FRANCE
SPAIN
PORTUGAL
Bordeaux
Avignon Marseille
Montpellier
Narbonne
Perpignan
Cerbère
Portbou
Figueres
GIRONA
Maçanet
Blanes
BARCELONA
Toulouse
Latour de Carol
Núria 658
Ribes
Puigcerdà
Andorra
La Pobla de Segur
LLEIDA
Sant Vicenç 665
TARRAGONA
Reus
Tortosa
Caspe
CASTELLÓ
VALÈNCIA
Gandia
Dénia
Benidorm
ALACANT
Xàtiva
Villena AV
Cartagena
MURCIA
Lorca
ALMERÍA
Maó
Sa Pobla
Inca
Manacor
Sóller
PALMA
Formentera
Eivissa
Sant Antoni
Pau
Oloron
Hendaye
Irún
Canfranc
Jaca
HUESCA
ZARAGOZA
AVE high-speed line
TERUEL
Requena / Utiel
ALBACETE
Cuenca
Calatayud
SORIA
PAMPLONA
Castejón de Ebro
SAN SEBASTIÁN
VITORIA
LOGROÑO
BILBAO
Miranda de Ebro
BURGOS
SANTANDER
Mataporquera
Venta de Baños
VALLADOLID
PALENCIA
GUADALAJARA
MADRID
Aranjuez
Alcázar de San Juan
Manzanares
Puertollano
CIUDAD REAL
TOLEDO
Linares-Baeza
Moreda
GRANADA
JAÉN
CÓRDOBA
Antequera Santa Ana
Antequera
Bobadilla
MÁLAGA
Fuengirola
La Línea
Gibraltar
Algeciras
SEVILLA
Dos Hermanas
Jerez de la Frontera
CÁDIZ
HUELVA
Zafra
Mérida
BADAJOZ
CÁCERES
Plasencia
Talavera de la Reina
SEGOVIA
Cercedilla
ÁVILA
Medina del Campo
SALAMANCA
ZAMORA
Puebla de Sanabria
LEÓN
Gijón
Avilés
Pravia
OVIEDO
Ponferrada
Monforte de Lemos
LUGO
OURENSE
Betanzos
Ferrol
A CORUÑA
Santiago de Compostela
PONTEVEDRA
Redondela
Vigo
Guillarei
Valença
Viana do Castelo
Braga 695
Guimarães 695a
Mirandela
Regua
Pocinho
Ermesinde
PORTO
Aveiro
Pampilhosa
Coimbra
Coimbra B
Figueira da Foz
Vilar Formoso
Guarda
Covilhã
Castelo Branco
Valencia de Alcántara
Tomar 699
Abrantes
Entroncamento
Caldas da Rainha
LISBOA
Sintra 699
Cascais 699
Barreiro
Setúbal 699
Évora
Casa Branca
Beja
Funcheira
Tunes
Lagos
Portimão
FARO
Vila Real de S. A
Ayamonte
Canarias

SPAIN

Operator: **Renfe Operadora** – unless otherwise indicated. www.renfe.es

Services: On long-distance trains first class is known as *Preferente* and second class as *Turista*; a 'super-first class' – *Club* – is additionally available on *AVE* trains between Madrid and Barcelona. Unless otherwise indicated (by '2' in the train column or [2] in the notes), all trains convey both first- and second-class seating accommodation.

🍸 indicates a buffet car (*cafetería*) or a mobile trolley service. ✕ indicates a full restaurant car service or the availability of hot meals served from the buffet car. Meals are served free of extra charge, on Mondays to Fridays, to holders of *Club* and *Preferente* tickets on all *AVE* trains and to holders of *Preferente* tickets on *Euromed* trains. Note that catering services may not be available throughout a train's journey, particularly in the case of trains with multiple origins/destinations.

Train categories:

Altaria (*Alta*): Talgo trains which can change gauge and run on the high-speed lines as well as the broad-gauge system.
Alta Velocidad Española (*AVE*): High-speed trains running on the standard-gauge lines.
Alvia: High-speed gauge-changing trains.
Arco: Quality day express trains.
Avant (*Av*): Medium-distance high-speed trains on the standard-gauge lines.
Estrella (*Estr*): Night trains, conveying 🛏, ▬, [1] and [2] as indicated.
Euromed (*Em*): *Alvia*-like trains running on the broad-gauge Barcelona - València - Alacant route.
Intercity (*IC*): *Alvia*-like trains offering *Turista* class only; also long-distance *MD*-like trains.
Talgo: Quality express trains using light, articulated stock.
Train à Grande Vitesse (*TGV*): French High-speed trains.
Trenhotel (*Hotel*): Quality night express trains (see Services, above).

▬ indicates coaches equipped with couchettes: for occupancy of these a standard supplement is payable in addition to the normal *Turista* fare. 🛏 indicates sleeping-cars with single, double, and 3- or 4-berth compartments. The *Turista* fare is payable plus a sleeping-car supplement corresponding to the type and standard of accommodation. ***Trenhotel*** services additionally convey *Gran Clase* accommodation: *de luxe* single- and double-occupancy compartments with *en suite* shower and toilet. *Preferente* fare is payable for travel in *Gran Clase* plus a sleeping-car supplement corresponding to the type and standard of accommodation.
Local (*Media Distancia*) and suburban (*Cercanías*) trains are shown without an indication of category except for some fast ***Tren Regional Diesel*** (*TRD*), ***R-598*** services and ***Media Distancia*** (*MD*).

Reservations: Reservations are compulsory for all journeys by services for which a train category (e.g. *D*, *TRD*) is shown in the timing column. Advance purchase of tickets is also available for travel by services for which a train number is shown.

Supplements: Higher fares, incorporating a supplement, are payable for travel by *Alaris, Altaria, Alvia, Arco, AVE, Euromed, InterCity, Talgo, TGV* and *Trenhotel* services.

Timings: Timings have been compiled from the latest information supplied by operators.

650 MADRID - ZARAGOZA - BARCELONA — High-speed services

km		*AVE*	*AVE*	*AVE*	*Av*	*AVE*	*AVE*	*AVE*	*AVE*	*AVE*	*Av*	*AVE*	*AVE*	*AVE*	*AVE*	*AVE*	*Av*	*AVE*	*AVE*	*AVE*	*AVE*	*AVE*	*AVE*	*Av*	*AVE*
		3263	**3053**	**3061**	**8087**	**3473**	**3063**	**3071**	**3271**	**3483**	**8477**	**3073**	**3081**	**3283**	**3083**	**3093**	**8507**	**3103**	**3993**	**3943**	**3113**	**3123**	**3333**	**8167**	**3143**
		①–⑤	①–⑤	①–④		⑥⑦	①–⑤	①–⑤	①–④	⑥⑦	①–⑤		①–⑤	①–④			⑥⑦							Ⓑ	Ⓑ
							f	**g**	**h**	**o**	**n**		**f**	**h**			**o**							**s**	
	Sevilla **660** d.	...	...	...	...	...	...	...	...	...	...	...	...	...	...	...	...	...	...	0850	...	...	...	...	...
	Málaga **660** d.	...	...	...	...	...	...	...	...	...	...	...	...	...	...	...	...	...	0840	|	...	...	...	...	...
0	**Madrid** Puerta de Atocha d.	...	0550	0610	...	0620	0630	0700	0720	...	...	0730	0800	0820	0830	0930	...	1030	|	|	1130	1230	1310	...	1430
64	Guadalajara - Yebes d.	...	|	|	...	|	|	|	|	...	...	|	|	|	|	|	...	|	|	|	|	|	1334	...	|
221	Calatayud d.	...	|	|	...	0716	0726	|	|	...	0735	0826	|	|	|	|	1035	|	|	|	1226	|	|	...	1526
307	**Zaragoza** Delicias d.	0620	0706	|	...	0742	0752	|	|	0800	0805	0852	|	0936	0946	1046	1105	1146	1236	1236	1252	1346	1432	...	1552
447	Lleida d.	0705	0750	|	0800	0826	|	|	|	0855	...	0937	|	|	|	1131	...	|	1322	1322	1337	1431	|	1600	|
526	Camp de Tarragona d.	0735	0819	|	0832	0854	|	|	|	0923	...	1005	|	|	1045	1159	...		1351	1351	1405	|	1531	1632	|
621	**Barcelona** Sants a.	0810	0855	0840	0908	0929	0920	0930	0950	0958	...	1040	1030	1105	1115	1234	...	1315	1425	1425	1440	1530	1606	1708	1721
	Girona **657** a.	...	...	...	...	1026	...	1026	...	...	...	1127¦	...	...	...	1321	...	...	...	...	1527	1619v	...	...	...
	Figueres Vilafant **657** a.	...	...	...	...	1040	...	1040	...	...	...	1143¦	...	...	...	1338	...	...	...	...	1543	1633v	...	...	...

	AVE	*Av*	*AVE*	*AVE*	*AVE*	*Av*	*AVE*	*AVE*	*Av*	*Av*	*AVE*	*AVE*	*AVE*	*AVE*	*AVE*	*Av*	*AVE*	*AVE*	*AVE*	*AVE*	*AVE*	*Av*	*AVE*	*AVE*	*AVE*
	3151	**8567**	**3153**	**19724** **9725**	**3161**	**8187**	**3163**	**3163**	**10563**	**3563**	**3171**	**3991**	**3941**	**3173**	**3181**	**8207**	**3945**	**3183**	**3191**	**11483**	**3193**	**8607**	**3201**	**3203**	**3211**
	①–⑤				Ⓑ		⑥⑦	①–⑤	④	⑤⑦	Ⓑ				Ⓑ		⑦		Ⓑ				①–⑤		④⑤⑦
	j			**P**	**q**						**p**				**k**	**x**				**A**	**T**				
Sevilla **660** d.	...	...	...	...	...	...	...	...	...	...	...	...	1450	...	...	...	1615	...	...	...	...	...	...	...	...
Málaga **660** d.	...	...	...	...	...	...	...	...	...	...	...	1435	|	...	...	...	|	...	...	...	...	...	...	...	...
Madrid Puerta de Atocha d.	1500	...	1530	1540	1600	...	1630	1630	1650	1650	1700	|	|	1730	1800	...	|	1830	1900	1905	1930	...	2000	2030	2125
Guadalajara - Yebes d.	|	...	|	|	|	...	|	|	|	|	|	|	|	1754	|	...	|	|	|	1928	|	...	|	2054	|
Calatayud d.	|	1600	1626	|	|	...	|	|	|	|	|	|	|	|	|	...	|	|	|	2007	|	2035	|	2125	|
Zaragoza Delicias d.	|	1630	1652	|	|	...	1746	1746	1805	1840	|	1831	1831	1852	|	...	|	1946	|	2033	2046	2105	|	2152	|
Lleida d.	|	...	1737	|	|	1800	|	|	...	...	|	1918	1918	1937	|	1955	|	|	|	...	2131	...	|	2237	|
Camp de Tarragona d.	|	...	1805	|	|	1832	1844	1844	...	...	|	1947	1947	2005	|	2027	2034	2045	|	...	2206	...	|	2305	|
Barcelona Sants a.	1730	....	1840	1813	1830	1908	1915	1915	...	...	1930	2022	2022	2040	2030	2103	2110	2120	2130	...	2240	...	2230	2340	2355
Girona **657** a.	...	...	1927	1903	...	...	...	2002	...	...	...	...	...	...	...	...	...	2209	...	...	...	...	...	...	...
Figueres Vilafant **657** a.	...	...	1943	1919	...	...	...	2018	...	...	...	...	...	...	...	...	...	2223	...	...	...	...	...	...	...

	Av	*AVE*	*AVE*	*AVE*	*AVE*	*AVE*	*AVE*	*Av*	*AVE*	*AVE*	*AVE*	*AVE*	*AVE*	*AVE*	*AVE*	*AVE*	*AVE*	*AVE*	*Av*	*AVE*	*AVE*	*AVE*	*AVE*	*AVE*	*Av*
	8476	**3252**	**3062**	**3260**	**3462**	**3270**	**3072**	**8496**	**11842**	**3070**	**3662**	**3082**	**3082**	**3080**	**3940**	**3990**	**3092**	**3092**	**8096**	**3102**	**3112**	**9730** **19730**	**3122**	**3132**	**8556**
	①–⑤	①–④	①–⑥	①–⑤	①–④	①–④		⑥⑦		①–⑤	①–⑤	①–⑤		①–⑥			①–⑥							Ⓑ	
	n			**g**	**h**	**h**	**T**	**o**	**A**	**p**				**z**								**Q**			
Figueres Vilafant **657** d.	...	...	...	...	...	...	...	...	...	...	0630	0655	...	...	...	...	0755	...	...	0855	...	1034	...	...	...
Girona **657** d.	...	...	...	...	...	...	...	...	...	...	0646	0711	...	...	...	...	0810	...	...	0910	...	1049	...	...	...
Barcelona Sants d.	...	0550	0605	0625	0640	0700	0705	...	...	0725	0740	0800	0800	0825	0830	0830	0900	0900	0910	1000	1100	1140	1200	1300	...
Camp de Tarragona d.	...	|	0638	|	|	|	|	...	...	0757	|	0833	0833	|	0905	0905	|	|	0947	1033	|	|	1233	|	...
Lleida d.	...	|	0704	|	|	|	|	...	...	|	|	0859	0859	|	0934	0934	|	|	1018	1059	|	|	1259	|	...
Zaragoza Delicias d.	0645	|	0748	|	0806	|	0831	0915	0900	|	|	0943	0943	|	1020	1020	1026	1026	...	1143	1226	|	1343	1426	1500
Calatayud d.	0715	|	|	|	|	|	|	0945	0925	|	|	1008	1008	|	|	|	|	|	...	|	|	|	1408	|	1530
Guadalajara - Yebes d.	...	|	0845	|	|	|	|	...	1005	|	|	|	|	|	|	|	|	|	...	1243	|	|	|	|	...
Madrid Puerta de Atocha a.	...	0820	0915	0855	0925	0930	0950	...	1035	1001	1010	1110	1110	1055	|	|	1145	1145	...	1310	1345	1413	1510	1545	...
Málaga **660** a.	...	...	...	...	...	...	...	...	...	...	...	...	...	...	|	1424	...	...	...	...	...	...	...	...	...
Sevilla **660** a.	...	...	...	...	...	...	...	...	...	...	...	...	...	...	1402	...	...	...	...	...	...	...	...	...	...

	AVE	*AVE*	*AVE*	*AVE*	*AVE*	*AVE*	*Av*	*AVE*	*AVE*	*AVE*	*AVE*	*AVE*	*AVE*	*Av*	*AVE*	*Av*	*AVE*	*Av*	*AVE*	*AVE*	*AVE*	*Av*	*AVE*	*AVE*	
	3142	**3152**	**3150**	**3942**	**3992**	**3162**	**8166**	**3160**	**3946**	**3172**	**3172**	**3170**	**10792**	**3792**	**3182**	**8186**	**3180**	**8606**	**3192**	**3190**	**3202**	**8206**	**3212**	**3222**	
			①–⑤				Ⓑ	Ⓑ	⑤		⑦	Ⓑ	④	⑤⑦			Ⓑ			④⑤⑦					
			j				**s**	**f**				**j**					**f**								
Figueres Vilafant **657** d.	...	...	...	...	...	1455	...	...	...	...	1545	...	...	...	1655	...	...	...	...	...	1855	...	...	2045	...
Girona **657** d.	...	...	...	...	...	1510	...	...	...	...	1600	...	...	...	1710	...	...	...	...	...	1910	...	...	2100	...
Barcelona Sants d.	1400	1500	1525	1550	1550	1600	1605	1625	1645	1700	1700	1725	...	...	1800	1805	1825	...	1900	1925	2000	2010	2115	2150	...
Camp de Tarragona d.	1433	|	|	1623	1623	1633	1642	|	1718	|	|	|	...	...	1833	1842	|	...	|	|	2033	2047	|	2223	...
Lleida d.	1459	|	|	1649	1649	1659	1713	|	|	|	|	|	...	...	1859	1913	|	...	|	|	2059	2118	|	2250	...
Zaragoza Delicias d.	1543	1626	|	1733	1733	1743	...	|	|	1826	1826	|	1900	1900	1943	...	|	1955	2026	|	2143	...	2243	2335	...
Calatayud d.	|	|	|	|	|	1808	...	|	|	|	|	|	|	|	|	...	|	2025	|	|	2208	...	|	...	...
Guadalajara - Yebes d.	1643	|	|	|	|	|	...	|	|	|	|	|	|	|	2043	...	|	...	|	|	|	...	|	...	...
Madrid Puerta de Atocha a.	1710	1745	1755	|	|	1910	...	1855	|	1945	1945	1955	2030	2030	2110	...	2055	...	2145	2155	2310	...	0002	...	...
Málaga **660** a.	...	...	...	|	2140	...	...	...	|	...	...	...	...	...	...	...	...	...	...	...	...	...	...	...	...
Sevilla **660** a.	...	...	...	2115	...	...	...	...	2155	...	...	...	...	...	...	...	...	...	...	...	...	...	...	...	...

A – From/to Alicant (Table **668**).
C – Ⓑ (⑤⑦ Sept. 16 - Oct. 13).
P – To Marseille (Table **49**).
Q – From Marseille (Table **49**).
T – From/Toledo (Table **679**).

f – Not Apr. 18.
g – Not Apr. 17, 18, 21.
h – Not Apr. 14 - 17, 21.
j – Not Apr. 14 - 18.
k – Not Apr. 14 - 18, 20.
n – Not Aug. 15, Nov. 1, Dec. 6, 9.
o – Also Aug. 15, Nov. 1, Dec. 6, 9.
p – Not Apr. 17, 18.
q – Not Apr. 17, 18, 20, 21, 22.
s – Not Aug. 4, 11, 15, 18, 25, Sept. 22, 23, Dec. 8.
v – Not ⑥.
x – Aug. 15, Nov. 1, Dec. 6.
z – Not Apr. 19.
¦ – ⑥⑦ only.

☛ *AVE* trains convey ✕ and 🍸.
Alvia trains convey 🍸.
Avant trains (*Av*) are *Turista* class only.

MADRID – LOGROÑO, PAMPLONA/IRUÑA, HUESCA – BARCELONA 650a

	Alvia	*Alvia*	*Alvia*	*Alvia*	*Alvia*	*Alvia*	*Alvia*	*Alvia*	*Alvia*	*Alvia*	*AVE*	*Alvia*	*Alvia*	*Alvia*	*Alvia*	*Alvia*	*IC*	*Alvia*	*Alvia*	*AVE*	*Alvia*		
	635	**10655**	**533**	**433**	**601**	**631**	**603**	**605**	**605**	**661**	**3363**	**10657**	**621**	**537**	**609**	**437**	**611**	**613**	**701**	**3393**	**801**		
	①–⑤	⑥	🍷		①–⑤	🍷	⑥	①–⑤	⑦	①–⑥	⑤⑦	⑦	**625**			⑧ h	⑤	④⑦	⑧		⑧		
	🍷	🍷 y	K	F	P	B			P	G	g	🍷 b	J	K		F		b					
Madrid Puerta de Atocha ....d.	...	...	...	...	0735	...	0940	1135	1135	...	1605	...	...	...	1505	...	1735	1735	1835	1905	1935	...	...
Guadalajara - Yebes ....d.	...	...	...	...	|	...	1007	1202	1202	...	|	...	...	...	1532	...	|	|	1901	1928	|	...	...
Calatayud ....d.	...	...	...	...	|	...	1055	1250	1250	...	|	...	...	...	1620	...	|	|	1948	2007	|	...	...
Logroño **653**...............a.	...	...	...	0909	|	1022	|	|	|	...	|	...	...	...	|	1752	|	|	2158	|	|	...	...
Pamplona/Iruña **653**...........a.	0625	0812	0913	|	1038	|	1252	1440	1440	1449	|	1625	1713	1754	1826	|	2043	2043	...	|	2240	...	...
Zaragoza Delicias...............d.	0810	1003	1113	1113	...	1215	...	...	...	1637	1727	1811	1906	1952	...	1952	...	...	...	2034	...	...	...
Huesca **670**...............a.	|	|	|	|	...	|	...	...	...	|	1810	|	|	|	...	|	...	...	...	2118	...	...	...
Lleida ....d.	0900	1056	1203	1203	...	1313	...	...	...	1732	...	|	1958	2051	...	2051	...	...	...	...	...	...	...
Camp de Tarragona...............d.	0930	1127	1238	1238	...	1343	...	...	...	1813	...	1924	2038	2128	...	2128	...	...	...	...	...	...	...
Barcelona Sants ....a.	1010	1205	1320	1320	...	1420	...	...	...	1850	...	2005	2120	2209	...	2209	...	...	...	...	...	...	...

	Alvia	*AVE*	*Alvia*	*Alvia*	*Alvia*		*Alvia*	*Alvia*	*Alvia*	*Alvia*	*Alvia*	*Alvia*	*Alvia*	*Alvia*	*Alvia*	*IC*	*Alvia*	*Alvia*	*Alvia*	*AVE*	*Alvia*	*Alvia*	
	802	**3272**	**702**	**800**	**600**		**534**	**434**	**602**	**602**	**622**	**10560**	**606**	**664**	**632**	**608**	**612**	**530**	**430**	**3593**	**610**	**10562**	
	①–⑤		①–⑥	①	⑥			①–⑥	①–⑤	⑦	**626**	⑥			🍷	⑦	⑤			⑤⑦	⑧	⑧	
	Q						K	F q		P	J	🍷 b		G	B			K	F	g		🍷 w	
Barcelona Sants ....d.	...	...	...	...	...	...	0730	0730	...	...	0930	1005	...	1210	1410	...	...	1530	1530	...	...	1840	...
Camp de Tarragona...............d.	...	...	...	...	...	...	0808	0808	...	...	1007	1043	...	1248	1447	...	...	1608	1608	...	...	1918	...
Lleida ....d.	...	...	...	...	...	...	0844	0844	...	...	1037	1115	...	1319	1517	...	...	1639	1639	...	...	1951	...
Huesca **670**...............d.	...	0800	...	...	...	...	|	|	...	...	|	|	...	|	|	...	...	|	|	1935	...	|	...
Zaragoza Delicias...............d.	...	0845	...	...	...	...	0934	0934	...	...	1128	1204	...	1414	1608	...	...	1729	1729	2020	...	2049	...
Pamplona/Iruña **653**...........d.	0635	|	...	0810	0900	...	1117	|	1130	1130	1315	1354	1535	1606	|	1807	1807	1920	|	|	1935	2231	...
Logroño **653**...............d.	|	|	0735	|	|	...	...	1122	|	|	...	...	|	...	1750	|	|	...	1923	|	|	...	...
Calatayud ....d.	|	0910	0936	|	1101	...	...	...	1324	1324	...	...	|	...	...	|	|	...	...	|	2134	...	...
Guadalajara - Yebes ....d.	|	0950	1022	|	1150	...	...	...	1412	1412	...	...	|	...	...	|	|	...	...	|	2224	...	...
Madrid Puerta de Atocha ....a.	0945	1020	1050	1120	1218	...	...	...	1440	1440	...	...	1838	...	...	2125	2125	...	...	2140	2253	...	...

B – (12) Valladolid - Barcelona and v.v. (Tables **653, 689**).
F – (12) Bilbao - Barcelona and v.v. (Table **653**).
G – (12) Gijón - Barcelona and v.v. (Table **685**).
J – (12) 🍷 Vigo and A Coruña - Barcelona and v.v. (Table **680**).
K – (12) Irún - Barcelona and v.v. (Table **653**).
P – Not July 28 - Sept. 2.

Q – Not July 29 - Sept. 3.

b – From/to Irún (Table **653**).
g – Also Aug. 14; not Aug. 16.
h – Daily June 22 - Sept. 7, also Nov. 2, Dec. 7.

k – Not Aug. 4, 11, 18, 25.
m – Not Aug. 4, 11, 18, 25, Sept. 1.
q – Daily June 23 - Sept. 8, also Nov. 3, Dec. 8.

w – To Vitoria/Gasteiz on ⑤ (Table **653**).
y – To/from Vitoria/Gasteiz (Table **653**).

MADRID - SORIA and ZARAGOZA 651

km	*For high-speed trains see Tables 650 and 650a*				*TRD* **17300**	*TRD* **17310**									*TRD* **17304**			*TRD* **17306**				*Estr* **370**			
		2	2		2	2	2		2		2	2	2	2	2	2		2		2					
		P	⑥⑦q		P	⑥⑦q	H		R		⑤y		⑤⑦h		⑤y	g				⑦		C			
0	**Madrid** Chamartín...............d.	...	...	...	0745	0814	0807	...	...	...	1432	...	...	...	1540	1545	...	1900	...	2002	...	2230	...	...	...
55	Guadalajara...............d.	...	...	...	0821	0850	0853	...	...	...	1509	1535	...	...	1621	1635	...	1937	...	2038	...	2308	...	...	...
138	Sigüenza ....d.	...	...	...	0906	0936	0950	...	...	...	1612	1638	...	...	1711	1737	...	2024	...	2142	...	2359	...	...	...
248	**Soria**...............a.	...	...	...	1030	1059	|	...	...	...	...	...	...	...	1835	|	...	2142	...	...	...	|	...	...	...
178	Arcos de Jalón ....d.	0650	0855	...	...	...	1018	...	1243	...	...	...	1750	...	...	1812	...	...	...	...	...	0026	...	...	...
241	Calatayud ....d.	0736	0941	...	...	...	1054	...	1329	...	...	...	1839	1839	...	1857	...	...	...	...	...	0105	...	...	...
339	**Zaragoza** Delicias ♣..........a.	0855	1106	...	...	...	1156	...	1439	...	...	...	1957	1957	...	2011	...	...	...	...	...	0215	...	...	...

For high-speed trains see Tables 650 and 650a	*Estr* **373**				*TRD* **17305**	*TRD* **17303**												*TRD* **17305**	*TRD* **33011**	*TRD* **33017**					
			2		2	2		2	2	2	2		2	2	2	2	2	2	2	2		2	2		
	C		Q		P	⑥⑦q		P	p	⑥⑦q			H	G	⑤y		⑤f	B	A	⑦			⑦		
Zaragoza Delicias ♥ ....d.	0312	...	...	...	...	...	...	0744	0857	0916	...	...	1359	...	...	1518	1518	...	...	...	...	2036	...	...	...
Calatayud...............d.	0427	...	...	...	...	...	...	0909	1021	1038	...	...	1458	...	...	1635	1635	...	...	...	...	2157	...	...	...
Arcos de Jalón...............d.	0508	...	...	...	...	...	...	0957	1107	1128	1220	...	1535	...	...	...	1723	...	...	...	...	2244	...	...	...
Soria ....d.	|	...	...	...	0743	0840	...	...	|	...	|	...	|	...	...	...	...	1655	1732	1822	...	...	...	...	...
Sigüenza ....d.	0536	...	0605	...	0905	1000	...	...	1143	...	1251	...	1607	1645	1700	...	...	1812	1850	1940	...	...	2150	...	...
Guadalajara...............d.	0629	...	0712	...	0955	1047	...	...	1245	...	1352	...	1710	1746	1758	...	...	1901	1936	2029	...	...	2248	...	...
Madrid Chamartín...............a.	0721	...	0824	...	1030	1122	...	...	1329	...	...	...	1755	...	1837	...	...	1937	2016	2106	...	...	2327	...	...

A – ①–⑥ (daily June 9 - Sept. 29).
B – ⑦ (not June 9 - Sept. 29).
C – ⑧: COSTA BRAVA – 🛏 1, 2 cl., 🛏 2 cl. (2) Madrid - Zaragoza - Barcelona and v.v.
G – ①②③④⑥⑦ (also Nov. 1, Dec. 6; not Oct. 31, Dec. 5).
H – To/from Barcelona (Table **652**).

P – ①–⑤ (not Aug. 15, Nov. 1, Dec. 6, 9).
Q – ①–⑤ (not Aug. 15, Nov. 1, Dec. 6).
R – ①–⑥ (not Aug. 15, Oct. 12, Nov. 1, Dec. 6, 9).

f – Also Oct. 31, Dec. 5; not Nov. 11.
g – To Lleida (Table **652**).
h – Also Aug. 15, Oct. 12, Dec. 9.

k – Also Aug. 15, Nov. 1, Dec. 6.
p – From Lleida on ①–⑤ (Table **652**).
q – Also Aug. 15, Nov. 1, Dec. 6, 9.
y – Also Oct. 31, Dec. 5; not Nov. 1, Dec. 6.

♥ – All services (except *Estr* **373**) call 7 - 8 minutes earlier at Zaragoza **Goya** and 5 minutes earlier at Zaragoza **Portillo**.
♣ – All services (except *Estr* **370**) call 4 - 5 minutes later at Zaragoza **Portillo** and 6 - 8 minutes later at Zaragoza **Goya**.

ZARAGOZA - BARCELONA 652

km	*For high-speed trains see Tables 650 and 650a*	2	2	2	2	*Hotel* **921**¶	2	2	2	2	2	2	2	2	2	2	2	2	2	2	2	2	2	*Estr* **370**
		①–⑥				G 🍷		①–⑤				⑥⑦					①–⑤	①–⑥	⑦					C
		h						f		H		y					h	h	j					
	Madrid Chamartín **651**.......d.	...	...	...	...	...	...	...	...	...	...	...	...	0817	...	...	...	...	...	...	...	1545	...	2230
0	**Zaragoza** Delicias ♣ ....d.	...	...	...	...	0632	...	0610	...	...	...	0705	...	1157	...	...	1515	...	...	1630	...	2012	2045	0220
114	Caspe ....d.	...	...	...	...	|	0715	|	...	...	...	|	...	1329	...	...	|	...	...	1803	...	|	2226	|
★	Lleida...............d.	...	...	...	0715	0730	|	0820	...	...	...	0920	1310	|	1545	...	1727	1748	1748	|	...	2240	...	|
239	Reus ....d.	0537	0643	0732	|	|	0917	...	1110	1210	1307	...	1437	1530	1714	1848	...	|	|	2008	2118	...	...	0530
257	Tarragona ....**672** d.	0552	0700	0747	|	0804t	0931	...	1125	1225	1324	...	1455	1548	1729	1904	...	|	|	2024	2134	...	...	0547
282	Sant Vicenç de Calders.... **672** d.	0615	0719	0810	0845	|	0949	...	1145	1245	1345	...	1517	1609	1747	1924	...	1913	1923	2043	2200	...	...	0608
342	**Barcelona** Sants .... **672** a.	0717	0809	0905	0935	0844	1035	...	1235	1340	1435	...	1606	1705	1835	2011	...	2005	2017	2136	2302	...	...	0705
345	Barcelona Pass. de Gràcia ....a.	0723	0815	0914	0944	...	1045	...	1244	1345	1444	...	1614	1714	1844	2017	...	2012	2023	2143	2307	...	...	...
350	**Barcelona** França ....a.	0733	0823	0922	0952	...	1055	...	1252	1353	1453	...	1623	1723	1852	2026	...	2020	2032	2152	2316	...	...	...

For high-speed trains see Tables 650 and 650a	2	2	2	2	2	2	2	2	2	2	2	2	2	2	2	2	2	2	2	2	*Hotel* **922**¶	2	*Estr* **373**	
	①–⑥	①–⑤		⑥													⑥⑦				G 🍷		C	
	f	f						H					①–⑤				y							
Barcelona França...............d.	...	...	0617	...	0650	0717	0847	0946	1147	...	1247	1347	...	1547	1648	1717	...	1847	1850	2018	...	2118	...	...
Barcelona Pass. de Gràcia....d.	...	...	0626	...	0659	0726	0856	0956	1156	...	1256	1355	...	1556	1656	1726	...	1855	1859	2026	...	2126	...	...
Barcelona Sants............**672** d.	...	...	0633	...	0706	0733	0903	1003	1203	...	1303	1403	...	1603	1703	1733	...	1903	1906	2033	2020	2133	2220	...
Sant Vicenç de Calders..**672** d.	...	...	0718	...	0807	0818	0948	1047	1248	...	1348	1446	...	1648	1746	1818	...	1947	2004	2118	|	2222	2317	...
Tarragona ....**672** d.	...	...	0739	...	|	0839	1009	1108	1308	...	1409	1507	...	1708	1808	1838	...	|	2036	2138	2103t	2243	2341	...
Reus ....d.	...	...	0754	...	|	0855	1027	1123	1326	...	1424	1529	...	1724	1827	1853	...	|	2050	2153	|	2258	2356	...
Lleida...............d.	...	0625	...	1025	0955	...	|	...	1455	1513	...	1646	1836	|	1953	|	2021	2111	...	...	2142	...	|	...
Caspe ....d.	0651	|	...	|	...	...	1224	...	...	|	...	...	|	1933	...	2053	|	...	...	...	|	...	|	...
Zaragoza Delicias ♥ ....a.	0832	0856	...	1253	...	...	1358	...	...	1726	...	...	2044	2103	...	...	2220	...	...	...	2238	...	0307	...
Madrid Chamartín **651** ....a.	...	1329	...	...	...	...	1737	...	...	...	...	...	...	...	...	...	...	...	...	...	...	...	0721	...

– ⑧: COSTA BRAVA – 🛏 1, 2 cl., 🛏 2 cl. (2) Madrid - Barcelona and v.v.
– GALICIA *Trenhotel* – 🛏, (1) (reclining) Barcelona - A Coruña and Vigo and v.v.
– Daily (not June 22 - Aug. 31), ①–⑤ Sept 1 - 29, not Sept. 11.
– Not Aug. 15, Nov. 1, Dec. 6, 9.

h – Not Aug. 15, Sept. 11, Oct. 12, Nov. 1, Dec. 6.
j – Also Aug. 15, Sept. 11, Oct. 12, Nov. 1, Dec. 6.
t – **Camp** de Tarragona.
y – Also Aug. 15, Nov. 1, Dec. 6, 9.

★ – Leida - Reus: *90 km.* Zaragoza - Lleida: *189 km.* Lleida - Sant Vicenç: *106 km.*

¶ – Via high speed line.
♥ – All trains (except *Hotel* **922** and *Estr* **373**) call 5 - 8 mins. earlier at Zaragoza **Goya** and 3 - 5 mins. earlier at Zaragoza **Portillo**.
♣ – All trains (except *Hotel* **921** and *Estr* **370**) call 4 - 5 mins. later at Zaragoza **Portillo** and 6 - 8 mins. later at Zaragoza **Goya**.

653 ZARAGOZA - IRÚN and BILBAO

km				*Alvia*	*Alvia*	*Alvia*	*Alvia*	*Alvia*	*Alvia*	*Alvia*		*Alvia*			*Alvia*	*Alvia*		*Alvia*		*Alvia*	*IC*				*Alvia*	*Alvia*	*Alvia*		*Hotel*
		18071	**16013**	**601**	**603**	**534**	**434**	**622**	**605**	**10560**	**18021**	**664**	**18073**	**18073**	**632**	**609**	**18023**	**530**	**16017**	**430**	**611**	**18075**	**18075**	**18077**	**10562**	**701**	**801**	**18079**	**922**
		2	2	**E**		**M**	**Q B**	**626**	**H**	🍷	2		2	2	**V**		2	**M**	2	**Q**	**T**	2	2	2	🍷			2	**G** 🍷
		①–⑥	①–⑤	①–⑤	⑥	🍷		**J**	Ⓑ	⑥		**A**			🍷			⑤**h**	①–⑥		④⑤⑦		⑦		Ⓑ	Ⓑ	Ⓑ		¶
	Barcelona Sants **652** d.	...	...	...	...	0730	0730	0930	...	1005	...	1210	...	...	1410	...	...	1530	...	1530	...	...	...	...	1840	...	...	...	2020
	Madrid PA ‡ **650a** ... d.	...	...	0735	0940	|	|	|	1135	|	...	|	...	...	|	1505	...	|	...	|	1735	...	...	...	|	1835	1935	...	|
0	**Zaragoza** Delicias ...... d.	0625	0625	|	|	0934	0934	1128	|	1204	1259	1414	1435	1418	1608	|	1652	1729	...	1729	|	1742	1742	1924	2049	|	|	2109	2250
94	Castejón de Ebro ★ ... d.	0729	0735	0945	1159	1028	1031	1224	|	1259	1406	|	1540	1545	1702	|	1748	1825	...	1828	|	1849	1851	2031	|	|	|	2215	0014
182	**Pamplona / Iruña** ...... d.	|	0839	1038	1252	1119	|	1317	1440	1356	1517	1608	|	1656	|	1826	1859	1922	1930	|	2043	|	1950	2138	2232	|	2240	|	|
234	Altsasu .... **689** d.	|	0918**y**	...	...	|	|	|	...	|	...	|	|	1736**y**	|	...	...	1953	2004**y**	|	|	|	2034**y**	...	|	|	...	|	|
275	Vitoria / Gasteiz **689** d.	|	0950	...	...	|	|	1410	...	|	...	1702	|	1808	|	...	...	|	2037	|	|	|	2110	...	2323**r**	|	...	|	|
321	San Seb / Don ❖ .... d.	|	...	...	...	1305	|	|	...	1550	...	|	|	...	|	...	...	2111	...	|	2226**x**	|	|	...	...	|	...	|	|
337	**Irún** .... **689** a.	|	...	...	...	1328	|	|	...	1611	...	|	|	...	|	...	...	2133	...	|	2245**x**	|	|	...	...	|	...	|	|
171	**Logroño 650a** .... d.	0839**z**	...	...	...	...	1124	|	...	...	...	|	1635	...	1751	...	...	...	...	1925	...	1945	|	...	...	2158	...	2312**c**	0102
242	Miranda de Ebro . **689** d.	...	...	...	...	...	1219	1431	...	...	...	1722	...	...	1848	...	...	...	...	2018	...	...	2135	...	...	...	...	...	...
347	**Bilbao** Abando.... **689** a.	...	...	...	...	...	1350	...	...	...	...	...	...	...	...	...	...	...	...	2150	...	...	...	...	...	...	...	...	...

		Alvia		*Alvia*	*Alvia*	*Alvia*		*Alvia*			*Alvia*	*Alvia*	*Alvia*	*Alvia*		*Alvia*	*Alvia*	*Alvia*			*Alvia*	*Alvia*	*Alvia*	*IC*	*Alvia*				*Hotel*
	18070	**635**	**18072**	**802**	**800**	**702**	**18074**	**10655**	**16007**	**600**	**533**	**433**	**602**	**631**	**18076**	**661**	**606**	**10657**	**18029**	**18029**	**621**	**537**	**437**	**608**	**610**	**16011**	**18078**	**18078**	**921**
	2	🍷	2	**K**			2	🍷	2 **f**		**M**	**Q**	**H**	**V**	2	**A**		🍷	2	2	**625**	**M**	**Q C**	**S**		2	2	2	**G** 🍷
	①–⑤	①–⑤		①–⑤	①	①–⑥		⑥	①–⑥	⑥	🍷		Ⓑ	🍷		①–⑥		⑦		**b**	**J**		Ⓑ	⑤⑦	Ⓑ	⑦	①–⑥		¶
Bilbao Abando .....**689** d.	...	...	...	...	...	...	...	...	...	...	...	0640	...	...	...	...	...	...	...	...	...	...	1528	...	...	...	...	...	...
Miranda de Ebro ...**689** d.	...	...	...	...	...	...	...	...	0720	...	...	0813	...	0925	...	1329	...	...	...	1502	1556	...	1657	...	...	...	...	...	...
Logroño 650a .... d.	...	...	0615**z**	...	...	0735	...	...	|	...	...	0909	...	1022	1415	|	...	...	1642**c**	|	|	...	1752	...	...	...	...	2018	0403
Irún ....**689** d.	...	...	|	...	0605	|	...	...	|	...	0710	|	...	|	|	|	...	1420	|	|	|	1555	|	1600**r**	...	...	...	|	|
San Seb / Don .... d.	...	...	|	...	0624	|	...	...	|	...	0728	|	...	|	|	|	...	1437	|	|	|	1613	|	1619**r**	...	...	...	|	|
Vitoria / Gasteiz ..**689** d.	...	...	|	...	|	|	...	0718	0750	...	|	|	...	|	|	1352	...	|	|	1530	1617	|	|	|	...	1905	1905	|	|
Altsasu ....**689** d.	...	...	|	...	|	|	...	|	0820**y**	...	0842	|	...	|	|	|	...	|	|	1601**y**	|	|	|	|	...	1936**y**	1936**y**	|	|
Pamplona / Iruña .... d.	...	0625	|	0635	0810	|	0743**z**	0812	0855	0900	0913	|	1130	|	|	1449	1535	1625	|	1638	1713	1754	|	1807	1935	2015	2015	|	|
Castejón de Ebro .... d.	0605	0717	0720	0725	|	|	0850	|	...	0952	1010	1010	|	1114	1510	|	|	|	1744	1744	1810	1848	1848	|	|	2112	2121	2121	0456
Zaragoza Delicias .... a.	0715	0807	0836	|	|	|	0956	1000	...	|	1110	1110	|	1212	1611	1635	|	1808	1851	1851	1904	1948	1948	|	|	2205	2229	2229	0629
Madrid PA ‡ **650a** ... a.	...	|	...	0945	1120	1050	...	|	...	1218	|	|	1440	|	...	|	1838	|	...	...	|	|	|	2125	2253	...	...	...	|
Barcelona Sants **652** .. a.	...	1010	...	...	...	...	...	1205	...	...	1320	1320	...	1420	...	1850	...	2005	...	...	2120	2209	2209	...	...	...	...	...	0844

A – [12] Barcelona - Gijón and v.v. (Table **685**).
B – ①–⑥ (daily June 23 - Sept. 8; also Nov. 3, Dec. 8).
C – Ⓑ (daily June 22 - Sept. 7; also Nov. 2, Dec. 7).
E – Not July 28 - Sept. 2.
G – GALICIA *Trenhotel* – 🛏, [1] (reclining) Barcelona - A Coruña and Vigo and v.v.
H – Not ⑦ July 28 - Sept. 2.
J – [12] 🍷 Barcelona - Vigo / A Coruña and v.v.
K – Not July 29 - Sept. 3.
M – [12] Barcelona - Irún and v.v.
Q – [12] Barcelona - Bilbao and v.v.
S – On ⑤ train number is *Alvia* **612**.

T – On ④⑦ train number is *Alvia* **613**.
V – [12] Barcelona - Valladolid and v.v. (Tables **650a, 689**). On ⑦ train **631** runs as **633**, departs Miranda de Ebro 1337, Logroño 1434, Castejón de Ebro 1527, arrives Zaragoza 1626, Barcelona 1835.

b – From Burgos Rosa de Lima on ①–⑥ (Table **689**).
c – ⑤⑥⑦ (also Oct. 31, Dec. 5).
f – From Miranda de Ebro, depart 0720 (Table **689**).
g – ⑤⑥⑦ (also Oct. 31, Dec. 5).
h – Not Aug. 2, 9, 16, 23.
k – Not Aug. 4, 11, 18, 25.

r – ⑤ only.
x – ④⑦.
y – Altsasu Pueblo (*230 km*).
z – ①–⑤.

¶ – Via high speed line.
★ – Calatayud - Castejón: *140 km*.
‡ – Full name is Madrid Puerta de Atocha.
❖ – Full name is San Sebastián / Donostia.

655 LLEIDA - LA POBLA DE SEGUR

FGC 2nd class

km		A		①–⑥	⑦		⑦		①–⑥		
0	**Lleida** .... d.	0715	...	0910	0910	...	1040	...	1730	...	2030
27	Balaguer .... d.	0744	...	0939	0939	...	1109	...	1759	...	2059
77	Tremp .... d.	...	...	1044	...	...	1214	...	...	...	...
90	**La Pobla de Segur** ... a.	...	...	1100	...	...	1230	...	...	...	...

	A		⑦		①–⑥		①–⑥	⑦		
La Pobla de Segur ... d.	...	...	...	...	1256	...	...	1730	...	...
Tremp .... d.	...	...	...	...	1311	...	...	1745	...	...
Balaguer .... d.	0800	...	1000	...	1416	...	1810	1850	...	2105
Lleida .... a.	0830	...	1030	...	1446	...	1839	1920	...	2134

A – ①–⑤ (not May 1, Aug. 15, Oct. 13, Dec. 8).

656 BARCELONA - PUIGCERDÀ - LATOUR DE CAROL

2nd class

km		①–⑤	①–⑤	①–⑤	①–⑤	⑥⑦	①–⑤	①–⑤	⑥⑦	①–⑤	⑥⑦	①–⑤	①–⑤	⑥⑦	①–⑤	⑥⑦	①–⑤	⑥⑦	①–⑤	⑥⑦	①–⑤	⑥⑦	①–⑤	⑥⑦	①–⑤	⑥⑦	①–⑤
		❖ f	f	f	f	j	f	f	j	f	j	f	f	j	f	j	f	j	f	j	f	j	f	j	f	j	f
0	**Barcelona** Sants .... d.	...	0511	0601	0622	0700	0701	0752	0756	0933	0936	1022	1103	1106	1203	1206	1303	1316	1403	1406	1510	1516	1610	1616	1703	1706	1731
	La Sagrera-Meridiana ... d.	...	0524	0614	0636	0713	0714	0805	0809	0946	0949	1035	1116	1119	1216	1219	1316	1329	1416	1419	1523	1529	1623	1629	1716	1719	1744
	Sant Andreu Arenal ...... d.	...	0526	0616	0639	0715	0716	0807	0811	0948	0951	1037	1118	1121	1218	1221	1318	1331	1418	1421	1525	1531	1625	1631	1718	1721	1746
33	Granollers - Canovelles ..... d.	...	0556	0645	0707	0740	0744	0838	0839	1016	1018	1111	1148	1149	1242	1245	1356	1401	1445	1450	1551	1558	1655	1700	1743	1747	1815
74	Vic .... d.	...	0638	0723	0744	0819	0824	0921	0921	1051	1053	1148	1231	1232	1321	1322	1444	1446	1521	1521	1627	1632	1732	1738	1814	1823	1902
90	Torelló .... d.	...	...	0737	0805	0839	...	0934	0935	1104	1106	1201	1244	1245	1334	1335	1457	1459	1539	1541	1643	1645	1745	1753	1829	1835	1916
110	Ripoll .... d.	...	...	0759	0827	0900	...	0957	0958	1125	1127	1223	1306	1307	1355	1356	1520	1523	1559	1601	1704	1706	1807	1815	1855	1856	1939
124	Ribes de Freser .... **658** a.	...	...	...	0843	0916	...	1011	1014	1143	1145	...	...	...	1411	1412	...	1538	...	...	1720	1725	...	...	1914	1915	...
145	La Molina .... a.	...	...	...	0909	0941	...	...	...	1207	1209	...	...	...	1437	1439	...	...	...	...	1752	1757	...	...	1947	1945	...
159	Puigcerdà .... a.	0801	...	...	0928	0959	...	...	...	1224	1226	...	...	...	1454	1456	...	...	...	...	1809	1814	...	...	2003	2001	...
163	**Latour de Carol** 🏛 .. **312** a.	0807	...	...	0934	1005	...	...	...	1230	1232	...	...	...	1500	1502	...	...	...	...	1815	1820	...	...	...	...	...

	①–⑤	①–⑤	⑥⑦	①–⑤	⑥⑦	⑥⑦	①–⑤	⑥⑦	①–⑤		
	f	f	j	f	j	j	f	j	f		
Barcelona Sants .... d.	1827	1857	1857	2012	2015	2045	2127	2206	2227	...	...
La Sagrera-Meridiana ... d.	1840	1910	1910	2025	2028	2058	2140	2219	2240	...	...
Sant Andreu Arenal ...... d.	1842	1912	1912	2027	2030	2100	2142	2221	2242	...	...
Granollers - Canovelles ..... d.	|	1939	1937	2054	2053	2128	2212	2250	2310	...	...
Vic .... d.	1935	2019	2019	2125	2124	2207	2250	2326	2346	...	...
Torelló .... d.	|	2039	2031	2141	2137	...	...	...	...	...	...
Ripoll .... d.	2005	2100	2052	2203	2159	...	...	...	...	...	...
Ribes de Freser .... **658** a.	|	2116	2108	...	...	...	...	...	...	...	...
La Molina .... a.	|	2140	2132	...	...	...	...	...	...	...	...
Puigcerdà .... a.	2057	2155	2148	...	...	...	...	...	...	...	...
Latour de Carol 🏛 .. **312** a.	...	...	...	...	...	...	...	...	...	...	...

			①–⑤	⑥⑦	①–⑤	①–⑤	⑥⑦	⑥⑦	①–⑤	①–⑤	⑥⑦
			f	j	f	f	j	j	f	f	j
Latour de Carol 🏛 **312** d.	...	...	...	...	...	...	...	...	...	...	...
Puigcerdà .... d.	...	...	...	...	...	0625	...	0655	0702	...	...
La Molina .... d.	...	...	...	...	...	|	...	0710	0717	...	...
Ribes de Freser ..... **658** d.	...	...	...	...	...	|	...	0735	0742	...	...
Ripoll .... d.	...	...	0636	...	...	0719	...	0752	0759	...	...
Torelló .... d.	...	...	0654	...	...	|	...	0812	0821	...	...
Vic .... d.	0548	0645	0707	0724	0727	0750	0803	0826	0834	0924	092
Granollers - Canovelles .. d.	0625	0724	0742	0803	0804	|	0842	0900	0908	1002	100
Sant Andreu Arenal ... a.	0651	0750	0806	0830	0832	0843	0907	0924	0930	1028	103
La Sagrera-Meridiana a.	0654	0753	0808	0833	0835	0847	0910	0927	0933	1031	103
Barcelona Sants .... a.	0707	0806	0821	0846	0850	0902	0922	0940	0947	1044	104

	①–⑤	⑥⑦		①–⑤	⑥⑦			①–⑤	⑥⑦		①–⑤	⑥⑦	①–⑤	①–⑤	⑥⑦	⑥⑦	①–⑤	⑥⑦	①–⑤	①–⑤	⑥⑦		⑥⑦	①–⑤	①–⑤	⑥⑦	
	f	j		f	j			f	j		f	j	f	f	f	j	f	j	f	f	j		j	f	f	j	
Latour de Carol 🏛 .. **312** d.	...	...	0848	...	...	...	1115	...	...	...	1345	1347	...	...	...	...	...	...	...	1700	1705	...	1853	1855	...	...	...
Puigcerdà .... d.	...	...	0854	...	...	...	1121	...	...	...	1351	1353	...	...	...	...	...	...	...	1706	1711	...	1859	1901	...	...	...
La Molina .... d.	...	...	0909	...	...	...	1136	...	...	...	1406	1408	...	...	...	...	...	...	...	1721	1726	...	1914	1916	...	...	...
Ribes de Freser .... **658** d.	...	...	0936	...	...	1109	1204	...	...	...	1433	1435	...	...	...	1647	...	...	...	1749	1754	...	1941	1943	...	...	...
Ripoll .... d.	0913	0915	0953	1043	...	1127	1222	...	...	1355	1450	1452	...	1607	...	1705	1712	...	...	1806	1811	1911	1958	2000	2107	...	...
Torelló .... d.	0933	0935	1016	1103	...	1148	1243	...	...	1415	1513	1515	...	1627	...	1726	1732	...	...	1827	1834	1933	2016	2024	2127	...	...
Vic .... d.	0949	0951	1029	1119	1122	1204	1258	1345	1352	1429	1526	1528	1602	1643	1649	1740	1748	1807	1814	1844	1849	1950	2034	2041	2143	2140	...
Granollers - Canovelles ..... d.	1032	1034	1057	1157	1159	1241	1327	1424	1429	1506	1555	1557	1639	1722	1729	1816	1825	1848	1850	1921	1918	2027	2109	2121	2220	2217	...
Sant Andreu Arenal ...... a.	1059	1100	1121	1223	1224	1309	1351	1452	1457	1534	1627	1621	1708	1751	1800	1842	1850	1920	1921	1956	1942	2057	2138	2151	2247	2244	...
La Sagrera-Meridiana ... a.	1102	1103	1124	1226	1227	1312	1354	1455	1500	1537	1630	1624	1711	1754	1803	1845	1853	1923	1924	1959	1945	2100	2141	2154	2250	2247	...
Barcelona Sants .... a.	1115	1116	1137	1239	1240	1325	1407	1508	1513	1550	1644	1637	1724	1807	1816	1858	1906	1937	1938	2013	1958	2116	2154	2207	2303	2300	...

f – Not Aug. 15, Sept. 11, 24, Nov. 1, Dec. 6, 25, 26.
j – Also Aug. 15, Sept. 11, 24, Nov. 1, Dec. 6, 25, 26.
❖ – Timing subject to confirmation. Please check local

BARCELONA - GIRONA - FIGUERES - PORTBOU / PERPIGNAN 657

Reservations are not compulsory on *Media Distancia* (*MD*) services on the Barcelona - Girona - Portbou - Cebère route. All stopping services convey 2nd class only.

km	km		*MD*	*TGV*		*MD*			*AVE*	*TGV*	*MD*	*MD*			*TGV*	*AVE*	*MD*	*MD*	*AVE*		*AVE*		*MD*	*MD*	*AVE*	*MD*	
			15900	**9700**		**15008**			**34253***	**9734**	**15056**	**15076**			**9703**	**3071**	**15908**	**15094**	**9720**		**3073**		**15078**	**15078**	**3093**	**15004**	
			①–⑤		①–⑤	①–⑤	⑥	①–⑤	①–⑤		⑥⑦	①–⑤	⑥⑦	①–⑤	**9702**	**34071***	⑥⑦	①–⑤	**9721**	⑥⑦	**34073***	①–⑤	①–⑤	⑥⑦	**34093***	①–⑤	⑥⑦
			p	**A P**	**p**	**p**		**p**		**H L**	**q**	**p**	**q**	**p**	**P**		**q**	**p**	**T**	**q**	⑥⑦	**p**	**p**	**q**		**p**	**q**
		Madrid ⊠ **630** ....d.	...	...	...	...	...	...	...	...	...	...	...	...	...	0700x	...	...	...	...	0730	...	...	...	0930	...	...
0	*0*	**Barcelona** Sants ... **666** d.	0556	0605	0616	0646	0646	0716	0720	0720	0746	0822	0846	0916	0920	0945	0949	1016	1024	1046	1050	1116	1146	1146	1244	1246	1246
3		Barcelona P de G ❖ ....d.	0601	|	0620	0651	0650	0720	|	|	0751	0827	0850	0920	|	|	0954	1021	|	1050	|	1120	1151	1151	|	1251	1250
31		Granollers Centre ....d.	|	|	0646	|	0716	0752	|	|	|	|	0917	0946	|	|	|	|	|	1116	|	1146	|	|	|	|	1316
72		Maçanet - Massanes **666** d.	0651	|	0722	0743	0752	0832	|	|	0843	0919	0957	1022	|	|	1049	1113	|	1152	|	1222	1243	1243	|	1343	1353
86		Caldes de Malavella ....d.	0702	|	0733	0754	0803	0843	|	|	0854	0930	1007	1033	|	|	1100	1124	|	1203	|	1233	1254	1253	|	1353	1403
102	*95*	**Girona** ....d.	0713	0646	0748	0805	0818	0858	0801	0801	0905	0941	1023	1049	1001	1026	1111	1135	1103	1218	1129	1248	1305	1305	1323	1404	1419
118		Flaçà ....d.	0726	|	0802	0818	0832	0912	|	|	0915	0954	1038	1104	|	|	1124	1148	|	1232	|	1302	1318	1318	|	1417	1434
143		Figueres .... § d.	0744	|	0827	0836	0857	0937	|	|	0937	1013	1102	1129	|	|	1143	1207	|	1257	|	1327	1336	1337	|	1437	1458
	129	Figueres Vilafant .... § d.	...	0703	|	...	|	|	0815	0818	|	|	|	|	1018	1040	|	|	1120	|	1143	|	...	|	1338	...	|
162		Llançà ....d.	...	|	0842	...	0912	0952	...	|	0950	1026	1116	1143	|	...	1156	1220	|	1312	...	1342	...	1350	...	...	1512
169		**Portbou** 🏛 .... **355** a.	...	|	0852	...	0922	1002	...	|	0957	1033	1126	1153	|	...	1203	1227	|	1323	...	1352	...	1357	...	...	1521
171		**Cerbère** 🏛 .... **355** a.	...	|	0857	...	0927	1007	...	|	...	...	1130	1157	|	...	...	...	|	1327	...	1357	...	...	...	...	1526
	177	**Perpignan** .... **355** a.	...	0730	...	...	...	...	...	0843	...	...	...	...	1044	...	...	...	1143	...	...	...	...	...	...	...	...

		TGV	*MD*	*MD*	*MD*	*MD*	*AVE*		*AVE*	*MD*	*MD*	*TGV*		*TGV*	*MD*	*MD*	*MD*	*AVE*	*MD*	*AVE*		*AVE*	*MD*	*MD*	*MD*	*AVE*	*MD*
		9704	**15910**	**15096**	**15096**	**15914**	**3113**		**3123**	**15012**	**15098**	**9707**		**9739**	**15080**	**15082**	**15922**	**9725**	**15084**	**3153**		**3163**	**15086**	**15088**	**15006**	**3183**	**15916**
	①–⑤		⑤⑦	①–⑤	⑥	⑦	**34113***		**34123***	Ⓑ		**9706**		**9738**	①–⑤	①–⑤	⑥⑦	**19724**	①–⑤	**34153***		**34163***	①–⑤	⑥⑦	Ⓑ	**34183***	
	p	**P**	**j**	**p**		**q**			Ⓑ			**P**		**L**	**p**	**p**	**q**	**M**	**p**			①–⑤	**p**	**q**			
Madrid ⊠ **630** .... d.	...	...	...	...	...	...	1130	...	1230	...	...	...	...	...	...	...	...	1540	...	1530	...	1630	...	...	...	1830	...
Barcelona Sants ... **666** d.	1316	1320	1346	1416	1416	1449	1450	1516	1540	1546	1616	1620	1716	1725	1746	1816	1819	1826	1846	1850	1916	1925	1946	2016	2046	2130	2146
Barcelona P de G ❖ .... d.	1320	|	1351	1421	1421	1454	|	1520	|	1551	1621	|	1720	|	1751	1821	1824	|	1851	|	1920	|	1951	2021	2051	|	2151
Granollers Centre .... d.	1346	|	|	|	|	|	|	1546	|	|	|	|	1746	|	|	|	|	|	|	|	1947	|	|	|	|	|	|
Maçanet - Massanes .**666** d.	1422	|	1443	1513	1513	1548	|	1622	|	1643	1713	|	1822	|	1843	1913	1920	|	1945	|	2026	|	2043	2113	2157	|	2250
Caldes de Malavella .... d.	1433	|	1454	1524	1524	1559	|	1633	|	1654	1724	|	1833	|	1854	1924	1931	|	1956	|	2037	|	2054	2124	2206	|	2301
Girona .... d.	1448	1401	1505	1535	1535	1610	1529	1648	1619	1703	1735	1701	1848	1804	1905	1935	1942	1905	2007	1929	2054	2004	2105	2135	2217	2209	2311
Flaçà .... d.	1502	|	1518t	1548	1548	1623	|	1702	|	...	1748	|	1902	|	1918	1948	1955	|	2020	|	2108	|	2118	2148	2229	|	2323
Figueres .... § d.	1527	|	1537t	1606	1607	1642	|	1727	|	...	1806	|	1927	|	1937	2006	2013	|	2038	|	2130	|	2138	2206	2246	|	2341
Figueres Vilafant .... § d.	|	1418	|	...	|	|	1543	|	1633	...	...	1718	|	1821	|	...	...	1922	...	1943	|	2018	...	...	...	2223	...
Llançà .... d.	1542	|	1550t	...	1620	1655	...	1742	...	...	...	|	1942	|	1950	...	...	|	...	...	2145	...	...	...	...	...	...
Portbou 🏛 .... **355** a.	1552	|	1557t	...	1627	1702	...	1751	...	...	...	|	1952	|	1957	...	...	|	...	...	2155	...	...	...	...	...	...
Cerbère 🏛 .... **355** a.	1557	|	...	...	...	...	...	1757	...	...	...	|	1957	|	...	...	...	|	...	...	...	...	...	...	...	...	...
Perpignan .... **355** a.	...	1443	...	...	...	...	...	...	...	...	...	1744	...	1844	...	...	...	1947	...	...	...	...	...	...	...	...	...

	MD	*MD*	*AVE*	*AVE*	*MD*	*MD*	*MD*		*AVE*	*MD*	*MD*	*AVE*		*MD*	*AVE*		*AVE*	*MD*	*TGV*		*MD*	*MD*	*AVE*		*AVE*	*TGV*	*MD*
	15010	**15046**	**3662**	**3082**	**15060**	**15060**	**15062**		**3092**	**15064**	**15066**	**3102**		**15068**	**9730**		**9741**	**15070**	**9711**		**15090**	**15002**	**3162**		**3172**	**9713**	**15072**
	①–⑤	①–⑥	**34662***	**34082***	①–⑤	⑥⑦	①–⑤	①–⑥	**34092***	⑦	①–⑥	**34102***			**19731**		**9740**		**9710**			①–⑤	**34162***		**34172***		⑥⑦
	p	**p**	①–⑤	①–⑤	**p**	**q**	**p**	**p**	①–⑥	**q**	**p**				**M**		**L**		**P**			**p**			⑦	**A P**	**q**
Perpignan .... **355** d.	...	...	...	...	...	...	...	...	...	...	...	...	...	...	1007	...	1109	...	1213	...	...	...	...	...	...	1513	...
Portbou 🏛 .... **355** d.	...	...	...	...	0623	...	...	0703	...	...	...	...	0833	...	|	1033	|	1127	|	1235	1327	...	...	1433	...	|	1527
Llançà .... d.	...	...	...	...	0630	...	...	0712	...	...	...	...	0842	...	|	1042	|	1135	|	1244	1335	...	...	1442	...	|	1535
Figueres Vilafant .... § d.	...	...	0630	0655	|	...	...	|	0755	...	...	0855	|	...	1034	|	1136	|	1245	|	|	...	1455	|	1545	1545	|
Figueres .... § d.	0544	0555	|	|	0643	0643	0713	0728	|	0749	0819	|	0858	0949	|	1058	|	1149	|	1300	1349	1419	|	1458	|	|	1549
Flaçà .... d.	0600	0615	|	|	0659	0659	0729	0750	|	0805	0835	|	0920	1005	|	1120	|	1205	|	1323	1405	1435	|	1520	|	|	1605
Girona .... d.	0614	0629	0646	0711	0713	0713	0743	0806	0810	0819	0849	0910	0936	1019	1049	1136	1151	1219	1301	1339	1419	1449	1510	1536	1600	1600	1619
Caldes de Malavella .... d.	0624	0640	|	|	0724	0724	0754	0820	|	0829	0859	|	0950	1029	|	1150	|	1229	|	1353	1429	1459	|	1550	|	|	1629
Maçanet - Massanes **666** d.	0635	0651	|	|	0735	0735	0805	0831	|	0839	0909	|	1001	1039	|	1201	|	1239	|	1404	1439	1509	|	1601	|	|	1639
Granollers Centre .... d.	|	|	|	|	|	|	|	0905	|	|	|	|	1035	|	|	1235	|	|	|	1437	|	|	|	1635	|	|	|
Barcelona P de G ❖ .... a.	0735	0749	|	|	0835	0835	0905	0934	|	0935	1005	|	1105	1135	|	1305	|	1335	|	1505	1535	1605	|	1705	|	|	1735
Barcelona Sants ... **666** a.	0739	0753	0725	0750	0839	0839	0909	0939	0848	0939	1009	0948	1109	1139	1127	1309	1229	1339	1340	1509	1539	1609	1548	1709	1638	1638	1739
Madrid ⊠ **630** .... a.	...	...	1010	1110	...	...	...	...	1145	...	...	1310	...	...	1413	...	...	...	...	...	...	...	1910	...	1945	...	...

	MD			*AVE*		*MD*	*MD*	*MD*	*MD*		*MD*	*TGV*	*AVE*	*MD*	*MD*		*TGV*			*MD*	*AVE*	*MD*		*TGV*	*AVE*		
	15072			**3182**		**15018**	**15018**	**15092**	**15092**		**15918**	**9743**	**3202**	**15074**	**15920**		**9715**			**15000**	**3222**	**15904**		**9717**	**9735**		
	①–⑤	⑤	Ⓑ	**34182***	⑥	①–⑤	⑦	①–⑤	⑥⑦	①–⑤	⑦		**34202***	Ⓑ	⑥	⑦	**9714**	①–⑤	⑥⑦	①–⑤	**34222***	①–⑤	⑥⑦		**9734**		
	p	**f**				**p**	**q**	**p**	**q**	**p**	**q**	**H L**				**q**	**P**	**p**	**q**	**p**	**k**	**p**	**q**	**P**	**T**		
Perpignan .... **355** d.	...	...	...	...	...	...	...	...	...	...	...	1810	...	...	...	...	1913	...	...	...	...	...	...	2125	2207	...	...
Portbou 🏛 .... **355** d.	...	...	1603	...	1633	...	...	...	1727	1733	1757	|	...	...	...	1839	|	1903	1941	...	...	2028	2028	|	|	...	...
Llançà .... d.	...	...	1612	...	1642	...	...	...	1735	1742	1805	|	...	...	...	1848	|	1912	1950	...	...	2036	2036	|	|	...	...
Figueres Vilafant .... § d.	...	...	|	1655	|	...	...	...	|	|	|	1838	1855	...	...	|	1945	|	|	...	2045	|	|	2150	2233	...	...
Figueres .... § d.	1549	...	1628	|	1658	1719	...	...	1749	1758	1819	|	|	1849	1856	1904	|	1928	2006	2029	|	2050	2049	|	|	...	...
Flaçà .... d.	1605	...	1650	|	1720	1735	...	...	1805	1820	1835	|	|	1905	1912	1926	|	1950	2030	2045	|	2106	2107	|	|	...	...
Girona .... d.	1619	1649	1706	1710	1736	1749	1749	1819	1819	1836	1849	1852	1910	1919	1926	1942	2001	2006	2046	2059	2100	2119	2121	2207	2248	...	...
Caldes de Malavella .... d.	1629	1659	1720	|	1750	1759	1759	1829	1829	1850	1859	|	|	1929	1936	1956	|	2020	2100	2109	|	2129	2134	|	|	...	...
Maçanet - Massanes **666** d.	1639	1709	1731	|	1801	1809	1809	1839	1839	1901	1909	|	|	1939	1946	2007	|	2031	2111	2119	|	2139	2145	|	|	...	...
Granollers Centre .... d.	|	|	1805	|	1835	|	|	|	|	1935	|	|	|	|	|	|	|	2105	2145	|	|	|	2219	|	|	...	...
Barcelona P de G ❖ .... a.	1735	1805	1835	|	1905	1905	1905	1935	1935	2004	2005	|	|	2035	2042	2105	|	2135	2215	2215	|	2235	2247	|	|	...	...
Barcelona Sants ... **666** a.	1739	1809	1839	1748	1909	1909	1909	1939	1939	2009	2009	1930	1948	2039	2046	2109	2040	2139	2219	2219	2138	2239	2251	2248	2326	...	...
Madrid ⊠ **630** .... a.	...	...	...	2110	...	...	...	...	...	...	...	...	2310	...	...	...	...	...	...	...	...	...	...	...	...	...	...

– From July 6.
– To commence on a date to be announced.
– To/from Lyon (Table **49**).
– To/from Marseille (Table **49**).
– To/from Paris (Table **13**).
– To/from Toulouse (Table **49**).

f – Also Aug. 14, Sept. 10.
j – Also Aug. 14, Sept. 10, 11, Oct. 13, Dec. 8.
k – To Zaragoza (Table **650**).
p – Not May 1, Aug. 15, Sept. 11, Oct. 13, Dec. 8.
q – Also May 1, Aug. 15, Sept. 11, Oct. 13, Dec. 8.
t – ⑦ (also May 1, Aug. 15, Sept. 11, Oct. 13, Dec. 8).

x – 0620 on ⑥⑦, also train numbers **3463** and **34463**.

❖ – Barcelona Passeig de Gràcia.
⊠ – Madrid Puerta de Atocha.
* – Train number for *Turista class (classified Av)*.

– **FIGUERES VILAFANT - FIGUERES BUS STATION (150m from Figueres).** *5 km.* By 🚌. Journey time: 15 - 20 minutes.

rom **Figueres Vilafant**: 0835 Ⓐ, 1020, 1050, 1125, 1150, 1255, 1345, 1550 Ⓐ, 1645 Ⓑ, 725, 1830, 1935, 1955, 2035 Ⓐ, 2240.

From **Figueres Bus Station**: 0600 Ⓐ, 0625 Ⓐ, 0725 ⚒, 0815, 0945, 1030, 1105, 1215, 1425 ⚒, 1515 ⑦, 1625, 1740, 1810, 1845, 1915, 2015, 2205.

2nd class VALL DE NÚRIA 658

ibes Enllaç - **Ribes** Vila - **Queralbs** - **Núria** rack railway

IGH SEASON:

⑦ (daily July 15 - Sept. 11), also Apr. 1, May 1, 20, June 24, Nov. 1:
rom Ribes: 0735 **v**, 0830 **n**, 0930 and hourly until 1730, also 1840 **c**, 2030 ⑤.
rom Núria: 0830, 0930 **n**, 1030 and hourly until 1830, also 1930 **c**, 2115 ⑤.

OW SEASON:

–⑤ (except dates above). No service from Nov. 4 (resumes early December)
om Ribes: 0750 **v**, 0940, 1120, 1300, 1455, 1645, 1830 ⑤, 2030 ⑤.
rom Núria: 0845, 1030, 1210, 1400, 1550, 1730, 1920 ⑤, 2115 ⑤.

ourney times **Ribes** – **Queralbs** (*6 km*) 24 minutes, **Ribes** – **Núria** (*12 km*) 44 minutes.
errocarrils de la Generalitat de Catalunya (FGC) ✆ +34 972 73 20 20. www.valldenuria.cat

– ⑤ (also July 27, Aug. 3-31, Sept. 1, 7, 11.
– Ski season only, also ⑥⑦ in June and July (daily July 29 - Sept. 1).   **v** – From Ribes Vila.

2nd class AEROPORT BARCELONA 659

Local rail service *Cercanías* (suburban) line **R2 Nord**. *14km*
Aeroport - Barcelona Sants – Barcelona Passeig de Gràcia
Journey time: 19 minutes Sants, 26 minutes Passeig de Gràcia

From Aeroport del Prat:
0542, 0608, 0638, 0708, 0738 and every 30 minutes until 2208, 2238, 2308, 2338.

From Barcelona Sants:
0513, 0535, 0609, 0639, 0709 and every 30 minutes until 2139, 2209, 2239, 2314.

660 MADRID - CÓRDOBA - SEVILLA and MÁLAGA — High-speed services

km		*Av*	*Av*	*AVE*	*AVE*	*AVE*	*AVE*	*AVE*	*AVE*	*Alvia*	*Alvia*	*Alta*	*AVE*	*Alta*	*AVE*	*AVE*	*Alvia*	*AVE*	*AVE*	*AVE*	*AVE*	*AVE*	*AVE*	*AVE*	*AVE*	*AVE*	*Alvia*	*AVE*	*AVE*
		2260	**2262**	**2070**	**2270**	**2072**	**2072**	**2080**	**2082**	**2084**	**2094**	**9366**	**2090**	**9218**	**3983**	**2092**	**2294**	**2100**	**2102**	**2110**	**3940**	**3990**	**2112**	**2120**	**2122**	**2130**	**4070**	**2140**	**2142**
		①–⑤	①–⑤	①–⑤		①–⑤	⑥	①–⑥		①–⑤	⑥⑦				①–⑥		⑥	①–⑥	①–⑤					Ⓑ					
		❦	❦	m		f	g	P				❦			V			w									Y		
	Barcelona Sants **650** . d.	...	...	...	...	...	...	...	...	...	...	...	...	...	...	...	...	...	...	...	0830	0830	...	...	...	...	...	...	...
0	**Madrid** Puerta de Atocha d.	0620	0620	0700	0730	0735	0739	0800	0825	0830	0915	0835	0900	0905	...	0935	0945	1000	1035	1100	│	│	1135	1200	1235	1300	1330	1400	1435
171	Ciudad Real d.	0720	0720	│	│	│	│	│	│	0922	1011	0937	0951	1007	1021	1026	│	│	│	│	1213	1213	│	│	1326	1351	1421	│	│
210	Puertollano d.	0738	0738	│	│	│	│	│	│	0937	1028	0953	1007	1023	1037	1044	│	│	│	│	1229	1229	│	│	1342	1407	1435	│	│
345	**Córdoba** d.	0830	0840	0844	│	│	│	0944	│	1020	1115	1039	1052	1110	1121	1127	1131	1144	│	1244	1319	1330	1324	1344	1425	1452	1517	1544	1619
470	**Sevilla** a.	0916	│	0930	0950	│	│	1030	│	1106	1202	│	1135	│	1205	│	│	1230	│	1330	1402	│	│	1430	│	1535	1605	1630	│
	Cádiz **671** a.	...	│	...	...	│	│	...	│	1238	1333	│	...	│	...	│	│	...	│	...	...	│	│	...	│	...	1745	...	│
	Huelva **671** a.	...	│	...	...	│	│	...	│	...	...	│	...	│	...	│	1320	...	│	...	...	│	│	...	│	...	...	...	│
419	Puente Genil - Herrera ¶ a.	...	0905	...	...	│	│	...	│	...	...	│	...	│	...	│	...	...	│	...	...	1351	│	...	1446	...	...	...	│
455	Antequera - Santa Ana § a.	...	0919	...	...	│	│	...	│	...	...	1117	...	1148	...	│	...	...	│	...	...	1402	1352	...	1459	...	...	...	│
	Algeciras **673** a.	...	│	...	...	│	│	...	│	...	...	1348	...	│	...	│	...	...	│	...	...	│	│	...	│	...	...	...	│
	Granada **673** a.	...	│	...	...	│	│	...	│	...	...	...	...	1330	...	│	...	...	│	...	...	│	│	...	│	...	...	...	│
513	**Málaga** María Zambrano a.	...	0945	...	...	1000	1009	...	1045	...	...	...	...	...	...	1217	...	...	1255	...	...	1424	1417	...	1525	...	...	...	1707

	AVE	*Alta*	*AVE*	*AVE*	*Alvia*	*IC*	*AVE*	*AVE*	*AVE*	*Alta*	*AVE*	*AVE*	*Alvia*	*AVE*	*AVE*	*Alvia*	*AVE*	*AVE*	*AVE*	*AVE*	*AVE*	*AVE*	*AVE*	*AVE*	*AVE*	*Av*	*AVE*		
	2150	**9330**	**2152**	**2160**	**2164**	**2364**	**2360**	**2162**	**2170**	**9234**	**2172**	**2180**	**2384**	**2382**	**2182**	**2184**	**3942**	**3992**	**3974**	**2190**	**2390**	**3946**	**2192**	**2200**	**2202**	**2410**	**2212**		
	Ⓑ		④⑤⑦			⑤	⑤				Ⓑ		Ⓑ	⑥	Ⓑ	⑤⑦			①⑤⑦	Ⓑ	Ⓑ	⑤				❦	Ⓑ		
	R	◐	j				q												E	k	S				T	T	A		
Barcelona Sants **650** .. d.	...	...	...	...	...	...	...	...	...	...	...	...	...	...	...	...	1550	1550	...	...	...	1645	...	...	...	...	...	...	...
Madrid Puerta de Atocha .d.	1500	1505	1535	1600	1615	1620	1630	1635	1700	1705	1735	1800	1805	1825	1830	1835	│	│	...	1900	1930	│	1935	2000	2035	2125	2135	...	...
Ciudad Real d.	│	│	│	│	│	│	│	│	1751	│	1826	│	│	1916	│	│	1936	1936	1942	1951	│	│	│	│	2127	2219	2230	...	...
Puertollano d.	│	│	│	│	│	│	│	│	1807	│	1842	│	│	1932	│	│	│	│	1957	2007	│	│	│	│	2142	2234	2247	...	...
Córdoba d.	│	1708	│	1744	│	│	1814	1819	1852	1909	1925	1944	1952	2015	│	│	2030	2040	2045	2052	│	2105	2119	2144	2227	2324	2329	...	...
Sevilla a.	1720	│	│	1830	│	1855	1900	│	1935	│	│	2030	│	│	│	│	2115	│	│	2135	2150	2155	│	2230	│	0010	│	...	...
Cádiz **671** a.	...	│	│	...	2013	│	...	│	...	│	│	...	│	│	│	2234	...	│	│	...	...	...	│	...	│	...	│	...	...
Huelva **671** a.	...	│	│	...	...	2023	...	│	...	│	│	...	2145	│	│	...	...	│	│	...	...	...	│	...	│	...	│	...	...
Puente Genil - Herrera ¶ a.	...	│	│	...	...	...	...	│	...	│	1946	...	...	2037	│	...	...	2104	2110	...	...	...	│	...	2248	...	2349	...	...
Antequera - Santa Ana § a.	...	1753	│	...	...	...	...	│	...	│	1959	...	...	2050	│	...	...	2118	2125	...	...	...	│	...	2302	...	0001	...	...
Algeciras **673** a.	...	2030	│	...	...	...	...	│	...	│	│	...	...	│	│	...	...	│	│	...	...	...	│	...	│	...	│	...	...
Granada **673** a.	...	...	│	...	...	...	...	│	...	2140	│	...	...	│	│	...	...	│	│	...	...	...	│	...	│	...	│	...	...
Málaga María Zambrano a.	...	...	1806	...	...	...	...	1907	...	...	2025	...	...	2115	2053	...	...	2140	2151	...	...	...	2207	...	2325	...	0025	...	...

	Av	*AVE*	*AVE*	*AVE*	*AVE*	*AVE*	*AVE*	*AVE*	*AVE*	*AVE*	*AVE*	*Alvia*	*AVE*	*AVE*	*Alvia*	*AVE*	*AVE*	*Alta*	*AVE*	*Alvia*	*Alta*	*Alta*	*Alvia*	*AVE*	*AVE*	*AVE*	*AVE*	*AVE*	*AVE*
	2261	**2063**	**2061**	**2073**	**2073**	**2271**	**2071**	**2083**	**2081**	**3993**	**3943**	**2285**	**2093**	**2091**	**2085**	**3971**	**2101**	**9219**	**2113**	**2095**	**9367**	**9367**	**2205**	**2111**	**2123**	**2121**	**2131**	**2143**	**2141**
	①–⑤	①–⑤	①–⑤	①–⑤	⑥		①–⑤	①–⑤				①–⑤		①–⑥	①–⑤	⑤⑥				⑥⑦	①–⑤	⑥⑦	⑥						Ⓑ
	T★	B	m	h	g			T						w		U						★							R
Málaga María Zambrano d.	...	0620	...	0710	0710	...	...	0800	...	0840	...	...	0900	...	...	0945	...	...	1105	...	...	...	...	...	1205	...	...	1405	...
Granada **673** d.	...	│	...	│	│	...	...	│	...	│	...	...	│	...	...	│	...	0910	│	...	...	...	...	...	│	...	...	│	...
Algeciras **673** d.	...	│	...	│	│	...	...	│	...	│	...	...	│	...	...	│	...	│	│	...	0843	0843	...	...	│	...	...	│	...
Antequera - Santa Ana § d.	...	0644	...	│	│	...	...	0823	...	0902	...	...	0926	...	...	1008	...	│	│	...	│	│	...	...	│	...	...	1429	...
Puente Genil - Herrera ¶ d.	...	0657	...	│	│	...	...	│	...	0916	...	...	│	...	...	1021	...	│	│	...	│	│	...	...	│	...	...	1442	...
Huelva **671** d.	...	│	...	│	│	...	...	│	...	│	...	0800	│	...	...	│	...	│	│	...	│	│	1025	...	│	...	...	│	...
Cádiz **671** d.	...	│	...	│	│	...	...	│	...	│	...	│	│	...	0815	│	...	│	│	0935	│	│	│	...	│	...	...	│	...
Sevilla d.	0610	│	0645	│	│	0715	0745	│	0845	│	0850	│	│	0945	0950	│	1045	│	│	1110	│	│	│	1145	│	1245	1345	│	1445
Córdoba d.	0653	0722	0729	│	│	0803	│	0856	0929	0944	0944	0950	0959	1028	1042	1051	1129	1132	1156	1159	1202	1202	1218	1229	1256	1328	│	1506	1529
Puertollano d.	0744	│	│	│	│	0845	│	│	│	│	│	│	1041	1110	1125	1135	│	│	│	1242	│	│	│	│	│	1413	│	1548	│
Ciudad Real d.	0759	│	│	│	│	0859	│	│	│	1041	1041	│	1057	1124	1140	1149	│	│	│	1257	│	│	│	│	│	1427	│	1603	│
Madrid Puerta de Atocha a.	0855	0905	0915	0935	0940	0955	1005	1040	1115	│	│	1140	1150	1220	1233	...	1315	1335	1340	1354	1405	1410	1410	1415	1440	1520	1605	1655	1715
Barcelona Sants **650** .. a.	...	...	...	...	...	...	...	...	...	1425	1425	...	...	...	...	...	...	...	...	...	...	...	...	...	...	...	...	...	...

	AVE	*AVE*	*AVE*	*Alvia*	*AVE*	*AVE*	*AVE*	*AVE*	*AVE*	*AVE*	*AVE*	*Alvia*	*Alta*	*AVE*	*Alvia*	*AVE*	*AVE*	*AVE*	*AVE*	*AVE*	*IC*	*AVE*	*AVE*	*Alta*	*Alvia*	*Av*	*AVE*	*AVE*	
	3991	**3941**	**2153**	**4181**	**2151**	**2163**	**3945**	**2361**	**2161**	**3973**	**2173**	**2365**	**9331**	**2171**	**2165**	**2183**	**3981**	**2181**	**2391**	**2193**	**2375**	**2191**	**2203**	**9237**	**2195**	**2411**	**2413**	**2213**	
			④⑤⑦	**4381**			⑦	⑦	Ⓑ	⑦		⑦					Ⓑ	Ⓑ	Ⓑ		⑦		④⑤⑦		⑤⑦		①–⑤	④⑤⑥⑦	
				Y				p		O			★				V	f	W							★	★		
Málaga María Zambrano d.	1435	...	1500	...	...	1605	...	...	...	1635	1700	...	...	...	...	1810	...	...	...	1905	...	...	2010	...	...	...	2035	2105	...
Granada **673** d.	│	...	│	...	...	│	...	...	...	│	│	...	...	...	...	│	...	...	...	│	...	...	│	1805	...	...	│	│	...
Algeciras **673** d.	│	...	│	...	...	│	...	...	...	│	│	...	1503	...	...	│	...	...	...	│	...	...	│	│	...	...	│	│	...
Antequera - Santa Ana § d.	1500	...	│	...	...	│	...	...	...	1658	1724	...	1733	...	...	│	...	...	...	1929	...	...	│	1949	...	...	2059	2129	...
Puente Genil - Herrera ¶ d.	1513	...	│	...	...	│	...	...	...	1711	1737	...	│	...	...	│	...	...	...	│	...	...	│	│	...	...	2113	2142	...
Huelva **671** d.	│	...	│	...	...	│	...	...	...	│	│	1620	│	...	...	│	...	...	...	│	1750	...	│	│	...	...	│	│	...
Cádiz **671** d.	│	...	│	1330	...	│	...	...	...	│	│	│	│	...	1640	│	...	...	...	│	│	...	│	│	1910	...	│	│	...
Sevilla d.	│	1450	│	1500	1545	│	1615	1625	1645	│	│	│	│	1745	│	│	1825	1845	1915	│	1919	1945	│	│	│	2100	│	│	...
Córdoba d.	1542	1542	│	1554	1629	1656	1700	1710	1729	1740	1802	1810	1815	1829	│	1900	1909	1929	│	2001	│	2029	│	2032	│	2149	2149	2206	...
Puertollano d.	1625	1625	│	1637	│	│	│	1752	│	1823	│	│	1919	│	│	│	1952	│	│	│	│	│	│	2121	│	2239	2239	2248	...
Ciudad Real d.	1639	1639	│	1653	│	│	│	1806	│	1837	│	│	1936	│	│	│	2005	│	│	│	│	│	│	2140	│	2255	2255	2303	...
Madrid Puerta de Atocha a.	│	│	1740	1751	1815	1840	│	1903	1915	...	1945	2001	2035	2015	2039	2045	...	2116	2135	2145	2158	2215	2235	2244	2319	2350	2350	2355	...
Barcelona Sants **650** .. a.	2022	2022	...	...	...	...	2110	...	...	...	...	...	...	...	...	...	...	...	...	...	...	...	...	...	...	...	...	...	...

A – Ⓑ (④⑤⑦ July 22 - Sept. 8).
B – ①–⑤ (①② July 22 - Sept. 8).
E – From València (dep. 1715).
K – From / to Santander (Table **684**).
O – To València (arr. 2101).
P – Not July 19 - Sept. 7, Nov. 2, Dec. 7, 9.
R – Not July 14 - Sept. 6, Nov. 1, Dec. 6.
S – Not July 1 - Sept. 20, Nov. 1, Dec. 6, 8.
T – From / to Toledo (Table **679**).
U – To València (arr. 1411).

V – From / to València (Table **668**).
W – Not July 1 - Sept. 20, Nov. 1, Dec. 6, 9.
Y – To / from León / Gijón (Table **685**).

f – Not Aug. 15, Sept. 9, Nov. 1, Dec. 6, 9.
g – Not Oct. 12, Nov. 9.
h – Not Aug. 15, Sept. 9.
j – Also Sept. 9, Dec. 9; not Aug. 15, Sept. 8, Dec. 8.
k – Not Aug. 15, Nov. 1, Dec. 6, 8.

m – Not Aug. 15, Nov. 1, Dec. 6.
p – Also Oct. 31, Dec. 5; not July 21, 28, Aug. 4, 11, 18, 25, Sept. 1.
q – Also Oct. 31, Nov. 3, Dec. 5, 9; not July 19, 26, Aug. 2, 9, 16, 23, 30, Nov. 1, Dec. 6.
w – Not Nov. 2, Dec. 7, 9.

★ – Also calls at Villanueva de CLP ❖ 23–24 mins after departing Córdoba.

◐ – Also calls at Villanueva de CLP ❖ 100 mins after departing Madrid.
❦ – Also calls at Villanueva de CLP ❖ 25–28 mins after departing Puertollano.
§ – ± *17 km* from Antequera.
¶ – ± *8 km* from Puente Genil.
☛ All trains convey 🍷. *AVE* trains also convey 🍴
❖ – Full name: Villanueva de Córdoba-Los Pedroches.

Madrid – Puertollano *Avant* high-speed shuttle services — *Turista* class; 🍷

		8260		8080		8100			8130	8140		8150		8170	8180	8190	8200		8220					
		A		E						A		E			D		Ⓑj							
Madrid Puerta de Atocha d.	...	0640	...	0805	...	1015	...	...	1315	1415	...	1545	...	1715	1815	1915	2015	...	2215	...	...	...	...	...
Ciudad Real d.	...	0736	...	0901	...	1111	...	...	1411	1511	...	1641	...	1812	1911	2011	2111	...	2311	...	...	...	...	...
Puertollano a.	...	0753	...	0918	...	1128	...	...	1428	1528	...	1658	...	1828	1928	2028	2128	...	2328	...	...	...	...	...

		8261		8271	8471	8081		8101		8121			8151	8161	8171	8181	8191		8211					
		D		D	A	D							E	A		⑦								
Puertollano d.	...	0625	...	0700	0750	0815	...	1015	...	1215	...	...	1515	1615	1715	1815	1915	...	2115	...	...	...	...	...
Ciudad Real d.	...	0642	...	0717	0807	0832	...	1032	...	1232	...	...	1532	1632	1732	1832	1932	...	2132	...	...	...	...	...
Madrid Puerta de Atocha a.	...	0742	...	0813	0903	0928	...	1128	...	1328	...	...	1628	1728	1828	1928	2028	...	2228	...	...	...	...	...

A – ①–⑤ (not Aug. 5 - 30, Nov. 1, Dec. 6). D – ①–⑤ (not Aug. 15, Nov. 1, Dec. 6). E – ①–⑥ (not Aug. 15, Nov. 1, Dec. 6). j – Not Aug. 15, Nov. 1, Dec. 6

Málaga – Córdoba – Sevilla *Avant* high-speed shuttle services — *Turista* class;

	8654	8664	8664	8694	8714	8744	8764	8784	8804
	A	A	C		A		E		
Málaga María Zambrano d.	...	0645	...	0915	...	1415	1615	1820	2015
Antequera - Santa Ana § d.	...	0711	...	0941	...	1441	1641	1844	2041
Puente Genil - Herrera ¶ d.	...	0725	...	0955	...	1455	1655	1858	2055
Córdoba a.	...	0750	...	1020	...	1520	1720	1922	2120
Córdoba d.	0650	0755	0755	1025	1255	1525	1725	1930	2125
Sevilla a.	0735	0840	0840	1110	1340	1610	1810	2015	2210

	8075	8085	8095	8095	8125	8155	8175	8195	8215	
	A	A	C	A			E			
Sevilla d.	0650	0800	0920	0920	1250	1540	1755	1935	2135	...
Córdoba a.	0735	0845	1005	1005	1335	1625	1840	2020	2220	...
Córdoba d.	0740	0850	1010	...	1340	1630	1845	2025	...	...
Puente Genil - Herrera ¶ d.	0803	0913	1033	...	1403	1653	1908	2048	...	...
Antequera - Santa Ana § d.	0817	0927	1047	...	1417	1707	1922	2102	...	...
Málaga María Zambrano a.	0845	0955	1115	...	1445	1735	1950	2130	...	...

A – ①–⑤ (not Aug. 15, Oct. 12, Nov. 1, Dec. 6, 9). C – ⑥⑦ (also Aug. 15, Oct. 12, Nov. 1, Dec. 6, 9). E – ①–⑤ (not Aug. 1 - 30, Oct. 12, Nov. 1, Dec. 6, 9). § – ± *17 km* from Antequera. ¶ – ± *8 km* from Puente Gen

MADRID - GRANADA, ALMERÍA and MÁLAGA 661

For other trains Madrid – Córdoba – Granada / Málaga and v.v. via the AVE high-speed line, see Table **660**

km		*MD* 17008	*MD* 13079		*Talgo* 276	*MD* 18030		*MD* 17041	*MD* 13083	*MD* 13035	*Talgo* 697	*MD* 13073	*Talgo* 278	*MD* 18032		*MD* 18034		*MD* 18036		*MD* 17000	*Hotel* 897		
		2 y	2		🍸	2		2	2	2	🍸	2	🍸	2		2		2		2	✕		
		①–⑤	E					C	E	E	N	E		①–⑤		⑧					R		
0	**Madrid** Chamartín .... **668a 669** d.	...	...	...	0800	0916	...	1258	...	...	...	...	1434	1545	...	1720	...	1918	...	2114	...	...	...
8	**Madrid** Atocha Cercanías **668a 669** d.	0713	...	...	0819	0929	...	1310	...	...	...	...	1453	1559	...	1734	...	1932	...	2128	...	...	...
57	Aranjuez .... **668a 669** d.	0751	...	...	|	1004	...	1342	...	...	...	...	|	1634	...	|	...	2010	...	2207	...	...	...
	Barcelona Sants **672** .... d.	|	...	...	|	|	...	|	...	...	0927	...	|	|	...	|	...	|	...	|	2000	...	...
	València Nord **668** .... d.	|	...	...	|	|	...	|	...	...	1245	...	|	|	...	|	...	|	...	|	2334	...	...
157	Alcázar de San Juan .... **678** d.	0840	...	...	0937	1102	...	1435	...	...	1545	...	1614	1723	...	1854	...	2101	...	2301	0242	...	...
206	Manzanares .... **678** d.	...	...	...	|	1126	...	1459	...	...	1609	...	1637	1747	...	1917	...	2124	...	...	|	...	...
323	Linares - Baeza .... a.	...	...	...	1117	1251	...	...	...	...	1735	...	1756	1911	...	2031	...	2241	...	...	0431	...	...
323	Linares - Baeza .... d.	...	...	...	1119	1252	...	...	...	...	1737	...	1801	1912	...	2031	...	2242	...	...	0441	...	...
441	Moreda .... d.	...	...	...	|	|	...	...	...	...	|	...	1933	|	...	|	...	|	...	...	|	...	...
499	**Granada** .... **673** a.	...	...	...	|	|	...	...	...	...	|	...	|	|	...	|	...	|	...	...	0730	...	...
466	Guadix .... **673** d.	...	...	...	1309	|	...	...	...	...	|	...	1956	|	...	|	...	|	...	...	...	...	...
565	**Almería** .... **673** a.	...	...	...	1422	|	...	...	...	...	|	...	2114	|	...	|	...	|	...	...	...	...	...
¶	**Jaén** .... d.	...	0640	...	...	1335	...	...	1435	1640	|	1835	...	1955	...	2117	...	2325	...	...	...	...	...
371	Andújar .... d.	...	0723	...	...	...	...	...	1519	1721	1817	1918	...	...	...	...	...	...	...	...	...	...	...
450	**Córdoba** .... a.	...	0812	...	...	...	...	...	1615	1813	1905	2013	...	...	...	...	...	...	...	...	...	...	...

	MD 18047		*MD* 18031		*MD* 18033	*Talgo* 277	*MD* 13001	*Talgo* 694		*MD* 13003	*MD* 17041		*MD* 18035	*MD* 13009	*MD* 18037	*MD* 13011	*Talgo* 279		*MD* 13017	*Hotel* 894			
	2 y		2		2	🍸	E 2	🍸	2	E 2	2		2	2	2	2	🍸		🍸	✕			
	①–⑤		①–⑤				①–⑤	N		⑥⑦	C			E		T			E	R			
Córdoba .... d.	...	...	...	...	...	...	0906	0950	...	1000	...	...	...	1451	...	1620	...	...	2045	...	...	...	...
Andújar .... d.	...	...	...	...	...	...	0959	1040	...	1056	...	...	...	1549	...	1717	...	...	2137	...	...	...	...
Jaén .... d.	...	...	0620	...	0830	...	1046	|	...	1143	...	...	1520	1634	1718	1811	...	...	2225	...	...	...	...
Almería .... **673** d.	...	...	|	...	|	0730	...	|	...	...	...	...	|	...	|	...	1536	...	...	...	...	...	...
Guadix .... **673** d.	...	...	|	...	|	0848	...	|	...	...	...	...	|	...	|	...	1654	...	...	...	...	...	...
Granada .... **673** d.	...	...	|	...	|	|	...	|	...	...	...	...	|	...	|	...	|	...	...	2130	...	...	...
Moreda .... d.	...	...	|	...	|	0910	...	|	...	...	...	...	|	...	|	...	|	...	...	|	...	...	...
Linares - Baeza .... a.	...	...	0700	...	0912	1040	...	1117	...	...	...	...	1602	...	1800	...	1859	...	...	2341	...	...	...
Linares - Baeza .... d.	...	...	0701	...	0913	1045	...	1120	...	...	...	...	1603	...	1801	...	1900	...	...	2353	...	...	...
Manzanares .... **678** d.	...	...	0817	...	1032	|	...	1236	...	...	1520	...	1723	...	1921	...	2019	...	...	|	...	...	...
Alcázar de San Juan .... **678** d.	0527	...	0843	...	1055	1223	...	1315	1355	...	1546	...	1745	...	1946	...	2044	...	...	0140	...	...	...
València Nord **668** .... a.	|	...	|	...	|	|	...	1602	|	...	|	...	|	...	|	...	|	...	...	0410	...	...	...
Barcelona Sants **672** .... a.	|	...	|	...	|	|	...	1939	|	...	|	...	|	...	|	...	|	...	...	0839	...	...	...
Aranjuez .... **668a 669** d.	0621	...	0936	...	1143	|	...	...	1447	...	1643	...	1830	...	2032	...	|	...	...	...	...	...	...
Madrid Atocha Cercanías **668a 669** a.	0656	...	1014	...	1214	1343	...	...	1526	...	1717	...	1905	...	2109	...	2213	...	...	...	...	...	...
Madrid Chamartín .... **668a 669** a.	...	...	1028	...	1231	1358	...	...	1541	...	1731	...	1919	...	2122	...	2227	...	...	...	...	...	...

C – To / from Ciudad Real (Table **678**).
D – From Sevilla (Table **671**).
E – To / from Cádiz (Table **671**).
G – ①–⑤ (not Aug. 15, Nov. 1, Dec. 6).
N – GARCÍA LORCA – 🛏12 🍸 Barcelona - Córdoba - Sevilla and v.v. (Table **672**).
R – ALHAMBRA *Trenhotel* – ⑧ (daily June 21 - Sept. 12): 🛏, 🛏1 (reclining) Barcelona - Granada and v.v.
T – Daily from Sevilla. From Cádiz on ①–⑤ (not Aug. 15, Nov. 1, Dec. 6). Table **671**.
y – Not Aug. 15, Nov. 1, Dec. 6.
¶ – Linares - Jaen: *59 km*. Jaen - Andújar: *54 km*.

2nd class MÁLAGA - TORREMOLINOS - FUENGIROLA 662

km					❦							
0	**Málaga** María Zambrano d.	0523	0558	0633	0653	and	2133	2203	2233	2303	2333	...
8	Málaga Aeropuerto ✈ ..... d.	0532	0607	0642	0702	every	2142	2212	2242	2312	2342	
16	**Torremolinos** .... d.	0543	0618	0653	0713	20	2153	2223	2253	2323	2353	...
20	Benalmádena .... d.	0554	0629	0704	0724	mins.	2204	2234	2304	2334	0004	...
31	**Fuengirola** .... a.	0606	0641	0716	0736	until	2216	2246	2316	2346	0016	...

				❦							
Fuengirola .... d.	0610	0645	0720	0740	and	2220	2250	2320	2350	0020	...
Benalmádena .... d.	0624	0659	0734	0754	every	2234	2304	2334	0004	0034	...
Torremolinos .... d.	0633	0708	0743	0803	20	2243	2313	2343	0013	0043	...
Málaga Aeropuerto ✈ .. d.	0644	0719	0754	0814	mins.	2254	2324	2354	0024	0054	...
Málaga María Zambrano a.	0652	0727	0802	0822	until	2302	2332	0002	0032	0102	...

❦ – 0653, 0733, 0813 from Málaga and 0740, 0820, 0900 from Fuengirola do not run on ①–⑤.

High-speed services MADRID - VALLADOLID 663

km		*Av* 4079	*Alvia* 4071	*Av* 8079	*Alvia* 4087	*Alvia* 4087	*Alvia* 4083	*Av* 8109	*IC* 4405	*Alvia* 4111	*Av* 8119	*Alvia* 4133	*AVE* 4149	*Alvia* 4141	*Alvia* 4155	*Alvia* 4155	*Av* 8359	*Alvia* 4167	*Alvia* 4167	*Av* 8169	*Av* 8179	*Alvia* 4183	*Alvia* 4181	*Alvia* 4197	*Av* 8299	*Av* 8399	*Alvia* 4201	*Av* 8219	
		①–⑤	①–⑥	①–⑤	①–⑥		①–⑥						①–⑤		4355	4355			⑧	①–⑤			4381	⑧	⑦		⑧		
			k	m 2			j	2		V	2		G				2		q	m 2	2		C	g T	y		p w	2	
	Alacant Terminal **668** d.	...	...	...	...	...	...	...	...	...	...	...	...	1100	1035x	...	...	...	...	...	...	1435	...	...	...	...	...	...	...
0	**Madrid** Chamartín .... d.	0710	0730	0738	0800	0800	0830	0945	1040	1105	1130	1325	1430	1440	1500	1500	1534	1605	1605	1615	1735	1805	1840	1855	1920	1945	2020e	2130	...
68	Segovia Guiomar ¶ ...... d.	0737	|	0806	0830	0830	|	1013	|	|	1158	|	|	1513	1530	1530	1602	1635	1635	1643	1803	1838	|	|	|	2013	|	2158	...
	A Coruña **680** .... a.	|	|	|	|	|	|	|	|	|	|	|	|	|	|	2114	|	|	|	|	|	|	|	|	|	|	|	|	...
	Pontevedra **680** .... a.	|	|	|	|	|	|	|	|	|	|	|	|	|	2203	...	|	|	|	|	|	|	|	|	|	|	|	|	...
180	**Valladolid** ⊠ .... a.	0811	0831	0843	0907	0907	0931	1050	1144	1208	1235	1438	1526	1550	...	...	1639	1723	1723	1720	1840	1925	1943	1955	2016	2050	2121e	2235	...
	Gijón Cercanías **681** . a.	...	1255	...	|	|	|	...	...	1621	...	|	...	2015	...	...	...	|	|	...	...	|	2353r	...	...	...	...	...	...
	Santander **681** .... a.	...	...	...	|	|	1255	...	...	...	...	1750	...	...	...	...	...	|	|	...	...	2247	...	...	...	...	...	...	...
	Bilbao Abando **689** ... a.	...	...	...	1247	|	...	...	...	...	...	...	...	...	...	...	...	|	2102	...	...	...	...	...	...	...	...	...	...
	Hendaye **689** .... a.	...	...	...	...	1351	...	...	...	...	...	...	...	...	...	...	...	2155	...	...	...	...	...	...	...	...	...	...	...

	Av 8278	*Av* 8478	*Av* 8088	*IC* 4060	*Av* 8288	*Alvia* 4076	*Av* 8098	*Alvia* 4072	*Alvia* 4070	*Alvia* 4092	*Alvia* 4086	*Alvia* 4086	*Av* 8138	*Alvia* 4084	*Alvia* 4284	*Alvia* 4100	*Av* 8158	*Alvia* 4142	*AVE* 4178	*Alvia* 4140	*Alvia* 4376	*Av* 8198	*Alvia* 4154	*Alvia* 4166	*Alvia* 4166	*Av* 8218	*Av* 8208	*Alvia* 4180	*Alvia* 4382
	①–⑤	①–⑤		①–⑤	①–⑤	①–⑤		①–⑤				①–⑥		4284	①–⑥				①–⑤		⑦	33398	⑧		⑧	①–⑥	⑦	4380	⑧
	m 2	m 2	2	G w	A	F T	2		C			q	2	①–⑥	f		2		G	V						2	y	①–⑥	t
Irún **689** .... d.	...	...	...	...	...	...	...	...	...	...	0825	...	...	...	...	...	...	...	...	...	1450	...	...	1620	...	...	...	t	...
Bilbao Abando **689** ..... d.	...	...	...	...	...	...	...	...	...	...	|	0857	...	...	...	...	...	...	...	...	|	...	...	|	1710	...	...	...	...
Santander **681** .... d.	...	...	...	...	...	...	...	0705	...	0905	|	|	...	...	...	...	...	1340	...	...	|	...	...	|	|	...	...	...	1850
Gijón Cercanías **681** ... d.	...	...	...	...	...	...	...	|	0700	|	|	|	...	...	...	1020	...	|	...	1400	|	...	...	|	|	...	...	1722	|
Valladolid ⊠ .... d.	0645	0715	0745	0810	0845	0909	0945	1025	1117	1245	1251	1251	1325	...	...	1440	1530	1654	1700	1820	1918	1956	...	2050	2050	2100	2105	2146c	2212
Pontevedra **680** .... d.	|	|	|	|	|	|	|	|	|	|	|	|	|	0740	...	|	|	|	|	|	|	|	1442	|	|	|	|	|	|
A Coruña **680** .... d.	|	|	|	|	|	|	|	|	|	|	|	|	|	|	0835	|	|	|	|	|	|	|	1535	|	|	|	|	|	|
Segovia Guiomar ¶ .... d.	0722	0752	0822	|	|	|	1022	1105	|	1325	1330	1330	1402	1412	1412	1519	1607	|	|	|	|	2033	2120	2130	2130	2137	2140	|	|
Madrid Chamartín .... a.	0750	0820	0850	0920	0941	1012	1050	1138	1222	1358	1400	1400	1430	1450	1440	1551	1635	1816	1756	1924	2030	2101	2148	2200	2200	2205	2206	2250c	2317
Alacant Terminal **668** .. a.	...	...	...	...	...	...	...	1506	...	1739	...	...	...	1846z	...	1932	...	...	...	...	...	...	...	...	...	...	...	...	...

A – Not July 15 - Sept. 13, Nov. 1, Dec. 6, 9.
C – From / to Cádiz (Table **671**).
F – Not Aug. 1 - 31, Oct. 25, Nov. 1, Dec. 6.
G – Not Aug. 1 - 31, Nov. 1, Dec. 6, 9.
T – To and from Vitoria / Gasteiz (Table **689**).
V – From / to València on dates shown in Table **668**.

c – 21 minutes earlier on ⑦.
e – 8 minutes earlier on ⑦.
f – From Ferrol (Table **682**).
g – Not Aug. 16, Oct. 24, 31, Nov. 1, Dec. 5, 6.
h – Also Aug. 15, Sept. 8.
j – Not Nov. 2, Dec. 7.
k – Not Sept. 9, Oct. 12, Nov. 2, 9, Dec. 7, 9.
m – Not Aug. 15, Nov. 1, Dec. 6.
p – Not Aug. 4, 11, 18, 25.
q – Daily May 25 - Sept. 15.
r – 2337 on ⑤.
t – Not Nov. 1, Dec. 6.
w – To / from León (Table **681**).
x – ⑦ only.
y – Not Aug. 1 - 31.
z – ⑥ only.

¶ – *4 km* from city centre.
☛ All trains convey 🍸. *AVE* trains also convey ✕.
⊠ – Full name is Valladolid Campo Grande.

664 BARCELONA - ANDORRA

From **Barcelona** Nord bus station: 0630*, 0700, 0730*, 1030, 1500, 1700*, 1900.
From **Andorra la Vella** bus station: 0600, 0815*, 1100, 1500, 1700*, 1915.
Journey 3 hr 15 min (*4 hours). Operator: Alsina Graells, Barcelona (ALSA) ✆ (+34) 91 327 05 40.

From **Barcelona Airport** ✈ (T1 and T2): 0730, 1100, 1300, 1500, 1730, 2000, 2300.
From **Barcelona** Sants railway station: 0615, 0815, 1145, 1345, 1545, 1815, 2045, 2345.
From **Andorra la Vella** bus station: 0615, 0815, 1115, 1315, 1515, 1815, 2015, 2215.
Journey 3 hours (3 hrs 30 mins to/from Barcelona ✈). Operator: Autocars Nadal ✆ +376 805 151.

665 BARCELONA - SITGES - SANT V de CALDERS 2nd class

Local rail service **Barcelona - Sitges - Sant Vicenç de Calders**.
From Barcelona Sants: 0606, 0636 and every 30 minutes until 2206; then 2306.
From Sant Vicenç: 0600, 0615 ⚒, 0632 Ⓐ, 0643 Ⓐ, 0658, 0732, 0751, 0816, 0831, 0903, 0933 and every 30 minutes until 2103, 2133 Ⓐ, then 2200.

Additional trains operate **Barcelona - Sitges** and v.v.

Journey times: **Barcelona – Sitges** (*34 km*) 30 minutes,
Barcelona – Sant Vicenç (*60 km*) 57 minutes.

666 BARCELONA - MATARÓ, BLANES and MAÇANET 2nd class

Cercanías (suburban) line **R1**. For faster services Barcelona - Maçanet via Granollers, see Table **657**.

Approximate journey times (in mins) to/from **Barcelona** Sants: Mataró (46), Arenys de Mar (57), Calella (69), Pineda de Mar (73), Malgrat de Mar (79), Blanes (84), Maçanet-Massanes (97).

Barcelona Sants – **Mataró** and v.v. *35 km*
Ⓐ: 4–6 trains per hour.
From Barcelona 0546–2354; from Mataró 0450–2313.
Ⓒ: 2–4 trains per hour.
From Barcelona 0612–0010; from Mataró 0457–2220.

Barcelona Sants – **Blanes** *67 km*
0612, 0642 and every 30 mins. until 2042, then 2112 Ⓒ, 2124 Ⓐ, 2142 Ⓒ, 2154 Ⓐ, 2213 Ⓒ, 2224 Ⓐ.
Blanes - **Barcelona** Sants
Ⓐ: 2 trains per hour, 0617–2115, 2155
Ⓒ: 2 trains per hour; 0603–2103, 2144.

Barcelona Sants – Blanes – **Maçanet-Massanes** *82 km*
Ⓐ: 0546 and hourly until 2045, 2124, 2154.
Ⓒ: 0612 and hourly until 2012, then 2042, 2142.
Maçanet-Massanes – Blanes – **Barcelona** Sants
Ⓐ: 0605, 0636, 0704, 0734, 0804 and hourly until 2103
Ⓒ: 0620, 0650, 0720 and hourly until 2020, then 2130.

667 ALACANT - BENIDORM - DÉNIA 2nd class

◐ *By tram (route L1)*									
Alacant Luceros ⊙ d.	...	0541	0611	every	1711	1811	1841	1941	2041
El Campello d.	...	0609	0639	hour	1739	1839	1909	2009	2109
La Vila Joiosa d.	0612	0635	0705	◐	1805	1905	1935	2035	2135
Benidorm a.	0630	0653	0723	until	1823	1923	1953	2053	2153
By train (route L9)									
Benidorm d.	0636	...	0736		1836	...	1959	2059	2159
Altea d.	0650	...	0750	every	1850	...	2013	2113	2211
Calpe d.	0712	...	0812	hour	1912	...	2035	2135	...
Gata d.	0739	...	0839	until	1939	...	2101	2201	...
Dénia a.	0753	...	0853		1953	...	2115	2215	...

By train (route L9)									
Dénia d.	...	...	0604		1804	1904	...	2026	...
Gata d.	...	...	0619	every	1819	1919	...	2041	...
Calpe d.	...	...	0646	hour	1846	1948	...	2111	...
Altea d.	0616	...	0708	until	1908	2014	...	2134	2216
Benidorm a.	0629	...	0721		1921	2027	...	2147	2229
✣ *By tram (route L1)*									
Benidorm d.	0635	0705	0735	every	1935	2035	2135	2205	2235
La Vila Joiosa d.	0653	0723	0753	hour	1953	2053	2153	2223	2253
El Campello d.	0723	0753	0823	✣	2023	2123	2223	2253	...
Alacant Luceros ⊙ a.	0751	0821	0851	until	2051	2151	2251	2321	...

◐ – Alacant - Benidorm runs every 30 minutes 0541 - 2141 (also 2319, 0119 night of ④⑤⑥ June 30 - Sept. 1).
✣ – Benidorm - Alacant runs every 30 minutes 0635 - 2205 (also 0113, 0313 night of ④⑤⑥ June 30 - Sept. 1).
⊙ – ± 400 m from Alacant Renfe station.

Operator: Tram Metropolitano / FGV ✆ 900 72 04 72
www.fgvalicante.com

668 MADRID - ALBACETE, ALACANT and VALÈNCIA

km		*AVE*	*AVE*		*AVE*	*AVE*	*Alvia*	*AVE*	*AVE*	*IC*	*AVE*	*AVE*	*AVE*	*AVE*	*AVE*	*Talgo*	*AVE*	*Alvia*	*AVE*	*AVE*	*Alvia*	*AVE*	*IC*	*Alvia*	*AVE*
		18024	**5270**	**5072**	**18018**	**5070**	**5080**	**5490**	**5094**	**5090**	**582**	**5102**	**5100**	**5110**	**5122**	**5120**	**694**	**5340**	**4092**	**5150**	**5152**	**4284**	**5162**	**584**	**4100**	**5160**
		①–⑤	①–⑤	①–⑥	⑥⑦	①–④				①–⑥	①–⑥		Ⓑ			①–④	🍷				①–⑤	⑥	Ⓑ			Ⓑ
		B	h		X	k	k	C	P	k			q			k	L		S			H			G	k
0	**Madrid** Puerta de Atocha d.	...	0710	0745	...	0740	0840	0910	0930	0940	...	1045	1040	1140	1230	1240	...	1410	1445	1540	1525	1555	1625	...	1645	1640
189	Cuenca Fernando Zóbel d.	...	0802	0837	...	|	|	1009	|	|	...	1138	|	1232	|	|	...	|	1548	1632	|	1657	|	...	1748	|
321	Requena/Utiel d.	...	0836	|	...	|	|	|	|	|	...	|	|	1306	|	|	...	|	|	1706	|	|	|	...	|	|
322*	**Albacete** d.	0806	|	0917	0918	|	|	|	1052	|	1100	1214	|	|	1352	|	1420	|	1626	|	|	1740	|	1650	1826	|
436	Villena AV d.	|	|	0959	|	|	|	|	|	|	|	1249	|	|	1427	|	|	|	1710	|	|	1824	|	|	1910	|
486	**Alacant** Terminal a.	|	|	1023	|	|	|	|	1142	|	|	1310	|	|	1448	|	|	|	1739	|	1730	1846	1845	|	1932	|
477	Xátiva d.	0928	|	...	1039	|	|	|	...	|	1205	...	|	|	...	|	1524	|	...	|	...	...	...	1756	...	|
391	**València** Joaquín Sorolla § a.	|	0900	...	|	0918	1018	1113	...	1120	|	...	1218	1330	...	1418	|	1545	...	1730	...	...	...	|	...	1818
	València Nord § a.	1011	...	...	1115	...	...	|	...	...	1243	...	...	...	...	...	1602	...	...	...	...	...	...	1835	...	...
	Sagunt a.	...	...	...	...	...	...	1141	...	...	...	...	...	...	...	...	|	...	...	...	...	...	...	...	...	...
	Castelló de la Plana **672** a.	...	...	...	...	...	...	1207	...	...	...	...	...	...	...	...	1654	...	...	...	...	...	...	...	...	...

	IC	*AVE*	*IC*	*AVE*	*AVE*	*AVE*	*AVE*	*Alvia*	*AVE*	*AVE*	*AVE*	*Hotel*
	5570	**5170**	**5036**	**5172**	**5180**	**5192**	**5392**	**4140**	**3981**	**5212**	**5410**	**894**
		Ⓑ	Ⓑ	Ⓑ		Ⓑ	⑥	Ⓑ	Ⓑ	Ⓑ		✕
	v		d					G	Y			Z
Madrid Puerta de Atocha d.	1710	1740	1748	1745	1840	1920	1920	2010	...	2105	2110	...
Cuenca Fernando Zóbel d.	1818	|	|	1838	|	|	2013	|	2121	2158	2203	...
Requena/Utiel d.	|	|	|	|	|	|	|	|	|	|	2238	...
Albacete d.	|	|	2011	1914	|	2040	2049	|	|	2234	|	0236
Villena AV d.	|	|	|	1949	|	|	2124	|	|	2309	|	|
Alacant Terminal a.	|	|	|	2010	|	2140	2145	|	|	2330	|	|
Xátiva d.	|	|	2113	...	|	...	...	|	|	...	|	|
València Joaquín Sorolla § a.	1926	1918	|	...	2018	...	...	2210	2215	...	2300	|
València Nord § a.	|	...	2153	...	...	...	...	|	...	...	...	0410
Sagunt a.	2006	...	...	...	...	...	...	2247	...	...	...	|
Castelló de la Plana **672** a.	2029	...	...	...	...	...	...	2312	...	...	...	0519

	AVE	*AVE*	*IC*	*AVE*	*AVE*	*AVE*	*AVE*	*Alvia*	*AVE*
	5261	**5063**	**5035**	**5071**	**5081**	**3983**	**5073**	**4111**	**5091**
	①–⑤	①–⑤	①–⑤	①–④		①–⑥	①–⑥	①–⑥	①–⑥
	k	h		E		Y	Q	G	J
Castelló de la Plana **672** d.	...	...	...	...	...	...	...	0721	...
Sagunt d.	...	...	...	...	...	...	...	0744	...
València Nord § d.	...	...	...	...	...	...	...	|	...
València Joaquín Sorolla § d.	0640	...	0620	0710	0800	0815	...	0820	0910
Xátiva d.	|	...	0658	|	|	|	...	|	|
Alacant Terminal d.	|	0605	|	|	|	|	0720	|	|
Villena AV d.	|	0627	|	|	|	|	|	|	|
Albacete d.	|	0708	0805	|	|	|	0810	|	|
Requena/Utiel d.	|	|	|	|	0823	|	|	|	|
Cuenca Fernando Zóbel d.	|	0750	|	|	0858	0908	|	|	|
Madrid Puerta de Atocha a.	0818	0843	1020	0848	0950	...	0932	1020	1048

	AVE	*AVE*	*AVE*	*Alvia*	*Alvia*	*AVE*	*AVE*	*Talgo*	*IC*	*AVE*	*AVE*	*Alvia*	*AVE*	*AVE*	*AVE*	*IC*		*AVE*	*AVE*	*AVE*	*AVE*	*Alvia*	*AVE*	*Alvia*	*IC*	*Hotel*
	5101	**5111**	**5093**	**4355**	**4141**	**5321**	**5123**	**697**	**583**	**5141**	**5151**	**4183**	**5161**	**5163**	**5171**	**5481**	**18027**	**5181**	**5191**	**5183**	**5391**	**5581**	**5211**	**5203**	**585**	**897**
	①–⑤		**5493**	⑦		Ⓑ	①–⑥	🍷					Ⓑ					Ⓑ	⑦						Ⓑ	✕
				H	G	k		L				S	k			v	A	k	q		k	C				Z
Castelló de la Plana **672** d.	...	...	...	...	...	...	...	1158	...	...	...	...	...	...	...	1632	...	...	...	...	...	1858	...	...	...	0036
Sagunt d.	...	...	...	...	...	...	...	|	...	...	...	...	...	...	...	1656	...	...	...	...	...	1921	...	...	...	|
València Nord § d.	...	...	...	...	...	...	...	1245	1348	...	...	...	...	...	...	|	1750	...	...	...	...	|	...	...	2045	0159
València Joaquín Sorolla § d.	1005	1110	...	...	...	1240	...	|	|	1410	1510	...	1610	...	1710	1730	|	1810	1910	...	1940	1955	2110	...	|	|
Xátiva d.	|	|	...	...	...	|	...	1326	1421	|	|	...	|	...	|	|	1826	|	|	...	|	|	|	...	2122	|
Alacant Terminal d.	|	|	0920	1035	1100	|	1240	|	|	|	|	1435	|	1610	|	|	|	|	|	1810	|	|	|	2010	|	|
Villena AV d.	|	|	0941	1058	1123	|	1301	|	|	|	|	1458	|	1631	|	|	|	|	|	|	|	|	|	2031	|	|
Albacete d.	|	|	1017	1143	1208	|	1337	1428	1524	|	|	1543	|	1707	|	|	1944	|	|	1900	|	|	|	2107	2229	0350
Requena/Utiel d.	1028	|	|	|	|	|	|	...	...	|	1533	|	|	|	|	|	...	|	|	|	|	|	2133	|	...	...
Cuenca Fernando Zóbel d.	1103	|	1053	1223	1245	|	1413	...	...	|	1607	|	|	1743	|	1834	...	|	|	|	|	2103	2207	2143	...	...
Madrid Puerta de Atocha a.	1155	1248	1147x	1326	1349	1418	1507	...	...	1545	1700	1718	1748	1835	1848	1940	...	1948	2048	2022	2124	2206	2300	2238	...	...

A – To Ciudad Real on ⑦ Table **678**.
B – From Ciudad Real on ① (Table **678**).
C – To/from Barcelona (Table **672**).
E – ①–④ (①–⑤ July 17 - Sept. 7).
G – From/to Gijón (Table **685**).
H – From/to Pontevedra (Table **680**).
J – ①–⑥ (daily July 17 - Sept. 7).
L – GARCÍA LORCA – 🛋 🍷 Barcelona - Sevilla and v.v. (Table **672**).
P – On ⑦ train runs as **5292**, d. Albacete 1059, a. Alacant 1157.
Q – On ⑥ train runs as **5473**, d. Albacete 0819, a. Madrid 0947.
S – From/to Santander (Table **684**).

X – ⑥⑦ (also Aug 15, Dec. 8).
Y – From/to Sevilla (Table **660**).
Z – ALHAMBRA *Trenhotel* – Ⓑ (daily June 21 - Sept. 12): 🛏, 🛋 (reclining) Barcelona - Castelló de la Plana - Albacete - Granada and v.v.

d – Not July 1 - Sept. 13, Nov. 1, Dec. 6.
h – Not Aug. 15, Oct. 13, Dec. 8.
j – Not July 20 - Sept. 8, Oct. 9.
k – Not July 17 - Sept. 7.
p – Not July 20 - Sept. 8, Nov. 1, Dec. 6.
q – Daily July 17 - Sept. 7.

t – Also July 2, 16, 17, Aug. 1, 2, 15.
v – To Vinaròs on ⑤; From Vinaròs on ⑦ (Table **672**).
x – 1158 on ⑥.
y – Not July 20 - Sept. 8, Oct. 9, Nov. 1, Dec. 6.

§ – Free 🚌 between València Joaquín Sorolla and València Nord, 0615 - 2330, every ± 10 minutes.
* – Albacete - Xátiva - València: *203 km*.
☛ Additional journey Ⓑ *AVE* **5193** dep. Alacant 1905 arr. Madrid 2113.

△ – *Cercanías* (suburban) line **C1**: **València - Gandia** and v.v. *62 km* 2nd class. Journey time: 54 - 60 minutes.

From **València** Nord
Ⓐ: 0611, 0641 and every 30 minutes until 1941; then 1956, 2033, 2041, 2111, 2141, 2211, 2241.
Ⓒ: 0641, 0741 and hourly until 2241.

From **Gandia**
Ⓐ: 0605, 0640, 0655, 0710, 0725, 0740, 0755, 0825, 0840, 0855, 0915, 0925 0955 and every 30 minutes until 2225.
Ⓒ: 0655, 0755 and hourly until 2055; then 2225.

MADRID - CARTAGENA 668a

km		*Alta* 220	*Alta* 222	*Talgo* 694	*Alta* 228	*MD* 18040	*Alaris* 584	*IC* 10146	*Alta* 224	*MD* 18042	*Alta* 226
		🍷	🍷	🍷	🍷				🍷		🍷
		b		A	Ⓑq		w	B		Ⓑ	Ⓑ
0	**Madrid** Chamartín ‡ d.	0713	0900	...	1234	1419	...	1555	1629	1818	1900
8	**Madrid** Atocha C ◧ ‡ d.	0730	0921	...	1251	1432	...	1609	1648	1832	1919
57	Aranjuez ‡ d.	|	|	...	|	1509	...	1649	|	1908	|
157	Alcázar de San Juan ‡ d.	0849	|	1315	1404	1604	1658	|	|	2000	2034
288	**Albacete** d.	0947	1132	1418	1502	1715	1759	|	1856	2106	2135
354	Hellín d.	1023	|	...	|	...	...	|	|	...	2215
466	Murcia **672** d.	1144	1326	...	1645	...	...	2006	2050	...	2331
531	**Cartagena** **672** a.	...	1412	...	1728	...	...	...	2138	...	0017

	MD 18047	*MD* 18041	*MD* 18049	*Alta* 221	*Alta* 223	*Talgo* 697	*Alta* 229	*MD* 18043	*Alta* 225	*IC* 10418	18027	*Alta* 227
	①-⑤	①-⑤	⑥⑦	🍷	🍷	🍷	🍷		🍷			🍷
	y	y		b		A	Ⓑ			C	w	Ⓑ
Cartagena **672** d.	...	...	...	0530	0850	...	1215x	...	1600	...	...	1820
Murcia **672** d.	...	...	...	0610	0936	...	1258	...	1647	1734	...	1905
Hellín d.	...	...	...	|	1049	...	|	...	|	|	...	2026
Albacete d.	0412f	0605	0730c	0753	1129	1430	1446	1740	1834	|	1946	2107
Alcázar de San Juan ‡ d.	0527	0711	0837	|	1235	1530	|	1851	1929	|	2106	2204
Aranjuez ‡ d.	0621	0807	0933	|	|	...	|	1948	|	2058	...	|
Madrid Atocha C ◧ ‡ a.	0656	0844	1008	1008	1402	...	1704	2020	2045	2144	...	2325
Madrid Chamartín ‡ a.	...	0858	1022	1025	1416	...	1718	2034	2100	2200	...	2340

A – GARCÍA LORCA – [12] 🍷 Sevilla - Alcázar - Albacete - Barcelona and v.v. (Table **672**).
B – ⑤: [2] Madrid - Murcia - Aguilas (arrive 2150).
C – ⑦: [2] Aguilas (depart 1555) - Murcia - Madrid.
b – ①-⑤ (not Aug. 1 - 31).
c – ⑥ (also Aug. 15, Dec. 8).
f – ① only.
q – Also ⑥ Aug. 3 - 31.
w – To / from València Nord (Table **668**).
x – ⑦ (daily Aug. 1 - 31).
y – Not Aug. 15, Dec. 8.
‡ – See also Table **661**.
◧ – Madrid **Atocha Cercanías**.

2nd class MADRID - CUENCA - VALÈNCIA 669

km		18160	18160	18160	18162	18162	14162	18164	18164	18768
		①-⑤	⑦	⑥	①-⑤	⑦	⑦	①-④	⑤⑥⑦	⑤
		m	w		m	w		g	h	k
0	**Madrid** Atocha Cercanías d.	*0625*	0630	0800	*1221*	1248	...	*1621*	1628	1754
8	Villaverde Bajo **677** d.	*0633*	0638	0808	*1229*	1256	...	*1629*	1638	1803
49	Aranjuez **661 668a** a.	*0709*	0712	0836	*1305*	1330	...	*1708*	1708	1832
49	Aranjuez **661 668a** d.	0715	0715	0837	1331	1331	...	1709	1709	1833
201	**Cuenca** d.	0921	0921	1043	1536	1536	1740	1915	1915	2048
327	Requena d.	1155	1155	1303	1756	1756	2010	2139	2139	...
399	**València** Sant Isidre ◧ a.	1255	1255	1408	1904	1904	2126	2240	2240	...

	18161	18161	18163	18163		18765	18165	18165	14163
	⑥⑦	①-⑤	⑤⑦	①-④		⑦	⑤⑥⑦	①-④	⑤
	w	m	h	g			h	g	k
València Sant Isidre ◧ d.	0655	0655	1012	1012	...	...	1514	1514	1700
Requena d.	0818	0818	1125	1125	...	...	1639	1639	1814
Cuenca d.	1045	1045	1410	1410	...	1745	1914	1914	2041
Aranjuez **661 668a** a.	1242	1242	1610	1610	...	1953	2114	2114	...
Aranjuez **661 668a** d.	1242	*1250*	1613	*1630*	...	1954	2116	*2132*	...
Villaverde Bajo **677** a.	1315	*1326*	1649	*1706*	...	2026	2149	*2208*	...
Madrid Atocha Cercanías a.	1323	*1334*	1657	*1715*	...	2035	2158	*2216*	...

g – Not Aug. 15.
h – Also Aug. 15.
k – Also Aug. 14, not Aug. 15.
m – Not Aug. 15, Dec. 8.
w – Also Aug. 15, Dec. 8.
▷ – València **Sant Isidre**.
¦ – 7 - 9 mins. later on ⑥⑦.
§ – 5 mins. later on ⑦.
◧ – *Renfe* rail tickets to / from València are valid on *MetroValencia* services between Sant Isidre and either Plaça d'Espanya (on Line 1) or Bailén (on Line 5) – both are adjacent to València Nord main railway station. Allow at least 15 minutes for the transfer. València Joaquín Sorolla is three station stops from Sant Isidre on either Line 1 or Line 5.

2nd class (except *AVE* trains) VALÈNCIA - TERUEL - ZARAGOZA - HUESCA - CANFRANC 670

km						18500	*IC* 18502		*IC* 18504	*AVE* 3363	*AVE* 3393	*IC* 18506	14530
		①-⑤	⑥⑦	①-⑤	⑥⑦								
		h	q	y	p				C	E			A
0	**València** Nord d.	...	...	...	...	...	0917	...	1230	...	...	1730	1903
34	Sagunt d.	...	...	...	...	...	0948	...	1303	...	...	1801	1937
65	Segorbe d.	...	...	...	...	...	1015	...	1331	...	...	1831	2013
171	**Teruel** d.	...	...	...	...	0633	1158	...	1512	...	...	2017	2213
242	Calamocha d.	...	...	...	...	0719	|	...	1554	...	...	2058	...
305	Cariñena d.	...	...	...	...	0812	1327	...	1639	...	...	2141	...
	Madrid ◇ **650** d.	...	...	...	...	|	|	...	|	1605	1905	|	...
359	**Zaragoza** Delicias d.	0624	0640	0840	0847	0900	1402	1541	1716	1727	2034	2224	...
361	**Zaragoza** Portillo d.	0627	0643	0843	0853	0911	1407	1545	1720	|	|	2228	...
363	**Zaragoza** Goya d.	0629	0645	0845	0855	0914	1409	1549	1723	|	|	2230	...
417	Tardienta d.	0710	0727	0932	0936	...	...	1629	...	|	2105	...	...
439	**Huesca** d.	0727	0748	0953	0959	...	...	1652	...	1810	2118	...	...
474	Ayerbe d.	...	0831	1036	1047	...	...	1738x	...	...	...	...	...
533	Sabiñánigo d.	...	0937	1143	1157	...	...	1841x	...	...	...	...	...
549	Jaca d.	...	0953	1159	1214	...	...	1902x	...	...	...	...	...
574	**Canfranc 324** a.	...	1026	1232	...	...	...	1937x	...	...	...	...	...

		14531	*IC* 18511	*AVE* 3272		*IC* 18523		*IC* 18515	18517		*AVE* 3593	
	①-⑤				①-⑤		⑥⑦			⑥⑦		
	h	B				k				p	E	
Canfranc 324 d.	...	...	...	...	0600	...	0845	...	...	...	...	1753
Jaca d.	...	...	...	...	0635	...	0920	...	...	1610	...	1828
Sabiñánigo d.	...	...	...	...	0650	...	0934	...	...	1625	...	1844
Ayerbe d.	...	...	...	...	0757	...	1045	...	...	1737	...	1953
Huesca d.	0640	...	...	0800	0845	...	1138	...	...	1827	1935	2041
Tardienta d.	0656	...	...	0812	0859	...	1152	...	...	1842	|	2055
Zaragoza Goya d.	0738	...	0806	|	0940	1107	1234	1704	1923	1935	|	2139
Zaragoza Portillo d.	0740	...	0808	|	0942	1110	1236	1707	1925	1939	|	2144
Zaragoza Delicias d.	0744	...	0813	0845	0945	1117	1240	1711	1935	1943	2020	2148
Madrid ◇ **650** a.	...	...	|	1020	...	|	...	|	|	...	2140	...
Cariñena d.	...	...	0855	...	...	1202	...	1751	2018	...	...	...
Calamocha d.	...	...	0938	...	...	1247	...	1844	2111	...	...	...
Teruel d.	...	0725	1023	...	...	1331	...	1929	2158	...	...	...
Segorbe d.	...	0914	1206	...	...	1518	...	2119	...	...	...	...
Sagunt d.	...	0949	1243	...	...	1548	...	2150	...	...	...	...
València Nord a.	...	1022	1312	...	...	1618	...	2219	...	...	...	...

A – ②④⑥⑦.
B – ①③⑤⑦.
C – From Cartagena on ①-⑤ and from Murcia on ⑥ (Table **672**).
E – ⑤⑦ (also Aug. 14; not Aug. 16).
h – Not Aug. 15, Nov. 1, Dec. 6, 25.
k – To Cartagena (Table **672**).
p – Also Aug. 15, Nov. 1, Dec. 6, 25.
q – Also Aug. 15, Nov. 1, Dec. 6.
x – Not Dec. 24, 31.
y – Not Aug. 15, Nov. 1, Dec. 6.
◇ – Madrid Puerta de Atocha.

CÓRDOBA - SEVILLA - HUELVA and CÁDIZ 671

km		*MD* 13000	*MD* 13002	*MD* 13030	*MD* 13099	*MD* 13079	*MD* 13037	*MD* 13020	*Alvia* 2084	*Alvia* 2084	*MD* 13008	*Alvia* 2294	*MD* 13010	*MD* 13032	*MD* 13032	*Alvia* 4070	*MD* 13014	*MD* 13039	*MD* 13083	*Alvia* 2164	*MD* 13035	*Talgo* 697	*IC* 394	*Alvia* 2384	*MD* 13095	*Alvia* 2184	*MD* 13073
		2f	2f	2f	2k	2	2f	2			2f		2	2	2f		2	2	2		2		2		2		2
		①-⑤	①-⑥	①-⑤	⑥⑦	J	①-⑤		①-⑤	⑥⑦	①-⑤	⑥			①-⑤	T			J		J	G		Ⓑ		⑤⑦	J
	Madrid PA ✣ **660** d.	...	...	...	...	...	...	...	0830	0915	...	0945	...	...	...	1330	...	...	...	1615	...	...	...	1805	...	1835	...
0	**Córdoba** **660** d.	...	...	0715	...	0814	...	0908	1020	1115	...	1131	...	1400	1400	1517	...	...	1620	|	1815	1910	...	1952	...	|	2015
51	Palma del Río d.	...	...	0744	...	0845	...	0940	|	|	...	|	...	1431	1431	|	...	...	1653	|	1845	|	...	|	...	|	2048
129	**Sevilla** **660** a.	...	...	0834	...	0933	...	1029	1106	1202	...	|	...	1520	1520	1605	...	...	1740	|	1936	2025	...	|	...	|	2133
129	**Sevilla** **673** § d.	0637	0745	0845	0845	0945	1000	1045	1109	1205	1245	|	1445	...	1545	1608	1645	1700	1745	|	1945	...	2045	|	2050	|	2150
204	La Palma del Condado d.	|	|	|	0949	|	1108	|	|	|	|	1254	|	...	|	|	|	1758	|	|	|	...	|	2120	2149	|	|
244	**Huelva** a.	|	|	|	1020	|	1138	|	|	|	|	1320	|	...	|	|	|	1834	|	|	|	...	|	2145	2218	|	|
145	Dos Hermanas **673** § d.	0651	0758	0858	...	0958	...	1058	|	|	1258	...	1500	...	1559	|	1658	...	1758	|	1958	...	2058	...	...	|	2203
162	Utrera § d.	0702	|	0908	...	|	...	1108	|	|	1308	...	|	...	1609	|	|	...	1808	|	|	...	2109	...	...	|	2213
224	Aeropuerto de Jerez d.	0736	|	0947	...	|	...	1143	|	|	1345	...	1545	...	|	|	1741	...	1844	|	|	...	|	...	...	|	2248
236	Jerez de la Frontera d.	0743	0846	0954	...	1046	...	1151	1204	1259	1353	...	1552	...	1651	1710	1749	...	1852	1937	2048	...	2148	...	...	2158	2256
251	Puerto de Santa María d.	0753	0855	1003	...	1055	...	1200	1213	1308	1402	...	1601	...	1700	1719	1758	...	1901	1946	2057	...	2157	...	...	2207	2305
270	San Fernando - Bahía Sur d.	0809	0911	1019	...	1110	...	1214	1228	1323	1418	...	1617	...	1714	1734	1813	...	1917	2001	2112	...	2212	...	...	2222	2321
285	**Cádiz** a.	0823	0923	1030	...	1123	...	1226	1238	1333	1430	...	1630	...	1726	1745	1825	...	1930	2013	2125	...	2223	...	...	2234	2335

	MD 13001	*MD* 13041	*Talgo* 694	*MD* 13003	*Alvia* 2285	*Alvia* 2085	*MD* 13005	*Alvia* 2095	*MD* 13007	*Alvia* 2205	*MD* 13009	*MD* 13011	*MD* 13011	*Alvia* 4181	*IC* 393	*MD* 13013	*MD* 13043	*MD* 13015	*Alvia* 2365	*Alvia* 2165	*MD* 13017	*MD* 13031	*MD* 13049	*Alvia* 2195	*MD* 13019	*MD* 13021	
	2fJ	2		2			2		2🍷f		2	2fJ	2	4381	2	2f	2	2			2	2	2		2	2	
	①-⑤		G	M	①-⑤	①-⑤		⑥⑦	①-⑤	⑥	J	①-⑤	J	T		①-⑤			⑦		J			⑤⑦			
Cádiz d.	0540	...	...	0640	...	0815	0840	0935	0940	...	1140	1240	...	1330	1412	1440	...	1540	...	1640	1740	1840	...	1910	1940	2040	...
San Fernando - Bahía Sur d.	0553	...	...	0651	...	0827	0851	0947	0951	...	1151	1251	...	1342	1423	1451	...	1551	...	1652	1751	1851	...	1922	1951	2052	...
Puerto de Santa María d.	0608	...	...	0706	...	0840	0905	1001	1006	...	1206	1306	...	1355	1436	1506	...	1606	...	1706	1805	1905	...	1936	2006	2106	...
Jerez de la Frontera ¦ d.	0617	...	...	0715	...	0850	0914	1011	1015	...	1215	1315	...	1405	1445	1515	...	1615	...	1716	1814	1914	...	1946	2015	2115	...
Aeropuerto de Jerez ¦ d.	0624	...	...	0723	...	|	|	|	1023	...	1223	|	...	|	|	1523	...	1623	...	|	1822	1921	...	|	|	|	...
Utrera § d.	0702	...	...	0801	...	|	|	|	|	...	|	1356	...	|	1525	|	...	1700	...	|	|	|	...	|	2102	2156	...
Dos Hermanas **673** § d.	0712	...	...	0811	...	|	1007	|	1107	...	1306	1406	...	|	1535	1606	...	1710	...	|	1906	2005	...	|	2112	2206	...
Huelva d.	|	0700	...	|	0800	|	|	|	|	1025	|	|	...	|	|	|	1500	|	1620	|	|	|	1900	|	|	|	...
La Palma del Condado d.	|	0730	...	|	0824	|	|	|	|	1047	|	|	...	|	|	|	1530	|	1647	|	|	|	1930	|	|	|	...
Sevilla **673** § a.	0728	0830	...	0826	|	0947	1022	1107	1120	|	1320	1420	...	1458	1549	1620	1627	1725	|	|	1920	2017	2030	|	2128	2220	...
Sevilla **660** d.	0745	...	0835	0838	|	0950	...	1110	...	|	1330	1503	1500	1500	...	...	...	1735	|	|	1925	2030	...	|	...	...	...
Palma del Río d.	0831	...	|	0926	|	|	...	|	...	|	1415	1552	1549	|	...	...	...	1823	|	|	2012	2121	...	|	...	...	...
Córdoba **660** a.	0904	...	0945	1000	0948	1040	...	1157	...	1216	1449	1621	1618	1552	...	...	...	1905	1810	|	2043	2152	...	|	...	...	...
Madrid PA ✣ **660** a.	...	...	...	...	1140	1233	...	1354	...	1410	...	...	...	1751	...	...	...	...	2001	2039	...	...	...	2319	...	...	...

– GARCÍA LORCA – [12] 🍷 Barcelona - València - Córdoba - Sevilla and v.v. (Table **672**).
– From / to Jaén (Table **661**).
– To Jaén on ⑥⑦ (Table **661**).
– To / from León / Gijón (Table **685**).
f – Not Aug. 15, Dec. 8.
k – Also Aug. 15, Dec. 8.
§ – Frequent suburban services operate Sevilla - Utrera and v.v.
¦ – Additional suburban services operate Jerez de la Frontera - Aeropuerto de Jerez and v.v.: depart Aeropuerto 0720 Ⓐ, 0820 Ⓒ, 1325, 1920; depart Jerez 0657 Ⓐ, 0757 Ⓒ, 1257, 1857.
✣ – Madrid Puerta de Atocha.

672 BARCELONA - VALÈNCIA - ALACANT - CARTAGENA

km		*MD*	*Alvia*				*Em*	*Em*		*Em*	*Talgo*	*Em*		*Talgo*		*Talgo*			*IC*	*Em*	*Talgo*	*Talgo*		*Em*	*Alvia*
		14123	**4111**	2	2	2	**1071**	**1081**		**1091**	**697**	**1101**		**1111**		**463**			**5481**	**1341**	**165**	**10541**		**1161**	**5581**
		2		①–⑤	⑥	①–⑥	①–⑥	①–④	2	⑤⑥			2		2	🍷	2	2	⑦	Ⓑ		⑤	2		
				v	**n**	**o**	**h**	**d**		**j**	**A**					**M**				**y**					
0	**Barcelona** França ... d.	...	...	...	...	0548	0634	0734	0747	...	0904	0934	0919	...	1047	...	...	1318	...	1404	...	...	1446	1534	1604
5	Barcelona Passeig de Gràcia d.	...	...	...	...	0556	|	|	0756	...	|	|	0927	...	1055	...	...	1326	...	|	...	...	1456	|	|
8	**Barcelona** Sants ... **652** d.	...	...	...	...	0603	0700	0800	0803	0900	0927	1000	0933	1100	1103	1200	...	1333	...	1430	1500	1530	1503	1600	1630
68	Sant Vicenç de Calders **652** d.	...	...	...	...	0648	|	|	0848	|	|	|	1019	|	1147	|	...	1416	...	|	|	|	1547	|	|
82	Altafulla - Tamarit ... d.	...	...	...	...	0658	|	|	0859	|	|	|	1030	|	1158	|	...	1426	...	|	|	|	1558	|	|
93	**Tarragona** ... **652** d.	...	...	...	...	0707	0754	0856	0909	0955	1027	1055	1041	1155	1207	1254	...	1435	...	1524	1555	1625	1608	1657	1720
103	Port Aventura ... d.	...	...	...	...	0720	|	|	0918	|	|	|	1049	|	1216	|	...	1443	...	|	|	|	1616	|	|
105	Salou ... d.	...	...	...	...	0724	|	|	0923	|	1039	|	1052	1204	1219	1307	...	1447	...	|	1606	|	1620	|	|
	Tortosa ... d.	...	...	0645	0751	|	|	|	|	|	|	|	|	|	|	|	1330	|	...	|	|	|	|	|	|
163	L'Aldea - Amposta ... d.	...	...	0658	0802	0807	|	|	1003	|	1107	|	1138	1237	1302	1335	1342	1532	...	|	1634	|	1710	|	|
176	Tortosa ... a.	...	...	|	|	0817	|	|	1012	|	|	|	1149	|	1312	|	|	1542	...	|	|	|	1720	|	|-
202	Vinaròs ... d.	...	...	0720	0828	...	|	|	...	|	1122	|	1227	1255	▬	1350	1404	▬	1550	|	1650	|	▬	|	1812
208	Benicarló - Peñíscola ... d.	...	...	0726	0833	...	|	|	...	|	1129	|	1233	1300	...	1355	1410	*IC*	1555	|	1656	|	...	|	1818
268	Benicàssim ... d.	...	...	0804	0914	...	|	|	...	|	|	|	1310	1330	...	1419	1447	**18523**	1623	|	1723	|	2	|	1846
280	Castelló de la Plana ... d.	...	0724	0815	0922	...	0915	1011	...	1117	1158	1215	1319	1339	2	1427	1456	🅁 2	1632	1643	1734	|	⑤	1812	1858
353	**València** Nord ... a.	...	0814r	0907	1019	...	0959r	1059r	...	1159r	1240	1259r	1412	1427	Ⓑ¶	1515	1550	**p**	1722r	1730r	1821	|	‡	1859r	1946r
353	**València** Nord ... **668** d.	0718	0820r	...	...	...	1005r	...	...	...	1245	1305r	...	1435	1502	1520	...	1635	1730r	...	1827	|	1705	1905r	1955r
409	Xátiva ... **668** d.	0752	|	...	...	...	|	...	...	...	1326	|	...	1523	1539	1608	...	1711	|	...	1906	1922	1744	|	|
	Madrid P de Atocha .. **668** a.	|	1020	...	...	...	|	...	...	...	|	|	...	|	|	|	...	|	1940	...	|	|	|	|	2206
	Sevilla **671** ... a.	|	...	...	...	...	|	...	...	...	2025	|	...	|	|	|	...	|	...	...	|	|	|	|	...
495	Elda - Petrer ... d.	0839	...	...	...	...	|	...	...	...	...	|	...	1611	1632	1652	...	1753	...	...	1946	|	1837	|	...
536	**Alacant** ... a.	0908	...	...	...	...	1140	...	...	...	...	1441	...	1647	1702	1721	...	1821	...	...	2019	2025	1908	2038	...
536	**Alacant** ... ¦ d.	0916	...	...	...	...	...	...	...	...	...	...	...	...	...	1731	...	1826	...	...	2039	...	...	...	...
614	Murcia ... **668a** ¦ a.	1028	...	...	...	...	...	...	...	...	...	...	...	...	...	1849	...	1930	...	...	2147	...	...	...	...
677	**Lorca** Sutullena ... ¦ a.	...	...	...	...	...	...	...	...	...	...	...	...	...	...	|	...	|	...	...	2252	...	...	...	...
679	**Cartagena** ... **668a** ¦ a.	...	...	...	...	...	...	...	...	...	...	...	...	...	...	1952	...	2018	...	...	...	...	...	...	...

		Talgo		*Em*		*IC*		*Hotel*	*Em*	
		1171		**1181**		**1391**		**897**	**1401**	
	2		2		2		2	✕	Ⓑ	2
								T		
Barcelona França ... d.	1618	...	...	1734	1748	...	1917	...	2004	2046
Barcelona Passeig de Gràcia d.	1626	...	...	|	1756	...	1925	...	|	2056
Barcelona Sants ... **652** d.	1633	1700	...	1800	1803	1930	1933	2000	2030	2103
Sant Vicenç de Calders **652** d.	1716	|	...	|	1848	|	2017	|	|	2147
Altafulla - Tamarit ... d.	1727	|	...	|	1900	|	2029	|	|	2159
Tarragona ... **652** d.	1738	1755	...	1854	1909	2025	2040	2059	2123	2208
Port Aventura ... d.	1747	|	...	|	1923	2033	2050	|	|	2219
Salou ... d.	1751	1807	...	|	1927	2038	2055	2118	|	2223
Tortosa ... d.	|	|	1835	|	|	|	|	|	|	|
L'Aldea - Amposta ... d.	1836	1841	1852	|	2017	2112	2142	|	|	2306
Tortosa ... a.	1847	|	|	|	2028	|	2151	|	|	2316
Vinaròs ... d.	...	1858	1914	|	▬	2129	...	|	|	...
Benicarló - Peñíscola ... d.	...	1904	1918	|	←	2135	...	|	|	...
Benicàssim ... d.	...	1933	1957	|	1958	2203	...	|	|	...
Castelló de la Plana ... d.	...	1947	→	2010	2020	2212	...	2236	2241	...
València Nord ... a.	...	2032	...	2055r	2117	2303	...	2319	2328r	...
València Nord ... **668** d.	...	2042	...	2104r	...	...	...	2334	...	...
Xátiva ... **668** d.	...	2126	...	|	...	...	...	|	...	...
Granada **661** ... a.	...	|	...	|	...	...	...	0730	...	...
Elda - Petrer ... d.	...	2224	...	|	...	...	...	...	...	...
Alacant ... a.	...	2247	...	2240	...	...	...	...	...	...
Alacant ... ¦ d.	...	2257e	...	...	...	...	...	...	...	...
Murcia ... **668a** ¦ a.	...	2357e	...	...	...	...	...	...	...	...
Cartagena ... **668a** ¦ a.	...	...	...	...	...	...	...	...	...	...

		Hotel	*Em*			*Em*			*IC*
	2	**894**	**1262**			**1282**			**18502**
	①–⑥	✕	①–⑥	2	2		2	2	①–⑥
	o	**T**	**h**						2**f**
Cartagena ... **668a** ¦ d.	...	...	...	...	...	...	...	...	...
Murcia ... **668a** ¦ d.	...	...	...	...	...	...	...	...	0555
Alacant ... ¦ a.	...	...	...	...	...	...	...	...	0718
Alacant ... d.	...	...	...	...	...	0655	...	...	0721
Elda - Petrer ... d.	...	...	...	...	...	|	...	...	0753
Granada **661** ... d.	...	2130	...	...	...	|	...	...	|
Xátiva ... **668** d.	...	|	...	...	...	|	...	...	0844
València Nord ... **668** a.	...	0410	...	...	...	0826r	...	...	0924
València Nord ... d.	...	0425	0640r	...	...	0834r	0820	...	...
Castelló de la Plana ... d.	...	0521	0717	...	...	0918	0933	...	...
Benicàssim ... d.	...	|	|	...	...	|	0941	...	...
Benicarló - Peñíscola ... d.	...	|	|	...	...	|	1018	...	...
Vinaròs ... d.	...	|	|	...	...	|	1024	...	...
Tortosa ... d.	0612	|	|	0748	0918	|	|	1049	...
L'Aldea - Amposta ... d.	0623	|	|	0800	0930	|	1048	1059	...
Tortosa ... a.	|	|	|	|	|	|	1100	|	...
Salou ... d.	0707	0648	|	0843	1014	|	...	1140	...
Port Aventura ... d.	0710	|	|	0845	1017	|	...	1143	...
Tarragona ... **652** d.	0721	0705	0836	0856	1027	1042	...	1154	...
Altafulla - Tamarit ... d.	0729	|	|	0904	1035	|	...	|	...
Sant Vicenç de Calders ... **652** d.	0743	|	|	0917	1049	|	...	1216	...
Barcelona Sants ... **652** a.	0835	0839	0939	1005	1140	1141	...	1305	...
Barcelona Passeig de Gràcia ... a.	0844	...	|	1014	1145	|	...	1313	...
Barcelona França ... a.	0853	...	1005	1023	1153	1205	...	1322	...

	Talgo	*Em*	*Alvia*	*IC*	*Talgo*	*IC*		*Em*		*Em*		*Talgo*	*Talgo*			*Em*	*IC*	*Talgo*	*Em*	*Talgo*			*Talgo*	*MD*	
	1102	**1112**	**5490**	**18504**	**460**	**1142**		**1152**		**1162**		**694**	**264**			**1182**	**5570**	**10458**	**1392**	**1202**	2	2	**1212**	**14202**	2
				①–⑥	🍷		2	Ⓑ	2	Ⓑ	2			2	2		⑤	⑦		①–⑥	Ⓑ	Ⓑ	⑦	2	Ⓑ
				2**f**	**L**			**y**				**A**								**m**	¶		**w**		
Cartagena ... **668a** ¦ d.	...	...	...	0740z	...	...	...	...	...	...	...	...	1255	...	...	...	...	...	...	...	...	...	...	1638	...
Lorca Sutullena ... ¦ d.	...	...	...	|	0820	...	...	...	...	...	...	...	|	...	...	...	...	...	...	...	...	...	...	|	...
Murcia ... **668a** ¦ d.	0635k	...	...	0834	0945	...	...	...	...	...	...	...	1353	...	...	...	...	...	...	...	...	...	1647	1732	...
Alacant ... ¦ a.	0745k	...	...	0944	1054	...	...	...	...	...	...	...	1453	...	...	...	...	...	...	...	...	...	1800	1840	...
Alacant ... d.	0800	0925	...	1000	1109	...	...	...	...	1420	...	...	1521	...	...	1617	...	1708	...	1822	1758	...	1820	1845	1944
Elda - Petrer ... d.	0828	|	...	1035	1137	...	...	...	...	|	...	...	1545	...	...	|	...	|	...	1848	1826	...	1850	1916	2015
Sevilla **671** ... d.	|	|	...	|	|	...	...	...	...	|	...	0835	|	...	...	|	...	|	...	|	|	...	|	|	|
Madrid P de Atocha .. **668** d.	|	|	0910	|	|	...	...	...	...	|	...	|	|	...	...	|	1710	|	...	|	|	...	|	|	|
Xátiva ... **668** d.	0917	|	|	1127	1216	...	...	...	...	|	...	1524	1625	...	...	|	|	1815	...	1929	1616	...	1931	2005	2106
València Nord ... **668** a.	0955	1055r	1113r	1205	1257	...	...	...	...	1554r	...	1602	1708	...	...	1755r	1926r	|	...	2014	1957	...	2018	2041	2145
València Nord ... d.	1005	1105r	1118r	▬	1308	1405	...	1505r	1450	1604r	...	1610	1715	...	1700	1805r	1940r	|	1935r	2020	...	2010	2024	...	...
Castelló de la Plana ... d.	1051	1144	1209	...	1352	1451	...	1546	1601	1647	...	1656	1803	...	1759	1847	2031	|	2016	2106	...	2104	2120	...	...
Benicàssim ... d.	1058	|	1219	...	1401	1500	...	|	1610	|	...	|	1811	...	1807	|	2038	|	|	2114	...	2112	2129	...	...
Benicarló - Peñíscola ... d.	1127	|	1248	...	1426	1533	...	|	1651	|	...	1727	1833	...	1848	|	2106	|	|	2142	...	2149	2157	...	...
Vinaròs ... d.	1133	|	1253	2	1431	1539	...	|	1656	|	...	1733	1838	...	1855	|	2110	|	|	2148	...	2155	2203	...	...
Tortosa ... d.	|	|	|	1324	|	|	1554	|	|	|	1725	|	|	1850	1936	|	...	|	|	|	...	|	|	...	...
L'Aldea - Amposta ... d.	1148	|	|	1336	1447	1555	1605	|	1721	|	1735	1748	1853	1903	1950	|	...	|	|	2206	...	2221	2219	...	...
Tortosa ... a.	|	|	|	|	|	|	|	|	1736	|	|	|	|	|	|	|	...	|	|	|	...	2230	|	...	...
Salou ... d.	1221	|	|	1413	1520	1630	1645	|	...	|	1818	1828	1927	1943	2035	|	...	|	|	2243	...	...	2250	...	...
Port Aventura ... d.	1223	|	|	1416	|	|	1647	|	...	|	1821	|	|	1947	2041	|	...	|	|	|	...	...	|	...	...
Tarragona ... **652** d.	1236	1309	1346	1428	1539	1641	1658	1710	...	1811	1830	1839	1940	1957	2100	2012	...	2100	2137	2247	...	...	2301	...	...
Altafulla - Tamarit ... d.	|	|	|	1435	|	|	1706	|	...	|	1838	|	|	2005	2108	|	...	|	|	|	...	...	|	...	...
Sant Vicenç de Calders **652** d.	|	|	|	1447	|	|	1718	|	...	|	1849	|	|	2017	2118	|	...	|	|	|	...	...	|	...	...
Barcelona Sants ... **652** a.	1339	1409	1440	1535	1637	1739	1805	1809	...	1910	1935	1939	2039	2105	2208	2111	...	2205	2237	2346	...	...	2350	...	...
Barcelona Passeig de Gràcia a.	...	|	|	1544	...	...	1814	|	...	|	1944	|	...	2111	2213	|	...	...	|	...	...	...	...	...	...
Barcelona França ... a.	...	1435	1504	1552	...	...	1822	1825	...	1935	1953	2005	...	2120	2222	2135	...	...	2306	...	...	...	...	...	...

Murcia – Cartagena

				Alta	*Alta*		*Talgo*	*IC*	*Alta*		*Alta*	
	①–⑤	①–⑤		**222**	**228**	①–⑤	**463**	**18523**	**224**		**226**	
	2§	2§	2		Ⓑ**x**	2§	**M**	2		2	Ⓑ**g**	
Murcia ... d.	0745	0950	1150	1404	1645	1745	1905	1935	2050	2105	2331	...
Cartagena ... d.	0834	1040	1240	1452	1728	1840	1952	2018	2135	2155	0017	...

	Alta	*IC*	*Alta*		*Alta*	*Talgo*		*Alta*	*MD*	*Alta*			
	221	**18504**	**223**		**229**	**264**	①–⑤	**225**	**14202**	**227**	①–⑤		
	C	①–⑤		2	⑦**q**		2§		2	Ⓑ**g**	2§	2	
Cartagena ... d.	0530	0740	0850	1050	1215	1255	1426	1600	1638	1820	1931	2200	...
Murcia ... a.	0608	0830	0934	1140	1256	1339	1516	1645	1727	1902	2028	2251	...

A – GARCÍA LORCA – [12] 🍷 Barcelona - Sevilla and v.v.
C – ①–⑤ (not Aug. 1 - 31).
L – [12] 🍷 Lorca - Barcelona.
M – [12] 🍷 Barcelona - Cartagena.
T – ALHAMBRA *Trenhotel* – Ⓑ (daily June 21 - Sept. 12): 🛏, [1] (reclining) Barcelona - Granada and v.v.

b – Not Nov. 1, Dec. 6.
d – Not Aug. 5 - Sept. 29.
e – Not June 22 - Sept. 21.
f – To Zaragoza (Table **670**).
g – Not Nov. 1, Dec. 6.
h – Not Sept. 24, Nov. 2, Dec. 7.
j – Also ①–④ Aug. 3 - Sept. 26. Also ⑦ from Sept. 29.
k – ①–⑥ (not June 24 - Sept. 24).
m – Also Sept. 22; not Sept. 24.
n – Also Aug. 15, Oct. 9, Nov. 1, Dec. 6.
o – Not Aug. 15, Sept. 11, Oct. 12, Nov. 1, Dec. 6, 25, 26.
p – From Zaragoza (Table **670**).
q – Daily Aug. 1 - 31.
r – València **Joaquín Sorolla**. Free 🚌 to València Nord.
t – Not ⑥ July 6 - Sept. 28. Also not Nov. 1, Dec. 6.
v – Not Aug. 15, Dec. 8.
w – Also Sept. 24; not Sept. 22.
x – Also ⑥ Aug. 3 - 31.
y – Also ⑥ July 6 - Sept. 28.
z – ①–⑤.
§ – Not Aug. 15, Nov. 1, Dec. 6, 9.
¶ – Not Aug. 15, Oct. 9.
‡ – Also Oct. 31, Dec. 5; not July 5 - Sept. 6, Nov. 1, Dec. 6.
¦ – Additional local trains operate between these stations.

2nd class SEVILLA and ALGECIRAS - MÁLAGA, GRANADA and ALMERÍA 673

For trains **Sevilla** – **Málaga** and v.v. via **Córdoba**, see Table **660**

km		MD 13920	MD 13063	MD 13900	Alta 9218	Alta 9367	MD 13902	MD 13922		MD 13904	MD 13065		MD 13906 ⑤⑦f	MD 13924	Alta 9331	MD 13061	MD 13077	MD 13908	MD 13926	Alta 9234	MD 13910		
0	**Sevilla** ¶ d.	0645	...	0740	...	...	1100	1155	...	1308	...	...	1510	1600	...	...	...	1725	1800	...	2005	...	...
15	Dos Hermanas ¶ d.	0700u	...	0754u	...	...	1114u	1208u	...	1322u	...	...	1524u	1614u	...	...	...	1739u	1814u	...	2019u	...	...
	Algeciras d.	│	0615	│	...	0843	│	│	...	│	1145	...	│	│	1503	...	1530	│	│	...	│	...	...
	San Roque - La Línea d.	│	0630	│	...	0858	│	│	...	│	1201	...	│	│	1518	...	1546	│	│	...	│	...	...
	Ronda d.	│	0753	│	...	1009	│	│	...	│	1332	...	│	│	1631	1650	1713	│	│	...	│	...	...
	Madrid Pta de Atocha **660** d.	│	│	│	0905	1405	│	│	...	│	│	...	│	│	2035	│	│	│	│	1705	│	...	...
167	Bobadilla **661** d.	│	0846	0919	│	...	1243	│	...	1448	1425	...	1645	│	...	1739	1801	1905	│	│	2145	...	...
236	**Málaga** M. Zambrano **661** a.	│	│	1015	│	...	1336	│	...	1547	│	...	1736	│	...	1847	│	1955	│	│	2236	...	...
	Antequera - Santa Ana § d.	0825	0856	...	1149	...	...	1337	...	...	1436	...	...	1738	...	...	1811	...	1941	│	...	...	...
183	Antequera d.	0839	0910	...	│	...	...	1351	...	...	1450	...	...	1752	...	...	1823	...	1955	2016	...	...	...
290	**Granada** **661** d.	1003	1055	...	1330	...	...	1512	...	...	1606	...	...	1915	...	...	1945	...	2116	2140	...	...	...
372	Guadix **661** d.	1112	...	...	...	...	...	1621	...	...	...	...	...	2019	...	...	...	...	2224	...	...	...	...
471	**Almería** **661** a.	1225	...	...	...	...	...	1746	...	...	...	...	...	2136	...	...	...	...	2343	...	...	...	...

km		MD 13062	MD 13901	MD 13941	MD 13057	Alta 9366		Alta 9219	MD 13903	MD 13943		MD 13905	MD 13064		MD 13907	Alta 9330	MD 13076	MD 13945	Alta 9237	MD 13909 ⑤⑦f	MD 13911	MD 13947	
0	**Almería** **661** d.	...	...	0620	...	...	...	...	...	0900	...	...	...	...	...	...	...	1500	...	...	...	1815	...
99	Guadix **661** d.	...	...	0740	...	...	...	...	...	1014	...	...	...	...	...	...	...	1616	...	...	...	1939	...
181	**Granada** d.	0645	...	0848	...	...	...	0910	...	1124	...	...	1245	...	...	...	1700	1732	1805	...	...	2056	...
288	Antequera d.	0800	...	1006	...	...	...	1029	...	1246	...	...	1422	...	...	...	1822	1851	│	...	...	2212	...
	Antequera - Santa Ana § d.	0818	...	1019	...	...	...	│	...	1259	...	...	1440	...	...	...	1840	1902	1949			2225	
	Málaga M. Zambrano **661** d.	│	0740	│	1005	...	...	│	1040	│	...	1408	│	...	1608	...	│	│	│	1900	2005	│	...
304	Bobadilla **661** d.	0825	0835	│	1100	...	...	│	1129	│	...	1502	1447	...	1747	...	1847	│	│	1956	2056	│	...
	Madrid Pta de Atocha **660** d.	│	│	│	│	0835	...	1335	│	│	...	│	│	...	│	1505	│	│	2244	│	│	│	...
376	Ronda d.	0918	│	│	1152	1221	...	...	│	│	...	│	1541	...	│	1858	1940	│	...	│	│	│	...
468	San Roque - La Línea d.	1045	│	│	...	1335	...	...	│	│	...	│	1725	...	│	2016	2102	│	...	│	│	│	...
480	**Algeciras** a.	1100	│	│	...	1348	...	...	│	│	...	│	1740	...	│	2030	2117	│	...	│	│	│	...
456	Dos Hermanas ¶ a.	...	1002s	1146s	...	...	...	...	1254s	1419s	...	1623s	...	...	1917s	...	...	2023s	...	2118s	2226s	2348s	...
471	**Sevilla** ¶ a.	...	1017	1205	...	...	...	...	1315	1437	...	1640	...	...	1933	...	...	2039	...	2135	2241	0003	...

f – Also Aug. 15; not Aug. 16.
s – Calls to set down only.
u – Calls to pick up only.
§ – ± *17 km* from Antequera.
¶ – Frequent suburban services run Sevilla - Dos Hermanas and v.v.

SFM 2nd class PALMA DE MALLORCA - INCA - SA POBLA and MANACOR 674

For services between Inca and sa Pobla, and Inca and Manacor change at Enllaç (5 *km* from Inca, 34 *km* from Palma)

km		Ⓐ	Ⓐ ◧		Ⓐ	Ⓒ	Ⓐ ◧		Ⓐ	Ⓒ	Ⓐ ◧		Ⓐ	Ⓒ	Ⓐ		and at the same		Ⓐ	Ⓒ	Ⓐ		Ⓐ	Ⓒ		
0	**Palma** d.	0545	0607	0615x	0635	0640	0650	0715x	0735	0740	0750	0815x	0835	0840	0855	0915x	minutes	2015	2035	2040	2055	2115x	2135	2140	2215x	...
7	Marratxi d.	0600	0615	0623	0643	0655	0658	0723	0743	0754	0758	0823	0843	0854	0903	0923	past	2023	2043	2054	2103	2123	2143	2154	2225	...
29	**Inca** d.	0625	0632	0644	0704	0720	0715	0744	0804	0815	0815	0844	0904	0915	0923	0944	each	2044	2104	2115	2123	2144	2204	2215	2250	...
***	sa Pobla a.	0642	...	│	*0723*	0736	...	│	*0823*	*0834*	...	│	*0923*	*0934*	...	│	hour	│	*2123*	*2134*	...	│	*2223*	*2234*	│	...
64	**Manacor** a.	...	...	*0718*	...	...	...	*0818*	...	...	...	*0916*	...	...	...	*1016*	until	*2116*	...	...	...	*2216*	...	...	2325	...

	Ⓐ	Ⓐ ◧		Ⓐ	Ⓐ	Ⓐ ◧		Ⓐ	Ⓒ	Ⓐ ◧		Ⓐ	Ⓒ	Ⓐ		Ⓐ	Ⓒ	and at the same	Ⓐ		Ⓐ	Ⓒ	Ⓐ			
Manacor d.	...	...	*0623*	...	0659	...	*0723*	...	...	...	*0823*	...	...	...	*0923*	...	...	minutes	...	*2023*	...	...	...	*2123*	...	2223
sa Pobla d.	...	...	│	*0656*	│	...	│	*0756*	*0807*	...	│	*0856*	*0907*	...	│	*0956*	*1007*	past	...	│	*2056*	*2107*	...	│	*2156*	│
Inca d.	0621	0650	0656	0716	0729	0733	0756	0816	0827	0833	0856	0916	0927	0936	0956	1016	1027	each	2036	2056	2116	2127	2136	2156	2216	2254
Marratxi d.	0645	0707	0716	0736	...	0750	0816	0836	0847	0850	0916	0936	0947	0956	1016	1036	1047	hour	2056	2116	2136	2147	2156	2216	2236	2318
Palma a.	0653	0715	0724z	0744	...	0758	0824z	0844	0901	0858	0924z	0944	1001	1004	1024z	1044	1101	until	2004	2124	2144	2201	2204	2230	2250	2333

x – 5 minutes earlier on Ⓒ.
z – 7 minutes later on Ⓒ.
◧ – Incaexprés.
*** – *19 km* Inca - sa Pobla.
Operator: Serveis Ferroviaris de Mallorca (SFM) ✆ +34 971 752 245.

PALMA DE MALLORCA - SÓLLER *28 km* Journey time: 55 minutes. **Operator**: Ferrocarril de Sóller (FS) ✆ +34 971 752 051.

Nov. - Feb.: 0800, 1050, 1305, 1515, 1900. Mar. - Oct.: 0800, 1010, 1050, 1215, 1330, 1510, 1930.

SÓLLER - PALMA DE MALLORCA

Nov. - Feb.: 0910, 1155, 1410, 1800. Mar. - Oct.: 0910, 1050, 1215, 1400, 1830.

A connecting tram service operates **Sóller - Port de Sóller**. 5 *km*. Journey time: 15–20 minutes. Not all services shown.

From Sóller: 0800, 0900, 1000, 1100, 1130, 1200, 1300, 1325, 1400, 1500, 1600, 1700, 1800, 1900, 2020.
From Port de Sóller: 0830, 0930, 1025, 1130, 1230, 1325, 1430, 1530, 1630, 1700, 1730, 1800, 1830, 1930, 2040.

🚌 MÁLAGA and ALGECIRAS - LA LÍNEA (for Gibraltar) 675

There are no cross-border 🚌 services: passengers to / from Gibraltar must cross the frontier on foot (walking-time about 5 minutes) and transfer to / from Gibraltar local 🚌 services

🚌 **MÁLAGA** bus stn – **LA LÍNEA** bus station (for **Gibraltar**)

From Málaga: 0700, 1130 ▽, 1400, 1630, 1915 ⑦.
From La Línea: 0850, 1030, 1630 ▽, 1900, 2045 ⑦.
Journey time: 3 hours. Operator: Automóviles Portillo, Málaga ✆ (+34) 902 020 052.
▽ – Journey operated by Alsina Graells (see Table **664** for contact details).

🚌 **ALGECIRAS** bus station - **LA LÍNEA** bus station (for **Gibraltar**) Route M-120

From Algeciras: Ⓐ: 0700 and every 30 minutes until 2130, also 2230.
⑥: every 45 mins 0700 – 2115, also 2230. †: every 45 mins 0800 – 2130, also 2230.
From La Línea: Ⓐ: 0700, 0745 and every 30 minutes until 2215, also 2315.
⑥: every 45 mins 0700 – 2200, also 2315. †: 0700, 0845 then every 45 mins until 2215, also 2315.
Journey time: 45 mins. Operator: Transportes Generales Comes SA, Algeciras ✆ (+34) 902 450 550.

DAMAS ☆ 🚌 SEVILLA - AYAMONTE - FARO - LAGOS 676

	Winter	Ⓒ	Ⓐ	⚒		†	⑥	Ⓐ	Ⓐ	†	⑥	†	⚒	Summer		⚒		Ⓐ	Ⓒ			†	⑥	Ⓐ
Sevilla ⊖ d.	Sept. 2 -	*0730*	0730	0930	1130		1300	*1300*	*1630*	*1630*	1730	1900	1930	June 28 -	*0730*	0930	1130	*1230*	*1330*	1530	*1730*	1900	1930	2030
Huelva d.	June 30	0900	0900	1100	1300	1430	1430	1530	1800	1900	1900	2030	2100	Sept. 1	0900	1100	1300	1400	1500	1700	1930	2030	2100	2200
Ayamonte a.		1000	1000	1200	1400	1530	1530	1630	1900	2000	2000	2130	2200		1000	1215	1415	1500	1600	1815	2030	2145	2215	2315

	Winter	⚒	Ⓐ			Ⓐ	⑥	†	Ⓐ	⑥	⑥	Ⓑ		Summer	Ⓐ			Ⓐ	†	⚒	†			Ⓐ
Ayamonte d.	Sept. 2 -	0645	0845	0930	1145	1400	1500	1515	1545	1615	1715	1730	1930	June 28 -	0645	*0845*	0930z	*1145*	*1400*	1530	1615	*1730*	1900	*1945*
Huelva d.	June 30	0745	0945	1030	1245	1500	1600	1615	1645	1715	1815	1830	2045	Sept. 1	0800	1000	1100	1300	1500	1700	1730	1830r	2000	2100
Sevilla ⊖ a.		0915	*1115*	1215	*1415*	*1645*	1715	1745	1815	1845	1945	*2045*	2215		0915	1115	1215	1415	1615	1815	1845	1945r	2115	2215

⛴ **Ayamonte - Vila Real de Santo António Guadiana** Journey time: 10 minutes. ✆ (+34) 959 470 617. July 1 - Sept. 15: every 30 mins (from Ayamonte 0930 - 2100 ⚒, 0930 - 2000 †). Sept. 16 - Apr. 30: hourly (from Ayamonte 0930 - 1930 ⚒, 1030 - 1830 †). May 1 - June 30: hourly (from Ayamonte 0930 - 2000 ⚒, 1030 - 1830 †).

INTERNATIONAL 🚌 SERVICE Joint EVA △ / DAMAS ☆ service *for international journeys only* No service Dec. 25, Jan. 1

		Winter		Summer			
Sevilla, Plaza de Armas ⊖ d.	→	0730	1615	→	0730	0800	1330	1615
Huelva d.	Winter	0845	1730	Summer	0845	0915	1445	1730
Ayamonte 🏛 ES d.		0930	1815		│	1000	│	1815•
Vila Real de Santo António 🏛 PT a.		0855	1740		│	0925	│	1740
Faro, Av. da República a.	Sept. 2 -	1010	1855	June 28 -	0920	1040	1520	1855
Albufeira, Alto dos Caliços a.	June 30	1055	1940	Sept. 1	1000	1125	1600	1940
Portimão, Largo do Dique a.		1130	2015		│	1200	│	2015
Lagos, Rossio de S. João a.		1200	2045		1045	1230	1645	2045

		Winter		Summer			
Lagos, Rossio de S. João d.	→	0630	1345	→	0615	0730	1230	1445
Portimão, Largo do Dique d.	Winter	0700	1415	Summer	│	0800	│	1515
Albufeira, Alto dos Caliços d.		0735	1450		0700	0835	1315	1550
Faro, Av. da República d.		0820	1535		0740	0920	1355	1635
Vila Real de Santo António 🏛 PT d.	Sept. 2 -	0935	1650	June 28 -	│	1035	│	1750
Ayamonte 🏛 ES a.	June 30	1100	1815	Sept. 1	│	1200•	│	1915
Huelva a.		1145	1905		1015	1245	1630	2000
Sevilla, Plaza de Armas ⊖ a.		1300	2015		1130	1400	1745	2115

r – 30 minutes later on ⚒.
z – 15 minutes later on Ⓒ.
• – Subject to confirmation.
☆ – DAMAS, Huelva ✆ +34 959 256 900. www.damas-sa.es
△ – EVA, Faro ✆ +351 289 899 700. www.eva-bus.com
⊖ – Sevilla Plaza de Armas bus station (± 2 km from Santa Justa rail station).
ES – Spain (Central European Time).
PT – Portugal (West European Time).
Huelva bus station is ± 1 km from the rail station.
Ayamonte bus station is ± 1.5 km from the ferry terminal.

677 MADRID - CÁCERES - BADAJOZ

km												*IC*	*IC*				*MD*	*IC*					
						17905		**17702**	**17014**	**17028**		**17900**	**17902**				**17012**	**17194**		**17018**	**17706**		
		2	2	2	2	2		2	2	2		2	2	2	2	2	2	2		2	2		
		①–⑤	①–⑤	⑥⑦		①–⑤		①–⑤	①–⑥	**T**		⑤⑥⑦	①–④		Ⓑ	Ⓑ				Ⓑ			
0	**Madrid** Chamartín d.	...	...	...	...	...	...	...	...	...	...	...	...	...	...	...	...	1600	...	...	...	...	...
8	**Madrid** Atocha Cercanías d.	...	...	...	...	...	...	0725	0807	...	...	1018	1018	...	...	...	1430	1619	...	1821	2028	...	...
16	Villaverde Bajo **669** d.	...	...	...	...	...	...	0733	|	...	...	|	|	...	...	...	|	|	...	|	2036	...	...
146	Talavera de la Reina d.	...	...	...	...	...	...	0900	0937	...	...	1155	1155	...	...	...	1608	1742	...	1953	2204	...	...
	Navalmoral de La Mata d.	...	...	...	...	...	...	...	1016	...	...	1231	1231	...	...	...	1643	1816	...	2028	...	...	...
278	Plasencia a.	...	...	...	...	...	...	...	1106	...	...	1310	1310	...	...	...	1733	|	...	2108	...	...	...
278	Plasencia d.	...	...	...	...	0708	...	...	1110	...	...	1313	1313	...	...	...	1736**z**	|	...	2111	...	...	...
*343**	**Cáceres** d.	0655	...	0810	...	0818	...	...	1219	1220	...	1416	1416	...	1640	...	1836**z**	1949	...	2220	...	...	...
	San Vicente de Alcántara d.	|	...	|	...	|	...	...	|	1333	...	|	|	...	|	...	...	|	...	...	...	...	...
430	Valencia de Alcántara d.	|	...	|	...	|	...	...	|	1348	...	|	|	...	|	...	...	|	...	...	...	...	...
409	Mérida a.	0746	...	0901	...	0921	...	...	1312	...	...	1508	1508	...	1733	...	...	2049	...	...	...	...	...
409	Mérida **678** d.	0754	0754	0908	0908	...	...	...	1315	...	...	1513	1513	1514	1741	1746	...	2054	...	...	...	...	...
469	**Badajoz** **678** a.	|	0841	|	0958	...	...	...	1359	...	...	|	|	1553	|	1834	...	2136	...	...	...	...	...
475	Zafra d.	0843	...	0957	...	...	...	...	...	...	...	1600	1600	...	1829	...	...	...	...	...	...	...	...
649	Sevilla a.	1133	...	1245	...	...	...	...	...	...	...	|	...	...	...	...	...	...	...	...	...	...	...
521	Fregenal de la Sierra d.	...	...	...	...	...	...	...	...	...	...	1640	...	...	...	...	...	...	...	...	...	...	...
660	Huelva a.	...	...	...	...	...	...	...	...	...	...	1911	...	...	...	...	...	...	...	...	...	...	...

					IC			*IC*									*IC*		*IC*				
	17703	**17705**	**17021**		**17197**			**17199**		**17707**		**17026**		**17709**	**17029**		**17907**		**17025**				
	❀ 2	2	2	2	2		2	2		2	2	2		2	2	2	2		2	2	2		
	①–⑤	⑥⑦	①–⑥	①–⑤	①–⑤		⑥	⑥⑦		①–⑤	Ⓑ			⑥⑦	**T**				Ⓑ				
Huelva d.	...	...	...	...	...	...	...	...	...	...	...	...	...	...	...	...	1050**x**	...	...	...	...	...	...
Fregenal de la Sierra d.	...	...	...	...	...	...	...	...	...	...	...	...	...	...	...	...	1329**x**	...	...	...	...	...	...
Sevilla d.	...	...	...	...	...	...	...	...	...	...	...	...	...	...	...	...	|	...	...	...	1708	...	...
Zafra d.	...	...	...	0655	...	...	0815	...	...	...	...	...	...	...	...	...	1410	...	...	...	1950	...	...
Badajoz **678** d.	...	...	...	|	0717	...	|	0845	...	...	1220	...	...	...	...	1420	|	...	1700	2000	|	...	...
Mérida **678** a.	...	...	...	0742	0753	...	0902	0922	...	...	1306	...	...	...	...	1503	1453	...	1738	2045	2043	...	...
Mérida d.	...	...	...	...	0758	...	...	0928	...	...	...	1316	...	...	...	...	1509	...	1743	...	2051	...	...
Valencia de Alcántara d.	...	...	...	...	|	...	...	|	...	...	...	|	...	...	1425	...	|	...	|	...	|	...	...
San Vicente de Alcántara d.	...	...	...	...	|	...	...	|	...	...	...	|	...	...	1440	...	|	...	|	...	|	...	...
Cáceres d.	...	...	0715	...	0854	...	...	1025	...	...	...	1416	...	...	1557	...	1604	...	1837	...	2148	...	...
Plasencia a.	...	...	0821	...	|	...	...	|	...	...	...	1523	...	...	...	...	1702	...	1941	...	...	...	...
Plasencia d.	...	...	0825	...	|	...	...	|	...	...	...	1525	...	...	...	...	1705	...	1944	...	...	...	...
Navalmoral de La Mata d.	...	...	0907	...	1020	...	...	1152	...	...	...	1609	...	...	...	...	1742	...	2027	...	...	...	...
Talavera de la Reina d.	0650	0840	0940	...	1056	...	...	1234	...	1505	...	1646	...	1750	...	...	1822	...	2103	...	...	...	...
Villaverde Bajo **669** a.	0814	1008	|	...	|	...	...	|	...	1628	...	|	...	1910	...	...	|	...	|	...	...	...	...
Madrid Atocha Cercanías a.	0827	1018	1107	...	1226	...	...	1353	...	1638	...	1819	...	1920	...	...	1951	...	2232	...	...	...	...
Madrid Chamartín a.	...	...	...	...	1242	...	...	1411	...	...	...	...	...	...	...	...	...	...	...	...	...	...	...

T – Not ②. **x** – ⑤⑥⑦. **z** – ⑤ only. ❀ – change of train is required at Fuenlabrada (a. 0754; d. 0756). * – Madrid - Cáceres via Plasencia *363 km*.

678 ALCÁZAR DE SAN JUAN - BADAJOZ

km		*MD*					*MD*	*MD*	*IC*	*MD*	
		17042					**18183**	**17041**	**18330**	**18083**	**18027**
		2	2	2	2	2	2	2	2	2	2 **A**
					Ⓑ	⑦	**h**	**f**		**k**	⑦
	Madrid AC § **661 668** d.	...	...	...	...	...	...	1310	...	...	...
	Albacete **668a** d.	...	...	...	...	...	1139	|	...	1902	1946
0	**Alcázar de San Juan** **661** d.	0715	...	...	...	...	1251	1435	1555	2014	2109
50	Manzanares **661** d.	0740	...	...	...	...	1318	1500	1618	2041	2138
114	Ciudad Real **660** d.	0820	...	...	...	...	1359	1546	1704	2122	2217
153	Puertollano **660** d.	...	...	1135	...	...	...	...	1736	...	...
265	Cabeza del Buey d.	...	0725**x**	1315	...	1545	...	...	1931	...	...
392	Mérida **677** a.	...	0906	1505	1746	1746	...	...	2132	...	...
451	**Badajoz** **677** a.	...	0958	1553	1834	1834	...	...	2216	...	...

		MD	*IC*		*MD*	*MD*				*MD*
	18024	**18081**	**18331**		**17041**	**18181**				**17043**
	2 **B**	2	2		2	2	2		2	2
	①	**j**			**f**	**g**				
Badajoz **677** d.	...	...	0656	...	...	...	1420	...	2000	...
Mérida **677** d.	...	...	0750	...	...	...	1510	...	2053	...
Cabeza del Buey d.	...	...	0933	...	...	...	1656	...	2233	...
Puertollano **660** d.	...	...	1118	...	...	...	1840	...	...	...
Ciudad Real **660** d.	0536	1012	1158	...	1440	1625	...	...	...	2222
Manzanares **661** d.	0614	1052	1243	...	1520	1712	...	...	...	2300
Alcázar de San Juan **661** a.	0642	1122	1309	...	1545	1740	...	...	...	2327
Albacete **668a** a.	0805	1229	...	...	|	1849	...	...	...	...
Madrid AC § **661 668** a.	...	...	...	...	1717	...	...	...	...	...

A – ⑦: [2] València - Albacete - Ciudad Real (Table **668**).
B – ①: [2] Ciudad Real - Albacete - València (Table **668**).
f – From / to Madrid **Chamartin** (Table **661**).
g – To Alacant (arrive 2033).
h – From Alacant (depart 1005).
j – To Alacant (arrive 1400).
k – From Alacant (depart 1728).
x – ①–⑥.
z – ⑥ only.
§ – Madrid Atocha Cercanías.

679 MADRID - TOLEDO, SEGOVIA, SALAMANCA and EL ESCORIAL

2nd class

km		*Av*	*Av*	*Av*	*Av*	*Av*	*AVE*	*AVE*	*Av*		*Av*	*Av*	*Av*	*Av*	*Av*	*Av*	*Av*		*Av*			
		8062	**8072**	**8082**	**2261**	**8292**	**3072**	**2083**	**8322**		**8132**	**8142**	**8152**	**8162**	**8172**	**8182**	**8192**		**8212**			
		M	**M**		**K**	⑥⑦	**H**	**J**				**A**		**C**		**M**						
0	**Madrid** Puerta de Atocha d.	0650	0750	0850	0920	0920	1008	1105	1220	...	1350	1450	1550	1650	1750	1850	1950	...	2150	...	...	...
75	**Toledo** a.	0723	0823	0923	0953	0953	1040	1138	1253	...	1423	1523	1623	1723	1823	1923	2023	...	2223	...	...	...

	Av	*Av*	*Av*	*Av*	*Av*	*Av*	*Av*		*Av*	*Av*		*Av*		*Av*	*Av*	*Av*	*AVE*	*AVE*	*Av*	*Av*			
	8063	**8273**	**8073**	**8283**	**8093**	**8103**	**8103**		**8123**	**8133**		**8153**		**8163**	**8173**	**8183**	**3193**	**2202**	**2410**	**8213**			
	M	**M**	**M**	**M**		**C**	⑥⑦							**D**		**E**	**H**	**J**	**K**				
Toledo d.	0625	0650	0725	0755	0925	1025	1025	...	1225	1325	...	1525	...	1618	1725	1825	1838	1920	2025	2130	...	...	...
Madrid Puerta de Atocha a.	0658	0723	0758	0828	0958	1058	1058	...	1258	1358	...	1558	...	1651	1758	1858	1910	1955	2058	2203	...	...	...

km		*Av*	*Av*	*Av*	*Av*	*Av*	*Av*	*Av*	*Av*	*Av*	*Av*	*Av*
		8079	**8109**	**8309**	**8119**	**8159**	**8359**	**8169**	**8179**	**8199**	**8399**	**8219**
		M		**E**		**M**		**M**		**M**		
0	**Madrid** Chamartín d.	0738	0945	1030	1130	1515	1534	1615	1720	1915	1945	2130
68	**Segovia** Guiomar a.	0805	1012	1058	1157	1543	1601	1642	1747	1943	2012	2157

	Av	*Av*	*Av*	*Av*	*Av*	*Av*	*Av*	*Av*	*Av*	*Av*	*Av*
	8078	**8278**	**8478**	**8088**	**8098**	**8138**	**8158**	**8188**	**8198**	**8218**	**8208**
	M	**M**	**M**							①–⑥	⑦**f**
Segovia Guiomar d.	0700	0722	0752	0822	1022	1402	1607	1830	2012	2137	2140
Madrid Chamartín a.	0728	0750	0828	0850	1050	1430	1635	1858	2040	2205	2206

km		**A**	**B**	**B**	**A**	**B**		⑤	**B**	**A**	**B**
0	**Madrid** Chamartín d.	...	0845	*1015*	*1116*	*1216*	...	*1547*	*1616*	*1846*	*1916*
58	Cercedilla d.	0700	0947	1132	1230	1332	...	1700	1732	2000	2032
100	**Segovia** a.	0737	1024	1208	1307	1409	...	1737	1808	2038	2110

	A	**B**	**B**			⑤	**B**	**A**	**B**	
Segovia d.	0750	1050	1250	1450	...	1750	1850	2050	2120	...
Cercedilla a.	0828	1128	1326	1527	...	1826	1926	2127	2157	...
Madrid Chamartín a.	*0935*	*1234*	*1435*	*1635*	...	*1935*	*2036*	*2235*	2254	...

km		*MD*	*MD*	*MD*	*MD*	*MD*	*MD*	*MD*	*MD*	*MD*	*MD*
		18201	**18203**	**18901**	**18903**	**18905**	**18907**	**18913**	**18919**	**18909**	**18911**
		T	⑦**j**	**P**		**P**			**U**		
0	**Madrid** Chamartín ◧ d.	...	...	0830	1114	1344	1545	1708	1838	2006	2113
122	Ávila ◧ d.	0705	0749	0956	1242	1512	1710	1835	2007	2136	2238
233	**Salamanca** a.	0831	0914	1109	1354	1623	1821	1946	2125	2241	2344

	MD	*MD*	*MD*	*MD*	*MD*	*MD*	*MD*	*MD*	*MD*	*MD*
	18910	**18900**	**18912**	**18902**	**18918**	**18904**	**18202**	**18906**	**18908**	**1820**
	P				**U**		**T**			⑦**j**
Salamanca d.	0550	0740	0945	1230	1452	1541	1640	1755	1959	2055
Ávila ◧ d.	0657	0848	1056	1341	1609	1649	1808	1905	2110	223
Madrid Chamartín ◧ a.	0828	1017	1224	1509	1741	1823	...	2039	2238	...

MADRID ATOCHA CERCANÍAS - VILLALBA - EL ESCORIAL. *45 km.* Line C8. Journey time: Villalba, 53 minutes; El Escorial, 66-67 minutes. Depart 14 minutes later from Madrid Chamartín arrive 15 minutes earlier at Madrid Charmartín. Additional services operate. From **Madrid Atocha Cercanías**: 0621 Ⓐ, 0635 Ⓒ, 0651 Ⓐ, 0709 Ⓐ, 0723 Ⓐ, 0737 Ⓒ, 0750 Ⓐ, 0835 Ⓒ 0839 Ⓐ, 0935 Ⓒ, 0941 Ⓐ, 1036, 1135, 1235, 1335, 1407 Ⓐ, 1436 Ⓒ, 1450 Ⓐ, 1521 Ⓐ, 1536 Ⓒ, 1547 Ⓐ, 1635, 1715 Ⓐ, 1736 Ⓒ, 1745 Ⓐ, 1827 Ⓐ, 1836 Ⓒ, 1847 Ⓐ, 1920, 1936, Ⓒ, 1944 Ⓐ 2036 Ⓐ, 2042 Ⓒ, 2139, 2236, 2334. From **El Escorial**: 0548, 0616 Ⓒ, 0631 Ⓐ, 0658 Ⓐ, 0706 Ⓐ, 0716 Ⓒ, 0736 Ⓐ, 0802 Ⓐ, 0817 Ⓒ, 0831 Ⓐ, 0915, 1015, 1115, 1215, 1315, 1414, 151 1601 Ⓐ, 1615 Ⓒ, 1624 Ⓐ, 1713, 1815, 1858 Ⓐ, 1912 Ⓐ, 1915 Ⓒ, 1930 Ⓐ, 1959 Ⓐ, 2013 Ⓒ, 2029 Ⓐ, 2115, 2215.

A – ①–⑤ (not Aug. 5 - 30, Nov. 1, Dec. 6).
B – ⑥⑦ (also Nov. 1, Dec. 6).
C – ①–⑤ (not Aug. 5 - 30, Nov. 1, Dec. 6).
D – ①–⑤ (not Aug. 15, Dec. 6).
E – ⑥⑦ (also Aug. 15, Nov. 1, Dec. 6).
H – From / to Barcelona (Table **650**).
J – From / to Málaga (Table **660**).
K – From / to Sevilla (Table **660**).
M – ①–⑤ (not Apr. 17, 18).
P – ①–⑥ (not Aug. 15, Oct. 12, Nov. 1, Dec. 6).
T – ①–⑥ (not Aug. 15, Oct. 12, Nov. 1, Dec. 6, 9).
U – ⑤⑥⑦ (also Oct. 31, Dec. 5).
f – Not July 30 - Aug. 31.
j – Also Aug. 15, Oct. 12, Nov. 1, Dec. 6, 9.
MD – Medium Distance Plus.
Av – ***Avant*** high-speed services. Single class.
◧ – See also Tables **680**, **681**, **68**

MADRID - ZAMORA - VIGO, PONTEVEDRA and A CORUÑA 680

For services to / from A Coruña via León, see Table **682**

km		MD 12512 2[R] ①-⑤ f	Av 9470 2 ①-⑤ f	MD 12414 [R] 2	Av 9480 2 ①-⑤ f	MD 12520 [R] 2	MD 12584 2 ①-⑤ f	MD 12418 [R] 2	MD 12525 [R] 2	Hotel 922 🍷 G	Av 9490 2 ①-⑤ f	Av 9410 2 ⑥⑦ k	MD 12422 2[R] ①-⑤ f	MD 12424 2[R]	2 h	Alvia 4075 ①-⑤	Alvia 4075 ①-⑤	2	Alvia 4085 ⑥	Alvia 4085 ⑥	MD 12532 [R] 2	MD 12428 2[R]	Av 9560 2 ①-⑤ f	MD 12430 2[R] ①-⑤ f	MD 12538 [R] 2
0	**Madrid** Chamartín **681 689** d.	...	...	...	...	...	...	...	...	...	...	...	...	...	...	0720	0720	...	0845	0845	...	...	...	...	...
121	Ávila **681 689** d.	...	...	...	...	...	...	...	...	...	...	...	...	...	...	|	|	...	|	|	...	...	...	...	...
	Irún **689** d.	...	...	...	...	...	...	...	...	...	...	...	...	...	...	◧	◧	...	◧	◧	...	...	...	...	...
	Barcelona Sants **652** d.	...	...	...	...	...	...	...	...	2020	...	...	...	...	...	|	|	...	|	|	...	...	...	...	...
	Miranda de Ebro **681 689** d.	...	...	...	...	...	...	...	...	|	...	...	...	...	...	|	|	...	|	|	...	...	...	...	...
207*	Medina del Campo **681 689** d.	...	...	...	...	...	...	...	...	|	...	...	...	...	...	0827	0827	...	0957	0957	...	...	...	...	...
297	**Zamora** d.	...	...	...	...	...	...	...	...	|	...	...	...	...	...	0917	0917	...	1046	1046	...	...	...	...	...
404	Puebla de Sanabria d.	...	...	...	...	...	...	...	...	|	...	...	...	...	...	|	|	...	1159	1159	...	...	...	...	...
547	**Ourense** d.	...	0700	...	0800	...	...	...	...	0921	0930	1000	...	...	1201	1205	1210	1330	1350	1354	...	...	1600	...	...
641	Guillarei d.	...	|	...	|	...	...	...	...	1049	|	|	...	...	1333	|	|	|	1454	|	...	...	|	...	...
	Vigo Guixar d.	0515	|	0620	|	0700	0818	0850	0940	|	|	|	1033	1213	|	|	|	|	|	|	1305	1355	|	1518	1545
666	Redondela de Galica d.	0527	|	|	|	0712	0830	|	0952	1110	|	|	|	1225	1357	|	|	|	1523	|	1318	1407	|	|	1558
678	**Vigo** Guixar a.	|	◧	|	◧	|	|	|	|	1121	◧	◧	|	|	1412	1332	◧	|	1535	◧	|	|	◧	|	|
684	**Pontevedra** d.	0546	|	0652	|	0732	0850	0921	1012	...	|	|	1105	1245	...	1405	|	|	1606	|	1338	1426	|	1548	1618
717	Vilagarcía de Arousa d.	0607	|	0714	|	0756	...	0945	1038	...	|	|	1126	1307	...	...	|	|	...	|	1400	1446	|	1610	1646
677§	Santiago de Compostela d.	0653	0738	0754	0840	0845	...	1018	1123	...	1008	1040	1203	1340	...	...	1252	1515	...	1434	1443	1525	1638	1645	1732
751§	**A Coruña** a.	0729	...	0828	0908	0924	...	1052	1157	...	...	1108	1237	1414	...	...	1323	...	...	1504	1522	1600	...	1718	1807

	MD 12434 2[R]	MD 12436 2[R]	Alvia 4125 b	Av 9570 2[R] ⑤⑥⑦ k	Arco 283 2 B	Arco 283 2 T	Arco 283 A	Av 9590 2	MD 12552 [R] 2	MD 12592 2 f ①-⑤	MD 12440 2[R]	Alvia 4155 4355 Ⓑ b	MD 12442 2[R]	Alvia 4155 4355 Ⓑ d	Alvia 622 🍷 P	Alvia 626 🍷 Q	Alvia 4175 🍷 ⑤	MD 18322 2 J	MD 12560 2 Ⓑ p	MD 12594 2[R] Ⓑ p	Hotel 851 ✕ C	Hotel 851 ✕ D
Madrid Chamartín **681 689** d.	...	...	1220	...	...	...	...	...	...	...	...	1500	...	1500	...	...	1630	...	...	...	2230	2230
Ávila **681 689** d.	...	...	|	...	...	...	...	...	...	...	...	|	...	|	...	...	|	...	...	...	0002	0002
Irún **689** d.	...	...	◧	...	...	0845	0845	...	...	...	...	◧	...	◧	...	...	◧	...	...	...	|	|
Barcelona Sants **652** d.	...	...	|	...	...	|	|	...	...	...	...	|	...	|	0930	0930	|	...	...	...	|	|
Miranda de Ebro **681 689** d.	...	...	|	...	1118	1118	1118	...	...	...	...	|	...	|	1432	1432	|	...	...	...	|	|
Medina del Campo **681 689** d.	...	...	1332	...	|	|	|	...	...	...	...	1612	...	1612	|	|	1737	1805	...	...	0053	0053
Zamora d.	...	...	1420	...	|	|	|	...	...	...	...	1701	...	1701	|	|	1826	1904	...	...	0149	0149
Puebla de Sanabria d.	...	...	1529	...	|	|	|	...	...	...	...	1809	...	1809	|	|	|	2025	...	...	0314	0314
Ourense d.	...	...	1715	1730	1838	1838	1843	1930	...	...	...	2001	...	1957	2112	2112	2116	...	...	...	0520	0540
Guillarei d.	...	...	...	|	1945	1945	|	|	...	...	...	|	...	2100	|	|	|	...	...	...	|	0651
Vigo Guixar d.	1702	1815	...	|	|	|	|	|	1845	1930	1955	|	2057	|	|	|	|	...	...	2228	|	|
Redondela de Galica d.	|	|	...	|	2007	2007	|	|	1858	1944	|	|	|	2119	2249	|	|	...	...	2241	|	0720
Vigo Guixar a.	|	|	...	◧	2017	2017	◧	◧	|	|	|	◧	|	2129	2300	◧	◧	...	...	|	|	0733s
Pontevedra d.	1733	1846	...	|	...	...	|	|	1922	2001	2024	|	2125	2203	...	|	|	...	...	2300	|	0825
Vilagarcía de Arousa d.	1753	1907	...	|	...	...	|	|	1945	...	2046	|	2150	...	...	|	|	...	...	2320	|	...
Santiago de Compostela d.	1827	1940	...	1810	...	...	1929	2010	2025	...	2119	2043	2228	...	...	2152	2157	...	2300	2354	0723	...
A Coruña a.	1901	2014	...	1838	...	...	2003	2038	2105	...	2153	2114	2302	...	...	2222	2228	...	2340	...	0805	...

km		MD 12551 2[R] ①-⑥ q	MD 18321 2 J	MD 12411 2[R] ①-⑤ f	Av 9071 2 ①-⑤ f	Alvia 621 🍷 R	Alvia 625 🍷 S	Alvia 4084 4284 ①-⑥ y	MD 12413 2[R]	MD 12585 2 f ①-⑤	MD 12417 2[R] ①-⑤ f	MD 12419 2[R]	Alvia 4084 4284 ①-⑥ b	Arco 280 A	Arco 280 2 T	Arco 280 2 B	MD 12521 [R] 2	Av 9101 2 ⑤⑥⑦ k	Alvia 4094 b	MD 12423 2[R] ①-⑤ f	MD 12425 2[R]	MD 12527 [R] 2	Av 9141 2 ①-⑤ f	MD 12429 [R] 2	Alvia 4144 🍷 ⑦
0	**A Coruña** d.	...	...	0535	0630	...	0812	...	0657	...	0755	0825	0835	0925	...	...	0940	1120	...	1035	1155	1240	...	1400	1420
74	Santiago de Compostela d.	0545	...	0614	0700	...	0842	...	0733	...	0830	0901	0905	0959	...	...	1023	1150	...	1111	1231	1321	1415	1436	1450
116	Vilagarcía de Arousa d.	0626	...	0649	|	...	|	...	0814	...	0904	0935	|	|	...	...	1101	|	...	1144	1302	1400	|	1514	|
149	**Pontevedra** d.	0650	...	0713	|	...	|	0740	0838	0905	0923	0957	|	|	...	...	1128	|	...	1203	1322	1425	|	1533	|
	Vigo Guixar d.	|	...	|	◧	0750	◧	0813	|	|	|	|	◧	◧	0920	0920	|	◧	...	|	|	|	◧	|	◧
167	Redondela de Galica d.	0714	...	0734	|	0801	|	0824	|	0926	|	|	|	|	0931	0931	1150	|	...	|	|	1447	|	|	|
179	**Vigo** Guixar a.	0727	...	0745	|	|	|	|	0915	0938	0953	1030	|	|	|	|	1203	|	...	1232	1354	1500	|	1603	|
192	Guillarei d.	...	...	...	|	|	|	0842	...	...	...	...	|	|	0947	0947	...	|	...	...	...	...	|	...	|
	Ourense d.	...	...	...	0738	0925	0925	0951	...	...	...	...	0951	1106	1106	1106	...	1228	1240	...	...	...	1453	...	1531
	Puebla de Sanabria d.	...	0728	...	...	|	|	1131	...	...	...	...	1131	|	|	|	...	...	1418	...	...	...	...	...	|
	Zamora d.	...	0845	...	...	|	|	1239	...	...	...	...	1239	|	|	|	...	...	1538	...	...	...	...	...	1821
	Medina del Campo **681 689** d.	...	0942	...	...	|	|	1332	...	...	...	...	1332	|	|	|	...	...	1638	...	...	...	...	...	1915
	Miranda de Ebro **681 689** a.	...	...	...	...	1555	1555	|	...	...	...	...	|	1817	1817	1817	...	...	|	...	...	...	...	...	|
	Barcelona Sants **652** a.	...	...	...	...	2120	2120	|	...	...	...	...	|	|	|	...	...	...	|	...	...	...	...	...	|
	Hendaye **689** a.	...	...	...	...	...	...	◧	...	...	...	...	◧	2052	2052	...	...	...	◧	...	...	...	...	...	◧
	Ávila **681 689** d.	...	...	...	...	...	...	|	...	...	...	...	|	...	...	...	...	...	|	...	...	...	...	...	|
	Madrid Chamartín **681 689** a.	...	...	...	...	...	...	1450	...	...	...	...	1450	...	...	...	...	...	1747	...	...	...	...	...	2019

	MD 12587 2 f ①-⑤	MD 12431 [R] 2	Av 9151 2 ①-⑤ f	2 h	Alvia 4154 🍷 Ⓑ	Alvia 4154 🍷 Ⓑ	MD 12531 [R] 2	2	Av 9181 2 ①-⑤	Av 9181 2 ⑥⑦	Hotel 921 🍷 G	MD 12435 [R] 2	MD 12437 [R] 2	MD 12539 [R] 2	Hotel 852 ✕ D	MD 12541 [R] 2	Av 9211 2	MD 12441 2[R]	Hotel 852 ✕ C	MD 12561 2[R] Ⓑ p
Coruña d.	...	1450	...	...	1535	...	1545	...	...	1815	...	1700	1755	1910	...	2020	2035	2108	2155	2215
antiago de Compostela d.	...	1526	1530	...	1605	...	1629	1725	1845	1845	...	1736	1831	1952	...	2100	2105	2144	2233	2252
Vilagarcía de Arousa d.	...	1559	|	...	|	...	1708	|	|	|	...	1810	1902	2037	...	2141	|	2223	|	...
Pontevedra d.	1605	1620	|	...	|	1442	1732	|	|	|	...	1831	1923	2101	2130	2204	|	2244	|	...
Vigo Guixar d.	|	|	◧	1430	◧	1515	|	|	◧	◧	1755	|	|	|	2220u	|	◧	|	|	...
Redondela de Galica d.	1622	|	|	1443	|	1526	1757	|	|	|	1805	|	|	2128	2236	2229	|	|	|	...
Vigo Guixar a.	1635	1650	|	|	|	|	1809	|	|	|	|	1903	1954	2138	|	2245	|	2316	|	...
Guillarei d.	...	...	|	1504	|	1543	...	|	|	|	1826	...	...	...	2258	...	|	...	|	...
urense d.	...	...	1608	1627	1650	1650	...	1911	1923	1923	1933	...	...	...	0035	...	2143	...	0035	...
uebla de Sanabria d.	...	...	...	...	1833	1833	...	...	...	...	|	...	...	...	0233	...	...	...	0233	...
amora d.	...	...	...	...	1946	1946	...	...	...	...	|	...	...	...	0400	...	...	...	0400	...
edina del Campo **681 689** d.	...	...	...	...	2038	2038	...	...	...	...	|	...	...	...	0541	...	...	...	0541	...
Miranda de Ebro **681 689** a.	...	...	...	...	|	|	...	...	...	...	|	...	...	...	|	...	...	...	|	...
Barcelona Sants **652** a.	...	...	...	...	|	|	...	...	...	...	0844	...	...	...	|	...	...	...	|	...
Hendaye **689** a.	...	...	...	...	◧	◧	...	...	...	...	...	...	...	...	|	...	...	...	|	...
vila **681 689** d.	...	...	...	...	|	|	...	...	...	...	...	...	...	...	0626	...	...	...	0626	...
adrid Chamartín **681 689** a.	...	...	...	...	2148	2148	...	...	...	...	...	...	...	...	0802	...	...	...	0802	...

– CAMINO DE SANTIAGO – [12] 🍷 Irún / Hendaye - Miranda de Ebro - A Coruña and v.v.
– CAMINO DE SANTIAGO – [2] Bilbao - Miranda de Ebro - Ourense - Vigo and v.v.
– RÍAS GALLEGAS *Trenhotel* – 🛏, [2] Madrid - A Coruña and v.v.
– RÍAS GALLEGAS *Trenhotel* – 🛏, [2] Madrid - Pontevedra and v.v.
– [12] 🍷 Barcelona - Vigo and v.v.
– GALICIA *Trenhotel* – 🛏, [1] (reclining) Barcelona - Vigo and v.v.
– [2] Valladolid - Medina del Campo - Puebla de Sanabria and v.v. (Table **689**).
– ③⑤⑦ [12] 🍷 Barcelona - Ourense - Vigo ❖.
– ①②④⑥ [12] 🍷 Barcelona - Ourense - A Coruña ❖.
– ①④⑥ [12] 🍷 Vigo - Ourense - Barcelona ❖.
– ②③⑤⑦ [12] 🍷 A Coruña - Ourense - Barcelona ❖.
– CAMINO DE SANTIAGO – [2] Irún / Hendaye - Miranda de Ebro - Ourense - Vigo and v.v.

b – To / from Ferrol (Table **682**).
d – From Alacant on ⑦ (Table **668**).
f – Not Aug. 15, Nov. 1, Dec. 6.
g – From Alacant on ⑥ (Table **668**).
h – To / from Ponferrada (Table **682**).
k – Also Aug. 15, Nov. 1, Dec. 6.
p – Not Aug. 14, Nov. 1, Dec. 6.
q – Not Aug. 15, Nov. 2, Dec. 7.
s – Calls to set down only.
u – Calls to pick up only.
y – To Alacant on ⑥ (Table **668**).

◐ – Via Lugo (Table **682**).

◧ – Via high-speed line.
* – *153 km* Madrid - Medina del Campo via high-speed line.
§ – *636 km* Madrid - Santiago de Compostela via high-speed line. *697 km* Madrid - A Coruña via high-speed line.
❖ – On days of indirect service, connections will be available between Ourense and Vigo / A Coruña and v.v. in the same timings.

681 MADRID - LEÓN

km			*Alvia*	*Alvia*		*IC*	*Alvia*	*Arco*	*Arco*		*Alvia*	*Alvia*	*Alvia*	*IC*	*Alvia*	*IC*	*IC*	*Alvia*	*Alvia*	*IC*		*IC*	*IC*	*Hotel*	
			4071	**4083**		**4405**	**4111**	**283**	**283**	**18215**	**4133**	**622**	**4141**	**4153**	**664**	**18003**	**4471**	**4183**	**4181**	**18005**	**18009**	**4201**	**4201**	**922**	
		2	①-⑥	①-⑥	2				2	2		**626**		2		2	**4571**		**4381**	2	2	⑦	①-⑤		
			k	**b**	**X**		**V**	**B J**	**K**			**L**	**m**	⑤**y**			⑧	**H**	**T**		⑤**j**	**p**		**G**	
0	**Madrid** Chamartín ... **680 689** d.	...	0730	0830	...	1040	1105	...	...	...	1325	...	1440	1523	...	1627	1700	1805	1840	1835	1912	2020	2020	...	...
121	Ávila ... **680 689** d.	...	◧	◧	...	◧	◧	...	...	...	◧	...	◧	◧	...	1757	◧	◧	◧	2004	2105	◧	◧	...	...
207	Medina del Campo . **680 689** d.	...	|	|	...	|	|	...	...	...	|	...	|	|	...	1843	|	|	|	2049	2157	|	|	...	...
249	**Valladolid** C. Grande ... **689** d.	0635	0833	0933	1053	1145	1210	...	...	1250	1440	...	1552	1626	...	1908	1802	1917	1945	2114	2225	2123	2123	...	...
286	Venta de Baños ... **689** d.	0706	|	|	1124	|	|	...	...	1325	|	...	|	|	...	1932	|	|	|	2137	...	|	|	...	...
	Barcelona Sants **652** ... d.	|	|	|	|	|	|	...	...	|	|	0930	|	|	1210	|	|	|	|	|	...	|	|	2020	...
	Irún **689** ... d.	|	|	|	|	|	|	0845	...	|	|	|	|	|	|	|	|	|	|	|	...	|	|	|	...
	Bilbao Abando **689** ... d.	|	|	|	|	|	|	|	0915	|	|	|	|	|	|	|	|	|	|	|	...	|	|	|	...
	Miranda de Ebro ... **689** d.	|	|	|	|	|	|	1118	1118	|	|	1432	|	|	1723	|	|	|	|	|	...	|	|	|	...
	Burgos Rosa de Lima **689** d.	|	|	|	|	|	|	1212	1212	|	|	1525	|	|	1815	|	|	|	|	|	...	|	|	0249	...
297	Palencia ... **689** d.	0718	0909	1013	1135	1217	1243	1302	1302	1339	1514	1613	1627	1708	1905	1954	1838	1956	2018	2149	...	2158	2158	0341	...
	Santander **684** ... a.	|	|	1255	1434	|	|	|	|	|	1750	|	|	2012	|	|	|	2238	|	|	...	|	|	|	...
420	**León** ... a.	0840	1014	...	...	1322	1342	1405	1405	1505	...	1716	1734	...	2011	2050	1941	...	2116**e**	2300	...	2305	2305	0445	...
	Gijón Cercanías **685** ... a.	1144	1255	...	...	|	1621	|	|	...	...	|	2015	...	2256**x**	...	|	...	2353**z**	...	...	...	...	|	...
	Ponferrada **682** ... a.	...	...	...	...	1459	...	1601	1601	...	...	1849	...	...	...	...	2125	...	...	...	...	...	...	0634	...
	Vigo Guixar **682** ... a.	...	...	...	...	1922	...	2017	2017	...	...	2300	...	...	...	...	...	...	...	...	...	...	...	1111	...
	A Coruña **682** ... a.	...	...	...	...	...	...	2003	...	...	...	2222	...	...	...	...	...	...	...	...	...	...	...	1052	...

	IC	*IC*	*IC*	*Alvia*	*Alvia*	*Alvia*	*Alvia*	*Alvia*	*IC*	*Arco*	*Arco*		*Alvia*	*Alvia*	*IC*		*IC*	*IC*	*Alvia*	*Alvia*	*Alvia*	*IC*	*Hotel*		
	4060	**18002**	**4360**	**2134**	**661**	**4092**	**4100**	**625**	**4384**	**280**	**280**	**18214**	**2194**	**4140**	**18006**	**18104**	**4460**	**4162**	**4180**	**4380**	**4382**	**4200**	**921**		
	①-⑤	2	①-⑤		①-⑥			**621**			2	2			2	2		⑦	①-⑤	⑦	⑧	⑦**r**			
	h			**T**		**H**	**m**	**L**		**B J**	**K**		**T**	**V**		**Y**	⑦	2	**g**		**g**	2	**G**		
A Coruña **682** ... d.	...	...	...	...	...	...	...	0812	...	0925	...	...	...	...	...	...	...	...	...	...	...	...	1800	...	...
Vigo Guixar **682** ... d.	...	...	...	...	...	...	...	0750	0825	0920	0920	...	...	...	...	...	...	...	...	...	...	...	1755	...	...
Ponferrada **682** ... d.	...	...	0650	...	...	...	...	1137	1241	1331	1331	...	...	...	...	...	1635	...	...	...	...	...	2222	...	...
Gijón Cercanías **685** ... d.	...	...	|	0700	0810	...	1020	|	|	|	|	...	...	1400	...	...	|	...	1722	1722	...	...	|	...	...
León ... d.	0630	0710	0830	0935	1037	...	1257	1312	1428	1525	1525	1530	...	1641	1705	...	1819	...	2004	|	...	2009	0012	...	...
Santander **684** ... d.	|	|	|	|	|	0905	|	|	|	|	|	|	1340	|	|	1540	|	1625	|	|	1850	|	|	...	...
Palencia ... **689** d.	0735	0816	0933	1040	1145	1200	1402	1416	1534	1629	1629	1659	1620	1742	1812	1839	1925	1920	2108	2047	2133	2113	0122	...	...
Burgos Rosa de Lima **689** d.	|	|	|	|	1237	|	|	1501	|	1718	1718	|	|	|	|	|	|	|	|	|	|	|	0215	...	...
Miranda de Ebro ... **689** a.	|	|	|	|	1328	|	|	1555	|	1817	1817	|	|	|	|	|	|	|	|	|	|	|	|	...	...
Bilbao Abando **689** ... a.	|	|	|	|	|	|	|	|	|	|	2003	|	|	|	|	|	|	|	|	|	|	|	|	...	...
Hendaye **689** ... a.	|	|	|	|	|	|	|	|	|	2052	...	|	|	|	|	|	|	|	|	|	|	|	|	...	...
Barcelona Sants **652** ... a.	|	|	|	|	1850	|	|	2120	|	...	...	|	|	|	|	|	|	|	|	|	|	|	0844	...	...
Venta de Baños ... **689** d.	|	0829	|	|	...	|	|	...	|	...	...	1709	|	|	1824	1850	|	|	|	|	|	|	...	...	...
Valladolid C. Grande ... **689** d.	0810	0853	1010	1117	...	1245	1440	...	1613	...	...	1739	1654	1820	1848	1916	2002	2002	2146	2125	2212	2149	...	...	...
Medina del Campo .. **680 689** a.	|	0916	|	|	...	|	|	...	|	...	...	...	|	|	1911	...	|	|	|	|	|	|	...	...	...
Ávila ... **680 689** a.	◧	1002	◧	◧	...	◧	◧	...	◧	...	...	...	◧	◧	1957	...	◧	◧	◧	◧	◧	|	...	...	...
Madrid Chamartín .. **680 689** a.	0920	1131	1115	1225	...	1358	1551	...	1730	...	...	...	1817	1924	2131	...	2115	2115	2250	2229	2317	2255	...	...	...

☛ **FOR NOTES**, SEE TABLE **682** BELOW.

682 LEÓN - VIGO, FERROL and A CORUÑA

km		*Alvia*	*MD*	*Hotel*	*Hotel*	*MD*		*MD*	*IC*	*MD*	*MD*	*Alvia*	*Arco*	*Arco*	*Arco*	*MD*	*Alvia*	*Alvia*	*Alvia*	*MD*	*IC*		
		4084	**12641**	**922**	**922**	**33641**		**12683**	**4405**	**12685**	**12685**	**4125**	**283**	**283**	**283**	**12687**	**4155**	**622**	**626**	**12647**	**4471**		
		4284	2	🍷		2	2	2		2	2		2	🍷	2	2					**4571**		
		A		**G**	**G**	⑥⑦				①-⑤	⑥⑦	**P**	**K**	**B**	**J**		**A**	**L**	**L**		⑧		
	Madrid Chamartín ... ‡ d.	①-⑥	...	...	...	...	...	...	1040	...	...	1220	...	...	...	...	1500	...	...	...	1700	...	...
	Barcelona Sants ... ‡ d.	...	...	2020	2020	...	...	...	|	...	...	|	...	...	...	...	|	0930	0930	...	|	...	...
	Irún ... ‡ d.	...	...	|	|	...	...	...	|	...	...	|	...	0845	0845	...	|	|	|	...	|	...	...
	Bilbao Abando ... ‡ d.	...	...	|	|	...	...	...	|	...	...	|	0915	|	|	...	|	|	|	...	|	...	...
0	**León** ... d.	...	...	0500	0500	...	0713	...	1327	...	...	|	1420	1420	1420	...	|	1721	1721	...	1946	...	...
52	Astorga ... d.	...	...	0534	0534	...	0751	...	1401	...	...	|	1501	1501	1501	...	|	1751	1751	...	2020	...	...
128	**Ponferrada** ... d.	...	...	0636	0636	...	0910	...	1500	...	...	|	1602	1602	1602	...	|	1850	1850	...	2125	...	...
238	Monforte de Lemos ... a.	...	...	0807	0807	...	1057	...	1637	...	...	1804	1732	1732	1732	...	|	2021	2021	...	...	...	...
238	Monforte de Lemos ... d.	...	0730**c**	0820	0827	0900	1102	...	1642	...	...	1806	1747	1747	1747	...	|	2026	2026	2040	...	...	...
285	Ourense ... **680** d.	...	|	|	0921	|	1201	...	1726	...	...	1725	1838	1843	1838	...	2001	2112	2112	|	...	...	...
416	**Vigo** Guixar ... **680** a.	...	|	|	1111	|	1412	...	1922	...	...	|	2017	|	2017	...	|	2300	|	|	...	...	...
309	Lugo ... d.	...	0824**c**	0913	...	0953	...	...	...	...	...	1859	...	|	...	...	|	...	|	2134	...	...	...
445	**Ferrol** ... d.	0715	|	|	...	|	...	1410	...	1718	1725	|	...	▲	...	1915	2236	...	▲	|	...	...	...
402	Betanzos - Infesta ... d.	0801	0955	1027	...	1119	...	1500	...	1811	1811	2005	...	|	...	2004	...	...	|	2245	...	...	...
428	**A Coruña** ... **680** a.	0825	1021	1052	...	1151	...	1525	...	1835	...	|	...	2003	...	2030	...	...	2222	2310	...	...	...
445	**Ferrol** ... a.	...	...	...	...	...	...	...	...	...	...	2047	...	...	...	...	...	...	...	...	...	...	...

	IC	*MD*	*MD*	*Alvia*	*Alvia*	*Alvia*	*IC*	*Alvia*	*Arco*	*Arco*	*Arco*	*MD*	*MD*	*Alvia*	*IC*		*MD*	*MD*	*Hotel*	*Hotel*	*MD*	*Alvia*	
	4360	**12680**	**12644**	**621**	**625**	**4084**	**4384**	**4094**	**280**	**280**	**280**	**12694**	**12682**	**4094**	**4460**		**12684**	**12696**	**921**	**921**	**12642**	**4155**	
		2				**4284**		**C**	🍷	2	2	2	2			2		2		🍷	2	**4355**	
	①-⑤	①-⑤		**L**	**L**	**A**		⑦	**B**	**J**	**K**	①-⑤	⑥⑦	**P**	⑦			⑥⑦	**G**	**G**		**A**	
Ferrol ... d.	...	...	...	...	...	①-⑥	...	...	...	...	...	...	...	0910	...	...	...	...	...	...	...	⑧	...
A Coruña ... **680** d.	...	0640	0700	...	0812	...	...	...	0925	...	...	...	1100	|	...	...	1430	...	...	1800	1930	2124	...
Betanzos - Infesta ... d.	...	0712	0725	...	|	...	...	...	|	...	...	1040	1130	0952	...	...	1459	1815	...	1822	2001	2154	...
Ferrol ... a.	...	0756	|	...	▲	0715	...	0910	▲	...	...	1125	1214	|	...	...	1546	1900	...	|	|	2236	...
Lugo ... d.	...	...	0851	...	|	|	...	1057	|	...	...	...	...	1057	...	...	...	...	...	1926	2135	...	...
Vigo Guixar ... **680** d.	...	...	|	0750	|	|	0825	|	|	0920	0920	...	...	|	...	1430	...	...	1755	|	|	...	...
Ourense ... **680** d.	...	...	|	0925	0925	0951	1018	1240	1106	1106	1106	...	...	1240	...	1628	...	...	1933	|	|	...	...
Monforte de Lemos ... a.	...	...	0954	1002	1002	|	1056	1149	1146	1146	1146	...	...	1149	...	1719	...	...	2013	2020	2228	...	...
Monforte de Lemos ... d.	...	...	...	1007	1007	|	1101	1151	1201	1201	1201	...	...	1151	...	1724	...	...	2041	2041	...	...	...
Ponferrada ... d.	0650	...	...	1137	1137	|	1241	|	1331	1331	1331	...	...	|	1635	1930	...	...	2222	2222	...	...	...
Astorga ... d.	0752	...	...	1237	1237	|	1343	|	1438	1438	1438	...	...	|	1737	2052	...	...	2324	2324	...	...	...
León ... a.	0825	...	...	1307	1307	|	1423	|	1510	1510	1510	...	...	|	1814	2131	...	...	2357	2357	...	...	...
Bilbao Abando ... ‡ a.	|	...	...	|	|	|	|	|	|	|	2003	...	...	|	|	...	...	...	|	|	...	...	...
Hendaye ... ‡ a.	|	...	...	|	|	|	|	|	2052	2052	...	...	...	|	|	...	...	...	|	|	...	...	...
Barcelona Sants ... ‡ a.	|	...	...	2120	2120	|	|	|	...	...	...	...	...	|	|	...	...	...	0844	0844	...	...	...
Madrid Chamartín ... ‡ a.	1115	...	...	...	...	1450	1730	1747	...	...	...	...	...	1747	2115	...	...	...	...	...	...	...	...

A – [12] Madrid - Ourense - A Coruña - Ferrol and v.v. (Table **680**).
B – CAMINO DE SANTIAGO – [12] 🍷 Irún / Hendaye - Monforte de Lemos - Santiago - A Coruña and v.v.
G – GALICIA *Trenhotel* – 🛏, [1] (reclining) Barcelona - A Coruña and Vigo and v.v.
H – [12] Alacant - Madrid - Santander and v.v. (Table **668**).
J – CAMINO DE SANTIAGO – [2] Irún / Hendaye - Monforte de Lemos - Vigo and v.v.
K – CAMINO DE SANTIAGO – [2] Bilbao - Monforte de Lemos - Vigo and v.v.
L – [12] 🍷 Barcelona - A Coruña and Vigo and v.v. For days of running see Table **680**.
P – [12] Madrid - Zamora - Ourense - Monforte de Lemos - Lugo - Ferrol and v.v. (Table **680**).
T – From / to Cádiz (Table **671**).
V – From / to València on dates shown in Table **668**.
X – Daily (①-⑤ July 1 - Aug. 31; not Aug. 15).
Y – Daily (⑧ July 1 - Aug. 31; not Aug. 15).

b – Not Nov. 2, Dec. 7.
c – ①-⑤.
e – Not ⑤.
g – Not Nov. 1, Dec. 6.
h – Not Aug. 1-31, Nov. 1, Dec. 6, 9.
j – Also Oct. 31, Dec. 5; not Nov. 1, Dec. 6.
k – Not Sept. 9, Oct. 12, Nov. 2, 9, Dec. 7, 9.
m – From / to Alacant (Table **668**).
p – Not Aug. 1-31.
r – Also Dec. 9.

x – Not ⑥.
y – Also Aug. 14; not Aug. 16
z – Not ⑥. 2337 on ⑤.

▲ – Via Santiago (Table **680**).
‡ – See Table **681**.
◧ – Via high-speed line (Table **663**).

683 LEÓN - BILBAO

FEVE narrow-gauge

1345 ✣ →	1410 →	1445 →	1535 →	1636 →	1717 →	1801 →	1935 →	2044 →	2130
León	San Feliz	La Vecilla	Cistierna	Guardo	Vado Cervera	Mataporquera	Espinosa	Balmaseda	**Bilbao** Concordia
2203 ✣	← 2138	← 2059	← 2018	← 1921	← 1841	← 1800	← 1623	← 1520	← 1430

✣ – Journey may be by 🚌 between León and Asunción-Universidad y León, due to construction of a new tunnel.

PALENCIA - SANTANDER 684

km			Alvia 4083		Alvia 4133		IC 4153	Alvia 4183			
		2		2		2	⑤j		2	2	
		E	A	D			2	B	J	⑤k	
	Madrid Chamartín **681 689** d.	...	0830	...	1325	...	1523	1805	...	...	...
	Valladolid C G **681 689** d.	0750	0933	1053	1440	1441	1626	1927	1700	1825	...
0	**Palencia** d.	0825	1013	1135	1514	1527	1708	2003	1740	1909	...
98	Aguilar de Campoo d.	0942	1120	1251	|	1647	1818	2111	1859	2025	...
110	Mataporquera **683** ‡ d.	0951	|	1300	|	1658	1827	|	1909	2040	...
129	Reinosa § d.	1006	1148	1315	|	1716	1845	2136	1924	2058	...
188	Torrelavega § d.	1100	1234	1405	1728	1826	1944	2222	2028	2156	...
218	**Santander** § a.	1123	1258	1434	1750	1905	2012	2247	2100	2224	...

		Alvia 4092	Alvia 4142		IC 4162	Alvia 4382		
	2							
	⑥⑦		🍷	2	⑦	Ⓑ	2	
	f	B		C	2	y	E	
Santander § d.	0705	0905	1340	1540	1625	1850	2018	...
Torrelavega § d.	0731	0932	1406	1608	1647	1915	2049	...
Reinosa § d.	0822	1020	|	1704	1740	2004	2152	...
Mataporquera **683** ‡ d.	0837	|	|	1718	1757	|	2207	...
Aguilar de Campoo d.	0848	1044	|	1726	1807	2028	2216	...
Palencia a.	1001	1158	1618	1838	1915	2131	2320	...
Valladolid C G **681 689** a.	1046	1243	1652	1916	2000	2210	2353	...
Madrid Chamartín **681 689** a.	...	1358	1816	...	2115	2317	...	...

A – ①–⑥ (not Nov. 2, Dec. 7).
B – From/to Alacant (Table **668**).
C – Daily (Ⓑ July 1 - Aug. 31) not Aug. 15.
D – Daily (①–⑤ July 1 - Aug. 31) not Aug. 15.
E – ⑥⑦ July 1 - Aug. 31 (also Aug. 15).
H – Daily. To Cádiz on Ⓑ (Table **671**).
J – ①②③④⑥⑦.
f – Also daily July 15 - Sept. 8.
g – Not Aug. 15, Sept. 8.
j – Also Aug. 14; not Aug. 16.
k – Also Aug. 16, Nov. 1, Dec. 6; not Aug. 14, Oct. 31, Dec. 5.
y – Not Nov. 1, Dec. 6.
‡ – Narrow gauge station is 600 metres.
§ – Additional local services operate between these stations.

LEÓN - OVIEDO - GIJÓN 685

km			Alvia 4071	Alvia 4111		Alvia 4141	IC 4151	Alvia 664	Alvia 4181	Alvia 4181
		2	①–⑥						⑤	⑦–④
			k	V		C	⑤f	A	Z	Z
	Barcelona Sants **681** d.	...	...	...	...	...	...	1210	...	...
	Madrid Chamartín **681** d.	...	0730	1105	...	1440	1545	|	1840	1840
0	**León** d.	0845	1019	1347	...	1745	|	2016	|	2121
109	Pola de Lena § a.	1039	|	|	...	1918	|	2151x	|	|
140	**Oviedo** ▽ § a.	1112	1226	1551	...	1945	2008	2222x	2313	2329
172	**Gijón** Cercanias § a.	1144	1255	1621	...	2015	2040	2256x	2337	2353

	Alvia 4070	Alvia 661	Alvia 4100	Alvia 4140	IC 4160		Alvia 4180	Alvia 4380	
	①–⑥	①–⑥			⑦	2	①–⑤	⑦	2
	Z	A	C	W		Q	g		P
Gijón Cercanias § d.	0700	0810	1020	1400	1605	1615	1722	1722	1945
Oviedo ▽ § d.	0725	0836	1047	1426	1632	1644	1749	1749	2015
Pola de Lena § d.	|	0902	1118	1455	|	1721	|	|	2051
León a.	0930	1032	1246	1636	|	1937	1959	|	2310
Madrid Chamartín **681** a.	1222	|	1556	1924	2100	...	2250	2229	...
Barcelona Sants **681** a.	...	1850	...	...	...	...	...	...	...

A – 12 Gijón - Barcelona and v.v. (Table **681**).
C – From/to Alacant (Table **668**).
P – ⑦ (daily July 1 - Aug. 31).
Q – ①–⑥ (not July 1 - Aug. 31).
V – From València on ①–⑥ (Table **668**).
W – to València on Ⓑ (Table **668**).
Z – From/to Cádiz (Table **671**).
f – Also Aug. 14, Oct. 31, Dec. 5; not Aug. 16, Nov. 1, Dec. 6.
g – Not Nov. 1, Dec. 6.
k – Not Sept. 9, Oct. 12, Nov. 2, 9, Dec. 7, 9.
x – Not ⑥.

▽ – **OVIEDO – AVILÉS** and v.v. ***Renfe Cercanías*** (suburban) service. *31 km.* Journey time: ± 38 minutes. **Additional services on Ⓐ.**
From Oviedo: Approximately 1 train each hour 0550 Ⓐ, 0616 Ⓐ, then 0716 until 2216. **From Avilés**: Approximately 1 train each hour 0641 Ⓐ, 0741 Ⓐ, then 0841 until 2311.

§ – **GIJÓN – OVIEDO – POLA de LENA** and v.v. ***Renfe Cercanías*** (suburban) service. *63 km.* Journey time: ± 78 minutes.
From Pola de Lena: Approximately 1–2 trains each hour from 0630 until 2200. **From Gijón**: Approximately 1–2 trains each hour from 0600 until 2230.

SAN SEBASTIÁN - BILBAO 686

EuskoTren (narrow gauge)

	Ⓐ	Ⓐ	Ⓒ					
San Sebastián ⊡ Amara d.	0550	0650	...	0750	0850		1950	2050
Zarautz d.	0620	0720	...	0820	0920		2020	2120
Zumaia d.	0629	0729	...	0829	0929	and	2029	2129
Eibar d.	0711	0811	0811	0911	1011	hourly	2111	2211
Durango d.	0742	0842	0842	0942	1042	until	2142	2241
Bilbao Bolueta ⊖ a.	0818	0918	0918	1018	1118		2218	...
Bilbao Atxuri § a.	0822	0922	0922	1022	1122		2222	...

	Ⓐ	Ⓐ	Ⓒ					
Bilbao Atxuri § d.	...	0600	...	0700	0800		2000	2100
Bilbao Bolueta ⊖ d.	...	0603	...	0703	0803		2003	2103
Durango d.	0540	0640	...	0740	0840	and	2040	2140
Eibar d.	0614	0714	...	0814	0914	hourly	2114	2214
Zumaia d.	0700	0800	0800	0900	1000	until	2200	...
Zarautz d.	0708	0808	0808	0908	1008		2208	...
San Sebastián ⊡ Amara a.	0738	0838	0838	0938	1038		2238	...

⊡ – San Sebastián/Donostia.
⊖ – Metro interchange.
§ – Bilbao Atxuri ⇆ Bilbao Concordia: ± *1000 m.* Linked by tram approx every 10 minutes, journey 6 minutes. Bilbao Concordia is adjacent to Bilbao Abando (*Renfe*).
Operator: EuskoTren. 2nd class, narrow gauge.
Distance: San Sebastian - Bilbao *108* km.

BILBAO - SANTANDER - OVIEDO - FERROL 687

FEVE (narrow gauge)

		Ⓐ			Ⓐ					
Bilbao Concordia § d.	...	...	...	0802	...	1302	...	...	1930	...
Marrón d.	...	0720	...	0940	...	1434	...	...	2106	...
Treto d.	...	0731	...	0950	...	1444	...	...	2116	...
Santander a.	...	0828	...	1059	...	1557	...	...	2213	...
Santander ▽ d.	...	...	0910	...	...	...	1610	...	...	...
Torrelavega ▽ d.	...	...	0937	...	...	...	1638	...	...	...
Cabezón de la Sal ▽ d.	...	...	1007	...	...	...	1707	...	...	...
Unquera d.	...	...	1044	...	...	...	1743	...	...	...
Llanes d.	0755	...	1113	...	1430	...	1813	...	...	...
Ribadesella d.	0832	...	1153	...	1507	...	1852	...	...	...
Oviedo a.	1029	...	1340	...	1706	...	2040	...	...	...

					Ⓐ			Ⓐ		
Oviedo d.	...	...	0905	...	1035	...	1535	...	1855	...
Ribadesella d.	...	...	1100	...	1237	...	1735	...	2054	...
Llanes d.	...	...	1139	...	1313	...	1814	...	2129	...
Unquera d.	...	...	1208	...	...	...	1843	...	...	...
Cabezón de la Sal ▽ d.	...	...	1249	...	...	...	1924	...	...	...
Torrelavega ▽ d.	...	...	1316	...	...	...	1949	...	...	...
Santander ▽ a.	...	...	1346	...	...	...	2017	...	...	...
Santander d.	0800	...	...	1400	...	1900	...	2035	...	...
Treto d.	0900	...	...	1503	...	2000	...	2133	...	...
Marrón d.	0911	...	...	1514	...	2011	...	2141	...	...
Bilbao Concordia § a.	1045	...	...	1645	...	2145	...	...	...	...

					Ⓐ					
Oviedo △ d.	...	...	0747	...	...	...	...	...	1447	...
Gijón Sanz Crespo △ d.	...	0731	|	0931	...	...	1131	1431	|	1831
Avilés △ d.	...	0814	|	1018	...	...	1218	1518	|	1918
Pravia △ d.	...	0844	0847	1048	...	...	1248	1548	1552	1948
Luarca d.	...	...	0956	...	...	...	...	...	1703	...
Navia d.	...	...	1021	...	...	...	...	...	1728	...
Ribadeo d.	0650	...	1112	...	...	1445	...	...	1817	...
Viveiro d.	0756	...	1220	...	...	1553	...	...	1923	...
Ortigueira d.	0832	...	1257	...	1500	1629	...	...	2000	...
Ferrol a.	0948	...	1409	...	1610	1739	...	...	2111	...

							Ⓐ			
Ferrol d.	...	...	0810	...	1030	...	1345	1518	...	1845
Ortigueira d.	...	...	0923	...	1143	...	1455	1631	...	1959
Viveiro d.	...	...	0959	...	1219	...	...	1707	...	2035
Ribadeo d.	...	...	1110	...	1324	...	...	1818	...	2147
Navia d.	...	...	1158	...	...	...	...	1907	...	...
Luarca d.	...	...	1223	...	...	...	...	1932	...	...
Pravia △ d.	0848	1148	1331	1348	...	1648	...	2049	2048	...
Avilés △ d.	0926	1226	|	1426	...	1726	...	|	2126	...
Gijón Sanz Crespo △ a.	1008	1308	|	1508	...	1808	...	|	2206	...
Oviedo △ a.	...	...	1429	...	...	...	...	2148	...	...

▽ – Additional trains run Santander - Cabezón de al Sal and v.v.
△ – Additional trains run Oviedo/Gijón - Pravia and v.v.
§ – Bilbao Concordia is adjacent to Bilbao Abando (*Renfe*).
Operator: FEVE. 2nd class, narrow gauge.

IRÚN - BILBAO - SANTANDER - GIJÓN 688

ALSA ★

🚌																									
	▽			♡	♡						♡			♡		♡						⊖			
	①–⑥			Ⓑ	⑥	①–⑥	⑦				Ⓑ	⑥		Ⓑ			⑤⑦					⑤⑦		⑦	
Irún RENFE rail station d.	...	...	...	0645	...	0745	...	...	0845	...	...	...	1100	...	1345	1445	...	...	1615	...	1830	...	2045	2115	2355
San Sebastián/Donostia d.	...	...	...	0710	...	0810	...	...	0910	...	...	...	1125	...	1410	1510	...	...	1640	...	1855	...	2110	2140	0020
Bilbao TermiBus d.	0600	...	0700	0830	0830	0930	0930	1000	1030	1130	1230	1230	1330	1430	1530	1630	1730	1730	1800	1845	2030	2115	2230	2300	0145
Santander d.	0715	0830	0830	0950	0950	1100	1115	1130	1215	1300	1350	1400	1530	1550	1700	1750	1900	1900	1930	2015	2200	2235	2350	0020	0330
Oviedo a.	1000*	1145	...	1205	1205	...	...	...	1530	...	1605	...	1845	1805	...	2005	2145	...	2230	2230	...	0050	...	...	0600
Gijón a.	0930	1215	...	1230	1230	...	...	...	1600	...	1635	...	1915	1835	...	2030	2215	...	2300	2300	...	0120	...	...	0700

🚌																									
						♡	♡				♡			♡				♡				▽		▽	▽
		①–⑥			①–⑥		①–⑥	⑤	⑦	①–⑥	①–⑥		⑤⑦				⑥	Ⓑ				Ⓑ	⑤⑦	⑤	⑦
Gijón d.	0014	...	...	...	...	0715	...	...	0815	0815	0915	1130	...	1315	...	1515	1545	1630	...	1715	...	1915	2015	2115	2115
Oviedo d.	0100	...	...	...	...	0745	...	...	0845	0845	0945	|	...	1345	...	|	1615	1700	...	1745	...	1945	2045	2145	2145
Santander d.	0345	0600	0700	0800	0930	1005	1200	...	1200	1230	1200	1400	1545	1605	1700	1900	1900	1920	...	2030	2100	2205	2340	0005	2359
Bilbao TermiBus d.	0515	0730	0840	0930	1100	1120	1315	1400	1400	1415	1315	1530	1745	1720	1830	2045	2030	2035	2045	2200	2230	2320	...	0120	0115
San Sebastián/Donostia a.	0640	0845	1000	...	1210	1230	...	1510	1600	1615	...	...	1855	1830z	1940	2155	...	2145r	2155	2310	...	...	...	...	0225
Irún RENFE rail station a.	0700	0915	1030	...	1240	1305	...	1545	1630	1645	...	...	1925	1905z	2010	2225	...	2220r	2225	2340	...	...	...	...	0300

♡ – *Clase Supra+* luxury coach.
▽ – *Clase Supra Economy* luxury coach.
⊖ – *Supra+ on ⑤, Supra Economy on ⑦.*
r – ①–④ only.
z – ⑥ only.
* – Calls after Gijon.
★ – ALSA: ✆ +34 913 270 540 www.alsa.es
Frequent services operate Bilbao - Santander and Oviedo - Gijon.

689 MADRID and SALAMANCA - BILBAO and IRÚN

km △		16007 ①-⑥ N 2	*MD* 16001 2	*Hotel* 310 ✕ B	*MD* 18316	*Alvia* 631 🍷 ①-⑥	17227 2	17201 ①-⑤ h 2	*MD* 18302 2	*Alvia* 4087 🍷	*Alvia* 4087 ①-⑥	*MD* 34321 2 Y	*Alvia* 661 ①-⑥ A	*MD-IC* 18061 2	*Alvia* 633 🍷 ⑦	18215 2 L	18029 2 Z	*Alvia* 621 🍷 Q	2 ①-⑤ t	
0	**Madrid** Chamartín ... 680 681 d.	...	...	...	...	...	...	...	...	0800	0800	...	...	0848	...	...	...	...	...	...
121	Ávila ... 680 681 d.	...	...	...	...	...	...	0700	...	|	|	...	...	1013	...	...	...	...	...	...
	Salamanca ... d.	...	...	0456	0600	...	...	|	0725	◧	◧	...	...	|	...	...	...	...	...	...
207	Medina del Campo ... 680 681 d.	...	...	0600	0639	...	0655	0748	0815	|	|	0943	...	1100	...	...	...	...	...	...
250	**Valladolid** Campo Grande ... 681 d.	...	...	0629	0705	0720	0730	0815	0850	0909	0909	1018	...	1125	1132	1250	...	...	...	...
286	Venta de Baños ... 681 d.	...	...	|	...	|	...	...	...	|	|	...	...	1152	|	1325	...	...	...	...
298	Palencia ... 681 d.	...	...	|	...	|	...	...	...	|	|	...	1145	1206	|	1337	...	1416	...	...
371	**Burgos** Rosa de Lima ... 681 d.	...	...	0748	...	0825	...	...	...	1023	1023	...	1237	1256	1240	...	1406j	1501	...	...
460	Miranda de Ebro ... 653 d.	0720	0830	0848	...	0925	...	...	...	1118	1130	...	1329	1353	1337	...	1502	1556	1715	...
565	**Bilbao** Abando ... 653 a.	|	|	|	...	|	...	...	...	|	1259	...	|	|	|	...	|	|	|	...
494	Vitoria / Gasteiz ... 653 d.	0750	0902	0912	...	|	...	...	...	1141	...	...	1352	1417	|	...	1530	1617	1740	...
	Barcelona Sants **653** ... a.	|	|	|	...	1420	...	...	...	|	...	...	1850	|	1835	...	|	2110	...	...
537	Altsasu ... 653 d.	0820n	0931	|	...	...	...	...	...	|	...	...	...	1445	...	...	1601n	...	...	...
624	**San Sebastián / Donostia** ... ▲ 653 d.	...	1049	1055	...	...	...	...	...	1320	...	...	...	1601	...	...	...	...	...	...
641	**Irún** ... ▲ 653 a.	...	1113	1117s	...	...	...	...	...	1345s	...	...	...	1625	...	...	...	...	...	...
643	Hendaye ... ▲ 653 a.	...	...	1128	...	...	...	...	...	1351	...	...	...	...	...	...	...	...	...	...

	MD 18306 2	*MD-IC* 18063 2	*Arco* 280 D	*Arco* 280 2 E	17221 2	*MD* 18314 2		18078 2 b ①-⑥	*Alvia* 4167 🍷	*Alvia* 4167 Ⓑ g	*IC* 4677 2 ⑥	33795 2 ⑤	*IC* 4177 🍷 ⑤	*Alvia* 4377 🍷 ⑦	*IC* 4677 2 ⑤	*Alvia* 4197 🍷 f ①-⑤	*IC* 18065 2 Ⓑ	*MD* 18312 2	*MD* 18007 2 Ⓑ	*Hotel* 921 🍷 G
Madrid Chamartín ... 680 681 d.	...	1222	...	...	...	...	...	...	1605	1605	...	1645	1740	1740	...	1855	1756	...	2030	...
Ávila ... 680 681 d.	...	1405	...	...	1510	...	...	...	|	|	...	1830	|	|	...	|	1940	...	2156	...
Salamanca ... d.	1345	|	...	...	|	1605	...	...	◧	◧	...	|	◧	◧	...	◧	|	2005	|	...
Medina del Campo ... 680 681 d.	1441	1452	...	...	1559	1644	...	...	|	|	...	1923	|	|	...	|	2027	2100	2242	...
Valladolid Campo Grande ... 681 d.	1505	1517	...	...	1632	1710	...	...	1725	1725	...	1953	1842	1842	...	1957	2052	2134	2307	...
Venta de Baños ... 681 d.	1529	1544	...	...	...	...	...	...	|	|	...	2021	|	|	...	|	2127	...	2332	...
Palencia ... 681 d.	1541	1557	1629	1629	...	...	...	...	|	|	...	2036	|	|	...	|	2138	...	2344	0122
Burgos Rosa de Lima ... 681 d.	...	1646	1718	1718	...	...	...	...	1835	1835	...	2131	1957	1957	...	2113	2238	...	...	0215
Miranda de Ebro ... 653 d.	...	1741	1827	1835	...	...	...	...	1933	1937	1940	2231	2050	2050	2058	2206	2334	...	...	|
Bilbao Abando ... 653 a.	...	|	|	2003	...	...	...	...	|	2102	2117	|	|	|	2232	|	|	...	...	|
Vitoria / Gasteiz ... 653 d.	...	1801	1845	...	...	...	...	1905	1954	...	...	2255	2114	2114	...	2228	2353	...	...	|
Barcelona Sants **653** ... a.	...	|	|	...	...	...	...	|	|	...	...	...	|	|	...	...	...	...	...	0844
Altsasu ... 653 d.	...	1829	1906	...	...	...	...	1936n	|	...	...	...	|	|	...	...	...	...	...	...
San Sebastián / Donostia ... ▲ 653 d.	...	1952	2025	...	...	...	...	...	2128	...	...	...	2250	2248	...	...	...	...	...	...
Irún ... ▲ 653 a.	...	2014	2046s	...	...	...	...	...	2149s	...	...	...	2309	...	...	...	...	...	...	...
Hendaye ... ▲ 653 a.	...	...	2052	...	...	...	...	...	2155	...	...	...	...	...	...	...	...	...	...	...

km		*Hotel* 922 G 🍷	*MD* 18000 2 ①-⑥	*MD* 18300 2 y ①-⑤	*Alvia* 4076 🍷 k ①-⑤	*MD* 18304 2	*IC* 18010 ①-⑥ 2	17218 2	*MD* 16000 2 ①-⑥	16013 ①-⑤ b 2	18071 Z 2 ①-⑥	*IC* 4586 2 ⑦	*Alvia* 4086 🍷	*Alvia* 4086 ①-⑥ g	*Arco* 283 2 E	*Arco* 283 D	*MD* 18308 2	*MD-IC* 18012 2	*Alvia* 622 🍷 Q	2 ①-⑤ t
0	**Irún** ... ▲ 653 d.	...	...	...	...	...	...	...	0640	...	...	...	0825	...	...	0845	...	1123	...	...
17	**San Sebastián / Donostia** ... ▲ 653 d.	...	...	...	...	...	...	...	0700	...	...	...	0842	...	...	0903	...	1141	...	...
104	Altsasu ... 653 d.	...	...	...	...	...	...	...	0819	0918n	0918n	...	|	...	...	1013	...	1302	...	...
	Barcelona Sants **653** ... d.	2020	...	...	...	...	...	...	|	|	|	...	|	...	...	|	...	|	0920	...
147	Vitoria / Gasteiz ... 653 d.	|	...	...	0640	...	0810	...	0848	0950	0950	...	1018	...	...	1035	...	1335	1403	1430
	Bilbao Abando ... 653 d.	|	...	...	|	...	|	...	...	...	|	0900	|	0900	0915	|	...	|	|	|
180	Miranda de Ebro ... 681 d.	|	...	...	0701	...	0831	...	...	...	1016	1038	1043	1043	1118	1118	...	1355	1425	1457
270	**Burgos** Rosa de Lima ... 681 d.	0249	...	...	0755	...	0928	...	...	...	1116	...	1136	1136	1212	1212	...	1446	1521	...
353	Palencia ... 681 d.	0338	0626	...	|	...	1027	...	...	...	...	...	|	|	1300	1300	1316	1537	1606	...
355	Venta de Baños ... 681 d.	...	0639	...	|	...	1038	...	...	...	...	...	|	|	...	...	1328	1550	...	...
391	**Valladolid** Campo Grande ... 681 d.	...	0704	0735	0909	0930	1102	1205	...	...	...	...	1251	1251	...	...	1353	1616	...	...
434	Medina del Campo ... 680 681 d.	...	0729	0812	|	0957	1127	1243	...	...	...	...	|	|	...	...	1422	1643	...	...
504	**Salamanca** ... a.	...	|	0905	◧	1036	|	|	...	...	...	...	◧	◧	...	...	1520	|	...	...
	Ávila ... 680 681 d.	...	0817	...	|	...	1214	1334	...	...	...	...	|	|	...	...	...	1730	...	...
	Madrid Chamartín ... 680 681 a.	...	1000	...	1012	...	1354	...	...	...	...	...	1400	1400	...	...	...	1910	...	...

	MD 34322 2 Y	**L** 18214 2	*MD-IC* 18014 2	*MD* 18318 2	33662 2 ⑦	*IC* 4176 🍷 ⑦	*Alvia* 664 A	17200 2	16015 2 b	*IC* 4666 2 ⑥	*Alvia* 4166 🍷	*Alvia* 4166 🍷 Ⓑ	*Alvia* 632 🍷	*MD* 18310 2	17226 2	*Hotel* 313 ✕ C	16017 2 N ①-⑥	16075 2 b ⑦	*MD* 16004 2	
Irún ... ▲ 653 d.	...	...	1315	...	...	1450	...	...	...	...	1620	...	...	...	...	1850	...	...	1937	...
San Sebastián / Donostia ... ▲ 653 d.	...	...	1333	...	...	1509	...	...	...	...	1639	...	...	...	...	1910	...	...	1957	...
Altsasu ... 653 d.	...	...	1454	...	...	|	...	...	1715n	...	|	...	...	...	...	|	2004n	2034n	2116	...
Barcelona Sants **653** ... d.	...	...	|	...	...	|	1210	...	|	...	|	...	1410	...	...	|	|	|	|	...
Vitoria / Gasteiz ... 653 d.	...	...	1528	...	1629	1650	1702	...	1749	...	1814	...	|	...	...	2046	2037	2110	2150	...
Bilbao Abando ... 653 d.	...	...	|	...	|	|	|	...	...	1656	|	1708	|	...	...	|	...	|	|	...
Miranda de Ebro ... 681 d.	...	...	1548	...	1653	1711	1723	...	...	1832	1840	1840	1853	...	...	2110	...	2135	2215	...
Burgos Rosa de Lima ... 681 d.	...	...	1644	...	1750	1805	1815	...	...	...	1934	1934	1945	...	...	2206	...	...	...	...
Palencia ... 681 d.	...	1656	1736	...	1849	|	1903	...	...	...	|	|	|	...	...	|	...	...	...	...
Venta de Baños ... 681 d.	...	1709	1746	...	1900	|	...	...	...	...	|	|	|	...	...	|	...	...	...	...
Valladolid Campo Grande ... 681 d.	1740	1739	1821	1905	1928	1918	...	2030	...	...	2050	2050	2056	2115	2230	2322	...	...	...	...
Medina del Campo ... 680 681 d.	1804	...	1845	1933	1958	|	...	2107	...	...	|	|	...	2150	2306	0011	...	...	...	...
Salamanca ... a.	...	...	|	2028	|	◧	...	|	...	...	◧	◧	...	2232	...	0057	...	...	...	...
Ávila ... 680 681 d.	...	...	1927	...	2050	|	...	2157	...	...	|	|	...	...	...	...	...	...	...	...
Madrid Chamartín ... 680 681 a.	...	...	2108	...	2243	2030	...	...	...	...	2200	2200	...	...	...	...	...	...	...	...

A – 🚃12 Gijón - Barcelona and v.v. (Table **685**).
B – SUD EXPRESSO / SUREX *Trenhotel* – 🛏 *Gran Clase/Gran Classe* (1, 2 berths), 🛏 *Preferente* (1, 2 berths), 🛏 *Turista* (4 berths), 🚃2 ✕ Lisboa (**310**) - Vilar Formoso (**311**) - Salamanca - Hendaye.
C – SUREX / SUD EXPRESSO *Trenhotel* – 🛏 *Gran Clase/Gran Classe* (1, 2 berths), 🛏 *Preferente* (1, 2 berths), 🛏 *Turista* (4 berths), 🚃2 ✕ Irún (**312**) - Salamanca - Vilar Formoso (**313**) - Lisboa.
D – CAMINO DE SANTIAGO – 🚃12 🍷 A Coruña / 🚃2 Vigo - Palencia - Miranda de Ebro - Irún / Hendaye and v.v.
E – CAMINO DE SANTIAGO – 🚃2 Vigo - Palencia - Miranda de Ebro - Bilbao and v.v.
G – GALICIA *Trenhotel* – 🛏, 🚃1 (reclining) Barcelona - A Coruña and Vigo and v.v.
L – To / from León (Table **681**).
N – To / from Pamplona (Table **653**).
Q – 🚃12 🍷 Vigo - Palencia - Barcelona and v.v.
Y – 🚃2 Puebla de Sanabria - Medina del Campo - Valladolid and v.v. (Table **680**).
Z – To / from Pamplona and Zaragoza (Table **653**).

b – From / to Castejón de Ebro and Pamplona / Iruña (Table **653**).

f – Not Aug. 16, Oct. 24, 31, Nov. 1, Dec. 5, 6.
g – Daily May 25 - Sept. 15.
h – Not Aug. 15, Nov.1, Dec. 6, 9.
j – ①-⑥.
k – Not Aug. 1 - 31, Oct. 25, Nov. 1, Dec. 6.
n – Altsasu Pueblo.
r – Not Aug. 15, Nov.1, Dec. 6. From Reinosa (Table **684**).
s – Calls to set down only.
t – Not July 25, Aug. 15, Oct. 25, Nov. 1, Dec. 6.
y – Not Aug. 15, Oct. 12, Nov.1, Dec. 6, 9.

◧ – Via high-speed line (Table **663**).
△ – Via Ávila.

▲ – **SAN SEBASTIÁN - IRÚN** and v.v. ***Renfe Cercanías*** (suburban) service. *17 km.* Journey time: ± 23 minutes.
From San Sebastián: Approximately 2 - 3 trains each hour from 0630 until 2300. **From Irún**: Approximately 2 - 3 trains each hour from 0522 until 2222.

▲ – **SAN SEBASTIÁN** (Amara) - **IRÚN** (Colón, near Renfe station) - **HENDAYE** (SNCF station) and v.v. ***EuskoTren*** (narrow-gauge) service. *22 km.* Journey time: ± 37 minutes.
From San Sebastián: 0555 Ⓐ, 0615 Ⓑ, 0645 Ⓐ, 0715, 0745 and every 30 mins until 2145, also 2315 ⑥ **s**. On ⑦ also 0015, 0115 **s**, 0215, 0315 **s**, 0415, 0515 **s**.
From Hendaye (A): 0647 Ⓐ, 0703 Ⓐ, 0733 Ⓐ, 0803, 0833 and every 30 mins until 2233. On ⑦ also 0003 **s**, 0103, 0203 **s**, 0303, 0403 **s**, 0503.
A – 4 minutes later from Irún. **s** – Summer only (late-June to mid-Sept).

NT 2nd class LEEDS - HALIFAX - BLACKPOOL and MANCHESTER 190

km		⚒	Ⓐ	⑥	⚒	Ⓐ	Ⓐ	Ⓐ	⚒	⚒	⚒	⚒	⚒	⚒	⚒	⚒	⚒		⚒	⚒	⚒	⚒	⚒	⚒	⚒
0	**Leeds** d.		0508	0535	0557	0608	0618	0623	0651	0708	0718	0723	0751	0805	0818	0826	0851		1805	1818	1823	1851	1905	1919	1951
15	Bradford Interchange d.		0531	0558	0618	0631	0641	|	0714	0728	0741	|	0814	0826	0841	|	0914	and	1826	1841	|	1914	1926	1942	2014
28	**Halifax** d.		0543	0610	0630	0643	0653	|	0726	0740	0753	|	0826	0838	0853	|	0926	at	1838	1853	|	1926	1938	1954	2026
	Dewsbury d.		|	|	|	|	|	0939	|	|	|	0739	|	|	|	0843	|	the	|	|	1841	|	|	|	|
42	Hebden Bridge d.		0559	0626	0646	0659	0709	0717	0743	0752	0805	0817	0842	0852	0905	0918	0942	same	1852	1905	1919	1942	1952	2010	2042
49	Todmorden d.		0607	0634	|	0707	0717	0724	0750	|	0812	0824	0850	|	0913	0925	0950	minutes	|	1913	1925	1950	|	2021	2050
63	Rochdale d.		0623	0650	|	0720	0733	0741	0805	|	0825	0841	0900	|	0923	0942	1000	past	|	1923	1941	2000	|	2037	2100
81	**Manchester** Victoria a.		0646	0713	|	0737	0754	0803	0823	|	0847	0902	0917	|	0941	1005	1017	each	|	1942	2006	2018	|	2100	2117
63	Burnley Manchester Road d.		...	...	0705	...	...	...	...	0811	...	...	...	0911	...	...	...	hour	1911	...	...	...	2011	...	...
72	Accrington d.		...	...	0714	...	...	...	...	0820	...	...	...	0920	...	...	...	until	1920	...	...	...	2020	...	...
81	Blackburn d.		...	...	0723	...	...	...	...	0829	...	...	...	0929	...	...	...		1929	...	...	...	2029	...	...
100	Preston 156 a.		...	...	0746	...	...	...	...	0852	...	...	...	0947	...	...	...	✤	1949	...	...	...	2047	...	...
129	**Blackpool North** 156 a.		...	...	0814	...	...	...	...	0921	...	...	...	1015	...	...	...		2017	...	...	...	2115	...	...

	⚒	⚒	⚒	⚒	⚒		⑦	⑦	⑦	⑦	⑦	⑦	⑦	⑦	⑦	⑦	⑦		⑦	⑦	⑦	⑦	⑦	⑦
Leeds d.	2005	2035	2105	2135	2235	...		0818	0851	0908	0951	1008	1051	1108	1151	1208	1251		1908	1951	2008	2051	2108	2135
Bradford Interchange d.	2026	2058	2126	2158	2258	...		0841	0912	0933	1014	1033	1113	1133	1214	1228	1314	and	1928	2014	2028	2114	2128	2158
Halifax d.	2038	2110	2138	2210	2310	...		0853	0925	0945	1026	1045	1125	1145	1228	1240	1326	at	1940	2026	2040	2127	2104	2210
Dewsbury d.	|	|	|	|	|	...		|	|	|	|	|	|	|	|	|	|	the	|	|	|	|	|	|
Hebden Bridge d.	2052	2126	2152	2234	2326	...		0909	0939	1001	1041	1101	1139	1201	1244	1252	1342	same	1952	2042	2052	2142	2152	2226
Todmorden d.	|	2134	|	2237	2334	...		0917	|	1009	|	1109	|	1209	1251	|	1350	minutes	|	2050	|	2151	|	2234
Rochdale d.	|	2150	|	2250	2350	...		0929	|	1021	|	1121	|	1221	1304	|	1403	past	|	2103	|	...	|	2250
Manchester Victoria a.	|	2214	|	2313	0008	...		0946	|	1038	|	1138	|	1238	1322	|	1420	each	|	2120	|	...	|	2313
Burnley Manchester Road d.	2111	...	2211	...	...	...		...	1000	...	1102	...	1200	...	...	1311	...	hour	2011	...	2111	...	2211	...
Accrington d.	2120	...	2220	...	...	...		...	1009	...	1111	...	1209	...	...	1320	...	until	2020	...	2120	...	2220	...
Blackburn d.	2129	...	2229	...	...	...		...	1018	...	1120	...	1218	...	...	1328	...		2029	...	2129	...	2229	...
Preston 156 a.	2148	...	2251	...	...	...		...	1040	...	1138	...	1236	...	...	1348	...	✤	2048	...	2147	...	2252	...
Blackpool North 156 a.	2213	...	2321	...	...	...		...	1108	...	1209	...	1307	...	...	1414	...		2114	...	2214	...	2332	...

	⚒	⚒	⚒	⑥	Ⓐ	⚒	⚒	⚒	⚒	⚒	⚒	⚒	⚒	⚒	⚒		⚒	⚒	⚒	⚒	⚒	⚒	⚒	⚒
Blackpool North 156 d.		...	0511	...	...	...	0611	...	...	...	0711	...	...	...	0811		...	...	...	1656	...	...	...	1811
Preston 156 d.		...	0537	...	...	...	0637	...	...	...	0737	...	...	...	0837	and	...	...	...	1725	...	...	...	1837
Blackburn d.		...	0555	...	...	...	0655	...	...	...	0755	...	...	...	0855	at	...	...	...	1753	...	...	...	1856
Accrington d.		...	0603	...	...	...	0703	...	...	...	0803	...	...	...	0903	the	...	...	...	1801	...	...	...	1904
Burnley Manchester Road d.		...	0612	...	...	...	0712	...	...	...	0812	...	...	...	0912	same	...	...	...	1812	...	...	...	1913
Manchester Victoria d.		0548	|	0608	0612	0636	|	0712	0726	0748	|	0816	0826	0848	|	minutes	1708	1725	1745	|	1811	1826	1848	|
Rochdale d.		0601	|	0626	0626	0652	|	0726	0746	0801	|	0830	0846	0901	|	past	1726	1746	1803	|	1827	1846	1902	|
Todmorden d.		0612	|	0643	0643	0709	|	0743	0803	0813	|	0842	0903	0913	|	each	1742	1803	1816	|	1842	1903	1913	|
Hebden Bridge d.		0619	0634	0650	0650	0716	0734	0750	0809	0820	0834	0849	0909	0920	0934	hour	1749	1809	1823	1834	1849	1909	1920	1935
Dewsbury d.		|	|	|	|	|	|	|	0843	|	|	|	0941	|	|	until	|	1841	|	|	|	1941	|	|
Halifax d.		0635	0647	0706	0706	0732	0747	0806	|	0832	0847	0906	|	0932	0946		1806	|	1835	1846	1906	|	1933	1947
Bradford Interchange d.		0652	0704	0723	0723	0749	0804	0823	|	0849	0904	0923	|	0949	1002	✤	1823	|	1852	1902	1923	|	1949	2004
Leeds a.		0713	0722	0744	0744	0810	0822	0845	0904	0910	0923	0944	1002	1010	1023		1845	1902	1914	1923	1945	2002	2011	2025

	⚒	⚒	⚒	⚒	⚒	⚒	Ⓐ	⑥	Ⓐ		⑦	⑦	⑦	⑦	⑦	⑦		⑦	⑦	⑦	⑦	⑦	⑦	⑦
Blackpool North 156 d.	...	...	1911	...	2031	...	...	...	...	...		...	0911	...	1011	...		...	1911	...	2011	...	2111	...
Preston 156 d.	...	...	1937	...	2056	...	...	...	...	...		...	0937	...	1037	...	and	...	1937	...	2037	...	2137	...
Blackburn d.	...	...	1955	...	2124	...	...	...	...	...		...	0955	...	1055	...	at	...	1955	...	2055	...	2155	...
Accrington d.	...	...	2003	...	2132	...	...	...	...	...		...	1003	...	1103	...	the	...	2003	...	2103	...	2203	...
Burnley Manchester Road d.	...	...	2012	...	2141	...	...	...	...	...		...	1012	...	1112	...	same	...	2012	...	2112	...	2212	...
Manchester Victoria d.	1916	1926	|	2026	|	2126	2226	2254	2321	...		0915	|	1015	|	1115	minutes	1915	|	2015	|	2115	|	2210
Rochdale d.	1930	1946	|	2046	|	2146	2246	2307	2341	...		0928	|	1028	|	1128	past	1928	|	2028	|	2128	|	2230
Todmorden d.	1942	2003	|	2103	|	2203	2303	2324	2358	...		0942	|	1042	|	1142	each	1942	|	2042	|	2142	|	2247
Hebden Bridge d.	1949	2009	2034	2110	2203	2210	2310	2331	0005	...		0949	1034	1049	1134	1149	hour	1949	2034	2049	2134	2148	2234	2254
Dewsbury d.	|	2041	|	|	|	|	|	|	|	...		|	|	|	|	|	until	|	|	|	|	|	|	|
Halifax d.	2006	|	2047	2127	2216	2227	2327	2347	0021	...		1006	1046	1106	1146	1206		2006	2047	2106	2147	2206	2247	2311
Bradford Interchange d.	2024	|	2104	2144	2233	2244	2344	0004	0038	...		1023	1102	1123	1202	1223	✤	2024	2104	2123	2204	2223	2304	2328
Leeds a.	2047	2102	2126	2207	2253	2306	0006	0027	0057	...		1045	1121	1145	1222	1245		2046	2123	2145	2225	2246	2323	2351

✤ – Timings may vary by ± 5 minutes.

NT 2nd class HULL - DONCASTER - SHEFFIELD 192

Subject to alteration July 28 - September 7.

km		Ⓐ	Ⓐ	Ⓐ	Ⓐ	Ⓐ	Ⓐ	Ⓐ	Ⓐ	Ⓐ	Ⓐ	Ⓐ	Ⓐ	Ⓐ	Ⓐ	Ⓐ	Ⓐ	Ⓐ	Ⓐ		⑥	⑥	⑥	⑥	⑥	⑥
0	**Hull** 181 d.		0520	0640	0803	0857	0957	1057	1157	1257	1357	1457	1557	1657	1743	1857	2003	2057	2220	...		0520	0640	0803	0857	0957
38	Goole d.		0547	0716	0830	0924	1024	1124	1224	1324	1424	1524	1624	1725	1821	1924	2036	2124	2253	...		0547	0716	0830	0924	1024
66	**Doncaster** 181 a.		0616	0746	0854	0949	1048	1148	1247	1347	1447	1548	1648	1747	1851	1948	2106	2147	2322	...		0616	0746	0857	0948	1047
66	**Doncaster** 193 d.		0628	0748	0856	0950	1049	1148	1249	1348	1449	1549	1649	1748	1901	1949	2107	2149	2324	...		0628	0748	0901	0949	1049
90	Meadowhall 193 d.		0655	0825	0916	1010	1110	1210	1310	1410	1510	1609	1709	1808	1929	2007	2134	2212	2354	...		0655	0825	0921	1008	1108
96	**Sheffield** 193 a.		0705	0833	0926	1019	1120	1219	1320	1420	1519	1620	1720	1819	1939	2018	2147	2221	0004	...		0705	0832	0931	1019	1120

	⑥	⑥	⑥	⑥	⑥	⑥	⑥	⑥	⑥	⑥	⑥	⑥		⑦	⑦	⑦	⑦	⑦	⑦	⑦		⑦	⑦	⑦	⑦	⑦
Hull 181 d.	1057	1155	1257	1357	1456	1557	1657	1742	1857	2003	2057	2217	...		0840	1050	1241	1330	1441	1531	...	1638	1732	183	2001	2140
Goole d.	1124	1223	1323	1424	1524	1624	1725	1821	1924	2036	2124	2220	...		0908	1118	1314	1403	1509	1602	...	1709	1802	1901	2034	2208
Doncaster 181 a.	1147	1247	1346	1447	1547	1648	1748	1855	1947	2106	2147	2319	...		0929	1146	1337	1426	1532	1627	...	1731	1831	1934	2059	2235
Doncaster 193 d.	1149	1249	1348	1448	1549	1649	1749	1905	1950	2107	2149	2321	...		0939	1148	1339	1429	1533	1629	...	1732	1834	1936	2101	2240
Meadowhall 193 d.	1208	1308	1408	1508	1608	1708	1808	1935	2008	2135	2212	2350	...		1000	1208	1359	1452	1552	1653	...	1753	1852	1957	2128	2304
Sheffield 193 a.	1220	1320	1420	1520	1622	1720	1821	1945	2018	2147	2212	2359	...		1008	1218	1408	1502	1601	1701	...	1801	1904	2006	2138	2315

	Ⓐ	Ⓐ	Ⓐ	Ⓐ	Ⓐ	Ⓐ	Ⓐ	Ⓐ	Ⓐ	Ⓐ	Ⓐ	Ⓐ	Ⓐ	Ⓐ	Ⓐ	Ⓐ	Ⓐ	Ⓐ		⑥	⑥	⑥	⑥	⑥	⑥	⑥
Sheffield 193 d.		0529	0741	0841	0941	1041	1141	1241	1341	1441	1541	1641	1741	1753	1841	1944	2115	2234	...		0529	0741	0841	0941	1041	1141
Meadowhall 193 d.		0535	0747	0847	0947	1047	1147	1247	1347	1447	1547	1647	1747	1759	1847	1950	2121	2240	...		0535	0747	0847	0947	1047	1147
Doncaster 193 a.		0606	0819	0915	1015	1114	1215	1315	1415	1517	1615	1717	1812	1835	1912	2012	2154	2312	...		0606	0819	0914	1014	1112	1214
Doncaster 181 d.		0610	0824	0918	1019	1119	1219	1319	1419	1519	1619	1719	1816	1839	1917	2017	2156	2315	...		0612	0824	0918	1019	1118	1219
Goole d.		0635	0843	0935	1038	1137	1235	1338	1437	1537	1638	1742	1836	1911	1937	2036	2222	2343	...		0637	0843	0938	1038	1137	1238
Hull 181 a.		0718	0913	1010	1110	1209	1308	1410	1511	1607	1709	1812	1908	1949	2008	2106	2257	...			0721	0915	1010	1110	1209	1310

	⑥	⑥	⑥	⑥	⑥	⑥	⑥	⑥	⑥	⑥	⑥		⑦	⑦	⑦	⑦	⑦	⑦	⑦	⑦	⑦	⑦	⑦	⑦	⑦	⑦
Sheffield 193 d.	1241	1341	1441	1541	1641	1741	1753	1841	1944	2115	2230	...		0845	...	1026	1228	1324	1428	1528	1628	1728	1828	2002	2124	2213
Meadowhall 193 d.	1247	1347	1447	1547	1647	1747	1759	1847	1950	2121	2236	...		0851	...	1032	1234	1330	1434	1534	1635	1734	1835	2009	2130	2219
Doncaster 193 a.	1315	1416	1516	1614	1712	1813	1837	1913	2015	2154	2309	...		0922	...	1051	1256	1402	1456	1556	1656	1755	1855	2029	2203	2238
Doncaster 181 d.	1319	1418	1519	1619	1719	1816	1839	1914	2016	2156	2310	...		0926	1019	1057	1258	1405	1500	1556	1656	1757	1856	2030	2206	2245
Goole d.	1338	1438	1537	1638	1742	1836	1911	1937	2036	2222	2338	...		0948	1040	1116	1317	1425	1519	1619	1715	1816	1922	2048	2225	2306
Hull 181 a.	1410	1509	1609	1709	1813	1909	1950	2009	2107	2259	...	...		1021	1118	1150	1354	1454	1557	1652	1748	1851	1956	2124	2258	2340

PORTUGAL

SEE MAP PAGE 321

Operator: CP – Comboios de Portugal (www.cp.pt).

Train categories: ***Alfa Pendular*** – *AP* – high-quality tilting express trains. ***Intercidades*** – *IC* – high-quality express trains linking the main cities of Portugal to Lisboa and Porto. ***Interregional*** – *IR* – 'semi-fast' links usually calling at principal stations only. ***Regional*** and ***Suburbano*** – local stopping trains (shown without train numbers).

Higher fares are payable for travel by *AP* and *IC* trains, also the international **Sud Expresso** service (Lisboa - Hendaye / Irún - Lisboa), and there is an additional supplement for travel by *AP* trains. The **Lusitania** *Hotel Train* service (Lisboa - Madrid and v.v.) is shown in Table **45**, special fares apply. International trains are classified *IN*.

Services: All services shown with a train number convey first and second class accommodation (on *Alfa Pendular* trains termed, respectively, *Conforto* and *Turística*) unless otherwise indicated. *Regional* and *Suburbano* trains convey second-class seating only.

AP, *IC*, *IR* and international trains convey a buffet car (*carruagem-bar*) and there is an at-seat service of meals to passengers in 1st class on *AP* and certain *IC* trains. Sleeping (🛏) and couchette (▬) cars are of the normal European types described on page 8.

Reservations: Reservations are **compulsory** for travel by *AP*, *IC* and *INT* trains, and also the *Sud Expresso* and *Lusitania*. Seat reservation is not normally available on other services.

Timings: Timings shown are the most recent available. Amendments to timetables may come into effect at short notice.

690 LISBOA - COIMBRA - PORTO

Reservations compulsory on *AP* and *IC* trains. For local trains Entroncamento - Coimbra / Coimbra - Aveiro see Table **699**. Local trains Aveiro - Porto run approx hourly.

km		*IC* 533	*AP* 121	*AP* 131	*IC* 521	*AP* 123	*IC* 511	*IC* 523	*AP* 182	*IC* 525	*AP* 125	*IC* 513	*AP* 133	*IC* 527	*AP* 135	*AP* 127	*IC* 621	*AP* 184	*IC* 515	*AP* 137	*IC* 721	*AP* 129	*IN* 310/35	*IC* 531
			Ⓐ		①–⑥	①–⑥					⚒				Ⓑ								S	
				△	n	n	◇					◇	△		h△		☆		◇	△	△		🅁	
	Faro **697** d.	...	...	...	...	...	...	...	0700	...	...	...	...	...	...	...	...	1505	...	...	...	...	...	...
0	**Lisboa** S Apolónia ▷ d.	...	0600	0700	0730	0800	0830	0930	|	1130	1200	1330	1400	1530	1600	1700	1730	|	1830	1900	1930	2000	2118	2130
7	**Lisboa** Oriente ▷ d.	...	0609	0709	0739	0809	0839	0939	1009	1139	1209	1339	1409	1539	1609	1709	1739	1809	1839	1909	1939	2009	2127	2139
31	Vila Franca de Xira ▷ d.	...	|	|	0752	|	0852	0952	|	1152	|	1352	|	1552	|	|	1752	|	1852	|	1952	|	|	2152
75	Santarém ▷ d.	...	|	|	0812	0838	0915	1012	|	1212	|	1415	|	1612	|	|	1812	|	1915	|	2012	2038	|	2212
107	**Entroncamento** ▷ d.	...	|	|	0830	0854	0932	1030	|	1230	|	1432	|	1630	|	|	1830	|	1932	|	2030	2054	2224	2230
131	Fátima ⊙ d.	...	|	|	|	|	0948	|	|	|	|	1448	|	|	|	|	|	|	1948	|	|	|	|	|
140	Caxarias ⊖ d.	...	|	|	|	|	0955	1050	|	|	|	1455	|	|	|	|	1850	|	1955	|	|	|	2245	2250
171	Pombal d.	...	|	|	0905	0925	1011	1107	|	1304	|	1511	|	1704	|	|	1907	|	2011	|	2105	2125	2309	2307
199	Alfarelos d.	...	|	|	|	|	1025	|	|	1318	|	1525	|	1718	|	|	|	|	2025	|	|	|	|	|
218	**Coimbra** B ▶ d.	0520	0745	0845	0930	0950	1039	1132	1145	1332	1345	1539	1545	1732	1745	1845	1932	1945	2039	2045	2130	2150	2337	2332
232	Pampilhosa d.	0532	|	|	|	|	1050	|	|	1342	|	1550	|	1742	|	|	|	|	2050	|	|	|	...	|
273	Aveiro d.	0553	0812	0912	1001	1016	...	1200	1212	1401	1412	...	1612	1801	1812	1912	2000	2012	...	2112	2201	2216	...	0000
318	Espinho d.	0618	|	|	1024	1036	...	1224	|	1424	|	...	|	1824	|	|	2024	|	...	|	2224	2236	...	0024
334	Vila Nova de Gaia d.	0629	0838	0939	1034	1045	...	1233	1238	1433	1438	...	1639	1833	1839	1938	2034	2038	...	2139	2235	2245	...	0033
337	**Porto** Campanhã ▽ a.	0635	0844	0946	1039	1052	...	1239	1244	1439	1444	...	1646	1839	1846	1944	2041	2044	...	2146	2246	2252	...	0039

		IN 313/32	*AP* 180	*AP* 130	*IC* 520	*AP* 120	*IC* 510	*IC* 620	*AP* 122	*IC* 720	*AP* 124	*IC* 524	*AP* 132	*IC* 512	*IC* 526	*AP* 186	*AP* 126	*IC* 528	*AP* 128	*AP* 134	*IC* 514	*IC* 530	*AP* 136	*IC* 532
		S			①–⑥	①–⑥			⚒		Ⓑ								Ⓑ				Ⓑ	
		🅁		△	n	n	◇	☆		△	b		△	◇						△	◇		h△	
Porto Campanhã ▽ d.	...	...	0547	0647	0652	0745	...	0852	0947	1052	1147	1252	1347	...	1452	1547	1647	1652	1745	1847	...	1952	2047	2200
Vila Nova de Gaia d.	...	...	0552	0652	0657	0750	...	0857	0952	1057	1152	1257	1352	...	1457	1552	1652	1657	1750	1852	...	1957	2052	2205
Espinho d.	...	...	|	|	0707	0800	...	0908	|	1107	|	1307	|	...	1507	|	|	1707	1800	|	...	2007	|	2216
Aveiro d.	...	...	0621	0721	0731	0821	...	0932	1021	1129	1221	1331	1421	...	1529	1621	1721	1731	1821	1921	...	2031	2121	2245
Pampilhosa d.	...	...	|	|	|	|	0905	|	|	1146	|	|	|	1505	1546	|	|	|	|	|	2005	|	|	2308
Coimbra B ▶ d.	...	0504	0647	0747	0801	0847	0919	1000	1047	1158	1247	1358	1447	1519	1558	1647	1747	1758	1847	1947	2019	2058	2147	2321
Alfarelos d.	...	|	|	|	|	|	0934	|	|	1211	|	|	|	1534	1611	|	|	|	|	|	2034	|	|	...
Pombal d.	...	0531	|	|	0826	0910	0949	1024	|	1226	|	1423	|	1549	1626	|	|	1823	1910	|	2049	2123	|	...
Caxarias ⊖ d.	...	0548	|	|	|	|	1005	1040	|	|	|	1439	|	1605	|	|	|	1839	|	|	2105	2139	|	...
Fátima ⊙ d.	...	|	|	|	|	|	1012	|	|	|	|	|	|	1612	|	|	|	|	|	|	2112	|	|	...
Entroncamento ▷ d.	...	0607	|	|	0858	0939	1027	1059	|	1258	|	1458	|	1627	1658	|	|	1858	1939	|	2127	2158	|	...
Santarém ▷ d.	...	|	|	|	0918	0957	1048	1119	|	1318	|	1518	|	1648	1718	|	|	1918	1957	|	2148	2218	|	...
Vila Franca de Xira ▷ d.	...	|	|	|	0940	|	1110	1140	|	1340	|	1540	|	1710	1740	|	|	1940	|	|	2210	2240	|	...
Lisboa Oriente ▷ a.	...	0720	0824	0922	0952	1031	1122	1152	1222	1352	1422	1552	1622	1722	1752	1824	1922	1952	2031	2122	2222	2252	2322	...
Lisboa S Apolónia ▷ a.	...	0730	|	0930	1000	1040	1130	1200	1230	1400	1430	1600	1630	1730	1800	|	1930	2000	2040	2130	2230	2300	2330	...
Faro **697** a.	...	...	1124	...	...	...	...	...	...	...	...	...	...	...	...	2124	...	...	...	...	...	...	...	...

S – SUD EXPRESSO / LUSITANIA – see Table **692**. International journeys only.

b – Not public holidays.
h – Not Aug. 15, Dec. 7.
n – Not Aug. 16, Dec. 8.

⊙ – *20 km* from Fátima (full name of station is Chão de Maçãs - Fatima).

◇ – Lisboa - Guarda and v.v. (Table **692**).
☆ – Lisboa - Porto - Guimarães and v.v. (Table **695a**).
△ – Lisboa - Porto - Braga and v.v. (Table **695**).
▷ – For other fast trains see Table **691**, for local trains see Table **699**.
▽ – Local services run Porto Campanhã - Porto São Bento.
▶ – Local trains run Coimbra B - Coimbra and v.v.
⊖ – 🚌 available Caxarias - Fátima. See www.rodotejo.pt for details.

691 LISBOA - ENTRONCAMENTO - COVILHÃ

km					*IC* 541		*IC* 543			*IC* 545	
		Ⓐ		⚒							
0	**Lisboa** Sta Apolónia ▷ d.	0548	...	0648	0816	*0948*	1316	1616	*1748*	1916	1948
7	**Lisboa** Oriente ▷ d.	0556	...	0656	0824	*0956*	1324	1624	*1756*	1924	1956
31	Vila Franca de Xira ▷ d.	0613	...	0713	0840	*1013*	1340	1640	*1815*	1940	2013
75	Santarém ▷ d.	0656	...	0756	0907	*1056*	1407	1707	*1857*	2007	2056
107	**Entroncamento** ▷ a.	0719	...	0819	0926	*1119*	1426	1727	*1920*	2026	2119
107	**Entroncamento** d.	▬	0748	...	0927	1153	1427	1728	1945	2026	*2145*
135	Abrantes d.	...	0823	...	0952	1228	1452	1800	2022	2052	*2218*
199	Ródão d.	...	0929	...	1042	1326	1549	1911	2126	2142	...
229	Castelo Branco a.	⚒	0957	...	1105	1353	1612	1952	2154	2205	...
229	Castelo Branco d.	0629	1000	...	1106	1423	1613	1955	...	2206	...
283	Fundaõ d.	0717	1048	...	1142	1517	1648	2043	...	2242	...
301	**Covilhã** a.	0733	1104	...	1156	1533	1702	2059	...	2256	...

		IC 540					*IC* 542		*IC* 544	
	①–⑥			Ⓐ						
Covilhã d.	*0454*a	0735	0850	...	...	*1300*	1435	...	1835	1845
Fundaõ d.	*0510*a	0750	0906	...	...	*1316*	1450	...	1850	1901
Castelo Branco a.	*0557*a	0824	0953	...	...	*1404*	1524	...	1924	1948
Castelo Branco d.	0600	0825	1008	...	...	*1410*	1525	*1819*	1925	...
Ródão d.	0628	0849	1042	...	...	*1438*	1549	*1847*	1949	...
Abrantes d.	0725	0939	1140	...	...	*1541*	1640	*1947*	2039	...
Entroncamento a.	0800	1007	1208	...	...	*1611*	1702	*2015*	2107	...
Entroncamento ▷ d.	0808	1008	...	1238	1342	1638	1703	2042	2108	...
Santarém ▷ d.	0829	1029	...	1304	1408	1704	1725	2108	2129	...
Vila Franca de Xira ▷ d.	0857	1056	...	1345	1445	1745	1752	2145	2156	...
Lisboa Oriente ▷ a.	0920	1111	...	1401	1501	1801	1811	2201	2211	...
Lisboa Sta Apolónia ▷ a.	0927	1119	...	1411	1511	1811	1820	2211	2219	...

a – ① (not public holidays).

▷ – For other fast trains see Table **690**, for local trains see Table **699**.

692 (LISBOA -) COIMBRA - GUARDA - VILAR FORMOSO

km		*IC* 511			*IC* 513				*IC* 515	*IN* 311	
							Ⓑ			S 🅁	
	Lisboa Sta Apolónia **690** d.	0830	...	...	1330	...	...	...	1830	2118	...
	Lisboa Oriente **690** d.	0839	...	...	1339	...	...	...	1839	2127	...
0	**Coimbra** ▶ d.	*1015*	...	1202	*1454*	...	1624	1807	*2015*b	|	...
2	**Coimbra** B d.	1039	...	1207	1539	...	1630	1815	2039	2337	...
16	Pampilhosa d.	1050	...	1219	1550	...	1648	1832	2050	|	...
51	Santa Comba Dão d.	1118	...	1250	1618	...	1722	1909	2118	0015	...
83	Nelas d.	1139	...	1315	1639	...	1749	1945	2139	|	...
95	Mangualde d.	1147	...	1324	1647	...	1758	1954	2147	0043	...
171	**Guarda** a.	1242	1302	1428	1744	1755	1902	2102	2244	0138	...
218	Vilar Formoso 🏛 a.	...	1345	...	...	1838	...	...	...	0205	...

	IN 312		*IC* 510		*IC* 512				*IC* 514	
	S 🅁	⚒				①–⑥	⑦d	①–⑥		
Vilar Formoso 🏛 d.	0225	...	*0622*z	*0944*y	...	...	*1534*	1707	...	...
Guarda d.	0254	0506	0710	1038	1310	1441	1624	1750	1810	...
Mangualde d.	0347	0603	0806	1147	1406	1537	1729	...	1906	...
Nelas d.	|	0614	0814	1157	1414	1548	1750	...	1914	...
Santa Comba Dão d.	0418	0641	0837	1227	1437	1618	1817	...	1937	...
Pampilhosa d.	|	0718	0905	1305	1505	1649	1850	...	2005	...
Coimbra B a.	0504	0731	0919	1319	1519	1702	1904	...	2019	...
Coimbra ▶ a.	|	0736	*0946*a	1330	*1551*a	1706	*1915*	...	*2041*a	...
Lisboa Oriente **690** a.	0720	...	1122	...	1722	...	2142	...	2222	...
Lisboa Sta Apolónia **690** a.	0730	...	1130	...	1730	...	2150	...	2230	...

S – SUD EXPRESSO / LUSITANIA – see Tables **46** / **690**.
a – Ⓐ only.
b – Ⓑ.

d – Also Dec. 8. Not Dec. 7.
y – †.
z – ①–⑥.

▶ – Local trains run Coimbra B - Coimbra and v.v.

LISBOA - CALDAS DA RAINHA - FIGUEIRA DA FOZ / COIMBRA 693

Linha do Oeste

km										
				Ⓐ						
	Lisboa Santa Apolónia	...	0551	...	...	1151	1351	1651	...	...
0	**Lisboa** Oriente ▷ d.	...	|	0641	0826	|	|	|	1726	1826
7	Entrecampos ▷ d.	...	0602	0650	0835	1202	1402	1702	1735	1835
9	Sete Rios ▷ d.	...	0605	0653	0838	1205	1405	1705	1738	1838
22	Agualva - Cacém ⊙ ▷ d.	...	0622	0715	0900	1222	1422	1722	1800	1900
26	Mira Sintra - Meleças ▷ d.	...	0627	0725	0925	1227	1427	1727	1835	1930
72	Torres Vedras d.	0627	0724	0830	1023	1326	1525	1825	1935	2028
95	Bombarral d.	0654	0747	0855	1047	1354	1547	1848	2000	...
114	**Caldas da Rainha** a.	0716	0810	0917	1109	1416	1609	1910	2022	...
	Leiria (below) a.	...	0930	...	...	1530	...	2030	...	...

	Ⓐ			Ⓐ					
Leiria (below) d.	...	...	...	...	...	1213	...	...	1813
Caldas da Rainha d.	...	0616	0723	0817	1116	1316	1616	1738	1918
Bombarral d.	...	0637	0746	0839	1137	1337	1637	1800	1940
Torres Vedras d.	0612	0700	0809	0902	1159	1400	1659	1824	2004
Mira Sintra - Meleças ▷ d.	0713	0802	0909	...	1301	1501	1800	1924	2106
Agualva - Cacém ⊙ ▷ a.	0727	0807	0927	...	1305	1505	1827	1957	2109
Sete Rios ▷ a.	0749	0826	0949	...	1323	1523	1849	2019	2123
Entrecampos ▷ a.	0752	0829*	0952	...	1327	1527	1855	2022	2127
Lisboa Oriente ▷ a.	0802	...	1002	...	|	|	1902	2032	|
Lisboa Santa Apolónia a.	...	...	...	...	1341	1541	...	...	2141

km		*IR* 801			*IR* 803			*IR* 805		
		①–⑥								
	Lisboa S Apolónia (above) d.	...	...	0551	...	...	1151	...	...	1651
0	**Caldas da Rainha** d.	0610	...	0831	1110	...	1431	1610	...	1931
13	São Martinho do Porto d.	0618	...	0843	1118	...	1443	1618	...	1943
47	Marinha Grande d.	0649	...	0921	1149	...	1521	1649	...	2021
57	Leiria d.	0658	...	0930	1158	...	1530	1658	...	2030
	Verride d.	0748	0756	...	1248	1249	...	1748	1749	...
104	Bifurcação de Lares ▽ a.	|	0803	...	|	1256	...	|	1756	...
111	**Figueira da Foz** a.	|	0815	...	|	1309	...	|	1809	...
118	Alfarelos ▽ d.	0756	...	...	1256	...	...	1756	...	...
138	**Coimbra** B ▽ a.	0810	...	...	1310	...	...	1810	...	...

			IR 802			*IR* 804			*IR* 806
									Ⓑ
Coimbra B ▽ d.	...	...	0851	...	...	1351	...	...	1851
Alfarelos ▽ d.	...	...	0905	...	...	1405	...	...	1905
Figueira da Foz d.	...	0858	|	...	1358	|	...	1858	|
Bifurcação de Lares ▽ d.	...	0911	|	...	1411	|	...	1911	|
Verride d.	...	0918	0921	...	1418	1421	...	1918	1921
Leiria d.	0713	...	1010	1213	...	1510	1813	...	2010
Marinha Grande d.	0723	...	1020	1223	...	1520	1823	...	2020
São Martinho do Porto d.	0756	...	1048	1256	...	1548	1856	...	2048
Caldas da Rainha a.	0808	...	1058	1308	...	1558	1908	...	2058
Lisboa S A'nia (above) a.	...	...	...	1541	...	...	2141	...	...

▷ – For suburban services see Table **699**.
▽ – See Table **693a**.
⊙ – Connections to / from Lisboa Rossio every 15 - 30 minutes (see Table **699**).
* – Terminal platforms (Entrecampos - Poente).

FIGUEIRA DA FOZ - COIMBRA 693a

km																								
		⚒	⚒	Ⓐ																				
0	**Figueira da Foz** d.	0558	0658	0740	...	0858	...	0958	1058	...	1158	1258	...	1358	1458	1558	...	1658	1758	...	1858	1958	...	2158
8	Bifurcação de Lares d.	0611	0711	0750	...	0911	...	1011	1111	...	1211	1311	...	1411	1511	1611	...	1711	1811	...	1911	2011	...	2211
	Verride d.	0620	0720	0757	...	0920	...	1020	1120	...	1220	1320	...	1420	1520	1620	...	1720	1820	...	1920	2020	...	2220
22	Alfarelos d.	0638	0738	0806	0812	0938	1031	1038	1138	1211	1238	1338	1411	1438	1538	1638	1704	1738	1838	1903	1938	2038	2119	2238
42	**Coimbra** B a.	0705	0805	0824	0832	1005	1052	1105	1205	1231	1305	1405	1431	1505	1605	1705	1725	1805	1905	1925	2005	2105	2141	2305
44	**Coimbra** a.	0715	0815	0837	0841	1015	1103	1115	1215	1240	1315	1415	1440	1515	1615	1715	1734	1815	1915	1938	2015	2115	2157	2315

			⚒	⚒											Ⓐ			Ⓑ		Ⓐ			Ⓑ	
Coimbra d.	...	0018	0524	0554	0654	0815	0854	0954	1015	1154	1254	1315	1354	1454	1554	1615	1654	1754	1815	1901	1915	1954	2015	2224
Coimbra B d.	...	0028	0533	0603	0703	0824	0903	1003	1024	1203	1303	1324	1403	1503	1603	1624	1703	1803	1824	1909	1924	2003	2024	2233
Alfarelos d.	...	0055	0606	0636	0736	0844	0937	1036	1044	1236	1336	1345	1436	1536	1636	1644	1736	1836	1844	1932	1944	2036	2045	2306
Verride d.	...	0106	0619	0649	0756	...	0949	1049	...	1249	1349	...	1449	1549	1649	...	1749	1849	...	1940	...	2049	...	2319
Bifurcação de Lares d.	...	0114	0626	0656	0803	...	0956	1056	...	1256	1356	...	1456	1556	1656	...	1756	1856	...	|	...	2056	...	2326
Figueira da Foz a.	...	0126	0639	0709	0815	...	1009	1109	...	1309	1409	...	1509	1609	1709	...	1809	1909	...	1955	...	2109	...	2339

PORTO - RÉGUA - POCINHO 694

km				*IR* 861	*IR* 863	*IR* 865	*IR* 867	*IR* 869	*IR* 871	*IR* 875	
			⚒								
0	**Porto** São Bento d.	0625	...	...	0910	...	...	1510	...	1925	...
3	**Porto** Campanhã d.	0630	...	0715	0915	1115	1315	1515	1715	1930	2155
12	Ermesinde d.	0642	...	0727	0927	1127	1327	1527	1727	1941	2205
50	Caíde d.	0728	0730	0807	1007	1207	1407	1607	1807	2014	2237
59	Livração d.	...	0745	0816	1016	1216	1416	1616	1816	2022	2251
64	Marco de Canaveses d.	...	0750	0822	1022	1222	1422	1622	1822	2028	2257
107	**Régua** a.	...	0845	0907	1108	1308	1507	1708	1907	2113	2352
	Pocinho (below) a.	...	...	1031	1239	...	1631	1847	2030	...	...

			IR 860	*IR* 864	*IR* 868	*IR* 870	*IR* 872	*IR* 878	*IR* 878	
	⚒				Ⓐ		⚒			
Pocinho (below) d.	...	...	...	0710	...	1118	1325	...	1725	1907
Régua d.	0512	0614	0650	0850	1050	1250	1450	1650	1850	2048
Marco de Canaveses d.	0609	0708	0736	0936	1136	1336	1536	1736	1936	2150
Livração d.	0615	0713	0743	0943	1143	1343	1543	1743	1943	2156
Caíde d.	0633	0731	0754	0954	1154	1354	1554	1754	1954	2212
Ermesinde d.	0714	0809	0825	1025	1225	1425	1625	1825	2025	2304
Porto Campanhã a.	0725	0821	0845	1035	1235	1435	1635	1835	2035	2315
Porto São Bento a.	0730	...	0850	...	...	1450	...	1850	...	2320

km		*IR* 861		*IR* 863		*IR* 867		*IR* 873	*IR* 871		
					△					△	
	Porto Campanhã d.	0715	...	0915	...	1315	...	1515	1715	...	...
0	**Régua** d.	0908	...	1115	...	1508	...	1723	1908	...	...
23	Pinhão d.	0936	...	1142	...	1536	...	1749	1934	...	...
36	Tua a.	0951	...	1159	1205	1551	...	1807	1950	1955	...
	Mirandela a.	|	...	|	1335	|	...	|	|	2115	...
68	**Pocinho** a.	1031	...	1239	...	1631	...	1847	2030	...	...

	IR 862		*IR* 870		*IR* 872	*IR* 876	*IR* 960			
		△			⚒	†		△		
Pocinho d.	0710	...	1118	...	1325	1508	1725	...	1907	...
Mirandela d.	|	0955	|	...	|	|	|	1800	|	...
Tua d.	0750	1142	1201	...	1406	1553	1806	1943	1949	...
Pinhaõ d.	0804	...	1215	...	1420	1607	1820	...	2003	...
Régua a.	0830	...	1241	...	1446	1633	1846	...	2029	...
Porto Campanhã a.	1035	...	1435	...	1635	1835	2035	...	2315g	...

g – Change at Regua and Caíde.
△ – By Taxi Tua - Cachão and v.v.

steam-hauled tourist train Regua - Tua and v.v.: ⑥ July 5 - Oct. 25, 2014 (also Aug. 15).
Régua d. 1522 → Tua a. 1634 / d. 1723 → Régua a. 1834. Trains also call at Pinhão (no timings given).

PORTO - BRAGA 695

km						*AP* 131								*AP* 133				*AP* 135					*AP* 137		*IC* 721	
																	Ⓐ	Ⓑh						Ⓐ		
	Lisboa Sta Ap. **690** d.	...	...	...	...	0700	...	...	...	...	...	...	...	1400	...	...	...	1600	...	...	...	...	1900	...	2000	...
0	**Porto** São Bento △ d.	0115	0645	0745	0845	|	0945	1045	1145	1245	1345	1445	1545	|	1645	1745	1815	|	1845	1915	1945	2045	|	2145	|	2245
3	**Porto** Campanhã △ d.	0120	0650	0750	0850	0946	0950	1050	1150	1250	1350	1450	1550	1646	1650	1750	1820	1846	1850	1920	1950	2050	2146	2150	2246	2250
12	Ermesinde △ d.	0132	0702	0802	0902	|	1002	1102	1202	1302	1402	1502	1602	|	1702	1802	1832	|	1902	1932	2002	2102	|	2202	|	2302
26	Trofa △ d.	0146	0716	0816	0916	|	1016	1116	1216	1316	1416	1516	1616	|	1716	1816	1844	|	1916	1944	2016	2116	|	2216	|	2316
35	Famalicão △ d.	0157	0727	0827	0927	1009	1027	1127	1227	1327	1427	1527	1627	1709	1727	1827	1852	1909	1927	1952	2027	2127	2209	2227	2309	2327
42	Nine △ d.	0205	0735	0835	0935	1015	1035	1135	1235	1335	1435	1535	1635	1715	1735	1835	1857	1915	1935	1957	2035	2135	2215	2235	2315	2335
57	**Braga** △ a.	0226	0756	0856	0956	1025	1056	1156	1256	1356	1456	1556	1656	1725	1756	1856	1909	1925	1956	2009	2056	2156	2225	2256	2325	2356

		AP 130								*IC* 720				*AP* 132							*AP* 134				*AP* 136	
	⚒			Ⓐ	Ⓒ	Ⓐ	Ⓐ												Ⓐ			Ⓐ			Ⓑh	
Braga ▽ d.	0534	0607	0634	0721	0734	0745	0804	0834	0934	1005	1034	1134	1234	1307	1334	1434	1534	1634	1721	1734	1807	1821	1834	1934	2007	2034
Nine ▽ d.	0554	0618	0654	0733	0754	0755	0824	0854	0954	1016	1054	1154	1254	1318	1354	1454	1554	1654	1733	1754	1818	1833	1854	1954	2018	2054
Famalicão ▽ d.	0602	0623	0702	0738	0802	0800	0832	0902	1002	1021	1102	1202	1302	1323	1402	1502	1602	1702	1738	1802	1823	1838	1902	2002	2023	2102
Trofa ▽ d.	0613	|	0713	0746	0813	0807	0843	0913	1013	|	1113	1213	1313	|	1413	1513	1613	1713	1746	1813	|	1846	1913	2013	|	2113
Ermesinde ▽ d.	0629	|	0729	0759	0829	0819	0859	0929	1029	|	1129	1229	1329	|	1429	1529	1629	1729	1759	1829	|	1859	1929	2029	|	2129
Porto Campanhã ▽ a.	0641	0647	0741	0811	0841	0831	0911	0941	1041	1052	1141	1241	1341	1347	1441	1541	1641	1741	1811	1841	1847	1911	1941	2041	2047	2141
Porto São Bento ▽ a.	0645	|	0745	0815	0845	0835	0915	0945	1045	|	1145	1245	1345	|	1445	1545	1645	1745	1815	1845	|	1915	1945	2045	|	2145
Lisboa Sta Ap. **690** a.	...	0930	...	...	...	...	...	...	...	1400	...	...	...	1630	...	...	...	...	...	...	2130	...	...	...	2330	...

d – Journey 55 minutes.
h – Not Apr. 18, 25, Aug. 15, Dec. 7.

△ – Additional journeys: 0615Ⓐ**d**, 0715Ⓐ, 0815Ⓐ**d**, 1215Ⓐ**d**, 1615Ⓐ**d**, 1715Ⓐ**d**. For other trains Porto - Nine see Table **696**.
▽ – Additional journeys: 0434, 0621Ⓐ**d**, 0821⑥**d**, 1321Ⓐ**d**, 2134Ⓒ, 2234Ⓐ, 2332. For other trains Nine - Porto see Table **696**.

695a PORTO - GUIMARÃES *60 km*

												IC 621
				Ⓐ				Ⓐ		Ⓐ		
Lisboa Sta Ap. **690** d.	...	...	...	...	...	...	...	...	...	...	...	1730
Porto São Bento ▷ d.	0720	0820	1020	1120	1220	1420	1620	1720	1820	1920	2020	|
Porto Campanhã ▷ d.	0725	0825	1025	1125	1225	1425	1625	1725	1825	1925	2025	2041
Ermesinde ▷ d.	0737	0837	1037	1137	1237	1437	1637	1737	1837	1937	2037	|
Trofa ▷ d.	0752	0852	1052	1152	1252	1452	1652	1752	1852	1952	2052	2100
Guimarães a.	0836	0936	1133	1236	1336	1533	1736	1836	1937	2037	2133	2138

		IC 620										
			Ⓐ						Ⓐ	Ⓐ	Ⓐ	
Guimarães d.	0648	0743	0748	0848	0948	1148	1348	1548	1712	1812	2012	2148
Trofa ▷ d.	0733	0824	0833	0933	1033	1233	1433	1633	1801	1901	2103	2233
Ermesinde ▷ d.	0749	|	0849	0949	1049	1249	1449	1649	1819	1919	2119	2249
Porto Campanhã ▷ a.	0801	0852	0901	1001	1101	1301	1501	1701	1831	1931	2131	2301
Porto São Bento ▷ a.	0805	|	0905	1005	1105	1305	1505	1705	1835	1935	2135	2305
Lisboa Sta Ap. **690** a.	...	1200	...	...	...	...	...	...	...	...	...	...

▷ – See also Tables **695** and **696**.

Additional trains: **Porto - Guimarães** 0620Ⓐ, 2120Ⓒ, 2220Ⓐ, 2320; **Guimarães - Porto** 0548Ⓐ, 1248Ⓐ, 1748Ⓒ, 1916Ⓐ, 1948 Ⓒ, 2248.

696 PORTO - VIANA DO CASTELO - VALENÇA - VIGO

km		IR 851			IN 421							IR 853				IR 855				IR 857		IN 423	IR 859	
		Ⓐ	Ⓐ			Ⓐ	Ⓒ	Ⓒ		Ⓐ				Ⓐ									Ⓐ	
0	**Porto** Campanhã ▷ d.	0610	0620	0650	0815	...	...	...	...	0820	0950	1310	1250	...	1350	1610	...	1650	...	1810	1850	1915	2010	2210
12	Ermesinde ▷ d.	0619	0632	0702	|	...	...	...	...	0832	1002	1321	1302	...	1402	1621	...	1702	...	1821	1902	|	2021	2221
23	Trofa ▷ d.	0630	0644	0716	|	...	...	...	...	0844	1016	1332	1316	...	1416	1632	...	1716	...	1832	1916	|	2032	2232
32	Famalicão ▷ d.	0638	0652	0727	|	...	...	...	...	0852	1027	1340	1327	...	1427	1640	...	1727	...	1840	1927	|	2040	2241
39	**Nine** ▷ a.	0644	0656	0735	|	...	...	...	...	0857	1035	1346	1335	...	1435	1646	...	1735	...	1846	1935	|	2047	2247
39	**Nine** d.	0644	0706	0747	|	...	...	...	...	0905	1055	1347	...	1400	1500	1647	...	1737	...	1848	1958	|	2048	2248
51	Barcelos d.	0654	0720	0804	|	...	...	...	...	0918	1108	1357	...	1413	1513	1659	...	1750	...	1858	2011	|	2104	2302
82	**Viana do Castelo** d.	0735	0824	0850	|	...	0943	...	...	1006	1151	1430	...	1456	1612	1734	...	1832	...	1931	2101	|	2138	2343
116	Vila Nova de Cerveira d.	0804	0912	...	|	...	1028	...	...	1053	...	1458	...	...	1655	1801	...	1914	...	1959	...	|	2205	...
130	**Valença** a.	0815	0927	...	|	...	1043	...	...	1108	...	1509	...	...	1710	1812	...	1929	...	2010	...	|	2216	...
130	**Valença** 🏛 PT d.	...	...	...	|	1000	...	1045	...	...	...	...	...	...	...	...	...	...	1944	...	...	|	...	...
134	Tui 🏛 ES d.	...	...	...	|	1107	...	1152	...	...	...	...	...	...	...	...	...	...	2051	...	...	|	...	...
162	Redondela **681** d.	...	...	...	|	1139	...	1224	...	...	...	...	...	...	...	...	...	...	2124	...	...	|	...	...
174	**Vigo** Guixar ◐ **681** a.	...	...	...	1130	1150	...	1235	...	...	...	...	...	...	...	...	...	...	2135	...	...	2230	...	...

						IR 850	IN 420			IR 852						IR 854				IR 856	IN 422			
			Ⓐ	Ⓐ	Ⓐ							Ⓐ		Ⓒ				Ⓒ						
Vigo Guixar ◐ **681** d.	...	...	...	...	...	...	0902	...	0955	...	...	...	...	...	...	...	...	...	...	...	1954	1812	...	...
Redondela **681** d.	...	...	...	...	...	...	|	...	1007	...	...	...	...	...	...	...	...	...	...	...	|	1824	...	...
Tui 🏛 ES d.	...	...	...	...	...	...	|	...	1039	...	...	...	...	...	...	...	...	...	...	...	|	1858	...	...
Valença 🏛 PT a.	...	...	...	...	...	...	|	...	0947	...	...	...	...	...	...	...	...	...	...	...	|	1806	...	...
Valença d.	...	...	...	0535	0615	0736	|	...	...	1018	1117	...	...	...	...	1425	1514	...	...	1749	|	...	1827	...
Vila Nova de Cerveira d.	...	...	...	0548	0630	0747	|	...	...	1029	1132	...	...	...	...	1435	1529	...	...	1800	|	...	1842	...
Viana do Castelo d.	...	0511	...	0627	0716	0816	|	0944	...	1057	1216	...	...	1350	...	1508	1617	...	1747	1834	|	...	1927	2022
Barcelos d.	...	0554	...	0719	0803	0853	|	1029	...	1129	1259	...	...	1437	...	1539	1700	...	1833	1917	|	...	...	2105
Nine a.	...	0608	...	0735	0817	0903	|	1044	...	1139	1313	...	...	1452	...	1548	1714	...	1847	1927	|	...	...	2119
Nine ▷ d.	...	...	0633	0732	0824	0904	|	1054	...	1139	...	1333	...	...	1454	1549	...	1733	1854	1928	|	...	...	2120
Famalicão ▷ d.	...	...	0638	0743	0832	0913	|	1102	...	1147	...	1338	...	...	1502	1557	...	1738	1902	1936	|	...	...	2129
Trofa ▷ d.	...	...	0646	0751	0843	0921	|	1113	...	1154	...	1346	...	...	1513	1605	...	1746	1913	1944	|	...	...	2137
Ermesinde ▷ d.	...	...	0659	0807	0859	0935	|	1129	...	1206	...	1359	...	...	1529	1619	...	1759	1929	1956	|	...	...	2151
Porto Campanhã ▷ a.	...	...	0710	0819	0910	0945	1017	1140	...	1215	...	1410	...	...	1540	1630	...	1810	1940	2005	2109	...	...	2200

◐ – New terminus (1 km from old station).

▷ – See also Table **695**.

ES – Spain (Central European Time).
PT – Portugal (West European Time).

697 LISBOA - PINHAL NOVO - TUNES - FARO

km		AP 180		IC 570		IC 572		IC 574		AP 186	
	Porto Campanhã **690** d.	0547	...	...	...	...	...	...	...	1547	...
	Coimbra B **690** d.	0647	...	...	...	...	...	...	...	1647	...
0	**Lisboa** Oriente ⊙ d.	0824	...	1020	...	1420	...	1720	...	1824	...
7	Entrecampos ⊙ d.	0831	...	1029	...	1429	...	1729	...	1831	...
9	Sete Rios ⊙ d.	|	...	1034	...	1434	...	1734	...	|	...
18	Pragal ⊙ d.	|	...	1045	...	1445	...	1745	...	|	...
47	Pinhal Novo ⊙ d.	0906	...	1106	...	1506	...	1806	...	1906	...
118	Grândola d.	|	...	1133	...	1533	...	1833	...	|	...
180	Funcheira d.	|	...	1208	...	1610	...	1908	...	|	...
264	**Tunes** ▷ d.	1056	...	1313	...	1722	...	2013	...	2056	...
269	Albufeira ▷ d.	1102	...	1318	...	1728	...	2019	...	2102	...
286	Loulé ▷ d.	1115	...	1330	...	1740	...	2033	...	2115	...
302	**Faro** ▷ a.	1124	...	1340	...	1750	...	2043	...	2124	...

	AP 182		IC 670		IC 672		AP 184		IC 674	
Faro ▷ d.	0700	...	0946	...	1341	...	1505	...	1735	...
Loulé ▷ d.	0711	...	0956	...	1351	...	1516	...	1752	...
Albufeira ▷ d.	0723	...	1008	...	1403	...	1528	...	1805	...
Tunes ▷ d.	0730	...	1016	...	1409	...	1535	...	1811	...
Funcheira d.	0823	...	1127	...	1512	...	|	...	1923	...
Grândola d.	0854	...	1204	...	1554	...	|	...	1959	...
Pinhal Novo ⊙ d.	0923	...	1233	...	1624	...	1723	...	2028	...
Pragal ⊙ a.	|	...	1249	...	1644	...	|	...	2044	...
Sete Rios ⊙ a.	|	...	1259	...	1653	...	|	...	2053	...
Entrecampos ⊙ a.	0957	...	1302	...	1657	...	1757	...	2057	...
Lisboa Oriente ⊙ a.	1004	...	1310	...	1705	...	1804	...	2105	...
Coimbra B **690** a.	1145	...	...	...	...	...	1945	...	...	...
Porto Campanhã **690** a.	1244	...	...	...	...	...	2044	...	...	...

LOCAL TRAINS LAGOS - TUNES - FARO

km			⚒								
0	**Lagos** d.	0614	0659	0900	1028	1253	1400	1701	1815	1919	...
18	Portimão d.	0633	0718	0919	1052	1312	1424	1720	1839	1938	...
29	Silves d.	0650	0734	0936	1110	1329	1440	1737	1902	1959	...
42	Algoz d.	0706	0750	0952	1127	1345	1456	1753	1918	2015	...
46	**Tunes** a.	0711	0755	0957	1132	1351	1502	1758	1923	2020	...
46	**Tunes** ▷ d.	0712	0800	0958	1133	1352	1503	1811	1924	2021	...
52	Albufeira ▷ d.	0722	0807	1008	1139	1403	1509	1817	1931	2028	...
69	Loulé ▷ d.	0738	0822	1023	1153	1418	1529	1833	1946	2049	...
85	**Faro** ▷ a.	0754	0838	1038	1208	1433	1545	1848	2002	2104	...

		⚒					Ⓐ	Ⓒ		
Faro ▷ d.	0717	0914	1020	1241	1617	1718	1757	1830	1925	2011
Loulé ▷ d.	0738	0931	1041	1258	1634	1740	1814	1853	1946	2033
Albufeira ▷ d.	0754	0947	1101	1318	1650	1756	1834	1912	2002	2101
Tunes ▷ a.	0759	0953	1106	1324	1656	1802	1839	1918	2007	2106
Tunes d.	0800	0958	1107	1325	1657	1803	1840	1925	2021	2107
Algoz d.	0806	1003	1113	1331	1702	1808	1846	1930	2027	2113
Silves d.	0821	1019	1133	1351	1718	1824	1901	1945	2042	2129
Portimão d.	0834	1034	1147	1405	1737	1839	1916	2000	2057	2143
Lagos a.	0853	1052	1206	1424	1755	1857	1939	2018	2115	2202

⊙ – See Table **698** for other fast trains, Table **699** for local services, including connections Barreiro - Pinhal Novo.

▷ – Also see other section of table above or below.

697a FARO - VILA REAL DE SANTO ANTÓNIO

km												
0	**Faro** △ d.	0736	0930	1134	1212	1445	1623	1729	1829	1908	2108	2200
10	Olhão △ d.	0747	0941	1150	1224	1457	1636	1741	1841	1920	2119	2212
32	Tavira △ d.	0818	1008	1220	1250	1523	1705	1809	1913	1948	2145	2238
56	**Vila Real** § a.	0846	1038	1249	1319	1551	1733	1837	1941	2016	2213	2306

		Ⓐ								
Vila Real § d.	0549	0617	0720	0905	1122	1327	1607	1740	1845	2044
Tavira △ d.	0614	0648	0749	0934	1152	1356	1637	1810	1914	2113
Olhão △ d.	0637	0713	0815	1004	1225	1425	1702	1842	1943	2141
Faro △ a.	0648	0724	0826	1015	1236	1437	1713	1853	1954	2151

△ – Additional journeys on Ⓐ: Faro - Tavira at 0657, 1041, 1349, 1534; Tavira - Faro at 0823, 1125, 1525, 1711.

§ – Vila Real de Santo António (± *1500m* from bus station/ferry terminal)

698 LISBOA - PINHAL NOVO - ÉVORA and BEJA

km		IC 590	IC 581	IC 592	IC 583	IC 594	IC 585	IC 596	IC 587	IC 598	IC 589
		Ⓐ	Ⓐ	Ⓐ	Ⓐ	Ⓒ	Ⓒ				
0	**Lisboa** Oriente ⊙ d.	0650	...	0850	...	0950	...	1650	...	1850	...
7	Entrecampos ⊙ d.	0659	...	0859	...	0959	...	1659	...	1859	...
9	Sete Rios ⊙ d.	0704	...	0904	...	1004	...	1704	...	1904	...
18	Pragal ⊙ d.	0715	...	0915	...	1015	...	1715	...	1915	...
47	**Pinhal Novo** ⊙ d.	0738	...	0938	...	1038	...	1738	...	1938	...
88	Vendas Novas d.	0809	...	1001	...	1101	...	1801	...	2001	...
122	Casa Branca a.	0822	...	1014	...	1122	...	1814	...	2014	...
122	Casa Branca d.	0823	0828	1015	1019	1123	1128	1815	1821	2015	2019
148	Évora a.	0833	|	1025	|	1133	|	1825	|	2025	|
185	**Beja** a.	...	0919	...	1110	...	1219	...	1915	...	2110

	IC 580	IC 690	IC 582	IC 692	IC 584	IC 694		IC 586	IC 696	IC 588	IC 790
	Ⓐ	Ⓐ	Ⓐ	Ⓐ	Ⓒ	Ⓒ					
Beja d.	0618	...	0815	...	0918	...	...	1611	...	1814	...
Évora d.	|	0702	|	0902	|	1002	...	|	1655	|	1902
Casa Branca a.	0707	0712	0907	0912	1007	1012	...	1700	1705	1904	1912
Casa Branca d.	...	0713	...	0913	...	1013	...	...	1706	...	1913
Vendas Novas d.	...	0727	...	0927	...	1027	...	...	1720	...	1927
Pinhal Novo ⊙ d.	...	0751	...	0951	...	1051	...	...	1751	...	1951
Pragal ⊙ a.	...	0814	...	1014	...	1114	...	...	1814	...	2014
Sete Rios ⊙ a.	...	0823	...	1023	...	1123	...	...	1824	...	2023
Entrecampos ⊙ a.	...	0827	...	1027	...	1127	...	...	1828	...	2027
Lisboa Oriente ⊙ a.	...	0835	...	1035	...	1135	...	...	1835	...	2035

⊙ – See Table **697** for other fast trains and Table **699** for local services, including connections Barreiro - Pinhal Novo.

OTHER LOCAL SERVICES 699

LISBOA - ESTORIL - CASCAIS

26 km (Estoril *24 km*)

Lisboa Cais do Sodre . d.	Ⓐ	0530	every	0700	every	1000	every	1700	every	2100	every	2200	every	0130	...	Ⓒ	0530	every	0800	0820	every	1900	1930	every	0130
Estoril . d.		0606	30	0729	12	1029	20	1729	12	2136	20	2236	30	0206	...		0606	30	0836	0856	20	1936	2006	30	0206
Cascais . a.		0610	mins	0733	mins	1033	mins	1733	mins	2140	mins	2240	mins	0210	...		0610	mins	0840	0900	mins	1940	2010	mins	0210

Cascais . d.	Ⓐ	0530	0600	0630	0652	0704	every	2040	2100	every	0130	...	Ⓒ	0530	0600	0630	0703	every	1903	every	2103	2130	every	0130
Estoril . d.		0534	0604	0634	0656	0708	12-20 ◧	2044	2104	30	0134	...		0534	0604	0634	0707	20	1907	30	2107	2134	30	0134
Lisboa Cais do Sodre . a.		0610	0640	0710	0725	0737	mins	2113	2140	mins	0210	...		0610	0640	0710	0743	mins	1943	mins	2143	2210	mins	0210

◧ – Every 12 minutes 0704 - 1004 and 1704 - 2040; every 20 minutes 1004 - 1704.

LISBOA ROSSIO - SINTRA

27 km

Lisboa Rossio . d.	Ⓐ	0608	every	2038	every	0108	Ⓒ	0608	every	0108
Monte Abraão . d.		0628	15	2058	30	0128		0628	30	0128
Agualva - Cacém . d.		0633	mins	2103	mins	0133		0633	mins	0133
Sintra . a.		0647		2117		0147		0647		0147

Sintra . d.	Ⓐ	0610	every	2040	every	0040	Ⓒ	0540	every	0040
Agualva - Cacém . d.		0623	15	2053	30	0053		0553	30	0053
Monte Abraão . d.		0629	mins	2059	mins	0059		0559	mins	0059
Lisboa Rossio . a.		0649		2119		0119		0619		0119

LISBOA ORIENTE - MIRA SINTRA-MELEÇAS

See also Table 693

Lisboa Oriente . d.	Ⓐ	0626		2026		2156	Ⓒ	0756		2056
Roma Areeiro . d.		0633		2033		2203		0803		2103
Entrecampos . d.		0635	every	2035	every	2205		0805	every	2105
Sete Rios . d.		0638	15	2038	30	2208		0808	30	2108
Monte Abraão . d.		0654	mins	2054	mins	2224		0824	mins	2124
Agualva - Cacém . d.		0700		2100		2230		0830		2130
Mira Sintra - Meleças . a.		0704		2104		2234		0834		2134

Mira Sintra - Meleças . d.	Ⓐ	0638		2023		2253	Ⓒ	0723		2023
Agualva - Cacém . d.		0642	every	2027	every	2257		0727	every	2027
Monte Abraão . d.		0648	15	2033	30	2303		0733	30	2033
Sete Rios . d.		0704	mins	2049	mins	2319		0749	mins	2049
Entrecampos . d.		0707		2052		2322		0752		2052
Roma Areeiro . d.		0709		2054		2324		0754		2054
Lisboa Oriente . a.		0717		2102		2332		0802		2102

LISBOA - PINHAL NOVO - SETÚBAL

Operator: Fertagus. CP tickets not valid.

Roma Areeiro . d.	Ⓐ	0043	0543		2243	2358	Ⓒ	0643		2343
Entrecampos . d.		0045	0545	and	2245	0000		0645	and	2345
Sete Rios . d.		0049	0549	every	2249	0004		0649	every	2349
Pragal . d.		0100	0600	hour	2300	0015		0700	hour	0000
Pinhal Novo . d.		0128	0628	until	2328	0043		0728	until	0028
Setúbal . a.		0141	0641		2341	0056		0741		0041

Setúbal . d.	Ⓐ	0548	0658		1858	1928	2018		0018	Ⓒ	0558		2258
Pinhal Novo . d.		0602	0712	and	1912	1942	2032	and	0032		0612	and	2312
Pragal . d.		0629	0739	every	1939	2009	2059	every	0059		0639	every	2339
Sete Rios . d.		0640	0750	hour	1950	2020	2110	hour	0110		0650	hour	2350
Entrecampos . d.		0644	0754	until	1954	2024	2114	until	0114		0654	until	2354
Roma Areeiro . a.		0646	0756		1956	2026	2116		0116		0656		2356

Additional journeys on Ⓐ: from Roma Areeiro 1813, 1913, 2013, from Setúbal 0628, 0728, 0828. *Fertagus* trains operate every 10 - 20 mins (30 evenings and Ⓒ) Roma Areeiro - Pragal - Coina.

Catamaran LISBOA - BARREIRO

Soflusa / Transtejo

From Lisboa Terreiro do Paço: By ⛴ journey time 20 minutes. *10* km

Ⓐ: 0545, 0610, 0640, 0700 and every 10 minutes until 0920, 0940, 0955 and every 30 minutes until 1555, 1615, 1630, 1650 and every 10 minutes 2010, 2030, 2050, 2110, 2125, 2155, 2225, 2255, 2330, 0000, 0100, 0200.

Ⓒ: 0545, 0615, 0645, 0715, 0755, 0825⑥, 0855, 0925⑥, 0955, 1025⑥, 1055, 1155, 1255, 1355, 1455, 1525, 1625, 1655, 1725, 1755, 1825, 1855, 1925, 1955, 2055, 2125, 2155, 2225, 0000, 0100, 0200.

From Barreiro Barcos: By ⛴ journey time 20 minutes. *10* km

Ⓐ: 0515, 0545, 0615, 0635 and every 10 minutes until 0855, 0900, 0910, 0925, 0940, 0955 and every 30 minutes until 1525, 1545, 1600, 1620 and every 10 minutes until 1940, 2005, 2020, 2040, 2100, 2125, 2155, 2225, 2300, 2330, 0030, 0130.

Ⓒ: 0515, 0545, 0620, 0650, 0725, 0755⑥, 0825, 0855⑥, 0925, 0955⑥, 1025, 1125, 1225, 1325, 1425, 1455, 1525, 1555, 1625, 1655, 1725, 1755, 1825, 1855, 1925, 2025, 2055, 2125, 2225, 2330, 0030, 0130.

BARREIRO - SETÚBAL

Most journeys continue to Praias do Sado A

km								
		Ⓐ						
0	**Barreiro** . d.	0555	0625	every 30 mins	2125	2232	2325	0029
15	Pinhal Novo . d.	0614	0644	(hourly on Ⓒ)	2144	2251	2344	0048
28	**Setúbal** . a.	0626	0656	until	2157	2303	2356	0100

	Ⓐ	Ⓒ	Ⓐ				Ⓐ			
Setúbal . d.	0508	0548	0618	0648	every 30 mins	2048	2122	2151	2248	2348
Pinhal Novo . d.	0520	0600	0630	0700	(hourly on Ⓒ)	2100	2136	2202	2300	0000
Barreiro . a.	0538	0618	0648	0718	until	2118	2154	2223	2318	0018

LISBOA - ENTRONCAMENTO - TOMAR

km																							
			Ⓐ	⚒		Ⓐ		Ⓐ	Ⓐ		Ⓐ		Ⓐ			Ⓐ§		Ⓐ§				Ⓐ	
0	**Lisboa** Santa Apolónia . ▷ d.	0015	0548	0648	0748	0848	0948	1048	1148	1248	1348	1448	1548	1616	1648	1718	1748	1816	1848	1948	2048	2148	2248
7	**Lisboa** Oriente . ▷ d.	0023	0556	0656	0756	0856	0956	1056	1156	1256	1356	1456	1556	1624	1656	1726	1756	1824	1856	1956	2056	2156	2256
31	Vila Franca de Xira . d.	0042	0613	0713	0813	0913	1013	1113	1213	1313	1413	1513	1613	1640	1715	1743	1815	1840	1915	2013	2113	2213	2313
75	Santarém . d.	0119	0656	0756	0856	0950	1056	1150	1256	1350	1456	1550	1656	1707	1757	1819	1857	1909	1957	2056	2150	2251	2350
107	Entroncamento . a.	0143	0719	0819	0919	1015	1119	1213	1320	1413	1519	1613	1719	1727	1820	1838	1920	1928	2020	2119	2213	2321	0013
130	**Tomar** . a.	...	0752	0849	0949	...	1152	1242	...	1442	1552	1652	1752	...	1854	1902	1954	2002	2054	2148	2252	2349	0042

		①–⑥	Ⓐ	Ⓐ§		Ⓐ§		①–⑥		Ⓐ			Ⓐ		Ⓐ					Ⓐ		Ⓐ	
Tomar . d.	...	...	0515	0605	0615v	0645	0711v	...	0802	...	1011	1111v	...	1315	...	1511	1611	1711	1811	1911	2011	...	2211
Entroncamento . d.	...	0415	0542	0626	0642	0706	0742	0808	0838	0942	1038	1142	1238	1342	1438	1542	1638	1742	1841	1943	2042	2145	2242
Santarém . d.	...	0441	0608	0647	0708	0728	0808	0829	0904	1008	1104	1208	1304	1408	1504	1608	1704	1808	1906	2009	2108	2207	2308
Vila Franca de Xira . d.	...	0518	0645	0716	0745	0759	0845	0857	0945	1045	1145	1245	1345	1445	1545	1645	1745	1845	1957	2045	2145	2245	2345
Lisboa Oriente . ▽ d.	...	0536	0704	0734	0804	0821	0904	0920	1004	1104	1204	1304	1404	1504	1604	1704	1804	1904	2020	2104	2204	2304	0004
Lisboa Santa Apolónia . ▽ a.	...	0543	0711	0741	0811	0828	0911	0927	1011	1111	1211	1311	1411	1511	1611	1711	1811	1911	2027	2111	2211	2311	0011

▷ – Additional local trains Santa Apolónia - Oriente on Ⓐ: hourly 0605 - 0005 (also every 30 minutes 0635 - 0935, 1635 - 1935).

▽ – Additional local trains Oriente - Santa Apolónia on Ⓐ: hourly 0647 - 0047 (also every 30 minutes 0717 - 1017, 1717 - 2017).

v – ⚒ only.

§ – *IR* train.

ENTRONCAMENTO - COIMBRA

km													
		†	Ⓐ		Ⓐ						Ⓐ		Ⓑ
0	**Entroncamento** . d.	...	0555	0655	0755	0905	1053	1253	1547	1740	1853	1955	2140
24	Fátima ⊙ . d.	...	0616	0716	0816	0926	1114	1314	1608	1807	1914	2016	2201
64	Pombal . d.	...	0648	0748	0848	0958	1146	1346	1640	1839	1947	2048	2233
91	Alfarelos . d.	0710	0712	0812	0919	1031	1211	1411	1704	1903	2012	2119	2256
111	**Coimbra B** . a.	0732	0732	0832	0941	1052	1231	1431	1725	1925	2032	2141	2317
111	**Coimbra B** . d.	0737	0737	0837	0949	1059	1236	1436	1731	1935	2038	2153	...
113	**Coimbra** . a.	0741	0741	0841	0953	1103	1240	1440	1734	1938	2041	2157	...

	⚒	Ⓐ					Ⓐ			Ⓑ
Coimbra . d.	0605	0715	0815	1015	1315	1615	1715	1815	1915	2015
Coimbra B . a.	0609	0719	0819	1019	1319	1619	1719	1819	1919	2019
Coimbra B . d.	0614	0724	0824	1024	1324	1624	1724	1824	1924	2024
Alfarelos . d.	0635	0745	0845	1045	1345	1645	1745	1845	1945	2045
Pombal . d.	0710	0818	0918	1118	1410	1718	1818	1918	2018	2110
Fátima ⊙ . d.	0744	0901	0950	1150	1450	1750	1901	1950	2050	2150
Entroncamento . a.	0804	0921	1011	1211	1511	1811	1921	2021	2111	2211

– Ⓐ only.

⊙ – Station is *20 km* from Fátima (full name of station is Chão de Maçãs - Fatima).

For fast trains Entroncamento - Coimbra B see Table **390**.

AVEIRO - COIMBRA

km													
					Ⓐ		Ⓐ		Ⓐ				
0	**Aveiro** . d.	0650	0750	0950	1050	1134	1224	1350	1450	1534	1750	1950	2150
41	Pampilhosa . d.	0726	0826	1026	1126	1210	1300	1426	1526	1610	1826	2026	2226
55	**Coimbra B** . a.	0741	0841	1041	1142	1226	1315	1441	1541	1628	1841	2041	2242
57	**Coimbra** . a.	0753	0846	1046	1151	1231	1324	1446	1551	1633	1852	2052	2246

		⚒								
Coimbra . d.	0632	0743	0846	1053	1343	1446	1643	1829	1943	2208
Coimbra B . d.	0636	0748	0851	1058	1348	1450	1648	1833	1948	2213
Pampilhosa . d.	0654	0805	0908	1115	1405	1507	1705	1856	2006	2230
Aveiro . a.	0731	0842	0945	1152	1442	1545	1742	1935	2043	2307

dditional trains: **Aveiro - Coimbra**: 0550⚒, 0734Ⓐ, 0850Ⓐ, 1648Ⓐ, 1850Ⓐ, 2050Ⓐ. **Coimbra - Aveiro**: 0543Ⓐ, 1005Ⓐ, 1143Ⓐ, 1243Ⓐ, 1542Ⓐ, 1744Ⓐ, 2043Ⓐ.

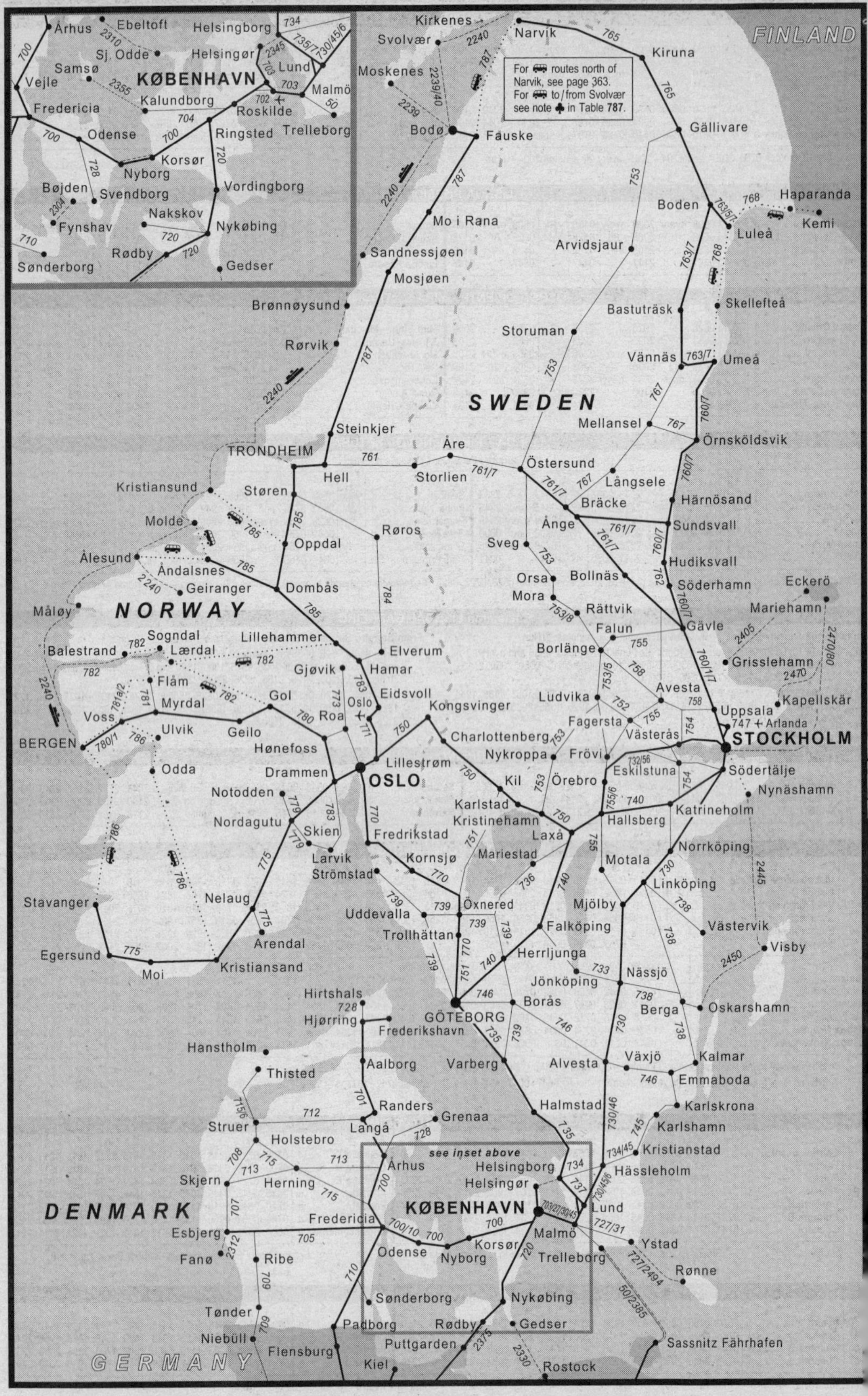
FINLAND
SWEDEN
NORWAY
DENMARK
GERMANY
KØBENHAVN
For routes north of Narvik, see page 363. For to/from Svolvær see note ♣ in Table 787.
Kirkenes
Svolvær
Narvik
Kiruna
Moskenes
Bodø
Fauske
Gällivare
Mo i Rana
Boden
Haparanda
Kemi
Luleå
Arvidsjaur
Sandnessjøen
Mosjøen
Skellefteå
Bastuträsk
Brønnøysund
Storuman
Rørvik
Vännäs
Umeå
Mellansel
Örnsköldsvik
Steinkjer
TRONDHEIM
Åre
Hell
Storlien
Östersund
Långsele
Kristiansund
Støren
Bräcke
Härnösand
Molde
Ånge
Sundsvall
Oppdal
Røros
Sveg
Ålesund
Åndalsnes
Hudiksvall
Geiranger
Dombås
Orsa
Bollnäs
Söderhamn
Eckerö
Mora
Måløy
Rättvik
Mariehamn
Gävle
Falun
Balestrand
Sogndal
Lærdal
Lillehammer
Elverum
Borlänge
Grisslehamn
Gjøvik
Hamar
Flåm
Eidsvoll
Avesta
Myrdal
Gol
Ludvika
Kapellskär
Voss
Oslo
Roa
Kongsvinger
Uppsala
Fagersta
Arlanda
BERGEN
Ulvik
Geilo
Charlottenberg
Västerås
STOCKHOLM
Hønefoss
Nykroppa
Frövi
Eskilstuna
Odda
Drammen
Lillestrøm
Södertälje
OSLO
Kil
Örebro
Nynäshamn
Notodden
Karlstad
Hallsberg
Katrineholm
Nordagutu
Kristinehamn
Skien
Fredrikstad
Laxå
Larvik
Kornsjø
Mariestad
Norrköping
Strömstad
Motala
Linköping
Stavanger
Nelaug
Mjölby
Uddevalla
Öxnered
Falköping
Västervik
Trollhättan
Arendal
Herrljunga
Visby
Egersund
Moi
Kristiansand
Jönköping
Nässjö
Hirtshals
GÖTEBORG
Borås
Berga
Oskarshamn
Hjørring
Frederikshavn
Hanstholm
Aalborg
Varberg
Alvesta
Växjö
Kalmar
Thisted
Emmaboda
Randers
Halmstad
Karlskrona
Grenaa
Struer
Langå
Karlshamn
Holstebro
Kristianstad
Århus
Helsingborg
Hässleholm
Skjern
Herning
Helsingør
Lund
Fredericia
Malmö
Esbjerg
Ystad
Odense
Nyborg
Korsør
Trelleborg
Fanø
Ribe
Rønne
Sønderborg
Nykøbing
Tønder
Padborg
Rødby
Gedser
Niebüll
Sassnitz Fährhafen
Flensburg
Puttgarden
Kiel
Rostock
Ebeltoft
Sj. Odde
Samsø
Vejle
Kalundborg
Roskilde
Ringsted
Bøjden
Svendborg
Vordingborg
Fynshav
Nakskov
see inset above

DENMARK

Operators: The principal operator is Danske Statsbaner (*DSB*): www.dsb.dk. Arriva Tog (*AT*) operate many local services in Jutland: www.mitarriva.dk. Additionally, local trains over the Øresund bridge are marketed as Øresundståg (*Øtåg*), and DSB Øresund operate the *Kystbanen* service between Helsingør and Malmö (Table 703).

Services: InterCity (*IC*) and InterCityLyn (*Lyn*) trains offer *Business* (1st class), *Standard* (2nd class), and on some services *Hvilepladser* ('quiet' seats) and *Familiepladser* ('family' seats). These services often consist of two or more portions for different destinations and care should be taken to join the correct portion. Other trains convey 1st and 2nd (standard) classes of accommodation unless otherwise shown.

Timings: Valid until **December 13, 2014** unless otherwise stated. Readers should note, however, that minor amendments may be made at any time, but particularly on and around the dates of public holidays (see **Holiday periods** below for known changes to schedules).

Reservations: Seat reservations (currently 30 DKK) are recommended for travel on *IC* and *Lyn* trains (especially at peak times) and may be purchased a maximum of two months and a minimum of 15 minutes before departure of the train from its *originating* station. Passengers may board the train without a reservation but are not guaranteed a seat. Reservations are also available on EuroCity (*EC*) trains. It is not possible to reserve seats on other types of train. Special reservation rules may apply during holiday periods.

Supplements: Supplements are payable for travel to and from Germany by InterCityExpress (*ICE*) and EuroCity (*EC*) trains.

Holiday periods: Danske Statsbaner services will be amended as follows: a ⑤ service will operate on June 4; a ⑥ service will operate on June 5; a ⑦ service will operate on June 8, 9.
Arriva services will be amended as follows: a ⑥ service will operate on June 5, 7; a ⑦ service will operate on June 8, 9.

KØBENHAVN - ODENSE - FREDERICIA - ÅRHUS — 700

km		*IC* 191 F	*IC* 807	*IC* 109 A	*Lyn* 11 F	*IC* 113 A	*IC* 917 S		*Lyn* 15 F	*IC* 117 A	*IC* 821 Z	*Lyn* 19 F		*IC* 121 A	*IC* 825 X	*Lyn* 23 F	*IC* 125 A	*IC* 829 X		*Lyn* 27 F	*IC* 129 A	*IC* 833 X	*Lyn* 29 F	*IC* 133 A	*IC* 837 X
				①–⑤	①–⑥	①–⑥			①–⑥			①–⑥													
0	**København** Lufthavn ... d.	0009	0151	...	...	0439	...	...	0530	0539	...	0630	...	0639	...	0730	0739	...	...	0830	0839	...	0930r	0939	...
11	**København** H **720** .. § d.	0030	0218	...	...	0500	0528	...	0550	0600	0628	0650	...	0700	0728	0750	0800	0828	...	0850	0900	0928	0950	1000	1028
31	Høje Taastrup **720** ... § d.	0045	0232	...	...	0513	0543	...	0603	0613	0643	0703	...	0713	0743	0803	0813	0843	...	0903	0913	0943	1003	1013	1043
42	Roskilde **720** .... § d.	0054	0244	...	...	0521	0551	...	|	0621	0651	|	...	0721	0751	|	0821	0851	...	|	0921	0951	|	1021	1051
75	Ringsted **720** .... d.	0118	0305	...	...	0538	0608	...	|	0638	0708	|	...	0738	0808	|	0838	0908	...	|	0938	1008	|	1038	1108
104	Slagelse .... d.	0138	0322	...	...	0555	0626	...	|	0655	0726	|	...	0755	0826	|	0855	0926	...	|	0955	1026	|	1055	1126
119	Korsør .... d.	0148	0331	...	...	0604	0635	...	|	0704	0735	|	...	0804	0835	|	0904	0935	...	|	1004	1035	|	1104	1135
143	Nyborg .... d.	0203	0344	0517	...	0617	0647	...	|	0717	0747	|	...	0817	0847	|	0917	0947	...	|	1017	1047	|	1117	1147
171	**Odense** .... a.	0224	0409	0530	...	0630	0700	...	0705	0730	0801	0805	...	0830	0901	0905	0930	1001	...	1005	1030	1101	1105	1130	1201
171	**Odense 728** .... d.	0226	0411	0533	0607	0633	0703	...	0707	0733	0803	0807	...	0833	0903	0907	0933	1003	...	1007	1033	1103	1107	1133	1203
221	Middelfart **710** .... d.	0254	0441	0557	|	0657	0727	...	|	0757	0827	|	...	0857	0927	|	0957	1027	...	|	1057	1127	|	1157	1227
231	**Fredericia** .... a.	0303	0450	0606	0636	0706	...	...	0736	0806	...	0836	...	0906	...	0936	1006	...	...	1036	1106	...	1136	1206	...
231	**Fredericia 705/10/5** .... d.	0305	...	0611	0638	0711	...	...	0738	0811	...	0838	...	0911	...	0938	1011	...	...	1038	1111	...	1138	1211	...
257	Vejle **715** .... d.	0320	...	0627	0654	0727	...	...	0754	0827	...	0854	...	0927	...	0954	1027	...	...	1054	1127	...	1154	1227	...
288	Horsens .... d.	0336	...	0643	0711	0743	...	...	0811	0843	...	0911	...	0943	...	1011	1043	...	...	1111	1143	...	1211	1243	...
317	Skanderborg **713** .... d.	0352	...	0658	0726	0758	...	...	0826	0858	...	0926	...	0958	...	1026	1058	...	...	1126	1158	...	1226	1258	...
340	**Århus 713 728** .... a.	0409	...	0712	0739	0812	...	...	0839	0912	...	0939	...	1012	...	1039	1112	...	...	1139	1212	...	1239	1312	...

	Lyn 41 F	*EC* 386	*IC* 137 A	*IC* 841 X	*Lyn* 43 F		*IC* 141 A	*IC* 845 X	*Lyn* 45 F	*IC* 145 A		*IC* 849 X	*Lyn* 47 A	*IC* 149 A		*IC* 853 X	*Lyn* 51 F	*ICE* 380	*IC* 153 A	*Lyn* 253		*IC* 857 Y	*Lyn* 55 F	*IC* 157 A	*Lyn* 257
		♦																♦		q					q
København Lufthavn .... d.	...	...	1039	...	1130	...	1139	...	1230	1239	...	...	1330	1339	...	...	1430	...	1439	1458	...	...	...	1539	1558
København H **720** .... § d.	1050	...	1100	1128	1150	...	1200	1228	1250	1300	...	1328	1350	1400	...	1428	1450	...	1500	1522	...	1528	1550	1600	1622
Høje Taastrup **720** .... § d.	1103	...	1113	1143	1203	...	1213	1243	1303	1313	...	1343	1403	1413	...	1443	1503	...	1513	|	...	1543	1603	1613	|
Roskilde **720** .... § d.	|	...	1121	1151	|	...	1221	1251	|	1321	...	1351	|	1421	...	1451	|	...	1521	|	...	1551	|	1621	|
Ringsted **720** .... d.	|	...	1138	1208	|	...	1238	1308	|	1338	...	1408	|	1438	...	1508	|	...	1538	|	...	1608	|	1638	|
Slagelse .... d.	|	...	1155	1226	|	...	1255	1326	|	1355	...	1426	|	1455	...	1526	|	...	1555	|	...	1626	|	1655	|
Korsør .... d.	|	...	1204	1235	|	...	1304	1335	|	1404	...	1435	|	1504	...	1535	|	...	1604	|	...	1635	|	1704	|
Nyborg .... d.	|	...	1217	1247	|	...	1317	1347	|	1417	...	1447	|	1517	...	1547	|	...	1617	1625	...	1647	|	1717	1725
Odense .... a.	1205	...	1230	1301	1305	...	1330	1401	1405	1430	...	1501	1505	1530	...	1601	1605	...	1630	1639	...	1701	1705	1730	1739
Odense 728 .... d.	1207	...	1233	1303	1307	...	1333	1403	1407	1433	...	1503	1507	1533	...	1603	1607	...	1633	1641	...	1703	1707	1733	1741
Middelfart **710** .... d.	|	...	1257	1327	|	...	1357	1427	|	1457	...	1527	|	1557	...	1627	|	...	1657	|	...	1727	|	1757	|
Fredericia .... a.	1236	...	1306	...	1336	...	1406	...	1436	1506	...	...	1536	1606	...	...	1636	...	1706	|	...	...	1736	1806	|
Fredericia 705/10/5 ..... d.	1238	1256	1311	...	1338	...	1411	...	1438	1511	...	...	1538	1611	...	...	1638	1656	1711	|	...	...	1738	1811	|
Vejle **715** .... d.	1254	1312	1327	...	1354	...	1427	...	1454	1527	...	...	1554	1627	...	...	1654	1712	1727	1723	...	...	1754	1827	1823
Horsens .... d.	1311	1330	1343	...	1411	...	1443	...	1511	1543	...	...	1611	1643	...	...	1711	1729	1743	|	...	...	1811	1843	|
Skanderborg **713** .... d.	1326	|	1358	...	1426	...	1458	...	1526	1558	...	...	1626	1658	...	...	1726	1744	1758	|	...	...	1826	1858	|
Århus 713 728 .... a.	1339	1400	1412	...	1439	...	1512	...	1539	1612	...	...	1639	1712	...	...	1739	1759	1812	1805	...	...	1839	1912	1905

	IC 861 Z	*Lyn* 59 F		*IC* 161 A	*IC* 865 Y	*Lyn* 63 F		*IC* 165 A	*IC* 869 Z	*Lyn* 65 F	*EN* 473 ⑥	*EN* 473 Ⓑ	*IC* 169 A	*IC* 873 Y	*Lyn* 69 A	*IC* 173 A	*IC* 877 W	*IC* 977 W		*Lyn* 73	*IC* 177	*IC* 881 Y	*IC* 179	*IC* 885	*IC* 189
											♦ 🅁	♦ 🅁						①–④		⑤–⑦					
København Lufthavn .... d.	...	...	...	1639	...	1730	...	1739	...	...	...	...	1839	...	1930	1939	...	...	...	2030	2039	...	2139	...	2306
København H **720** .... § d.	1628	1650	...	1700	1728	1750	...	1800	1828	1850	1724	1846	1900	1928	1950	2000	2028	2028	...	2050	2100	2128	2200	2228	2328
Høje Taastrup **720** .... § d.	1643	1703	...	1713	1743	1803	...	1813	1843	1903	|	|	1913	1943	2003	2013	2043	2043	...	2103	2113	2143	2213	2243	2344
Roskilde **720** .... § d.	1651	|	...	1721	1751	|	...	1821	1851	|	1745	1911	1921	1951	|	2021	2051	2051	...	|	2121	2151	2221	2251	2353
Ringsted **720** .... d.	1708	|	...	1738	1808	|	...	1838	1908	|	|	|	1938	2008	|	2038	2108	2108	...	|	2138	2208	2238	2308	0017
Slagelse .... d.	1726	|	...	1755	1826	|	...	1855	1926	|	|	|	1955	2026	|	2055	2126	2126	...	|	2155	2226	2255	2325	0034
Korsør .... d.	1735	|	...	1804	1835	|	...	1904	1935	|	|	|	2004	2035	|	2104	2135	2135	...	|	2204	2235	2304	2335	0043
Nyborg .... d.	1747	|	...	1817	1847	|	...	1917	1947	|	|	|	2017	2047	|	2117	2147	2147	...	|	2217	2247	2317	2348	0055
Odense .... a.	1801	1805	...	1830	1901	1905	...	1930	2001	2005	1855	2028	2030	2101	2105	2130	2201	2201	...	2205	2230	2301	2336	0011	0117
Odense 728 .... d.	1803	1807	...	1833	1903	1907	...	1933	2003	2007	...	...	2033	2103	2107	2133	2203	2203	...	2207	2233	2303	2339	0013	0119
Middelfart **710** .... d.	1827	|	...	1857	1927	|	...	1957	2027	|	...	...	2057	2127	|	2157	2227	2233	...	|	2257	2327	0004	0039	0144
Fredericia .... a.	...	1836	...	1906	...	1936	...	2006	...	2036	...	...	2106	...	2136	2206	...	2240	...	2236	2306	...	0014	0048	0155
Fredericia 705/10/5 ..... d.	...	1838	...	1911	...	1938	...	2011	...	2038	...	...	2111	...	2138	2211	...	...	...	2238	2311	...	0016	...	0157
Vejle **715** .... d.	...	1854	...	1927	...	1954	...	2027	...	2054	...	...	2127	...	2154	2227	...	...	...	2254	2330	...	0032	...	0213
Horsens .... d.	...	1911	...	1943	...	2011	...	2043	...	2111	...	...	2143	...	2211	2245	...	...	...	2310	2349	...	0049	...	0231
Skanderborg **713** .... d.	...	1926	...	1958	...	2026	...	2058	...	2126	...	...	2158	...	2226	2302	...	...	...	2326	0007	...	0106	...	0248
Århus 713 728 .... a.	...	1939	...	2012	...	2039	...	2112	...	2139	...	...	2212	...	2239	2320	...	...	...	2342	0024	...	0123	...	0305

	IC 190 F	*IC* 100	*IC* 800	*IC* 102	*IC* 802	*Lyn* 2	*IC* 804	*IC* 8004	*IC* 810	*IC* 8002 S	*IC* 904	*Lyn* 208	*Lyn* 6	*IC* 108		*Lyn* 10 A	*IC* 808 Y	*IC* 908 S	*Lyn* 212	*EN* 472 ①–⑥	*IC* 112 A	*Lyn* 14 F	*IC* 7/812 E	*IC* 814 Z	*EN* 472 ⑦	*ICE* 381
		①–⑥	①–⑤	⑦	①–⑥		①–⑤	q		①–⑤	①–⑤	q	①–⑤			①–⑤	①–⑤	⑥⑦	q	♦ 🅁		①–⑥	⑦	①–⑥	♦ 🅁	♦
Århus 713 728 .... d.	0149	...	...	...	...	0419	...	...	...	...	...	0554	0540	0600g	...	0627	...	...	0654	...	0700	0727	...	...	...	0756
Skanderborg **713** .... d.	0205	...	...	...	...	0433	...	...	...	...	...	|	0555	0616g	...	0641	...	...	|	...	0716	0741	...	...	...	|
Horsens .... d.	0220	...	...	...	...	0448	...	...	...	...	...	|	0610	0630g	...	0655	...	...	|	...	0730	0755	...	...	...	0824
Vejle **715** .... d.	0237	...	...	...	...	0505	...	...	...	...	...	0636	0626	0647g	...	0712	...	...	0738	...	0747	0812	0803	...	...	0841
Fredericia 715 .... a.	0255	...	...	...	...	0523	...	...	...	...	...	|	0642	0704g	...	0729	...	...	|	...	0804	0829	0823	...	...	0858
Fredericia 705 710 .... d.	0305	0358	...	...	0506	0528	0536	...	0606	...	...	|	0647	0709	...	0734	...	...	|	...	0809	0834	0827	...	...	...
Middelfart **710** .... d.	0312	0406	...	...	0514	|	0544	...	0614	0623	...	|	|	0717	...	|	0745	0745	|	...	0817	|	0845	0845	...	...
Odense .... a.	0340	0433	...	...	0541	0558	0610	...	0645	0649	...	0720	0717	0743	...	0804	0811	0811	0820	...	0843	0905	0911	0911	...	...
Odense 728 .... d.	0342	0437	0513	0546	0546	0600	0615	0628	0647	0656	0715	0722	0727	0746	...	0806	0815	0816	0822	0817	0846	0907	0916	0916	0920	...
Nyborg .... d.	0401	0455	0527	0600	0600	0614	0629	0642	0701	0710	0728	0737	0744	0800	...	|	0827	0831	0837	|	0900	|	0931	0931	|	...
Korsør .... d.	0415	0508	0540	0613	0613	|	0642	|	0714	|	0741	|	|	0813	...	|	0840	0844	|	|	0913	|	0944	0944	|	...
Slagelse .... d.	0425	0520	0551	0623	0623	0633	0652	0701	0723	0729	0750	|	|	0823	...	|	0849	0854	|	|	0923	|	0954	0954	|	...
Ringsted **720** .... a.	0444	0539	0609	0639	0639	|	0709	|	0739	|	0811	|	|	0839	...	|	0911	0910	|	|	0939	|	1010	1010	|	...
Roskilde **720** .... § a.	0506	0555	0624	0656	0656	|	0725	|	0756	|	0827	|	|	0855	...	|	0927	0926	|	0944	0955	|	1026	1026	1031	...
Høje Taastrup **720** ... § a.	0519	0603	0634	0704	0704	0707	0733	|	0805	|	0835	|	0839	0904	...	0907	0935	0935	|	|	1004	1007	1035	1035	|	...
København H **720** ... § a.	0537	0618	0651	0720	0721	0722	0750	0754	0823	0826	0852	0847	0856	0918	...	0922	0951	0951	0942	1008	1018	1022	1051	1051	1054	...
København Lufthavn .... a.	0557	0637	...	0740	...	0740	...	...	...	...	...	0908	...	0936	...	...	...	...	1001	...	1037	1041	...	...	...	...

FOR NOTES SEE NEXT PAGE

700 ÅRHUS - FREDERICIA - ODENSE - KØBENHAVN

	IC 116	*Lyn* 18	*IC* 816	*IC* 120	*Lyn* 24	*IC* 820	*IC* 124	*Lyn* 26	*IC* 826	*IC* 128	*Lyn* 28	*IC* 828		*IC* 132	*Lyn* 40	*IC* 834	*IC* 136	*Lyn* 42	*IC* 838	*IC* 140	*EC* 387	*Lyn* 44	*IC* 842	*IC* 144	*Lyn* 46
	A	F	Y	A	F	Z	A	F	X	A	F	X		A	F	X	A	F	X	A	♦	F	X	A	F
Århus 713 728 d.	0800	0827	...	0900	0927	...	1000	1027	...	1100	1127	...	...	1200	1227	...	1300	1327	...	1400	1424	1427	...	1500	1527
Skanderborg **713** d.	0816	0841	...	0916	0941	...	1016	1041	...	1116	1141	...	...	1216	1241	...	1316	1341	...	1416	|	1441	...	1516	1541
Horsens d.	0830	0855	...	0930	0955	...	1030	1055	...	1130	1155	...	...	1230	1255	...	1330	1355	...	1430	1451	1455	...	1530	1555
Vejle **715** d.	0847	0912	...	0947	1012	...	1047	1112	...	1147	1212	...	...	1247	1312	...	1347	1412	...	1447	1509	1512	...	1547	1612
Fredericia 715 a.	0904	0929	...	1004	1029	...	1104	1129	...	1204	1229	...	...	1304	1329	...	1404	1429	...	1504	1525	1529	...	1604	1629
Fredericia 705 710 d.	0909	0934	...	1009	1034	...	1109	1134	...	1209	1234	...	...	1309	1334	...	1409	1434	...	1509	...	1534	...	1609	1634
Middelfart **710** d.	0917	|	0945	1017	|	1045	1117	|	1145	1217	|	1245	...	1317	|	1345	1417	|	1445	1517	...	|	1545	1617	|
Odense a.	0943	1005	1011	1043	1105	1111	1143	1205	1211	1243	1305	1311	...	1343	1405	1411	1443	1505	1511	1543	...	1605	1611	1643	1705
Odense 728 d.	0946	1007	1016	1046	1107	1116	1146	1207	1216	1246	1307	1316	...	1346	1407	1416	1446	1507	1516	1546	...	1607	1616	1646	1707
Nyborg d.	1000	|	1031	1100	|	1131	1200	|	1231	1300	|	1331	...	1400	|	1431	1500	|	1531	1600	...	|	1631	1700	|
Korsør d.	1013	|	1044	1113	|	1144	1213	|	1244	1313	|	1344	...	1413	|	1444	1513	|	1544	1613	...	|	1644	1713	|
Slagelse d.	1023	|	1054	1123	|	1154	1223	|	1254	1323	|	1354	...	1423	|	1454	1523	|	1554	1623	...	|	1654	1723	|
Ringsted **720** a.	1039	|	1110	1139	|	1210	1239	|	1310	1339	|	1410	...	1439	|	1510	1539	|	1610	1639	...	|	1710	1739	|
Roskilde **720** § a.	1055	|	1126	1155	|	1226	1255	|	1326	1355	|	1426	...	1455	|	1526	1555	|	1626	1655	...	|	1726	1755	|
Høje Taastrup **720** § a.	1104	1107	1135	1204	1207	1235	1304	1307	1335	1404	1407	1435	...	1504	1507	1535	1604	1607	1635	1704	...	1707	1735	1804	1807
København H **720** § a.	1118	1122	1151	1218	1222	1251	1318	1322	1351	1418	1422	1451	...	1518	1522	1551	1618	1622	1651	1718	...	1722	1751	1818	1822
København Lufthavn a.	1137	1141	...	1237	...	...	1337	1341	...	1437	...	...	...	1537	1541	...	1637	...	...	1737	...	1741	...	1837	1841

	IC 846	*IC* 844	*IC* 148	*Lyn* 50	*IC* 850	*IC* 152	*Lyn* 54	*IC* 852	*IC* 156	*Lyn* 56	*IC* 856	*IC* 160	*Lyn* 60	*IC* 860	*IC* 164	*Lyn* 64	*IC* 864	*IC* 168	*IC* 772	*Lyn* 68	*IC* 868	*IC* 172	*IC* 176	*IC* 180	
	X	X	A	F	X	A	F	Z	A	F	Y	A	F	Z	A	F	Y	A		F	Z	A	A	A	
	①–⑤	⑥⑦																	①–⑥	⑦					
Århus 713 728 d.	...	...	1600	1627	...	1700	1727	...	1800	1827	...	1900	1927	...	2000	2027	...	2100	...	2127	...	2200	2300	0000	...
Skanderborg **713** d.	...	...	1616	1641	...	1716	1741	...	1816	1841	...	1916	1941	...	2016	2041	...	2116	...	2141	...	2216	2316	0016	...
Horsens d.	...	...	1630	1655	...	1730	1755	...	1830	1855	...	1930	1955	...	2030	2055	...	2130	...	2155	...	2230	2330	0030	...
Vejle **715** d.	...	...	1647	1712	...	1747	1812	...	1847	1912	...	1947	2012	...	2047	2112	...	2147	2203	2212	...	2247	2350	0050	...
Fredericia 715 a.	...	...	1704	1729	...	1804	1829	...	1904	1929	...	2004	2029	...	2104	2129	...	2204	2223	2229	...	2306	0009	0109	...
Fredericia 705 710 d.	...	...	1709	1734	...	1809	1834	...	1909	1934	...	2009	2034	...	2109	2134	...	2209	2225	2234	...	2311	0014	0112	...
Middelfart **710** d.	1645	1645	1717	|	1745	1817	|	1845	1917	|	1945	2017	|	2045	2117	|	2145	2217	2232	|	2245	2318	0021	0122	...
Odense a.	1711	1711	1743	1805	1811	1843	1905	1911	1943	2005	2011	2043	2105	2111	2143	2205	2211	2243	2257	2307	2315	2347	0051	0152	...
Odense 728 d.	1713	1716	1746	1807	1816	1846	1907	1916	1946	2007	2016	2046	2107	2116	2146	2207	2216	2246	...	2309	2319	2349	0053	...	...
Nyborg d.	1727	1731	1800	|	1831	1900	|	1931	2000	|	2031	2100	|	2131	2200	|	2231	2302	...	|	2333	0003	0111	...	...
Korsør d.	1740	1744	1813	|	1844	1913	|	1944	2013	|	2044	2113	|	2144	2213	|	2244	2316	...	|	2346	0017	0125	...	...
Slagelse d.	1749	1754	1823	|	1854	1923	|	1954	2023	|	2054	2123	|	2154	2223	|	2254	2326	...	|	2355	0026	0136	...	...
Ringsted **720** a.	1811	1810	1839	|	1910	1939	|	2010	2039	|	2110	2139	|	2210	2239	|	2311	2353	...	|	0012	0043	0154	...	...
Roskilde **720** § a.	1827	1826	1855	|	1926	1955	|	2026	2055	|	2126	2155	|	2226	2255	|	2328	0000	...	|	0029	0100	0214	...	...
Høje Taastrup **720** § a.	1835	1835	1904	1907	1935	2004	2007	2035	2104	2107	2135	2204	2207	2235	2304	2307	2336	0007	...	0022	0037	0108	0223	...	...
København H **720** § a.	1850	1851	1918	1922	1951	2018	2022	2051	2118	2122	2151	2218	2222	2251	2318	2322	2355	0035	...	0048	0059	0140	0240	...	...
København Lufthavn a.	...	...	1937	1941	...	2037	...	...	2137	2141	...	2237	2241	...	2337	2341	...	0057	...	...	...	0220c	0255	...	...

A – From/to Aalborg on some days (see Table **701**).
E – From/to Esbjerg on some days (Table **705**).
F – From/to Frederikshavn on some days. A change of train may be necessary at Aalborg (see Table **701**).
S – From/to Sønderborg on some days (Table **710**).
W – From/to Esbjerg and Padborg on some days (see Tables **705/10**).
X – From/to Esbjerg, Sønderborg/Flensburg on some days (see Tables **705/10**).
Y – From/to Esbjerg and Sønderborg on some days (see Tables **705/10**).
Z – From/to Esbjerg and Flensburg on some days (see Tables **705/10**).

c – ⑥⑦ only.
g – ⑥ only.
q – ①–⑤ Dec. 16 - June 27, Aug. 18 - Dec. 12 (not Apr. 14-16, May 30, June 6).
r – ⑤⑥⑦ only.
♦ – For days of running and composition see Table **710**.
§ – *IC* and *Lyn* trains are not available for local journeys. Frequent local trains run between Roskilde and København.

701 ÅRHUS - AALBORG - FREDERIKSHAVN

2nd class only (*IC* & *Lyn* 1st & 2nd class)

km		*IC* 191	*IC* 101		*Lyn* 7		*IC* 107		*IC* 109	*Lyn* 11	*IC* 113	*Lyn* 15		*IC* 117		*Lyn* 19		*IC* 121	*Lyn* 23	*IC* 125	*Lyn* 27	*IC* 129	*Lyn* 29		*IC* 133		*Lyn* 41
			①–⑤	⑥⑦	①–⑤	⑦	①–⑤	⑥		①–⑥		①–⑥	⑦			①–⑥	⑤⑦							①–⑤		①–⑤	
0	**Århus 712** d.	0418	0520	0544	0548	...	0620	0642	0720	0748	0820	0848	...	0920	...	0948	...	1020	1048	1120	1148	1220	1248	...	1320	...	1348
46	Langå **712** d.	0446	0547	0611	|	...	0647	0711	0747	|	0847	|	...	0947	...	|	...	1047	|	1147	|	1247	|	...	1347	...	|
59	Randers d.	0456	0556	0620	0620	...	0656	0720	0756	0820	0856	0920	...	0956	...	1020	...	1056	1120	1156	1220	1256	1320	...	1356	...	1420
91	Hobro d.	0513	0613	0636	0638	...	0713	0737	0813	0838	0913	0938	...	1013	...	1038	...	1113	1138	1213	1238	1313	1338	...	1413	...	1438
140	**Aalborg** a.	0552	0652	0717	0709	...	0752	0817	0852	0909	0952	1009	...	1052	...	1109	...	1152	1209	1252	1309	1352	1409	...	1452	...	1509
140	**Aalborg** d.	0556**k**	*0656*	0720**g**	*0720*	0759	0759	0820	...	0920	...	1020	1020	...	...	1120**h**	1120	...	1220**h**	...	1320**h**	...	1420**c**	1420	...	1500	1520**j**
188	Hjørring **728** d.	0636**k**	*0738*	0801**g**	*0801*	0846	0846	0905	...	1003	...	1102	1103	...	...	1202**h**	1202	...	1302**h**	...	1402**h**	...	1502**c**	1502	...	1539	1605**j**
225	**Frederikshavn** a.	0708**k**	*0810*	0831**g**	*0833*	0911	0914	0930	...	1030	...	1127	1128	...	...	1231**h**	1231	...	1327**h**	...	1431**h**	...	1527**c**	1530	...	1606	1634**j**

		IC 137	*Lyn* 43			*IC* 141	*Lyn* 45		*IC* 145	*Lyn* 47	*IC* 149	*Lyn* 51	*IC* 153	*Lyn* 55	*IC* 157	*Lyn* 59	*IC* 161	*Lyn* 63		*IC* 165	*Lyn* 65/7		*IC* 169	*Lyn* 69		*IC* 173	
	①–⑤			①–⑤	①–⑤			①–⑤										Ⓑ	⑥		Ⓑ	⑥		⑦	⑥⑦		
Århus 712 d.	...	1420	1448	...	...	1520	1548	...	1620	1648	1720	1748	1820	1848	1920	1948	2020	2048	...	2120	2148	...	2220	2248	...	2326	...
Langå **712** d.	...	1447	|	...	...	1547	|	...	1647	|	1747	|	1847	|	1947	|	2047	|	...	2147	|	...	2247	|	...	2353	...
Randers d.	...	1456	1520	...	...	1556	1620	...	1656	1720	1756	1820	1856	1920	1956	2020	2056	2120	...	2156	2220	...	2256	2320	...	0002	...
Hobro d.	...	1513	1538	...	...	1613	1638	...	1713	1738	1813	1838	1913	1938	2013	2038	2113	2138	...	2213	2238	...	2313	2338	...	0020	...
Aalborg a.	...	1552	1609	...	...	1652	1709	...	1752	1809	1852	1909	1952	2009	2052	2109	2152	2209	...	2252	2309	...	2352	0009	...	0100	...
Aalborg d.	1549	...	1620**c**	1620	1649	...	1720	1749	...	*1820*	...	1920	...	2020	...	2120	...	2220	2220	...	2319	2319	...	...	0020	...	...
Hjørring **728** d.	1640	...	1705**c**	1705	1740	...	1802	1839	...	*1902*	...	2002	...	2103	...	2205	...	2301	2301	...	2358	2358	...	...	0102	...	...
Frederikshavn a.	1708	...	1735**c**	1735	1811	...	1826	1911	...	*1932*	...	2026	...	2132	...	2233	...	2328	2328	...	0027	0027	...	...	0131	...	...

	Lyn 10	*IC* 112	*Lyn* 14	*IC* 116			*Lyn* 18	*IC* 120			*Lyn* 24	*IC* 124		*Lyn* 26			*IC* 128	*Lyn* 28	*IC* 132	*Lyn* 40	*IC* 136	*Lyn* 42	*IC* 140	*Lyn* 44	*IC* 144	*Lyn* 46	*IC* 148
	①–⑤	①–⑥	①–⑥		①–⑤	⑤–⑦	①–⑥		①–⑤	Ⓑ	①–⑥		①–⑤			①–⑤											
Frederikshavn d.	...	...	0437**a**	...	0510	0535	0536**n**	...	0602	0624	0629**g**	...	0707	0731**c**	...	0754	...	0834	...	0934	...	1039	...	1134	...	1239	...
Hjørring **728** d.	...	...	0506**a**	...	0539	0602	0602**n**	...	0640	0704	0704**g**	...	0738	0806**c**	...	0826	...	0906	...	1006	...	1106	...	1206	...	1306	...
Aalborg a.	...	...	0550**a**	...	0627	0646	0646**n**	...	0725	0752	0752**g**	...	0830	0850**c**	...	0907	...	0950	...	1050	...	1150	...	1250	...	1350	...
Aalborg d.	0501	0518	0601	0618	...	...	0701	0718	...	...	0801	0818	...	0901	...	...	0918	1001	1018	1101	1118	1201	1218	1301	1318	1401	1418
Hobro d.	0532	0558	0632	0658	...	...	0732	0758	...	...	0832	0858	...	0932	...	...	0958	1032	1058	1132	1158	1232	1258	1332	1358	1432	1458
Randers d.	0548	0615	0648	0714	...	...	0748	0815	...	...	0848	0915	...	0948	...	...	1015	1048	1115	1148	1215	1248	1315	1348	1415	1448	1515
Langå **712** d.	|	0625	|	0723	...	...	|	0825	...	...	|	0925	...	|	...	...	1025	|	1125	|	1225	|	1325	|	1425	|	1525
Århus 712 a.	0620	0652	0720	0752	...	...	0820	0852	...	...	0920	0952	...	1020	...	...	1052	1120	1152	1220	1252	1320	1352	1420	1452	1520	1552

	Lyn 50	*IC* 152	*Lyn* 54		*IC* 156		*Lyn* 56	*IC* 160		*Lyn* 60	*IC* 164			*Lyn* 62	*IC* 168		*Lyn* 68	*IC* 172		*Lyn* 72	*IC* 176		*IC* 180		*IC* 184	*IC* 190	
				⑤		①–⑤			①–⑤			①–⑤		Ⓑ		⑥	Ⓑ		⑥⑦	①–⑤							
Frederikshavn d.	1334**h**	...	1434**q**	1437	...	1456	1534**h**	...	1547	1635**h**	...	1651	1737	...	...	1832	1832**r**	...	1937	1937	...	2032	...	2140	...	2256	...
Hjørring **728** d.	1406**h**	...	1506**q**	1506	...	1540	1606**h**	...	1640	1706**h**	...	1740	1806	...	...	1906	1906**r**	...	2006	2006	...	2106	...	2206	...	2324	...
Aalborg a.	1450**h**	...	1550**q**	1550	...	1623	1650**h**	...	1723	1750**h**	...	1823	1850	...	...	1950	1950**r**	...	2050	2050	...	2150	...	2250	...	2400	...
Aalborg d.	1501	1518	1601	...	1618	...	1701	1718	...	1801	1818	...	...	1901	1918	...	2001	2018	...	2101	2118	...	2218	...	2318	0005	...
Hobro d.	1532	1558	1632	...	1658	...	1732	1758	...	1832	1858	...	...	1932	1958	...	2032	2058	...	2132	2158	...	2258	...	2358	0045	...
Randers d.	1548	1615	1648	...	1715	...	1748	1815	...	1848	1915	...	...	1948	2015	...	2048	2115	...	2148	2215	...	2315	...	0015	0103	...
Langå **712** d.	|	1625	|	...	1725	...	|	1825	...	|	1925	...	...	|	2025	...	|	2125	...	|	2225	...	2325	...	0025	0114	...
Århus 712 a.	1620	1652	1720	...	1752	...	1820	1852	...	1920	1952	...	...	2020	2052	...	2120	2152	...	2220	2252	...	2352	...	0056	0143	...

a – ①–⑤ only.
c – ⑥⑦ only.
g – ⑥ only.
h – Connection on ⑤.
j – Connection on Ⓑ.
k – Connection on ⑦.
n – ①–④ only.
q – Daily **except** ⑤.
r – Connection on ①–⑤.

HELSINGØR - KØBENHAVN - KØBENHAVN LUFTHAVN (KASTRUP) ✈ - MALMÖ 703

Principal regular interval services are shown as minutes past each hour only. Additional services operate at peak times.

km													A	B	C	D	A	B	C	D	A	B	C	D		E	F	E	F	E	F
0	**Helsingør** d.	...	...	...	...	...	...	...	0438	0458	0516	0530	43	...	45	...	03	...	05	...	23	...	25	...	2000	05	...	25	...	45	...
43	Østerport d.	0101	0201	0301	0401	0430	0450	0510	0521	0541	0601	to	21	21	30	30	41	41	50	50	01	01	10	10	to	50	01j	10	21j	30	41j
46	**København H** a.	0108	0208	0308	0408	0437	0457	0517	0528	0548	0608	2000	28	28	37	37	48	48	57	57	08	08	17	17	2400	57	08j	17	28j	37	48j
46	**København H** d.	0112	0212	0312	0412	0440	0500	0520	0532	0552	0612		32	32	40	40	52	52	00	00	12	12	20	20		00	12	20	32	40	52
58	Lufthavn (Kastrup) a.	0126	0226	0326	0426	0452	0512	0532	0546	0606	0626	▶▶▶	46	46	52	52	06	06	12	12	26	26	32	32	▶▶▶	12	26	32	46	52	06
93	**Malmö C** a.	0146	0246	0346	0446	...	...	...	0606	0626	0646		06	06	...	...	26	26	...	...	46	46	...	...		...	46	...	06	...	26

						G	K	H	J	G	K	H	J	G	K	H	J		L	M	L	M	L	M				
Malmö C d.	0033	0133	0233	0333	0400	13	13	...	...	33	33	...	...	53	53	...	...	1900	...	13	...	33	...	53	...	...	...	...
Køb Lufthavn (Kastrup) ✈ d.	0054	0154	0254	0354	to	34	34	42	42	54	54	02	02	14	14	22	22	to	22	34	42	54	02	14	...	...	...	...
København H a.	0108	0208	0308	0408	1900	48	48	56	56	08	08	16	16	28	28	36	36	2400	36	48	56	08	16	28	...	...	...	...
København H d.	0112	0212	0312	0412		52	52	01	01	12	12	21	21	32	32	41	41		41	52r	01	12r	21	32r	...	...	...	...
Østerport a.	0119	0219	0319	0419	▶▶▶	59	59	08	08	19	19	28	28	39	39	48	48	▶▶▶	48	59r	08	19r	28	39r	...	...	...	...
Helsingør a.	...	...	...	...		36	...	...	54	56	...	...	14	16	...	...	34		34	...	54	...	14	...	...	...	...	...

A – ①–⑤: 0543 - 1943; ⑥⑦: 0843 - 1943.
B – ⑥⑦: 0621 - 0901.
C – ⑥⑦: 0545 - 0825.
D – ①–⑤: 0601 - 2001; ⑥⑦: 0901 - 2001.
E – Daily: 2005 - 0005.
F – Daily: 2041 - 0021.
G – ①–⑤: 0413 - 1853; ⑥⑦: 0833 - 1853.
H – ①–⑤: 0442 - 1902; ⑥⑦: 0842 - 1902.
J – ⑥⑦: 0442 - 0822.
K – ⑥⑦: 0413 - 0813.
L – Daily: 1922 - 0022.
M – Daily: 1913 - 2333.
j – No departure at 2341, 0001, 0021 (starts from København H).
r – No arrival at 2339, 2359, 0019 (terminates at København H).

KØBENHAVN - KALUNDBORG 704

Valid May 3 - August 17. From July 26 to August 3 the change between train and bus takes place at Lejre (between Roskilde and Hvalsø) instead of Hvalsø. Train times remain the same.

km			A	B	C	D	E		F	G	H	N		P	Q	R		F	G	R	N		S	T	V		F	G	V	N			
0	**København H** d.	①-⑤	36	🚌	...	06	🚌	...	24	🚌	...	36	⑥	24	🚌	...	...	24	🚌	...	36	⑦	24	🚌	...	...	24	🚌	...	36	...	...	...
20	Høje Taastrup d.		51	...	...	21	...	...	39	...	...	51		39	...	...	...	39	...	...	51		39	...	...	...	39	...	...	51	...	...	...
31	**Roskilde** d.		03	...	...	33	...	...	53	...	...	05		50	...	...	...	53	...	...	05		50	...	...	...	53	...	...	05	...	...	...
	Hvalsø a.		18	25	...	48	55	...	07	13	...	19		05	11	...	...	07	13	...	19		05	11	...	...	07	13	...	19	...	...	...
67	Holbæk d.		...	50	57	...	20	...	...	38	51	...		...	36	51	...	...	38	51	...		...	36	51	...	...	38	51	...	...	...	...
111	**Kalundborg 2355** a.		...	...	37	...	...	...	...	...	32	...		...	...	32	...	...	...	32	...		...	...	32	...	...	...	32	...	...	...	...

		j	k	m	n	p		q	r	t	v		w	x	y		z	x	y	r	t	v		a	z	b	c		z	b	r	t	v
Kalundborg 2355 d.	①-⑤	00	🚌	...	🚌	...	...	🚌	...	...	...	⑥	00	🚌	...	...	00	🚌	...	...	...	...	⑦	00	00	🚌	...	...	00	🚌	...	...	...
Holbæk d.		41	48	...	18	...	...	53	...	...	...		38	53	...	...	41	53	...	...	...	...		38	41	53	...	...	41	53	...	...	...
Hvalsø d.		...	13	19	43	49	...	18	24	24	24		...	18	24	...	...	18	24	24	24	24		...	...	18	24	...	...	18	24	24	24
Roskilde d.		...	...	33	...	03	...	...	40	40	40		...	...	39	...	...	...	39	40	40	40		...	...	...	39	...	...	...	40	40	40
Høje Taastrup a.		...	...	44	...	14	...	...	52	52	51		...	...	49	...	...	...	49	52	52	51		...	...	...	49	...	...	...	52	52	51
København H a.		...	...	01	...	31	...	...	10	15	18		...	...	05	...	...	...	05	10	15	18		...	...	...	05	...	...	...	10	15	18

A – ①–⑤: 0436 - 1836.
B – ①–⑤: 0525 - 1925.
C – ①–⑤: 0457 - 1957.
D – ①–⑤: 0506 - 1806.
E – ①–⑤: 0555 - 1855.
F – Daily: 1924 - 2324.
G – Daily: 2013 - 0013.
H – ①–⑤: 2051 - 0051.
N – Daily: 0036 only.
P – ⑥: 0524 - 1824. 1724 departure runs 4 minutes **earlier** throughout.
Q – ⑥: 0611 - 1911.
R – ⑥: 0551 - 0051.
S – ⑦: 0624 - 1824.
T – ⑦: 0711 - 1911.
V – ⑦: 0651 - 0051.
a – ⑦: 0600 - 1900.
b – ⑦: 0653 - 2353.
c – ⑦: 0724 - 2024.
j – ①–⑤: 0500 - 2300.
k – ①–⑤: 0448 - 1948.
m – ①–⑤: 0519 - 2019.
n – ①–⑤: 0518 - 1918.
p – ①–⑤: 0549 - 1949.
q – ①–⑤: 2053 - 2353.
r – Daily: 2124 - 2224.
t – Daily: 2324 only.
v – Daily: 0024 only.
w – ⑥: 0500 - 1900.
x – ⑥: 0553 - 2353.
y – ⑥: 0624 - 2024.
z – ⑥⑦: 2000 - 2300.

FREDERICIA - ESBJERG 705

2nd class only (*IC* & *Lyn* 1st & 2nd class)

km						*IC* 821		*IC* 825		*IC* 829		*IC* 833		*IC* 837		*IC* 841		*IC* 845		*IC* 849		*IC* 853		*IC* 857		*IC* 861	
			①–⑥	①–⑤				①–⑥																Ⓑ			
	København H 700 d.	*0030*	...	...	...	0628	...	0728	...	0828	...	0928	...	1028	...	1128	...	1228	...	1328	...	1428	...	1528	...	1628	...
	Odense 700 d.	*0226*	...	...	...	0803	...	0903	...	1003	...	1103	...	1203	...	1303	...	1403	...	1503	...	1603	...	1703	...	1803	...
	Middelfart 700 d.	*0254*	...	...	...	0827	...	0927	...	1027	...	1127	...	1227	...	1327	...	1427	...	1527	...	1627	...	1727	...	1827	...
	Århus 700 d.	|	...	0610	0635j	|	0741	|	0841	|	0941	|	1041	|	1141	|	1241	|	1341	|	1441	|	1541	|	1641	|	1741
0	**Fredericia 700/10** d.	0315	0542	0714	0743	|	0843	|	0943	|	1043	|	1143	|	1243	|	1343	|	1443	|	1543	|	1643	|	1743	|	1843
20	Kolding 710 d.	0333	0557	0730	0757	0842	0857	0942	0957	1042	1057	1142	1157	1242	1257	1342	1357	1442	1457	1546	1557	1642	1657	1742	1757	1842	1857
33	Lunderskov 710 d.	0342	0605	0738	0806	|	0906	|	1006	|	1106	|	1206	|	1306	|	1406	|	1506	|	1606	|	1706	|	1806	|	1906
44	Vejen d.	0351	0613	0746	0813	0856	0913	0956	1013	1056	1113	1156	1213	1256	1313	1356	1413	1456	1513	1600	1613	1656	1713	1756	1813	1856	1913
72	Bramming 709 a.	0415	0635	0810	0836	0910	0936	1010	1036	1110	1136	1210	1236	1310	1336	1413	1436	1513	1536	1613	1636	1713	1736	1810	1836	1910	1936
88	**Esbjerg 709** a.	0427	0647	0821	0847	0922	0947	1022	1047	1122	1147	1222	1247	1322	1347	1426	1447	1526	1547	1626	1647	1726	1747	1822	1847	1922	1947

	IC 865		*IC* 869		*IC* 873		*IC* 877		*IC* 881 ⑥	*IC* 881 Ⓑ	
København H 700 d.	1728	...	1828	...	1928	...	2028	...	2128	...	...
Odense 700 d.	1903	...	2003	...	2103	...	2203	...	2303	...	...
Middelfart 700 d.	1927	...	2027	...	2127	...	2227	...	2327	...	...
Århus 700 d.	|	1841	|	1941	|	2041	|	2141	|	...	*2300*
redericia 700/10 d.	|	1943	|	2043	|	2143	|	2243	|	2333	0027
olding 710 d.	1942	1957	2042	2057	2142	2157	2246	2257	2347	2347	0042
underskov 710 d.	|	2006	|	2106	|	2206	|	2306	|	|	0050
'ejen d.	1956	2013	2056	2113	2156	2213	2300	2313	0003	0003	0058
ramming 709 a.	2010	2036	2110	2136	2210	2236	2314	2336	0019	0019	0121
:sbjerg 709 a.	2022	2047	2122	2147	2222	2247	2326	2347	0031	0031	0132

	IC 890 ①–⑥	*IC* 890 ⑦	*Lyn* 806 ①–⑤	t	*IC* 808 ①–⑤		*IC* 814 ①–⑥	*IC* 812 ⑦		*IC* 816	
Esbjerg 709 d.	0152	0152	0556	0612	0644	0721	0740	0742	0821	0837	0921
Bramming 709 d.	0204	0204	0606	0623	0655	0732	0751	0753	0832	0850	0932
Vejen d.	0226	0226	0621	0645	0710	0754	0808	0808	0854	0907	0954
Lunderskov 710 d.	0234	0234	|	0652	|	0802	|	|	0902	|	1002
Kolding 710 d.	0243	0243	0636	0702	0730	0812	0830	0825	0912	0930	1012
Fredericia 700/10 a.	0258	0258	|	0717	|	0826	|	|	0926	|	1026
Århus 700 a.	|	|	|	0828v	|	0932r	|	|	1031r	|	1131r
Middelfart 700 a.	*0312*	0312	|	...	0745	...	0845	0845	...	0945	...
Odense 700 a.	*0340*	0340	0717	...	0811	...	0911	0911	...	1011	...
København H 700 a.	*0537*	0537	0856	...	0951	...	1051	1051	...	1151	...

	IC 820		*IC* 824		*IC* 828		*IC* 832		*IC* 836		*IC* 840		*IC* 844/6		*IC* 848		*IC* 852		*IC* 856		*IC* 860		*IC* 862/4		*IC* 866/8		
sbjerg 709 d.	0944	1021	1044	1121	1144	1221	1244	1321	1344	1421	1444	1521	1544	1621	1644	1721	1744	1821	1844	1921	1944	2021	2042	2121	2142	2257	2351
ramming 709 d.	0955	1032	1055	1132	1155	1232	1255	1332	1355	1432	1455	1532	1555	1632	1655	1732	1755	1832	1855	1932	1955	2032	2053	2132	2153	2311	0002
ejen d.	1010	1054	1110	1154	1210	1254	1310	1354	1410	1454	1510	1554	1610	1654	1710	1754	1810	1854	1910	1954	2010	2054	2108	2154	2208	2336	0025
underskov 710 d.	|	1102	|	1202	|	1302	|	1402	|	1502	|	1602	|	1702	|	1802	|	1902	|	2002	|	2102	|	2202	|	2345	0033
olding 710 d.	1030	1112	1130	1212	1230	1312	1330	1412	1430	1512	1530	1612	1630	1712	1730	1812	1830	1912	1930	2012	2030	2112	2130	2212	2230	2354	0042
redericia 700/10 a.	|	1126	|	1226	|	1326	|	1426	|	1526	|	1626	|	1726	|	1826	|	1926	|	2026	|	2126	|	2226	|	0008	0056
Århus 700 a.	|	1231r	|	1331r	|	1428	|	1528	|	1628	|	1728	|	1828	|	1928	|	2028	|	2128	|	2228	|	2328	|	*0123*	...
Middelfart 700 a.	1045	...	1145	...	1245	...	1345	...	1445	...	1545	...	1645	...	1745	...	1845	...	1945	...	2045	...	2145	...	2245	...	...
Odense 700 a.	1111	...	1211	...	1311	...	1411	...	1511	...	1611	...	1711	...	1811	...	1911	...	2011	...	2111	...	2211	...	2315	...	...
København H 700 a.	1251	...	1351	...	1451	...	1551	...	1651	...	1751	...	1851	...	1951	...	2051	...	2151	...	2251	...	2355	...	0059	...	...

- Depart 0641 ①–⑤ until June 27 and from Aug. 18 (not Apr. 14 - 16, May 30, June 6).
- Arrive 3 – 4 minutes earlier on ①–⑤ until June 27 and from Aug. 18 (not Apr. 14 - 16, May 30, June 6).
- Runs 8 – 10 minutes later on ⑥⑦ (daily June 29 - Aug. 16; also Apr. 14 - 21, May 16, 29, 30, June 5 - 9).

v – Arrive 0833 on ⑥⑦ (daily June 29 - Aug. 16; also Apr. 14 - 21, May 16, 29, 30, June 5 - 9).

ESBJERG - SKJERN 707

)perator: *AT* 2nd class only

km																			⑥								
0	**Esbjerg 705** ⊗ d.	Ⓐ	0517	0602	0638	0739	0840	0930	1030	and	1530	1630	1730	1930	2130	...	Ⓒ	0503	0703	...	0903	and every	2103	...	2303
17	Varde ⊗ d.		0537	0630	0702	0803	0900	0954	1054	hourly	1554	1654	1754	1954	2154	...		0523	0723	...	0923	two hours	2123	...	2323
60	**Skjern 708/13** a.		0616	0714	0739	0841	0937	1034	1134	until	1634	1734	1834	2034	2234	...		0600	0800	...	1000	until	2200	...	2400

																⑥	⑥	†						
kjern 708/13 d.	Ⓐ	0525	0622	0645	0809	0946	1046	and	1546	1646	1746	1846	2046	2241	...	Ⓒ	0511	0625	0710	0825	1005	and every	2005	2205	...
ırde ⊗ d.		0605	0701	0729	0901	1029	1129	hourly	1629	1729	1829	1929	2129	2324	...		0551	0702	0750	0902	1043	two hours	2043	2243	...
:bjerg 705 ⊗ a.		0625	0723	*0800*	0923	1051	1151	until	1651	1751	1851	1951	2151	2344	...		0610	0724	0810	0924	1102	until	2102	2302	...

- Additional services operate Esbjerg - Varde and v.v.

708 SKJERN - STRUER

Operator: *AT* 2nd class only

km																									
																	⑥	⑥	†						
0	**Skjern 707/13** d.	Ⓐ	0442	0624	0716	0800	0847	0947	1047		1547	1646	1847	2047	2247	...	Ⓒ	0458	0602	0658	...	0802		2002	...	2202
23	Ringkøbing a.	Ⓐ	0500	0645	0734	0819	0906	1006	1106	and	1606	1708	1906	2106	2306	...	Ⓒ	0517	0621	0717	...	0821	and every	2021	...	2221
23	Ringkøbing d.	Ⓐ	0501	0646	0737	0820	0910	1010	1110	hourly	1610	1710	1910	2110	2310	...	Ⓒ	0518	0621	0718	...	0821	two hours	2021	...	2221
71	Holstebro a.	Ⓐ	0544	0726	0817	0902	0954	1054	1154	until	1654	1754	1954	2154	2350	...	Ⓒ	0601	0702	0801	...	0902	until	2102	...	2302
71	Holstebro **715** d.	Ⓐ	0553	0731	0818	0903	0955	1055	1155		1655	1755	1955	2203	2350	...	Ⓒ	0602	0703	0802	...	0903		2103	...	2303
86	**Struer 715** a.	Ⓐ	0607	0744	0833	0916	1008	1108	1208		1708	1808	2008	2216	0004	...	Ⓒ	0616	0716	0816	...	0917		2117	...	2317

																		⑥							
Struer 715 d.	Ⓐ	0500	0523	0632	0730	0900	1009	1109		1509	1609	1709	1909	2109	2251	...	Ⓒ	0501	0701	...	0848		2048	...	2248	...
Holstebro **715** a.	Ⓐ	0512	0536	0645	0744	0915	1021	1121	and	1521	1621	1721	1921	2121	2303	...	Ⓒ	0516	0716	...	0901	and every	2101	...	2301	...
Holstebro d.	Ⓐ	0513	0545	0652	0817	0922	1022	1122	hourly	1522	1622	1722	1922	2122	2304	...	Ⓒ	0517	0717	...	0902	two hours	2102	...	2302	...
Ringkøbing a.	Ⓐ	0554	0624	0736	0900	1004	1104	1204	until	1604	1704	1804	2004	2204	2348	...	Ⓒ	0557	0757	...	0942	until	2142	...	2342	...
Ringkøbing d.	Ⓐ	0555	0625	0737	0911	1011	1111	1211		1611	1711	1811	2011	2211	2349	...	Ⓒ	0558	0758	...	0943		2143	...	2343	...
Skjern 707/13 a.	Ⓐ	0614	0644	0756	0931	1031	1131	1231		1631	1731	1831	2031	2231	0008	...	Ⓒ	0621	0821	...	1002		2202	...	0002	...

709 ESBJERG - TØNDER - NIEBÜLL

2nd class only Operator: *AT*

A change of trains at Tønder may be necessary on some journeys

km																									
		⑥	Ⓐ	Ⓐ	Ⓐ	Ⓐ	⑥	†	Ⓐ		Ⓐ	⑥		Ⓐ	⑥		Ⓐ	⑥		Ⓐ		Ⓐ			
0	**Esbjerg 705** ⊗ d.	0508	0508	...	0627	...	0709	0709	0808	0909	1009	1009	1109	1209	1209	1309	1409	1409	1509	1609	1709	1809	1909	2009	2209
16	Bramming **705** ⊗ d.	0522	0522	...	0641	...	0723	0723	0822	0923	1023	1023	1123	1223	1223	1323	1423	1423	1523	1623	1723	1823	1923	2023	2223
33	Ribe ⊗ d.	0543	0549	...	0700	...	0743	0743	0843	0943	1043	1043	1143	1243	1243	1343	1443	1443	1543	1643	1743	1843	1943	2043	2243
80	**Tønder** a.	0631	0641	...	0749	...	0831	0831	0931	1031	1131	1131j	1231	1331	1331j	1431	1531	1531j	1631	1731	1831	1931	2031	2131	2331
80	**Tønder** d.	...	...	0722	...	0834	0834	...	...	1034	...	...	1234	1334	...	1434	1534	...	1634	...	1834	...	2034	...	...
97	Niebüll **821** a.	...	...	0741	...	0853	0853	...	...	1053	...	...	1253	1353	...	1453	1553	...	1653	...	1853	...	2053	...	...

	⑥	Ⓐ	⑥	Ⓐ	Ⓐ	†	⚒	†	Ⓐ		Ⓐ	⑥		Ⓐ	⑥		Ⓐ	⑥		Ⓐ		Ⓐ		
Niebüll **821** d.	...	...	...	...	0701	...	0807	...	...	1007	...	...	1207	1310	...	1407	1507	...	1607	...	1807	...	2007	...
Tønder a.	...	...	...	...	0719	...	0824	...	...	1024	...	...	1224	1327	...	1424	1524	...	1624	...	1824	...	2024	...
Tønder d.	0535	0609	0635	0650	...	0735	0835	0835	0935	1035	1135	1135j	1235	1335	1335j	1435	1535	1535j	1635	1735	1835	1935	2035	2235
Ribe ⊗ d.	0625	0702	0725	0742	...	0825	0925	0925	1025	1125	1225	1225	1325	1425	1425	1525	1625	1625	1725	1825	1925	2025	2125	2325
Bramming **705** ⊗ a.	0644	0720	0744	0800	...	0844	0944	0944	1044	1144	1244	1244	1344	1444	1444	1544	1644	1644	1744	1844	1944	2044	2144	2344
Esbjerg 705 ⊗ a.	0659	0735	0759	0815	...	0859	0959	0959	1059	1159	1259	1259	1359	1459	1459	1559	1659	1659	1759	1859	1959	2059	2159	2359

j – June 28 - Sept. 6.

⊗ – Additional services operate Esbjerg - Ribe and v.v.

710 FREDERICIA - SØNDERBORG and FLENSBURG (- HAMBURG)

km		*IC* 5727	*IC* 807	*Lyn* 2		*IC* 109	*IC* 5747	*IC* 917	*IC* 5721	*IC* 5721	*Lyn* 19	*ICE* 381		*IC* 925	*IC* 5729	*IC* 933	*IC* 5737	*IC* 941	*IC* 5745		*IC* 145	*EC* 387	*IC* 949	*IC* 5753	*IC* 957
		①–⑥		①–⑤		①–⑤			①–⑥	⑦	①–⑥	♦x		♣	♠	♣	♠	♣	♠			♦y	♣	♠	
	København H **700** d.	...	0218	...	...	...	...	0528	0628	...	0650	...	...	0728	0828	0928	1028	1128	1228	...	1300	...	1328	1428	1528
	Odense **700** d.	...	0411	...	...	0533	...	0703	0803	...	0807	...	...	0903	1003	1103	1203	1303	1403	...	1433	...	1503	1603	1703
	Århus **700** d.	...	|	0419	...	|	...	|	|	...	|	0756	...	|	|	|	|	|	|	...	|	1424	|	|	|
0	**Fredericia 700** d.	...	0450	0523	0532	0606	0633	|	|	0834	0836	0900	...	|	|	|	|	|	|	...	1506	1527	|	|	|
*	Middelfart **700** d.	...	...	...	|	...	|	0727	0827	|	...	|	...	0927	1027	1127	1227	1327	1427	...	...	|	1527	1627	1727
20	Kolding **705** d.	...	...	...	0548	...	0646	0746	0846	0846	...	0913	...	0946	1046	1146	1246	1346	1446	...	...	1540	1550	1646	1746
33	Lunderskov **705** d.	...	...	...	0555	...	0654	0754	0854	0854	...	|	...	0954	1054	1154	1254	1354	1454	...	...	|	1558	1654	1754
60	Vojens d.	...	...	...	0615	...	0715	0813	0915	0915	...	|	...	1013	1115	1213	1315	1413	1511	...	...	|	1615	1715	1813
95	Tinglev d.	0619	...	...	0637	...	0737	0834	0937	0937	...	|	...	1034	1137	1234	1337	1434	1534	...	...	|	1636	1737	1834
136	**Sønderborg** a.	|	...	...	0711	...	|	0908	|	|	...	|	...	1108	|	1308	|	1508	|	...	...	|	1709	|	1908
110	Padborg 🏛 a.	0635	...	...	...	...	0752	...	0952	0952	...	1010	...	...	1152	...	1352	...	1552	...	...	1640	...	1752	...
122	**Flensburg** 🏛 **823** a.	0647	...	...	...	...	0804	...	1004	1004	...	1022	...	...	1203	...	1404	...	1604	...	...	1651	...	1804	...
302	*Hamburg Hbf* **823** a.	...	...	...	...	...	...	...	...	...	...	1230	...	...	...	...	...	...	...	...	...	1853	...	...	...

	IC 5761	*IC* 965	*IC* 5769	*EN* 473	*EN* 473	*IC* 973	*IC* 173	*IC* 981	*IC* 179	
			♧	⑥ ♦🅁	Ⓑ ♦🅁	♧	♤	♧		
København H **700** d.	1628	1728	1828	1724	1846	1928	2028	2128	2200	...
Odense **700** d.	1803	1903	2003	1855	2028	2103	2203	2303	2339	...
Århus **700** d.	|	|	|	|	|	|	|	|	|	...
Fredericia 700 d.	|	|	|	|	|	|	|	|	0014	0027
Middelfart **700** d.	1827	1927	2027	|	|	2127	2227	2327	...	|
Kolding **705** d.	1846	1946	2046	1953	2110	2146	2242	2342	...	0042
Lunderskov **705** d.	1854	1954	2054	|	|	2154	2250	2350	...	0050
Vojens d.	1915	2013	2115	|	|	2213	2308	0015	...	...
Tinglev d.	1937	2034	2137	|	|	2234	2332	0037	...	...
Sønderborg a.	|	2108	|	|	|	2308	|	0111	...	...
Padborg 🏛 a.	1952	...	2152	2118	2224	...	2343	...	...	...
Flensburg 🏛 **823** a.	2004	...	2203	2133	2238	...	...	...	...	...
Hamburg Hbf **823** a.	...	...	...	0001	0031	...	...	...	...	...

	IC 8002		*IC* 908	*EN* 472	*EN* 472		*IC* 5722	*IC* 916	*IC* 5720	*IC* 924
	①–⑤	①–⑤		①–⑥ ♦🅁	⑦ ♦🅁	⑦	①–⑥		♥	♣
Hamburg Hbf **823** d.	...	...	...	0355	0348	...	...	...	...	...
Flensburg 🏛 **823** d.	...	...	...	0553	0636	...	0656	...	0856	...
Padborg 🏛 d.	...	0542	...	0607	0707	...	0710	...	0910	...
Sønderborg d.	0449	|	0553	|	|	...	|	0753	|	0953
Tinglev d.	0523	0554	0628	|	|	0717	0722	0828	0923	1028
Vojens d.	0543	0616	0647	|	|	0738	0745	0847	0944	1047
Lunderskov **705** d.	0600	0635	0711	|	|	0758	0811	0911	1011	1111
Kolding **705** d.	0609	0644	0729	0732	0837	0807	0830	0930	1030	1130
Middelfart **700** a.	0623	|	0745	|	|	|	0845	0945	1045	1145
Fredericia 700 a.	|	0659	|	|	|	0820	|	|	|	|
Århus **700** a.	|	...	|	|	|	...	|	|	|	|
Odense **700** a.	0649	...	0811	0817	0920	...	0911	1011	1111	1211
København H **700** a.	0826	...	0951	1008	1054	...	1051	1151	1251	1351

	IC 5728	*EC* 386	*IC* 132	*IC* 932	*IC* 5736	*IC* 940	*IC* 5744	*ICE* 380	*IC* 148	*IC* 948	*IC* 952	*IC* 5752	*IC* 852	*IC* 5752	*IC* 956	*IC* 5760	*IC* 860	*IC* 964	*IC* 5768	*IC* 868	*IC* 5726	*IC* 2370/6	*IC* 176		
	♠	♦z		♣	♠	♣	♠	♦y		♣	B	A		⑤⑥	♥			♧	♧	Ⓑ	Ⓑ	Ⓑ		Ⓑ	
Hamburg Hbf **823** d.	...	0930	...	...	...	...	...	1330	...	...	...	...	...	...	...	...	...	...	...	...	...	...	...	...	...
Flensburg 🏛 **823** d.	1056	1124	...	...	1256	...	1456	1532	...	...	...	1656	...	1656	...	1856	...	...	2056	...	2212	...	...	...	...
Padborg 🏛 d.	1110	1148	...	...	1310	...	1510	1550	...	...	...	1710	...	1710	...	1910	...	...	2115	...	2228	...	...	...	...
Sønderborg d.	|	|	...	1153	|	1353	|	|	...	1553	1624	|	...	|	1753	|	...	1953	|	...	|	2159	...	2344	...
Tinglev d.	1122	|	...	1228	1322	1428	1522	|	...	1628	1706	1722	...	1722	1828	1922	...	2028	2128	...	2239	2245	...	0025	...
Vojens d.	1145	|	...	1247	1345	1447	1545	|	...	1647	1726	1745	...	1745	1847	1945	...	2047	2151	...	...	2304	...	0046	...
Lunderskov **705** d.	1211	|	...	1311	1411	1511	1611	|	...	1711	...	1811	...	1811	1911	2011	...	2111	2211	...	...	2324	...	0108	...
Kolding **705** d.	1230	1242	...	1330	1430	1530	1630	1639	...	1730	...	1820	1830	1830	1930	2020	2030	2130	2220	2230	...	2332	...	0117	...
Middelfart **700** a.	1245	|	...	1345	1445	1545	1645	|	...	1745	...	|	1845	1845	1945	|	2045	2145	|	2245	...	|	...	|	...
Fredericia 700 a.	|	1254	1309	|	|	|	|	1653	1709	|	...	1833	|	|	|	2033	|	|	2233	|	...	2345	0014	0132	...
Århus **700** a.	|	1400	|	|	|	|	|	1759	|	|	...	...	|	|	|	...	|	|	...	|	...	...	|	...	...
Odense **700** a.	1311	...	1343	1411	1511	1611	1711	...	1743	1811	...	...	1911	1911	2011	...	2111	2211	...	2315	...	...	0051	...	...
København H **700** a.	1451	...	1518	1551	1651	1751	1851	...	1918	1951	...	...	2051	2051	2151	...	2251	2355	...	0059	...	...	0240	...	...

♦ – **NOTES** (LISTED BY TRAIN NUMBER)

380/1 – 🚃12 and 🍷 Berlin - Hamburg - Århus and v.v.

386/7 – 🚃12 and 🍷 Århus - Fredericia - Hamburg and v.v.

472 – *City Night Line* – 🛏 1, 2 cl. and 🛌 2 cl. (4 / 6 berth) Basel (**472/1272**) - Frankfurt - København; 🛏 1, 2 cl., 🛌 2 cl. and 🚃2 [reclining] Amsterdam (**40457**) - Köln - København; 🛏 1, 2 cl. and 🛌 2 cl. Praha (**40456**) - København. For passengers making international journeys only.

473 – *City Night Line* – 🛏 1, 2 cl. and 🛌 2 cl. (4 / 6 berth) København (**473/1273**) - Frankfurt - Basel; 🛏 1, 2 cl., 🛌 2 cl. and 🚃2 [reclining] København (**40453**) - Köln - Amsterdam; 🛏 1, 2 cl. and 🛌 2 cl. København (**50473**) - Praha. For passengers making international journeys only.

A – ①②③④⑦ only. **B** – ① from Mar. 17.

x – Not Mar. 22, 23, Apr. 5, 6, 18 - 22, May 18 - 20.

y – ②–⑦ (also Mar. 3, 10; not Mar. 22, 23, Apr. 17 - 20, May 17, 18).

z – ②–⑦ (also Mar. 3, 10; not Apr. 18 - 22, May 18 - 20).

♣ – On ① (not Dec. 16 - Mar. 10) subject to alteration owing to engineering work. Service retimed and diverted to Flensburg including partial replacement by 🚌.

♠ – On ① (not Dec. 16 - Mar. 10) subject to alteration owing to engineering work. Service retimed and diverted to Sønderborg including partial replacement by 🚌.

♥ – On ① (not Dec. 16 - Mar. 10) subject to alteration owing to engineering work. Service retimed including partial replacement by 🚌.

♧ – On ⑥ subject to alteration owing to engineering work. Service retimed including partial replacement by 🚌.

♤ – ①–⑥ only. On ⑥ subject to alteration owing to engineering work. Service retimed includi[ng] partial replacement by 🚌.

* – Middelfart - Kolding: *23 km*.

Operator: *AT* 2nd class only (*IC* & *Lyn* 1st & 2nd class)

ÅRHUS - VIBORG - STRUER 712

km		Ⓐ						♣								♣					Ⓒ	⑥	⑥	⑥	†
	København H **700** ... d.		...	...	...	...	...	...	...	...	...	...	...	...	...	...	...	...	...	...		...	...	...	...
0	**Århus 700** ⊗ d.		0512	0624	0736	0836	0936	1036	1136	1236	1336	1436	1536	1636	1736	1836	1936	2036	2136	2236		...	0534	0636	...
46	Langå **701** ⊗ a.		0542	0655	0807	0906	1006	1106	1206	1306	1406	1506	1606	1706	1806	1906	2006	2106	2206	2306		...	0604	0706	...
46	Langå ⊗ d.		0546	0659	0813	0913	1013	1113	1213	1313	1413	1513	1613	1713	1813	1913	2013	2113	2213	2313		...	0613	0713	...
86	Viborg ⊗ d.		0622	0733	0843	0943	1043	1143	1243	1343	1443	1543	1643	1743	1843	1943	2043	2143	2243	2343		0543	0643	0743	0743
116	Skive d.		0646	0756	0914	1014	1114	1214	1314	1414	1514	1614	1714	1814	1914	2014	2107	2214	2314	0008		0614	0714	0814	0814
148	**Struer 715 716** a.		0716	0819	0941	1041	1141	1241	1341	1441	1541	1641	1741	1841	1941	2041	...	2241	2341	0031		0641	0741	0841	0841

																					621	**625**	**653**	**657**
			†	⑥	♣	♣				⑥	†				♣					♣	①–⑥	⑦	①–⑤	⑥⑦
København H **700** ... d.	...	...	...	...	...	...	...	...	...	...	...	...	...	...	...	...	...	...	...		0700	0800	1500	1600
Århus 700 ⊗ d.	0736	0836	0936	0936	1036	1136	1236	1336	1436	1536	1536	1636	1736	1836	1936	2036	2136	2236	2336	DSB	1036	1136	1836	1936
Langå **701** ⊗ a.	0806	0906	1006	1006	1106	1206	1306	1406	1506	1606	1606	1706	1806	1906	2006	2106	2206	2306	0006	*IC/Lyn*	1106	1206	1906	2006
Langå ⊗ d.	0813	0913	1013	1013	1113	1213	1313	1413	1513	1613	1613	1713	1813	1913	2013	2113	2213	2313	0013	services	1113	1213	1913	2013
Viborg ⊗ d.	0843	0943	1043	1043	1143	1243	1343	1443	1543	1643	1643	1743	1843	1943	2043	2143	2243	2343	0042	▶▶▶▶	1143	1243	1943	2043
Skive d.	0914	1014	1107	1114	1214	1314	1414	1514	1614	1707	1714	1814	1914	2014	2114	2214	2314	0008	...		1214	1314	2014	2114
Struer 715 716 a.	0941	1041	...	1141	1241	1341	1441	1541	1641	...	1741	1841	1941	2041	2141	2241	2341	0031	...		1241	1341	2041	2141

	Ⓐ						♣								♣						Ⓒ	⑥	⑥	⑥	†
Struer 715 716 d.		0454	0535	0637	0719	0821	0921	1021	1121	1221	1321	1421	1521	1621	1721	1821	1921	2021	...	2221		...	0521	0621	...
Skive d.		0517	0558	0703	0742	0844	0944	1044	1144	1244	1344	1444	1544	1644	1744	1844	1944	2044	2144	2244		...	0544	0644	...
Viborg ⊗ d.		0540	0621	0729	0808	0908	1008	1108	1208	1308	1408	1508	1608	1708	1808	1908	2008	2108	2208	2308		0526	0608	0708	0708
Langå ⊗ a.		0611	0652	0800	0839	0939	1039	1139	1239	1339	1439	1539	1639	1739	1839	1939	2039	2139	2239	2339		0555	0639	0739	0739
Langå **701** ⊗ d.		0615	0701	0804	0843	0943	1046	1143	1243	1343	1443	1543	1643	1743	1846	1943	2043	2143	2243	2343		0600	0643	0743	0743
Århus 700 ⊗ a.		0647	0733	0835	0915	1015	1116	1215	1315	1415	1515	1615	1715	1815	1916	2015	2115	2215	2315	0015		0632	0715	0815	0815
København H **700** ... a.		...	...	...	...	...	...	...	...	...	...	...	...	...	...	...	...	...	...	...		...	...	...	...

																					628	**654**	**660**	**660**
			♣		⑥	†				♣		⑥	♣							♣		⑥	①–⑤	⑦
Struer 715 716 d.	0721	0821	0921	1021	1121	...	1221	1321	1421	1521	1621	...	1721	1821	1921	2021	2121	2221	2321		0921	1521	1721	1721
Skive d.	0744	0844	0944	1044	1144	1144	1244	1344	1444	1544	1644	1744	1744	1844	1944	2044	2144	2244	2344	DSB	0944	1544	1744	1744
Viborg ⊗ d.	0808	0908	1008	1108	1208	1208	1308	1408	1508	1608	1708	1808	1808	1908	2008	2108	2208	2308	0007	*IC/Lyn*	1008	1608	1808	1808
Langå ⊗ a.	0839	0939	1039	1139	1239	1239	1339	1439	1539	1639	1739	1839	1839	1939	2039	2139	2239	2339	...	services	1039	1639	1839	1839
Langå **701** ⊗ d.	0843	0943	1046	1143	1243	1243	1343	1443	1543	1643	1743	1843	1846	1943	2043	2143	2243	2343	...	▶▶▶▶	1046	1646	1846	1846
Århus 700 ⊗ a.	0915	1015	1116	1215	1315	1315	1415	1515	1615	1715	1815	1915	1916	2015	2115	2215	2315	0015	...		1116	1715	1916	1916
København H **700** ... a.	...	...	...	...	...	...	...	...	...	...	...	...	...	...	...	...	...	...	...		1422	2022	2222	2222

♣ – Runs as DSB *Lyn* service on some days/dates – see panel (and heading).
⊗ – Additional services operate Århus - Viborg and v.v.

See **Table 715** below for direct services Struer - Herning - København and v.v.

Operator: *AT* 2nd class only

ÅRHUS - HERNING - SKJERN 713

km		Ⓐ															Ⓒ	⑥									
0	**Århus 700** ⊗ d.		0500	0600	0710	0809	0849	and at	1409	1449	1509	1609	1809	2009	2109	2314		0509	0709	0809	0909	1009	and	1909	2009	2109	2314
23	Skanderborg **700** ⊗ d.		0520	0620	0731	0831	0909	the same	1431	1509	1531	1631	1831	2031	2131	2336		0531	0731	0831	0931	1031	every	1931	2031	2131	2336
53	Silkeborg ⊗ d.		0549	0651	0803	0903	0938	minutes	1503	1538	1603	1703	1903	2103	2203	0011		0603	0803	0903	1003	1103	two	2003	2103	2203	0011
94	**Herning** ⊗ a.		0633	0733	0847	0947	1008	past	1547	1608	1647	1747	1947	2147	2247	0047		0647	0847	0947	1047	1147	hours	2047	2147	2247	0047
94	**Herning 715** d.		0642	0751	0850	0949	...	each hour	1549	...	1652	*1752*	1950	2150	*2320*	...		*0717*	*0917*	...	*1117*	...	until	*2117*	...	*2317*	...
136	**Skjern 707 708** a.		0721	0830	0930	1028	...	until	1628	...	1728	*1828*	2027	2227	*2357*	...		*0753*	*0953*	...	*1153*	...		*2153*	...	*2353*	...

	Ⓐ															Ⓒ	⑥	⑥	†								
Skjern 707 708 d.		0525	0703	0743	0845	...	0942	and at	...	1542	1640	1740	1843	2043	2243		*0506*	*0622*	*0706*	*0822*	...	*1014*	and	...	*1814*	2014	*2214*
Herning 715 a.		0602	0740	0820	0920	...	1019	the same	...	1619	1720	1820	1920	2120	2320		*0545*	*0659*	*0745*	*0859*	...	*1051*	every	...	*1851*	2051	*2251*
Herning ⊗ d.		0603	0802	0821	0921	1008	1021	minutes	1608	1621	1721	1821	1921	*2153*	2321		0621	0721	0821	0921	1021	1121	two	1821	1921	2053	2321
Silkeborg ⊗ d.		0638	0840	0904	1004	1040	1104	past	1640	1704	1804	1904	2004	*2234*	2358		0704	0804	0904	1004	1104	1204	hours	1904	2004	2134	2358
Skanderborg **700** ⊗ a.		0701	0903	0931	1031	1103	1131	each hour	1703	1731	1831	1931	2031	*2303*	0025		0731	0831	0931	1031	1131	1231	until	1931	2031	2203	0025
Århus 700 ⊗ a.		0722	0923	0953	1053	1123	1153	until	1723	1753	1853	1953	2053	*2325*	0045		0753	0853	0953	1053	1153	1253		1953	2053	2223	0045

⊗ – Additional services operate Århus - Herning and v.v.

2nd class only (*IC* & *Lyn* 1st & 2nd class)

FREDERICIA - STRUER - THISTED 715

km		*IC* **791**	*IC* **807**					*Lyn* **15**		*Lyn* **721**	*Lyn* **719**	*Lyn* **23**		*Lyn* **727**	*Lyn* **29**		*Lyn* **741**	*Lyn* **43**		*Lyn* **745**	*Lyn* **47**		*Lyn* **751**	*Lyn* **55**	*Lyn* **755**
				①–⑤	⑥	①–⑤	⑥	①–⑥		⑦	①–⑥														①–④
	København H **700** ... d.	*0030*	0218	...	...	...	...	0550	...	...	0650	0750	...	0850	0950	...	1050	1150	...	1250	1350	...	1450	1550	1550
	Odense **700** d.	*0226*	0411	...	...	...	...	0707	...	0807	0807	0907	...	1007	1107	...	1207	1307	...	1407	1507	...	1607	1707	1707
0	**Fredericia 700** d.	0314	0456	0502	0502	0614	0641	0738	0742	0841	0841	0938	0941	1042	1138	1141	1241	1338	1341	1441	1538	1541	1641	1738	1741
26	Vejle **700** d.	0331	0510	0523	0523	0631	0702	0753	0801	0902	0902	0953	1002	1102	1153	1202	1302	1353	1402	1502	1553	1602	1702	1753	1802
99	Herning a.	0426	...	0628	0625	0734	0801	...	0901	1001	1001	...	1101	1201	...	1301	1401	...	1501	1601	...	1701	1801	...	1901
99	Herning **713** d.	0428	...	0636	0636	0746	0803	...	0903	1003	1003	...	1103	1203	...	1303	1403	...	1503	1603	...	1703	1803	...	1903
140	Holstebro **708** d.	0500	...	0715	0717	0834	0835	...	0935	1035	1035	...	1135	1235	...	1335	1435	...	1535	1635	...	1735	1835	...	1935
155	**Struer 708** a.	0514	...	0729	0731	0845	0847	...	0947	1047	1047	...	1147	1247	...	1347	1447	...	1547	1647	...	1747	1847	...	1947
229	*Thisted* **716** a.	...	...	...	...	...	...	...	...	...	...	...	...	1407c	...	...	...	...	...	...	...	...	...	...	...

		Lyn **759**	*Lyn* **63**		*Lyn* **765**	*Lyn* **69**		*IC* **777**	*Lyn* **773**
	⑤–⑦						Ⓑ	①–④	⑤–⑦
København H **700** ... d.	...	1650	1750	...	1850	1950	...	2028	2050
Odense **700** d.	...	1807	1907	...	2007	2107	...	2203	2207
Fredericia 700 d.	1741	1841	1938	1941	2041	2138	2141	2244	2244
Vejle **700** d.	1802	1902	1953	2002	2102	2153	2202	2304	2304
Herning a.	1901	2001	...	2101	2201	...	2302	2358	2358
Herning **713** d.	1903	2003	...	2103	2203	...	2303	0003	0003
Holstebro **708** d.	1935	2035	...	2135	2235	...	2335	0035	0035
Struer 708 a.	1947	2047	...	2147	2247	...	2347	0047	0047
Thisted **716** a.	...	2207	...	...	...	...	...	...	...

	Lyn **706**	*Lyn* **710**		*IC* **112**	*Lyn* **714**	*IC* **712**		*IC* **116**		*Lyn* **18**	*Lyn* **722**
	①–⑤	①–⑤	①–⑤		①–⑥	⑦	①–⑤				⑥⑦
Thisted **716** d.	...	...	...	...	...	...	...	...	...	...	0655
Struer 708 d.	0428	0531	0538	...	0618	0618	0640	...	0716	...	0819
Holstebro **708** d.	0441	0545	0553	...	0632	0632	0654	...	0733	...	0833
Herning **713** a.	0515	0611	0628	...	0701	0701	0729	...	0803	...	0902
Herning d.	0524	0613	0630	...	0703	0703	0734	...	0804	...	0904
Vejle **700** d.	0622	0708	0731	0747	0803	0803	0833	0847	0903	0912	1002
Fredericia 700 a.	0638	0724	0750	0804	0823	0823	0854	0904	0924	0929	1022
Odense **700** a.	0717	0804	...	0843	0905	0911	...	0943	...	1005	1105
København H **700** a.	0856	0922	...	1025	1029	1051	...	1125	...	1129	1222

	Lyn **724**		*Lyn* **26**	*Lyn* **726**		*Lyn* **40**	*Lyn* **742**		*Lyn* **44**	*Lyn* **746**			*Lyn* **50**	*Lyn* **754**		*Lyn* **56**	*Lyn* **760**		*Lyn* **64**	*IC* **772**	*Lyn* **68**	*IC* **172**		*IC* **176**	
	①–⑤																				⑦				
Thisted **716** d.	0656	...	...	...	...	...	...	...	...	...	...	...	...	1455c	...	...	...	...	...	...	...	...	...	...	...
Struer 708 d.	0820	0918	...	1018	1118	...	1218	1318	...	1418	...	1518	...	1618	1718	...	1818	1918	...	2018	...	...	2149	...	...
Holstebro **708** d.	0833	0933	...	1033	1133	...	1233	1333	...	1433	...	1533	...	1633	1733	...	1833	1933	...	2033	...	...	2204	...	...
Herning **713** a.	0902	1003	...	1102	1203	...	1302	1403	...	1502	...	1603	...	1702	1803	...	1902	2003	...	2102	...	...	2238	...	...
Herning d.	0904	1004	...	1104	1204	...	1304	1404	...	1504	...	1604	...	1704	1804	...	1904	2004	...	2104	...	...	2240	...	...
Vejle **700** d.	1003	1103	1112	1203	1303	1312	1403	1501	1512	1603	...	1703	1712	1803	1903	1912	2003	2103	2112	2203	2212	2247	2354j	2350	...
Fredericia 700 a.	1023	1123	1129	1223	1324	1329	1423	1522	1529	1623	...	1724	1729	1823	1924	1929	2023	2124	2129	2223	2229	2306	0015	0009	...
Odense **700** a.	1105	...	1205	1305	...	1405	1505	...	1605	1705	...	...	1805	1905	...	2005	2105	...	2205	2257g	2307	2347	...	0051	...
København H **700** a.	1222	...	1329	1422	...	1529	1622	...	1729	1829	...	...	1929	2022	...	2129	2229	...	2329	...	0048	0140	...	0240	...

– ⑥⑦ only. g – ①–⑥ only. j – Arrive 2344.

716 STRUER - THISTED
2nd class only (*Lyn* 1st & 2nd class) Operator: *AT* (*Lyn* trains: *DSB*)

km		Ⓐ													Ⓒ											
														759							727				759	
														K		⑥	⑥	†			K				K	
0	Struer 708/12/5 ....d.		0446	0540	0730	0950	1151	1251	1351	1451	1551	1651	1850	2050	2250	0524	0650	0726	0850	1050	1250	1450	1650	1850	2050	2250
74	Thisted ....a.		0608	0727	0919	1107	1308	1409	1509	1609	1709	1809	2007	2207	0007	0641	0807	0846	1007	1207	1407	1607	1807	2007	2207	0007

	Ⓐ														Ⓒ											
			724														722				754					
			K													⑥	K				K					
Thisted ....d.		0612	0656	0756	0955	1211	1314	1414	1514	1614	1714	1855	2055	2255	...	0529	0655	0855	1055	1255	1455	1655	1855	2055	2255	...
Struer 708/12/5 ....a.		0729	0818	0914	1114	1339	1440	1539	1639	1739	1839	2014	2214	0015	...	0649	0814	1014	1214	1414	1614	1814	2014	2214	0015	...

K – 12 København - Struer - Thisted and v.v. InterCityLyn (*Lyn*) service (see Table **715**).

720 KØBENHAVN - RØDBY - PUTTGARDEN (- HAMBURG)

km										*ICE*				*ICE*				*ICE*				*EC*			
		4201	2201							38				36				34	2229	1229		238	1233		
		①–⑤	①–⑤	⑥⑦	①–⑤	⑥⑦	①–⑤	①–⑤	⑥⑦	B		①–⑥				①–⑥				①–⑥		C	W		
0	**København** H **700/4** ....d.	...	0440	0511	0540	0611	0642	0709	0711	0742	0811	0842	0911	0942	1011	1042	1111	1142	1211	1242	1311	1342	1342	1411	1442
20	Høje Taastrup **700/4** ....d.	...	0455	0527	0555	0627	0655	0725	0727	0758	0827	0857	0927	0958	1027	1057	1127	1158	1227	1257	1327	1358	1357	1427	1457
31	Roskilde **700/4** ....d.	...	0504	0537	0605	0637	0704	0734	0737	|	0837	|	0937	|	1037	|	1137	|	1237	|	1337	|	|	1437	|
64	Ringsted **700** ....d.	...	0523	0556	0624	0656	0722	0753	0756	|	0856	|	0956	|	1056	|	1156	|	1256	|	1356	|	|	1456	|
91	Næstved ....d.	...	0543	0616	0650	0716	0742	0814	0816	0833	0916	0933	1016	1033	1116	1133	1216	1233	1316	1333	1416	1433	1433	1516	1533
118	Vordingborg ....d.	...	0603	0637	0710	0737	0803	0835	0837	0848	0937	0948	1037	1048	1137	1148	1237	1248	1337	1348	1437	1448	1448	1537	1548
147	Nykøbing (Falster) .... ⊙ d.	0512	0637	0701	0737	0800	0827	0903	0903	0912	1003	1008	1103	1112	1203	1208	1303	1312	1412	1412	1503	1512	1508	1603	1608
183	**Rødby** .... ⛴ ▲ a.	0540	0702	...	...	...	...	...	...	0935	...	...	...	1135	...	...	...	1335	1435e	1435r	...	1535	1535a	...	...
202	**Puttgarden** .... ⛴ ▲ a.	...	...	...	...	...	...	...	...	1036	...	...	...	1236	...	...	...	1436	...	...	...	1636	...	...	...
291	*Lübeck* **825** ....a.	...	...	...	...	...	...	...	...	1137	...	...	...	1337	...	...	...	1537	...	...	...	1737	...	...	...
353	*Hamburg Hbf* **825** ....a.	...	...	...	...	...	...	...	...	1216	...	...	...	1416	...	...	...	1616	...	...	...	1816	...	...	...

				ICE								*EC*													
				32	2247						1249	30					4261								
	①–⑤	⑥⑦	①–⑤		①–⑤	⑥⑦	①–⑤	⑧		①–⑤	Q	D		⑧		⑦		⑦		⑦				⑥⑦	P
København H § **700/4** .... d.	1509	1511	1537	1542	1609	1611	1637	1642	1711	1737	1742	1742	1811	1842	1904	1942	2004	2042	2104	2142	2204	2311	0014	0118	...
Høje Taastrup § **700/4** .... d.	1525	1527	1554	1558	1625	1627	1654	1657	1727	1754	1757	1758	1827	1857	1920	1957	2020	2057	2120	2157	2220	2325	0029	0131	...
Roskilde § **700/4** .... d.	1534	1537	1606	|	1634	1637	1706	|	1737	1806	|	|	1837	|	1929	|	2029	|	2129	|	2229	2333	0038	0143	...
Ringsted § **700** .... d.	1553	1556	1624	|	1653	1656	1724	|	1756	1824	|	|	1856	|	1954	|	2054	|	2154	|	2256	0001	0104	0204	0211
Næstved § .... d.	1614	1616	1643	1633	1714	1716	1743	1733	1816	1843	1833	1833	1916	1933	2014	2033	2114	2133	2214	2233	2316	0021	0123	...	0231
Vordingborg .... d.	1635	1637	1703	1648	1735	1737	1803	1748	1837	1903	1848	1848	1937	1948	2034	2048	2134	2148	2234	2248	2336	0041	0141	...	...
Nykøbing (Falster) .... ⊙ d.	1703	1703	1727	1712	1806	1803	1827	1808	1903	1927	1912	1912	2003	2008	2058	2109	2206	2208	2258	2309	2400	0105	0204	...	...
Rødby .... ⛴ ▲ a.	...	...	...	1735	1834	...	...	...	...	...	1935	1935	...	...	...	...	2235	...	...	...	...	...	...	...	...
Puttgarden .... ⛴ ▲ a.	...	...	...	1836	...	...	...	...	...	...	...	2036	...	...	...	...	...	...	...	...	...	...	...	...	...
Lübeck **825** .... a.	...	...	...	1937	...	...	...	...	...	...	...	2137	...	...	...	...	...	...	...	...	...	...	...	...	...
Hamburg Hbf **825** .... a.	...	...	...	2016	...	...	...	...	...	...	...	2216	...	...	...	...	...	...	...	...	...	...	...	...	...

																				EC					*ICE*
									4208				1214							31	1226				33
	①–⑤	⑥⑦	①–⑤	①–⑤	①–⑤	①–⑤			①–⑤	①–⑤	⑥⑦	①–⑤	①–⑤			①–⑥		①–⑥		E	N		①–⑥		
Hamburg Hbf **825** .... d.	...	...	...	...	...	...	...	...	...	...	...	...	...	...	...	...	...	...	...	0725	...	...	...	...	0928
Lübeck **825** .... d.	...	...	...	...	...	...	...	...	...	...	...	...	...	...	...	...	...	...	...	0806	...	...	...	...	1006
Puttgarden .... ⛴ ▲ d.	...	...	...	...	...	...	...	...	...	...	...	...	...	...	...	...	...	...	...	0908	...	...	...	...	1108
Rødby .... ⛴ ▲ d.	...	...	...	...	...	...	...	...	0614	...	...	...	0716	...	...	...	...	...	...	1010	1010	...	...	...	1210
Nykøbing (Falster) .... ⊙ d.	0434	0438	0444	0509	0534	0544	0610	...	0642	0651	0710	0710	0744	...	0810	0841	0910	0941	1010	1041	1041	1110	1141	1210	1241
Vordingborg .... d.	0459	0502	0504	0534	0559	0604	0634	...	0706	0711	0734	0736	0804	...	0834	0904	0934	1004	1034	1104	1104	1134	1204	1234	1304
Næstved .... d.	0526	0523	0521	0555	0627	0621	0655	...	0723	0732	0755	0757	0821	...	0855	0921	0955	1021	1055	1121	1121	1155	1221	1255	1321
Ringsted **700** .... d.	0546	0543	|	0614	0649	|	0716	...	|	0751	0816	0818	|	...	0916	|	1016	|	1116	|	|	1216	|	1316	|
Roskilde **700/4** .... a.	0604	0600	|	0631	0706	|	0735	...	|	0810	0835	0838	|	...	0937	|	1035	|	1135	|	|	1235	|	1335	|
Høje Taastrup **700/4** .... a.	0618	0608	0559	0640	0718	0700	0747	...	0801	0821	0847	0850	0859	...	0947	0959	1047	1059	1147	1159	1159	1247	1259	1347	1359
København H **700/4** .... a.	0636	0625	0615	0657	0736	0717	0805	...	0819	0839	0905	0909	0915	...	1005	1015	1105	1114	1205	1214	1215	1305	1315	1405	1414

									ICE					*ICE*				*ICE*			*EC*				
	2234				2242			2246	35/380					37				39			239		4274		
		①–⑥		①–⑥		①–⑤	⑥⑦		B			⑧				⑦					C			P	
Hamburg Hbf **825** .... d.	...	...	...	...	...	...	...	...	1328	...	...	...	...	1528	...	...	...	1728	...	...	1928	...	...	...	...
Lübeck **825** .... d.	...	...	...	...	...	...	...	...	1406	...	...	...	...	1606	...	...	...	1806	...	...	2006	...	...	...	...
Puttgarden .... ⛴ ▲ d.	...	...	...	...	...	...	...	...	1508	...	...	...	...	1708	...	...	...	1908	...	...	2108	...	...	...	...
Rødby .... ⛴ ▲ d.	1246j	...	...	...	1444c	...	...	1544a	1610	...	...	...	...	1810	...	...	...	2010	...	...	2210	...	2244	...	...
Nykøbing (Falster) .... ⊙ d.	1310	1341	1410	1441	1510	1541	1541	1610	1641	...	1710	1741	1810	1841	1910	1941	2010	2041	2110	2210	2241	...	2310	...	...
Vordingborg .... d.	1334	1404	1434	1504	1534	1604	1604	1634	1704	...	1734	1804	1834	1904	1934	2004	2034	2104	2134	2234	2304	...	2333	...	...
Næstved .... d.	1355	1421	1455	1521	1555	1621	1621	1655	1721	...	1755	1821	1855	1921	1955	2021	2055	2121	2155	2255	2321	...	2353	0124	...
Ringsted **700** .... d.	1416	|	1516	|	1616	1636	|	1716	|	...	1816	|	1916	|	2016	|	2116	|	2216	2316	|	...	0016	0144	0155
Roskilde **700/4** .... a.	1435	|	1535	|	1635	|	|	1735	|	...	1835	|	1935	|	2035	|	2140	|	2240	2340	|	...	0040	...	0214
Høje Taastrup **700/4** .... a.	1447	1459	1547	1559	1647	1659	1659	1747	1759	...	1847	1859	1947	1959	2047	2059	2149	2159	2250	2349	2351	...	0050	...	0223
København H **700/4** .... a.	1505	1515	1605	1615	1705	1714	1715	1805	1814	...	1905	1915	2005	2014	2105	2115	2206	2214	2306	0009	0019	...	0114	...	0240

B – 12 and 🍸 København - Berlin and v.v.
C – June 6 - Aug. 24.
D – Apr. 11 - Oct. 26.
E – Apr. 12 - Oct. 27.
N – ①–⑥ Jan. 7 - Apr. 11, Oct. 28 - Dec. 13.
P – ⑦ Apr. 13 - Sept. 21.
Q – ⑧ Jan. 6 - Apr. 10, Oct. 27 - Dec. 12.
W – ①–⑥ Dec. 16 - June 12, Aug. 25 - Dec. 13 (not June 6, 7).

a – ①–⑤ only.
c – ⑥⑦ only.
e – ⑦ only.
j – ⑥ June 21 - Aug. 16.
r – ⑥ (①–⑥ June 14 - Aug. 23).

⊙ – Trains run approximately hourly (more frequent on ①–⑤) Nykøbing (Falster) - Nakskov and v.v., journey 45 minutes. Operator: Regionstog A/S.
▲ – Through trains are conveyed by ⛴ Rødby - Puttgarden and v.v. ✕ on board ship. Passengers to/from Rødby or Puttgarden may be required to leave or join the train on board the train-ferry. See **Table 2375** for other available sailings.

727 KØBENHAVN - YSTAD - RØNNE

Valid June 1 - December 13

km				B	C	D	E	D	G		
0	**København** H ....d.	0636	...	1043	1445	1645	1845	2045	2245	...	...
11	Kastrup ✈ ....d.	0649	...	1056	1458	1658	1858	2058	2258	...	...
76	**Ystad** ....a.	0749	...	1149	1549	1749	1949	2149	2349	...	...
	Ystad ⛴ ....d.	*0830*	...	*1230*	*1630*	*1830*	*2030*	*2230*	*0020*	...	...
	Rønne ⛴ ....a.	*0950*	...	*1350*	*1750*	*1950*	*2150*	*2350*	*0140*	...	...

			B	C	D	E	D	G		
Rønne ⛴ ....d.	*0630*	...	*1030*	*1430*	*1630*	*1830*	*2030*	*2230*	...	...
Ystad ⛴ ....a.	*0750*	...	*1150*	*1550*	*1750*	*1950*	*2150*	*2350*	...	...
Ystad ....d.	0809	...	1209	1609	1809	2009	2209	0009	...	...
Kastrup ✈ ....a.	0905	...	1305	1705	1909	2105	2309	0111	...	...
København H ....a.	0920	...	1319	1720	1924	2120	2323	0123	...	...

B – Daily June 1 - Sept. 1; ①④⑤⑥⑦ Sept. 4 - 29; ⑤⑥⑦ Oct. 4 - 19; ⑥ Oct. 25 - Dec. 13 (not Oct. 5)
C – June 1, 6 - 9, 13 - 15, 20 - 22, 27 - 30; ①③④⑤⑥⑦ July 2 - Aug. 4; ⑤⑥⑦ Aug. 8 - Oct. 19; ⑤⑦ Oct. 24 - Dec. 12 (not Sept. 27, Oct. 4).
D – June 2 - 5, 10 - 12, 16 - 19, 23 - 26; ② July 1 - 29; ①②③④ Aug. 5 - Dec. 11.
E – June 1, 6 - 9, 13 - 15, 20 - 22, 27 - 30; ①③④⑤⑥⑦ July 2 - Aug. 4; ⑤⑥⑦ Aug. 8 Dec. 13.
G – June 1, 6, 7, 9, 13 - 15, 20 - 22, 27 - 30; ③④⑤⑥⑦ July 2 - Aug. 3; ⑤⑥⑦ Aug. 8 - 31

BRANCH LINES in Denmark 728

2nd class only

ÅRHUS - GRENAA: Subject to alteration until Oct. 17 — 69 km

	①–⑥	①–⑥			and				
Århus......d.	0507	0607	...	0707	hourly	2207	...	2332	...
Grenaa....a.	0623	0723	...	0823	until	2323	...	0049	...

	①–⑤	①–⑤	①–⑥	①–⑥		and			
Grenaa....d.	0459	0529	0629	0729	0829	hourly	2229	...	2329
Århus......a.	0616	0646	0746	0846	0946	until	2346	...	0046

ODENSE - SVENDBORG: — 48 km

	①–⑤	①–⑥	①–⑤		①–⑤		①–⑥	and		①–⑥		and		⑥⑦
Odense..........d.	0453	0522	0553	0622	0653	0722	0753	hourly	1622	1653	1722	hourly	2322	0022
Svendborg.....a.	0534	0604	0634	0704	0734	0804	0834	until	1704	1734	1804	until	0004	0104

	①–⑤	①–⑤	①–⑥	①–⑥		and	①–⑥			and		⑥⑦	①–⑤	⑥⑦
Svendborg.....d.	0511	0541	0611	0641	0711	hourly	1741	1811	1911	hourly	2311	0011	0011	0111
Odense..........a.	0554	0622	0654	0722	0754	until	1822	1854	1954	until	2354	0054	0107	0154

HJØRRING - HIRTSHALS: Nordjyske Jernbaner A/S — 18 km — Journey 22 minutes

From **Hjørring**:

①–⑤: 0450, 0543, 0606, 0636, 0706, 0740, 0808, 0906, 1006, 1106, 1206, 1306, 1334, 1406, 1434, 1506, 1539, 1606, 1639, 1706, 1739, 1806, 1906, 2106, 2208, 2306.

⑥: 0706, 0806 and hourly until 1706, then 1806, 1906, 2106, 2208, 2306.

⑦: 0742, 0842, 1006, 1106, 1206, 1306, 1406, 1606, 1706, 1806, 1906, 2106, 2208, 2306.

From **Hirtshals/Color Line**:

①–⑤: 0515, 0609, 0638, 0706, 0743, 0811, 0836, 0936, 1036, 1136, 1236, 1337, 1409, 1437, 1509, 1541, 1609, 1641, 1709, 1741, 1809, 1836, 2010, 2136, 2236, 2332.

⑥: 0706, 0836 and hourly until 1536, then 1736, 1836, 2010, 2136, 2236, 2332.

⑦: 0808, 0908, 1036, 1136, 1236, 1336, 1436, 1636, 1736, 1836, 2010, 2136, 2236, 2332.

ICELAND

There are no railways in Iceland but bus services serve most major settlements, though long-distance services in the eastern part of the country operate in summer only. There are no services to the far northwest in 2014. Principal services enabling a circuit of the country (along road number 1) and some other important routes are shown below. Additional information may be obtained from the websites of the operators as shown in the footnotes. For a complete listing of all routes, including local services and ferries, see www.nat.is and www.ferdamalastofa.is. Buses have scheduled stops in all settlements (often at N1 filling stations) but may also stop on demand at any point along the route (confirm with operator).

Winter timings: Only *STR* and a few shorter routes shown in 'Other Services' below operate. *STR* winter timings shown are valid **Jan. 5 - May 14 or 31, 2014** (depending on route; expected to be similar from September, 2014). No long-distance services operate on Dec. 24, 25, 31, Jan. 1.

Summer timings: In addition to *STR* services, many more routes are run by private operators, with bus passes available for the *STA/SBA* and *RE/SBA* networks, respectively.

Tourist excursions are also available all year. All schedules may change at short notice - contact operators for latest timings. Confirm timings, particularly in winter, as in adverse weather conditions buses may be delayed or cancelled.

Public holidays: In 2014 are Jan. 1, Apr. 17, 18, 20, 21, 24, May 1, 29, June 8, 9, 17, Dec. 25, 26.

PRINCIPAL BUS SERVICES 729

REYKJAVÍK - AKUREYRI

km	operator	WINTER	STR	STR		SUMMER	STR	STA	STR
	route number		57	57			57	60	57
			WXb	⑧W			H	B	H
0	Reykjavík (BSÍ terminal)....... ■ d.		0840z	...	...		0840z	1515h	...
7	Reykjavík (Mjódd)............... ■ d.		0900	1730	...		0900	|	1730
426	Akureyri (Hof)........................ a.		1514y	2344	...		1529y	2030r	2359

operator	WINTER	STR	STR		SUMMER	STA	STR	STR
route number		57	57			60a	57	57
		⑧W	W			B	H	H
Akureyri (Hof)........................d.		1045	1635	...		0730r	1015	1620
Reykjavík (Mjódd)............ ■ a.		1659	2249	...		|	1644	2249
Reykjavík (BSÍ terminal) ... ■ a.		...	...	...		1255h	...	...

Additional local STR services operate Reykjavík (Mjódd) - Borgarnes (Hyrnan) and v.v. (4-8 services per day, journey ± 1h 23 mins., 82 *km*). No service on Dec. 25, Jan. 1, and afternoons of Dec. 24, 31.

INTERIOR HIGHLAND ROUTE: Additional tourist services operate Reykjavik - Akureyri via Thingvellir/Selfoss - Geysir - Gulfoss - Kjölur (with sightseeing stops):

Reykjavík BSÍ d. 0800 → Akureyri (**r**) a. 1830. Akureyri (**r**) d. 0800 → Reykjavík BSÍ a. 1830. Daily June 18 - Sept. 7. Operator: *SBA* route 610. *448 km* via Selfoss.

Reykjavík Harpa d. 0730 → Akureyri (**r**) a. 2030. Akureyri (**r**) d. 0730 → Reykjavík Harpa a. 2030. Daily June 20 - Sept. 5. Operator: *STA* route F35/F35a. *427 km* via Thingvellir, return via Selfoss. Change buses in Kerlingarfjöll (cabins) a. 1300/d. 1530 in both directions.

AKUREYRI - EGILSSTADIR - HÖFN

km	operator	WINTER	STR		SUMMER	SBA		STR		STR
	route number		56			62		56		56
			Y			K§		G		G
0	Akureyri (Hof).......................d.		1515	...		0800r	...	1150	...	1535y
103	Reykjahlid (Mývatn)...... (N1) d.		1645	...		1000	...	1320	...	1705
266	Egilsstadir.................. (q) ❦ d.		1845	...		1300k	...	...	...	1905
533	Höfn í Hornafirdi ....(N1) ❦ a.		...	...		1730	...	...	...	...

operator	WINTER	STR		SUMMER	STR		STR		SBA
route number		56			56		56		62a
		Y			G		G		K§
Höfn í Hornafirdi....(N1) ❦ d.		...	...		...	...	...	...	0800
Egilsstadir.............. (q) ❦ d.		0910	...		0910	...	...	...	1300k
Reykjahlíd (Mývatn) ...(N1) d.		1110	...		1110	...	1325	...	1525
Akureyri (Hof)...................a.		1240	...		1240	...	1455	...	1715r

❦ – No through service in winter. Additional local services run all year on separate routes Egilsstadir - Reydarfjördur (299 *km*) - Breiddalsvík (365 *km*) and v.v. (2-3 services per day), and Djúpivogur (430 *km*) - Höfn and v.v. (5 services per week). Operator: *SVA*.

HÖFN - REYKJAVÍK

km	operator	WINTER	STR	STR	STR	SUMMER	STA	STR	RE	RE	STR
	route number		51	51	51		12a	51	19	20a	51
			†W	AW	ⒶW		T§	H	R§	S§	H
0	Höfn í Hornafirdi (N1) d.		1025v	1155v	...		0730	0735v	0800	...	1605v
135	Skaftafell..................d.		1220	1350	...		1135	0935	1215	1230	1805
275	Vík í Mýrdal .... (N1) d.		1430c	1545c	1600		1410	1200c	...	1530	2030c
456	Reykjavík (Mjódd) . ■ a.		1715	...	1845		|	1445f	...	|	2315
461	Reykjavík (BSÍ)..... ■ a.		...	...	...		1815h	...	...	1935	...

operator	WINTER	STR	STR	STR	SUMMER	STA	RE	STR	RE	STR
route number		51	51	51		12	20	51	19	51
		†W	ⒶW	AW		T§	R§	H	R§	H
Reykjavík (BSÍ)........ ■ d.		...	...	...		0730h	0800	*0840*a	...	...
Reykjavík (Mjódd).... ■ d.		1130	1300	...		|	|	0900	...	1730
Vík í Mýrdal..........(N1) d.		1445c	1545c	1615		1200	1400	1200c	...	2030c
Skaftafell .... d.		1650	...	1820		1420	1600	1410	1730	2240
Höfn í Hornafirdi ...(N1) a.		1835v	...	2005v		1800	...	1555v	1930	0025

Additional local STR services operate (Hvolsvöllur (N1) -) Selfoss (Fossnesti) - Reykjavík (Mjódd) and v.v. Hvolsvöllur - Selfoss - Mjódd (3-8 services per day, journey ± 1h 40 mins., 100 *km*). Selfoss - Mjódd (8-12 services per day, journey 53 min, 52 *km*). No service on Dec. 25, Jan. 1, and afternoons of Dec. 24, 31.

OTHER SERVICES

gilsstadir - Seydisfjördur: 27 *km*, journey ± 35 minutes, operator *FAS*. Services connect with Smyril Line ferry (Table **2285**). Confirm departure point with operator.
rom Egilsstadir (**q**) 0900Ⓐ, 1030⑥**x**, 1640Ⓐ. Additional journey Apr. 1 - June 10, Aug. 26 - Oct. 28 at 1100②. Additional journeys June 19 - Aug. 21 at 1100④, 1300⑥⑦.
rom Seydisfjördur (**j**) 0755Ⓐ, 0940⑥**x**, 1550Ⓐ. Additional journeys Apr. 1 - June 10, Aug. 26 - Oct. 28 at 1015**n**. Additional journeys June 19 - Aug. 21 at 1015④**n**, 1215⑥⑦.

eykjavík BSÍ - Keflavík Airport: 50 *km*, journey ± 45 minutes, (*flybus*) operator *RE*. Departures several times per day, connecting with all flights.
Additional services 🄡 (*airportexpress*) operated by *IE* between Reykjavík Laekjartorg and Keflavík Airport, connecting with all flights.

eykjavík BSÍ - Blue Lagoon: 48 *km*, journey ± 45 minutes, operator *RE*. Departures several times per day, also infrequent departures from Keflavík airport.

eykjavík BSÍ - Thingvellir - Geysir - Gullfoss (**Golden Circle**): Operator *RE* route 6/6a (with sightseeing stops). Departures June 13 - Sept. 14 from Reykjavík at 1000, arriving back in Reykjavík at 845. See also *SBA* and *STA* Reykjavík - Kjölur - Akureyri services.

Daily excursions also available from different operators during winter.

– ②⑤ only.
– ①–⑤ June 18 - Aug. 31.
– June 1 - circa Sept. 13.
– May 18 - circa Sept. 13.
K – June 1 - Sept. 10.
R – June 13 - Sept. 7.
S – June 14 - Sept. 8.
T – June 2 - Sept. 10.
– Jan. 5 - May 17 (not Dec. 24, 25, 31, Jan. 1). Similar timings expected from circa Sept. 14.
– On Dec. 24, 31 only to Borgarnes (a. 1023).
– ①③⑤† Jan. 5 - May 31 (not Dec. 24, 25, 31, Jan. 1). Similar timings expected from circa Sept. 14.
– † only. STR route 57 to Akureyri; change bus in Mjódd.
– Change bus in Borgarnes on ⑥ (a. 1023/d. 1028).
– Change bus in Vík í Mýrdal.
– Change to route 52 at Selfoss Fossnesti (a. 1348/d. 1352).
– Reykjavík Harpa concert hall.
– Seydisfjördur Herdubreid.

k – Egilsstadir camping site (400 metres south of tourist information).
n – Seydisfjördur Smyril Line terminal.
q – Egilsstadir tourist information.
r – Akureyri Hafnarstraeti 77/82 (500 metres south of *STR* bus stop at Hof concert hall).
v – Höfn STR bus stop at Víkurbraut/Heppuskóli (600 metres south of N1).
x – Not June 19 - Aug. 21.
y – For connection between *STR* services 57 and 56 d. 1515 or 1535 to Mývatn/Egilsstadir contact operator/bus driver.
z – ⑦ and holidays only.
§ – With sightseeing stops.
N1 – Bus stop is at N1 filling station.

■ Reykjavík terminals

Harpa concert hall (*STA*, city centre/old harbour); Laekjartorg (*IE*, centre near old harbour); *BSÍ* bus terminal (*RE* and *STR* route 57 on † mornings, southern side of city centre); Mjódd (*STR*, 7 *km* southeast of city centre).
STR city service 3 connects Hlemmur/city centre to Mjódd via Harpa, Laekjartorg and bus stop at BSÍ every 15-30 minutes (journey 28 mins., 18 mins. from BSÍ); no city services on † mornings.

Operators:
FAS Ferdathjónusta Austurlands + 354 472 1515 www.visitseydisfjordur.com/bus-service-fas/
IE Iceland Excursions + 354 540 1313 www.grayline.is
RE Reykjavik Excursions + 354 580 5400 www.re.is
SBA SBA - Nordurleid + 354 550 0700 www.sba.is
STA Sterna + 354 551 1166 www.sterna.is
STR Straetó + 354 540 2700 www.straeto.is
SVA Straetisvagnar Austurlands + 354 471 2320 www.fjardabyggd.is

SWEDEN

SEE MAP PAGE 342

Operators: Most services are operated by **SJ AB** (*SJ*) - Swedish State Railways - formerly part of Statens Järnvägar: www.sj.se. There is, however, a number of other operators that run services shown within the European Rail Timetable; these are indicated by their initials in the relevant table heading, or at the top of each train column where more than one operator runs services on the same route.

AEX – Arlanda Express (A-Train AB)	*IB* – Inlandsbanan AB	*NT* – Norrtåg	*Øtåg* – Øresundståg
SKJB – Skandinaviska Jernbanor	*ST* – Svenska Tågkompaniet AB	*Tågab* – Tågåkeriet i Bergslagen AB	*VEO* – Veolia Transport (Snälltåget)

The Regional Public Transport Authority is responsible for many local services, known collectively as Länstrafik (*LT*). Those shown within these pages are abbreviated as follows:

JLT – Jönköpings Länstrafik	*KLT/ÖT* – Kalmar Läns Trafik / ÖstgötaTrafiken	*Skåne* – Skånetrafiken
V – Västtrafik	*VTAB* – Värmlandstrafik	*XT* – X-Trafik

Services: Trains convey first and second classes of accommodation, unless otherwise shown. The fastest trains are classified *Snabbtåg (Sn)* and *InterCity (IC)*. Sleeping cars (🛏) are of two basic types with a range of supplements: older cars (those without showers) have one berth in first class, two or three berths in second class. Newer cars either have compartments with shower and WC (one or two berth, first class only) or have shower and WC available in the car (one or two berths in first class, two berths in second class). Couchette cars (▬) have six berths and are second class only. Refreshment services (✕, 🍸, Bistro or Shop) may be available for part of the journey only.

Timings: Valid until **December 13, 2014** except where shown otherwise. Alterations may be made on and around the dates of public holidays.

Tickets: Through journeys between Länstrafik and SJ AB, Veolia Transport or Svenska Tågkompaniet are possible with a combined ticket known as 'Resplus'. Similarly, Arlanda Express may be combined with SJ AB journeys. However, Veolia Transport and Svenska Tågkompaniet have their own fare structures and tickets cannot be combined with those of SJ AB.

Reservations: Seat reservation is compulsory on all *Snabbtåg* and night trains, and for through journeys to København (excluding local and *Skåne* services). Reserved seats are not labelled and, if occupied, must be claimed by presenting the seat ticket on the train.

Supplements: Special supplements are payable for travel on *Snabbtåg* high-speed trains.

730 STOCKHOLM - MALMÖ - KØBENHAVN

km																										
		Sn	*Sn*	*Sn*	*Sn*			*IC*	*Sn*			*Sn*	*VEO*		*Sn*			*Sn*		*Sn*			*Sn*	*VEO*		*Sn*
		519	**521**	**521**	**523**			**201**	**525**			**527**	**3941**		**529**			**531**		**533**			**535**	**3933**		**537**
		R ✕	R ✕	R ✕	R ✕				R ✕			R ✕	✕		R ✕			R ✕		R ✕			R ✕	✕		R ✕
		Ⓐp	A	Ⓐq	Ⓐ	Ⓐq	Ⓐq	B		Ⓐ	⑥			⚒		⑥	†	C	⚒		Ⓐ	Ⓒ	C	†	Ⓑq	⑥
0	**Stockholm** Central ‡ d.	0521	0621	0621	0721	0751	0759	0806	0821	0851	0859	0921	0925	0940	1021	1051	1059	1121	1140	1221	1240	1251	1321	1325	1340	1421
15	Flemingsberg ‡ d.	|	|	|	0732	|	0810	|	|	|	|	0932	|	0951	|	|	1110	1132	1151	|	1251	|	1332	|	1351	|
36	Södertälje Syd ‡ d.	0539	0639	0639	|	0809	0821	0826	0839	0909	0917	|	0946	1003	1039	1109	1122	|	1203	1239	1301	1309	|	1346	1403	1439
*	Katrineholm **740 754** d.	|	|	|	|	|	|	|	|	|	|	|	|	|	|	|	|	|	|	|	|	|	|	|	|	|
103	Nyköping d.	|	|	|	|	|	0901	|	|	|	|	|	|	1047	|	|	1203	|	1244	|	1347	|	|	|	1444	|
162	**Norrköping** d.	0635	0735	0735	0835	0913	0943	0939	0935	1014	1022	1035	1051	1128	1135	1211	1241	1235	1328	1335	1426	1414	1435	1451	1528	1535
209	Linköping d.	0700	0800	0800	0900	0941	1013	1007	1000	1042	1050	1100	1119	...	1200	1241	1310	1300	...	1400	...	1440	1500	1519	...	1600
241	**Mjölby 755** d.	|	0814	0814	|	...	...	|	1014	...	...	|	|	...	1214	...	...	|	...	1414	...	...	|	|	...	1614
277	Tranås d.	|	|	|	0928	...	...	|	|	...	...	|	|	...	|	...	...	|	...	|	...	...	|	|	...	|
329	**Nässjö 733** d.	0748	0851	0851	0951	...	...	1112	1051	...	...	1148	1217	...	1251	...	...	1348	...	1451	...	...	1548	1617	...	1651
416	Alvesta d.	0822	0925	0925	1025	...	...	1157	1125	...	...	1222	1258	...	1325	...	...	1422	...	1525	...	...	1622	1656	...	1725
514	Hässleholm **745/6** a.	0902	1002	1002	1102	...	...	1242	1202	...	...	1302	1341s	...	1402	...	...	1502	...	1602	...	...	1659	1755s	...	1802
581	Lund **745/6** § a.	0935s	1035s	1035s	1135s	...	...	1322s	1235s	...	...	1335s	1424s	...	1435s	...	...	1535s	...	1635s	...	...	1732s	1829s	...	1945s
597	**Malmö** C **745/6** § a.	0947	1047	1047	1147	...	...	1339	1247	...	...	1347	1440	...	1447	...	...	1547	...	1647	...	...	1747	1845	...	2000
597	**Malmö** C **703** d.	0959	1057	...	...	...	...	...	1250	...	...	...	...	...	1458	...	...	...	...	1657	...	...	...	...	...	2006
632	København (Kastrup) ✈ **703** a.	1017s	1118s	...	...	...	...	...	1309s	...	...	...	...	...	1518s	...	...	...	...	1717s	...	...	...	...	...	2025s
644	**København** H **703** a.	1032	1133	...	...	...	...	...	1323	...	...	...	...	...	1532	...	...	...	...	1731	...	...	...	...	...	2040

	Sn				*Sn*	*IC*			*VEO*	*Sn*		*Sn*	*Sn*	*Sn*	*Sn*	*Sn*		*Sn*				*Sn*				
	537			**10207**	**539**	**207/9**			**3943**	**541**		**505**	**513**	**543**	**507**	**507**		**545**				**547**			**1**	
	R ✕				R ✕				✕	R ✕		R ✕	R ✕	R ✕	R ✕	R ✕		R ✕				R ✕			R	
	Ⓑ	Ⓐ		④⑤t	Ⓑ	D	Ⓐm	Ⓐn	M		K	Ⓑv	♦	⑤†k	Ⓐq	†q		⊡	⑥n	L	⑤q	Z	†q	Ⓑq	♦	
Stockholm Central ‡ d.	1421	1440	1451	1459	1521	1536	1551	1555	1605	1621	1644	1706	1721	1721	1740	1740	1744	1821	1851	1859	1859	1921	1940	2044	2125	2151
Flemingsberg ‡ d.	|	1451	|	|	|	|	|	|	|	|	|	|	1732	1732	|	|	1756	|	|	|	|	|	|	2055	|	2202
Södertälje Syd ‡ d.	1439	1503	1510	1520	1539	1558	1609	1615	1624	1639	1705	|	|	|	|	|	1808	1839	1909	1922	1922	1939	1959	2106	2150u	2214
Katrineholm **740 754** d.	|	|	|	|	|	|	|	|	|	|	|	|	|	|	|	|	|	|	|	|	|	|	|	|	2250	|
Nyköping d.	|	1547	|	|	|	|	|	|	|	|	|	|	|	|	|	|	1849	|	|	|	|	|	|	2147	|	2254
Norrköping d.	1535	1627	1615	1710	1635	1710	1715	1739	1727	1735	1823	|	1835	1835	|	|	1927	1935	2012	2027	2026	2035	2102	2226	2339	2332
Linköping d.	1600	...	1641	1737	1700	1737	1739	1806	1803	1800	1850	|	1900	1900	|	|	1954	2000	2042	2054	2053	2100	2132	2254	0012	2359
Mjölby 755 d.	1614	...	...	|	|	|	...	...	|	1814	...	|	|	|	|	|	...	2014	...	...	...	|	...	...	|	...
Tranås d.	|	...	...	|	|	|	...	...	|	|	...	|	1928	1928	|	|	...	|	...	...	...	|	...	...	|	...
Nässjö 733 d.	1651	...	...	1844	1748	1844	...	...	1900	1851	...	|	1951	1951	|	|	...	2051	...	...	...	2148	...	...	0234j	...
Alvesta d.	1725	...	...	1930	1822	1930	...	...	1939	1925	...	1958	...	2025	2031	2031	...	2125	...	...	...	2222	...	...	0327	...
Hässleholm **745/6** a.	1802	...	...	2012	1902	2012	...	...	2022	2002	...	2033	...	2102	2106	2106	...	2202	...	...	...	2259	...	...	0435s	...
Lund **745/6** § a.	1835s	...	...	2052s	1935s	2052s	...	...	2102s	2035s	...	2109s	...	2135s	2138s	2138s	...	2235s	...	...	...	2332s	...	...	0527s	...
Malmö C **745/6** § a.	1847	...	...	2108	1947	2108	...	...	2115	2047	...	2122	...	2147	2154	2154	...	2247	...	...	...	2344	...	...	0541	...
Malmö C **703** d.	...	...	...	...	1958	...	...	...	...	...	...	...	...	...	2158	...	...	...	...	...	...	...	...	...	...	...
København (Kastrup) ✈ **703** a.	...	...	...	...	2017s	...	...	...	...	...	...	...	...	...	2217	...	...	...	...	...	...	...	...	...	...	...
København H **703** a.	...	...	...	...	2032	...	...	...	...	...	...	...	...	...	2232	...	...	...	...	...	...	...	...	...	...	...

				Sn			*Sn*	*Sn*	*Sn*		*Sn*	*Sn*			*Sn*		*Sn*		*IC*	*Sn*	*Sn*		*VEO*	*Sn*		
				510			**512**	**522**	**500**		**516**	**524**			**526**		**528**		**200**	**530**	**530**		**3940**	**532**		
				R ✕			R ✕	R ✕	R ✕		R ✕	R ✕			R ✕		R ✕			R ✕	R ✕		✕	R ✕		
	Ⓐ	Ⓐq	Ⓐ	Ⓐq	Ⓐ	⚒	♦	E	Ⓐp	⑥	♦	Ⓐq	Ⓐq	Ⓒ		†	⚒	Ⓒ	B	F	⑥k			C	⑤q	Ⓒ
København H **703** d.	...	...	...	...	...	...	...	...	...	...	...	...	...	...	...	...	...	...	...	0828	...	...	...	...	...	...
København Kastrup ✈ **703** d.	...	...	...	...	...	...	...	...	...	...	...	...	...	...	...	...	...	...	...	0842u	...	...	...	...	...	...
Malmö C **703** a.	...	...	...	...	...	...	...	...	...	...	...	...	...	...	...	...	...	...	...	0859	...	...	...	...	...	...
Malmö C **745/6** § d.	...	...	...	...	...	...	...	0511	0542	...	...	0611	...	...	0711	...	0811	...	0803	0911	0911	...	0920	1011	...	...
Lund **745/6** § d.	...	...	...	...	...	...	...	0523u	0554u	...	...	0623u	...	...	0723u	...	0823u	...	0815u	0923u	0923u	...	0930u	1023u	...	...
Hässleholm **745/6** d.	...	...	...	...	...	...	...	0556	0627	...	...	0656	...	...	0756	...	0856	...	0902	0956	0956	...	1005	1056	...	...
Alvesta **746** d.	...	...	...	...	...	...	...	0631	|	...	...	0734	...	...	0831	...	0934	...	0947	1031	1031	...	1049	1134	...	...
Nässjö 733 d.	...	...	...	...	...	...	0644	0705	|	...	0806	0808	...	...	0905	...	1008	...	1030	1105	1105	...	1129	1208	...	...
Tranås d.	...	...	...	...	...	...	0706	|	|	...	0828	|	...	...	|	...	|	...	|	|	|	...	|	|	...	...
Mjölby 755 d.	...	...	...	...	...	...	|	0742	|	...	|	|	...	...	0942	...	|	...	|	1142	1142	...	|	|	...	...
Linköping d.	0500	0600	0608	0625	0644	0724	0738	0800	|	0800	0900	0900	...	0922	1000	1005	1100	1118	1134	1200	1200	...	1231	1300	1315	1315
Norrköping 754 d.	0527	0627	0640	0650	0715	0751	0803	0824	|	0828	0924	0924	0932	0950	1024	1032	1124	1145	1203	1224	1224	1232	1258	1324	1343	1343
Nyköping d.	0607	|	0724	|	0756	|	|	|	|	0909	|	|	1015	|	|	1113	|	|	|	|	|	1315	|	|	|	|
Katrineholm **740 754** a.	|	|	|	|	|	|	|	|	|	|	|	|	|	|	|	|	|	|	|	|	|	|	|	|	|	|
Södertälje Syd ‡ a.	0646	0731	0805	0745	0840	0856	0900	0919	|	0950	|	1018	1056	1052	1118	1155	|	1250	1310	1318	1318	1355	1410	1419	1447	1447
Flemingsberg ‡ a.	0656	0742	0816	0756	0851	|	0911	|	|	1001	1026	|	1107	|	|	1206	1225	|	|	|	|	1406	|	|	|	|
Stockholm Central ‡ a.	0709	0754	0831	0809	0905	0920	0924	0939	0954	1020	1039	1039	1120	1116	1139	1224	1239	1316	1335	1339	1339	1420	1435	1439	1509	1516

♦ – NOTES (LISTED BY TRAIN NUMBER)

- **1** – Ⓑ Mar. 31 - Oct. 31: 🛏, ▬, (2) and 🍸 Stockholm - Malmö.
- **512** – Ⓐ Aug. 10 - Dec. 13: (12) and ✕ Jönköping - Nässjö - Stockholm. From Aug. 25 runs 5–7 minutes later Södertälje Syd - Stockholm (train number **518**).
- **513** – Ⓑ Aug. 10 - Dec. 13: (12) and ✕ Stockholm - Nässjö - Jönköping.
- **516** – ⑥ Aug. 10 - Dec. 13: (12) and ✕ Jönköping - Nässjö - Stockholm.

- **A** – ⚒ June 29 - Aug. 9; ⑥ Aug. 10 - Dec. 13.
- **B** – ①⑤ June 29 - Aug. 10; ⑤ Aug. 11 - Dec. 13.
- **C** – Daily June 29 - Aug. 9; Ⓑ Aug. 10 - Dec. 13.
- **D** – ④⑤† June 29 - Aug. 17; † Aug. 18 - Dec. 13 (not Nov. 1).
- **E** – ① June 29 - Aug. 9; Ⓐ Aug. 10 - Dec. 13.
- **F** – Ⓑ June 29 - Aug. 9; daily Aug. 10 - Dec. 13.
- **K** – Daily June 28 - Sept. 28; Ⓒ Sept. 29 - Dec. 13.
- **L** – ①②③④† Aug. 25 - Dec. 13.
- **M** – ①④⑤⑥† only.
- **Z** – ①②③④† Aug. 10 - Dec. 13.
- **a** – Ⓐ only.

- **j** – Arrive 0142.
- **k** – June 29 - Aug. 9.
- **m** – Aug. 10 - 24.
- **n** – Aug. 25 - Dec. 13.
- **p** – Sept. 1 - Dec. 13.
- **q** – Aug. 10 - Dec. 13.
- **s** – Stops to set down only.
- **t** – Aug. 18 - Dec. 13.
- **u** – Stops to pick up only.
- **v** – Aug. 17 - Dec. 13.

- ⊡ – Runs 5 minutes later Lund - Malmö ①–④ until Aug. 7.
- ‡ – Most trains on this table may not be used for local journeys between Stockholm ar[d] Södertälje Syd or v.v. Local trains run every 30 mins Stockholm Central - Södertä[lje] Hamn - Södertälje Centrum and v.v. (journey 42 mins). 🚌 Södertälje Syd - Södertä[lje] Centrum runs every 30 mins.
- § – Frequent local trains run Lund - Malmö and v.v.
- * – Södertälje Syd: *0 km* - Katrineholm: *95 km* - Norrköping: *143 km*.

KØBENHAVN - MALMÖ - STOCKHOLM 730

		Sn		Sn	Sn	Sn			Sn	Sn			Sn		Sn		IC	Sn		VEO	VEO	Sn	Sn	Sn	Sn	
		534		536	536	536			538	538			540		542		204/6	544		3942	3944	504	546	548	550	2
		🅁✗		🅁✗	🅁✗	🅁✗			🅁✗	🅁✗			🅁✗		🅁✗			🅁✗		✗	✗	🅁✗	🅁✗	🅁✗	🅁✗	🅁
	Q			G	Ⓐq	†k	Ⓐ		K	H	Ⓑq	†q	Ⓑ			Ⓑq	④⑤†		Ⓑ	J	†	Ⓑv		†q	Ⓑ	♦
København H 703 d.	...	...	...	...	1116	1135	...	...	...	1229	...	...	...	...	1429	...	...	...	...	...	...	...	1629	...	1836	...
København Kastrup ✈ **703** d.	...	...	...	...	1129u	1150u	...	...	...	1242u	...	...	...	...	1442u	...	...	...	...	...	...	...	1642u	...	1850u	...
Malmö C 703 a.	...	...	...	...	1155	1209	...	...	...	1259	...	...	...	...	1459	...	...	...	...	...	...	...	1702	...	1908	...
Malmö C 745/6 § d.	...	1111	...	1211	1211	1211	...	...	1311	1311	...	...	1411	...	1511	...	1502	1611	...	1604	1604	1638	1711	1833	1911	2237
Lund **745/6** § d.	...	1123u	...	1223u	1223u	1223u	...	...	1323u	1323u	...	...	1423u	...	1523u	...	1515u	1623u	...	1615u	1615u	1650u	1723u	1845u	1923u	2249u
Hässleholm **745/6** d.	...	1156	...	1256	1256	1256	...	...	1356	1356	...	...	1456	...	1556	...	1559	1656	...	1658u	1658u	1723	1756	1918	1956	2335u
Alvesta **746** d.	...	1231	...	1335	1335	1335	...	...	1431	1431	...	...	1531	...	1631	...	1645	1734	...	1742	1742	|	1831	1953	2031	0037
Nässjö 733 d.	...	1305	...	1408	1408	1408	...	...	1505	1505	...	...	1605	...	1705	...	1729	1808	...	1828	1828	|	1905	2027	2105	0132
Tranås d.	...	|	...	|	|	|	...	...	|	|	...	...	1628	...	|	...	|	|	...	|	|	|	|	|	2128	|
Mjölby 755 d.	...	1342	...	|	|	|	...	...	1542	1542	...	...	|	...	1742	...	|	|	...	|	|	|	1942	|	|	|
Linköping d.	1322	1400	1405e	1500	1500	1500	...	1517	1600	1600	...	1624	1700	1726	1800	...	1840	1900	1905	1926	1926	|	2000	2119	2200	0336j
Norrköping 754 d.	1350	1424	1432	1524	1524	1524	1532	1545	1624	1624	1632	1652	1724	1754	1824	1831	1911	1924	1932	1954	1954	|	2024	2144	2224	0408
Nyköping d.	|	|	1515	|	|	|	1617	|	|	|	1720	|	|	|	|	1919	|	|	2017	|	|	|	|	|	|	|
Katrineholm **740 754** a.	|	|	|	|	|	|	|	|	|	|	|	|	|	|	|	|	|	|	|	|	|	|	|	|	|	0442
Södertälje Syd ‡ a.	1452	1518	1559	|	|	|	1700	1649	1719	1719	1805	1756	1818	1857	1919	2001	2032y	|	2057	2101	2101	|	2118	|	2318	0540s
Flemingsberg ‡ a.	|	|	1610	1626	1626	1626	1711	|	|	|	1817	|	|	|	|	2011	|	2026	2107	|	|	|	|	|	|	|
Stockholm Central ‡ a.	1516	1539	1624	1639	1639	1639	1724	1709	1739	1739	1831	1816	1839	1916	1939	2024	2059y	2039	2121	2125	2131	2054	2139	2258	2339	0609

♦ – **NOTES** (LISTED BY TRAIN NUMBER)

2 – Ⓑ Mar. 31 - Oct. 31: 🛏, 🛏, (2) and 🍸 Malmö - Stockholm.

G – ⚒ June 29 - Aug. 9; † Aug. 10 - Dec. 13.
H – ⚒ June 29 - Aug. 9; Ⓒ Aug. 10 - Dec. 13.
J – ①④⑤⑥ only.
K – † June 29 - Aug. 9; Ⓐ Aug. 10 - Dec. 13.
Q – ①-④ Aug. 10 - Dec. 13.

e – † only.
j – Arrive 0246.
k – June 29 - Aug. 9.

q – Aug. 10 - Dec. 13.
s – Stops to set down only.
u – Stops to pick up only.
v – Aug. 17 - Dec. 13.
y – Arrive Södertälje Syd 2046s, Stockholm 2116 from Aug. 10.

‡ – Most trains on this table may not be used for local journeys between Stockholm and Södertälje Syd or v.v. Local trains run every 30 mins Stockholm Central - Södertälje Hamn - Södertälje Centrum and v.v. (journey 42 mins). 🚌 Södertälje Syd - Södertälje Centrum runs every 30 mins.

§ – Frequent local trains run Malmö - Lund.

Operator: *Skåne* MALMÖ - YSTAD - SIMRISHAMN 732

km		Ⓒ	Ⓐ	Ⓐ	⑥	Ⓐ		Ⓐ		⚒			and at the			⚒	†	⚒	⑤⑥	①-④	†	⑤⑥	①-④	
0	**Malmö C** d.	0108	...	0508	...	0538	0608	0638	0708	0725	0808	0838	same mins.	2108	2138	2208	2208	2238	2308	2315	2315	2338	2344	0008
70	Ystad a.	0158	0500	0600	0600	0628	0658	0728	0758	0828	0858	0928	past each	2158	2228	2258	2258	2328	2358	2358	2358	0028	0028	0058
116	Simrishamn a.	...	0540	0640	0640	...	0740	...	0840	...	0940	...	hour until	2240	...	2340	...	...	0040	0040	...	...	...	...

	②-⑤	Ⓒ	Ⓐ		Ⓐ		Ⓐ		Ⓐ			and at the				⚒		⚒		⚒		Ⓒ	⚒
Simrishamn d.	0049	0049	...	...	...	0549a	...	0649d	...	0749	...	same mins.	1849	...	1949	...	2049	...	2149	...	2249	...	2349
Ystad d.	0130	0132	0432	0532	0602	0632	0702	0732	0802	0832	0902	past each	1932	2002	2032	2102	2132	2202	2232	2302	2332	0002	0032
Malmö C a.	...	0237	0521	0621	0651	0721	0751	0821	0851	0921	0951	hour until	2021	2051	2121	2151	2221	2251	2314r	2351	0021d	0051	0121f

a – Ⓐ only. d – ⚒ only. f – ⑤⑥ only. r – Arrive 2321 on ⑤⑥.

STOCKHOLM - ESKILSTUNA - ARBOGA 732

km		2		2				2		2		2			2		2										
		Ⓐq	Ⓐ	⚒	Ⓐ	⑥	Ⓐ						Ⓐq			M	Ⓐ	Ⓐ		Ⓐp	†q	Ⓐ		Ⓐ	Ⓒ	①-④	⑤⑥
0	**Stockholm** C d.	...	0629	...	0755	0851	0855	...	1044	...	1244	...	1344	1444	...	1544	...	1625	1651	1725	1751	1755	1855	2040	2155	2255	2325
36	Södertälje Syd d.	...	0651	...	0817	0913	0917	...	1106	...	1306	...	1406	1506	...	1606	...	1648	1713	1748	1814	1819	1917	2102	2217	2317	2347
67	Läggesta ● d.	...	0708	...	0834	0930	0935	...	1123	...	1323	...	1423	1524	...	1624	...	1706	1730	1806	1832	1836	1934	2119	2234	2334	0004
83	Strängnäs d.	0618	0722	...	0843	0939	0944	...	1132	...	1332	...	1433	1533	...	1634	...	1724	1739	1816	1842	1845	1943	2128	2243	2343	0013
115	Eskilstuna a.	0640	0738	...	0859	0955	1000	...	1148	...	1348	...	1449	1549	...	1649	...	1742	1755	1834	1900	1859	1959	2144	2259	2359	0029
115	Eskilstuna d.	0648	...	0759	...	...	...	1010	...	1205	...	1405	...	...	1559	...	1700	...	1759	1837	...	1902	2002	2147	...	...	...
141	Kungsör d.	0702	...	0813	...	...	...	1024	...	1219	...	1419	...	...	1613	...	1714	...	1813	1851	...	1916	2016	2201	...	...	...
159	**Arboga 756** a.	0713	...	0824	...	...	...	1035	...	1230	...	1430	...	...	1624	...	1725	...	1824	1902	...	1927	2027	2212	...	...	...
	Örebro **756** a.	...	...	...	...	...	...	...	...	...	...	...	...	...	...	...	...	...	...	1928	...	...	...	2234p	...	...	...

							2				2			2		2			2		2		2				
	Ⓐp	Ⓐ	Ⓐp	Ⓐ	⑥	Ⓐ	Ⓐ	Ⓐ	⑥	Ⓐ	⚒	Ⓒ	Ⓐ					Ⓑq			Ⓐ	M					
Örebro **756** d.	...	...	0602	...	...	...	...	...	...	...	...	...	...	...	...	...	...	...	...	...	...	...	...	...	...	...	...
rboga 756 d.	...	0547p	|	0624	...	...	0724	...	...	...	0920	...	...	1120	...	1320	...	...	1520	...	1627	...	1734	...	...	1935	2125
ungsör d.	...	0557p	|	0634	...	...	0734	...	...	...	0930	...	...	1130	...	1330	...	...	1530	...	1638	...	1744	...	...	1945	2135
skilstuna a.	...	0613p	0642	0650	...	...	0750	...	...	...	0946	...	...	1146	...	1346	...	...	1546	...	1654	...	1800	...	...	2001	2151
skilstuna d.	0516	0616	0645	0652	0652	0715	...	0805	0905	0912	...	1005	1012	...	1205	...	1401	1501	...	1601	...	1701	...	1810	...	2005	2201b
trängnäs d.	0532	0632	|	0710	0710	0732	...	0821	0921	0928	...	1021	1028	...	1221	...	1417	1517	...	1617	...	1717	...	1830	...	2021	2217b
äggesta ● d.	0540	0640	|	0723	0723	0742	...	0829	0929	0937	...	1029	1036	...	1229	...	1425	1525	...	1625	...	1725	...	1845	...	2029	2225b
ödertälje Syd d.	0557	0701	|	0741	0741	0800	...	0846	0946	0954	...	1046	1053	...	1246	...	1443	1543	...	1642	...	1742	...	1901	...	2046	2242b
tockholm C a.	0620	0724	0735	0805	0805	0824	...	0909	1009	1019	...	1109	1116	...	1309	...	1505	1605	...	1705	...	1805	...	1924	...	2109	2309b

– Ⓐ June 29 - Aug. 9; Ⓑ Aug. 10 - Dec. 13.
– Ⓑ only.
– Aug. 4 - Dec. 13.
– Aug. 10 - Dec. 13.

● – Summer only narrow gauge service operates Mariefred - Läggesta (nedre) - Taxinge-Näsby and v.v. Operator: Östra Södermanlands Järnväg, Box 53, SE-647 22 Mariefred. ✆ +46 (0)159 210 00, fax +46 (0)159 211 15.

perator: *V* (except *Sn* trains) SKÖVDE - JÖNKÖPING - NÄSSJÖ 733

2nd class only except where shown

km				*Sn*		*Sn*																							
				512/8		516																							
		Ⓐ	Ⓐ	ⒶS	Ⓐ	⑥S	Ⓐq	⚒	Ⓐq	Ⓐ		⚒	⑥		Ⓐ	Ⓐy		⑥	Ⓐy	⚒		Ⓑ	Ⓑ		Ⓑ	Ⓑ		Ⓑy	W
0	**Skövde 740** d.	0448	...	...	0557	...	0612	0656	0723	...	0855	0925	...	1054	1128	...	1256	1330	1350	...	1455	1547	...	1653	1802	...	1854	2054	2159
	Göteborg d.	|	...	...	|	...	|	|	|	0650	|	|	0855	|	|	1055	|	|	|	1255	|	|	1500	|	|	1705	|	|	|
30	Falköping **740** d.	0506	0511	...	0617	...	0631	0716	0743	0818	0916	0943	1015	1116	1146	1218	1316	1347	1408	1415	1516	1605	1616	1716	1820	1827	1917	2119	2218
00	Jönköping a.	...	0552	...	0701	...	0715	0758	0828	0901	1000	...	1100	1200	...	1300	1400	...	...	1500	1600	...	1702	1800	...	1912	2002	2201	2302
00	Jönköping d.	...	0554	0610	0706	0725	...	0806	...	0905	1006	...	1104	1204	...	1304	1404	...	...	1504	1603	...	1704	1804	...	1913	2005	2205	2307
43	**Nässjö 730** a.	...	0625	0637	0739	0757	...	0843	...	0944	1040	...	1140	1240	...	1340	1440	...	...	1540	1640	...	1741	1840	...	1944	2040	2241	2340

																										Sn	
																										513	
	Ⓐ	Ⓐ	Ⓐq	Ⓐ	⑥	⚒	⚒		Ⓐ	Ⓐ		Ⓐy	⑥	⚒		Ⓐy	Ⓐy		Ⓐq	Ⓑ	Ⓑ			Ⓑ	Ⓑ		ⒷS	
issjö 730 d.	0447	0545	...	0715	0715	0818	...	0919	1017	...	1116	...	1218	...	1316	1416	...	1516	...	1616	...	1716	...	1816	...	1920	2003	2118
nköping a.	0519	0620	...	0749	0749	0851	...	0953	1050	...	1150	...	1257	...	1350	1450	...	1550	...	1650	...	1752	...	1850	...	1953	2032	2149
nköping d.	0521	0631	0728	0758	0758	0901	...	1000	1100	...	1200	1300	1300	...	1400	1500	...	1600	1632	1702	...	1801	...	1853	...	2002	...	2204
lköping **740** a.	0606	0715	0812	0845	0846	0943	0955	1046	1144	1150	1244	1344	1344	1411	1444	1543	1550	1645	1716	1742	1756	1844	...	1944	1954	2046	...	2247
Göteborg a.	|	|	|	|	|	1105	|	|	1305	|	|	|	1505	|	|	1700	|	|	|	1905	|	|	...	2105	|	|	...	|
övde 740 a.	0628	0735	0834	0906	0909	...	1014	1105	...	1207	1306	1403	...	1428	1503	...	1607	1705	1741	...	1813	1905	...	...	2015	2108	...	2311

– Aug. 10 - Dec. 13: (12) and ✗ Jönköping - Nässjö - Stockholm and v.v. 🅁. Operator: *SJ*.
– Daily June 28 - Aug. 17; ⑥ Aug. 18 - Dec. 13.

q – Aug. 10 - Dec. 13.
y – Aug. 18 - Dec. 13.

734 KRISTIANSTAD - HÄSSLEHOLM - HELSINGBORG

2nd class only Operator: *Skåne*

km																										
		Ⓐ	Ⓐ	Ⓐ	Ⓐ	Ⓐ		✕	Ⓐ		Ⓐ		Ⓐ								Ⓐ		Ⓐ		Ⓐ	
0	**Kristianstad 745** d.	...	0402	0502	...	0538	0602	...	0638	0702	0738	0802	0838	0902	1002	1102	...	1202	1302	1402	1438	1502	1538	1602	1638	1702
30	Hässleholm **745** d.	...	0423	0523	...	0557	0623	...	0657	0723	0757	0823	0857	0923	1023	1123	...	1223	1323	1423	1457	1523	1557	1623	1657	1723
30	Hässleholm d.	...	0501	...	0531	0601	...	0631	0701	0731	0801	0831	0901	0931	1031	1131	...	1231	1331	1431	1501	1531	1601	1631	1701	1731
83	Åstorp d.	0512	0540	...	0612	0640	...	0712	0740	0812	0840	0912	0940	1012	1112	1212	...	1312	1412	1512	1540	1612	1640	1712	1740	1812
107	**Helsingborg** a.	0535	0603	...	0635	0703	...	0735	0803	0835	0903	0935	1003	1035	1135	1235	...	1335	1435	1535	1603	1635	1703	1735	1803	1835

	Ⓐ							H	Ⓒ	Ⓒ
Kristianstad 745 d.	1738	1802	1902	2002	2102	2202	2302	0002	...	...
Hässleholm **745** d.	1757	1823	1923	2023	2123	2223	2323	0023	...	...
Hässleholm d.	1801	1831	1931	2031	2131	2231	2331	...	0031	0131
Åstorp d.	1840	1912	2012	2112	2212	2312	0012	...	0112	0212
Helsingborg a.	1903	1935	2035	2135	2235	2335	0035	...	0135	0235

	Ⓐ	Ⓐ	✕	Ⓐ	Ⓐ			Ⓐ		Ⓐ
Helsingborg d.	0417	0447	0517	...	0547	...	0617	0647	0717	0747	0817
Åstorp d.	0440	0511	0540	...	0611	...	0640	0711	0740	0811	0840
Hässleholm a.	0518	0548	0618	...	0648	...	0718	0748	0818	0848	0918
Hässleholm **745** d.	0531	0558	...	0631	0658	...	0731	0758	0831	0858	0931
Kristianstad 745 a.	0552	0619	...	0652	0719	...	0752	0819	0852	0919	0952

							Ⓐ		Ⓐ		Ⓐ		Ⓐ									✕		Ⓒ	H	
Helsingborg d.	0917	1017	1117	1217	...	1317	1347	1417	1447	1517	1547	1617	1647	1717	...	1817	1917	2017	2117	...	2217	2317	...	0017	...	...
Åstorp d.	0940	1040	1140	1240	...	1340	1411	1440	1511	1540	1611	1640	1711	1740	...	1840	1940	2040	2140	...	2240	2340	...	0040	...	...
Hässleholm a.	1018	1118	1218	1318	...	1418	1448	1518	1548	1618	1648	1718	1748	1818	...	1918	2018	2118	2218	...	2318	0018	...	0118	...	...
Hässleholm **745** d.	1031	1131	1231	1331	...	1431	1458	1531	1558	1631	1658	1731	1758	1831	...	1931	2031	2131	2231	...	2331	...	0031	...	0156	...
Kristianstad 745 a.	1052	1152	1252	1352	...	1452	1519	1552	1619	1652	1719	1752	1819	1852	...	1952	2052	2152	2252	...	2352	...	0052	...	0217	...

H – ②③④⑤⑥† only.

735 GÖTEBORG - MALMÖ - KØBENHAVN

Operator: *Øtåg* (except *Sn* trains)

km																										
					Sn 481			*Sn* 483	*Sn* 483			*Sn* 485		*Sn* 487	*Sn* 487			*Sn* 489	*Sn* 489			*Sn* 491	*Sn* 491			*Sn* 493
		Ⓐ	Ⓐ	✕	Ⓐq			✕q	p			q		†q	p			q	m			q	p			✕q
0	**Göteborg** C ▲ d.	...	...	0540a	0625	0640d	0740	0825	0825	0840	0940	1025	1040	1125	1125	1140	1240	1325	1325	1340	1440	1525	1525	1540	1640	1725
28	Kungsbacka ▲ d.	...	...	0558a	|	0658d	0758	|	|	0858	0958	|	1058	|	|	1158	1258	|	|	1358	1458	|	|	1558	1658	|
76	Varberg ▲ d.	...	...	0619a	|	0719d	0819	|	|	0919	1019	|	1119	|	|	1219	1319	|	|	1419	1519	|	|	1619	1719	|
106	Falkenberg ▲ d.	...	...	0634a	|	0734d	0834	|	|	0934	1034	|	1134	|	|	1234	1334	|	|	1434	1534	|	|	1634	1734	|
150	**Halmstad** ▲ d.	0504	0604	0704	0731	0804	0904	0931	0931	1004	1104	1129	1204	1229	1229	1304	1404	1429	1429	1504	1604	1631	1631	1704	1804	1831
173	Laholm d.	0514	0614	0714	|	0814	0914	|	|	1014	1114	|	1214	|	|	1314	1414	|	|	1514	1614	|	|	1714	1814	|
185	Båstad d.	0522	0622	0722	|	0822	0922	|	|	1022	1122	|	1222	|	|	1322	1422	|	|	1522	1622	|	|	1722	1822	|
210	Ängelholm d.	0541	0641	0741	|	0841	0941	|	|	1041	1141	|	1241	|	|	1341	1441	|	|	1541	1641	|	|	1741	1841	|
237	**Helsingborg** a.	0608	0708	0808	0819	0908	1008	1017	1017	1108	1208	1217	1308	1317	1317	1408	1508	1519	1519	1608	1708	1719	1719	1808	1908	1917
237	**Helsingborg 737** d.	0612	0712	0812	0821	0912	1012	1020	1020	1112	1212	1220	1312	1320	1320	1412	1512	1521	1521	1612	1712	1721	1721	1812	1912	1920
259	Landskrona **737** d.	0623	0723	0823	|	0923	1023	|	|	1123	1223	|	1323	|	|	1423	1523	|	|	1623	1723	|	|	1823	1923	|
290	Lund **737** a.	0639	0739	0839	0847s	0939	1039	1042s	1042s	1139	1239	1242s	1339	1342s	1342s	1439	1539	1547s	1547s	1639	1739	1747s	1747s	1839	1939	1942s
306	**Malmö** C **737** a.	0651	0751	0851	0859	0951	1051	1054	1054	1151	1251	1254	1351	1354	1354	1451	1551	1559	1559	1651	1751	1759	1759	1851	1951	1954
306	**Malmö** C **703** d.	0653	0753	0853	...	0953	1053	...	1104	1153	1253	...	1353	...	1358	1453	1553	...	1605	1653	1753	...	1805	1853	1953	...
341	København (Kastrup) ✈ **703** a.	0713	0813	0913	...	1013	1113	...	1124s	1213	1313	...	1413	...	1417s	1513	1613	...	1625s	1713	1813	...	1825s	1913	2013	...
353	**København** H **703** a.	0728	0828	0928	...	1028	1128	...	1139	1228	1328	...	1428	...	1432	1528	1628	...	1640	1728	1828	...	1840	1928	2028	...

	Sn 493		*Sn* 495		*Sn* 497					
	p		†q		Ⓑq				✕	
Göteborg C ▲ d.	1725	1740	1825	1840	1925	1940	2040	2140	2240	2340
Kungsbacka ▲ d.	|	1758	|	1858	|	1958	2058	2158	2258	2358
Varberg ▲ d.	|	1819	|	1919	|	2019	2119	2220	2320	0020
Falkenberg ▲ d.	|	1834	|	1934	|	2034	2134	2234	2334	0034
Halmstad ▲ d.	1831	1904	1931	2004	2031	2104	2204	2255	2355	0055
Laholm d.	|	1914	|	2014	|	2114	2214	...	...	...
Båstad d.	|	1922	|	2022	|	2122	2222	...	...	...
Ängelholm d.	|	1941	|	2041	|	2141	2241	...	...	...
Helsingborg a.	1917	2008	2017	2108	2117	2208	2308	...	...	...
Helsingborg 737 d.	1920	2012	2020	2112	2120	2212	2312	...	...	...
Landskrona **737** d.	|	2023	|	2123	|	2223	2323	...	...	...
Lund **737** a.	1942s	2039	2042s	2139	2142s	2239	2339	...	...	...
Malmö C **737** a.	1954	2051	2054	2151	2157	2251	2351	...	...	...
Malmö C **703** d.	2004	2053	...	2153	...	2253	...	...	...	...
København (Kastrup) ✈ **703** a.	2025s	2113	...	2213	...	2313	...	...	...	...
København H **703** a.	2040	2128	...	2228	...	2328	...	...	...	...

						Sn 480			*Sn* 482		*Sn* 484
	Ⓐ	Ⓐ	Ⓐ	Ⓐ	✕	Ⓐq	✕		⑥q		Ⓑq
København H **703** d.	...	...	...	...	...	...	0532	0632	...	0732	...
København (Kastrup) ✈ **703** d.	...	...	...	...	...	...	0546	0646	...	0746	...
Malmö C **703** a.	...	...	...	...	...	...	0606	0706	...	0806	...
Malmö C **737** d.	...	...	...	...	0508a	0605	0608	0708	0804	0808	0905
Lund **737** d.	...	...	...	...	0520a	0617u	0620	0720	0816u	0820	0917u
Landskrona **737** d.	...	...	...	...	0535a	|	0635	0735	|	0835	|
Helsingborg 737 a.	...	...	...	...	0548a	0641	0648	0748	0841	0848	0941
Helsingborg d.	...	...	...	...	0553a	0643	0653	0753	0843	0853	0943
Ängelholm d.	...	...	...	...	0614a	|	0714	0814	|	0914	|
Båstad d.	...	...	...	...	0636a	|	0736	0836	|	0936	|
Laholm d.	...	...	...	...	0643a	|	0743	0843	|	0943	|
Halmstad ▲ d.	0505	0535	0605	0635	0705	0731	0805	0905	0931	1005	1031
Falkenberg ▲ d.	0522	0552	0622	0652	0722	|	0822	0922	|	1022	|
Varberg ▲ d.	0538	0608	0638	0708	0737	|	0837	0937	|	1037	|
Kungsbacka ▲ d.	0600	0630	0700	0730	0800	|	0900	1000	|	1100	|
Göteborg C ▲ a.	0620	0650	0720	0750	0820	0835	0920	1020	1030	1120	1130

		Sn 486	*Sn* 486			*Sn* 488	*Sn* 488			*Sn* 490	*Sn* 490		*Sn* 492			*Sn* 494	*Sn* 494			*Sn* 496	*Sn* 496		*Sn* 498			
		p	⑥q			p	q			p	✕q		†q			p	q			p	Ⓑq		Ⓑq		✕	
København H **703** d.	0832	0916	...	0932	1032	1116	...	1132	1232	1317	...	1332	...	1432	1532	1617	...	1632	1732	1816	...	1832	...	2032	2232	...
København (Kastrup) ✈ **703** d.	0846	0929u	...	0946	1046	1129u	...	1146	1246	1329u	...	1346	...	1446	1546	1629u	...	1646	1746	1829u	...	1846	...	2046	2246	...
Malmö C **703** a.	0906	0955	...	1006	1106	1155	...	1206	1306	1356	...	1406	...	1506	1606	1654	...	1706	1806	1855	...	1906	...	2106	2306	...
Malmö C **737** d.	0908	1005	1005	1008	1108	1205	1205	1208	1308	1405	1405	1408	1505	1508	1608	1700	1700	1708	1808	1905	1905	1908	2005	2108	2308	...
Lund **737** d.	0920	1017u	1017u	1020	1120	1217u	1217u	1220	1320	1417u	1417u	1420	1517u	1520	1620	1712u	1712u	1720	1820	1917u	1917u	1920	2017u	2120	2320	...
Landskrona **737** d.	0935	|	|	1035	1135	|	|	1235	1335	|	|	1435	|	1535	1635	|	|	1735	1835	|	|	1935	|	2135	2335	...
Helsingborg 737 a.	0948	1041	1041	1048	1148	1241	1241	1248	1348	1441	1441	1448	1541	1548	1648	1741	1741	1748	1848	1941	1941	1948	2041	2148	2348	...
Helsingborg d.	0953	1043	1043	1053	1153	1243	1243	1253	1353	1443	1443	1453	1543	1553	1653	1743	1743	1753	1853	1943	1943	1953	2043	2153	2353	...
Ängelholm d.	1014	|	|	1114	1214	|	|	1314	1414	|	|	1514	|	1614	1714	|	|	1814	1914	|	|	2014	|	2214	0014	...
Båstad d.	1036	|	|	1136	1236	|	|	1336	1436	|	|	1536	|	1636	1736	|	|	1836	1936	|	|	2036	|	2236	0036	...
Laholm d.	1043	|	|	1143	1243	|	|	1343	1443	|	|	1543	|	1643	1743	|	|	1843	1943	|	|	2043	|	2243	0043	...
Halmstad ▲ d.	1105	1131	1131	1205	1305	1330	1330	1405	1505	1531	1531	1605	1631	1705	1805	1831	1831	1905	2005	2031	2031	2105	2131	2305	0056	...
Falkenberg ▲ d.	1122	|	|	1222	1322	|	|	1422	1522	|	|	1622	|	1722	1822	|	|	1922	2022	|	|	2122	|	2322	...	...
Varberg ▲ d.	1137	|	|	1237	1337	|	|	1437	1537	|	|	1637	|	1737	1837	|	|	1937	2037	|	|	2137	|	2337	...	...
Kungsbacka ▲ d.	1200	|	|	1300	1400	|	|	1500	1600	|	|	1700	|	1800	1900	|	|	2000	2100	|	|	2200	|	0000	...	...
Göteborg C ▲ a.	1220	1230	1230	1320	1420	1430	1430	1520	1620	1635	1635	1720	1735	1820	1920	1935	1935	2020	2120	2135	2135	2220	2235	0020	...	...

a – Ⓐ only.
d – ✕ only.
m – July 5 - Aug. 9.
p – June 29 - Aug. 9.
q – Aug. 10 - Dec. 13.
s – Stops to set down only.
u – Stops to pick up only.
▲ – Additional services operate on Ⓐ Göteborg - Halmstad and v.v.

736 HALLSBERG - LIDKÖPING - HERRLJUNGA

2nd class only Operator: V

km																												
		Ⓐ	Ⓐ	Ⓐ	⑥	Ⓐp	Ⓒ	Ⓐ	Ⓐ	†	⑥	Ⓐ	⑥		†	†	⑥p	Ⓐ	⑥q	Ⓐ	Ⓐp	⑥	†	Ⓐ	Ⓐ	†	Ⓐp	⑤
	Örebro C 755/6 d.	...	...	...	...	...	...	0755	...	...	...	...	...	...	...	...	...	...	...	...	...	...	...	1624	...	...	...	...
0	**Hallsberg 740** d.	...	...	...	...	...	...	0815	...	...	...	...	1151	...	1300	...	...	...	...	...	...	1614	...	1645	...	1851	1904	...
30	Laxå **740** d.	...	...	...	...	...	...	0831	...	...	...	...	1207	...	1316	...	...	...	...	...	...	1630	...	1701	...	1907	1920	...
92	Mariestad d.	...	0530	0700	...	0757	0835	0918	1008	...	1142	1221	1251	...	1403	1409	1430	1440	1538	1546	1702	1720	1722	1755	...	2012j	2009	200[illegible]
146	Lidköping a.	...	0611	0748	...	0852	0916	1007	1104	...	1230	1309	...	...	...	1450	1511	1522	1619	1642	1756	1809	1802	1843	...	2100	2057f	205[illegible]
146	Lidköping d.	0535	0626	0758	0805	0902	0917	1009	1110	1155	1243	1315	...	...	...	1452	1513	1524	1628	1705	...	...	1805	...	2006	...	...	...
201	**Herrljunga 740** a.	0621	0704	0846	0855	0950	0957	1056	1157	1244	1335	1403	...	...	...	1533	1559	1605	1706	1750	...	...	1843	...	2051	...	...	...
	Göteborg C 740 a.	...	0755	...	...	...	1055	1155	...	1335	1425	...	...	...	...	1625	1655	1655	1755	...	...	...	1935	...	...	...	...	...

	Ⓐ	Ⓐp	Ⓐ	Ⓐ	⑥	Ⓐ	†	⑥	Ⓐ	⑥	⑥	Ⓐp	†	Ⓐ	Ⓐ	Ⓐ	Ⓐp	†	⑥	Ⓐp	Ⓐq	⑥p	Ⓐ	†	Ⓐ	⑥q	†q	Ⓐ
Göteborg C 740 d.	...	...	...	...	...	...	...	...	0925	...	1105	...	1125	...	1300	...	...	1405	1455	...	...	1705	1725	1750	...	1900	2000	...
Herrljunga 740 d.	...	...	...	0705	...	0909	...	1000	1020	...	1153	1203	1213	...	1348	1418	...	1500	1543	1613	1613	1755	1824	1844	1912	1948	2059	21[illegible]
Lidköping a.	...	...	...	0752	...	0959	...	1045	1101	...	1233	1246	1252	...	1430	1505	...	1548	1625	1659	1659	1834	1906	1923	1957	2028	2139	21[illegible]
Lidköping d.	...	0517	0614	0755	0925	1010	1044	1046	1106	...	1235	...	1254	1321	1431	...	1542	1556	1627	1702	1702	1836	1907	1926	...	2030	...	...
Mariestad d.	0550	0612	0655	0846	1015	1100	1133	1136	1147	1257	1319	...	1336	1412	1522	...	1634	1646	1715	1751	1749	1919	1949	2007	...	2112	...	...
Laxå **740** d.	0636	...	...	...	1103	...	1221	...	...	1344	...	...	...	1504	...	...	...	1735	...	1837	...	...	...	...	...	...	...	...
Hallsberg 740 a.	0652	...	...	...	1119	...	1237	...	...	1404	...	...	...	1521	...	...	...	1751	...	1857	...	...	...	...	...	...	...	...
Örebro C 755/6 a.	0713	...	...	...	...	...	...	...	...	...	...	...	...	1548	...	...	...	...	...	...	...	...	...	...	...	...	...	...

f – ⑤ only.
j – Arrive 1954.
p – Aug. 18 - Dec. 13.
q – June 29 - Aug. 17.

KØBENHAVN - LUFTHAVN (KASTRUP) ✈ - MALMÖ - HELSINGBORG 737

Operator: *Skåne* (Ø – *Øtåg*)

km		ØⒶ	Ⓐ2	Ø	2	ØⒶ	Ⓐ2	Ⓐ2	Ø	2	ØⒶ	Ⓐ2	ØⒶr	Ø	2	ØⒶ	Ⓐ2	Ø	2	Ø	2	Ø	2	Ø	2	Ø	2
	København H **703** d.	...	...	0532	...	...	...	...	0632	...	0700r	...	0720	0732	...	0800r	...	0832	...	0932	...	1032	...	1132	...	1232	...
	Lufthavn (Kastrup) **703** d.	...	...	0546	...	...	...	...	0646	...	0714r	...	0734	0746	...	0814r	...	0846	...	0946	...	1046	...	1146	...	1246	...
0	**Malmö** C **703 735** d.	0508	0514	0608	0614	0638	0644	0700	0708	0714	0738	0744	0800	0808	0814	0838	0844	0908	0914	1008	1014	1108	1114	1208	1214	1308	1314
16	Lund **735** d.	0520	0526	0620	0626	0650	0656	0712	0720	0726	0750	0756	0812	0820	0826	0850	0856	0920	0926	1020	1026	1120	1126	1220	1226	1320	1326
48	Landskrona **735** d.	0535	0550	0635	0650	0705	0720	0728	0735	0750	0805	0820	0828	0835	0850	0905	0920	0935	0950	1035	1050	1135	1150	1235	1250	1335	1350
69	**Helsingborg 735** a.	0548	0607	0648	0707	0720	0739	0743	0748	0807	0820	0839	0843	0848	0907	0920	0939	0948	1007	1048	1107	1148	1207	1248	1307	1348	1407

	Ø	2	Ⓐ2	Ø	2	ØⒶ	Ⓐ2	ØⒶ	Ø	2	ØⒶ	Ⓐ2	ØⒶ	Ø	2	ØⒶ	Ⓐ2	ØⒶ	Ø	2	Ⓐ2	Ø	2	Ø	2	Ø
København H **703** d.	1332	...	...	1432	...	1500	...	1520	1532	...	1600	...	1620	1632	...	1700	...	1720	1732	...	...	1832	...	1932	...	2032
Lufthavn (Kastrup) **703** d.	1346	...	...	1446	...	1514	...	1534	1546	...	1614	...	1634	1646	...	1714	...	1734	1746	...	...	1846	...	1946	...	2046
Malmö C **703 735** d.	1408	1414	1444	1508	1514	1538	1544	1600	1608	1614	1639	1644	1703	1708	1714	1738	1744	1800	1808	1814	1844	1908	1914	2008	2014	2108
Lund **735** d.	1420	1426	1456	1520	1526	1550	1556	1612	1620	1626	1651	1656	1714	1720	1726	1750	1756	1812	1820	1826	1856	1920	1926	2020	2026	2120
Landskrona **735** d.	1435	1450	1520	1535	1550	1605	1620	1628	1635	1650	1707	1720	1730	1735	1750	1805	1820	1828	1835	1850	1920	1935	1950	2035	2050	2135
Helsingborg 735 a.	1448	1507	1539	1548	1607	1620	1639	1643	1648	1707	1720	1739	1745	1748	1807	1820	1839	1843	1848	1907	1939	1948	2007	2048	2107	2148

	2	Ø	2	Ø	2	Ø	2H	Ø	Ⓒ	
København H **703** d.	...	2132	...	2232	...	2332	...	2352	...	...
Lufthavn (Kastrup) **703** d.	...	2146	...	2246	...	2346	...	0006	...	...
Malmö C **703 735** d.	2114	2208	2214	2308	2314	0008	0014	0029	0114	...
Lund **735** d.	2126	2220	2226	2320	2326	0020	0026	0039	0126	...
Landskrona **735** d.	2150	2235	2250	2335	2350	0035	0050	...	0150	...
Helsingborg 735 a.	2207	2248	2307	2348	0007	0048	0107	...	0207	...

	ØⒶ	Ⓐ2	ØⒶ	2	Ø	ØⒶr	Ⓐ2	ØⒶ	2	Ø
Helsingborg 735 d.	0508	0521	0540	0551	0612	0615	0621	0640	0651	0712
Landskrona **735** d.	0521	0539	0552	0609	0623	0626	0639	0652	0709	0723
Lund **735** d.	0541	0604	0610	0634	0641	0646	0704	0710	0734	0741
Malmö C **703 735** a.	0551	0614	0620	0644	0651	0656	0714	0720	0744	0751
Lufthavn (Kastrup) **703** a.	0613	...	0641r	...	0713	0721	...	0741r	...	0813
København H **703** a.	0628	...	0656r	...	0728	0736	...	0756r	...	0828

	ØⒶr	Ⓐ2	ØⒶ	2	Ø	Ⓐ2	Ⓐ2	ØⒶ	2	Ø	Ⓐ2	2	Ø	2	Ø	2	Ø	2	Ø	2	Ø	2	Ø	ØⒶ	Ⓐ2	ØⒶ
Helsingborg 735 d.	0715	0721	0740	0751	0812	0815	0824	0840	0851	0912	0921	0951	1012	1051	1112	1151	1212	1251	1312	1351	1412	1451	1512	1515	1524	1540
Landskrona **735** d.	0726	0739	0752	0809	0823	0826	0842	0852	0909	0923	0939	1009	1023	1109	1123	1209	1223	1309	1323	1409	1423	1509	1523	1526	1542	1552
Lund **735** d.	0746	0804	0810	0834	0841	0846	0907	0910	0934	0941	1004	1034	1041	1134	1141	1234	1241	1334	1341	1434	1441	1534	1541	1546	1607	1610
Malmö C **703 735** a.	0756	0814	0820	0844	0851	0856	0917	0920	0944	0951	1014	1044	1051	1144	1151	1244	1251	1344	1351	1444	1451	1544	1551	1556	1617	1620
Lufthavn (Kastrup) **703** a.	0821	...	0841r	...	0913	...	...	...	...	1013	...	...	1113	...	1213	...	1313	...	1413	...	1513	...	1613	1621	...	1641
København H **703** a.	0836	...	0856r	...	0928	...	...	...	...	1028	...	...	1128	...	1228	...	1328	...	1428	...	1528	...	1628	1636	...	1656

	2	Ø	ØⒶ	Ⓐ2	ØⒶ	2	Ø	ØⒶ	Ⓐ2	ØⒶ	2	Ø	Ⓐ2	2	Ø	2	Ø	2	Ø	2	Ø	2	Ø	⚒2	Ⓒ2	Ⓒ2
Helsingborg 735 d.	1551	1612	1615	1621	1640	1651	1712	1715	1724	1740	1751	1812	1821	1851	1912	1951	2012	2051	2112	2151	2212	2251	2312	2351	0047	0147
Landskrona **735** d.	1609	1623	1626	1639	1652	1709	1723	1726	1742	1752	1809	1823	1839	1909	1923	2009	2023	2109	2123	2209	2223	2309	2323	0009	0105	0205
Lund **735** d.	1634	1641	1646	1704	1710	1734	1741	1746	1807	1810	1834	1841	1904	1934	1941	2034	2041	2134	2141	2234	2241	2337	2341	0034	0130	0230
Malmö C **703 735** a.	1644	1651	1656	1714	1720	1744	1751	1756	1817	1820	1844	1851	1914	1944	1951	2044	2051	2144	2151	2244	2251	2347	2351	0044	0144	0244
Lufthavn (Kastrup) **703** a.	...	1713	1721	...	...	...	1813	...	...	...	...	1913	...	...	2013	...	2113	...	2213	...	2313	...	...	...	...	...
København H **703** a.	...	1728	1736	...	...	...	1828	...	...	...	...	1928	...	...	2028	...	2128	...	2228	...	2328	...	...	...	...	...

H – ②③④⑤⑥† only.
r – Aug. 10 - Dec. 13.
Ø – Operated by *Øtåg*.

South-eastern SECONDARY LINES 738

km	Operator: *KLT/ÖT*	Ⓐ									Ⓑ
0	Västervik d.	0541	0739	...	1006	1205	...	1405	1601	1803	2002
77	Åtvidaberg d.	0648	0845	...	1112	1313	...	1513	1710	1910	2111
116	Linköping a.	0731	0921	...	1145	1345	...	1545	1745	1942	2142

Operator: *KLT/ÖT*	Ⓐ									Ⓑ
Linköping d.	0543	...	0811	1013	1213	1413	1603	1803	...	2123
Åtvidaberg d.	0617	...	0844	1044	1245	1445	1641	1839	...	2200
Västervik a.	0727	...	0949	1149	1349	1553	1747	1944	...	2304

km	Operator: *KLT/ÖT*	Ⓐ	Ⓐ	⑥						Ⓑ	Ⓑ
0	Linköping d.	...	0534	...	0823	1023	1223	1423	1621	1825	2023
41	Rimforsa d.	...	0611	...	0905	1105	1304	1504	1704	1904	2106
123	Hultsfred d.	0620	0712	0712	1004	1208	1405	1608	1808	2003	2203
159	Berga a.	0644	0737	0737	1032	1232	1431	1632	1832	2028	...
159	Berga d.	0649	0742	0742	1037	1237	1436	1637	1837	2033	...
235	Kalmar **746** a.	0748	0845	0845	1135	1335	1534	1736	1935	2129	...

Operator: *KLT/ÖT*	Ⓐ	Ⓐ	⑥						Ⓑ	Ⓑ
Kalmar **746** d.	...	0544	...	0839	1036	1236	1436	1636	1836	2125
Berga a.	...	0641	...	0935	1133	1333	1533	1733	1933	2221
Berga d.	...	0646	...	0940	1138	1338	1538	1738	1938	2226
Hultsfred d.	0540	0712	0712	1004	1203	1404	1604	1804	2004	2249
Rimforsa d.	0642	0811	0811	1104	1303	1505	1703	1904	2105	...
Linköping a.	0717	0845	0845	1139	1338	1540	1742	1939	2139	...

km	Operator: *JLT*	2Ⓐ		2Ⓐ	2Ⓒ	2Ⓐ		2	2Ⓑ	2F	2N
0	Nässjö d.	0659	...	0916	0916	←	...	1316	1525	1721	1721
83	Hultsfred d.	0811	...	1034	1035	1112	...	1436	1641	1843	1845
120	Berga d.	...	...	→	1101	1141	...	1508	1709	...	1912
149	Oskarshamn a.	...	...	...	1121	1201	...	1528	1729	...	1932

Operator: *JLT*	2Ⓐ	2Ⓐ	2Ⓒ		2		2		2Ⓑw	2y
Oskarshamn d.	0530	...	0840	...	1238	...	1647	...	...	1848
Berga d.	0552	...	0902	...	1300	...	1709	...	...	1910
Hultsfred d.	0624	0929	0929	...	1327	...	1735	...	1936	1936
Nässjö a.	0738	1042	1042	...	1439	...	1847	...	2047	2047

F – ⑧ June 29 - Aug. 16.
N – ⑥ June 29 - Aug. 16; daily Aug. 17 - Dec. 13.
w – June 29 - Aug. 16.
y – Aug. 17 - Dec. 13.

VARBERG - UDDEVALLA 739

Operator: *V* (except *Sn* trains) 2nd class only

km		†z	Ⓐ	Ⓐ	Ⓐ	Ⓐ	⑥	†	Ⓐ	Ⓐ	Ⓐr	Ⓒ	Ⓐ	*Sn* **463** Sp		†	Ⓒ	Ⓐ	Ⓐ	Ⓒ	Ⓐ	Ⓐr	Ⓑ	⑥	*Sn* **467** SⒷq	Ⓑ		†
0	**Varberg 735** d.	0200	...	...	0612	...	...	...	0713	...	0813	0844g	0950	...	*1044*g	1144	1244g	...	1342	...	1442	1542	1642	*1542*	...	1842a	1943	2144
84	Borås **746** a.	0310	...	...	0725	...	...	...	0825	...	0927	0954g	1101	...	*1156*g	1252	1354g	...	1452	...	1555	1655	1755	*1655*	...	1952a	2102	2257
84	Borås d.	...	0554	0656	...	0757	0756	0758	...	0859	...	1002	...	...	1225	...	1400	1400	1458q	1610	1617	1657	1758	1800	...	2005	...	...
127	Herrljunga **740** a.	...	0632	0738	...	0838	0838	0836	...	0940	...	1038	...	...	1303	...	1438	1438	1539q	1649	1658	1740	1838	1838	...	2040	...	...
127	Herrljunga d.	...	0648	0748r	...	0852	0921	...	...	0951t	...	1052	...	1245	1321	...	1454	1459t	1606q	1721	1721	1753	1854e	1854	1927	2052	...	...
191	Vänersborg d.	...	0733	0831r	...	0940	1004	...	...	1034t	...	1135	...	1328	1404	...	1539	1551t	1656q	1805	1805	1838	1940e	1940	2013	2135	...	...
195	Öxnered **750** d.	...	0739	0839r	...	0946	1010	...	...	1040t	...	1141	...	|	1410	...	1545	1557t	1702q	1811	1811	1844	1946e	1946	|	2141	...	...
217	Uddevalla C a.	...	0757	0855r	...	1002	1026	...	...	1056t	...	1157	...	1357	1426	...	1606	1613t	1718q	1827	1827	1900	2002e	2002	2035	2157	...	...

	Ⓐ	⑥	Ⓐ	*Sn* **462** SⒶq	Ⓐ	*Sn* **460** S⑥q	⑥	⑥	Ⓐ	Ⓐ	⑥	Ⓒ	Ⓐ	†		Ⓐq	Ⓒ		Ⓐ	Ⓒ	Ⓐr	Ⓒ	*Sn* **466** Sp	Ⓑ	Ⓑ	Ⓑ	†z
Uddevalla C d.	...	...	0517	0532	0616	0700	...	0725	...	0824	...	0924	...	...	1158	1325	1328	...	1539	1545	1617	1723	1802	...	1916	...	...
Öxnered **750** d.	...	...	0533	|	0632	|	...	0741	...	0840	...	0940	...	...	1214	1341	1344	...	1555	1602	1634	1740	|	...	1933	...	...
Vänersborg d.	...	...	0540	0556	0638	0719	...	0747	...	0846	...	0949	...	...	1221	1350	1351	...	1602	1610	1642	1749	1828	...	1939	...	...
Herrljunga **746** a.	...	...	0628	0636	0736	0759	...	0832	...	0941	...	1039	...	...	1305	1437	1437	...	1652	1657	1738	1839	1911	...	2031	...	...
Herrljunga d.	0540r	...	0648	...	0749	▬	0819	0923	*0852*	1016	...	1054	...	...	1321	1519	1452	1605y	1721	1721	1753	1855g	...	1930	2054	...	...
Borås **746** a.	0620r	...	0725	...	0826	†	0858	1000	*0927*	1053	...	1131	...	...	1358	1556	1528	1648y	1756	1758	1828	1932g	...	2003	2130	...	...
Borås d.	0628	0700	0728	...	0830r	0900	...	...	1000	...	1100	...	1201	1300	1400g	1558	...	1658	1758	...	...	...	...	2004	...	2200	0040
Varberg **735** a.	0743	0812	0843	...	0942r	1012	...	...	1113	...	1213	...	1313	1412	1512g	1713	...	1811	1913	...	...	...	...	2114	...	2313	0152

GÖTEBORG - UDDEVALLA - STRÖMSTAD

km			m		Y			m	Ⓐ	Ⓒ	
0	**Göteborg** C ▲ d.	0640	0840	1040	1240	...	1440	1640	1840	1840	...
89	Uddevalla C ▲ a.	0749	0949	1149	1349	...	1549	1749	1949	1949	...
89	Uddevalla C d.	0802	1000	1202	1400	...	1600	1800	2000	2007	...
173	Skee d.	0914	1125	1314	1518	...	1718	1928	2112	2119	...
180	**Strömstad** a.	0921	1132	1321	1530	...	1725	1935	2119	2126	...

	⚒	⚒t	†z			m		Y		
Strömstad d.	0641	0820	0837	1034	...	1219	1427	1626	...	1835
Skee d.	0648	0827	0844	1041	...	1226	1434	1634	...	1842
Uddevalla C a.	0759	0955	0955	1152	...	1355	1548	1751	...	1953
Uddevalla C ▲ d.	0805	1005	1005	1205	...	1405	1605	1805	...	2005
Göteborg C ▲ a.	0915	1115	1115	1315	...	1518	1718	1915	...	2115

– (12) and ✕ Stockholm - Herrljunga - Uddevalla and v.v. Ⓡ. Train **462** runs as train **10462** from Aug. 25.
– Daily Aug. 10 - 17; Ⓑ Aug. 18 - Dec. 13.
– Ⓐ only.
– † only.
– ⑥ only.
– June 29 - Aug. 16.

n – Aug. 17 - Dec. 13.
p – June 29 - Aug. 9.
q – Aug. 10 - Dec. 13.
r – Aug. 18 - Dec. 13.
t – June 29 - Aug. 17.
y – Ⓐ Aug. 10 - Dec. 13.
z – June 29 - Aug. 10.

▲ – Additional services **Göteborg - Uddevalla and v.v.**: Operator: Västtrafik.
From **Göteborg** C: 0540Ⓐ, 0740Ⓐ, 0840**n**, 0940⚒, 1140⚒, 1240**p**, 1240⑥**r**, 1340⚒, 1540⚒, 1640**n**, 1710Ⓐ, 1740Ⓑ, 1940Ⓑ, 2040.
From **Uddevalla**: 0535Ⓐ, 0605Ⓐ, 0619Ⓐ, 0705⚒, 0805†, 0905⚒, 1005**r**, 1105⚒, 1305⚒, 1405**n**, 1505⚒, 1705Ⓑ, 1805**p**, 1805⑥**r**, 1905Ⓑ.

740 STOCKHOLM - HALLSBERG - GÖTEBORG

For additional services Stockholm - Hallsberg and v.v. see Table 750. For long distance sleeper trains see Table 767

km																									
		Sn		Sn			Sn		Sn	Sn			Sn	Sn	Sn		Sn	IC		Sn	Sn		SKJB	Sn	Sn
		401	117	421	157	157	423		415	425	163	193	427	463	429	167	431	103		433	453	171	7075	435	435
		R✕		R✕			R✕		R✕	R✕	⊡	⊡	R✕	R✕	R✕	⊡	R✕			R✕	R✕	⊡		R✕	R✕
		H	Ⓐq	Ⓐ	M	⑥	Ⓐq		Ⓒ	Ⓐ	Ⓑ	⑥	B	♦			Ⓑq	†J		Ⓐq	A		⑥	Ⓐq	†q
0	**Stockholm** C **730** ▲ d.	0606	...	0614	...	...	0714	...	0814	0814	0649a	0719	0914	1006	1014	0919	1114	1136	...	1214	1214	1119	1255	1314	1314
15	Flemingsberg ‡ ▲ d.	|	...	|	...	...	0725	...	|	|	|	|	0925	|	|	|	|	|	...	|	|	|	|	1325	1325
36	Södertälje Syd ‡ ▲ d.	|	...	0632	...	...	|	...	0832	0832	V	V	|	1024	1032	V	1132	1157	...	1232	1232	V	|	|	|
131	Katrineholm **730** ▲ d.	|	...	0710	...	...	0810	...	0910	0910	|	|	1010	|	1110	|	1211	|	...	1310	1310	|	|	1410	1410
197	**Hallsberg 755/6** ▲ a.	|	...	|	...	...	0835	...	|	|	|	|	|	1125	|	|	|	1315	...	|	|	|	1422	|	|
	Örebro C **755/6** d.	|	0623	|	0718	0718	|	...	|	|	0854	0918	|	|	|	1118	|	|	...	|	|	1318	|	|	|
197	**Hallsberg** d.	|	0645	|	0740	0740	0837	...	|	|	0920	0940	|	1125	|	1140	|	1315	...	|	|	1340	1424	|	|
227	Laxå **736** d.	|	|	|	0754	0754	|	...	|	|	0948	0954	|	|	|	1154	|	|	...	|	|	1354	|	|	|
272	Töreboda d.	|	|	|	0815	0815	|	...	|	|	1010	1015	|	|	|	1215	|	|	...	|	|	1416	|	|	|
311	**Skövde** § d.	|	0730	0816	0836	0836	0919	...	1015	1016	1033	1033	1114	1208	1214	1235	1314	1426	...	1414	1414	1435	1516	1514	1514
341	Falköping § d.	|	0752	|	0853	0853	|	...	|	|	1051	1051	|	|	|	1250	|	|	...	|	|	1454	|	|	|
375	Herrljunga **736/9** § d.	|	|	0844	0912	0912	|	...	1042	|	1114	1114	|	1245	1240	1309	|	|	...	|	1444	1509	|	1544	|
	Uddevalla C **739** a.	|	|	|	|	|	|	...	|	|	|	|	|	1357	|	|	|	|	...	|	|	|	|	|	|
410	Alingsås § a.	|	|	|	0934	0933	|	...	|	1055s	1134	1134	|	...	|	1334	1353s	|	...	1454s	|	1529	1559s	|	|
455	**Göteborg** C § a.	0855	0900	0925	1005	1005	1025	...	1125	1125	1205	1205	1225	...	1325	1405	1425	1555	...	1525	1525	1600	1630	1630	1630

	IC	Sn		Sn	SKJB	Sn	Sn	197		SKJB		Sn	Sn	Sn	Sn	Sn	IC		Sn	Sn	Sn	Sn		Sn	Sn
	105	437	175	439	7073	441	411	199	179	7079		413	467	473	443	10443	109		405	407	445	455	183	447	449
		R✕	⊡	R✕		R✕	R✕	⊡				R✕	R✕	R✕	R✕	R✕			R✕	R✕	R✕	R✕	⊡	R✕	R✕
	⑤			C	④⑤	Ⓑ	⑥	A	Ⓐq	†		K	♦	⑥q	D	E	†		F	L	Ⓑ	⑥		G	Ⓑ
Stockholm C **730** ▲ d.	1325	1414	1319	1514	1506	1614	1614	1519	1524	1559	...	1636	1640	1706	1714	1714	1725	...	1736	1736	1814	1814	1719	1914	2014
Flemingsberg ‡ ▲ d.	|	|	|	|	|	|	|	|	|	|	...	|	|	|	|	|	|	...	|	|	|	|	|	1925	|
Södertälje Syd ‡ ▲ d.	1347	1432	V	1532	|	1632	1632	V	V	|	...	|	|	1724	1732	1732	1757	...	|	|	1832	1832	V	|	2032
Katrineholm **730** ▲ d.	|	1510	|	|	|	1710	1710	|	|	|	...	|	|	1806	1810	1810	|	...	|	|	1910	1910	|	2010	2110
Hallsberg 755/6 ▲ a.	1456	|	|	1631	|	|	|	|	|	1726	...	|	|	|	|	|	1908	...	|	|	|	|	|	|	2134
Örebro C **755/6** d.	|	|	1518	|	|	|	|	1718	1718	|	...	|	|	|	|	|	|	...	|	|	|	|	1918	|	|
Hallsberg d.	1458	|	1540	1631	|	|	|	1740	1740	1728	...	|	|	|	|	|	1908	...	|	|	|	|	1940	|	2136
Laxå **736** d.	|	|	1604	|	|	|	|	1754	1802	|	...	|	|	|	|	|	|	...	|	|	|	|	1954	|	|
Töreboda d.	|	|	1616	|	|	|	|	1814	|	|	...	|	1830	|	|	|	|	...	|	|	|	|	2015	|	|
Skövde § d.	1550	1614	1641	1715	1730	1814	1814	1836	1836	1828	...	|	1847	1917	1914	1914	2001	...	|	|	2014	2014	2034	2114	2218
Falköping § d.	|	|	1657	|	|	|	|	1853	1853	|	...	|	1904	|	|	|	|	...	|	|	|	|	2054	|	|
Herrljunga **736/9** § d.	1634	|	1714	1744	|	|	1841	1910	1910	|	...	|	1927	|	|	|	|	...	|	|	2044	|	2113	|	|
Uddevalla C **739** a.	|	|	|	|	|	|	|	|	|	|	...	|	2035	|	|	|	|	...	|	|	|	|	|	|	|
Alingsås § a.	1700s	1654s	1734	|	1813s	|	|	1930	1930	1912s	...	|	...	|	1954s	1954s	|	...	|	|	|	2054s	2133	2154s	|
Göteborg C § a.	1730	1725	1805	1825	1855	1925	1925	2000	2000	1955	...	1930	...	2030	2025	2030	2130	...	2030	2035	2125	2125	2205	2225	2325

	Sn	Sn	Sn	Sn			Sn	Sn		Sn	Sn	SKJB		Sn		SKJB	Sn				Sn	IC		SKJB	Sn
	420	402	400	462	164	160	10422	422		424	460	7074	168	426		7070	428	172	22172		430	102		7078	432
	R✕	R✕	R✕	R✕		⊡	R✕	R✕		R✕	R✕		⊡	R✕			R✕				R✕				R✕
	Ⓐp	H	Ⓐm	♦	Ⓐq	R	Ⓐt	N		Ⓐq	♦	⑥				④⑤	B	w	h			†J		†	
Göteborg C § d.	0505	0555	0600	...	0545	0555	0630	0635	...	0735	...	0750	0755	0835	...	0855	0935	0955	0955	...	1035	1030	...	1100	1135
Alingsås § d.	0532u	|	|	...	0613	0625	0700u	0700u	...	|	...	0819u	0825	0901u	...	0925u	|	1025	1025	...	1100u	|	...	1132u	|
Uddevalla C **739** d.	|	|	|	0532	|	|	|	|	...	|	0700	|	|	|	...	|	|	|	|	...	|	|	...	|	|
Herrljunga **736/9** § d.	0546	|	|	0642	0650	0646	|	|	...	|	0806	|	0846	|	...	|	1011	1046	1050	...	|	|	...	|	|
Falköping § d.	0602	|	|	0657	0707	0702	|	|	...	|	0822	|	0902	|	...	|	|	1102	1107	...	|	|	...	|	|
Skövde § d.	0618	|	|	0714	0724	0720	0738	0738	...	0838	0842	0905	0920	0939	...	1009	1038	1120	1124	...	1139	1149	...	1218	1239
Töreboda d.	|	|	|	0732	0742	0738	|	|	...	|	|	|	0938	|	...	|	|	1138	1142	...	|	|	...	|	|
Laxå **736** d.	|	|	|	|	0804	0804	|	|	...	|	|	|	1004	|	...	|	|	1204	1204	...	|	|	...	|	|
Hallsberg a.	0705	|	|	0808	0820	0820	|	|	...	|	0930	0955	1020	|	...	1058	|	1220	1220	...	|	1242	...	1307	|
Örebro C **755/6** a.	|	|	|	|	0842	0842	|	|	...	|	|	|	1042	|	...	|	|	1242	1242	...	|	|	...	|	|
Hallsberg 755/6 ▲ d.	0707	|	|	0810	|	|	|	|	...	|	0932	0957	|	|	...	1100	|	|	|	...	|	1244	...	1309	|
Katrineholm **730** ▲ d.	0733	|	|	|	|	|	0850	0850	...	0950	|	|	|	1050	...	|	1150	|	|	...	1250	|	...	|	1350
Södertälje Syd ‡ ▲ a.	|	|	|	0915	V	V	0926	0926	...	1025	1037	|	V	1126	...	|	|	V	V	...	1326	1359	...	|	1426
Flemingsberg ‡ ▲ a.	0821	|	|	|	|	|	|	|	...	|	|	|	|	|	...	|	1233	|	|	...	|	|	...	|	|
Stockholm C **730** ▲ a.	0835	0846	0850	0935	1035	1043	0946	0946	...	1046	1101	1124	1243	1146	...	1235	1246	1435	1443	...	1346	1425	...	1452	1446

		Sn	Sn	IC				Sn	Sn	Sn	Sn				Sn	IC	Sn				Sn	Sn		Sn	
	176	434	436	104	190	180		438	470	440	406		184	194	442	108	444		188	22186	446	466	150	450	
	⊡	R✕	R✕		⊡	⊡		R✕	R✕	R✕	R✕		⊡	⊡	R✕		R✕		⊡		R✕	R✕		R✕	
			C	⑤q	⑥	Ⓑ			⑥q	Ⓑq	Q		S	T		†	Ⓑq		X	†j		♦	Z	Ⓑq	
Göteborg C § d.	1155	1235	1335	1330	1355	1355	...	1435	1525	1535	1600	...	1555	1555	1630	1655	1735	...	1755	1800	1835	...	1855	2035	...
Alingsås § d.	1225	|	1400u	|	1425	1425	...	1500u	|	1600u	|	...	1625	1625	|	|	|	...	1825	1829	1900u	...	1925	|	...
Uddevalla C **739** d.	|	|	|	|	|	|	...	|	|	|	|	...	|	|	|	|	|	...	|	|	|	1802	|	|	...
Herrljunga **736/9** § d.	1244	1311	|	|	1444	1444	...	|	|	|	|	...	1652	1646	1706	|	|	...	1846	1851	|	1917	1945	2111	...
Falköping § d.	1302	|	|	|	1502	1503	...	|	|	|	|	...	1709	1702	|	|	|	...	1902	1908	|	1933	2005	|	...
Skövde § d.	1320	1338	1438	1449	1520	1521	...	1538	1634	1638	|	...	1725	1720	1734	1806	1838	...	1920	1925	1938	1948	2025	2138	...
Töreboda d.	1338	|	|	|	1538	1541	...	|	|	|	|	...	1742	1738	|	|	|	...	1938	1942	|	|	2044	|	...
Laxå **736** d.	1404	|	|	|	1604	1604	...	|	|	|	|	...	1804	1804	|	|	|	...	2004	2004	|	|	2112	|	...
Hallsberg a.	1420	|	|	1540	1620	1620	...	|	|	|	|	...	1820	1820	|	1900	1923	...	2020	2020	|	2035	2127	2227	...
Örebro C **755/6** a.	1442	|	|	|	1642	1643	...	|	|	|	|	...	1842	1842	|	|	|	...	2042	2042	|	|	2150	|	...
Hallsberg 755/6 ▲ d.	|	|	|	1542	|	|	...	|	|	|	|	...	|	|	|	1902	1925	...	|	|	|	2037	...	2229	...
Katrineholm **730** ▲ d.	|	1450	1549	|	|	|	...	1650	1749	1750	|	...	|	|	1850	|	1950	...	|	|	2050	|	...	|	...
Södertälje Syd ‡ ▲ a.	V	1526	|	1654	V	V	...	1726	1830	1826	|	...	V	V	1926	2010	|	...	V	V	2126	2145	...	2326	...
Flemingsberg ‡ ▲ a.	|	|	1631	|	|	|	...	|	|	|	|	...	|	|	|	|	2033	...	|	|	|	|	...	|	...
Stockholm C **730** ▲ a.	1643	1546	1646	1720	1843	1913	...	1746	1850	1846	1901	...	2035	2043	1946	2032	2046	...	2243	2243	2146	2205	...	2346	...

▲ – **Stockholm - Hallsberg and v.v. regional services** (2nd class only): **Valid until June 29 - August 17**

	Ⓐ	Ⓐ	⑥	†	Ⓐ	⑥	Ⓑ	Ⓐk	Ⓐ	⚒J	†J	Ⓐ	Ⓐ
Stockholm C d.	0640	0836	0929	1029	1229	1329	1436	1529	1629	1729	1729	1929	2214
Flemingsberg d.	0651	0847	0941	1040	1240	1340	1447	1540	1640	1740	1745	1940	2227
Södertälje Syd d.	0702	0859	0953	1052	1252	1352	1458	1551	1651	1753	1803	1952	2239
Flen d.	0736	0935	1030	1128	1328	1428	1534	1631	1728	1827	1839	2027	2313
Katrineholm d.	0750	0950	1043	1141	1341	1441	1550	1645	1741	1842	1854	2041	2325
Hallsberg a.	0828	1021	1116	1213	1413	1513	1622	1720	1820	1915	1929	2113	2358

	Ⓐm	⑥	Ⓐ	†	Ⓐ	⑥		†	⚒	Ⓐ	†	Ⓐ	
Hallsberg d.	0714	0838	0945	1049	1147	1245	...	1445	1549	1650	1729	1848	...
Katrineholm d.	0802	0911	1018	1122	1219	1318	...	1518	1621	1722	1800	1921	...
Flen d.	0815	0923	1030	1134	1231	1330	...	1530	1633	1734	1811	1933	...
Södertälje Syd d.	0851	0959	1107	1210	1306	1406	...	1606	1708	1810	1846	2010	...
Flemingsberg d.	0903	1010	1118	1221	1317	1417	...	1617	1719	1821	1858	2021	...
Stockholm C a.	0916	1024	1131	1235	1331	1431	...	1631	1731	1835	1911	2035	...

♦ – **NOTES** (LISTED BY TRAIN NUMBER)

460 – ⑥ Aug. 10 - Dec. 13: (12) and ✕ Uddevalla - Herrljunga - Stockholm.
462 – Ⓐ Aug. 10 - Dec. 13: (12) and ✕ Uddevalla - Herrljunga - Stockholm. Train number **10462** from Aug. 25.
463 – June 29 - Aug. 9: (12) and ✕ Stockholm - Herrljunga - Uddevalla.
466 – June 29 - Aug. 9: (12) and ✕ Uddevalla - Herrljunga - Stockholm.
467 – Ⓑ Aug. 10 - Dec. 13: (12) and ✕ Stockholm - Herrljunga - Uddevalla.

A – Daily June 29 - Aug. 9; Ⓒ Aug. 10 - Dec. 13.
B – Daily June 29 - Aug. 9; ⚒ Aug. 10 - Dec. 13.
C – Daily June 29 - Aug. 9; Ⓑ Aug. 10 - Dec. 13.
D – ⚒ June 29 - Aug. 9; Ⓐ Aug. 10 - Sept. 28.
E – † June 29 - Sept. 28; Ⓑ Sept. 29 - Dec. 13.
F – ⑤ Aug. 10 - 24; Ⓐ Aug. 25 - Sept. 28.
G – Ⓑ June 29 - July 5, Aug. 3 - Dec. 13.
H – ①–④ Aug. 18 - Dec. 13.
J – June 29 - Aug. 9.
K – ⑤ Aug. 10 - 17; Ⓐ Aug. 18 - Dec. 13.
L – † Aug. 10 - Dec. 13 (also Ⓐ Sept. 29 - Nov. 30). Train number **10405** from Sept. 29.
M – Ⓐ June 29 - Aug. 24; ①②④ Aug. 25 - Dec. 13. Train number **10157** from Aug. 25.
N – Ⓐ June 29 - Aug. 9; ⚒ Aug. 10 - 17; ⑥ Aug. 18 - Dec. 13.
Q – ①–④ Aug. 10 - Dec. 13. Train number **10406** from Aug..25.
R – ⑥ (also Ⓐ June 29 - Aug. 9).
S – ①–④ Aug. 10 - 24; Ⓑ Aug. 25 - Dec. 13.
T – Daily June 29 - Aug. 9; ⑤⑥† Aug. 10 - 24; ⑥ Aug. 25 - Dec. 13.
V – Via Västerås – see Table **756**.
X – Daily **except** † July 7 - Aug. 3.
Z – ①②③④† Aug. 10 - Dec. 13.

a – Ⓐ only.
h – July 12 - Aug. 3.
j – July 7 - Aug. 3.
k – July 28 - Aug. 17.
m – Not July 7 - Aug. 9.
p – Not July 7 - Aug. 3.
q – Aug. 10 - Dec. 13.
s – Stops to set down only.
t – Aug. 18 - Dec. 13.
u – Stops to pick up only.
w – Not July 12 - Aug. 3.
y – June 29 - Aug. 16.

Sn – High speed train. Special supplement payable.
▲ – For Stockholm - Hallsberg and v.v. regional services see panel.
‡ – From Stockholm stops to pick up, to Stockholm stops to set down only.
⊡ – Times vary on some dates (earliest departure, latest arrival times shown). Train number **10xxx** or **22xxx** on some dates.

§ – Local services **Skövde - Göteborg and v.v.**: Operator: Västtrafik.
From **Skövde**: 0448Ⓐ, 0533Ⓐ**q**, 0601Ⓐ**y**, 0641Ⓐ, 0704Ⓐ, 0732⑥, 0836†, 1125⑥, 1330Ⓐ**t**, 1532Ⓒ, 1537Ⓐ**y**, 1736⑥, 2239⑤⑥**t**, 2239**y**.
From **Göteborg** C: 0025Ⓒ, 0900Ⓐ, 1500⑥, 1525Ⓐ**q**, 1635Ⓐ, 1955, 2055⑤⑥**t**, 2055**y**, 2200①②③④†**y**, 2255.

KØBENHAVN - MALMÖ - KRISTIANSTAD - KARLSKRONA 745

Operator: *Øtåg*

km		Ⓐ	Ⓐ	Ⓐ																							
0	**København** H **703/30** d.	...	...	...	0552	0612	0652	0712	0752	0812	0852	0912	0952	1012	1052	1112	1152	1212	1252	1312	1352	1412	1452	1512	1552	1612	1652
12	Kastrup ✈ **703/30** d.	...	...	...	0606	0626	0706	0726	0806	0826	0906	0926	1006	1026	1106	1126	1206	1226	1306	1326	1406	1426	1506	1526	1606	1626	1706
47	**Malmö** C **703** a.	..	...	...	0626	0646	0726	0746	0826	0846	0926	0946	1026	1046	1126	1146	1226	1246	1326	1346	1426	1446	1526	1546	1626	1646	1726
47	**Malmö** C **730/46** d.	...	0529	0548	0629	0648	0729	0748	0829	0848	0929	0948	1029	1048	1129	1148	1229	1248	1329	1348	1429	1448	1529	1548	1629	1648	1729
63	Lund **730/46** d.	...	0541	0600	0641	0700	0741	0800	0841	0900	0941	1000	1041	1100	1141	1200	1241	1300	1341	1400	1441	1500	1541	1600	1641	1700	1741
81	Eslöv **746** d.	...	|	0610	|	0710	|	0810	|	0910	|	1010	|	1110	|	1210	|	1310	|	1410	|	1510	|	1610	|	1710	|
130	Hässleholm **730/46** a.	...	0612	0636	0712	0736	0812	0836	0912	0936	1012	1036	1112	1136	1212	1236	1312	1336	1412	1436	1512	1536	1612	1636	1712	1736	1812
130	Hässleholm **734** d.	0512	0612	...	0712	...	0812	...	0912	...	1012	...	1112	...	1212	...	1312	...	1412	...	1512	...	1612	...	1712	...	1812
160	**Kristianstad 734** a.	0532	0632	...	0732	...	0832	...	0932	...	1032	...	1132	...	1232	...	1332	...	1432	...	1532	...	1632	...	1732	...	1832
160	**Kristianstad** d.	0539	0639	...	0739d	...	0839	...	0939a	...	1039	...	1139d	...	1239	...	1339	...	1439	...	1539	...	1639	...	1739	...	1839
191	Sölvesborg d.	0558	0658	...	0758d	...	0858	...	0958a	...	1058	...	1158d	...	1258	...	1358	...	1458	...	1558	...	1658	...	1758	...	1858
222	**Karlshamn** d.	0619	0719	...	0819d	...	0919	...	1019a	...	1119	...	1219d	...	1319	...	1419	...	1519	...	1619	...	1719	...	1819	...	1919
260	Ronneby d.	0647	0747	...	0847d	...	0947	...	1047a	...	1147	...	1247d	...	1347	...	1447	...	1547	...	1647	...	1747	...	1847	...	1947
290	**Karlskrona** a.	0712	0812	...	0912d	...	1012	...	1112a	...	1212	...	1312d	...	1412	...	1512	...	1612	...	1712	...	1812	...	1912	...	2012

København H **703/30** d.	1712	1752	1812	1852	1912	1952	2012	2052	2112	2152	2252
Kastrup ✈ **703/30** d.	1726	1806	1826	1906	1926	2006	2026	2106	2126	2206	2306
Malmö C **703** a.	1746	1826	1846	1926	1946	2026	2046	2126	2146	2226	2326
Malmö C **730/46** d.	1748	1829	1848	1929	1948	2029	2048	2129	2148	2229	2329
Lund **730/46** d.	1800	1841	1900	1941	2000	2041	2100	2141	2200	2241	2341
Eslöv **746** d.	1810	|	1910	|	2010	|	2110	|	2210	|	|
Hässleholm **730/46** a.	1836	1912	1936	2012	2036	2112	2136	2212	2236	2312	0012
Hässleholm **734** d.	...	1912	...	2012	...	2112	...	2212	...	2312	0012
Kristianstad 734 a.	...	1932	...	2032	...	2132	...	2232	...	2332	0032
Kristianstad d.	...	1939b	...	2039	...	2139b	...	2239	...	...	...
Sölvesborg d.	...	1958b	...	2058	...	2158b	...	2258	...	...	...
Karlshamn d.	...	2019b	...	2119	...	2219b	...	2319	...	...	...
Ronneby d.	...	2047b	...	2147	...	2247b	...	2347	...	...	...
Karlskrona a.	...	2112b	...	2212	...	2312b	...	0012	...	...	...

Karlskrona d.	...	...	0447a	...	0547d	...	0647a	...	0747	...
Ronneby d.	...	...	0508a	...	0608d	...	0708a	...	0808	...
Karlshamn d.	...	...	0536a	...	0636d	...	0736a	...	0836	...
Sölvesborg d.	...	...	0557a	...	0657d	...	0757a	...	0857	...
Kristianstad a.	...	...	0618a	...	0718d	...	0818a	...	0918	...
Kristianstad 734 d.	0524	...	0624	...	0724	...	0824	...	0924	...
Hässleholm **734** a.	0542	...	0642	...	0742	...	0842	...	0942	...
Hässleholm **730/46** d.	0544	0622	0644	0722	0744	0822	0844	0922	0944	1022
Eslöv **746** d.	|	0647	|	0747	|	0847	|	0947	|	1047
Lund **730/46** d.	0617	0701	0717	0801	0817	0901	0917	1001	1017	1101
Malmö C **730/46** a.	0629	0711	0729	0811	0829	0911	0929	1011	1029	1111
Malmö C **703** d.	0633	0713	0733	0813	0833	0913	0933	1013	1033	1113
Kastrup ✈ **703/30** a.	0653	0733	0753	0833	0853	0933	0953	1033	1053	1133
København H **703/30** a.	0708	0748	0808	0848	0908	0948	1008	1048	1108	1148

Karlskrona d.	0847d	...	0947	...	1047d	...	1147	...	1247	...	1347	...	1447	...	1547	...	1647b	...	1747	...	1847b	...	1947	...	2047b	2147
Ronneby d.	0908d	...	1008	...	1108d	...	1208	...	1308	...	1408	...	1508	...	1608	...	1708b	...	1808	...	1908b	...	2008	...	2108b	2208
Karlshamn d.	0936d	...	1036	...	1136d	...	1236	...	1336	...	1436	...	1536	...	1636	...	1736b	...	1836	...	1936b	...	2036	...	2136b	2236
Sölvesborg d.	0957d	...	1057	...	1157d	...	1257	...	1357	...	1457	...	1557	...	1657	...	1757b	...	1857	...	1957b	...	2057	...	2157b	2257
Kristianstad a.	1018d	...	1118	...	1218d	...	1318	...	1418	...	1518	...	1618	...	1718	...	1818b	...	1918	...	2018b	...	2118	...	2218b	2318
Kristianstad 734 d.	1024	...	1124	...	1224	...	1324	...	1424	...	1524	...	1624	...	1724	...	1824	...	1924	...	2024	...	2124	...	2224	2324
Hässleholm **734** a.	1042	...	1142	...	1242	...	1342	...	1442	...	1542	...	1642	...	1742	...	1842	...	1942	...	2042	...	2142	...	2242	2342
Hässleholm **730/46** d.	1044	1122	1144	1222	1244	1322	1344	1422	1444	1522	1544	1622	1644	1722	1744	1822	1844	1922	1944	2022	2044	2122	2144	2222	2244	2344
Eslöv **746** d.	|	1147	|	1247	|	1347	|	1447	|	1547	|	1647	|	1747	|	1847	|	1947	|	2047	|	2147	|	2247	|	|
Lund **730/46** d.	1117	1201	1217	1301	1317	1401	1417	1501	1517	1601	1617	1701	1717	1801	1817	1901	1917	2001	2017	2101	2118	2201	2217	2301	2317	0016
Malmö C **730/46** a.	1129	1211	1229	1311	1329	1411	1429	1511	1529	1611	1629	1711	1729	1811	1829	1911	1929	2011	2029	2111	2129	2211	2229	2311	2329	0028
Malmö C **703** d.	1133	1213	1233	1313	1333	1413	1433	1513	1533	1613	1633	1713	1733	1813	1833	1913	1933	2013	2033	2113	2133	2213	2233	2313	2333	0033
Kastrup ✈ **703/30** a.	1153	1233	1253	1333	1353	1433	1453	1533	1553	1633	1653	1733	1753	1833	1853	1933	1953	2033	2053	2133	2153	2233	2253	2333	2353	0053
København H **703/30** a.	1208	1248	1308	1348	1408	1448	1508	1548	1608	1648	1708	1748	1808	1848	1908	1948	2008	2048	2108	2148	2208	2248	2308	2348	0008	0108

a – Ⓐ only. b – Ⓑ only. d – ⚒ only.

KØBENHAVN, MALMÖ and GÖTEBORG - KALMAR 746

km		Øtåg Ⓐ	Øtåg Ⓐ	Øtåg Ⓐ	Ⓐ	Øtåg	Øtåg Ⓐ	Øtåg	Øtåg Ⓐ	⑥	Øtåg Ⓐ	Øtåg Ⓒ	Ⓐ	Øtåg Ⓐ	Øtåg	Øtåg	†	Øtåg	⑥	Øtåg Ⓐ	Ⓐ	Øtåg	Øtåg Ⓐ	Ⓑ	Øtåg	Øtåg Ⓑ	Øtåg
0	**København** H **703** d.	...	...	0612	...	0712	0812	0912	1012	...	1112	1112	...	1212	1312	1412	...	1512	...	1612	...	1712	1812	...	1912	2012	2112
12	Kastrup ✈ **703** d.	...	...	0626	...	0726	0826	0926	1026	...	1126	1126	...	1226	1326	1426	...	1526	...	1626	...	1726	1826	...	1926	2026	2126
47	**Malmö** C **703** a.	...	...	0646	...	0746	0846	0946	1046	...	1146	1146	...	1246	1346	1446	...	1546	...	1646	...	1746	1846	...	1946	2046	2146
47	**Malmö** C **730/45** d.	...	0548	0648	...	0748	0848	0948	1048	...	1148	1148	...	1248	1348	1448	...	1548	...	1648	...	1748	1848	...	1948	2048	2148
63	Lund **730/45** d.	...	0600	0700	...	0800	0900	1000	1100	...	1200	1200	...	1300	1400	1500	...	1600	...	1700	...	1800	1900	...	2000	2100	2200
80	Eslöv **745** d.	...	0610	0710	...	0810	0910	1010	1110	...	1210	1210	...	1310	1410	1510	...	1610	...	1710	...	1810	1910	...	2010	2110	2210
130	Hässleholm **730/45** d.	...	0636	0740	...	0840	0940	1040	1140	...	1240	1240	...	1340	1440	1540	...	1640	...	1740	...	1840	1940	...	2040	2140	2240
181	Älmhult d.	...	0700	0803	...	0903	1003	1103	1203	...	1303	1303	...	1403	1503	1603	...	1703	...	1803	...	1903	2003	...	2103	2203	2303
	Göteborg C ▲ d.	...	|	|	0605	|	|	|	|	1005	|	|	1105	|	|	|	1400	|	1510	|	1605	|	|	1805	|	|	|
	Borås ▲ d.	...	|	|	0659	|	|	|	|	1059	|	|	1159	|	|	|	1454	|	1604	|	1704	|	|	1859	|	|	|
	Limmared d.	...	|	|	0727	|	|	|	|	1128	|	|	1227	|	|	|	1522	|	1631	|	1732	|	|	1931	|	|	|
	Värnamo d.	...	|	|	0808	|	|	|	|	1210	|	|	1307	|	|	|	1609	|	1715	|	1818	|	|	2013	|	|	|
228	Alvesta **730** a.	...	0720	0824	0836	0924	1024	1124	1224	1234	1324	1324	1333	1424	1524	1624	1636	1724	1742	1824	1845	1924	2024	2040	2124	2224	2324
228	Alvesta ▲ d.	0608	0721	0826	0838	0935	1035	1136	1235	1235	1326	1339	1339	1439	1535	1635	1640	1735	1748	1838	1850	1935	2026	2043	2135	2232	2326
245	**Växjö** ▲ d.	0621	0732	0838	0852	0947	1048	1147	1247	1253	1337	1350	1353	1451	1548	1647	1652	1747	1804	1850	1902	1947	2038	2057	2147	2244	2337
302	Emmaboda a.	0656	0806	...	0927	1024	...	1223	1330	1327	1413	1426	1428	1527	1627	1726a	1728	1825	1839	...	1934	2026	...	2131	2224	...	0008
302	Emmaboda ● d.	0656	0806	...	0929	1030	...	1224	1330	1330	1413	1426	1432	1527	1627	1730a	1730	1830	1841	...	1936	2026	...	2133	2224	...	0009
330	Nybro d.	0711	0821	...	0944	1043	...	1242	1344	1345	1429	1443	1446	1548	1643	1743a	1745	1843	1855	...	1951	2040	...	2148	2238	...	0023
359	**Kalmar** a.	0733	0838	...	0959	1059	...	1258	1400	1401	1445	1504	1503	1605	1659	1759a	1801	1900	1910	...	2006	2057	...	2204	2255	...	0040

km		Øtåg Ⓐ	Ⓐ	Øtåg Ⓐ	Øtåg Ⓐ	Øtåg	⑥	Øtåg Ⓐ	Øtåg ⑥	Øtåg	Ⓐ	Øtåg Ⓐ	Øtåg	Ⓑ	Øtåg Ⓐ	Øtåg	Øtåg Ⓑ	⑥	Øtåg Ⓑ	Øtåg ⑥	Ⓑ	Øtåg Ⓐ	Øtåg	Øtåg Ⓑ	Øtåg	Øtåg Ⓑ	Øtåg Ⓐ
	Kalmar d.	...	0500	...	0557	0700	0800	0805	...	0900	1000	...	1100	1150	...	1300	1402a	1458	1455	1517	1557	...	1700	1800a	1904	...	2100
	Nybro d.	...	0516	...	0611	0715	0816	0820	...	0914	1016	...	1114	1206	...	1314	1416a	1514	1511	1531	1615	...	1714	1814a	1920	...	2114
	Emmaboda ● a.	...	0531	...	0628	0729	0831	0834	...	0929	1030	...	1129	1220	...	1329	1432a	1529	1525	1545	1629	...	1729	1829a	1934	...	2130
	Emmaboda d.	...	0533	...	0628	0729	0833	0834	...	0929	1032	...	1129	1223	...	1329	1432a	1531	1525	1545	1634	...	1729	1829a	1934	...	2130
	Växjö ▲ d.	0521	0607	0615	0706	0809	0907	0908	0920	1009	1105	1120	1209	1257	1313	1410	1509	1607	1609	1620	1707	1718	1809	1905	2010	2120	2209
	Alvesta ▲ a.	0531	0619	0626	0720	0821	0920	0920	0931	1021	1118	1130	1221	1310	1326	1421	1520	1620	1621	1631	1720	1731	1821	1917	2021	2131	2221
0	Alvesta **730** d.	0533	0622	0633	0733	0833	0922	0933	0933	1033	1120	1133	1233	1312	1333	1433	1533	1622	1633	1633	1722	1733	1833	1933	2033	2133	...
49	Värnamo d.	|	0647	|	|	|	0947	|	|	|	1145	|	|	1336	|	|	|	1646	|	|	1749	|	|	|	|	|	...
110	Limmared d.	|	0727	|	|	|	1028	|	|	|	1229	|	|	1416	|	|	|	1728	|	|	1827	|	|	|	|	|	...
149	Borås ▲ a.	|	0757	|	|	|	1058	|	|	|	1256	|	|	1445	|	|	|	1757	|	|	1857	|	|	|	|	|	...
222	**Göteborg** C ▲ a.	|	0855	|	|	|	1155	|	|	|	1350	|	|	1550	|	|	|	1855	|	|	1955	|	|	|	|	|	...
	Älmhult d.	0552	...	0652	0752	0852	...	0952	0952	1052	...	1152	1252	...	1352	1452	1552	...	1652	1652	...	1752	1852	1952	2052	2152	...
	Hässleholm **730/45** a.	0618	...	0718	0818	0918	...	1018	1018	1118	...	1218	1318	...	1418	1518	1618	...	1718	1718	...	1818	1918	2018	2118	2218	...
	Eslöv **745** a.	0647	...	0747	0847	0947	...	1047	1047	1147	...	1247	1347	...	1447	1547	1647	...	1747	1747	...	1847	1947	2047	2147	2247	...
	Lund **730/45** a.	0659	...	0759	0859	0959	...	1059	1059	1159	...	1259	1359	...	1459	1559	1659	...	1759	1759	...	1859	1959	2059	2159	2259	...
	Malmö C **730/45** a.	0711	...	0811	0911	1011	...	1111	1111	1211	...	1311	1411	...	1511	1611	1711	...	1811	1811	...	1911	2011	2111	2211	2311	...
	Malmö C **703** d.	0713	...	0813	0913	1013	...	1113	1113	1213	...	1313	1413	...	1513	1613	1713	...	1813	1813	...	1913	2013	2113	2213	2313	...
	Kastrup ✈ **703** a.	0733	...	0833	0933	1033	...	1133	1133	1233	...	1333	1433	...	1533	1633	1733	...	1833	1833	...	1933	2033	2133	2233	2333	...
	København H **703** a.	0748	...	0848	0948	1048	...	1148	1148	1248	...	1348	1448	...	1548	1648	1748	...	1848	1848	...	1948	2048	2148	2248	2348	...

– CONNECTING SERVICES **Emmaboda - Karlskrona and v.v.** (2nd class only): Operator: *LT*

km		Ⓐ§	⚒		⚒			⚒§			⚒§			⚒§	Ⓑ	§		Ⓑ	Ⓑ§	⑥§		Ⓑ	§		Ⓑ	†§	
0	Emmaboda d.	0634	0734	...	0839	0934	...	1034	1150	...	1234	...	1334	1432	1534	1634	...	1734	1834	1842	...	1950	2034	...	2136	2229	...
57	Karlskrona a.	0716	0817	...	0921	1017	...	1117	1233	...	1317	...	1417	1517	1617	1717	...	1817	1917	1925	...	2033	2117	...	2219	2312	...

	Ⓐ	⚒	⚒		⚒	†	⚒			⚒			⚒	Ⓑ			Ⓑ			Ⓑ			Ⓑ		†h	
arlskrona a.	0543	0643	0743	...	0830	0843	0943	...	1043	1140	1243	...	1343	1443	...	1543	1643	...	1743	1843	...	1940	2043	...	2125	...
mmaboda d.	0624	0724	0824	...	0911	0923	1024	...	1125	1220	1324	...	1424	1524	...	1624	1724	...	1824	1924	...	2021	2124	...	2206	...

– Ⓐ only.
– Until Aug. 16.

§ – Runs up to 20 minutes later from Aug. 17.
▲ – Additional trains run Göteborg - Borås and v.v., and Alvesta - Växjö and v.v.

747 STOCKHOLM - STOCKHOLM ARLANDA ✈

Arlanda Express. Operator: A-Train AB (*AEX*)

Journey time: 20 minutes. All services stop at Arlanda Södra (17 minutes from Stockholm, 2 minutes from Arlanda Norra). Södra serves terminals 2, 3 and 4; Norra serves terminal 5.

From **Stockholm** Central: 0435, 0505, 0520, 0535, 0550, 0605, 0620, 0635, 0650 and at the same minutes past each hour until 2205, then 2220, 2235, 2305, 2335, 0005, 0035.

From **Arlanda** Norra: 0505, 0535, 0550, 0605, 0620, 0635, 0650 and at the same minutes past each hour until 2205, then 2220, 2235, 2250, 2305, 2335, 0005, 0035, 0105.

Minor alterations to schedules are possible at peak times

750 STOCKHOLM - HALLSBERG - KARLSTAD - OSLO

Valid June 29 - August 9

km		*VTAB*	*VTAB*	*VTAB*	*VTAB*	*ST*		*IC*	*Sn*	*VTAB*	*VTAB*	*VTAB*		*Sn*	*ST*	*VTAB*	*VTAB*	*VTAB*	*VTAB*	*Tågab*	*IC*	*ST*	*VTAB*	*Sn*	*ST*	*VTAB*	*Sn*		*Sn*	*VTAB*
								51	**627**					**633**							**55**			**643**			**645**		**647**	
		2	2	2	2				R✕	2	2	2		R✕		2	2	2	2				2	R✕		2	R✕		R✕	2
		Ⓐ	Ⓐ	Ⓐ	Ⓐ	Ⓒ			⚒	Ⓒ	Ⓐ	Ⓐ			†	Ⓐ	Ⓐ	Ⓐ	⑥	♠		Ⓐ	Ⓐ	Ⓑ	†	†	⑥		Ⓑ	
0	**Stockholm** C **730/40** d.	...	...	...	...	...	...	0829	0951	...	...	...	...	1225	...	...	...	...	...	...	1525	...	...	1710	...	...	1825	...	1925	...
36	Södertälje Syd **730/40** d.	...	...	...	...	...	...	0849u	1010u	...	...	...	...	1244u	...	...	...	...	...	...	1545j	...	...	1728u	...	...	1843u	...	1944u	...
131	Katrineholm **730/40** .. d.	...	...	...	...	...	...	0932	|	...	...	...	...	1328	...	...	...	...	...	...	1628	...	...	|	...	...	1921	...	2027	...
197	**Hallsberg 740** a.	...	...	...	...	...	...	1000	1120	...	...	...	...	1355	...	...	...	...	...	...	1656	...	...	1826	...	...	1945	...	2055	...
197	**Hallsberg** d.	...	...	0614	...	0712g	...	1002	1122	...	...	1324	...	1357	...	...	...	...	...	...	1658	1718	...	1828	1856	...	1947	...	2057	...
261	Degerfors d.	...	...	0644	...	0745g	...	1038	1149	...	...	1352	...	1427	...	...	...	...	...	...	1727	1751	...	1853	1925	...	2013	...	2124	...
287	Kristinehamn d.	...	0613	0703	...	0805g	...	1055	1203	...	...	1406	...	1442	...	1511	1607	1634	...	1858	1742	1810	...	1906	1940	...	2028	...	2139	...
327	**Karlstad 751** a.	...	0643	0728	...	0830g	...	1114	1225	...	...	1433	...	1505	...	1538	1631	1701	...	1921	1817	1836	...	1928	2004	...	2047	...	2201	...
327	**Karlstad** d.	0532	0645	0737	0841	0843	...	1119	...	1239	1245	1437	...	...	1527	1547	1631	1708	1726	...	1820	...	1850	1933	...	2017	...	...	...	2220
347	Kil d.	0545	0659	0755	0900	0904	...	1134	...	1252	1305	1451	...	...	1540	1602	1648	1726	1744	...	1837	...	1903	1952	...	2031	...	...	...	2236
395	Arvika d.	0621	0741	0835	0937	0938	...	1201	...	1324	1343	1525	...	...	1614	1635	1725	1800	1819	...	1903	...	1936	2020	...	2104	...	...	...	2308
430	Charlottenberg ▦ a.	0647	0807	0901	1001	1002	...	1225	...	1351	1409	1553	...	...	1642	1658	1755	1827	1844	...	1926	...	2001	...	...	2132	...	...	...	2333
472	Kongsvinger a.	0717	...	...	1029	1038	...	1254	...	...	...	...	...	...	1722	1726	...	...	...	...	1953	...	...	...	...	...	...	...	...	...
572	**Oslo** Sentral a.	*0856§*	...	...	*1156§*	1204	...	1424	...	...	...	...	...	...	1844	*1856§*	...	...	...	...	2124	...	...	...	...	...	...	...	...	...

	Sn	*ST*	*Sn*	*VTAB*	*VTAB*	*VTAB*	*Sn*	*Sn*	*VTAB*	*VTAB*	*Tågab*	*IC*	*VTAB*	*Sn*	*VTAB*	*Sn*	*VTAB*	*Sn*	*VTAB*	*ST*	*VTAB*	*Sn*	*Sn*	*VTAB*	*IC*	*VTAB*	*VTAB*	*VTAB*	*ST*	*VTAB*
	622		**624**				**636**	**626**				**50**		**632**		**634**		**640**				**642**	**10642**		**58**					
	R✕		R✕	2	2	2	R✕	R✕	2	2			2	R✕	2	R✕	2	R✕	2		2	R✕	R✕	2		2	2	2		2
	⑥	⑥	Ⓐ	Ⓐ	Ⓐ	Ⓒ	Ⓐ	⑥	Ⓐ	⑥	♠		Ⓐ	⚒	Ⓐ	†	Ⓒ	⑥	Ⓐ	Ⓒ	Ⓐ	†	Ⓐ	Ⓐ		Ⓐ	⑥	Ⓐ	†	Ⓐ
Oslo Sentral d.	...	...	...	...	...	...	...	...	*0604§*	...	...	0732	...	...	*1004§*	...	...	...	...	1346	...	...	...	...	1541	*1704§*	...	...	1936	...
Kongsvinger d.	...	...	...	...	...	...	...	...	0735	...	...	0852	...	...	1133	...	...	...	...	1503	...	...	...	...	1704	1833	...	...	2054	...
Charlottenberg ▦ d.	...	...	...	0623	0652	0750	...	...	0808	0829	...	0920	1003	...	1203	...	1401	...	1420	1531	1531	...	...	1609	1738	1905	1930	2030	2133	2138
Arvika d.	...	...	...	0648	0714	0815	0833	0839	0837	0854	...	0942	1029	...	1228	...	1426	...	1442	1554	1554	...	...	1634	1757	1936	1955	2052	2154	2200
Kil d.	...	...	...	0727	0748	0858	0858	0904	0927	0932	...	1009	1105	...	1305	...	1502	...	1520	1630	1630	...	...	1718	1829	2017	2034	2127	2229	2235
Karlstad 751 a.	...	...	...	0739	0801	0911	0911	0918	0941	0945	...	1027	1117	...	1318	...	1514	...	1533	1643	1643	...	...	1737	1844	2029	2047	2140	2242	2250
Karlstad d.	0644	0724	0730	0742	0802	...	0928	0928	...	...	1014	1030	1121	1254	...	1327	...	1524	1539	1645e	1644	1736	1736	1741	1846	...	...	2143	...	...
Kristinehamn d.	0706	0748	0755	0807	0828	...	0948	0948	...	...	1037	1050	1147	1313	...	1344	...	1546	1605	1709e	1708	1756	1756	1806	1909	...	...	2211	...	...
Degerfors d.	0720	0803	0809	...	...	...	1001	1001	...	...	...	1110	1205	1329	...	1405	...	1600	...	1727e	1727	1810	1810	...	1926	...	...	...	...	...
Hallsberg a.	0750	0831	0839	...	...	...	1030	1030	...	...	...	1140	1233	1358	...	1431	...	1636	...	1755e	1757	1839	1842	...	1956	...	...	...	...	...
Hallsberg 740 d.	0752	...	0841	...	...	...	1032	1032	...	...	...	1142	...	1400	...	1433	...	1638	...	...	...	1841	1844	...	1958	...	...	...	...	...
Katrineholm **730/40** a.	0819	...	0907	...	...	...	1056	1056	...	...	...	1210	...	1426	...	1456	...	1706	...	...	...	1907	1910	...	2026	...	...	...	...	...
Södertälje Syd **730/40** a.	0902s	...	0949s	...	...	...	1133	1133s	...	...	...	1256s	...	1510	...	1533s	...	1748s	...	...	...	1949s	1951s	...	2113s	...	...	...	...	...
Stockholm C **730/40** a.	0924	...	1016	...	...	...	1154	1154	...	...	...	1320	...	1533	...	1554	...	1809	...	...	...	2009	2020	...	2135	...	...	...	...	...

e – † only.
g – ⑥ only.
j – Ⓒ only (stops to pick up only).
s – Stops to set down only.
u – Stops to pick up only.
♠ – [12] Göteborg - Mora and v.v. – see Tables **751/3/8**.
Sn – High speed train. Special supplement payable.
§ – Operated by Norges Statsbaner (NSB).

751 KARLSTAD - GÖTEBORG

km									*Tågab*		
		Ⓐ		⚒				Ⓑ		G	H
0	**Karlstad 750** d.	0611	0814	1016	1214	...	1411	1612	1815	1926	2210
19	Kil d.	0628	0829	1033	1229	...	1425	1627	1830	1941	2225
70	Säffle d.	0659	0859	1108	1300	...	1458	1700	1903	2010	2259
87	Åmål d.	0709	0909	1118	1310	...	1507	1709	1913	2019	2309
128	Mellerud d.	0734	0934	1142	1335	...	1535	1734	1937	|	2333
169	Öxnered a.	0759	0954	1202	1359	...	1555	1758	1957	2102	2353
179	Trollhättan a.	0805	1000	1208	1405	...	1601	1805	2005	2108	2359
251	**Göteborg** C a.	0845	1035	1240	1440	...	1645	1845	2040	2145	0030

			Tågab							
	Ⓐ	Ⓐ	G		⚒				Ⓑ	
Göteborg C d.	0510	0715	0745	0915	1115	...	1315	1515	1715	1915
Trollhättan d.	0544	0752	0824	0952	1152	...	1352	1552	1752	1952
Öxnered d.	0550	0800	0831	1000	1200	...	1400	1600	1800	2000
Mellerud d.	0609	0821	|	1021	1222	...	1421	1620	1825	2021
Åmål d.	0633	0844	0912	1045	1245	...	1444	1647	1849	2044
Säffle d.	0643	0859	0922	1056	1300	...	1500	1700	1901	2059
Kil a.	0720	0931	0958	1128	1331	...	1530	1730	1932	2130
Karlstad 750 a.	0734	0947	1011	1145	1346	...	1546	1745	1946	2146

G – June 29 - Aug. 9: [12] Göteborg - Mora and v.v. – see Tables **750/3/8**.
H – ①②③④† only.
p – June 29 - Aug. 9.

752 VÄSTERÅS - LUDVIKA

Operator: *ST* 2nd class only

km																									
		Ⓐ	Ⓐ	Ⓒ		Ⓐ	Ⓐq	Ⓐ	Ⓒ	Ⓐq		Ⓐq			Ⓐq		Ⓐ			Ⓐq		Ⓐq		Ⓐ	Ⓐ
0	**Västerås 756** d.	0615	0715	0715	...	0815	0915	1015	1115	1115	...	1215	1315	...	1415	1515	1615	1715	...	1815	1915	2015	...	2127	2227
80	Fagersta C d.	0712	0810	0812	...	0912	1010	1112	1212	1210	...	1310	1412	...	1510	1612	1710	1812	...	1910	2012	2110	...	2228	2324
129	**Ludvika** a.	0755	...	0854	...	0954	...	1154	1254	...	...	...	1454	...	...	1654	...	1854	...	...	2054	...	...	2310	...

	Ⓐ	Ⓐ	Ⓒ	Ⓐq	Ⓐ	Ⓒx	Ⓐq		Ⓐ	Ⓒ	Ⓐq	Ⓐq			Ⓐ		Ⓐq			Ⓐq	Ⓐ	Ⓐ	Ⓐ	
Ludvika d.	...	0607	0707	...	0807	0907	...	...	1007	1107	...	...	...	1307	...	1507	...	1707	...	...	1907	...	2107	...
Fagersta C d.	0532	0650	0750	0750	0850	0950	0950	...	1050	1150	1150	1250	...	1350	1450	1550	1650	1750	...	1850	1950	2050	2150	...
Västerås 756 a.	0625	0745	0845	0845	0945	1045	1045	...	1145	1245	1245	1345	...	1445	1545	1645	1745	1845	...	1945	2045	2146	2257	...

q – Aug. 10 - Dec. 13.
x – Not July 7 - Aug. 3.

753 KRISTINEHAMN - MORA - ÖSTERSUND - GÄLLIVARE

INLANDSBANAN **2014 service**

km		W		♠	C
0	**Kristinehamn 750** d.	...	...	1045	...
40	Nykroppa d.	...	...	1122	...
131	Grängesberg d.	...	...	1229	...
146	Ludvika d.	...	...	1247	...
296	**Mora 758** d.	1345	...	1427	1451
310	Orsa d.	1359	...	...	1505
433	Sveg d.	1530	...	...	1733
617	**Östersund** C a.	1830	...	...	2104

	C	W	♠	
Östersund C d.	0751	0820	...	...
Sveg d.	1117	1125	...	...
Orsa d.	1332	1313	...	...
Mora 758 d.	1346	1330	1523j	...
Ludvika d.	...	...	1700	...
Grängesberg d.	...	...	1710	...
Nykroppa d.	...	...	1819	...
Kristinehamn 750 a.	...	...	1855	...

km		D	
0	**Östersund** C d.	0705	...
115	Ulriksfors d.	0912	...
244	Vilhelmina d.	1105	...
312	Storuman d.	1302	...
384	Sorsele d.	1431	...
473	Arvidsjaur d.	1607	...
646	Jokkmokk d.	1934	...
746	**Gällivare** a.	2146	...

	E	
Gällivare d.	0730	...
Jokkmokk d.	0917	...
Arvidsjaur d.	1309	...
Sorsele d.	1448	...
Storuman d.	1550	...
Vilhelmina d.	1731	...
Ulriksfors d.	1941	...
Östersund C a.	2124	...

All rail services operated by Railbus.
C – June 2 - Aug. 24.
D – June 2 - Aug. 23.
E – June 3 - Aug. 24.
W – Until June 1.
j – depart 1511 on ⑥.
♠ – June 29 - Aug. 9: [12] Göteborg - Mora and v.v. – see Tables **750/1/8**. Operated by *Tågab*.
🚂 – Steam train operates ⑤⑥ July 11 - Aug. 9, 2014 Arvidsjaur - Slagnäs and v.v. (*53 km*) depart 1745, arrive back 2200. Contact: Arvidsjaur Järnvägsförening ✆ +46 (0)730 81 93 69.
Operator: Inlandsbanan AB, Box 561, 831 27, Östersund. ✆ +46 (0)771 53 53 53, fax +46 (0)63 19 44 06.

754 NORRKÖPING - VÄSTERÅS - SALA

2nd class only

km		Ⓐ	⚒	Ⓐn		Ⓐ		Ⓐn		Ⓐn			
	Linköping **730** d.	...	0604a	0906	1006	1106	1206	1306	1406	1506	1606	1806	2006
0	**Norrköping 730** d.	...	0632a	0936	1036	1136	1236	1334	1436	1536	1636	1836	2036
48	Katrineholm **730** d.	...	0658a	1002	1102	1202	1302	1400	1502	1602	1702	1902	2102
71	Flen **730** d.	...	0710a	1015	1115	1215	1315	1413	1515	1615	1715	1915	2115
112	Eskilstuna d.	0546	0752	1052	1152	1252	1352	1452	1552	1652	1752	1952	2152
160	**Västerås** a.	0619	0825	1125	1225	1325	1425	1525	1625	1725	1825	2025	2225
160	**Västerås** d.	0622	0827	1127	1227	1327	1427	1527	1627	1727	1827	2027b	...
199	Sala **758** a.	0647	0852	1152	1252	1352	1452	1552	1652	1752	1852	2052b	...

	Ⓐ		Ⓐn			Ⓐn				Ⓐn	Ⓑ	Ⓑ
Sala **758** d.	...	0709a	0809	0909d	1109	1209	1309	1509	1709	1809	1909	21[illegible]
Västerås a.	...	0733a	0833	0933d	1133	1233	1333	1533	1733	1833	1933	21[illegible]
Västerås d.	0529	0735	0835	0935	1135	1235	1335	1535	1735	1835	1935	21[illegible]
Eskilstuna d.	0603	0809	0909	1009	1209	1309	1409	1609	1809	1909	2009	22[illegible]
Flen **730** d.	0637	0844	0944	1045	1244	1344	1444	1645	1844	1945	2045	...
Katrineholm **730** d.	0650	0858	0959	1058	1258	1358	1458	1658	1858	1958	2058	...
Norrköping 730 a.	0714	0922	1023	1122	1322	1422	1522	1722	1922	2022	2122	...
Linköping **730** a.	0742	0952	1052	1152	1352	1452	1552	1752	1948	2049	2149	...

a – Ⓐ only.
b – Ⓑ only.
d – ⚒ only.
n – From Aug. 4.

Operator: *ST*

MJÖLBY - HALLSBERG - ÖREBRO - GÄVLE 755

km		Ⓐq	Ⓐ	Ⓐ	⚒q	⚒q	Ⓐ	Ⓐ	Ⓐ	Ⓐz	⑥	Ⓐq		q		Ⓐq	⚒z		Ⓐq		Ⓐq	Ⓑ	Ⓑ	Ⓐq	Ⓑ	†	Ⓐ	Ⓑ
0	**Mjölby 730** d.	...	...	...	...	...	...	0600	...	...	...	...	0812d	...	1012	...	...	1212	...	1412	...	...	1612	...	1812	...	...	2012
27	Motala d.	...	...	...	...	...	...	0614	...	...	...	...	0826d	...	1026	...	...	1226	...	1426	...	...	1626	...	1826	...	...	2026
96	**Hallsberg** a.	...	...	...	...	...	...	0657	...	...	...	...	0906d	...	1106	...	...	1306	...	1506	...	...	1706	...	1906	...	...	2106
	Hallsberg 736/56 d.	...	...	...	0530a	0635	0659	0711	0734	0805	...	...	0926d	1038c	1120	...	1250a	1318	...	1518	1635	1650a	1738	1837	1940	1934	1934	2120
121	**Örebro C 736/56** a.	...	...	...	0548a	0653	0717	0729	0752	0823	...	...	0943d	1056c	1138	...	1308a	1336	...	1537	1653	1708a	1756	1855	1958	1952	1952	2138
	Örebro C d.	...	...	...	0550a	0700	0718	...	0800	0855	0900	0900	1000d	1100	1201	1300	1310	1358	1500	1559	1658	1710	1800	1900	2000	1955	1955	2205
146	Frövi d.	...	...	...	0606a	0714	0732	...	0814	0910	0914	0914	1014d	1114	1215	1314	1324	1414	1514	1614	1712	1724	1814	1914	2014	2011	2011	2219
204	Kopparberg d.	...	...	...	0656a	0757	|	...	0900	|	|	0957	1058d	1200	1301	1400	|	1502	1559	1700	1800	|	1857	1959	2056	|	|	2301
232	Grängesberg d.	...	...	...	0717a	0818	|	...	0920	|	|	1018	1122d	1220	1320	1419	|	1521	1618	1719	1819	|	1919	2018	2119	|	|	2320
247	Ludvika d.	...	...	0629	0729a	0829	|	...	0931	|	|	1029	1133d	1233	1331	1429	|	1531	1629	1730	1831	|	1929	2032	2136	|	|	2332
295	**Borlänge** a.	...	...	0656	0758a	0900	|	...	0957	|	|	1100	1202d	1300	1357	1456	|	1558	1656	1756	1858	|	1956	2058	2202	|	|	2358
	Borlänge 758 d.	0603	...	0708	0808	0904a	|	...	1005	|	|	...	1212	...	1405	1502	|	1605	1700	1805	1918	|	2013	...	2222	|	|	...
317	Falun **758** d.	0624	...	0729	0827	0921a	|	...	1025	|	|	...	1230	...	1427	1520	|	1625	1717	1826	1945	|	2029	...	2238	|	|	...
	Fagersta d.	|	0600	|	|	...	0815	...	|	0955	0957	...	|	...	|	|	1405	|	|	|	...	1807	|	...	...	2106	2122	...
	Avesta Krylbo d.	|	0628	|	|	...	0838	...	|	1021	1025	...	|	...	|	|	1429	|	|	|	...	1831	|	...	...	2130	2147	...
371	Storvik d.	0710	0719	0812	0912	...	0917	...	1111	1057	1102	...	1312	...	1510	1602	1518	1712	1802	1910	...	1915	2112r	...	...	2208	2228	...
385	Sandviken d.	0721	0735	0823	0923	...	0928	...	1123	1108	1113	...	1324	...	1522	1613	1530	1723	1813	1921	...	1926	2126r	...	...	2219	2239	...
408	**Gävle 760** a.	0741	0751	0848	0938	...	0943	...	1138	1123	1128	...	1338	...	1540	1628	1545	1738	1828	1936	...	1942	2141r	...	...	2234	2254	...

km		Ⓐ	Ⓐ	Ⓐ	⚒	Ⓐq		Ⓐq	⚒		†	Ⓐq		Ⓐy	Ⓐq		q	Ⓐz		Ⓐq	Ⓐq	Ⓑ	Ⓑ	Ⓐq	Ⓑ	†	Ⓐ	Ⓑ
0	**Gävle 760** d.	...	0430	...	...	0518	0615d	0720	0827	0822d	1026	...	1020	1226	...	1222	...	1426	1420	1510	...	1629	1622	1714	1820	1825	1843	2022
23	Sandviken d.	...	0446	...	...	0534	0636d	0736	0844	0838d	1042	...	1036	1243	...	1238	...	1442	1436	1528	...	1645	1638	1735	1835	1842	1900	2038
37	Storvik d.	...	0456	...	...	0544	0646d	0746	0854	0848d	1052	...	1046	1254	...	1248	...	1453	1446	1538	...	1655	1648	1745	1846	1853	1911	2048
95	Avesta Krylbo d.	...	0534	...	...	|	|	|	0931	|	1131	...	|	1333	...	|	...	1533	|	|	...	1734	|	|	|	1933	1951	|
130	Fagersta d.	...	0600	...	...	|	|	|	0955	|	1156	...	|	1403	...	|	...	1558	|	|	...	1801	|	|	|	1958	2015	|
	Falun **758** d.	...	|	0455e	...	0626	0728d	0829	|	0929d	|	1034	1130	|	...	1329	...	|	1529	1621	...	|	1728	1836	1926	...	...	2131r
	Borlänge 758 a.	...	|	0511e	...	0643	0745d	0845	|	0946d	|	1054	1147	|	...	1346	...	|	1546	1637	...	|	1745	1852	1943	...	...	2148r
	Borlänge d.	...	|	0519	0550	0700	0800d	0902	|	0959	|	1100	1202	|	1300	1401	1502	|	1602	...	1700	|	1802	1900	2002	...	...	...
	Ludvika d.	...	|	0552	0624	0730	0829d	0930	|	1030	|	1131	1231	|	1330	1429	1531	|	1629	...	1729	|	1829	1928	2030	...	...	...
	Grängesberg d.	...	|	0602	0635	0740	0839d	0941	|	1040	|	1143	1243	|	1341	1439	1541	|	1641	...	1740	|	1841	1940	2041	...	...	...
	Kopparberg d.	...	|	0621	0657	0758	0859d	0959	|	1058	|	1202	1301	|	1400	1502	1559	|	1700	...	1800	|	1900	1959	2059	...	...	...
202	Frövi d.	...	0643	0705	0744	0843	0945d	1046	1042	1144	1240	1246	1348	1447	1444	1544	1644	1642	1744	...	1843	1849	1944	2041	2144	...	...	...
228	**Örebro C** a.	...	0659	0719	0759	0857	1000d	1100	1056	1159	1254	1303	1402	1501	1458	1558	1701	1656	1758	...	1858	1904	1959	2057	2158	...	...	...
	Örebro C 736/56 d.	0619	0701	0724	0813	0859	1012	...	1057a	1217	...	...	1412	1502	*1518*	1610	...	1658	1817	...	...	1905	2016	...	2201	...	...	...
252	**Hallsberg 736/56** a.	0637	0721	0744	0831	0917	1029	...	1114a	1236	...	...	1429	1518	*1538*	1627	...	1717	1835	...	...	1922	2035	...	2219	...	...	...
	Hallsberg d.	0647	...	...	0845	...	1045	...	...	1246	...	...	1445	...	...	1644	...	...	1844b	...	...	...	2044	...	...	...	...	...
	Motala d.	0725	...	...	0926	...	1127	...	...	1326	...	...	1526	...	...	1724	...	...	1924b	...	...	...	2124	...	...	...	...	...
	Mjölby 730 a.	0741	...	...	0942	...	1143	...	...	1342	...	...	1541	...	...	1740	...	...	1940b	...	...	...	2140	...	...	...	...	...

a – Ⓐ only. **b** – Ⓑ only. **c** – Ⓒ only. **d** – ⚒ only. **e** – ① only. **q** – From Aug. 10. **r** – From July 14. **y** – Not Aug. 11 - 17, Sept. 8 - 14. **z** – Not Aug. 11 - 17.

STOCKHOLM - VÄSTERÅS - ÖREBRO - HALLSBERG 756

km		Ⓐq	Ⓐ	Ⓐ	⑥	Ⓐq		Ⓐq		Ⓐq		Ⓐn	⚒q		q	⚒n	Ⓐq		Ⓐp	Ⓐ		Ⓐp	⚒q	Ⓑ	⚒
0	**Stockholm C** ⊡ d.	...	0554§	0654§	0724§	0824	0924§	1006	1124§	1206	1324§	1424§	1424	1524§	1624	1624§	1654	1724§	1725	1824§	1924§	2040	2124	2224§	2324§
72	Enköping ⊡ d.	...	0635	0738	0805	0905	1005	1053	1205	1253	1405	1505	1505	1605	1708	1708	1739	1806	|	1905	2008	|	2205	2305	0005
107	**Västerås 752** ⊡ d.	...	0654	0759	0825	0923	1025	1109	1225	1325	1425	1525	1525	1622	1731	1731	1759	1825	|	1929	2030	|	2219	2325	0019
141	Köping d.	...	0710	0817	0841	0939	1041	1129	1241	1341	1441	1541	1541	1638	1749	1749	1818	1841	|	1946	2048	|	...	2341	...
159	Arboga **757** d.	...	0726	0829	0853	0951	1053	1141	1253	1353	1453	1553	1553	1650	1801	1801	1829	1853	1902	1959	2100	2213	...	2353	...
205	**Örebro C 736/55** ▲ d.	0623	0750	0854	0918	1017	1118	1205	1318	1418	1518	1618	1618	1718	1827	1829	1856	1918	1928	2023	2130	2236	...	0016	...
230	**Hallsberg 736/55** ▲ a.	0643	0810	0914	0938	1037	1138	1226	1338	1438	1538	1639	1639	1738	1847	1852	1916	1938	...	2043	2150	2256	...	0036	...
	Göteborg C a.	0900	...	1205	1205	...	1405	...	1600	...	1805	...	...	2000	...	...	...	2205	...	...	...	...	...	...	...

	Ⓐ	Ⓐ	Ⓐp	Ⓐq	Ⓐ	⑥	Ⓐ	Ⓐ	Ⓒ	⑥q	Ⓐq		Ⓐq		Ⓐq		Ⓐ	⑥	Ⓑ	†q	Ⓐn	Ⓐq			Gq
Göteborg C d.	...	...	...	...	...	...	...	0545t	0555g	...	...	0755	...	0955	...	1155	...	1355	1355	...	...	...	1555	1755j	1855
allsberg 736/55 ▲ d.	...	0514	0539	0544	0609	0715	0722	0822	0822	0914	0920	1022	1133	1222	1322	1422	1522	1622	1623	1715	1724	1730	1822	2022	2130
rebro C 736/55 ▲ d.	...	0537	0602	0607	0632	0738	0745	0845	0845	0937	0943	1045	1157	1245	1345	1445	1545	1645	1702	1737	1746	1753	1845	2045	2150
rboga 757 d.	...	0600	|	0630	0659	0801	0806	0906	0906	1001	1004	1106	1218	1306	1406	1506	1606	1706	1725	1800	1807	1818	1906	2106	...
öping d.	...	0610	|	0640	0709	0811	0816	0916	0916	1011	1014	1116	1228	1316	1416	1516	1616	1716	1735	1810	1818	1829	1916	2116	...
ästerås 752 ⊡ d.	0534	0633	|	0704	0734	0834	0841	0941	0941	1034	1053	1141	1253	1341	1441	1541	1641	1741	1804	1834	1841	1853	1941	2141	...
nköping ⊡ d.	0551	0650	|	0721	0751	0851	0855	0955	0955	1051	1107	1155	1307	1355	1455	1555	1655	1755	1821	1851	1855	1907	1955	2155	...
tockholm C ⊡ a.	0635§	0735§	0735	0805	0835§	0935§	0935§	1035§	1035§	1135	1153	1235§	1353	1435§	1535	1635§	1735§	1835§	1905§	1935	1935§	1953	2035§	2235§	...

– ①②③④† only.
– ⑥ only.
– Depart 1800 on †.
n – Until Aug. 9.
p – From Aug. 4.
q – From Aug. 10.
t – Depart 0555 July 12 - Aug. 3.
§ – July 12 - Aug. 3 Stockholm depart 5 minutes **earlier**, arrive 8 minutes **later**.
▲ – Svenska Tågkompaniet AB also operate services Hallsberg - Örebro and v.v.
⊡ – Additional services operate **Stockholm - Västerås** and v.v.

Valid June 29 - August 9

STOCKHOLM - BORLÄNGE - FALUN and MORA 758

km		*IC* **32** ⑤⑥§	*Sn* **690** ①–④§		*IC* **16** †§	*Sn* **666** ⚒§		*Tågab* **G**	*IC* **36** Ⓑ§	*IC* **38** ⑥§		*IC* **22** ⑤§	*IC* **46** †§	*Sn* **674** A§		*Sn* **676** C§	*IC* **26** ⑤§	*Sn* **698** ⑥k	*IC* **48** n§	*IC* **48** Ⓑk		*IC* **28** †§
0	**Stockholm C 760** ♠ d.	0745	0746	...	0945	0946	...	...	1145	1145	...	1345	1345	1346	...	1546	1545	1746	1745	1745	...	1945
39	Arlanda C ✈ **760** ◧ ♠ d.	0806	0805	...	1006	1005	...	...	1206	1206	...	1406	1406	1405	...	1605	1606	1805	1806	1806	...	2006
69	Uppsala **760** ◧ ♠ d.	0824	0824	...	1024	1024	...	...	1224	1224	...	1424	1424	1424	...	1624	1624	1824	1824	1824	...	2024
131	Sala **754** d.	0900	0900	...	1100	1100	...	...	1300	1300	...	1500	1500	1500	...	1700	1700	1900	1900	1900	...	2100
164	Avesta Krylbo d.	0921	0921	...	1120	1119	...	...	1321	1321	...	1521	1521	1520	...	1720	1721	1919	1921	1921	...	2121
229	**Borlänge 755** ● a.	1010	1010	...	1202	1200	...	1315	1410	1410	...	1614	1609	1600	...	1810	1810	2000	2006	2006	...	2203
253	Falun **755** ● a.	|	|	...	1221	1219	...	|	|	|	...	1633	|	1629	...	1830	1830	|	|	|	...	2226
	Leksand a.	1050	1050	...	...	...	...	1345	1439	1449	...	...	1653	...	...	...	...	2041	2046	2046	...	...
	Rättvik a.	1109	1109	...	...	...	...	1405	1458	1511	...	...	1710	...	...	...	...	2058	2104	2104	...	...
	Mora 753 a.	1134	1134	...	...	...	...	1427	1523	1536	...	...	1735	...	...	...	...	2123	2129	2129	...	...

	IC **41** Ⓐ	*IC* **15** ⑥		*IC* **43** ⑥	*IC* **17** ①	*Sn* **669** B	*IC* **21** ⑥	*Sn* **673** Ⓐ		*Sn* **691** ①–④	*IC* **31** ⑤⑥	*IC* **33** †		*IC* **25** †	*Sn* **681** ⚒	*Tågab* **G** ⑥	*Tågab* **G** Ⓑ	*IC* **39** Ⓐ	*IC* **37** ⑥	*IC* **10039** †		*IC* **40** †
ora 753 d.	0626	...	...	0830	...	...	...	...	...	1230	1230	1238	...	...	...	1511	1523	1633	1633	1644	...	1827
ättvik d.	0650	...	...	0854	...	...	...	...	...	1253	1253	1302	...	...	...	1541	1547	1657	1657	1707	...	1851
ksand d.	0708	...	...	0913	...	...	...	...	...	1315	1315	1321	...	...	...	1600	1602	1717	1718	1728	...	1910
Falun 755 ● d.	|	0738	...	|	0938	0938	1124	1141	...	|	|	|	...	1537	1537	|	|	|	|	|	...	|
orlänge 755 ● d.	0753	0757	...	0957	0957	0957	1147	1200	...	1357	1357	1357	...	1556	1601	1628	1628	1757	1757	1757	...	1953
esta Krylbo d.	0841	0841	...	1041	1041	1041	1241	1242	...	1441	1441	1441	...	1641	1642	...	...	1841	1841	1841	...	2041
la 754 d.	0900	0900	...	1100	1100	1100	1300	1300	...	1500	1500	1500	...	1700	1700	...	...	1900	1900	1900	...	2100
psala 760 ◧ ♠ a.	0934	0934	...	1134	1134	1134	1334	1334	...	1534	1534	1534	...	1734	1734	...	...	1934	1934	1934	...	2134
anda C ✈ 760 ◧ ♠ a.	0953	0953	...	1153	1153	1153	1353	1353	...	1553	1553	1553	...	1753	1753	...	...	1953	1953	1953	...	2153
ockholm C 760 ♠ a.	1016	1016	...	1216	1216	1216	1416	1414	...	1614	1616	1616	...	1816	1814	...	...	2016	2016	2016	...	2216

perator: *ST* (except *Tågab*)

BORLÄNGE - MORA

km		Ⓐ		†	⚒	†		Ⓑ	⚒			Ⓑ
0	**Borlänge** d.	0640	0851	1020	1210	1212	...	1429	1628	1820	...	2217
43	Leksand d.	0711	0925	1051	1241	1243	...	1500	1702	1851	...	2248
63	Rättvik d.	0726	0941	1108	1256	1301	...	1517	1717	1908	...	2303
03	**Mora 753** ♣ a.	0749	1004	1131	1319	1324	...	1544	1740	1931	...	2326
04	Morastrand ♣ a.	0753	1008	1135	1323	1328	...	1548	1744	1935	...	2330

	Ⓐ	⑥	Ⓑ		†	⑥	Ⓑ	Ⓐ	†	⚒	Ⓑ
Morastrand ♣ d.	0505	0628	0828	1025	1213	1427	1429	1620	1623	1825	2034
Mora 753 ♣ d.	0510	0632	0832	1029	1217	1431	1433	1624	1627	1829	2038
Rättvik d.	0533	0655	0855	1052	1240	1454	1458	1647	1650	1852	2103
Leksand d.	0548	0710	0911	1107	1257	1509	1515	1702	1708	1907	2119
Borlänge 755 a.	0620	0742	0945	1139	1333	1541	1547	1734	1740	1939	2151

– ①②③④⑥ only. **B** – ②③④⑤† only. **C** – ①②③④† only.
– (12) Göteborg - Mora and v.v. – see Tables **750/1/3**.
– June 29 - July 11. **j** – July 12 - Aug. 3.
– From Aug. 4. **n** – Until Aug. 3.
♣ – Local journeys are not permitted Mora - Morastrand and v.v.
♠ – Frequent local services operate Stockholm - Uppsala and v.v.
● – Additional services operate Borlänge - Falun and v.v.
◧ – From Stockholm calls to pick up only; to Stockholm calls to set down only.
§ – July 12 - Aug. 3 Stockholm depart 5 minutes **earlier**. Train number **10xxx** or **100xx**.

760 STOCKHOLM - SUNDSVALL - UMEÅ

Valid June 29 - August 9

For additional services Stockholm - Gävle and v.v. see Table 761. For local services Gävle - Sundsvall and v.v. see Table 762. For sleeper services see Table 767

km		NT	NT	NT	NT	Sn	Sn	Sn	Sn	NT	Sn	Sn	NT	NT	Sn	Sn	NT	Sn	Sn	Sn	NT	NT	IC	Sn	Sn	Sn	NT
						20560	10560	20564	10564		20568	10568			20572	10572		20576	10576	10576			10008	10580	20584	10584	
		2	2	2	2	Ⓡ✕	Ⓡ✕	Ⓡ✕	Ⓡ✕	2	Ⓡ✕	Ⓡ✕	2	2	Ⓡ✕	Ⓡ✕	2	Ⓡ✕	Ⓡ✕	Ⓡ✕	2	2	10010	Ⓡ✕	Ⓡ✕	Ⓡ✕	2
		Ⓐ	Ⓐ		Ⓐ	Ⓐv	Ⓐw	v	w		v	⚒w	Ⓐ	F	Ⓐv	w		Ⓑm	G	⑤y	†	⚒	⑤	H	v	w	Ⓑ
0	**Stockholm** C ....d.	...	...	...	...	0617	0622	0817	0822	...	1017	1022	...	...	1217	1222	...	1417	1422	1422	...	...	1455	1622f	1817	1822	...
39	Arlanda C ✈ .....‡ d.	...	...	...	...	0641	0641	0841	0841	...	1041	1041	...	...	1241	1241	...	1441	1441	1441	...	...	1521	1641	1841	1841	...
69	Uppsala ....‡ d.	...	...	...	...	0700	0700	0900	0900	...	1100	1100	...	...	1300	1300	...	1500	1500	1500	...	...	1547	1700	1900	1900	...
182	**Gävle** C ....d.	...	...	...	...	0748	0748	0948	0948	...	1148	1148	...	...	1348	1348	...	1548	1548	1548	...	...	1646	1748	1948	1948	...
260	Söderhamn ....d.	...	...	...	...	0833	0833	1035	1035	...	1233	1233	...	...	1433	1433	...	1635	1635	1635	...	...	1739	1835	2035	2035	...
314	Hudiksvall ....d.	...	...	...	...	0901	0903n	1101	1101n	...	1301	1303n	...	...	1501	1503n	...	1703	1703	1703	...	...	1815	1903	2103	2103	...
402	**Sundsvall** ....a.	...	...	...	...	...	1008y	...	1207y	...	...	1407y	...	...	...	1607y	...	1807	1807	1807	...	...	1925	2004	2202	2202	...
402	**Sundsvall** ....d.	...	0549	0755	0910	...	1014y	...	...	1219	...	...	1406	1508	...	1615y	1655	...	...	1813	1806	1902	...	2007	...	...	2212
470	Härnösand ....d.	...	0644	0851	1004	...	1110y	...	...	1315	...	...	1457	1601	...	1713y	1757	...	...	1913	1901	2003	...	2109	...	...	2310
516	Kramfors ....d.	0553	0711	0916	1037	...	1132y	...	...	1339	...	...	1521	1622	...	1739y	1824	...	...	1935	1924	2026	...	2131	...	...	2341
603	Örnsköldsvik C .....d.	0639	0751	0956	1116	...	1215y	...	...	1416	...	...	1605	1716	...	1821y	1907	...	...	2012	2006	2124	...	2207	...	...	...
713	**Umeå** Östra .... ♠ a.	0736	0851	1052	1217	...	1304y	...	...	1511	...	...	1708	1813	...	1913y	2004	...	...	2054	2104	2221	...	2249	...	...	...
715	**Umeå** C .... ♠ a.	0741	0855	1056	1221	...	1308y	...	...	1515	...	...	1712	1818	...	1917y	2008	...	...	2058	2108	2225	...	2253	...	...	...

	Sn	NT	Sn	Sn		NT	NT	Sn	Sn		NT	Sn		NT	Sn		NT	Sn	IC	Sn		NT	NT	NT	NT	
	10563		10567	10567				10573	10571			10575			10579			10583	10011	10587						
	Ⓡ✕	2	Ⓡ✕	Ⓡ✕		2	2	Ⓡ✕	Ⓡ✕		2	Ⓡ✕		2	Ⓡ✕		2	Ⓡ✕		Ⓡ✕		2	2	2	2	
	E	Ⓐ	Ⓐ	©y		Ⓐ	Ⓐ	†k	Ⓐ		F							Ⓑ	†			Ⓐk		Ⓑ	⑥	
Umeå C .... ♠ d.	...	...	0515y	...	...	0545	0645	...	...	...	0752	0905y	...	1056	...	...	1245	...	...	1505	...	1540	1625	1729	1837	...
Umeå Östra .... ♠ d.	...	...	0518y	...	...	0549	0649	...	...	...	0756	0908y	...	1100	...	...	1249	...	...	1510	...	1545	1629	1733	1842	...
Örnsköldsvik C ....d.	...	0514	0605y	...	...	0654	0749	...	...	...	0857	0955y	...	1157	...	...	1347	...	...	1556	...	1648	1732	1831	1947	...
Kramfors ....d.	...	0603	0639y	...	...	0735	0830	...	...	...	0938	1027y	...	1234	...	...	1431	...	...	1632	...	1733	1815	1911	2035	...
Härnösand ....d.	...	0626	0704y	...	...	0757	0853	...	...	...	1002	1052y	...	1258	...	...	1455	...	...	1655	...	1756	1838	1944	2106	...
Sundsvall ....a.	...	0723	0755y	...	...	0850	0947	...	...	...	1057	1143y	...	1348	...	...	1546	...	...	1748	...	1847	1936	2038	2159	...
Sundsvall ....d.	0600	...	0800y	0800	...	...	...	0959	0952y	...	...	1151y	...	...	1351y	...	...	1551	1620	1751	...	...	...	...	...	...
Hudiksvall ....d.	0701	...	0858n	0858	...	...	...	1058	1058n	...	...	1258n	...	...	1458n	...	...	1658	1730	1858	...	...	...	...	...	...
Söderhamn ....d.	0729	...	0929	0929	...	...	...	1129	1129	...	...	1329	...	...	1529	...	...	1729	1806	1929	...	...	...	...	...	...
Gävle C ....d.	0814	...	1014	1014	...	...	...	1214	1214	...	...	1414	...	...	1614	...	...	1814	1856	2014	...	...	...	...	...	...
Uppsala ....‡ a.	0859	...	1059	1059	...	...	...	1259	1259	...	...	1459	...	...	1659	...	...	1859	1955	2059	...	...	...	...	...	...
Arlanda C ✈ ....‡ a.	0917	...	1117	1117	...	...	...	1317	1317	...	...	1517	...	...	1717	...	...	1917	2022	2117	...	...	...	...	...	...
Stockholm C ....a.	0938	...	1138	1138	...	...	...	1338	1338	...	...	1538	...	...	1738	...	...	1938	2046	2138	...	...	...	...	...	...

761 STOCKHOLM and SUNDSVALL - ÖSTERSUND - TRONDHEIM

For additional services Stockholm - Gävle and v.v. see Table 760. For sleeper services see Table 767

km		NT	NT	NT	NT	IC	IC	IC			NT		NT	NT		Sn	IC	Sn	Sn	NT			Sn	Sn		NT	NT
						10080	80	80								10594	84	574	10574				10578	578			
		2	2	2	2						2		2	2		Ⓡ✕		Ⓡ✕	Ⓡ✕	2			Ⓡ✕	Ⓡ✕		2	2
			Ⓐx	Ⓐ		v	C	⚒q	Ⓐq	⚒				Ⓐ		⑥v	⑤†q	⑥q	⑥r	D	⑤q	Ⓑq	Ⓑv	Ⓑt			Ⓐ
0	**Stockholm** C ....d.	...	...	...	...	0809	0813	0813	0716	0922	...	1118	...	...	1318	1417	1358	1422	1422	...	1514	1616	1647	1652	1918	...	...
39	Arlanda C ✈ ....d.	...	...	...	...	0835u	0835u	0835u	0735	0941	...	1141	...	...	1341	1441u	1420u	1441u	1441u	...	1535	1635u	1711u	1711u	1941	...	...
69	Uppsala ....d.	...	...	...	...	0904u	0904u	0904u	0754	1000	...	1200	...	...	1400	1500u	1447u	1500u	1500u	...	1555	1652	1730u	1730u	2000	...	...
182	**Gävle** C ....d.	...	...	...	...	1000	1000	1000	0843	1046	...	1250	...	...	1446	1548	1545	1548	1548	...	1651	1744	1825	1825	2050	...	...
281	Bollnäs ....d.	...	...	...	...	1054	1054	1054	...	...	...	...	...	...	...	1639	1640	|	|	...	...	1838	1916	1916	...	...	...
344	Ljusdal ....d.	...	...	...	...	1134	1134	1134	...	...	...	...	...	...	...	1715	1717	|	|	...	...	1916	1951	1951	...	...	...
	Sundsvall ....d.	0508	...	0743	1010	|	|	|	...	...	1215	...	1408	1630	...	|	|	1801	1810	1820	...	...	|	|	...	2018	2216
450	Ånge ....d.	0622	0805	0900	1137	1235	1235	1235	...	...	1337	...	1521	1748	...	1811	|	1909	1925	1933	...	...	2049	2049	...	2136	2331
480	Bräcke ....d.	0639	0823	0917	1154	1258	1258	1258	...	...	1354	...	1538	1805	...	1829	1835	1932	1943	1950	...	...	2107	2107	...	2155b	...
551	**Östersund** C ....a.	0727	0912	1007	1238	1341	1341	1341	...	...	1444	...	1630	1857	...	1911	1916	2013	2024	2050	...	...	2155	2155	...	2244b	...
551	**Östersund** C **753** d.	0729	▬	1009x	1240	1344	1344	...	...	...	...	...	1633	▬	...	...	...	...	...	...	...	...	...	...	...	2246b	...
656	Åre ....d.	0844	...	1120x	1352	1505	1505	...	...	...	...	...	1747	...	...	...	...	...	...	...	...	...	...	...	...	0002b	...
665	Duved ....d.	0853	2	1128x	1359	...	...	...	...	...	...	...	1757	2	...	...	...	...	...	...	...	...	...	...	...	0010b	...
713	Storlien ▦ ....a.	0929	0935	...	...	...	...	...	...	...	...	...	1830	1835	...	...	...	...	...	...	...	...	...	...	...	...	...
819	**Trondheim 787** ...a.	...	1110	...	...	...	...	...	...	...	...	...	...	2010	...	...	...	...	...	...	...	...	...	...	...	...	...

km					NT		Sn		NT	NT	NT	Sn		Sn	Sn	NT			NT	NT	NT	NT		IC	NT		NT
							565					569		573	10573									85			
					2		Ⓡ✕		2	2	2	Ⓡ✕		Ⓡ✕	Ⓡ✕	2		2	2	2	2	2			2	2	2
		Ⓐq	Ⓐ	⑥	Ⓐ	Ⓐp	Ⓐq	⑥	Ⓐx	†	⚒	A		†q	†k	B	Ⓐq			Ⓐ	Ⓑ		Ⓑq		Ⓐ		
	Trondheim 787 ...d.	...	...	...	...	...	...	...	...	...	...	...	...	...	...	...	...	0750	...	...	...	...	...	...	...	1650	...
	Storlien ▦ ....d.	...	...	...	...	...	...	...	...	...	...	...	...	...	...	...	...	0925	0939	...	...	...	...	...	...	1825	1840
	Duved ....d.	...	...	...	...	...	...	...	...	...	0607	...	...	...	...	...	...	▬	1013	1200x	...	1500	...	...	...	...	1914
	Åre ....d.	...	...	...	...	...	...	...	...	...	0616	...	...	...	...	...	...	...	1022	1209x	...	1509	...	1553p	...	...	1923
	Östersund C ....a.	...	...	...	...	...	...	...	...	...	0725	...	...	...	...	...	...	...	1133	1318x	...	1617	...	1715p	...	...	2034
	Östersund C **753** d.	...	...	...	...	...	0547	...	0620	...	0727	0743	...	0750	0750	0930	...	...	1134	1320	1516	1620	...	1725	1923	...	2037
	Bräcke ....d.	...	...	...	...	...	0627	...	0712	...	0815	0823	...	0830	0830	1015	...	...	1223	1411	1607	1707	...	1807	2011	...	2128
0	Ånge ....d.	...	...	...	0557	...	0644	...	0728	0821	0834	0841	...	0848	0848	1033	...	...	1241	1429	1627	1725	...	1827	2029	...	2145
94	**Sundsvall** ....a.	...	...	...	0716	...	|	...	...	0935	0953	|	...	0955	0955	1145	...	...	1353	1552	1751	1849	...	|	2142	...	230[illegible]
	Ljusdal ....d.	...	0542q	...	...	...	0743	0743q	...	...	...	0940	...	|	|	▬	...	...	▬	▬	...	...	...	1927	...	...	...
	Bollnäs ....d.	...	0618q	...	...	...	0817	0819q	...	...	...	1014	...	|	|	...	...	...	p	⑤q	...	...	...	2010	...	...	...
	Gävle C ....d.	0616	0717	0717	...	0914	0914	0918	...	...	...	1114	1118	1214	1214	1318	1418	1510	1711	1715	...	...	1911	2110	...	...	...
	Uppsala ....a.	0706	0806	0806	...	0959	0959s	1006	...	...	...	1159s	1206	1259s	1259s	1406	1506	1559	1758	1813	...	...	1959	2204s	...	...	...
	Arlanda C ✈ ....a.	0723	0827	0823	...	1017	1017s	1023	...	...	...	1217s	1223	1317s	1317s	1423	1523	1617	1817	1832	...	...	2017	2223s	...	...	...
	Stockholm C ....a.	0745	0846	0846	...	1038	1038	1045	...	...	...	1238	1245	1338	1338	1445	1545	1638	1838	1853	...	...	2038	2246	...	...	...

762 GÄVLE - SUNDSVALL

Journey ± 2 hours 15 minutes, 2nd class only.

From **Gävle**: 0513Ⓐ, 0908Ⓐ**y**, 1157Ⓐ**y**, 1405Ⓐ, 1610Ⓐ, 1719Ⓑ, 1906†, 2120Ⓐ.

From **Sundsvall**: 0536Ⓐ, 0830Ⓐ**y**, 1216Ⓐ**y**, 1443Ⓐ, 1642Ⓐ, 1925Ⓐ, 2024Ⓐ, 2026†.

Subject to alteration from Aug. 10.

All services stop at Söderhamn and Hudiksvall.

Operator: *XT*.

763 UMEÅ - LULEÅ

2nd class only. Operator: *N*[illegible]

km		⑥	Ⓐ	†		⑥	Ⓐ	†
0	**Umeå** Östra **762** ......d.	1116	1120	1120	...	1712	1718	1839
2	**Umeå** C **762** .... ♣ d.	1119	1134	1123	...	1715	1722	1844
33	Vännäs .... ♣ d.	1148	|	1150	...	1741	|	1910
142	Bastuträsk ....d.	1321	1320	1336	...	1845	1845	2022
269	Älvsbyn ....d.	1509	1510	1511	...	2135	2145	2251
315	Boden **765** ....a.	1541	1542	1547	...	2208	2220	2324
351	**Luleå 765** ....a.	1613	1614	1621	...	2239	2250	2355

	Ⓐ	Ⓐ	⑥		†	©
Luleå 765 ....d.	0602	0950	0950	...	1224	180[illegible]
Boden **765** ....d.	0634	1021	1021	...	1305	190[illegible]
Älvsbyn ....d.	0709	1106	1106	...	1346	195[illegible]
Bastuträsk ....d.	0852	1247	1248	...	1539	215[illegible]
Vännäs .... ♣ d.	|	|	1412	...	1716	232[illegible]
Umeå C **762** .... ♣ a.	1013	1436	1436	...	1739	234[illegible]
Umeå Östra **762** ...a.	1017	1440	1440	...	1742	234[illegible]

765 LULEÅ - NARVIK

km		NT				IC		NT	NT		NT	
			94	10094		96						
		2	Ⓡ	Ⓡ		2		2	2		2	
			♦	♦					⑥		Ⓑ	
0	**Luleå 763** .... d.	0545	0553	0553	...	1036	...	1334	1457	...	1614	...
36	Boden **763** .... d.	0612	0638	0638	...	1108	...	1402	1544	...	1640	...
204	Gällivare **753** .... d.	0809	0858	0858	...	1310	...	1603	1802	...	1848	...
304	**Kiruna** .... a.	0915	1011	1011	...	1422	...	1709	1922	...	1958	...
304	**Kiruna** .... d.	...	1029	1029	...	1439	...	...	...	...	...	...
397	Abisko Östra .... d.	...	1225z	1245z	...	1605	...	...	...	...	...	...
406	Björkliden .... d.	...	1242	1319	...	1622	...	...	...	...	...	...
426	Vassijaure .... ◇ d.	...	|	|	...	1644	...	...	...	...	...	...
433	Riksgränsen ▦ .... d.	...	1319	1400	...	1655	...	...	...	...	...	...
473	**Narvik 787** .... a.	...	1412	1458	...	1756	...	...	...	...	...	...

	NT		NT	NT		IC	IC			NT	
						95	10095		93		
	2		2	2		2	2		Ⓡ	2	
	⚒			†		♦	♦		♦		
Narvik 787 .... d.	...	...	...	...	...	1043	...	...	1240	...	...
Riksgränsen ▦ . d.	...	...	...	...	...	1140	...	...	1329	...	...
Vassijaure ..... ◇ d.	...	...	...	...	...	1151	...	...	|	...	...
Björkliden .... d.	...	...	...	...	...	1211	1211	...	1407	...	...
Abisko Östra ..... d.	...	...	...	...	...	1227	1227	...	1424	...	...
Kiruna .... a.	...	...	...	...	...	1345	1345	...	1529	...	...
Kiruna .... d.	0551	...	0941	1042	...	1358	1359	...	1546	1735	...
Gällivare **753** ..... d.	0709	...	1051	1213	...	1511	1511	...	1659	1848	...
Boden **763** .... a.	0908	...	1244	1416	...	1729	1729	...	1914	2046	...
Luleå 763 .... a.	0935	...	1310	1443	...	1808	1808	...	1946	2113	...

FOR NOTES SEE NEXT PAGE

LONG DISTANCE SLEEPER TRAINS 767

	10094 R ♦	10094 R ♦	94 R ♦	94 R ♦	10092 R ♦	92 R ♦	72 R ♦	10094 R ♦	94 R ♦	
Malmö C **730** d.	...	...	...	...	...	...	...	...	...	...
Göteborg d.	...	...	...	...	1825j	1825	1825j	...	...	...
Herrljunga d.	...	...	...	...	1925j	1925	1925j	...	...	...
Skövde d.	...	...	...	...	2000j	2000	2000j	...	...	...
Hallsberg d.	...	...	...	...	2100j	2100	2100j	...	...	...
Stockholm C a.	...	...	...	...	2233j	2233	2233j	...	...	...
Stockholm C d.	1750	1750	1755	1755	2235	2235	2235	...	...	...
Arlanda C ✈ d.	1821u	1821u	1821u	1821u	2306u	2306u	2306u	...	...	...
Uppsala d.	1844u	1844u	1844u	1844u	2327	2327	2327	...	...	...
Gävle a.	1943	1943	1943	1943	0027	0027	0027	...	...	...
Gävle d.	1952	1952	1952	1952	0030	0030	0030	...	...	...
Söderhamn d.	2053	2053	2053	2053	0116	0116	0116	...	...	...
Hudiksvall d.	2128	2128	2128	2128	0150	0150	0150	...	...	...
Sundsvall a.	2240	2240	2240	2240	0253	0253	0253	←	←	...
Sundsvall d.	2253	→	2253	→	0308	0308	0327	0327	0327	...
Härnösand d.	2348	...	2348	...	0410	0410	|	|	|	...
Kramfors d.	0017	...	0017	...	0438	0438	|	|	|	...
Ånge d.	|	...	|	...	|	|	0457	0457	0457	...
Bräcke d.	|	...	|	...	|	|	0521	0521	0521	...
Östersund C a.	|	...	|	...	|	|	0632	0632	0632	...
Östersund C d.	|	...	|	...	|	|	0632	0632	0632	...
Åre a.	|	...	|	...	|	|	0809s	0809s	0809s	...
Duved a.	|	...	|	...	|	|	0833	0833	0833	...
Storlien 🏛 a.	|	...	|	...	|	|	...	...	...	...
Långsele d.	|	...	|	...	|	|	...	...	...	...
Mellansel d.	|	...	|	...	|	|	...	...	...	...
Örnsköldsvik d.	0116	...	0116	...	0537	0537	...	...	...	...
Umeå C a.	0214	...	0214	...	0644	0644	...	...	...	...
Umeå C d.	0221	...	0221	...	0650	0650	...	...	...	...
Bastuträsk d.	0400	...	0400	...	0847	0847	...	...	...	...
Älvsbyn d.	0537	...	0537	...	1027	1027	...	...	...	...
Boden a.	0614	...	0614	...	1104	1104	...	...	...	...
Luleå a.	0706	...	0640	...	1155	1155	...	...	...	...
Narvik **765** a.	1458	...	1412	...	...	...	...	...	...	...

		71 R ♦	10073 R ♦		91 R ♦		10073 R ♦	93 R ♦		
Narvik **765** d.	...	...	...	...	...	...	...	1240	...	...
Luleå d.	...	...	...	...	1639	...	...	1825	...	...
Boden d.	...	...	...	...	1736	...	...	1936	...	...
Älvsbyn d.	...	...	...	...	1811	...	...	2022	...	...
Bastuträsk d.	...	...	...	...	1952	...	...	2201	...	...
Umeå C a.	...	...	...	...	2128	...	...	2327	...	...
Umeå C d.	...	...	...	...	2132	...	...	2356	...	...
Örnsköldsvik d.	...	...	...	...	2245	...	...	0100	...	...
Mellansel d.	...	...	...	...	|	...	...	|	...	...
Långsele d.	...	...	...	...	|	...	...	|	...	...
Storlien 🏛 d.	...	...	...	...	|	...	...	|	...	...
Duved d.	...	1950	1950	...	|	...	...	|	...	...
Åre d.	...	2012u	2012u	...	|	...	...	|	...	...
Östersund C a.	...	2143	2143	...	|	...	...	|	...	...
Östersund C d.	...	2235	2235	...	|	...	...	|	...	...
Bräcke d.	...	2326	2326	...	|	...	...	|	...	...
Ånge d.	...	2348	2348	...	|	...	...	|	...	...
Kramfors d.	...	|	|	...	2332	...	...	0158	...	...
Härnösand d.	...	|	|	...	0004	...	...	0225	...	...
Sundsvall a.	...	0058	0058	...	0103	...	←	0325	...	...
Sundsvall d.	...	0145	→	...	0145	...	0355	0355	...	...
Hudiksvall d.	...	0258	...	...	0258	...	0507	0507	...	...
Söderhamn d.	...	0331	...	...	0331	...	0542	0542	...	...
Gävle a.	...	0424	...	...	0424	...	0649	0649	...	...
Gävle d.	...	0426	...	...	0426	...	0653	0653	...	...
Uppsala a.	...	0532	...	...	0532	...	0832s	0832s	...	...
Arlanda C ✈ a.	...	0606	...	...	0606	...	0852s	0852s	...	...
Stockholm C a.	...	0630	...	...	0630	...	0916	0916	...	...
Stockholm C d.	...	0640j	...	...	0640j	...	...	...	...	...
Hallsberg a.	...	0844j	...	...	0844j	...	...	...	...	...
Skövde a.	...	1000j	...	...	1000j	...	...	...	...	...
Herrljunga a.	...	|	...	...	|	...	...	...	...	...
Göteborg a.	...	1140j	...	...	1140j	...	...	...	...	...
Malmö C **730** a.	...	...	...	...	...	...	...	...	...	...

♦ – **NOTES FOR TABLES 760 – 767** (LISTED BY TRAIN NUMBER)

71 – [sleeper] and [couchette] Duved - Sundsvall (**91**) - Göteborg; [2nd class] and 🍸 Duved - Sundsvall.
72 – [sleeper] and [couchette] Göteborg (**92**) - Sundsvall - Duved; [2nd class] and 🍸 Sundsvall - Duved; [sleeper], [couchette], [2nd class] and ✕ Stockholm (**92/10092**) - Sundsvall - Duved.
91 – [sleeper], [couchette], [2nd class] and ✕ Luleå - Stockholm (- Göteborg, not July 18 - 26); [sleeper] and [couchette] Duved (**71**) - Sundsvall - Göteborg; [2nd class] and 🍸 Duved - Sundsvall.
92 – May 19 - July 11, Aug. 4 - Dec. 13: [sleeper], [couchette], [2nd class] and ✕ Göteborg - Stockholm - Luleå; [sleeper] and [couchette] Göteborg - Sundsvall (**72**) - Duved; [2nd class] and 🍸 Sundsvall - Duved.
93 – [sleeper], [couchette], [2nd class] and ✕ / 🍸 Narvik - Luleå - Stockholm; [sleeper], [couchette], [2nd class] and ✕ Duved (**71**) - Sundsvall - Stockholm.
94 – Aug. 18 - Dec. 13: [sleeper], [couchette], [2nd class] and ✕ / 🍸 Stockholm - Luleå - Narvik; [sleeper], [couchette], [2nd class] and ✕ Stockholm - Sundsvall (**72**) - Duved.
95 – ⑤⑥† June 29 - Aug. 17; daily Aug. 18 - Dec. 13: [2nd class] Narvik - Luleå.
10073 – [sleeper], [couchette], [2nd class] and ✕ Duved - Sundsvall (**93**) - Stockholm.
10092 – July 12 - Aug. 3: [sleeper], [couchette], [2nd class] and ✕ (Göteborg, not July 19 - 27 -) Stockholm - Luleå; [sleeper] and [couchette] Göteborg - Sundsvall (**72**) - Duved; [2nd class] and 🍸 Sundsvall - Duved.
10094 – June 29 - Aug. 17: [sleeper], [couchette], [2nd class] and ✕ / 🍸 Stockholm - Luleå - Narvik: [sleeper], [couchette], [2nd class] and ✕ Stockholm - Sundsvall (**72**) - Duved.
10095 – ①②③④ June 29 - Aug. 17: [2nd class] Björkliden - Luleå.

A – ⚒ June 29 - July 6; daily July 7 - Aug. 9; ⑥ Aug. 10 - Dec. 13.
B – Daily June 29 - July 6; Ⓒ July 7 - Aug. 17; daily Aug. 18 - Dec. 13.
C – Daily June 29 - July 11; ⚒ Aug. 4 - 9.
D – Ⓑ June 29 - July 6; † July 7 - Aug. 17; Ⓑ Aug. 18 - Dec. 13.
E – Ⓐ (also ⑥ July 7 - Aug. 3).
F – Daily June 29 - July 6; Ⓒ July 7 - Aug. 9.

G – ①②③④† June 29 - July 10, Aug. 4 - 9.
H – Ⓑ June 29 - July 11; daily July 12 - Aug. 3; Ⓑ Aug. 4 - 9. Train number **20580** July 12 - Aug. 3.

f – Depart 1617 July 12 - Aug. 3.
j – Not July 19 - 27.
k – June 29 - July 6.
m – July 11 - Aug. 3.
n – Not July 7.
p – June 29 - Aug. 9.
q – Aug. 10 - Dec. 13.
r – June 29 - July 11, Aug. 4 - 9.
s – Stops to set down only.
t – June 29 - July 11, Aug. 4 - Dec. 13.
u – Stops to pick up only.
v – July 12 - Aug. 3.
w – Not July 12 - Aug. 3.
x – Not July 7 - Aug. 17.
y – Not July 7 - Aug. 3.
z – Arrive 1148.

Sn – High speed train. Special supplement payable.
◇ – Ticket point.
‡ – From Stockholm stops to pick up only, to Stockholm stops to set down only.
♠ – Local journeys are not permitted Umeå C - Umeå Östra and v.v.
♣ – Additional services operate Umeå - Vännäs and v.v.

🚌 UMEÅ - LULEÅ - HAPARANDA - KEMI 768

For validity date periods see footnotes. All stops refer to bus stations except where shown

	NET ①-⑤	*NET* ①-⑥	*NET* ①-⑤	*LN* ①-⑤	*NET* ①-⑥	*VS* ⑥⑦	*NET* ①-⑤	*VS* ①-⑤	*LN*	*NET* ①-⑤	*VS* ⑥	*VS* ①-⑤	*LN* ①-⑤	*NET* ①-⑥	*VS* ①-⑤	*LN* ①-⑤		*LN* ⑥⑦	*NET* ①-⑤	*VS* ⑥	*NET* ①-⑥	*LN* ⑥⑦	*LN* ①-⑤	*NET* ①-⑤	*NET* ①-⑥	*LN* ⑦	*LN* ①-⑤	*LN* ①-⑥	*VS* ①-⑤
Jmeå d.	...	...	...	...	...	...	...	...	...	...	...	...	...	...	...	0515	...	0545	...	...	...	0730	0730	...	...	0900	0900	...	...
Skelleftea d.	...	...	...	...	...	...	...	...	0535	...	...	...	0635	...	...	0740	...	0800	...	...	...	0950	0955	...	...	1115	1125	...	...
Piteå d.	...	...	...	...	...	...	...	...	0700	...	...	...	0805	...	...	0905	...	0925	...	...	...	1115	1120	...	...	1240	1250	...	...
Luleå a.	...	...	...	...	...	...	...	...	0800	...	...	...	0905	...	...	1005	...	1025	...	...	...	1210	1215	...	...	1335	1345	...	...
Luleå d.	...	...	...	0515	...	...	...	...	0820	...	...	...	0950	...	...	1050	...	1050	...	...	...	1230	1245	...	...	1350	1400	1510	...
Haparanda 🏛 d.	0515	0615	0715	0755	0815	0855	0915	1030	1035	1115	1120	1200	1215	1215	1300	1315	...	1315	1315	1353	1415	1500	1515	1515	1615	1635	1645	1745	1805
Tornio 🏛 ... ⊡ d.	0625	0725	0825	...	0925	1005	1025	1145	...	1225	1235	1315	...	1325	1405	...	...	...	1425	1500	1525	...	...	1625	1725	...	...	...	1920
Kemi ⊡ a.	0700	0800	0900	...	1000	1035	1100	1220	...	1300	1310	1350	...	1400	1455	...	...	...	1500	1535	1600	...	...	1700	1800	...	...	...	1950

	VS ⑦	*NET* ①-⑤	*LN*	*NET* ①-⑤	*LN* ①-⑤	*LN* ⑥⑦	*LN* ⑦	*LN* ①-⑤	*LN*	*LN* ①-⑤	*LN*	
Jmeå d.	...	...	1215	...	1420	1430	...	1525	1630	1725	1930	...
Skelleftea d.	...	...	1420	...	1625	1635	...	1755	1835	1955	2135	...
Piteå d.	...	...	1535	...	1740	1750	...	1925	1950	2120	2250	...
Luleå a.	...	...	1625	...	1830	1840	...	2015	2040	2215	2340	...
Luleå d.	...	...	1635	...	1840	...	1855	...	2110	...	...	...
Haparanda 🏛 d.	1820	1815	1850	2015	2055	...	2110	...	2325	...	...	...
Tornio 🏛 ... ⊡ d.	1930	1925	...	2125	...	...	...	...	...	...	...	...
Kemi ⊡ a.	1958	2000	...	2200	...	...	...	...	...	...	...	...

	LN	*LN* ①-⑤	*LN* ①-⑤	*LN* ⑥⑦	*NET* ①-⑤	*NET* ①-⑤	*LN* ①-⑤	*LN* ⑥	*VS* ①-⑤	*NET* ①-⑥	*LN*	*NET* ①-⑤	*VS* ①-⑤
Kemi ⊡ d.	...	...	...	...	0605	0705	...	...	0745	0805	...	0905	0920
Tornio 🏛 ⊡ d.	...	...	...	...	0635	0735	...	...	0825	0835	...	0935	0955
Haparanda 🏛 d.	...	0440	0530	...	0545	0645	0650	0725	0735	0745	0825	0845	0858
Luleå a.	...	0700	0750	...	...	...	0945	0950	...	...	1045	...	...
Luleå d.	0540	0710	0800	0800	...	...	1000	...	...	...	1055	...	...
Piteå d.	0635	0805	0855	0855	...	...	1105	...	...	...	1150	...	...
Skelleftea d.	0750	0920	1015	1015	...	...	1230	...	...	...	1305	...	...
Umeå a.	0945	1115	1210	1210	...	...	1435	...	...	...	1500	...	...

	NET ①-⑥	*LN* ①-⑤	*LN* ⑥⑦	*VS* ①-⑤	*VS* ⑥	*NET* ①-⑤	*LN*	*NET* ①-⑤	*VS* ①-⑤	*LN*	*NET* ①-⑥	*NET* ①-⑤	*LN* ①-⑤	*NET* ①-⑥	*VS* ⑥	*LN* ①-⑤	*NET* ①-⑤	*VS* ①-⑤	*LN* ⑥⑦	*LN* ①-⑤	*NET* ①-⑥	*LN* ⑦	*VS* ⑥⑦	*VS* ①-⑤	*NET* ①-⑤	*NET* ①-⑤	*VS* ⑥	*VS* ①	*VS* ②-⑥
Kemi ⊡ d.	1005	...	...	1125	1125	1205	...	1305	1320	...	1405	1505	...	1605	1625	...	1705	1720	...	...	1805	...	1850	1855	2005	2205	2245	0110	0115
Tornio 🏛 ... ⊡ d.	1035	...	...	1150	1200	1235	...	1335	1355	...	1435	1535	...	1635	1700	...	1735	1755	...	...	1835	...	1925	1930	2035	2235	2315	0140	0145
Haparanda 🏛 d.	0945	1000	1050	1055	1105	1145	1230	1245	1300	1345	1345	1445	1510	1545	1605	1610	1645	1700	1710	1720	1745	1810	1830	1835	1945	2145	2220	0045	0050
Luleå a.	...	1235	1310	...	...	...	1450	...	...	1610	...	...	1750	...	...	1845	...	...	1940	1955	...	2040	...	...	...	...	...	...	...
Luleå d.	...	1300	1320	...	...	...	1500	...	...	1635	...	...	1810	...	...	1910	...	...	2005	2010	...	2055	...	...	...	...	...	...	...
Piteå d.	...	1405	1415	...	...	...	1555	...	...	1750	...	...	1915	...	...	2010	...	...	2105	2110	...	2150	...	...	...	...	...	...	...
Skelleftea d.	...	1535	1530	...	...	...	1715	...	...	1925	...	...	2025	...	...	2130	...	...	2225	2230	...	2300	...	...	...	...	...	...	...
Umeå a.	...	1740	1725	...	...	...	1910	...	...	2130	...	...	...	...	...	2340	...	...	0040	...	...	...	...	...	...	...	...	...	...

⊡ – Finnish time.

Approximate walking distances:
Haparanda bus station - Tornio bus station 800 metres;
Kemi railway station - Kemi bus station 200 metres.

Operators:
LN – Länstrafiken Norrbotten, routes 20 / 100, valid **June 15 - December 13, 2014**; www.ltnbd.se
NET – NET-Matkat, route 70, valid **from June 8, 2014**; www.netmatkat.com
VS – Veljekset Salmela, valid **August 8, 2013 - May 31, 2014** (international rail tickets valid); www.veljeksetsalmela.fi

See also www.matkahuolto.fi

NORWAY

SEE MAP PAGE 342

Operator: Norges Statsbaner (NSB) www.nsb.no

Services: All trains convey second class seating accommodation. Many services, as identified in the notes, also convey *NSB Komfort* accommodation (see below). Sleeping-cars (🛏) have one- and two-berth compartments; the sleeper supplement is 850 NOK per compartment (for two people travelling together, or sole use for single travellers). Most long distance express trains convey a bistro car (✕) serving hot and cold meals, drinks and snacks. 🍸 indicates that drinks and light refreshments are available from automatic vending machines.

Timings: NSB services are valid **June 15 - December 13**, 2014 (unless otherwise stated).

Reservations: Seat reservation is highly recommended on long-distance routes Oslo - Kristiansand - Stavanger (Table **775**), Oslo - Bergen (Table **780**), Oslo - Trondheim / Åndalsnes (Table **785**) and Trondheim - Bodø (Table **787**).

NSB Komfort: *NSB Komfort* is a dedicated area provided on many trains with complimentary tea / coffee and newspapers; a supplement of 90 NOK is payable per single journey.

770 OSLO - HALDEN - GÖTEBORG

All trains convey *NSB Komfort* and 🍸

July 28 - August 17 all trains are replaced by 🚌 Oslo - Moss and v.v. During this period journey times are extended by up to 30 minutes (earlier departures from Oslo).

km	Norwegian train number	139		101	103	105	107	109	111	113	115	117	119	121	141	123	143	125	127	129	131	133	135	137
	Swedish train number					391						395							399					
				Ⓐ	Ⓐ	①–⑥		⚒n		⚒n				k	Ⓐb		Ⓐb	k		Ⓑb		Ⓑb		Ⓑb
0	**Oslo** Sentral d.	0002	...	0356	0602	0702	0802	0902	1002	1102	1202	1302	1402	1502	1528	1602	1628	1702	1802	1902	2002	2102	2202	2302
60	Moss d.	0052	...	0446	0644	0745	0844	0944	1044	1144	1244	1344	1444	1546	1614	1645	1713	1745	1844	1944	2044	2144	2244	2344
69	Rygge ✈ d.	0059	...	0453	0651	0752	0851	0951	1051	1151	1251	1351	1451	1553	1621	1652	1720	1752	1851	1951	2051	2151	2251	2351
94	Fredrikstad d.	0119	...	...	0711	0812	0911	1016	1112	1211	1311	1411	1511	1616	1642	1713	1741	1812	1911	2011	2112	2211	2311	0011
109	Sarpsborg d.	0133	...	...	0729	0825	0929	1033	1126	1225	1325	1425	1529	1633	1656	1727	1755	1826	1925	2028	2126	2225	2325	0025
137	**Halden** ★ d.	0152	...	...	0748	0846	0948	1052	1145	1244	1344	1446	1548	1652	1720	1746	1820	1845	2002**z**	2047	2145	2244	2344	0044
268	Öxnered **751** d.	...	...	...	...	1001	...	...	...	...	...	1601	...	...	...	...	...	...	2116	...	...	...	...	...
278	Trollhättan **751** d.	...	...	...	...	1007	...	...	...	...	...	1608	...	...	...	...	...	...	2122	...	...	...	...	...
350	**Göteborg 751** a.	...	...	...	...	1040	...	...	...	...	...	1650	...	...	...	...	...	...	2200	...	...	...	...	...

Swedish train number										390						394					398			
Norwegian train number	102	154	104	142	156	106	144	108	110	112	114	116	118	120	122	124	126	128	130	132	134	136		138
	Ⓐ	⑥	Ⓐ	Ⓐb	†	⚒	Ⓐb	⚒n		①–⑥		⚒n		k				k		Ⓑb		Ⓑb		
Göteborg 751 d.	...	...	...	...	...	...	...	...	...	0655	...	...	...	...	...	1300	...	...	...	...	1755	...	...	...
Trollhättan **751** d.	...	...	...	...	...	...	...	...	...	0735	...	...	...	...	...	1336	...	...	...	...	1834	...	...	...
Öxnered **751** d.	...	...	...	...	...	...	...	...	...	0742	...	...	...	...	...	1342	...	...	...	...	1840	...	...	...
Halden ★ d.	0400	0500	0502	0533	0600	0602	0633	0700	0802	0910	1005	1103	1202	1302	1402	1510	1605	1703	1802	1902	2005	2102	...	2202
Sarpsborg d.	0422	0520	0524	0553	0620	0624	0654	0721	0824	0930	1026	1125	1224	1324	1424	1530	1626	1725	1825	1924	2026	2124	...	2224
Fredrikstad d.	0436	0534	0538	0608	0634	0638	0709	0736	0838	0944	1040	1139	1238	1338	1438	1544	1640	1739	1839	1938	2040	2138	...	2238
Rygge ✈ d.	0454	0552	0556	0626	0652	0656	0727	0756	0856	1002	1058	1157	1256	1356	1456	1602	1658	1757	1857	1956	2058	2156	...	2256
Moss d.	0503	0601	0608	0635	0701	0708	0736	0808	0908	1012	1108	1208	1308	1408	1508	1612	1711	1808	1908	2008	2108	2208	...	2308
Oslo Sentral a.	0552	0651	0651	0722	0751	0751	0822	0851	0949	1052	1149	1249	1349	1449	1549	1652	1751	1849	1951	2049	2149	2249	...	2349

b – Not June 30 - Aug. 10.
k – Not July 5, 6, 12, 13, 19, 20, 26, 27, Aug. 2, 3, 9, 10.
n – Not July 5, 12, 19, 26, Aug. 2, 9.
z – Arrives 1944.
★ – 🏛 at Kornsjø (*km169*).

771 OSLO - OSLO GARDERMOEN ✈

See also Table 783

Operated by Flytoget AS.
Special fares apply.
✆ +47 815 00 777.

Daily services (journey time: 22 minutes)
Trains call at Lillestrøm 10 minutes from Oslo
From Oslo Sentral every 20 minutes 0440 - 0000.
From Gardermoen every 20 minutes 0530 - 0050.

Additional services on Ⓑ (journey time: 19 minutes)
Non-stop services
From Oslo Sentral every 20 minutes: 0610 - 2230 on Ⓐ, 1210 - 2310 on ⑦.
From Gardermoen every 20 minutes: 0640 - 2300 on Ⓐ, 1240 - 2340 on ⑦.

773 OSLO - GJØVIK

All trains convey *NSB Komfort* and 🍸

km			h				Ⓐ				ⒶⒶ▲
0	**Oslo** S d.	0002	0702	0902	1102	1302	1502	1612	1702	1902	2102	2302
56	Roa d.	0103	0800	0959	1158	1358	1600	1705	1803	1959	2158	0003
70	Jaren d.	0119	0816	1015	1214	1414	1616	1722	1819	2015	2214	0019
99	Eina d.	0142**x**	0840	1039	1238	1437	1639	1750	1842	2039	2238	0042
110	Raufoss d.	0152	0850	1049	1248	1447	1649	1801	1852	2049	2248	0052
122	**Gjøvik** a.	0202	0900	1059	1258	1457	1659	1811	1902	2059	2258	0102

	Ⓐ	⊙	Ⓐ⊠	Ⓐ								
Gjøvik d.	0431	0528	0543	0631	0733	0932	1131	1327	1530	1729	1932	2131
Raufoss d.	0442	0539	0554	0641	0744	0943	1142	1338	1541	1740	1943	2142
Eina d.	0452**x**	0549	0604	0650	0754	0953	1152	1348	1551	1751	1953	2152
Jaren d.	0515	0612	0627	0713	0817	1016	1215	1412	1615	1818	2016	2215
Roa d.	0531	0628	0644	0730	0833	1032	1231	1429	1631	1834	2032	2231
Oslo S a.	0628	0728	0744	0830	0930	1128	1330	1530	1730	1930	2130	2328

h – Not June 28, 29, July 5, 6, 12, 13; 19, 20, 26, 27, Aug. 2, 3.
x – Stops on request only.
⊙ – ⑥⑦ (not June 28 - Aug. 3).
▲ – Runs 29 – 36 minutes **earlier** June 23 - Aug. 1.
⊠ – June 23 - Aug. 1 departs Gjøvik 0547, Raufoss 0558, Eina 0608, Jaren 0639, Roa 0656, arrives Oslo 0804.

775 OSLO - KRISTIANSAND - STAVANGER

km		701	707	715	715	719	723	727	731	735	735	745
		Ⓐ	⚒	⚒		Ⓑ		⑤⑦	◇		⑤⑦¶	Ⓑ
		✕⊡	✕⊡	✕⊡	✕⊡	✕⊡	✕⊡	✕⊡	✕⊡	✕⊡	✕⊡	♣✕
0	**Oslo** Sentral § d.	...	...	0725	...	...	1101	1325	1525	1725	1725	2223
41	Drammen § d.	...	...	0800**u**	...	...	1135**u**	1400**u**	1600**u**	1800**u**	1800**u**	2300**u**
87	Kongsberg § d.	...	...	0836	...	...	1215	1435	1636	1836	1836	2343
134	Nordagutu d.	...	...	0911	...	...	1252	|	1716	1912	1912	0020**x**
151	Bø d.	...	...	0925	...	...	1307	1522	1730	1926	1926	0037
209	Neslandsvatn d.	...	...	1010	...	...	1354	1609	1814	2013	2013	0126**x**
225	Gjerstad d.	...	...	1023	...	...	1410	1622	1826	2026	2026	0142**x**
270	Nelaug d.	...	...	1056	...	...	1447	1656	1859	2059	2059	0221**x**
353	**Kristiansand** a.	...	...	1154	...	...	1550	1754	1957	2157	2157	0331
353	**Kristiansand** d.	0515	0803	1204	1204	1404	1606	...	2009	...	2210	0355
465	Moi d.	0643	0934	1334	1334	1534	1736	...	2140	...	2341	0531**x**
514	Egersund ◇ d.	0721	1020	1412	1412	1615	1816	...	2220	...	0024	0611
573	Sandnes S ◇ d.	0758**z**	1100**z**	1513**z**	1513**z**	1713**z**	1900**z**	...	2258**z**	...	0100**z**	0713**z**
587	**Stavanger** ◇ a.	0812	1112	1527	1527	1727	1912	...	2312	...	0113	0727

	702	706	710	716	720	724	728	732	732	736	744
	Ⓐ	⑥	♥	Ⓐ		⑦	Ⓑ		⑤⑦	Ⓑ	Ⓑ
	✕⊡	✕⊡	✕⊡	✕⊡	✕⊡	✕⊡	✕⊡	✕⊡	✕⊡	✕⊡	♣✕
Stavanger ◐ d.	...	...	0525	0841	1011	1241	1423	1623	1623	1923	2242
Sandnes S ◐ d.	...	...	0539**v**	0856**v**	1026**v**	1256**v**	1439**v**	1638**v**	1638**v**	1938**v**	2256**v**
Egersund ◐ d.	...	...	0626	0939	1119	1339	1525	1727	1727	2021	2340
Moi d.	...	...	0710	1019	1159	1417	1603	1813	1813	2059	0022
Kristiansand a.	...	...	0839	1147	1329	1546	1738	1943	1943	2230	0154
Kristiansand d.	0534	0649	0847	...	1344	1558	1755	...	1958	...	0219
Nelaug d.	0634	0749	0947	...	1449	1658	1858	...	2057	...	0336**x**
Gjerstad d.	0708	0823	1023	...	1527	1732	1932	...	|	...	0413**x**
Neslandsvatn d.	0721	0836	1036	...	1542	1745	1945	...	|	...	0427**x**
Bø d.	0803	0924	1118	...	1627	1831	2031	...	2219	...	0515
Nordagutu d.	0818	0938	1133	...	1641	|	2045	...	|	...	0530**x**
Kongsberg ‡ d.	0859	1011	1212	...	1718	1917	2119	...	2311	...	0608
Drammen ‡ a.	0932**s**	1050**s**	1252**s**	...	1751**s**	1950**s**	2152**s**	...	2357**s**	...	0650**s**
Oslo S ‡ a.	1005	1127	1327	...	1827	2027	2227	...	0035	...	0727

Nelaug - Arendal

km		Ⓐ	⑥	⑦	⚒				⑤⑦		Ⓑ	
0	Nelaug d.	0636	0755	0950	1100	...	1455	...	1700	1900	2100	...
36	Arendal a.	0711	0830	1025	1135	...	1530	...	1735	1935	2135	...

	Ⓐ	⑥					⑤⑦			Ⓑ	
Arendal d.	0550	0705	...	0905	...	1405	1615	1815	...	2015	...
Nelaug a.	0625	0740	...	0940	...	1440	1650	1850	...	2050	...

b – Not June 30 - Aug. 8.
e – Not July 5, 12, 19, 26, Aug. 2, 9.
r – Not July 6, 13, 20, 27, Aug. 3, 10.
s – Stops to set down only.
u – Stops to pick up only.
v – Stops on request to pick up only.
x – Stops on request.
z – Stops on request to set down only.

◇ – June 21 - Oct. 4 by 🚌 Egersund - Sandnes (a. 2337) - Stavanger (a. 2358).
¶ – On ⑤ by 🚌 Egersund - Sandnes (a. 0140) - Stavanger (a. 0159).
♥ – On ⑦ by 🚌 Stavanger - Sandnes - Egersund.
♣ – Conveys 🛏 and [2]. Reservation recommended.
⊡ – Reservation recommended. Conveys *NSB Komfort*.
⊗ – On ⑥ operated by 🚌 Vigrestad ▷ - Egersund.
⊖ – On ①–⑤ operated by 🚌 Vigrestad ▷ - Egersund.
★ – By 🚌 Vigrestad ▷ - Egersund and v.v.
▷ – Vigrestad is located 25 km from Egersund. Journey time extended by 17 – 22 minutes.

§ – Other local trains **Oslo** S - **Drammen** (35 – 36 minutes) - **Kongsberg** (75 – 81 minutes): 0009, 0609 Ⓐ, 0709, 0809 **r**, 0909, 1009 **r**, 1109, 1209 **r**, 1309, 1409, 1509, 1549 Ⓐ **b**, 1609, 1709, 1809, 1909 **e**, 2009, 2109 **e**, 2209 and 2309 **e**.

‡ – Other local trains **Kongsberg** - **Drammen** (42 – 45 minutes) - **Oslo** S (76 – 81 minutes): 0435 Ⓐ, 0535, 0552 Ⓐ **b**, 0635 **r**, 0650 Ⓐ **b**, 0735, 0835 **r**, 0935, 1035 **r**, 1135, 1233, 1335, 1435, 1535, 1635, 1733, 1835, 1935 **e**, 2035, 2133 **e** and 2235.

◇ – Other local trains **Egersund** - **Sandnes** S (51 – 57 minutes) - **Stavanger** (67 – 73 minutes): 0457 Ⓐ, 0527 Ⓐ, 0558 Ⓐ, 0628 ⚒, 0658 Ⓐ, 0728 ⚒, 0825 ⚒, 0925, 1026, 1126, 1230, 132[illegible] 1427, 1458 Ⓐ, 1528, 1558 Ⓐ, 1629, 1659 Ⓐ, 1728, 1824, 1929, 2029, 2110 ⑥ ★, 2130 Ⓑ, 2210 ⑥ ★, 2230 Ⓑ, 2309 ⑥ ★ and 2325 Ⓑ. **Subject to alteration June 30 - July 20.**

◐ – Other local trains **Stavanger** - **Sandnes** S (16 minutes) - **Egersund** (68 – 72 minutes): 0500 Ⓐ, 0531 Ⓐ, 0601 ⚒, 0701 ⚒, 0801 ⚒, 0901, 1001, 1101, 1201, 1301, 1331 Ⓐ, 1401, 1431 Ⓐ, 1501, 1531 Ⓐ, 1601, 1631 Ⓐ, 1701, 1801, 1901, 2001, 2101 ⊗, 2201 ⊗, 2301 Ⓑ [illegible] and 2331 ★. **Subject to alteration June 30 - July 20.**

PORSGRUNN - NOTODDEN 779

No service on ©

km		Ⓐ	Ⓐb	Ⓐ	Ⓐ	Ⓐb	Ⓐ	Ⓐ	Ⓐ
0	**Porsgrunn** . 783 d.	...	0641	0753	0953b	1153	1353	1553b	...
9	Skien .... 783 d.	0533	0652	0802	1003	1203	1403	1603	1803
43	Nordagutu .... a.	0602	0723	0831	1032	1232	1432	1631	1832
43	Nordagutu .... d.	0603	0724	0835	1033	1233	1433	1632	1833
62	**Notodden** .... a.	0622	0743	0854	1052	1252	1452	1651	1852

	Ⓐ	Ⓐb	Ⓐ	Ⓐ	Ⓐb	Ⓐ	Ⓐ	Ⓐ
Notodden .... d.	0643	0812	0908	1108	1308	1508	1708	1908
Nordagutu .... a.	0702	0834	0927	1127	1327	1527	1727	1927
Nordagutu .... d.	0703	0837	0928	1128	1328	1528	1728	1928
Skien .... 783 a.	0737	0907	0958	1158	1358	1558	1758	1958
Porsgrunn .... 783 a.	0746	0916	1010b	1210	1410	1610b	*1826*b	...

b – Not June 30 - Aug. 8.

OSLO - BERGEN 780

Subject to alteration on Sept. 27

km		609 B ⊡	61 ✕⊡	1849 ★	601 ✕⊡	607 ⑦C ⊡	63 ✕⊡		605 Ⓑ N✕	
0	**Oslo** Sentral .... 783 d.	0643	0805	...	1201	...	1601	...	2323	...
41	Drammen .... 783 d.	0720u	0839u	...	1237u	...	1638u	...	0002u	...
112	Hønefoss .... d.	0816	0931	...	1338	...	1741	...	0103	...
208	Nesbyen .... d.	0932	1040	...	1453	...	1850	...	0221	...
225	Gol .... d.	0946	1053	...	1507	...	1903	...	0235	...
250	Ål .... d.	1006	1116	...	1530	1705	1925	...	0259	...
275	Geilo .... d.	1031	1137	...	1551	1727	1946	...	0322	...
286	Ustaoset .... d.	...	1148	...	1603	1740	1957	...	0334	...
324	Finse .... d.	1136	1215	1241	1631	1812	2026	...	0407	...
354	**Myrdal** .... 781 a.	1205	1239	1307	1656	1841	2051	...	0435	...
403	**Voss** .... 781 a.	1300	1338	...	1739	1926	2134	...	0524	...
443	Dale .... 781 a.	...	1414	...	1815	|	2210	...	0559	...
480	Arna .... 781 a.	...	1446s	...	1847	2032s	2246	...	0637s	...
489	**Bergen** .... 781 a.	...	1459	...	1900	2044	2259	...	0651	...

	62 ✕⊡	1848 ★	🚌 ①–⑤ D	602 ✕⊡	604 ⑤E ⊡	64 ✕⊡	610 B ⊡		606 Ⓑ N✕
Bergen .... 781 d.	0757	...	1135	1159z	1410	1559	...	...	2259
Arna .... 781 d.	0809	...	1150	1211z	1424u	1611u	...	...	2311
Dale .... 781 d.	0840	...	1225	1242z	|	|	...	...	2348
Voss .... 781 d.	0910	...	1301	1314	1531	1711	1750	...	0021
Myrdal .... 781 d.	0952	1005	...	1358	1625	1757	1842	...	0106
Finse .... d.	1018	1033	...	1428	1658	1825	1919	...	0140
Ustaoset .... d.	1044	...	...	1458	1728	1851	|	...	0210
Geilo .... d.	1056	...	...	1511	1741	1904	2010	...	0225
Ål .... d.	1116	...	...	1531	1800	1924	2031	...	0257
Gol .... d.	1135	...	...	1551	...	1945	2050	...	0319
Nesbyen .... d.	1147	...	...	1604	...	1957	2104	...	0332
Hønefoss .... d.	1256	...	...	1719	...	2109	2227	...	0454
Drammen .... 783 a.	1350s	...	...	1825s	...	2208s	2326s	...	0551s
Oslo Sentral .... 783 a.	1427	...	...	1905	...	2245	0005	...	0627

B – Until Sept. 26.
C – From Oct. 5.
D – Sept. 1 – 26.
E – From Oct. 3.
N – Conveys 🛏 and 🛏2. Reservation recommended. Subject to alteration on Sept. 26.
s – Trains stop to set down only.
u – Trains stop to pick up only.
z – Not ①–⑤ Sept. 1 – 26.
★ – Daily July 14 - Aug. 17; ⑥⑦ Aug. 23 - Sept. 21.
⊡ – Reservation recommended. Conveys *NSB Komfort*.

MYRDAL - VOSS - BERGEN and FLÅM 781

SERVICE JUNE 15 - SEPT. 28. *All services are subject to alteration on Sept. 27.*

km		Ⓐ	605 ①–⑥ ✕◇	⊖	Ⓐ	Ⓐy ✣	✣	Ⓐ ✣	✣	Ⓐ ✣		✣	609 ◇	61 ✕◇	Ⓐ				601 ✕◇			⑤	63 ✕◇	⑥	Ⓑ ◧
	Oslo Sentral **780** ..... d.	...	2323p	...	...	...	...	...	...	...	...	...	0643	0805	...	...	...	...	1201	...	...	...	1601	...	...
0	**Myrdal** .... d.	...	0436	...	...	...	...	...	...	0956	0956	1111	1213	1243	1322	1322	1440	1553	1658	1719	...	1941	2053	...	...
18	Mjølfjell .... d.	...	|	...	...	0747	...	...	...	1014x	1014x	1128x	|	|	|	|	|	|	|	1741	...	1959x	|	...	...
49	**Voss** .... a.	...	0524	...	...	0821	...	...	...	1051	1051	1205	1300	1338	1412	1412	1528	1633	1739	1819	...	2034	2134	...	...
49	**Voss** .... d.	0504	0529	0608	0721	0836	0836	0923	1040	1125	...	1239	...	1341	1439	...	1539	1638	1742	1841	1941	...	2138	2154	2239
89	Dale .... d.	0535	0559	0645	0752	0910	0910	1000	1114	1202	...	1313	...	1414	1514	...	1614	1714	1815	1915	2019	...	2210	2225	2316
104	Vaksdal .... d.	0554	|	0700	0807	0931	0931	1015	1129	1227	...	1329	...	|	1529	...	1630	1730	|	1931	2037	...	|	2244	2332
126	Arna .... ‡ d.	0613	0637s	0721	0832	0949	0949	1035	1148	1245	...	1348	...	1446s	1548	...	1648	1748	1849	1950	2058	...	2248	2303	2350
135	**Bergen** .... ‡ a.	0623	0651	0731	0843	0959	0959	1046	1158	1255	...	1358	...	1459	1558	...	1658	1758	1900	2000	2108	...	2259	2313	2400

	①–⑥ ⊖		Ⓐ	B	62 ✕◇		✣	Ⓐ ✣	🚌 ①–⑤ D	602 ✕◇		✣	Ⓐ		64 ✕◇	Ⓐ	610 ◇		⑤	Ⓐ		Ⓐ		606 Ⓑ◧ ✕◇	⑥
Bergen .... ‡ d.	0009	...	0531	0651	0757	0844	0959	1059	1135	1159z	...	1259	1359	1514	1559	1614	...	1659	1659	1759	1900	2029	2159	2259	2320
Arna .... ‡ d.	0019	...	0549	0701	0809	0854	1009	1109	1150	1211z	...	1309	1409	1525	1611u	1625	...	1709	1709	1809	1910	2039	2210	2311	2330
/aksdal .... d.	0036	...	0615	0719	|	0911	1030	1128	|	|	...	1329	1429	1545	|	1646	...	1729	1729	1830	1930	2057	2228	|	2347
Dale .... d.	0054	...	0630	0734	0840	0926	1044	1143	1225	1242z	...	1344	1444	1600	|	1701	...	1745	1745	1845	1946	2113	2243	2348	0002
Voss .... a.	0125	...	0703	0810	0908	0958	1115	1216	1301	1311z	...	1415	1515	1632	1710	1734	...	1816	1816	1916	2017	2149	2314	0019	0033
Voss .... d.	...	...	0706y	0829	0910	1003	1120	...	...	1314	1346	1440	...	...	1711	...	1750	...	1821	...	...	...	...	0021	...
Mjølfjell .... d.	...	...	0737y	0900x	|	1033x	|	...	...	|	|	1515x	...	...	|	...	|	...	1854x	...	...	...	...	|	...
Myrdal .... a.	...	...	...	0918	0950	1051	1159	...	...	1355	1428	1533	...	...	1755	...	1830	...	1913	...	...	...	...	0104	...
Oslo Sentral **780** ...... a.	...	...	...	...	1427	...	...	...	...	1905	...	...	...	...	2245	...	0005	...	...	...	...	...	...	0627	...

Myrdal - Flåm ⊠

km										L	
0	Myrdal .... d.	0939	1058	1213	1327	1443	1559	1715	1835	1948	2100
20	Flåm .... a.	1035	1155	1310	1425	1540	1655	1810	1930	2045	2150

									L	
Flåm .... d.	0835	0945	1105	1220	1335	1450	1605	1725	1840	1955
Myrdal .... a.	0927	1043	1201	1315	1431	1546	1703	1817	1936	2048

– Until Sept. 26.
– Sept. 1 – 26.
– Until Aug. 31.
p – Previous day.
s – Stops to set down only.
u – Stops to pick up only.
x – Stops on request.
y – Not June 23 - Aug. 15.
z – Not ①–⑤ Sept. 1 – 26.
◇ – Reservation recommended.
◧ – Subject to alteration on Sept. 26.
⊖ – Subject to alteration on Sept. 28.
‡ – Additional local services operate.
✣ – Operated by 🚌 Voss - Bergen and v.v. on ①–⑤ Sept. 1 – 26. Please confirm timings locally.
⊠ – **Operator**: Flåm Utvikling AS. ✆ + 47 57 63 21 00. 30 % discount for rail pass holders.

⛴ FLÅM - GUDVANGEN and 🚌 GUDVANGEN - VOSS 781a

May 1 - Sept. 30

	⛴	🚌	⛴ B		⛴	🚌	⛴	🚌	⛴	
låm .... d.	0900	...	1100	...	1320	...	1510	...	1800	...
iudvangen .... a.	1125	...	1320	...	1530	...	1730	...	1950	...
iudvangen .... d.	...	1140	...	...	...	1540	...	1745	...	...
oss .... a.	...	1255	...	...	...	1655	...	1900	...	...

	🚌 ①–⑤	⛴	🚌	⛴		⛴ B	🚌	⛴	🚌 ①–⑤	⛴
Voss .... d.	0830	...	1005	...	...	...	1440	...	1610	...
Gudvangen .... a.	0920e	...	1115	...	...	...	1540	...	1710	...
Gudvangen .... d.	...	1030	...	1145	...	1330	...	1545	...	1740
Flåm .... a.	...	1255	...	1410	...	1545	...	1750	...	1930

– June 20 - Aug. 20.
e – Bus stop on E16 main road.

⛴ / 🚌 LILLEHAMMER and GOL - FLÅM - BALESTRAND - BERGEN 782

May 1 - Sept. 30

	⛴ A	⛴ ⚒	🚌	⛴ ⑦E	⛴	🚌	🚌 h	🚌 s	🚌 Ⓑ	🚌	🚌 ⑤⑦	🚌 s
illehammer skysst. d.	...	...	...	...	...	1030	...	...	...	...	...	...
Sogndal ⊕ .... d.	...	...	0755	...	...	|	1430	...	1715	...	...	...
Kaupangersenteret. d.	...	...	0810	...	...	|	1445	...	1730	...	...	...
Øvre Årdal ◇ ..... d.	...	*0535*e	*0740*	...	...	|	1430	...	*1705*	*1850*	*2030*	...
Fodnes .... d.	...	*0630*e	0835	...	...	|	1515	...	1755	1940	2120	...
ol Skysstasjon ...... d.	...	|	|	...	...	|	|	1325	|	|	|	1900
ærdal Rådhuset ..... d.	...	*0615*e	0845	...	...	|	1525	1525	1805	|	|	2105
aupangersenteret... d.	...	*0646*e	|	...	...	|	|	1600	|	2000	2140	2140
ogndal ⊕ .... d.	...	0705	|	1040	...	|	|	1620	|	2015	2155	2205
Flåm .... d.	0600	|	0930	|	1530	1620	1620	|	1850	...	...	|
eikanger .... d.	0730	0730	|	1110	1630	|	|	1645	|	...	...	2230
alestrand .... d.	0800	0750	|	1130	1655	|	|	1735	|	...	...	2310
Voss .... a.	...	|	1035	|	|	1730	1730	...	2000	...	...	...
ergen ⊡ .... a.	...	1150	1225	1520	2045	1915	1915	...	2145	...	...	...

	⛴ A	🚌 s	🚌 k	🚌	⛴	🚌 s	🚌	⛴ ⑥	🚌	⛴ D	🚌 Ⓑ
Bergen ⊡ .... d.	...	...	0845	0845	0800	...	...	1415	1530	1630	1715
Voss .... d.	...	...	1035	1035	|	...	...	|	1725	|	1900c
Balestrand .... d.	0830	1000	|	|	1150	1310	...	1820	|	2020	|
Leikanger .... d.	0900	1045	|	|	1220	1350	...	1835	|	2045	|
Flåm .... a.	1030	|	1145	1145	1325	|	...	|	1835	|	2020
Sogndal ⊕ .... d.	...	1135	|	|	...	1430	1430	1900	|	2120	|
Kaupangersenteret ... d.	...	1150	|	|	...	1445	1445	...	|	...	|
Lærdal Rådhuset ...... a.	...	1225	1245	|	...	1525	|	...	1920	...	2105
Gol skysstasjon .... a.	...	1415	|	|	...	1715	|	...	|	...	|
Fodnes .... a.	...	...	1300	|	...	...	1515	...	1935	...	2115
Øvre Årdal ◇ .... a.	...	...	1345	|	...	...	*1600*	...	*2025*	...	*2200*
Kaupangersenteret . a.	...	...	1320	|	...	...	...	...	2000	...	2140
Sogndal ⊕ .... a.	...	...	1335	|	...	...	...	...	2015	...	2155
Lillehammer skysst . a.	...	...	...	1735	...	...	...	...	...	...	...

– ①–⑤ June 16 - Aug. 15.
– ①–⑤ (also ⑦ to June 15 / from Aug. 17).
– ⑦ to June 15 / from Aug. 17.
– 1910 on ⑦.
– Ⓐ only. By 🚌 to Sogndal kai.
h – Change 🚌 at Håbakken (a. 1535, d. 1545).
k – Change 🚌 at Håbakken (a. 1230, d. 1235).
s – Change 🚌 at Sogndal.
◇ – Øvre Årdal Farnes.
⊕ – 🚌: Sogndal skysstasjon. ⛴: Sogndal kai.
⊡ – 🚌: Bus station. ⛴: Strandkaiterminal.

🚌 operators: Nettbuss Sogn Billag ✆ +47 57 67 66 00.
NOR-WAY Bussekspress ✆ +47 815 44 444.
⛴ operator: Norled AS ✆ +47 5186 8700.

783 LILLEHAMMER - OSLO - SKIEN

All trains convey *NSB Komfort* and 🍷

km		Ⓐ	Ⓐ	Ⓐ	Ⓒ	Ⓐ	⑥	Ⓑ	⑥	⚒	Ⓑ	⑥	⚒		⚒		Ⓐ	Ⓑr		Ⓐ	⑦		Ⓑ		Ⓑ	
						t	▲			n⊙			t	♣	n⊡	♥	t	⊡⊖		⊙	t		t			
0	**Lillehammer** ...... 785 d.	...	0408	0519	0519	0610	0610	0710	0710	0810	0911	0911	1010	1109	1209	1304	...	1410	1512	1611	1611	1713	1812	1913	2012t	2110
58	**Hamar** .... 785 d.	...	0456	0607	0607	0703	0703	0801	0801	0903	1003	1003	1103	1203	1303	1356	...	1502	1601	1703	1703	1803	1903	2002	2103t	2200
117	Eidsvoll .... d.	...	0541	0652	0652	0752	0752	0852	0852	0952	1052	1052	1152	1252	1352	1452	...	1552	1652	1752	1752	1852	1952	2052	2152	2252
133	Oslo ✈ ● ....771 785 d.	...	0603	0703	0703	0803	0803	0903	0903	1003	1103	1103	1203	1303	1403	1503	...	1603	1703	1803	1803	1903	2003	2103	2203	2303
164	Lillestrøm .....771 785 d.	...	0616	0716	0716	0816	0816	0916	0916	1016	1116	1116	1216	1316	1416	1516	...	1616	1716	1816	1816	1916	2016	2116	2216	2316
185	**Oslo** Sentral 771 785 a.	...	0626	0726	0726	0826	0826	0926	0926	1026	1126	1126	1226	1326	1426	1526	...	1626	1726	1826	1826	1926	2026	2126	2226	2326
185	**Oslo** Sentral .... d.	0539	0639	0739	0739	0839	0839	0939	0939	1039	1139	1139	1239	1339	1439	1539	1605	1639	1739	1839	1839	1939	2039	2139	2239	2339
225	Drammen .... d.	0615	0715	0815	0815	0915	0915	1015	1015	1115	1215	1215	1315	1415	1515	1615	1644	1715	1815	1915	1915	2015	2115	2215	2315	0015
259	Holmestrand .... d.	0639	0739	0839	0839	0939	0939	1039	1039	1139	1239	1239	1339	1439	1539	1639	1705	1739	1839	1939	1939	2039	2139	2239	2339	0039
273	Skoppum .... d.	0649	0749	0849	0849	0949	0949	1049	1049	1149	1249	1249	1349	1449	1549	1649	1719	1749	1849	1949	1949	2049	2149	2249	2349	0049
289	Tønsberg .... d.	0701	0801	0901	0901	1001	1001	1101	1101	1201	1301	1301	1401	1501	1601	1701	1731	1801	1901	2001	2001	2101	2201	2301	0001	0101
308	Torp ✈ .... d.	0715	0815	0915	0915	1015	1015	1115	1115	1215	1315	1315	1415	1515	1615	1715	1752	1815	1915	2015	2015	2115	2215	2315	0015	|
313	**Sandefjord** .... d.	0722	0822	0922	0922	1022	1022	1122	1122	1222	1322	1322	1422	1522	1622	1722	1758	1822	1922	2022	2022	2122	2222	2322	0022	0122
332	Larvik .... a.	0736	0836	0936	0936	1036	1036	1136	1136	1236	1336	1336	1436	1536	1636	1736	1812	1836	1936	2036	2036	2136	2236	2336	0036	0136
332	Larvik .... d.	0740*	0840*	0944	0940*	1044	1040*	1140*	1137	1240*	1340*	1337	1440*	1540*	1644	1744	1813	1840*	1944	2040*	2044	2144	2237	2337	0037	0137
366	Porsgrunn .... 779 d.	0800*	0900*	1019	1000*	1118	1100*	1200*	1212	1300*	1400*	1412	1500*	1600*	1718	1819	1847	1900*	2021	2100*	2118	2218	2311	0011	0111	0211
375	**Skien** .... 779 a.	0818*	0918*	1027	1018*	1126	1118*	1218*	1220	1318*	1418*	1420	1518*	1618*	1726	1827	1855	1918*	2030	2118*	2126	2226	2319	0019	0119	0219

	Ⓐ	Ⓐ		⚒		⚒	Ⓐ	Ⓒ	⚒	Ⓐ	Ⓒ	⚒	⑦	Ⓑ	⑥	Ⓑ	⚒	⑦	Ⓑ	⚒	⑦	Ⓑ		Ⓑ		Ⓐ
				◇		n			t			n⊙	t	d	n	r	⊖		r⊡			t		⊠		
Skien ....779 d.	...	0341	0441	0538	0632	0725	0825*	0835	0925*	1025*	1025	1125*	1125	1224	1225*	1325	1425*	1437c	1520*	1620*	1636	1725*	1825*	1925*	2025*	2125*
Porsgrunn ....779 d.	...	0350	0450	0547	0643	0734	0843*	0844	0943*	1043*	1034	1143*	1134	1233	1243*	1334	1443*	1446c	1543*	1643*	1645	1743*	1843*	1943*	2043*	2143*
Larvik .... a.	...	0423	0523	0621	0718	0807	0907*	0918	1007*	1107*	1107	1207*	1207	1307	1307*	1407	1507*	1518c	1607*	1707*	1718	1807*	1907*	2007*	2107*	2207*
Larvik .... d.	...	0424	0524	0622	0719	0819	0919	0919	1019	1119	1119	1219	1219	1319	1319	1419	1519	1519	1619	1719	1719	1819	1919	2019	2119	2219
Sandefjord .... d.	...	0438	0538	0638	0738	0838	0938	0938	1038	1138	1138	1238	1238	1338	1338	1438	1538	1538	1638	1738	1738	1838	1938	2038	2138	2238
Torp ✈ .... d.	...	0442	0542	0642	0742	0842	0942	0942	1042	1142	1142	1242	1242	1342	1342	1442	1542	1542	1642	1742	1742	1842	1942	2042	2142	2242
Tønsberg .... d.	...	0459	0559	0659	0759	0859	0959	0959	1059	1159	1159	1259	1259	1359	1359	1459	1559	1559	1659	1759	1759	1859	1959	2059	2159	2259
Skoppum .... d.	...	0509	0609	0709	0809	0909	1009	1009	1109	1209	1209	1309	1309	1409	1409	1509	1609	1609	1709	1809	1809	1909	2009	2109	2209	2309
Holmestrand .... d.	...	0519	0619	0719	0819	0919	1019	1019	1119	1219	1219	1319	1319	1419	1419	1519	1619	1619	1719	1819	1819	1919	2019	2119	2219	2319
Drammen .... d.	...	0547	0647	0747	0847	0947	1047	1047	1147	1247	1247	1347	1347	1447	1447	1547	1647	1647	1747	1847	1847	1947	2047	2147	2247	2347
Oslo Sentral .... a.	...	0621	0721	0821	0921	1021	1121	1121	1221	1321	1321	1421	1421	1521	1521	1621	1721	1721	1821	1921	1921	2021	2121	2221	2321	0021
Oslo Sentral .771 785 d.	...	0634	0734	0834	0934	1034	1134	1134	1234	1334	1334	1434	1434	1534	1534	1634	1734	1734	1834	1934	1934	2034	2134	2234	2334	...
Lillestrøm ......771 785 d.	...	0645	0745	0845	0945	1045	1145	1145	1245	1345	1345	1445	1445	1545	1545	1645	1745	1745	1845	1945	1945	2045	2145	2245	2345	...
Oslo ✈ ● ....771 785 d.	...	0659	0759	0859	0959	1059	1159	1159	1259	1359	1359	1459	1459	1559	1559	1659	1759	1759	1859	1959	1959	2059	2159	2259	2359	...
Eidsvoll .... d.	...	0709	0809	0909	1009	1109	1209	1209	1309	1409	1409	1509	1509	1609	1609	1709	1809	1809	1909	2009	2009	2109	2209	2309	0009	...
Hamar ....785 d.	0657	0757	0901	1000n	1059	1158	1302	1302	1357	1500	1500	1600	1600	1702	1702	1801	1902	1902	2001	2104	2104	2159	2303	2357	0055	...
Lillehammer ....785 a.	0744	0844	0947	1046n	1145	1244	1355	1355	1444	1547	1547	1646	1646	1748	1748	1847	1957	1957	2047	2155	2155	2244	2348	0042	0140	...

c – 11 minutes earlier July 6 - Aug. 10.
d – Runs daily June 29 - Aug. 15.
n – Not July 5, 12, 19, 26, Aug. 2, 9.
r – Not July 6, 13, 20, 27, Aug. 3, 10.
t – Not June 30 - Aug. 10.

* – By 🚌 Larvik - Skien and v.v.
● – Oslo Lufthavn Gardermoen.
⊠ – Does not run Skien - Drammen June 30 - Aug. 10.
⊖ – Through train service to / from Skien June 30 - Aug. 9.
♣ – Through train service to Skien on ⑥⑦ July 5 - Aug. 10.

⊡ – On ①–⑤ June 30 - Aug. 8 does not run Lillehammer - Eidsvoll and v.v.
⊙ – On ①–⑤ June 30 - Aug. 8 does not run Drammen - Skien and v.v.
▲ – Also ①–⑤ June 30 - Aug. 8; on July 5, 12, 19, 26, Aug. 2, 9 does not run Drammen - Skien.
♥ – On ⑦ July 6 - Aug. 10 by 🚌 Larvik (d. 1740) - Porsgrunn (d. 1800) - Skien.

784 HAMAR - RØROS - TRONDHEIM

km		Ⓐ	⑥	Ⓐ	⚒b	Ⓐ	Ⓑ	Ⓒ		Ⓑb	Ⓑ	
0	**Hamar** .... d.	...	...	0810	1011	1210	1210	...	1607	1811	2017	...
32	Elverum .... d.	...	...	0833	1036	1235	1235	...	1633	1834	2042	...
64	Rena .... d.	...	...	0855	1059	1257	1257	...	1656	1859	2104	...
120	Koppang .... d.	...	...	0937	1141	1339	1339	...	1737	1941	2146	...
273	**Røros** .... a.	...	...	1130	1337	1531	1531	...	1932	2133	2339	...
273	**Røros** .... d.	0505	0703	...	...	1537	...	1630	1937	...	...	...
384	Støren .... 785 d.	0640	0833	...	...	1710	...	1802	2108	...	...	...
435	**Trondheim S** ...... 785 a.	0735	0928	...	...	1800	...	1855	2200	...	...	...

	Ⓐ	⚒b	Ⓐ		Ⓑb	⑦		Ⓐ	⑦
Trondheim S.... 785 d.	...	...	0545	0950	...	1345	...	1625	2040
Støren .... 785 d.	...	...	0640	1041	...	1439	...	1722	2133
Røros .... a.	...	...	0813	1212	...	1610	...	1857	2305
Røros .... d.	0419	0617	0818	1217	1410	1626	1626	...	...
Koppang .... d.	0611	0809	1015	1416	1605	1817	1817	...	...
Rena .... d.	0653	0854	1059	1458	1656	1859	1859	...	...
Elverum .... d.	0715	0916	1121	1520	1718	1921	1921	...	...
Hamar .... a.	0740	0941	1146	1545	1743	1946	1946	...	...

b – Does not run on ①–⑤ June 23 - Aug. 15.

785 OSLO - LILLEHAMMER - ÅNDALSNES and TRONDHEIM

km		407	41	2341	311	2343	45	2345	47	2347	327	329	405
		Ⓐt		2351		Ⓐ		2355	Ⓑ	Ⓑ	ⒷL	Ⓑn	Ⓑ
		R	R	R		R	R	R	R	R			R
		✕⊡	✕⊡	🍷	🍷⊡	🍷	✕⊡	🍷	✕⊡	🍷	🍷⊡	🍷⊡	✕N
0	**Oslo** Sentral...... 783 d.	...	0802	...	0934	...	1402	...	1602	...	1734	1834	2256
21	Lillestrøm .... 783 d.	...	0813u	...	0945	...	1414u	...	1614u	...	1745	1845	2321u
52	Oslo ✈ ⊖ .... 783 d.	...	0828u	...	0959	...	1429u	...	1630u	...	1759	1859	2340u
127	**Hamar** .... 783 d.	...	0925	...	1059	...	1526	...	1726	...	1902	2001	0040
185	**Lillehammer** ..... 783 d.	...	1012	...	1145	1205	1612	...	1813	...	2007	2055	0134
243	Ringebu .... d.	...	1056	...	...	1255	1654	...	1856	...	2054	2137	0221
267	Vinstra .... d.	...	1111	...	...	1313	1711	...	1913	...	2111	2154	0240
298	Otta .... d.	...	1136	...	...	1335	1736	...	1937	...	2136	2219	0309
344	Dombås .... d.	...	1207	1209	...	1407	1808	1833	2009	2011	2207	2250	0359
458	**Åndalsnes** .... a.	...	|	1333v	...	1526	|	1957v	|	2128	...	...	|
430	Oppdal .... d.	0645	1305	...	...	...	1913	...	2106	...	...	...	0504
502	Støren .... 784 d.	0735	1355	...	...	...	2005	...	2156	...	...	...	0559
553	**Trondheim S** .... 784 a.	0830	1445	...	...	...	2048	...	2240	...	...	...	0650

	308	2340	316	2342	42	2344	44	2346	46	406
	⚒	Ⓐ		2352		Ⓑ	Ⓑ	2356		Ⓑ
		R		R	R	R	R	R	R	R
	🍷⊡	🍷	🍷⊡	🍷	✕⊡	🍷	✕⊡	🍷	✕⊡	✕N
Trondheim S . 784 d.	...	...	...	...	0823	...	1424	...	1618	2313
Støren .... 784 d.	...	...	...	...	0907	...	1509	...	1702	0003
Oppdal .... d.	...	...	...	...	1003	...	1601	...	1753	0103
Åndalsnes .... d.	...	0739	...	0927z	|	1531	|	1659z	|	|
Dombås .... d.	0513	0903	...	1056	1101	1654	1701	1827	1853	0224
Otta .... d.	0545	0933	...	...	1135	...	1735	...	1936	0306
Vinstra .... d.	0609	0956	...	...	1156	...	1756	...	1957	0330
Ringebu .... d.	0625	1012	...	...	1213	...	1813	...	2014	0347
Lillehammer .. 783 d.	0710	1057	1109	...	1257	...	1900	...	2058	0435
Hamar .... 783 d.	0801	...	1203	...	1341	...	1944	...	2141	0531
Oslo ✈ ⊖ .... 783 d.	0903	...	1303	...	1432s	...	2033s	...	2232s	0626
Lillestrøm .... 783 d.	0916	...	1316	...	1449s	...	2049s	...	2249s	0649
Oslo Sentral ... 783 a.	0926	...	1326	...	1503	...	2104	...	2304	0704

🚌					Ⓐ	Ⓐ	⑥	Ⓑ			Ⓑ	Ⓑ¶
Åndalsnes .... d.	0625r	1000	1340	1345	1540	1550	1555	1800	2005	2015	2130	2130
Molde .... a.	0750	1125	|	1510	|	1715	1715	1925	|	2135	2250	|
Ålesund .... a.	...	...	1540	...	1740	...	...	...	2205	...	...	2345

🚌	Ⓐ			⚒	Ⓑ	Ⓑ			Ⓑ	
Ålesund .... d.	...	0705	...	...	...	1300	1430	...	...	...
Molde .... d.	0610	|	0755	1000	1335	|	|	1515	2015	2200
Åndalsnes .... a.	0735	0915	0920	1120	1500	1510	1640	1640	2130	2315

🚌	⚒		Ⓐ		Ⓑ		⑤⑦		Ⓑ			
Oppdal skysstasjon .... d.	0530	...	1050	...	1315	...	1815	...	2120	...	...	...
Kristiansund .... a.	0915	...	1425	...	1635	...	2125	...	0030	...	...	...

🚌	Ⓐ		Ⓐ				⑤⑦		Ⓑ	
Kristiansund .... d.	0625	...	1040	...	1405	...	1635	...	2120	...
Oppdal skysstasjon a.	0940	...	1540	...	1730	...	2010	...	0035	...

L – June 30 - Aug. 10 only.
N – Conveys 🛏 and 🛏2.
R – Reservation recommended.

n – Not June 30 - Aug. 10.
r – 0630 on ⑥⑦.
s – Stops to set down only.
t – Not June 16 - Aug. 8.

u – Stops to pick up only.
v – 5–6 minutes earlier from Aug. 25.
z – 6 minutes later from Aug. 25.

⊡ – Conveys *NSB Komfort*.
⊖ – Oslo Lufthavn Gardermoen (see also Table **771**).
¶ – Journey is by taxi and is only available for passengers from train **2347** (please inform the on train staff).

786 SOUTHWEST NORWAY 🚌 LINKS

BERGEN - TRONDHEIM (Operator: NOR-WAY Bussekspress ✆ +47 815 44 444)
Bergen ⊡ d. 1620 → Oppdal a. 0440 → Trondheim a. 0642.
Trondheim d. 2230 → Oppdal d. 0032 → Bergen ⊡ a. 1220.

BERGEN - ÅLESUND (Operator: NOR-WAY Bussekspress ✆ +47 815 44 444)
From Bergen ⊡ at 0800 daily (Ålesund a. 1745) and 1220 Ⓑ (Ålesund a. 2215 ①–⑤ / 2240 ⑦).
From Ålesund at 0815 ①–⑤ / 0845 ⑥ (Bergen ⊡ a. 1810) and 1110 daily (Bergen ⊡ a. 2015).

BERGEN - KRISTIANSAND (Operator: NOR-WAY Bussekspress ✆ +47 815 44 444)
Bergen ⊡ d. 0825 → Odda d. 1120 → Haukeli a. 1300, d. 1455 → Kristiansand ⊡ a. 1900.
Kristiansand ⊡ d. 0845 → Haukeli a. 1250, d. 1455 → Odda a. 1655 → Bergen ⊡ a. 2005.

BERGEN - STAVANGER (Operator: NOR-WAY Bussekspress ✆ +47 815 44 444)
Journey time: 4 hrs 30 m – 5 hrs. From Bergen ⊡ at 0900 ⚒, 1115 ⑦, 1130 ⑥, 1300, 1445 Ⓐ, 1500 ⑦, 1600 ⑥, 1615 Ⓐ, 1700 ⑦ and 1930 ⑦. From Stavanger ⊙ at 0845 ⑥, 0915 Ⓐ, 1015 Ⓐ, 1045 ⑥⑦, 1245 ⑥, 1315 Ⓑ, 1510 Ⓐ, 1515 ⑥⑦, 1715 ⑦ and 1835 Ⓑ.

BERGEN - ODDA ★ 🚌/⛴ *Journey time: 2 hrs 45 m – 2 hrs 55 m.*
From Bergen ⊡ at 0825, 1155 Ⓑ and 2055 Ⓑ. From Odda ⊡ at 0530 ⚒, 1710 and 2040 Ⓑ

VOSS - ODDA ★ *Journey time: 2 hrs – 2 hrs 10 m.*
From Voss at 0913, 1120 ⚒, 1250, 1550 ⚒, 1740 and 2155 Ⓑ.
From Odda ⊡ at 0630 ⚒, 0720, 1225, 1410 ⚒, 1715 and 2035 Ⓑ.

VOSS - ULVIK ★ *Journey time: 55 – 65 minutes. A change of bus may be required.*
From Voss at 0755 Ⓐ, 0913 Ⓐ, 1005, 1120 ⚒, 1440 Ⓐ, 1550 ⚒, 1740, 1905 Ⓑ and 2155 Ⓑ
From Ulvik ⊡ at 0610 Ⓐ, 0730 Ⓐ, 0830, 1045, 1330 Ⓐ, 1515, 1820 Ⓑ, 2130 ⑦ and 2140 Ⓐ

⊡ – Bus station.
⊙ – Stavanger Byterminalen.

★ – Operator: Tide Buss AS / Skyss ✆ +47 55 55 90 70.

TRONDHEIM - BODØ and NARVIK 787

km		1781	1783	475		469	473	1785	471		1791	479	477
		Ⓐ	Ⓐ		🚌	⑥	Ⓐ	Ⓐ t		🚌	Ⓐ	Ⓑ t	Ⓑ
		🍷	🍷	N R	◇	🍷	🍷 R	🍷	✕ R	◇♥	🍷	🍷 R	🍷 R
0	**Trondheim** S ...d.	...	...	2340	...	...	...	...	0738	...	...	...	1602
33	Værnes ✈ ‡ .....d.	...	...	0006	...	...	...	...	0811	...	...	...	1630u
34	Stjørdal ....d.	...	...	0011	...	...	...	...	0819	...	...	...	1636u
126	Steinkjer ....d.	...	...	0129	...	...	...	...	0946	...	...	...	1801u
220	Grong ....d.	...	...	0240	...	...	...	...	1053	...	...	...	1909
406	Mosjøen ....d.	...	...	0457	...	0607	0650	...	1309	...	...	1645	2130
498	Mo i Rana.........d.	...	...	0608	...	0708	0800	...	1420	...	...	1747	2238
648	Rognan.............d.	0542	0642	0802	...	...	0953	1145	1615	...	1745	1936	...
	Bodø ⊖ ....d.	|	|	|	0715	...	|	|	|	1505	|	|	...
674	Fauske ....a.	0603	0703	0825	0820	...	1013	1206	1637	1615	1804	1956	...
674	Fauske ....d.	0603	0703	0830	0850	...	1015	1206	1646	1645	1811	2001	...
	Narvik ⊡ ♣..a.	|	|	|	1330	...	|	|	|	2130	|	|	...
729	**Bodø**...............a.	0642	0742	0915	...	...	1055	1253	1728	...	1848	2040	...

	478	470	1792	1784		472	1790	474		476
		Ⓐ t	Ⓐ S	Ⓐ t	🚌		Ⓐ	Ⓑ	🚌	
	🍷 R	🍷 R	🍷	🍷	◇	✕ R	🍷	🍷 R	◇	N R
Bodø............d.	...	0747	0747	1013	...	1215	1605	1730	...	2110
Narvik ⊡ ♣d.	...	|	|	|	0700	|	|	|	1610	|
Fauske ....a.	...	0828	0828	1059	1155	1255	1644	1809	2110	2154
Fauske ....d.	...	0828	0828	1059	1210	1258	1646	1809	2125	2158
Bodø ⊖.....a.	...	|	|	|	1320	|	|	|	2230	|
Rognan..........d.	...	0847	0847	1119	...	1320	1705	1832	...	2219
Mo i Rana......d.	0715	1032	...	...	...	1531	...	2018	...	0020
Mosjøen.........d.	0827	1138	...	...	...	1641	...	2122	...	0140
Grong ....d.	1050	...	...	...	...	1907	...	...	...	0426
Steinkjer ....d.	1157	...	...	...	...	2016	...	...	...	0540
Stjørdal..........d.	1318	...	...	...	...	2133	...	...	...	0705
Værnes ✈ ‡ ..d.	1320	...	...	...	...	2135	...	...	...	0707
Trondheim ....a.	1347	...	...	...	...	2205	...	...	...	0747

Local services Trondheim - Steinkjer and v.v.

km	▶	Ⓐ	⚒					Ⓐ z		Ⓐ w			Ⓑ
0	**Trondheim** S ...d.	0610	0710	0910	1110	1310	1510	1545	1710	1810	1910	2110	2310
31	Hell ● ....d.	0641	0743	0941	1141	1341	1541	1617	1741	1841	1941	2141	2341
33	Værnes ✈ ‡ ●..d.	0643	0745	0943	1143	1343	1543	1619	1743	1843	1943	2143	2343
34	Stjørdal.............d.	0652	0752	0952	1152	1352	1552	1623	1752	1852	1952	2152	2347
126	**Steinkjer**..........a.	0816	0916	1119	1316	1516	1716	1744	1916	2016	2116	2313	0105

▶	Ⓐ								Ⓐ w	
Steinkjer.......d.	0528	0728	0928	1128	1328	1528	1728	1925	2028	2128
Stjørdal..........d.	0652	0852	1052	1252	1452	1652	1852	2052	2152	2252
Værnes ✈ ‡ ●d.	0654	0854	1054	1254	1454	1654	1854	2054	2154	2254
Hell ● ....d.	0657	0857	1057	1257	1457	1657	1857	2057	2157	2257
Trondheim S.a.	0732	0932	1132	1332	1532	1732	1932	2132	2227	2332

N – Conveys 🛏, 2 and ✕.
R – Reservation recommended.
S – June 23 - Aug. 15 only.

t – Not June 23 - Aug. 15.
u – Stops to pick up only.
w – Not June 16 - Aug. 8.
z – Not June 30 - Aug. 8.

♥ – On ⑦ Bodø d. 1645, Fauske a. 1750, d. 1810, Narvik a. 2300.
● – Trains stop on request.
⊡ – Bus station.
⊖ – Bodø Sentrumsterminalen.
‡ – Station for Trondheim Airport.
◇ – Operator: Saltens Bilruter Nordlandsbuss.

▶ – Additional services on Ⓐ Trondheim - Stjørdal - Steinkjer and v.v.:
From Trondheim at 0515 **w**, 0810 **w**, 1010 **w**, 1210, 1410, 1445 **w** and 1610.
From Steinkjer at 0600 **z**, 0628, 0657 **w**, 0828, 1028 **w**, 1228 **w**, 1428, 1628 **w** and 1828.

♣ – 🚌 **Narvik - Svolvær** (Lofoten). Operator: Veolia Transport. *253 km.*
Journey time: 4 hrs 5 m - 4 hrs 30 m.
From Narvik at 0920 ⑥, 0940 Ⓐ, 1200 ⑦ and 1530.
From Svolvær sentrum at 0950, 1510 ⚒ and 1655 ⑦.

LAPLAND 🚌 LINKS 789

Subject to alteration on and around the dates of public holidays

Narvik – Tromsø – Alta

Operator: Torghatten

km		①–⑤	①–⑥		Ⓑ	Ⓑ	Ⓑ		Ⓑ		⑦
0	**Narvik** bus station ......d.	0520	...	...	1250	...	...	...	...	1520	1840
	Narvik rail station ....d.	|	...	...	|	...	...	...	←	1527	1845
181	Nordkjosbotn ....d.	0825	0825	...	1615	1620	1620	...	1620	1845	2200
252	**Tromsø** Prostneset .d.	0930	0930	...	→	|	|	1600	1730	1950	2305
241	Lyngseidet...............a.	...	...	...	...	1731	|	1730	...	...	...
465	**Alta**.............................a.	...	...	...	...	...	2223	2223	...	...	...

km		①–⑤			①–⑥	①–⑤		⑦	⑦	⑦
0	**Alta**...........................d.	...	...	...	1055	...	...	1410	...	...
224	Lyngseidet..................d.	...	...	...	1545	1545	...	1910	1910	...
293	**Tromsø** Prostneset.d.	0615	1000	...	1725	|	1600	2050	|	1915
	Nordkjosbotn ....d.	0730	1105	...	...	1653	1705	...	2018	2020
	Narvik rail station ....a.	1028	|	...	...	...	|	...	...	|
	Narvik bus station ......a.	1035	1415	...	...	...	2010	...	...	2325

Alta – Hammerfest – Karasjok – Kirkenes

Operator: Boreal Transport

km		Ⓑ	①–⑤	①–⑤ ◇	①③	⑤⑦		①–④	①–④ ◇	⑤⑦	⑤⑦ ◇
0	**Alta**...........................d.	...	0635	...	...	...	...	1430	...	1500	...
	Hammerfest ....d.	...	|	0710	...	...	...	|	1500	|	1540
87	Skaidi ....a.	...	0800	0805	...	...	...	1605	1600	1635	1635
87	Skaidi ....d.	...	0810	0810	...	...	...	1615	1615	1645	1645
	Hammerfest ....a.	...	0905	|	...	...	...	1710	|	1740	|
112	Olderfjord ....d.	...	...	0845	...	...	...	...	1650	...	1720
212	Honningsvåg ★.......a.	...	...	1025	...	...	...	...	1830	...	1900
174	Lakselv.........................d.	...	...	1010	...	...	...	...	1755	...	1835
248	Karasjok ....d.	...	...	1125	1200	1410	...	...	1910	...	1950
429	Tanabru.........................d.	0830	...	...	1500	1715	...	...	...	...	...
571	**Kirkenes**......................a.	1050	...	...	1720	1935	...	...	...	...	...

km		①–⑤ ◇	①–⑤		W	①–④ ◇	①–④	⑤⑦ ◇	⑤⑦	Ⓑ
	Kirkenes....................d.	...	...	...	0805	...	...	...	...	1510
	Tanabru........................d.	...	...	...	1035	...	...	...	...	1800
	Karasjok ....d.	0515	...	...	1310	1350	...	1430	...	...
	Lakselv..........................d.	0725	...	...	...	1520	...	1605	...	...
	Honningsvåg ★.......d.	0640	...	...	...	1440	...	1510	...	...
	Olderfjord ....d.	0845	...	...	...	1650	...	1720	...	...
0	Hammerfest ....d.	|	0810	...	...	|	1615	|	1640	...
57	Skaidi ....a.	0905	0905	...	...	1710	1710	1740	1735	...
57	Skaidi ....d.	0915	0915	...	...	1720	1720	1750	1750	...
	Hammerfest ....a.	1010	|	...	...	1815	|	1845	|	...
144	**Alta**.............................a.	...	1035	...	...	...	1840	...	1915	...

Rovaniemi – Muonio – Tromsø

km	*Operator:*	G	E	G
0	**Rovaniemi** bus station d.	0800	1130	1710
	Rovaniemi rail station d.	0820	1100	1715
157	Kittilä ....d.	1040	1335	1925
238	Muonio ....d.	1300**z**	1505	2040
327	Karesuvanto ....d.	1435	1625**b**	...
440	Kilpisjärvi ⊡ .... FI d.	1625	1810**b**	...
535	Nordkjosbotn .... NO d.	...	1830**b**	...
608	**Tromsø** Prostneset .... a.	...	1930**b**	...

	G	E	G
Tromsø Prostneset .. d.	...	0730**e**	...
Nordkjosbotn ...... NO d.	...	0830**e**	...
Kilpisjärvi ⊡ .... FI d.	...	1110**e**	1315
Karesuvanto ....d.	...	1240**e**	1515
Muonio ....d.	0850	1410	1700**f**
Kittilä..........................d.	1015	1535	1835
Rovaniemi rail station a.	1215**x**	1730	2035**x**
Rovaniemi bus station a.	1215	1740	2040

Rovaniemi – Karasjok, Nordkapp, Tanabru, Kirkenes and Murmansk

km	*Operator:*	G	G	G	G	G	G	E	P	E	G/L
		①–⑤	①–⑤		①–⑤	⑥⑦	Y		①–⑥		Ⓑ
0	**Rovaniemi** bus station d.	0530	...	0800	...	...	...	1145	1520	1720	2000
	Rovaniemi rail station d.	|	...	0820	...	...	...	1100	1525	1700	2010
130	Sodankylä.....................d.	0735	...	1020	...	...	...	1345	1730	1915	2200
305	Ivalo .... FI d.	1005	1100	1250	1300	1400	1600j	1625f	1935	2130	0015
345	Inari..................... FI d.	...	1135	...	1340	1440	|	1700	...	2200	...
461	Karasjok............ NO a.	...	...	...	...	▬	|	1755	...	|	...
536	Lakselv, Statoil........ a.	...	...	...	...	...	|	1855**h**	...	|	...
	Honningsvåg .... a.	...	...	...	...	...	|	2135**h**	...	|	...
735	**Nordkapp** .... a.	...	...	...	...	*S*	|	2220**h**	...	|	...
	Tanabru......... NO a.	...	...	...	...		|	...	...	2355**r**	...
	Kirkenes, Europris NO d.	...	...	...	...	1500j	|	...	...	...	...
	Murmansk .... RU a.	...	...	...	...	2200**v**	2250	...	...	...	...

Operator:	P		E	G	G	G/L	E	E	S	G	G
	①–⑥			①–⑤	Y	①–⑥	A				
Murmansk .... RU d.	...	...	...	...	0700	...	...	...	0700**v**	...	...
Kirkenes .... NO a.	...	...	...	...	|	...	...	...	1000**j**	...	...
Tanabru.......... NO d.	...	...	0330**t**	...	|	...	...	...	...	...	...
Nordkapp ....d.	...	...	|	...	|	...	0100	...	...	...	...
Honningsvåg ....d.	...	...	|	...	|	...	0510**g**	...	...	...	...
Lakselv, Statoil.........d.	...	...	|	...	|	...	0810	...	...	...	...
Karasjok............. NO d.	...	...	|	...	|	...	0915	0915	...	...	...
Inari...................... FI d.	...	...	0715	1105	|	...	1210	1210	...	1415	...
Ivalo .... FI d.	0530	...	0820	1140	1150j	1215	1320f	1320f	...	1450	1615
Sodankylä.....................d.	0755	...	1035	...	...	1500	1550	1550	...	...	1845
Rovaniemi rail station . a.	0945**x**	...	1210	...	...	1715	1730	1730	...	...	2030
Rovaniemi bus station a.	0950	...	1220	...	...	1710	1735	1735	...	...	2035

Operator codes: *E* – Eskelisen Lapin Linjat. *G* – Gold Line. *L* – Liikenne O. Niemelä. *M* – Murmanskavtotrans. *P* – Pikakuljetus Rovaniemi. *S* – Pasvikturist AS.

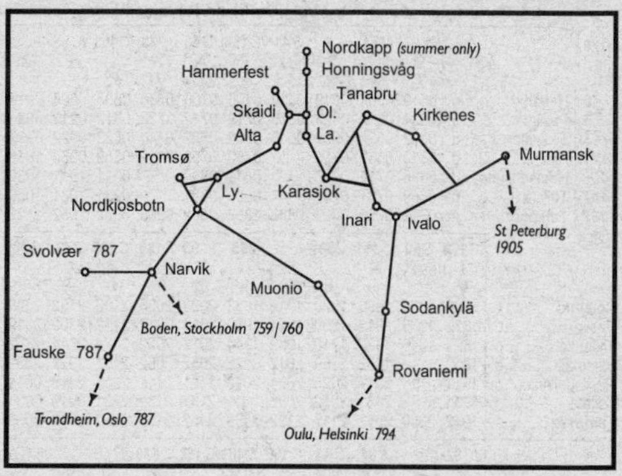

A – June 2 - Aug. 23.
Q – From Aug. 18.
R – June 3 - Aug. 18.
S – June 2 - Aug. 17.
T – May 19 - Aug. 17.
W – ①③⑤⑦.
Y – ①③⑤.
b – Runs Muonio - Tromsø June 1 - Sept. 20 only.
e – June 2 - Sept. 21 only.
f – Arrives 35 minutes earlier.
g – Arrives 0140.
h – June 1 - Aug. 22.
j – 60 minutes earlier from Oct. 27.
r – ③④⑤⑦ (daily June 1 - Sept. 12).
t – ①④⑤⑥ (daily June 2 - Sept. 13).
v – Murmansk Vorovskogo Street.

x – Stops on request.
z – Arrives 1200.

⊡ – Trekking centre (Retkeilykeskus).
◇ – Two routes: Hammerfest - Olderfjord - Karasjok and v.v.; Hammerfest - Olderfjord - Honningsvåg and v.v.
★ – **Honningsvåg - Nordkapp** and v.v. *34 km.* Journey 35–45 minutes.
From Honningsvåg (Nordkapphuset) at 1130 **Q**, 1145 **T**, 1400 **S**, 1600 **S**, 1900 **S** and 2130 **S**
From Nordkapp at 0015 **R**, 1330 **Q**, 1345 **T**, 1630 **S**, 1815 **S** and 2115 **S**.

FI – Finland (East European Time).
NO – Norway (Central European Time).
RU – Russia (Moskva Time).

FINLAND

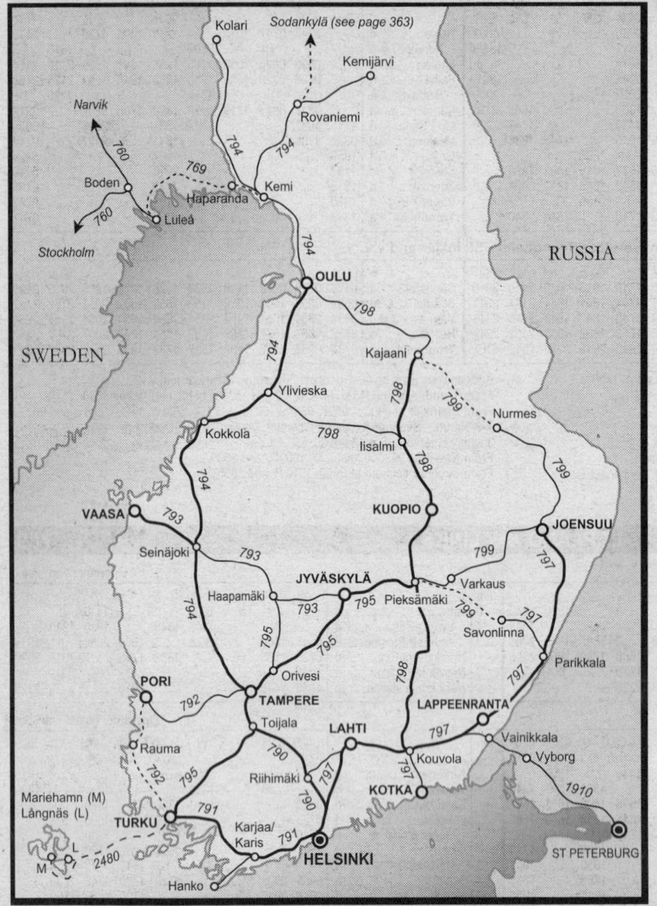

Operator: VR – VR-Yhtymä Oy www.vr.fi

Tickets and train types: For all except purely local journeys, tickets are always sold for travel by a specific train or combination of trains. Please note that travel classes in Finland are referred to as *Extra* (1st) and *Eco* (2nd). There are four different pricing-scales, corresponding to each of the following train types (in descending order of cost):

- **S 220 Pendolino** (e.g. *S* **123**) – high-speed tilting trains (220 km/h), with *Extra* and *Eco* class seats. Reservation compulsory.
- **InterCity** (e.g. *IC* **124**) – quality fast trains between major centres, with *Extra* and *Eco* class seats, all reservable.
- **Express**, *pikajunat* (train number only shown, e.g. **128**) – other fast trains, with *Eco* class seats, all reservable. Night expresses convey sleeping-cars and *Eco* class seats only (marked ★ in the tables).
- **Regional**, *taajamajunat* (no train number shown) – stopping-trains, normally with *Eco* class seats only.

S 220, InterCity and Express tickets include a seat reservation when purchased in advance.

Rail tickets are **not** valid on 🚌 services (except Kemi - Tornio). However, special combined train / bus fares are available on certain routes.

Services: ✕ indicates a train with a restaurant car.

Trains marked 🍸 convey a *MiniBistro* trolley service.

A variable supplement is payable for travel in sleeping-cars (🛏) in addition to the appropriate *Eco* class **Express** fare – the price to be paid depends on the date of travel and the type of accommodation required. A higher supplement is charged for occupancy of a single-berth cabin.

Timings: Timings are valid, unless otherwise indicated, **JUNE 16 - DECEMBER 13**, 2014.

In these tables Ⓐ = ①-⑤, ⚒ = ①-⑥.

Changes to the normal service pattern are likely to occur on and around the dates of public holidays (June 21, Nov. 1, Dec. 6). On June 20 services generally run as on ⑥.

790 HELSINKI - TAMPERE

For through journeys to / from **Oulu** and **Rovaniemi**, see Table **794**. For through journeys to / from **Jyväskylä** and **Pieksämäki**, see Table **795**.

km			*S* 81		*S* 41	*IC* 163	*IC* 63	*IC* 43	*IC* 165	*IC* 85		*S* 45	*IC* 47	*IC* 169	*IC* 87		*IC* 49	*IC* 173	*S* 89	*IC* 175		*S* 53	*IC* 55	*S* 91	*IC* 197		*S* 57
		2	[R] ✕	2	[R] ✕	🍸	✕	✕	🍸	🍸	2	[R] ✕	✕	🍸	🍸	2	✕	✕	[R] ✕	🍸	2	[R] ✕	✕	[R] ✕	🍸	2	[R] ✕
		Ⓐ	Ⓐ	⚒	⚒	Ⓐ	⑥⑦	Ⓐ	⚒					‡					Ⓑ	§					◧		Ⓑ
0	**Helsinki** d.	0519	0606	0619	0630	0706	0706	0730	0806	0906	0919	0930	1006	1106	1206	1219	1306	1406	1430	1506	1519	1530	1606	1630	1706	1719	1730
3	Pasila d.	0524	0612	0624	0636	0712	0712	0736	0812	0912	0924	0936	1012	1112	1212	1224	1312	1412	1436	1512	1524	1536	1612	1636	1712	1724	1736
16	Tikkurila ⊙ d.	0532	0622	0632	0646	0722	0722	0746	0822	0922	0932	0946	1022	1122	1222	1232	1322	1422	1446	1522	1532	1546	1622	1646	1722	1732	1746
71	Riihimäki d.	0613	0652	0713	|	0752	0752	|	0852	0952	1013	|	1052	1152	1252	1313	1352	1452	|	1552	1613	|	1652	|	1752	1813	|
108	Hämeenlinna d.	0636	0711	0736	|	0811	0811	|	0911	1011	1036	|	1111	1211	1311	1336	1411	1511	|	1611	1636	|	1711	|	1811	1836	|
147	Toijala d.	0659	0731	0759	|	0831	0831	|	0931	1031	1059	|	1131	1231	1331	1359	1431	1531	|	1631	1659	|	1731	|	1831	1859	|
187	**Tampere** a.	0722	0752	0822	0800	0852	0852	0905	0952	1052	1122	1100	1152	1252	1352	1422	1452	1552	1600	1652	1722	1700	1752	1800	1852	1922	1900

	IC 179	*S* 59	*IC* 181	263		265	*IC* 93	*S* 183	*IC* 185	273	*IC* 189	
	🍸	[R] ✕	✕		2		✕	[R] ✕	✕		🍸	
	♥		Ⓑ	★	Ⓑ	★	Ⓑ	⑥	◐	★		
Helsinki d.	1806	1830	1906	1823	1919	1852	2006	2006	2106	2152	2306	...
Pasila d.	1812	1836	1912	1830	1924	1900	2012	2012	2112	2200	2312	...
Tikkurila ⊙ d.	1822	1846	1922	1910	1932	1944	2022	2022	2122	2244	2322	...
Riihimäki d.	1852	|	1952	1959	2012	2022	2052	2052	2152	2322	2352	...
Hämeenlinna d.	1911	|	2011	2025	2034	2048	2111	2111	2211	2348	0011	...
Toijala d.	1931	|	2031	2050	2056	|	2131	2131	2231	0015	0031	...
Tampere a.	1952	2000	2052	2117	2122	2138	2152	2152	2252	0042	0052	...

	266	*IC* 160	270	*IC* 162	274			272	*S* 80	*IC* 40		*S* 42
				✕		2	2		[R] ✕	✕	2	[R] ✕
	★	Ⓐ	★	⚒	★	Ⓐ	⚒	★	Ⓐ	⚒		⚒
Tampere d.	0437	0533	0543	0604	0612	0632	...	0636	0700	0707	0732	0800
Toijala d.	0504	0554	0610	0626	0639	0655	...	0737	|	0728	0755	|
Hämeenlinna d.	0531	0615	0637	0647	0706	0718	...	0804	|	0749	0818	|
Riihimäki d.	0556	0635	0702	0707	0732	0740	0752	0832	|	0809	0852	|
Tikkurila ⊙ a.	0631	0702	0746	0737	|	...	0828	0910	0815	0837	0928	0915
Pasila a.	0658	0711	0824	0746	0852	...	0836	0952	0824	0846	0936	0924
Helsinki a.	0706	0717	0832	0752	0900	...	0841	1000	0830	0852	0941	093

	IC 82		*S* 84	*S* 44	*IC* 166	*S* 46	*IC* 168	*IC* 170	*IC* 48		*IC* 174	*IC* 196	*IC* 50		*S* 52	*IC* 88	*S* 62	*IC* 180		*IC* 54	*S* 56	*IC* 90		*IC* 184	*IC* 58	*S* 60	*S* 94
	✕	2	[R] ✕	[R] ✕	🍸	[R] ✕	🍸	🍸	✕	2	🍸	🍸	✕	2	[R] ✕	🍸	[R] ✕	🍸	2	✕	[R] ✕	🍸	2	✕	✕	[R] ✕	[R] ✕
	⚒	⚒	⚒	⚒	♥	¶					◇	□						△									
Tampere d.	0807	0832	0855	0900	0907	1000	1007	1107	1207	1237	1307	1407	1507	1537	1600	1607	1700	1707	1737	1807	1900	1907	1937	2007	2107	2207	230
Toijala d.	0828	0855	|	|	0928	|	1028	1128	1228	1300	1328	1428	1528	1600	|	1628	|	1728	1800	1828	|	1928	2000	2028	2128	2228	232
Hämeenlinna d.	0849	0918	|	|	0949	|	1049	1149	1249	1323	1349	1449	1549	1623	|	1649	|	1749	1823	1849	|	1949	2023	2049	2149	2249	234
Riihimäki d.	0909	0952	|	|	1009	|	1109	1209	1309	1352	1409	1509	1609	1652	|	1709	|	1809	1852	1909	|	2009	2052	2109	2209	2309	000
Tikkurila ⊙ a.	0937	1028	1010	1015	1037	1115	1137	1237	1337	1428	1437	1537	1637	1728	1715	1737	1815	1837	1928	1937	2015	2037	2128	2137	2237	2337	003
Pasila a.	0946	1036	1019	1024	1046	1124	1146	1246	1346	1436	1446	1546	1646	1736	1724	1746	1824	1846	1936	1946	2024	2046	2136	2146	2246	2346	004
Helsinki a.	0952	1041	1025	1030	1052	1130	1152	1252	1352	1441	1452	1552	1652	1741	1730	1752	1830	1852	1941	1952	2030	2052	2141	2152	2252	2352	005

Regional trains (2nd class only) HELSINKI - RIIHIMÄKI and v.v.

km											
				Ⓐ	⚒	⚒		⚒			
0	**Helsinki** d.	0031	0131	0519	0619	0719	0748	0819	0919		2319
3	Pasila d.	0036	0136	0524	0624	0724	0753	0824	0924	and	2324
16	Tikkurila ⊙ d.	0052	0152	0532	0632	0732	0802	0832	0932	hourly	2332
37	Järvenpää d.	0116	0216	0546	0646	0746	0818	0846	0946	until	2346
59	Hyvinkää d.	0135	0235	0600	0700	0800	0837	0900	1000		0000
71	**Riihimäki** a.	0144	0244	0608	0708	0808	0846	0908	1008		0008

		⑥⑦	Ⓐ			⚒					
Riihimäki d.	0414	0514	0527	0614	0714	0752	0852		2052	2214	233
Hyvinkää d.	0423	0523	0536	0623	0723	0800	0900	and	2100	2223	234
Järvenpää d.	0441	0541	0551	0641	0741	0814	0914	hourly	2114	2241	000
Tikkurila ⊙ d.	0505	0605	0607	0658	0758	0828	0928	until	2128	2258	003
Pasila a.	0520	0620	0617	0707	0807	0836	0936		2136	2307	004
Helsinki a.	0525	0625	0623	0712	0812	0841	0941		2141	2312	005

♥ – To / from Pori (Table **792**).
⊙ – For Helsinki ✈ Vantaa.
‡ – Train number **199** on ⑦.
§ – Train number **195** on ⑥.
◧ – Train number **177** on ⑥.
◐ – Train number **187** on ⑥.
¶ – Train number **64** on ⑦.
◇ – Train number **194** on ⑥.
□ – Train number **176** on ⑥.
△ – Train number **190** on ⑥.
★ – Overnight train to / from northern Finland. Conveys 🛏, 2 and ✕. For through cars and days of running see Table **794**.

HELSINKI - TURKU and HANKO 791

Subject to alteration on June 28, July 12

km		🚌	IC 941	IC 943	IC 979	IC 945	IC 947	IC 949		IC 951	IC 953	IC 955		IC 957		IC 959		IC 961		IC 963	IC 965		IC 967	IC 969	IC 973	🚌
			🍷	🍷	🍷	🍷	🍷	🍷	2	🍷	🍷	🍷	2	🍷	2	🍷	2	🍷	2	🍷	🍷	2	🍷	🍷		
		E	D	⚒	Ⓐ		⚒		⚒		Ⓑ			Ⓑ	Ⓐ		Ⓐ	Ⓑ			Ⓑ	Ⓑ	A		G	H
0	**Helsinki** d.	0520	0520	0700	0802	0902	1002	1102	1132	1202	1302	1402	1432	1502	1532	1602	1632	1702	1732	1802	1902	1932	2002	2102	2302	2315
3	Pasila d.	|	0526	0706	0808	0908	1008	1108	1137	1208	1308	1408	1437	1508	1537	1608	1637	1708	1737	1808	1908	1937	2008	2108	2308	|
20	Espoo d.	|	0539	0719	0821	0921	1021	1121	|	1221	1321	1421	|	1521	|	1621	|	1721	|	1821	1921	|	2021	2121	2321	2345
87	Karjaa / Karis ★ d.	|	0619	0804	0901	1001	1101	1201	1241	1301	1401	1501	1541	1601	1641	1701	1741	1801	1841	1901	2001	2041	2101	2201	0005	|
138	Salo d.	|	0655	0830	0930	1030	1130	1230	...	1330	1430	1530	...	1630	...	1730	...	1830	...	1930	2030	...	2130	2230	0032	0055
194	**Turku** a.	0730	0732	0900	1000	1100	1200	1300	...	1400	1500	1600	...	1700	...	1800	...	1900	...	2000	2100	...	2200	2300	0102	0150
197	Turku satama a.	0740	0741	...	...	...	...	...	...	...	...	...	...	...	...	*1819*	...	1912	...	2016	...	...	...	...	...	...

		IC 942		IC 944		IC 946			IC 948	IC 950	IC 952	IC 954	IC 956		IC 958	IC 960	IC 962		IC 964	IC 966	IC 968		IC 970		IC 972	IC 974
	2	🍷	2	🍷	2	🍷	2	2	🍷	🍷	🍷	🍷	🍷	2	🍷	🍷	🍷	2	🍷	🍷	🍷	2	🍷		🍷	🍷
	Ⓐm	Ⓐ	Ⓐ	Ⓐ	Ⓐ	F	⑦	⑥k	Ⓐ		⚒	p		⚒	Ⓑ		Ⓑ			Ⓑ			B			
Turku satama d.	...	...	...	...	...	...	...	...	0742	0830	...	...	...	...	...	...	...	...	...	...	...	...	...	...	1945	2035
Turku d.	...	0537	...	0625	...	0704	...	...	0800	0900	1000	1100	1200	...	1300	1400	1500	...	1600	1700	1800	...	1900	...	2000	2100
Salo d.	...	0609	...	0657	...	0736	...	...	0832	0932	1032	1132	1232	...	1332	1432	1532	...	1632	1732	1832	...	1932	...	2032	2132
Karjaa / Karis ★ d.	0532	0635	0654	0724	0738	0802	0756	0850	0858	0958	1058	1158	1258	1315	1358	1458	1558	1615	1658	1758	1858	1915	1958	...	2058	2158
Espoo a.	|	0714	|	0805	|	0841	0850	|	0938	1038	1138	1238	1338	|	1438	1538	1638	|	1738	1838	1938	|	2038	...	2138	2238
Pasila a.	0639	0728	0756	0819	0841	0856	0914	0953	0952	1052	1152	1252	1352	1423	1452	1552	1652	1723	1752	1852	1952	2023	2052	...	2152	2252
Helsinki a.	0644	0734	0802	0825	0846	0902	0919	0958	0958	1058	1158	1258	1358	1428	1458	1558	1658	1728	1758	1858	1958	2028	2058	...	2158	2258

A – ①②③④⑦ (not June 19).
B – Ⓑ from July 13 (also July 4, 6).
D – ①–⑤ July 14 - Aug. 8 (also June 16, July 7); daily from Aug. 11.
E – ①–⑤ June 17 - July 11 (not July 7).
F – ⚒ from July 14 (also June 16, 20, July 5, 7).
G – Daily from July 13 (also July 4, 5, 6).
H – June 16 - July 12 (not July 4, 5, 6).
k – Also June 20; not June 21.
m – Not June 17 - July 11.
p – Not June 21, 22, 29, July 13.

★ – **KARJAA / KARIS - HANKO** and v.v. *50 km*. 2nd class only. Journey: 40 minutes.
From Karjaa at 0733 ⑦, 0810 ⚒, 1010, 1310, 1510, 1710, 1910 and 2210.
From Hanko at 0638, 0910, 1210, 1410, 1610, 1810 and 2110.

TAMPERE and TURKU - PORI 792

2nd class only (except where shown) — *Subject to alteration on June 20, 21*

km			🚌		🚌		🚌			IC 179	
		A	ⒶB	C	ⒶD	C	ⒶD			ⒷH	
0	**Tampere** d.	0807	0815	1207	1215	1407	1415	1607	1807	2007	2207
135	**Pori** a.	0943	0950	1340	1350	1540	1550	1745	1945	2143	2343

			🚌	IC 166	🚌			🚌		
	⚒	⚒	ⒶB	CH	ⒶD	C	C	ⒶB		
Pori d.	0510	0605	0710	0710	1010	1010	1405	1410	1605	1810
Tampere a.	0646	0741	0845	0852	1145	1146	1542	1545	1746	1946

km	⊠	⚒🚌	🚌	🚌	🚌	🚌	🚌	🚌	🚌	🚌	🚌
0	**Turku** bus station d.	0600	0815	1100	...	1500	1500	1730	1800	...	2030
90	Rauma bus station d.	|	0945	1230	1610	|	1640	1855	|	1945	2205
139	**Pori** bus station a.	0815	1035	1315	1705	1715	...	...	2015	2050	2250

⊠	🚌	🚌	🚌	⚒🚌	🚌	🚌	🚌	🚌	🚌	🚌
Pori bus station d.	0600	0800	...	1030	1200	...	1700	2000	2005	...
Rauma bus station d.	0650	|	1040	1135	1250	1535	1800	|	2110	2210
Turku bus station a.	0830	1015	1220	...	1415	1700	1925	2215	...	2345

A – ⑥ to Aug. 9 (also June 20, July 14–18; not June 21; ⚒ from Aug. 11.
B – Ⓐ June 16 - Aug. 8 (not June 20, July 14–18).
C – ⑥⑦ to Aug. 3 (also June 20, July 14–18; not June 21); daily from Aug. 9.
D – Ⓐ June 16 - Aug. 8 (also June 21; not June 20, July 14–18).
H – (12) and 🍷 Helsinki - Tampere - Pori and v.v.
⊠ – Selected services only (many additional 🚌 services operate).

JYVÄSKYLÄ - SEINÄJOKI - VAASA 793

2nd class only (except where shown)

Services to / from Vaasa are subject to alteration on June 21, July 26, 27

km		⚒	‡	¶
0	**Jyväskylä** d.	0734	1028	1628
78	Haapamäki d.	0843	1142	1742
151	Alavus d.	0949	1253	1853
196	**Seinäjoki** a.	1021	1325	1925
270	**Vaasa** a.	*1136*	1436	*2034*

	‡	¶	Ⓑ
Vaasa d.	*0920*	1520	*1800*
Seinäjoki d.	1034	1634	1934
Alavus d.	1107	1707	2007
Haapamäki d.	1216	1820	2116
Jyväskylä a.	1327	1931	2227

				S 61				449		S 57	S 59
	Ⓐ◇	⚒		R♥						ⒷH	H
Seinäjoki d.	0747	0928	1038	1227	1338	...	1633	1818	1933	2023	2115
Vaasa a.	0845	1029	1136	1322	1436	...	1734	1908	2034	2110	2202

	S 440	S 44					S 62				
	ⒶH	⚒H					H				Ⓑ
Vaasa d.	0550	0700	0731	0920	...	1220	1500	1520	1625	1800	1925
Seinäjoki a.	0637	0747	0832	1018	...	1318	1544	1618	1723	1901	2023

– (12) and ✕ Helsinki - Vaasa and v.v. R.
– Subject to alteration on June 28, July 5.
– Subject to alteration on June 29, July 6.
◇ – From Tampere (Table **794**).
♥ – Daily. On Ⓐ runs Helsinki (**45**) - Seinäjoki (**61**) - Vaasa. Conveys ✕.

TAMPERE - VAASA, OULU, KOLARI and ROVANIEMI 794

Subject to alteration on June 20, 21, 22, 28, July 12, 26, Aug. 2

km		403	273		S 41	411	401		IC 63	IC 43	711	S 45	S 45	S 45	405		IC 47	IC 49	IC 173	S 53	IC 55	S 57	S 59	S 59	IC 181	263	265
		2	★⊕	2	R✕	2		🚌	✕	✕	2✕	R✕	R✕	R✕	2	🚌	✕	✕	✕	R✕	✕	R✕	R✕	R✕	✕	★	★
		⚒	n◇	Ⓐ	⚒	⑦	⚒	Ⓐm	⑥⑦	Ⓐ	K	Ⓐ		⑥	Ⓑ	⑦L	▲		Ⓑ			Ⓑ			A	J	n
	Helsinki **790** d.	...	2152	...	0630	...	...	...	0706	0730	...	0930	0930	0930	...	...	1006	1306	1406	1530	1606	1730	1830	1830	1906	1823	1852
0	**Tampere** d.	...	0115	0548	0804	...	...	...	0909	0909	...	1104	1104	1104	...	...	1200	1500	1600	1704	1800	1904	2004	2004	2100	2134	2211
75	Parkano d.	...	0211	0645	|	...	...	...	0947	0947	...	|	|	|	...	...	1238	1543	1645	|	1843	1938	|	|	2144	|	2306
59	Seinäjoki a.	...	0302	0739	0920	...	...	...	1024	1024	...	1213	1213	1213	...	...	1315	1626	1729	1810	1920	2019	2108	2108	2221	2331	0008
59	Seinäjoki **793** d.	...	0304	0747	0922	...	...	...	1033	1033	...	1227	1217	1217	...	...	1333	1630	...	1813	1936	2023	2112	2115	...	2333	0010
	Vaasa 793 a.	...	|	0845	|	...	...	...	|	|	...	1322	|	|	...	...	|	|	...	|	|	2110	|	2202	...	|	|
92	Kokkola d.	0415	0453	▬	1022	1022	...	...	1153	1153	...	▬	1323	1323	...	...	1456	1756	...	1929	2053	...	2215	...	...	0137r	0133
71	Ylivieska d.	0532	0617	...	1130	1130	...	...	1302	1302	...	...	1433	1433	...	...	1606	1913	...	2046	2208	...	2324	...	...	0324	0303
93	**Oulu** a.	0740	0827	...	1303z	1303	...	...	1438	1438z	...	...	1609z	1609	...	...	1750	2053	...	2246	0024	...	0120	...	...	0505	0500
93	**Oulu** d.	...	0835	...	▬	...	1310	...	...	...	1445	...	...	1622	1622	...	1757	2057b	...	...	...	...	...	...	...	0535	0505
99	Kemi d.	...	0948	🚌	🚌	...	1412	...	...	...	1544	🚌	...	1736	1736	...	1857	2200b	...	...	...	...	...	...	...	0649	0617
08	**Kolari** a.	...	|	Ⓐm	⑥	...	|	...	...	...	|	Ⓑ	...	|	|	...	|	|	...	...	...	...	...	...	...	0952	|
13	**Rovaniemi** a.	...	1120	1135	1200	...	1532	1545	...	...	1658	1725	...	1858	1858	1935	2025	2314b	...	...	...	...	...	...	...	...	0736f
96	Kemijärvi ⊡ a.	...	...	1250	1320	...	...	1700	...	...	...	1840	...	...	...	2050	...	...	...	...	...	...	...	...	...	...	0900

	IC 40	S 440	S 42	S 44	S 64	S 46	IC 48	404	IC 50	IC 50	S 52	S 62		IC 54	S 56		710	IC 58	408	S 60	S 60	410		266	270	272	274
	✕	R✕	R✕	R✕	R✕	R✕	✕	2	✕	✕	R✕	R✕	🚌	✕	R✕	🚌	2✕	✕	2	R✕	R✕	2	🚌	★⊕	★	★	★
	Ⓐ	Ⓐ	⚒	⚒	⑦	⚒		Ⓐ	⚒❖	⑦			⑥s	❖		Ⓐ	K		Ⓐ	⑦	Ⓑ		Ⓑ	n⊠	G	H	n
Kemijärvi ⊡ d.	...	...	...	...	...	...	...	...	...	...	...	...	0800	...	...	1030	...	...	...	...	...	...	1540	...	...	...	1915
Rovaniemi d.	...	...	...	...	...	...	...	...	0625	...	...	...	0915	0930	...	1145	1220	...	1425	1425	...	1620	1700	1745	...	...	2055e
Kolari d.	...	...	...	...	...	...	...	...	|	...	...	...	...	|	...	▬	|	...	|	|	...	|	...	|	1805	1805	|
Kemi d.	...	...	...	...	...	...	...	...	0746	...	...	...	...	1053	...	...	1338	...	1541	1541	...	1739	...	1922	2109	2109	2221
Oulu a.	...	...	...	...	...	...	...	...	0850	...	...	...	...	1151	...	...	1455	...	1637	1637	...	1845	...	2037	2218	2218	2324
Oulu d.	...	...	...	...	...	0410	0550	...	0855	0855	1030v	...	...	1155	1334v	...	...	1508v	...	1644	1644v	1848	...	2108	2250	2250	2338
Ylivieska d.	...	...	...	...	...	0619	0739	...	1042	1042	1213	...	...	1345	1517	IC	...	1648	...	1826	1826	2052	...	2303	0048	0048	0113
Kokkola d.	...	...	0530	...	0725	0738	0856	...	1156	1156	1328	...	...	1500	1632	**184**	...	1758	...	1932	1932	2215	...	0022	0211	0211	0225
Vaasa **793** d.	...	0550	|	0700	|	|	|	...	|	|	|	1500	...	|	|	✕	...	|	...	|	|	...	...	|	|	|	|
Seinäjoki **793** a.	...	0637	0641	0747	0844	0844	1024	...	1324	1324	1444	1544	...	1622	1738	Ⓑ	...	1924	...	2046	2046	...	...	0151	0350	0350	0404
Seinäjoki d.	0538	0639	0643	0749	0847	0847	1038	1210	1338	1338	1447	1546	...	1638	1741	1826	...	1938	...	2050	2050	...	...	0153	0352	0352	0406
Parkano d.	0616	|	0717	0823	|	|	1118	1302	1418	1418	|	|	...	1717	|	1910	...	2016	...	|	|	...	...	0311	|	|	|
Tampere a.	0653	0748	0752	0856	0956	0956	1156	1350	1456	1456	1553	1653	...	1759	1853	1952	...	2059	...	2200	2200	...	...	0403	0535	0535	0550
Helsinki **790** a.	0852	0930	0930	1030	1130	1130	1352	...	1652	1652	1730	1830	...	1952	2030	2152	...	2252	...	2352	2352	...	...	0706	0832	1000	0900

– ①②③④⑦ (not June 19).
– ⑥ (also June 19; not June 21).
– ④⑦ (not June 19).
– ③⑤⑥ (also June 19; not June 20, 21).
– From / to Kuopio (Table **798**).
– From Aug. 10.
– Ⓑ only.
– Arrives 2020.
– Departs 0755.

m – Runs 10–20 minutes later until Aug. 5.
n – Not June 20, 21.
r – Arrives 0122.
s – Also ①–⑤ until Aug. 5.
v – On ①–④ July 14 - Aug. 7 operated by 🚌 Oulu - Ylivieska (departs Oulu 19–38 minutes earlier).
z – On ①–④ July 14 - Aug. 7 operated by 🚌 Ylivieska - Oulu (arrives 21–32 minutes later).

▲ – On ①–④ July 14 - Aug. 7 by 🚌 Ylivieska - Oulu (a. 1815; train runs Oulu - Rovaniemi in normal timings, so no connection between bus and train at Oulu).
❖ – On ①–④ July 14 - Aug. 7 by 🚌 Oulu - Ylivieska (departs Oulu 25–30 minutes earlier; train runs Rovaniemi - Oulu in normal timings, so no connection between train and bus at Oulu).
★ – Conveys 🛏, (2) and ✕.
⊕ – Conveys 🛏 Turku - Tampere - Rovaniemi and v.v. See Table **790**.
◇ – Subject to alteration on July 11, Aug. 1, 15, Sept. 5, 12, Oct. 3, 17, Nov. 14, 21, 28.
⊠ – Subject to alteration on July 12, Aug. 2, 16, Sept. 6, 13, Oct. 4, 18, Nov. 15, 22, 29.
⊡ – 🚌 services operate to / from the bus station.

795 TURKU - TAMPERE - PIEKSÄMÄKI

km		903	S81	IC163	IC905	IC165		909	IC85	IC47	IC911	IC87	IC49	IC917	IC173	S89		S53	IC921	923	S91	S91	S59	IC927	931	IC93	933
		2	🅁✕	‡🍸	✕	🍸	2	2	🍸	✕	✕	🍸	✕	IC919	✕	🅁✕	2	🅁✕	✕	2	🅁✕	🅁✕	🅁✕	✕	2	✕	2
		Ⓐ	K Ⓐ			⚒								✕L		K Ⓑ						Ⓑ		K		Ⓑ	R
0	**Turku** d.	0600	...	...	0700	...	...	0905	...	...	1005	...	...	1305	...	...	...	...	1505	1605	...	...	...	1805	2005	...	2105
66	Loimaa d.	0639	...	...	0741	...	...	0944	...	...	1044	...	...	1344	...	...	...	...	1544	1644	...	...	...	1844	2044	...	2147
	Helsinki **790**. d.	|	0606	0706	|	0806	...	|	0906	1006	|	1206	1306	|	1406	1430	...	1530	|	|	1630	1630	1830	|	|	2006	|
128	Toijala **790** d.	0720	0731	0831	0825	0931	...	1025	1031	1131	1125	1331	1431	1425	1531	|	...	|	1625	1725	|	|	|	1925	2125	2131	2234
168	**Tampere** **790** a.	0742	0752	0852	0847	0952	...	1047	1052	1152	1147	1352	1452	1447	1552	1600	...	1700	1647	1747	1800	1800	2000	1947	2147	2152	2300
168	**Tampere** d.	...	0809	...	0905	...	1005	...	1109	...	1205	1409	...	1505	...	1609	1617	...	1709	...	1818	1818	...	2009	...	2209	...
210	Orivesi d.	...	|	...	0930	...	1031	...	|	...	1230	|	...	1530	...	|	1643	...	1734	...	1843	1843	...	2034	...	2235	...
282	Haapamäki a.	...	|	...	|	...	1124	...	|	...	|	|	...	|	...	|	1736	...	|	...	|	|	...	|	...	|	...
266	Jämsä d.	...	0909	...	1006	...	...	...	1209	...	1306	1514	...	1606	...	1716	...	...	1821	...	1919	1919	...	2110	...	2311	...
323	Jyväskylä d.	...	0938	...	1045r	...	...	...	1239	...	1345r	1544	...	1645r	...	1745	...	...	1855	...	1953	1957	...	2153	...	2341	...
403	**Pieksämäki** a.	...	1025	...	1134	...	...	...	...	...	1434	...	...	1734	...	1827	...	...	1954	...	...	2045	...	2242b	...	...	...

	904	S80	906	IC82	S84	S84	910	IC912	IC912	IC168	IC916	IC48		IC176	IC922	IC50	IC88	924	IC928	IC54	IC90	930		IC184	IC934	IC58	S94
	2 T	🅁✕	2	✕	🅁✕	🅁✕	2	✕	✕	🍸	✕	✕	2	IC196	✕	✕	🍸	2	✕	✕	🍸	2	2	✕	✕	✕	🅁✕
		Ⓐ	Ⓐ	⚒	K Ⓐ	⚒	⚒	K ⚒						🍸					L								K
Pieksämäki d.	...	...	...	...	0635	...	...	0718	...	...	0924	...	...	...	1220	...	...	...	1520	...	...	...	...	...	1827	...	2049b
Jyväskylä d.	...	0520	...	0622	0719	0719	...	0813	0813	...	1015	...	...	...	1313	...	1417	...	1613	...	1721	...	...	...	1916	...	2133
Jämsä d.	...	0554	...	0654	0748	0748	...	0845	0845	...	1051	...	...	...	1351	...	1449	...	1651	...	1757	...	...	...	1948	...	2202
Haapamäki d.	...	|	...	|	|	|	...	|	|	...	|	...	1224	...	|	...	|	...	|	...	|	...	1829	...	|	...	|
Orivesi d.	...	|	...	|	0823	0823	...	0920	0920	...	1126	...	1320	...	1426	...	|	...	1726	...	|	...	1925	...	2023	...	|
Tampere a.	...	0650	...	0750	0847	0847	...	0944	0944	...	1150	...	1345	...	1450	...	1545	...	1750	...	1850	...	1950	...	2047	...	2256
Tampere **790** d.	0556	0700	0711	0807	0855	0855	0911	1011	1011	1007	1211	1207	...	1407	1511	1507	1607	1611	1811	1807	1907	1911	...	2007	2111	2107	2307
Toijala **790** d.	0623	|	0735	0828	|	|	0935	1035	1035	1028	1235	1228	...	1428	1535	1528	1628	1635	1835	1828	1928	1935	...	2028	2135	2128	2328
Helsinki **790** a.	|	0830	|	0952	1025	1025	|	|	|	1152	|	1352	...	1552	|	1652	1752	|	|	1952	2052	|	...	2152	|	2252	0052
Loimaa d.	0706	...	0813	...	...	...	1013	1113	1113	...	1313	...	...	...	1613	...	...	1713	1915	...	...	2013	...	...	2215	...	...
Turku a.	0750	...	0850	...	...	...	1055	1150	1150	...	1355	...	...	...	1655	...	...	1750	1955	...	...	2055	...	...	2252	...	...
Turku Satama a.	0802	...	...	...	...	...	...	...	...	...	...	...	...	...	...	...	...	1819	2007	...	...	...	...	...	...	...	...

K – To / from Kuopio (Table **798**).
L – To / from Oulu (Table **798**).
R – (2) Turku - Tampere; 🛏 Turku - Tampere (**273**) - Rovaniemi.
T – (2) Tampere - Turku; 🛏 Rovaniemi (**266**) - Tampere - Turku.
b – Ⓑ only.
r – Arrives 9 minutes earlier.
‡ – Train number **63** on ⑥⑦.

797 HELSINKI - KOUVOLA - JOENSUU

km		IC69		IC1	IC71	IC3		IC73	IC5		IC109	S7	S117		IC77	IC77	IC111		IC11	S79	IC113					
		K✕	2	✕	J✕	✕	2	D✕	✕	2	🍸	🅁✕	🅁✕	2	C✕	§✕	✕	2	✕	🅁✕	✕	2		2		2
		Ⓐ	⚒R				R			◇		Ⓑ¶	⑥T	Ⓐ		Ⓑ	Ⓑ	R		C		Ⓑ				
0	**Helsinki** d.	0512	...	0712	0812	1012	...	1112	1252	1319	1412	1512	1512	1541	1612	1612	1712	...	1812	1912	2012	2241	Other	0641	and	2241
3	Pasila d.	0518	...	0718	0818	1018	...	1118	1300	1324	1418	1518	1518	1547	1618	1618	1718	...	1818	1918	2018	2246	local	0646	hourly	2246
16	Tikkurila ⊙ d.	0528	...	0728	0828	1028	...	1128	1312	1332	1428	1528	1528	1556	1628	1628	1728	...	1828	1928	2028	2255	trains	0655	until	2255
104	**Lahti** d.	0614	0705	0808	0908	1108	1155	1208	1401	1455	1508	1602	1602	1651	1708	1708	1808	1855	1908	2002	2108	2343	→	0742		2342
166	**Kouvola** a.	0645	0743	0838	0938	1138	1245	1238	1433	1533	1538	1630	1630	1733	1738	1738	1838	1933	1938	2030	2138	0021		...		...
166	**Kouvola** d.	...	...	0840	...	1140	...	...	1436	...	1540	1636	1636	...	...	1746	...	...	1940	...	2140	...		...		...
252	Lappeenranta d.	...	...	0922	...	1222	...	...	1522	...	1620	1717	1717	...	...	1828	...	...	2022	...	2222	...		...		...
288	Imatra d.	...	...	0948	...	1248	...	...	1550	...	...	1747	1745	...	...	1854	...	...	2053	...	2246	...		...		...
352	Parikkala d.	...	...	1029	...	1329	...	...	1633	...	...	|	...	...	...	1935	...	...	2134	...	...	...		...		...
482	**Joensuu** a.	...	...	1140	...	1440	...	...	1747	...	...	1930	...	...	...	2046	...	...	2245	...	...	...		...		...

			IC102	IC104	S2		S70	IC4	IC100	IC74		IC6	IC68	IC8	S118	S76		IC114	IC10	IC66	IC78	IC12				
	2	2	✕	✕	🅁✕	2	🅁✕	✕	✕	H✕	2	✕	E✕	✕	🅁✕	🅁✕	2	🍸	✕	K✕	J✕	✕		2		2
	⚒	Ⓐ	Ⓐ	⚒	⚒	R	J⚒	⚒	⑦		R				⑦T	K	◇			Ⓑ						
Joensuu d.	...	...	...	...	0528	...	...	0617	...	...	...	0917	...	1217	...	...	...	...	1517	...	...	1817		...		...
Parikkala d.	...	...	...	...	0638	...	...	0731	...	...	...	1031	...	1331	...	...	...	...	1631	...	...	1933		...		...
Imatra d.	...	...	...	0612	0715	...	...	0812	0812	...	...	1112	...	1412	1507	...	...	...	1712	...	...	2014		...		...
Lappeenranta d.	...	...	...	0638	0738	...	...	0838	0838	...	...	1138	...	1440	1538	...	...	1638	1738	...	...	2041		...		...
Kouvola a.	...	...	...	0718	0816	...	...	0918	0918	...	...	1218	...	1520	1616	...	...	1718	1818	...	...	2124	❖	...		...
Kouvola d.	0500	0537	0622	0722	0818	0821	0830	0922	0922	1122	1114	1222	1422	1522	1618	1630	1621	1722	1822	1922	2022	2126		...		...
Lahti d.	0540	0611	0654	0754	0848	0905	0900	0954	0954	1154	1203	1254	1454	1554	1648	1700	1706	1754	1854	1954	2054	2200	Other	0917	and	2317
Tikkurila ⊙ a.	0627	0707	0732	0832	0920	...	0932	1032	1032	1232	...	1332	1532	1632	1720	1732	1828	1832	1932	2032	2132	2251	local	1005	hourly	0005
Pasila a.	0635	0717	0741	0841	0929	...	0941	1041	1041	1241	...	1341	1541	1641	1729	1741	1836	1841	1941	2041	2141	2301	trains	1014	until	0014
Helsinki a.	0640	0723	0748	0848	0936	...	0948	1048	1048	1248	...	1348	1548	1648	1736	1748	1841	1848	1948	2048	2148	2308	→	1019		0019

Branch lines **KOUVOLA - KOTKA** and **PARIKKALA - SAVONLINNA** (2nd class only).

km		⚒					Ⓑ		⚒					Ⓑ
0	**Kouvola** d.	0632	0845	1252	1543	1750	2152	**Kotka** satama d.	0725	1022	1427	1632	1922	2245
51	**Kotka** a.	0714	0927	1334	1625	1832	2234	**Kotka** d.	0728	1025	1430	1634	1925	2248
52	**Kotka** satama a.	0717	0930	1337	1627	1835	2237	**Kouvola** a.	0811	1108	1513	1717	2008	2331

km		⚒				Ⓑ			⚒					Ⓑ
0	**Parikkala** d.	0734	1034	1334	1640	1940	2140	**Savonlinna** d.	0540	0930	1230	1530	1830	2041
33	Retretti d.	0802	1102	1402	1708	2008	2208	Retretti d.	0601	0951	1251	1551	1851	|
59	**Savonlinna** a.	0827	1127	1427	1733	2033	2233	**Parikkala** a.	0633	1023	1323	1623	1923	2129

Local trains **RIIHIMÄKI - LAHTI** and v.v.
59 km. Journey time: 40 – 41 minutes. 2nd class only.

From Riihimäki at 0013, 0613 ⚒, 0713, 0813 and hourly until 2213. The services from Riihimäki at 0613, 1113, 1413 and 1813 continue to Kouvola (see main table).

From Lahti at 0452 Ⓐ, 0544 Ⓐ, 0628 ⑥ **v**, 0706 ⚒, 0806, 090 and hourly until 2206. The services from Lahti at 0906, 1206 and 1706 start from Kouvola (see main table).

C – To Kuopio (also Kajaani on Ⓑ) (Table **798**).
D – To Kuopio (also Kajaani on ⑥) (Table **798**).
E – From Kuopio (also Kajaani on ⑦) (Table **798**).
H – From Kuopio (also Kajaani on ⚒) (Table **798**).
J – To / from Kajaani (Table **798**).
K – To / from Kuopio (Table **798**).
R – From / to Riihimäki.
T – From Aug. 16.
v – Also June 20; not June 21.
◇ – Via Riihimäki.
§ – Train number **9** Kouvola - Joensuu.
¶ – Conveys (12) Helsinki - Kouvola (**75**) - Kuopio (Table **798**
⊙ – For Helsinki ✈ Vantaa.
❖ – Also from Lahti at 0617 ⑥⑦, 0711 Ⓐ, 0717 ⑥⑦ and 081

798 KOUVOLA - KUOPIO - OULU

Subject to alteration June 19 – 22, 28, 2

km		719	IC69	711	S81	IC71	713	IC73	715	IC707	IC919	IC917	S75	IC917	S89	IC77	IC709	S79	S79	IC927
		2	✕	2✕	🅁✕	✕	2	✕	2✕	✕	✕	✕	🅁✕	✕	🅁✕	✕	✕	🅁✕	🅁✕	T✕
		⚒	⚒	R	Ⓐ				Ⓑ		⑥T	Ⓑ T	Ⓑ‡	Ⓑ T	Ⓑ		Ⓑ		Ⓑ	Ⓑ
	Helsinki **797** d.	...	0512e	...	0606	0812	...	1112	...	*1412*	...	...	1512	...	1430	1612	*1712*	1912	1912	...
0	**Kouvola** d.	...	0703	...	|	0951	...	1252	...	1545	...	...	1639	...	|	1756	1845	2037	2037	...
113	Mikkeli d.	...	0810	...	|	1058	...	1358	...	1659	...	...	1744	...	|	1905	1957	2139	2139	...
	Tampere **795** d.	...	|	...	0809	|	...	|	...	|	1505	1505	|	...	1609	|	|	|	|	2009
184	Pieksämäki d.	...	0855	...	1027	1144	...	1444	...	1742	1749	1749	1824	←	1829	2001t	2052t	2220	2220	2245
273	**Kuopio** d.	...	0950	1000	1115	1248	...	1543	1543	...	1850	1847	1915	1930	1920	2100	2147	2314	2316	2340
358	Iisalmi d.	...	...	1101	...	1348	...	1643v	1643	...	1959	→	...	2058	...	2158b	...	...	0010	...
441	Kajaani d.	0550	...	1153	...	1438	1508	1731v	1734	...	2119z	...	...	2119	...	2245b	...	...	0055	...
484	Paltamo d.	0624	...	1223	...	...	1538	...	1804	...	2151	...	...	2151f	...	...	...	...	...	...
633	**Oulu** a.	0813	...	1409	...	...	1721	...	2000	...	2331	...	...	2331f	...	...	...	...	...	...

	IC700	S70	S84	S70	IC912	IC74	IC74	714	IC68	IC68	IC928	S76	IC928	IC706	IC66	718	IC78	710	S94	712
		🅁✕	🅁✕	🅁✕	T✕	✕	✕	✕	✕	✕	✕	🅁✕	✕	✕	✕	2	✕	2✕	🅁✕	2
	⚒	⚒	Ⓐ	⚒	⚒	⚒		⚒	⑦		T		T		Ⓑ			R	Ⓑ	Ⓑ¶
Oulu d.	...	...	...	...	...	...	...	0613	...	...	0935	...	...	...	...	1207	...	1518	...	1930
Paltamo d.	...	...	...	...	...	...	...	0751	...	...	1107	...	...	...	...	1354	...	1651	...	2113
Kajaani d.	...	0355	...	...	...	0620	...	0907z	0907	...	1155t	...	...	...	...	1435	1511	1737	...	2155
Iisalmi d.	...	0442	...	←	...	0715	...	0959	0959	...	1246	...	←	...	...	...	1607	1831	...	...
Kuopio d.	0410	0534	0539	0545	0617	0817	0817	1104	1115t	1115	1348	1354	1407	...	1602	...	1715t	1929	1950	...
Pieksämäki d.	0512	→	0635	0642	0718	0921	0921	...	1216	1216	→	1444	1520t	1516	1700	...	1822t	...	2049	...
Tampere **795** a.	|	...	0847	|	0944	|	|	...	|	|	...	|	1750	|	|	...	|	...	2256	...
Mikkeli d.	0559	...	|	0722	...	1007	1007	...	1303	1303	...	1524	...	1603	1746	...	1907	...	|	...
Kouvola a.	0703	...	|	0820	...	1109	1109	...	1408	1408	...	1622	...	1709	1902	...	2008	...	|	...
Helsinki **797** a.	*0848*	...	1025	0948	...	1248	1248	...	1548	1548	...	1748	...	*1848*	2048	...	2148	...	0052	...

IISALMI - YLIVIESKA

km		⚒	h
0	**Iisalmi** d.	0420	164
99	Haapajärvi d.	0528	174
154	**Ylivieska** a.	0605	182

	h		Ⓑ
Ylivieska d.	1356	...	210
Haapajärvi d.	1430	...	213
Iisalmi a.	1533	...	225

R – To / from Rovaniemi (Table **794**).
T – From / to Turku (Table **795**).
b – Kuopio - Kajaani on Ⓑ only.
e – Ⓐ only.
f – On ①–⑤ July 14 - Sept. 26 by 🚌 Kajaani - Oulu (a. 0005).
h – Not July 26.
t – Arrives 7 – 13 minutes earlier.
v – Kuopio - Kajaani on ⑥ only.
z – Arrives 30 – 35 minutes earlier.
‡ – Train number **7** Helsinki - Kouvola
¶ – By 🚌 on ①–⑤ July 14 - Sept. 2

PIEKSÄMÄKI - JOENSUU - NURMES - KAJAANI — 799

2nd class only

km		🚌 Ⓐ			🚌 Ⓐ			🚌			Ⓑ	
0	**Pieksämäki** d.	0655	...	1148	1235	...	1453	1640	1833	...	2100	...
49	Varkaus d.	0750	...	1223	1310	...	1528	1725	1907	...	2135	...
183	**Joensuu** ⊙ a.	1000	...	1357	...	...	1702	1920	2041	...	2309	...

			🚌 ⚒						Ⓑ	
Joensuu ⊙ d.	0700	...	0910	...	1221	...	1526	...	1832	...
Varkaus d.	0836	...	1120	...	1400	...	1705	...	2010	...
Pieksämäki a.	0909	...	1155	...	1433	...	1738	...	2043	...

km		🚌 Ⓐ	🚌 ⚒		🚌 ⑦w	🚌 ⚒	🚌 ⚒	🚌 Ⓐ	🚌		🚌 ⑤⑦	🚌 Ⓐ
0	**Joensuu** ⊙ d.	0710	0900	1147	1210	1405	1520	...	1630	1755	2105	2115
104	Lieksa ⊙ a.	0855	|	1306	|	|	1705	1720	|	1914	|	2245
160	Nurmes ⊙ a.	...	1055	1353	1400	1610	...	1805	1830	2001	2315	...
274	**Kajaani** bus station a.	...	1300	...	1600	1805	...	...	2030	...	...	...

	🚌 Ⓐ		🚌 Ⓐ	🚌 ⑥	🚌 ⑦	🚌 Ⓑ	🚌	🚌		🚌
Kajaani bus station d.	...	...	0545r	0615	...	...	...	1050	...	1710
Nurmes ⊙ d.	...	0640	0750r	0810	0915	...	...	1245	1540	1905
Lieksa ⊙ d.	0550	0726	|	|	1005	1005	1300	|	1626	1950
Joensuu ⊙ a.	0740	0845	1010	1010	1150	1150	1440	1450	1745	2130

🚌 **PIEKSÄMÄKI – SAVONLINNA** *123 km* Journey time: 1 hr 55 m - 2 hrs 5 m
From Pieksämäki at 1830⑤ (also ⑦ from Aug. 10) and 2100⑦ until Aug. 3.
From Savonlinna at 1530⑤ (also ⑦ from Aug. 10) and 1830⑦ until Aug. 3.

r – Until Aug. 8 departs Kajaani 0610, Nurmes 0810.
w – Also ⑤ from Aug. 15.

⊙ – 🚌 timings are at the bus station.

GERMANY

Operator: Principal operator is Deutsche Bahn AG (DB) www.bahn.de
Many regional services are run by private operators – these are specified in the table heading (or by footnotes for individual trains).

Services: Trains convey first- and second-class seating accommodation unless otherwise shown (by '2' in the column heading, a footnote or a general note in the table heading). Overnight sleeping car (🛏) and couchette (▬) trains do not necessarily convey seating accommodation - refer to individual footnotes for details. Descriptions of sleeping and couchette cars appear on page 8.

There are various categories of trains in Germany. The type of train is indicated by the following letter codes above each column (or by a general note in the table heading):

ICE	**InterCity Express**	German high-speed (230 – 320 km/h) train.
EC	**EuroCity**	International express train.
IC	**InterCity**	Internal express train.
TGV	**Train à Grande Vitesse**	French high-speed (320 km/h) train.
RJ	**Railjet**	Austrian high-speed train.
IRE	**InterRegio Express**	Regional express train.
RE	**Regional Express**	Semi-fast train.
RB	**Regional Bahn**	Stopping train.
S-Bahn		Suburban stopping train.

Overnight services:

CNL	**City Night Line**	Quality overnight express train. Most services convey *Deluxe* sleeping cars (1/2 berth) with en-suite shower and WC, *Economy* sleeping cars (1/2/4 berth), couchettes (4/6 berth) and reclining seats. Reservation compulsory. See also page 8.
EN	**Euro Night**	International overnight express train. See also page 8.
D	**Durchgangszug**	Or **Schnellzug** – other express train (day or night).

Other long-distance service operators:

ALX	**alex**	Regional express train operated by *Vogtlandbahn* on the routes München - Oberstdorf / Lindau and München - Regensburg - Hof (also international services München - Regensburg - Schwandorf - Furth im Wald - Praha).
HKX	**Hamburg-Köln-Express**	Operates fast services on the Hamburg - Köln route (see Table **800a** below). **DB tickets not valid**.
X	**InterConnex**	Fast services, operated by *Veolia Verkehr*, on the Warnemünde - Rostock - Berlin - Leipzig route. **DB tickets not valid**.

Timings: Valid **JUNE 15 - DECEMBER 13**, 2014 (except where shown otherwise).

Many long distance trains operate on selected days only for part of the journey. These are often indicated in the train composition footnote by showing the dated journey segment within brackets. For example '(12) Leipzig - Hannover (- Dortmund ⑦)' means that the train runs daily (or as shown in the column heading) between Leipzig and Hannover, but only continues to Dortmund on Sundays. Additional footnotes / symbols are often used to show more complex running dates, e.g. '(12) (München ⊡ -) Nürnberg - Hamburg' means that the train runs only on dates in note ⊡ between München and Nürnberg, but runs daily (or as shown in the column heading) between Nürnberg and Hamburg. Please note that international overnight trains that are not intended for internal German journeys are not usually shown in the German section (refer to the International section).

Engineering work may occasionally disrupt services at short notice (especially at weekends and during holiday periods), so it is advisable to check timings locally before travelling.

Tickets: There are three standard levels of fares, corresponding to travel by (in ascending order of price): ○ Regional trains. ○ *IC* / *EC* trains. ○ High-speed *ICE* (also *TGV* / *RJ*) trains. A 'Sprinter' supplement (€ 16.50 in first class, € 11.50 in second class) is also payable for travel by limited stop *ICE* ***SPRINTER*** trains **1090 – 1097**. A variable supplement (*Aufpreis*) is payable for travel by overnight *CNL* and *EN* trains, the cost of which depends on the type of accommodation required (sleeper, couchette or reclining seat).

Catering: Two types of catering are indicated in the tables: 🍸 Bordbistro – hot and cold drinks, snacks and light meals; ✕ Bordrestaurant – full restaurant car service (bordbistro also available). First class passengers on *ICE* and *IC* trains benefit from an at-seat service. On overnight trains 🍸 indicates that drinks and light snacks are available, usually from the sleeping or couchette car attendant (the refreshment service may only be available to sleeping and couchette car passengers).

Reservations: Reservation is compulsory for travel by *CNL* and *ICE* ***SPRINTER*** trains, also any other trains marked 🅁. Optional reservations are available on *ICE* / *EC* / *IC* trains (€ 4).

Holidays: Jan. 1, Apr. 18, 21, May 1, 29, June 9, Oct. 3, Dec. 25, 26 are German national public holidays (trains marked ⚒ or Ⓐ do not run). In addition there are other regional holidays as follows: June 19 – Fronleichnam (Corpus Christi), Aug. 15 – Mariä Himmelfahrt (Assumption), Oct. 31 – Reformationstag (Reformation Day), Nov. 1 – Allerheiligen (All Saints Day) and Nov. 19 – Buß und Bettag. On these days the regional service is usually that applicable on ⑦ (please refer to individual footnotes).

HAMBURG - KÖLN — 800a

Hamburg-Köln-Express (HKX)

km		*HKX* **1800** A	*HKX* **1802**	*HKX* **1804** ④–⑦
0	**Hamburg** Altona d.	0635	1138j	1637
7	**Hamburg** Hbf d.	0649	1151	1650
228	Osnabrück Hbf d.	0844	1344	1844
278	Münster (Westf) Hbf d.	0909	1409	1909
351	Gelsenkirchen Hbf d.	0950	1450	1950
361	**Essen** Hbf d.	1004	1504	2004
380	Duisburg Hbf d.	1018	1518	2018
404	**Düsseldorf** Hbf d.	1034	1534	2034
444	**Köln** Hbf a.	1057	1557	2057

	HKX **1801** A	*HKX* **1803** B	*HKX* **1805** ②–⑦
Köln Hbf d.	0701	1201	1701
Düsseldorf Hbf d.	0727	1227	1727
Duisburg Hbf d.	0742	1242	1742
Essen Hbf d.	0755	1255	1755
Gelsenkirchen Hbf d.	0805	1305	1805
Münster (Westf) Hbf d.	0847	1347	1847
Osnabrück Hbf d.	0914	1414	1914
Hamburg Hbf a.	1105	1608	2105
Hamburg Altona a.	1122	1622	2122

A – ①⑤⑥ only.
B – ①④⑤⑥⑦ only.

j – 1136 June 14 - July 27.

Operator: Hamburg-Köln-Express GmbH. ✆ +49 (0) 221 677 8020. www.hkx.de
Special fares payable (**DB tickets are not valid**). 🍸.

☛ See Table **800** for DB services.

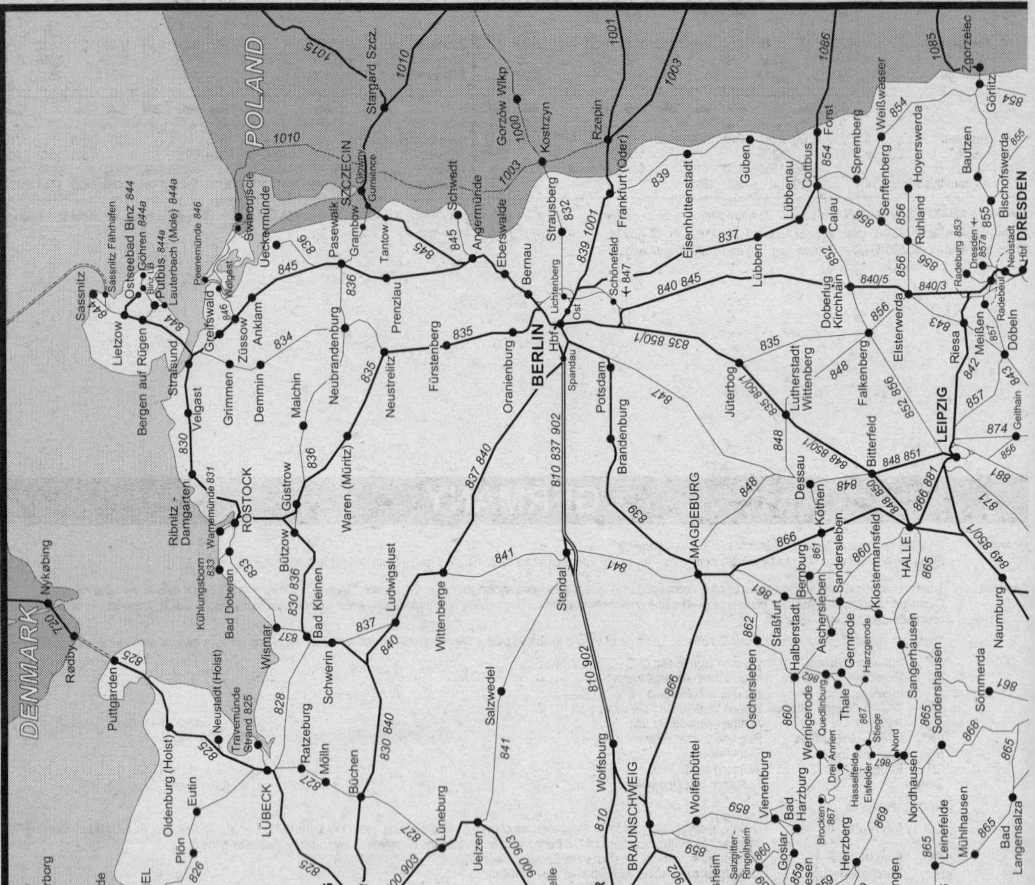
DENMARK
POLAND
NETHERLANDS
Table 800 shows all long-distance trains which pass through the Ruhr area below. Local RE and S-Bahn services are shown in Table 802.
For more detail of the Ruhr area see inset
HAMBURG
BERLIN
HANNOVER
BREMEN
MAGDEBURG
LEIPZIG
DRESDEN
HALLE
KASSEL
DORTMUND
DÜSSELDORF
KÖLN
ESSEN
DUISBURG
BOCHUM
WUPPERTAL
HAGEN
KIEL
LÜBECK
ROSTOCK
SZCZECIN
BRAUNSCHWEIG
BIELEFELD
MÜNSTER (Westf)
AACHEN
BONN
MÖNCHENGLADBACH
KREFELD
OBERHAUSEN
GELSENKIRCHEN
Frankfurt (Oder)
Cottbus
Görlitz
Stralsund
Schwerin
Wismar
Lüneburg
Uelzen
Celle
Osnabrück
Göttingen
Erfurt
Westerland
Flensburg
Husum
Cuxhaven
Emden
Norddeich Mole
Oldenburg
Wilhelmshaven
Puttgarden
Sassnitz
Binz
Stendal
Wolfsburg
Wittenberge
Potsdam
Brandenburg
Dessau
Bitterfeld
Lutherstadt Wittenberg
Nordhausen
Paderborn
Hamm
Soest
Rheine
Bad Bentheim
Emmerich
Venlo
Groningen
Leeuwarden
Zwolle
Apeldoorn
Arnhem
Nijmegen
Deventer
Enschede
Hengelo
Kostrzyn
Rzepin
Forst
Zgorzelec
Stargard Szcz.
Swinoujście
Helgoland
Nykøbing
Rødby
Tønder

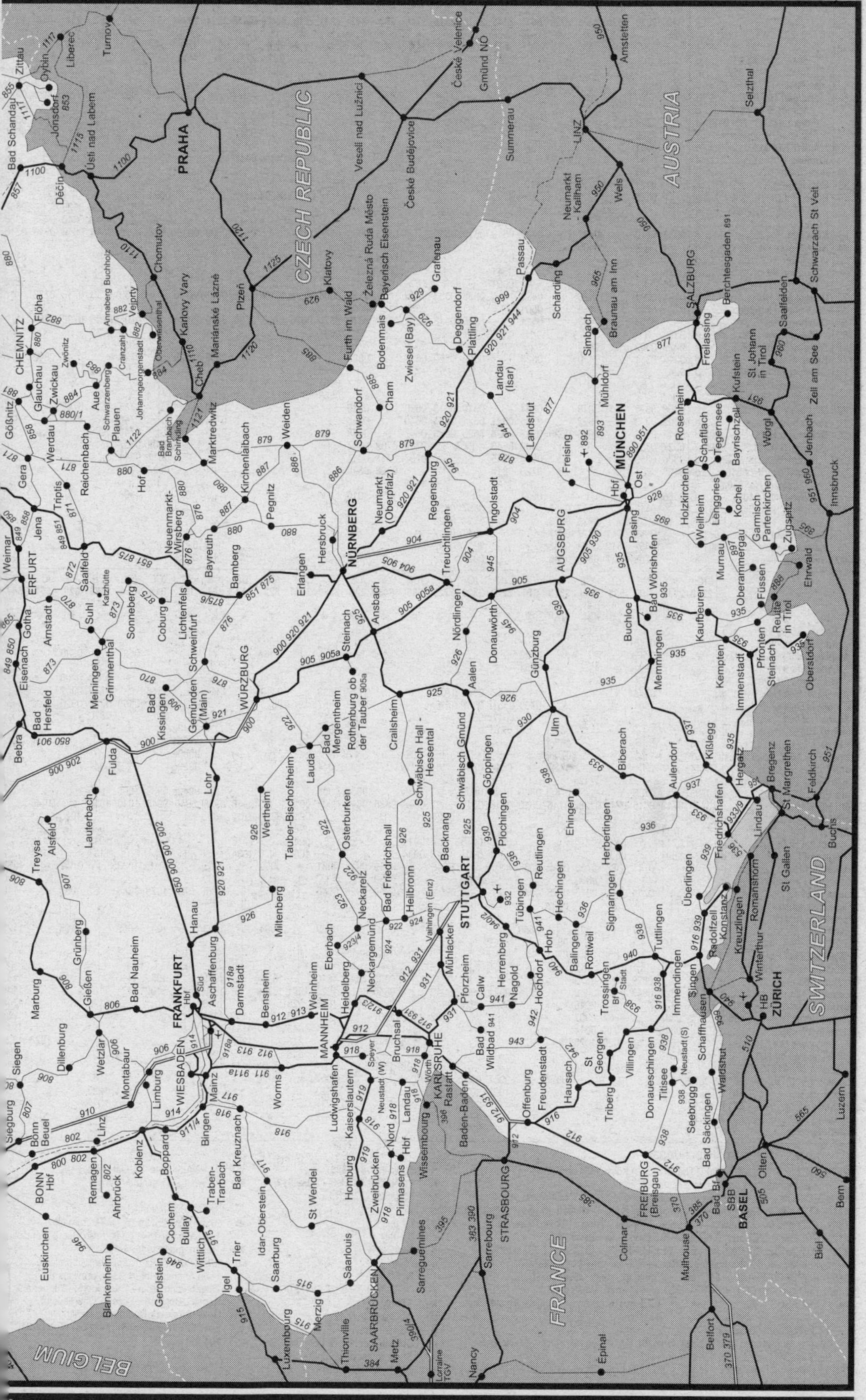

CZECH REPUBLIC
AUSTRIA
SWITZERLAND
FRANCE
BELGIUM
PRAHA
FRANKFURT
MÜNCHEN
NÜRNBERG
STUTTGART
WÜRZBURG
AUGSBURG
MANNHEIM
KARLSRUHE
SAARBRÜCKEN
STRASBOURG
BASEL
ZÜRICH
SALZBURG
LINZ
CHEMNITZ
ERFURT
WIESBADEN
BONN
Koblenz
Mainz
Darmstadt
Heidelberg
Regensburg
Ingolstadt
Ulm
Passau
Plzeň
Cheb
Karlovy Vary
Chomutov
Ústí nad Labem
Děčín
Liberec
České Budějovice
Innsbruck
Kufstein
Freilassing
Lindau
Bregenz
Konstanz
Friedrichshafen
Freiburg (Breisgau)
Offenburg
Mulhouse
Colmar
Metz
Nancy
Luxembourg
Trier
Kaiserslautern
Ludwigshafen
Heilbronn
Bamberg
Bayreuth
Hof
Plauen
Zwickau
Gera
Jena
Weimar
Eisenach
Fulda
Bebra
Hanau
Aschaffenburg
Gießen
Marburg
Siegen
Limburg
Rosenheim
Landshut
Plattling
Kempten
Lindau
Garmisch Partenkirchen
Berchtesgaden

800 KOBLENZ - KÖLN - DORTMUND - HAMBURG

km			ICE 949	IC 2020	ICE 1020	IC 2228	IC 2228	ICE 541*	IC 2445	IC 2214	IC 2314	ICE 1745	ICE 853	ICE 843	IC 2331	CNL 418	CNL 40478	IC 60478	IC 2224	ICE 1095	ICE 553	ICE 543	ICE 222	ICE 918	ICE 618	ICE 1018
			①		Ⓐ	①	Ⓐ	①-⑥	①-⑥	Q			①-⑥		B	R	R			①-④	①-⑥		♣	⑤f	①-⑤	⑦
			◇		✕	🍷	🍷	✕	d D	🍷	🍷♦	✕♦	✕	✕	N	🍷♦	🍷♦	2	K 🍷	t R	✕	✕	A 🍷	🍷	🍷	🍷
	*Basel SBB 🚢 **912***	d.	...	...	...	...	...	...	🍷	...	...	...	...	...	...	...	2213	2213	...	⚡✕	...	...	...	...	...	...
	*Karlsruhe Hbf **912***	d.	...	...	...	...	...	...	...	...	...	...	...	...	...	...	0029	0029	...	...	...	...	...	...	0348	0348
	*München Hbf **904 930***	d.	...	...	...	...	...	...	...	...	...	...	...	...	...	2250	|	|	...	...	...	...	...	...	2350p	2350p
	*Stuttgart Hbf **912***	d.	...	...	...	...	...	...	...	...	...	...	...	...	...	0135	|	|	...	...	...	...	...	...	0221	0221
	*Nürnberg Hbf **920***	d.	...	...	...	...	...	...	...	...	...	...	...	...	...	|	|	|	...	...	...	...	...	...	|	|
	*Frankfurt (Main) Hbf **910/1***	d.	...	2324	...	...	...	...	...	...	...	...	...	...	...	|	|	|	...	...	...	...	0510t	0510	0544	0544
	Frankfurt Flughafen ✈ §	d.	...	2338	...	...	...	...	...	...	...	...	...	...	...	|	|	0341	...	...	...	...	0525t	0525	0601	0601
	*Mainz Hbf **911***	d.	...	0001	...	...	...	...	...	...	...	...	...	...	...	|	|	|	...	...	...	...	|	|	|	|
0	**Koblenz** Hbf	d.	...	0057	...	...	...	...	...	...	...	...	...	...	...	0446s	0446s	0448	...	...	0547	...	|	|	|	|
18	Andernach	d.	...	0109	...	...	...	...	...	...	...	...	...	...	...	|	|	|	...	...	|	...	|	|	|	|
39	Remagen	d.	...	0121	...	...	...	...	...	...	...	...	...	...	...	|	|	|	...	...	|	...	|	|	|	|
59	**Bonn** Hbf	d.	...	0135	...	...	...	...	...	...	...	...	...	...	...	0520s	0520s	0522	...	...	0621	...	|	|	|	|
	Köln/Bonn Flughafen ✈	d.	...	|	...	...	...	...	...	...	...	...	...	...	...	|	|	|	...	...	|	...	0629t	0629	|	0652
93	**Köln** Hbf	a.	...	0156	...	...	...	...	...	...	...	...	...	...	...	0543s	0543s	0543	...	...	0642	...	0640t	0640	0705	0705
93	**Köln** Hbf	d.	0033	0210	...	0400	...	0429	0510	0510	0510	...	0545	0529	0541	|	|	0546	0609	0616	0648	0626	0646	0646	0713	0710
94	**Köln** Messe/Deutz	d.	|	|	...	0405	...	|	|	|	|	...	|	|	|	|	|	|	|	|	|	|	|	|	|	|
	Solingen Hbf	d.	|	|	...	|	...	|	0528	|	|	...	0604	|	|	|	|	|	|	|	|	|	|	|	|	0730
	Wuppertal Hbf	d.	0125	|	...	|	...	|	0541	|	|	...	0617	|	|	|	|	|	|	|	0716	|	|	|	|	0743
	Hagen Hbf	d.	0145	|	...	|	...	|	0601	|	|	...	0634	|	|	|	|	|	|	|	0734	|	|	|	|	0801
133	**Düsseldorf** Hbf	d.	0104	0234	...	0426	...	0453	|	0533	0533	0546	|	0553	0606	0610s	0610s	0612	0633	0639u	|	0653	0713	0713	0739	|
140	Düsseldorf Flughafen ✈	d.	|	0242	...	0433	...	0501	|	|	|	0553	|	0600	0613	|	|	|	|	|	|	|	|	|	|	|
157	**Duisburg** Hbf	d.	|	0254	...	0443	...	0511	|	0546	0546	0604	|	0610	0626	0626	0626	0626	0646	0651u	|	0708	0726	0728	0751	|
165	Oberhausen Hbf	d.	0236	|	...	|	...	|	|	|	|	|	|	|	0633	...	...	...	|	|	|	|	0732	|	|	|
167	Mülheim (Ruhr) Hbf	d.	0227	0302	...	0451	...	|	|	|	|	|	|	|	|	...	...	...	|	|	|	|	...	|	|	|
176	**Essen** Hbf	d.	0218	0311	...	0459	...	0523	|	0559	0559	0617	|	0623	|	...	...	...	0659	0703u	|	0723	...	0741	0802	|
	Gelsenkirchen Hbf	d.	0247	|	...	|	...	|	|	|	|	|	|	|	0645	...	...	...	|	|	|	|	...	|	...	|
	Wanne-Eickel Hbf	d.	|	|	...	|	...	|	|	|	|	|	|	|	0651	...	...	...	|	|	|	|	...	|	...	|
	Recklinghausen Hbf	d.	|	|	...	|	...	|	|	|	|	|	|	|	0659	...	...	...	|	|	|	|	...	|	...	|
192	Bochum Hbf	d.	0208	0322	...	0510	...	0534	|	0610	0610	0630	|	0635	|	...	...	...	0710	|	|	0735	...	0752	...	|
210	**Dortmund** Hbf	a.	0309	0333	...	0522	...	0545	0621	0621	0621	0640	|	0646	|	...	...	...	0721	|	|	0746	...	0802	...	0821
210	**Dortmund** Hbf **805**	d.	0311	0336	...	0525	0525	0547	0628	0625	0625	0643	|	0648	|	...	...	...	0725	|	|	0748	...	...	...	...
	Hamm (Westf) **805**	a.	0327	0353	...	|	|	0602	0643	|	|	0702	0702	0707	|	...	...	...	|	|	0802	0807	...	...	...	...
	Hamm (Westf)	d.	0330	0355	...	|	|	0604	0645	|	|	0707	0711	0711	|	...	...	...	|	|	0811	0811	...	...	...	...
	*Hannover Hbf **810***	a.	0458	|	...	|	|	0728	0818	|	|	|	0828	0828	|	...	...	...	|	|	0928	0928	...	...	...	...
	*Leipzig Hbf **866***	a.	|	|	...	|	|	|	1118	|	|	1148	|	|	|	...	...	...	|	|	|	|	...	...	...	...
	*Berlin Hbf **810***	a.	0655	|	...	|	|	0911	...	|	|	...	1010	1010	|	...	...	...	|	|	1108	1108	...	...	...	...
266	Münster (Westf) Hbf **801**	d.	...	0416	...	0557	0557	...	...	0657	0657	...	...	...	0727	...	...	...	0758	|	...	...	...	...	...	...
316	Osnabrück Hbf **801**	d.	...	0456z	...	0623	0623	...	...	0723	0723	...	...	...	...	...	...	...	0824	|	...	...	...	...	...	...
438	**Bremen** Hbf **801**	d.	...	0555	0717	0727	0727	...	...	0817	0817	...	...	...	...	...	...	...	0917	|	...	...	...	...	...	...
553	**Hamburg** Hbf **801**	a.	...	0651	0812	0833	0833	...	...	0912	0912	...	...	...	...	...	...	...	1012	0945	...	...	...	...	...	...
560	**Hamburg** Altona	a.	...	0706	0827	0846	0846	...	...	0927	...	...	...	...	...	...	...	...	...	0959	...	...	...	...	...	...

		IC 2212	IC 2443	ICE 618	ICE 855	ICE 845	IC 2333	ICE 616	IC 2220	IC 2320	ICE 1223	ICE 555	ICE 545	ICE 226	IC 2310	IC 2441	ICE 822	ICE 857	ICE 847	IC 131	ICE 818	ICE 614	ICE 1028	ICE 820	ICE 557	ICE 547
			①-⑥	⑥		◧	E			⊡							①-⑥				⑦			Ⓐ		
		🍷♦	d D	🍷	✕	✕	N 🍷	🍷	🍷♦	🍷	🍷♦	✕	✕	A 🍷	🍷♦	D 🍷	🍷	✕	✕	🍷♦	🍷	🍷	✕	🍷	✕	✕
*Basel SBB 🚢 **912***	d.	...	🍷	...	...	...	...	...	...	...	...	...	...	...	...	...	...	...	...	...	...	...	...	...	...	...
*Karlsruhe Hbf **912***	d.	...	...	0348	...	...	...	...	...	...	...	...	...	...	...	...	...	...	...	...	...	...	...	...	...	...
*München Hbf **904 930***	d.	...	...	2350p	...	...	...	0323	...	...	...	...	...	...	...	...	0446n	...	...	...	...	0527	...	0545	...	...
*Stuttgart Hbf **912***	d.	...	...	0221	...	...	...	0551	...	...	...	...	...	...	...	...	|	...	...	...	...	0751	...	|	...	...
*Nürnberg Hbf **920***	d.	...	...	|	...	...	...	|	...	...	...	...	...	...	...	...	0600	...	...	...	...	|	0530	0700	...	...
*Frankfurt (Main) Hbf **910/1***	d.	...	...	0544	...	...	...	|	0542r	0542	0702a	...	...	0727	0638	...	0810	...	...	...	0816	|	0742	0909	...	...
Frankfurt Flughafen ✈ §	d.	...	...	0601	...	...	...	0709	0557r	0557	0715a	...	...	0743	0657	...	0825	...	...	...	0832	0909	0758	0925	...	...
*Mainz Hbf **911***	d.	...	...	|	...	...	...	|	0617r	0617	|	...	...	|	0717	...	|	...	...	...	|	|	0820	|	...	...
Koblenz Hbf	d.	0605	...	|	...	...	0642j	|	0713	0713	|	...	...	|	0813	...	|	...	...	0842e	|	|	0913	|	...	...
Andernach	d.	0618	...	|	...	...	0656j	|	|	|	|	...	...	|	|	...	|	...	...	0856e	|	|	|	|	...	...
Remagen	d.	0631	...	|	...	...	0708j	|	|	|	|	...	...	|	|	...	|	...	...	0908e	|	|	|	|	...	...
Bonn Hbf	d.	0644	...	|	...	...	0722j	|	0744	0744	|	0825v	...	|	0844	...	|	...	...	0922e	|	|	0944	|	...	...
Köln/Bonn Flughafen ✈	d.	|	...	|	...	0712a	|	|	|	|	|	|	...	|	|	...	|	...	...	|	|	|	|	|	...	...
Köln Hbf	a.	0705	...	0705	...	|	0742j	0805	0805	0805	|	0845v	...	0832	0905	...	|	...	...	0942e	0939	1005	1005	|	...	...
Köln Hbf	d.	0710	0713	0715	0748	0728c	0746	0810	0810	0810	|	0848	0828	0846	0908	0910	|	0948	0928	0946	0943	1010	1010	|	1048	...
Köln Messe/Deutz	d.	|	|	|	|	0730a	|	|	|	|	0824	|	|	|	|	0914	0917	|	|	|	|	|	|	1020	|	...
Solingen Hbf	d.	|	0731	|	|	|	|	|	0829	0829	|	|	|	|	|	0931	|	|	|	|	|	|	1030	|	|	...
Wuppertal Hbf	d.	|	0743	|	0817	|	|	|	0843	0843	|	0916	|	|	|	0943	|	1016	|	|	|	|	1043	|	1116	...
Hagen Hbf	d.	|	0801	|	0834	|	|	|	0901	0901	|	0934	|	|	|	1001	|	1034	|	|	|	|	1101	|	1134	...
Düsseldorf Hbf	d.	0733	|	0741	|	0753	0812	0833	|	|	0845	|	0853	0913	0931	|	0939	|	0953	1012	1016z	1033	|	1042	|	1053
Düsseldorf Flughafen ✈	d.	|	|	|	|	0800	|	|	|	|	|	|	0900	|	|	|	|	|	1000	|	|	|	|	|	|	1100
Duisburg Hbf	d.	0746	|	0754	|	0810	0826	0846	|	|	0904z	|	0910	0926	0946	|	0952	|	1010	1026	1029	1046	|	1055	|	1110
Oberhausen Hbf	d.	|	|	|	|	|	0833	|	|	|	|	|	|	0932	|	|	|	|	|	1033	|	|	|	|	|	|
Mülheim (Ruhr) Hbf	d.	|	|	|	|	|	|	|	|	|	|	|	|	...	|	|	|	|	|	|	|	|	|	|	|	|
Essen Hbf	d.	0759	|	0817	|	0823	|	0859	|	|	0917	|	0923	...	0959	|	1004	|	1023	|	1041	1059	|	1105	|	112
Gelsenkirchen Hbf	d.	|	|	|	|	|	0845	|	|	|	|	|	|	...	|	|	|	|	|	1045	|	|	|	...	|	|
Wanne-Eickel Hbf	d.	|	|	|	|	|	0851	|	|	|	|	|	|	...	|	|	|	|	|	1051	|	|	|	...	|	|
Recklinghausen Hbf	d.	|	|	|	|	|	0859	|	|	|	|	|	|	...	|	|	|	|	|	1059	|	|	|	...	|	|
Bochum Hbf	d.	0810	|	0829	|	0835	|	0910	|	|	0930	|	0935	...	1010	|	1016k	|	1035	|	1052	1110	|	...	|	113
Dortmund Hbf	a.	0821	0821	0843	|	0846	|	0921	0921	0921	0940	|	0946	...	1021	1021	1030k	|	1046	|	1102	1121	1121	...	|	114
Dortmund Hbf **805**	d.	0825	0828	...	|	0848	|	...	0925	0925	0942	|	0948	...	1025	1028	...	|	1048	|	...	...	1125	...	|	114
Hamm (Westf) **805**	a.	|	0843	...	0902	0907	|	...	|	|	1002	1002	1007	...	|	1043	...	1102	1107	|	...	...	|	...	1202	120
Hamm (Westf)	d.	|	0845	...	0911	0911	|	...	|	|	...	1011	1011	...	|	1045	...	1111	1111	|	...	...	|	...	1211	121
*Hannover Hbf **810***	a.	|	1018	...	1028	1028	|	...	|	|	...	1128	1128	...	|	1218	...	1228	1228	|	...	...	|	...	1328	132
*Leipzig Hbf **866***	a.	|	1318	...	|	|	|	...	|	|	...	|	|	...	|	1518	...	|	|	|	...	...	|	...	|	|
*Berlin Hbf **810***	a.	|	...	...	1210	1210	|	...	|	|	...	1308	1308	...	|	...	...	1411	1411	|	...	...	|	...	1511	151
Münster (Westf) Hbf **801**	d.	0859	...	...	...	...	0927	...	0957	0957	...	...	...	...	1057	...	...	...	...	1127	...	...	1157	...	...	...
Osnabrück Hbf **801**	d.	0925	...	...	...	...	...	...	1023	1023	...	...	...	...	1123	...	...	...	...	...	...	...	1223	...	...	...
Bremen Hbf **801**	d.	1017	...	...	...	...	...	...	1117	1117	...	...	...	...	1217	...	...	...	...	...	...	...	1317	...	...	...
Hamburg Hbf **801**	a.	1112	...	...	...	...	...	...	1212	1212	...	...	...	...	1312	...	...	...	...	...	...	...	1412	...	...	...
Hamburg Altona	a.	...	...	...	...	...	...	...	...	1227	...	...	...	...	...	...	...	...	...	...	...	...	1427	...	...	...

♦ – **NOTES** (LISTED BY TRAIN NUMBER)

131 – [12] and 🍷 (Luxembourg / Trier ①-⑥ -) Köln - Münster - Emden. Runs with train number **231** on ②③④⑥ from Oct. 28.
418 – POLLUX – 🛏 1, 2 cl., ▬ 2 cl., [2] (reclining) and 🍷 München - Amsterdam.
1223 – [12] and 🍷 (Darmstadt Hbf, d. 0637 Ⓐ -) Köln - Paderborn - Kassel - München.
1745 – [12] and ✕ Düsseldorf - Paderborn - Kassel - Erfurt - Leipzig - Dresden.
2212 – RÜGEN – [12] and 🍷 Koblenz - Stralsund - Ostseebad Binz.
2220 – Daily to Oct. 19; ⑤⑦ from Oct. 24. FEHMARN – [12] and 🍷 Frankfurt - Koblenz - Köln - Hamburg - Lübeck (- Fehmarn-Burg until Oct. 19).
2310 – NORDFRIESLAND – [12] and 🍷 Frankfurt - Köln - Westerland.
2314 – Until Oct. 26. DEICHGRAF – [12] and 🍷 Köln - Westerland.
40478 – PEGASUS – 🛏 1, 2 cl., ▬ 2 cl., [2] (reclining) and 🍷 Zürich - Amsterdam.

A – To Amsterdam (Table **28**).
B – ⑤⑥ to Aug. 9 (also June 19; not June 20); ④-⑦ Aug. 15 - Oct. 23 (also Nov. 1; not Aug. 21).
D – To Dresden (Table **842**).
E – Daily to Nov. 1; ①-⑥ from Nov. 3.

K – To Kiel (Table **820**).
N – To Norddeich Mole (Table **812**).
Q – From Oct. 27.

a – Ⓐ only.
c – © only.
d – Not Oct. 4.
e – ①-⑥ only.
f – Not Oct. 3.
j – ①-⑤ (not June 19, Oct. 3).
k – ⑥ only.
n – 0443 until July 12.
p – Previous day.
r – Daily to Oct. 19; ⑤ from Oct. 24.
s – Stops to set down only.
t – ①-④ (not June 19).
u – Stops to pick up only.

v – ①-⑥ (not June 19, Oct. 3, Nov. 1).
z – Arrives 8 – 11 minutes earlier.

⊡ – ①②③④⑥ from Oct. 20.
♣ – ①②③④⑥ to Nov. 6; ①-④ from Nov. 10.
* – Train number **1541** on ⑥ (also Oct. 3; not Oct.
◧ – Train number **1045** on ©.
⚡ – *ICE SPRINTER*. R, supplement payable.
◇ – From Aachen Hbf (d. 2349, previous day). Train routing: Köln - Düsseldorf - Wuppertal - Hagen - Bochum - Essen - Oberhausen - Gelsenkirchen - Dortmund - Berlin.
§ – Frankfurt Flughafen Fernbahnhof (Tables **910** and **911**).

See page 367 for Table **800a** (HKX services)

KOBLENZ - KÖLN - DORTMUND - HAMBURG 800

	ICE 128 A🍷	IC 2010 Ⓐr T	IC 2010 ⑤f T	IC 2010 ⑦	IC 2018 ⑥ ♦	IC 2216 🍷♦	ICE 202 ①–④ d🍷	IC 2049 ⑤⑥j D🍷	IC 2249 ⑦ D🍷	ICE 728 🍷	IC 1959 ⑤f D	IC 2359 ⑦ 🍷	ICE 859 🍴	ICE 849 🍴	IC 133 🍷♦	ICE 612 🍷	IC 2226 🍷♦	ICE 726 ①–⑥ 🍷	ICE 559 🍴	ICE 549 🍴	ICE 126 P A🍷	IC 2218 🍷	ICE 200 ⑤⑦ b🍷	ICE 1200 ⑥ 🍷	IC 2047 Ⓑm D🍷
Basel SBB **912** d.	...	...	...	...	...	...	0713	...	...	...	...	...	...	...	...	...	...	...	...	...	...	...	0913‡	0913‡	...
Karlsruhe Hbf **912** d.	...	...	...	...	...	...	0900	...	...	...	...	...	...	...	...	...	...	...	...	...	...	...	1100‡	1100‡	...
München Hbf **904 930** d.	...	...	...	...	...	...	|	...	...	0647n	...	...	...	...	...	0728	...	0750n	...	...	...	...	|	|	...
Stuttgart Hbf **912** d.	...	0714	0714	...	0714	0737	|	...	...	|	...	...	...	...	...	0951	...	|	...	...	...	0937	|	|	...
Nürnberg Hbf **920** d.	...	|	|	...	|	|	|	...	...	0802	...	...	...	...	...	|	0729t	0900	...	...	...	|	|	|	...
Frankfurt (Main) Hbf **910/1** d.	0929	|	|	...	|	|	|	...	...	1010	...	...	...	...	...	|	0942	1110	...	...	1129	|	|	|	...
Frankfurt Flughafen ✈ § d.	0943	|	|	...	|	|	1009	...	...	1025	...	...	...	...	...	1109	0958	1125	...	...	1143	|	1209	1209	...
Mainz Hbf **911** d.	|	0848	0848	...	0848	0920	|	...	...	|	...	...	...	...	...	|	1020	|	...	...	|	1120	|	|	...
Koblenz Hbf d.	|	0943	0943	...	0943	1013	|	...	...	|	...	...	...	...	1042	|	1113	|	...	...	|	1213	|	|	...
Andernach d.	|	0956	0956	...	0956	|	|	...	...	|	...	...	...	...	1056	|	|	|	...	...	|	|	|	|	...
Remagen d.	|	1008	1008	...	1008	|	|	...	...	|	...	...	...	...	1108	|	|	|	...	...	|	|	|	|	...
Bonn Hbf d.	|	1022	1022	...	1022	1044	|	...	...	|	...	...	...	...	1122	|	1144	|	1222e	...	|	1244	|	|	...
Köln/Bonn Flughafen ✈ d.	|	|	|	...	|	|	|	...	...	|	...	...	...	1112a	|	|	|	|	|	...	|	|	|	|	...
Köln Hbf a.	1032	1042	1042	...	1042	1105	1105	...	...	|	...	...	...	|	1142	1205	1205	|	1242e	...	1232	1305	1305	1305	...
Köln Hbf d.	1042	1046	1046	1046	1046	1110	1110	1110	1113	|	1120	1120	1148	|	1146	1210	1210	|	1248	...	1245	1310	1314	1310	1313
Köln Messe/Deutz d.	|	|	|	|	|	|	|	1114	|	1117	|	|	|	1128a	|	|	|	1217	|	...	|	|	|	|	|
Solingen Hbf d.	|	|	|	|	|	|	1130	1131	1131	|	|	|	|	|	|	|	1230	|	|	...	|	|	|	1330	1331
Wuppertal Hbf d.	|	|	|	|	|	|	1143	1143	1143	|	|	|	1216	|	|	|	1243	|	1316	...	|	|	|	1343	1343
Hagen Hbf d.	|	|	|	|	|	|	1201	1201	1201	|	|	|	1234	|	|	|	1301	|	1334	...	|	|	|	1401	1401
Düsseldorf Hbf d.	1114	1115	1118	1118	1118	1133	|	|	|	1139	1146	1146	|	1153	1212	1233	|	1239	|	1253	1313	1333	1339	|	|
Düsseldorf Flughafen ✈ d.	|	...	|	|	|	|	|	|	|	|	1153	1153	|	1200	|	|	|	|	|	1300	|	|	|	|	|
Duisburg Hbf d.	1128	...	1133	1133	|	1146	|	|	|	1152	1204	1204	|	1210	1226	1246	|	1251	|	1310	1326	1346	1352	|	|
Oberhausen Hbf d.	1133	...	|	|	|	|	|	|	|	|	|	|	|	|	1233	|	|	|	|	|	1332	|	|	|	|
Mülheim (Ruhr) Hbf d.	...	...	|	|	|	|	|	|	|	|	|	|	|	|	|	|	|	|	|	|	...	|	|	|	|
Essen Hbf d.	...	...	1145	1145	|	1159	|	|	|	1204	1217	1217	|	1223	|	1259	|	1302	|	1323	...	1359	1402	|	|
Gelsenkirchen Hbf d.	...	...	|	|	1148	|	|	|	|	|	|	|	|	|	1245	|	|	...	|	|	...	|	...	|	|
Wanne-Eickel Hbf d.	...	...	|	|	|	|	|	|	|	|	|	|	|	|	1251	|	|	...	|	|	...	|	...	|	|
Recklinghausen Hbf d.	...	...	|	|	1159	|	|	|	|	|	|	|	|	|	1259	|	|	...	|	|	...	|	...	|	|
Bochum Hbf d.	...	...	1156	1156	|	1210	|	|	|	1216	1231	1231	|	1235	|	1310	|	...	|	1335	...	1410	...	|	|
Dortmund Hbf a.	...	...	1207	1207	|	1221	1221	1221	1221	1230	1242	1241	|	1246	|	1321	1321	...	|	1346	...	1421	...	1421	1421
Dortmund Hbf **805** d.	...	...	1211	1211	|	1225	...	1228	1228	...	1244	1244	|	1248	|	...	1325	...	|	1348	...	1425	...	...	1428
Hamm (Westf) **805** a.	...	...	1232	1232	|	|	...	1243	1243	...	|	1302	1302	1307	|	...	|	...	1402	1407	...	|	...	...	1443
Hamm (Westf) d.	...	...	1234	1234	|	|	...	1245	1245	...	|	1307	1311	1311	|	...	|	...	1411	1411	...	|	...	...	1445
Hannover Hbf **810** a.	...	...	1401	1401	|	|	...	1418	1418	...	◇	◇	1428	1428	|	...	|	...	1528	1528	...	|	...	...	1618
Leipzig Hbf **866** a.	...	...	|	|	|	|	...	1718	1718	...	1748	|	|	|	|	...	|	...	|	|	...	|	...	...	1918
Berlin Hbf **810** a.	...	...	1552	1552	|	|	...	...	...	...	...	1900	1612	1612	|	...	|	...	1711	1711	...	|	...	...	...
Münster (Westf) Hbf **801** d.	...	...	...	...	1228	1257	...	...	...	...	...	...	...	...	1327	...	1359	...	...	...	...	1459	...	...	...
Osnabrück Hbf **801** d.	...	...	...	...	...	1323	...	...	...	...	...	...	...	...	...	...	1425	...	...	...	...	1525	...	...	...
Bremen Hbf **801** d.	...	...	...	...	...	1417	...	...	...	...	...	...	...	...	...	...	1518	...	...	...	...	1617	...	...	...
Hamburg Hbf **801** a.	...	...	...	...	...	1512	...	...	...	...	...	...	...	...	...	...	1612	...	...	...	...	1712	...	...	...
Hamburg Altona a.	...	...	...	...	...	...	...	...	...	...	...	...	...	...	...	...	...	...	...	...	...	1727	...	...	...

	IC 2151 🍷	ICE 951 🍴	ICE 941 🍴	IC 2339 ⑤f N🍷	IC 2335 G N🍷	ICE 610 🍷	IC 2024 🍷♦	ICE 722 🍷	ICE 651 🍴	ICE 641 🍴	ICE 124 A🍷	IC 1920 ⑦	IC 1216 ⑤f S🍷	IC 2312 🍷	ICE 1108 ⑥ 🍷	ICE 1741 Ⓑ D🍴	ICE 720 🍷	ICE 953 Ⓑ 🍴	ICE 943 🍴	IC 2006 ⑥ 🍷♦	IC 2014 ⑤f ♦🍷	IC 2004 ⑦ 🍷♦	IC 2004 ①–④ E🍷	ICE 518 🍷	ICE 1026 🍴
Basel SBB **912** d.	...	...	...	...	...	...	...	...	...	...	...	...	...	...	1113	...	...	...	...	...	...	...	...	...	...
Karlsruhe Hbf **912** d.	...	...	...	...	...	...	...	...	...	...	...	...	...	...	1300‡	...	...	...	...	1221v	...	1221v	...	...	...
München Hbf **904 930** d.	...	...	...	...	...	0928	...	0950n	...	...	...	...	0848	...	|	...	1050n	...	...	|	...	|	...	1130	...
Stuttgart Hbf **912** d.	...	...	...	...	...	1151	...	|	...	...	...	...	1114	1137	|	...	|	...	...	|	1209	|	...	1351	...
Nürnberg Hbf **920** d.	...	...	...	...	...	|	0928	1100	...	...	...	...	|	|	|	...	1200	...	...	|	|	|	...	|	...
Frankfurt (Main) Hbf **910/1** d.	...	...	...	...	...	|	1142	1310	...	...	1329	1215	|	|	|	...	1410	...	...	|	|	|	...	|	1344
Frankfurt Flughafen ✈ § d.	...	...	...	...	...	1309	1158	1325	...	...	1343	1228	|	|	1409	...	1424	...	...	|	|	|	...	1509	1358
Mainz Hbf **911** d.	...	...	...	...	...	|	1220	|	...	...	|	1248	1248	1320	|	...	|	...	...	1341	1341	1341	...	|	1420
Koblenz Hbf d.	...	...	...	...	...	|	1313	|	...	...	|	1343	1343	1413	|	...	|	...	...	1443	1443	1443	1443	|	1513
Andernach d.	...	...	...	...	...	|	|	|	...	...	|	1356	1356	|	|	...	|	...	...	1456	1456	1456	1456	|	|
Remagen d.	...	...	...	...	...	|	|	|	...	...	|	1408	1408	|	|	...	|	...	...	1508	1508	1508	1508	|	|
Bonn Hbf d.	...	...	...	...	...	|	1344	|	1425	...	|	1422	1422	1444	|	...	|	...	...	1522	1522	1522	1522	|	1544
Köln/Bonn Flughafen ✈ d.	...	...	...	...	...	|	|	|	|	1412	|	|	|	|	|	...	|	...	...	|	|	|	|	|	|
Köln Hbf a.	...	...	...	...	...	1405	1405	|	1445	|	1432	1442	1442	1505	1505	...	|	...	...	1542	1542	1542	1542	1605	1605
Köln Hbf d.	...	1348	...	1338	1346	1410	1410	|	1448	|	1446	1445	1445	1510	1510	1510	|	1548	...	1546	1546	1546	1546	1610	1610
Köln Messe/Deutz d.	...	|	...	|	|	|	|	1417	|	1430	|	|	|	|	|	1514	1530	|	...	|	|	|	|	|	|
Solingen Hbf d.	...	|	...	|	|	|	1430	|	|	|	|	|	|	|	1530	1531	|	|	...	|	|	|	|	|	1629
Wuppertal Hbf d.	...	1417	...	|	|	|	1443	|	1516	|	|	|	|	|	1543	1544	|	1616	...	|	|	|	|	|	1643
Hagen Hbf d.	...	1434	...	|	|	|	1501	|	1534	|	|	|	|	|	1601	1601	|	1634	...	|	|	|	|	|	1701
Düsseldorf Hbf d.	1346	|	1353	1408	1413	1433	|	1440	|	1453	1514	1518	1518	1533	|	|	1551	|	1556	1611	1612	1612	1612	1633	|
Düsseldorf Flughafen ✈ d.	1353	|	1400	|	|	|	|	|	|	1500	|	|	|	|	|	|	|	|	|	|	|	|	|	|	|
Duisburg Hbf d.	1404	|	1410	1424	1428	1446	|	1453	|	1510	1529	1533	1533	1546	|	|	1605	|	1610	1624	1626	1626	1626	1646	|
Oberhausen Hbf d.	|	|	|	|	1435	|	|	|	|	|	1534	|	|	|	|	|	|	|	|	|	1633	1633	1633	|	|
Mülheim (Ruhr) Hbf d.	|	|	|	|	|	|	|	|	|	|	...	|	|	|	|	|	|	|	|	1630s	|	|	|	|	|
Essen Hbf d.	1417	|	1423	1437	|	1459	|	1503	|	1523	...	1545	1545	1559	|	|	1617	|	1623	1639	|	|	|	1659	|
Gelsenkirchen Hbf d.	|	|	|	1448	1446	|	|	...	|	|	...	|	|	|	|	|	|	|	|	|	1645	1645	1645	|	|
Wanne-Eickel Hbf d.	|	|	|	|	1452	|	|	...	|	|	...	|	|	|	|	|	|	|	|	|	1651	1651	1651	|	|
Recklinghausen Hbf d.	|	|	|	1459	1500	|	|	...	|	|	...	|	|	|	|	|	|	|	|	|	1659	1659	1659	|	|
Bochum Hbf d.	1430	|	1435	|	|	1510	|	...	|	1535	...	1556	1556	1610	|	|	1629k	|	1635	1652	|	|	|	1710	|
Dortmund Hbf a.	1441	|	1446	|	|	1521	1521	...	|	1546	...	1608	1608	1621	1621	1621	1643k	|	1646	1703	|	|	|	1721	1721
Dortmund Hbf **805** d.	1443	|	1448	|	|	...	1525	...	|	1548	...	1611	1611	1625	...	1628	...	|	1648	...	|	|	|	...	1725
Hamm (Westf) **805** a.	1502	1502	1507	|	|	...	|	...	1602	1607	...	1632	1632	|	...	1643	...	1702	1707	...	|	|	|	...	|
Hamm (Westf) d.	1507	1511	1511	|	|	...	|	...	1611	1611	...	1634	1634	|	...	1645	...	1711	1711	...	|	|	|	...	|
Hannover Hbf **810** a.	◇	1628	1628	|	|	...	|	...	1728	1728	...	1801	1801	|	...	1818	...	1828	1828	...	|	|	|	...	|
Leipzig Hbf **866** a.	1946	|	|	|	|	...	|	...	|	|	...	|	|	|	...	2118	...	|	|	...	|	|	|	...	|
Berlin Hbf **810** a.	...	1810	1810	|	|	...	|	...	1908	1908	...	1951	1951	|	...	...	...	2012	2012	...	|	|	|	...	|
Münster (Westf) Hbf **801** d.	...	...	...	1529	1528	...	1557	...	...	...	...	...	...	1657	...	...	...	...	...	...	1727	1727	1727	...	1758
Osnabrück Hbf **801** d.	...	...	...	...	...	...	1623	...	...	...	...	...	...	1723	...	...	...	...	...	...	...	...	...	...	1824
Bremen Hbf **801** d.	...	...	...	...	...	...	1717	...	...	...	...	...	...	1817	...	...	...	...							1917
Hamburg Hbf **801** a.	...	...	...	...	...	...	1812	...	...	...	...	...	...	1912	...	...	...	...							2012
Hamburg Altona a.	...	...	...	...	...	...	1827	...	...	...	...	...	...	1927	...	...	...	...							2027

*See Table **802** for Rhein-Ruhr local RE and S-Bahn services*

♦ – **NOTES** (LISTED BY TRAIN NUMBER)

133 – 🚃12 and 🍷 Luxembourg / Trier - Koblenz - Emden - Norddeich Mole.
2004 – ⑦ (also Oct. 3). BODENSEE – 🚃12 and 🍷 Konstanz - Karlsruhe - Mannheim - Koblenz - Emden.
2006 – ⑥ (also June 19). BODENSEE – 🚃12 and 🍷 Konstanz - Karlsruhe - Mannheim - Dortmund.
2014 – 🚃12 and 🍷 Stuttgart - Mannheim - Emden.
2018 – ⑥ to Oct. 18 (also June 19). NORDERNEY – 🚃12 Stuttgart - Mannheim - Emden - Norddeich Mole.
2024 – 🚃12 and 🍷 Passau - Regensburg - Köln - Hamburg.
2216 – 🚃12 and 🍷 Stuttgart - Köln - Hamburg - Stralsund (- Greifswald Ⓐ).
2226 – 🚃12 and 🍷 (Passau ⑥ **z** -) (Regensburg ②–⑥ **c** -) (Nürnberg ①–⑥ **t** -) Frankfurt - Köln - Kiel.

A – To Amsterdam (Table **28**).
D – To Dresden (Table **842**).
E – ①–④ (also June 20; not June 18, 19, Oct. 2). To Emden (Table **812**).
G – ①②③④⑥⑦ (also June 20, Oct. 3; not June 18, Oct. 2).
N – To Norddeich Mole (Table **812**).
P – Daily until Nov. 2; ⑤ from Nov. 7.
S – From Salzburg (Table **890**).

T – From Tübingen Hbf (d. 0611).

a – Ⓐ only.
b – Also Oct. 2; not Oct. 3.
c – Not June 21, Aug. 16, Oct. 4.
d – Not Oct. 2.
e – ①–⑥ only.
f – Also June 18, Oct. 2; not June 20, Oct. 3.
j – Also Oct. 2.
k – ⑥ only.
m – Not Oct. 3.
n – 3–7 minutes **earlier** until July 12.
r – Not June 19, 20.
s – Stops to set down only.
t – ①–⑥ (not Oct. 4).
v – 1219 Aug. 2 - Sept. 14.
z – Also June 19, Aug. 15, Oct. 3; not June 21, Aug. 16, Oct. 4.

◇ – Via Paderborn / Kassel / Erfurt (Tables **805** and **850**).
‡ – 8–11 minutes **earlier** July 31 - Sept. 14.
§ – Frankfurt Flughafen Fernbahnhof (Tables **910** and **911**).

800 KOBLENZ - KÖLN - DORTMUND - HAMBURG

	ICE 628	ICE 653	ICE 643	IC 2012	EC 8	ICE 106	ICE 626	ICE 1226	ICE 122	ICE 955	ICE 945	IC 137	IC 137	ICE 516	IC 2022	ICE 624	ICE 655	ICE 645	IC 118	EC 6	EC 6	IC 2041	ICE 606	ICE 104	ICE 622
							Ⓐ	⑥			Ⓑ	Ⓑ									Ⓑ	⑦	①–⑥		Ⓑ
	🍸	✕	✕	✕♦	✕♦	🍸	🍸	🍸	A🍸	✕	✕	🍸♦	🍸♦	🍸	✕	🍸	✕	✕	♦	✕♦	✕♦	🍸	✕	A🍸	🍸
Basel SBB 🏛 **912** d.	...	...	...	...	1220‡	1313	...	...	...	...	...	...	...	...	...	...	...	...	...	1420‡	1420‡	...	...	1513	...
Karlsruhe Hbf **912** d.	...	...	...	...	1412‡	1500‡	...	...	...	...	...	...	...	...	...	...	...	...	...	1612‡	1612‡	...	...	1700	...
München Hbf **904 930** d.	1148n	...	...	...	│	│	1250n	1250n	...	...	...	...	...	1328	...	1350n	...	...	...	│	│	...	...	│	1450n
Stuttgart Hbf **912** d.	│	...	...	1314	│	│	│	│	...	...	...	...	...	1551	...	│	...	...	1512	│	│	...	...	│	│
Nürnberg Hbf **920** d.	1300	...	...	│	│	│	1400	1400	...	...	...	...	...	│	...	1500	...	...	│	│	│	...	...	│	1600
Frankfurt (Main) Hbf **910/1** d.	1510	...	...	│	│	│	1610	1610	1629	...	...	...	...	│	1544	1710	...	...	│	│	│	...	...	│	1810
Frankfurt Flughafen ✈ § d.	1525	...	...	│	│	1609	1623	1624	1643	...	...	...	...	1709	1558	1725	...	...	│	│	│	...	...	1809	1825
Mainz Hbf **911** d.	│	...	...	1448	1520	│	│	│	│	...	...	...	...	│	1620	│	...	...	1648	1720	1720	...	...	│	│
Koblenz Hbf d.	│	...	...	1543	1613	│	│	│	│	...	...	1642	...	│	1713	│	...	...	1743	1813	1813	...	...	│	│
Andernach d.	│	...	...	1556	│	│	│	│	│	...	...	1656	...	│	│	│	...	...	1756	│	│	...	...	│	│
Remagen d.	│	...	...	1608	│	│	│	│	│	...	...	1708	...	│	│	│	...	...	1808	│	│	...	...	│	│
Bonn Hbf d.	│	...	...	1622	1644	│	│	│	│	...	...	1722	...	│	1744	│	...	...	1822	1844b	1844b	...	...	│	│
Köln/Bonn Flughafen ✈ d.	│	...	1612a	│	│	│	│	│	│	...	...	│	...	│	│	│	...	1812	│	│	│	...	...	│	│
Köln Hbf a.	│	...	│	1642	1705	1705	│	│	1739b	...	...	1742	...	1805	1805	│	...	│	1842	1905b	1905b	...	...	1905	│
Köln Hbf d.	│	1648	│	1646	1710	1710	│	│	1746b	1748	...	1745	1745	1810	1810	│	1848	│	1845	1910b	1910b	1913	1913	1917	│
Köln Messe/Deutz d.	1617	│	1630a	│	│	│	1717	1730	│	│	...	│	│	│	│	1816	│	1827	│	│	│	│	│	│	1923
Solingen Hbf d.	│	│	│	│	│	1730	│	│	│	│	...	│	│	│	1830	│	│	│	│	│	│	1931	1931	│	│
Wuppertal Hbf d.	│	1716	│	│	│	1743	│	│	│	1816	...	│	│	│	1843	│	1916	│	│	│	│	1943	1944	│	│
Hagen Hbf d.	│	1734	│	│	│	1801	│	│	│	1834	...	│	│	│	1901	│	1934	│	│	│	│	2001	2002	│	│
Düsseldorf Hbf d.	1642	│	1653	1715	1733	│	1739	1753	1814	│	1753	1817z	1817z	1833	│	1837	│	1853	1911	1933	1933	│	│	1940	1946
Düsseldorf Flughafen ✈ d.	│	│	1700	│	│	│	│	1800	│	│	1800	│	│	│	│	│	│	1900	│	│	│	│	│	│	│
Duisburg Hbf d.	1655	│	1710	1729j	1746	│	1752	1810	1826	│	1810	1830	1830	1846	│	1850	│	1910	1924	1946	1946	│	│	1953	2004
Oberhausen Hbf d.	│	│	│	│	│	│	│	│	1832	│	│	1837	1837	│	│	│	│	│	│	│	│	│	│	1958	│
Mülheim (Ruhr) Hbf d.	│	│	│	1736r	│	│	│	│	...	│	│	│	│	│	│	│	│	│	│	│	│	│	│	...	│
Essen Hbf d.	1707	│	1723	1745	1759	│	1802	1823	...	│	1823	│	│	1859	│	1903	│	1923	1936	1959	1959	│	│	...	2017
Gelsenkirchen Hbf d.	...	│	│	│	│	│	...	│	...	│	│	1849	1849	│	│	│	│	│	1946	│	│	│	│	...	│
Wanne-Eickel Hbf d.	...	│	│	│	│	│	...	│	...	│	│	│	│	│	│	│	│	│	1952	│	│	│	│	...	│
Recklinghausen Hbf d.	...	│	│	│	│	│	...	│	...	│	│	1900	1900	│	│	│	│	│	2000	│	│	│	│	...	│
Bochum Hbf d.	...	│	1735	1757	1810	│	...	1835	...	│	1835	│	│	1910	│	1916	│	1935	│	2010	2010	│	│	...	2029
Dortmund Hbf a.	...	│	1746	1808	1821	1821	...	1846	...	│	1846	│	│	1921	1921	1930	│	1946	│	2021	2021	2021	2021	...	2040
Dortmund Hbf **805** d.	...	│	1748	1828	1825	...	...	1848	...	│	1848	│	│	...	1925	...	│	1948	│	...	2025	2028	...	...	...
Hamm (Westf) **805** a.	...	1802	1807	1843	│	...	...	1906	...	1902	1907	│	│	...	│	...	2002	2007	│	...	│	2043	...	...	...
Hamm (Westf) d.	...	1811	1811	1845	│	...	...	...	...	1911	1911	│	│	...	│	...	2011	2011	│	...	│	2045	...	...	...
Hannover Hbf **810** a.	...	1928	1928	2018	│	...	...	...	...	2028	2028	│	│	...	│	...	2128	2128	│	...	│	2218	...	...	...
Leipzig Hbf **866** a.	...	│	│	2320w	│	...	...	...	...	│	│	│	│	...	│	...	│	│	│	...	│	...	...	...	...
Berlin Hbf **810** a.	...	2108	2108	...	│	...	...	...	...	2222	2222	│	│	...	│	...	2308	2308	│	...	│	...	...	...	...
Münster (Westf) Hbf **801** d.	...	...	...	...	1859	...	...	...	...	...	...	1928	1928	...	1957	...	...	...	2029	...	2057	...	...	...	...
Osnabrück Hbf **801** d.	...	...	...	...	1925	...	...	...	...	...	...	...	...	...	2023	...	...	...	...	...	2123	...	...	...	...
Bremen Hbf **801** d.	...	...	...	...	2018	...	...	...	...	...	...	...	...	...	2117	...	...	...	...	...	2218	...	...	...	...
Hamburg Hbf **801** a.	...	...	...	...	2112	...	...	...	...	...	...	...	...	...	2212	...	...	...	...	...	2314	...	...	...	...
Hamburg Altona a.	...	...	...	...	2127e	...	...	...	...	...	...	...	...	...	2227	...	...	...	...	...	2329	...	...	...	...

	ICE 957	ICE 947	EC 114	ICE 26	ICE 514	ICE 1220	ICE 620	ICE 120	ICE 657	IC 2318	IC 2318	ICE 1102	ICE 102	ICE 102	ICE 528	ICE 1522	ICE 512	ICE 526	CNL 457	IC 1910	IC 2210	ICE 100	ICE 524	ICE 22	ICE 522
	⑤⑦					Ⓒ	Ⓐ	⊡	⑦		Ⓑq	⑥	Ⓑ	①–⑤				Ⓑ	Ⓡ	⑦	Ⓑq				c
	y✕	p✕	🍸♦	H✕	🍸	G🍸	🍸	A🍸	✕	🍸	🍸	🍸	🍸	🍸	🍸	✕	🍸	🍸	🍸♦	🍸	🍸	🍸	🍸	H✕	🍸
Basel SBB 🏛 **912** d.	...	...	...	...	...	...	...	...	...	...	...	1713	1713	1713	...	...	...	...	...	...	...	1913‡	...	...	...
Karlsruhe Hbf **912** d.	...	...	...	...	...	...	...	...	...	...	...	1900‡	1900‡	1900‡	...	...	...	...	...	...	...	2101‡	...	...	...
München Hbf **904 930** d.	...	...	1346	...	1528	1550n	1550n	...	...	...	...	│	│	│	1647n	1616n	1727	1748	...	1620	...	│	1850n	...	1948n
Stuttgart Hbf **912** d.	...	...	1609	...	1751	│	│	...	...	1741	1741	│	│	│	│	│	1951	│	...	1914	1918t	│	│	...	│
Nürnberg Hbf **920** d.	...	...	│	1528	│	1700	1700	...	...	│	│	│	│	│	1800	1734	│	1900	...	│	│	│	2000	1928	2102
Frankfurt (Main) Hbf **910/1** d.	...	...	│	1742	│	1910	1910	1929	...	│	│	│	│	│	2010	1944	│	2110	...	│	│	│	2210	2146	2310
Frankfurt Flughafen ✈ § d.	...	...	│	1758	1909	1925	1923	1943	...	│	│	2009	2009	2009	2025	1958	2109	2125	...	│	│	2209	2225	2159	2329
Mainz Hbf **911** d.	...	...	1746	1820	│	│	│	│	...	1920	1920	│	│	│	│	2020	│	│	...	2048	2120	│	│	2220	│
Koblenz Hbf d.	...	...	1843	1913	│	│	│	│	...	2013	2013	│	│	│	│	2113	│	│	...	2143	2213	│	│	2313	│
Andernach d.	...	...	1856	│	│	│	│	│	...	│	│	│	│	│	│	│	│	│	...	2156	│	│	│	│	│
Remagen d.	...	...	1908	│	│	│	│	│	...	│	│	│	│	│	│	│	│	│	...	2208	│	│	│	│	│
Bonn Hbf d.	...	...	1922	1944	│	│	│	│	2025	2044	2044	│	│	│	│	2144	│	│	...	2222	2244	│	│	2344	│
Köln/Bonn Flughafen ✈ d.	...	...	│	│	│	│	│	│	│	│	│	│	│	│	│	│	│	│	...	│	│	│	2328	│	│
Köln Hbf a.	...	...	1942	2005	2005	│	│	2039	2045	2105	2105	2105	2105	2105	│	2205	2205	│	...	2242	2305	2305	│	0005	0034
Köln Hbf d.	1948	1926r	1946	2010	2010	│	│	2046	2048	...	2110	2110	2110	2110	│	2210	2210	│	2228	2245	...	2310	│	0010	0039
Köln Messe/Deutz d.	│	│	│	│	│	2017	2029	│	│	...	│	│	│	│	2117	│	│	2217	│	│	...	│	2339	│	│
Solingen Hbf d.	│	│	│	2030	│	│	│	│	│	...	│	│	2129	2129	│	2229	│	│	│	│	...	│	│	│	│
Wuppertal Hbf d.	2016	│	│	2043	│	│	│	│	2116	...	│	│	2143	2143	│	2243	│	│	2314	│	...	│	│	│	│
Hagen Hbf d.	2034	│	│	2101	│	│	│	│	2134	...	│	│	2201	2201	│	2301	│	│	│	│	...	│	│	│	│
Düsseldorf Hbf d.	│	1953	2010	│	2033	2040	2051	2113	│	...	2133	2133	│	│	2139	│	2233	2239	2202*	2309	...	2333	0001	0034	0102
Düsseldorf Flughafen ✈ d.	│	2000	│	│	│	│	│	│	│	...	│	│	│	│	│	│	│	│	│	│	...	2340	│	│	0110
Duisburg Hbf d.	│	2010	2024	│	2046	2052	2104	2126	│	...	2146	2146	│	│	2152	│	2247	2252	2146*	2322	...	2350	0014	0047	0120
Oberhausen Hbf d.	│	│	│	│	│	│	│	2132	│	...	│	│	│	│	│	│	│	│	│	│	...	│	│	│	│
Mülheim (Ruhr) Hbf d.	│	│	2029s	│	│	│	│	...	│	...	│	│	│	│	│	│	│	│	│	2329	...	│	│	│	│
Essen Hbf d.	│	2023	2039	│	2059	2104	2118	...	│	...	2159	2159	│	│	2204	│	2307z	2304	│	2338	...	0003	0027	0059	0132
Gelsenkirchen Hbf d.	│	│	│	│	│	│	│	...	│	...	│	│	│	│	│	│	│	│	│	│	...	│	│	│	│
Wanne-Eickel Hbf d.	│	│	│	│	│	│	│	...	│	...	│	│	│	│	│	│	│	│	│	│	...	│	│	│	│
Recklinghausen Hbf d.	│	│	│	│	│	│	│	...	│	...	│	│	│	│	│	│	2327	│	│	│	...	│	│	│	│
Bochum Hbf d.	│	2035	2049	│	2110	2116	2130	...	│	...	2210	2210	│	│	2216	│	│	2314	│	2348	...	0013	0037	0111	0142
Dortmund Hbf a.	│	2046	2100	2120	2121	2130	2141	...	│	...	2221	2221	2221	2221	2230	2321	│	2325	│	2359	...	0024	0048	0121	0153
Dortmund Hbf **805** d.	│	2048	...	2125	...	2132w	...	...	│	...	2225w	2228	...	2228	...	...	│	...	2356	...	...	...	...	...	...
Hamm (Westf) **805** a.	2102	2107	...	│	...	2147w	...	...	2202	...	│	2248	...	2248	...	...	│	...	│	...	...	...	...	...	...
Hamm (Westf) d.	2111	2111	...	│	...	2149w	...	...	2211	...	│	2250	...	2250	...	...	│	...	0014	...	...	...	...	...	...
Hannover Hbf **810** a.	2228	2228	...	│	...	2317w	...	...	2328	...	│	0018	...	0018	...	...	│	...	│	...	...	...	...	...	...
Leipzig Hbf **866** a.	│	│	...	│	...	...	...	...	│	...	│	...	...	...	...	...	│	...	│	...	...	...	...	...	...
Berlin Hbf **810** a.	0010	0010	...	│	...	...	...	...	0111	...	│	...	...	...	...	...	│	...	0423	...	...	...	...	...	...
Münster (Westf) Hbf **801** d.	...	...	...	2200	...	...	...	...	...	...	2254w	...	...	...	...	...	2356	...	...	...	...	...	...	...	...
Osnabrück Hbf **801** d.	...	...	...	2227	...	...	...	...	...	...	...	...	...	...	...	...	...	...	...	...	...	...	...	...	...
Bremen Hbf **801** d.	...	...	...	2321	...	...						...	...	...	...	...	...	...	...	...	...	...	...	...	...
Hamburg Hbf **801** a.	...	...	...	0015	...	...						...	...	...	...	...	...	...	...	...	...	...	...	...	...
Hamburg Altona a.	...	...	...	...	...	...						...	...	...	...	...	...	...	...	...	...	...	...	...	...

See Table ***802*** *for Rhein - Ruhr local RE and S-Bahn services*

♦ – **NOTES** (LISTED BY TRAIN NUMBER)

6 – (12) and ✕ Zürich - Basel - Dortmund (- Hamburg Ⓑ).
8 – (12) and ✕ Zürich - Basel - Hamburg (- Kiel ⑦). Train number **2** on ⑦.
114 – WÖRTHERSEE – (12) and 🍸 Klagenfurt - Villach - Salzburg - Dortmund.
118 – (12) Salzburg - Innsbruck - Bregenz - Lindau - Ulm - Münster.
137 – (12) (Luxembourg / Trier ⑦ -) (Koblenz Ⓑ -) Köln - Münster (- Emden ♥).
457 – KOPERNIKUS – 🛏 1, 2 cl., ▬ 2 cl. and (2) Amsterdam - Köln - Dresden - Praha (Table **28**); 🛏 1, 2 cl., ▬ 2 cl. and (2) (*CNL* **40457** – BOREALIS) Amsterdam - Köln - København (Table **50**); 🛏 1, 2 cl., ▬ 2 cl. and (2) (*EN* **447** – JAN KIEPURA) Amsterdam - Berlin - Warszawa (Table **24**). For overnight journeys only.
2012 – ALLGÄU – (12) and ✕ Oberstdorf - Stuttgart - Köln - Hannover (- Magdeburg ⊖ -) (- Leipzig ⑦).

A – To Amsterdam (Table **28**).
G – From Garmisch (Table **895**) on ⑥.
H – From Wien (Tables **950**/**920**).

a – ①–⑤ only.
b – Not June 14 - July 11.
c – Not June 19.
e – ①–⑥ only.
j – 1733 on ⑤⑦ (also Oct. 2; not Oct. 3).
n – Departs up to 6 minutes **earlier** until July 12.
p – Not Oct. 2.
q – Not Oct. 3.
r – ①②③④⑥ (also Oct. 3; not Oct. 2).
s – Stops to set down only.
t – 1937 on ⑤⑦ (also June 19).
w – ⑦ only.
y – Also Oct. 2; not Oct. 3.
z – Arrives 9 minutes earlier.

⊖ – ①④⑤⑦ (also Oct. 1; not Oct. 3).
⊡ – ④⑤⑦ only.
♥ – Daily to Oct. 24; Ⓑ from Oct. 26.
* – Calls before Köln.
‡ – 3–11 minutes **earlier** July 31 - Sept. 14.
§ – Frankfurt Flughafen Fernbahnhof (Tables **910** and **911**).

HAMBURG - DORTMUND - KÖLN - KOBLENZ 800

km		*ICE* 523 Ⓐ 🍷	*ICE* 1123 ⑥ 🍷	*ICE* 948 ①	*ICE* 511 ① 🍷	*ICE* 23 ✗♦	*CNL* 456 🅁 🍷♦	*ICE* 925 Ⓒ 🍷	*ICE* 525 Ⓐ 🍷	*ICE* 101 🍷	*IC* 2319 ⚒ 🍷	*IC* 2338 ①–⑤ d	*ICE* 813 ①–⑤ d🍷	*ICE* 527 ①–⑥ G🍷	*ICE* 1521 ✗	*ICE* 513 Ⓐ 🍷	*ICE* 1013 🍷	*ICE* 815 ①–⑤ d🍷	*EC* 115 🍷♦	*ICE* 529 🍷	*ICE* 103 🍷	*EC* 7 Z✗	*IC* 119 ♦	*ICE* 646 Ⓐ ✗	*ICE* 656 Ⓐ ✗
	Hamburg Altona d.	...	...	...	...	...	...	...	...	...	...	...	...	...	...	...	...	...	...	...	...	0428e	...	...	...
	Hamburg Hbf 801 d.	...	...	...	...	...	...	...	...	...	...	...	...	...	...	...	...	...	...	...	...	0442e	...	...	...
	Bremen Hbf 801 d.	...	...	...	...	...	...	...	...	...	...	...	...	...	...	...	...	...	...	...	...	0540e	...	...	...
	Osnabrück Hbf 801 d.	...	...	...	...	...	...	...	...	...	...	...	...	...	...	...	...	...	...	...	...	0637e	...	...	...
	Münster (Westf) Hbf 801 d.	...	...	...	...	...	...	...	...	...	0503g	...	...	...	...	...	0601	...	0631	...	...	0703e	0727	...	...
	Berlin Hbf **810** d.	...	...	0037	...	...	0027	...	...	...	|	...	...	...	...	...	|	...	|	...	...	|	|	0422	0422
	Leipzig Hbf **866** d.	...	...	|	...	...	|	...	...	...	|	...	...	...	...	...	|	...	|	...	...	|	|	|	|
	Hannover Hbf **810** d.	...	...	0232	...	...	|	...	...	...	|	...	...	...	...	...	|	...	|	...	0540	|	|	0621	0621
	Hamm (Westf) a.	...	...	0402	...	...	0425	...	...	...	|	...	...	...	...	...	|	...	|	...	0713	|	|	0748	0748
0	Hamm (Westf) 805 d.	...	...	0404	...	...	|	...	...	...	|	...	...	...	...	0606	|	...	|	...	0715	|	|	0752	0754
	Dortmund Hbf 805 a.	...	...	0420	...	...	0447	...	...	...	0533g	...	...	...	...	0624	0633	...	|	...	0732	0733e	|	0809	|
	Dortmund Hbf d.	0406	0423	0422	0437	0437	|	0502	0524	0537	0537	0552	0600	0624	0636	0638	0638	0652	|	0724	0737	0737	|	0812	|
	Bochum Hbf d.	0417	0434	0434	|	0448	|	0513	0538	|	0549	0603	|	0638	|	0649	0649	0704	|	0738	|	0749	|	0824	|
	Recklinghausen Hbf d.	|	|	|	|	|	|	|	|	|	|	|	|	|	|	|	|	|	0700	|	|	|	0758	|	|
	Wanne-Eickel Hbf d.	|	|	|	|	|	|	|	|	|	|	|	|	|	|	|	|	|	0709	|	|	|	0806	|	|
	Gelsenkirchen Hbf d.	|	|	|	|	|	|	|	|	|	|	|	|	|	|	|	|	|	0715	|	|	|	0812	|	|
	Essen Hbf d.	0428	0445	0444	|	0459	|	0526	0553	|	0600	0614	|	0653	|	0700	0700	0715	|	0753	|	0800	0823	0836	|
	Mülheim (Ruhr) Hbf d.	|	|	|	|	|	|	|	|	|	|	0622	|	|	|	|	|	|	|	|	|	|	0831	|	|
	Oberhausen Hbf d.	|	|	|	|	|	|	|	|	|	|	|	|	|	|	|	|	|	0727	|	|	|	|	|	|
	Duisburg Hbf d.	0440	0458	0456	|	0512	0710*	0538	0608	|	0612	0633	|	0708	|	0712	0712	0728	0734	0808	|	0812	0838	0849	|
	Düsseldorf Flughafen ✈ d.	|	|	0507	|	|	|	|	|	|	|	|	|	|	|	|	|	|	|	|	|	|	|	0859	|
	Düsseldorf Hbf d.	0455	0513	0518	|	0527	0654*	0553	0621	|	0627	0652	|	0721	|	0727	0727	0747	0751	0821	|	0827	0852	0908	|
48	**Hagen** Hbf d.	|	|	|	0457	|	|	|	|	0557	|	|	0622	|	0657	|	|	|	|	|	0757	|	|	|	0824
75	Wuppertal Hbf d.	|	|	|	0514	|	0538	|	|	0614	|	|	0638	|	0714	|	|	|	|	|	0814	|	|	|	0841
93	Solingen Hbf d.	|	|	|	0527	|	|	|	|	0627	|	|	0651	|	0727	|	|	|	|	|	0827	|	|	|	|
120	**Köln** Messe/Deutz a.	0515	0533	|	|	|	|	0615	0642	|	|	|	|	0742	|	|	|	0808	|	0842	|	|	|	0928	|
121	**Köln** Hbf a.	|	|	0540	0545	0550	0614	|	|	0646	0650	0715	0709	|	0746	0749	0749	|	0815	|	0846	0850	0915	|	0909
	Köln Hbf d.	|	|	0543	0555	0553	...	|	|	0655	0653	0718	0720	|	0753	0755	0755	|	0818	|	0855	0853	0918	|	...
	Köln/Bonn Flughafen ✈ a.	0529	0545	0603	|	|	...	0629	|	|	|	|	|	|	|	|	|	0819	|	|	|	|	|	0942	...
	Bonn Hbf d.	|	|	...	|	0614	...	|	|	|	0714	0737	|	|	0814	|	|	|	0837	|	|	0914	0937	...	...
	Remagen d.	|	|	...	|	|	...	|	|	|	|	0751	|	|	|	|	|	|	0851	|	|	|	0951	...	...
	Andernach d.	|	|	...	|	|	...	|	|	|	|	0803	|	|	|	|	|	|	0903	|	|	|	1003	...	...
	Koblenz Hbf a.	|	|	...	|	0646	...	|	|	|	0746	0816	|	|	0846	|	|	|	0916	|	|	0946	1016	...	...
	Mainz Hbf **911** a.	|	|	...	|	0737	...	|	|	|	0837	...	|	|	0937	|	|	|	1015	|	|	1037	1111	...	...
	Frankfurt Flughafen ✈ § a.	0634	0634	...	0650	0759	...	0734	0734	0750	|	...	0826	0834	0959	0850	0850	0926	|	0934	0950	|	|	...	...
	Frankfurt (Main) Hbf **910/1** a.	0648	0648	...	|	0813	...	0748	0748	|	|	...	0841	0848	1013	|	|	0941	|	0948	|	|	|	...	...
	Nürnberg Hbf **920** a.	0859	0859	...	|	1027	...	0959	0959	|	|	...	...	1059	1224	|	|	...	|	1159	|	|	|	...	...
	Stuttgart Hbf **912** a.	|	|	...	0808	...	...	|	|	|	1018	...	...	|	|	1008	1008	...	1153	|	|	|	1246	...	...
	München Hbf **904 930** a.	1016	1016	...	1027	...	...	1115	1115	|	...	...	...	1216t	1350v	1227	1227	...	1411	1321	|	|	...	...	...
	Karlsruhe Hbf **912** a.	...	...	...	...	...	...	...	...	0858‡	...	...	...	...	...	...	...	...	...	...	1058	1147‡	...	...	...
	Basel SBB 🏛 **912** a.	...	...	...	...	...	...	...	...	1047‡	...	...	...	...	...	...	...	...	...	...	1247	1335z	...	...	...

	ICE 621 ①–⑥ 🍷	*ICE* 1121 ⑦ 🍷	*ICE* 1094 ♥🅁 ✗	*ICE* 121 ①–⑥ A🍷	*ICE* 515 🍷	*ICE* 27 ✗♦	*IC* 2005 ①–⑥ E🍷	*IC* 2005 ⑤⑥ B🍷	*ICE* 923 ⑦ 🍷	*ICE* 946 ①–⑥ ✗	*ICE* 956 ①–⑥ ✗	*ICE* 105 A🍷	*EC* 9 Z✗	*IC* 2013 ✗♦	*ICE* 644 ①–⑥ ✗	*ICE* 654 ✗	*ICE* 625 ⑦ 🍷	*ICE* 625 ⑧d 🍷	*ICE* 825 ⑥c 🍷	*IC* 2023 ✗	*ICE* 517 🍷	*ICE* 927 ⑦ 🍷	*IC* 1936 L🍷	*ICE* 944 ✗	*ICE* 954 ①–⑥ ✗
Hamburg Altona d.	...	...	0558	...	0511	...	...	...	...	...	...	...	0630k	...	...	...	...	...	...	0732	...	...	...	...	...
Hamburg Hbf 801 d.	...	...	0612	...	0525	...	...	...	...	...	...	...	0646	...	...	...	...	...	...	0746	...	...	...	...	...
Bremen Hbf 801 d.	...	...	|	...	0633	...	...	...	...	...	...	...	0744	...	...	...	...	...	...	0844	...	...	...	...	...
Osnabrück Hbf 801 d.	...	...	|	...	0733	...	...	...	...	...	...	...	0837	...	...	...	...	...	...	0937	...	...	...	...	...
Münster (Westf) Hbf 801 d.	...	...	|	...	0801	...	0832	0832	...	...	...	...	0903	...	...	...	...	...	0946j	1003	...	...	1032	...	...
Berlin Hbf **810** d.	...	...	|	...	|	...	|	|	...	0536	0536	...	|	...	0647	0647	...	...	|	|	...	...	|	0746	0746
Leipzig Hbf **866** d.	...	...	|	...	|	...	|	|	...	|	|	...	|	0436g	|	|	...	...	|	|	...	...	|	|	|
Hannover Hbf **810** d.	...	...	|	...	|	...	|	|	...	0731	0731	...	|	0740	0831	0831	...	...	|	|	...	...	|	0931	0931
Hamm (Westf) a.	...	...	|	...	|	...	|	|	...	0848	0848	...	|	0912	0948	0948	...	...	|	|	...	...	|	1048	1048
Hamm (Westf) 805 d.	...	...	|	...	|	...	|	|	...	0852	0854	...	|	0914	0952	0954	1002	...	|	|	...	...	|	1052	1054
Dortmund Hbf 805 a.	...	...	|	...	0833	...	|	|	...	0909	|	...	0933	0932	1009	|	1020	...	|	1033	...	...	|	1109	|
Dortmund Hbf d.	0816r	0824	|	...	0837	0837	|	|	0912	0912	|	...	0937	0952	1012	|	1024	...	|	1036	1037	1103	|	1112	|
Bochum Hbf d.	0829r	0838	|	...	|	0848	|	|	0924	0924	|	...	0949	1003	1024	|	1038	...	|	|	1049	|	|	1124	|
Recklinghausen Hbf d.	|	|	|	...	|	|	0901	0901	|	|	|	...	|	|	|	|	|	...	1025	|	|	|	1101	|	|
Wanne-Eickel Hbf d.	|	|	|	...	|	|	0909	0909	|	|	|	...	|	|	|	|	|	...	|	|	|	|	1109	|	|
Gelsenkirchen Hbf d.	|	|	|	...	|	|	0915	0915	|	|	|	...	|	|	|	|	|	...	1036	|	|	|	1115	|	|
Essen Hbf d.	0840	0853	0853s	...	|	0859	|	|	0936	0936	|	...	1000	1014	1036	|	1053	1053	1053	|	1100	|	|	1136	|
Mülheim (Ruhr) Hbf d.	|	|	|	...	|	|	|	|	|	|	|	...	|	1022	|	|	|	|	|	|	|	|	|	|	|
Oberhausen Hbf d.	|	|	|	0900	|	|	0927	0927	|	|	|	1000	|	|	|	|	|	|	|	|	|	|	1127	|	|
Duisburg Hbf d.	0856	0908	|	0908	|	0913	0934	0934	0949	0949	|	1008	1012	1030	1049	|	1108	1108	1108	|	1112	|	1134	1149	|
Düsseldorf Flughafen ✈ d.	|	|	|	|	|	|	|	|	|	0959	|	|	|	1040	1059	|	|	|	|	|	|	|	|	1159	|
Düsseldorf Hbf d.	0913	0921	0916s	0923	|	0927	0949	0949	1008	1006	|	1022	1027	1050	1106	|	1121	1121	1121	|	1127	|	1149	1206	|
Hagen Hbf d.	|	|	|	|	0857	|	|	|	|	...	0924	|	|	|	...	1024	|	|	|	1057	|	1124	|	...	1124
Wuppertal Hbf d.	|	|	|	|	0914	|	|	|	|	...	0941	|	|	|	...	1041	|	|	|	1114	|	1141	|	...	1141
Solingen Hbf d.	|	|	|	|	0927	|	|	|	|	...	|	|	|	|	...	|	|	|	|	1127	|	|	|	...	|
Köln Messe/Deutz a.	0934	0942	|	0943	|	|	|	|	1028	...	|	|	|	|	...	|	1142	1142	1142	|	|	|	|	...	|
Köln Hbf a.	|	|	0941	|	0946	0950	1015	1015	|	...	1009	1045	1050	1115	...	1109	|	|	|	1146	1149	1209	1212	...	1209
Köln Hbf d.	|	|	...	|	0955	0953	1018	1018	|	...	...	1055	1053	1118	...	1112e	|	|	|	1153	1155	1215	...	...	...
Köln/Bonn Flughafen ✈ a.	|	|	...	|	|	|	|	|	|	...	...	|	|	|	...	|	|	|	|	|	|	1229	...	...	...
Bonn Hbf d.	|	|	...	|	|	1014	1037	1037	|	...	...	|	1114	1137	...	1132e	|	|	|	1214	|	|	...	...	...
Remagen d.	|	|	...	|	|	|	1051	1051	|	...	...	|	|	1151	...	...	|	|	|	|	|	|	...	...	...
Andernach d.	|	|	...	|	|	|	1103	1103	|	...	...	|	|	1203	...	...	|	|	|	|	|	|	...	...	...
Koblenz Hbf a.	|	|	...	|	|	1046	1116	1116	|	...	...	|	1146	1216	...	...	|	|	|	1246	|	|	...	...	...
Mainz Hbf **911** a.	|	|	...	|	|	1137	...	1215	|	...	...	|	1237	1311	...	...	|	|	|	1337	|	|	...	...	...
Frankfurt Flughafen ✈ § a.	1026	1034	...	1034	1050	1159	...	|	1134	...	...	1150	|	|	...	...	1234	1234	1234	1359	1250	1326	...	...	...
Frankfurt (Main) Hbf **910/1** a.	1041	1048	...	1050	|	1213	...	|	1148	...	...	|	|	|	...	...	1248	1248	1248	1412	|	1344	...	...	...
Nürnberg Hbf **920** a.	1259	1259	...	...	|	1427	...	|	1400	...	...	|	|	|	...	...	1459	1459	1459	...	|	1559	...	...	...
Stuttgart Hbf **912** a.	|	|	...	...	1208	...	...	|	|	...	...	|	|	1446	...	...	|	|	|	...	1408	|	...	...	...
München Hbf **904 930** a.	1415	1415	...	...	1427	...	...	|	1515	...	...	|	|	...	...	...	1615	1615	1615	...	1627	1715v	...	...	...
Karlsruhe Hbf **912** a.	...	...	...	...	...	...	...	1334	...	...	...	1258	1347‡	...	...	...	...	...	...	...	...	...	...	...	...
Basel SBB 🏛 **912** a.	...	...	...	...	...	...	...	...	...	...	...	1447	1535z	...	...	...	...	...	...	...	...	...	...	...	...

♦ – **NOTES** (LISTED BY TRAIN NUMBER)

3/7 – 🚃12 and ✗ Dortmund - Regensburg - Passau - Linz - Wien.
15 – WÖRTHERSEE – 🚃12 and 🍷 Münster - Salzburg - Klagenfurt.
19 – 🚃12 Münster - Ulm - Lindau - Bregenz - Innsbruck.
56 – KOPERNIKUS – 🛏 1, 2 cl., 🛌 2 cl. and 🚃2 Praha - Dresden - Köln - Amsterdam (Table **28**);
🛏 1, 2 cl., 🛌 2 cl. and 🚃2 (*CNL* **40473** – BOREALIS) København - Amsterdam (Table **50**).
🛏 1, 2 cl., 🛌 2 cl. and 🚃2 (*EN* **446** – JAN KIEPURA) Warszawa - Berlin - Amsterdam (Table **24**).
For overnight journeys only.
013 – ALLGÄU – 🚃12 and ✗ (Leipzig ① -) (Magdeburg ①–⑥ **h** -) Hannover - Köln - Koblenz - Stuttgart - Ulm - Oberstdorf.

– From Amsterdam (Table **28**).
– ⑤⑥ (also June 18, 19, Oct. 2; not June 20). BODENSEE – 🚃12 and 🍷 Emden - Karlsruhe - Konstanz. Arrives Karlsruhe 1338 Aug. 1 - Sept. 13.
– From Emden (Table **812**). On June 20 starts from Münster.
– To Garmisch (Table **895**) on ⑥.
– From Emden (Table **812**) on ①–⑥ (daily until Oct. 25).
– To Zürich (Tables **510**).

c – Also June 19, Oct. 3; not June 21, Oct. 4.
d – Not June 19, Oct. 3.
e – ①–⑥ only.
g – ① only.
h – Not Oct. 4.
j – Departs Münster 0955 June 14 – 28, Sept. 6 – 27 and from Oct. 25.
k – 0621 on ①–⑤ June 16 - July 25.
r – ⑥ only.
s – Stops to set down only.
t – 1210 on ⑥.
v – 3 – 9 minutes later until July 12.
z – 19 – 20 minutes later July 31 - Sept. 14.

♥ – ①–④ (not June 19). *ICE* ***SPRINTER***. Supplement payable.
* – Arrival times. Calls after Köln.
‡ – 11 – 12 minutes later July 31 - Sept. 14.
§ – Frankfurt Flughafen Fernbahnhof (Tables **910** and **911**).

800 HAMBURG - DORTMUND - KÖLN - KOBLENZ

	IC	ICE	ICE	IC	ICE	IC	ICE	ICE	ICE	ICE	ICE	IC	ICE	ICE	ICE	IC	ICE	IC	ICE	IC	IC	IC	ICE	ICE	ICE
	2156	**1742**	**107**	**2313**	**123**	**1911**	**642**	**652**	**629**	**1025**	**519**	**134**	**942**	**952**	**721**	**2046**	**109**	**2217**	**125**	**2011**	**2011**	**2017**	**640**	**650**	**723**
		①–⑥	⑦			⑤⑦			Ⓑ							⑥k	Ⓑb			①–④	⑦	⑤f			Ⓑ
	🍷	🍴	🍷	🍷	A🍷	v🍷	🍴	🍴	🍷	🍴	🍷	🍷♦	🍴	🍴	🍷	D🍷	🍷	🍷♦	A🍷	T	🍷		🍴	🍴	🍷
Hamburg Altona . . . d.	...	...	...	0832	...	...	...	...	...	0932	...	...	...	...	...	...	...	...	...	...	...	...	...	...	...
Hamburg Hbf . . . **801** d.	...	...	...	0846	...	...	...	...	...	0946	...	...	...	...	...	...	...	1046	...	...	...	...	...	...	...
Bremen Hbf . . . **801** d.	...	...	...	0944	...	...	...	...	...	1044	...	...	...	...	...	...	...	1144	...	...	...	...	...	...	...
Osnabrück Hbf . . . **801** d.	...	...	...	1037	...	...	...	...	...	1137	...	...	...	...	...	...	...	1237	...	...	...	...	...	...	...
Münster (Westf) Hbf . . . **801** d.	...	...	...	1103	...	...	...	...	...	1202	...	1232	...	...	...	...	...	1303	...	...	...	...	...	...	...
Berlin Hbf **810** . . . d.	...	...	...	|	...	...	0847	0847	...	|	...	|	0946	0946	...	...	...	|	...	...	1008	...	1047	1047	...
Leipzig Hbf **866** . . . d.	0603	0640	...	|	...	...	|	|	...	|	...	|	|	|	...	0840	...	|	...	...	|	...	|	|	...
Hannover Hbf **810** . . . d.	|	0940	...	|	...	...	1031	1031	...	|	...	|	1131	1131	...	1140	...	|	...	...	1156	1156	1231	1231	...
Hamm (Westf) . . . a.	1052	1113	...	|	...	...	1148	1148	...	|	...	|	1248	1248	...	1312	...	|	...	...	1324	1324	1348	1348	...
Hamm (Westf) . . . **805** d.	1056	1115	...	|	...	...	1152	1154	...	|	...	|	1252	1254	...	1314	...	|	...	...	1326	1326	1352	1354	...
Dortmund Hbf . . . **805** a.	1115	1132	...	1133	...	...	1209	|	...	1233	...	|	1309	|	...	1332	...	1333	...	...	1348	1347	1409	|	...
Dortmund Hbf . . . d.	1117	1137	1137	1137	...	1152	1212	|	1224w	1236	1237	|	1312	|	1324h	1337	1337	1337	...	...	1352	1352	1412	|	1424t
Bochum Hbf . . . d.	1130	|	|	1149	...	1203	1224	|	1238w	|	1249	|	1324	|	1338h	|	|	1349	...	...	1403	1403	1424	|	1438t
Recklinghausen Hbf . . . d.	|	|	|	|	...	|	|	|	|	|	|	1301	|	|	|	|	|	|	...	...	|	|	|	|	|
Wanne-Eickel Hbf . . . d.	|	|	|	|	...	|	|	|	|	|	|	1309	|	|	|	|	|	|	...	...	|	|	|	|	|
Gelsenkirchen Hbf . . . d.	|	|	|	|	...	|	|	|	|	|	|	1315	|	|	|	|	|	|	...	...	|	|	|	|	|
Essen Hbf . . . d.	1141	|	|	1200	...	1214	1236	|	1253	|	1300	|	1336	|	1353	|	|	1400	...	...	1414	1414	1436	|	1453
Mülheim (Ruhr) Hbf . . . d.	|	|	|	|	...	1222	|	|	|	|	|	|	|	|	|	|	|	|	...	...	1422	1422	|	|	|
Oberhausen Hbf . . . d.	|	|	|	|	1226	|	|	|	|	|	|	1327	|	|	|	|	|	|	1426	...	|	|	|	|	|
Duisburg Hbf . . . d.	1155	|	|	1212	1234	1229	1249	|	1308	|	1312	1334	1349	|	1408	|	|	1412	1434	...	1430	1430	1449	|	1508
Düsseldorf Flughafen ✈ . . . d.	1206	|	|	|	|	|	1259	|	|	|	|	|	1359	|	|	|	|	|	|	...	|	|	1459	|	|
Düsseldorf Hbf . . . d.	1212	|	|	1227	1248	1252	1308	|	1321	|	1327	1349	1406	|	1421	|	|	1428	1448	1451	1451	1451	1508	|	1521
Hagen Hbf . . . d.	...	1158	1157	|	|	|	|	1224	|	1257	|	|	...	1324	|	1357	1357	|	|	|	|	|	|	1424	|
Wuppertal Hbf . . . d.	...	1215	1214	|	|	|	|	1241	|	1314	|	|	...	1341	|	1414	1414	|	|	|	|	|	|	1441	|
Solingen Hbf . . . d.	...	1227	1227	|	|	|	|	|	|	1327	|	|	...	|	|	1426	1427	|	|	|	|	|	|	|	|
Köln Messe/Deutz . . . a.	...	1243	|	|	|	|	1328	|	1342	|	|	|	...	|	1442	|	|	|	|	|	|	|	1528a	|	1542
Köln Hbf . . . a.	...	1248	1246	1250	1312	1315	|	1309	|	1346	1349	1412	...	1409	|	1445	1446	1450	1512	1515	1515	1515	|	1509	|
Köln Hbf . . . d.	...	...	1255	1253	1328	1318	|	1312	|	1353	1355	1418	...	...	|	...	1455	1453	1528	1518	1518	1518	|	...	|
Köln/Bonn Flughafen ✈ . . . a.	...	...	|	|	|	|	1344	|	|	|	|	|	...	...	|	...	|	|	|	|	|	|	1544a	...	|
Bonn Hbf . . . d.	...	...	|	1314	|	1337	...	1332	|	1414	|	1437	...	...	|	...	|	1514	|	1537	1537	1537	...	...	|
Remagen . . . d.	...	...	|	|	|	1351	...	...	|	|	|	1451	...	...	|	...	|	|	|	1551	1551	1551	...	...	|
Andernach . . . d.	...	...	|	|	|	1403	...	...	|	|	|	1503	...	...	|	...	|	|	|	1603	1603	1603	...	...	|
Koblenz Hbf . . . a.	...	...	|	1346	|	1416	...	...	|	1446	|	1516	...	...	|	...	|	1546	|	1616	1616	1616	...	...	|
Mainz Hbf **911** . . . a.	...	...	|	1437	|	1511	...	...	|	1537	|	...	...	...	|	...	|	1637	|	1711	1711	1711	...	...	|
Frankfurt Flughafen ✈ § . . . a.	...	...	1350	|	1416	|	...	...	1434	1559	1450	...	...	...	1534	...	1550	|	1616	|	|	|	...	...	1634
Frankfurt (Main) Hbf **910/1** . a.	...	...	|	|	1430	|	...	...	1448	1613	|	...	...	...	1548	...	|	|	1630	|	|	|	...	...	1648
Nürnberg Hbf **920** . . . a.	...	...	|	|	...	|	...	...	1659	...	|	...	...	...	1759	...	|	|	...	|	|	|	...	...	1859
Stuttgart Hbf **912** . . . a.	...	...	|	1622	...	1646	...	...	|	...	1608	...	...	...	|	...	|	1825	...	1846	1846	1846e	...	...	|
München Hbf **904 930** . . . a.	...	...	|	...	...	...	...	...	1818	...	1827	...	...	...	1916•	...	|	...	...	...	...	2124	...	...	2016
Karlsruhe Hbf **912** . . . a.	...	...	1456‡	...	...	...	...	...	...	...	...	...	...	...	...	...	1658	...	...	...	...	...	...	...	...
Basel SBB 🏛 **912** . . . a.	...	...	1647	...	...	...	...	...	...	...	...	...	...	...	...	...	1847	...	...	...	...	...	...	...	...

	IC	IC	ICE	IC	IC	ICE	ICE	ICE	IC	IC	ICE	IC	ICE	ICE	ICE	ICE	ICE	IC	ICE	IC	ICE	ICE	ICE	ICE	IC
	2027	**2327**	**611**	**132**	**2019**	**940**	**950**	**725**	**2048**	**2311**	**127**	**1915**	**548**	**558**	**1228**	**1224**	**727**	**2229**	**613**	**130**	**848**	**858**	**929**	**729**	**2440**
					⑥						G	⑤⑦			①–⑤	⑥⑦	Ⓑ						⑥	Ⓑ	
	🍷♦	🍷♦	🍷	🍷♦	♦	🍴	🍴	🍷	D🍷	🍷♦	A🍷	fH	🍴	🍴	d♦ 🍷	j♦ 🍷	🍷	🍷♦	🍷	🍷♦	🍴	🍴	🍷	🍷	D🍷
Hamburg Altona . . . d.	1132	...	...	...	...	...	...	...	...	...	...	...	...	...	...	...	...	...	...	...	...	...	...	...	...
Hamburg Hbf . . . **801** d.	1146	1146	...	...	...	...	...	...	...	1246	...	...	...	...	...	...	...	1346	...	...	...	...	...	...	...
Bremen Hbf . . . **801** d.	1244	1244	...	...	...	...	...	...	...	1344	...	...	...	...	...	...	...	1444	...	...	...	...	...	...	...
Osnabrück Hbf . . . **801** d.	1337	1337	...	...	...	...	...	...	...	1437	...	...	...	...	...	...	...	1537	...	...	...	...	...	...	...
Münster (Westf) Hbf . . . **801** d.	1403	1403	...	1431	1431	...	...	...	...	1503	...	...	...	...	...	...	...	1603	...	1631	...	...	...	...	...
Berlin Hbf **810** . . . d.	|	|	...	|	|	1146	1146	...	...	|	...	1206	1247	1247	...	...	...	|	...	|	1346	1346	...	...	...
Leipzig Hbf **866** . . . d.	|	|	...	|	|	|	|	...	1040	|	...	|	|	|	...	...	...	|	...	|	|	|	...	...	1240
Hannover Hbf **810** . . . d.	|	|	...	|	|	1331	1331	...	1340	|	...	1356	1431	1431	...	...	...	|	...	|	1531	1531	...	...	1540
Hamm (Westf) . . . a.	|	|	...	|	|	1448	1448	...	1512	|	...	1524	1548	1548	...	...	...	|	...	|	1648	1648	...	...	1712
Hamm (Westf) . . . **805** d.	|	|	...	|	|	1452	1454	...	1514	|	...	1526	1552	1554	1556	1556	...	|	...	|	1652	1654	...	...	1714
Dortmund Hbf . . . **805** a.	1433	1433	...	|	|	1509	|	...	1532	1533	...	1548	1609	|	1614	1614	...	1633	...	|	1709	|	...	...	1732
Dortmund Hbf . . . d.	1436	1436	1437	|	|	1512	|	1524w	1537	1537	...	1552	1612	|	1616	1616	...	1636	1637	|	1712	|	...	...	1737
Bochum Hbf . . . d.	|	|	1449	|	|	1524	|	1538w	|	1549	...	1603	1625	|	1629	1629	...	|	1649	|	1724	|	...	...	|
Recklinghausen Hbf . . . d.	|	|	|	1500	1500	|	|	|	|	|	...	|	|	|	|	|	...	|	|	1700	|	|	...	...	|
Wanne-Eickel Hbf . . . d.	|	|	|	1508	1508	|	|	|	|	|	...	|	|	|	|	|	...	|	|	1708	|	|	...	...	|
Gelsenkirchen Hbf . . . d.	|	|	|	1514	1514	|	|	|	|	|	...	|	|	|	|	|	...	|	|	1715	|	|	...	...	|
Essen Hbf . . . d.	|	|	1500	|	|	1536	|	1553	|	1600	...	1614	1636	|	1640	1640	1653	|	1700	|	1736	|	1742	1753	|
Mülheim (Ruhr) Hbf . . . d.	|	|	|	|	|	|	|	|	|	|	...	1622	|	|	|	|	|	|	|	|	|	|	|	|	|
Oberhausen Hbf . . . d.	|	|	|	1527	1527	|	|	|	|	|	1626	|	|	|	|	|	|	|	|	1727	|	|	|	|	|
Duisburg Hbf . . . d.	|	|	1512	1534	1534	1549	|	1608	|	1612	1634	1630	1649	|	1654	1656	1707	|	1712	1734	1749	|	1756	1808	|
Düsseldorf Flughafen ✈ . . . d.	|	|	|	|	|	1559	|	|	|	|	|	|	1657s	|	|	|	|	|	|	|	1759	|	|	|	|
Düsseldorf Hbf . . . d.	|	|	1527	1549	1549	1606	|	1621	|	1627	1648	1651	1712z	|	1708	1711	1720	|	1727	1749	1806	|	1813	1821	|
Hagen Hbf . . . d.	1457	1457	|	|	|	...	1524	|	1557	|	|	|	|	1624	|	|	|	1657	|	|	...	1724	|	|	1757
Wuppertal Hbf . . . d.	1514	1514	|	|	|	...	1541	|	1614	|	|	|	|	1641	|	|	|	1714	|	|	...	1741	|	|	1814
Solingen Hbf . . . d.	1527	1527	|	|	|	...	|	|	1626	|	|	|	|	|	|	|	|	1727	|	|	...	|	|	|	1826
Köln Messe/Deutz . . . a.	|	|	|	|	|	...	|	1642	1642	|	|	|	1734*	|	1728	|	1742	|	|	|	...	|	1833	1842	|
Köln Hbf . . . a.	1546	1546	1549	1612	1612	...	1609	|	1648	1650	1712	1715	|	1709	...	1733r	|	1746	1749	1812	...	1809	|	|	1845
Köln Hbf . . . d.	1553	1553	1556	1618q	1618	...	...	|	...	1653	1720	1718	|	...	...	...	|	1753	1755	1818	...	...	|	|	...
Köln/Bonn Flughafen ✈ . . . a.	|	|	|	|	|	...	...	|	...	|	|	|	1746*	...	...	...	|	|	|	|	...	...	|	|	...
Bonn Hbf . . . d.	1614	1614	|	1637q	1637	...	...	|	...	1714	|	1737	...	...	...	...	|	1814	|	1837	...	...	|	|	...
Remagen . . . d.	|	|	|	1651q	1651	...	...	|	...	|	|	1751	...	...	...	...	|	|	|	1851	...	...	|	|	...
Andernach . . . d.	|	|	|	1703q	1703	...	...	|	...	|	|	1803	...	...	...	...	|	|	|	1903	...	...	|	|	...
Koblenz Hbf . . . a.	1646	1646	|	1716q	1716	...	...	|	...	1746	|	1816	...	...	...	...	|	1846	|	1916	...	...	|	|	...
Mainz Hbf **911** . . . a.	1737	1737	|	...	1815	...	...	|	...	1837	|	1911	...	...	...	...	|	1937	|	...	...	...	|	|	...
Frankfurt Flughafen ✈ § . . . a.	1759	1759	1650	...	|	...	...	1734	...	|	1816	|	...	...	...	...	1834	1959	1850	...	...	...	1934	1934	...
Frankfurt (Main) Hbf **910/1** . a.	1813	1813	|	...	|	...	...	1748	...	|	1830	|	...	...	...	...	1848	2013	|	...	...	...	1948	1948	...
Nürnberg Hbf **920** . . . a.	2027	2027	|	...	|	...	...	1959	...	|	...	|	...	...	...	...	2059	2226b	|	...	...	...	2159	2159	...
Stuttgart Hbf **912** . . . a.	...	...	1808	...	1958	...	...	|	...	2023	...	2046	...	...	...	...	|	...	2008	...	...	...	|	|	...
München Hbf **904 930** . . . a.	...	...	2027	...	...	...	...	2115y	...	...							2212	...	2226	...	...	...	2316	2316	...
Karlsruhe Hbf **912** . . . a.	...	...	...	...	...	...	...	...	...	...							...	...	...	...	...	...	...	...	...
Basel SBB 🏛 **912** . . . a.	...	...	...	...	...	...	...	...	...	...							...	...	...	...	...	...	...	...	...

*See Table **802** for Rhein-Ruhr local RE and S-Bahn services*

♦ – **NOTES** (LISTED BY TRAIN NUMBER)

130 – [12] and 🍷 Norddeich Mole - Emden - Koblenz (- Trier / Luxembourg ⑥).
132 – Ⓑ to Oct. 17 (not June 19); daily from Oct. 19. [12] and 🍷 Norddeich Mole - Emden - Köln (- Koblenz - Trier / Luxembourg Ⓑ **q**).
134 – [12] and 🍷 Norddeich Mole - Münster - Koblenz - Trier / Luxembourg.
1224 – [12] and 🍷 München - Kassel - Paderborn - Düsseldorf (- Köln ⑥).
1228 – [12] and 🍷 München - Kassel - Paderborn - Düsseldorf - Wiesbaden.
2019 ⑥ to Oct. 18 (also June 19). NORDERNEY – [12] Norddeich Mole - Emden - Stuttgart.
2027 – ①–④ to July 3 (also June 15); daily from Oct. 6 (not Oct. 10, 11, 17, 18, 19, 24, 31). [12] and 🍷 Hamburg - Regensburg - Passau.
2217 – [12] and 🍷 (Greifswald Ⓐ -) Stralsund - Hamburg - Köln - Stuttgart.
2229 – [12] and 🍷 Kiel - Köln - Frankfurt (- Nürnberg Ⓑ **b**) (- Passau ⑤ **p**).
2311 – NORDFRIESLAND – [12] and 🍷 Westerland - Heidelberg - Stuttgart.
2327 – July 4 - Oct. 5 (also June 14, 20, 21, 22, 27, 28, 29, Oct. 10, 11, 17, 18, 19, 24, 31). LÜBECKER BUCHT – [12] and 🍷 Fehmarn-Burg - Lübeck - Köln - Frankfurt - Nürnberg - Passau.

A – From Amsterdam (Table **28**).
D – From Dresden (Table **841**).
G – Daily to Nov. 2; ⑤ from Nov. 7.
H – To Tübingen Hbf on ⑦ (a. 2150).
T – ①–④ (not June 18, 19, Oct. 2). To Tübingen Hbf (a. 1950).

a – ①–⑤ only.
b – Ⓑ (not Oct. 3).
d – Not June 19, 20, Oct. 3.
e – Not Aug. 1 - Sept. 12.
f – Also June 18, Oct. 2; not June 20, Oct. 3.
h – ⑤⑦ only.
j – Also June 19, 20, Oct. 3.
k – Also Oct. 3; not Oct. 4.
p – Also June 18, Aug. 14, Oct. 2; not June 20, Aug. 15, Oct. 3.

q – Ⓑ (not June 19).
r – ⑥ only.
s – Stops to set down only.
t – ①②③④⑦ (not Oct. 2).
v – Also Oct. 2; not Oct. 3.
w – ⑦ only.
y – 2120 on ①–⑤ until July 11.
z – On ⑥ (also June 19, 20, Oct. 3) Düsseldorf a. 1706, d. 1715. On ⑦ Düsseldorf a. 1706, d. 1708.

* – On ⑦ Köln Messe/Deutz a. 1728, Köln/Bonn Flughafen a. 1742.
• – 1919 until July 12.
‡ – 12 minutes later July 31 - Sept. 14.
§ – Frankfurt Flughafen ✈ Fernbahnho
(Tables **910** and **911**).

HAMBURG - DORTMUND - KÖLN - KOBLENZ 800

	IC 2213 🍷♦	IC 1917 ⑦	ICE 129 A🍷	ICE 821 Ⓑm 🍷	ICE 546 🍴	ICE 556 🍴	ICE 556 Ⓐ 🍴	ICE 1029 🍴	ICE 615 🍷	IC 2332 E 🍷	IC 2334 ②–④ G🍷	ICE 846 Q 🍴	ICE 1046 ⑤f C🍴	ICE 856 🍴	ICE 1746 D🍴	ICE 605 🍷	IC 2442 Ⓑd D🍷	IC 2215 J 🍷	IC 2315 🍷♦	ICE 227 A🍷	ICE 544 H🍴	ICE 554 🍴		IC 2321 Y 🍷	IC 2221 🍷♦
Hamburg Altona d.	...	...	...	...	...	...	...	1532	...	...	...	...	...	...	...	...	...	1632	...	...	...	...	...	1732	...
Hamburg Hbf 801 d.	1446	...	...	...	...	...	...	1546	...	...	...	...	...	...	...	...	...	1646	1646	...	...	...	...	1746	1746
Bremen Hbf 801 d.	1544	...	...	...	...	...	...	1644	...	...	...	...	...	...	...	...	...	1744	1744	...	...	...	...	1844	1844
Osnabrück Hbf 801 d.	1637	...	...	...	...	...	...	1737	...	...	...	...	...	...	...	...	...	1837	1837	...	...	...	...	1937	1937
Münster (Westf) Hbf 801 d.	1703	...	...	...	...	...	...	1802	...	1832	1832	...	...	...	...	...	...	1903	1903	...	...	...	...	2003	2003
Berlin Hbf **810** d.	|	1358	...	...	1447	1447	1447	|	...	|	|	1546	1546	1546	...	...	...	|	|	...	1647	1647	...	|	|
Leipzig Hbf **866** d.	|	|	...	...	|	|	|	|	...	|	|	|	|	|	1410	...	1440	|	|	...	|	|	...	|	|
Hannover Hbf **810** d.	|	1556	...	...	1631	1631	1631	|	...	|	|	1731	1731	1731	◇	...	1740	|	|	...	1831	1831	...	|	|
Hamm (Westf) a.	|	1724	...	...	1748	1748	1748	|	...	|	|	1848	1848	1848	1852	...	1912	|	|	...	1948	1948	...	|	|
Hamm (Westf) 805 d.	|	1726	...	...	1752	1754	1754	|	...	|	|	1852	1852	1854	1856	...	1914	|	|	...	1952	1954	...	|	|
Dortmund Hbf 805 a.	1733	1748	...	...	1809	|	|	1833	...	|	|	1909	1909	|	1914	...	1932	1933	1933	...	2009	|	...	2033	2033
Dortmund Hbf d.	1737	1752	...	1815w	1812	|	|	1836	1837	|	|	1912	1912	|	1916	1924	1937	1937	1937	...	2012	|	...	2037	2037
Bochum Hbf d.	1749	1803	...	1829w	1824	|	|	|	1849	|	|	1924	1924	|	1929	1938	|	1949	1949	...	2024	|	...	2049	2049
Recklinghausen Hbf d.	|	|	...	|	|	|	|	|	|	1901	1901	|	|	|	|	|	|	|	|	...	|	|	...	|	|
Wanne-Eickel Hbf d.	|	|	...	|	|	|	|	|	|	1909	1909	|	|	|	|	|	|	|	|	...	|	|	...	|	|
Gelsenkirchen Hbf d.	|	|	...	|	|	|	|	|	|	1915	1915	|	|	|	|	|	|	|	|	...	|	|	...	|	|
Essen Hbf d.	1800	1814	...	1841	1836	|	|	|	1900	|	|	1936	1936	|	1940	1950	|	2000	2000	...	2036	|	...	2100	2100
Mülheim (Ruhr) Hbf d.	|	1822	...	|	|	|	|	|	|	|	|	|	|	|	|	|	|	|	|	...	|	|	...	|	|
Oberhausen Hbf d.	|	|	1826	|	|	|	|	|	|	1927	1927	|	|	|	|	|	|	|	|	2026	|	|	...	|	|
Duisburg Hbf d.	1812	1830	1834	1854	1849	|	|	|	1912	1934	1934	1949	1949	|	1955	2004	|	2012	2012	2034	2049	|	...	2112	2112
Düsseldorf Flughafen ✈ d.	|	|	|	|	1904	|	|	|	|	|	|	1959	|	|	2006	2014	|	|	|	|	2059	|	...	|	|
Düsseldorf Hbf d.	1827	1851	1848	1908	1911	|	|	|	1927	1949	1949	2008	2015	|	2013	2022	|	2027	2027	2048	2108	|	...	2127	2127
Hagen Hbf d.	|	|	|	|	...	1824	1824	1857	|	|	|	|	...	1924	...	|	1957	|	|	|	|	2024	...	|	|
Wuppertal Hbf d.	|	|	|	|	...	1841	1841	1914	|	|	|	|	...	1941	...	|	2014	|	|	|	|	2041	...	|	|
Solingen Hbf d.	|	|	|	|	...	|	|	1927	|	|	|	|	...	|	...	|	2026	|	|	|	|	|	...	|	|
Köln Messe/Deutz a.	|	|	|	1928	...	|	|	|	|	|	|	|	...	|	...	2042	|	|	|	|	2128	|	...	|	|
Köln Hbf a.	1850	1915	1912	|	...	1909	1909	1946	1949	2012	2012	2033	...	2009	...	|	2045	2050	2050	2112	2133	2109	...	2150	2150
Köln Hbf d.	1853	1918	1920	|	...	1912q	1912	1953	1957	...	...	...	...	2018q	...	|	...	2053	2053	2128	...	...	...	2153	2153
Köln/Bonn Flughafen ✈ a.	|	|	|	|	...	|	|	|	|	...	...	...	...	|	...	|	...	|	|	|	...	...	...	|	|
Bonn Hbf d.	1914	1937	|	|	...	1932q	1937	2014	|	...	...	...	...	2038q	...	|	...	2114	2114	|	...	...	...	2214	2214
Remagen d.	|	1951	|	|	...	...	|	|	|	...	...	...	...	...	...	|	...	|	|	|	...	...	...	|	|
Andernach d.	|	2003	|	|	...	...	2001	|	|	...	...	...	...	...	...	|	...	|	|	|	...	...	...	|	|
Koblenz Hbf a.	1946	2016	|	|	...	...	2013	2046	|	...	...	...	...	...	...	|	...	2146	2146	|	...	...	...	2246	2246
Mainz Hbf **911** a.	2037	2111	|	|	...	...	...	2141	|	...	...	...	...	...	...	|	...	2237	2237	|	...	...	...	2337z	2337
Frankfurt Flughafen ✈ § a.	|	|	2016	2034	...	...	...	2159	2050	...	...	...	...	...	...	2150	...	2259	2259	2216	...	...	...	2359z	2359
Frankfurt (Main) Hbf **910/1** a.	|	|	2030	2048	...	...	...	2213	|	...	...	...	...	...	...	|	...	2311	2311	2230	...	...	...	0013z	0013
Nürnberg Hbf **920** a.	|	|	...	2259h	...	...	...	0037	|	...	...	...	...	...	...	|	...	...	...	...	...	...	...	...	...
Stuttgart Hbf **912** a.	2222	|	...	|	...	...	...	...	2208	...	...	...	...	...	...	|	...	...	...	...	...	...	...	...	...
München Hbf **904 930** a.	...	|	...	0017h	...	...	...	...	0027	...	...	...	...	...	...	|	...	...	...	...	...	...	...	...	...
Karlsruhe Hbf **912** a.	...	2224x	...	...	...	...	...	...	...	...	...	...	...	...	...	2300‡	...	...	...	...	...	...	...	...	...
Basel SBB 🛃 **912** a.	...	...	...	...	...	...	...	...	...	...	...	...	...	...	...	0056r	...	...	...	...	...	...	...	...	...

	IC 2330 R 🍷	ICE 619 🍷	ICE 844 🍴	ICE 854 Ⓑ 🍴	ICE 854 ⑦v 🍴	IC 2354 ⑤f 🍷	IC 1952 ⑦ D	IC 2307 🍷	IC 2444 Ⓑd D🍷	ICE 542 🍴	ICE 552 🍴	CNL 419 🅁 🍷♦	CNL 40419 🅁 🍷♦	IC 61419 2	ICE 223 T A🍷	IC 2225 K🍷	IC 2009 ⑦	ICE 842 🍴	ICE 852 ⑦ 🍴	IC 2446 ⑦ D🍷	IC 2309 P 🍷	IC 2309 S 🍷		ICE 540 ⑤–⑦ 🍴	IC 2021
Hamburg Altona d.	...	...	...	...	...	...	...	1832	...	...	...	...	...	...	...	...	...	...	...	...	2032	2032	...	...	2232
Hamburg Hbf 801 d.	...	...	...	...	...	...	...	1846	...	...	...	...	...	...	...	1946	...	...	...	...	2046	2046	...	...	2246
Bremen Hbf 801 d.	...	...	...	...	...	...	...	1944	...	...	...	...	...	...	...	2044	...	...	...	...	2144	2144	...	...	2344
Osnabrück Hbf 801 d.	...	...	...	...	...	...	...	2037	...	...	...	...	...	...	...	2137	...	...	...	...	2238	2238	...	...	0045
Münster (Westf) Hbf 801 d.	2032	...	...	...	...	...	...	2103	...	...	...	...	...	...	...	2203	...	...	...	...	2304	2304	...	...	0113
Berlin Hbf **810** d.	|	...	1746	1746	1746	1458	...	|	...	1847	1847	...	...	...	...	|	...	1946	1946	...	|	|	...	2107	|
Leipzig Hbf **866** d.	|	...	|	|	|	|	1610	|	1640	|	|	...	...	...	...	|	...	|	|	1840	|	|	...	|	|
Hannover Hbf **810** d.	|	...	1931	1931	1931	◇	◇	|	1940	2031	2031	...	...	...	...	|	...	2131	2131	2140	|	|	...	2301	|
Hamm (Westf) a.	|	...	2048	2048	2048	2052	2052	|	2110	2148	2148	...	...	...	...	|	...	2248	2248	2310	|	|	...	0026	0131
Hamm (Westf) 805 d.	|	...	2052	2054	2054	2056	2056	|	2112	2152	2154	...	...	...	...	|	...	2252	2254	2312	|	|	...	0028	0133
Dortmund Hbf 805 a.	|	...	2109	|	|	2115	2115	2133	2132	2209	|	...	...	...	...	2233	...	2309	|	2332	2333	2333	...	0047	0149
Dortmund Hbf d.	|	2058	2112	|	|	2117	2117	2137	2137	2212	|	...	...	...	...	2237	...	2312	|	2337	...	2337	...	0051	0152
Bochum Hbf d.	|	2111	2124	|	|	2130	2130	2149	|	2224	|	...	...	...	...	2249	...	2324	|	|	...	2349	...	0103	0203
Recklinghausen Hbf d.	2101	|	|	|	|	|	|	|	|	|	|	...	...	...	...	|	...	|	|	|	...	|	...	|	|
Wanne-Eickel Hbf d.	2109	|	|	|	|	|	|	|	|	|	|	...	...	...	...	|	...	|	|	|	...	|	...	|	|
Gelsenkirchen Hbf d.	2115	|	|	|	|	|	|	|	|	|	|	...	...	...	...	|	...	|	|	|	...	|	...	|	|
Essen Hbf d.	|	2125	2136	|	|	2140	2140	2200	|	2236	|	...	...	...	...	2300	...	2336	|	|	...	2359	...	0114	0215
Mülheim (Ruhr) Hbf d.	|	|	|	|	|	|	|	|	|	|	|	...	...	...	...	|	...	|	|	|	...	|	...	|	|
Oberhausen Hbf d.	2127	|	|	|	|	|	|	|	|	|	|	...	...	...	2258	|	...	|	|	|	...	|	...	|	|
Duisburg Hbf d.	2134	2139	2151	|	|	2156	2156	2212	|	2249	|	2257	2257	2257	2306	2312	...	2349	|	|	...	0012	...	0128	0229
Düsseldorf Flughafen ✈ d.	|	|	2200	|	|	2208	2208	|	|	2259	|	|	|	|	|	|	...	2359	|	|	...	|	...	0138	0239
Düsseldorf Hbf d.	2148	2155	2209	|	|	2216	2216	2227	|	2308	|	2313u	2313u	2313	2320	2327	...	0008	|	|	...	0027	...	0147	0247
Hagen Hbf d.	|	|	|	2124	2124	|	|	|	2157	|	2224	|	|	|	|	|	...	|	2324	2357	...	|	...	|	|
Wuppertal Hbf d.	|	|	|	2141	2141	|	|	|	2214	|	2241	|	|	|	|	|	...	|	2341	0014	...	|	...	|	|
Solingen Hbf d.	|	|	|	|	|	|	|	|	2226	|	2254	|	|	|	|	|	...	|	|	0026	...	|	...	|	|
Köln Messe/Deutz a.	|	|	|	|	|	|	|	|	|	|	|	|	|	|	|	|	...	|	|	|	...	|	...	|	|
Köln Hbf a.	2212	2219	2231	2209	2209	2240	2240	2250	2245	2330	2313	|	|	2337	2343	2349	...	0030	0012	0045	...	0050	...	0209	0309
Köln Hbf d.	...	2230	...	...	2218	...	...	2253	...	...	2318q	2346u	2346u	2346	...	...	2353	...	...	...	...	...	...	0214b	0351
Köln/Bonn Flughafen ✈ a.	...	2240	...	...	|	...	...	|	...	...	|	|	|	|	...	...	|	...	...	...	...	...	...	0225b	|
Bonn Hbf d.	...	|	...	...	2238	...	...	2314	...	...	2339q	0007u	0007u	0007	...	...	0014	...	...	...	...	...	...	...	0416
Remagen d.	...	|	...	...	|	...	...	2328	...	...	...	|	|	|	...	...	|	...	...	...	...	...	...	...	0431
Andernach d.	...	|	...	...	|	...	...	2341	...	...	...	|	|	|	...	...	|	...	...	...	...	...	...	...	0444
Koblenz Hbf a.	...	|	...	...	2313	...	...	2354	...	...	...	0040u	0040u	0038	...	...	0046	...	...	...	...	...	...	...	0458
Mainz Hbf **911** a.	...	|	...	...	...	...	...	...	...	...	...	|	|	0136j	...	...	0141	...	...	...	...	...	...	...	0626
Frankfurt Flughafen ✈ § a.	...	2345	...	...	...	...	...	...	...	...	...	|	|	0154	...	...	0202	...	...	...	...	...	...	...	0646
Frankfurt (Main) Hbf **910/1** a.	...	2400	...	...	...	...	...	...	...	...	...	|	|	|	...	...	0217	...	...	...	...	...	...	...	0702
Nürnberg Hbf **920** a.	...	|	...	...	...	...	...	...	...	...	...	|	|	|	...	...	...	...	...	...	...	...	...	...	...
Stuttgart Hbf **912** a.	...	0320	...	...	...	...	...	...	...	...	...	0417	|	|	...	...	...	...	...	...	...	...	...	...	...
München Hbf **904 930** a.	...	0602	...	...	...	...	...	...	...	...	...	0710	|	|	...	...	...	...	...						
Karlsruhe Hbf **912** a.	...	0152y	...	...	...	...	...	...	...	...	...	...	0437	0437	...	...	...	...	...						
Basel SBB 🛃 **912** a.	...	...	...	...	...	...	...	...	...	...	...	...	0647	0647	...	...	...	...	...						

*See Table **802** for Rhein-Ruhr local RE and S-Bahn services*

♦ – **NOTES** (LISTED BY TRAIN NUMBER)

19 – POLLUX – 🛏 1, 2 cl., 🛏 2 cl. and 💺2 (reclining) Amsterdam - München.
213 – RÜGEN – 🚃12 and 🍷 Ostseebad Binz - Stralsund - Köln - Stuttgart.
221 – Daily until Oct. 19; ⑤⑦ from Oct. 24. FEHMARN – 🚃12 and 🍷 (Until Oct. 19: Fehmarn-Burg -) Lübeck - Hamburg - Frankfurt.
315 – Until Oct. 26. DEICHGRAF – 🚃12 and 🍷 Westerland - Frankfurt.
0419 – PEGASUS – 🛏 1, 2 cl., 🛏 2 cl. and 💺2 (reclining) Amsterdam - Zürich.

– From Amsterdam (Table **28**).
– To Neuss Hbf (a. 2027) and Mönchengladbach Hbf (a. 2041).
– From Dresden (Table **842**).
– Daily to Oct. 27; ①⑤⑦ from Oct. 31.
– ②–④ from Oct. 28. From Norddeich Mole (Table **812**).
– On ⑦ continues to Düren (a. 2153) and Aachen Hbf (a. 2216).
– From Oct. 27.
– From Kiel (Table **820**).

P – Daily to Oct. 24; Ⓑ from Oct. 26.
Q – ①②③④⑥⑦ (also Oct. 3; not Oct. 2).
R – ④–⑦ to Aug. 24 (also June 18); ③–⑦ Aug. 27 - Oct. 22; ⑦ from Oct. 26 (also Oct. 31). From Norddeich Mole (Table **812**).
S – ⑤–⑦ to Oct. 24 (also Oct. 2); ⑤⑦ from Oct. 26.
T – ⑤⑦ to Nov. 2; ⑦ from Nov. 9.
Y – ①②③④⑥ from Oct. 20.

b – Mornings of ①⑥⑦ until Oct. 20.
d – Not Oct. 3.
f – Also Oct. 2; not Oct. 3.
h – Frankfurt - München on ④⑤⑦ (also June 18; not June 19, Oct. 3).
j – Not the mornings of June 15, 16, 22, 23.
m – Not June 19, Oct. 3.
q – Ⓑ only.

r – Karlsruhe - Basel on ①②③④⑦ (not Oct. 2). Basel **Badischer Bf**.
u – Stops to pick up only.
v – Also Oct. 3.
w – ⑦ only.
x – 2239 Aug. 3 - Sept. 14.
y – 0158 on the mornings July 18 - Sept. 30.
z – Koblenz - Frankfurt on ①–④ only.

◇ – Via Erfurt / Kassel / Paderborn (Tables **850** and **805**).
‡ – 2309 July 31 - Sept. 14.
§ – Frankfurt Flughafen Fernbahnhof (Tables **910** and **911**).

801 Local services MÜNSTER - OSNABRÜCK and BREMEN - HAMBURG

See Table **800** for fast trains

MÜNSTER (Westf) - **OSNABRÜCK** and v.v. Operated by WestfalenBahn. Journey time: 36 minutes. Trains call at **Lengerich** (Westf), 22 minutes from Münster, 14 minutes from Osnabrück.
From Münster (Westf) Hbf at 0503 Ⓐ, 0603 ⚒, 0634 Ⓐ, 0703, 0734 Ⓐ, 0803, 0903 and hourly until 1603; then 1634 Ⓐ, 1703, 1734 Ⓐ, 1803, 1903, 2003, 2103, 2203 and 2303.
From Osnabrück Hbf at 0519 Ⓐ, 0549 Ⓐ, 0619 ⚒, 0649 Ⓐ, 0719, 0749 Ⓐ, 0819, 0919 and hourly until 1619; then 1649 Ⓐ, 1719, 1749 Ⓐ, 1819, 1919, 2019, 2119, 2219 and 2319.

OSNABRÜCK - BREMEN and v.v. SEE TABLE **815**.

BREMEN - HAMBURG and v.v. Operated by *metronom*. Journey time: 69 – 88 minutes. Trains call at **Rotenburg** (Wümme), 21 – 29 minutes from Bremen, 47 – 56 minutes from Hamburg.
From Bremen Hbf at 0004 Ⓒ, 0500, 0528 Ⓐ, 0600, 0626 Ⓐ, 0631 Ⓒ, 0700, 0733, 0800, 0833 and at 00 and 33 minutes past each hour until 2000, 2033; then 2100, 2133 ⑤–⑦ **f**, 2200 and 2306. **From Hamburg** Hbf at 0015 ①, 0038 Ⓒ, 0508 †, 0514 ⑥, 0532 ⚒, 0559 Ⓐ, 0615 Ⓒ, 0637, 0715, 0738, 0815, 0838 and at 15 and 38 minutes past each hour until 2115, 2138; then 2238.

f – Also Oct. 2.

802 RHEIN – RUHR LOCAL SERVICES

RE / RB services

Services in this table (pages 376 – 378) are shown route by route. Sub-headings indicate the route number and principal stations served.

RE1 Aachen - Köln - Düsseldorf - Dortmund - Hamm (- Paderborn: Table 805) ⊡ *RE6* Düsseldorf - Dortmund - Bielefeld (- Minden) ⊡

km			m		m		m		m		m			m		m							⑤⑥f
0	**Aachen** Hbf.. **807 910** d.	...	...	...	...	0451e	...	0551	...	0651	...		1751	...	1851	...	1951	...	...	2051	2151	2251	2351	2351
31	Düren .... **807** d.	...	...	...	...	0517e	...	0617	...	0717	...		1817	...	1917	...	2017	...	...	2117	2217	2317	0017	0017
70	**Köln** Hbf ...... **807 910** a.	...	...	...	...	0544e	...	0644	...	0744	...		1844	...	1944	...	2044	...	...	2144	2244	2344	0044	0044
70	**Köln** Hbf .... d.	...	...	...	...	0549	...	0649	...	0749	...	and at	1849	...	1949	...	2049	...	...	2149	2249	2349	0049	0049
71	**Köln** Messe/Deutz ...... d.	...	...	...	...	0552	...	0652	...	0752	...		1852	...	1952	...	2052	...	...	2152	2252	2352	0051	0052
83	Leverkusen Mitte .... d.	...	...	...	...	0604	...	0704	...	0804	...	the same	1904	...	2004	...	2104	...	...	2204	2304	0004	...	0104
110	**Düsseldorf** Hbf .... d.	0422c	...	0522	...	0622	0654e	0722	0754r	0822	0854		1922	1954	2022	2054	2122	2154	...	2222	2322	0022	...	0122
117	Düsseldorf Flughafen ✈ d.	0428c	...	0528	...	0628	0702e	0728	0802r	0828	0902	minutes	1928	2002	2028	2102	2128	2202	...	2228	2328	0028	...	0128
134	**Duisburg** Hbf .... d.	0438	...	0538	...	0638	0715e	0738	0814r	0838	0914		1938	2014	2038	2114	2138	2214	...	2238	2338	0038	...	0138
144	Mülheim (Ruhr) Hbf...... d.	0444	...	0544	...	0644	0721e	0744	0820r	0844	0920	past each	1944	2020	2044	2120	2144	2221	...	2244	2344	0044	...	0144
153	**Essen** Hbf........ d.	0453	...	0553	...	0653	0729e	0753	0829r	0853	0929		1953	2029	2053	2129	2153	2229	...	2253	2353	0053	...	0153
169	Bochum Hbf........ d.	0505	...	0605	...	0705	0740e	0805	0840r	0905	0940	hour until	2005	2040	2105	2140	2205	2240	...	2305	0005	0105	...	0205
187	**Dortmund** Hbf........ d.	0517	0554	0617	0654	0717	0754	0817	0854	0917	0954		2017	2054	2117	2154	2217	2254	...	2317	0017	0117	...	0217
218	**Hamm** (Westf) ..... **810** d.	0545	0615	0636t	0715	0736	0815	0836	0915	0936	1015		2036	2115	2145	2215	2245	2313	2322	2345	0045	0145	...	0245
268	Gütersloh Hbf ...... **810** d.	...	0649	*0718*e	0749	*0818*r	0849	*0918*	0949	*1018*	1049		*2118*	2149	...	2249	...	...	2355	...	...	...	...	...
285	**Bielefeld** Hbf....... **810** a.	...	0658	*0732*e	0758	*0832*r	0858	*0932*	0958	*1032*	1058		*2132*	2158	...	2258	...	...	0008	...	...	...	...	...

						⚒rm		m		m		m		✣	m		m		m		m		⑤⑥f	m
Bielefeld Hbf........ **810** d.	0002	...	...	...	*0527*e	0558	*0627*e	0658	*0727*e	0758	*0827*r	0858	*0927*		1858	*1927*	1958	*2027*	2058	...	2158	...	...	2258
Gütersloh Hbf .... **810** d.	0014	...	...	...	*0538*e	0608	*0638*e	0708	*0738*e	0808	*0838*r	0908	*0938*		1908	*1938*	2008	*2038*	2108	...	2208	...	...	2308
Hamm (Westf)....... **810** d.	0044	0315	0415	0515	0615h	0644	0722j	0744	0822	0844	0922	0944	1022		1944	2022	2044	2115	2144	2215	2244	2315	2315	2344
Dortmund Hbf........... d.	▬	0345	0445	0545	0645	0706	0745	0806	0845	0906	0945	1006	1045	and at	2006	2045	2106	2145	2206	2245	2304	2345	2345	0004
Bochum Hbf............... d.	...	0356	0456	0556	0656	0718	0756	0818	0856	0918	0956	1018	1056		2018	2056	2118	2156	2218	2256	▬	2356	2356	...
Essen Hbf................. d.	...	0409	0509	0609	0709	0731	0809	0831	0909	0931	1009	1031	1109	the same	2031	2109	2131	2209	2231	2309	...	0009	0009	...
Mülheim (Ruhr) Hbf...... d.	...	0415	0515	0615	0715	0738	0815	0838	0915	0938	1015	1038	1115		2038	2115	2138	2215	2238	2315	...	0015	0015	...
Duisburg Hbf............. d.	...	0422	0522	0622	0722	0746	0822	0846	0922	0946	1022	1046	1122	minutes	2046	2122	2146	2222	2246	2322	...	0020	0023	...
Düsseldorf Flughafen ✈ d.	...	0432	0532	0632	0732	0756	0832	0856	0932	0956	1032	1056	1132		2056	2132	2156	2232	2256	2332	...	...	0032	...
Düsseldorf Hbf.......... d.	...	0437	0540	0640	0740	0804	0840	0904	0940	1004	1040	1104	1140	past each	2104	2140	2204	2240	2304	2340	...	...	0040	...
Leverkusen Mitte .... d.	Ⓐe	...	0555	0655	0755	...	0855	...	0955	...	1055	...	1155		...	2155	...	2255	...	2355	...	...	0055	...
Köln Messe/Deutz .... d.	0509	...	0609	0709	0809	...	0909	...	1009	...	1109	...	1209	hour until	...	2209	...	2309	...	0009	0047	...	0109	...
Köln Hbf .... a.	0512	...	0612	0712	0812	...	0912	...	1012	...	1112	...	1212		...	2212	...	2312	...	0012	0049	...	0112	...
Köln Hbf .... **807 910** d.	0515	...	0615	0715	0815	...	0915	...	1015	...	1115	...	1215		...	2215	...	2315	...	0015	0050	...	0115	...
Düren .... **807** d.	0539	...	0639	0739	0839	...	0939	...	1039	...	1139	...	1239		...	2239	...	2339	...	0039	0128	...	0139	...
Aachen Hbf... **807 910** a.	0607	...	0707	0807	0907	...	1007	...	1107	...	1207	...	1307		...	2307	...	0007	...	0107	0154	...	0207	...

RE2 Düsseldorf - Essen - Gelsenkirchen - Münster ⊡ *RB42* Essen - Münster

km		⚒r	Ⓐe	⚒r	⚒r		⚒r					●											⑤⑥f	
0	**Düsseldorf** Hbf .... d.	...	...	0506	...	0606	...	0706	...	0806	...		1806	...	1906	...	2006	...	2106	...	2206	...	2306	...
7	Düsseldorf Flughafen ✈ d.	...	...	0513	...	0613	...	0713	...	0813	...	and at	1813	...	1913	...	2013	...	2113	...	2213	...	2313	...
24	**Duisburg** Hbf.............. d.	...	...	0524	...	0624	...	0724	...	0824	...		1824	...	1927	...	2027	...	2124	...	2224	...	2324	...
34	Mülheim (Ruhr) Hbf...... d.	...	...	0530	...	0630	...	0730	...	0830	...	the same	1830	...	1934	...	2036	...	2130	...	2230	...	2330	...
43	**Essen** Hbf.................. d.	0444	0518	0544	0618	0644	0718	0744	0818	0844	0918	minutes	1844	1918	1944	2018	2044	2118	2144	2218	2244	2318	2344	2344
53	Gelsenkirchen Hbf ...... d.	0453	0526	0553	0626	0653	0726	0753	0826	0853	0926		1853	1926	1953	2026	2053	2126	2153	2226	2253	2326	2353	2353
58	Wanne-Eickel Hbf .... d.	0458	0531	0558	0631	0658	0731	0758	0833	0858	0931	past each	1858	1931	1958	2031	2058	2131	2158	2231	2258	2331	2358	2358
68	Recklinghausen Hbf.... d.	0505	0539	0605	0639	0705	0739	0805	0841	0905	0939	hour until	1905	1939	2005	2039	2105	2139	2205	2239	2305	2339	0006	0006
84	Haltern am See .... d.	0516	0550	0616	0650	0716	0750	0816	0852	0916	0950		1916	1950	2016	2050	2116	2150	2216	2250	2316	2350	0017	0017
97	Dülmen........................ d.	0525	0559	0625	0659	0725	0759	0825	0901	0925	0959		1925	1959	2025	2059	2125	...	2225	...	2325	...	0026	0026
126	**Münster** (Westf) Hbf.... a.	0550	0622	0650	0722	0750	0822	0852	0924	0950	1022		1950	2022	2050	2122	2150	...	2250	...	2350	...	0050	0050

			⚒r	⚒r	⚒r	Ⓐe	⚒r		⚒r			⚒r										⑤⑥f		⑤⑥f
Münster (Westf) Hbf.....d.	0210	...	0410	...	0510	0536	...	0610	0636	...	0710	0736	...	0810	0836		2010	2036	2110	...	2210	2210	2310	2310
Dülmen.......................d.	0233	...	0433	...	0533	0558	...	0633	0658	...	0731	0758	...	0833	0858	and at	2033	2058	2133	...	2233	2233	2333	2333
Haltern am See ....d.	0243	...	0443	0507	0543	0607	0607	0643	0707	0707	0741	0807	0807	0843	0907		2043	2107	2143	2207	2243	2243	2343	2343
Recklinghausen Hbf.....d.	0254	...	0454	0518	0554	0618	0618	0654	0718	0718	0752	0818	0818	0854	0918	the same	2054	2118	2154	2218	2254	2254	2354	2354
Wanne-Eickel Hbf........d.	0303	...	0502	0527	0602	0627	0627	0702	0727	0727	0800	0827	0827	0902	0927		2102	2127	2202	2227	2303	2303	0003	0003
Gelsenkirchen Hbf ....d.	0308	...	0508	0532	0608	0632	0632	0708	0732	0732	0806	0832	0832	0908	0932	minutes	2108	2132	2208	2232	2308	2308	0008	0008
Essen Hbf..................a.	0317	...	0517	0542	0617	0642	0642	0717	0742	0742	0815	0842	0842	0917	0942	past each	2117	2142	2217	2242	2317	2317	0017	0017
Mülheim (Ruhr) Hbf.......a.	...	...	0526	...	0626	...	...	0726	...	...	0824	...	...	0926	...	hour until	2126	...	2226	...	...	2326	...	0026
Duisburg Hbf.............a.	...	...	0533	...	0633	...	...	0733	...	...	0831	...	...	0933	...		2133	...	2233	...	...	2333	...	0033
Düsseldorf Flughafen ✈.a.	...	...	0545	...	0645	...	...	0745	...	...	0845	...	...	0945	...		2145	...	2245	...	...	2345	...	0045
Düsseldorf Hbf ....a.	...	...	0553	...	0653	...	...	0753	...	...	0853	...	...	0953	...		2153	...	2253	...	...	2353	...	0053

RE3 Düsseldorf - Duisburg - Gelsenkirchen - Dortmund - Hamm ⊡ ◇

km		Ⓐe			⊖						
0	**Düsseldorf** Hbf .... d.	0445	0545	0645		1845	1945	2045	2145	2245	2345
7	Düsseldorf Flughafen ✈ .. d.	0453	0553	0653		1853	1953	2053	2153	2253	2353
24	**Duisburg** Hbf .... d.	0510	0610	0710	and	1910	2010	2110	2210	2310	0010
32	Oberhausen Hbf .... d.	0516	0616	0716	hourly	1916	2016	2116	2216	2316	0016
48	Gelsenkirchen Hbf .... d.	0529	0629	0729		1929	2029	2129	2229	2329	0029
53	Wanne-Eickel Hbf .... d.	0534	0634	0734	until	1934	2034	2134	2234	2334	0034
57	Herne .... d.	0538	0638	0738		1938	2038	2138	2238	2338	0038
78	**Dortmund** Hbf.............. a.	0557	0657	0757		1957	2057	2157	2257	2357	0057
109	**Hamm** (Westf) .... a.	0628	0728r	0828		2028	*2145*	*2245*	*2345*	*0045*	*0145*

Hamm (Westf)................ d.	*0215*c	0530e	0630e	0730r	0830		2030	*2115*	*2215*
Dortmund Hbf................ d.	0303	0603	0703	0803	0903		2103	2203	2303
Herne .... d.	0320	0620	0720	0820	0920	and	2120	2220	2320
Wanne-Eickel Hbf .... d.	0324	0624	0724	0824	0924	hourly	2124	2224	2324
Gelsenkirchen Hbf .... d.	0329	0629	0729	0829	0929		2129	2229	2329
Oberhausen Hbf .... d.	0343	0643	0743	0843	0943	until	2143	2243	2343
Duisburg Hbf .... a.	0348	0648	0748	0848	0948		2148	2248	2248
Düsseldorf Flughafen ..... a.	0401	0701	0801	0901	1001		2201	2301	0001
Düsseldorf Hbf .... a.	0412	0712	0812	0912	1012		2212	2312	0012

RE11 Mönchengladbach - Duisburg - Dortmund ⊡ *RB33* Mönchengladbach - Duisburg

km		⚒r								
0	**Mönchengladbach** Hbf .. d.	0522	0622	0637	and at	2122	2137	2222	2237	2337
9	Viersen .... d.	0530	0630	0645		2130	2145	2230	2245	2345
24	Krefeld Hbf .... d.	0542	0642	0659	the same	2142	2159	2242	2259	2359
45	**Duisburg** Hbf .... a.	0558	0658	0724		2158	2224	2258	2324	0024
55	Mülheim (Ruhr) Hbf........ a.	0605	0705	...	minutes	2205	...	2305	...	...
64	**Essen** Hbf .... a.	0612	0712	...	past each	2212	...	2312	...	...
80	Bochum Hbf.................... a.	0624	0724	...	hour until	2224	...	...	...	...
98	**Dortmund** Hbf............... a.	0637	0737	...		2237	...	...	...	...

	Ⓐe	⚒r						
Dortmund Hbf............... d.	...	0521	...	0621	...	and at	2221	...
Bochum Hbf.................... d.	...	0533	...	0633	...		2233	...
Essen Hbf .... d.	...	0546	...	0646	...	the same	2246	...
Mülheim (Ruhr) Hbf........ d.	...	0552	...	0652	...	minutes	2252	...
Duisburg Hbf .... d.	0506	0600	0636	0700	0736		2300	2336
Krefeld Hbf .... d.	0531	0618	0700	0718	0800	past each	2318	0000
Viersen .... d.	0544	0633	0713	0733	0813	hour until	2333	0013
Mönchengladbach Hbf . a.	0551	0641	0720	0741	0820		2341	0020

c – Ⓒ (also June 19).
e – Ⓐ (not June 19).
f – Also June 18, Oct. 2.
h – 0622 on Ⓐ (not June 19).
j – 0718 on † (also June 19, Nov. 1).
m – To / from Minden (Table **811**).
r – ⚒ (not June 19, Nov. 1).
t – 0640 on ⑥ (not Nov. 1); 0645 on † (also June 19, Nov. 1).
⊡ – See note and shaded panel on page 377.
✣ – The 1422 from Hamm runs 4 minutes later Köln Hbf - Aachen on Ⓐ **e**.
⊖ – The 1345 and 1745 from Düsseldorf arrive Hamm 4 minutes later on ⑦
● – Trains may depart Duisburg / Mülheim 3 – 6 minutes later on certain days
◇ – Operated by **eurobahn** Keolis Deutschland GmbH & Co. KG.

RE4 Aachen - Mönchengladbach - Düsseldorf - Wuppertal - Dortmund ⊡ *RE13* Venlo - Mönchengladbach - Düsseldorf - Wuppertal - Hamm ⊡ ◇

km			⚒r	⚒r		⚒r																		
0	**Aachen** Hbf .... **473** d.	0253	0413	...	0513	...	0613	...	0713	0737	...		1737	...	1813	1837	...	1913	...	2013	...	2113	...	2237
14	Herzogenrath .... **473** d.	0307	0427	...	0527	...	0627	...	0727	0752	...		1752	...	1827	1852	...	1927	...	2027	...	2127	...	2252
58	Rheydt Hbf .... d.	0341	0503	...	0603	...	0703	...	0803	0830	...		1830	...	1903	1930	...	2003	...	2103	...	2203	...	2330
	Venlo 🏛 .... d.	│	│	0505	│	0605	│	0705	│	│	0805	and at	│	1805	│	│	1905	│	2005	│	2105	│	2205	│
	Kaldenkirchen .... d.	│	│	0510	│	0610	│	0710	│	│	0810		│	1810	│	│	1910	│	2010	│	2110	│	2210	│
	Viersen .... d.	│	│	0527	│	0627	│	0727	│	│	0827	the same	│	1827	│	│	1927	│	2027	│	2127	│	2227	│
62	**Mönchengladbach** Hbf d.	0349	0510	0545j	0610	0645j	0710	0745j	0810	0836	0845j		1836	1845j	1910	1936	1945j	2010	2045j	2110	2145j	2210	2236	2336
79	Neuss Hbf .... d.	0403	0524	0557	0624	0657	0724	0757	0824	...	0857	minutes	...	1857	1924	...	1957	2024	2057	2124	2157	2224	...	...
90	**Düsseldorf** Hbf .... a.	0413	0534	0608	0634	0708	0734	0808	0834	...	0908		...	1908	1934	...	2008	2034	2108	2134	2208	2234	...	...
90	**Düsseldorf** Hbf .... d.	d	0540e	0612e	0640r	0712	0740	0812	0840	...	0912	past each	...	1912	1940	...	2012	2040	...	2140	...	2240	...	...
117	**Wuppertal** Hbf .... d.	...	0602e	0632e	0702r	0732	0802	0832	0902	...	0932		...	1932	2002	...	2032	2102	...	2202	...	2302	...	...
144	**Hagen** Hbf .... **804** d.	...	0630e	0658e	0730r	0758	0830	0858	0930	...	0958	hour until	...	1958	2030	...	2055	2130	...	2230	...	2330	...	...
159	Witten .... d.	...	0641e	│	0741r	│	0841	│	0941	...	│		...	│	2041	...	│	2141	...	2241	...	2341	...	...
175	**Dortmund** Hbf .... d.	...	0651e	│	0751r	│	0851	│	0951	...	│		...	│	2051	...	│	2151	...	2251	...	2351	...	...
	Schwerte (Ruhr) **804** d.	...	...	0708e	...	0808e	...	0908r	...	...	1008		...	2008	...	...	*2131*	...	...	...	...	...	...	...
	Unna .... d.	...	...	0720e	...	0820e	...	0920r	...	...	1020		...	2020	...	...	*2143*	...	...	...	...	...	...	...
	Hamm (Westf) .... d.	...	...	0734e	...	0834e	...	0934r	...	...	1034		...	2034	...	...	*2157*	...	...	...	...	...	...	...

km		⚒r	⚒r																					
0	**Hamm** (Westf) .... d.	...	...	...	...	0625e	...	0725e	...	...	0825e	...	...	0925r	...	1025	...		1925	...	...	...	...	...
19	Unna .... d.	...	...	...	...	0637e	...	0737e	...	...	0837e	...	...	0937r	...	1037	...		1937	...	...	...	...	...
35	Schwerte (Ruhr) **804** d.	...	...	...	...	0649e	...	0749e	...	...	0849e	...	...	0949r	...	1049	...		1949	...	...	...	...	...
	Dortmund Hbf .... d.	...	...	...	0609e	│	0709r	│	...	0809	│	...	0909	│	1009	│	...	and at	│	...	2009	...	2109	2209
	Witten .... d.	...	...	...	0619e	│	0719r	│	...	0819	│	...	0919	│	1019	│	...		│	...	2019	...	2119	2219
48	**Hagen** Hbf .... **804** d.	...	...	0602e	0632e	0702r	0732r	0802	...	0832	0902	...	0932	1002	1032	1102	...	the same	2002	...	2032	...	2132	2232
75	**Wuppertal** Hbf .... d.	...	...	0625e	0658e	0725r	0758r	0825	...	0858	0925	...	0958	1025	1058	1125	...		2025	...	2058	...	2158	2258
102	**Düsseldorf** Hbf .... a.	...	...	0645e	0719e	0745r	0819r	0845	...	0919	0945	...	1019	1045	1119	1145	...	minutes	2045	...	2119	...	2219	2319
102	**Düsseldorf** Hbf .... d.	0548	0622	0648r	0722	0748	0822	0848	...	0922	0948	...	1022	1048	1122	1148	...		2048	...	2122	2148	2222	2322
113	Neuss Hbf .... d.	0601	0636	0701r	0736	0801	0836	0901	...	0936	1001	...	1036	1101	1136	1201	...	past each	2101	...	2136	2201	2236	2336
130	**Mönchengladbach** Hbf d.	0625j	0649	0725j	0749	0825j	0849	0925j	0922	0949	1025j	1022	1049	1125j	1149	1225j	1222		2125j	2122	2149	2225j	2249	2349
139	Viersen .... d.	0633	│	0733	│	0833	│	0933	│	│	1033	│	│	1133	│	1233	│	hour until	2133	│	│	2233	│	│
157	Kaldenkirchen .... a.	0650	│	0750	│	0850	│	0950	│	│	1050	│	│	1150	│	1250	│		2150	│	│	2250	│	│
167	**Venlo** 🏛 .... a.	0656	│	0756	│	0856	│	0956	│	│	1056	│	│	1156	│	1256	│		2156	│	│	2256	│	│
	Rheydt Hbf .... d.	...	0654	...	0754	...	0854	...	0926	0954	...	1026	1054	...	1154	...	1226		...	2126	2154	...	2254	2354
	Herzogenrath .... **473** d.	...	0729	...	0829	...	0929	...	1008	1029	...	1108	1129	...	1229	...	1308		...	2208	2229	...	2329	0029
	Aachen Hbf .... **473** a.	...	0745	...	0845	...	0945	...	1023	1045	...	1123	1145	...	1245	...	1323		...	2223	2245	...	2345	0045

RE5 Koblenz - Bonn - Köln - Düsseldorf - Duisburg - Emmerich ⊡

km		⚒r◐		Ⓐe	◐	⚒r															◐	◐		◐	◐
0	**Koblenz** Hbf .... d.	0426	...	0516	0526	0616	0716	0816	0916	1016	1116	1216	1316	1416	1516	1616	1716	1816	1916	2016	2026	2126	...	2226	2326
18	Andernach .... d.	0444	...	0528	0544	0628	0728	0828	0928	1028	1128	1228	1328	1428	1528	1628	1728	1828	1928	2028	2044	2144	...	2244	2344
29	Bad Breisig .... d.	0454	...	0535	0554	0635	0735	0835	0935	1035	1135	1235	1335	1435	1535	1635	1735	1835	1935	2035	2054	2154	...	2254	2354
39	Remagen .... d.	0511j	...	0543	0611j	0643	0743	0843	0943	1043	1143	1243	1343	1443	1543	1643	1743	1843	1943	2043	2111j	2211j	...	2311j	0011j
59	**Bonn** Hbf .... d.	0531	...	0601	0631	0701	0801	0901	1001	1101	1201	1301	1401	1501	1601	1701	1801	1901	2001	2101	2131	2231	...	2331	0031
93	**Köln** Hbf .... a.	0601	...	0628	0701	0728	0828	0928	1028	1128	1228	1328	1428	1528	1628	1728	1828	1928	2028	2128	2201	2301	...	0001	0101
93	**Köln** Hbf .... ♥ d.	▬	0631r	0631	▬	0731	0831	0931	1031	1131	1231	1331	1431	1531	1631	1731	1831	1931	2031	2131	...	▬	2349	▬	...
106	Leverkusen Mitte .... d.	...	0645r	0645	...	0745	0845	0945	1045	1145	1245	1345	1445	1545	1645	1745	1845	1945	2045	2145	...	...	0004	...	...
133	**Düsseldorf** Hbf .... d.	...	0703r	0703	...	0803	0903	1003	1103	1203	1303	1403	1503	1603	1703	1803	1903	2003	2103	2203	...	2323	0022	...	...
140	Düsseldorf Flughafen ✈ d.	...	0710r	0710	...	0810	0910	1010	1110	1210	1310	1410	1510	1610	1710	1810	1910	2010	2110	2209	...	2331	0028	...	...
157	**Duisburg** Hbf .... d.	0620	0720	0720	0820	0820	0920	1020	1120	1220	1320	1420	1520	1620	1720	1820	1920	2020	2120	2220	...	2344	0036	0044	...
165	Oberhausen Hbf .... d.	0628	0728	0728	0828	0828	0928	1028	1128	1228	1328	1428	1528	1628	1728	1828	1928	2028	2128	2228	...	2352	...	0051	...
192	Wesel .... d.	0700	0756	0756	0856	0856	0956	1056	1156	1256	1356	1456	1556	1656	1756	1856	1956	2056	2156	2256	...	0022	...	0119	...
226	**Emmerich** .... a.	0725	0821	0821	0925	0925	1021	1125	1221	1325	1421	1525	1621	1725	1821	1925	2021	2125	2228	2328	...	...	...	0152	...

	Ⓐe	◐	⚒r		⚒r														◐		◐	◐			
mmerich .... d.	...	...	0433e	0533	0533	0636	0740	0836	0940	1036	1140	1236	1340	1436	1540	1636	1740	1836	...	1940	...	...	2036	2140	2236
Vesel .... d.	...	...	0506e	0606	0606	0706	0806	0906	1006	1106	1212	1306	1412	1506	1612	1706	1812	1906	...	2012	...	...	2106	2206	2309
)berhausen Hbf .... d.	...	...	0534e	0634	0634	0734	0834	0934	1034	1134	1234	1334	1434	1534	1634	1734	1834	1934	...	2034	...	...	2134	2234	2337
uisburg Hbf .... d.	...	...	0542	0640	0642	0742	0842	0942	1042	1142	1242	1342	1442	1542	1642	1742	1842	1942	...	2042	...	...	2140	2240	2343
üsseldorf Flughafen ✈ d.	...	...	0550	▬	0650	0750	0850	0950	1050	1150	1250	1350	1450	1550	1650	1750	1850	1950	...	2050	...	...	*2203*	*2303*	*0003*
üsseldorf Hbf .... d.	...	...	0558	...	0658	0758	0858	0958	1058	1158	1258	1358	1458	1558	1658	1758	1858	1958	...	2058	...	...	*2212*	*2312*	*0012*
everkusen Mitte .... d.	...	...	0614	...	0714	0814	0914	1014	1114	1214	1314	1414	1514	1614	1714	1814	1914	2014	...	2114	...	...	▬	...	...
öln Hbf .... ★ a.	...	...	0629	...	0729	0829	0929	1029	1129	1229	1329	1429	1529	1629	1729	1829	1929	2029	...	2129	...	...	◐	...	...
öln Hbf .... d.	0532	0556	0632	0732	0732	0832	0932	1032	1132	1232	1332	1432	1532	1632	1732	1832	1932	2032	2056	*2138*	2156	2256	2356	...	...
onn Hbf .... d.	0557	0627	0657	0757	0757	0857	0957	1057	1157	1257	1357	1457	1557	1657	1757	1857	1957	2057	2127	*2208*	2227	2327	0027	...	...
emagen .... d.	0615	0654j	0715	0815	0815	0915	1015	1115	1215	1315	1415	1515	1615	1715	1815	1915	2015	2115	2154j	*2235*	2254j	2354j	0054j	...	...
ad Breisig .... d.	0623	0702	0723	0823	0823	0923	1023	1123	1223	1323	1423	1523	1623	1723	1823	1923	2023	2123	2202	...	2302	0002	0102c	...	...
ndernach .... d.	0630	0713	0730	0830	0830	0930	1030	1130	1230	1330	1430	1530	1630	1730	1830	1930	2030	2130	2213	...	2313	0013	0113c	...	...
oblenz Hbf .... a.	0642	0731	0742	0842	0842	0942	1042	1142	1242	1342	1442	1542	1642	1742	1842	1942	2042	2142	2231	...	2331	0031	0131c	...	...

RE7 Köln - Wuppertal - Hagen - Hamm - Münster (- Rheine: Table 812) ⊡

km		Ⓐe									
0	**Köln** Hbf .... d.	...	0521e	0621r	0721		1921	2021	2121	2221	2352
1	**Köln** Messe/Deutz ...... d.	...	0524e	0624r	0724	and	1924	2024	2124	2224	2355
28	Solingen Hbf .... d.	...	0543e	0643r	0743		1943	2043	2143	2243	0021
46	**Wuppertal** Hbf .... d.	...	0556e	0656r	0756	hourly	1956	2056	2156	2256	0037
73	**Hagen** Hbf .... d.	0521	0621	0721	0821		2021	2121	2221	2321	...
86	Schwerte (Ruhr) .... d.	0531	0631	0731	0831	until	2031	2131	2231	2331	...
102	Unna .... d.	0543	0643	0743	0843		2043	2143	2243	2343	...
121	**Hamm** (Westf) .... d.	0559	0659	0759	0859		2059	2159	2259	0010z	...
157	**Münster** (Westf) Hbf .... a.	0622	0722	0822	0922		2122	2229	2329	0040	...

	Ⓐe	⚒r								
Münster (Westf) .... d.	...	...	0529e	0634		2034	...	...	2134	2234
Hamm (Westf) .... d.	...	0501	0601	0701	and	2101	...	...	2201	2301
Unna .... d.	...	0514	0614	0714		2114	...	...	2214	2314
Schwerte (Ruhr) .... d.	...	0527	0627	0727	hourly	2127	...	...	2227	2327
Hagen Hbf .... d.	0439	0539	0639	0739		2139	...	2232	2237	2337
Wuppertal Hbf .... d.	0504	0604	0704	0804	until	2204	2221	2321	...	...
Solingen Hbf .... d.	0515	0615	0715	0815		2215	2238	2338	...	...
Köln Messe/Deutz ... a.	0534	0634	0734	0834		2234	2301	0001	...	...
Köln Hbf .... a.	0538	0639	0738	0838		2238	2305	0005	...	...

Düsseldorf and Köln - Krefeld - Kleve ⊖

km		⚒r	⚒r					✣		
0	**Düsseldorf** Hbf .... d.	...	0609	...	0709	...	0809		...	2309
•	**Köln** Hbf .... d.	0542	│	0642	│	0742	│	and at	2242	│
•	Neuss Hbf .... d.	0607	│	0707	│	0807	│		2307	│
7•	**Krefeld** Hbf .... d.	0625	0636	0725	0736	0825	0836	the same	2325	2336
57	Geldern .... d.	...	0702	...	0802	...	0902	minutes	...	0002
66	Kevelaer .... d.	...	0708	...	0808	...	0908		...	0008
72	Weeze .... d.	...	0717	...	0817	...	0917	past each	...	0014
79	Goch .... d.	...	0723	...	0823	...	0923	hour until	...	0020
92	**Kleve** .... a.	...	0735	...	0835	...	0935		...	0032

	⚒r								
Kleve .... d.	0526	...	0625	...	0721	...		2221	...
Goch .... d.	0539	...	0638	...	0738	...	and at	2238	...
Weeze .... d.	0545	...	0645	...	0745	...		2245	...
Kevelaer .... d.	0551	...	0651	...	0751	...	the same	2251	...
Geldern .... d.	0558	...	0658	...	0758	...	minutes	2258	...
Krefeld Hbf .... d.	0626	0635	0726	0735	0826	0835	past each	2326	2335
Neuss Hbf .... d.	│	0653	│	0753	│	0853		│	2353
Köln Hbf .... a.	│	0718	│	0818	│	0918	hour until	│	0018
Düsseldorf Hbf .... a.	0652	...	0752	...	0852	...		2352	...

- Remagen - Koblenz on the mornings of Ⓒ (also June 19).
- To Düsseldorf Flughafen Terminal (a. 0425).
- Ⓐ (not June 19).
- Arrives 8–9 minutes earlier.
- ⚒ (not June 19, Nov. 1).
- Arrives 2357.

– Düsseldorf - Kleve is operated by NordWestBahn GmbH.
- Operated by Mittelrheinbahn.

✣ – The 2209 from Düsseldorf departs Weeze 2314, Goch 2320, arrives Kleve 2332.
♥ – Trains also call at Köln Messe/Deutz (3 minutes after Köln Hbf).
★ – Trains also call at Köln Messe/Deutz (4 minutes before Köln Hbf).
• – Distances from Köln Hbf: Neuss *36 km*, Krefeld *54 km*.
◇ – *RE13* services operated by **eurobahn** Keolis Deutschland GmbH & Co. KG.
⊡ – See shaded panel for a summary of the principal Rhein – Ruhr *RE* routes.

	RE1	*RE2*	*RE3*	*RE4*	*RE5*	*RE6*	*RE7*	*RE11*	*RE13*
Aachen Hbf	●	...	...	●	...	...	...	...	...
Köln Hbf	●	...	...	│	●	...	●	...	...
Mönchengladbach Hbf	│	...	...	●	│	...	│	●	●
Düsseldorf Hbf	●	●	●	●	●	●	│	│	●
Duisburg Hbf	●	●	●	│	●	●	│	●	│
Essen Hbf	●	●	│	│	...	●	│	●	│
via Gelsenkirchen	│	●	●	│	...	│	│	│	│
via Wuppertal and Hagen ..	│	│	│	●	...	│	●	│	●
Dortmund Hbf	●	│	●	●	...	●	│	●	│
Hamm (Westf)	●	│	●	...	...	●	●	...	●
Münster (Westf) Hbf	...	●	...	...	...	...	●	...	...

802 RHEIN – RUHR LOCAL SERVICES

RE / RB services

RE8 / RB27 Mönchengladbach - Köln - Königswinter - Koblenz

km		Ⓐe	⚒r	⚒r		⚒r						▲								Ⓑw				
0	**Mönchengladbach** ⊖ d.	0440	0503e	0540	0603e	0640	0703e	0740	0803e	0840	...	and at	1340	...	1440	1503e	and at	1740	1803e	1840	1903e	*1940*	*2040*	*2140*
3	Rheydt Hbf ⊖ d.	0444	0507e	0544	0607e	0644	0707e	0744	0807e	0844	...		1344	...	1444	1507e		1744	1807e	1844	1907e	*1944*	*2044*	*2144*
22	Grevenbroich ⊖ d.	0502	0528e	0602	0628e	0702	0728e	0802	0828e	0902	...		1402	...	1502	1528e		1802	1828e	1902	1928e	*2002*	*2102*	*2202*
56	**Köln** Hbf ⊖ a.	0535	0600e	0635	0700e	0735	0800e	0835	0900e	0935	...		1435	...	1535	1600e		1835	1900e	1935	2000e	*2035*	*2135*	*2235*
56	**Köln** Hbf **807** d.	0538	0601t	0638	0701t	0738	0801t	0838	0901t	0938	1001t	the same	1438	1501t	1538	1601t	the same	1838	1901t	1938	2001t	2101	2201	2301
57	**Köln** Messe/Deutz d.	0541	0604t	0641	0704t	0741	0804t	0841	0904t	0941	1004t		1441	1504t	1541	1604t		1841	1904t	1941	2004t	2104	2204	2304
71	Köln/Bonn Flughafen ✈ d.	0551	|	0651	|	0751	|	0851	|	0951	|	minutes	1451	|	1551	|	minutes	1851	|	1951	|	|	|	|
83	Troisdorf **807** d.	0601	0623	0701	0723	0801	0823	0901	0923	1001	1023		1501	1523	1601	1623		1901	1923	2001	2023	2123	2223	2323
92	**Bonn** Beuel d.	0611	0633	0711	0733	0811	0833	0911	0933	1011	1033	past each	1511	1533	1611	1633	past each	1911	1933	2011	2033	2133	2233	2333
100	Königswinter d.	0620	0643	0720	0743	0820	0843	0920	0943	1020	1043		1520	1543	1620	1643		1920	1943	2020	2043	2143	2243	2343
105	Bad Honnef d.	0626	0649	0726	0749	0826	0849	0926	0949	1026	1049	hour until	1526	1549	1626	1649	hour until	1926	1949	2026	2049	2149	2249	2349
115	Linz (Rhein) d.	0637	0702	0735t	0802	0835	0902	0935	1002	1035	1102		1535	1602	1635	1702		1935	2002	2035	2102	2202	2302	0002
122	Bad Hönningen d.	0642	0709	0740t	0809	0840	0909	0940	1009	1040	1109		1540	1609	1640	1709		1940	2009	2040j	2109	2209	2309	...
138	Neuwied **914** d.	0655	0724	0752t	0824	0852	0924	0952	1024	1052	1124		1552	1624	1652	1724		1952	2024	2052j	2124	2224	2324	...
◊153	**Koblenz** Hbf **914** a.	0716	0740	0813t	0840	0913	0940	1013	1040	1113	1140		1613	1640	1713	1740		2013	2040	2113j	2140	2240	2340	...

	⚒r			Ⓐe		Ⓐe	⑥k		⚒r													Ⓑd		
Koblenz Hbf **914** d.	...	...	0518r	0537	0618r	0637	0647	0718	0747	0818	0847		1218	1247	1318	1347	1418		1818	1847	1918	1947	2018	2118
Neuwied **914** d.	...	...	0533r	0557	0633r	0657	0708	0733	0808	0833	0908		1233	1306	1333	1408	1433		1833	1908	1933	2008	2033	2133
Bad Hönningen d.	...	...	0546r	0611	0646r	0711	0719	0746	0819	0846	0919	and at	1246	1317	1346	1419	1446	and at	1846	1919	1946	2019	2046	2146
Linz (Rhein) d.	0453	...	0553	0618	0653	0718	0724	0753	0824	0853	0924		1253	1322	1353	1424	1453		1853	1924	1953	2024	2053	2153
Bad Honnef d.	0503	...	0603	0629	0703	0729	0733	0803	0833	0903	0933	the same	1303	1333	1403	1433	1503	the same	1903	1933	2003	2033	2103	2203
Königswinter d.	0509	...	0609	0635	0709	0735	0739	0809	0839	0909	0939		1309	1339	1409	1439	1509		1909	1939	2009	2039	2109	2209
Bonn Beuel d.	0518	...	0618	0646	0718	0746	0749	0818	0849	0918	0949	minutes	1318	1349	1418	1449	1518	minutes	1918	1949	2018	2049	2118	2218
Troisdorf **807** d.	0528	...	0628	0659	0728	0759	0759	0828	0859	0928	0959		1328	1359	1428	1459	1528		1928	1959	2028	2059	2128	2228
Köln/Bonn Flughafen ✈ d.	|	...	|	0708	|	0808	0808	|	0908	|	1008	past each	|	1408	|	1508	|	past each	|	2008	|	2108	|	|
Köln Messe/Deutz d.	0550	0619	0650	0719	0750	0819	0819	0850	0919	0950	1019	hour until	1350	1419	1450	1519	1550	hour until	1950	2019	2050	2119	2150	2250
Köln Hbf **807** a.	0553	0622	0653	0722	0753	0822	0822	0853	0922	0953	1022		1353	1422	1453	1522	1553		1953	2022	2053	2122	2153	2253
Köln Hbf ⊖ d.	0559e	0625	0659e	0725	0759e	0825	0825	...	0925	...	1025		...	1425	1459e	1525	1559e		1959e	2025	...	2125	*2225*	*2325*
Grevenbroich ⊖ d.	0630e	0655	0730e	0755	0830e	0855	0855	...	0955	...	1055		...	1455	1530e	1555	1630e		2030e	2055	...	2155	*2255*	*2355*
Rheydt Hbf ⊖ d.	0651e	0715	0751e	0815	0851e	0915	0915	...	1015	...	1115		...	1515	1551e	1615	1651e		2051e	2115	...	2215	*2315*	*0015*
Mönchengladbach ⊖ a.	0656e	0720	0756e	0820	0856e	0920	0920	...	1020	...	1120		...	1520	1556e	1620	1656e		2056e	2120	...	2220	*2320*	*0020*

S-Bahn 13 Köln - Köln/Bonn Flughafen ✈ - Troisdorf

				Ⓒz		Ⓒz	Ⓐe		Ⓐe	Ⓒz	Ⓐe			Ⓐe	Ⓒz	Ⓐe							
Köln Hbf d.	0011	0041	0241	0241	0341	0341	0421	0441	0501	0511	0521	0541	and at the same minutes past each hour until	2001	2011	2021	2041	2111	2141	2211	2241	2311	2341
Köln Messe/Deutz d.	0013	0043	0243	0243	0343	0343	0423	0443	0503	0513	0523	0543		2003	2013	2023	2043	2113	2143	2213	2243	2313	2343
Köln/Bonn Flughafen ✈ d.	0026	0056	0255	0256	0355	0356	0436	0456	0516	0526	0536	0556		2016	2026	2036	2056	2126	2156	2226	2256	2326	2356
Troisdorf a.	0036	0108	...	0308	...	0408	0448	0508	0528	0536	0548	0608		2028	2036	2048	2108	2136	2208	2236	2308	2336	0008

					Ⓒz		Ⓒz		Ⓐe	Ⓒz	Ⓐe			Ⓐe	Ⓒz	Ⓐe							
Troisdorf d.	0023	0053	0123	...	0303	...	0403	...	0513	0523	0533	0553	and at the same minutes past each hour until	2013	2023	2033	2053	2123	2153	2223	2253	2323	2353
Köln/Bonn Flughafen ✈ d.	0034	0104	0134	...	0314	0314	0414	0414	0524	0534	0544	0604		2024	2034	2044	2104	2134	2204	2234	2304	2334	0004
Köln Messe/Deutz a.	0046	0116	0146	...	0326	0326	0426	0426	0536	0546	0556	0616		2036	2046	2056	2116	2146	2216	2246	2316	2346	0016
Köln Hbf a.	0049	0119	0149	...	0329	0329	0429	0429	0539	0549	0559	0619		2039	2049	2059	2119	2149	2219	2249	2319	2349	0019

Dortmund - Unna - Soest ✣

km			Ⓒz	⚒r	⚒r	Ⓐe		Ⓐe		Ⓐe		Ⓐe			Ⓐe		Ⓐe		Ⓐe				
0	**Dortmund** Hbf **805** d.	0007	0107	0507	0607	0637	0707	0737	0807	0837	0907	0937	and at the same minutes past each hour until	1707	1737	1807	1837	1907	1937	2007	2107	2207	2307
23	Unna d.	0032	0132	0532	0632	0702	0732	0802	0832	0902	0932	1002		1732	1802	1832	1902	1932	2002	2032	2132	2232	2332
53	**Soest** **805** a.	0054	0154	0554	0654	0724	0754	0824	0854	0924	0954	1024		1754	1824	1854	1924	1954	2024	2054	2154	2254	2354

		Ⓒz	Ⓒz	⚒r	Ⓐe	⚒r	Ⓐe		Ⓐe		Ⓐe		Ⓐe			Ⓐe		Ⓐe					
Soest **805** d.	0003	0103	...	0503	0533	0603	0633	0703	0733	0803	0833	0903	0933	and at the same minutes past each hour until	1703	1733	1803	1833	1903	2003	2103	2203	2303
Unna d.	0027	0127	0237	0527	0557	0627	0657	0727	0757	0827	0857	0927	0957		1727	1757	1827	1857	1927	2027	2127	2227	2327
Dortmund Hbf **805** a.	0051	0151	0302	0551	0621	0651	0721	0751	0821	0851	0921	0951	1021		1751	1821	1851	1921	1951	2051	2151	2251	2351

RB 53 Dortmund - Schwerte - Iserlohn

km		Ⓐe	Ⓐe	Ⓐe		Ⓐe		Ⓐe			Ⓐe		Ⓐe		Ⓐe		Ⓐe		Ⓐe		Ⓐe			
0	**Dortmund** Hbf d.	0523	0553	0623	0653	0723	0753	0823	0853	and at the same minutes past each hour until	1523	1553	1623	1653	1723	1753	1823	1853	1923	1953	2023	2053	2153	232
18	Schwerte (Ruhr) d.	0545	0615	0645	0715	0745	0815	0842	0915		1542	1615	1645	1715	1745	1815	1842	1915	1942	2015	2042	2115	2215	2345
38	**Iserlohn** a.	0608	0638	0708	0738r	0808	0838	...	0938		...	1638	1708	1738	1808	1838	...	1938	...	2038	...	2138	2238	000

	Ⓐe	Ⓐe	Ⓐe		Ⓐe		Ⓐe		Ⓐe			Ⓐe		Ⓐe		Ⓐe		Ⓐe		Ⓐe			
Iserlohn d.	...	0523	...	0617e	0647	0717r	0747	0817	...	0917	and at the same minutes past each hour until	...	1617	1647	1717	1747	1817	...	1917	...	2017	2117	2217	232
Schwerte (Ruhr) d.	0520	0550	0620	0650	0720	0750	0820	0850	0920	0950		1620	1650	1720	1750	1820	1850	1920	1950	2020	2050	2150	2250	234
Dortmund Hbf a.	0539	0609	0639	0709	0739	0809	0839	0909	0939	1009		1639	1709	1739	1809	1839	1909	1939	2009	2039	2109	2209	2309	...

BONN - REMAGEN (*20 km*) - AHRBRÜCK (*48 km*) and v.v.

From Bonn Hbf at 0749 ⚒r, 0849 and hourly until 2049; then 2149 ⑥k.
Trains depart Remagen 22 minutes later. Journey time from Bonn: 67 minutes.

From Ahrbrück at 0703 ⚒r, 0803 and hourly until 2003 (also 2103 and 2203 to Remagen only). Journey time to Remagen 44 minutes, Bonn 65 minutes.

DUISBURG - MOERS - XANTEN and v.v. (45 km, journey time: 44 – 47 minutes) ⊠

From Duisburg Hbf at: 0556 ⚒r, 0710 ⚒r, 0810, 0910 and hourly until 2310.

From Xanten at: 0458 ⚒r, 0558 ⚒r, 0658, 0800, 0900 and hourly until 1600; then 1704, 1804, 1900, 2000, 2100 and 2200.

Trains call at Moers, 18 minutes from Duisburg, 27 – 28 minutes from Xanten.

OTHER USEFUL S-BAHN LINKS

Services operate every 20 minutes (every 30 minutes evenings and weekends)

Service	*Route (journey time in minutes)*
S1	Solingen Hbf - Düsseldorf Hbf (22) - Düsseldorf Flughafen ✈ (35) - Duisburg Hbf (53) - Essen Hbf (72) - Bochum Hbf (90) - Dortmund Hbf (11
S3	Oberhausen Hbf - Mülheim Hbf (8) - Essen Hbf (17).
S9	Essen Hbf - Wuppertal Hbf (46).
S11	Düsseldorf Flughafen Terminal ✈ - Düsseldorf Hbf (12) - Neuss Hbf (31) Köln Hbf (82).

d – Ⓑ (also Nov. 1); runs daily Koblenz - Linz.
e – Ⓐ (not June 19).
j – Linz - Koblenz on † (also June 19, Nov. 1).
k – Not Nov. 1.
r – ⚒ (not June 19, Nov. 1).
t – 2 – 3 minutes later on Ⓐ (not June 19).

v – Also June 19, Nov. 1.
w – Also Nov. 1.
z – Also June 19.
⊠ – Operated by Nord West Bahn GmbH.
✣ – Operated by **eurobahn** Keolis Deutschland GmbH & Co. KG (2nd class only).
◊ – Via Koblenz-Lützel (*159 km* via Ehrenbreitstein).

▲ – On Ⓐ (not June 19) the 1040, 1140 and 1240 from Mönchengladbach run 2 – 5 minutes later Linz (Rhein) - Koblenz Hbf.
⊖ – Additional journeys Mönchengladbach - Köln and v.v.
From Mönchengladbach Hbf at 0040 Ⓒ**z**, 0440 ⑥**k**, 0540 †**v**, 0640 †**v** 1840 ⑥**k**, 2240 and 2340. **From Köln** Hbf at 0025, 0525 ⚒**r**, 0725 Ⓒ 0825 †**v**, 0925 †**v** and 2125 ⑥**k**.

803 DORTMUND and MÜNSTER - ENSCHEDE

2nd class onl

km	△	Ⓐe	⚒r							
0	**Dortmund** Hbf d.	0552	0652	0752r	0852		1852	1952	2052	2152
44	Dülmen d.	0640	0740	0840r	0940	and	1940	2040	2140	2240
61	Coesfeld (Westf) d.	0705	0800	0900	1000	hourly	2000	2100	2153	2253
96	Gronau (Westf) d.	0739	0839	0939	1039	until	2039	2139q	...	...
103	**Enschede** a.	0750	0850	0950	1050		2050	2150q	...	...

△	Ⓐe	⚒r	⚒r	⚒r					
Enschede d.	...	...	0556e	0656	...	0756		1956	205
Gronau (Westf) d.	...	0525e	0620	0708	...	0820	and	2020	210
Coesfeld (Westf) d.	0506	0603	0703	0803	0803	0903	hourly	2103	...
Dülmen d.	0520	0617	0717	0817	0817	0917	until	2117	...
Dortmund Hbf a.	0607	0707	0807	0907	0907	1007		2207	...

km	△	Ⓐe	Ⓐe	⚒r						⑤⑥f
0	**Münster** (Westf) Hbf d.	0508	0608	0708	...	0808	and	2108	2208	2308
56	Gronau (Westf) d.	0609	0709	0809	0809	0909	hourly	2209	2309	0004
63	**Enschede** a.	0620	0720	0820	0820	0920	until	2220	2320	...

△	⚒r	⚒r						⑤⑥f	⑤⑥
Enschede d.	...	0626	0726p	0826	and	2126	2226	2226	232
Gronau (Westf) d.	0544	0644	0744	0844	hourly	2144	2237	2244	234
Münster (Westf) Hbf a.	0644	0744	0844	0944	until	2244	...	2344	004

e – Ⓐ (not June 19).
f – Also June 18, Oct. 2.
p – ①–⑥ only.
q – Coesfeld - Enschede on ⑦ (also June 19, Oct. 3, Nov. 1).
r – ⚒ (not June 19, Nov. 1).
△ – German holiday dates apply.

HAGEN - KASSEL 804

RE services

km		Ⓐe	Ⓐe	⑥k	Ⓐe	⑥h			Ⓒz												Ⓒz	Ⓐe			d
0	**Hagen** Hbf 802 d.	...	0505	...	0603	0613	0713	0813	...	0913	1013	1113	1213	1313	1413	1513	1613	1713	1813	1913	2013	2013	2113	2213	*2321*
14	Schwerte (Ruhr) 802 d.	...	0515	...	0613	0623	0723	0823	...	0923	1023	1123	1223	1323	1423	1523	1623	1723	1823	1923	2023	2023	2123	2223	2349
57	Arnsberg (Westf) d.	...	0545	...	0646	0656	0756	0856	...	0956	1056	1156	1256	1356	1456	1556	1656	1756	1856	1956	2056	2056	2156	2256	0020
77	Meschede d.	...	0603	...	0705	0715	0815	0915	...	1015	1115	1215	1315	1415	1515	1615	1715	1815	1915	2015	2115	2115	2215	2315	0038
85	Bestwig d.	...	0610	0623	0714	0723	0823	0923	...	1023	1123	1223	1323	1423	1523	1623	1723	1823	1923	2023	2123	2124	2224	2322	0045
100	Brilon Wald d.	...	0624	0638	0733	0738	0838	0938	...	1038	1138	1238	1338	1438	1538	1638	1738	1838	1938	2038	2138	2138	2237	...	...
126	Marsberg d.	...	0650	0700	0800	0800	0900	1000	...	1100	1200	1300	1400	1500	1600	1700	1800	1900	2000	2100	2200	...	...	...	...
151	Warburg (Westf) a.	...	0709	0719	0819	0819	0919	1019	...	1119	1219	1319	1419	1519	1619	1719	1819	1919	2019	2119	2219	...	...	...	...
151	Warburg (Westf) 805 d.	0624	0721	0721	...	...	0921	...	1024	1129	...	1323	...	1523	...	1723	...	1923	*2024*	...	...	...	...	...	...
177	Hofgeismar d.	0638	0739	0739	...	...	0939	...	1038	1144	...	1339	...	1539	...	1739	...	1939	*2038*	...	...	...	...	...	...
202	**Kassel** Wilhelmshöhe 805 a.	0655	0757	0757	...	...	0957	...	1056	1209	...	1358	...	1557	...	1757	...	1956	*2055*	...	...	...	...	...	...

	⚒r	⚒r	Ⓐe	⑥h		Ⓐe	⑥h	Ⓐe								†z	⚒e	Ⓒz				†w	⚒r		
Kassel Wilhelmshöhe 805 d.	...	...	...	...	...	...	...	0702	...	0800	...	1000	...	1200	...	1352	1354	1502	...	1600	...	1800	1801	2000	*2102*
Hofgeismar d.	...	...	...	...	...	...	...	0719	...	0818	...	1018	...	1218	...	1421	1422	1519	...	1618	...	1818	1819	2018	*2119*
Warburg (Westf) 805 a.	...	...	...	...	...	...	...	0733	...	0835	...	1035	...	1235	...	1436	1437	1533	...	1636	...	1836	1836	2035	*2133*
Warburg (Westf) d.	...	...	0530	0538	...	0630	0638	▬	0738r	0838	0938	1038	1138	1238	1338	1438	1438	...	1538	1638	1738	1838	1838	2038	2138
Marsberg d.	...	...	0552	0600	...	0649	0700	...	0800r	0900	1000	1100	1200	1300	1400	1500	1500	...	1600	1700	1800	1900	1900	2100	2200
Brilon Wald d.	...	...	0620	0622	...	0715	0722	...	0822r	0922	1022	1122	1222	1322	1422	1522	1522	...	1622	1722	1822	1922	1922	2122	2222
Bestwig d.	0436	0536	0636	0636	0636	0736	0736	0736	0836	0936	1036	1136	1236	1336	1436	1536	1536	...	1636	1736	1836	1936	1936	2136	2236
Meschede d.	0443	0543	0643	0643	0643	0743	0743	0743	0843	0943	1043	1143	1243	1343	1443	1543	1543	...	1643	1743	1843	1943	1943	2143	2243
Arnsberg (Westf) d.	0501	0601	0701	0701	0701	0801	0801	0801	0901	1001	1101	1201	1301	1401	1501	1601	1601	...	1701	1801	1901	2001	2001	2201	2301
Schwerte (Ruhr) 802 d.	0535	0635	0735	0735	0735	0835	0835	0835	0935	1035	1135	1235	1335	1435	1535	1635	1635	...	1735	1835	1935	2035	2035	2235	2335
Hagen Hbf 802 a.	0545	0645	0745	0745	0745	0845	0845	0845	0945	1045	1145	1245	1345	1445	1545	1645	1645	...	1745	1845	1945	2045	2045	2245	2345

d – From Dortmund Hbf (d. 2323).
e – Not June 19.
h – Not Nov. 1.
k – Also June 19; not Nov. 1.
r – ⚒ (not June 19, Nov. 1).
w – Also June 19, Nov. 1.
z – Also June 19.

DORTMUND and MÜNSTER - PADERBORN - KASSEL 805

km		◇ Ⓐe	◇ Ⓐe	◇ ⑥h	◇ Ⓐe	◇ Ⓒz		*ICE* 1745 D✕	*RE* 10109	◇ Ⓐe	◇ Ⓒz	◇ Ⓐe	◇ Ⓒz	*RE* 10113	◇ Ⓐe	◇ Ⓒz		*ICE* 1223 E🍷	◇ Ⓐe	◇ Ⓒz	*RE* 10117	◇ Ⓐe	◇ Ⓒz	◇ Ⓐe	◇ Ⓒz
	Köln Hbf 800 802 d.	...	...	...	...	...	...	...	0549	...	...	...	...	0749	...	...	...	0824d	...	...	0949	...	...	...	...
	Düsseldorf Hbf 800 802 d.	...	...	...	...	...	...	0546	0622	...	...	...	...	0822	...	...	...	0845	...	...	1022	...	...	...	...
0	**Dortmund** Hbf 802 d.	0450	...	...	...	...	...	0643	0717	...	...	...	...	0917	...	...	...	0942	...	...	1117	...	...	...	...
	Münster (Westf) Hbf 802 d.	|	0510	0510	0610	0610	0634	|	|	0710	0710	0810	0810	|	0910	0910	0934	|	1010	1010	|	1110	1110	1210	1210
31	Hamm (Westf) 802 a.	0507	0537	0537	0637	0637	0659	0702	0736	0737	0737	0837	0837	0936	0937	0937	0959	1002	1037	1037	1136	1137	1137	1237	1237
31	Hamm (Westf) d.	0512	0546	0552	0646	0652	...	0707	0741	0746	0752	0846	0852	0941	0946	0952	...	1007	1046	1052	1141	1146	1152	1246	1252
57	Soest 802 d.	0525	0602	0608	0702	0708	...	0722	0755	0802	0808	0902	0908	0955	1002	1008	...	1022	1102	1108	1155	1202	1208	1302	1308
77	Lippstadt d.	0535	0614	0620	0714	0720	...	0733	0806	0814	0820	0914	0920	1006	1014	1020	...	1033	1114	1120	1206	1214	1220	1314	1320
109	**Paderborn** Hbf 809 811 d.	0550	0642	0642	0739	0744	...	0749	0822	0842	0842	0939	0942	1025	1042	1042	...	1049	1139	1140	1225	1242	1242	1339	1340
126	Altenbeken 809 811 d.	0602	0654	0654	...	...	...	0804	...	0854	0854	...	0954	...	1054	1054	...	1103	...	...	...	1254	1254	...	...
163	Warburg (Westf) 804 d.	0624	0716	0716	...	...	...	0826	...	0916	0916	...	1024j	...	1116	1116	...	1125	...	...	...	1316	1316	...	...
214	**Kassel** Wilhelmshöhe 804 a.	0655	*0757*	*0757*	...	...	...	0857	...	*0957*	*0957*	...	1056	...	...	...	...	1156	...	...	...	*1358*	*1358*	...	...

	IC 2359 ⑦ B🍷	*IC* 1959 ⑤n K	*RE* 10121	◇ Ⓐe	◇ Ⓒz	◇ Ⓐe	◇ Ⓒz		*IC* 2151 L🍷	*RE* 10125	◇ Ⓐe	◇ Ⓒz	◇ Ⓐe	◇ Ⓒz	*RE* 10129	◇ Ⓐe	◇ Ⓒz	◇ Ⓐe	◇ Ⓒz	*RE* 10133	◇	◇	◇	◇	◇ ⑤⑥ v
Köln Hbf 800 802 d.	1120	1120	1149	...	...	...	...	...	...	1349	...	...	...	...	1549	...	...	...	...	1749	...	...	...	...	...
Düsseldorf Hbf 800 802 d.	1146	1146	1222	...	...	...	...	...	1346	1422	...	...	...	...	1622	...	...	...	...	1822	...	...	...	...	...
Dortmund Hbf 802 d.	1244	1244	1317	...	...	...	...	...	1443	1517	...	...	...	...	1717	...	...	...	...	1917	...	...	...	...	...
Münster (Westf) Hbf 802 d.	|	|	|	1310	1310	1410	1410	1434	|	|	1510	1510	1610	1610	|	1710	1710	1810	1810	|	*1934*	*2034*	*2134*	*2234*	*2234*
Hamm (Westf) 802 a.	1302	|	1336	1337	1337	1437	1437	1459	1502	1536	1537	1537	1637	1637	1736	1737	1737	1837	1837	1936	*1959*	*2059*	*2159*	*2259*	*2259*
Hamm (Westf) d.	1307	|	1341	1346	1352	1446	1452	...	1507	1541	1546	1552	1646	1652	1741	1746	1752	1846	1852	1944	2007	2107	2207	2307	2307
Soest 802 d.	1322	1322	1355	1402	1408	1502	1508	...	1522	1555	1602	1608	1702	1708	1755	1802	1808	1902	1908	1958	2023	2123	2223	2323	2323
Lippstadt d.	1333	1333	1406	1414	1420	1514	1520	...	1533	1606	1614	1620	1714	1720	1806	1814	1820	1914	1920	2009	2035	2135	2235	2335	2335
Paderborn Hbf 809 811 d.	1349	1349	1425	1442	1442	1539	1540	...	1549	1625	1642	1642	1739	1740	1825	1842	1842	1942	1942	2025	2100	2200	2300	2359	0002
Altenbeken 809 811 d.	1404	1404	...	1454	1454	...	...	...	1604	...	1654	1654	...	...	...	1854	1854	1954	1954	...	...	2211	...	...	0014
Warburg (Westf) 804 d.	1426	1426	...	1516	1516	...	...	...	1626	...	1716	1716	...	...	...	1916	1916	2024j	2024j	...	...	2236	...	...	0037
Kassel Wilhelmshöhe 804 a.	1457	1457	...	*1557*	*1557*	...	...	...	1657	...	*1757*	*1757*	...	...	...	*1956*	*1956*	2055	2055	...	...	...	...	...	...

	◇ ⑥h	◇ Ⓐe	◇	*RE* 10114 ⚒r	◇ Ⓐe	◇	*RE* 10116	◇ Ⓒz	◇ Ⓐe	◇ Ⓒz	◇ Ⓐe	*RE* 10120	*IC* 2156 L🍷		◇ Ⓒz	◇ Ⓐe	◇ Ⓒz	◇ Ⓐe	*RE* 10124	◇ Ⓒz	◇ Ⓐe	◇ Ⓒz	◇ Ⓐe	*RE* 10128 10158	◇ Ⓒz
Kassel Wilhelmshöhe 804 d.	...	...	...	...	...	...	...	...	0702	*0800*	*0800*	...	0859	...	...	...	*1000*	*1000*	...	...	...	*1200*	*1200*	...	...
Warburg (Westf) 804 d.	...	...	...	...	0614	0639r	...	...	0739	0839	0839	...	0934	...	...	...	1039	1039	...	...	...	1239	1239	...	...
Altenbeken 809 811 d.	...	...	...	...	0638	0702r	...	...	0802	0902	0902	...	0956	...	...	...	1102	1102	...	...	...	1302	1302	...	...
Paderborn Hbf 809 811 d.	0513	0521	0621	0638	0651	0721	0738	0816	0821j	0916	0921j	0938	1010	...	1016	1021	1116	1121j	1138	1216	1221	1316	1321j	1338	1416
Lippstadt d.	0536	0544	0644	0653	0714	0744	0753	0836	0844	0936	0944	0953	1026	...	1036	1044	1136	1144	1153	1236	1244	1336	1344	1353	1436
Soest 802 d.	0548	0556	0656	0704	0726	0756	0804	0848	0856	0948	0956	1004	1037	...	1048	1056	1148	1156	1204	1248	1256	1348	1356	1404	1448
Hamm (Westf) a.	0606	0614	0714	0718	0744	0814	0818	0906	0914	1006	1014	1018	1052	...	1106	1114	1206	1214	1218	1306	1314	1406	1414	1418	1506
Hamm (Westf) 802 d.	0620	0620	0720	0722	0750	0820	0822	0920	0920	1020	1020	1022	1056	1059	1120	1120	1220	1220	1222	1320	1320	1420	1420	1422	1520
Münster (Westf) Hbf 802 a.	0647	0647	0747	|	0817	0847	|	0947	0947	1047	1047	|	|	1122	1147	1147	1247	1247	|	1347	1347	1447	1447	|	1547
Dortmund Hbf 802 a.	...	...	...	0743	...	...	0843	...	...	...	...	1043	1115	...	...	...	...	...	1243	...	...	...	...	1443	...
Düsseldorf Hbf 800 802 a.	...	...	...	0837	...	...	0937	...	...	...	...	1137	1212	...	...	...	...	...	1337	...	...	...	...	1537	...
Köln Hbf 800 802 a.	...	...	...	0912	...	...	1012	...	...	...	...	1212	...	...	...	...	...	...	1412	...	...	...	...	1612	...

	◇ Ⓐe	*ICE* 1224 ⑥⑦ M🍷	*ICE* 1228 ①–⑤ A🍷		◇ Ⓒz	◇ Ⓐe	*RE* 10132	◇ Ⓒz	◇ Ⓐe	◇ Ⓒz	◇ Ⓐe	*RE* 10136	*ICE* 1746 D✕		◇ Ⓒz	◇ Ⓐe	◇ Ⓒz	◇ Ⓐe	*RE* 10140	*IC* 2354 ⑤f B🍷	*IC* 1952 ⑦ K	◇	◇	◇	◇
Kassel Wilhelmshöhe 804 d.	...	1402	1402	...	...	...	...	1502	...	*1600*	*1600*	...	1701	...	...	...	*1801t*	*1801*	...	1900	1900	...	*2000*	2102	...
Warburg (Westf) 804 d.	...	1433	1433	...	1438	1438	...	1539j	...	1639	1639	...	1734	...	...	...	1839	1839	...	1934	1934	...	2039	2134	...
Altenbeken 809 811 d.	...	1456	1456	...	1502	1502	...	1602	...	1702	1702	...	1756	...	...	...	1902	1902	...	1956	1956	...	2102	2157	...
Paderborn Hbf 809 811 d.	1421	1510	1510	...	1516	1521j	1538	1616	1621	1716	1721j	1738	1810	...	1816	1821	1916	1921j	1938	2010	2010	2016	2116	2210	2311
Lippstadt d.	1444	1526	1526	...	1536	1544	1553	1636	1644	1736	1744	1753	1826	...	1836	1844	1936	1944	1953	2026	2026	2039	2139	2228	2334
Soest 802 d.	1456	1537	1537	...	1548	1556	1604	1648	1656	1748	1756	1804	1837	...	1848	1856	1948	1956	2004	2037	2037	2051	2151	2240	2346
Hamm (Westf) a.	1514	1552	1552	...	1606	1614	1618	1706	1714	1806	1814	1818	1852	...	1906	1914	2006	2014	2018	2052	2052	2109	2209	2256	0004
Hamm (Westf) 802 d.	1520	1556	1556	1559	1620	1620	1622	1720	1720	1820	1820	1822	1856	1859	1920	1920	2020	2020	2022	2056	2056	2120	*2259*	2304	*0052*
Münster (Westf) Hbf 802 a.	1547	|	|	1622	1647	1647	|	1747	1747	1847	1847	|	|	1922	1947	1947	2047	2047	|	|	|	2147	*2329*	|	*0119*
Dortmund Hbf 802 a.	...	1614	1614	...	...	...	1643	...	...	...	...	1843	1914	...	...	...	...	...	2043	2115	2115	...	...	2321	...
Düsseldorf Hbf 800 802 a.	...	1709	1706	...	...	...	1737	...	...	...	...	1937	2013	...	...	...	...	...	2137	2214	2214	...	...	...	...
Köln Hbf 800 802 a.	...	1733k	1728d	...	...	...	1812	...	...	...	...	2012	...	...	...	...	...	...	2212	2240	2240	...	...	...	...

A – ①–⑤ (not June 19, 20, Oct. 3). 🚃12 and 🍷 München - Nürnberg - Kassel - Düsseldorf - Wiesbaden.
B – 🚃12 and 🍷 Köln - Kassel - Erfurt - Halle - Berlin and v.v.
D – 🚃12 and ✕ Düsseldorf - Kassel - Erfurt - Leipzig - Dresden and v.v.
E – 🚃12 and 🍷 (Darmstadt - Frankfurt Ⓐ -) Köln - Kassel - Nürnberg - München.
K – 🚃12 Köln - Kassel - Erfurt - Leipzig - Dresden and v.v.
L – 🚃12 and 🍷 Düsseldorf - Kassel - Erfurt - Leipzig and v.v.
M – ⑥⑦ (also June 19, 20, Oct. 3). 🚃12 and 🍷 München - Nürnberg - Kassel - Düsseldorf (- Köln ⑥).

d – Köln **Messe/Deutz**.
e – Not June 19.
f – Also Oct. 2; not Oct. 3.
h – Not Nov. 1.
j – Arrives 6–8 minutes earlier.
k – ⑥ only.
n – Also June 18, Oct. 2; not June 20, Oct. 3.
r – ⚒ (not June 19, Nov. 1).
t – *1800* on † (also June 19, Nov. 1).

v – Also June 18, Oct. 2.
z – Also June 19.

◇ – Operated by **eurobahn** Keolis Deutschland GmbH & Co. KG (2nd class only).

806 FRANKFURT - GIESSEN - KASSEL and SIEGEN

FRANKFURT - GIESSEN - KASSEL

km		RE 4170	RE 4150	IC 2388	RE 4152	IC 2376	RE 4154	IC 2170	IC 2374	IC 2174	RE 4156	IC 2372	RE 4158	IC 2370	RE 4160	IC 2276	IC 2286	RE 4162	IC 2274	RE 4164	IC 2272	IC 2272	IC 2172	RE 4166	RE 4168
		†z	⚒t	①–⑥				Ⓒ	A	⑤f		⊗		◧		①–⑥	⑦				①–⑤	⑥m	⑦		
				B 🍷		N 🍷		G ✕	🍷	R 🍷		🍷		🍷		🍷	R		🍷		n 🍷		S 🍷		
	Karlsruhe Hbf **912** ... d.	...	...	...	...	0702h	...	...	0910y	0910x	...	1110c	...	1310	...	1510y	1510x	...	1710x	...	1910x	...	...	...	...
	Heidelberg Hbf **912** . d.	...	...	...	...	0746h	...	0846p	0946	0946	...	1146c	...	1346	...	1546	1546	...	1746	...	1946	...	1946	...	...
0	**Frankfurt (Main)** Hbf ¶ d.	0508	0522	0649	0718	0852	0922	0958	1052	1052	1122	1252	1322	1450	1522	1650	1652	1720	1849	1922	2052	2052	2052	2122	2324
34	Friedberg (Hess) ...... ¶ d.	0530	0545	0715	0745	0915	0945	1021	1115	1115	1145	1315	1345	1515	1545	1715	1715	1745	1915	1945	2115	2115	2115	2145	2345
66	**Gießen** .... ¶ d.	0604	0604	0735	0804	0935	1004	1040	1135	1135	1204	1335	1404	1535	1604	1735	1735	1804	1935	2004	2135	2135	2135	2204	0007
96	Marburg (Lahn) .... ¶ d.	0620	0620	0750	0820	0950	1020	1056	1150	1150	1220	1350	1420	1550	1620	1750	1750	1820	1950	2020	2150	2150	2150	2220	0031
118	Stadtallendorf .... d.	0635	0635	|	0835	|	1035	|	|	|	1235	|	1435	|	1635	|	|	1835	|	2035	|	|	|	2235	0046
138	Treysa .... d.	0649	0649	0814	0849	1014	1049	|	1214	1214	1249	1414	1449	1614	1649	1814	1814	1849	2014	2049	2214	2214	2214	2249	0101
166	Wabern...................... d.	0707	0707	0833	0907	1034	1107	|	1233	1233	1307	1433	1507	1633	1707	1833	1833	1907	2033	2107	2233	2233	2233	2307	...
196	**Kassel** Wilhelmshöhe . a.	0726	0726	0852	0926	1053	1126	1153	1253	1253	1326	1452	1526	1652	1726	1853	1853	1926	2053	2126	2254	2254	2254	2326	...
200	**Kassel** Hbf .... a.	0734	0734	|	0934	|	1134	|	|	|	1334	|	1534	|	1734	|	|	1934	|	2134	...	...	...	2334	...
	Hannover Hbf **900** ... a.	...	...	0958	...	1156	...	1256	1356	1356	...	1556	...	1756	...	1956	1956	...	2156v	...	...	...	...	...	...
	Hamburg Hbf **900** .... a.	...	...	...	...	1328j	...	1428	1529	1532	...	1732j	...	1928j	...	2128r	2128	...	2328w	...	...	...	...	...	...
	Stralsund Hbf **830** ... a.	...	...	...	...	1630j	...	...	...	...	...	2030j	...	2231q	...	...	...	...	...	...	...	...	...	...	...

	RE 4171	RE 4151	IC 2273	RE 4173	RE 4153	IC 2271	IC 2275	RE 4155	IC 2277	RE 4157	IC 2279	RE 4159	IC 2371	RE 4161	IC 2373	RE 4163	IC 2375	IC 2385	IC 2191	RE 4165	IC 2377	RE 4167	IC 2379	IC 1999	RE 4169
	Ⓐt	⑥	Ⓐt	Ⓐt	Ⓒz	⊡	⑤d		⊕								⑦	①–⑥	⑥⑦				⑤d	⑦	
			🍷			🍷	S 🍷		🍷		K 🍷		K 🍷		🍷		🍷	B 🍷	E ✕		L 🍷		🍷	B	
Stralsund Hbf **830** .... d.	...	...	...	...	...	...	...	...	...	...	0527g	...	...	...	0927j	...	...	...	...	...	1325j	...	1527j	...	...
Hamburg Hbf **900** ..... d.	...	...	...	...	...	...	...	...	0624e	...	0828k	...	1028j	...	1228j	...	1428j	...	1527	...	1627j	...	1828j	...	...
Hannover Hbf **900** .... d.	...	...	...	...	...	0601b	0601	...	0801e	...	1001e	...	1201	...	1401	...	1601	1601	1704	...	1801	...	2001	2101	...
Kassel Hbf .... d.	0400	0423	...	0611	0615	|	|	0823	|	1023	|	1223	|	1423	|	1623	|	|	|	1823	|	2023	|	|	2223
Kassel Wilhelmshöhe .. d.	0405	0429	0502	0617	0621	0703	0703	0829	0903	1029	1103	1229	1303	1429	1503	1629	1703	1703	1805	1829	1903	2029	2103	2203	2229
Wabern........................ d.	0423	0448	0522	0639	0645	0722	0722	0848	0922	1048	1122	1248	1322	1448	1522	1648	1722	1722	|	1848	1922	2048	2122	2225	2251
Treysa .... d.	0441	0506	0539	0700	0703	0739	0739	0906	0939	1106	1139	1306	1339	1506	1539	1706	1739	1739	|	1906	1939	2106	2139	2243	2309
Stadtallendorf.............. d.	0455	0519	|	0716	0718	|	|	0919	|	1119	|	1319	|	1519	|	1719	|	|	|	1919	|	2119	|	2300	2323
Marburg (Lahn) .... ¶ d.	0512	0535	0604	0734	0734	0804	0804	0935	1004	1135	1204	1335	1404	1535	1604	1735	1804	1804	1901	1935	2004	2135	2204	2314	2339
Gießen .... ¶ d.	0536	0553	0623	0753	0753	0823	0823	0953	1023	1153	1223	1353	1423	1553	1623	1753	1823	1823	1919	1953	2023	2153	2223	2333	0008
Friedberg (Hess) .... ¶ d.	0600	0612	0642	0812	0812	0842	0842	1012	1042	1212	1242	1412	1442	1612	1642	1812	1842	1842	1937	2012	2042	2212	2242	2356	0036
Frankfurt (Main) Hbf. ¶ a.	0625	0634	0707	0837	0837	0907	0907	1034	1108	1234	1305	1434	1505	1637	1705	1837	1905	1905	2000	2034	2105	2234	2304	0022	0059
Heidelberg Hbf **912** .. a.	...	...	0812	...	...	1012	1012	...	1212c	...	1412	...	1612	...	1812	...	2012	2012a	...	...	2246d	...	...	...	...
Karlsruhe Hbf **912** .... a.	...	...	0850x	...	...	1050x	...	...	1250c	...	1450§	...	1650¦	...	1852•	...	2051	2051a	...	...	2326d	...	...	...	...

FRANKFURT - GIESSEN - SIEGEN

km																										
			◇	◇	◇		◇		◇	◇	◇		◇			◇	◇		◇		◇		◇		◇	◇
		†z	⚒t	Ⓐt	⑥	Ⓐt	⚒t		Ⓐt	Ⓐt	Ⓒz		⚒t	Ⓐ	Ⓒ		Ⓐt		⚒t							Ⓐt
0	**Frankfurt** (Main) Hbf ‡ d.	0508	*0522*	0552	0622	0630	*0718*	0748	0815	0815	0822	0831	*0922*	0952	0952	1022	1022	1031	*1122*	1152	1222	1231	*1322*	1352	1422	1422
34	Friedberg (Hess)..... ‡ d.	0530	*0545*	0615	0645	0657	*0745*	0815	0845	0845	0845	0859	*0945*	1015	1015	1045	1045	1059	*1145*	1215	1245	1259	*1345*	1415	1445	1445
38	Bad Nauheim .... ‡ d.	0535	|	0619	|	0701	|	0819	|	|	|	0903	|	1019	1019	|	|	1103	|	1219	|	1303	|	1419	|	|
66	**Gießen** .... ‡ a.	0602	*0602*	0640	0702	0724	*0802*	0835	0902	0902	0902	0928	*1002*	1035	1035	1102	1102	1128	*1202*	1235	1302	1328	*1402*	1435	1502	1502
66	**Gießen** .... **906** ‡ d.	0604	0611	0652	0709	0740	0809	0839	0909	0909	0909	0940	1009	1039	1046	1109	1109	1140	1209	1239	1309	1340	1409	1439	1509	1509
	Marburg (Lahn) ... ‡ a.	0619	|	|	|	|	|	0905	0938	|	|	|	|	1105	1115	|	1138	|	|	1305	|	|	|	1505	|	1538
79	Wetzlar .... **906** d.	...	0621	0703	0718	0750	0818	...	...	0918	0918	0950	1018	...	...	1118	...	1150	1218	...	1318	1350	1418	...	1518	...
101	Herborn .... d.	...	0633	0730	0733	0812	0833	...	...	0933	0933	1012	1033	...	...	1133	...	1212	1233	...	1333	1412	1433	...	1533	...
107	Dillenburg................... d.	...	0638	0738	0738	0822	0838	...	...	0938	0938	1022	1038	...	...	1138	...	1222	1238	...	1338	1422	1438	...	1538	...
139	**Siegen**...................... a.	...	0705	0805	0805	...	0905	...	...	1005	1005	...	1105	...	...	1205	...	...	1305	...	1405	...	1505	...	1605	...

		◇		◇	◇			◇		◇	◇		◇	◇		◇		◇		◇					◇	
					Ⓐt	Ⓑ	⑥	Ⓐt	Ⓐt	†z	Ⓐt			Ⓐt		Ⓑ						Ⓐt				
Frankfurt (Main) Hbf ‡ d.	1431	*1522*	1552o	1622	1622	1631	1631	...	1701	*1720*	1730	1752	1822	1822	1831	*1922*	1952	2021	2031	*2122*	2152	2152	2228	2228	*2324*	0032
Friedberg (Hess) ......‡ d.	1459	*1545*	1615	1645	1645	1657	1659	...	1725	*1745*	|	1815	1845	1845	1859	*1945*	2015	2045	2059	*2145*	2215	2215	2256	2256	*2345*	0058
Bad Nauheim..........‡ d.	1503	|	1619	|	|	1701	1703	...	1730	|	1758	1819	|	|	1903	|	2019	|	2103	|	2219	2219	2300	2300	|	0102
Gießen....................‡ a.	1528	*1602*	1635	1702	1702	1725	1728	...	1748	*1802*	|	1835	1902	1902	1928	*2002*	2035	2102	2128	*2202*	2236	2236	2324	2324	*0004*	0126
Gießen............**906** ‡ d.	1540	1609	1639	1709	1708	1740	1740	1747	1749	1809	|	1839	1909	1909	1940	2009	2039	2109	2140	2211	2239	2240	2328	2329	0011	0132
Marburg (Lahn).....‡ a.	|	|	1705	|	1738	|	|	|	1815	|	|	1905	|	1938	|	|	2105	|	|	|	2305	|	2356	|	|	0159
Wetzlar...............**906** d.	1550	1618	...	1718	...	1750	1750	1758	...	1818	1821	...	1918	...	1950	2018	...	2118	2150	2220	...	2250	...	2340	0021	...
Herborn .... d.	1612	1633	...	1733	...	1812	1812	...	...	1833	1835	...	1933	...	2012	2033	...	2133	2212	2233	...	2312	...	0002	0044	...
Dillenburg .... d.	1622	1638	...	1738	...	1822	1822	...	...	1838	1839	...	1938	...	2022	2038	...	2138	2222	2238	...	2320	...	0010	0051	...
Siegen .... a.	...	1705	...	1805	...	...	...	...	...	1905	1905	...	2005	...	...	2105	...	2205	...	2305	...	...	...	...	0121	...

				◇			◇	◇					◇				◇		◇		◇	◇		◇		◇
		Ⓐt	Ⓐt	Ⓐt	Ⓐt	Ⓐt	⑥	Ⓐt	⑥	Ⓐt	Ⓐt	†z	⚒t	Ⓐt	⚒t				⚒t			Ⓐt		⚒t		
Siegen .... d.	...	...	...	0457	...	...	0554	0600	...	...	...	...	0654	...	...	...	0754	...	0854	...	0954	...	...	1054	...	1154
Dillenburg .... d.	...	...	0512	0525	...	...	0617	0626	...	0644	...	0702	0728	...	0733	...	0817	...	0917	0933	1017	...	...	1117	1133	1217
Herborn .... d.	...	...	0520	0530	...	...	0622	0631	...	0652	...	0709	0734	...	0740	...	0822	...	0922	0940	1022	...	...	1122	1140	1222
Wetzlar...............**906** d.	...	...	0542	0547	...	...	0637	0648	...	0716	...	0731	0751	...	0802	...	0837	...	0937	1002	1037	...	...	1137	1202	1237
Marburg (Lahn).....‡ d.	0359	0440	|	|	0538	0623	|	|	0634	|	0702	|	|	...	|	...	|	0849	|	|	|	1021	1049	|	|	|
Gießen............**906** ‡ a.	0428	0510	0554	|	0604	0649	0646	0658	0704	0727	0733	0743	0801	...	0814	...	0846	0918	0946	1014	1046	1051	1118	1146	1214	1246
Gießen....................‡ d.	0430	0514	...	|	0607	0652	0654	0705	0709	0736	0736	*0753*	...	0809	0828	0828	0854	0922	*0953*	1028	1054	1054	1122	*1153*	1228	1254
Bad Nauheim..........‡ d.	0452	0538	...	0611	0624	|	|	0723	0733	0755	0755	|	...	0826	0853	0853	|	0938	|	1053	|	|	1138	|	1253	|
Friedberg (Hess) ......‡ d.	0456	0542	...	|	0630	0712	0712	0728	0738	0759	0759	*0812*	...	0830	0858	0858	0912	0942	*1012*	1058	1112	1112	1142	*1212*	1258	1312
Frankfurt (Main) Hbf ‡ a.	0528	0607	...	0641*	0658	0737	0734	0753	0807	0825	0825	*0837*	...	0858	0927	0927	0934	1007	*1034*	1127	1134	1134	1207	*1234*	1327	1334

	◇		◇		◇		◇		◇	◇		◇		◇	◇			◇		◇		◇			◇	
	Ⓐt									Ⓐt		Ⓑ			Ⓐu	Ⓒ	Ⓐ	Ⓑ					Ⓐt			
Siegen .... d.	...	...	1254	...	1354	...	1454	...	1554	...	...	1654	...	1754	...	...	...	1854	...	1954	...	2054	...	...	2309	...
Dillenburg .... d.	...	...	1317	1333	1417	...	1517	1533	1617	...	...	1717	1733	1817	...	...	...	1917	1933	2017	...	2117	2233	...	2333	...
Herborn .... d.	...	...	1322	1340	1422	...	1522	1540	1622	...	...	1722	1740	1822	...	...	...	1922	1940	2022	...	2122	2240	...	2338	...
Wetzlar...............**906** d.	...	...	1337	1402	1437	...	1537	1602	1637	...	...	1737	1802	1837	...	...	...	1937	2002	2037	...	2137	2302	...	2351	...
Marburg (Lahn).....‡ d.	1221	1249	|	|	|	1449	|	|	|	1621	1649	|	|	|	1818	1840	1849	|	|	|	2049	|	|	2249	|	2339
Gießen............**906** ‡ a.	1251	1318	1346	1414	1446	1518	1546	1614	1646	1651	1718	1746	1814	1846	1851	1911	1918	1946	2014	2046	2117	2146	2314	2318	0001	0004
Gießen....................‡ d.	1254	1322	*1353*	1428	1454	1522	*1553*	1628	1654	1654	1722	*1753*	1828	1854	1854	1922	1922	*1953*	2028	2054	2118	*2153*	2322	2322	...	0008
Bad Nauheim..........‡ d.	|	1338	|	1453	|	1538	|	1653	|	|	1738	|	1853	|	|	1938	1938	|	2053	|	2140	|	2345	2345	...	0031
Friedberg (Hess) ......‡ d.	1312	1342	*1412*	1458	1512	1542	*1612*	1658	1712	1712	1742	*1812*	1858	1912	1912	1942	1942	*2012*	2058	2112	2143	*2212*	2348	2348	...	0036
Frankfurt (Main) Hbf ‡ a.	1334	1407	*1434*	1527	1535	1606	*1637*	1727	1735	1735	1806	*1837*	1927	1934	1934	2007	2007	*2034*	2127	2134	2207	*2234*	0010	0010	...	0059

A – ①②③④⑥⑦ (also Oct. 3; not Oct. 2).
B – To / from Berlin (Table **810**).
E – WATTENMEER – [12] and ✕ Westerland - Frankfurt.
G – WATTENMEER – [12] and ✕ (Stuttgart ⑥**p** -) Frankfurt - Westerland.
K – To Konstanz on dates in Table **916**.
L – From Ostseebad Binz (Table **844**).
N – To Ostseebad Binz on dates in Table **844**.
R – To Rostock (Table **830**).
S – From / to Stuttgart (Table **912**).

a – Ⓐ only. Arrives Karlsruhe 2057 July 31 - Sept. 12.
b – ① (also June 20; not June 18, Oct. 2).
c – Ⓒ only.
d – ⑤ (also June 18, Oct. 2; not June 20, Oct. 3).
e – ①–⑥ only.
f – ⑤ (also Oct. 2; not Oct. 3).
g – ①–⑥ from July 28 (not Oct. 4).
h – ①–⑥ (not Oct. 4).
j – From July 28.
k – ①–⑥ from July 28.
m – Also Oct. 3; not Oct. 4.
n – Not June 20, Oct. 3.
o – 1547 on ①–⑤ July 14 - Aug. 22.
p – ⑥ (also Oct. 3; not Aug. 2 - Sept. 13).
q – ⑤⑦ from Aug. 1 (also Oct. 2; not Oct. 3).
r – ⑤⑥ (also Oct. 2).
t – Not June 19.
u – Not June 19, July 14 - Aug. 22.
v – ⑤⑦ (also June 18, Oct. 2; not Oct. 3).
w – ⑦ only.
x – Not July 31 - Sept. 14.
y – Not ①–④ July 31 - Sept. 11.
z – Also June 19.

⊗ – Does not run Karlsruhe - Heidelberg on ⑥ Aug. 2 - Sept. 13.
⊕ – Does not run Heidelberg - Karlsruhe on ⑥⑦ Aug. 2 - Sept. 14.
⊡ – ①②③④⑥ (also June 20, Oct. 3; not June 18, Oct. 2).
◧ – From Konstanz (Table **916**). Train number **2270** on ⑤⑦ (also June 18, Oct. 2; not Oct. 3).
§ – Not ⑦ Aug. 3 - Sept. 14.
¦ – Not ①–⑤ July 31 - Sept. 12.
• – Not ⑤ Aug. 1 - Sept. 12. Arrives up to 17 minutes later July 31 - Sept. 14.
* – July 14 - Aug. 22 terminates at Frankfurt (Main) **West** (a. 0635).
◇ – Operated by Hessische Landesbahn GmbH.
¶ – See also Frankfurt - Siegen panel.
‡ – See also Frankfurt - Kassel panel.

AACHEN - KÖLN - SIEGEN 807

RE / RB services

km	SEE NOTE ▲	Ⓒz		Ⓒz	⑥k	Ⓐe	Ⓐe	Ⓐe	⚒r	Ⓐe	Ⓐe	⚒r	Ⓐe		Ⓐe		⚒r							
0	**Aachen** Hbf .... 802 910 d.	...	...	...	...	...	...	...	...	...	0518	...	0618	...	0718	...	0818	...	0918		1918	...	...	...
31	Düren .... 802 d.	...	...	0303	...	...	...	...	0453	...	0545	...	0645	...	0745	...	0845	...	0945		1945	...	...	...
70	**Köln** Hbf .... 802 910 a.	...	...	0340	...	...	...	...	0530	...	0612	...	0712	...	0812	...	0912	...	1012		2012	...	...	...
70	**Köln** Hbf .... 802 910 d.	0023	...	0341	...	...	0431	...	0531	...	0623	0623	0723	0723	0823	0823	0923	0923	1023	and	2023	2123	2223	2323
71	**Köln** Messe/Deutz 802 910 d.	0026	...	0343	...	...	0433	...	0533	...	0626	0626	0726	0726	0826	0826	0926	0926	1026		2026	2126	2226	2326
91	Troisdorf .... 802 d.	0041	...	0409	...	...	0454	...	0554	...	0641	0641	0741	0741	0841	0841	0941	0941	1041	hourly	2041	2141	2241	2341
95	Siegburg/Bonn .... 910 d.	0046	...	0414	...	...	0459	...	0559	...	0646	0646	0746	0746	0846	0846	0946	0946	1046		2046	2146	2246	2346
102	Hennef (Sieg) .... d.	0050	...	0419	...	...	0506	...	0606	...	0650	0650	0750	0750	0850	0850	0950	0950	1050	until	2050	2150	2250	2350
114	Eitorf .... d.	0059	...	0432	...	...	0518	...	0618	...	0659	0659	0759	0759	0859	0859	0959	0959	1059		2059	2159	2259	2359
136	Au (Sieg) .... d.	0116	...	0454	0500	0515	0541	0545	0639	0650	0716	0716	0816	0816	0916	0916	1016	1016	1116		2116	2216	2316	0016
142	Wissen (Sieg) .... d.	0124	...	...	0507	0522	...	0552	...	0657	0722	0722	0822	0822	0922	0922	1022	1022	1122		2122	2224	2324	0024
154	Betzdorf (Sieg) .... d.	0138	...	...	0521	0536	...	0606	...	0711	0731	0731	0831	0831	0931	0931	1031	1031	1131		2131	2238	2338	0038
171	**Siegen** .... ▲ a.	0200	...	...	0547	0606	...	0636	...	0739	0750	0750	0850	0850	0950	0950	1050	1050	1150		2150	2300	2400	0100

SEE NOTE ▲	†V	⚒r	Ⓐe		Ⓐe		⚒r									Ⓑw	Ⓐe	⑥S
Siegen .... ▲ d.	0004	0454	0454	0608	0608	0708	0708	0809		1809	1909	2009	2109	2209	...	2314	2314	2359
Betzdorf (Sieg) .... d.	0026	0515	0515	0628	0628	0728	0728	0828		1828	1928	2028	2128	2228	...	2336	2337	0022
Wissen (Sieg) .... d.	0039	0528	0528	0637	0637	0737	0737	0837		1837	1937	2037	2137	2237	...	▬	2349	0034
Au (Sieg) .... d.	0047	0537	0537	0643	0643	0743	0743	0843	and	1843	1943	2043	2143	2243	2320	...	2357	0042
Eitorf .... d.	▬	0557	0557	0700	0700	0800	0800	0900		1900	2000	2100	2200	2300	2339	...	...	...
Hennef (Sieg) .... d.	...	0609	0609	0709	0709	0809	0809	0909	hourly	1909	2009	2109	2209	2309	2353	...	...	...
Siegburg/Bonn .... 910 d.	...	0614	0614	0714	0714	0814	0814	0914		1914	2014	2114	2214	2314	2359	...	...	...
Troisdorf .... 802 d.	Ⓐe	0618	0618	0718	0718	0818	0818	0918	until	1918	2018	2118	2218	2318	0003	0023	...	...
Köln Messe/Deutz .... 802 910 d.	0533	0633	0633	0733	0733	0833	0833	0933		1933	2033	2133	2234	2333	0027	0047	...	...
Köln Hbf .... 802 910 a.	0536	0636	0636	0736	0736	0836	0836	0936		1936	2036	2136	2236	2336	0029	0049	...	...
Köln Hbf .... 802 910 d.	0547	...	0647	...	0747	...	0847	0947		1947	*2047*e	...	...	...	0030z	0050	...	...
Düren .... 802 d.	0614	...	0714	...	0814	...	0914	1014		2014	*2114*e	...	...	...	0107z	0128	...	...
Aachen Hbf .... 802 910 a.	0644	...	0744	...	0844	...	0944	1044		2044	*2146*e	...	...	...	...	0154	...	...

S – From Nov. 29.
V – † until Nov. 23 (also June 19, Nov. 1).

e – Ⓐ (not June 19).
k – Not Nov. 1.
r – Not June 19, Nov. 1.
w – Also Nov. 1.
z – Ⓒ (also June 19).

▲ – **July 7 - Aug. 18** all trains are replaced by 🚌 between Niederschelden (*km 165*) and Siegen. Journey times extended by up to 20 minutes (earlier departures from Siegen).

ESSEN - HAGEN - SIEGEN 808

ABELLIO Rail NRW

km		Ⓒz	Ⓐe	Ⓐe	Ⓐe	Ⓐe	Ⓒz	Ⓐe		⚒r				⚒r		★	⚒r				⚒r				
0	**Essen** Hbf .... ⊡ d.	...	...	...	...	...	...	...	0634e	...	0734e	...	0834r	...	0934	and at	...	1734	...	1834	...	1934	...	...	...
16	Bochum Hbf .. ⊡ d.	...	...	...	...	...	...	...	0647e	...	0747e	...	0847r	...	0947		...	1747	...	1847	...	1947	...	...	...
30	Witten Hbf .... ⊡ d.	...	...	...	...	...	...	...	0657e	...	0757e	...	0857r	...	0957	the same	...	1757	...	1857	...	1957	...	...	...
45	**Hagen** Hbf .... ⊡ a.	...	...	...	...	...	...	...	0709e	...	0809e	...	0909r	...	1009		...	1809	...	1909	...	2009	...	...	...
45	**Hagen** Hbf .... d.	0024	...	...	0540	0610	0615	0640	0715	0740	0815	0840	0915	0940	1015	minutes	1740	1815	1840	1915	1940	2015	2115	2215	2315
75	Altena (Westf) ... d.	0050	...	...	0605	0636	0640	0705	0740	0805	0840	0905	0940	1005	1040		1805	1840	1905	1940	2005	2040	2140	2240	2340
84	Werdohl .... d.	0059	...	...	0614	0645	0649	0714	0749	0814	0849	0914	0949	1014	1049	past each	1814	1849	1914	1949	2014	2049	2149	2249	2349
106	Finnentrop .... d.	0117	0502	0558	0631	0703	0707	0731	0807	0831	0907	0931	1007	1031	1107		1831	1907	1931	2007	2031	2107	2207	2307	0007
119	Lennestadt ♥ ... d.	0129	0515	0610	0643	0715	0718	0743	0818	0843	0918	0943	1018	1043	1118	hour until	1843	1918	1943	2018	2043	2119	2219	2319	0019
141	Kreuztal .... d.	0152	0537	0633	0706	0738	0737	0806	0837	0906	0937	1006	1037	1106	1137		1906	1937	2006	2037	2106	2142	2242	2342	0042
152	**Siegen** .... a.	0204	0550	0644	0719	0750	0748	0819	0848	0919	0948	1019	1048	1119	1148		1919	1948	2020	2048	2121	2154	2254	2354	0054

	⚒r	Ⓐe	⚒r		Ⓐe		Ⓐe			⚒r		♣	⚒r					⚒r							
Siegen .... d.	...	0402	0503	...	0543	0612	0635	0712	...	0743	0812		1543	1612	...	1643	1712	1744	1812	1844	1912	2011	2111	2211	2311
Kreuztal .... d.	...	0413	0514	...	0554	0622	0647	0722	...	0754	0822	and at	1554	1622	...	1654	1722	1755	1822	1855	1922	2022	2122	2222	2323
Lennestadt ♥ .... d.	...	0436	0537	...	0617	0641	0710	0741	...	0817	0841		1617	1641	...	1717	1741	1818	1841	1918	1941	2045	2145	2245	2347
Finnentrop .... d.	0453	0453	0553	0553	0630	0653	0730	0754	...	0830	0853	the same	1630	1653	...	1730	1753	1831	1853	1931	1953	2058	2158	2258	2400
Werdohl .... d.	0510	0510	0610	0610	0647	0710	0747	0810	...	0847	0910		1647	1710	...	1747	1810	1848	1910	1948	2010	2115	2215	2315	...
Altena (Westf) .... d.	0518	0518	0618	0618	0655	0718	0755	0818	...	0855	0918	minutes	1655	1718	...	1755	1818	1856	1918	1956	2018	2123	2223	2323	...
Hagen Hbf .... a.	0546	0546	0646	0646	0724	0746	0824	0846	...	0924	0946		1724	1746	...	1824	1846	1924	1946	2024	2046	2152	2252	2352	...
Hagen Hbf ..... ⊡ d.	...	...	0651e	...	...	0751e	...	0851r	...	...	0951	past each	...	1751	...	...	1851	...	1951	...	...	...	...	...	...
Witten Hbf ..... ⊡ d.	...	...	0702e	...	...	0802e	...	0902r	...	...	1002		...	1802	...	...	1902	...	2002	...	...	...	...	...	...
Bochum Hbf ... ⊡ d.	...	...	0714e	...	...	0814e	...	0914r	...	...	1014	hour until	...	1814	...	...	1914	...	2014	...	...	...	...	...	...
Essen Hbf ..... ⊡ a.	...	...	0729e	...	...	0829e	...	0929r	...	...	1029		...	1829	...	...	1929	...	2029	...	...	...	...	...	...

	⚒r									
Essen Hbf .... d.	0507	0607	0707	and	1907	2007	2107	2207	2307	...
Bochum Hbf .... d.	0521	0621	0721	hourly	1921	2021	2121	2221	2321	...
Witten Hbf .... d.	0533	0633	0733	until	1933	2033	2133	2233	2333	...
Hagen Hbf .... a.	0546	0646	0746		1946	2046	2146	2246	2346	...

	⚒r								
Hagen Hbf .... d.	0517	0617	0717	and	1917	2017	2117	2217	2317
Witten Hbf .... d.	0531	0631	0731	hourly	1931	2031	2131	2231	2331
Bochum Hbf .... d.	0542	0642	0742	until	1942	2042	2142	2242	2342
Essen Hbf .... a.	0556	0656	0756		1956	2056	2156	2256	2356

e – Ⓐ (not June 19).
r – ⚒ (not June 19, Nov. 1).
z – Also June 19.
★ – The 1040, 1240, 1440 and 1640 from Hagen run daily.
♣ – The 0843, 1043, 1243 and 1443 from Siegen run daily.
⊡ – See also panel below main table.
♥ – Lennestadt - Altenhundem.

PADERBORN - HAMELN - HANNOVER - HANNOVER FLUGHAFEN ✈ 809

S-Bahn 5

km							Ⓐ	⑥			⚒	†				⚒	†				⚒	†			
0	**Paderborn** Hbf ..... 805 811 d.	...	...	...	...	...	0512	...	...	...	0615	...	...	0715	...	0815	...	...	0915	...	1015	...	...	1115	...
17	Altenbeken .... 805 811 d.	...	...	...	...	...	0524	...	...	...	0627	...	...	0727	...	0827	...	...	0927	...	1027	...	...	1127	...
56	Bad Pyrmont .... d.	0005	...	...	0505r	...	0602	0605	...	0635e	0702	0705	0735e	0802	...	0902	0905	...	1002	...	1102	1105	...	1202	...
75	Hameln .... a.	0019	...	...	0519r	...	0616	0618	...	0649e	0716	0718	0749e	0816	...	0916	0918	...	1016	...	1116	1118	...	1216	...
75	Hameln .... d.	0020	0420e	0450e	0520	0550r	0620	0620	0620	0650r	0720	0720	0750r	0820	0850r	0920	0920	0950r	1020	1050r	1120	1120	1150r	1220	1250r
133	**Hannover** Hbf .... a.	0103	0503e	0533e	0603	0633r	0703	0703	0703	0733r	0803	0803	0833r	0903	0933r	1003	1003	1033r	1103	1133r	1203	1203	1233r	1303	1333r
133	**Hannover** Hbf .... d.	0105	0505	0535	0605	0635	0705	0705	0705	0735	0805	0805	0835	0905	0935	1005	1005	1035	1105	1135	1205	1205	1235	1305	1335
148	**Hannover** Flughafen ✈ .... a.	0123	0523	0553	0623	0653	0723	0723	0723	0753	0823	0823	0853	0923	0953	1023	1023	1053	1123	1153	1223	1223	1253	1323	1353

	⚒	†				⚒	†				⚒	†				Ⓐ	Ⓒ				Ⓐ	Ⓒ			
Paderborn Hbf .... 805 811 d.	1215	...	...	1315	...	1415	...	...	1515	...	1615	...	...	1715	...	1815	...	...	1915	...	2015	...	...	2115	...
Altenbeken .... 805 811 d.	1227	...	...	1327	...	1427	...	...	1527	...	1627	...	...	1727	...	1827	...	...	1927	...	2027	...	...	2127	...
Bad Pyrmont .... d.	1302	1305	1335e	1402	...	1502	1505	...	1602	1635e	1702	1705	...	1802	1835e	1902	1905	...	2002	...	2102	2105	...	2202	2305
Hameln .... a.	1316	1318	1349e	1416	...	1516	1518	...	1616	1649e	1716	1718	...	1816	1849e	1916	1918	...	2016	...	2116	2118	...	2216	2318
Hameln .... d.	1320	1320	1350r	1420	1450r	1520	1520	1550r	1620	1650r	1720	1720	1750	1820	1850	1920	1920	1950	2020	2050b	2120	2120	...	2220	2320
Hannover Hbf .... a.	1403	1403	1433r	1503	1533r	1603	1603	1633r	1703	1733r	1803	1803	1833	1903	1933	2003	2003	2033	2103	2133b	2203	2203	...	2303	0003
Hannover Hbf .... d.	1405	1405	1435	1505	1535	1605	1605	1635	1705	1735	1805	1805	1835	1905	1935	2005	2005	2035	2105	2135	2205	2205	2235	2305	0005
Hannover Flughafen ✈ .... a.	1423	1423	1453	1523	1553	1623	1623	1653	1723	1753	1823	1823	1853	1923	1953	2023	2023	2053	2123	2153	2223	2223	2253	2323	0023

				⚒		⚒					†	⚒				†	⚒				†	⚒			
Hannover Flughafen ✈ .... d.	0006	0036	0106	0436e	0506	0536	0536	0606	0636	0706	0736	0736	0806	0836	0906	0936	0936	1006	1036	1106	1136	1136	1206	1236	1306
Hannover Hbf .... a.	0023	0053	0123	0453e	0523	0553	0553	0623	0653	0723	0753	0753	0823	0853	0923	0953	0953	1023	1053	1123	1153	1153	1223	1253	1323
Hannover Hbf .... d.	...	0100	...	0455e	0525e	0555	...	0625r	0655	0725r	0755	0755	0825r	0855	0925r	0955	0955	1025r	1055	1125r	1155	1155	1225r	1255	1325r
Hameln .... a.	...	0144	...	0540e	0610e	0640	...	0710r	0740	0810r	0840	0840	0910r	0940	1010r	1040	1040	1110r	1140	1210r	1240	1240	1310r	1340	1410r
Hameln .... d.	...	...	...	0544	0611e	0644	...	0711e	0744	...	0841	0844	...	0944	...	1041	1044	...	1144	...	1241	1244	1311e	1344	...
Bad Pyrmont .... d.	...	...	...	0600	0625e	0700	...	0725e	0800	...	0855	0900	...	1000	...	1055	1100	...	1200	...	1255	1300	1325e	1400	...
Altenbeken .... 805 811 d.	...	...	...	0633	...	0733	...	...	0833	...	...	0933	...	1033	...	...	1133	...	1233	...	...	1333	...	1433	...
Paderborn Hbf .... 805 811 a.	...	...	...	0646	...	0746	...	...	0846	...	...	0946	...	1046	...	...	1146	...	1246	...	...	1346	...	1446	...

	†	⚒				†	⚒				Ⓒ	Ⓐ				Ⓒ	Ⓐ								
Hannover Flughafen ✈ .... d.	1336	1336	1406	1436	1506	1536	1536	1606	1636	1706	1736	1736	1806	1836	1906	1936	1936	2006	2036	2106	2136	2206	2236	2306	2336
Hannover Hbf .... a.	1353	1353	1423	1453	1523	1553	1553	1623	1653	1723	1753	1753	1823	1853	1923	1953	1953	2023	2053	2123	2153	2223	2253	2323	2353
Hannover Hbf .... d.	1355	1355	1425r	1455	1525r	1555	1555	1625	1655	1725	1755	1755	1825	1855	1925	1955	1955	2025r	2055	2125e	2155	...	2255	...	2355
Hameln .... a.	1440	1440	1510r	1540	1610r	1640	1640	1710	1740	1810	1840	1840	1910	1940	2010	2040	2040	2110r	2140	2210e	2240	...	2340	...	0040
Hameln .... d.	1441	1444	...	1544	1611e	1641	1644e	...	1744	1811e	1841	1844	...	1944	...	2041	2044	...	2144	...	2241	...	2341	...	...
Bad Pyrmont .... d.	1455	1500	...	1600	1625e	1655	1700e	...	1800	1825e	1855	1900	...	2000	...	2055	2100	...	2200	...	2255	...	2355	...	...
Altenbeken .... 805 811 d.	...	1533	...	1633	...	...	1733e	...	1833	...	...	1933	...	2033	...	...	2133	...	2233	...	...	...	...	...	...
Paderborn Hbf .... 805 811 a.	...	1546	...	1646	...	...	1746e	...	1846	...	...	1946	...	2046	...	...	2146	...	2246	...	...	...	...	...	...

– Ⓑ only.
e – Ⓐ only.
r – ⚒ only.

810 HAMM and BAD BENTHEIM - HANNOVER - BERLIN

km		CNL 457 🅁 B🍷		ICE 949 ① Y	ICE 649 Ⓐ ✕§	IC 2447 ① D	ICE 841 ①–⑥ L✕	IC 2241 ①–⑥ M	ICE 541* ①–⑥ ✕	ICE 541* ✕	EC 249 ①–⑥ C	IC 2445 ①–⑥ h D	ICE 843 ✕	ICE 853 ①–⑥ ✕	IC 2343 ⑦	IC 2243 ①–⑥ ⊙✕	ICE 543 ✕	ICE 553 ①–⑥ K✕	IC 2388 ①–⑥ F🍷	IC 2443 ①–⑥ h D	ICE 845 Ⓐ ✕	ICE 1045 Ⓒ ✕	ICE 855 ✕	IC 141 ✕
	Bonn Hbf **800** d.	...	...	...	...	...	...	...	...	...	...	🍷	...	...	...	...	...	0621	...	🍷	...	...	...	...
	Köln Hbf **800** d.	2228	...	0033	...	...	...	...	0429	...	...	0510	0529	0545	...	...	0626	0648	...	0713	...	0728	0748	...
	Wuppertal Hbf **800** d.	2314	...	0125	...	...	...	...	|	...	...	0541	|	0617	...	...	|	0716	...	0743	◐	|	0817	...
	Düsseldorf Hbf **800** d.	2202	...	0104	...	...	...	...	0453	...	...	|	0553	|	...	...	0653	|	...	|	0753	0753	|	...
	Dortmund Hbf **800** d.	2356	...	0311	...	...	...	...	0547	...	...	0628	0648	|	...	...	0748	|	...	0828	0848	0848	|	...
0	**Hamm** (Westf) **802** d.	0014	...	0330	...	...	...	...	0604	...	...	0645	0711	0711	...	...	0811	0811	...	0845	0911	0911	0911	...
50	Gütersloh Hbf **802** d.	|	...	0351	...	...	...	...	0629	...	...	0705	|	|	...	...	|	|	...	0905	|	|	|	...
67	**Bielefeld** Hbf **802 811** d.	0043	...	0403	...	0517	...	...	0640	...	...	0717	0738	0738	...	...	0838	0838	...	0917	0938	0938	0938	...
81	Herford **811** d.	|	...	0413	...	0527	...	...	|	...	...	0727	|	|	...	...	|	|	...	0927	|	|	|	...
	Amsterdam C **22** d.	|	...	|	...	|	...	...	|	...	...	|	|	|	...	...	|	|	...	|	|	|	|	0701
	Bad Bentheim 🏛 **811** d.	|	...	|	...	|	...	...	|	...	...	|	|	|	...	0721	|	|	...	|	|	|	|	0928
	Rheine **811** d.	|	...	|	...	|	...	...	|	...	...	|	|	|	...	0735	|	|	...	|	|	|	|	0942
	Osnabrück Hbf **811** d.	|	...	|	...	|	...	0604	|	...	...	|	|	|	0804	0805	|	|	...	|	|	|	|	1008
	Bünde (Westf) **811** d.	|	...	|	...	|	...	0626	|	...	...	|	|	|	0826	0826	|	|	...	|	|	|	|	|
97	Bad Oeynhausen **811** d.	|	...	|	...	0537	...	0639	|	...	...	0737	|	|	0839	0839	|	|	...	0937	|	|	|	1039
112	Minden (Westf) **811** d.	|	...	0430	...	0549	...	0649	|	...	...	0749	|	|	0849	0849	|	|	...	0949	|	|	|	1049
177	**Hannover** Hbf **811** a.	|	...	0458	...	0618	...	0718	0728	...	...	0818	0828	0828	0918	0918	0928	0928	...	1018	1028	1028	1028	1118
177	**Hannover** Hbf d.	|	...	0501	0527	0636	0631	0721	0731	0731	...	0836	0831	0831	0921	0921	0931	0931	1018	1036	1031	1031	1031	1121
	Magdeburg Hbf **866** a.	|	...	|	|	0755	|	|	|	|	...	0955	|	|	|	|	|	|	|	1155	|	|	|	|
	Leipzig Hbf **866** a.	|	...	|	|	0918	|	|	|	|	...	1118	|	|	|	|	|	|	|	1318	|	|	|	|
252	Wolfsburg **902** d.	|	...	0534	0620	...	0704	0755	|	|	...	...	0905	0905	0955	0955	|	|	1052	...	1105	1105	1105	1155
327	Stendal **838** d.	|	...	0606	0648	...	0734	0827	|	|	0850	...	|	|	1027	1027	|	|	|	...	|	|	|	1227
419	**Berlin** Spandau **838 902** a.	|	...	0640	0721	...	0806	0901	0855	0855	0927	...	0955	0955	1101	1101	1052	1052	1151	...	1155	1155	1155	1301
435	**Berlin** Hbf **838 902** a.	0423	...	0655	0735	...	0823	0915	0911	0911	0937	...	1010	1010	1115	1115	1108	1108	1206	...	1210	1210	1210	1315
440	**Berlin** Ostbahnhof **838 902** a.	...	...	0707	0749	...	0834	0926	0922	0922	...	...	1023	1023	1126	1126	1120	1120	1217	...	1223	1223	1223	1326

	ICE 545 ✕	ICE 555 ✕	IC 2441 D🍷	ICE 847 ✕	ICE 857 ✕	IC 1931 ⑤ U	IC 143 ✕	ICE 547 ✕	ICE 557 ✕	IC 2010 ⑤v H	IC 2010 ⑦	IC 2049 ⑤⑥z D🍷	IC 2249 ⑦ D🍷	ICE 849 ✕	ICE 859 ✕	IC 145 ✕	ICE 549 ✕	ICE 559 ✕	IC 2047 Ⓑb D🍷	ICE 941 ✕	ICE 951 ✕	IC 147 ✕	ICE 641 ✕	ICE 651 ✕
Bonn Hbf **800** d.	...	0825t	...	...	...	...	...	...	...	1022	...	...	...	...	...	...	...	1222e	...	...	...	...	...	1425
Köln Hbf **800** d.	0828	0848	0910	0928	0948	...	...	...	1048	1046	1046	1110	1113	...	1148	...	...	1248	1313	...	1348	...	...	1448
Wuppertal Hbf **800** d.	|	0916	0943	|	1016	...	...	...	1116	|	|	1143	1143	◐	1216	...	...	1316	1343	...	1417	...	◐	1516
Düsseldorf Hbf **800** d.	0853	|	|	0953	|	...	...	1053	|	1118	1118	|	|	1153	|	...	1253	|	|	1353	|	...	1453	|
Dortmund Hbf **800** d.	0948	|	1028	1048	|	...	...	1148	|	1211	1211	1228	1228	1248	|	...	1348	|	1428	1448	|	...	1548	|
Hamm (Westf) **802** d.	1011	1011	1045	1111	1111	...	...	1211	1211	1234	1234	1245	1245	1311	1311	...	1411	1411	1445	1511	1511	...	1611	1611
Gütersloh Hbf **802** d.	|	|	1105	|	|	...	...	|	|	1255	1255	1305	1305	|	|	...	|	|	1505	|	|	...	|	|
Bielefeld Hbf **802 811** d.	1038	1038	1117	1138	1138	...	...	1238	1238	1305	1305	1317	1317	1338	1338	...	1438	1438	1517	1538	1538	...	1638	1638
Herford **811** d.	|	|	1127	|	|	...	...	|	|	1315	1315	1327	1327	|	|	...	|	|	1527	|	|	...	|	|
Amsterdam C **22** d.	|	|	|	|	|	...	0901	|	|	|	|	|	|	|	|	1101	|	|	|	|	|	1301	|	|
Bad Bentheim 🏛 **811** d.	|	|	|	|	|	...	1128	|	|	|	|	|	|	|	|	1328	|	|	|	|	|	1528	|	|
Rheine **811** d.	|	|	|	|	|	...	1142	|	|	|	|	|	|	|	|	1342	|	|	|	|	|	1542	|	|
Osnabrück Hbf **811** d.	|	|	|	|	|	...	1208	|	|	|	|	|	|	|	|	1408	|	|	|	|	|	1608	|	|
Bünde (Westf) **811** d.	|	|	|	|	|	...	1229	|	|	|	|	|	|	|	|	|	|	|	|	|	|	1629	|	|
Bad Oeynhausen **811** d.	|	|	1137	|	|	...	|	|	|	|	|	1337	1337	|	|	1439	|	|	1537	|	|	|	|	|
Minden (Westf) **811** d.	|	|	1149	|	|	...	1249	|	|	|	|	1349	1349	|	|	1449	|	|	1549	|	|	1649	|	|
Hannover Hbf **811** a.	1128	1128	1218	1228	1228	...	1318	1328	1328	1401	1401	1418	1418	1428	1428	1518	1528	1528	1618	1628	1628	1718	1728	1728
Hannover Hbf d.	1131	1131	1236	1231	1231	...	1321	1331	1331	1404	1404	1436	1436	1431	1431	1521	1531	1531	1636	1631	1631	1721	1731	1731
Magdeburg Hbf **866** a.	|	|	1355	|	|	...	|	|	|	|	|	1555	1555	|	|	|	|	|	1755	|	|	|	|	|
Leipzig Hbf **866** a.	|	|	1518	|	|	...	|	|	|	|	|	1718	1718	|	|	|	|	|	1918	|	|	|	|	|
Wolfsburg **902** d.	|	|	...	1305	1305	...	1355	|	|	1438	1438	...	...	1505	1505	1555	|	|	...	1705	1705	1755	|	|
Stendal **838** d.	|	|	...	|	|	1407	1427	|	|	|	|	...	...	|	|	1627	|	|	...	|	|	1827	|	|
Berlin Spandau **838 902** a.	1254	1254	...	1355	1355	1442	1501	1453	1453	1540	1540	...	...	1555	1555	1701	1653	1653	...	1755	1755	1901	1853	1853
Berlin Hbf **838 902** a.	1308	1308	...	1411	1411	1453	1515	1511	1511	1552	1552	...	...	1612	1612	1715	1711	1711	...	1810	1810	1915	1908	1908
Berlin Ostbahnhof **838 902** a.	1321	1321	...	1423	1423	...	1526	1523	1523	...	...	...	...	1623	1623	1726	1722	1722	...	1823	1823	1926	1920	1920

	IC 1216 ⑤v J🍷	IC 1920 ⑦ R	ICE 1741 Ⓑ D✕	ICE 943 ✕	ICE 953 Ⓑ ✕	IC 149 ✕	ICE 643 ✕	ICE 653 ✕	IC 2012 A✕	ICE 945 Ⓑ ✕	ICE 955 ✕	IC 241 Ⓑ ✕	IC 241 ⑦ ✕	ICE 645 ✕	ICE 655 ✕	IC 2041 ⑦ 🍷	ICE 947 x✕	ICE 957 ⑤⑦ f✕	ICE 1220 ⑦ E🍷	IC 243 ⑦ ✕	ICE 657 ⑦ ✕		ICE 102 ①–⑤ Q🍷	ICE 1102 ⑥ Q🍷
Bonn Hbf **800** d.	1422	1422	...	...	...	...	...	...	1622	...	...	...	...	...	...	...	...	...	...	...	2025	...	...	...
Köln Hbf **800** d.	1445	1445	1510	...	1548	...	...	1648	1646	...	1748	...	...	...	1848	1913	1926r	1948	2017d	...	2048	...	2110	2110
Wuppertal Hbf **800** d.	|	|	1544	...	1616	...	◐	1716	|	...	1816	...	...	◐	1916	1943	|	2016	|	...	2116	...	2143	|
Düsseldorf Hbf **800** d.	1518	1518	|	1556	|	...	1653	|	1715	1753	|	...	...	1853	|	|	1953	|	2040	...	|	...	|	2133
Dortmund Hbf **800** d.	1611	1611	1628	1648	|	...	1748	|	1828	1848	|	...	...	1948	|	2028	2048	|	2132	...	|	...	2228	2228
Hamm (Westf) **802** d.	1634	1634	1645	1711	1711	...	1811	1811	1845	1911	1911	...	...	2011	2011	2045	2111	2111	2149	...	2211	...	2250	2250
Gütersloh Hbf **802** d.	1655	1655	1705	|	|	...	|	|	1905	|	|	...	...	|	|	2105	|	|	2210	...	|	...	2310	2310
Bielefeld Hbf **802 811** d.	1706	1706	1716	1738	1738	...	1838	1838	1917	1938	1938	...	...	2038	2038	2117	2138	2138	2220	...	2238	...	2320	2320
Herford **811** d.	1715	1715	1726	|	|	...	|	|	1927	|	|	...	...	|	|	2127	|	|	|	...	|	...	2330	2330
Amsterdam C **22** d.	|	|	|	|	|	1501	|	|	|	|	|	1701	1701	|	|	|	|	|	|	1901	|	...	|	|
Bad Bentheim 🏛 **811** d.	|	|	|	|	|	1728	|	|	|	|	|	1928	1928	|	|	|	|	|	|	2128	|	...	|	|
Rheine **811** d.	|	|	|	|	|	1742	|	|	|	|	|	1942	1942	|	|	|	|	|	|	2142	|	...	|	|
Osnabrück Hbf **811** d.	|	|	|	|	|	1808	|	|	|	|	|	2008	2008	|	|	|	|	|	|	2208	|	...	|	|
Bünde (Westf) **811** d.	|	|	|	|	|	|	|	|	|	|	|	2029	2029	|	|	|	|	|	|	|	|	...	|	|
Bad Oeynhausen **811** d.	|	|	1737	|	|	1839	|	|	1937	|	|	|	|	|	|	2137	|	|	|	2240	|	...	|	|
Minden (Westf) **811** d.	|	|	1749	|	|	1849	|	|	1949	|	|	2049	2049	|	|	2149	|	|	2247	2252	|	...	2346	2348
Hannover Hbf **811** a.	1801	1801	1818	1828	1828	1918	1928	1928	2018	2028	2028	2118	2118	2128	2128	2218	2228	2228	2317	2326	2328	...	0018	0018
Hannover Hbf d.	1804	1804	1836	1831	1831	1921	1931	1931	2036p	2031	2031	...	2121	2131	2131	...	2231	2231	...	...	2331	...	...	...
Magdeburg Hbf **866** a.	|	|	1955	|	|	|	|	|	2155p	|	|	...	|	|	|	...	|	|	...	...	|	...	...	...
Leipzig Hbf **866** a.	|	|	2118	|	|	|	|	|	2320w	|	|	...	|	|	|	...	|	|	...	...	|	...	...	...
Wolfsburg **902** d.	1838	1838	...	1905	1905	1955	|	|	...	2105	2105	...	2155	|	|	...	2305	2305	...	...	0005	...	...	...
Stendal **838** d.	|	|	...	|	|	2027	|	|	...	2134	2134	...	2227	|	|	...	|	|	...	...	|	...	...	...
Berlin Spandau **838 902** a.	1941	1941	...	1958	1958	2101	2053	2053	...	2207	2207	...	2301	2254	2254	...	2355	2355	...	...	0057	...	...	...
Berlin Hbf **838 902** a.	1951	1951	...	2012	2012	2115	2108	2108	...	2222	2222	...	2318	2308	2308	...	0010	0010	...	...	0111	...	...	...
Berlin Ostbahnhof **838 902** a.	...	...	...	2023	2023	2126	2121	2121	...	2235	2235	...	...	2319	2319	...	...	...	...	...	0122	...	...	...

A – ALLGÄU – (12) and ✕ Oberstdorf - Ulm - Stuttgart - Mainz - Koblenz - Köln - Hannover (- Magdeburg ①④⑤⑦ **p**) (- Leipzig ⑦).
B – KOPERNIKUS – 🛏 1, 2 cl., 🛏 2 cl. and (2) Amsterdam - Dresden - Praha (Table **28**). Conveys 🛏 1, 2 cl., 🛏 2 cl. and (2) (*EN* **447** – JAN KIEPURA) Amsterdam - Berlin - Warszawa (Table **24**). For overnight journeys only.
C – WAWEL – (12) Hamburg - Berlin - Cottbus - Forst 🏛 - Wrocław.
D – To Dresden (Table **842**).
E – (12) and 🍷 München - Frankfurt - Köln Messe/Deutz - Hannover.
F – (12) and 🍷 Frankfurt - Gießen - Kassel - Hannover - Berlin.
H – From Tübingen via Stuttgart (Tables **911/2**).
J – (12) and 🍷 Salzburg - München - Stuttgart - Mainz - Köln - Berlin.
K – From Koblenz Hbf (d. 0547).
L – (12) and ✕ (Oldenburg ① -) (Bremen Ⓐ -) Hannover - Berlin.
M – From Münster (Westf) Hbf (d. 0538). Conveys ✕ on ①⑥.
Q – (12) and 🍷 Basel - Karlsruhe - Köln - Hannover.
R – From Frankfurt (Table **911**).
U – ⑤ from Aug. 1 (also Oct. 2; not Oct. 3). From Hamburg (Tables **900/841**).
Y – From Aachen Hbf (d. 2349, previous day). Conveys ✕ Hannover - Berlin.

b – Not Oct. 3.
d – Köln **Messe/Deutz**.
e – ①–⑥ only.
f – Also Oct. 2; not Oct. 3.
h – Not Oct. 4.
p – ①④⑤⑦ (also Oct. 1; not Oct. 3).
r – ①②③④⑥ (also Oct. 3; not Oct. 2).
t – ①–⑥ (not June 19, Oct. 3, Nov. 1).
v – Also June 18, Oct. 2; not June 20, Oct. 3.
w – ⑦ only.
x – Not Oct. 2.
z – Also Oct. 2.

***** – Train number **1541** on ⑥ (also Oct. 3; not Oct. 4).
§ – Also calls at Braunschweig Hbf (d. 0601).
⊙ – Also calls at Ibbenbüren (d. 0748).
◐ – From Köln/Bonn Flughafen ✈ (Table **800**).

BERLIN - HANNOVER - HAMM and BAD BENTHEIM — 810

km		CNL 456 Ⓡ B🍷	ICE 948 ①		ICE 103 L🍷		ICE 656 Ⓐ ✗	ICE 646 Ⓐ ✗	IC 242 ①–⑥ ✗	ICE 956 ①–⑥ ✗	ICE 946 ①–⑥ ✗	IC 2013 A✗	ICE 654 ✗	ICE 644 ①–⑥ ✗	IC 240 ①–⑥ ✗	ICE 954 ①–⑥ ✗	ICE 944 ✗	ICE 1742 ①–⑥ ✗	ICE 652 ✗	ICE 642 ✗	IC 148 ✗	ICE 952 ✗	ICE 942 ✗	IC 2046 ⑥k D🍷
0	**Berlin** Ostbahnhof . 838 902 d.	0016	0026	...	...	...	0411	0411	...	0525	0525	...	0636	0636	0625	0735	0735	...	0836	0836	0825	0935	0935	...
5	**Berlin** Hbf .... 838 902 d.	0027	0037	...	...	...	0422	0422	...	0536	0536	...	0647	0647	0636	0746	0746	...	0847	0847	0836	0946	0946	...
21	**Berlin** Spandau ...... 838 902 d.	|	0052	...	...	...	0439	0439	...	0551	0551	...	0702	0702	0652	0801	0801	...	0902	0902	0852	1001	1001	...
113	Stendal .... 838 d.	|	0126	...	...	...	0516	0516	...	0626	0626	...	|	|	0734	|	|	...	|	|	0934	|	|	...
188	Wolfsburg .... 902 d.	|	0156	...	...	...	0548	0548	...	0656	0656	...	|	|	0805	0856	0856	...	|	|	1005	1056	1056	...
	Leipzig Hbf **866** .... d.	|	|	...	...	...	|	|	...	|	|	0436g	|	|	|	|	|	0640	|	|	|	|	|	0840
	Magdeburg Hbf **866** .... d.	|	|	...	...	...	|	|	...	|	|	0601h	|	|	|	|	|	0802	|	|	|	|	|	1002
263	**Hannover** Hbf .... a.	|	0228	...	...	...	0618	0618	...	0728	0728	0723h	0828	0828	0837	0928	0928	0924	1028	1028	1037	1128	1128	1123
263	**Hannover** Hbf .... 811 d.	|	0232	...	0540	...	0621	0621	0640	0731	0731	0740	0831	0831	0840	0931	0931	0940	1031	1031	1040	1131	1131	1140
328	Minden (Westf) .... 811 d.	|	0302	...	0612	...	0651	0651	0712	|	|	0812	|	|	0912	|	|	1013	|	|	1112	|	|	1212
343	Bad Oeynhausen .... 811 d.	|	|	...	|	...	|	|	0722	|	|	0822	|	|	|	|	|	1023	|	|	1122	|	|	1222
359	Bünde (Westf) .... 811 d.	|	|	...	|	...	|	|	|	|	|	|	|	|	0932	|	|	|	|	|	|	|	|	|
396	**Osnabrück** Hbf .... 811 d.	|	|	...	|	...	|	|	0753	|	|	|	|	|	0953	|	|	|	|	|	1153	|	|	|
444	Rheine .... 811 d.	|	|	...	|	...	|	|	0821	|	|	|	|	|	1021	|	|	|	|	|	1221	|	|	|
465	Bad Bentheim 🏛 .... 811 a.	|	|	...	|	...	|	|	0834	|	|	|	|	|	1034	|	|	|	|	|	1234	|	|	|
655	*Amsterdam C* **22** .... a.	|	|	...	|	...	|	|	1100	|	|	|	|	|	1300	|	|	|	|	|	1500	|	|	|
	Herford .... 811 d.	|	0322	...	0632	...	0711	0711	...	|	|	0833	|	|	...	|	|	1034	|	|	...	|	|	1233
	Bielefeld Hbf .... 802 811 d.	0355	0332	...	0641	...	0721	0721	...	0822	0822	0842	0922	0922	...	1022	1022	1043	1122	1122	...	1222	1222	1242
	Gütersloh Hbf .... 802 d.	|	0342	...	0651	...	|	|	...	|	|	0852	|	|	...	|	|	1053	|	|	...	|	|	1252
	Hamm (Westf) .... 802 a.	0425	0402	...	0713	...	0748	0748	...	0848	0848	0912	0948	0948	...	1048	1048	1113	1148	1148	...	1248	1248	1312
	Dortmund Hbf **800** .... a.	0447	0420	...	0732	...	|	0809	...	|	0909	0932	|	1009	...	|	1109	1132	|	1209	...	|	1309	1332
	Düsseldorf Hbf **800** .... a.	0654	0514	...	|	...	|	0906	...	|	1006	1046	|	1106	...	|	1206	|	|	1306	...	|	1406	|
	Wuppertal Hbf **800** .... a.	0538	|	...	0812	...	0839	◐	...	0939	...	|	1039	...	...	1139	...	1213	1239	◐	...	1339	...	1412
	Köln Hbf **800** .... a.	0614	0540	...	0846	...	0909	...	...	1009	...	1115	1109	...	...	1209	...	1248	1309	...	...	1409	...	1445
	Bonn Hbf **800** .... a.	...	◐	...	...	...	...	...	...	...	...	1135	1132e	...	...	...	...	...	1332	...	...	...	...	...

	IC 2011 ⑦ S🍷	IC 2017 ⑤v Q	ICE 650 ✗	ICE 640 ✗	IC 146 ✗	ICE 950 ✗	ICE 940 ✗	IC 2048 D🍷	IC 1915 ⑤⑦ vS	ICE 558 ✗	ICE 548 ✗	IC 144 ✗	ICE 858 ✗	ICE 848 ✗	IC 2440 D🍷	IC 2385 ⑥r F🍷	IC 2385 Ⓐ P🍷	IC 1917 ⑦ K	ICE 556 X✗	ICE 546 ✗	IC 142 ✗	ICE 856 ✗	ICE 846 ♣ ✗	ICE 1046 ⑤f G✗
Berlin Ostbahnhof .. 838 902 d.	...	...	1036	1036	1025	1135	1135	...	...	1236	1236	1225	1335	1335	...	1326	1344	...	1436	1436	1425	1535	1535	1535
Berlin Hbf .... 838 902 d.	1008	...	1047	1047	1036	1146	1146	...	1206	1247	1247	1236	1346	1346	...	1338	1355	1358	1447	1447	1436	1546	1546	1546
Berlin Spandau .... 838 902 d.	1018	...	1102	1102	1052	1201	1201	...	1217	1302	1302	1252	1401	1401	...	1353	1409	1410	1502	1502	1452	1601	1601	1601
Stendal .... 838 d.	|	...	|	|	1134	|	|	...	|	|	|	1334	|	|	...	1440j	|	1449	|	|	1534	|	|	|
Wolfsburg .... 902 d.	1121	...	|	|	1205	1256	1256	...	1321	|	|	1405	1456	1456	...	1511	1511	1521	|	|	1605	1656	1656	1656
Leipzig Hbf **866** .... d.	|	...	|	|	|	|	|	1040	|	|	|	|	|	|	1240	|	|	|	|	|	|	|	|	|
Magdeburg Hbf **866** .... d.	|	...	|	|	|	|	|	1202	|	|	|	|	|	|	1402	|	|	|	|	|	|	|	|	|
Hannover Hbf .... a.	1153	...	1228	1228	1237	1328	1328	1323	1353	1428	1428	1437	1528	1528	1523	1545	1545	1553	1628	1628	1637	1728	1728	1728
Hannover Hbf .... 811 d.	1156	1156	1231	1231	1240	1331	1331	1340	1356	1431	1431	1440	1531	1531	1540	...	...	1556	1631	1631	1640	1731	1731	1731
Minden (Westf) .... 811 d.	|	|	|	|	1312	|	|	1412	|	|	|	1512	|	|	1612	...	...	|	|	|	1712	|	|	|
Bad Oeynhausen .... 811 d.	|	|	|	|	|	|	|	1422	|	|	|	1522	|	|	1622	...	...	|	|	|	|	|	|	|
Bünde (Westf) .... 811 d.	|	|	|	|	1332	|	|	|	|	|	|	|	|	|	|	...	...	|	|	|	1732	|	|	|
Osnabrück Hbf .... 811 d.	|	|	|	|	1353	|	|	|	|	|	|	1553	|	|	|	...	...	|	|	|	1753	|	|	|
Rheine .... 811 d.	|	|	|	|	1421	|	|	|	|	|	|	1621	|	|	|	...	...	|	|	|	1821	|	|	|
Bad Bentheim 🏛 .... 811 a.	|	|	|	|	1434	|	|	|	|	|	|	1634	|	|	|	...	...	|	|	|	1834	|	|	|
Amsterdam C **22** .... a.	|	|	|	|	1700	|	|	|	|	|	|	1900	|	|	|	...	...	|	|	|	2100	|	|	|
Herford .... 811 d.	1244	1244	|	|	...	|	|	1433	1444	|	|	...	|	|	1633	...	...	1644	|	|	...	|	|	|
Bielefeld Hbf .... 802 811 d.	1253	1253	1322	1322	...	1422	1422	1442	1453	1522	1522	...	1622	1622	1642	...	...	1653	1722	1722	...	1822	1822	1822
Gütersloh Hbf .... 802 d.	1303	1303	|	|	...	|	|	1452	1503	|	|	...	|	|	1652	...	...	1703	|	|	...	|	|	|
Hamm (Westf) .... 802 a.	1324	1324	1348	1348	...	1448	1448	1512	1524	1548	1548	...	1648	1648	1712	...	...	1724	1748	1748	...	1848	1848	1848
Dortmund Hbf **800** .... a.	1348	1347	|	1409	...	|	1509	1532	1548	|	1609	...	|	1709	1732	...	...	1748	|	1809	...	|	1909	1909
Düsseldorf Hbf **800** .... a.	1442	1442	|	1506	...	|	1606	|	1642	|	1710z	...	|	1806	|	...	...	1842	|	1911	...	|	2006	2015
Wuppertal Hbf **800** .... a.	|	|	1439	◐	...	1539	...	1612	|	1639	◐	...	1739	...	1812	...	...	|	1839	...	...	1939	|	...
Köln Hbf **800** .... a.	1515	1515	1509	...	...	1609	...	1648	1715	1709	...	...	1809	...	1845	...	...	1915	1909	...	...	2009	2033	...
Bonn Hbf **800** .... a.	1535	1535	...	...	...	...	...	...	1735	...	...	...	...	...	...	...	...	1935	1932q	...	...	2038q	...	...

	IC 2442 Ⓑb D🍷	ICE 554 ✗	ICE 544 C✗	IC 140 ✗	EC 248 Ⓑ H	ICE 854 Ⓑ T✗	ICE 844 ✗	IC 2444 Ⓑb D🍷	ICE 552 ✗	ICE 542 ✗	IC 2242 M	90516 ‡	IC 1999 ⑦ F	ICE 852 ⑦ ✗	ICE 842 ✗	ICE 832 J ✗	ICE 932 ⑤m O✗	IC 2446 ⑦ D🍷	IC 1932 ⑦ R	IC 2240 ⑦ N✗	IC 1938 ⑦ E	ICE 540 ✗	ICE 540 ⑤–⑦ ✗	ICE 850 ⑦ O✗
Berlin Ostbahnhof .. 838 902 d.	...	1636	1636	1625	1701	1735	1735	...	1836	1836	1825	...	...	1935	1935	1935	1935	...	...	2025	...	2056	2056	2139
Berlin Hbf .... 838 902 d.	...	1647	1647	1636	1711	1746	1746	...	1847	1847	1836	...	1907	1946	1946	1946	1946	...	...	2036	2056	2107	2107	2150
Berlin Spandau .... 838 902 d.	...	1702	1702	1652	1724	1801	1801	...	1902	1902	1852	...	1920	2001	2001	2001	2001	...	1954	2052	2109	2121	2121	2204
Stendal .... 838 d.	...	|	|	1734	1758	|	|	...	|	|	1934	...	|	|	|	|	|	...	2032	2134	2145	2155	2155	2244
Wolfsburg .... 902 d.	...	|	|	1805	...	1856	1856	...	|	|	2005	...	2021	2056	2056	2056	2056	...	2104	2205	...	2223	2223	2313
Leipzig Hbf **866** .... d.	1440	|	|	|	...	|	|	1640	|	|	|	...	|	|	|	|	|	1840	|	|	...	|	|	|
Magdeburg Hbf **866** .... d.	1602	|	|	|	...	|	|	1802	|	|	|	...	|	|	|	|	|	2002	|	|	...	|	|	|
Hannover Hbf .... a.	1723	1828	1828	1837	...	1928	1928	1923	2028	2028	2037	...	2053	2128	2128	2128	2128	2123	2140	2236	...	2256	2256	2344
Hannover Hbf .... 811 d.	1740	1831	1831	1840	...	1931	1931	1940	2031	2031	2040	...	...	2131	2131	...	...	2140	...	2240	...	...	2301	...
Minden (Westf) .... 811 d.	1812	|	|	1912	...	|	|	2012	|	|	2112	...	...	|	|	...	...	2212	...	2312	...	...	|	...
Bad Oeynhausen .... 811 d.	1822	|	|	1922	...	|	|	2022	|	|	2122	...	...	|	|	...	...	2222	...	2322	...	...	|	...
Bünde (Westf) .... 811 d.	|	|	|	|	...	|	|	|	|	|	2135	2146	...	|	|	...	...	|	...	2335	...	...	|	...
Osnabrück Hbf .... 811 d.	|	|	|	1953	...	|	|	|	|	|	2159	2214	...	|	|	...	...	|	...	2358	...	...	|	...
Rheine .... 811 d.	|	|	|	2021	...	|	|	|	|	|	...	2248	...	|	|	...	...	|	...	...	...	...	|	...
Bad Bentheim 🏛 .... 811 a.	|	|	|	2034	...	|	|	|	|	|	...	2303	...	|	|	...	...	|	...	...	...	...	|	...
Amsterdam C **22** .... a.	|	|	|	2300	...	|	|	|	|	|	...	...	...	|	|	...	...	|	...	...	...	...	|	...
Herford .... 811 d.	1833	|	|	...	...	|	|	2033	|	|	...	...	...	|	|	...	...	2233	...	...	...	...	2346	...
Bielefeld Hbf .... 802 811 d.	1842	1922	1922	...	...	2022	2022	2042	2122	2122	...	...	...	2222	2222	...	...	2242	...	...	...	...	2356	...
Gütersloh Hbf .... 802 d.	1852	|	|	...	...	|	|	2052	|	|	...	...	...	|	|	...	...	2252	...	...	...	...	0007	...
Hamm (Westf) .... 802 a.	1912	1948	1948	...	...	2048	2048	2110	2148	2148	...	...	...	2248	2248	...	...	2310	...	...	...	...	0026	...
Dortmund Hbf **800** .... a.	1932	|	2009	...	...	|	2109	2132	|	2209	...	...	...	|	2309	...	...	2332	...	...	...	...	0047	...
Düsseldorf Hbf **800** .... a.	|	|	2106	...	...	|	2207	|	|	2306	...	...	...	|	0006	...	...	|	...	...	...	...	0145	...
Wuppertal Hbf **800** .... a.	2012	2039	|	...	...	2139	|	2212	2239	|	...	...	...	2339	|	...	...	0012	...	...	...	...	|	...
Köln Hbf **800** .... a.	2045	2109	2133	...	...	2209	2231	2245	2313	2330	...	...	...	0012	0030	...	...	0045	...	...	...	...	0209	...
Bonn Hbf **800** .... a.	...	...	...	...	...	2236w	...	...	2339q	...	...	...	...	...	...	...	...	...	...	...	...	...	◐	...

A – ALLGÄU – [12] and ✗ (Leipzig ① -) (Magdeburg ①–⑥ **h** -) Hannover - Köln - Stuttgart - Oberstdorf.
B – KOPERNIKUS – 🛏 1, 2 cl., ▬ 2 cl. and [2] Praha - Dresden - Köln - Amsterdam (Table **28**).
Conveys 🛏 1, 2 cl., ▬ 2 cl. and [2] (*EN* **446** – JAN KIEPURA) Warszawa - Berlin - Amsterdam (Table **24**).
For overnight journeys only.
C – On ⑦ continues to Düren (a. 2153) and Aachen Hbf (a. 2216).
D – From Dresden (Table **842**).
E – To Hamburg (Tables **841/900**). Terminates at Uelzen until July 27.
F – [12] Berlin - Kassel - Gießen - Frankfurt.
G – To Neuss Hbf (a. 2027) and Mönchengladbach Hbf (a. 2041).
H – WAWEL – [12] Wrocław - Forst 🏛 - Cottbus - Berlin - Hamburg.
J – ①②③④⑥ (not Oct. 2). To Bremen Hbf (Table **813**).
K – To Karlsruhe (Tables **911/2**).
L – To Basel (Table **912**).
M – Continues to Münster (Westf) Hbf (a. 2225) on Ⓑ. Conveys 🍷 on ⑤⑦.
N – To Münster (Westf) Hbf (a. 0024).
O – To Oldenburg via Bremen (Table **813**).
P – [12] Berlin - Kassel - Gießen - Frankfurt - Karlsruhe.
Q – [12] Hannover - Köln - Stuttgart - München.
R – [12] Stralsund - Berlin - Bremen - Oldenburg.
S – To Stuttgart (Tables **911/2**).

T – To Koblenz Hbf (a. 2313) on ⑦ (also Oct. 3).
X – To Koblenz Hbf (a. 2013) on Ⓐ.

b – Not Oct. 3.
e – ①–⑥ only.
f – Also Oct. 2; not Oct. 3.
g – ① only.
h – ①–⑥ (not Oct. 4).
j – Arrives 1427.
k – Also Oct. 3; not Oct. 4.
m – Also Oct. 2.
q – Ⓑ only.
r – Also Oct. 3.
v – Also June 18, Oct. 2; not June 20, Oct. 3.
w – ⑦ (also Oct. 3).
z – 1706 on ⑥⑦ (also June 19, 20, Oct. 3).

♣ – ①②③④⑥⑦ (also Oct. 3; not Oct. 2).
◐ – Continues to Köln/Bonn Flughafen on dates in Table **800**.
‡ – Operated by WestfalenBahn.

811 Regional services BIELEFELD and BAD BENTHEIM - HANNOVER and PADERBORN

See Table 810 for faster *ICE*/*IC* services Bielefeld / Bad Bentheim - Hannover and v.v.

km		⚒	⚒¶	⚒	⚒¶		⚒n	¶			¶			¶		A	A¶	B	A	A¶	B	♣		¶
0	Bad Bentheim d.	...	...	...	...	...	...	0557e	...	...	0657r	...	...	0757r	...	...	0857	...	...	0957	...		...	1857
21	**Rheine** d.	...	...	...	0514	...	...	0614e	0638	...	0714r	...	...	0814	0838	...	0914	...	...	1014	1038		...	1914
43	Ibbenbüren d.	...	...	...	0528	...	...	0628e	0654	...	0728r	...	...	0828	0854	...	0928	...	...	1028	1054	and in	...	1928
69	**Osnabrück** Hbf d.	...	0448	0513	0548	...	...	0648	0716	...	0748	...	...	0848	0916	...	0948	...	...	1048	1116	the same	...	1948
106	Bünde (Westf) d.	...	0512	0539	0612	...	E	0712	0738	E	0812	...	D	0912	0938	D	1012	...	D	1112	1138	pattern	D	2012
	Bielefeld Hbf d.	0424	|	|	|	0624	0659	|	|	0759	|	0824	0859	|	|	0959	|	1024	1059	|	|	every	1959	|
120	Herford a.	0431	0526	|	0626	0631	0707	0726	|	0807	0826	0831	0907	0926	|	1007	1026	1031	1107	1126	|	two hours	2007	2026
120	Herford d.	0433	0537	|	0637	0633	0708	0737	|	0808	0837	0833	0908	0937	|	1008	1037	1033	1108	1137	|	until	2008	2037
134	**Bielefeld** Hbf a.	|	0548	|	0648	|	|	0748	|	|	0848	|	|	0948	|	|	1048	|	|	1148	|		|	2048
	Löhne d.	0440	...	0550	...	0640	0714	...	0751	0814	...	0840	0914	...	0951	1014	...	1040	1114	...	1151		2014	...
	Bad Oeynhausen d.	0445	...	0555	...	0645	0719	...	0756	0819	...	0845	0919	...	0956	1019	...	1045	1119	...	1156		2019	...
	Minden (Westf) a.	0457	...	0606	...	0657	0730	...	0807	0830	...	0857	0930	...	1007	1030	...	1057	1130	...	1207		2030	...
	Minden (Westf) d.	0507	...	0607	...	0707	*0735*	...	0808	*0835*	...	0907	*0935*	...	1008	*1035*	...	1107	*1135*	...	1208		*2035*	...
	Hannover Hbf a.	0550	...	0650	...	0750	*0830*	...	0851	*0930*	...	0950	*1030*	...	1051	*1130*	...	1150	*1230*	...	1251		*2130*	...
	Braunschweig Hbf **866** a.	0641	...	0741	...	0841	...	...	0941	...	...	1041	...	...	1141	...	...	1241	...	...	1341		...	...

			¶		⚒n	¶		Ⓑw	¶		¶
Bad Bentheim d.	...	...	1957	...	...	2057	...	...	2157	...	2312
Rheine d.	...	...	2014	2038	...	2114	...	...	2214	...	2329
Ibbenbüren d.	...	...	2028	2054	...	2128	...	...	2228	...	2344
Osnabrück Hbf d.	...	...	2048	2116	...	2148	...	...	2248	...	0002
Bünde (Westf) d.	...	D	2112	2138	D	2212	...	D	2312	...	...
Bielefeld Hbf d.	2024	2059	|	|	2159	|	2224	2259	|	2327	...
Herford a.	2031	2107	2126	|	2207	2226	2231	2307	2326	2335	...
Herford d.	2033	2108	2137	|	2208	2237	2233	2308	2337	2336	...
Bielefeld Hbf a.	|	|	2148	|	|	*2248*	|	|	2348	|	...
Löhne d.	2040	2114	...	2151	2214	▬	2240	2314	▬	2343	...
Bad Oeynhausen d.	2045	2119	...	2156	2219	...	2245	2319	...	2348	...
Minden (Westf) a.	2057	2130	...	2207	2230	...	2257	2330	...	2400	...
Minden (Westf) d.	2107	*2135*	...	2208	...	2235	...	...	2335	...	...
Hannover Hbf a.	2150	*2230*	...	2251	...	2330	...	...	0030	...	...
Braunschweig Hbf **866** a.	2241	...	...	2341	...	...	...	...	...	...	...

km			Ⓒz	Ⓐ¶	Ⓐt	⚒¶	⚒	⚒¶	⚒n
	Braunschweig Hbf **866** d.	...	...	...	...	...	0420	...	...
0	**Hannover** Hbf d.	0028	...	...	...	...	0509	...	*0528*
65	Minden (Westf) a.	0123	...	...	...	...	0554	...	*0623*
65	Minden (Westf) d.	...	0127	...	0528	...	0555	...	0628
80	Bad Oeynhausen d.	...	0138	...	0539	...	0606	...	0639
86	Löhne d.	...	0143	...	0544	...	0611	...	0644
	Bielefeld Hbf d.	...	|	...	|	0509	|	0609	|
96	Herford a.	...	0149	...	0549	0520	|	0620	0649
96	Herford d.	...	0150	...	0550	0533	|	0633	0650
110	**Bielefeld** Hbf a.	...	0201	...	0557	|	|	|	0657
	Bünde (Westf) d.	...	...	...	D	0546	0622	0646	D
	Osnabrück Hbf d.	...	...	0514	...	0614	0647	0714	...
	Ibbenbüren d.	...	...	0530	...	0630	0707	0730	...
	Rheine d.	...	...	0548	...	0648	0723	0748	...
	Bad Bentheim a.	...	...	0603	...	0703	...	0803	...

	⚒	¶	⚒n	B	A¶	A	B	A¶	A	♥		¶			¶			¶	⚒n		¶	Ⓑ		
Braunschweig Hbf **866** d.	0520	...	...	0620	...	...	0720	...	...		1820	...	...	1920	...	...	2020	...	...	2120	...	2220	...	...
Hannover Hbf d.	0609	...	*0628*	0709	...	*0728*	0809	...	*0828*		1909	...	*1928*	2009	...	*2028*	2109	...	*2128*	2209	...	2309	2328	...
Minden (Westf) a.	0659	...	*0723*	0751	...	*0823*	0853	...	*0923*	and in	1951	...	*2023*	2053	...	*2123*	2151	...	*2223*	2253	...	2352	0023	...
Minden (Westf) d.	0702	...	0728	0752	...	0828	0902	...	0928	the same	1952	...	2028	2102	...	2128	2152	...	2228	2302	...	...	...	0030
Bad Oeynhausen d.	0714	...	0739	0804	...	0839	0914	...	0939	pattern	2004	...	2039	2114	...	2139	2204	...	2239	2314	...	...	...	0042
Löhne d.	0719	...	0744	0811	...	0844	0919	...	0944	every	2011	...	2044	2119	...	2144	2211	...	2244	2319	...	...	...	0047
Bielefeld Hbf d.	|	0709	|	|	0809	|	|	0909	|	two hours	|	2009	|	|	2109	|	|	2209	|	|	2309	...	...	|
Herford a.	0725	0720	0749	|	0820	0849	0925	0920	0949	until	|	2020	2049	2125	2120	2149	|	2220	2249	2325	2320	...	...	0053
Herford d.	0727	0733	0750	|	0833	0850	0927	0933	0950		|	2033	2050	2127	2133	2150	|	2233	2250	2327	2333	...	...	0054
Bielefeld Hbf a.	0739	|	0757	|	|	0857	0936	|	0957		|	|	2057	2136	|	2157	|	|	2257	2336	|	...	...	0105
Bünde (Westf) d.	...	0746	D	0821	0846	D	...	0946	D		2021	2046	D	...	2146	E	2221	2246	E	...	2346	...	...	...
Osnabrück Hbf d.	...	0814	...	0847	0914	...	...	1014	...		2047	2114	...	...	2214	...	2246	2314	...	...	0012	...	...	...
Ibbenbüren d.	...	0830	...	0907	0930	...	...	1030	...		2107	2130	...	...	2230	...	...	2330	...	...	...	...	...	...
Rheine d.	...	0848	...	0923	0948	...	...	1048	...		2123	2148	...	...	2248	...	...	2346	...	...	...	...	...	...
Bad Bentheim a.	...	0903	...	...	1003	...	...	1103	...		...	2203	...	...	2303	...	...	...	...	...	...	...	...	...

BIELEFELD - PADERBORN - HOLZMINDEN - KREIENSEN ⊖ and OTTBERGEN - GÖTTINGEN ★ ⊖

km			Ⓐ	Ⓐ	⑥	Ⓐ	⑥	⚒	⚒																⚒
0	**Bielefeld** Hbf d.	...	0432	0528	0539	0616	0639	0739	0839	0939	1039	1139	1234	1339	1439	1539	1639	1739	1839	...	1939	...	2039	2139	2239
44	**Paderborn** Hbf a.	...	0538	0643	0646	0729	0746	0846	0946	1046	1146	1246	1346	1446	1546	1646	1746	1846	1946	...	2046	...	2146	2246	2346
	Change trains	Ⓐ	⚒	Ⓐ	⚒		d	d	d											†	Ⓐ	Ⓒ		⑤–⑦	
44	**Paderborn** Hbf 805 809 d.	0453	0553	...	0653	...	0753	0853	0953	1053	1153	1253	1353	1453	1553	1653	1753	1853	1953	1953	2053	2106	2206	2315	...
61	Altenbeken 805 809 d.	0507	0607	...	0707	...	0807	0907	1007	1107	1207	1307	1407	1507	1607	1707	1807	1907	2007	2007	2107	2119	2219	2329	...
92	Ottbergen ★ d.	0534	0634	...	0734	...	0834	0934	1034	1134	1234	1334	1434	1534	1634	1734	1834	1934	2034	2034	2134	2145	2249	2355	...
102	Höxter Rathaus d.	0544	0644	...	0744	...	0844	0944	1044	1144	1244	1344	1444	1544	1644	1744	1844	1944	2044	2044	2144	2153	2257	0004	...
110	Holzminden a.	0553	0653	...	0753	...	0853	0953	1053	1153	1253	1353	1453	1553	1653	1753	1853	1953	2053	2053	2153	2202	2306	0012	...
110	Holzminden d.	*0629*	0654k	0711	0758	0758	...	0958	...	1158	...	1358	...	1558	1654e	1754f	...	1958	...	2128	...	...	...	...	...
154	**Kreiensen** a.	*0703*	0728k	0745	0832	0832	...	1032	...	1232	...	1432	...	1632	1728e	1828f	...	2032	...	2202	...	...	...	...	...

			Ⓐ		⚒	⚒											Ⓐ	Ⓒ		Ⓐ					†
Kreiensen d.	...	...	...	...	...	0627e	0709e	0754r	0923	...	1123	...	1323	...	1523	...	1650	1723	...	1829	...	1923	...	2125	2238
Holzminden a.	...	...	...	...	...	0700e	0742e	0827r	0956	...	1156	...	1356	...	1556	...	1723	1756	...	1902	...	1956	...	2158	2311
Holzminden d.	...	...	0454	...	0604	0704	0804	0904	1004	1104	1204	1304	1404	1504	1604	1704	...	1804	1804	1904	1904	2004	2104	2204	2316
Höxter Rathaus d.	...	...	0504	...	0614	0714	0814	0914	1014	1114	1214	1314	1414	1514	1614	1714	...	1814	1814	1914	1914	2014	2114	2214	2325
Ottbergen ★ d.	...	...	0516	...	0626	0726	0826	0926	1026	1126	1226	1326	1426	1526	1626	1726	...	1826	1826	1926	1926	2026	2126	2228	2335
Altenbeken 805 809 d.	...	...	0542	...	0652	0752	0852	0952	1052	1152	1252	1352	1452	1552	1652	1752	...	1852	1852	1952	1952	2052	2152	2254	0001
Paderborn Hbf 805 809 a.	...	...	0555	...	0705	0805	0905	1005	1105	1205	1305	1405	1505	1605	1705	1805	...	1905	1905	2005	2005	2105	2205	2307	0015
Change trains	Ⓐ	⑥	Ⓐ	⑥	⚒	⚒																⚒			
Paderborn Hbf d.	0504	0513	0604	0613	0713	0813	0913	1013	1113	1213	1313	1413	1513	1613	1713	1813	...	...	1913	...	2013	2113	2213	...	...
Bielefeld Hbf a.	0606	0616	0706	0716	0821	0916	1021	1116	1216	1316	1416	1516	1616	1716	1816	1921	...	...	2016	...	2116	2216	2316	...	...

MÜNSTER - BIELEFELD ⊡ ♠ and BIELEFELD - DETMOLD - ALTENBEKEN ⊡

km		⚒n		⚒n			⚒n				
0	**Bielefeld** Hbf ♠ d.	0749	0849	0949	1049	1249	1349	1449	1649	1849	2049
11	Oerlinghausen d.	0803	0903	1003	1103	1303	1403	1503	1703	1903	2103
22	Lage d.	0813	0913	1013	1113	1313	1413	1513	1713	1913	2113
31	Detmold a.	0820	0920	1020	1120	1320	1420	1520	1720	1920	2120
60	**Altenbeken** a.	...	0946v	1046	...	...	1446	1546v	...	1946v	2146n

	⚒n			⚒n			⚒n				⚒n
Altenbeken d.	...	...	1013v	1113	...	...	1513	1613v	...	2013v	2213
Detmold d.	0740	0840	1040	1140	1240	1440	1540	1640	1840	2040	2240
Lage d.	0750	0850	1050	1150	1250	1450	1550	1650	1850	2050	2250
Oerlinghausen d.	0800	0900	1100	1200	1300	1500	1600	1700	1900	2100	2300
Bielefeld Hbf ♠ a.	0811	0911	1111	1211	1311	1511	1611	1711	1911	2111	2311

HERFORD - PADERBORN ¶

km		Ⓐt		⚒n					Ⓒz
0	**Herford** d.	0530	...	0633	0733	and	2133	2233	2233
8	Bad Salzuflen d.	0537	...	0640	0740	hourly	2140	2240	2240
19	Lage d.	0549	...	0652	0752	until	2152	2252	2252
28	Detmold d.	0559	...	0702	0802		2202	2258	2302
57	Altenbeken 805 809 a.	0624	...	0727	0827		2227	...	2327
74	**Paderborn** Hbf 805 809 a.	0638	...	0741	0841		2241	...	2341

	Ⓐt	⚒n			✣	L			
Paderborn Hbf 805 809 d.	...	0518	...	0621	and	2021	2121	...	...
Altenbeken 805 809 d.	...	0530	...	0633	hourly	2033	2133	...	...
Detmold d.	0458	0558	...	0701	until	2101	2201	...	...
Lage d.	0506	0606	...	0709		2109	2209	...	...
Bad Salzuflen d.	0517	0617	...	0720		2120	2220	...	...
Herford a.	0524	0624	...	0727		2127	2227	...	...

A – Train runs hourly.
B – Train runs every **two** hours.
D – From / to Düsseldorf (Table **802**).
E – From / to Dortmund (Table **802**).
L – To Bielefeld Hbf (a. 2248).

c – Not Nov. 1.
d – Daily.
e – Ⓐ only.
f – 4 minutes later on Ⓒ.
k – ⑥ only.
n – ⚒ (not June 19, Nov. 1).
r – ⚒ only.

t – Not June 19.
v – † (also June 19, Nov. 1).
w – Also Nov. 1.
z – Also June 19.

¶ – Operated by Westfalen Bahn.
⊖ – Operated by Nord West Bahn. 2nd class only.
⊡ – Operated by **eurobahn** Keolis Deutschland GmbH & Co. KG.
✣ – The 1221 from Paderborn runs 3–4 minutes later Detmold - Herford on Ⓐ (not June 19).

♥ – Bielefeld d. 1012 / 1212 / 1812 (not 1009 / 1209 / 1809; arrives Herford 1022 / 1222 / 1822).
♣ – On ⑦ (also June 18, Oct. 2) the 1057 from Bad Bentheim departs Herford 1232, arrives Bielefeld 1243. On ①–④ (not June 18, Oct. 2) the 1057 from Bad Bentheim departs Herford 1240, arrives Bielefeld 1251. The 1357 from Bad Bentheim departs Herford 1534, arrives Bielefeld 1545.
★ – **OTTBERGEN - GÖTTINGEN** ⊖. *63 km.* Journey: 79–83 minutes (102 minutes for train marked ‡). **From Ottbergen** at 0535 ⚒, 0635 ⚒, 0735, 0835 ⚒, 0935, 1035 ⚒, 1135, 1235 ⑥, 1235 Ⓐ ‡, 1335 Ⓒ, 1535, 1635 Ⓐ, 1735, 1835 Ⓐ, 1935 and 2035. **From Göttingen** at 0604 ⚒, 0703, 0803 ⚒, 0903, 1003 ⚒, 1103, 1203 ⚒, 1303 Ⓒ, 1402 ⑥, 1503, 1603 Ⓐ, 1703, 1803 Ⓐ, 1903, 2003 Ⓐ and 2103.
♠ – **MÜNSTER - BIELEFELD** ⊡. *76 km.* Journey: 91–102 minutes. **From Münster (Westf)** at 0607 Ⓐ **t**, 0717 ⚒**n**, 0817, 0917 ⚒**n**, 1017, 1117 ⚒**n**, 1217, 1417, 1517 ⚒**n**, 1617, 1717 ⚒**n**, 1817, 1917 ⚒**n**, 2017, 2117 ⚒**n** and 2217 ⑥ **c**. **From Bielefeld Hbf** at 0608 ⑥ **c**, 0614 Ⓐ **t**, 0708 ⚒**n**, 0814, 0914 ⚒**n**, 1014, 1114 ⚒**n**, 1214, 1314 ⚒**n**, 1414, 1514 ⚒**n**, 1614, 1714 ⚒**n**, 1814, 1914 ⚒**n** and 2014.

MÜNSTER - EMDEN - NORDDEICH 812

RE services except where shown

km				*IC* 2438				*IC* 2331					*IC* 2333					*IC* 231	*IC* 131	*IC* 2432				*IC* 2018	
		Ⓐ	⚒	①–⑥ e🍷	⚒		Ⓐt H		A				Q 🍷					G 🍷	D 🍷	D 🍷	Ⓒ	Ⓐ		⑥ ◆	
	Luxembourg **915**.... d.	...	...	...	...	...	...	...	...	...	...	...	...	...	...	...	...	...	0620x	0620v	...	...	...	...	...	...
	Koblenz Hbf **800**.... d.	...	...	...	...	...	...	...	...	...	...	...	...	0642a	...	...	...	...	0842	0842n	...	...	...	...	0943	...
	Köln Hbf **800 802**... d.	...	...	...	...	...	...	...	0541	...	...	0621r	...	0746	...	...	0821	...	0946	0946	...	...	...	1021	1046	...
	Düsseldorf Hbf **800** d.	...	...	...	...	...	...	...	0606	...	...	|	...	0812	...	...	|	...	1012	1012	...	...	...	|	1118	...
0	**Münster** (Westf) Hbf.. d.	0502	...	...	0602	...	0624	0702	0731	0805	...	0824	0905	0931	1005	...	1024	1105	1131	1131	...	1205	1205	1224	1231	...
15	Greven................ d.	0513	...	...	0613	...	0637	0713	|	0814	...	0833	0914	|	1014	...	1033	1114	|	|	...	1214	1214	1233	|	...
26	Emsdetten............. d.	0522	...	...	0622	...	0646	0722	|	0822	...	0840	0922	|	1022	...	1040	1122	|	|	...	1222	1222	1240	|	...
39	**Rheine**................ d.	0534	0534	...	0634	...	0658	0734	0756	0834	...	0851	0934	0956	1034	...	1051	1134	1156	1156	...	1234	1234	1251	1258	...
70	Lingen (Ems).......... d.	0555	0555	...	0655	...	...	0755	0815	0855	...	...	0955	1015	1055	...	...	1155	1215	1215	...	1255	1255	...	|	...
90	Meppen................ d.	0610	0610	...	0710	...	...	0810	0829	0910	...	...	1010	1029	1110	...	...	1210	1229	1229	...	1310	1329c	...	|	...
136	Papenburg (Ems)...... d.	0643	0643	...	0743	...	...	0843	0856	0943	...	...	1043	1056	1143	...	...	1243	1256	1256	...	1343	1403	...	|	...
153	Leer (Ostfriesl).... **813** d.	0655	0655	0715	0755	0824	...	0855	0909	0955	1024	...	1055	1109	1155	1224	...	1255	1309	1309	1323	1355	1415	...	|	1424
180	**Emden** Hbf........ **813** a.	0712	0712	0731	0812	0840	...	0912	0925	1012	1040	...	1112	1125	1212	1240	...	1312	1325	1325	1339	1412	1432	...	1416	1440
180	**Emden** Hbf........ **813** d.	...	...	0742	...	0842	...	...	0942	...	1042	...	...	1142	...	1242	...	...	1328	...	1342	...	...	...	1422	1442
209	Norden.............. **813** d.	...	...	0808	...	0906	...	...	1005	...	1106	...	...	1205	...	1306	...	...	1351	...	1408	...	...	...	1447	1506
215	**Norddeich**......... **813** a.	...	...	0814	...	0912	...	...	1011	...	1112	...	...	1211	...	1312	...	...	1357	...	1414	...	...	...	1454	1512
	Norddeich Mole **813** a.	...	...	0820	...	0916	...	...	1016	...	1116	...	...	1217	...	1316	...	...	1404	...	1420	...	...	...	1500	1516

		IC 133					*IC* 2335					*IC* 2014	*IC* 2004	*IC* 2036					*IC* 137	*IC* 2034						
							◧ 🍷					⑤ 🍷◆	🍷◆	Ⓑd 🍷		⑥			N 🍷	🍷						¶
Luxembourg **915**.... d.	...	0820h	...	...	...	...	...	...	...	...	...	...	...	...	...	...	...	...	1419z	...	...	...	...	...	...	...
Koblenz Hbf **800**..... d.	...	1042	...	...	...	...	...	...	...	...	...	1443	1443	...	...	...	...	...	1642b	...	...	...	...	...	...	...
Köln Hbf **800 802**... d.	...	1146	...	...	1221	...	1346g	...	...	1421	...	1546	1546	...	...	...	1621	...	1745	...	...	...	1821	...	...	...
Düsseldorf Hbf **800**. d.	...	1212	...	...	|	...	1413g	...	...	|	...	1612	1612	...	...	...	|	...	1817	...	...	...	|	...	...	...
Münster (Westf) Hbf... d.	1305	1331	1405	...	1424	1505	1531	1605	...	1624	1705	1731	1731	...	1805	...	1824	1905	1931	...	2005	...	2024	2105	2211	2311
Greven..................... d.	1314	|	1414	...	1433	1514	|	1614	...	1633	1714	|	|	...	1814	...	1833	1914	|	...	2014	...	2033	2114	2222	2324
Emsdetten................. d.	1322	|	1422	...	1440	1522	|	1622	...	1640	1722	|	|	...	1822	...	1840	1922	|	...	2022	...	2040	2122	2231	2332
Rheine.................... d.	1334	1356	1434	...	1451	1534	1556	1634	...	1651	1734	1756	1756	...	1834	...	1851	1934	1956	...	2034	...	2051	2134	2252j	2343
Lingen (Ems).............. d.	1355	1415	1455	...	...	1555	1615	1655	...	...	1755	1815	1815	...	1855	...	...	1955	2015	...	2055	...	...	2155	2313	...
Meppen..................... d.	1410	1429	1510	...	...	1610	1629	1710	...	...	1810	1829	1829	...	1910	...	...	2010	2029	...	2110	...	...	2210	2327	...
Papenburg (Ems)........ d.	1443	1456	1543	...	...	1643	1656	1743	...	...	1843	1856	1856	...	1943	...	...	2043	2056	...	2143	...	...	2243	2359	...
Leer (Ostfriesl) .....**813** d.	1455	1509	1555	1624	...	1655	1709	1755	1824	...	1855	1909	1909	1923	1955	2024	...	2055	2109	2123	2155	2224	...	2255	0011	...
Emden Hbf..........**813** a.	1512	1525	1612	1640	...	1712	1725	1812	1840	...	1912	1925	1925	1939	2012	2040	...	2112	2125	2139	2212	2240	...	2312	0028	...
Emden Hbf..........**813** d.	...	1542	...	1642	...	...	1728	...	1842	...	...	...	...	1942	...	2042	...	...	...	2142	...	2242	...	...	...	...
Norden.................**813** d.	...	1607	...	1706	...	...	1751	...	1906	...	...	...	...	2008	...	2106	...	...	...	2208	...	2306	...	...	...	...
Norddeich...........**813** a.	...	1613	...	1712	...	...	1757	...	1912	...	...	...	...	2014	...	2112	...	...	...	2214	...	2312	...	...	...	...
Norddeich Mole..**813** a.	...	1618	...	1716	...	...	1805	...	1916	...	...	...	...	2020	...	2116	...	...	...	...	...	...	...	...	...	...

							IC 2035	*IC* 2005						*IC* 2037	*IC* 1936					*IC* 134						*IC* 2019
	¶ ⚒r	Ⓐt		⚒		⚒	①–⑥ e🍷	①–⑥ 🍷◆	Ⓐ	Ⓒ				①–⑥ e🍷	M 🍷					🍷					Ⓐ	⑥ ◆
Norddeich Mole..**813** d.	...	...	...	...	...	...	...	...	...	...	...	...	...	0736	...	...	...	0839	...	0952	...	...	1039	...	...	1136
Norddeich...........**813** d.	...	...	...	...	...	...	0536	...	...	...	...	0641	...	0739	...	...	...	0841	...	0955	...	...	1041	...	...	1139
Norden...................**813** d.	...	...	...	...	...	...	0543	...	...	...	...	0647	...	0746	...	...	...	0847	...	1004	...	...	1047	...	...	1146
Emden Hbf..........**813** a.	...	...	...	...	...	...	0607	...	...	...	...	0715	...	0814	...	...	...	0915	...	1026	...	...	1115	...	...	1213
Emden Hbf..........**813** d.	...	...	...	0449	...	0549	0609	0634	0642	0649	...	0717	0749	0816	0834	0849	...	0917	0949	1034	1049	...	1117	1149	1224	1234
Leer (Ostfriesland) **813** d.	...	...	...	0506	...	0606	0626	0653	0658	0706	...	0734	0806	0833	0853	0906	...	0934	1006	1053	1106	...	1134	1206	1241	1253
Papenburg (Ems)....... d.	...	...	...	0516	...	0616	...	0704	0709	0716	...	...	0816	...	0904	0916	...	...	1016	1104	1116	...	...	1216	1251	1304
Meppen.................... d.	...	...	...	0550	...	0650	...	0731	0743	0750	...	...	0850	...	0931	0950	...	...	1050	1131	1150	...	...	1250	1325	1331
Lingen (Ems)............. d.	...	...	...	0604	...	0704	...	0744	0804	0804	...	...	0904	...	0944	1004	...	...	1104	1144	1204	...	...	1304	→	1344
Rheine.................... d.	0452	0606	0617	0628	0706	0729	...	0804	0829	0829	0906	...	0929	...	1004	1029	1106	...	1129	1204	1229	1306	...	1327	...	1404
Emsdetten................. d.	0502	0614	0627	0636	0714	0737	...	|	0837	0837	0914	...	0937	...	|	1037	1114	...	1137	|	1237	1314	...	1337	...	|
Greven...................... d.	0511	0621	0635	0644	0721	0745	...	|	0845	0845	0921	...	0945	...	|	1045	1121	...	1145	|	1245	1321	...	1345	...	|
Münster (Westf) Hbf... a.	0525	0632	0650	0654	0732	0756	...	0829	0856	0856	0932	...	0956	...	1029	1056	1132	...	1156	1229.	1256	1332	...	1356	...	1429
Düsseldorf Hbf **800**. a.	...	|	...	...	|	...	...	0946	...	...	|	...	...	...	1146	...	|	...	...	1346	...	|	...	...	...	1546
Köln Hbf **800 802**... a.	...	0838	...	...	0938	...	...	1015	...	...	1138	...	...	...	1212	...	1338	...	...	1412	...	1538	...	...	...	1612
Koblenz Hbf **800**..... a.	...	...	...	...	...	...	...	1116	...	...	...	...	...	...	...	...	...	...	...	1516	...	...	...	...	...	1716
Luxembourg **915**.... a.	...	...	...	...	...	...	...	...	...	...	...	...	...	...	...	...	...	...	...	1744h	...	...	...	...	...	...

	IC 132						*IC* 130					*IC* 2435	*IC* 2332	*IC* 2334					*IC* 2330							
	E 🍷	Ⓐ	Ⓒ				🍷					D 🍷	S 🍷	②–④ L🍷					B 🍷							¶
Norddeich Mole..**813** d.	1136	...	...	...	1239	...	1352k	...	...	1439	...	1536	...	1558	...	...	1639	...	1758	...	1839	...	...	2039	...	...
Norddeich...........**813** d.	1139	...	...	...	1241	...	1357k	...	...	1441	...	1539	...	1601	...	...	1641	...	1801	...	1841	...	...	2041	...	...
Norden...................**813** d.	1146	...	...	...	1247	...	1407k	...	...	1447	...	1550	...	1608	...	...	1647	...	1808	...	1847	...	...	2047	...	...
Emden Hbf..........**813** a.	1213	...	...	...	1315	...	1429k	...	...	1515	...	1614	...	1630	...	...	1715	...	1830	...	1915	...	...	2115	...	...
Emden Hbf..........**813** d.	1234	...	1249	...	1317	1349	1434	1449	...	1517	1549	1616	1634	1634	1649	...	1717	1749	1834	1849	1917	1949	2049	2117	2214	...
Leer (Ostfriesland) **813** d.	1253	...	1306	...	1334	1406	1453	1506	...	1534	1606	1633	1653	1653	1706	...	1734	1806	1853	1906	1934	2006	2106	2134	2230	...
Papenburg (Ems)....... d.	1304	←	1316	...	...	1416	1504	1516	...	...	1616	...	1704	1704	1716	...	...	1816	1904	1916	...	2016	2116	...	2240	...
Meppen.................... d.	1331	1337	1350	...	...	1450	1531	1550	...	...	1650	...	1731	1731	1750	...	...	1850	1931	1950	...	2050	2150	...	2313	...
Lingen (Ems)............. d.	1344	1351	1404	...	...	1504	1544	1604	...	...	1704	...	1744	1744	1804	...	...	1904	1944	2004	...	2104	2204	...	2327	...
Rheine.................... d.	1404	1429j	1429	1506	...	1529	1604	1629	1706	...	1729	...	1804	1804	1829	1906	...	1929	2004	2029	...	2129	2229	...	2349	2352
Emsdetten................. d.	|	1437	1437	1514	...	1537	|	1637	1714	...	1737	...	|	|	1837	1914	...	1937	|	2037	...	2137	2237	...	...	0002
Greven...................... d.	|	1445	1445	1521	...	1545	|	1645	1721	...	1745	...	|	|	1845	1921	...	1945	|	2046	...	2146	2245	...	...	0011
Münster (Westf) Hbf... a.	1429	1456	1456	1532	...	1556	1629	1656	1732	...	1756	...	1829	1829	1856	1932	...	1956	2029	2056	...	2156	2256	...	...	0025
Düsseldorf Hbf **800**. a.	1546	...	...	|	...	...	1746	...	|	...	...	...	1946	1946	...	|	...	...	2146	...	...	...	...	...	...	...
Köln Hbf **800 802**... a.	1612	...	...	1738	...	...	1812	...	1938	...	...	...	2012	2012	...	2138	...	...	2212	...	...	...	...	...	...	...
Koblenz Hbf **800**..... a.	1716q	...	...	...	...	...	1916	...	...	...	...	...	...	...	...	...	...	...	...	...	...	...	...	...	...	...
Luxembourg **915**.... a.	1939y	...	...	...	...	...	2139p	...	...	...	...	...	...	...	...	...	...	...	...	...	...	...	...	...	...	...

◆ – **NOTES** (LISTED BY TRAIN NUMBER)

2004 – ①②③④⑦ (also June 20, Oct. 3; not June 18, 19, Oct. 2). BODENSEE – [12] and 🍷 (Konstanz - Karlsruhe ⑦**w** -) Koblenz - Münster - Emden.

2005 – ①–⑥ (not June 20). BODENSEE – [12] and 🍷 Emden - Münster - Köln - Koblenz (- Karlsruhe - Konstanz ⑤⑥**f**).

2014 – ⑤ (also June 18, Oct. 2; not June 20, Oct. 3). [12] and 🍷 Stuttgart - Emden.

2018/9 – ⑥ to Oct. 18 (also June 19). NORDERNEY – [12] Stuttgart - Mannheim - Münster - Norddeich Mole and v.v.

– ⑤⑥ to Aug. 9 (also June 19; not June 20); ④–⑦ Aug. 15 - Oct. 23 (also Nov. 1; not Aug. 21).
– ④–⑦ to Aug. 24 (also June 18); ③–⑦ Aug. 27 - Oct. 22; ⑦ from Oct. 26 (also Oct. 31).
– Daily to Oct. 27; ①⑤⑦ from Oct. 31.
– Ⓑ to Oct. 17 (not June 19); daily from Oct. 19.
– ②③④⑥ from Oct. 28.
– From Hagen (Table **802**).
– ②–④ from Oct. 28.
– Daily to Oct. 25; ①–⑥ from Oct. 27.
– Daily to Oct. 24; Ⓑ from Oct. 26.
– Daily to Nov. 1; ①–⑥ from Nov. 3.
– Daily to Oct. 27; ①⑤⑦ from Oct. 31.
– ①–⑤ (not June 19, Oct. 3).
– Ⓑ only.

c – Arrives 1309.
d – Not Oct. 3.
e – Not Oct. 4.
f – Also June 18, 19, Oct. 2; not June 20.
g – On ⑤ (also June 18, Oct. 2; not June 20, Oct. 3) Köln d. 1338, Düsseldorf d. 1408.
h – Until June 27 and from Nov. 22 does not run Luxembourg - Trier and v.v.
j – Arrives 9–11 minutes earlier.
k – 15–20 minutes earlier on ⑥ to Oct. 18.
n – Runs Trier - Koblenz - Köln on ①–⑥ to Oct. 27 (also ①⑤ from Oct. 31).
p – ⑥ June 28 - Nov. 15; runs Koblenz - Trier on ⑥ to Dec. 13.
q – Ⓑ (not June 19).
r – ⚒ (not June 19, Nov. 1).
t – Not June 19.
v – ①–⑥ June 28 - Oct. 27 (also ①⑤ Oct. 31 - Nov. 21).
w – Also Oct. 3.
x – From Nov. 22 does not run Luxembourg - Trier.
y – Ⓑ June 29 - Nov. 21; runs Koblenz - Trier on Ⓑ (not June 19).
z – ⑦ June 29 - Nov. 16; runs Trier - Koblenz on ⑦ to Dec. 7.
◧ – Train number **2339** on ⑤ (also June 18, Oct. 2; not June 20, Oct. 3).
¶ – Operated by WestfalenBahn.

813 NORDDEICH - EMDEN - BREMEN - HANNOVER

km		RE 4401	♣	ICE 841	ICE 841	RE 4403	IC 2235	IC 2235	RE 4405	RE 4407	ICE 533	RE 4407	IC 2035	IC 2035	RE 4409	ICE 535	RE 4411	IC 2037	RE 4413	ICE 537	RE 4415	IC 2039	RE 4417	ICE 1139	RE 4419
			Ⓐ	①	Ⓐ		①–⑥				①–⑥		①–⑥	m											
				✕	✕		z 🍷	🍷	B		✕		z 🍷	🍷	B	✕		🍷	B	✕		🍷	B	🍷	
	Norddeich Mole .. **812** d.	...	...	...	...	...	...	...	...	...	...	...	...	...	...	...	...	0736z	...	...	0839	0936	...	...	1039
0	**Norddeich** .... **812** d.	...	...	...	...	...	...	...	...	...	...	...	0536	...	...	...	0641	0739z	...	...	0841	0939	...	...	1041
6	Norden .... **812** d.	...	...	...	...	...	...	...	...	...	...	...	0543	...	...	...	0647	0746z	...	...	0847	0946	...	...	1047
35	**Emden** Hbf .... **812** d.	...	...	...	...	...	0416	...	...	0517	...	...	0609	...	...	...	0717	0816	...	...	0917	1016	...	...	1117
62	Leer (Ostfriesland) **812** a.	...	...	...	...	...	0433	...	...	0534	...	...	0626	...	...	...	0734	0833	...	...	0934	1033	...	...	1134
62	Leer (Ostfriesland) .... d.	...	...	...	...	...	0441	...	...	0541	...	...	0634	...	...	...	0741	0841	...	...	0941	1041	...	...	1141
101	Bad Zwischenahn ...... d.	...	...	...	...	...	0513	...	...	0612	...	...	0712	...	...	...	0812	0913	...	...	1012	1113	...	...	1212
116	**Oldenburg** (Oldb) .... a.	...	...	...	...	...	0523	...	...	0623	...	...	0723	...	...	...	0823	0923	...	...	1023	1123	...	...	1223
116	**Oldenburg** (Oldb) .... d.	...	0406b	0442e	...	...	0535n	...	...	0635	0641	...	0735	0735	...	...	0835	0935	...	...	1035	1135	...	...	1235
147	Delmenhorst .... d.	...	0431	0500	...	...	0554	...	...	0654	0659	...	0754	0754	...	...	0854	0954	...	...	1054	1154	...	...	1254
161	**Bremen** Hbf .... a.	...	0444	0510	...	...	0605	...	...	0705	0709	←	0805	0805	...	...	0905*	1005	...	...	1105*	1205	...	...	1305*
161	**Bremen** Hbf .... d.	0418	...	0512	0512	0518	0609	0609	0618	→	0714	0718	0810	0810	0818	0914	0918	1009	1018	1114	1118	1209	1218	1314	1318
196	Verden (Aller) .... d.	0442	...	0532	0532	0542	0629	0629	0642	...	|	0742	0830	0830	0842	|	0942	1029	1042	|	1142	1229	1242	|	1342
227	Nienburg (Weser) .... d.	0504	...	|	|	0604	0647	0647	0704	...	|	0804	0847	0847	0904	|	1004	1047	1104	|	1204	1247	1304	|	1404
283	**Hannover** Hbf .... a.	0538	...	0615	0615	0638	0714	0714	0738	...	0814	0838	0914	0914	0938	1014	1038	1113	1138	1214	1238	1313	1338	1414	1438
	Magdeburg Hbf **866** . a.	...	...	|	|	...	0857	0857	...	...	|	...	1057	...	...	|	...	1257	...	|	...	1457	...	|	...
	Berlin Hbf **810** .... a.	...	...	0823	0823	...	|	|	...	...	|	...	|	...	...	|	...	|	...	|	...	|	...	|	...
	Leipzig Hbf **866** .... a.	...	...	...	...	...	1019	1019	...	...	|	...	1219	...	...	|	...	1419	...	|	...	1619	...	|	...
	Nürnberg Hbf **900** a.	...	...	...	...	...	...	...	...	...	1124	...	...	...	...	1324	...	...	...	|	...	...	...	|	...
	München Hbf **900** a.	...	...	...	...	...	...	...	...	...	1248	...	...	...	...	1517	...	...	...	1659	...	...	...	1900	...

	IC 2431	RE 4421	ICE 631	RE 4423	IC 2433	RE 4425	ICE 633	RE 4427	IC 2435	IC 2435	RE 4429	ICE 635	ICE 635	RE 4431	IC 2437	RE 4433	RE 4435		IC 2439	RE 4437	♣	RE 4439		RE 4441	♣
							¶		♥			Ⓑ d	⑦ w												
	C 🍷	B	✕		🍷	B	✕		🍷	🍷	B	✕	✕		🍷	B			🍷	B					
Norddeich Mole ... **812** d.	...	...	...	1239	...	...	...	1439	1536	...	...	...	...	1639	...	...	1839	...	...	...	...	2039	...	...	...
Norddeich .... **812** d.	...	...	...	1241	...	...	...	1441	1539	...	...	...	...	1641	...	...	1841	...	...	...	...	2041	...	...	...
Norden .... **812** d.	...	...	...	1247	...	...	...	1447	1550	...	...	...	...	1647	...	...	1847	...	...	...	...	2047	...	...	...
Emden Hbf .... **812** d.	1218	...	...	1317	1415j	...	...	1517	1616	1616	...	...	...	1717	1816	...	1917	...	2016	...	...	2117	...	...	...
Leer (Ostfriesland) . **812** a.	1235	...	...	1334	1433j	...	...	1534	1633	1633	...	...	...	1734	1833	...	1934	...	2033	...	...	2134	...	...	...
Leer (Ostfriesland) .... d.	1241	...	...	1341	1441	...	...	1541	1641	1641	...	...	...	1741	1841	...	1941	...	2041	...	...	2141	...	...	...
Bad Zwischenahn .... d.	1313	...	...	1412	1513	...	...	1612	1713	1713	...	...	...	1812	1913	...	2012	...	2113	...	2145	2212	...	...	2345
Oldenburg (Oldb) .... a.	1323	...	...	1423	1523	...	...	1623	1723	1723	...	...	...	1823	1923	...	2023	...	2123	...	2157	2223	...	...	2357
Oldenburg (Oldb) .... d.	1335	...	...	1435	1535	...	...	1635	1735	1735	...	...	...	1835	1935	...	2035	...	2135	...	2206	2235	...	...	0006v
Delmenhorst .... d.	1354	...	...	1454	1554	...	...	1654	1754	1754	...	...	...	1854	1954	...	2054	...	2154	...	2231	2254	...	...	0031
Bremen Hbf .... a.	1405	...	...	1505*	1605	...	...	1705*	1805	1805	...	...	...	1905*	2005	...	2105*	...	2205	...	2244	2305	...	...	0044
Bremen Hbf .... d.	1409	1418	1514	1518	1609	1618	1714	1718	1809	1809	1818	1914	1914	1918	2009	2018	2118	...	...	2218	...	2311	...	0011	...
Verden (Aller) .... d.	1429	1442	|	1542	1629	1642	|	1742	1829	1829	1842	|	|	1942	2029	2042	2142	...	...	2242	...	2344	...	0042	...
Nienburg (Weser) .... d.	1447	1504	|	1604	1647	1704	|	1804	1847	1847	1904	|	|	2004	2047	2104	2204	...	...	2304	...	0006	...	0104	...
Hannover Hbf .... a.	1513	1538	1614	1638	1713	1738	1814	1838	1913	1913	1938	2014	2014	2038	2113	2138	2238	...	...	2338	...	0039	...	0138	...
Magdeburg Hbf **866** .. a.	1657	...	|	...	1857	...	|	...	2057	2057	...	|	|	...	2300q	...	...	...	...	...	...	...	...	...	...
Berlin Hbf **810** .... a.	1825	...	|	...	|	...	|	...	|	|	...	|	|	...	...	...	...	...	...	...	...	...	...	...	...
Leipzig Hbf **866** .... a.	...	...	|	...	2019	...	|	...	2220	2220	...	|	|	...	...	...	...	...	...	...	...	...	...	...	...
Nürnberg Hbf **900** . a.	...	...	1924	...	...	...	|	...	...	...	...	2324	2324	...	...	...	...	...	...	...	...	...	...	...	...
München Hbf **900** . a.	...	...	2117	...	...	...	2300	...	...	...	...	...	0051	...	...	...	...	...	...	...	...	...	...	...	...

	RE 4442	RE 4440	IC 2438	RE 4402	RE 4404	IC 2436	RE 4406	ICE 636	RE 4408	IC 2434	RE 4410	ICE 634	RE 4412	IC 2432	IC 2432	RE 4414	ICE 1132	RE 4416	IC 2430	RE 4418	ICE 630	RE 4420	IC 2038	RE 4422	ICE 538
	⚒		①–⑥					Ⓐ				①–⑥			♥										
		B	z 🍷		B	🍷		✕	B	◇ 🍷		✕	B	C 🍷	C 🍷		🍷	B	◇ 🍷		✕	B	◇ 🍷		✕
München Hbf **900** . d.	...	...	...	...	...	...	...	...	...	...	...	0513r	...	...	...	...	0653	...	...	...	0905	...	...	...	1045
Nürnberg Hbf **900** . d.	...	...	...	...	...	...	...	...	...	...	...	0632	...	...	...	...	|	...	...	...	|	...	...	...	1235
Leipzig Hbf **866** .... d.	...	...	...	...	...	...	...	...	...	0540t	...	|	...	...	...	...	|	...	0940	...	|	...	1140	...	|
Berlin Hbf **810** .... d.	...	...	...	...	...	...	...	...	...	|	...	|	...	0731	0731	...	|	...	|	...	|	...	|	...	|
Magdeburg Hbf **866** .. d.	...	...	...	...	...	0503z	...	...	...	0700t	...	|	...	0901	0901	...	|	...	1100	...	|	...	1300	...	|
Hannover Hbf .... d.	...	0421	...	0521	0618‡	0645	0721	0745	0821	0845	0921	0945	1021	1045	1045	1121	1145	1221	1245	1321	1345	1421	1445	1521	1545
Nienburg (Weser) .... d.	...	0454	...	0554	0654	0713	0754	|	0854	0913	0954	|	1054	1113	1113	1154	|	1254	1313	1354	|	1454	1513	1555	|
Verden (Aller) .... d.	...	0516	...	0616	0716	0730	0816	|	0916	0931	1016	|	1116	1130	1130	1216	|	1316	1330	1416	|	1516	1530	1616	|
Bremen Hbf .... a.	...	0539	...	0639	0739	0750	0839	0844*	0939	0950	1039	1044*	1139	1150	1150	1239	1244*	1339	1350	1439	1444*	1539	1550	1639	1644*
Bremen Hbf .... d.	*0415*a	...	0553	0653	...	0753	0853	...	...	0953	1053	...	...	1153	1153	1253	...	...	1353	1453	...	...	1553	1653	...
Delmenhorst .... d.	*0428*a	...	0604	0703	...	0804	0903	...	...	1004	1103	...	...	1204	1204	1303	...	...	1404	1503	...	...	1604	1703	...
Oldenburg (Oldb) .... a.	*0453*a	...	0623	0723	...	0823	0923	...	...	1023	1123	...	...	1223	1223	1323	...	...	1423	1523	...	...	1623	1723	...
Oldenburg (Oldb) .... d.	0533	...	0626	0733	...	0833	0933	...	...	1033	1133	...	...	1233	1233	1333	...	...	1433	1533	...	...	1633	1733	...
Bad Zwischenahn .... d.	0544	...	0637	0744	...	0844	0944	...	...	1044	1144	...	...	1244	1244	1344	...	...	1444	1544	...	...	1644	1744	...
Leer (Ostfriesland) .... a.	0614	...	0707	0814	...	0914	1014	...	...	1114	1214	...	...	1315	1315	1414	...	...	1515	1614	...	...	1715	1814	...
Leer (Ostfriesland) . **812** d.	0624	...	0715	0824	...	0922	1024	...	...	1122	1224	...	...	1323	1323	1424	...	...	1523	1624	...	...	1723	1824	...
Emden Hbf .... **812** d.	0642	...	0742	0842	...	0938	1042	...	...	1138	1242	...	...	1339	1342	1442	...	...	1539	1642	...	...	1739	1842	...
Norden .... **812** d.	0706	...	0808	0906	...	...	1106	...	...	...	1306	...	...	...	1408	1506	...	...	...	1706	...	...	...	1906	...
Norddeich .... **812** a.	0712	...	0814	0912	...	...	1112	...	...	...	1312	...	...	...	1414	1512	...	...	...	1712	...	...	...	1912	...
Norddeich Mole ... **812** a.	0716	...	0820	0916	...	...	1116	...	...	...	1316	...	...	...	1420	1516	...	...	...	1716	...	...	...	1916	...

	RE 4424	IC 2036	RE 4426	RE 4426	ICE 536	RE 4428	IC 2034	IC 1934	RE 4430	ICE 776	RE 4430	RE 4432	IC 2032	IC 2032	RE 4434	ICE 832	ICE 932	IC 1932	RE 4434	RE 4434	RE 4436	ICE 732	ICE 532	RE 4438	ICE 850
				⑥				⑦		Ⓑ q			Ⓑ q			⊡	⑤ p	⑦		⑥		⑤⑥	⊖		⑦
	B	◇ 🍷			✕	B	◇ 🍷	🍷		F ✕		B	◇ 🍷			✕	✕	S				A ✕	✕		
München Hbf **900** . d.	...	...	...	...	1240	...	...	...	...	...	...	...	...	...	...	...	...	...	...	...	...	1812	1812	...	...
Nürnberg Hbf **900** . d.	...	...	...	...	1435	...	...	...	...	...	...	...	...	...	...	...	...	...	...	...	...	1934	1934	...	...
Leipzig Hbf **866** .... d.	...	1340q	...	...	|	...	1540q	1605	...	...	...	...	1740	...	...	...	...	...	...	...	...	|	|	...	...
Berlin Hbf **810** .... d.	...	|	...	...	|	...	|	|	...	...	...	...	|	...	...	1946	1946	1954k	...	...	...	|	|	...	2150
Magdeburg Hbf **866** .. d.	...	1500q	...	...	|	...	1700q	1727	...	...	...	...	1900	...	...	|	|	|	...	...	...	|	|	...	|
Hannover Hbf .... d.	1621	1645	1721	1721	1745	1821	1845	1901	1921	1950	...	2021	2045	2045	2121	2141	2141	2143	...	...	2221	2250	2250	2321	2349
Nienburg (Weser) .... d.	1654	1713	1754	1754	|	1854	1913	1929	1954	|	...	2054	2113	2113	2154	2211	2211	2211	...	...	2254	2319	2319	2354	0017
Verden (Aller) .... d.	1716	1730	1816	1816	|	1916	1930	1948	2016	|	...	2116	2130	2130	2216	2228	2228	2229	...	...	2316	2337	2337	0016	0035
Bremen Hbf .... a.	1739	1750	1839	1839	1844*	1939	1950	2009	2039	2047	←	2139	2150	2150	2239	2248	2247	2247	...	...	2347	2356	2357	0047	0056
Bremen Hbf .... d.	...	1753	1853	1853	...	...	1953	2011	→	2050	2054	...	2153	2153	...	...	2249	2249	2253x	2253	...	...	2359	...	0058
Delmenhorst .... d.	...	1804	1903	1903	...	...	2004	2022	...	|	2104	...	2204	2204	...	...	2300	2300	2304	2304	...	...	0011	...	0110
Oldenburg (Oldb) .... a.	...	1823	1923	1923	...	...	2023	2040	...	2115	2123	...	2223	2223	...	...	2319	2318	2323	2323	...	...	0029	...	0128
Oldenburg (Oldb) .... d.	...	1833	1933	1933	...	...	2033	2042	...	...	2133	...	2233	...	...	...	...	...	...	2333	...	...	...	...	...
Bad Zwischenahn .... d.	...	1844	1944	1944	...	...	2044	2055	...	...	2144	...	2244	...	...	...	...	...	...	2344	...	...	...	...	...
Leer (Ostfriesland) .... a.	...	1915	2014	2014	...	...	2115	2130	...	...	2214	...	2315	...	...	...	...	...	...	0014	...	...	...	...	...
Leer (Ostfriesland) . **812** d.	...	1923	2024	2024	...	...	2123	2138	...	...	2224	...	2323	...	...	...	...	...	...	0024	...	...	...	...	...
Emden Hbf .... **812** d.	...	1942	2040	2042	...	...	2142	2154	...	...	2242	...	2339	...	...	...	...	...	...	0040	...	...	...	...	...
Norden .... **812** d.	...	2008q	...	2106	...	...	2208	...	...	...	2306	...	...	...	...	...	...	...	...	...	...	...	...	...	...
Norddeich .... **812** a.	...	2014q	...	2112	...	...	2214	...	...	...	2312	...	...	...	...	...	...	...	...	...	...	...	...	...	...
Norddeich Mole ... **812** a.	...	2020q	...	2116	...	...	...	...	...	...	...	...	...	...	...	...	...	...	...	...	...	...	...	...	...

A – ⑤⑥ (also June 19, Oct. 2). From Garmisch (Table **895**) on ⑥ to Nov. 8 (also June 19, Oct. 3; not Oct. 4).
B – To / from Bremerhaven (Table **815**).
C – To / from Cottbus (Table **838**).
F – From Frankfurt (Table **900**).
S – From Stralsund (Table **845**).

a – Ⓐ only. Bremen d. 0412 July 21 - Sept. 1.
b – 0401 June 17 - July 18.

d – Not June 19.
e – 0438 June 23 - July 14.
j – 3 minutes later on ⑥ until Oct. 18.
k – Berlin **Spandau**.
m – Not Oct. 4.
n – 0531 June 17 - July 19.
p – Also Oct. 2.
q – Ⓑ (not Oct. 3).
r – ①–⑤ (not June 19, Aug. 15, Oct. 3).
t – ①–⑥ only.

v – 0001 on the mornings June 17 - July 20.
w – Also June 18, Aug. 14, Oct. 2.
x – 2249 on ①–④ July 21 - Aug. 28.
z – ①–⑥ (not Oct. 4).

‡ – 0621 on Ⓒ.
¶ – Train number **1133** on ⑥.
⊡ – ①②③④⑥ (not Oct. 2).

⊖ – ①②③④⑦ (not June 19, Oct. 2). On ⑦ runs with train number **1032** a[illegible] runs 6–7 minutes **earlier** Hannover - Oldenburg.
♥ – Daily to Oct. 27; ①⑤⑦ from Oct. 31
◇ – Departs Leipzig 3 minutes later until Sept. 27.
* – Connects with train in previous colum[illegible]
♣ – Operated by Nord West Bahn.

Nord West Bahn — OSNABRÜCK - OLDENBURG - WILHELMSHAVEN — 814

km																										
		⚒	Ⓐ		Ⓐ								Ⓐ				Ⓐ		Ⓐ							†
0	**Osnabrück** Hbf .... d.	...	0459	0601	0631	0701	0801	0901	1001	1101	1201	1301	1326	1401	1501	1601	1626	1701	1726	1801	1901	2001	2101	2201	2253	2253
20	Bramsche .... d.	...	0518	0617	0648	0717	0817	0917	1017	1117	1217	1317	1348	1417	1517	1617	1648	1717	1748	1817	1917	2017	2117	2217	2313	2313
50	Quakenbrück .... d.	...	0540	0640	0710	0740	0840	0940	1040	1140	1240	1340	1410	1440	1540	1640	1710	1740	1810	1840	1940	2040	2140	2240	2340	2340
72	Cloppenburg .... d.	...	0556	0656	0726	0756	0856	0956	1056	1156	1256	1356	1426	1456	1556	1656	1726	1756	1826	1856	1956	2056	2156	2256	2356	2356
113	**Oldenburg** (Oldb) .... a.	...	0629	0729	0759	0829	0929	1029	1129	1229	1329	1429	1459	1529	1629	1729	1759	1829	1859	1929	2029	2129	2229	2329	0029	0029
113	**Oldenburg** (Oldb) .... d.	0536	0636	0736	...	0836	0936	1036	1136	1236	1336	1436	...	1536	1636	1736	...	1836	...	1936	2036	2136	2236	2336	...	0036
143	Varel (Oldb) .... d.	0559	0659	0759	...	0859	0959	1059	1159	1259	1359	1459	...	1559	1659	1759	...	1859	...	1959	2059	2159	2259	2359	...	0059
165	**Wilhelmshaven** Hbf ...... a.	0619	0719	0819	...	0919	1019	1119	1219	1319	1419	1519	...	1619	1719	1819	...	1919	...	2019	2119	2219	2319	0019	...	0119

	Ⓐ	⚒	Ⓐ	⚒	Ⓐ							Ⓐ		⑥	Ⓑ		Ⓐ		Ⓐ							
Wilhelmshaven Hbf .... d.	...	0444	...	0544	*0613*	0644	0744	0844	0944	1044	1144	...	1244	*1329*e	1344	1444	...	1544	...	1644	1744	1844	1944	2044	2144	2313
Varel (Oldb) .... d.	...	0501	...	0601	*0630*	0701	0801	0901	1001	1101	1201	...	1301	1401	1401	1501	...	1601	...	1701	1801	1901	2001	2101	2201	2330
Oldenburg (Oldb) .... a.	...	0525	...	0625	*0653*	0725	0825	0925	1025	1125	1224	...	1325	1425	1425	1525	...	1625	...	1725	1825	1925	2025	2125	2225	2353
Oldenburg (Oldb) .... d.	0406	0529	0559	0629	0659	0729	0829	0929	1029	1129	1229	1259	1329	1429	1429	1529	1559	1629	1659	1729	1829	1929	2029	2129	2229	2359f
Cloppenburg .... d.	0438	0606	0636	0706	0736	0806	0906	1006	1106	1206	1306	1336	1406	1506	1506	1606	1636	1706	1736	1806	1906	2006	2106	2206	2306	0033f
Quakenbrück .... d.	0453	0621	0651	0721	0751	0821	0921	1021	1121	1221	1321	1351	1421	1521	1521	1621	1651	1721	1751	1821	1921	2021	2121	2221	2321	...
Bramsche .... d.	0516	0641	0716	0741	0816	0841	0941	1041	1141	1241	1341	1416	1441	1541	1541	1641	1716	1741	1816	1841	1941	2041	2141	2241	2341	...
Osnabrück Hbf .... a.	0535	0658	0735	0758	0835	0858	0958	1058	1158	1258	1358	1435	1458	1558	1558	1658	1735	1758	1835	1858	1958	2058	2158	2258	2358	...

e – Change trains at Sande (a. *1336*, d. 1350).

f – Oldenburg - Cloppenburg on ⑤⑥ (not Oct. 3).

RE services — OSNABRÜCK - BREMEN - BREMERHAVEN - CUXHAVEN — 815

km																										
		⚒¶	⚒	ⒶH	¶	⚒	H		H		H		H		H		H		H		H		¶	Ⓒ	Ⓐ	¶
0	**Osnabrück** Hbf.. **800** d.	...	0421	...	...	0537	*0637*r	0737	*0837*	0937	*1037*	1137	*1237*	1337	*1437*	1537	*1637*	1737	*1837*	1937	*2037*	2137	...	2234	2252	...
53	Diepholz .... d.	...	0454	...	...	0606	*0706*r	0806	*0906*	1006	*1106*	1206	*1306*	1406	*1506*	1606	*1706*	1806	*1906*	2006	*2106*	2206	...	2303	2321	...
122	**Bremen** Hbf....... **800** a.	...	0548	...	...	0652	*0752*r	0852	*0952*	1052	*1152*	1252	*1352*	1452	*1552*	1652	*1752*	1852	*1952*	2052	*2152*	2252	...	2349	0007	...
122	**Bremen** Hbf.............. d.	0541	...	0556	0641	0656	0756	0856	0956	1056	1156	1256	1356	1456	1556	1656	1756	1856	1956	2056	2156	...	2312	...	...	0012
143	Osterholz-Scharmbeck d.	0557	...	0610	0657	0710	0810	0910	1010	1110	1210	1310	1410	1510	1610	1710	1810	1910	2010	2110	2210	...	2328	...	...	0028
185	**Bremerhaven** Hbf...... a.	0625	...	0630	0725	0730	0830	0930	1030	1130	1230	1330	1430	1530	1630	1730	1830	1930	2030	2130	2230	...	2357	...	...	0057
188	**Bremerhaven**-Lehe .. a.	0630	...	0635g	0730	0735h	0835	0935	1035	1135	1235	1335	1435	1535	1635	1735	1835	1945j	2035	2135	2235	...	0002	...	...	0102

	Ⓒ¶		⚒	⚒¶	ⒶH	⚒	⚒		H		H		H		H		H		H		H		H	¶		¶
Bremerhaven-Lehe ... d.	0008	...	...	0407	0523	...	0623	...	0723	0823	0923	1023	1123	1223	1323	1423	1523	1623	1723	1823	1923	2023	2123	2158	...	2258
Bremerhaven Hbf ..... d.	0012	...	...	0412	0528	...	0628	...	0728	0828	0928	1028	1128	1228	1328	1428	1528	1628	1728	1828	1928	2028	2128	2203	...	2303
Osterholz-Scharmbeck. d.	0043	...	...	0444	0550	...	0650	...	0750	0850	0950	1050	1150	1250	1350	1450	1550	1650	1750	1850	1950	2050	2150	2233	...	2333
Bremen Hbf .... a.	0100	...	...	0504	0603	...	0703	...	0803	0903	1003	1103	1203	1303	1403	1503	1603	1703	1803	1903	2003	2103	2203	2250	...	2350
Bremen Hbf ....**800** d.	...	...	0507	...	...	0607	0707	0707	*0807*	0907	*1007*	1107	*1207*	1307	*1407*	1507	*1607*	1707	*1807*	1907	*2007*	2107	*2207*	...	2312	...
Diepholz .... d.	...	...	0549	...	...	0649	0749	0749	*0849*	0949	*1049*	1149	*1249*	1349	*1449*	1549	*1649*	1749	*1849*	1949	*2049*	2149	*2254*	...	0000	...
Osnabrück Hbf ...**800** a.	...	...	0620	...	...	0720	0820	0820	*0920*	1020	*1120*	1220	*1320*	1420	*1520*	1621	*1721*	1820	*1920*	2020	*2120*	2220	*2326*	...	0032	...

Bremerhaven - Cuxhaven ⊡

km		Ⓐ	⚒					Ⓐ		
0	**Bremerhaven** Hbf..... d.	0504	0636	0736	0836	and	2036	2136	2236	...
3	Bremerhaven-Lehe.... d.	0510	0641	0741	0841	hourly	2041	2141	2241	...
43	**Cuxhaven** .... a.	0557	0727	0827	0927	until	2127	2227	2327	...

	Ⓐ	⚒						Ⓐ	
Cuxhaven .... d.	0509	0639	0739	0839	and	1939	2039	2139	2239
Bremerhaven-Lehe........... a.	0548	0718	0818	0918	hourly	2018	2119	2218	2318
Bremerhaven Hbf........... a.	0553	0723	0823	0923	until	2023	2123	2223	2323

H – From / to Hannover (Table **813**).

g – 0645 on ①.

h – 0745 on ⑥.

j – 1935 on Ⓒ.

r – ⚒ only.

⊡ – Operated by Elbe-Weser.

¶ – Operated by Nord West Bahn (2nd class only).

☛ Additional stopping trains operate Bremen Hbf - Bremerhaven-Lehe (operated by Nord West Bahn): **From Bremen Hbf** at 0741 and hourly until 2141. **From Bremerhaven-Lehe** at 0453 Ⓐ, 0537 ⚒, 0556 Ⓐ, 0637, 0656 Ⓐ, 0737, 0837 and hourly until 2037.

metronom; Elbe-Weser — HAMBURG - CUXHAVEN and BREMERHAVEN — 818

km																										
	❖	‡	Ⓐ‡	⚒	‡	Ⓐ	⚒	‡	†	⚒		⚒														
0	**Hamburg** Hbf .... ⊖ d.	0028	0448	...	0528	*0602*	...	0628	...	0706	0806	0906	1006	1106	1206	1306	1406	1506	1606	1706	1806	1906	2006	2106	2206	2306
12	**Hamburg** Harburg ⊖ d.	0041	0501	...	0541	0624	...	0641	...	0724	0824	0924	1024	1124	1224	1324	1424	1524	1624	1724	1824	1924	2024	2124	2224	2324
33	**Buxtehude** .... ⊖ d.	0106	0526	...	0606	0638	...	0706	...	0738	0838	0938	1038	1138	1238	1338	1438	1538	1638	1738	1838	1938	2038	2138	2238	2338
54	Stade .... ⊖ d.	0127	0547	0550	0627	0656	0656	0727	0736	0756	0856	0956	1056	1156	1256	1357	1456	1556	1656	1756	1856	1956	2056	2156	2256	2356
102	Otterndorf .... d.	...	...	0632	...	0736	0736	...	0816	0836	0936	1036	1136	1236	1336	1438	1536	1636	1736	1836	1936	2036	2136	2236	2336	0036
116	**Cuxhaven** .... a.	...	...	0645	...	0750	0750	...	0830	0850	0950	1050	1150	1250	1350	1451	1550	1650	1750	1850	1950	2050	2150	2250	2350	0050

❖	Ⓐ	⚒	Ⓐ		Ⓐ	⑥	Ⓑ	⑥															‡	Ⓒ	Ⓐ	‡
Cuxhaven .... d.	0434	0510	0551	0610	0651	0710	0751	0810	0910	1010	1110	1210	1310	1410	1510	1610	1710	1810	1910	2010	2110	...	...	2210	2238	...
Otterndorf .... d.	0445	0521	0602	0621	0702	0721	0802	0821	0921	1021	1121	1221	1321	1421	1521	1621	1721	1821	1921	2021	2121	...	...	2221	2250	...
Stade .... ⊖ d.	0527	0603	0644	0703	0744	0803	0844	0903	1003	1103	1203	1303	1403	1503	1603	1703	1803	1903	2003	2103	2203	...	2235	2303	2332	2335
Buxtehude .... ⊖ d.	0546	0621	0702	0721	0802	0821	0902	0921	1021	1121	1221	1321	1421	1521	1621	1721	1821	1921	2021	2121	2221	...	2255	2321	...	2355
Hamburg Harburg . ⊖ a.	0600	0636	0717	0736	0817	0836	0917	0936	1036	1136	1236	1336	1436	1536	1636	1736	1836	1936	2036	2136	2236	...	2320	2336	...	0020
Hamburg Hbf .... ⊖ a.	*0619*	0657	0734	0758	0835	0852	0940	0957	1058	1155	1258	1356	1453	1556	1659j	1756	1900	1956	2058	2157	2257	...	2334	2354	...	0034

km	△	⚒		Ⓐ	Ⓐ	Ⓐ	Ⓒ	Ⓐ	Ⓒ	Ⓐ	Ⓒ	Ⓐ	Ⓐ	Ⓒ	Ⓐ⊠	Ⓒ	Ⓐ	Ⓐ	Ⓒ	Ⓐ	Ⓐ	Ⓒ	Ⓐ	Ⓐ	Ⓒ	Ⓐ
	Hamburg Hbf ..... ¶ d.	...	...	*0448*	*0548*	*0628*	*0648*	*0848*	*0858*	*1048*	*1058*	*1148*	*1248*	*1258*	*1408*	*1458*	*1508*	*1608*	*1658*	*1708*	*1808*	*1858*	*1908*	*2008*	*2058*	*2108*
0	Buxtehude .... d.	...	...	0537	0637	0717	0737c	0937	0942	1137	1142	1237	1337	1342	1450	1542	1550	1650	1742	1750	1850	1942	1950	2050	2142	2150
39	Bremervörde .... a.	...	...	0620	0721	0820	0820c	1020	1023	1220	1223	1320	1420	1423	1532	1623	1632	1732	1823	1832	1932	2023	2032	2132	2223	2232
39	Bremervörde .... d.	0538	0638	0638	0738	0838	0838	1038	1038	1238	1238	1338	1438	1438	1538	1638	1638	1738	1838	1838	1938	2038	...	...	...	...
78	**Bremerhaven** Hbf a.	0620	0720	0720	0820	0920	0920	1120	1120	1320	1320	1420	1520	1520	1620	1720	1720	1820	1920	1920	2020	2120	...	...	...	...

△	Ⓐ	⚒	†	⚒	Ⓐ	Ⓒ	Ⓐ	Ⓒ	Ⓐ	Ⓒ	Ⓐ	Ⓒ	Ⓐ	Ⓐ⊠	Ⓒ	Ⓐ	Ⓐ	Ⓒ	Ⓐ	Ⓐ	Ⓒ		⚒	†	Ⓒ	Ⓐ
Bremerhaven Hbf . d.	0536	...	...	0636	0736	0736	0836	0936	1036	1136	1236	1336	1336	1436	1536	1536	1636	1736	1736	1836	1936	1936	2036	2136	2236	2354
Bremervörde .... a.	0620	...	...	0720	0820	0820	0920	1020	1120	1220	1320	1420	1420	1520	1620	1620	1720	1820	1820	1920	2020	2020	2120	2220	2320	0036
Bremervörde .... d.	0625	0625	0630	0725	0825	0830	0925	1030	1125	1230	1325	1430	1440	1540	1630	1640	1740	1830	1840	1940	2030	...	...	...	...	...
Buxtehude .... a.	0709	0709	0714	0809	0909	0914	1009	1114	1209	1314	1409	1514	1526	1626	1714	1726	1826	1914	1926	2026	2114	...	...	...	...	...
Hamburg Hbf ...... ¶ a.	*0754*	*0754*	*0814*	*0854*	*0954*	*1004*	*1054*	*1204*	*1254*	*1404*	*1454*	*1604*	*1614*	*1714*	*1804*	*1814*	*1914*	*2004*	*2014*	*2114*	*2204*	...	...	...	...	...

– On † Buxtehude d. 0742, Bremervörde a. 0823.

– 1654 on ⑦ from Aug. 3.

⊠ – Change trains at Bremervörde on ⑤ (also Oct. 2).

‡ – Hamburg S-Bahn (2nd class only).

⊖ – Additional S-Bahn trains operate.

❖ – Operated by *metronom*.

△ – Operated by Elbe-Weser GmbH.

¶ – Connections shown are Hamburg S-Bahn services. Faster connections, operated by *metronom*, may be available (see Hamburg - Cuxhaven panel).

RE services except where shown — HAMBURG - KIEL — 820

km	SEE NOTE ▲			▲						*IC* 2224	*ICE* 76	*IC* 2226	*ICE* 74	*ICE* 892	*ICE* 974	*EC* 2
			⚒								v		❖	Ⓑ	Ⓑ b	⑦
										N	Z	F	Z	L	S	C
0	**Hamburg** Hbf **823** d.	0028	0520	0620	and	2220	2323	...	also	1015	1538	1615	1738	1901j	2041	2115
37	Elmshorn........ **823** d.	0100	0551	0650	hourly	2250	2353	...		|	|	|	|	|	|	|
73	Neumünster .. **823** d.	0133	0618	0716	until	2316	0019	...		1103	1626	1703	1826	1952	2129	2203
111	**Kiel** Hbf ....a.	0200	0638	0737		2337	0039	...		1121	1644	1721	1844	2010	2148	2222

SEE NOTE ▲				▲						*ICE* 973	*ICE* 73	*ICE* 791	*ICE* 77	*IC* 2229	*ICE* 1173	*IC* 2225
	Ⓐ									①–⑥		①–⑥			n	
										d S	◇Z	L	◇Z	F	◇K	N
Kiel Hbf .... d.	0404	0521	0621	0721	and	2221	2323	...	also	0612	0712	0753	1112	1238	1712	1838
Neumünster ... **823** d.	0425	0542	0642	0742	hourly	2242	2343	...		0631	0730	0811	1130	1257	1730	1857
Elmshorn .... **823** d.	0457	0609	0709	0809	until	2309	0009	...		|	|	|	|	|	|	|
Hamburg Hbf **823** a.	0531	0637	0737	0837		2337	0038	...		0718	0820	0903	1218	1343	1820	1943

C – 🚃 and ✕ Zürich - Basel - Koblenz - Köln - Kiel.

F – 🚃 and 🍷 Nürnberg - Frankfurt - Köln - Kiel and v.v.

K – 🚃 and ✕ Kiel - Frankfurt - Karlsruhe (- Basel ⑤⑥).

L – 🚃 Leipzig - Berlin - Kiel and v.v.

N – 🚃 and 🍷 Köln - Kiel and v.v.

S – 🚃 and ✕ Kiel - Frankfurt - Stuttgart and v.v.

Z – 🚃 and ✕ Kiel - Frankfurt - Basel - Zürich and v.v.

b – Not Oct. 3. 14–20 minutes later June 15 - July 27.

d – Not Oct. 4. 20–23 minutes **earlier** June 14 - July 26.

j – 1858 June 15 - July 27.

n – Not ①–④ June 16 - July 24.

v – Not June 14 - July 27.

◇ – 20–27 minutes **earlier** June 14 - July 27.

❖ – 17–19 minutes later June 14 - July 27.

▲ – July 14 - Aug. 24 most regional services run from / to Hamburg Altona (not Hbf). See page 563 for details.

821 HAMBURG - WESTERLAND

Nord-Ostsee-Bahn (*IC* trains operated by DB)

km		◇	◇	◇	◇	◇	◇	◇	◇	◇	◇	◇	*IC*• 2314	◇	◇	*IC*• 2074	*IC*• 2072	◇	◇	◇	*IC*• 2310	◇	◇	◇	*IC*• 2170
			Ⓐ		Ⓒ		Ⓐ		◧			S	S 🍷	W		Ⓒ D ✕	Ⓐ D ✕			S	F 🍷	W	⑥S		K ✕
	Köln Hbf **800** d.	...	...	...	...	...	...	...	...	...	...	...	0510	...	...	...	...	...	...	...	0908	...	...	...	...
	Berlin Hbf **840** d.	...	...	...	...	...	...	...	...	...	...	...	|	...	...	0820	0820	...	...	...	|	...	...	...	...
	Hamburg Hbf... **820** d.	...	...	...	...	...	*0500‡*	...	*0620**	*0720**	*0820**	*0843**	0915	*0920**	*1020**	1048	1048	*1120**	*1220**	*1243**	1315	*1320**	1405	*1420**	1448
0	**Hamburg** Altona d.	...	...	...	...	...	0524	...	0633	0733	0833	0902	|	0933	1033	|	|	1133	1233	1303	|	1333	|	1433	|
30	Elmshorn **820** d.	...	...	...	...	...	0545	...	0655	0755	0855	0922	|	0955	1055	|	|	1155	1255	1322	|	1355	1432	1455	|
64	Itzehoe d.	...	0503	...	0538	...	0612	...	0721	0821	0921	0950	1014t	1021	1121	1142	1142	1221	1321	1344	1414t	1421	1456	1521	1540
123	Heide (Holst) a.	...	0547	...	0622	...	0656	...	0756	0856	0956	1027	1050	1056	1156	1216	1216	1256	1356	1428	1450	1458	1531	1556	1616
123	Heide (Holst) d.	...	0549	...	0623	...	0702	...	0802	0902	1002	1029	1052	1102	1202	1218	1218	1302	1402	1429	1452	1502	1532	1602	1618
157	Husum d.	0558	0615	0630	0649	0658	0730	0730	0830	0930	1030	1100j	1119	1130	1230	1242	1242	1330	1430	1500	1519	1530	1600	1630	1643
197	Niebüll a.	0628	...	0658	...	0728	0758	0758	0858	0958	1058	1129	1145	1158	1258	1307	1307	1400	1458	1528	1545	1558r	1628	1658	1709
197	Niebüll d.	0631	...	0701	...	0731	0801	0801	0901	1001	1101	1131	1201	1201	1301	1331	1331	1401	1501	1531	1601h	1601r	1631	1701	1731
237	**Westerland** (Sylt) a.	0705	...	0735	...	0805	0835	0835	0937	1035	1135	1207	1234	1235	1337	1404	1406	1435	1535	1605	1634h	1635r	1705	1735	1804

	◇	◇	◇	◇	◇	◇	◇	◇	◇	◇
										⑥
Köln Hbf **800** d.	...	...	...	...	...	...	...	...	...	...
Berlin Hbf **840** d.	...	...	...	...	...	...	...	...	...	...
Hamburg Hbf.... **820** d.	*1520**	*1620**	*1720**	*1820**	*1920**	*2020**	*2120**	...	*2220**	*2323**
Hamburg Altona d.	1533	1633	1733	1833	1933	2033	2133	...	2233	2351
Elmshorn **820** d.	1555	1655	1755	1855	1955	2055	2155	...	2255	0012
Itzehoe d.	1621	1721	1821	1921	2021	2121	2221	...	2321	0036
Heide (Holst) a.	1656	1756	1856	1956	2056	2203	2304	...	0003	0116
Heide (Holst) d.	1702	1802	1902	2002	2102	2204	2307	...	0004	0117
Husum d.	1730	1830	1930	2030	2130	2232	2333	2336	0030	0142
Niebüll a.	1758	1858	1958	2058	2158	2300	...	0004	...	...
Niebüll d.	1801	1901	2001	2101	2201	2301	...	0005	...	...
Westerland (Sylt) a.	1835	1935	2035	2135	2235	2335	...	0037	...	...

	◇		◇	◇	◇	◇	◇	◇	◇	*IC*• 2311	◇
			Ⓐ	Ⓐ		⊙				H 🍷	
Westerland (Sylt) d.	0000	...	...	0423	...	0522	0622	0722	0822	0926	0952
Niebüll a.	0031	...	...	0453	...	0559	0659	0759	0859	0959	1029
Niebüll d.	0032	...	...	0454	...	0601	0701	0801	0901	1013	1031
Husum d.	0102	...	0423	0522	0525	0631	0731	0831	0931	1041	1101
Heide (Holst) a.	...	...	0448	...	0550	0656	0756	0856	0956	1102	1127
Heide (Holst) d.	...	...	0450	...	0552	0702	0802	0902	1002	1104	1128
Itzehoe d.	...	...	0537	...	0637	0737	0837	0937	1037	1155t	1203
Elmshorn **820** d.	...	...	0602	...	0702	0802	0902	1002	1102	|	1226
Hamburg Altona a.	...	...	0625	...	0725	0825	0925	1025	1125	|	1248
Hamburg Hbf **820** a.	...	...	*0637**	...	*0737**	*0837**	*0937**	*1037**	*1137**	1242	*1311‡*
Berlin Hbf **840** a.	...	...	...	...	...	...	...	...	...	|	...
Köln Hbf **800** a.	...	...	...	...	...	...	...	...	...	1650	...

	◇	◇	◇	*IC*• 2171	*IC*• 2191	*IC*• 2193	◇	◇	◇	*IC*• 2315	◇	*IC*• 2073	◇	◇	◇	◇	◇	◇	◇	◇		◇	◇	◇	◇
		⑥S		⑤ J ✕	⑥⑦ L ✕	N ✕		S	W	S G 🍷		D ✕							P	⑤⑥ W					
Westerland (Sylt) d.	1022	1056	1122	1156	1156	1156	1222	1252	1322	1326	1422	1456	1522	1622	1722	1822	1922	2022	2022	...	...	2122	...	2200	2300
Niebüll a.	1059	1129	1159	1229	1229	1229	1259	1329	1359	1359	1459	1529	1559	1659	1759	1859	1959	2059	2059	...	...	2159	...	2231	2331
Niebüll d.	1101	1131	1201	1245	1245	1245	1301	1331	1401	1413	1501	1545	1601	1701	1801	1901	2001	2101	2101	...	...	2201	...	...	2332
Husum d.	1131	1157	1231	1312	1312	1312	1331	1404	1431	1441	1531	1612	1631	1731	1831	1931	2031	2129	2131	2132	...	2229	2244	...	0002
Heide (Holst) a.	1156	1219	1256	1333	1333	1333	1356	1429	1456	1502	1556	1633	1656	1756	1856	1956	2056	...	2156	2200	...	...	2309	...	...
Heide (Holst) d.	1202	1220	1302	1335	1335	1335	1402	1431	1502	1504	1602	1635	1702	1802	1902	2002	2102	...	2202	2205	...	...	2310	...	...
Itzehoe d.	1237	1256	1337	1412	1412	1412	1437	1517	1537	1555t	1637	1712	1737	1837	1937	2037	2147	...	2247	2249	2322	...	2354	...	...
Elmshorn **820** d.	1302	1320	1402	|	|	|	1502	1541	1602	|	1702	|	1802	1902	2002	2102	2214	...	2314	2314	2353	...	...	...	...
Hamburg Altona a.	1325	|	1425	|	|	|	1525	1604	1625	|	1725	|	1825	1925	2025	2125	2235	...	2335	2335	0020	...	...	...	...
Hamburg Hbf.... **820** a.	*1337**	1347	*1437**	1510	1510	1510	*1537**	*1614**	*1637**	1642	*1737**	1811	*1837**	*1937**	*2037**	*2137**	*2258‡*	...	*0001‡*	*0001‡*	*0038**	...	...	...	...
Berlin Hbf **840** a.	...	...	...	...	...	...	...	...	...	|	...	2035	...	...	...	...	...	...	...	...	...	...	...	...	...
Köln Hbf **800** a.	...	...	...	...	...	...	...	...	...	2050	...	...	...	...	...	...	...	...	...	...	...	...	...	...	...

D – UTHLANDE – From / to Dresden on dates in Table **840**.
F – NORDFRIESLAND – (12) and 🍷 Frankfurt - Köln - Westerland.
G – DEICHGRAF – (12) and 🍷 Westerland - Köln - Frankfurt.
H – NORDFRIESLAND – (12) and 🍷 Westerland - Köln - Stuttgart.
J – ⑤ (also Oct. 2). WATTENMEER – (12) and ✕ Westerland - Hannover - Frankfurt - Stuttgart.
K – Daily to Oct. 26; ④–⑦ from Oct. 30. WATTENMEER – (12) and 🍷 (Stuttgart ⑥ **z** -) (Frankfurt ♥ -) Hannover - Westerland.
L – WATTENMEER – (12) and ✕ Westerland - Hannover - Frankfurt.
N – ①–④ to Oct. 27 (not Oct. 2); ① from Nov. 3. WATTENMEER – (12) and ✕ Westerland - Hannover - Göttingen.
P – Daily to Oct. 30; ①②③④⑦ from Nov. 2.
S – Until Oct. 26.
W – From Oct. 27.

h – From Nov. 3 Niebüll d. 1547, Westerland a. 1621.

j – Arrives 1052.
r – On Oct. 27 – 31 Niebüll a. 1606, d. 1616, Westerland a. 1651. On Nov. 1, 2 Niebüll a. 1606, d. 1631, Westerland a. 1705.
t – Arrives 12 – 16 minutes earlier.
z – Also Oct. 3.

* – Change trains at Elmshorn. **July 14 - Aug. 24** Hamburg Hbf connections are subject to alteration (see page 563).
‡ – S-Bahn connection Hamburg Hbf - Hamburg Altona and v.v.
♥ – ①⑥⑦ to Oct. 26 (also Oct. 3); ⑥⑦ from Nov. 1.
• – Until Oct. 26 conveys (2) to / from Dagebüll Mole (Table **822**).
◧ – Change trains at Husum on ⑥⑦ from Nov. 1.
⊙ – Change trains at Husum on Ⓒ.
◇ – Operated by Nord-Ostsee-Bahn GmbH.

822 SCHLESWIG-HOLSTEIN BRANCH LINES

NEUMÜNSTER - HEIDE - BÜSUM *See note* ⊠

km		⚒		⚒	⑥		Ⓐ																		
0	Neumünster d.	...	...	...	0537	...	0537	...	0737	...	0937	...	1137	...	1337	...	1537	...	1737	...	1937	...	...	...	2137
63	Heide a.	...	...	...	0646	...	0710	...	0846	...	1046	...	1246	...	1446	...	1646	...	1846	...	2046	...	...	...	2246
63	Heide d.	0451	...	0601	0701	0701	...	0801	0901	1001	1101	1201	1301	1401	1501	1601	1701	1801	1901	2001	2101	...	2208	...	...
87	Büsum a.	0517	...	0627	0727	0727	...	0827	0927	1027	1127	1227	1327	1427	1527	1627	1727	1827	1927	2027	2127	...	2234	...	...

	⚒	⚒		⚒	⑥																				
Büsum d.	...	0521	...	0631	0631	...	0731	0831	0931	1031	1131	1231	1331	1431	1531	1631	1731	1831	1931	2031	2131	...	2238	...	...
Heide a.	...	0547	...	0657	0657	...	0757	0857	0957	1057	1157	1257	1357	1457	1557	1657	1757	1857	1957	2057	2157	...	2304	...	...
Heide d.	0517	...	...	...	0717	0717	...	0917	...	1117	...	1317	...	1517	...	1717	...	1917	...	2117	...	...	2317	...	...
Neumünster a.	0625	...	...	...	0825	0825	...	1025	...	1228	...	1425	...	1625	...	1825	...	2025	...	2225	...	...	0025	...	...

HUSUM - BAD ST PETER ORDING

km		Ⓐ								
0	Husum d.	0436	0536	0636	and	1836	1936	2036	2136	2236
21	Tönning d.	0501	0601	0701	hourly	1901	2001	2101	2201	2301
43	Bad St Peter Ording a.	0527	0627	0727	until	1927	2027	2127	2227	2327

	Ⓐ								
Bad St Peter Ording d.	0533	0633	0733	and	1933	2033	2133	2233	2333
Tönning d.	0604	0704	0804	hourly	2004	2104	2204	2304	0004
Husum a.	0625	0725	0825	until	2025	2125	2225	2325	0025

NIEBÜLL - DAGEBÜLL MOLE *See note* ⊡

km	*Until Oct. 26*				⊗	★	★		★	★		⊖
	Hamburg Hbf a.	...	...	...	...	0915	1048	...	1315	1448	...	...
	Niebüll a.	...	...	...	...	1145	1307	...	1545	1709	...	...
0	Niebüll neg d.	0735	0905	1010	1135	1205	1335	1435	1605	1720	1815	1910
14	Dagebüll Mole a.	0754	0924	1029	1154	1221	1354	1454	1624	1739	1834	1929

Until Oct. 26		★		★	★	★		✣		¶	■
Dagebüll Mole d.	0820	0935	1035	1200	1340	1500	1635	1725	1840	1935	2025
Niebüll neg a.	0839	0954	1054	1226	1357	1519	1654	1744	1856	1955	2044
Niebüll d.	...	1013	...	1245	1413	1545	...	...	...	...	...
Hamburg Hbf a.	...	1242	...	1510	1642	1811	...	...	...	...	...

km	*From Oct. 27*	♥	Ⓐ		Ⓐ		Ⓐ					⑤–⑦
0	Niebüll neg d.	0635	0735	0905	1010	1125	1235	1335	1435	1603	1805	1905
14	Dagebüll Mole a.	0655	0754	0924	1029	1144	1254	1354	1454	1619	1824	1924

From Oct. 27	♥	Ⓐ		Ⓐ		Ⓐ					♣
Dagebüll Mole d.	0705	0815	0930	1035	1150	1305	1415	1500	1625	1835	1935
Niebüll neg a.	0724	0834	0949	1054	1209	1324	1431	1519	1644	1854	1955

◇ – ⑤–⑦ to June 29; ⑤ July 4 - Sept. 5; ⑤–⑦ Sept. 12 - Oct. 11.
⊖ – ⑤–⑦ (also Oct. 2). On ⑥⑦ July 5 - Sept. 7 Niebüll d. 1935, Dagebüll Mole a. 1954.
⊗ – ①–④ to Oct. 9 (also ⑥⑦ July 5 - Sept. 7); daily Oct. 12 – 26.
■ – ⑥⑦ July 5 - Sept. 7.
¶ – Daily to July 4; ①–⑤ July 7 - Sept. 5; daily from Sept. 8. By 🚌 on ①–④ (not Oct. 2).
♥ – Daily. By 🚌 on Ⓒ.
♣ – Daily. By 🚌 on ①–④.
‡ – 10 minutes later on ⑥⑦ July 5 - Sept. 7.

✣ – On ⑥⑦ July 5 - Sept. 7 Dagebüll Mole d. 1745, Niebüll a. 1801.
★ – Conveys (2) (*IC*) from / to Hamburg and beyond (Table **821**).
⊠ – **Operator**: Nordbahn Eisenbahngesellschaft.
⊡ – **Operator**: Norddeutsche Eisenbahngesellschaft Niebüll GmbH. ✆ +49 (0) 4661 980 880. Niebüll neg station is situated a short distance from the Niebüll DB station forecourt. **Additional journeys until Oct. 26**: Niebüll neg → Dagebüll Mole at 0635 Ⓐ, 0635 Ⓒ 🚌, 1105 ◇ and 1305 ‡. Dagebüll Mole → Niebüll neg at 0705 Ⓐ and 0705 Ⓒ 🚌, 1125 ◇ and 1245 ‡.

RE / RB services except where shown — HAMBURG - NEUMÜNSTER - FLENSBURG — 823

For overnight service Basel / Amsterdam / Praha - København via Flensburg, see Table **54**. Connecting trains from / to Hamburg Hbf are subject to alteration July 14 - Aug. 24 (see page 563).

km																										
								ICE 388		EC 386					ICE 380								IC 1284		
		①–⑥		⚒	Ⓒ ⊖	Ⓐ	⊕		Q 🍷		‡ A◇				H◇					⊠	✣		⑦ M		♥
0	**Hamburg** Hbf .... **820** d.	2323p	...	...	0520k	0520	0620	0720	0808	0843	0930	0920	1043	1120	1243	1330	1320	1443	1520	1643	1720	1843	1920	2032	2052	2220
37	Elmshorn .... **820** d.	2353p	...	...	0551k	0551	0650	0750	|	0910	|	0950	1110	1150	1310	|	1350	1510	1550	1710	1750	1910	1950	|	2119	2250
73	Neumünster .... **820** d.	0033	...	0533	0635	0656	0733	0835	0902	0933	1022	1035	1133	1235	1333	1422	1435	1533	1635	1733	1835	1933	2033	2120	2143	2333
112	Rendsburg .... **824** d.	0103	...	0603	0708	0727	0803	0908	0928	1003	1048	1108	1203	1308	1403	1449	1508	1603	1708	1803	1908	2003	2103	2149	2215	0003
136	Schleswig .... **824** d.	0121	...	0621	0725	0744	0821	0925	0943	1019	1102	1125	1219	1325	1419	1505	1525	1619	1725	1819	1925	2019	2121	2204	2231	0021
174	**Flensburg** .... a.	0152	...	0652	0753	0814	0847	0953	1008	1045	1122	1153	1245	1353	1445	1525	1553	1645	1753	1845	1953	2045	2152	2226	2256	0052

									ICE 381		IC 1981						EC 387								
	⑥r	⚒	①–⑥ v	⊡	⊡				H◇		⑤f M						◧ A◇					⑥e	Ⓑd		⑥e	Ⓑ
Flensburg .... d.	0003	0409	0509	0609	0709	0809	0909	1009	1024	1109	1126	1209	1309	1409	1509	1609	1653	1709	1809	1909	2009	2109	2209	...	2233	2309
Schleswig ....**824** d.	0032	0437	0537	0634	0737	0834	0937	1034	1045	1137	1148	1234	1337	1434	1537	1634	1716	1737	1834	1937	2034	2137	2237	...	2301	2337
Rendsburg ....**824** d.	0102	0456	0556	0650	0756	0850	0956	1050	1101	1156	1205	1250	1356	1450	1556	1650	1733	1756	1850	1956	2056	2156	2256	...	2320	2356
Neumünster ....**820** a.	0134	0526	0626	0721	0826	0921	1026	1121	1134	1226	1230	1321	1426	1521	1626	1721	1758	1826	1921	2026	2126	2226	2326	2343	0018*	0026
Elmshorn ....**820** a.	...	0607	0707	0745	0907	0945	1107	1145	|	1307	|	1345	1507	1545	1707	1745	|	1907	1945	2107	2207	2307	...	0008	...	...
Hamburg Hbf ......**820** a.	...	0637	0737	0814	0937	1014	1137	1214	1231	1337	1316	1414	1537	1614	1737	1814	1853	1937	2014	2137	2237	2337	...	0038	...	...

A – To / from Århus (Tables **700** / **710**).
H – 🚄12 and 🍷 Berlin - Padborg - Århus and v.v.
M – From / to München (Table **900**).
Q – ①–⑥ July 15 - Aug. 5 (also Aug. 10 – 12, Sept. 7 – 9).

d – Also June 21, 28, Dec. 13.
e – Not June 21, 28, Dec. 13.
f – Also Oct. 2; not Oct. 3.
k – ⑥ only.
p – Previous day.
r – Also Oct. 3.
v – Also June 22, 29.

* – By 🚌 from Rendsburg.
‡ – Not July 15 - Aug. 5, Aug. 10, 11, 12, 7, 8, 9.
⊠ – Runs 2 – 7 minutes later Neumünster - Flensburg on ①–④ June 16 - July 24.
✣ – Runs 9 – 12 minutes earlier June 14 - July 27.
◇ – Does not run between Flensburg and Århus on certain dates (see Table **710**).
◧ – Runs as *ICE* **389** July 14 - Aug. 4 (also Aug. 9 – 11, Sept. 6 – 8).

⊖ – On ⑦ (not June 22, 29) by 🚌 Neumünster - Rendsburg (then train, running 19 – 21 minutes later Rendsburg - Flensburg).
⊕ – On ⑦ (not June 22, 29) by 🚌 Neumünster (d. 0722) - Rendsburg (a. 0806; then train departing Rendsburg 0814, Schleswig 0828, arriving Flensburg 0851).
♥ – On ⑥ (not June 21, 28, Dec. 13) by 🚌 Neumünster - Rendsburg (then train, running 19 – 23 minutes later Rendsburg - Flensburg).
⊡ – On ⑦ (not June 22, 29) runs up to 30 minutes **earlier** Flensburg - Rendsburg, then by 🚌 to Neumünster.

RB services — KIEL - HUSUM and FLENSBURG — 824

km	SEE NOTE ▲	①–⑥	⚒w								c
0	**Kiel** Hbf .... d.	0001	0346	0501r	0556r	0701r	0801	and	2101	2201y	2301
40	Rendsburg . **823** d.	0033	0427	0533	0633	0733	0833	hourly	2133	2233	2333
65	Schleswig .. **823** d.	0051	0445	0551	0651	0751	0851	until	2151	2251	2351
102	**Husum** .... ▲ a.	0124	0518	0624	0724	0824	0924		2224	2324	0024

SEE NOTE ▲	⚒								Ⓑ
Husum .... ▲ d.	0423	0530	0635	0735	and	2035	2135	2235	2335
Schleswig .... **823** d.	0455	0602	0707	0807	hourly	2107	2207	2307	0007
Rendsburg .... **823** d.	0515	0622	0727	0827	until	2127	2227	2327	0027
Kiel Hbf .... a.	0549	0654f	0759f	0859		2159	2259z	2359z	0059

km		Ⓐ	⚒	Ⓐ	Ⓒ						
0	**Kiel** Hbf .... d.	0403	0520	0620	0642	0742	and	2042	2142	2242	2342
29	Eckernförde ...... d.	0432	0552	0650	0710	0810	hourly	2110	2210	2311	0011
50	Süderbrarup ...... d.	0451	0612	0709	0730	0830	until	2130	2234	2330	0030
81	**Flensburg** .... a.	0519	0639	0736	0756	0856		2156	2300	2357	0057

	⚒		Ⓒ	Ⓐ					
Flensburg .... d.	0447	0544	0703	0703	0803	and	2103	2208	2323
Süderbrarup .... d.	0513	0611	0729	0730	0829	hourly	2129	2234	2351
Eckernförde .... d.	0532	0630	0749	0749	0849	until	2149	2253	0011
Kiel Hbf .... a.	0604	0700	0816	0816	0916		2216	2318	0038

c – On ⑥ July 5 - Dec. 6 by 🚌 Kiel (d. 2306) - Rendsburg (then train, running 26 minutes later Rendsburg - Husum).
f – 20 – 25 minutes later on ⑦ to June 15 / from July 6 (by 🚌 from Rendsburg).
r – 16 – 21 minutes earlier on ⑦ to June 15 / from July 6 (by 🚌 to Rendsburg)
w – Runs 6 – 15 minutes later on June 21, 28.
y – 2140 on ⑥ July 5 - Dec. 6 (by 🚌 to Rendsburg).
z – 20 minutes later on ⑥ July 5 - Dec. 6 (by 🚌 from Rendsburg).
▲ – Evening / early morning services (1930 - 0500) between Schleswig and Husum are subject to alteration **July 14 - Aug. 4**. During this period services may be operated by 🚌 for all or part of journey (journey time extended by up to 32 minutes; earlier departures from Husum).

RB / RE services — HAMBURG - LÜBECK - PUTTGARDEN and TRAVEMÜNDE — 825

km			⚒	⊠								J	ⒷG
0	**Hamburg** Hbf . d.	0028	0505	0605	and	2005	2112	2212	2323			1101	2104
40	Bad Oldesloe .. d.	0054	0530	0630	hourly	2030	2136	2236	2347		also	|	|
63	**Lübeck** Hbf .... a.	0112	0548	0648	until	2048	2154	2254	0006			1137	2140

			⚒	⊠						H	E
Lübeck Hbf .... d.	0016	0408	0504	0608	and	2208	2308	...		0816	1416
Bad Oldesloe .... d.	0033	0426	0522	0625	hourly	2225	2325	...	also	|	|
Hamburg Hbf .... a.	0103	0508	0547	0650	until	2250	2350	...		0853	1453

km		Ⓐ	⚒						
0	**Lübeck** Hbf .... d.	0503	0603	0703	0803*	and	2203*	2303	...
18	Travemünde Skandinavienkai .... a.	0519	0619	0719	0819	hourly	2219	2319	...
21	**Travemünde** Strand .... a.	0525	0625	0725	0825	until	2225	2325	...

	Ⓐ	⚒								
Travemünde Strand .... d.	0534	0634	0734	...	0834	and	2234	...	2334
Travemünde Skandinavienkai ..... d.	0539	0639	0739	...	0839	hourly	2239	...	2339
Lübeck Hbf .... a.	0556	0656	0756	...	0858	until	2258	...	2356

km																										
					EC 31					ICE 33							IC 2220	ICE 35					ICE 37			
					M			L	Ⓒk	🍷							F🍷	B🍷		r	L	Ⓒk	🍷			
0	**Hamburg** Hbf .... d.	...	...	...	0725	...	...	...	0835v	0928	...	...	...	...	...	...	1230	1328	...	...	...	1425v	1528	...	...	...
63	**Lübeck** Hbf .... d.	0612	0712	0712	0806	0812	0912	0912	0920	1006	1012	1112	1112	1212	1308j	1308j	1314	1406	1412	1512	1512	1516	1606	1612	1712	1712
93	Neustadt (Holst) ..... a.	0658b	0752	|	|	0851	0952r	|	|	|	1051	1152	|	1251	1345z	|	|	|	1451	1552	|	|	|	1651	1752	|
115	Oldenburg (Holst) ...... d.	...	...	0816	0839	...	...	1016	1016	1039	...	...	1216	...	...	1405z	1417	1439	...	...	1616	1616	1639	...	...	1816
144	Fehmarn-Burg .... a.	...	...	0840	|	...	...	1040	1042	|	...	...	1240	...	...	1428z	1442	|	...	...	1640	1642	|	...	...	1840
151	**Puttgarden** 🚢 .... a.	...	...	0855h	0905	...	...	1055p	1058	1105	...	...	1255k	...	...	1440k	...	1505	...	...	1655f	1658	1705	...	...	1855
	København H **720** .. a.	...	...	...	1214	...	...	...	...	1414	...	...	...	...	...	...	...	1814	...	...	...	...	2014	...	...	...

	ICE 39				EC 239					
	🍷				S					
amburg Hbf .... d.	1728v	...	...	...	1928	...	...	...	...	...
übeck Hbf .... d.	1806	1812	1912	1912	2006	2012	2112	2112	2212	2312
Neustadt (Holst) ...... a.	|	1851	1952	|	|	2051	2152	|	2251	2345
ldenburg (Holst) .... d.	1839	...	...	2016	2039	...	...	2216	...	0017
ehmarn-Burg .... a.	|	...	...	2040	|	...	...	2240	...	0040
uttgarden 🚢 .... a.	1905	...	...	2055k	2105	...	...	2255	...	0055
København H **720** .. a.	2214	...	...	...	0014	...	...	...	...	...

							IC 2327			ICE 38		
		Ⓐ					A			B🍷		Ⓒk
København H **720** a.	...	...	...	...	...	...	...	...	...	0742	...	...
Puttgarden 🚢 .... d.	0519	0620	...	0720	...	...	...	0915h	...	1042	...	1113
Fehmarn-Burg .... d.	0530	0631	...	0731	...	...	0908	0931	...	|	...	1128
Oldenburg (Holst) .... d.	0553	0654	...	0754	...	...	0933	0954	...	1107	...	1154
Neustadt (Holst) ... d.	0623	|	0717e	|	0817	0923r	|	|	1017	|	1123	|
Lübeck Hbf .... a.	0654	0754	0754	0854	0854	0954	1034	1054	1054	1137	1154	1242
Hamburg Hbf .... a.	...	...	...	...	...	...	1115	...	...	1216	...	1328c

			ICE 36					ICE 34		IC 2221			EC 234					ICE 32				EC 30				
	L		🍷		k	R		🍷		F🍷			S		Ⓒk	L		🍷				k				
København H **720** .. a.	...	...	0942	...	...	...	...	1142	...	...	...	...	1342	...	...	...	...	1542	...	...	...	1742	...	...	...	...
uttgarden 🚢 .... d.	1115p	...	1242	...	1309	...	...	1442	...	...	1515k	...	1642	...	1710	1715f	...	1842	...	1915	...	2042	...	2115k	...	...
ehmarn-Burg .... d.	1131	...	|	...	1320	1331	...	|	...	1508	1531	...	|	...	1725	1731	...	|	...	1931	...	|	...	2131	...	...
ldenburg (Holst) .... d.	1154	...	1307	...	1343	1354	...	1507	...	1533	1554	...	1707	...	1751	1754	...	1907	...	1954	...	2107	...	2154	...	...
Neustadt (Holst) ...... d.	|	1217t	|	1314z	|	|	1417	|	1523r	|	|	1617	|	1723r	|	|	1817t	|	1923	|	2017	|	2123	|	2217	2317
übeck Hbf .... a.	1254	1254	1337	1354	1454	1454	1454	1537	1554	1634	1654	1654	1737	1754	1842	1854	1854	1937	1954	2054	2054	2137	2155	2254	2254	2348
amburg Hbf .... a.	...	...	1416	...	...	...	...	1616	...	1716q	...	...	1816	...	1934	...	...	2016	...	...	...	2216	...	...	...	...

– July 4 - Oct. 5 (also June 14, 20, 21, 22, 27, 28, 29, Oct. 10, 11, 17, 18, 19, 24, 31). LÜBECKER BUCHT – 🚄12 Fehmarn-Burg - Köln - Frankfurt - Passau.
– 🚄12 and 🍷 Berlin - Hamburg - København and v.v.
– Daily to Sept. 15; ⑤⑦ from Sept. 19 (also Oct. 2). *ICE* **1081**. To München (Table **900**). Runs up to 21 minutes **earlier** June 14 - July 27.
– Until Oct. 19. FEHMARN – 🚄12 Frankfurt - Köln - Fehmarn-Burg and v.v. Also runs Frankfurt - Köln - Lübeck and v.v. on ⑤⑦ from Oct. 24.
– Ⓑ (not Oct. 3). *ICE* **584**. From München (Table **900**). Runs 3 minutes later June 15 - July 27.
– ①–⑥ (not Oct. 4). *ICE* **585**. To München (Table **900**). June 14 - July 26 Lübeck d. 0805, Hamburg a. 0846.
– Daily to Sept. 15; ⑤⑦ from Sept. 19 (also Oct. 2). *ICE* **784**. From München / Nürnberg (Table **900**). June 14 - July 27 Hamburg d. 1112, Lübeck a. 1156.

L – Ⓐ (daily from Oct. 27).
M – Until Oct. 27.
R – From Oct. 27.
S – June 6 - Aug. 24.

b – 0651 on Ⓒ.
c – 1339 July 19 - Aug. 24.
e – 0723 on Ⓒ.
f – Ⓐ until Oct. 24.
h – Ⓐ (daily until Oct. 31).
j – 1312 from Oct. 27.
k – Until Oct. 26.

p – Ⓐ to Oct. 24; ⑥⑦ from Nov. 1.
q – 1728 July 14 - Aug. 25 (also ⑦ from Oct. 26).
r – 4 – 9 minutes **earlier** on Ⓒ until Oct. 26.
t – 6 minutes later on Ⓒ until Oct. 26.
v – 7 – 15 minutes **earlier** July 14 - Aug. 24.
z – 7 – 12 minutes later from Oct. 27.

* – 2 minutes earlier on Ⓒ until Oct. 26.
⊠ – **Additional journeys** on Ⓐ Hamburg - Lübeck: From Hamburg Hbf at 0635 and hourly until 2035. From Lübeck Hbf at 0543 and hourly until 1943.

826 KIEL - LÜBECK

RE/RB services

km		Ⓒ	Ⓐ	Ⓒ	Ⓐ							
0	**Kiel** Hbf .... d.	0543	0544	0643	0644	0744	and	1944	2044	2143	2243	2343
33	Plön .... d.	0615	0615	0713	0715	0815	hourly	2015	2115	2215	2315	0015
47	Eutin .... d.	0629	0629	0727	0729	0829	until	2029	2131	2229	2329	0029
80	**Lübeck** Hbf ...... a.	0658	0652	0752	0752	0852		2052	2153	2258	2358	0058

	⑥	Ⓐ	Ⓒ	Ⓐ							
Lübeck Hbf ... d.	0501	0504	0601	0606	0704	0806	and	2006	2106	2201	2301
Eutin .... d.	0529	0529	0629	0629	0729	0829	hourly	2029	2131	2229	2329
Plön .... d.	0544	0544	0643	0645	0745	0845	until	2045	2145	2244	2344
Kiel Hbf .... a.	0617	0615	0715	0715	0815	0915		2115	2216	2317	0017

Other stopping trains Kiel - Lübeck and v.v. (journey 86 – 88 minutes): **From Kiel** Hbf at 0604 Ⓐ, 0704 and hourly until 2004. **From Lübeck** Hbf at 0628 Ⓐ, 0728 and hourly until 2028.

827 LÜBECK - BÜCHEN - LÜNEBURG

RB services

km		Ⓐ					✣				
0	**Lübeck** Hbf .... d.	0505	0605	0707	0809	0909		2109	2219	2323	...
9	Lübeck Flughafen ✈ ... d.	0515	0615	0716	0819	0919	and	2119	2229	2333	...
22	Ratzeburg .... d.	0528	0628	0730	0830	0930		2130	2243	2344	...
31	Mölln (Lauenburg) .... d.	0535	0635	0737	0837	0937	hourly	2137	2250	2351	...
50	Büchen .... a.	0546	0646	0749	0848	0949	until	2149	2302	0003	...
50	Büchen .... d.	0555	0652	0750	0859	0950		2150	2322	...	...
79	**Lüneburg** .... a.	0618	0716	0815	0922	1015		2215	2345	...	...

	⚒	Ⓐ	Ⓒ					⊠		
Lüneburg .... d.	0521	0628	0628	0745	0826	0945	1031		2038	2245
Büchen .... a.	0543	0650	0650	0808	0848	1008	1053	and	2100	2308
Büchen .... d.	0555	0655	0710	0810	0910	1010	1110		2110	2324
Mölln (Lauenburg) .... d.	0609	0709	0722	0822	0922	1022	1122	hourly	2122	2336
Ratzeburg .... d.	0617	0717	0732	0832	0932	1032	1132	until	2132	2345
Lübeck Flughafen ✈ d.	0625	0725	0741	0841	0941	1041	1141		2141	2354
Lübeck Hbf .... a.	0636	0736	0752	0852	0952	1052	1152		2152	0004

✣ – The 1009, 1209, 1409, 1609, 1809 and 2009 from Lübeck run 11 – 20 minutes later Büchen - Lüneburg (arriving 1126, 1326, 1533, 1733, 1933 and 2133 respectively).

⊠ – The following services run 7 – 15 minutes later Lüneburg - Büchen: Departures from Lüneburg at 1145, 1345, 1438, 1545, 1638, 1745, 1838 and 1945 (then at the same minutes past each hour Büchen - Lübeck). Also, Lüneburg d. 1230 (not 1231).

828 LÜBECK - BAD KLEINEN

RE/RB services

km		Ⓐ	ⒶS		S		S		S		S		S		P		N		A
0	**Lübeck** Hbf .... d.	0502	0602	0704	0802	0904	1002	1104	1202	1304	1402	1504	1602	1704	1802	1904	2002	2104	2306
39	Grevesmühlen. d.	0537	0637	0740	0837	0940	1037	1140	1237	1340	1437	1540	1637	1740	1837	1940	2037	2140	2341
62	**Bad Kleinen** ... a.	0551	0655	0755	0855	0955	1055	1155	1255	1355	1455	1555	1655	1755	1855	1955	2055	2155	2359

	ⒶA	Ⓐ	Ⓐ	N		S		S		S		S		S		S		S	
Bad Kleinen ..... d.	0432	0518	0603	0703	0803	0903	1003	1103	1203	1303	1403	1503	1603	1703	1803	1903	2003	2103	2203
Grevesmühlen .. d.	0446	0540	0617	0721	0817	0921	1017	1121	1217	1321	1417	1521	1617	1721	1817	1921	2017	2121	2221
Lübeck Hbf ...... a.	0523	0623	0655	0756	0854	0956	1054	1156	1254	1356	1454	1556	1654	1756	1854	1956	2054	2156	2256

A – From / to Schwerin (Table **830**).
N – To / from Neubrandenburg (Table **836**).
P – To Pasewalk (Table **836**).
S – To / from Szczecin (Table **836**).

830 HAMBURG - ROSTOCK - STRALSUND

km		*RE*	*RE*	*RE*	*RE*	*RE*	*RE*	*RE*	*RE*	*IC*	*RE*	*RE*	*RE*	*IC*	*IC*	*RE*	*RE*	*IC*	*RE*	*RE*	*IC*	*RE*	*RE*	*IC*	*IC*
		13001	**13003**	**13190**	**4301**	**13005**	**4393**	**4305**	**13007**	**2184**	**4307**	**4307**	**13009**	**2182**	**2238**	**4309**	**13011**	**2212**	**4311**	**13013**	**2376**	**4313**	**13015**	**2216**	**2174**
			Ⓐ **d**	Ⓐ			Ⓐ **d**				Ⓒ	Ⓐ			E										⑤ **f**
		S	S	L		S			S	🍷♦			S	🍷♦	♦		S	🍷♦		S	🍷♦		S	🍷♦	A 🍷
0	**Hamburg** Hbf .... d.	...	...	...	...	...	*0528*	0634	...	0744	0823	0835	...	0944	...	1027	...	1117	1225v	...	1344	1425	...	1517	1544
47	Büchen .... d.	...	...	...	0503a	...	*0559*	0705	...	|	0903	0905	...	|	...	1101	...	|	1305	...	|	1505	...	|	|
123	**Schwerin** Hbf **836 837** d.	...	...	0413	0552	...	0704	0753	...	0837	0953	0953	...	1037	1054	1153	...	1210	1353	...	1437	1553	...	1614	1637
140	Bad Kleinen ... **836 837** d.	...	...	0426	0605	...	0716	0805	...	|	1005	1005	...	|	1107	1205	...	|	1405	...	|	1605	...	|	1650
181	Bützow .... **836** d.	...	...	...	0630	...	0741	0830	...	0911	1030	1030	...	1111	1132	1230	...	1244	1430	...	1511	1630	...	1648b	1713
211	**Rostock** Hbf .... a.	...	...	...	0651	...	0802	0851	...	0932	1051	1051	...	1132	1152	1252	...	1303	1452	...	1532	1651	...	1706	1733
211	**Rostock** Hbf .... d.	0454	0554	...	...	0701	...	...	0901	0938	...	...	1101	1138	...	...	1301	1317	...	1501	1538	...	1701	1717	...
240	Ribnitz-D'garten West . d.	0516	0618	...	...	0724	...	...	0922	1000	...	...	1122	1200	...	...	1322	1339	...	1522	1600	...	1722	1739	...
265	Velgast .... d.	0540	0640	...	...	0740	...	...	0940	1016	...	...	1140	1216	...	...	1340	1354	...	1540	1616	...	1740	1754	...
283	**Stralsund** Hbf .... a.	0555	0655	...	...	0755	...	...	0955	1031	...	...	1155	1231	...	...	1355	1411	...	1555	1630	...	1755	1811	...
	Ostseebad Binz **844** a.	...	...	...	...	...	...	...	...	1134	...	...	...	...	...	...	...	1517	...	...	1721k	...	...	...	...

	RE	*RE*	*RE*	*IC*	*RE*	*RE*	*IC*	*IC*	*RE*	*IC*	*RE*
	4315	**4315**	**13017**	**2372**	**4317**	**13019**	**2188**	**2270**	**4319**	**2286**	**4321**
	Ⓒ	Ⓐ					①–④	⑤⑦		⑦	
			S	🍷♦		S	c	🍷♦		A	
Hamburg Hbf .... d.	1622	1634	...	1743	1835	...	1944	1944	2032	2146	2249
Büchen .... d.	1705	1705	...	|	1905	...	|	|	2105	2210	2319
Schwerin Hbf **836 837** d.	1753	1753	...	1837	1953	...	2037	2037	2153	2244	0007
Bad Kleinen ... **836 837** d.	1805	1805	...	1850	2005	...	|	|	2205	|	0018
Bützow .... **836** d.	1830	1830	...	1913	2030	...	2111	2111	2230	2318	0044
Rostock Hbf .... a.	1851	1851	...	1933	2051	...	2132	2132	2251	2338	0103
Rostock Hbf .... d.	...	...	1901	1938	...	2101	...	2138	...	...	...
Ribnitz-Damgarten West d.	...	...	1922	2000	...	2122	...	2200	...	...	...
Velgast .... d.	...	...	1940	2016	...	2140	...	2217	...	...	...
Stralsund Hbf .... a.	...	...	1955	2030	...	2155	...	2231	...	...	...
Ostseebad Binz **844** .a.	...	...	...	...	...	...	...	...	...	...	...

	RE	*RE*	*IC*	*RE*	*RE*	*IC*	*RE*	*RE*	*IC*
	4300	**4330**	**2189**	**4302**	**13000**	**2279**	**13002**	**4304**	**2217**
	Ⓐ		①–⑥		Ⓐ **d**	①–⑥			
			e		S	e ♦	S		🍷♦
Ostseebad Binz **844** .... d.	...	...	...	...	...	🍷	...	...	...
Stralsund Hbf .... d.	...	...	...	...	0453	0527	0558	...	0727
Velgast .... d.	...	...	...	...	0508	0541	0613	...	0741
Ribnitz-Damgarten West .... d.	...	...	...	...	0526	0555	0632	...	0755
Rostock Hbf .... a.	...	...	...	...	0548	0619	0655	...	0815
Rostock Hbf .... d.	...	...	0458	0505	...	0625	...	0707	0825
Bützow .... **836** d.	...	...	0519	0527	...	0646	...	0728	0846
Bad Kleinen .... **836 837** d.	...	...	0544	0552	...	|	...	0753	|
Schwerin Hbf ...... **836 837** d.	0353	0457	0601	0604	...	0722	...	0805	0922
Büchen .... d.	0448	0552	0634	0658	...	|	...	0857	|
Hamburg Hbf .... a.	0520	0625	0701	0729	...	0816	...	0928	1016

	RE	*RE*	*IC*	*RE*	*RE*	*IC*	*RE*	*RE*	*IC*	*IC*	*RE*	*RE*	*IC*	*RE*	*RE*	*RE*	*IC*	*RE*	*RE*	*IC*	*RE*	*RE*	*RE*	*RE*	*RE*
	13004	**4306**	**2373**	**13006**	**4308**	**2213**	**13008**	**4310**	**2239**	**2377**	**13010**	**4312**	**2379**	**13012**	**4314**	**13038**	**1989**	**13014**	**4316**	**2185**	**13016**	**4318**	**13018**	**4320**	**13195**
									E				B			①–④	⑦			⑦					
	S		🍷♦	S		🍷♦	S		♦	🍷♦	S		🍷♦	S			N			H 🍷	S		S		L
Ostseebad Binz **844** .d.	...	...	...	...	...	1029	...	...	...	1225	...	...	...	...	...	...	...	1707	...	...	...	...	...	...	...
Stralsund Hbf .... d.	0800	...	0927	1000	...	1127	1200	...	...	1325	1400	...	1527	1600	...	1700	1727	1800	...	1927	2000	...	2201	...	...
Velgast .... d.	0815	...	0941	1015	...	1141	1215	...	...	1341	1415	...	1541	1615	...	1711	1741	1815	...	1941	2015	...	2216	...	...
Ribnitz-Damgarten West d.	0832	...	0955	1032	...	1155	1232	...	...	1400	1432	...	1555	1632	...	1737	1800	1833	...	1955	2033	...	2233	...	...
Rostock Hbf .... a.	0855	...	1019	1055	...	1219	1255	...	...	1419	1455	...	1619	1655	...	1757	1819	1855	...	2019	2055	...	2255	...	...
Rostock Hbf .... d.	...	0907	1025	...	1107	1244	...	1307	1405	1425	...	1507	1625	...	1707	*1808*	1825	...	1907	2025	...	2107	...	2307	...
Bützow .... **836** d.	...	0928	1046	...	1128	1304	...	1328	1427	1446	...	1528	1646	...	1728	*1830*	1846	...	1928	2046	...	2128	...	2328	...
Bad Kleinen ... **836 837** d.	...	0953	|	...	1153	|	...	1353	1449	|	...	1553	|	...	1753	*1856*	|	...	1953	|	...	2153	...	2353	0005
Schwerin Hbf **836 837** d.	...	1005	1122	...	1205	1338	...	1405	1500	1522	...	1605	1722	...	1805	*1909*	1922	...	2005	2122	...	2203	...	0003	0017
Büchen .... d.	...	1059	|	...	1258	|	...	1454	...	|	...	1658	|	...	1854	...	|	...	2054	|	...	...	...	...	...
Hamburg Hbf .... a.	...	1131	1216	...	1330z	1431	...	1536r	...	1616	...	1732t	1816	...	1924z	...	2016	...	2123	2216	...	...	...	...	...

♦ – **NOTES** (LISTED BY TRAIN NUMBER)

2182 – Daily to Oct. 11; ①–⑥ from Oct. 13. [12] and 🍷 (Kassel Ⓐ -) (Hannover ①–⑥ -) Hamburg - Stralsund. June 14 - July 27 runs as *IC* **2088** and starts from Hamburg.
2184 – ①–⑥ to Oct. 3; ①–⑤ from Oct. 6. [12] and 🍷 (Hannover Ⓐ -) Hamburg - Ostseebad Binz.
2212 – RÜGEN – [12] and 🍷 Koblenz - Köln - Hamburg - Ostseebad Binz.
2213 – RÜGEN – [12] and 🍷 Ostseebad Binz - Hamburg - Köln - Koblenz - Heidelberg - Stuttgart.
2216 – [12] and 🍷 Stuttgart - Koblenz - Köln - Hamburg - Stralsund (- Greifswald Ⓐ **d**).
2217 – [12] and 🍷 (Greifswald Ⓐ **d** -) Stralsund - Hamburg - Köln - Koblenz - Stuttgart.
2238 – WARNOW – [12] Leipzig - Magdeburg - Stendal - Rostock (- Warnemünde ●).
2239 – WARNOW – [12] (Warnemünde ● -) Rostock - Stendal - Magdeburg - Leipzig.
2270 – ⑤⑦ (also Oct. 2; not Oct. 3). SCHWARZWALD – [12] and 🍷 Konstanz - Karlsruhe - Frankfurt - Hannover - Hamburg - Stralsund. June 15 - July 27 runs as *IC* **2280** and starts from Hamburg.
2279 – [12] and 🍷 Stralsund - Hamburg - Hannover - Frankfurt - Karlsruhe - Konstanz. June 14 - July 26 runs as *IC* **2087** and terminates at Hamburg.
2372 – [12] and 🍷 (Karlsruhe Ⓒ -) Frankfurt - Hannover - Hamburg - Stralsund. June 14 - July 27 runs as *IC* **2288** and starts from Hamburg.
2373 – [12] and 🍷 Stralsund - Hamburg - Hannover - Frankfurt - Karlsruhe. June 14 - July 27 runs as *IC* **2289** and terminates at Hamburg.
2376 – [12] and 🍷 (Karlsruhe ①–⑥ **e** -) Frankfurt - Hannover - Hamburg - Stralsund (- Ostseebad Binz on dates in note **k**). June 14 - July 27 runs as *IC* **2086** and starts from Hamburg.
2377 – [12] and 🍷 Ostseebad Binz - Hamburg - Hannover - Frankfurt (- Karlsruhe ⑤ **p**). June 14 - July 27 runs as *IC* **2287** and terminates at Hamburg.
2379 – [12] and 🍷 Stralsund - Hamburg - Hannover (- Göttingen ⑤⑦ **y**) (- Frankfurt ⑤ **f**). June 14 - July 27 runs as *IC* **2289** and terminates at Hamburg.

A – [12] Karlsruhe - Frankfurt - Hannover - Hamburg - Rostock.
B – Daily to Oct. 10; Ⓑ from Oct. 12.
E – Daily June 13 - Aug. 31; ⑤–⑦ Sept. 5 - Oct. 19 (also Oct. 2; not Oct. 3), ⑤ from Oct. 24.
H – To Hannover (Table **900**).
L – To / from Lübeck (Table **828**).
N – To Nürnberg (Table **900**).
S – To / from Sassnitz (Table **844**).

a – Ⓐ only.
b – Ⓑ only.
c – Not Oct. 2.
d – Not Oct. 31.
e – Not Oct. 4.
f – Also Oct. 2; not Oct. 3.
k – ⑥ to Nov. 1 (also Oct. 3); ⑤⑥ from Nov. 7.
p – Also June 18, Oct. 2; not June 20, Oct. 3.
r – 1525 on Ⓐ.
t – 1726 on Ⓐ.
v – 1223 July 14 - Aug. 24.
z – 5 minutes later July 14 - Aug. 24.

● – Until Oct. 19 (**2238** arrives 1213; **2239** departs 1343).

ROSTOCK - WARNEMÜNDE 831

S-Bahn

ROSTOCK - WARNEMÜNDE and v.v. *13 km*. Journey time: 21 minutes. Additional services run at peak times on Ⓐ (not Oct. 31).

From Rostock Hbf at 0433, 0448 Ⓐ **e**, 0503, 0518 Ⓐ **e**, 0533, 0548 Ⓐ **e**, 0603, 0618 Ⓐ **e**, 0633, 0648 Ⓐ **e**, 0703, 0718 Ⓐ **e**, 0733, 0748 Ⓐ **e**, 0803, 0818, 0833, 0848 and at 03, 18, 33 and 48 minutes past each hour until 2003, 2018, 2033, 2048; then 2103, 2133, 2203, 2233, 2303, 2333 and 0003.

From Warnemünde at 0403, 0433, 0448 Ⓐ **e**, 0503, 0518 Ⓐ **e**, 0533, 0548 Ⓐ **e**, 0603, 0618 Ⓐ **e**, 0633, 0648 Ⓐ **e**, 0703, 0718 Ⓐ **e**, 0733, 0748 Ⓐ **e**, 0804, 0818 Ⓐ **e**, 0833, 0848, 0903, 0918, 0933, 0948 and at 03, 18, 33 and 48 minutes past each hour until 2003, 2018, 2033, 2048; then 2103, 2133, 2203, 2233, 2303, 2333 and 0003.

e – Not Oct. 31.

BERLIN - KOSTRZYN 832

Niederbarnimer Eisenbahn (2nd class only)

km		Ⓐ							
0	**Berlin** Lichtenberg ...... d.	0537	0637	0737	and in the same pattern every two hours until	1837	1937	2037	2137
23	Strausberg ...... d.	0555	0655	0755		1855	1955	2055	2155
47	Müncheberg (Mark) ¶ .. d.	0613	0713	0813		1913	2013	2113	2212
80	**Kostrzyn** 🏛 ...... a.	0654	0744	0854		1944	2054	2144	...

	Ⓐ							
Kostrzyn 🏛 ...... d.	0508	0602	0711	and in the same pattern every two hours until	1802	1911	2002	2111
Müncheberg (Mark) ¶ d.	0549	0649	0749		1849	1949	2049	2149
Strausberg ...... d.	0610	0710	0810		1910	2010	2110	2210
Berlin Lichtenberg ... a.	0628	0728	0828		1928	2028	2128	2228

¶ – Station for the Buckower Kleinbahn (operates ⓒ May - September).

WISMAR - ROSTOCK 833

RE services

km		⚒e	Ⓐe				
0	**Wismar** ...... d.	0442	0542	0642	and hourly until	2042	2142
22	Neubukow ...... d.	0511	0611	0711		2111	2211
41	Bad Doberan ▲ ...... d.	0530	0630	0730		2130	2230
57	**Rostock** Hbf ...... a.	0551	0651	0751		2151	2250

	Ⓐe		⚒e				
Rostock Hbf ...... d.	0412	0506	0606	0706	and hourly until	2006	2106
Bad Doberan ▲ ...... d.	0432	0532	0632	0732		2032	2132
Neubukow ...... d.	0451	0551	0651	0751		2051	2151
Wismar ...... a.	0515	0615	0715	0815		2115	2215

e – Not Oct. 31.

▲ – **BAD DOBERAN - OSTSEEBAD KÜHLUNGSBORN WEST**. All services worked by steam locomotive. 2nd class only. Journey time: 39–46 minutes.
Operator: Mecklenburgische Bäderbahn Molli GmbH, Am Bahnhof, 18209 Bad Doberan. ✆ +49 (0) 38293 431331, Fax +49 (0) 38293 431332. **Service until Oct. 31**, 2014.
From **Bad Doberan** at 0835 Ⓐ **e**, 0936, 1036 and hourly until 1636; then 1745 and 1845. From **Kühlungsborn West** at 0640 Ⓐ **e**, 0828, 0935, 1035 and hourly until 1735.

STRALSUND - NEUBRANDENBURG - NEUSTRELITZ 834

km																Ⓑ			Ⓑ			Ⓑ			
0	**Stralsund** Hbf ...... d.	...	...	...	0502	0602r	0702	0802r	0902	1002r	1102	1202r	1302	1402	1502	1602	...	1702	1802	...	1902	2002	...	2102	...
23	Grimmen ...... d.	...	...	...	0523	0623r	0723	0823r	0923	1023r	1123	1223r	1323	1423	1523	1623	...	1723	1823	...	1923	2023	...	2123	...
47	Demmin ...... d.	...	...	...	0546	0646r	0746	0846r	0946	1046r	1146	1246r	1346	1446	1546	1646	...	1746	1846	...	1946	2046	...	2146	...
89	**Neubrandenburg** ...... a.	...	...	...	0629	0729r	0829	0929r	1029	1129r	1229	1329r	1429	1529	1629	1729	...	1829	1929	...	2029	2129	...	2229	...
89	**Neubrandenburg** ...... d.	0426	...	0529	0630	0731	0830	0931	1030	1131	1230	1331	1430	1531	1630	1731	1731	1830	1931	1931	2030	2131	...	...	2234
124	**Neustrelitz** Hbf ...... a.	0454	...	0557	0657	0757	0857	0957	1057	1157	1257	1357	1457	1557	1657	1757	1757	1857	1957	1957	2057	2157	...	...	2305
	Berlin Hbf **835** ...... a.	0614	...	...	0814	...	1014	...	1214	...	1414	...	1614	...	1814	...	...	2014	...	...	2215	...	...	...	...

									⊡		Ⓑ			Ⓑ			Ⓑ			Ⓑ			Ⓑ	S	⑤⑥h
Berlin Hbf **835** ...... d.	...	...	...	0544	...	0744	...	0944	...	1144	...	...	1344	...	...	1544	...	...	1744	...	...	1944	...	2144	2311
Neustrelitz Hbf ...... d.	0455	...	0603	0702	0803	0902	1003	1102	1203	1302	1403	1403	1502	1603	1603	1702	1803	1803	1902	2003	2003	2102	2203	2306	0025
Neubrandenburg ...... a.	0524	...	0630	0730	0829	0930	1029	1130	1229	1330	1430	1430	1530	1629	1629	1730	1829	1829	1930	2029	2029	2130	2229	2333	0053
Neubrandenburg ...... d.	...	0533	0632r	0732	0832r	0932	1032r	1132	1232	1332	1432	...	1532	1632	...	1732	1832	...	1932	2032	...	2132	...	...	...
Demmin ...... d.	...	0609	0709r	0809	0909r	1009	1109r	1209	1309	1409	1509	...	1609	1709	...	1809	1909	...	2009	2109	...	2209	...	...	...
Grimmen ...... d.	...	0629	0729r	0829	0929r	1029	1129r	1229	1329	1429	1529	...	1629	1729	...	1829	1929	...	2029	2129	...	2229	...	...	...
Stralsund Hbf ...... a.	...	0650	0750r	0850	0950r	1050	1150r	1250	1354	1450	1550	...	1650	1750	...	1850	1950	...	2050	2150	...	2250	...	...	...

S – ①②③④⑦ (not Oct. 2). h – Also Oct. 2. r – ①–⑥ only. ⊡ – Change trains at Neubrandenburg on ⑦.

ROSTOCK - BERLIN - LUTHERSTADT WITTENBERG and FALKENBERG 835

km		*RE*	*RE*	*RE*	*RE*	*ICE*	*RE*	*RE*	*ICE*	*RE*	*RE*	*RE*	*RE*	*RE*	*RE*	*EC*	*X*	*RE*	*RE*	*RE*	*RE*	*RE*	*RE*	*RE*	*RE*
		18523	**18503**	**4353**	**18505**	**1207**	**4355**	**18507**	**1509**	**4357**	**18509**	**4359**	**18511**	**4361**	**18513**	**179**	**68904**	**4363**	**18515**	**4365**	**18517**	**18591**	**4367**	**18519**	**4369**
		ⓒ H		Ⓐ d		Ⓐ M✕			⑥ k M✕							⑥ P ✕	⊠ L					C			
	Warnemünde ...... 831 d.	...	...	...	...	...	...	...	0801	...	...	...	...	...	...	...	1407	...	...	...	...	1807	...	...	...
0	**Rostock** Hbf ...... 831 d.	...	...	0434	...	0621	0634	...	0821	0834	...	1034	...	1234	...	1422	1433	1459	...	1634	...	1831	1834	...	2034
34	Güstrow ...... d.	...	...	0457	...	|	0657	...	|	0857	...	1057	...	1257	...	|	1457	|	...	1657	...	|	1857	...	2057
85	Waren (Müritz) ...... d.	...	...	0535	...	0706	0735	...	0906	0935	...	1135	...	1335	...	1507	1530	1540	...	1735	...	1914	1935	...	2135
	Stralsund Hbf **834** ...... d.	...	...	|	0502	|	|	0702	|	|	0902	|	1102	|	1302	|	|	|	1502	|	1702	|	|	1902	|
	Neubrandenburg **834** ...... d.	...	0426	|	0630	|	|	0830	|	|	1030	|	1230	|	1430	|	|	|	1630	|	1830	|	|	2030	|
121	**Neustrelitz** Hbf ...... a.	...	0454	0555	0657	0723	0755	0857	0923	0955	1057	1155	1257	1355	1457	1525	1549	1600	1657	1755	1857	1934	1955	2057	2155
121	**Neustrelitz** Hbf ...... d.	...	0500	0601	0701	0725	0801	0901	0925	1001	1101	1201	1301	1401	1501	1527	1551	1601	1701	1801	1901	1936	2001	2101	2201
141	Fürstenberg (Havel) ...... d.	...	0514	0614	0715	|	0814	0915	|	1014	1115	1214	1315	1414	1515	|	|	1614	1715	1814	1915	1950	2014	2115	2214
162	Gransee ...... d.	...	0528	0628	0728	|	0828	0928	|	1028	1128	1228	1328	1428	1528	|	|	1628	1728	1828	1928	|	2028	2128	2228
191	Oranienburg ...... d.	...	0547	0646	0747	|	0846	0947	|	1046	1147	1246	1347	1446	1547	|	|	1646	1747	1846	1947	2019	2046	2147	2246
218	**Berlin** Gesundbrunnen ...... d.	...	0610	0710	0810	0828	0910	1010	1028	1110	1210	1310	1410	1510	1610	1630	1654	1710	1810	1910	2010	2043	2110	2211	2310
223	**Berlin** Hbf ...... a.	...	0614	0714	0814	0832	0914	1014	1032	1114	1214	1314	1414	1514	1614	1634	1658	1714	1814	1914	2014	2048	2114	2215	2314
223	**Berlin** Hbf ...... △ d.	0025	0616	0716	0816	0840	0916	1016	1042	1116	1216	1316	1416	1516	1616	1648	1704	1716	1816	1916	2016	...	2116	2217	...
231	**Berlin** Südkreuz ...... △ d.	0036	0624	0724	0824	0845	0924	1024	1047	1124	1224	1324	1424	1524	1624	1653	1708	1724	1824	1924	2024	...	2124	2226	...
276	Luckenwalde ...... d.	0115	0657	0754	0857	...	0954	1057	...	1154	1257	1354	1457	1554	1657	...	...	1754	1858	1954	2057	...	2154	2304	...
289	Jüterbog ...... d.	0123	0705	0802	0905	...	1002	1105	...	1202	1305	1402	1505	1602	1705	...	...	1802	1906	2002	2105	...	2202	2312	...
338	**Falkenberg** (Elster) ...... a.	|	0747	|	0947	...	|	1147	...	|	1347	|	1547	|	1747	...	...	|	1947	|	2147	...	|	2354	...
321	**Lutherstadt Wittenberg** △ a.	0139	...	0829	...	...	1029	...	...	1229g	...	1429	...	1629g	...	...	...	1830g	...	2029	...	...	2229	...	...

	RE	*RE*	*RE*	*RE*	*RE*	*RE*	*RE*	*RE*	*X*	*EC*	*RE*	*RE*	*RE*	*RE*	*RE*	*RE*	*ICE*	*RE*	*RE*	*ICE*	*RE*	*RE*	*RE*	*RE*	*RE*
	4350	**18504**	**4352**	**18506**	**18590**	**4354**	**18508**	**4356**	**68903**	**178**	**18510**	**4358**	**18512**	**4360**	**18514**	**4362**	**1508**	**18516**	**4364**	**1506**	**18518**	**4366**	**18520**	**18522**	**18524**
	Ⓐ		H		D				⊠ L	⑥ P ✕							Ⓐ M✕			⑦ M✕			S		⑤⑥ h
Lutherstadt Wittenberg .. △ d.	...	...	0527	...	...	0728	...	0927	...	...	...	1127	...	1327	...	1527y	...	...	1727z	...	...	1927v	...	2126j	...
Falkenberg (Elster) ...... d.	...	*0410e*	|	0612	...	|	0812	|	...	...	1012	|	1212	|	1412	|	...	1612	|	...	1812	|	2012	|	...
Jüterbog ...... d.	...	0455	0555	0655	...	0756	0855	0955	...	...	1055	1155	1255	1355	1455	1555	...	1655	1755f	...	1855	1955	2055	2154	...
Luckenwalde ...... d.	...	0503	0603	0703	...	0804	0903	1003	...	...	1103	1203	1303	1403	1503	1603	...	1703	1803f	...	1903	2003	2103	2201	...
Berlin Südkreuz ...... △ d.	...	0535	0635	0735	...	0835	0935	1035	1044	1110	1135	1235	1335	1435	1535	1635	1713	1735	1835f	1913	1935	2035	2135	2243	...
Berlin Hbf ...... △ a.	...	0542	0642	0742	...	0842	0942	1042	1050	1115	1142	1242	1342	1442	1542	1642	1719	1742	1842f	1919	1942	2042	2142	2251	...
Berlin Hbf ...... d.	0444	0544	0644	0744	0816	0844	0944	1044	1059	1120	1144	1244	1344	1445	1544	1644	1723	1744	1845	1923	1944	2044	2144	2253	2311
Berlin Gesundbrunnen ...... d.	0449	0549	0649	0749	0822	0849	0949	1049	1105	1126	1149	1249	1349	1450	1549	1649	1729	1749	1850	1929	1949	2049	2149	2257	2316
Oranienburg ...... d.	0510	0610	0710	0810	0844	0910	1010	1110	|	|	1210	1310	1410	1511	1610	1710	|	1810	1911	|	2010	2110	2210	...	2337
Gransee ...... d.	0529	0630	0729	0830	|	0929	1030	1129	|	|	1230	1329	1430	1529	1630	1729	|	1830	1929	|	2030	2129	2230	...	2357
Fürstenberg (Havel) ...... d.	0544	0644	0744	0844	0913	0944	1044	1144	|	|	1244	1344	1444	1544	1644	1744	|	1844	1944	|	2044	2144	2244	...	0010
Neustrelitz Hbf ...... a.	0558	0658	0758	0858	0926	0958	1058	1158	1205	1224	1258	1358	1458	1558	1658	1758	1827	1858	1958	2027	2058	2158	2258	...	0024
Neustrelitz Hbf ...... d.	0605	0702	0805	0902	0928	1005	1102	1200	1208	1226	1302	1405	1502	1605	1702	1805	1829	1902	2005	2029	2102	2205	2306	...	0025
Neubrandenburg **834** ...... a.	|	0730	|	0930	|	|	1130	|	|	|	1330	|	1530	|	1730	|	|	1930	|	|	2130	|	2333	...	0053
Stralsund Hbf **834** ...... a.	|	0850	|	1050	|	|	1250	|	|	|	1450	|	1650	|	1850	|	|	2050	|	|	2250	|	...	...	...
Waren (Müritz) ...... d.	0630	...	0830	...	0948	1030	...	1218	1230	1247	...	1430	...	1630	...	1830	1848	...	2030	2048	...	2230	...	...	...
Güstrow ...... d.	0702	...	0902	...	|	1102	...	|	1302	|	...	1502	...	1702	...	1902	|	...	2102	|	...	2302	...	...	...
Rostock Hbf ...... 831 a.	0723	...	0923	...	1034	1123	...	1300	1323	1329	...	1523	...	1723	...	1923	1931	...	2123	2131	...	2323	...	...	...
Warnemünde ...... 831 a.	...	...	...	...	1057	...	...	...	1351	...	...	...	...	...	...	...	1945	...	...	...	...	...	...	...	...

C – ⓒ to Nov. 2; ⑦ from Nov. 9.
D – ⓒ to Nov. 2; ⑥ from Nov. 8.
H – To / from Halle (Table **848**) on ⓒ.
L – From / to Leipzig Hbf (Table **851**).
M – To / from München (via Jena and Nürnberg) – see Table **851**.
P – ⑥ until Nov. 1. [12] and ✕ Praha - Dresden - Berlin - Rostock and v.v.
S – Daily Falkenberg - Berlin Hbf; ①②③④⑦ (not Oct. 2) Berlin Hbf - Neubrandenburg.

d – Daily Berlin Hbf - Lutherstadt Wittenberg.
e – Ⓐ only.
f – 2–4 minutes later on ⑤ (also June 18, Oct. 2; not June 20, Oct. 3).
g – 9–13 minutes later from Sept. 28.
h – Also Oct. 2.
j – 2121 on ⑥ from Oct. 4.
k – Also Oct. 3; not Oct. 4.

v – 1924 on ⑦ from Sept. 28.
y – 1518 on ⑦ from Sept. 28.
z – 1722 from Sept. 28.

△ – See Tables **850/1** for *ICE* / *IC* services Berlin - Lutherstadt Wittenberg and v.v.
⊠ – Operated by Veolia Verkehr. **DB tickets not valid**.

836 LÜBECK and SCHWERIN - PASEWALK - SZCZECIN and UECKERMÜNDE
DB (*RE* services); OLA ‡

km				Ⓐa				Ⓐ	Ⓒ																⑦
0	**Lübeck** Hbf 828 d.	...	...	...	...	...	...	0602	...	...	0802	...	1002	...	1202	...	1402	...	1602	...	1802	...	...	2002	...
	Schwerin Hbf 830/7 d.	...	...	0442	...	0552	...	|	0641	0753	|	0953	|	1153	|	1353	|	1553	|	1753	|	1953	...	|	2153
62	Bad Kleinen 828 830/7 d.	...	...	0504	...	0605	...	0704	0704	0805	0904	1005	1104z	1205	1304	1405	1504	1605	1704	1805	1904	2005	...	2104	2205
103	Bützow 830 d.	...	...	0534	...	0634	...	0743	0734	0834	0934	1034	1134	1234	1334	1434	1534	1634	1734	1834	1934	2034	...	2134	2234
117	Güstrow a.	...	...	0543	...	0643	...	0753	0743	0843	0943	1043	1143	1243	1343	1443	1543	1643	1743	1843	1943	2043	...	2143	2243
117	Güstrow d.	...	...	0558	...	0708	...	0758	0758	0908	0958	1108	1158	1308	1358	1508	1558	1708	1758	1908	1958	...	2108	2158	2308
146	Teterow d.	...	...	0625	...	0735	...	0825	0825	0935	1025	1135	1225	1335	1425	1535	1625	1735	1825	1935	2025	...	2135	2225	2335
160	Malchin d.	...	0535a	0636	...	0746	...	0836	0836	0946	1036	1146	1236	1346	1436	1546	1636	1746	1836	1946	2036	...	2146	2236	2346
204	**Neubrandenburg** a.	...	0610a	0711	...	0825	...	0911	0911	1025	1111	1225	1311	1425	1511	1625	1711	1825	1911	2025	2111	...	2225	2311	0021
204	**Neubrandenburg** d.	0516a	0611h	0712	0712	0832h	...	0912	0912	1032	1112	1232	1312	1433	1512	1632	1712	1832	1912	2032	2134	...	...	...	...
257	**Pasewalk** a.	0601a	0700h	0801	0801	0916h	...	1001	1001	1116	1201	1316	1401	1517	1601	1716	1801	1916	2005	2116	2219	...	...	...	...
257	**Pasewalk** d.	0602	0714	0802	0802	0922h	0922	1002	1002	1122	1202	1322	1402	1522	1602	1722	1802	1922	2005	2122	...	...	...	...	...
287	Ueckermünde ⊙ a.	|	0754	|	|	0954h	0954	|	|	1154	|	1354	|	1554	|	1754	|	1954	|	2154	...	...	...	...	...
284	Grambow d.	0624	...	0824	0824	...	...	1024	1024	...	1224	...	1424	...	1624	...	1824	...	2027	...	...	...	...	...	...
294	Szczecin Gumience 🏛 d.	0634	...	0843	0843	...	...	1034	1034	...	1234	...	1439	...	1639	...	1834	...	2037	...	...	...	...	...	...
299	**Szczecin** Główny a.	0640	...	0849	0849	...	...	1040	1040	...	1240	...	1445	...	1645	...	1840	...	2043	...	...	...	...	...	...

		Ⓐa		Ⓐa	⑥		Ⓐ																⑦	
Szczecin Główny d.	...	...	...	0459	...	...	...	0659	...	...	0859	...	1059	...	1259	...	1459	...	1659	...	...	1859	...	...	2059
Szczecin Gumience 🏛 d.	...	...	...	0505	...	...	...	0705	...	...	0905	...	1105	...	1305	...	1505	...	1705	...	...	1905	...	...	2105
Grambow d.	...	...	...	0515	...	...	...	0715	...	...	0915	...	1115	...	1315	...	1515	...	1715	...	...	1915	...	...	2115
Ueckermünde ⊙ ★ d.	...	...	...	|	0559	0559a	0655	|	0759h	0759	|	0959	|	1159	|	1403	|	1559	|	1759	...	|	2003	2003	|
Pasewalk ★ a.	...	...	...	0538	0632	0632a	0728	0738	0832h	0832	0938	1032	1138	1236	1338	1439	1538	1636	1738	1832	...	1938	2036	2036	2138
Pasewalk d.	...	...	...	0543	▬	0643h	...	0743	0843h	...	0943	1043	1143	1243	1343	1444	1543	1643	1743	1843	...	1947	2043	2043	2145
Neubrandenburg a.	...	...	...	0627	...	0728h	...	0827	0928h	...	1027	1128	1227	1328	1427	1528	1627	1728	1827	1928	...	2029	2128	2128	2231
Neubrandenburg d.	...	0443	0526	0639	0639	0735	...	0839	0935	...	1039	1135	1239	1335	1439	1535	1639	1735	1839	1935	...	2039	...	2135	...
Malchin d.	...	0522	0608	0718	0718	0808	...	0918	1008	...	1118	1208	1318	1408	1518	1608	1718	1808	1918	2008	...	2118	...	2208	...
Teterow d.	...	0533	0623	0733	0733	0823	...	0933	1023	...	1133	1223	1333	1423	1533	1623	1733	1823	1933	2023	...	2133	...	2223	...
Güstrow a.	...	0556	0646	0756	0756	0846	...	0956	1046	...	1156	1246	1356	1446	1556	1646	1756	1846	1956	2046	...	2156	...	2246	...
Güstrow d.	0505	0608	0708	0808	0808	0908	...	1008	1108	...	1208	1308	1408	1508	1608	1708	1808	1908	2008	...	2108	2208	...	2308	...
Bützow 830 a.	0515	0618	0718	0818	0818	0918	...	1018	1118	...	1218	1318	1418	1518	1618	1718	1818	1918	2018	...	2118	2218	...	2318	...
Bad Kleinen 828 830/7 a.	0550	0648	0752	0848	0848	0952	...	1048	1152	...	1248	1352	1456	1552	1648	1752	1848	1952	2048	...	2152	2248	...	2352	...
Schwerin Hbf 830/7 a.	0602	|	0803	|	|	1003	...	|	1203	...	|	1403	|	1603	|	1803	|	2003	|	...	2203	2301	...	0003	...
Lübeck Hbf 828 a.	...	0756	...	0956	0956	...	...	1156	...	...	1356	...	1556	...	1756	...	1956	...	2156	...	...	...	...	...	...

a – Ⓐ (not Oct. 31).
h – ①–⑤ only.
z – Departs 1056 daily to Aug. 31, ⑤–⑦ Sept. 5 - Oct. 19 (also Oct. 2; not Oct. 3) and ⑤ from Oct. 24.
★ – Additional journey: Ueckermünde Stadthafen d. 2203, Pasewalk a. 2236.
⊙ – Ueckermünde Stadthafen.

837 WISMAR - SCHWERIN - BERLIN - COTTBUS
DB (*RE* services); Ostdeutsche Eisenbahn

km		◇	◇	◇	◇	◇	◇	◇ ⚒	◇	◇	EC 249 A		◇	◇		◇	◇		◇	◇		◇	IC 2239 L	◇		IC 2431 Ⓑ E 🍷
0	**Wismar** d.	...	...	...	...	0425a	...	0525	...	...	...	0621	0734	...	0845	0934	...	1045	1134	...	1245	1333	...	...	1430	
16	Bad Kleinen a.	...	...	...	...	0439a	...	0539	...	...	...	0636	0748	...	0900	0948	...	1100	1148	...	1259	1348	...	...	1445	...
16	Bad Kleinen 830/6 d.	...	...	...	...	0440a	...	0556	...	...	...	0636	0800	...	0901	1000	...	1101	1200	...	1301	1400	1449	...	1501	...
32	**Schwerin** Hbf. 830/6 d.	...	...	...	...	0515	...	0610	...	...	...	0649	0815	...	0913	1015	...	1113	1215	...	1313	1415	1502	...	1513	...
72	Ludwigslust 840 d.	...	...	...	...	0548	...	0648j	...	...	...	0713	0848	...	0946	1048	...	1146	1248	...	1337	1448	1527	...	1546	...
116	Wittenberge 840 d.	0412	...	0512r	...	0612	...	0712	0712	0812	...	▬	0912	1012	▬	1112	1212	▬	1312	1412	▬	1512	1548	1612	▬	...
207	Nauen d.	0504	...	0604r	...	0704	...	0804	0804	0904	...	◇	1004	1104	◇	1204	1304	◇	1404	1504	◇	1604	|	1704	◇	...
	Stendal ⊡ d.	|	0447	|	0526r	|	0631	|	|	|	0850h	0831	|	|	1031	|	|	1231	|	|	1431	|	1619	|	1631	...
	Rathenow ‡ d.	|	0505	|	0605	|	0705	|	|	|	|	0910	|	|	1110	|	|	1310	|	|	1510	|	...	|	1710	...
229	**Berlin** Spandau 840 ‡ d.	0519	0551	0619r	0651	0719	0751	0819	0819	0919	0929h	0951	1019	1119	1151	1219	1319	1351	1421	1519	1551	1619	...	1719	1751	...
241	**Berlin** Zoo d.	0528	|	0628	|	0728	|	0828	0828	0928	|	|	1028	1128	|	1228	1328	|	1429	1528	|	1628	...	1728	|	...
245	**Berlin** Hbf 840 ‡ d.	0533	0601	0633	0701	0733	0801	0833	0833	0934	0941	1001	1033	1133	1201	1233	1334	1401	1435	1534	1601	1633	...	1734	1801	1829
250	**Berlin** Ostbahnhof d.	0544	...	0644	...	0744	...	0844	0844	0945	|	...	1044	1144	...	1244	1345	...	1445	1544	...	1644	...	1745	...	1839
283	Königs Wusterhausen d.	0610	...	0710	...	0810	...	0910	0910	1010	|	...	1110	1210	...	1310	1410	...	1510	1610	...	1710	...	1810	...	1905
329	Lübben (Spreewald) d.	0632	...	0732	...	0832	...	0932	0932	1032	|	...	1132	1232	...	1332	1432	...	1532	1632	...	1732	...	1832	...	1927
340	Lübbenau (Spreew) d.	0638	...	0738	...	0839	...	0939	0939	1039	1050	...	1139	1239	...	1339	1439	...	1539	1639	...	1739	...	1839	...	1935
370	**Cottbus** a.	0701	...	0800	...	0859	...	0959	0959	1059	1104	...	1159	1259	...	1359	1459	...	1559	1659	...	1759	...	1859	...	1950

	◇	◇		◇	◇		◇		◇	
Wismar d.	1534k	...	1645	1734	...	1845	1934	2045	2134	2245
Bad Kleinen a.	1548k	...	1700	1748	...	1900	1948	2100	2148	2300
Bad Kleinen 830/6 d.	1600	...	1701	1800	...	1901	2000	2101	2200	2301
Schwerin Hbf 830/6 d.	1615	...	1713	1815	...	1913	2012	2113	2215	2312
Ludwigslust 840 d.	1648	...	1746	1848	...	1946	2049j	2146	2248	...
Wittenberge 840 d.	1712	1812	▬	1912	2012	▬	2113	▬	2312	...
Nauen d.	1804	1904	◇	2004	2104	◇	2205	◇	0008	...
Stendal ⊡ d.	|	|	1831	|	|	2031	|	2231	|	...
Rathenow ‡ d.	|	|	1910	|	|	2110	|	2305	|	...
Berlin Spandau 840 ‡ d.	1819	1919	1951	2019	2119	2151	2220	2345	0024	...
Berlin Zoo d.	1828	1928	|	2028	2128	|	2229	|	0032	...
Berlin Hbf 840 ‡ d.	1833	1933	2001	2033	2133	2201	2234	2355	0041	...
Berlin Ostbahnhof d.	1844	1944	...	2044	2144	...	2245	...	0051	...
Königs Wusterhausen d.	1910	2010	...	2110	2210	...	2314	...	0116	...
Lübben (Spreewald) d.	1933	2032	...	2132	2232	...	2349	...	0152	...
Lübbenau (Spreew) d.	1940	2039	...	2139	2239	...	2356	...	0158	...
Cottbus a.	2000	2059	...	2159	2259	...	0017	...	0221	...

	◇ Ⓒ	◇ Ⓐ	◇ ⚒♥	◇	◇	◇ ★	◇ ⑦w	IC 2432 G 🍷	◇	◇	IC 2238 L
Cottbus d.	...	...	0350	...	0500	0536	0600	0605	...	0700	...
Lübbenau (Spreew) d.	...	...	0412	...	0522	0557	0622	0621	...	0722	...
Lübben (Spreewald) d.	...	...	0418	...	0528	0603	0628	0629	...	0728	...
Königs Wusterhausen d.	...	...	0442	...	0552	0627	0652	0652	...	0752	...
Berlin Ostbahnhof d.	0415	0415	0505	...	0615	0651	0715	0720	...	0815	...
Berlin Hbf 840 ‡ d.	0425	0425	0515	0600	0625	0701	0725	0727	0800	0825	...
Berlin Zoo d.	0431	0431	0521	|	0631	0731e	0731	...	|	0831	...
Berlin Spandau 840 ‡ d.	0440	0440	0530	0613	0640	0740	0740	...	0813	0840	...
Rathenow ‡ a.	|	|	|	0654	|	|	|	...	0852	|	...
Stendal ⊡ a.	|	|	|	0727	|	|	|	...	0927	|	0936
Nauen d.	0454	0454	0544	▬	0654	0754	0754	...	▬	0854	|
Wittenberge 840 d.	0550	0550	0650f	...	0754	0850	0850	...	...	0950	1011
Ludwigslust 840 d.	0614	0614	0714	0814	...	0914	0914	...	1014	...	1031
Schwerin Hbf 830/6 d.	0646	0656f	0746	0846	...	0946	0946	...	1046	...	1054
Bad Kleinen 830/6 a.	0658	0708	0758	0858	...	0958	0958	...	1058	...	1105
Bad Kleinen d.	0701	0709	0807	0901	...	1007	1007	...	1110	...	...
Wismar a.	0716	0724	0821	0916	...	1021	1021	...	1125	...	...

km		◇	◇	◇	◇	◇	◇	◇	◇	◇	◇	◇	◇	EC 248 B	◇	◇	◇	◇	◇	◇	◇	◇	◇ Ⓑ	◇	◇	◇
	Cottbus d.	0800	...	0900	1000	...	1100	1200	...	1300	1400	...	1500	1555	1600	...	1700	1800	...	1900	...	2000	2000	2100	...	2300
	Lübbenau (Spreew) d.	0822	...	0922	1022	...	1122	1222	...	1322	1422	...	1522	1612	1622	...	1722	1822	...	1922	...	2022	2022	2122	...	2322
	Lübben (Spreewald) d.	0828	...	0928	1028	...	1128	1228	...	1328	1428	...	1528	|	1629	...	1728	1828	...	1928	...	2028	2028	2128	...	2328
	Königs Wusterhausen d.	0852	...	0952	1052	...	1152	1252	...	1352	1452	...	1552	|	1652	...	1752	1852	...	1952	...	2052	2052	2152	...	0006
	Berlin Ostbahnhof d.	0915	...	1015	1117	...	1215	1315	...	1415	1515	...	1615	1701	1715	...	1815	1915	...	2015	...	2115	2115	2215	...	0033
0	**Berlin** Hbf 840 ‡ d.	0925	1000	1025	1128	1200	1225	1325	1403t	1425	1525	1602	1625	1711	1725	1801	1825	1925	2001	2025	2100	2125	2125	2225	2309	0044
	Berlin Zoo d.	0931	|	1031	1133	|	1231	1331	|	1431	1531	|	1631	|	1731	|	1831	1931	|	2031	|	2131	2131	2231	|	0050
12	**Berlin** Spandau 840 ‡ d.	0940	1013	1040	1142	1213	1240	1340	1416t	1440	1540	1613	1640	1724q	1740	1813	1840	1940	2013	2040	2113	2140	2140	2240	2321	0059
70	Rathenow ‡ a.	|	1051	|	|	1251	|	|	1451	|	|	1653	|	|	|	1853	|	|	2053	|	2158	|	|	|	2400	0135
104	**Stendal** ⊡ a.	|	1127	|	|	1327	|	|	1527	|	|	1727	|	1758q	|	1927	|	|	2127	|	...	|	|	|	0018	...
	Nauen d.	0954	▬	1054	1156	▬	1254	1354	▬	1454	1554	▬	1654	...	1754	▬	1854	1954	▬	2054	...	2154	2154	2301	...	...
	Wittenberge 840 d.	1050	...	1150	1251	...	1350	1450	...	1550	1650	...	1750	...	1850	...	1950	2050	⊗	2150	...	2250	2250	0003	...	...
	Ludwigslust 840 d.	1114	1214	...	1315	1414	...	1514	1614	...	1714	1814	...	...	1914	2014c	...	2114	2208	...	...	2314	2314	...	...	...
	Schwerin Hbf. 830/6 d.	1146	1246	...	1346	1446	...	1546	1646	...	1746	1846	...	...	1946	2046	...	2146	2249f	...	...	2344	2346	...	...	...
	Bad Kleinen 830/6 a.	1158	1258	...	1358	1458	...	1558	1658	...	1758	1858	...	...	1958	2058	...	2158	2301	...	...	...	2358	...	...	...
	Bad Kleinen d.	1207	1301	...	1407	1501	...	1607	1701	...	1807	1901	...	...	2007	2101	...	2207	2302	...	...	...	0021	...	...	...
	Wismar a.	1221	1316	...	1421	1516	...	1621	1716	...	1821	1916	...	...	2021	2116	...	2221	2317	...	...	...	0034	...	...	...

A – WAWEL – 🚃12 (Hamburg ①–⑥ -) Berlin - Cottbus - Forst 🏛 - Wrocław.
B – WAWEL – 🚃12 Wrocław - Forst 🏛 - Cottbus - Berlin (- Hamburg Ⓑ).
E – Ⓑ (not Oct. 3). 🚃12 Emden - Bremen - Hannover - Magdeburg - Berlin - Cottbus.
G – ①–⑥ (not Oct. 4). 🚃12 Cottbus - Berlin - Magdeburg - Hannover - Bremen - Emden (- Norddeich Mole on dates in Table **813**).
L – Daily June 13 - Aug. 31; ⑤–⑦ Sept. 5 - Oct. 19 (also Oct. 2; not Oct. 3); ⑤ from Oct. 24. WARNOW – 🚃12 Leipzig - Magdeburg - Rostock (- Warnemünde ●) and v.v.

a – Ⓐ only.
c – Ⓒ only.
e – Arrives 0706.
f – Arrives 10–12 minutes earlier.
h – ①–⑥ only.
j – Arrives 7–8 minutes earlier.
k – On Ⓐ Wismar d. 1541, Bad Kleinen a. 1556.
q – Ⓑ only.
r – ⚒ only.
t – On † Berlin Hbf d. 1401, Berlin Spandau d. 1413.
w – Also Oct. 4.
● – Until Oct. 19.
★ – ①–⑥ (not Oct. 4).
⊗ – Change trains at Schwerin on ⑥.
◇ – Operated by Ostdeutsche Eisenbahn.
⊡ – See Table **810** for fast *IC* / *ICE* trains Stendal - Berlin and v.v.
♥ – Runs daily Cottbus - Berlin Zoo and Schwerin - Wismar
‡ – Additional journeys (◇) Rathenow - Berlin Hbf and v.v. **From Rathenow** at 0357 Ⓐ, 0805, 1005, 1205, 1405, 1605, 1805, 2005 and 2205. **From Berlin Hbf** at 0500 Ⓐ, 0700, 0900, 1100, 1300, 1500, 1702, 1900 and 2200.

MAGDEBURG - BERLIN - FRANKFURT (ODER) - COTTBUS — 839

RE services

km																						
															P🍷				B	w♣					
0	**Magdeburg** Hbf d.	...	...	...	...	0525	0606	...	0708	...		1608	...	1659	1708	...	1808	...	1854	1908	2008	2108	2208	2325
79	**Brandenburg** Hbf d.	0425	0500	0525	0600	0625j	0700	0725j	0800	0825	and at	1700	1725	1741	1800	1825	1900	1925	|	2000	2100	2158	2258	0025
114	Potsdam Hbf d.	0455	0525	0555	0625	0655	0725	0755	0825	0855	the same	1725	1755	1800	1825	1855	1925	1955	2011	2025	2125	2225	2325	0055
123	Berlin Wannsee d.	0502	0532	0602	0632	0702	0732	0802	0832	0902	minutes	1732	1802	1808	1832	1902	1932	2002	2023	2032	2132	2232	2332	0102
138	**Berlin** Zoo d.	0515	0545	0615	0645	0715	0745	0815	0845	0915	past	1745	1815	|	1845	1915	1945	2015	2034	2045	2145	2245	2345	0114
142	**Berlin** Hbf **1001** d.	0521	0551	0621	0651	0721	0751	0821	0851	0921	each hour	1751	1821	1829	1851	1921	1951	2021	2040	2051	2151	2251	2351	...
147	**Berlin** Ostbahnhof **1001** d.	0533	0603	0633	0703	0733	0803	0833	0903	0933	until	1803	1833	1836	1903	1933	2003	2033	2051	2103	2203	2303	0003	...
194	Fürstenwalde (Spree) d.	0609	0636	0709	0736	0809	0836	0909	0936	1009		1836	1909	...	1936	2009	2036	2117	...	2139	2239	2339	0039	...
228	**Frankfurt (Oder)** **1001** a.	0626	0701	0726	0801	0826	0901	0926	1001	1026		1901	1926	...	2001	2026	2101	2134	...	2205	2305	0005	0105	...

		Ⓒ					B		Ⓒ♣	N🍷		C			⊡							B		⑤⑥f
Frankfurt (Oder) **1001** d.	0030	0030	...	0356	...	0456	0533	0600	...	...	0633	0700	0733	0800		1833	1900	1933	2000	2033	2130	2236	2330	2330
Fürstenwalde (Spree) d.	0054	0054	...	0421	...	0521	0549	0624	...	...	0649	0724	0749	0824	and at	1849	1924	1949	2024	2049	2154	2301	2354	2354
Berlin Ostbahnhof **1001** d.	0129	0129	...	0457	0529	0559	0629	0659	0708	0720	0729	0759	0829	0859	the same	1929	1959	2029	2059	2129	2229	2338	0029	0029
Berlin Hbf **1001** d.	0141	0141	...	0509	0541	0611	0641	0711	0721	0731	0741	0811	0841	0911	minutes	1941	2011	2041	2111	2141	2241	2348	0041	0041
Berlin Zoo d.	0145	0147	...	0515	0547	0617	0647	0717	0727	|	0747	0817	0847	0917	past	1947	2017	2047	2115	2147	2247	2354	0047	0047
Berlin Wannsee d.	...	0159	...	0529	0559	0629	0659	0729	0738	0746	0759	0829	0859	0929	each hour	1959	2029	2059	...	2159	2259	0006	0059	0059
Potsdam Hbf d.	...	0208	...	0538	0608	0638	0708	0738	0746	0754	0808	0838	0908	0938	until	2008	2038	2108	...	2208	2308	0014	0108	0108
Brandenburg Hbf d.	...	0235	0420	0559	0635	0659	0735	0759	|	0815	0835	0859	0935	0959		2035	2059	2137	...	2235	2337	0041	0135	0137
Magdeburg Hbf a.	...	...	0518	0650	...	0750	...	0850	0905	0858	...	0950	...	1050		...	2150	2233	...	...	0026	...	...	0223

Frankfurt (Oder) - Cottbus

km		Ⓐ		Ⓐ			B			
0	**Frankfurt (Oder)** d.	0410	0534	0604	0634	and	2034	2136	2309	...
23	Eisenhüttenstadt d.	0433	0554	0619	0654	hourly	2054	2157	2330	...
48	Guben d.	0454	0615	0636	0715	until	2115	2217	2351	...
86	**Cottbus** a.	0528	0651	0657	0751		2151	2252	0026	...

	⚒B		ⒶC					B		
Cottbus d.	0412	0509	0551	0609	and	1909	2009	2110	...	2309
Guben d.	0447	0546	0615	0646	hourly	1946	2046	2145	...	2346
Eisenhüttenstadt d.	0508	0606	0636	0706	until	2006	2106	2206	...	0006
Frankfurt (Oder) a.	0530	0628	0657	0728		2028	2127	2228	...	0027

B – [12] Brandenburg - Berlin - Frankfurt (Oder) - Cottbus and v.v.
C – [12] Cottbus - Frankfurt (Oder) - Berlin - Magdeburg.
N – *IC* **2432**. [12] (Cottbus ①–⑥ **e** -) Berlin - Hannover - Bremen - Emden.
P – *IC* **2431**. [12] Emden - Bremen - Hannover - Berlin (- Cottbus Ⓑ **q**).

e – Not Oct. 4.
f – Also Oct. 2, 30.
j – 5 minutes later on Ⓐ.
q – Not Oct. 3.
w – ⑤–⑦ (also Oct. 2).

⊡ – The 1600 from Frankfurt (Oder) departs Berlin Ostbahnhof 1656 (not 1659), Berlin Hbf 1708 (1711).
♣ – *HARZ-BERLIN-EXPRESS.* [2] Berlin - Halberstadt - Thale (Table **862**) / Vienenburg (Table **860**) and v.v. Operated by Veolia Verkehr Sachsen-Anhalt GmbH. **DB tickets not valid.**

HAMBURG - BERLIN - DRESDEN — 840

km		*D* 60457	*EC* 171	*ICE* 1627	*ICE* 1607	*EC* 173	*ICE* 793	*ICE* 1709	*ICE* 1709	*EC* 175	*ICE* 791	*ICE* 1209	*ICE* 209	*EC* 177	*ICE* 1713	*ICE* 38 381	*EC* 379	*ICE* 1507	*ICE* 1615	*ICE* 919	*ICE* 1719	*EC* 179	*ICE* 901	*IC* 1918	*IC* 2071
				⑥h	Ⓐ			⑥h	Ⓑq			◇							△	⑤f				⑤u	
		A	✕♦	M✕	✕	✕♦		M✕	✕	✕♦	K	M✕	M✕	✕♦	✕	B	✕♦	✕	M✕	M✕	✕	✕♦	✕		✕
0	**Hamburg** Altona d.	...	...	0546	0546	0614	0652	0752	0752	0814	...	0942	1036	...	1152	...	...	1242	1352	1421	1451	...	1552	...	1615
7	**Hamburg** Hbf **830** d.	...	...	0600	0600	0628	0706	0806	0806	0828	0906	1000	1051	...	1206	1239	...	1258	1406	1438	1505	...	1606	...	1630
54	Büchen **830** d.	...	...	|	|	0656	|	|	|	0856	|	|	|	...	|	|	...	|	|	|	|	...	|	...	1656
122	Ludwigslust **837** d.	...	...	0644	0644	0722	|	|	|	0922	|	|	|	...	|	|	...	1345	|	1524	|	...	|	...	1722
167	Wittenberge **837** d.	...	...	|	0701	0742	|	|	|	0942	|	|	|	...	|	|	...	1402	|	1543	|	...	|	...	1742
280	**Berlin** Spandau **837** d.	...	...	|	0741	0826	0839	0939	0939	1026	1039	1133	|	...	1339	|	...	1440	1539	1626	|	...	1739	1744	1826
292	**Berlin** Hbf **837** a.	...	...	0743	0750	0834	0848	0948	0948	1035	1048	1143	1234	...	1348	1427	...	1449	1548	1636	1644	...	1749	1752	1836
292	**Berlin** Hbf **845** d.	...	0646	0754	|	0846	0852	0952	|	1046	1051	1152	1243	1246	...	|	1444	1452	1552	1639	1652	1648	|	1757	1846
300	**Berlin** Südkreuz **845** d.	0459	0653	0801	0758	0853	0859	0959	1001	1053	1059	1159	1250	1253	...	1440o	1453	1459	1559	1644	1659	1655	1756p	1805	1853
	Leipzig Hbf **851** a.	|	|	0904	...	|	1004	1104	...	|	1215	1304	1357	|	...	...	|	1604	1704	...	1804	|	...	|	|
432	Elsterwerda **843 845** d.	|	0816n	...	...	|	...	...	...	|	...	...	...	1416n	...	...	|	...	...	...	...	1816n	...	|	2016n
489	**Dresden** Hbf **843** a.	0659	0852	...	...	1052	...	...	...	1252	...	...	...	1452	...	...	1652	...	...	...	...	1852	...	2014	2052

	ICE 1517	*ICE* 1721	*ICE* 1721	*IC* 2073	*IC* 2073	*IC* 2077	*ICE* 893	*ICE* 1723	*ICE* 1723	*ICE* 905	*ICE* 907
		Ⓑq	⑦	③⑥	⊡	③		Ⓑq	⑤f		⑤⑦
	E✕	✕	✕	D✕	D✕	✕	✕	✕	✕	✕	¶✕
Hamburg Altona d.	1652	1752	1752	...	...	...	1852	1940y	1940y	2104	2222
Hamburg Hbf **830** d.	1706	1806	1806	1827	1827	...	1906	2001	2001	2121	2243
Büchen **830** d.	|	|	|	1856	1856	...	|	|	|	|	|
Ludwigslust **837** d.	1749	|	|	1922	1922	...	|	2046	2046	2204	|
Wittenberge **837** d.	|	|	|	1942	1942	...	|	|	|	2222	|
Berlin Spandau **837** d.	|	1939	1939	2026	2026	...	2039	2139	2139	2300	0014
Berlin Hbf **837** a.	1849	1948	1948	2035	2035	...	2048	2149	2149	2315	0025
Berlin Hbf **845** d.	1852	1952	1952	2038	2043	2046	2052	2152	2152	|	|
Berlin Südkreuz **845** d.	1859	1957	1959	2043	2053	2053	2059	2157	2159	2326o	0033
Leipzig Hbf **851** a.	2004	...	2104	...	|	|	2204b	...	2304	...	...
Elsterwerda **843 845** d.	...	...	...	...	|	|	...	...	...	...	...
Dresden Hbf **843** a.	...	...	...	...	2301	2301j	...	...	...	...	...

	ICE 1618	*ICE* 1518	*ICE* 1706	*ICE* 1616	*ICE* 794	*IC* 2076	*IC* 2072	*IC* 2074	*IC* 2070
	Ⓐ	①–⑥	①	②–⑦		④	Ⓐ	Ⓒ	
	✕	✕	M✕	✕	✕	✕	D✕	D✕	✕
Dresden Hbf **843** d.	...	...	...	...	...	0604k	0604t	0604v	0654
Elsterwerda **843 845** d.	...	...	...	...	...	|	|	|	0746n
Leipzig Hbf **851** d.	...	...	0551	0551z	0651e	|	|	|	|
Berlin Südkreuz **845** d.	0507	0545	0659	0659	0803	0808	0810	0810	0908
Berlin Hbf **845** a.	|	|	0704	0704	0809	0815	0815	0815	0915
Berlin Hbf **837** d.	0515	0553	0712	0712	0816	...	0820	0820	...
Berlin Spandau **837** d.	0526	0603	0722	0722	0827	...	0831	0831	...
Wittenberge **837** d.	0605	0644	|	|	|	...	0914	0914	...
Ludwigslust **837** d.	0623	0701	|	|	|	...	0935	0935	...
Büchen **830** d.	|	|	|	|	|	...	1002	1002	...
Hamburg Hbf **830** a.	0708	0745	0853	0853	0957	...	1025	1025	...
Hamburg Altona a.	0722	0759	0908	0907	1015	...	...	...	...

	ICE 1516	*ICE* 1614	*ICE* 1724	*EC* 178	*ICE* 35 380	*ICE* 1612	*ICE* 1512	*EC* 176	*ICE* 1722	*IC* 1919	*ICE* 890	*EC* 378	*ICE* 1608	*ICE* 892	*EC* 174	*ICE* 706	*ICE* 1708	*EC* 172	*ICE* 1604	*IC* 1970	*EC* 170	*ICE* 1720	*ICE* 1720	*ICE* 898	*D* 60456
										⑦			⊕				⑤–⑦		Ⓑ	⑦		⑥	Ⓑ		
	N✕	G✕	✕	✕♦	B	M✕	M✕	✕♦	✕			✕♦	M✕	K	✕♦	✕	✕	✕♦	✕		✕♦	✕	✕	✕	A
Dresden Hbf **843** d.	...	...	...	0904	...	...	...	1104	...	1245g	...	1304	...	...	1504	...	...	1704	...	...	1904	...	...	...	2053
Elsterwerda **843 845** d.	...	...	...	|	...	...	...	|	...	|	...	1346n	...	...	|	...	...	|	...	...	1946n	...	...	...	|
Leipzig Hbf **851** d.	0751	0851e	0951q	|	...	1051	1200	|	...	|	1351r	|	1451	1551	|	...	1751	|	...	...	|	1951	1951	...	|
Berlin Südkreuz **845** d.	0859	1001	1103	1110	1114o	1202	1303	1310	...	1456	1500	1510	1600	1659	1710	1807p	1902	1910	2004	...	2108	2100	2100	2246	2346o
Berlin Hbf **845** a.	0904	1006	1108	1115	|	1207	1308	1315	...	1501	1505	1515	1606	1704	1715	|	1908	1915	|	...	2115	2105	2105	|	...
Berlin Hbf **837** d.	0924	1016	1112	...	1125	1216	1312	1324	1416	1507	1524	...	1616	1712	1724	1816	1912	1924	2016	2021	...	2124	2124	2255	...
Berlin Spandau **837** d.	|	1027	1122	...	|	1227	1322	1334	1427	1517	|	...	1627	1723	1734	1827	1922	1934	2027	2031	...	2134	2134	|	...
Wittenberge **837** d.	|	|	|	...	|	|	|	1418	|	...	1610	...	|	|	1818	|	|	2018	|	2117	...	2214	2214	|	...
Ludwigslust **837** d.	|	|	|	...	|	|	|	1438	|	...	1628	...	|	|	1838	|	|	2038	|	2137	...	2231	2231	|	...
Büchen **830** d.	|	|	|	...	|	|	|	1506	|	...	|	...	|	|	1906	|	|	2106	|	|	...	|	|	|	...
Hamburg Hbf **830** a.	1101	1157	1255	...	1318	1357	1454	1528	1557	...	1710	...	1758	1854	1928‡	1958	2054	2133	2158	2225	...	2313	2313	0033	...
Hamburg Altona a.	1116	1216	1316	...	...	1413	1513	1541	1619	...	1721	...	1810	...	1943‡	2013	2111	2148	2213	2247	...	2329	2348	0048	...

♦ – **NOTES** (LISTED BY TRAIN NUMBER)

170/1 – [12] and ✕ Budapest - Bratislava - Břeclav - Praha - Děčín - Berlin and v.v.
172/3 – [12] and ✕ Villach - Wien - Břeclav - Praha - Děčín - Berlin - Hamburg and v.v.
174/5 – [12] and ✕ Budapest - Bratislava - Břeclav - Praha - Děčín - Berlin - Hamburg and v.v.
176 – [12] and ✕ Brno - Praha - Děčín - Berlin - Hamburg. Arrives Hamburg Altona 1545 June 14 - July 27. Departs Dresden 1103 Sept. 15 - Nov. 16.
177 – [12] and ✕ Berlin - Děčín - Praha - Brno - Břeclav - Bratislava.
178/9 – [12] and ✕ Praha - Děčín - Berlin (- Rostock ♣) and v.v.
378 – [12] and ✕ Bratislava - Břeclav - Brno - Praha - Děčín - Dresden - Berlin - Stralsund (- Ostseebad Binz ♥).
379 – [12] and ✕ (Ostseebad Binz ♥ -) Stralsund - Berlin - Dresden - Děčín - Praha - Brno.

A – [2] Praha - Děčín - Bad Schandau - Berlin and v.v.; 🛏 1, 2 cl., ▬ 2 cl. and [2] (*CNL* **456/7** [R] – KOPERNIKUS) Praha - Dresden - Berlin - Köln - Amsterdam and v.v.
B – [12] (**35/8**) Berlin - Hamburg - Puttgarden - København and v.v.; [12] (**380/1**) Berlin - Hamburg - Flensburg - Århus and v.v.
D – UTHLANDE – To / from Westerland (Table **821**).
E – [12] and ✕ Hamburg - Berlin - Jena - Nürnberg - München; conveys [12] and ✕ (**1717**) Hamburg - Lutherstadt Wittenberg - Erfurt (Table **850**).
G – From Nürnberg / Saalfeld on dates in Table **851**.
K – From / to Kiel on dates in Table **820**.
M – [12] and ✕ München - Nürnberg - Jena - Berlin - Hamburg and v.v.

N – From Eisenach (Table **850**).

b – Ⓑ only.
e – ①–⑥ only.
f – Also Oct. 2; not Oct. 3.
g – 1237 from Sept. 21.
h – Also Oct. 3.
j – 2255 Sept. 17 - Nov. 12.
k – 0545 from Sept. 18.
n – Until Sept. 26.

o – Berlin **Ostbahnhof**.
p – Until Sept. 27.
q – Ⓑ (not Oct. 3).
r – 1344 from Sept. 28.
t – ①②③⑤ (not Oct. 3). 0545 from Sept. 15.
u – Also June 18, Oct. 2; not June 20, Oct. 3.
v – ⑥ (also Oct. 3). 0545 from Sept. 20.
y – 1945 June 15 - July 27.
z – ②–⑤ only.

‡ – July 14 - Aug. 24 arrives Hamburg Hbf 1933, Altona 1944.
⊡ – ①②④⑤⑦. Arrives Dresden 2255 on ⑦ (also ①②④⑤ Sept. 15 - Nov. 14).
¶ – ⑤⑦ (also Oct. 2; not Oct. 3). Train number **1727** on ⑦.
◇ – Runs 2–4 minutes earlier Hamburg Hbf - Leipzig from Sept. 28.
△ – From Sept. 28 does not call at Berlin Spandau and then runs 3–4 minutes earlier Berlin Hbf - Leipzig.
⊕ – On ⑦ from Sept. 28 runs as train **1628** and 8–9 minutes later Leipzig - Berlin Hbf.
♣ – ⑥ until Nov. 1 (see Table **835**).
♥ – See Table **844** for running dates.

841 MAGDEBURG - STENDAL - UELZEN and WITTENBERGE

RE / RB services except where shown

km																										
		⚒	Ⓐe					N		C												Ⓑd				
0	**Magdeburg** Hbf ... d.	0349	...	0508	0553	0608	0708	0756	0808	0857	0903	0908	1008	1103	1108	1208	1303	1308	1408	1503	1508	1603	1608	1703	1708	1808
58	Stendal ... a.	0435	...	0555	0633	0655	0755	0832	0855	0934	0943	0955	1055	1143	1155	1255	1343	1355	1455	1543	1555	1643	1655	1743	1755	1855
58	Stendal ... d.	0438	0458	0558	0636	0658e	0758	0833	0911	0936	0944	0958	...	1144	1158	1258e	1344	1358	1503e	1544	1558	1644	1658e	1744	1758	1858e
113	**Wittenberge** ... a.	|	0537	0637	|	0737e	0837	0908	|	1009	|	1037	...	|	1237	1337e	|	1437	1541e	|	1637	|	1737e	|	1837	1937e
116	Salzwedel ... d.	0519	...	...	0714	...	...	...	0952	...	1014	...	...	1214	...	...	1414	...	...	1614	...	1714	...	1814	...	...
167	**Uelzen** ... a.	0551	...	...	0746	...	...	...	...	...	1046	...	...	1246	...	...	1446	...	...	1646	...	1749	...	1847	...	...

					⊙		
Magdeburg Hbf ... d.	1903	1908	2008	2108	2138	2214	2318
Stendal ... a.	1943	1955	2055	2155	2219	2302	0005
Stendal ... d.	1944	1958	2100b	2200	2228b	...	...
Wittenberge ... a.	|	2037	2139b	2239	|	...	...
Salzwedel ... d.	2014	...	...	...	2309b	...	...
Uelzen ... a.	2046	...	...	...	...	...	...

					⚒					N					
Uelzen ... d.	...	...	...	...	0619	...	...	...	0902	...	...	...	1102	...	...
Salzwedel ... d.	...	...	0554	...	0651	...	...	...	0934	...	1014	...	1134	...	...
Wittenberge ... d.	...	0517e	|	0617e	|	0717	0817e	0918	|	1007	|	1117	|	...	1317
Stendal ... a.	...	0555e	0634	0655e	0719	0755	0855e	0955	1006	1045	1055	1155	1206	...	1355
Stendal ... d.	0456	0556	0643	0658	0723	0756	0856	0956	1010	...	1056	1156	1210	1256	1356
Magdeburg Hbf ... a.	0543	0643	0725	0744	0804	0843	0943	1043	1051	...	1143	1243	1251	1343	1443

					C					Ⓑd			Ⓐe					
Uelzen ... d.	1302	...	...	1502	...	...	...	1702	...	1802	...	1902	...	...	...	2103	...	...
Salzwedel ... d.	1334	...	...	1534	...	...	...	1735	...	1838	...	1934	...	2014	...	2135	...	...
Wittenberge ... d.	|	1422e	1517	|	1548	1617e	1717	|	1822e	|	1917	|	2007	|	2117	|	2227b	2317
Stendal ... a.	1409	1458e	1555	1606	1619	1655e	1755	1806	1859e	1919	1955	2006	2045	2055	2155	2216	2305b	2355
Stendal ... d.	1410	1458	1556	1610	1621	1656	1756	1810	1859	...	1956	2010	...	2056	2156	2217	2306	...
Magdeburg Hbf ... a.	1451	1544	1643	1651	1659	1743	1843	1851	1944	...	2043	2051	...	2144	2244	2257	2353	...

	IRE 18596	*IRE* 18598	*EC* 248	*IC* 1938
	L▲	⑦▲	ⒷA	⑦
Berlin Hbf ... d.	0654*	1337*	1711	2056
Stendal ... d.	0753	1427	1806	2150
Salzwedel ... d.	0841	1455	1836	2232
Uelzen ... a.	0905s	1532s	1858	2258
Lüneburg ... a.	0930s	1553s	1914	2327h
Hamburg Hbf ... a.	1004	1628	1944	0008h

	EC 249	*IC* 1931	*IRE* 18597	*IRE* 18599
	L A	⑤f	P▲	R▲
Hamburg Hbf ... d.	0658	1149	1636	1811
Lüneburg ... d.	0737	1221	1713u	1850u
Uelzen ... d.	0758	1250	1730u	1913u
Salzwedel ... d.	0823	1323	1817	1955
Stendal ... a.	0848	1404	1904	2041
Berlin Hbf ... a.	0937	1453	1955*	2140*

A – WAWEL – [12] Wrocław - Forst 🚉 - Cottbus - Berlin - Hamburg and v.v.
C – *IC* **2238/9**. Daily June 13 - Aug. 31; ⑤–⑦ Sept. 5 - Oct. 19 (also Oct. 2; not Oct. 3); ⑤ from Oct. 24. WARNOW – [12] Leipzig - Magdeburg - Schwerin - Rostock (- Warnemünde until Oct. 19) and v.v.
L – ①–⑥ only.
N – ①–⑥ (not Oct. 4, Nov. 1).
P – ①–④ (not Oct. 2).
R – ⑤–⑦ (also Oct. 2).

b – Ⓑ (not Oct. 3, 31).
d – Not Oct. 3.
e – Ⓐ (not Oct. 31).

f – ⑤ from Aug. 1 (also Oct. 2; not Oct. 3).
h – Uelzen - Hamburg from Aug. 3.
s – Calls to set down only.
u – Calls to pick up only.

* – Also calls at Berlin Ostbahnhof, Berlin Zoo and Berlin Spandau.
⊙ – Change trains at Stendal on ⑦.
▲ – Revised service operates June 14 - July 27 as follows:
On ①–⑥ Berlin Hbf 0654 → Stendal 0747 → Hamburg Hbf 0933;
on ⑦ Berlin Hbf 1337 → Stendal 1429 → Hamburg Hbf 1627;
on ①–⑤ Hamburg Hbf 1636 → Stendal 1841 → Berlin Hbf 1937;
on ⑥⑦ Hamburg Hbf 1831 → Stendal 2042 → Berlin Hbf 2140.

842 LEIPZIG - DRESDEN

Sept. 15 - Nov. 16 *ICE / IC* services do not call at Dresden Neustadt.

km		*RE* 17051	*RE* 17053	*RE* 17053	*RE* 17055	*ICE* 1747	*CNL* 459	*IC* 61459	*RE* 17057	*IC* 2043	*ICE* 1749	*RE* 17059	*ICE* 1543	*RE* 17061	*IC* 2447	*RE* 17063	*ICE* 1545	*IC* 2235	*RE* 17065	*IC* 2445	*ICE* 1745	*RE* 17067	*RE* 17069	*IC* 2443
		①–⑥	①–⑥		①–⑥	①	Ⓡ			①–⑤	Ⓒ	①–⑥	Ⓐ		①–⑥	①–⑥	①–⑥	⑦		①–⑥		①–⑥		
		a	a		a	✕	C🍷	2 E		G🍷	✕	a	✕		e B	a	e✕	R🍷		e K 🍷	M ✕	a		K🍷
	Frankfurt Flughafen § **850** .. d.	...	...	...	...	...	...	...	...	...	...	...	...	...	...	...	...	...	...			...	...	...
	Frankfurt (Main) Hbf **850** .... d.	...	...	...	...	...	0054‡	...	...	...	...	...	...	...	...	...	0618	...	...	...	...	...	...	...
0	**Leipzig** Hbf ... d.	...	0503	...	0603	0626	|	0650	0703	0726	0753	0803	0826	0903	0926	1003	1026	1026	1103	1126	1150	1203	1303	1326
26	Wurzen ... d.	...	0521	...	0621	|	|	|	0721	|	|	0821	|	0921	|	1021	|	|	1121	|	|	1221	1321	|
53	Oschatz ... d.	...	0538	...	0638	|	|	|	0738	|	|	0838	|	0938	|	1038	|	|	1138	|	|	1238	1338	|
66	Riesa ... d.	0446	0546	0546	0646	0702	0725	0727	0746	0802	0825	0846	0902	0946	1002	1046	1102	1102	1146	1202	|	1246	1346	1402
102	Coswig ... **843 856 857** d.	0515	0615	0615	0715	|	|	|	0815	|	|	0915	|	1015	|	1115	|	|	1215	|	|	1315	1415	|
110	Radebeul Ost ... **857** d.	0521	0621	0621	0721	|	|	|	0821	|	|	0921	|	1021	|	1121	|	|	1221	|	|	1321	1421	|
116	**Dresden** Neustadt ... **856/7** a.	0527	0627	0627	0727	0731	|	|	0827	0831	0854	0927	0931	1027	1031	1127	1131	1131	1227	1231	|	1327	1427	1431
120	**Dresden** Hbf ... **843 856 857** a.	0534	0634	0634	0734	0738	0803	0803	0834	0838	0901	0934	0938	1034	1038	1134	1138	1138	1234	1238	1301	1334	1434	1438

	RE 17071	*ICE* 1547	*RE* 17073	*IC* 2441	*RE* 17075	*ICE* 1549	*RE* 17077	*IC* 2049 2249	*IC* 1959	*RE* 17079	*ICE* 1641	*RE* 17081	*IC* 2047	*RE* 17083	*ICE* 1643	*RE* 17085	*ICE* 1741		*IC* 2155	*IC* 2435	*RE* 17091	*RE* 17089	*ICE* 1657	
									⑤n				Ⓑr				Ⓑ		⑤f	⑥	⑥⑦	①–⑤	Ⓑ	
		✕		K🍷		✕		K🍷	M		✕		K🍷		✕		K✕	⊖	🍷	S🍷			¶	⊖
Frankfurt Flughafen § **850** ... d.	...	1011	...	...	...	1211	...	...	...	...	1411	...	...	...	1611	...	...	...	1811	...	...	...	1902	...
Frankfurt (Main) Hbf **850** ... d.	...	|	...	...	...	|	...	...	...	...	|	...	...	...	|	...	...	...	|	...	...	...	1919	...
Leipzig Hbf ... d.	1403	1426	1503	1526	1603	1626	1703	1726	1750	1803	1826	1903	1926	2003	2026	2103	2126	2205	2232	2232	2303	2303	2313j	0006
Wurzen ... d.	1421	|	1521	|	1621	|	1721	|	|	1821	|	1921	|	2021	|	2121	|	2250	|	|	2321	2321	|	0044
Oschatz ... d.	1438	|	1538	|	1638	|	1738	|	|	1838	|	1938	|	2038	|	2138	|	2307	|	|	2338	2338	|	0100
Riesa ... d.	1446	1502	1546	1602	1646	1702	1746	1802	1832	1846	1902	1946	2002	2046	2102	2146	2202	...	2304	2304	2346	2346	2356	...
Coswig ... **843 856 857** d.	1515	|	1615	|	1715	|	1815	|	|	1915	|	2015	|	2115	|	2215	|	...	|	|	|	0017	|	...
Radebeul Ost ... **857** d.	1521	|	1621	|	1721	|	1821	|	|	1921	|	2021	|	2121	|	2221	|	...	|	|	|	|	|	...
Dresden Neustadt ... **856/7** a.	1527	1531	1627	1631	1727	1731	1827	1831	1902	1927	1931	2027	2031	2127	2131	2227	2231	...	2333	2333	|	|	|	...
Dresden Hbf ... **843 856 857** a.	1534	1538	1634	1638	1734	1738	1834	1838	1913	1934	1938	2034	2038	2134	2138	2234	2238	...	2341	2341	0024	0036	0027	...

			ICE 1644		*RE* 17050		*RE* 17052	*ICE* 1654	*ICE* 1642	*RE* 17054		*IC* 2046	*RE* 17056	*ICE* 1640	*RE* 17058	*IC* 2048	*RE* 17060	*ICE* 1548	*RE* 17062	*IC* 2440	*RE* 17064		*RE* 17066	*ICE* 1746
	①–⑤		①–⑤	⑦w	①–⑥			①–⑥	Ⓑ	①–⑥		①–⑥			①–⑥				①–⑥				①–⑥	
	a ⊖		a	⊖	a			W✕	✕	a		d K		✕	a	K🍷		✕	a	K🍷			a	M✕
Dresden Hbf ... **843 856 857** d.	...	...	0420	...	0415	...	0515	0544	0619	0615	...	0719	0715	0819	0815	0919	0915	1019	1015	1119	1115	...	1215	1255
Dresden Neustadt ... **856/7** d.	...	...	0427	...	0422	...	0522	0551	0626	0622	...	0726	0722	0826	0822	0926	0922	1026	1022	1126	1122	...	1222	|
Radebeul Ost ... **857** d.	...	...	|	...	0428	...	0528	|	|	0020	...	|	0728	|	0828	|	0928	|	1028	|	1128	...	1228	|
Coswig ... **843 856 857** d.	...	...	|	...	0437	...	0537	|	|	0637	...	|	0737	|	0837	|	0937	|	1037	|	1137	...	1237	|
Riesa ... d.	...	...	0456	...	0505	...	0605	0621	0655	0705	...	0755	0805	0855	0905	0955	1005	1055	1105	1155	1205	...	1305	1332
Oschatz ... d.	0339	...	|	0458	0514	...	0614	|	|	0714	...	|	0814	|	0914	|	1014	|	1114	|	1214	...	1314	|
Wurzen ... d.	0356	...	|	0515	0530	...	0630	|	|	0730	...	|	0830	|	0930	|	1030	|	1130	|	1230	...	1330	|
Leipzig Hbf ... a.	0435	...	0535	0554	0551	...	0651	0704	0725	0751	...	0825	0851	0925	0951	1025	1051	1125	1151	1225	1251	...	1351	1408
Frankfurt (Main) Hbf **850** ... a.	...	...	|	...	...	...	...	1037	|	...	...	...	...	|	...	...	...	|	...	...	...	...	...	...
Frankfurt Flughafen § **850** ... a.	...	...	0949	...	...	...	...	1055	1149	...	...	...	...	1348	...	...	...	1549	...	...	...	...	...	...

	IC 2442	*RE* 17068	*ICE* 1544	*RE* 17070	*IC* 1952	*IC* 2444	*RE* 17072	*ICE* 1542	*RE* 17074	*IC* 2446	*RE* 17076		*RE* 17078	*IC* 2030	*RE* 17080	*ICE* 1540	*RE* 17082	*IC* 61458	*CNL* 458		*RE* 17086		*RE* 17088	*RE* 17090
					⑦									Ⓑr		⑦			Ⓡ				①–⑥	⑦
	K🍷		✕		M	K🍷		✕		K🍷				H🍷		✕		2 E	C🍷	⊖				
Dresden Hbf ... **843 856 857** d.	1319	1315	1419	1415	1456	1519	1515	1619	1615	1719	1715	...	1815	1855	1915	1954	2015	2104	2104	...	2215	...	2315	2327
Dresden Neustadt ... **856/7** d.	1326	1322	1426	1422	|	1526	1522	1626	1622	1726	1722	...	1822	1902	1922	2001	2022	|	|	...	2222	...	2322	|
Radebeul Ost ... **857** d.	|	1328	|	1428	|	|	1528	|	1628	|	1728	...	1828	|	1928	|	2028	|	|	...	2228	...	2328	|
Coswig ... **843 856 857** d.	|	1337	|	1437	|	|	1537	|	1637	|	1737	...	1837	|	1937	|	2037	|	|	...	2237	...	2337	|
Riesa ... d.	1355	1405	1455	1505	1532	1555	1605	1655	1705	1755	1805	...	1905	|	2005	2031	2105	2142	2142	...	2305	...	0005	0005
Oschatz ... d.	|	1414	|	1514	|	|	1614	|	1714	|	1814	...	1914	|	2014	|	2114	|	|	2158	2314	...	...	...
Wurzen ... d.	|	1430	|	1530	|	|	1630	|	1730	|	1830	...	1930	|	2030	|	2130	|	|	2215	2330	...	...	...
Leipzig Hbf ... a.	1425	1451	1525	1551	1608	1625	1651	1725	1751	1825	1851	...	1951	2000	2051	2101	2151	2225	|	2254	2351	...	...	...
Frankfurt (Main) Hbf **850** ... a.	...	...	1940	...	...	...	...	|	...	...	...	...	...	...	...	...	...	...	0359‡	...	...	...	...	...
Frankfurt Flughafen § **850** ... a.	...	...	2007k	...	...	...	...	2149	...	...	...	...	...	...	...	...	...	...	...	...	...	...	...	...

B – [12] (Bielefeld ① -) Hannover - Dresden.
C – CANOPUS – 🛏 1, 2 cl., ▬ 2 cl. and [2] (reclining) Praha - Dresden - Basel - Zürich and v.v.
E – [2] Praha - Děčín - Bad Schandau - Dresden - Erfurt and v.v.
G – ①–⑤ (not Oct. 3, 31, Nov. 19). From Magdeburg (Table **866**).
H – To / from Hannover (Table **866**).
K – [12] Köln - Dortmund - Hannover - Magdeburg - Dresden and v.v.
M – [12] Düsseldorf - Kassel - Erfurt - Dresden and v.v.
R – ⑦ (also Oct. 4). [12] and 🍷 Bremen - Hannover - Magdeburg - Dresden.
S – ⑥ (also Oct. 3). [12] and 🍷 Emden - Bremen - Hannover - Magdeburg - Dresden.
W – To Wiesbaden (Table **911**). Sept. 15 – 27 Dresden Hbf d. 0538. Sept. 29 - Nov. 15 Dresden Hbf d. 0556, Riesa d. 0636. From Nov. 17 Dresden Hbf d. 0556, Dresden Neustadt d. 0603, Riesa d. 0636.

a – Not Oct. 3, 31, Nov. 19.
d – Not Oct. 4, 31, Nov. 19.
e – Not Oct. 4.
f – Also Oct. 2; not Oct. 3.
j – 2323 from Sept. 28.
k – ⑥ only.
n – Also June 18, Oct. 2; not June 20, Oct. 3.
r – Not Oct. 3.
w – Also Oct. 3, 31, Nov. 19.

‡ – Frankfurt (Main) **Süd**.
¶ – From Wiesbaden (Table **911**).
⊖ – S-Bahn service (from / to the underground platforms at Leipzig Hbf).
§ – Frankfurt Flughafen Fernbahnhof ✈.

ELSTERWERDA - CHEMNITZ and DRESDEN — 843

RE / RB services except where shown

km																									
		Ⓐ	Ⓐ		Ⓐ		Ⓐ		Ⓐe		Ⓐe		Ⓐe		Ⓐ		Ⓐ			Ⓐe			Ⓑ		
0	**Elsterwerda** d.	...	0455	...	0603	...	0703	0803	...	1003	...	1203	...	1403	1503	1603	1703	...	1803	1903	...	2018	...	2214	...
24	Riesa a.	...	0520	...	0628	...	0728	0828	...	1028	...	1228	...	1428	1528	1628	1728	...	1828	1928	...	2043	...	2239	...
24	Riesa d.	0440	0540	0540	0640	0640	0740	0840	0940	1040	1140	1240	1340	1440	1540	1640	1740	1740	1840	1940	...	2048	2140	2240	...
50	Döbeln Hbf d.	0503	0603	0603	0703	0703	0803	0903	1003	1103	1203	1303	1403	1503	1603	1703	1803	1803	1903	2003	...	2111	2203	2303	...
91	**Chemnitz** Hbf a.	0544	0644	0644	0744	0744	0844	0944	1044	1144	1244	1344	1444	1544	1644	1744	1844	1844	1944	2044	...	2152	2244	2344	...

	Ⓐ		Ⓐ		Ⓐe		Ⓐe		Ⓐe		Ⓐ			Ⓐ		Ⓐe		Ⓑ	Ⓐe		Ⓒz	Ⓐ			
Chemnitz Hbf d.	0406	0506	0506	0606	0706	0806	0906	1006	1106	1206	1306	1406	1506	1506	1606	1706	1806	1906	1906	2006	2006	2106	...	2235	...
Döbeln Hbf d.	0447	0547	0547	0647	0747	0847	0947	1047	1147	1247	1347	1447	1547	1547	1647	1747	1847	1947	1947	2047	2047	2147	...	2315	...
Riesa a.	0510	0610	0610	0710	0810	0910	1010	1110	1210	1310	1410	1510	1610	1610	1710	1810	1910	2010	2010	2110	2110	2210	...	2338	...
Riesa d.	0511	...	0615	0715	...	0915	...	1115	...	1315	1415	1515	...	1615	1715	1815	1915	...	2015	...	2115	2215	...	...	...
Elsterwerda a.	0533	...	0638	0738	...	0938	...	1138	...	1338	1438	1538	...	1638	1738	1838	1938	...	2040	...	2139	2238	...	...	...

km																								
		Ⓐ	Ⓐ		Ⓐ																		⑥⑦	①–⑤
0	**Elsterwerda-Biehla** d.	0440	0540	...	0640	0740	...	0940	...	1140	...	1340	...	1540	...	1740	...	1940	...	2140	...	2323	...	...
2	Elsterwerda a.	0443	0543	...	0643	0743	...	0943	...	1143	...	1343	...	1543	...	1743	...	1943	...	2143	...	2326	...	...
2	Elsterwerda d.	0444	0544	0544	0644	0744	...	0944	...	1144	...	1344	...	1544	...	1744	...	1944	...	2144	...	...	2344	2344
41	Coswig **842 856/7** d.	0523	0623	0623	0723	0823	...	1023	...	1223	...	1423	...	1623	...	1823	...	2023	...	2223	...	...	|	0023
59	**Dresden** Hbf **842 856/7** a.	0544	0644	0644	0744	0844	...	1044	...	1244	...	1444	...	1644	...	1844	...	2044	...	2244	...	...	0040	0046

		Ⓐ	ⒶS	T						Ⓐ					⑥⑦	①–⑤
Dresden Hbf **842 856/7** d.	0509	0609	0651	0709	...	0909	1109	1309	1509	1609	1709	1909	2109	...	2309	2309
Coswig **842 856/7** d.	0531	0631	0717	0731	...	0931	1131	1331	1531	1631	1731	1931	2131	...	|	2331
Elsterwerda a.	0610	0710	0810	0810	...	1010	1210	1410	1610	1710	1810	2010	2210	...	2354	0010
Elsterwerda d.	0617	0717	0817	0817	...	1017	1217	1417	1617	1717	1817	2017	...	...	...	...
Esterwerda-Biehla a.	0620	0720	0820	0820	...	1020	1220	1420	1620	1720	1820	2020	...	...	...	...

S – Until Sept. 12.
T – Ⓒ to Sept. 7; daily from Sept. 13.

e – Not Oct. 31, Nov. 19.
z – Also Oct. 31, Nov. 19.

STRALSUND - OSTSEEBAD BINZ / SASSNITZ — 844

RE / RB services except where shown

km																									
													IC 61259 ⑥ L			*IC* 2184 ◆					*IC* 2357 ⑥ ◆	*IC* 2353 ⑥ ◆			*ICE* 1714 ⑥ ◆
		Ⓐt			Ⓐt	Ⓐt	Ad	A			Ad	A					Ad	A					Ad	A	
	Rostock Hbf **830** d.	...	...	0454	...	0554	...	...	0701	...	...	...	...	0901	...	0938	...	...	1101	...	...	...	...	...	...
0	**Stralsund** Hbf d.	0504	...	0604	...	0704	0704	...	0804	...	0904	...	...	1004	...	1042	1104	...	1204	...	1242	1242	1304	...	1357
29	Bergen auf Rügen d.	0533	...	0633	...	0733	0733	...	0833	...	0933	...	1016	1033	...	1107	1133	...	1233	...	1307	1307	1333	...	1421
39	Lietzow (Rügen) d.	0541	...	0641	0644	0741	0741	0744	0841	0844	0941	0944	|	1041	1044	|	1141	1144	1241	1244	|	|	1341	1344	|
	Ostseebad Binz a.	|	...	|	0657	|	|	0757	|	0857	0955	|	1042	|	1057	1134	1155	|	|	1259	1334	1334	1355	|	1442
51	**Sassnitz** a.	0555	...	0655	...	0755	0755	...	0855	...	...	0957	...	1055	...	...	...	1157	1255	...	...	...	...	1357	...

			IC 2212 ♀◆					*IC* 2376 ◆	*IC* 2355 D ◆					*EC* 378 H ✕◆					*ICE* 1606 ⑤ ◆						
				Ad	A					Ad	A				Ad	A				Ad	A				Ⓑ
Rostock Hbf **830** d.	1301	...	1317	...	...	1501	...	1538	...	...	...	1701	...	...	...	...	1901	...	...	...	...	2101	...	...	...
Stralsund Hbf d.	1404	...	1424	1504	...	1607	...	1632	1642	1704	...	1804	...	1833	1904	...	2007	...	2059	2106	...	2204	...	...	2306
Bergen auf Rügen d.	1433	...	1452	1533	...	1636	...	1656	1707	1733	...	1833	...	1857	1933	...	2036	...	2123	2135	...	2233	...	...	2334
Lietzow (Rügen) d.	1441	1444	|	1541	1544	1644	1647	|	|	1741	1744	1841	1844	|	1941	1944	2044	2047	|	2143	2146	2241	2244	...	...
Ostseebad Binz a.	|	1457	1517	1555	|	|	1700	1721	1732	1755	|	|	1857	1921	1955	|	|	2100	2143	2157	|	|	2257	...	...
Sassnitz a.	1455	...	...	...	1557	1658	...	...	...	...	1757	1855	...	...	...	1957	2058	...	...	...	2159	2255	...	...	...

km																									
													IC 2356 C ◆					*IC* 2213 ♀◆	*EC* 379 J ✕◆					*IC* 2377 ◆	*ICE* 1715 ⑥⑦ ◆
		Ⓐt				Ⓐt	⚒t				A	Ad				A	Ad					A	Ad		
	Sassnitz d.	0400	...	0505	...	...	0607	...	...	0707	...	0807	...	...	0907	1003	...	...	...	...	1107	1203	...	...	...
0	**Ostseebad Binz** d.	|	...	|	...	0605	|	...	0705	|	0805	|	0843	0905	|	|	1007	1029	1043	1105	|	|	1207	1225	1245
12	Lietzow (Rügen) d.	0414	...	0519	...	0618	0621	...	0718	0721	0818	0821	|	0918	0921	1017	1021	|	|	1118	1121	1217	1221	|	|
22	Bergen auf Rügen d.	0423	...	0528	...	...	0630	...	...	0730	...	0830	0908	...	0930	...	1030	1055	1107	...	1130	...	1230	1256	1309
51	**Stralsund** Hbf a.	0451	...	0556	...	...	0658	...	...	0758	...	0858	0930	...	0958	...	1058	1118	1130	...	1158	...	1258	1319	1333
	Rostock Hbf **830** a.	0548	...	0655	...	...	...	...	...	0855	...	...	...	...	1055	...	...	1219	...	...	1255	...	...	1419	...

													IC 61258 ⑥ L												
			A	Ad			A	Ad			A	Ad				A	Ad			A	Ad				
Sassnitz d.	...	1307	1403	...	...	1507	1603	...	1704	...	1803	...	...	...	1903	2003	...	...	2107	2205	...	...	...	...	...
Ostseebad Binz d.	1305	|	|	1407	1505	|	|	1607	|	1707	|	1807	1845	1905	|	|	2007	2107	|	|	2207	...	...	...	...
Lietzow (Rügen) d.	1318	1321	1417	1421	1518	1521	1617	1621	1718	1721	1817	1821	|	1919	1922	2017	2022	2120	2123	2219	2223	...	...	...	...
Bergen auf Rügen d.	...	1330	...	1430	...	1530	...	1630	...	1730	...	1830	1909	...	1931	...	2031	...	2132	...	2232	...	...	...	...
Stralsund Hbf a.	...	1358	...	1458	...	1558	...	1658	...	1758	...	1858	...	...	1959	...	2059	...	2200	...	2300	...	...	...	...
Rostock Hbf **830** a.	...	1455	...	...	...	1655	...	...	...	1855	...	...	...	...	2055	...	...	...	2255	...	...	...	...	...	...

◆ – **NOTES** (LISTED BY TRAIN NUMBER)

378 – [12] and ✕ Bratislava - Praha - Berlin - Ostseebad Binz.
379 – [12] and ✕ Ostseebad Binz - Berlin - Praha - Brno.
1606 – ⑤ until Oct. 31 (not Oct. 3). [12] and ✕ München - Nürnberg - Leipzig - Berlin - Ostseebad Binz.
1714 – ⑥ until Nov. 1 (also Oct. 3). [12] and ✕ Nürnberg - Leipzig - Berlin - Ostseebad Binz.
1715 – ⑥⑦ to Nov. 1 (also Oct. 3). [12] and ✕ Ostseebad Binz - Berlin - Halle - Nürnberg - München.
2184 – ①–⑥ to Oct. 3; ①–⑤ from Oct. 6. [12] (Hannover Ⓐ -) Hamburg - Ostseebad Binz.
2212 – RÜGEN – [12] and ♀ Koblenz - Köln - Hamburg - Ostseebad Binz.
2213 – RÜGEN – [12] and ♀ Ostseebad Binz - Hamburg - Köln - Stuttgart.
2353 – ⑥ July 5 - Sept. 6. [12] Erfurt - Halle - Berlin - Ostseebad Binz.
2355/6 – [12] and ♀ Frankfurt - Erfurt - Halle - Berlin - Ostseebad Binz and v.v.
2357 – ⑥ until Oct. 18 (also Oct. 3; not July 5 - Sept. 6, Oct. 4). [12] Leipzig - Berlin - Ostseebad Binz.
2376 – ⑥ to Nov. 1 (also Oct. 3); ⑤⑥ from Nov. 7. [12] and ♀ Karlsruhe - Frankfurt - Hannover - Hamburg - Ostseebad Binz. June 14 - July 26 runs as *IC* **2086** and starts from Hamburg.
2377 – [12] and ♀ Ostseebad Binz - Hamburg - Hannover - Frankfurt (- Karlsruhe ⑤**f**). June 14 - July 27 runs as *IC* **2287** and terminates at Hamburg.

A – Daily to Oct. 10; ①–⑤ from Oct. 13 (not Oct. 31).
C – Daily to Nov. 2; ⑥⑦ from Nov. 8.
D – Daily to Nov. 1; ⑤⑥ from Nov. 7.
H – Daily until Sept. 13; ⑤⑥ Sept. 19 - Nov. 1 (also Oct. 2).
J – Daily until Sept. 14; ⑥⑦ Sept. 20 - Nov. 2 (also Oct. 3).
L – ⑥ July 5 - Aug. 30. [2] Erfurt - Halle - Berlin - Ostseebad Binz and v.v. Conveys 🛏 1, 2 cl., ▬ 2 cl., [2] (*CNL* **1251/1250** – SIRIUS) Zürich - Basel - Ostseebad Binz and v.v. (Table **912**).

d – Runs daily Stralsund - Bergen auf Rügen and v.v.
f – Also June 18, Oct. 2; not June 20, Oct. 3.
t – Not Oct. 31.

BERGEN AUF RÜGEN - PUTBUS - LAUTERBACH and RÜGENSCHE BÄDERBAHN — 844a

Preßnitztalbahn

km	*SEE NOTE* ★		v								v
0	**Bergen** auf Rügen d.	0740	0840	0940	1040	1140	1340	1540	1740	1940	2040
10	**Putbus** a.	0749	0849	0949	1049	1149	1349	1549	1749	1949	2049
12	**Lauterbach** Mole a.	0754	...	0954	1054	1154	1354	1554	1754	1954v	...

SEE NOTE ★	Ⓐt	Ⓒz		v						
Lauterbach Mole d.	0604	0704	0800	...	1000	1104	1304	1504	1704	1904
Putbus d.	0611	0711	0811	0854	1011	1111	1311	1511	1711	1911
Bergen auf Rügen a.	0620	0720	0820	0903	1020	1120	1320	1520	1720	1920

ÜGENSCHE BÄDERBAHN **SERVICE UNTIL OCTOBER 4, 2014** Please note that Binz Lokalbahn station is situated 2½ km from Ostseebad Binz DB station.

km			r					r		r	r
0	**Lauterbach** Mole d.	...	...	...	1122r	1322r	1522r	...	1722r	1922	...
2	**Putbus** a.	...	...	...	1129r	1329r	1529r	...	1729r	1929	...
2	**Putbus** d.	0808	...	1008	1208	1408	1608	...	1808	2008	...
14	Binz Lokalbahn ♥ d.	0840	0944	1040	1240	1440	1640	1744	1840	2040	2244
22	Sellin (Rügen) Ost ♥ d.	0909	1013	1109	1309	1509	1709	1813	1909	2109	2313
27	**Göhren** (Rügen) ♥ a.	0923	1027	1123	1323	1523	1723	1827	1923	2123	2327

	r					r		r		r
Göhren (Rügen) ♥ d.	0849	0953	1153	1353	1553	1649	1753	1849	1953	2149
Sellin (Rügen) Ost ♥ d.	0907	1011	1211	1411	1611	1707	1811	1907	2011	2207
Binz Lokalbahn ♥ d.	0933	1040	1240	1440	1640	1733	1840	1936	2040	2233
Putbus a.	...	1106	1306	1506	1706	...	1906	2002	2106	...
Putbus d.	...	1111r	1311r	1511r	1711r	...	1911r	...	...	...
Lauterbach Mole a.	...	1117r	1317r	1517r	1717r	...	1917r	...	...	...

– May 29 - Oct. 4.
– Not Oct. 31.
v – May 29 - Sept. 7.
z – Also Oct. 31.
★ – Additional journeys **May 29 - Sept. 7** Bergen - Putbus - Lauterbach: **From Bergen** at 1240, 1440, 1640 and 1840. **From Lauterbach** at 1200, 1400, 1600, 1800 and 2000.
♥ – Additional journeys **from May 29** Binz Lokalbahn - Göhren: **From Binz** at 1144, 1344 and 1544. **From Göhren** at 1049, 1249 and 1449.

845 ELSTERWERDA - BERLIN - STRALSUND

RE/RB services except where shown

km		Ⓐ	IC 2217 Ⓐd P	¶			①–⑥ e	IC 61259 ⑥ H	Ⓐ			ⒸY		Ⓐ		IC 2357 ⑥E	IC 2353 ⑥D			ICE 1714 ⑥B ✕				
0	**Elsterwerda** 840 d.	...	...	...	...	0418h	...	...	0537z	...	...	...	0626z	0722z	...	...	...	...	0826z	...	...	1026z	...	...
20	Doberlug-Kirchhain d.	...	...	...	...	0447	...	...	0552	...	...	...	0647	0740	...	...	...	...	0847	...	...	1047	...	...
132	**Berlin** Südkreuz 840 d.	...	...	...	0520a	0624	...	0713	0724	0724	...	...	0824	0924	0924	0915	0915	...	1024	1059	1124	1224	...	1324
140	**Berlin** Hbf 840 d.	...	...	...	0528	0633	...	0725	0733	0733	...	0808	0833	0933	0933	0937	0937	...	1033	1108	1133	1233	...	1332
145	**Berlin** Gesundbrunnen d.	...	...	...	0533	0638	...	0732	0739	0739	0805	0815	0838	0939	0939	0943	0943	...	1038	1116	1138	1238	...	1339
166	Bernau (b. Berlin) d.	...	...	...	0548	0653	...	|	0753	0753	0822	0831	0853	0953	0953	0959	0959	...	1053	|	1153	1253	...	1353
188	Eberswalde Hbf d.	...	...	0506	0603	0708	...	|	0808	0808	0840	0846	0908	1008	1008	1014	1014	...	1108	1144	1208	1308	...	1408
214	Angermünde a.	...	...	0526	0622	0728	...	|	0827	0827	0855	0902	0928	1027	1027	1031	1031	...	1128	|	1227	1328	...	1427
214	Angermünde d.	...	...	0533	0633	0733	0732	|	0833	0833	0857	0904	0933	1033	1033	1033	1033	1045	1133	|	1233	1333	1332	1433
237	**Schwedt** (Oder) a.	...	...	|	0656	|	|	|	0856	0856	|	|	|	1056	1056	|	|	|	|	|	1256	|	|	1454
	Tantow 🏛 d.	...	...	|	...	|	0810	|	...	...	0929	|	|	...	...	|	|	1123	|	|	...	|	1410	...
	Szczecin Gumience 🏛 d.	...	...	|	...	|	0823	|	...	...	0943	|	|	...	...	|	|	1136	|	|	...	|	1423	...
	Szczecin Głowny a.	...	...	|	...	|	0829	|	...	...	0949	|	|	...	...	|	|	1142	|	|	...	|	1429	...
251	Prenzlau d.	...	...	0601	...	0801	...	|	...	...	...	0928	1001	...	...	1056	1056	...	1201	1223	...	1401	...	...
276	**Pasewalk** d.	0422	...	0619	...	0818	...	|	...	...	...	|	1018	...	...	1112	1112	...	1222	1239	...	1418	...	...
319	Anklam d.	0455	...	0649	...	0849	...	|	...	...	...	|	1049	...	...	1138	1138	...	1253	1305	...	1449	...	...
335	Züssow 846 d.	0509	...	0704	...	0903	...	0920	...	...	...	1018	1103	...	...	1155	1155	...	1305	1317	...	1503	...	...
353	Greifswald 846 d.	0525	0704	0720	...	0919	...	0932	...	...	...	1031	1119	...	...	1208	1208	...	1321	1331	...	1519	...	...
384	**Stralsund** Hbf 846 a.	0547	0724	0743	...	0942	...	...	...	...	...	1051	1140	...	...	1226	1226	...	1345	1352	...	1540	...	...

	IC 2355 G🍷	⑤f		T		EC 378 F✕			Ⓐ		ICE 1606 Ⓑ L✕			Ⓐ			⑤⑥ v		Ⓒ	Ⓐ	⑦		①–⑥	
Elsterwerda 840 d.	...	...	1224z	...	...	1346z	1424z	...	1537z	...	...	1624z	...	1737z	...	1826z	1826z	...	...	1922z	...	2026z	...	...
Doberlug-Kirchhain d.	...	...	1245	...	...	|	1445	...	1552	...	...	1645	...	1752	...	1847	1847	...	...	1940	...	2047	...	...
Berlin Südkreuz 840 d.	1314	...	1424	...	1524	1510	1624	...	1724	1724	1800	1824	...	1924	1924	2024	2024	...	2124	2124	...	2224	...	2321
Berlin Hbf 840 d.	1337	...	1433	...	1533	1537	1633	...	1734	1734	1820	1833	...	1933	1933	2033	2033	...	2133	2133	...	2233	...	2333
Berlin Gesundbrunnen d.	1343	1429	1440	...	1539	1543	1639	1716	1740	1740	1826	1838	...	1938	1938	2038	2038	...	2138	2138	...	2238	...	2339
Bernau (b. Berlin) d.	1359	1446	1455	...	1553	1559	1654	1731	1754	1754	|	1853	...	1953	1953	2053	2053	...	2153	2153	...	2253	...	2353
Eberswalde Hbf d.	1414	1502	1510	...	1608	1614	1709	1749	1808	1808	1852	1908	...	2008	2008	2108	2108	...	2208	2208	...	2313	...	0012
Angermünde a.	1431	1518	1529	...	1627	1631	1729	1805	1827	1827	1908	1928	...	2027	2027	2128	2128	...	2229	2229	...	2332	...	...
Angermünde d.	1433	1524	1533	1532	1633	1633	1733	1807	1833	1833	1909	1933	1932	2033	2033	2133	2133	2132	2233	*2233*	2233	2333	2338	...
Schwedt (Oder) a.	|	|	|	|	1656	|	|	|	1856	1856	|	|	|	2056	2056	|	|	|	2256	*2256*	|	2356	|	...
Tantow 🏛 d.	|	1602	|	1610	...	|	|	1847	...	...	|	|	2016	...	...	|	|	2210	...	...	|	...	|	...
Szczecin Gumience 🏛 d.	|	1615	|	1623	...	|	|	1906	...	...	|	|	2029	...	...	|	|	2223	...	...	|	...	|	...
Szczecin Głowny a.	|	1621	|	1629	...	|	|	1912	...	...	|	|	2035	...	...	|	|	2229	...	...	|	...	|	...
Prenzlau d.	1456	...	1601	...	...	1656	1801	...	...	...	1932	2001	...	...	...	2201	2201	...	...	...	2301	...	0007	...
Pasewalk d.	1512	...	1622	...	...	1712	1818	...	...	...	1949	2022	...	...	...	2217	2223	...	...	...	2318	...	0023	...
Anklam d.	1538	...	1653	...	...	1738	1849	...	...	...	2014	2053	...	...	...	...	2254	...	...	...	2349	...	...	...
Züssow 846 d.	1553	...	1706	...	...	1751	1903	...	...	...	|	2106	...	...	...	...	2307	...	...	...	0003	...	...	...
Greifswald 846 d.	1606	...	1722	...	...	1804	1919	...	...	...	2035	2122	...	...	...	...	2322	...	...	...	0019	...	...	...
Stralsund Hbf 846 a.	1624	...	1743	...	...	1823	1940	...	...	...	2054	2143	...	...	...	...	2343	...	...	...	0040	...	...	...

km		Ⓐ	Ⓒ	Ⓐ	①				Ⓐ		Ⓐ			ICE 1609 Ⓐ S✕	①–⑥ e				IC 2356 G🍷				EC 379 C✕	
	Stralsund Hbf 846 d.	...	...	...	0323	...	...	...	0414	...	...	...	0614	0705	...	...	0814	...	0936	...	1014	...	1140	...
	Greifswald 846 d.	...	...	...	0342	...	...	...	0435	...	...	...	0635	0726	...	...	0835	...	0956	...	1035	...	1202	...
	Züssow 846 d.	...	...	...	0356	...	...	...	0452	...	...	...	0652	0739	...	...	0852	...	1010	...	1052	...	1214	...
	Anklam d.	...	...	...	0408	...	...	...	0505	...	...	...	0705	0751	...	...	0905	...	1022	...	1105	...	1226	...
	Pasewalk d.	...	...	...	0435	0435	...	...	0543j	...	...	...	0743j	0817	...	...	0943j	...	1049	...	1143j	...	1252	...
	Prenzlau d.	...	...	...	0452	0452	...	...	0600	...	0659	...	0800	0833	...	...	1000	...	1104	...	1200	...	1308	...
0	**Szczecin** Głowny d.	...	...	...	|	|	...	...	|	0611	|	...	|	|	0835	...	|	1014	|	...	|	1223	|	...
5	Szczecin Gumience 🏛 d.	...	...	...	|	|	...	...	|	0617	|	...	|	|	0841	...	|	1020	|	...	|	1229	|	...
24	Tantow 🏛 d.	...	...	...	|	|	...	...	|	0630	|	...	|	|	0853	...	|	1032	|	...	|	1241	|	...
	Schwedt (Oder) d.	...	...	...	|	|	0508	0508	|	|	|	0708	|	|	|	0908	|	|	|	1108	|	|	|	1308
64	Angermünde a.	...	...	...	0519	0519	0530	0530	0626	0707	0726	0730	0826	0854	0928	0930	1026	1113	1126	1130	1226	1320	1329	1329
	Angermünde d.	...	...	0433	...	...	0533	0533	0633	0710	...	0733	0833	0856	...	0932	1033	...	1128	1133	1233	...	1331	1336
	Eberswalde Hbf d.	...	0449	0454	...	...	0554	0554	0654	0726	...	0754	0854	0914	...	0953	1054	...	1146	1154	1254	...	1348	1356
	Bernau (b. Berlin) d.	...	0509	0509	...	...	0610	0610	0709	0742	...	0809	0909	|	...	1007	1109	...	1201	1209	1309	...	1406	1412
	Berlin Gesundbrunnen d.	0407	0524	0524	...	...	0625	0625	0724	0756	...	0823	0924	0945	...	1023	1124	...	1217	1224	1324	...	1421	1426
	Berlin Hbf 840 d.	0413	0532	0532	...	...	0632	0632	0732	...	...	0831	0932	0949○	...	1032	1132	...	1221○	1231	1332	...	1426○	1432
	Berlin Südkreuz 840 d.	0421	0541	0541	...	...	0639	0641	0741	...	...	0838	0941	0957	...	1039	1141	...	1244	1239	1341	...	1451	1439
	Doberlug-Kirchhain d.	0554	0718	0718	...	...	...	0825	0918	...	...	...	1118	...	...	...	1318	...	...	...	1518	...	...	...
	Elsterwerda 840 a.	0612z	0735z	0735z	...	...	...	0842z	0935z	...	...	...	1135z	...	...	...	1335z	...	...	...	1535z	...	...	...

	Ⓐ		ICE 1715 N ✕			Ⓐ	⑤f				Ⓐ		IC 1932 ⑦ A			IC 2216 Ⓐd P			ⒸY	IC 61258 ⑥ H				Ⓒ
Stralsund Hbf 846 d.	...	1214	1339	...	...	...	...	1414	...	...	...	1614	1705	...	...	1813	1023	...	1915	...	...	2014	...	...
Greifswald 846 d.	...	1235	1402	...	...	...	...	1435	...	...	...	1635	1726	...	...	1832	1844	...	1936	2001	...	2035	...	...
Züssow 846 d.	...	1252	1415	...	...	...	...	1452	...	...	...	1652	|	...	...	...	1859	...	1950	2014	...	2052	...	...
Anklam d.	...	1305	1427	...	...	...	...	1505	...	...	...	1705	1748	...	...	...	1912	...	|	|	...	2105	...	...
Pasewalk d.	...	1343j	1453	...	...	...	...	1543j	...	...	...	1743j	1814	...	...	...	1943	...	|	|	...	2143j	...	...
Prenzlau d.	...	1400	1509	...	...	...	...	1600	...	...	...	1800	1831	...	...	...	2000	...	2039	|	...	2200	...	...
Szczecin Głowny d.	...	|	|	1431	...	...	...	|	1631	...	...	|	|	1824	...	...	|	1952	|	|	...	|	...	...
Szczecin Gumience 🏛 d.	...	|	|	1437	...	...	...	|	1637	...	...	|	|	1830	...	...	|	1958	|	|	...	|	...	...
Tantow 🏛 d.	...	|	|	1449	...	...	...	|	1649	...	...	|	|	1847	...	...	|	2012	|	|	...	|	...	...
Schwedt (Oder) d.	1308	|	|	|	1508	1508	...	|	|	1708	1708	|	|	|	1908	...	|	|	|	|	2108	|	2307	2307
Angermünde a.	1329	1426	|	1526	1530	1530	←	1627	1728	1730	1730	1826	1853	1926	1930	...	2027	2044	2102	|	2130	2226	2328	2328
Angermünde d.	1336	1433	|	→	1533	1533	1610	1633	...	1733	1733	1833	1855	...	1933	...	2033	2049	2103	|	2133	2233	2333	2333
Eberswalde Hbf d.	1356	1454	1546	...	1554	1554	1627	1654	...	1754	1754	1854	1911	...	1954	...	2054	2109	2126j	|	2154	2254	2354	2354
Bernau (b. Berlin) d.	1412	1509	|	...	1609	1609	1644	1709	...	1809	1809	1909	1927	...	2009	...	2109	2124	2141	|	2209	2309	0009	0009
Berlin Gesundbrunnen d.	1426	1524	1617	...	1625	1625	1705	1724	...	1824	1824	1925	1940	...	2024	...	2124	2140	2156	2207	2224	2324	0024	0026
Berlin Hbf 840 d.	1432	1532	1622○	...	1632	1632	...	1732	...	1832	1832	1932	...	...	2032	...	2132	...	2200	2215	2232	2332	...	0030
Berlin Südkreuz 840 d.	1441	1540	1644	...	1639	1641	...	1741	...	1839	1841	1941	...	...	2039	...	2141	...	...	2220	2239	2339	...	...
Doberlug-Kirchhain d.	1625	1718	...	...	...	1825	...	1918	...	...	2025	2118	...	...	...	...	2318	...	...	...	...	...	...	...
Elsterwerda 840 a.	1642z	1735z	...	...	...	1842z	...	1935z	...	...	2042z	2135z	...	...	...	...	2335z	...	...	...	...	...	...	...

A – [12] Stralsund - Berlin Spandau - Hannover - Bremen - Oldenburg.
B – ⑥ until Nov. 1 (also Oct. 3). [12] and ✕ Nürnberg - Leipzig - Berlin - Ostseebad Binz.
C – [12] and ✕ (Ostseebad Binz ♣ -) Stralsund - Dresden - Praha - Brno.
D – ⑥ July 5 - Sept. 6. [12] Erfurt - Halle - Berlin - Ostseebad Binz.
E – ⑥ (also Oct. 3; not July 5 - Sept. 6, Oct. 4). From Leipzig via Halle (Table **850**). Continues to Ostseebad Binz (Table **844**) until Oct. 18.
F – [12] and ✕ Bratislava - Praha - Dresden - Stralsund (- Ostseebad Binz ♣).
G – [12] and 🍷 Frankfurt - Halle - Berlin - Stralsund (- Ostseebad Binz ♣) and v.v.
H – ⑥ July 5 - Aug. 30. [2] Erfurt - Halle - Berlin - Ostseebad Binz and v.v. Conveys 🛏 1, 2 cl., ▬ 2 cl. and [2] (*CNL* **1251**/**1250** – SIRIUS) Zürich - Basel - Ostseebad Binz and v.v. (Table **912**).
L – Ⓑ (not Oct. 3). [12] and ✕ München - Nürnberg - Leipzig - Berlin - Stralsund. Continues to Ostseebad Binz (Table **844**) on ⑤ until Oct. 31 (not Oct. 3). Berlin Südkreuz d. 1807 from Sept. 28.
N – ⑥⑦ to Nov. 2 (also Oct. 3); ⑦ from Nov. 9. [12] and ✕ (Ostseebad Binz ♥ -) Stralsund - Berlin - Halle - Nürnberg - München.

P – [12] and 🍷 Greifswald - Hamburg - Köln - Stuttgart and v.v.
S – [12] and ✕ Stralsund - Berlin - Leipzig - Nürnberg - München.
T – ①②③④⑥⑦ (also Oct. 3; not Aug. 14, Oct. 2, Nov. 10).
Y – Until Nov. 2.

a – Ⓐ only.
d – Not Oct. 31.
e – Not Oct. 3.
f – Also Aug. 14, Oct. 2, Nov. 10; not Oct. 3).
h – Until Sept. 26. 0425 on ⑥⑦.
j – Arrives 8 minutes earlier.
v – Also Oct. 2.
z – Until Sept. 26.

○ – Arrival time.
¶ – Change trains at Angermünde on ②–⑥ (not Oct. 4).
♣ – See Table **844** for running dates to / from Ostseebad Binz.
♥ – Until Nov. 1

Usedomer Bäderbahn (2nd class only) — STRALSUND - ZÜSSOW - ŚWINOUJŚCIE — Service until Oct. 5 — 846

km																		
0	Stralsund Hbf ..... 845 d.	0526e	0614	0726	0814	0921	1014	1121	1214	1326	1414	1526	1614	1726	1823	1926	2014	2206
31	Greifswald .... 845 d.	0550e	0635	0750	0835	0945	1035	1145	1235	1350	1435	1550	1635	1750	1844	1950	2035	2231
49	Züssow .... 845 d.	0607e	0707	0807	0907	1003	1107	1203	1307	1407	1507	1607	1707	1807	1907	2007	2107	2246
67	Wolgast .... d.	0630	0730	0830	0930	1030	1130	1230	1330	1430	1530	1630	1730	1830	1930	2030	2130	2306
77	Zinnowitz ▲ .... d.	0649	0749	0847	0952	1052	1152	1252	1352	1452	1552	1652	1752	1849	1949	2049	2149	2324
104	Seebad Heringsdorf .... d.	0730	0830	0942	1042	1142	1242	1342	1442	1542	1642	1742	1842	1930	2030	2130	2230	2359
106	Seebad Ahlbeck .... d.	0735	0835	0946	1046	1146	1246	1346	1446	1546	1646	1746	1846	1935	2035	2135	2235	...
110	Świnoujście Centrum a.	0740	0840	0951	1051	1151	1251	1351	1451	1551	1651	1751	1851	1940	2040	2140	2240	...

	Ⓐ		Ⓐ	Ⓒ														
Świnoujście Centrum .. d.	0418	0518	0554	0618	0718	0818	0900	1000	1100	1200	1300	1400	1500	1600	1700	1800	1918	2018
Seebad Ahlbeck .... d.	0424	0524	0600	0624	0724	0824	0906	1006	1106	1206	1306	1406	1506	1606	1706	1806	1924	2024
Seebad Heringsdorf ..... d.	0433	0533	0609	0633	0733	0833	0918	1018	1118	1218	1318	1418	1518	1618	1718	1818	1933	2033
Zinnowitz ▲ .... d.	0512	0612	0649	0712	0812	0909	1009	1109	1209	1309	1409	1509	1609	1709	1809	1912	2012	2112
Wolgast .... d.	0529	0629	0708	0729	0829	0929	1029	1129	1229	1329	1429	1529	1629	1729	1829	1929	2029	2129
Züssow .... 845 a.	0547	0647	0729	0747	0847	0947	1047	1147	1247	1347	1447	1547	1647	1747	1847	1947	2047	2147
Greifswald .... 845 a.	0602	0719	0744	0802	0917	1002	1117	1202k	1317	1408	1517	1616	1717	1815	1917	2002	2119	2203
Stralsund Hbf ...... 845 a.	0627	0743	0809	0827	0942	1027	1140	1227k	1344	1432	1540	1641	1740	1840	1940	2027	2141	...

e – Ⓐ only.
k – 16 minutes later on ⑥.
t – Not July 14 - Aug. 22.
z – Ⓒ (daily July 12 - Aug. 24).

▲ – **Zinnowitz - Peenemünde** and v.v. (*12 km,* journey 14 minutes).
From Zinnowitz at 0431 Ⓐ, 0512 Ⓐ, 0612, 0659 Ⓐ t, 0712 Ⓒ z, 0812, 0912 and hourly until 2112.
From Peenemünde at 0452 Ⓐ, 0530 Ⓐ, 0630, 0717 Ⓐ t, 0730 Ⓒ z, 0830, 0930 and hourly until 2130.

RE services — BERLIN SCHÖNEFELD ✈ - BERLIN - DESSAU — 847

km			Ⓐ																		A					
0	Berlin Schönefeld ✈ ¶ d.	0442	0544	0644	0744	0844	0944	1044	1144	1244	1344	1444	1544	1644	1744	1844	1945	2044	2144	2244	2244		0526		2226	2324
19	Berlin Ostbahnhof .... d.	0501	0603	0703	0803	0903	1003	1103	1203	1303	1403	1503	1603	1705	1803	1903	2004	2103	2203	2303	2303		0545	and	2245	2345
24	Berlin Hbf .... ¶ d.	0513	0615	0715	0815	0915	1015	1115	1215	1315	1415	1515	1615	1716	1815	1915	2015	2115	2215	2315	2315	also	0557	hourly	2257	2357
28	Berlin Zoo .... d.	0518	0621	0721	0821	0921	1021	1121	1221	1321	1421	1521	1621	1722	1821	1921	2021	2121	2221	2321	2321		0602	until	2302	0001
43	Berlin Wannsee .... d.	0534	0634	0734	0834	0934	1034	1134	1234	1334	1434	1534	1634	1734	1834	1934	2034	2134	2234	2334	2334		...		...	...
95	Bad Belzig .... a.	0615	0715	0815	0915	1015	1115	1215	1315	1415	1515	1615	1715	1815	1915	2015	2115	2215	2315	0015	0015		...		...	...
139	Roßlau (Elbe) ..... 848 a.	0647	0745	0847	0945e	1047	1145e	1247	1345e	1447	1545e	1647	1745e	1847	1945e	2047	2145e	2247	2347h	...	0047		...		...	...
144	Dessau Hbf .... 848 a.	0651	0750	0851	0950e	1051	1150e	1251	1350e	1451	1550e	1651	1750e	1851	1950e	2051	2150e	2251	2351h	...	0051		...		...	...

			①–⑥																			Ⓐ	Ⓒ				
Dessau Hbf .... 848 d.	...	0408e	0509	...	0609e	0709	0810e	0909	1010e	1109	1210e	1309	1410e	1509	1610e	1709	1810e	1909	2010e	2109	2217	2311		...		...
Roßlau (Elbe) .... 848 d.	...	0412e	0514	...	0614e	0714	0815e	0914	1015e	1114	1215e	1314	1415e	1514	1615e	1714	1815e	1914	2015e	2114	2222	2316		...		...
Bad Belzig .... d.	0346e	0446	0546	0546	0646	0746	0846	0946	1046	1146	1246	1346	1446	1546	1646	1746	1846	1946	2046	2146	2254	2348		...	V	...
Berlin Wannsee .... d.	0428e	0528	0628	0628	0728	0828	0928	1028	1128	1228	1328	1428	1528	1628	1728	1828	1928	2028	2128	2228	2338	0030		...		...
Berlin Zoo .... d.	0441	0541	0641	0641	0741	0841	0941	1041	1141	1241	1341	1441	1541	1641	1741	1841	1941	2041	2141	2241	2350	0042		0400	and	2101
Berlin Hbf .... ¶ d.	0447	0547	0647	0647	0747	0847	0947	1047	1147	1247	1347	1447	1547	1647	1747	1847	1947	2047	2147	2247	2356	0049	also	0407	hourly	2107
Berlin Ostbahnhof ..... d.	0458	0558	0658	0658	0758	0858	0958	1058	1158	1258	1358	1458	1558	1658	1758	1858	1958	2058	2158	2256	0005	0059		0418	until	2118
Berlin Schönefeld ✈ ¶ a.	0521	0621	0721	0721	0821	0921	1017	1121	1221	1323	1421	1521	1621	1721	1821	1921	2021	2121	2221	...	...	...		0437		2139

A – ①②③④⑦ (not Oct. 2).
V – Timings may vary by up to 3 minutes.
e – Ⓐ only.
h – † only.
¶ – Services also run Berlin Schönefeld ✈ - Berlin Hbf via Südkreuz (journey: 32 minutes).
From Berlin Schönefeld at 0503, 0603 Ⓐ, 0703, 0801 Ⓐ, 0903, 1003 ⚒, 1103 and hourly until 2103.
From Berlin Hbf at 0430, 0530 Ⓐ, 0630, 0730 ⚒, 0830 and hourly until 2030.

RE / RB services — MAGDEBURG - DESSAU - LEIPZIG and HALLE — 848

km		ⒸB	Ⓒ																						
0	Magdeburg Hbf .... d.	...	...	...	...	...	...	0512	...	...	0612r	...	...	0717	...	...	0817	...	...	0917	...	...	1017	...	...
	Falkenberg (Elster) .... d.	...	...	...	...	...	...	|	0522k	...	|	0624e	...	|	0724	...	|	...	...	|	0924	...	|	...	...
	Lutherstadt Wittenberg ..... d.	0139	...	0441	0408e	0509	0546	|	0611h	0646	|	0711	0746	|	0811	0846	|	0911	0946	|	1011	1046	|	1111	1146
56	Roßlau (Elbe) .... 847 d.	|	...	|	0438e	0541	|	0604	0641h	|	0704r	0741	|	0810	0841	|	0904	0941	|	1010	1041	|	1104	1141	|
61	Dessau Hbf .... 847 a.	0208	...	|	0443e	0546	|	0608	0646h	|	0708r	0746	|	0815	0846	|	0908	0946	|	1015	1046	|	1108	1146	|
61	Dessau Hbf .... d.	0209	...	|	0447	0553	|	0610	0654	|	0712	0754	|	...	0854	|	0913	0954	|	...	1054	|	1113	1154	|
87	Bitterfeld .... a.	0225	...	0512	0510	0616	0617	0628	0717	0717	0730	0817	0817	...	0917	0917	0930	1017	1017	...	1117	1117	1130	1217	1217
87	Bitterfeld .... d.	0226	0234	0513	0520	0620	0620	0629	0722	0720	0731	0822	0820	...	0920	0922	0931	1022	1020	...	1120	1122	1131	1222	1220
	Halle (Saale) Hbf .... a.	0245	|	0538	|	0645	|	|	|	0745	|	|	0845	...	0945	|	|	|	1045	...	1145	|	|	|	1245
120	Leipzig Hbf .... a.	...	0301	...	0548	...	0648	0652	0750	...	0754	0850	...	...	...	0950	0954v	1050	...	...	...	1150	1154	1250	...

km																									
	Magdeburg Hbf .... d.	1117	...	...	1217	...	...	1317	...	...	1417	...	...	1517	...	...	1617	...	...	1717	...	...	1817	...	...
0	Falkenberg (Elster) .... d.	|	...	...	|	1224	...	|	...	...	|	...	...	|	1524	...	|	...	...	|	1724	...	|	1824e	...
54	Lutherstadt Wittenberg ..... d.	|	1211	1246	|	1311	1346	|	1411	1446	|	1511	1546	|	1611	1646	|	1711	1744	|	1811	1846	|	1911	1946
86	Roßlau (Elbe) .... 847 d.	1210	1241	|	1304	1341	|	1410	1441	|	1504	1541	|	1610	1641	|	1704	1741	|	1810	1841	|	1904	1941	|
91	Dessau Hbf .... 847 a.	1215	1246	|	1308	1346	|	1415	1446	|	1508	1546	|	1615	1646	|	1708	1746	|	1815	1846	|	1908	1946	|
91	Dessau Hbf .... d.	...	1254	|	1313	1354	|	...	1454	|	1513	1554	|	...	1654	|	1713	1754	|	...	1854	|	1913	1954	|
117	Bitterfeld .... a.	...	1317	1317	1330	1417	1417	...	1517	1517	1530	1617	1617	...	1717	1717	1730	1817	1817	...	1917	1917	1930	2017	2017
117	Bitterfeld .... d.	...	1320	1322	1331	1422	1420	...	1520	1522	1531	1622	1620	...	1720	1722	1731	1822	1820	...	1920	1922	1931	2022	2020
147	Halle (Saale) Hbf .... a.	...	1345	|	|	|	1445	...	1545	|	|	|	1645	...	1745	|	|	|	1845	...	1945	|	|	|	2045
	Leipzig Hbf .... a.	...	...	1350	1354	1450	...	...	...	1550	1554	1650	...	...	...	1750	1754	1850	...	...	...	1950	1954	2052	...

Magdeburg Hbf .... d.	1917	...	2012	...	...	...	2117	...	...	2317
Falkenberg (Elster) .... d.	|	1924	|	...	...	...	|	2124	...	|
Lutherstadt Wittenberg ..... d.	|	2011	|	2056	2140	...	|	2211	2244	|
Roßlau (Elbe) .... 847 d.	2010	2041	2057	|	|	...	2210	2241	|	0010
Dessau Hbf .... 847 a.	2015	2046	2101	|	|	...	2215	2246	|	0015
Dessau Hbf .... d.	...	...	2104	|	|	2154	▬	2254	|	▬
Bitterfeld .... a.	...	...	2127	2127	2211	2217	...	2315	2315	...
Bitterfeld .... d.	...	...	2130	2130	...	2220	2220	2315	2322	2320
Halle (Saale) Hbf .... a.	...	...	|	2155	...	2245	|	|	2347	|
Leipzig Hbf .... a.	...	...	2158	...	...	...	2245	2339	...	2345

		Ⓐe	Ⓐe	Ⓐe	ⒸR		Ⓒz		Ⓐe	⚒r
Leipzig Hbf .... d.	...	0408	...	...	...	...	...	0508z	...	...
Halle (Saale) Hbf .... d.	...	|	0415	...	0427	...	0515	|	...	0546e
Bitterfeld .... a.	...	0437	0439	...	0451	...	0539	0537z	...	0610e
Bitterfeld .... d.	...	0442	0442	...	0452	...	0542	0542z	...	0612e
Dessau Hbf .... a.	...	|	0505	...	|	...	|	0605z	...	0636e
Dessau Hbf .... 847 d.	0438	|	0514	0520	|	0538	|	0614	0625	0642
Roßlau (Elbe) .... 847 d.	0444	|	0520	0525	|	0544	|	0620	0630	0651
Lutherstadt Wittenberg ... d.	|	0514	0552	|	0524	|	0614	0650	|	|
Falkenberg (Elster) .... a.	|	...	0636	|	...	|	...	...	|	|
Magdeburg Hbf .... a.	0538	...	...	0620	...	0638	...	...	0720	0742

Leipzig Hbf .... d.	0608	...	...	...	0708	0805	0808	...	...	...	0908	1005	1008	...	...	...	1108	1205	1208	...	...	...	1308	1405	1408
Halle (Saale) Hbf .... d.	|	0615	...	0715	|	|	|	0815	...	0915	|	|	|	1015	...	1115	|	|	|	1215	...	1315	|	|	|
Bitterfeld .... a.	0637	0639	...	0739	0737	0827	0837	0839	...	0939	0937	1027	1037	1039	...	1139	1137	1227	1237	1239	...	1339	1337	1427	1437
Bitterfeld .... d.	0642	0642	...	0742	0742	0828	0842	0842	...	0942	0942	1028	1042	1042	...	1142	1142	1228	1242	1242	...	1342	1342	1428	1442
Dessau Hbf .... a.	|	0705	...	|	0805	0846	|	0905	...	|	1005	1046	|	1105	...	|	1205	1246	|	1305	...	|	1405	1446	|
Dessau Hbf .... 847 d.	|	0714	0742	|	0814	0849	|	0914	0942	|	1014	1049	|	1114	1142	|	1214	1249	|	1314	1342	|	1414	1449	|
Roßlau (Elbe) .... 847 d.	|	0720	0749	|	0820	0854	|	0920	0949	|	1020	1054	|	1120	1149	|	1220	1254	|	1320	1349	|	1420	1454	|
Lutherstadt Wittenberg ..... d.	0714	0752	|	0814	0850	|	0914	0950	|	1014	1052	|	1114	1150	|	1214	1250	|	1314	1352	|	1414	1450	|	1514
Falkenberg (Elster) .... a.	...	0836	|	...	...	|	...	...	|	...	1136	|	...	...	|	...	...	|	...	1436	|	...	...	|	...
Magdeburg Hbf .... a.	...	...	0842	...	...	0942	...	...	1042	...	...	1142	...	...	1242	...	...	1342	...	...	1442	...	...	1542	...

Leipzig Hbf .... d.	...	...	...	1508	1605	1608	...	...	...	1708	1805	1808	...	...	...	1908	2005	2008	...	...	2108	2219	2322	...	...
Halle (Saale) Hbf .... d.	1415	1446e	1515	|	|	|	1615	1646e	1715	|	|	|	1815	...	1915	|	|	|	2015	2113	|	|	|	2326	...
Bitterfeld .... a.	1439	1510e	1539	1537	1627	1637	1639	1710e	1739	1737	1827	1837	1839	...	1939	1937	2027	2037	2039	2137	2146	2249	2348	2350	...
Bitterfeld .... d.	1442	1512e	1542	1542	1628	1642	1642	1712e	1742	1742	1828	1842	1842	...	1942	1942	2028	2042	2042	2150	2147	2250	▬	2357	2355
Dessau Hbf .... a.	1505	1536e	|	1605	1646	|	1705	1736e	|	1805	1846	|	1905	...	|	2005	2046	|	2105	|	2210	2306	⑤–⑦	0021	|
Dessau Hbf .... 847 d.	1514	1542	|	1614	1649	|	1714	1742	|	1814	1849	|	1914	2003	|	2014h	2048	|	2114	|	2213g	2307	2317	...	|
Roßlau (Elbe) .... 847 d.	1520	1549	|	1620	1654	|	1720	1749	|	1820	1854	|	1920	2009	|	2020h	2053	|	2120	|	2217g	2311	2322	...	|
Lutherstadt Wittenberg ..... d.	1552	|	1614	1655	|	1714	1752	|	1814	1850	|	1914	1952	|	2014	2050h	|	2114	2152	2222	2248g	|	2352	...	0028
Falkenberg (Elster) .... a.	1636	|	...	1744e	|	...	1836	|	...	...	|	...	2036	|	...	...	|	...	2236b	...	...	|	...	...	...
Magdeburg Hbf .... a.	...	1642	...	...	1742	...	...	1842	...	...	1942	...	...	2103	...	...	2142	...	...	...	...	0006	...	...	...

– From Berlin (Table **835**).
– To Berlin and Rostock (Table **835**).
b – Ⓑ (not Oct. 3, 31).
e – Ⓐ (not Oct. 31).
g – ①–④ only.
h – ①–⑥ only.
k – ①–⑥ (not Oct. 4, Nov. 1).
r – ⚒ (not Oct. 31).
v – 0956 on ⑥ from Oct. 4 (also Oct. 3).
z – Ⓒ (also Oct. 31).

849 Local services LEIPZIG and HALLE - EISENACH and SAALFELD *RB services*

See Tables **850** and **851** for faster *ICE* and *IC* trains.

km																								⑤⑥j	H
0	**Halle** (Saale) Hbf d.	0423a	0523	...	0623	...	0723	...	0823	...	0923	...		1823	...	1923	...	2023	...	2123	...	2223	...	...	*2325*
32	Weißenfels d.	0453a	0553	...	0653	...	0753	...	0853	...	0953	...		1853	...	1953	...	2053	...	2153	...	2253	...	...	0003
46	Naumburg (Saale) Hbf d.	0503	0603	0607	0703	0709t	0803	0814	0903	0914	1003	...	and in	1903	1914	2003	...	2103	...	2203	...	2303	2319	2319	0013
59	Großheringen d.	0513	0613	|	0713	|	0813	|	0913	|	1013	1022	the same	1913	|	2013	2022	2113	2122	2213	2222	2313	|	|	0023
	Jena Paradies ◧ d.	|	|	0642	|	0741t	|	0848	|	0948	|	1048		|	1948	|	2048	|	2148	|	2248	|	2352	2352	|
	Jena-Göschwitz ◧ d.	|	|	0647	|	0753	|	0853	|	0953	|	1053	pattern	|	1953	|	2053	|	2153	|	2253	|	2357	2359	|
	Rudolstadt (Thür) ◧ d.	|	|	0715	|	0821	|	0921	|	1021	|	1121		|	2021	|	2121	|	2221	|	2321	|	...	0027	|
	Saalfeld (Saale) ◧ a.	|	|	0723	|	0832	|	0932	|	1032	|	1132	every	|	2033	|	2131	|	2231	|	2331	|	...	0036	|
87	Weimar 858 d.	0541	0641	...	0741	...	0841	...	0941	...	1041	...	**two** hours	1941	...	2041	...	2141	...	2241	...	2341	...	...	0048
108	**Erfurt** Hbf 858 a.	0557	0658	...	0758	...	0858	...	0958	...	1058	...	until	1958	...	2058	...	2158	...	2257	...	2358	...	...	0104
108	**Erfurt** Hbf d.	0601	0700	...	0800	...	0900	...	1000	...	1100	...		2005	...	2100	...	2206	...	2329	...	0024	...	...	...
136	Gotha d.	0623	0723	...	0826	...	0923	...	1026	...	1123	...		2030	...	2126	...	2230	...	2354	...	0046	...	...	...
165	**Eisenach** a.	0644	0744	...	0847	...	0944	...	1047	...	1144	...		2052	...	2147	...	2254	...	0015	...	0108	...	...	...

km					Ⓒz																L				⊕
	Eisenach d.	0409a	0501	...	...	0610	...	0710	...	0813	...	0910		...	1710	...	1813	...	1910	...	2013	...	2113	...	2218
	Gotha d.	0432a	0525	...	...	0632	...	0732	...	0835	...	0932		...	1732	...	1835	...	1932	...	2035	...	2135	...	2242
	Erfurt Hbf a.	0452a	0547	...	...	0654	...	0754	...	0856	...	0954	and in	...	1754	...	1856	...	1954	...	2056	...	2156	...	2302
	Erfurt Hbf 858 d.	0457	0601	...	...	0703	...	0801	...	0901	...	1001		...	1801	...	1901	...	2001	...	2101	...	2201	...	2313
	Weimar 858 d.	0515	0619	...	...	0719	...	0819	...	0919	...	1019	the same	...	1819	...	1919	...	2019	...	2119	...	2219	...	2330
0	**Saalfeld** (Saale) ◧ d.	|	|	0546	0629	|	0729	|	0827	|	0927	|	pattern	1727	|	1827	|	1940	|	2028	|	2122	|	2243	|
10	Rudolstadt (Thür) ◧ d.	|	|	0555	0638	|	0738	|	0836	|	0936	|		1736	|	1836	|	1949	|	2037	|	2131	|	2252	|
42	Jena-Göschwitz ◧ d.	|	|	0623	0705	|	0805	|	0905	|	1005	|	every	1805	|	1905	|	2010	|	2105	|	2158v	|	2318	|
47	**Jena** Paradies ◧ d.	|	|	0628	0710	|	0810	|	0910	|	1010	|	**two** hours	1810	|	1910	|	2015	|	2110	|	2215	|	2323	|
75	Großheringen d.	0538	0643	|	|	0743	|	0843	0935	0943	|	1043	until	|	1843	1935	1943	2039	2043	2135	2143	|	2243	2347	2352
	Naumburg (Saale) Hbf d.	0548	0654	0700	0743	0754	0843	0854	...	0954	1043	1054		1843	1854	...	1954	...	2054	...	2154	2247	2254	...	0002
	Weißenfels d.	0559	0705	*0744*a	...	0805	...	0905	...	1005	...	1105		...	1905	...	2005	...	2105	...	2203	...	2305	...	0012
	Halle (Saale) Hbf a.	0630	0737	*0820*a	...	0837	...	0937	...	1037	...	1137		...	1937	...	2037	...	2137	...	*2238*	...	2337	...	0042

LEIPZIG - WEISSENFELS Journey time: 39–46 minutes. On Oct. 31 services between Leipzig and Weißenfels run as on ⑦.

From Leipzig Hbf at 0419 Ⓐ, 0505 Ⓒ, 0519 Ⓐ, 0619 Ⓐ, 0647 Ⓒ, 0719 Ⓐ, 0847, 0947 Ⓐ, 1047, 1147 Ⓐ, 1247, 1344 Ⓐ, 1447, 1547 Ⓐ, 1647, 1747 Ⓐ, 1847, 1947 Ⓐ, 2047 and 2321.
From Weißenfels at 0426, 0526 Ⓐ, 0626, 0726 Ⓐ, 0826, 0926 Ⓐ, 1026, 1140 Ⓐ, 1226, 1326 Ⓐ, 1427, 1524 Ⓐ, 1626, 1726 Ⓐ, 1826, 1926 Ⓐ, 2026 and 2205.

EISENACH - BEBRA Journey time: 36–40 minutes. Operated by CANTUS Verkehrsgesellschaft (2nd class only).

From Eisenach at 0440 Ⓐ, 0530 Ⓐ, 0614 ⚒, 0712 ⚒, 0812, 0912 ⚒, 1012, 1112 Ⓐ, 1212, 1312 Ⓐ, 1412, 1512 Ⓐ, 1612, 1712 Ⓐ, 1812, 1912 Ⓐ, 2012, 2112 Ⓐ and 2212 Ⓒ.
From Bebra at 0506 Ⓐ, 0606 ⚒, 0659 Ⓐ, 0706 Ⓒ, 0723 Ⓐ, 0806 ⑥, 0906, 1006 Ⓐ, 1106, 1206 Ⓐ, 1306 Ⓒ, 1315 Ⓐ, 1406 Ⓐ, 1506, 1606 Ⓐ, 1706, 1807 Ⓐ, 1906, 2006 Ⓐ and 2106.

H – From Leipzig Hbf (d. 2321).
L – To Leipzig Hbf (a. 2249).

a – Ⓐ (not Oct. 31).

j – Also Oct. 2, 30.
t – On Ⓒ (also Oct. 31) Naumburg d. 0714, Jena d. 0748.
v – On ⑤⑦ (also Oct. 2; not Oct. 3) Jena Göschwitz a. 2158, d. 2209.
z – Also Oct. 31.

⊕ – Change trains at Erfurt on Ⓒ until Nov. 2 (also on Oct. 31).
◧ – See also Table **875**.

850 BERLIN and LEIPZIG - ERFURT - KASSEL and FRANKFURT

Other regional services: Table **835** Berlin - Lutherstadt Wittenberg. Table **848** Lutherstadt Wittenberg - Halle. Table **849** Leipzig / Halle - Erfurt - Eisenach - Bebra.

km		*IC* 1950	*IC* 1950	*IC* 2256	*IC* 2256	*IC* 2158	*ICE* 1003	*ICE* 1644	*IC* 2156	*ICE* 1605	*ICE* 1654	*ICE* 297	*ICE* 297	*ICE* 1005 1525	*ICE* 1642	*ICE* 1627	*IC* 2252	*ICE* 1207	*ICE* 1640	*ICE* 1609 1709	*ICE* 1009	*IC* 2250	*ICE* 1509	*ICE* 1548
		①	①–⑤	①	①–⑥	①–⑥	①–⑥	①–⑥		①–⑥	①–⑥	⑦N	⑦M							①–⑥	⑦			
			a		e	e			D			E	E											
				🍷	🍷	🍷	⊖🍷	🍴	🍷	⊖🍴	🍴	🍴	🍴	⊖🍷	🍴	⊖🍴	🍷	⊖🍴	🍴	⊖🍴	⊖🍷	🍷	⊖🍴	🍴
	Berlin Hbf 851 902 d.	0031	...	...	...	...	0437	...	...	0548	...	0551	0557	0639	...	0754	...	0840	...	0952	0952	...	1042	...
	Berlin Südkreuz 851 d.	0038	...	...	...	...	0443	...	...	0555	...	0557	0603	0646	...	0801	...	0847	...	0959	0959	...	1049	...
	Lutherstadt Wittenberg 851 d.	0114	...	...	...	...	0519	...	...	0632	...	|	|	0722	...	0836	...	|	...	1035	1035	...	|	...
	Bitterfeld 851 d.	0131	...	...	...	...	0536	...	...	0648	...	|	|	0739	...	|	...	0937	...	|	|	...	1137	...
	Halle (Saale) Hbf 851 d.	0152	...	...	...	...	0557	...	...	|	...	|	|	0800	...	|	...	1000	...	|	|	...	1200	...
	Dresden Hbf 842 d.	|	...	...	...	...	|	0420p	...	|	0544v	|	|	|	0619b	|	...	|	0819	|	|	...	|	1019
0	**Leipzig** Hbf 851 d.	0226x	...	0359	...	0500	|	0548	0603	0704	0711	0703	0711	|	0737z	0904	0911	|	0937z	1104	1104	1111	|	1135y
40	Weißenfels d.	|	...	|	...	|	|	|	0631	...	|	|	|	|	|	...	|	|	|	...	...	|	|	1216
54	Naumburg (Saale) Hbf 851 a.	|	...	0434	...	0535	0628	0624	|	...	|	|	|	0829	0825	...	|	1029	1025	...	...	|	1229	1225
54	Naumburg (Saale) Hbf d.	|	...	0436	...	0537	...	0634	|	...	|	|	|	...	0836	...	|	...	1036	...	...	|	...	1236
95	Weimar 858 d.	0335	...	0502	...	0602	...	0701	0707	...	|	|	|	...	0902	...	|	...	1102	...	...	|	...	1302
117	**Erfurt** Hbf 858 d.	0354	...	0518	0518	0618	...	0718	0726	...	0825	0825	0825	...	0918	...	1025	...	1118	...	...	1225	...	1318
144	Gotha d.	0411	...	0534	0534	0635	...	0734	0742	...	|	|	|	...	0934	...	|	...	1134	...	...	|	...	1334
173	**Eisenach** d.	0426	...	0549	0549	0652	...	0749	0757	...	0852	0855	0855	...	0949	...	1052	...	1149	...	...	1252	...	1349
	Bebra 901 d.	0500	0500	|	|	|	...	|	0822	...	|	|	|	...	|	...	|	...	|	...	...	|	...	|
	Kassel Wilhelmshöhe 901 a.	|	|	|	|	|	...	|	0856	...	|	|	|	...	|	...	|	...	|	...	...	|	...	|
230	Bad Hersfeld 901 d.	0511	0511	0618	0618	|	...	0818	...	...	|	|	|	...	1018	...	|	...	1218	...	...	|	...	1418
272	Fulda 900/1/2 d.	0540	0540	0644	0644	0744	...	0844	...	...	0944	0950	0950	...	1044	...	1144	...	1244	...	...	1344	...	1444
353	Hanau Hbf 900/1/2 d.	0623	0623	|	|	|	...	|	...	...	|	|	|	...	|	...	|	...	|	...	...	|	...	|
372	**Frankfurt** (Main) Süd a.	|	|	0737	0737	|	...	0937	...	...	|	|	|	...	1137	...	|	...	1336	...	...	|	...	1537
376	**Frankfurt** (Main) Hbf 900/1/2 a.	0642	0642	|	|	0837	...	|	...	...	1037	1044	1044	...	|	...	1237	...	|	...	...	1437	...	|
	Frankfurt Flughafen ✈ § a.	...	...	0750	0750	0855	...	0949	...	...	1055	...	...	...	1149	...	1255	...	1348	...	...	1455	...	1549
	Wiesbaden Hbf 911 a.	...	...	...	...	0931	...	...	...	...	1131	...	...	...	...	...	1331	...	...	...	...	1531	...	...

	ICE 1209	*ICE* 1558	*IC* 2356	*ICE* 209	*ICE* 1746	*IC* 2207	*IC* 2154	*IC* 1958	*ICE* 1511	*ICE* 1544	*IC* 2354	*IC* 1952	*IC* 1956	*ICE* 1615	*ICE* 1554	*ICE* 1594	*IC* 1956	*ICE* 919 1515 1715	*ICE* 1542	*ICE* 1617	*IC* 2152	*ICE* 1517	*ICE* 1717	*ICE* 1717
								⑦			⑤f	⑦	⑦			Ⓑ	⑦							⑦
	△				D						D	D	K	△		R	K			△		H	H	H
	⊖🍴	🍴	G🍷	⊖🍴	🍴	⊖	🍷		⊖🍴	🍴	🍷		🍷	⊖🍴	🍴	🍴	🍷	⊖	🍴	⊖🍴	🍷	⊖🍴	🍴	🍴
Berlin Hbf 851 902 d.	1152	...	1239	1243	...	1352	...	...	1440	...	1458	...	1539	1552	...	...	...	1639	...	1752	...	1852	1852	1852
Berlin Südkreuz 851 d.	1159	...	1246	1250	...	1358	...	...	1447	...	1505	...	1545	1559	...	...	...	1646	...	1759	...	1859	1859	1859
Lutherstadt Wittenberg 851 d.	1235	...	1321	|	...	1435	...	...	|	...	|	...	1622	1635	...	...	...	|	...	1836	...	1935	1938t	1938
Bitterfeld 851 d.	|	...	1337	|	...	|	...	...	1537	...	|	...	1639	|	...	...	...	1737	...	|	...	|	1955	1955
Halle (Saale) Hbf 851 d.	|	...	1400	|	...	|	...	...	1600	...	1612	...	1700	|	...	...	...	1800	...	|	...	|	2015	2015
Dresden Hbf 842 d.	|	...	|	|	1255	|	...	...	|	1419	|	1456	|	|	...	...	...	|	1619	|	...	|	|	|
Leipzig Hbf 851 d.	1304	1311	|	1402	1410	1504	1511	1537	|	1537z	|	1610	|	1704	1711	1711	...	|	1737z	1904	1911	2012	|	|
Weißenfels d.	...	|	1423	|	|	...	|	1609	|	|	1638	|	1728	...	|	|	...	|	|	...	|	|	|	|
Naumburg (Saale) Hbf 851 a.	...	|	1431	1437	|	...	|	1618	1629	1625	|	|	|	...	|	|	...	1829	1825	...	|	2047	2051	2051
Naumburg (Saale) Hbf d.	...	|	1433	...	|	...	|	1620	...	1635	|	|	|	...	|	|	...	...	1836	...	|	...	2053	2053
Weimar 858 d.	...	|	1500	...	1510	...	|	1649	...	1702	1711	1711	1802	...	|	|	...	...	1902	...	2011	...	2118	2118
Erfurt Hbf 858 d.	...	1425	1518	...	1526	...	1625	1706	...	1718	1726	1726	1818	...	1825	1825	←	...	1918	...	2029	...	2133	2135
Gotha d.	...	|	1534	...	1543	...	|	1727	...	1734n	1743	1743	1843	...	|	|	1845	...	1934	...	2046	...	...	2152
Eisenach d.	...	1452	1549	...	1559	...	1652	1745	...	1749	1759	1759	→	...	1852	1852	1900	...	1949	...	2101	...	...	2208
Bebra 901 d.	...	|	|	...	1623	...	|	|	...	|	1823	1823	...	...	|	|	|	...	|	...	|	...	...	|
Kassel Wilhelmshöhe 901 a.	...	|	|	...	1658	...	|	|	...	|	1856	1856	...	...	|	|	|	...	|	...	|	...	...	|
Bad Hersfeld 901 d.	...	|	1618	...	...	...	|	|	...	1818	...	...	...	...	|	|	|	...	2018	...	|	...	...	2238
Fulda 900/1/2 d.	...	1544	1644	...	...	...	1744	1838	...	1844	...	...	...	...	1944	1944	1953	...	2044	...	2157t	...	...	2304
Hanau Hbf 900/1/2 d.	...	|	|	...	...	...	|	|	...	|	...	...	...	...	|	|	|	...	2125	...	2240	...	...	2345
Frankfurt (Main) Süd a.	...	|	1737	...	...	...	|	1935	...	|	...	...	...	...	|	|	|	...	2138	...	|	...	...	|
Frankfurt (Main) Hbf 900/1/2 a.	...	1637	|	...	...	...	1837	|	...	1940	...	...	...	...	2037	2037	2052	...	|	...	2254	...	...	2400
Frankfurt Flughafen ✈ § a.	...	1655	1749	...	...	...	1855	1948	...	2007k	...	...	...	...	2055	...	...	...	2149	...	...	...	...	...
Wiesbaden Hbf 911 a.	...	1731	...	...	...	...	1931	...	...	...	...	...	...	...	2131	...	...	...	...	...	...	...	...	...

FOR NOTES SEE NEXT PAGE →

FRANKFURT and KASSEL - ERFURT - LEIPZIG and BERLIN 850

Other regional services: Table **835** Berlin - Lutherstadt Wittenberg. Table **848** Lutherstadt Wittenberg - Halle. Table **849** Leipzig / Halle - Erfurt - Eisenach - Bebra.

	ICE 1721	IC 2150	ICE 893	ICE 1619	IC 61458	CNL 458	IC 61258	CNL 1258
	⑦	⑦	Ⓑ	⑥		R		R ¶
	H		H		L	A	⊙	B ⊙
	✕	🍷	✕	🍷	2	🍷	2	🍷
Berlin Hbf 851 902 d.	1952	...	2052	2052	...	...	2215	2215
Berlin Südkreuz 851 d.	1959	...	2059	2059	...	...	2222	2222
Lutherstadt Wittenberg 851 d.	2035	...	2135	2135	...	...	2256	2256u
Bitterfeld 851 d.	|	...	|	|	...	...	2314	2314u
Halle (Saale) Hbf 851 d.	|	...	|	|	...	...	2335	2335u
Dresden Hbf 842 d.	|	...	|	|	2104	2104	|	|
Leipzig Hbf 851 d.	2104	2114	2204	2204	2235	2235	|	|
Weißenfels d.	...	|	...	...	|	|	|	|
Naumburg (Saale) Hbf 851 a.	...	2150	...	...	2313	|	0005	|
Naumburg (Saale) Hbf d.	...	2152	...	...	2315	2315u	0007	0007u
Weimar 858 d.	...	2217	...	...	2347	2347u	0033	0033u
Erfurt Hbf 858 d.	...	2234	...	...	0003	0120u	0049	0120u
Gotha d.	...	2252	...	...	...	|	...	|
Eisenach d.	...	2307	...	...	...	|	...	|
Bebra 901 d.	...	|	...	...	...	|	...	|
Kassel Wilhelmshöhe 901 a.	...	|	...	...	...	|	...	|
Bad Hersfeld 901 d.	...	2338	...	...	...	|	...	|
Fulda 900/1/2 d.	...	0004	...	...	...	|	...	|
Hanau Hbf 900/1/2 d.	...	0049	...	...	...	|	...	|
Frankfurt (Main) Süd a.	...	|	...	...	...	0359	...	0359
Frankfurt (Main) Hbf 900/1/2 a.	...	0104	...	...	...	...	...	...
Frankfurt Flughafen ✈ § a.	...	...	...	...	...	...	...	...
Wiesbaden Hbf 911 a.	...	...	...	...	...	...	...	...

km		CNL 1259	IC 61259	CNL 459	IC 61459	ICE 1516	IC 2302	ICE 1716	IC 2357	IC 2353	IC 2153
		R		R			①	②–⑤	⑥	⑥	Ⓐ
		B ⊙	⊙	A	L	H		q	J	O	
		🍷	2	🍷	2	✕	⊖		G		🍷
	Wiesbaden Hbf 911 d.	...	...	...	...	...	...	...	...	...	...
0	**Frankfurt** Flughafen ✈ § d.	...	...	...	...	...	...	...	...	...	...
	Frankfurt (Main) Hbf 900/1/2 d.	...	...	...	...	...	...	...	...	...	0452g
11	**Frankfurt** (Main) Süd d.	0054	...	0054	...	...	...	...	...	...	|
—	Hanau Hbf 900/1/2 d.	|	...	|	...	...	...	...	...	...	0508g
	Fulda 900/1/2 d.	|	...	|	...	...	...	...	...	...	0551g
	Bad Hersfeld 901 d.	|	...	|	...	...	...	...	...	...	0621g
0	**Kassel** Wilhelmshöhe 901 d.	|	...	|	...	...	...	...	...	...	|
54	Bebra 901 d.	|	...	|	...	...	...	...	...	...	|
99	**Eisenach** d.	|	...	|	...	0553	...	...	...	...	0658
128	Gotha d.	|	...	|	...	0610	...	...	...	...	0714
155	**Erfurt** Hbf 858 d.	0345s	0442	0345s	0511	0628	...	...	...	0639	0732
177	Weimar 858 d.	0457s	0459	0527s	0529	0645	...	...	...	0654	0749
218	Naumburg (Saale) Hbf a.	0523s	0523	0552s	0552	0708	...	...	...	0725	|
218	Naumburg (Saale) Hbf 851 d.	|	0525	|	0554	0710	0724	0724	...	0725	|
232	Weißenfels d.	|	|	|	|	|	|	|	...	0735	|
	Leipzig Hbf 851 a.	|	|	0636	0636	0746	|	|	0731	|	0846
	Dresden Hbf 842 a.	|	|	0803	0803	|	|	|	|	|	...
264	**Halle** (Saale) Hbf 851 d.	0557s	0559	...	...	|	0803t	0803t	0803t	0803	...
294	Bitterfeld 851 d.	0618s	0621	...	...	|	0824	0824	0824	0824	...
331	Lutherstadt Wittenberg 851 d.	0635s	0637	...	...	0823	|	|	|	|	...
421	**Berlin** Südkreuz 851 a.	0711	0711	...	...	0857	0913	0913	0913	0913	...
429	**Berlin** Hbf 851 902 a.	0719	0719	...	...	0904	0920	0920	0920	0920	...

	ICE 1614	ICE 1545	ICE 1514	IC 2157	ICE 1612	ICE 1745	ICE 1512	IC 2355	IC 2355	ICE 1557	ICE 1597	IC 2208	ICE 1547	ICE 208	IC 2159	ICE 1608 1628	ICE 1549	ICE 1508	IC 1953	ICE 1651	ICE 1606	IC 1953	IC 1959	IC 2359
	①–⑥	①–⑥	Ⓐ					①–⑥	⑦	①–⑥									⑤m			⑤m	⑤m	⑦
						D		e	w	R						⊕			K		♣	K	D	D
	⊖✕	✕	⊖✕	🍷	⊖✕	✕	⊖✕	G 🍷	G 🍷	✕	🍷	⊖	✕	⊖✕	🍷	⊖✕	✕	⊖✕	🍷	✕	⊖✕	🍷		🍷
Wiesbaden Hbf 911 d.	...	...	...	...	...	...	...	...	...	...	0823c	...	...	...	1023	...	...	...	...	1223	...	...	...	...
Frankfurt Flughafen ✈ § d.	...	...	...	...	...	...	...	0810	...	...	0901	...	1011	...	1102	...	1211	...	...	1302	...	...	...	...
Frankfurt (Main) Hbf 900/1/2 d.	...	0618	...	0720	...	...	...	|	0802	0919	0919	...	|	...	1119	...	|	...	1302	1319	...	...	...	...
Frankfurt (Main) Süd d.	...	|	...	|	...	...	...	0821	|	|	|	...	1022	...	|	...	1222	...	|	|	...	...	...	...
Hanau Hbf 900/1/2 d.	...	0634	...	|	...	...	...	|	|	|	|	...	|	...	|	...	|	...	|	|	...	...	...	...
Fulda 900/1/2 d.	...	0714	...	0814	...	...	...	0914	0856	1014	1014	...	1114	...	1214	...	1314	...	1400	1414	...	...	...	...
Bad Hersfeld 901 d.	...	0740	...	|	...	...	...	0940	0922	|	|	...	1140	...	|	...	1340	...	1426	|	...	...	...	...
Kassel Wilhelmshöhe 901 d.	...	|	...	|	...	0859	...	|	|	|	|	...	|	...	|	...	|	...	|	|	...	...	1459	1459
Bebra 901 d.	...	|	...	|	...	0933	...	|	|	|	|	...	|	...	|	...	|	...	|	|	...	...	1535	1535
Eisenach d.	...	0809	...	0906	...	0958	...	1009	1009j	1106	1106	...	1209	...	1306	...	1409	...	1457	1506	...	...	1559	1559
Gotha d.	...	0824	...	|	...	1014	...	1024	1024	|	|	...	1224	...	|	...	1424	...	1513	|	...	←	1614	1614
Erfurt Hbf 858 d.	...	0841	...	0934	...	1031	...	1041	1041	1134	1134	...	1241	...	1334	...	1441	...	1527	1534	...	1540	1631	1631
Weimar 858 d.	...	0859	...	|	...	1048	...	1059	1059	|	|	...	1259	...	|	...	1459	...	→	|	...	1557	1648	1648
Naumburg (Saale) Hbf a.	...	0923	...	|	...	|	...	1124	1124	|	|	...	1323	...	|	...	1523	...	...	|	...	1623	|	|
Naumburg (Saale) Hbf 851 d.	...	0935h	0929	|	...	|	...	1126	1126	|	|	...	1335	1329	|	...	1532	1529	...	|	...	1626	|	|
Weißenfels d.	...	|	|	|	...	|	...	1136	1136	|	|	...	|	|	|	...	1543	|	...	|	...	|	|	|
Leipzig Hbf 851 a.	0851	1021r	|	1046	1051	1148	1200	|	|	1246	1246	1251	1421r	|	1446	1451	1621r	|	...	1646	1651	|	1748	|
Dresden Hbf 842 a.	|	1138e	|	...	|	1301	|	|	|	...	...	|	1538	|	...	|	1738	|	...	...	|	|	1913	|
Halle (Saale) Hbf 851 d.	|	...	1003	...	|	...	|	1200	1200	...	...	|	...	1403	...	|	...	1603	...	...	|	1700	...	1746
Bitterfeld 851 d.	|	...	1024	...	|	...	|	1222	1222	...	...	|	...	1424	...	|	...	1624	...	...	|	|	...	|
Lutherstadt Wittenberg 851 d.	0923	...	|	...	1123	...	|	1238	1238	...	...	1323	...	|	...	1523	...	|	...	...	1723	|	...	|
Berlin Südkreuz 851 a.	0958	...	1111	...	1159	...	1301	1312	1312	...	...	1358	...	1513	...	1558	...	1711	...	...	1758	1809	...	1852
Berlin Hbf 851 902 a.	1006	...	1118	...	1207	...	1308	1319	1319	...	...	1407	...	1520	...	1606	...	1719	...	...	1805	1820	...	1900

	ICE 1641	ICE 906 1206 1506	IC 1955	IC 2251	ICE 708 1008	IC 2151	ICE 1643	ICE 1004 1504	IC 2204	ICE 296	IC 2253	IC 2155	IC 2255	ICE 1502	ICE 1702	ICE 1657	ICE 1657	ICE 1000 1600	IC 2257	ICE 1647	ICE 1500	ICE 1500	IC 2259	IC 2259
			⑤m						①–④	⑥	Ⓑ	⑤f	T		⑤m		Ⓑ	⑤⑦	⑥	Ⓑ	F	⑤⑦	Ⓑq	⑤⑦
					⊕	D			Y	E		◇										f▲		d
	✕	⊖✕		🍷	⊖🍷	🍷	✕	⊖🍷		⊡✕	🍷	🍷	🍷	⊖✕	⊖✕	✕	✕	f⊖	🍷	✕	⊖	⊖	🍷	🍷
Wiesbaden Hbf 911 d.	...	...	...	1423	...	...	...	...	...	...	1623	...	...	...	...	1823	1823	...	...	...	...	...	2023	2023
Frankfurt Flughafen ✈ § d.	1411	...	...	1502	...	...	1611	...	...	...	1702	1811	1811	...	...	1902	1902	...	...	...	...	...	2102	2102
Frankfurt (Main) Hbf 900/1/2 d.	|	...	1418	1520	...	...	|	...	1617	1713	1720	|	|	...	...	1919	1919	...	2022	2022	...	...	2118	2118
Frankfurt (Main) Süd d.	1422	...	|	|	...	...	1622	...	|	|	|	1822	1822	...	...	|	|	...	|	|	...	...	|	|
Hanau Hbf 900/1/2 d.	|	...	1438	|	...	...	|	...	1636	|	|	|	|	...	...	|	|	...	2038	2038	...	...	|	|
Fulda 900/1/2 d.	1514	...	1522	1614	...	...	1714	...	1721	1811	1814	1914	1914	...	...	2014	2014	...	2117	2117	...	...	2214	2214
Bad Hersfeld 901 d.	1540	...	|	|	...	...	1740	...	1753	|	|	1940	1940	...	...	|	|	...	2142	2142	...	...	|	|
Kassel Wilhelmshöhe 901 d.	|	...	|	|	...	1659	|	...	|	|	|	|	|	...	...	|	|	...	|	|	...	...	|	|
Bebra 901 d.	|	...	|	|	...	1735	|	...	1802	|	|	|	|	...	...	|	|	...	|	|	...	...	|	|
Eisenach d.	1609	...	|	1706	...	1758	1809	...	...	1904	1906	2009	2009	...	...	2107	2107	...	2214	2214	...	...	2308	2308
Gotha d.	1624	...	1632	|	...	1813	1824	...	...	|	|	2024	2024	...	...	2122	2122	...	2229	2229	...	...	2323	2323
Erfurt Hbf 858 d.	1641	...	1656	1734	...	1830	1841	...	...	1933	1934	2041	2041	...	...	2140	2140	...	2246	2246	...	...	2338	2342
Weimar 858 d.	1659	...	1712	|	...	1848	1859	...	...	|	1952	2059	2059	...	...	2157	2157	...	2303	2303	...	...	...	2359
Naumburg (Saale) Hbf a.	1723	...	1738	|	...	|	1923	...	...	|	|	2122	2122	...	...	|	|	...	2329	2329	...	...	...	0023
Naumburg (Saale) Hbf 851 d.	1734	1729	1740	|	...	|	1935	1929	...	|	|	2124	2133	2129	2135	|	|	2234	2339	2339	2335	2335	...	0025
Weißenfels d.	|	|	1751	|	...	|	|	|	...	|	|	|	2144	|	|	|	|	|	|	|	|	|	...	|
Leipzig Hbf 851 a.	1821r	|	1818	1846	1851	1946	2021r	|	...	2046	2048	2215	2250	2204	|	2256	2256	2308	0046	0047	0010	0010	...	0058
Dresden Hbf 842 a.	1938	|	...	...	|	...	2138	|	...	|	...	2341	|	|	|	...	0027	|	|	|	...	|	...	...
Halle (Saale) Hbf 851 d.	...	1803	...	...	|	...	...	2003	...	|	...	...	2206*	|	2208	...	...	|	0011*	0011*	...	|	...	...
Bitterfeld 851 d.	...	1824	...	...	|	...	...	2024	...	|	...	...	...	|	2228	...	...	|	...	...	...	|	...	...
Lutherstadt Wittenberg 851 d.	...	|	...	...	1923	...	...	|	...	|	...	...	...	|	2245	...	...	2349	...	...	...	0046	...	...
Berlin Südkreuz 851 a.	...	1911	...	...	1958	...	...	2112	...	2158	...	...	...	2310	2321	...	...	0023	...	...	...	0121	...	...
Berlin Hbf 851 902 a.	...	1919	...	...	2005	...	...	2120	...	2206	...	...	...	2317	2328	...	...	0030	...	...	...	0128	...	...

A – CANOPUS – 🛏 1, 2 cl., ▬ 2 cl., (2) (reclining) and 🍷 Praha - Basel - Zürich and v.v.
B – SIRIUS – 🛏 1, 2 cl., ▬ 2 cl., (2) (reclining) and 🍷 Berlin - Basel - Zürich and v.v.
D – To / from Düsseldorf or Köln (Tables **800/805**).
E – (12) and ✕ Interlaken - Basel - Karlsruhe - Berlin and v.v.
F – ①②③④⑥ (also Oct. 3; not Oct. 2).
G – To / from Stralsund (Table **845**), also Ostseebad Binz on dates in Table **844**.
H – From / to Hamburg (Table **840**).
J – ⑥ (also Oct. 3; not July 5 - Sept. 6, Oct. 4).
K – To / from Karlsruhe (Table **912**).
L – From / to Praha (Table **1100**).
M – Until Sept. 21.
N – From Sept. 28.
O – ⑥ July 5 - Sept. 6. To Ostseebad Binz (Tables **844/5**).
R – To / from Saarbrücken (Table **919**).
T – ①②③④⑦ (not June 18, Oct. 2).
Y – ①–④ (not June 18, 19, Oct. 2).

a – Not June 19, 20, Oct. 3.
b – Ⓑ only.
c – Ⓒ (also June 19).
d – Also Oct. 2; not Oct. 3.
e – Not Oct. 4.
f – Also Oct. 2; not Oct. 3.
g – ① only.
h – 9–10 minutes earlier on ⑥ (also Oct. 3).
j – Arrives 0951.
k – ⑥ only.
m – Also June 18, Oct. 2; not June 20, Oct. 3.
n – ①–⑥ only.
p – ①–⑤ (not Oct. 3, 31, Nov. 19).
q – Not Oct. 3.
r – 6–8 minutes earlier from Sept. 28.
s – Stops to set down only.
t – Arrives 6–10 minutes earlier.
u – Stops to pick up only.
v – 0538 Sept. 15–27; 0556 from Sept. 29.

w – Also Oct. 4.
x – 0235 until Sept. 22.
y – 1141 from Sept. 28.
z – 3–4 minutes later from Sept. 28.

⊡ – From Oct. 4 arrives Leipzig 2055, Berlin Südkreuz 2202, Berlin Hbf 2209.
◇ – Also runs on June 18 Frankfurt Flughafen - Leipzig.
△ – 2–5 minutes earlier from Sept. 28.
♣ – 7–10 minutes later from Sept. 28.
⊕ – 7–10 minutes later on ⑦ from Sept. 28.
▲ – From Sept. 28 Leipzig a. 0020, Lutherstadt Wittenberg d. 0102, Berlin Südkreuz a. 0136, Berlin Hbf a. 0143.
⊙ – From / to Ostseebad Binz on ⑥ July 5 - Aug. 30 (Tables **844/5**).
¶ – Train number **1250** on ⑥ July 5 - Aug. 30.
◧ – Train number **1251** on ⑥ July 5 - Aug. 30.
* – Arrival time (calls before Leipzig).
⊖ – See Table **851** for further details.
§ – Frankfurt Flughafen Fernbahnhof.

851 BERLIN - LEIPZIG - SAALFELD - NÜRNBERG

Other regional services: Table **835** Berlin - Lutherstadt Wittenberg. Table **848** Lutherstadt Wittenberg - Leipzig / Halle. Table **849** Leipzig / Halle - Saalfeld.

km		ICE 985		ICE 1501	ICE 1603	ICE 1644	ICE 1003	ICE 1605	ICE 297	ICE 1642	ICE 1525	ICE 1005	ICE 1703	ICE 1627	ICE 1697	X 68902	ICE 1640	ICE 1207	ICE 793	ICE 1609	ICE 1009	ICE 1709	ICE 1548	ICE 1509	ICE 791
		Ⓐt		Ⓐu	①	①–⑥	①–⑥	①–⑥	⑦⊠		⑥	Ⓑ	Ⓐ		⑥b			RQ		Ⓐ	⑦	⑥r			
		✕		✕	✕	⊖	🍸	✕	⊖✕	⊖	✕	🍸	✕	✕	P🍸	△	⊖	✕		S✕	🍸	✕	⊖	R✕	L
	Hamburg Hbf **840** d.	...	...	...	...	...	...	...	...	...	...	...	...	0600r	...	...	...	...	0706	...	...	0806	...	...	0906
0	**Berlin** Hbf **850** d.	...	...	...	...	...	0437	0548	0557	...	0639	0639	0652	0754	0754	0757	...	0840	0852	0952	0952	0952	...	1042	1051
8	**Berlin** Südkreuz **850** d.	...	...	...	...	...	0443	0555	0603	...	0646	0646	0658	0801	0801	0805	...	0847	0859	0959	0959	0959	...	1049	1059
98	Lutherstadt Wittenberg **850** d.	...	...	...	...	...	0519	0632	|	...	0722	0722	0735	0836	0836	|	...	|	0935	1035	1035	1035	...	|	1135
135	Bitterfeld **850** d.	...	...	...	...	...	0536	0648	|	...	0739	0739	|	|	|	|	...	0937	|	|	|	|	...	1137	|
	Halle (Saale) Hbf **850** d.	...	...	...	...	...	0557	|	|	...	0800	0800	|	|	|	|	...	1000	|	|	|	|	...	1200	|
168	**Leipzig** Hbf a.	...	...	...	...	...	|	0704	0704	...	|	|	0804	0904	0904	0922	...	|	1004	1104	1104	1104	...	|	1215
168	**Leipzig** Hbf **850** d.	...	...	...	0512	0548	|	0715	...	0737‡	|	|	...	0915	0915	...	0937‡	|	...	1115	1115	1115	1135‡	|	...
222	Naumburg (Saale) Hbf **850** d.	...	...	...	0548	0624	0630	|	...	0825	0831	0831	...	|	|	...	1025	1031	...	|	|	|	1225	1231	...
261	**Jena** Paradies d.	...	...	...	0614	...	0657	0814	...	...	0900	0900	...	1014	1014	...	...	1100	...	1214	1214	1214	...	1300	...
308	**Saalfeld** (Saale) **875** d.	...	...	...	0647	...	0729	0847	...	...	|	|	...	1047	1047	...	...	|	...	1247	1247	1247	...	|	...
395	Lichtenfels **875** d.	...	...	0628	0749	...	0832	0949	...	...	|	|	...	1149	1149	...	...	|	...	1349	1349	1349	...	|	...
427	**Bamberg** **875** d.	...	...	0647	0808	...	0849	1007	...	...	|	|	...	1207	1207	...	...	1251	...	1407	1407	1407	...	1451	...
465	Erlangen **875** d.	0608	...	0708	0830	...	0909	1028	...	...	|	|	...	1228	1228	...	...	|	...	1428	1428	1428	...	|	...
489	**Nürnberg** Hbf **875** a.	0625	...	0725	0849	...	0925	1047	...	...	1124	1124	...	1247	1247	...	...	1325	...	1447	1447	1447	...	1525	...
	Augsburg Hbf **905** a.	|	...	|	1007	...	|	1207	...	...	1237	1237	...	1407	...	...	...	|	...	1607	1607	1607	...	|	...
	München Hbf **904 905** a.	0747	...	0850	1041	...	1049	1241	...	...	1311	1311	...	1441	...	...	...	1450	...	1641	1641	1641	...	1655	...

	ICE 1209	ICE 1699	IC 2356	ICE 209	IC 2207	ICE 1544	ICE 1511	ICE 1507	ICE 1615	ICE 1542	ICE 919	ICE 1515	ICE 1719	X 68904	ICE 1617	ICE 1617	ICE 1617	ICE 1717	ICE 1517	ICE 1721	ICE 893	ICE 1619	CNL 1247	ICE 1723	IC 1903
	◇	⑤m							⊗		⑤f	★				Ⓑ	⑤⑦			⑦	Ⓑ	⑥	🅁	⑤f	⑦
	Q✕	◇P	⊖🍸	N✕		⊖	✕	✕	✕	⊖	✕	S✕	✕	R△	✕	⊗✕	f⊗	⊖✕	✕	✕	✕	🍸	A🍸	✕	🍸
Hamburg Hbf **840** d.	1000	🍸	...	1051	...	...	...	1258	1406	...	1438	...	1505	...	...	...	✕	1706	1706	1806	1906	...	...	2001	...
Berlin Hbf **850** d.	1152	1152	1239	1243	1352	...	1440	1452	1552	...	1639	1639	1652	1704	1752	1752	1752	1852	1852	1952	2052	2052	2104	2152	2153
Berlin Südkreuz **850** d.	1159	1159	1246	1250	1358	...	1447	1459	1559	...	1646	1646	1659	1710	1759	1759	1759	1859	1859	1959	2059	2059	|	2159	2159
Lutherstadt Wittenberg **850** d.	1235	1235	1321	|	1435	...	|	1535	1635	...	|	|	1735	|	1836	1836	1836	1938j	1935	2035	2135	2135	|	2235	2235
Bitterfeld **850** d.	|	|	1337	|	|	...	1537	|	|	...	1737	1737	|	|	|	|	|	1955	|	|	|	|	|	|	|
Halle (Saale) Hbf **850** d.	|	|	1400	|	|	...	1600	|	|	...	1800	1800	|	|	|	|	|	2015	|	|	|	|	|	|	|
Leipzig Hbf a.	1304	1304	|	1357	1504	...	|	1604	1704	...	|	|	1804	1831	1904	1904	1904	|	2004	2104	2204	2204	|	2304	2304
Leipzig Hbf **850** d.	1315	1315	|	1402	1515	1537‡	|	...	1715	1737‡	|	|	...	...	...	1915	1915	|	2012	...	...	...	|	...	...
Naumburg (Saale) Hbf **850** d.	|	|	1431	1439	|	1625	1631	...	|	1825	1831	1831	...	...	...	1951	1951	2051	2057j	...	...	...	|	...	...
Jena Paradies d.	1414	1414	...	1505	1614	...	1700	...	1814	...	1900	1900	...	...	...	2017	2017	...	2123	...	...	...	|	...	...
Saalfeld (Saale) **875** d.	1447	1447	...	|	1647	...	|	...	1847	...	|	|	...	...	...	2049	2050	...	2156	...	...	...	|	...	...
Lichtenfels **875** d.	1549	1549	...	|	1749	...	|	...	1949	...	|	|	...	...	...	...	2151	...	2254	...	...	...	|	...	...
Bamberg **875** d.	1607	1607	...	|	1807	...	1851	...	2007	...	2051	2051	...	...	...	...	2209	...	2310	...	...	...	|	...	...
Erlangen **875** d.	1630	1630	...	|	1827	...	|	...	2028	...	|	|	...	...	...	...	2230	...	2334	...	...	...	|	...	...
Nürnberg Hbf **875** a.	1649	1649	...	1724	1847	...	1925	...	2047	...	2125	2125	...	...	...	...	2249	...	2354	...	...	...	|	...	...
Augsburg Hbf **905** a.	1807	...	...	|	2007	...	|	...	2210	...	|	|	...	...	...	...	0007	...	|	...	...	...	0625	...	...
München Hbf **904 905** a.	1842	...	...	1850	2041	...	2048	...	2243	...	2247	2247	...	...	...	...	0041	...	0114	...	...	...	0705	...	...

	ICE 1706	ICE 1616	ICE 794	CNL 1246	ICE 1516	IC 2302	ICE 1614	ICE 1614	ICE 1614	X 68903	ICE 1724	ICE 1714	ICE 1514	ICE 1545	ICE 1612	ICE 1612	ICE 1512	IC 2355	IC 2208	ICE 890	ICE 208	ICE 1547	ICE 1608	ICE 1698	ICE 892
	①	②–⑤	①–⑥	🅁		①	①	Ⓐ	①–⑥		Ⓑq	⑥r	Ⓐ	Ⓐ	①–⑥								⊕	⑥d	
	✕⊙	✕	✕	A🍸	⊖✕		✕	✕	✕	R△	✕	S✕	✕	⊖	✕	✕	✕	⊖🍸			N✕	⊖	✕	P🍸	L
München Hbf **904 905** d.	0002	...	...	2215	...	...	...	...	...	...	...	...	...	...	0458	...	0716k	...	0711	...	0916k	...	0919	...	...
Augsburg Hbf **905** d.	0030	...	...	2250	...	...	...	...	...	...	...	...	...	...	0531	...	|	...	0748	...	|	...	0954	...	...
Nürnberg Hbf **875** d.	0205	...	...	|	...	0405	0504	...	...	...	...	0610	0618	...	0701	0701	0834	...	0906	...	1034	...	1106	1106	...
Erlangen **875** d.	0222	...	...	|	...	0424	0527	...	...	...	...	0630	0635	...	0720	0720	|	...	0926	...	|	...	1126	1126	...
Bamberg **875** d.	0243	...	...	|	...	0444	0549	...	...	...	...	0652	0658	...	0752	0752	0908	...	0952	...	|	...	1152	1152	...
Lichtenfels **875** d.	0302	...	...	|	...	0504	0608	...	...	...	...	0709	0717	...	0811	0811	|	...	1011	...	|	...	1211	1211	...
Saalfeld (Saale) **875** d.	0404	...	...	|	...	0607	0709	0709	...	...	...	0811	0821	...	0913	0913	|	...	1113	...	|	...	1313	1313	...
Jena Paradies d.	0436	...	...	|	...	0640	0741	0741	...	...	...	0845	0857	...	0946	0946	1054	...	1146	...	1257	...	1346	1346	...
Naumburg (Saale) Hbf **850** d.	0502	...	...	|	0710	0724c	0807	0807	...	...	...	0913	0929	0935	|	|	1119	1126	|	...	1329	1335	|	|	...
Leipzig Hbf **850** a.	0546	...	...	|	0746	|	0842	0842	...	...	...	0946	|	1021§	1042	1042	1156	|	1242	...	|	1421§	1442	1442	...
Leipzig Hbf d.	0551	0551	0651	|	0751	|	0851	0851	0851	0932	0951	0951	|	...	1051	1051	1200	|	1251	1351z	|	...	1451	1451	1551
Halle (Saale) Hbf **850** d.	|	|	|	|	|	0803j	|	|	|	|	|	|	1003	...	|	|	|	1200	|	|	1403	...	|	|	|
Bitterfeld **850** d.	|	|	0708	|	|	0824	|	|	|	|	|	|	1024	...	|	|	|	1222	|	|	1424	...	|	|	|
Lutherstadt Wittenberg **850** d.	0623	0623	0725	|	0823	|	0923	0923	0923	|	1023	1023	|	...	1123	1123	|	1238	1323	1423	|	...	1523	1523	1623
Berlin Südkreuz **850** a.	0657	0657	0800	|	0857	0913	0958	0958	0958	1042	1057	1057	1111	...	1159	1159	1301	1312	1358	1458	1513	...	1558	1558	1657
Berlin Hbf **850** a.	0704	0704	0809	0813	0904	0920	1006	1006	1006	1050	1108	1104	1118	...	1207	1207	1308	1319	1407	1505	1520	...	1606	1606	1704
Hamburg Hbf **840** a.	0853	0853	0957	...	1101	...	1157	1157	1157	...	1255	...	...	...	1357	1357	1454	...	...	1710	...	...	1758	...	1854

	ICE 1508	ICE 1549	ICE 1606	ICE 1696	ICE 1708	ICE 1506	ICE 1206	ICE 906	ICE 1641	ICE 1008	ICE 708	X 68905	ICE 1720	ICE 1004	ICE 1504	ICE 1643	ICE 296	ICE 1602	ICE 1502	ICE 1702	IC 2255	ICE 1600	ICE 1500	ICE 1500	ICE 1647
			♣	⑦♣		♥	⊡	⑤m		①–⑥	⑦			Ⓑ	⑥		⑥✣			⑤m	T	⑤⑦f	W	⑤⑦f	¶
	R✕	⊖	S✕	P🍸	✕	R✕	✕	✕	⊖	🍸	♣✕	△	✕	🍸	✕	⊖	⊖✕	✕	✕	✕		◐	✕	▲✕	⊖
München Hbf **904 905** d.	1116v	...	1117	...	...	1315k	1315k	1315k	...	1319	1319	...	...	1449	1449	...	...	1616k	1716k	1716k	...	1739	1916k	1916k	...
Augsburg Hbf **905** d.	|	...	1154	...	...	|	|	|	...	1354	1354	...	...	1522	1522	...	...	|	|	|	...	1813	|	|	...
Nürnberg Hbf **875** d.	1234	...	1306	1306	...	1434	1434	1434	...	1504	1504	...	...	1634	1634	...	...	1737	1835	1835	...	1935	2035	2035	...
Erlangen **875** d.	|	...	1326	1326	...	|	|	|	...	1522	1522	...	...	|	|	...	...	1752	|	|	...	1952	2052	2052	...
Bamberg **875** d.	1308	...	1352	1352	...	1508	1508	1508	...	1552	1552	...	...	1708	1708	...	...	1812	1908	1908	...	2012	2113	2113	...
Lichtenfels **875** d.	|	...	1411	1411	...	|	|	|	...	1611	1611	...	...	|	|	...	...	1831	|	|	...	2031	2131	2131	...
Saalfeld (Saale) **875** d.	|	...	1513	1513	...	|	|	|	...	1713	1713	...	...	|	|	...	...	1936	2023	2023	...	2138	2237	2237	...
Jena Paradies d.	1457	...	1546	1546	...	1657	1657	1657	...	1746	1746	...	...	1857	1857	...	...	2009	2055	2055	...	2209	2309	2309	...
Naumburg (Saale) Hbf **850** d.	1529	1532	|	|	...	1729	1729	1729	1734	|	|	...	...	1929	1929	1935	...	2036	2129	2135	2133	2234	2335	2335	2339
Leipzig Hbf **850** a.	|	1621§	1642	1642	...	|	|	|	1821§	1842	1842	...	...	|	|	2021§	...	2114	2204	|	|	2308	0010	0010	|
Leipzig Hbf d.	|	...	1651	1651	1751	|	|	|	...	1851	1851	1922	1951	|	|	...	2051	2123	2209	|	|	2318	...	0014	|
Halle (Saale) Hbf **850** d.	1603	...	|	|	|	1803	1803	1803	...	|	|	|	|	2003	2003	...	|	|	|	2208	2206	|	...	|	0011
Bitterfeld **850** d.	1624	...	|	|	|	1824	1824	1824	...	|	|	|	|	2024	2024	...	|	2141	|	2228	...	|	...	|	...
Lutherstadt Wittenberg **850** d.	|	...	1723	1723	1823	|	|	|	...	1923	1923	|	2023	|	|	...	|	2159	|	2245	...	2349	...	0046	...
Berlin Südkreuz **850** a.	1711	...	1758	1758	1859	1911	1911	1911	...	1958	1958	2036	2058	2112	2112	...	2158	2235	2310	2321	...	0023	...	0121	...
Berlin Hbf **850** a.	1719	...	1805	1805	1908	1919	1919	1919	...	2005	2005	2042	2105	2120	2120	...	2206	2242	2317	2328	...	0030	...	0128	...
Hamburg Hbf **840** a.	...	...	...	...	2054n	...	...	...	...	...	...	...	2313	...	...	...	...	...	...	...	...	...	...	...	...

A – CAPELLA – Conveys 🛏 1, 2 cl., 🛏 2 cl. and (2). Also calls at Hildesheim, Braunschweig, Magdeburg, Brandenburg, Potsdam, Berlin Wannsee, Berlin Zoo and Berlin Ostbahnhof (see footnote in Table **905** for timings).
L – From / to Kiel on dates in Table **820**.
N – From / to Innsbruck via Kufstein (Table **951**).
P – To / from Passau (Table **920**).
Q – To Mittenwald via Garmisch on dates in Table **895**.
R – From / to Rostock or Warnemünde on dates in Table **835**.
S – From / to Ostseebad Binz or Stralsund on dates in Tables **844/5**.
T – ①②③④⑦ (not June 18, Oct. 2).
W – ①②③④⑥ (also Oct. 3; not Oct. 2).

b – Also Oct. 3; not Oct. 4.
c – Arrives 0704 (connects with train **1516** in previous column).
d – Also June 19, Oct. 3; not June 21, Oct. 4.
f – Also Oct. 2; not Oct. 3.
j – Arrives 7–10 minutes earlier.
k – Departs up to 6 minutes earlier until July 12.
m – Also June 18, Oct. 2; not June 20, Oct. 3.

n – ⑤–⑦ only.
q – Not Oct. 3.
r – ⑥ (also Oct. 3).
t – Not June 19, Aug. 15.
u – Not June 19.
v – 1113 until July 12; 1104 on ⑥ from July 19.
z – 1344 from Sept. 28.

★ – ①②③④⑥⑦ (also Oct. 3; not Oct. 2). Train number **1715** on ⑥⑦ (also Oct. 3).
♥ – ①②③④⑦ (also June 20, Oct. 3; not June 18, Oct. 2).
⊡ – ⑥⑦ until Nov. 2; ⑥ from Nov. 8. Train number **1526** on ⑥ from July 19. From Mittenwald via Garmisch until Nov. 2 (Table **895**).
‡ – 3–6 minutes later from Sept. 28.
§ – 6–8 minutes earlier from Sept. 28.
⊠ – From Sept. 28 departs Berlin Hbf 0551, Berlin Südkreuz 0557, arrives Leipzig 0659.
✣ – From Oct. 4 departs Leipzig 2101, arrives Berlin Südkreuz 2202, Berlin Hbf 2209.
◇ – Timings Hamburg - Berlin - Leipzig are up to 2–9 minutes earlier from Sept. 28.
⊗ – Timings Berlin - Leipzig are 4–9 minutes earlier from Sept. 28.
⊕ – On ⑦ from Sept. 28 runs with train number **1628** and timings are 8–11 minutes later Leipzig - Berlin Hbf.
♣ – From Sept. 28 timings Leipzig - Berlin Hbf are 7–11 minutes later.
▲ – From Sept. 28 Leipzig a. 0020, d. 0031, Lutherstadt d. 0102, Berlin Südkreuz a. 0136, Berlin Hbf a. 0143.
◐ – Train number **1000** on ⑦. Conveys ✕ on ⑤ (also Oct. 2), 🍸 on ⑦.
¶ – Runs as *IC* **2257** on ⑥.
⊙ – Conveys ✕ from Leipzig.
△ – Operated by Veolia Verkehr. DB tickets **not** valid.
⊖ – See Table **850** for further details.

COTTBUS - LEIPZIG — 852

RE / RB services

km		⚒									
0	**Cottbus** d.	0505	0705	0905	1105	1305	1505	1705	1905	2003	2308
24	Calau (Niederl) d.	0522	0722	0922	1122	1322	1522	1722	1922	2021	2325
46	Finsterwalde d.	0535	0735	0935	1135	1335	1535	1735	1935	2035	2340
56	Doberlug-Kirchhain d.	0543	0743	0943	1143	1343	1543	1743	1943	2043	2347
79	Falkenberg 856 d.	0600	0800	1000	1200	1400	1600	1800	2000	2110	0015
97	Torgau 856 d.	0613	0813	1013	1213	1413	1613	1813	2013	...	...
124	Eilenburg 856 d.	0634	0834	1034	1234	1434	1634	1834	2034	...	...
149	**Leipzig** Hbf 856 a.	0656	0856	1056	1257	1457	1656	1857	2056	...	...

		⚒								
Leipzig Hbf 856 d.	...	*0600*	0705	0905	1105	1305	1505	1705	1905	2105
Eilenburg 856 d.	...	*0628*	0728	0928	1128	1328	1528	1728	1928	2128
Torgau 856 d.	...	*0650*	0750	0950	1150	1350	1550	1750	1950	2150
Falkenberg 856 d.	0523	0726	0804	1004	1204	1404	1604	1804	2004	2204
Doberlug-Kirchhain d.	0546	0746	0818	1018	1218	1418	1618	1818	2018	2218
Finsterwalde d.	0553	0753	0825	1025	1225	1425	1625	1825	2025	2225
Calau (Niederl) d.	0607	0807	0838	1038	1238	1438	1638	1838	2038	2238
Cottbus a.	0626	0826	0855	1055	1255	1455	1655	1855	2055	2255

☛ **Other stopping trains**: Cottbus → Falkenberg at 0603 Ⓐ, 0803, 1203, 1403, 1603 and 1803. Falkenberg → Cottbus at 0423 Ⓐ, 0623 Ⓐ, 0855, 1255, 1455, 1655 and 1855.

STEAM TRAINS IN SACHSEN — 853

km		Ⓐe							A	
0	Radebeul Ost **842 857** d.	0456	...	0826	1020	1258	1428	1726	1858	...
8	Moritzburg d.	0525	...	0854	1050	1326	1458	1754	1925	...
16	Radeburg a.	0546	...	...	1115	...	1523	...	...	...

	Ⓐe								A
Radeburg d.	0611	...	...	...	1136	...	1546	...	...
Moritzburg d.	0634	...	0903	...	1204	1335	1614	1803	1934
Radebeul Ost **842 857** a.	0701	...	0930	...	1231	1402	1641	1831	2001

km		High season ♠ →		🍷	C	🍷		C d		🍷		C d		🍷		C d		C 🍷	Low season ♣ →	🍷	🍷	🍷	🍷	🍷	🍷
0	Zittau d.		0837	0900	1000	1100	...	1200	...	1300	...	1400	...	1500	...	1600	...	1700		0900	...	...	1300	...	...
9	Bertsdorf d.		0931f	0931	1039	1131	1131	1236	1239	1331	1331	1436	1439	1531	1531	1636	1636	1731		0931	1030	1131	1331	1430	1531
12	Kurort Oybin a.		|	0942	1050	1142	|	|	1250	1342	|	|	1450	1542	|	1647	|	1742		0942	|	1142	1342	|	1542
13	Kurort Jonsdorf a.		0942	...	...	...	1142	1247	...	...	1342	1447	...	...	1542	...	1647	...		...	1041	...	...	1441	...

	High season ♠ →		🍷		C d		🍷		C d		🍷		C d		🍷	C d		C 🍷	Low season ♣ →	🍷	🍷	🍷	🍷	🍷	🍷
Kurort Jonsdorf d.		0953	...	...	1107	1153	...	...	1307	1353	...	...	1507	1553	...	...	1719	...		...	1055	...	...	1455	...
Kurort Oybin d.		|	0954	1104	|	|	1154	1304	|	|	1354	1504	|	|	1554	1704	|	1754		0954	|	1154	1354	|	1554
Bertsdorf d.		1004	1006	1115	1118	1204	1206	1315	1318	1404	1406	1515	1518	1604	1606	1718	1733	1806		1005	1105	1206	1405	1505	1606
Zittau a.		...	1033	...	1147	...	1233	...	1347	...	1433	...	1547	...	1633	1747	1800	1833		...	...	1234	...	...	1634

Operators: Radebeul – SDG Sächsische Dampfeisenbahngesellschaft mbH, Lößnitzgrundbahn, Am Bahnhof 1, 01468 Moritzburg. ✆ +49 (0) 35207 89290. www.loessnitzgrundbahn.de
Zittau – SOEG - Sächisch Oberlausitzer Eisenbahngesellschaft mbH, Bahnhofstraße 41, 02763 Zittau. ✆ +49 (0) 3583 540540. www.soeg-zittau.de

A – Apr. 5 - Nov. 2.
C – © Apr. 5 - Nov. 2 (also May 2, 30, June 19, 20, Aug. 15, Oct. 31).
d – Diesel train.
e – Not Feb. 17–28, Apr. 18–25, May 30, July 21 - Aug. 29, Oct. 20–31, Nov. 19.
f – Arrives 0906.
♠ – High season: Feb. 14 - Mar. 2 and Apr. 4 - Nov. 2.
♣ – Low season: Jan. 7 - Feb. 13, Mar. 3 - Apr. 3 and Nov. 28 - Dec. 13 (no service Nov. 3–27).

SEUSSLITZ - DRESDEN - BAD SCHANDAU — 853a

Apr. 11 - Nov. 2, 2014

Subject to alteration on May 1, 15, Aug. 15, 16, 17. Contact the operator for service details on these dates.

	E			A		C	A		E	A	B	H
Seußlitz d.	...	...	...	...	...	...	...	...	...	...	1315	...
Meißen d.	...	...	...	...	...	...	0930	...	...	...	1445	1445
Radebeul d.	...	...	...	...	...	...	1115	...	...	...	1630	1630
Dresden ⊡ d.	...	0930	1000	1015	...	1200	1315	1400	...	1600	1800	1800
Pillnitz d.	...	1100	1150	|	1230	1350	1500	1550	1700	1750	...	...
Pirna d.	1015	1205	...	1240	1330	...	...	...	1805	...	...	...
Königstein d.	1215	1415	...	1445	1530	...	...	...	...	...	...	...
Bad Schandau a.	1300	...	...	1545	1615	...	...	...	...	...	...	...

	B	H				C	A	E			A	A
Bad Schandau d.	...	...	...	0930	...	...	...	1320	...	...	...	1615
Königstein d.	...	...	...	1000	...	...	...	1350	...	1450	...	1645
Pirna d.	...	...	...	1120	...	...	...	1515	...	1610	...	1800
Pillnitz d.	...	...	...	1200	1205	1405	1515	1555	1605	1650	1805	1845
Dresden ⊡ d.	0945	0945	...	...	1305	1505	1630	...	1705	1755	1905	1945
Radebeul d.	1045	1045	...	...	...	...	1730	...	...	...	...	...
Meißen d.	1145	1145	...	...	...	...	1830	...	...	...	...	...
Seußlitz a.	1240	...	...	...	...	...	...	...	...	...	...	...

A – May 2 - Oct. 5.
B – ⑤–⑦ May 2 - Oct. 5 (also May 29, June 9).
C – ⑤–⑦ Apr. 11–27 (also Apr. 21); daily May 2 - Oct. 5; ⑤–⑦ Oct. 10 - Nov. 2.
E – May 2 - Oct. 5 (not July 14, 28, Aug. 11, 25).
H – ②–⑦ May 2 - Oct. 5 (also June 9).
⊡ – Dresden Terrassenufer.

Operator: Sächsische Dampfschiffahrts GmbH & Co. Conti Elbschiffahrts KG. Hertha-Lindner Straße 10, D-01067 Dresden. ✆ +49 (0) 351 866 090.

FORST - COTTBUS - GÖRLITZ - ZITTAU — 854

ODEG ★ 2nd class only

km		Ⓐe	Ⓐ	Ⓐe	⚒r								Ⓐe											Ⓐe		
0	**Cottbus** d.	...	0504	0504	...	...	0604	0704	0804	0904	1004	1104	1104	1204	1304	1404	1504	1604	1704	1804	1904	2004	2104	2204	...	2304
24	Spremberg d.	...	0522	0522	...	...	0622	0722	0822	0922	1022	1121	1122	1222	1322	1422	1522	1622	1722	1822	1921	2022	2122	2222	...	2322
42	Weißwasser d.	0436	...	0536	0536	...	0636	0736	0836	0936	1036	...	1136	1236	1336	1436	1536	1636	1736	1836	...	2036	2136	2236	...	2340
72	Horka d.	0500	...	0600	0600	...	0700	0800	0900	1000	1100	...	1200	1300	1400	1500	1600	1700	1800	1900	...	2100	2200	2300	...	0001
93	**Görlitz** a.	0516	...	0616	0616	...	0716	0816	0916	1016	1116	...	1216	1316	1416	1516	1616	1716	1816	1916	...	2116	2216	2316	...	0016
93	**Görlitz** d.	0518	...	0618	0618	...	0720	0820	0920	1020	1120	...	1220	1320	1420	1520	1620	1720	1820	1920	...	2120	2220	...	...	...
127	**Zittau** a.	0553	...	0653	0653	...	0755	0855	0955	1055	1155	...	1255	1355	1455	1555	1655	1755	1855	1955	...	2155	2255	...	...	...

	Ⓐ							Ⓐe												Ⓐe
Zittau d.	...	...	0500r	0600	0702	0802	0902	1003	...	1102	1202	1302	1402	1502	1602	1702	...	1902	2102	2202
Görlitz a.	...	...	0538r	0638	0740	0840	0940	1039	...	1140	1240	1340	1440	1540	1640	1740	...	1940	2140	2240
Görlitz d.	0345	0444	0544	0644	0744	0844	0944	1045	...	1144	1244	1344	1444	1544	1644	1744	...	1944	2144	2244
Horka d.	0400	0500	0600	0700	0800	0900	1000	1101	...	1200	1300	1400	1500	1600	1700	1800	...	2000	2200	2300
Weißwasser d.	0424	0521j	0621	0721	0821	0921	1021	1121	...	1221	1321	1421	1521	1621	1721	1821	...	2021	2221	2321
Spremberg d.	0438	0538	0638	0738	0838	0938	1038	1138	1138	1238	1338	1438	1538	1638	1738	1838	1938	2038	2238	...
Cottbus a.	0455	0555	0655	0755	0855	0955	1055	1155	1155	1255	1355	1455	1555	1655	1755	1855	1955	2055	2255	...

e – Not Oct. 31, Nov. 19
j – 0524 on ⑥.
r – ⚒ (not Oct. 31, Nov. 19).

★ – Ostdeutsche Eisenbahn GmbH ✆ +49 (0) 3581 764 89 10. www.odeg.de

FORST (Lausitz) - **COTTBUS** and v.v. *22 km.* Journey time: 18 minutes. See also Table **1086**.
From Forst at 0433 Ⓐ, 0533, 0633 and hourly until 2133. **From Cottbus** at 0507 Ⓐ, 0607, 0707, 0807, 0907, 1007, 1104, 1207 and hourly until 2107; then 2207 ①②③④⑦ and 2307 ⑤⑥.

DRESDEN - GÖRLITZ and ZITTAU — 855

RE / RB services

km		©z	Ⓐe	Ⓐe	⚒e	⚒e																		A	B	
0	**Dresden** Hbf d.	0048	0413	0413	0537	0609	0637	0709	0809	0909	1009	1109	1209	1309	1409	1509	1609	1709	1809	1909	2009	2137	2237	2309	2330	2337
4	Dresden Neustadt d.	0054	0420	0420	0544	0615	0644	0715	0815	0915	1015	1115	1215	1315	1415	1515	1615	1715	1815	1915	2015	2144	2244	2315	2338	2344
41	Bischofswerda d.	0129	0459	0502	0621	0645	0719	0745	0845	0945	1045	1145	1245	1345	1445	1545	1645	1745	1845	1945	2045	2215	2324	2345	0007	0019
79	Ebersbach (Sachs) d.	|	0538	|	0701	|	|	0816	|	1016	|	1216	|	1416	|	1616	|	1816	|	2016	|	2245	|	0016	0035	|
83	Neugersdorf d.	|	0542	|	0705	|	|	0820	|	1020	|	1220	|	1420	|	1620	|	1820	|	2020	|	2249	|	0020	0039	|
105	**Zittau** a.	|	0605	|	0728	|	|	0839	|	1039	|	1239	|	1439	|	1639	|	1839	|	2039	|	2308	|	0039	0058	|
	Liberec **1117** a.	|	...	|	...	|	|	0918	|	...	|	1321	|	...	|	1718	|	...	|	2118	|	...	|	...	...	|
	Bautzen d.	0144	...	0517	...	0658	0734	T	0858	...	1058	...	1258	...	1458	T	1658	...	1858	...	2058	...	2339	...	...	0033
	Löbau (Sachs) d.	0201	...	0536	...	0712	0754	...	0912	...	1112	...	1312	...	1512	...	1712	...	1912	...	2112	...	2358	...	...	0052
	Görlitz a.	0219	...	0557	...	0727	0814	...	0927	...	1127	...	1327	...	1527	...	1727	...	1927	...	2127	...	0019	...	...	0113
	Wroclaw Gł **1085** a.	...	...	...	...	...	...	...	1134	...	...	...	1533	...	...	...	...	...	2133	...	...	...	...	...	...	...

km		⚒e		⚒e		⚒e																				
	Wroclaw Gł **1085** d.	...	...	...	...	...	...	...	0639	...	...	...	...	...	...	1239	...	...	...	...	...	...	1839	...	...	...
0	**Görlitz** d.	...	0445	...	0543	0643	...	0745	0843	...	0945	1025	...	1225	...	1443	...	1625	...	1825	...	1945	2043	...	...	2245
24	Löbau (Sachs) d.	...	0506	...	0558	0658	...	0806	0858	...	1006	1040	...	1240	...	1458	...	1640	...	1840	...	2006	2058	...	...	2306
46	Bautzen d.	...	0524	...	0612	0713	...	0824	0912	...	1024	1054	...	1254	T	1512	...	1654	...	1854	...	2024	2112	...	T	2324
	Liberec **1117** d.	...	|	...	|	|	...	|	|	0838	|	|	...	|	1238	|	...	|	1635	|	...	|	|	...	2035	|
	Zittau d.	0354	|	0514	|	|	0721	|	|	0921	|	|	1121	|	1321	|	1521	|	1721	|	1921	|	|	2031	2121	|
	Neugersdorf d.	0417	|	0533	|	|	0740	|	|	0940	|	|	1140	|	1340	|	1540	|	1740	|	1940	|	|	2055	2140	|
	Ebersbach (Sachs) d.	0423	|	0537	|	|	0745	|	|	0945	|	|	1145	|	1345	|	1545	|	1745	|	1945	|	|	2101	2145	|
65	Bischofswerda d.	0500	0540	0607	0624	0724	0815	0840	0924	1015	1040	1107	1215	1307	1415	1524	1615	1707	1815	1907	2015	2040	2124	2140	2215	2340
102	Dresden Neustadt a.	0533	0614	0635	0651	0751	0842	0913	0951	1042	1113	1134	1242	1334	1442	1551	1642	1734	1842	1934	2042	2113	2151	2213	2242	0013
106	**Dresden** Hbf a.	0541	0621	0642	0659	0758	0849	0920	0957	1049	1120	1143	1249	1343	1449	1557	1649	1743	1849	1943	2049	2120	2157	2220	2249	0020

– ①–④ (also Oct. 3, 31; not Oct. 2, 30).
– ⑤–⑦ (also Oct. 2, 30; not Oct. 3, 31).
– To / from Tanwald (Table **1141**) on ⑥⑦ (also Oct. 28, Nov. 17).
e – Not Oct. 31, Nov. 19.
z – Also Oct. 31, Nov. 19.

☛ **Other stopping trains**: Dresden Hbf → Görlitz at 0537 ⑥, 0837, 1037, 1237, 1437, 1637, 1837 and 2037. Görlitz → Dresden Hbf at 0605, 1145, 1345, 1545 and 1745. Dresden Hbf → Zittau at 0737, 0937, 1137, 1337, 1537, 1737 and 1937. Zittau → Dresden Hbf at 0631, 0831, 1031, 1231, 1431, 1631 and 1831.

856 DRESDEN and LEIPZIG - RUHLAND - COTTBUS and HOYERSWERDA

RE services

km	km									⊠	⊠													
	0	**Dresden** Hbf .. 842 843 857 d.	...	...	0550	...	...	0650	0750	...		1550	...	...	1650	1750	...	...	1850	1950	...	...	2050	2150
	18	Coswig .... 842 843 857 d.	...	...	0608	...	...	0708	0808	...		1608	...	...	1708	1808	...	...	1908	2008	...	...	2108	2208
0		**Geithain** .... 874 d.	...	...	|	...	0502	|	|	...		|	...	1502	|	|	...	1702	|	|	...	1902	|	|
45		Leipzig-Connewitz ★ .... d.	...	...	|	...	0550	|	|	...	each train	|	...	1550	|	|	...	1750	|	|	...	1950	|	|
51		**Leipzig** Hbf ★ ... 852 874 d.	...	...	|	...	0600	|	|	...		|	...	1600	|	|	...	1800	|	|	...	2000	|	|
76		Eilenburg .... 852 d.	...	...	|	...	0628	|	|	...	runs every	|	...	1628	|	|	...	1828	|	|	...	2028	|	|
103		Torgau .... 852 d.	...	...	|	...	0650	|	|	...		|	...	1650	|	|	...	1850	|	|	...	2050	|	|
121		Falkenberg (Elster) .... 852 d.	0411e	E	|	0611e	0712t	|	|	0811r	two hours	|	1611b	1712t	|	|	1811b	1912t	|	|	2011e	2112t	|	|
145		Elsterwerda-Biehla .... d.	0430e	0522	|	0630e	0734	|	|	0830r		|	1630b	1734	|	|	1830b	1934	|	|	2030e	2134	|	|
171	73	Ruhland .... a.	0452e	0553	0655	0652e	0756	0757	0855	0852r	until	1655	1652b	1756	1757	1855	1852b	1956	1957	2055	2052e	2156	2157	2255
171	73	Ruhland .... d.	0506	0558	0656	0706	0802	0800	0856	0906		1656	1706	1802	1800	1856	1906	2002	2000	2056	2106	2202	2200	2256
196		**Hoyerswerda** .... a.	|	|	0719	|	0824	|	0919	|		1719	|	1824	|	1919	|	2024	|	2119	|	2224	|	2319
	86	Senftenberg .... d.	0517	0610	...	0717	...	0810	...	0917		...	1717	...	1810	...	1917	...	2010	...	2117	...	2210	...
	120	**Cottbus** .... 852 a.	0548	0644	...	0749	...	0839	...	0948		...	1748	...	1839	...	1948	...	2039	...	2148	...	2239	...

	Ⓐ								⊡		⊡													
Cottbus .... 852 d.	0415	...	0515	...	0607	...	0715	...	0807v	...		1515	...	1606	...	1715	...	1806	...	1915	...	2006	...	2206
Senftenberg .... d.	0446	...	0544	...	0638	...	0744	...	0838	...		1544	...	1638	...	1744	...	1838	...	1944	...	2038	...	2239
Hoyerswerda .... d.	|	0440	|	0533	|	0640	|	0733	|	0840		|	1533	|	1640	|	1733	|	1840	|	1933	|	2040	|
Ruhland .... a.	0457	0501	0553	0554	0648	0701	0753	0756	0848	0901	each train	1553	1556	1648	1701	1753	1756	1848	1901	1953	1956	2048	2101	2249
Ruhland .... d.	0505	0502	0602	0601	0705e	0702	0802	0801	0905r	0902		1602	1601	1705b	1702	1802	1801	1905b	1902	2002	2001	2105e	2102	2259
Elsterwerda-Biehla .... d.	0528	|	|	0625	0728e	|	|	0825	0928r	|	runs every	|	1625	1728b	|	|	1825	1928b	|	|	2025	2128e	|	2322
Falkenberg (Elster) ..... 852 d.	0549	|	|	0658t	0749e	|	|	0858t	0949r	|		|	1658t	1749b	|	|	1858t	1949b	|	|	2058t	2149e	|	L
Torgau .... 852 d.	...	|	|	0712	...	|	|	0912	...	|	two hours	|	1712	...	|	|	1912	...	|	|	2112	...	|	...
Eilenburg .... 852 d.	...	|	|	0734	...	|	|	0934	...	|		|	1734	...	|	|	1934	...	|	|	2134	...	|	...
Leipzig Hbf ★ .... 852 874 d.	...	|	|	0800	...	|	|	1000	...	|	until	|	1800	...	|	|	2000	...	|	|	2200	...	|	...
Leipzig-Connewitz ★ .... d.	...	|	|	0810	...	|	|	1010	...	|		|	1810	...	|	|	2010	...	|	|	2210	...	|	...
Geithain .... 874 a.	...	|	|	0856	...	|	|	1056	...	|		|	1856	...	|	|	2056	...	|	|	2256	...	|	...
Coswig .... 842 843 857 d.	...	0551	0651	...	...	0751	0851	...	...	0951		1651	...	...	1751	1851	...	...	1951	2051	...	...	2151	...
Dresden Hbf ... 842 843 857 a.	...	0608	0708	...	...	0808	0908	...	...	1008		1708	...	...	1808	1908	...	...	2008	2108	...	...	2208	...

E – From Elsterwerda (d. 0519).
L – To Elsterwerda (a. 2326).
b – Ⓑ only.
e – Ⓐ only.
r – ⚒ only.
t – Arrives 8–10 minutes earlier.
v – Subsequent departures are at 1006, 1206 and 1406.
⊠ – The 1211 and 1411 from Falkenberg run daily throughout.
⊡ – The 1206 and 1406 from Cottbus run daily throughout.
★ – Trains also call at Leipzig MDR, Bayerischer Bahnhof, Wilhelm-Leuschner-Platz and Markt.

857 BAD SCHANDAU - DRESDEN - MEISSEN - LEIPZIG

RB / S-Bahn services

km	S-Bahn					✥		✥			①–⑥	⑦	①–⑥	⑦	①–⑤	⑥	⑦	①–⑤	
0	**Bad Schandau** ⊡ ..... 1100 d.	...	0445e	0515	0545r	0615	0645		2011	2045	2115	2115	2145	2145	2215	2215	2215	...	2315
23	Pirna .... d.	0438	0508	0538	0608	0638	0708	and at	2038	2108	2138	2138	2208	2208	2238	2238	2238	2308	2338
40	**Dresden** Hbf 842/3 856 1100 d.	0501	0531	0601	0631	0701	0731	the same	2101	2131	2201	2201	2231	2231	2301	2301	2301	2331	0001
44	**Dresden** Neustadt .. 842 856 d.	0508	0538	0608	0638	0708	0738	minutes	2108	2138	2208	2208	2238	2237	2308	2308	2307	2338	0007
50	Radebeul Ost .... d.	0516k	0546	0616	0646	0716	0746	past each	2116	2146	2216	2216	2246	2301*	2316	2316	2331*	2346	0031*
58	Coswig .... 842/3 856 d.	0527k	0557	0627	0657	0727	0757	hour until	2127	2157	2227	2226	2257	2321*	2327	2326	2351*	2357	0051*
68	**Meißen** .... a.	0535k	0605	0635	0705	0735	0805		2135	2205	2235	2252*	2305	2339*	2335	2352*	0009*	0005	0110*

S-Bahn	Ⓐd										⑦			⑥	①–⑤	⑦ 🚌	⑥ 🚌	①–⑤	
Meißen .... d.	...	...	0449k	0519k	0549	0619		2049	2119	2149	2219	2219k	2249k	2319	2319	2316	...	2349	...
Coswig .... 842/3 856 d.	...	0428k	0458k	0528	0558	0628	and at	2058	2128	2158	2233	2228k	2258k	2329	2328	2335	2335	2358	...
Radebeul Ost .... d.	...	0440k	0510k	0540	0610	0640	the same	2110	2140	2210	|	2240k	2310k	|	2340	2354	2354	0010	...
Dresden Neustadt .... 842 856 d.	...	0451	0521	0551	0621	0651	minutes	2121	2151	2221	|	2251	2321	|	2351	0013	0013	0021	0021
Dresden Hbf 842/3 856 1100 d.	0429	0459	0529	0559	0629	0659	past each	2129	2159	2229	2249	2259	2329	2342	2357	...	...	0029	0029
Pirna .... d.	0451	0521	0551	0621	0651	0721	hour until	2151	2221	2250	...	2321	2350	...	...	...	...	0051	0051
Bad Schandau ⊡ ...... 1100 a.	0513	0543	0613r	0643	0713	0743		2213	2243	...	...	2343	...	...	...	...	...	0113	0113

Service alterations until Aug. 23

Services Bad Schandau - Pirna and v.v. are subject to alteration Mar. 16 - Aug. 23. Certain trains are replaced by 🚌 between Bad Schandau and Pirna with journey times extended by up to 15 minutes (earlier departures from Bad Schandau). Southbound rail services between Pirna and Bad Schandau are also subject to extended journey times during this period.

km	SEE NOTE ⊠									⑤⑥	
0	**Meißen** .... d.	...	0720e	0920	1120	1320	1520	1720	1920	2120	...
21	Nossen .... d.	0555e	0755	0955	1155	1355	1555	1755	1955	2155	...
29	Roßwein .... d.	0605e	0805	1005	1205	1405	1605	1805	2005	2205	...
40	Döbeln Hbf .... d.	0624	0824	1024	1224	1424	1624	1824	2024	2224	2224
53	Leisnig .... d.	0636	0836	1036	1236	1436	1636	1836	2036	2236	2236
68	Großbothen .... d.	0653	0853	1053	1253	1453	1653	1853	2053	2251	2251
75	Grimma ob Bf .... d.	0700	0900	1100	1300	1500	1700	1900	2100	2258	2258
106	**Leipzig** Hbf .... a.	0736	0936	1136	1336	1536	1736	1936	2136	2333	2333

SEE NOTE ⊠								Ⓐe		⑤⑥	
Leipzig Hbf .... d.	0608	0808	1008	1208	1408	1608	1808	1908	2108	2108	2310
Grimma ob Bf .... d.	0645	0845	1045	1245	1445	1645	1845	1945	2145	2145	2353
Großbothen .... d.	0652	0852	1052	1252	1452	1652	1852	1952	2152	2152	2359
Leisnig .... d.	0706	0906	1106	1306	1506	1706	1906	2006	2206	2206	0014
Döbeln Hbf .... d.	0722	0922	1122	1322	1522	1722	1922	2020	2220	2222	0027
Roßwein .... d.	0736	0936	1136	1336	1536	1736	1936	...	...	2236	...
Nossen .... d.	0748	0948	1148	1348	1548	1748	1948	...	...	2245	...
Meißen .... a.	0815	1015	1215	1415	1615	1815	2015	...	...	...	...

d – Ⓐ (not Oct. 31, Nov. 19; runs daily until Aug. 23).
e – Ⓐ (not Oct. 31, Nov. 19).
k – ①–⑥ only.
r – ⚒ (not Oct. 31, Nov. 19; runs daily until Aug. 23).
* – By 🚌.
⊠ – **Service from July 7**. Until July 6 trains are replaced by 🚌 Leisnig - Großbothen and v.v. (journey times extended by up to 38 minutes; earlier departures Meißen - Leisnig).
✥ – Bad Schandau d. 0811 / 1011 / 1211 / 1411 / 1611 / 1811 (not at 15 minutes past the hour).
⊡ – A frequent ferry services links the railway station with Bad Schandau town centre. **Operator**: Oberelbische Verkehrsgesellschaf Pirna - Sebnitz mbH. ✆ +49 (0) 3501 7920.

857a DRESDEN - DRESDEN FLUGHAFEN ✈

S-Bahn

km									①–⑥	⑦	①–⑥	⑦
0	**Dresden** Hbf .... d.	0408	0438	0508	0538	0608	and every	2138	2208	2238	2244	2308	2314
4	**Dresden** Neustadt ...... d.	0415	0445	0515	0545	0615	30 minutes	2145	2215	2245	2251	2315	2321
15	**Dresden** Flughafen ✈ a.	0429	0500	0530	0602	0632	until	2202	2229	2302	2304	2332	2334

Dresden Flughafen ✈ .... d.	0444	0514	and every	2314	2344
Dresden Neustadt .... a.	0456	0526	30 minutes	2326	2356
Dresden Hbf .... a.	0504	0534	until	2334	0004

858 CHEMNITZ / ZWICKAU - GERA - ERFURT

RB / RE services

km		Ⓒz‡	⚒r‡	Ⓐr‡		⚒rG	G		G		G		G		G		G		G	G				‡
0	**Chemnitz** Hbf .... 880 d.	...	...	...	...	*0530*	...	...	*0730*	...	*0930*	...	*1130*	...	*1330*	...	*1530*	...	*1730*	...	...	*1930*	...	...
32	Glauchau (Sachs) .... 880 d.	...	...	...	...	0607	...	...	0807	...	1007	...	1207	...	1407	...	1607	...	1807	...	...	2007	...	...
	Zwickau (Sachs) Hbf .. 881 d.	...	...	...	0603	|	...	0803	|	1003	|	1203	|	1403	|	1603	|	1803	|	...	2003	|	...	...
	Werdau .... 881 d.	...	...	...	0611	|	...	0811	|	1011	|	1211	|	1411	|	1611	|	1811	|	...	2011	|	...	...
48	Gößnitz .... 881 a.	...	...	...	0625	0621	...	0825	0821	1025	1021	1225	1221	1425	1421	1625	1621	1825	1821	...	2025	2021	...	...
48	Gößnitz .... d.	...	...	...	▬	0628	0628	▬	0828	▬	1028	▬	1228	▬	1428	▬	1628	▬	1828	...	...	2028	...	...
83	**Gera** Hbf .... a.	...	...	...	...	0659	0659	...	0859	...	1059	...	1259	...	1459	...	1659	...	1859	...	...	2059	...	...
83	**Gera** Hbf .... d.	...	0432	0508	0559	0705	0705	0805	0905	1005	1105	1205	1305	1405	1505	1605	1705	1805	1905	2005	...	2105	2205	2345
123	Jena-Göschwitz .... d.	0413	0506	0543	0627	0733	0733	0833	0933	1033	1133	1233	1333	1433	1533	1633	1733	1833	1933	2033	...	2133	2233	0018
128	**Jena** West .... d.	0419	0512	0550	0633	0739	0739	0839	0939	1039	1139	1239	1339	1439	1539	1639	1739	1839	1939	2039	...	2139	2239	0024
151	Weimar .... 849 850 d.	0436	0533	0612	0652	0757	0757	0857	0957	1057	1157	1257	1357	1457	1557	1657	1757	1857	1957	2057	...	2157	2257	0044
172	**Erfurt** Hbf .... 849 850 a.	0450	*0557*	0628	0705	0810	0810	0910	1010	1110	1210	1310	1410	1510	1610	1710	1810	1910	2010	2110	...	2210	2310	*010*

	‡		†z	⚒r	Ⓐr			G		G		G		G		G		G		G	ⒷG		G	G
Erfurt Hbf .... 849 850 d.	0031	...	0439	0449	0541	...	0645	0749	0849	0949	1049	1149	1249	1349	1449	1549	1649	1749	1849	1949	1949	2049	2149	225
Weimar .... 849 850 d.	0050	...	0452	0504	0555	...	0700	0805	0905	1005	1105	1205	1305	1405	1505	1605	1705	1805	1905	2005	2005	2105	2205	230
Jena West .... d.	0110	...	0509	0521	0615	...	0723	0823	0923	1023	1123	1223	1323	1423	1523	1623	1723	1823	1923	2023	2023	2123	2223	232
Jena-Göschwitz .... d.	0116	...	0514	0526	0622	...	0728	0828	0928	1028	1128	1228	1328	1428	1528	1628	1728	1828	1928	2028	2028	2128	2228	233
Gera Hbf .... a.	0146	...	0542	0553	0650	...	0756	0856	0956	1056	1156	1256	1356	1456	1556	1656	1756	1856	1956	2056	2056	2156	2256	235
Gera Hbf .... d.	...	...	0549	...	0658	0658	▬	0858	▬	1058	▬	1258	▬	1458	▬	1658	▬	1858	▬	...	2058	▬	...	...
Gößnitz .... a.	...	...	0622	...	0728	0728	...	0928	...	1128	...	1328	...	1528	...	1728	...	1928	...	...	2128	...	...	...
Gößnitz .... 881 d.	...	...	...	...	0735	0735	0734	0935	0934	1135	1134	1335	1334	1535	1534	1735	1734	1935	1934	...	2135	2134	...	...
Werdau .... 881 d.	...	...	...	...	|	|	0748	|	0948	|	1148	|	1348	|	1548	|	1748	|	1948	...	|	2148	...	...
Zwickau (Sachs) Hbf ... 881 a.	...	...	...	...	|	|	0756	|	0956	|	1156	|	1356	|	1556	|	1756	|	1956	...	|	2156	...	...
Glauchau (Sachs) .... 880 a.	...	...	...	...	0748	0748	...	0948	...	1148	...	1348	...	1548	...	1748	...	1948	...	...	2148	...	...	...
Chemnitz Hbf .... 880 a.	...	...	...	...	*0825*	*0825*	...	*1025*	...	*1225*	...	*1425*	...	*1625*	...	*1825*	...	*2025*	...	...	*2225*	...	...	...

G – To / from Göttingen (Table 865).
r – Not Oct. 31.
z – Also Oct. 31.
‡ – Operated by Erfurter Bahn.

German national public holidays are on Jan. 1, Apr. 18, 21, May 1, 29, June 9, Oct. 3, Dec. 25, 26

RB services

BRAUNSCHWEIG - BAD HARZBURG, GOSLAR and HERZBERG — 859

km		Ⓐ								Ⓒ	Ⓐ			Ⓐ										Ⓑ		
0	**Braunschweig** Hbf ... d.	0513	0626	0644	0826	0907	1026	1107	1226	1307	1322	1426	1507	1551	1626	1638	1707	1826	1907	2026	2107	...	...	2222	...	...
12	Wolfenbüttel ... d.	0522	0636	0653	0836	0916	1036	1116	1236	1316	1331	1436	1516	1601	1636	1650	1716	1836	1916	2036	2116	...	...	2231	...	...
39	Vienenburg ... **860** d.	0548	0702	0721	0902	0942	1102	1142	1302	1342	1356	1502	1542	1627	1702	1716	1742	1902	1942	2102	2142	2153	...	2256	...	...
47	**Bad Harzburg 860** a.	|	0711	|	0911	|	1111	|	1311	|	|	1511	|	1635	1711	|	|	1911	|	2111	|	2201	...	|	...	...
58	**Goslar** ... **860** a.	0601	...	0734	...	0955	...	1155	...	1355	1410	...	1555	...	...	1729	1755	...	1955	...	2155	...	...	2310	...	...

km		Ⓐ	Ⓐ	⚒	⚒	⚒							Ⓒ	Ⓐ												
0	**Goslar** ... **860** d.	0452	0526	...	0627	...	0809	...	1009	...	1209	...	1409	1423	...	1609	...	1809	...	2009	...	...	2214	...	...	...
	Bad Harzburg 860 d.	|	0547	0547	|	0651	|	0851	|	1051	|	1251	|	|	1451	|	1651	|	1851	|	2051	...	|	...	...	...
13	Vienenburg ... **860** d.	0505	0555	0555	0639	0701	0821	0901	1021	1101	1221	1301	1421	1436	1501	1621	1701	1821	1901	2021	2101	...	2226	...	...	...
40	Wolfenbüttel ... d.	0529	0620	0620	0703	0726	0846	0926	1046	1126	1246	1326	1446	1500	1526	1646	1726	1846	1926	2046	2126	...	2251	...	...	...
52	**Braunschweig** Hbf ... a.	0538	0629	0629	0712	0736	0855	0936	1055	1136	1255	1336	1455	1509	1536	1655	1736	1855	1936	2055	2136	...	2300	...	...	...

km		Ⓐ	Ⓐ			⚒			⚒			⚒			Ⓐ			Ⓐ			Ⓐ			Ⓐ		B
0	**Braunschweig** Hbf ... d.	0503	0603	0703	0803	0803	0903	1003	1003	1103	1203	1203	1303	1403	1403	1503	1603	1603	1703	1803	1803	1903	2005	2005	...	2205
31	Salzgitter-Ringelheim . d.	0529	0629	0729	0829	0829	0929	1029	1029	1129	1229	1229	1329	1429	1429	1529	1629	1629	1729	1829	1829	1929	2029	2029	...	2226
52	Seesen ... d.	0545	0645	0745	0844	0845	0945	1044	1045	1145	1244	1245	1345	1444	1445	1545	1644	1645	1745	1844	1845	1945	2044	2045	...	2242
71	Osterode (Harz) Mitte . d.	0607	0707	0807	...	0907	1007	...	1107	1207	...	1309	1407	...	1507	1607	...	1707	1807	...	1907	2007	...	2107	...	...
83	**Herzberg** (Harz) ... a.	0621	0721	0821	...	0921	1021	...	1121	1221	...	1325	1421	...	1521	1621	...	1721	1821	...	1921	2021	...	2121	...	...

	ⒶB	Ⓐ	Ⓐ	ⒸB	Ⓐ	Ⓒ	⚒			⚒			⚒			Ⓐ			Ⓐ			Ⓐ			Ⓐ	
Herzberg (Harz) ... d.	...	0534	0634	...	0730	0734	0834	...	0934	1034	...	1134	1234	...	1334	1434	...	1534	1634	...	1734	1834	...	1934	2034	...
Osterode (Harz) Mitte . d.	...	0547	0647	...	0745	0747	0847	...	0947	1047	...	1147	1247	...	1347	1447	...	1547	1647	...	1747	1847	...	1947	2047	...
Seesen ... d.	0513	0613	0713	0713	0813	0813	0913	0913	1013	1113	1113	1213	1313	1313	1413	1513	1513	1613	1713	1713	1813	1913	1913	2013	2113	2113
Salzgitter-Ringelheim . d.	0529	0629	0729	0729	0829	0829	0929	0929	1029	1129	1129	1229	1329	1329	1429	1529	1529	1629	1729	1729	1829	1929	1929	2029	2129	2129
Braunschweig Hbf ... a.	0551	0651	0751	0751	0851	0851	0951	0951	1051	1151	1151	1251	1351	1351	1451	1551	1551	1651	1751	1751	1851	1951	1951	2051	2151	2151

km		Ⓐ	Ⓐ																B	¶	
0	**Bad Harzburg** ... **860** d.	...	0618	0743	0820	0936	1022	1136	1222	1336	1422	1536	1622	1736	1822	1936	2022	...	...	...	...
11	Goslar ... **860** d.	0532	0632	0757	0835	0957	1035	1157	1235	1357	1435	1557	1635	1757	1835	1957	2035	...	...	...	...
34	Seesen ... d.	0551	0651	0817	0854	1017	1054	1217	1254	1417	1454	1617	1654	1817	1854	2017	2054	...	2243	...	...
48	Bad Gandersheim ... d.	0601	0701	0827	0904	1027	1104	1227	1304	1427	1504	1627	1704	1827	1904	2027	2104	...	2253	...	...
54	**Kreiensen** ... a.	0606	0706	0832	0911	1032	1111	1232	1311	1432	1511	1632	1711	1832	1911	2032	2111	...	2301	...	...
54	**Kreiensen** ... **903** d.	*0623*	*0723*	0839	*0919*	1039	*1119*	1239	*1319*	1439	*1519*	1639	*1719*	1839	*1919*	2039	*2119*	...	...	2323	...
73	Northeim (Han) ... **903** d.	*0637*	*0737*	0855	*0933*	1055	*1133*	1255	*1333*	1455	*1533*	1655	*1733*	1855	*1933*	2055	*2133*	...	...	2337	...
93	**Göttingen** ... **903** a.	*0649*	*0749*	0909	*0947*	1109	*1147*	1309	*1347*	1509	*1547*	1709	*1747*	1909	*1947*	2109	*2147*	...	...	2349	...

B – 🚌 Braunschweig - Seesen - Kreiensen and v.v.

¶ – Operated by *metronom*.

	⚒¶	ⒶB	Ⓐ	¶	Ⓐ	ⒸB	⚒														
Göttingen ... **903** d.	0409	...	*0504*	0607	...	...	*0707*	*0809*	0848	*1009*	1048	*1209*	1248	*1409*	1448	*1609*	1648	*1809*	1848	*2009*	2051
Northeim (Han) ... **903** d.	0423	...	*0517*	0620	...	...	*0720*	*0823*	0902	*1023*	1102	*1223*	1302	*1423*	1502	*1623*	1702	*1823*	1902	*2023*	2105
Kreiensen ... **903** a.	0437	...	*0530*	0633	...	...	*0733*	*0837*	0917	*1037*	1117	*1237*	1317	*1437*	1517	*1637*	1717	*1837*	1917	*2037*	2120
Kreiensen ... d.	...	0457	0542	...	0641	0657	0750	0842	0923	1042	1123	1242	1323	1442	1523	1642	1723	1842	1923	2042	2123
Bad Gandersheim ... d.	...	0502	0548	...	0646	0702	0755	0848	0928	1048	1128	1248	1328	1448	1528	1648	1728	1848	1928	2048	2128
Seesen ... d.	...	0512	0558	...	0657	0712	0806	0858	0939	1058	1139	1258	1339	1458	1539	1658	1739	1858	1939	2058	2139
Goslar ... **860** a.	...	...	0617	...	0716	...	0825	0917	0957	1117	1157	1317	1357	1517	1557	1717	1757	1917	1957	2117	2157
Bad Harzburg ... **860** a.	...	...	0633	...	0742	...	0840	0930	1017	1130	1217	1330	1417	1530	1617	1730	1817	1930	2017	2130	...

DB (*RE* services); *HEX* ◇

HANNOVER - BAD HARZBURG - HALLE — 860

km		Ⓐ	Ⓒ	Ⓐ	Ⓒ	Ⓐ	⚒	⚒										Ⓐ		Ⓐ	Ⓒ		Ⓐ		Ⓒ	Ⓐ
0	**Hannover** Hbf ... d.	...	...	...	...	...	0546	...	...	0651	...	0748	0855	...	0948	1055	...	...	1148	1255	1255	...	...	1348	1449	1449
36	**Hildesheim** Hbf ... d.	...	...	...	...	...	0614	...	...	0721	...	0814	0921	...	1014	1121	...	...	1214	1321	1321	...	...	1414	1519	1519
70	Salzgitter-Ringelheim d.	...	...	...	...	...	0643	...	...	0744	...	0843	0944	...	1043	1144	...	...	1243	1344	1344	...	...	1443	1544	1544
89	Goslar **859** ... d.	...	...	...	...	0610	0658	0703	...	0759	...	0858	0959	...	1058	1159	...	...	1258	1359	1359	...	...	1458	1559	1559
100	**Bad Harzburg 859** ... a.	...	...	...	...	|	0711	|	...	0809	...	0911	1009	...	1111	1209	...	...	1311	1409	1409	...	...	1511	1609	1609
100	**Bad Harzburg 859** ... d.	...	...	...	...	*0547*	...	*0651*	...	0815	*0851*	▬	1015	*1051*	▬	1215	*1251*	...	▬	1415	1415	*1451*	...	▬	1615	1615
108	Vienenburg **859** ... d.	...	...	...	...	0620	...	0713	...	0824	0911	...	1024	1111	...	1224	1311	...	...	1424	1424	1511	...	...	1624	1624
124	Ilsenburg ... d.	...	...	0447	0623	0631	...	0727	...	0835	0927	...	1035	1127	...	1235	1327	...	...	1435	1435	1527	...	...	1635	1635
133	Wernigerode ... d.	...	...	0459	0634	0642	...	0738	...	0843	0938	...	1043	1138	...	1243	1338	...	...	1443	1443	1538	...	...	1643	1643
157	**Halberstadt** ... a.	...	...	0515	0650	0656	...	0754	...	0856	0954	...	1056	1154	...	1256	1354	...	Ⓒ	1456	1456	1554	...	Ⓒ	1656	1656
157	**Halberstadt** ... d.	0436	0514	0517	0652	0702	...	...	0813	0902	...	1013	1102	...	1213	1302	...	1403	1413	1459	1502	...	1603	1613	1702	1702
189	Aschersleben ... d.	0509	0547	0547	0721	0728	...	...	0843	0925	...	1043	1126	...	1243	1325	...	1443j	1443	1522	1525	...	1643j	1643	1725	1725
200	Sandersleben (Anh) ... d.	0522	0602	0602	0729	0735	...	...	0858	0932	...	1058	1134	...	1258	1332	...	1458	1458	1535	1532	...	1658	1658	1732	1732
217	Könnern ... d.	0535	0618	0618	0742	0746	...	...	0912	0943	...	1112	1144	...	1312	1343	...	1516	1512	1547	1547	...	1716	1712	1743	1747
247	**Halle** (Saale) Hbf ... a.	0605	0654	0645	0804	0804	...	...	0943	1000	...	1143	1200	...	1343	1400	...	1549	1543	1605	1605	...	1749	1743	1800	1805

		Ⓐ										
Hannover Hbf ... d.	...	...	1548	1655	...	1748	1855	...	1948	2045	2045	2148
Hildesheim Hbf ... d.	...	...	1614	1721	...	1814	1921	...	2014	2109	2109	2214
Salzgitter-Ringelheim . d.	...	...	1643	1744	...	1843	1944	...	2043	2131	2131	2243
Goslar **859** ... d.	...	...	1658	1759	...	1858	1959	...	2058	2147f	2152f	2257
Bad Harzburg 859 ... a.	...	...	1711	1809	...	1911	2009	...	2111	|	2204	▬
Bad Harzburg 859 ... d.	*1651*	...	▬	1815	*1851*	▬	2015	*2051*	...	|	...	...
Vienenburg **859** ... d.	1711	...	...	1824	1911	...	2024	2107	...	2157	...	...
Ilsenburg ... d.	1727	...	...	1835	1927	...	2035	2121	...	2209	...	2311
Wernigerode ... d.	1738	...	...	1843	1938	...	2043	2133	...	2221	...	2322
Halberstadt ... a.	1754	...	Ⓒ	1856	1954	...	2056	2150	...	2233	...	2339
Halberstadt ... d.	**A**	1801	1813	1902	...	2013	2109	...	...	2238	...	...
Aschersleben ... d.	...	1843j	1843	1925	...	2043	2130	...	...	2259	...	...
Sandersleben (Anh) ... d.	...	1900	1900	1932	...	2100	2137	...	...	2307	...	...
Könnern ... d.	...	1914	1914	1943	...	2120	2148	...	...	2317	...	...
Halle (Saale) Hbf ... a.	...	1945	1945	2000	...	2149	2205	...	...	2334	...	...

	Ⓐ	Ⓐ	Ⓐ	⑥	Ⓒ	Ⓐ	Ⓐ		Ⓒ
Halle (Saale) Hbf ... d.	...	...	...	...	...	0419	*0508*	0601	0623
Könnern ... d.	...	...	...	...	...	0436	0545	0617	0652
Sandersleben (Anh) ... d.	...	...	...	...	...	0449	0601	0627	0706
Aschersleben ... d.	...	...	...	...	...	0500	0615	0635	0721
Halberstadt ... a.	...	...	...	...	...	0528	0643	0656	0750
Halberstadt ... d.	...	0441	...	0457	...	0538	▬	0703	▬
Wernigerode ... d.	...	0502	...	0515	...	0555	...	0718	...
Ilsenburg ... d.	...	0518	...	0533	...	0606	...	0727	...
Vienenburg **859** ... d.	...	0531	...	0547	...	0623	...	0739	...
Bad Harzburg 859 ... a.	...	|	...	|	...	|	...	0747	...
Bad Harzburg 859 ... d.	...	|	0540	|	...	|	0642	0752	0845
Goslar **859** ... d.	0457	0542	0554	0559	0605	0640	0656	0806	0859
Salzgitter-Ringelheim ... d.	0511	...	0608	...	0616	0652	0710	0817	0913
Hildesheim Hbf ... d.	0543	...	0639	...	0640	0720	0743	0843	0943
Hannover Hbf ... a.	0609	...	0707	...	0706	0747	0810	0906	1010

	Ⓐ																	Ⓐ								
Halle (Saale) Hbf ... d.	0630	...	0800	0812	...	1001	1010	...	1201	1212	...	1401	1412	...	1601	1612	...	1718	1801	...	1812	...	2021	2048	2248	...
Könnern ... d.	0704	...	0817	0842	...	1017	1042	...	1217	1242	...	1417	1443	...	1619	1643	...	1747	1817	...	1842	...	2037	2120	2320	...
Sandersleben (Anh) ... d.	0718	...	0827	0901	...	1027	1101	...	1227	1301	...	1427	1501	...	1629	1701	...	1801	1827	...	1901	...	2047	2138	2334	...
Aschersleben ... d.	0729	...	0835	0918	...	1035	1118	...	1235	1318	...	1435t	1523j	...	1636	1718	...	1823j	1835	...	1918	...	2055	2151	2358j	...
Halberstadt ... a.	0757	...	0856	0947	**B**	1056	1147	...	1256	1347	...	1457	1552	...	1656	1747	...	1852	1856	...	1947	...	2115	2220	0027	...
Halberstadt ... d.	...	0804	0903	▬	1004	1103	▬	1204	1303	▬	1404	1503	▬	1604	1703	▬	1804	...	1903	...	▬	2004	2118	2237	...	0032
Wernigerode ... d.	...	0822	0918	...	1022	1118	...	1222	1318	...	1422	1518	...	1622	1718	...	1822	...	1918	...	...	2022	2133	2255	...	0050
Ilsenburg ... d.	...	0836	0926	...	1036	1126	...	1236	1326	...	1436	1526	...	1636	1726	...	1836	...	1926	...	...	2036	2141	2306	...	0100
Vienenburg **859** ... d.	...	0849	0938	...	1049	1138	...	1249	1338	...	1449	1538	...	1649	1738	...	1849	...	1938	...	...	2049	2153	...	...	...
Bad Harzburg 859 ... a.	...	*0911*	0946	...	*1111*	1146	...	*1311*	1346	...	*1511*	1546	...	*1711*	1746	...	*1911*	...	1946	...	...	*2111*	2201	...	...	...
Bad Harzburg 859 ... d.	...	...	0952	1045	...	1152	1245	...	1352	1445	...	1552	1645	...	1752	1845	...	...	1952	2045	...	▬	2207	...	...	...
Goslar **859** ... d.	...	...	1006	1059	...	1206	1259	...	1406	1459	...	1606	1659	...	1806	1859	...	...	2006	2059	...	...	2219	...	...	...
Salzgitter-Ringelheim . d.	...	...	1017	1113	...	1217	1313	...	1417	1513	...	1617	1713	...	1817	1913	...	...	2017	2113	...	...	...	...	...	...
Hildesheim Hbf ... d.	...	...	1043	1143	...	1243	1343	...	1443	1543	...	1643	1743	...	1843	1943	...	...	2043	2143	2207	2307	...	...	...	...
Hannover Hbf ... a.	...	...	1106	1210	...	1306	1410	...	1506	1610	...	1706	1810	...	1906	2010	...	...	2106	2210	2238	2338	...	...	...	...

BERNBURG - HALLE

	Ⓐ	⑥		Ⓒ	Ⓐ					⊕	⑥
Bernburg ... ◧ d.	0612	0634	0818	1018	1022	1218	1418	1618	1818	2044	2318
Könnern ... ◧ a.	0635	0657	0841	1041	|	1241	1441	1641	1841	2107	2341
Halle (Saale) Hbf ... a.	0706	0730	0916	1116	1104	1316	1516	1716	1913	2119	0012

	Ⓐ	Ⓒ				Ⓐ	Ⓒ	Ⓐ	Ⓒ		
Halle (Saale) Hbf ... d.	0508	0700	0912	1112	1312	1412	1512	1612	1712	1931	2218
Könnern ... ◧ d.	0539	0737	0943	1143	1343	1446	1543	1646	1750j	2006	2247
Bernburg ... ◧ a.	0604	0802	1007	1207	1407	1510	1607	1710	1814	2031	2311

A – To Berlin via Magdeburg on ⑤–⑦ (also Oct. 2). See Tables **862**/**839**.
B – From Berlin via Magdeburg on Ⓒ. See Tables **839**/**862**.
f – Arrives 2142.

j – Arrives 10–12 minutes earlier.
t – 1438 on Ⓐ.

⊕ – Change trains at Könnern on Ⓒ.

◇ – *Harz Elbe Express*. Operated by Veolia Verkehr.
◧ – Other services Bernburg - Könnern and v.v.: From Bernburg at 0508 Ⓐ, 0637 Ⓐ and 1718 Ⓐ. From Könnern at 0708 Ⓐ and 1750 Ⓐ.

861 MAGDEBURG - SANGERHAUSEN - ERFURT and DESSAU - ASCHERSLEBEN *RE / RB services*

Magdeburg - Erfurt and Aschersleben

km		⚒t		Ⓐt	Ⓐt										Ⓐt	⑦	Ⓒz	Ⓐt			Ⓐt					
0	**Magdeburg** Hbf d.	...	...	...	0512	0612	0712	0826	0912	1026	1112	1226	1312	1426	1457	...	1512	1534	1626	1712	1712	1826	1912	2026	2112	2250
17	Schönebeck (Elbe) d.	...	...	...	0526	0625	0726	0838	0926	1038	1126	1238	1326	1438	1514	...	1526	1546	1638	1726	1726	1838	1926	2038	2126	2310
37	Staßfurt d.	...	...	...	0550	0651	0750	0853	0950	1053	1150	1253	1350	1453	1534	...	1550	1607	1653	1750	1750	1853	1950	2053	2150	2332
44	Güsten d.	...	...	...	0557	0658	0757	0858	0957	1058	1157	1258	1357	1458	1541	...	1557	1614	1658	1759	1803	1858	1957	2058	2157	2339
	Aschersleben a.	...	...	0537	0609	|	0809	|	1009	|	1209	|	1409	|	|	1544	1609	1626	|	1810	|	|	2009	|	2209	2351
60	Sandersleben d.	...	...	0547	▬	0712	▬	0912	▬	1112	▬	1312	▬	1512	1554	1554	▬	▬	1712	▬	1816	1912	...	2112	...	...
66	Hettstedt d.	...	...	0554	...	0719	...	0919	...	1119	...	1319	...	1519	1601	1601	...	...	1719	...	1823	1919	...	2119	...	...
75	Klostermansfeld d.	...	...	0603	...	0728	...	0928	...	1128	...	1328	...	1528	1610	1610	Ⓐt	Ⓒz	1728	...	1832	1928	...	2128	...	...
97	**Sangerhausen** d.	0356	0546	0623	0640	0749	0838	0949	1038	1149	1238	1349	1436	1549	1629	1629	1636	1638	1749	1838	1902	1949	...	2148	...	...
142	Sömmerda d.	0438	0632	0702	0725	0830	0924	1030	1124	1230	1324	1430	1524	1630	...	...	1724	1724	1830	1924	...	2030	...	2230	...	...
167	**Erfurt** Hbf a.	0458	0654	0719	0744	0847	0944	1047	1144	1247	1344	1447	1544	1647	...	...	1744	1744	1847	1944	...	2047	...	2247	...	...

	Ⓐt	Ⓐt	Ⓒz	Ⓐt	Ⓐt		Ⓒz	Ⓐt							Ⓐt	Ⓒz		Ⓐt	Ⓒz						Ⓒz	
Erfurt Hbf d.	...	...	...	...	...	0506	...	0613	0706	0816	0916	1016	1116	1216	1314	1316	1415	1514	1516	1615	1716	1816	1916	2016	2116	2314
Sömmerda d.	...	...	...	...	...	0524	...	0634	0729	0836	0933	1036	1133	1236	1331	1333	1435	1531	1533	1635	1733	1836	1933	2036	2136	2336
Sangerhausen d.	...	...	...	0510	...	0609	...	0723	0818	0922	1018	1122	1218	1322	1418	1418	1518	1618	1618	1722	1818	1922	2018	2122	2230	0022
Klostermansfeld d.	...	...	...	0529	...	0629	...	▬	0837	▬	1037	▬	1237	▬	1437	1437	▬	1637	1637	▬	1837	▬	2037	▬	...	...
Hettstedt d.	...	...	...	0538	...	0639	...		0846	...	1046	...	1246	...	1446	1446	...	1646	1646	...	1846	...	2046	...	...	...
Sandersleben d.	...	...	...	0551	...	0653	...	Ⓐt	0853	...	1053	...	1253	...	1453	1453	...	1653	1653	...	1853	...	2053	...	...	...
Aschersleben d.	0447	0529	0547	|	0623	|	0745	0747	|	0947	|	1147	|	1347	|	|	1547	|	|	1747	|	1947	|	2145	...	...
Güsten d.	0459	0541	0559	0604	0635	0707	0759	0759	0907	0959	1107	1159	1307	1359	1507	1507	1559	1707	1707	1759	1907	1959	2107	2159	...	...
Staßfurt d.	0508	0552	0608	0611	0644	0714	0808	0808	0914	1008	1114	1208	1314	1408	1514	1514	1608	1714	1714	1808	1914	2008	2114	2208	...	...
Schönebeck (Elbe) d.	0529	0613	0629	0626	0706	0729	0829	0829	0929	1029	1129	1229	1329	1431	1529	1529	1629	1729	1729	1829	1929	2029	2129	2230	...	...
Magdeburg Hbf a.	0540	0625	0640	0639	0717	0740	0840	0840	0940	1040	1140	1240	1340	1441	1540	1540	1640	1740	1740	1840	1940	2040	2140	2247	...	...

Dessau - Aschersleben

km		Ⓐt	Ⓐt	Ⓒz	Ⓐt		Ⓐt	Ⓒz	Ⓐt								Ⓐt	Ⓒz								
0	**Dessau** Hbf d.	...	0419	0454	0523	0600	0645	0712	0732	0800	0858	1000	1058	1200	1258	1400	1458	1458	1600	1658	1800	1858	2000	2112	2147	2315
21	Köthen a.	...	0442	0517	0549	0623	0714	0734	0752	0823	0919	1023	1119	1223	1319	1423	1519	1519	1623	1719	1823	1919	2023	2134	2214	2337
21	Köthen d.	...	0451	0520	0550	0633	0720	0735	0753	0833	0920	1033	1120	1233	1320	1433	1520	1520	1633	1720	1833	1920	2033	2135	...	2338
42	Bernburg d.	0432	0512	0542	0609	0653	0742	0756	0812	0853	0942	1053	1142	1253	1342	1453	1542	1542	1653	1742	1853	1942	2053	2156	...	2359
54	Güsten d.	0443	0522	0553	0619	0703	0753	0809	0823	0903	0953	1103	1153	1303	1353	1503	1553	1553	1703	1753	1903	1953	2103	2209	...	0010
66	**Aschersleben** a.	0454	0533	0604	0630	0714	*0809*	0821	0831	0914	*1009*	1114	*1209*	1314	*1409*	1514	1604	*1609*	1714	*1810*	1914	*2009*	2114	2221	...	0022

		Ⓐt			Ⓒz	Ⓐt								Ⓐt	Ⓒz										
Aschersleben d.	0433	0515	0558	0649	0745	*0747*	0849	*0947*	1049	*1147*	1249	*1347*	1449	1537	*1547*	1649	*1747*	1849	*1947*	*2046*	...	2145	...	...	...
Güsten d.	0444	0527	0609	0702	0802	0802	0902	1002	1102	1202	1302	1402	1502	1549	1602	1702	1802	1902	2002	2110	...	2202	...	...	...
Bernburg d.	0455	0538	0619	0713	0813	0813	0913	1013	1113	1213	1313	1413	1513	1600	1613	1713	1813	1913	2013	2121	...	2213	...	...	...
Köthen a.	0517	0600	0638	0735	0834	0834	0935	1034	1135	1234	1335	1434	1535	1622	1634	1735	1834	1935	2034	2142	...	2235	...	...	...
Köthen d.	0518	0601	0640	0736	0835	0835	0936	1035	1136	1235	1336	1435	1536	1635	1635	1736	1835	1936	2035	2143	2224	2238	...	...	...
Dessau Hbf a.	0542	0628	0704	0758	0856	0856	0958	1056	1158	1256	1358	1456	1558	1656	1656	1758	1856	1958	2056	2205	2246	2254	...	...	...

t – Not Oct. 31.

z – Also Oct. 31.

862 MAGDEBURG - HALBERSTADT - THALE *HEX ◇*

km		Ⓐt							Ⓒ ▲			Ⓐ													
	Berlin Ostbf **839** d.	...	...	...	...	...	...	...	0708	...	...	...	...	...	...	...	...	...	...	...	...	...	...	...	...
0	**Magdeburg** Hbf d.	0429	...	...	0544	0710	0810	0910	0910	1010	1110	1110	...	1210	1310	1410	1510	1610	1710	1810	1910	2007	2137	2224	2318
39	Oschersleben (Bode) d.	0507	...	...	0625	0742	0842	0942	0942	1042	1142	1142	...	1242	1342	1442	1542	1642	1742	1842	1942	2045	2218	2303	2357
59	**Halberstadt** a.	0524	...	...	0642	0758	0858	0958	0958	1058	1158	1158	...	1258	1358	1458	1558	1658	1758	1858	1958	2102	2234	2320	0014
59	**Halberstadt** d.	0530	0530	0607	0706	0806	0906	1006	1006	1108	...	1206	1206	1306	1406	1506	1606	1706	1806	1906	2006	2112	2241	...	0026
77	Quedlinburg a.	0546	0546	0623	0723	0823	0923	1023	1023	1125	...	1223	1223	1323	1423	1523	1623	1723	1823	1923	2023	2129	2256	...	0041
77	Quedlinburg d.	0547	0547	0630	0730	0830	0930	1030	1030	1130	...	1230	1230	1330	1430	1530	1630	1730	1830	1930	2030	2130	2257	...	0042
87	**Thale** Hbf a.	0559	0559	0642	0742	0842	0942	1042	1042	1142	...	1242	1242	1342	1442	1542	1642	1742	1842	1942	2042	2142	2309	...	0053

	Ⓐt										Ⓐ								⑤–⑦ b▲						
Thale Hbf d.	...	...	0505	...	0617	0717	0817	0917	1017	1117	1117	...	1217	1317	1417	1517	1617	1717	1717	1817	1917	2017	2117	2155	2345
Quedlinburg a.	...	...	0517	...	0628	0728	0828	0928	1028	1128	1128	...	1228	1328	1428	1528	1628	1728	1728	1828	1928	2028	2128	2206	2356
Quedlinburg d.	...	...	0517	...	0633	0733	0833	0933	1033	1133	1133	...	1233	1333	1433	1533	1633	1733	1733	1833	1933	2033	2133	2207	2357
Halberstadt a.	...	...	0535	...	0649	0749	0849	0949	1049	1149	1149	...	1249	1349	1449	1549	1649	1749	1749	1849	1949	2049	2149	2224	0013
Halberstadt d.	0333	0443	0540	0601	0701	0801	0901	1001	1101	...	1201	1201	1301	1401	1501	1601	1701	1801	1801	1901	2001	2103	2155	...	...
Oschersleben (Bode) d.	0349	0459	0556	0617	0717	0817	0917	1017	1117	...	1217	1217	1317	1417	1517	1617	1717	1817	1817	1917	2017	2119	2212	...	...
Magdeburg Hbf a.	0423	0537	0635	0644	0745	0844	0944	1044	1144	...	1244	1244	1344	1444	1544	1644	1744	1844	1844	1944	2056	2145	2252	...	...
Berlin Ostbf **839** a.	...	...	...	...	...	...	...	...	...	...	...	...	...	...	...	...	...	...	2051	...	...	...	...	...	...

b – Also Oct. 2.
t – Not Oct. 31.

▲ – *HARZ-BERLIN-EXPRESS*. **DB tickets not valid for journeys from / to Berlin.** Conveys [2] Berlin - Halberstadt - Vienenburg and v.v. (Table **860**).
◇ – *Harz Elbe Express*. Operated by Veolia Verkehr Sachsen-Anhalt GmbH.

863 BRAUNSCHWEIG - HILDESHEIM - HAMELN - BÜNDE *Nord West Bahn ★*

km		Ⓐ	⚒	⚒	Ⓐ			Ⓐ			Ⓐ			Ⓐ			Ⓐ			Ⓐ			Ⓐ			
0	**Hildesheim** Hbf d.	...	0537	0634	0634	0737	0834	0834	0937	1034	1034	1137	1234	1234	1337	1434	1434	1537	1634	1634	1737	1834	1834	1937	2034	2137
18	Elze a.	...	0553	0650	0650	0753	0850	0850	0953	1050	1050	1153	1250	1250	1353	1450	1450	1553	1650	1650	1753	1850	1850	1953	2050	2153
18	Elze d.	...	0602	0702	0702	0802	0902	0902	1002	1102	1102	1202	1302	1302	1402	1502	1502	1602	1702	1702	1802	1902	1902	2002	2102	2202
47	**Hameln** d.	0529	0629	0727	0729	0829	0927	0929	1029	1127	1129	1229	1327	1329	1429	1527	1529	1629	1727	1729	1829	1927	1929	2029	2127	2227
71	Rinteln d.	0546	0646	...	0746	0846	...	0946	1046	...	1146	1246	...	1346	1446	...	1546	1646	...	1746	1846	...	1946	2046	...	...
88	Vlotho d.	0602	0702	...	0802	0902	...	1002	1102	...	1202	1302	...	1402	1502	...	1602	1702	...	1802	1902	...	2002	2102	...	...
100	Löhne (Westf) **811** a.	0613	0713	...	0813	0913	...	1013	1113	...	1213	1313	...	1413	1513	...	1613	1713	...	1813	1913	...	2013	2113	...	...
110	**Bünde** (Westf) **811** a.	0626	0725e	...	0825	...	...	1025	...	...	1225	1325e	...	1425	...	...	1625	1725e	...	1825	...	...	...	...	...	...

	⚒	Ⓐ	⚒	⚒		Ⓐ			Ⓐ			Ⓐ			Ⓐ			Ⓐ			Ⓐ			Ⓐ		
Bünde (Westf) **811** d.	...	...	...	0632e	...	0732	...	0832e	...	...	1032e	...	...	1232e	1332	...	1432e	...	...	1632e	1732	...	1832e	...	...	...
Löhne (Westf) **811** d.	...	0545	...	0645	...	0745	...	0845	0945	...	1045	1145	...	1245	1345	...	1445	1545	...	1645	1745	...	1845	1945	...	2045
Vlotho d.	...	0559	...	0659	...	0759	...	0859	0959	...	1059	1159	...	1259	1359	...	1459	1559	...	1659	1759	...	1859	1959	...	2059
Rinteln d.	...	0610	...	0710	...	0810	...	0910	1010	...	1110	1210	...	1310	1410	...	1510	1610	...	1710	1810	...	1910	2010	...	2110
Hameln d.	0528	0628	0628	0728	0728	0828	0828	0928	1028	1028	1128	1228	1228	1328r	1428	1428	1528	1628	1628	1728	1828	1828	1928	2028	2028	2128
Elze a.	0553	0653	0653	0753	0753	0852	0852	0953	1052	1052	1153	1252	1252	1353r	1452	1452	1553	1652	1652	1753	1852	1852	1953	2052	2052	2153
Elze d.	0602	0702	0702	0802	0802	0907	0907	1002	1107	1107	1202	1307	1307	1402r	1507	1507	1602	1707	1707	1802	1907	1907	2002	2107	2107	2202
Hildesheim Hbf a.	0620	0720	0720	0820	0820	0925	0925	1020	1125	1125	1220	1325	1325	1420r	1525	1525	1620	1725	1725	1820	1925	1925	2020	2125	2125	2220

Regional trains **BRAUNSCHWEIG - HILDESHEIM** ⊠

km		Ⓐ	Ⓐ	⚒							Ⓐ				Ⓐ	Ⓒ										
0	**Braunschweig** Hbf d.	0542	0642	0742	...	1042	...	1342	...	1542	1642	...	1842	...	2042	2142	...	...	...	...	...	...	...	...	...	...
43	**Hildesheim** Hbf a.	0615	0715	0815	...	1115	...	1415	...	1615	1715	...	1915	...	2115	2215	...	...	...	...	...	...	...	...	...	...

	Ⓐ	⚒	Ⓐ		Ⓒ	Ⓐ	Ⓒ		Ⓐ	Ⓒ	Ⓐ	Ⓐ	Ⓒ	Ⓐ	Ⓒ	Ⓐ										
Hildesheim Hbf d.	0545	0645	0745	...	0945	1045	1145	...	1345	1445	1545	1645	1743	1845	1945	2045	...	...	...	...	...	...	...	...	...	...
Braunschweig Hbf a.	0618	0718	0818	...	1018	1118	1218	...	1418	1518	1618	1718	1816	1918	2018	2118	...	...	...	...	...	...	...	...	...	...

e – Ⓐ only.
r – On Ⓐ (not July 31 - Sept. 10, Oct. 27 - Nov. 7) Hameln d. 1335, Elze a. 1402, d. 1403, Hildesheim a. 1422.

★ – Bünde - Hildesheim operated by Nord West Bahn.
⊠ – Operated by DB. For faster *ICE* trains see Table **902**.

CANTUS Verkehrsgesellschaft (2nd class only) — GÖTTINGEN - KASSEL local services — 864

km		Ⓐ	⑥	⑥	Ⓐ	Ⓒ	Ⓐ	⚒		⚒			Ⓒ	Ⓐ			Ⓐ	Ⓒ	Ⓑ	Ⓐ	Ⓒ	Ⓑ	⚒	Ⓑ	⚒◇	Ⓒ
0	**Göttingen** 908 d.	0442	0444	0543	0600	0703	0714	0814	0914	1018	1114	1218	1314	1335	1418	1514	1614	1618	1714	1814	1818	1914	2014	2118	2214	2359
20	Eichenberg 908 a.	0456	0458	0557	0613	0717	0728	0828	0928	1032	1128	1232	1328	1350	1432	1528	1628	1632	1728	1828	1832	1928	2028	2132	2228	0014
20	Eichenberg 865 d.	0508	0502	0603	0623	0723	0733	0833	0933	1033	1133	1233	1333	1356	1433	1533	1633	1633	1733	1833	1833	1933	2033	2133	2234	0015
43	Hann Münden 865 d.	0528	0523	0623	0644	0743	0753	0853	0953	1053	1153	1253	1353	1416	1453	1553	1653	1653	1753	1853	1853	1953	2053	2153	2255	0035
67	**Kassel** Hbf ⊡ 865 a.	0549	0543	0643	0703	0803	0813	0913	1013	1113	1213	1313	1413	1437	1513	1613	1713	1713	1813	1913	1913	2013	2113	2213	2318	0055

	Ⓐ	Ⓐ	⑥	Ⓐ	Ⓒ	⚒	†	⚒	⚒				Ⓐt			Ⓑ	Ⓐt				Ⓑ	⚒			Ⓐ	Ⓒ
Kassel Hbf ⊡ 865 d.	0416	0535	0546	0625	0636	0746	0846	0846	0946	1046	1146	1246	1317	1346	1446	1546	1614	1646	1746	1846	1946	2046	2146	...	2314	2346
Hann Münden 865 d.	0436	0555	0606	0645	0656	0806	0906	0906	1006	1106	1206	1306	1339	1406	1506	1606	1635	1706	1806	1906	2006	2106	2206	...	2334	0006
Eichenberg 865 a.	0456	0615	0626	0705	0715	0826	0926	0926	1026	1126	1226	1326	1401	1426	1526	1626	1655	1726	1825	1926	2026	2126	2226	...	2355	0026
Eichenberg 908 d.	0458	0624	0627	0707	0722	0832	0927	0932	1032	1127	1232	1327	...	1432	1527	1632	1700	1727	1832	1927	2032	2127	2227	...	0003	0027
Göttingen 908 a.	0513	0637	0640	0721	0735	0845	0940	0945	1045	1140	1245	1340	...	1445	1540	1645	1713	1740	1845	1940	2045	2140	2240	...	0016	0040

t – Not June 19.　◇ – Runs 5–6 minutes later on ⑥.　⊡ – See Tables **804**, **806** and **901** for connecting trains to / from Kassel Wilhelmshöhe.

RE / RB services — ERFURT and HALLE - LEINEFELDE - KASSEL and GÖTTINGEN — 865

km		Ⓐe	Ⓐ	Ⓐ		Ⓐe	Ⓐ	Ⓒ						A	k				A	k				A	
0	**Erfurt** Hbf 849 850 d.	...	...	...	0430	0500	...	...	0613	...	0623	0709	...	0812	...	0831	0908	...	1012	...	1031	1108	...	1212	...
27	Gotha 849 850 d.	...	...	...	0501	|	...	...	0636	...	|	◇	...	0836	...	|	◇	...	1036	...	|	◇	...	1236	...
48	Bad Langensalza d.	...	...	0450	0513	0556	...	...	0648	...	0710	0759	...	0848	...	0914	0959	...	1048	...	1114	1159	...	1248	...
67	Mühlhausen (Thür) d.	...	...	0506	0526	0613	...	...	0701	...	0726	0815	...	0901	...	0926	1015	...	1101	...	1126	1215	...	1301	...
	Halle (Saale) Hbf ◧ d.	...	...	|	|	|	0444	0446	|	...	|	|	0704	|	...	|	|	0904	|	...	|	|	1104	|	...
	Lutherstadt Eisleben ◧ d.	...	...	|	|	|	0514	0520	|	...	|	|	0733	|	...	|	|	0933	|	...	|	|	1133	|	...
	Sangerhausen ◧ d.	...	...	|	|	|	0534	0543	|	...	|	|	0753	|	...	|	|	0953	|	...	|	|	1153	|	...
	Nordhausen ◧ d.	...	0445	|	|	|	0609	0621	|	0703	|	|	0821	|	0903	|	|	1021	|	1103	|	|	1221	|	1303
94	**Leinefelde** a.	...	0527	0531	0545	0636	0648	0654	0717	0747	0750	0838	0854	0917	0947	0950	1038	1054	1117	1147	1150	1238	1254	1317	1347
94	**Leinefelde** d.	0426	...	0532	0548	...	0649	0655	0719	...	0751	...	0855	0919	...	0953	...	1055	1119	...	1153	...	1255	1319	...
110	Heilbad Heiligenstadt d.	0440	...	0547	0559	...	0703	0706	0730	...	0801	...	0906	0930	...	1004	...	1106	1130	...	1204	...	1306	1330	...
144	**Göttingen** a.	|	...	|	0625	...	|	|	0752	...	|	...	|	0952	...	|	...	|	1152	...	|	...	|	1352	...
125	Eichenberg 864 d.	0454	...	0602	...	...	0718	0718	...	...	0816	...	0918	...	...	1018	...	1118	...	...	1218	...	1318	...	...
148	Hann Münden 864 d.	0528	...	0622	...	...	0736	0736	...	...	0833	...	0936	...	...	1036	...	1136	...	...	1236	...	1336	...	...
172	**Kassel** Hbf 864 a.	0549	...	0643	...	...	|	|	...	...	|	...	|	...	...	|	...	|	...	...	|	...	|	...	...
176	**Kassel** Wilhelmshöhe 864 a.	...	...	0657	...	...	0753	0753	...	...	0852	...	0953	...	...	1056	...	1153	...	...	1255	...	1356j	...	...

				A					A			⑦E			A					A		⚒	⊖	G	
Erfurt Hbf 849 850 d.	1231	1308	...	1412	...	1431	1508	...	1612	...	1630	...	1708	...	1812	...	1830	1908	...	2012	2031	...	...	2112	2140
Gotha 849 850 d.	|	◇	...	1436	...	|	◇	...	1636	...	|	...	◇	...	1836	...	|	◇	...	2036	|	...	...	2139	|
Bad Langensalza d.	1314	1359	...	1448	...	1514	1559	...	1648	...	1714	...	1759	...	1848	...	1914	1959	...	2048	2114	...	...	2151	2224
Mühlhausen (Thür) d.	1326	1415	...	1501	...	1526	1615	...	1701	...	1726	...	1815	...	1901	...	1926	2014	...	2101	2126	...	...	2205	2240
Halle (Saale) Hbf ◧ d.	|	|	1304	|	...	|	|	1504	|	...	|	1605	|	1704	|	...	|	...	1904	|	|	...	2004	|	...
Lutherstadt Eisleben ◧ d.	|	|	1333	|	...	|	|	1533	|	...	|	1636	|	1733	|	...	|	...	1933	|	|	...	2033	|	...
Sangerhausen ◧ d.	|	|	1353	|	...	|	|	1553	|	...	|	1654	|	1753	|	...	|	...	1953	|	|	...	2055	|	...
Nordhausen ◧ d.	|	|	1421	|	1503	|	|	1621	|	1703	|	1725t	|	1821	|	1903	|	...	2020	|	|	...	2134	|	...
Leinefelde a.	1350	1438	1454	1517	1548	1550	1638	1654	1717	1747	1750	1754	1838	1854	1917	1947	1950	...	2056	2117	2144	...	2217	2222	...
Leinefelde d.	1353	...	1455	1519	...	1553	...	1655	1719	...	1751	1756	...	1855	1919	...	1953	...	2057	2119	2150	...	...	2224	...
Heilbad Heiligenstadt d.	1404	...	1506	1530	...	1604	...	1706	1730	...	1802	1808	...	1906	1930	...	2004	...	2107	2130	2201	...	...	2234	...
Göttingen a.	|	...	|	1552	...	|	...	|	1752	...	|	|	...	|	1952	...	|	...	|	2150	|	...	...	2256	...
Eichenberg 864 d.	1418	...	1518	...	...	1618	...	1718	...	...	1815	|	...	1918	...	...	2018	...	2118	...	2212	2234	...	...	...
Hann Münden 864 d.	1436	...	1536	...	...	1636	...	1736	...	...	1832	|	...	1936	...	...	2036	...	2136	...	...	2255	...	...	...
Kassel Hbf 864 a.	|	...	|	...	...	|	...	|	...	...	|	|	...	|	...	...	|	...	2153	...	...	2318	...	...	...
Kassel Wilhelmshöhe 864 a.	1455	...	1553	...	...	1655	...	1753	...	...	1852	1854	...	1953	...	...	2053	...	...	...	...	...	...	...	...

km				Ⓐe	A	Ⓐ	Ⓒ		Ⓐ		k	A				k	A					A			
0	**Kassel** Wilhelmshöhe 864 d.	...	...	...	...	...	...	...	0704	...	...	...	0804	...	0906	...	...	1005	...	1107	...	...	1204	...	1306
	Kassel Hbf 864 d.	...	...	0416	...	0600	0605	...	|	...	...	...	|	...	|	...	...	|	...	|	...	...	|	...	|
23	Hann Münden 864 d.	...	...	0436	...	0616	0621	...	0724	...	...	...	0821	...	0922	...	...	1022	...	1123	...	...	1221	...	1322
46	Eichenberg 864 d.	...	...	0510	...	0634	0639	...	0744	...	...	...	0840	...	0941	...	...	1040	...	1141	...	...	1240	...	1341
	Göttingen d.	...	...	|	0604	|	|	...	|	...	...	0808	|	...	|	...	1008	|	...	|	...	1208	|	...	|
61	Heilbad Heiligenstadt d.	...	0444e	0524	0628	0648	0652	...	0758	...	...	0830	0852	...	0955	...	1030	1052	...	1155	...	1230	1252	...	1355
77	**Leinefelde** a.	...	0459e	0538	0639	0702	0702	...	0807	...	...	0840	0902	...	1005	...	1040	1102	...	1205	...	1240	1302	...	1405
77	**Leinefelde** d.	0445e	0501	0539	0640	0703	0703	0719e	0808	0808	0811	0842	0903	0919	1007	1011	1042	1103	1119	1207	1211	1242	1303	1319	1407
119	**Nordhausen** ◧ d.	0530	|	0623*	|	0737	0737	|	|	|	0853	|	0937	|	|	1053	|	1137	|	|	1253	|	1337	|	|
157	Sangerhausen ◧ d.	0600	|	0658	|	0804	0804	|	|	|	...	|	1004	|	|	...	|	1204	|	|	...	|	1404	|	|
179	Lutherstadt Eisleben ◧ d.	0618	|	0718	|	0822	0822	|	|	|	...	|	1022	|	|	...	|	1222	|	|	...	|	1422	|	|
217	**Halle** (Saale) Hbf ◧ d.	0651	|	0748	|	0851	0851	|	|	|	...	|	1051	|	|	...	|	1251	|	|	...	|	1451	|	|
—	Mühlhausen (Thür) d.	...	0525	...	0659	...	...	0742	0831	0831	...	0859	...	0942	1031	...	1059	...	1142	1231	...	1259	...	1342	1431
0	Bad Langensalza d.	...	0537	...	0709	...	...	0758	0843	0843	...	0909	...	0958	1043	...	1109	...	1158	1243	...	1309	...	1358	1443
	Gotha 849 850 a.	...	0550	...	0721	...	...	⊙	|	|	...	0921	...	⊙	|	...	1121	...	⊙	|	...	1321	...	⊙	|
38	**Erfurt** Hbf 849 850 a.	...	0617	...	0745	...	...	0845	0927	0927	...	0945	...	1045	1127	...	1145	...	1245	1327	...	1345	...	1445	1527

	Ⓒ¶	Ⓐb	A					A			⑤F			A				G		G					
Kassel Wilhelmshöhe 864 d.	...	...	...	1405	...	1507	...	...	1604	...	1704	1707	...	...	1805	...	1907	...	2002	...	2106	...	...	...	...
Kassel Hbf 864 d.	...	1317	...	|	...	|	...	...	|	...	|	|	...	...	|	...	|	...	|	...	|	...	...	2146	...
Hann Münden 864 d.	...	1339	...	1422	...	1523	...	...	1621	...	|	1724	...	...	1821	...	1923	...	2021	...	2122	...	...	2206	...
Eichenberg 864 d.	...	1406	...	1440	...	1541	...	...	1640	...	|	1741	...	...	1840	...	1941	...	2040	...	2141	...	...	2241	...
Göttingen d.	...	|	1408	|	...	|	...	1608	|	...	|	|	...	1808	|	...	|	2008	|	2108	|	...	...	|	2308
Heilbad Heiligenstadt d.	...	1420	1430	1452	...	1555	...	1630	1652	...	1749	1755	...	1830	1852	...	1955	2030	2052	2132	2155	...	...	2253	2332
Leinefelde a.	...	1433	1440	1502	...	1605	...	1640	1702	...	1759	1805	...	1840	1902	...	2005	2040	2102	2142	2205	...	...	2303	2343
Leinefelde d.	1411	1434	1442	1503	1519	1607	1611	1642	1703	1719	1801	1807	1811	1842	1903	1919	2007	2042	2103	2145	2223	2236	2236w	...	...
Nordhausen ◧ d.	1453f	1515f	|	1537	|	|	1654	|	1737	|	1831k	|	1853	|	1937	|	|	|	2139f	|	|	2317	2321	...	...
Sangerhausen ◧ d.	...	...	|	1604	|	|	...	|	1804	|	1904	|	...	|	2004	|	|	|	2206f	|	|	...	2353	...	...
Lutherstadt Eisleben ◧ d.	...	...	|	1622	|	|	...	|	1822	|	1921	|	...	|	2022	|	|	|	2223f	|	|	...	0012	...	...
Halle (Saale) Hbf ◧ d.	...	...	|	1651	|	|	...	|	1851	|	1949	|	...	|	2051	|	|	|	2253f	|	|	...	0050	...	...
Mühlhausen (Thür) d.	...	...	1459	...	1542	1631	...	1659	...	1742	...	1831	...	1859	...	1942	2031	2059	...	2203	2242	...	...	...	...
Bad Langensalza d.	...	...	1509	...	1558	1643	...	1709	...	1758	...	1843	...	1909	...	1958	2043	2109	...	2213	2258	...	...	...	...
Gotha 849 850 a.	...	...	1521	...	⊙	|	...	1721	...	⊙	...	|	...	1921	...	⊙	|	2121	...	2224	|	...	...	...	...
Erfurt Hbf 849 850 a.	...	...	1545	...	1645	1728	...	1745	...	1845	...	1928	...	1945	...	2045	2122	2146	...	2250	2336	...	...	...	...

			Ⓐe			Ⓐe						Ⓐe		Ⓒz	Ⓐe	⑦	①–⑥	†z	Ⓐe						
Halle (Saale) Hbf d.	0016	...	...	...	0535	0628	0804	...	1004	...	1204	1234	1404	1434	1434	1544	1604	1634	1634	1804	...	2034	2104	2204	2234
Lutherstadt Eisleben d.	0057	...	...	...	0612	0702	0833	...	1033	...	1233	1319	1433	1515	1519	1613	1633	1715	1719	1833	...	2115	2133	2245	2303
Sangerhausen d.	0117	...	0409	...	0633	0728	0855	...	1055	...	1255	1339	1455	1539	1539	1635	1655	1739	1739	1855	...	2135	2153	2305	2322
Nordhausen d.	...	...	0442	...	0706	0801	0928	...	1128	...	1328	1412	1528	1612	1612	1708	1728	1812	1812	1928	...	...	2225	...	2355

	Ⓐe		⑥	Ⓐe		⚒r						Ⓐe	Ⓒz	Ⓐe	Ⓐe	Ⓒz			Ⓐe	Ⓒz		L	⑤d		
Nordhausen d.	...	...	0421	0421	...	0623*	...	0823	...	1023	...	1223	1223	1253	1423	1423	...	...	1623	1623	...	1823	1823	...	2053
Sangerhausen d.	0345	0431	0455	0458	...	0658	...	0858	...	1058	...	1258	1258	1329	1458	1458	1520	...	1658	1658	...	1858	1919v	...	2129
Lutherstadt Eisleben d.	0405	0451	0515	0518	...	0718	...	0918	...	1118	...	1314	1318	1349	1514	1519	1539	...	1714	1719	...	1919	1939	...	2149
Halle (Saale) Hbf a.	0443	0531	0548	0548	...	0748	...	0948	...	1148	...	1348	1348	1430	1548	1551	1618	...	1748	1748	...	1948	2018	...	2230

A – From / to Glauchau (Table **858**).
E – *IC* **1948** – (12) Leipzig Hbf (d. 1526) - Halle - Kassel - Frankfurt.
F – ⑤ (also Oct. 2; not Oct. 3). *IC* **1951** – (12) Frankfurt - Kassel - Halle - Leipzig Hbf (a. 2029).
G – From / to Gera (Table **858**).
L – ①②③④⑥⑦ (also June 20, Oct. 3; not June 18, Oct. 2).

b – Not July 21 - Aug. 29, Oct. 6 – 17, 31.
d – Also June 18, Oct. 2; not June 20, Oct. 3.
e – Ⓐ (not Oct. 31).
f – 4 – 8 minutes later from Oct. 6.
j – 1353 on Ⓒ.
k – Until Oct. 5.
r – Not Oct. 31.
t – 1723 from Oct. 12.
v – Arrives 1856.
w – † only.
z – Also Oct. 31.

* – 0625 from Oct. 6.
¶ – Ⓒ (also Oct. 31; runs daily July 19 - Aug. 31, Oct. 3 – 19).
⊖ – Change trains at Nordhausen on ⑥. From Oct. 6 Nordhausen d. 2130, Leinefelde a. 2214.
◇ – Connecting trains Gotha - Bad Langensalza (journey time: 18 minutes): Gotha d. 0737, 0937, 1137, 1337, 1537, 1737 and 1937.
⊙ – Connecting trains Bad Langensalza - Gotha (journey time: 19 minutes): Bad Langensalza d. 0801, 1001, 1201, 1401, 1601, 1801 and 2001.
◧ – See panel below main table for other services Halle - Nordhausen.

866 HANNOVER - MAGDEBURG - LEIPZIG

See panels below main table for other regional / S-Bahn trains

km		IC 2043	IC 2233	IC 2447	IC 2235	IC 2445	IC 2035	IC 2443	IC 2037	IC 2441	IC 2039	IC 2049	IC 2049	IC 2249	IC 1949	IC 2431	IC 2239	IC 2047	IC 2433	ICE 1741	IC 2435	IC 2012	IC 2012	IC 2437	RE 17647
		①–⑤	Ⓐ	①–⑥		①–⑥	①–⑥					①–⑥	⑤⑥	⑦	⑤			Ⓑ		Ⓑ		T	⑦	Ⓑ	
		d	⊙	e		e	e						b		f	C	A	p				D	D	p	
		🍷	🍷		🍷	🍷	🍷	🍷	🍷	🍷	🍷	🍷	🍷	🍷	🍷	🍷		🍷	🍷	🍴	🍷	🍴	🍴		
	Köln Hbf **800** d.	...	...	...	...	0510	...	0713e	...	0910	...	...	1110	1113	...	...	...	1313	...	1510	...	1646	1646	...	...
	Dortmund Hbf **800** d.	...	...	...	...	0628	...	0828e	...	1028	...	...	1228	1228	...	...	...	1428	...	1628	...	1828	1828	...	...
	Bielefeld Hbf **810** d.	...	...	0517g	...	0717	...	0917e	...	1117	...	...	1317	1317	...	...	...	1517	...	1716	...	1917	1917	...	...
	Norddeich **813** d.	...	...	|	...	|	0536	|	0739e	|	0939	...	|	|	...	...	...	|	...	|	1539‡	|	|	...	...
	Emden Hbf **813** d.	...	...	|	0416e	|	0609	|	0816	|	1016	...	|	|	...	1218	...	|	1415y	|	1616	|	|	1816	...
	Oldenburg (Oldb) **813** d.	...	...	|	0535v	|	0735	|	0935	|	1135	...	|	|	...	1335	...	|	1535	|	1735	|	|	1935	...
	Bremen Hbf **813** d.	...	...	|	0609	|	0810	|	1009	|	1209	...	|	|	...	1409	...	|	1609	|	1809	|	|	2009	...
0	**Hannover** Hbf d.	...	0507	0636	0736	0836	0936	1036	1135	1236	1335	1436	1436	1436	1510	1535	...	1636	1735	1836	1935	2036	2036	2135	...
35	Peine d.	...	|	|	|	|	|	|	|	|	|	|	|	|	1533	|	...	|	|	|	|	|	|	2156	...
61	**Braunschweig** Hbf d.	...	0608	0711	0810	0911	1010	1111	1210	1311	1410	1511	1511	1511	1550	1610	...	1711	1810	1911	2010	2111	2111	2212	...
97	Helmstedt d.	...	0632	|	0832	|	1032	|	1232	|	1432	|	|	|	1612	1632	...	|	1832	|	2032	|	|	2235	...
145	**Magdeburg** Hbf a.	...	0657	0755	0857	0955	1057	1155	1257	1355	1457	1555	1555	1555	1637	1657	...	1755	1857	1955	2057	2155	2155	2300	...
145	**Magdeburg** Hbf d.	0600	0703	0759	0903	0959	1103	1159	1303	1359	1503	1559	1559	1559	1641	1659	1703	1759	1903	1959	2103	...	2200	...	2307
	Berlin Hbf **839** a.	|	|	|	|	|	|	|	|	|	|	|	|	|	|	1825	|	|	|	|	|	...	|	...	|
195	Köthen d.	0630	0732	0830	0932	1030	1132	1230	1332	1430	1532	1630	1630	1630	1710	...	1732	1830	1932	2030	2132	...	2233	...	2347
231	**Halle** (Saale) Hbf a.	0651	0753	0851	0953	1051	1153	1251	1353	1451	1553	1651	1651	1651	1729	...	1753	1851	1953	2051	2153	...	2254	...	0015
231	**Halle** (Saale) Hbf d.	0653	0755	0853	0955	1053	1155	1253	1355	1453	1555	1653	1653	1653	1731	...	1755	1853	1955	2053	2155	...	2256	...	*0025*
249	Leipzig/Halle Flughafen ✈ a.	0704	0805r	0904	1005r	1104	1205r	1304	1405r	1504	1605r	1704	1704	1704	|	...	1805r	1904	2005r	2103	2205	...	2306	...	*0036*
268	**Leipzig** Hbf a.	0718	0819	0918	1019	1118	1219	1318	1419	1518	1619	1718	1718	1718	1753	...	1819	1918	2019	2118	2220	...	2320	...	*0050*
	Dresden Hbf **842** a.	0838	...	1038	1138w	1238	...	1438	...	1638	...	1838	1838	1838	...	...	...	2038	...	2238	2341j	...	...	...	...

	IC 2436	IC 2013	IC 2013	IC 2434	ICE 1742	IC 2238	IC 2432	IC 2046	IC 2046	IC 2430	IC 2048	IC 2038	IC 2440	IC 2036	IC 2442	IC 2442	IC 2034	IC 1934	IC 2444	IC 2444	IC 2032	IC 2446	IC 2446	IC 2230	IC 2232
	①–⑥	①	①–⑥	①–⑥	①–⑥			①–⑥	⑥					Ⓑ		Ⓑ	Ⓑ	⑦		Ⓑ	Ⓑ		⑦	Ⓑ	L
	e	E	e E			A	B	h	k					p		p	p			p	p			p	
		🍴	🍴	🍷	🍴		🍷	🍷	🍷	🍷	🍷	🍷	🍷	🍷	🍷	🍷	🍷	🍷	🍷	🍷	🍷	🍷	🍷	🍷	
Dresden Hbf **842** d.	...	...	...	...	...	...	...	0719	0719	...	0919	...	1119	...	1319	1319	...	...	1519	1519	...	1719	1719	1855	...
Leipzig Hbf d.	...	0436	...	0540•	0640	0740•	...	0840	0840	0940•	1040	1140•	1240	1340•	1440	1440	1540•	1605	1640	1640	1740•	1840	1840	2006*	2140
Leipzig/Halle Flughafen ✈ d.	...	0450	...	0554r	0654	0754r	...	0854	0854	0954r	1054	1154r	1254	1354r	1454	1454	1554r	1619	1654	1654	1754r	1854	1854	2020*	2154
Halle (Saale) Hbf a.	...	0501	...	0605	0705	0805	...	0905	0905	1005	1105	1205	1305	1405	1505	1505	1605	1630	1705	1705	1805	1905	1905	2031*	2206
Halle (Saale) Hbf d.	...	0503	...	0607	0707	0807	...	0907	0907	1007	1107	1207	1307	1407	1507	1507	1607	1633	1707	1707	1807	1907	1907	2037	2213
Köthen d.	...	0525	...	0628	0728	0828	...	0928	0928	1028	1128	1228	1328	1428	1528	1528	1628	1654	1728	1728	1828	1928	1928	2058	2234
Berlin Hbf **839** d.	...	|	...	|	|	|	0731	|	|	|	|	|	|	|	|	|	|	|	|	|	|	|	|	|	|
Magdeburg Hbf a.	...	0556	...	0656	0756	0855	0858	0956	0956	1056	1156	1256	1356	1456	1556	1556	1656	1722	1756	1756	1856	1956	1956	2126	2307
Magdeburg Hbf d.	0503	0601	0601	0700	0802	...	0901	1002	1002	1100	1202	1300	1402	1500	1602	1602	1700	1727	1802	1802	1900	2002	2002	2131	...
Helmstedt d.	0528	0628	0628	0727	|	...	0927	|	|	1127	|	1327	|	1527	|	|	1727	|	|	|	1927	|	|	|	...
Braunschweig Hbf d.	0551	0651	0651	0750	0851	...	0950	1050	1050	1150	1250	1350	1450	1550	1650	1650	1750	1816	1850	1850	1950	2050	2050	2218	...
Peine d.	0606	|	|	|	|	...	|	|	|	|	|	|	|	|	|	|	|	|	|	|	|	|	|	|	...
Hannover Hbf a.	0626	0723	0723	0823	0924	...	1023	1123	1123	1223	1323	1423	1523	1623	1723	1723	1823	1851	1923	1923	2023	2123	2123	2250	...
Bremen Hbf **813** a.	0750	|	|	0950	|	...	1150	...	|	1350	|	1550	|	1750	...	|	1950	2009	...	|	2150	...	|	...	...
Oldenburg (Oldb) **813** a.	0823	|	|	1023	|	...	1223	...	|	1423	|	1623	|	1823	...	|	2023	2040	...	|	2223	...	|	...	...
Emden Hbf **813** a.	0938	|	|	1138	|	...	1339	...	|	1539	|	1739	|	1939	...	|	2139	2154	...	|	2339	...	|	...	...
Norddeich **813** a.	...	|	|	...	|	...	1414‡	...	|	...	|	...	|	2014	...	|	2214	...	...	|	...	...	|	...	...
Bielefeld Hbf **810** a.	...	0840	0840	...	1041	...	...	...	1240	...	1440	...	1640	...	...	1840	...	...	...	2040	...	...	2240	...	...
Dortmund Hbf **800** a.	...	0932	0932	...	1132	...	...	...	1332	...	1532	...	1732	...	...	1932	...	...	...	2132	...	...	2332	...	...
Köln Hbf **800** a.	...	1115	1115	...	1248	...	...	...	1445	...	1648	...	1845	...	...	2045	...	...	...	2245	...	...	0045	...	...

Other regional trains **HANNOVER - BRAUNSCHWEIG** (most trains start from / continue to Bielefeld or Rheine – see Table **811**)

			⚒¶						
Hannover Hbf d.	0012	...	0448	0555	0655	and	2255	...	...
Peine d.	0038	...	0514	0624	0724	hourly	2324	...	...
Braunschweig Hbf a.	0055	...	0530	0641	0741	until	2341	...	...

	⚒								
Braunschweig Hbf d.	0420	...	0520	0620	and	2320	...	...	...
Peine d.	0437	...	0537	0637	hourly	2337	...	...	...
Hannover Hbf a.	0505	...	0605	0705	until	0005	...	...	...

Other regional trains **BRAUNSCHWEIG - MAGDEBURG** (calling at all stations)

	⑦w		Ⓐ¶	Ⓒ		Ⓐ		Ⓐ		Ⓐ		Ⓐ	Ⓒ	Ⓐ	Ⓐ		Ⓐ		Ⓐ			Ⓑ	⑥	Ⓑp	
Braunschweig Hbf d.	0107	...	0531	0541	...	0617	0717	0817	0917	1017	1117	1217	1317	1320	1417	1517	1617	1717	1817	1917	2017	2117	2147	2217	2347
Helmstedt d.	0136	...	0601	0610	0610	0646	0746	0846	0946	1046	1146	1246	1346	1348	1446	1546	1646	1746	1846	1946	2046	2146	2216	2246	0017
Magdeburg Hbf a.	0218	...	...	0652	0652	0728	0828	0928	1028	1128	1228	1328	1428	1428	1528	1628	1728	1828	1928	2028	2128	2228	2258	2328	...

	⑥	Ⓐ	⑦	⑥m	Ⓐ			Ⓒ	Ⓐ		Ⓐ		Ⓐ		Ⓐ		Ⓒ	Ⓐ		Ⓒ	Ⓐ				
Magdeburg Hbf d.	0253	0433	0503	0508	0533	0633	0733	...	0833	0933	1033	1133	1233	1333	1433	1533	...	1633	1733	...	1833	1933	2033	2203	2313
Helmstedt d.	0334	0514	0544	0545	0614	0714	0814	0913	0914	1014	1114	1214	1314	1414	1514	1614	1713	1714	1814	1913	1914	2014	2114	2244	2354
Braunschweig Hbf a.	0402	0542	0611	0612	0642	0742	0842	0942	0942	1042	1142	1242	1342	1442	1542	1642	1742	1742	1842	1940	1940	2042	2142	2313	...

Other regional / S-Bahn trains **MAGDEBURG - HALLE - LEIPZIG** (SEE NOTE ⊠)

	Ⓐt	Ⓐt		Ⓒz	Ⓐt		Ⓐt																	
Magdeburg Hbf d.	0407	...	...	0452	0456	...	0526	...	...	0607	...	...	and at	2007	...	...	2107	...	...	2207	...	...	2307	...
Schönebeck (Elbe) d.	0420	...	...	0503	0506	...	0539	...	...	0620	...	...	the same	2020	...	...	2120	...	...	2220	...	...	2320	...
Köthen d.	0447	...	...	0523	0525	...	0610	...	...	0647	...	...	minutes	2047	...	...	2147	...	...	2247	...	...	2347	...
Halle (Saale) Hbf ⊠ a.	0515	...	...	0550	0550	...	0638	...	...	0715	...	...	past each	2115	...	...	2218	...	...	2315	...	...	0015	...
Halle (Saale) Hbf ⊠ ... **881** ■ d.	...	0519	0549	...	...	0614	...	0649	...	...	0719	0749	hour until	...	2119	2149	...	2247	...	...	2349	...	...	0025
Leipzig Hbf **881** ■ a.	...	0554	0624	...	...	0639	...	0724	...	...	0754	0824		...	2154	2224	...	2314	...	...	0015	...	...	0050

		Ⓐt			Ⓐt			Ⓐt																
Leipzig Hbf **881** ■ d.	0340	...	...	...	0443	0505	...	0535	0605	...	...	0635	0705	...	and at	2035	2105	...	...	2205	...	...	2335	...
Halle (Saale) Hbf ⊠ ... **881** ■ a.	0407	...	...	...	0517	0540	...	0610	0640	...	...	0710	0740	...	the same	2110	2140	...	...	2240	...	...	0001	...
Halle (Saale) Hbf ⊠ d.	...	0444	...	...	...	...	0544	...	...	0644	...	...	...	0744	minutes	...	...	2144	...	...	2251	...	...	0020
Köthen d.	...	0513	0513	...	...	...	0613	...	...	0713	...	...	...	0813	past each	...	...	2213	...	...	2316	...	...	0047
Schönebeck (Elbe) d.	...	0538	0538	...	...	...	0638	...	...	0738	...	...	...	0838	hour until	...	...	2238	...	...	2342	...	...	0111
Magdeburg Hbf a.	...	0550	0550	...	...	...	0651	...	...	0751	...	...	...	0851		...	...	2252	...	...	2354	...	...	0124

A – WARNOW – [12] Leipzig - Magdeburg (- Rostock / Warnemünde ♣) and v.v.
B – From Cottbus (Table **838**) on ①–⑥ (not Oct. 4).
C – To Cottbus (Table **838**) on Ⓑ (not Oct. 3).
D – ALLGÄU – [12] Oberstdorf - Stuttgart - Koblenz - Köln - Hannover - Magdeburg (- Leipzig ⑦).
E – ALLGÄU – [12] (Leipzig ① -) Magdeburg - Hannover - Köln - Koblenz - Stuttgart - Oberstdorf.
L – ①②③④⑦ (not Oct. 2, 30).
T – ①④⑤⑦ (also Oct. 1; not Oct. 3).

b – Also Oct. 2.
d – Not Oct. 3, 31, Nov. 19.
e – ①–⑥ (not Oct. 4).
f – Also Oct. 2; not Oct. 3.
g – ① only.
h – Not Oct. 4, 31, Nov. 19.
j – ⑥ (also Oct. 3).
k – Also Oct. 3; not Oct. 4.
m – Also Oct. 3.
p – Not Oct. 3.

r – From Sept. 28.
t – Not Oct. 31.
v – ①–⑥ (not Oct. 4). Departs 0531 June 17 - July 19.
w – ⑦ (also Oct. 4).
y – 1418 on ⑥ until Oct. 18.
z – Also Oct. 31.

‡ – Daily until Oct. 27; ①⑤⑦ from Oct. 31.
• – 3 minutes later until Sept. 27.
* – 4 minutes later from Sept. 28.
⊙ – Also calls at Hildesheim Hbf (d. 0531).
¶ – [12] Hannover - Braunschweig - Helmstedt.
♣ – Daily Leipzig - Magdeburg and v.v. Runs to / from Warnemünde (via Rostock) daily June 13 - Aug. 31 and ⑤–⑦ Sept. 5 - Oct. 19 (also Oct. 2; not Oct. 3). Runs to / from Rostock on ⑤ from Oct. 24. See also Tables **830**, **837** and **84**
■ – See Table **881** for S-Bahn service Halle - Leipzig/Halle Flughafen - Leipzig - Zwickau and v.v.
⊠ – The official minimum connecting time between trains at Halle is 7 minutes.

HARZER SCHMALSPURBAHNEN — 867

2nd class only

Nordhausen - Wernigerode: *Die Harzquerbahn*; Eisfelder Talmühle - Stiege - Alexisbad - Quedlinburg: *Die Selketalbahn*; Drei Annen Hohne - Brocken: *Die Brockenbahn*

Summer service Apr. 26 - Nov. 2, 2014

km			🚂	🚂	🚂	🚂	🚂 B	🚂	🚂	🚂 B	🚂	
0	**Wernigerode** § ....d.	0725	0855	0942	1025	1155	...	1325	1455	...	1625	1625
15	Drei Annen Hohne ....a.	0802	0932	1019	1102	1232	...	1402	1532	...	1702	1702
15	Drei Annen Hohne ◇ d.	0810	0945	1030	1115	1240	1245	1415	1551	1540	1716	1718
20	Schierke .... ◇ a.	|	0957	1042	1127	|	1257	1427	1603	|	1728	|
20	Schierke .... ◇ d.	|	1005	1050	1135	|	1313	1440	1621	|	1748	|
34	**Brocken** .... ◇ a.	|	1036	1121	1206	|	1344	1530	1652	|	1819	|
19	Elend......................d.	0822	▬	▬	...	1252	▬	...	...	1552	...	1730
28	Sorge ....d.	0841	...	...	...	1311	...	...	...	1611	...	1749
31	Benneckenstein ....d.	0850	...	🚋	...	1320	...	...	...	1620	...	1758
44	Eisfelder Talmühle ...a.	0919	Ⓒ	Ⓐ	...	1349	...	...	...	1650	...	1827
44	Eisfelder Talmühle ...d.	...	0943	*0943*	...	...	1402	...	...	1702	...	*1834*
50	Ilfeld ....d.	...	0959	0959	...	...	1417	...	...	1717	...	*1849*
61	**Nordhausen** Nord § a.	...	1022*	1022*	...	...	1438t	...	...	1739	...	*1913**

		◇	🚂 B	🚂	🚂		🚂	🚂	🚂	🚂	🚋	
Nordhausen Nord §.. d.		*0854**	1025	...	...	1325	...	...	...	...	1754*	...
Ilfeld .... d.		*0917*	1047	...	...	1346	...	...	...	...	1815	*1817*
Eisfelder Talmühle .... a.		*0931*	1101	...	...	1400	...	...	...	...	▬	*1831*
Eisfelder Talmühle .... d.		0938	1108	...	...	▬	1408	...	...	...	...	1838
Benneckenstein .... d.		1008	1138	...	...	...	1438	...	...	...	...	1908
Sorge .... d.		1016	1146	...	...	...	1446	...	...	...	...	1916
Elend......................... d.		1035	1206	...	...	🚂 B	1506	...	...	...	🚂	1936
Brocken .... ◇ d.		|	|	1136	1314	1451	|	1622	1707	1749	1831	|
Schierke.................. a.		|	|	1216	1354	1521	|	1702	1746	1829	1901	|
Schierke............. ◇ d.		|	|	1224	1355	1522	|	1703	1747	1830	1902	|
Drei Annen Hohne . ◇ a.		1046	1217	1236	1407	1533	1517	1714	1759	1841	1913	1947
Drei Annen Hohne .... d.		1108	...	1253	1423	...	1553	1723	1808	1853	1923	1954
Wernigerode § .... a.		1145	...	1333	1503	...	1633	1800	1845	1930	2000	2030

km		🚂	◧	🚂		🚂	◧				◧	🚂
0	**Quedlinburg** § ....d.	...	0830	1030	...	*1340*	...	...	1530	...	1753	1943
8	**Gernrode** ....a.	...	0845	1045	...	*1355*	...	...	1545	...	1808	1958
8	**Gernrode** ....d.	0734	0846	1046	...	1357	1502	...	1546	...	1809	▬
18	Mägdesprung ....d.	0805	0918	1117	...	1429	1533	...	1618	...	1843	...
	Harzgerode ....d.	|	|	|	1209	|	|	1620	|	...	|	1841
23	Alexisbad.................a.	0819	0932	1131	1219	1443	1547	1630	1632	...	1857	1851
23	Alexisbad.................d.	0826	0939	*1133*	1225	1456	▬	▬	1633	1634	1904	1859
26	**Harzgerode** ....a.	0835	|	*1143*	|	|	...	...	|	1643	1913	|
26	Silberhütte ....d.	▬	0950	▬	1236	1507	...	...	1644	▬	▬	1910
30	Straßberg (Harz) .....d.	...	1001	...	1247	1521	...	...	1655	...	...	1921
35	Güntersberge ....d.	...	1010	...	1256	1530	🚂	...	1704	...	...	1930
	Hasselfelde ....d.	1012	|	...	|	|	1610	...	|	1758	...	|
44	Stiege.....................a.	1025	1026	...	1312	1546	1623	...	1720	1811	...	1946
44	Stiege.....................d.	...	1027	...	1327	1547	1624	...	1725	1812	...	1947
48	**Hasselfelde** ....a.	...	|	...	|	1600	|	🚂 B	1738	|	...	|
53	Eisfelder Talmühle ...d.	...	1051	1103	1402r	...	1644	1702	...	1834	1915	2014
59	Ilfeld ....d.	...	...	1118	1417	...	...	1717	...	1849	1929	2029
70	**Nordhausen** Nord § a.	...	...	1139	1438t	...	...	1739	...	1913*	1952	2053*

			◇		🚂 B	◧					🚂	
Nordhausen Nord §.. d.		0825	0854*	...	1025	...	1225	1325	...	1625	...	...
Ilfeld .... d.		0849	0917	...	1047	...	1246	1346	...	1646	...	...
Eisfelder Talmühle .... d.		0903	0932	...	1101	1106	1301	1401	...	1700	1702	...
Hasselfelde .... d.		▬	|	1012	▬	|	|	|	1440	▬	|	...
Stiege........................ a.		...	0953	1025	...	1126	1322	1422	1453	...	1723	...
Stiege........................ d.		...	0954	1031	...	1127	1323	1423	1454	...	1733	1725
Hasselfelde .... a.		...	1007	|	...	|	|	1436	|	...	|	1738
Güntersberge............ d.		...	▬	1047	...	1145	1341	...	1510	...	1749	▬
Straßberg (Harz)........ d.		...	...	1057	...	1155	1350	...	1520	...	1758	...
Silberhütte .... d.		...	🚂	1109	...	1206	1402	...	1531	...	1810	◧
Harzgerode .... d.		...	0845	|	...	|	|	...	|	...	⊙	1923
Alexisbad.................. a.		...	0855	1119	🚂	1217	1412	...	1542	◧	1820	1933
Alexisbad.................. d.		...	0902	1133	1146	1224	1413	...	1549	1602	1827	1940
Harzgerode .... a.		...	|	1143	|	|	|	...	1558	|	⊙	|
Mägdesprung............. d.		...	0919	...	1201	1238	1430	...	...	1619	1842	1955
Gernrode .... a.		◧	0950	...	1231	1308	1500	...	...	1649	1912	2025
Gernrode .... d.		0759	0959	...	...	1309	1501	...	...	1659	1913	...
Quedlinburg §.......... a.		0815	1015	...	...	1325	1516	...	...	1715	1928	...

B – 🚃2 Brocken - Nordhausen and v.v.

r – Arrives 1349.

t – Arrives *1523** on schooldays (change trains at Ilfeld).

◧ – Steam train on ④⑤⑥ (also June 8).

🚂 – Steam train.

🚋 – Nordhausen Stadtbahn.

* – Nordhausen **Bahnhofsplatz**.

§ – Adjacent to DB station.

◇ – Change trains at Ilfeld on Ⓐ.

⊙ – Connecting trains: Harzgerode d. 1812 → Alexisbad a. 1822. Alexisbad d. 1826 → Harzgerode a. 1836.

◇ – Additional journeys (🚂) Drei Annen Hohne - Brocken and v.v.: From Drei Annen Hohne at 1200, 1339, 1506 and 1647. From Brocken at 1051, 1221, 1359 and 1540.

Operator: Harzer Schmalspurbahnen GmbH. Friedrichstraße 151, 38855 Wernigerode. ✆ + 49 (0) 3943 5580. Fax + 49 (0) 3943 558 148.

ERFURT - NORDHAUSEN — 868

RE / *RB* services

km		Ⓐ																	
0	**Erfurt** Hbf...................d.	0450	0604	0703	0803	0903	1003	1103	1203	1303	1403	1503	1603	1703	1803	1903	2003	...	2145
27	Straußfurt ....d.	0517	0626	0730	0825	0930	1025	1130	1225	1330	1425	1530	1625	1730	1825	1930	2025	...	2211
60	Sondershausen...........d.	0553	0658	0804	0858	0958	1058	1158	1258	1358	1458	1558	1658	1758	1858	1958	2058	...	2248
80	**Nordhausen**...............a.	0615	0715	0825	0920	1015	1120	1215	1320	1415	1520	1615	1720	1815	1920	2015	2120	...	2309

	Ⓐ	Ⓐ																
Nordhausen................d.	0422	0529	...	0637	0724	0831	0935	1031	1135	1231	1335	1431	1535	1631	1735	1831	1935	...	2140
Sondershausen............d.	0445	0552	...	0658	0747	0858	0958	1058	1158	1258	1358	1458	1558	1658	1758	1858	1958	...	2201
Straußfurt ....d.	0517	0626	...	0730	0825	0930	1025	1130	1225	1330	1425	1530	1625	1730	1825	1930	2025	...	2232
Erfurt Hbf....................a.	0542	0651	...	0751	0854	0951	1054	1151	1254	1351	1454	1551	1654	1751	1854	1951	2054	...	2257

☛ Subject to alteration from Oct. 6.

NORDHAUSEN - GÖTTINGEN — 869

RB services

km		①	⚒																Ⓑ
0	**Nordhausen**...............d.	0438	0538	0638	0738	0838	0938	1038	1138	1238	1338	1438	1538	1638	1738	1838	1938	2038	2142
20	Walkenried ....d.	0500	0603	0703	0803	0903	1003	1103	1203	1303	1403	1503	1603	1703	1803	1903	2003	2103	2203
23	Bad Sachsa ....d.	0506	0608	0708	0808	0908	1008	1108	1208	1308	1408	1508	1608	1708	1808	1908	2008	2108	2208
37	Bad Lauterberg ⊡ ......d.	0516	0619	0719	0819	0919	1019	1119	1219	1319	1419	1519	1619	1719	1819	1919	2019	2119	2219
43	Herzberg (Harz) ....d.	0523	0626	0726	0826	0926	1026	1126	1226	1329	1426	1526	1626	1726	1826	1926	2026	2126	2226
70	Northeim (Han)..... **903** a.	0547	0650	0750	0850	0950	1050	1150	1250	1353	1450	1550	1650	1750	1850	1950	2050	2150	2250
90	**Göttingen** .... **903** a.	0605	0712	0808h	*0909*	1008	*1109*	1208	*1309*	1410	*1509*	1608	*1709*	1808	*1909*	2008k	*2109*	2207	2308

	Ⓐ	⚒	Ⓐ	Ⓒ														⑤–⑦
öttingen .... **903** d.	*0409*	0538j	0638	0638	0749	*0848*	0949	*1048*	1149	*1248*	1349	*1448*	1549	*1648*	1749	*1848*	1949	*2051*	2149
lortheim (Han)...... **903** d.	0506	0606	0702	0706	0806	0906	1006	1106	1206	1306	1406	1506	1606	1706	1806	1906	2006	2109	2206
lerzberg (Harz) ....d.	0530	0630	0730	0730	0830	0930	1030	1130	1230	1330	1430	1530	1630	1730	1830	1930	2030	2133	2230
ad Lauterberg ⊡ ....d.	0536	0636	0736	0736	0836	0936	1036	1136	1236	1336	1436	1536	1636	1736	1836	1936	2036	2139	2236
ad Sachsa.................d.	0547	0647	0747	0747	0847	0947	1047	1147	1247	1347	1447	1547	1647	1747	1847	1947	2047	2150	2247
Valkenried ....d.	0552	0652	0752	0752	0852	0952	1052	1152	1252	1352	1452	1552	1652	1752	1852	1952	2052	2205v	2252
lordhausen................a.	0616	0715	0815	0815	0915	1015	1115	1215	1315	1415	1515	1615	1715	1815	1915	2015	2115	2227	2314

h – 0810 on ①.

j – 0546 on ⑥.

k – 2010 on ⑦.

v – Arrives 2155.

⊡ – Bad Lauterberg im Harz Barbis.

ERFURT - MEININGEN - SCHWEINFURT - WÜRZBURG — 870

DB (*RE* services); *STB*; *EB*

km		▽			▽ Ⓐt		▽ Ⓐt	▽			▽		▽		▽		▽		▽			▽		▽	
0	**Erfurt** Hbf............ **872** d.	0010	...	...	0406	0502	...	0648	0734	...	0849	0934	1049	1134	1249	1334	1449	1534	1649	1734	1830	1849	1934	2049	2213
23	Arnstadt Hbf .... **872** d.	0031	...	...	0427	0519	...	0710	0751	...	0911	0951	1111	1151	1311	1351	1511	1551	1711	1751	1847	1911	1951	2111	2232
31	Plaue (Thür) ....d.	0040	...	...	0435	0525	...	0721	0758	...	0921	0958	1121	1158	1321	1358	1521	1558	1721	1758	1853	1921	1958	2121	2239
37	Gräfenroda ....d.	0045	...	...	0440	0530	...	0726	0803	...	0926	1003	1126	1203	1326	1403	1526	1603	1726	1803	1858	1926	2003	2126	2244
53	Oberhof (Thür) ....d.	0059	...	...	0455	0543	...	0744	0815	...	0944	1015	1144	1215	1344	1415	1544	1615	1744	1815	1910	1944	2015	2144	2255
58	Zella-Mehlis ....d.	0104	...	...	0505	0548	...	0751	0819	...	0950	1019	1150	1219	1351	1419	1551	1619	1751	1819	1915	1951	2019	2151	2300
64	Suhl...........................d.	0111	...	...	0514	0554	...	0758	0825	...	0958	1025	1158	1225	1358	1425	1558	1625	1758	1825	1920	1958	2025	2158	2305
84	Grimmenthal .... **873** a.	0127	...	...	0535	0607	0629	0814	0836	...	1014	1036	1214	1236	1414	1436	1614	1636	1814	1836	1938	2014	2036	2214	2316
92	**Meiningen** .... **873** a.	0134	...	...	0544	|	0635	0821	*0848*	...	1021	*1048*	1221	*1248*	1421	*1448*	1621	*1648*	1821	*1848*	1949	2021	*2048*	2221	2322
					▬	|		▬	|		▬	|	▬	|	▬	|	▬	|	▬	|	▬		|	▬	
			◇ Ⓐe	◇	▽ Ⓐt	|	◇ ⚒r	◇	|	◇ ⚒r	◇	|	◇	|	◇	|	◇	|	◇	|	◇		|	◇ Ⓐe	
	Meiningen .... **873** d.	...	0416	0529	0549	|	0646e	0741	*0822*	0838e	0945	*1022*	1145	*1222*	1345	*1422*	1545	*1622*	1745	*1822*	1945	...	*2022*	2145	...
84	Grimmenthal .... **873** d.	...	|	|	0555	0608	|	|	0836	|	|	1036	|	1236	|	1436	|	1636	|	1836	|	...	2036	|	...
110	Mellrichstadt ....d.	...	0439	0552	...	0626	0712	0809	0849	0912	1009	1049	1209	1249	1409	1449	1609	1649	1809	1849	2009	...	2049	2208	...
124	Bad Neustadt (Saale) ..d.	...	0448	0605	...	0637	0722	0818	0857	0922	1018	1057	1218	1257	1418	1457	1618	1657	1818	1857	2018	...	2057	2217	...
134	Münnerstadt................d.	...	0456	0613	...	0646	0731	0828	0904	0931	1028	1104	1228	1304	1428	1504	1628	1704	1828	1904	2028	...	2104	2225	...
149	Ebenhausen (Unterfr) ..d.	...	0506	0630	...	0700	0744	0841	0917	0943	1041	1117	1241	1317	1441	1517	1641	1717	1841	1917	2041	...	2117	2241	...
163	**Schweinfurt** Hbf . **876** a.	...	*0521*	0642	...	0714	0754	0854	0926	0954	1054	1126	1254	1326	1454	1526	1654	1726	1854	1926	2054	...	2126	2254	...
206	**Würzburg** Hbf ..... **876** a.	...	...	*0722*	...	0744	*0820*	*0922*	0955	*1020*	*1122*	1155	*1320*	1355	*1521*	1555	*1722*	1755	*1921*	1955	*2122*	...	2157	*0015*	...

\- Ⓐ (not June 19, Aug. 15).

\- Not June 19, Aug. 15.

t – Not Oct. 31.

▽ – Operated by Süd Thüringen Bahn (2nd class only).

◇ – Operated by Erfurter Bahn (2nd class only).

870 WÜRZBURG - SCHWEINFURT - MEININGEN - ERFURT

DB (*RE* services); *STB*; *EB*

							◇	◇	◇	◇		◇		◇		◇		◇		◇		◇		◇	◇
				⚒v			⚒r	Ⓐe	Ⓒz	⚒r														Ⓐe	
Würzburg Hbf ...... **876** d.	...	...	...	0458	...	...	...	*0604*	*0604*	*0738*	0801	*0835*	1001	*1035*	1201	*1235*	1401	*1435*	1601	*1636*	1801	*1836*	2001	*2035*	*2143*
Schweinfurt Hbf .... **876** d.	...	...	...	0529	0534	...	0618	0648	0703	0806	0830	0906	1030	1106	1230	1304	1430	1506	1630	1704	1830	1904	2030	2104	2226
Ebenhausen (Unterf) .... d.	...	...	...	▬	0544	...	0633	0701	0720	0816	0840	0920	1040	1120	1240	1319	1440	1520	1640	1719	1840	1919	2040	2120	2243
Münnerstadt .... d.	...	...	...	...	0553	...	0645	0712	0731	0827	0849	0931	1049	1131	1249	1331	1449	1531	1649	1731	1849	1931	2049	2131	2254
Bad Neustadt (Saale) ... d.	...	...	...	...	0601	...	0654	0722	0740	0836	0857	0940	1057	1140	1257	1340	1457	1540	1657	1740	1857	1940	2057	2140	2303
Mellrichstadt .... d.	...	...	...	...	0610	...	0709	0731	0748	0848	0906	0948	1106	1148	1306	1348	1506	1548	1706	1748	1906	1948	2106	2148	2311
Grimmenthal .... **873** a.	...	...	...	...	0625	...	|	|	|	|	0919	|	1119	|	1319	|	1519	|	1719	|	1919	|	2120	|	|
Meiningen .... **873** a.	...	...	...	...	|	...	0732e	0756	0816	0912e	*0932*	1016	*1132*	1216	*1332*	1416	*1532*	1616	*1732*	1816	*1932*	2016	*2132*	2216	2335
					|		▬				|	▬	|	▬	|	▬	|	▬	|	▬	|	▬	|	▬	
	▽		▽	▽	|		▽				|	▽	|	▽	|	▽	|	▽	|	▽	|	▽	|	▽	
	Ⓐt				|																				
Meiningen .... **873** d.	0411	0509	0526	0615	|	0711	0733	...	...	...	*0906*	0933	*1106*	1133	*1306*	1333	*1506*	1533	*1706*	1733	*1906*	1933	*2106*	2133	...
Grimmenthal .... **873** d.	0418	0516	0537	0621	0626	0719	0740	...	...	...	0920	0940	1120	1140	1320	1340	1520	1540	1720	1740	1920	1940	2121	2140	...
Suhl .... d.	0435	0528	0554	...	0637	0731	0758	...	...	...	0931	0958	1131	1158	1331	1358	1531	1558	1731	1758	1931	1958	2133	2158	...
Zella-Mehlis .... d.	0441	0534	0602	...	0644	0737	0805	...	...	...	0937	1005	1137	1205	1337	1405	1537	1605	1737	1805	1937	2005	2139	2205	...
Oberhof (Thür) .... d.	0447	0539	0607	...	0649	0743	0810	...	...	...	0943	1010	1143	1210	1343	1410	1543	1610	1743	1810	1943	2010	2144	2210	...
Gräfenroda .... d.	0501	0551	0622	...	0659	0753	0826	...	...	...	0953	1026	1153	1226	1353	1426	1553	1626	1753	1826	1953	2026	2154	2226	...
Plaue (Thür) .... d.	0507	0555	0633	...	0704	0758	0837	...	...	...	0958	1038	1158	1238	1358	1438	1558	1638	1758	1838	1958	2038	2159	2242j	...
Arnstadt Hbf .... **872** d.	0517	0604	0641	...	0711	0806	0846	...	...	...	1006	1046	1206	1246	1406	1446	1606	1646	1806	1846	2006	2046	2207	2250	...
Erfurt Hbf .... **872** a.	0537	0623	0656	...	0725	0822	0907	...	...	...	1022	1107	1222	1307	1422	1507	1622	1707	1822	1907	2021	2107	2222	2309	...

e – Ⓐ (not June 19, Aug. 15).
j – Arrives 2231.
t – Not Oct. 31.
r – Not June 19, Aug. 15.
v – Not June 19, Aug. 15, Nov. 1.
z – Also June 19, Aug. 15.
▽ – Operated by Süd Thüringen Bahn (2nd class only).
◇ – Operated by Erfurter Bahn (2nd class only).

871 LEIPZIG - GERA - SAALFELD

Erfurter Bahn; 2nd class only

km																									
				Ⓐt	⑥	Ⓐt	Ⓐt																		
0	**Leipzig** Hbf ...... d.	0012	...	...	...	...	0506	...	0625	0726	0826	0926	1026	1126	1226	1326	1426	1526	1626	1726	1826	1926	2026	2126	...	2230
45	Zeitz .... d.	0052	...	...	...	0439	0547	...	0705	0805	0905	1005	1105	1205	1305	1405	1505	1605	1705	1805	1905	2005	2107	2205	...	2313
72	**Gera** Hbf .... a.	0115	...	...	...	0504	0617	...	0730	0830	0930	1030	1130	1230	1330	1430	1530	1630	1730	1830	1930	2030	2132	2230	...	2337
72	**Gera** Hbf .... d.	...	...	0454	0525	0525	0620	0620	0732	0832	0932	1032	1132	1232	1332	1432	1532	1632	1732	1832	1932	2035	2135	2302	...	...
84	Weida .... d.	...	...	0505	0537	0537	0632	0632	0746	0846	0946	1046	1146	1246	1346	1446	1546	1646	1746	1846	1946	2049	2152j	2316	...	...
99	Triptis .... d.	...	...	0518	0551	0551	0646	0646	0800	0900	1000	1100	1200	1300	1400	1500	1600	1700	1800	1900	1959	2103	2205	2330	...	...
108	Neustadt (Orla) .. d.	...	...	0525	0558	0559	0653	0653	0807	0907	1007	1107	1207	1307	1407	1507	1607	1707	1807	1907	2007	2110	2214	2337	...	...
139	**Saalfeld** (Saale) a.	...	...	0556	0625	0626	0720	0720	0829	0935	1029	1135	1229	1335	1429	1535	1630	1735	1830	1941	2030	2137	2237	0005	...	...

	Ⓐt			Ⓐt	⚒t		Ⓐt																		
Saalfeld (Saale) . d.	...	...	...	...	0515	...	0550	0620	0728	0824	0929	1024	1130	1224	1329	1424	1529	1624	1730	1824	1939	2026	...	2142	...	2242
Neustadt (Orla) ... d.	...	...	...	...	0542	...	0623	0654j	0752	0851	0952	1051	1152	1251	1352	1451	1552	1651	1752	1851	2007j	2053	...	2215j	...	2308
Triptis .... d.	...	...	...	...	0552	...	0631	0702	0800	0900	1000	1100	1200	1300	1400	1500	1600	1700	1800	1900	2015	2103	...	2223	...	2315
Weida .... d.	...	...	...	...	0609	...	0646	0715	0814	0914	1014	1114	1214	1314	1414	1514	1614	1716	1814	1914	2028	2116	...	2236	...	2330
Gera Hbf .... a.	...	...	...	...	0622	...	0657	0727	0825	0926	1025	1126	1225	1326	1425	1526	1625	1727	1825	1926	2039	2128	...	2247	...	2342
Gera Hbf .... d.	0350	...	0511	0541	0631	0631	...	0731	0831	0931	1031	1131	1231	1331	1431	1530	1631	1731	1831	1931	2042	...	...	2248	...	...
Zeitz .... d.	0415	...	0537	0607	0655	0655	...	0755	0855	0955	1055	1155	1255	1355	1455	1555	1655	1755	1855	1955	2107	...	...	2313	...	...
Leipzig Hbf ...... a.	0453	...	0616	0644	0733	0733	...	0833	0933	1033	1133	1233	1333	1433	1533	1633	1733	1833	1933	2033	2145	...	...	2351	...	...

km									
0	**Gera** Hbf .... d.	0557	0802	1002	1202	1402	1602	1802	...
12	Weida .... d.	0608	0815	1015	1215	1415	1615	1815	...
84	**Hof** Hbf .... a.	0721	0926	1125	1325	1525	1725	1925	...

Hof Hbf .... d.	0833	1033	1233	1433	1633	1833	2033
Weida .... d.	0945	1145	1345	1545	1745	1945	2147
Gera Hbf ...... a.	0956	1156	1356	1556	1756	1956	2158

j – Arrives 6–7 minutes earlier.
t – Not Oct. 31.

872 ERFURT - SAALFELD and ROTTENBACH - KATZHÜTTE

DB; Erfurter Bahn★; 2nd class only

km											
0	**Erfurt** Hbf .... **870** d.	0630	*0738*	0841	*0939*	1041	and in	*1939*	2041	*2213*	*2304*
23	Arnstadt Hbf .... **870** d.	0646	0802	0900	1003	1100	the same	2003	2100	2235	2331
38	Stadtilm .... d.	0657	0815	0913	1016	1113	pattern	2015	2114	2247	2344
54	Rottenbach .... d.	0709	0828	0931	1027	1131	every	2027	2127	2301	2356
62	Bad Blankenburg .... d.	0716	0835	0939r	1034	1138	**two** hours	2034	2134	2309	0003
70	**Saalfeld** (Saale) .... a.	0723	0842	0946r	1042	1146	until	2041	2142	2317	0011

Saalfeld (Saale) ..... d.	0604	0705	0810	0916	and in	1810z	1916	2043	2244
Bad Blankenburg .... d.	0611	0718	0817	0923	the same	1817	1923	2050	2251
Rottenbach .... d.	0620	0725	0829	0930	pattern	1829	1930	2058	2302
Stadtilm .... d.	0632	0739	0843	0942	every	1843	1942	2115	2314
Arnstadt Hbf .... **870** a.	0645	0752	0856	0955	**two** hours	1856	1955	2128	2327
Erfurt Hbf .... **870** a.	0706	*0818*	0915	*1018*	until	1915	*2018*	2144	2343

km													
					✣				□			⑤⑦
0	Rottenbach .... d.	0631	0729	0841	0941	1041	and	1641	1741	1841	1941	2041
15	Obstfelderschmiede .. a.	0655	0751	0905	1005	1105	hourly	1705	1805	1905	2005	2105
25	Katzhütte .... a.	0712	0809	0922	1022	1122	until	1722	1822	1922	2022	2122

							⊗			⑤⑦
Katzhütte .... d.	0626	0743	0836	0936	1036	and	1736	1836	1936	2036
Obstfelderschmiede d.	0643	0801	0853	0953	1053	hourly	1753	1853	1953	2053
Rottenbach .... a.	0705	0823	0917	1017f	1117	until	1817	1917	2017	2117

f – 1023 on Ⓒ until Oct. 5.
r – 6 minutes later on Ⓒ until Oct. 5.
z – 1804 on Ⓒ until Oct. 5.
✣ – Runs 8–10 minutes later on Ⓒ until Oct. 5.
□ – Runs 7–9 minutes **earlier** on Ⓒ until Oct. 5.
⊗ – Runs 9–11 minutes **earlier** on Ⓒ until Oct. 5.
★ – Erfurt - Saalfeld operated by Erfurter Bahn. Rottenbach - Katzhütte operated by DB.

☛ **Oberweißbacher Bergbahn**. Obstfelderschmiede - Lichtenhain - Cursdorf. Journey time: 29–44 minutes. **From Obstfelderschmiede** at 0625, 0700, 0730 and every 30 minutes until 1730 then 1808, 1830, 1908, 1930. **From Cursdorf** at 0614, 0644, 0710, 0734, 0814, 0844 and every 30 minutes until 1944.

873 EISENACH - MEININGEN - SONNEBERG

Süd Thüringen Bahn (2nd class only)

km																										
		Ⓐt		Ⓐt	Ⓐt										Ⓒz	Ⓐt		Ⓒz	Ⓐt							
0	**Eisenach** .... d.	...	...	0400	0450	...	0607	0715	0815	0915	1015	1115	1215	1315	1415	1415	1515	1615	1615	1715	1815	1915	2015	2115	2220	2311
27	Bad Salzungen .... d.	...	...	0423	0522	...	0641	0741	0841	0941	1041	1141	1241	1341	1441	1441	1541	1641	1641	1741	1841	1941	2041	2141	2249	2334
41	Wernshausen .... d.	...	...	0438	0538	...	0657	0757	0857	0957	1057	1157	1257	1357	1457	1457	1557	1657	1657	1757	1857	1957	2057	2157	2303	...
61	**Meiningen** .... a.	...	...	0501	0601	...	0714	0814	0914	1014	1114	1214	1314	1414	1514	1514	1614	1714	1714	1814	1914	2014	2114	2214	2320	...
61	**Meiningen** .... **870** d.	0404	...	0549	0615	0615	0719	0822	0919	1022	1119	1222	1319	1422	1519	1519	1622	1719	1719	1822	1919	2022	2119	...	...	...
68	Grimmenthal ...... **870** d.	0411	...	0556	0631	0631	0731	0831	0931	1031	1131	1231	1331	1431	1531	1542k	1631	1731	1742k	1831	1931	2031	2131	...	...	...
82	Themar .... d.	0430	...	0609	0644	0644	0744	0844	0944	1044	1144	1244	1344	1444	1544	1554	1644	1744	1754	1844	1944	2044	2144	...	...	...
94	Hildburghausen .... d.	0443	...	0621	0701	0701	0801	0901	1001	1101	1201	1301	1401	1501	1601	1605	1701	1801	1805	1901	2001	2101	2155	...	...	...
109	**Eisfeld** .... d.	0514k	...	0643	0716	0716	0815	0916	1015	1116	1215	1316	1415	1516	1615	1620	1716	1815	1820	1916	2015	2115	2210	...	...	...
141	**Sonneberg** (Thür) Hbf a.	0558	...	0727	0800	0800	...	1000	...	1200	...	1400	...	1600	...	...	1800	...	...	2000	...	...	...	...	...	...

	Ⓐt		Ⓐt																
Sonneberg (Thür) Hbf d.	...	...	...	...	0600	...	0802	...	1002	...	1202	...	1401	...	1602	...	1802	...	2002
Eisfeld .... d.	0401	...	0540	...	0645	0745	0845	0945	1045	1145	1245	1345	1445	1545	1645	1745	1845	1945	2045
Hildburghausen .... d.	0416	...	0555	...	0659	0759	0859	0959	1059	1159	1259	1359	1459	1600j	1659	1759j	1859	1959	2059
Themar .... d.	0427	...	0610	...	0711	0811	0911	1011	1111	1211	1311	1411	1511	1611j	1711	1811j	1911	2011	2111
Grimmenthal .... **870** d.	0440	...	0629	...	0726	0829	0926	1029	1126	1229	1326	1429	1526	1629	1726	1829	1926	2029	2126
Meiningen .... **870** a.	0446	...	0635	...	0732	0835	0932	1035	1132	1235	1332	1435	1532	1635	1732	1835	1932	2035	2132
Meiningen .... d.	0448	0549	0639	0639	0739	0839	0939	1039	1139	1239	1339	1439	1539	1639	1739	1839	1939	2039	2139
Wernshausen .... d.	0506	0608	0657	0657	0757	0857	0957	1057	1157	1257	1357	1457	1557	1657	1757	1857	1957	2057	2157
Bad Salzungen .... d.	0520	0622	0711	0711	0811	0911	1011	1111	1211	1311	1411	1511	1611	1711	1811	1911	2011	2111	2211
Eisenach .... a.	0544	0647	0740	0740	0840	0940	1040	1140	1240	1340	1440	1540	1640	1740	1840	1940	2040	2140	2236

j – 6–7 minutes later on Ⓐt.
k – Arrives 17 minutes earlier.
t – Not Oct. 31.
z – Also Oct. 31.

874 LEIPZIG - CHEMNITZ

RE services

km							
			⚒r				
0	**Leipzig** Hbf .... **856** d.	0526	0626	0726		2126	2337
33	Bad Lausick .... d.	0550	0650	0750	and	2150	0001
44	Geithain .... **856** d.	0559	0659	0759	hourly	2159	0009
66	Burgstädt .... d.	0614	0714	0814	until	2214	0024
81	**Chemnitz** Hbf .... a.	0625	0725	0825		2225	0036

		⚒r				
Chemnitz Hbf .... d.	0423	0533	0633		2033	2244
Burgstädt .... d.	0435	0544	0644	and	2044	2255
Geithain .... **856** d.	0450	0600	0700	hourly	2100	2310
Bad Lausick .... d.	0458	0607	0707	until	2107	2321
Leipzig Hbf ...... **856** a.	0520	0633	0733		2133	2350

r – Not Oct. 31, Nov. 19.

RE / RB services — Regional services NÜRNBERG - LICHTENFELS - SONNEBERG and JENA — 875

See Table **851** for faster *ICE* and *IC* services Nürnberg - Erlangen - Bamberg - Lichtenfels - Saalfeld - Jena and v.v.

km																										
		2	Ⓐe 2	Ⓐe	W	J	W	J	W	J	W	J	W	J	Ⓐe S	W	Ⓐe	J	W	J	W	L			⑥h	
0	**Nürnberg** Hbf .... **921** d.	0049	0447	...	0541	0642	0740	0841	0941	1041	1141	1241	1341	1441	1509	1541	1608	1641	1741	1841	1941	2041	2141	2247	2247	2346
8	Fürth (Bay) Hbf ... **921** d.	0057	0455	...	0548	0649	0747	0848	0948	1048	1148	1248	1348	1448	1516	1548	1615	1648	1748	1848	1948	2048	2148	2253	2253	2353
24	Erlangen .... d.	0114	0512	...	0600	0701	0800	0900	1000	1100	1200	1300	1400	1500	1527	1600	1627	1700	1800	1900	2000	2100	2200	2305	2305	0005
39	Forchheim (Oberfr) .... d.	0126	0524	...	0609	0709	0809	0909	1009	1109	1209	1309	1409	1509	1536	1609	1636	1709	1809	1909	2009	2109	2209	2314	2314	0013
62	**Bamberg** .... a.	0146	0543	...	0624	0730	0824	0924	1024	1124	1224	1324	1424	1524	1555	1624	1653	1724	1824	1924	2024	2124	2224	2329	2329	0029
62	**Bamberg** .... **876** d.	...	...	0553	0627	0736	0835	0936	1035	1136	1235	1336	1435	1536	1558	1635	1655	1736	1835	1936	2035	2136	2238	2344	2344	0031
94	Lichtenfels .... **876** a.	...	...	0617	0653	0754	0852	0954	1052	1154	1252	1358	1452	1554	1623	1652	1720	1754	1852	1954	2053	2154	2303	0009	0009	0057
94	Lichtenfels .... d.	...	...	0618	0659	0804	0904	1004	1104	1204	1304	1404	1504	1604	1625	1704	1722	1804	1904	2004	2104	2205	2309	0010	0010	...
114	**Coburg** .... d.	...	...	0644	0722	0821	0921	1021	1121	1221	1321	1421	1521	1621	1645	1721	1743	1821	1921	2021	2121	2221	2329	0029	0030	...
135	**Sonneberg** (Thür) Hbf a.	...	...	0706	0746	0842	0942	1042	1142	1242	1342	1442	1542	1642	1706	1742	1805	1842	1942	2042	2142	2242	2350	...	0051	...

		Ⓐe	Ⓒz	Ⓐe	K	Ⓐe K	Ⓐe W	Ⓒz S	Ⓐe S	J	W	J	W	J	W	J	W	J	W	J	W	J	W	J		2
Sonneberg (Thür) Hbf d.	...	0413	...	...	0512	...	0610	0610	...	0714	0812	0912	1012	1112	1212	1312	1412	1512	1612	1712	1812	1912	2012	2112	2212	...
Coburg .... d.	0400h	0434	...	0509	0533	0612	0638	0632	...	0741	0839	0939	1039	1139	1239	1341	1439	1539	1639	1740	1839	1939	2039	2140	2239	...
Lichtenfels .... a.	0416h	0454	...	0529	0554	0637	0657	0650	...	0757	0856	0957	1056	1157	1256	1357	1456	1557	1656	1757	1856	1957	2056	2159	2300	...
Lichtenfels .... **876** d.	0417r	0456	0456	0533	0600	0640	0658	0703	0721	0804	0903	1004	1103	1204	1303	1404	1503	1604	1703	1804	1903	2004	2103	2207	*2324*	...
Bamberg .... **876** a.	0442r	0522	0522	0559	0625	0701	0720	0730	0749	0820	0921	1020	1121	1220	1321	1420	1521	1620	1721	1820	1921	2020	2121	2231	*2349*	...
Bamberg .... d.	0446	0526	0529	0603	0630	0704	0733	0733	0801	0836	0936	1036	1136	1236	1336	1436	1536	1636	1736	1836	1936	2036	2136	2236	...	0015
Forchheim (Oberfr) ..... d.	0459	0545	0545	0617	0647	0719	0747	0747	0814	0850	0950	1050	1150	1250	1350	1450	1550	1650	1750	1850	1950	2050	2150	2249	...	0033
Erlangen .... d.	0510	0555	0555	0628	0656	0730	0757	0757	0824	0900	1000	1100	1200	1300	1400	1500	1600	1700	1800	1900	2000	2100	2200	2257	...	0045
Fürth (Bay) Hbf ..... **921** d.	0522	0609	0609	0641	0708	0743	0809	0809	0840	0912	1012	1112	1212	1312	1412	1512	1611	1712	1811	1912	2012	2112	2212	2309	...	0101
Nürnberg Hbf ...... **921** a.	0530	0616	0616	0649	0716	0751	0816	0816	0846	0919	1019	1119	1219	1319	1419	1519	1618	1719	1818	1919	2019	2119	2219	2317	...	0110

km																									
			Ⓐe							Ⓒu	Ⓐt		Ⓒz	Ⓐe		Ⓐe	Ⓒz					v	⑥h	⑤⑦j	⑤f
	Nürnberg Hbf (see above) d.	...	...	...	0642	...	0841	...	1041	...	...	1241	...	...	1441	1509	...	1641	...	1841	...	2041	2041	2041	2041
0	**Bamberg** .... d.	0506	0553	...	0736	0801	0936	1003	1136	1203	1203	1336	1403	1403	1536	1558	1603	1736	1816	1936	2016	2136	2136	2136	2136
32	Lichtenfels .... d.	0542	0617	0641	0800	0831	1000	1030	1200	1238	1244	1400	1430	1430	1600	1630	1630	1800	1842	2000	2042	2202	2202	2214	2214
56	Kronach .... d.	0603	...	0702	0812	0850	1012	1051	1212	1300	1307	1412	1451	1459	1612	1651	1651	1812	1903	2012	2103	2222	2223	2234	2235
119	**Saalfeld** (Saale) .... **849** d.	0701	...	0801	0906	0949	1106	1149	1306	1357	1405	1506	1549	1556	1706	1749	1749	1908	2001	2106	2201	...	2319	...	2334
129	Rüdolstadt (Thür) .... **849** d.	0709	...	...	0914	...	1114	...	1314	...	...	1514	...	...	1714	...	...	1917	...	2114	...	...	...	...	...
161	Jena-Göschwitz .... **849** d.	0729	...	...	0934	...	1134	...	1334	...	...	1534	...	...	1734	...	...	1942	...	2134	...	...	...	...	...
166	**Jena** Paradies .... **849** a.	0733	...	...	0938	...	1138	...	1338	...	...	1538	...	...	1738	...	...	1946	...	2138	...	...	...	...	...

	Ⓐe	Ⓐe	Ⓐe	Ⓒz	Ⓐe																				
Jena Paradies .... **849** d.	...	...	...	...	...	0620	...	0820	...	1020	...	1220	...	1420	...	1620	...	1820	...	2022	...	...	...	...	...
Jena-Göschwitz .... **849** d.	...	...	...	...	...	0624	...	0824	...	1024	...	1224	...	1424	...	1624	...	1824	...	2027	...	...	...	...	...
Rüdolstadt (Thür) .... **849** d.	...	...	...	...	...	0646	...	0846	...	1046	...	1246	...	1446	...	1646	...	1846	...	2049	...	...	...	...	...
Saalfeld (Saale) .... **849** d.	...	...	...	0535	0603	0654	0812	0854	1013	1054	1212	1254	1412	1454	1612	1654	1812	1854	2006	2057	2206	...	...	...	...
Kronach .... d.	0537	0613	0633	0633	0702	0747	0909	0947	1110	1147	1309	1347	1509	1547	1709	1747	1909	1947	2102	2150	2303	...	...	...	...
Lichtenfels .... a.	0557	0633	0652	0653	0719	0800	0929	1000	1129	1200	1329	1400	1529	1600	1729	1800	1929	2000	2121	2202	2323	...	...	...	...
Bamberg .... a.	0625	0701	...	0730	0749	0820	0957	1020	1157	1220	1357	1420	1557	1620	1757	1820	1957	2020	2148	2231	2349	...	...	...	...
Nürnberg Hbf (see above) . a.	0716	0751	...	0816	0846	0919	...	1119	...	1319	...	1519	...	1719	...	1919	...	2119	...	2317	...	...	...	...	...

J – Conveys 🚲12 Nürnberg - Lichtenfels - Jena and v.v. (see panel below main table).
K – Conveys 🚲12 Kronach - Lichtenfels - Nürnberg (see panel below main table).
L – Conveys 🚲12 Nürnberg - Lichtenfels - Kronach (- Saalfeld ⑤⑥ **g**) (see panel below main table).
S – Conveys 🚲12 Nürnberg - Lichtenfels - Saalfeld (see panel below main table).
W – Conveys 🚲12 Nürnberg - Bamberg - Würzburg and v.v. (see Table **876**).

e – Not June 19.
f – Also June 18, Oct. 2; not Oct. 3.
g – Also June 18, Oct. 2; not Oct. 3, Nov. 1.
h – ⑥ (not Nov. 1).
j – Also June 18, 19, Oct. 2, Nov. 1.

r – ⚒ (not June 19, Nov. 1).
t – Not June 10–20, July 30 - Sept. 15, Oct. 27–31.
u – Runs daily June 7–22, July 30 - Sept. 15 and Oct. 25 - Nov. 2.
v – ①②③④⑥ (not June 18, 19, Oct. 2, Nov. 1).
z – Also June 19.

RE / RB services — WÜRZBURG - BAMBERG - HOF — 876

km																										
		‡Ⓐe																								
0	**Bamberg** ..... **851 875** d.	...	*0506*	...	*0553*e	*0553*e	*0736*	*0736*	0838	0838	*0936*	*0936*	1038	1038	*1136*	*1136*	1238	1238	*1336*	*1336*	1438	1438	*1536*	*1536*	1638	1638
32	Lichtenfels .... **851 875** d.	0459	0548	...	0656	0656e	0806	0806	0859	0859	1006	1006	1059	1059	1206	1206	1259	1259	1406	1406	1459	1459	1606	1606	1659	1659
62	Kulmbach .... d.	0523	0611	...	0718	0718e	0826	0826	0918	0918	1026	1026	1118	1118	1226	1226	1318	1318	1426	1426	1518	1518	1626	1626	1718	1718
74	Neuenmarkt-Wirsberg a.	0534	0623	...	0726	0726e	0833	0833	0926	0926	1033	1033	1126	1126	1233	1233	1326	1326	1433	1433	1526	1526	1633	1633	1726	1726
74	Neuenmarkt-Wirsberg d.	0534	0627	0634	0727	0732	0835	0838	0928	0932	1035	1038	1128	1132	1235	1238	1327	1332	1435	1438	1528	1532	1635	1638	1728	1732
96	**Bayreuth** Hbf .... a.	0554	|	0657	|	0756	|	0856	|	0955	|	1056	|	1155	|	1256	|	1355	|	1456	|	1555	|	1656	|	1755
103	Münchberg .... **880** d.	...	0655	...	0755	...	0859	...	0955	...	1059	...	1155	...	1259	...	1355	...	1459	...	1555	...	1659	...	1755	...
116	Schwarzenbach .... d.	...	0707	...	0806	...	0909	...	|	...	1109	...	|	...	1309	...	|	...	1509	...	|	...	1709	...	|	...
127	**Hof** Hbf .... **880** a.	...	0718	...	0819	...	0920	...	1018	...	1120	...	1018	...	1320	...	1422	...	1522	...	1618	...	1720	...	1822	...

									‡	‡		
Bamberg ...... **851 875** d.	*1736*	*1736*	1838	1838	*1936*	*1936*	2038	2038	2139	...	2241	2241
Lichtenfels .... **851 875** d.	1806	1806	1859	1859	2006	2006	2059	2059	2209	...	2312	2312
Kulmbach .... d.	1826	1826	1918	1918	2026	2026	2119	2119	2231	...	2337	2337
Neuenmarkt-Wirsberg a.	1833	1833	1926	1926	2033	2033	2128	2128	2243	...	2349	2349
Neuenmarkt-Wirsberg d.	1835	1838	1928	1932	2035	2038	2130	2132	2243	2246	2350	2350
Bayreuth Hbf .... a.	|	1856	|	1955	|	2057	|	2157	2303	|	0015	|
Münchberg .... **880** d.	1859	...	1955	...	2059	...	2157	...	...	2314	...	*0036*t
Schwarzenbach .... d.	1909	...	|	...	2109	...	2209	...	...	2327	...	*0045*t
Hof Hbf .... **880** a.	1920	...	2019	...	2123	...	2222	...	...	2339	...	*0057*t

Hof Hbf .... **880** d.	...	0523	...	0636	0736	...	...	0836	0936
Schwarzenbach .... d.	...	0531	...	0645	|	...	...	0845	|
Münchberg .... **880** d.	...	0540	...	0656	0754	...	...	0856	0954
Bayreuth Hbf .... d.	0543	|	0701	|	|	0801	0900	|	|
Neuenmarkt-Wirsberg .... a.	0608	0604	0720	0725	0821	0826	0920	0925	1021
Neuenmarkt-Wirsberg .... d.	...	0616	0727	0727	0831	0831	0927	0927	1031
Kulmbach .... d.	...	0626	0736	0736	0839	0839	0936	0936	1039
Lichtenfels .... **851 875** a.	...	0648	0755	0755	0859	0859	0955	0955	1059
Bamberg .... **851 875** a.	...	*0720*j	0818	0818	*0921*	*0921*	1018	1018	*1121*

																										‡
Hof Hbf .... **880** d.	...	...	1036	1136	...	...	1236	1336	...	...	1436	1536	...	...	1636	1736	...	...	1836	1936	...	...	2036	*2136*v	...	2252
Schwarzenbach .... d.	...	...	1045	|	...	...	1245	|	...	...	1445	|	...	...	1645	|	...	...	1845	|	...	...	2045	|	...	2303
Münchberg .... **880** d.	...	...	1056	1154	...	...	1256	1354	...	...	1456	1554	...	...	1656	1754	...	...	1856	1954	...	...	2056	*2153*v	...	2316
Bayreuth Hbf .... d.	1001	1100	|	|	1201	1259	|	|	1401	1500	|	|	1601	1700	|	|	1801	1900	|	|	2001	2100	|	|	2204	...
Neuenmarkt-Wirsberg a.	1026	1120	1125	1221	1226	1320	1325	1421	1426	1520	1525	1621	1626	1720	1725	1821	1826	1920	1925	2021	2026	2120	2125	2230	2230	...
Neuenmarkt-Wirsberg d.	1031	1127	1127	1231	1231	1327	1327	1431	1431	1527	1527	1631	1631	1727	1727	1831	1831	1927	1927	2031	2031	...	2127	2233	2233	...
Kulmbach .... d.	1039	1136	1136	1239	1239	1336	1336	1439	1439	1536	1536	1639	1639	1736	1736	1839	1839	1936	1936	2039	2039	...	2136	2246	2246	...
Lichtenfels .... **851 875** a.	1059	1155	1155	1259	1259	1355	1355	1459	1459	1555	1555	1659	1659	1755	1755	1859	1859	1955	1955	2059	2059	...	2156	2306	2306	...
Bamberg ...... **851 875** a.	*1121*	1218	1218	*1321*	*1321*	1418	1418	*1521*	*1521*	1618	1618	*1721*	*1721*	1818	1818	*1921*	*1921*	2018	2018	*2121*	*2121*	...	2219	...	*2349*	...

WÜRZBURG - BAMBERG

km																										
			Ⓒz		Ⓐd	⚒r		Ⓐd																		Ⓒz
0	**Würzburg** Hbf ... **870** d.	0023	0023	...	...	0458	0604	0635	0738	0835	0935	1035	1135	1235	1338	1435	1538	1636	1738	1836	1938	2035	2139	2236	2302	2302
43	Schweinfurt Hbf.. **870** d.	0053	0054	...	0437	0544	0636	0659	0802	0900	1000	1059	1200	1259	1402	1459	1602	1659	1802	1859	2002	2059	2202	2300	2332	2333
68	Haßfurt .... d.	...	0110	...	0455	0600	0653	0712	0816	0912	1014	1112	1214	1312	1416	1512	1616	1712	1816	1912	2016	2112	2216	2317	...	2348
100	**Bamberg** .... a.	...	0132	...	0520	0622	0716	0730	0932	0930	1032	1130	1232	1330	1432	1530	1632	1730	1832	1930	2032	2130	2232	2338	...	0011
	Nürnberg Hbf **875** .. a.	...	...	...	...	...	...	0816	...	1019	...	1219	...	1419	...	1618	...	1818	...	2019	...	2219	...	...	...	...

		Ⓒz		Ⓐd	Ⓒz	Ⓐd																Ⓑb				
Nürnberg Hbf **875** ... d.	...	...	...	...	...	...	0541	...	0740	...	...	0941	...	1141	...	1341	...	1541	...	1741	...	1941	...	...	...	...
Bamberg .... d.	0034	0034	...	0448	0451	0553	0629	0725	0826	0840	0925	1026	1125	1226	1325	1426	1525	1626	1725	1826	1925	2026	2040	2140	...	2304
Haßfurt .... d.	0056	0056	...	0508	0513	0617	0644	0742	0843	0901	0942	1043	1142	1243	1342	1443	1542	1643	1742	1843	1942	2043	2101	2201	...	2326
Schweinfurt Hbf ... **870** d.	0112	0113	...	0524	0530	0639	0658	0757	0857	0918	0957	1057	1157	1257	1357	1457	1557	1657	1757	1857	1957	2057	2118	2218	...	2344
Würzburg Hbf ..... **870** a.	...	0144	...	0548	0602	0716	0722	0820	0922	0951	1020	1122	1220	1320	1420	1521	1620	1722	1821	1921	2020	2122	2150	2251	...	0015

– Also Nov. 1.
– Not June 19, Aug. 15.
– Ⓐ (not June 19).
0730 on Ⓒ (also June 19).

r – Not June 19, Aug. 15, Nov. 1.
t – Change trains at Trebgast (a. 2354, d. *0011*).
v – Change trains at Trebgast (a. *2215*, d. 2225).
z – Also June 19, Aug. 15.

‡ – Operated by *agilis* (2nd class only).

877 LANDSHUT - MÜHLDORF - SALZBURG

RB services

km		⑥k	Ⓐe								
0	**Landshut** (Bay) Hbf .... d.	...	...	0609r	0836	1036	1237	1436	1636	1836	2036
55	Mühldorf (Oberbay) ..... a.	...	...	0712r	0928	1128	1328	1528	1728	1928	2128
55	Mühldorf (Oberbay) ..... d.	0601	0606	0743	0943	1143	1343	1543	1743	1943	2146
120	Freilassing .... 890/1 a.	0700	0711	0841	1041	1242	1441	1641	1841	2041	2240
126	**Salzburg** Hbf .... 890/1 a.	0720	0729n	0855	1052	1320	1452	1652	1852	2120	2250

	Ⓐe	⚒r								
Salzburg Hbf. 890/1 d.	0453	...	0703v	0907	1107	1311	1507	1707	1907	...
Freilassing ..... 890/1 d.	0529	...	0720	0920	1120	1321	1520	1720	1920	2119f
Mühldorf (Oberbay) ... a.	0622	...	0814	1014	1214	1414	1614	1814	2014	2214f
Mühldorf (Oberbay) ... d.	...	0633	0830	1030	1230	1430	1630	1830	2030	2240
Landshut (Bay) Hbf .. a.	...	0723	0921	1121	1321	1521	1721	1921	2121	2329

e – Not June 19, Aug. 15.
f – ⑤ only.
k – Not Nov. 1.
n – 0750 on Dec. 8.
r – ⚒ (not June 19, Aug. 15, Nov. 1).
v – 0650 on ⑥ (also Oct. 3; not Nov. 1); 0641 on ⑦ (also June 19, Aug. 15, Nov. 1).

878 MÜNCHEN - REGENSBURG

DB (*RE* services); *ALX*

km		ALX ⚒rP	N	ALX	N	ALX	ALX P	N	ALX	N	ALX P	ALX ⑤f	N	ALX	N	ALX	ALX P	N	ALX	N	ALX	ALX ⑦		ALX	ALX
0	**München** Hbf ...... 944 d.	0455	0544	0644	0744	0844	0901	0944	1044	1144	1244	1244	1344	1444	1544	1604	1702	1743	1844	1944	2044	2044	2144	2244	0004
42	Freising .... 944 d.	0518	0608	0709	0808	0909	|	1008	1109	1208	1309	1309	1408	1509	1608	1629	1728	1808	1909	2008	2109	2109	2208	2309	0028
76	Landshut (Bay) Hbf 944 d.	0538	0635	0731	0832	0931	0944	1032	1132	1232	1332	1332	1432	1531	1632	1650	1749	1832	1932	2032	2132	2132	2231	2335	0050
99	Neufahrn (Niederbay) .. d.	|	0652	0748	0849	0948	|	1049	1148	1249	1348	1348	1449	1548	1649	|	|	1849	1948	2049	2148	2148	2247	2351	0106
138	**Regensburg** Hbf .... a.	0614	0717	0811	0914	1011	1020	1114	1211	1314	1411	1411	1514	1611	1716	1726	1825	1916	2011	2114	2211	2211	2319	0018	0133
	Schwandorf 879 885 a.	0649	...	0846	...	1050	1059	...	1246	...	1447	1447	...	1646	...	1759	1902	...	2047	...	2252	2252	...	...	...
	Hof Hbf 879 .... a.	...	...	1019	...	1220	...	...	1419	...	...	1619	...	1819	...	1937	...	...	2220	...	...	0026	...	...	...

	ALX ⚒r	ALX	Ⓐe	ALX Ⓒz	ALX Ⓐe	ⒶeN	ALX	N	ALX P	ALX	N	ALX	N	ALX P	ALX	N	ALX	N	ALX P	N	ALX	ALX	N	ALX P	N
Hof Hbf 879 .... d.	...	...	...	...	...	...	0535	...	...	0740	...	0940	...	...	1140	...	1340	...	...	...	1740	1843w	...	...	...
Schwandorf 879 885 . d.	...	0501r	...	...	...	...	0703v	...	0902	0909	...	1109	...	1303	1309	...	1509	...	1708	...	1909	2009w	...	2104	...
Regensburg Hbf .... d.	0442	0546	0622	0646	0653	0702	0747	0844	0951	0951	1044	1146	1244	1341	1346	1444	1546	1644	1746	1844	1946	2046	2050	2141	2245
Neufahrn (Niederbay) ... d.	0508	0610	0648	0711	|	0728	0811	0911	1014	1014	1111	1211	1311	|	1411	1511	1611	1711	1811	1911	2011	2111	2120	|	2317
Landshut (Bay) Hbf 944 d.	0527	0628	0707	0729	0732	0747	0827	0929	1030	1030	1129	1227	1329	1419	1428	1529	1627	1729	1827	1929	2027	2127	2138	2220	2335
Freising .... 944 d.	0548	0649	0731	0751	|	0810	0848	0951	1050	1050	1149	1248	1349	|	1449	1549	1648	1749	1849	1951	2048	2147	2210	2241	2357
München Hbf .... 944 a.	0615	0715	0757	0819	0819	0835	0915	1016	1116	1116	1217	1317	1417	1503	1516	1617	1715	1817	1915	2017	2115	2217	2235	2305	0023

N – To / from Nürnberg (Table **921**).
P – (12) München - Schwandorf - Furth im Wald 🚃 - Praha and v.v. See also Tables **57** and **885**.
e – Not June 19, Aug. 15.
f – Also June 18, Aug. 14, Oct. 2; not June 20, Aug. 15, Oct. 3.
r – ⚒ (not June 19, Aug. 15, Nov. 1).
v – 0707 on Ⓐ (not June 19, Aug. 15).
z – Also June 19, Aug. 15.
w – ⑦ only.
ALX – Operated by Vogtlandbahn. 🍷.

879 REGENSBURG - HOF

DB (*RE* services); *ALX*; Vogtlandbahn

km		2		Ⓐt	2	ALX	2	ALX	2	2 Ⓒc	ALX	⑤f	2	ALX ⑤f	H	2	ALX	ALX		2	ALX	2	ALX	ALX ⑦	
	München Hbf 878 .... d.	...	...	...	...	0644	...	0844	...	...	1044	...	...	1244	...	...	1444	1604	...	...	1844	...	2044	2044	...
0	**Regensburg** Hbf . 885 d.	...	0628	0730	0731c	0821	0931	1021	1131	1131	1221	1322	1331	1419	1431	1531	1621	1734	1828	1931	2021	2133	2221	2221	2326
42	Schwandorf .... 885 a.	...	0654	0756	0800c	0846	1000	1050	1159	1159	1246	1348	1400	1447	1458	1600	1646	1759	1855	2000	2047	2202	2252	2252	2356
42	Schwandorf .... d.	0502e	0655	...	0802	0847	1002	1051	1202	1202	1247	1349	1402	1451	1459	1602	1647	1800	1905	2002	2049	2205	...	2256	2357
86	Weiden (Oberpf) .... d.	0542	0721	...	0842	0914	1042	1117	1241	1242	1314	1419	1442	1517	1521	1642	1714	1826	1928	2042	2115	2245	...	2322	0032
137	Marktredwitz .... 880 a.	0623	0753	...	0924	0949	1124	1152	...	1324	1349	1453	1524	1552	1552	1724	1749	1901	1959	2124	2152	2327	...	2357	...
179	**Hof** Hbf .... 880 a.	*0704*	0819	...	*1004*	1019	*1204*	1220	...	*1404*	1419	1519	*1604*	1619	1619	*1804*	1819	1937	2024	*2205*	2220	*0006*	...	0026	...

	ALX ⚒r	Ⓐe	2 Ⓒz	ALX		ALX	2	ALX	2	ALX	2	2 Ⓐe	ALX	2	ALX ⑤f		2	2 ⑦	ALX	2	ALX ⑦		2		2
Hof Hbf .... 880 d.	...	0420	...	0535	0627	0740	*0756*	0940	*0956*	1140	*1156*	...	1340	*1356*	1443	1540	*1556*	*1632*	1740	*1756*	1843	1940	*2056*	...	*2223*
Marktredwitz .... 880 d.	...	0450	...	0601	0708	0807	0835	1007	1035	1207	1235	...	1407	1435	1509	1604	1635	1700	1807	1835	1909	2004	2135	...	2335
Weiden (Oberpf) .... d.	*0415*e	0524	0522	0638	0743	0841	0915	1042	1115	1243	1315	1321	1442	1515	1544	1638	1715	1735	1842	1915	1943	2035	2217	...	0014
Schwandorf .... a.	*0454*e	0547	0602	0702v	0807	0908	0953	1108	1153	1307	1353z	1401	1508	1553	1608	1701	1753	1803	1908	1953	2008	2058	2256	...	...
Schwandorf .... 885 d.	0501	0548	0604	0703v	0810	0909	1002	1109	1202	1309	1402z	1402	1509	1602	1609	1702	1805h	1805	1909	2002	2009	2111	...	2303	...
Regensburg Hbf .. 885 a.	0536	0615	0634	0737	0837	0938	1033	1137	1233	1338	1433z	1433	1536	1633	1637	1731	1837h	1837	1937	2033	2037	2140	...	2332	...
München Hbf 878 ..... a.	0715	...	...	0915	...	1116	...	1317	...	1516	...	...	1715	...	...	...	...	...	2115	...	2217	...	...	...	...

H – ①②③④⑥⑦ (also June 20, Aug. 15, Oct. 3; not June 18, Aug. 14, Oct. 2).
c – Ⓒ (also June 19).
e – Ⓐ (not June 19, Aug. 15).
f – Also June 18, Aug. 14, Oct. 2; not June 20, Aug. 15, Oct. 3.
h – ①–⑥ only.
r – Not June 19, Aug. 15, Nov. 1.
t – Not June 19.
v – On Ⓐ (not June 19, Aug. 15) Schwandorf a. 0705, d. 0707.
z – Ⓒ (also June 19, Aug. 15).
ALX – Operated by Vogtlandbahn. 🍷.

880 NÜRNBERG - HOF - DRESDEN

IRE / RE / RB services

km			Ⓐ		⚒			Ⓐ				C									C				
0	**Nürnberg** Hbf .... ● d.	...	...	...	...	...	...	0544	0544	0544	*0642*	0648	0648	0748	0748	*0842*	0848	0948	0948	*1042*	1048	1048	1148	1148	*1242*
28	Hersbruck (r Pegnitz) .... ● d.	...	...	...	...	...	...	0605	0605	0605	|	0705	0705	0806	0806	|	0905	1005	1005	|	1105	1105	1205	1205	|
67	Pegnitz .... ● a.	...	...	...	...	...	...	0630	0630	0630	|	0730	0730	0831	0831	|	0930	1030	1030	|	1130	1130	1230	1230	|
67	Pegnitz .... d.	...	...	...	...	...	...	0633	0633	0638	|	0732	0736	0833	0838	|	0936	1033	1038	|	1132	1136	1233	1238	|
	Bayreuth Hbf .... d.	...	...	...	...	...	...	|	|	0656	*0731*	|	0756	|	0855	*0931*	0956	|	1055	*1131*	|	1156	|	1255	*133*
	Münchberg .... 876 d.	...	...	...	...	...	...	|	|	...	*0805*	|	...	|	...	*1005*	▬	|	...	*1205*	|	...	|	...	*140*
94	Kirchenlaibach .... d.	...	...	...	...	...	...	0649	0649	...	|	0747	...	0849	...	|	...	1049	...	|	1147	...	1249	...	|
125	Marktredwitz .... 879 d.	...	...	...	...	...	...	0706	0706	...	|	0803	...	0906	...	|	...	1106	...	|	1203	...	1306	...	|
167	**Hof** Hbf .... 876 879 a.	...	...	...	...	...	...	0728	0728	...	*0823*	*0904*	...	0928	...	*1023*	...	1128	...	*1224*	*1304*	...	1328	...	*142*
167	**Hof** Hbf .... 881 d.	...	0425	...	0530	0627	...	0730	▬	...	0827	▬	...	0930	...	1027	...	1130	...	1227	▬	...	1330	...	1427
215	Plauen (Vogtl) ob Bf ..... 881 d.	...	0457	...	0558	0658	...	0758	...	...	0858	...	...	0958	...	1058	...	1158	...	1258	...	...	1358	...	1458
240	Reichenbach (Vogtl) ob Bf 881 d.	...	0514	...	0615	0715	...	0815	...	...	0915	...	...	1015	...	1115	...	1215	...	1315	...	...	1415	...	1515
263	**Zwickau** (Sachs) Hbf .... d.	...	0530	0538	0631	0731	0738	0831	0838	...	0931	0938	...	1031	...	1131	1138	1231	...	1331	1338	...	1431	...	1531
279	Glauchau (Sachs) .... 858 d.	...	0540	0554	0640	0741	0754	0840	0854	...	0941	0954	...	1040	...	1141	1154	1240	...	1341	1354	...	1440	...	1541
311	**Chemnitz** Hbf .... 858 d.	0430	0602	0630	0702	0802	0830	0902	0930	...	1002	1030	...	1102	...	1202	1230	1302	...	1402	1430	...	1502	...	1602
324	Flöha .... d.	0443	0613	0643	0713	0813	0843	0913	0943	...	1013	1043	...	1113	...	1213	1243	1313	...	1413	1443	...	1513	...	1613
350	Freiberg (Sachs) .... d.	0508	0631	0708	0729	0831	0908	0929	1007	...	1031	1108	...	1129	...	1231	1308	1329	...	1431	1508	...	1529	...	163
390	**Dresden** Hbf .... a.	0551	0703	0751	0801	0903	0951	1001	...	...	1103	1151	...	1201	...	1303	1351	1401	...	1503	1551	...	1601	...	170

						C					C											◇			
Nürnberg Hbf .... ● d.	1248	1248	1348	1348	*1442*	1448	1448	1548	1548	*1642*	1648	1648	1746	1746	*1842*	1848	1848	1948	1948	2055	2055	...	2148	2148	225
Hersbruck (r Pegnitz) .... ● d.	1305	1305	1405	1405	|	1505	1505	1605	1605	|	1705	1705	1805	1805	|	1905	1905	2005	2005	2112	2112	...	2205	2205	231
Pegnitz .... ● a.	1330	1330	1430	1430	|	1530	1530	1630	1630	|	1730	1730	1830	1830	|	1930	1930	2030	2030	2137	2137	...	2230	2230	233
Pegnitz .... d.	1332	1336	1433	1438	|	1532	1536	1633	1638	|	1732	1736	1833	1838	|	1932	1936	2033	2038	2139	2144	...	2234	2241	233
Bayreuth Hbf .... d.	|	1356	|	1455	*1531*	|	1556	|	1655	*1731*	|	1756	|	1855	*1931*	|	1956	|	2055	2159	|	...	|	2258	235
Münchberg .... 876 d.	|	...	|	...	*1605*	|	...	|	...	*1805*	|	▬	|	...	*2005*	|	▬	|	...	...	|	...	|	...	003
Kirchenlaibach .... d.	1347	...	1449	...	|	1547	...	1649	...	|	1747	...	1849	...	|	1949	...	2050	...	...	2158	...	2252	...	|
Marktredwitz .... 879 d.	1403	...	1506	...	|	1603	...	1706	...	|	1803	...	1906	...	|	2017	...	2107	...	...	2215	...	2313	...	|
Hof Hbf .... 876 879 a.	*1504*v	...	1528	...	*1623*	*1704*	...	1728	...	*1823*	*1904*	...	1928	...	*2024*	2046f	...	2129	...	...	2236	...	2343	...	005
Hof Hbf .... 881 d.	▬	...	1530	...	1627	▬	...	1730	...	1827	▬	...	*1939*	...	2027	▬	...	*2134*	...	...	▬	*2247*	...	...	...
Plauen (Vogtl) ob Bf ...... 881 d.	...	...	1558	...	1658	...	...	1758	...	1858	...	...	*2017*	...	2058	...	...	*2213*	...	...	...	2340	...	...	...
Reichenbach (Vogtl) ob Bf. 881 d.	...	...	1615	...	1715	...	...	1815	...	1915	...	...	...	...	2115	...	...	...	...	...	...	0004	...	...	...
Zwickau (Sachs) Hbf .... d.	1538	...	1631	...	1731	1738	...	1831	...	1931	1938	2038	...	...	2131	2138	2243	...	...	...	2338	...	...	...	...
Glauchau (Sachs) .... 858 d.	1554	...	1640	...	1741	1754	...	1840	...	1941	1954	2054	...	...	2141	2154	2259	...	...	...	2354	...	...	...	...
Chemnitz Hbf .... 858 d.	1630	...	1702	...	1802	1830	...	1902	...	2002	2030	2130	...	...	2202	2230	2331	...	...	...	0025	...	...	...	...
Flöha .... d.	1643	...	1713	...	1813	1843	...	1913	...	2013	2043	2143	...	...	2213	2243	2343	...	...	...	...	...	...	...	...
Freiberg (Sachs) .... d.	1708	...	1729	...	1831	1908	...	1929	...	2031	2108	2208	...	...	2231	2308	0007	...	...	...	...	...	...	...	...
Dresden Hbf .... a.	1751	...	1801	...	1903	1951	...	1958	...	2103	2151	2251e	...	...	2303	2351	...	...	...	...	...	...	...	...	...

C – To Cheb (Table **1121**).
e – Ⓐ (not Oct. 31, Nov. 19).
f – ⑤ (not Oct. 3).
v – *1444* on Ⓐ (not June 19).
◇ – Operated by Vogtlandbahn.
● – Most trains between Nürnberg and Pegnitz convey portions for two separate destinations. Passengers should take care to join the correct portion for their destination.

DRESDEN - HOF - NÜRNBERG — 880

IRE / RE services

km			Ⓐt					Ⓐ			†	⚒		C										C	
0	**Dresden** Hbf	d.	...	...	...	...	...	...	0453	0507	...	...	0556	...	...	0653	0707	0756	...	0853	0907	0956	...	...	...	1053
40	Freiberg (Sachs)	d.	...	...	...	...	...	0450	0525	0550	...	...	0627	...	...	0725	0750	0827	...	0925	0950	1027	...	...	...	1125
66	Flöha	d.	...	...	...	...	...	0513	0545	0613	...	...	0643	...	...	0745	0813	0843	...	0945	1013	1043	...	...	...	1145
79	**Chemnitz** Hbf	858 d.	...	...	0410	...	...	0530	0555	0630	...	...	0655	...	...	0755	0830	0855	...	0955	1030	1055	...	...	...	1155
111	Glauchau (Sachs)	858 d.	...	...	0442	...	...	0602	0616	0702	...	...	0718	...	...	0816	0902	0918	...	1016	1102	1118	...	...	...	1216
127	**Zwickau** (Sachs) Hbf	d.	...	...	0459	0509	...	0619	0627	0719	...	...	0727	...	...	0827	0919	0927	...	1027	1119	1127	...	...	...	1227
150	Reichenbach (Vogtl) ob Bf	881 d.	...	...	▬	0527	...	▬	0643	▬	...	...	0745	...	...	0843	▬	0945	...	1043	...	1145	...	...	...	1243
175	Plauen (Vogtl) ob Bf	881 d.	...	...	...	0545	...	...	0700	...	...	*0745*	0802	...	...	0900	...	1002	...	1100	...	1202	...	...	...	1300
223	**Hof** Hbf	881 a.	...	...	...	0617	...	...	0732	⚒r	...	*0825*	0830	...	...	0932	...	1030	...	1132	...	1230	...	...	...	1332
223	**Hof** Hbf	876 879 d.	...	0420	0518	▬	0627	...	▬	0736	...	0832	0832	...	*0856*	*0936*	...	1032	...	*1136*	...	1232	...	...	*1256*	*1336*
	Marktredwitz	879 d.	...	0442	0549	...	0655	...	...	|	...	0855	0855	...	0956	|	...	1055	...	|	...	1255	...	...	1356	|
	Kirchenlaibach	d.	...	0506	0606	...	0711	...	...	|	...	0911	0911	...	1012	|	...	1111	...	|	...	1311	...	...	1412	|
	Münchberg	876 d.	...	|	|	...	|	...	...	0754	...	|	|	...	|	*0954*	...	|	...	*1154*	...	|	...	...	|	*1354*
295	**Bayreuth** Hbf	d.	0502	|	|	0605	|	0712	0803	0829	0903	|	|	1003	|	*1029*	1103	|	1203	*1229*	...	|	1310	1403	|	*1429*
322	Pegnitz	a.	0523	0527	0622	0627	0731	0735	0823	|	0921	0927	0927	1023	1027	|	1121	1127	1223	|	...	1327	1335	1423	1427	|
322	Pegnitz	d.	0529	0529	0630	0630	0738	0738	0830	|	0930	0930	0930	1030	1030	|	1130	1130	1230	|	...	1338	1338	1430	1430	|
361	Hersbruck (r Pegnitz)	d.	0552	0552	0654	0654	0759	0759	0856	|	0956	0956	0956	1056	1056	|	1156	1156	1256	|	...	1359	1359	1456	1456	|
389	**Nürnberg** Hbf	a.	0607	0607	0710	0710	0817	0817	0914	0918	1014	1014	1014	1114	1114	*1118*	1214	1214	1314	*1318*	...	1417	1417	1514	1514	*1518*

			Ⓒ	Ⓐ							C						C						◇			
Dresden Hbf	d.	1107	...	1156	...	...	1253	1307	1356	...	...	1453	1507	1556	1653	1707	...	...	1756	1853	1907	1953	...	2107	2207e	2307
Freiberg (Sachs)	d.	1150	...	1227	1250	...	1325	1350	1427	...	...	1525	1550	1627	1725	1750	...	...	1827	1925	1950	2025	...	2150	2250	2350
Flöha	d.	1213	...	1243	1313	...	1345	1413	1443	...	...	1545	1613	1643	1745	1813	...	...	1843	1945	2013	2045	...	2213	2313	0013
Chemnitz Hbf	858 d.	1230	...	1255	1330	...	1355	1430	1455	...	...	1555	1630	1655	1755	1830	...	...	1855	1955	2030	2055	...	2230	2331	0025
Glauchau (Sachs)	858 d.	1302	...	1318	1402	...	1416	1502	1518	...	...	1616	1702	1718	1816	1902	...	...	1918	2016	2102	2118	...	2302	0003	...
Zwickau (Sachs) Hbf	d.	1319	...	1327	1419	...	1427	1519	1527	...	...	1627	1719	1727	1827	1919	...	...	1927	2027	2119	2128	2208	2319	0020	...
Reichenbach (Vogtl) ob Bf	881 d.	▬	...	1345	▬	...	1443	▬	1545	...	...	1643	▬	1745	1843	▬	...	...	1945	2043	▬	▬	2230	...	...	...
Plauen (Vogtl) ob Bf	881 d.	...	*1345*	1402	...	...	1500	...	1602	...	...	1700	...	1802	1900	...	...	...	2002	2100	...	...	2255	...	...	...
Hof Hbf	881 a.	...	*1425*	1430	...	...	1532	...	1630	...	...	1732	...	1830	1932	...	...	...	2030	2132	...	‡	...	...	...	...
Hof Hbf	876 879 d.	...	1432	1432	...	*1456*	*1536*	...	1632	...	*1656*	*1736*	...	1832	*1936*	...	*1856*	...	2032	...	2136	2223	...	...	...	...
Marktredwitz	879 d.	...	1455	1455	...	1556	|	...	1655	...	1756	|	...	1855	|	...	1956	...	2055	...	|	2257	...	...	...	...
Kirchenlaibach	d.	...	1511	1511	...	1612	|	...	1711	...	1812	|	...	1911	|	...	2012	...	2111	...	|	2321	...	...	...	...
Münchberg	876 d.	...	|	|	...	|	*1554*	...	|	...	|	*1754*	...	|	*1954*	...	|	...	|	...	2153	...	...	...	...	...
Bayreuth Hbf	d.	1503	|	|	1603	|	*1629*	1703	|	1803	|	*1829*	1903	|	*2029*	2003	|	2103	|	...	2228	...	...	...	...	...
Pegnitz	a.	1521	1527	1527	1623	1627	|	1721	1727	1823	1827	|	1921	1927	|	2023	2027	2121	2127	...	2247	...	...	...	...	...
Pegnitz	d.	1530	1530	1530	1630	1630	|	1730	1730	1830	1830	|	1930	1930	|	2030	2030	2130	2130	...	2248	...	...	...	...	...
Hersbruck (r Pegnitz)	d.	1556	1556	1556	1656	1656	|	1756	1756	1856	1856	|	1956	1956	|	2109j	2109j	2154	2154	...	2315	...	...	...	...	...
Nürnberg Hbf	a.	1614	1614	1614	1714	1714	*1718*	1814	1814	1914	1914	*1918*	2014	2014	*2119*	2124	2124	2214	2214	...	2330	...	...	...	...	...

C – From Cheb (Table **1121**).
e – Ⓐ (not Oct. 31, Nov. 19).
j – Arrives 2055.
r – Not June 19, Nov. 1.
t – Not June 19.
◇ – Operated by Vogtlandbahn.
‡ – Operated by agilis. 2nd class only.

ZWICKAU - LEIPZIG - HALLE — 881

S-Bahn 5

km																								
0	**Zwickau** (Sachs) Hbf	858 d.	...	...	0348	...	0503e	0513	0603	...	0703e	0713	0803	...	0903		1903	1913	2003	...	2103e	2113	...	2213
9	Werdau	858 d.	...	...	0358	...	0511e	0524	0611	...	0711e	0724	0811	...	0911	and in	1911	1924	2011	...	2111e	2124	...	2224
29	Gößnitz	858 d.	...	...	0414	...	0526e	0540	0626	...	0726e	0740	0826	...	0926	the same	1926	1940	2026	...	2126e	2141	...	2241
44	Altenburg	d.	...	...	0432	0502	0538	0602	0638	0702	0738	0802	0838	0902	0938	pattern	1938	2002	2038	2102	2138	2157	...	2257
80	Leipzig-Connewitz ★	d.	0026	0330	0510	0540	0610	0640	0710	0740	0810	0840	0910	0940	1010	every	2010	2040	2110	2140	2210	2239	2325	2339
85	**Leipzig** Hbf ★	866 d.	0037	0340	0520	0550	0620	0650	0720	0750	0820	0850	0920	0950	1020	**two** hours	2020	2050	2120	2150	2220	2248	2335	2348
104	Leipzig/Halle Flughafen ✈	866 d.	0051	0355	0536	0608	0635	0708	0735	0808	0835	0908	0935	1008	1035	until	2035	2108	2135	2204	2235	...	2350	...
122	**Halle** (Saale) Hbf	866 a.	0102	0407	0546	...	0648	...	0746	...	0846	...	0946	...	1046		2046	...	2146	...	2246	...	0001	...

Halle (Saale) Hbf	866 d.	...	0025	0414	...	0514	...	0614	...	0714		...	1814	...	1914	...	2014	...	2114	...	...	...	2247	2349
Leipzig/Halle Flughafen ✈	866 d.	...	0037	0426	0456	0526	0556	0626	0656	0726	and in	1756	1826	1856	1926	1956	2026	2056	2126	2156	2227	...	2259	0001
Leipzig Hbf ★	866 d.	0010	0051	0442	0510	0540	0610	0640	0710	0740	the same	1810	1840	1910	1940	2010	2040	2110	2140	2210	2241	2310	2315	0016
Leipzig-Connewitz ★	d.	0021	0101	0452	0520	0550	0620	0650	0720	0750	pattern	1820	1850	1920	1950	2020	2050	2120	2150	2220	2254	2320	2325	0026
Altenburg	d.	0107	...	0523e	0605	0621	0656	0721	0805	0821	every	1856	1921	2005	2021	2056	2121	2156	2221	2256	...	0008	...	...
Gößnitz	858 d.	...	...	0535e	0617	0634e	...	0734	0817	0834	**two** hours	...	1934	2017	2034	...	2134	...	2233	...	...	0020	...	...
Werdau	858 d.	...	...	0549e	0634	0648e	...	0748	0834	0848	until	...	1948	2034	2048	...	2148	...	2251	...	...	0038	...	...
Zwickau (Sachs) Hbf	858 a.	...	...	0557e	0646	0656e	...	0756	0845	0856		...	1956	2045	2056	...	2156	...	2302	...	...	0048	...	...

HOF - WERDAU ◇

km			Ⓐ							
0	**Hof** Hbf	880 d.	0557	0707	...	1107	...	...	...	...
	Cheb **1122**	d.	|	|	...	|	...	1406	1606	1806
48	Plauen (Vogt) ob Bf	880 d.	0639	0739	0939	1139	1339	1539	1739	1939
73	Reichenbach (Vogt) ob Bf	880 d.	0655	0755	0955	1155	1355	1555	1755	1955
90	**Werdau**	a.	0706	0806	1006	1206	1406	1606	1806	2006

Werdau	d.	0751	0951	1151	1351	1551	1751	1851	2051
Reichenbach (Vogt) ob Bf	880 a.	0802	1002	1202	1402	1602	1802	1902	2102
Plauen (Vogt) ob Bf	880 a.	0821	1019	1221	1421	1621	1821	1919	2119
Cheb **1122**	a.	...	|	1353	1553	1753	...	|	|
Hof Hbf	880 a.	...	1052	...	...	...	...	1952	2152

d – Not Oct. 31, Nov. 19.
e – Ⓐ (not Oct. 31).
★ – All trains also call at Leipzig MDR, Leipzig Bayerischer Bahnhof, Leipzig Wilhelm-Leuschner-Platz and Leipzig Markt.
◇ – Operated by Vogtlandbahn (2nd class only).

CHEMNITZ - VEJPRTY - CHOMUTOV — 882

DB (RB services); ČD

km				Ⓒz	⑥⑦	①–⑤	Ⓒz						
0	**Chemnitz** Hbf	880 d.	0536	0736	0836	0836	0936	1136	1336	1536	1636	1836	2036
13	Flöha	880 d.	0547	0747	0847	0847	0947	1147	1347	1547	1647	1847	2047
31	Zschopau	d.	0609	0809	0907	0909	1009	1209	1409	1609	1709	1909	2109
57	Annaberg-Buchholz ¶	d.	0646	0846	0941	0944	1046	1246	1445	1646	1745	1946	2146
64	Cranzahl ⊖	d.	0659	0900	1000j	0957	1058	1259	1457	1659	1800	2005z	2159v
74	Bärenstein (Annab)	a.	...	0911c	1012	...	...	...	...	...	1812c	...	...
75	Vejprty 🏛	a.	...	0914c	1014	...	...	...	...	...	1814c	...	...
75	Vejprty 🏛	d.	...	...	1019	...	...	...	...	...	*1819*c	...	...
133	**Chomutov**	a.	...	...	1135	...	...	...	...	...	*1941*c	...	...

						★		①–⑤	⑥⑦		
Chomutov	d.	...	...	*0803*c	...	...	...	...	1621	...	...
Vejprty 🏛	a.	...	...	*0930*c	...	...	...	...	1739	...	...
Vejprty 🏛	d.	...	...	0943c	...	...	...	...	1743	1843c	...
Bärenstein (Annab)	d.	...	...	0945c	...	...	...	...	1745	1845c	...
Cranzahl ⊖	d.	0557	0759	0959	1157	1357z	1557	1759	1803	1857c	1949
Annaberg-Buchholz ¶	d.	0610	0811	1011	1210	1410	1610	1811	1813	1910	2010
Zschopau	d.	0645	0845	1045	1245	1445	1645	1845	1847	1945	2045
Flöha	880 a.	0708	0908	1108	1308	1508	1708	1908	1908	2008	2108
Chemnitz Hbf	880 a.	0719	0919	1119	1319	1519	1719	1919	1919	2019	2119

⊖ – **Cranzahl - Kurort Oberwiesenthal** *Fichtelbergbahn* (17 km, narrow gauge steam). Journey: 60–65 minutes. **Service suspended Nov. 3–27.**
Operator: SDG Sächsische Dampfeisenbahngesellschaft GmbH, Bahnhofstraße 7, 09484 Kurort Oberwiesenthal. ✆ + 49 (0) 37348 151 0.
From **Cranzahl** at 1002, 1145, 1323, 1521, 1637 ⊡ and 1813. From **Kurort Oberwiesenthal** at 0835, 1015, 1158, 1336, 1449 ⊡ and 1650.

– ⑥⑦ only.
– Arrives 0951.
v – ⑤⑥ (also Oct. 2, 30, Nov. 18).
z – Ⓒ (also Oct. 31, Nov. 19).
★ – On Ⓐ (not Oct. 31, Nov. 19) an additional service runs from Cranzahl (d. 1459) to Chemnitz (a. 1619).
⊡ – ⑥⑦ (daily June 28 - Oct. 5; also Oct. 31).
¶ – Annaberg-Buchholz unterer Bf.

CHEMNITZ - AUE — 883

RB services

km												
0	**Chemnitz** Hbf	d.	0605	0810	0910	1110	1310	1510	1710	1910	2110	2245
27	Thalheim	d.	0658	0857	0958	1157	1357	1557	1757	1957	2157	2324
36	Zwönitz	d.	0709	0908	1009	1208	1408	1608	1808	2008	2208	2335
47	Lößnitz unt Bf. ⊗	d.	0719	0918	1019	1218	1418	1618	1818	2018	2218	2346
51	**Aue** (Sachs)	a.	0724	0923	1024	1223	1423	1623	1823	2023	2223	2351

			Ⓐe								Ⓒz	Ⓐe	Ⓒz	
Aue (Sachs)	d.	0410	0526	0629	0828	0929	1128	1328	1528	1728	1829	1928	2029	2128
Lößnitz unt Bf ⊗	d.	0415	0531	0634	0833	0934	1133	1333	1533	1733	1834	1933	2034	2133
Zwönitz	d.	0427	0543	0646	0845	0946	1145	1345	1545	1745	1846	1945	2046	2145
Thalheim	d.	0438	0558	0658	0858	0958	1158	1358	1558	1758	1858	1958	2058	2158
Chemnitz Hbf	a.	0516	0636	0740	0940	1040	1240	1440	1640	1840	1940	2040	2140	2236

– Not Oct. 31, Nov. 19.
z – Also Oct. 31, Nov. 19.
⊗ – Trains stop on request only.

884 ZWICKAU - JOHANNGEORGENSTADT - KARLOVY VARY

DB; ČD (2nd class only)

km		Ⓐt			⊠					
0	**Zwickau** (Sachs) Hbf . d.	0507	...	0607	and	1907	2007	2107	2207	2307
27	Aue (Sachs) .... d.	0540	0540	0640	hourly	1940	2040	2140	2241	2339
37	Schwarzenberg (Erzg) . d.	0555	0555	0655	until	1955	2055	2155	2254	...
56	**Johanngeorgenstadt**. a.	0620	0620	0720		2020	2120	2220	...	...

	Ⓐt	Ⓐt				⊡			
Johanngeorgenstadt ...... d.	...	0429	...	0529	0629	and	1929	2029	2129
Schwarzenberg (Erzg) ...... d.	0354	0455	0455	0555	0655	hourly	1955	2055	2155
Aue (Sachs) .... d.	0409	0509	0509	0609	0709	until	2009	2109	2209
Zwickau (Sachs) Hbf .... a.	0441	0541	0541	0641	0741		2041	2141	2241

km	See note ▶	Ⓐ		Ⓐ	Ⓒ¶		¶			Ⓒ	
0	**Johanngeorgenstadt**. d.	...	0725	0925	1025	1237	1437	1623	2040	2040	...
1	Potučky 🏛 .... d.	0600	0728	0929	1032	1244	1442	1626	2050	2050	...
28	Nejdek .... d.	0700	0819	1019	1118	1334	1536	1714	2135	2138	2224
44	**Karlovy Vary** .... a.	0726	0845	1045	1145	1401	1602	1740	...	2204	2250
47	**Karlovy Vary** dolní ... a.	*0734*	0854	1054	1151	1407	1608	1747	...	2210	...

See note ▶				¶	Ⓐ	Ⓒ	Ⓐ	Ⓒ¶		
Karlovy Vary dolní .... d.	0540e	0746	0945	1258	1345	1430	1707	1806	2103	...
Karlovy Vary .... d.	0546	0752	0951	1306	1351	1436	1713	1813	2111	...
Nejdek .... d.	0618	0819	1019	1333	1425	1505	1740	1839	2137	2221
Potučky 🏛 .... d.	0708	0906	1106	1423	1519	1602	1824	1924	...	2304
Johanngeorgenstadt ...... a.	0710	0908	1108	1425	1521	1604	1826	1926	...	...

e – Ⓐ only.
t – Not Oct. 31, Nov. 19).

⊠ – On Ⓒ (also Oct. 31, Nov. 19) the 1207 from Zwickau does not run Schwarzenberg - Johanngeorgenstadt.
⊡ – On Ⓒ (also Oct. 31, Nov. 19) no service from Johanngeorgenstadt at 1329 (starts from Schwarzenberg, d. 1355).
¶ – On ⑥⑦ operates as a through service Zwickau - Johanngeorgenstadt - Karlovy Vary and v.v.

▶ – Czech holiday dates apply (see page 2).

885 REGENSBURG - SCHWANDORF - FURTH IM WALD - PLZEŇ

DB (*RE* / *RB* services); ČD

km				2	2	**351**	2	2		2	**353**	2	2	2	2	2	**355**	2		2	**357**	2	2	2	2
				Ⓐe	Ⓐe	‡			¶		‡	Ⓐe	Ⓐe	Ⓒz	Ⓒz		‡🍷	Ⓐe	¶		‡🍷				⑤⑥f
	München Hbf **878** .... d.	...	...	...	...	0455r	...	...	...	...	0901	...	...	...	...	...	1244	...	...	...	1702	...	...	...	...
0	**Regensburg** Hbf . **879** d.	...	...	*0521*	...	0623r	...	*0730*	*0831*	*0931*	1031	*1131*	...	*1131*	*1231*	*1331*	1419	*1531*	*1631*	*1734*	1835	*1931*	*2031*	*2221*	*2221*
42	**Schwandorf** .... **879** d.	...	...	0555	0633	0705	...	0803	0905	1004	1107	1202	...	1207	1306	1406	1507	1604	1705	1804	1909	2007	2111	2306	2306
90	Cham (Oberpf) .... d.	...	...	0635	0716	0736	0839	0854	0940	1039	1135	1243	1247	1257	1339	1439	1535	1654	1740	1839	1938	2047	2146	2341	2342
109	**Furth im Wald** 🏛 .... a.	...	...	0652	0734	0749	0856	▬	0956	1056	1149	...	1305	1321	1356	1456	1549	1712	1758	1856	1951	2103	2202	...	2359
				▬	▬	|				▬	|			▬	▬	▬	|	▬	▬		|	▬			
		2	2	2Ⓐ	2	|	2	2		2	|			2	2Ⓐ	2	|	2Ⓐ	2	2	|	Ⓐ2			
109	**Furth im Wald** 🏛 .... d.	...	...	...	...	0750	0900	...	...	...	1150	...	...	...	...	...	1550	...	...	*1859*	1952	...	...	...	...
131	Domažlice .... d.	0337	0530	0605	0731	0810	0922	0939	...	1131	1210	...	...	1340	1428	1532	1610	1630	1739	1932	2012	2231	...	...	...
190	**Plzeň** Hlavni .... a.	0451	0649	0734	0847	0857	...	1049	...	1251	1257	...	...	1449	1545	1649	1657	1749	1847	2049	2059	2333	...	...	...
	Praha Hlavní **1120** .. a.	...	...	...	...	1044	...	...	...	...	1444	...	...	...	...	...	1844	...	...	...	2244	...	...	...	...

							2	2	**356**	2	2		**354**	2		2	**352**		2	2	2	**350**	2	2	2
							Ⓐ		‡🍷				‡🍷			Ⓐ	‡		Ⓐ		Ⓐ	‡			
Praha Hlavní **1120** .... d.	...	...	...	...	...	...	...	...	0515	...	...	...	0915	...	...	...	1315	...	...	...	...	1715	...	...	...
Plzeň Hlavni .... d.	...	...	...	...	...	...	0510	0610	0700	*0710*	0810	...	1100	1110	1310	1410	1500	*1506*	1610	1710	1810	1900	1910	2110	2300
Domažlice .... d.	...	...	...	...	...	...	0629	0723	0746	0827	0925	...	1146	1223	1422	1530	1546	1630	1731	1819	1919	1946	2024	2219	0005
Furth im Wald 🏛 .... a.	...	...	...	...	...	...	▬	▬	0810	0850	▬	...	1210	▬	▬	▬	1610	1653	▬	▬	▬	2012	▬	...	...
	2Ⓐe	Ⓐt¶	Ⓒv¶	‡🍷	⑥h2	Ⓐe2	2	2	|	2	¶	2	|	2Ⓒz	2	2	|	2Ⓒz	2	2	2	|	2		
Furth im Wald 🏛 .... d.	0443	0555	0609	...	0653	0657	...	0755	0812	0901	1002	1101	1212	1256	1401	1501	1612	1704	...	1800	1901	2014	2108	...	...
Cham (Oberpf) .... d.	0458	0612	0625	...	0710	0715	0715	0812	0826	0917	1017	1117	1226	1317	1417	1517	1627	1718	1718	1817	1917	2028	2124	...	...
Schwandorf .... **879** a.	0533	0651	0658	0703k	...	0754	0754	0844	0854	0955	1055	1155	1255	1357	1456	1555	1657	1757	1757	1856	1956	2056	2201	...	...
Regensburg Hbf .. **879** a.	*0615*	*0731*	...	0737	...	*0832*	*0832*	...	0929	*1033*	*1132*	*1233*	1331	*1433*	*1530*	*1633*	1737	*1837*	*1837*	*1930*	*2033*	2133	*2236*	...	...
München Hbf **878** ..... a.	...	...	...	0915	...	...	...	...	1116	...	...	...	1503	...	...	...	1915	...	...	...	...	2305	...	...	...

e – Not June 19, Aug. 15.
f – Not Aug. 15, Oct. 3, Nov. 1.
h – Not Nov. 1.
k – 0707 on Ⓐ (not June 19, Aug. 15).
r – ⚒ (not June 19, Aug. 15, Nov. 1).
t – Not June 19.
v – Also June 19.
z – Also June 19, Aug. 15.
¶ – From / to Nürnberg (Table **886**).
‡ – Train category *ALX* in Germany (operated by Vogtlandbahn).

886 NÜRNBERG - SCHWANDORF and WEIDEN

RE services

km		Ⓐt		Ⓐt		f						Ⓒv	Ⓐt		Ⓐt	f	Ⓐt									
0	**Nürnberg** Hbf .... ◧d.	0434	0536	0631	0648	0748	0848	0948	1048	1136	1248	1348	1353	1448	1536	1553	1636	1648	1736	1753	1848	1936	2055	2148	2255	0017
28	Hersbruck (r Pegnitz) ◧d.	0449	0551	0650	0712	0812	0912	1012	1112	1151	1312	1412	1412	1512	1551	1612	1651	1712	1751	1812	1912	1951	2117	2212	2315	0033
56	Sulzbach-Rosenberg . d.	0515	0619	0718	0733	0833	0933	1033	1133	1219	1333	1433	1433	1533	1619	1634	1719	1733	1819	1833	1933	2019	2138	2238	2339	0059
68	Amberg .... d.	0526	0627	0731	0743	0843	0943	1043	1143	1229	1342	1443	1443	1543	1630	1643	1729	1744	1830	1843	1943	2030	2146	2246	2347	0106
94	**Schwandorf** .... a.	0543	0644	0745	0757	0901	0957	1057	1157	1243	1358	1457	1457	1557	1644	1657	1744	1758	1846	1857	1957	2044	2200	2301	0003	...

	Ⓐt	⚒r	†w	Ⓐt	⚒r	†w	Ⓐt	Ⓐtf	Ⓒvf	Ⓐt				f												
Schwandorf .... d.	0412	0509	0516	0544	0557	0609	0644	0703	0709	0714	0809	0909	1009	1109	1209	1309	1409	1509	1609	1709	1809	1911	2009	2110	2209	0008
Amberg .... d.	0428	0526	0532	0559	0615	0626	0700	0721	0734	0734	0824	0924	1024	1124	1224	1324	1424	1524	1626	1726	1825	1925	2024	2124	2224	0023
Sulzbach-Rosenberg .. d.	0437	0535	0541	0607	0626	0634	0707	0732	0741	0741	0832	0932	1032	1132	1232	1335	1432	1532	1637	1734	1836	1932	2032	2132	2235	...
Hersbruck (r pegnitz) .. d.	0503	0607	0607	|	0648	0707	|	0752	0808	0808	0907	1007	1107	1207	1307	1407	1507	1607	1707	1807	1907	2007	2109	2202	2315	...
Nürnberg Hbf .... a.	0518	0621	0621	0651	0706	0722	0751	0808	0823	0823	0922	1022	1122	1222	1322	1422	1522	1622	1722	1822	1922	2022	2124	2218	2330	...

km		Ⓐt							
0	**Nürnberg** Hbf .... ◧d.	0434	0536	0631	0737	0836	and	2036	2255
28	Hersbruck (r Pegnitz) ◧d.	0449	0551	0650	0751	0851	hourly	2051	2315
97	**Weiden** (Oberpf) .... a.	0542	0645	0745	0845	0945	until	2145	0007

	⚒r									
Weiden (Oberpf) .... d.	0506	0610	and	1509	1609	1709	1809	1910	2010	2213
Hersbruck (r Pegnitz) .... a.	0606	0706	hourly	1606	1706	1806	1906	2006	2106	2306
Nürnberg Hbf .... a.	0621	0722	until	1622	1722	1822	1922	2022	2124	2330

f – To / from Furth im Wald (Table **885**).
r – Not June 19, Nov. 1.
t – Not June 19.
v – Also June 19.
w – Also June 19, Nov. 1.
◧ – Certain trains from Nürnberg and Hersbruck convey portions for two separate destinations. Passengers should take care to join the correct portion for their destination.

887 BAYREUTH - WEIDEN

Operated by *agilis* (2nd class only)

km		Ⓐt	Ⓐt											Ⓐt	Ⓒv												
0	**Bayreuth** Hbf .. d.	0507	0540	0630	0730	0742	0830	0930	0940	1030	1130	1140	1230	1311	1330	1340	1430	1530	1540	1630	1730	1740	1830	1930	2031	2230	0002
19	Kirchenlaibach a.	0528	0557	0646	0743	0758	0845	0943	0956	1045	1143	1156	1245	1333	1343	1356	1445	1543	1556	1645	1743	1756	1845	1946	2047	2246	0018
19	Kirchenlaibach d.	0535	...	0654	0751	...	0851	0951	...	1051	1151	...	1251	...	1350	1356t	1451	1551	...	1651	1751	...	1851	1951	2052	...	...
59	**Weiden** .... a.	0603	...	0725	0825	...	0925	1025	...	1125	1225	...	1325	...	1427	1427t	1525	1625	...	1725	1825	...	1925	2025	2120	...	...

	Ⓐt	Ⓐt			Ⓐt																			Ⓒv		
Weiden .... d.	...	0522	...	0633t	...	0737	0837	...	0937	1037	...	1137	1237	...	1335	1437	...	1537	1637	...	1737	1837	1937	...	2133	...
Kirchenlaibach .... a.	...	0557	...	0707t	...	0806	0906	...	1006	1107	...	1206	1306	...	1408	1506	...	1606	1706	...	1806	1906	2006	...	2203	...
Kirchenlaibach .... d.	0509	0609	0657	0713	0802	0815	0913	1002	1015	1113	1202	1215	1313	1402	1415	1513	1602	1615	1713	1802	1815	1913	2014	2117	2205	2326
Bayreuth Hbf .... a.	0524	0625	0716	0728	0818	0828	0928	1018	1028	1128	1218	1228	1328	1418	1428	1528	1618	1628	1728	1818	1828	1928	2030	2134	2220	2343

t – Ⓐ (not June 19).
v – Also June 19.

888 KEMPTEN - REUTTE IN TIROL - GARMISCH-PARTENKIRCHEN

RB services; 2nd class only

km											
0	**Kempten** (Allgäu) Hbf .... d.	0540	0734	0934	1134	1334	1534	1634	1734	1951	2253
18	Oy-Mittelberg .... d.	0607	0801	1001	1201	1401	1601	1701	1801	2018	2323
24	Nesselwang .... d.	0620	0812	1012	1212	1412	1612	1712	1812	2029	2335
31	Pfronten-Ried .... d.	0629	0822	1022	1222	1422	1622	1722	1822	2038	2345
33	**Pfronten-Steinach** 🏛 .... d.	0634	0828	1031	1227	1427	1627	1731	1831	2042	2348
38	Vils in Tirol 🏛 .... d.	0643k	0837	1040	1236	1436	1636	1740	1840	2051	...
48	**Reutte in Tirol** .... a.	0657k	0851	1054	1250	1450	1650	1754	1854	2105	...
	Change trains							n⊠			
48	**Reutte in Tirol** .... d.	0701	0901	1101	1301	1501	1701	1801	1901	2107	...
68	Lermoos .... d.	0725	0925	1125	1325	1525	1725	1825	1925	2131	...
71	Ehrwald Zugspitzbahn 🏛 ... d.	0731	0931	1131	1331	1531	1731	1831	1931	2137	...
93	**Garmisch**-Partenkirchen ... a.	0757	0957	1157	1357	1557	1757	1857	1956	2203	...

	k	⑥⑦c						n		
Garmisch-Partenkirchen d.	0637	0704	0804	1004	1204	1404	1604	1657g	1804	2004
Ehrwald Zugspitzbahn 🏛 d.	0702	0731	0831	1031	1231	1431	1631	1731	1831	2031
Lermoos .... d.	0705	0734	0834	1034	1234	1434	1634	1734	1834	2034
Reutte in Tirol .... a.	0736	0800	0900	1100	1300	1500	1700	1800	1900	2100
	▬									
Change trains		⑥⑦c								
Reutte in Tirol .... d.	0709e	0804	0907	1109	1309	1509	1707	1807	1903	2110
Vils in Tirol 🏛 .... d.	0723e	0818	0921	1123	1323	1523	1721	1821	1917	2124
Pfronten-Steinach 🏛 .... d.	0734	0834	0934	1134	1334	1534	1734	1834	1927	2137
Pfronten-Ried .... d.	0738	0838	0938	1138	1338	1538	1738	1838	1931	2141
Nesselwang .... d.	0748	0848	0948	1148	1348	1548	1748	1848	1940	2151
Oy-Mittelberg .... d.	0802	0902	1002	1202	1402	1602	1802	1902	1950	2201
Kempten (Allgäu) Hbf ..... a.	0828	0928	1028	1228	1428	1628	1828	1928	2018	2228

c – ⑥⑦ (also June 19, Aug. 15, Dec. 8).
e – ①–⑤ (not June 19, Aug. 15, Dec. 8).
g – 1704 on ①–⑤ (not June 19, Aug. 15).
k – ①–⑥ (not June 19, Aug. 15, Nov. 1, Dec. 8).
n – Not Dec. 8.
⊠ – On ⑥⑦ (also June 19, Aug. 15) Reutte d. 1826, Lermoos d. 1852, Ehrwald d. 1858, Garmisch a. 1929

Bayerische Oberlandbahn; DB

MÜNCHEN - SALZBURG

km																								
						RJ		RJ		EC		RJ		EC			RJ		EC		RJ			
		◇		◇	◇	265	◇	61	◇	111	◇	63	◇	217	◇	◇	65	◇	113	◇	6[illegible]			
		①–⑤		⑥⑦	①–⑤	①–⑥										①–⑤								
		t		z	t	e ✕		B ✕		✕ ♦		B ✕		🍷 ♦		t	B ✕		✕ ♦		B ✕			
	Frankfurt (Main) Hbf **912** d.	...	...	...	...	...	...	...	...	...	...	0517c	...	...	...	...	...	...	0822	...	...	...	...	[illegible]
	Stuttgart Hbf **930** d.	...	...	...	...	...	...	...	...	...	...	0656c	...	0758	...	...	...	...	0958	...	...	...	...	[illegible]8
0	**München** Hbf **951** d.	...	...	0544	0600	0624	0655	0731	0755	0818	0854	0934	0955	1018	1055	1129	1134	1155	1218	1255	1334	1355	...	1418
10	München Ost **951** d.	...	...	0552	0608	0633	0704	|	0804	0826	0904	|	1004	1026	1104	1137	|	1204	1226	1304	|	1404	1412	1426
65	Rosenheim **951** d.	0534	...	0631	0641	0702	0735	0807	0835	0857	0935	|	1035	1057	1135	1212	|	1235	1257	1335	|	1435	1441	1457
82	Bad Endorf d.	0545	...	0642	0652	|	0746	|	0846	|	0946	|	1046	|	1146	1224	|	1246	|	1346	|	1446	1454	|
90	Prien am Chiemsee d.	0551	...	0648	0658	|	0752	|	0852	0913	0952	|	1052	1113	1152	1234	|	1252	1313	1352	|	1452	1502	1513
118	Traunstein d.	0614	...	0711	0728j	|	0818	|	0924j	0933	1018	|	1124j	1133	1218	1257	|	1324j	1333	1418	|	1515	1526	1533
147	Freilassing **891** d.	0634	...	0730	0748	|	0841	|	0944	0952	1046	|	1144	1152	1244	...	|	1344	1352	1446	|	1535	1546	1552
153	**Salzburg** Hbf 🏛 **891** a.	0641	...	0738	0756	0759	0852	0902	0953	1000	1055	1102	1153	1200	1253	...	1302	1353	1400	1455	1502	1541	...	1600
	Wien Westbahnhof **950** a.	...	...	...	...	1030	...	1130	...	...	...	1330	...	...	...	...	1530	...	...	...	1730	...	...	...

			RJ		EC				RJ		EC	EC		IC			EC					EN	EN	
	◇	◇	69	◇	219	◇	◇	◇	261	◇	117	1217	◇	1269	◇	◇	391	◇	◇	◇		463	499	◇
		①–⑤				①–⑤		①–⑤			Ⓑ	⑥		Ⓑ	⑥	Ⓑ						Ⓡ	Ⓡ	
		t	✕		🍷 ♦	t		t	✕		🍷 ♦	🍷 ♦		K 🍷			🍷 ♦					🍷 ♦	🍷 ♦	
Frankfurt (Main) Hbf **912** d.	...	...	...	...	1220	...	...	...	...	...	1420	...	...	...	...	...	1620	...	...	...	...	...	...	...
Stuttgart Hbf **930** d.	...	...	...	...	1358	...	...	...	...	...	1558	1558	...	1653r	...	...	1758	...	...	...	...	...	...	...
München Hbf **951** d.	1455	1529	1534	1555	1618	1635	1655	1729	1734	1755	1818	1818	1855	1918	1955	1955	2018	2044	2144	2244	...	2340	2340	2350
München Ost **951** d.	1504	1537	|	1604	1626	1643	1704	1737	|	1804	1826	1826	1904	1926	2004	2004	2027	2052	2152	2252	...	|	|	2358
Rosenheim **951** d.	1535	1612	|	1635	1657	1713	1735	1812	|	1835	1857	1857	1935	1957	2035	2035	2058	2131	2231	2331	...	|	|	0035
Bad Endorf d.	1546	1624	|	1646	|	1725	1746	1824	|	1846	|	|	1946	|	2046	2046	2109	2142	2242	2342	...	|	|	0046
Prien am Chiemsee d.	1552	1631	|	1652	1713	1732	1752	1831	|	1852	1913	1913	1952	2013	2052	2052	2116	2148	2248	2348	...	|	|	0052
Traunstein d.	1618	1654	|	1724j	1733	1753	1818	1854	|	1924j	1933	1933	2018	2033	2119	2124j	2136	2211	2311	0011	...	|	|	0115
Freilassing **891** d.	1646	...	|	1744	1752	...	1846	...	|	1944	1952	1952	2040	2052	2141	2148	2155	2231	2331	0031	...	|	|	0135
Salzburg Hbf 🏛 **891** a.	1655	...	1702	1753	1800	...	1855	...	1902	1953	2000	2000	2052	2059	2153	2158	2203	2238	2338	0038	...	0118	0118	0142
Wien Westbahnhof **950** a.	...	...	1930	...	...	...	...	...	2130	...	...	...	...	...	...	...	...	...	...	...	...	0545h	...	...

		EN	EN			IC			IC	IC				EC		RJ			IC	EC		RJ		EC
	◇	462	498	◇	◇	1296	◇	◇	1268	1216	◇	◇	◇	390	◇	260	◇	◇	2082	218	◇	262	◇	114
	①–⑤	Ⓡ	Ⓡ	①–⑤		①–⑥	①–⑤		⊡	⑤	①–⑤	①–⑤	⑥⑦				①–⑤							
	t	🍷 ♦	🍷 ♦	t		🍷	t		K 🍷	🍷 ♦	t	t	z	🍷 ♦		✕	t		✕ ♦	🍷 ♦		✕		🍷 ♦
Wien Westbahnhof **950** d.	...	0011h	...	...	...	...	...	...	...	...	...	...	...	...	...	0630	...	...	...	...	...	0830	...	...
Salzburg Hbf 🏛 **891** d.	0405	0428	0428	0448	0515	0545	0600	0612	0643	0643	0647	*0703*	0712	0800	0812	0856	...	0912	...	1000	1012	1056	1112	1200
Freilassing **891** d.	0413	|	|	0456	0524	0553	0608	0623	0651	0651	0654	0724	0724	0808	0824	|	...	0924	0945	1008	1024	|	1124	1208
Traunstein d.	0432	|	|	0515	0544	0610	0627	0643	0709	0709	0716	0747	0747	0826	0847	|	0905	0947	1005	1025	1047	|	1147	1225
Prien am Chiemsee d.	0454	|	|	0538	0606	0628	0649	0705	0728	0728	0744	0808	0808	0844	0909	|	0927	1009	1026	1044	1109	|	1209	1244
Bad Endorf d.	0500	|	|	0544	0612	0636	0655	0711	0736	0736	0751	0815	0815	|	0915	|	0933	1015	1034	|	1115	|	1215	|
Rosenheim **951** d.	0514	|	|	0600	0629	0651	0712	0729	0750	0750	0806	0829	0829	0903	0929	|	0951	1029	1047	1103	1129	|	1229	1303
München Ost **951** a.	0541	|	|	0632	0657	0719	0739	0756	0817	0817	0841	0856	0856	0931	0956	|	1019	1056	1115	1131	1156	|	1256	1331
München Hbf **951** a.	0551	0610	0610	0642	0711	0730	0749	0806	0829	0829	0850	0906	0906	0941	1005	1025	1029	1106	...	1141	1206	1225	1306	1341
Stuttgart Hbf **930** a.	...	...	...	...	...	1001	...	...	1107	1107	...	...	...	1201	...	...	...	...	...	1401	...	...	...	1600
Frankfurt (Main) Hbf **912** a.	...	...	...	...	...	1140	...	...	...	...	...	...	...	1340	...	...	...	...	...	1540	...	...	...	...

		RJ			EC		RJ		EC		RJ					RJ	RJ		EC		RJ		
	◇	60	◇	◇	112	◇	62	◇	216	◇	64	◇	◇		◇	66	66	◇	110	◇	68	◇		◇
			①–⑤									①–⑤					⑤⑥ p							
		B ✕	t		✕ ♦		B ✕		🍷 ♦		B ✕	t				B ✕	B ✕		✕ ♦		B ✕			
Wien Westbahnhof **950** d.	...	1030	...	...	...	...	1230	...	...	...	1430	...	...	...	...	1630	1630	...	...	...	1830	...	...	...
Salzburg Hbf 🏛 **891** d.	1212	1256	...	1311	1400	1412	1456	1512	1600	1612	1656	...	1712	...	1812	1856	1856	1912	2000	2020	2056	2120	...	2300
Freilassing **891** d.	1224	|	...	1324	1408	1424	|	1524	1608	1624	|	...	1724	...	1824	|	|	1923	2008	2028	|	2128	...	2310
Traunstein d.	1247	|	1309	1347	1425	1447	|	1547	1625	1647	|	1705	1747	...	1847	|	|	1947	2025	2049	|	2149	...	2329
Prien am Chiemsee d.	1309	|	1342	1409	1444	1509	|	1609	1644	1709	|	1727	1809	...	1909	|	|	2009	2044	2111	|	2211	...	2351
Bad Endorf d.	1315	|	1349	1415	|	1515	|	1615	|	1715	|	1733	1815	...	1915	|	|	2016	|	2117	|	2217	...	2357
Rosenheim **951** d.	1329	|	1402	1429	1503	1529	|	1629	1703	1729	|	1751	1829	...	1929	|	|	2032	2103	2131	2151	2232	...	0011
München Ost **951** a.	1356	|	1429	1456	1531	1556	|	1656	1731	1756	|	1819	1856	...	1956	|	|	2105	2131	2204	|	2305	...	0045
München Hbf **951** a.	1406	1425	1438	1505	1541	1606	1632	1706	1741	1805	1825	1829	1906	...	2006	2025	2025	2115	2141	2214	2226	2315	...	0055
Stuttgart Hbf **930** a.	...	...	...	...	1800	...	...	...	2001	...	...	...	...	...	...	...	2300	...	...	...	...	...	...	...
Frankfurt (Main) Hbf **912** a.	...	...	...	...	1940	...	...	...	...	...	...	...	...	...	...	...	0042	...	...	...	...	...	...	...

♦ – **NOTES** (LISTED BY TRAIN NUMBER)

10/1 – [12] and ✕ Klagenfurt - Villach - München and v.v.
12/3 – [12] and ✕ Klagenfurt - Villach - München - Frankfurt and v.v.; [12] Zagreb (**212/3**) - Dobova 🏛 - Ljubljana - Jesenice 🏛 - Villach - München - Frankfurt and v.v.
14 – WÖRTHERSEE – [12] and 🍷 Klagenfurt - München - Mannheim - Köln - Dortmund.
15 – WÖRTHERSEE – [12] and 🍷 Münster - Köln - Mannheim - München - Klagenfurt.
17 – [12] and 🍷 Frankfurt - Salzburg - Villach - Klagenfurt.
216/7 – [12] and 🍷 Graz - Selzthal - Bischofshofen - Salzburg - Mannheim - Saarbrücken and v.v.
218/9 – [12] and 🍷 Graz - Selzthal - Bischofshofen - Salzburg - Frankfurt and v.v.
90 – [12] and 🍷 (Linz ①–⑥ -) Salzburg - Frankfurt.
91 – [12] and 🍷 Frankfurt - Salzburg (- Linz Ⓑ).
462/3 – KÁLMÁN IMRE – 🛏 1, 2 cl., 🛏 2 cl., [2] and 🍷 Budapest - Wien - München and v.v.
498/9 – LISINSKI – 🛏 1, 2 cl., 🛏 2 cl., [2] and 🍷 Zagreb - Dobova 🏛 - Ljubljana - Jesenice 🏛 - Villach - München and v.v.
1216 – ⑤ (also June 18, Oct. 2; not June 20, Oct. 3). [12] and 🍷 Salzburg - Mannheim - Mainz - Köln - Dortmund - Berlin.
1217 – [12] and 🍷 Karlsruhe - Salzburg - Villach - Klagenfurt.
082/3 – KÖNIGSSEE – [12] and ✕ Berchtesgaden - Augsburg - Hamburg and v.v.

B – To / from Budapest (Table **1250**).
K – To / from Karlsruhe (Table **931**).

c – Ⓒ (also June 19). Departs Frankfurt 0522 on ⑦ (also Oct. 3, June 19).
e – Not Dec. 8.
h – Wien **Hütteldorf**.
j – Arrives 9–11 minutes earlier.
p – Also June 18, Oct. 2.
r – 1655 July 31 - Sept. 14.
t – Not June 19, Aug. 15, Oct. 3.
z – Also June 19, Aug. 15, Oct. 3.

⊡ – ①②③④⑥ (also June 20, Oct. 3; not June 18, Oct. 2).
◇ – *Meridian* regional service (operated by Bayerische Oberlandbahn GmbH).

Berchtesgadener Land Bahn *

SALZBURG - FREILASSING - BERCHTESGADEN 891

km																									
		①–⑤																							⑤–⑦
		t											A												b
0	**Salzburg** Hbf **890** d.	*0611*	*0650*j	*0741*	*0812*	0911	...	and at	1411	...	1511	1541	...	1611	...	1711	...	1811	...	1912	1911e	2033	*2141*	2229	2325
6	Freilassing **890** a.	*0623*	*0702*j	*0753*	*0820*	0923	...	the same	1423	...	1523	1553	...	1623	...	1723	...	1823	...	1919	1924e	2044	*2153*	2240	2336
6	Freilassing d.	0632	0717	0800	0846	0929	0947	minutes	1427	1447	1537	...	1607	1629	1647	1729	1747	1829	1847	...	1947	2047	2200	2245	2339
21	Bad Reichenhall d.	0651	0738	0821	0911	0946	1004	past each	1444	1504	1559	...	1626	1646	1704	1746	1804	1846	1904	...	2004	2104	2217	2304	2356
39	**Berchtesgaden** Hbf a.	0724	0807	0854	0939	...	1037	hour until	...	1537	...	...	1656	...	1737	...	1837	...	1937	...	2037	2133	2245	2332	0024

	①–⑤	①–⑥																							
	t	m				A																			
erchtesgaden Hbf d.	0535g	0620	0707	...	0820	0835	0920	...	1020	...	and at	...	1420	...	1520	...	1620	...	1720	...	1820	...	1920	2020	2209
ad Reichenhall d.	0604	0655	0737	0811	0851	0910	0953	1011	1051	1111	the same	1410	1451	1516	1549	1603	1653	1711	1751	1811	1851	1916	1951	2051	2243
reilassing a.	0620	0711	0754	0827	0911	0928	1013	1027	1113	1127	minutes	1426	1513	1532	1606	1624	1713	1727	1813	1827	1913	1932	2013	2113	2303
reilassing **890** d.	0623	*0717*n	*0807*	0837	...	*0944*	...	1037	...	1137	past each	1437	*1535*	1537	*1624*a	1637	...	1737	...	1837	...	1937	2015	*2137*k	2305v
alzburg Hbf **890** a.	0635	*0729*n	*0820*	0850	...	*0953*	...	1050	...	1150	hour until	1450	*1541*	1550	*1637*a	1650	...	1750	...	1850	...	1950	2028	*2150*k	2316v

– *IC* **2082/3**: KÖNIGSSEE – [12] and ✕ Berchtesgaden - München Ost - Hamburg and v.v. Train category *RE* Berchtesgaden - Freilassing and v.v. Operated by DB.

– ①–⑤ (not June 19, Aug. 15, Dec. 8).
– Also June 19.
– ①–⑥ (not June 19, Aug. 15, Nov. 1).
– ① (also June 20).

j – On ⑦ (also June 19, Aug. 15, Nov. 1, Dec. 8) Salzburg d. *0641*, Freilassing a. *0656*.
k – On ⑦ (also June 19, Aug. 15, Dec. 8) Freilassing d. *2148*, Salzburg a. *2158*. On Nov. 1 Freilassing d. *2141*, Salzburg a. *2153*.
m – Not June 19, Aug. 15, Oct. 3, Nov. 1.
n – Not Dec. 8.
t – Not June 19, Aug. 15, Oct. 3.

v – On ①–④ (except on June 19) change trains at Freilassing (d. *2309*, Salzburg Hbf a. *2320*).

***** – Services to / from Bad Reichenhall or Berchtesgaden are operated by Berchtesgadener Land Bahn GmbH (Salzburg AG / Arriva). 2nd class only. Other trains are operated by either DB or ÖBB.

892 FLUGHAFEN MÜNCHEN ✈ (S-Bahn services S1, S8)

2nd class only

km		S8	S8	S8	S8		S8	S1	S8	S1	S8	S1	S8		S1	S8	S1	S8	S1	S8	S8
0	**München** Pasing ... d.	0005	0045	0125	0305	and every	0445	...	0505	...	0525	...	0545	and at the	...	2245	...	2305	...	2325	2345
7	**München** Hbf (low level) ... d.	0015	0055	0135	0315	20 minutes	0455	0503	0515	0523	0535	0543	0555	same minutes	2243	2255	2303	2315	2323	2335	2355
11	**München** Ost ... d.	0024	0104	0144	0324	until	0504	|	0524	|	0544	|	0604	past each	|	2304	|	2324	|	2344	0004
44	**München Flughafen** Terminal ✈ a.	0055	0135	0215	0355		0535	0546	0555	0606	0615	0626	0635	hour until	2326	2335	2346	2355	0006	0015	0035

km*		S8	S8	S8	S8		S8	S1	S8	S1	S8	S1	S8		S1	S8	S1	S8	S1	S8	S1
0	**München Flughafen** Terminal ✈ d.	0004	0044	0124	0404	and every	0544	0551	0604	0611	0624	0631	0644	and at the	2251	2304	2311	2324	2331	2344	2351
	München Ost ... a.	0035	0115	0155	0435	20 minutes	0615	|	0635	|	0655	|	0715	same minutes	|	2335	|	2355	|	0015	|
41	**München** Hbf (low level) ... a.	0045	0125	0205	0445	until	0625	0637	0645	0657	0705	0717	0725	past each	2337	2345	2357	0005	0017	*0027*	0037
	München Pasing ... a.	0055	0135	0215	0455		0635	...	0655	...	0715	...	0735	hour until	...	2355	...	0015	...	*0037*	...

* – Via Neufahrn (b Freising).

☛ Many **S1** trains from München Hbf are combined with a Freising service - travel in the rear portion for the Airport.

893 MÜNCHEN - MÜHLDORF - SIMBACH

km			Ⓐe	Ⓒz	⚒r			⊡						Ⓐe	Ⓒz	Ⓐe		Ⓐe		Ⓐe		Ⓐe		⊙		
0	**München** Hbf ... d.	...	0603	0606	0706	0807z	0907	1007	1107	1207	1307	1407	1506	1522	1607	1626	1707	1725	1806	1831	1907	1948	2027	2129	2228	2356
10	**München** Ost ... d.	...	0616	0617	0716	0816	0917	1017	1117	1217	1317	1417	1515	1532	1617	1638	1717	1739	1817	1840	1917	1957	2038	2139	2238	0005
85	**Mühldorf** (Oberbay) .. a.	...	0722	0722	0816	0919	1016	1118	1216	1316	1417	1516	1620	1627	1718	1731	1819	1829	1919	1931	2020	2058	2140	2236	2336	0105
		⚒r	|	|	◇			|					Ⓒz	|		◇	Ⓒz	|		◇				|		
85	**Mühldorf** (Oberbay) .. d.	0637	0737	0737	0830	0937	1037	1137	1227	1337	1437	1537	1634	1634	...	1737	1837	1833	...	1937	2037	...	2146	2247	2341	...
124	**Simbach** (Inn) ... a.	0713	0813	0813	0859	1013	1113	1213	1258	1413	1513	1613	1714	1714	...	1813	1913	1907	...	2013	2113	...	2217	2318	0013	...

			Ⓐe		⑥k	Ⓐe	Ⓐe	Ⓒz					⊡									Ⓐ	Ⓒz	⊙	◐	
Simbach (Inn) ... d.	...	...	0507	...	0545	0554	0648	0648	...	0749	0900	0949	1049	1149	1259	1349	1449	1549	...	1649	1749	1839	1849	1949	2049	2149
Mühldorf (Oberbay) ... a.	...	...	0540	...	0616	0628	0723	0723	...	0822	0932	1021	1123	1221	1332	1421	1524	1622	...	1722	1822	1917	1922	2022	2122	2227
	⚒r	①–⑥	Ⓐe	Ⓒz	|	|	|	Ⓒz	Ⓐe				|					Ⓒz	Ⓐe				Ⓒz	|	|	
Mühldorf (Oberbay) ... d.	0430	0522	0546	0623	0623	0637	0731	0731	0739	0830	0937	1042	1138	1238	1340	1429	1538	1630	1633	1737	1842	...	1940	2032	2146	...
München Ost ... a.	0523	0625	0640	0725	0725	0722	0822	0826	0844	0926	1045	1141	1246	1341	1443	1525	1645	1725	1745	1845	1944	...	2043	2140	2247	...
München Hbf ... a.	0533	0636	0652	0737	0737	0734	0837	0837	0855	0937	1055	1155	1256	1351	1454	1536	1655	1736	1754	1856	1955	...	2055	2152	2257	...

e – Not June 19, Aug. 15.
k – Not Nov. 1.
r – Not June 19, Aug. 15, Nov. 1.
z – Ⓒ (also June 19, Aug. 15).
⊡ – Change trains at Mühldorf on Ⓒ (also June 19, Aug. 15).
⊙ – Change trains at Mühldorf on † (also June 19, Aug. 15, Nov. 1).
◐ – Change trains at Mühldorf on ⑥**k**.
◇ – Daily from Mühldorf.

895 MÜNCHEN - GARMISCH - INNSBRUCK

DB; ÖBB (2nd class only in Austria)

km									*ICE* **527** ⑥D		*ICE* **583** ⑥L			*ICE* **1207** ⑥jK					*ICE* **1209** ⑤fK						
		Ⓐe		Ⓒz																					
0	**München** Hbf ... d.	0453	...	0532	0632	0732	0832	0932	1032	1132	1213	1232	1253	1332	1432	1455	1532	1632	1732	1832	1848	1932	2032	2132	2232	2332
7	München Pasing ... d.	0500	...	0539	0639	0739	0840	0939	1039	1139	|	1239	|	1339	1439	|	1539	1639	1739	1839	|	1939	2039	2139	2240	2339
40	Tutzing ... d.	0529	...	0602	0702	0802	0902	1002	1102	1202	|	1302	1324	1402	1501	1522	1602	1701	1802	1901	1921	2001	2102	2202	2302	0002
54	Weilheim (Oberbay) ... d.	0545	...	0612	0712	0812	0912	1012	1112	1212	|	1312	|	1412	1512	|	1612	1712	1812	1912	|	2012	2112	2212	2312	0012
75	Murnau ... d.	0605	...	0628	0728	0828	0928	1028	1128	1228	1310	1328	1355	1428	1528	1554	1628	1728	1828	1929	1957	2028	2128	2228	2328	0028
101	**Garmisch**-Partenk. ... a.	0630	...	0654	0754	0854	0954	1054	1154	1254	1337	1354	1428	1454	1555	1622	1655	1754	1854	1955	2022	2054	2154	2254	2353	0054
101	**Garmisch**-Partenk. ... d.	0632	0632	...	*0802*	0906	1002	1102	*1203*	1302	...	1402	...	1502	*1602*	1624	1702	1802	1902	*2002*	2026	2102	2202	2302	0002	0102**g**
118	**Mittenwald** ... a.	0653	0653	...	*0823*	0927	1023	1123	*1223*	1323	...	1423	...	1523	*1623*	1653	1723	1823	1923	*2023*	2053	2123	2223	2323	0023	0123**g**
118	**Mittenwald** 🏛 ... d.	0655	0655	...	*0826*	0936	1026	1136**v**	*1226*	1336**v**	...	1426	...	1536	*1626*	...	1736**v**	1826	1936	*2026*	...	...	...	...	...	...
125	Scharnitz 🏛 ... ⊡ d.	0703	0703	...	*0834*	0944	1034	1144**v**	*1234*	1344**v**	...	1434	...	1544	*1634*	...	1744**v**	1834	1944	*2034*	...	...	...	...	...	...
135	Seefeld in Tirol ... ⊡ d.	0716	0716	...	*0846*	0955	1046	1155**v**	*1246*	1355**v**	...	1446	...	1555	*1646*	...	1755**v**	1846	1955	*2046*	...	...	...	...	...	...
160	**Innsbruck** Hbf ... ⊡ a.	0753	0753	...	*0923*	*1053*t	1123	...	*1323*	...	...	1523	...	*1653*t	*1723*	...	...	1923	*2053*t	*2123*	...	...	...	...	...	...

										ICE **586** ⑥P		*ICE* **1206** QK				*ICE* **1220** ⑥D			*ICE* **732** ⑥B							
	⚒r	Ⓐe	Ⓒz	Ⓐe	Ⓐe	Ⓒz																				
Innsbruck Hbf ... ⊡ d.	...	...	...	...	...	...	*0638*	...	0838	...	*0908*t	...	*1038*	...	1238	...	...	*1438*	...	*1508*t	1638	...	*1838*	*1908*t	2038	...
Seefeld in Tirol ... ⊡ d.	...	...	...	...	...	...	*0715*	...	0915	...	1003	...	*1115*	1203**v**	1315	...	1403**v**	*1515*	...	1603	1715	1803**v**	*1915*	2003	2115	...
Scharnitz 🏛 ... ⊡ d.	...	...	...	...	...	...	*0728*	...	0928	...	1014	...	*1128*	1214**v**	1328	...	1414**v**	*1528*	...	1614	1728	1814**v**	*1928*	2014	2128	...
Mittenwald 🏛 ... a.	...	...	...	...	...	...	*0735*	...	0935	...	1022	...	*1135*	1222**v**	1335	...	1422**v**	*1535*	...	1622	1735	1822**v**	*1935*	2022	2135	...
Mittenwald ... d.	...	0530	0536	0603	0634	0634	*0736*	0836	0936	...	1036	1054	*1136*	1236	1336	...	1436	*1536*	...	1636	1736	1836	*1936*	2036	2136	2236
Garmisch-Partenk. ... a.	...	0551	0557	0630	0700	0700	*0757*	0900	1000	...	1057	1119	*1157*	1300	1400	...	1500	*1557*	...	1700	1800	1900	*1957*	2057	2157	2257
Garmisch-Partenk. ... d.	0500	0559	0607	0635	0702	0707	0807	0907	1005	1037	1107	1121	1207	1307	1407	1413	1507	1607	1624	1707	1807	1907	2005	2107	2207	2307
Murnau ... d.	0524	0627	0632	0655	0730	0732	0832	0932	1033	1105	1132	1151	1232	1332	1432	1444	1531	1631	1653	1732	1833	1932	2031	2132	2232	2332
Weilheim (Oberbay) ... d.	0541	0646	0649	0711	0747	0749	0849	0949	1050	|	1149	|	1249	1349	1449	|	1549	1650	|	1750	1851	1950	2049	2149	2249	2349
Tutzing ... d.	0555	0700	0700	|	0800	0800	0900	1000	1100	1139	1200	|	1300	1400	1500	1516	1600	1700	1721	1800	1901	2000	2100	2200	2300	0000
München Pasing ... a.	0614	0719	0719	0741	0819	0819	0919	1019	1120	|	1219	1248	1319	1419	1519	|	1619	1719	|	1819	1919	2019	2119	2219	2319	0019
München Hbf ... a.	0621	0726	0726	0748	0826	0826	0926	1026	1127	1215	1226	1257	1326	1426	1526	1544	1626	1726	1756	1826	1926	2026	2126	2226	2326	0026

MÜNCHEN - TUTZING - KOCHEL

km		Ⓐe	⚒r	Ⓐe						Ⓒz	Ⓐe				Ⓐe	Ⓒz	Ⓐe	Ⓒz	Ⓐe	Ⓒz	Ⓒz	Ⓐe		◇			
0	**München** Hbf . d.	0532	0559	0632	0659	0759	0900	0959	1059	1159	*1232*	1259	1359	1459	1556	1559	1656	1659	1756	1759	1859	1900	1959	2032	*2132*	2232	*2332*
7	München Pasing d.	0539	0605	0639	0705	0805	0907	1005	1105	1205	*1239*	1305	1405	1506	1604	1605	1704	1705	1804	1805	1905	1906	2005	2039	*2139*	*2240*	*2339*
40	Tutzing ... d.	0602	0628	0704	0733	0830**h**	0933	1033	1133	1233	1310	1333	1433	1533	1632	1634	1732	1734	1832	1834	1934	1932	2032**h**	2104	2204	2304	0004
75	**Kochel** ... a.	0636	0708	0737	0808	0908	1008	1108	1208	1308	1346	1412**b**	1508	1608	1708	1708	1808	1808	1908	1908	2008	2008	2108	2138	2238	2338	0038

	Ⓐe	⚒r	†s	⚒r	Ⓐe	Ⓐe	Ⓒz	Ⓐe						Ⓒz	Ⓐe	Ⓒz	Ⓐe			Ⓐe							
Kochel ... d.	0437	0511	0511	0545	0615	0645	0645	0715	0745	0845	0945	1045	1145	1245	1300	1345	1352	1445	1545	1615	1645	1745	1845	1945	2116	2216	2316
Tutzing ... a.	0510	0547	0547	0625	0652	0725	0725	0753	0828	0924	1024	1124	1224	1323	1333	1424	1424	1524	1625	1653	1725	1825	1926	2026	2153	2253	2353
München Pasing a.	*0541*	0614	0618	0657	0719	0753	0800	0819	0902	0952	1052	1152	1252	1351	1402	1452	1452	1552	1652	*1719*	1752	1852	1953	2052	*2219*	*2319*	*0019*
München Hbf ... a.	*0549*	0621	0625	0705	0726	0800	0808	0826	0909	1000	1100	1200	1300	1400	1409	1501	1500	1600	1700	*1726*	1800	1900	2000	2059	*2226*	*2326*	*0026*

B – ⑥ to Nov. 8 (also June 19, Oct. 3; not Oct. 4). ZUGSPITZE – (12) and ✕ Garmisch - Nürnberg - Bremen.
D – WETTERSTEIN – (12) and 🍸 Dortmund - Köln - Frankfurt - Nürnberg - Garmisch and v.v.
K – KARWENDEL – (12) and ✕ Berlin - Halle - Nürnberg - Garmisch - Mittenwald and v.v.
L – ⑥ (also June 19, Oct. 3; not Oct. 4). WERDENFELSERLAND – (12) and ✕ Hamburg - Nürnberg - Garmisch.
P – ⑥ until Nov. 8. WERDENFELSERLAND – (12) and ✕ Garmisch - Nürnberg - Hamburg.
Q – ⑥⑦ until Nov. 2. Train number **1526** on ⑥ from July 19.
b – 1407 on Ⓒ (also June 19, Aug. 15).
e – Not June 19, Aug. 15.
f – ⑤ to Oct. 31 (not Oct. 3).
g – Mornings of ①⑦ (also June 20, Aug. 16, Oct. 4).
h – 2–3 minutes later on Ⓒ (also June 19, Aug. 15).
j – ⑥ to Nov. 1 (also Oct. 3).
r – Not June 19, Aug. 15, Nov. 1.
s – Also June 19, Aug. 15, Nov. 1.
t – ①–⑤ (not June 19, Aug. 15, Dec. 8).
v – ⑥⑦ (also June 19, Aug. 15, Dec. 8).
z – Also June 19, Aug. 15.
◇ – Change trains at Tutzing on Ⓐ (not June 19, Aug. 15
⊡ – Additional journeys Scharnitz - Seefeld - Innsbruck and v.v.: **From Scharnitz** at 0003, 0633, 0733⚒, 0803⚒, 0903, 1303, 1403Ⓐ, 1503, 1703, 1803Ⓐ, 1903 and 2133. **From Innsbruck** Hbf at 0708⚒, 0808, 1208, 1308Ⓐ, 1408, 1608, 1708Ⓐ, 1808, 2008 and 2308.

A rack railway operates between Garmisch-Partenkirchen and the Zugspitz mountain: departures at 0815 and hourly to 1415, returning from Bf Zugspitzplatt at 0930 and hourly to 1630. All trains call at Eibsee (30 minutes from Garmisch, 45 minutes from Zugspitzplatt). Service may be suspended in bad weather conditions – please check locally before travelling. Cable cars ru between Eibsee and Zugspitzgipfel (Eibsee-Seilbahn) and between Zugspitzplatt and Zugspitzgipfel summit (Gletscherbahn). **Operator**: Bayerische Zugspitzbahn AG ✆ + 49 (0) 88 21 7970

897 MURNAU - OBERAMMERGAU

RB services

km		⑥k	Ⓐe							Ⓐt	Ⓒw	Ⓐt	Ⓒw				
0	**Murnau** ... d.	0553	0600	0648	0742	0842	0942	1042	1142	1235	1242	1325	1342	1442	and	2242	2334
12	Bad Kohlgrub ... d.	0612	0619	0707	0802	0902	1002	1102	1202	1254	1302	1343	1402	1502	hourly	2302	2353
24	**Oberammergau** ... ♥ a.	0631	0638	0726	0821	0921	1021	1121	1221	1313	1321	1402	1421	1521	until	2321	0012

	Ⓐe	⑥k	Ⓐe							Ⓐt	Ⓒw	Ⓐt	Ⓒw				
Oberammergau ... ♥ d.	0508	0549	0556	0644	0739	0839	0939	1039	1139	1230	1239	1319	1339	1439	and	2239	2330
Bad Kohlgrub ... d.	0530	0611	0618	0706	0801	0901	1001	1101	1201	1253	1301	1342	1401	1501	hourly	2301	2352
Murnau ... a.	0548	0628	0636	0724	0819	0919	1019	1119	1219	1312	1319	1401	1419	1519	until	2319	0010

e – Not June 19, Aug. 15.
k – Not Nov. 1.
t – Not June 10–20, July 30 - Sept. 15, Oct. 27–31.
w – Ⓒ (daily June 7–22, July 30 - Sept. 15 and Oct. 25 - Nov. 2).
♥ – All trains call at Unterammergau (*km 20*) 4–6 minutes from Oberammergau.

NÜRNBERG and FRANKFURT - HAMBURG 900

km	*Subject to alteration June 14 - July 27* SEE NOTE ❖	*ICE* 990 ①	*IC* 2178 Ⓐ	*CNL* 1286 [R] 🍷♦	*IC* 2184 Ⓐ 🍷♦	*EN* 490 ♦	*IC* 2186 Ⓐ ◐🍷	*CNL* 478 [R] ✕♦	*ICE* 988 ①–⑥ §✕	*IC* 2182 ①–⑥ T⊗	*ICE* 672 ①–⑥ n Q	*ICE* 1676 ⑦m Q✕	*ICE* 888 Ⓐ ✕	*IC* 1074 ①–⑥ ⊖🍷	*ICE* 784 ◇ ✕	*ICE* 634 ①–⑥ ✕	*IC* 2388 ①–⑥ 🍷♦	*ICE* 670 ②–④ ⊡✕	*ICE* 674 E ✕	*ICE* 886 ✕	*ICE* 772 ✕	*ICE* 1082 ✕	*ICE* 1132 🍷
	Basel SBB **912** 🏛 d.	...	...	...	...	...	...	2213	...	🍷	✕	...	...	...	...	...	...	...	0511b	...	...	...	...
	Karlsruhe Hbf **912** d.	...	...	...	...	...	...	0029	...	...	...	...	...	...	...	...	...	0651r	0651r	...	...	...	...
	Stuttgart Hbf **912** d.	2305p	...	...	...	...	...	│	...	...	...	...	...	0502	...	...	...	│	│	...	0726	...	...
	Mannheim Hbf **912** d.	2351p	...	...	...	...	...	│	...	...	...	...	...	0605	...	...	...	0716	0716	...	0806	...	...
	Frankfurt Flughafen Fernbf ✈ **912** d.	0029	...	...	...	...	...	│	...	...	0539	0539	...	0642	...	...	...	│	│	...	0842	...	...
	Frankfurt (Main) Hbf ... **850 901 902** d.	0055	...	...	...	...	...	│	0504	...	0555	0555	...	0658	...	...	0649	0758	0758	...	0858	...	...
	Hanau Hbf **850 901 902** d.	0113	...	...	...	...	...	│	0520	...	0611	0611	...	│	...	...	│	│	│	...	│	...	...
	München Hbf **904 905** d.	│	...	2215	...	...	...	│	│	...	│	│	0410•	│	0513t	0513t	│	│	│	0611k	│	0653	0653
	Augsburg Hbf **905** d.	│	...	2250	...	...	...	│	│	...	│	│	│	│	│	│	◧	│	│	│	│	0732	0732
0	**Nürnberg** Hbf **920 921** d.	│	...	│	...	0115	...	│	│	...	│	│	0534	│	0632	0632	│	│	│	0733	│	│	│
102	**Würzburg** Hbf **920 921** d.	│	...	│	...	0211	...	│	│	...	│	│	0630	│	0729	0729	│	│	│	0830	│	0929	0929
195	Fulda **850 901 902** d.	0158	...	│	...	│	...	│	0604	...	0653	0653	0707	│	0803	0803	│	│	│	0904	│	1003	1003
285	**Kassel** Wilhelmshöhe **901 902** d.	│	...	│	...	│	...	│	0636	0623a	0724	0725	0739	0824	0836	0836	0854	0922	0922	0936	1022	1036	1036
330	Göttingen **902 903** d.	0325	...	│	...	0509	0548g	0613s	0656	0645a	0743	0746	0759	│	0856	0856	0917	0943	0943	0956	1043	1056	1056
430	**Hannover** Hbf **903** a.	0421	...	0525s	...	0613	0655g	0702s	0732	0756a	0817	0820	0832	0920	0932	0932	0958	1017	1017	1032	1117	1132	1132
430	**Hannover** Hbf **903** d.	0424	0458	│	0555	0616	0700	│	0736	0759	0820	0823	0836	0923	0936	0945	...	1020	1020	1036	1120	1136	1145
	Bremen Hbf **813** a.	│	│	0644	│	│	│	│	│	│	│	│	│	│	│	1044	...	│	│	│	│	│	1244
471	Celle **903** d.	│	0518	│	0619	│	0720	│	│	0819	│	│	│	│	│	...	...	│	│	│	│	│	...
523	Uelzen **903** d.	│	0542	│	0642	│	0742	│	│	0842	│	│	│	│	│	...	...	│	│	│	│	│	...
559	Lüneburg **903** d.	0515	0559	│	0658	│	0758	│	│	0902	│	│	│	│	│	...	...	│	│	1128	│	│	...
608	**Hamburg** Hbf **903** a.	0549	0633	0755	0729	0750	0828	0836	0855	0932	0935	0939	0953	1037	1055	...	...	1135	1135	1156	1235	1253	...
615	**Hamburg** Altona a.	...	0649	0809	...	0804	0842	0851	...	...	0950	0954	1008	1050	...	...	...	1150	...	1211	1250	1308	...

Subject to alteration June 14 - July 27 SEE NOTE ❖	*IC* 2376 ⊗ 🍷♦	*ICE* 78 ⊠ Z✕	*ICE* 882 ✕	*IC* 2170 Ⓒ A✕	*IC* 2170 ★ A✕	*IC* 2170 ①F A✕	*IC* 2180 ①♠ ✕	*ICE* 770 ✕	*ICE* 680 ✕	*ICE* 630 ✕	*IC* 2374 D 🍷	*IC* 2174 ⑤f R🍷	*ICE* 76 ✕♦	*ICE* 880 ✕	*IC* 1972 ⑤f ⊗	*ICE* 1228 🍷♦	*ICE* 578 ✕	*ICE* 588 ✕	*ICE* 538 ✕	*IC* 2372 ⊗ T🍷	*ICE* 74 ✕♦	*ICE* 788 ✕	*IC* 2082 ✕♦
Basel SBB **912** 🏛 d.	...	0706r	...	...	...	...	...	...	...	...	...	...	0906r	...	...	...	...	...	...	...	1106r	...	...
Karlsruhe Hbf **912** d.	0702e	0851r	...	...	...	...	...	...	...	...	0910y	0910x	1051r	...	...	...	...	...	...	1110c	1251r	...	...
Stuttgart Hbf **912** d.	│	│	...	0804h	...	...	...	0926	...	...	│	│	│	...	...	...	1126	...	...	│	│	...	...
Mannheim Hbf **912** d.	│	0916	...	│	...	...	...	1006	...	...	│	│	1116	...	...	...	1206	...	...	│	1316	...	...
Frankfurt Flughafen Fernbf ✈ **912** d.	│	│	...	│	...	...	...	1042	...	...	│	│	│	...	...	...	1242	...	...	│	│	...	...
Frankfurt (Main) Hbf ... **850 901 902** d.	0852	0958	...	0958	...	1022	1022	1058	...	...	1052	1052	1158	...	1217	...	1258	...	...	1252	1358	...	...
Hanau Hbf **850 901 902** d.	│	│	...	│	...	1039	1039	│	...	...	│	│	│	...	1238	...	│	...	...	│	│	...	...
München Hbf **904 905** d.	│	│	0816•	│	...	│	│	│	0905	0905	│	│	│	1016•	│	1050v	│	1045	1045	│	│	1216•	1117o
Augsburg Hbf **905** d.	◧	│	│	◧	...	│	│	│	0938	0938	◧	◧	│	│	│	│	│	1121	1121	◧	│	│	1230
Nürnberg Hbf **920 921** d.	│	│	0933	│	...	│	│	│	│	│	│	│	│	1133	│	1200	│	1235	1235	│	│	1333	│
Würzburg Hbf **920 921** d.	│	│	1030	│	...	│	│	│	1129	1129	│	│	│	1230	│	1301j	│	1329	1329	│	│	1430	1438
Fulda **850 901 902** d.	│	│	1104	│	...	1121	1122	│	1203	1203	│	│	│	1304	1320	1332	│	1403	1403	│	│	1504	1518
Kassel Wilhelmshöhe **901 902** d.	1055	1122	1136	1155	...	1158	1158	1222	1236	1236	1255	1255	1322	1336	1359	1400	1422	1436	1436	1454	1522	1536	1554
Göttingen **902 903** d.	1117	1143	1156	1217	...	1219	1220	1243	1256	1256	1317	1317	1343	1356	1420	...	1443	1456	1456	1517	1543	1556	1615
Hannover Hbf **903** a.	1156	1217	1232	1256	...	1258	1258	1317	1332	1332	1356	1356	1417	1432	1459	...	1517	1532	1532	1556	1617	1632	1654
Hannover Hbf **903** d.	1159	1220	1236	1259	1259	1300	1300	1320	1336	1345	1359	1359	1420	1436	1502	...	1520	1536	1545	1559	1620	1636	1657
Bremen Hbf **813** a.	│	│	│	│	│	│	│	│	│	1444	│	│	│	│	│	...	│	│	1644	│	│	│	│
Celle **903** d.	1219	│	│	1320	1320	1320	1320	│	│	...	1419	1419	│	│	1521	...	│	│	...	1619	│	│	1718
Uelzen **903** d.	1242	│	│	1343	1343	1343	1343	│	│	...	1442	1442	│	│	1543	...	│	│	...	1642	│	│	1742
Lüneburg **903** d.	1258	│	│	1400	1400	1400	1400	│	│	...	1502	1502	│	│	1559	...	│	│	...	1703	│	│	1758
Hamburg Hbf **903** a.	1328	1335	1354	1428	1428	1428	1428	1435	1454	...	1529	1532	1535	1554	1629	...	1635	1653	...	1732	1735	1754	1828
Hamburg Altona a.	...	1350	1409	...	...	...	1443	1450	1508	...	1548	...	...	1609	1644	...	1650	1711	...	...	...	1808	1844

Subject to alteration June 14 - July 27 SEE NOTE ❖	*IC* 1986 ⑥ ♦	*ICE* 576 ✕	*ICE* 586 G✕	*ICE* 536 ✕	*IC* 2370 ⊗ 🍷♦	*IC* 1951 ⑤f ♦	*ICE* 72 Z✕	*EC* 248 Ⓑ ♦	*ICE* 786 ✕	*IC* 1284 ⑦ ♦	*ICE* 974 Ⓑq ✕♦	*ICE* 574 ⑥♣ ✕	*ICE* 584 Ⓑ L✕	*ICE* 1084 ⑥ ✕	*ICE* 776 Ⓑq N✕	*IC* 2276 ①–⑥ 🍷	*IC* 2276 ⑤⑥ w🍷	*IC* 2286 ⑦ R	*IC* 2386 ①–④ u	*ICE* 70 Ⓑ ✕	*ICE* 70 ⑥ ✕	*ICE* 1522 ✕	*ICE* 90 ✕♦
Basel SBB **912** 🏛 d.	...	...	...	...	...	...	1306r	...	...	...	...	...	...	...	...	...	...	...	...	1506r	1506r	...	...
Karlsruhe Hbf **912** d.	...	...	...	...	1310	...	1451r	...	...	...	...	...	...	...	...	1510y	1510z	1510x	...	1651r	1651r	...	...
Stuttgart Hbf **912** d.	...	1326	...	...	│	...	│	...	...	...	1526	1526	...	...	...	│	│	│	...	│	│	...	...
Mannheim Hbf **912** d.	...	1406	...	...	│	...	1516	...	...	...	1606	1606	...	...	...	│	│	│	...	1716	1716	...	...
Frankfurt Flughafen Fernbf ✈ **912** d.	...	1442	...	...	│	...	│	...	...	...	1642	1642	...	...	...	│	│	│	...	│	│	...	...
Frankfurt (Main) Hbf ... **850 901 902** d.	...	1458	...	...	1450	1517	1558	...	...	...	1658	1658	...	...	1716	1650	1650	1652	...	1758	1758	...	...
Hanau Hbf **850 901 902** d.	...	│	...	...	│	1540	│	...	...	...	│	│	...	...	1741	│	│	│	...	│	│	...	...
München Hbf **904 905** d.	...	│	1240	1240	│	│	│	...	1416•	1351	│	│	1516•	1516•	│	│	│	│	...	│	│	1616•	...
Augsburg Hbf **905** d.	...	│	1321	1321	◧	│	│	...	│	1425	│	│	│	│	│	◧	◧	◧	...	│	│	│	...
Nürnberg Hbf **920 921** d.	1325	│	1435	1435	│	│	│	...	1533	│	│	│	1633	1633	│	│	│	│	...	│	│	1734	1728
Würzburg Hbf **920 921** d.	1422	│	1529	1529	│	│	│	...	1630	1636	│	│	1729	1729	│	│	│	│	...	│	│	1825	1830j
Fulda **850 901 902** d.	1525	│	1603	1603	│	1625	│	...	1704	1717	│	│	1803	1810j	│	│	│	│	...	│	│	...	1907
Kassel Wilhelmshöhe **901 902** d.	1601	1622	1636	1636	1654	1700	1722	...	1736	1756	1822	1822	1836	1843	1853	1857	1857	1857	...	1922	1922	...	1940
Göttingen **902 903** d.	1622	1643	1656	1656	1717	...	1743	...	1756	1817	1843	1843	1856	1903	1912	1918	1918	1918	...	1943	1943	...	│
Hannover Hbf **903** a.	1659	1717	1732	1732	1756	...	1817	...	1832	1856	1917	1917	1932	1939	1947	1956	1956	1956	...	2017	2017	...	2032
Hannover Hbf **903** d.	1702	1720	1736	1745	1759	...	1820	...	1836	1901	1920	1920	1936	1942	1950	...	1959	1959	2000	2020	2020	...	2036
Bremen Hbf **813** a.	1811	│	│	1844	│	...	│	...	│	│	│	│	│	│	2047	...	│	│	│	│	│	...	│
Celle **903** d.	│	│	│	...	1819	...	│	...	│	1921	│	│	│	│	...	...	2019	2019	2020	│	│	...	│
Uelzen **903** d.	│	│	│	...	1842	...	│	1900	│	1943	│	│	│	│	...	...	2042	2042	2042	│	2057	...	│
Lüneburg **903** d.	│	│	│	...	1858	...	│	1916	│	1959	2012	2012	│	│	...	...	2058	2058	2058	│	2114	...	│
Hamburg Hbf **903** a.	1907	1835	1853	...	1928	...	1935	1944	1953	2028	2038	2038	2054	2103	...	...	2128	2128	2128	2138	2145	...	2153
Hamburg Altona a.	1921	1850	1908	...	...	...	1950	2001	2009	...	...	2053	...	2119	...	...	...	...	2143	2153	2201	...	2208

♦ – **NOTES** (LISTED BY TRAIN NUMBER)

4/6 – [12] and ✕ Zürich - Basel - Hamburg - Kiel.
0 – [12] and ✕ Wien - Linz - Passau - Regensburg - Hamburg.
48 – WAWEL – [12] Wrocław - Cottbus - Berlin - Stendal - Hamburg.
78 – KOMET – 🛏 1, 2 cl., ▬ 2 cl. and [2] (reclining) Zürich - Hamburg. On the mornings of ②–⑥ Göttingen a. 0541, Hannover a. 0630. On the mornings of ⑥ Hamburg Hbf a. 0812, Altona a. 0827. On the mornings of ① June 16 - July 21 Hamburg Hbf a. 0915, Altona a. 0936.
90 – HANS ALBERS – 🛏 1, 2 cl., ▬ 2 cl. and [2] Wien - Passau - Regensburg - Hamburg; [2] (*D* **60490**) Nürnberg - Hamburg. On ①–④ June 16 - July 24 arrives Hamburg Hbf 0851, Altona 0903. On ⑤ June 20 - July 25 arrives Hamburg Hbf 0836, Altona 0850.
74 – [12] and ✕ Stuttgart - Kiel.
228 – [12] and 🍷 München - Kassel - Paderborn - Düsseldorf. Train number **1224** on ⑥⑦ (also June 19, 20, Oct. 3).
284 – [12] München - Flensburg. From Schwarzach on dates in Table **960**.
286 – PYXIS – Conveys 🛏 1, 2 cl., ▬ 2 cl., [2] (reclining) and 🍷.
951 – [12] Frankfurt - Kassel - Leinefelde - Halle - Leipzig.
986 – ROTTALER LAND – [12] Passau - Regensburg - Hamburg. Also calls at Gemünden, d. 1447.
82 – KÖNIGSSEE – [12] and ✕ Berchtesgaden - München - Hamburg; conveys [12] Oberstdorf (**2084**) - Augsburg (**2082**) - Hamburg.
84 – [12] and 🍷 Hannover - Rostock - Stralsund - Ostseebad Binz.
70 – SCHWARZWALD – [12] and 🍷 Konstanz - Karlsruhe - Hamburg (- Stralsund ⑤⑦ **f**). Train number **2270** on ⑤⑦ (also June 18, Oct. 2; not Oct. 3).
76 – [12] and 🍷 (Karlsruhe ①–⑥ **e** -) Frankfurt - Hamburg - Stralsund (- Ostseebad Binz on dates in Table **844**).
88 – [12] and 🍷 Frankfurt - Gießen - Hannover - Berlin.

A – WATTENMEER – To Westerland (Table **821**).
D – ①②③④⑥⑦ (also Oct. 3; not Oct. 2).
E – ①⑤⑥⑦ (also June 18, 19, Oct. 2). To Kiel Hbf, a. 1244 (1307 June 14 - July 27).
F – Until Oct. 20.
G – From Garmisch (Table **895**) on ⑥ to Nov. 8.
L – To Lübeck (Table **825**).
N – To Oldenburg (Table **813**).
Q – From Wiesbaden Hbf (Table **911**).
R – To Rostock (Table **830**).
T – To Stralsund (Table **830**).
Z – From Zürich (Table **510**).

a – Ⓐ only.
b – ⑥ (also June 19, Oct. 3). Basel **Bad Bf.** 0506 Aug. 2 - Sept. 13.
c – Ⓒ (not ⑥ Aug. 2 - Sept. 13).
e – ①–⑥ (not Oct. 4).
f – Also Oct. 2; not Oct. 3.
g – ① (not June 16 - July 21).
h – ⑥ (also Oct. 3; not Aug. 2 - Sept. 13).
j – Arrives 8–9 minutes earlier.
k – 0600 on ① to July 7; 0609 on ① from July 14.
m – Also June 20, 21, Oct. 4.
n – Not June 20, 21, Oct. 4.
o – München **Ost**.
p – Previous day.
q – Not Oct. 3.
r – 6–11 minutes **earlier** July 31 - Sept. 14.

s – Stops to set down only.
t – Ⓐ (not June 19, Aug. 15).
u – Not Oct. 2.
v – 3 minutes **earlier** until July 12.
w – Also Oct. 2.
x – Not Aug. 1 - Sept. 14.
y – Not ①–④ July 31 - Sept. 11.
z – 1501 Aug. 1 - Sept. 13.

⊖ – Not Oct. 4.
⊡ – Not June 18, 19, Oct. 2.
♣ – Also Oct. 3.
◧ – Via Gießen (Table **806**).
★ – ②–⑦ to Oct. 26; ④–⑦ from Oct. 30.
♠ – ① from Oct. 27 (also runs Hannover - Hamburg on ②③ from Oct. 28).
◇ – Train number **684** on ①②③④⑥ from Sept. 16 (not Oct. 2). To Lübeck on dates in Table **825**.
◐ – Train number **2176** on ① from July 28.
§ – On ① runs as train *ICE* **1188** and continues to Kiel Hbf (a. 1010).
⊠ – On ⑤–⑦ June 14 - July 27 continues to Kiel Hbf (a. 1510), not calling at Hamburg Altona.
• – 2–7 minutes **earlier** until July 12.
⊗ – Terminates at Hannover June 14 - July 27.
❖ – **June 14 - July 27** timings and stopping patterns between Hannover and Hamburg are subject to alteration. Certain *IC* services (as indicated) do not run between Hannover and Hamburg. *ICE* services are subject to extended journey times of up to 21 minutes. Please confirm timings locally.

900 NÜRNBERG and FRANKFURT - HAMBURG

	ICE	IC	ICE	ICE	IC	IC	ICE	IC	ICE	ICE	ICE	ICE	ICE	ICE	ICE	ICE	ICE	ICE	ICE	ICE	ICE	ICE	ICE
Subject to alteration June 14 - July 27	**1090**	**1980**	**572**	**582**	**2274**	**2274**	**376**	**1938**	**782**	**532**	**592**	**782**	**532**	**570**	**580**	**580**	**292**	**580**	**1172**	**272**	**780**	**992**	**698**
SEE NOTE ✣	Ⓑ	⑦			⑤⑦	⑦	⑤⑦	⑦C	⌧	★		⌧	★	⑦	①–⑤	⑦	⑦	⑦	⑥p	Ⓐ	⑦	⑦	⑤u
	H✕		✕	✕	s🍷	🍷	v♦	B	✕	✕	✕	✕	✕	✕	✕	✕	✕♦	✕	Z✕	Z✕	✕	✕	✕
Basel SBB **912** 🚌 d.	...	...	...	...	...	...	1706	...	...	...	...	...	...	...	...	...	1813r	...	1813r	1813r	...	...	...
Karlsruhe Hbf **912** d.	...	...	...	...	1710x	1710x	1851r	...	...	...	...	...	...	...	...	...	2000r	...	2000r	2000r	...	...	...
Stuttgart Hbf **912** d.	1651	...	1726	...	|	|	|	...	...	...	1851	...	...	1926	...	...	|	...	|	|	...	2051	2051
Mannheim Hbf **912** d.	1732	...	1806	...	|	|	1916	...	...	...	1932	...	...	2006	...	...	2032	...	2032	2032	...	2132	2132
Frankfurt Flughafen Fernbf ✈ **912** d.	|	...	1842	...	|	|	|	...	...	...	|	...	...	2042	...	...	|	...	|	|	...	|	|
Frankfurt (Main) Hbf ... **850 901 902** d.	1813	...	1858	...	1849	1849	1958	...	...	...	2013	...	...	2058	...	...	2113	...	2113	2113	...	2222	2222
Hanau Hbf **850 901 902** d.	|	...	1914	...	|	|	|	...	...	...	2029	...	...	2114	...	...	2129	...	2129	2129	...	2238	2238
München Hbf **904 905** d.	|	1552	|	1706	|	|	|	...	1812	1812	|	...	...	|	1854	1854	|	...	|	|	2016	|	|
Augsburg Hbf **905** d.	|	1625	|	1738	◧	◧	|	...	|	|	|	...	...	|	1932	1932	|	...	|	|	|	|	|
Nürnberg Hbf **920 921** d.	|	|	|	|	|	|	|	...	1934	1934	|	...	...	|	|	|	|	...	|	|	2136	|	|
Würzburg Hbf **920 921** d.	|	1835	|	1929	|	|	|	...	2030	2030	|	...	...	|	2131	2131	|	...	|	|	2232	|	|
Fulda **850 901 902** d.	|	1914	|	2003	|	|	|	...	2104	2104	|	...	...	|	2204	2204	2211	...	2211	2211	2306	2323	2323
Kassel Wilhelmshöhe **901 902** d.	|	1951	2025	2036	2056	2056	2122	...	2136	2136	2140	←	←	2225	...	2236	2243	←	2243	2243	2338	2357	0035
Göttingen **902 903** d.	|	2012	2046	2056	2117	2117	2143	...	2155	2155	2159	2205	2205	2245	...	2255	2301	2306	2306	2305	...	0047	...
Hannover Hbf **903** a.	2021	2051	2119	2132	2156	2156	2217	...	→	→	...	2240	2240	2318	...	→	...	2341	2341	0002	...	0146	...
Hannover Hbf **903** d.	...	2055	2122q	2136	...	2159	2220	...	...	...	...	2244	2250	2321	...	...	...	2345	2344	0005	...	0149	...
Bremen Hbf **813** a.	...	|	|	|	...	|	|	...	...	...	...	|	2357	|	...	...	...	|	|	|	...	|	...
Celle **903** d.	...	2119	|	|	...	2219	2240	...	...	...	...	|	...	|	...	...	...	0005	|	0027	...	|	...
Uelzen **903** d.	...	2142	|	|	...	2242	2303	2309	...	...	...	2322	...	|	...	...	...	0027	0023	0050	...	|	...
Lüneburg **903** d.	...	2158	2214q	|	...	2258	2319	2334	...	...	...	2339	...	0015	...	...	...	0044	0041	0106	...	|	...
Hamburg Hbf **903** a.	...	2227	2243q	2253	...	2328	2351	0008	...	...	...	0008	...	0045	...	...	...	0113	0111	0137	...	0308	...
Hamburg Altona a.	...	2242	2258q	2309	...	2343	0006	0023	...	...	...	0023	...	0059	...	...	...	0129	0125	0152	...	0324	...

	ICE	ICE	ICE	ICE	ICE	IC	IC	ICE	ICE	IC	ICE	ICE	ICE	ICE	IC	EC	ICE	ICE	ICE	ICE	ICE	ICE	ICE
Subject to alteration June 14 - July 27	**271**	**591**	**591**	**781**	**781**	**2275**	**2271**	**581**	**571**	**2179**	**1097**	**783**	**71**	**71**	**2277**	**249**	**983**	**297**	**983**	**533**	**583**	**973**	**573**
SEE NOTE ✣	①	Ⓐ	①–⑥	①	①–⑥	⑤a	①–④		①–⑥	Ⓐ	①–⑤	①–⑥	Ⓒ	Ⓐ	①–⑥	①–⑥	⑦	⑦	⑦	①–⑥	①–⑥	①–⑥	⑦m
	♦	✕	✕	✕	✕	🍷	n🍷	✕	d✕		D✕	♠✕	✕	✕	♦	♦	△✕	✕	✕	N✕	G✕	dK	✕
Hamburg Altona d.	...	0332	...	...	...	...	...	...	0502	0454	0552	0541	0557	0604	0609	...	0642	...	...	...	0642	✕	0708
Hamburg Hbf **903** d.	0025	0346	...	...	...	...	...	0453	0516	0523	0607	0555b	0611	0618	0624	0658k	0656	...	...	...	0701	0723	0723
Lüneburg **903** d.	|	0418	...	...	...	...	...	0526	0547	0555	|	|	0642	0648	0655	0737	|	...	...	...	|	|	|
Uelzen **903** d.	|	0435	...	...	...	...	...	0543e	|	0615	|	|	0659	|	0714	0756	|	...	...	...	|	|	|
Celle **903** d.	|	0457	...	...	...	...	...	|	|	0638	|	|	0721	|	0738	...	|	...	...	...	|	|	|
Bremen Hbf **813** d.	|	|	...	...	...	...	...	|	|	|	|	|	|	|	|	...	|	...	...	0714	|	|	|
Hannover Hbf **903** a.	0147	0517	...	...	...	...	...	0621	0638	0657	0719	0723	0739	0738	0758	...	0816	...	...	0814	0823	0838	0838
Hannover Hbf **903** d.	0150	0520	0520	0526	...	0601	0601	0626	0641	...	0722	0726	0741	0741	0801	...	0819	...	...	0826	0826	0841	0841
Göttingen **902 903** d.	0247	0555	0555	0602	...	0640	0640	0702	0717	...	|	0802	0817	0817	0840	...	0856	...	...	0902	0902	0917	0917
Kassel Wilhelmshöhe **901 902** d.	|	0616	0616	0623	...	0703	0703	0723	0738	...	|	0827	0838	0838	0903	...	0917	...	←	0923	0923	0938	0938
Fulda **850 901 902** d.	0418	0647	0647	0656	0656	|	|	0755	|	...	|	0858	|	|	|	...	0946	0950	0955	0955	0955	|	|
Würzburg Hbf **920 921** d.	|	|	|	0729	0729	|	|	0831	|	...	|	0930	|	|	|	...	→	|	1031	1031	1031	|	|
Nürnberg Hbf **920 921** a.	|	|	|	0824	0824	◧	◧	0924	|	...	|	1024	|	|	◧	...	...	|	1124	1124	1124	|	|
Augsburg Hbf **905** a.	|	|	|	|	|	|	|	1037	|	...	|	|	|	|	|	...	...	|	|	|	|	|	|
München Hbf **904 905** a.	|	|	|	0952	0952	|	|	1110	|	...	|	1150	|	|	|	...	...	|	1248	1248	1248	|	|
Hanau Hbf **850 901 902** d.	0506	0730	0730	...	...	|	|	...	|	...	|	...	|	|	|	...	...	|	...	...	...	|	|
Frankfurt (Main) Hbf ... **850 901 902** a.	0529	0745	0745	...	...	0907	0907	...	0900	...	0928	...	1000	1000	1108	...	...	1044	...	...	...	1100	1100
Frankfurt Flughafen Fernbf ✈ **912** a.	0550	|	|	...	...	|	|	...	0916	...	...	...	|	|	|	...	...	|	...	...	...	1116	1116
Mannheim Hbf **912** a.	0625	0827	0827	...	...	|	|	...	0954	...	...	...	1043	1043	|	...	...	1127	...	...	...	1154	1154
Stuttgart Hbf **912** a.	|	0908	0908	...	...	1112	|	...	1035	...	...	...	|	|	|	...	...	|	...	...	...	1235	1235
Karlsruhe Hbf **912** a.	0650y	...	...	...	...	...	1050x	...	...	...	...	...	1108t	1108t	1250h	...	...	1158t	...	...	...	...	...
Basel SBB **912** a.	0847	...	...	...	...	...	...	...	...	...	...	...	1254t	1254t	...	...	...	1347	...	...	...	...	...

	IC	ICE	ICE	ICE	ICE	IC	ICE	ICE	ICE	ICE	IC	ICE	IC	ICE	ICE	IC	ICE	ICE	ICE	IC	ICE	ICE	IC
Subject to alteration June 14 - July 27	**2083**	**91**	**1521**	**91**	**73**	**2279**	**535**	**1085**	**585**	**575**	**1987**	**1223**	**1979**	**787**	**75**	**2371**	**537**	**587**	**577**	**1931**	**789**	**77**	**2373**
SEE NOTE ✣						①–⑥		⑦m	①–⑥		⑥		⑤f			⊗				⑤A			⊗
	✕♦	✕♦	✕	✕♦	✕♦	⊗♦	✕	✕	dL	✕	♦	🍷♦	⊗	✕	Z✕	🍷♦	✕	✕	✕	B	✕	✕♦	T🍷
Hamburg Altona d.	0714	0747	...	...	...	🍷	...	0847	✕	0907	0857	...	0915	0947	1009	1014	...	1047	1109	...	1147	...	...
Hamburg Hbf **903** d.	0729	0803	...	...	0824	0828	...	0901	0901	0924	0912	...	0929	1001	1024	1028	...	1101	1124	1149	1201	1224	1228
Lüneburg **903** d.	0801	|	...	...	|	0900	...	|	|	|	0943	...	0959	|	|	1059	...	|	|	1221	|	|	1259
Uelzen **903** d.	0817	|	...	...	|	0917	...	|	|	|	1004	...	1016	|	|	1114	...	|	|	1246	|	|	1314
Celle **903** d.	0840	|	...	...	|	0939	...	|	|	|	|	...	1040	|	|	1138	...	|	|	...	|	|	1338
Bremen Hbf **813** d.	|	|	...	...	|	|	0914	|	|	|	|	...	|	|	|	|	1114	|	|	...	|	|	|
Hannover Hbf **903** a.	0900	0921	...	...	0938	0958	1014	1021	1021	1038	1043	...	1058	1121	1138	1158	1214	1223	1238	...	1321	1338	1358
Hannover Hbf **903** d.	0903	0926	...	...	0941	1001	1026	1026	1026	1041	1046	...	1101	1126	1141	1201	1226	1226	1241	...	1326	1341	1401
Göttingen **902 903** d.	0944	1003	...	...	1017	1041	1102	1102	1102	1117	1126	...	1142	1202	1217	1240	1302	1302	1317	...	1402	1417	1440
Kassel Wilhelmshöhe **901 902** d.	1006	1025	...	...	1038	1103	1123	1123	1123	1138	1149	1158	1204	1223	1238	1303	1323	1323	1338	...	1423	1438	1503
Fulda **850 901 902** d.	1043	1057	...	←	|	|	1155	1155	1155	|	1232	1228	1241	1255	|	|	1355	1355	|	...	1455	|	|
Würzburg Hbf **920 921** d.	1122	1128	1132	1135	|	|	1231	1231	1231	|	1336	1307j	|	1329	|	|	1431	1431	|	...	1529	|	|
Nürnberg Hbf **920 921** a.	|	→	1224	1227	|	◧	1324	1324	1324	|	1432	1400	|	1424	|	◧	|	|	|	...	1624	|	◧
Augsburg Hbf **905** a.	1331	...	|	...	|	|	1440	1440	1440	|	...	|	|	|	|	|	1626	1626	|	...	|	|	|
München Hbf **904 905** a.	1410o	...	1350g	...	|	|	1517	1517	1517	|	...	1515	|	1557	|	|	1659	1659	|	...	1747	|	|
Hanau Hbf **850 901 902** d.	...	...	...	...	|	|	...	...	...	|	...	...	|	...	|	|	...	...	|	...	...	|	|
Frankfurt (Main) Hbf ... **850 901 902** a.	...	...	...	...	1200	1305	...	...	...	1300	...	...	1336	...	1400	1505	...	...	1500	...	...	1600	1705
Frankfurt Flughafen Fernbf ✈ **912** a.	...	...	...	...	|	|	...	...	...	1316	...	...	...	...	|	|	...	...	1516	...	...	|	|
Mannheim Hbf **912** a.	...	...	...	...	1243	|	...	...	...	1354	...	...	...	...	1443	|	...	...	1554	...	...	1643	|
Stuttgart Hbf **912** a.	...	...	...	...	|	|	...	...	...	1435	...	...	...	...	|	|	...	...	1635	...	...	|	|
Karlsruhe Hbf **912** a.	...	...	...	...	1308t	1450§	...	...	...	...	...	...	...	...	1508t	1650‡	...	...	...	...	...	1708t	1852¦
Basel SBB **912** a.	...	...	...	...	1454t	...	...	...	...	...	...	...	...	...	1654t	...	...	...	...	...	...	1854t	...

♦ – **NOTES** (LISTED BY TRAIN NUMBER)

73/7 – 🚃 and ✕ Kiel - Hamburg - Basel - Zürich.
91 – 🚃 and ✕ Hamburg - Regensburg - Passau - Linz - Wien.
249 – WAWEL – 🚃 Hamburg - Stendal - Berlin - Cottbus - Wrocław.
271 – 🚃 Hamburg - Basel - Bern - Interlaken. ✕ Frankfurt - Interlaken.
292 – 🚃 and ✕ Zürich - Basel - Berlin.
376 – 🚃 and ✕ Interlaken - Bern - Basel - Frankfurt - Hamburg.
1223 – 🚃 and 🍷 Köln - Düsseldorf - Paderborn - Kassel - München.
1987 – ROTTALER LAND – 🚃 Hamburg - Passau. Also calls at Gemünden (d. 1301).
2083 – KÖNIGSSEE – 🚃 Hamburg - Berchtesgaden; conveys 🚃 Hamburg - Augsburg (**2085**) - Oberstdorf.
2277 – 🚃 and 🍷 Hamburg - Frankfurt (- Karlsruhe ⑥ **h**).
2279 – 🚃 and 🍷 Stralsund - Hamburg - Karlsruhe - Konstanz.
2371 – 🚃 and 🍷 Hamburg - Karlsruhe (- Konstanz ⑦).

A – ⑤ from Aug. 1 (also Oct. 2; not Oct. 3).
B – To / from Berlin (Tables **841**/**810**).
C – From Aug. 3.
D – ①–⑤ (not June 19, Oct. 3). *ICE* ***SPRINTER***. To Darmstadt Hbf (a. 0953). Ⓡ and supplement payable for journeys to Frankfurt and Darmstadt.
G – To Garmisch (Table **895**) on ⑥ (also June 19, Oct. 3; not Oct. 4).
H – Ⓑ (not June 19, Oct. 3). *ICE* ***SPRINTER***. Ⓡ and supplement payable. To Berlin (Table **902**).
K – From Kiel (Table **820**).
L – From Lübeck (Table **825**).
N – From Oldenburg (Table **813**).
T – From Stralsund (Table **830**).
Z – From / to Zürich (Table **510**).

a – Also June 18, Oct. 2; not June 20, Oct. 3.
b – 0601 on ⑥.
d – Not Oct. 4.
e – ①–⑥ only.
f – Also Oct. 2; not Oct. 3.
g – 1359 until July 12.
h – ⑥ (also Oct. 3; not Aug. 2 - Sept. 13).
j – Arrives 1257.
k – On ①–⑤ June 16 - July 25 starts from Hamburg **Harburg** (d. 0715).
m – Also Oct. 4.
n – Also June 20; not June 18, Oct. 2.
o – München **Ost**.

p – Also Oct. 3.
q – Not Oct. 3.
r – 8–11 minutes **earlier** July 31 - Sept. 14.
s – Also June 18, Oct. 2; not Oct. 3.
t – 7–12 minutes later July 31 - Sept. 14.
u – Also June 19, Oct. 2; not Oct. 3.
v – Also Oct. 2; not Oct. 3.
x – Not July 31 - Sept. 14.
y – 6 minutes later Aug. 4 - Sept. 8.

⊗ – Starts from Hannover June 14 - July 27.
§ – Not ⑦ Aug. 3 - Sept. 14.
‡ – Not ①–⑤ July 31 - Sept. 12.

¦ – Not ⑤ Aug. 1 - Sept. 12. Arrives up to 17 minutes later July 31 - Sept. 14.
△ – 5–7 minutes later Hannover - Fulda on June 22.
♠ – Does not run Hamburg - Hannover on ①–⑤ June 16 - July 25.
⌧ – Runs 5–8 minutes **earlier** Göttingen - Hamburg on ⑦ (connection at Göttingen with train **592** not available). Train number **1182** on ⑥ (also June 19, Oct. 3).
★ – From Garmisch (Table **895**) on ⑥ to Nov. 8 (also June 19, Oct. 3; not Oct. 4). To Oldenburg (Table **813**) on ①②③④⑦ (not June 19, Oct. 2). Train number **732** on ⑤⑥ (also June 19, Oct. 2). Train number **1032** on ⑦. Runs 6–8 minutes **earlier** Göttingen - Bremen on ⑦ (connection at Göttingen with train **592** not available).
◧ – Via Gießen (Table **806**).
✣ – **June 14 - July 27** timings and stopping patterns between Hamburg and Hannover are subject to alteration. Certain *IC* services (as indicated) do not run between Hamburg and Hannover. *ICE* services are subject to extended journey times of up to 30 minutes (earlier departures from Hamburg Altona and Hamburg Hbf). Please confirm timings locally.

HAMBURG - FRANKFURT and NÜRNBERG 900

Subject to alteration June 14 - July 27 SEE NOTE ❖	ICE 1139	ICE 1189	ICE 579	IC 1981	ICE 881	ICE 79	IC 2375	IC 2385	ICE 631	ICE 1081	ICE 771	IC 2171	IC 2191	IC 2193	IC 2281	ICE 883	ICE 1183	ICE 1171	IC 1948	IC 2377	ICE 633	ICE 683	IC 1073
				⑤⑦			⑦	①–⑥		◇		⑤y	⑥⑦	J	②–④	②–④			⑦	⊗	⊙	Ⓑ	Ⓑr
	🍷	✕	✕	♣	✕	Z✕	⊗🍷	B🍷	✕	✕	✕	A✕	A✕	A✕	R✕	d✕	✕♦	✕	♦	O🍷	✕	✕	🍷
Hamburg Altona d.	...	1247	1309	...	1339	1409	1414	...	...	...	1509	...	...	...	1514	1547	...	1609	...	...	...	1647	1708
Hamburg Hbf **903** d.	...	1301	1324	1327	1353	1424	1428	...	...	1501	1524	1527	1527	1527	1528	1601	1601	1624	...	1627	...	1701	1722
Lüneburg **903** d.	...	|	|	1358	1426	|	1459	...	...	|	|	1557	1557	1557	1559	|	|	|	...	1659	...	|	|
Uelzen **903** d.	...	|	|	1414	1442	|	1515	...	...	|	|	1618	1618	1618	1620	|	|	|	...	1714	...	|	|
Celle **903** d.	...	|	|	|	1505	|	1539	...	...	|	|	1640	1640	1640	1642	|	|	|	...	1737	...	|	|
Bremen Hbf **813** d.	1314	|	|	|	|	|	|	...	1514	|	|	|	|	|	|	|	|	|	...	|	1714	|	|
Hannover Hbf **903** a.	1414	1423	1438	1451	1523	1538	1558	...	1614	1623	1638	1659	1700	1659	1700	1721	1721	1738	...	1757	1814	1823	1836
Hannover Hbf **903** d.	1426	1426	1441	1454	1526	1541	1601	1601	1626	1626	1641	1703	1704	1703	1703	1726	1726	1741	...	1801	1826	1826	1839
Göttingen **902 903** d.	1503	1503	1517	1534	1602	1617	1640	1640	1702	1702	1717	1744	1744	1814	1814	1802	1802	1817	...	1840	1902	1902	|
Kassel Wilhelmshöhe **901 902** d.	1525	1525	1538	1558	1623	1638	1703	1703	1723	1723	1738	1806	1805	...	...	1823	1823	1838	1856	1903	1923	1923	1937
Fulda **850 901 902** d.	1557	1557	|	1632	1655	|	|	|	1755	1755	|	1840	|	...	...	1855	1855	|	1933	|	1955	1955	|
Würzburg Hbf **920 921** d.	1631	1631	|	1714	1729	|	|	|	1831	1831	|	|	|	...	...	1929	1929	|	|	|	2031	2031	|
Nürnberg Hbf **920 921** a.	|	|	|	|	1824	|	◧	◧	1924	1924	|	|	◧	...	...	2024	2024	|	|	◧	|	|	|
Augsburg Hbf **905** a.	1826	1826	|	1929	|	|	|	|	2041	2041	|	|	|	...	...	|	|	|	|	|	2226	2226	|
München Hbf **904 905** a.	1900	1900	|	2002	1950e	|	|	|	2117	2117	|	|	|	...	...	2150	2150	|	|	|	2300	2300	|
Hanau Hbf **850 901 902** d.	...	...	|	...	...	|	|	|	...	...	|	1935	|	...	...	...	...	|	2016	|	...	...	|
Frankfurt (Main) Hbf **850 901 902** a.	...	...	1700	...	...	1800	1905	1905	...	...	1900	1950	2000	...	...	...	...	2000	2040	2105	...	...	2100
Frankfurt Flughafen Fernbf ✈ **912** a.	...	...	1716	...	...	|	|	|	...	...	1916	|	...	...	...	...	...	|	...	|	...	...	2116
Mannheim Hbf **912** a.	...	...	1754	...	...	1843	|	|	...	...	1954	|	...	...	...	...	...	2043	...	|	...	...	2154
Stuttgart Hbf **912** a.	...	...	1835	...	...	|	|	|	...	...	2035	2155	...	...	...	...	...	|	...	|	...	...	2250
Karlsruhe Hbf **912** a.	...	...	...	...	...	1908t	2051	2051h	...	...	...	...	...	...	...	...	...	2108t	...	2326f	...	...	...
Basel SBB **912** a.	...	...	...	...	...	2054t	...	...	...	...	...	...	...	...	...	...	...	2300k	...	...	...	...	...

Subject to alteration June 14 - July 27 SEE NOTE ❖	ICE 773	IC 2173	ICE 1185	ICE 885	ICE 1173	IC 2379	IC 2379	ICE 635	ICE 685	ICE 635	ICE 685	ICE 775	IC 1999	IC 2175	ICE 887	ICE 1587	IC 1989	IC 2150	CNL 479	EN 491	CNL 1287	IC 61287	IC 2185
	⑥s	Ⓑr	⑥	Ⓑ		G	⑤f	Ⓑb		⑦¶	⑦	⑤⑦	⑦	♠	Ⓑq	⑥p	⑦	①	Ⓡ		Ⓡ	Ⓐ	⑦
	✕	🍷	✕	✕	K✕	T🍷	T⊗ 🍷	✕	✕	✕	✕	a✕	B	✕	N✕	N✕	T		✕♦	♦	🍷♦	m 2	T🍷
Hamburg Altona d.	1709	1714	1747	1747	...	...		...	1847	...	1847	1909	...	1914	1947	1947	...	...	1957⁝	2020	2112	2112	...
Hamburg Hbf **903** d.	1724	1728	1801	1801	1824	1828	1828	...	1901	...	1901	1924	...	1928	2001	2001	2028	...	2011⁝	2034	2126	2126	2228
Lüneburg **903** d.	|	1757	|	|	|	1859	1859	...	|	...	|	|	...	2000	|	|	2100	...	|	|	|	|	2300
Uelzen **903** d.	|	1819	|	|	|	1914	1914	...	|	...	|	|	...	2017	|	|	2116	...	|	|	|	|	2317
Celle **903** d.	|	1841	|	|	|	1938	1938	...	|	...	|	|	...	2040	|	|	2140	...	|	|	|	|	2340
Bremen Hbf **813** d.	|	|	|	|	|	|	|	1914	|	1914	|	|	...	|	|	|	|	...	|	|	|	|	|
Hannover Hbf **903** a.	1838	1904	1921	1921	1938	1957	1957	2014	2023	2014	2023	2038	...	2059	2121	2121	2158	...	|	2225	|	2300	2358
Hannover Hbf **903** d.	1841	1909w	1926	1926	1941	2001w	2001	2026	2026	2026	2026	2041	2101	...	2126	2137	2210	...	2216u	2227	2323u	...	...
Göttingen **902 903** d.	1917	2022w	2002	2002	2017	2039w	2040	2102	2102	2102	2102	2117	2142	...	2202	2214	2300j	...	2332u	2327	|	...	...
Kassel Wilhelmshöhe **901 902** d.	1938	2043w	2023	2027	2038	...	2103	2123	2123	2123	2123	2138	2203	...	2223	2235	2323	...	|	|	|	...	...
Fulda **850 901 902** d.	|	...	2055	2059	|	...	|	2155	2155	2155	2155	|	|	...	2256	2306	0006j	0004	|	|	|	...	...
Würzburg Hbf **920 921** d.	|	...	2134	2134	|	...	|	2231	2231	2231	2231	|	|	...	|	|	0043	|	|	0226	|	...	...
Nürnberg Hbf **920 921** a.	|	...	2227	2227	|	...	◧	2324	2324	2324	2324	|	◧	...	|	|	0141	|	|	0321	|	...	...
Augsburg Hbf **905** a.	|	...	|	|	|	...	|	...	...	|	|	|	|	...	|	|	...	|	|	...	0625	...	...
München Hbf **904 905** a.	|	...	2355	2355	|	...	|	...	...	0051	0051	|	|	...	|	|	...	|	|	...	0705	...	...
Hanau Hbf **850 901 902** d.	|	...	...	...	|	...	|	...	...	...	...	|	|	...	2340	2352	...	0049	|	...	...	...	...
Frankfurt (Main) Hbf **850 901 902** a.	2100	...	...	...	2200	...	2304	...	...	...	...	2300	0022	...	2355	0008	...	0104	|	...	...	...	...
Frankfurt Flughafen Fernbf ✈ **912** a.	2116	...	...	...	|	...	...	...	...	...	...	|	...	...	0021	0023	...	...	|	...	...	...	...
Mannheim Hbf **912** a.	2154	...	...	...	2243	...	...	...	...	...	...	|	...	...	...	...	...	...	|	...	...	...	...
Stuttgart Hbf **912** a.	2250	...	...	...	|	...	...	...	...	...	...	0049v	...	...	...	...	...	...	|	...	...	...	...
Karlsruhe Hbf **912** a.	...	...	...	...	2308t	...	...	...	...	...	...	...	...	...	...	...	...	...	0437	...	...	...	...
Basel SBB **912** a.	...	...	...	...	0100c	...	...	...	...	...	...	...	...	...	...	...	...	...	0647	...	...	...	...

♦ – **NOTES** (LISTED BY TRAIN NUMBER)

479 – KOMET – 🛏 1, 2 cl., ▬ 2 cl., (2) and ✕ Hamburg - Zürich.

491 – HANS ALBERS – 🛏 1, 2 cl., ▬ 2 cl. and (2) Hamburg - Passau - Wien. (2) (*D* **60491**) Hamburg - Nürnberg. Ⓡ for journeys beyond Nürnberg. From Nov. 1 departs Hamburg Altona 2035, Hamburg Hbf 2052.

1183 – ①⑤⑥⑦ (also Oct. 2, June 18, 19; not Oct. 3). (12) and ✕ Kiel Hbf (d. 1441 to July 27; 1449 from July 28) - Hamburg - München.

1287 – PYXIS – Conveys 🛏 1, 2 cl., ▬ 2 cl. and (2) (reclining). On ①⑦ June 15 - July 27 Hamburg Altona d. 2003, Hamburg Hbf d. 2021. On ②–⑥ June 14 - July 26 Hamburg Altona d. 2110, Hamburg Hbf d. 2124.

1948 – (12) Leipzig - Halle - Nordhausen - Frankfurt.

A – WATTENMEER – From Westerland (Table **821**).
B – From Berlin (Table **810**).
G – From July 28.
– ①–④ to Oct. 27 (not Oct. 2); ① from Nov. 3.
K – From Kiel (Table **820**).
– To Wiesbaden (Table **911**).
– From Ostseebad Binz via Stralsund (Tables **844** / **830**).

R – ②–④ from Oct. 28
T – From Stralsund (Table **830**).
Z – To Zürich (Table **510**).

a – Also Oct. 2; not Oct. 3.
b – Not June 19.
c – Karlsruhe - Basel on ⑤⑥ (also Oct. 2); arrives 0106 Aug. 1 - Sept. 14.
d – Also Oct. 3; not June 18, 19, Oct. 2.
e – 1958 until July 12.

f – ⑤ (also June 18, Oct. 2; not June 20, Oct. 3).
h – Ⓐ only. Arrives 2057 July 31 - Sept. 12.
j – Arrives Göttingen 2249, Fulda 2358.
k – ⑦ only. 2313 Aug. 3 - Sept. 14.
m – Not ① June 16 - July 21. On ②–⑤ June 17 - July 25 departs Hamburg Altona 2110, Hamburg Hbf 2124.
p – Also June 19, 20, Oct. 3.
q – Not June 19, 20, Oct. 3.
r – Not Oct. 3.
s – Also Oct. 3.
t – 7–12 minutes later July 31 - Sept. 14.

u – Stops to pick up only.
v – Frankfurt - Stuttgart on ⑦ only.
w – ⑦ only.
y – Also Oct. 2.
¶ – Also June 18, Aug. 14, Oct. 2.
♠ – ①②③④⑦ (not Oct. 2).
⊙ – Train number **1133** on ⑥.
◇ – Train number **681** on ①②③④⑥ from Sept. 16 (not Oct. 2). From Lübeck on dates in Table **825**.
⊗ – Starts from Hannover June 14 - July 27.
◧ – Via Gießen (Table **806**).

♣ – ⑤⑦ (also Oct. 2; not Oct. 3). From Flensburg (Table **823**) on ⑤ (also Oct. 2). Train number **1983** on ⑦.

⁝ – On ①–⑤ to July 25 departs Hamburg Altona 1903, Hamburg Hbf 1918. On ⑦ to July 27 departs Hamburg Altona 1909, Hamburg Hbf 1925. On ⑦ from Aug. 3 departs Hamburg Altona 2011, Hamburg Hbf 2025. On ⑥ departs Hamburg Altona 2013, Hamburg Hbf 2027.

❖ – **June 14 - July 27** timings and stopping patterns between Hamburg and Hannover are subject to alteration. Certain *IC* services (as indicated) do not run between Hamburg and Hannover. *ICE* services are subject to extended journey times of up to 23 minutes (earlier departures from Hamburg Altona and Hamburg Hbf). Please confirm timings locally.

RE / RB services — Local services FRANKFURT - FULDA - KASSEL 901

Other *ICE / IC* services: Table **850** for Bebra - Kassel Wilhelmshöhe and v.v., also Frankfurt - Fulda - Bad Hersfeld and v.v. Tables **900** / **902** for Frankfurt - Fulda - Kassel Wilhelmshöhe and v.v.

km						A	
0	**Frankfurt** (Main) Hbf **921** d.	0526	and hourly until	2026	2126	2226	2326
10	Offenbach (Main) Hbf **921** d.	0538		2038	2138	2238	2338
23	Hanau Hbf **921** d.	0548		2048	2148	2248	2348
104	**Fulda** a.	0648		2148	2250	2348	0048

		ⒶeB	†z	⚒r	ⒶeB						
Fulda d.	0401	0438	0508	0515	0600	0608	0708	0808	0908	and hourly until	2309
Hanau Hbf **921** d.	0500	0539	0609	0616	0656	0709	0809	0909	1009		0009
Offenbach (Main) Hbf **921** d.	0509	0548	0617	0624	|	0717	0817	0921	1017		0017
Frankfurt (Main) Hbf **921** a.	0520	0558	0628	0636	0716	0728	0828	0932	1028		0028

FULDA - KASSEL (SEE NOTE ♠)

km		Ⓐe	Ⓐe		Ⓐe	ⒸzG										Ⓒz	Ⓐe						G		ⒶB
0	**Fulda** d.	...	0548	0616	0644	0655	0719	0819	0919	1019	1119	1219	1319	1419	1519	1619	1619	1719	1819	1919	2019	2122e	2221	2301	2357
42	Bad Hersfeld d.	0511	0616	0644	0714	0721	0747	0847	0947	1047	1147	1247	1347	1447	1547	1647	1647	1747	1847	1947	2047	2149	2250	2329	0027
56	Bebra d.	0525	0627	0657	0727	0731	0758	0857	0958	1057	1158	1257	1358	1457	1558	1657	1657	1758	1857	1958	2058	2200	2301	2340	0040
62	Rotenburg (Fulda) d.	0531	0633	0703	0733	...	0804	0903	1004	1103	1204	1303	1404	1503	1604	1703	1703	1804	1903	2004	2104	2206	...	...	...
84	Melsungen d.	0550	0653	0723	0753	...	0824	0923	1024	1123	1224	1323	1424	1523	1624	1723	1722	1824	1923	2024	2124	2225	...	...	...
110	**Kassel** Wilhelmshöhe **804/6** a.	0609	0712	0742	0811	...	0842	0942	1042	1142	1242	1342	1442	1542	1642	1742	1744	1842	1942	2042	2142	2249	...	...	...
114	**Kassel** Hbf **804/6** a.	0616	0718	0748	0818	...	0848	0948	1048	1148	1248	1348	1448	1548	1648	1748	1754	1848	1948	2053	2150	2254	...	...	...

		ⒶB	ⒶB	⚒r	Ⓒz	Ⓐe		G															Ⓑ	⚒r	†z
assel Hbf **804/6** d.	...	...	...	0506	0605	0629	0709	...	0810j	0910	1010	1110	1210	1310	1410	1510	1610	1710	1810	1910	2010	2105t	2210	2309	2335
assel Wilhelmshöhe **804/6** d.	...	...	...	0510	0614	0633	0713	...	0814	0914	1014	1115	1214	1314	1414	1514	1614	1715	1814	1914	2014	2115	2214	2315	2341
elsungen d.	...	...	...	0529	0634	0650	0733	...	0833	0932	1033	1132	1233	1332	1433	1532	1633	1733	1833	1933	2033	2132	2233	2336	0000
otenburg (Fulda) d.	...	...	...	0549	0653	0710	0752	...	0852	0951	1052	1151	1252	1351	1452	1551	1652	1751	1852	1951	2052	2151	2252	2356	0019
ebra d.	0315	0359	0522	0558	0700	0717	0800	0815	0859	0958	1059	1158	1259	1358	1459	1558	1659	1758	1859	1958	2059	2159	2300f	0008	0034
ad Hersfeld d.	0325	0409	0531	0608	0709	0727	0810	0826	0908	1008	1108	1208	1308	1408	1508	1608	1708	1808k	1908	2008	2108h	2209	2311f	0022	0045
ulda a.	0354	0436	0558	0637	0737	0755	...	0854	0937	1037	1137	1237	1337	1437	1537	1637	1737	1837k	1937	2037	2137h	2237	...	...	...

– To Bebra on Ⓐ**e** (see following panel).
– Ⓐ (not June 19). (12) Bebra - Fulda - Frankfurt and v.v.
– To / from Göttingen (Table **908**).

e – Ⓐ (not June 19).
f – 4–5 minutes later on ①–⑤.
h – 3 minutes later on Ⓒ**z**.
j – 0806 on † (also June 19).

k – On † (also June 19) Bad Hersfeld d. 1807, Fulda a. 1840.
r – Not June 19.
t – 2110 on Ⓐ (not June 19).

z – Also June 19.

♠ – Operated by CANTUS Verkehrsgesellschaft (except trains marked with note **B**). 2nd class only.

902 FRANKFURT - BRAUNSCHWEIG - BERLIN

km		ICE 649	ICE 876	ICE 1096	ICE 1092	ICE 696	ICE 874	ICE 1674	IC 2388	ICE 694	ICE 374	ICE 692	ICE 372	ICE 690	ICE 370	ICE 598	ICE 278	ICE 596	ICE 276	ICE 296	ICE 1090	ICE 594	ICE 274	ICE 592	ICE 292
		Ⓐ	①–⑥	①	D	① d	①–⑥	⑦	①–⑥				♠						Ⓑ	⑥	Ⓑ w	⑥ u		s	⑦
		✕	✕	⚡✕	⚡✕	✕	✕	✕	🍷	✕	✕	✕	✕	✕	✕	✕	✕	✕	✕	✕	⚡✕	✕	✕	✕	Z✕
	Interlaken Ost **560** d.	...	...	...	...	...	...	...	...	...	...	...	0600	...	0800	...	1000	...	1200	1200	...	...	...	...	...
	Bern **560** d.	...	...	...	...	...	...	...	...	...	...	...	0704	...	0904	...	1104	...	1304	1304	...	...	...	...	...
	Basel SBB **912** d.	...	...	...	...	...	0412**b**	...	...	...	0608‡	...	0813‡	...	1013‡	...	1213‡	...	1413‡	1413‡	...	...	1613‡	...	1813‡
	Karlsruhe Hbf **912** d.	...	...	0500‡	...	...	0558‡	0558‡	...	...	0800‡	...	1000‡	...	1200‡	...	1400‡	...	1600‡	1600‡	...	...	1801‡	...	2000‡
	Ulm Hbf **930** d.	...	...	|	...	...	|	|	...	...	|	0751**a**	|	0951	|	1151	|	1351	|	|	1551	1551	|	1751	|
	Stuttgart Hbf **912** d.	...	...	|	...	...	|	|	...	0651	|	0851	|	1051	|	1251	|	1451	|	|	1651	1651	|	1851	|
	Mannheim Hbf **912** d.	...	...	0528	...	...	0632	0632	...	0732	0832	0932	1032	1132	1232	1332	1432	1532	1632	1632	1732	1732	1832	1932	2032
0	**Frankfurt** (Main) Hbf **850 900** d.	...	0510**g**	0614	0614	...	0713	0713	0649	0813	0913	1013	1113	1213	1313	1413	1513	1613	1713	1713	1813	1813	1913	2013	2113
23	Hanau Hbf **850 900** d.	...	0526**g**	|	|	...	0729	0729	|	0829	0929	1029	1129	1229	1329	1429	1529	1629	1729	|	|	1829	1929	2029	2129
104	Fulda **850 900** d.	...	0610**g**	|	|	...	0811	0811	**G**	0911	1011	1111	1211	1311	1411	1511	1611	1711	1811	1811	|	1911	2011	|	2211
194	**Kassel** Wilhelmshöhe **900** d.	...	0643	|	|	0743	0843	0843	0854	0943	1043	1143	1243	1343	1443	1543	1643	1743	1843	|	|	1944	2043	2140	2243
239	Göttingen **900** d.	...	0703	|	|	0804	0903	0904	0917	1003	1103	1203	1303	1403	1503	1603	1703	1803	1903	|	|	2004	2103	2201	2303
	Hannover Hbf **900** a.	...	|	|	|	|	|	|	0958	|	|	|	|	|	|	|	|	|	|	|	2021	|	|	|	|
317	Hildesheim Hbf **863** d.	*0531*	0734	|	|	0834	0934	0935	|	1034	1134	1234	1334	1434	1534	1634	1734	1834	1934	**E**	|	2034	2134	2234	2334
360	**Braunschweig** Hbf **863** d.	0601	0759	|	|	0900	0959	1000	|	1059	1159	1259	1359	1459	1559	1659	1759	1859	1959	|	|	2059	2159	2259	2359
392	Wolfsburg **810** d.	0620	0817	|	|	0918	1017	1018	1052	|	1217	|	1417	|	1617	|	1817	|	2017	|	|	2117	2217	2317	0017
559	**Berlin** Spandau **810** a.	0721	0911	0939	0939	1010	1111	1113	1151	1207	1311	1407	1511	1607	1711	1807	1911	2007	2111	|	2145	2212	2311	0020	0111
575	**Berlin** Hbf **810** a.	0735	0925	0953	0953	1026	1125	1127	1206	1222	1325	1422	1525	1622	1725	1822	1925	2022	2126	2206**j**	2156	2227	2325	0032	0125
580	**Berlin** Ostbahnhof **810** a.	0749	0937	1004	1004	1037	1136	1139	1217	1234	1336	1434	1536	1635	1737	1834	1936	2034	2137	...	...	2238	2336	...	0136

	ICE 275	ICE 593	ICE 1091	ICE 297	ICE 277	ICE 595	ICE 279	ICE 597	ICE 371	ICE 599	ICE 373	ICE 691	IC 2385	ICE 375	ICE 693	ICE 377	ICE 397	ICE 695	ICE 1093	ICE 877	ICE 1677	IC 1999	ICE 697	ICE 697	ICE 879
	Ⓐ	Ⓒ c	Ⓐ n	⑦	①–⑥								①–⑥			Ⓑ	⑥	⑥ z	Ⓑ v	Ⓑ	⑥	⑦	Ⓑ	⑤⑦	⑦
	✕	✕	⚡✕	✕	✕	✕	✕	✕	✕	✕	✕	✕	🍷	✕	✕	✕	✕	✕	⚡✕	✕	✕		✕	m✕	✕
Berlin Ostbahnhof **810** d.	0421	0520	...	...	0621	0723	0821	0923	1021	1123	1221	1323	1344**r**	1421	1523	1621	...	1723	1753	1821	1820	...	1923	1923	2021
Berlin Hbf **810** d.	0432	0531	0606	0557**k**	0632	0734	0832	0934	1032	1134	1232	1334	1355**r**	1432	1534	1632	1631	1734	1804	1832	1831	1907	1934	1934	2032
Berlin Spandau **810** d.	0446	0545	0617	|	0646	0748	0846	0948	1046	1148	1246	1348	1409**r**	1446	1548	1646	1644	1748	1818	1846	1845	1920	1948	1948	2046
Wolfsburg **810** d.	0540	0642	|	|	0740	|	0940	|	1140	|	1340	|	1511	1540	|	1740	1740	|	|	1940	1940	2021	|	|	2140
Braunschweig Hbf **863** d.	0558	0701	|	|	0758	0858	0958	1058	1158	1258	1358	1458	|	1558	1658	1758	1758	1858	|	1958	1959	|	2058	2058	2158
Hildesheim Hbf **863** d.	0625	0725	|	**E**	0825	0925	1025	1125	1225	1325	1425	1525	|	1625	1725	1825	1825	1925	|	2025	2025	|	2125	2125	2225
Hannover Hbf **900** d.	|	|	|	|	|	|	|	|	|	|	|	|	1601	|	|	|	|	|	|	|	|	2101	|	|	|
Göttingen **900** d.	0655	0755	|	|	0855	0955	1055	1155	1255	1355	1455	1555	1640	1655	1755	1855	1855	1955	|	2055	2056	2142	2155	2155	2255
Kassel Wilhelmshöhe **900** d.	0716	0816	|	|	0916	1016	1116	1216	1316	1416	1516	1616	1703	1716	1816	1916	1916	2016	|	2116	2117	2203	2214	2216	2316
Fulda **850 900** d.	0747	0847	|	0950	0947	1047	1147	1247	1347	1447	1547	1647	**G**	1747	1847	1947	1947	2047	|	2147	2148	**G**	...	2247	2347
Hanau Hbf **850 900** d.	0829	0929	|	|	1029	1129	1229	1329	1429	1529	1629	1729	|	1829	1929	2029	2029	|	|	2229	2232	|	...	2329	0029
Frankfurt (Main) Hbf **850 900** a.	0844	0944	0942	1044	1044	1144	1244	1344	1444	1544	1644	1744	1905	1844	1944	2044	2044	2142	2142	2248	2250	0022	...	2344	0048
Mannheim Hbf **912** a.	0927	1027	1027	1127	1127	1227	1327	1427	1527	1627	1727	1827	|	1927	2027	2127	2127	2227	2227	2348	2348	...	...	...	0149
Stuttgart Hbf **912** a.	|	1108	1108	|	|	1308	|	1508	|	1708	|	1908	|	|	2108	|	|	2308	2308	|	|	...	...	...	|
Ulm Hbf **930** a.	|	1207	1207	|	|	1407	|	1607	|	1807	|	2007**q**	|	|	2207	|	|	...	0010**t**	|	|	...	...	...	|
Karlsruhe Hbf **912** a.	0958¦	...	...	1158¦	1158¦	...	1358¦	...	1558¦	...	1758¦	...	2051**p**	1958¦	...	2158¦	2158¦	...	...	0013**y**	0013**y**	...	...	...	0220**y**
Basel SBB **912** a.	1147	...	...	1347	1347	...	1547	...	1747	...	1947	...	...	2147¦	...	2357	2357	...	...	...	...	...	...	...	...
Bern **560** a.	1256	...	...	1456	1456	...	...	...	1856	...	2056	...	...	...	...	...	...	...	...	...	...	...	...	...	...
Interlaken Ost **560** a.	1357	...	...	1557	1557	...	...	...	1957	...	2157	...	...	...	...	...	...	...	...	...	...	...	...	...	...

D – ②–④ (not June 18, 19, Oct. 2). From Darmstadt Hbf (d. 0543).
E – Via Erfurt (Table **850**).
G – Via Gießen (Table **806**).
Z – From Zürich HB (d. 1700).

a – Ⓐ only.
b – ① only. Basel **Badischer Bahnhof**. 0411 Aug. 4 - Sept. 8.
c – Also June 19.
d – Also June 20.
g – ① only.

j – 2209 from Oct. 4.
k – 0551 from Sept. 28.
m – Also Oct. 2; not Oct. 3.
n – Not June 19.
p – Ⓐ only. Arrives 2057 July 31 - Sept. 12.
q – Ⓑ (not Oct. 3).
r – 16–18 minutes **earlier** on ⑥ (also Oct. 3).
s – Also calls at Stendal (d. 2346).
t – Stuttgart - Ulm on ⑦ only.
u – Also June 19, Oct. 3.

v – Not June 20, Oct. 3.
w – Not June 19, Oct. 3.
y – 12–14 minutes later on the mornings July 18 - Sept. 29.
z – Also June 20, Oct. 3.

‡ – Departs up to 12 minutes **earlier** July 31 - Sept. 14.
¦ – Arrives 11–12 minutes later July 31 - Sept. 14.
♠ – On ⑤–⑦ (also Oct. 2; not Oct. 3) runs with train number **392** and terminates at Berlin Hbf (a. 1522).
⚡ – *ICE* ***SPRINTER***. 🅁 and supplement payable.

903 Local services GÖTTINGEN - HANNOVER - UELZEN - HAMBURG

metronom

Services below are operated by ***metronom*** (except trains **A**, **B**, **C**, **D** and **E**). For faster *ICE* and *IC* services see Table **900**. SUBJECT TO ALTERATION JUNE 14 - JULY 27 (SEE NOTE ⊠)

km	SEE NOTE ⊠																										
				⚒		① A🍷	Ⓐ A🍷	h	Ⓐ B🍷																	Ⓐ	Ⓒ
0	**Göttingen** d.	...	...	0409	0504	0548	0548	0607	0645	...	0707	0809	0907	1009	1107	1209	1307	1409	1507	1609	1707	1809	1907	2009	2108	2207	2207
20	Northeim (Han) d.	...	...	0423	0517	0600	0600	0620	0658	...	0720	0823	0920	1023	1120	1223	1320	1423	1520	1623	1720	1823	1920	2023	2121	2220	2220
39	Kreiensen d.	...	...	0438	0534	0613	0613	0634	0712	...	0734	0838	0934	1038	1134	1238	1334	1438	1534	1638	1734	1838	1934	2038	2134	2234	2234
58	Alfeld (Leine) d.	...	...	0450	0547	0625	0625	0647	0725	...	0747	0850	0947	1050	1147	1250	1347	1450	1547	1650	1747	1850	1947	2050	2147	2247	2247
75	Elze (Han) d.	...	...	0503	0558	0636	0636	0658	0736	...	0758	0903	0958	1103	1158	1303	1358	1503	1558	1703	1758	1903	1958	2103	2158	2258	2258
108	**Hannover** Hbf. a.	...	...	0526	0623	0655	0655	0723	0756	...	0824	0926	1023	1126	1223	1326	1423	1526	1623	1726	1823	1926	2025	2126	2223	2323	2323
108	**Hannover** Hbf. d.	...	...	0540	0640	0700	—	0740	0759	...	0840	0940	1040	1140	1240	1340	1440	1540	1640	1740	1840	1940**k**	2040	2140	2248	2340	2351
149	Celle d.	...	...	0606	0706	0720	...	0806	0819	...	0906	1006	1106	1206	1306	1406	1506	1606	1706	1806	1906	2006**k**	2106	2206	2317	0006	0019
201	Uelzen a.	...	...	0638	0738	0740	...	0838	0840	...	0938	1038	1138	1238	1338	1438	1538	1638	1738	1838	1938	2038**k**	2138	2238	2348	0038	0048
						|			|												|				—		
				d																				⑦	①–⑥		
201	Uelzen d.	0501	0606	0704	...	0742	0802	...	0842	0902	1002	1101	1201	1301	1401	1501	1601	1701	1801	1903	2001	2101	2201	2252	2307	...	...
214	Bad Bevensen d.	0509	0614	0713	...	|	0810	...	0850	0910	1010	1109	1209	1309	1409	1509	1609	1709	1809	1911	2009	2109	2209	2300	2315	...	...
237	Lüneburg d.	0524	0629	0728	...	0758	0828	...	0902	0928	1028	1131**j**	1228	1328	1428	1528	1628	1728	1828	1929	2028	2128	2228	2322**j**	2329	...	...
256	Winsen (Luhe) d.	0535	0641	0740	...	|	0839	...	|	0939	1039	1142	1239	1339	1439	1539	1639	1739	1839	1940	2039	2139	2239	2337	2344	...	...
286	**Hamburg** Hbf a.	0556	0702	0802	...	0828	0901	...	0932	1001	1101	1204	1301	1401	1502	1601	1701	1801	1902	2001	2101	2201	2301	0010	0020	...	...

SEE NOTE ⊠																											
				①–⑤	⑥⑦ L	P								C✕	②–④ D✕			⑦ E🍷							⚒	†	
Hamburg Hbf d.	...	...	...	0545	0552	0652	0753	0854	0954	1054	1154	1255	1357	1527	1528	1454	1554	1728	1656	1755	1855	1954	...	2057	2158	2158	2334
Winsen (Luhe) d.	...	...	...	0606	0613	0713	0815	0917	1017	1117	1217	1318	1419	|	|	1517	1617	|	1719	1818	1918	2017	...	2119	2220	2220	0008
Lüneburg d.	...	...	...	0617	0624	0724	0826	0933	1033	1133	1233	1333	1432	1557	1559	1533	1633	1757	1733	1833	1933	2033	...	2131	2231	2231	0023
Bad Bevensen d.	...	...	...	0632	0642	0742	0844	0948	1048	1148	1248	1348	1446	1609	1611	1548	1648	1809	1748	1848	1948	2048	...	2146	2246	2246	0037
Uelzen a.	...	...	...	0640	0650	0750	0852	0956	1056	1156	1256	1356	1454	1616	1618	1556	1656	1817	1756	1856	1956	2056	...	2153	2253	2253	0045
														|	|			|							|	|	
	⚒		h	Ⓐ	Ⓒ																	Ⓒ	Ⓐ				
Uelzen d.	...	0513**v**	0609	0651	0709	0809	0909	1009	1109	1209	1309	1409	1509	1618	1620	1609	1709	1819	1809	1909	2009	2111	2126	2217	2303	2312	...
Celle d.	0447	0547	0647	0747**t**	0746	0847	0947	1047	1147	1247	1347	1447	1547	1640	1642	1647	1747	1841	1847	1947	2047	2148	2200**f**	2251	2337	0002	...
Hannover Hbf a.	0514	0614	0714	0814	0812	0914	1014	1114	1214	1314	1414	1514	1614	1659	1700	1714	1814	1904	1914	2014	2114	2215	2226**f**	2317	0002	0028	...
Hannover Hbf d.	0536	0636	0736	0833	0833	0936	1033	1136	1233	1336	1433	1536	1633	1703	1703	1736	1833	1909	1936	2033	2133**r**	2236	2236	2336	...	...	...
Elze (Han) d.	0558	0658	0758	0855	0855	0958	1055	1158	1255	1358	1455	1558	1655	1722	1722	1758	1855	1929	1958	2055	2158	2258	2258	2358	...	...	...
Alfeld (Leine) d.	0610	0710	0810	0906	0906	1010	1106	1210	1306	1410	1506	1610	1706	1733	1733	1810	1906	1940	2010	2106	2210	2310	2310	0010	...	...	...
Kreiensen d.	0623	0723	0823	0919	0919	1023	1119	1223	1319	1423	1519	1623	1719	1746	1746	1823	1919	1953	2023	2119	2223	2323	2323	0023	...	...	...
Northeim (Han) d.	0637	0737	0837	0933	0933	1037	1133	1237	1333	1437	1533	1637	1733	1759	1759	1837	1933	2007	2037	2133	2237	2337	2337	0037	...	...	...
Göttingen a.	0649	0749	0849	0947	0947	1049	1147	1249	1347	1449	1547	1649	1747	1814	1814	1849	1947	2020	2049	2147	2249	2349	2349	0049	...	...	...

A – *IC* **2176** (operated by DB).
B – *IC* **2182** (operated by DB). From Kassel Wilhelmshöhe (d. 0623). June 16 - July 25 does not run Hannover - Hamburg.
C – ①–④ to Oct. 27 (not Oct. 2); ① from Nov. 3. *IC* **2193** (operated by DB). From Westerland (Table **821**).
D – ②–④ from Oct. 28. *IC* **2281** (operated by DB).
E – *IC* **2173** (operated by DB). To Kassel Wilhelmshöhe (a. 2043).
L – Runs 2–5 minutes later Hamburg - Uelzen on ⑦.

P – On ⑦ departs Hamburg 0653, Winsen 0716, Lüneburg 0730, Bad Bevensen 0745, arrives Uelzen 0752.

d – Daily.
f – 3–4 minutes later from Nov. 3.
h – Change trains at Hannover on Ⓐ.
j – Arrives 7 minutes earlier.
k – On ⑥ Hannover d. 1946, Celle d. 2012, Uelzen a. 2048.

r – 2136 on Ⓐ (not June 19, 20, 30).
t – Arrives 0728.
v – ⚒ only.

⊠ – **June 14 - July 27** northbound timings Lüneburg - Hamburg / southbound timings Hamburg - Uelzen may vary by up to 8 minutes (earlier departures possible).

MÜNCHEN - INGOLSTADT - NÜRNBERG 904

km		ICE	ICE	ICE	ICE	ICE	ICE	ICE	ICE	ICE	ICE	ICE	ICE	ICE	ICE	ICE	ICE	ICE	ICE	ICE	ICE	ICE	ICE	ICE
		888	822	684	634	820	886	886	728	1512	726	882	724	208	722	880	720	1224	1508	628	788	626	1206	624
	SEE NOTE ▶	Ⓐ	①–⑥	784	Ⓐt	Ⓐ	①	②–⑦			①–⑥							1228				‡	1506*	
			K	Ⓐt	H	K			K		K		K	B	K		K	♠	R	K		K	DR	K
		✕	🍷	✕	✕	🍷	✕	✕	🍷	✕	🍷	✕	🍷	✕	🍷	✕	🍷	🍷	✕	🍷	✕	🍷	✕	🍷
0	**München** Hbf ▶ d.	0410	0446	0513	0513	0545	0609	0611	0647	0716	0750	0816	0849	0916	0950	1016	1050	1050	1116y	1148	1216	1250	1315	1350
81	**Ingolstadt** Hbf d.	0456	0528	0558	0558	0630	0655	0659	0732v	0800	│	0901	│	1000	│	1101	│	│	1200	│	1301	│	1400	│
171	**Nürnberg** Hbf a.	0526	0555	0629	0629	0657	0725	0730	0759	0831	0857	0930	0957	1031	1057	1130	1157	1157	1231	1257	1330	1357	1431	1457
	Würzburg Hbf **900 920** a.	0627	0653	0727	0727	0753	0827	0827	0853	│	0953	1027	1053	│	1153	1227	1253	1253	│	1353	1427	1453	│	1553
	Frankfurt (Main) Hbf **920** a.	│	0804	│	...	0904	│	│	1004	│	1104	│	1204	│	1304	│	1404	...	│	1504	│	1604	│	1704
	Leipzig Hbf **851** a.	│	...	│	...	...	│	│	...	1156	...	│	...	│	...	│	...	...	│	...	│	...	│	...
	Berlin Hbf **851** a.	│	...	│	...	...	│	│	...	1308	...	│	...	1520	...	│	...	...	1719	...	│	...	1919	...
	Hamburg Hbf **900** a.	0953j	...	1055j	...	...	1156j	1156j	...	...	...	1354j	...	...	...	1554j	...	...	...	...	1754j	...	...	...

	ICE	ICE	ICE	ICE	ICE	ICE	ICE	ICE	ICE	ICE	ICE	ICE	ICE	ICE	ICE	ICE	ICE	ICE	ICE	ICE		ICE	ICE	
	786	622	584	1084	620	1220	1522	1602	528	1502	526	782	524	1500	1500	522	780	520	922	1620		920	1520	
SEE NOTE ▶		1222	Ⓑ	⑥	Ⓐ	Ⓒ					Ⓑ	1182		W	⑤⑦	x	⑦	①–④	⑤⑦	⑥s		⊡	⑤⑥	
		K	L		K	G K	K		K		K	☆	K		f⊠	K	A	p	f			⊖	m⊖	
	✕	🍷	✕	✕	🍷	🍷	✕	✕	🍷	✕	🍷	✕	🍷	✕	✕	🍷	✕	🍷	✕	✕		✕	✕	
München Hbf ▶ d.	1416	1450	1516	1516	1550	1550	1616	1616	1647	1716	1748	1812	1850	1916	1916	1948	2016	2050	2050	2050	...	2255	2255	...
Ingolstadt Hbf d.	1501	│	1600	1600	│	│	1658	1658	1730	1800	│	1901	│	2000	2000	2032	2101	2133	2133	│	...	2337	2337	...
Nürnberg Hbf a.	1530	1557	1630	1630	1657	1657	1730	1730	1757	1831	1857	1931	1957	2031	2031	2059	2132	2200	2202	2202	...	0009	0009	...
Würzburg Hbf **900 920** a.	1627	1653	1727	1727	1753	1753	1825	│	1853	│	1953	2027	2053	│	│	2153	2229	2255	2255	2255	...	...	...	...
Frankfurt (Main) Hbf **920** a.	│	1804	│	│	1904	1904	1936	│	2004	│	2104	│	2204	│	│	2305	...	0004	0004	0004	...	...	...	...
Leipzig Hbf **851** a.	│	...	│	│	...	...	...	2114	...	2204	...	│	...	0010	0010	...	...	...	...	...	...	...	...	...
Berlin Hbf **851** a.	│	...	│	│	...	...	...	2242	...	2317	...	│	...	...	0128	...	...	...	...	...	...	...	...	...
Hamburg Hbf **900** a.	1953j	...	2054j	2103j	...	...	...	...	...	...	...	0008	...	...	...	...	...	...	...	...	...	...	...	...

	ICE		ICE	ICE	ICE	ICE	ICE	ICE	ICE	ICE	ICE	ICE	ICE	ICE	ICE	ICE	ICE	ICE	ICE	ICE	ICE	ICE	ICE	ICE
	823		985	827	1501	521	781	1123	523	1003	925	525	783	783	527	983	583	533	529	1521	621	1207	623	1223
	Ⓐt		Ⓐt	Ⓐ	Ⓐ		①–⑥	⑥	Ⓐ	①–⑥	Ⓒ	Ⓐ	①–⑤	⑥	①–⑥	⑦	①–⑥	①–⑥			1121		923	
			M	K	E	K	N	K	K		K	K	⊗		KG		G	O	K	K	K	RD	K	♠
	🍷		✕	🍷	✕	🍷	✕	🍷	🍷	🍷	🍷	🍷	✕	✕	🍷	✕	✕	✕	🍷	✕	🍷	✕	🍷	🍷
Hamburg Hbf **900** d.	...	...	...	...	...	...	...	...	...	...	...	...	0555	0601h	...	0656h	0701h	...	...	...	...	...	...	...
Berlin Hbf **851** d.	...	...	...	...	...	...	...	...	...	0437	...	...	│	│	...	│	│	...	...	...	...	0840	...	...
Leipzig Hbf **851** d.	...	...	...	...	...	...	...	...	...	│	...	...	│	│	...	│	│	...	...	...	...	│	...	...
Frankfurt (Main) Hbf **920** d.	...	...	...	0456	...	0551	...	0654	0654	│	0754	0754	│	│	0854	│	│	...	0954	1018	1054	│	1154	...
Würzburg Hbf **900 920** d.	...	...	...	0604	...	0704	0729	0804	0804	│	0904	0904	0930	0930	1004	1031	1031	1031	1104	1132	1204	│	1307	1307
Nürnberg Hbf d.	0558	...	0628	0702	0729	0802	0827	0902	0902	0928	1002	1002	1027	1027	1102	1128	1128	1128	1202	1227	1302	1328	1403	1403
Ingolstadt Hbf d.	0627	...	0700	0731	0802	│	0901	│	│	1002	│	│	1101	1101	│	1201	1201	1201	│	1301	│	1401	│	│
München Hbf a.	0711	...	0747	0816	0850	0920	0952	1016	1016	1049	1115	1115	1150	1150	1216e	1248	1248	1248	1321	1350b	1415	1450	1515	1515

	ICE	ICE	ICE	ICE	ICE	ICE	ICE	ICE	ICE	ICE	ICE	ICE	ICE	ICE	ICE	ICE	ICE		ICE		ICE	ICE		ICE
	787	625	1509	627	789	629	209	721	881	723	1511	725	883	727	1515	729	885		821		685	635		1517
		825		927		Ⓑ				Ⓑ			1183	Ⓑ	1715§	929	1185		♣		⑦	⑦¶		
		u K	R	K		K	B	K		K		K		K	J	K			K					
	✕	🍷	✕	🍷	✕	🍷	✕	🍷	✕	🍷	✕	🍷	✕	🍷	✕	🍷	✕		🍷		✕	✕		✕
Hamburg Hbf **900** d.	1001h	...	...	...	1201h	...	...	...	1353	...	...	...	1601h	...	...	...	1801h	...	...	...	1901	...	...	...
Berlin Hbf **851** d.	│	...	1042	...	│	...	1243	...	│	...	1440	...	│	...	1639	...	│	...	...	...	│	...	...	1852
Leipzig Hbf **851** d.	│	...	│	...	│	...	1402	...	│	...	│	...	│	...	│	...	│	...	...	...	│	...	...	2012
Frankfurt (Main) Hbf **920** d.	│	1254	│	1354	│	1454	│	1554	│	1654	│	1754	│	1854	│	1954	│	...	2054	...	│	...	...	│
Würzburg Hbf **900 920** d.	1329	1404	│	1504	1529	1604	│	1704	1729	1804	│	1904	1929	2004	│	2104	2134	...	2204	...	2231	2231	...	│
Nürnberg Hbf d.	1427	1502	1528	1602	1627	1702	1728	1802	1827	1902	1928	2002	2027	2103	2129	2202	2230	...	2302	...	2331	2331	...	2357
ngolstadt Hbf d.	1501	│	1601	│	1701	│	│	1831	1901	│	2001	│	2101	│	2202	2231	2303	...	2331	...	0004	0004	...	0030
München Hbf a.	1557	1615	1655	1715b	1747	1818	1850	1916b	1950b	2016	2048	2115g	2150	2212	2247	2316	2355	...	0017	...	0051	0051	...	0114

RE services via the high-speed line (SEE NOTE ❖). *Timings may vary by up to 24 minutes until July 12.*

km		Ⓐt	⑥c	†w	⑥c	Ⓐt	Ⓐt	Ⓒz	⑥c	Ⓐt	Ⓒz	Ⓒz	Ⓐt	Ⓒ	Ⓒz	Ⓐt	⑤d	Ⓒz	Ⓒz	Ⓐt	Ⓒz	Ⓒz	Ⓐt	T	Y
0	**München** Hbf d.	0456	0507	0555	0656	0704	*0901*	0905	1010	1105	1109	*1300*	1308	1409	*1500*	1508	*1559*	1605	*1655*	*1657*	1808	*1900*	1907	2106	*2128*
50	Pfaffenhofen (Ilm) d.	0522	0533	0621	0722	0730	*0932*	0931	1033	1131	1132	*1331*	1331	1432	*1531*	1531	*1629*	1631	*1725*	*1727*	1831	*1930*	1930	2132	*2205*
81	**Ingolstadt** Hbf d.	0546	0605¦	0705•	0805•	0805¦	1005	1005¦	1105	1205¦	1205¦	1405	1405¦	1506	1605	1605¦	1707	1707	1805	1805	1906	2005	2005¦	2201	2236
171	**Nürnberg Hbf** a.	0635	0648	0748	0848	0848	1048	1048	1148	1248	1248	1448	1448	1549	1648	1648	1751	1751	1848	1848	1949	2048	2048	2244	2319

	Ⓐt	Ⓐt	Ⓒz	Ⓐt	⑥c	Ⓒz	Ⓐt	Ⓐt	Ⓒz	⑥c	Ⓐt	Ⓒz	Ⓒz	Ⓐt	⑤d	Ⓒz	Ⓐt	Ⓐt	Ⓒz	Ⓒz	Ⓐt	Ⓒz	T	Y	⑤⑥q
ürnberg Hbf d.	0510	0607	0632	0732	0810	0910	0910	1110	1110	1210	1310	1310	1510	1510	1607	1610	...	1710	1710	1810	1910	1910	2110	2140	2340
ngolstadt Hbf d.	0559	0655	0720	0819	0906¦	1006¦	0955	1205¦	1205¦	1306¦	1406¦	1355	1555	1555	1651	1705¦	1705	1805¦	1755	1905¦	2005¦	1955	2206¦	2225	0034¦
'faffenhofen (Ilm) d.	0623	*0733*	0742	0844	0935	1035	*1035*	1233	1233	1335	1435	*1435*	*1635*	*1701*	...	1732	1732	1833	*1834*	1935	2033	*2033*	2231	*2302*	0058
ünchen Hbf a.	0651	*0803*	0809	0907	0958	1058	*1106*	1256	1303	1403	1458	*1506*	*1706*	*1739*	...	1758	1805	1856	*1904*	2002	2056	*2104*	2259	*2340*	0126

RE services via EICHSTÄTT and TREUCHTLINGEN. *Timings between München and Treuchtlingen may vary by up to 12 minutes until July 12.*

km				◧	Ⓐt		◧		◧		◧		◧		◐		◐		◐		Ⓐ	Ⓒ			
0	**München** Hbf d.	0030	...	...	0522	...	0622	0727	0827	0927	1026	1125	1227	1327	1427	1527	1623	1724	1827	1924	2020	2027	2128	2229	2330
50	Pfaffenhofen (Ilm) d.	0107	...	...	0559	...	0659	0804	0904	1004	1103	1202	1304	1404	1504	1604	1701	1801	1904	2001	2102	2104	2205	2306	0007
81	**Ingolstadt** Hbf d.	0131	...	0528	0628	0628	0730	0830	0930	1030	1130	1230	1330	1430	1530	1630	1730	1830	1930	2030	2130	2130	2230	2330	0031
108	Eichstätt Bahnhof ♥ d.	...	...	0555	0656	0656	0756	0856	0956	1057	1156	1256	1356	1456	1556	1656	1756	1857	1956	2056	2156	2156	2256	...	...
137	Treuchtlingen a.	...	...	0619	0719	0719	0820	0919	1020	1120	1220	1319	1420	1519	1620	1719	1820	1920	2020	2119	2220	2220	2319	...	...
137	Treuchtlingen **905** d.	...	...	0624	0725	0725	0829	0925	1029	1125	1229	1325	1429	1525	1625	1725	1825	1925	2025	2125	*2225*	2225	2325	...	...
146	Weißenburg (Bay) **905** d.	...	...	0632	0732	0732	0836	0932	1036	1131	1236	1332	1436	1532	1632	1732	1832	1931	2032	2132	*2232*	2232	2332	...	...
199	**Nürnberg** Hbf **905** a.	...	...	0717	0817	0817	0920	1017	1120	1217	1320	1417	1520	1617	1717	1817	1917	2017	2117	2217	*2317*	2317	0017	...	...

	Ⓒz	Ⓐt	⚒n	†w	Ⓐt	Ⓒz	⚒n	†w		◧		◧	Ⓒz	Ⓐt	◧		◐		◐		◐		◐		
ürnberg Hbf **905** d.	...	...	*0435*	0439	0521	0538	*0630*	0639	0737	0839	0937	1039	1137	1137	1239	1336	1439	1538	1639	1738	1839	1938	2039	2139	2342
'eißenburg (Bay) **905** d.	...	...	*0518*	0523	0605	0622	*0716*	0723	0821	0923	1021	1123	1221	1221	1323	1421	1523	1622	1723	1822	1923	2022	2123	2223	0025
'euchtlingen **905** a.	...	...	*0525*	0530	0613	0629	*0723*	0730	0828	0930	1028	1130	1228	1228	1330	1428	1530	1630	1730	1830	1930	2030	2130	2230	0033
'euchtlingen d.	...	0451	0532	0532	0629	0634	0735	0735	0835	0935	1035	1135	1235	1240	1336	1435	1535	1635	1735	1835	1935	2035	2135	2235	...
ichstätt Bahnhof ♥ d.	...	0515	0556	0556	0654	0657	0759	0759	0859	0959	1059	1159	1259	1303	1400	1459	1559	1659	1759	1859	1959	2059	2159	2259	...
golstadt Hbf d.	0528	0535	0631¦	0631¦	0734¦	0734¦	0831	0831	0931	1031	1131	1231	1331	1335	1431	1531	1631	1731	1834¦	1931	2031	2132	2234	2334	...
'affenhofen (Ilm) d.	0555	0600	0658	0658	0802	0802	0903	0903	1002	1101	1202	1301	1402	1408	1501	1601	1701	1801	1902	2001	2101	2159	2302	0003	...
ünchen Hbf a.	0633	0638	0736	0736	0840	0840	0941	0941	1040	1139	1240	1339	1440	1446	1539	1640	1739	1838	1940	2039	2139	2237	2340	0041	...

– To Kassel (Table **900**).
– From / to Innsbruck via Kufstein (Table **951**).
– From / to Mittenwald via Garmisch on dates in Table **895**.
– Ⓐ (not June 19). From Lichtenfels (Table **851**).
– From / to Garmisch on dates in Table **895**.
– To Bremen (Table **900**/**813**).
– From Ostseebad Binz / Stralsund on dates in Tables **845**/**4**.
– To / from Köln, Essen or Dortmund (Tables **800** / **910**).
– To Lübeck (Table **825**).
– From Erlangen (Table **851**).
– From Fulda (also Hannover on ①). See Table **900**.
– From Oldenburg via Bremen (Tables **813**/**900**).
– To / from Rostock or Warnemünde on dates in Table **835**.
– ⑤–⑦ (also June 19).
– ①②③④⑥ (also Oct. 3; not Oct. 2).
– ①–④ (not June 19).

– 3–9 minutes later until July 12.
– Not Nov. 1.

d – Not Aug. 15, Oct. 3.
e – 1210 on ⑥.
f – Also Oct. 2; not Oct. 3.

g – 2120 on ①–⑤ until July 11.
h – 6–8 minutes **earlier** June 14 - July 27.
j – 7–12 minutes later June 14 - July 27.
m – Also Oct. 2.
n – Not June 19, Aug. 15, Nov. 1.
p – Not Oct. 2.
q – Also June 18, Aug. 14, Oct. 2.
r – Also June 18, Oct. 2; not June 20, Oct. 3.
s – Also Oct. 3.
t – Not June 19, Aug. 15.
u – Not June 21, Oct. 4.
v – 0730 until July 12.
w – Also June 19, Aug. 15, Nov. 1.
x – Not June 19.
y – 1113 until July 12; 1104 on ⑥ from July 19.
z – Also June 19, Aug. 15.

⊡ – ①②③④⑦ (not Oct. 2).
¶ – ⑦ (also June 18, Aug. 14, Oct. 2). From Bremen (Table **900**).
♣ – ④⑤⑦ (also June 18; not June 19, Oct. 3).

* – Train number **906** on ⑤**r**. Train number **1526** on ⑥ from July 19.
§ – Train number **919** on ⑤**f**.
‡ – Not Oct. 3. Train number **1226** on ⑥, **926** on ⑦.
¦ – Arrives 9–14 minutes earlier.
• – Arrives 20–21 minutes earlier.
◧ – Change trains at Treuchtlingen on ⚒**n**.
◐ – Change trains at Treuchtlingen on Ⓐ**t**.
⊗ – June 16 - July 25 starts from Hannover Hbf, d. 0726 (connecting train departs Hamburg Hbf 0607).
☆ – Conveys 🛏12 (*ICE* **532**/**732**/**1032**) (Garmisch ⑥ **G** -) München - Hannover - Bremen.
♠ – 🛏12 Köln - Paderborn - Kassel - München and v.v.
♥ – Connecting trains (operated by Bayerische Regiobahn) run Eichstätt Bahnhof - Eichstätt Stadt (*5 km*).
❖ – Regional services call at Kinding and Allersberg (located 112 and 146 km from München respectively).
▶ – Until July 12 *ICE* services may depart München up to 9 minutes **earlier**.
⊖ – Until July 12 Ingolstadt d. 2341, Nürnberg a. 0013.
⊠ – From Sept. 28 arrives Leipzig 0020, Berlin 0143.

905 MÜNCHEN - AUGSBURG - NÜRNBERG and WÜRZBURG

See Table **904** for services via Ingolstadt. See Table **905a** for local trains Treuchtlingen - Würzburg.

ICE and *IC* services

	ICE	ICE	ICE	IC	ICE	ICE	ICE	ICE	IC	ICE	ICE	ICE	IC	ICE	IC	IC	ICE	ICE	ICE	ICE	ICE	ICE	ICE	CNL	CNL
	1706	**1612**	**1082**	**2208**	**680**	**1608**	**588**	**1606**	**2082**	**586**	**1008**	**708**	**1284**	**1004 1504**	**2206**	**1980**	**902**	**582**	**582**	**1000 1600**	**1000 1600**	**580**	**580**	**1286**	**1246**
	①	①–⑥				⊕					①–⑥	⑦	⑦		Ⓐt	⑦	Ⓐt	Ⓐt	©z			①–⑤	⑦		
			⊖		⊖		⊖	S	A	G⊖			F			♣				Ⓑh	⑤⑦f	Q		D	B⊙
		✕	✕		✕	✕	✕	✕	✕	✕	🍸	✕		🍸			✕	✕	✕	✕‡	✕‡	✕	✕	R🍸	R🍸
München Ost ... d.	...	...	...	...	...	...	...	...	1117	...	...	...	...	...	...	...	...	...	...	...	...	...	...	2146	2146
München Hbf ... 930 d.	0002	0458	0653	0711	0905	0919	1045	1117	|	1240	1319	1319	1351	1449	1540	1552	1641	1706	1706	1739	1739	1854	1854	2215	2215
München Pasing ... 930 d.	|	0506	0702	0719	0913	0927	1054	1125	1132	1249	1327	1327	1359	1457	1548	1600	1649	|	1715	1748	1748	1902	1902	|	|
Augsburg Hbf ... 930 d.	0030	0531	0732	0748	0938	0954	1121	1154	1230*	1321j	1354	1354	1425	1522	1613	1625	1714	1738	1738	1813	1813	1932	1932	2250	2250
Donauwörth ... d.	0049	0551	0752	0808	|	|	|	|	1249	|	|	|	1444	|	1633	1644	1733	|	|	1833	1833	1952	1952	|	|
Treuchtlingen ... d.	0111	0614	|	|	|	|	|	|	1310	|	|	|	1506	|	1654	1707	1754	|	|	1855	1855	2012	2012	|	|
Nürnberg Hbf ... 900 920 a.	0146	0654	|	0858	|	1100	1229	1300	|	1429	1459	1459	|	1628	1728	|	1829	|	|	1930	1930	|	|	|	|
Leipzig Hbf **851** ... a.	0546	1042	|	1242	|	1442	|	1642v	|	|	1842	1842v	|	|	...	|	...	|	|	...	2308	|	|	|	|
Berlin Hbf **851** ... a.	0704	1207	|	1407	|	1606	|	1805v	|	|	2005	2005v	|	2120	...	|	...	|	|	...	0030	|	|	|	0813
Würzburg Hbf ... 900 920 a.	...	...	0927	...	1127	...	1327	...	1436	1527	...	...	1634	...	...	1830	...	1927	1927	...	...	2129	2129	|	...
Hamburg Hbf **900** ... a.	...	...	1253e	...	1454e	...	1653e	...	1828	1853e	...	...	2028	...	...	2227	...	2253e	2253e	...	...	...	0113	0755	...

	ICE	CNL	CNL	IC	ICE	ICE	ICE	ICE	ICE	ICE	IC	ICE	ICE	ICE	ICE	ICE	ICE	ICE	IC	IC	ICE	ICE	ICE	ICE	ICE
	981	**1247**	**1287**	**2201**	**989**	**1603**	**581**	**1605**	**1525**	**1005**	**2083**	**1627**	**585 1085**	**1609 1709**	**1009**	**587**	**1209**	**1189**	**1981**	**2207**	**681 1081**	**1615**	**633 1133**	**683**	**1617**
	Ⓐt			Ⓐt	Ⓐt	①		①–⑥	⑥	Ⓑ					⑦				⑤⑦					Ⓑ	⑤⑦
		B◇	D								A		L⊖	①–⑥		⊖	J	⊖	f N		⊖		E		p
	✕	R🍸	R🍸		✕	✕	✕	✕	✕	🍸	✕	✕	✕	S✕	🍸	✕	✕	✕			✕	✕	✕	✕	✕
Hamburg Hbf **900** ... d.	...	...	2126k	...	...	...	0453	...	...	...	0729	...	0901g	...	...	1101g	...	1301g	1327p	...	1501g	...	...	1701g	...
Würzburg Hbf ... 900 920 d.	...	...	|	...	...	...	0831	...	...	...	1122	...	1231	...	...	1431	...	1631	1714	...	1831	...	2031	2031	...
Berlin Hbf **851** ... d.	...	2104	|	...	...	...	|	0548	0639	0639	|	0754	|	0952	0952	|	1152r	|	|	1352	|	1552r	|	|	1752r
Leipzig Hbf **851** ... d.	...	|	|	...	...	0512	|	0715	|	|	|	0915	|	1115	1115	|	1315r	|	|	1515	|	1715r	|	|	1915r
Nürnberg Hbf ... 900 920 d.	...	|	|	0547	0615	0857	0930	1057	1130	1130	|	1257	1330	1457	1457	|	1657	|	|	1857	1930	2057	|	|	2254
Treuchtlingen ... d.	...	|	|	0622	0651	|	|	|	|	|	1250	|	|	|	|	|	|	|	1844	|	|	|	|	|	2329
Donauwörth ... d.	0557	|	|	0644	0711	|	|	|	|	|	1312	|	|	|	|	1608	|	1808	1907	|	2022	2151	2208	2208	2349
Augsburg Hbf ... 930 a.	0618	0625	0625	0705	0731	1007	1037	1207	1237	1237	1331	1407	1440	1607	1607	1626	1807	1826	1929	2007	2041	2210	2226	2226	0007
München Pasing ... 930 a.	0645	|	|	0733	0758	1031	1100	1231	1302	1302	1357	1431	1507	1631	1631	1649	1831	1850	1953	2031	2108	2233	2250	2250	0031
München Hbf ... 930 a.	0655	0705	0705	0742	0807	1041	1110	1241	1311	1311	|	1441	1517	1641	1641	1659	1842	1900	2002	2041	2117	2243	2300	2300	0041
München Ost ... a.	...	0727	0727	...	...	...	...	...	...	...	1410	...	...	...	...	...	...	...	...	...	...	...	...	...	...

RE services

km																										
		©z	⚒d		⚒d		⚒d H	⚒d		⚒d		⚒d		Ⓐt		Ⓐt	⑥w H		Ⓐt H	Ⓐt		©z H	Ⓐt			
0	**München** Hbf ... 930 d.	0200	...	0534	...	0736	...	...	0936	1036	1136	1236	1336	1436	1536	1617	1634	1735	1811	...	1936	...	2036	2101	2201	2301
7	München Pasing 930 d.	0206	...	0541	...	0743	...	...	0943	1043	1144	1243	1343	1443	1542	1624	1643	1742	1818	...	1943	...	2043	2107	2209	2307
62	**Augsburg** Hbf ... 930 a.	0246	...	0619	...	0819	...	...	1019	1119	1218	1319	1419	1519	1619	1705	1719	1819	1904	...	2019	...	2119	2148	2244	2348
62	**Augsburg** Hbf ... d.	0315	0509	0628	0720	0828	0840	0923	1028	1126	1224	1327	1429	1525	1628	1719	1732	1828	1918	1921	2028	2118	2126	2154	2254	0001
103	Donauwörth ... d.	0357	0558n	0659	0758	0858	0905	1000	1059	1158	1300	1358	1459	1558	1659	1759j	1757	1859	1939	1958	2059	2139	2158	2235	2332	0040
137	Treuchtlingen ... a.	0417	0620	0720	0820	0920	|	1020	1120	1220	1320	1420	1520	1620	1720	1821	1816	1920	|	2020	2120	2159	2220	2255	...	...
137	Treuchtlingen ... 904 d.	0418	0624	0725	0829	0925	|	1029	1125	1229	1325	1429	1525	1625	1725	1825	1817	1925	|	2025	2125	2200	2225	2325	...	...
146	Weißenburg (Bay) 904 d.	0424	0632	0732	0836	0932	|	1036	1131	1236	1332	1436	1532	1632	1732	1832	|	1931	|	2032	2132	|	2232	2332	...	...
199	**Nürnberg** Hbf ... 904 a.	0507	0717	0817	0920	1017	0953	1120	1217	1320	1417	1520	1617	1717	1817	1917	1848	2017	2026	2117	2217	2232	2317	0017	...	...

	©z	Ⓐt	©z	Ⓐt	⚒d		⚒d	H	⊗	⚒d		⚒d		⚒d		Ⓐt		Ⓐt	H		Ⓐt		Ⓐt		©z	
Nürnberg Hbf ... 904 d.	0053	...	...	...	0435	0521b	0630	0718	0737	0839	0937	1039	1137	1239	1336	1439	1538	1639	1733	1738	1839	1938	2039	2139	...	...
Weißenburg (Bay) 904 d.	0135	...	...	...	0518	0605b	0716	|	0821	0923	1021	1123	1221	1323	1421	1523	1622	1723	|	1822	1923	2022	2123	2223	...	...
Treuchtlingen ... 904 a.	0141	...	...	...	0525	0613b	0723	0748	0828	0930	1028	1130	1228	1330	1428	1530	1630	1730	|	1830	1930	2030	2130	2230	...	...
Treuchtlingen ... d.	0142	...	...	...	0526	0634	0731y	0749	0834	0935	1034	1135	1234	1335	1434	1535	1634	1735	|	1834	1935	2034	2135	2235t	2235	...
Donauwörth ... d.	0205	0414	0511	0528	0604n	0658	0754	0807	0858	0958	1058	1158	1258	1358	1458	1558	1658	1758	1821	1858	1958	2058	2158	2256t	2258	2328
Augsburg Hbf ... a.	0228	0453	0551	0612	0640	0728	0826	0829	0928	1031	1128	1229	1328	1432	1528	1636	1726	1836	1842	1927	2031	2128	2236	...	2328	0006
Augsburg Hbf ... 930 d.	...	0502	0606	0615	0651t	0739	...	0839	0939	1039	1139	1239	1339	1439	1539	...	1739	...	...	1939	2039	2139	...	...	2339	...
München Pasing ... 930 a.	...	0541	0645	0653	0728t	0813	...	0913	1013	1113	1213	1313	1413	1514	1613	...	1813	...	...	2013	2115	2222	...	...	0022	...
München Hbf ... 930 a.	...	0549	0652	0702	0738t	0821	...	0921	1021	1121	1221	1321	1421	1522	1621	...	1821	...	...	2021	2123	2230	...	...	0030	...

A – KÖNIGSSEE – (12) and ✕ Berchtesgaden - Freilassing - Augsburg - Hamburg and v.v.; conveys (12) Oberstdorf (**2084/5**) - Augsburg - Hamburg and v.v.
B – CAPELLA. Conveys 1, 2 cl., 2 cl. and (2) (reclining).
D – PYXIS. Conveys 1, 2 cl., 2 cl. and (2) (reclining).
E – From Bremen (Table **900**).
F – To Flensburg (Table **823**). From Schwarzach June 22 - Sept. 14 (Tables **960/951**). Also calls at Gunzenhausen (d. 1519) and Ansbach (d. 1536).
G – From Garmisch (Table **895**) on ⑥ to Nov. 8.
H – From / to Lindau and Oberstdorf (Table **935**).
J – To Mittenwald via Garmisch (Table **895**) on ⑤ (not Oct. 3).
L – From Lübeck (Table **825**) on ①–⑥ (not Oct. 4).
N – Also calls at Ansbach (d. 1814) and Gunzenhausen (d. 1830). From Flensburg (Table **823**) on ⑤ (also Oct. 2). Train number **1983** on ⑦.
Q – To Fulda (Table **900**).
S – To / from Stralsund on dates in Table **845**.

b – 16–17 minutes later on © (also June 19, Aug. 15).
d – Not June 19, Aug. 15, Nov. 1.
e – 9–14 minutes later June 14 - July 27.
f – Also Oct. 2; not Oct. 3.
g – 7–8 minutes **earlier** June 14 - July 27.
h – Not Oct. 3.
j – Arrives 8 minutes earlier.
k – 2021 on ①⑦ June 15 - July 27; 2124 on ②–⑥ June 14 - July 26.
n – Arrives 14–17 minutes earlier.
p – 1306 on ⑦ June 15 - July 27.
r – 4–9 minutes earlier from Sept. 28.
t – Ⓐ (not June 19, Aug. 15).
v – 7–11 minutes later from Sept. 28.
w – Not Nov. 1.
y – 0725 on ⑥.
z – Also June 19, Aug. 15.

* – Arrives 1202.
‡ – Conveys 🍸 on ⑦.
♣ – Also calls at Gunzenhausen (d. 1720) and Ansbach (d. 1736). On June 15, 22 Hamburg a. 223
⊗ – Change trains at Donauwörth on © (also June 19, Aug. 15).
⊕ – On ⑦ from Sept. 28 runs as train **1628** and arrives Leipzig 1453, Berlin 1614.
⊙ – Also calls at Hildesheim Hbf (a. 0509), Braunschweig Hbf (a. 0534), Magdeburg Hbf (a. 0629) Brandenburg Hbf (a. 0710), Potsdam Hbf (a. 0730) Berlin Wannsee (a. 0739), Berlin Zoo (a. 0806) and Berlin Ostbahnhof (a. 0824).
◇ – Also calls at Berlin Ostbahnhof (d. 2052), Berlin Zoo (d. 2114), Berlin Wannsee (d. 2153), Potsdam Hbf (d. 2201), Brandenburg Hbf (d. 2221), Magdeburg Hbf (d. 2305), Braunschweig Hbf (d. 2355) and Hildesheim Hbf (d. 0020).
⊖ – Conveys (12) München - Hannover - Bremen and v.v. (Table **900**).

905a TREUCHTLINGEN - WÜRZBURG

RB services (except train A

km																										
		⚒r	©z	Ⓐt	Ⓐt	©z		⑥k						Ⓐt	A✕										©z	Ⓐ
0	**Treuchtlingen** ... d.	...	0502	0512	0614	0626	0705t	0725	0825	0925	1025	1125	1225	1306	1310	1325z	1425	1525	1625	1725	1826	1925	2025	2125	2225	222
24	Gunzenhausen ... d.	...	0515	0527	0626	0638	0719t	0738	0838	0938	1038	1138	1238	1318	1324	1338z	1438	1538	1638	1738	1839	1938	2038	2138	2238	223
51	Ansbach ... a.	...	0535	0547	0645	0658	0739t	0758	0858	0958	1058	1158	1258	1339	1342	1358z	1458	1558	1658	1758	1859	1958	2058	2159	2258	225
51	Ansbach ... d.	0440	0536	0606	0701	0710	0810	0810	0910	1010	1110	1210	1311	...	1344	1410	1510	1610	1710	1810	1910	2010	2110	2210t	2310	...
83	Steinach (b Rothenb) ◐ d.	0503	0559	0628	0723	0732	0832	0832	0932	1032	1132	1232	1332	...	1404	1432	1532	1632	1732	1832	1932	2032	2132	2232t	2332	...
140	**Würzburg** Hbf ... a.	0547	0642	0713	0810	0816	0918	0918	1016	1118	1216	1318	1416	...	1436	1518	1616	1718	1816	1918	2018	2118	2218	2316t	0016	...

	⚒r	Ⓐt	©z	Ⓐt	Ⓐt	©z					A✕	©z	Ⓐt											†w	⚒
Würzburg Hbf ... d.	0430	...	0531	0541	0632	0641	0739	0841	0941	1041	1122	1141	1141	1241	1341	1441	1541	1641	1741	1841	1941	2041	2141	2241	230
Steinach (b Rothenb) ◐ ... d.	0512	...	0614	0624	0716	0724	0824	0924	1024	1124	1156	1224	1224	1326	1424	1524	1624	1724	1824	1924	2024	2124	2224	2324	234
Ansbach ... a.	0535	...	0636	0646	0737	0746	0846	0946	1046	1146	1215	1246	1247	1347	1446	1546	1646	1746	1846	1946	2046	2146	2246	2347	000
Ansbach ... d.	0537	0610	0654	0711	0754	0754	0854	0954	1054	1154	1217	1254	1317	1354	1454	1554	1654	1754	1854	1954	2054	2154	2247	...	001
Gunzenhausen ... d.	0556	0629	0715	0730	0815	0815	0915	1015	1115	1215	1234	1315	1336	1415	1515	1615	1715	1815	1915	2015	2115	2215	2306	...	002
Treuchtlingen ... a.	0609	0643	0730	0744	0830	0830	0930	1030	1130	1230	1248	1330	1350	1430	1530	1630	1730	1830	1930	2030	2130	2230	2321	...	004

◐ – Local trains **STEINACH** (b Rothenb) - **ROTHENBURG OB DER TAUBER** and v.v. 2nd class only *12 km* Journey time: 14 minutes
From Steinach at 0517 ⚒r, 0617 ©z, 0631 Ⓐt, 0726 Ⓐt, 0735 ©z, 0835, 0935, 1035, 1135, 1235, 1335, 1435, 1535, 1635, 1735, 1835 ©z, 1845 Ⓐt, 1935, 2035 and 2235.
From Rothenburg ob der Tauber at 0445 ⚒r, 0541 ©z, 0606 Ⓐt, 0657 Ⓐt, 0706 ©z, 0806, 0906, 1006, 1106, 1206, 1309, 1406, 1506, 1606, 1706, 1806, 1906, 2006 and 2206.

A – *IC* **2082**/3. KÖNIGSSEE – (12) and ✕ Berchtesgaden - Augsburg - Hamburg and v.v.; (12) Oberstdorf (**2084/5**) - Augsburg - Hamburg and v.v.
k – Not Nov. 1.
r – Not June 19, Nov. 1.
t – Ⓐ (not June 19).
v – Not June 19.
w – Also June 19.
z – © (also June 1

DB (*RE* services); VEC★; HLB★ GIESSEN - KOBLENZ; LIMBURG - FRANKFURT and WIESBADEN 906

km	⊠		⚒r	⚒r								†t
0	**Gießen** .... **807** d.	...	0618	0716	0916	1116	1316	1516	1716	1916	2021	2116
13	Wetzlar .... **807** d.	...	0630	0727	0927	1127	1327	1527	1727	1927	2033	2127
36	Weilburg .... d.	...	0656	0743	0943	1143	1343	1543	1743	1943	2058	2143
65	**Limburg** (Lahn).... a.	...	0732	0807	1007	1207	1407	1607	1807	2007	2135	2207
			◧ d	|	|	|	|	|	|	|	◧ ⚒r	|
65	**Limburg** (Lahn).... d.	0645	0745	0808	1008	1208	1408	1608	1808	2008	2145	2208
68	Diez .... d.	0649	0749	0812	1012	1212	1412	1612	1812	2012	2149	2212
91	Nassau (Lahn)...... d.	0715	0815	0831	1031	1231	1431	1631	1831	2031	2215	2231
99	Bad Ems.............. d.	0725	0825	0838	1038	1238	1438	1638	1838	2038	2225	2238
112	Niederlahnstein .... d.	0743	0843	0849	1049	1249	1449	1649	1849	2049	2243	2249
117	**Koblenz** Hbf........ a.	0752	0852	0858	1058	1258	1458	1658	1859	2059	2250	2258

⊠	Ⓐe							Ⓒz	Ⓐe		
Koblenz Hbf..... d.	0510	0658	0905	1105	1305	1505	1705	1905	1919	2110	2319
Niederlahnstein . d.	0517	0704	0911	1111	1311	1511	1711	1911	1925	2117	2326
Bad Ems........... d.	0533	0718	0921	1121	1321	1521	1721	1921	1938	2133	2341
Nassau (Lahn)... d.	0542	0728	0928	1128	1328	1528	1728	1928	1944	2142	2350
Diez .... d.	0609	0745	0945	1145	1345	1545	1745	1945	2003	2209	0016
Limburg (Lahn). a.	0613	0749	0949	1149	1349	1549	1749	1949	2008	2213	0019
	◧ Ⓐe	|	|	|	|	|	|	|	◧ d		
Limburg (Lahn). d.	0618	0750	0950	1150	1350	1550	1750	1950t	2023	...	...
Weilburg .... d.	0655	0815	1015	1215	1415	1615	1815	2015t	2100	...	...
Wetzlar ....**807** a.	0719	0831	1031	1231	1431	1631	1831	2031t	2125	...	...
Gießen ....**807** a.	0731	0842	1042	1242	1442	1642	1842	2042t	2138	...	...

Limburg - Niedernhausen - Frankfurt and Wiesbaden

km		⚒r	Ⓐe	Ⓐe	⑥	Ⓐe	Ⓒz	Ⓐe	Ⓐe	Ⓐe	⚒r	Ⓐe			Ⓐe			Ⓐe		Ⓐe	Ⓐe	Ⓒz	Ⓐe		Ⓐe	Ⓒz
0	**Limburg** (Lahn)......... d.	0418	0448	0518	0518	0555	0618	0625	0638	0655	0718	0755	0818	0918	0955	1018	1118	1155	1218	1248	1318	1318	1355	1418	1518	1518
21	Bad Camberg............ d.	0441	0511	0541	0541	0614	0641	0644	0703	0714	0741	0814	0841	0941	1014	1041	1141	1214	1241	1311	1341	1341	1414	1441	1541	1541
30	Idstein....................... d.	0451	0521	0551	0551	0621	0651	0651	0713	0721	0751	0821	0851	0951	1021	1051	1151	1221	1251	1321	1351	1351	1421	1451	1551	1551
38	Niedernhausen........‡a.	0457	0527	0557	0559	0627	0657	0657	0722	0727	0757	0827	0857	0959	1027	1057	1159	1227	1257	1329	1357	1359	1427	1457	1557	1559
	Wiesbaden Hbf..... a.	|	*0555*	*0625*	0625	*0655*	*0725*k	|	0743	|	*0825*	*0857*	*0925*	1025	|	*1125*	1225	|	*1325*	1357	*1425*	1425	|	*1525*	*1627*	1625
70	**Frankfurt** (Main) Hbf ‡ a.	0528	0558	0628	...	0658	0728	0728	...	0758	0828	0858	0928	...	1058	1128	...	1258	1330	...	1428	...	1458	1528	1632	...

	Ⓐe		Ⓐe	Ⓐe	Ⓒz	Ⓐe					
Limburg (Lahn) .... d.	1555	1618	1655	1718	1718	1755	1818	1918	2018	2118	2218
Bad Camberg .... d.	1614	1641	1714	1741	1741	1814	1841	1941	2041	2141	2241
Idstein .... d.	1621	1651	1721	1751	1751	1821	1851	1951	2051	2151	2251
Niedernhausen .... ‡ a.	1627	1657	1727	1757	1759	1827	1857	1959	2058	2158	2258
Wiesbaden Hbf...... a.	|	*1727*	*1757*	*1827*	1825	*1857*	*1925*	2025b	...	...	...
Frankfurt (Main) Hbf ‡ a.	1658	1728	1758	1828	...	1858	1928	...	...	...	...

km			Ⓐe	Ⓒz	Ⓐe	Ⓐe	Ⓒz	Ⓐe		Ⓐe
	Frankfurt (Main) Hbf..........‡ d.	...	0601	0631	0643	0731	...	...	0831	0857
0	**Wiesbaden** Hbf..............d.	0531h	*0601*	*0636*k	*0650*	*0720*	0736k	0801	*0836*r	|
20	Niedernhausen..................‡ d.	0601	0631	0701	0718	0801	0801	0831	0901	0931
28	Idstein.................................d.	0608	0638	0708	0725	0808	0808	0838	0908	0938
37	Bad Camberg.......................d.	0617	0647	0717	0734	0817	0817	0847	0917	0945
58	**Limburg** (Lahn)...................a.	0640	0710	0740	0759	0840	0840	0910	0940	1003

			Ⓐe			Ⓐe	Ⓐe	Ⓒz		Ⓐe		Ⓐe	Ⓒz	Ⓐe	Ⓐe	Ⓐe	Ⓒz	Ⓐe		Ⓐe	Ⓐe	Ⓒz				
Frankfurt (Main) Hbf ‡ d.	...	1031	1101	...	1231	1301	1331	...	1431	1501		1601	1631	...	1701	1730	...	1801	1831	1901	1931	...	2031	...	...	...
Wiesbaden Hbf...... d.	0936	*1036*	|	1136	*1236*	|	*1336*	1336	*1436*	*1501*	1536	*1606*	*1636*	1636	*1706*	*1736*	1736	*1806*	*1836*	|	*1936*	1936	*2036*e	...	...	...
Niedernhausen ....‡ d.	1001	1101	1131	1201	1301	1331	1401	1401	1501	1531	1601	1631	1701	1701	1731	1801	1801	1831	1901	1931	2001	2001	2101	2203	2303	0003
Idstein .... d.	1008	1108	1138	1208	1308	1338	1408	1408	1508	1538	1608	1638	1708	1708	1738	1808	1808	1838	1908	1938	2008	2008	2108	2210	2310	0010
Bad Camberg .... d.	1017	1117	1145	1217	1317	1345	1417	1417	1517	1545	1617	1645	1717	1717	1745	1817	1817	1845	1917	1945	2017	2017	2117	2219	2319	0019
Limburg (Lahn) .... a.	1040	1140	1203	1240	1340	1403	1440	1440	1540	1603	1640	1703	1740	1740	1803	1840	1840	1903	1940	2003	2040	2040	2140	2242	2342	0042

b – Ⓑ only.
d – Daily.
e – Ⓐ (not June 19).
h – ⚒ (not June 19). 0536 on ⑥.
k – ⑥ only.
r – ⚒ (not June 19).

t – † (also June 19).
z – Also June 19.

◧ – Change trains at Limburg.
⊠ – Additional stopping trains operate.

★ – VEC: Vectus Verkehrsgesellschaft. HLB: Hessische Landesbahn.
‡ – **Additional S-Bahn *S2* services** Frankfurt - Niedernhausen and v.v. Journey: 35 minutes. **From Frankfurt** (Main) Hbf (underground platforms): On ⚒ (not June 19) every 30 minutes 0522–2322; on † (also June 19) hourly 0522–1222, then every 30 minutes 1252–2322. **From Niedernhausen**: On ⚒ (not June 19) every 30 minutes 0433–2303; on † (also June 19) hourly 0503–1203, then every 30 minutes 1233–2303.

Hessische Landesbahn GIESSEN - FULDA 907

km		Ⓐe	Ⓐe	⑥	Ⓐe	⚒e	⑥	Ⓐe		⚒d		⚒d		Ⓐe	C		Ⓐe	Ⓒz		Ⓐe	Ⓒz		†z	Ⓐe		
0	**Gießen** .... d.	...	0524	...	0617	...	0744	0747	0844	0947	1044	1147	1241	1346	1347	1444	1544	1547	1644	1744	1747	1844	1947	1947	2047	2209
23	Grünberg (Oberhess). d.	...	0549	...	0709	...	0811	0817	0911	1013	1111	1213	1311	1411	1413	1511	1611	1613	1711	1811	1813	1911	2013	2017	2114	2237
60	Alsfeld (Oberhess) ..... d.	0515	0633	0649	0749	0749	0849	0849	0949	1049	1149	1249	1349	1449	1449	1549	1649	1649	1749	1849	1849	1949	2045	2058	2148	2311
79	Lauterbach (Hess) ..... d.	0529	0649	0703	0803	0803	0903	0903	1003	1103	1203	1303	1403	1503	1503	1603	1703	1703	1803	1903	1903	2003	...	...	...	...
106	**Fulda** .... a.	0602	0719	0729	0829	0829	0929	0929	1029	1129	1229	1329	1429	1529	1529	1629	1729	1729	1829	1929	1929	2029	...	...	...	...

	Ⓐe	Ⓐe	⑥	Ⓐe	⑥	Ⓐe	Ⓐe	⑥		⚒d	Ⓐe	Ⓒz	⚒d		⚒d	Ⓐe	Ⓒz		Ⓐe	Ⓒz	Ⓒz	Ⓐe		Ⓐe		†z
ulda .... d.	...	...	...	0533	...	0610	0653	0735	0835	0934	1034	1035	1134	1234	1334	1434	1435	1534	1634	1635	1734	1735	1835	1935	2035	2134
auterbach (Hess) ...... d.	...	...	...	0612j	...	0654j	0723	0805	0905	1005	1105	1105	1205	1305	1405	1505	1505	1605	1705	1705	1805	1805	1905	2005	2100	2200
lsfeld (Oberhess)...... d.	0415	0532	0616	0631	0712	0719j	0757j	0819	0919	1019	1119	1119	1219	1319	1419	1519	1519	1619	1719	1719	1819	1819	1919	2018	2113	2213
rünberg (Oberhess).. d.	0456	0614	0651	0705	0747	0753	0838	0850	0953	1050	1153	1153	1250t	1353	1450t	1553	1553	1650t	1753	1753	1850	1853	1953	...	...	...
ießen .... a.	0521	0640	0716	0729	0816	0818	0906	0915	1018	1115	1218	1218	1315	1418v	1515	1615	1618	1715	1815	1818	1915	1915	2018	...	...	...

C – Ⓒ to Nov. 1 (also June 19); ⑥ from Nov. 8.
d – Daily until Nov. 1.
e – Not June 19.
j – Arrives 10–12 minutes earlier.
t – 3 minutes later on Ⓐ (not June 19).
v – 1416 on Ⓐ (not June 19).
z – Also June 19.

CANTUS Verkehrsgesellschaft (2nd class only) GÖTTINGEN - BEBRA 908

km		Ⓐ	⑥	Ⓐ	F	⚒		Ⓐ						Ⓐ	Ⓒ		Ⓐ			◇
0	**Göttingen**. **864** d.	0442	0543	0600	0703	0814	0914	1040	1114	1240	1314	1440	1514	1614	1640	1714	1814	1914	2014	2214
20	Eichenberg **864** d.	0458	0558	0618	0718k	0830	0930	1054	1130	1254	1330	1454	1530	1630	1654	1730	1830	1930	2030	2230
35	Bad Sooden ⊡ d.	0509	0608	0628	0728k	0840	0940	1105	1140	1305	1340	1505	1540	1640	1705	1740	1840	1940	2040	2239
49	Eschwege .... a.	0520	0619	0639	0739k	0852	0952	1116	1152	1316	1352	1516	1552	1651	1716	1751	1851	1952	2051	2250
49	Eschwege ... ★ d.	0525	0624	0644	0747	0921	1018	1121	1218	1321	1418	1521	1618	1656	1721	1756h	1856	1957h	2056	2256
87	**Bebra** .... ★ a.	0553	0651	0712	0814	0949	1047	1149	1247	1349	1447	1549	1647	1724	1749	1824h	1924	2028h	2124	2324

	Ⓐ	⑥	Ⓐ	G	⚒		Ⓐ							Ⓐ	Ⓒ	Ⓐ				F
ebra ....d.	0523	0622	0633	0731	0832	0905r	1003	1105	1203	1305	1403	1505	1603	1705	1705	1803	1905	2003	2103	2303
schwege ....a.	0553	0650	0700	0800	0900	0934r	1031	1134	1231	1334	1431	1534	1631	1734	1734	1831	1934	2031	2131	2331
schwege ....d.	0558	0655	0705	0805	0905	1005	1036	1205	1236	1405	1436	1605	1636	1739	1805	1836	2005	2036	2136	2336
ad Sooden ⊡ .d.	0609	0707	0716	0816	0916	1016	1047	1216	1247	1416	1447	1616	1647	1750	1816	1847	2016	2047	2147	2347
chenberg **864** d.	0624	0722	0732	0832	0932	1032	1100	1232	1300	1432	1500	1632	1700	1806	1832	1900	2032	2100	2206	0003
öttingen . **864** a.	0637	0735	0745	0845	0945	1045	1113	1245	1313	1445	1513	1645	1713	1820	1845	1913	2045	2113	2219	0016

F – To / from Fulda (Table **901**).
G – From Fulda (Table **901**) on Ⓒ (also June 19).
h – 19–23 minutes later on Ⓒ.
k – 3 minutes later on Ⓒ.
r – On Ⓒ Bebra d. 0932, Eschwege a. 1000.
★ – Additional journey on Ⓒ: Eschwege d. 0821, Bebra a. 0849.
◇ – Runs 4–5 minutes later on ⑥ (also Oct. 3).
⊡ – Bad Sooden-Allendorf.

DB (*RB* services); EB ★ WÜRZBURG - SCHWEINFURT - BAD KISSINGEN - GEMÜNDEN 909

km				Ⓐe	Ⓒz	Ⓐe						⊠								⚒r	Ⓒz	
0	**Würzburg** Hbf........ **870 876** d.	...	*0458*v	...	*0604*	*0635*	...	...	0801	*0835*	...	and in the same	1601	*1636*	*1645*e	1801	*1836*	...	2001	*2035*	*2035*	*2143*
43	**Schweinfurt** Hbf .... **870 876** d.	0450	0534	0618	0703	0703	0732	...	0830	0906	0930	pattern every	1630	1704	1730	1830	1904	1930	2030	2104	2146	2226
57	Ebenhausen (Unterf) ...... **870** d.	0510	0549	0631	0718	0718	0745	...	0843	0918	0945	**two hours**	1643	1717	1745	1843	1917	1945	2043	2118	2159	2240
66	**Bad Kissingen**.....................a.	0519	0600	0643	0727	0727	0755	...	0853	0927	0955	until	1653	1726	1755	1853	1926	1955	2053	2127	2209	2250

	Ⓐ	Ⓐe	Ⓐe		Ⓐe	Ⓐe							✥				Ⓐe			⚒r		
ad Kissingen......................d.	0459	0539	0618	0645	0706	0728	0805	0825	0901	1005	1026	1101	and in the same	1805	1826	1901	1929	2005	2101	2148	...	2230
enhausen (Unterf) .... **870** a.	0508	0548	0627	0654	0715	0737	0813	0834	0910	1013	1035	1110	pattern every	1813	1835	1910	1937	2013	2110	2157	...	2239
hweinfurt Hbf ..... **870 876** a.	0521	0603	0642	0714	0727	0754	0829	0854	0926	1029	1054	1126	**two hours**	1829	1854	1926	1954	2029	2126	2211	...	2254
ürzburg Hbf......... **870 876** a.	*0548*e	*0648*	*0722*	0744	*0814*	*0820*	...	*0922*	0955	...	*1122*	1155	until	...	*1921*	1955	*2020*	*2122*	2157	*2251*	...	*0015*

	⚒r	Ⓐe	†z	Ⓐe	Ⓒz			Ⓐe	Ⓒz	Ⓐe	Ⓐe	Ⓒz	Ⓐe	Ⓐe	Ⓒz		Ⓐe	Ⓒz
Schweinfurt Hbf ♥ ...d.	...	...	...	0703	...	0930	1130	...	1330	...	1506	1530	1600	1704	1730	1930	2104	2146
d Kissingen............d.	0543	0612	0650	0732	0801	1001	1201	1256	1401	1434	1532	1601	1631	1732	1801	2001	2132	2214
mmelburg ....d.	0612h	0657j	0713	0822j	0822	1022	1222	1322	1422	1458	1558	1622	1658	1758	1822	2023	2153	2235
münden (Main) ....a.	0648h	0734	0744	0854	0854	1054	1254	1354	1454	1534	1634	1654	1734	1834	1854	2054	...	2308

km		Ⓐe	Ⓐe	Ⓐe	⚒r				Ⓒz	Ⓐe		Ⓐe		Ⓐe		Ⓐe	Ⓒz	Ⓐe
0	**Gemünden** (Main) ......d.	...	...	0620	0704	...	0904	1104	1304	1313	1504	1605	1705	1805	1905	...	2104	2104
28	Hammelburg...............d.	0547	0617	0659	0736	0736	0936	1136	1336	1359	1536	1636	1736	1836	1936	2036	2136	2203j
47	**Bad Kissingen**...........a.	0610	0640	0722	0759	0759	0959	1159	1359	1421	1559	1658	1759	1859	1959	2058	2159	2225
	Schweinfurt Hbf ♥ ..a.	0642	0727	0754	0829	0829	1029	1229	1429	...	1629	...	1829	1954	2029	...	2254	2254

e – Ⓐ (not June 19, Aug. 15).
h – On ⑥ departs Hammelburg 0607, arrives Gemünden 0639.
j – Arrives 19–27 minutes earlier.
r – Not June 19, Aug. 15.
v – ⚒ (not June 19, Aug. 15, Nov. 1).
z – Also June 19, Aug. 15.

⊠ – Schweinfurt Hbf d. 1304 (not 1306; Ebenhausen d. 1316).
✥ – Bad Kissingen d. 1204 (not 1205) and 1604 (not 1605).

– Erfurter Bahn (2nd class only).

♥ – See panel above for full service

910 AACHEN - KÖLN - FRANKFURT via high-speed line

See Tables **800**/**911** for services via Bonn and Koblenz. See Table **20** for *Thalys* services Paris - Brussels - Aachen - Köln.

km		*ICE*	*ICE*		*ICE*		*ICE*	*ICE*	*ICE*	*ICE*		*ICE*	*ICE*	*ICE*	*ICE*	*ICE*	*ICE*	*ICE*	*ICE*	*ICE*	*ICE*	*ICE*	*ICE*	*ICE*
		827	**827**		**521**		**523**	**1123**	**511**	**511**		**711**	**811**	**925**	**525**	**101**	**813**	**527**	**1013**	**11**	**11**	**815**	**529**	**103**
		Ⓐ					Ⓐ	⑥	①			①–⑤	①–⑤	Ⓒ	Ⓐ		①–⑤	①–⑥	⊖	①–⑤	⑥⑦	①–⑤		
					🍷		🍷	🍷	🍷	🍷		a 🍷	d 🍷	🍷	🍷	🍷	d 🍷	G 🍷	M 🍷	d 🍷	c 🍷	d 🍷	🍷	H 🍷
	Dortmund Hbf **800** d.	...	...	...	...	...	0406	0423	0437	...	...	...	...	0502	0524	0537	0600	0624	0638	...	...	0652	0724	0737
	Essen Hbf **800** d.	...	...	...	...	...	0428	0445	│	...	...	...	...	0526	0553	│	│	0653	0700	...	...	0715	0753	│
	Amsterdam Centraal **28** d.	...	...	...	...	...	│	│	│	...	...	...	...	│	│	│	│	│	│	...	...	│	│	│
	Düsseldorf Hbf **800** d.	...	...	...	...	...	0455	0513	◐	...	...	...	...	0553	0621	◐	◐	0721	0727	...	...	0747	0821	◐
	Brussels Midi/Zuid **21 400** d.	...	...	...	...	...	│	│	│	...	...	...	...	│	│	│	│	│	│	0625	0625	│	│	│
	Aachen Hbf **802 807** d.	...	...	...	...	...	│	│	│	...	...	...	...	│	│	│	│	│	│	0740	0740	│	│	│
	Köln Hbf **802 807** a.	...	...	...	...	...	│	│	0545	...	...	...	...	│	│	0646	0709	│	0749	0815	0815	│	│	0846
0	**Köln** Hbf **802 807** d.	0314	0314	...	0422	...	│	│	0555	0555	...	0611	0619	│	│	0655	0720	│	0755	0820	0820	│	│	0855
1	**Köln** Messe/Deutz **802** d.	│	│	...	│	...	0518	0535	│	│	...	│	│	0618	0644	│	│	0744	│	│	│	0810	0844	│
	Köln/Bonn Flughafen ✈ **802** d.	0326	0326	...	│	...	0531	0547	│	│	...	│	│	0631	│	│	│	│	│	│	│	0821	│	│
25	Siegburg/Bonn 🚃 **807** d.	0336	0336	...	0437	...	0542	│	0611	0611	...	0626	0636	0642	│	0711	0736	│	0811	│	0836	0836	│	0911
88	Montabaur d.	0401	0401	...	0457	...	0602	│	│	│	...	0646	0656	0702	│	│	0756	│	│	│	0856	0856	│	│
110	Limburg Süd d.	0412	0412	...	0508	...	0613	│	│	│	...	0657	0707	0713	│	│	0807	│	│	│	0907	0907	│	│
	Wiesbaden Hbf a.	│	│	...	│	...	│	│	│	│	...	0719	│	│	│	│	│	│	│	│	│	│	│	│
	Mainz Hbf a.	│	│	...	│	...	│	│	│	│	...	0744	│	│	│	│	│	│	│	│	│	│	│	│
169	**Frankfurt** Flughafen Fernbf ✈ a.	0435	0435	...	0527	...	0634	0634	0650	0650	...	│	0726	0734	0734	0750	0826	0834	0850	0910	0926	0926	0934	0950
180	**Frankfurt** (Main) Hbf a.	0448	0448	...	0545	...	0648	0648	│	│	...	│	0741	0748	0748	│	0841	0848	│	0924	0941	0941	0948	│
	Nürnberg Hbf **920** a.	0659	...	...	0759	...	0859	0859	│	│	...	│	...	0959	0959	│	...	1059	│	...	...	...	1159	│
	Mannheim Hbf **912** a.	│	...	...	│	...	│	│	0723	0723	...	0824	...	│	│	0823	...	│	0923	...	...	...	│	1023
	Karlsruhe Hbf **912** a.	│	...	...	│	...	│	│	│	│	...	│	...	│	│	0858‡	...	│	│	...	...	...	│	1058
	Basel SBB **912** a.	│	...	...	│	...	│	│	│	│	...	│	...	│	│	1047‡	...	│	│	...	...	...	│	1247
	Stuttgart Hbf **912** a.	│	...	...	│	...	│	│	0808	0808	...	0924	...	│	│	...	...	│	1008	...	...	...	│	...
	München Hbf **904 930** a.	0816	...	...	0920	...	1016	1016	1027	1027	...	...	...	1115	1115	...	...	1216e	1227	...	...	...	1321	...

	ICE	*ICE*	*ICE*	*ICE*	*ICE*	*ICE*	*ICE*	*ICE*	*ICE*	*ICE*	*ICE*	*ICE*	*ICE*	*ICE*	*ICE*	*ICE*	*ICE*	*ICE*	*ICE*	*ICE*	*ICE*	*ICE*	*ICE*	*ICE*
	621	**1121**	**121**	**515**	**623**	**923**	**105**	**505**	**625**	**825**	**517**	**15**	**627**	**927**	**107**	**1107**	**123**	**629**	**519**	**817**	**721**	**109**	**109**	**125**
	①–⑥	⑦	①–⑥		①–⑥	⑦			Ⓑ **d**	⑥ **k**			①–⑥	⑦	⑦	①–⑥		Ⓑ				Ⓑ **q**		
	🍷	🍷	🍷	A 🍷	🍷	🍷	🍷	🍷	🍷	M 🍷	🍷	🍷	🍷	🍷	🍷	🍷	🍷	🍷	🍷	🍷	🍷	🍷	🍷	🍷
Dortmund Hbf **800** d.	0816r	0824	...	0837	...	0912	...	...	1024w	...	1037	...	...	1103	1137	...	...	1224w	1237	...	1324z	1337	...	...
Essen Hbf **800** d.	0840	0853	...	│	...	0936	...	...	1053	1053	1100	...	...	│	│	...	...	1253	1300	...	1353	│	...	...
Amsterdam Centraal **28** d.	│	│	0704	│	...	│	0804	...	│	│	│	...	...	│	│	...	1034	│	│	...	│	│	...	1234
Düsseldorf Hbf **800** d.	0913	0921	0923	◐	0945	1008	1022	...	1121	1121	1127	...	...	◐	◐	1234	1248	1321	1327	...	1421	◐	...	1448
Brussels Midi/Zuid **21 400** d.	│	│	│	│	│	│	│	...	│	│	│	1025	...	│	│	│	│	│	│	...	│	│	...	│
Aachen Hbf **802 807** d.	│	│	│	│	│	│	│	...	│	│	│	1139	...	│	│	│	│	│	│	...	│	│	...	│
Köln Hbf **802 807** a.	│	│	│	0946	1012	│	1045	...	│	│	1149	1215	...	1209	1246	│	1312	│	1349	...	│	1446	...	1512
Köln Hbf **802 807** d.	│	│	│	0955	1019	│	1055	1055	│	│	1155	1220	1214	1215	1255	│	1328	│	1355	1420	│	1455	1455	1528
Köln Messe/Deutz **802** d.	0937	0944	0945	│	│	1030	│	│	1144	1144	│	│	│	│	│	1256	│	1344	│	│	1444	│	│	│
Köln/Bonn Flughafen ✈ **802** d.	│	│	│	│	1031	│	│	│	│	│	│	│	1231	1231	│	│	│	│	│	│	│	│	│	│
Siegburg/Bonn 🚃 **807** d.	│	│	│	1011	1042	1044	1111	1111	│	│	1211	│	│	│	1311	1311	│	│	1411	1436	│	1511	1511	│
Montabaur d.	│	│	│	│	1102	1104	│	│	│	│	│	│	1258	1258	│	│	│	│	│	1456	│	│	│	│
Limburg Süd d.	│	│	│	│	1113	1115	│	│	│	│	│	│	1308	1308	│	│	│	│	│	1507	│	│	│	│
Wiesbaden Hbf a.	│	│	│	│	│	│	│	│	│	│	│	│	│	│	│	│	│	│	│	│	│	│	│	│
Mainz Hbf a.	│	│	│	│	│	│	│	│	│	│	│	│	│	│	│	│	│	│	│	│	│	│	│	│
Frankfurt Flughafen Fernbf ✈ a.	1026	1034	1034	1050	1134	1134	1150	1150	1234	1234	1250	1310	1326	1326	1350	1350	1416	1434	1450	1526	1534	1550	1550	1616
Frankfurt (Main) Hbf a.	1041	1048	1050	│	1148	1148	│	│	1248	1248	│	1324	1344	1344	│	│	1430	1448	│	1541	1548	│	│	1630
Nürnberg Hbf **920** a.	1259	1259	...	│	1400	1400	│	│	1459	1459	│	...	1559	1559	│	│	...	1659	│	...	1759	│	│	...
Mannheim Hbf **912** a.	│	│	...	1123	│	│	1223	1223	│	│	1323	...	│	│	1423	1423	...	│	1523	...	│	1623	1623	...
Karlsruhe Hbf **912** a.	│	│	...	│	│	│	1258	1258	│	│	│	...	│	│	1456‡	1456‡	...	│	│	...	│	1658	1658	...
Basel SBB **912** a.	│	│	...	│	│	│	1447	1447	│	│	│	...	│	│	1647	1647	...	│	│	...	│	1847	1847	...
Stuttgart Hbf **912** a.	│	│	...	1208	│	│	...	...	│	│	1408	...	│	│	...	...	...	│	1608	...	│	...	...	...
München Hbf **904 930** a.	1415	1415	...	1427	1515	1515	...	...	1615	1615	1627	...	1715t	1715t	...	...	...	1818	1827	...	1916t	...	...	...

	ICE	*ICE*	*ICE*	*ICE*	*ICE*	*ICE*	*ICE*	*ICE*	*ICE*	*ICE*	*ICE*	*ICE*	*ICE*	*ICE*	*ICE*	*ICE*	*ICE*	*ICE*	*ICE*	*ICE*	*ICE*	*ICE*		*ICE*
	723	**611**	**17**	**725**	**201**	**127**	**1228**	**727**	**613**	**819**	**929**	**729**	**1103**	**203**	**129**	**821**	**821**	**615**	**19**	**605**	**605**	**227**		**619**
	Ⓑ					**T**	①–⑤	Ⓑ		Ⓑ	⑥	Ⓑ	⑦	①–⑥		Ⓑ **d**	**Q**				**R**			
	🍷	🍷	🍷	🍷	🍷	🍷	a L	🍷	🍷	🍷	🍷	🍷	🍷	🍷	🍷	N 🍷	🍷	🍷	🍷	🍷	🍷	🍷		🍷
Dortmund Hbf **800** d.	1424p	1437	...	1524w	...	...	1616	...	1637	...	...	...	...	...	...	1815w	1815w	1837	...	1924	1924	...	...	2058
Essen Hbf **800** d.	1453	1500	...	1553	...	...	1640	1653	1700	...	1742	1753	...	...	...	1841	1841	1900	...	1950	1950	...	...	2125
Amsterdam Centraal **28** d.	│	│	...	│	...	1434	│	│	│	...	│	│	...	...	1634	│	│	│	...	│	│	1834	...	│
Düsseldorf Hbf **800** d.	1521	1527	...	1621	1634	1648	1708	1720	1727	...	1813	1821	...	...	1848	1908	1908	1927	...	2022	2022	2048	...	2155
Brussels Midi/Zuid **21 400** d.	│	│	1425	│	│	│	│	│	│	...	│	│	...	...	│	│	│	│	1825	│	│	│	...	│
Aachen Hbf **802 807** d.	│	│	1539	│	│	│	│	│	│	...	│	│	...	...	│	│	│	│	1939	│	│	│	...	│
Köln Hbf **802 807** a.	│	1549	1615	│	│	1712	│	│	1749	...	│	│	...	...	1912	│	│	1949	2015	│	│	2112	...	2219
Köln Hbf **802 807** d.	│	1556	1620	│	│	1720	│	│	1755	1819	│	│	1855	1855	1920	│	│	1957	2028	│	│	2128	...	2230
Köln Messe/Deutz **802** d.	1544	│	│	1644	1657	│	1730	1744	│	│	1835	1844	│	│	│	1930	1930	│	│	2046	2046	│	...	│
Köln/Bonn Flughafen ✈ **802** d.	│	│	│	│	│	│	│	│	│	│	│	│	│	│	│	│	│	│	│	│	│	│	...	2242
Siegburg/Bonn 🚃 **807** d.	│	1611	1636	│	1711	│	1744	│	1811	1836	│	│	1911	1911	│	1944	1944	2012	│	2100	2100	│	...	2253
Montabaur d.	│	│	1656	│	│	│	1804	│	│	1856	1905	│	│	│	│	2004	2004	│	│	2120	2120	│	...	231
Limburg Süd d.	│	│	1707	│	│	│	1818	│	│	1907	1916	│	│	│	│	2015	2015	│	│	2131	2131	│	...	2324
Wiesbaden Hbf a.	│	│	│	│	│	│	1840	│	│	│	│	│	│	│	│	│	│	│	│	│	│	│	...	│
Mainz Hbf a.	│	│	│	│	│	│	...	│	│	│	│	│	│	│	│	│	│	│	│	│	│	│	...	│
Frankfurt Flughafen Fernbf ✈ a.	1634	1650	1726	1734	1750	1816	...	1834	1850	1926	1934	1934	1950	1950	2016	2034	2034	2050	2116	2150	2150	2216	...	234
Frankfurt (Main) Hbf a.	1648	│	1741	1748	│	1830	...	1848	│	1941	1948	1948	│	│	2030	2048	2048	│	2130	│	│	2230	...	240
Nürnberg Hbf **920** a.	1859	│	...	1959	│	...	...	2059	│	...	2159	2159	│	│	...	...	2259	│	...	│	│	...	...	│
Mannheim Hbf **912** a.	│	1723	...	│	1823	...	...	│	1923	...	│	│	2023	2023	...	...	│	2123	...	2223	2223	...	...	010
Karlsruhe Hbf **912** a.	│	│	...	│	1858	...	...	│	│	...	│	│	2100	2100‡	...	...	│	│	...	2300‡	2300‡	...	...	0152
Basel SBB **912** a.	│	│	...	│	2047	...	...	│	│	...	│	│	2250	2300‡	...	...	│	│	...	...	0056b	...	...	│
Stuttgart Hbf **912** a.	│	1808	...	│	...	...	...	│	2008	...	│	│	...	...	...	...	│	2208	...	...	...	...	...	032
München Hbf **904 930** a.	2016	2027	...	2115j	...	...	...	2212	2226	...	2316	2316	...	...	...	...	0017	0027	...	...	...	...	...	060

A – From Hamburg (Table **800**).
G – Continues to Garmisch (Table **895**) on ⑥.
H – From Hannover (Table **810**).
L – 🚃12 and 🍷 Kassel - Paderborn - Dortmund - Wiesbaden.
M – From Münster (Table **800**).
N – To Würzburg (Table **920**).
Q – ④⑤⑦ (also June 18; not June 19, Oct. 3).
R – ①②③④⑦ (not Oct. 2).
T – Daily to Nov. 2; ⑤ from Nov. 7.

a – Not June 19, 20, Oct. 3.
b – Basel **Badischer Bahnhof**.
c – Also June 19, Oct. 3.
d – Not June 19, Oct. 3.
e – 1210 on ⑥.
j – 2120 on ①–⑤ until July 11.
k – Also June 19, Oct. 3; not June 21, Oct. 4.
p – ①②③④⑦ (not Oct. 2).
q – Not Oct. 3.
r – ⑥ only.
t – 3 minutes later until July 12.
w – ⑦ only.

y – 0158 on the mornings July 18 - Sept. 30.
z – ⑤⑦ only.

‡ – 9–13 minutes later July 31 - Sept. 14.
⊖ – On Ⓐ conveys 🚃12 (*ICE* **513**) Hamm - Dortmund - München (Table **800**).
◐ – Via Wuppertal (Table **800**).

🚃 – Light-rail services **Bonn Hbf** - **Siegburg/Bonn**. Journey: 24–25 minutes. Operator: SWB Bus und Bahn.

Bonn Hbf → Siegburg/Bonn
On Ⓐ: 0017, 0047, 0132, 0402, 0432, 0452, 0512, 0532, 0542, 0552, 0602, 0613, 0623 and every 10 minutes until 1933; 1947, 2002 and every 15 minutes until 2247; then 2317 and 2347.
On ⑥: 0017, 0047, 0132, 0402, 0432, 0502, 0532, 0602, 0617, 0632 and every 15 minutes until 0932; 0943, 0958 and every 15 minutes until 2028; 2047, 2102 and every 15 minutes until 2247; then 2317 and 2347.
On †: 0017, 0047, 0132, 0432, 0517, 0547 and every 30 minutes until 1017; 1032, 1047 and every 15 minutes until 2247; then 2317 and 2347.

Siegburg/Bonn → Bonn Hbf
On Ⓐ: 0032, 0102, 0132, 0202, 0454, 0514, 0534, 0554, 0604 and every 10 minutes until 1914; 1922, 1937, 1952, 1957, 2007, 2022 and every 15 minutes until 2322; then 2352.
On ⑥: 0032, 0102, 0132, 0202, 0452, 0522, 0552, 0622, 0637, 0652, 0707, 0722, 0737, 0752, 0808, 0823 and every 15 minutes until 1908; 1922, 1937 and every 15 minutes until 2322; then 2352.
On †: 0032, 0102, 0132, 0202, 0502, 0552, 0622 and every 30 minutes until 1052; 1107, 1122 and every 15 minutes until 2322; then 2352.

FRANKFURT - KÖLN - AACHEN via high-speed line — 910

See Tables **800**/**911** for services via Koblenz and Bonn. See Table **20** for *Thalys* services Köln - Aachen - Brussels - Paris.

km		ICE 222	ICE 918	ICE 1018	ICE 618	ICE 618	ICE 716	ICE 18	ICE 18	ICE 616	ICE 1223	ICE 226	ICE 1126	ICE 604	ICE 822	ICE 818	ICE 818	ICE 614	ICE 820	ICE 128	ICE 202	ICE 1202	ICE 728	ICE 16
		①–④	⑤f	⑦	①–⑤	⑥	①–⑤	⑦	①–⑥		Ⓐ		①–④		①–⑥		⑦		Ⓐ		R	⑤⑥		
		s🍷	🍷	🍷	🍷	🍷	a	🍷	🍷	🍷	D🍷	🍷	E🍷	🍷	🍷	🍷	🍷	🍷	🍷	🍷	🍷	y🍷	🍷	🍷
	München Hbf **904 930** d.	...	...	2350p	2350p	2350p	...	...	...	0323	...	...	...	...	0446n	...	...	0527	0545	...	...	...	0647n	...
	Stuttgart Hbf **912** d.	...	...	0221	0221	0221	...	...	...	0551	...	...	...	...	│	...	...	0751	│	...	...	...	│	...
	Basel SBB **912** d.	...	...	│	│	│	...	...	...	│	...	...	...	0515b	│	...	...	│	│	...	0713v	0713	│	...
	Karlsruhe Hbf **912** d.	...	...	0348	0348	0348	...	...	...	│	...	...	...	0700‡	│	...	...	│	│	...	0900	0900	│	...
	Mannheim Hbf **912** d.	...	...	0440	0440	0440	...	...	...	0636	...	...	...	0736	│	...	...	0836	│	...	0936	0936	│	...
	Nürnberg Hbf **920** d.	...	...	│	│	│	...	...	...	│	...	...	...	│	0600	...	...	│	0700	...	│	│	0802	...
	Frankfurt (Main) Hbf d.	0510	0510	0544	0544	0544	...	0625	0629	│	0702	0727	0727	│	0810	0816	0816	│	0909	0929	│	│	1010	1016
	Frankfurt Flughafen Fernbf ✈ d.	0525	0525	0601	0601	0601	...	0638	0643	0709	0715	0743	0743	0809	0825	0832	0832	0909	0925	0943	1009	1009	1025	1032
0	**Mainz** Hbf d.	│	│	│	│	│	0607	│	│	│	│	│	│	│	│	│	│	│	│	│	│	│	│	│
10	**Wiesbaden** Hbf d.	│	│	│	│	│	0624	│	│	│	│	│	│	│	│	│	│	│	│	│	│	│	│	│
65	Limburg Süd d.	0544	0544	│	0620	0620	0645	0657	│	│	0734	│	│	│	│	0851	0851	│	│	│	│	│	│	1051
87	Montabaur d.	0556	0556	│	0631	0631	0656	0708	│	│	0746	│	│	│	│	0902	0902	│	│	│	│	│	│	1102
150	Siegburg/Bonn 🚋 **807** d.	0618	0618	0641	0651	0651	│	│	│	0749	0808	│	│	0849	│	0923	0923	0949	│	│	1049	1049	│	│
166	Köln/Bonn Flughafen ✈ **802** a.	0627	0627	0650	│	│	│	│	0726	│	│	│	│	│	│	│	│	│	│	│	│	│	│	1126
180	**Köln** Messe/Deutz **802** a.	│	│	│	│	│	│	│	│	│	0822	│	│	0903	0914	│	│	│	1013	│	│	1103	1114	│
181	**Köln** Hbf **802 807** a.	0640	0640	0705	0705	0705	0728	0739	0739	0805	│	0832	0832	│	│	0939	0939	1005	│	1032	1105	│	│	1139
181	**Köln** Hbf **802 807** d.	0646	0646	0710	0713	0715	...	0743	0743	0810	│	0846	...	│	│	...	0943	1010	│	1042	1110v	│	│	1143
251	**Aachen** Hbf **802 807** a.	│	│	│	│	│	...	0816	0816	│	│	│	...	│	│	...	│	│	│	│	│	│	│	1216
	Brussels Midi/Zuid **21 400** a.	│	│	│	│	│	...	0935	0935	│	│	│	...	│	│	...	│	│	│	│	│	│	│	1335
	Düsseldorf Hbf **800** a.	0710	0710	◐	0736	0739	...	...	...	0831	0843	0911	...	0925	0937	...	1005	1031	1040	1111	◐	1125	1137	...
	Amsterdam Centraal **28** a.	0927	│	│	│	│	...	...	...	│	│	1127	...	...	│	...	│	│	│	1327	│	...	│	...
	Essen Hbf **800** a.	...	0739	│	0802	0804	...	...	...	0857	0915	...	...	...	1002	...	1039	1057	1105	...	│	...	1202	...
	Dortmund Hbf **800** a.	...	0802	0821	...	0843	...	...	...	0921	0940	...	...	...	1030r	...	1102	1121	...	...	1221v	...	1230	...

	ICE 612	ICE 726	ICE 126	ICE 200	ICE 1200	ICE 724	ICE 610	ICE 722	ICE 124	ICE 108	ICE 1108	ICE 720	ICE 14	ICE 518	ICE 628	ICE 816	ICE 106	ICE 626	ICE 826	ICE 926	ICE 1226	ICE 122	ICE 712	ICE 516
		①–⑥	T	Ⓑ	⑥					Ⓑ	⑥							Ⓐ	Ⓐ	⑦	⑥		①–⑤	
	🍷	🍷	🍷	🍷	🍷	🍷	🍷	🍷	🍷	🍷	🍷	🍷	🍷	🍷	🍷	🍷	🍷	🍷	🍷	🍷	🍷	🍷	a🍷	🍷
München Hbf **904 930** d.	0728	0750n	...	...	...	0849n	0928	0950n	...	...	...	1050n	...	1130	1148n	...	...	1250n	1250n	1250n	1250n	...	...	1328
Stuttgart Hbf **912** d.	0951	│	...	...	...	│	1151	│	...	...	...	│	...	1351	│	...	...	│	│	│	│	...	1434	1551
Basel SBB **912** d.	│	│	...	0913‡	0913‡	│	│	│	...	1113	1113	│	...	│	│	...	1313	│	│	│	│	...	│	│
Karlsruhe Hbf **912** d.	│	│	...	1100‡	1100‡	│	│	│	...	1300‡	1300‡	│	...	│	│	...	1500‡	│	│	│	│	...	│	│
Mannheim Hbf **912** d.	1036	│	...	1136	1136	│	1236	│	...	1336	1336	│	...	1436	│	...	1536	│	│	│	│	...	1533	1636
Nürnberg Hbf **920** d.	│	0900	...	│	│	1000	│	1100	...	│	│	1200	...	│	1300	...	│	1400	1400	1400	1400	...	│	│
Frankfurt (Main) Hbf d.	│	1110	1129	│	│	1210	│	1310	1329	│	│	1410	1429	│	1510	1517	│	1610	1610	1610	1610	1629	│	│
Frankfurt Flughafen Fernbf ✈ d.	1109	1125	1143	1209	1209	1225	1309	1325	1343	1409	1409	1424	1443	1509	1525	1532	1609	1623	1627	1624	1624	1643	│	1709
Mainz Hbf d.	│	│	│	│	│	│	│	│	│	│	│	│	│	│	│	│	│	│	│	│	│	│	1617	│
Wiesbaden Hbf d.	│	│	│	│	│	│	│	│	│	│	│	│	│	│	│	│	│	│	│	│	│	│	1645	│
Limburg Süd d.	│	│	│	│	│	1244	│	│	│	│	│	1443	│	│	│	1551	│	│	1646	1643	1643	│	1707	│
Montabaur d.	│	│	│	│	│	1256	│	│	│	│	│	1454	│	│	│	1602	│	│	1656	1654	1654	│	1718	│
Siegburg/Bonn 🚋 **807** d.	1149	│	│	1249	1249	1318	1349	│	│	1449	1449	1514	│	1549	│	1623	1649	│	1716	1714	1714	│	1738	1749
Köln/Bonn Flughafen ✈ **802** a.	│	│	│	│	│	1326	│	│	│	│	│	│	│	│	│	│	│	│	│	│	│	│	1747	│
Köln Messe/Deutz **802** a.	│	1214	│	│	│	│	│	1414	│	1503	│	1527	│	│	1614	│	│	1714	│	│	1727	│	│	│
Köln Hbf **802 807** a.	1205	│	1232	1305	1305	1339	1405	│	1432	│	1505	│	1539	1605	│	1639	1705	│	1732	1732	│	1739z	1801	1805
Köln Hbf **802 807** d.	1210	│	1245	1314t	1310	...	1410	│	1446	│	1510	│	1543	1610	│	...	1710	│	...	...	│	1746z	...	1810
Aachen Hbf **802 807** a.	│	│	│	│	│	...	│	│	│	│	│	│	1616	│	│	...	│	│	...	...	│	│	...	│
Brussels Midi/Zuid **21 400** a.	│	│	│	│	│	...	│	│	│	│	│	│	1735	│	│	...	│	│	...	...	│	│	...	│
Düsseldorf Hbf **800** a.	1231	1237	1311	1336t	◐	...	1431	1438	1511	1526	◐	1549	...	1631	1640	...	◐	1737	...	...	1750	1812	...	1831
Amsterdam Centraal **28** a.	│	│	1527	│	│	...	│	│	1727	...	│	│	...	│	│	...	│	│	...	...	│	2027	...	│
Essen Hbf **800** a.	1257	1302	...	1402t	│	...	1457	1503	...	...	│	1615	...	1657	1707	...	│	1802	...	...	1821	...	...	1857
Dortmund Hbf **800** a.	1321	...	...	...	1421	...	1521	...	...	...	1621	1643r	...	1721	...	...	1821	...	...	...	1846	...	...	1921

	ICE 624	ICE 814	ICE 504	ICE 104	ICE 622	ICE 1222	ICE 812	ICE 10	ICE 812	ICE 514	ICE 1220	ICE 620	ICE 120	ICE 912	ICE 102	ICE 1102	ICE 528	ICE 810	ICE 512	ICE 526	ICE 100	ICE 524	ICE 1110	ICE 522
		①–⑤			Ⓑ	⑥	Ⓑd		Ⓑd		Ⓒ	Ⓐ	Q	①–③	Ⓑ	⑥				Ⓑ			⑦	s
	🍷	d🍷	🍷	🍷	🍷	🍷	🍷	🍷	🍷	🍷	G🍷	🍷	🍷	🍷	N🍷	H🍷	🍷	🍷	M🍷	🍷	🍷	🍷	🍷	🍷
München Hbf **904 930** d.	1350n	...	...	...	1450n	1450n	...	...	...	1528	1550n	1550n	...	...	...	...	1647n	...	1727	1748	...	1850n	1928	1948n
Stuttgart Hbf **912** d.	│	...	...	...	│	│	...	...	...	1751	│	│	...	...	...	...	│	...	1951	│	...	│	2151	│
Basel SBB **912** d.	│	...	1513	1513	│	│	...	...	...	│	│	│	...	...	1713	1713	│	...	│	│	1913‡	│	│	│
Karlsruhe Hbf **912** d.	│	...	1700	1700	│	│	...	...	...	│	│	│	...	...	1900‡	1900‡	│	...	│	│	2101‡	│	│	│
Mannheim Hbf **912** d.	│	...	1736	1736	│	│	...	...	...	1836	│	│	...	...	1936	1936	│	...	2036	│	2136	│	2232	│
Nürnberg Hbf **920** d.	1500	...	│	│	1600	1600	...	...	...	│	1700	1700	...	...	│	│	1800	...	│	1900	│	2000	│	2102
Frankfurt (Main) Hbf d.	1710	1717	│	│	1810	1810	1816	1829	...	│	1910	1910	1929	1929	│	│	2010	2016	│	2110	│	2210	│	2310
Frankfurt Flughafen Fernbf ✈ d.	1725	1732	1809	1809	1825	1824	1832	1843	...	1909	1925	1923	1943	1943	2009	2009	2025	2031	2109	2125	2209	2225	2310	2329
Mainz Hbf d.	│	│	│	│	│	│	│	│	...	│	│	│	│	│	│	│	│	│	│	│	│	│	│	│
Wiesbaden Hbf d.	│	│	│	│	│	│	│	│	...	│	│	│	│	│	│	│	│	│	│	│	│	│	│	│
Limburg Süd d.	│	1751	│	│	│	1843	1851	│	←	│	│	1942	│	│	│	│	│	2050	│	│	│	2244	│	2348
Montabaur d.	│	1802	│	│	│	1854	1900	│	1907	│	│	1953	│	│	│	│	│	2101	│	│	│	2256	│	2359
Siegburg/Bonn 🚋 **807** d.	│	1823	1849	1849	│	1914	→	1923	1929	1949	│	2014	│	│	2049	2049	│	2121	2149	│	2249	2318	2349	0020
Köln/Bonn Flughafen ✈ **802** a.	│	│	│	│	│	│	...	│	1937	│	│	│	│	│	│	│	│	2129	│	│	│	2326	│	│
Köln Messe/Deutz **802** a.	1813	│	│	│	1914	│	...	│	│	│	2014	2027	│	│	│	│	2113	│	│	2214	│	2337	│	│
Köln Hbf **802 807** a.	│	1839	1905	1905	│	1930	...	1939	1956	2005	│	│	2039	2039	2105	2105	│	2143	2205	│	2305	│	0005	0034
Köln Hbf **802 807** d.	│	...	...	1917	│	...	...	1943	...	2010	│	│	2046	...	2110	2110	│	...	2210	│	2310	│	...	0039
Aachen Hbf **802 807** a.	│	...	...	│	│	...	...	2016	...	│	│	│	│	...	│	│	│	...	│	│	│	│	...	│
Brussels Midi/Zuid **21 400** a.	│	...	...	│	│	...	...	2135	...	│	│	│	│	...	│	│	│	...	│	│	│	│	...	│
Düsseldorf Hbf **800** a.	1835	...	...	1938	1943	...	...	...	...	2031	2038	2049	2111	...	◐	2131	2137	...	2231	2237	2331	2359	...	0100
Amsterdam Centraal **28** a.	│	...	...	2156	│	...	...	...	...	│	│	│	2327	...	│	│	│	...	│	│	│	│	...	│
Essen Hbf **800** a.	1900	...	...	...	2015	...	...	...	...	2057	2102	2116	...	...	│	2157	2202	...	2258	2302	0001	0025	...	0130
Dortmund Hbf **800** a.	1930	...	...	...	2040	...	...	...	...	2121	2130	2141	...	...	2221	2221	2230	...	...	2325	0024	0048	...	0153

– (12) and 🍷 Darmstadt Hbf (d. 0637) - Dortmund - Paderborn - Kassel.
– From Würzburg (Table **920**).
– From Garmisch (Table **895**) on ⑥. To Hannover (Table **810**) on ⑦.
– To Hannover (Table **810**).
– To Münster (Table **800**).
– To Hannover (Table **810**) on ①–⑤.
– ④⑤⑦ only.
– ①②③④⑦ (not Oct. 2).
– Daily until Nov. 2; ⑤ from Nov. 7.

– Not June 19, 20, Oct. 3.
– Not ⑥. Basel **Badischer Bahnhof**. Departs 0503 on ⑦ to Sept. 28, 0506 on ⑦ from Oct. 5, 0511 on ①–⑤ July 31 - Sept. 12.
– Not June 19, Oct. 3.

f – Not Oct. 3.
n – Departs up to 7 minutes **earlier** until July 12.
p – Previous day.
r – ⑥ only.
s – Not June 19.
t – ⑤⑦ (also Oct. 2; not Oct. 3).
v – ①–④ (not Oct. 2).
y – Also Oct. 2.
z – Not June 14 - July 11.

‡ – 8 – 11 minutes earlier July 31 - Sept. 14.
◐ – Via Wuppertal (Table **800**).

🚋 – Frequent light-rail services operate from / to Bonn Hbf. See page 422.

911 KOBLENZ - MAINZ - MANNHEIM and FRANKFURT

km		IC	IC		ICE	ICE		IC		ICE	ICE	IC	IC	ICE	ICE	ICE	EC	EC	IC	IC	ICE	IC	EC	ICE
		61419	**2009**		**672**	**991**		**2021**		**23**	**711**	**2317**	**2319**	**1597**	**1597**	**1521**	**115**	**7**	**2159**	**119**	**27**	**2005**	**9**	**1651**
			⑦		¶	Ⓐ					①–⑤	⑥k	⚒	Ⓒu								⑤⑥		
		2⊡			H✕	✕		◇		A✕	a🍷		🍷	L🍷	L🍷	✕	🍷♦	Z✕	L🍷	♦	A✕	🍷♦	Z✕	L✕
	Hamburg Hbf **800** d.	...	...	...	...	...	...	2246	...	...	...	...	...	...	...	...	...	0442h	...	...	...	...	0646	...
	Dortmund Hbf **800** d.	...	...	...	...	...	...	0152	...	0437	...	...	0537	...	...	0636	...	0737	...	...	0837	...	0937	...
	Köln Hbf **800** d.	2346	2353	...	...	...	...	0351	...	0553	0611	...	0653	...	...	0753	0818	0853	...	0918	0953	1018	1053	...
	Bonn Hbf **800** d.	0007	0014	...	...	...	...	0416	...	0614	|	...	0714	...	...	0814	0837	0914	...	0937	1014	1037	1114	...
0	**Koblenz** Hbf **914** d.	0040	0048	...	...	...	...	0530	...	0648	|	...	0748	...	...	0848	0918	0948	...	1018	1048	1118	1148	...
61	Bingen (Rhein) Hbf **914** d.	|	0124	...	...	...	...	0609	...	|	|	...	|	...	...	|	0952	|	...	1052	|	1152	|	...
	Wiesbaden Hbf **917a** d.	|	|	...	0458	0523	...	|	...	|	0732	0732	|	0823	...	|	|	|	1023	|	|	|	|	1223
91	**Mainz** Hbf **914 917a** a.	0136o	0141	...	0509	0534	...	0626	...	0737	0744	0744	0837	0834	...	0937	1015	1037	1034	1111	1137	1215	1237	1234
91	**Mainz** Hbf **911a 917a** d.	0138o	0143	...	0511	0539	...	0628	...	0739	0746	0746	0839	0843	0843	0939	1017	1039	1043	1113	1139	1217	1239	1243
117	**Frankfurt** Flughafen ✈ ◧ **917a** a.	0154	0202	...	0531	|	...	0646	...	0759	|	|	|	0859	0859	0959	|	|	1100	|	1159	|	|	1300
128	**Frankfurt** (Main) Hbf **917a** a.	|	0217	...	0550	|	...	0702	...	0813	|	|	|	0912	0912	1013	|	|	1113	|	1213	|	|	1313
	Nürnberg Hbf **920** a.	|	...	...	...	|	...	...	...	1027	|	|	|	...	...	1224	|	|	...	|	1427	|	|	...
	Worms Hbf **911a** d.	|	...	...	...	0608g	...	...	...	...	|	|	|	...	...	|	1045g	|	...	|	...	1245g	|	...
	Mannheim Hbf **911a** a.	0233	...	...	...	0622	...	...	...	...	0824	0824	0921	...	...	|	1100	1121	...	1152	...	1307	1321	...
	Stuttgart Hbf **912** a.	|	...	...	...	0708	...	...	...	...	0924	0924	1018	...	...	|	1153	|	...	1246	...	|	|	...
	München Hbf **930** a.	|	...	...	...	0927	...	...	...	...	...	...	...	...	...	1350y	1411	|	...	...	...	|	|	...
	Karlsruhe Hbf **912** a.	0437	...	...	...	...	...	...	...	...	...	...	...	...	...	...	...	1147x	...	...	...	1334	1347x	...
	Basel SBB **912** a.	0647	...	...	...	...	...	...	...	...	...	...	...	...	...	...	...	1335x	...	...	...	...	1535x	...

	IC	IC	IC	IC	IC	ICE	IC	IC	IC	IC	IC	IC	IC	ICE	IC	IC	IC	IC	IC	ICE	IC	IC	IC	IC
	2013	**2023**	**2313**	**2251**	**1911**	**1025**	**2217**	**2253**	**2011**	**2017**	**2027**	**2019**	**2311**	**1657**	**1915**	**2229**	**2213**	**2259**	**1917**	**1029**	**2215**	**2315**	**2221**	**2321**
					⑤⑦					⑤f		⑥			⑤⑦			Ⓑq	⑦		R	S		①–④
	✕♦	✕	🍷	L🍷	d🍷	✕	🍷♦	🍷♦	♦	N	🍷♦	♦	E🍷	✕♦	v♦	🍷♦	🍷♦	🍷♦	B	✕	🍷	E🍷	🍷♦	T🍷
Hamburg Hbf **800** d.	...	0746	0846	...	...	0946	1046	...	...	...	1146	...	1246	...	...	1346	1446	...	...	1546	1646	1646	1746	1746
Dortmund Hbf **800** d.	0952	1036	1137	...	1152	1236	1337	...	1352w	1352	1436	...	1537	...	1552	1636	1737	...	1752	1836	1937	1937	2037	2037
Köln Hbf **800** d.	1118	1153	1253	...	1318	1353	1453	...	1518	1518	1553	1618	1653	...	1718	1753	1853	...	1918	1953	2053	2053	2153	2153
Bonn Hbf **800** d.	1137	1214	1314	...	1337	1414	1514	...	1537	1537	1614	1637	1714	...	1737	1814	1914	...	1937	2014	2114	2114	2214	2214
Koblenz Hbf **914** d.	1218	1248	1348	...	1418	1448	1548	...	1618	1618	1648	1718	1748	...	1818	1848	1948	...	2018	2048	2148	2148	2248	2248
Bingen (Rhein) Hbf **914** d.	1252	|	|	...	1452	|	|	...	1652	1652	|	1752	|	...	1852	|	|	...	2052	2124	|	|	|	|
Wiesbaden Hbf **917a** d.	|	|	|	1423	|	|	|	1623	|	|	|	|	|	1823	|	|	|	2023	|	|	|	|	|	|
Mainz Hbf **914 917a** a.	1311	1337	1437	1434	1511	1537	1637	1634	1711	1711	1737	1815	1837	1834	1911	1937	2037	2034	2111	2141	2237	2237	2337	2337
Mainz Hbf **911a 917a** d.	1313	1339	1439	1443	1513	1539	1639	1643	1713	1713	1739	1817	1839	1843	1913	1939	2039	2043	2113	2143	2239	2239	2339	2339
Frankfurt Flughafen ✈ ◧ **917a** a.	|	1359	|	1459	|	1559	|	1659	|	|	1759	|	|	1900	|	1959	|	2100	|	2159	2259	2259	2359	2359
Frankfurt (Main) Hbf **917a** a.	|	1412	|	1515	|	1613	|	1715	|	|	1813	|	|	1913	|	2013	|	2113	|	2213	2311	2311	0013	0013
Nürnberg Hbf **920** a.	|	...	|	...	|	...	|	...	|	|	2027	|	|	...	|	2226q	|	...	|	0037	...	...	...	...
Worms Hbf **911a** d.	|	...	|	...	|	...	|	...	|	|	...	1845g	|	...	|	...	|	...	|	...	...	...	...	...
Mannheim Hbf **911a** a.	1352	...	1521	...	1552	...	1721	...	1752	1752	...	1901	1921	...	1952	...	2121	...	2152	...	...	...	...	...
Stuttgart Hbf **912** a.	1446	...	1622	...	1646	...	1825	...	1846	1846j	...	1958	2023	...	2046	...	2222	...	|	...	...	...	...	...
München Hbf **930** a.	...	...	...	...	...	...	...	...	...	2124	...	...	...	...	...	...	...	...	|	...	...	...	...	...
Karlsruhe Hbf **912** a.	...	...	...	...	...	...	...	...	...	...	...	...	...	...	...	...	...	...	2224x	...	...	...	...	...
Basel SBB **912** a.	...	...	...	...	...	...	...	...	...	...	...	...	...	...	...	...	...	...	...	...	...	...	...	...

km		ICE	ICE	IC	IC	IC	IC	IC	ICE	IC	IC	IC	IC	IC	ICE	ICE	IC	IC	IC	IC	IC	IC	IC	IC
		887	**1587**	**60478**	**2220**	**2320**	**2310**	**1114**	**1028**	**2018**	**2010**	**2158**	**2216**	**2226**	**1654**	**1654**	**2218**	**2024**	**1920**	**1216**	**2252**	**2312**	**2006**	**2004**
		①–⑥	⑦╏			★	⊖	①–⑤		⑥	Ⓐn				⑦	①–⑥			⑦	⑤f			⑥u	⑦
		♣H	H	2⊡	🍷♦	🍷	E🍷	§	✕	♦	♦	♦	🍷♦	🍷♦	✕	✕♦	🍷	P🍷	B	🍷♦	L🍷	🍷	🍷♦	🍷♦
	Basel SBB **912** d.	...	...	2213	...	...	...	...	...	...	...	...	...	...	...	...	...	...	...	...	...	...	...	...
	Karlsruhe Hbf **912** d.	...	...	0029	...	...	...	...	...	...	...	...	...	...	...	...	...	...	...	...	...	...	1221•	1221•
	München Hbf **930** d.	...	...	|	...	...	...	...	...	...	...	...	...	...	...	...	...	...	...	0848	...	...	|	|
	Stuttgart Hbf **912** d.	...	...	|	...	...	...	0630	...	0714	0714	...	0737	...	...	...	0937	...	...	1114	...	1137	|	|
0	**Mannheim** Hbf **911a** d.	...	...	0256	...	...	...	0734	...	0808	0808	...	0839	...	...	...	1039	...	...	1208	...	1239	1258	1258
24	Worms Hbf **911a** d.	...	...	|	...	...	...	|	...	|	|	...	|	...	...	...	|	...	...	|	...	|	1315g	1315g
	Nürnberg Hbf **920** d.	...	...	|	...	...	...	|	0530	|	|	...	|	0729e	...	...	|	0928	...	|	...	|	|	|
	Frankfurt (Main) Hbf **917a** d.	0009	0013	|	0542	0542	0638	|	0742	|	|	0842	|	0942	1042	1044	|	1142	1215	|	1242	|	|	|
	Frankfurt Flughafen ✈ ◧ **917a** d.	0027	0042	0341	0557	0557	0657	|	0758	|	|	0858	|	0958	1058	1058	|	1158	1228	|	1258	|	|	|
70	**Mainz** Hbf **911a 917a** a.	0044	0059	|	0615	0615	0715	0815	0818	0846	0846	0915	0918	1018	1115	1115	1118	1218	1246	1246	1315	1318	1339	1339
70	**Mainz** Hbf **914 917a** d.	0046	0101	|	0617	0617	0717	...	0820	0848	0848	0917	0920	1020	1117	1117	1120	1220	1248	1248	1317	1320	1341	1341
80	**Wiesbaden** Hbf **917a** a.	0057	0113	|	|	|	|	...	|	|	|	0931	|	|	1131	1131	|	|	|	|	1331	|	|	|
	Bingen (Rhein) Hbf **914 917a** d.	...	...	|	0635	0635	|	...	|	0906	0906	...	|	|	...	...	|	|	1306	1306	...	|	1406	1406
	Koblenz Hbf **914 917a** a.	...	...	0446	0711	0711	0811	...	0911	0941	0941	...	1011	1111	...	...	1211	1311	1341	1341	...	1411	1441	1441
	Bonn Hbf **800** a.	...	...	0520	0742	0742	0842	...	0942	1020	1020	...	1042	1142	...	...	1242	1342	1420	1420	...	1442	1520	1520
	Köln Hbf **800** a.	...	...	0543	0805	0805	0905	...	1005	1042	1042	...	1105	1205	...	...	1305	1405	1442	1442	...	1505	1542	1542
	Dortmund Hbf **800** a.	...	...	...	0921	0921	1021	...	1121	...	1207f	...	1221	1321	...	...	1421	1521	1608	1608	...	1621	1703	...
	Hamburg Hbf **800** a.	...	...	...	1212	1212	1312	...	1412	...	...	...	1512	1612	...	...	1712	1812	...	...	...	1912	...	...

♦ – **NOTES** (LISTED BY TRAIN NUMBER)

8 – [12] and ✕ Zürich - Basel - Hamburg (- Kiel ⑦). Train number **2** on ⑦.
26 – [12] and ✕ Wien - Liz - Passau - Regensburg - Dortmund - Hamburg.
114 – WÖRTHERSEE – [12] and 🍷 Klagenfurt - Villach - Salzburg - München - Dortmund.
115 – WÖRTHERSEE – [12] and 🍷 Münster - München - Salzburg - Villach - Klagenfurt.
118/9 – [12] Innsbruck - Bregenz - Lindau - Ulm - Stuttgart - Münster and v.v.
1216 – [12] and 🍷 Salzburg - Dortmund - Berlin.
1654 – [12] and ✕ Dresden - Leipzig - Erfurt - Frankfurt - Wiesbaden.
1657 – [12] and ✕ Wiesbaden - Frankfurt - Leipzig (- Dresden Ⓑ).
1915 – [12] Berlin - Dortmund - Stuttgart. Continues to Tübingen Hbf (a. 2150) on ⑦.
2004 – ⑦ (also Oct. 3). BODENSEE – [12] and 🍷 Konstanz - Karlsruhe - Münster - Emden.
2005 – ⑤⑥ (also June 18, 19, Oct. 2; not June 20). BODENSEE – [12] and 🍷 Emden - Münster - Karlsruhe - Konstanz. Aug. 1 - Sept. 13 arrives Mannheim 1258, Karlsruhe 1338.
2006 – BODENSEE – [12] and 🍷 Konstanz - Karlsruhe - Dortmund.
2010 – LORELEY – [12] Tübingen Hbf (d. 0611) - Stuttgart - Düsseldorf (- Dortmund - Berlin ⑤**f**).
2011 – ①②③④⑦ (not June 18, 19, Oct. 2). [12] (Berlin ⑦ -) Düsseldorf - Koblenz - Stuttgart. Continues to Tübingen (a. 1950) on ①–④ (not June 18, 19, Oct. 2). Conveys 🍷 on ⑦.
2012/3 – ALLGÄU – [12] and ✕ Oberstdorf - Kempten - Ulm - Stuttgart - Köln - Dortmund - Hannover (- Magdeburg - Leipzig ♣) and v.v.
2014 – [12] and 🍷 Stuttgart - Münster - Emden.
2018/9 – ⑥ to Oct. 18 (also June 19). NORDERNEY – [12] Stuttgart - Münster - Emden - Norddeich Mole and v.v.
2027 – [12] and 🍷 Hamburg - Regensburg - Passau. July 4 - Oct. 5 (also June 14, 20, 21, 22, 27, 28, 29, Oct. 10, 11, 17, 18, 19, 24, 31) runs with train number **2327** and starts from Fehmarn-Burg (Table **825**).
2158 – [12] (Leipzig ①–⑥**e** -) Frankfurt - Wiesbaden. Conveys 🍷 on ①–⑥**e**.
2213 – RÜGEN – [12] and 🍷 Ostseebad Binz - Stralsund - Rostock - Hamburg - Stuttgart.
2216 – [12] and 🍷 Stuttgart - Hamburg - Rostock - Stralsund (- Greifswald Ⓐ).
2217 – [12] and 🍷 (Greifswald Ⓐ -) Stralsund - Rostock - Hamburg - Stuttgart.
2220 – Daily to Oct. 19; ⑤ from Oct. 24. FEHMARN – [12] and 🍷 Frankfurt - Köln - Hamburg - Lübeck (- Fehmarn-Burg until Oct. 19).
2221 – Daily until Oct. 19; ⑤⑦ from Oct. 24. FEHMARN – [12] and 🍷 (Until Oct. 19: Fehmarn-Burg -) Lübeck - Hamburg - Köln - Frankfurt.
2226 – [12] and 🍷 (Passau ⑥**z** -) (Regensburg ♥ -) (Nürnberg ①–⑥**e** -) Frankfurt - Köln - Kiel.
2229 – [12] and 🍷 Kiel - Köln - Frankfurt (- Nürnberg Ⓑ**q**) (- Passau ⑤**m**).
2253 – [12] and 🍷 Wiesbaden - Frankfurt (- Leipzig Ⓑ).
2259 – [12] and 🍷 Wiesbaden - Frankfurt - Erfurt (- Leipzig ⑤⑦**d**).
2318 – [12] and 🍷 Stuttgart - Köln (- Dortmund Ⓑ**q**) (- Münster ⑦).

A – [12] and ✕ Dortmund - Regensburg - Passau - Linz - Wien and v.v.
B – From / to Berlin (Table **810**).
E – From / to Westerland (Table **821**).
H – To / from Hamburg (Table **900**).
L – To / from Leipzig (Table **850**).
N – From Hannover (Table **810**).
P – From Passau (Table **920**).
R – From Oct. 27.
S – Until Oct. 26.
T – From Oct. 20.
Z – To / from Zürich (Tables **510**).

a – Not June 19, 20, Oct. 3.
b – Ⓑ only.
c – 3–10 minutes **earlier** July 31 - Sept. 14.
d – Also Oct. 2; not Oct. 3.
e – ①–⑥ (not Oct. 4).
f – ⑤ (also June 18, Oct. 2; not June 20, Oct. 3).
g – Not July 26 - Sept. 7.

╏ – Also June 20, 21, Oct. 4.
♣ – Not June 20, 21, Oct. 4.
• – 1219 Aug. 2 - Sept. 14.
‡ – 1610 until July 12.
§ – ①–⑤ (not June 19, Oct. 3). Arrives Mainz 0836 July 28 - Sept. 5.
¶ – Train number **1676** on ⑦ (also June 20, 21, Oct. 4).
★ – ①②③④⑥ from Oct. 20.
♥ – ②–⑥ (not June 21, Aug. 16, Oct. 4).
◇ – Also calls at Boppard Hbf (d. 0543).
⊖ – Also calls at Boppard Hbf (d. 0757).
⊙ – Also calls at Boppard Hbf (d. 0043).
⊕ – Train number **1010** on ⑤⑥ (also Oct. 2). Train number **1190** on ⑦. Also conveys ✕ on ①–④ (not Oct. 2).
♣ – See Table **866** for running dates to / from Magdeburg and Leipzig.
⊡ – From / to Duisburg (Table **800**). For *City Night Line* cars (🛏 1, 2 cl., 🛌 2 cl. and [2]) see Table **912**.
◧ – Frankfurt Flughafen Fernbahnhof.

h – ①–⑥ only.
j – Not Aug. 1 - Sept. 12.
k – Also June 19, Oct. 3.
m – Also June 18, Aug. 14, Oct. 2; not June 20, Aug. 15, Oct. 3.
n – Not June 19, 20.
o – Not June 15, 16, 22, 23.
q – Ⓑ (not Oct. 3).
r – 1937 on ⑤⑦ (also June 19).
t – Not June 14 - July 11.
u – Also June 19.
v – Also June 18, Oct. 2; not June 20, Oct. 3.
w – ⑦ only.
x – 11–20 minutes later July 31 - Sept. 14.
y – 1359 until July 12.
z – Also June 19, Aug. 15, Oct. 3; not June 21, Aug. 16, Oct. 4.

MANNHEIM and FRANKFURT - MAINZ - KOBLENZ — 911

	IC 2014 ⑤f 🍷♦	ICE 1026 ✗	IC 2012 ✗♦	IC 2250 L🍷	EC 8 ✗♦	IC 2022 ✗	ICE 712 ①–⑤ a🍷	IC 118 ♦	ICE 1558 L✗	EC 6 Z✗	EC 114 🍷♦	IC 2316 Ⓑ	ICE 26 ✗♦	IC 2154 L🍷	IC 2318 🍷♦	ICE 1522 ✗	IC 1910 ⑦ 🍷	ICE 1554 L✗	IC 2210 Ⓑq 🍷	IC 2096 ⑦	ICE 22 A✗		ICE 510 ⊕ 🍷	IC 2020 ⊙
Basel SBB **912** d.	...	...	...	...	1220c	...	...	...	...	1420c	...	...	...	...	...	...	...	...	...	...	...	...	...	...
Karlsruhe Hbf **912** d.	...	...	...	...	1412c	...	...	...	...	1612c	...	...	...	...	...	...	...	...	...	...	...	...	...	...
München Hbf **930** d.	...	...	...	...	|	...	...	...	...	|	1346	...	...	...	...	1616‡	1620	...	...	...	...	...	1928	...
Stuttgart Hbf **912** d.	1209	...	1314	...	|	...	1434	1512	...	|	1609	1636	...	...	1741	|	1914	...	1918r	2035	...	...	2151	...
Mannheim Hbf **911a** d.	1258	...	1408	...	1439	...	1533	1608	...	1639	1658	1738	...	...	1839	|	2008	...	2039	2138	...	...	2232	...
Worms Hbf **911a** d.	1315g	...	|	...	|	...	|	|	...	|	1714g	|	...	...	|	|	|	...	|	|	...	...	|	...
Nürnberg Hbf **920** d.	|	...	|	...	|	...	|	|	...	|	|	|	1528	...	|	1734	|	...	|	|	1928	...	|	...
Frankfurt (Main) Hbf **917a** d.	|	1344	|	1442	|	1544	|	|	1642	|	|	|	1742	1842	|	1944	|	2042	|	|	2146	...	|	2324
Frankfurt Flughafen ✈ ◧ **917a** d.	|	1358	|	1458	|	1558	|	|	1658	|	|	|	1758	1858	|	1958	|	2058	|	|	2159	...	2313	2338
Mainz Hbf **911a 917a** a.	1339	1418	1446	1515	1518	1618	1615	1646	1715	1718	1744	1815	1818	1915	1918	2018	2046	2115	2118	2215	2218	...	2330	2359
Mainz Hbf **914 917a** d.	1341	1420	1448	1517	1520	1620	1617	1648	1717	1720	1746	1817	1820	1917	1920	2020	2048	2117	2120	...	2220	...	2332	0001
Wiesbaden Hbf **917a** a.	|	|	|	1531	|	|	1631	|	1731	|	|	1831	|	1931	|	|	|	2131	|	...	|	...	2343	|
Bingen (Rhein) Hbf **914 917a** d.	1406	|	1506	...	|	|	|	1706	...	|	1806	...	|	...	|	|	2106	...	|	...	|	...	...	0018
Koblenz Hbf **914 917a** a.	1441	1511	1541	...	1611	1711	|	1741	...	1811	1841	...	1911	...	2011	2111	2141	...	2211	...	2311	...	...	0055
Bonn Hbf **800** a.	1520	1542	1620	...	1642	1742	|	1820	...	1842t	1920	...	1942	...	2042	2142	2220	...	2242	...	2342	...	...	0133
Köln Hbf **800** a.	1542	1605	1642	...	1705	1805	1801	1842	...	1905t	1942	...	2005	...	2105	2205	2242	...	2305	...	0005	...	...	0156
Dortmund Hbf **800** a.	...	1721	1808	...	1821	1921	...	...	...	2021	2100	...	2120	...	2221q	2321	2359	...	...	...	0121	...	...	0333
Hamburg Hbf **800** a.	...	2012	...	...	2112	2212	...	...	...	2314b	...	...	0015	...	...	...	...	...	...	...	...	...	...	0651

← FOR NOTES SEE PREVIOUS PAGE

RE / RB services

Local services MAINZ - MANNHEIM and MAINZ - SPEYER - KARLSUHE — 911a

SUBJECT TO ALTERATION JULY 26 - SEPT. 7 (services between Germersheim and Karlsruhe are also subject to alteration Sept. 8 – 14)

km			Ⓐe	⚒r	Ⓐe		⚒r				Ⓐe							Ⓐe			Ⓐe			Ⓐe	Ⓒz	Ⓐe
0	**Mainz** Hbf **911** d.	0022	0456	0515	0545	0552b	0622	0656	0722r	0752	0813	0822e	0852	0952	1013	1052	1152	1213	1252	1352	1413	1452	1554	1613	1613	1628
46	Worms Hbf **911** a.	0106	0540	0555	0614	0633b	0706	0739	0806r	0836	0839	0903e	0936	1036	1039	1136	1236	1239	1336	1436	1439	1536	1636	1639	1639	1717
46	Worms Hbf **911** d.	...	0541	0556	0615	0635	0712	0746	0816	0848	0840	0916	0948	1048	1040	1148	1249	1240	1348	1448	1440	1548	1648	1640	1640	1717
67	Ludwigshafen Hbf **918** d.	...	0558	0616	0636	0653	0732	0804	0837	0909	0856	0937	1009	1109	1056	1209	1309	1256	1409	1509	1456	1609	1709	1655	1656	1737
87	Speyer Hbf **918** d.	...	|	|	0655	|	|	|	|	|	0913	|	|	|	1113	|	|	1313	|	|	1513	|	|	|	1714	|
101	Germersheim **918** a.	...	|	|	0709	|	|	|	|	|	0921	|	|	|	1121	|	|	1321	|	|	1521	|	|	|	1721	|
138	**Karlsruhe** Hbf a.	...	|	|	...	|	|	|	|	|	0953	|	|	|	1152	|	|	1352	|	|	1552	|	|	1748h	1752	|
70	**Mannheim** Hbf **911** a.	...	0603	0621	...	0658	0737	0811	0842	0914	...	0942	1014	1114	...	1214	1314	...	1414	1514	...	1614	1714	1700	...	1742

		Ⓐe				Ⓐe		Ⓑb			
Mainz Hbf **911** d.	1652	1718	1752	1813	1852	1922	1952	2013	2052	2152	2325
Worms Hbf **911** a.	1736	1744	1836	1839	1936	2006	2036	2039	2136	2240	0006
Worms Hbf **911** d.	1749	1746	1848	1840	1948	2018	2048	2040	2148	2241	0007
Ludwigshafen Hbf **918** d.	1809	1801	1909	1856	2009	2038	2109	2057	2209	2302	0023
Speyer Hbf **918** d.	|	1818	|	1915	|	|	|	2114	|	|	|
Germersheim **918** a.	|	1830	|	1923	|	|	|	2122	|	|	|
Karlsruhe Hbf a.	|	...	|	1952	|	|	|	2152	|	|	|
Mannheim Hbf **911** a.	1814	...	1914	...	2014	2043	2114	...	2214	2307	0029

		⚒r	Ⓐe	⑥k	Ⓐe	Ⓐe		⚒r	Ⓐe	
Mannheim Hbf **911** d.	0012	0430	0500	0527	0534	0550	...	0618	...	0650
Karlsruhe Hbf d.	|	|	|	|	|	|	...	|	...	|
Germersheim **918** d.	|	|	|	|	|	|	...	|	0620	|
Speyer Hbf **918** d.	|	|	|	|	|	|	...	|	0632	|
Ludwigshafen Hbf **918** d.	0017	0436	0505	0533	0541	0558	...	0624	0655	0659
Worms Hbf **911** a.	0039	0454	0523	0551	0559	0615	...	0644	0711	0718
Worms Hbf **911** d.	...	0455	0525	0553	0600	0622	0622	0653	0712	0725
Mainz Hbf **911** a.	...	0537	0607	0636	0637	0706	0706	0737	0746	0807

	Ⓐe	Ⓒz	Ⓐe		Ⓐe	Ⓐe						Ⓐe			Ⓐe									Ⓐe		
Mannheim Hbf **911** d.	...	0744	0748	0844	...	0916	0944	1044	...	1144	1244	...	1344	1444	...	1544	1644	...	1744	1844	...	1944	2044	...	2144	2248
Karlsruhe Hbf d.	...	|	|	|	0808	|	|	|	1008	|	|	1208	|	|	1408	|	|	1608	|	|	1808	|	|	2008	|	|
Germersheim **918** d.	0718	|	|	|	0838	|	|	|	1038	|	|	1238	|	|	1438	|	|	1638	|	|	1838	|	|	2038	|	|
Speyer Hbf **918** d.	0728	|	|	|	0847	|	|	|	1047	|	|	1247	|	|	1447	|	|	1647	|	|	1847	|	|	2047	|	|
Ludwigshafen Hbf **918** d.	0750	0750	0755	0850	0904	0921	0950	1050	1104	1150	1250	1304	1350	1450	1504	1550	1650	1704	1750	1850	1904	1950	2050	2105	2150	2253
Worms Hbf **911** a.	0804	0816	0816	0914	0919	0937	1014	1111	1119	1214	1311	1319	1414	1514	1519	1614	1714	1719	1813	1913	1919	2014	2114	2119	2213	2312
Worms Hbf **911** d.	0805	0825	0825	0925	0920	0955	1025	1125	1120	1225	1325	1320	1425	1525	1520	1625	1725	1720	1825	1925	1920	2025	2125	2120	2225	2315
Mainz Hbf **911** a.	0836	0907	0907	1007	0947	1036	1107	1207	1147	1307	1407	1347	1507	1608	1547	1707	1807	1747	1907	2007	1947	2107	2207	2147	2307	2400

b – Ⓑ (also Nov. 1). e – Ⓐ (not June 19). h – Not July 28 - Sept. 12. Via Hockenheim. k – Not Nov. 1. r – ⚒ (not June 19, Nov. 1). z – Also June 19.

FRANKFURT - BASEL and STUTTGART — 912

km	km		ICE 619 ♣	ICE 879 ①	CNL 479 🅁 🍷♦	CNL 40419 🅁 🍷♦	IC 61419 D2	CNL 419 🅁 🍷♦	CNL 1258 🅁◇ 🍷♦	IC 60458 Ⓐ 2	IC 60458 Ⓒ 2	ICE 3 Ⓐ ✗	2	①–⑤ 2	RJ 63 Ⓒ ♦	IC 2099 ①–⑤ d	ICE 991 Ⓐ A✗	ICE 271 ① N✗	ICE 271 ⚒ N✗	2	TGV 9578 ①–⑥ 🅁♦	①–⑤ 2	IC 181 ①–⑤ d	EC 217 🍷♦	ICE 511 🍷
		Berlin Hbf **810** d.	...	2032p	...	...	...	...	2215	...	...	...	...	...	...	...	...	...	...	...	...	...	...	...	...
		Hamburg Hbf **800 900** d.	...	|	2011z	...	...	...	|	...	...	...	...	...	...	...	...	0025c	...	...	...	...	...	...	...
		Hannover Hbf **810 900** d.	...	|	2216	...	...	...	|	...	...	...	...	...	...	...	...	0150	...	...	...	...	...	...	...
		Dortmund Hbf **800** d.	2058	|	|	...	...	...	|	...	...	...	...	...	...	...	...	|	...	...	...	...	...	...	0437g
		Köln Hbf **800 910** d.	2230	|	|	2346	2346	2346	|	...	...	...	...	...	...	...	...	|	...	...	...	...	...	...	0555
		Koblenz Hbf **911** d.	|	|	|	0040	0040	0040	|	...	...	...	...	...	...	...	...	|	...	...	...	...	...	...	|
		Mainz Hbf **911** d.	|	|	|	|	0138b	|	|	...	...	...	...	...	...	...	0539	|	...	...	...	...	...	...	|
0	0	**Frankfurt** (Main) Hbf **913** d.	0005	0109	|	|	|	|	|	0402j	0402j	...	...	...	0517r	0520	|	0538e	0538e	...	...	...	0556	...	|
		Frankfurt Flughafen ✈ ◧ d.	0028	|	|	0156	0156	0156	|	|	|	...	...	...	0539	|	|	0555e	0555e	...	...	...	|	...	0653
78		**Mannheim** Hbf **913** a.	0104	0149	|	|	0233	|	0443s	0443	0443	...	...	...	0611	|	0622	0625e	0625e	...	...	...	|	...	0723
78		**Mannheim** Hbf **913** d.	0106	0152	|	|	0404	|	|	0445	0445	...	...	...	0613	|	0630	0627e	0627e	...	...	...	|	0712	0731
	28	Darmstadt Hbf **913** d.	|	|	|	|	|	|	|	|	|	...	...	...	|	0537	|	|	|	...	...	...	0613	|	|
	50	Bensheim **913** d.	|	|	|	|	|	|	|	|	|	...	...	...	|	0550	|	|	|	...	...	...	0625	|	|
	64	Weinheim **913** d.	|	|	|	|	|	|	|	|	|	...	...	...	|	0600	|	|	|	...	...	...	0636	|	|
	87	**Heidelberg** Hbf **913 931** d.	0119	|	|	|	|	|	0458s	0500	0500	...	...	...	|	0615	|	|	|	...	...	...	0655	|	|
	120	Bruchsal **913 931** d.	0136	|	|	|	|	|	|	0523	0523	...	...	...	|	|	|	|	|	...	...	...	|	|	|
		Vaihingen (Enz) **931** d.	0248	|	|	|	|	|	|	|	|	...	...	...	|	|	|	|	|	...	...	...	|	|	|
		Stuttgart Hbf **931** a.	0320	|	|	|	|	0417	|	|	|	...	...	...	0652	0700	0708	|	|	...	...	...	0737	0754	0808
		München Hbf **930** a.	0602	|	|	|	|	0710	|	|	|	...	...	...	0910	...	0927	|	|	...	...	...	|	1011	1027
138	141	**Karlsruhe** Hbf **913 916** d.	0152a	0220	0437s	0437s	0439	...	0540s	0542	0551	0556	...	...	...	...	...	0656	0656	...	0733	...	|	...	...
169	172	Baden-Baden **916** d.	...	...	|	|	|	...	|	|	0610	0612	...	...	...	...	...	0714	0714	...	|	...	|	...	...
209		Offenburg **916** ☆ d.	...	...	0519s	0519s	0521	...	0620s	0622	0629	0629	0632	0704	...	...	...	0730	0730	0734	|	0804	⊙	...	...
	217	Kehl 🏛 d.	...	...	|	|	|	...	|	|	|	|	0653	0722	...	...	...	|	|	0752	|	0822	|	...	...
	225	**Strasbourg** a.	...	...	|	|	|	...	|	|	|	|	0704	0734	...	...	...	|	|	0805	0811	0834	|	...	...
272		**Freiburg** (Brsg) Hbf ☆ d.	...	...	0555s	0555s	0558	...	0705s	0707	0702	0702	...	...	...	...	...	0802	0802	...	...	...	|	...	...
30*		**Basel** Bad Bf 🏛 ☆ a.	...	...	0636	0636	0636	...	0746	0746	0735	0735	...	...	...	...	...	0835	0835	...	...	...	|	...	...
35*		**Basel** SBB ☆ a.	...	...	0647	0647	0647	...	0754	0754	0747	0747	...	...	...	...	...	0847	0847	...	...	...	|	...	...
		Zürich HB **510** a.	...	...	0834t	0834t	...	...	0917	...	...	0900	...	...	...	...	...	...	...	...	...	...	1055	...	...

– **NOTES** (LISTED BY TRAIN NUMBER)

3 – Ⓒ (also June 19). (12) and ✗ Frankfurt - Salzburg - Wien - Budapest.
17 – (12) and 🍷 Saarbrücken - Salzburg - Bischofshofen - Graz.
19 – POLLUX – 🛏 1, 2 cl., ▬ 2 cl., (2) (reclining) and 🍷 Amsterdam - München.
79 – KOMET – Conveys 🛏 1, 2 cl., ▬ 2 cl., (2) (reclining) and 🍷.
258 – SIRIUS – 🛏 1, 2 cl., ▬ 2 cl., (2) (reclining) and 🍷 (Ostseebad Binz ♥ -) Berlin - Basel - Zürich. Train number **1250** on ⑥ July 5 - Aug. 30. Conveys 🛏 1, 2 cl., ▬ 2 cl. and (2) (*CNL* **458** – CANOPUS) Praha - Dresden - Leipzig - Erfurt - Zürich.
578 – (12) and 🍷 Stuttgart - Strasbourg - Paris.
0419 – PEGASUS – 🛏 1, 2 cl., ▬ 2 cl., (2) (reclining) and 🍷 Amsterdam - Zürich.

– From Wiesbaden Hbf (d. 0523).
– From Duisburg (Table **800**).
– To Interlaken (Table **560**).

a – Arrival time (calls before Vaihingen). 0158 on the mornings July 18 - Sept. 30.
b – Not the mornings of June 15, 16, 22, 23.
c – 0012 on June 16, 23.
d – Not June 19, Oct. 3.
e – 3 – 4 minutes **earlier** July 26 - Sept. 13
g – ① only.
j – Frankfurt (Main) **Süd**.
p – Previous day.
r – 0522 on † (also June 19).
s – Stops to set down only.
t – 0820 on ⑥⑦.
y – 0232 on the mornings July 21 - Sept. 29.
z – 1918 on ①–⑤ to July 25; 2027 on ⑥. 1925 on ⑦ to July 27; 2025 on ⑦ from Aug. 3.

♣ – (12) Dortmund - Frankfurt - Mannheim - Karlsruhe - Stuttgart - München.
◇ – On the mornings of Ⓒ arrives Offenburg 0627, Freiburg 0700, Basel Bad Bf 0735, Basel SBB 0747.
♥ – ⑥ July 5 - Aug. 30.
⊙ – Via Schaffhausen (Table **940**).
☆ – See panel on page 426 for other local services.
◧ – Frankfurt Flughafen Fernbahnhof.
* – Distance via Katzenberg Tunnel (3 km further via the original route).

912 FRANKFURT - BASEL and STUTTGART

	ICE 5	IC 2053	CNL 473		IC 2273	ICE 711	IC 2317	ICE 591	ICE 999	ICE 101	TGV 9576		EC 113	IC 2319	ICE 1013	ICE 275		ICE 571	IC 2275	IC 2271	ICE 1091	ICE 593	ICE 103		ICE 71
	⊗	①–⑤	[R]	①–⑤	Ⓐn	①–⑤	⑥k	①–⑥	⑦	⊗		⑥⑦		⚒	⊖	⊗	①–⑤	①–⑥	⑤f		Ⓐn	Ⓒc		⑥⑦	⊗
	✕	m S	🍷◆	2	L🍷	m🍷	B	✕	✕	🍷	[R]◆	2	✕◆	🍷	M🍷	N✕	2	g✕	🍷	🍷◆	✕	✕	🍷	2	✕
Berlin Hbf **810** d.	...	...	...	...	...	...	...	...	...	...	...	...	...	...	...	0432a	...	...	...	...	0606*	0531	...	...	...
Hamburg Hbf **800 900** d.	...	...	0029	...	...	...	...	0346a	...	...	...	...	...	...	...	│	...	0516•	...	...	│	│	...	...	0618h
Hannover Hbf **810 900** d.	...	...	│	...	...	...	...	0520	...	...	...	...	...	...	...	│	...	0641	0601	0601	│	│	0540	...	0741
Dortmund Hbf **800** d.	...	...	│	...	...	...	...	│	...	0537	...	...	...	0537	0638	│	...	│	│	│	│	│	0737	...	│
Köln Hbf **800 910** d.	...	...	│	...	...	0611	...	│	...	0655	...	...	...	0653	0755	│	...	│	│	│	│	│	0855	...	│
Koblenz Hbf **911** d.	...	...	│	...	...	│	...	│	...	│	...	...	...	0748	│	│	...	│	│	│	│	│	│	...	│
Mainz Hbf **911** d.	...	...	│	...	...	0746	0746	│	...	│	...	...	...	0839	│	│	...	│	│	│	│	│	│	...	│
Frankfurt (Main) Hbf **913** d.	0650	...	│	...	0714	│	│	0750	0750	│	...	...	0822	│	│	0850	...	0905	0920	0920	0950	0950	│	...	1005
Frankfurt Flughafen ✈ d.	│	...	│	...	│	│	│	│	│	0753	...	...	│	│	0853	│	...	0920	│	│	│	│	0953	...	│
Mannheim Hbf **913** a.	0727	...	0750s	...	│	0824	0824	0827	0827	0823	...	...	│	0921	0923	0927	...	0954	│	│	1027	1027	1023	...	1043
Mannheim Hbf **913** d.	0736	0753	│	...	│	0826	0826	0830	0830	0836	...	...	│	0923	0931	0936	...	0956	│	│	1030	1030	1036‡	...	1045
Darmstadt Hbf **913** d.	│	│	│	...	0731	│	│	│	│	│	...	...	0838	│	│	│	...	│	0937	0937	│	│	│	...	│
Bensheim **913** d.	│	│	│	...	0746	│	│	│	│	│	...	...	0850	│	│	│	...	│	0950	0950	│	│	│	...	│
Weinheim **913** d.	│	│	│	...	0758	│	│	│	│	│	...	...	0900	│	│	│	...	│	1000	1000	│	│	│	...	│
Heidelberg Hbf **913 931** d.	│	0806	│	...	0814	0838	0838	│	│	│	...	...	0914	0936	│	│	...	│	1014	1014	│	│	│	...	│
Bruchsal **913 931** d.	│	│	│	...	0836	│	│	│	│	│	...	...	│	│	│	│	...	│	│	1036	│	│	│	...	│
Vaihingen (Enz) **931** d.	│	│	│	...	│	0905	0906	│	│	│	...	...	│	│	│	│	...	│	1055	│	│	│	│	...	│
Stuttgart Hbf **931** a.	│	0846	│	...	│	0924	0924	0908	0908	│	...	...	0954	1018	1008	│	...	1035	1112	│	1108	1108	│	...	│
München Hbf **930** a.	│	▬	│	...	│	...	...	1127	1127	│	...	...	1210	...	1227	│	...	...	...	│	1327	1327	│	...	│
Karlsruhe Hbf **913 916** d.	0800	...	0816s	...	0850	...	...	...	...	0900	0933	...	...	...	...	1000	...	...	...	1050	...	...	1100	...	1110
Baden-Baden **916** d.	│	2	│	...	...	...	...	...	...	0917	│	...	...	...	...	│	...	...	...	...	...	...	│	...	1126
Offenburg **916** ☆ d.	0829	0834	0856s	0904	...	...	...	...	...	0933	│	1004	...	...	...	1029	1034	...	...	...	...	...	1129	1204	│
Kehl 🏛 d.	│	0852	│	0922	...	...	...	...	...	│	│	1022	...	...	...	│	1051	...	...	...	...	...	│	1224	│
Strasbourg a.	│	0904	│	0934	...	...	...	...	...	│	1011	1034	...	...	...	│	1104	...	...	...	...	...	│	1236	│
Freiburg (Brsg) Hbf ☆ d.	0901	...	0937s	...	...	...	...	...	...	1004	...	...	...	...	...	1101	...	...	...	...	...	...	1201	...	1212
Basel Bad Bf 🏛 ☆ a.	0934	...	1014	...	...	...	...	...	...	1037	...	...	...	...	...	1134	...	...	...	...	...	...	1234	...	1245
Basel SBB ☆ a.	0947	...	1030	...	...	...	...	...	...	1047	...	...	...	...	...	1147	...	...	...	...	...	...	1247	...	1254
Zürich HB **510** a.	1100	...	...	...	...	...	...	...	...	...	...	...	...	...	...	...	...	...	...	...	...	...	...	...	...

	IC 2293	EC 115	EC 7	ICE 515	ICE 297	ICE 277	IC 119	ICE 973	ICE 573	IC 2277	ICE 595	ICE 505		ICE 73	TGV 9574		EC 219	IC 2005	EC 9	ICE 517	ICE 279	IC 2013	ICE 575	IC 2279	IC 2055
			⊕		⑦⊗	①–⑥		①–⑥	⑦¶	Ⓒ			①–⑤	⊗		⑥⑦		⑤⑥	⊕		⊗				⑤f
	🍷	🍷◆	✕	🍷	N✕	⊗N	◆	g K	✕	🍷◆	✕	🍷◆	2	K✕	[R]P	2	🍷◆	🍷◆	✕	🍷	✕	✕◆	✕	🍷◆	S
Berlin Hbf **810** d.	...	...	...	...	0557r	0632	...	✕	...	...	0734	...	...	...	...	...	...	...	...	...	0832	...	...	...	...
Hamburg Hbf **800 900** d.	...	...	0442e	0525	│	│	...	0723•	0723•	0624y	│	...	...	0824•	...	...	...	...	0646	...	│	...	0924•	0828e	...
Hannover Hbf **810 900** d.	...	...	│	│	│	│	...	0841	0841	0801y	│	...	...	0941	...	...	...	...	│	...	│	0740	1041	1001e	...
Dortmund Hbf **800** d.	...	...	0737	0837	│	│	...	│	│	│	│	...	...	│	...	...	...	...	0937	1037	│	0952	│	│	...
Köln Hbf **800 910** d.	...	0818	0853	0955	│	│	0918	│	│	│	│	1055	...	│	...	...	...	1018	1053	1155	│	1118	│	│	...
Koblenz Hbf **911** d.	...	0918	0948	│	│	│	1018	│	│	│	│	│	...	│	...	...	...	1118	1148	│	│	1218	│	│	...
Mainz Hbf **911** d.	...	1017	1039	│	│	│	1113	│	│	│	│	│	...	│	...	...	...	1217	1239	│	│	1313	│	│	...
Frankfurt (Main) Hbf **913** d.	1020	│	│	│	1050	1050	│	1105	1105	1120	1150	│	...	1205	...	...	1220	│	│	│	1250	│	1305	1320	...
Frankfurt Flughafen ✈ d.	│	│	│	1053	│	│	│	1120	1120	│	│	1153	...	│	...	...	│	│	│	1253	│	│	1320	│	...
Mannheim Hbf **913** a.	│	1100	1121	1123	1127	1127	1152	1154	1154	│	1227	1223	...	1243	...	...	│	1307	1321	1323	1327	1352	1354	│	...
Mannheim Hbf **913** d.	│	1102	1123	1131	1136	1136	1154	1156	1156	│	1230	1236‡	...	1245	...	...	│	1309	1323	1331	1336	1354	1356	│	1424
Darmstadt Hbf **913** d.	1037	│	│	│	│	│	│	│	│	1137	│	│	...	│	...	...	1237	│	│	│	│	│	│	1337	│
Bensheim **913** d.	│	│	│	│	│	│	│	│	│	1150	│	│	...	│	...	...	1250	│	│	│	│	│	│	1350	│
Weinheim **913** d.	1056	│	│	│	│	│	│	│	│	1200	│	│	...	│	...	...	1300	│	│	│	│	│	│	1400	│
Heidelberg Hbf **913 931** d.	1110	│	│	│	│	│	1206	│	│	1214	│	│	...	│	...	...	1314	│	│	│	│	1406	│	1414	1437
Bruchsal **913 931** d.	│	│	│	│	│	│	│	│	│	1236	│	│	...	│	...	...	│	│	│	│	│	│	│	1436	│
Vaihingen (Enz) **931** d.	│	1137	│	│	│	│	│	│	│	│	│	│	...	│	...	...	│	│	│	│	│	│	│	│	1505
Stuttgart Hbf **931** a.	1150	1153	│	1208	│	│	1246	1235	1235	│	1308	│	...	│	...	...	1354	│	│	1408	│	1446	1435	│	1523
München Hbf **930** a.	...	1411	│	1427	│	│	▬	▬	...	│	1528	│	...	│	...	...	1611	│	│	1627	│	▬	▬	│	...
Karlsruhe Hbf **913 916** d.	...	...	1149	...	1200	1200	...	①–⑤	...	1250	...	1300	...	1310	1333	...	...	1336	1349	...	1400	...	①–⑤	1452	...
Baden-Baden **916** d.	...	...	1207	...	│	│	2	2	...	...	...	│	...	1326	│	...	...	1356	1407	...	│	2	2	1516e	...
Offenburg **916** ☆ d.	...	...	│	...	1229	1229	1234	1304	...	...	...	1329	1334	│	│	1403	...	1415	│	...	1429	1434	1504	1534e	...
Kehl 🏛 d.	...	...	│	...	│	│	1252	1322	...	...	...	│	1352	│	│	1422	...	...	│	...	│	1452	1522	...	...
Strasbourg a.	...	...	│	...	│	│	1304	1334	...	...	...	│	1404	│	1411	1434	...	...	│	...	│	1504	1535	...	...
Freiburg (Brsg) Hbf ☆ d.	...	...	1255	...	1301	1301	...	...	...	...	...	1401	...	1412	...	...	...	...	1455	...	1501	...	...	...	...
Basel Bad Bf 🏛 ☆ a.	...	...	1327	...	1334	1334	...	...	...	...	...	1434	...	1445	...	...	...	...	1527	...	1534	...	...	...	...
Basel SBB ☆ a.	...	...	1335	...	1347	1347	...	...	...	...	...	1447	...	1454	...	...	...	...	1535	...	1547	...	...	...	...
Zürich HB **510** a.	...	...	1500	...	...	...	...	...	...	...	...	...	...	1600	...	...	...	...	1700	...	...	...	...	...	...

	ICE 597	ICE 107	ICE 1107	TGV 9580	ICE 75	TGV 9580	IC 2299	EC 117	IC 2351	IC 2313	ICE 519	ICE 371	ICE 577	IC 1911	IC 2371	ICE 599	ICE 109		ICE 77	TGV 9572	EC 391	IC 2217	ICE 611	ICE 373	
		⑦⊗	①–⑥	[R]	⊗	[R]	⑥	Ⓑ	⑤⑦			⊗		⑤⑦				①–⑤ 2	⊗	⑥⑦				⊗	
	✕	🍷	⊗D	🍷◆	✕	🍷◆	🍷	🍷◆	f S	🍷	🍷	N✕	✕	v🍷	E🍷	✕	🍷	...	K✕	[R]P	🍷◆	🍷◆	🍷	N✕	2
Berlin Hbf **810** d.	0934	...	🍷	...	...	...	...	...	...	...	...	1032	...	...	...	1134	...	...	...	...	...	...	...	1232	...
Hamburg Hbf **800 900** d.	│	...	...	...	1024•	...	...	...	...	0846	...	│	1124•	...	1028◊	│	...	...	1224•	...	...	1046	...	│	...
Hannover Hbf **810 900** d.	│	...	...	...	1141	...	...	...	...	│	...	│	1241	...	1201	│	...	...	1341	...	...	│	...	│	...
Dortmund Hbf **800** d.	│	1137	...	...	│	...	...	...	...	1137	1237	│	│	1152	│	│	1337q	...	│	...	...	1337	1437	│	...
Köln Hbf **800 910** d.	│	1255	1256d	...	│	...	...	...	...	1253	1355	│	│	1318	│	│	1455	...	│	...	...	1453	1556	│	...
Koblenz Hbf **911** d.	│	│	│	...	│	...	...	...	...	1348	│	│	│	1418	│	│	│	...	│	...	...	1548	│	│	...
Mainz Hbf **911** d.	│	│	│	...	│	...	...	...	...	1439	│	│	│	1513	│	│	│	...	│	...	...	1639	│	│	...
Frankfurt (Main) Hbf **913** d.	1350	│	│	1401	1405	...	1420	1420	...	│	│	1450	1505	│	1520	1550	│	...	1605	...	1620	│	│	1650	...
Frankfurt Flughafen ✈ d.	│	1353	1353	│	│	...	│	│	...	│	1453	│	1520	│	│	│	1553	...	│	...	│	│	1653	│	...
Mannheim Hbf **913** a.	1427	1423	1423	1437	1443	...	│	│	...	1521	1523	1527	1554	1552	│	1627	1623	...	1643	...	│	1721	1723	1727	...
Mannheim Hbf **913** d.	1430	1434	1434	1440	1445	...	│	│	1518	1523	1531	1536	1556	1554	│	1630	1636‡	...	1645	...	│	1723	1731	1736	...
Darmstadt Hbf **913** d.	│	│	│	│	│	...	1437	1437	│	│	│	│	│	│	1537	│	│	...	│	...	1637	│	│	│	...
Bensheim **913** d.	│	│	│	│	│	...	│	1450	│	│	│	│	│	│	1550	│	│	...	│	...	1650	│	│	│	...
Weinheim **913** d.	│	│	│	│	│	...	1456	1500	│	│	│	│	│	│	1600	│	│	...	│	...	1700	│	│	│	...
Heidelberg Hbf **913 931** d.	│	│	│	│	│	...	1510	1514	│	1536	│	│	│	1606	1614	│	│	...	│	...	1714	1736	│	│	...
Bruchsal **913 931** d.	│	│	│	│	│	...	│	│	│	│	│	│	│	│	1636	│	│	...	│	...	│	│	│	│	...
Vaihingen (Enz) **931** d.	│	│	│	│	│	...	│	│	│	1605	│	│	│	│	│	│	│	...	│	...	│	1808	│	│	...
Stuttgart Hbf **931** a.	1508	│	│	│	│	...	1550	1554	1612	1622	1608	│	1635	1646	│	1708	│	...	│	...	1754	1825	1808	│	...
München Hbf **930** a.	1728	│	│	│	│	←	▬	1811	...	...	1827	│	▬	▬	│	1927	│	...	│	...	2011	▬	2027	│	...
Karlsruhe Hbf **913 916** d.	...	1500	1500	1502	1510	1513	...	...	...	...	...	1600	①–⑤	...	1652	...	1700	...	1710	1733	...	①–⑤	...	1800	...
Baden-Baden **916** d.	...	│	│	→	1526	1535	2	...	...	...	...	│	2	2	1717w	...	│	...	1726	│	...	2	...	│	...
Offenburg **916** ☆ d.	...	1529	1529	...	│	│	1604	...	...	...	...	1629	1634	1704	1733w	...	1729	1734	│	│	...	1804	...	1829	1834
Kehl 🏛 d.	...	│	│	...	│	│	1622	...	...	...	...	│	1652	1722	...	...	│	1758	│	│	...	1822	...	│	1852
Strasbourg a.	...	│	│	...	│	1601	1634	...	...	...	...	│	1704	1734	...	...	│	1815	│	1811	...	1834	...	│	1904
Freiburg (Brsg) Hbf ☆ d.	...	1601	1601	...	1612	...	...	...	...	...	...	1701	...	...	...	...	1801	...	1812	...	...	...	...	1901	...
Basel Bad Bf 🏛 ☆ a.	...	1634	1634	...	1645	...	...	...	...	...	...	1734	...	...	...	...	1834	...	1845	...	...	...	...	1934	...
Basel SBB ☆ a.	...	1647	1647	...	1654	...	...	...	...	...	...	1747	...	...	...	...	1847	...	1854	...	...	...	...	1947	...
Zürich HB **510** a.	...	...	...	...	1800	...	...	...	...	...	...	...	...	...	...	...	...	...	2000	...	...	...	...	...	...

Regional trains **OFFENBURG - BASEL** (German holiday dates apply). **SERVICE FROM SEPT. 29** (SEE PAGE 563 FOR SERVICE UNTIL SEPT. 28). On Nov. 1 services run as on ⑦.

	†	Ⓐ	Ⓐ		①–⑥	⚒	Ⓐ			⚒																
Offenburg d.	0049	0428	0525	...	...	0549	0634	...	...	0706	0807	0907	1007	1107	1204	1307	1404	1507	1607	1707	1807	1907	2007	2043	...	224
Freiburg (Brsg) Hbf a.	0131	0528	0625	...	...	0649	0729	...	...	0756	0855	0955	1055	1155	1250	1355	1450	1555	1656	1756	1856	1955	2055	2142	...	234
Freiburg (Brsg) Hbf d.	0132	0529	0628	0628	...	0710	0734	...	0815	0815	0915	1015	1115	1215	1315	1415	1515	1615	1715	1815	1915	2015	...	2145	...	234
Müllheim (Baden) d.	0152	0550	0655	0655	...	0731	0751	...	0835	0835	0935	1035	1135	1235	1337	1435	1535	1635	1735	1835	1935	2035	...	2212	...	001
Basel Bad Bf 🏛 a.	0220	0625	0732	0732	0745	0806	0813	0819	0911	0911	1011	1111	1211	1311	1412	1511	1611	1711	1811	1911	2011	2111	...	2249	2319	004
Basel SBB a.	...	*0654*	...	...	0754	...	0820	0824	*0924*	*0924*	*1024*	*1124*	*1224*	*1324*	*1424*	*1524*	1620§	1720§	1820§	*1924*	*2024*	*2124*	...	...	2324	...

FOR NOTES SEE NEXT PAGE →

FRANKFURT - BASEL and STUTTGART — 912

	ICE	IC	IC	IC	ICE	ICE	ICE	TGV		IC	IC	IC	ICE	IC	ICE	IC	ICE	IC	IC	IC	ICE	ICE	ICE	ICE	ICE
	579	**2017**	**2011**	**2373**	**691**	**201**	**79**	**9570**		**2295**	**2019**	**2311**	**613**	**2264**	**375**	**2264**	**771**	**1915**	**2375**	**2385**	**693**	**203**	**1103**	**1171**	**1171**
		⑤f					⊗	R		Ⓑq	⑥			Ⓑb	⊗	Ⓑb		⑤⑦	⑦	Ⓐ		①–⑥	⑦	⊗	⑦⊗
	✕		◆	A🍷	✕	D🍷	✕	[R]P	2	🍷	◆	J🍷	🍷	🍷◆	✕	🍷◆	✕	f T	🍷	🍷	✕	⊗🍷	🍷	✕	✕
Berlin Hbf **810** d.	...	...	1008w	...	1334	...	...	...	...	...	...	...	...	...	1432	...	...	1206	...	1355	1534	...	...	...	...
Hamburg Hbf **800 900** d.	1324•	...	│	1228◊	│	...	1424•	...	...	...	...	1246	...	...	│	...	1524•	│	1428◊	│	│	...	...	1624•	1624•
Hannover Hbf **810 900** d.	1441	1156	1156w	1401	│	...	1541	...	...	...	...	│	...	...	│	...	1641	1356	1601	1601	│	...	...	1741	1741
Dortmund Hbf **800** d.	│	1352	1352w	│	│	...	│	...	...	...	...	1537	1637	...	│	...	│	1552	│	│	│	...	...	│	│
Köln Hbf **800 910** d.	│	1518	1518	│	│	1657d	│	...	...	...	1618	1653	1755	...	│	...	│	1718	│	│	│	1855	1855	│	│
Koblenz Hbf **911** d.	│	1618	1618	│	│	│	│	...	...	...	1718	1748	│	...	│	...	│	1818	│	│	│	│	│	│	│
Mainz Hbf **911** d.	│	1713	1713	│	│	│	│	...	...	...	1817	1839	│	...	│	...	│	1913	│	│	│	│	│	│	│
Frankfurt (Main) Hbf **913** d.	1705	│	│	1720	1750	│	1805	...	...	1820	│	│	│	...	1850	...	1905	│	1920	1920	1950	│	│	2005	2005
Frankfurt Flughafen ✈ ◧ d.	1720	│	│	│	│	1753	│	...	...	│	│	│	1853	...	│	...	1920	│	│	│	│	1953	1953	│	│
Mannheim Hbf **913** a.	1754	1752	1752	│	1827	1823	1843	...	...	│	1901	1921	1923	...	1927	...	1954	1952	│	│	2027	2023	2023	2043	2043
Mannheim Hbf **913** d.	1756	1754	1754	│	1830	1836‡	1845	...	...	│	1903	1923	1931	...	1936	...	1956	1954	│	│	2030	2036	2036‡	2045	2045
Darmstadt Hbf **913** d.	│	│	│	1737	│	│	│	...	...	1837	│	│	│	...	│	...	│	│	1937	1937	│	│	│	│	│
Bensheim **913** d.	│	│	│	1750	│	│	│	...	...	1850	│	│	│	...	│	...	│	│	1950	1950	│	│	│	│	│
Weinheim **913** d.	│	│	│	1800	│	│	│	...	...	1900	│	│	│	...	│	...	│	│	2000	2000	│	│	│	│	│
Heidelberg Hbf **913 931** d.	│	1806	1806	1814	│	│	│	...	...	1914	1916	1936	│	...	│	...	│	2006	2014	2014	│	│	│	│	│
Bruchsal **913 931** d.	│	│	│	1836o	│	│	│	...	...	│	│	│	│	...	│	...	│	│	2036	2036j	│	│	│	│	│
Vaihingen (Enz) **931** d.	│	│	│	│	│	│	│	...	...	│	│	2005	│	...	│	...	│	│	│	│	│	│	│	│	│
Stuttgart Hbf **931** a.	1835	1846¦	1846	│	1908	│	│	...	...	1954	1958	2023	2008	...	│	...	2035	2046	│	│	2108	│	│	│	│
München Hbf **930** a.	▬	2124	...	│	2129q	│	│	...	...	2213	...	...	2226	...	│	...	▬	...	│	│	2327	│	│	│	│
Karlsruhe Hbf **913 916** d.	①–⑤	...	...	1852o	...	1900	1910	1933	...	...	...	...	...	1955	2000	...	...	...	2051	2051j	...	2100	2102	2108	2112
Baden-Baden **916** d.	2	...	...	...	...	│	1926	│	...	...	...	...	...	│	2018	...	2	...	...	...	...	→	2119	...	2129
Offenburg **916** ☆ d.	1904	...	...	...	...	1929	│	│	2004	...	...	...	...	2026	2034	...	2104	...	...	...	...	...	2135	...	2145
Kehl 🏛 d.	1922	...	...	...	...	│	│	│	2022	...	...	...	...	│	│	...	2122	...	...	...	...	...	│	...	│
Strasbourg a.	1934	...	...	...	...	│	│	2011	2034	...	...	...	...	│	│	←	2134	...	...	...	...	...	│	...	│
Freiburg (Brsg) Hbf ☆ d.	...	...	...	...	...	2001	2012	...	...	...	...	...	...	2100	2106	2112	...	...	...	...	...	...	2208	...	2217
Basel Bad Bf 🏛 ☆ a.	...	...	...	...	...	2034	2045	...	...	...	...	...	...	→	2138	2152	...	...	...	...	...	...	2242	...	2251
Basel SBB ☆ a.	...	...	...	...	...	2047	2054	...	...	...	...	...	...	...	2147	...	...	...	...	...	...	...	2250	...	2300
Zürich HB **510** a.	...	...	...	...	...	...	2200	...	...	...	...	...	...	...	...	...	...	...	...	...	...	...	...	...	...

	ICE	IC	IC	IC	ICE	ICE	ICE		IC	IC	IC	ICE	ICE	ICE	ICE	IC	ICE	IC	ICE	ICE	ICE	ICE	ICE	ICE	IC
	203	**2171**	**2297**	**2213**	**615**	**377**	**397**		**1917**	**1956**	**1073**	**773**	**695**	**1093**	**1093**	**2377**	**605**	**1973**	**1173**	**1173**	**605**	**877**	**1677**	**775**	**2395**
	①–⑥	⑤z				Ⓑ⊗	⑥⊗		⑦	⑦	Ⓑq	⑥y	⑥k	Ⓑb	⑦	⑤f	⊗	⑦	⊗	⑤⑥z	♠⊗	Ⓑ	⑥	⑦	⑥
	⊗🍷	J✕	Y	🍷◆	🍷	✕	✕	2		🍷◆	🍷	✕	✕	✕	✕	A🍷	🍷◆		K✕	⊗K	🍷◆	✕	✕	✕	🍷
Berlin Hbf **810** d.	...	...	...	...	...	1632	1631	...	1358	1539	...	...	1734	1804*	1804*	...	...	...	...	✕	...	1832	1831	...	...
Hamburg Hbf **800 900** d.	...	1527	...	1446	...	│	│	...	│	│	1722•	1724•	│	│	│	1627◊	...	...	1824•	1824•	...	│	│	1924•	...
Hannover Hbf **810 900** d.	...	1703	...	│	...	│	│	...	1556	│	1839	1841	│	│	│	1801	...	...	1941	1941	...	│	│	2041	...
Dortmund Hbf **800** d.	...	│	...	1737	1837	│	│	...	1752	│	│	│	│	│	│	│	1924	...	│	│	...	│	│	│	...
Köln Hbf **800 910** d.	...	│	...	1853	1957	│	│	...	1918	│	│	│	│	│	│	│	2046d	...	│	│	...	│	│	│	...
Koblenz Hbf **911** d.	...	│	...	1948	│	│	│	...	2018	│	│	│	│	│	│	│	│	...	│	│	...	│	│	│	...
Mainz Hbf **911** d.	...	│	...	2039	│	│	│	...	2113	│	│	│	│	│	│	│	│	...	│	│	...	│	│	│	...
Frankfurt (Main) Hbf **913** d.	...	2015	2020	│	│	2050	2050	...	│	2058	2105	2105	2150	2150	2150	2154	│	2154	2205	2205	...	2300	2300	2308	2308
Frankfurt Flughafen ✈ ◧ d.	...	│	│	│	2053	│	│	...	│	│	2120	2120	│	│	│	│	2153	│	│	│	...	2317	2317	│	│
Mannheim Hbf **913** a.	...	│	│	2121	2123	2127	2127	...	2152	│	2154	2154	2227	2227	2227	│	2223	│	2243	2243	...	2348	2348	│	│
Mannheim Hbf **913** d.	...	│	│	2123	2131	2136	2136	...	2158	│	2156	2156	2230	2230	2230	│	2236	│	2245	2245	...	2350	2350	│	│
Darmstadt Hbf **913** d.	...	2037	2037	│	│	│	│	...	│	2121	│	│	│	│	│	2211	│	2211	│	│	...	│	│	2325	2327
Bensheim **913** d.	...	2050	2050	│	│	│	│	...	│	2135	│	│	│	│	│	2223	│	2223	│	│	...	│	│	│	2341
Weinheim **913** d.	...	2100	2100	│	│	│	│	...	│	2146	│	│	│	│	│	2233	│	2233	│	│	...	│	│	│	│
Heidelberg Hbf **913 931** d.	...	2114	2114	2136	│	│	│	...	│	2206	2210	2210	│	│	│	2248	│	2248	│	│	...	│	│	0004	0004
Bruchsal **913 931** d.	...	│	│	│	│	│	│	...	│	2231	│	│	│	│	│	2310	│	│	│	│	...	│	│	│	│
Vaihingen (Enz) **931** d.	...	│	│	2205	│	│	│	...	│	│	│	│	│	│	│	│	│	2320	│	│	...	│	│	0033	0032
Stuttgart Hbf **931** a.	...	2155	2155	2222	2208	│	│	...	│	│	2250	2250	2308	2308	2308	│	│	2338	│	│	...	│	│	0049	0049
München Hbf **930** a.	←	...	...	...	0027	│	│	...	│	│	...	...	...	...	0131	│	│	...	│	│	←	│	│	...	...
Karlsruhe Hbf **913 916** d.	2112	...	...	...	...	2200	2200	...	2224x	2252	...	...	...	...	...	2326	2300	...	2308	2312	2312	0013t	0013t	...	...
Baden-Baden **916** d.	2129	...	...	...	...	2218	2218	...	...	...	...	...	...	...	...	...	→	...	...	2328	2330	...	...	...	...
Offenburg **916** ☆ d.	2145	...	...	...	...	2237	2237	2325	...	...	...	...	...	...	...	...	...	...	...	2345	2350	...	...	...	...
Kehl 🏛 d.	│	...	...	...	...	│	│	2348	...	...	...	...	...	...	...	...	...	...	...	│	│	...	...	...	...
Strasbourg a.	│	...	...	...	...	│	│	2400	...	...	...	...	...	...	...	...	...	...	...	│	│	...	...	...	...
Freiburg (Brsg) Hbf ☆ d.	2217	...	...	...	...	2311	2311	...	...	...	...	...	...	...	...	...	...	...	...	0017	0022	...	...	...	...
Basel Bad Bf 🏛 ☆ a.	2251	...	...	...	...	2346	2346	...	...	...	...	...	...	...	...	...	...	...	...	0050	0056	...	...	...	...
Basel SBB ☆ a.	2300	...	...	...	...	2357	2357	...	...	...	...	...	...	...	...	...	...	...	...	0100	...	...	...	...	...
Zürich HB **510** a.	...	...	...	...	...	...	...	...	...	...	...	...	...	...	...	...	...	...	...	...	...	...	...	...	...

◆ – **NOTES** (LISTED BY TRAIN NUMBER) for pages 426 and 427

13 – [12] and ✕ Frankfurt - Salzburg - Villach - Klagenfurt; [12] Frankfurt - Villach (**213**) - Ljubljana - Zagreb.
15 – WÖRTHERSEE – [12] and 🍷 Münster - München - Salzburg - Villach - Klagenfurt.
17 – [12] and 🍷 Frankfurt - München - Salzburg - Klagenfurt.
19 – [12] Münster - Ulm - Lindau - Bregenz - Innsbruck.
19 – [12] and 🍷 Frankfurt - München - Salzburg - Bischofshofen - Selzthal - Graz.
91 – [12] and 🍷 Frankfurt - München - Salzburg (- Linz Ⓑ).
73 – AURORA – 🛏 1, 2 cl., ▬ 2 cl., [2] and 🍷 København - Flensburg - Basel (Table **54**). Train number **1273/1275** on the mornings of ⑦. Departs Hamburg 0001 on ⑦. Starts from Flensburg July 14 - Aug. 11 (also on Sept. 7, 8).
05 – [12] and 🍷 Köln - Basel; conveys [12] and 🍷 (*ICE* **105**) Amsterdam - Köln - Basel.
05 – [12] and 🍷 Dortmund - Karlsuhe (- Basel Bad Bf ♠).
956 – [12] and 🍷 Berlin - Halle - Erfurt - Frankfurt - Karlsruhe.
005 – ⑤⑥ (also June 18, 19, Oct. 2; not June 20). BODENSEE – [12] and 🍷 Emden - Münster - Konstanz. Aug. 1 - Sept. 13 Mannheim a. 1258, d. 1302, Karlsruhe d. 1340, Baden-Baden d. 1359, Offenburg a. 1416.
011 – ①②③④⑦ (not June 18, 19, Oct. 2). [12] (Berlin ⑦ -) Düsseldorf - Stuttgart. Continues to Tübingen (a. 1950) on ①–④ (not June 18, 19, Oct. 2). Conveys 🍷 on ⑦.
013 – ALLGÄU – [12] and ✕ Hannover - Dortmund - Stuttgart - Ulm - Oberstdorf.
019 – ⑥ to Oct. 18 (also June 19). NORDERNEY – [12] Norddeich Mole - Münster - Stuttgart.
213 – RÜGEN – [12] and 🍷 Ostseebad Binz - Stralsund - Rostock - Hamburg - Stuttgart.
217 – [12] and 🍷 (Greifswald Ⓐ -) Stralsund - Rostock - Hamburg - Köln - Stuttgart.
264 – BADEN-KURIER – [12] and 🍷 München - Stuttgart - Basel. Runs 7–9 minutes later July 31 - Sept. 14.
271 – ①②③④⑥ (also June 20, Oct. 3; not June 18, Oct. 2). [12] and 🍷 (Hannover ⊡ -) Kassel - Gießen - Frankfurt - Karlsruhe. Does not run Heidelberg - Karlsruhe July 31 - Sept. 13.
277 – [12] and 🍷 (Hamburg ⑥**y** -) Kassel - Karlsruhe. Does not run Heidelberg - Karlsruhe Aug. 2 - Sept. 14.
279 – [12] and 🍷 (Stralsund ①–⑥ **g** -) (Hamburg - Hannover ①–⑥ -) Kassel - Frankfurt - Karlsruhe (- Konstanz ①–⑥). Does not run Stralsund - Hamburg - Hannover June 14 - July 26. Does not run Heidelberg - Karlsruhe on ⑦ Aug. 3 - Sept. 14.
576 – [12] and 🍷 München - Stuttgart - Strasbourg - Paris.
580 – [12] and 🍷 Frankfurt - Strasbourg - Mulhouse - Lyon - Marseille. July 31 - Sept. 14 Karlsruhe a. 1512, d. 1515 and does not call at Baden Baden.

– From Stralsund (Table **830**).
– ⑥ (also June 19, Oct. 3). From Wiesbaden Hbf (d. 0732). July 26 - Sept. 6 Vaihingen d. 0909, Stuttgart a. 0928.
– From Düsseldorf Hbf (Table **910**).
– To Konstanz (Table **916**) on ⑦. Does not run Heidelberg - Karlsruhe on ①–⑤ July 31 - Sept. 12.
– From Westerland (Table **821**).
– From Kiel (Table **820**).
– From Kassel (Table **806**). Does not run Heidelberg - Karlsruhe July 31 - Sept. 12.
– From Münster (Table **800**).

N – To Interlaken via Bern (Table **560**).
P – [12] and 🍷 Stuttgart - Strasbourg - Paris.
R – ①–⑤ (also June 22, Aug. 17, Sept. 28, Oct. 5).
S – From Saarbrücken (Table **919**).
T – To Tübingen Hbf (a. 2150) on ⑦.
Y – ①②③④⑥⑦ (not Oct. 2). Runs with train number **2397** and conveys ✕ on ④⑦ (also June 18); conveys 🍷 on ⑥.

a – Ⓐ only.
b – Not June 20, Oct. 3.
c – Also June 19.
d – Köln **Messe/ Deutz**.
e – ①–⑥ only.
f – Also June 18, Oct. 2; not June 20, Oct. 3.
g – ①–⑥ (not Oct. 4).
h – 0548 June 14 - July 27; 0611 on © from Aug. 2.
j – 3–6 minutes later July 31 - Sept. 12.
k – Also June 20, Oct. 3.
m – Not June 19, 20, Oct. 3.
n – Not June 19.
o – Not ⑤ Aug. 1 - Sept. 12. Timings may be up to 18 minutes later July 31 - Sept. 14.
q – Ⓑ (not Oct. 3).
r – 0551 from Sept. 28.
s – Stops to set down only.
t – 0027 on the mornings July 18 - Sept. 29.
v – Also Oct. 2; not Oct. 3.
w – ⑦ only.
x – 2239 Aug. 3 - Sept. 14.
y – ⑥ (also Oct. 3).
z – Also Oct. 2.

¶ – Also Oct. 4.
◊ – From July 28.
♠ – ①②③④⑦ (not Oct. 2).
⊡ – ①–④ (also June 20; not June 18, Oct. 2).
⊖ – On Ⓐ conveys [12] (*ICE* **513**) Hamm - Dortmund - München (Table **800**).
* – [R] and supplement payable for journeys from Berlin.
§ – On ⑥⑦ change trains at Basel Badischer Bf (arrives Basel SBB 4 minutes later).
• – 20–23 minutes **earlier** June 14 - July 26.
‡ – 10 minutes **earlier** July 31 - Aug. 14.
⊗ – July 31 - Sept. 14 Karlsruhe - Basel timings are up to 13 minutes later.
⊕ – July 31 - Sept. 14 timings Karlsruhe - Basel are 7–20 minutes later.
¦ – Not Aug. 1 - Sept. 12.
☆ – See panel on page 426 for other local services.
◧ – Frankfurt Flughafen Fernbahnhof.

912 BASEL and STUTTGART - FRANKFURT

km	km		ICE 618	ICE 1096	IC 1074	ICE 874	ICE 874	ICE 616	IC 2278	ICE 604	ICE 674	ICE 674	IC 2296	ICE 604	ICE 604	ICE 604	ICE 694	IC 1114	IC 2376		ICE 676	ICE 772	IC 2018	IC 2010	IC 2265
				①⊗	①–⑥	①⊗	◐⊗		①–⑤	⑦⊗	⑥h	⊗	①–⑥	⑦⊗	①–⑤	⊗		Ⓐn	①–⑥		Ⓐn		⑥	Ⓐr	①–⑥
			⊖	✕	e🍷	✕	✕	🍷	m	D🍷	⊗✕	¶✕	e♣	D🍷	⊗D	D🍷	✕		eA	2	⊗✕	✕	♦	♦	🍷♦
		Zürich HB **510** d.	...	...	...	...	...	...	...	...	...	...	...	...	🍷	...	...	...	🍷	...	...	...	...	...	...
		Basel SBB ☆ d.	...	...	...	...	...	...	...	...	...	...	...	...	...	...	...	...	...	...	...	...	...	...	...
		Basel Bad Bf ☆ d.	...	...	...	0412	...	...	...	0506o	0511	...	...	...	0515	...	...	...	...	...	0545	...	...	...	0553
		Freiburg (Brsg) Hbf ☆ d.	...	...	...	0447	...	...	...	0539	0546	...	...	...	0552	...	...	...	...	...	0622	...	...	...	0643
	0	**Strasbourg** ♥ d.	...	...	...	|	...	...	...	|	|	...	...	...	|	...	...	...	...	0622	|	...	...	...	|
	8	Kehl ♥ d.	...	...	...	|	...	...	...	|	|	...	...	...	|	...	...	...	...	0634	|	...	...	...	|
	29	Offenburg **916** ☆ ♥ d.	...	...	...	0520	...	...	...	0612	0618	...	...	...	0626	...	...	...	...	0652	0657	...	...	...	0731
	—	Baden-Baden **916** d.	...	...	...	0536	...	...	...	0628	0634	...	...	←	0642	...	...	...	...	...	0714	...	...	...	0749
		Karlsruhe Hbf **913 916** d.	0348	0500	...	0558	0558	...	0615	0644	0651	0651	...	0700	0700	0700	...	...	0702	...	0736	...	...	...	0804
		München Hbf **930** d.	2350	|	...	|	|	0323	|	→	|	|	...	|	|	|	...	...	|	...	|	...	...	...	...
0	0	**Stuttgart** Hbf **931** d.	0221	|	0502	|	|	0551	|	...	|	|	0602	|	|	|	0651	0630	|	...	|	0726	0714	0714	...
29	29	Vaihingen (Enz) **931** d.	0252	|	0519	|	|	|	|	...	|	|	0620	|	|	|	|	0648	|	...	|	|	|	|	...
		Bruchsal **913 931** d.	0407	|	|	|	|	|	0633	...	|	|	|	|	|	|	|	|	0724	...	|	|	|	|	...
	92	**Heidelberg** Hbf **913 931** d.	0428	|	0547	|	|	|	0654	...	|	|	0658	|	|	|	|	0721	0746	...	|	|	0755	0755	...
		Weinheim **913** d.	|	|	|	|	|	|	|	...	|	|	0714	|	|	|	|	|	0800	...	|	|	|	|	...
		Bensheim **913** d.	|	|	|	|	|	|	|	...	|	|	0728	|	|	|	|	|	0809	...	|	|	|	|	...
		Darmstadt Hbf **913** d.	|	|	|	|	|	|	|	...	|	|	0742	|	|	|	|	|	0824	...	|	|	|	|	...
107	109	**Mannheim** Hbf **913** a.	0438	0526	0559	0623	0623	0628	0709	...	0714	0714	|	0723	0723	0723	0729	0732	|	...	0800	0804	0806	0806	...
107		**Mannheim** Hbf **913** d.	0440	0528	0605	0632	0632	0636	0711	...	0716	0716	|	0736	0736	0736	0732	0734	|	...	...	0806	0808	0808	...
179		**Frankfurt** Flughafen ✈ a.	0512	|	0638	|	|	0706	|	...	|	|	|	0806	0806	0806	|	|	|	...	...	0838	|	|	...
		Frankfurt (Main) Hbf **913** a.	0533	0608	0652	0708	0708	|	0752	...	0752	0752	0802	|	|	|	0808	|	0840	...	...	0853	|	|	...
		Mainz Hbf **911** a.	|	|	|	|	|	|	...	...	|	|	...	|	|	|	|	0815c	|	...	...	|	0846	0846	...
		Koblenz Hbf **911** a.	|	|	|	|	|	|	...	...	|	|	...	|	|	|	|	...	|	...	...	|	0941	0941	...
		Köln Hbf **800 910** a.	0705	|	|	|	|	0805	...	...	|	|	...	0903d	0903d	0903d	|	...	|	...	...	|	1042	1042	...
		Dortmund Hbf **800** a.	0843x	|	|	|	|	0921	...	...	|	|	...	...	...	...	|	...	|	...	...	|	...	1207f	...
		Hannover Hbf **810 900** a.	...	|	0920	|	|	...	...	...	1017	1017	...	...	...	...	|	...	1156	...	...	1117	...	1401f	...
		Hamburg Hbf **800 900** a.	...	|	1037•	|	|	...	...	...	1135•	1135•	...	...	...	...	|	...	1328◊	...	...	1235•	...	|	...
		Berlin Hbf **810** a.	...	0953*	...	1125	1125	...	...	...	...	...	...	...	...	...	1222	...	...	...	...	...	...	1552f	...

	ICE 374	ICE 614	IC 2216	IC 2294	IC 2170	ICE 78		ICE 1202	ICE 202	ICE 202	ICE 692	IC 2374	IC 2174	ICE 770		ICE 372	ICE 612	IC 2218	IC 1296		TGV 9571	ICE 76	ICE 200	ICE 1200	ICE 690
	⊗			ⒷT	⑥	⊗		⑤⑥	⊡	✣		■	⑤R		①–⑤	♠⊗						⊗	Ⓑ⊗	⑥⊗	
	✕	🍷	🍷♦	🍷	✕♦	✕	2	uD	🍷	🍷	✕	🍷	🍷	✕	2	N✕	🍷	🍷	G🍷	2	P🅁	K✕	Y🍷	🍷	✕
Zürich HB **510** d.	...	...	...	...	...	0600	...	🍷	...	...	...	...	...	...	...	...	...	...	...	...	...	0800	...	...	...
Basel SBB ☆ d.	0608	...	...	...	...	0706	...	0713	0713	...	...	...	...	...	...	0813	...	...	...	...	...	0906	0913	0913	...
Basel Bad Bf ☆ d.	0618	...	...	...	...	0715	...	0722	0722	...	...	...	...	...	...	0823	...	...	...	...	...	0915	0923	0923	...
Freiburg (Brsg) Hbf ☆ d.	0652	...	...	...	...	0749	...	0755	0755	...	...	...	...	...	...	0857	...	...	...	...	...	0949	0957	0957	...
Strasbourg ♥ d.	|	...	...	...	...	|	0750	|	|	...	...	...	...	...	0852	|	...	...	...	0922	0947	|	|	|	...
Kehl ♥ d.	|	...	...	...	...	|	0804	|	|	...	...	...	...	...	0904	|	...	...	...	0934	|	|	|	|	...
Offenburg **916** ☆ ♥ d.	0724	...	...	...	...	|	0822	0827	0827	...	...	...	...	...	0922	0930	...	...	...	0952	|	|	1030	1030	...
Baden-Baden **916** d.	0742	...	...	...	...	0834	...	0843	0843	...	...	...	...	...	...	|	...	...	...	...	|	1034	|	|	...
Karlsruhe Hbf **913 916** d.	0800	...	...	...	...	0851	...	0900	0900	0900	...	0910	0910	...	...	1000	...	...	...	...	1025	1051	1100	1100	...
München Hbf **930** d.	|	0527	...	0539n	...	|	...	|	|	|	0632a	|	|	...	...	|	0728	...	0748y	...	...	|	|	|	0828
Stuttgart Hbf **931** d.	|	0751	0737	0805	0804	|	...	|	|	|	0851	|	|	0926	...	|	0951	0937	1005	...	...	|	|	|	1051
Vaihingen (Enz) **931** d.	|	|	0755	|	|	|	...	|	|	|	|	|	|	|	...	|	|	0955	|	...	...	|	|	|	|
Bruchsal **913 931** d.	|	|	|	|	|	|	...	|	|	|	|	0924	0924	|	...	|	|	|	|	...	...	|	|	|	|
Heidelberg Hbf **913 931** d.	|	|	0825	0846	0846	|	...	|	|	|	|	0946	0946	|	...	|	|	1025	1046	...	...	|	|	|	|
Weinheim **913** d.	|	|	|	0900	0900	|	...	|	|	|	|	1000	1000	|	...	|	|	|	1100	...	...	|	|	|	|
Bensheim **913** d.	|	|	|	0909	0909	|	...	|	|	|	|	1009	1009	|	...	|	|	|	1109	...	...	|	|	|	|
Darmstadt Hbf **913** d.	|	|	|	0924	0924	|	...	|	|	|	|	1024	1024	|	...	|	|	|	1124	...	...	|	|	|	|
Mannheim Hbf **913** a.	0823	0828	0837	|	|	0914	...	0923‡	0923‡	0923‡	0929	|	|	1004	...	1023	1028	1037	|	...	...	1114	1123	1123	1129
Mannheim Hbf **913** d.	0832	0836	0839	|	|	0916	...	0936	0936	0936	0932	|	|	1006	...	1032	1036	1039	|	...	...	1116	1136	1136	1132
Frankfurt Flughafen ✈ a.	|	0906	|	|	|	|	...	1006	1006	1006	|	|	|	1038	...	|	1106	|	|	...	...	|	1206	1206	|
Frankfurt (Main) Hbf **913** a.	0908	|	|	0940	0940	0952	...	|	|	|	1008	1040	1040	1053	...	1108	|	|	1140	...	...	1153	|	|	1208
Mainz Hbf **911** a.	|	|	0918	...	|	|	...	|	|	|	|	|	|	|	...	|	|	1118	...	...	...	|	|	|	|
Koblenz Hbf **911** a.	|	|	1011	...	|	|	...	|	|	|	|	|	|	|	...	|	|	1211	...	...	...	|	|	|	|
Köln Hbf **800 910** a.	|	1005	1105	...	|	|	...	1103d	1105	1105	|	|	|	|	...	|	1205	1305	...	...	...	|	1305	1305	|
Dortmund Hbf **800** a.	|	1121	1221	...	|	|	...	...	1221	...	|	|	|	|	...	|	1321	1421	...	...	...	|	...	1421	|
Hannover Hbf **810 900** a.	|	...	|	...	1256	1217	...	...	...	...	|	1356	1356	1317	...	|	...	|	...	...	...	1417	...	...	|
Hamburg Hbf **800 900** a.	|	...	1512	...	1428	1335•	...	...	...	...	|	1529	1532	1435•	...	|	...	1712	...	...	...	1535•	...	...	|
Berlin Hbf **810** a.	1325	...	...	...	...	...	...	...	...	...	1422	...	...	...	...	1525	...	...	...	...	...	...	...	...	1622

	IC 2058	IC 1953	IC 2372	IC 1216	ICE 578		ICE 370	ICE 610	IC 2312	EC 390	IC 2006	IC 2004	IC 2014	ICE 74	ICE 108	ICE 1108	ICE 598	IC 2370	IC 2012	ICE 576		ICE 278	ICE 518	EC 8	EC 218
	⑤f	⑤f	Ⓒ⊕	⑤f			⊗				⑥△	⑦△	⑤f	⊗	Ⓑ⊗	⑥⊗						⊗		⊗	
	♦	🍷♦	A🍷	G🍷	✕	2	N✕	🍷	🍷	🍷♦	🍷♦	🍷♦	♦🍷	K✕	D🍷	🍷	✕	🍷♦	✕♦	✕	2	N✕	🍷	✕♦	🍷♦
Zürich HB **510** d.	...	...	...	...	...	...	...	...	...	...	...	...	...	1000	...	...	...	...	...	...	...	...	...	1100	...
Basel SBB ☆ d.	...	...	...	...	...	...	1013	...	...	...	...	...	...	1106	1113	1113	...	...	...	...	...	1213	...	1220	...
Basel Bad Bf ☆ d.	...	...	...	...	...	...	1023	...	...	...	...	...	...	1115	1123	1123	...	...	...	...	...	1223	...	1228	...
Freiburg (Brsg) Hbf ☆ d.	...	...	...	...	...	...	1057	...	...	...	...	...	...	1149	1157	1157	...	...	...	...	...	1257	...	1304	...
Strasbourg ♥ d.	...	...	...	...	...	1052	|	...	...	...	...	...	...	|	|	|	...	...	...	...	1252	|	...	|	...
Kehl ♥ d.	...	...	...	...	...	1104	|	...	...	...	...	...	...	|	|	|	...	...	...	...	1304	|	...	|	...
Offenburg **916** ☆ ♥ d.	...	...	...	...	...	1122	1130	...	...	...	1139	1139	...	|	1230	1230	...	1223	...	...	1322	1330	...	|	...
Baden-Baden **916** d.	...	...	...	...	...	...	|	...	...	...	1202	1202	...	1234	|	|	...	1245	...	...	...	|	...	1352	...
Karlsruhe Hbf **913 916** d.	...	1110	1110	...	...	...	1200	...	...	...	1221	1221	...	1251	1300	1300	...	1310	...	...	...	1400	...	1412	...
München Hbf **930** d.	...	|	|	0848	...	...	|	0928	...	0946	|	|	...	|	|	|	1028	|	...	...	...	|	1130	|	1146
Stuttgart Hbf **931** d.	1039	|	|	1114	1126	...	|	1151	1137	1205	|	|	1209	|	|	|	1251	|	1314	1326	...	|	1351	|	1405
Vaihingen (Enz) **931** d.	1056	|	|	|	|	...	|	|	1155	|	|	|	1226	|	|	|	|	|	|	|	...	|	|	|	|
Bruchsal **913 931** d.	|	1124	1124	|	|	...	|	|	|	|	|	|	|	|	|	|	|	1324	|	|	...	|	|	|	|
Heidelberg Hbf **913 931** d.	1125	1146	1146	1155	|	...	|	|	1225	1246	|	|	|	|	|	|	|	1346	1355	|	...	|	|	|	144
Weinheim **913** d.	|	1200	1200	|	|	...	|	|	|	1300	|	|	|	|	|	|	|	1400	|	|	...	|	|	|	150
Bensheim **913** d.	|	1209	1209	|	|	...	|	|	|	1309	|	|	|	|	|	|	|	1409	|	|	...	|	|	|	150
Darmstadt Hbf **913** d.	|	1224	1224	|	|	...	|	|	|	1324	|	|	|	|	|	|	|	1424	|	|	...	|	|	|	152
Mannheim Hbf **913** a.	1139	|	|	1206	1204	...	1223	1228	1237	|	1250	1250	1256	1314	1323	1323	1329	|	1406	1404	...	1423	1428	1437	|
Mannheim Hbf **913** d.	...	|	|	1208	1206	...	1232	1236	1239	|	1258	1258	1258	1316	1336	1336	1332	|	1408	1406	...	1432	1436	1439	|
Frankfurt Flughafen ✈ a.	...	|	|	|	1238	...	|	1306	|	|	|	|	|	|	1406	1406	|	|	|	1438	...	|	1506	|	|
Frankfurt (Main) Hbf **913** a.	...	1240	1240	|	1253	...	1308	|	|	1340	|	|	|	1353	|	|	1408	1440	|	1453	...	1508	|	|	154
Mainz Hbf **911** a.	...	|	|	1246	|	...	|	|	1318	...	1339	1339	1339	|	|	|	|	|	1446	|	...	|	|	1518	...
Koblenz Hbf **911** a.	...	|	|	1341	|	...	|	|	1411	...	1441	1441	1441	|	|	|	|	|	1541	|	...	|	|	1611	...
Köln Hbf **800 910** a.	...	|	|	1442	|	...	|	1405	1505	...	1542	1542	1542	|	1503d	1505	|	|	1642	|	...	|	1605	1705	...
Dortmund Hbf **800** a.	...	|	|	1608	|	...	|	1521	1621	...	1703	...	...	|	...	1621	|	|	1808	|	...	|	1721	1821	...
Hannover Hbf **810 900** a.	...	|	1556	1801	1517	...	|	...	|	...	...	...	...	1617	...	...	|	1756	2018	1717	...	|	...	|	...
Hamburg Hbf **800 900** a.	...	|	1732◊	|	1635•	...	|	...	1912	...	...	...	...	1735•	...	...	|	1928◊	...	1835•	...	|	...	2112	...
Berlin Hbf **810** a.	...	1820	...	1951	...	...	1725	...	...	...	...	...	...	...	...	...	1822	...	...	...	...	1925	...	...	...

Regional trains **BASEL - OFFENBURG** (German holiday dates apply). **SERVICE FROM SEPT. 29** (SEE PAGE 563 FOR SERVICE UNTIL SEPT. 28). On Nov. 1 service run as on ⑦.

km		①–⑥		Ⓐ													Ⓐ	Ⓒ	①–⑤	⑥				①–⑥		
0	**Basel** SBB d.	0532	...	0604	...	0737§	0837§	0935	1035	1135	1235	1335	1435	1535	1637§	1737§	1809	1835	1837	1909	...	1935	...	2109	...	224
5	**Basel** Bad Bf d.	0538	0549	0625	0634	0748	0848	0948	1048	1148	1248	1348	1448	1548	1648	1748	1826	1848	1848	1926	...	1948	...	2115	2126	225
37	Müllheim (Baden) d.	—	0620	0649	0706	0823	0923	1023	1123	1223	1323	1423	1523	1623	1723	1823	1855	1923	1923	1955	...	2023	2054	...	2158	233
66	**Freiburg** (Brsg) Hbf a.	...	0646	0718	0736	0847	0944	1044	1144	1244	1344	1444	1544	1644	1744	1844	1923	1944	1944	2021	...	2044	2122	...	2219	000
66	**Freiburg** (Brsg) Hbf d.	0555	0656	0722	0803	0903	1003	1103	1203	1307	1403	1507	1603	1703	1803	1903	1925	2003	...	...	2028	...	2125	...	2225	001
129	**Offenburg** a.	0645	0745	0814	0851	0953	1053	1153	1253	1353	1450	1553	1650	1751	1850	1949	2021	2050	...	...	2124	...	2221	...	2318	011

FOR NOTES SEE NEXT PAGE →

BASEL and STUTTGART - FRANKFURT 912

		TGV 9573	TGV 9583	ICE 72	TGV 9583	ICE 106	ICE 596	ICE 712	IC 2276	IC 118	ICE 974	ICE 574		ICE 276	ICE 296	ICE 516	EC 6	IC 2292	EC 114	ICE 70		ICE 504	ICE 1090	ICE 594	IC 2316
			[R]	⊗	[R]	⊗		①–⑤			Ⓑb	⑥t		Ⓑ⊗	⑥⊗		⊗			⊗	①–⑤		Ⓑs	⑥h	Ⓑ
	2	P [R]	🍷◆	✕	🍷◆	🍷	✕	m🍷	🍷◆	◆	K✕	✕	2	N✕	N✕	🍷	✕	🍷	🍷◆	✕	2	🍷◆	✕	✕	◆
Zürich HB **510** d.	...	...	...	1200	...	...	...	...	...	...	...	...	...	...	...	...	1300	...	...	...	...	...	...	...	...
Basel SBB ☆ d.	...	...	...	1306	...	1313	...	...	...	...	...	...	...	1413	1413	...	1420	...	...	1506	...	1513	...	...	...
Basel Bad Bf ☆ d.	...	...	...	1315	...	1323	...	...	...	...	...	...	...	1423	1423	...	1428	...	...	1515	...	1523	...	...	...
Freiburg (Brsg) Hbf ☆ d.	...	...	...	1349	...	1357	...	...	...	...	...	...	...	1457	1457	...	1504	...	...	1549	...	1557	...	...	...
Strasbourg ♥ d.	1322	1347	1355	│	...	│	...	...	...	...	...	...	1452	│	│	...	│	...	...	│	1522	│	...	...	...
Kehl ♥ d.	1334	│	│	│	...	│	...	...	...	...	...	...	1504	│	│	...	│	...	...	│	1534	│	...	...	...
Offenburg 916 ☆ ♥ d.	1352	│	│	│	...	1430	...	...	...	...	...	...	1522	1530	1530	...	│	...	...	│	1552	1630	...	...	...
Baden-Baden 916 d.	...	│	1425	1434	←	│	...	...	...	...	...	...	...	│	│	...	1552	...	...	1634	...	│	...	...	...
Karlsruhe Hbf 913 916 d.	...	1425	1446	1451	1454	1500	...	...	1510	...	...	...	...	1600	1600	...	1612	...	...	1651	...	1700	...	...	...
München Hbf **930** d.	...	...	→	│	│	│	1228	...	│	...	...	...	...	│	│	1328	│	...	1346	│	...	│	1428	1428	...
Stuttgart Hbf 931 d.	...	...	...	│	│	│	1451	1434	│	1512	1526	1526	...	│	│	1551	│	1605	1609	│	...	│	1651	1651	1636
Vaihingen (Enz) 931 d.	...	...	...	│	│	│	│	1452	│	│	│	│	...	│	│	│	│	│	1626	│	...	│	│	│	│
Bruchsal 913 931 d.	...	...	...	│	│	│	│	│	1524	│	│	│	...	│	│	│	│	1646	│	│	...	│	│	│	│
Heidelberg Hbf 913 931 d.	...	...	...	│	│	│	│	1518	1546	1555	│	│	...	│	│	│	│	1700	│	│	...	│	│	│	1720
Weinheim 913 d.	...	...	...	│	│	│	│	│	1600	│	│	│	...	│	│	│	│	1709	│	│	...	│	│	│	│
Bensheim 913 d.	...	...	...	│	│	│	│	│	1609	│	│	│	...	│	│	│	│	1724	│	│	...	│	│	│	│
Darmstadt Hbf 913 d.	...	...	...	│	│	│	│	│	1624	│	│	│	...	│	│	│	│	│	│	│	...	│	│	│	│
Mannheim Hbf 913 a.	...	...	...	1514	1518	1523	1529	1531	│	1606	1604	1604	...	1623	1623	1628	1637	│	1656	1714	...	1723‡	1729	1729	1736
Mannheim Hbf 913 d.	...	...	...	1516	1521	1536	1532	1533	│	1608	1606	1606	...	1632	1632	1636	1639	│	1658	1716	...	1736	1732	1732	1738
Frankfurt Flughafen ✈ ◧ a.	...	...	...	│	│	1606	│	│	│	│	1638	1638	...	│	│	1706	│	│	│	│	...	1806	│	│	│
Frankfurt (Main) Hbf 913 a.	...	...	...	1553	1558	│	1608	│	1640	│	1653	1653	...	1708	1708	│	│	1740	│	1753	...	│	1808	1808	│
Mainz Hbf **911** a.	...	...	...	│	...	│	│	1615	│	1646	│	│	...	│	│	│	1718	...	1744	│	...	│	│	│	1815
Koblenz Hbf **911** a.	...	...	...	│	...	│	│	│	│	1741	│	│	...	│	│	│	1811	...	1841	│	...	│	│	│	...
Köln Hbf **800 910** a.	...	...	...	│	...	1705	│	1801	│	1842	│	│	...	│	│	1805	1905p	...	1942	│	...	1905	│	│	...
Dortmund Hbf **800** a.	...	...	...	│	...	1821	│	...	│	...	│	│	...	│	│	1921	2021	...	2100	│	...	...	│	│	...
Hannover Hbf **810 900** a.	...	...	...	1817	...	...	│	...	1956	...	1917	1917	...	│	│	...	│	...	...	2017	...	...	2021*	│	...
Hamburg Hbf **800 900** a.	...	...	...	1935•	...	...	│	...	2128j	...	2038•	2038•	...	│	│	...	2314q	...	...	2138¦	...	...	│	│	...
Berlin Hbf **810** a.	...	...	...	...	...	...	2022	...	...	...	...	...	...	2126	2206	...	...	...	...	...	...	...	2156*	2227	...

	IC 2274	ICE 572			ICE 274	ICE 514	IC 2318	IC 2052	EC 112		TGV 9575	ICE 376		ICE 102	ICE 1102	ICE 592	IC 2172	IC 2272	ICE 570	IC 1910		ICE 1172	ICE 272	ICE 292	ICE 512
				①–⑤	⊗			Ⓑs				★		Ⓑ★	⑥★		⑦	①–⑤	⑦	⑦	①–⑤	⑥t	Ⓐ⊗	⑦⊗	
	🍷◆	✕	2	2	✕	🍷	🍷◆	◆	✕◆	2	[R]◆	N✕	2	🍷◆	🍷	✕	⊠🍷	g◆	✕	🍷	2	⊗✕	✕	✕	M🍷
Zürich HB **510** d.	...	...	...	...	...	...	...	...	...	...	...	...	...	...	...	...	...	...	...	...	...	1700	1700	1700	...
Basel SBB ☆ d.	...	...	...	...	1613	...	...	...	...	...	...	1706	...	1713	1713	...	...	...	...	...	...	1813	1813	1813	...
Basel Bad Bf ☆ d.	...	...	...	...	1623	...	...	...	...	...	...	1715	...	1723	1723	...	...	...	...	...	...	1823	1823	1823	...
Freiburg (Brsg) Hbf ☆ d.	...	...	...	...	1656	...	...	...	...	...	...	1749	...	1756	1756	...	...	...	...	...	...	1857	1857	1857	...
Strasbourg ♥ d.	...	...	1622	1652	│	...	...	...	...	1723	1747	│	1751	│	│	...	...	...	...	...	1852	│	│	│	...
Kehl ♥ d.	...	...	1634	1704	│	...	...	...	...	1734	│	│	1804	│	│	...	...	...	...	...	1904	│	│	│	...
Offenburg 916 ☆ ♥ d.	...	...	1652	1722	1728	...	...	...	...	1752	│	│	1822	1827	1827	...	...	...	...	...	1922	1930	1930	1930	...
Baden-Baden 916 d.	...	...	...	...	1744	...	...	...	...	...	│	1834	...	1843	1843	...	...	...	...	...	...	│	│	│	...
Karlsruhe Hbf 913 916 d.	1710	...	...	...	1801	...	...	...	...	...	1825	1851	...	1900	1900	...	...	1910	...	...	...	2000	2000	2000	...
München Hbf **930** d.	│	...	...	...	│	1528	...	...	1546	...	...	│	...	│	│	1628	...	│	...	1620	...	│	│	│	1727
Stuttgart Hbf 931 d.	│	1726	...	...	│	1751	1741	1755	1805	...	...	│	...	│	│	1851	1855	│	1926	1914	...	│	│	│	1951
Vaihingen (Enz) 931 d.	│	│	...	...	│	│	│	│	│	...	...	│	...	│	│	│	1914	│	│	│	...	│	│	│	│
Bruchsal 913 931 d.	1724	│	...	...	│	│	│	│	│	...	...	│	...	│	│	│	│	1924	│	│	...	│	│	│	│
Heidelberg Hbf 913 931 d.	1746	│	...	...	│	│	1825	│	1846	...	...	│	...	│	│	│	1946	1946	│	1955	...	│	│	│	│
Weinheim 913 d.	1800	│	...	...	│	│	│	│	1900	...	...	│	...	│	│	│	2000	2000	│	│	...	│	│	│	│
Bensheim 913 d.	1809	│	...	...	│	│	│	│	1909	...	...	│	...	│	│	│	2009	2009	│	│	...	│	│	│	│
Darmstadt Hbf 913 d.	1824	│	...	...	│	│	│	│	1924	...	...	│	...	│	│	│	2023	2023	│	│	...	│	│	│	│
Mannheim Hbf 913 a.	│	1804	...	...	1823	1828	1837	1845	│	...	...	1914	...	1923	1923	1929	│	│	2004	2006	...	2023	2023	2023	2028
Mannheim Hbf 913 d.	│	1806	...	...	1832	1836	1839	...	│	...	...	1916	...	1936	1936	1932	│	│	2006	2008	...	2032	2032	2032	2036
Frankfurt Flughafen ✈ ◧ a.	│	1838	...	...	│	1906	│	...	│	...	...	│	...	2006	2006	│	│	│	2038	│	...	│	│	│	2106
Frankfurt (Main) Hbf 913 a.	1840	1853	...	...	1908	│	│	...	1940	...	...	1953	...	│	│	2008	2040	2040	2052	│	...	2108	2108	2108	│
Mainz Hbf **911** a.	│	│	...	...	│	│	1918	...	...	...	...	│	...	│	│	│	...	...	│	2046	...	│	│	│	│
Koblenz Hbf **911** a.	│	│	...	...	│	│	2011	...	...	...	...	│	...	│	│	│	...	...	│	2141	...	│	│	│	│
Köln Hbf **800 910** a.	│	│	...	...	│	2005	2105	...	...	...	...	│	...	2105	2105	│	...	...	│	2242	...	│	│	│	2205
Dortmund Hbf **800** a.	│	│	...	...	│	2121	2221b	...	...	...	...	│	...	2221	2221	│	...	...	│	2359	...	│	│	│	...
Hannover Hbf **810 900** a.	2156k	2119	...	...	│	...	...	...	...	...	...	2217z	...	0018	0018	│	...	...	2318	...	...	2341	0002	│	...
Hamburg Hbf **800 900** a.	2328w	2243v	...	...	│	...	...	...	...	...	...	2351z	...	...	...	│	...	...	0045•	...	...	0111	0137	│	...
Berlin Hbf **810** a.	...	...	...	...	2325	...	...	...	...	...	...	...	...	...	...	0032	...	...	...	...	...	...	...	0125	...

♦ – **NOTES** (LISTED BY TRAIN NUMBER)

– [12] and ✕ Zürich - Dortmund - Hamburg (- Kiel ⑦). Train number **2** on ⑦.
02 – [12] and 🍷 Basel - Dortmund (- Hannover ①–⑤).
12 – [12] and ✕ Klagenfurt - Villach - Salzburg - Frankfurt; [12] Zagreb (**212**) - Ljubljana - Villach (**112**) - Frankfurt.
14 – WÖRTHERSEE – [12] and 🍷 Klagenfurt - Villach - Salzburg - München - Dortmund.
18 – [12] Salzburg - Innsbruck - Bregenz - Lindau - Ulm - Stuttgart - Münster.
18 – [12] and 🍷 Graz - Selzthal - Bischofshofen - Salzburg - Frankfurt.
90 – [12] and 🍷 (Linz ①–⑥ -) Salzburg - München - Frankfurt.
04 – [12] and 🍷 Basel - Köln; conveys [12] and 🍷 (*ICE* **104**) Basel - Köln - Amsterdam.
953 – [12] and 🍷 Karlsruhe - Frankfurt - Erfurt - Halle - Berlin. Aug. 1 - Sept. 12 departs Karlsruhe 1107.
004 – ⑦ (also Oct. 3). BODENSEE – [12] and 🍷 Konstanz - Karlsruhe - Münster - Emden.
006 – ⑥ (also June 19). BODENSEE – [12] and 🍷 Konstanz - Karlsruhe - Dortmund.
010 – LORELEY – [12] Tübingen Hbf (d. 0611) - Stuttgart - Düsseldorf (- Dortmund - Berlin ⑤ **f**).
012 – ALLGÄU – [12] and ✕ Oberstdorf - Ulm - Stuttgart - Dortmund - Hannover.
014 – [12] and 🍷 Stuttgart - Münster - Emden.
018 – ⑥ to Oct. 18 (also June 19). NORDERNEY – [12] Stuttgart - Münster - Norddeich Mole.
052 – [12] Stuttgart - Saarbrücken.
058 – [12] Stuttgart - Saarbrücken. Does not call at Vaihingen July 4 - Aug. 29, Sept. 19, 26, Oct. 24, 31.
70 – ⑥ (also Oct. 3; not Aug. 2 - Sept. 13). WATTENMEER – [12] and ✕ Stuttgart - Frankfurt - Gießen - Hamburg - Westerland.
216 – [12] and 🍷 Stuttgart - Hamburg - Rostock - Stralsund (- Greifswald Ⓐ).
265 – ①–⑥ (not June 21, Oct. 4). BADEN-KURIER – [12] and 🍷 Basel - Stuttgart - München. July 31 - Sept. 13 Basel d. 0600, Freiburg d. 0651, Offenburg d. 0725, Baden-Baden d. 0742, Karlsruhe a. 0758.
272 – [12] and 🍷 Karlsruhe - Frankfurt - Kassel. Does not run Karlsruhe - Heidelberg July 31 - Sept. 12.
274 – [12] and 🍷 Karlsruhe - Frankfurt - Kassel (- Hannover ⑤⑦ **k**) (- Hamburg ⑦). Does not run Karlsruhe - Heidelberg July 31 - Sept. 14.
276 – [12] Karlsruhe - Frankfurt - Hannover (- Hamburg ⑤–⑦ **j**). On ⑦ runs with train number **2286** and continues to Rostock (Table **830**). Does not run Karlsruhe - Heidelberg on ①②③④⑦ July 31 - Sept. 14. On ⑤⑥ Aug. 1 - Sept. 13 Karlsruhe d. 1501, Bruchsal d. 1515. Conveys 🍷 on ①–⑥.
16 – [12] Stuttgart - Wiesbaden Hbf (a. 1831).
18 – [12] and 🍷 Stuttgart - Köln (- Dortmund Ⓑ **b**) (- Münster ⑦).
70 – SCHWARZWALD – [12] and 🍷 Konstanz - Frankfurt - Hamburg. On ⑤⑦ (also June 18, Oct. 2; not Oct. 3) runs with train number **2270** and continues to Stralsund (Table **830**).
75 – [12] and 🍷 Paris - Strasbourg - Stuttgart - München.
83 – [12] and 🍷 Marseille - Lyon - Mulhouse - Strasbourg - Frankfurt.

– To Stralsund (Table **830**).
– To Düsseldorf (Table **910**).
– From Salzburg (Table **890**).
– To Kiel (Table **820**).
– To Münster (Table **800**).
– From Interlaken via Bern (Table **560**).

P – [12] and 🍷 Paris - Strasbourg - Stuttgart.
R – ⑤ (also Oct. 2; not Oct. 3). To Rostock (Table **830**). Does not run Karlsruhe - Heidelberg Aug. 1 - Sept. 12.
T – Ⓑ (daily July 27 - Sept. 19; not Oct. 3).
Y – To Essen (Table **800**) on ⑤⑦ (also Oct. 2; not Oct. 3).

a – Ⓐ only.
b – Ⓑ (not Oct. 3).
c – 0836 July 28 - Sept. 5.
d – Köln **Messe/Deutz**.
e – Not Oct. 4.
f – ⑤ (also June 18, Oct. 2; not June 20, Oct. 3).
g – Not June 20, Oct. 3.
h – Also June 19, Oct. 3.
j – ⑤–⑦ (also Oct. 2).
k – ⑤⑦ (also June 18, Oct. 2; not Oct. 3).
m – Not June 19, 20, Oct. 3.
n – Ⓐ (not June 19).
o – 0503 until Sept. 28.
p – Not June 14 - July 11.

q – Ⓑ only.
r – Not June 19, 20.
s – Not June 19, Oct. 3.
t – Also Oct. 3.
u – Also Oct. 2.
v – Not Oct. 3. 2254 June 14 - July 27.
w – ⑦ only.
x – ⑥⑦ only. Arrives 0821 on ⑦.
y – ①–⑥ only.
z – ⑤⑦ (also Oct. 2; not Oct. 3). Arrives Hamburg 2358 June 15 - July 27.

◊ – From July 28.
⊡ – ①–④ (not Oct. 2).
❖ – ①②③④⑦ (not Oct. 2).

■ – ①②③④⑥⑦ (also Oct. 3; not Oct. 2). On ①–④ July 31 - Sept. 11 does not run Karlsruhe - Heidelberg.
¦ – 2152 June 14 - July 27. 2145 on ⑥ from Aug. 2.
⊠ – To Kassel (Table **806**). On June 22, July 6, 27, Sept. 21, 28, Oct. 5, 26, Nov. 2 departs Stuttgart 1903 and does not call at Vaihingen.
⊖ – Train number **1018** on ⑥ (from München). [12] München - Stuttgart - Karlsruhe - Mannheim - Frankfurt - Essen / Dortmund.
♣ – Train number **2396** (✕) on ①⑤ (also June 19; not Oct. 3).
◐ – Train number **1674** on ⑦ (arrives Berlin Hbf 1127).
¶ – Train number **670** on ②–④ (not June 18, 19, Oct. 2).
♠ – On ⑤–⑦ (also Oct. 2; not Oct. 3) runs with train number **392**.
§ – On Ⓒ depart Basel SBB 2 minutes earlier and change at Basel Bad Bf.
⊕ – On ⑥ Aug. 2 - Sept. 13 does not run Karlsruhe - Heidelberg.
△ – Aug. 2 - Sept. 14 departs Karlsruhe 1219, arrives Mannheim 1256.
⊗ – July 31 - Sept. 14 timings Basel - Karlsruhe are up to 12 minutes **earlier**.
★ – July 31 - Sept. 14 departures Basel Bad Bf - Karlsruhe are up to 11 minutes **earlier** and does not call at Baden Baden.
• – 10–20 minutes later June 14 - July 27.
‡ – 10–11 minutes later July 31 - Sept. 14.
♥ – Additional trains Strasbourg - Kehl - Offenburg: From Strasbourg at 0005, 0722 ①–⑤, 0822 ①–⑤, 1422 ①–⑤ and 1822 ①–⑤.
* – [R] and supplement payable for journeys to Hannover / Berlin.
☆ – See panel on page 428 for other local services.
◧ – Frankfurt Flughafen Fernbahnhof.

912 BASEL and STUTTGART - FRANKFURT

	IC	IC	EC	IC	IC		TGV	CNL	ICE	ICE	IC		ICE	ICE	ICE	IC		IC	ICE	RJ	CNL	CNL	IC	CNL	CNL
	2210	2210	216	1976	182		9577	472	100	590	2096		4	1110	510	2050		60459	990	66	1259	478	60478	40478	418
	①–④	⑤⑦		⑥⑦	①–⑤		Ⓑ	Ⓡ	⊗		⑦		⊗	⑦		⑦			A	⑤⑥	Ⓡ	Ⓡ		Ⓡ	Ⓡ
	a 🍷	v 🍷	🍷♦			2	Ⓡ♦	🍷♦	🍷	✕♦		2	✕	🍷	🍷♦	S	2	2	✕	✕♦	🍷♦	🍷♦	D 2	🍷♦	🍷♦
Zürich HB **510** d.	...	...	...	...	1705	...	...	...	...	...	...	...	1900	...	...	...	...	...	...	...	1942	2042	...	2042	...
Basel SBB ☆ d.	...	...	...	...	|	...	...	1826	1913	...	...	...	2013	...	...	...	...	2113	...	...	2113	2213	2213	2213	...
Basel Bad Bf ☆ d.	...	...	...	...	|	...	...	1837	1923	...	...	...	2023	...	...	...	...	2122	...	...	2122u	2223u	2223	2223u	...
Freiburg (Brsg) Hbf ☆ d.	...	...	...	...	|	...	...	1915u	1956	...	...	...	2057	...	...	...	...	2158	...	...	2158u	2300u	2300	2300u	...
Strasbourg d.	...	...	...	...	|	1922	1947	|	|	...	...	2022	|	...	...	...	2152	|	...	...	|	|	|	|	...
Kehl d.	...	...	...	...	⊙	1934	|	|	|	...	...	2034	|	...	...	...	2204	|	...	...	|	|	|	|	...
Offenburg **916** ☆ d.	...	...	...	...	|	1952	|	1954u	2028	...	...	2052	2130	...	...	...	2222	2230	...	...	2230u	2344u	2344	2344u	...
Baden-Baden **916** d.	...	...	...	...	|	...	|	|	2044	...	...	...	|	...	...	...	...	|	...	...	|	|	0009	|	...
Karlsruhe Hbf **913 916** d.	...	...	...	...	|	...	2026	2035u	2101	...	...	...	2200	...	...	...	...	2304	...	...	2304u	0029u	0029	0029u	...
München Hbf **930** d.	...	...	1746	...	|	...	...	|	|	1828	...	...	|	1928	1928	...	...	|	2045	2045	|	|	|	|	2250
Stuttgart Hbf **931** d.	1918	1937	2005	2009	2020	...	...	|	|	2051	2035	...	|	2151	2151	2209	...	|	2305	2305	|	|	|	|	0135
Vaihingen (Enz) **931** d.	|	1955	|	|	|	...	...	|	|	|	2053	...	|	|	|	2226	...	|	|	|	|	|	|	|	|
Bruchsal **913 931** d.	|	|	|	|	|	...	...	|	|	|	|	...	|	|	|	|	...	|	|	|	|	|	0048	|	|
Heidelberg Hbf **913 931** d.	2025t	2025	|	2050	2107	...	...	|	|	|	2121	...	|	|	|	2255	...	2333	|	|	2333u	|	0110	|	|
Weinheim **913** d.	|	|	|	2104	2122	...	...	|	|	|	|	...	|	|	|	|	...	|	|	|	|	|	|	|	|
Bensheim **913** d.	|	|	|	2114	2132	...	...	|	|	|	|	...	|	|	|	|	...	|	|	|	|	|	|	|	|
Darmstadt Hbf **913** d.	|	|	|	2127	2145	...	...	|	|	|	|	...	|	|	|	|	...	|	|	|	|	|	|	|	|
Mannheim Hbf **913** a.	2037	2037	2048	|	|	...	...	|	2124	2129	2136	...	2223	2229	2229	2306	...	2346	2344	2344	|	|	0126	|	|
Mannheim Hbf **913** d.	2039	2039	...	|	|	...	...	2104u	2136	2132	2138	...	2236	2232	2232	...	...	...	2351	2351	2359u	|	0256	|	|
Frankfurt Flughafen ✈ ◧. a.	|	|	...	|	|	...	...	|	2206	|	|	...	|	2304	2304	...	...	...	0023	0023	|	|	0339	0339	0339
Frankfurt (Main) Hbf **913** a.	|	|	...	2144	2202	...	...	|	|	2208	|	...	2315	|	|	...	...	...	0042	0042	|	|	|	|	|
Mainz Hbf **911** a.	2118	2118	...	...	...	...	...	|	|	|	2215	...	...	|	2330	...	...	...	|	...	|	|	|	|	|
Koblenz Hbf **911** a.	2211	2211	...	...	...	...	...	|	|	|	...	...	...	|	...	...	...	...	|	...	|	|	0446	0446	0446
Köln Hbf **800 910** a.	2305	2305	...	...	...	...	...	|	2305	|	...	...	...	0005	...	...	...	...	|	...	|	|	0543	0543	0543
Dortmund Hbf **800** a.	...	...	...	...	...	...	...	|	0024	|	...	...	...	...	...	...	...	...	|	...	|	|	...	...	...
Hannover Hbf **810 900** a.	...	...	...	...	...	...	...	|	...	0146	...	...	...	...	...	...	...	...	0421g	...	|	0702b	...	...	...
Hamburg Hbf **800 900** a.	...	...	...	...	...	...	...	0355	...	0308	...	...	...	...	...	...	...	...	0549g	...	|	0836b	...	...	...
Berlin Hbf **810** a.	...	...	...	...	...	...	...	...	...	...	...	...	...	...	...	...	...	...	...	...	0719	...	...	...	...

♦ – **NOTES** (LISTED BY TRAIN NUMBER)

66 – ⑤⑥ (also June 18, Oct. 2). [12] and ✕ Budapest - Wien - Salzburg - Frankfurt.
216 – [12] and 🍷 Graz - Selzthal - Bischofshofen - Salzburg - Saarbrücken.
418 – POLLUX – 🛏 1, 2 cl., ▬ 2 cl., [2] and 🍷 München - Amsterdam.
472 – AURORA – 🛏 1, 2 cl., ▬ 2 cl., [2] and 🍷 Basel - Hamburg - Flensburg - København (Table **54**). Terminates at Flensburg on the mornings July 14 - Aug. 11 (also on Sept. 7, 8). Train number **1272** on ⑥. Departs Karlsruhe 2026 July 31 - Sept. 14.
478 – KOMET – 🛏 1, 2 cl., ▬ 2 cl., [2] (reclining) and 🍷 Zürich - Hamburg.
510 – [12] and 🍷 München - Wiesbaden Hbf (a. 2343). Train number **1010** on ⑤⑥ (also Oct. 2). Train number **1190** on ⑦. Also conveys ✕ on ①–④ (not Oct. 2).
590 – [12] and ✕ München - Frankfurt (- Kassel ♣) (- Hannover - Hamburg ⑦). Train number **698** on ⑤ (also June 19, Oct. 2; not Oct. 3). Train number **992** on ⑦.
1259 – SIRIUS – 🛏 1, 2 cl., ▬ 2 cl., [2] (reclining) and 🍷 Zürich - Erfurt - Halle - Berlin (on ⑤ July 4 - Aug. 29 runs Zürich - Berlin - Ostseebad Binz with train number **1251**). Conveys 🛏 1, 2 cl., ▬ 2 cl. and [2] (*CNL* 459 – CANOPUS) Zürich - Leipzig - Dresden - Praha.
9577 – Ⓑ (also June 21, Aug. 16, Sept. 27, Oct. 4). [12] and 🍷 Paris - Strasbourg - Stuttgart.
40478 – PEGASUS – 🛏 1, 2 cl., ▬ 2 cl., [2] (reclining) and 🍷 Zürich - Amsterdam.

a – Not June 19.
b – Arrives Hannover 0630 on the mornings of ②–⑥. Arrives Hamburg 0812 on the mornings of ⑥. Arrives Hamburg 0915 on the mornings of ① June 16 - July 21.
g – ① only.
t – Arrives 2002.
u – Stops to pick up only.
v – Also June 19; not Oct. 3.

♣ – ⑤⑦ (also June 19, Oct. 2; not Oct. 3).
⊗ – July 31 - Sept. 14 timings Basel - Karlsruhe are 7 – 11 minutes **earlier**.
⊙ – Via Schaffhausen (Table **940**).
☆ – See panel on page 428 for other local services.
◧ – Frankfurt Flughafen Fernbahnhof.

A – ①②③④⑦ (not June 18, Oct. 2). Train number **1590** on ④ (also June 17, Oct. 1; not June 19).
D – To Duisburg (Table **800**).
S – To Saarbrücken (Table **919**).

913 Local trains FRANKFURT - HEIDELBERG - KARLSRUHE

RE / RB / S-Bahn services

See Table **912** for *ICE / IC* services

FRANKFURT - DARMSTADT - HEIDELBERG and MANNHEIM

	Ⓐe	Ⓐe		Ⓒz	Ⓐe	†z	⚒e		Ⓐe	⑦	①–⑥				Ⓐe		Ⓐe		Ⓒz	Ⓐe				
Frankfurt (Main) Hbf d.	...	0506	0606	...	0633	0706	0706	0806	0834	0906	0906	1006	and	1706	1735	1806	1833	1906	2006	2034	2106	2206	2312	0006
Darmstadt Hbf d.	0426	0530	0630	...	0653	0730	0734	0830	0853	0930	0930	1030	hourly	1730	1757	1830	1853	1930	2030	2056	2130	2230	2331	0029
Bensheim d.	0452	0557	0655	...	0709	0755	0757	0859	0909	0955	0959	1059	until	1759	1826	1859j	1909	1959	2058	2110	2155	2255	2355	0055
Weinheim (Bergstr) d.	0508	0612	0710	...	0722	0810	0811	0914	0922	1010	1014	1114		1814	1842	1914	1922	2014	2117	2123	2210	2310	0010	0110
Mannheim Friedrichsfeld a.	0521	0624	0723	0732	0732	0823	0824	0927	|	1023	1027	1127		1827	1856	1927	|	2027	2130	2132	2223	2323	0023	0123
Mannheim Hbf a.	*0545*	*0644*	|	0743	0742	*0842*	*0842*	*0942*	0940	*1042*	*1042*	*1142*		*1842*	1910	*1942*	1940	*2042*	*2143*	*2143*	*2242*	*2343*	|	0138
Heidelberg Hbf a.	0532	0634	0736	...	...	0837	0834	0939	...	1037	1039	1139		1838	...	1939	...	2039	2141	2143	2237	2335	0035	...

	Ⓐe		Ⓐe		Ⓒz	Ⓐe		Ⓐe						Ⓐe			Ⓐe				⚒e	†z		
Heidelberg Hbf d.	0424	0525	...	0625	...	...	0725	...	0821	0921	and	1421	1525	...	1621	1724	...	1821	1921	2021	2124	2127	2221	2324
Mannheim Hbf d.	|	*0515*	0602	*0612*	0716	0720	|	0820	*0816*	*0916*	hourly	*1416*	*1516*	1620	*1616*	*1716*	1820	*1816*	*1916*	*2016*	*2116*	*2116*	*2216*	*2316*
Mannheim Friedrichsfeld d.	0434	0534	|	0635	0726	0731	0735	|	0832	0932	until	1432	1535	|	1632	1734	|	1832	1932	2032	2135	2136	2232	2335
Weinheim (Bergstr) d.	0448	0548	0620	0648	...	...	0745	0839	0845	0945		1446	1545	1639	1645	1745	1839	1845	1945	2045	2149	2150	2245	2349
Bensheim d.	0503	0603	0636	0703	...	...	0800	0851	0900	1000		1500	1600	1652	1700	1800	1852	1900	2000	2100	2204	2204	2259	0004
Darmstadt Hbf d.	0531	0630	0658	0730	...	...	0830	0906	0930	1030		1530	1630	1707	1730	1830	1907	1930	2030	2130	2230	2230	2330	0030
Frankfurt (Main) Hbf a.	0550	0648	0716	0748	...	...	0848	0924	0948	1048		1548	1648	1724	1748	1848	1924	1948	2048	2148	2248	2248	2348	0048

FRANKFURT - BIBLIS - WORMS and MANNHEIM *SEE NOTE* ⊠

	⚒e	⚒e			⚒e	⚒e				⚒e	⚒e			Ⓐe	Ⓐe			Ⓐe	Ⓐe			Ⓐe	Ⓐe	
Frankfurt (Main) Hbf d.	0609	...	0710	...	0810	...	0913	...	and in the same	1610	...	1713	...	1810	...	1913	...	2010	...	2113	...	2210	...	231
Biblis d.	0657	0700	0758	0804	0858	0904	0958	1004	pattern every	1658	1707	1758	1804	1858	1904	1958	2004	2058	2104	2158	2204	2258	2305	235
Worms Hbf a.	|	0710	|	0814	|	0914	|	1014	two hours until	|	1717	|	1814	|	1913	|	2014	|	2114	|	2214	|	2315	|
Mannheim Hbf a.	0719	...	0819	...	0919	...	1019	...		1719	...	1819	...	1919	...	2019	...	2119	...	2219	...	2319	...	001

km				Ⓐe		⚒e	⚒e				⚒e	⚒e			Ⓐe	Ⓐe			Ⓐe	Ⓐe			Ⓐe	Ⓐe
	Mannheim Hbf d.	0009	...	...	0532	...	0639	...	0739	and in the same	...	1639	...	1739	...	1839	...	1939	...	2039	...	2139	...	223
0	**Worms** Hbf d.	|	...	0535	|	0643	|	0744	|	pattern every	1644	|	1744	|	1844	|	1944	|	2044	|	2144	|	2244	|
10	Biblis d.	0034	...	0545	0559	0653	0659	0754	0759	two hours until	1654	1659	1754	1759	1854	1859	1954	1959	2054	2059	2154	2159	2254	230
63	**Frankfurt** (Main) Hbf a.	0132	...	...	0645	...	0747	...	0845		...	1747	...	1845	...	1947	...	2045	...	2147	...	2245	...	234

MANNHEIM - HEIDELBERG - KARLSRUHE

S-Bahn				†w	⑥k	Ⓐe	Ⓒz	Ⓐe										Ⓒz	Ⓐe							
Mannheim Hbf ⊡ d.	0007	...	0457	0535	*0536*	0544	*0637*	0647	0729	0830	0930	1030	1130	1230	1330	1430	1530	1630	1630	1730	1830	1930	2030	2137	2237	225
Heidelberg Hbf ⊡ d.	0024	...	0517	0558	0558	0603	0706	0706	0748	0848	0948	1048	1148	1248	1348	1448	1548	1648	1648	1748	1848	1948	2048	2155	2255	231
Bruchsal d.	0053	...	0544	0625	0625	0630	0732	0733	0817	0915	1015	1115	1215	1315	1415	1515	1615	1715	1716	1815	1915	2015	2116	2221	2321	234
Karlsruhe Hbf a.	0112	...	0601	0646	0646	0648	0750	0750	0833	0936	1032	1132	1232	1336	1432	1532	1632	1732	1736	1832	1932	2032	2133	2235	2335	240

S-Bahn				Ⓐe	⑥k	†w	Ⓐe	Ⓒz	Ⓐe	Ⓐe															
Karlsruhe Hbf d.	0012	...	0327	0534	0611	0614	0620	0725	0728	0754	0828	0928	1028	1128	1228	1328	1428	1528	1628	1728	1828	1928	2028	2128	2228	232
Bruchsal d.	0026	...	0344	0558	0633	0632	0638	0744	0744	0814	0844	0944	1044	1144	1244	1344	1444	1543	1644	1744	1844	1944	2044	2143	2244	234
Heidelberg Hbf ⊡ d.	0054	...	0413	0634	0709f	0659	0709	0813	0813	0843	0913	1013	1113	1213	1313	1413	1513	1613	1713	1813	1913	2013	2114	2214	2314	001
Mannheim Hbf ⊡ a.	0114	...	0429	0651	0725	*0719*	0725	0829	0829	0901	0929	1029	1129	1229	1329	1429	1529	1629	1729	1829	1929	2029	2132	2232	2332	003

e – Not June 19.
f – Arrives 0700.
j – 1855 on ⑥.
k – Not Nov. 1.
w – Also June 19, Nov. 1.
z – Also June 19.
⊠ – July 26 - Sept. 7 timings may vary by up to 3 minutes on certain journeys.
⊡ – See also Tables **918**, **919**, **923** and **924**.

Local trains KOBLENZ - WIESBADEN - FRANKFURT and KOBLENZ - MAINZ - FRANKFURT 914

Neuwied - Koblenz - St Goarshausen - Wiesbaden - Frankfurt (*Rechte Rheinstrecke*) ❖

km		Ⓐe	⚒r	Ⓐe								Ⓐe		Ⓐe								Ⓒz	Ⓐe	Ⓒz	Ⓐe	
0	**Neuwied** 802 d.	0437	...	0537	...	0637z	0737	0837	0937	1037	1137	...	1237	...	1337	1437	1537	1637	1737	1837	1937	2037	2037	2137	2137	2237
15	**Koblenz** Hbf 802 906 d.	0454	...	0552	...	0654	0754	0854	0954	1054	1154	1224	1254	1324	1354	1454	1554	1654	1754	1854	1954	2054	2054	2154	2154	2254
20	Niederlahnstein 906 d.	0500	...	0558	...	0700	0800	0900	1000	1100	1200	1230	1300	1330	1400	1500	1600	1700	1800	1900	2000	2100	2100	2200	2200	2300
26	Braubach d.	0506	...	0604	...	0706	0806	0906	1006	1106	1206	1236	1306	1336	1406	1506	1606	1706	1806	1906	2006	2106	2106	2206	2206	2306
38	Kamp-Bornhofen d.	0517	...	0615	...	0717	0817	0917	1017	1117	1217	1247	1317	1347	1417	1517	1617	1717	1817	1917	2017	2117	2117	2217	2217	2317
50	St Goarshausen d.	0527	...	0625	...	0727	0827	0927	1027	1127	1227	1257	1327	1357	1427	1527	1627	1727	1827	1927	2027	2127	2127	2227	2227	2327
61	Kaub d.	0536	...	0636	0636	0736	0836	0936	1036	1136	1236	1306	1336	1406	1436	1536	1636	1736	1836	1936	2036	2136	2136	2236	2236	2336
67	Lorch (Rhein) d.	0542	...	0642	0642	0742	0842	0942	1042	1142	1242	1312	1342	1412	1442	1542	1642	1742	1842	1942	2042	2142	2142	2242	2242	...
79	Rüdesheim (Rhein) d.	0553	0553	0653	0653	0753	0853	0953	1053	1153	1253	1323	1353	1423	1453	1553	1653	1753	1853	1953	2053	2153	2153	2253	2253	...
109	**Wiesbaden** Hbf a.	0625	0625	0725	0725	0825	0925	1025	1125	1225	1325	1355	1425	1455	1525	1625	1725	1825	1925	2025	2125	2225	2225	2325	2325	...
109	**Wiesbaden** Hbf d.	0632	0632	0732	0732	0832	0932	1032	1132	1232	1332	...	1432	...	1532	1632	1732	1832	1932	2032	2132	2232	*2235*	2333	*2345*	...
150	**Frankfurt** (Main) Hbf a.	0705	0705	0805	0805	0905	1005	1105	1205	1305	1405	...	1505	...	1605	1705	1805	1905	2005	2105	2205	2305	*2318*	0005	*0043*	...

	Ⓐe	Ⓐe		⚒r										Ⓐe		Ⓐe		Ⓐe		Ⓐe					Ⓐe	Ⓒz
Frankfurt (Main) Hbf d.	...	...	*0442e*	0553e	0653	0753	0853	0953	1053	1153	1253	1353	1453	1523	1553	1622	1653	1723	1753	1823	1853	1953	2053	2153	*2242*	2253
Wiesbaden Hbf a.	...	...	*0524e*	0628e	0728	0828	0928	1028	1128	1228	1328	1428	1528	1558	1628	1658	1728	1758	1828	1858	1928	2028	2128	2228	*2324*	2328
Wiesbaden Hbf d.	...	...	0533e	0633	0733	0833	0933	1033	1133	1233	1333	1433	1533	1603	1633	1703	1733	1803	1833	1903	1933	2033	2133	2233	2333	2333
Rüdesheim (Rhein) d.	...	0531	0606e	0706	0806	0906	1006	1106	1206	1306	1406	1506	1606	1636	1706	1736	1806	1836	1906	1936	2006	2106	2206	2306	0004	0006
Lorch (Rhein) d.	...	0540	0615e	0715	0815	0915	1015	1115	1215	1315	1415	1515	1615	1645	1715	1745	1815	1845	1915	1945	2015	2115	2215	2315	...	0015g
Kaub d.	0450	0550	0623	0723	0823	0923	1023	1123	1223	1323	1423	1523	1623	1653	1724	1753	1823	1854	1924	1954	2023	2123	2223	2323	...	0023g
St Goarshausen d.	0458	0558	0631	0731	0831	0931	1031	1131	1231	1331	1431	1531	1631	1701	1732	1801	1831	1902	1932	2002	2031	2131	2231	...	...	...
Kamp-Bornhofen d.	0509	0609	0642	0742	0842	0942	1042	1142	1242	1342	1442	1542	1642	1712	1743	1812	1842	1913	1943	2013	2042	2142	2242	...	...	...
Braubach d.	0520	0620	0653	0753	0853	0953	1053	1153	1253	1353	1453	1553	1653	1723	1754	1823	1853	1924	1954	2024	2053	2153	2253	...	...	...
Niederlahnstein 906 d.	0526	0626	0659	0759	0859	0959	1059	1159	1259	1359	1459	1559	1659	1729	1800	1829	1859	1930	2000	2030	2059	2159	2259	...	...	...
Koblenz Hbf 802 906 a.	0533	0633	0706	0806	0906	1006	1106	1206	1306	1406	1506	1606	1706	1736	1806	1836	1906	1936	2006	2036	2106	2206	2306	...	...	...
Neuwied 802 a.	0556	...	0726	0826	0926	1026	1126	1226	1326	1426	1526	1626	1726	...	1826	...	1926	...	2026	...	2126	2226	2326	...	...	...

Koblenz - Bingen - Mainz - Frankfurt (*Linke Rheinstrecke*) ⊠

km		Ⓐe	⚒d	Ⓐe		Ⓐe			Ⓐe			Ⓐe			Ⓐe			Ⓐe			Ⓐe					
0	**Koblenz** Hbf d.	0504	0553	0606	0653	0706	0753	0853	0902	0953	1053	1102	1153	1253	1302	1353	1453	1502	1553	1653	1702	1753	1853	1953	2053	2153
19	Boppard Hbf d.	0517	0608	0620	0708	0720	0808	0908	0919	1008	1108	1119	1208	1308	1319	1408	1508	1519	1608	1708	1719	1808	1908	2008	2108	2208
24	Boppard-Bad Salzig d.	|	0612	|	0712	|	0812	0912	|	1012	1112	|	1212	1312	|	1412	1512	|	1612	1712	|	1812	1912	2012	2112	2212
34	St Goar d.	|	0620	|	0720	|	0820	0920	|	1020	1120	|	1220	1320	|	1420	1520	|	1620	1720	|	1820	1920	2020	2120	2220
41	Oberwesel d.	0531	0626	0634	0726	0734	0826	0926	0934	1026	1126	1134	1226	1326	1334	1426	1526	1534	1626	1726	1734	1826	1926	2026	2126	2226
47	Bacharach d.	|	0631	|	0730	|	0830	0930	|	1030	1130	|	1230	1330	|	1430	1530	|	1630	1730	|	1830	1930	2030	2130	2230
61	Bingen (Rhein) Hbf a.	0544	0644	0646	0743	0746	0843	0943	0946	1043	1143	1146	1243	1343	1346	1443	1543	1546	1643	1743	1746	1843	1942	2043	2143	2242
61	Bingen (Rhein) Hbf d.	0545	0654	0647	0752	0747	0854	0955	0947	1055	1155	1147	1255	1354	1347	1455	1554	1547	1655	1755	1747	1855	1943	2055	2157	2244
62	Bingen (Rhein) Stadt d.	|	0657	|	0755	|	0857	0958	|	1058	1158	|	1258	1357	|	1458	1557	|	1658	1758	|	1858	1945	2058	2200	2246
73	Ingelheim d.	0555	0707	0656	0805	0756	0907	1008	0956	1108	1208	1156	1308	1407	1356	1508	1607	1556	1708	1808	1756	1908	1955	2108	2210	2301
91	**Mainz** Hbf a.	0608	0725	0708	0823	0808	0926	1026	1008	1126	1226	1208	1326	1425	1408	1526	1625	1608	1726	1826	1808	1926	2013	2126	2227	2318
119	Frankfurt Flughafen ◨ a.	0634	...	0734	...	0834	...	...	1034	...	...	1234	...	...	1434	...	...	1634	...	...	1834	...	...	...	...	...
130	**Frankfurt** (Main) Hbf a.	0649	...	0751	...	0849	...	...	1049	...	...	1249	...	...	1449	...	...	1649	...	...	1849	...	...	...	...	...

	⚒h		Ⓐe			Ⓐe			Ⓐe			Ⓐe			Ⓐe		Ⓐe		Ⓐe		Ⓐe		Ⓐe			
Frankfurt (Main) Hbf d.	...	...	0706	...	...	0908	...	...	1108	...	...	1308	...	...	1508	...	1608	...	1708	...	1808	...	1858	...	...	...
Frankfurt Flughafen ◨ d.	...	...	0721	...	...	0924	...	...	1124	...	...	1324	...	...	1524	...	1623	...	1721	...	1823	...	1909	...	...	...
Mainz Hbf ¶ d.	0532e	0632	0751	0721	0832	0951	0932	1032	1151	1132	1232	1351	1332	1432	1551	1532	1654	1632	1751	1732z	1851	1832	1933	1933z	2032	2132
Ingelheim ¶ d.	0550e	0650	0803	0740	0850	1003	0951	1050	1203	1150	1250	1403	1350	1450	1603	1551	|	1650	1803	1750z	1903	1851	1952	1952z	2050	2151
Bingen (Rhein) Stadt ¶ d.	0600e	0700	|	0751	0900	|	1003	1100	|	1205	1306	|	1400	1500	|	1603	|	1700	|	1800v	|	1903	2003	2003z	2100	2201
Bingen (Rhein) Hbf ¶ a.	0603e	0703	0811	0754	0902	1011	1005	1102	1211	1208	1310	1411	1402	1502	1611	1605	1712	1702	1811	1802v	1911	1905	2006	2006z	2102	2204
Bingen (Rhein) Hbf d.	0610	0710	0812	0816	0910	1012	1016	1110	1212	1216	1311	1412	1416	1510	1612	1616	1713	1716	1812	1816	1912	1916	...	2010	2111	2210
Bacharach d.	0622	0722	|	0828	0922	|	1028	1122	|	1228	1324	|	1428	1522	|	1628	|	1728	|	1828	|	1928	...	2022	2123	2222
Oberwesel d.	0627	0727	0824	0833	0927	1024	1033	1127	1224	1233	1329	1424	1433	1527	1624	1633	1725	1733	1824	1833	1924	1933	...	2027	2128	2227
St Goar d.	0633	0733	|	0839	0933	|	1039	1133	|	1239	1335	|	1439	1533	|	1639	|	1739	|	1839	|	1939	...	2033	2134	2233
Boppard-Bad Salzig d.	0641	0741	|	0847	0941	|	1047	1141	|	1247	1343	|	1447	1541	|	1647	|	1747	|	1847	|	1947	...	2041	2142	2241
Boppard Hbf d.	0645	0745	0839	0851	0945	1039	1051	1145	1239	1251	1347	1439	1451	1545	1639	1651	1740	1751	1839	1851	1939	1951	...	2045	2146	2245
Koblenz Hbf a.	0702	0802	0853	0908	1002	1053	1108	1202	1253	1308	1404	1453	1508	1602	1653	1708	1753	1808	1853	1908	1953	2008	...	2101	2202	2301

d – ⚒ (not June 19, Nov. 1). Runs daily Bingen (Rhein) Hbf - Mainz Hbf.
e – Ⓐ (not June 19).
g – Rüdesheim - Kaub on the mornings of ① (also June 20, Oct. 4).
h – Not June 19, Nov. 1.
r – Not June 19.
v – 5–6 minutes later on Ⓐ (not June 19).
z – Ⓒ (also June 19).

❖ – Operated by VIAS GmbH.
¶ – Additional journeys Mainz Hbf - Bingen (Rhein) Hbf: 0007 and 2232.
◨ – Frankfurt Flughafen Regionalbahnhof ✈.
⊠ – Stopping services Koblenz - Mainz and v.v. are operated by Mittelrheinbahn. See Table **911** for long-distance *ICE / IC* services. See Table **917a** for S-Bahn service Mainz - Frankfurt Flughafen ✈ - Frankfurt (Main) Hbf and v.v.

2014 service; KD (see shaded panel) KÖLN - KOBLENZ - MAINZ 914a

◐		A	A⛴	K	D	C	E	A	Q	J	G
750	**Köln** (Rheingarten) d.	...	...	...	...	...	...	...	0930	0930	...
1600	**Bonn** d.	...	...	...	...	...	0730	...	1230	1230	...
1300	Bad Godesberg d.	...	...	...	...	...	0800	...	1300	1300	...
900	Königswinter Fähre d.	...	...	...	...	...	0815	...	1330	1330	...
750	Bad Honnef (Rhein) d.	...	...	...	...	...	0835	...	1350	1350	...
400	Remagen d.	...	...	...	...	...	0910	...	1420	1420	...
750	Linz am Rhein d.	...	...	...	...	...	0930	...	1450	1450	...
1500	Bad Breisig d.	...	...	...	0800	...	1000	...	...	1520	...
400	Bad Hönningen d.	...	...	...	0805	...	1005	...	...	1525	...
1200	Andernach d.	...	...	...	0850	...	1050	...	...	...	...
2200	**Koblenz** ⊙ a.	...	...	...	1040	...	1250	...	...	...	...
2200	**Koblenz** ⊙ d.	...	0900	0945	1100	...	1300	1400	...	...	1810
600	Winningen (Mosel) a.	...	|	1055	|	...	1430	|	...	...	|
800	Cochem (Mosel) a.	...	|	1500	|	...	...	|	...	...	|
150	Oberlahnstein d.	...	0940	...	1140	...	...	1440	...	...	1845
450	Braubach d.	...	1005	...	1205	...	...	1505	...	...	1910
400	**Boppard** d.	0900	1100	...	1300	1400	...	1600	...	...	2000
400	Kamp-Bornhofen d.	0910	1110	...	1310	1410	...	1610	...	...	...
300	Bad Salzig d.	0925	1125	...	1325	1425	...	1625	...	...	...
450	**St Goarshausen** ★ d.	1010	1210	...	1410	1510	...	1710	...	...	...
250	**St Goar** ★ d.	1020	1220	...	1420	1520	...	1720	...	...	...
450	Oberwesel d.	1050	1250	...	1450	1550	...	1750	...	...	...
900	Kaub d.	1105	1305	...	1505	1605	...	1805	...	...	...
600	Bacharach d.	1130	1330	...	1530	1630	...	1830	...	...	...
900	Assmannshausen d.	1230	1430	...	1630	1730	...	1930	...	...	...
400	**Bingen** (Rhein) ♥ d.	1300	1500	...	1700	1800	...	2000	...	...	...
900	**Rüdesheim** (Rhein) ♥ d.	1315	1515	...	1715	1815	...	2015	...	...	...
1500	Wiesbaden-Biebrich d.	...	...	...	1905	2005r	...	...	...	...	...
1600	**Mainz** a.	...	...	...	1930	2030r	...	...	...	...	...

	L	A	D‡	C	E		A	G	K	A⛴
Mainz d.	...	...	0845	0945v	...	...	...	...	...	...
Wiesbaden-Biebrich d.	...	...	0905	1005v	...	...	...	...	...	...
Rüdesheim ♥ d.	...	0915	1015	1115	...	...	1415	1415	...	1615
Bingen (Rhein) ♥ d.	...	0930	1030	1130	...	...	1430	1430	...	1630
Assmannshausen d.	...	0945	1045	1145	...	...	1445	1445	...	1645
Bacharach d.	...	1015	1115	1215	...	...	1515	1515	...	1715
Kaub d.	...	1025	1125	1225	...	...	1525	1525	...	1725
Oberwesel d.	...	1035	1135	1235	...	...	1535	1535	...	1735
St Goar ★ d.	...	1055	1155	1255	...	...	1555	1555	...	1755
St Goarshausen ★ d.	...	1105	1205	1305	...	...	1605	1605	...	1805
Bad Salzig d.	...	1130	1230	1330	...	...	1630	1630	...	1830
Kamp-Bornhofen d.	...	1140	1240	1340	...	...	1640	1640	...	1840
Boppard d.	...	1150	1250	1350	...	...	1650	1650	...	1850
Braubach d.	...	1220	1320	...	...	...	...	1720	...	1920
Oberlahnstein d.	...	1240	1340	...	...	...	...	1740	...	1940
Cochem (Mosel) d.	...	|	|	...	...	...	...	|	1540	|
Winningen (Mosel) d.	...	|	|	...	1540	...	...	|	1845	|
Koblenz ⊙ a.	...	1310	1410	...	1700	...	...	1810	2000	2010
Koblenz ⊙ d.	...	...	1430	...	1705	...	...	...	...	...
Andernach d.	...	...	1540	...	1805					
Bad Hönningen d.	...	...	1615‡	...	1830					
Bad Breisig d.	...	...	1620	...	1840					
Linz am Rhein d.	1450	...	1650	...	1905					
Remagen d.	1500	...	1700	...	1915					
Bad Honnef (Rhein) d.	1525	...	1725	...	1940					
Königswinter Fähre d.	1540	...	1740	...	2000					
Bad Godesberg d.	1545	...	1745	...	2010					
Bonn d.	1615	...	1815	...	2030					
Köln (Rheingarten) a.	1800	...	2000	...	...					

Köln-Düsseldorfer Deutsche Rheinschiffahrt AG, Frankenwerft 35, D-50667 Köln.
✆ +49 (0) 221 20 88 318
Fax +49 (0) 221 20 88 345
A special service operates on "Rhein in Flammen" days

– Mar. 29 - Oct. 26.
– Apr. 18 - Oct. 26.
– Apr. 18 - Oct. 5.
– ① July 7 - Sept. 8.
– ①⑤⑥⑦ Mar. 29 - Apr. 14; daily Apr. 18 - Oct. 6; ①⑤⑥⑦ Oct. 10–26.
– ①②③④⑦ Apr. 20 - Oct. 5.
– ⑤–⑦ May 30 - Oct. 5.

L – ⑤⑥ Apr. 18 - Oct. 25 (also Oct. 12, 19, 26).
Q – Daily Apr. 18 - Oct. 5; ⑤–⑦ Oct. 10–26.
r – Daily July 1 - Aug. 31; ④–⑦ Sept. 4 - Oct. 26.
v – Daily July 1 - Sept. 1; ①⑤⑥⑦ Sept. 5 - Oct. 26.
⛴ – Operated by paddlesteamer *Goethe* Apr. 18 - Oct. 5.

‡ – Change boats at Bad Hönningen on ①②③④⑦.
⊙ – Koblenz (Konrad-Adenauer-Ufer).
◐ – Distance in metres from rail station to river landing stage.
★ – A frequent ferry service operates St Goar - St Goarshausen and v.v. Operator: Rheinschifffahrt Goar. ✆ + 49 (0) 6771 26 20.
♥ – Passenger ferry Bingen - Rüdesheim and v.v. Operator: Bingen-Rüdesheimer Fahrgastschiffahrt. ✆ + 49 (0) 6721 30808 10. Service **May 1 - Oct. 31**: From Bingen at 0700 and hourly until 2100. From Rüdesheim at 0730 and hourly until 2130.

915 KOBLENZ - TRIER - LUXEMBOURG and SAARBRÜCKEN

RE / RB services except where shown

km		⑥h	Ⓐt	Ⓐt	Ⓐt K	⑥h	①–⑤ A		Ⓐt K	Ⓒz K	⚒r		⚒r		⚒r		Ⓐt M	⚒r								K
	Emden Hbf **812** d.	...	...	...	...	...	...	...	...	...	...	...	...	...	...	...	...	...	...	...	...	...	...	...	...	...
	Köln Hbf **800 802** d.	...	...	...	...	...	...	...	...	...	...	...	...	...	...	...	...	...	...	...	...	...	...	...	...	...
0	**Koblenz** Hbf d.	...	...	...	...	...	...	...	...	...	...	...	0557	...	...	0622	...	0722	...	0822	0840	...	0940	1022	...	1122
47	Cochem (Mosel) d.	...	...	...	...	0503	0503	...	...	...	...	0610	0634	...	...	0721	...	0758	...	0857	0929	...	1029	1058	...	1158
59	Bullay d.	...	...	...	...	0515	0516	...	...	...	...	0621	0644	...	...	0733	...	0808	...	0908	0940	...	1040	1108	...	1208
76	Wittlich Hbf d.	...	...	...	...	0531	0534	...	...	...	...	0637	0658	...	...	0748	...	0821	...	0920	0955	...	1055	1121	...	1221
112	**Trier** Hbf a.	...	...	...	...	0606	0615	...	...	...	...	0711	0728	...	...	0824	...	0846	...	0945	1036	...	1136	1146	...	1246
112	**Trier** Hbf ⊙ d.	0348	0406	0522	0527	...	0624	0620	0634	...	0701	...	0730	0730	0801	—	0831	—	0901	0946	—	1101	...	1148	1201	1248
	Luxembourg ⊙ a.	|	|	|	|	...	0724	|	|	...	|	...	|	|	|	...	|	⚒r	|	|	...	|	...	|	|	|
135	Saarburg d.	0414	0426	0540	0552	...	...	0641	0659	...	0725	...	0748	0748	0825	...	0849	K	0925	1004	K	1125	...	1206	1225	1306
161	Merzig (Saar) d.	0441	0445	0559	0621	...	...	0701	0723	0729	0751	...	0808	0808	0851	0851	0907	0923	0951	1022	1123	1151	...	1224	1251	1325
173	Dillingen (Saar) d.	0453	0456	0609	0632	...	...	0710	0733	0738	0801	...	0817	0817	0902	0902	0916	0932	1002	1030	1132	1202	...	1232	1302	1336
177	Saarlouis Hbf d.	0457	0500	0613	0635	...	...	0714	0736	0741	0804	...	0821	0821	0905	0905	0920	0935	1005	1034	1135	1205	...	1236	1305	1340
190	Völklingen d.	0508	0511	0624	0645	...	...	0722	0746	0750	0815	...	0831	0831	0916	0916	0928	0944	1016	1042	1144	1216	...	1244	1316	1348
200	**Saarbrücken** Hbf a.	0522	0523	0634	0657	...	...	0733	0754	0759	0828	...	0841	0841	0928	0928	0938	0953	1028	1052	1153	1228	...	1254	1328	1358

							IC 134 N🍷	K			⑥	*IC* 132 Ⓑt N🍷	Ⓐt K				Ⓑ	*IC* 130 ⑥ N🍷	Ⓐt K							♣
Emden Hbf **812** d.	...	...	...	...	...	...	1034	...	...	...	...	1234	...	...	...	...	...	1434	...	...	...	...	...	...	...	...
Köln Hbf **800 802** d.	...	...	...	...	...	...	1418	...	...	...	...	1618	...	...	...	...	...	1818	...	...	...	...	...	...	...	...
Koblenz Hbf d.	...	1222	1240	...	1340	1422	1524	...	1622	...	1722	1724	...	...	1822	...	1923	1924	...	...	2022	2040	...	2140	2222	2325
Cochem (Mosel) d.	...	1258	1329	...	1429	1458	1558	...	1658	...	1758	1758	...	...	1858	...	1959	1958	...	...	2058	2129	...	2229	2258	0014
Bullay d.	...	1308	1340	...	1440	1508	1610	...	1708	...	1808	1810	...	...	1908	...	2010	2010	...	...	2108	2140	...	2240	2308	0023
Wittlich Hbf d.	...	1321	1355	...	1455	1521	1624	...	1721	...	1821	1824	...	...	1921	...	2024	2024	...	...	2121	2155	...	2255	2321	0037
Trier Hbf a.	...	1346	1436	...	1536	1546	1649	...	1746	...	1846	1849	...	...	1946	...	2049	2049	...	...	2146	2236	...	2336	2351	0103
Trier Hbf ⊙ d.	1301	1348	—	1501	...	1548	1657b	1654	1748	1801	...	1851b	1854	1901	1948	2001	2051b	2051b	2054	2101	2148	...	2301	...	*0001*	...
Luxembourg ⊙ a.	|	|	...	|	...	|	1744b	|	|	|	...	1939b	|	|	|	|	2139b	2139b	|	|	|	...	|	...	|	...
Saarburg d.	1325	1406	K	1525	...	1606	...	1712	1806	1825	...	...	1912	1925	2006	2025	...	...	2112	2125	2206	...	2326	...	*0026*	...
Merzig (Saar) d.	1350	1424	1523	1551	...	1624	...	1730	1824	1851	...	...	1930	1951	2024	2051	...	...	2130	2151	2224	...	2349	...	*0053*	...
Dillingen (Saar) d.	1400	1432	1532	1602	...	1632	...	1738	1832	1902	...	...	1938	2002	2032	2102	...	...	2138	2202	2232	...	2358	...	...	...
Saarlouis Hbf d.	1404	1436	1535	1605	...	1636	...	1742	1836	1905	...	...	1942	2005	2036	2105	...	...	2142	2205	2236	...	0002	...	...	...
Völklingen d.	1414	1444	1544	1616	...	1644	...	1750	1844	1916	...	...	1950	2016	2044	2116	...	...	2149	2216	2244	...	0009	...	...	...
Saarbrücken Hbf a.	1426	1453	1553	1628	...	1652	...	1758	1853	1928	...	...	1959	2028	2053	2128	...	...	2159	2227	2254	...	0019	...	...	...

		Ⓐt	Ⓐt	⚒r	Ⓐt		Ⓒz	Ⓐt	*IC* 131 ①–⑥ ¶🍷		⚒r			*IC* 133 N🍷	K◇				K			K			K	*IC* 137 ⑦ 🍷
Saarbrücken Hbf d.	0120	...	...	...	0434	...	0533	0549	...	...	0623	0702	0732	...	0817	0904	...	0932	1001	...	1104	1201	1304	...	1401	...
Völklingen d.	0131	...	...	...	0441	...	0541	0556	...	...	0634	0710	0743	...	0825	0911	...	0943	1008	...	1111	1208	1311	...	1408	...
Saarlouis Hbf d.	0141	...	...	...	0450	...	0551	0607	...	...	0645	0718	0753	...	0834	0920	...	0953	1016	...	1120	1218	1320	...	1416	...
Dillingen (Saar) d.	0145	...	...	...	0453	...	0554	0611	...	...	0648	0722	0757	...	0838	0923	...	0957	1019	...	1123	1222	1323	...	1419	...
Merzig (Saar) d.	0156	...	...	...	0505	...	0602	0620	...	...	0659	0730	0807	...	0846	0932	...	1007	1027	...	1132	1232	1332	...	1427	...
Saarburg d.	—	...	...	...	0532	...	0630	0641	...	...	0725	0749	0833	...	—	0951	...	1033	1045	...	1151	1252	1351	...	1445	...
Luxembourg ⊙ d.	...	...	...	...	|	...	|	|	0620b	...	|	|	|	0820b	...	|	...	|	|	...	|	|	|	...	|	1419b
Trier Hbf ⊙ a.	...	...	...	...	0601	...	0700	0702	0706b	...	0753	0811	0900	0906b	...	1011	...	1059	1104	...	1211	1311	1411	...	1504	1506b
Trier Hbf d.	...	0340	0505	0520	...	0613	...	...	0708	0720	...	0813	...	0908	0920	1013	1020	...	...	1120	1213	1312	1413	1420	...	1508
Wittlich Hbf d.	...	0406	0532	0557	...	0636	...	...	0733	0757	...	0836	...	0933	0957	1036	1057	...	...	1157	1236	1336	1436	1457	...	1533
Bullay d.	⚒r	0418	0546	0612	...	0649	...	...	0747	0812	...	0849	...	0947	1012	1049	1112	...	...	1212	1249	1349	1449	1512	...	1547
Cochem (Mosel) d.	0430	0430	0556	0627	...	0658	...	...	0758	0826	...	0858	...	0958	1026	1058	1126	...	...	1226	1258	1358	1458	1526	...	1558
Koblenz Hbf a.	0520	0520	0636	0721	...	0737	...	...	0835	0918	...	0937	...	1035	1118	1137	1218	...	...	1318	1337	1437	1537	1618	...	1635
Köln Hbf **800 802** a.	...	...	...	...	...	...	...	...	0942	...	...	...	...	1142	...	...	...	...	...	...	...	...	...	...	...	1742
Emden Hbf **812** a.	...	...	...	...	...	...	...	...	1325	...	...	...	...	1525	...	...	...	...	...	...	...	...	...	...	...	2125

				Ⓐt K	Ⓒz K	Ⓑ	⑥	Ⓐt M				K	† K	Ⓑq					K							Ⓑq
Saarbrücken Hbf d.	...	1504	1532	1601	1601	...	...	1623	1632	1704	1732	1801	1801	...	...	1832	1905	...	2004	...	2032	...	2115	2234	2321	2343
Völklingen d.	...	1511	1543	1608	1608	...	...	1632	1643	1711	1743	1808	1808	...	...	1843	1912	...	2011	...	2043	...	2123	2241	2332	2354
Saarlouis Hbf d.	...	1520	1553	1616	1617	...	...	1643	1653	1720	1753	1816	1816	...	...	1853	1921	...	2021	...	2053	...	2131	2251	2342	0006
Dillingen (Saar) d.	...	1523	1557	1619	1620	...	...	1647	1657	1723	1757	1819	1819	...	...	1857	1924	...	2025	...	2057	...	2135	2254	2346	0009
Merzig (Saar) d.	...	1532	1607	1627	1631	...	...	1657	1707	1732	1807	1827	1827	...	...	1907	1932	...	2034	...	2107	...	2144	2303	2356	0021
Saarburg d.	...	1551	1633	1645	...	...	...	1726	1733	1751	1833	1846	1846	...	...	1933	1952	...	2054	...	2133	...	2206	2328	...	0040
Luxembourg ⊙ d.	...	|	|	|	...	1619b	*1619*b	|	|	|	|	|	|	...	...	|	|	...	|	...	|	...	|	|	...	|
Trier Hbf ⊙ a.	...	1611	1700	1705	...	1707b	*1707*b	1753	1800	1811	1900	1908	1908	...	...	2000	2012	...	2115	...	2200	...	2228	2400	...	0103
Trier Hbf d.	1520	1613	...	...	...	1709	1713	...	...	1813	...	...	1913	1913	1920	...	2013	2113	...	2120	...	2220	...	...	...	...
Wittlich Hbf d.	1557	1636	...	...	...	1734	1736	...	...	1837	...	...	1938	1938	1957	...	2036	2136	...	2157	...	2257	...	...	...	...
Bullay d.	1612	1649	...	...	...	1748	1749	...	...	1849	...	...	1950	1950	2012	...	2049	2149	...	2212	...	2312	...	...	...	...
Cochem (Mosel) d.	1626	1658	...	...	...	1758	1758	...	...	1858	...	...	1959	1959	2026	...	2058	2158	...	2226	...	2325	...	...	...	...
Koblenz Hbf a.	1718	1737	...	...	...	1837	1837	...	...	1938	...	...	2038	2038	2118	...	2137	2237	...	2318	...	...	...	...	...	...
Köln Hbf **800 802** a.	...	...	...	...	...	...	...	...	...	...	...	...	...	...	...	...	...	...	...	...	...	...	...	...	...	...
Emden Hbf **812** a.	...	...	...	...	...	...	...	...	...	...	...	...	...	...	...	...	...	...	...	...	...	...	...	...	...	...

Complete service TRIER - LUXEMBOURG and v.v. SERVICE JUNE 28 - NOV. 21 (SEE PAGE 563 FOR SERVICE TO JUNE 27).

km	🏛 at Igel	B		①–⑤	①–⑤	①–⑥ h	①–⑤	⑦ q	①–⑤ t				①–⑥						♥		Ⓑ ♥	⑥ h		Ⓑ	⑥ ♥	
0	**Trier** Hbf d.	0007	...	0535	0624	0640	0655	0702	0724	0752	0852	0952	1056	1152	1252	1352	1457	1552	1657	1752	1851	1851	1952	2051	2051	2152
51	**Luxembourg** a.	0101	...	0633	0724	0747	0753v	0807	0824	0850	0947	1049	1144	1249	1349	1449	1544	1649	1744	1845	1939	1939	2045	2139	2139	2245

🏛 at Wasserbillig	①–⑤	①–⑥ ♥	①–⑤		♥						⑦ ♥	①–⑥			①–⑤ a	⑥⑦ w	①–⑤	①–⑤ a	⑥⑦ w	①–⑤					⑥⑦ w	①–⑤ a
Luxembourg d.	0517	0620	0634	0710	0820	0914	1023	1114	1212	1314	1419	1419	1514	1619	1708	1717	1738	1808	1817	1838	1917	2017	2117	...	2248	2250
Trier Hbf a.	0606	0706	0734	0806	0906	1006	1108	1206	1306	1406	1506	1508	1606	1707	1806	1806	1832	1904	1905	1932	2006	2106	2206	...	2356	2356

A – ①–⑤ June 30 - Nov. 21.
B – June 29 - Nov. 17.
K – To / from Kaiserslautern (Table **919**).
M – To / from Mannheim (Table **919**).
N – From / to Norddeich Mole (Table **812**).

a – Not Aug. 15.
b – June 28 - Nov. 21.
h – Not Nov. 1.
q – Also Nov. 1.
r – Not June 19, Nov. 1.
t – Not June 19.
v – 0807 on Aug. 15.
w – Also Aug. 15.
z – Also June 19.

¶ – On ②③④⑥ from Oct. 28 runs with train number **231** and continues to Norddeich Mole.
♣ – ①②③④⑦.
◇ – Runs 2–4 minutes later on ①–⑤.
♥ – *IC* train (see main Table).
⊙ – See also panel below main table.

BULLAY - TRABEN-TRARBACH *13 km* Journey time: 20 minutes

From Bullay at 0655 ⚒r, 0817, 0917 and hourly until 2217.
From Traben-Trarbach at 0619 ⚒r, 0721, 0843, 0943 and hourly until 2143.

TRIER - PERL - METZ

km		⑥⑦	⑥⑦		⑥⑦	⑥⑦
0	**Trier** Hbf d.	0958	1958	**Metz** d.	0758	1812
49	Perl 🏛 d.	1042	2042	Hagondange d.	|	1825
70	Thionville a.	1110	2111	Thionville d.	0820	1834
82	Hagondange a.	|	|	Perl 🏛 d.	0852	1910
100	**Metz** a.	1136	2136	**Trier** Hbf a.	0932	1952

Other local *RB* services **Trier** - **Perl** and v.v. Journey time: 47–48 minutes.

From Trier Hbf at 0508 Ⓐt, 0553 Ⓐt, 0708 ⚒r, 0808, 0908 Ⓐt, 1008, 1108 Ⓐt, 1208, 1322 Ⓐt, 1408, 1508 Ⓐt, 1608, 1708, 1808, 1908 Ⓐt, 2008 and 2208.

From Perl at 0501 Ⓐt, 0601 ⚒r, 0631 Ⓐt, 0647 Ⓐt, 0801, 0901, 1001 Ⓐt, 110[illegible] 1201 Ⓐt, 1301, 1431 Ⓐt, 1501, 1601 Ⓐt, 1701, 1801, 1901, 2001 Ⓐt and 2101.

KARLSRUHE - OFFENBURG - KONSTANZ — 916

IRE / RE services except where shown

km		Ⓐe	⑥x	Ⓒz								IC 2005 ⑤⑥f E🍷		IC 2279 ①-⑥ G🍷			IC 2371 ⑦ B🍷	IC 2364 ①-⑤ a S				† q	✕r ●	⑤† wd
0	**Karlsruhe** Hbf .. 912 943 ⊠ d.	...	0500	...	0607	0704	0809	0909	1009	1109	1209	1309	1336b	1409	1452	1509	1609	1652	1733	1809	1909	2009	2116	2116	2221
23	Rastatt .... 943 ⊠ d.	...	0513	...	0619	0718	0823	0923	1023	1123	1223	1323	|	1423	1505	1523	1623	1706	1747	1823	1923	2023	2129	2129	2240
31	Baden-Baden .... 912 ⊠ d.	...	0519	...	0625	0726	0830	0930	1030	1130	1230	1330	1356b	1430	1516	1530	1630	1717	1754	1830	1930	2030	2136	2136	2247
71	**Offenburg** .... 912 942 d.	0523	0554j	...	0658	0758	0859	0959	1059	1159	1259	1359	1418	1459	1536	1559	1659	1735	1813	1859	1959	2107j	2205	2205	2323j
104	Hausach .... 942 d.	0548	0619	...	0723	0818	0921	1018	1121	1218	1321	1418	1439	1521	1555	1618	1721	1755	▬	1921	2018	2131	2228	2229	2348
114	Hornberg (Schwarzw) .... d.	0556	0627	...	0731	0826	0930	1026	1130	1226	1330	1426	1448	1530	1603	1626	1730	1803	...	1930	2026	2139	2236	2237	2356
127	Triberg .... d.	0609	0640	...	0744	0839	0944	1039	1144	1239	1344	1439	1503	1544	1617	1639	1744	1817	...	1944	2039	2152	2249	2250	0009
142	St Georgen (Schwarzw) .... d.	0625	0655	...	0759	0854	0958	1054	1158	1253	1358	1454	1520	1558	1632	1654	1758	1832	...	1958	2054	2206	2304	2304	0023
157	Villingen (Schwarzw) ..... 938 d.	0636	0705	0705	0808	0904	1009	1104	1209	1303	1409	1504	1531	1609	1642	1704	1809	1842	...	2009	2104	2215	2313	2313	0032
171	Donaueschingen .... 938 d.	0654j	0714	0714	0817	0913	1018	1113	1218	1313	1418	1513	1542	1618	1653	1713	1818	1853	...	2018	2113	2224	2323	...	...
190	Immendingen .... 938 d.	0706	0726	0726	0828	|	1029	|	1229	|	1429	|	1554	1629	1704	|	1829	1904	...	2029	2123	2236	2335	...	...
206	Engen .... 940 d.	0719	0738	0738	0841	|	1041	|	1242	|	1442	|	|	1642	|	|	1842	|	1948	2042	|	2248	|	...	...
220	**Singen** .... 939 940 d.	0735	0752	0752	0853	0953j	1053	1153j	1253	1353j	1453	1553j	1626j	1653	1726	1753j	1853	1926	2002	2053	2155j	2302	2356	...	...
230	Radolfzell .... 939 d.	0746	0800	0800	0900	1000	1100	1200	1300	1400	1500	1600	1634	1700	1734	1800	1900	1934	2012	2100	2202	2311	0003	...	...
250	**Konstanz** .... a.	0810	0816	0816	0916	1016	1116	1216	1316	1416	1516	1616	1650	1716	1751	1816	1916	1951	2035	2116	2217	2330	0018	...	...

	IC 2365 Ⓐe S🍷	✕r	✕r	Ⓐe	Ⓒz	●			IC 2004 ⑦v E🍷	IC 2006 ⑥z D🍷	IC 2370 A🍷										⑤† m	⊕		⑤ u	
Konstanz .... d.	...	...	0502e	0524	0551	0638	0735	0838	0909	0909	1006	1038	1138	1238	1338	1438	1538	1638	1738	1838	1938	2038	2159	2159	2322
Radolfzell .... 939 d.	...	...	0516e	0545j	0606	0655	0753	0855	0923	0923	1025	1055	1153	1255	1353	1455	1553	1655	1753	1855	1953	2055	2223	2223	2346
Singen .... 939 940 d.	...	...	0530j	0557	0614	0705	0814j	0905	0932	0932	1034	1105	1214j	1305	1414j	1505	1614j	1705	1814j	1905	2014j	2105	2234	2234	0000
Engen .... 940 d.	...	...	0539	|	|	0715	|	0914	|	|	|	1114	|	1314	|	1514	|	1714	|	1914	|	2114	2250	2250	0013
Immendingen .... 938 d.	...	...	0552	0618	0635	0728	|	0928	0953	0953	1056	1128	|	1328	|	1528	|	1728	|	1928	|	2127	2307	2307	...
Donaueschingen .... 938 d.	...	*0505*	0603	0630	0645	0740	0845	0939	1005	1005	1107	1139	1245	1339	1445	1539	1645	1739	1845	1939	2045	2140	2319	2319	...
Villingen (Schwarzw) ..... 938 d.	...	0535	0612	0641	0655	0750	0855	0949	1016	1016	1117	1149	1255	1349	1455	1549	1655	1749	1855	1949	2055	2150	2328	2329	...
St Georgen (Schwarzw) .... d.	...	0544	0621	0650	0703	0759	0904	0958	1026	1026	1126	1158	1303	1358	1503	1558	1703	1758	1903	1958	2103	2158	...	2338	...
Triberg .... d.	...	0558	0635	0705	0718	0814	0918	1012	1042	1042	1141	1212	1318	1413	1518	1612	1718	1812	1918	2012	2118	2213	...	2353	...
Hornberg (Schwarzw) .... d.	...	0612	0649	0718	0731	0828	0927	1027	1057	1057	1155	1227	1327	1427	1527	1627	1727	1827	1927	2027	2131	2226	...	0006	...
Hausach .... 942 d.	...	0621	0657	0727	0739	0836	0939	1035	1105	1105	1203	1235	1339	1435	1539	1635	1739	1835	1939	2035	2139	2234	...	0014	...
Offenburg .... 912 942 a.	0558	0647	0719	0747	0758	0858	0958	1058	1125	1125	1221	1258	1358	1458	1558	1658	1758	1858	1958	2058	2158	2300	...	0039	...
Baden-Baden .... 912 a.	0615	0723	0800e	0819	0827	0927t	1027	1127	1200	1200	1240	1327	1427	1527	1627	1727	1827	1927	2027	2127	2227q	2346	...	...	...
Rastatt .... 943 a.	0622	0730	0806e	0825	0833	0933t	1033	1133	|	|	1250	1333	1433	1533	1633	1733	1833	1933	2033	2133	2233q	2352	...	...	...
Karlsruhe Hbf .... 912 943 a.	0635	0749	0821e	0839	0849	0949t	1049	1149	1219	1219	1307	1349	1449	1549	1649	1749	1849	1949	2049	2149	2249q	0005	...	...	...

A – SCHWARZWALD – 🛏12 and 🍷 Konstanz - Heidelberg - Frankfurt - Hannover - Hamburg (- Stralsund ⑤⑦ h). Train number **2270** on ⑤⑦ (also June 18, Oct. 2; not Oct. 3). Terminates at Hannover June 14 - July 27.
B – 🛏12 and 🍷 Hamburg - Hannover - Frankfurt - Heidelberg - Konstanz. Starts from Hannover June 15 - July 27.
D – BODENSEE – 🛏12 and 🍷 Konstanz - Mannheim - Köln - Dortmund.
E – BODENSEE – 🛏12 and 🍷 Konstanz - Mannheim - Köln - Emden and v.v.
G – SCHWARZWALD – 🛏12 and 🍷 Stralsund - Hamburg - Hannover - Kassel - Frankfurt - Heidelberg - Konstanz. Starts from Hannover June 14 - July 26.
S – From / to Stuttgart (Table **931**).

a – Not June 19, 20, Aug. 1, 8, 15, 22, 29, Sept. 5, 12, Oct. 3.
b – 3–4 minutes later Aug. 1 - Sept. 6.
d – Runs daily Karlsruhe - Hausach.
e – Ⓐ (not June 19).
f – Also June 18, 19, Oct. 2; not June 20.
h – Also Oct. 2; not Oct. 3.
j – Arrives 8–12 minutes earlier.
m – Also June 19, Oct. 2, Nov. 1.
q – † (also June 19, Nov. 1).

r – Not June 19, Nov. 1.
t – 3–6 minutes later on Ⓐ (not June 19).
u – Not Oct. 3.
v – Also Oct. 3.
w – Also June 19, Nov. 1.
x – Not Nov. 1.
z – Also June 19.

● – Change trains at Offenburg on Ⓐ (not June 19).
⊕ – Change trains at Offenburg on ⑤.
⊠ – Timings Karlsruhe - Offenburg and v.v. are subject to alteration July 31 - Sept. 14 (departures may be up to 6 minutes **earlier** / arrivals up to 9 minutes later).

FRANKFURT - MAINZ - IDAR OBERSTEIN - SAARBRÜCKEN — 917

RB / RE services

SERVICE TO JULY 27 AND FROM SEPT. 5. See page 563 for service July 28 - Sept. 4.

km		Ⓐe	Ⓐe	✕r	✕r											⑤f			⊖					Ⓐe	★
0	**Frankfurt** (Main) Hbf .... ‡ d.	...	...	...	...	...	0725	0825	...	1025	...	1225	...	1425	...	1529	1625	...	1734	1825	...	2025	...	2225	...
11	Frankfurt Flughafen ✈ § .... ‡ d.	...	...	...	...	...	0737	0837	...	1037	...	1237	...	1437	...	|	1638	...	|	1837	...	2037	...	2237	...
39	**Mainz** Hbf .... ‡ d.	...	0510	...	b	0655	0800	0900	1000	1100	1155	1300	1355	1500	1555	1608	1700	1755	1808	1900	1955	2100	2205	2300	2338
80	Bad Kreuznach .... d.	*0501*	0542	...	0632e	0737	0826	0926	1026	1126	1225	1326	1424	1526	1624	1645	1726	1824	1845	1926	2024	2126	2244	2326	0019
102	Bad Sobernheim .... d.	*0523*	0603	...	0654	0755	0844	0944	1044	1144	1245	1344	1445	1544	1645	1708	1744	1845	1908	1944	2045	2144	2307	2344	0042
117	Kirn .... d.	*0540*	0619	...	0712	0805	0854	0954	1054	1154	1255	1354	1455	1554	1655	1727	1754	1855	1927	1954	2055	2154	2323	2354	0058
131	Idar-Oberstein .... d.	*0558*	0635	0635	0729	0816	0905	1005	1105	1205	1307	1405	1506	1605	1706	1744	1805	1906	1944	2005	2106	2205	2340	0005	0115
155	Türkismühle .... d.	0634	0704	0704	0759	0837	0926	1026	1126	1226	1328	1426	1526	1626	1726	...	1826	1926	...	2026	2126	2226	...	0026	...
170	St Wendel .... d.	0651	0723	0723	0818	0850	0938	1038	1138	1238	1340	1438	1538	1638	1738	...	1838	1938	...	2038	2138	2238	...	0038	...
179	Ottweiler (Saar) .... d.	0658	0733	0733	0826	0858	0945	1045	1145	1245	1347	1445	1545	1645	1745	...	1845	1945	...	2045	2145	2245	...	0045	...
184	Neunkirchen (Saar) .... d.	0705	0740	0740	0833	0905	0952	1052	1152	1252	1353	1452	1552	1652	1752	...	1852	1952	...	2052	2152	2252	...	0052	...
205	**Saarbrücken** Hbf .... a.	0722	0800	0800	0854	0924	1011	1111	1211	1311	1413	1511	1611	1711	1811	...	1911	2012	...	2111	2212	2311	...	0111	...

		Ⓐe	Ⓐe	✕v																Ⓑw	Ⓐe			
Saarbrücken Hbf .... d.	0115	0348	...	0446	0546	0651	0749	0851	0949	1051	1149	1251	1349	1451	1549	1651	1749	1849	1935	2035	2105	...	2135	2235	2343
Neunkirchen (Saar) .... d.	0144	0404	...	0504	0602	0708	0807	0908	1008	1108	1208	1308	1408	1508	1608	1708	1808	1908	2002	2108	2134	...	2214	2322j	0010
Ottweiler (Saar) .... d.	0151	0410	...	0510	0608	0713	0813	0913	1013	1113	1213	1313	1413	1513	1613	1713	1813	1913	2009	2115	2141	...	2221	2329	0017
St Wendel .... d.	0202	0417	...	0517	0616	0720	0820	0920	1020	1120	1220	1320	1420	1520	1620	1720	1820	1920	2020	2125	2151	2202	2233	2337	0028
Türkismühle .... d.	...	0428	...	0528	0627	0731	0831	0931	1031	1131	1231	1331	1431	1531	1631	1731	1831	1931	2037	2141	...	2222	2253	2353	...
Idar-Oberstein .... d.	...	0449	...	0549	0648	0752	0852	0952	1052	1152	1252	1352	1452	1552	1652	1752	1852	1952	2103	▬	...	2251f	...	...	...
Kirn .... d.	...	0500	0505	0600	0659	0803	0903	1003	1103	1203	1303	1403	1503	1603	1703	1803	1903	2003	2117	...	...	...	...	...	...
Bad Sobernheim .... d.	...	0509	0523	0610	0709	0812	0913	1012	1112	1212	1312	1412	1512	1612	1712	1812	1912	2012	2131	...	...	...	...	...	...
Bad Kreuznach .... d.	...	0528	0602	0631	0731	0832	0934	1032	1133	1232	1333	1432	1533	1632	1733	1832	1933	2033	2152	2247	...	...	...	...	...
Mainz Hbf .... ‡ a.	...	0557	0639	0657	0757	0857	1005	1057	1205	1257	1405	1457	1605	1657	1805	1857	2005	2105	2219	2324	...	...	...	...	...
Frankfurt Flughafen ✈ § ..... ‡ a.	...	0620	|	0720	0820	0920	...	1120	...	1320	...	1520	...	1720	...	1920	...	...	...	...	...	...	...	...	...
Frankfurt (Main) Hbf .... ‡ a.	...	0636	0724	0736	0836	0936	...	1136	...	1336	...	1536	...	1736	...	1936	...	...	...	...	...	...	...	...	...

b – From Bingen (Table **918**).
e – Ⓐ (not June 19).
f – ⑤ (not Oct. 3).
j – Arrives 2302.
r – Not June 19, Nov. 1.
v – Not June 19.
w – Also Nov. 1.
⊖ – ①-④ (not June 19).
★ – ⑤-⑦ (also June 19).
‡ – See also Tables **911 / 914 / 917a**.
§ – Frankfurt Flughafen Regionalbahnhof.

FRANKFURT - FRANKFURT FLUGHAFEN ✈ - MAINZ - WIESBADEN — 917a

S-Bahn 8 / 9

				✕r	✕r		✕r	†z	✕r	⊠	✕r	†z	✕r	✕r		†z	✕r		✕r		†z	✕r		⊠
Frankfurt (Main) Hbf ▽ d.	0017	0117	0317	0417	0502	0517	0532	0547	0547	and at	1232	1247	1247	1302	1317	1331*	1332	1347	1402	1417	1431*	1432	1447	and at
Frankfurt Flughafen .. ¶ d.	0029	0129	0329	0429	0514	0529	0544	0559	0559	the same	1244	1259	1259	1314	1329	1344	1344	1359	1414	1429	1444	1444	1459	the same
Mainz Hbf .... d.	0057	0157	0400	0457	|	0557	|	|	0627	minutes	|	|	1327	|	1357	|	|	1435j	|	1457	|	|	1527	minutes
Mainz-Kastel .... d.	|	|	|	|	0538	|	0608	0623	|	past each	1308	1323	|	1338	|	1408	1408	|	1438	|	1508	1508	|	past each
Wiesbaden Hbf .... a.	0110	0210	0413	0510	0548	0610	0618	0633	0640	hour until	1318	1333	1340	1348	1410	1418	1418	1448	1448	1510	1518	1518	1540	hour until

	✕r		†z	✕r									
Frankfurt (Main) Hbf ▽ d.	2002	2017	2031*	2032	2047	2117	2131*	2147	2217	2231*	2247	2317	2331*
Frankfurt Flughafen .. ¶ d.	2014	2029	2044	2044	2059	2129	2144	2159	2229	2244	2259	2329	2344
Mainz Hbf .... d.	|	2057	|	|	2127	2157	|	2227	2257	|	2327	2357	|
Mainz-Kastel .... d.	2038	|	2108	2108	|	|	2208	|	|	2308	|	|	0008
Wiesbaden Hbf .... a.	2048	2110	2118	2118	2140	2210	2218	2240	2310	2318	2340	0010	0018

			✕r	†z	✕r		✕r	✣
Wiesbaden Hbf .... d.	0245	0345	0415	0426	0441	0445	0511	and at
Mainz-Kastel .... d.	|	|	|	0434	0449	|	0519	the same
Mainz Hbf .... d.	0302	0402	0432	|	|	0502	|	minutes
Frankfurt Flughafen ¶ d.	0335	0432	0502	0502	0517	0532	0547	past each
Frankfurt (Main) Hbf. a.	0346	0443	0513	0513	0528	0543	0558	hour until

	✕r	†z	✕r		✕r				✕r		✕r														
Wiesbaden Hbf .... d.	1115	1126	1141	1145	1211	1215	1241	1245	1311	and at	1911	1915	1941	1945	2015	2041	2045	2115	2141	2145	2215	2241	2245	2345	0045
Mainz-Kastel .... d.	|	1134	1149	|	1219	|	1249	|	1319	the same	1919	|	1949	|	|	2049	|	|	2149	|	|	2249	|	|	|
Mainz Hbf .... d.	1132	|	|	1202	|	1232	|	1302	|	minutes	|	1932	|	2002	2032	|	2102	2132	|	2202	2232	|	2302	0002	0102
Frankfurt Flughafen .. ¶ d.	1202	1202	1217	1232	1247	1302	1317	1332	1347	past each	1947	2002	2017	2032	2102	2117	2132	2202	2217	2232	2302	2317	2332	0032	0132
Frankfurt (Main) Hbf .. a.	1213	1213	1228	1243	1258	1313	1329	1343	1358	hour until	1958	2013	2029	2043	2113	2129	2143	2213	2229	2243	2313	2329	2343	0043	0143

j – Arrives 1425.
r – Not June 19.
z – Also June 19.
▽ – From the underground platforms.
¶ – Frankfurt Flughafen Regionalbahnhof ✈.
✣ – Wiesbaden Hbf d. 0614 (not 0615).
* – Departs from the main station (not underground platforms).
⊠ – The 0947 ✕r, 1147 ✕r, 1547, 1747 and 1947 from Frankfurt (Main) Hbf run 8 minutes later Mainz Hbf - Wiesbaden Hbf. On ⑥ the 0747 from Frankfurt (Main) Hbf runs 8 minutes later Mainz Hbf - Wiesbaden Hbf.

918 RHEINLAND-PFALZ LOCAL SERVICES *RB / S-Bahn services*

PIRMASENS - SAARBRÜCKEN

km		Ⓐe	⚒r	Ⓐe	⚒r	†w				
0	**Pirmasens** Hbf d.	0515	0552	*0622*	*0732*	0732	0832	and hourly until	1932	2032
7	Pirmasens Nord d.	0522	0602	0641	0743	0743	0843		1943	2043
31	Zweibrücken Hbf d.	0552	0640	0713	0813	0813	0913		2013	2113
67	**Saarbrücken** Hbf a.	0636	0722	0752	0851	0851	0951		2051	2151

	Ⓒz	⚒r	Ⓐe						
Saarbrücken Hbf d.	0045	0602	0633	0704	0807	and hourly until	1907	2007	2107
Zweibrücken Hbf d.	0128	0643	0712	0745	0845		1945	2045	2145
Pirmasens Nord a.	0157	0715	0741	0815	0915		2015	2115	2215
Pirmasens Hbf a.	0205	*0728*k	0753	0826	0926		2026	2126	2226

PIRMASENS - LANDAU (Pfalz) - NEUSTADT (Weinstr)

km		Ⓐe	⑥p	Ⓐe	Ⓐe		†w	⚒r								†w	⚒r							
0	**Pirmasens** Hbf d.	0440	0542	0544	0622	0702	0802	0802	0902	1002	1102	1202	1302	1402	1502	1602	1602	1702	1802	1902	2002	...	...	...
7	Pirmasens Nord d.	0452	0555	0609	0634	0718	0818	0818	0918	1018	1118	1218	1318	1418	1518	1618	1618	1718	1818	1918	2018	...	...	...
55	**Landau** (Pfalz) Hbf a.	0548	0658	0708	0735	0818	0915	0918	1018	1118	1218	1318	1418	1518	1618	1715	1718	1818	1918	2018	2118	2140	...	...
73	**Neustadt** (Weinstr) Hbf a.	*0615*	*0801*	0732	0757	*0845*	*0945*	*0945*	*1044*	*1145*	*1245*	*1345*	*1445*	*1545*	*1646*	*1746*	*1746*	*1845*	*1945*	*2045*	...	2202	...	...

	Ⓐe		Ⓐe	⑥p		Ⓐe	†w	⑥p				D	†EM											
Neustadt (Weinstr) Hbf d.	*0426*	...	*0529*	*0612*	...	0659	0700	0716	...	...	*0816*	*0916*	0916	*1016*	*1116*	*1216*	*1316*	*1416*	*1516*	*1616*	*1716*	*1816*	*1916*	*2016*
Landau (Pfalz) Hbf d.	0528	...	0608	0641	...	0712	0721	0737	0741	...	0841	0941	0941	1041	1141	1241	1341	1441	1541	1641	1741	1841	1941	2041
Pirmasens Nord a.	0632	...	0715	0740	...	...	...	...	0840	...	0940	1040	1040	1140	1240	1340	1440	1540	1640	1740	1840	1940	2040	2140
Pirmasens Hbf a.	0657	...	0728	0757	...	...	...	...	0857	...	0957	1057	1057	1157	1257	1357	1457	1557	1657	1757	1857	1957	2057	2157

BINGEN - KAISERSLAUTERN - PIRMASENS

km		Ⓐe	Ⓐe	⚒r	⚒r		ⒶeS							◇						†w		⚒r	⑤⑥f	Ⓒz
0	**Bingen** (Rhein) Hbf d.	...	...	...	0549	...	0612	0649	...	0755	...	0855	...	and at the same minutes past each hour until	1755	...	1855	...	1955	2102	...	2210	...	...
16	Bad Kreuznach d.	...	0506	...	0610	...	0631	0710	...	0816	...	0916	...		1816	...	1916	...	2016	2131	...	2230	2249	...
43	Rockenhausen d.	...	0534	...	0639	...	...	0740	...	0855	...	0955	...		1855	...	1955	...	2055	2159	...	...	2317	...
79	**Kaiserslautern** Hbf a.	...	0609	...	0717	...	...	0819	...	0926q	...	1026	...		1926	...	2026	...	2130	2237	...	...	2349	...
79	**Kaiserslautern** Hbf d.	0516	...	0626	...	0735	...	...	0835	...	0935	...	1035		...	1935	...	2035	...	...	2300	...	...	0030
108	Pirmasens Nord a.	0553	...	0707	...	0806	...	...	0906	...	1006	...	1106		...	2006	...	2107	...	...	2332	...	...	0101
115	**Pirmasens** Hbf a.	0608	...	0719	...	0818	...	...	0918	...	1018	...	1118		...	2018	...	2118	...	...	2341	...	...	0111

	⚒r	⚒r	Ⓐe	Ⓐe	J																			
Pirmasens Hbf d.	...	...	0531	...	0640	...	0732t	...	0841	...	and at the same minutes past each hour until	1441	...	1541	...	1641	...	1741	...	1841	...	1941	...	2041
Pirmasens Nord d.	...	...	0538	...	0648	...	0750	...	0850	...		1450	...	1550	...	1650	...	1750	...	1850	...	1950	...	2050
Kaiserslautern Hbf a.	...	...	0609	...	0720	...	0826	...	0926	...		1526	...	1626	...	1726	...	1828	...	1927	...	2026	...	2126
Kaiserslautern Hbf d.	0521	0556	*0625*	0640	...	0737	...	0832	...	0932		...	1532	...	1638	...	1738	...	1838	...	1932	...	2032	*2142*
Rockenhausen d.	0555	0636	*0656*	0713	...	0812	...	0901	...	1001		...	1601	...	1708	...	1808	...	1908	...	2001	...	2101	*2213*
Bad Kreuznach d.	0642	0717	*0725*	0743	...	0841	...	0941	...	1041		...	1641	...	1741	...	1841	...	1941	...	2041	...	2132	*2253*
Bingen (Rhein) Hbf a.	0701	0736	...	0803	...	0901	...	1001	...	1101		...	1701	...	1801	...	1901	...	2001	...	2101	...	2151	...

NEUSTADT (Weinstr) - KARLSRUHE and WISSEMBOURG

km		Ⓐe	Ⓐe	Ⓐe	⚒r	⚒r	⚒r	Ⓐe	†w	⑥p							D	†E		D	†E			Ⓐe	Ⓒz
0	**Neustadt** (Weinstr) Hbf d.	0426	...	*0507*	0529	0612	0636e	0659	0700	0709	0736	0809	0836	0909v	0936	1009	1036	1044	1109	1136	1145	1209	1236	1305	1309
18	Landau (Pfalz) Hbf d.	0448	...	*0536*	0555	0634	0655e	0713	0722	0722	0758	0822	0858	0922	0958	1022	1058	1058	1122	1158	1159	1222	1258	1319	1322
31	Winden (Pfalz) d.	0504	0505	0555	0603	0651	0706	0722	0731	0731	0809	0831	0909	0931	1009	1031	1109	1108	1131	1209	1208	1231	1309	1331	1331
47	**Wissembourg** 🏛 ◐ a.	|	0521	0615	|	|	0726	|	|	|	0827	|	0927	|	1028	|	1128	1128	|	1228	1228	|	1327	|	|
44	Wörth (Rhein) d.	0519	...	...	0617	0709	...	0735	0744	0744	...	0844	...	0944	...	1044	...	...	1144	...	...	1244	...	1344	1344
58	**Karlsruhe** Hbf a.	0533	...	...	0636	0726	...	0753	0754	0754	...	0854	...	0954	...	1054	...	...	1154	...	...	1254	...	1354	1354

			✤								⑥p
Neustadt (Weinstr) Hbf d.	1336	1409	and at the same minutes past each hour until	1909	1936	2009	2104	*2136*	2226	2333	2333
Landau (Pfalz) Hbf d.	1358	1422		1922	1958	2022	2122	*2158*	2248	2354	2355
Winden (Pfalz) d.	1409	1431		1931	2009	2031	2131	2229	2304	...	0004
Wissembourg 🏛 ◐ a.	1428	|		|	2028	|	|	|	|	...	|
Wörth (Rhein) d.	...	1444		1944	...	2044	2144	2244	2320	...	0017
Karlsruhe Hbf a.	...	1454		1954	...	2054	2154	2256	2337	...	0027

	Ⓐe	Ⓐe	⚒r		Ⓒz	Ⓐe		Ⓐe
Karlsruhe Hbf d.	0430	...	0601	...	0707	0716	...	0805
Wörth (Rhein) d.	0447	...	0617	...	0716	0736	...	0816
Wissembourg 🏛 ◐ d.	|	0526	|	0626e	|	|	0733r	|
Winden (Pfalz) d.	0502	0553	0631	0647e	0728	0748	0757r	0829
Landau (Pfalz) Hbf d.	0518	0607	0645	0701	0741	0757	0807	0838
Neustadt (Weinstr) Hbf a.	0540	0628	0705	0722	0801	0811	0826	0851

	Ⓒz						Ⓐe	Ⓒz	†E	D	Ⓐe	Ⓒz	†E	D							⑥p			
Karlsruhe Hbf d.	0807	...	0907	and at the same minutes past each hour until	1507	...	1601	1607	...	...	1705	1707	...	...	1807	...	1907	...	2007	...	...	2107	2207	2314
Wörth (Rhein) d.	0817	...	0916		1516	...	1616	1616	...	...	1716	1716	...	...	1816	...	1916	...	2016	...	...	2116	2216	2324
Wissembourg 🏛 ◐ d.	|	0833	|		|	1533	|	|	1633	1633	|	|	1733	1733	|	1833	|	1933	|	2033	2103	|	|	|
Winden (Pfalz) d.	0829	0853	0929		1529	1553	1629	1629	1653	1653	1729	1729	1753	1753	1829	1853	1929	1953	2029	2053	2123	2131	2229	2336
Landau (Pfalz) Hbf d.	0838	0903	0938		1538	1603	1638	1638	1702	1703	1738	1738	1802	1803	1838	1903	1938	2003	2038	2103	2131	2140	2238	2344
Neustadt (Weinstr) Hbf a.	0851	0924	0951		1551	1624	1651	1651	1714	1724	1751	1751	1816	1824	1851	1924	1951	2024	2053	2124	...	2202	2259	2359

GERMERSHEIM - SPEYER - MANNHEIM - HEIDELBERG

km			Ⓐe	Ⓐe	Ⓐe	⑥p	Ⓐe	Ⓐe	Ⓒz	Ⓐe														
0	**Germersheim** ‡ d.	0409e	0517	0555	0620	0622	0643	0704	0703	0725	0749z	0812	0849	0912	0949	1012	and at the same minutes past each hour until	1549	1612	1649	1712	1749	1812	184
14	Speyer Hbf ‡ d.	0423	0535	0609	0632	0635	0659	0714	0716	0738	0802	0825	0902	0925	1002	1025		1602	1625	1702	1725	1802	1825	190
23	Schifferstadt ‡ d.	0439	0551	0627	0640	0648	0711	|	0729	0801h	0811	0835	0911	0935	1011	1035		1611	1635	1711	1735	1811	1835	191
34	Ludwigshafen Hbf ‡ d.	0451	0607	0640	0648	0659	0725	|	0740	0814	0821	0848	0921	0948	1021	1048		1621	1648	1720	1749	1821	1848	192
37	**Mannheim** Hbf ⊡ a.	0456	*0621*	0645	*0705*	0705	...	0734	0747	0818	0825	0853	0926	0953	1026	1053		1626	1653	1726	1753	1826	1853	192
54	**Heidelberg** Hbf ⊡ a.	0514	*0639*	0704	*0723*	0723	...	0748	*0823*	0844	0844	0916r	0944	1016r	1044	1116r		1644	1716r	1744	1816e	1845	1916e	194

Germersheim ‡ d.	1912	1949	2012	...	2049	2120	*2120*	2154	2252	...	2322
Speyer Hbf ‡ d.	1925	2002	2025	...	2102	2135	*2135*	2209	2305	...	2335
Schifferstadt ‡ d.	1935	2011	2034	2045	2119	2149	2149	2228	2314	2317	2349
Ludwigshafen Hbf ‡ d.	1948	2021	...	2057	2128	2200	2200	2241	...	2329	0000
Mannheim Hbf ⊡ a.	1953	2026	...	2103	2134	2206	2206	2249	...	2334	0006
Heidelberg Hbf ⊡ a.	2016e	2045	...	2123	2153	...	2223	2313	...	2353	0023

	Ⓐe			Ⓐe	Ⓒz	Ⓐe	⚒r			
Heidelberg Hbf ⊡ d.	0505	0534r	...	*0602*	*0634*	0644	0709	0742e	0813	0843
Mannheim Hbf ⊡ d.	0526	0554	...	0632	0656	0705	0730	0804	0831	090
Ludwigshafen Hbf ‡ d.	0531	0600	0612	0638	0703	0712	0737	0810	0836	091
Schifferstadt ‡ d.	0546	0611	0627	0652	0717	0730	0755	0824	0846	092
Speyer Hbf ‡ d.	0559	...	0637	0704	0726	0740	0804	0833	0855	093
Germersheim ‡ a.	0612	...	0652	0719	0740	0754	0818	0845	0908	094

																	Ⓑb	⑥p				Ⓑb	⑥
Heidelberg Hbf ⊡ d.	0913	0943r	1013	1043r	and at the same minutes past each hour until	1613	1643r	1713	1743	1813	1843r	1913	1943e	2013	2037	...	2114	*2144*	2144	2214	*2244*	...	*2314*	231
Mannheim Hbf ⊡ d.	0931	1004	1031	1104		1631	1704	1731	1804	1831	1904	1931	2004	2031	2056	...	2138	2208	2208	2240	2312	...	2335	233
Ludwigshafen Hbf ‡ d.	0936	1010	1036	1110		1636	1710	1736	1810	1836	1910	1936	2010	2036	2103	...	2143	2215	2215	2246	2317	...	2340	234
Schifferstadt ‡ d.	0946	1024	1046	1124		1646	1724	1746	1823	1846	1924	1946	2024	2046	2114	2124	2158	2230	2233	2305	2327	2333	2355	235
Speyer Hbf ‡ d.	0955	1033	1055	1132		1656	1733	1756	1832	1856	1933	1956	2033	2056	...	2133	2207	2243	2243	2314	...	2343	0008	000
Germersheim ‡ a.	1008	1046	1108	1145		1708	1745	1808	1845	1908	1945	2008	2045	2108	...	2145	2220	2255	2255	2328	...	2356	0021	002

WÖRTH (Rhein) - GERMERSHEIM

km				Ⓐe	Ⓐe		Ⓐe	Ⓒz	Ⓐe	Ⓒz	Ⓐe	Ⓒz	Ⓐe	Ⓒz	Ⓐe	Ⓒz	Ⓐe	Ⓐe	Ⓒz	Ⓐe		Ⓐe	Ⓒ
0	**Wörth** (Rhein) d.	0030	...	0539	0614	0625	0708	0725	0731	0825	0835	0925	0935	1025	1035	1125	1135	1218	1225	1234	and at the same minutes past each hour until	1918	192
27	**Germersheim** a.	0101	...	0606	0642	0657	0741	0757	0803	0857	0907	0957	1007	1057	1107	1157	1207	1244	1257	1307		1944	195

	Ⓐe	Ⓒz	Ⓐe			
Wörth (Rhein) d.	1934	2025	2035	2120	2220	2328
Germersheim a.	2007	2057	2107	2153	2253	0003

	Ⓒz		⑥p	Ⓐe	⑥p	Ⓐe	⑥p	Ⓐe	Ⓐe	Ⓒz	Ⓐe	Ⓐe	Ⓒz	Ⓐe	Ⓒ
Germersheim d.	0027	...	0437	0440	0519	0550	0601	0616	0655	0701	0725	0756	0801	0850	090
Wörth (Rhein) a.	0058	...	0508	0515	0551	0623	0634	0650	0728	0734	0758	0828	0834	0922	093

	Ⓐe	Ⓒz	Ⓐe	Ⓒz	Ⓐe	Ⓒz	Ⓐe	Ⓐe		Ⓒz	Ⓐe	Ⓐe	Ⓒz	Ⓐe	Ⓐe	Ⓒz	Ⓐe	Ⓐe	Ⓒz				
Germersheim d.	0950	1001	1050	1101	1150	1201	1214	1250	and at the same minutes past each hour until	1601	1614	1650	1701	1714	1741	1801	1814	1850	1901	1950	2050	2150	23
Wörth (Rhein) a.	1022	1034	1122	1133	1221	1234	1240	1321		1634	1640	1721	1734	1740	1814	1834	1840	1922	1934	2022	2122	2222	00

D – ⚒ to Oct. 18 (not June 19); daily from Oct. 20.
E – † to Oct. 19 (also June 19).
J – On † (also June 19, Nov. 1) Pirmasens Hbf d. 0641, Pirmasens Nord d. 0652, Kaiserslautern a. 0724.
M – From Mannheim Hbf (d. 0848).
S – To Saarbrücken (Table **917**).

b – Also Nov. 1.
e – Ⓐ (not June 19).
f – Not Oct. 3, Nov. 1.
h – Arrives 0748.
k – *0757* on ⑥ (not Nov. 1).
p – Not Nov. 1.

q – 0929 on † to Oct. 26 (also June 19).
r – ⚒ (not June 19, Nov. 1).
t – 0741 on † (also June 19, Nov. 1).
v – 0906 on † (also June 19, Nov. 1).
w – Also June 19, Nov. 1.
z – Ⓒ (also June 19).

✤ – On †w: Neustadt d. 1706 (not 1709).
◇ – Kaiserslautern d. 1738 (not 1735; arrives Pirmasens Nord 1809, Pirmasens Hbf 181
⊡ – See also Tables **913**, **919**, **923** and **924**.
‡ – See also Table **911a**.
◐ – For Strasbourg connections see Table 39

RB services — WIESBADEN - MAINZ - DARMSTADT - ASCHAFFENBURG — 918a

km		⚒r	Ⓐt	⚒r	Ⓐt		Ⓐt										Ⓐt		Ⓐt							
0	**Wiesbaden** Hbf d.	...	...	0538	0607	0638	0707	0738	0838	0938	1038	1138	1238	1338	1438	1538	1607	1638	1707	1738	1838	1938	2038	2138	2238	2338
10	**Mainz** Hbf d.	...	...	0550	|	0650	|	0750	0850	0950	1050	1150	1250	1350	1450	1550	|	1650	|	1750	1850	1950	2050	2150	2250	2350
43	Darmstadt Hbf a.	...	...	0622	0650	0722	0750	0823	0922	1022	1122	1222	1322	1422	1522	1622	1650	1722	1750	1822	1922	2022	2122	2222	2322	0022
43	Darmstadt Hbf d.	0452	0549	0632	0703	0732	0800	0832r	0932	1032r	1132	1232r	1332	1432r	1532	1632r	1700	1732	1800	1832t	1932	2032t	2132t	...	...	...
87	**Aschaffenburg** Hbf a.	0535	0631	0713	0745	0813	0842	0913r	1013	1113r	1213	1313r	1413	1513r	1613	1713r	1742	1813	1843	1913t	2013	2113t	2213t	...	...	...

	Ⓐt	Ⓐt	Ⓐt		Ⓐt		Ⓐt									Ⓐt		Ⓐt		Ⓐt		Ⓐt				
Aschaffenburg Hbf d.	...	...	0510	0542r	0606	0640r	0716	0746	0846r	0946	1046r	1146	1246r	1346	1446r	1516	1546	1616	1646r	1716	1746	1816	1846t	1946	2046t	...
Darmstadt Hbf a.	...	...	0552	0623r	0651	0727r	0759	0827	0927r	1027	1127r	1227	1327r	1427	1527r	1559	1627	1659	1727r	1759	1827	1859	1927t	2027	2127t	...
Darmstadt Hbf d.	0440	0540	0607	0640	0706	0740	0806	0840	0940	1040	1140	1240	1340	1440	1540	1606	1640	1706	1740	1806	1840	1906	1940	2040	2140	2240
Mainz Hbf d.	0513	0613	|	0713	|	0813	|	0913	1013	1113	1213	1313	1413	1513	1613	|	1713	|	1813	|	1913	|	2013	2113	2213	2313
Wiesbaden Hbf a.	0525	0625	0655	0725	0755	0825	0855	0925	1025	1125	1225	1325	1425	1525	1625	1655	1725	1755	1825	1855	1925	1955	2025	2125	2225	2325

r – ⚒ (not June 19). t – Ⓐ (not June 19).

RE / S-Bahn services except where shown — SAARBRÜCKEN - MANNHEIM (- FRANKFURT) — 919

km		*IC* 2051 Ⓐt	Ⓐt	*EC* 217 G🍷		*IC* 2053 ①–⑤ nS	*ICE* 1557 ①–⑥ L		T	Ⓐt	¶	T		*ICE* 9551 ①–⑥ R✕		Ⓐt T	M	*TGV* 9553 R🍷				M	◇	*IC* 2055 ①–⑤ nQ	*IC* 2059 ⑥z
0	**Saarbrücken** Hbf d.	0440	0448	0531	0551	0619	0642	...	0658	0740	...	0801	...	0858	0903	0940	0957	1057	...	1102	...	1201	...	1249	1249
31	Homburg (Saar) Hbf d.	0502	0519	0552	0620	0641	0703	0650r	0726	0804	0743	0827	0856	|	0928	1004	1021	|	1056	1124	1156	1227	1243	1312	1312
67	**Kaiserslautern** Hbf a.	0525	0550	0615	0651	0700	0725	0721r	0754	0826	0814	0854	0929	0935	0954	1026	1048	1133	1128	1152	1229	1254	1314	1332	1332
		|	◧	|	▬	|	|	|	◧	|	|	◧	|	|	◧	|	◧	|	|	◧	|	◧	|	|	|
		|	Ⓐt	|		|	|	|		|	|		|	|		|		|	|		|		|	|	|
67	**Kaiserslautern** Hbf d.	0527	0602	0617	0619	0702	0727	0732	0758	0827	0832	0858	0931	0937	0958	1027	1058	1135	1129	1158	1232	1258	1324	1334	1334
100	Neustadt (Weinstr) Hbf d.	0552	0632	0641	0651	0727	0750	0805	0830	0850	0905	0930	1005j	|	1030	1050	1130	|	1205	1230	1305	1330	1405j	1358	1358
128	Ludwigshafen Hbf 918 d.	0612	0700	0705	0720	0746	|	0829	0857	|	0929	0957	1029	|	1057	|	1157	|	1228	1257	1329	1357	1429	|	|
131	**Mannheim** Hbf 918 a.	0616	0705	0709	0725	0751	0811	0834	0903	0912	0934	1003	1034	1017	1103	1112	1203	1215	1234	1303	1334	1403	1434	1421	1421
131	**Mannheim** Hbf 918 ▽ d.	0618	0707	...	0729	0753	0813	0838	0907	*0930*	0938	1007	1038	1021	1107	*1130*	1207	1218	1238	1307	1338	1407	1438	1424	1423
	Heidelberg Hbf 918 a.	|	0723	...	0744	0804	|	0854	0923	*0944*	0954	1023	1054	|	1123	*1144*	1223	|	1254	1323	1354	1423	1454	1435	|
191	Darmstadt Hbf ▽ a.	0653	...	...	...	...	0846	...	...	...	...	...	...	|	...	...	...	|	...	...	...	...	...	...	1504
219▲	**Frankfurt** (Main) Hbf ▽ a.	0712	...	...	...	...	0904	...	...	...	...	...	...	1058	...	...	...	1258	...	...	...	...	...	...	1524

		IC 2351 ⑤⑦ fS		K		*ICE* 9555 ⊠ R✕			M			*IC* 2057 ⑤⑦ f	⊙	T	*TGV* 9557 Ⓑ R🍷		⑥k	Ⓑq		T	*ICE* 9559 R✕			T	
Saarbrücken Hbf d.	1301	1345	...	1401	...	1459	1503	...	1601	...	1656	1733	...	1801	1858	...	1901	1903	...	2001	2058	...	2103	2201¦	2301
Homburg (Saar) Hbf d.	1327	1408	1346	1427	1444	|	1527	1556	1627	...	1721	1754	1745	1826	|	1856	1927	1929	1945	2027	|	...	2128	2225¦	2331
Kaiserslautern Hbf a.	1354	1428	1417	1454	1515	1535	1554	1630	1654	...	1751	1820	1815	1853	1935	1929	1954	2000	2016	2054	2134	...	2203	2254¦	0002
	◧	|	|	◧	|	|	◧	|	◧		◧	|	|	◧	|	|	◧		|	◧	|		◧	◧	◧
		|	|		|	|		|				|	|		|	|	d		|		|				
Kaiserslautern Hbf d.	1358	1430	1433	1458	1531	1537	1558	1633	1658	1732	1758	1824	1832	1858	1937	1931	1958	...	2032	2058	2136	2141	2232	2302	0006
Neustadt (Weinstr) Hbf d.	1430	1454v	1505	1530	1605j	|	1630	1705	1730	1805	1830	1848	1905	1930	|	2005j	2030	...	2102	2130	|	2210	2300	2330	0035
Ludwigshafen Hbf 918 d.	1457	|	1528	1557	1628	|	1657	1729	1759	1828	1857	|	1928	1957	|	2029	2057	...	2128	2200	|	2241	2329	0000	0104
Mannheim Hbf 918 a.	1503	1515	1534	1603	1634	1617	1703	1734	1804	1834	1903	1910	1934	2003	2016	2034	2103	...	2134	2206	2217	2249	2334	0006	0109
Mannheim Hbf 918 ▽ d.	1507	*1523*	1538	1607	1638	1619	1707	1738	1807	1838	1907	1912	1938	2007	2018	2038	2107	...	2137	2207	2221	2257	2336	0007	0116
Heidelberg Hbf 918 a.	1523	*1534*	1554	1623	1654	|	1723	1754	1823	1854	1923	|	1954	2023	|	2054	2123	...	2153	2223	|	2313	2353	0023	0132
Darmstadt Hbf ▽ a.	...	...	...	...	...	|	...	...	...	...	...	1947	...	...	|	...	...	...	...	...	|	...	...	...	...
Frankfurt (Main) Hbf ▽ a.	...	...	...	...	...	1658	...	...	...	...	...	2004	...	...	2058	...	...	...	...	...	2258	...	...	...	...

	⚒r		*ICE* 9558 ①–⑤ R✕		*TGV* 9568 ⑥ R🍷				*IC* 2308 ①			*TGV* 9556 ‡ R🍷				*IC* 2058 ⑤f S			Ⓐt		*ICE* 9554 R✕				Ⓐt T
Frankfurt (Main) Hbf ▽ d.	...	...	0600	...	0654	...	...	...	0749	...	...	0857	...	...	...	...	...	...	...	...	1301	...	...	...	...
Darmstadt Hbf ▽ d.	...	...	|	...	|	...	...	...	0812	...	...	|	...	...	...	...	...	...	...	...	|	...	...	...	...
Heidelberg Hbf 918 d.	0413	0534r	|	0634	|	0704	0733	0804	|	0833	0903	|	0933	1003	1033	1125	1133	1203	*1213*	1233	|	1303	1333	1403	*1413*
Mannheim Hbf 918 ▽ a.	0429	0551r	0636	0651	0736	0719	0751	0820	0846	0851	0920	0939	0951	1020	1051	1139	1151	1220	*1229*	1251	1337	1320	1351	1420	*1429*
Mannheim Hbf 918 d.	0431	0554	0640	0656	0739	0720	0756	0826	0848	0856	0926	0942	0956	1026	1056	1143	1156	1226	1246	1256	1341	1326	1356	1426	1446
Ludwigshafen Hbf 918 d.	0438	0600	|	0703	|	0725	0803	0832	|	0903	0931	|	1003	1031	1103	|	1203	1231	|	1303	|	1331	1403	1431	|
Neustadt (Weinstr) Hbf d.	0506	0632	|	0732	|	0802j	0832	0858	0911	0932	1004j	|	1032	1100	1132	1208	1232	1300	1308	1332	|	1404j	1432	1500	1508
Kaiserslautern Hbf a.	0535	0659	0720	0759	0821	0829	0859	0926	0932	0959	1029	1021	1059	1128	1159	1230	1259	1328	1330	1359	1421	1429	1459	1528	1530
	◧	◧	|	◧	|	|	◧		|	◧	|	|	◧	|	◧	|	◧	|	|	◧	|	|	◧	|	|
	d	M	|		|	|	T		|		|	|	K	|		|	T	|	|		|	|	T	|	|
Kaiserslautern Hbf d.	0543	0711	0722	0803	0823	0841	0903	...	0934	1003	1036	1023	1103	1138	1203	1232	1305	1341	1331	1404	1423	1442	1504	1541	1531
Homburg (Saar) Hbf d.	0620	0745c	|	0831	|	0913	0931	...	0955	1030	1107	|	1130	1211	1230	1256	1332	1414	1354	1432	|	1513	1531	1613	1554
Saarbrücken Hbf a.	0656	0816c	0758	0857	0901	...	0957	...	1017	1055	...	1100	1157	...	1257	1320	1359	...	1421	1456	1500	...	1557	...	1621

			IC 2056 ①–④ m	*IC* 2258 ⑤⑦ f			*IC* 2054 Ⓐt			*TGV* 9552 R🍷			*IC* 2052 Ⓑp S			*ICE* 9550 Ⓑ R✕			*EC* 216 G🍷		*ICE* 1594 Ⓑ⊡ L✕			*IC* 2050 ⑦ S	
Frankfurt (Main) Hbf ▽ d.	...	...	...	1446	...	...	1554	...	...	1658	...	...	...	...	...	1901	...	...	...	...	2054	...	...	...	...
Darmstadt Hbf ▽ d.	...	...	...	1503	...	...	1611	...	...	|	...	...	...	...	...	|	...	...	...	...	2111	...	...	...	...
Heidelberg Hbf 918 d.	1433	1503	1521	|	1535	1603	|	1636	1703	|	1733	1803	*1825*	1833	1903	|	1933	2003	*2013*	2037	|	2144	2214	2255	2314
Mannheim Hbf 918 ▽ a.	1451	1520	1537	1537	1551	1620	1646	1654	1720	1740	1751	1820	*1837*	1851	1920	1937	1951	2020	*2029*	2055	2146	2202	2232	2306	2332
Mannheim Hbf 918 d.	1456	1526	1539	1539	1556	1626	1648	1656	1726	1743	1756	1826	1849	1856	1926	1941	1956	2026	2050	2056	2148	2208	2240	2308	2335
Ludwigshafen Hbf 918 d.	1503	1531	|	|	1603	1631	1654	1703	1731	|	1804	1831	1854	1903	1931	|	2003	2032	|	2103	|	2215	2246	|	2340
Neustadt (Weinstr) Hbf d.	1532	1604j	1600	1600	1632	1700	1712	1732	1805j	|	1832	1900	1912	1932	2004j	|	2032	2058	2112	2132	2210	2246	2322	2331	0016
Kaiserslautern Hbf a.	1559	1630	1622	1622	1659	1728	1733	1759	1830	1822	1859	1928	1933	1959	2029	2021	2059	2126	2133	2159	2231	2314	2351	2353	0044
	◧	|	|	|	◧	|	|	◧	|	|	◧		|	◧	|	|	◧		|	◧	|		◧	|	
		|	|	|	T	|	|	|	|	|	A		|		|	|			|		|			|	
Kaiserslautern Hbf d.	1603	1641	1624	1624	1703	1742	1737	*1808*	1840	1824	1903	...	1935	2005	2041	2023	2104	...	2135	2210	2233	...	0002	2355	...
Homburg (Saar) Hbf d.	1631	1714	1646	1646	1730	1814	1803	1858	1911	|	1930	...	1957	2032	2113	|	2131	...	2157	2238	2255	...	0033	0017	...
Saarbrücken Hbf a.	1657	...	1707	1707	1757	...	1824	1929	...	1901	1957	...	2018	2056	...	2100	2157	...	2218	2303	2316	...	0105	0039	...

– To Trier (Table **915**) on ⚒ (not Aug. 15, Sept. 4, Nov. 1).
– 🚃12 and 🍷 Graz - Salzburg - München - Stuttgart - Saarbrücken and v.v.
– From / to Koblenz via Trier (Table **915**).
– 🚃12 and ✕ Saarbrücken - Frankfurt - Erfurt - Leipzig and v.v.
– From / to Merzig (Table **915**).
– To Stuttgart (Table **912**) on ⑤ (also June 18, Oct. 2).
– From / to Paris (Table **390**). 🅁 for international journeys.
– To / from Stuttgart (Table **912**).
– From / to Trier (Table **915**).

– On ①–⑤ Homburg d. 0750, Saarbrücken a. 0819.
– Daily.
– Also June 18, Oct. 2; not June 20, Oct. 3.
– Arrives 8 – 12 minutes earlier.
– Not Nov. 1.
– Not June 18, 19, Oct. 2.
– Not June 19, 20, Oct. 3.
– Not June 19, Oct. 3.
– Also Nov. 1.

r – ⚒ (not June 19, Nov. 1).
t – Not June 19.
v – ⑤⑦ to Aug. 3 (also June 18; not June 20); ⑦ from Aug. 10.
z – Also June 19, Oct. 3; not Oct. 4.

‡ – On ⑥ runs as *ICE* **9566** (Frankfurt d. 0901, Mannheim a. 0937, d. 0941).
¦ – 2–3 minutes later until Aug. 2.
⊡ – Runs 6 – 10 minutes later Mannheim - Saarbrücken from Aug. 3.
⊠ – On ⑥ runs as *TGV* **9565** (🍷).
¶ – On Ⓐ (not June 19) passengers travelling from Homburg or Kaiserslautern to Heidelberg should move to the front portion of the train at Mannheim.
⊙ – On Ⓑ (also Nov. 1) passengers from Homburg or Kaiserslautern travelling to Heidelberg should move to the front portion of the train at Mannheim.
◇ – On ①–④ (not June 19) passengers travelling from Homburg or Kaiserslautern to Heidelberg should move to the front portion of the train at Mannheim.
◧ – Change trains at Kaiserslautern.
▽ – See also Table **912** (*ICE* trains) and Table **913** (local trains).
▲ – *209 km* for trains running non-stop Mannheim - Frankfurt.

920 FRANKFURT - NÜRNBERG - PASSAU (- WIEN)

See Table 921 for other regional trains

km		Ⓐt ◐	Ⓒz ◐	ICE 827 Ⓐ 🍷	ICE 521 🍷	ICE 21 ✕	ICE 523 Ⓐ 🍷	ICE 1123 ⑥ 🍷	ICE 925 Ⓒ 🍷	ICE 525 Ⓐ 🍷	ICE 23 ✕	ICE 527 ①–⑥ G🍷	ICE 529 🍷	ICE 1521 ✕	ICE 91 ✕	ICE 621 ①–⑥ 🍷	ICE 1697 ⑥c B🍷	ICE 1121 ⑦ 🍷	ICE 623 ①–⑥ 🍷	ICE 923 ⑦ 🍷	ICE 27 ✕	IC 1987 ⑥	ICE 625 Ⓑu 🍷	ICE 825 ⑥m M🍷
	Hamburg Hbf 800 900 d.	...	...	...	...	...	...	...	...	...	...	...	...	...	0803h	...	...	...	...	...	...	0912	...	...
	Dortmund Hbf 800 d.	...	...	...	...	...	0406	0423	0502	0524	0437	0624	0724	0636	|	0816k	...	0824	...	0912	0837	|	1024w	...
	Essen Hbf 800 d.	...	...	...	...	...	0428	0445	0526	0553	0459	0653	0753	|	|	0840	...	0853	...	0936	0859	|	1053	1053
	Düsseldorf Hbf 800 d.	...	...	...	...	...	0455	0513	0553	0621	0527	0721	0821	|	|	0913	...	0921	0945	1008	0927	|	1121	1121
	Köln Hbf 800 910 d.	...	...	0314	0422	...	|	|	|	|	0553	|	|	0753	|	|	...	|	1019	|	0953	|	|	|
	Köln Messe/Deutz 910 d.	...	...	|	|	...	0518	0535	0618	0644	|	0744	0844	|	|	0937	...	0944	|	1030	|	|	1144	1144
	Bonn Hbf 800 d.	...	...	|	|	...	|	|	|	|	0614	|	|	0814	|	|	...	|	|	|	1014	|	|	|
	Koblenz Hbf 911 d.	...	...	|	|	...	|	|	|	|	0648	|	|	0848	|	|	...	|	|	|	1048	|	|	|
	Mainz Hbf 911 d.	...	...	|	|	...	|	|	|	|	0739	|	|	0939	|	|	...	|	|	|	1139	|	|	|
0	Frankfurt Flughafen ✈ § d.	...	...	0437	0535	...	0637	0637	0737	0737	0802	0837	0937	1002	|	1029	...	1037	1137	1137	1202	|	1237	1237
11	Frankfurt (Main) Hbf d.	...	...	0456	0551	0622	0654	0654	0754	0754	0819*	0854	0954	1018	|	1054	...	1054	1154	1154	1221	|	1254	1254
35	Hanau Hbf d.	...	...	|	|	0638	|	|	|	|	0835*	|	|	1035	|	|	...	|	|	|	1238	|	|	|
57	Aschaffenburg Hbf d.	...	...	0524	0624	0652	0724	0724	0824	0824	|	0924	1024	|	|	1124	...	1124	1224	1224	|	|	1324	1324
136	Würzburg Hbf a.	...	...	0602	0702	0731	0802	0802	0902	0902	0925*	1002	1102	1125	1128	1202	...	1202	1301	1303	1331	1331	1402	1402
136	Würzburg Hbf 900 d.	...	...	0604	0704	0733	0804	0804	0904	0904	0933	1004	1104	1132	1135	1204	...	1204	1307	1307	1333	1336	1404	1404
238	Nürnberg Hbf 900 a.	...	...	0659	0759	0827	0859	0859	0959	0959	1027	1059	1159	1224	1227	1259	...	1259	1400	1400	1427	1432	1459	1459
238	Nürnberg Hbf d.	...	...	0702	0802	0830	0902	0902	1002	1002	1030	1102	1202	1227	1230	1302	1305	1302	1403	1403	1430	1435	1502	1502
	München Hbf 904 a.	...	...	0816	0920	|	1016	1016	1115	1115	|	1216r	1321	1350b	|	1415	|	1415	1515	1515	|	|	1615	1615
339	Regensburg Hbf d.	0657	0716	...	...	0927	...	...	...	...	1127	...	...	...	1327	...	1404	...	...	...	1527	1536	...	...
379	Straubing d.	0722	0741	...	...	|	...	...	...	...	|	...	...	...	|	...	|	...	...	...	|	1558	...	...
404	Plattling 944 d.	0738	0756	...	...	1000	...	...	...	...	1200	...	...	...	1400	...	1440	...	...	...	1600	1612	...	...
456	Passau Hbf 🏛 944 a.	0833	0836	...	...	1033	...	...	...	...	1233	...	...	...	1433	...	1510	...	...	...	1633	1644	...	...
	Linz Hbf 950 a.	...	...	...	...	1143	...	...	...	...	1343	...	...	...	1543	...	...	...	...	...	1743	...	...	...
	Wien Westbahnhof 950 a.	...	...	...	...	1308	...	...	...	...	1508	...	...	...	1708	...	...	...	...	...	1908	...	...	...

	ICE 627 ①–⑥ 🍷	ICE 927 ⑦ 🍷	ICE 29 ✕	ICE 629 Ⓑ 🍷	ICE 1699 ⑤f B🍷	ICE 721 🍷	ICE 229 ✕	ICE 723 Ⓑ 🍷	ICE 725 🍷	IC 2027 ¶ 🍷	ICE 727 Ⓑ 🍷	ICE 929 ⑥ 🍷	ICE 729 Ⓑ 🍷	IC 2229 Ⓑn 🍷	IC 2229 ⑤d 🍷	IC 2165 ⑦ R	RE 59299 ♥	ICE 821 Ⓑq 🍷	ICE 821 T 🍷	ICE 685 ✕	ICE 1625 ⑥ ✕	ICE 1029 ✕	EN 421 Ⓡ N🍷	EN 491 Ⓡ L🍷
Hamburg Hbf 800 900 d.	...	...	...	...	...	...	...	...	...	1146	...	...	...	1346	1346	...	...	...	...	...	...	1546	...	2034g
Dortmund Hbf 800 d.	...	1103	...	1224w	...	1324e	...	1424y	1524w	1436	...	...	...	1636	1636	...	...	1815w	1815w	...	...	1836	...	|
Essen Hbf 800 d.	...	|	...	1253	...	1353	...	1453	1553	|	1653	1742	1753	|	|	...	...	1841	1841	...	...	|	...	|
Düsseldorf Hbf 800 d.	...	|	...	1321	...	1421	...	1521	1621	|	1720	1813	1821	|	|	...	...	1908	1908	...	...	|	...	|
Köln Hbf 800 910 d.	1214	1215	...	|	...	|	...	|	|	1553	|	|	|	1753	1753	...	...	|	|	...	...	1953	2002	|
Köln Messe/Deutz 910 d.	|	|	...	1344	...	1444	...	1544	1644	|	1744	1835	1844	|	|	...	...	1930	1930	...	...	|	|	|
Bonn Hbf 800 d.	|	|	...	|	...	|	...	|	|	1614	|	|	|	1814	1814	...	...	|	|	...	...	2014	2034	|
Koblenz Hbf 911 d.	|	|	...	|	...	|	...	|	|	1648	|	|	|	1848	1848	...	...	|	|	...	...	2048	2113	|
Mainz Hbf 911 d.	|	|	...	|	...	|	...	|	|	1739	|	|	|	1939	1939	...	...	|	• |	...	...	2143	2210	|
Frankfurt Flughafen ✈ § d.	1329	1329	...	1437	...	1537	...	1637	1737	1802	1837	1937	1937	2002	2002	...	...	2037	2037	...	2102	2202	2233	|
Frankfurt (Main) Hbf d.	1354	1354	1416	1454	...	1554	1621	1654	1754	1818	1854	1954	1954	2018	2018	...	...	2054	2054	...	2118	2218	2300	|
Hanau Hbf d.	|	|	1439	|	...	|	1638	|	|	1835	|	|	|	2035	2035	...	...	|	|	...	2135	2235	|	|
Aschaffenburg Hbf d.	1424	1424	|	1524	...	1624	1652	1724	1824	1849	1924	2024	2024	2049	2049	...	...	2124	2124	...	2149	2249	|	|
Würzburg Hbf a.	1502	1502	1531	1602	...	1702	1731	1802	1902	1931	2002	2102	2102	2129	2129	...	...	2202	2202	...	2233	2341	0224	0224
Würzburg Hbf 900 d.	1504	1504	1533	1604	...	1704	1733	1804	1904	1933	2004	2104	2104	2131	2131	...	...	▬	2204	2231	2235	2343	0226	0226
Nürnberg Hbf 900 a.	1559	1559	1627	1659	...	1759	1827	1859	1959	2027	2059	2159	2159	2226	2226	...	...	...	2259	2324	2328	0037	0321	0321
Nürnberg Hbf d.	1602	1602	1630	1702	1705	1802	1830	1902	2002	2031	2103	2202	2202	...	2235	2235	2257	...	2302	...	...	...	0324	0324
München Hbf 904 a.	1715b	1715b	|	1818	|	1916b	|	2016	2115j	|	2212	2316	2316	...	|	|	|	◐	0017	...	...	...	|	|
Regensburg Hbf d.	...	...	1727	...	1803	...	1927	...	...	2133	...	...	...	...	2340	2340	0005	0009	...	...	...	...	0430	0430
Straubing d.	...	...	|	...	|	...	|	...	...	2155	...	...	...	...	0003	0003	...	0036	...	...	...	...	|	|
Plattling 944 d.	...	...	1800	...	1839	...	2000	...	...	2209	...	...	...	...	0018	0018	...	0050	...	...	...	...	|	|
Passau Hbf 🏛 944 a.	...	...	1833	...	1911	...	2033	...	...	2242	...	...	...	...	0048	0048	...	0147p	...	...	...	...	0532	0532
Linz Hbf 950 a.	...	...	1943	...	...	...	2143	...	...	...	...	...	...	...	...	...	...	...	...	...	...	...	0647	0647
Wien Westbahnhof 950 a.	...	...	2108	...	...	...	2308	...	...	...	...	...	...	...	...	...	...	...	...	...	...	...	0844	0844

B – 🚃 and 🍷 Berlin - Leipzig - Passau. See also Table 851.
G – To Garmisch (Table 895) on ⑥.
L – HANS ALBERS – 🛏 1, 2 cl., 🛌 2 cl. and 🚃 Hamburg - Wien.
M – From Münster (Table 800).
N – 🛏 1, 2 cl., 🛌 2 cl. and 🚃 Köln - Wien.
R – 🚃 Karlsruhe - Stuttgart - Nürnberg - Passau. Also calls at Neumarkt (Oberpf), d. 2259.
T – ④⑤⑦ (also June 18; not June 19, Oct. 3).

b – 3–9 minutes later until July 12.
c – Also Oct. 3; not Oct. 4.
d – Also June 18, Aug. 14, Oct. 2; not June 20, Aug. 15, Oct. 3.
e – ⑤⑦ only.
f – Also June 18, Oct. 2; not June 20, Oct. 3.
g – 2052 from Nov. 1.
h – 0753 June 14 - July 27.
j – 2120 on ①–⑤ until July 11.
k – ⑥ only.
m – Also June 19, Oct. 3; not June 21, Oct. 4.
n – Not Oct. 3.
p – 0128 on ①⑦ (also June 20, Aug. 16, Oct. 4).
q – Not June 19, Oct. 3.
r – 1210 on ⑥.
t – Not June 19, Aug. 15.
u – Not June 19, Oct. 3.
w – ⑦ only.
y – ①②③④⑦ (not Oct. 2).
z – Also June 19, Aug. 15.

* – 2–3 minutes later on ⑦.
¶ – Train number 2327 July 4 - Oct. 5 (also June 14, 20, 21, 22, 27, 28, 29, Oct. 10, 11, 17, 18, 19, 24, 31).
♥ – Also calls at Neumarkt (Oberpf), d. 2319.
◐ – Operated by agilis.
§ – Frankfurt Flughafen Fernbahnhof.

921 Local trains FRANKFURT - WÜRZBURG - NÜRNBERG - REGENSBURG - PASSAU

RE / RB services

For faster ICE / IC trains see Table 920 above. Neumarkt - Regensburg - Plattling trains are operated by agilis.

km			Ⓒz	Ⓐt	†y	⚒r	Ⓐr	Ⓒy								Ⓒy	Ⓐr		Ⓒy	Ⓐr			†y	⚒r		
0	Frankfurt (Main) Hbf d.	...	0442k	0442	0530	0634	0726	0730	0834	0930	1034	1130	1234	1330	1434	1530	1534	1634	1730	1734	1834	1930	2034	2034	2130	2236
4	Frankfurt (Main) Süd d.	...	0448k	0448	0536	0640	0733	0736	0840	0936	1040	1136	1240	1336	1440	1536	1540	1640	1736	1740	1840	1936	2040	2040	2136	2242
10	Offenbach (Main) Hbf d.	...	|	|	|	0645	0738	|	0845	|	1045	|	1245	|	1445	|	1545	1645	|	1745	1845	|	2045	2045	|	2248
24	Hanau Hbf d.	...	0513k	0513	0614	0659	0759	0759	0859	0959	1059	1159	1259	1359	1459	1559	1559	1659	1759	1759	1859	1959	2059	2059	2159	2259
46	Aschaffenburg Hbf d.	0459	0601	0604	0710	0717	0817	0817	0917	1017	1117	1217	1317	1417	1517	1617	1617	1717	1817	1817	1917	2017	2117	2131f	2220	2322
84	Lohr Bahnhof d.	0531	0633	0636	0741	0743	0843	0843	0943	1043	1143	1243	1343	1443	1543	1643	1643	1743	1843	1843	1943	2043	2143	2204	2252	2355
96	Gemünden (Main) d.	0543	0645	0654	0752	0800	0900	0900	1000	1100	1200	1300	1400	1500	1556	1700	1656	1756	1900	1858	2000	2100	2158	2216	2304	0007
109	Karlstadt (Main) d.	0553	0654	0703	0802	0808	0908	0908	1008	1108	1208	1308	1408	1508	1607	1708	1707	1807	1908	1908	2008	2108	2206	2224	2314	0017
136	Würzburg Hbf a.	0617	0720	0720	0824	0824	0924	0924	1024	1124	1224	1324	1424	1524	1624	1724	1722	1822	1924	1924	2024	2124	2222	2241	2336	0038

km		⚒r		⚒r	Ⓐr									⑥⊡												
0	Würzburg Hbf d.	0438	...	0536	0607	...	0637	0742	0842	0942	1042	1142	1242	1336	1342	1442	1542	1642	1742	1842	1942	2042	...	2148	2304	001
23	Kitzingen d.	0456	...	0554	0623	...	0655	0801	0901	1001	1101	1201	1301	|	1401	1501	1601	1701	1801	1901	2001	2101	...	2208	2323	0031
61	Neustadt (Aisch) Bf d.	0519	0548	0616	0648	0648	0717	0826	0926	1026	1126	1226	1324	1407	1426	1526	1626	1726	1826	1926	2026	2126	2143	2239	2346	...
94	Fürth (Bay) Hbf d.	0546	0615	0644	0711	0711	0740	0847	0947	1047	1147	1247	1347	|	1447	1547	1647	1747	1847	1947	2047	2147	2212	2308	0016	...
102	Nürnberg Hbf a.	0553	0622	0652	0719	0719	0749	0854	0954	1054	1154	1254	1354	1432	1454	1554	1654	1754	1854	1954	2054	2154	2219	2315	0023	...

	⚒d	Ⓐt																				L				
Nürnberg Hbf d.	...	0554	0621	0735	...	0817	0934	...	1017	1136	...	1217c	1336	...	1417	1536	...	1617g	1736	...	1817	1936	...	2021	2136	...
Neumarkt (Oberpf) d.	0445k	0619	0706	0759	0806	0906	0959	1006	1106	1159	1206	1306c	1359	1406	1506	1559	1606	1705	1759	1806	1906	1959	2006	2106	2159	2206
Regensburg Hbf a.	0538k	0659	0758	0838	0858	0959	1038	1058	1159	1238	1258	1357c	1438	1458	1558	1638	1658	1756	1838	1858	1958	2038	2058	2158	2238	2258
Regensburg Hbf d.	0540	0702	0801	0844	0901	1001	1044	1101	1201	1244	1301	1359	1444	1501	1601	1644	1701	1758	1844	1901	2001	...	2101	2201	2245	2301
München Hbf 878 a.	|	0835	|	1016	|	|	1217	|	|	1417	|	|	1617	|	|	1817	|	|	2017	|	|	...	|	|	0023	|
Straubing d.	0607	...	0827	...	0927	1027	...	1127	1227	...	1327	1430	...	1527	1627	...	1727	1829	...	1927	2027	...	2128	2227	...	232
Plattling a.	0623	...	0844	...	0944	1044	...	1144	1244	...	1344	1448	...	1544	1644	...	1744	1846	...	1944	2044	...	2144	2243	...	234
Plattling 944 d.	0642	...	0901	...	1005	1103	...	1205	1303	...	1405	1503	...	1605	1703	...	1805	1903	...	2005	2103	...	2157	2305	...	...
Passau Hbf 944 a.	0718	...	0934	...	1039	1138	...	1239	1338	...	1439	1538	...	1640	1738	...	1839	1937	...	2039	2139	...	2230	2340	...	...

L – To Landshut (Table 878).

c – Ⓒ (daily June 7–22, July 30 - Sept. 15, Oct. 25 - Nov. 2; also Nov. 19).
d – Not June 19, Aug. 15, Nov. 1.
f – Arrives 2116.
g – 1636 on Ⓐ (not June 19).
h – Gemünden - Würzburg on the mornings of ⑥⑦ (not Oct. 4).
k – ⑥ only.
r – Not June 19.
t – Not June 19, Aug. 15.
y – Also June 19.
z – Also June19, Aug. 15.
⊡ – IC 1987: 🚃 Hamburg - Passau.

See Table **921** *for other regional trains*

(WIEN -) PASSAU - NÜRNBERG - FRANKFURT — 920

	ICE	ICE	ICE	RE	RE	ICE	IC	IC	IC	IC	ICE	ICE	IC	ICE	ICE	ICE	ICE	ICE	ICE	ICE	IC	ICE	ICE	ICE
	1126	**1028**	**822**	**59296**	**59292**	**820**	**2162**	**2226**	**2226**	**2226**	**728**	**726**	**2024**	**724**	**1698**	**722**	**228**	**720**	**1696**	**628**	**1986**	**28**	**626**	**1226**
	①–④		①–⑥	©	Ⓐ	Ⓐ	①	⑥h	②–⑥	①–⑥		①–⑥			⑥d				⑦		⑥		Ⓐ	⑥
	🍷	✕	🍷	★	♥	🍷	A¶	🍷¶	b🍷¶	e🍷	🍷	🍷	🍷	🍷	B🍷	🍷	✕	🍷	B🍷	🍷		✕	🍷	🍷
Wien Westbahnhof 950 ...... d.	...	...	...	...	...	...	...	...	...	...	...	...	...	...	...	...	0652	...	...	...	...	0852	...	...
Linz Hbf 950 ...... d.	...	...	...	...	...	...	...	...	...	...	...	...	...	...	...	...	0817	...	...	...	...	1017	...	...
Passau Hbf 🚌 ...... **944** d.	...	...	...	...	...	...	0511	0511	...	...	...	...	0718	...	0846	...	0924	...	1046	...	1112	1124	...	...
Plattling ...... **944** d.	...	...	...	...	...	...	0544	0544	...	...	...	...	0751	...	0916	...	0958	...	1116	...	1145	1158	...	...
Straubing ...... d.	...	...	...	...	...	...	0558	0558	...	...	...	...	0806	...	|	...	|	...	|	...	1159	|	...	...
Regensburg Hbf ...... d.	...	...	...	0530	0530	...	0622	0622	0622	...	...	...	0827	...	0951	...	1029	...	1153	...	1223	1229	...	...
München Hbf **904** ...... d.	...	...	0446t	|	|	0545	|	|	|	...	0647t	0750t	|	0849t	|	0950t	|	1050t	|	1148t	|	|	1250t	1250t
Nürnberg Hbf ...... a.	...	...	0555	0640	0642	0657	0721	0721	0721	...	0759	0857	0925	0957	1053	1057	1125	1157	1253	1257	1320	1326	1357	1357
Nürnberg Hbf ...... **900** d.	...	0530	0600	...	...	0700	...	0729	0729	0729	0802	0900	0928	1000	...	1100	1128	1200	...	1300	1325	1329	1400	1400
Würzburg Hbf ...... **900** a.	...	0624	0653	...	...	0753	...	0824	0824	0824	0853	0953	1024	1053	...	1153	1224	1253	...	1353	1420	1424	1453	1453
Würzburg Hbf ...... d.	0555	0626	0655	...	...	0755	...	0826	0826	0826	0855	0955	1027	1055	...	1155	1227	1257	...	1355	1422	1427	1455	1455
Aschaffenburg Hbf ...... d.	0636	0708	0736	...	...	0836	...	|	|	|	0936	1036	|	1136	...	1236	|	1336	...	1436	|	|	1536	1536
Hanau Hbf ...... d.	|	|	|	...	...	|	...	0920	0920	0920	|	|	1120	|	...	|	|	|	...	|	|	1520	|	|
Frankfurt (Main) Hbf ...... a.	0717	0736	0804	...	...	0904	...	0936	0936	0936	1004	1104	1136	1204	...	1304	1340	1404	...	1504	|	1536	1604	1604
Frankfurt Flughafen ✈ § ...... a.	0740	0755	0822	...	...	0922	...	0955	0955	0955	1022	1122	1155	1222	...	1322	...	1422	...	1522	|	...	1620	1621
Mainz Hbf **911** ...... a.	|	0818	|	...	...	|	...	1018	1018	1018	|	|	1218	|	...	|	...	|	...	|	|	...	|	|
Koblenz Hbf **911** ...... a.	|	0911	|	...	...	|	...	1111	1111	1111	|	|	1311	|	...	|	...	|	...	|	|	...	|	|
Bonn Hbf **800** ...... a.	|	0942	|	...	...	|	...	1142	1142	1142	|	|	1342	|	...	|	...	|	...	|	|	...	|	|
Köln Messe/Deutz **910** ...... a.	|	|	0914	...	...	1013	...	|	|	|	1114	1214	|	|	...	1414	...	1527	...	1614	|	...	1714	1727
Köln Hbf **800 910** ...... a.	0832	1005	|	...	...	|	...	1205	1205	1205	|	|	1405	1339	...	|	...	|	...	|	|	...	|	|
Düsseldorf Hbf **800** ...... a.	...	|	0937	...	...	1040	...	|	|	|	1137	1237	|	...	...	1438	...	1549	...	1640	|	...	1737	1750
Essen Hbf **800** ...... a.	...	|	1002	...	...	1105	...	|	|	|	1202	1302	|	...	...	1503	...	1615	...	1707	|	...	1802	1821
Dortmund Hbf **800** ...... a.	...	1121	1030k	...	...	...	...	1321	1321	1321	1230	...	1521	...	...	...	...	1643k	...	...	|	...	...	1846
Hamburg Hbf **800 900** ...... a.	...	1412	...	...	...	...	...	1612	1612	1612	...	...	1812	...	...	...	...	...	...	...	1907	...	...	...

	ICE	ICE	ICE	ICE	ICE	ICE	ICE	ICE	ICE	ICE	ICE	ICE	ICE	ICE	ICE	ICE	ICE	ICE	ICE		RE		EN	EN
	826	**926**	**624**	**26**	**622**	**1222**	**1220**	**620**	**90**	**1522**	**528**	**526**	**22**	**524**	**522**	**20**	**520**	**922**	**1620**		**4091**	◐	**420**	**490**
	Ⓐ	⑦			Ⓑ	⑥	©	Ⓐ				Ⓑ			r		①–④	⑤⑦	⑥s				[R]	[R]
	🍷	🍷	🍷	✕	🍷	🍷	H🍷	🍷	✕	✕	🍷	🍷	✕	🍷	🍷	✕	m🍷	c✕	✕				N🍷	L🍷
Wien Westbahnhof 950 ...... d.	...	...	...	1052	...	...	...	...	1252	...	...	...	1452	...	...	1652	...	...	...	...	...	...	2000	2000
Linz Hbf 950 ...... d.	...	...	...	1217	...	...	...	...	1417	...	...	...	1617	...	...	1817	...	...	...	...	...	...	2152	2152
Passau Hbf 🚌 ...... **944** d.	...	...	...	1324	...	...	...	...	1524	...	...	...	1724	...	...	1924	...	...	...	...	2210	...	2306	2306
Plattling ...... **944** d.	...	...	...	1358	...	...	...	...	1558	...	...	...	1758	...	...	1958	...	...	...	...	2244	2311	|	|
Straubing ...... d.	...	...	...	|	...	...	...	...	|	...	...	...	|	...	...	|	...	...	...	...	...	2327	|	|
Regensburg Hbf ...... d.	...	...	...	1429	...	...	...	...	1629	...	...	...	1830	...	...	2029	...	...	...	...	...	2355	0013	0013
München Hbf **904** ...... d.	1250t	1250t	1350t	|	1450t	1450t	1550t	1550t	|	1616t	1647t	1748	|	1850t	1948t	|	2050t	2050t	2050t	...	...	...	|	|
Nürnberg Hbf ...... a.	1357	1357	1457	1525	1557	1557	1657	1657	1725	1730	1757	1857	1925	1957	2059	2125	2200	2202	2202	...	...	...	0112	0112
Nürnberg Hbf ...... **900** d.	1400	1400	1500	1528	1600	1600	1700	1700	1728	1734	1800	1900	1928	2000	2102	2128	2205	2205	2205	...	...	...	0115	0115
Würzburg Hbf ...... **900** a.	1453	1453	1553	1624	1653	1653	1753	1753	1822	1825	1853	1953	2024	2053	2153	2226	2255	2255	2255	...	...	...	0209	0209
Würzburg Hbf ...... d.	1455	1455	1555	1627	1655	1655	1755	1755	1830	1827	1855	1955	2027	2055	2155	2229	2257	2257	2257	...	...	...	0211	0211
Aschaffenburg Hbf ...... d.	1536	1536	1636	|	1736	1736	1836	1836	|	|	1936	2036	|	2136	2236	2310	2336	2336	2336	...	...	...	|	|
Hanau Hbf ...... d.	|	|	|	1720	|	|	|	|	|	1920	|	|	2120	|	2250	2324	|	|	|	...	...	...	|	|
Frankfurt (Main) Hbf ...... a.	1604	1604	1704	1736	1804	1804	1904	1904	|	1936	2004	2104	2136	2204	2305	2339	0004	0004	0004	...	...	...	0602	|
Frankfurt Flughafen ✈ § ...... a.	1620	1621	1722	1755	1822	1822	1922	1921	|	1956	2022	2122	2157	2222	2322	...	...	...	...	...	...	...	0626	|
Mainz Hbf **911** ...... a.	|	|	|	1818	|	|	|	|	|	2018	|	|	2218	|	|	...	...	...	...	...	...	...	0646	|
Koblenz Hbf **911** ...... a.	|	|	|	1911	|	|	|	|	|	2111	|	|	2311	|	|	...	...	...	...	...	...	...	0745	|
Bonn Hbf **800** ...... a.	|	|	|	1942	|	|	|	|	|	2142	|	|	2342	|	|	...	...	...	...	...	...	...	0819	|
Köln Messe/Deutz **910** ...... a.	|	|	1813	|	1914	|	2014	2027	|	|	2113	2214	|	2337	|	...	...	...	...	...	...	...	|	|
Köln Hbf **800 910** ...... a.	1732	1732	|	2005	|	1930	|	|	|	2205	|	|	0005	|	0034	...	...	...	...	...	...	...	0842	|
Düsseldorf Hbf **800** ...... a.	...	...	1835	|	1943	...	2038	2049	|	|	2137	2237	0032	2359	0100	...	...	...	...	...	...	...	...	|
Essen Hbf **800** ...... a.	...	...	1900	|	2015	...	2102	2116	|	|	2202	2302	0057	0025	0130	...	...	...	...	...	...	...	...	|
Dortmund Hbf **800** ...... a.	...	...	1930	2120	2040	...	2130	2141	|	2321	2230	2325	0121	0048	0153	...	...	...	...	...	...	...	...	|
Hamburg Hbf **800 900** ...... a.	...	...	...	0015	...	...	...	...	2153j	...	...	...	...	...	...	...	...	...	...	...	...	...	...	0750g

A – To Karlsruhe via Stuttgart (Table **925**).
B – [12] and 🍷 Passau - Leipzig - Berlin. See also Table **851**.
H – From Garmisch (Table **895**) on ⑥. To Hannover (Table **810**) on ⑦.
L – HANS ALBERS – 🛏 1, 2 cl., ▬ 2 cl. and [2] Wien - Hamburg.
N – 🛏 1, 2 cl., ▬ 2 cl. and [2] Wien - Köln.

b – Not June 21, Aug. 16, Oct. 4.
c – Also Oct. 2; not Oct. 3.
d – Also June 19, Oct. 3; not June 21, Oct. 4.
e – Not Oct. 4.
g – 0836 on ⑤ June 20 - July 25; 0851 on ①–④ June 14 - July 24.
h – Also June 19, Aug. 15, Oct. 3; not June 21, Aug. 16, Oct. 4.

j – 2203 June 14 - July 27.
k – ⑥ only.
m – Not Oct. 2.
r – Not June 19.
s – Also Oct. 3.
t – Departs up to 7 minutes **earlier** until July 12.

★ – © (also June 19, Aug. 15). Also calls at Neumarkt (Oberpf), d. 0618.
♥ – Ⓐ (not Jun e 19, Aug. 15). Also calls at Neumarkt (Oberpf), d. 0620.
¶ – Also calls at Neumarkt (Oberpf), d. 0700.
§ – Frankfurt Flughafen Fernbahnhof ✈.
◐ – Operated by *agilis*.

RE / RB services

Local trains PASSAU - REGENSBURG - NÜRNBERG - WÜRZBURG - FRANKFURT — 921

For faster *ICE / IC* trains see Table **920** above. Plattling - Regensburg - Neumarkt trains are operated by *agilis*.

Passau Hbf ...... **944** d.	*0522*	...	*0604*h	*0725*	...	*0826*	*0916*	...	*1026*	*1116*	...	*1224*	*1316*	...	*1426*	*1516*	...	*1626*	*1715*	...	*1823*	*1916*	...	*2025*	*2128*	...
Plattling ...... **944** a.	*0558*	...	*0640*h	*0759*	...	*0859*	*0950*	...	*1059*	*1150*	...	*1259*	*1349*	...	*1459*	*1551*	...	*1659*	*1751*	...	*1857*	*1951*	...	*2058*	*2200*	...
Plattling ...... d.	0609	...	0710	0811	...	0907	1011	...	1108	1211	...	1311	1411	...	1511	1611	...	1711	1811	...	1911	2011	...	2111	2210	...
Straubing ...... d.	0625	...	0728	0827	...	0924	1027	...	1124	1227	...	1327	1427	...	1527	1627	...	1727	1827	...	1927	2027	...	2127	2226	...
München Hbf **878** ... d.	|	0544	|	|	0744	|	|	0944	|	|	1144	|	|	1344	|	|	1544	|	|	1743	|	|	1944	|	|	...
Regensburg Hbf ...... a.	0652	0717	0753	0852	0914	0955	1052	1114	1155	1253	1314	1354	1452	1514	1553	1653	1716	1752	1852	1916	1953	2053	2114	2152	2252	...
Regensburg Hbf ...... d.	0656	0719	0756	0856	0919	0957	1056	1119	1158	1256	1319	1356	1456	1519	1556	1656	1719	1757	1856	1919	1956	2056	2119	2156	...	2323
Neumarkt (Oberpf) ...... d.	0750	0800	0852	0950	1000	1052	1150	1200	1253	1350	1400	1452	1550	1600	1652	1750	1800	1852	1950	2000	2050	2150	2200	2250	...	0020
Nürnberg Hbf ...... a.	...	0825	*0942*	...	1027	*1142*	...	1225	*1342*	...	1427	*1542*	...	1626	*1742*	...	1826	*1942*	...	2025	*2142*	...	2225	*2338*	...	0044

				⚒r													Ⓐr									
Nürnberg Hbf ...... d.	0101	...	...	0443	...	0605	0705	0805	0905	1005	1105	1205	1305	1405	1505	1605	1625	1705	1805	1905	2005	2105	2206	2239	...	2335
Fürth (Bay) Hbf ...... d.	0109	...	...	0451	...	0611	0711	0811	0911	1011	1111	1211	1311	1411	1511	1611	1632	1711	1811	1911	2011	2111	2212	2247	...	2344
Neustadt (Aisch) Bf ...... d.	0138	...	...	0521	...	0634	0734	0834	0934	1034	1134	1234	1334	1434	1534	1634	1701	1734	1834	1934	2034	2134	2235	2316	...	0013
Kitzingen ...... d.	...	...	...	0543	...	0657	0757	0857	0957	1057	1157	1257	1357	1457	1557	1657	1726	1757	1857	1957	2057	2157	2258	...	...	0035
Würzburg Hbf ...... a.	...	...	...	0603	...	0716	0817	0915	1015	1115	1215	1315	1415	1515	1615	1715	1747	1815	1915	2015	2115	2221	2316	...	...	0053

	Ⓐr	⚒r	†		©z	⑥	Ⓐr								©y	Ⓐr							†y	⚒r		
Würzburg Hbf ...... d.	0421	0512	0517	...	0611	0611	0634	0734	0834	0934	1034	1134	1234	1334	1434	1434	1534	1634	1734	1834	1934	2034	2136	2139	...	2323
Karlstadt (Main) ...... d.	0443	0534	0541	...	0633	0633	0649	0749	0849	0949	1049	1149	1249	1349	1449	1449	1549	1649	1749	1849	1949	2049	2153	2201	...	2346
Gemünden (Main) ...... d.	0455	0545	0553	...	0645	0645	0704	0804	0904	1004	1104	1204	1304	1404	1504	1504	1604	1704	1804	1904	2003	2104	2205	2212	...	2357
Lohr Bahnhof ...... d.	0505	0555	0603	...	0655	0655	0715	0815	0916	1015	1115	1215	1315	1415	1515	1515	1615	1715	1815	1915	2014	2115	2215	2223	...	0007
Aschaffenburg Hbf ...... d.	0542	0640j	0637	*0717*	0726	0742	0743	0843	0943	1043	1143	1243	1343	1443	1543	1543	1643	1743	1843	1943	2043	2143	2243	2256	*2313*	0040
Hanau Hbf ...... d.	0604	0704	...	0755	...	0804	0804	0904	1003	1104	1203	1304	1403	1504	1603	1604	1704	1803	1904	2003	2104	2203	2303	...	2346	...
Offenbach (Main) Hbf .. d.	0613	0713	...	0804	...	0813	0813	0913	|	1113	|	1313	|	1513	|	1613	1713	|	1913	|	2113	|	|	...	0001x	...
Frankfurt (Main) Süd .. a.	0616	0716	...	0809	...	0816	0816	0916	1025	1116	1225	1316	1425	1516	1625	1617	1716	1825	1916	2025	2117	2225	2325	...	|	...
Frankfurt (Main) Hbf .. a.	0624	0724	...	0815	...	0824	0824	0924	1032	1124	1232	1324	1432	1524	1632	*1628*	1724	1832p	1924	2032	2124	2232	2332	...	0016	...

– On © (also June 19, Aug. 15) Passau d. *0627*, Plattling a. *0701*.
– Arrives 0629.
– 1840 on † (also June 19).
– Not June 19.

x – Offenbach (Main) **Marktplatz**.
y – Also June 19
z – Also June 19, Aug. 15.

922 WÜRZBURG - HEILBRONN - STUTTGART *RE services*

km		Ⓒz	Ⓐe	Ⓐe		Ⓐe		Ⓐe				D						
0	**Würzburg** Hbf d.	...	...	...	0637	...	0837	0937	1037	1237	1437	1537	1637	1737	1837	1937	2037	2137
43	Lauda d.	...	...	*0532*	0710	...	0910	1008	1110	1310	1510	1608	1710	1807	1910	2007	2110	2207
78	Osterburken d.	...	0502	0616	0733	0802	0933	1032	1133	1333	1533	1631	1733	1830	1933	2030	2133	2230
94	Möckmühl d.	...	0519	0632	0745	0819	0945	1043	1145	1344	1545	1643	1745	1841	1945	2042	2145	2242
116	Bad Friedrichshall ⊖ d.	...	0544	0657	0801	0845	1001	1101	1201	1401	1601	1700	1801	1858	2001	2058	2202	2258
122	Neckarsulm d.	...	0552	0703	0806	0850	1006	1105	1206	1406	1606	1704	1806	1903	2006	2103	2207	2303
127	**Heilbronn** Hbf **924** d.	0554	0559	0712	0812	0856	1012	1111	1212	1412	1612	1713	1812	1909	2012	2108	2211	2309
140	Lauffen (Neckar) **924** d.	0604	0610	|	|	0904	|	|	|	|	|	|	|	|	|	2117	2219	2318
180	**Stuttgart** Hbf **924** a.	0643	0651	0747	0853	0943	1053	1146	1253	1453	1653	1758	1853	1949	2053	2158	2254	2356

	Ⓐe	Ⓒz	Ⓐe					D				Ⓒz	Ⓐe					⊠
Stuttgart Hbf **924** d.	0452	0456	0558	0659h	0907	1107	1307	1409	1504	1555	1704	1805	1809	1907	1942	2102	2315	2315
Lauffen (Neckar) **924** d.	0527	0532	|	0739	|	|	|	|	|	|	|	|	|	|	2017	2135	2351	2351
Heilbronn Hbf **924** d.	0538	0544	0641	0749	0945	1145	1345	1446	1545	1645	1745	1845	1844	1945	2027	2151	0001	0011
Neckarsulm d.	0544	0549	|	0755	0950	1150	1350	1451	1550	1650	1750	1850	1849	1950	2031	2156	...	0016
Bad Friedrichshall ⊖ d.	0549	0554	0649	0800	0955	1155	1355	1456	1555	1655	1755	1855	1854	1955	2036	2201	...	0022
Möckmühl d.	0605	0611	0713	0817	1012	1213	1412	1513	1612	1713	1812	1913	1918	2012	2059	2218	...	0047
Osterburken d.	0616	0622	0727	0828	1027	1227	1427	1527	1627	1727	1827	1927	1930	2027	2127v	2229	...	0104
Lauda d.	0643	0650	0750	0851	1050	1250	1450	1550	1650	1750	1850	1953	1953	2050	2155p	2253	...	...
Würzburg Hbf a.	0724	0720	0820	0921	1121	1321	1521	1621	1721	1821	1921	2024	2024	2121	...	2325	...	...

D – ⑤⑦ (also June 19, Nov. 1).

e – Not June 19.
h – 0702 on Ⓐ (not June 19).
p – ①②③④⑦ (not June 18, Oct. 2).
v – Arrives 2115.
z – Also June 19.

⊠ – ⑤–⑦ (also June 18, 19, Oct. 2). Change trains at Heilbronn on ⑤⑥ (also June 18, Oct. 2).
⊖ – Bad Friedrichshall-Jagstfeld.

923 MANNHEIM - EBERBACH - OSTERBURKEN *S-Bahn*

km			Ⓐe	†w	Ⓐe	⑥k	Ⓐe	Ⓐe	Ⓐe	Ⓒz								⑥t
0	**Mannheim** Hbf ¶ **924** d.	0007	0416	0457	*0457*	0536	...	0607	*0629*	0637	0729*	0838		2038	2137	2257	2257
17	**Heidelberg** Hbf ¶ **924** d.	0026	0434	0520	0555	0555	...	0631	0655	0655	0755	0855		2055	2201	2316	2316
28	Neckargemünd **924** d.	0039	0448	0534	0609	0609	...	0645	0709	0709	0809	0909	and	2109	2215	2336	2336
34	Neckarsteinach d.	0045	0454	0540	0615	0615	...	0651	0715	0715	0815	0915		2115	2221	2342	2342
41	Hirschhorn (Neckar) d.	0052	0501	0547	0622	0622	...	0658	0722	0722	0822	0922	hourly	2122	2228	2349	2349
50	Eberbach **924** d.	0059	0510	0553	0629	0629	...	0714f	0729	0729	0829	0929		2129	2235	2356	2356
69	Mosbach-Neckarelz **924** d.	0118	0535	0616	0648	0648	0709	0733	0748	0748	0848	0948	until	2148	2258	0014	0014
72	Mosbach (Baden) d.	0122	0539	0620	0652	0652	0714	0738	0752	0752	0852	0952		2152	2302	0018	0018
101	**Osterburken** a.	...	0612	...	0723	0723	0751	...	0823	0823	0923	1023		2223	2333	...	0049

	⚒r	Ⓐe	Ⓐe		Ⓐe		Ⓒz	Ⓐe		⚒r						⑥k	
Osterburken d.	...	...	0513	0536k	0604	...	0632	0643	...	0706e	0736		1836	1936	2036	2139	2239
Mosbach (Baden) d.	0435	0510	0543	0605	0633	0705	0705	0718	...	0735	0805		1905	2005	2105	2208	2308
Mosbach-Neckarelz **924** d.	0440	0526g	0548	0610	0638	0710	0710	0724	0729	0740	0810	and	1910	2010	2110	2213	2313
Eberbach **924** d.	0459	0545	0607	0629	0657	0729	0729	...	0743	0759	0829		1929	2029	2129	2232	2332
Hirschhorn (Neckar) d.	0506	0552	0614	0636	0704	0736	0736	...	|	0806	0836	hourly	1936	2036	2136	2239	2339
Neckarsteinach d.	0512	0559	0620	0642	0710	0742	0742	...	|	0812	0842		1942	2042	2142	2245	2345
Neckargemünd **924** d.	0519	0605	0627	0649	0718	0749	0749	...	|	0819	0849	until	1949	2049	2149	2252	2352
Heidelberg Hbf ¶ **924** a.	0533	0619	0640	0702	0732	0802	0802	...	0809	0832	0902		2002	2103	2203	2306	0006
Mannheim Hbf ¶ **924** a.	0551	0635	0702	0719	0751	0820	0820	...	0824	0851	0920		2020	2132	2232	2332	0030

e – Ⓐ (not June 19).
f – Arrives 0705.
g – Arrives 0514.
k – ⑥ (not Nov. 1).
r – Not June 19, Nov. 1.
t – Also June 18, Oct. 2, 31.
w – Also June 19, Nov. 1.
z – Also June 19.

* – Change trains at Heidelberg on Ⓒ (also June 19).
¶ – See also Tables **913**, **918**, **919**.

924 MANNHEIM - HEILBRONN - STUTTGART *RE / RB / S-Bahn services*

km		⚒r	Ⓐe		Ⓐe		Ⓐe	Ⓒz	Ⓐe	Ⓒz		Ⓐe	Ⓒz		Ⓐe	Ⓒz		Ⓐe	Ⓒz		Ⓐe	Ⓒz	Ⓐe		
0	**Mannheim** Hbf **923** d.	...	0629	...	0736	0835	0935	0935	1135	1135	1235	1335	1335	1435	1536	1535	1635	1735	1735	1835	1935	1935	2035	2142	2257
17	**Heidelberg** Hbf **923** d.	...	0642	...	0749	0849	0949	0949	1149	1149	1249	1349	1349	1449	1549	1549	1649	1749	1749	1849	1949	1949	2049	2158	2316
28	Neckargemünd **923** d.	...	0653	...	|	|	|	|	|	|	|	|	|	|	|	|	|	|	|	|	|	|	|	|	2330
50	Eberbach **923** d.	...	|	...	0813	0914	1014	1018	1214	1218	1314	1414	1418	1514	1614	1618	1714	1814	1818	1914	2014	2018	2114	2223	2348
69	Mosbach-Neckarelz **923** d.	0616	0726	0751	0828	0928	1028	1032	1228	1232	1328	1428	1432	1529	1628	1632	1728	1828	1832	1928	2028	2032	2127	2237	0002
87	Bad Friedrichshall ⊖ **922** d.	0636	0741	0811	0841	0942	1042	1045	1242	1245	1342	1442	1445	1542	1642	1648	1742	1842	1845	1942	2042	2045	2142	2250	0016
93	Neckarsulm d.	0644	0746	0818	0846	0947	1047	1050	1247	1250	1347	1447	1450	1547	1647	1653	1747	1847	1850	1947	2047	2050	2147	2255	0021
98	**Heilbronn** Hbf **922** a.	0651	0752	0824	0850	0951	1051	1054	1251	1254	1351	1451	1454	1551	1651	1657	1751	1851	1854	1951	2054	2054	2151	2259	0026
98	**Heilbronn** Hbf **922** d.	0653	*0758*	0826	*0856*	*0956*e	*1056*	1056	*1256*	1256	*1356*e	*1456*	1456	*1556*e	*1656*	1659	1754e	*1856*	1856	*2012*	*2108*	*2108*	*2211*	*2309*	...
111	Lauffen (Neckar) **922** d.	0704	*0806*	0837	*0904*	*1004*e	*1104*	1104	*1304*	1304	*1404*e	*1504*	1504	*1604*e	*1704*	1707	1802e	*1904*	1904	|	*2117*	*2117*	*2219*	*2318*	...
151	**Stuttgart** Hbf **922** a.	0743	*0843*	0915	*0943*	*1043*e	*1146*	1146	*1343*	1343	*1443*e	*1543*	1543	*1643*e	*1743*	1743	1839e	*1943*	1943	*2053*	*2158*	*2158*	*2254*	*2356*	...

	Ⓐe	Ⓒz			Ⓒz	Ⓐe		Ⓒz	Ⓐe	Ⓒz	Ⓐe		Ⓒz	Ⓐe		Ⓒz	Ⓐe			Ⓒz	Ⓐe		⊙		
Stuttgart Hbf **922** d.	...	0545	*0614*b	*0659*h	0813	*0813*	*0915*e	1015	*1015*	1215	*1215*	*1315*e	1415	*1415*	*1515*e	1613	*1613*	1715e	1745	1815	*1815*	*1914*e	2015	*2102*	2215
Lauffen (Neckar) **922** d.	...	0621	0649e	*0739*	0850	*0850*	*0953*e	1050	*1050*	1251	*1251*	*1353*e	1450	*1450*	*1553*e	1650	*1650*	1753e	1820	1850	*1850*	*1953*e	2051	*2135*	2251
Heilbronn Hbf **922** a.	...	0630	0659e	*0748*	0901	*0901*	*1001*e	1101	*1101*	1301	*1301*	*1401*e	1501	*1501*	*1601*e	1701	*1701*	1801e	1829	1901	*1901*	*2001*e	2101	*2146*	2301
Heilbronn Hbf **922** d.	0456	0631	0700	0806	0904	0906	1006	1104	1106	1304	1306	1406	1504	1505	1605	1704	1705	1805	1830	1904	1906	2006	2105	2221	2301
Neckarsulm d.	0500	0636	0705	0811	0909	0911	1011	1109	1111	1309	1311	1411	1509	1511	1611	1709	1711	1811	1836	1909	1911	2011	2109	2228	2306
Bad Friedrichshall ⊖ **922** d.	0504	0643	0710	0816	0914	0916	1016	1114	1116	1314	1316	1417	1514	1516	1616	1714	1716	1816	1843	1914	1916	2016	2113	2235	...
Mosbach-Neckarelz **923** d.	0518	0705	0729	0829	0927	0929	1029	1127	1129	1327	1329	1430	1528	1529	1629	1727	1729	1829	1906	1927	1929	2029	2129	2254	...
Eberbach **923** d.	0532	...	0743	0843	0941	0943	1043	1141	1143	1341	1343	1443	1541	1543	1643	1741	1743	1843	...	1941	1943	2043	2143	...	...
Neckargemünd **923** d.	|	...	|	|	|	|	|	|	|	|	|	|	|	|	|	|	|	|	...	|	|	|	|	...	...
Heidelberg Hbf **923** a.	0556	...	0809	0909	1009	1009	1109	1209	1209	1409	1409	1509	1609	1609	1709	1809	1809	1909	...	2009	2009	2109	2208	...	...
Mannheim Hbf **923** a.	0612	...	0824	0924	1024	1024	1124	1224	1224	1424	1424	1524	1624	1624	1724	1824	1824	1924	...	2022	2024	2124	2222	...	...

Local services MANNHEIM - SINSHEIM

	Ⓐe	Ⓒz	Ⓑq	⑥k	†w	⚒r		†w	⚒r	◐	‡	
Mannheim Hbf d.	*0544*	*0535*	*0707*e	0707	0807	*0807*	and	1907	*1907*	2007	2107	2207
Heidelberg Hbf d.	0612	0631	0731	0734	0831	0834	hourly	1931	1934	2031	2131	2231
Neckargemünd d.	0626	0646	0746	0746	0846	0846		1946	1946	2046	2146	2246
Sinsheim (Elsenz) Hbf a.	0657	0708	0808	0808	0908	0908	until	2008	2008	2107	2208	2308

		Ⓒz	Ⓐe	◐	◐		◐	‡	
Sinsheim (Elsenz) Hbf d.	0549t	0649	0649	0747v	0849	and	1949	2049	2149
Neckargemünd d.	0611	0711	0711	0811	0911	hourly	2011	2111	2211
Heidelberg Hbf a.	0625	0726	0726	0826	0926		2026	2124	2226
Mannheim Hbf a.	*0651*	0751	0746	0851	0951	until	2055	2202	*2302*

HEIDELBERG - SINSHEIM - HEILBRONN (special engineering work timetable operates in 2014)

km		Ⓐe	Ⓐe	Ⓐe	Ⓐe 🚌	Ⓒz 🚌	Ⓐe	Ⓐe	Ⓒz 🚌	Ⓐe	Ⓒz 🚌		Ⓒz 🚌	Ⓐe	❖	Ⓒz 🚌	Ⓐe	Ⓒz 🚌	Ⓐe	🚌	🚌		◇	🚌
0	**Heidelberg** Hbf ■ d.	...	...	...	...	...	...	0731	...	...	...	...	...	1004	and at	...	1904	...	1958	...	...	...	2323	...
12	Neckargemünd ■ d.	...	...	...	...	...	...	0746	...	...	...	...	...	1016	the same	...	1916	...	2015	...	...	...	2334	...
32	Sinsheim (Elsenz) Hbf ■ d.	0448	0533	0612	0624	0713	0716	0810	0813	0911	0913	...	1013	1038	minutes	1913	1938	2013	2042	2117	2217	...	2355	0010
49	Bad Rappenau d.	0504	0557	0633	0659	0742	0733	0832	0842	0932	0942	...	1042	1055	past each	1942	1955	2042	2107	2146	2246	...	...	0039
55	Bad Wimpfen-Hohenstadt d.	*0518**	*0611**	*0646**	0707	0750	*0746**	*0846**	0850	*0946**	0950	...	1050	*1111**	hour until	1950	*2011**	2050	*2116**	2154	2254	...	...	0047
58	Bad Friedrichshall ⊖ ⊠ d.	|	|	|	|	|	|	|	|	|	|	...	|	|		|	|	|	|	|	|	...	...	|
64	Neckarsulm ⊠ d.	*0543**	*0637**	*0712**	0739	0815	*0811**	*0911**	0915	*1011**	1015	...	1115	*1136**		2015	*2036**	2115	*2149**	2219	2319	...	...	0112
69	**Heilbronn** Hbf ⊠ a.	...	...	...	...	...	...	...	...	...	...	...	...	...		...	...	...	...	...	...	...	...	0124

	Ⓐe 🚌	Ⓐe	Ⓐe	Ⓐe	Ⓐe 🚌	Ⓒz 🚌	Ⓐe	Ⓒz 🚌	Ⓐe	Ⓒz 🚌	♥	Ⓐe	Ⓒz 🚌	Ⓒz 🚌	Ⓐe	Ⓒz 🚌	Ⓐe	Ⓒz 🚌	Ⓐe	Ⓐe 🚌	Ⓒz 🚌		🚌	🚌
Heilbronn Hbf ⊠ d.	0438	...	...	...	...	...	...	...	...	...	and at	...	...	...	...	...	...	...	...	...	...	...	...	...
Neckarsulm ⊠ d.	0452	...	*0520**	*0601**	0635	0640	*0717**	0745	*0817**	0840	the same	*1717**	1740	1840	*1842**	1940	*1942**	2040	*2042**	2117	2140	...	2240	2315
Bad Friedrichshall ⊖ ⊠ d.	|	...	|	|	|	|	|	|	|	|		|	|	|	|	|	|	|	|	|	|	...	|	|
Bad Wimpfen-Hohenstadt d.	|	...	*0545**	*0626**	0700	0705	*0742**	|	*0842**	0905	minutes	*1742**	1805	1905	*1907**	2005	*2007**	2105	*2107**	2142	2205	...	2305	2340
Bad Rappenau d.	0521	0528	0604	0646	0710	0715	0800	0814	0900	0915	past each	1800	1815	1915	1924	2015	2024	2115	2124	2152	2215	...	2315	2350
Sinsheim (Elsenz) Hbf ■ d.	...	0545	0620	0715f	0742	0744	0817	0843	0917	0944		1817	1844	1944	1945	2044	2041	2144	2143	2221	2244	2249	2344	0015
Neckargemünd ■ d.	...	...	|	0741	...	...	0841	...	0941	...	hour until	1840	...	...	...	...	...	...	...	...	...	2311	...	...
Heidelberg Hbf ■ a.	...	...	0648	0755	...	...	0856	...	0954	...		1854	...	...	...	...	...	...	...	...	...	2326	...	...

b – Ⓐ (not June 19). Change at Bietigheim-Bissingen (a. *0629*, d. 0633).
e – Ⓐ (not June 19).
f – Arrives 0704.
h – *0702* on Ⓐ (not June 19).
k – Not Nov. 1.
q – Also Nov. 1.
r – Not June 19, Nov. 1.
t – 0547 on ⑥ (not Nov. 1).
v – 0749 on Ⓒ (also June 19).
w – Also June 19, Nov. 1.
z – Also June 19.

* – By 🚌 Bad Rappenau - Neckarsulm and v.v.
◐ – Change trains at Heidelberg on ⚒r.
‡ – Change trains at Heidelberg on Ⓐe
⊙ – Change trains at Heilbronn on Ⓐe.
⊖ – Bad Friedrichshall-Jagstfeld.
◇ – From Mannheim Hbf (d. 2310).

❖ – Heidelberg d. 1603 / 1703 (not 1604 / 1704).
♥ – Timings Sinsheim - Heidelberg may vary by up to 2 minutes.
■ – See also Mannheim - Sinsheim panel above.
⊠ – For connecting trains from / to Neckarsulm see main Mannheim - Heilbronn panel, also Table **922**.

STUTTGART - BACKNANG / AALEN - NÜRNBERG 925

RE services except where shown

km				IC 2061				IC 2063			IC 2065			IC 2067			IC 2069			IC 2161				IC 2163		
			Ⓐt	Ⓐt	⚒r	2														Ⓑq		Ⓒz	Ⓐt			
	Karlsruhe Hbf **931** .. d.	...	...	...	...	...	...	0706e	...	...	0906	...	...	1106	...	...	1306	...	...	1506	...	...	...	1706	...	...
0	**Stuttgart** Hbf ‡ d.	...	0543	0605	0620t	...	0641f	0807	0822	0841f	1007	1022	1041f	1207	1222	1241f	1407	1422	1441f	1607	1619k	1641	1658	1807	1819k	1841f
31	Backnang d.	...	0607	|	|	...	0706f	|	|	0906f	|	|	1106f	|	|	1306j	|	|	1506f	|	|	1706	1725	|	|	1906f
73	Schwäbisch H-H ⊡ a.	...	0653	|	|	...	0747j	|	|	0947f	|	|	1147f	|	|	1347f	|	|	1547f	|	|	1747	1758	|	|	1947f
73	Schwäbisch H-H ⊡ d.	...	0654	|	|	...	0759	|	|	0959	|	|	1159	|	|	1359	|	|	1559	|	|	1759	1759	|	|	1959
	Schwäbisch Gmünd ‡ d.	...	|	0642	0705	...	|	0842	0905	|	1040	1105	|	1240	1305	|	1440	1505	|	1640	1705	|	|	1840	1905	|
	Aalen ‡ a.	...	|	0657	0725	...	|	0857	0925	|	1055	1125	|	1255	1325	|	1455	1525	|	1655	1725	|	|	1855	1925	|
	Aalen d.	...	|	0659	▬	0728	|	0859	0928	|	1057	1128	|	1257	1328	|	1457	1528	|	1657	1728	|	|	1857	1928	|
	Ellwangen d.	...	|	0710	...	0748	|	0910	0948	|	1108	1149	|	1308	1349	|	1508	1549	|	1708	1748	|	|	1908	1948	|
100	Crailsheim d.	0606	0714	0726	⚒r	0812	0818	0926	1012	1018	1125	1212	1218	1325	1412	1418	1525	1612	1618	1725	1812	1818	1818	1925	2012	2018
146	Ansbach d.	0641	0745	0750	0754	...	0850	0950	...	1050	1150	...	1250	1350	...	1450	1550	...	1650	1750	...	1850	1850	1950	...	2050
190	**Nürnberg** Hbf a.	0718	...	0818	0835	...	0925	1018	...	1125	1218	...	1325	1418	...	1525	1618	...	1725	1818	...	1925	1925	2018	...	2125

				IC 2165				IC 2167				
	Ⓒz	Ⓒz	Ⓐt	⑤⑦ s P		Ⓒz	Ⓐt	⑦		⑥d	Ⓑq	
Karlsruhe Hbf **931** .. d.	...	...	...	1906	...	...	...	2106	...	...	...	...
Stuttgart Hbf ‡ d.	1945*	...	1958	2007	2022	2057	2058	2207	2232	2245*	2258	2358
Backnang d.	2022	...	2025	|	|	2123	2125	|	|	2325	2325	0026
Schwäbisch H-H ⊡ a.	2054	...	2102	|	|	2202	2202	|	|	0001	0001	0102
Schwäbisch H-H ⊡ d.	...	2059	2103	|	|	2203	2203	|	|	0002	0002	0103
Schwäbisch Gmünd ‡ d.	...	|	|	2040	2105	|	|	2243	2316	|	|	|
Aalen ‡ a.	...	|	|	2055	2125	|	|	2258	2338	|	|	|
Aalen d.	...	|	|	2057	2128	|	|	2300	2344	|	|	|
Ellwangen d.	...	|	|	2108	2148	|	|	2311	0004	|	|	|
Crailsheim d.	...	2121	2121	2125	2209	2222	2222	2329	0020	0020	0020	0121
Ansbach d.	...	...	...	2150	...	...	...	2354	...	...	...	...
Nürnberg Hbf a.	...	...	...	2218	...	...	...	0020	...	...	...	...

km						IC 2164				
		Ⓐt	Ⓐt	Ⓒz	Ⓐt	Ⓐt	Ⓐt	Ⓒz	Ⓐt	Ⓒz
0	**Nürnberg** Hbf d.	...	...	...	...	0538	...	...	...	...
44	Ansbach d.	...	...	...	...	0603	...	...	...	...
90	Crailsheim d.	0452	0514	0552	0552	0632	0634	0635	0646	0651
111	Ellwangen d.	|	0530	|	|	0648	|	|	0710	0712
127	**Aalen** a.	|	0550	|	|	0658	|	|	0727	0732
127	**Aalen** ‡ d.	|	0600	|	|	0701	|	|	0735	0735
152	Schwäbisch Gmünd ‡ d.	|	0621	|	|	0718	|	|	0754	0754
	Schwäbisch H-H ⊡ a.	0510	|	0610	0611	|	0652	0653	|	|
	Schwäbisch H-H ⊡ d.	0511	|	0611	0618	|	0653	0702	|	|
	Backnang d.	0551	|	0651	0705	|	0736	0737	|	|
203	**Stuttgart** Hbf ‡ a.	0618	0714	0718	0735	0753	0803	0815*	0843	0837
	Karlsruhe Hbf **931** .. a.	...	...	...	...	0853	...	...	...	...

			IC 2162			IC 2160			IC 2068				IC 2066			IC 2064			IC 2062			IC 2060				IC 1968
			①–⑥ n Q							Ⓒz	Ⓐt											⑤⑦ s			2	⑦
Nürnberg Hbf d.	0636	...	0739	0833k	...	0939	1036	...	1139	1236	1236	...	1339	1436	...	1539	1636	...	1739	1836	...	1939	...	2036	...	2140
Ansbach d.	0707	...	0807	0907	...	1007	1107	...	1207	1307	1310	...	1407	1507	...	1607	1707	...	1807	1907	...	2007	...	2107	...	2207
Crailsheim d.	0742	0752	0835	0942	0952	1035	1142	1152	1235	1342	1343	1352	1435	1542	1552	1635	1742	1752	1835	1942	1952	2035	2042z	2142	2149	2235
Ellwangen d.	|	0812	0851	|	1012	1051	|	1212	1251	|	|	1412	1451	|	1612	1651	|	1812	1851	|	2012	2051	2112	|	2207	2251
Aalen a.	|	0832	0901	|	1032	1101	|	1232	1301	|	|	1432	1501	|	1632	1701	|	1832	1901	|	2032	2101	2132	|	2221	2301
Aalen ‡ d.	|	0835	0903	|	1035	1103	|	1235	1303	|	|	1435	1503	|	1635	1703	|	1835	1903	|	2035	2103	2135	|	2222	2303
Schwäbisch Gmünd ‡ d.	|	0854	0920	|	1054	1120	|	1254	1320	|	|	1454	1520	|	1654	1720	|	1854	1920	|	2054	2120	2154	|	2240	2320
Schwäbisch H-H ⊡ a.	0759	|	|	0959	|	|	1159	|	|	1359	1401	|	|	1559	|	|	1759	|	|	1959	|	|	|	2159	|	|
Schwäbisch H-H ⊡ d.	0812f	|	|	1012f	|	|	1212	|	|	1412	1414	|	|	1612f	|	|	1812f	|	|	2003b	|	|	|	2203	|	|
Backnang d.	0851	|	|	1051	|	|	1251	|	|	1451	1451	|	|	1651	|	|	1851	|	|	2051	|	|	|	2251	|	|
Stuttgart Hbf ‡ a.	0918	0937	0953	1118	1137	1153	1318	1337	1353	1518	1518	1537	1553	1718	1743c	1753	1918	1937	1953	2118	2137	2153	2237	2318	2329	2355
Karlsruhe Hbf **931** .. a.	...	...	1053	...	...	1253	...	...	1453	...	...	...	1653	...	...	1853	...	...	2053	...	...	2259	...	...	...	...

P – To Passau on ⑦ (Table **920**).
Q – From Passau on ① (Table **920**).

b – 2012 on Ⓒ (also June 19).
c – 1737 on Ⓒ (also June 19).
d – Also Oct. 3.
e – ①-⑥ (not June 19, Oct. 4).
f – 2 minutes later on Ⓐ (not June 19).

j – 5 minutes later on Ⓐ (not June 19).
k – 3 minutes later on Ⓒ (also June 19).
n – Not Oct. 4.
q – Not Oct. 3.
r – Not June 19, Nov. 1.
s – Also June 18, Oct. 2; not June 20, Oct. 3.
t – Ⓐ (not June 19).
z – Ⓒ (also June 19).

⊡ – Schwäbisch Hall-Hessental.
* – From the S-Bahn (underground) platforms.
‡ – Other *RE* trains Stuttgart - Schwäbisch Gmünd - Aalen and v.v.
From Stuttgart Hbf at 0032, 0453 Ⓐ**t**, 0532 Ⓐ**t**, 0650 Ⓐ**t**, 0719 Ⓐ**t**, 0722 Ⓒ**z**, 0922, 1122, 1322, 1449 Ⓐ**t**, 1522, 1549 Ⓐ**t**, 1636 Ⓐ**t**, 1649 Ⓐ**t**, 1719 Ⓐ**t**, 1722 Ⓒ**z**, 1748 Ⓐ**t**, 1846 Ⓐ**t**, 1922, 2122, 2332 Ⓐ**t** and 2336 Ⓒ**z**.
From Aalen at 0426 Ⓐ**t**, 0503 Ⓐ**t**, 0518 Ⓐ**t**, 0533 Ⓐ**t**, 0535 Ⓒ**z**, 0627 Ⓐ**t**, 0635 Ⓒ**z**, 0706 Ⓐ**t**, 0805 Ⓐ**t**, 0935, 1135, 1335, 1535, 1605 Ⓐ**t**, 1708 Ⓐ**t**, 1735, 1805 Ⓐ**t** and 1935.

HEILBRONN / ASCHAFFENBURG - CRAILSHEIM and AALEN - DONAUWÖRTH / ULM 926

RE / *RB* services

ASCHAFFENBURG - LAUDA - CRAILSHEIM ⊠

km		Ⓐt	Ⓒz							
0	**Aschaffenburg** Hbf d.	...	...	0644	0922	1122	1322	1522	1722	1922k
38	Miltenberg d.	...	...	0750	0959	1159	1359	1559	1759	1959
69	Wertheim d.	...	0626	0828j	1035	1235	1435	1635	1835	2035
93	Tauberbischofsheim d.	0545	0653	0900	1100	1300	1500	1700	1900	2101
100	**Lauda** a.	0555	0702	0906	1106	1306	1506	1706	1906	2106
100	**Lauda** d.	0608	0713	0913	1113	1313	1513	1713	1913	2113
110	Bad Mergentheim d.	0620	0725	0925	1125	1325	1525	1725	1925	2124
169	**Crailsheim** a.	0726	0830	1028	1228	1428	1628	1828	2028	...

	Ⓐt	Ⓒz	Ⓐt								
Crailsheim d.	...	...	0520	0731	0931	1131	1328s	1531	1731	1931	...
Bad Mergentheim d.	...	...	0636	0833v	1033	1233	1433	1633	1833	2033	2053t
Lauda a.	...	...	0647	0843v	1043	1243	1443	1643	1843	2043	2104t
Lauda d.	...	0614	0702	0853	1053	1253	1453	1653	1853	▬	2110
Tauberbischofsheim d.	0515*	0624	0712	0900	1059	1259	1459	1659	1859	...	2120
Wertheim d.	0600	0700	0800p	0921	1121	1321	1521	1721	1921	...	2147
Miltenberg d.	0636	0740	0840	0959	1159	1359	1559	1759	1959	2035	2222
Aschaffenburg Hbf a.	0712	0830	0930	1037	1237	1437	1637	1837	2034z	2121	2307

HEILBRONN - CRAILSHEIM ⊠

km		Ⓐt	Ⓒz	Ⓐt		Ⓒz	Ⓐt	Ⓒz	Ⓐt
0	**Heilbronn** Hbf d.	0550	0803	0805	and every	1803	1805	2003	2005
27	Öhringen d.	0618	0825	0827	**two** hours	1825	1827	2025	2027
54	Schwäbisch Hall d.	0642	0851	0851	until	1851	1851	2051	2051
61	Schwäbisch Hall-H ⊡ a.	0649	0858	0859		1858	1858	2058	2058
88	**Crailsheim** a.	0713	0921	0922		1921	1921	2121	2121

	Ⓐt		Ⓐt	Ⓒz		Ⓐt	Ⓒz	Ⓒz	Ⓐt
Crailsheim d.	0552	0634	0838	0838	and every	1838	1838	2038	2038
Schwäbisch Hall-H ⊡ d.	0612	0658	0858	0900	**two** hours	1858	1900	2103	2106
Schwäbisch Hall d.	0619	0705	0905	0906	until	1905	1906	2110	2112
Öhringen a.	0643	0728	0928	0930		1928	1930	2136	2136
Heilbronn Hbf a.	0718	0751	0951	0952		1951	1952	2220	2220

AALEN - DONAUWÖRTH

km		Ⓐt	Ⓐt	Ⓒz	Ⓐt	Ⓐt	Ⓐt			Ⓐt		Ⓐt	Ⓒz	Ⓐt	Ⓐt		Ⓐt		Ⓐt		Ⓐt					
0	**Aalen** d.	...	...	0531	...	0603	0625	...	0735	0835	0935	1035	1135	1135	1235	1335	1435	1535	1635	1735	1835	1935	2035	...	...	...
39	Nördlingen a.	...	...	0613	...	0638	0706	...	0813	0913	1013	1113	1213	1219	1313	1413	1513	1613	1713	1813	1913	2013	2113	...	...	...
39	Nördlingen d.	0518	0600	0614	0624	0639	0707	...	0814	0914	1014	1114	1214	1221	1314	1414	1514	1614	1714	1814	1914	2014	2114	...	...	...
68	**Donauwörth** a.	0546	0632	0644	0651	0706	0734	...	0844	0944	1044	1144	1244	1248	1344	1444	1544	1645	1744	1845	1944	2045	2145	...	...	...

	Ⓐt		Ⓐt		Ⓒz	Ⓐt	Ⓐt		Ⓐt		Ⓐt		Ⓐt		Ⓐt		Ⓐt	Ⓐt	Ⓐt		Ⓐt			Ⓐt	Ⓒz	
Donauwörth d.	...	...	0608	...	0703	0708	0803	0903	1003	1103	1203	1303	1403	1503	1603	1703	1745	1803	1845	1903	2003	2103	...	2211	2242	...
Nördlingen a.	...	...	0638	...	0739	0739	0831	0931	1031	1131	1236	1331	1431	1531	1631	1731	1812	1831	1912	1931	2031	2131	...	2238	2309	...
Nördlingen d.	0532	...	0641	0641	0744	0744	0844	0944	1044	1144	1244	1344	1444	1544	1644	1744	...	1844	...	1944	...	2134	...	...	...	...
Aalen a.	0614	...	0721	0721	0826	0826	0926	1026	1126	1226	1326	1426	1526	1626	1726	1826	...	1926	...	2026	...	2215	...	...	...	...

AALEN - ULM ⊠ ⊖

km		Ⓐt	⑥w	Ⓐt	Ⓐt	Ⓒz	Ⓐt			Ⓐt			⚒r													
0	**Aalen** d.	0442	0529	0554	0625	0633	0702	0733	0833	0907	0933	1033	1107	1133	1307	1333	1507	1533	1633	1706	1733	1833	1907	1933	2039b	2133
23	Heidenheim d.	0506	0552	0617	0647	0659	0725	0756h	0859	0923	0955	1059	1123	1154	1323	1354	1523	1554	1659	1722	1754	1859	1923	1953	2107	2155
73	**Ulm** Hbf a.	0555	0642	0710	0743	0744	0756	0844	0944	0954	1044	1144	1154	1244	1354	1444	1554	1644	1744	1754	1844	1944	1954	2044	2151	2246

	Ⓐt	Ⓐt	Ⓐt	Ⓒz	Ⓐt	Ⓒz	Ⓐt			⚒r																
Ulm Hbf d.	0430	0542	0603	0609	0648	0713	0803	0813	0913	1000	1013	1113	1200	1213	1313	1400	1413	1513	1600	1613	1713	1800	1813	1913	2013	2220
Heidenheim d.	0520	0630	0656	0658	0800	0800	0835	0859	1005	1032	1059	1205	1232	1259	1403	1432	1459	1605	1634	1659	1805	1832	1859	2003	2059	2308
Aalen a.	0545	0651	0721	0721	0823	0823	0851	0924	1027	1050	1124	1227	1250	1324	1426	1450	1525	1627	1650	1724	1827	1850	1924	2026	2124	2331

– 2035 on † (also June 19, Nov. 1).
– 0800 on Ⓒ (also June 19).
– 0835 on Ⓐ (not June 19).
– 1928 on Ⓒ (also June 19).
– Arrives 0738.

r – Not June 19, Nov. 1.
s – 1334 on ①–⑤ Aug. 4 - Sept. 12 (also June 16, 17, 18, 20, Oct. 27–31). 1331 on Ⓒ (also June 19).
t – Ⓐ (not June 19).
v – 3 minutes later on Ⓐ (not June 19).

w – Not Nov. 1.
y – Also June 19, Nov. 1.
z – Ⓒ (also June 19).
* – By 🚌.

⊠ – 2nd class only.
⊡ – Schwäbisch Hall-Hessental.
⊖ – **Additional journeys** Aalen - Ulm and v.v.
From Aalen at 0516 Ⓐ**t**, 1233, 1433, 2107 †**y**.
From Ulm at 0455 Ⓐ**t**, 1630 Ⓐ**t**, 2000 †**y**.

928 MÜNCHEN - BAYRISCHZELL, LENGGRIES and TEGERNSEE

Bayerische Oberlandbahn GmbH

km		■	Ⓒz					Ⓒz					Ⓐe				Ⓐe								⑤⑥v	A
0	**München** Hbf . d.	0005	0605	...	0705t	...	0805	0830	0905	0927	1005	1105	1205	1230	1305	1405	1505	1530	1605	1705	1805	1905	2005	2105	2205	2305	*2305*
37	Holzkirchen ..... d.	0032	0632	...	0732	...	0832	0858	0932	0958	1032	1132	1232	1302	1332	1432	1532	1558	1632	1732	1832	1932	2032	2132	2232	2332	2336
61	Schliersee .... d.	0059	0659	...	0759	...	0859	0926	0959	1026	1059	1159	1259	1330	1359	1459	1559	1626	1659	1759	1859	1959	2059	2159	2259	2359	0004
78	**Bayrischzell** ... a.	0123	0723	...	0823	...	0923	...	1023	...	1123	1223	1323	1354	1423	1523	1623	...	1723	1823	1923	2023	2123	2223	2323	0023	0028

km				Ⓐe	Ⓒz	Ⓐe		Ⓒz						Ⓐe				Ⓐe								⑤⑥v	A
0	**München** Hbf . d.	*0005*	0605	0628	0705	0730	0805	0830	0905	0927	1005	1105	1205	1230	1305	1405	1505	1530	1605	1705	1805	1905	2005	2105	*2205*	*2305*	2305
37	Holzkirchen ..... d.	0034	0632j	0704	0734	0803	0834	0902	0934	1002	1034	1134	1234	1304	1334	1434	1534	1602	1634	1734	1834	1934	2034	2134	2234	2334	2334
47	Schaftlach .... d.	0047	0647	0717	0748	0817	0847	0916	0947	1017	1047	1147	1247	1317	1347	1447	1547	1617	1647	1747	1847	1947	2047	2147	2247	2347	2347
57	Bad Tölz .... d.	0100	0700	0730	0801	0830	0900	0929	1000	1030	1100	1200	1300	1330	1400	1500	1600	1630	1700	1800	1900	2000	2100	2200	2300	0000	0000
67	**Lenggries** ...... a.	0111	0712	0741	0812	0841	0911	0940	1011	1041	1111	1211	1311	1341	1411	1511	1611	1641	1711	1811	1911	2011	2111	2211	2311	0011	0011

km				Ⓐe	Ⓒz	Ⓐe		Ⓒz						Ⓐe				Ⓐe								⑤⑥v	A
0	**München** Hbf . d.	*0005*	0605	0628	0705	0730	0805	0830	0905	0927	1005	1105	1205	*1230*	1305	1405	1505	1530	1605	1705	1805	1905	2005	2105	*2205*	*2305*	2305
37	Holzkirchen ..... d.	0034	0632j	0704	0734	0803	0834	0902	0934	1002	1034	1134	1234	*1304*	1334	1434	1534	1602	1634	1734	1834	1934	2034	2134	2234	2334	2334
47	Schaftlach .... d.	0048	0648	0718	0748	0818	0848	0917	0948	1018	1048	1148	1247	1316	1348	1448	1548	1618	1648	1747	1848	1948	2048	2148	2248	2348	2348
59	**Tegernsee** ...... a.	0109	0709	0739	0809	0839	0909	0938	1009	1039	1109	1209	1309	1339	1409	1509	1609	1639	1709	1809	1909	2009	2109	2209	2309	0009	0009

	⚒r	Ⓐe		Ⓐe	Ⓒz	Ⓐe	⚒r	⊖					Ⓒz	Ⓐe				Ⓒz		Ⓒz							
Bayrischzell.....d.	...	0449	0534	0607	0634	0633	0706e	0733	0834	0934	1034	1134	1234	1234	1334z	1434	1534	...	1634	...	1734	...	1834	1934	2034	2134	2234
Schliersee.........d.	0444	0516	0602	0636	0702	0702	0734	0802	0902	1002	1102	1202	1302	1302	1402	1502	1602	1634	1702	1734	1802	...	1902	2002	2102	2202	2302
Holzkirchen.......d.	0510	0544	0630	0705	0730	0732	0803	0830	0930	1030	1130	1230	1330	1332	1430	1530	1630	1704	1730	1804	1830	...	1930	2030	2130	2230	2330
München Hbf...a.	0535	0612	0655	0735	0755	0800	0831	0856	0956	1055	1155	1255	1355	1357	1455	1556	1656	1732	1756	1831	1855	...	1955	2055	2155	2255	2355

	⚒r	Ⓐe		Ⓐe	Ⓒz	Ⓐe	⚒r						Ⓒz	Ⓐe				Ⓒz		Ⓒz	Ⓐe	Ⓒz			⊡	⊗	
Lenggries ....d.	0431f	0503	0550	0623	0648	0648	0718	0748	0848	0948	1048	1148	1248	1248	1348	1448	1548	1618	1648	1718	1748	1748	1848	1948	2048	2148	2248
Bad Tölz...........d.	0443f	0515	0602	0635	0702	0702	0731	0802	0902	1002	1102	1202	1302	1304	1402	1502	1602	1632	1702	1732	1804	1802	1902	2002	2102	2202	2302
Schaftlach.........d.	0454	0531	0618	0648	0718	0716	0747	0818	0918	1018	1118	1218	1318	1317	1418	1518	1618	1649	1718	1749	1818	1818	1918	2018	2118	2218	2318
Holzkirchen.......a.	0504	0541	0628	0657	0728	0725	0757	0828	0928	1028	1128	1228	1328	1326	1428	1528	1628	1658	1728	1758	1828	1828	1928	2028	2128	2228	2328
München Hbf...a.	0535	0612	0655	0731	0755	0800	0831	0856	0956	1055	1155	1255	1355	1357	1455	1556	1656	1732	1756	1831	1855	1855	1955	2055	2155	2255	*2355*

	⑥h	Ⓐe		Ⓐe	Ⓒz		⚒r						Ⓒz	Ⓐe				Ⓒz		Ⓒz	Ⓐe	Ⓒz			⊡	⊕	
Tegernsee ....d.	0433	0508	0554	0622	0654	...	0724	0754	0854	0954	1054	1154	1254	1252	1354	1454	1554	1624	1654	1724	1752	1754	1854	1954	2054	2154	2254
Schaftlach.........a.	0452	0528	0615	0642	0715	...	0746	0815	0915	1015	1115	1215	1315	1312	1415	1515	1615	1646	1715	1746	1812	1815	1915	2015	2115	2215	2315
Holzkirchen.......a.	0504	0541	0628	0657	0728	...	0757	0828	0928	1028	1128	1228	1328	1326	1428	1528	1628	1658	1728	1758	1828	1828	1928	2028	2128	2228	2328
München Hbf...a.	0535	0612	0655	0731	0755	...	0831	0856	0956	1055	1155	1255	1355	1357	1455	1556	1656	1732	1756	1831	1855	1855	1955	2055	2155	2255	*2355*

A – ①②③④⑦ (also Aug. 15; not June 18, Aug. 14, Oct. 2).
e – Ⓐ (not June 19, Aug. 15).
f – 4 minutes **earlier** on ⑥.
h – Not Nov. 1.
j – 0634 on Ⓒ (also June 19, Aug. 15).
r – Not June 19, Aug. 15, Nov. 1.
t – 0703 on Ⓐ (not June 19, Aug. 15).
v – Also June 18, Aug. 14, Oct. 2; not Aug. 15.
z – Ⓒ (also June 19, Aug. 15).
■ – Change trains at Schliersee on Ⓐ (not June 19, Aug. 15).
⊖ – Change trains at Holzkirchen on Ⓐ (not June 19, Aug. 15).
⊡ – Change trains at Holzkirchen on ①②③④⑦ (also Aug. 15, Oct. 3, Nov. 1; not June 18, Aug. 14, Oct. 2).
⊗ – Change trains at Holzkirchen on ①–⑥ (not June 19, Aug. 15, Oct. 3).
⊕ – Change trains at Holzkirchen on ⑤⑥ (also June 18, Aug. 14, Oct. 2; not Aug. 15, Oct. 3).

929 PLATTLING - BAYERISCH EISENSTEIN - PLZEŇ

Waldbahn ⊠; ČD; 2nd class only

km					773					775						777									779
				Ⓐ	◇	Ⓐ	Ⓐe	⑥h		◇			v			◇		Ⓐ							◇
0	**Plattling** ......d.	...	...	...	...	...	0520	0601	0659	...	0806	0906	...	1006	1106	...	1206	...	...	1306	...	1406	...	1506	...
9	Deggendorf Hbf ......d.	...	...	...	...	...	0531	0611	0709	...	0816	0916	...	1016	1116	...	1216	...	...	1316	...	1416	...	1516	...
33	Gotteszell ......d.	...	...	...	...	...	0554	0630	0733	...	0835	0935	...	1035	1135	...	1235	...	...	1335	...	1435	...	1535	...
48	Regen ......d.	...	...	...	...	...	0609	0644	0748	...	0849	0949	...	1049	1149	...	1249	...	...	1349	...	1449	...	1549	...
58	Zwiesel (Bay) ......d.	...	...	...	...	...	0623	0658	0800	...	0900	1000	...	1100	1200	...	1300	...	...	1401	...	1500	...	1600	...
72	**Bayerisch Eisenstein** ☆ 🏛 a.	...	...	...	...	...	0636	0711	0813	...	0913	1013	...	1113	1213	...	1313	...	...	1414	...	1513	...	1613	...
72	**Železná Ruda-Alžbětín** ☆ 🏛 d.	...	0410	...	...	0550	▬	▬	...	0845	0917	...	1045	▬	...	1245	...	1330	...	...	1445c	...	1526j	...	1645
76	Železná Ruda Město ......d.	...	0417	...	...	0557	...	...	...	0852	0923	...	1052	...	...	1252	...	1338	...	...	1452c	...	1535j	...	1652
79	Špičák ......d.	...	0422	...	...	0602	...	...	...	0903	0927	...	1103	...	...	1303	...	1344	...	...	1503c	...	1542j	...	1703
131	**Klatovy** ......a.	...	0518	...	...	0710	Ⓐ	...	...	0956	...	...	1156	...	...	1356	...	1441	...	...	1556c	...	1639j	...	1756
131	**Klatovy** ......d.	0358	...	0530	0606	...	0806	0846	...	1006	...	...	1206	1246	...	1406	...	...	1446	...	1606	...	1646	...	1806
141	Švihov u Klatov ......d.	0410	...	0541	0615	...	0815	0858	...	1015	...	...	1215	1258	...	1415	...	...	1458	...	1615	...	1658	...	1815
170	**Plzeň** Hlavni ......a.	0457	...	0630	0656	...	0856	0947	...	1056	...	...	1256	1345	...	1456	...	...	1545	...	1656	...	1745	...	1856
	Praha Hlavní **1120** ......a.	...	...	...	0844	...	...	...	...	1244	...	...	...	...	...	1644	...	...	...	...	...	...	...	...	2044

				Ⓐ						
Plattling ......d.	1606	...	1706	...	1806	...	1906	2006	2102	2310
Deggendorf Hbf ......d.	1616	...	1716	...	1816	...	1916	2016	2111	2319
Gotteszell ......d.	1635	...	1735	...	1835	...	1935	2035	2130	2338
Regen ......d.	1649	...	1749	...	1849	...	1949	2049	2144	2353
Zwiesel (Bay) ......d.	1700	...	1800	...	1900	...	2000	2100	2153	0003
Bayerisch Eisenstein ☆ 🏛 . a.	1713	...	1813	...	1913	...	2013	2113	...	...
Železná Ruda-Alžbětín ☆ 🏛 . d.	...	1730	1814	1821	...	1930	...	...	...	...
Železná Ruda Město ......d.	...	1738	1820	1827	...	1938	...	...	...	...
Špičák ......d.	...	1744	1824	1835	...	1944	...	...	...	...
Klatovy ......a.	...	1841	...	1933	...	2041	...	...	...	...
Klatovy ......d.	...	*1846*	...	1946	...	2046	...	...	...	...
Švihov u Klatov ......d.	...	*1858*	...	1958	...	2058	...	...	...	...
Plzeň Hlavni ......a.	...	*1946*	...	2045	...	2146	...	...	...	...
Praha Hlavní **1120** ......a.	...	...	...	...	...	...	...	...	...	...

	⚒r	Ⓐe	Ⓒz	Ⓐe	Ⓒz	Ⓐ	Ⓐe		
Praha Hlavní **1120** ......d.	...	...	...	...	...	...	...	...	...
Plzeň Hlavni ......d.	...	...	...	...	...	...	...	...	0524
Švihov u Klatov ......d.	...	...	...	...	...	...	...	...	0615
Klatovy ......a.	...	...	...	...	...	...	...	...	0627
Klatovy ......d.	...	...	...	...	...	0431	...	...	0651
Špičák ......d.	...	...	...	...	...	0527	...	...	0747
Železná Ruda Město ......d.	...	...	...	...	...	0532	...	...	0752
Železná Ruda-Alžbětín ☆ 🏛 ......a.	...	...	...	...	...	0537	...	...	0759
Bayerisch Eisenstein ☆ 🏛 ......d.	...	...	...	...	...	▬	0705	0744	...
Zwiesel (Bay) ......d.	0416	0529	0552	0622	0655	...	0722	0759	...
Regen ......d.	0426	0539	0602	0631	0705	...	0732	0808	...
Gotteszell ......d.	0440	0555	0617	0645	0721	...	0751	0822	...
Deggendorf Hbf ......d.	0501	0614	0645	0710	0739	0739	0815	0845	...
Plattling ......a.	0510	0623	0654	0719	0748	0748	0825	0854	...

						778						776							774					772	
		k				◇			v			◇		Ⓐ		k			◇					◇	
Praha Hlavní **1120** ......d.	...	...	...	...	...	0715	...	...	...	...	...	1115	...	...	...	...	...	...	1515	...	...	...	...	1915	...
Plzeň Hlavni ......d.	...	0702	...	0810	...	0902	...	...	1102	1212	...	1302	...	*1412*	...	1502	...	...	1702	...	...	1812	*1910*	2102	2258
Švihov u Klatov ......d.	...	0743	...	0858	...	0943	...	...	1143	1258	...	1343	...	*1458*	...	1546	...	...	1743	...	...	1858	*1958*	2143	2345
Klatovy ......a.	...	0752	...	0911	...	0952	...	...	1152	1311	...	1352	...	*1511*	...	1555	...	...	1752	...	...	1911	*2011*	2152	2357
Klatovy ......d.	...	0802	...	0920j	...	1002	...	...	1202	▬	...	1402	...	1514	...	1601	...	...	...	1802	...	▬	2020	▬	▬
Špičák ......d.	...	0902	0933	1026j	...	1102	...	...	1302	...	...	1502	...	1611	...	1704	...	1833	...	1902	...	...	2114	...	...
Železná Ruda Město ......d.	...	0909	0937	1032j	...	1109	...	...	1309	...	...	1509	...	1617	...	1710	...	1837	...	1909	...	...	2118	...	...
Železná Ruda-Alžbětín ☆ 🏛 . a.	...	0915	0943	1038j	...	1115	...	...	1315	w	...	1515	...	1623	...	1716	...	1843	...	1915	...	...	2124	...	...
Bayerisch Eisenstein ☆ 🏛 . d.	0840	...	0944	...	1041	...	1144	1244	...	1344	1444	...	1544	...	1644	...	1744	1844	...	...	1944	2044	...	2139	...
Zwiesel (Bay) ......d.	0859	...	0959	...	1059	...	1159	1259	...	1400	1459	...	1559	...	1659	...	1759	1859	...	...	1959	2059	...	2154	...
Regen ......d.	0908	...	1008	...	1108	...	1208	1308	...	1409	1508	...	1608	...	1708	...	1808	1908	...	...	2008	2108	...	2204	...
Gotteszell ......d.	0922	...	1022	...	1122	...	1222	1322	...	1423	1522	...	1622	...	1723	...	1822	1922	...	...	2022	2131	...	2218	...
Deggendorf Hbf ......d.	0945	...	1045	...	1145	...	1245	1345	...	1445	1545	...	1645	...	1745	...	1845	1945	...	...	2045	2150	...	2236	232[illegible]
Plattling ......a.	0954	...	1054	...	1154	...	1254	1354	...	1454	1554	...	1654	...	1754	...	1854	1954	...	...	2054	2159	...	2245	233[illegible]

ZWIESEL - GRAFENAU and BODENMAIS ⊠

ZWIESEL - GRAFENAU *32 km.* Journey time: 47–49 minutes.
From Zwiesel (Bay) at 0702 Ⓒ**z**, 0713 Ⓐ**e**, 0902, 1102, 1304, 1502, 1702 and 1902. **From Grafenau** at 0805, 1000, 1200, 1400, 1600, 1800 and 2000.

ZWIESEL - BODENMAIS *15 km.* Journey time: 20 minutes.
From Zwiesel (Bay) at 0624 Ⓐ**e**, 0802 ⚒**r**, 0902, 1002, 1102, 1202, 1303, 1402, 1502, 1602, 1702, 1802, 1902, 2002 and 2202.
From Bodenmais at 0559 Ⓐ**e**, 0649 Ⓐ**e**, 0729 ⑥**h**, 0829, 0929, 1029, 1129, 1229, 1329, 1429, 1529, 1629, 1729, 1829, 1929 and 2029.

c – Ⓒ only.
e – Not June 19, Aug. 15.
h – Not Nov. 1.
j – June 14 - Sept. 21.
k – Change trains at Klatovy on Ⓐ.
r – Not June 19, Aug. 15, Nov. 1.
v – Change trains at Klatovy on Ⓐ from Sept. 8.
w – Change trains at Zwiesel on Ⓐ (not June 19, Aug. 15).
z – Also June 19, Aug. 15.
◇ – Also conveys 🚃 Praha - Klatovy and v.v.
⊠ – Operated by *Regentalbahn - Die Länderbahn* (under contract from *DB Regi*
☆ – Bayerisch Eisenstein (German) / Železná Ruda-Alžbětín (Czech) is the same station.

STUTTGART - MÜNCHEN 930

km		RB 19353		ICE 619	CNL 419 🅁 A🍷	IC 60419 2	IC 2091 ①	IC 2095 ②–⑤ c	RE 19201 Ⓐt	RB 19297 Ⓒz	IC 2291 Ⓐt 🍷	RB 19301 Ⓐt	RE 19203 Ⓒz	RJ 63 Ⓒz ✗♦	ICE 699 Ⓐt ✗	IRE 4241 Ⓐt L	IRE 4221 Ⓒz L	ICE 991 Ⓐ ✗♦	RB 19307 Ⓒz	RE 19205 Ⓐt	EC 217 🍷♦	IRE 4223 L	ICE 511 🍷	IC 2265 🍷♦
	Dortmund Hbf **800** d.	...	...	2058	...	...	...	...	...	...	...	...	...	...	...	...	...	...	...	...	...	...	0437g	...
	Köln Hbf **800 910** d.	...	...	2230	2346	...	...	...	...	...	...	...	...	...	...	...	...	...	...	...	...	...	0555	...
	Frankfurt (Main) Hbf **912** d.	...	...	0005	|	...	...	...	...	...	...	...	...	0517b	...	...	...	...	...	...	...	...	|	...
	Frankfurt Flughafen ✈ **912** d.	...	...	0028	0156	...	...	...	...	...	...	...	...	0539	...	...	...	...	...	...	...	...	0653	...
	Mannheim Hbf **912** d.	...	...	0106	|	...	...	...	...	...	...	...	...	0613	...	...	...	0630	...	...	0712	...	0731	...
	Heidelberg Hbf **912** d.	...	...	0119	|	...	...	...	...	...	...	...	...	|	...	...	...	|	...	...	|	...	|	...
	Karlsruhe Hbf **931** d.	...	...	0211	|	...	...	...	...	...	0455	...	...	|	...	...	...	|	...	...	|	...	|	0806r
0	**Stuttgart** Hbf **936** ◇ d.	0022	...	0336	|	0435	0503	...	0529	0531	0553	0608	0631	0656	0656	0659	0702	0712	0717	0732	0758	0802	0812	0853r
22	Plochingen **936** ◇ d.	0042	...	0353	0449s	0451	0518	...	0548	0549	0609	0630	0649	|	|	0713	0716	|	0736	0751	|	0816	|	0909
42	Göppingen ◇ d.	0101	...	|	0502s	0504	0531	...	0602	0607	0621	0649	0707	|	|	0725	0727	|	0754	0807	|	0827	|	0921
61	Geislingen (Steige) ◇ d.	0126	...	|	0517s	0519	0544	...	0622	0629	|	0711	0724	|	|	0736	0738	|	0815	0823	|	0840	|	|
94	**Ulm** Hbf **945** ◇ d.	0158j	...	0442	0542s	0544	0609	0609	0649	0700	0656	0740	0749	0756	0756	0758	0759	0809	0847	0848	0856	0902	0909	0956
118	Günzburg **945** d.	...	...	0458	0559s	0601	0627	0627	...	...	0710	...	...	|	0811	...	...	|	...	...	0910	...	|	|
180	**Augsburg** Hbf **905** d.	...	...	0532	0633s	0636	0659	0659	...	...	0742	...	...	0839	0842	...	...	0855	...	...	0942	...	0955	1044
235	München Pasing **905** a.	...	...	0553	|	|	0721	0721	...	...	0804	...	...	0901	0903	...	...	0918	...	...	|	...	1018	1106
242	**München** Hbf **905** a.	...	...	0602	0710	0710	0730	0730	...	...	0813	...	...	0910	0913	...	...	0927	...	...	1011	...	1027	1115
	Salzburg Hbf **890** a.	...	...	...	...	...	...	...	...	...	...	...	...	1102	...	...	...	...	...	...	1200	...	...	...

	ICE 999 ⑦ ✗	ICE 591 ①–⑥ ♦✗	EC 113 ✗♦	IRE 4225 L	ICE 1013 ⊖ M🍷	IC 2093 ⑤f 🍷	ICE 1091 Ⓐt B✗	ICE 593 Ⓒz B✗	EC 115 🍷♦	IRE 4227 4247 L	ICE 515 H🍷	IC 2261 🍷	IC 119 ♦	ICE 595 B✗	EC 219 🍷♦	IRE 4229 L	ICE 517 🍷	IC 2013 ✗♦	ICE 597 B✗	EC 117 Ⓑ 🍷♦	EC 1217 ⑥ 🍷♦	IRE 4231 L	ICE 519 🍷	IC 1269 Ⓑ 🍷
Dortmund Hbf **800** d.	...	...	...	...	0638	...	...	...	...	...	0837	...	...	...	...	...	1037	0952	...	...	...	...	1237	...
Köln Hbf **800 910** d.	...	...	...	...	0755	...	...	...	0818	...	0955	...	0918	...	...	...	1155	1118	...	...	...	...	1355	...
Frankfurt (Main) Hbf **912** d.	0750	0750	0822	...	|	...	0950	0950	|	...	|	...	|	1150	1220	...	|	|	1350	1420	...	...	|	...
Frankfurt Flughafen ✈ **912** d.	|	|	|	...	0853	...	|	|	|	...	1053	...	|	|	|	...	1253	|	|	|	...	...	1453	...
Mannheim Hbf **912** d.	0830	0830	|	...	0931	...	1030	1030	1102	...	1131	...	1154	1230	|	...	1331	1354	1430	|	...	...	1531	...
Heidelberg Hbf **912** d.	|	|	0914	...	|	...	|	|	|	...	|	...	1206	|	1314	...	|	1406	|	1514	...	...	|	...
Karlsruhe Hbf **931** d.	|	|	|	...	|	...	|	|	|	...	|	1206r	|	|	|	...	|	|	|	|	1505k	...	|	1606r
Stuttgart Hbf **936** ◇ d.	0912	0912	0958	1002	1012	1053	1112	1112	1158	1202	1212	1253r	1257	1312	1358	1402	1412	1454	1512	1558	1558	1602	1612	1653r
Plochingen **936** ◇ d.	|	|	|	1016	|	1109	|	|	|	1216	|	1309	|	|	|	1416	|	1510	|	|	|	1616	|	1709
Göppingen ◇ d.	|	|	|	1027	|	1121	|	|	|	1227	|	1321	1326	|	|	1427	|	1524	|	|	|	1627	|	1721
Geislingen (Steige) ◇ d.	|	|	|	1040	|	|	|	|	|	1240	|	|	1339	|	|	1440	|	|	|	|	|	1640	|	|
Ulm Hbf **945** ◇ d.	1009	1009	1056	1102	1109	1156	1209	1209	1256	1302	1309	1356	1401	1409	1456	1502	1509	1602	1609	1656	1656	1703	1709	1756
Günzburg **945** d.	|	|	1110	...	|	|	|	|	1310	...	|	|	...	|	1510	...	|	...	|	1710	1710	...	|	|
Augsburg Hbf **905** d.	1056	1056	1142	...	1155	1244	1255	1255	1342	...	1355	1439	...	1455	1542	...	1555	...	1655	1742	1742	...	1755	1839
München Pasing **905** a.	1118	1118	|	...	1218	1307	1318	1318	|	...	1418	1501	...	1519	|	...	1618	...	1719	|	|	...	1818	1901
München Hbf **905** a.	1127	1127	1210	...	1227	1316	1327	1327	1411	...	1427	1511	...	1528	1611	...	1627	...	1728	1811	1811	...	1827	1911
Salzburg Hbf **890** a.	...	...	1400	...	...	...	...	...	1600	...	...	...	...	...	1800	...	...	...	...	2000	2000	...	...	2059

	IRE 4233 Ⓐt L	ICE 599 B✗	EC 391 🍷♦	IRE 4235 L	ICE 611 🍷	IC 2011 ①–④ ♦	IC 2267 🍷	IC 2017 ⑤f	ICE 691 Ⓑn B✗	TGV 9575 ⑥ 🍷♦	TGV 9575 Ⓑ 🍷♦	IC 2295 Ⓑn 🍷	IRE 4237 F	ICE 613 🍷	RE 19245	IC 1915 ⑦ T	IC 2269 ♣	IC 2269 ⑦	ICE 693 B✗	RB 19347	ICE 615 🍷	RB 19349	ICE 1093 ⑦ B✗	RB 19351
Dortmund Hbf **800** d.	...	...	...	...	1437	...	...	1352	...	...	...	...	...	1637	...	1552	...	...	...	...	1837	...	...	...
Köln Hbf **800 910** d.	...	...	...	...	1556	1518	...	1518	...	...	...	...	...	1755	...	1718	...	...	...	...	1957	...	...	...
Frankfurt (Main) Hbf **912** d.	...	1550	1620	...	|	|	...	|	1750	...	...	1820	...	|	...	|	...	...	1950	...	|	...	2150	...
Frankfurt Flughafen ✈ **912** d.	...	|	|	...	1653	|	...	|	|	...	...	|	...	1853	...	|	...	...	|	...	2053	...	|	...
Mannheim Hbf **912** d.	...	1630	|	...	1731	1754	...	1754	1830	...	...	|	...	1931	...	1954	...	...	2030	...	2131	...	2230	...
Heidelberg Hbf **912** d.	...	|	1714	...	|	1806	...	1806	|	...	...	1914	...	|	...	2006	...	...	|	...	|	...	|	...
Karlsruhe Hbf **931** d.	...	|	|	...	|	|	1806r	|	|	1828	1828	|	...	|	...	|	2006r	2006r	|	...	|	...	|	...
Stuttgart Hbf **936** ◇ d.	1702	1712	1758	1802	1812	1850	1853r	1856y	1912	1912	1919	1958	2002	2012	2028	2050	2053r	2053r	2112	2131	2212	2231	2312	2332
Plochingen **936** ◇ d.	1716	|	|	1816	|	1904	1909	1915	|	|	|	|	2016	|	2046	2106	2108	2108	|	2151	|	2252	|	2353
Göppingen ◇ d.	1727	|	|	1827	|	...	1921	|	|	|	|	|	2027	|	2104	...	2120	2120	|	2209	|	2312	|	0013
Geislingen (Steige) ◇ d.	1740	|	|	1840	|	...	|	1938	|	|	|	|	2040	|	2125	...	2133	2133	|	2232	|	2336	|	0037
Ulm Hbf **945** ◇ d.	1802	1809	1856	1902	1909	...	1956	2002	2009	2010	2017	2056	2102	2109	2151	...	2155	2157	2209	2302	2309	0007	0012	0109
Günzburg **945** d.	...	|	1910	...	|	...	|	|	|	|	|	2110	...	|	...	...	...	2213	|	...	|	...	0028	...
Augsburg Hbf **905** d.	...	1855	1942	...	1955	...	2039	2047	2055	2058	2103	2142	...	2155	...	...	...	2244	2255	...	2355	...	0059	...
München Pasing **905** a.	...	1918	|	...	2018	...	2101	|	2120	|	|	2205	...	2216	...	...	...	2307	2318	...	0017	...	0121	...
München Hbf **905** a.	...	1927	2011	...	2027	...	2111	2124	2129	2127	2136	2213	...	2226	...	...	...	2316	2327	...	0027	...	0131	...
Salzburg Hbf **890** a.	...	...	2203	...	...	...	...	...	...	...	...	...	...	...	...	...	...	...	...	...	...	...	...	...

Regional trains ULM - MÜNCHEN

		Ⓐd		Ⓐd		Ⓐd									Ⓐd	Ⓒp								
Ulm Hbf d.	...	0446	0523	0549	0621	0644	0723	0823	0923	1023	1124	1223	1324	1423	1517	1523	1623	1723	1824	1923	2023	2123	2221	2323
Günzburg d.	...	0504	0542	0608	0640	0704	0742	0842	0942	1042	1142	1242	1342	1442	1536	1542	1642	1742	1842	1942	2042	2142	2240	2341
Augsburg Hbf a.	...	0559	0633	0700	0733	0802	0833	0933	1033	1133	1233	1333	1433	1533	1628	1633	1733	1833	1933	2033	2133	2233	2333	...
Augsburg Hbf d.	0539	0606	0639	0705	0739	0806	0839	0939	1039	1139	1239	1339	1439	1539	1640	1640	1739	1839	1939	2039	2139	2239	2339	...
München Pasing a.	0613	0641	0713	0739	0813	0843	0913	1013	1113	1213	1313	1413	1514	1613	1714	1714	1813	1913	2013	2115	2222	2313	0022	...
München Hbf a.	0621	0649	0721	0747	0821	0850	0921	1021	1121	1221	1321	1421	1522	1621	1722	1722	1821	1921	2021	2123	2230	2321	0030	...

– **NOTES** (LISTED BY TRAIN NUMBER)

3 – [12] and ✗ Frankfurt - Salzburg - Wien - Budapest.
13 – [12] and ✗ Frankfurt - Salzburg - Villach - Klagenfurt; conveys [12] Frankfurt - Villach (**213**) - Ljubljana - Zagreb.
5 – WÖRTHERSEE – [12] and 🍷 Münster - Köln - Koblenz - Salzburg - Villach - Klagenfurt.
7 – [12] and 🍷 Frankfurt - Salzburg - Villach - Klagenfurt.
9 – [12] Münster - Köln - Koblenz - Ulm - Lindau - Bregenz - Innsbruck.
7 – [12] and 🍷 Saarbrücken - Salzburg - Bischofshofen - Selzthal - Graz.
9 – [12] and 🍷 Frankfurt - Salzburg - Bischofshofen - Selzthal - Graz.
1 – [12] and 🍷 Frankfurt - Salzburg (- Linz Ⓑ).
1 – [12] and ✗ (Hamburg Ⓐ -) Hannover - Frankfurt - München.
1 – [12] and ✗ Wiesbaden - Mainz - München.
17 – [12] and 🍷 Karlsruhe - Stuttgart - Salzburg - Villach - Klagenfurt.
11 – ①–④ (not June 18, 19, Oct. 2). [12] Düsseldorf - Köln - Koblenz - Stuttgart - Plochingen - Nürtingen (a. 1917) - Reutlingen Hbf (a. 1937) - Tübingen Hbf (a. 1950).
13 – ALLGÄU – [12] and ✗ Hannover - Dortmund - Köln - Koblenz - Ulm - Kempten - Oberstdorf.
65 – BADEN-KURIER – [12] and 🍷 (Basel ①–⑥ **m** -) Karlsruhe - Stuttgart.
75 – [12] and 🍷 Paris - Strasbourg - München. 🅁 for international journeys.

– POLLUX – 🛏 1, 2 cl., 🛏 2 cl., [2] and 🍷 Amsterdam - Köln - München. Conveys on dates in Table **32** 🛏 1, 2 cl., 🛏 2 cl. and [2] (*CNL* **40451** – CASSIOPEIA) Paris - München.
– From Berlin (Table **902**).
– To Friedrichshafen (Table **933**).
– From Hamburg (Table **800**).
– To Lindau (Table **933**).
– From Münster (Table **800**).
– To Nürtingen (a. 2118), Reutlingen Hbf (a. 2137) and Tübingen Hbf (a. 2150).

b – 0522 on † (also June 19).
c – Not June 19, 20, Aug. 15, Oct. 3.
d – Not June 19, Aug. 15.
f – Also June 18, Oct. 2; not June 20, Oct. 3.
g – ① only.
j – ①⑥⑦ (also June 19, 20, Oct. 3).
k – 1504 Aug. 2 - Sept. 13.
m – Not June 21, Oct. 4.
n – Not Oct. 3.
p – Also June 19, Aug. 15.
r – July 31 - Sept. 14 departs Karlsruhe 6 minutes earlier, departs Stuttgart 2 minutes later.
s – Arrival time. Stops to set down only.
t – Not June 19.
y – Not Aug. 1 - Sept. 12.
z – Also June 19.

♣ – ①②③④⑦ (not June 18, Oct. 2). Train number **1969** on ①–⑤ July 31 - Sept. 12.
⊖ – On Ⓐ conveys [12] (*ICE* **513**) Hamm - Dortmund - München (Table **800**).
◇ – See panel below for other regional trains Stuttgart - Ulm.

		Ⓒz	Ⓐt			Ⓒz	Ⓐt
Stuttgart Hbf d.	0831	0917	0931	and in	1831	1917	1930
Plochingen d.	0849	0936	0949	the same	1849	1936	1948
Göppingen d.	0907	0954	1007	pattern	1907	1955	2006
Geislingen (Steige) d.	0924	1015	1024	every two	1924	2016	2023
Ulm Hbf a.	0949	1047	1049	hours until	1949	2047	2049

930 MÜNCHEN - STUTTGART

	RB 19296	ICE 616 🍸	RB 19300	RE 19200 Ⓐt		IC 2268 ① 🍸	IC 2268 Ⓐt 🍸	IC 2010 Ⓐ ♦	RE 19202 ©z	RB 19310 Ⓐt	ICE 614 🍸	IRE 4240 Ⓐt L	IRE 4220 ©z F	IC 2294 Ⓐt 🍸	RE 19206 Ⓐt	RB 19316 ©z	TGV 9576 Ⓐ 🍸♦	TGV 9576 © 🍸♦	ICE 692 Ⓐ B✕	IC 2266 ①–⑥ m🍸	ICE 612 🍸	IRE 4222 4224 L	IC 1296 ①–⑥ 🍸	ICE 690 B✕
Salzburg Hbf **890** d.	...	...	...	...	...	...	...	...	...	...	...	...	...	...	...	...	...	...	...	...	...	...	0545	...
München Hbf **905** d.	...	0323	...	...	...	0443	...	...	...	...	0527	...	...	0539	...	...	0627	0629	0632	0646	0728	...	0748	0828
München Pasing **905** d.	...	0333	...	...	...	0451	...	...	...	...	0535	...	...	0547	...	...	|	|	0640	0655	0737	...	|	0837
Augsburg Hbf **905** d.	...	0357	...	...	...	0516	...	...	...	...	0602	...	...	0612	...	...	0657	0706	0706	0721	0803	...	0817	0903
Günzburg **945** d.	...	|	...	...	...	0546	...	...	...	...	|	...	...	0641	...	...	|	|	|	|	|	...	0847	|
Ulm Hbf **945** ◇ d.	0411	0440	0455	0523	...	0602	0602	...	0601	0613	0651	0654	0654	0659	0706	0709	0743	0751	0751	0804	0851	0854	0904	0951
Geislingen (Steige) ◇ d.	0435	|	0525	0554	...	0625	0625	...	0625	0643	|	0717	0717	0722	0732	0737	|	|	|	|	|	0917	|	|
Göppingen ◇ d.	0457	|	0548	0609	...	0639	0639	...	0644	0707	|	0729	0729	|	0751	0757	|	|	|	0838	|	0929	|	|
Plochingen **936** ◇ d.	0518	|	0607	0623	...	0651	0651	0655	0705	0722	|	|	0740	0746	0805	0815	|	|	|	0850	|	0940	|	|
Stuttgart Hbf **936** ◇ a.	0538	0537	0626	0643	...	0707	0707	0710	0724	0738	0747	0756	0756	0801	0824	0832	0839	0847	0847	0907	0947	0956	1001	1047
Karlsruhe Hbf **931** a.	...	|	...	...	...	0753k	0753k	|	...	...	|	...	...	|	...	...	0930	0930	|	0953k	|	...	|	|
Heidelberg Hbf **912** a.	...	|	...	...	...	...	...	0753	...	...	|	...	...	0844	...	...	...	...	|	...	|	...	1044	|
Mannheim Hbf **912** a.	...	0628	...	...	...	...	...	0806	...	...	0828	...	...	|	...	...	...	...	0929	...	1028	...	|	1129
Frankfurt Flughafen ✈ **912** a.	...	0706	...	...	...	...	...	|	...	...	0906	...	...	|	...	...	...	...	|	...	1106	...	|	|
Frankfurt (Main) Hbf **912** a.	...	|	...	...	...	...	...	|	...	...	|	...	...	0940	...	...	...	...	1008	...	|	...	1140	1208
Köln Hbf **800 910** a.	...	0805	...	...	...	...	...	1042	...	...	1005	...	...	...	...	...	...	...	...	...	1205	...	...	...
Dortmund Hbf **800** a.	...	0921	...	...	...	...	...	1207f	...	...	1121	...	...	...	...	...	...	...	...	...	1321	...	...	...

	IC 1268 ⊖ 🍸	IC 1216 ⑤f 🍸		ICE 610 🍸	IRE 4226 4232 L	EC 390 🍸♦	ICE 598 B✕	IC 2012 ✕♦	ICE 518 🍸	IRE 4228 L	EC 218 🍸♦	ICE 596 B✕	IC 118 ♦	IC 2260 🍸	ICE 516 🍸	IRE 4230 L	EC 114 🍸♦	ICE 1090 Ⓑb B*✕	ICE 594 ⑥h B✕	IRE 4244 Ⓐt	IC 2362 ⑤f 🍸	ICE 514 🍸	IRE 4234 4246 L	EC 112 ✕♦
Salzburg Hbf **890** d.	0643j	0643	...	...	...	0800	...	...	...	...	1000	...	...	...	...	...	1200	...	...	...	...	...	...	1400
München Hbf **905** d.	0848	0848	...	0928	...	0946	1028	...	1130	...	1146	1228	...	1247	1328	...	1346	1428	1428	...	1443	1528	...	1546
München Pasing **905** d.	0856	0856	...	0937	...	|	1037	...	1138	...	|	1237	...	1255	1337	...	|	1437	1437	...	1451	1537	...	|
Augsburg Hbf **905** d.	0921	0921	...	1003	...	1017	1103	...	1203	...	1217	1303	...	1321	1403	...	1417	1503	1503	...	1521	1603	...	1617
Günzburg **945** d.	|	|	...	|	...	1048	|	...	|	...	1247	|	...	|	|	...	1448	|	|	...	|	|	...	1648
Ulm Hbf **945** ◇ d.	1004	1004	...	1051	1054	1104	1151	1157	1251	1254	1304	1351	1356	1404	1451	1454	1504	1551	1551	1554	1604	1651	1654	1703
Geislingen (Steige) ◇ d.	|	|	...	|	1117	|	|	|	|	1317	|	|	1420	|	|	1517	|	|	|	1617	|	|	1717	|
Göppingen ◇ d.	1038	1038	...	|	1129	|	|	1235	|	1329	|	|	1433	|	|	1529	|	|	|	1629	|	|	1729	|
Plochingen **936** ◇ d.	1050	1050	...	|	1140	|	|	1249	|	1340	|	|	|	1449	|	1540	|	|	|	1640	1649	|	1740	|
Stuttgart Hbf **936** ◇ a.	1107	1107	...	1147	1156	1201	1247	1305	1347	1356	1401	1447	1458	1504	1547	1556	1600	1647	1647	1656	1704	1747	1756	1800
Karlsruhe Hbf **931** a.	1153k	|	...	|	...	|	|	|	|	...	|	|	|	1550k	|	...	|	|	|	...	1753k	|	...	|
Heidelberg Hbf **912** a.	...	1153	...	|	...	1244	|	1353	|	...	1444	|	1553	...	|	...	|	|	|	...	...	|	...	1844
Mannheim Hbf **912** a.	...	1206	...	1228	...	|	1329	1406	1428	...	|	1529	1606	...	1628	...	1656	1729	1729	...	...	1828	...	|
Frankfurt Flughafen ✈ **912** a.	...	|	...	1306	...	|	|	|	1506	...	|	|	|	...	1706	...	|	|	|	...	...	1906	...	|
Frankfurt (Main) Hbf **912** a.	...	|	...	|	...	1340	1408	|	|	...	1540	1608	|	...	|	...	|	1808	1808	...	...	|	...	1940
Köln Hbf **800 910** a.	...	1442	...	1405	...	...	...	1642	1605	...	...	...	1842	...	1805	...	1942	...	...	...	...	2005	...	...
Dortmund Hbf **800** a.	...	1608	...	1521	...	...	...	1808	1721	...	...	...	...	...	1921	...	2100	...	...	...	...	2121	...	...

	IC 1910 ⑦ 🍸	ICE 592 B✕	IC 1910 ⑦ 🍸	IC 2264 🍸♦	IC 2094 ①–⑤ a	ICE 512 M🍸	IRE 4236 L	EC 216 🍸♦	ICE 590 ⊡ ✕	IC 2092 Ⓑn 🍸	RE 19246	ICE 1110 ⑦ 🍸	ICE 510 ♥ Q🍸	IRE 4238 ©z L	RB 19354 Ⓐt	RB 19356 ©z	ICE 990 P ✕	RJ 66 ⑤⑥ ✕♦	RB 19360 ©z	RE 19248	IC 2090 ⑦	IC 60418 2	CNL 418 Ⓡ A🍸	ICE 618 ‡
Salzburg Hbf **890** d.	...	...	...	...	...	...	...	1600	...	...	...	...	...	...	...	...	...	1856	...	...	...	...	...	...
München Hbf **905** d.	1620	1628	...	1648	1711	1727	...	1746	1828	1845	...	1928	1928	...	...	...	2045	2045	...	...	2151	2250	2250	2350
München Pasing **905** d.	1628	1637	...	1656	1719	1736	...	|	1837	1853	...	1937	1937	...	...	...	2053	2053	...	...	2159	|	|	2358
Augsburg Hbf **905** d.	1653	1703	...	1721	1745	1803	...	1817	1903	1918	...	2003	2003	...	...	...	2118	2118	...	...	2224	2320	2320u	0021
Günzburg **945** d.	1728	|	...	|	1816	|	...	1847	|	1948	...	|	|	...	...	...	|	|	...	...	2253	2353	2353u	0051
Ulm Hbf **945** ◇ d.	1744	1751	←	1804	1834	1851	1854	1904	1951	2004	2009	2051	2051	2054	2104	2109	2204	2204	2209	2242	2310	0010	0010u	0109
Geislingen (Steige) ◇ d.	1808	|	1816	|	...	|	1917	|	|	|	2033	|	|	2117	2133	2137	|	|	2239	2308	|	0034	0034u	|
Göppingen ◇ d.	→	|	1830	1838	...	|	1929	|	|	2038	2050	|	|	2129	2155	2157	|	|	2301	2324	2344	0048	0048u	|
Plochingen **936** ◇ d.	...	|	|	1850	...	|	1940	|	|	2050	2109	|	|	2140	2213	2215	|	|	2321	2341	2356	0102	0102u	0153
Stuttgart Hbf **936** ◇ a.	...	1847	1858	1907	...	1947	1956	2001	2047	2107	2128	2147	2147	2156	2231	2232	2300	2300	2340	0001	0011	0116	|	0210
Karlsruhe Hbf **931** a.	...	|	|	1953k	...	|	...	|	|	2153k	...	|	|	...	...	...	|	|	...	...	...	...	|	0330
Heidelberg Hbf **912** a.	...	|	1953	...	...	|	...	|	|	...	...	|	|	...	...	...	|	|	...	...	...	...	|	0426
Mannheim Hbf **912** a.	...	1929	2006	...	...	2028	...	2048	2129	...	...	2229	2229	...	...	...	2344	2344	...	...	...	...	|	0438
Frankfurt Flughafen ✈ **912** a.	...	|	|	...	...	2106	...	...	|	...	...	2304	2304	...	...	...	0023	0023	...	...	...	...	0339	0512
Frankfurt (Main) Hbf **912** a.	...	2008	|	...	...	|	...	...	2208	...	...	|	...	...	...	...	0042	0042	...	...	...	...	|	0533
Köln Hbf **800 910** a.	...	...	2242	...	...	2205	...	...	...	...	...	0005	...	...	...	...	...	...	...	...	...	...	0543	0705
Dortmund Hbf **800** a.	...	...	2359	...	...	...	...	...	...	...	...	...	...	...	...	...	...	...	...	...	...	...	...	0843

Regional trains MÜNCHEN - ULM

		©w		⚒v																				
München Hbf d.	0007	0007	...	...	...	0534	0639	0736	0836	0936	1036	1136	1236	1336	1436	1536	1634	1735	1836	1936	2036	2101	2201	230
München Pasing d.	0014	0014	...	...	...	0541	0646	0743	0843	0943	1043	1144	1243	1343	1443	1542	1643	1742	1843	1943	2043	2107	2209	230
Augsburg Hbf a.	0049	0049	...	...	...	0619	0721	0819	0919	1019	1119	1218	1319	1419	1519	1619	1719	1819	1919	2019	2119	2148	2244	234
Augsburg Hbf d.	...	0053	...	...	0524	0625	0725	0825	0925	1025	1125	1222	1325	1425	1525	1625	1725	1825	1925	2025	2125	2151	2251	235
Günzburg d.	...	0148	...	0529	0616	0716	0819	0927r	1016	1116	1216	1321	1416	1519	1616	1716	1821	1916	2017	2116	2216	2242	2342	004
Ulm Hbf a.	...	0206	...	0547	0635	0735	0840	0946	1035	1135	1235	1339	1435	1539	1635	1735	1840	1935	2036	2135	2235	2302	0002	010

♦ – **NOTES** (LISTED BY TRAIN NUMBER)

66 – ⑤⑥ (also June 18, Oct. 2). [12] and ✕ Budapest - Wien - Frankfurt.
112 – [12] and ✕ Klagenfurt - Villach - Salzburg - Frankfurt; conveys [12] Zagreb (**212**) - Ljubljana - Frankfurt.
114 – WÖRTHERSEE – [12] and 🍸 Klagenfurt - Villach - Salzburg - Koblenz - Köln - Dortmund.
118 – [12] Salzburg - Innsbruck - Bregenz - Lindau - Ulm - Koblenz - Köln - Münster.
216 – [12] and 🍸 Graz - Selzthal - Bischofshofen - Salzburg - Saarbrücken.
218 – [12] and 🍸 Graz - Selzthal - Bischofshofen - Salzburg - Frankfurt.
390 – [12] and 🍸 (Linz ①–⑥ -) Salzburg - Frankfurt.
2010 – Ⓐ (not June 19, 20). LORELEY – [12] Tübingen Hbf (d. 0611) - Reutlingen Hbf (d. 0623) - Nürtingen (d. 0642) - Plochingen - Stuttgart - Koblenz - Düsseldorf (- Dortmund - Berlin ⑤**f**).
2012 – ALLGÄU – [12] and ✕ Oberstdorf - Kempten - Ulm - Köln - Dortmund - Hannover.
2264 – BADEN-KURIER – [12] and 🍸 München - Karlsruhe (- Basel Ⓑ**q**).
9576 – [12] and 🍸 München - Strasbourg - Paris. Ⓡ for international journeys.

A – POLLUX – 🛏 1, 2 cl., ▬ 2 cl., [2] and 🍸 München - Köln - Amsterdam. Conveys on dates in Table **32** 🛏 1, 2 cl., ▬ 2 cl. and [2] (*CNL* **40418** – CASSIOPEIA) München - Paris.
B – To Berlin (Table **902**).
F – From Friedrichshafen (Table **933**).
L – From Lindau (Table **933**).
M – To Münster (Table **800**).
P – ①②③④⑦ (not June 18, Oct. 2). Train number **1590** on ④ (also June 17, Oct. 1; not June 19).
Q – To Wiesbaden (Table **911**).

a – Not June 19, 20, Aug. 15, Oct. 3.
b – Not June 19, Oct. 3.
c – Mornings of ⑥⑦ only. Arrives 0821 on ⑦.
h – Also June 19, Oct. 3.
j – ①②③④⑥ (also June 20, Oct. 3; not June 18, Oct. 2).
k – 6–12 minutes later July 31 - Sept. 13.
m – Not June 21.
n – Not Oct. 3.
q – Not June 20, Oct. 3.
r – Arrives 0916.
t – Not June 19.
u – Stops to pick up only.
v – Not June 19, Aug. 15, Nov. 1.
w – Also June 19, Aug. 15.
z – Also June 19.

⊖ – ①②③④⑥⑦ (also June 20, Oct. 3; not June 18, Oct. 2).
♥ – Train number **1010** on ⑤⑥ (also Oct. 2). Train number **1190** on ⑦. Also conveys ✕ on ①–④ (not Oct. 2).
‡ – Train number **1018** on ⑥.
⊡ – On ⑤ (also June 19, Oct. 2; not Oct. 3) runs with train number **698** and continues to Kassel (Table **900**). On ⑦ runs with train number **992** and continues to Hamburg (Table **900**).
* – Ⓡ and supplement payable for journeys to Berlin.
❖ – Timings may vary by 1–2 minutes.
◇ – See panel below for other regional trains Ulm - Stuttgart.

		Ⓐt	©z	❖		Ⓐt	©
Ulm Hbf d.	0809	0909	0909	and in	1809	1909	190
Geislingen (Steige) d.	0832	0933	0937	the same	1832	1932	193
Göppingen d.	0850	0951	0957	pattern	1850	1954	195
Plochingen d.	0909	1009	1015	every **two**	1909	2013	201
Stuttgart Hbf a.	0928	1028	1032	hours until	1928	2032	203

 German national public holidays are on Jan. 1, Apr. 18, 21, May 1, 29, June 9, Oct. 3, Dec. 25, 26

KARLSRUHE - STUTTGART (also local trains HEIDELBERG - STUTTGART) 931

See Table **32** for full details of international *TGV* services from / to Paris. See Table **912** for fast trains Heidelberg - Stuttgart and v.v.

km	km		*ICE*	*IC*	*IRE*	*IC*	*IRE*	*RE*	*IC*	*IC*	*IC*	*RE*	*IC*	*IC*	*IRE*	*RE*	*IC*	*RE*	*IRE*	*TGV*	*RE*	*IC*	*RE*	*IC*	*IRE*
			619	**2291**	**19011**	**2363**	**4901**	**19503**	**2365**	**2367**	**2063**	**19525**	**2369**	**2265**	**4903**	**19505**	**2065**	**19527**	**4905**	**9571**	**19507**	**2067**	**19531**	**2261**	**4907**
				Ⓐt	Ⓐt	①-⑥	Ⓐt	Ⓒz	Ⓐt	①-⑤	①-⑥	Ⓒz	①-⑤	✣				19529					19533	✣	
			R			n🍷			O🍷	a🍷	h N		a	B🍷			N			P🍷		N		🍷	
0		**Karlsruhe** Hbf .... d.	0211	0455	...	0559	0601	...	0637	0658	0706	0719	0741e	0806	0805	...	0906	0919	1005	1028	...	1106	1119	1206	1205
26		Pforzheim .... d.	|	|	0546	|	0624	...	|	|	0727	0743	|	|	0826	...	0927	0943	1026	|	...	1127	1143	|	1226
	0	**Heidelberg** Hbf **912** d.	|	|	|	|	|	0610	|	|	|	|	|	|	|	0810	|	|	|	|	1010	|	|	|	|
	33	Bruchsal .... **912** d.	|	0513	|	0617**x**	|	0632	0654**x**	0719	|	|	0758**x**	0819**x**	|	0833	|	|	|	|	1033	|	|	1219**x**	|
39	*65*	Mühlacker .... d.	|	|	0555	|	0632	0656	|	|	0737	0755	|	|	0834	0859	0937	0955	1034	|	1059	1137	1155	|	1234
47	*73*	Vaihingen (Enz) .... **912** d.	0248	0532	0602	|	0639	0705	|	|	0746	0804	|	|	0841	0907	0946	1004	1041	|	1107	1146	1204	|	1241
86	*112*	**Stuttgart** Hbf .... **912** a.	0320	0549	0619	0648	0657	0740	0725	0750	0803	0839	0829	0849	0858	0939	1003	1039	1058	1104**r**	1139	1203	1239	1249	1258
		München Hbf **930** .... a.	0602	0813	...	...	...	...	...	...	...	...	...	1115	...	...	...	...	...	...	...	...	...	1511	...

	RE	*IC*	*IC*	*IRE*	*TGV*	*RE*	*EC*	*IC*	*IC*	*IRE*	*RE*	*IC*	*IC*	*IRE*	*TGV*	*RE*	*IC*	*RE*	*IC*	*IRE*	*TGV*	*RE*	*IC*	*RE*	*RE*
	19509	**2069**	**2263**	**4909**	**9573**	**19511**	**1217**	**2161**	**1269**	**4911**	**19513**	**2163**	**2267**	**4913**	**9575**	**19515**	**2165**	**19547**	**2269**	**4915**	**9577**	**19517**	**2167**	**19551**	**19553**
			⑤f				⑥	Ⓑq	Ⓑ✣				✣					19549	Ⓑ✣		Ⓑd		Ⓑy		
		N	✣🍷		P🍷		A🍷	N	S🍷			N	🍷		P🍷		L		G🍷		P🍷		◇T		
Karlsruhe Hbf .... d.	...	1306	1406	1405	1428	...	1505	1506	1606	1605	...	1706	1806	1805	1828	...	1906	1919	2006	2005	2029	...	2106	2208	2321
Pforzheim .... d.	...	1327	|	1426	|	...	|	1527	|	1626	...	1727	|	1826	|	...	1927	1943	|	2026	|	...	2127	2231	2343
Heidelberg Hbf . **912** d.	1210	|	|	|	|	1410	|	|	|	|	1610	|	|	|	|	1810	|	|	|	|	|	2010	|	|	|
Bruchsal .... **912** d.	1233	|	1419**x**	|	|	1433	1518**x**	|	1619**x**	|	1633	|	1819**x**	|	|	1833	|	|	2019**x**	|	|	2030	|	|	|
Mühlacker .... d.	1259	1337	|	1434	|	1459	|	1537	|	1634	1659	1737	|	1834	|	1859	1937	1955	|	2034	|	2055	2137	2243	2356
Vaihingen (Enz) ..... **912** d.	1307	1346	|	1441	|	1507	|	1546	|	1641	1707	1746	|	1841	|	1907	1946	2007	|	2041	|	2103	2146	2252	0005
Stuttgart Hbf .... **912** a.	1339	1403	1449	1458	1504**b**	1539	1554	1603	1649	1658	1739	1803	1849	1858	1904	1939	2003	2039	2049	2058	2105**b**	2142	2203	2325	0040
München Hbf **930** ..... a.	...	...	...	...	...	...	1811	...	1911	...	...	...	2111	...	2136**c**	...	...	...	2316**w**	...	...	...	...	...	...

km		*RE*	*ICE*	*IC*	*RE*	*TGV*	*RE*	*IC*	*RE*	*RE*	*IC*	*RE*	*TGV*	*IRE*	*IC*	*IC*	*RE*	*IRE*	*IC*	*IC*	*RE*	*TGV*	*IRE*	*IC*	*IC*
		19556	**618**	**2376**	**19500**	**9578**	**19522**	**2268**	**19524**	**19526**	**2164**	**19502**	**9576**	**4902**	**2266**	**2162**	**19504**	**4904**	**1268**	**2160**	**19506**	**9574**	**4906**	**2262**	**2068**
			1018	Ⓐt		①-⑥	Ⓐt	Ⓐt	Ⓒz	Ⓐt	①-⑥				①-⑥	①-⑥			⊠					⑤f	
			R	¶		P🍷		H🍷			h N		P🍷		j⊠🍷	n J			S🍷	N		P🍷		⊠🍷	N
	München Hbf **930** .... d.	...	2350	...	...	...	...	0443**g**	...	...	...	...	0627•	...	0646	...	...	...	0848**v**	...	...	...	...	...	...
0	**Stuttgart** Hbf .... **912** d.	0019	0221	0545	0614	0655**k**	0626	0711	0717	0722	0759	0819	0855	0900	0911	0959	1019	1059	1111	1159	1219	1255**k**	1259	1311	1359
29	Vaihingen (Enz) .... **912** d.	0052	0252	0603	0645	|	0704	|	0750	0753	0816	0850	|	0916	|	1016	1050	1115	|	1216	1250	|	1315	|	1416
	Mühlacker .... d.	0101	|	0611	0700	|	0714	|	0759	0801	0823	0900	|	0922	|	1023	1100	1121	|	1223	1300	|	1321	|	1423
66	Bruchsal .... **912** d.	|	|	|	0728	|	|	0740*	|	|	|	0929	|	|	0940**x**	|	1129	|	1140**x**	|	1329	|	|	1340**x**	|
	Heidelberg Hbf **912** a.	|	|	|	0748	|	|	|	|	|	|	0949	|	|	|	|	1149	|	|	|	1349	|	|	|	|
	Pforzheim .... d.	0114	|	0622	...	|	0728	|	0813	0814	0834	...	|	0930	|	1034	...	1130	|	1234	...	|	1330	|	1434
87	**Karlsruhe** Hbf .... a.	0137	0330	0645	...	0730	0752	0753*	0838	0838	0853	...	0930	0953	0953	1053	...	1153	1153	1253	...	1330	1353	1353	1453

	RE	*IRE*	*IC*	*IC*	*RE*	*IC*	*TGV*	*IRE*	*IC*	*IC*	*IC*	*IC*	*IC*	*RE*	*TGV*	*IRE*	*IC*	*RE*	*RE*	*IC*	*RE*	*IRE*	*IC*	*IC*	*RE*
	19508	**4908**	**2260**	**2066**	**19510**	**2364**	**9572**	**4910**	**2362**	**2362**	**2366**	**2360**	**2064**	**19514**	**9570**	**4912**	**2264**	**19548**	**19550**	**2062**	**19516**	**4914**	**2092**	**2060**	**19552**
			⊠			①-⑤	⑥⑦		⑤f	①-④	⑦z	①-⑤			E		⊠	Ⓒz	Ⓐt				Ⓑq	Ⓑy	**19554**
			🍷	N		u O	P🍷		🍷⊠	§⊠	🍷	a🍷	N		P🍷		Y🍷			N			⊠🍷	D	
München Hbf **930** ..... d.	...	...	1247	...	...	...	...	...	1443	...	...	...	...	...	...	...	1648	...	...	...	...	...	1845	...	...
Stuttgart Hbf .... **912** d.	1419	1459	1508	1559	1617	1641	1655**k**	1659	1708	1708	1708	1734	1759	1819	1855**k**	1859	1911	1918	1922	1959	2016	2059	2111	2159	2219
Vaihingen (Enz) ..... **912** d.	1450	1515	|	1616	1650	|	|	1715	|	|	|	|	1816	1850	|	1915	|	1950	1953	2016	2051	2115	|	2216	2254
Mühlacker .... d.	1500	1521	|	1623	1700	|	|	1721	|	|	|	|	1823	1900	|	1921	|	1959	2001	2023	2100	2121	|	2224	2303
Bruchsal .... **912** d.	1529	|	1537**x**	|	1729	1712**x**	|	|	1737**x**	1737**x**	1738	1804	|	1929	|	|	1940**x**	|	|	|	2129	|	2140**x**	|	|
Heidelberg Hbf . **912** a.	1549	|	|	|	1749	|	|	|	|	|	|	|	|	1949	|	|	|	|	|	|	2156	|	|	|	|
Pforzheim .... d.	...	1530	|	1634	...	|	|	1730	|	|	|	|	1834	...	|	1930	|	2013	2014	2034	...	2130	|	2234	2317
Karlsruhe Hbf .... a.	...	1553	1550	1653	...	1731	1730	1753	1753	1753	1753	1821**x**	1853	...	1930	1953	1953	2038	2038	2053	...	2153	2153	2259	2340

A – [12] and 🍷 Karlsruhe - Stuttgart - Salzburg - Klagenfurt. Aug. 2 - Sept. 13 departs Karlsruhe 1504.
B – From Basel (Table **912**) on ①–⑥ (not June 21, Oct. 4).
D – [12] (Nürnberg ⑤⑦ **m** -) Stuttgart - Karlsruhe.
E – ①–⑤ (also June 22, Aug. 17, Sept. 28, Oct. 5).
G – Ⓑ (not June 20, Oct. 3). [12] Karlsruhe - Stuttgart (- Ulm ♣ -) (- München ⑦). Train number **1969** on ①–⑤ July 31 - Sept. 12.
H – [12] and 🍷 (München ① -) Ulm - Stuttgart - Karlsruhe.
J – [12] (Passau ① -) Nürnberg - Stuttgart - Karlsruhe.
L – [12] Karlsruhe - Stuttgart (- Nürnberg ⑤⑦ **m**) (- Passau ⑦).
N – [12] Karlsruhe - Stuttgart - Nürnberg and v.v.
O – To / from Offenburg (Table **916**).
P – From / to Paris via Strasbourg (Table **32**). Ⓡ for international journeys.
R – From / to Dortmund or Essen via Frankfurt (Tables **800**/**912**).
S – From / to Salzburg (Table **890**).
T – To Nürnberg on ⑦ (Table **925**).
Y – To Basel (Table **912**) on Ⓑ (not June 20, Oct. 3).

a – Not June 19, 20, Oct. 3.
b – 13 – 14 minutes later July 31 - Sept. 14.
c – 2127 on ⑥.
d – Also June 21, Aug. 16, Sept. 27, Oct. 4.
e – 0731 July 31 - Sept. 12.
f – Also June 18, Oct. 2; not June 20, Oct. 3.
g – ① only.
h – Not June 19, Oct. 4.
j – Not June 21.
k – 15 minutes earlier July 31 - Sept. 14.
m – Also June 18, Oct. 2; not June 20, Oct. 3.
n – Not Oct. 4.
q – Not Oct. 3.
r – 1112 on June 19, Sept. 26, Oct. 3.
t – Not June 19.
u – Not June 19, 20, Aug. 1, 8, 15, 22, 29, Sept. 5, 12, Oct. 3.

v – ①②③④⑥⑦ (also June 20, Oct. 3; not June 18, Oct. 2).
w – ⑦ only.
x – Not July 31 - Sept. 14.
y – Not June 20, Oct. 3.
z – Also June 19.
• – 0629 on Ⓒ.
* – 4 – 6 minutes later July 31 - Sept. 12.
♣ – ①②③④⑦ (not June 18, Oct. 2).
¶ – Train number **2368** on ①.
◇ – Train number **2385** on ①–④ (not June 18, Oct. 2).
§ – ①–④ (not June 18, 19, Oct. 2). Train number **1962** July 31 - Sept. 11.
✣ – July 31 - Sept. 14 departs Karlsruhe 6 minutes earlier, arrives Stuttgart 2 minutes later
⊠ – July 31 - Sept. 14 arrives Karlsruhe 9 – 12 minutes later.

S-Bahn 2/3

STUTTGART - STUTTGART FLUGHAFEN / MESSE ✈ 932

20 km. Journey time: 27 minutes. On June 19, Nov. 1 services run as on ⑦.

From Stuttgart Hbf at 0455 Ⓐ, 0515 Ⓐ, 0525, 0545 Ⓑ, 0555 ⚒, 0615 Ⓐ, 0625, 0645 Ⓑ, 0655 ⚒, 0715 Ⓐ, 0725, 0745, 0755, 0815, 0825, 0845, 0855 and then at 15, 25, 45, and 55 minutes past each hour until 1815, 1825, 1845, 1855; then 1915 Ⓐ, 1925, 1945 Ⓐ, 1955, 2015 Ⓐ, 2025, 2045 Ⓐ, 2055, 2115 Ⓐ, 2125, 2155, 2225, 2255, 2325, 2355 and 0025.

From Stuttgart Flughafen / Messe ✈ at 0508, 0518 Ⓐ, 0538 ⚒, 0548 Ⓑ, 0608, 0618 Ⓐ, 0638 ⚒, 0648 Ⓑ, 0708, 0718 Ⓐ, 0738 ⚒, 0748 Ⓑ, 0808, 0818, 0838, 0848 and then at 08, 18, 38 and 48 minutes past each hour until 1808, 1818, 1838, 1848; then 1908, 1918, 1938, 1948 Ⓐ, 2008, 2018 Ⓐ, 2038, 2048 Ⓐ, 2108, 2118 Ⓐ, 2138, 2148 Ⓐ, 2208, 2238, 2308, 2338 and 0008.

IRE / RE services (except trains **C** and **D**)

ULM - FRIEDRICHSHAFEN - LINDAU 933

km		Ⓒz	Ⓐe	⊕	B			B			B			B	C		B			B					S2
	Stuttgart Hbf **930** .... d.	...	...	...	...	0659**k**	0802	...	...	1002	...	...	1202	...	1257	1402	...	...	1602	...	1702**e**	1802	...	2002	...
0	**Ulm** Hbf .... d.	0550	0552	0707**h**	0805	0812	0912	1004	1012	1112	1205	1212	1312	1405	1411	1512	1605	1612	1712	1805	1812	1917	2012	2112	2212
37	Biberach (Riß) .... d.	0618	0621	0733**h**	0825	0835	0935	1025	1035	1135	1225	1235	1335	1425	1433	1535	1626	1635	1735	1825	1835	1940	2035	2138	2238
62	Aulendorf .... d.	0638	0640	0753	|	0855	0955	|	1055	1155	|	1254	1355	1442**z**	1451	1554	|	1654	1754	|	1855	2002	2055	2157	2258
84	Ravensburg .... d.	0651	0653	0806	0852	0908	1008	1052	1108	1208	1252	1307	1408	1456	1505	1607	1652	1707	1807	1852	1908	2015	2108	2210	2311
95	Meckenbeuren .... d.	0658	0701	0814	|	0916	1016	|	1116	1216	|	1314	1416	|	1513	1614	|	1714	1815	|	1916	2022	2116	2219	2318
99	Friedrichshafen Flughafen ✈ d.	0702	0706	|	0901	|	|	1101	|	|	1301	|	|	1505	|	|	1701	|	|	1900	|	|	|	2224	2322
103	Friedrichshafen Stadt ▲ ...... a.	0707	0715	0822	0906	0924	1023	1106	1123	1224	1306	1323	1424	1510	1521	1624	1706	1723	1824	1905	1924	2030	2124	2229	2328
103	Friedrichshafen Stadt ... **939** d.	*0728*	0728	0828	...	0928	1029	...	1128	1229	...	1328	1429	...	1535	1629	...	1728	1829	...	1929	2037	2132	*2234*	*2344*
127	**Lindau** Hbf 🏛 .... **939** a.	*0750*	0750	0857	...	0952	1055	...	1151	1255	...	1351	1455	...	1554	1655	...	1751	1855	...	1951	2100	2156	*2256*	*0016*

	◇	Ⓐe			⊕	B			B		D	zB	eB			B			B			B		B	2
Lindau Hbf 🏛 .... **939** d.	...	0509	0559	0701	0803**k**	...	0906	1006	...	1102	1202	...	...	1302	1405	...	1500	1606	...	1702	1806	...	1902	*2012*	*2134*
Friedrichshafen Stadt .... **939** a.	...	0544	0622	0727	0827	...	0927	1027	...	1127	1219	...	...	1327	1427	...	1527	1627	...	1727	1828	...	1927	*2035*	*2209*
Friedrichshafen Stadt ▲ ...... d.	0521	0549	0628	0732	0832	0850	0931	1032	1049	1131	1233	1245	1250	1331	1432	1450	1531	1632	1650	1731	1832	1847	1932	2050	2231
Friedrichshafen Flughafen ✈ d.	|	|	0632	|	|	0855	|	|	1054	|	|	1250	1255	|	|	1455	|	|	1655**z**	|	|	1852	|	|	2236
Meckenbeuren .... d.	0529	|	0637	0739	0839	|	0938	1039	|	1138	1241	|	|	1338	1439	|	1538	1639	|	1738	1839	|	1939	2056	2241
Ravensburg .... d.	0537	0601	0645	0747	0846	0905	0945	1046	1104	1145	1250	1259	1305	1345	1446	1505	1545	1646	1705	1745	1846	1901	1946	2103	2250
Aulendorf .... d.	0552	|	0700**k**	0803	0901	|	1001	1101	|	1201	1306	1314	|	1401	1501	|	1601	1701	|	1801	1901	1915	2001	2117	2305
Biberach (Riß) .... d.	0610	0627	0720	0820	0920	0930	1020	1120	1129	1220	1322	1330	1330	1420	1520	1530	1620	1720	1730	1820	1920	1930	2020	2133	2325
Ulm Hbf .... a.	0642	0651	0745	0845	0945	0953	1045	1145	1153	1245	1345	1352	1353	1445	1545	1553	1645	1745	1753	1845	1945	1952	2045	2158	2359
Stuttgart Hbf **930** .... a.	0756**z**	0756	...	0956	...	...	1156	...	...	1356	1458	...	...	1556	...	...	1756	...	...	1956	...	...	2156**z**	...	...

– To / from Basel (Table **939**).
– *IC* **119**: [12] Münster - Köln - Lindau - Bregenz - Innsbruck.
– *IC* **118**: [12] Salzburg - Innsbruck - Bregenz - Lindau - Köln - Münster.
– To Singen (Table **939**).

e – Ⓐ (not June 19).
h – On Ⓐ **e**: Ulm d. 0712, Biberach d. 0736.
k – 3 minutes later on Ⓒ (also June 19).
z – Ⓒ (also June 19).

◇ – Runs 1 – 3 minutes **earlier** on Ⓐ **e**.
⊕ – Change trains at Friedrichshafen Stadt on Ⓐ **e**.
▲ – Regular services operate to / from Friedrichshafen Hafen.

935 MÜNCHEN, AUGSBURG and ULM - OBERSTDORF and LINDAU *RE/RB services except where shown*

For services to/from Bad Wörishofen see panel at foot of page (also on page 445). For regional services Memmingen - Lindau (via Kißlegg) see Table **937**.

km		©z	Ⓐe	Ⓐe	ALX ⚒rL	ALX ⚒rL		Ⓐe	Ⓐt	Ⓐe	Ⓐe	©z	©z		★			†w	⚒r	©k	©k	EC 196 ♥	ALX			
0	**München** Hbf ⊡ d.	...	...	...	0448	0448	...	...	...	...	0553	0553	...	...	...	...	0653	...	...	...	...	0717	0720	...	...	0753
7	München Pasing d.	...	...	...	0455	0455	...	...	...	...	0600	0600	...	...	...	...	0700	...	...	...	...	|	0727	...	...	0800
42	Geltendorf d.	...	...	...	0517	0517	...	...	...	...	0622	0622	...	...	...	...	0722	...	...	...	...	|	|	...	...	0822
56	Kaufering d.	...	...	...	0526	0526	...	...	...	...	0631	0631	...	...	...	...	0731	...	...	...	...	|	0756	...	...	0831
	Nürnberg Hbf **905** d.	...	...	...	|	|	...	...	...	...	|	|	...	...	...	...	|	...	...	...	...	|	|	...	...	|
	Augsburg Hbf d.	...	...	0501	|	|	...	...	...	0548	|	|	...	0618	0618	0703	|	...	...	...	...	|	|	0730	0815	|
68	Buchloe a.	...	...	0533	0534	0534	...	...	...	0620	0640	0640	...	0648	0648	0735	0738	←	←	...	...	0756	0804	0802c	0843	0840
68	Buchloe d.	...	...	▬	0536	0536	...	...	...	0631	0641	0652	0643	0649	0649	→	0739	0746	0749	...	...	0758	0807	0818	▬	0846
88	Kaufbeuren d.	...	...	...	0549	0549	0554	...	...	|	|	|	0655	0700	0700	▬	0753	0758	0801	...	...	|	0821	|	...	0900
94	Biessenhofen d.	...	...	...	0554	0554	0600	...	...	|	|	|	0701	0704	0704	...	0800	0806	0806	...	...	|	|	|	...	0905
100	Marktoberdorf d.	...	...	...	|	|	0610	...	...	|	|	|	0712	|	|	...	|	0817	0817	...	...	|	|	|	...	0915
131	**Füssen** a.	...	...	...	|	|	0649	...	...	|	|	|	0752	|	|	...	|	0855	0855	...	...	|	|	|	...	0954
	Türkheim (Bay) d.	...	...	...	|	|	▬	...	...	0638	0700j	0658	...	|	|	...	|	▬	▬	...	...	|	|	0825	...	...
	Mindelheim d.	...	...	©k	|	|	...	...	...	0648	0713	0708	...	|	|	...	|	Ⓐe	Ⓐe	...	...	|	|	0835	...	...
	Ulm Hbf d.	...	...	0509	|	|	...	...	0549	|	|	|	...	|	|	0618k	|	0659	0659	0717	0717	|	|	|	0819	...
	Memmingen a.	...	...	0554	|	|	Ⓐe	...	0644	0709	0733	0729	...	|	|	0721k	|	0759	0759	0800	0800	|	|	0855	0855	...
	Memmingen **937** d.	...	...	0556	|	|	*0559*	...	0646	...	...	...	...	|	|	0723	|	0802	0802	0802	0802	|	|	▬	0904	...
131	**Kempten** Hbf a.	...	...	0620	0621	0621	*0633*	...	0717	...	...	...	...	0725	0725	0757	0822	0826	0826	0827	0827	0839	0848	...	0925	...
131	**Kempten** Hbf d.	0514	0522	...	0625	0625	0651	...	...	...	...	...	...	0727	0727	0800	...	0828	0828	0828	0828	0841	0852	ALX	...	...
152	Immenstadt a.	0526	0535	...	0641	0641	0708	◄	...	...	...	...	...	0742	0742	0814	...	0842	0842	0842	0842	|	0907	◄	...	...
152	Immenstadt d.	0527	0538	...	0645	0656	0713	0715	...	...	...	...	...	0747	0748	0820	...	0844	0850	0850	0844	|	0911	0914	...	...
	Sonthofen d.	|	|	...	|	0705	|	0730	...	...	...	...	...	|	0758	0829	...	|	0900	0900	|	|	|	0922	...	...
	Oberstdorf a.	|	|	...	|	0728	|	0748	...	...	...	...	...	|	0816	0851	...	|	0918	0918	|	|	|	0939	...	...
197	Hergatz **937** d.	0600	0612	...	0725	...	0752	...	...	...	...	...	...	0819	...	...	...	0921	...	...	0916	|	0946	...	...	...
203	Wangen (Allgäu) **937** a.	|	|	...	|	...	0756	...	...	...	...	...	...	|	...	...	...	0926	...	...	|	|	|	...	...	...
220	**Lindau** Hbf **937** a.	0615	0626	...	0743	...	...	...	...	...	...	...	...	0834	...	...	...	...	...	...	0931	0947	1003	...	...	...

			†w			ALX	◐								ALX	◐					EC 194 ♥				ALX	◐
München Hbf ⊡ d.	...	0820	0840	0853	...	0919	...	...	0953	...	1020	1053	...	...	1119	...	...	1153	...	1220	1233	1253	...	...	1319	...
München Pasing d.	...	0827	0847	0900	...	0927	...	...	1000	...	1027	1100	...	...	1127	...	...	1200	...	1227	|	1300	...	...	1327	...
Geltendorf d.	...	0849	|	0922	...	|	...	...	1022	...	1049	1122	...	...	|	...	...	1222	...	1249	|	1322	...	...	|	...
Kaufering d.	...	0900	|	0931	...	0955	...	...	1031	...	1059	1131	...	...	1155	...	...	1231	...	1259	|	1331	...	...	1355	...
Nürnberg Hbf **905** d.	0718	|	|	|	...	|	...	...	|	...	|	|	...	...	|	...	...	|	...	|	|	|	...	...	|	...
Augsburg Hbf d.	0831	|	|	|	0903	|	0930	1015	|	1030	|	|	1103	...	|	1130	1215	|	1229	|	|	|	1303	...	|	1330
Buchloe a.	0852	0908	|	0939	0935c	1003	0959c	1043	1040	1052	1108	1138	1135c	...	1203	1159c	1243	1240	1252	1308	1315	1338	1335c	...	1403	1401c
Buchloe d.	0854	0911	|	0941f	0947	1005	1006	...	1046	1054	1111	1139	1147	...	1205	1206	...	1246	1254	1309	1317	1339	1347	...	1405	1406
Kaufbeuren d.	0906	|	|	0954f	1000	1018	|	...	1059	1106	|	1153	1200	...	1218	|	...	1259	1306	|	|	1353	1400	...	1418	|
Biessenhofen d.	|	|	|	1000	1006	|	|	...	1104	|	|	1159	1206	...	|	|	...	1304	|	|	|	1402	1406	...	|	|
Marktoberdorf d.	|	|	0950	|	1016	|	|	...	1114	|	|	|	1216	...	|	|	...	1314v	|	|	|	|	1416	...	|	|
Füssen a.	|	|	1027	|	1055	|	|	...	1154	|	|	|	1255	...	|	|	...	1354v	|	|	|	|	1455	...	|	|
Türkheim (Bay) d.	|	0918	...	|	▬	|	1014	...	▬	|	1118	|	▬	...	|	1214	...	▬	|	1316	|	|	▬	...	|	1414
Mindelheim d.	|	0930	...	|	...	|	1032j	...	...	|	1130	|	Ⓐe	...	|	1232j	...	...	|	1334j	|	|	...	...	|	1429
Ulm Hbf d.	|	|	...	|	0919	|	|	...	1019	|	|	|	1119	1119	|	|	...	1219	|	|	|	|	1317	1317	|	|
Memmingen a.	|	0951	...	|	0954	|	1053	...	1055	|	1151	|	1200	1200	|	1253	...	1255	|	1354	1344	|	1355	1355	|	1456
Memmingen **937** d.	|	▬	...	|	1002	|	▬	...	1104	|	▬	|	1202	1202	|	▬	...	1304	|	▬	1346	|	1402	1402	|	▬
Kempten Hbf a.	0928	...	...	1025f	1026	1046	...	...	1126	1128	...	1222	1226	1226	1246	...	...	1326	1328	...	|	1424	1426	1426	1446	...
Kempten Hbf d.	0931	...	...	...	1031	1047	ALX	...	...	1131	...	...	1231	1231	1247	ALX	...	...	1331	...	|	...	1431	1431	1447	ALX
Immenstadt a.	0945	◄	...	...	1045	1102	◄	...	...	1145	◄	...	1245	1245	1302	◄	...	...	1345	◄	|	...	1445	1445	1502	◄
Immenstadt d.	0947	0951	...	...	1051	1106	1115	...	...	1147	1151	...	1247	1251	1306	1319	...	...	1347	1351	|	...	1447	1451	1506	1514
Sonthofen d.	|	1001	...	...	1102	|	1123	...	...	|	1201	...	|	1302	|	1330	...	...	|	1401	|	...	|	1501	|	1522
Oberstdorf a.	|	1023	...	...	1120	|	1140	...	...	|	1219	...	|	1320	|	1349	...	...	|	1419	|	...	|	1519	|	1539
Hergatz **937** d.	1019	...	...	...	...	1144	...	...	...	1219	...	...	1323	...	1344	...	...	...	1419	...	|	...	1518	...	1544	...
Wangen (Allgäu) **937** a.	|	...	...	...	...	|	...	...	...	|	...	...	1328	...	|	...	...	...	|	...	|	...	|	...	|	...
Lindau Hbf **937** a.	1034	...	...	...	...	1200	...	...	...	1234	...	...	...	...	1400	...	...	...	1434	...	1447	...	1532	...	1600	...

	IC 2085 H								ALX	ALX	RE 2013 A✗	◐					EC 192 ♥	Ⓐe	©z	Ⓐe	©z		ALX Ⓐe	◐	ALX ©z	
München Hbf ⊡ d.	...	...	1353	...	1420	1452	...	...	1519	...	...	...	...	1552	...	1620	1633	...	1652	1652	...	...	1713	...	1719	...
München Pasing d.	...	...	1400	...	1427	1459	...	...	1527	...	...	...	...	1559	...	1627	|	...	1659	1659	...	...	1720	...	1727	...
Geltendorf d.	...	...	1422	...	1449	1522	...	...	|	...	...	...	...	1622	...	1649	|	...	1722	1722	...	...	|	...	|	...
Kaufering d.	...	...	1431	...	1459	1531	...	...	1555	...	...	...	...	1631	...	1659	|	...	1731	1732	...	...	1750	...	1755	...
Nürnberg Hbf **905** d.	...	...	|	...	|	|	...	...	|	...	...	...	...	|	...	|	|	...	|	|	...	...	|	...	|	...
Augsburg Hbf d.	1356	1415	|	1430	|	|	1503	...	|	...	...	1531	1615	|	1630	|	|	1703	|	|	1703	...	|	1729	|	1815
Buchloe a.	1422	1443	1440	1452	1508	1538	1535c	...	1603	...	...	1559c	1643	1640	1652	1708	1715	1735	1738	1741	1735c	...	1759	1759c	1803	1843
Buchloe d.	1423	...	1446	1454	1511	1539	1547	...	1605	...	...	1606	1653e	1646	1654	1709	1717	1736	1739	1742	1747	...	1802	1806	1805	▬
Kaufbeuren d.	1438	...	1459	1506	|	1553	1600	...	1618	...	...	|	|	1659	1706	|	|	1749	1753	1756	1800	...	1816	|	1818	...
Biessenhofen d.	|	...	1504	|	|	1600	1606	...	|	...	...	|	|	1704y	|	|	|	1806j	1800	1801	1806	...	|	|	|	...
Marktoberdorf d.	|	...	1514	|	|	|	1616	...	|	...	...	|	|	1714y	|	|	|	1816	|	|	1818	...	|	|	|	...
Füssen a.	|	...	1554	|	|	|	1655	...	|	...	...	|	|	1755	|	|	|	1855	|	|	1856	...	|	|	|	...
Türkheim (Bay) d.	|	...	▬	|	1518	|	▬	...	|	...	...	1614	1700e	...	|	1716	|	...	|	|	▬	...	|	1814	|	...
Mindelheim d.	|	...	...	|	1530	|	Ⓐt	...	|	...	...	1635j	1707e	...	|	1734j	|	...	|	|	...	...	|	1830	|	...
Ulm Hbf d.	|	...	1419	|	|	|	1519	1519	|	...	1615	|	...	...	|	|	|	...	|	|	1717	1717	|	|	|	...
Memmingen a.	|	...	1455	|	1551	|	1555	1555	|	...	1643	1655	...	...	|	1756	1744	...	|	|	1757	1757	|	1851	|	...
Memmingen **937** d.	|	...	1504	|	▬	|	1602	1602	|	...	1645	...	...	...	|	▬	1746	...	|	|	1801	1801	|	▬	|	...
Kempten Hbf a.	1509	...	1526	1528	...	1622	1626	1626	1646	...	1707	...	...	...	1728	...	|	...	1822	1829	1825	1825	1846	ALX	1846	ALX
Kempten Hbf d.	1511	...	...	1531	...	...	1631	1631	1647	...	1709	...	...	...	1731	...	|	...	...	...	1832	1832	1847	Ⓐe	1847	©z
Immenstadt a.	1527	...	...	1545	◄	...	1645	1645	1702	◄	1724	...	...	...	1745	◄	|	...	...	...	1846	1846	1902	◄	1902	◄
Immenstadt d.	1542	...	...	1547	1551	...	1647	1651	1706	1714	1740	...	...	...	1747	1751	|	...	...	...	1848	1851	1908	1915	1906	1915
Sonthofen d.	1552	...	...	|	1601	...	|	1701	|	1722	1752	...	...	...	|	1801	|	...	...	...	|	1902	|	1923	|	1923
Oberstdorf a.	1611	...	...	|	1619	...	|	1719	|	1739	1812	...	...	...	|	1819	|	...	...	...	|	1920	|	1940	|	1940
Hergatz **937** d.	...	...	...	1619	...	...	1724	...	1744	...	...	...	...	...	1819	...	|	...	...	...	1922	...	1948	...	1944	...
Wangen (Allgäu) **937** a.	...	...	...	|	...	...	1729	...	|	...	...	...	...	...	|	...	|	...	...	...	|	...	|	...	|	...
Lindau Hbf **937** a.	...	...	...	1634	...	...	...	...	1800	...	...	...	...	...	1834	...	1847	...	...	...	1937	...	2009	...	2000	...

A – ALLGÄU – 🚃12 (*IC* **2013**) Hannover - Dortmund - Köln - Stuttgart - Ulm (*RE* **2013**) - Oberstdorf.
H – NEBELHORN – 🚃12 Hamburg (**2083**) - Augsburg (**2085**) - Oberstdorf.
L – Runs daily from Kempten.
R – ⑤–⑦ (also June 19).

c – Connects with train in preceding column.
e – Ⓐ (not June 19, Aug. 15).
f – On © (also June 19, Aug. 15) Buchloe d. 0939, Kaufbeuren d. 0953, Kempten a. 1022.

j – Arrives 8–12 minutes earlier.
k – © (also June 19).
r – Not June 19, Aug. 15, Nov. 1.
t – Not June 19.
v – 3 minutes later on Ⓐ (not June 19, Aug. 15).
w – Also June 19, Aug. 15, Nov. 1.
y – 3 minutes later on † (also June 19, Aug. 15, Nov. 1).
z – Also June 19, Aug. 15.

⊖ – 4 minutes later on © (also June 19, Aug. 15).

★ – Change trains at Immenstadt on Ⓐ (not June 19, Aug. 15).
♥ – 🚃12 and ✗ München - Bregenz - St Gallen - Zürich (Table **75**).
◄ – Detached from train in previous column at Immenstadt.
◐ – Conveys 🚃12 Augsburg - Türkheim - Bad Wörishofen (see panel below).
♣ – Additional journeys Türkheim - Bad Wörishofen: 0525 Ⓐ **e**, 0600 Ⓐ **e**, 0627 Ⓐ **e**, 0726 Ⓐ **e** and 2247 **R**.
⊡ – Most trains in Table **935** use platforms 27–36 at München Hbf (minimum connecting time from other services is 10 minutes).

ALX – Operated by Vogtlandbahn. 🍸.

AUGSBURG - TÜRKHEIM - BAD WÖRISHOFEN

km		⊖																							R	
0	**Augsburg** Hbf d.	...	...	...	...	0930	...	...	1130	...	...	1330	...	...	1531	...	...	1729	...	...	1930	...	...	2131	...	2331
40	Buchloe d.	...	...	...	...	1006	...	...	1206	...	...	1406	...	...	1606	...	...	1806	...	...	2006	...	...	2209	...	0009
48	Türkheim (Bay) ♣ d.	0658	0816	0847	0920	1017	1047	1120	1217	1247	1320	1417	1447	1520	1617	1647	1719	1817	1847	1920	2017	2047	2121	2219	2321	0020
53	**Bad Wörishofen** ♣ a.	0704	0822	0853	0926	1023	1053	1126	1223	1253	1326	1423	1453	1526	1623	1653	1725	1823	1853	1926	2023	2053	2128	2226	2328	0026

RE / RB services except where shown MÜNCHEN, AUGSBURG and ULM - OBERSTDORF and LINDAU 935

For services to / from Bad Wörishofen see panel at foot of page (also on page 444). For regional services Memmingen - Lindau (via Kißlegg) see Table **937**.

					EC			*ALX*									*ALX*							*ALX*		
					190															⑤–⑦	⑤–⑦					
					♥				◐							◐				**R**	**R**				◐	
München Hbf ⊡ d.	1752	1820	...	...	1833	1852	...	1919	...	...	1952	2020	...	...	...	...	2119	...	...	...	...	2220	...	2319	...	0001
München Pasing d.	1759	1827	...	...	│	1859	...	1927	...	...	1959	2027	...	...	...	...	2127	...	...	...	...	2227	...	2327	...	0008
Geltendorf d.	1822	1849	...	...	│	1922	...	│	...	...	2022	2050	...	...	...	...	2148	...	...	...	...	2249	...	2348	...	0030
Kaufering d.	1831	1859	...	...	│	1931	...	1955	...	...	2031	2101	...	...	...	...	2158	...	...	...	...	2259	...	2358	...	0040
Nürnberg Hbf **905** d.	│	│	1733	1733	│	│	...	│	...	...	│	│	...	...	...	...	│	...	...	...	...	│	...	│	...	│
Augsburg Hbf d.	│	│	1845	1845	│	│	1903	│	1930	2015	│	│	2050	2050	...	2131	│	...	2233	2233	...	│	...	│	2331	│
Buchloe a.	1840	1907	1905**c**	1905	1915	1939	1935**c**	2003	1959**c**	2043	2040	2110	2109**c**	2109	...	2203	2206**c**	...	2305	2305	...	2307**c**	...	0006	0003**c**	0049
Buchloe d.	1846	1909	1912	1912	1917	1941	1947	2005	2006	▬	2050	2112	2114	2114	...	2209	2207	...	2310	2310	...	2312	...	0007	0009	...
Kaufbeuren d.	1859	│	1923	1923	│	1954	2000	2018	│	...	2102	│	2125	2125	...	│	2221	2227	2321	2321	2329	│	...	0020	│	...
Biessenhofen d.	1904	│	│	│	│	2000	2006	│	│	...	2108	│	2130	2130	...	│	│	2236	2325	2325	2334	│	...	0025	│	...
Marktoberdorf d.	1914	│	│	│	│	│	2016	│	│	...	2119	│	│	│	...	│	│	2246	│	│	2346	│	...	│	│	...
Füssen a.	1954	│	│	│	│	│	2055	│	│	...	2158	│	│	│	...	│	│	2326	│	│	0026	│	...	│	│	...
Türkheim (Bay) d.	▬	1916	│	│	│	│	▬	│	2014	...	...	2119	│	│	...	2217	│	▬	│	│	...	2319	...	│	0017	...
Mindelheim d.	...	1934**j**	│	│	│	│	...	│	2030	...	...	2130	│	│	...	2230	│	...	│	│	...	2330	...	│	0027	...
Ulm Hbf d.	1819	│	│	│	│	│	1919	│	│	2019	...	│	│	│	2119	│	│	2221	│	│	...	│	2323	│	│	...
Memmingen a.	1855	1955	│	│	1944	│	1955	│	2051	2055	...	2151	│	│	2159	2251	│	2255	│	│	...	2352	0003	│	0047	...
Memmingen **937** d.	1902	2005	│	│	1946	│	2002	│	▬	2105	...	...	│	│	2200	...	│	2257	│	│	...	...	0004	│	...	...
Kempten Hbf a.	1927	│	1946	1946	│	2026	2026	2046	...	2129	...	...	2152	2152	2230	...	2250	2323	2347	2347	...	...	0029	0052	...	...
Kempten Hbf d.	1931	│	1949	1949	│	...	...	2048	...	...	...	...	2154	2154	...	...	2254	2324	...	2349	...	...	...	...	...	...
Immenstadt a.	1945	◇	2003	2003	│	...	...	2103	...	...	...	...	2208	2208	...	...	2309	2340	...	0003	...	...	...	...	...	...
Immenstadt d.	1951	│	2005	2015	│	...	...	2106	2111	...	...	...	2211	2214	...	...	2310	2346	...	0005	...	...	...	...	...	...
Sonthofen d.	2001	│	│	2025	│	...	...	│	2121	...	...	...	│	2224	...	...	│	2356	...	│	...	...	...	...	...	...
Oberstdorf a.	2019	│	│	2049	│	...	...	│	2139	...	...	...	│	2242	...	...	│	0014	...	│	...	...	...	...	...	...
Hergatz **937** d.	...	2106	2038	...	│	...	...	2144	...	...	...	...	2250	...	...	...	2347	...	...	0039	...	...	...	...	...	...
Wangen (Allgäu) **937** a.	...	2100	│	...	│	...	...	│	...	...	...	...	│	...	...	...	│	...	...	│	...	...	...	...	...	...
Lindau Hbf **937** a.	...	2121	2052	...	2047	...	...	2201	...	...	...	...	2304	...	...	...	0004	...	...	0053	...	...	...	...	...	...

km	*km*																									
				ALX												*ALX*	*ALX*									
			Ⓐ e	⚒ r	Ⓐ e		Ⓐ e		Ⓐ e	Ⓐ t	Ⓐ e			Ⓐ e				⚒ r	⚒ r	⚒ r	†w	†w	†w		†w	
0		**Lindau** Hbf **937** d.	...	...	...	...	...	*0443*e	...	...	...	...	...	...	...	...	0520	...	0610	...	...	0624	...	...	...	0707
		Wangen (Allgäu) **937** d.	...	...	...	...	...	│	...	...	...	...	...	...	...	...	│	...	│	...	...	│	...	...	...	0730
23		Hergatz **937** d.	...	...	...	...	...	*0457*e	...	...	...	...	...	...	...	...	0538	...	0624	...	...	0639	...	...	...	0724
	0	**Oberstdorf** d.	...	...	...	...	...	│	...	0501	...	...	...	...	...	0542	│	0624	│	...	...	│	0631	...	...	│
	13	Sonthofen d.	...	...	...	...	...	│	...	0520	...	...	...	...	...	0601	│	0643	│	...	...	│	0655	...	...	│
	21	Immenstadt a.	...	...	...	...	...	*0531*e	...	0529	...	...	...	...	...	0611**c**	0616**c**	0652	0659	...	...	0714	0707	...	...	◇
	21	Immenstadt d.	...	...	...	...	...	*0532*e	...	0536	...	...	...	...	0623	▶	0629	▶	0703	...	...	0717	0717	...	...	│
	42	**Kempten** Hbf a.	...	...	...	...	...	*0545*e	...	0552	...	...	...	...	0638	...	0646	...	0718	...	...	0731	0731	...	...	│
	42	**Kempten** Hbf d.	...	0446	...	0529	0522	0548	...	0556	0601	...	...	...	0641	...	0648	...	0722	...	...	0734	0734	0734	0737	│
85	*77*	Memmingen **937** a.	...	│	...	0554	│	│	...	0621	│	...	...	...	0708	...	│	...	│	...	...	0800	0800	0800	│	0813
85	*77*	Memmingen d.	0452	│	0526	0556	│	│	0553	0622	│	0626	...	0647	0710	...	│	...	│	0739	0739	0804	0804	0804	│	0815
	129	**Ulm** Hbf a.	│	│	│	0643	│	│	│	0720	│	│	...	│	0743	...	│	...	│	│	│	0839	0839	0839	│	│
112		Mindelheim d.	0514	│	0549	▬	│	│	0614	▬	│	0648	...	0713	...	...	│	...	│	0800	0800	▬	▬	...	│	0836
123		Türkheim (Bay) d.	0522	│	0558	Ⓐ e	│	│	0623	...	│	0656**g**	...	0722	...	...	│	...	│	0810	0809	Ⓒ z	Ⓐ e	...	│	0844
		Füssen d.	│	│	│	0453	│	│	│	...	│	│	0600	│	...	...	│	...	│	│	│	0702	0704	...	│	│
		Marktoberdorf d.	│	│	│	0535	│	│	│	...	│	│	0644	│	...	...	│	...	│	│	│	0746	0749	...	│	│
		Biessenhofen d.	│	0513	│	0543	0549	│	│	...	0627	│	0652	│	...	...	│	...	0745	│	│	0754	0757	...	0803	│
		Kaufbeuren d.	│	0519	│	0548	0554	0619	│	...	0634	│	0657	│	...	...	0717	...	0751	│	│	0759	0802	...	0808	│
131		Buchloe a.	0529	0530**c**	0605	...	0606**c**	0632	0630**c**	Ⓒ z	0647	0704**g**	0709**c**	0729	...	...	0730**c**	...	0802	0817	0817	0812**c**	0815**c**	...	0819**c**	0851
131		Buchloe d.	0535	0533	0610	...	0608	0633	0640	0648	0648	0712	0712	0739	...	...	0732	...	0805	0820	0824	0824	0824	...	0820	0853
171		**Augsburg** Hbf a.	0607	│	│	...	0641	│	0712	0716	0716	│	0744	0811	...	...	│	...	0829	│	0856	0856	0856	...	│	│
		Nürnberg Hbf **905** a.	...	│	│	...	...	│	...	...	...	│	...	...	...	...	│	...	0953	│	...	...	...	...	│	│
		Kaufering d.	...	0541	0618	...	...	0641	...	...	...	0720	...	...	...	...	0741	...	...	0829	...	...	...	...	0829	0901
		Geltendorf d.	...	│	0628	...	...	0650	...	...	...	0730	...	...	...	...	│	...	...	0838	...	...	...	...	0838	0910
		München Pasing a.	...	0610	0651	...	...	0711	...	...	...	0756	...	...	...	...	0809	...	...	0857	...	...	...	...	0857	0933
		München Hbf ⊡ a.	...	0618	0700	...	...	0719	...	...	...	0804	...	...	...	...	0819	...	...	0904	...	...	...	...	0904	0941

					ALX	*ALX*				*EC*					*IC*	*IC*	*ALX*	*ALX*				*EC*				
										191					**2084**	**2012**						**193**				
							Ⓐ e			♥					**H**	**A** ✕			Ⓒ z			♥				
Lindau Hbf **937** d.	...	0725	...	...	...	0758	...	...	...	0912	...	0925	...	...	...	...	...	0958	1019	...	...	1112	...	1125	...	...
Wangen (Allgäu) **937** d.	...	│	...	...	...	│	0829	...	...	│	...	│	...	...	...	...	...	│	│	...	...	│	...	│	...	...
Hergatz **937** d.	...	0739	...	...	...	0815	0839	...	...	│	...	0941	...	...	...	...	...	1015	1033	...	...	│	...	1139	...	...
Oberstdorf d.	0734**f**	│	...	...	0822	│	│	0837	...	│	0904	│	...	...	0940	0946	1024	│	│	1039	...	│	1143	│	...	...
Sonthofen d.	0758	│	...	...	0839	│	│	0901	...	│	0934	│	...	...	1000	1013	1041	│	│	1102	...	│	1201	│	...	...
Immenstadt a.	0807	0814	...	...	0847	0851	0914	0910	...	│	0943	1015	...	...	1009	1021	1049	1051	1108	1111	...	│	1210	1214	...	...
Immenstadt d.	▶	0817	...	...	▶	0901	0917	0917	...	│	▬	1017	...	...	1027	1036	▶	1101	1117	1117	...	│	▶	1217	...	...
Kempten Hbf a.	...	0830	...	...	▬	0915	0931	0931	...	│	...	1030	...	...	1043	1052	▬	1115	1131	1131	...	│	▬	1230	...	...
Kempten Hbf d.	...	0832	0835	...	...	0916	0934	0934	0941	│	...	1032	...	...	1045	1055	...	1116	1134	1134	1141	│	...	1232	1235	...
Memmingen **937** a.	...	│	0857	...	◧	│	0958	0958	│	1013	...	│	...	...	│	1123	◧	│	1158	1158	│	1213	...	│	1257	...
Memmingen d.	...	│	0904	...	0907	│	1005	1005	│	1015	1005	│	...	...	│	1127	1107	│	1204	1204	│	1215	1205	│	1304	...
Ulm Hbf a.	...	│	0939	...	│	│	1039	1039	│	│	│	│	...	...	│	1155	│	│	1239	1239	│	│	│	│	1339	...
Mindelheim d.	...	│	▬	...	0932	│	...	▬	│	│	1037**j**	│	...	...	│	...	1132	│	...	▬	│	│	1237**j**	│	▬	...
Türkheim (Bay) d.	...	│	...	...	0946	│	...	...	│	│	1045	│	...	...	│	...	1146	│	...	...	│	│	1245	│	...	...
Füssen d.	...	│	0806	...	│	│	...	0905	│	│	│	│	1006	...	│	...	│	│	...	1105	│	│	│	│	1206	...
Marktoberdorf d.	...	│	0850	...	│	│	...	0949	│	│	│	│	1050	...	│	...	│	│	...	1147	│	│	│	│	1250	...
Biessenhofen d.	...	│	0858	...	│	│	...	0957	1005	│	│	│	1058	...	│	...	│	│	...	1156	1205	│	│	│	1258	...
Kaufbeuren d.	...	0856	0903	...	│	0943	...	1002	1010	│	│	1056	1103	...	1115	...	│	1143	...	1201	1210	│	│	1256	1303	...
Buchloe a.	...	0907	0914	...	0952	0954**c**	...	1015	1021**c**	1041	1052	1107	1114	...	1129	...	1152	1154**c**	...	1213	1221**c**	1241	1252	1307	1314	...
Buchloe d.	...	0909	0919	0918	1000	0955	...	1024	1022	1043	1053	1109	1119	1118	1131	...	1200	1155	...	1224	1222	1243	1253	1309	1319	1318
Augsburg Hbf a.	...	0930	│	0945	1029	│	...	1056	│	│	│	1130	│	1145	1156	...	1229	│	...	1256	│	│	│	1330	│	1345
Nürnberg Hbf **905** a.	...	...	│	...	...	│	...	...	│	│	│	...	│	...	...	...	...	│	...	...	│	│	│	...	│	...
Kaufering d.	...	...	0929	...	...	1003	...	..	1029	│	1101	...	1129	...	...	...	...	1203	...	...	1230	│	1301	...	1329	...
Geltendorf d.	...	...	0938	...	...	│	...	...	1038	│	1110	...	1138	...	...	...	...	│	...	...	1238	│	1310	...	1338	...
München Pasing a.	...	...	0958	...	...	1033	...	...	1058	│	1133	...	1158	...	...	...	...	1233	...	...	1258	│	1333	...	1357	...
München Hbf ⊡ a.	...	...	1005	...	...	1041	...	...	1105	1128	1141	...	1205	...	...	...	...	1241	...	...	1305	1328	1341	...	1404	...

– ALLGÄU – 🚃12 and ✕ Oberstdorf - Stuttgart - Köln - Hannover.
– NEBELHORN – 🚃12 Oberstdorf - Augsburg (**2082**) - Hamburg.
– ⑤–⑦ (also June 19).

– Change trains at Buchloe on ⑥ (not Nov. 1).
– Connects with train in preceding column.
– Ⓐ (not June 19, Aug. 15).
– 0739 on Ⓒ (also June 19, Aug. 15).
– On Ⓒ (also June 19, Aug. 15) Türkheim d. 0659, Buchloe a. 0706.
– Arrives 11 minutes earlier.

r – Not June 19, Aug. 15, Nov. 1.
t – Not June 19.
w – Also June 19, Aug. 15, Nov. 1.
z – Also June 19, Aug. 15.

◐ – Conveys 🚃12 Augsburg - Türkheim - Bad Wörishofen (see panel page 444).
◧ – Conveys 🚃12 Bad Wörishofen - Türkheim - Augsburg (see panel below).
◇ – Via Kißlegg (Table **937**).

▶ – Attached to train in the next column at Immenstadt.
♥ – 🚃12 and ✕ München - Bregenz - St Gallen - Zürich and v.v. (Table **75**).
♣ – Additional journeys Bad Wörishofen - Türkheim: 0510 Ⓐ **e**, 0612 Ⓐ **e**, 0709 Ⓐ **e**, 0758 Ⓐ **e**, 2308 **R**.
⊡ – Most trains in Table **935** use platforms 27 – 36 at München Hbf (minimum connecting time from / to other services is 10 minutes).

ALX – Operated by Vogtlandbahn. 🍸.

BAD WÖRISHOFEN - TÜRKHEIM - AUGSBURG

	Ⓐ e		Ⓒ z																						**R**	
Bad Wörishofen ♣ d.	0545	0645	0739	0833	0907	0932	1034	1107	1132	1234	1303	1332	1428	1507	1532	1634	1703	1731	1828	1904	1932	2028	2107	2133	2231	2333
Türkheim (Bay) ♣ a.	0552	0652	0746	0840	0914	0939	1041	1114	1139	1241	1310	1339	1435	1514	1539	1641	1710	1737	1835	1911	1939	2035	2114	2139	2238	2339
Buchloe a.	...	...	0753	...	...	0952	...	...	1152	...	...	1352	...	...	1552	...	...	1752	...	...	1952	...	...	2152	...	2352
Augsburg Hbf a.	...	...	0829**b**	...	...	1029	...	...	1229	...	...	1429	...	...	1629	...	...	1829	...	...	2029	...	...	2244	...	0043

935 LINDAU and OBERSTDORF - ULM, AUGSBURG and MÜNCHEN

RE/RB services except where shown

For services from / to Bad Wörishofen see pages 444 and 445. For regional services Lindau - Memmingen (via Kißlegg) see Table **937**.

	ALX	*ALX*	Ⓐe							*ALX*	*ALX*			*EC* **195** ♥						*ALX*	*ALX*		Ⓒz	Ⓐe	Ⓐe	★ Ⓒz
Lindau Hbf ... **937** d.	...	1158	...	...	...	...	1325	...	...	...	1358	...	...	1512	...	1525	...	...	...	1558	1624z	...	...	...	1657	1714
Wangen (Allgäu) **937** d.	...	|	1230	...	...	...	|	...	...	...	|	...	...	|	...	|	...	...	...	|	1630e	...	...	...	|	|
Hergatz ... **937** d.	...	1215	1240	...	...	...	1339	...	...	...	1415	...	...	|	...	1539	...	...	...	1615	1639	...	...	...	1711	1728
Oberstdorf ... d.	1224	|	|	1239f	...	1335	|	...	...	1424	|	1441	...	|	1540	|	...	...	1622	|	|	1637	...	1704	|	|
Sonthofen ... d.	1241	|	|	1302	...	1401	|	...	...	1441	|	1501	...	|	1601	|	...	...	1639	|	|	1701	...	1730	|	|
Immenstadt ... a.	1249	1251	1314	1311	...	1410	1414	...	...	1449	1451	1510	...	|	1610	1614	...	...	1647	1651	1714	1710	...	1739	1746	1803
Immenstadt ... d.	▶	1301	1317	1317	...	▶	1417	...	...	▶	1501	1517	...	|	▶	1617	...	...	▶	1701	▶	1717	...	▶	1749	▬
Kempten Hbf ... a.	▬	1315	1331	1331	...	▬	1430	...	...	▬	1515	1531	...	|	▬	1630	...	...	▬	1715	▬	1731	...	▬	1803	...
Kempten Hbf ... d.	...	1316	1334	1334	1341	...	1432	1435	...	...	1516	1534	1541	|	...	1632	1635	...	...	1716	...	1734	1738	...	1809	...
Memmingen ... **937** a.	◧	|	1359	1359	|	...	|	1456	...	◧	|	1558	|	1613	...	|	1704	...	...	|	◧	1759	|	...	|	...
Memmingen ... d.	1307	|	1404	1404	|	1408	|	1504	...	1507	|	1602	|	1615	1605	|	1705	...	...	|	1707	1804	|	...	|	1806
Ulm Hbf ... a.	|	|	1439	1439	|	|	|	1539	...	|	|	1641	|	|	|	|	1739	...	...	|	|	1840	|	...	|	|
Mindelheim ... d.	1332	|	...	▬	|	1430	|	▬	...	1532	|	▬	|	|	1637j	|	▬	...	...	|	1731	▬	|	...	|	1830
Türkheim (Bay) ... d.	1346	|	...	...	|	1439	|	...	...	1546	|	...	|	|	1645	|	...	...	†w	|	1746	...	|	...	|	1838
Füssen ... d.	|	|	...	1305	|	|	|	1406	...	|	|	1505	|	|	|	|	1606	...	1634	|	|	1705	|	...	|	|
Marktoberdorf ... d.	|	|	...	1351	|	|	|	1450	...	|	|	1548	|	|	|	|	1650	...	1718	|	|	1749	|	...	|	|
Biessenhofen ... d.	|	|	...	1359	1405	|	|	1458	...	|	|	1557	1605	|	|	|	1658	...	|	|	|	1757	1805	...	1831	|
Kaufbeuren ... d.	|	1343	...	1404	1410	|	1456	1503	...	|	1543	1602	1610	|	|	1656	1703	...	|	1743	|	1803	1810	...	1836	|
Buchloe ... a.	1352	1354c	...	1417	1421c	1445	1507	1514	...	1552	1554c	1614	1621c	1641	1652	1707	1714	...	|	1754	1752c	1815	1821c	...	1848	1845c
Buchloe ... d.	1400	1355	...	1424	1422	1453	1509	1519	1518	1600	1555	1624	1622	1643	1653	1709	1719	1719	|	1755	1800	1824	1822	1822	1849	1851
Augsburg Hbf ... a.	1429	|	...	1456	|	|	1530	|	1545	1629	|	1656	|	|	|	1730	|	1746	|	|	1829	1856	|	|	1914	|
Nürnberg Hbf **905** ... a.	...	|	...	...	|	|	...	|	...	...	|	...	|	|	|	1848h	|	...	|	|	...	...	|	|	2026	|
Kaufering ... d.	...	1403	...	...	1430	1501	...	1529	...	...	1603	...	1629	|	1701	...	1729	...	|	1803	...	...	1831	1831	...	1900
Geltendorf ... d.	...	|	...	...	1438	1510	...	1538	...	...	|	...	1638	|	1710	...	1738	...	|	|	...	...	1840	1840	...	1910
München Pasing ... a.	...	1433	...	...	1458	1533	...	1558	...	...	1633	...	1658	|	1733	...	1758	...	1811	1833	...	...	1910	1910	...	1933
München Hbf ... ⊡ a.	...	1441	...	...	1505	1541	...	1605	...	...	1641	...	1705	1728	1741	...	1805	...	1820	1841	...	...	1917	1917	...	1941

	†w	⑥h	Ⓐe		*ALX*	*ALX*	Ⓐt					*ALX*	*ALX*	◧	*EC* **197** ♥			⑤–⑦ R	⑤–⑦ R		◧		*ALX*			
Lindau Hbf ... **937** d.	...	...	...	...	...	1758	...	...	...	1905	...	...	1954	...	2016	...	...	...	2107	...	...	...	2209	...	...	2310
Wangen (Allgäu) **937** d.	...	...	...	...	...	|	1819	...	...	|	...	...	|	...	|	...	...	...	|	...	...	...	|	...	...	|
Hergatz ... **937** d.	...	...	...	...	...	1815	1839	...	...	1919	...	...	2010	...	|	...	...	...	2121	...	...	...	2227	...	...	2324
Oberstdorf ... d.	1726	1740	1740	...	1824	|	|	1839	1906	|	1942	2020	|	...	|	...	2102	...	|	...	...	2228	|	...	2326	|
Sonthofen ... d.	1750	1801	1801	...	1841	|	|	1902	1933	|	2001	2037	|	...	|	...	2121	...	|	...	...	2252	|	...	2345	|
Immenstadt ... a.	1801	1810	1810	...	1849	1851	1914	1911	1942	1954	2010	2045	2047	...	|	...	2130	...	2156	...	...	2301	2305	...	2356	2359
Immenstadt ... d.	1807	1817	1817	...	▶	1901	▶	1917	▶	1957	2017	▶	2055	...	|	...	2137	...	2157	...	...	▬	2306	...	0003	0003
Kempten Hbf ... a.	1821	1831	1831	...	▬	1915	▬	1931	▬	2011	2031	▬	2109	...	2122	...	2153	...	2211	...	...	...	2323	...	0018	0018
Kempten Hbf ... d.	1829	1836	1834	1834	...	1916	...	1934	...	2012	2034	...	2113	...	2124	...	2155	...	2212	2212	...	...	2325	2334	...	...
Memmingen ... **937** a.	|	|	1856	1856	◧	|	...	1959	...	|	2058	...	|	...	|	...	2221	...	|	|	...	...	|	2400	...	...
Memmingen ... d.	|	|	1904	1904	1907	|	...	2004	2008	|	2105	...	|	2107	|	2208	2222	...	|	|	2307	...	|	0001	...	...
Ulm Hbf ... a.	|	|	1939	1939	|	|	...	2039	|	|	2155b	...	|	|	|	|	2315	...	|	|	|	...	|	0043	...	...
Mindelheim ... d.	|	|	▬	▬	1932	|	...	...	2030	|	...	...	|	2132	|	2233	...	...	|	|	2332	...	|	▬	...	...
Türkheim (Bay) ... d.	|	|	...	...	1946	|	...	...	2039	|	...	...	|	2146	|	2241	...	...	|	|	2346	...	|	...	...	...
Füssen ... d.	|	|	1806	...	|	|	1905	...	|	|	...	2034	|	|	|	|	...	2138	|	|	|	2238	|	...	...	...
Marktoberdorf ... d.	|	|	1850	...	|	|	1948	...	|	|	...	2117	|	|	|	|	...	2220	|	|	|	2320	|	...	...	...
Biessenhofen ... d.	|	|	1858	...	|	|	1956	...	|	|	...	2126	|	|	|	|	...	2228	2233	2233	|	2329	2351	...	...	...
Kaufbeuren ... d.	1852	1858	1903	...	|	1943	2010j	...	|	2038	...	2131	2141	|	|	|	...	2233	2238	2238	|	2334	2356	...	...	...
Buchloe ... a.	1902	1909	1914	...	1952	1954c	2022	...	2045	2048c	...	...	2153	2152c	2203c	2248	...	...	2248c	2248c	2352	...	0008	←	...	...
Buchloe ... d.	1903	1910	1919	1918	2000	1955	2024	...	2052	2052	...	...	2155	2215	2205	2251	...	...	2253	2253	→	...	0009	0011	...	...
Augsburg Hbf ... a.	1922	1930	|	1945	2029	|	2056	...	|	2121g	...	...	|	2244	|	|	...	...	2321	2321	...	...	|	0043	...	...
Nürnberg Hbf **905** ... a.	...	...	|	...	...	|	...	...	|	2232z	...	...	|	...	|	|	...	...	...	...	...	...	|	...	...	...
Kaufering ... d.	...	...	1929	...	...	2003	...	...	2101	...	...	...	2203	...	|	2301	...	...	...	...	...	...	0017	...	...	...
Geltendorf ... d.	...	...	1938	...	...	|	...	...	2110	...	...	...	|	...	|	2310	...	...	...	...	...	...	0027	...	...	...
München Pasing ... a.	...	...	1958	...	...	2033	...	...	2133	...	...	...	2233	...	|	2333	...	...	...	...	...	...	0049	...	...	...
München Hbf ... ⊡ a.	...	...	2005	...	...	2041	...	...	2141	...	...	...	2241	...	2245	2341	...	...	...	...	...	...	0057	...	...	...

R – ⑤–⑦ (also June 19).

b – 2139 on Ⓒ (also June 19).
c – Connects with train in preceding column.
e – Ⓐ (not June 19, Aug. 15).
f – 1244 on Ⓒ (also June 19).
g – 2116 on Ⓒ (also June 19, Aug. 15).
h – ⑥ (not Nov. 1).

j – Arrives 10 – 11 minutes earlier.
t – Not June 19.
w – Also June 19, Aug. 15, Nov. 1.
z – Ⓒ (also June 19, Aug. 15).

★ – Runs 11 minutes later on ⑥ (not Nov. 1). Runs 17 minutes **earlier** on Aug. 15, Oct. 3.
▶ – Attached to train in the next column at Immenstadt.

♥ – (12) and ✕ Zürich - St Gallen - Bregenz - München (Table **75**).
◧ – Conveys (12) Bad Wörishofen - Türkheim - Augsburg (see panel on page 445).
⊡ – Most trains in Table **935** use platforms 27 – 36 at München Hbf (minimum connecting time to other services is 10 minutes).

ALX – Operated by Vogtlandbahn. 🍸.

936 STUTTGART - TÜBINGEN - AULENDORF

DB (*IRE* / *RB* services); HzL

km		2Ⓐt		2Ⓐt	2Ⓒz	Ⓐt‡	Ⓐt	Ⓒz‡	Ⓐt	Ⓒz	‡		‡		‡		‡		‡		‡		‡		‡	‡
0	**Stuttgart** Hbf ... ★ d.	...	...	...	...	...	...	...	...	...	...	0816	...	1016	...	1216	...	1416	...	1616	...	1816	...	2016	...	...
57	Reutlingen ... ★ d.	...	...	...	...	...	...	...	0645	...	...	0849	...	1049	...	1249	...	1449	...	1649	...	1849	...	2049	...	...
71	**Tübingen** Hbf ... ★ d.	...	...	...	...	0546	...	0607	0656	0658	0727	0900	0928	1100	1128	1300	1328	1500	1528	1700	1728	1900	1928	2100	2135	2235
96	Hechingen ... d.	...	...	...	...	0616	...	0631	0718	0719	0753	0920	0952	1120	1152	1320	1352	1520	1552	1720	1752	1920	1952	2120	2203	2259
113	Balingen (Württ) ... d.	...	...	...	...	0639	...	0647	0733	0733	0809	0935	1007	1135	1207	1335	1407	1535	1607r	1735	1807	1935	2007	2132	2218	2314
131	Albstadt-Ebingen ... d.	...	...	...	...	0657	0701	0704	0747	0747	0832	0947	1032	1147	1232	1347	1432	1547	1632	1747	1832	1948	2032	2149	2235	2331
158	**Sigmaringen** ... a.	...	...	...	...	...	0725	...	0812	0811	0856	1011	1056	1211	1256	1411	1456	1611	1656	1811	1856	2011	2056	2210	...	...
158	**Sigmaringen** ... **938** d.	0540	...	0646	0652	...	0727	...	0813	0813	*0903*	1012	*1103*	1212	*1303*	1412	*1503*	1612	*1703*	1812	*1903*	2013	*2105*	2213	...	...
175	Herbertingen ... **938** d.	0555	...	0708j	0708	...	0743	...	0825	0825	*0917*	1025	*1117*	1225	*1317*	1424	*1517*	1625	*1717*	1825	*1917*	2027	*2121*	2230	...	...
184	Bad Saulgau ... d.	0609	...	0724j	0724j	...	...	...	0834	0834	*0929*	1034	*1129*	1234	*1329*	1433	*1529*	1634	*1729*	1834	*1929*	2036	*2137*	2239	...	...
203	**Aulendorf** ... d.	0625	...	0740	0740	...	...	...	0850	0850	*0944*	1050	*1144*	1250	*1344*	1448	*1544*	1650	*1744*	1850	*1944*	2051	*2153*	2254	...	...

	‡	Ⓐt	⑥k‡	Ⓐt‡	Ⓐt	Ⓐt‡	Ⓒz‡	2Ⓐt		‡		‡		‡		‡		‡		‡		‡	2	2		2
Aulendorf ... d.	...	...	...	...	0552	...	...	0633	0705	*0812*	0912	*1012*	1112	*1212*	1312	*1412*	1512	*1612*	1712	*1812*	1912	*2012*	2119	2203	...	2313
Bad Saulgau ... d.	...	...	...	...	0608	...	...	0650	0721	*0835*	0928	*1035*	1128	*1235*	1328	*1435*	1528	*1635*	1728	*1835*	1928	*2036*	2136	2220	...	2330
Herbertingen ... **938** d.	...	...	...	...	0617	...	...	0702	0730	*0844*	0937	*1044*	1137	*1244*	1337	*1444*	1537	*1644*	1737	*1844*	1938	*2046*	2145	2233	...	2339
Sigmaringen ... **938** a.	...	...	...	...	0630	...	...	0718	0746	*0859*	0949	*1059*	1149	*1259*	1349	*1459*	1549	*1659*	1749	*1859*	1949	*2100*	2201	2248	...	2355
Sigmaringen ... d.	...	0542	...	...	0631	...	...	...	0750	0903	0950	1103	1150	1305	1350	1503	1550	1703	1750	1905	1950	2105	...	...	...	...
Albstadt-Ebingen ... d.	0501	0605	0626	0634	0655	0703	0726	...	0812	0928	1011	1128	1211	1329	1411	1528	1611	1728	1811	1929	2011	2129	...	...	...	...
Balingen (Württ) ... d.	0519	0619	0646	0700	...	0734	0751	...	0827	0952	1027	1152	1227	1352	1427	1552	1627	1752	1827	1952	2027	2148	...	...	...	...
Hechingen ... d.	0535	0634	0701	0718	...	0752	0807	...	0839	1007	1039	1207	1239	1407	1439	1607	1639	1807	1840	2007	2039	2203	...	...	...	...
Tübingen Hbf ... ★ a.	0601	0653	0725	0743	...	0816	0830	...	0857	1030	1057	1230	1257	1430	1457	1630	1657	1830	1857	2030	2057	2226	...	...	...	...
Reutlingen ... ★ a.	...	0707	...	...	...	...	...	...	0908	...	1108	...	1308	...	1508	...	1708	...	1908	...	2108f	...	...	...	...	...
Stuttgart Hbf ... ★ a.	...	0743	...	...	...	...	...	...	0943	...	1143	...	1343	...	1543	...	1743	...	1943	...	2143f	...	...	...	...	...

Other services Stuttgart - Tübingen

km			Ⓐt	Ⓒz	Ⓐt				
0	**Stuttgart** Hbf ... **930** d.	0048	0522	*0531*	0616	0722	0822		2322
22	Plochingen ... **930** d.	0107	0541	0558	0637	0742	0844	and	2344
35	Nürtingen ... d.	0120	0552	0609	0649	0755	0855	hourly	2355
57	Reutlingen Hbf ... d.	0137	0608	0627	0706	0812	0912	until	0012
71	**Tübingen** Hbf ... a.	0150	0619	0641	0718	0823	0923		0023

		Ⓒz	Ⓐt	Ⓒz	Ⓐt		Ⓒz	Ⓐt					
Tübingen Hbf ... d.	0537	0622	0625	0732	0737	0837	0932	0937	1037		2037	2136	2236
Reutlingen Hbf ... d.	0547	0632	0636	0743	0748	0848	0943	0948	1048	and	2048	2150	2250
Nürtingen ... d.	0604	0649	0652	0759	0804	0904	0959	1004	1104	hourly	2104	2206	2306
Plochingen ... **930** d.	0618	0700	0704	0818	0818	0918	1018	1018	1118	until	2118	2218	2318
Stuttgart Hbf ... **930** a.	0638	0718	0723	0838	0838	0938	1038	1038	1138		2138	2238	2338

f – ⑤–⑦ (also June 18, 19, Oct. 2).
j – Arrives 7 minutes earlier.
k – Not Nov. 1.

r – 1612 on Ⓐ (not June 19).
t – Not June 19.
z – Also June 19.

★ – See panel below main table for other services.
‡ – Operated by Hohenzollerische Landesbahn. 2nd class only.

RE / RB services; 2nd class only — MEMMINGEN - FRIEDRICHSHAFEN and AULENDORF — 937

km		Q	Ⓐe	Ⓒz							M	
0	**Memmingen** 935 d.	...	0625	...	...	...	...	...	...	...	2005	2103
32	Leutkirch d.	...	0703	0727	...	...	...	...	...	...	2038	2140
43	Kißlegg d.	0541	0713	0742	0946	1145	1337	1546	1738	1937	2047	2149
56	Wangen (Allgäu) 935 d.	0552	0731	0754	1001	1204	1401	1601	1801	2001	2101	2200
62	Hergatz 935 d.	0557	0737	0800	1006	1209	1406	1606	1806	2006	2106	2205
85	**Lindau** Hbf 935 a.	...	0754	0817	1022	1227	1422	1623	1822	2023	2121	2222
109	**Friedrichshafen** ⊖ a.	...	0826	0907	1106	1306	1507	1707*	1907	2125	2209	2323

	Ⓐe	⑥k	M								
Friedrichshafen ⊖ d.	...	...	0623	0702e	0847	1050	1239n	1450	1650	1850	...
Lindau Hbf 935 d.	...	0602	0707	0741y	0936	1136	1336	1538	1736	1936	2310
Hergatz 935 d.	0615	0618	0724	0759	0954	1154	1354	1555	1754	1954	2327
Wangen 935 d.	0620	0623	0730	0804	1007	1207	1402	1607	1802	2002	2332
Kißlegg d.	0631	0633	0741	0816	1018	1218	1413	1618	1813	2013	2345
Leutkirch d.	0640	0642	0750	...	...	...	...	...	...	...	2354
Memmingen 935 a.	0707	0707	0813	...	...	...	...	...	...	...	...

km		Ⓐe	⑥k	L	s		Ⓒz								Ⓐe		
0	**Memmingen** d.	...	...	...	...	0900	...	1100	...	1300	...	1500	...	1700	...	1900	...
32	Leutkirch d.	0540	0622	...	...	0924	...	1124	...	1325	...	1524	...	1724	1815	1924	...
43	Kißlegg d.	0550	0636	0715	0822	0934	1026	1134	1226	1334	1426	1534	1626	1734	1827	1934	2050
63	Bad Waldsee d.	0615	0652	0736	0840	0950	1042	1150	1242	1350	1444	1550	1642	1750	1843	1950	2106
73	**Aulendorf** a.	0623	0700	0744	0848	0958	1050	1158	1250	1358	1452	1558	1650	1758	1851	1958	2114

	ⒶeJ	Ⓒz				Ⓒz	Ⓒw	Ⓐt							Ⓐe		H
Aulendorf d.	0554	0710	0757e	0906	1002	1108	1202	1202	1308	1402	1508	1602	1708	1802	1906	2004	2201
Bad Waldsee d.	0609	0718	0805e	0914	1009	1116	1209	1209	1316	1409	1516	1609	1716	1809	1914	2012	2209
Kißlegg d.	0628	0738	0825	0931	1026	1131	1226	1226	1331	1426	1531	1626	1731	1826	1931	2028	2227
Leutkirch d.	...	...	0833	...	1035	...	1235	1246	...	1435	...	1635	...	1835	...	2037	...
Memmingen a.	...	...	0859	...	1059	...	1259	1316	...	1459	...	1659	...	1859	...	2101	...

H – To Wangen (a. 2242) and Hergatz (a. 2247).
J – To Wangen (a. 0643) and Hergatz (a. 0648).
L – From Hergatz (d. 0653) and Wangen (d. 0658).
M – (12) München - Lindau and v.v. (Table 935).
Q – 12 minutes later on Ⓐe.
e – Ⓐ (not June 19).
k – Not Nov. 1.
n – 1250 on Ⓒw.
s – 3–4 minutes later on Ⓐe.
t – Not June 10–20, July 31 - Sept. 12, Oct. 27–31.
w – Ⓒ (daily June 7–22, July 31 - Sept. 14, Oct. 25 - Nov. 2).
y – 0739 on Ⓒ (also June 19).
z – Also June 19.
* – Change trains at Lindau on Ⓐ (not June 19).
⊖ – **Friedrichshafen Stadt**. See also Tables **933/9**.

DB (RE / RB services); HzL — ULM and ROTTWEIL - NEUSTADT (Schwarzw) - FREIBURG — 938

km		Ⓒz	Ⓐe	Ⓐe‡	◧	‡	Ⓐe	Ⓒz			2		2		2		2		2		2	†v2		2	
0	**Ulm** Hbf d.	...	...	...	...	...	0556	0605	...	0810	0915	1015	1115	1215	1315	1415	1515	1615	1715	1815	1915	1915	2015	2115	2217
16	Blaubeuren d.	...	...	...	...	...	0612	0617	...	0821	0927	1026	1127	1226	1327	1426	1527	1626	1727	1826	1928	1928	2027	2133	2233
34	Ehingen (Donau) d.	...	...	...	...	...	0631	0631	...	0834	0943	1039	1143	1239	1343	1439	1543	1639	1743	1839	1943	1943	2039	2152	2248
76	Herbertingen 937 d.	...	...	...	...	...	0708	0708	...	0907	1014	1107	1214	1307	1414	1507	1614	1707	1814	1907	2015	2015	2108	2227	2320
93	**Sigmaringen** 937 a.	...	...	...	...	...	0723	0723	...	0922	1029	1122	1228	1322	1428	1522	1629	1722	1828	1922	2031	2031	2126	2241	2335
93	**Sigmaringen** d.	...	...	...	...	...	0731	0728	...	0928	▬	1128	▬	1328	▬	1528k	▬	1728	▬	1928	▬	2032	▬	▬	▬
135	Tuttlingen d.	...	...	...	...	...	0818j	0812	...	1016j	...	1216j	...	1416j	...	1616j	...	1816j	...	2016j	...	2110	...	...	...
145	Immendingen 916 d.	...	...	...	...	...	0826	0824j	...	1024	...	1224	...	1424	...	1624	...	1824	...	2024	⊕‡	2118	...	Ⓐe‡	Ⓒz‡
	Rottweil d.	...	...	0557	0702	0754	|	|	0911	|	1111	|	1311	|	1511	|	1711	|	1911	|	2111	|	...	2157	2253
	Trossingen Bahnhof ▲ d.	...	...	0607	0713	0804	|	|	0920	|	1120	|	1320	|	1520	|	1720	|	1920	|	2121	|	...	2208	2304
	Villingen (Schwarzw) 916 d.	0604	0620	0628	0738	0825	|	|	0938	|	1138	|	1338	|	1538	|	1738	|	1938	|	2137	|	2215	2228	2325
164	Donaueschingen 916 a.	0614	0640	0645	0749	0841	0839	0839	0949	1037	1149	1237	1349	1437	1549	1637	1749	1837	1949	2037	...	2139	2223	2244	2341
164	Donaueschingen d.	0615	0642	...	0750	...	0848	0848	0950	1048	1150	1248	1350	1448	1550	1648	1750	1848	1950	2048	...	...	...	...	...
204	**Neustadt** (Schwarzw) a.	0652	0726	...	0826	...	0926	0926	1026	1126	1226	1325	1426	1526	1626	1726	1826	1926	2026	2126	...	...	...	...	...

km		Ⓒz2	Ⓐe2	⚒r‡	Ⓐe	Ⓐe‡	‡	Ⓐe	Ⓒz															Ⓒz‡	
0	**Neustadt** (Schwarzw) d.	...	...	...	...	0626	...	...	...	0732	0833	0933	1033	1133	1232	1331k	1433	1533	1633	1733	1833	1933	2033	...	2202
40	Donaueschingen a.	...	...	...	...	0705	...	...	...	0809	0910	1009	1110	1209	1310	1409	1510	1609	1710	1809	1910	2009	2110	...	2240
40	Donaueschingen 916 d.	...	...	0505	0515	0708	0715z	0717	0720	0810	0919	1010	1119	1210	1319	1410	1519	1610	1719	1810	1919	2010	2113	2118*	2249
54	Villingen (Schwarzw) 916 d.	...	...	0525	|	0725	0736	|	|	0822	|	1022	|	1222	|	1422	|	1622	|	1822	|	2022	2122	2141j	2307
69	Trossingen Bahnhof ▲ d.	...	...	0541	|	▬	0754	|	|	0835	|	1035	|	1235	|	1435	|	1635	|	1835	|	2035	2142e	2158	...
81	**Rottweil** a.	...	...	0551	|	...	0806	|	|	0844	|	1044	|	1244	|	1444	|	1644	|	1844	|	2044	2153e	2210	...
	Immendingen 916 d.	...	...	▬	0530	...	...	0733	0734	▬	0934	▬	1134	▬	1334	▬	1534	▬	1734	▬	1934	...	...	...	...
	Tuttlingen d.	...	...	...	0538	...	...	0751h	0747j	...	0947j	...	1147j	...	1347j	...	1547j	...	1747j	...	1947j	...	...	...	...
	Sigmaringen a.	...	...	Ⓒz2	0620	2	...	0829	0823	2	1025	2	1225	2	1425	2	1625	2	1825	2	2025	...	...	...	...
	Sigmaringen 937 d.	0525	0526	0617	0631	0727	...	0830	0830	0924	1030	1124	1230	1323	1430	1524	1630	1725	1830	1925	2032	...	...	...	...
	Herbertingen 937 d.	0539	0541	0632	0643	0743	...	0846	0846	0939	1046	1139	1246	1339	1446	1539	1646	1739	1846	1939	2047	...	...	...	...
	Ehingen (Donau) d.	0607	0612	0704	0717	0815	...	0918	0918	1012	1118	1212	1318	1412	1518	1612	1718	1812	1918	2012	2121	...	...	...	...
	Blaubeuren d.	0627	0630	0721	0732	0833	...	0930	0930	1027	1130	1227	1330	1427	1530	1627	1730	1827	1930	2027	2135	...	...	...	...
	Ulm Hbf a.	0644	0641	0738	0744	0844	...	0942	0942	1039	1142	1239	1342	1439	1542	1639	1742	1839	1942	2039	2147	...	...	...	...

km		Ⓐe	Ⓐe	⚒r	Ⓐe	Ⓐe	Ⓐe	Ⓒz	Ⓐe	Ⓒz	Ⓐe	Ⓑ												
0	**Neustadt** (Schwarzw) d.	🚌	0529	0558	🚌	0631	0642	0656	...	0708	...	0731	0801	...	0831	...	and at the same minutes past each hour until	1931	...	2031	...	2131	...	2223
	Seebrugg d.	0459	|	|	0601	|	|	|	0641	|	0705	|	|	...	|	0839		|	1939	|	2021	|	...	|
5	Titisee d.	0531	0536	0605	0633	0638	0649	0703	0708	0715	0731	0738	0808	...	0838	0908		1938	2008	2038	2048	2138	...	2230
36	**Freiburg** (Brsg) Hbf a.	...	0615	0643	...	0718	0738	0741	0748	...	...	0818	0848	...	0918	0948		2018	2048	2118	...	2218	...	2313

km		Ⓐe	Ⓐe	Ⓐe	Ⓐe	Ⓒz	Ⓒz	Ⓐe	Ⓐe											🚌				
0	**Freiburg** (Brsg) Hbf d.	...	0538	...	0640	0638	...	0710	...	0742	...	0810	0840	and at the same minutes past each hour until	1810	1840	1910	1940	2010	...	...	2110	2225	2325
31	Titisee d.	0608	0615	0630	0719	0722	0724	0749	0752	0819	...	0849	0919		1849	1919	1949	2019	2049	2055	2058	2149	2301	0001
50	**Seebrugg** a.	0633	|	0658	|	0749	|	|	0818	|	...	0916	|		1916	|	2015	|	|	2129	|	|	|	|
	Neustadt (Schwarzw) a.	...	0621	...	0725	...	0730	0755	...	0825	...	...	0925		...	1925	...	2025	2055	...	2104	2155	2307	0007

e – Ⓐ (not June 19).
h – Arrives 0740.
j – Arrives 5–7 minutes earlier.
k – 2 minutes later on Ⓒ (also June 19).
r – Not June 19, Nov. 1.
v – Also June 19, Nov. 1.
z – Ⓒ (also June 19).
* – Change trains at Villingen on † (also June 19, Nov. 1).
◧ – Change trains at Villingen on Ⓐ (not June 19).
⊕ – Runs 8–9 minutes later on Ⓐ (not June 19).
‡ – Operated by Hohenzollerische Landesbahn (HzL). 2nd class only.
▲ – Connecting services run to / from Trossingen Stadt (operated by HzL). Journey time: 5 minutes.

IRE / RB services — LINDAU - SCHAFFHAUSEN - BASEL — 939

km		①–⑤			Ⓐe	Ⓐe	Ⓒz	2	U	2	U	2	U	2	U	2	U	2	U	2		2	2	2	U2
0	**Lindau** Hbf 933 d.	...	...	...	0509	0637	0654	0701b	0834	0906	1037	1102	1237	1302	1427k	1500y	1637	1702	1837	1902	...	2012	2103	2134	2244
24	**Friedrichshafen** Stadt 933 d.	0440	...	...	0547	0702	0713	0739	0913	0938	1113	1138	1313	1338	1513	1538	1713	1738	1913	1933	...	2036	2129	2236	2333
58	Überlingen d.	0516	...	...	0624	0730	0734	0813	0935	1012	1135	1212	1335	1412	1535	1612	1735	1812	1933	2011	...	2113	2158	2316	0010
83	Radolfzell 916 d.	0540	0637	...	0650	0752	0753	0842	0953	1042	1153	1242	1353	1442	1553	1642	1753	1842	1953	2042	...	2140	2217	2341	0034
93	**Singen** 916 a.	0548	0647	...	0702	0759	0800	0856	1000	1056	1200	1256	1400	1456	1600	1656	1800	1856	2000	2056	...	2148	2232	2350	0042
		|	Ⓒz	Ⓐe		|	|	①–⑤	|	①–⑤	|	①–⑤	|	①–⑤	|	B	|	Ⓑ	|		⑥c2				
93	**Singen** 🏛 940 d.	0559	0700	0702	...	0802	0802	0902	1002	1102	1202	1302	1402	1502	1602	1702	1802	1902	2002	2102	...	2206	2236	0006	...
112	**Schaffhausen** 🏛 940 d.	0612	0715	0715	...	0815	0815	0915	1015	1115	1215	1315	1415	1515	1615	1715	1815	1915	2015	2115	...	2224	2254	0024	...
131	Erzingen (Baden) 🏛 d.	0626	0729	0729	...	0829	0829	0929	1029	1129	1229	1329	1429	1529	1629	1729	1829	1929	2029	2129	...	2306	2336	...	...
151	Waldshut d.	0641	0742	0742	...	0842	0842	0942	1042	1142	1242	1342	1442	1542	1642	1742	1842	1942	2042	2148	2258	...	...	...	...
174	Bad Säckingen d.	0654	0756	0756	...	0856	0856	0956	1056	1156	1256	1356	1456	1556	1656	1756	1856	1956	2056	2210	2320	...	...	...	...
191	Rheinfelden (Baden) d.	0704	0806	0806	...	0907	0907	1007	1107	1207	1307	1407	1507	1607	1707	1807	1907	2007	2107	2225	2335	...	...	...	...
206	**Basel** Bad Bf a.	0715	0816	0816	...	0916	0916	1016	1116	1216	1316	1416	1516	1616	1716	1816	1916	2016	2122	2240	2350	...	...	...	...

				2Ⓐe		Ⓒz	ⒸzU	ⒶeU	①–⑤	U	E	U	①–⑤	U	①–⑤	U		①–⑤	U	Ⓑ	U	Ⓑ			2
Basel Bad Bf d.	...	...	...	...	0511e	...	0614	0635	0741	0841	0941	1041	1141	1241	1341	1441	...	1541	1641	1741	1841	1941	2041	...	2152
Rheinfelden (Baden) d.	...	...	...	...	0525e	...	0628	0645	0750	0850	0950	1050	1150	1250	1350	1450	...	1550	1650	1750	1850	1950	2050	...	2206
Bad Säckingen d.	...	...	...	...	0541e	...	0644	0656	0800	0900	1000	1100	1200	1300	1400	1500	...	1600	1700	1800	1900	2000	2100	...	2222
Waldshut d.	...	...	...	...	0604	0604g	0711	0711	0814	0914	1014	1114	1214	1314	1414	1514	...	1614	1714	1814	1914	2014	2114	...	2252
Erzingen (Baden) 🏛 d.	...	...	...	0531h	0627	0627g	0728	0728	0827	0927	1027	1127	1227	1327	1427	1527	...	1627	1727	1827	1927	2027	2127	2146	2311
Schaffhausen 🏛 940 d.	...	...	0528	0559	0641	0641g	0741	0741	0841	0941	1041	1141	1241	1341	1441	1541	...	1641	1741	1841	1941	2041	2141	2230	2337
Singen 🏛 940 a.	...	...	0547	0618	0655	0655g	0755	0755	0855	0955	1055	1155	1255	1355	1455	1555	...	1655	1755	1855	1955	2055	2155	2249	...
	Ⓐe2	Ⓐe2	Ⓒz2	|		|	|	|	2d	|	2d	|	2d	|	2d	|	2	2d	|	2d	|	d		
Singen 916 d.	0423	0538	0610	0619	...	0658	0757	0757	0902	0957	1102	1157	1302	1357	1502	1557	1610	1702	1757	1902	1957	2102	2219	2302	...
Radolfzell 916 d.	0432	0546	0620	0627	...	0709	0806	0806	0914	1006	1114	1206	1314	1406	1514	1606	1618	1714	1806	1928	2006	2118	2227	2315	...
Überlingen d.	0456	0610	0644	0655	...	0740	0824	0824	0942	1024	1142	1224	1342	1424	1542	1624	1645	1742	1824	1954	2026	2141	2250	2343	...
Friedrichshafen Stadt 933 a.	0541	0648	0723	0738	...	0822	0843	0843	1021	1042	1221	1243	1421	1443	1621	1643	1722	1821	1842	2027	2045	2220	2323	0020	...
Lindau Hbf 933 a.	0621	0736	0750	0822	...	0857	0907	0907	1055	1122	1255	1351j	1455	1522	1655	1723	1751	1855	1923	2100	2127	2256	0016	...	...

B – Daily to Nov. 7; Ⓑ from Nov. 9.
E – Daily to Nov. 7; ①–⑤ from Nov. 10.
U – From / to Ulm (Table **933**).
b – 0703 on Ⓒ (also June 19).
c – Not Nov. 1.
d – Daily.
e – Ⓐ (not June 19).
g – † (also June 19, Nov. 1).
h – Not Aug. 1.
j – 1322 on Ⓒ¶.
k – 1437 on Ⓒ¶.
y – 1502 on Ⓒ¶.
z – Also June 19.
¶ – Ⓒ (daily June 7–22, July 31 - Sept. 14, Oct. 25 - Nov. 2).

940 STUTTGART - SINGEN - SCHAFFHAUSEN - ZÜRICH

km																									
		◇			IC 181	IC 181			IC 183		IC 185		IC 187		IC 281		IC 283			IC 285	IC 285				
		Ⓐe	Ⓒe	Ⓐe	E F															Ⓑq			2		
0	**Stuttgart** Hbf .... 942 d.	0516	0618	0618	0758	...	0818	0918	0953	1018	1153	1218	1353	1418	1550	1618	1750	1818	1918	1953	...	2018	...	2118	2225
26	Böblingen .... 942 d.	0538	0638	0638	|	...	0838	0938	1015	1038	1215	1238	1415	1438	1615	1638	1816	1838	1938	2015	...	2038	...	2138	2245
42	Herrenberg .... 942 d.	0547	0650	0650	|	...	0850	0948	|	1050	|	1250	|	1450	|	1650	|	1850	1948	|	...	2050	...	2148	2259
57	Eutingen im Gäu .. 942 d.	0600	0705	0705	|	...	0907	1004	|	1107	|	1307	|	1507	|	1707	|	1907	2004	|	...	2107	...	2204	2314
67	Horb .... d.	0608	0714	0717	0841	...	0917	1012	1041	1117	1241	1317	1441	1517	1641	1717	1841	1917	2012	2041	...	2117	...	2213	2322
110	Rottweil .... d.	0641	0744	0753	0910	...	0951	1047	1110	1151	1310	1351	1510	1551	1710	1751	1910	1951	2047	2110	...	2150	2156	2249z	2353
138	Tuttlingen .... d.	0722	0805	0816	0928	...	1014	...	1128	1214	1328	1414	1528	1614	1728	1814	1928	2014	...	2128	...	...	2221	▬	0014
157	Engen .... 916 d.	0737	0821	0830	|	...	1030	...	|	1230	|	1430	|	1630	|	1830	|	2030	...	|	...	...	|	...	0029
172	**Singen** .... 916 a.	0746	0833	0840	0949	...	1040	...	1149	1240	1349	1440	1549	1640	1749	1840	1949	2040	...	2149	...	...	2301n	...	0039
172	**Singen** .... 939 d.	0802	0836	0902	0957	0957	1106	...	1157	1306	1357	1506	1557	1706	1757	1906	1957	2102	...	2157	2157	...	...	2306	...
191	**Schaffhausen** 🏛 . 939 a.	0814	0854	0914	1011	1011	1124	...	1211	1324	1411	1524	1611	1724	1811	1924	2011	2114	...	2211	2211	...	...	2324	...
191	**Schaffhausen** 🏛 ... ★ d.	...	...	...	1018	1018	...	...	1218	...	1418	...	1618	...	1818	...	2018	...	...	2218	2218	...	...	2342	...
239	**Zürich** HB .... ★ a.	...	...	...	1055	1055	...	...	1255	...	1455	...	1655	...	1855	...	2055	...	...	2255	2255	...	...	0021	...

						IC 284	IC 284			IC 282		IC 280		IC 186		IC 184		IC 182		IC 180	IC 180			
	Ⓐe		Ⓐe		Ⓒz	Ⓐe	①–⑥		Ⓒz	Ⓐe								F			Ⓑq		Ⓒz	Ⓐe
Zürich HB .... ★ d.	...	...	...	...	...	...	0705	0705	...	...	0905	...	1105	...	1305	...	1505	...	1705	...	1905	1905	2005	...	...
Schaffhausen 🏛 .... ★ a.	...	...	...	...	...	...	0743	0743	...	...	0943	...	1143	...	1343	...	1543	...	1743	...	1943	1943	2043	...	...
Schaffhausen 🏛 . 939 d.	...	...	0528	...	0658	0700	0745	0745	0830	0858	0945	1030	1145	1230	1345	1430	1545	1630	1745	1830	1945	1945	2104	...	...
Singen .... 939 a.	...	...	0547	...	0718	0721	0802	0802	0849	0911	1002	1049	1202	1249	1402	1449	1602	1649	1802	1849	2002	2002	2123	...	...
Singen .... 916 d.	...	...	0551	...	0721	0726	0809	▬	0919	0919	1009	1119	1209	1319	1409	1519	1609	1719	1809	1919	...	2009	▬	2130	...
Engen .... 916 d.	...	...	0600	...	0730	0735	|	...	0928	0928	|	1128	|	1328	|	1528	|	1728	|	1928	...	|	...	2139	...
Tuttlingen .... d.	...	...	0614	...	0745	0749	0832	...	0945	0945	1032	1145	1232	1345	1432	1545	1632	1745	1832	1945	...	2032	...	2153	...
Rottweil .... d.	0503	0603	0638	0700j	0810	0810	0849	0909	1010	1010	1049	1210	1249	1410	1449	1610	1649	1810	1849	2010	...	2049	2115k	2215	...
Horb .... d.	0537	0642	0710	0740	0846	0846	0922	0945	1046	1046	1122	1246	1322	1446	1522	1646	1722	1846	1922	2046	...	2122	2151	2246	...
Eutingen im Gäu ... 942 d.	0553	0653	|	0757	0857	0857	|	0957	1057	1057	|	1257	|	1457	|	1657	|	1857	|	2057	...	|	2159	2257	2257
Herrenberg .... 942 d.	0612	0712	0727	0812	0912	0912	|	1012	1112	1112	|	1312	|	1512	|	1712	|	1912	|	2112	...	|	2212	2312	2317
Böblingen .... 942 d.	0622	0722	0736	0822	0922	0922	0948	1022	1122	1122	1148	1322	1348	1522	1548	1722	1748	1922	1948	2122	...	2148	2230	2322	2330
Stuttgart Hbf .... 942 a.	0642	0742	0757	0842	0942	0942	1010	1042	1142	1142	1210	1342	1410	1542	1610	1742	1810	1942	2010	2142	...	2210	2255	2342	2355

km										
0	**Schaffhausen** .... d.	0540	0618	and at the same	2018	2040	2140	2240	2342
28	Bülach .... d.	0600	|	minutes past	|	2100	2200	2300	0002
48	**Zürich** HB .... a.	0621	0655	each hour until	2055	2121	2221	2321	0021

Zürich HB .... d.	0605	0640	and at the same	2105	2140	2240	2340	0017
Bülach .... d.	|	0701	minutes past	|	2201	2301	0001	0040
Schaffhausen .... a.	0643	0721	each hour until	2143	2221	2321	0021	0107

E – ①–⑥ only.
F – From / to Frankfurt (Table 912).
e – Not June 19.
j – 0702 on Ⓐ (not June 19).
k – ⑥ only.
n – Change trains at Immendingen (a. 2229, d. 2236).
q – Also Nov. 29, Dec. 6, 13.
z – Ⓒ (also June 19).
◇ – Operated by Hohenzollerische Landesbahn Rottweil - Singen. 2nd class only.
★ – See panel below main table for other services.

941 TÜBINGEN - HORB - PFORZHEIM - BAD WILDBAD

RB services (2nd class only)

km		Ⓐe	Ⓐe	⑥k	Ⓐe	Ⓐe	Ⓒz				
0	**Horb** .... d.	0440	...	0600	0613	0648	0653	0753	and	1953	2151§
15	Hochdorf (b. Horb) .... d.	0451	0604	0611	0624	0659	0704	0804	hourly	2004	2220
25	Nagold .... d.	0506	0615	0622	0634	0715	0714	0814	until	2014	2235
34	Wildberg (Württ) .... d.	0514	0623	0629	0647	0722	0722	0822		2022	2243
45	Calw .... d.	0524	0633	0640	0657	0739	0732	0834		2034	2253
52	Bad Liebenzell .... d.	0532	0643	0652	0705	0750	0740	0843		2043	2300
71	**Pforzheim** Hbf .... a.	0552	0703	0712	0725	0810	0800	0905		2105	2320

	Ⓐe							A
Pforzheim Hbf .... d.	0637	0754	0849	and	1949	2049	2150	2347
Bad Liebenzell .... d.	0708j	0816	0913	hourly	2013	2110	2210	0007
Calw .... d.	0722j	0823	0922	until	2022	2117	2217	0014
Wildberg (Württ) .... d.	0734	0834	0934		2034	2127	2227	0023
Nagold .... d.	0742	0842	0942		2042	2134	2234	0030
Hochdorf (b. Horb) .... d.	0753	0853	0953		2053	2145	2253j	...
Horb .... a.	0805	0905	1005		2105	2212‡	2305	...

km		Ⓐe	Ⓐe	Ⓐe	Ⓒz		Ⓒz					Ⓐe					Ⓐe			Ⓐe			Ⓒz		
0	**Tübingen** Hbf .... d.	0535	0558	0630	0642	0805	0835	1005	1035	1204	1235	1304	1405	1435	1605	1635	1704	1803	1835	1933	2006	2035	2133	...	2236
32	**Horb** .... a.	0603	0635	0706	0711	0836	0908	1036	1107	1236	1307	1341	1436	1507	1636	1707	1741	1836	1908	2006	2036	2107	2206	...	2315

	Ⓐe		Ⓐe	Ⓒz	Ⓐe	Ⓐe	Ⓒz							Ⓐe					Ⓐe						Ⓒz
Horb .... d.	0455	...	0617	0640	0648	0730	0750	0848	0924	1048	1124	1248	1324	1417	1448	1524	1648	1724	1817	1848	1924	2048	2124	...	2249
Tübingen Hbf .... a.	0526	...	0651	0720	0727	0801	0824	0924	0954	1124	1154	1324	1354	1454	1524	1554	1724	1754	1854	1924	1954	2124	2154	...	2316

km	SEE NOTE ▶	Ⓐe	Ⓐe	⑥k						
0	**Pforzheim** Hbf .... d.	0514	0647	0647	0747	and	2147	2217	2321	0017
23	**Bad Wildbad** Bf .... d.	0545	0713	0719	0819	hourly	2219	2249	2351	0049
25	**Bad Wildbad** Kurpark a.	0547	0715	0722	0822	until	2222	2252	2353	0052

SEE NOTE ▶	Ⓐe	⚒r	Ⓐe		⊠			
Bad Wildbad Kurpark .... d.	0532	0635	0657	0735	and	2135	2245	2345
Bad Wildbad Bf .... d.	0536	0641	0701	0739	hourly	2139	2249	2351
Pforzheim Hbf .... a.	0609	0711	0732	0810	until	2210	2320	0020

A – ⑤–⑦ (also June 18, 19, Oct. 2).
e – Not June 19.
j – Arrives 8 – 10 minutes earlier.
k – Not Nov. 1.
r – Not June 19, Nov. 1.
z – Also June 19.
§ – Change trains at Eutingen im Gäu (a. 2158, d. 2208) and Hochdorf (a. 2212).
‡ – Change trains at Hochdorf (d. 2151) and Eutingen im Gäu (a. 2155, d. 2204).
⊠ – The 1235 from Bad Wildbad Kurpark runs only on Ⓒ (also June 19). See also note ▶.
▶ – S-Bahn route **S6**. Additional journeys on Ⓐe: **From Pforzheim** Hbf at 0612, 0705, 1227, 1317, 1617, 1717, 1817 and 1917. **From Bad Wildbad** Kurpark at 0505, 0601, 0805, 0905, 1215, 1305, 1605, 1705 and 1805.

942 STUTTGART - FREUDENSTADT - OFFENBURG

DB (*RE/RB* services); OSB★; 2nd class only

km					Ⓐe																		Ⓒz	Ⓐe
0	**Stuttgart** Hbf .... 940 d.	...	...	...	0518	0618	0718	0818	0918	1018	...	1118	1218	1318	1418	1518	1618	1718	1818	1918	...	2018	2118	2225	2235‡
26	Böblingen .... 940 d.	...	...	...	0538	0638	0738	0838	0938	1038	...	1138	1238	1338	1438	1538	1638	1738	1838	1938	...	2038	2138	2245	2259
42	Herrenberg .... 940 d.	...	...	...	0547	0650	0748	0850	0948	1050	...	1148	1250	1348	1450	1548	1650	1748	1850	1948	...	2050	2148	2259	2317
57	Eutingen im Gäu .. 940 d.	...	...	...	0635	0708	0808	0908	1008	1108	...	1208	1308	1408	1508	1608	1708	1808	1908	2008	...	2108	2208	2318	2333
62	Hochdorf (b. Horb) ...... d.	...	...	...	0643	0712	0812	0912	1012	1112	...	1212	1312	1412	1512	1612	1712	1812	1912	2012	...	2112	2212	2322	2337
87	**Freudenstadt** Hbf ...... a.	...	...	...	0711	0741	0841	0941	1041	1141	...	1241	1341	1441	1541	1641	1741	1841	1941	2041	...	2140	2241	2347	0001
																							▬		
	Change trains	Ⓐe	Ⓐe	⑥c							Ⓐj	Ⓒh									⑤†f	Ⓐe			
87	**Freudenstadt** Hbf .. ★ d.	0533	0640	0643	...	0743	0843	0943	1043	1143	1220	1243	1343	1443	1543	1643	1743	1843	1943	2043	...	2143	...	...	...
103	Alpirsbach .... ★ d.	0550	0657	0659	...	0759	0859	0959	1059	1159	1237	1259	1359	1459	1559	1659	1759	1859	1959	2059	...	2159	...	...	...
112	Schiltach .... ★ d.	0601	0708	0711	...	0811	0911	1011	1111	1211	1254	1311	1411	1511	1611	1711	1811	1911	2011	2111	...	2211	...	...	...
122	Wolfach .... ★ d.	0612	0719	0722	...	0822	0922	1022	1122	1222	1305	1322	1422	1522	1622	1722	1822	1922	2022	2122	...	2222	...	...	...
126	Hausach .... 916 ★ a.	0616	0723	0726	...	0826	0926	1026	1126	1226	1309	1326	1426	1526	1626	1726	1826	1926	2026	2126	2139	2226	2234	...	...
159	**Offenburg** .... 916 ★ a.	0647	0747	0754	...	0854	0954	1054	1154	1254	1340	1354	1454	1554	1654	1754	1854	1954	2054	...	2158	...	2300	...	...

		Ⓐe		Ⓐe	⑥c	Ⓐe	Ⓒz					Ⓐe	Ⓒz								Ⓐe				
Offenburg .... 916 ★ d.	...	0446	...	0558	0554	0701	0704	0804	0904	1004	1104	1159	1204	1304	1404	1504	1604	1704	1804	1904	2004	...	...	...	2226
Hausach .... 916 ★ d.	...	0521	...	0627	0631	0730	0731	0831	0931	1031	1131	1231	1231	1331	1431	1531	1631	1731	1831	1931	2031	...	...	...	2253
Wolfach .... ★ d.	...	0526	...	0632	0636	0735	0736	0836	0936	1036	1136	1236	1236	1336	1436	1536	1636	1736	1836	1936	2036	...	...	...	2258
Schiltach .... ★ d.	...	0536	...	0643	0647	0747	0747	0847	0947	1047	1147	1248	1247	1347	1447	1547	1647	1747	1847	1947	2047	...	...	...	2309
Alpirsbach .... ★ d.	...	0550	...	0700	0700	0800	0800	0900	1000	1100	1200	1300	1300	1400	1500	1600	1700	1800	1900	2000	2100	...	...	...	2321
Freudenstadt Hbf ... ★ a.	...	0607	...	0717	0717	0817	0817	0917	1017	1117	1217	1317	1317	1417	1517	1617	1717	1817	1917	2017	2117	...	...	...	2338
Change trains	Ⓐe	Ⓐe	Ⓒz	Ⓐe	Ⓒz		d						d								d		Ⓒz	Ⓐe	
Freudenstadt Hbf .... d.	0519	0615	0619	0719	0719	...	0819	0919	1019	1119	1219	...	1319	1419	1519	1619	1719	1819	1919	2019	2119	...	2219	2219	...
Hochdorf (b. Horb) .... d.	0546	0642	0645	0748	0748	...	0844	0944	1044	1148	1244	...	1344	1444	1548	1644	1744	1844	1948	2044	2151	...	2245	2245	...
Eutingen im Gäu ... 940 a.	0550	0646	0649	0753	0753	...	0849	0949	1049	1153	1249	...	1349	1449	1553	1649	1749	1849	1953	2049	2155	...	2249	2249	...
Herrenberg .... 940 a.	0609	0710	0710	0811	0811	...	0911	1011	1111	1211	1311	...	1411	1511	1611	1711	1811	1911	2011	2111	2212	2217	2311	2312	...
Böblingen .... 940 a.	0622	0722	0722	0822	0822	...	0922	1022	1122	1222	1322	...	1422	1522	1622	1722	1822	1922	2022	2122	...	2230	2322	2330	...
Stuttgart Hbf .... 940 a.	0642	0742	0742	0842	0842	...	0942	1042	1142	1242	1342	...	1442	1542	1642	1742	1842	1942	2042	2142	...	2255	2342	2355	...

c – Not Nov. 1.
d – Daily.
e – Not June 19.
f – Also June 19, Oct. 2, Nov. 1.
h – Ⓒ (daily June 7 – 22, July 31 - Sept. 14 and Oct. 25 - Nov. 2).
j – Not June 10 – 20, July 31 - Sept. 12, Oct. 27 – 31.
z – Also June 19.
‡ – Departs from the underground platforms.
★ – Freudenstadt - Offenburg operated by Ortenau-S-Bahn GmbH. Services Freudenstadt - Hausach and v.v. are Subject to alteration July 26 - Sept. 14 (trains replaced by 🚌).

KARLSRUHE - FREUDENSTADT 943

S-Bahn (2nd class only)

km		Ⓐe	Ⓐe	⑥k	Ⓐe	Ⓒz										Ⓒz		†w					
	Karlsruhe Bahnhofsvorplatz d.	0431	0509	0511	...	0611	0711z	0811z	0911	1011	1111		2011	2111	2211	2311		...	...	...	...	...	...
0	**Karlsruhe** Hbf .... 916 d.	|	|	|	0611	|	0707e	*0809*j	|	|	|		|	|	|	|		0806	1010	1210	1410	1610	1810
24	Rastatt .... 916 d.	0503	0534	0538	0634	0638	0738	0838	0938	1038	1138	and	2038	2138	2238	2338	also	0829	1029	1229	1429	1629	1829
40	Gernsbach Bf .... d.	0525	0556	0600	0655	0700	0800	0900	1000	1100	1200		2100	2200	2300	0000		0844	1044	1244	1444	1644	1844
51	Forbach (Schwarzw) .... d.	0544	0613	0618	0718	0718	0818	0918	1018	1118	1218	hourly	2118	2218	2317	0018	faster	0900	1100	1300	1500	1700	1900
61	Schönmünzach .... d.	0556	0625	0631	0729	0729	0829	0929	1029	1129	1229		2129	2229	2331	0033	trains	0911	1111	1311	1511	1711	1911
74	Baiersbronn Bf .... d.	0612	0642	0649	0749	0750	0849	0949	1049	1149	1249	until	2149	2245	2347	0050	at	0922	1122	1322	1522	1722	1922
79	**Freudenstadt** Stadt .... a.	0619	0649	0656	0756	0757	0856	0956	1056	1156	1256		2156	2253	2355	0057		0929	1129	1329	1529	1729	1929
82	**Freudenstadt** Hbf .... a.	0625	0705	0707	0807	0807	0907	1007	1112	1215	1307		2207	2258	0001	0103		0937	1137	1337	1537	1737	1937

	Ⓐe	Ⓐe	Ⓒz	Ⓐe	Ⓐe	Ⓒz	Ⓐe	Ⓒz									Ⓐe	⚒r					Ⓒz
Freudenstadt Hbf .... d.	0443	0524	0601	0613	0648	0653	0745	0753	...	0853		2053	2153	2302	...		0720	0823	1023	1223	1423	1623	1823
Freudenstadt Stadt .... d.	0449	0530	0607	0620	0654	0703	0803	0803	...	0903		2103	2203	2308	...	also	0730	0830	1030	1230	1430	1630	1830
Baiersbronn Bf .... d.	0458	0539	0616	0628	0702	0711	0811	0811	...	0911	and	2111	2211	2316	...		0738	0838	1038	1238	1438	1638	1838
Schönmünzach .... d.	0513	0555	0631	0645	0729	0729	0829	0829	...	0929		2129	2229	2332	...	faster	0749	0849	1049	1249	1449	1649	1849
Forbach (Schwarzw) .... d.	0524	0612	0643	0701	0742	0742	0842	0842	...	0942	hourly	2142	2242	2343	...	trains	0801	0901	1101	1259	1501	1701	1901
Gernsbach Bf .... d.	0541	0631	0659	0728	0800	0800	0900	0900	...	1000		2200	2300	0000	...		0815	0915	1115	1313	1515	1715	1915
Rastatt .... 916 d.	0557	0706t	0722	0754	0822	0822	0922	0922	...	1022	until	2222	2322	0022	...	at	0831	0931	1131	1331	1531	1731	1931
Karlsruhe Hbf .... 916 a.	0614	0726	|	0816	|	|	|	|	...	|		|	|	|	...		0848	0949	1148	1348	1548	1749	1949
Karlsruhe Bahnhofsvorplatz a.	...	...	0745	...	0845	0845	0945	0945	...	1045		2245	2345	0045	...		...	...	...	...	...	...	...

e – Ⓐ (not June 19).
j – Ⓐ (not June 19); change trains at Rastatt.
k – Not Nov. 1.
r – Not June 19, Nov. 1.
t – Arrives 0653.
w – Also June 19, Nov. 1.
z – Ⓒ (also June 19).

MÜNCHEN - PASSAU 944

RE services

km		Ⓐe	⚒r	Ⓐe	Ⓐe	Ⓒz											Ⓐe						Ⓒz	Ⓐe
0	**München** Hbf .... 878 d.	...	*0455*	0524	0604	0624	0724	0824	0924	1024	1124	1224	1324	1424	1524	1622	*1642*	1723	1824	1924	2024	2123	2325	2325
42	Freising .... 878 d.	...	*0518*	0549	0628	0651	0748	0848	0948	1048	1148	1248	1348	1448	1548	1648	1713	1749	1847	1948	2048	2148	2349	2349
76	Landshut (Bay) Hbf .... 878 d.	...	0543	0613	0650	0714	0809	0909	1014	1109	1212	1314	1414	1510	1613	1709	1744	1814	1910	2013	2111	2211	0013	0031j
121	Landau (Isar) .... d.	...	0625	0701v	0737	0743	0845	0944	1048	1144	1244	1343	1448	1544	1649	1744	1823	1848	1942	2045	2143	2247	0042	0101
139	Plattling .... a.	...	0640	0714	0750	0755	0857	0953	1100	1153	1256	1354	1500	1554	1700	1755	1836	1900	1954	2056	2155	2303	0054	0112
139	Plattling .... 920 d.	0600	0642	0725	0800	0802	0901	1005	1103	1205	1303	1405	1503	1605	1703	1805	...	1903	2005	2103	2157	2305	0055	0113
191	**Passau** Hbf .... 920 a.	0633	0718	0759	0833	0836	0934	1039	1138	1239	1338	1439	1538	1640	1738	1839	...	1937	2039	2139	2230	2340	0128	0147

	⚒r		Ⓐe	Ⓒz	Ⓐe																			
Passau Hbf .... 920 d.	0442	0522	0604	0627	0646	...	0725	0826	0916	1026	1116	1224	1316	1426	1516	1626	1715	1823	1916	2025	2128	...	2210	...
Plattling .... 920 a.	0514	0558	0640	0701	0720	...	0759	0859	0950	1059	1150	1259	1349	1459	1551	1659	1751	1857	1951	2058	2200	...	2244	...
Plattling .... d.	0521	0600	0642	0702	0723	...	0802	0901	1001	1102	1202	1301	1401	1502	1601	1702	1801	1902	2003	2100	2202	...	2249	...
Landau (Isar) .... d.	0533	0612	0655	0714	0735	...	0814	0913	1012	1114	1212	1313	1413	1515	1611	1714	1812	1915	2013	2112	2216	...	2301	...
Landshut (Bay) Hbf .... 878 d.	0608	0647	0726	0749	0807	...	0849	0948	1048	1147	1248	1349	1448	1547	1648	1748	1849	1949	2049	2148	2248	...	2329	2335
Freising .... 878 d.	0629	0709	0748	0810	0829	...	0910	1010	1110	1210	1310	1410	1510	1610	1710	1810	1911	2011	2110	2210	2310	...	...	2357
München Hbf .... 878 a.	0655	0736	0815	0835	0855	...	0937	1035	1135	1235	1335	1435	1535	1636	1735	1835	1935	2035	2135	2235	2336	...	...	0023

e – Not June 19, Aug. 15.
j – Arrives 0012.
r – Not June 19, Aug. 15, Nov. 1.
v – Arrives 0649.
z – Also June 19, Aug. 15.

REGENSBURG - INGOLSTADT - DONAUWÖRTH - ULM 945

agilis

km		Ⓐe		Ⓒz	Ⓐe	◇	Ⓒz	Ⓐe		Ⓒz	Ⓐe		Ⓒz	Ⓐe		Ⓒz	Ⓐe		Ⓒz	Ⓐe		Ⓒz	Ⓐe			
0	**Regensburg** Hbf ... ‡ d.	...	0452e	0557	0544	...	0759	0832	0845	1000	0945	1045	1200	1220	1245	1400	1345	1445	1600	1545	1645	1800	1745	1845	2045	2222
46	Neustadt (Donau) ... ‡ d.	...	0534e	0638	0632	0731z	0838	0906	0931	1038	1027	1131	1238	1259	1323t	1438	1427	1531	1638	1630	1731	1838	1831	1931	2128r	2302
74	**Ingolstadt** Hbf ... ‡ a.	...	0553e	0654	0651	0752z	0854	0926	0952	1054	1051	1151	1254	1317	1351	1454	1453	1551	1654	1654	1752	1854	1852	1951	2152	2323
74	**Ingolstadt** Hbf .... d.	0507	0607	0707	0702	0809	0907	0933	1002t	1107	1109	1209	1307	1323	1409	1507	1509	1609	1707	1708	1809	1907	1909	2035r	2240	2336
95	Neuburg (Donau) .... d.	0528	0626	0722	0728	0824	0922	0946	1024k	1122	1128	1224k	1322	1345	1424k	1522	1528	1624k	1722	1723	1824k	1922	1928	2052t	2258	2351
127	**Donauwörth** .... a.	0553	0653	0747	0753	0853	0947	1014	1053	1147	1153	1253	1347	1413	1453	1547	1553	1653	1747	1748	1853	1947	1953	2124	2323	0021
127	**Donauwörth** .... d.	0603	0703	0750	0803	0903	0950	1015	1103	1150	1203	1302	1350	1415	1503	1550	1603	1703	1750	1803	1901r	1950	2016	2138	2337	...
153	Dillingen (Donau) .... d.	0639	0724h	0807	0824	0924	1007	1036	1124h	1207	1224	1324h	1407	1436	1524h	1607	1624	1724h	1807	1824	1924k	2007	2040	2159h	2358	...
176	Günzburg .... 930 a.	0655	0741h	0823	0841	0942	1023	1052	1142k	1223	1241	1342h	1423	1452	1542h	1623	1641	1742k	1824	1841	1942	2023	2056	2221	0014	...
200	**Ulm** Hbf .... 930 a.	0716	0810	0845	0910	1010	1040	1114	1210	1240	1310	1410	1440	1514	1610	1640	1710	1810	1844	1910	2010	2040	2115	*2302*	0033	...

	Ⓐe	Ⓐe		Ⓐe	Ⓒz		Ⓐe	Ⓒz		Ⓐe	Ⓒz		Ⓐe	Ⓒz		Ⓐe	Ⓒz		Ⓐe	Ⓒz		Ⓐe	Ⓒz	Ⓐe		
Ulm Hbf .... 930 ◐ d.	0450	0533	0555z	*0630*	0718	0745	0831	0918	0944	1044	1118	1142r	1231	1318	1344	1444	1518	1544	1644	1718	1744	1831	1918	1944	1944z	*2221*
Günzburg .... 930 ◐ d.	0509	0551	0614z	*0650*	0736	0804	0851	0936	1004	1114	1136	1204	1251	1336	1404	1514	1536	1604	1714	1736	1804	1851	1936	2005	2004z	*2243*
Dillingen (Donau) ..... ◐ d.	0524	0607	0631z	*0707*	0752	0829	0907	0952	1022t	1130	1152	1229	1307	1352	1422t	1530	1552	1629	1730	1752	1829	1907	1952	2021	2029z	2301
Donauwörth .... ◐ a.	0545	0629	0653z	*0730*	0812	0850	0927	1013	1050	1153	1212	1251	1328	1412	1450	1553	1612	1651	1754	1812	1851	1927	2012	2042	2051z	2323
Donauwörth .... d.	0554	0631	0701	0807	0814	0859t	0928	1014	1101	1202	1214	1302	1328	1414	1502	1602	1615	1702	1800	1814	1902	1940	2014	2043	2138	2338
Neuburg (Donau) .... d.	0627	0704	0730r	0837	0837	0928r	1002	1037	1130r	1229	1237	1328t	1404	1437	1530r	1630	1637	1733	1829	1837	1929r	2008	2037	2108	2205	0004
Ingolstadt Hbf .... a.	0648	0723	0748	0853	0851	0949	1023	1051	1149	1248	1251	1349	1426	1451	1549	1647	1651	1750	1849	1851	1949	2022	2056	2125	2222	0021
Ingolstadt Hbf .... ‡ d.	0705	0730	0805	0905	0905	1005	1032	1105	1205	1318	1305	1405	1432	1505	1605	1705	1705	1805	1906	1905	2005	2030	2105	*2206*	...	...
Neustadt (Donau) ..... ‡ d.	0729	0752	0827	0927	0921	1027	1048	1121	1227	1339	1321	1427	1449	1521	1627	1727	1721	1827	1927	1921	2027	2047	2121	*2227*	...	...
Regensburg Hbf ..... ‡ a.	0811	0835	0910	1010	0953	1110	1131	1155	1310	1421	1355	1510	1533	1555	1711	1810	1754	1910	2010	1954	2110	2129	2156	*2312*	...	...

– Ⓐ (not June 19, Aug. 15).
– 5–7 minutes later on Ⓐ (not June 19, Aug. 15).
– 2–4 minutes later on Ⓐ (not June 19, Aug. 15).
– 2–4 minutes later on Ⓒ (also June 19, Aug. 15).
– 5–9 minutes later on Ⓒ (also June 19, Aug. 15).
– Ⓒ (also June 19, Aug. 15).

◇ – On Ⓐ**e**: Ingolstadt d. 0807, Neuburg d. 0826, Donauwörth d. 0901, Dillingen d. 0930, Günzburg a. 0947, Ulm a. 1010.

‡ – **Additional journeys** Regensburg - Neustadt (Donau) - Ingolstadt and v.v.
From Regensburg Hbf at 0609 Ⓐ**e**, 0713 Ⓐ**e**, 0745 Ⓐ**e**, 1145 Ⓐ**e**, 1614 Ⓐ**e**, 1727 Ⓐ**e** and 1945 Ⓐ**e**.
From Ingolstadt Hbf at 0520 Ⓐ**e**, 0600 Ⓐ**e**, 0605 Ⓒ**z**, 0627 Ⓐ**e**, 1106 Ⓐ**e**, 1506 Ⓐ**e**, 1622 Ⓐ**e** and 2206 Ⓒ**z**.

◐ – **Additional journey** on Ⓐ**e**: Ulm Hbf d. 2044 → Günzburg d. 2115 → Dillingen d. 2132 → Donauwörth a. 2153.
Additional journey (daily): Ulm Hbf d. 2255 → Günzburg d. 2318 → Dillingen d. 2334 → Donauwörth a. 2400.

KÖLN - GEROLSTEIN - TRIER 946

RE / RB services — *Subject to alteration from July 25*

km				⊡			⑥v		†w				⑥v		†w			Ⓒz	Ⓐe				Ⓒz	†w	⚒r		
0	**Köln** M/Deutz . d.	...	...	0605	0715h	0815h	0855	0915	0955	1015	1115	1215	1255	1315	1355	1415	1515	1615	1615	1715	1815	1915	1959	2005	2015	2105	2205
1	**Köln** Hbf .... d.	...	...	0611	0721h	0821h	0905	0921	1005	1021	1121	1221	1305	1321	1405	1421	1521	1621	1621	1721	1821	1921	2005	2011	2027	2111	2211
41	Euskirchen ...... d.	...	...	0656	0800	0900	0943	1000	1043	1100	1200	1300	1341	1400	1441	1500	1600	1700	1700	1800	1900	2000	2041	2100	2110	2200	2300
56	Mechernich ...... d.	...	...	0707	0811	0909	0952	1011	1052	1109	1211	1309	|	1411	|	1509	1611	1709	1709	1811	1909	2011	|	2111	2121	2211	2311
65	Kall .... d.	...	...	0716	0819	0917	1000	1019	1100	1117	1219	1317	1359	1419	1459	1517	1619	1717	1717	1819	1917	2019	2059	2120	2132	2220	2320
81	Blankenheim ... d.	...	...	0732	0835	0932	|	1035	|	1132	1235	1332	|	1435	|	1532	1635	1732	1732	1835	1932	2035	|	2136	2149	2236	2336
94	Jünkerath .... d.	0539v	0654e	0745	0846	0946	|	1046	|	1146	1246	1346	|	1446	|	1546	1646	1746	1746	1846	1946	2046	|	2150	2203	2250	2350
113	**Gerolstein** ...... a.	0555v	0710e	0802	0902	1002	1034	1101	1134	1202f	1302	1402	1434	1502	1534	1602	1702	1758	1802	1902	2002	2102	2134	2214	2223	2307	0007
113	**Gerolstein** ...... d.	0559	0712g	0803	0902	1003	1035	1101j	1135	1203f	1303	1403	1435	1503	1535	1603	1703	1759	1803	1903	2003	2103	2135	2229	2229	...	...
143	Bitburg-Erdorf.. d.	0633	0758	0841	0941	1041	1100	1133j	1159	1241f	1341	1441	1500	1541	1600	1641	1741	1833	1841	1941	2041	2141	2200	2300	2300	...	...
182	**Trier** Hbf .... a.	0718	0839	0927	1027	1127	1140	1227	1240	1327	1427	1527	1540	1627	1640	1727	1826	1927	1927	2026	2127	2227	2240	2347	2347	...	...

	⚒r	⚒r	Ⓐe	Ⓒz	Ⓐe	Ⓒz	⑥v		†w				⑥v		†w							Ⓒz	Ⓐe				
ier Hbf .... d.	...	...	...	0541	0556	0623v	0726	0731	0826	0835	0935	1035	1126	1135	1226	1235	1335	1435	1535	1632	1735	1826	...	1831	1935	2031	2235
burg-Erdorf ... d.	...	...	...	0615	0658	0710v	0757	0817	0857	0917	1018	1117	1157	1218	1258	1317	1418	1517	1618	1717	1818	1857	...	1917	2018	2117	2321
erolstein .... a.	...	...	...	0647	0732	0746v	0821	0854	0921	0953	1053	1153	1221	1253	1322	1353	1453	1553	1653	1753	1853	1921	...	1953	2053	2153	2355
erolstein .... d.	0445	0549	0644	0650	0736	0756	0822	0856	0922	0956	1056	1156	1222	1256	1323	1356	1456	1556	1656	1756	1856	1922	1923	1956	2056	2156	0001
nkerath .... d.	0502	0606	0709	0709	0813b	0813	|	0913	|	1013	1113	1213	|	1313	|	1413	1513	1613	1713	1813	1913	|	1945	2009	2113	2217	0018
ankenheim ..... d.	0516	0620	0725	0725	0826	0826	|	0926	|	1026	1126	1226	|	1326	|	1426	1526	1626	1726	1826	1926	|	1958	2023	...	2231	...
ll .... d.	0533	0636	0740	0740	0841	0841	0859	0940	0959	1041	1140	1241	1259	1340	1359	1441	1540	1641	1740	1841	1940	1959	2012	2039	...	2247	...
echernich .... d.	0541	0645	0748	0748	0848	0848	0906	0948	1006	1048	1148	1248	1306	1348	1406	1448	1548	1648	1748	1848	1948	2006	2019	2047	...	2256	...
skirchen .... d.	0557	0657	0802	0802j	0902	0902j	0917	1002	1017	1102	1202	1300	1317	1400	1417	1502	1602	1702	1802	1902	2002	2017	2030	2107	...	2307	...
öln Hbf .... a.	0639	0739	0839	0839j	0939	0939j	0952	1039	1052	1139	1239	1339	1352	1439	1452	1539	1639	1739	1839	1939	2039k	2052	2112	2151	...	2351	...
öln M/Deutz ... a.	0644	0745	0845	0845j	0945	0945j	0957	1044	1057	1144	1244	1344	1357	1444	1457	1544	1644	1744	1845	1944	2044k	2057	2117	2157	...	2357	...

– Arrives 0753.
– Ⓐ (not June 19).
– On † (also June 19, Nov. 1) Gerolstein a. 1158, d. 1159, Bitburg d. 1233.
g – 0719 on ⑥ (not Nov. 1); 0724 on † (also June 19, Nov. 1).
h – 10 minutes **earlier** on † (also June 19, Nov. 1).
j – 2–12 minutes later on † (also June 19, Nov. 1).
k – 5 minutes later on ⑥ (not Nov. 1).
r – Not June 19, Nov. 1.
v – ⑥ (not Nov. 1).
w – Also June 19, Nov. 1.
z – Also June 19.
⊡ – On ⑥ (not Nov. 1) Euskirchen - Jünkerath timings are 4–5 minutes later. On † (also June 19, Nov. 1) Gerolstein d. 0802, Bitburg d. 0833.

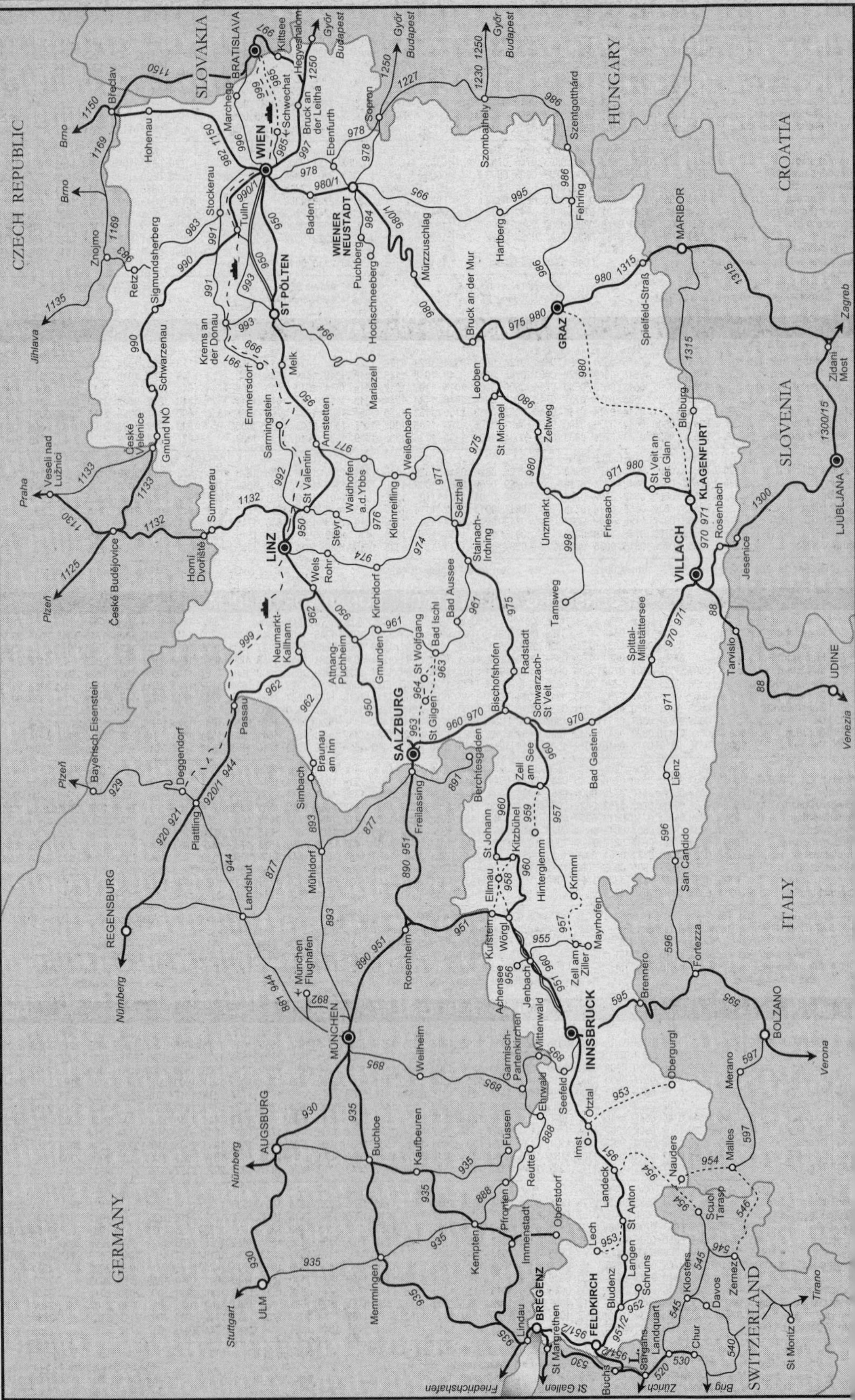

A list of Scenic Rail Routes appears elsewhere in the timetable – see Contents page

AUSTRIA

Operator: Except where otherwise stated, rail services are operated by Österreichische Bundesbahnen (**ÖBB**) www.oebb.at

Timings: **Valid until Dec. 13, 2014**. unless stated otherwise in individual tables. See page 2 for public holiday dates.

Services: Trains convey both first- and second-class seating unless footnotes show otherwise or there is a '2' in the train column. Overnight sleeping car (🛏) or couchette (▬) trains do not necessarily convey seating accommodation - refer to individual footnotes for details. Descriptions of sleeping and couchette cars appear on page 8.

Train categories:

RJ	**Railjet**	Austrian high-speed train. Conveys first and economy (2nd) class. *Business class* also available to first class ticket holders (supplement payable).
ICE	**InterCity Express**	German high-speed train.
EC	**EuroCity**	International express train.
IC	**InterCity**	Internal or international express train.
D	**Schnellzug**	Ordinary fast train.
EN	**EuroNight**	(also *CNL*) Overnight express train. Special fares payable.
WB	**Westbahn**	Wien - Linz - Salzburg private operator (special fares – ÖBB tickets are not valid).
REX	**Regional Express**	Semi-fast regional train.
	Regional / S-Bahn	Local stopping trains – no category or train number shown.

Reservations: Seats may be reserved on all express trains (*RJ, ICE, ÖEC/EC, IC, CNL, EN, D*).

Catering: Three types of catering are indicated in the tables: ✕ – Restaurant car; ⊗ – Bordbistro; 🍷 – At seat trolley service.

WIEN - LINZ - SALZBURG 950

km		⚒ 2	2 S	*EC* 390 ①–⑥ F⊗	⚒ 2	*RJ* 364 ①–⑥ e✕	Ⓐ 2	*WB* 900 ⚒ ★🍷	*IC* 540 🍷	*RJ* 660 ✕	*RJ* 260 ✕	*WB* 902 ★🍷	*ICE* 228 Q✕	*IC* 542 🍷	*RJ* 160 ✕	*RJ* 560 ✕	*WB* 904 ★🍷	*IC* 860 ✕	*RJ* 262 ✕	*WB* 906 ★🍷	*ICE* 28 Q✕	*IC* 690 V🍷	5914 P 2	*RJ* 162 B✕	*RJ* 562 ①–⑥ h✕
0	**Wien** Westbahnhof d.	...	...	...	...	0530	...	0540	0556	0630	0630	0640	0652	0656	0730	0730	0740	0748	0830	0840	0852	0856	...	0930	0930
6	**Wien** Hütteldorf ● d.	...	...	...	...	|	...	0546	0604	|	|	0646	|	0704	|	|	0746	0756	|	0846	|	0904	...	|	|
30	Tullnerfeld 993 d.	...	...	...	...	|	...	|	0616	|	|	|	|	0716	|	|	|	0809	|	|	|	0916	...	|	|
60	**St Pölten** Hbf 993 d.	...	...	...	0432	0556	...	0608	0632	0656	0656	0708	0721	0732	0756	0756	0808	0826	0856	0908	0921	0932	0859	0956	0956
120	Amstetten d.	...	*0429*	...	0535	|	0613	0633	0700	|	|	0733	|	0800	|	|	0833	0857	|	0933	|	1000	0946	|	|
157	St Valentin 976 d.	...	0512	...	0610	|	0635	|	0716	|	|	|	|	0816	|	|	|	0915	|	|	|	1016	1016	|	|
182	**Linz** Hbf 976 a.	...	0537	...	0635	0645	0651	0659	0730	0745	0745	0759	0815	0830	0845	0845	0859	0930	0945	0959	1015	1030	1035	1045	1045
182	**Linz** Hbf 962 d.	0504	0544	0632	...	0647	0658	0700	0732	0747	0747	0800	0817	0832	0847	0847	0900	0932	0947	1000	1017	1032	1038	1047	1047
207	**Wels** Hbf 962 d.	0521	0612	0645	...	|	0723	0713	0745	|	|	0813	0832	0845	|	|	0913	0945	|	1013	1032	1045	1055	|	|
	Passau Hbf 962 ⊞ a.	|	0730	|	...	|	0836	|	|	|	|	|	0918	|	|	|	|	|	|	|	1118	|	1156	|	|
237	Attnang-Puchheim d.	0544	...	0700	...	|	...	0727	0800	|	|	0827	...	0900	|	|	0927	1001	|	1027	...	1100	...	|	|
242	Vöcklabruck d.	0549	...	0706	...	|	...	|	0806	|	|	|	...	0906	|	|	|	1007	|	|	...	1106	...	|	|
307	**Salzburg** Hbf a.	0648	...	0748	...	0752	...	0810	0848	0852	0852	0910	...	0948	0952	0952	1010	1048	1052	1110	...	1148	...	1152	1152
	München Hbf 890 a.	...	...	0941	...	|	...	...	...	|	1025	...	...	|	|	|	...	|	1225	...	...	...	...	|	|
	Innsbruck Hbf 951 a.	...	...	...	...	0938	...	...	...	1054	...	...	...	1336z	1138	1138	...	1256	...	...	...	...	...	1340	1340
	Zürich HB 520 a.	...	...	...	...	1320	...	...	...	...	...	...	...	...	1520	|	...	|	...	...	...	...	...	1720	|
	Bregenz 951 a.	...	...	...	...	...	...	...	...	...	...	...	...	...	...	1417	...	1547	...	...	...	...	...	...	1617

	WB 908 ★🍷	*IC* 546 ◇ 🍷	*RJ* 60 B✕	*RJ* 862 ✕	*WB* 910 ★🍷	*ICE* 26 R✕	*IC* 548 🍷	*RJ* 564 ✕	*WB* 912 ★🍷	*IC* 864 🍷	*RJ* 62 B✕	*WB* 914 ★🍷	*ICE* 90 E✕	*IC* 642 🍷	*RJ* 166 ✕	*RJ* 566 ✕	*WB* 916 ★🍷	*IC* 866 🍷	*RJ* 64 B✕	*WB* 918 ★🍷	*ICE* 22 R✕	*IC* 692 K🍷	*RJ* 168 ✕	*WB* 920 ★🍷	*IC* 644 🍷
Wien Westbahnhof d.	0940	0956	1030	1030	1040	1052	1056	1130	1140	1156	1230	1240	1252	1256	1330	1330	1340	1356	1430	1440	1452	1456	1530	1540	1556
Wien Hütteldorf ● d.	0946	1004	|	|	1046	|	1104	|	1146	1204	|	1246	|	1304	|	|	1346	1404	|	1446	|	1504	|	1546	1604
Tullnerfeld 993 d.	|	1016	|	|	|	|	1116	|	|	1216	|	|	|	1316	|	|	|	1416	|	|	|	1516	|	|	1616
St Pölten Hbf 993 d.	1008	1032	1056	1056	1108	1121	1132	1156	1208	1232	1256	1308	1321	1332	1356	1356	1408	1432	1456	1508	1521	1532	1556	1608	1632
Amstetten d.	1033	1100	|	|	1133	|	1200	|	1233	1300	|	1333	|	1400	|	|	1433	1500	|	1533	|	1600	|	1633	1700
St Valentin 976 d.	|	1116	|	|	|	|	1216	|	|	1316	|	|	|	1416	|	|	|	1516	|	|	|	1616	|	|	1716
Linz Hbf 976 a.	1059	1130	1145	1145	1159	1215	1230	1245	1259	1330	1345	1359	1415	1430	1445	1445	1459	1530	1545	1559	1615	1630	1645	1659	1730
Linz Hbf 962 d.	1100	1132	1147	1147	1200	1217	1232	1247	1300	1332	1347	1400	1417	1432	1447	1447	1500	1532	1547	1600	1617	1632	1647	1700	1732
Wels Hbf 962 d.	1113	1145	|	|	1213	1232	1245	|	1313	1345	|	1413	1432	1445	|	|	1513	1545	|	1613	1632	1645	|	1713	1745
Passau Hbf 962 ⊞ a.	|	|	|	|	|	1318	|	|	|	|	|	|	1518	|	|	|	|	|	|	|	1718	|	|	|	|
Attnang-Puchheim d.	1127	1200	|	|	1227	...	1300	|	1327	1400	|	1427	...	1500	|	|	1527	1600	|	1627	...	1700	|	1727	1800
Vöcklabruck d.	|	1206	|	|	|	...	1306	|	|	1406	|	|	...	1506	|	|	|	1606	|	|	...	1706	|	|	1806
Salzburg Hbf a.	1210	1248	1252	1252	1310	...	1348	1352	1410	1448	1452	1510	...	1548	1552	1552	1610	1648	1652	1710	...	1748	1752	1810	1848
München Hbf 890 a.	...	...	1425	|	...	...	...	|	...	|	1632	...	...	...	|	|	...	|	1825	...	...	...	|	...	...
Innsbruck Hbf 951 a.	...	...	...	1454	...	...	...	1539	...	1654	...	...	...	...	1738	1738	...	1854	...	...	...	...	1940	...	...
Zürich HB 520 a.	...	...	...	...	...	...	...	...	...	|	...	...	...	...	2120	|	...	...	...	...	...	...	2320	...	...
Bregenz 951 a.	...	...	...	...	...	...	...	...	...	1923	...	...	...	...	...	2017	...	...	...	...	...	...	...	...	...

	RJ 66 C✕	*RJ* 868 ✕	*WB* 922 ★🍷	*ICE* 20 Q✕	*IC* 646 🍷	*RJ* 662 ✕	*WB* 924 ★🍷	*IC* 648 🍷	*RJ* 68 B✕	*RJ* 762 Ⓑq ✕	*WB* 926 ★🍷	*IC* 744 N🍷	*RJ* 764 ✕	*WB* 928 ★🍷	*WB* 928 ⑤⑥† ★🍷	*IC* 746 🍷	*EN* 490 H	*RJ* 42 B✕	*WB* 930 † ★🍷	2	*EN* 944 A	*IC* 748 🍷	*EN* 466 G	*EN* 246 ♥	*EN* 462 🅁 D
Wien Westbahnhof d.	1630	1630	1640	1652	1656	1730	1740	1756	1830	1830	1840	1856	1930	1940	1940	1956	2000	2030	2040	...	2056	2156	2240	2256	...
Wien Hütteldorf ● d.	|	|	1646	|	1704	|	1746	1804	|	|	1846	1904	|	1946	1946	2004	2009	|	2046	...	2104	2204	|	|	0011
Tullnerfeld 993 d.	|	|	|	|	1716	|	|	1816	|	|	|	1916	|	|	|	2016	|	|	|	...	2117	2216	|	|	|
St Pölten Hbf 993 d.	1656	1656	1708	1721	1732	1756	1808	1832	1856	1856	1908	1932	1956	2008	2008	2032	2037	2056	2108	...	2134	2232	2309	2332	0053
Amstetten d.	|	|	1733	|	1800	|	1833	1900	|	|	1933	2000	|	2033	2033	2100	2110	|	2133	...	2205	2300	|	0008	|
St Valentin 976 d.	|	|	|	|	1816	|	|	1916	|	|	|	2016	|	|	|	2116	2134	|	|	...	2223	2316	|	0030	|
Linz Hbf 976 a.	1745	1745	1759	1815	1830	1845	1859	1930	1945	1945	1959	2030	2045	2059	2059	2130	2150	2145	2159	...	2238	2330	0002	0045	0158
Linz Hbf 962 d.	1747	1747	1800	1817	1832	1847	1900	1932	1947	1947	2000	2032	2047	...	2100	2132	2152	2147	...	2204	2240	...	0005	0048	0201
Wels Hbf 962 d.	|	|	1813	1832	1845	|	1913	1945	|	|	2013	2045	|	...	2113	2145	2209	|	...	2227	2253	...	0018	0105	0218
Passau Hbf 962 ⊞ a.	|	|	|	1918	|	|	|	|	|	|	|	|	|	...	|	|	2304	|	...	|	|	...	|	|	|
Attnang-Puchheim d.	|	|	1827	...	1900	|	1927	2000	|	|	2027	2100	|	...	2127	2200	...	|	...	2255	2308	...	|	0124	0238
Vöcklabruck d.	|	|	|	...	1906	|	|	2006	|	|	|	2106	|	...	|	2206	...	|	...	...	2314	...	|	|	|
Salzburg Hbf a.	1852	1852	1910	...	1948	1952	2010	2048	2052	2052	2110	2148	2152	...	2210	2248	...	2252	...	...	2356	...	0116	0212	0326
München Hbf 890 a.	2025	|	...	...	...	|	...	...	2226	|	...	...	|	...	...	...	...	...	...	...	...	...	|	|	0610
Innsbruck Hbf 951 a.	...	2055	...	...	...	2138	...	...	...	2258	...	...	2352	...	...	...	...	...	...	...	...	...	0335	0519	...
Zürich HB 520 a.	...	...	...	...	...	|	...	...	...	...	...	...	...	...	...	...	...	...	...	...	...	...	0720	|	...
Bregenz 951 a.	...	...	...	...	...	0010	...	...	...	...	...	...	...	...	...	...	...	...	...	...	...	...	...	0823	...

Regional trains WIEN - MELK - AMSTETTEN - ST VALENTIN (2nd class only)

km		⚒	ⒶT	⚒			Ⓐ		P							Ⓐt		Ⓐt		Ⓐt		Ⓐt			
0	**Wien** Westbahnhof d.	...	0412	*0442*	0600	...	0700	*0716*	...	0900	1100	1200	1300	1400	1500	1608	1600	1708	1700	1808	1800	1908	1900	2104	0000
6	**Wien** Hütteldorf ● d.	...	0419	*0451*	0608	...	0708	*0723*	...	0908	1108	1208	1308	1408	1508	1616	1608	1716	1708	1816	1808	1916	1908	2112	0013
61	**St Pölten** Hbf a.	...	0519	*0552*	0651	...	0751	*0823*	...	0951	1151	1251	1351	1451	1551	1643	1651	1743	1751	1843	1851	1943	1951	2214	0103
61	**St Pölten** Hbf d.	0432	0521	0559	0659	0735	0759	0835	0859	0959	1159	1259	1359	1459	1559	1645	1659	1745	1759	1845	1859	1945	1959	2235	0105
85	Melk d.	0456	0541	0621	0721	0758	0819	0858	0915	1019	1219	1319	1419	1519	1619	1703	1719	1803	1819	1903	1919	2003	2019	2259	0125
94	Pöchlarn d.	0504	0548	0629	0729	0808	0826	0905	0923	1027	1227	1327	1427	1527	1627	1711	1727	1811	1827	1911	1927	2011	2027	2306	0132
107	Ybbs an der Donau d.	0516	0557	0642	0742	0826	0837	...	0932	1042	1242	1342	1442	1542	1642	1725	1742	1825	1842	1925	1940	2025	2042	2318	0140
124	Amstetten a.	0528	0608	0653	0753	0838	0848	...	0944	1053	1253	1353	1453	1553	1653	1737	1753	1837	1853	1937	1951	2037	2053	2330	0151
163	**St Valentin** a.	0608	*0630*	0739	0839	...	0939	...	1013	1139	1339	1439r	1539	1639r	1739	1809	1839r	1909	1939	2009	2039r	...	...	...	...

– [12] Wien - Salzburg; conveys 🛏 1, 2 cl., ▬ 2 cl. and [2] (*EN* **237**) Wien - Villach - Tarvisio ⊞ - Venezia

– From Budapest (Table **1250**).

– [12] and ✕ Budapest - München (- Frankfurt ⑤⑥ **m**).

– KÁLMÁN IMRE – 🛏 1, 2 cl., ▬ 2 cl. and [2] Budapest - München.

– [12] and ✕ Wien - Nürnberg - Hannover - Hamburg.

– ①–⑥ (not Apr. 21, June 9). [12] and ⊗ Linz - München - Stuttgart - Frankfurt.

– 🛏 1, 2 cl., ▬ 2 cl. and [2] Budapest - Wien - Zürich.

– HANS ALBERS – 🛏 1, 2 cl., ▬ 2 cl. and [2] Wien - Hannover - Hamburg; conveys 🛏 1, 2 cl., ▬ 2 cl. and [2] (*EN* **420**) Wien - Frankfurt - Köln. 🅁 for journeys to Germany.

– To Klagenfurt (Table **970**).

N – Conveys [2] Wien - Salzburg (**1516**) - Saalfelden (Table **960**).

P – May 1 - Oct. 26. [2] Wien Franz-Josefs-Bf (d. 0728) - Passau. *Einfach-Raus-Ticket* not valid.

Q – [12] and ✕ Wien - Nürnberg - Frankfurt.

R – [12] and ✕ Wien - Nürnberg - Frankfurt - Köln - Dortmund.

S – From Garsten (Table **976**).

T – To Kleinreifling (Table **977**).

V – To Villach (Table **970**).

e – Not Apr. 21, June 9, Dec. 8.

h – ①–⑥ (daily Feb. 3 - Apr. 26 and from Nov. 3; also June 8; not Apr. 17, 21, May 28, June 6, 9).

m – Also Apr. 17, 20, 30, May 28, June 8, 18, Oct. 2.

q – Not Apr. 20, June 8.

r – ⚒ only.

t – Also calls at Tullnerfeld (13 minutes after Wien Hütteldorf; via high-speed line).

z – Ⓒ only. Via Zell am See (Table **960**).

♥ – Conveys 🛏 1, 2 cl., ▬ 2 cl. and [2].

◇ – On Ⓒ conveys [12] Wien - Attnang-Puchheim - Stainach-Irdning (Table **961**).

★ – Operated by *Westbahn*. Special fares payable (ÖBB tickets **not** valid).

● – See note on page 452.

950 SALZBURG - LINZ - WIEN

	EN 463	WB 901	EN 247	IC 821	WB 903	EN 467	IC 823	EN 945	EN 491	WB 905	RJ 767	IC 541	WB 907	RJ 49	IC 543	WB 909	RJ 765	RJ 265	IC 545	WB 911	RJ 61	IC 861	WB 913	RJ 663	IC 693
	Ⓡ	Ⓐ			⚒		Ⓐ			⚒				①–⑥				①–⑥	⊖						
	D	★🍷	♥	🍷	★🍷	G	🍷	A	H	★🍷	✕	🍷	★🍷	N✕	🍷	★🍷	✕	d✕	🍷	★🍷	B✕	🍷	★🍷	✕	K🍷
Bregenz **951** d.	...	...	2146	...	...	...	...	...	...	...	...	...	...	...	...	...	...	...	...	...	...	...	...	0547	...
Zürich HB **520** d.	...	...	|	...	...	2240	...	...	...	...	...	...	...	...	...	...	...	...	...	...	...	...	...	|	...
Innsbruck Hbf **951** d.	...	...	0044	...	...	0221	...	...	...	...	...	...	...	0505	...	...	0609	...	...	...	...	0705	...	0820	...
München Hbf **890** d.	2340	...	|	...	...	|	...	...	...	...	...	...	...	|	...	...	|	0624	...	...	0731	|	...	|	...
Salzburg Hbf d.	0213	...	0341	...	...	0434	...	0505	...	0550	0604	0612	0650	0708	0712	0750	0808	0808	0812	0850	0908	0912	0950	1008	1012
Vöcklabruck d.	|	...	|	...	...	|	...	0547	...	|	|	0654	|	|	0754	|	|	|	0854	|	|	0954	|	|	1054
Attnang-Puchheim d.	0304	...	0432	...	...	|	...	0553	...	0634	0650	0700	0734	|	0800	0834	|	|	0900	0934	|	1000	1034	|	1100
Passau Hbf **962** 🛃 d.	|	...	|	...	...	|	...	|	0535	|	|	|	|	|	|	|	|	|	|	|	|	|	|	|	|
Wels Hbf **962** d.	0323	...	0451	...	...	0537	...	0610	0632	0648	|	0715	0748	|	0815	0848	|	|	0915	0948	|	1015	1048	|	1115
Linz Hbf **962** a.	0338	...	0507	...	...	0552	...	0624	0647	0659	0713	0727	0759	0813	0827	0859	0913	0913	0927	0959	1013	1027	1059	1113	1127
Linz Hbf **976** d.	0340	0500	0510	0530	0600	0604	0608	0628	0650	0700	0715	0730	0800	0815	0830	0900	0915	0915	0930	1000	1015	1030	1100	1115	1130
St Valentin **976** d.	0359	|	0528	0546	|	|	0625	0644	0708	|	|	0746	|	|	0846	|	|	|	0946	|	|	1046	|	|	1146
Amstetten d.	0422	0527	0550	0602	0627	|	0642	0702	0734	0727	|	0802	0827	|	0902	0927	|	|	1002	1027	|	1102	1127	|	1202
St Pölten Hbf **993** d.	0500	0552	0633	0630	0652	0701	0710	0733	0811	0752	0805	0830	0852	0905	0930	0952	1005	1005	1030	1052	1105	1130	1152	1205	1230
Tullnerfeld **993** a.	|	|	|	0643	|	|	0723	0748	|	|	|	0843	|	|	0943	|	|	|	1043	|	|	1143	|	|	1243
Wien Hütteldorf ● a.	0545	0615	0700	0655	0715	0724	0735	0801	0835	0815	|	0855	0915	|	0955	1015	|	|	1055	1115	|	1155	1215	|	1255
Wien Westbahnhof a.	...	0622	0708	0704	0722	0734	0744	0810	0844	0822	0830	0904	0922	0930	1004	1022	1030	1030	1104	1122	1130	1204	1222	1230	1304

	ICE 21	WB 915	RJ 863	RJ 63	IC 549	WB 917	RJ 161	IC 641	ICE 23	WB 919	RJ 65	IC 865	WB 921	RJ 563	IC 643	ICE 91	WB 923	RJ 67	IC 867	WB 925	RJ 165	RJ 565	IC 691	ICE 27	WB 927
	Q✕	★🍷	✕	M✕	🍷	★🍷	✕	🍷	R✕	★🍷	B✕	🍷	★🍷	✕	🍷	E✕	★🍷	B✕	🍷	★🍷	B✕	✕	K🍷	R✕	★🍷
Bregenz **951** d.	...	...	0639	...	...	...	...	...	...	...	...	0809	...	...	...	...	...	...	...	...	...	1140	...	...	...
Zürich HB **520** d.	...	...	|	...	...	...	0640	...	...	...	...	|	...	...	...	...	...	...	...	...	1040	|	...	...	...
Innsbruck Hbf **951** d.	...	...	0905	...	...	...	1022	...	...	...	...	1105	...	1220	...	...	...	...	1305	...	1420	1420	...	...	...
München Hbf **890** d.	...	...	|	0934	...	...	|	...	...	...	1134	|	...	|	...	...	...	1334	|	...	|	|	...	...	...
Salzburg Hbf d.	...	1050	1108	1108	1112	1150	1208	1212	...	1250	1308	1312	1350	1408	1412	...	1450	1508	1512	1550	1608	1608	1612	...	1650
Vöcklabruck d.	...	|	|	|	1154	|	|	1254	...	|	|	1354	|	|	1454	...	|	|	1554	|	|	|	1654	...	|
Attnang-Puchheim d.	...	1134	|	|	1200	1234	|	1300	...	1334	|	1400	1434	|	1500	...	1534	|	1600	1634	|	|	1700	...	1734
Passau Hbf **962** 🛃 d.	1038	|	|	|	|	|	|	|	1238	|	|	|	|	|	|	1438	|	|	|	|	|	|	|	1638	|
Wels Hbf **962** d.	1129	1148	|	|	1215	1248	|	1315	1329	1348	|	1415	1448	|	1515	1529	1548	|	1615	1648	|	|	1715	1729	1748
Linz Hbf **962** a.	1143	1159	1213	1213	1227	1259	1313	1327	1343	1359	1413	1427	1459	1513	1527	1543	1559	1613	1627	1659	1713	1713	1727	1743	1759
Linz Hbf **976** d.	1145	1200	1215	1215	1230	1300	1315	1330	1345	1400	1415	1430	1500	1515	1530	1545	1600	1615	1630	1700	1715	1715	1730	1745	1800
St Valentin **976** d.	|	|	|	|	1246	|	|	1346	|	|	|	1446	|	|	1546	|	|	|	1646	|	|	|	1746	|	|
Amstetten d.	|	1227	|	|	1302	1327	|	1402	|	1427	|	1502	1527	|	1602	|	1627	|	1702	1727	|	|	1802	|	1827
St Pölten Hbf **993** d.	1242	1252	1305	1305	1330	1352	1405	1430	1442	1452	1505	1530	1552	1605	1630	1642	1652	1705	1730	1752	1805	1805	1830	1842	1852
Tullnerfeld **993** a.	|	|	|	|	1343	|	|	1443	|	|	|	1543	|	|	1643	|	|	|	1743	|	|	|	1843	|	|
Wien Hütteldorf ● a.	|	1315	|	|	1355	1415	|	1455	|	1515	|	1555	1615	|	1655	|	1715	|	1755	1815	|	|	1855	|	1915
Wien Westbahnhof a.	1308	1322	1330	1330	1404	1422	1430	1504	1508	1522	1530	1604	1622	1630	1704	1708	1722	1730	1804	1822	1830	1830	1904	1908	1922

	RJ 869	RJ 69	IC 829	IC 649	5927	WB 929	RJ 167	RJ 567	IC 741	ICE 29	WB 931	RJ 261	IC 961	WB 933	RJ 169	RJ 569	IC 941	ICE 229	RJ 661	IC 943		RJ 363	EC 391		
			Ⓒ		P									⑤⑥†									Ⓑ		⑤⑥
	✕	✕	◇	🍷	2	★🍷	✕	✕	🍷	Q✕	★🍷	✕	✕	★🍷	✕	✕	🍷	Q✕	✕	🍷	2	✕	⊗F	2	w 2
Bregenz **951** d.	...	...	...	...	...	...	...	1340	...	...	...	...	1403	...	...	1540	...	...	...	...	...	...	...	...	...
Zürich HB **520** d.	...	...	...	...	...	...	1240	|	...	...	...	...	|	...	1440	|	...	...	...	...	...	1640	...	...	...
Innsbruck Hbf **951** d.	1505	...	...	...	...	...	1622	1622	1424z	...	...	...	1705	...	1822	1822	...	...	1905	...	...	2022	...	...	...
München Hbf **890** d.	|	1534	...	...	...	...	|	|	|	...	...	1734	|	...	|	|	...	...	|	...	...	|	2018	...	...
Salzburg Hbf d.	1708	1708	...	1712	...	1750	1808	1808	1812	...	1850	1908	1912	1950	2008	2008	2012	...	2108	2112	...	2208	2212	2227	2327
Vöcklabruck d.	|	|	...	1754	...	|	|	|	1854	...	|	|	1954	|	|	|	2054	...	|	2154	...	|	2254	2338	0038
Attnang-Puchheim d.	|	|	1754	1800	...	1834	|	|	1900	...	1934	|	2000	2034	|	|	2100	...	|	2200	...	|	2300	2342	0042
Passau Hbf **962** 🛃 d.	|	|	|	|	1719	|	|	|	|	1838	|	|	|	|	|	|	|	2038	|	|	...	|	|	...	...
Wels Hbf **962** d.	|	|	1809	1815	1818	1848	|	|	1915	1929	1948	|	2015	2048	|	|	2115	2129	|	2215	...	|	2315	...	...
Linz Hbf **962** a.	1813	1813	1821	1827	1836	1859	1913	1913	1927	1943	1959	2013	2027	2059	2113	2113	2127	2143	2213	2227	...	2313	2327	...	...
Linz Hbf **976** d.	1815	1815	1823	1830	1839	1900	1915	1915	1930	1945	2000	2015	2030	2100	2115	2115	2130	2145	2215	...	2252	2315	...	...	...
St Valentin **976** d.	|	|	1839	1846	1859	|	|	|	1946	|	|	|	2046	|	|	|	2146	|	|	...	2323	|	...	...	...
Amstetten d.	|	|	1856	1902	1921	1927	|	|	2002	|	2027	|	2104	2127	|	|	2202	|	|	...	2355	|	...	...	...
St Pölten Hbf **993** d.	1905	1905	1924	1930	2013	1952	2005	2005	2030	2042	2052	2105	2135	2152	2205	2205	2230	2242	2305	...	...	0005	...	...	...
Tullnerfeld **993** a.	|	|	|	1943	...	|	|	|	2043	|	|	|	2150	|	|	|	2243	|	|	...	...	|	...	...	...
Wien Hütteldorf ● a.	|	|	1946	1955	...	2015	|	|	2055	|	2115	|	2203	2215	|	|	2255	|	|	...	...	|	...	...	...
Wien Westbahnhof a.	1930	1930	1956	2004	...	2022	2030	2030	2104	2108	2122	2130	2212	2222	2230	2230	2304	2308	2330	...	...	0030	...	...	...

Regional trains ST VALENTIN - AMSTETTEN - MELK - WIEN (2nd class only)

	Ⓐt	Ⓒ	Ⓐt	Ⓐt	⑥g		Ⓐt	⑥g		⊕	T										P		Ⓒ		
St Valentin d.	...	...	0434	0502	0502	0521v	0538	0538	0624	0721r	*0821*r	1021e	1121c	1221r	1321	1421r	1521	1621r	1721	1821	1859	...	...	...	*2121*
Amstetten d.	0400	0400	0505	0533	0533	0557	0618	0618	0706	0756	0906	1106	1206	1306	1406	1506	1606	1706	1806	1906	1921	...	1957v	...	2207
Ybbs an der Donau d.	0412	0412	0518	0545	0545	0609	0631	0631	0719	0807	0920	1120	1220	1320	1420	1520	1620	1720	1820	1920	1935	...	2010v	...	2219
Pöchlarn d.	0419	0419	0527	0552	0552	0622	0641	0641	0732	0820	0934	1134	1234	1334	1434	1534	1634	1734	1834	1934	1947	1954	2023	2054e	2229
Melk d.	0426	0426	0534	0559	0559	0629	0648	0648	0739	0826	0940	1140	1240	1340	1440	1540	1640	1740	1840	1940	1955	2001	2030	2101e	2236
St Pölten Hbf a.	0446	0446	0554	0620	0620	0654	0714	0714	0800	0846	1000	1200	1300	1400	1500	1600	1700	1800	1900	2000	2013	2024	2053	2124e	2257
St Pölten Hbf d.	0448	0450	0557	0622	0633	...	0716	0719	*0806*r	0908	1008	1208	1308	1408	1508	1608	1708	1808	1908r	2008	...	*2038*e	...	2138	2308
Wien Hütteldorf ● a.	0512	0539	0621	0647	0721	...	0743	0809	*0859*r	0951	1051	1251	1351	1451	1551	1651	1751	1851	1951r	2051	...	*2146*e	...	2246	0016
Wien Westbahnhof a.	0520	0548	0630	0656	0730	...	0752	0818	*0908*r	1000	1100	1300	1400	1500	1600	1700	1800	1900	2000r	2100	...	*2156*e	...	2256	0026

A – [12] Salzburg - Wien; conveys 🛏 1, 2 cl., ▬ 2 cl. and [2] (*EN* **236**) Venezia - Tarvisio 🛃 - Villach - Wien (Table **88**).
B – To Budapest (Table **1250**).
D – KÁLMÁN IMRE – 🛏 1, 2 cl., ▬ 2 cl. and [2] München - Budapest.
E – [12] and ✕ Hamburg - Nürnberg - Regensburg - Passau - Wien.
F – Ⓑ (not Apr. 20, June 8). [12] and ⊗ Frankfurt - Stuttgart - München - Linz.
G – 🛏 1, 2 cl., ▬ 2 cl. and [2] Zürich - Wien - Budapest.
H – HANS ALBERS – 🛏 1, 2 cl., ▬ 2 cl. and [2] Hamburg - Hannover - Passau - Wien; conveys 🛏 1, 2 cl., ▬ 2 cl. and [2] (*EN* **421**) Köln - Frankfurt - Wien. Ⓡ for journeys from Germany.
K – From Klagenfurt (Table **970**).
M – [12] and ✕ München - Budapest. Starts from Frankfurt on ⑥⑦ (also Apr. 18, 21, May 1, 29, June 9, 19, Oct. 3).
N – ①–⑥ (not Apr. 21, June 9). [12] and ✕ Innsbruck - Wien - Hegyeshalom 🛃 - Budapest.
P – May 1 - Oct. 26. [2] Passau - Wien Franz-Josefs-Bf (a. 2155). *Einfach-Raus-Ticket* not valid.
Q – [12] and ✕ Frankfurt - Nürnberg - Regensburg - Passau 🛃 - Wien.
R – [12] and ✕ Dortmund - Köln - Frankfurt - Nürnberg - Regensburg - Passau 🛃 - Wien.
T – From Kleinreifling (Table **977**).

c – Ⓒ only.
d – Not Apr. 21, June 9, Dec. 8.
e – Ⓐ only.
g – Not Nov. 1.
r – ⚒ only.
t – Also calls at Tullnerfeld (12 – 14 minutes before Wien Hütteldorf; via high-speed line).
v – † only.
w – Also Apr. 20, 30, May 28, June 8, 18, Aug. 14, Dec. 7.
z – Ⓒ only. Via Zell am See (Table **960**).

⊖ – Conveys [2] Saalfelden (**1501**) - Salzburg - Wien (Table **960**).
♥ – Conveys 🛏 1, 2 cl., ▬ 2 cl. and [2].
◇ – Conveys [12] Stainach-Irdning - Attnang-Puchheim - Wien (Table **961**).
⊕ – From Linz Hbf (d. 0655) on ⚒.
★ – Operated by *Westbahn*. Special fares payable (ÖBB tickets **not** valid).
● – S-Bahn trains operate every 10 – 15 minutes to / from Wien Heiligenstadt (journey time: 21 – 23 minutes). See panel below for local trains between Wien Hütteldorf and Hauptbahnhof via Meidling. Approximately 10 trains per hour operate Wien Meidling - Hauptbahnhof - Mitte - Praterstern - Floridsdorf and v.v. for most of the day.

			Ⓐ		Ⓐ		⁘	
Wien Hütteldorf d.	0022	...	0554	0622	0657	0722	and	2322
Wien Meidling a.	0034	...	0606	0634	0709	0734	hourly	2334
Wien Hauptbahnhof a.	0040	...	0613	0641	0716	0741	until	2341

	Ⓐ		Ⓐ		⁘			
Wien Hauptbahnhof d.	0526	0622	0645	0722	and	2122	2212	234
Wien Meidling d.	0533	0628	0652	0728	hourly	2128	2218	235
Wien Hütteldorf a.	0545	0640	0705	0740	until	2140	2231	000

⁘ – Additional trains on Ⓐ: From Wien Hütteldorf at 1254 and hourly until 1754. From Wien Hauptbahnhof at 0551, 0745, 1345, 1445, 1545, 1645 and 1745.

SALZBURG and MÜNCHEN - INNSBRUCK - BREGENZ - LINDAU 951

km		EN 466		EN 464	EN 246	RJ 760				RJ 362			IC 118	EC 81	RJ 364		RJ 660		EC 85	RJ 160	RJ 560	IC 860	EC 87	RJ 162	RJ 562	
								⚒				⚒		¶				⚒							①–⑥	⑦j
		♦	2	♦	N	✕	2	2	2	✕	2	2	🍷♦	A✕	✕	2	✕	2	✕♦	✕	✕	✕	✕♦	B✕	y✕	2
	Wien Westbf **950** ... d.	2240	...	...	2256	...	...	...	...	...	...	...	...	...	0530h	...	0630	...	...	0730	0730	0748	...	0930	0930	...
	Linz Hbf **950** ... d.	0005	...	...	0048	...	...	...	...	...	...	...	...	...	0647h	...	0747	...	...	0847	0847	0932	...	1047	1047	...
0	**Salzburg** Hbf ... d.	0140	...	...	0306	...	...	...	...	...	...	...	0700	...	0756	...	0900	...	...	0956	0956	1100	...	1156	1156	...
	München Hbf **890** ‡ d.	|	...	...	|	...	...	...	...	...	...	...	|	0738	|	...	|	...	0938	|	|	|	1138	|	|	...
	München Ost **890** ‡ d.	|	...	...	|	...	...	...	...	...	...	...	|	0747	|	...	|	...	0947	|	|	|	1147	|	|	...
	Rosenheim .. **890** ‡ d.	|	...	...	|	...	...	...	...	...	...	...	|	0819	|	...	|	...	1019	|	|	|	1219	|	|	...
120	Kufstein 🏛 ... ‡ d.	|	...	...	|	...	0514	0613	0619b	...	0649	...	0814	0841	|	0848e	1014	...	1041	|	|	1214	1241	|	|	...
134	Wörgl Hbf ... **960** d.	|	...	...	|	*0530*	0536	0630	0636	...	0700	...	0823	0851	|	0900e	1023	...	1051	|	|	1223	1251	|	|	...
159	Jenbach ▲ ... **960** d.	|	...	...	|	*0550*	0558	0651	0658	...	0720	0728	0838	0906	|	0920e	1038	...	1106	|	|	1237	1306	|	|	...
193	**Innsbruck** Hbf ... **960** a.	0335	...	...	0519	*0619*	0632	0721	0732	...	0747	0802	0854	0923	0938	0947e	1054	...	1123	1138	1138	1256	1323	1340	1340	...
193	**Innsbruck** Hbf ... d.	0341	...	0453	0523	0630	0637r	...	...	0740	▬	0807	0902	...	0944	0957	▬	1057	...	1144	1144	1301	...	1344	1344	...
239	Ötztal ... d.	|	...	|	0551	0701	0732r	...	...	0804	...	0906	0931	...	1008	1039	...	1131	...	1208	1208	1329	...	1408	1408	...
248	Imst-Pitztal ... d.	|	...	|	0602	0712	0747r	...	...	0814	...	0917e	0941	...	1018	1049	...	1143	...	1218	1218	1341	...	1418	1418	...
265	Landeck - Zams ... d.	|	...	0545	0622	0727	0802r	...	...	0828	...	0934e	0954	...	1034	1104	...	1158	...	1232	1232	1355	...	1432	1432	...
293	St Anton am Arlberg.. d.	|	...	0610	0648	0751	▬	...	...	0852	...	...	1019	...	1058	▬	...	...	...	1256	1256	1419	...	1456	1456	...
304	Langen am Arlberg ... d.	|	...	0620	0659	0800	...	...	...	0902	...	...	1030	...	1108	...	2	...	...	1306	1306	1429	...	1506	1506	...
329	Bludenz ... **952** d.	0526	0539	0706	0735	0830	①–⑤	...	...	0930	...	...	1102	...	1135	Ⓐ	1139	...	...	1333	1333	1500	...	1533	1533	...
350	**Feldkirch** ... **952** a.	0540	0559	0721	0749	0842	a 2	...	...	0941	2	...	1113	...	1146	2	1159	...	...	1344	1344	1512	...	1544	1544	...
350	**Feldkirch** ... **952** d.	0545	0600	0738	0755	0847	0849	...	...	0943	0947	...	1115	...	1148	1150	1200	...	...	1348	1353	1517	...	1548	1553	1553
369	**Buchs** 🏛 ... **952** a.	0601	|	0753	|	|	0911	...	...	0958	|	...	|	...	1206	|	|	...	...	1406	|	|	...	1606	|	|
	Zürich HB **520** ... a.	0720	|	0920	|	|	...	...	...	1120	|	...	|	...	1320	|	|	...	...	1520	|	|	...	1720	|	|
375	Dornbirn ... **952** d.	...	0629	...	0815	0906	...	...	...	...	1009	...	1132	...	...	1211	1229	...	...	...	1407	1536	...	...	1607	1607
387	**Bregenz** 🏛 ... **952** a.	...	0644	...	0823	0917	...	...	...	...	1018	...	1140	...	...	1220	1244	...	...	...	1417	1547	...	...	1617	1617
397	**Lindau** Hbf 🏛 ... **952** a.	...	...	...	*0901*	*0932*	...	...	...	...	1031	...	1153	...	...	1233	1257	...	...	...	*1432*	...	...	...	*1632*	1632

	RJ 862		EC 89	RJ 564	EC 164		IC 864		IC 1281	EC 83	RJ 166	RJ 566	IC 866		EC 189	RJ 168		ICE 209	RJ 868		RJ 662		CNL 485	RJ 762	RJ 764	
		⚒				Ⓐ			⑥					Ⓐ			⚒						R ❖	Ⓑq		
	✕	2	A✕	✕	✕♦	2	🍷	2	♦	A✕	✕	✕	🍷	2	✕	✕	2	L✕	✕	2	✕	2	🍷♦	✕	✕	2
Wien Westbf **950** ... d.	1030	...	...	1130	...	...	1156	...	...	...	1330	1330	1356	...	...	1530	...	...	1630	...	1730	...	...	1830	1930	...
Linz Hbf **950** ... d.	1147	...	...	1247	...	...	1332	...	...	...	1447	1447	1532	...	...	1647	...	...	1747	...	1847	...	...	1947	2047	...
Salzburg Hbf ... d.	1300	...	...	1356	...	...	1500	...	...	...	1556	1556	1700	...	...	1756	...	...	1900	...	1956	...	...	2100	2156	...
München Hbf **890** ‡ d.	|	...	1338	|	...	...	|	...	1519	1538	|	|	|	...	1738	|	...	1901	|	...	|	...	2108	|	|	...
München Ost **890** ‡ d.	|	...	1347	|	...	...	|	...	|	1547	|	|	|	...	1747	|	...	1910	|	...	|	...	|	|	|	...
Rosenheim ... **890** ‡ d.	|	...	1419	|	...	...	|	...	1559	1619	|	|	|	...	1819	|	...	1941	|	...	|	...	2145	|	|	...
Kufstein 🏛 ... ‡ d.	1414	...	1441	|	...	*1453*	1614	...	1624	1641	|	|	1814	...	1841	|	...	2004	2014	2019	|	2119	2207	2214	2308	...
Wörgl Hbf ... **960** d.	1423	...	1451	|	1500	*1504*	1623	...	1635	1651	|	|	1823	...	1851	|	...	2015	2023	2036	|	2136	2217	2223	2318	...
Jenbach ▲ ... **960** d.	1438	...	1506	|	1516	*1524*	1638	...	...	1706	|	|	1838	...	1906	|	1928	2031	2038	2058	|	2158	2233	2238	2332	...
Innsbruck Hbf ... **960** a.	1454	...	1523	1539	1535	*1549*	1654	...	...	1723	1738	1737	1854	...	1923	1940	2002	2051	2055	2132	2138	2232	2254	2258	2352	...
Innsbruck Hbf ... d.	...	1457	...	...	1543	1623	1657	1701	...	...	1744	1744	...	1857	...	1944	2007	...	...	...	2144	2237r	...	...	...	0006
Ötztal ... d.	...	1531	...	...	1607	1702	|	1731	...	...	1808	1808	...	1931	...	2008	2100	...	...	...	2208	2316r	...	...	...	0057
Imst-Pitztal ... d.	...	1541	...	...	1617	1713	|	1741	...	...	1818	1818	...	1941	...	2018	2112	...	...	...	2218	2326r	...	...	...	0108
Landeck - Zams ... d.	...	1556	...	...	1630	1728	1741	1757	...	...	1832	1832	...	1956	...	2032	2129	...	...	...	2232	2341r	...	...	...	0124
St Anton am Arlberg .. d.	...	...	...	...	1654	▬	1806	...	...	...	1856	1856	...	...	...	2056	▬	...	...	...	2256	...	...	...	...	...
Langen am Arlberg ... d.	...	...	...	...	1704	...	|	...	...	...	1906	1906	...	...	...	2106	...	...	...	...	2306	...	...	...	...	...
Bludenz ... **952** d.	...	...	...	...	1731	...	1845	...	...	...	1933	1933	...	...	...	2133	...	...	...	...	2333	...	...	...	...	...
Feldkirch ... **952** a.	...	...	...	...	1742	2	1856	...	...	...	1944	1944	...	...	...	2144	2	...	...	...	2344	...	...	...	...	...
Feldkirch ... **952** d.	...	...	...	...	1744	1747	1858	...	...	...	1948	1953	...	...	...	2151	2150	...	...	...	2347	...	...	...	...	...
Buchs 🏛 ... **952** a.	...	...	...	...	1758	|	|	...	...	...	2006	|	...	...	...	2206	|	...	...	...	|	...	...	...	...	...
Zürich HB **520** ... a.	...	...	...	...	1920	|	|	...	...	...	2120	|	...	...	...	2320	|	...	...	...	|	...	...	...	...	...
Dornbirn ... **952** d.	...	...	...	...	...	1809	1914	...	...	...	...	2007	...	...	...	...	2210	...	...	...	0002	...	...	...	...	...
Bregenz 🏛 ... **952** a.	...	...	...	...	...	1818	1923	...	...	...	...	2017	...	...	...	...	2219	...	...	...	0010	...	...	...	...	...
Lindau Hbf 🏛 ... **952** a.	...	...	...	...	...	1832	*2005*	...	...	...	...	*2032*	...	...	...	...	2232	...	...	...	...	...	...	...	...	...

km		CNL 484	RJ 49			RJ 765		IC 861		ICE 208		RJ 663		RJ 863		RJ 161	EC 82		IC 865	IC 1284			EC 163	RJ 563	EC 88	IC 867
		R ◇	①–⑥				⚒		⚒				①–⑤					①–⑤		⑦	⚒					
		🍷♦	p B ✕	2	2	✕	2	🍷	2	L✕	2	✕	a 2	✕	2	✕	✕	a 2	🍷	♦	2	2	✕♦	✕	A✕	🍷
	Lindau Hbf 🏛 ... **952** d.	...		...	...	...	...	...	...	...	...	...	...	*0624*	0727	...	...	...	...	...	...	0927	...	...	...	...
	Bregenz 🏛 ... **952** d.	...	...	...	...	...	...	...	...	...	...	0547	...	0639	0740	...	...	...	0809	...	...	0940	...	...	...	...
	Dornbirn ... **952** d.	...	...	...	...	...	...	...	...	...	...	0556	...	0653	0751	...	...	...	0822	...	...	0951	...	...	...	...
	Zürich HB **520** ... d.	...	...	...	...	...	...	...	...	...	...	|	...	|	|	0640	...	...	|	...	...	|	0840	...	...	...
	Buchs 🏛 ... **952** d.	...	...	...	...	...	...	...	...	...	...	|	0617	|	|	0754	...	0819	|	...	...	|	0959	...	...	...
	Feldkirch ... **952** a.	...	...	...	...	...	...	...	...	...	...	0610	0639	0709	0812	0812	...	0841	0846	...	...	1012	1014	...	...	...
	Feldkirch ... **952** d.	...	...	...	...	...	...	...	...	...	...	0615	▬	0711	▬	0815	...	▬	0851	...	...	▬	1016	...	...	...
	Bludenz ... **952** d.	...	...	...	...	...	...	...	...	...	...	0628	...	0726	...	0828	...	...	0912	...	...	...	1029	...	...	...
	Langen am Arlberg ... d.	...	...	...	...	...	...	...	...	...	...	0654	...	|	...	0854	...	...	0943	...	...	...	1055	...	...	...
	St Anton am Arlberg.. d.	...	...	...	...	...	...	...	...	...	...	0705	...	|	...	0905	...	2	|	...	...	...	1105	...	...	...
	Landeck - Zams ... d.	...	...	0404r	0434	...	0535e	...	0604	...	0647	0729	...	0821	...	0929	...	0950	1017	...	1102	...	1129	...	...	...
	Imst-Pitztal ... d.	...	...	0426r	0451	...	0550e	...	0619	...	0711	0742	*IC*	|	...	0942	...	1005	|	...	1117	...	1142	...	...	...
	Ötztal ... d.	...	...	0437r	0504	...	0604	...	0631	...	0722	0753	**515**	|	*IC*	0953	...	1018	|	...	1128	...	1153	...	...	...
	Innsbruck Hbf ... a.	...	...	0526r	0553	...	0653	...	0702	...	0801	0816		0902	**1280**	1016	...	1058	1102	...	1202	2	1216	...	...	...
0	**Innsbruck** Hbf ... **960** d.	0436	0505	0528	...	0609	0658	0705	...	0709	*0813*e	0820	0824	0905	⑥	1022	1036	...	1105	...	...	1210	1224	1220	1236	1305
34	Jenbach ▲ ... **960** d.	0458	0524	0602	...	0626	0732	0722	...	0730	*0839*e	|	0846	0922	♦	|	1055	...	1122	...	...	1236	1245	|	1255	1322
59	Wörgl Hbf ... **960** d.	0516	0538	0628	...	0641	...	0737	...	0747	*0857*e	|	0900	0937	1024	|	1110	...	1137	1222	...	1257	1300	|	1310	1337
73	Kufstein 🏛 ... ‡ d.	0527	0546	0641	...	0651	...	0746	...	0758	*0907*e	|	...	0946	1044	|	1120	...	1146	1234	...	1310	...	|	1320	1346
107	Rosenheim ... **890** ‡ a.	0550	|	...	...	|	...	|	...	0817	...	|	...	|	1107	|	1139	...	|	1255	...	...	...	|	1339	|
162	**München** Ost **890** ‡ a.	|	|	...	...	|	...	|	...	0848	...	|	...	|	|	|	1210	...	|	|	...	...	...	|	1410	|
172	**München** Hbf **890** ‡ a.	0630	|	...	...	|	...	|	...	0900	...	|	...	|	1149	|	1221	...	|	1333	...	...	...	|	1421	|
	Salzburg Hbf ... a.	...	0658	...	...	0802	...	0858	...	...	...	1003	...	1058	...	1203	...	...	1258	...	...	...	...	1403	...	1458
	Linz Hbf **950** ... a.	...	0813	...	...	0913	...	1027	...	...	...	1113	...	1213	...	1313	...	...	1427	...	...	...	...	1513	...	1627
	Wien Westbf **950** ... a.	...	0930	...	...	1030	...	1204	...	...	...	1230	...	1330	...	1430	...	...	1604	...	...	...	...	1630	...	1804

♦ – **NOTES** (LISTED BY TRAIN NUMBER)

5 – 🚃12 and ✕ München - Brennero 🏛 - Bolzano/Bozen - Verona - Bologna.

7 – 🚃12 and ✕ München - Brennero 🏛 - Bolzano/Bozen - Verona - Venezia.

18 – 🚃12 Salzburg (*IC* **962**) - Innsbruck (*IC* **118**) - Lindau - Ulm - Stuttgart - Köln - Münster.

63/4 – 🚃12 and ✕ Zürich - Kitzbühel - Schwarzach - Selzthal - Graz and v.v.

84/5 – LUPUS – 🛏 1, 2 cl., 🛌 2 cl. and 🚃2 Roma - Brennero 🏛 - München and v.v. For overnight journeys from / to Italy only.

64 – 🛏 1, 2 cl., 🛌 2 cl. and 🚃2 Graz - Selzthal - Schwarzach - Zürich. Train number **1364** on the mornings Sept. 2–28. Conveys from Schwarzach 🛏 1, 2 cl.*, 🛌 2 cl.* and 🚃2 Beograd (**414**) - Zagreb - Ljubljana - Villach - Schwarzach (**464**) - Zürich.

66 – 🛏 1, 2 cl., 🛌 2 cl. and 🚃2 Budapest - Wien - Zürich.

280 – ⑥ Dec. 28 - Mar. 29; ⑥ June 28 - Sept. 13. 🚃12 Zell am See - Wörgl - München.

281 – ⑥ Dec. 21 - Apr. 5; ⑥ June 21 - Sept. 13. 🚃12 München - Wörgl - Schwarzach.

284 – ⑦ Jan. 5 - Apr. 6; ⑦ June 22 - Sept. 14. 🚃12 Schwarzach - Wörgl - München - Hamburg - Flensburg.

– 🚃12 and ✕ Verona - Bolzano/Bozen - Brennero 🏛 - München and v.v.

– From / to Budapest (Table **1250**).

– To / from Berlin via Nürnberg (Table **851**).

– Conveys 🛏 1, 2 cl., 🛌 2 cl. and 🚃2.

– Not Apr. 21, May 29, June 9, 19, Dec. 8.

– Ⓑ only.

e – Ⓐ only.

h – ①–⑥ (not Apr. 21, June 9, Dec. 8).

j – Also Apr. 17, 21, May 28, June 6, 9; not Feb. 9 - Apr. 20, Nov. 9 - Dec. 7.

k – Also June 19, Aug. 15.

m – Not June 19, Aug. 15.

p – Not Apr. 21, June 9.

q – Not Apr. 20, June 8.   r – ⚒ only.

y – ①–⑥ (daily Feb. 3 - Apr. 26 and from Nov. 3; also June 8; not Apr. 17, 21, May 28, June 6, 9).

* – 🛏 1, 2 cl. and 🛌 2 cl. from Zagreb.

❖ – Subject to alteration Aug. 8, 9, 14–18, Oct. 12, 31. Nov. 1, 2, 7, 8, 9.

◇ – Subject to alteration Aug. 9, 10, 15–19, Nov. 1, 2, 3, 8, 9.

¶ – On ①–⑤ continues to Bologna. On ⑥⑦ Mar. 29 - Nov. 2 runs with train number **1289** and continues to Venezia.

▲ – Aug. 15–31 *RJ*, *EC* and *IC* services may not call at Jenbach.

‡ – See panel below for *Meridian* regional services (operated by Bayerische Oberlandbahn GmbH) München - Kufstein and v.v. German holiday dates apply.

München Hbf ... d.	0644	0744	0844	and	1844	1944	2044	*2144*	*2244*
München Ost ... d.	0652	0752	0852	hourly	1852	1952	2052	*2152*	*2252*
Rosenheim ... d.	0728	0830	0931	until	1931	2035	2135	2235	2335
Kufstein ... a.	0756	0857	0958		1958	2102	2202	2302	0002

	Ⓐm	Ⓒk							
Kufstein ... d.	0550	0558	0702	and	1902	1959	2058	2158	2341
Rosenheim ... d.	0618	0632	0732	hourly	1932	2026	2125	2225	0005
München Ost ... a.	0651	0705	0805	until	2005	*2105*	*2204*	*2305*	*0045*
München Hbf ... a.	0700	0715	0815		2016	*2115*	*2214*	*2315*	*0055*

951 LINDAU - BREGENZ - INNSBRUCK - MÜNCHEN and SALZBURG

	RJ 565	*RJ* 165	*EC* 80	*RJ* 869	†	Ⓐ	*RJ* 567	*RJ* 167	*EC* 84	*IC* 961	*RJ* 569	*RJ* 169
	✕	✕♦	A✕	✕	2	2	✕	✕	✕♦	✕	✕	✕
Lindau Hbf ⊞ ..... 952 d.	*1125*	...	...	...	...	...	*1325*	...	...	...	*1525*	...
Bregenz ⊞ .... 952 d.	1140	...	...	...	...	...	1340	...	...	1403	1540	...
Dornbirn .... 952 d.	1150	...	...	...	...	...	1350	...	...	1413	1550	...
Zürich HB 520 .... d.	|	1040	...	...	...	...	|	1240	...	|	|	1440
Buchs ⊞ .... 952 d.	|	1154	...	...	...	...	|	1354	...	|	|	1554
Feldkirch .... 952 a.	1205	1209	...	...	...	...	1405	1409	...	1436	1605	1609
Feldkirch .... 952 d.	1215	1215	...	...	...	...	1415	1415	...	1446	1615	1615
Bludenz .... 952 d.	1228	1228	...	...	...	...	1428	1428	...	1500	1628	1628
Langen am Arlberg .... d.	1254	1254	...	...	...	...	1454	1454	...	|	|	|
St Anton am Arlberg .. d.	1305	1305	...	...	...	...	1505	1505	...	1537	1701	1701
Landeck - Zams .... d.	1329	1329	...	...	1350	1402	1529	1529	...	1602	1725	1725
Imst-Pitztal .... d.	1342	1342	...	...	1405	1417	1542	1542	...	1616	1742	1742
Ötztal .... d.	1353	1353	...	...	1422	1428	1553	1553	...	1627	1753	1753
Innsbruck Hbf .... a.	1416	1416	...	...	1502	1502	1616	1616	...	1657	1816	1816
Innsbruck Hbf ..... 960 d.	1420	1420	1436	1505	...	...	1622	1622	1636	1705	1822	1822
Jenbach ▲ .... 960 d.	|	|	1455	1522	...	...	|	|	1655	1722	|	|
Wörgl Hbf .... 960 d.	|	|	1510	1537	...	...	|	|	1710	1737	|	|
Kufstein ⊞ .... ‡ d.	|	|	1520	1546	...	...	|	|	1720	1746	|	|
Rosenheim .... 890 ‡ a.	|	|	1539	|	...	...	|	|	1739	|	|	|
München Ost 890 ‡ a.	|	|	1610	|	...	...	|	|	1810	|	|	|
München Hbf 890 ‡ a.	|	|	1624	|	...	...	|	|	1821	|	|	|
Salzburg Hbf .... a.	1603	1603	...	1658	...	...	1803	1803	...	1858	2003	2003
Linz Hbf 950 .... a.	1713	1713	...	1813	...	...	1913	1913	...	2027	2113	2113
Wien Westbf 950 .... a.	1830	1830	...	1930	...	...	2030	2030	...	2212	2230	2230

	EC 86	*IC* 119	*RJ* 661		*RJ* 363	*EC* 188 ¶			*RJ* 365		*EN* 247	*EN* 465		*EN* 467
	✕♦	🍷♦	✕	2	✕	A✕	2	2	✕	2	N	♦	2	♦
Lindau Hbf ⊞ ..... 952 d.	...	1601	...	1727	...	...	...	1927	...	...	*2104*	...	2332	...
Bregenz ⊞ .... 952 d.	...	1611	...	1740	...	...	...	1940	...	...	2146	...	2345	...
Dornbirn .... 952 d.	...	1621	...	1750	...	...	...	1951	...	...	2156	...	2353	...
Zürich HB 520 .... d.	...	|	...	|	1640	...	...	|	1840	...	|	2040	|	2240
Buchs ⊞ .... 952 d.	...	|	...	|	1759	...	...	|	1954	...	|	2205	|	2358
Feldkirch .... 952 a.	...	1638	...	1809	1814	...	...	2012	2009	...	2212	2223	0012	0014
Feldkirch .... 952 d.	...	1640	...	▬	1816	...	...	▬	2015	...	2227	2242	...	0016
Bludenz .... 952 d.	...	1656	...	...	1829	...	...	...	2028	...	2242	2258	...	0032
Langen am Arlberg .... d.	...	1728	...	⚒	|	...	...	...	2054	...	2310	2331	...	|
St Anton am Arlberg .. d.	...	1738	...	2	1905	...	...	2	2105	...	2320	2341	...	|
Landeck - Zams .... d.	...	1805	...	1902	1929	...	...	2045	2129	...	2348	0009	...	|
Imst-Pitztal .... d.	...	1822	...	1917	1942	...	...	2100	2142	...	0002	|	...	|
Ötztal .... d.	...	1832	...	1928	1953	...	...	2111	2153	...	0013	|	...	|
Innsbruck Hbf .... a.	...	1901	...	2002	2016	...	...	2200	2216	...	0039	0054	...	0213
Innsbruck Hbf ..... 960 d.	1836	...	1905	2013e	2022	2036	2128	...	...	2228	0044	0056	...	0221
Jenbach ▲ .... 960 d.	1855	...	1922	2039e	|	2055	2202	...	...	2302	|	0119	...	|
Wörgl Hbf .... 960 d.	1910	...	1937	2100e	|	2110	2228	...	...	2325	|	0136	...	|
Kufstein ⊞ .... ‡ d.	1920	...	1946	2110e	|	2120	2241	...	...	2338	|	...	...	|
Rosenheim .... 890 ‡ a.	1939	...	|	...	|	2139	...	...	...	...	|	...	...	|
München Ost 890 ‡ a.	2010	...	|	...	|	2210	...	...	...	...	|	...	...	|
München Hbf 890 ‡ a.	2021	...	|	...	|	2221	...	...	...	...	|	...	...	|
Salzburg Hbf .... a.	...	...	2103	...	2206	...	...	...	...	...	0258	...	...	0416
Linz Hbf 950 .... a.	...	...	2213	...	2313	...	...	...	...	...	0507	...	...	0552
Wien Westbf 950 .... a.	...	...	2330	...	0030	...	...	...	...	...	0708	...	...	0734

♦ – **NOTES** (LISTED BY TRAIN NUMBER)

84 – [12] and ✕ Bologna - Verona - Bolzano/Bozen - Brennero ⊞ - München.
86 – [12] and ✕ Venezia - Verona - Bolzano/Bozen - Brennero ⊞ - München.
119 – [12] Münster - Köln - Stuttgart - Ulm - Lindau - Innsbruck.
165 – [12] and ✕ Zürich - Wien - Budapest.
465 – 🛏 1, 2 cl., ▬ 2 cl. and [2] Zürich - Schwarzach - Selzthal - Graz. Train number **1365** Sept. 1–27. Conveys 🛏 1, 2 cl.*, ▬ 2 cl.* and [2] Zürich - Schwarzach (**415**) - Villach - Ljubljana - Zagreb - Beograd.
467 – 🛏 1, 2 cl., ▬ 2 cl. and [2] Zürich - Budapest.

A – [12] and ✕ Verona - Bolzano/Bozen - Brennero ⊞ - München.
N – Conveys 🛏 1, 2 cl., ▬ 2 cl. and [2].
e – Ⓐ only.
***** – 🛏 1, 2 cl. and ▬ 2 cl. to Zagreb.
¶ – On ①–⑤ starts from Bologna. Train number **1288** on ⑥⑦ Mar. 29 - Nov. 2 (starts from Venezia).
‡ – See panel on page 453 for other regional services Kufstein - München.
▲ – Aug. 15–31 *RJ*, *EC* and *IC* services may not call at Jenbach.

952 VORARLBERG LOCAL SERVICES

2nd class only (except where shown)

BLUDENZ - BREGENZ - LINDAU ⊖ △

		Ⓐ																									
Bludenz .... d.	...	0509	0605	0637	0656	0730	0800	0839	0939	1009	1109	1209	1300	1339	1430	1539	1600	1630	1700	1800	1809	1909	1939	2039	...	2239	0039
Feldkirch .... d.	0500	0530	0618	0651	0713	0747	0817	0900	1000	1030	1130	1230	1317	1400	1447	1600	1617	1647	1717	1817	1830	1930	2000	2100	2230	2300	0100
Dornbirn .... d.	0529	0559	0639	0710	0734	0809	0839	0929	1029	1059	1159	1259	1339	1429	1509	1629	1639	1709	1739	1839	1859	1959	2029	2129	2259	2329	0129
Bregenz ⊞ .... d.	0545	0615	0649	0721	0746	0819	0849	0945	1045	1115	1214	1315	1349	1445	1519	1645	1648	1719	1749	1849	1915	2020	2045	2145	2315	2344	0144
Lindau Hbf ⊞ .. a.	0556	0629	0658	0733	0759	0831	0901	0957	1057	1127	*1233*	1327	1401	1457	1531	1657	...	1732	1801	1901	1927	2032	2057	2157	2327	...	...

											Ⓐd			Ⓐd							Ⓐd							
Lindau Hbf ⊞ .. d.	...	...	0624	0657	*0754*	0831	0901	1001	1101	1157	1227	1301	1401	1427	...	1459	1627	1701	1757	1827	1901	1957	2031	2104	2227	2301	...
Bregenz ⊞ .... d.	0514	0610	0644	0710	0814	0844	0914	1014	1114	1210	1240	1314	1414	1440	1510	1514	1640	1714	1810	1840	1914	2010	2044	2114	2240	2314	0014
Dornbirn .... d.	0530	0621	0700	0721	0830	0900	0930	1030	1130	1221	1251	1330	1430	1451	1521	1530	1651	1730	1821	1851	1930	2021	2100	2130	2251	2330	0030
Feldkirch .... d.	0601	0644	0731	0744	0901	0931	1001	1101	1201	1244	1314	1401	1501	1514	1544	1601	1714	1801	1844	1914	2001	2044	2130	2201	2314	0001	0101
Bludenz .... a.	0621	0659	0751	0759	0921	0951	1021	1121	1221	1259	1329	1421	1521	1529	1559	1621	1729	1821	1859	1929	2021	2059	...	2221	2329	0021	0121

ST MARGRETHEN - BREGENZ - LINDAU △

km		Ⓒ	Ⓐ		Ⓐ		*EC* 191 ♥			*EC* 193 ♥					*EC* 195 ♥						*EC* 197 ♥					
0	St Margrethen ⊞ ...... d.	0625	0625	0655	0725	0755	0842	0855	0955	1042	1055	1155	1255	1355	1442	1455	1555	1655	1755	1855	1942	1955	2055	2155	2255	2355
12	**Bregenz** ⊞ .... a.	0640	0640	0710	0740	0810	0853	0910	1010	1053	1110	1210	1310	1410	1453	1510	1610	1710	1810	1910	1953	2010	2110	2210	2310	0010
22	**Lindau** Hbf ⊞ .... a.	0650	*0658*	*0733*	*0759*	*0831*	0905	*0932*	*1031*	1105	*1127*	*1233*	*1327*	*1432*	1505	*1531*	*1632*	*1732*	*1832*	*1927*	2005	*2032*	*2127*	*2232*	*2327*	...

				Ⓐ				*EC* 196 ♥						*EC* 194 ♥		Ⓐ		Ⓐ			*EC* 192 ♥			*EC* 190 ♥		
Lindau Hbf ⊞ .... d.	...	...	*0624*	*0657*	*0727*	*0831*	*0927*	0954	*1031*	*1125*	*1227*	*1325*	*1427*	1454	*1525*	1605	*1627*	*1701*	*1727*	*1827*	1854	*1927*	*2031*	2054	*2131*	*2227*
Bregenz ⊞ .... d.	0542	0617	0647	0717	0747	0849	0947	1006	1049	1147	1247	1347	1449	1506	1547	1617	1647	1717	1747	1847	1906	1949	2047	2106	2147	2247
St Margrethen ⊞ .... a.	0558	0634	0704	0734	0804	0904	1004	1018	1104	1204	1304	1404	1504	1518	1604	1634	1704	1734	1804	1904	1918	2004	2104	2118	2204	2304

FELDKIRCH - BUCHS ⊖

km		A	A	A B	A	A		A	A	A	A	
0	**Feldkirch** .... d.	0533	0649	0714	0749	0849	...	1612	1645	1715	1815	...
16	Schaan-Vaduz d.	0552	0708	0733	0808	0908	...	1634	1704	1734	1834	...
19	**Buchs** ⊞ .... a.	0555	0711	0736	0811	0911	...	1637	1707	1737	1837	...

	A	A	A		A		A	A	A	A	A
Buchs ⊞ .... d.	0617	0716	0819	...	1234	...	1619	1649	1719	1819	1849
Schaan-Vaduz .... d.	0620	0719	0822	...	1237	...	1622	1652	1722	1822	1852
Feldkirch .... a.	0639	0737	0841	...	1256	...	1641	1711	1741	1841	1911

BLUDENZ - SCHRUNS

Operated by Montafonerbahn. *12 km*. Journey time: 19 minutes.

From Bludenz at 0538 Ⓐ, 0631 ⚒, 0704, 0738, 0804, 0838, 0938, 1038, 1138, 1204 ⚒, 1238, 1304 ⚒, 1338, 1438, 1538, 1604, 1632, 1704, 1738, 1804, 1838, 1938, 2038, 2138, 2245, 2338.
From Schruns at 0500 Ⓐ, 0537 ⚒, 0630, 0703, 0737, 0803, 0903, 1003, 1103, 1137 ⚒, 1203, 1237 ⚒, 1303, 1403, 1503, 1537, 1603, 1631, 1703, 1737, 1803, 1903, 2003, 2103, 2210, 2310

A – ①–⑤ (not Apr. 21, May 29, June 9, 19, Dec. 8).
B – From Bludenz (d. 0646).
d – Runs daily Lindau - Bregenz.
♥ – [12] and ✕ Zürich - München and v.v. See Table **75**.
⊖ – Local trains. See Table **951** for long distance trains.
△ – Austrian holiday dates apply.

953 🚌 IMST - ÖTZTAL - OBERGURGL and ST ANTON - LECH

ÖBB-Postbus

km	🚌 Route 4194											Ⓒ	Ⓐ	Ⓐ	Ⓒ	Ⓒ	Ⓐ	Ⓒ	Ⓐ	Ⓒ	Ⓐ		
0	**Imst** (Terminal Post) .... d.	0605	0632	...	...	0805	0855	...	1000	1115	1155	1230	1235	1340	1400	1450	1510	1530	1600	1630	1645	1800	1915
13	**Ötztal** (Bahnhof) .... a.	0622	0649	...	...	0822	0909	...	1017	1132	1212	1247	1252	1357	1417	1507	1527	1544	1617	1647	1702	1817	1932
13	**Ötztal** (Bahnhof) .... d.	0623	0700	0715	0800	0825	0910	0940	1020	1135	1215	1248	1300	1400	1420	1510	1535	1545	1618	1648	1705	1818	1935
21	Oetz (Posthotel Kassel) .... d.	0637	0714	0728	0813	0839	0924	0954	1034	1149	1229	1302	1314	1414	1434	1524	1549	1559	1632	1702	1719	1832	1949
54	Sölden (Postamt) .... d.	0725	0802	0817	0902	0927	1012	1042	1122	1237	1317	1350	1402	1502	1522	1612	1637	1647	1720	1750	1807	1920	2037
58	Zwieselstein (Gh Neue Post) .... d.	0733	0810	0825	0910	0935	1020	1050	1130	1245	1325	1358	1410	1510	1530	1620	1645	1655	1728	1758	1815	1928	2045
68	**Obergurgl** (Zentrum) .... a.	0748	0825	0840	0925	0950	1035	1105	1145	1300	1340	1413	1425	1525	1545	1635	1700	1710	1743	1813	1830	1943	2100

🚌 Route 4194	Ⓐ								Ⓐ	Ⓒ	Ⓐ	Ⓒ											
Obergurgl (Zentrum) .... d.	...	...	...	0650	0750	0845	1015	1115	1205	1215	1305	1315	1345	...	1515	1545	1615	1645	1715	1745	1815	...	1915
Zwieselstein (Gh Neue Post) .... d.	...	0550	...	0705	0805	0900	1030	1130	1220	1230	1320	1330	1400	...	1530	1600	1630	1700	1730	1800	1830	...	1930
Sölden (Postamt) .... d.	0525	0600	...	0715	0815	0910	1040	1140	1230	1240	1330	1340	1410	...	1540	1610	1640	1710	1740	1810	1840	...	1940
Oetz (Posthotel Kassel) .... d.	0612	0647	...	0807	0907	1002	1132	1232	1322	1332	1424	1432	1502	...	1632	1702	1732	1802	1832	1902	1932	...	2032
Ötztal (Bahnhof) .... a.	0622	0657	...	0817	0917	1012	1142	1242	1332	1342	1432	1442	1512	...	1642	1712	1742	1812	1842	1912	1942	...	2042
Ötztal (Bahnhof) .... d.	...	0700	...	0820	0920	1015	1145	1245	1335	1345	1435	1445	1515	...	1645	...	1745	...	1845	...	1945	...	2045
Imst (Terminal Post) .... a.	...	0715	...	0835	0935	1030	1200	1300	1350	1400	1450	1500	1530	...	1700	...	1800	...	1900	...	2000	...	2100

🚌 Route 92: **ST ANTON AM ARLBERG - LECH** *20 km* Journey time: 30 minutes Service **June 7 - Sept. 28.**

From St Anton Bahnhof at 0726, 0910, 1110, 1310, 1510 and 1710.
From Lech Landbrugg at 0810, 1010, 1210, 1410, 1610 and 1810.

☛ All services call at St Christoph a. Arlberg and Zürs (Posthaus

LANDECK - NAUDERS - SCUOL and MALLES 954

Landeck - Nauders

Routes 4218/4220									
Landeck-Zams Bahnhof d.	0650	0805	1005	1212	1405	1505	1605	1805	1905
Ried im Oberinntal d.	0718	0833	1033	1240	1433	1533	1633	1833	1933
Nauders Dorf a.	0758	0913	1113	1320	1513	1613	1713	1913	2013
Nauders Mühle a.	0800	0915	1115	1322	1515	1615	1715	1915	2015

						⚒			
Nauders Dorf d.	0605	0845	0945	1145	1345	1445	1545	1645	1755
Nauders Mühle d.	0607	0847	0947	1147	1347	1447	1547	1647	1757
Ried im Oberinntal d.	0648	0928	1028	1228	1428	1528	1628	1728	1838
Landeck-Zams Bahnhof a.	0713	0953	1053	1253	1453	1553	1653	1753	1903

Scuol Tarasp - Nauders - Malles

	⚒	⚒	⚒									
Scuol Tarasp Staziun d.	...	0630	...	...	0730	...	and at	1830	...	...	1930	...
Martina Cunfin 🏛 d.	...	0655	0703	...	0755	0803	the same	1855	1903	...	2001	2003
Nauders Mühle 🏛 d.	...	...	0716	...	...	0816	minutes	...	1916	...	...	2016
Reschenpass/Passo di Resia 🏛 d.	0620	...	0720	...	...	0820	past each	...	1920	...	...	2020
Resia d.	0623	...	0723	...	...	0823	hour until	...	1923	...	...	2023
Malles Stazione **597** a.	0653	...	0753	...	...	0853		...	1953	...	...	2053

	⚒	⚒										⚒
Malles Stazione **597** d.	0601	...	...	0701	...	and at	1801	...	...	1901	...	2001
Resia d.	0631	...	...	0731	...	the same	1831	...	...	1931	...	2031
Passo di Resia/Reschenpass 🏛 d.	0634	...	...	0734	...	minutes	1834	...	...	1934	...	2034
Nauders Mühle 🏛 d.	0640	...	...	0740	...	past each	1840	...	...	1940	...	...
Martina Cunfin 🏛 d.	0651	0701	...	0751	0801	hour until	1851	1901	...	1951	2001	...
Scuol Tarasp Staziun a.	...	0728	...	...	0828		...	1928	...	...	2036	...

Operators

Landeck - Nauders: ÖBB-Postbus GmbH, Landeck. ✆ +43 (0) 5442 64 422.

Scuol Tarasp - Martina: Auto Da Posta, Svizra. CH-7550 Scuol. ✆ +41 (0) 58 453 28 28.

Martina - Nauders - Malles: Servizi Autobus Dolomiti (SAD). Corso Italia 13N, I-39100 Bolzano. ✆ +39 0471 450 111.

JENBACH - MAYRHOFEN 955

2nd class only   Narrow gauge   Zillertalbahn *

km																🚂 A
0	**Jenbach** Zillertalbahnhof § d.	0628	0652	0737	0810	0844		1610	1644	1710	1744	1815	1848	1948		1017
11	Fügen-Hart d.	0646	0709	0754	0829	0859	and at	1629	1659	1729	1759	1832	1904	2004		1047
13	Uderns d.	0649	0713	0800	0833	0903	the same	1633	1703	1733	1803	1836	1908	2008	also	1052
17	Kaltenbach-Stumm d.	0656	0720	0807	0840	0910	minutes	1640	1710	1740	1810	1843	1915	2015		1104
21	Aschau im Zillertal d.	0703	0727	0813	0846	0916	past each	1646	1716	1746	1816	1849	1920	2020		1119
25	**Zell am Ziller** d.	0712	0736	0820	0855	0925	hour until	1655	1725	1755	1822	1855	1927	2027		1130
32	**Mayrhofen** a.	0724	0748	0833	0906	0936		1706	1736	1806	1833	1906	1938	2038		1149

																🚂 A
Mayrhofen d.	0541	0607	0637	0731	0821	0851		1621	1651	1721	1751	1851	1951	...		1437
Zell am Ziller d.	0552	0619	0649	0741	0833	0903	and at	1633	1703	1733	1803	1903	2003	...		1454
Aschau im Zillertal d.	0558	0625	0655	0747	0839	0909	the same	1639	1709	1739	1809	1909	2009	...	also	1503
Kaltenbach-Stumm d.	0605	0632	0702	0754	0846	0916	minutes	1646	1716	1746	1816	1916	2016	...		1519
Uderns d.	0611	0638	0712	0800	0852	0922	past each	1652	1722	1752	1823	1923	2023	...		1533
Fügen-Hart d.	0616	0645	0716	0804	0858	0927	hour until	1658	1727	1758	1829	1928	2028	...		1540
Jenbach Zillertalbahnhof § a.	0634	0703	0733	0821	0916	0943		1716	1743	1814	1845	1943	2043	...		1605

A – May 31 - Oct. 5 (also May 3, 10, 11, 17, 24).

🚂 – Steam train. Special fares apply.

§ – Adjacent to ÖBB station.

* – Zillertaler Vehrkehrsbetriebe, Austraße 1, A-6200 Jenbach. ✆ +43 (0) 5244 606 0.

JENBACH - ACHENSEE 956

2nd class only   *Achenseebahn*

Narrow gauge rack railway operated by steam locomotives. Special fares apply. **Service May 29 - Oct. 5, 2014***.

km									
0	**Jenbach** Achensee-Bahnhof § d.	0815	1000	1045	1200	1345	1500	1645	...
5	Maurach d.	0850	1038	1123	1238	1423	1538	1723	...
7	**Achensee** Seespitz-Bahnstation a.	0900	1050	1135	1250	1435	1550	1735	...

Achensee Seespitz-Bahnstation d.	0915	1105	1220	1405	1520	1600	...	1740
Maurach d.	0925	1115	1230	1415	1530	1610	...	1750
Jenbach Achensee-Bahnhof § a.	0957	1147	1302	1447	1602	1642	...	1822

§ – Adjacent to ÖBB station.

Operator: Achenseebahn AG, A-6200 Jenbach: ✆ +43 (0) 5244 62243, Fax +43 (0) 5244 622435.

* – Service May 1–28 and Oct. 6 - Nov. 2: **Jenbach** → **Achensee** at 1100, 1300 and 1500; **Achensee** → **Jenbach** at 1200, 1400 and 1600.

ZELL AM SEE - KRIMML and 🚌 KRIMML - MAYRHOFEN 957

2nd class only

ZELL AM SEE - KRIMML ⊡

km					🚂 S		🚂 S				Ⓐ	Ⓒ
0	**Zell am See** Lokalbahn d.	0630	0800	0900	0918	1000	←	1100	and	1900	2000	2050
29	Mittersill d.	0723	0848	0948	1038	1048	1108	1148	hourly	1948	2048	2138
39	Bramberg d.	0737	0904	1004	→	1104	1131	1204	until	2004	2104	2154
53	**Krimml** a.	0758	0923	1023	...	1123	1203	1223		2023	2123	2213

		Ⓐ					🚂 S		🚂 S			
Krimml d.	0533	0603	0640	0733	and	1433	1453	1533	...	1633	1733	1833
Bramberg d.	0552	0621	0658	0751	hourly	1451	1523	1551	←	1651	1751	1851
Mittersill d.	0608	0638	0720	0808	until	1508	1545	1608	1615	1708	1808	1908
Zell am See Lokalbahn a.	0655	0725	0805	0855		1555	→	1655	1728	1755	1855	1955

🚌 Krimml Bahnhof - Krimml Wasserfälle and v.v. Route **671**. *3 km.* Journey time: 5–6 minutes.

From Krimml Bahnhof at 0802, 0836 Ⓐ, 0838 Ⓒ **R**, 0929, 1029, 1046, 1129, 1229, 1329, 1429, 1446, 1529, 1629 and 1729.

From Krimml Wasserfälle at 0823, 0900 Ⓐ, 1023, 1100, 1123, 1223, 1323, 1423, 1500, 1523, 1623 and 1723.

🚌 routes **673** and **4094**: KRIMML - KÖNIGSLEITEN - MAYRHOFEN (summer service **valid June 7 - October 5**)

km			R			R			R	
0	**Krimml** Bahnhof d.	...	*0836**	...	...	*1429*	...	...	*1629*	...
3	Krimml Wasserfälle d.	...	0847	...	...	1435	...	...	1635	...
16	Königsleiten Dorfbahn d.	...	0909	1000	1100	1453a	1502a	1600	1657	1715
25	**Gerlos** Gasthaus Oberwirt d.	0821	...	1013	1113	...	1513	1613	...	1728
45	Zell am Ziller Bf **955** a.	0856	...	1053	1153	...	1553	1653	...	1801
53	**Mayrhofen** Bahnhof **955** a.	0909	...	...	1206	...	...	1706	...	1809

		R			R		R		
Mayrhofen Bahnhof **955** d.	0820	...	0920	...	...	1440	...	...	1840
Zell am Ziller Bahnhof **955** d.	0835	...	0935	1327	...	1455	...	1616	1855
Gerlos Gasthaus Oberwirt d.	0917	...	1017	1402	...	1534	...	1654	1928
Königsleiten Dorfbahn d.	0930	0948	1030	1415	1458	1547	1658	1707	...
Krimml Wasserfälle a.	...	1012	...	...	1522	...	1722	...	...
Krimml Bahnhof a.	...	*1028*	...	...	*1528*	...	*1728*	...	...

R – July 5 - Sept. 7.
S – ④ June 5 - Sept. 25 (also ②③ July 8 - Aug. 27; also Sept. 6). Steam train with special fares.

a – Königsleiten Almdorf.

* – *0838* on Ⓒ.

⊡ – Narrow gauge railway. **Operator**: Pinzgauer Lokalbahn. Trains call at Mittersill and Bramberg on request only.

🚌 WÖRGL - ELLMAU - KITZBÜHEL and ST JOHANN 958

ÖBB-Postbus routes **4006**, **4060**, **4902**

	⚒	Ⓐ¶	⑥z	⚒	Ⓐ	⑥z	⚒	†	⚒		⚒	Ⓐ	⚒	Ⓑr	⚒		⚒	†	⚒	Ⓐ		⚒	Ⓐ	Ⓑr
Wörgl Hauptbahnhof d.	...	0545	...	0640	0743	0743	...	...	0905	...	1120	1210	1210	...	...	...	1405	...	1610	...	...	1740	1835	...
Söll (Dorf) ♥ d.	...	0605	0612	0658	0805	0810	...	0917	0937	...	1140	1240	1240	1240	...	...	1437	1545	1640	...	...	1810	1905	1905
Scheffau am Wilden Kaiser ★ d.	...	0612	0621	...	0812	0817	...	0927	0947	...	1150	1250	1250	1250	...	...	1447	1555	1650	...	...	1820	1913	1913
Ellmau (Dorf) d.	0622	0621	0633	...	0821	0826	0900	0942	1002	...	1205	1305	1305	1305	1315	...	1502	1610	1705	1715	...	1835	1924	1924
Kitzbühel Bahnhof a.	0650	|	|	...	|	|	0924	|	|	...	|	|	...	|	1345	...	|	|	|	1745	...	|	|	|
St Johann in Tirol Bahnhof a.	...	0639	0650	...	0839	0844	...	1000	1020	...	1223	1323	...	1323	...	...	1520	1628	1723	...	...	1853	1940	1940

	Ⓐ	⚒	Ⓐ	⚒	⚒	†	⚒	⚒		⚒	⚒	Ⓐ	⑥z		⚒	⚒	Ⓐ	Ⓑr	Ⓐ	⚒	⚒	Ⓐ	Ⓐ	Ⓐ
St Johann in Tirol Bahnhof d.	...	0535	0535	...	0725	0750	...	0855	1055	1055	...	1235	...	1340	1340	1555	...	1655	1655	...	1755	1755	...	1855
Kitzbühel Bahnhof d.	...	|	|	...	|	|	0803	|	|	|	1215	|	...	|	|	|	1620	|	|	...	|	|	1815	|
Ellmau (Dorf) d.	...	0552	0552	...	0747	0812	0833	0917	1117	1117	1245	1302	1305	1402	1402	1617	1650	1717	1717	...	1817	1817	1843	1917
Scheffau am Wilden Kaiser ★ d.	...	0559	0559	...	0753	0818	...	0923	1123	1123	...	1308	1311	1408	1408	1623	...	1723	1723	...	1823	1823	...	1923
Söll (Dorf) ♥ d.	0550	0612	0615	0715	0810	0832	...	0940	1137	1140	...	1325	1325	1422	1425	1645e	...	1737	1745	1745	1837	1840	...	1940
Wörgl Hauptbahnhof a.	0620	...	0645	0750	0840	...	...	1010	...	1210	...	1355	1352	...	1455	1715	...	...	1808	1808	...	1903	...	2003

e – Arrives 1637.
¶ – Also Nov. 1.
z – Not Nov. 1.
★ – Scheffau am Wilden Kaiser Am Trattenbach.
r – Runs 5–10 minutes later during school holiday periods.

♥ – 🚌 **KUFSTEIN** Bahnhof → **SÖLL** Dorf (journey time: 27–29 minutes): 0540 ⚒, 0640 Ⓐ, 0735 Ⓐ, 0740 ⑥**z**, 0840, 1010, 1110, 1210 Ⓐ, 1300 Ⓒ, 1310 Ⓐ, 1410 Ⓐ, 1510 Ⓒ, 1524 Ⓐ, 1610 ⚒, 1710 Ⓐ, 1740 Ⓒ, 1810 Ⓐ and 1907 Ⓐ.
🚌 **SÖLL** Dorf → **KUFSTEIN** Bahnhof (journey time: 25–29 minutes): 0610 ⚒, 0710 Ⓐ, 0812 ⚒, 0915 Ⓒ, 0940 Ⓐ, 1040, 1140, 1240 Ⓐ, 1330 Ⓒ, 1337 Ⓐ, 1440 Ⓐ, 1540 Ⓒ, 1551 Ⓐ, 1640 ⑥**z**, 1642 Ⓐ, 1742 Ⓐ, 1810 †, 1840 ⚒ and 1934 Ⓐ.

959 🚌 ZELL AM SEE - HINTERGLEMM

ÖBB-Postbus Route **680**

km		⚒	E	E		E		E		A		A		A	
0	**Zell am See** Bahnhof .... d.	0610p	0655	0820	0920	1020	1120	1220	1320	1420	1520	1620	1720	1820	1920
20	Saalbach Schattberg............. a.	0637	0725	0852	0952	1052	1152	1252	1352	1452	1552	1652	1752	1852	1952
23	**Hinterglemm** Ellmauweg...... a.	0643	0731	0858	0958	1058	1158	1258	1358	1458	1558	1658	1758	1858	1958

	⚒	E			E		E		E		A		A		A
Hinterglemm Ellmauweg....... d.	0611	0657	0750	...	0920	1020	1120	1220	1320	1420	1520	1620	1720	1820	1915
Saalbach Schattberg.............. d.	0618	0703	0800	...	0930	1030	1130	1230	1330	1430	1530	1630	1730	1830	1921
Zell am See Bahnhof............ a.	0648p	0735	0834	...	1004	1104	1204	1304	1404	1504	1604	1704	1804	1904	1953

A – Ⓐ (daily Dec. 15 - Apr. 25 and June 20 - Oct. 3).
E – ⚒ (daily Dec. 15 - Apr. 26 and June 20 - Oct. 4).

p – Zell am See Postplatz (not Bahnhof).

Information: ✆ +43 (0) 6542 5444-18

960 SALZBURG - SCHWARZACH - INNSBRUCK

km			*EN* **464** ⊠		⚒	⚒	Ⓒ	Ⓐ	*IC* **590**	⚒		*IC* **1280** ⑥**N**		*EC* **85**	⚒	*IC* **592**	⚒	*IC* **1284** ⑦**M**		*EC* **111**	Ⓐ	*IC* **542** Ⓒ		
		2	**A**	2	2	2	2	2	✕⊖	2	2		2		2	🍷⊖	2		2	✕⊖	2	🍷	2	2
	Wien Westbahnhof **950** ..... d.	...	...	...	...	...	...	...	...	...	...	...	...	...	...	...	...	...	...	...	...	0656	...	...
0	**Salzburg** Hbf.**951 970 975** ‡ d.	0021	...	...	...	...	0425	0441	0612	...	...	...	0708	...	...	0812	...	...	0908	1012	...	1015	...	...
29	Golling-Abtenau .... **970** ‡ d.	0059	...	...	...	...	0505	0505	0633	...	...	...	0734	...	...	0833	...	...	0934	1033	...	1038	...	...
53	**Bischofshofen**.... **970 975** ‡ d.	0124	0158c	...	...	...	0529	0529	0654	...	...	...	0756	...	...	0854	...	...	0956	1054	...	1102	...	...
61	St Johann im Pongau . **970** ‡ d.	0134	|	...	...	...	0539	0539	0703	...	...	...	0804	...	...	0903	...	...	1004	1103	...	1111	...	...
67	**Schwarzach - St Veit**.. **970** ‡ d.	0139	0226	...	...	...	0547	0547	0709	0712	...	...	0811	...	...	0909	0912	1005	1012	1109	1112	1119	...	...
99	**Zell am See** .... d.	...	|	...	...	...	0623	0623	▬	0745	...	0839	0845	...	...	...	0945	1035	1045	▬	1145	1148	...	...
113	Saalfelden .... d.	...	|	0412	0530	0554	0636	0636	Ⓐ	0756	...	0850	0856	...	...	...	0954	1046	1056	...	1156	1158	...	...
131	Hochfilzen............................. d.	...	|	0429	0547	0614	0653	0653	2	0814	...	0906	0914	...	1014	...	...	1102	1114	...	1214	|	...	...
148	St Johann in Tirol .... d.	...	|	0445	0603	0632	0710	0710	0757	0832	0918	0923	0932	...	1032	...	...	1118	1132	*EC*	1232	1228	...	1318
157	**Kitzbühel** .... d.	...	|	0453	0611	0641	0718	0718	0806	0841	0926	0931	0941	...	1041	...	...	1127	1141	**87**	1241	1236	...	1326
166	Kirchberg in Tirol .... d.	...	|	0502	0622	0652	0727	0727	0817	0852	0934	0943	0952	...	1052	...	...	1139	1152		1252	1244	...	1334
192	Wörgl Hbf .... **951** a.	...	|	0529	0647	0721	0752	0752	0846	0921	0959	1011	1021	1051	1121	...	...	1207	1221	1251	1321	1305	1336	1359
217	Jenbach.......................... **951** a.	...	|	0549	*0708*r	*0749*e	0812	0812	*0904*	*0957*	1019	...	*1057*	1104	*1157*	...	...	...	*1257*	1304	...	|	1357	1419
251	**Innsbruck** Hbf.............. **951** a.	...	0449	0619	*0737*r	*0817*e	0840	0837	*0923*	*1032*	1047	...	...	1123	*1232*	...	...	...	...	1323	...	1336	1432	1447

		IC **690**	*EC* **164**	⚒	Ⓐ		*EC* **113**	⚒	Ⓐ		*EC* **115**	*IC* **518**	Ⓐ			Ⓐ	*IC* **692**		Ⓑ	Ⓐ		*EC* **117** **1217**		*REX* **1516** ¶
	2	🍷	**Z**✕	2	2	2	✕⊖	2	2	2	⊗⊖	**G**🍷	2	2	2	2	🍷⊖	2	2	2	2	⊗⊖	2	2
Wien Westbahnhof **950** ...... d.	...	0856	...	...	...	...	...	...	...	...	...	...	...	...	...	...	1456	...	...	...	...	...	...	1856
Salzburg Hbf..**951 970 975** ‡ d.	1108	1212	...	...	...	1308	1412	...	...	1508	1612	...	...	...	1708	1742	1812	...	...	...	1908	2012	...	2211
Golling-Abtenau .... **970** ‡ d.	1134	1233	...	...	...	1334	1433	...	...	1534	1633	...	...	...	1734	1810	1833	...	...	...	1934	2033	...	2237
Bischofshofen..... **970 975** ‡ d.	1156	1254	1250	...	...	1356	1454	...	...	1556	1654	1650	...	...	1756	1835	1854	...	...	...	1956	2054	...	2259
St Johann im Pongau .. **970** ‡ d.	1204	1303	1259	...	...	1404	1503	...	...	1604	1703	1659	...	...	1804	1845	1903	...	...	...	2004	2103	...	2307
Schwarzach - St Veit... **970** ‡ d.	1211	1309	1312j	...	...	1412	1509	1512	...	1611	1709	1712j	...	...	1813	1851	1909	1912	1912	...	2011	2109	2112	2315
Zell am See .... d.	1245	▬	1343	...	...	1445	▬	1545	...	1645	▬	1743	...	...	1846	1927	...	1948	1948	...	2045	...	2148	2350
Saalfelden .... d.	1256	...	1352	1356e	...	1456	...	1556	...	1656	...	1752	1756	...	1856	1937	...	2000	2001	...	2056	...	2200	0001
Hochfilzen............................. d.	1314	...	|	1414	...	1514	...	1614	1702	1714	...	|	1814	1902	1914	...	...	...	2017	2102	2114	...	...	...
St Johann in Tirol .... d.	1332	*EC*	1420	1432	1518	1532	*EC*	1632	1718	1732	*EC*	1820	1832	1918	1932	...	...	...	2035	2118	2132	...	...	...
Kitzbühel .... d.	1341	**89**	1428	1441	1526	1541	**83**	1641	1726	1741	**189**	1828	1841	1926	1941	...	...	...	2044	2126	2141	...	...	...
Kirchberg in Tirol .... d.	1352		1436	1452	1534	1552		1652	1734	1752		1836	1852	1934	1952	...	...	...	2053	2134	2152	...	...	...
Wörgl Hbf .... **951** a.	1421	1451	1458	1521	1559	1621	1651	1721	1759	1821	1851	1858	1921	1959	2021	...	...	...	2121	2159	2221	...	...	...
Jenbach.......................... **951** a.	*1457*	1504	1514	*1557*	1619	*1657*	1704	*1757*	1819	*1857*	1904	1914	*1957*	2019	*2057*	...	...	...	*2157*	2219	*2257*	...	...	...
Innsbruck Hbf.............. **951** a.	...	1523	1535	*1632*	1647	...	1723	*1832*	1847	...	1923	1936	*2032*	2047	*2132*	...	...	...	*2232*	2247	*2332*	...	...	...

	EN **465** ✣	⚒	⚒	*REX* **1501** §		⚒	Ⓐ		⚒	Ⓐ	*IC* **861**			*IC* **515**	*EC* **114**	Ⓐ	Ⓒ	⚒	*IC* **865**			⚒	*EC* **163**	*IC* **691**
	A	2	2	2	2	2	2	2	2	2	🍷	2	2	**G**🍷	⊗⊖	2	2	2	🍷	2	2	2	**Z**✕	🍷⊖
Innsbruck Hbf.............. **951** d.	0056	...	...	...	...	...	*0513*	...	*0528*	*0528*	0705	...	0713	0824	...	0849	0849	*0928*	1105	...	1113	*1128*	1224	...
Jenbach.......................... **951** d.	0119	...	...	...	...	...	*0539*	...	*0602*	*0602*	0722	...	0741	0846	...	0915	0915	*1002*	1122	...	1139	*1202*	1245	...
Wörgl Hbf .... **951** d.	0138	...	...	...	...	0538	0601	...	0631	0631	0735	0738	0802	0902	...	0938	0938	1038	1135	1138	1200	1238	1302	...
Kirchberg in Tirol .... d.	|	...	...	...	...	0608	0631	...	0701	0701	▬	0808	0828	0924	...	1008	1008	1108	▬	1208	1226	1308	1324	...
Kitzbühel .... d.	|	...	...	...	...	0619	0642	...	0712	0712	...	0819	0838	0932	...	1019	1019	1119	...	1219	1234	1319	1332	...
St Johann in Tirol .... d.	|	...	...	...	...	0628	0652	...	0721	0721	...	0828	0845	0940	...	1028	1028	1128	...	1228	1241	1328	1340	...
Hochfilzen............................. d.	|	...	...	...	...	0646	0710	...	0739	0741	*IC*	0846	...	|	...	1046	1046	1146	*EC*	1246	...	1346	|	...
Saalfelden .... d.	|	...	0458	0554	0705	0705	0727	0735	...	0800	**693**	0905	...	1008	...	1105	1105	1205	**112**	1305	...	1402e	1408	...
Zell am See .... d.	|	...	0508	0604	0715	0715	...	0748	...	0813	🍷⊖	0915	...	1019	...	1115	1121j	1215	✕⊖	1315	...	...	1419	...
Schwarzach - St Veit... **970** ‡ d.	0324	0423	0542	0640	0749	0749	...	0824	...	0847	0850	0949	...	1056j	1050	1149	1157	1247	1250	1349	...	...	1456j	1450
St Johann im Pongau .. **970** ‡ d.	|	0428	0548	0647	0755	0755	...	0829	...	...	0856	0955	...	1102	1056	1155	1202	...	1256	1355	...	...	1502	1456
Bischofshofen..... **970 975** ‡ d.	0336c	0439	0558	0656	0804	0804	...	0840	...	...	0905	1004	...	1110	1105	1204	1211	...	1305	1404	...	...	1510	1505
Golling-Abtenau .... **970** ‡ d.	...	0503	0620	0718	0825	0825	...	0904	...	...	0925	1025	...	...	1125	1225	1231	...	1325	1425	...	...	...	1525
Salzburg Hbf..**951 970 975** ‡ a.	...	0540	0645	0745	0851	0851	...	0940	...	...	0948	1051	...	...	1148	1251	1256	...	1348	1451	...	...	...	1548
Wien Westbahnhof **950** ...... a.	...	...	...	1104	...	...	...	...	...	...	1304	...	...	...	...	...	...	...	...	...	...	...	...	1904

	IC **867**		Ⓐ		Ⓐ	*IC* **741** Ⓒ	*RJ* **869**		Ⓐ	Ⓐ		*EC* **110**	*IC* **1281** ⑥**P**	*IC* **961**				*RJ* **661**	⚒	Ⓐ	Ⓒ	Ⓐ		
	🍷	2	2	2	2	🍷	✕	2	2	2	2	✕⊖		✕	2	2	2	✕	2	2	2	2	2	2
Innsbruck Hbf.............. **951** d.	1305	...	1313	1328	...	1424	1505	...	1513	*1528*	...	...	...	1705	...	1713	*1728*h	1905	...	1913	*1928*	*1952*	*2128*	*2328*
Jenbach.......................... **951** d.	1322	...	1339	1402	...	|	1522	...	1539	*1602*	...	...	...	1722	...	1741	*1802*h	1922	...	1939	*2002*	*2017*	*2202*	*0002*
Wörgl Hbf .... **951** d.	1335	1338	1400	1424	1438	1455	1535	1538	1600	1638	...	...	1647	1735	1738	1802	1838	1935	1938	2000	2038	2044	2238	0029
Kirchberg in Tirol .... d.	...	1408	1426	...	1508	1517	▬	1608	1626	1708	...	...	1719	...	1807	1828	1908	▬	2008	2026	2108	2110	2308	0057
Kitzbühel .... d.	...	1419	1434	...	1519	1526	...	1619	1634	1719	...	...	1729	...	1818	1836	1919	...	2019	2034	2119	2119	2319	0105
St Johann in Tirol .... d.	...	1428	1441	...	1528	1534	...	1628	1642	1728	...	...	1737	...	1827	1844	1928	...	2028	2042	2128	2127	2328	0114
Hochfilzen............................. d.	...	1446	...	...	1546	|	*IC*	1646	1656	1746	...	...	1758	...	1844	1858	1946	*IC*	2046	2100	2146	2143	2346	0130
Saalfelden .... d.	...	1505	...	...	1605	1604	**591**	1705	...	1805	1805	...	1813	...	1903	...	2005	**593**	2103k	2117	2203	2202	0003	0147
Zell am See .... d.	...	1515	...	...	1615	1615	🍷⊖	1715	...	1815	1815	...	1825	...	1914	...	2015	✕⊖	...	...	...	2214	...	...
Schwarzach - St Veit... **970** ‡ d.	...	1549	...	...	1647	1654j	1650	1749	...	1849	1849	1852	1854	...	1949	...	2047	2050	...	...	...	2247	...	...
St Johann im Pongau .. **970** ‡ d.	...	1555	...	...	...	1700	1656	1755	...	...	...	1858	...	...	1955	...	...	2056	...	...	...	...	...	...
Bischofshofen..... **970 975** ‡ d.	...	1604	...	...	...	1709	1705	1804	...	...	...	1907	...	...	2004	...	...	2105	...	...	...	...	...	...
Golling-Abtenau........... **970** ‡ d.	...	1625	...	...	...	1731	1725	1825	...	...	...	1927	...	...	2025	...	...	2125	...	...	...	...	...	...
Salzburg Hbf..**951 970 975** ‡ a.	...	1651	...	...	...	1756	1748	1851	...	...	...	1950	...	...	2051	...	...	2148	...	...	...	...	...	...
Wien Westbahnhof **950** ...... a.	...	...	...	...	...	2104	...	...	...	...	...	...	...	...	...	...	...	...	...	...	...	...	...	...

A – ZÜRICHSEE – 🛏 1, 2 cl., ▬ 2 cl. and (2) Graz - Feldkirch - Buchs 🛃 - Zürich and v.v. Conveys from / to Schwarzach 🛏 1, 2 cl.*, ▬ 2 cl.* and (2) Beograd - Zagreb - Ljubljana - Villach - Schwarzach - Zürich and v.v.
G – From / to Graz (Table **975**).
M – ⑦ Jan. 5 - Apr. 6; ⑦ June 22 - Sept. 14. (12) Schwarzach - München - Flensburg.
N – ⑥ Dec. 28 - Mar. 29; ⑥ June 28 - Sept. 13. (12) Zell am See - Wörgl - München.
P – ⑥ Dec. 21 - Apr. 5; ⑥ June 21 - Sept. 13. (12) München - Wörgl - Schwarzach.
Z – (12) and ✕ Graz - Selzthal - Bischofshofen - Innsbruck - Buchs 🛃 - Zürich and v.v.

c – Not Sept. 2 – 28.
e – Ⓐ only.
h – On Ⓐ departs Innsbruck *1743*, Jenbach *1809*.
j – Arrives 7 – 8 minutes earlier.
k – ⑥ (not Nov. 1).
r – 10 – 11 minutes later on ⑥.
v – ⚒ only.

* – 🛏 1, 2 cl. and ▬ 2 cl. from / to Zagreb.
¶ – Train *IC* **744** Wien - Salzburg.
§ – Train *IC* **545** Salzburg - Wien.
⊖ – See Table **970** for further details.
⊠ – Train number **1364** on the mornings of Sept. 2 – 28.
✣ – Train number **1365** on the mornings of Sept. 2 – 28.

‡ – See panel below main table for other local stopping trains.

	⚒				
Freilassing ....**890** d.	0529	0607v	0707		2207
Salzburg Hbf........**890** d.	0543	0621	0721	and	2221
Golling-Abtenau .... d.	0620	0659	0759	hourly	2259
Bischofshofen........... d.	0645	0724	0824	until	2324
St Johann im Pongau . d.	0655	0734	0834		2334
Schwarzach - St Veit.. a.	0700	0739	0839		2339

Schwarzach - St Veit.. d.	0524	...	0624		2224
St Johann im Pongau . d.	0529	...	0629	and	2229
Bischofshofen........... d.	0540	...	0640	hourly	2240
Golling-Abtenau .... d.	0604	...	0704	until	2304
Salzburg Hbf........**890** a.	0640	...	0740		2340
Freilassing ....**890** a.	0658	...	0753		2353

ATTNANG-PUCHHEIM - STAINACH-IRDNING — 961

2nd class only

km		⚒		Ⓐ									ⒸA											
	Wien Westbahnhof **950** d.	...	...	...	...	...	...	...	...	...	...	...	0956	...	...	...	...	...	...	...	...	...	...	...
0	**Attnang-Puchheim** d.	...	...	0449	...	0602	0715	0811	0911	1011	1111	1211	1211	1311	1411	1511	1611	1711	1811	1911	2005	2105	...	...
12	**Gmunden** d.	...	...	0505	...	0621	0732	0826	0932	1026	1132	1226	1226	1332	1426	1532	1626	1732	1826	1932	2023	2123	...	...
17	Altmünster am Traunsee d.	...	...	0512	...	0627	0738	0832	0938	1032	1138	1232	1232	1338	1432	1538	1632	1738	1832	1938	2029	2130	...	...
22	Traunkirchen d.	...	...	0518	...	0633	0744	0838	0944	1038	1144	1238	1238	1344	1438	1544	1638	1744	1838	1944	2035	2135	...	...
27	Ebensee Landungsplatz d.	...	...	0524	...	0641	0752	0844	0952	1044	1152	1244	1244	1352	1444	1552	1644	1752	1844	1952	2042	2143	...	...
44	**Bad Ischl** d.	...	...	0549	...	0706	0820	0903	1020	1103	1220	1303	1303	1420	1503	1620	1703	1820	1903	2020	2103	2207	...	...
54	Bad Goisern d.	...	...	...	...	0720	0833	0913	1033	1113	1233	1313	1313	1433	1513	1633	1713	1833	1913	2033	2116	...	...	...
64	Hallstatt ⊡ d.	...	...	...	...	0732	0848	0925	1048	1125	1248	1325	1325	1448	1525	1648	1725	1848	|	|	|	...	...	...
67	Obertraun-Dachsteinhöhlen d.	...	...	...	...	0735	0851	0928	1051	1128	1251	1328	1328	1451	1528	1651	1728	1851	1928	2051	2131	...	...	...
78	**Bad Aussee** d.	0503	0632	...	...	0749	...	0942	...	1142	...	1342	1342	...	1542	...	1742	...	1942	2104	2143	...	...	...
93	Bad Mitterndorf d.	0521	0650	...	...	0805	...	0959	...	1159	...	1359	1359	...	1559	...	1759	...	1959	...	...	...	...	...
108	**Stainach-Irdning** a.	0538	0707	...	...	0818	...	1015	...	1215	...	1415	1415	...	1615	...	1815	...	2015	...	...	...	...	...

			Ⓐ	⚒	⚒											ⒸB	Ⓒ	Ⓐ				Ⓒ	Ⓐ	
Stainach-Irdning d.	...	...	...	...	0611	...	0713	...	0940	...	1140	...	1340	...	1540	1540	...	...	1740	...	...	1940	1940	2047
Bad Mitterndorf d.	...	...	...	...	0629	...	0730	...	0959	...	1159	...	1359	...	1559	1559	...	...	1759	...	...	1959	1959	2104
Bad Aussee d.	...	0457	...	0604	0650	0650	0811r	...	1016	...	1216	...	1416	...	1616	1616	...	...	1816	...	...	2016	2016	2121
Obertraun-Dachsteinhöhlen d.	...	0509	...	0616	0702	0702	0824	0904	1028	1104	1228	1304	1428	1504	1628	1628	1704	1704	1828	1905	...	2028	...	...
Hallstatt ⊡ d.	...	|	...	|	0706	0706	0828	0907	1032	1107	1232	1307	1432	1507	1632	1632	1707	1707	1832	|	...	|	...	...
Bad Goisern d.	...	0525	...	0631	0720	0720	0842	0922	1043	1122	1243	1322	1443	1522	1643	1643	1722	1722	1843	1922	...	2043	...	...
Bad Ischl d.	0435	0538	0600	0644	0733	0733	0853	0935	1053	1135	1253	1335	1453	1535	1653	1653	1735	1740	1853	1935	...	2053	...	...
Ebensee Landungsplatz d.	0458	0602	0624	0710	0800	0800	0913	1001	1113	1201	1313	1401	1513	1601	1713	1713	1801	1801	1913	2001	...	2114	...	...
Traunkirchen d.	0506	0609	0633	0718	0808	0808	0919	1009	1119	1209	1319	1409	1519	1609	1719	1719	1809	1809	1919	2009	...	2120	...	...
Altmünster am Traunsee d.	0512	0615	0639	0724	0814	0814	0925	1016	1125	1216	1325	1416	1525	1616	1725	1725	1816	1816	1925	2016	...	2131	...	...
Gmunden d.	0519	0621	0645	0732	0826	0826	0931	1026	1131	1226	1331	1426	1531	1626	1731	1731	1826	1826	1931	2023	...	2137	...	...
Attnang-Puchheim a.	0535	0639	0703	0748	0842	0842	0945	1044	1146	1244	1346	1444	1546	1644	1746	1746	1844	1844	1946	2041	...	2155	...	...
Wien Westbahnhof **950** a.	...	...	...	...	...	...	...	...	...	...	...	...	...	...	...	1956	...	...	...	...	...	...	...	...

A – (12) Wien (**546**) - Attnang-Puchheim - Stainach.
B – (12) Stainach - Attnang-Puchheim (**829**) - Wien.

d – Runs daily Apr. 28 - Oct. 31.
r – Arrives 0748.

⊡ – ⛴ services operate Hallstatt Bahnhof - Hallstatt Markt. Journey: 8 minutes. **Operator**: Hallstättersee-Schifffahrt Hemetsberger KG ✆ +43 (0) 6134 8228.
From Hallstatt Bahnhof at 0706 ⚒, 0735 ⚒, 0830 ⚒ **d**, 0905, 0930, 1035, 1105, 1130, 1235, 1305, 1330, 1435, 1505, 1530, 1635, 1705, 1730 and 1850.
From Hallstatt Markt at 0650 ⚒, 0720 ⚒, 0815 ⚒ **d**, 0850, 0915, 1015, 1050, 1115, 1215, 1250, 1315, 1415, 1450, 1515, 1615, 1650, 1715 and 1815.

LINZ - PASSAU and SIMBACH — 962

km										*ICE* 228					*ICE* 28	5914					*ICE* 26				
		⚒ 2	⚒ 2	G2	2	Ⓐ A2	Ⓐ 2	Ⓒ 2	Ⓒ 2	✕	2	2	2	Ⓐ 2	✕	⊖2	2	2	2	⚒ 2	D✕	2	2	⚒ 2	⚒ 2
	Wien Westbahnhof **950** d.	...	...	...	...	...	...	...	...	0652	...	...	...	...	0852	0728f	...	...	...	...	1052	...	...	...	...
0	**Linz** Hbf **950** d.	0454	...	0544	0600	0658	...	0736	...	0817	0851	...	0951	...	1017	1038	1051	...	1151	...	1217	1251	...	1351	...
25	**Wels** Hbf **950** d.	0518	...	0612	0621	0723	...	0755	...	0832	0909	...	1009	...	1032	1055	1110	...	1209	...	1232	1309	...	1409	...
54	Neumarkt-Kallham d.	0545	0620	0642	0645	0751	0811	0824	0832	|	0936	0939	1033	1039	|	1117	1139	1140	1233	1239	|	1336	1339	1433	1439
	Ried im Innkreis d.	|	0643	|	0710	|	0831	|	0855	|	|	1001	|	1101	|	|	1201	|	|	1301	|	|	1401	|	1501
	Braunau am Inn a.	|	0719	|	0740	|	0907	|	0940	|	|	1040	|	1140	|	|	1240	|	|	1340	|	|	1440	|	1540
	Simbach (Inn) 🏛 a.	|	...	|	0744	|	*0945*	|	0945	|	|	1045	|	1145	|	|	1245	|	|	1345	|	|	1445	|	1545
92	Schärding d.	0623	...	0718	...	0824	...	0856	...	|	1010	...	1101	...	|	1144	...	1216	1301	...	|	1410	...	1501	...
106	**Passau** Hbf a.	0634	...	0730	...	0836	...	0908	...	0918	1023	...	1113	...	1118	1156	...	1228	1313	...	1318	1423	...	1513	...
	Nürnberg Hbf **920** a.	...	...	...	...	...	...	...	...	1125	...	...	...	...	1326	...	...	...	...	...	1525	...	...	...	...
	Frankfurt (Main) Hbf **920** a.	...	...	...	...	...	...	...	...	1340	...	...	...	...	1536	...	...	...	...	...	1736	...	...	...	...

	ICE 90					*ICE* 22								*ICE* 20						*IC* 746		*EN* 420 490	*EN* 944		
	H✕	2	2	2	⚒ 2	D✕	Ⓐ 2	Ⓐ 2	2	2	Ⓐ 2	2	2	✕	Ⓐ 2	Ⓐ 2	2	2	2	🍷	2	◇		2	Ⓐ 2
Wien Westbahnhof **950** d.	1252	...	...	...	...	1452	...	...	...	...	...	...	...	1652	...	...	...	...	...	1956	...	2000	2056	...	...
Linz Hbf **950** d.	1417	1451	...	1551	...	1617	1625	1636	1651	...	1725	1751	1752	1817	1851	...	1951	...	2051	2132	...	2152	2240	...	...
Wels Hbf **950** d.	1432	1510	...	1609	...	1632	1642	1654	1709	...	1742	1809	1818	1832	1909	...	2009	...	2109	2143	2148	2209	2251	2257	...
Neumarkt-Kallham d.	|	1539	1540	1633	1639	|	1704	1720	1736	1739	1809	1833	1840	|	1936	1939	2036	2039	2136	...	2216	|	...	2324	2327
Ried im Innkreis d.	|	1601	|	|	1701	|	|	1737	|	1801	|	|	1901	|	|	2001	|	2105	|	...	2237	|	...	|	2347
Braunau am Inn a.	|	1640	|	|	1740	|	|	1809	|	1840	|	|	1940	|	|	2040	|	2141	|	...	2311	|	...	|	...
Simbach (Inn) 🏛 a.	|	1645	|	|	1745	|	|	...	|	1845	|	|	1945	|	|	2045	|	2145	|	...	...	|	...	|	...
Schärding d.	|	...	1616	1701	...	|	1732	...	1810	...	1843	1901	...	|	2010	...	2110	...	2210	...	...	2251	...	2358	...
Passau Hbf a.	1518	...	1628	1713	...	1718	...	...	1823	...	1856	1913	...	1918	2023	...	2123	...	2223	...	...	2304	...	...	...
Nürnberg Hbf **920** a.	1725	...	...	...	...	1925	...	...	...	...	...	...	...	2125	...	...	...	...	...	...	...	0112	...	...	...
Frankfurt (Main) Hbf **920** a.	...	...	...	...	...	2136	...	...	...	...	...	...	...	2339	...	...	...	...	...	...	...	0602	...	...	...

km					*EN* 421 491																*ICE* 21				
		⚒ 2	Ⓐ 2	2	◇	⚒ 2	† 2	2	⚒ 2	Ⓐ 2	Ⓐ 2	2	† 2	⚒ 2	Ⓐ 2	2	2	Ⓒ 2	2	2	✕	Ⓐ 2	2	2	2
	Frankfurt (Main) Hbf **920** d.	...	...	...	2300	...	...	...	...	...	...	...	...	...	...	...	...	...	...	...	0622	...	...	...	...
	Nürnberg Hbf **920** d.	...	...	...	0324	...	...	...	...	...	...	...	...	...	...	...	...	...	...	...	0830	...	...	...	...
	Passau Hbf d.	...	0408	0424c	0535	...	...	0539	0606	...	0622	...	...	0647	...	...	0807	...	0933	...	1038	...	1044	...	1136
	Schärding d.	0357	0421	0437	0548	...	...	0552	0619	...	0635	...	...	0700	...	...	0820	...	0946	...	|	...	1057	...	1149
0	**Simbach** (Inn) 🏛 d.	|	|	|	|	...	...	|	|	...	|	...	...	|	0718	...	|	0817	|	0919	|	1019	|	1119	|
2	**Braunau** am Inn d.	|	|	|	|	0513	0528	|	|	0610	|	0629	0629	|	0723	0751	|	0821	|	0923	|	1023	|	1123	|
39	Ried im Innkreis d.	|	|	|	|	0552	0604	|	|	0643	|	0710	0710	|	0755	0831	|	0855	|	1001	|	1101	|	1201	|
61	Neumarkt-Kallham d.	0431	0451	0513	|	0614	0622	0626	0648	0702	0706	0728	0730	0736	0812	0850	0854	0912	1019	1024	|	1119	1126	1219	1224
90	**Wels** Hbf **950** d.	0458	0516	0541	0632	0639	...	0654	0718	...	0729	...	0758	0807	0835	...	0922	0935	...	1052	1129	...	1152	...	1252
115	**Linz** Hbf **950** a.	0520	0532	0603	0647	0654e	...	0709	0743	...	0747	...	...	0823	0855	...	0938	0955	...	1109	1143	...	1208	...	1308
	Wien Westbahnhof **950** a.	...	...	...	0844	...	...	...	...	...	...	...	...	...	...	...	...	...	...	...	1308	...	...	...	...

	ICE 23					*ICE* 91					*ICE* 27			5927		*ICE* 29			*IC* 961		*IC* 941	*ICE* 229			*IC* 943
	D✕	⚒ 2	2	2	2	H✕	⚒ 2	⚒ 2	2	2	D✕	⚒ 2	2	⊖2	2	✕	2	2	✕	2	🍷	✕	Ⓐ 2	2	
Frankfurt (Main) Hbf **920** d.	0819v	...	...	...	...	...	...	...	...	...	1221	...	...	...	...	1416	...	...	...	...	...	1621	...	...	...
Nürnberg Hbf **920** d.	1030	...	...	...	...	1230	...	...	...	...	1430	...	...	...	...	1630	...	...	...	...	...	1830	...	...	...
Passau Hbf d.	1238	...	1244	1333	...	1438	...	1444	...	1536	1638	...	1644	1719	...	1838	...	1851	...	...	...	2038	...	2051	...
Schärding d.	|	...	1257	1346	...	|	...	1457	...	1549	|	...	1657	1730	...	|	...	1904	...	...	...	|	...	2104	...
Simbach (Inn) 🏛 d.	|	1219e	|	|	1319	|	1419	|	1519	|	|	1619	|	|	1719	|	1819	|	...	1919	...	|	2019	|	...
Braunau am Inn d.	|	1223	|	|	1323	|	1423	|	1523	|	|	1623	|	|	1723	|	1823	|	...	1923	...	|	2023	|	...
Ried im Innkreis d.	|	1301	|	|	1401	|	1501	|	1601	|	|	1701	|	|	1801	|	1901	|	...	2001	...	|	2101	|	...
Neumarkt-Kallham d.	|	1319	1326	1419	1424	|	1519	1526	1619	1624	|	1719	1726	1755	1824	|	1924	1937	...	2024	...	|	2119	2137	...
Wels Hbf **950** d.	1329	...	1352	...	1452	1529	...	1552	...	1652	1729	...	1752	1818	1852	1929	1952	2006	2015	2051	2115	2129	...	2204	2215
Linz Hbf **950** a.	1343	...	1408	...	1509	1543	...	1608	...	1708	1743	...	1808	1836	1909	1943	2009	2022c	2027	...	2127	2143	...	...	2227
Wien Westbahnhof **950** a.	1508	...	...	...	...	1708	...	...	...	...	1908	...	...	2155f	...	2108	...	...	2212	...	2304	2308	...	...	...

– From Amstetten (Table **950**).
– To / from Dortmund (Table **800**).
– From Garsten (Table **976**).
– To / from Hamburg (Table **900**).

c – Ⓒ only.
e – Ⓐ only.
f – Wien **Franz-Josefs-Bahnhof**.
v – 0821 on ⑦.

⊖ – May 1 - Oct. 26. (2) Wien Franz-Josefs-Bf - Tulln - St Pölten - Passau and v.v. *Einfach-Raus-Ticket* not valid.
◇ – 🛏 1, 2 cl., couchette 2 cl. and (2) (*EN* **420**/**1**) Wien - Nürnberg - Frankfurt - Köln and v.v.; 🛏 1, 2 cl., couchette 2 cl. and (2) (*EN* **490**/**1** – HANS ALBERS) Wien - Nürnberg - Hamburg and v.v. Ⓡ for journeys to Germany.

963 SALZBURG and ST WOLFGANG - STROBL - BAD ISCHL

Routes 150, 546

km	Route 150	⚒	†	Ⓐ	⑥z		⚒		k	Ⓐm	Ⓒ	Ⓐ	⚒	Ⓒ	Ⓐ	⚒	Ⓒ	Ⓐ	Ⓐ	Ⓒ	Ⓐ		†	Ⓐ	⑥z
0	**Salzburg** Hbf △ d.	0555	...	*0625*	0645	0815	0915	1015	1115	1115	1215	1220	1320r	1415	1420	1520r	1615	1625	1725	1815	1820	1915	2015	2015	2215
32	St Gilgen (Busbahnhof) d.	0645	0650	0730	0735	0910	1010	1110	1210	1220	1310	1315	1410	1510	1510	1610	1710	1710	1810	1910	1910	2005	2058	2105	2258
45	Strobl (Busbahnhof) d.	0703	0706	0748	0751	0928	1028	1128	1228	1235	1328	1333	1428	1528	1528	1628	1728	1728	1828	1928	1928	2021	2113	2121	2313
57	**Bad Ischl** Bahnhof a.	0725	0725	0810	0810	0950	1050	1150	1250	1257	1350	1355	1450	1550	1550	1650	1750	1750	1850	1947	1950	2040	2130	2140	2330

Route 150	⚒	Ⓐ	Ⓐ		⚒	Ⓐ	Ⓒ	†	⚒		k	Ⓐm	Ⓒ	Ⓐ	⑥z	Ⓐ		⚒		⚒		Ⓐ		⑥z	⚒
Bad Ischl Bahnhof d.	0504	...	...	0611	0646	0740	0746	0824	0924	1024	1124	1124	1224	1224	1324	1336	1424	1524	1624	1724	1824	1924	2024	...	...
Strobl (Busbahnhof) d.	0520	0550	0615	0631	0707	0801	0807	0845	0945	1045	1145	1145	1245	1245	1345	1357	1445	1545	1645	1745	1845	1945	2040	...	...
St Gilgen (Busbahnhof) d.	0535	0605	0629	0645	0727	0821	0827	0905	1005	1105	1205	1220	1305	1315	1405	1415	1505	1605	1705	1805	1905	2005	2054	2105	2205
Salzburg Hbf △ a.	0619	0649	0715	0731	0819	0913	0919	0953	1057	1157	1257	1307	1357	1407	1457	1507	1557	1657	1757	1857	1953	2053	...	2153	2253

km	Route 546	Ⓐ	⚒	⚒	Ⓒ	†	Ⓐ	Ⓐ	Ⓐ		Ⓐ	Ⓒ	Ⓐ		Ⓐ		Ⓐ			Ⓐ	Ⓒ	Ⓐ	Ⓒ		
0	**St Wolfgang** ⊡ ‡... ♥ d.	0500	0557	0648	0735	0735	0740	0748	0900	0913	1013	1013	1100	1213	1318	1413	1513	1613	1713	1713	1813	1813	1828	1913	2003
7	Strobl (Busbahnhof) ♥ d.	0513	0612	0703	0747	0748	|	0800	|	0927	|	1028	|	1228	1333	1428	1528	1628	1727	1728	|	1828	1842	1927	2017
19	**Bad Ischl** Bahnhof a.	0533	0639	0730	...	0810	0812	...	0932	...	1045	1050	1132	1250	1400	1450	1555	1650	...	1755	1845	1850	...	...	...

Route 546	Ⓐ	⚒	⚒		Ⓐ	Ⓐ	Ⓒ	Ⓐ			⚒			Ⓐ			Ⓐ	Ⓒ		Ⓐ				
Bad Ischl Bahnhof d.	0605	0645	...	0823	0913	...	0913	1023	...	1113	1223	...	1330	1423	...	1513	1613	...	1713	1823	...	1913	...	...
Strobl (Busbahnhof) d.	0630	0708	0808	|	|	0930	0935	1045	1045	1135	1245	1245	1355	1445	1445	1535	1635	1645	1735	1845	1845	|	1930	2040
St Wolfgang ⊡ ‡ a.	0645	0723	0823	0853	0943	0945	0950	1100	1100	1150	1300	1300	1410	1500	1500	1550	1650	1700	1750	1900	1900	1943	1945	2055

k – ⑥ to June 28 (also Feb. 10 – 14, Apr. 14 – 18, 22, May 2, 30, June 10); ⚒ July 5 - Sept. 6; ⑥ from Sept. 13 (also Sept. 24; not Nov. 1).
m – Not Feb. 10 – 14, Apr. 14 – 22, May 2, 30, June 10, July 7 - Sept. 5, Sept. 24.
r – 5 minutes **earlier** on ⑥.
z – Not Nov. 1.

△ – All services also call at Mirabellplatz.
⊡ – St Wolfgang Schafbergbahnhof. All services also call at St Wolfgang Markt.
♥ – Additional services St Wolfgang - Strobl: 1028 Ⓐ, 1113 Ⓒ, 1313 Ⓒ and 1513 Ⓒ.
‡ – The **Schafbergbahn** narrow-gauge steam rack railway operates St Wolfgang - Schafbergspitze (*6 km*). Services operate subject to demand and weather conditions **Apr. 19 - Oct. 26**, 2014. 2nd class only. Special fares payable. Journey time: 45 minutes each way. ✆ +43 (0) 6138 2232 0.

964 STROBL - ST GILGEN (WOLFGANGSEE)

Service June 19 - Sept. 7

			⛴			⛴			⛴			⛴					
Strobl Schiffstation ⊡ d.	...	0845	...	0925	1025	...	1125	1225	...	1325	1425	...	1525	1625	1725	1820	1920
St Wolfgang Markt d.	...	|	...	|	|	1125	|	|	1325	1400	1500	1525	1600	1700	1800	1835	1933
St Wolfgang Schafbergbahnhof ‡ d.	0830	0910	0935	0955	1055	1133	1155	1255	1333	1408	1508	1533	1608	1708	1808	1845	1941
St Wolfgang Markt d.	|	0918	0945	1005	1105	|	1205	1305	|	|	|	|	|	|	|	...	...
St Gilgen Schiffstation ● a.	0855	0955	1015	1045	1145	1215	1245	1345	1415	1445	1545	1615	1645	1745	1845	...	...

					⛴			⛴			⛴			⛴			
St Gilgen Schiffstation ● d.	...	...	0900	1000	1030	1100	1200	1230	1300	1400	1430	1500	1600	1630	1700	1800	1850
St Wolfgang Markt d.	...	...	|	|	|	|	|	|	|	|	|	|	|	|	|	|	1925
St Wolfgang Schafbergbahnhof ‡ d.	0825	0902	0937	1037	1109	1137	1237	1309	1337	1437	1509	1537	1637	1709	1737	1837	1935
St Wolfgang Markt d.	|	0910	0950	1050	1117	1150	1250	1317	1350	1450	1517	1550	1650	1717	1750	1850	...
Strobl Schiffstation ⊡ a.	0840	0925	1015	1115	...	1215	1315	...	1415	1515	...	1615	1715	...	1815	1915	...

‡ – See note under Table **963**.
⊡ – Approximately 400 metres from Strobl Busbahnhof.
● – Approximately 500 metres from St Gilgen Busbahnhof.
⛴ – July 5 - Aug. 31 (subject to weather conditions). Operated by paddle-steamer *Kaiser Franz Josef I*. Supplement payable (€1).

969 TAUERN TUNNEL CAR - CARRYING TRAINS

BÖCKSTEIN - MALLNITZ-OBERVELLACH *11 km.* Transit time: 11 minutes. Passengers without cars are also conveyed. ✆ 05-1717. E-mail: autoschleuse.tauernbahn@pv.oebb.at
From Böckstein at 0620, 0720 and hourly until 2320. **From Mallnitz-Obervellach** at 0550, 0650 and hourly until 2250.

970 SALZBURG - VILLACH - KLAGENFURT

km		*EN* 499 🅁 L	*EN* 944 🅁 ♦	*EN* 234 2	⚒ 2	*D* 415 ♦	2	⚒ 2	2	Ⓐ 2	*IC* 590 ✕	*IC* 592 🍷	*EC* 111 ✕	*IC* 690 🍷	Ⓐ 2	*RJ* 632	*EC* 113 ✕♦	Ⓐ 2	*EC* 115 ⊗♦		*IC* 692 🍷		*EC* 117 ⊗♦
	Wien Westbahnhof **950** d.	...	2056	...	...	...	...	...	...	...	...	...	...	0856	...	...	...	...	...	...	1456	...	...
	München Hbf **890** d.	2340	|	...	...	...	...	...	...	...	...	...	0818	|	...	...	1218	...	1418	...	|	...	1818
0	**Salzburg** Hbf 960 975 d.	0134	0134	...	...	...	...	...	...	...	0612	0812	1012	1212	...	...	1412	...	1612	...	1812	...	2012
29	Golling-Abtenau 960 d.	|	|	...	...	...	...	...	...	...	0633	0833	1033	1233	...	...	1433	...	1633	...	1833	...	2033
53	**Bischofshofen** 960 975 d.	|	|	...	...	...	...	...	...	...	0654	0854	1054	1254	...	...	1454	...	1654	...	1854	...	2054
61	St Johann im Pongau 960 d.	|	|	...	...	...	...	...	...	...	0703	0903	1103	1303	...	...	1503	...	1703	...	1903	...	2103
67	**Schwarzach - St Veit** 960 d.	0226	0226	...	...	0427	...	...	...	0533	0711	0911	1111	1311	...	...	1511	...	1711	...	1911	...	2111
86	Bad Hofgastein d.	|	|	...	...	0444	...	...	...	0549	0729	0929	1129	1329	...	...	1529	...	1729	...	1929	...	2129
97	Bad Gastein d.	|	|	...	...	0501	...	...	...	0600	0742	0942	1142	1342	...	...	1542	...	1742	...	1942	...	2142
113	Mallnitz-Obervellach d.	|	|	...	...	0516	...	0647	...	...	0756	0956	1156	1356	...	...	1556	1740	1756	...	1956	...	2156
146	Spittal-Millstättersee 971 d.	0327	0327	...	...	0542	...	0717	0723	...	0820	1020	1220	1420	...	...	1620	1809	1820	...	2020	...	2220
182	**Villach** Hbf 971 a.	0351	0351	...	...	0605	...	...	0748	...	0843	1043	1243	1443	...	...	1643	...	1843	...	2043	...	2243
182	**Villach** Hbf 971 d.	...	...	0418	0458	...	0620	...	0750	...	0846	1046	1246	...	1450	1514	1649	...	1846	...	2046	...	2248
198	Velden am Wörthersee 971 d.	...	...	|	0513	...	0635	...	0801	...	0857	1057	1257	...	1505	1525	1700	...	1857	...	2057	...	2259
207	Pörtschach am Wörthersee 971 d.	...	...	|	0521	...	0643	...	|	...	0904	1104	1304	...	1513	|	1707	...	1904	...	2104	...	2306
220	**Klagenfurt** Hbf 971 a.	...	...	0439	0536	...	0656	...	0816	...	0912	1112	1315	...	1526	1537	1718	...	1915	...	2115	...	2317

	EN 236 🅁 ♦	*EN* 498 🅁 L		Ⓐ 2	1501 2S		⚒ 2		*IC* 693 🍷	*EC* 114 ⊗♦	*EC* 112 ✕♦		*IC* 691 🍷	*RJ* 533	Ⓐ 2	*IC* 591 🍷	Ⓐ 2	*EC* 110 ✕		*IC* 593 ✕		*EC* 173	*D* 414 ♦
Klagenfurt Hbf 971 d.	...	...	...	...	...	...	...	...	0645	0842	1027	...	1245	1423	1432	...	1532	1642	...	1845	...	2218	...
Pörtschach am Wörthersee 971 d.	...	...	...	...	...	...	...	...	0655	0855	1040	...	1255	|	1446	...	1546	1655	...	1855	...	|	...
Velden am Wörthersee 971 d.	...	...	...	...	...	...	...	...	0702	0902	1047	...	1302	1436	1454	...	1554	1702	...	1902	...	|	...
Villach Hbf 971 a.	...	...	...	...	...	...	...	...	0713	0913	1058	...	1313	1446	1509	...	1609	1713	...	1913	...	2240	...
Villach Hbf 971 d.	0146	0146	...	...	...	...	0528	...	0716	0916	1116	...	1316	...	...	1516	1612	1716	...	1916	...	...	2316
Spittal-Millstättersee 971 d.	0209	0209	...	...	...	...	0604	...	0740	0940	1140	...	1340	...	...	1540	1644	1740	...	1940	...	...	2341
Mallnitz-Obervellach d.	|	|	...	...	...	...	0633	...	0804	1004	1204	...	1404	...	...	1604	1714	1804	...	2004	...	...	0010
Bad Gastein d.	|	|	...	0606	...	...	...	...	0817	1017	1217	...	1417	...	...	1617	...	1817	...	2017	...	...	0027
Bad Hofgastein d.	|	|	...	0617	...	...	...	...	0830	1030	1230	...	1430	...	...	1630	...	1830	...	2030	...	...	0041
Schwarzach - St Veit 960 d.	0320	0320	...	0633	0640	...	...	...	0850	1050	1250	...	1450	...	...	1650	...	1852	...	2050	...	...	0057
St Johann im Pongau 960 a.	|	|	...	...	0646	...	...	...	0855	1055	1255	...	1455	...	...	1655	...	1857	...	2055	...	...	...
Bischofshofen 960 975 a.	|	|	...	...	0654	...	...	...	0903	1103	1303	...	1503	...	...	1703	...	1905	...	2103	...	...	...
Golling-Abtenau 960 a.	|	|	...	...	0717	...	...	...	0924	1124	1324	...	1524	...	...	1724	...	1926	...	2124	...	...	...
Salzburg Hbf 960 975 a.	0409	0409	...	...	0745	...	...	...	0948	1148	1348	...	1548	...	...	1748	...	1950	...	2148	...	...	...
München Hbf **890** a.	|	0610	...	...	|	...	...	...	|	1341	1541	...	|	...	...	...	...	2141	...	...	...	...	...
Wien Westbahnhof **950** a.	0810	...	...	...	1104	...	...	...	1304	...	...	...	1904	...	...	...	...	...	...	...	...	...	...

♦ – **NOTES** (LISTED BY TRAIN NUMBER)

112 – [12] and ✕ Klagenfurt - München - Stuttgart - Frankfurt; [12] Zagreb (**212**) - Villach (**112**) - Frankfurt.
113 – [12] and ✕ Frankfurt - Stuttgart - München - Klagenfurt; [12] Frankfurt - Villach (**213**) - Zagreb.
114 – WÖRTHERSEE – [12] and ⊗ Klagenfurt - München - Stuttgart - Köln - Dortmund.
115 – WÖRTHERSEE – [12] and ⊗ Münster - Köln - Stuttgart - München - Klagenfurt.
117 – [12] and ⊗ (Frankfurt Ⓑ / Karlsruhe ⑥ -) Stuttgart - München - Salzburg - Klagenfurt. Train number **1217** on ⑥ (also Apr. 18, 20, June 8).
236 – 🛏 1, 2 cl., ▬ 2 cl. and [2] Venezia - Tarvisio ▦ - Villach - Salzburg - Wien.
944 – 🛏 1, 2 cl., ▬ 2 cl. and [2] Wien - Salzburg - Villach - Tarvisio ▦ - Venezia.
414 – [2] Beograd - Zagreb - Ljubljana - Villach - Schwarzach (**464***) - Innsbruck - Feldkirch - Zürich; 🛏 1, 2 cl. and ▬ 2 cl. Zagreb - Ljubljana - Villach - Schwarzach (**464***) - Innsbruck - Feldkirch - Zürich.
415 – [2] Zürich (**465**‡) - Feldkirch - Innsbruck - Schwarzach (**415**) - Villach - Ljubljana - Zagreb - Beograd; 🛏 1, 2 cl. and ▬ 2 cl. Zürich (**465**‡) - Feldkirch - Innsbruck - Schwarzach (**415**) - Villach - Ljubljana - Zagreb.

L – LISINSKI – 🛏 1, 2 cl., ▬ 2 cl. and [2] Zagreb - Dobova ▦ - Ljubljana - Jesenice ▦ - Villach - München and v.v.
S – [2] Saalfelden - Schwarzach - Salzburg (*IC* **545**) - Wien

* – Train number **1364** Sept. 2 – 28.
‡ – Train number **1365** Sept. 1 – 27.

LIENZ - VILLACH - KLAGENFURT - FRIESACH (- WIEN) 971

	EN 234 ★ 2		EC 172 ✕	U 2	2		⚒ 2	2	D 734 Ⓐ 2	2	2	⚒ 2	IC 590 ◐ ✕	2		Ⓐ 2	IC 592 ◐ 🍸	2	D 736 ⑥ 2			Ⓐ 2	EC 111 ◐ ✕		2
Lienz d.	...	...	...	...	...	...	...	0524	0547	...	0621	...	...	0727	...	0832	...	0923	0950	...	...	...	...	...	1124
Spittal-Millstättersee a.	...	...	...	...	...	...	...	0627	0633	...	0721	...	...	0828	...	0929	...	1027	1038	...	...	...	...	...	1227
Spittal-Millstättersee 970 d.	...	...	...	0448r	0530e	...	0602	0630	0637	0642e	0723	0731	0820	0831	...	0931	1020	1031	1044	...	...	1131	1220		1236
Villach Hbf 970 a.	...	...	...	0521r	0558e	...	0635	0656	0701	0716e	0748	0804	0843	0904	...	1004	1043	1104	1108	...	...	1204	1243	...	1309
		⚒ 2				2	Ⓐ 2		RJ 534 ✕			⚒ 2		EC 102 ✕	2	⚒ 2		Ⓐ 2	RJ 538 d✕	2	Ⓐ 2	⚒ 2		Ⓐ 2	RJ 630 ✕
Villach Hbf 970 d.	0418	0458	0526	0529	0604	0620	0641	0659e	0714	0720	0750	0820	0846	0914	0920	1020	1046	1050	1114	1120	1150	1220	1246	1250	1314
Velden am Wörthersee . 970 d.	|	0513	|	0544	|	0635	0654	0711e	0725	0735	0801	0835	0857	|	0935	1035	1057	1105	1125	1135	1205	1235	1257	1305	|
Pörtschach am W'see ⊡ 970 d.	|	0521	|	0552	|	0643	0700	|	|	0743	|	0843	0904	0929	0943	1043	1104	1113	|	1143	1213	1243	1304	1313	1329
Klagenfurt Hbf 970 a.	0439	0536	0547	0605	0625	0656	0710	0728e	0737	0756	0816	0856	0912	0937	0956	1056	1112	1126	1137	1156	1226	1256	1315	1326	1337
Klagenfurt Hbf 980 d.	0440	...	0549	0607	0627	0704	...	...	0739	0804	0817	0904	...	0939	1004	1104	...	1128	1139	1204	1228	1310	...	1328	1339
St Veit an der Glan 980 d.	|	...	0602	0627	0640	0724	...	...	0753	0824	0831	0924	...	0953	1024	1124	...	1147	1153	1224	1247	1330	...	1347	1353
Friesach 980 a.	|	...	|	0659	0703	0756	...	...	|	0856	...	0956	...	1016	1056	1156	...	...	|	1256	...	1402	...	...	1416
Wien Meidling 980 a.	0833	...	0927	...	...	...	...	...	1127	...	...	...	...	1327	...	...	...	...	1527	...	...	...	...	...	1727

			⚒ 2	IC 690 ◐	2			⚒ 2	EC 113 ◐ ✕	2	RJ 530 ✕			RJ 738 ⑦¶ ✕	⚒ 2	EC 115 ◐ ⊗		2		⚒ 2	IC 692 ◐ 🍸	2	2	EC 117 1217 Ⓐ ⊗	
Lienz d.	...	...	1224	...	1322	...	...	1423	...	1524	1550	...	...	...	1625	...	...	1725	...	1823	...	1923	2025	...	...
Spittal-Millstättersee a.	...	...	1327	...	1427	...	...	1527	...	1627	1638	...	...	...	1726	...	...	1828	...	1927	...	2027	2126	...	...
Spittal-Millstättersee 970 d.	...	...	1331	1420	1431	...	...	1531	1620	1631	1644	...	...	...	1731	1820	...	1831	...	1931	2020	2031	2131	2220	...
Villach Hbf 970 a.	...	...	1404	1443	1504	...	...	1604	1643	1704	1709	...	...	...	1804	1843	...	1904	...	2004	2043	2104	2204	2243	...
	2	Ⓐ 2	⚒ 2	Ⓐ 2	RJ 632 ✕	2	Ⓐ 2	⚒ 2		Ⓐ 2		2	Ⓐ 2		⚒ 2		Ⓑ 2	IC 30 V🍸	2	⚒ 2		2	⚒ 2		2
Villach Hbf 970 d.	1320	1350	1420	1450	1514	1520	1550	1620	1649	1650	1714	1720	1750	1814	1820	1846	1850	1914	1920	2020	2046	2120	2220	2248	2350
Velden am Wörthersee . 970 d.	1335	1405	1435	1505	1525	1535	1605	1635	1700	1705	|	1735	1805	|	1835	1857	1905	1925	1935	2035	2057	2135	2235	2259	0005
Pörtschach am W'see ⊡ 970 d.	1343	1413	1443	1513	|	1543	1613	1643	1707	1713	1729	1743	1813	1829	1843	1904	1913	|	1943	2043	2104	2143	2243	2306	0013
Klagenfurt Hbf 970 a.	1356	1426	1456	1526	1537	1556	1626	1656	1718	1726	1737	1756	1826	1837	1856	1915	1926	1937	1956	2056	2115	2156	2256	2317	0026
Klagenfurt Hbf 980 d.	1404	1428	1504	1528	1539	1604	1628	1704	...	1728	1739	1804	1828	1839	1858	...	1928	1939	2004	2104	...	2204	2304	...	0028
St Veit an der Glan 980 d.	1424	1447	1524	1547	1553	1624	1647	1724	...	1747	1753	1824	1847	1853	1918	...	1947	1953	2024	2124	...	2224	2324	...	0047
Friesach 980 a.	1456	...	1556	...	|	1656	...	1756	...	...	1816	1856	...	1918	1950	...	...	|	2056	2156	...	2256	2356	...	...
Wien Meidling 980 a.	...	...	...	...	1927	...	...	...	...	...	2127	...	...	2227	...	...	...	2327	...	...	...	...	...	...	...

km																									
				⚒ 2	⚒ 2		2	⚒ 2	IC 693 ◐ 🍸	⚒ 2	⚒⊖ U 2	2	EC 114 ◐ ⊗	2	2	IC 31 V 🍸	EC 112 ◐ ✕	⚒ 2	2	RJ 531 ✕		Ⓐ 2	IC 691 ◐ 🍸	⚒ 2	Ⓐ 2
	Wien Meidling 980 d.	...	...	...	...	...	...	...	...	...	...	...	...	...	...	0630	...	...	...	0830	...	...	...	...	...
0	**Friesach** 980 d.	...	...	...	...	...	0521	0545	...	0611	0643	0708	...	0808	0908	|	...	1008	1108	1145	...	...	...	1208	...
33	St Veit an der Glan 980 d.	...	...	0509	...	...	0556	0616	...	0645	0718	0742	...	0842	0942	1009	...	1042	1142	1209	...	1212	...	1242	1312
53	**Klagenfurt** Hbf 980 a.	...	...	0528	...	...	0615	0631	...	0704	0738	0800	...	0900	1000	1021	...	1100	1200	1221	...	1230	...	1300	1330
53	**Klagenfurt** Hbf 970 d.	...	...	0530	0602	...	0622	0633	0645	0712	0745	0802	0842	0902	1002	1023	1027	1102	1202	1223	...	1232	1245	1302	1332
66	Pörtschach am W ⊡ 970 d.	...	...	0543	0616	...	0636	0646	0655	0725	0757	0816	0855	0916	1016	|	1040	1116	1216	1232	...	1246	1255	1316	1346
75	Velden am Wörthersee 970 d.	...	...	0550	0624	...	0644	0653	0702	0731	0804	0824	0902	0924	1024	1036	1047	1124	1224	|	...	1254	1302	1324	1354
91	**Villach** Hbf 970 a.	...	...	0606	0639	...	0659	0710	0713	0747	0820	0839	0913	0939	1039	1046	1058	1139	1239	1246	...	1309	1313	1339	1409
		⚒ 2	2		d 2	Ⓐ 2				d 2		⚒ 2		2		⚒ 2			2		⚒ 2			d 2	
91	**Villach** Hbf 970 d.	0528	...	0616e	0656	...	...	...	0716	0756	...	0856	0916	0956	...	1056	1116	1156	1156	1253	1257	...	1316	1356	...
127	Spittal-Millstättersee 970 a.	0602	...	0650e	0729	...	...	...	0738	0829	...	0929	0938	1029	...	1129	1138	1229	1229	1316	1330	...	1338	1429	...
127	Spittal-Millstättersee d.	...	0627	...	...	0736	...	...	...	0831	...	0931	...	1031	...	1131	...	1231	1231	1319	1331	...	...	1431	...
195	**Lienz** a.	...	0727	...	...	0827	...	...	...	0936	...	1032	...	1137	...	1237	...	1335	1335	1406	1434	...	...	1535	...

	2	RJ 533 ✕	Ⓐ 2	⚒ 2	Ⓐ 2	2	RJ 535 ✕		Ⓐ 2	EC 110 ◐ ✕	⚒ 2	Ⓐ 2	2	EC 103 ✕	Ⓐ 2	IC 593 ◐ ✕	⚒ 2	Ⓐ 2	2	RJ 537 ✕	⚒ 2	EC 173 ✕	⚒ 2	2	EN 235 ★ 2
Wien Meidling 980 d.	...	1030	...	...	...	...	1230	...	...	...	...	...	...	1430	...	...	...	...	...	1630	...	1830	...	...	1930
Friesach 980 d.	1308	|	...	1408	...	1508	1545	...	...	...	1608	...	1708	|	...	...	1808	...	1908	1945	2008	2140	2144	...	2259
St Veit an der Glan 980 d.	1342	1409	1412	1442	1512	1542	1609	...	1612	...	1642	1712	1742	1809	1812	...	1842	1912	1942	2009	2042	2204	2217	...	|
Klagenfurt Hbf 980 a.	1400	1421	1430	1500	1530	1600	1621	...	1630	...	1700	1730	1800	1821	1830	...	1900	1930	2000	2021	2100	2216	2235	...	2335
Klagenfurt Hbf 970 d.	1402	1423	1432	1502	1532	1602	1623	...	1632	1642	1702	1732	1802	1823	1832	1845	1902	1932	2002	2023	2102	2218	2236	2318	2338
Pörtschach am W'see ⊡ 970 d.	1416	|	1446	1516	1546	1616	1632	...	1646	1655	1716	1746	1816	|	1846	1855	1916	1946	2016	2032	2116	|	2251	2333	|
Velden am Wörthersee . 970 d.	1424	1436	1454	1524	1554	1624	|	...	1654	1702	1724	1754	1824	1836	1854	1902	1924	1954	2024	|	2124	|	2258	2341	|
Villach Hbf 970 a.	1439	1446	1509	1539	1609	1639	1646	...	1709	1713	1739	1809	1839	1846	1909	1913	1939	2009	2039	2046	2139	2240	2313	2356	0001
		⚒ 2	IC 591 ◐	d 2			D 735 B 2	Ⓐ 2			d 2			⚒ 2			d 2			⚒ 2	Ⓑ 2	Ⓑ 2			
Villach Hbf 970 d.	...	1456	1516	1556	1612	...	1650	1656	1710	1716	1756	1810	...	1856	...	1916	1956	...	...	2056	2156	2256	...	...	...
Spittal-Millstättersee 970 a.	...	1529	1538	1629	1637	...	1716	1729	1734	1738	1829	1836	...	1929	...	1938	2030	...	...	2129	2229	2329	...	...	...
Spittal-Millstättersee d.	...	1531	...	1640	...	...	1719	1731	...	...	1831	...	...	1931	...	...	2031	...	...	2131	...	...	...	...	...
Lienz a.	...	1635	...	1741	...	...	1810	1836	...	...	1936	...	...	2038	...	...	2132	...	...	2230	...	...	...	...	...

B – Ⓑ (not Apr. 20, May 1, 29, June 8, 19, Aug. 15, Dec. 7).
U – To / from Unzmarkt (Table **980**).
V – 12 Venezia - Tarvisio - Villach - Wien and v.v.
d – Daily.
e – Ⓐ only.
r – ⚒ only.
★ – See Table **980** for through cars to / from Roma and Milano.
◐ – See Table **970** for further details.
¶ – Also Apr. 21, June 9, Dec. 8; not Apr. 20, June 8, Dec. 7.
⊖ – Change trains at Klagenfurt on Ⓐ to July 4 / from Sept. 8.
⊡ – Pörtschach am Wörthersee.

2nd class only LINZ - SELZTHAL - LIEZEN 974

km																									
		⚒	Ⓐ		L			IC 503 G🍸	L		L	©	Ⓐ	L	⚒	Ⓐ		IC 601 G🍸		Ⓐ			Ⓐ		
0	**Linz** Hbf d.	0506	0536	0633	0714	0736	0836	0914	1058	1136	1258	1336	1405	1458	1536	1607	1636	1714	1736	1810	1858	1936	2036	2136	2336
28	Rohr - Bad Hall d.	0540	0609	0709	0736	0810	0910	0935	1121	1209	1321	1409	1430	1521	1609	1631	1709	1735	1809	1834	1921	2009	2109	2209	0009
32	Kremsmünster d.	0546	0616	0715	|	0815	0915	|	1125	1214	1325	1414	1435	1525	1614	1636	1714	|	1814	1838	1925	2014	2114	2214	0014
51	Kirchdorf a. d. Krems d.	0604	0633	0734	0750	0835	0934	0949	1140	1232	1340	1435	1451	1540	1632	1653	1732	1750	1833	1853	1939	2033	2132	2232	0032
68	Hinterstoder ★ d.	0625	...	0754	0807	0856	...	|	1201	...	1401	1457	1513	1601	...	1714	...	|	...	1914	2001	2103	...	...	...
82	Windischgarsten d.	0639	...	...	0821	0910	...	1020	1215	...	1415	1511	1527	1615	...	1728	...	1819	...	1928	2015	2118	...	...	...
87	Spital am Pyhrn d.	0646	...	...	0827	0915	...	1026	1221	...	1421	1516	1532	1621	...	1735	...	1826	...	1934	2021	2124	...	...	...
104	**Selzthal** a.	0702	...	...	0843	...	...	1041	1239	...	1439	...	...	1639	...	1752	...	1841	...	...	2039	2141	...	...	...

	⚒	Ⓐ		⚒		⚒	Ⓐ	©		IC 502 G🍸					L		L	Ⓐ		IC 600 G🍸				Ⓐ	
Selzthal d.	...	0428	...	...	...	0547	0615	0615	0721	0918	...	...	1121	...	1321	...	1521	...	...	1718	...	...	1921	...	...
Spital am Pyhrn d.	...	0445	...	...	...	0604	0632	0632	0738	0934	...	1044	1140	...	1340	...	1540	...	1643	1734	...	...	1940	2043	...
Windischgarsten d.	...	0452	...	...	...	0610	0640	0640	0744	0940	...	1050	1146	...	1346	...	1546	...	1649	1740	...	...	1947	2049	...
Hinterstoder ★ d.	...	0505	...	...	...	0625	0654	0654	0758	|	...	1105	1200	...	1400	...	1600	...	1703	|	...	...	2000	2103	...
Kirchdorf a. d. Krems d.	0428	0526	0526	0556	0627	0646	0717	0725	0821	1011	1026	1126	1221	1326	1421	1526	1621	1655	1726	1811	1826	1926	2021	2126	2126
Kremsmünster d.	0445	0546	0546	0616	0645	0703	0731	0746	0836	|	1045	1145	1236	1345	1436	1545	1636	1715	1745	|	1846	1945	2036	2145	2145
Rohr - Bad Hall d.	0449	0550	0550	0620	0650	0708	0737	0750	0840	1025	1049	1149	1240	1349	1440	1549	1640	1719	1750	1825	1850	1949	2040	2149	2149
Linz Hbf a.	0524	0623	0623	0654	0728h	0735	0803	0824	0903	1047	1124	1224	1303	1424	1503	1624	1703	1754	1824	1847	1924	2024	2103	2224	2224

G – To / from Graz (Table **975**).
L – To / from Liezen on Ⓐ (Table **975**).
h – 0724 on ©.
k – Not Nov. 1.
★ – 🚌 services operate Hinterstoder rail station - Hinterstoder town centre and v.v. Journey time: 18 – 20 minutes. Operated by Riedler Reisen & Touristik GmbH. **From Hinterstoder rail station** at 0645 ⑥ **k**, 0810, 1205, 1405, 1515 Ⓐ, 1605 and 1715. **From Hinterstoder town centre** at 0555 Ⓐ, 0625 ⚒, 0737, 1135, 1335, 1535 and 1635.

975 SALZBURG - BISCHOFSHOFEN - SELZTHAL - GRAZ

SUBJECT TO ALTERATION SEPT. 1–28

km		⚒ 2	EN 465 h A	⚒ 2	⚒ 2	EN 1365 T A	Ⓐ 2	Ⓐ 2	2	IC 719 ⊗	Ⓐ 2	2	IC 513 🍷	IC 503 🍷	EC 102 ✕	2	EC 111 ✕	IC 515 🍷	Ⓐ 2L	2	EC 217 S⊗	Ⓐ 2L	Ⓑ 2	EC 113 ✕	EC 163 Z✕
0	**Salzburg** Hbf .... 960 970 d.	...	...	...	...	...	...	...	...	0615	...	...	0815	...	...	...	1012	...	...	...	1215	...	...	1412	...
	Innsbruck Hbf 960 .... d.	...	0056	...	...	0056	...	...	...	|	...	...	|	...	...	...	|	0824	...	...	|	...	...	|	1224
53	**Bischofshofen** ..... 960 970 a.	...	0336	...	...	|	...	...	...	0702	...	...	0902	...	...	...	1052	1110	...	...	1302	...	...	1452	1510
53	**Bischofshofen** .... d.	...	0338	...	...	|	...	...	...	0713	...	0741v	0913	...	...	...	...	1113	...	...	1313	...	...	...	1513
77	Radstadt .... d.	...	|	...	...	|	...	...	0610	0736	...	0809	0936	...	...	...	...	1136	...	...	1336	...	...	...	1536
94	Schladming .... d.	...	0416	0500	...	|	...	...	0629	0752	...	0831	0952	...	...	1031	...	1152	...	1231	1352	...	1431	...	1552
133	**Stainach-Irdning** .... d.	0427	0447	0541	...	|	...	...	0710	0821	...	0912	1021	...	...	1112	...	1221	...	1312	1421	...	1512	...	1621
145	Liezen .... d.	0438	|	0553	...	|	...	...	0726	0833	0905	0926	1033	...	...	1126	...	1233	1305	1326	1433	1505	1526	...	1633
	Linz Hbf 974 .... d.	|	|	|	...	|	...	...	|	|	|	|	|	0914	...	|	...	|	|	|	|	|	|	...	|
152	**Selzthal** .... a.	0444	0504	0559	...	|	...	...	0733	0840	0912	0933	1040	1041	...	1133	...	1240	1312	1333	1440	1512	1533	...	1640
152	**Selzthal** .... d.	0451	0513	0606	...	|	0716	...	0739	0846	━	0939	1048	1048	...	1139	...	1248	━	1339	1446	━	1539	...	1648
158	Stadt Rottenmann .... d.	0458	|	0613	...	|	0722	...	0745	0853	...	0945	|	|	...	1145	...	|	...	1345	1453	...	1545	...	|
169	Trieben .... d.	0506	|	0621	...	|	0729	...	0753	|	RJ	0953	|	|	...	1153	...	|	RJ	1353	|	RJ	1553	...	|
215	St Michael .... a.	0540	0550	0655	...	|	0802	...	0828	0921	534	1028	1121	1121	...	1228	...	1321	538	1428	1521	630	1628	...	1721
215	St Michael .... 980 d.	0541	0551	0701	0706	|	0803	...	0833	0922	✕	1033	1122	1122	...	1233	...	1322	✕	1433	1522	✕	1633	...	1722
225	Leoben Hbf .... 980 d.	0551	0601	0709	0715	0728	0811	0818	0841	0930	0934	1041	1130	1130	1134	1241	...	1330	1334	1441	1530	1534	1641	...	1730
	Bruck a. d. Mur .... 980 a.	|	0612	|	0728	0741	0824	|	0853	|	0944	1053	|	|	1144	1253	...	|	1344	1453	|	1544	1653	...	|
	Wien Meidling 980 .... a.	|	|	|	...	|	...	|	...	|	1127	...	|	|	1327	...	...	|	1527	...	|	1727	...	...	|
293	**Graz** Hbf .... 980 a.	0645	0700	0801	...	0830	...	0903	...	1014	...	...	1214	1214	...	...	...	1414	...	...	1614	...	...	...	1814

	Ⓐ 2	2	IC 611 🍷	IC 601 🍷	RJ 530 ✕	2	Ⓐ 2	EC 219 F⊗	EC 117 1217 ⊗	2
Salzburg Hbf .... 960 970 d.	...	...	1615	...	...	...	1642	1815	2012	...
Innsbruck Hbf 960 .... d.	...	...	|	...	...	...	|	|	|	...
Bischofshofen .... 960 970 a.	...	...	1702	...	...	...	1733	1902	2052	...
Bischofshofen .... d.	...	...	1713	...	...	...	1741	1913	━	2100
Radstadt .... d.	...	...	1736	...	...	...	1810	1936	...	2130
Schladming .... d.	...	1631	1752	...	...	1831	...	1952	...	2149
Stainach-Irdning .... d.	...	1712	1821	...	...	1912	...	2021	...	2234b
Liezen .... d.	1705	1726	1833	...	...	1926	...	2033	...	...
Linz Hbf 974 .... d.	|	|	|	1714	...	|	...	|	...	...
Selzthal .... a.	1712	1733	1840	1841	...	1933	...	2040	...	...
Selzthal .... d.	━	1739	1848	1848	...	1939	...	2046	...	...
Stadt Rottenmann .... d.	...	1745	|	|	...	1945	...	2053	...	...
Trieben .... d.	RJ	1753	|	|	...	1953	...	|	IC	...
St Michael .... a.	632	1828	1921	1921	...	2028	...	2121	30	...
St Michael .... 980 d.	✕	1833	1922	1922	...	2033	...	2122	🍷	...
Leoben Hbf .... 980 d.	1734	1841	1930	1930	1934	2041	...	2130	2134	...
Bruck a. d. Mur .... 980 a.	1744	1853	|	|	1944	2053	...	|	2144	...
Wien Meidling 980 .... a.	1927	...	|	|	2127	...	...	|	2327	...
Graz Hbf .... 980 a.	...	...	2014	2014	...	...	...	2214	...	...

	⚒ 2	⚒ 2	Ⓐ 2	⚒ 2	EC 218 F⊗	2	IC 31 🍷	IC 502 🍷	IC 512 🍷	2
Graz Hbf .... 980 d.	...	...	...	...	0545	...	...	0745	0745	...
Wien Meidling 980 .... d.	...	...	...	...	|	...	0630	|	|	...
Bruck a. d. Mur .... 980 d.	...	...	0536	0613	|	0708	0815	|	|	0908
Leoben Hbf .... 980 d.	...	...	0549	0625	0631	0721	0825	0831	0831	0921
St Michael .... 980 a.	...	...	0556	...	0637	0728	━	0837	0837	0928
St Michael .... d.	...	...	0600	...	0638	0731	...	0838	0838	0931
Trieben .... d.	...	...	0636	...	|	0805	...	|	|	1005
Stadt Rottenmann .... d.	...	...	0644	...	0708	0812	Ⓐ	|	|	1012
Selzthal .... a.	...	...	0650	...	0713	0818	2L	0911	0911	1018
Selzthal .... d.	...	0544	━	...	0719	0823	0845	0918	0919	1023
Linz Hbf 974 .... a.	...	|	...	...	|	|	|	1047	|	|
Liezen .... d.	...	0552	...	...	0727	0832	0852	...	0927	1032
Stainach-Irdning .... d.	...	0604	2	...	0737	0845	...	...	0937	1045
Schladming .... d.	0506	0648	0648	...	0810	0928	...	...	1010	1128
Radstadt .... d.	0525	0706	0706	...	0826	...	...	...	1026	...
Bischofshofen .... a.	0554	0735	0735	...	0848	...	...	...	1048	...
Bischofshofen ... 960 970 d.	0558	0740	0740	...	0857	...	...	...	1057	...
Innsbruck Hbf 960 .... a.	|	|	|	...	|	...	...	...	|	...
Salzburg Hbf ...... 960 970 a.	0645	0840	0840	...	0944	...	...	...	1144	...

	RJ 531 ✕	EC 164 Z🍷	EC 112 ✕	Ⓑ 2	RJ 533 ✕	EC 216 S⊗	2	RJ 535 ✕	IC 518 🍷	IC 591 🍷	2	Ⓐ 2L	⚒ 2	EC 103 ✕	IC 600 🍷	IC 610 🍷	Ⓐ 2	Ⓑ 2	⚒ 2	RJ 537 ✕	IC 718 ⊗	2	2	EN 1364 Y A	EN 464 e A
Graz Hbf .... 980 d.	...	0945	...	...	...	1145	...	...	1345	...	...	...	1501	...	1545	1545	...	...	1701	...	1745	1825	...	2056	2224
Wien Meidling 980 .... d.	0830	|	...	...	1030	|	...	1230	|	...	...	...	|	1430	|	|	...	...	|	1630	|	|	...	|	|
Bruck a. d. Mur .... 980 d.	1015	|	...	1108	1215	|	1308	1415	|	...	1508	...	|	1615	|	|	...	1708	|	1815	|	1908	...	2155	2317
Leoben Hbf .... 980 d.	1025	1031	...	1121	1225	1231	1321	1425	1431	...	1521	...	1557	1625	1631	1631	...	1721	1801	1825	1831	1921	...	2214	2331
St Michael .... 980 a.	...	1037	...	1128	━	1237	1328	━	1437	...	1528	...	1605	...	1637	1637	...	1728	1809	...	1837	1928	...	|	2338
St Michael .... d.	...	1038	...	1131	...	1238	1331	...	1438	...	1531	...	1608	...	1638	1638	...	1731	1810	...	1838	...	1931	|	2340
Trieben .... d.	...	|	...	1205	...	|	1405	...	|	...	1605	...	1644	...	|	|	...	1805	1846	...	|	...	2005	|	|
Stadt Rottenmann .... d.	...	|	...	1212	Ⓐ	1308	1412	Ⓐ	|	...	1612	...	1652	...	|	|	...	1812	1854	...	1908	...	2012	|	|
Selzthal .... a.	...	1111	...	1218	2L	1313	1418	2L	1511	...	1618	...	1658	...	1711	1711	...	1818	1900	...	1913	...	2018	|	0017
Selzthal .... d.	...	1119	...	1223	1244	1319	1423	1444	1519	...	1623	1644	...	...	1718	1719	...	1823	...	...	1919	...	2023	|	0029
Linz Hbf 974 .... a.	...	|	...	|	|	|	|	|	|	...	|	|	...	...	1847	|	...	|	...	...	|	...	|	|	|
Liezen .... d.	...	1127	...	1232	1251	1327	1432	1451	1527	...	1632	1651	...	...	...	1727	...	1832	...	...	1927	...	2032	|	|
Stainach-Irdning .... d.	...	1137	...	1245	...	1337	1445	...	1537	...	1645	...	...	...	...	1737	...	1845	...	...	1937	...	2045	|	0046
Schladming .... d.	...	1210	...	1328	...	1410	1528	...	1610	...	1728	...	...	...	...	1810	...	1929	...	...	2010	...	2127	|	0118
Radstadt .... d.	...	1226	...	...	...	1426	...	...	1626	...	...	...	...	...	...	1826	1920	1952	...	...	2026	...	2147k	|	|
Bischofshofen .... a.	...	1248	...	...	...	1448	...	...	1648	...	...	...	...	...	...	1848	1950	...	...	...	2048	...	...	|	0156
Bischofshofen ...... 960 970 d.	...	1250	1305	...	...	1457	...	...	1650	1705	...	...	...	...	...	1857	2004	...	...	...	2057	...	...	|	0158
Innsbruck Hbf 960 .... a.	...	1535	|	...	...	|	...	...	1936	|	...	...	...	...	...	|	|	...	...	...	|	...	...	0449	0449
Salzburg Hbf .... 960 970 a.	...	...	1348	...	...	1544	...	...	...	1748	...	...	...	...	...	1944	2051	...	...	...	2144	...	...	...	...

A – ZÜRICHSEE – 🛏 1, 2 cl., ▬ 2 cl. and (2) Graz - Innsbruck - Buchs 🏛 - Zürich and v.v.
F – (12) and ⊗ Graz - München - Stuttgart - Frankfurt and v.v.
L – To / from Linz (Table **974**).
S – (12) and ⊗ Graz - München - Stuttgart - Saarbrücken and v.v.
T – Sept. 2–28 only.
Y – Sept. 1–27 only.
Z – (12) and ✕ Zürich - Buchs 🏛 - Innsbruck - Graz and v.v.
b – Ⓑ only.
e – Not Sept. 1–27.
h – Not Sept. 2–28.
k – ⑥ only.
v – ⚒ only.

976 LINZ - STEYR - KLEINREIFLING - WEISSENBACH

2nd class only

km		⚒	⚒				Ⓐ	⚒		Ⓐ		Ⓐ	⚒		Ⓐ	⚒	Ⓐ		Ⓐ	⚒	Ⓐ		Ⓐ			
0	**Linz** Hbf ...... 950 992 d.	0433	0514	0616	0646	0752	0830	0852	0952	1030	1152	1222	1252	1352	1422	1452	1530	1552	1622	1652	1730	1752	1822	1952	2152	2252
17	Enns .... 992 d.	0451	0532	0633	0704	0810	|	0910	1010	|	1210	1240	1310	1410	1440	1510	|	1610	1640	1710	|	1810	1840	2010	2210	2310
25	St Valentin .... 950 a.	0458	0539	0640	0711	0817	0844	0917	1017	1044	1217	1246	1317	1417	1447	1517	1544	1617	1647	1717	1744	1817	1847	2017	2217	2317
25	St Valentin .... d.	0509	0540	0649	0721	0821	0851	0921	1021	1051	1221	1251	1321	1421	1451	1521	1551	1621	1651	1721	1751	1821	1851	2021	2225	2321
45	**Steyr** .... d.	0532	0605	0714	0755t	0846	0912	0946	1046	1112	1246	1312	1346	1446	1512	1546	1612	1646	1712	1746	1812	1846	1912	2046	2250	2346
47	Garsten .... a.	0535	0608	0717	0758	0849	0915	0949	1049	1115	1249	1315	1349	1449	1515	1549	1615	1649	1715	1749	1815	1849	1915	2048	2253	2349
47	Garsten .... d.	0536	...	...	0759	0850c	0916	...	1050c	1116	1250c	1316	1350e	1450c	1516	...	1616	1650c	1716	...	1816	1850c	1916	2049	...	...
67	Losenstein .... d.	0601	...	...	0822	0917c	0937	...	1117c	1137	1317c	1337	1423e	1517c	1537	...	1637	1717c	1737	...	1841	1917c	1937	2112	...	...
89	Kastenreith .... 977 a.	0628	...	...	0848z	0941c	1004	...	1141c	1204	1341c	1404	1447e	1541c	1603	...	1703	1741c	1803	...	1905	1941c	2003	2135	...	...
92	**Kleinreifling** ...... 977 a.	0633	...	...	0852z	0946c	1008	...	1146c	1208	1346c	1408	1451e	1546c	1607	...	1707	1746c	1807	...	1909	1946c	2007	2139	...	...
106	Weißenbach ⊡ .. 977 a.	0648e	...	...	0907e	...	...	...	...	...	...	...	...	...	1622	...	1722	...	1822	...	1924	...	...	...	...	...

	P	Ⓐ	⚒		⚒			Ⓐ		Ⓐ		⚒	Ⓐ		⚒	Ⓐ		⚒		Ⓐ	Ⓐ	⑥k	Ⓐ			
Weißenbach ⊡ .... 977 d.	...	...	...	...	...	0603e	...	...	...	0940	...	...	...	...	...	1340	...	...	...	...	1641	...	1738	...	...	...
Kleinreifling .... 977 d.	...	0437	0512	...	...	0618	...	0754	0812c	0954	1015c	...	1154	1215c	...	1354	1415c	...	1608y	...	1708	...	1753	1815c	...	2021
Kastenreith .... 977 d.	...	0441	0516	...	...	0622	...	0758	0816c	0958	1019c	...	1158	1219c	...	1358	1419c	...	1612y	...	1712	...	1757	1819c	...	2025
Losenstein .... d.	...	0505	0540	...	...	0647	...	0822	0843c	1022	1044c	...	1222	1244c	...	1422	1444c	...	1644	...	1744	...	1821	1844c	...	2050
Garsten .... a.	...	0526	0600	...	...	0709	...	0843	0907c	1043	1107c	...	1243	1307c	...	1443	1507c	...	1707	...	1807	...	1843	1907c	...	2113
Garsten .... d.	0443	0527	0600	0611	0637	0709	0809	0843	0909	1043	1109	1209	1243	1309	1409	1443	1509	1609	1709	1743	1809	1809	1843	1909	2009	2114
Steyr .... d.	0447	0531	0605	0615	0642	0714	0814	0847	0914	1047	1114	1214	1247	1314	1414	1447	1514	1614	1714	1747	1814	1814	1847	1914	2014	2118
St Valentin .... a.	0508	0554	0621	0639	0705	0737	0837	0907	0937	1107	1137	1237	1307	1337	1437	1507	1537	1637	1737	1807	1837	1837	1907	1937	2037	2139
St Valentin .... 950 d.	0512	0555	0624	0642	0713	0743	0843	0915	0943	1116	1143	1243	1316	1343	1443	1516	1543	1643	1743	1816	1843	1916	1916	1943	2043	2143
Enns .... 992 d.	0519	0601	|	0648	0720	0750	0850	|	0950	|	1150	1250	|	1350	1450	|	1550	1650	1750	|	1850	|	|	1950	2050	2150
Linz Hbf .... 950 992 a.	0537	0616	0640	0704	0738	0807	0907	0930	1007	1130	1207	1307	1330	1407	1507	1530	1607	1707	1807	1830	1907	1930	1930	2007	2107	2207

P – To Passau (Table **962**).
c – © only.
e – Ⓐ only.
k – Not Nov. 1.
t – Arrives 0745.
y – 7 minutes later on ©.
z – 4 minutes later on ©.
⊡ – Weißenbach-St Gallen.

AMSTETTEN - KLEINREIFLING - SELZTHAL 977

2nd class only

km		⚒	ⒶL	W	ⒶL	⚒	Ⓒ	Ⓒ	Ⓐ	Ⓐ	Ⓒ	Ⓐ		Ⓐ		Ⓐ		ⒶS	⑥k	Ⓐ	⑥k	Ⓑw	ⒶS	†	Ⓐ	
0	**Amstetten** .... d.	0512	...	0621	...	0713	0805	0905	0905	1005	1105	1105	1205	1305	1405	1505	1605	...	...	1705	1803	1805	...	1903	1915	2005
23	Waidhofen a. d. Ybbs. d.	0550	...	0703f	...	0740	0831	0931	0931	1030	1131	1131	1231	1331	1431	1531	1631	...	...	1731	1831	1831	...	1931	1944	2030
41	Weyer .... d.	0609	...	0729	...	...	0850	0949	0949	...	1149	1149	1249	1349	1449	1558	1649	...	...	1749	1850	1849	...	1950	2010	...
44	Kastenreith .... **976** d.	0613	0629	0733	0848	...	0856	0953	0952	...	1153	1152	1253	1352	1453	1601	1653	1704	...	1752	1854	1853	1906	1954	2014	...
47	**Kleinreifling** ...... **976** a.	0617	0633	0737	0852	...	0859	0957	*1008*	...	1157	*1208*	1257	*1408*	1457	*1607*	1657	1707	1801	*1807*	1858	1857	1909	1958	2018	...
61	Weißenbach-St Gallen a.	...	0648	...	0907	...	0917	...	...	...	...	...	1312r	...	1512c	*1622*	...	1722	1815	*1822*	...	1912z	1924	...	...	...
119	**Selzthal** .... a.	...	...	...	...	...	1019	...	...	...	...	...	...	...	...	...	...	...	...	...	...	...	...	...	...	...

	⚒	⚒	Ⓐ	⑥k	Ⓐ	ⒶL		Ⓐ	W	⚒	Ⓐ	Ⓒ	Ⓐ	Ⓐ	Ⓒ	Ⓐ	Ⓐ	Ⓒ	Ⓐ		Ⓐ	Ⓐ	Ⓒ	†	Ⓐ	Ⓒ
Selzthal .... d.	...	...	...	...	...	...	...	...	...	...	...	...	...	...	...	...	...	...	...	...	...	...	1644	...	...	...
Weißenbach-St Gallen. d.	...	...	...	...	...	0603	...	0706	...	...	*0940*	...	...	...	...	...	*1340*	1346	...	1546c	*1641*	*1738*	1747	...	*1941*	1943
Kleinreifling .... **976** d.	...	...	0522	0600	...	0618	0633	0721	0802	...	*0954*	1002	...	*1154*	1202	1302	*1354*	1402	1502	1602c	1658	*1753*	1802	1902	1958	1958
Kastenreith .... **976** d.	...	...	0526	0604	...	0622	0637	0725	0806	...	1006	1006	...	1206	1206	1306	1406	1406	1506	1606	1706	1806	1806	1906	2006	2006
Weyer .... d.	...	...	0530	0608	...	...	0641	0728	0810	...	1010	1010	...	1210	1210	1310	1410	1410	1510	1610	1710	1810	1810	1910	2010	2010
Waidhofen a. d. Ybbs.. d.	0500	0525	0550	0628	0629	...	0701	...	0831	0931	1031	1031	1131	1231	1231	1331	1431	1431	1531	1631	1731	1831	1831	1931	2031	2031
Amstetten .... a.	0528	0554	0619	0655	0655	...	0729	...	0857	0957	1055	1055	1155	1255	1255	1355	1455	1455	1555	1655	1755	1855	1855	1955	2055	2055

L – From / to Linz (Table 976).
S – From St Valentin (Table 976).
W – From / to Wien (Table 950).
c – Ⓒ only.
f – Arrives 0654.
k – Not Nov. 1.
r – *1314* on Ⓐ (change trains at Kleinreifling).
w – Also Nov. 1.
z – † only.

WIEN and WIENER NEUSTADT - SOPRON 978

2nd class only

WIEN - EBENFURTH - SOPRON (operated by GySEV ◐)

km	*GySEV* ★	Ⓐ	Ⓐ		Ⓐ		Ⓐ		Ⓐ		Ⓐ		Ⓐ‡	Ⓐ	Ⓑ‡		Ⓐ‡	Ⓐ								
0	**Wien** Hbf .... d.	0532	0632	0732	0832	0932	*1022*	1132	1232	1332	1432	1532	*1550*	1632	*1650*	1732	*1750*	*1822*	*1922*	...	2032	...	...	...	...	...
4	**Wien** Meidling .... d.	0539	0639	0739	0839	0940	1040	1140	1240	1340	1440	1540	1600	1640	1700	1740	1800	1840	1940	...	2040	...	...	...	...	...
42	Ebenfurth .... d.	0615	0715	0815	0915	1015	1115	1215	1315	1415	1515	1615	|	1715	|	1815	|	1915	2015	...	2115	...	...	...	...	...
74	**Sopron** 🏛 .... a.	0652	0752	0852	0952	1052	1152	1252	1352	1452	1552	1652	1701	1752	1801	1852	1901	1952	2052	...	2152	...	...	...	...	...

GySEV ★	Ⓐ	Ⓐ	Ⓐ‡	Ⓐ	Ⓐ	Ⓐ‡			‡									Ⓐ		Ⓐ						
Sopron 🏛 .... d.	0414	0438	0500	0514	0538	0600	0614	0638	0700	0714	0738	0838	0938	1038	1138	1238	1338	1438	1538	1638	1738	...	1938	...	...	...
Ebenfurth .... d.	0456	0519	|	0556	0619	|	0656	0719	|	0756	0819	0919	1019	1119	1219	1319	1419	1519	1619	1719	1819	...	2019	...	...	...
Wien Meidling .... a.	0526	0549	0600	0626	0649	0700	0726	0749	0800	0826	0849	0949	1049	1149	1249	1349	1449	1549	1649	1749	1849	...	2049	...	...	...
Wien Hbf .... a.	...	0556	*0610*	*0641*	0656	*0716*	*0741*	0756	*0816*	*0841*	0856	0956	*1058*	*1158*	1256	1356	1456	1556	1656	1756	*1858*	...	2056	...	...	...

WIEN - WIENER NEUSTADT - SOPRON (operated by ÖBB)

km		⚒	Ⓑ	⚒		Ⓐ						Ⓐ		Ⓐ		Ⓐ				Ⓐ		Ⓐ		Ⓐ		
	Wien Meidling .... d.	*0515*	*0603*	*0630*	*0716e*	*0830*	*0930*	*1030*	*1130*	*1230*	*1330*	*1403*	*1430*	*1503*	*1530*	1600	*1630*	1700b	*1729*	1800	*1830*	*1903*	*1930*	*2003*	*2103*	*2158*
0	**Wiener Neustadt** Hbf. d.	0608	0638	0708	0803	0903	1003	1103	1203	1303	1403	1433	1503	1533	1603	1633	1703	1733	1803	1833	1903	1939	2003	2039	2139	2239
16	Mattersburg .... d.	0632	0702	0732	0825	0925	1025	1125	1225	1325	1425	1447	1525	1547	1625	1647	1725	1747	1825	1847	1925	2003	2025	2103	2203	2303
33	**Sopron** 🏛 .... a.	0645	0715	0747	0841	0941	1041	1141	1241	1341	1441	1501	1541	1601	1641	1701	1741	1801	1841	1901	1941	2018	2041	2118	2218	2318

	Ⓐ	Ⓐ	Ⓐ	Ⓐ	⚒	Ⓐ		Ⓐ		Ⓐ		Ⓐ											Ⓐ			
Sopron 🏛 .... d.	0416	0446	0500	0516	0546	0600	0616	0646	0700	0716	0747	0846	0946	1046	1146	1246	1346	1446	1546	1646	1746	1846	1946	2046	2146	2246
Mattersburg .... d.	0432	0502	0515	0532	0602	0615	0632	0702	0715	0732	0803	0903	1003	1103	1203	1303	1403	1503	1603	1703	1803	1903	2003	2103	2203	2303
Wiener Neustadt Hbf a.	0454	0524	0528	0554	0624	0628	0654	0724	0728	0754	0826	0926	1026	1126	1226	1326	1426	1526	1626	1726	1826	1926	2026	2126	2226	2326
Wien Meidling .... a.	*0531*	...	0600	*0630*	...	0700	*0743*	...	0800	*0830*	*0857r*	*0957*	*1057*	*1157*	*1257*	*1357*	*1457*	*1557*	*1657*	*1757*	*1857*	*1957*	*2057*	*2157*	*2257*	*0049*

b – Change trains at Wiener Neustadt on ⑥.
e – *0729* on Ⓒ.
r – ⚒ only.
‡ – Via Wiener Neustadt (see panel below; operated by ÖBB).
◐ – GySEV: Györ-Sopron-Ebenfurti Vasút (in German translates as Raab-Oedenburg-Ebenfurter Eisenbahn – ROeEE).

☛ **Additional journeys** Wiener Neustadt → Sopron on Ⓐ: 0538, 1239, 1339, 1439, 1539, 1639, 1739 and 1839.

WIEN and GRAZ - KLAGENFURT - VILLACH 980

km							🚌 851	*RJ* 551	*RJ* 554	*IC* 31	🚌 853	*RJ* 553		*EC* 151	*RJ* 558	*RJ* 531	*RJ* 555 Ⓐ	*RJ* 15555 Ⓒ		🚌 855	*RJ* 557	*EC* 158	*RJ* 533	🚌 857	*RJ* 559
		⚒ 2	⚒ 2	⚒ 2	2	2	☆	✕	✕	V🍷	☆	✕	2	E✕	✕	L✕	✕	✕	2	☆	✕	✕	✕	☆	✕
0	**Wien** Meidling ● .... **981** d.	...	...	...	...	...	...	0603	...	0630	...	0703	...	0803	...	0830	0903	0903	...	...	1003	...	1030	...	1103
45	**Wiener Neustadt** Hbf .. **981** a.	...	...	...	...	...	...	0628	...	0654	...	0728	...	0828	...	0854	0928	0928	...	...	1028	...	1054	...	1128
45	**Wiener Neustadt** Hbf .. **981** d.	...	...	...	...	...	...	0631	...	0656	...	0731	...	0831	...	0856	0931	0931	...	...	1031	...	1056	...	1131
100	Semmering .... **981** d.	...	...	...	...	...	...	|	...	|	...	|	...	0915	...	|	|	1015	...	...	1115	...	|	...	|
114	Mürzzuschlag .... **981** d.	...	0526	...	0621	...	...	0730	...	|	...	0830	...	0930	...	|	1030	1030	...	...	1130	...	|	...	1230
	Graz Hbf .... **975** d.	...	|	*0500e*	|	*0625r*	0630	|	0725	|	0800	|	*0825*	|	0925	|	|	|	*1025*	1030	|	1125	|	1200	|
154	**Bruck** an der Mur .... a.	...	0607	*0546e*	0702	*0701r*	|	0756	0801	0813	|	0856	*0901*	0956	1001	1013	1056	1056	*1101*	|	1156	1201	1213	|	1256
154	**Bruck** an der Mur ..... **975** ‡ d.	0439	0609	0613	0709	0708	|	0758	...	0815	|	0858	0908	0958	...	1015	1058	1058	1108	|	1158	...	1215	|	1258
208	**Graz** Hbf .... ‡ a.	|	0656	|	0756	|	|	0833	...	|	|	0933	|	1033	...	|	1133	1133	|	|	1233	...	|	|	1333
170	Leoben Hbf .... **975** d.	0453	▬	0626	...	0721	|	...	...	0827	|	...	0921	...	...	1027	...	...	1121	|	...	...	1227	|	...
◧	St Michael .... **975** a.	0501	...	|	...	0728	|	...	...	|	|	...	0928	...	...	|	...	...	1128	|	...	...	|	|	...
◧	St Michael .... d.	0508	...	|	...	0734	|	...	...	|	|	...	0934	...	...	|	...	...	1134	|	...	...	|	|	...
201	Knittelfeld .... d.	0528	...	0648	...	0752	|	...	...	0847	|	...	0952	...	...	1047	...	...	1152	|	...	...	1247	|	...
209	Zeltweg .... d.	0535	⚒	0654	...	0759	|	...	...	|	|	...	0959	...	...	|	...	...	1159	|	...	...	|	|	...
216	Judenburg .... d.	0543	2	0702	...	0807	|	...	...	0900	|	...	1007	...	...	1100	...	...	1207	|	...	...	1300	|	...
235	Unzmarkt .... d.	0559	0608	0718	...	0823	|	...	...	0914	|	...	1023	...	...	1114	...	...	1223	|	...	...	1314	|	...
272	Friesach .... **971** a.	...	0642	...	...	0856e	|	...	...	|	|	...	1056e	...	...	1144	...	...	1256e	|	...	...	|	|	...
305	St Veit an der Glan ...... **971** a.	...	0716	...	...	...	|	...	...	1007	|	...	...	...	...	1207	...	...	...	|	...	...	1407	|	...
325	**Klagenfurt** Hbf ..... **970 971** a.	...	0738	...	...	...	0830	...	...	1021	1000	...	...	...	...	1221	...	...	...	1230	...	...	1421	1400	...
363	**Villach** Hbf .... **970 971** a.	...	0820k	...	...	...	...	...	...	1046	...	...	...	...	...	1246	...	...	...	...	...	...	1446	...	...

		RJ 651	*RJ* 654	*RJ* 535	🚌 859	*RJ* 653		*RJ* 655	*RJ* 658	*EC* 103	*RJ* 657		🚌 951	⚒	*EC* 159	*RJ* 752	*RJ* 537	*RJ* 659		🚌 953	Ⓐ	*RJ* 751		*EC* 173	
	2	✕	✕	✕	☆	✕	2	✕	✕	P✕	✕	2	☆	2	J✕	✕	✕	✕	2	☆	2	✕	2	H✕	2
Vien Meidling ● .... **981** d.	...	1203	...	1230	...	1303	...	1403	...	1430	1503	...	...	...	1603	...	1630	1703	...	...	...	1803	...	1830	...
Viener Neustadt Hbf ... **981** a.	...	1228	...	1254	...	1328	...	1428	...	1454	1528	...	...	...	1628	...	1654	1728	...	...	...	1828	...	1854	...
Viener Neustadt Hbf ... **981** d.	...	1231	...	1256	...	1331	...	1431	...	1456	1531	...	...	...	1631	...	1656	1731	...	...	...	1831	...	1856	...
'emmering .... **981** d.	...	1315	...	|	...	|	...	|	...	|	1615	...	...	...	|	...	|	1814	...	...	...	|	...	|	...
lürzzuschlag .... **981** d.	...	1330	...	|	...	1430	...	1530	...	|	1630	...	...	...	1730	...	|	1830	...	...	...	1930	...	|	...
Graz Hbf .... **975** d.	*1225*	|	1325	|	1415	|	*1425*	|	1525	|	|	*1625*	1630	1701	|	1725	|	|	*1825*	1845	1901	|	*1925*	|	...
ruck an der Mur .... a.	*1301*	1356	1401	1413	|	1456	*1501*	1556	1601	1613	1656	*1701*	|	|	1756	1801	1813	1856	*1901*	|	|	1956	*2001*	2013	...
ruck an der Mur ...... **975** ‡ d.	1308	1358	...	1415	|	1458	1508	1558	...	1615	1658	1708	|	|	1758	...	1815	1858	1908	|	|	1958	2008	2015	...
Graz Hbf .... ‡ a.	|	1433	...	|	|	1533	|	1633	...	|	1733	|	|	|	1833	...	|	1933	|	|	|	2033	|	|	...
eoben Hbf .... **975** d.	1321	...	...	1427	|	...	1521	...	...	1627	...	1721	|	1758	...	...	1827	...	1921	|	1956	...	2021	2027	...
St Michael .... **975** a.	1328	...	...	|	|	...	1528	...	...	|	...	1728	|	|	...	...	|	...	1928	|	2003	...	2028	|	←
St Michael .... d.	1334	...	...	|	|	...	1534	...	...	|	...	1734	|	|	...	...	|	...	1934	|	2009	...	2034	|	2034
nittelfeld .... d.	1352	...	...	1447	|	...	1552	...	...	1647	...	1752	|	1821	...	...	1847	...	1952	|	2027	...	→	2047	2052
eltweg .... d.	1359	...	...	|	|	...	1559	...	...	|	...	1759	|	1827	...	...	|	...	1959	|	2034	...	...	|	2059
ıdenburg .... d.	1407	...	...	1500	|	...	1607	...	...	1700	...	1807	|	1835	...	...	1900	...	2007	|	2042	...	...	|	2107
nzmarkt .... d.	1423	...	...	1514	|	...	1623	...	...	1714	...	1823	|	1851	...	...	1914	...	2022	|	2057	...	...	|	2122
riesach .... **971** a.	1456e	...	...	1544	|	...	1656e	...	...	|	...	1856b	|	...	...	...	1944	...	...	|	...	...	...	2139	...
t Veit an der Glan .... **971** a.	...	...	...	1607	|	...	...	...	...	1807	...	...	|	...	...	...	2007	...	...	|	...	...	...	2202	...
lagenfurt Hbf .... **970 971** a.	...	...	...	1621	1615	...	...	...	...	1821	...	...	1830	...	...	...	2021	...	...	2045	...	...	...	2216	...
illach Hbf .... **970 971** a.	...	...	...	1646	...	...	...	...	...	1846	...	...	...	...	...	...	2046	...	...	...	...	...	...	2240	...

OR NOTES SEE NEXT PAGE →

980 WIEN and GRAZ - KLAGENFURT - VILLACH

	RJ 753		EN 235	RJ 755	EN 1237	EC 757		REX 1975
			A		⑤D		⑤–⑦	
	✕	2	R	✕	R	✕	2	2
Wien Meidling ● ... 981 d.	1903	...	1930	2003	2030	2103	...	2303
Wiener Neustadt Hbf ... 981 a.	1928	...	1954	2028	2055	2128	...	2329
Wiener Neustadt Hbf ... 981 d.	1931	...	1956	2031	2057	2131	...	2331
Semmering ... 981 d.	|	...	|	|	|	|	...	0026
Mürzzuschlag ... 981 d.	2030	...	|	2130	|	2230	...	0040
Graz Hbf ... 975 d.	|	2025	|	|	|	|	2224t	...
Bruck an der Mur ... a.	2056	2101	2123	2156	2220	2256	2301t	...
Bruck an der Mur ... 975 ‡ d.	2058	2108	2125	2158	2222	2258	2308	...
Graz Hbf ... ‡ a.	2133	|	|	2233	|	2333	|	...
Leoben Hbf ... 975 d.	...	2121	2140	...	2236	...	2321	...
St Michael ... 975 a.	...	2128	|	...	|	...	|	...
St Michael ... d.	...	2134	|	...	|	...	|	...
Knittelfeld ... d.	...	2152	2203	...	|	...	2344	...
Zeltweg ... d.	...	2159	|	...	|	...	2350	...
Judenburg ... d.	...	2207	|	...	|	...	2358	...
Unzmarkt ... d.	...	2222	|	...	|	...	0014	...
Friesach ... 971 a.	...	...	2258	...	|	...	...	...
St Veit an der Glan ... 971 a.	...	...	|	...	|	...	...	...
Klagenfurt Hbf ... 970 971 a.	...	...	2335	...	0019	...	...	...
Villach Hbf ... 970 971 a.	...	...	0001	...	0043	...	...	...

			EC 278	EN 1236		EN 234		RJ 552			EC 172	RJ 551
	⚒	⚒		B	⚒	A	⚒	⚒	⚒	⚒		
	2	2	G✕	R	2	R	2	✕	2	2	H✕	✕
Villach Hbf ... 970 971 d.	...	...	...	0344	...	0418	...	...	...	...	0526	...
Klagenfurt Hbf ... 970 971 d.	...	...	...	0409	...	0440	...	...	...	...	0549	...
St Veit an der Glan ... 971 d.	...	...	...	|	...	|	...	...	0501	...	0602	...
Friesach ... 971 d.	...	...	...	|	...	|	...	...	0527	...	|	...
Unzmarkt ... d.	0446	...	...	|	0527	|	0549	...	0608	...	|	...
Judenburg ... d.	0502	...	...	|	0543	|	0605	...	0624	...	|	...
Zeltweg ... d.	0510	...	...	|	0552	|	0613	...	0632	...	|	...
Knittelfeld ... d.	0516	...	...	|	0558	|	0619	...	0638	...	|	...
St Michael ... a.	0535	...	...	|	|	|	|	...	0657	...	|	...
St Michael ... 975 d.	0546	0541	...	|	|	|	|	...	0706	0701	|	...
Leoben Hbf ... 975 d.	0554	0551	...	0608	0623	0627	0643	...	0715	0709	0733	...
Graz Hbf ... ‡ d.	|	|	0537	|	|	|	|	0625	|	|	|	...
Bruck an der Mur ... 975 ‡ a.	0608	|	0613	0621	|	0639	0655	0701	0728	|	0744	...
Bruck an der Mur ... d.	...	|	0615	0624	|	0641	0709	0703	...	|	0746	0758
Graz Hbf ... 975 a.	...	0645	|	|	0715	|	0756	|	...	0801	|	0833
Mürzzuschlag ... 981 d.	...	...	0646	|	...	0708	...	0733	...	...	|	...
Semmering ... 981 d.	...	...	|	|	...	|	...	0747	...	...	|	...
Wiener Neustadt Hbf. 981 a.	...	...	0745	0751	...	0802	...	0828	...	...	0902	...
Wiener Neustadt Hbf. 981 d.	...	...	0747	0755	...	0804	...	0832	...	...	0904	...
Wien Meidling ● ... 981 a.	...	...	0816	0904y	...	0833	...	0857	...	...	0927	...

	🚌 850		RJ 554			RJ 556	🚌 852	RJ 534	EC 151	RJ 558	🚌 854		RJ 650	EC 102	RJ 557	EC 158	🚌 856		RJ 652	RJ 538	RJ 651	RJ 654	🚌 858		RJ 656
	①m																								
	☆	2	✕	2	2	✕	☆	✕	✕	✕	☆	2	✕	P✕	✕	J✕	☆	2	✕	✕	✕	✕	☆	2	✕
Villach Hbf ... 970 971 d.	...	...	...	0529	...	...	...	0714	...	...	...	...	...	0914	...	...	...	...	...	1114	...	...	...	...	...
Klagenfurt Hbf ... 970 971 d.	0620	...	...	0607	...	...	0720	0739	...	...	0920	...	...	0939	...	...	1120	...	...	1139	...	...	1330	...	...
St Veit an der Glan ... 971 d.	|	...	...	0627	...	...	|	0753	...	...	|	...	...	0953	...	...	|	...	...	1153	...	...	|	...	...
Friesach ... 971 d.	|	...	...	0700	...	...	|	|	...	...	|	0903e	...	1017	...	...	|	1103e	...	|	...	...	|	1303e	...
Unzmarkt ... d.	|	0656	...	0733	0737	...	|	0847	...	...	|	0937	...	1047	...	...	|	1137	...	1247	...	...	|	1337	...
Judenburg ... d.	|	0712	...	...	0753	...	|	0901	...	...	|	0953	...	1101	...	...	|	1153	...	1301	...	...	|	1353	...
Zeltweg ... d.	|	0720	...	...	0801	...	|	|	...	...	|	1001	...	|	...	...	|	1201	...	|	...	...	|	1401	...
Knittelfeld ... d.	|	0726	...	...	0807	...	|	0914	...	...	|	1007	...	1114	...	...	|	1207	...	1314	...	...	|	1407	...
St Michael ... a.	|	|	...	...	0826	...	|	|	...	...	|	1026	...	|	...	...	|	1226	...	|	...	...	|	1426	...
St Michael ... 975 d.	|	|	...	...	0833	...	|	|	...	...	|	1033	...	|	...	...	|	1233	...	|	...	...	|	1433	...
Leoben Hbf ... 975 d.	|	0747	...	...	0841	...	|	0934	...	...	|	1041	...	1134	...	...	|	1241	...	1334	...	...	|	1441	...
Graz Hbf ... ‡ d.	|	|	0725	...	|	0825	|	|	...	0925	|	|	1025	|	...	1125	|	|	1225	|	...	1325	|	|	1425
Bruck an der Mur ... 975 ‡ a.	|	0758	0801	...	0853	0901	|	0944	...	1001	|	1053	1101	1144	...	1201	|	1253	1301	1344	...	1401	|	1453	1501
Bruck an der Mur ... d.	|	0809	0803	...	0858	0903	|	0946	0958	1003	|	1058	1103	1146	1158	1203	|	1258	1303	1346	1358	1403	|	1458	1503
Graz Hbf ... 975 a.	0820	0856	|	...	0933	|	0920	|	1033	|	1120	1133	|	|	1233	|	1320	1333	|	|	1433	|	1530	1533	|
Mürzzuschlag ... 981 d.	...	...	0833	...	...	0933	...	|	...	1033	...	...	1133	|	...	1233	...	...	1333	|	...	1433	...	...	1533
Semmering ... 981 d.	...	...	|	...	...	0947	...	|	...	|	...	...	1147	|	...	|	...	...	1347	|	...	|	...	...	|
Wiener Neustadt Hbf ... 981 a.	...	...	0928	...	...	1028	...	1102	...	1128	...	...	1228	1302	...	1328	...	...	1428	1502	...	1528	...	...	1628
Wiener Neustadt Hbf ... 981 d.	...	...	0932	...	...	1032	...	1104	...	1132	...	...	1232	1304	...	1332	...	...	1432	1504	...	1532	...	...	1632
Wien Meidling ● ... 981 a.	...	...	0957	...	...	1057	...	1127	...	1157	...	...	1257	1327	...	1357	...	...	1457	1527	...	1557	...	...	1657

	RJ 630	RJ 655	RJ 658		RJ 750	RJ 15750	🚌 950	RJ 632	EC 159	RJ 752		RJ 754	🚌 952	RJ 530	D 15030	RJ 751	EC 150		RJ 738		RJ 756	🚌 954	IC 30		
					Ⓐ	Ⓒ									⑦z				⑦z					⚒	⑤–⑦
	✕	✕	✕	2	✕	✕	☆	✕	✕	✕	2	✕	☆	L✕	2	✕	E✕	2	✕	2	✕	☆	V🍷	2	2
Villach Hbf ... 970 971 d.	1314	...	...	...	...	...	...	1514	...	...	...	...	...	1714	...	...	...	...	1814	...	...	...	1914	...	...
Klagenfurt Hbf ... 970 971 d.	1339	...	...	...	...	...	1545	1539	...	...	...	...	1745	1739	...	...	...	...	1839	...	...	1945	1939	...	...
St Veit an der Glan ... 971 d.	1353	...	...	...	...	...	|	1553	...	...	...	...	|	1753	...	...	...	...	1853	...	...	|	1953	...	...
Friesach ... 971 d.	1417	...	...	1503e	...	...	|	|	...	...	1703e	...	|	1817	...	...	...	1903b	1919	...	...	|	|	...	...
Unzmarkt ... d.	1447	...	...	1537	...	...	|	1647	...	...	1737	...	|	1847	1856	...	...	1937	|	...	...	|	2047	2108	2137
Judenburg ... d.	1501	...	...	1553	...	...	|	1701	...	...	1753	...	|	1901	1910	...	...	1953	2001	...	...	|	2101	2125	2153
Zeltweg ... d.	|	...	...	1601	...	...	|	|	...	...	1801	...	|	|	1918	...	...	2001	|	...	...	|	|	2133	2201
Knittelfeld ... d.	1514	...	...	1607	...	...	|	1714	...	...	1807	...	|	1914	1924	...	...	2007	2014	...	...	|	2114	2139	2207
St Michael ... a.	|	...	...	1626	...	...	|	|	...	...	1826	...	|	|	|	...	...	2026	|	←	...	|	|	▬	2226
St Michael ... 975 d.	|	...	...	1633	...	...	|	|	...	...	1833	...	|	|	|	...	...	2033	|	2033	...	|	|	...	2233
Leoben Hbf ... 975 d.	1534	...	...	1641	...	...	|	1734	...	...	1841	...	|	1934	1945	...	...	→	2034	2041	...	|	2134	RJ	2241
Graz Hbf ... ‡ d.	|	...	1525	|	1625	1625	|	|	...	1725	|	1825	|	|	|	...	1925	...	|	|	2025	|	|	755	|
Bruck an der Mur ... 975 ‡ a.	1544	...	1601	1653	1701	1701	|	1744	...	1801	1853	1901	|	1944	|	...	2001	...	2044	2053	2101	|	2144	✕	2253
Bruck an der Mur ... d.	1546	1558	1603	1658	1703	1703	|	1746	1758	1803	1858	1903	|	1946	|	1958	2003	...	2046	2058	2103	|	2146	2158	2258
Graz Hbf ... 975 a.	|	1633	|	1733	|	|	1745	|	1833	|	1933	|	1945	|	2030	2033	|	...	|	2133	|	2145	|	2233	2333
Mürzzuschlag ... 981 d.	|	...	1633	...	1733	1733	...	|	...	1833	...	1933	...	|	...	...	2033	...	|	...	2133	...	|	...	...
Semmering ... 981 d.	|	...	1647	...	|	1747	...	|	...	1847	...	|	...	|	...	...	|	...	|	...	|	...	|	...	...
Wiener Neustadt Hbf ... 981 a.	1702	...	1728	...	1828	1828	...	1902	...	1928	...	2028	...	2102	...	...	2128	...	2202	...	2228	...	2302	...	...
Wiener Neustadt Hbf ... 981 d.	1704	...	1732	...	1832	1832	...	1904	...	1932	...	2032	...	2104	...	...	2132	...	2204	...	2232	...	2304	...	...
Wien Meidling ● ... 981 a.	1727	...	1757	...	1857	1857	...	1927	...	1957	...	2057	...	2127	...	...	2157	...	2227	...	2257	...	2327	...	...

Local stopping trains **BRUCK AN DER MUR - GRAZ - SPIELFELD-STRASS** (for international services Graz - Spielfeld Straß - Maribor - Ljubljana / Zagreb see Table **1315**).

km				Ⓐ				◇									◇			⚒			⚒	⚒	
	Bruck a. d. Mur ... d.	0457	0609	0650	0709	0809	0909	0958	1009	1109	1209	1309	1409	1509	1609	1709	1758	1809	1909	2009	2109	2209	2209	2309	...
	Graz Hbf ... a.	0544	0656	0730	0756	0856	0956	1033	1056	1156	1256	1356	1456	1556	1656	1756	1833	1856	1956	2056	2156	2256	2256	2356	...
0	Graz Hbf ... 1315 d.	0558	0708	0738	0808	0908	1008	1038	1108	1208	1308	1408	1508	1608	1708	1808	1838	1908	2008	2108	2208	...	2308	...	0008
9	Flughafen Graz ✈ ... d.	0610	0720	0750	0820	0920	1020	|	1120	1220	1320	1420	1520	1620	1720	1820	|	1920	2020	2120	2220	...	2320	...	0020
35	Leibnitz ... d.	0636	0750	0820	0850	0950	1047	1059	1150	1250	1350	1450	1550	1650	1750	1847	1859	1950	2047	2147	2247	...	2347	...	0047
47	Spielfeld-Straß 🛃 ... 1315 a.	0648	0800	0830	0900	1000	1100	1108	1200	1300	1400	1500	1600	1700	1800	1900	1908	2000	2057	2157	2257	...	2357	...	0057

						⚒						◇									◇		⚒		⚒
Spielfeld-Straß 🛃 ... 1315 d.	...	...	0439	0504	...	0529	0609	0709	0809	0909	1009	1048	1109	1209	1309	1409	1509	1609	1709	1809	1848	1909	2009	2109	2209
Leibnitz ... d.	...	...	0450	0515	...	0540	0620	0720	0820	0920	1020	1058	1120	1220	1320	1420	1520	1620	1720	1820	1858	1920	2020	2120	2220
Flughafen Graz ✈ ... d.	...	...	0518	0542	...	0608	0649	0748	0848	0948	1048	|	1148	1248	1348	1448	1548	1648	1748	1848	|	1948	2048	2148	2248
Graz Hbf ... 1315 a.	...	...	0530	0555	...	0620	0702	0800	0900	1000	1100	1120	1200	1300	1400	1500	1600	1700	1800	1900	1920	2000	2100	2200	2300
Graz Hbf ... d.	0005	...	...	0559e	0611	...	0708	0805	0905	1005	1105	1125	1205	1305	1405	1505	1605	1705	1805	1905	1925	2005	2105	2205	2305
Bruck a. d. Mur ... a.	0051	...	...	0641e	0657	...	0754	0851	0951	1051	1151	1201	1251	1351	1451	1551	1651	1751	1851	1951	2001	2051	2151	2251	2351

A – 🛏 1, 2 cl., ▬ 2 cl. and [2] Roma - Bologna - Venezia - Wien and v.v.; 🛏 1, 2 cl. and ▬ 2 cl. Milano - Venezia - Wien and v.v.

B – Fom Villach on ⑦ Apr. 13 - Sept. 28 (also ⑤ June 20 - Aug. 29; also Apr. 22, May 2, 30, June 10). Previous night from Livorno. 🛏 1, 2 cl., ▬ 2 cl. and [2] Livorno - Pisa - Firenze - Bologna - Wien. Train number **1238** on ⑤ June 20 - Aug. 29 (also Apr. 22, May 2, 30, June 10).

D – ⑤ Apr. 11 - Sept. 26 (also ③ June 18 - Aug. 27; also Apr. 20, 30, May 28, June 8). 🛏 1, 2 cl., ▬ 2 cl. and [2] Wien - Bologna - Firenze - Pisa - Livorno.

E – EMONA – [12] and ✕ Ljubljana - Maribor - Spielfeld-Straß 🛃 - Graz - Wien and v.v.

G – GUSTAV KLIMT – [12] and ✕ Graz - Wien - Břeclav 🛃 - Praha.

H – VINDOBONA – [12] and ✕ Villach - Břeclav 🛃 - Praha - Dresden - Berlin - Hamburg and v.v.

J – CROATIA – [12] and ✕ Zagreb - Maribor - Spielfeld-Straß 🛃 - Graz - Wien and v.v.

L – To / from Lienz (Table **971**).

P – POLONIA – [12] and ✕ Villach - Wien - Břeclav 🛃 - Ostrava - Warszawa and v.v.

R – 🅁 for journeys from / to Italy.

V – [12] and 🍷 Wien - Villach - Tarvisio 🛃 - Udine - Venezia and v.v.

b – Ⓑ only.

e – Ⓐ only.

k – Change trains at Klagenfurt on Ⓐ to July 4 / from Sept. 8.

m – Not Apr. 21, June 9, Dec. 8.

r – On † departs Graz *0611*, arrives Bruck a. d. Mur *0657*.

t – Sept. 5–27 departs Graz 2205, arrives Bruck a. d. Mur 2251.

y – 0828 on ⑦.

z – Also Apr. 21, June 9, Dec. 8; not Apr. 20, June 8, Dec. 7.

◇ – *EC* train (see main panel, also Table **1315**).

‡ – For other local journeys see panel below main table.

◧ – Leoben - St Michael is *10 km*. St Michael - Knittelfeld is *22 km*.

● – See Tables **981/2** for S-Bahn trains to / from Wien Hbf, Mitte, Praterstern and Floridsdorf. See Table **985** for S-Bahn connections to / from Wien Flughafen ✈. U-bahn line **U6** provides a direct link Wien Meidling - Westbahnhof - Spittelau - Floridsdorf and v.v.

☆ – **ÖBB** *Intercitybus*. Rail tickets valid. 1st and 2nd class. 🍷 in first class. Number of seats limited so reservation is recommended.

Local trains WIEN - WIENER NEUSTADT - MÜRZZUSCHLAG 981

Wien - Wiener Neustadt

km		⚒P	⚒	ⒶP		⚒P		⚒		⚒P			⊡			P				M		P		
0	**Wien** Praterstern....... **980/2** d.	0437	0456	0526	0544	0556	0614	0626	0644	0656	0714	0744		2014	2044	2114	2135	2144	2214	2244	2247	2344	2347	0047
2	**Wien** Mitte............... **980/2** d.	0441	0500	0530	0548	0600	0618	0630	0648	0700	0718	0748	and at	2018	2048	2118	2139	2148	2218	2248	2251	2348	2351	0051
5	**Wien** Hbf.................. **980/2** d.	0449	0508	0538	0556	0608	0626	0638	0656	0708	0726	0756	the same	2026	2056	2126	2147	2156	2226	2256	2259	2356	2359	0059
9	**Wien** Meidling ● ...... **980/2** d.	0456	0515	0546	0605	0616	0635	0646	0705	0716	0735	0805	minutes	2035	2105	2135	2158	2205	2235	2303	2307	0003	0007	0107
21	Mödling............................d.	0509	0527	0557	0617	0627	0647	0657	0717	0727	0747	0817	past each	2047	2117	2147	|	2217	2247	|	2325	|	0025	0125
32	Baden...............................d.	0516	0534	0604	0624	0634	0654	0704	0724	0734	0754	0824	hour until	2054	2124	2154	2215	2224	2254	2316	2337	0017	0037	0137
54	**Wiener Neustadt** Hbf. **980/2** a.	0537	0556	0620	0643	0651	0716	0720	0746	0750	0816	0846		2116	2146	2216	2228	2246	2316	2329	0003	0029	0103	0203

	⚒	ⒶM	⚒	Ⓐ	Ⓐ		M		Ⓐ		P		P		P			⊡				⚒P		
Wiener Neustadt ...... **980/2** d.	0430	0501	0504	0520	0534	0604	0616	...	0620	0634	0647	...	0704	0720	0734	0810	0840		2110	2140	2149	2240	2243	2343
Baden...............................d.	0452	|	0524	0540	0554	0624	|	...	0640	0654	|	...	0724	0740	0754	0832	0902	and at	2132	2202	2219	2302	2311	0011
Mödling............................d.	0501	|	0531	0548	0601	0631	|	0638	0648	0701	|	...	0731	0748	0801	0839	0909	the same	2139	2209	2232	2309	2329	0032
Wien Meidling ● .... **980/2** a.	0513	0531	0543	0558	0613	0643	0646	0655	0658	0713	0716	0723	0743	0758	0813	0852	0922	minutes	2152	2222	2249	2322	2346	0049
Wien Hbf.................. **980/2** a.	0519	0540	0549	0604	0619	0649	...	0701	0704	0719	...	0728	0749	0804	0819	0858	0928	past each	2158	2228	2255	2328	2352	0055
Wien Mitte................ **980/2** a.	0527	0548	0557	0612	0627	0657	...	0709	0712	0727	...	0736	0757	0812	0827	0906	0936	hour until	2206	2236	2303	2336	2400	0103
Wien Praterstern .... **980/2** a.	0531	0552	0601	0616	0631	0701	...	0713	0716	0731	...	0740	0801	0816	0831	0910	0940		2210	2240	2307	2340	0004	0107

Wiener Neustadt - Mürzzuschlag

km		⚒	⚒			Ⓐ															Ⓐ			
	Wien Meidling ....d.	0456	0546e	0616r	0716r	0746	0805	0905	1005	1105	...	1205	1305	1416t	1533k	1633k	1716t	1816t	...	1905	...	2035	2135	2303	0003
0	**Wiener Neustadt** Hbf .. **980** d.	0538	0634	0700	0800	0835	0900	1000	1100	1200	...	1300	1400	1500	1600	1700	1800	1900	...	2000	2110	2135	2235	2331	0031
14	Neunkirchen NÖ ....d.	0548	0644	0711	0811	0846	0911	1011	1111	1211	...	1311	1411	1511	1611	1711	1811	1911	...	2011	2121	2146	2246	2342	0042
27	Gloggnitz ....d.	0601	0657	0724	0824	0859	0924	1024	1124	1224	...	1324	1424	1524	1624	1724	1824	1924	...	2024	2134	2159	2259	2354	0055
34	Payerbach-Reichenau ....a.	0610	0706	0733	0833	0908	0933	1033	1133	1233	1236	1333	1433	1533	1633	1733	1833	1933	1936	2033	2143	2208	2308	0001	0104
55	Semmering .... **980** a.	...	*0732*	...	*0905*	...	...	*1105*	...	...	1305	...	...	*1605*	...	*1805*	...	...	2005	...	...	...	...	0026	...
69	**Mürzzuschlag** .... **980** a.	...	...	...	...	...	...	...	...	...	1321e	...	...	...	...	...	...	...	2021	...	...	...	...	0040	...

	Ⓐ	Ⓒ	Ⓐ		†		⚒	⚒		⚒															
Mürzzuschlag............. **980** d.	0348	0510	0513	...	0538	...	0608	...	...	...	...	...	...	...	...	...	1337e	...	...	...	...	...	...	...	...
Semmering .... **980** d.	0403	0525	0527	...	0554	...	0624	...	...	0752	...	...	*0952*	...	*1152*	...	1352	...	...	...	*1652*	...	*1852*	...	...
Payerbach-Reichenau ....d.	0430	0552	0552	0615	0624	0627	0654	0657	0729	0821	0824	0924	1024	1124	1224	1324	1421	1424	1524	1624	1724	1824	1924	2024	2158
Gloggnitz ....d.	0439	0600	0600	0624	...	0636	...	0706	0738	...	0833	0933	1033	1133	1233	1333	...	1433	1533	1633	1733	1833	1933	2033	2219
Neunkirchen NÖ ....d.	0450	|	|	0635	...	0647	...	0717	0749	...	0844	0944	1044	1144	1244	1344	...	1444	1544	1644	1744	1844	1944	2044	2229
Wiener Neustadt Hbf ... **980** a.	0459	0614	0614	0645	...	0657	...	0727	0759	...	0854	0954	1054	1154	1254	1354	...	1454	1554	1654	1754	1854	1954	2054	2239
Wien Meidling ....a.	0531	0646	0646	0716	...	0743	...	0813	0843j	...	0952	1052	1152	1252	1352	1452	...	1543n	1643n	1743n	1843n	1943n	2043n	...	2322v

M – To / from Mürzzuschlag (see panel below main table).
P – To / from Payerbach-Reichenau (see panel below main table).

e – Ⓐ only.
j – 0852 on †.

k – 28 minutes **earlier** on Ⓒ.
n – 9 minutes later on Ⓒ.
r – 11 minutes **earlier** on †.
t – 11 minutes **earlier** on Ⓒ.
v – ⚒ only.

⊡ – For through services to / from Payerbach-Reichenau see panel below main table.
● – See panel on page 452 for S-Bahn trains from / to Wien Hütteldorf. See Table **985** for S-Bahn connections to Wien Flughafen ✈. U-bahn line **U6** provides a direct link Wien Meidling - Westbahnhof - Spittelau.

WIEN - BŘECLAV 982

Austrian Holiday dates apply

km		2⚒	2	*EC* **78** ✕	*EC* **104** ♠✕	2	*EC* **278** G✕	*EC* **172** A✕	2	2⚒	2	*EC* **70** ✕	2⚒	*EC* **102** ♠✕	2	*EC* **72** ✕	2Ⓐ	2	*EC* **74** ✕	2Ⓐ	2	*EC* **76** ✕	2	2	2
	Wiener Neustadt Hbf **980/1** d.	...	0520e	...	....	0720	0747	0904	0910	1010	1110	1204	1210	1304	1310	1404	1440	1510	1604	1640	1710	1804	1910	2010	2140
0	**Wien** Meidling........... **980/1** d.	0459	0559	...	0741	0759	0824	0931	0953	1053	1153	1231	1253	1331	1353	1431	1523	1553	1631	1723	1753	1831	1953	2053	2223
	Wien Simmering ....d.	|	|	...	0754	|	0855	0945	|	|	|	1253	|	1345	|	1453	|	|	1653	|	|	1853	|	|	|
4	**Wien** Hbf..................... **981** d.	0505	0605	...	|	0805	|	|	0959	1059	1159	|	1259	|	1359	|	1529	1559	|	1729	1759	|	1959	2059	2229
7	**Wien** Mitte.................. **981** d.	0513	0613	...	|	0813	|	|	1007	1107	1207	|	1307	|	1407	|	1537	1607	|	1737	1807	|	2007	2107	2237
9	**Wien** Praterstern.......... **981** d.	0517	0617	0650	|	0817	|	|	1011	1111	1211	|	1311	|	1411	|	1541	1611	|	1741	1811	|	2011	2111	2241
14	**Wien** Floridsdorf ⊡..............d.	0525	0625	0700	|	0825	|	|	1019	1119	1219	|	1319	|	1419	|	1549	1619	|	1749	1819	|	2019	2119	2249
40	Gänserndorf.........................d.	0549	0649	|	|	0849	|	|	1043	1143	1243	|	1343	|	1443	|	1612	1643	|	1812	1843	|	2043	2143	2314
74	Hohenau 🏛 ....a.	0622	0722	|	|	0920	|	|	1114	1216	1316	|	1416	|	1514	|	1643	1714	|	1843	1914	|	2116	2216	2346
92	**Břeclav** 🏛...........................a.	...	...	0753	0853	0936	0953	1053	1130	...	...	1353	...	1453	1530c	1553	1703	1730c	1756	1858	1930c	1953	...	...	...
	Praha hlavní **1150** ....a.	...	...	1121	...	...	1321	1421	...	...	...	1721	...	...	...	1921	...	...	2121	...	...	2321	...	...	...

	2Ⓐ	2⚒	2	2⚒	*EC* **71** ✕	2	*EC* **73** ✕	2	*EC* **75** ✕	2	*EC* **103** ♠✕	2⚒	*EC* **77** ✕	2	2⚒	2	*EC* **173** A✕	2Ⓐ	*EC* **279** ✕	2	*EC* **105** ♠✕	2Ⓐ	2	*EC* **79** ✕	2
Praha hlavní **1150** ....d.	...	...	...	...	0439z	...	0639	...	0839	...	...	...	1039	...	...	...	1339	...	1439	...	...	...	...	1839	...
Břeclav 🏛..........................d.	...	0555	...	...	0802	...	1002	1026	1202	1226	1302	...	1402	...	...	1626c	1702	1726	1802	1826c	1902	1926	2026c	2202	...
Hohenau 🏛..........................d.	0439	0610	0639	0709	|	0839	|	1041	|	1241	|	1339	|	1439	1539	1641	|	1741	|	1841	|	1941	2041	|	2239
Gänserndorf.........................d.	0512	0643	0712	0742	|	0912	|	1113	|	1313	|	1412	|	1512	1612	1713	|	1813	|	1913	|	2013	2113	|	2312
Wien Floridsdorf ⊡..............a.	0535	0705	0735	0805	|	0935	|	1135	|	1335	|	1435	|	1535	1635	1735	|	1835	|	1935	|	2035	2135	2254	2335
Wien Praterstern .... **981** a.	0543	0713	0743	0813	|	0943	|	1143	|	1343	|	1443	|	1543	1643	1743	|	1843	|	1943	|	2043	2143	2303	2343
Wien Mitte..................... **981** a.	0547	0717	0747	0817	|	0947	|	1147	|	1347	|	1447	|	1547	1647	1747	|	1847	|	1947	|	2047	2147	...	2347
Wien Hbf....................... **981** a.	0555	0725	0755	0825	|	0955	|	1155	|	1355	|	1455	|	1555	1655	1755	|	1855	|	1955	|	2055	2155	...	2355
Wien Simmering ....a.	|	|	|	|	0902	|	1102	|	1302	|	1402	|	1502	|	|	|	1802	|	1902	|	2002	|	|	...	|
Wien Meidling............ **980/1** a.	0602	0732	0802	0832	0924	1002	1124	1202	1324	1402	1424	1502	1524	1602	1702	1802	1824	1902	1922	2002	2017	2102	2202	...	0002
Wiener Neustadt Hbf **980/1** a.	0643	0816	0846	0916	0955	1046	1155	1246	1355	1446	1454	1546	1555	1646	1746	1846	1854	1946	...	2046	w	2146	2246	...	0029

A – VINDOBONA – (12) and ✕ Villach - Praha - Dresden - Berlin - Hamburg and v.v.
G – From Graz (Table **980**).

c – Ⓒ only.
e – Ⓐ only.

w – To Wien Westbahnhof (a. 2034).
z – ①–⑥ (not Apr. 21, Nov. 17).

♠ – To / from Warszawa (Table **99**).
⊡ – U-Bahn line **U6** provides a direct link Wien Westbahnhof - Spittelau - Floridsdorf and v.v.

WIEN - RETZ - ZNOJMO 983

2nd class only; Austrian holiday dates apply

km		A	⚒		G	⑥h		⚒		⚒		†	⚒	⚒		Ⓐ	◇	Ⓐ	⚒	Ⓐ		Ⓐ			
0	**Wien** Meidling.............. **991** d.	...	0544	0644	0744	0744	0817	0944	1044	1144	1232	...	1244	1344	1444	1544	1644	1714	1744	1814	1844	1944	2044	2250	...
4	**Wien** Hbf...................... **991** d.	...	0550	0650	0750	0750	0823	0950	1050	1150	1238	...	1250	1350	1450	1550	1650	1720	1750	1820	1850	1950	2050	2256	...
7	**Wien** Mitte.................... **991** d.	...	0558	0658	0758	0758	0831	0958	1058	1158	1246	...	1258	1358	1458	1558	1658	1728	1758	1828	1858	1958	2058	2304	...
9	**Wien** Praterstern........... **991** d.	...	0602	0702	0802	0802	0835	1002	1102	1202	1250	...	1302	1402	1502	1602	1702	1732	1802	1832	1902	2002	2102	2308	...
14	**Wien** Floridsdorf ⊡...... **991** d.	...	0610	0710	0810	0810	0843	1010	1110	1210	1257	1310	1310	1410	1510	1610	1710	1740	1810	1840	1910	2010	2110	2315	2332
34	Stockerau .... **991** d.	...	0628	0728	0828	0828	0914	1028	1128	1228	...	1328	1328	1428	1528	1628	1728	1802	1828	1902	1928	2028	2128	...	2349
60	Hollabrunn ....d.	...	0645	0745	0845	0845	0940	1045	1145	1245	...	1345	1345	1445	1545	1645	1745	1824	1845	1924	1945	2045	2153	...	0010
90	**Retz** 🏛..............................d.	0617	0712	0815	0912	0916	...	1112	1215	1312	...	1415	1415	1512	1615	1712	1815	1853	1912	1953	2012	2112	2220	...	0036
96	Šatov 🏛 ....d.	0625	...	0823	...	0924	...	...	1223	...	...	1423	1423	...	1623	...	1823	...	...	...	...	...	...	...	...
107	**Znojmo** ....a.	0636	...	0834	...	0935	...	...	1234	...	...	1434	1434	...	1634	...	1834	...	...	...	...	...	...	...	...

	Ⓐ	⚒		⚒	A		⚒		⑥h	⚒		⚒	Ⓐ	Ⓒ		⚒		⚒		Ⓐ	⚒	†	Ⓑq	⑥h	
Znojmo ....d.	...	...	...	...	0653	...	...	0856	0956	...	...	...	1256	1256	...	...	1456	...	1656	...	1856	1856	...	...	...
Šatov 🏛 ....d.	...	...	...	...	0704	...	...	0907	1007	...	...	...	1307	1307	...	...	1507	...	1707	...	1907	1907	...	...	...
Retz 🏛................................d.	0417	0510	0552	0635	0715	0715	0817	0917	1017	1017	...	1217	1317	1317	...	1417	1517	1617	1717	1817	1917	1917	2017	2017	...
Hollabrunn ....d.	0444	0538	0620	0706	0744	0744	0844	0944	1044	1044	1149	1244	1344	1344	...	1444	1544	1644	1744	1844	1944	1944	2044	2044	...
Stockerau .... **991** d.	0501	0556	0640	0728	0801	0801	0901	1001	1101	1101	1216	1301	1401	1401	...	1501	1601	1701	1801	1901	2001	2001	2101	2101	...
Wien Floridsdorf ⊡....... **991** a.	0517	0617	0702	0747	0817	0817	0917	1017	1117	1117	1244	1317	1417	1417	1430	1517	1617	1717	1817	1917	2017	2017	2117	2117	2127
Wien Praterstern .... **991** a.	0525	0625	0710	0755	0825	0825	0925	1025	1125	1125	1252	1325	1425	...	1437	1525	1625	1725	1825	1925	2025	*2037*	2125	...	2134
Wien Mitte..................... **991** a.	0529	0629	0714	0759	0829	0829	0929	1029	1129	1129	1256	1329	1429	...	1441	1529	1629	1729	1829	1929	2029	*2041*	2129	...	2138
Wien Hbf....................... **991** a.	0537	0637	*0725*	0807	0837	0837	0937	1037	1137	1137	1304	1337	1437	...	1449	1537	1637	1737	1837	1937	2037	*2049*	2137	...	2146
Wien Meidling............... **991** a.	0544	0644	*0732*	0814	0844	0844	0944	1044	1144	1144	1311	1344	1444	...	1456	1544	1644	1744	1844	1944	2044	*2056*	2144	...	2153

A – ①–⑥ (not Apr. 21).
G – ⚒ (daily Apr. 28 - Oct. 31).

h – Not Nov. 1.
q – Also Nov. 1.

◇ – Change trains at Retz on Ⓒ.
⊡ – U-Bahn line **U6** provides a direct link Wien Westbahnhof - Spittelau - Floridsdorf and v.v.

984 WIENER NEUSTADT - PUCHBERG am Schneeberg - HOCHSCHNEEBERG *2nd class only*

WIENER NEUSTADT - PUCHBERG am Schneeberg *28 km.* Journey time: 44 – 46 minutes.
From Wiener Neustadt at 0038 †, 0611 Ⓐ, 0737, 0837 **A**, 0937, 1037 **E**, 1137, 1237 **E**, 1337, 1437 **E**, 1537, 1637, 1737, 1837 Ⓑ **q**, 1937, 2037 Ⓑ **q** and 2137.
From Puchberg at 0455 Ⓐ, 0525 Ⓐ, 0555 ⚒, 0624 Ⓐ, 0638 Ⓒ, 0647 Ⓐ, 0738, 0838, 0938 **C**, 1038, 1138 **E**, 1238, 1338 **E**, 1438, 1538 **E**, 1638, 1738, 1838, 1938 Ⓑ **q** and 2038 ⑤⑥ **t**.

PUCHBERG am Schneeberg - **HOCHSCHNEEBERG** *Schneebergbahn* (narrow-gauge rack railway). *9 km.* Journey time: ± 40 minutes.
Services run **Apr. 26 - Oct. 26, 2014** subject to demand and weather conditions. **Operator**: NÖ Schneebergbahn GmbH, Bahnhofplatz 1, A-2734 Puchberg. ✆ +43 (0) 2636 3661 20.
From Puchberg at 0900, 1030, 1200, 1400, 1530. **From Hochschneeberg** at 0945, 1115, 1315, 1445, 1615. Additional trains operate during July and August, also at other times when there is sufficient demand. A steam service operates on ⑦ June 29 - Aug. 31 (also Aug. 15): Departs Puchberg 1120, departs Hochschneeberg 1515 (journey time ± 80 minutes – special fares apply).

A – Ⓐ (daily Apr. 22 - Oct. 31).
C – Ⓒ Apr. 26 - Oct. 26.
E – ⚒ (daily Apr. 22 - Oct. 31).
q – Not Apr. 20, June 8, Dec. 7.
t – Also Apr. 20, 30, May 28, June 8, 18, Aug. 14, Oct. 31, Dec. 7.

985 FLUGHAFEN WIEN ✈ Schwechat *CAT ★; S-Bahn (2nd class only)*

km		★	★	★		★	★															
0	**Wien** Praterstern ....d.	CAT	...	...	and	...	...	S-Bahn	0426	0450	0520	0550	0611	0641	0711	0741	0811	0841	and at	2211	2241	2341
2	**Wien** Mitte.................d.	→	0536	0606	every	2236	2306	→	0430	0454	0524	0554	0615	0645	0715	0745	0815	0845	the same	2215	2245	2345
	Wien Meidling ▲.....d.		|	|	30	|	|		|	*0441*	*0511*	*0541*	*0559*	*0635*	*0702*	*0732*	*0802*	*0832*	minutes	*2202*	*2232*	*2332*
	Wien Hbf ▲............d.		|	|	minutes	|	|		|	*0447*	*0517*	*0547*	*0605*	*0641*	*0708*	*0738*	*0808*	*0838*	past each	*2208*	*2238*	*2338*
3	**Wien** Rennweg..........d.		|	|	until	|	|		0433	0457	0527	0557	0618	0648	0718	0748	0818	0848	hour until	2218	2248	2348
21	**Flughafen Wien** ✈ ....a.		0552	0622		2252	2322		0456	0519	0549	0619	0642	0711	0744	0811	0845	0911		2245	2311	0011
		★	★	★		★	★															
0	**Flughafen Wien** ✈ ....d.	CAT	0606	0636	and	2306	2336	S-Bahn	0538	0608	0638	0708	0722	0738	0808	0843	0917	0942	and at	2242	2317	0017
18	**Wien** Rennweg..........a.	→	|	|	every	|	|	→	0600	0630	0700	0730	0745	0800	0830	0906	0939	1006	the same	2306	2339	0039
20	**Wien** Hbf ▲............a.		|	|	30	|	|		*0610*	*0640*	*0710*	*0740*	*0755*	*0810*	*0837*	*0919*	*0949*	*1019*	minutes	*2319*	*2349*	*0058*
24	**Wien** Meidling ▲.....a.		|	|	minutes	|	|		*0617*	*0647*	*0717*	*0747*	*0802*	*0817*	*0844*	*0926*	*0956*	*1026*	past each	*2326*	*2356*	*0105*
	Wien Mitte.................a.		0622	0652	until	2322	2352		0603	0633	0703	0733	0748	0803	0833	0909	0942	1009	hour until	2309	2342	0042
	Wien Praterstern ....a.		...	...		...	...		0607	0637	0707	0737	0752	0807	0837	0913	0946	1013		2313	2346	0046

★ – *City Airport Train (CAT)*. Non-stop service with special fares.
▲ – Shaded timings are connecting services – change at Rennweg (cross platform).

🚌 *Vienna Airport Lines*: Wien Westbahnhof (Europaplatz) – Wien Meidling (Dörfelstraße) – Flughafen Wien ✈ and v.v.
🚌 From **Wien Westbahnhof**: 0510, 0540 and every 30 minutes until 2240, 2310. Journey time: 45 minutes (from Westbahnhof), 30 minutes (from Meidling).
🚌 From **Flughafen Wien** ✈: 0004, 0605, 0635 and every 30 minutes until 2305, 2335. Journey time: 30 minutes (to Meidling), 45 minutes (to Westbahnhof).

🚌 ÖBB-Postbus / Slovak Lines: **Bratislava**, AS Mlynské nivy (bus station) – **Flughafen Wien** ✈ and v.v. Journey time: 60 minutes.
Reservation recommended ✆ +43 (0) 810 222 333-6 or +421 18 211.
🚌 From **Bratislava** AS Mlynské nivy at 0440, 0530, 0600, 0700, 0730 ①–⑤, 0800, 0830, 0900, 0930 ①–⑤, 1000, 1100, 1200, 1300, 1400, 1500, 1600, 1700, 1800, 1900, 2000 and 2200.
🚌 From **Flughafen Wien** ✈ at 0630, 0815, 0830, 0940, 1030, 1130, 1230, 1300 ①–⑤, 1330, 1430, 1500 ①–⑤, 1530, 1630, 1730, 1800, 1830, 1930, 2030, 2130, 2230 and 2330.

986 GRAZ - SZENTGOTTHÁRD - SZOMBATHELY *ÖBB, GySEV •; 2nd class only*

km					A ✗									Ⓐ		Ⓐ		Ⓐ		Ⓐ		⚒		Ⓐ		
0	**Graz** Hbf.............☆ d.	0008	...	...	0608	0708	0808	0908	1008	1108	1208	1308	1408	1438	1508	1538	1608	1638	1708	1738	1808	1838	1908	1938	2008	2108
29	Gleisdorf..............☆ d.	0047	...	...	0650	0750	0850	0950	1050	1150	1250	1350	1450	1513	1550	1613	1650	1713	1750	1813	1850	1913	1950	2013	2050	2150
53	Feldbach...............☆ d.	0111	...	...	0715	0814	0914	1014	1114	1214	1314	1414	1514	1529	1614	1629	1714	1729	1814	1829	1914	1929	2014	2029	2114	2214
62	Fehring.................☆ d.	0121	...	...	0727	0824	0925	1024	1125	1233t	1325	1429	1525	1538	1624	1638	1725	1738	1824	1838	1925	1941	2024	2040	2125	2224
82	Szentgotthárd 🏛....... a.	▬	...	...	0746	▬	0947	...	1147	1255	1347	1450e ▬	1547c ▬	*1603*	...	*1702*	1747c	*1802*	...	*1903*	1947c	2002e	...	2101	2147	...
					|									d		d		d				d		d		
82	Szentgotthárd 🏛....... d.	0506	0606	0706	0811	0836	1006	...	1206	1306	1406	1436	1536	1636	...	1736	...	1836	...	...	...	2006	...	2106	2236	...
110	Körmend...............d.	0530	0630	0730	0829	0900	1030	...	1230	1330	1430	1500	1600	1700	...	1800	...	1900	...	...	...	2030	...	2130	2300	...
146	**Szombathely**...........a.	0553	0653	0753	0848	0923	1053	...	1253	1353	1453	1523	1623	1723	...	1823	...	1927	...	...	...	2053	...	2153	2323	...

			⚒																				B ✗			
Szombathely .... d.	...	...	0436	0506	...	...	0606	0636	0706	...	0906	...	1106	1236	1306	1336	1406	1436	1536	1636	1736	1836	1912	2036	2136	2236
Körmend.................. d.	...	...	0501	0531	...	...	0631	0701	0731	...	0931	...	1131	1301	1331	1401	1431	1501	1601	1701	1801	1901	1930	2101	2201	2301
Szentgotthárd 🏛........ a.	...	...	0524	0554	...	...	0654 ▬	0724 ▬	0754	...	0954	...	1154	1324 ▬	1354	1424	1458	1524	1624	1724	1824 ▬	1924 ▬	1950	2124 ▬	2224	2324
	Ⓐ		Ⓐ	†	Ⓐ	⚒	Ⓐ H							F							W	⚒	|	⚒		
Szentgotthárd 🏛........ d.	*0446*	0516k	*0532*	0616	*0619*	0640k	...	...	0816	...	1016	...	1210	1300	1406	...	*1510*e	1616	1716e	1813	...	...	2020	...	...	...
Fehring................⊡ d.	0511	0539	0557	0639	0644	0703	0730	0739	0839	0939	1039	1139	1239	1329	1429	...	1539	1639	1739	1835	1839	1939	2044	2139	...	...
Feldbach..............⊡ d.	0522	0550	0606	0650	0654	0715	0742	0750	0850	0950	1050	1150	1250	1350	1450	...	1550	1650	1750	...	1850	1950	2054	2150	...	...
Gleisdorf..............⊡ d.	0540	0613	0626	0713	0713	0738	0802	0813	0913	1013	1113	1213	1313	1413	1513	...	1613	1713	1813	...	1913	2013	2114	2213	...	...
Graz Hbf ....⊡ a.	0615	0653	0703	0753	0748	0816	0837	0853	0953	1053	1153	1253	1353	1453	1553	...	1653	1753	1853	...	1953	2053	2153	2253	...	...

A – 🚃12 Graz (**4700**) - Szentgotthárd (*IC* **917**) - Budapest.
B – 🚃12 Budapest (*IC* **916**) - Szentgotthárd (**4737**) - Graz.
F – Change trains at Fehring on Ⓐ.
H – From Hartberg (Table **995**).
W – From Wiener Neustadt (Table **995**).
c – Ⓒ only.
d – Daily.
e – Ⓐ only.
k – ⑥ (not Nov. 1).
t – Arrives 1224.
✗ – Ⓡ and supplement payable in Hungary.
• – Szentgotthárd - Szombathely operated by Györ-Sopron-Ebenfurti Vasút (GySEV).
☆ – Additional journeys Graz Hbf - Fehring at 1238 Ⓐ, 1338 Ⓐ, 2208 ⚒ and 2308 ⚒.
⊡ – Additional journeys Fehring - Graz at 0409 Ⓐ, 0439 and 0615 ⚒.

990 WIEN - GMÜND - ČESKÉ VELENICE *2nd class only*

km			⚒									Ⓐ	Ⓐ		Ⓐ		Ⓐ	Ⓒ	Ⓐ	⚒	⚒	†		
0	**Wien** Franz-Josefs-Bf..... **991** d.	0622	0627	0725	0923	1029	1123	1229	1326	1429	1522	1555	1558	1624	1648	1657	1719	1719	1755	1820	1921	1921	1956	2047
1	Wien Spittelau .... ● **991** d.	0625	0630	0728	0925	1032	1125	1232	1329	1432	1525	1558	1601	1627	1651	1700	1723	1723	1759	1823	1924	1924	1958	2050
3	Wien Heiligenstadt.....△ **991** d.	0628	0633	0731	0929	1035	1129	1235	1332	1435	1528	1601	1604	1631	1654	1704	1726	1726	1802	1826	1928	1928	2002	2054
33	Tulln a. d. Donau .... **991** d.	0650	0655	0753	0955	1056	1155	1256	1358	1456	1551	1624	1631	1654	|	|	1752	1752	1824	1852	|	1952	2028	2116
44	Absdorf-Hippersdorf....... **991** d.	0700	0704	0802	1003	1105	1203	1305	1406	1506	1603	|	1639	1703	|	|	1801	1805	1833	1903	1959	|	2036	2125
79	Eggenburg.............................d.	0731	0748	0831	1042	1134	1242	1335	1444	1535	1641	1653	1718	1735	1750	1756	1845	1845	1903	1934	2026	2026	2117	2152
89	Sigmundsherberg..................d.	0740	0757	0839	1052	1143	1252	1344	1453	1543	1649	1701	1728	1743	1758	1805	1855	1855	1911	1942	2035	2035	2127	2201
121	Göpfritz ....d.	0803	...	0904	...	1209	...	1411	...	1610	...	1727	...	1812	...	1830	...	...	1935	...	2100	2100	...	2224
138	Schwarzenau.........................d.	0817	...	0917	...	1223	...	1425	...	1624	...	1741	...	1826	...	1844	...	...	1951	...	2114	2114	...	2237
162	**Gmünd** NÖ ....a.	0838	...	0939	...	1244	...	1447	...	1646	...	1804	...	1847	...	1906	...	...	2012	...	2135	2135	...	2258
162	**Gmünd** NÖ 🏛.......................d.	0841	...	0942	...	1247	...	1449	...	1649	...	...	...	1849	...	...	...	...	...	...	2138	*2138*	...	...
164	České Velenice 🏛.... **1130/3** a.	0845	...	0946	...	1251	...	1453	...	1653	...	...	...	1853	...	...	...	...	...	...	2142	*2142*	...	...

	Ⓐ	⚒	Ⓐ	†	Ⓐ	⚒		Ⓒ	Ⓐ	⚒		⚒											†	
České Velenice 🏛 ..... **1130/3** d.	...	...	...	...	...	...	...	...	...	...	0618	...	...	0905	...	1109	...	1312	...	1508	...	1729	...	1906
Gmünd NÖ 🏛........................a.	...	...	...	...	...	...	...	...	...	...	0622	...	...	0909	...	1113	...	1316	...	1512	...	1733	...	1910
Gmünd NÖ ....d.	...	0348	...	...	0420	...	...	0516	0531	...	0624	...	...	0911	...	1115	...	1318	...	1515	...	1735	...	1929
Schwarzenau..........................d.	...	0410	...	...	0441	...	...	0538	0553	...	0645	...	...	0937	...	1137	...	1339	...	1537	...	1758	...	1952
Göpfritz................................d.	...	0423	...	...	0456	...	...	0552	0606	...	0659	...	...	0952	...	1150	...	1352	...	1550	...	1812	...	2007
Sigmundsherberg....................d.	0410	0448	0509	0505	0522	0529	0616	0616	0630	0643	0723	0805	0908	1016	1108	1217	1308	1418	1508	1616	1708	1836	1908	2035
Eggenburg.............................d.	0420	0457	0517	0514	|	0538	0625	0625	|	0653	0731	0814	0917	1025	1117	1225	1317	1426	1517	1625	1717	1846	1917	2043
Absdorf-Hippersdorf........ **991** d.	0501	|	|	0548	|	0608	0654	0654	|	0729	0800	0856	0954	1054	1154	1254	1354	1455	1554	1657	1757	1920	1954	2112
Tulln a. d. Donau .... **991** d.	0510	0532	0553	0558	|	0617	0703	0703	|	0738	0809	0906	1004	1103	1204	1303	1404	1504	1604	1706	1807	1930	2004	2122
Wien Heiligenstadt..... △ **991** a.	0534	0555	0614	0623	0619	0644	0724	0724	0729	0759	0830	0930	1028	1124	1228	1324	1428	1526	1628	1727	1831	1952	2028	2143
Wien Spittelau .... ● **991** a.	0537	0558	0617	0626	0622	0647	0728	0728	0733	0802	0833	0934	1031	1127	1231	1328	1431	1529	1631	1730	1834	1956	2031	2146
Wien Franz-Josefs-Bf..... **991** a.	0540	0601	0620	0629	0625	0650	0731	0731	0735	0805	0836	0937	1034	1131	1234	1331	1434	1533	1634	1733	1837	1959	2034	2149

△ – S-Bahn trains run every 10 – 15 minutes from / to Wien Hütteldorf (journey time: 21 – 23 minutes).
● – Direct U-bahn links: Line **U4** – Wien Mitte - Spittelau. Line **U6** – Wien Meidling - Westbahnhof - Spittelau - Floridsdorf.

2nd class only — WIEN - KREMS an der Donau - EMMERSDORF — 991

km		⚒	†	Ⓐ	P		©									Ⓐ		Ⓐ		Ⓐ				
0	**Wien Franz-Josefs-Bf** .... 990 d.	0553	0616	0651	0728	0751	0851	0951	1051	1151	1251	1351	1451	1551	1651	1716	1750	1826	1851	1922w	1951	2051	2151	2302
1	Wien Spittelau .... ● 990 d.	0556	0619	0654	|	0754	0854	0954	1054	1154	1254	1354	1454	1554	1654	1719	1753	1830	1854	|	1954	2054	2154	2304
3	Wien Heiligenstadt..... △ 990 d.	0559	0623	0657	0734	0757	0857	0957	1057	1157	1257	1357	1457	1557	1657	1723	1756	1833	1857	|	1957	2057	2157	2308
33	Tulln a. d. Donau .... 990 d.	0621	0644	0723	0800	0819	0919	1019	1119	1219	1319	1419	1519	1619	1719	|	1818	1856	1919	|	2019	2119	2219	2345
44	Absdorf-Hippersdorf .... 990 d.	0632	0656	0732	...	0828	0928	1028	1128	1228	1328	1428	1528	1628	1728	|	1828	1905	1928	1953	2028	2129	2228	...
76	**Krems** a. d. Donau .... a.	0714	0722	0804	...	0855	0954	1054	1154	1254	1354	1454	1554	1654	1759	1818	1854	1938	1954	2018	2054	2203	2256	...

	Ⓐ	⚒	Ⓐ	Ⓐ		Ⓐ		Ⓐ	Ⓑz													P		
Krems a. d. Donau .... d.	0425	0452	0517	0543	0614	0644	0726	0741	0815	0902	1002	1102	1201	1301	1400	1502	1601	1702	1802	1902	2001	...	2102	...
Absdorf-Hippersdorf .... 990 d.	0456	0529	|	0614	0648	0722	|	0808	0852	0928	1028	1128	1228	1328	1428	1528	1628	1728	1828	1928	2028	...	2128	...
Tulln a. d. Donau .... 990 d.	0506	0538	|	0624	0658	0730	0804	|	0902	0937	1037	1137	1237	1337	1437	1537	1637	1737	1837	1937	2037	2126	2137	2242
Wien Heiligenstadt..... △ 990 a.	0526	0604	0610	0648	0720	0755	0825	|	0923	0958	1058	1158	1258	1358	1458	1558	1658	1758	1858	1958	2058	2148	2158	2319
Wien Spittelau .... ● 990 a.	0530	0608	0613	0651	0724	0758	0828	|	0926	1001	1101	1201	1301	1401	1501	1601	1701	1801	1901	2001	2101	2152	2201	2323
Wien Franz-Josefs-Bf ..... 990 a.	0533	0611	0616	0655	0727	0801	0831	0838w	0929	1004	1104	1204	1304	1404	1504	1604	1704	1804	1904	2004	2104	2155	2204	2325

WIEN Meidling - STOCKERAU - ABSDORF-HIPPERSDORF ✣

km		Ⓐ	◧	©	©	©	©	©	©	
0	**Wien** Meidling.............. 983 d.	0605	0647	0847	1047	1247	1447	1647	1847	1947
4	**Wien** Hbf...................... 983 d.	0611	0653	0853	1053	1253	1453	1653	1853	1953
7	**Wien** Mitte..................... 983 d.	0619	0701	0901	1101	1301	1501	1701	1901	2001
9	**Wien** Praterstern............ 983 d.	0623	0705	0905	1105	1305	1505	1705	1905	2005
14	**Wien** Floridsdorf........... 983 d.	0631	0713	0913	1113	1313	1513	1713	1913	2013
35	Stockerau ....983 ✣ d.	0658	0744	0945	1145	1345	1545	1745	1945	2045
52	**Absdorf-Hippersdorf** ...... ✣ a.	*0718*	0758	1000	1200	1400	1600	1800	2000	2100

	Ⓐ	Ⓐ	Ⓐ	©	©	©	©	©	©	
Absdorf-Hippersdorf.. ✣ d.	0500	*0627*	*0724*	0830	1030	1230	1430	1630	1830	2030
Stockerau ....983 ✣ d.	0516	0646	0746	0846	1046	1246	1446	1646	1846	2046
Wien Floridsdorf .... 983 a.	0544	0714	0814	0914	1114	1314	1514	1714	1914	2114
Wien Praterstern......... 983 a.	0552	0722	0822	0922	1122	1322	1522	1722	1922	2122
Wien Mitte .... 983 a.	0556	0726	0826	0926	1126	1326	1526	1726	1926	2126
Wien Hbf.................... 983 a.	0604	0734	0834	0934	1134	1334	1534	1734	1934	2134
Wien Meidling............ 983 a.	0611	0741	0841	0941	1141	1341	1541	1741	1941	2141

KREMS - EMMERSDORF ⊠

km		©R		©R		©R			
0	**Krems** an der Donau ....d.	1000	...	1300	...	1600	...	...	...
18	**Spitz** an der Donau ....d.	1036	...	1336	...	1636	...	...	...
34	**Emmersdorf** an der Donau...... ⊡ a.	1110	...	1410	...	1710	...	...	...

	©R		©R		©R			
Emmersdorf an der Donau... ⊡ d.	1140	...	1440	...	1740	...	...	...
Spitz an der Donau ....d.	1217	...	1517	...	1817	...	...	...
Krems an der Donau ....a.	1250	...	1550	...	1850	...	...	...

P – May 1 - Oct. 26. (2) Wien - St Pölten - Linz - Passau and v.v. *Einfach-Raus-Ticket* not valid.

R – © Apr. 12 - Oct. 26 (daily June 28 - Sept. 28). Special fares payable.

w – Wien **Westbahnhof**. z – Also Nov. 1.

◧ – Change trains at Stockerau on Ⓐ.

● – Direct U-bahn links: Line **U4** – Wien Mitte - Spittelau. Line **U6** – Wien Meidling - Westbahnhof - Spittelau - Floridsdorf.

△ – S-Bahn trains run every 10 – 15 minutes from / to Wien Hütteldorf (journey time: 21 – 23 minutes).

✣ – **Additional journeys** on Ⓐ Stockerau - Absdorf-Hippersdorf and v.v. (journey time: 14 – 16 minutes). **From Stockerau** at 0434, 0532, 0550, 0906, 1106, 1306, 1406, 1506, 1606, 1706, 1806, 1906 and 2006. **From Absdorf-Hippersdorf** at 0530, 0838, 1038, 1238, 1338, 1438, 1538, 1642, 1738, 1838 and 1938.

⊠ – Krems - Emmersdorf operated by NÖVOG (special fares payable). ✆ +43 (0) 2742 360 990-99. A connecting 🚌 service operates Emmersdorf - Melk and v.v. Journey time: 10 minutes. From Emmersdorf at 1125 and 1725. From Melk at 1115 and 1715.

2nd class only — LINZ and ST VALENTIN - GREIN - SARMINGSTEIN — 992

km		Ⓐ	Ⓐ	⚒								⚒		Ⓐ	⚒	Ⓐ	Ⓐ		Ⓐ	Ⓐ	Ⓐ	©	Ⓐ	Ⓐ	
0	**Linz** Hbf .... 976 d.	...	0525	*0616*	*0646*	...	0834	...	1034	...	*1230*	*1330*	1434	*1452*	*1530*	*1530*	1604	1634	1704	*1730*	*1752*	*1830*	1834	1934	*2030*
17	Enns.................... 976 d.	...	0542	*0633*	*0704*	...	0849	...	1049	...	|	|	1449	*1510*	|	|	1619	1649	1719	|	*1810*	|	1849	1949	|
	St Valentin ....d.	0502	|	0648	0719	...	|	...	|	...	1250	1350	|	1522	1550	1550	|	|	|	1750	1822	1850	|	|	2050
34	Perg ....d.	0526	0609	0713	0744	...	0914	...	1114	...	1314	1414	1514	1545	1614	1614	1644	1714	1745	1814	1845	1914	1914	2014	2113
55	Grein-Bad Kreuzen .....d.	0601	0644	0744	0816	...	0945	...	1145	...	1345	1445	1545	1613	1644	1645	1714	1745	1816	1845	1915	1945	1945	2043	2142
57	Grein Stadt ....d.	0604	0648	0747	0819	...	0948	...	1148	...	1348	1448	1548	...	...	1648	...	1748	1819	1847	1918	1948	1948	2046	...
62	St Nikola-Struden........a.	0610	0655	0753	0825	...	0954	...	1154	...	1354	1455	1554	...	...	1654	...	1754	1825	...	1924	1954	1954	2052	...
65	Sarmingstein..............a.	0615	...	...	...	...	...	...	...	...	...	...	...	...	...	...	...	...	1830	...	...	1959	1959	2057	...

km		Ⓐ	Ⓐ		Ⓐ	⚒		Ⓐ				Ⓐ	©	⚒		Ⓐ	Ⓐ	©	Ⓐ	Ⓐ	Ⓐ	©	Ⓐ	Ⓑ	
0	Sarmingstein..............d.	...	0511	0525	...	...	0627	...	...	...	...	...	...	...	...	...	...	...	...	...	...	...	1900	...	...
3	St Nikola-Struden........d.	...	0516	0530	...	...	0632	0702	...	0804	1004	1204	1204	1304	1404	1502	1604	1604	...	1704	1804	1804	1904	...	1933
8	Grein Stadt ....d.	0403	0523	0537	...	...	0639	0710	...	0811	1011	1211	1211	1311	1411	1510	1611	1611	...	1711	1811	1811	1911	1911	1940
10	Grein-Bad Kreuzen .....d.	0407	0526	0540	0601	0612	0644	0714	...	0815	1015	1215	1215	1315	1415	1515	1615	1615	1644	1715	1815	1815	1915	1915	1945
31	Perg ....d.	0435	0554	0610	0630	0641	0713	0744	...	0844	1044	1244	1244	1344	1444	1544	1644	1644	1714	1744	1844	1844	1944	1944	2014
49	**St Valentin** ....a.	0458	|	0632	|	0705	|	0807	...	|	|	|	1307	1407	|	|	|	1707	1738	1807	|	1907	2007	2007	2036
	Enns.................... 976 a.	*0518*	0613	*0647*	0652	|	0739	|	...	0907	1107	1307	|	|	1507	1607	1707	|	*1749*	|	1907	|	|	|	*2049*
	Linz Hbf .... 976 a.	*0537*	0630	*0704*	0709	*0730*	0754	*0830*	...	0922	1122	1322	*1330*	*1430*	1522	1622	1722	*1730*	*1807*	*1830*	1922	*1930*	*2030*	*2030*	*2107*

2nd class only — ST PÖLTEN - KREMS and TULLN — 993

km		Ⓐ	Ⓐ	⚒	⚒	†		⚒				©	Ⓐ	©	Ⓐ		Ⓐ			Ⓐ					
0	**St Pölten** Hbf ....d.	0424	0604	0635	0706	0739	0809	0831	0908	1002	1112	1202	1250	1312	1331	1415	1450	1512	1602	1650	1712	1802	1912	2012	2110
10	Herzogenburg ....d.	0438	0613	0648	0716	0759	0818	0843	0926	1011	1126	1211	1259	1326	1340	1425	1500	1526	1611	1700	1726	1811	1926	2026	2124
30	**Krems** a. d. Donau ......a.	0508	0640	0720	0745	0829	0845	0917	0956	1036	1156	1236	1324	1356	1410	1450	1528	1556	1636	1728	1756	1836	1956	2058	2152

	Ⓐ	Ⓐ	⚒	⚒	†	⚒	⚒	⚒	†	Ⓐ															
Krems a. d. Donau ....d.	0430	0459	0539	0604	0609	0616	0643	0722	0724	0754	0838	0920	1001	1120	1201	...	1335	1415	1520	1601	1720	1801	...	1920	2020
Herzogenburg ....d.	0500	0531	0610	0632	0640	0648	0713	0753	0753	|	0908	0947	1032	1147	1232	...	1401	1446	1547	1632	1747	1832	...	1947	2050
St Pölten Hbf ....a.	0517	0544	0626	0644	0656	0703	0722	0808	0808	0825	0919	0956	1046	1156	1246	...	1409	1500	1556	1646	1756	1846	...	1956	2100

km		Ⓐ	⚒	⚒	Ⓐ	⚒			⚒		Ⓐ		Ⓐ		Ⓐ		Ⓐ		Ⓐ		P		
0	**St Pölten** Hbf .... 950 d.	0347	0408	0518	0554	0613	...	0735	0835	0935	1035	1135	1235	1335	1435	1535	1635	1735	1835	1935	2026	...	...
10	Herzogenburg ....d.	0356	0422	0532	0615	0639	...	0757	0849	0949	1049	1149	1249	1349	1449	1549	1649	1749	1849	1949	2045	...	...
40	Tullnerfeld.............................. 950 a.	0428	0456	0604	0650	0718	...	0829	0927	1027	1127	1227	1327	1427	1527	1627	1727	1827	1927	2027	|	...	...
40	Tullnerfeld.....................................d.	0429	0457	0618	0653	0727	...	0830	0933	1033	1133	1233	1333	1433	1533	1633	1733	1833	1933	2033	|	...	...
47	**Tulln** a. d. Donau .... 990/1 a.	0437	0506	0625	0701	0735	...	0838	0941	1041	1141	1241	1341	1441	1541	1641	1741	1841	1941	2041	2124	...	...
80	**Wien** Franz-Josefs-Bf ● ...... 990/1 a.	...	...	0700	0753	0825	...	0925	1025	1125	1225	1325	1425	1525	1625	1725	1825	1925	2025	2125	2155	...	...

	Ⓐ	Ⓐ		⚒	⚒	⚒	⚒	P		Ⓐ		Ⓐ		Ⓐ		Ⓐ		Ⓐ		Ⓐ			
Wien Franz-Josefs-Bf ●........ 990/1 d.	...	...	...	...	0534	0602	0630	0728*	0732	0832	0932	1032	1132	1232	1332	1432	1532	1628	1732	1832	1932	...	...
Tulln a. d. Donau .... 990/1 d.	0401	0448	...	0555	0619	0646	0714	0806	0820	0920	1020	1120	1220	1320	1420	1520	1620	1720	1820	1920	2020	...	...
Tullnerfeld..a.	0409	0456	...	0603	0629	0653	0721	|	0827	0927	1027	1127	1227	1327	1427	1527	1627	1727	1827	1927	2027	...	...
Tullnerfeld.............................. 950 d.	0410	0457	...	0604	0630	0654	0722	|	0832	0932	1032	1132	1232	1332	1432	1532	1632	1732	1832	1932	2032	...	...
Herzogenburg ....d.	0447	0535	...	0643	0704	0730	0803	0846	0911	1011	1111	1211	1311	1411	1511	1611	1711	1811	1911	2011	2108	...	...
St Pölten Hbf.......................... 950 a.	0501	0548	...	0652	0715	0747	0819	0855	0925	1025	1125	1225	1325	1425	1525	1625	1725	1825	1925	2025	2123	...	...

P – May 1 - Oct. 26. (2) Wien Franz-Josefs-Bf - St Pölten - Linz - Passau and v.v. *Einfach-Raus-Ticket* not valid.

● – Trains also call at Wien Heiligenstadt and Spittelau.

* – Does not call at Spittelau.

Narrow gauge 2nd class only — ST PÖLTEN - MARIAZELL — 994

km				★	⑥N	S[R]					
0	**St Pölten** Hbf ....d.	0636	0740	0840	0910	0910	1040	1240	1440	1640	1840
12	Ober Grafendorf ....d.	0652	0800	0900	0930	0935	1100	1300	1500	1700	1900
31	Kirchberg a. d. Pielach.d.	0720	0830	0930	1002	1012	1130	1330	1530	1730	1930
43	Frankenfels............ ⊗ d.	0738	0848	0948	1024	|	1148	1348	1548	1748	1948
48	Laubenbachmühle.......d.	0748	0858	0958	1038	1058	1158	1358	1558	1758	1956
67	Gösing.........................d.	0820	0930‡	1030	1113	1136	1230	1430	1630	1830	...
80	Mitterbach...................d.	0845	0955‡	1055	1140	1208	1255	1455	1655	1855	...
84	**Mariazell** ....a.	0852	1002‡	1102	1147	1217	1302	1502	1702	1902	...

					⑥N	S[R]	★	‡		
Mariazell ....d.	...	0857	1157	1357	1447	1447	1557	1647	1757	1907
Mitterbach.....................d.	...	0904	1204	1404	1454	1455	1604	1654	1804	1914
Gösing...........................d.	...	0930	1230	1430	1522	1525	1630	1720	1830	1940
Laubenbachmühle....d.	0802	1002	1302	1502	1557	1612	1702	1802	1902	2010
Frankenfels......... ⊗ d.	0811	1011	1311	1511	1606	|	1711	1811	1911	...
Kirchberg a. d. Pielach d.	0830	1030	1330	1530	1628	1645	1730	1830	1930	...
Ober Grafendorf.......d.	0900	1100	1400	1600	1702	1725	1800	1900	2000	...
St Pölten Hbf ....a.	0919	1119	1419	1619	1724	1749	1819	1919	2019	...

– ⑥ (also July 6, 20, Aug. 3, 15, 17, 31; not Oct. 4 - Nov. 22). Traditional loco-hauled electric train. Conveys (12) and ✕.

– Runs on June 8, 22, July 13, 27, Aug. 10, 24, Sept. 14, 28. Steam train with special fares. Conveys (12) and ✕. [R].

‡ – Not Oct. 27 - Nov. 28.

★ – Runs daily. On © from June 28 (not Nov. 1 – 23) also conveys first class panorama cars with special fares which include food and drink served at your seat ([R]).

⊗ – Trains call at Frankenfels on request only.

Operator: NÖVOG. ✆ +43 (0) 2742 360 990 99. www.noevog.at/mariazellerbahn

995 (WIEN -) WIENER NEUSTADT - FEHRING — 2nd class only

km		⚒A	Ⓐ	Ⓐ	Ⓒ		Ⓐ			†	Ⓐ	G	Ⓐ			⚒	Ⓑ	
0	**Wien** Meidling .... **980/1** d.	...	*0456*	*0716*	0729	*0930*	*0930*	*1130*	*1330*	*1330*	1433	*1530*	1600	1700	1729	*1830*	*1930*	*2103*
44	**Wiener Neustadt** Hbf. **980/1** d.	...	0541	0800	0800	1000	1000	1200	1400	1400	1500	1600	1630	1730	1800	1900	2003	2137
99	Friedberg .... d.	...	0647j	0902j	0902j	1101j	1101j	1301	1502j	1502j	1553	1702j	1721	1823	1902j	1953	2059	2248
126	Hartberg .... d.	0620	0725j	0935	0935	1132	1133	1338	1534	1535	...	1735	1754	1857b	1935	*2028*e	2132	...
157	Fürstenfeld .... d.	0652	0759	1009	1009	...	1206	1412	...	1609	...	1809	...	...	2007	...	...	...
177	**Fehring** .... a.	0722	0828	1037	1036	...	1235	1442	...	1636	...	1837	...	...	2036	...	...	...

	Ⓐ	Ⓐ	⚒	Ⓐ		Ⓐ	⚒			Ⓐ			†			Ⓒ	Ⓐ
Fehring .... d.	...	...	...	0510	...	...	0622	0729	0927	1118	...	1327	1527	...	...	1727	1727
Fürstenfeld .... d.	...	...	...	0539	...	...	0653	0758	0954	1149	...	1356	1554	...	...	1754	1754
Hartberg .... d.	...	0431	0527	0611	...	...	0725	0829	1026	1227	1227	1429	1627	1627	...	1827	1827
Friedberg .... d.	0402	0505	0601	0644	0644	0710	0800	0902	1102	1302	1302	1502	1702	1702	...	1902	1902
Wiener Neustadt Hbf .... **980/1** a.	0457	0559	0659	0744	0744	0758	0857	0959	1155	1355	1355	1555	1758	1758	...	1958	1958
Wien Meidling .... **980/1** a.	*0531*	0630	0730	*0828*	*0828*z	0830	*0927*	1028	*1227*	*1427*	*1427*	*1627*	*1827*	*1827*	...	2028	*2043*

A – To Graz on Ⓐ (Table **986**).
G – To Graz (Table **986**).

b – Ⓑ only.
e – Ⓐ only.
j – Arrives 6–9 minutes earlier.
z – *0833* on †.

996 WIEN - BRATISLAVA via Marchegg — 2nd class only

km								Ⓐn		
0	**Wien** Hbf .... d.	0521	0625	0725	0821		1821	1921	2021	2221
4	**Wien** Simmering ⊖ .... d.	0528	0632	0732	0828	and	1828	1928	2028	2228
47	Marchegg 🏛 .... d.	0607	0707	0807	0907	hourly	1907	2007	2107	2307
53	Devínska Nová Ves 🏛 .... d.	0615	0715	0815	0915	until	1915	2015	2115	2315
66	**Bratislava** hlavná .... a.	0627	0727	0827	0927		1927	2027	2127	2327

Bratislava hlavná .... d.	0543	0642	0743		1843	2043	2243
Devínska Nová Ves 🏛 .... d.	0556	0656	0756	and	1856	2056	2256
Marchegg 🏛 .... d.	0606	0706	0806	hourly	1906	2106	2306
Wien Simmering ⊖ .... a.	0641	0741	0841	until	1941	2141	2341
Wien Hbf .... a.	0648	0748	0848		1948	2148	2348

n – Not June 30 - Aug. 29.

⊖ – For U-Bahn connections (line U3) from / to Wien Mitte and Wien Westbahnhof.

☛ **Until Nov. 8** the following trains run to / from Bratislava **Lamač** (not hlavná), located approximately 5 km from hlavná station: From Wien Hbf at 0625, 1021, 1421 and 1521; from Bratislava hlavná at 0743, 1143, 1543, 1643 and 1743 (departing Lamač 6 minutes later); the 1621 from Wien Hbf requires a change of train at Devínska.

997 WIEN - BRATISLAVA via Bruck an der Leitha — 2nd class only; Austrian holiday dates apply

km					Ⓐ	Ⓐ	Ⓒ	Ⓐ	Ⓐ		Ⓐ		Ⓐ		Ⓐ		Ⓐ		Ⓐ		Ⓐ			
0	**Wien** Meidling .... d.	0035r	...	...	0503	0551	*0647*	0651	0751	0851	0951	1051	1151	1251	1351	1451	1551	1651	1751	*1847*	*1947*	2051	...	2235r
4	**Wien** Hbf .... d.	0042	...	0500	0512	0600	0700	0700	0800	0900	1000	1100	1200	1300	1400	1459	1559	1659	1759	1900	2000	2100	...	2242
45	Bruck an der Leitha .... d.	0122	...	0529	0552	0630	0730	0730	0830	0930	1030	1130	1230	1330	1430	1530	1630	1730	1830	1930	2030	2130	...	2322
73	Kittsee 🏛 .... a.	0147	...	0553	0615	0654	0754	0754	0854	0954	1054	1154	1254	1354	1454	1554	1654	1754	1854	1954	2054	2154	...	2347
78	**Bratislava** - Petržalka 🏛 ☆ ... a.	0153	...	0559	0621	0700	0800	0800	0900	1000	1100	1200	1300	1400	1500	1600	1700	1800	1900	2000	2100	2200	...	2353

	Ⓐ	Ⓐ	Ⓒ	Ⓐ	Ⓐ	Ⓐ		Ⓐ		Ⓐ		Ⓐ		Ⓐ		Ⓐ		Ⓐ		Ⓐ		Ⓐ		
Bratislava - Petržalka 🏛 ☆ .... d.	0424	...	0424	0451	0531	0609	0631	0649	...	0731	0831	0931	1031	1131	1231	1331	1431	1531	1631	1731	1831	1931	2031	2230
Kittsee 🏛 .... d.	0430	...	0430	0456	0536	0615	0636	0658	...	0736	0836	0936	1036	1136	1236	1336	1436	1536	1636	1736	1836	1936	2036	2236
Bruck an der Leitha .... d.	0455	0459	0459	0524	0602	0640	0702	0726	0731	0802	0902	1002	1102	1202	1302	1402	1502	1602	1702	1802	1902	2002	2103	2301
Wien Hbf .... a.	...	0528	0528	0553	0630	0720	0730	...	0800	0830	0928	1028	1128	1228	1328	1428	1528	1628	1728	1828	1928	2028	2129	2341
Wien Meidling .... a.	...	0537	0537	*0607*	0638	0727t	0738	...	*0814*	0838	0938	1038	1138	1238	1338	1438	1538	1638	1738	*1844*	*1947*	2038	*2147*	2351t

r – Starts from Wien Hütteldorf (departs 13 minutes earlier).
t – Continues to Wien Hütteldorf (arrives 13 minutes later).

☆ – Bus 93 links Petržalka station with Bratislava hlavná every 5–10 minutes (journey time is approximately 12 minutes).

998 UNZMARKT - TAMSWEG — 2nd class only; Narrow gauge

km		Ⓐ		④B 🚂	Ⓒ 🚌	Ⓐ	②A 🚂		Ⓒ 🚌		Ⓐ	④B 🚂	Ⓒ 🚌	Ⓐ		Ⓐ 🚌	Ⓒ	🚌
0	**Unzmarkt** .... d.	0719	0923	...	1118	1123	...	1323	1518	...	1523	...	1718	1723	1923	...	1923	2125
27	Murau-Stolzalpe .... d.	0800	1000	1015	1200	1200	1250	1400	1558	1600	1600	1655	1800	1810	1958	2000	2000	2205
34	St Lorenzen .... d.	0811	1011	1035	1212	1211	1310	1411	...	1611	1611	1715	1812	1821	...	2008s	2011	2213s
44	Stadl an der Mur .... d.	0825	1025	1105	1225	1225	1343	1425	...	1625	1625	1745	1825	1835	...	2019s	2025	2224s
65	**Tamsweg** .... a.	0855	1055	1153	1252	1255	1431	1455	...	1655	1655	1830	1852	1905	...	2040	2055	2245

	Ⓐ	Ⓐ	Ⓒ	Ⓒ 🚌	Ⓐ		Ⓒ 🚌	D	Ⓐ	④B 🚂	Ⓐe		Ⓐ	②A 🚂		Ⓐ 🚌	🚌	Ⓒ 🚌
Tamsweg .... d.	...	0655	0705	0910	0905	1105	1310	1305	...	1335	1355	1505	1505	1615	1710	1815	...	1910
Stadl an der Mur .... d.	...	0723	0733	0930	0933	1133	1330	1333	...	1425	1425	1533	1533	1710	1738	1835	...	1930
St Lorenzen .... d.	...	0737	0747	0945	0947	1147	1345	1347	...	1446	1438	1547	1547	1732	1752	1848	...	1945
Murau-Stolzalpe .... d.	0615	0802	0802	1000	1002	1202	1400	1402	1402	1500	1450	1559	1602	1745	1806	1900	2000	2000
Unzmarkt .... a.	0653	0840	0840	1040	1040	1240	1440	1440	1440	...	...	...	1640	...	1840	...	2040	2040

A – June 17 - Sept. 16.
B – June 19 - Sept. 18.
D – Ⓐ July 7 - Sept. 5 (also Apr. 14–18, 22, June 10).

e – Not Apr. 14–22, June 10, July 7 - Sept. 5.
s – Stops to set down only.

🚂 – Steam train. Special fares payable.

Operator: Steiermärkische Landesbahnen.

999 Danube shipping: BUDAPEST - BRATISLAVA - WIEN - LINZ - PASSAU — *2014 service*

Hydrofoil services. 🍸.	E Ⓡ♠	W Ⓡ♠	B Ⓡ◇	Q ⊙	E Ⓡ♠	E Ⓡ♠	P ⊙	Y ⊙	T Ⓡ♠
Wien Reichsbrücke ▲ .... d.	...	...	0900	0945	...	...	1600	1730	...
Wien Schwedenplatz ▲ .. d.	0830	0900	|	|	1230	1630	|	|	2030
Bratislava .... d.	0945	1015	|	1115	1345	1745	1730	1900	2145
Budapest § .... a.	...	...	1430	...	...	...	...	...	...

Hydrofoil services. 🍸.	Z ⊙	E Ⓡ♠	A Ⓡ◇	E Ⓡ♠	W Ⓡ♠	R ⊙	S ⊙	E Ⓡ♠	T Ⓡ♠
Budapest § .... d.	...	...	0900	...	...	...	...	...	...
Bratislava .... d.	0900	1030	|	1430	1600	1600	1730	1830	2230
Wien Schwedenplatz .... a.	|	1200	|	1600	1730	|	|	2000	2400
Wien Reichsbrücke ▲ .... a.	1045	...	1530	...	...	1745	1915	...	...

All sailings convey ✕	C ⊡	C ◐	⑦N ⊖	K ◐	D ◐Ⓡ	K ⊡	K ◐	K ◐	
Wien Reichsbrücke ▲ .... d.	...	...	...	...	0830	...	...	...	...
Tulln .... d.	...	...	0900n	...	1120	...	...	...	...
Krems an der Donau ...... d.	1010	1015	1220	1315	1400	1540	1545	...	...
Dürnstein .... d.	1040	1050	1250	1345	1430	1610	1620	...	...
Spitz an der Donau .... d.	1140	1145	1345	1450r	...	1705	1720	1730	...
Melk .... a.	1300	1320	1510	1605	...	1825	...	1850	...
Grein .... d.	...	...	1820	...	...	...	...	...	...
Linz Lentos .... a.	...	...	2220	...	...	...	...	...	...

All sailings convey ✕	K ⊡	K ◐		C ◐	C ⊡	⑥N ⊖	D ◐Ⓡ	K ◐	K ◐
Linz Lentos .... d.	...	...	...	...	...	0900	...	...	...
Grein .... d.	...	...	...	...	...	1200	...	...	...
Melk .... d.	0825	1100	...	1350	1350	1440	...	1625	...
Spitz an der Donau .... d.	0910	1200t	...	1440	1445	1520	...	1710	1725
Dürnstein .... d.	0940	1230	...	1510	1515	1600	1640	...	1750
Krems an der Donau .... d.	1005	1250	...	1530	1535	1620	1700	...	1810
Tulln .... d.	...	...	...	...	...	1820q	1900	...	...
Wien Reichsbrücke ▲ .... a.	...	...	...	...	...	2030q	2100	...	...

All sailings convey ✕	⊖H	⊖N		⊖M
Linz Lentos .... d.	...	...	...	1420
Schlögen .... d.	...	1425	...	1755
Obernzell .... d.	...	1615	...	1935
Passau Liegestelle 11 🏛 d.	1500	1715	...	2040
Deggendorf .... a.	2000	...	...	...

All sailings convey ✕	⊖L		⊖N	⊖G
Deggendorf .... d.	...	...	...	1000
Passau Liegestelle 11 🏛 d.	0900	...	1200	1330
Obernzell .... d.	0945	...	1245	...
Schlögen .... a.	1110	...	1410	...
Linz Lentos .... a.	1410	...	...	...

A – ②④⑥ June 3 - Sept. 27.
B – ③⑤⑦ June 4 - Sept. 28.
C – Apr. 12 - Oct. 26.
D – Runs on May 11, 25, June 8, 29, July 13, 27, Aug. 10, 24, 31, Sept. 14, 28.
E – Apr. 11 - Nov. 2.
G – ④⑥ May 29 - Oct. 2 (not June 21, July 26, Aug. 2, 23, 30).
H – ④ May 29 - Oct. 2 (not July 10).
K – May 1 - Oct. 5.

L – ②–⑦ Apr. 25 - Oct. 5 (also Oct. 11, 18, 25).
M – ②③④⑥⑦ Apr. 26 - Oct. 5 (also Oct. 11, 18, 25; not May 10, June 19, Aug. 14).
N – Apr. 26 - Oct. 5.
P – ⑤–⑦ Sept. 19 - Oct. 26.
Q – ③–⑦ Apr. 19 - June 29; daily July 1 - Aug. 31; ③–⑦ Sept. 3 - 28; ⑤–⑦ Oct. 3 - 26.
R – ③–⑦ Sept. 3 - 28; ⑤–⑦ Oct. 3 - 26.
S – ③–⑦ Apr. 19 - June 29; daily July 1 - Aug. 31.
T – ⑤⑥ Apr. 25 - Sept. 27.
W – Ⓒ Apr. 12 - 21; daily Apr. 25 - Sept. 30; ⑥⑦ Oct. 4 - Nov. 2.
Y – ③–⑦ Apr. 23 - June 29; daily July 1 - Aug. 31; ⑤–⑦ Sept. 5 - 14.
Z – ③–⑦ Apr. 23 - June 29; daily July 1 - Aug. 31; ⑤–⑦ Sept. 5 - Oct. 26.

n – Not May 11, June 22, Aug. 31, Sept. 14.
q – Not June 21, Aug. 30.
r – Arrives 1435.
t – Arrives 1140.

§ – Nemzetközi Hajóállomás (International shipping terminal).

▲ – DDSG operates Wien sightseeing cruises Schwedenplatz - Reichsbrücke and v.v. Daily Apr. 1 - Oct. 26.
From Schwedenplatz (duration 1 h 55 m via Schleuse Freudenau at 1030 and 1400 (also 1130 and 1500 Apr. 19 - Sept. 28).
From Reichsbrücke (duration 1 h 20 m via Schleuse Nußdorf) at 1230 and 1600 (also 1330 and 1700 Apr. 19 - Sept. 28).

Operators:
⊡ – Brandner Schiffahrt GmbH, Ufer 50, A-3313 Wallsee. ✆ +43 (0) 7433 25 90 21, Fax +43 (0) 7433 25 90 25.
◐ – DDSG Blue Danube Schiffahrt GmbH, Handelskai 265, A-1020 Wien. ✆ +43 (0) 1 588 80, Fax +43 (0) 1 588 80 440.
⊖ – Wurm und Köck, Höllgasse 26, D-94032 Passau. ✆ +49 (0) 851 92 92 92, Fax +49 (0) 851 355 18.
⊙ – SPaP - LOD – Slovenská Plavba a Prístavy - Lodná Osobná Doprava a.s., Fajnorovo nábrežie 2, 811 02 Bratislava. Reservation recommended. Check-in 15 minutes before departure. Bratislava: ✆ +421 2 529 32 226, Fax +421 2 529 32 231.
◇ – MAHART PassNave, H-1056 Budapest, Belgrád rakpart. Check-in 60 minutes before departure. Budapest: ✆ +36 1 484 4013, Fax +36 1 266 4201.
♠ – *Twin City Liner.* DDSG Blue Danube GmbH, Handelskai 265, A-1020 Wien. Check-in 30 minutes before departure. ✆ +43 (0) 1 588 80. Internet booking: www.twincityliner.com

POLAND

Operators: *EC, EIC, EN, MP, TLK* trains are operated by PKP Intercity www.intercity.pl. *IR, RE* and most local trains are operated by Przewozy Regionalne (PR) www.przewozyregionalne.pl Certain local services are operated by regional companies owned by local government: e.g. Koleje Dolnośląskie, Koleje Mazowieckie, Koleje Śląskie, Koleje Wielkopolskie.

Services: **PKP InterCity**: Note reservation is compulsory ([R]) on all services operated by PKP InterCity (*EC, EIC, EN, MP, TLK*):

EC and *EIC* trains are fast premium-rate trains on long-distance routes (*EC* or *EuroCity* trains run on international routes) - first and second class seats, higher rate of fares apply and a supplement is payable for pass holders. *EC* and *EIC* trains normally convey ✕ or 🍸 for at least part of the route.

TLK trains are lower-cost long distance trains with first and second class seats (also sleepers and couchettes on nights routes as shown in the tables). *TLK* is short for *Twoje Linie Kolejowe* (Your Railway Lines). Certain trains convey 🍸 but it is not possible to identify these in the tables.

MP is the classification (within Poland) for other international trains; *TLK* fares apply within Poland. Note that Russian/Ukrainian sleeping car services cannot be used for journeys in or between Poland and Germany unless seating cars are also conveyed. *EN* trains are *EuroNight* services with 'global' fares which include the sleeping accommodation.

Przewozy Regionalne and other local operators:

IR (InterRegio) and *RE (Regional Express)* trains are semi-fast trains operated by Przewozy Regionalne on longer distance routes, with second class seats. Fares are cheaper than *TLK* services but slightly higher than local *Regio* trains.

All other trains are local *R* (*Regio*) trains, second class only, calling at all or most stations en route. No train category is shown in our tables for these trains. They are operated by Przewozy Regionalne unless otherwise shown in the table heading or by a footnote. Fares on *Regio* trains are the cheapest available.

Timings: Valid until **August 31, 2014** except where shown otherwise. However, alterations are possible at any time. Public holidays in 2014 are Jan. 1, 6, Apr. 20, 21, May 1, 3, June 8, 19, Aug. 15, Nov. 1, 11, Dec. 25, 26. Many trains are subject to alteration or cancellation at Christmas and Easter. Engineering work can often affect schedules; major changes are shown in the tables where possible but other changes may occur at short notice. A number of long-distance trains running only in high summer (particularly to coastal resorts) are not shown due to lack of space. Note that train numbers often change en route by one or two digits. In station names, Gł. is short for Główny or Główna, meaning main station. Descriptions of sleeping (🛏) and couchette (▬) cars appear on page 8.

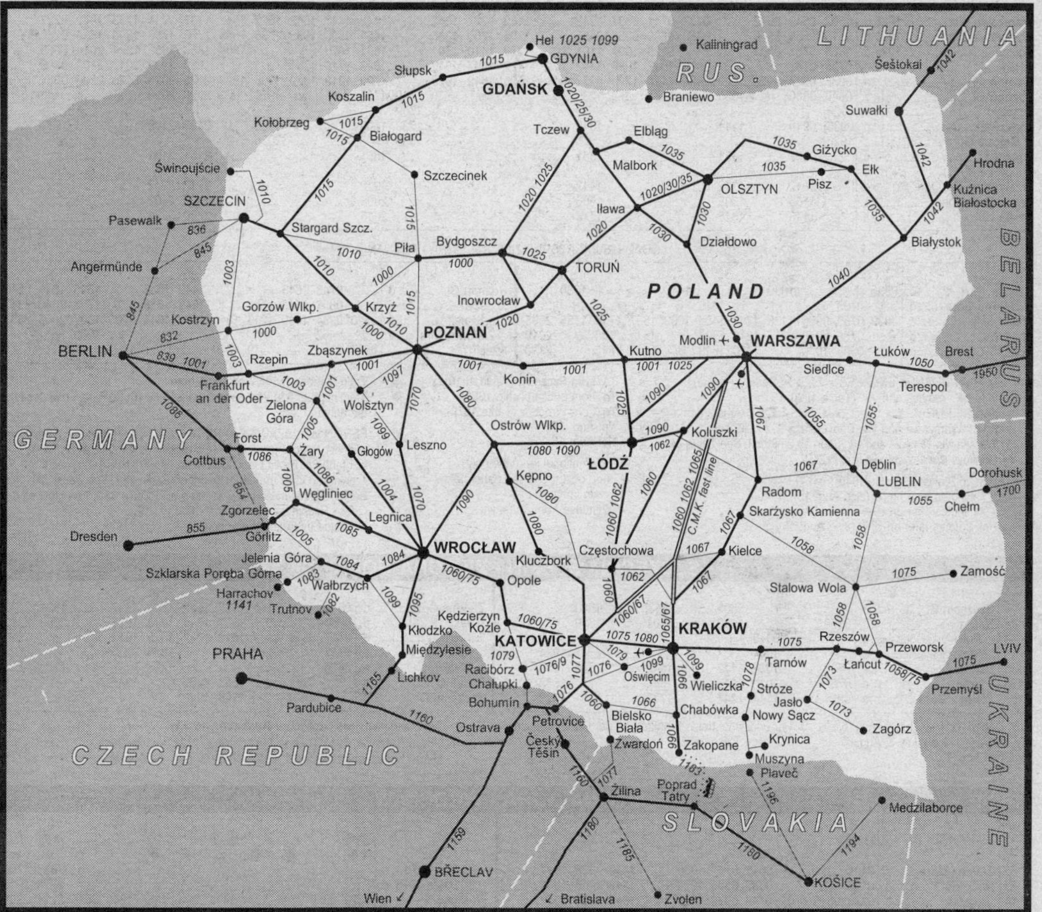

KOSTRZYN - KRZYŻ - POZNAŃ and BYDGOSZCZ 1000

km		TLK 83104 H					①–⑤ z							TLK 85162 K			①–⑤ z					①–⑤ z	⑦ w		⑧z		TLK 88200
0	**Kostrzyn** ....d.	...	...	...	...	0530	...	0646	0905	...	...	1059	...	...	1300	...	...	1514	...	...	1618	...	...	1815	...	2110	...
43	Gorzów Wlkp......d.	...	...	...	...	0611	...	0727	0945	...	...	1140	...	...	1341	...	...	1556	...	...	1659	...	...	1855	...	2151	2345
103	Krzyż .... **1010** d.	...	...	0623	...	0715	0715	0820	1038	1047	...	1233	...	...	1433	1446	...	1649j	1713	...	1751	1820	...	1947	2026	2243	0038
186	**Poznań** ... **1010** a.	...	...	|	...	0832	|	...	...	|	...	...	...	...	...	|	...	1805j	|	...	...	|	...	...	|	...	...
163	Piła Gł...............d.	0544	0559	0716	0736	...	0808	...	...	1140	1200	...	1438	1522	...	1539	1547	...	1806	1809	...	1913	2033	...	2118	...	...
248	**Bydgoszcz** ....a.	0700	0727	...	0904	...	...	...	...	...	1329	...	1617	1642	...	...	1720	...	...	1939	...	...	2216	...	...	...	...

	TLK 88203			①–⑥ y						①–⑤ z					①–⑤ z			TLK 58163 K					⑧	①–⑤ z	⑥⑦ w	TLK 18109 J	
Bydgoszcz ....d.	...	...	...	...	...	0531	0738	...	...	...	...	1130	...	...	...	...	...	1454	...	...	1625	...	1844	...	1948	2050	...
Piła Gł...............d.	...	...	...	0605	...	0701	0901	0907	...	1140	...	1306	1340	...	1440	...	1550	1605	1708	...	1751	...	2008	2010	2120	2200	...
Poznań ... **1010** d.	...	...	...	|	...	...	...	|	0850r	|	...	...	|	...	|	...	|	...	|	...	...	1854	...	|	...	...	...
Krzyż .... **1010** d.	0409	0515	0630	0658	0850	...	...	1000	1007k	1233	1318	...	1433	1502	1533	1620	1642	...	1801	1823	...	2026	...	2103	...	...	...
Gorzów Wlkp......d.	0505	0610	0726	...	0946	...	...	...	1101k	...	1414	...	...	1557	...	1715	...	...	...	1917	...	2123	...	...	...	...	...
Kostrzyn ....a.	...	0650	0806	...	1027	...	...	...	1137k	...	1454	...	...	1638	...	1755	...	...	...	1957	...	2200	...	...	...	...	...

H – To Warszawa (Table **1025**) and Przemyśl (Table **1058**).
J – From Białystok (Table **1040**).
K – To/from Kołobrzeg (Table **1015**).

j – 8–9 minutes later until Aug. 5.
k – 12–13 minutes later until Aug. 5; 20–21 minutes later on Aug. 6.

n – Not Aug. 31.
r – Depart 0903 until Aug. 6.
w – Also Aug. 15.

y – Not Aug. 16.
z – Not Aug. 15.

1001 BERLIN - POZNAŃ - WARSZAWA

km		*TLK*	*TLK*	*EIC*	*IR*	*EIC*	*EIC*	*EIC*	*EN*	*EC*	*IR*	*TLK*	*TLK*	*EC*	*IR*	*TLK*	*EC*		*IR*	*EIC*	*EC*	*EIC*	*TLK*	*EC*
		81200	**71102**	**6103**	**72110**	**7100**	**8102**	**7104**	**447**	**41**	**81120**	**81100**	**77106**	**43**	**71104**	**82160**	**45**		**81108**	**6101**	**55**	**8100**	**71100**	**47**
		81201	**71103**	**6102**	**72111**	**7101**	**8103**	**7105**	**71010**	**71006**	**81121**	**81101**		**71004**	**71105**	**82161**	**71002**		**81109**	**6100**	**75000**	**8101**	**71101**	**71000**
				①-⑤	①-⑥	①-⑥	①-⑤	①-⑥	⑦	①-⑥			①-⑥							Ⓑ		Ⓑ	§	Ⓑ
		Z		z	u	y	z	y	J▽	❀		b	y	❀		u	❀			♠	G	z		❀
0	**Berlin** Hbf ⊖ d.	...	...	...	...	...	...	...	0637	0637	...	...	...	0937	...	...	1337	...	...	...	1537	...	...	1737
5	**Berlin** Ostbahnhof ⊖ d.	...	...	...	...	...	...	...	0650	0650	...	...	...	0950	...	...	1350	...	...	...	1550	...	...	1750
87	Frankfurt an der Oder 🏛 ⊖ d.	...	...	...	...	...	...	...	0745	0745	...	...	...	1045	...	...	1445	...	...	...	1645	...	...	1845
98	Kunowice 🏛 ⊖ d.	...	...	...	...	...	...	...	|	|	...	...	...	|	...	...	|	...	...	...	|	...	...	|
110	Rzepin ▷ d.	...	...	...	...	...	...	...	0810	0810	...	...	...	1108	...	...	1508	...	...	...	1708	...	...	1908
•58	**Zielona Góra** ▷ d.	...	...	...	...	0530	...	...	|	|	...	...	1037	|	...	...	|	...	...	...	|	...	1743k	|
185	Zbąszynek ▷ d.	...	...	...	...	0614	...	...	0852	0852	...	...	1122	1146	...	...	1546	...	...	...	1746	...	1828k	1946
191	Zbąszyń ▷ d.	...	...	...	...	|	...	...	|	|	...	...	1129	|	...	...	|	...	...	...	|	...	1835k	|
266	**Poznań** Gł. ▷ a.	s	...	w	...	0659	s	...	0933	0933	s	s	1220	1227	...	s	1626	...	s	w	1826	s	1926	2026
266	**Poznań** Gł. d.	0234	0544	0632	0620	0702	0734	0830	0936	0936	1008	1127	...	1230	1330	1430	1630	...	1732	1754	...	1835	1933	2030
366	Konin d.	0409	0651	0720	0731	|	|	0922	1028	1028	1118	1238	...	1321	1433	1539	1719	...	1838	1843	...	|	2042	2120
445	Kutno **1025** d.	0508	0742	|	0834	|	0909	1005	1114	1114	1208	1337	...	1404	1526	1627	1801	...	1941	|	...	2006	2135	2203
572	**Warszawa** Cent. **1025** a.	0637	0903	0912	0957	0940	1016	1115	1222	1222	1335	1457	...	1510	1650	1746	1908	...	2106	2035	...	2115	2255	2309
577	**Warszawa** Wsch. **1025** a.	0649	0916	0924	1018	0953	1028	1128	1235	1235	1358	1510	...	1522	1703	1758	1933	...	2126	2048	...	2130	2308	2322

	TLK	*EC*	*EIC*	*EC*	*EIC*	*IR*	*TLK*	*EC*		*IR*	*TLK*	*EIC*	*TLK*	*EC*	*IR*	*EIC*	*EIC*	*EIC*	*EC*	*EN*	*IR*	*TLK*	*TLK*	
	17100	**46**	**1800**	**54**	**1600**	**18106**	**28160**	**44**		**17104**	**18100**	**1704**	**70107**	**42**	**18122**	**1602**	**1700**	**1802**	**40**	**446**	**27120**	**17102**	**18200**	
	17101	**17001**	**1801**	**57001**	**1601**	**18107**	**28161**	**17003**		**17105**	**18101**	**1705**		**17005**	**18123**	**1603**	**1701**	**1803**	**17007**	**17011**	**27121**	**17103**	**18201**	
	§	①-⑥	①-⑤		①-⑥							Ⓑ	Ⓑ			①-⑥	Ⓑ	Ⓑ	Ⓑ	⑥	Ⓑ			
		❀	z	G	y		u	❀		♣	b	z	z	❀		y	z	z	❀	J▽	u		Z	
Warszawa Wsch. **1025** d.	0502	0542	0642	...	0737	0747	0837	0942	...	1152	1222	1342	...	1442	1447	1542	1622	1642	1737	1737	1733	1842	2222	...
Warszawa Cent. **1025** d.	0515	0555	0655	...	0750	0800	0850	0955	...	1205	1250	1355	...	1455	1500	1555	1635	1655	1750	1750	1800	1855	2235	...
Kutno **1025** d.	0635	0701	0803	...	|	0925	1007	1101	...	1329	1410	1501	...	1601	1620	|	|	1803	1856	1856	1924	2014	0008	...
Konin d.	0725	0742	|	...	0939	1017	1056	1142	...	1422	1507	1542	...	1643	1713	1744	|	|	1939	1939	2017	2100	0106	...
Poznań Gł. a.	0836	0827	0928	...	1026	1124	1209	1227	...	1525	1612	1628	...	1726	1818	1829	1906	1929	2025	2025	2125	2204	0231	...
Poznań Gł. ▷ d.	0840	0830	s	1030	w	s	s	1230	...	...	s	...	1640	1729	s	w	1909	s	2028	2028	...	...	s	...
Zbąszyń ▷ d.	0928j	|	...	|	...	...	...	|	...	...	...	...	1732	|	...	...	|	...	|	|	...	...	...	...
Zbąszynek ▷ d.	0935j	0910	...	1111	...	...	...	1310	...	...	...	...	1739	1809	...	...	1953	...	2109	2109	...	...	...	...
Zielona Góra ▷ a.	1026j	|	...	|	...	...	...	|	...	...	...	...	1836	|	...	...	2036	...	|	|	...	...	...	...
Rzepin ▷ d.	...	0951	...	1151	...	...	...	1351	...	...	...	...	...	1851	...	...	...	...	2151	2151	...	...	...	...
Kunowice 🏛 ⊖ d.	...	|	...	|	...	...	...	|	...	...	...	...	...	|	...	...	...	...	|	|	...	...	...	...
Frankfurt an der Oder 🏛 ⊖ d.	...	1012	...	1212	...	...	...	1412	...	...	...	...	...	1912	...	...	...	...	2212	2212	...	...	...	...
Berlin Ostbahnhof ⊖ a.	...	1106	...	1306	...	...	...	1506	...	...	...	...	...	2006	...	...	...	...	2306	2400	...	...	...	...
Berlin Hbf ⊖ a.	...	1116	...	1318	...	...	...	1516	...	...	...	...	...	2016	...	...	...	...	2320	0024	...	...	...	...

LOCAL TRAINS RZEPIN/ZIELONA GORA - POZNAŃ

			‡		‡			‡	‡	q	
Rzepin d.	0535	...	...	1030	...	...	1446	...	...	1630	...
Zielona Góra d.	|	0705	...	|	...	1410	|	...	...	|	...
Zbąszynek d.	0639	0753	0905	1135	1205	1457	1602	1607	1710	1735	2005
Zbąszyń d.	...	0759	0910	...	1210	1503	...	1613	1715	...	2010
Poznań Gł. a.	...	0908	1010	...	1310	1613	...	1712	1815	...	2110

			‡			‡	‡			‡	‡
Poznań Gł. d.	...	0748	1043	...	...	1440	1535	...	1645	1940	2246
Zbąszyń d.	...	0857	1143	...	...	1540	1638	...	1755	2040	2347
Zbąszynek d.	0510	0904	1149	1215	1515	1546	1644	1705	1807	2046	2353
Zielona Góra a.	|	0952	...	|	|	...	...	|	1909	...	...
Rzepin a.	0614	...	...	1319	1619	...	...	1809	...	...	...

G – BERLIN GDANSK EXPRESS – (12) ✕ Berlin - Poznań - Gdansk - Gdynia and v.v. (Table **1020**).
J – JAN KIEPURA – 🛏 1, 2 cl., ▬ 2 cl., (2) 🍸 Amsterdam - Köln - Warszawa and v.v. Conveys 🛏 1, 2 cl. Basel - Warszawa - Moskva and v.v. (journey 2 nights). See Table **24**.
Z – Conveys 🛏 1, 2 cl., ▬ 2 cl., (2).

b – From/to Białystok (Table **1040**).
j – 3–7 minutes later on ⑦ (also Aug. 15).
k – 5–7 minutes later on ①–⑥.
q – Runs 2 hours later on ⑥⑦ (also Aug. 15).

s – To/from Szczecin (Table **1010**).
u – To/from Lublin (Table **1055**).
w – To/from Wrocław (Table **1070**).
y – Not Aug. 16.
z – Not Aug. 15.

▽ – International journeys only.
▷ – For local trains see panel below main table.
• – Distance from Zbąszynek.

♣ – Train number **17106/7** on some dates.
♠ – Train number **6105/4** on some dates. July 16 - 20 runs 8 minutes later throughout.
❀ – BERLIN WARSZAWA EXPRESS – (12) ✕ 🅁, Berlin - Warszawa and v.v. Special fares apply. On certain dates calls at Berlin Lichtenberg, Berlin Gesundbrunnen (via Kostrzyn); not call at Frankfurt (Oder), Berlin Ostbahnhof, Berlin Hbf. See Table **56**.
⊖ – Berlin - Frankfurt an der Oder: see also Table **839**. Frankfurt an der Oder - Rzepin: see also Table **1003**.
‡ – Operated by Koleje Wielkopolskie.

1003 SZCZECIN - RZEPIN - ZIELONA GÓRA

km											
0	**Szczecin** Gł. d.	...	...	...	0805	...	1243j	...	1540	...	...
104	Kostrzyn d.	0659	...	...	1032	...	1501	...	1800	...	...
	Frankfurt/Oder d.	|	...	0949	|	...	|	...	|	1913	...
	Kunowice 🏛 d.	|	...	1004	|	...	|	...	|	1924	...
136	Rzepin a.	0739	...	1008	1112	...	1542	...	1840	1932	...
136	Rzepin d.	0752	...	1013	1113	...	1544	...	...	1933	...
207	**Zielona Góra** a.	0924	...	1144	1247	...	1723	...	...	2109	...

		p								
Zielona Góra d.	0618	...	...	1339	1539	1643	1732	...	1921	2130
Rzepin a.	0750	...	...	1511	1711	1818	1905	...	2053	2311
Rzepin d.	0807	0814	...	1512	1712	1819	1912	...	...	...
Kunowice 🏛 d.	0815	|	...	|	|	1828	|	...	...	...
Frankfurt/Oder a.	0826	|	...	|	|	1838	|	...	...	...
Kostrzyn d.	...	0909	...	1603	1803	...	1957	...	...	...
Szczecin Gł. a.	...	1053k	...	1758	1946	...	...	...	...	...

j – Depart 1219 on July 2, Aug. 6.
k – Arrive 1131 on July 2, Aug. 6.
z – Not Aug. 15.

For additional trains Frankfurt an der Oder - Rzepin see Table **1001**.

Additional services **Szczecin - Kostrzyn and v.v.**:
From Szczecin: 0613 ①–⑥ **z**, 1441 ①–⑥ **z**, 1722 ①–⑥ **z**, 2013.
From Kostrzyn: 0410 ①–⑥ **z**, 0527, 0643 ①–⑥ **z**, 1322 ①–⑥ **z**.

1004 ZIELONA GÓRA - WROCŁAW

km		*TLK*										
		83266			r	r				⑦		
				z	♠	y						
0	**Zielona Góra** d.	0101	...	...	0613	0747	1000	...	1510	1655	1917	...
23	Nowa Sól d.	0125	...	...	0633	0808	1020	...	1545	1716	1938	...
54	Glogów d.	0233	0515	0622	0743	0922	1128	1430	1647	1829	2048	...
154	**Wrocław** Gł a.	0422	0716	0823	0946	1131	1327	1632	1847	2025	2249	...
	Katowice **1075** a.	0809	...	...	...	...	...	...	...	...	...	...
	Kraków **1075** a.	1022f	...	...	...	...	...	...	...	...	...	...

										TLK	*TLK*
										38207	**38267**
	①-⑥				①-⑤						
	z♠		♠	♣	z	♣	♣			x	w
Kraków **1075** d.	...	...	...	...	...	...	...	...	...	1633	1700
Katowice **1075** d.	...	...	...	...	...	...	...	...	...	1838	1913
Wrocław Gł d.	0522	0650	0845	1254	1411	1449	1655	1849	2044	2224	2301
Glogów d.	0734	0900	1100	1505	1621	1659	1905	2059	2256	0019	0106
Nowa Sól d.	0829	...	1154	1558	...	1753	1958	...	...	0110j	0200k
Zielona Góra a.	0849	...	1214	1619	...	1813	2018	...	...	0128j	0218k

f – July 1 - 25 arrive 1029.
j – 15 minutes later on Aug. 31.
k – 20 minutes later Aug. 28 - 30.
r – From Rzepin (Table **1003**).
w – Until Aug. 29.
x – From Aug. 30.
z – Not Aug. 15.
♣ – Subject to retiming Aug. 27 - 30 Nowa Sól - Zielona Góra and v.v.
♠ – Subject to retiming Aug. 28 - 31 Nowa Sól - Zielona Góra and v.v.

1005 ZIELONA GÓRA - WEGLINIEC - JELENIA GÓRA

km												
		⊖	⊖			⊖		⊖		⊖		⊖
			x	p	a	x	❀	x	t	a	a	
0	**Zielona Góra** d.	...	...	0635	0635	...	...	...	1309	...	1545	...
54	Zary ▷ d.	...	0542a	0732	0733	0930	1213	...	1409	1542	1643	...
67	Żagań ▷ a.	...	|	|	0745	|	|	...	1421	|	...	...
94	Wegliniec d.	0502	0656	0833	...	1036	1306	1450	...	1634	...	1757
118	Zgorzelec Miasto d.	0523	0717	0851	...	1057	...	1509	...	...	...	1818
120	Zgorzelec d.	|	0728	|	...	1111	...	1523	...	...	...	1829
144	Lubań Śląski d.	0554	0759	0919	...	1142	...	1553	...	...	...	1900
196	**Jelenia Góra** a.	0712	0910k	1035	...	1253j	...	1718	...	...	...	2011

	⊖		⊖	⊖			⊖		⊖		⊖
	a	t		x	a	❀	x	a	x	p	
Jelenia Góra d.	...	...	0536	0931	...	...	1320	...	1533	1644	1905
Lubań Śląski d.	...	...	0646	1040	...	...	1435	...	1644j	1754	2023
Zgorzelec d.	0605	...	0732	|	...	...	1516	...	|	|	2102
Zgorzelec Miasto d.	0608	...	0735	1110	...	...	1519	...	1715j	1821	2105
Wegliniec d.	0636	...	0757	1139	...	1353	1540	...	1737j	1846	2126
Żagań ▷ d.	|	0911	...	...	1355	|	|	...	...	|	...
Zary ▷ d.	0727	0925	...	...	1409	1445	1649	1715	...	1937	...
Zielona Góra a.	...	1022	...	...	1506	...	...	1812	...	2039	...

a – ①–⑤ (not Aug. 15).
j – 14–20 minutes later ①–⑤ (not Aug. 15).
k – Arrive 0922 ①–⑤ (not Aug. 15).
p – ⑥⑦ (also Aug. 15).
t – To/from Legnica (Table **1086**).

x – July 15 - 18, 21 - 24 replaced by 🚌 Lubań Śląski - Jelenia Góra (times may vary).
y – Also Aug. 15.
z – Not Aug. 15.

❀ – *EC* WAWEL – see Table **1086**.
▷ – See also Table **1086**.
⊖ – Operated by Koleje Dolnośląskie.
☛ Local 🚌 service 'P' links Görlitz Bahnhof with Zgorzelec Miasto station every 30 mins (journey 22 mins).

Additional services:
Zielona Góra - Zary - Żagań: 1913 Ⓑ **z**, 2115⑥⑦ **y**
Żagań - Zary - Zielona Góra: 0455, 1730 ⑦.

SZCZECIN - POZNAŃ 1010

km																								
		EIC	*TLK*	*TLK*		*IR*	*TLK*	*TLK*		*IR*	*TLK*		*TLK*	*IR*		*TLK*	*EIC*	*TLK*		*IR*	*TLK*	*TLK*		*TLK*
		8102	**87104**	**84100**		**81120**	**83100**	**81100**		**84109**	**82161**		**83157**	**81109**		**86151**	**8100**	**87100**		**87105**	**83261**	**83250**		**81201**
		8103				**81121**		**81101**		**84108**	**82160**		**83156**	**81108**		**86150**	**8101**			**87104**	**83260**			**81200**
		M	**M**	⑥	**M**		**p**	**b**			**u**	**M**				♣	Ⓑ**z**			**T**	**B**	**A x**		**A**
	Świnoujście .... d.	...	...	...	...	...	...	...	0754	0857	0952	...	1207	1244	...	1429**z**	...	...	...	1708	1723	...	...	2055
0	**Szczecin** Gł. .... **1015** d.	0455	0541	0541	0547	0709	0738	0827	0946	1038	1130	1135	1340	1434	1510	1603	1556	1727	1755	1851	1924	2019	...	2302
15	Szczecin Dąbie .... **1015** d.	0511	0558	0558	0603	0723	0754	0844	1002	1054	1147	1152	1356	1448	1527	1619	1612	1743	1810	1908	1943	2035	...	2320
40	Stargard Szczeciński ... **1015** d.	0527	0614	0614	0624	0740	0811	0902	1025	1111	1205	1217	1413	1507	1551	1636	1628	1804	1834	1926	2002	2053	...	2339
130	Krzyż .... **1000** d.	0620	0712	0712	0741	0840	0913	1005	1138	1209	1307	1341	1514	1610	1711	1735	1720	1903	1955	2022	2107	2157	...	0109
213	**Poznań** Gł. .... **1000** a.	0724	0819	0819	0901	0953	1022	1116	1305	1317	1418	1513	1628	1719	1836	1843	1823	2010	2111	2128	2220	2309	...	0227
	Wrocław Gł. **1070** .... a.	|	...	|	...	|	1334**k**	|	...	|	|	...	|	|	...	2143**n**	|	...	...	...	|	|	...	|
	Warszawa Cent. **1001** .... a.	1016	...	|	...	1335	|	1457	...	|	1746	...	▽	2106	...	...	2115	...	...	...	|	|	...	0637
	Katowice **1075 1080** .... a.	...	...	1343	...	...	1643**k**	...	...	1919	...	...	|	...	...	...	...	...	...	...	0458**r**	|	...	...
	Kraków Gł **1075 1080** .... a.	...	...	...	...	...	1851**k**	...	...	...	...	...	0005	...	...	...	...	...	...	...	0709**r**	0553	...	...

	TLK	*TLK*	*IR*		*TLK*		*TLK*	*TLK*	*EIC*	*TLK*	*IR*		*TLK*	*IR*		*TLK*	*TLK*		*IR*	*TLK*	*EIC*	*TLK*	*TLK*	
	48255	**18201**	**78105**		**38261**		**38251**	**68151**	**1800**	**78103**	**18107**		**28160**	**48107**		**38157**	**18100**		**18122**	**38101**	**1802**	**78105**	**48101**	
		18200						♣	**1801**		**18106**		**28161**			♣	**18101**		**18123**		**1803**			
	S	**A**	**T**		**B**		**A**		**M**	§			**u**			§	**b**			**p**	Ⓑ**y**	**M**	⑦	
Kraków Gł. **1075 1080** .... d.	...	...	...	...	2134	...	0035	...	...	...	...	...	...	...	...	0741	...	...	...	1005**j**	...	...	...	...
Katowice **1075 1080** .... d.	2016	...	...	...	2345	...	|	...	...	...	...	...	...	0757	...	|	...	...	...	1219**j**	...	...	1503	...
Warszawa Cent. **1001** .... d.	|	2222	...	...	|	...	|	...	0655	...	0800	...	0850	|	...	▽	1250	...	1500	|	1655	...	|	...
Wrocław Gł. **1070** .... d.	|	|	...	...	|	...	|	0514	|	...	|	...	|	|	...	|	|	...	|	1524	|	...	|	...
Poznań Gł. .... **1000** d.	0225	0234	0557	...	0628	0644	0734	0842	0941	1039	1137	...	1235	1430	1342	1450	1633	1656	1830	1841	1941	2042	2042	...
Krzyż .... **1000** d.	0329	0403	0709	...	0747	0803	0843	0949	1043	1146	1244	...	1345	1542	1459	1600	1743	1807	1937	1953	2044	2148	2148	...
Stargard Szczeciński .... **1015** d.	0430	0503	0809	...	0850	0919	0941	1046	1133	1244	1342	...	1444	1643	1611	1657	1842	1924	2037	2051	2134	2244	2244	...
Szczecin Dąbie .... **1015** d.	0449	0521	0826	...	0914	0941	0958	1106	1150	1301	1359	...	1502	1700	1632	1714	1901	1948	2054	2109	2151	2302	2302	...
Szczecin Gł. .... **1015** a.	0505	0539	0841	...	0932	0959	1017	1123	1207	1318	1415	...	1519	1716	1649	1730	1920	2005	2110	2127	2209	2318	2318	...
Świnoujście .... a.	0645	0741	1017	...	1137	1205	...	1258**z**	...	...	1606	...	1700	1853	...	1914**z**	...	...	...	...	...	...	...	...

km											
		N	⑦	**N**		⑥⑦**y**	**M**			Ⓑ	
0	**Świnoujście** .... d.	0444	0541	0625	0754	1043	1310	1547	1800	2030	...
101	Szczecin Dąbie .... a.	0624	0718	0807	0925	1224	1447	1721	1937	2210	...
116	**Szczecin** Gł. .... a.	0650	0734	0823	0941	1241	1503	1738	1954	2226	...

	N		⑥⑦**v**			**Q**			Ⓑ	
Szczecin Gł. .... d.	0420	0520	0747	1017	...	1306	1547	...	1801	2057
Szczecin Dąbie .... d.	0437	0544	0803	1033	...	1322	1603	...	1822	2119
Świnoujście .... a	0614	0714	0943	1205	...	1454	1740	...	2008	2257

km											
0	**Szczecin** Gł. .... d.	...	...	0757	...	1120	...	1436	...	1846	...
12	Szczecin Dąbie .... d.	...	...	0813	...	1137	...	1452	...	1902	...
37	Stargard Szczeciński .. d.	0449	...	0839	...	1157	...	1519	...	1924	...
102	Kalisz Pomorski .... d.	0602	...	0945	...	1302	...	1636	...	2030	...
146	Wałcz .... d.	0648	...	1030	...	1346	...	1720	...	2115	...
176	**Piła** Główna .... a.	0716	...	1100	...	1415	...	1748	...	...	...

									①–⑥	⑦
Piła Główna .... d.	...	...	0745	...	1312	...	1524	...	1810	1810
Wałcz .... d.	0357	...	0812	...	1348	...	1551	...	1837	1837
Kalisz Pomorski .... d.	0440	...	0855	...	1434	...	1639	...	1914	1914
Stargard Szczeciński . d.	0558	...	1007	...	1548	...	1750	...	2021	2023
Szczecin Dąbie .... d.	0619	...	1028	...	1614	...	1811	...	...	2043
Szczecin Gł. .... d.	0636	...	1046	...	1632	...	1827	...	...	2100

A – Conveys 1, 2 cl., 2 cl., 2.
B – 1, 2 cl., 2 Świnoujście - Szczecin - Poznań - Kraków - Przemyśl and v.v. (Table **1075**).
M – ①–⑤ (not Aug. 15).
N – ①–⑥ (not Aug. 15).
Q – ①–⑤ (not Aug. 6, 15).
S – ⑥⑦ (also Aug. 15, 18; not Aug. 31).
T – ⑥⑦ (also Aug. 15; not Aug. 16).
b – To / from Białystok (Table **1040**).
j – 10 – 11 minutes later on some dates.
k – 19 – 21 minutes later on some dates.
n – Arrive 2119 July 16 - 20; 2148 Aug. 31.
p – To / from Przemyśl (Table **1075**).
r – Arrive 29 – 35 minutes earlier on Aug. 31.
u – To / from Lublin (Table **1055**).
v – Also Aug. 15.
x – Not Aug. 30, 31.
y – Not Aug. 15.
z – Not Aug. 31.
§ – 12 – 16 minutes later on Aug. 4.
▽ – Via Łódź (Table **1025**).
♣ – Train number variations on Aug. 31: **38157** runs as **38107**; **68151** runs as **68101**; **86150** runs as **86100**.

SZCZECIN - KOSZALIN - GDYNIA - GDAŃSK 1015

km																								
		TLK	*TLK*	*TLK*	*EIC*		*TLK*	*TLK*		*TLK*	*TLK*		*TLK*			*TLK*	*TLK*		*TLK*		*TLK*		*TLK*	
		65251	**48251**	**85102**	**8330**		**83108**	**38253**		**81104**	**45103**		**85100**			**38103**	**84200**		**83258**		**82250**		**75109**	
		65250			**8331**						**45102**					⊖					**A**		**75108**	
		Az	**Az**	**G**			**K**	**Dz**		**E**	**H**♣		**G**			**J**	**A**	**q**	**Dz**	**p**	**uz**	Ⓑ	**Y**	
0	**Szczecin** Gł. .... § d.	...	...	0556	...	0730	...	...	...	1001	...	1232	1400	...	1543	...	1748	...	...	...	...	...	...	2005
15	Szczecin Dąbie .... § d.	...	...	0615	...	0745	...	...	...	1019	...	1247	1416	...	1600	...	1805	...	...	...	...	...	...	2021
40	Stargard Szczeciński .... § d.	...	...	0636	...	0808	...	...	...	1036	...	1314	1433	...	1626	...	1825	...	...	...	...	...	...	2054
*231	**Poznań** Gł. .... d.	0040	0317	|	...	|	...	0500	0537	|	1045	|	|	1225	|	1436	|	1502	...	1519	...	1656	1739	|
*135	Piła Gł. .... d.	0216	0517	|	...	|	...	0652	0737	|	1232	|	|	1435	|	1628	|	1714	...	1800**r**	...	1856	1919	|
*64	Szczecinek .... d.	0320	0624	|	...	|	...	0805	0852	|	1330	|	|	1545	|	1729	|	1818	...	1917	...	2004	2027	|
151	Białogard .... a.	0414	0731	0802	...	0950	...	0908	0953	1202	1426	1452	1553	1646	1817	1823	1956	1923	...	2030	...	2105	2123	2230
151	Białogard .... d.	0416	0733	0803	...	0958	...	0910	0955	1203	1429	1505	1554	1648	1820	1825	2010	1934	...	2035	...	2106	2129	2230
187	Kołobrzeg .... a.	|	0800	|	...	|	...	0938	1038	|	|	|	|	1730	|	1856	|	2010	...	2119	...	|	|	|
**43	Kołobrzeg .... d.	|	...	|	0735	|	1005	...	...	|	|	|	|	...	|	...	|	...	2015	...	2040	|	|	|
175	**Koszalin** .... d.	0441	...	0819	0828	1018	1054	...	...	1220	1448	1535	1611	...	1850	...	2042	...	2105	...	2130	2130	2150	2249
242	Słupsk .... d.	0547	...	0903	0920	1106	1155	...	...	1306	1539	1634	1700	...	1952	...	2135	...	2200	...	2230	...	2245	...
294	Lębork .... d.	0638	...	0937	1001	...	1237	...	...	1343	1629	...	1736	...	...	...	2219	...	2238	...	2307	...	2334	...
353	**Gdynia** Gł. .... a.	...	...	1020	1040	...	1320	...	...	1427	1713	...	1820	...	...	...	2302	...	2324	...	2354	...	0017	...
353	**Gdynia** Gł. .... ▷ d.	...	...	1038	1058	...	1331	...	...	1437	...	...	1840	...	...	...	2312	...	2334	...	0020	...	...	...
362	Sopot .... ▷ a.	...	...	1050	1108	...	1342	...	...	1447	...	...	1854	...	...	...	2323	...	2345	...	0032	...	...	...
374	**Gdańsk** Gł. .... ▷ a.	...	...	1108	1125	...	1359	...	...	1504	...	...	1914	...	...	...	2342	...	0004	...	0054	...	...	...
	Warszawa C. **1025/30** .... a.	...	...	...	1619	...	1914	...	...	...	...	...	...	...	...	...	...	...	...	...	...	...	...	...

			TLK	*TLK*		*TLK*	*TLK*	*TLK*	*TLK*	*TLK*	*TLK*				*TLK*		*TLK*		*TLK*	*TLK*		*TLK*	*EIC*	*TLK*
			57109	**28251**		**38259**	**38209**	**48201**	**83102**	**58101**	**84102**				**18105**		**38109**		**84250**	**58103**		**83252**	**3831**	**56250**
			57108				♣				**84103**								♠					**56251**
	y		**Z**	**Az**		**Dz**	**D**	**A**	**J**	**G**	**H**♣				**E**	Ⓑ	**K**		**A**	**G**		**Az**	**z**	**Az**
Warszawa C. **1025/30** .... d.	...	...	...	...	...	...	2305	...	...	...	...	...	...	...	...	...	0926	...	...	...	...	...	1335	...
Gdańsk Gł. .... ▷ d.	...	...	...	0312	...	0400	0505	0534	...	0924	...	...	...	...	1300	...	1421	...	...	1643	...	...	1809	...
Sopot .... ▷ d.	...	...	...	0333	...	0420	0526	0554	...	0942	...	...	...	...	1318	...	1439	...	...	1700	...	...	1826	...
Gdynia Gł. .... ▷ a.	...	...	...	0343	...	0429	0536	0604	...	0952	...	...	...	...	1328	...	1448	...	...	1710	...	...	1835	...
Gdynia Gł. .... d.	...	...	0415	0357	...	0441	0552	0614	...	1008	...	...	...	...	1356	...	1459	...	...	1722	...	...	1852	...
Lębork .... d.	...	...	0510	0442	...	0601	0652	0705	...	1057	...	...	...	...	1442	...	1602	...	...	1820	...	...	1934	2314
Słupsk .... d.	...	0450	0546	0525	...	0652	0730	0753	...	1132	1222	1235	...	...	1517	...	1639	1800	...	1856	...	...	2010	2350
Koszalin .... d.	0418	0549	0632	0625	...	0755	0825	0848	...	1221	1314	1338	1529	...	1611	1718	1734	1848	...	1941	...	...	2103	0037
Kołobrzeg .... a.	|	|	|	0711	...	0851	0910	|	...	|	|	|	|	...	|	|	1822	|	...	|	...	...	2153	|
Kołobrzeg .... d.	|	|	|	...	0802	...	...	|	1000	|	|	|	|	1445	|	|	...	|	1858	|	1911	1944	...	|
Białogard .... a.	0437	0616	0650	...	0838	...	...	0904	1033	1236	1331	1359	1551	1521	1628	1741	...	1908	1926	1957	1951	2021	...	0054
Białogard .... d.	0438	0618	0654	...	0840	...	...	0906	1039	1238	1338	1403	1555	1528	1629	1751	...	1910	1927	1958	2004	2032	...	0056
Szczecinek .... d.	|	|	0748	...	0952	...	...	|	1141	|	1444	|	|	1642	|	1859	...	|	2026	|	2117	2143	...	0151
Piła Gł. .... d.	|	|	0853	...	1105	...	...	|	1238	|	1543	|	|	1758	|	2011	...	|	2133	|	...	2240	...	0249
Poznań Gł. .... a.	|	|	1043	...	1311	...	...	|	1425	|	1726	|	|	2002	|	2211	...	|	2318	|	...	0024	...	0426
Stargard Szczeciński .... § d.	0616	0758	...	...	...	...	...	1035	...	1402	...	1537	1740	...	1759	...	...	2054	...	2119	...	...	...	...
Szczecin Dąbie .... § a.	0641	0822	...	...	...	...	...	1101	...	1419	...	1603	1805	...	1817	...	...	2115	...	2136	...	...	...	...
Szczecin Gł. .... § a.	0658	0839	...	...	...	...	...	1117	...	1437	...	1630	1834	...	1838	...	...	2131	...	2154	...	...	...	...

A – Conveys 1, 2 cl., 2 cl., 2.
D – 1, 2 cl., 2 cl., 12 Kołobrzeg - Gdynia - Bydgoszcz - Warszawa - Kielce - Kraków and v.v.
E – 12 Szczecin - Gdańsk - Białystok and v.v.
G – 12 Szczecin - Gdańsk - Olsztyn and v.v.
H – 12 Katowice - Ostrów Wlkp - Poznań - Gdynia and v.v.
J – 12 Kraków - Katowice - Wrocław - Poznań - Kołobrzeg and v.v.
K – 12 Kołobrzeg - Gdynia - Gdańsk - Warszawa - Kraków and v.v. (Table **1030**).
Y – ①⑤⑦ (also Aug. 14; not Aug. 15).
Z – ①⑤⑥ (also Aug. 14; not Aug. 16).
p – July 16 - 20.
q – Not July 16 - 20.
r – Arrive 1736.
u – To / from Lublin (Table **1055**).
y – Not Aug. 15.
z – Not Aug. 31.
♠ – Retimed on Aug. 31.
⊖ – Retimed July 16 - 20.
* – Distance from Białogard.
** – Distance from Koszalin.
§ – See also Table **1010**.
▷ – Frequent local trains runs between Gdynia and Gdansk.
♣ – Train number variations: **38209** runs as **38203** on Aug. 31; **45103/2** runs as **45153/2** on ⑥ (also Aug. 15); **84102/3** runs as **84152/3** on ⑦ (also Aug. 16)..

1020 GDYNIA - GDAŃSK - BYDGOSZCZ - POZNAŃ

km		①-⑥ q			TLK 56102/56103	EC 54/57000 B	TLK 57104/57105 ①⑥ v	TLK 57102/57103		IR 56110/56111 j		①-⑥ q		TLK 56106/56107 ⑧ q		IR 57110/57111			TLK 56104/56105	TLK 56100/56101				IR 57114/57115 ⑤ w	TLK 57100/57101 ⑧ q	TLK 56260/56261 ♣ K
0	**Gdynia** Gł. ▷ d.	...	...	...	0455	0642	...	0813	...	...	...	...	...	1209	...	...	...	...	...	1539	...	...	...	...	1825	2215
9	Sopot ▷ d.	...	...	...	0508	0655	...	0826	...	...	...	...	...	1220	...	...	...	...	...	1549	...	...	...	...	1837	2227
21	**Gdańsk** Gł. ▷ d.	...	...	...	0534	0717	...	0848	...	...	...	...	...	1242	...	...	...	...	...	1611	...	...	...	...	1901	2252
53	Tczew ▷ d.	...	...	...	0557	0736	...	0911	...	...	...	...	...	1306	...	...	...	...	...	1634	...	...	...	...	1924	2318
181	**Bydgoszcz** Gł. ▷ a.	...	...	...	0718	0844	...	1032	...	...	...	...	...	1427	...	...	...	...	...	1755	...	...	...	...	2046	0045
181	**Bydgoszcz** Gł. d.	0539	0642	...	0721	0847	...	1039	1049	...	1248	...	1336	1436	...	...	1454	...	...	1758	1837	...	2014	...	2049	0048
•198	**Olsztyn** Gł. d.	|	|	...	|	|	0640	|	|	0840	|	...	|	|	...	1150	|	...	1432	|	|	...	|	1720	|	|
•129	Iława d.	|	|	...	|	|	0739	|	|	0937	|	...	|	|	...	1248	|	...	1532	|	|	...	|	1818	|	|
•35	**Toruń** Gł. d.	|	|	0635	|	|	0931	|	|	1135	|	1258	|	|	...	1432	|	1613	1738	|	|	1843	|	2020	|	|
227	Inowrocław d.	0632	0731	0736	0752	0917	1015	1110	1132	1218	1330	1344	1425	1508	...	1514	1544	1701	1824	1840	1924	1939	2103	2108	2123	0126
283	Gniezno d.	0719	...	0846	0836	0956	1100	1151	1228	1300	...	1434	...	1550	...	1605	1640	1750	1906	1921	...	2026	...	2150	2206	0210
334	**Poznań** Gł. a.	0819	...	0935	0909	1027	1133	1232	1318	1333	...	1530	...	1623	...	1640	1734	1840	1940	1955	...	2123	...	2225	2241	0244
	Wrocław **1070** a.	...	...	...	1214	...	...	...	...	...	...	...	...	1943p	...	...	...	...	...	2321r	...	...	...	...	...	0642n

	TLK 65261/65260 ♣ K	TLK 45255 Az	①-⑥ q	TLK 75100/75101 N		IR 75106/75107 P		TLK 65101/65100	TLK 65104/65105			IR 75110/75111	TLK 65107/65106 N		TLK 75102/75103			IR 65111/65110	TLK 65103/65102 y	TLK 75104/75105 ⑤⑦ w		EC 55/75000 B			
Wrocław **1070** d.	2354t	...	...	...	...	...	...	0635	...	...	...	...	0920	...	...	...	...	...	1343	...	...	...	...	...	...
Poznań Gł. d.	0350	...	0539	0625	...	0723	0744	0944	0959	1032	...	1222	1235	1346	1441	1516	...	1635	1643	1723	1746	1830	1945	...	...
Gniezno d.	0422	...	0634	0702	...	0757	0838	1020	1034	1124	...	1258	1310	1436	1519	1608	...	1708	1719	1757	1838	1859	2035	...	...
Inowrocław d.	0504	0527	0734	0742	0755	0839	0929	1100	1126	1221	...	1345	1352	1534	1558	1657	1705	1747	1801	1842	1939	1935	2128	2135	...
Toruń Gł. d.	|	|	0825	|	|	0924	|	|	1222	1311	...	1430	|	1621	|	...	|	1841	|	1935	2030	|	2219	|	...
Iława d.	|	|	...	|	|	1048	|	|	1353	...	...	1612	|	...	|	...	|	2015	|	2105	...	|	...	|	...
Olsztyn Gł. a.	|	|	...	|	|	1143	|	|	1458	...	...	1718	|	...	|	...	|	2117	|	2201	...	|	...	|	...
Bydgoszcz Gł. a.	0536	0602	...	0813	0843	...	1011	1131	...	...	...	...	1424	...	1630	...	1750	...	1833	...	...	2006	...	2224	...
Bydgoszcz Gł. ▷ d.	0539	0605	...	0817	...	...	...	1134	...	...	...	...	1429	...	1633	...	...	...	1839	...	...	2009	...	...	...
Tczew ▷ d.	0705	0728	...	0943	...	...	...	1256	...	...	...	...	1605	...	1757	...	...	...	2001	...	...	2114	...	...	...
Gdańsk Gł. ▷ a.	0730	0753	...	1007	...	...	...	1320	...	...	...	...	1629	...	1820	...	...	...	2025	...	...	2132	...	...	...
Sopot ▷ a.	0755	0820	...	1029	...	...	...	1342	...	...	...	...	1652	...	1842	...	...	...	2058	...	...	2157	...	...	...
Gdynia Gł. ▷ a.	0805	0830	...	1038	...	...	...	1351	...	...	...	...	1702	...	1851	...	...	...	2109	...	...	2205	...	...	...

A – Conveys 🛏 1, 2 cl., ▬ 2 cl., 🚃2 .
B – BERLIN GDANSK EXPRESS 🚃12 ✕ Gdynia - Poznań - Berlin and v.v. (Table **1001**).
K – 🛏 1, 2 cl., ▬ 2 cl., 🚃12 (Hel, until Aug. 30 -) Gdynia - Wrocław and v.v. Conveys 🛏 1, 2 cl. Berlin - Kaliningrad and v.v. on dates in Table **51**.
N – ①–⑥ (not Aug. 16).
P – ⑥⑦ (also Aug. 15; not Aug. 16).

j – To Jelenia Gora (Table **1084**).
k – To / from Katowice (Table **1025**).
n – Departure time varies (0621 - 0702).
p – Arrival time varies (1931 - 1952).
q – Not Aug. 15.
r – Arrive 2341 July 16 - 20.
t – Depart 2326 on some dates.
v – Also Aug. 15; not Aug. 16.

w – Also Aug. 14; not Aug. 15.
y – July 16 - 20 runs up to 17 minutes later to Bydgoszcz.
z – Not Aug. 31.
♣ – Train number varies on some dates.
• – Distance from Inowrocław.
▷ – See also Table **1025**. Frequent local services run between Gdynia and Gdansk (see Table **1035**).

1025 GDYNIA - GDAŃSK - BYDGOSZCZ - WARSZAWA / ŁODŹ

km		TLK 83258/83259 Kq	TLK 51108	EIC 5102/5103	TLK 83104 D	EIC 5104/5105 ⑧ q	TLK 5304/5305	TLK 52102 L	TLK 53102/53103	TLK 53108 ♣ P		TLK 54160/54161	TLK 51110	TLK 52100/52101 L	TLK 83108/83109 K	TLK 52112/52113 L	IR 51114	TLK 53256/53257 w	EIC 5130/5131	TLK 51112 ⑦		TLK 84200/84201 B	TLK 83208 ♣ J
	Hel d.	...	...	...	...	...	...	...	...	...	...	0724	...	...	...	...	...	...	1500	...	...	...	...
0	**Gdynia** Gł. ▷ d.	2334	...	0420	...	0612	0719	...	0744	...	...	0932	...	...	1331	1445	1532	1616	1717	...	...	2312	2321
9	Sopot ▷ d.	2345	...	0429	...	0622	0730	...	0755	...	...	0942	...	...	1342	1455	1542	1626	1727	...	...	2323	2333
21	**Gdańsk** Gł. ▷ d.	0009	...	0449	...	0645	0751	...	0817	...	...	1002	...	...	1402	1515	1603	1654	1747	...	...	2347	0000
53	Tczew ▷ d.	0036	...	0509	...	0704	0814	...	0841	...	...	1025	...	...	1424	1538	1640	1721	1808	...	...	0011	0026
181	**Bydgoszcz** Gł. ▷ a.	0201	...	0619	...	0812	|	...	1007	...	...	1145	...	...	|	1658	1806	1856	1919	...	...	0139	0153
181	**Bydgoszcz** Gł. d.	0208	0512	0621	0716	0821	|	0913	1022	1119	...	1206	1357	1518	|	1719	1821	1917	1921	1958	...	0156	0214
232	**Toruń** Gł. d.	|	0601	|	0805	|	|	1002	1113	1208	...	1255	1447	1607	|	1813	1913	2018	|	2050	...	0242	0303
287	Włocławek d.	|	0642	|	0846	|	≋	1044	1155	1249	...	1337	1528	1648	≋	1857	1955	2105	|	2130	...	0322	0347
	Poznan Gł d.	|	|	|	|	|	|	|	|	|	...	|	|	|	|	|	|	|	|	|	...	|	|
	Konin d.	|	|	|	|	|	|	|	|	|	...	|	|	|	|	|	|	|	|	|	...	|	|
342	Kutno d.	0436	0727	0826	0924	1023	|	1124	1235	1329	...	1416	1607	1734	|	1937	2036	2147	2122	2209	...	0402	0431
469	**Warszawa** Centralna a.	|	0850	0935	1047	1135	1226	1247	|	1453	...	|	1730	1858	1914	2101	|	2325	2236	2335	...	|	0600
474	**Warszawa** Wschodnia a.	|	0903	0948	1059	1148	1209x	1300	|	1506	...	|	1743	1911	1855x	2113	|	2338	2249	2348	...	|	0629
410	**Łódź** Kaliska a.	0624	...	...	...	...	|	...	1407	...	...	1554	...	...	|	...	2209	|	...	...	...	0536	|
	Częstochowa **1060/62** a.	0919	...	...	...	...	|	...	1708	...	...	1907	...	...	|	...	...	|	...	...	...	0829	◧
	Katowice **1060** a.	|	...	...	...	...	|	...	|	...	...	2026k	...	...	|	...	...	|	...	...	...	0958	|
	Kraków **1062/65** a.	1141	...	...	...	...	1542	...	1919	...	...	...	...	...	2252	...	...	0519	...	...	...	...	1215
	Zakopane **1066** a.	...	...	...	...	...	...	...	...	...	...	...	...	...	...	...	...	0925	...	...	...	...	...

	EIC 1531	TLK 38109 K	IR 15102/15103	TLK 25100/25101 L	TLK 38256/38257 ♣	TLK 15110/15111	TLK 25112/25113 L	TLK 45160/45161 ♣	TLK 35108/35109 P		EIC 1504/1505 ⑧ q	TLK 25102/25103 L	EIC 1502/1503	TLK 15112/15113 ⑤ q	TLK 18108/18109 E	TLK 35102/35103	EIC 3504/3505	TLK 35104/35105 R		TLK 38258/38259 Kw	TLK 38208/38209 ♣ J	TLK 48200/48201 B	
Zakopane **1066** d.	...	...	...	...	2142	...	...	...	...	...	...	...	...	...	...	...	...	...	...	...	...	...	...
Kraków **1062/65** d.	...	0555	...	...	0134	...	...	...	...	...	...	...	...	...	...	1153	1407	...	...	1650	1716	...	...
Katowice **1060** d.	...	|	...	...	|	...	...	0817	...	...	...	...	...	...	...	|	|	...	...	|	|	1925	...
Częstochowa **1060/62** d.	...	|	...	...	|	...	...	0946	...	...	...	...	...	...	...	1357	|	...	...	1917	◧	2059	...
Łódź Kaliska d.	...	|	0600j	...	|	...	...	1237	...	...	...	...	...	...	...	1707	|	...	...	2212	|	2345	...
Warszawa Wschodnia d.	0547	0941z	|	0637	0732	0847	1037	|	1237	...	1347	1433	1547	1532	1656	|	1730z	1837	...	|	2250	|	...
Warszawa Centralna d.	0600	0926	|	0700	0755	0900	1100	|	1300	...	1400	1505	1600	1608	1708	|	1720	1905	...	|	2305	|	...
Kutno d.	0709	|	0751	0824	0915	1023	1226	1418	1431	...	1509	1628	1709	1732	1831	1842	|	2032	...	2351	0038	0122	...
Konin d.	|	|	|	|	|	|	|	|	|	...	|	|	|	|	|	|	|	|	...	|	|	|	...
Poznan Gł a.	|	|	|	|	|	|	|	|	|	...	|	|	|	|	|	|	|	|	...	|	|	|	...
Włocławek d.	|	≋	0831	0904	0956	1104	1307	◐	1511	...	|	1708	|	1809	1909	1922	≋	2111	...	|	0123	0203	...
Toruń Gł. d.	|	|	0932	0951	1048	1156	1358	|	1557	...	|	1752	|	1853	1956	2008	|	2155	...	|	0210	0247	...
Bydgoszcz Gł a.	0907	|	1016	1034	1138	1243	1443	1629	1641	...	1708	1835	1905	1933	2040	2053	|	2240	...	0206	0253	0326	...
Bydgoszcz Gł. ▷ d.	0909	|	1026	...	1204	...	1459	1645	...	...	1704	...	1907	...	...	2108	|	...	...	0211	0308	0340	...
Tczew ▷ d.	1018	1355	1154	...	1334	...	1625	1804	...	...	1819	...	2015	...	...	2231	2107	...	...	0331	0435	0505	...
Gdańsk Gł. ▷ a.	1039	1418	1222	...	1401	...	1648	1827	...	...	1838	...	2035	...	...	2255	2127	...	...	0355	0501	0529	...
Sopot ▷ a.	1059	1439	1242	...	1430	...	1708	1851	...	...	1902	...	2105	...	...	2319	2149	...	...	0420	0526	0550	...
Gdynia Gł. ▷ a.	1108	1448	1251	...	1441	...	1717	1900	...	...	1911	...	2114	...	...	2329	2158	...	...	0429	0536	0604	...
Hel a.	1323	...	...	...	...	...	...	2120v	...	...	...	...	...	...	...	...	...	...	...	...	...	...	...

B – 🛏 1, 2 cl., ▬ 2 cl., 🚃12 (Hel, until Aug. 30 -) Gdynia - Katowice - Bielsko Biała and v.v.
D – 🚃12 Piła (Table **1000**) - Bydgoszcz - Warszawa - Przemyśl (Table **1058**).
E – 🚃12 Białystok (Table **1040**) - Warszawa - Bydgoszcz - Piła (Table **1000**).
J – 🛏 1, 2 cl., ▬ 2 cl., 🚃12 Kołobrzeg (also Hel until Aug. 30) - Gdynia - Bydgoszcz - Warszawa - Kielce - Kraków and v.v.
K – To / from Kołobrzeg (Table **1015**).
L – To / from Lublin (Table **1055**).
P – To / from Przemyśl (Table **1058**).
R – To / from Rzeszów (Table **1058**).

j – Depart 0623 or 0628 some dates.
k – Arrive 1955 on some dates.
q – Not Aug. 15.
t – Until July 31.
v – Not Aug. 31.
w – Not Aug. 30, 31.
x – Calls at Wschodnia before Centralna.
z – Calls at Wschodnia after Centralna.
♣ – Train number varies on some dates.

▷ – See also Table **1020**. Frequent local services run between Gdynia and Gdansk.
⊖ – Timings may vary.
◧ – Via Kielce (Table **1067**).
≋ – Via Malbork and Iława (Table **1030**).

GDYNIA - GDAŃSK - IŁAWA - MALBORK - WARSZAWA 1030

For the full service Gdynia - Gdansk - Warszawa (including trains via Bydgoszcz) see Table **1025**

km			TLK 54104 54105 b	IR 56110	EIC 5304 5305	EIC 5108	EIC 8330 8331		TLK 83108 83109		TLK 51100 51101	
	Kołobrzeg **1015**	d.	...	...	...	...	0735	...	1005	...	...	...
0	**Gdynia** Gł. ▶	d.	...	...	0719	...	1058	...	1331	...	...	...
9	Sopot ▶	d.	...	...	0730	...	1108	...	1342	...	...	...
21	**Gdańsk** Gł. ▶	d.	...	...	0751	...	1128	...	1402	...	...	...
53	Tczew ▶	d.	...	...	0814	...	1149	...	1424	...	...	...
72	Malbork ▶	d.	...	...	0840	...	1209	...	1450	...	...	...
•	**Olsztyn** ▶	d.	0712	0840	|	1243	|	1430	|	1600	1922	2022
141	Iława Gł. ▶	d.	|	0936	0953	|	1322	|	1622	|	|	|
201	Działdowo	d.	0822	...	|	1347	|	1554	1709	1726	2035	2141
251	Ciechanów	d.	0904	...	|	1424	1456	...	1753	...	2115	...
305	Modlin ✈ ▷	d.	0940	...	|	1503	|	...	1827	...	2149	...
345	**Warszawa** Wschodnia ▷	a.	1009	...	1209	1527	1548	...	1855	...	2216	...
350	**Warszawa** Centralna ▷	a.	1020	...	1226	...	1619	...	1914	...	2225	...
	Katowice **1060**	a.	1524j	...	|	...	|	...	|	...	...	...
	Kraków Gł. **1065**	a.	...	...	1542	...	1944	...	2252	...	...	...
	Zakopane **1066**	a.	...	...	...	...	...	...	...	...	...	...

			TLK 15100 15101	TLK 38108 38109			EIC 3830 3831	EIC 1509	Ⓑ q	TLK 45104 45105 b	EIC 3504 3505
Zakopane **1066**	d.	...	...	...	...	...	...	...	...	...	...
Kraków Gł. **1065**	d.	...	...	0555	...	...	1005	...	...	...	1407
Katowice **1060**	d.	...	...	|	...	...	|	...	...	1131	|
Warszawa Centralna ▷	d.	...	0700	0926	...	...	1335	...	...	1705	1720
Warszawa Wschodnia ▷	d.	...	0710	0941	...	...	1358	1417	...	1714	1730
Modlin ✈ ▷	d.	...	0737	1008	...	...	|	1442	...	1744	|
Ciechanów	d.	...	0812	1041	...	...	1450	1520	...	1831	|
Działdowo	d.	0545	0858	1124	...	1506	1532	1556	1755	1911	|
Iława Gł. ▶	d.	|	|	1210	1227	|	1616	|	|	|	1940
Olsztyn ▶	a.	0705	1005	|	1332	1632	|	1700	1915	2018	|
Malbork ▶	d.	...	...	1334	...	...	1723	...	...	...	2048
Tczew ▶	d.	...	...	1355	...	...	1743	...	...	...	2107
Gdańsk Gł. ▶	a.	...	...	1418	...	...	1804	...	...	...	2127
Sopot ▶	a.	...	...	1439	...	...	1826	...	...	...	2149
Gdynia Gł. ▶	a.	...	...	1448	...	...	1835	...	...	...	2158
Kołobrzeg **1015**	a.	...	...	1820	...	...	2153r	...	...	...	...

b – To / from Bielsko Biała (Table **1060**).
j – Arrive 1543 from Aug. 11.
q – Not Aug. 15.
r – Not Aug. 31.
▶ – For additional trains Gdynia - Gdansk - Iława (- Olsztyn) see Table **1035**. Frequent local trains run between Gdynia and Gdańsk operated by *SKM* (every 10 - 30 minutes).
• – Olsztyn - Działdowo: *84 km.*
▷ – For other trains Warszawa - Modlin ✈ see panel on right.

Warszawa Centralna - Modlin ✈ Operator *KM*, journey 36 minutes

From Warszawa Centralna:
0320, 0420, 0515, 0615, 0721, 0815, 0920, 1015, 1115, 1215, 1310, 1415, 1518, 1615, 1715, 1815, 1915, 2017, 2114, 2215.

From Modlin ✈:
0421, 0524, 0620, 0724, 0821, 0917, 1014, 1121, 1221, 1323, 1421, 1517, 1621, 1721, 1817, 1917, 2018, 2121, 2219.

A 🚌 connects the rail station with the terminal. Additional slower trains run Modlin ✈ to Warszawa Gdánska, with metro connection to city centre.

GDYNIA - GDAŃSK - EŁBLAG - OLSZTYN - BIAŁYSTOK 1035

km					TLK 54108 54109 G		TLK 85102 85103		TLK 81104 81105		TLK 85100 85101		①–⑥ y
	Szczecin Gł. **1015**	d.	...	...	...	...	0556	...	1001	...	1400	...	...
0	**Gdynia** Gł. ▶	d.	0440	0541	0654	0900	1038	1310	1437	1550	1840	1905	2102
9	Sopot ▶	d.	0452	0554	0705	0909	1050	1319	1447	1600	1854	1915	2115
21	**Gdańsk** Gł. ▶	d.	0521	0618	0735	0932	1111	1335	1509	1616	1918	1935	2134
53	Tczew ▶	d.	0549	0702	0759	1013	1134	1406	1533	1653	1941	2019	2220
72	Malbork ▶	d.	0615	0726	0820	1036	1154	1427	1554	1717	2001	2052	2244
101	**Ełblag**	d.	|	0752	0844	1102	1217	|	1618	1744	2025	2119	2317
	Iława Gł. ▶	a.	0728	...	|	...	|	1541	|	...	|	...	...
	Iława Gł.	d.	0739	...	|	...	|	1549	|	...	|	...	...
*200	**Olsztyn**	a.	0835	...	1030	...	1343	1652	1754	...	2153	...	...
200	**Olsztyn**	d.	...	...	1038	...	...	...	1808	...	...	...	...
319	Giżycko	d.	...	...	1241	...	...	...	2012	...	...	...	...
366	Ełk	a.	...	...	1338	...	...	...	2102	...	...	...	...
366	Ełk	d.	...	...	1354	...	...	...	2114	...	...	...	...
470	**Białystok**	a.	...	...	1523	...	...	...	2236	...	...	...	...

			TLK 58100 58101		TLK 18104 18105			TLK 58102 58103			TLK 45108 45109 G	
Białystok	d.	...	...	...	0539	...	...	...	...	...	1431	...
Ełk	a.	...	...	...	0702	...	...	...	...	...	1556	...
Ełk	d.	...	...	...	0714	...	...	...	...	...	1616	...
Giżycko	d.	...	...	...	0805	...	...	...	...	...	1706	...
Olsztyn	a.	...	...	...	0959	...	...	...	...	...	1901	...
Olsztyn	d.	...	0644	0910	1004	...	...	1402	...	...	1906	2001
Iława Gł.	a.	...	|	1010	|	...	...	|	...	...	|	2057
Iława Gł. ▶	d.	...	|	1020	|	...	...	|	...	...	|	2107
Ełblag	d.	0541	0813	|	1142	1154	1435	1535	1755	1928	2043	|
Malbork ▶	d.	0610	0835	1127	1210	1223	1507	1557	1823	2002	2106	2214
Tczew ▶	d.	0634	0857	1148	1231	1246	1532	1617	1853	2026	2128	2236
Gdańsk Gł. ▶	a.	0703	0921	1215	1255	1328	1609	1640	1928	2103	2153	2302
Sopot ▶	a.	0729	0942	1244	1318	1357	1632	1700	1956	2127	2217	2327
Gdynia Gł. ▶	a.	0740	0952	1255	1328	1409	1645	1710	2008	2140	2227	2339
Szczecin Gł. **1015**	a.	...	1437	...	1838	...	...	2154	...	...	...	...

LOCAL SERVICES OLSZTYN - EŁK - BIAŁYSTOK

km						Ⓑ			p	q			
0	**Olsztyn**	d.	...	0908	1054	...	1335	...	1712	1735	1734	...	2045
45	Szczytno	d.	...	|	1140	...	|	...	|	|	1814	...	|
102	Pisz	d.	...	|	1247	...	|	...	|	|	1922	...	|
	Giżycko	d.	...	1059	|	...	1526	...	1903	1934	|	...	2236
157	Ełk	d.	0542	1142	1426	1457	1614	1726	1952	2018	2101	...	2319
261	**Białystok**	a.	0727	...	...	1641	...	1911	...	...	...	...	...

							x				Ⓑ	
Białystok	d.	...	...	...	...	...	1043	...	1458	...	1716	...
Ełk	d.	0341	0504	0747	0819	...	1222	1240	1652	1714	1854	...
Giżycko	d.	|	0549	0831	|	...	...	1324	...	1759	...	...
Pisz	d.	0521	|	|	0959	...	...	|	...	|	...	...
Szczytno	d.	0628	|	|	1107	...	...	|	...	|	...	...
Olsztyn	a.	0707	0740	1022	1145	...	...	1529	...	2001	...	...

G – 🚃12 Gdynia - Gdańsk - Olsztyn - Białystok - Warszawa - Częstochowa - Katowice and v.v.
p – Not July 2 - 9.
q – ①–⑤ July 2 - 9.
x – On July 4, 5 partially replaced by 🚌 (d. 1022).
y – Not Aug. 15.
▶ – For additional trains Gdynia - Gdansk - Iława (- Warszawa) see Table **1030**. Frequent local trains run between Gdynia and Gdańsk operated by *SKM* (every 10 - 30 minutes).
* – *210 km* via Iława.

WARSZAWA - BIAŁYSTOK 1040

km			TLK 10010 10011 H		TLK 45108 45109 K		TLK 81100 81101 S		TLK 10100 10101 Ⓑ q		TLK 61102 61103
0	**Warszawa** Centralna	d.	0709	...	1100	...	1502	...	1710	...	2100
5	**Warszawa** Wschodnia	d.	0720	...	1115	...	1522	...	1719	...	2119
184	**Białystok**	a.	1017	...	1419	...	1819	...	2008	...	0005
	Ełk **1035**	a.	...	...	1556	...	...	...	...	...	...

		TLK 10110 10111 n		TLK 16102 16103		TLK 18100 18101 S		TLK 54108 54109 K		TLK 10012 10013 H
Ełk **1035**	d.	...	...	...	...	...	...	1354	...	...
Białystok	d.	0410	...	0549	...	0907	...	1540	...	1805
Warszawa Wschodnia	a.	0659	...	0849	...	1203	...	1845	...	2058
Warszawa Centralna	a.	0710	...	0900	...	1230	...	1855	...	2115

H – HAŃCZA – 🚃12 Warszawa - Białystok - Suwałki (- Šeštokai, from July 25) and v.v.
K – 🚃12 Gdynia - Gdańsk - Olsztyn - Ełk - Białystok - Warszawa - Częstochowa - Katowice and v.v.
S – To / from Szczecin via Poznań (Table **1010**).
n – ①–⑥ (not Aug. 16).
q – Not Aug. 15.

PKP, BCh, LG

(WARSZAWA) - BIAŁYSTOK - VILNIUS and HRODNA 1042

km	2nd class (except train H)		51001 192	①–⑤ y		TLK 10010 10011	11007 194			Ⓑ	Ⓑ	11009 196
0	*Warszawa Cent.* **1040**	d.	...	...	...	0709	...	...	...	...	...	...
5	*Warszawa Wsch.* **1040**	d.	...	...	...	0720	...	...	...	...	...	...
184	**Białystok**	d.	0542	0633	...	1032	1134	1345	1451	1613	2013	2030
225	Sokółka	d.	0634	0730	...	1114	1210	1429	1530	1705	2053	2106
324	**Suwałki**	a.	|	0903	...	1244	|	|	1710	|	2226	|
377	Šeštokai 🏛 ◐	§ a.	|	...	...	1404j	|	|	...	|	...	|
471	**Kaunas** 1811	§ a.	|	...	...	...	|	|	...	|	...	|
575	**Vilnius** 1811	§ a.	|	...	...	...	|	|	...	|	...	|
241	Kuźnica Białostocka 🏛	a.	0651	...	...	...	1224	1446	...	1722	...	2120
241	Kuźnica Białostocka 🏛	d.	0801	...	...	...	1324	...	...	...	...	2220
268	**Hrodna** 🏛	‡ a.	0948	...	...	...	1511	...	...	...	...	0007

		①–⑥	191 11002		①–⑤ y	193 11014			TLK 10012 10013	195 15000	
Hrodna 🏛	‡ d.	...	0550	...	...	1120	...	...	...	1655	...
Kuźnica Białostocka 🏛	a.	...	0536	...	...	1107	...	...	...	1642	...
Kuźnica Białostocka 🏛	d.	...	0709	...	...	1227	...	1611	...	1757	...
Vilnius 1811	§ d.	...	|	...	...	|	...	|	...	|	...
Kaunas 1811	§ d.	...	|	...	...	|	...	|	...	|	...
Šeštokai 🏛 ◐	§ d.	...	|	...	...	|	...	|	1420j	|	...
Suwałki	d.	0514	|	...	0936	|	...	|	1540	|	1728
Sokółka	d.	0647	0724	...	1115	1245	...	1628	1711	1811	1901
Białystok	a.	0727	0801	...	1202	1322	...	1711	1750	1846	1941
Warszawa Wsch. **1040**	a.	..	...	...	...	...	...	...	2058	...	...
Warszawa Cent. **1040**	a.	...	...	...	...	...	...	...	2115	...	...

H – HAŃCZA – 🚃12 Warszawa - Białystok - Suwałki (- Šeštokai, from July 25) and v.v.
j – From July 25.
y – Not Aug. 15.
§ – Lithuanian time (Polish time + 1 hour).
‡ – Belarus time (Polish time + 1 hour in summer; + 2 in winter), see page 2.
◐ – 🏛 = Trakiszki (Poland) / Mockava (Lithuania); ticketing point is Mockava.

1050 WARSZAWA - TERESPOL - BREST

km			TLK		◇		◇				◇		◇		MP	◇		TLK		◇	IR	MP	◇	MP
		①–⑤	11101					①–⑤				①–⑤	①–⑤		10			11103		①–⑤	11117	116		453
		uy		✣		u		y	✣			uy	x	u	⊠			⑧y	✣	x	⑤⑦z	⊠		⊠
0	**Warszawa** Centralna d.	...	0711g	...	...	...	...	...	...	...	...	...	...	...	1612g	...	...	...	...	...	...	2103	...	0342
5	**Warszawa** Wschodnia d.	...	|	...	0744	...	0941	...	...	...	1342	...	1448	...	|	1641	...	1823	...	1741	2033	2130	2141	0423
93	Siedlce a.	...	0821	...	0906	...	1106	...	...	...	1506	...	1611	...	1717	1806	...	1922	...	1906	2132	2226	2307	|
93	Siedlce d.	...	0823	...	*0925*	...	*1125*	...	...	...	*1525*	...	*1626*	...	1718	*1823*	...	1924	...	2023	2133	2227	2308	|
121	Łuków d.	0754	0844	...	*0957*	1002	*1157*	1215	...	1504	*1557*	1609	*1658*	1705	1738	*1855*	1859	1944	...	2053	2156	2250	2337	|
173	Biała Podlaska d.	0852	0931	...	...	1102	...	1313	...	1604	...	1709	...	1804	1824	...	1957	2028	...	...	2255	2332	...	|
210	Terespol 🏛 a.	0935	1006	1125	...	1145	...	1355	1530	1646	...	1750	...	1847	1859	...	2040	2103	2159	...	2336	0006	...	0644
217	**Brest** Tsentralny 🏛 ‡ a.	...	...	1143	...	...	...	...	1548	...	...	...	...	...	2111	...	...	...	2218	...	...	0230	...	0912
	Moskva **1950** a.	...	...	...	...	...	...	...	...	...	...	...	...	...	1145	...	...	...	...	...	...	...	...	2358

	MP	MP	◇	MP		◇		◇			TLK	◇		◇		TLK		◇		IR	◇			TLK
	452	115	①–⑥	9							11110			①–⑤		11150	①–⑤	①–⑥		11114				11112
	⊠	⊠		⊠	u		✣			u	①–⑤		u	x	✣	⑥⑦	y		u	⑤⑦z		✣		⑧y
Moskva **1950** d.	0743	...	...	1650	...	...	...	...	...	...	...	...	...	...	...	...	...	...	...	...	...	...	...	...
Brest Tsentralny 🏛 ‡ d.	2115	0240	...	0532	...	...	0701	...	...	...	...	...	...	...	1310	...	...	...	...	...	...	1732	...	...
Terespol 🏛 d.	2113	0238	...	0530	0647	...	0719	...	0856	1132	1228	...	1319	...	1328	1414	1424	...	1520	1731	...	1750	1855	1936
Biała Podlaska d.	|	0314	...	0602	0729	...	...	...	0938	1214	1303	...	1401	...	...	1449	1505	...	1602	1806	...	...	1937	2013
Łuków d.	|	0401	0529	0646	0829	*0842*	...	*1042*	1038	1313	1349	*1442*	1500	*1545*	...	1537	1605	*1640*	1701	1851	*1940*	...	2034	2100
Siedlce a.	|	0423	0601	0710	...	*0915*	...	*1116*	...	...	1411	*1516*	...	*1618*	...	1557	...	*1713*	...	1914	*2013*	...	...	2122
Siedlce d.	|	0424	0602	0711	...	0927	...	1127	...	...	1413	1527	...	1626	...	1559	...	1726	...	1914	2026	...	...	2124
Warszawa Wschodnia a.	2342	0530	0703	0802	...	1051	...	1251	...	...	1516	1651	...	1751	...	1700	...	1854	...	2016	2151	...	...	2223
Warszawa Centralna a.	0020	0540	0714	...	...	...	...	...	...	...	...	...	...	...	...	...	...	...	...	...	...	...	...	2234

g – Warszawa **Gdańska**.
u – From / to Lublin or Chełm (Table **1055**).
x – Not May 1.
y – Not May 1, 2.
z – Also Apr. 30; not May 2.

✣ – Subject to confirmation.
◇ – Operated by Koleje Mazowieckie. Trains runs approx hourly Warszawa - Siedlce, approx every 2 hours Siedlce - Łuków.
‡ – Belarus time (Polish time +1 hour in summer; +2 in winter).

⊠ – Conveys only sleeping car passengers to / from Brest and points east thereof. For composition and days of running see **International** section (Tables **24 / 56 / 94**).

1055 WARSZAWA - LUBLIN - CHEŁM - DOROHUSK

km				TLK			IR	TLK	IR		TLK		IR		TLK	TLK	MP		TLK	TLK	TLK		TLK	IR
				62201 62203 62205			72111	83105	62121		52103		12107		53109	62103	68 12011		82101	32101	52101		52113	12125
							①–⑥						①–⑤											⑦
				w	t		y	bh	w		b	t	p	t	bh	w	K	t	s	k	b		b	
0	**Warszawa** Centralna d.	...	...	0630g	...	...	1003g	1056g	...	...	1255g	...	...	...	1512g	...	1645g	...	1755g	...	1912g	...	2107g	...
5	**Warszawa** Wschodnia d.	...	...	|	...	...	|	|	...	...	|	...	1359	...	|	...	|	...	|	...	|	...	|	2201
•62	Łuków d.	...	...	|	0834	...	|	|	...	...	|	1318	|	1503	|	...	|	1719	|	...	|	...	|	|
104	Dęblin d.	...	0606	0825	0941	...	1129	1225	...	...	1423	1430	1520	1610	1639	...	1819	1826	1918	...	2042	...	2241	2321
125	Puławy Miasto d.	...	0629	0842	1005	...	1144	1241	1351	...	1441	1455	1536	1633	1655	1746	1836	1850	1934	2022	2058	...	2257	2338
175	**Lublin** a.	...	0728	0936	1058	...	1225	1322	1426	...	1523	1547	1612	1725	1738	1821	1913	1942	2009	2056	2133	...	2334	0015
175	**Lublin** d.	0524	0734	...	1110	...	...	...	...	1440	...	1549	1614	1750	...	...	1918	1951	...	...	...	2231	...	...
249	Chełm a.	0636	0846	...	1224	...	...	...	...	1553	...	1702	1728	1902	...	...	2016	2104	...	...	...	2344	...	...
270	**Dorohusk** 🏛 a.	0659	...	...	1253	...	...	...	...	...	...	1724	...	1925	...	...	2036	...	...	...	...	...	...	...

	TLK	MP			TLK	IR		TLK		TLK		TLK		TLK		IR		IR	TLK	TLK		IR	TLK	
	25100 25101	67 21010			28100 28101	21102		26102		25112 25113		35108 35109		25102 25103		26100 26122		27120 27121	35104 35105	23102		21122	26200 26202 26204	
			①–⑤			①–⑤									①–⑤			⑧				⑦		
		K	qt		s	p	t	w		b		h		b	qt	w	t		bh	k			w	
Dorohusk 🏛 a.	...	0353	...	0443	...	...	...	...	0642	...	...	...	...	...	...	...	...	...	...	...	1506	...	...	1809
Chełm d.	...	0416	0352	0506	...	0538	0606	...	0706	...	...	...	1030	...	1219	...	1330	...	...	...	1530	1656	...	1832
Lublin a.	...	0513	0504	0619	...	0652	0721	...	0818	...	...	...	1143	...	1331	...	1442	...	...	...	1642	1752	...	1945
Lublin d.	0425	0525	0540	...	0625	0706	0738	0814	...	0822	...	1025	...	1225	1334	1415	1448	1525	1629	1650	1658	1802	1950	2005
Puławy Miasto d.	0458	0559	0631	...	0700	0744	0830	0850	...	0901	...	1102	...	1302	1425	1450	1540	1559	1704	1726	1750	1838	2027	2057
Dęblin d.	0513	0615	0654	...	0716	0800	0902	...	...	0918	...	1119	...	1319	1455	...	1604	1614	1722	...	1811	1854	2044	2120
Łuków a.	|	|	0753	...	|	|	1001	...	...	|	...	|	...	|	1554	...	1709	|	|	...	...	|	|	...
Warszawa Wschodnia a.	0634	0739	...	...	0830	0939	...	...	...	1035	...	1234	...	1433	...	...	...	1730	1839	...	...	2033	2216	...
Warszawa Centralna a.	0658	...	...	...	0841	...	...	...	...	1045	...	1254	...	1443	...	...	...	1755	1855	...	...	...	2258	...

K – KYÏV EKSPRES / KIEV EXPRESS – 🛏 1, 2 cl. Warszawa - Kyïv and v.v. (Table **1700**). International journeys only.

b – From / to Bydgoszcz (Table **1025**).
g – Warszawa **Gdańska**.
h – From / to Przemyśl (Table **1058**).
k – From / to Kraków.
p – Not May 1.
q – Not May 1, 2.
s – From / to Szczecin (Table **1010**).
t – From / to Terespol (Table **1050**).
w – From / to Wrocław (Table **1067**).
y – From / to Poznań (Table **1001**).
• – Distance from Dęblin.

1058 LUBLIN - STALOWA WOLA - RZESZÓW - PRZEMYŚL

km								TLK			TLK
								83105			53109
				①–⑤					①–⑤		
				q				E	q		B
	Warszawa Cent. **1055** d.	...	...	...	...	...	...	1055g	...	...	1512g
	Warszawa Wsch. **1055** d.	...	...	...	...	...	...	|	...	...	|
0	**Lublin** d.	...	...	...	...	...	...	1343	...	...	1751
•	Skarżysko Kamienna d.	...	...	...	...	...	...	|	...	...	|
103	Stalowa Wola Rozwadów a.	...	...	...	...	...	...	|	...	...	|
103	Stalowa Wola Rozwadów d.	0740	...	1013	...	1431	1545	|	1835	...	|
	Rzeszów a.	|	...	|	...	|	|	1701	|	...	2053
	Rzeszów 1075 d.	|	0946	|	1450	|	|	1713	|	2002	2105
178	Przeworsk 1075 d.	0926	1024	1159	1527	1616	1730	1739	2021	2041	2131
193	Jarosław 1075 d.	...	1043	...	1540	...	...	1751	...	2055	2143
228	**Przemyśl** 1075 a.	...	1135	...	1630	...	...	1831	...	2146	2229

		TLK			TLK		TLK			
		35108			33204		35104			
			①–⑤							
		B	q				F			
Przemyśl 1075 d.	...	0502	...	0730	1126	...	...	...	1548	1921
Jarosław 1075 d.	...	0545	...	0825	1209	...	...	...	1644	2011
Przeworsk 1075 d.	0535	0557	0704	0838	1221	1236	...	1630	1657	2025
Rzeszów 1075 a.	|	0626	|	0919	1249	|	...	|	1738	2105
Rzeszów d.	|	0641	|	...	...	|	1316	|	...	...
Stalowa Wola Rozwadów a.	0722	|	0851	...	...	1423	|	1817	...	...
Stalowa Wola Rozwadów d.	...	|	...	...	...	...	|	...	...	...
Skarżysko Kamienna d.	...	|	...	...	...	...	|	...	...	...
Lublin a.	...	1000	...	...	...	...	1617	...	...	...
Warszawa Wsch. **1055** a.	...	1234	...	...	...	...	1839	...	...	...
Warszawa Cent. **1055** a.	...	1254	...	...	...	...	1855	...	...	...

LOCAL SERVICES LUBLIN - STALOWA WOLA - RZESZÓW

km	🚌 service	①–⑥									
0	**Lublin** d.	p	...	...	0600	...	1146	...	1626	...	2015
103	Stalowa Wola Rozwadów d.	0458	0532	...	0754	...	1339	...	1812	...	2157
132	Tanobrzeg d.	0527	0602	...	0822	...	1406	...	1839	...	...
204	**Rzeszów** a.	0639	0715	...	0930	...	1530	...	1950	...	...

🚌 service						⑧q				
Rzeszów d.	...	0446	...	0947	...	1428	...	1555	1728	...
Tanobrzeg d.	...	0615	...	1055	...	1539	...	1710	1842	...
Stalowa Wola Rozwadów d.	0535	0658	...	1132	...	1611	...	1739	1918	...
Lublin a.	0729	0850	...	1311	...	...	...	...	2056	...

B – (12) Gdynia (Table **1025**) - Bydgoszcz - Warszawa - Rzeszów - Przemyśl and v.v.
E – (12) Piła - Bydgoszcz (Table **1025**) - Warszawa - Rzeszów - Przemyśl.
F – (12) Rzeszów - Lublin - Warszawa - Bydgoszcz (Table **1025**).

g – Warszawa **Gdańska**.
p – Not May 2, 3.
q – Not May 1, 2.
• – Skarżysko Kamienna - Stalowa Wola Rozwadów = *125 km*.

Subject to alteration from June 1

WARSZAWA / ŁÓDŹ - KATOWICE - OPOLE - WROCŁAW 1060

For other trains Warszawa - Wrocław see Table **1090**

km		*TLK*	*EC*	*EIC*	*IR*	*TLK*	*EC*	*TLK*	*TLK*	*EC*	*TLK*		*TLK*	*EIC*	*EIC*	*EIC*	*TLK*	*TLK*	*TLK*		*TLK*	*MP*	*MP*		*TLK*
		14104	**103**	**1400**	**14121**	**14150**	**131**	**54111**	**54104**	**105**	**16106**		**14102**	**1404**	**1608**	**4409**	**54101**	**14108**	**14106**		**54108**	**407**	**407**		**54201**
		14105	**14001**	**1401**	**16113**	**14151**	**14009**		**54105**	**14003**	**16107**		**14103**	**1405**	**1609**			**14109**	**14107**		**54109**	**14011**	**14011**		
				①–⑥	Ⓑ			n										Ⓑ							
			P	**y**			**B**	**d**	**o**	**S**			**b**				**D**	**w**			**Q**	**C p**	**C q**		**A**
	Gdańsk Gł. **1025** d.	...	...	...	...	...	...	...	...	...	...	...	...	...	...	...	1055	...	...	...	0736**z**	...	...	...	2223
0	**Warszawa** Wschodnia d.	0552	0557	0804	0809	0747	0943	...	1025	1132	1214	...	1419	1403	1611	...	|	1656	1802	...	1837	1956	2007	...	|
5	**Warszawa** Centralna d.	0605	0610	0829	0834	0800	0956	...	1038	1153	1245	...	1432	1417	1623	...	|	1710	1820	...	1850	2009	2020	...	|
	Łódź Kaliska d.	|	|	|	|	|	|	1015	|	|	|	...	|	|	|	...	1645	|	|	...	|	|	|	...	0420
	Koluszki d.	0741	|	|	|	0939	|	|	1212	|	1419	...	1610	|	|	...	|	1848	|	...	2022	|	|	...	|
	Piotrków Trybunalski d.	0809	|	|	|	1008	|	1117	1254	|	1447	...	1638	|	|	...	1749	1916	|	...	2052	|	|	...	0529
	Częstochowa d.	0930	|	|	|	1128	|	1241	1415	|	1610	...	1804	|	|	...	1924	2046	|	...	2228	|	|	...	0701
259	Zawiercie d.	1003	0840	1059	1121	...	1241	1322	1450	1426	1643	...	1840	1702	1910	...	1957	...	2105	...	2303	2258	2305	...	0736
294	Sosnowiec Gł. d.	1039	0912	1132	1156	...	1311	1354	1522	1456	1717	...	1915	1736	1944	...	2033	...	2141	...	2342	2335	2338	...	0813
302	**Katowice** a.	1049	0921	1142	1205	...	1320	1404	1531	1505	1727	...	1925	1754	1954	...	2043	...	2151	...	2352	2345	2353	...	0823
302	**Katowice** **1075** d.	...	...	1145	1210	...	...	...	1536	...	...	...	...	1749	2006	2021	...	...	2156	...	...	...	...	...	0828
347	Rybnik ▷ a.	...	...	|	|	...	...	...	|	...	...	...	...	|	|	|	...	...	2310	...	...	...	...	...	|
319	Tychy ▷ d.	...	...	1205	|	...	...	...	1556	...	...	...	...	1809	|	2040	...	...	...	...	...	...	...	...	0849
357	**Bielsko Biała** ▷ a.	...	...	1243	|	...	...	...	1634	...	...	...	...	1847	|	2106	...	...	...	...	...	...	...	...	0930
330	Gliwice **1075** d.	...	...	...	1240	...	...	...	...	...	...	...	...	...	2038	...	...	...	...	...	...	...	...	...	...
410	Opole Gł **1075** d.	...	...	...	...	...	...	...	...	...	...	...	...	...	2159	...	...	...	...	...	...	...	...	...	...
492	**Wrocław** Gł. **1075** a.	...	...	...	...	...	...	...	...	...	...	...	...	...	2245	...	...	...	...	...	...	...	...	...	...

	TLK	*MP*		*EIC*	*TLK*		*EIC*	*TLK*	*TLK*	*TLK*	*TLK*	*EC*	*TLK*	*EC*		*TLK*	*EIC*	*TLK*		*EC*	*TLK*		*TLK*	*EIC*	
	41100	**406**		**4104**	**45108**		**6108**	**45100**	**41106**	**61106**	**45104**	**104**	**41102**	**130**		**45110**	**4100**	**41104**		**102**	**41150**		**45200**	**6106**	
	41110	**41010**			**45109**		**6109**		**41107**			**41002**		**41008**			**4101**	**41152**		**41000**	**41151**			**6107**	
	①–⑥															m	Ⓑ				⑦			⑦	
	y	**C**			**Q**		**y**	**D**			**o**	**S**	**b**	**B**		**d**	**w**			**P**			**A**		
Wrocław Gł. **1075** d.	...	...	...	...	...	...	0556	...	...	...	...	...	...	...	...	...	...	...	...	...	...	...	...	1716	...
Opole Gł. **1075** d.	...	...	...	...	...	...	0645	...	...	...	...	...	...	...	...	...	...	...	...	...	...	...	...	1804	...
Gliwice **1075** d.	...	...	...	...	...	...	0757	...	...	...	...	...	...	...	...	...	...	...	...	...	...	...	...	1916	...
Bielsko Biała ▷ d.	...	...	...	0504	...	...	|	...	...	...	1029	...	...	...	...	...	1525	...	...	...	...	...	1858	|	...
Tychy ▷ d.	...	...	...	0543	...	...	|	...	...	...	1110	...	...	...	...	...	1604	...	...	...	...	...	1940	|	...
Rybnik ▷ d.	...	...	...	|	...	...	|	...	0825	...	|	...	...	...	...	...	|	...	...	...	...	...	|	|	...
Katowice **1075** a.	...	...	...	0558	...	...	0827	...	0938	...	1125	...	...	...	...	...	1619	...	...	...	...	...	1955	2008	...
Katowice d.	...	0414	...	0601	0521	...	0830	0838	0942	1010	1130	1236	1306	1436	...	1611	1622	1705	...	1831	...	...	2000	2013	...
Sosnowiec Gł. d.	...	0426	...	0612	0532	...	0841	0849	0953	1021	1141	1247	1317	1447	...	1622	1633	1715	...	1842	...	...	2012	2024	...
Zawiercie d.	...	0501	...	0647	0618	...	0913	0922	1032	1057	1215	1321	1354	1521	...	1659	1707	1752	...	1914	...	...	2052	2101	...
Częstochowa d.	0512	|	...	|	0655	...	|	0956	|	1145	1248	|	1429	|	...	1733	|	1828	...	|	1951	...	2128	|	...
Piotrków Trybunalski d.	0650	|	...	|	0824	...	|	1125	|	1320	1415	|	1607	|	...	1921	|	2003	...	|	2123	...	2300	|	...
Koluszki d.	0721	|	...	|	0858	...	|	|	|	1349	1454	|	1641	|	...	|	|	2036	...	|	2152	...	|	|	...
Łódź Kaliska a.	|	|	...	|	|	...	|	1230	|	|	|	|	|	|	...	2038	|	|	...	|	|	...	0006	|	...
Warszawa Centralna a.	0857**g**	0805**g**	...	0923	1038**g**	...	1145	|	1317	1525**g**	1631**g**	1609**g**	1825**g**	1817**g**	...	...	1955	2222**g**	...	2155	2323	...	|	2333	...
Warszawa Wschodnia a.	...	...	...	...	|	...	1158	|	1332	...	...	...	...	...	...	...	2034	...	...	2207	2336	...	|	2345	...
Gdańsk Gł. **1025** a.	...	...	...	...	2121**z**	...	...	1804	...	...	...	...	...	...	...	...	...	...	...	...	...	...	0541	...	...

A – 🛏 1, 2 cl., 🛏 2 cl., [12] (Hel △) - Gdynia - Gdańsk - Katowice - Bielsko Biała and v.v.
B – VARSOVIA – [12] ✕ Warszawa - Budapest and v.v.
C – CHOPIN – 🛏 1, 2 cl., 🛏 2 cl., [2] Warszawa - Bratislava / Budapest / Praha / Wien and v.v.
D – [12] (Hel △) - Gdynia - Gdańsk - Bydgoszcz - Łódz - Katowice and v.v. (Table **1025**).
P – POLONIA – [12] ✕ Warszawa - Wien - Villach and v.v.
Q – [12] Gdynia - Gdańsk - Olsztyn - Ełk - Białystok - Warszawa - Częstochowa - Katowice and v.v.
S – SOBIESKI – [12] ✕ Warszawa - Wien and v.v.

b – From / to Białystok (Table **1040**).
d – From / to Bydgoszcz (Table **1025**).
g – Warszawa **Gdańska**.
m – ⑤⑦ (also Apr. 30; not May 2).
n – ①⑥ (also May 1; not May 3).
o – From / to Olsztyn (Table **1030**).
p – Until June 13.
q – From June 14.
w – Not May 1, 2.
y – Not May 2, 3.
z – Via Białystok and Olsztyn (Table **1035**).
△ – Runs to / from Hel on dates in Table **1025**.
▷ – For local trains Katowice - Bielsko Biała and Rybnik see Tables **1077 / 79**.

ŁÓDŹ - KRAKÓW 1062

km		*TLK*				*TLK*				*TLK*
		73105				**53103**				**83107**
		p y		✣		**g z**	✣	✣		**s y**
0	**Łódź** Kaliska **1060** d.	0848	...	1028	...	1404	1551	1715	...	2019
7	Łódź Chojny d.	0857	...	1038	...	1414	1601	1725	...	2029
59	Tomaszów Mazowieki d.	0948	...	|	...	|	|	|	...	2118
67	Piotrków Trybunalski **1060** d.	|	...	1204	...	1506	1732	1848	...	|
153	**Częstochowa** **1060** d.	|	...	1342	...	1647	1916	2039	...	|
•299	**Kraków** Gł. a.	1214	...	...	...	1859	...	...	...	2343

			TLK		*TLK*		*TLK*		
			38106		**35102**		**37104**		
	✣		**s y**		**g**		**p y**		
Kraków Gł. d.	...	...	0736	...	1216	...	1518	...	...
Częstochowa d.	0459	...	|	...	1413	...	|	...	...
Piotrków Trybunalski d.	0657	...	|	...	1602**r**	...	|	...	...
Tomaszów Mazowieki d.	|	...	1013	...	|	...	1748	...	...
Łódź Chojny a.	0818	...	1101	...	1654	...	1836	...	...
Łódź Kaliska a.	0828	...	1109	...	1704	...	1844	...	...

– To / from Gdynia via Gdańsk (Table **1025**).
– To / from Poznań (Table **1025**).
– 16 - 20 minutes earlier from June 1.
– To / from Szczecin via Poznań (Tables **1010 / 25**).
y – Not June 7, 8.
z – Runs 10 - 20 minutes later from June 1.
✣ – Subject to confirmation.
• – *273 km* via Tomaszów Mazowieki.

WARSZAWA - KRAKÓW 1065

Via CMK high-speed line (ticketing route is via Idzikowice). For trains via Kielce (including night trains) see Table **1067**.

km		*TLK*		*EIC*		*EIC*		*TLK*		*EIC*		*EIC*		*EIC*	*EIC*		*EIC*		*IR*	*TLK*		*EIC*	
		13100		**1300**		**1312**		**13104**		**131**		**5304**		**1302**	**1310**		**1304**		**13122**	**83108**		**1318**	
		13101		**1301**		**1313**		**13105**		**1315**		**5305**		**1303**	**1311**		**1305**		**13123**	**83109**		**1319**	
				①–⑤						①–⑤				Ⓑ								Ⓑ	
				y						**y**		**n**		**y**	**M**					**k**		**y**	
	Gdańsk Gł. **1030** d.	...	...	...	...	...	...	...	...	...	...	0805	...	...	...	...	...	...	...	1334	...	...	...
0	**Warszawa** Wschodnia d.	0422	...	0602	...	0759	...	0948	...	1032	...	1209	...	1606	1616	...	1757	...	1807	1817	...	2002	...
5	**Warszawa** Centralna d.	0435	...	0615	...	0824	...	1005	...	1048	...	1235	...	1619	1629	...	1815	...	1825	1845	...	2015	...
297	**Kraków** Gł. a.	0801**z**	...	0921**z**	...	1127	...	1347**z**	...	1419	...	1542	...	1929	1953	...	2124	...	2149	2245	...	2325	...

	TLK	*EIC*		*IR*		*EIC*		*EIC*		*TLK*		*EIC*		*EIC*		*EIC*	*EIC*		*EIC*		*TLK*		*EIC*
	38108	**3102**		**31120**		**3104**		**35100**		**31104**		**3504**		**3108**		**3100**	**3138**		**3114**		**31100**		**3112**
				31121		**3105**		**35101**				**3505**				**3101**	**3139**		**3115**		**31101**		**3113**
		①–⑤												①–⑤		Ⓑ	⑥						
	k	**y**		**w**								**n**		**y**		**y**	**w**						**M**
Kraków Gł. d.	0532	0615	...	0705	...	0830	...	1005	...	1150	...	1355	...	1436	...	1609**x**	1609**x**	...	1824	...	1931	...	2030
Warszawa Centralna a.	0919**g**	0928	...	1051	...	1140	...	1336	...	1532**g**	...	1715	...	1758	...	1916	1916	...	2145	...	2314	...	2337
Warszawa Wschodnia a.	|	...	...	1108	...	1153	...	1359	...	...	...	1728	...	...	...	1929	1929	...	2157	...	2328	...	2350
Gdańsk Gł. **1030** a.	1350	...	...	...	...	...	...	...	...	...	...	2132	...	...	...	...	...	...	...	...	...	...	...

– ⑤⑦ (also Apr. 30; not May 2).
– Warszawa **Gdańska**.
– To / from Kołobrzeg (Table **1015**).
– To / from Gdynia (Table **1030**).
w – Also May 1; not May 3.
x – Depart 1548 from June 2.
y – Not May 1, 2.
z – Arrive 6 – 13 minutes later from June 5.

1066 KRAKÓW and KATOWICE - ZAKOPANE

Services are subject to partial 🚌 replacement. Timings may vary

km				*TLK*		*TLK*				*IR*		*IR*		*EIC*			*TLK*					
				33109		**33107**				**43126**		**63126**		**3301**			**33101**					
										43127		**63127**										
		🚌	◇	🚌		🚌		◇						🚌	◇		🚌		◇	◇	◇	
		①–⑥	Z	m		m				n		p					⑥q					
	Warszawa Cent **1065 1067** d.	...	...	...	...	...	...	...	...	...	...	...	...	...	...	...	...	...	...	...	...	...
	Katowice d.	...	...	...	...	...	...	...	...	0815	...	...	...	...	...	...	...	...	...	...	...	...
	Bielsko Biała d.	...	...	...	...	...	...	...	...	0913	...	...	...	...	...	...	...	...	...	...	...	...
0	**Kraków** Gł. d.	...	0512	0525	...	0645	...	0747	...	|	...	...	...	1145	1220	...	1415	...	1550	1638	1900	...
5	Kraków Płaszów d.	...	0529	|	...	|	...	0806	...	|	...	...	...	|	1238	...	|	...	1608	1655	1917	...
68	Sucha Beskidzka d.	0415	0716	|	...	|	...	0951	...	1104	...	1158	...	|	⊖	...	|	...	1752	⊖	2112	...
103	Chabówka a.	⊖	...	|	...	|	...	...	...	1144	...	1239	...	|	⊖	...	|	...	...	⊖	...	...
105	Rabka Zdroj d.	⊖	...	0640	...	0800	...	...	...	1158	...	1253	...	1300	⊖	...	1530	...	...	⊖	...	...
103	Chabówka d.	⊖	...	|	...	|	...	...	...	1202	...	1257	...	|	⊖	...	|	...	...	⊖	...	...
126	Nowy Targ d.	⊖	...	0706	...	0826	...	...	...	1230	...	1326	...	1325	⊖	...	1555	...	...	⊖	...	...
147	**Zakopane** a.	0650	...	0810	...	0930	...	...	...	1254	...	1349	...	1430	1722	...	1700	...	...	2145	...	...

					TLK						*EIC*				*IR*		*IR*		*TLK*		*TLK*	
					33110						**3302**				**36126**		**34126**		**33116**		**33118**	
															36127		**34127**					
	◇	◇	◇		🚌		◇	◇	◇		🚌		◇						🚌		🚌	
			①–⑥		⑦r			Z					⑧		n		p		m		m	
Zakopane d.	...	...	0415	...	0845	...	...	...	1340	...	1520	...	1604	...	1620	...	1620	...	1905	...	2240	...
Nowy Targ d.	...	...	⊖	...	0948	...	...	...	⊖	...	1623	...	⊖	...	1642	...	1642	...	2010	...	2310	...
Chabówka a.	...	...	⊖	...	|	...	...	...	⊖	...	|	...	⊖	...	1709	...	1709	...	|	...	|	...
Rabka Zdroj d.	...	...	⊖	...	1015	...	...	...	⊖	...	1650	...	⊖	...	1723	...	1723	...	2035	...	2343	...
Chabówka d.	...	...	⊖	...	|	...	...	...	⊖	...	|	...	⊖	...	1728	...	1728	...	|	...	|	...
Sucha Beskidzka d.	0354	0531	⊖	...	|	...	1052	1400	⊖	...	|	...	⊖	...	1809	...	1809	...	|	...	|	...
Kraków Płaszów a.	0537	0714	0907	...	|	...	1236	1545	1821	...	|	...	2048	...	|	...	|	...	|	...	|	...
Kraków Gł. a.	0555	0735	0924	...	1130	...	1254	1603	1841	...	1805	...	2106	...	|	...	|	...	2150	...	0125	...
Bielsko Biała a.	...	...	...	...	...	...	...	...	...	...	...	...	...	...	2001	...	2001	...	...	...	...	...
Katowice a.	...	...	...	...	...	...	...	...	...	...	...	...	...	...	2057	...	2057	...	...	...	...	...
Warszawa Cent **1065 1067** a.	...	...	...	...	...	...	...	...	...	...	...	...	...	...	...	...	...	...	...	...	...	...

Z – ①–⑤ (not May 1, 2).
m – May 1, 4 only.
n – May 1, 3 only.
p – May 2, 4 only.

q – Also May 1.
r – Also May 2.
y – Not May 1, 2.

◇ – Subject to partial bus replacement.
⊖ – Timings unknown.

1067 WARSZAWA and LUBLIN - KIELCE - KRAKÓW

km	*For fast trains to Kraków see Table* **1065**		*TLK*		*TLK*			*TLK*				*TLK*		*IR*			*TLK*	*TLK*		*TLK*		*TLK*	
			23100		**83203**			**26102**				**13107**		**26101**			**12109**	**23103**		**12111**		**13261**	
			23101					**26103**						**26123**						⑧		⑤	
					k															m		Gp	
0	**Warszawa** Wschodnia d.	...	...	...	...	...	...	...	...	...	...	1200	...	...	...	...	1600	...	...	2000	...	2357x	...
4	**Warszawa** Centralna d.	...	...	...	...	...	...	...	...	...	...	|	...	...	...	...	|	...	...	|	...	2335	...
•	**Lublin** d.	...	0514	...	...	...	...	0814	...	...	...	|	...	1415	...	...	|	1650	...	|	...	|	...
107	Radom d.	...	0639	...	0820	...	...	0943	...	...	...	1407	...	1546	...	...	1759	1816	...	2201	...	0203	...
148	Skarżysko Kamienna **1058** d.	0603	0706	...	0848	...	...	1013	...	...	...	1435	...	1616	1741	...	1826	1843	...	2230	...	0232	...
192	Kielce d.	0656	0747	...	0938	1024	...	1107	...	1334	1431	1518	...	1721	1833	...	1913	1924	...	2311	...	0312	...
	Katowice a.	|	|	...	|	|	...	1330	...	1741	|	|	...	1931	|	...	...	|	...	...	...	|	...
	Wrocław Gł **1075** a.	|	|	...	|	|	...	1632	...	...	|	|	...	2234	|	...	...	|	...	...	...	|	...
324	**Kraków** Gł. a.	0911	0943	...	1140	1244	...	...	...	...	1652	1715	...	...	2053	...	...	2113	...	...	...	0503	...
	Zakopane **1066** a.	...	...	...	...	...	...	...	...	...	...	...	...	...	...	...	...	...	...	...	...	...	...

	TLK	*TLK*		*TLK*			*IR*					*TLK*		*TLK*			*TLK*	*TLK*				*TLK*	
	21108	**32102**		**21110**			**62120**					**62102**		**31106**			**32100**	**38202**				**31260**	
												62103		**31107**			**32101**	**38203**				①	
				n														k				Gq	
Zakopane **1066** d.	...	...	...	...	...	...	...	...	...	...	...	...	...	...	...	...	...	...	...	...	...	...	...
Kraków Gł. d.	...	0637	0713	...	...	...	...	...	1052	...	...	...	...	1445	1453	...	1631	1719	...	1901	...	0154	...
Wrocław Gł **1075** d.	...	|	|	...	...	...	0627	...	|	...	...	1024	...	|	|	...	|	|	...	|	...	|	...
Katowice d.	...	|	|	...	...	0726	0921	...	|	...	1114	1314	...	|	|	...	|	|	...	|	...	|	...
Kielce d.	0620	0829	0928	1023	...	1114	1148	...	1309	...	1459	1539	...	1633	1710	...	1825	1915	...	2116	...	0336	...
Skarżysko Kamienna **1058** d.	0703	0913	...	1110	...	...	1232	...	...	...	...	1620	...	1713	...	...	1907	1959	...	...	...	0416	...
Radom d.	0729	0939	...	1136	...	...	1239	...	...	...	...	1650	...	1738	...	...	1932	2027	...	...	...	0444	...
Lublin a.	|	1122	...	|	...	...	1426	...	...	...	...	1821	...	|	...	...	2056	|	...	...	...	|	...
Warszawa Centralna a.	|	...	...	|	...	...	...	...	...	...	...	...	...	|	...	...	...	2240	...	...	...	|	...
Warszawa Wschodnia a.	0934	...	...	1346	...	...	...	...	...	...	...	...	...	1935	...	...	...	2230z	...	...	...	0713	...

G – 🛏 1, 2 cl., ▬ 2 cl., (2) Warszawa - Kraków and v.v.; 🛏 1, 2 cl., ▬ 2 cl., (2) Warszawa - Kraków - Krynica and v.v.

k – To / from Kołobrzeg (Table **1015**).
m – Not May 1, 2.
n – Not May 2, 3.
p – Also Apr. 30; not May 2).
q – Also May 2.

x – Calls at Warszawa Centralna before Wschodnia.
z – Calls at Warszawa Wschodnia before Centralna.
* – Estimated time.
• – Lublin - Radom: *128 km*.

1070 POZNAŃ - WROCŁAW

km		*TLK*	*TLK*		*TLK*			*TLK*		*EIC*	*TLK*			*TLK*	*IR*		*TLK*	*TLK*		*EIC*	*TLK*			*TLK*
		83204	**56201**		**73102**			**56103**		**1601**	**83100**			**76110**	**56111**		**83102**	**56107**		**1603**	**86100**			**5610**[illegible]
		83205	**56200**		**73103**			**56102**		**1600**	**83101**				**56110**		**83103**	**56106**		**1602**				**5610**[illegible]
		A	J		P	j		K		R	C			R	B		M	KT		R	Ts			K
	Warszawa Cent. **1001** ... ◧ d.	...	...	...	...	...	...	...	...	0745	...	...	...	...	...	...	...	...	...	1554	...	...	...	...
0	**Poznań** Gł. d.	0154	0247	...	0629	0643	...	0928	0937	1028	1040	1057	...	1230	1336	...	1431	1702	...	1829	1838	1929	...	2020
69	Leszno d.	△	△	...	0742	0805	...	1035	1058	1131	1151	1225	...	1337	1448	...	1539	1809	...	1932	1954	2050	...	2129
165	**Wrocław** Gł. a.	0507	0617	...	0917	0957	...	1214	1243	1257	1336	1425	...	1509	1643	...	1726	1951	...	2056	2134	2237	...	2302

	EIC		*TLK*		*TLK*		*TLK*		*TLK*		*IR*	*TLK*			*EIC*	*TLK*		*TLK*			*TLK*		*TLK*	*TLK*
	6103		**68101**		**65101**		**65107**		**38102**		**65110**	**65103**			**6101**	**38100**		**37102**			**67111**		**38204**	**6520**[illegible]
	6102				**65100**		**65106**		**38103**		**65111**	**65102**			**6100**	**38101**		**37103**					**38205**	**6520**[illegible]
	Q		Rs		K		KR		M		B	K			T	C		P	j		T		A	J
Wrocław Gł. d.	0353	...	0514	0520	0633	...	0919	...	1138	...	1259	1340	...	1427	1511	1603	...	1723	1838	...	2018	...	2341	2354
Leszno d.	0517	...	0706	0745	0813	...	1059	...	1312	...	1444	1519	...	1646	1637	1744	...	1858	2027	...	2158	...	△	△
Poznań Gł. a.	0627	...	0826	0915	0926	...	1217	...	1426	...	1610	1640	...	1821	1747	1908	...	2016	2203	...	2313	...	0313	0351
Warszawa Cent. **1001** .. ◧ a.	0906	...	...	...	...	...	...	...	...	...	...	...	...	...	2027	...	...	...	...	...	...	...	...	...

A – 🛏 1, 2 cl., ▬ 2 cl., (2) Szczecin - Poznań - Wrocław - Katowice - Kraków and v.v. (Table **1075**).
B – (2) Olsztyn - Poznań - Wrocław - Jelenia Góra and v.v.
C – (12) Szczecin - Poznań - Kraków and v.v.
J – 🛏 1, 2 cl., ▬ 2 cl., (12) Gdynia - Wrocław and v.v. (Table **1020**).
K – (12) Gdynia - Poznań - Wrocław and v.v. (Table **1020**).
M – (12) Kraków - Katowice - Wrocław - Poznań - Kołobrzeg and v.v.

P – (12) Poznań - Wrocław - Katowice - Kraków and v.v. (Table **1075**).
Q – ①–⑤ (not May 1, 2).
R – ①–⑥ (not May 2, 3).
T – ⑧ (not May 1, 2).

j – To / from Jelenia Góra (Table **1084**).
s – To / from Szczecin.

▽ – Via Jarocin (Table **1080**).
△ – Via Ostrów Wlkp.
◧ – For other trains Warszawa - Wrocław see Table **1090**.

RZESZÓW - JASŁO - ZAGÓRZ 1073

Service until Mar. 31

km			Ⓑ	①–⑤		Ⓑ				
0	**Rzeszów** d.	...	0457	...	...	...	...	1550	...	...
9	Boguchwała d.	...	0510	...	...	...	...	1603	...	...
71	**Jasło** d.	...	0639	0705	...	1507	...	1728	...	...
94	Krosno d.	...	...	0737	...	1539	...	...	...	...
133	Sanok d.	...	...	0843	...	1644	...	...	...	...
139	Nowy Zagórz a.	...	...	0851	...	1652	...	...	...	...
140	**Zagórz** a.	...	...	0854	...	1655	...	...	...	...

	①–⑤	⑥⑦		①–⑥		①–⑤	Ⓑ		
Zagórz d.	...	...	...	0507	...	1306	...	...	...
Nowy Zagórz d.	...	...	...	0510	...	1309	...	...	...
Sanok d.	...	...	...	0518	...	1317	...	...	...
Krosno d.	...	...	...	0622	...	1422	...	...	...
Jasło d.	0448	0523	...	0655	...	1455	1513	...	...
Boguchwała d.	0611	0656	...	...	...	...	1640	...	...
Rzeszów a.	0625	0710	...	...	...	...	1654	...	...

WROCŁAW - KATOWICE - KRAKÓW - PRZEMYŚL 1075

For other trains Poznań - Katowice / Kraków see Tables **1080** (via Ostrów Wlkp) and **1025** (via Łódź)

km		①–⑥				TLK 83261 Bt					TLK 83204 W E	TLK 63106 R	IR 62120 w		TLK 33207	TLK 63104 63105		IR 63120		TLK 73102 73103		TLK 62102 62103 w			TLK 53109
	Świnoujście **1010** d.	...	...	...	...	1703	...	...	...	...	...	...	...	...	...	...	...	...	...	...	...	...	...	...	...
	Szczecin Gł. **1010** d.	...	...	...	...	1927	...	...	...	...	2300	...	...	...	...	...	...	...	...	...	...	...	...	...	...
	Poznań Gł. **1070** d.	...	...	...	...	2235	...	...	...	...	0154	...	...	...	...	...	...	...	...	0629	...	...	...	...	...
0	**Wrocław** Gł. **1060** d.	...	...	...	...	|	...	...	...	...	0522	0522	0627	...	...	0710	...	0836	...	0927	...	1024	...	...	...
42	Brzeg d.	...	...	...	...	◐	...	...	...	...	0601	0601	0704	...	...	0744	...	0909	...	1000	...	1059	...	...	...
82	Opole Gł. **1060** d.	...	...	...	...	|	...	...	...	...	0628	0628	0729	...	...	0809	...	0937	...	1026	...	1124	...	...	...
162	Gliwice **1060** d.	...	...	...	...	|	...	...	...	...	0749	0749	0845	...	...	0933	...	1049	...	1143	...	1239	...	...	...
190	**Katowice** **1060** a.	...	...	...	...	0406	...	...	...	...	0821	0821	0916	...	...	1003	...	1123	...	1213	...	1309	...	...	...
190	**Katowice** d.	...	...	...	...	0416	0511	...	...	0735	0826	0826	...	...	...	1008	...	1126	...	1218	...	...	...	...	...
268	**Kraków** Gł. a.	...	...	...	...	0626	0721	...	...	0951	1051	1051	...	...	...	1215	...	1325	...	1425	...	...	...	...	...
268	**Kraków** Gł. **1078** d.	...	...	...	...	0740	0724	0751	...	...	...	...	...	...	1140	1303	...	...	...	1453	...	...	1518	...	...
273	Kraków Płaszów **1078** d.	...	...	...	...	0748	0732	0757	...	...	...	...	...	...	1147	1310	...	...	...	1459	...	...	1525	...	...
346	Tarnów **1078** d.	0430	0538	...	0755	0936	...	0941	...	...	...	...	...	...	1324	1455	...	...	...	1637	1712	...	1735	...	...
379	Dębica d.	0526	0626	...	0847	1021	...	1026	...	...	...	...	...	...	1419	1538	...	...	...	1719	1807	...	1844	...	...
426	**Rzeszów** **1058** d.	0623	0726	0730	0946	1116	...	1124	1245	...	...	...	...	1450	1517	1630	...	...	1656	1811	1906	...	1943	2002	2105
463	Przeworsk **1058** d.	0701	...	0808	1024	1143	...	...	1323	...	...	...	...	1527	1543	1659	...	...	1742	...	1945	...	...	2041	2131
478	Jarosław **1058** d.	0714	...	0822	1043	1156	...	...	1337	...	...	...	...	1540	1555	1713	...	...	1755	...	1959	...	...	2055	2143
•	Zamość a.	|	...	|	|	|	...	...	|	...	...	...	...	|	|	|	...	...	|	...	|	...	...	|	|
513	**Przemyśl** **1058** a.	0812	...	0914	1135	1256	...	...	1428	...	...	...	...	1630	1634	1753	...	...	1846	...	2055	...	...	2146	2229

			TLK 33101 Ⓑ d	TLK 83100 83101	TLK 63102 63103 Ⓑd	TLK 33105 Zx		IR 64104 64120 ⑤⑦v	TLK 83102 83103 k	IR 64122 ⑤⑦ .q	TLK 64100
Świnoujście **1010** d.	...	...	...	...	...	...	...	...	...	...	...
Szczecin Gł. **1010** d.	...	...	...	0742	...	...	...	...	...	...	...
Poznań Gł. **1070** d.	...	...	...	1040	...	...	...	...	1431	...	...
Wrocław Gł. **1060** d.	...	...	...	1339	1524	...	...	1638	1729	1822	1927
Brzeg d.	...	...	...	1414	1601	...	...	1714	1803	1856	2001
Opole Gł. **1060** d.	...	...	...	1439	1629	...	...	1741	1830	1923	2028
Gliwice **1060** d.	...	...	...	1554	1746	...	...	1854	1951	2044	2144
Katowice **1060** a.	...	...	...	1626	1817	...	...	1925	2020	2114	2216
Katowice d.	...	1544	...	1633	1822	...	1912	...	2030	...	...
Kraków Gł. a.	...	1802	...	1848	2034	...	2141	...	2235	...	...
Kraków Gł. **1078** d.	1700	...	1816	1920	...	2059	...	...	...	...	...
Kraków Płaszów **1078** d.	1708	...	1824	1928	...	2107	...	...	...	...	...
Tarnów **1078** d.	1917	...	2010	2105	...	2250	...	...	...	...	...
Dębica d.	2015	...	2058	2152	...	2334	...	...	...	...	...
Rzeszów **1058** d.	2110	...	2154	2247	...	0031	...	...	...	...	...
Przeworsk **1058** d.	...	...	2221	2314	...	0058	...	...	...	...	...
Jarosław **1058** d.	...	...	2239	2327	...	0110	...	...	...	...	...
Zamość a.	...	...	|	|	...	|	...	...	...	...	...
Przemyśl **1058** a.	...	...	2322	0010	...	0158	...	...	...	...	...

	IR 46121 ①⑥ u		TLK 46101	TLK 38102 38103 k	TLK 33114 Z	TLK 33110 ①–⑥ y			TLK 38100 38101
Przemyśl **1058** d.	...	...	...	...	0211	0328	...	...	0454
Zamość d.	...	...	...	...	|	|	...	...	|
Jarosław **1058** d.	...	...	...	...	0257	0413	...	...	0539
Przeworsk **1058** d.	...	...	...	...	0310	0425	...	...	0552
Rzeszów **1058** d.	...	...	...	...	0344	0457	...	0515	0625
Dębica d.	...	...	...	...	0440	0549	...	0626	0719
Tarnów **1078** d.	...	...	...	...	0529	0637	...	0726	0823
Kraków Płaszów **1078** d.	...	...	...	...	0709	0808	...	0938	1014
Kraków Gł. **1078** a.	...	...	...	...	0716	0814	...	0946	1020
Kraków Gł. d.	...	0332	...	0617	...	...	0938	...	1040
Katowice a.	...	0543	...	0827	...	...	1156	...	1247
Katowice **1060** d.	0510	...	0628	0831	...	...	...	...	1253
Gliwice **1060** d.	0613	...	0659	0904	...	...	...	...	1330
Opole Gł. **1060** d.	0739	...	0819	1031	...	...	...	...	1453
Brzeg d.	0804	...	0843	1056	...	...	...	...	1518
Wrocław Gł. **1060** a.	0839	...	0928	1131	...	...	...	...	1555
Poznań Gł. **1070** a.	...	...	...	1426	...	...	...	...	1908
Szczecin Gł. **1010** a.	...	...	...	...	...	...	...	...	2152
Świnoujście **1010** a.	...	...	...	...	...	...	...	...	...

	TLK 35108	TLK 26102 26103 w	TLK 37102 37103		IR 36120 36121			TLK 36104 36105	TLK 36101 Ⓑd		IR 26101 26123 w		TLK 33204	TLK 38205 T E	TLK 36107 S					TLK 38260 38261 C					
Przemyśl **1058** d.	0502	...	...	...	...	0730	...	0956	...	...	...	...	1126	...	...	1212	1330	...	...	1626	...	1745	...	1921	2147
Zamość d.	|	...	...	...	...	|	...	|	...	...	...	...	|	...	...	|	|	...	...	|	...	|	...	|	|
Jarosław **1058** d.	0545	...	...	...	...	0825	...	1041	...	...	...	...	1209	...	...	1302	1420	...	...	1713	...	1836	...	2011	2237
Przeworsk **1058** d.	0557	...	...	...	...	0838	...	1053	...	...	...	...	1221	...	...	1315	1434	...	...	1727	...	1848	...	2025	2251
Rzeszów **1058** d.	0626	...	0805	...	...	0919	...	1124	...	...	...	1202	1252	...	...	1413	1526	...	1705	1803	...	1925	1940	2105	...
Dębica d.	...	...	0903	...	...	...	...	1216	...	...	...	1259	1344	...	...	1511	1643	...	1809	1903	...	...	2038	...	...
Tarnów **1078** d.	...	...	1003	...	...	...	...	1301	...	...	...	1345	1431	...	...	1612	1733	...	1858	1957	...	...	2134	...	...
Kraków Płaszów **1078** d.	...	...	1136	...	...	...	...	1443	...	...	...	1536	1630	...	...	...	...	...	2114	2145	...	...	2338	...	...
Kraków Gł. **1078** a.	...	...	1142	...	...	...	...	1449	...	...	...	1543	1637	...	...	...	...	...	2122	2152	...	...	2346	...	...
Kraków Gł. d.	...	...	1210	1348	1408	...	...	1516	1611	1622	...	...	...	1754	1754	...	...	2045	...	2210	...	...	...	...	...
Katowice a.	...	...	1413	1559	1616	...	...	1722	1817	1836	...	...	...	2007	2007	...	...	2257	...	0023	...	...	...	...	...
Katowice **1060** d.	...	1337	1418	...	1626	...	...	1732	1830	...	1936	...	...	2012	2012	...	...	...	...	0026	...	...	...	...	...
Gliwice **1060** d.	...	1408	1450	...	1658	...	...	1802	1902	...	2010	...	...	2047	2047	...	...	...	...	|	...	...	...	...	...
Opole Gł. **1060** d.	...	1530	1612	...	1820	...	...	1926	2030	...	2134	...	...	2215	2215	...	...	...	...	|	...	...	...	...	...
Brzeg d.	...	1555	1638	...	1845	...	...	1950	2056	...	2159	...	...	2242	2242	...	...	...	...	◐	...	...	...	...	...
Wrocław Gł. **1060** a.	...	1632	1714	...	1921	...	...	2027	2140	...	2234	...	...	2320	2320	...	...	...	...	|	...	...	...	...	...
Poznań Gł. **1070** a.	...	...	2016	...	...	...	...	...	...	...	...	...	...	0313	...	...	...	...	...	0621	...	...	...	...	...
Szczecin Gł. **1010** a.	...	...	...	...	...	...	...	...	...	...	...	...	...	0641	...	...	...	...	...	0917	...	...	...	...	...
Świnoujście **1010** a.	...	...	...	...	...	...	...	...	...	...	...	...	...	...	...	...	...	...	...	1149	...	...	...	...	...

B – 🛏 1, 2 cl., 🛌 2 cl., 🚃 Świnoujście - Szczecin - Poznań - Przemyśl.
C – 🛏 1, 2 cl., 🛌 2 cl., 🚃 Przemyśl - Poznań - Szczecin - Świnoujście. Timings may vary on certain dates.
E – 🛏 1, 2 cl., 🛌 2 cl., 🚃 Szczecin - Poznań - Wrocław - Katowice - Kraków and v.v.
G – Runs on uneven dates in Apr., May; even dates in June.
H – Runs on even dates in Apr., May; uneven dates in June.
L – LVIV EXPRESS – 🛏 2 cl. Kraków (**33105**) - Przemyśl (**35/51**) - Lviv.
M – LVIV EXPRESS – 🛏 2 cl. Lviv (**52/36**) - Przemyśl (**33114**) - Kraków.
R – ②③④⑤⑦ May 6 - June 1 (also Apr. 27, 29, 30).
S – ①②③④⑥ May 5 - 31 (also Apr. 28, 29).
T – ⑤⑦ (also Apr. 30, May 1 - 3, June 2 - 12, 14; not June 6, 8). Train number **38207/38209** on May 1 - 3, June 3 - 12, 14.
W – ⑤⑦ (also Apr. 30, May 1 - 3, June 2 - 13). Train number **83206** on May 1 - 4, June 3 - 14.
Z – Conveys 🛏 2 cl. Kraków - Przemyśl - Lviv and v.v. (see panel on right).

d – Not May 1, 2.
k – From / to Kołobrzeg (Table **1015**).
q – Also Apr. 30.
t – Not May 26.
u – Also May 1; not May 3.
v – Also Apr. 30; not May 2.

w – To / from Lublin (Table **1067**).
x – Not June 14.
y – Not May 2, 3.

• – *276 km* from Rzeszów.
◐ – Via Ostrów Wlkp. (Table **1080**).
‡ – Ukrainian (East European) time.

PRZEMYŚL - LVIV

km		33011 35 36*SH* G L	33001 51 36*SH* H L
	Kraków Gł. (see above) d.	2059	2059
0	**Przemyśl** d.	0249	0356
13	Medyka 🏛 d.	|	|
20	Mostiska II 🏛 ‡ d.	0451	0600
98	**Lviv** ‡ a.	0603	0715

	52 35*SH* 33002 H M	36 35*SH* 33012 G M
Lviv ‡ d.	2259	2359
Mostiska II 🏛 ‡ d.	0045	0145
Medyka 🏛 d.	|	|
Przemyśl a.	0020	0116
Kraków Gł. (see above) a.	0716	0716

1076 KATOWICE and KRAKÓW - BOHUMÍN - OSTRAVA

km		*EC* 103 ✕⁄ P	*EC* 131 ✕⁄ B	*EC* 105 ✕⁄		*MP* 407 C	*MP* 402 407 K	*MP* 407 444 S	*MP* 402 442 W	
	Warszawa Cent. **1060** d.	0610	0956	1153	...	2009	...	2009	...	...
0	**Katowice** d.	0924	1324	1524	...	2350	...	2350	...	...
•116	**Kraków** Gł. ▷ d.	|	|	|	...	|	2159	|	2159	...
•51	Oświecim ▷ d.	|	|	|	...	|	2341	|	2341	...
74	Zebrzydowice 🏛 d.	1023	1423	1623	...	0053	0102	0053	0102	...
45	Rybnik ▷ d.	|	|	|	...	|	|	|	|	...
82	Racibórz ▷ d.	|	|	|	...	|	|	|	|	...
102	Chałupki ▷ d.	|	|	|	...	|	|	|	|	...
Δ94	Bohumín 🏛 a.	1040	1440	1640	...	0111	0119	0111	0119	...
94	Bohumín 🏛 **1160** d.	1052	1452	1652	...	0210	0210	0258	0337	...
102	**Ostrava** hlavní **1160** a.	1059	1459	1659	...	0217	0217	0305	0344	...
	Praha hlavní **1160** a.	|	...	|	...	|	|	0649	0737	...
	Wien Meidling **1150** a.	1424	...	2017	...	0617	0617	...	...	...
	Wien Westbf **1150** a.	...	...	2034	...	0634	0634	...	...	...

	MP 445 406 S	*MP* 406 C	*MP* 406 403 K	*MP* 443 403 W		*EC* 104 ✕⁄	*EC* 130 ✕⁄ B	*EC* 102 ✕⁄ P	
Wien Westbf **1150** d.	...	2212	2212	...	...	...	...	...	...
Wien Meidling **1150** d.	...	2231	2231	...	...	0741	...	1331	...
Praha hlavní **1160** d.	2153	|	|	2226	...	|	...	|	...
Ostrava hlavní **1160** d.	0139	0211	0211	0217	...	1101	1301	1701	...
Bohumín 🏛 **1160** a.	0146	0219	0219	0224	...	1108	1308	1708	...
Bohumín 🏛 d.	0254	0254	0306	0306	...	1120	1320	1720	...
Chałupki ▷ d.	|	|	|	|	...	|	|	|	...
Racibórz ▷ d.	|	|	|	|	...	|	|	|	...
Rybnik ▷ d.	|	|	|	|	...	|	|	|	...
Zebrzydowice 🏛 d.	0317	0317	0326	0326	...	1138	1338	1738	...
Oświecim ▷ a.	|	|	0445	0445	...	|	|	|	...
Kraków Gł. ▷ a.	|	|	0636	0636	...	|	|	|	...
Katowice a.	0411	0411	...	...	...	1233	1433	1828	...
Warszawa Cent. **1060** a.	0805**g**	0805**g**	...	...	...	1609**g**	1817**g**	2155	...

B – From/to Budapest.
C – CHOPIN – 🛏 1, 2 cl., ▬ 2 cl., ⊏2⊐ Warszawa - Wien and v.v. Conveys 🛏 1, 2 cl., ▬ 2 cl., ⊏2⊐ Warszawa - Bratislava - Budapest and v.v.; 🛏 1, 2 cl. Moskva - Wien and v.v.
K – 🛏 1, 2 cl. Kraków - Wien and v.v. (also ▬ 2 cl. Mar. 27 - Sept. 22 from Kraków, Mar. 28 - Sept. 23 from Wien); 🛏 1, 2 cl., ▬ 2 cl. Kraków - Bratislava - Budapest and v.v.
P – POLONIA – ⊏12⊐ ✕ Warszawa - Wien - Villach and v.v.
S – 🛏 1, 2 cl., ▬ 2 cl., ⊏2⊐ Warszawa - Praha and v.v.
W – SILESIA – 🛏 1, 2 cl., ▬ 2 cl., ⊏2⊐ Kraków - Praha and v.v.

g – Warszawa **Gdańska**.
• – Distance from Zebrzydowice.
⁄ – Supplement payable.
▷ – For local trains see Tables **1079** and **1099**.
Δ – *106 km* via Chałupki.

TRAIN NAMES:
EC **104/105** SOBIESKI
EC **130/131** VARSOVIA

1077 KATOWICE - BIELSKO BIAŁA - ZWARDOŃ - ŽILINA

Koleje Śląskie, 2nd class

km			Ⓒ								①–⑥				
0	**Katowice** **1060** d.	0526	0630	0833	0952	1126	1300	1430	1541	1649	1736	1830	1930	2032	2159
17	Tychy d.	0549	0650	0856	1016	1149	1323	1453	1605	1713	1759	1853	1953	2055	2225
44	Czechowice Dziedzice d.	0616	0713	0925	1048	1217	1354	1522	1636	1745	1841	1920	2024	2124	2254
55	**Bielsko Biała** **1060** d.	0640	0732	0945	1108	1246	1414	1542	1656	1805	1901	1940	2052	2144	2314
76	Zywiec a.	0711	0801	1020	1139	1316	1452	1613	1727	1836	1932	2015	2132	2215	2346
113	**Zwardoń** a.	0827	0855	1124	1247	1420	1553	1714	1830	1943	...	2122	...	2316	0047

					D		D					Ⓒ		①–⑥	
Zwardoń d.	...	0420	0532	0623	...	0858	...	1134	1325	1440	1619	1639	1735	...	1953
Zywiec d.	0326	0520	0632	0725	0843	0958	1115	1234	1427	1548	1729	1759	1838	1953	2055
Bielsko Biała **1060** d.	0400	0554	0707	0759	0917	1037	1155	1308	1502	1627	1803	1835	1912	2036	2129
Czechowice Dziedzice d.	0422	0613	0726	0819	0937	1056	1215	1327	1522	1646	1822	1850	1931	2055	2149
Tychy d.	0450	0641	0755	0850	1010	1126	1248	1356	1553	1714	1851	1915	2000	2124	2221
Katowice **1060** a.	0509	0700	0814	0910	1030	1145	1308	1427	1613	1733	1910	1932	2019	2145	2241

					Ⓐ		
Bielsko Biała d.	...	...	1414	...	...	...	...
Czech. Dziedzice d.	0622	...	1434	...	1549	...	1745
Zebrzydowice d.	0705	...	1515	...	1639	...	1829
Cieszyn ★ a.	0738	...	1548	...	1712		1902

			Ⓐ				
Cieszyn ★ d.	0609	...	1420	...	1555	...	1720
Zebrzydowice d.	0648	...	1502	...	1634	...	1759
Czech. Dziedzice a.	0722	...	1535	...	1710	...	1834
Bielsko Biała a.	0748	...	...	...	...	...	...

A – ①–⑤ (not May 1, 8, Aug. 29, Sept. 1, 15, Nov. 17).
C – ⑥⑦ (also May 1, 8, Aug. 29, Sept. 1, 15, Nov. 17).
D – ①–⑤ (not May 1, 2).
b – Ⓑ until July 4 (not Apr. 18, 20, May 1, 8, July 6, 13, 20, 27, Aug. 3, 10, 17, 24, 29, 31, Sept. 14, Nov. 16).
★ – Cieszyn station (Poland) is situated ± 1500 metres from Český Těšín station (Czech Republic).

ZWARDÓN - ŽILINA Operator: ZSSK (Slovak Railways)

km					A	
0	**Zwardoń** 🏛 d.	0642	...	1541	1642	1950
22	Čadca **1160** a.	0726	...	1626	1731	2024
52	**Žilina** **1160** a.	0808	...	1712	1812	2112

	C		A		
Žilina **1160** d.	*0448*	1348	1448	1648	1748**b**
Čadca 🏛 **1160** d.	0544	1436	1536	1726	1836
Zwardoń 🏛 a.	0618	1509	1609	...	1909

1078 KRAKÓW - NOWY SĄCZ - KRYNICA

km		Wy	Xy	z	*TLK* 33263 P	Wy	Vy	R	qy	Sy	Ty
	Warszawa C. **1067** d.	...	...	...	2335	...	...	...	...	...	...
0	**Kraków** Gł. **1075** d.	...	...	0518	0508	...	...	1423	1630	1820	...
5	Kraków Płaszów **1075** d.	...	...	0524	0607	...	...	1429	1638	1828	...
78	Tarnów **1075** a.	...	...	0752	0846	...	...	1631	1809	2022	...
78	Tarnów d.	0427	0544	0801	0856	1332	1447	1640	1810	2038	2212
136	Stróze d.	0555	0701	0916	1002	1456	1608	1809	1914	2157	2325
167	**Nowy Sącz** d.	0636	0743	0957	1045	1532	1703	1850	1955	2239	0008
217	Muszyna d.	...	...	1117	1205	1652	1823	2011**e**	...	...	...
228	**Krynica** a.	...	...	1135	1223	1710	1841	2029**e**	...	...	...

	x	y	Yy	Xy	Wy	Xy	Xy	Wy		*TLK* 33260 Q
Krynica d.	...	0455**d**	0551	...	...	...	1415	1752	...	1936
Muszyna d.	...	0523**d**	0619	...	...	...	1443	1820	...	2007
Nowy Sącz d.	0443	0702	0728	1132	1419	1453	1551	1929	...	2115
Stróze d.	0523	0742	0807	1212	1458	1534	1631	2008	...	2157
Tarnów a.	0625	0853	0925	1325	1627	1659	1743	2120	...	2302
Tarnów **1075** d.	0626	0906	...	...	...	1701	1744	...	...	2307
Kraków Płaszów **1075** a.	0753	1113	...	...	...	1847	1935	...	...	0050
Kraków Gł. **1075** a.	0803	1121	...	...	...	1856	1944	...	...	0149
Warszawa C. **1067** a.	...	...	...	...	...	...	...	...	...	0713**v**

P – From Warszawa on ⑤ (also Apr. 30, May 3; not May 2): 🛏 1, 2 cl., ⊏2⊐ Warszawa - Kraków - Krynica.
Q – ⑦ (also May 1): 🛏 1, 2 cl., ⊏2⊐ Krynica - Kraków - Warszawa.
R – Daily Apr. 27 - May 3; ⑥⑦ May 4 - June 14.
S – ⑤⑥⑦ (also Apr. 28 - May 1).
T – ⑤⑦ (also Apr. 28 - May 1).
V – ⑦ (also Apr. 28 - May 2).
W – Apr. 28 - 30.
X – ⑥⑦ (also Apr. 28 - May 2).
Y – ⑥ (also Apr. 28 - May 2).
d – ⑥ only.
e – ⑦ only.
q – Not May 2, June 13.
v – Warszawa Wschodnia.
x – Replaced by 🚌 on ②–⑤ from May 6.
y – Replaced by 🚌 on ①–④ from May 5.
z – Replaced by 🚌 on ①–⑤ from May 5.
* – *TLK* train (see Table **1075**).

1079 LOCAL SERVICES IN SILESIA

2nd class

KATOWICE - OSWIECIM

Operator: Koleje Śląskie

km		Ⓐ						Ⓑd	Ⓐ		Ⓐ	
0	Katowice d.	0535	0743	0933	...	1235	1432	1534	1638	1827	2040	...
33	Oswiecim d.	0641	0844	1033	...	1335	1537	1633	1738	1932	2140	...
54	Czech. Dziedzice a.	0725	0929	1117	...	1420	1622	...	1822	2016	2224	...

		Ⓐ				Ⓐ					Ⓐ
Czech. Dziedzice d.	...	0556	0753	0945	...	1246	...	1452	1647	...	1844
Oswiecim d.	...	0642	0845	1034	...	1336	1435	1546	1738	...	1932
Katowice a.	...	0743	0945	1135	...	1435	1535	1650	1839	...	2033

KATOWICE - RYBNIK - RACIBÓRZ

Operator: Koleje Śląskie

km								Ⓑd		Ⓐ			Ⓐ
0	**Katowice** d.	0420	0620	0722	0953	1120	1326	1418	1527	1619	1722	1920	2120
45	Rybnik d.	0528	0728	0829	1100	1229	1432	1528	1633	1728	1828	2028	2223
81	**Racibórz** a.	0625	0821	0921	1157	1322	1524	1621	1726	1821	1921	2120	2315

			Ⓐ				Ⓐ			Ⓐ		
Racibórz d.	0444	0643	0744	0844	1044	1238	1344	1440	1544	1744	1939	2139
Rybnik d.	0537	0739	0843	0937	1138	1333	1438	1534	1637	1837	2035	2231
Katowice a.	0637	0840	0942	1038	1238	1438	1539	1636	1739	1936	2136	2336

Additional journeys on Ⓐ: Katowice d. 0520 → Rybnik d. 0628 → Racibórz a. 0721; Racibórz d. 0544 → Rybnik d. 0637 → Katowice a. 0739.

RACIBÓRZ - CHAŁUPKI

Operator: Koleje Śląskie

km		Ⓐ									
0	Racibórz d.	0553	...	1057	...	1459	...	1756	...	1959	...
22	Chałupki △ a.	0629	...	1133	...	1535	...	1832	...	2035	...

	Ⓐ									
Chałupki △ d.	0431	...	0639	...	1239	...	1635	...	1842	...
Racibórz a.	0458	...	0706	...	1305	...	1702	...	1909	...

(WROCŁAW -) OPOLE - KEDZIERZYN-KOŹLE - RACIBÓRZ

Operator: Przewozy Regionalne

km		d	d		d	d	d	Ⓐ	d	Ⓐ	d	
	Wrocław Gł d.	...	...	...	0743	*0946*	*1146*	*1246*	1442	*1645*	1843	
0	Opole d.	*0500*a	*0559*	...	0906	*1106*	*1306*	*1406*	1606	*1806*	2006	...
42	Kedzierzyn-Koźle d.	0556	0656	...	1002	1202	1402	1502	1702	1902	2102	...
74	Racibórz a.	0648	0748	...	1054	1254	1454	1554	1753	1954	2152	...

	d	Ⓐ	d		d		d	Ⓐ	d	d	d
Racibórz d.	0500	0600	0710	...	1010	...	1310	1408	1508	1708	1912
Kedzierzyn-Koźle a.	0546	0646	0754	...	1054	...	1354	1452	1552	1754	1956
Opole a.	*0652*	*0752*	0852	...	1152	...	*1501*	*1553*	*1652*	1849	*2101*
Wrocław Gł a.	*0813*	*0921*	1013	...	1313	...	*1616*	...	*1830*	2010	*2217*

a – Ⓐ only.
d – Not Apr. 20.
△ – Chałupki station is situated ± 1600 metres from Stary Bohumín, where a 🚌 service runs approx every 30 minutes from the main square (náměsti Svobody) to Bohumín (journey 15 mins) and Ostrava (journey 45 mins).

POZNAŃ - OSTRÓW - KATOWICE - KRAKÓW 1080

For other trains Poznań - Katowice - Kraków (via Wrocław) see Table **1075**; for Poznań - Kraków via Łódź see Table **1025**.

km												
				TLK 84100							*TLK* 54102	*TLK* 83260
			⊖				⊖			⊖		
			①–⑤	⑥ **z**								
			y								**g**	**C**
	Szczecin Gł. **1010** d.	...	...	0540	...	...	...	...	...	...	...	1927
0	**Poznań** Gł. d.	...	...	0832	1050	...	...	1450	...	...	1732	2235
67	Jarocin d.	...	...	0928	1158	...	...	1558	...	...	1835	2333
114	Ostrów Wlkp. d.	...	...	1005	1256	...	...	1656	...	...	1915	0021
160	Kępno d.	...	...	1040	1338	...	...	1741	...	...	1947	0056
	Częstochowa ✣ d.	...	...	|	|	...	...	|	...	...	|	|
201	Kluczbork d.	0743	...	1127	1431	1436	...	1836	1852	...	2027	|
252	Lubliniec d.	0856	0940	1232	...	1543	1600	...	2004	2007	2134	|
	Gliwice d.	...	|	|	...	...	|	...	...	|	2242	|
302	Bytom d.	...	1104	|	...	...	1725	...	...	2142	|	|
320	**Katowice** a.	...	1130	1418	...	...	1752	...	...	2211	2312	0406
398	**Kraków** Gł. a.	...	...	...	...	...	...	...	...	...	...	0630

	TLK 45103					*TLK* 48101				*TLK* 38261
			⊖				⊖		⊖	
			①–⑤			⑦				
	g		**y**							**D**
Kraków Gł. d.	...	...	...	...	...	...	...	...	...	2210
Katowice d.	0441	...	1135	...	...	1431	1740	...	2045	0028
Bytom d.	|	...	1208	...	...	|	1813	...	2119	|
Gliwice d.	0513	...	|	...	...	|	|	...	|	|
Lubliniec d.	0607	0934	1329	1334	...	1557	1933	2018	2238	|
Kluczbork d.	0718	1038	...	1438	1448	1712	...	2130	...	|
Częstochowa ✣ d.	|	...	...	...	|	|	...	...	...	|
Kępno d.	0818	...	...	...	1549	1829	...	...	...	0421
Ostrów Wlkp. d.	0853	...	...	...	1652	1905	...	...	...	0437
Jarocin d.	0931	...	...	...	1740	1946	...	...	...	0524
Poznań Gł. a.	1025	...	...	...	1846	2037	...	...	...	0621
Szczecin Gł. **1010** a.	...	...	...	...	...	2328	...	...	...	0917

2nd class — LOCAL TRAINS POZNAŃ / WROCŁAW - OSTRÓW WLKP - ŁÓDŹ

		①–⑥	⑦				⑧			
Poznań Gł. d.	...	...	...	0910	1249	1450	...	1650	1855	2059
Jarocin d.	...	0645	...	1031	1403	1558	...	1758	2008	2208
Wrocław Gł. **1090** d.	...	|	...	|	|	|	1406	|	|	|
Ostrów Wlkp. **1090** d.	0446	0800**t**	0800	1135**t**	1457**t**	1643	1648	1902**t**	2056	2257
Kalisz **1090** d.	0512	0810	0826	1200	1522	...	1716	1927	...	...
Łódź Kaliska **1090** a.	0717	1046	1031	1423	1727	...	1921	2135	...	...

		P								
Łódź Kaliska **1090** d.	...	0511	...	0712	1000	...	1336	...	1658	1906
Kalisz **1090** d.	...	0714	...	0918	1205	...	1540	...	1904	2112
Ostrów Wlkp. **1090** d.	0617	0745	0750	1003**t**	1259**t**	1431	1606	1652	1939**t**	2137
Wrocław Gł. **1090** a.	|	0951	|	|	|	|	1839	|	|	...
Jarocin d.	0705	...	0839	1051	1346	1520	...	1740	2028	...
Poznań Gł. a.	0812	...	0947	1207	1456	1632	...	1846	2136	...

C – 🛏 1, 2 cl., 🛌 2 cl., (2) Świnoujście - Szczecin - Poznań - Kraków - Przemyśl. Timings may vary on certain dates.
D – 🛏 1, 2 cl., 🛌 2 cl., (2) Przemyśl - Kraków - Poznań - Szczecin - Świnoujście. Timings may vary on certain dates.
P – ①–⑥ (not May 1, 3).
g – To / from Gdynia (Table **1015**).
t – Arrive 10 – 30 minutes earlier.
y – Not May 1, 2.
z – Not May 3.
✣ – Częstochowa **Stradom**.
⊖ – Operated by Koleje Slaskie.

JELENIA GÓRA - TRUTNOV 1082

km										
			Bw		**B**		**B**			
0	**Jelenia Góra** d.	...	...	...	1118	...	1716	...	...	...
27	Sędzisław d.	...	0739	...	1203	...	1810	...	...	...
43	Lubawka 🏛 d.	...	0808	...	1232	...	1833	...	...	...
48	Královec 🏛 d.	...	0817	...	1241	...	1842	...	...	...
65	**Trutnov** hlavní a.	...	0850	...	1309	...	1910	...	...	...

		B		**B**		**Bw**			
Trutnov hlavní d.	...	0910	...	1454	...	1929	...	...	...
Královec 🏛 d.	...	0942	...	1524	...	1958	...	...	...
Lubawka 🏛 d.	...	0950	...	1532	...	2006	...	...	...
Sędzisław d.	...	1020	...	1602	...	2027	...	...	...
Jelenia Góra a.	...	1058	...	1636	...	...	...	...	...

B – ⑥⑦ from May 3 (also May 1, 2). Operated by Koleje Dolnośląskie (in Czech Republic by GW Train Regio).
w – From / to Wrocław.

JELENIA GORA - SZKLARSKA POREBA GÓRNA 1083

Operator: *KD*

Rail service suspended during track reconstruction. *32* km. 🚌 service (subject to confirmation) runs as follows, journey approx 55 minutes:
From Jelenia Góra: 0735, 0950, 1500, 1840. From Szklarska Poreba Górna: 0835, 1400, 1725, 1937.

JELENIA GÓRA - WAŁBRZYCH - WROCŁAW 1084

km												
					IR		*TLK*			⊖		*TLK*
		①–⑥		①–⑥	65110		61100			⑥⑦		62200
		n		**n**	**y**		**B**	**p**	**n**	**k**		**A**
0	**Jelenia Góra** d.	0519	0624	0747	1012	1137	1257	1541	1738	1834	1941	2102
27	Sedzisław d.	0550	0655	0817	1044	1208	1324	1614	1808	1901	2011	2133
47	Wałbrzych Gł. d.	0630	0730	0841	1109	1233	1344	1645	1832	1924	2032	2155
78	Jaworzyna Śląska d.	0721	0812	0918	1147	1310	1420	1723	1914	2000	2110	2238
127	**Wrocław** Gł. a.	0811	0900	1008	1237	1401	1502	1813	2003	2040	2157	2323
	Warszawa C. △ a.	...	...	...	...	...	2206**g**	...	...	...	...	0625**g**

		TLK		⊖		*TLK*			*IR*		
	①–⑤	16201		⑥⑦		16100			56110		
	m	**A**		**k**	**p**	**B**	**n**		**y**		⑧**m**
Warszawa C. △ d.	...	2305	...	...	...	0530	...	...	...	...	...
Wrocław Gł. d.	0451	0643	0718	0813	1015	1225	1252	1524	1701	1906	2106
Jaworzyna Śląska d.	0535	0727	0807	0853	1107	1304	1340	1613	1750	1959	2157
Wałbrzych Gł. d.	0621	0814	0847	0934	1150	1346	1424	1653	1831	2041	2238
Sedzisław d.	0644	0836	0910	0955	1214	1405	1447	1716	1855	2105	2259
Jelenia Góra a.	0716	0907	0942	1025	1251	1433	1520	1750	1927	2148	2330

A – 🛏 1, 2 cl., 🛌 2 cl., (12) Warszawa - Katowice - Jelenia Góra and v.v.
B – (12) Warszawa - Łódź - Jelenia Góra and v.v.
g – Warszawa **Gdańska**.
h – Also May 1.
k – Also May 1, 2.
m – Not May 1, 2.
n – Not May 1, 3.
p – To / from Poznań (Table **1070**).
y – To / from Olsztyn (Table **1020**).
⊖ – Operated by Koleje Dolnośląskie.
△ – **1060** via Katowice; **1070** via Poznań; **1090** via Łódź.

Additional trains Wałbrzych - Wroclaw:
From Wałbrzych at 0339 ①–⑤ **m**, 0434 ①–⑥ **n**, 0532, 0630 ⑦ **h**, 0958 ①–⑤ **m**, 1455 ①–⑤ **m**.
From Wroclaw: 0545 ①–⑤ **m**, 1410 ①–⑤ **m**, 1607, 1757 ⑧ **m**, 2106 ⑥ **k**, 2305.

GÖRLITZ - WROCŁAW 1085

km												
		⊖	⊖	*RE*	⊖	*EC*	*RE*	⊖	⊖	⊖	*RE*	⊖
				5791		249	5793				5795	
		①–⑤		66012			66014				66016	
		h		🚌		**A**	🚌				🚌	
	Dresden **855** d.	...	...	0809	...	...	1209	...	...	...	1809	...
0	**Görlitz** 🏛 d.	...	...	0933	...	...	1333	...	...	...	1933	...
2	Zgorzelec 🏛 d.	...	*0733*	0938	*1118*	...	1338	*1402*	*1516*	...	1938	*2058*
30	Węgliniec d.	0407	0805	1000	1145	1320	1400	1432	1636	1802	2000	2133
55	Bolesławiec d.	0424	0824	1018	1202	1336	1416	1449	1653	1816	2016	2149
99	Legnica **1086** d.	0458	0858	1049	1235	1404	1446	1522	1726	1841	2046	2224
165	**Wrocław** Gł. **1086** a.	0554	0951	1135	1329	1448	1533	1616	1819	1932	2133	2314

	RE	⊖	⊖	⊖	*EC*	*RE*	⊖	⊖	*RE*	⊖	⊖
	5790				248	5792			5794		
	66001					66003			66005		
	🚌				**A**	🚌			🚌	**h**	
Wrocław Gł. **1086** d.	0631	0828	...	1140	1214	1236	1426	1543	1836	2010	2143
Legnica **1086** d.	0718	0923	...	1234	1259	1325	1522	1643	1925	2106	2241
Bolesławiec d.	0748	0956	...	1309	1327	1354	1555	1718	1954	2134	2318
Węgliniec d.	0810	1013	1208	1326	1343	1411	1611	1737	2011	2147	2336
Zgorzelec 🏛 d.	0833	...	1232	*1356*	...	1432	...	*1811*	2032	*2218*	...
Görlitz 🏛 a.	0837	...	...	...	...	1437	...	...	2037	...	...
Dresden **855** a.	0957	...	...	...	...	1557	...	...	2157	...	...

A – WAWEL – (12) Berlin - Wrocław and v.v. For dates from / to Hamburg see Table **58**.
h – Not May 1, 2.
⊖ – Operated by Koleje Dolnośląskie.

COTTBUS - FORST - WROCŁAW 1086

km											
			⊖		*EC*		⊖	⊖		⊖	⊖
		①–⑤		⑥⑦	249	🚌	①–⑤				
		h		**k**	**A**	**z**	**h**				
	Berlin Hbf. **838** d.	...	...	...	0941	...	...	...	...	...	...
0	**Cottbus** **854** d.	*0607*	...	*0807*	1115	...	...	...	*1607*	...	...
22	Forst 🏛 **854** a.	*0626*	...	*0825*	1134	...	...	...	*1626*	...	...
22	Forst d.	0635	...	0845	1134	...	...	...	1635	...	...
36	Tuplice d.	0650	...	0901	|	...	...	...	1650	...	...
57	Żary d.	0712	0749	0922	1212	1414	...	1552	1711	1750	2025
	Wegliniec d.	|	|	|	1320	|	...	|	|	|	|
70	Żagań d.	0724	0802	0934	▽	1426	...	1604	1724	1802	2037
144	Legnica **1085** d.	...	0926	...	1403	1555	1619	1740	...	1929	2208
210	**Wrocław** Gł. **1085** a.	...	1013	...	1448	...	1711	1829	...	2025	...

			⊖		⊖	*EC*		⊖	⊖		⊖
	①–⑤	⑥⑦	①–⑤	🚌		248	🚌		①–⑤	🚌	
	h	**k**	**h**	**z**		**A**			**h**		
Wrocław Gł. **1085** d.	...	...	*0512*	...	1120	1214	...	1445	1618	...	2101
Legnica **1085** d.	...	...	0609	0722	1216	1259	...	1537	1716	1723	2204
Żagań d.	0538	0750	0740	0852	1340	▽	1537	1703	...	1853	2328
Wegliniec d.	|	|	|	|	|	1354	|	|	...	|	|
Żary d.	0550	0802	0752	0904	1353	1443	1549	1715	...	1905	2340
Tuplice d.	0611	0823	...	...	...	|	1610	...	...	...	...
Forst a.	0626	0838	...	...	...	1525	1625	...	...	...	...
Forst 🏛 **854** d.	*0633*	*0933*	...	...	...	1525	*1633*	...	...	...	...
Cottbus **854** a.	*0651*	*0951*	...	...	...	1543	*1651*	...	...	...	...
Berlin Hbf. **838** a.	...	...	...	...	...	1708	...	...	...	...	...

A – WAWEL – (12) Berlin - Wrocław and v.v. For dates from / to Hamburg see Table **58**.
h – Not May 1, 2.
k – Also May 1.
z – From / to Zielona Góra (Table **1005**).
⊖ – Operated by Koleje Dolnośląskie.
▽ – Via Table **1085**.

1090 WARSZAWA - ŁÓDŹ - WROCŁAW

VIA SOCHACZEW. Includes full daytime service Warszawa - Wrocław via all routes; for night train see Table **1060**.

km		*TLK* 16100 16101 j	*EIC* 1601 1600 C	*TLK* 16102 16103 b		*TLK* 16110 16111	*EIC* 1603 1602 C		*TLK* 16104 16105 Ⓑh	
0	**Warszawa** Wschodnia d.	0517	...	0853	...	1250	1541	...	1706	...
4	**Warszawa** Centralna d.	0530	0745	0930	...	1308	1554	...	1730	...
58	Sochaczew d.	0610	|	1009	...	1346	|	...	1808	...
145	**Łódź** Kaliska ▷ d.	0747	◧	1154	...	1550	◧	...	1943	...
257	Kalisz ▷ d.	0940	|	1341	...	1742	|	...	2129	...
281	Ostrów Wlkp ▷ d.	1001	|	1403	...	1805	|	...	2151	...
382	**Wrocław** Gł. ▷ a.	1200	1257	1603	...	2013	2056	...	2345	...

	EIC 6103 6102 A	*TLK* 61105 61104 C		*TLK* 61111 61110		*TLK* 61103 61102 b		*EIC* 6101 6100 Ⓑh	*TLK* 61100 61101 j	
Wrocław Gł. ▷ d.	0353	0542	...	0925	...	1356	...	1511	1529	...
Ostrów Wlkp ▷ d.	|	0745	...	1127	...	1556	...	|	1731	...
Kalisz ▷ d.	|	0808	...	1148	...	1616	...	|	1759	...
Łódź Kaliska ▷ d.	◧	0959	...	1340	...	1806	...	◧	1950	...
Sochaczew d.	|	1131	...	1508	...	1943	...	|	2125	...
Warszawa Centralna a.	0906	1217g	...	1603g	...	2025g	...	2027	2206g	...
Warszawa Wschodnia a.	0918	...	...	...	...	...	...	2040	...	...

WARSZAWA - ŁÓDŹ VIA KOLUSZKI

km		*TLK* 19100 19101	*TLK* 19102 19103	*TLK* 19104 19105	*IR* 10121 10120	*IR* 10123 10222	*TLK* 19106 19107		*IR* 10125 10124	*TLK* 19109 19108	*TLK* 19150 19151 D	*IR* 10127 10126	*TLK* 19152 19153 D	*TLK* 19110 19111	*TLK* 19154 19155 D		*TLK* 19120 19121 D	*TLK* 19112 19113 D	*TLK* 19156 19157	*IR* 10131 10130		*TLK* 19114 19115	*IR* 10129 10128 B	*TLK* 19116 19117
0	**Warszawa** Wschodnia d.	0416	0655	0848	...	...	1124	...	...	...	1409	...	1512	1557	1626	...	1701	1742	1812	...	...	2007	...	2050
4	**Warszawa** Centralna d.	0430	0753	0913	1012	1105	1137	...	1225	1349	1422	1518	1523	1611	1639	...	1718	1755	1830	1922	...	2022	2048	2148
70	Skierniewice d.	0655	0909	1028	1118	1213	1250	...	1345	1504	1539	1631	1638	1729	1752	...	1831	|	1946	2035	...	2136	2159	2259
109	Koluszki d.	0719	0941	1052	1142	1235	1315	...	1410	1528	1603	1655	1703	1759	1818	...	1855	1931	2010	2057	...	2200	2226	2324
137	**Łódź** Chojny a.	0749	1017	1122	1210	1302	1351	...	1442	1559	1632	1722	1736	1830	1846	...	1934	2008	2040	2123	...	2229	2253	2352
144	**Łódź** Kaliska a.	0757	1025	1130	1217	1310	1359	...	1450	1606	1640	1729	1744	1839	1854	...	1942	2016	2048	2130	...	2237	2300	2359

	TLK 91151 91150 D	*TLK* 91101 91100	*TLK* 91153 91152 D	*TLK* 91121 91120 D		*TLK* 91155 91154	*IR* 10133 10132	*TLK* 91103 91102 k	*IR* 10135 10134	*TLK* 91105 91104		*TLK* 91107 91106		*IR* 10137 10136	*IR* 10139 10138	*TLK* 91111 91110		*TLK* 91157 91156 D		*TLK* 91113 91112	*IR* 10141 10140	*TLK* 91115 91114		*TLK* 91117 91116
Łódź Kaliska d.	0414	0444	0512	0534	...	0637	0702	0805	0842	0920	...	1137	...	1300	1410	1523	...	1626	...	1733	1831	1934	...	2139
Łódź Chojny d.	0424	0455	0523	0545	...	0647	0710	0814	0844	0930	...	1147	...	1308	1419	1534	...	1636	...	1742	1839	1954	...	2148
Koluszki d.	0453	0526	0553	0618	...	0714	0736	0845	0917	1002	...	1222	...	1334	1447	1609	...	1704	...	1817	1921	2013	...	2219
Skierniewice d.	0518	0551	0618	0643	...	0739	0800	0908	0950	1027	...	1251	...	1357	1523	|	...	1729	...	1841	1955	2039	...	2245
Warszawa Centralna a.	0632	0701	0731	0753	...	0845	0857	1009	1102	|	...	|	...	1457	1637	1804g	...	1932	...	1950	2112	2151	...	2349
Warszawa Wschodnia a.	0643	0728	0743	...	...	...	...	1021	...	1150	...	1413	...	...	...	...	...	1944	...	2029	...	2202	...	2359

A – ①–⑤ (not May 1, 2).
B – ⑤⑦ (also Apr. 30; not May 2).
C – ①–⑥ (not May 2, 3).
D – ①–⑤ (not May 1).
b – From / to Białystok (Table **1040**).
g – Warszawa **Gdańska**.
h – Not May 1, 2.
j – To / from Jelenia Góra (Table **1084**).
k – Not May 1 - 4.
▷ – For local trains see Table **1080**.
▽ – Via Katowice (Table **1060**).
◧ – Via Poznań (Table **1070**).

1095 WROCŁAW - KŁODZKO - MIEDZYLESIE

km		①–⑤ y					L	z	z		Ⓑy	
0	**Wrocław** Gł. d.	0445	0622	0750	1007	...	1220	1349	1558	1650	1754	1936
72	Kamieniec Ząbkowicki d.	0655	0749	0928	1132	...	1358	1531	1732	1813	1924	2100
94	Kłodzko Gł. a.	0724	0815	1000	1200	...	1427	1602	1801	1842	1953	2129
94	Kłodzko Gł. **1165** d.	0725	0816	...	...	1205	1430	...	1802	1843	...	2130
130	**Międzylesie** 🏛 **1165** a.	0812	0901	...	...	1250	1517	...	1847	1929	...	2215
	Letohrad **1165** a.	...	0941	...	...	1329	...	...	...	2001	...	...

	①–⑤ y		z	L		①–⑤ y	L		L	
Letohrad **1165** d.	...	...	...	...	0906	...	...	...	...	...
Międzylesie **1165** d.	0413	0533	0652	0904	1050	1341	1528	...	1802	1933
Kłodzko Gł. **1165** a.	0456	0616	0735	0946	1133	1425	1611	...	1853	2025
Kłodzko Gł. d.	0457	0617	0745	0947	...	1436	...	1615	1857	2026
Kamieniec Ząbkowicki d.	0522	0642	0813	1008	...	1501	...	1641	1925	2047
Wrocław Gł. a.	0649	0814	0937	1138	...	1627	...	1821	2103	2230

L – To / from Lichkov (Table **1165**). **y** – Not May 1, 2. **z** – Not May 1, 3.

1097 POZNAN - WOLSZTYN

Operator: Koleje Wielkopolskie

All services (except 🚂) currently operated by 🚌 – times may vary

km		Ⓐ			①–⑥				🚂 K		🚂 K
0	**Wolsztyn** d.	0434	0551	0836	1145	...	1354	1553	1735	1940	2315
81	**Poznań** Gł. a.	0601	0721	1003	1322	...	1421	1736	1919	2115	0037

	Ⓐ	①–⑥	Ⓒ	🚂 K	🚂 K					
Poznań Gł. d.	0519	0635	0840	1010	1145	...	1356	1538	1749	1953
Wolsztyn a.	0710	0808	1012	1142	1318	...	1532	1705	1916	2120

K – May 3 only: Special fares payable.

🚂 – Normally hauled by steam locomotive (not guaranteed). See www.parowozy.com.pl www.thewolsztynexperience.org.

1099 OTHER LOCAL SERVICES

2nd class only

GDYNIA - HEL

77 km, journey 1 hr 50 mins - 2 hrs

June 21 - 28, 2013:

Gdynia Główna depart: 0556, 0708, 1054, 1216, 1346, 1540, 1630, 1917, 2046.

Hel depart: 0428, 0636, 0800, 0948, 1300, 1413, 1602, 1750, 1837.

June 29 - Sept. 1, 2013:

Gdynia Główna depart: 0526, 0736, 0903, 1031, 1207, 1318, 1532, 1638, 1854, 2024, 2247.

Hel depart: 0427, 0614, 0822, 0948, 1059, 1255, 1458, 1556, 1633, 1754, 2003.

KRAKÓW - KRAKÓW BALICE AIRPORT ✈

12 km, journey 19–20 mins

Kraków Główny depart:

Kraków Balice ✈ depart:

Balice ✈ rail station is 200m from the international air terminal. A free shuttle bus operates.

Service currently suspended for construction of new station and terminal building. Reopening expected mid - late 2015.

KRAKÓW - OŚWIĘCIM (for Auschwitz-Birkenau Memorial and Museum)

VIA TRZEBINIA 65 km Journey 1 hr 45 mins - 1 hr 50 mins

Kraków Główny depart: 0557, 0643, 0838, 1018, 1128, 1312 ①–⑤ **z**, , 1451, 1549, 1726, 1817 ①–⑤ **z**, 1935, 2138.

Oświęcim depart: 0336, 0419, 0502 ①–⑤ **z**, 0532, 0644, 0850, 1048, 1226, 1342, 1427 ①–⑤ **z**, 1544, 1639, 1830, 1935.

KRAKÓW - WADOWICE

62 km, journey 1 hr 50 mins

Kraków Główny depart: 1220 ⑦, 1432, 1753 Ⓑ.

Wadowice depart: 0658 ①–⑥, 1634, 1940 ⑦.

Wadowice is the birthplace of Pope John Paul II.

KRAKÓW - WIELICZKA (for Salt Mine)

15 km, journey 25–30 mins

Kraków Główny depart: 0451 ①–⑥, 0535, 0626, 0712, 0734, 0843, 1049, 1132 ①–⑤ **z**, 1250 1428, 1539, 1624 ①–⑤ **z**, 1726 ①–⑤ **z**, 1836, 1935, 2026.

Wieliczka Rynek depart: 0523 ①–⑥, 0617, 0707, 0810, 0846, 0953, 1136, 1245 ①–⑤ **z**, 1416, 1523, 1559, 1642, 1749 ①–⑤ **z**, 1826 ①–⑤ **z**, 1909, 2016.

LESZNO - WOLSZTYN - ZBĄSZYNEK

Operator: *Koleje Wielkopolskie*

	🚌 y				🚌 H		🚌		🚌	🚌 r
Leszno d.	0550	...	0952	...	1345	...	1446	...	1643	1837
Wolsztyn d.	0649	...	1105	...	1444	...	1545	...	1756	1936
Zbąszyń a.	0722	...	...	...	1511	...	1619	...	...	...
Zbąszynek a.	0729	...	...	...	1518	...	1626	...	...	...

		🚌	🚌 J		🚌 v			🚌		r
Zbąszynek d.	...	0655	0757	...	0943	...	...	1555	...	...
Zbąszyń d.	...	0701	0804	...	0949	...	...	1601	...	...
Wolsztyn d.	0607	0730	0831	...	1016	1316	...	1628	...	1943
Leszno a.	0726	0829	0930	...	1129	1436	...	1734	...	2043

WAŁBRZYCH - KŁODZKO

51 km, journey 1 hr 25 mins

Wałbrzych Główny depart: 0620 ①–⑥ **n**, 0852, 1428, 1701 ①–⑤ **z**, 1837 ⑥⑦ **p**.

Kłodzko Główne depart: 0550, 1004, 1449 ①–⑤ **q**, 1649 ⑥⑦ **p**, 2028 Ⓑ **z**.

Operator: Koleje Dolnośląskie.

H – ①–⑤ (also May 3; not May 1, 2).
J – ①–⑤ (not May 1, 2).
n – Not May 2, 3.
p – Also May 1.
q – Not May 1.
r – Not May 11.
v – May 3 only.
y – Not May 12.
z – Not May 1, 2.

CZECH REPUBLIC

Services: Operator: České Dráhy (ČD), www.cd.cz. Railway infrastructure and timetables is the responsibility of Správa železniční dopravní cesty (SŽDC), www.szdc.cz. All daytime trains convey first and second classes of travel unless otherwise shown by '2' at the top of the column or by a note (which may be in the table heading).

Timings: Valid **December 15, 2013 - December 13, 2014**. Certain trains are cancelled or curtailed during the Christmas and New Year period.

Reservations: It is possible to reserve seats on most Express trains.

Supplements: SuperCity (*SC*) trains are operated by tilting *Pendolino* units and have a compulsory reservation fee of 200 CZK or €7.00.

Station names: hlavní = main; západ = west; východ = east; horní = upper; dolní = lower; střed = centre, starý = old; město = town; předměstí = suburban; nádraží = station.

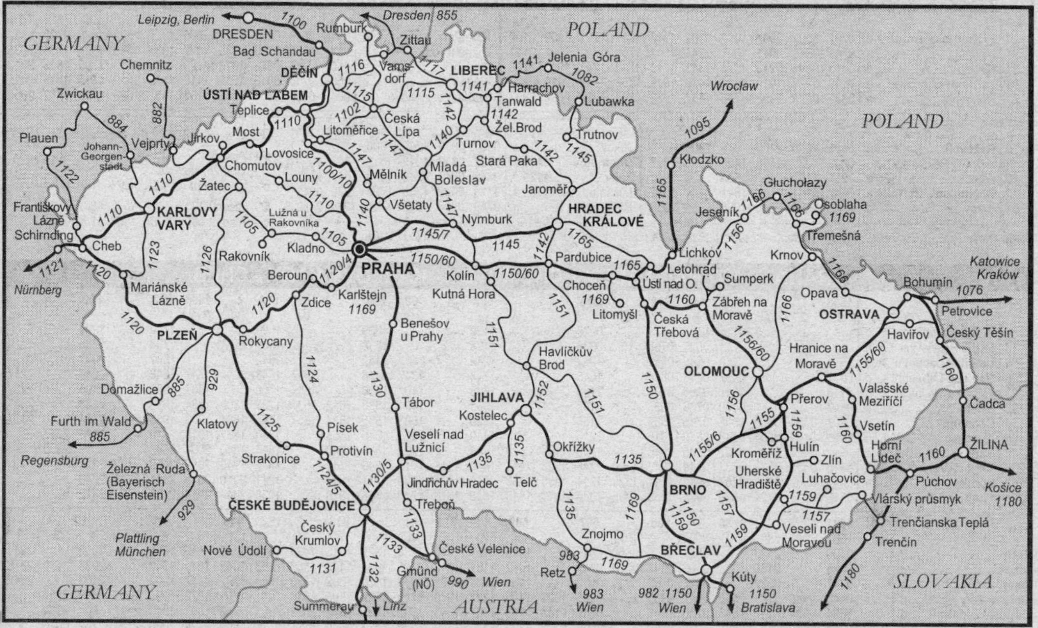

PRAHA - ÚSTÍ NAD LABEM - DĚČÍN - DRESDEN — 1100

km	Praha - Ústí : see also 1110	EN 476	440	2	EC 178 ✕	692	EC 176 ✕	690	EC 378 ✕	688	EC 174 ✕	686	EC 172 ✕	684	682	1171	EC 170 ✕	680	678	EN* 456	676	674	672	670
		♦	♦		♦		♦		♦		♦		♦		Ⓐr		♦		Ⓐ	CP		Ⓐr		
0	**Praha** hlavní ▷ d.	0429	0515	...	0629	0646	0829	0846	1029	1046	1229	1246	1429	1446	1546	...	1629	1646	1746	1829	1846	1946	2046	2329
3	**Praha** Holešovice ▷ d.	0439	0526	...	0639	0656	0839	0856	1039	1056	1239	1256	1439	1456	1556	...	1639	1656	1756	1839	1856	1956	2056	2339
27	Kralupy nad Vltavou d.	|	0549	...	|	0718	|	0918	|	1118	|	1318	|	1518	1618	...	|	1718	1818	|	1918	2018	2118	0000
66	Roudnice nad Labem d.	|	0611	...	|	0743	|	0943	|	1143	|	1343	|	1543	1643	...	|	1743	1843	|	1943	2043	2143	0024
84	Lovosice d.	|	0624	...	|	0758	|	0958	|	1158	|	1358	|	1558	1658	...	|	1758	1858	|	1958	2058	2158	0037
106	**Ústí nad Labem** hlavní ▷ a.	0540	0640	...	0740	0814	0940	1014	1140	1214	1340	1414	1540	1614	1714	...	1740	1814	1914	1940	2014	2114	2213	0052
106	**Ústí nad Labem** hlavní ▶ d.	0542	...	0700	0742	0816	0942	1016	1142	1216	1342	1416	1542	1616	...	1727	1742	1816	1916	1942	2016	*2118*	2216	0054
129	**Děčín** ▶ a.	0600	...	0728	0758	0832	0958	1032	1158	1232	1358	1432	1558	1632	...	1743	1758	1832	1932	1958	2032	*2133*	2232	0109
129	**Děčín** 🏛 ⊖ d.	0604	...	...	0800	...	1000	...	1200	...	1400	...	1600	...	...	...	1800	...	...	2000	...	...	...	...
151	Bad Schandau 🏛 ⊖ 857 d.	|	...	...	0817	...	1017	...	1217	...	1417	...	1617	...	...	...	1817	...	...	2017	...	...	...	...
191	**Dresden** Hbf 857 a.	0649	...	...	0845	...	1045	...	1245	...	1445	...	1645	...	...	...	1845	...	...	2047	...	...	...	...

	671	673	675	677	EN* 457	1172	679	EN* 459	681	EC 171 ✕	683	EC 173 ✕	685	EC 175 ✕	687	EC 177 ✕	689	EC 379 ✕	691	EC 179 ✕		441	EN 477	2
			Ⓐ		P		Ⓐr	C		♦		♦		♦		♦		♦		♦		♦	♦	
Dresden Hbf 857 d.	...	...	...	...	0706	...	...	0806	...	0906	...	1106	...	1306	...	1506	...	1706	...	1906	...	...	2106	...
Bad Schandau 🏛 ⊖ 857 d.	...	...	...	...	0738	...	...	0838	...	0938	...	1138	...	1338	...	1538	...	1738	...	1938	...	...	|	...
Děčín 🏛 ⊖ a.	...	...	...	...	0753	...	...	0853	...	0953	...	1153	...	1353	...	1553	...	1753	...	1953	...	...	2153	...
Děčín ▶ d.	0424	0524	0624	0724	0756	0816	...	0856	0924	0956	1124	1156	1324	1356	1524	1556	1724	1756	1924	1956	2037	...	2156	2233
Ústí nad Labem hlavní ▶ a.	0438	0538	0638	0738	0811	0832	...	0914	0938	1011	1138	1211	1338	1411	1538	1611	1738	1811	1938	2011	2105	...	2211	2300
Ústí nad Labem hlavní ▷ d.	0440	0540	0640	0740	0813	...	0842	0917	0940	1013	1140	1213	1340	1413	1540	1613	1740	1813	1940	2013	...	2113	2213	2302
Lovosice d.	0458	0558	0658	0758	|	...	0858	|	0958	|	1158	|	1358	|	1558	|	1758	|	1958	|	...	2132	|	2324
Roudnice nad Labem d.	0512	0612	0712	0812	|	...	0912	|	1012	|	1212	|	1412	|	1613	|	1812	|	2012	|	...	2144	|	2336
Kralupy nad Vltavou d.	0537	0637	0737	0837	|	...	0937	|	1037	|	1237	|	1437	|	1637	|	1837	|	2037	|	...	2208	|	...
Praha Holešovice ▷ a.	0559	0659	0759	0859	0917	...	0959	1021	1059	1117	1259	1317	1459	1517	1659	1717	1859	1917	2059	2117	...	2230	2317	...
Praha hlavní ▷ a.	0609	0709	0809	0909	0927	...	1009	1031	1109	1127	1309	1327	1509	1527	1709	1727	1909	1927	2109	2127	...	2240	2327	...

ADDITIONAL LOCAL TRAINS DĚČÍN - DRESDEN AND V.V.

			W					S		
Litomerice město d.	...	...	...	...	...	...	...	1611	...	...
Ústí n. L. hlavní d.	...	...	0918	...	...	...	...	1647	...	...
Děčín 🏛 ⊖ d.	0640	0840	0936	1040	1240	1440	1640	1710	1840	2040
Bad Schandau a.	0708	0908	0951	1108	1308	1508	1708	1727	1908	2108
Bad Schandau 857 d.	*0715*	*0915*	0952	*1115*	*1315*	*1515*	*1715*	1729	*1915*	*2115*
Dresden Hbf ◇ 857 a.	*0759*	*0959*	1020	*1159*	*1359*	*1559*	*1759*	1810	*1959*	*2159*

		S					W			
Dresden Hbf ◇ 857 d.	*0559*	0747	*0759*	*0959*	*1159*	*1359*	1600	*1559*	*1759*	*1959*
Bad Schandau 857 a.	*0643*	0825	*0843*	*1043*	*1243*	*1443*	1626	*1643*	*1843*	*2043*
Bad Schandau d.	0650	0826	0850	1050	1250	1450	1627	1650	1850	2050
Děčín 🏛 ⊖ a.	0717	0844	0917	1117	1317	1517	1643	1717	1917	2117
Ústí n. L. hlavní a.	...	0904	...	...	...	...	1659	...	...	...
Litomerice město a.	...	0940	...	...	...	...	...	...	...	...

♦ – **NOTES** (LISTED BY TRAIN NUMBERS)

70/1 – HUNGARIA – 🚃12 ✕ Budapest - Bratislava - Brno - Praha - Dresden - Berlin and v.v.

72/3 – VINDOBONA – 🚃12 ✕ Villach - Wien - Brno - Praha - Dresden - Berlin - Hamburg and v.v.

74/5 – JAN JESENIUS – 🚃12 ✕ Budapest - Bratislava - Brno - Praha - Dresden - Berlin - Hamburg and v.v.

76 – JOHANNES BRAHMS – 🚃12 ✕ Brno - Praha - Dresden - Berlin - Hamburg.

77 – SLOVENSKÁ STRELA – 🚃12 ✕ Berlin - Dresden - Praha - Brno - Bratislava.

78/9 – ALOIS NEGRELLI – 🚃12 ✕ Praha - Dresden - Berlin (- Rostock on dates in Table **835**) and v.v.

78 – SLOVENSKÁ STRELA – 🚃12 ✕ Bratislava - Brno - Praha - Dresden - Berlin - Stralsund ◐.

79 – CARL MARIA VON WEBER – 🚃12 ✕ (Binz ◐) - Stralsund - Berlin - Dresden - Praha - Brno.

40/1 – EXCELSIOR – 🛏 1, 2 cl., ▬ 2 cl., 🚃12 Cheb - Karlovy Vary - Praha - Žilina - Košice and v.v.

76/7 – METROPOL – 🛏 1, 2 cl., ▬ 2 cl., 🚃2 (⊖) Budapest - Bratislava - Brno - Praha - Dresden - Berlin and v.v.; 🛏 1, 2 cl., ▬ 2 cl., 🚃2 (⊖) Wien Westbf - Brno - Praha - Dresden - Berlin and v.v.

– CANOPUS – 🚃2 Praha - Dresden - Leipzig - Erfurt and v.v.; 🛏 1, 2 cl., ▬ 2 cl., 🚃2 (🅁) Praha - Leipzig - Erfurt - Frankfurt Sud - Basel - Zürich and v.v. See Table **54**.

P – PHOENIX – 🚃2 Praha - Dresden - Berlin and v.v.; 🛏 1, 2 cl., ▬ 2 cl., 🚃2 (🅁) Praha - Dresden - Berlin - Köln - Amsterdam and v.v.; 🛏 1, 2 cl., ▬ 2 cl. Praha - Berlin - København and v.v. See Table **54**.

S – ⑥⑦ Apr. 5 - Nov. 2 (also Apr. 18-21, May 1, 29, June 9, Oct. 3, 31).

W – ⑥⑦ Nov. 29 - Dec. 13.

r – Not May 2, 9, Oct. 27.

◐ – Extended to/from Binz on dates in Table **844**.

▶ – Ústí nad Labem - Děčín: see also Table **1115** and foot of Table **1110**.

▷ – For other non-stop trains Praha - Ústí nad Labem and v.v. see Table **1110**.

◇ – Local trains continue to/from Meissen.

⊖ – Routeing point for international tickets: Schöna.

⊖ – 🅁 Berlin - Děčín and v.v.

* – *CNL* in Germany.

Other local services:
Praha M'kovo - Lovosice: every 1-2 hours.
Lovosice - Ústí nad Labem: hourly.

1102 LOVOSICE - LITOMĚŘICE - ČESKÁ LIPA
Local trains, 2nd class

km										
0	Lovosice 1100 d.	0601	0801	1001	1201	1401	1601	1801	2001	2213
8	Litoměřice horní d.	0616	0816	1016	1216	1416	1616	1816	2016	2226
50	Česká Lípa a.	0725	0923	1123	1323	1523	1723	1923	2123	...

		Ⓐ									
Česká Lípa d.	...	0443	0633	0833	1033	1233	1433	1633	1833	2033	...
Litoměřice horní d.	0022	0559	0740	0940	1140	1340	1540	1740	1940	2141	2211
Lovosice 1100 a.	0035	0615	0753	0953	1153	1353	1553	1753	1953	2154	2227

Also: Lovosice - Litoměřice horní: 0040, 0500, 0638Ⓐ, 0737, 0828, 0936, 1029, 1136, 1229, 1336, 1429, 1457Ⓐ, 1536, 1629, 1701Ⓐ, 1736, 1829, 1901Ⓐ, 1936, 2029, 2139, 2237Ⓐ, 2326.
Litoměřice horní - Lovosice: 0501, 0528Ⓐ, 0640Ⓐ, 0659Ⓐ, 0759, 0844Ⓐ, 0911, 0959, 1111, 1159, 1311, 1359, 1439Ⓐ, 1511, 1559, 1639Ⓐ, 1759, 1839Ⓐ, 1859Ⓐ, 1959, 2113, 2211.

1105 PRAHA - RAKOVNIK - CHOMUTOV - JIRKOV

km			2◧		2◧			2Ⓐ			⑦e
0	Praha Masarykovo d.	0702	0802	0902	1002	1302	1502	1617	1702	1902	2102
31	Kladno a.	0741	0841	0941	1041	1341	1541	1708	1741	1941	2141
31	Kladno d.	0743	*0846*	0943	*1046*	1343	1543	1710	1743	1943	2143
64	Lužná u Rakovnika a.	0819	*0927*	1019	*1127*	1419	1619	1752	1819	2019	2219
73	Rakovník a.	0832	*0948*	1032	*1148*	1432	1632	1804	1832	2032	2232

	⚒n	2			2◐			2◐		⑦e
Rakovník d.	0516	0618	0722	0922	*1006*	1322	1522	*1606*	1722	1922
Lužná u Rakovnika d.	0527	0632	0735	0935	*1021*	1335	1535	*1621*	1735	1935
Kladno a.	0603	0711	0813	1013	*1103*	1413	1613	*1703*	1813	2013
Kladno d.	0608	0715	0815	1015	1115	1415	1615	1715	1815	2015
Praha Masarykovo a.	0646	0754	0852	1052	1152	1452	1652	1752	1852	2052

km	2nd class	Ⓒ					
0	Rakovník d.	*0806*	*1006*	1406	...	1806	...
9	Lužná u Rakovnika d.	0823	1023	1418	1423	1818	1823
50	Žatec 1126 d.	0911	1109	...	1509	...	1911
75	Chomutov 1126 a.	0942	1141	...	1541	...	1942
81	Jirkov a.	...	1156	...	1556	...	1956

	Ⓐ	Ⓒ			⑦e	R
Jirkov d.	0551	0800	1200	1600	...	...
Chomutov 1126 d.	0602	0812	1212	1612	1812	*1928*
Žatec 1126 d.	0643	0843	1243	1643	1843	2001
Lužná u Rakovnika a.	0729	0929	1329	1729	1929	2043
Rakovník a.	0749	*0948*	*1348*	*1748*	*1944*	2059

R – ⑤⑥ (also Apr. 20, 30, May 1, 7, 8, Oct. 26, 27).
e – Also Apr. 21, Oct. 28, Nov. 17; not Apr. 20, Oct. 26, Nov. 16.
n – ①–⑥ (not Apr. 21, July 5, Nov. 17).
◧ – Also at 1202, 1402, 1602, 1802, 2002.
◐ – Also at *0806*, *1207*, *1406*, *1806*, *2033*.

For journeys Praha - Chomutov and v.v. change at Lužná u Rakovnika (lower table); for through trains via Ústí n. L. see Table **1110**.

1110 PRAHA - ÚSTI NAD LABEM - CHOMUTOV - KARLOVY VARY - CHEB

km		1688				440	612		610			608		1694	606		1696	604		1698	602		600		
		2	2	Ⓐ		E		Ⓐ			2Ⓐ	m		2Ⓐ			Ⓐ		Ⓒ	2Ⓐ		2			
0	Praha hlavní ▶ d.	...	...	...	...	0515	0729	...	0929	...	...	1129	...	...	1329	...	...	1529	...	...	1729	...	1929	...	...
3	Praha Holešovice ▶ d.	...	...	...	...	0526	0738	...	0938	...	...	1138	...	...	1338	...	...	1538	...	...	1738	...	1938	...	...
106	Ústí nad Labem hl ▶ a.	...	...	...	...	0640	0842	...	1042	...	...	1242	...	...	1442	...	...	1642	...	...	1842	...	2042	...	...
106	Ústí nad Labem hl d.	0057	...	...	0457	0648	0848	...	1048	...	...	1248	...	1347	1448	...	1547	1648	...	1747	1848	...	2048	...	2217
123	Teplice v Čechách d.	0118	...	...	0517	0706	0906	...	1106	...	...	1306	...	1407	1506	...	1607	1706	...	1807	1906	...	2106	...	2237
152	Most d.	0147	...	...	0600	0733	0933	...	1133	...	...	1333	...	1434	1533	1612	1637	1733	1808	1834	1933	...	2133	...	2307
177	Chomutov d.	0207	0405	0505	0625	0755	0955	...	1155	...	...	1355	...	1503	1555	1634	1657	1755	1834	1903	1955	...	2154	2156	2327
196	Klášterec nad Ohří d.	▬	0439	0534	0643	0810	1010	...	1210	...	...	1410	...	1515	1610	1655	...	1810	1855	1918	2010	...	▬	2217	...
236	Karlovy Vary ⊙ a.	...	0524	0620	0727	0846	1046	...	1246	...	...	1446	...	1601	1646	1740	...	1846	1940	2004	2046	...	...	2300	...
236	Karlovy Vary ⊙ d.	0418	*0531*	0622	0731	0849	1049	1200	1249	1308	1411	1449	1517	*1611*	1649	1744	...	1849	1943	2012	2049	2122	2222	...	...
262	Sokolov d.	0444	*0557*	0649	0757	0911	1111	1229	1311	1335	1438	1511	1544	*1639*	1711	1814	...	1911	2010	2039	2111	2148	2248	...	...
291	Cheb a.	0518	*0629*	0724	0829	0938	1138	1305	1338	1410	1513	1538	1618	*1713*	1738	1848	...	1938	2044	2114	2138	2222	2322	...	...

	601	1691	603		1695		605		607		609		611			613			615		441				
	Ⓐt	Ⓐ		2	2Ⓐ	Ⓐ		2Ⓐ			m	Ⓐ		Ⓐ	Ⓒ		2Ⓐ				E		2	2	2
Cheb d.	...	0400	...	0423	...	0527	0616	0652	0816	...	1016	1121	1216	*1238*	1322	1416	*1433*	1544	1616	*1706*x	1816	...	2003	...	2241
Sokolov d.	...	0425	...	0456	...	0602	0642	0750	0842	...	1042	1154	1242	*1315*	1354	1442	*1507*	1618	1642	*1740*	1842	...	2038	...	2316
Karlovy Vary ⊙ a.	...	0447	...	0522	...	0627	0702	0816	0902	...	1102	1220	1302	*1343*	1420	1502	*1533*	1645	1702	*1817*	1902	...	2103	...	2342
Karlovy Vary ⊙ d.	...	0448	*0448*	...	0558	0647	0705	...	0905	1022	1105	1222	1305	1422	1422	1505	1538	...	1705	1822	1905	2022	▬	2257	...
Klášterec nad Ohří d.	...	0534	*0534*	...	0643	0730	0743	...	0943	1107	1143	1307	1343	1507	1507	1543	1623	...	1743	1907	1943	2107	Ⓐ	2354	...
Chomutov d.	0457	0553	0600	...	0700	...	0800	...	1000	1126	1200	1326	1400	1526	1526	1600	1643*	...	1800	1926	2000	2132	2252	0016	...
Most d.	0522	...	0622	...	0721	...	0822	...	1022	1149	1222	1349	1422	1549	1549	1622	...	...	1822	1949	2022	2204	2315	...	...
Teplice v Čechách d.	0550	...	0650	...	0748	...	0850	...	1050	...	1250	...	1450	...	...	1650	...	...	1850	...	2050	2237			
Ústí nad Labem hl a.	0607	...	0707	...	0810	...	0907	...	1107	...	1307	...	1507	...	...	1707	...	...	1907	...	2107	2258			
Ústí nad Labem hl. ▶ d.	0613	...	0713	...	...	...	0913	...	1113	...	1313	...	1513	...	...	1713	...	...	1913	...	2113	...			
Praha Holešovice ▶ a.	0717	...	0817	...	...	...	1017	...	1217	...	1417	...	1617	...	...	1817	...	...	2017	...	2230	...			
Praha hlavní ▶ a.	0727	...	0827	...	...	...	1027	...	1227	...	1427	...	1627	...	...	1827	...	...	2027	...	2240	...	...	...	...

Timings may vary by up to 30 mins until July 30

km	*via Louny (2 cl.)*	Ⓒ	Ⓐ
0	Praha Masarykovo d.	0717	1620
47	Slaný d.	0813	1731
90	Louny d.	0858	1825
115	Most a.	0925	...

via Louny (2 cl.)	Ⓐ	Ⓒ
Most d.	...	1644
Louny d.	0528	1715
Slaný d.	0625	1801
Praha Masarykovo a.	0734	1859

Local trains (2 cl.)				⊡
Děčín ▶ d.	0528	and	1928	2037
Ústí n. L. hlavní ▶ d.	0557	hourly	1957	2117
Teplice v Čechách d.	0617	⊡	2017	2137
Most a.	0650	until	2050	2210

Local trains (2 cl.)				△
Most d.	0504	and	2004	2104
Teplice v Čechách d.	0537	hourly	2037	2137
Ústí n. L. hlavní ▶ d.	0600	⊖	2100	2158
Děčín ▶ a.	0628	until	2128	...

E – EXCELSIOR – 🛏 1, 2 cl., 🛌 2 cl., 🍴 Cheb - Karlovy Vary - Praha - Žilina - Košice and v.v.
m – Conveys on dates in Table **95** 🛏 1, 2 cl. Cheb - Karlovy Vary - Praha (**405/4**) - Moskva and v.v.
t – Not May 2, 9, Oct. 27.
x – 1718 on Ⓐ.
▶ – For other non-stop trains see Table **1100**.
⊙ – Known locally as Karlovy Vary horní (upper).
⊡ – Also Děčín - Ústí at 0456, 0602Ⓐ, 0702Ⓐ, 2121, 2233.
⊖ – Also Ústí - Děčín at 0449, 0530, 1432Ⓐ, 2233.
△ – Also at 2204.
* – Change at Kadaň Pruneřov.

1115 ÚSTÍ NAD LABEM - DĚČÍN - ČESKÁ LIPA - LIBEREC
2nd class

km		1999	1161	◇	1163	1165	1167	1169	1171	1173	1175
				◧							Ⓑh
0	Ústí nad Labem hl. § d.	...	0727	...	0927	1127	1327	1527	1727	1927	2118
23	Děčín § d.	0526	0745	0841	0945	1145	1345	1545	1745	1945	2135
54	Česká Lipa a.	0608	0820	0926	1020	1220	1420	1620	1820	2020	2211
54	Česká Lipa d.	...	0822	...	1022	1222	1422	1622	1822	2022	...
113	Liberec a.	...	0943	...	1143	1343	1543	1743	1943	2130	...

	1174	1172	1170	1168		1166	1164	1162	1160	
	⚒n				◐					
Liberec d.	...	0628	0828	1028	...	1228	1428	1628	1828	...
Česká Lipa a.	...	0733	0933	1133	...	1333	1533	1733	1933	...
Česká Lipa d.	0610	0739	0939	1139	1230	1339	1539	1739	1939	2225
Děčín § d.	0647	0816	1016	1216	1314	1416	1616	1816	2016	2314
Ústí nad Labem hl. § a.	0704	0832	1032	1232	...	1432	1632	1832	2032	...

h – Not Apr. 20, Nov. 16.
n – ①–⑥ (not Apr. 21, July 5, Nov. 17).
◧ – Every 2 hours 0841 - 2041.
◐ – 0626 and every 2 hours 0830 - 2030.
§ – See also Table **1100** and foot of Table **1110**.

1116 DĚČÍN - RYBNIŠTĚ - RUMBURK - DOLNÍ POUSTEVNA
2nd class

km								Ⓐc			
0	Děčín d.	0611	0815	1015	1215	1415	1615	1702	1815	2015	2236
25	Česká Kamenice ⊖ d.	0649	0849	1049	1249	1449	1649	1745	1849	2046	2308
50	Rybniště a.	0727	0925	1126	1326	1527	1726	1826	1920	2117	2337
61	Rumburk a.	0740	0939	1142	1339	1540	1741	1842	1934	2131	2351
88	Dolní Poustevna a.	0829	1027	1230	1426	1632	1829	...	2028	*2216*	...

	Ⓐ							Ⓐc		
Dolní Poustevna d.	...	...	...	0922	1125	1321	1524r	...	1724	1924
Rumburk d.	0358	0616	0816	1013	1216	1416	1615	1715	1816	2016
Rybniště d.	0415	0630	0830	1030	1230	1430	1630	1728	1830	2030
Česká Kamenice ⊖ d.	0446	0710	0910	1110	1310	1510	1710	1810	1910	2104
Děčín a.	0519	0744	0944	1144	1344	1544	1744	1850	1944	2134

c – Change at Jedlová (41 km from Děčín).
r – *1530* on Ⓐ.
⊖ – Heritage journeys to Kamenický Šenov run at 1115, 1315, 1515 on Ⓒ June 28 - Sept. 7 (see www.kzc.cz)

1117 RYBNIŠTĚ - VARNSDORF - ZITTAU - LIBEREC
2nd class

km		Ⓐ			Ⓐ	Ⓒ	⊖					⊖					⊖						⊖		
0	Rybniště d.	0413	...	0632	...	...	...	0832	...	1032	...	...	...	1332	...	1532	...	...	1732	...	1832	...	...	2032	...
11	Varnsdorf 🏛 d.	0432	0552	0652	0731	0806	...	0852	0952	1052	1152	...	1252	1357	1452	1552	...	1652	1749	1756	1852	2006	...	2049	2137
29	Zittau 🏛 d.	0451	0619	0719	0751	0825	0845	0919	1019	1119	1215	1245	1319	1419	1519	1615	1645	1719	...	1819	1919	2025	2045	...	2157
56	Liberec a.	0525	0655	0755	0824	...	0918	0955	1055	1155	...	1321	1355	1455	1555	...	1718	1755	...	1855	1955	...	2118	...	2229
	Tanwald **1141** a.	...	...	...	...	...	1013c	...	...	...	...	...	...	...	...	...	1812c	...	...	...	...	...	...	...	...

					⊖	Ⓐ	Ⓒ				⊖						⊖					⊖		⚒	
Tanwald **1141** d.	...	...	...	...	...	...	...	...	...	...	1140c	...	...	...	...	...	...	...	...	...	...	1940c	...	...	...
Liberec d.	0502	0602	0702	0802	0838	0857	...	1002	1102	1202	1238	...	1402	1502	...	1602	1635	...	...	1802	1902	2035	...	2252	...
Zittau 🏛 d.	0546	0646	0746	0846	0910	0946	0946	1046	1146	1246	1310	1313	1446	1546	...	1646	1710	1713	...	1846	1946	2110	2113	2327	...
Varnsdorf 🏛 d.	0604	0703	0804	0903	...	1004	1004	1103	1203	1304	...	1331	1504	1603	...	1704	...	1731	1804	1903	2004	...	2131	2344	...
Rybniště a.	0621	...	0821	...	...	1021	1021	...	...	1321	...	...	1521	...	...	1721	...	...	1821	...	2021	...	...	...	...

c – Ⓒ only.
⊖ – From/to Dresden (Table **855**). 1, 2 class.
Operator: Vogtlandbahn *Trilex*. Trains marked ⊖ are operated by ČD.

PRAHA - PLZEŇ - MARIÁNSKÉ LÁZNĚ - CHEB — 1120

km					Ex				SC•	Ex		SC•				Ex					Ex					
			768		356	766	778	764	516	354	762	512	776	760		352	758	774		756	350	754	772	752	770	750
			⚒	Ⓐ	🍷				🅁	🍷		🅁			2				2					Ⓑ		Ⓑ
			n		M	⊡	z		🍷	M		🍷	z		u	M		k			M		k	h		h
0	Praha hlavní .... 1124 d.	...	...	...	0515	0615	0715	0815	0840	0915	1015	1040	1115	1215	...	1315	1415	1515	...	1615	1715	1815	1915	2015	2115	2340
4	Praha Smíchov .... 1124 d.	...	...	...	0523	0623	0723	0823	0849	0923	1023	1049	1123	1223	...	1323	1423	1523	...	1623	1723	1823	1923	2023	2123	2348
43	Beroun .... 1124 d.	...	...	...	0552	0652	0752	0852	|	0952	1052	|	1152	1252	...	1352	1452	1552	...	1652	1752	1852	1952	2052	2152	0017
52	Zdice.................. 1124 d.	...	...	...	|	0700	|	0900	|	|	1100	|	|	1300	...	|	1500	|	...	1700	|	1900	|	2100	|	0024
91	Rokycany.......................d.	...	...	...	0630	0730	0830	0930	|	1030	1130	|	1230	1330	...	1430	1530	1630	...	1730	1830	1930	2030	2130	2230	0051
114	**Plzeň** hlavní...................a.	...	...	...	0650	0750	0850	0950	1006	1050	1150	1206	1250	1350	...	1450	1550	1650	...	1750	1850	1950	2050	2150	2250	0111
114	**Plzeň** hlavní...................d.	...	0606	0635	...	0806	...	...	1008	...	...	1208	...	1406	...	...	1606	...	...	1806	...	2006	...	...	...	...
147	Stříbro...........................d.	...	0630	0711	...	0830	...	...	1029	...	...	1229	...	1430	...	...	1630	...	...	1830	...	2030	...	...	...	...
190	Mariánské Lázně..........d.	0553	0708	0810	...	0908	...	...	1056	...	...	1256	...	1505	1631	...	1708	...	1840	1908	...	2105	...	...	...	...
220	**Cheb** .... 1122 a.	0623	0728	0840	...	0928	...	...	1114	...	...	1317	...	1525	1702	...	1728	...	1910	1928	...	2128	...	...	...	...
229	Františkovy Lázně 1122 a.	...	...	...	...	...	...	...	1124	...	...	1327	...	...	...	...	...	...	...	...	...	...	...	...	...	...

					Ex					Ex	SC•				SC•		Ex						Ex		
	751	771	753	773	755	351	2	757	775	759	353	511	761		777	515	763	355		765	779		767	357		
	⚒		⚒									🅁		Ⓐ		🅁		🍷						🍷		Ⓐ
	n		n	k		M‡	u		z		M	🍷		u	z	🍷		M	u		z	u	⊡	M		
Františkovy Lázně.. 1122 d.	...	...	...	...	...	...	...	...	...	...	...	1236	...	...	...	1436	...	...	...	...	...	...	...	...	...	...
Cheb..................... 1122 d.	...	...	0431	...	0633	...	0648	0833	...	1033	...	1246	...	1318	...	1446	...	...	1519	1633	...	1718	1833	...	2003	2236
Mariánské Lázně ....d.	...	...	0455	...	0655	...	0720	0855	...	1055	...	1304	...	1349	...	1504	...	...	1550	1655	...	1749	1855	...	2034	2307
Stříbro ....d.	...	...	0530	...	0730	...	...	0930	...	1130	...	1332	...	...	...	1532	...	...	...	1730	...	...	1930	...	...	...
Plzeň hlavní ....a.	...	...	0555	...	0755	...	...	0955	...	1155	...	1353	...	...	...	1553	...	...	...	1755	...	...	1955	...	...	...
Plzeň hlavní ....d.	0407	0507	0607	0707	0807	0907	...	1007	1107	1207	1307	1355	1407	...	1507	1555	1607	1707	...	1807	1907	...	2007	2109	...	...
Rokycany...........................d.	0430	0530	0630	0730	0830	0930	...	1030	1130	1230	1330	|	1430	...	1530	|	1630	1730	...	1830	1930	...	2030	2131	...	...
Zdice .... 1124 d.	0458	0558	0658	|	0858	|	...	1058	|	1258	|	|	1458	...	|	|	1658	|	...	1858	1958	...	2058	|	...	...
Beroun.................... 1124 d.	0507	0607	0707	0807	0907	1007	...	1107	1207	1307	1407	|	1507	...	1607	|	1707	1807	...	1907	2007	...	2107	2207	...	...
Praha Smíchov ...... 1124 a.	0536	0636	0736	0836	0936	1036	...	1136	1236	1336	1436	1511	1536	...	1636	1711	1736	1836	...	1936	2036	...	2136	2236	...	...
Praha hlavní.......... 1124 a.	0544	0644	0744	0844	0944	1044	...	1144	1244	1344	1444	1519	1544	...	1644	1719	1744	1844	...	1944	2044	...	2144	2244	...	...

M – 🚌12 Praha - Regensburg - München and v.v. (Tables **76**, **885**).
h – Not Apr. 20, Nov. 16.
k – To/from Klatovy (Table **929**).
n – ①–⑥ (not Apr. 21, July 5, Nov. 17).
u – To/from Karlovy Vary (Table **1110**).
z – To/from Klatovy and Železná Ruda (Table **929**).

⊡ – Conveys 🛏 1, 2 cl. Cheb - Plzeň - Praha (**441/0**) - Žilina - Košice and v.v.

• – *SUPERCITY PENDOLINO* tilting train, 🅁, 🍷, reservation fee CZK 200. From/to Bohumín or Ostrava via Olomouc, Pardubice (Table **1160**). Between Plzeň and Františkovy Lázně reservation is only compulsory in 1st class.

‡ – Starts from Schwandorf on ⑦ and dates in Table **885**.

TRAIN NAMES:
350/3 ALBERT EINSTEIN, **351/2** JAN HUS, **354/7** FRANZ KAFKA, **355/6** KAREL ČAPEK.

CHEB - MARKTREDWITZ - NÜRNBERG — 1121

*27 km**												
Cheb .... d.	0627	0827	0935	1024	1227	1335	1427	1627	1735	1827	1935	2024
Schirnding 🏛 .... d.	0640	0840	|	1037	1240	|	1440	1640	|	1840	|	2037
Marktredwitz.... a.	0652	0852	0955	1049	1252	1355	1452	1652	1755	1852	1955	2049
Nürnberg **880** a.	*0817*	*1014*	1114	*1214*	*1417*	1514	*1614*	*1814*	1914	*2014*	2124	*2214*

Nürnberg **880** d.	0648	*0748*	*0948*	1048	*1148*	*1348*	1448	*1548*	1648	*1746*	*1948*
Marktredwitz... d.	0804	0908	1113	1204	1308	1508	1604	1708	1804	1908	2113
Schirnding 🏛 ... d.	|	0920	1125	|	1320	1520	|	1720	|	1920	2125
Cheb .... a.	0825	0933	1138	1225	1333	1533	1625	1733	1825	1933	2138

z – Also Apr. 18-21, May 1, 29, June 9, 19, Oct. 3.
* – Cheb - Schirnding = 13 km, Cheb - Marktredwitz = 27 km.

Additional journey: Nürnberg d. *0544*, Marktredwitz d. 0737 (0713 on ⑥⑦ **z**), Cheb a. 0802 (0738 on ⑥⑦ **z**).

Local journeys Cheb - Marktredwitz are operated by Vogtlandbahn (2nd cl. only).

CHEB - FRANTIŠKOVY LÁZNĚ - PLAUEN — 1122

2nd class

km			⊖		⊖		⊖		⊖		
0	**Cheb** .... ▶ d.	0955	1006	1215	1406	1415	1606	1624	1806	1815	2015
9	Františkovy Lázně... ▶ d.	1004	1014	1224	1414	1424	1614	1633	1814	1824	2024
28	Aš město...................a.	1031	|	1251	|	1451	|	1700	|	1851	2051
27	Bad Brambach 🏛 ....d.	...	1038	...	1438	...	1638	...	1838	...	...
76	**Plauen** .... a.	...	1135	...	1535	...	1735	...	1935	...	...

	Ⓐ	⊖		⊖		⊖			⊖	
Plauen.........................d.	...	0824	...	1224	...	1424	...	...	1624	...
Bad Brambach 🏛.........d.	...	0922	...	1322	...	1522	...	...	1722	...
Aš město ....d.	0909	|	1127	|	1327	|	1527	1708	|	1922
Františkovy Lázně ▶ d.	0937	0947	1155	1347	1355	1547	1555	1736	1747	1950
Cheb 1110............. ▶ a.	0945	0954	1203	1354	1403	1554	1603	1744	1754	1958

⊖ – Operator: Vogtlandbahn.

▶ – For *SC* trains see Table **1120**. Additional local trains Cheb - Františkovy Lázně: **From Cheb**: 0505 Ⓐ, 0545 Ⓐ, 0647, 0811 Ⓐ, 1520 Ⓐ, 2235. **From Františkovy Lázně**: 0514 Ⓐ, 0540 Ⓒ, 0620 Ⓐ, 0722 Ⓐ, 0757 Ⓒ, 0820 Ⓐ, 2127.

KARLOVY VARY - MARIÁNSKÉ LÁZNĚ — 1123

Operator: GW TrainRegio. 2nd class

km										
0	**Karlovy Vary** dolní (lower) ... d.	0617	0904	1057	1258	1503	1708	1924	2123	...
33	Bečov nad Teplou.................d.	0650	0938	1131	1332	1537	1742	2000	2159	...
53	**Mariánské Lázně** ....a.	0739	1027	1220	1421	1626	1831	2049	2248	...

Mariánské Lázně ....d.	0558	0832	1038	1225	1428	1634	1909	2108	...
Bečov nad Teplou..............d.	0651	0923	1132	1315	1519	1725	2000	2159	...
Karlovy Vary dolní (lower). a.	0724	0956	1205	1349	1554	1759	2033	2232	...

PRAHA - BEROUN - PŘÍBRAM - PISEK - ČESKÉ BUDĚJOVICE — 1124

2nd class

For direct trains Praha - České Budějovice see Table **1130**

km		1254	1252	1250		1248	1246	1244	1242	1240
		Ⓐ	①x		◧	Ⓒ	Ⓐ	⑤f		
0	**Praha** hlavní................ 1120 d.	...	0545	0745	*0815*	0945	1145	1340	1545	1745
4	Praha Smichov .... 1120 d.	...	0553	0753	*0823*	0953	1153	1348	1553	1753
43	Beroun .... 1120 d.	...	0622	0822	0859	1022	1222	1417	1622	1822
52	Zdice .... 1120 d.	...	0630	0830	0910	1030	1230	1425	1630	1830
82	Přibram..............................d.	...	0659	0859	0948	1059	1259	1459	1659	1859
100	Březnice ....d.	...	0718	0918	1013	1118	1318	1518	1718	1918
142	Pisek ....d.	0559	0759	0959	...	1159	1359	1559	1759	1959
155	Protivín...................... 1125 d.	0614	0814	1014	...	1214	1414	1614	1814	2014
192	**České Budějovice** ...... 1125 a.	0644	0844	1044	...	1244	1444	1644	1844	2044r

	1241	1241	1243		1245	1247	1249	1251	1253
	①x			◧	⑤f			⑦e	
České Budějovice ... 1125 d.	0510	...	0710	...	1110	1310	1510	1710	1910
Protivín .... 1125 d.	0544	0544	0744	...	1144	1344	1544	1744	1944
Pisek ....d.	0558	0558	0758	...	1158	1358	1558	1758	1956
Březnice ....d.	0639	0639	0839	1143	1239	1439	1639	1839	...
Přibram.................................d.	0659	0659	0859	1210	1301	1459	1659	1901	...
Zdice .... 1120 d.	0729	0729	0929	1249	1333	1529	1729	1933	...
Beroun....................... 1120 d.	0737	0737	0937	1300	1342	1537	1737	1942	...
Praha Smichov .... 1120 a.	0806	0806	1006	*1336*	1411	1606	1806	2011	...
Praha hlavní............. 1120 a.	0814	0814	1014	*1344*	1419	1614	1814	2019	...

– Also Apr. 21, Oct. 28, Nov. 17; not Apr. 20, Oct. 26, Nov. 16.
– Also Apr. 30, May 7; not May 2, 9.
– ⑤–⑦ (also Apr. 21, 30, May 1, 7, 8, Oct. 27, 28, Nov. 17).

x – Also Apr. 22, Oct. 29, Nov. 18; not Apr. 21, Oct. 27, Nov. 17.
◧ – Runs every 2 hours (change at Beroun): from Praha 0815 - 1615, from Březnice 0943 - 1943. Most journeys extend to/from Protivin.

PLZEŇ - ČESKÉ BUDĚJOVICE — 1125

km		623	661	663	665	667	669	625	627	629
		⚒n						h		⑤⑦r
0	**Plzeň** hlavní ....d.	...	0603	0803	1003	1203	1403	1603	1803	2003
34	Nepomuk................................d.	...	0631	0831	1031	1231	1431	1631	1831	2031
59	Horaždovice předměstí ....d.	...	0652	0852	1052	1252	1452	1652	1852	2052
76	Strakonice ....d.	0500	0708	0908	1108	1308	1508	1708	1908	2108
99	Protivín........................ 1124 d.	0519	0727	0927	1127	1327	1527	1727	1927	2127
136	**České Budějovice** ...... 1124 a.	0554	0756	0956	1156	1356	1556	1756	1956	2156
	Jihlava **1135**......................a.	0833	1033	1233z	1433	1633	1833	2031b	...	...
	Brno **1135** ....a.	1036	1236	1436z	1636	1836	2036	...	...	...

	628	626	624	668	666	664	662	660	
			h					⑤⑦r	2Ⓑ
Brno **1135** ....d.	...	...	...	0720	0920z	1120	1320	1520	...
Jihlava **1135** ....d.	...	0525x	0725	0925	1125z	1325	1525	1725	...
České Budějovice ... 1124 d.	0604	0804	1004	1204	1404	1604	1804	2004	2242
Protivín .... 1124 d.	0633	0833	1033	1233	1433	1633	1833	2033	2327
Strakonice...........................d.	0653	0853	1053	1253	1453	1653	1853	2053	2350
Horaždovice předměstí ......d.	0709	0909	1109	1309	1509	1709	1909	2109	...
Nepomuk ....d.	0729	0929	1129	1329	1529	1729	1929	2129	...
Plzeň hlavní.......................a.	0757	0957	1157	1357	1557	1757	1957	2157	...

– Ⓑ (not Apr. 20, Nov. 16).
– To/from Havlíčkův Brod on dates in Table **1152**.
– ①–⑥ (not Apr. 21, July 5, Nov. 17).

r – Also Apr. 21, 30, May 7, Oct. 28, Nov. 17; not Apr. 20, May 2, 9, Oct. 26, Nov. 16.
x – Ⓐ (also May 3, 10, Oct. 28).
z – ⑤⑥⑦ (daily May 30 - Sept. 14), also Apr. 21, 30, May 1, 7, 8, Oct. 28, Nov. 17.

1126 PLZEŇ - CHOMUTOV - MOST *2nd class*

km		1798 Ⓐ	1192	1190	1188	1186	1184	1182 Ⓑh	1180 ⑦e	
0	**Plzeň** hlavní d.	...	0605	1005	1205	1405	1605	1805	2005	...
59	Blatno u Jesenice d.	0454	0710	1110	1310	1510	1710	1908	2110	...
107	Žatec **1105** d.	0551	0802	1202	1402	1602	1802	2002	2202	...
130	Chomutov **1110** d.	0617	0829	1229	1429	1629	1829	2029	2229	...
155	**Most** **1110** a.	...	0850	1250	1450	1650	1850	2050	2250	...

	1181 ⚒n	1183	1185		1187	1189	1191	1193 ⑦e	1797 Ⓐ
Most **1110** d.	0505	0705	0905	...	1305	1503	1705	1905	1905
Chomutov **1110** d.	0528	0728	0928	...	1328	1527	1728	1928	1928
Žatec **1105** d.	0553	0753	0953	...	1353	1553	1753	1953	1954
Blatno u Jesenice d.	0646	0845	1045	...	1445	1645	1845	2045	2049
Plzeň hlavní a.	0752	0952	1152	...	1552	1752	1952	2152	...

e – Also Apr. 21, Oct. 28, Nov. 17; not Apr. 20, Oct. 26, Nov. 16.
h – Not Apr. 20, Nov. 16.
n – ①–⑥ (not Apr. 21, July 5, Nov. 17).

1130 PRAHA - TÁBOR - ČESKÉ BUDĚJOVICE

km		1839 2	1541	633 ⚒ n	635		637 ⚒ n	1543		641	643 Ⓐ	1545	645	647		649	651	653 Ⓑ h	655	657		659		
0	**Praha** hlavní d.	...	0533	0633	0733	...	0833	0933	...	1133	1233	1333	1433	1533	...	1633	1733	1833	1933	2033	...	2233	...	...
49	Benešov u Prahy d.	...	0614	0714	0814	...	0914	1014	...	1214	1314	1414	1514	1614	...	1714	1814	1914	2014	2114	...	2314	...	...
103	**Tábor** d.	0617	0701	0801	0901	...	1001	1101	...	1301	1401	1501	1601	1701	...	1801	1901	2001	2101	2201	...	0001	...	...
130	Veselí nad Lužnicí ▷ d.	0651	0729	0829	0929	...	1029	1129	...	1329	1429	1529	1629	1729	...	1829	1929	2029	2132	2229	...	0034	...	...
169	**České Budějovice** ▷ a.	0730	0801	0901	1001	...	1101	1201	...	1401	1501	1601	1701	1801	...	1901	2001	2101	2203	2301	...	0112	...	...
	Linz Hbf **1132** a.	...	1024	...	...	...	...	1424	...	...	...	1824	...	...	...	...	...	...	...	...	...	...	...	...

	630 ⚒ n‡	656 ⚒ n	654	652 ⚒ n		650	648 Ⓐ	646		644	642	1540		640	638	636	1542		632	630	2 Ⓐ	2	2	
Linz Hbf **1132** d.	...	...	...	...	...	...	...	...	...	...	...	1135	...	...	...	...	1535	...	...	...	...	...	...	...
České Budějovice ▷ d.	0338	0457	0557	0657	...	0757	0857	0957	...	1157	1257	1357	...	1457	1557	1657	1757	...	1857	1957	2029	2240	...	...
Veselí nad Lužnicí ▷ d.	0422	0529	0629	0729	...	0829	0929	1029	...	1229	1329	1429	...	1529	1629	1729	1829	...	1929	2029	2133	2325	2333	...
Tábor d.	0459	0559	0659	0759	...	0859	0959	1059	...	1259	1359	1459	...	1559	1659	1759	1859	...	1959	2059	2207	...	0007	...
Benešov u Prahy d.	0550	0650	0750	0850	...	0950	1050	1150	...	1350	1450	1550	...	1650	1750	1850	1950	...	2050	2150	...	...	...	...
Praha hlavní a.	0631	0731	0831	0931	...	1031	1131	1231	...	1431	1531	1631	...	1731	1831	1931	2031	...	2131	2231	...	...	...	...

h – Not Apr. 20, Nov. 16.
n – ①–⑥ (not Apr. 21, July 5, Nov. 17).
▷ – See also Table **1135**.
‡ – Train number **8200** České Budějovice - Tábor.
For train names Praha - Linz see Table **1132**.

1131 ČESKÉ BUDĚJOVICE - ČESKÝ KRUMLOV - NOVÉ ÚDOLÍ

km		P	Q			R		S	◇		Ⓐ	
0	**České Budějovice** d.	0531	0604	0806	1006	1206	1406	1453	1606	1811	2007	2244
31	Český Krumlov d.	0623	0657	0857	1057	1257	1457	1543	1659	1902	2056	2332
68	Horní Planá a.	0719	0759	0959	1159	1359	1559	...	1759	1958	...	...
96	**Nové Údolí** a.	...	...	1044	1244c	1444	1644	...	1844r	...	...	...

	Ⓐ		P	N	◇	R				T
Nové Údolí d.	...	...	...	...	0913v	1113	1313c	1513	1713	...
Horní Planá d.	...	...	0720	0759	0959	1159	1359	1559	1759	...
Český Krumlov d.	0432	0603	0836	0857	1057	1300	1457	1700	1903	2116
České Budějovice a.	0519	0658	0929	0947	1147	1349	1547	1749	1952	2205

N – Ⓒ (daily June 28 - Aug. 31).
P – Ⓐ (not June 30 - Aug. 29).
Q – Ⓒ to June 22 (not Apr. 5-13); daily June 28 - Aug. 31, also Oct. 6, 7, 13, 14.
R – Ⓐ (daily Apr. 14 - Oct. 27).
S – Ⓐ (not Apr. 17, 18, June 30 - Aug. 29, Oct. 27-29).
T – Ⓐ (daily Apr. 14 - Sept. 19).
c – Ⓒ (daily Apr. 19 - Sept. 14), also Apr. 5, 6, 12, 13; not Aug. 2.
r – Apr. 19 - Sept. 14 (also Ⓒ Sept. 20 - Oct. 26); not Aug. 3.
v – Ⓒ (daily Apr. 19 - Sept. 14), not Aug. 3.
◇ – Timings vary on Aug. 3.

1132 ČESKÉ BUDĚJOVICE - LINZ

km		2	2	1541	3883 2	1543	3885 2	1545	2	3889 2	2
	Praha hlavní **1130** d.	...	...	0533	...	0933	...	1333	...	...	...
0	**České Budějovice** d.	0559	...	0812	1011	1212	1400	1612	...	1806	2013
50	Rybnik d.	0658	...	0858	1059	1258	1456	1658	...	1857	2113
64	Summerau ⊞ a.	0713	...	0912	1115	1312	1510	1712	...	1912	...
64	Summerau d.	...	0716	0914	1117	1314	1512	1714	1810	1914	...
73	Freistadt d.	...	0724	0922	1125	1322	1520	1723	1819	1922	...
126	**Linz** Hbf a.	...	0825	1024	1224	1424	1624	1824	1924	2025	...

	2	3882 2	3884 2	1540	3886 2	1542	2Ⓐ	2Ⓐ	3890
Linz Hbf d.	...	0721	0915	1135	1315	1535	1652	...	1935
Freistadt d.	...	0821	1018	1235	1420	1633	1744	...	2040
Summerau a.	...	0830	1027	1243	1429	1642	1753	...	2049
Summerau ⊞ d.	0726	0841	1042	1245	1438	1645	...	1818	2059
Rybnik d.	0741	0859	1100	1259	1456	1659	...	1835	2115
České Budějovice a.	0842	0952	1152	1343	1552	1743	...	1931	2212
Praha hlavní **1130** a.	...	...	...	1631	...	2031	...	...	...

TRAIN NAMES: **1540/1** – F. A. GERSTNER, **1542/3** – ANTON BRUCKNER.

1133 ČESKÉ BUDĚJOVICE - ČESKÉ VELENICE - (WIEN) *2nd class only*

km		Ⓐ	Ⓐ			N		Ⓑh		Ⓐ	
0	České Budějovice d.	0510	0636	0808	1008	1208	1408	1608	1808	2008	2246
50	České Velenice ⊞ a.	0558	0729	0856	1056	1256	1456	1656	1856	2056	2333
	České Velenice . **990** d.	*0618*	...	*0905*	*1109*	*1312*	*1508*	*1729*	*1906*	...	...
	Gmünd NÖ **990** a.	*0622*	...	*0909*	*1113*	*1316*	*1512*	*1733*	*1910*	...	...
	Wien FJB **990** a.	*0836*	...	*1131*	*1331*	*1533*	*1733*	*1959*	*2149*	...	...

	Ⓐ		Ⓐ		Ⓐ		Ⓑh		N	
Wien FJB **990** d.	...	...	...	*0622*	...	*1029*	*1229*	*1429*	*1624*	*1921*
Gmünd NÖ **990** d.	...	...	...	*0841*	...	*1247*	*1449*	*1649*	*1849*	*2138*
České Velenice. **990** a.	...	...	...	*0845*	...	*1251*	*1453*	*1653*	*1853*	*2142*
České Velenice ⊞ d.	0400	0459	0630	0903	1103	1303	1503	1703	1903	2144
České Budějovice a.	0450	0552	0720	0952	1152	1352	1552	1752	1952	2231

VESELÍ NAD LUŽNICÍ - ČESKÉ VELENICE *For connections Praha - Veselí nad Lužnicí see Table* **1130**. *For connections České Velenice - Wien see Table* **990**.

km			Ⓐ	Ⓒ			E				Ⓒ	Ⓐ
0	Veselí nad Lužnicí d.	0457	0556	0733	0933	1133	1333	1533	1733	1933	2150	2230
21	Třeboň d.	0523	0618	0759	0959	1159	1359	1559	1759	1959	2214	2256
55	České Velenice a.	0600	0702	0840	1040	1240	1440	1640	1840	2040	2255	2336

	Ⓐ	Ⓐd	Ⓒ		E					t
České Velenice d.	0609	0649	0719	0919	1119	1319	1519	1719	1919	2213
Třeboň d.	0649	0759	0759	0959	1159	1359	1559	1759	1959	2255
Veselí nad Lužnicí a.	0712	0823	0823	1023	1223	1423	1623	1823	2023	2319

E – Ⓐ (daily Apr. 14 - Sept. 19).
N – Ⓐ (also ⑥ July 5 - Aug. 30).
d – Not Apr. 17, 18, June 30 - Aug. 29, Oct. 27-29.
h – Not Apr. 20, Nov. 16.
t – To Tábor (Table **1130**), arrive 0007.

1135 ČESKÉ BUDĚJOVICE - JIHLAVA - BRNO

km		1869 2Ⓐ	621 A	623	661	663 H	665	667	669	2	625 Ⓑh
	Plzeň **1125** d.	...	...	...	0603	0803	1003	1203	1403	...	1603
0	**České Budějovice** d.	...	0412	0612	0807	1007	1212	1407	1607	...	1807
39	Veselí nad Lužnicí ▷ d.	...	0445	0645	0845	1045	1245	1445	1645	...	1845
65	Jindřichův Hradec ▷ d.	...	0516	0716	0916	1116	1316	1516	1716	...	1916
117	Kostelec u Jihlavy ▲ d.	...	0615	0815	1015	1215	1415	1615	1815	...	2013
132	**Jihlava** a.	...	0633	0833	1033	1233	1433	1633	1833	...	2031
132	**Jihlava** d.	0530	0639	0839	1039	1239	1439	1639	1839	1930	▽
161	Okříšky d.	0603	0707	0907	1107	1307	1507	1707	1907	2019	...
173	Trebíč d.	0620	0723	0923	1123	1323	1523	1723	1923	2046	...
236	**Brno** hlavní a.	0737	0836	1036	1236	1436	1636	1836	2036	2211	...

	626 Ⓐ	624	668	666 H	664	662	660	622	620 Ⓑh
Brno hlavní d.	...	...	0720	0920	1120	1320	1520	1720	1920
Trebíč d.	...	...	0831	1031	1231	1431	1631	1831	2037
Okříšky d.	...	...	0846	1046	1246	1446	1646	1846	2052
Jihlava a.	...	▽	0919	1119	1319	1519	1719	1919	2119
Jihlava d.	0525	0725	0925	1125	1325	1525	1725	1934s	...
Kostelec u Jihlavy ▲ d.	0543	0743	0943	1143	1343	1543	1743	1953s	...
Jindřichův Hradec ▷ d.	0643	0843	1043	1243	1443	1643	1843	2056s	...
Veselí nad Lužnicí ▷ d.	0715	0915	1115	1315	1515	1715	1915	2126s	...
České Budějovice a.	0750	0950	1147	1350	1550	1750	1950	2158s	...
Plzeň **1125** a.	0957	1157	1357	1557	1757	1957	2157s	...	...

CONNECTIONS OKŘÍŠKY - ZNOJMO

km		Ⓐ	Ⓐ	⚒				Ⓑv			
0	Okříšky d.	0443	0610	0710	0917	1117	1317	1517	1717	1920	...
32	Moravské Budějovice a.	0518	0645	0744	0952	1152	1352	1554	1752	1959	...
70	Znojmo a.	0630	0730	0847	1047	1247	1447	1647	1847	...	...

	Ⓐ	Ⓐ	⚒			⑦	Ⓐ			z
Znojmo d.	0423	0530	*0701*	0904	1104	1304	*1304*	1504	1704	190
Moravské Budějovice d.	0522	0623	0803	1003	1203	1403	1427	1603	1803	194
Okříšky a.	0557	0703	0839	1039	1239	1439	1503	1639	1839	201

A – ① (also Apr. 22, Oct. 29, Nov. 18; not Apr. 21, Oct. 27, Nov. 17) from České Budějovice; ①–⑥ (not Apr. 21, July 5, Nov. 17) from Jihlava.
H – ⑤⑥⑦ (daily May 30 - Sept. 14), also Apr. 21, 30, May 1, 7, 8, Oct. 28, Nov. 17.
h – Not Apr. 20, Nov. 16.
s – ⑤⑦ (also Apr. 21, 30, May 7, Oct. 28, Nov. 17; not Apr. 20, May 2, 9, Oct. 26, Nov. 16).
v – Not Apr. 20, Oct. 26, Nov. 16.
z – To Jihlava, arrive 2106.
▷ – Additional trains: from Veselí nad Lužnicí 0742, 0942, 1142 Ⓐ, 1342, 1542 Ⓑ **h**, 1742, 1942 Ⓐ, 2142, 2328 Ⓐ; from Jindřichův Hradec 0542, 0730, 0940, 1140, 1340 Ⓐ, 1540 Ⓑ **h**, 1740, 1940, 2222 Ⓐ. Journey 35 minutes.
▽ – To / from Havlíčkův Brod on dates in Table **1152**.
▲ – Connections Kostelec - Telč (journey 36 minutes, *23* km
From Kostelec: 0636 Ⓐ, 0820, 1018, 1111 Ⓐ, 1316, 1421 Ⓐ, 1512 Ⓒ, 1522 Ⓐ, 1710, 1818 ⑦, 1910 ⚒, 2019 ⑦, 2128 Ⓐ.
From Telč: 0403 ⚒, 0516 Ⓐ, 0618 ⑥, 0718 Ⓑ, 0803 Ⓐ, 0902 Ⓒ, 0935 Ⓐ, 1204, 1327 Ⓐ, 1404 Ⓒ, 1441 Ⓐ, 160 1655 ⑦, 1804 ⚒, 1910 ⑦, 2028 Ⓐ.

2nd class PRAHA - MLADÁ BOLESLAV - TURNOV - (LIBEREC) 1140

km			1148	1146		1144	1142	1140	1940		
			T	T		T	T				ⓑh
0	**Praha** hlavní	d.	0548	0725	0925	1148	1325	1525	1725	1925	2106	2106
34	Neratovice	d.	0632	0800	1000	1232	1400	1600	1800	2000	2149	2149
40	Všetaty	d.	0643	0807	1007	1243	1407	1607	1807	2007	2157	2157
72	**Mladá Boleslav**	a.	0718	0835	1035	1321	1435	1635	1835	2035	2232	2232
72	**Mladá Boleslav**	d.	...	0838	1038	*1347*	1438	1638	1838	2038	...	2240
88	Mnichovo Hradiště	d.	...	0858	1058	*1409*	1458	1658	1858	2058	...	2259
102	**Turnov**	a.	...	0912	1112	*1428*	1512	1712	1912	2116	...	2315
	Turnov **1142**	d.	...	*0920*	*1120*	...	*1520*	*1720*	*1920*	*2120*	...	*2318*
	Liberec **1142**	a.	...	*0957*	*1157*	...	*1557*	*1757*	*1957*	*2157*	...	*2356*

		1941	1141	1143		1145	1147	1149	1151		
		Ⓐ		T			T	T	T		Ⓒ
Liberec **1142**	d.	*0400*	*0602*	*0802*	...	*1202*	*1402*	*1602*	*1802*	...	*2031*
Turnov **1142**	a.	*0438*	*0639*	*0839*	...	*1239*	*1439*	*1639*	*1839*	...	*2113*
Turnov	d.	0441	0644	0844	*0922*	1244	1444	1644	1844	...	2122
Mnichovo Hradiště	d.	0459	0658	0858	*0940*	1258	1458	1658	1858	...	2140
Mladá Boleslav	a.	0519	0715	0915	*1000*	1315	1515	1715	1915	...	2200
Mladá Boleslav	d.	0521	0724	0924	1037	1324	1524	1724	1924	2037	2207
Všetaty	d.	0550	0751	0951	1120	1351	1551	1751	1951	2121	2248
Neratovice	d.	0558	0800	1000	1130	1400	1600	1800	2000	2130	2257
Praha hlavní	a.	0634	0834	1034	1211	1434	1639	1834	2034	2211	2334

T – To/from Tanwald on dates in Table **1142**. **h** – Not Apr. 20, Nov. 16.

2nd class LIBEREC - TANWALD - HARRACHOV - SZKLARSKA POREBA GÓRNA 1141

km				s⊖			⊖	Ⓒd	b		s⊖			⊖			s⊖			⊖	Ⓒd				
0	**Liberec**	▷ d.	0637	...	0757	0837	...	0922	0922	1002	...	1117	1237	...	1317	1437	...	1517	1637	...	1720	1717**a**	1757	1917	2032
12	Jablonec nad Nisou	▷ d.	0656	...	0816	0856	...	0941	0941	1021	...	1136	1256	...	1336	1456	...	1536	1656	...	1740	1736**a**	1816	1936	2054
27	**Tanwald**	▷ a.	0732	...	0852	0932	...	1013	1013	1053	...	1212	1332	...	1412	1534	...	1612	1734	...	1812	1812**a**	1852	2016	2126
27	**Tanwald**	d.	0738	...	0855**s**	0938	...	...	1018	1055**s**	...	1218	1334	...	1418	1536	...	1618	1736	...	...	1818	...	2018	...
34	Kořenov	d.	0754	0756	0919**s**	0954	0956	...	1039	1119**s**	...	1239	1350	1352	1439	1552	1554	1639	1752	1754	...	1839	...	2039	...
39	Harrachov	d.	...	0804	0926**s**	1012**s**	1004	...	1046	1126**s**	1128	1246	...	1401	1446	...	1603	1646	...	1803	...	1846	...	2046**x**	...
55	**Szklarska Poreba Górna**	◇ a.	...	0829	...	...	1030	...	...	...	1153	...	...	1426	...	...	1628	...	...	1828	...	...	...	...	...

				Ⓐ	s⊖			⊖	b	Ⓒd		s⊖			⊖			s⊖			⊖	b	Ⓒd	
Szklarska Poreba Górna	◇ d.	...	...	...	0840	...	...	1040	...	...	...	1225	...	...	1435	...	...	1635	...	...	1840	...	...	...	...
Harrachov	d.	...	...	...	0909	...	0943**s**	1108	1110	...	1150**s**	1253	1258	...	1503	1505	...	1703	1705	...	1908	1910	...	...	2120**x**
Kořenov	d.	...	0757	...	0916	0918**s**	0958	...	1118	...	1158**s**	...	1306	1358	...	1512	1558	...	1712	1758	...	1918	...	...	2128
Tanwald	d.	...	0816	...	...	0936**s**	1016	...	1136	...	1216**s**	...	1325	1416	...	1531	1616	...	1731	1816	...	1936	...	...	2147
Tanwald	▷ d.	0700	0820	0900	...	0940	1020	...	1140	1140	1220	...	1340	1420	...	1540	1620	...	1738	1820	...	1940	1940	2020	2153
Jablonec nad Nisou	▷ d.	0737	0857	0942	...	1022	1057	...	1215	1215	1257	...	1417	1457	...	1617	1657	...	1817	1857	...	2011	2011	2055	2229
Liberec	▷ a.	0756	0916	1001	...	1041	1116	...	1234	1234	1316	...	1436	1516	...	1636	1716	...	1836	1916	...	2030	2030	2118	2247

a – Ⓐ only.
b – Change at Tanwald on Ⓒ.
d – To/from Dresden (Table **855**, 1,2 class).
s – Jan. 11 - Mar. 16, ⑥⑦ Apr. 26 - June 22 (also May 1, 2, 8, June 19, 20), daily June 28 - Aug. 31, ⑥⑦ Sept. 6 - Oct. 26, also Oct. 28.
x – ⑤⑥ only.

◇ – 🚌 = Jakuszyce. For connections to/from Jelenia Góra see Table **1083**.
⊖ – Operator: GW Train Regio.
▷ – Additional journeys Liberec - Tanwald:
From Liberec: 0516, 0557, 0717, 1152 Ⓐ, 1357, 1557, 1837, 2135, 2233.
From Tanwald: 0345 Ⓐ, 0420, 0500, 0540, 0620, 0740, 1300 Ⓐ, 1500, 1700, 2256 ⑤⑥.

2nd class LIBEREC - HRADEC KRÁLOVÉ - PARDUBICE 1142

km			1261	1263		1275	1277
0	**Liberec**	d.	0400	0602		1802	2002
38	Turnov	d.	0439	0642		1842	2042
52	Železný Brod ★	d.	0456	0700	and	1900	2100
76	Stará Paka	d.	0525	0727	every	1927	2127
107	Dvůr Králové n. L.	d.	0600	0800	**two**	2000	2201
122	Jaroměř	d.	0618	0819	hours	2020	2221
139	**Hradec Králové**	a.	0633	0834	until	2035	2238
139	**Hradec Králové** ▶	d.	0638	0838		2038	2241
161	**Pardubice** ▶	a.	0700	0900		2100	2310

		1276	1274		1262	1260
Pardubice ▶	d.	0500	0700		1900	2100
Hradec Králové ▶	a.	0522	0721	and	1921	2121
Hradec Králové	d.	0526	0725	every	1925	2125
Jaroměř	d.	0542	0742	**two**	1942	2144
Dvůr Králové n. L.	d.	0559	0759	hours	1959	2200
Stará Paka	d.	0631	0831	until	2031	2235
Železný Brod ★	d.	0700	0900		2100	2301
Turnov	d.	0720	0920		2120	2318
Liberec	a.	0757	0957		2157	2356

		△		d		ⓑh	ⓑh
Praha hl **1140**	d.	...	0725	0925	1325	1525	*1725*
Turnov	d.	...	0919	1119	1519	1719	1926
Železný Brod	d.	0702	0937	1137	1537	1737	1946
Tanwald	a.	0728	1004	1207	1604	1804	2012
		⚒	▽	⑥u	d	d	
Tanwald	d.	0425	0625	0752	1345	1545	1746
Železný Brod	a.	0453	0652	0819	1413	1619	1819
Turnov	a.	...	...	0836	1436	1636	1836
Praha hl **1140**	a.	...	...	1034	1639	1834	2034

d – Change at Turnov on Ⓐ.
h – Not Apr. 20, Nov. 16.
u – ⑥ (also ①–⑤ July 1 - Aug. 29), also May 1, 8, Oct. 28.
△ – Also 0902, 1102Ⓒ, 1302, 1414Ⓐ, 1502, 1702, 1902⑤–⑦, 2102, 2302Ⓐ.
▽ – Also 0505 Ⓐ, 0825, 1025, 1225, 1428, 1625, 1825 ⑤–⑦, 2025, 2231Ⓐ.
★ – For Pardubice - Tanwald change at Železný Brod (see right hand panel).

▶ – Additional trains **Hradec Kralové - Pardubice** and v.v. Journey 25 - 30 minutes:
From Hradec Kralové: 0025, 0529, 0603, 0708, 0729 ⑥, 0733 Ⓐ, 0803, 0908, 0929 Ⓐ, 1003, 1108, 1129, 1203, 1308, 1308, 1329, 1403, 1508, 1529, 1603, 1708, 1729, 1803, 1908, 1929 Ⓒ, 2003, 2108, 2204.
From Pardubice: 0027 Ⓐ, 0127 Ⓒ, 0529, 0605 Ⓐ, 0622, 0637 Ⓐ, 0713 Ⓐ, 0730 Ⓒ, 0747 Ⓐ, 0806 ⑥, 0822, 0929, 1022, 1129, 1206, 1222, 1329, 1406, 1422, 1529, 1602, 1622, 1726, 1802, 1822, 1930, 2022, 2131, 2248.

PRAHA - HRADEC KRÁLOVÉ - TRUTNOV 1145

km			1780	941	1782	921	943	1784	923	945	1786	925	1788	927	947	1790	929	935	1792	931	949	951	1796	953	955	957
				Ⓐ	2Ⓒ			2			2Ⓐ		2		Ⓐ	2		L	2							
0	**Praha** hlavní	d.	...	0511	...	0611	0711	...	0811	0911	...	1011	...	1211	1311	...	1411	1511	...	1611	1711	1811	...	1911	2011	2211
35	Lysá nad Labem	▷ d.	...	0543	...	0643	0743	...	0843	0943	...	1043	...	1243	1343	...	1443	1543	...	1643	1743	1843	...	1943	2043	2243
50	Nymburk	▷ d.	...	0556	...	0656	0756	...	0856	0956	...	1056	...	1256	1356	...	1456	1556	...	1656	1756	1856	...	1956	2056	2256
57	Poděbrady	▷ d.	...	0602	...	0702	0802	...	0902	1002	...	1102	...	1302	1402	...	1502	1602	...	1702	1802	1902	...	2002	2102	2302
116	**Hradec Králové**	a.	...	0651	...	0751	0851	...	0951	1051	...	1151	...	1351	1451	...	1551	1651	...	1751	1851	1951	...	2051	2151	2348
116	**Hradec Králové**	d.	0601	...	0701	0804	...	0901	1004	...	1101	1204	1301	1404	...	1501	1604	...	1701	1804	...	...	2001	...	...	...
137	Jaroměř	d.	0617	...	0718	0820	...	0917	1020	...	1117	1220	1317	1420	...	1517	1620	...	1717	1820	...	...	2020	...	...	...
189	**Trutnov** hlavní	a.	0720	...	0821	0920	...	1021	1120	...	1220	1320	1420	1520	...	1621	1720	...	1820	1920	...	...	2120	...	...	...

		952	1781	950	1783	934	932	1785	948	930	1787	928	1789	946	926	1791	944	924	1793	942	922	1795	940	920		
		Ⓐ	⚒n		2	L		2			2Ⓐ		2	Ⓐ		2			2			2Ⓒ			2	2
rutnov hlavní	d.	...	0438	...	0540	...	0640	0743	...	0841	0941	1040	1141	...	1241	1341	...	1440	1541	...	1640	1741	...	1840	...	...
aroměř	d.	...	0541	...	0641	...	0741	0844	...	0941	1044	1141	1244	...	1341	1444	...	1541	1644	...	1741	1844	...	1941	...	...
radec Králové	a.	...	0558	...	0658	...	0755	0858	...	0955	1058	1155	1258	...	1355	1459	...	1555	1659	...	1755	1858	...	1955	...	...
radec Králové	d.	0508	...	0608	...	0708	0808	...	0908	1008	...	1208	...	1308	1408	...	1508	1608	...	1708	1808	...	1908	2008	...	...
oděbrady	▷ d.	0554	...	0654	...	0754	0854	...	0954	1054	...	1254	...	1354	1454	...	1554	1654	...	1754	1854	...	1954	2054	2147	...
ymburk	▷ d.	0602	...	0702	...	0802	0902	...	1002	1102	...	1302	...	1402	1502	...	1602	1702	...	1802	1902	...	2002	2102	2206	2301
ysá nad Labem	▷ d.	0613	...	0713	...	0813	0913	...	1013	1113	...	1313	...	1413	1513	...	1613	1713	...	1813	1913	...	2013	2113	2225	2325
raha hlavní	a.	0645	...	0745	...	0845	0945	...	1045	1145	...	1345	...	1445	1545	...	1645	1745	...	1845	1945	...	2045	2145	2301	0001

– To/from Letohrad (Table **1165**). **n** – ①–⑥ (not Apr. 21, July 5, Nov. 17). ▷ – See also Table **1147**.

DĚČÍN - ÚSTÍ NAD LABEM - MĚLNÍK - KOLÍN and RUMBURK - KOLÍN 1147

km			781	783		793	795
			⚒n				ⓑh
0	**Ústí** n. L západ	d.	0447	0647		1647	1847
2	**Ústí** n. L Střekov	d.	0452	0652		1652	1852
27	Litoměřice město	d.	0511	0711	and	1711	1911
63	**Mělník**	d.	0540	0740	every	1740	1940
73	Všetaty	d.	0548	0748	**two**	1748	1948
85	Stará Boleslav	d.	0557	0757	hours	1757	1957
96	Lysá nad Labem §	d.	0606	0806	until	1806	2006
11	Nymburk §	d.	0619	0819		1819	2019
18	Poděbrady §	d.	0626	0826		1826	2026
34	**Kolín**	d.	0640	0840		1840	2040
	⊖						
0	**Děčín** hlavní	d.	0604	0802	1202	1402	1602	1802
28	**Ústí** n. L Střekov	a.	0643	0844	1244	1444	1644	1844

		794	792		782	780
		⚒n				ⓑh
Kolín	d.	0714	0914		1914	2114
Poděbrady §	d.	0728	0928		1928	2128
Nymburk §	d.	0736	0936	and	1936	2136
Lysá nad Labem §	d.	0747	0947	every	1947	2147
Stará Boleslav	d.	0754	0954	**two**	1954	2154
Všetaty	d.	0809	1009	hours	2009	2205
Mělník	d.	0817	1017	until	2017	2213
Litoměřice město	d.	0846	1046		2046	2242
Ústí n. L Střekov	a.	0904	1104		2104	2300
Ústí n. L západ	a.	0909	1109		2109	2305
⊖						
Ústí n. L Střekov	d.	0655	0913	1313	1513	1713	1913
Děčín hlavní	a.	0734	0955	1355	1555	1755	1955

RUMBURK - ČESKA LIPÁ - KOLÍN

							E
Rumburk	d.	0459**a**	0711	1115**c**	1310	1512	1715
Česka Lipá	d.	0624	0824	1224	1424	1624	1824
Mladá Boleslav	d.	0722	0922	1322	1522	1722	1922
Nymburk §	d.	0749	0949	1349	1549	1749	1949
Poděbrady §	d.	0757	0957	1357	1557	1757	1957
Kolín	a.	0810	1010	1410	1610	1810	2010
							E
Kolín	d.	0746	0946	1346	1546	1746	1946
Poděbrady §	d.	0800	1000	1400	1600	1800	2000
Nymburk §	d.	0808	1008	1408	1608	1808	2008
Mladá Boleslav	a.	0833	1033	1433	1633	1833	2033
Česka Lipá	a.	0936	1136	1536	1736	1936	2136
Rumburk	a.	1039	1242**c**	1640	1842	2042	...

– ⑤⑥⑦ (daily May 30 - Sept. 14), also Apr. 21, May 1, 8, Oct. 28, Nov. 17.
– Ⓐ only.
– Ⓒ only.

h – Not Apr. 20, Nov. 16.
n – ①–⑥ (not Apr. 21, July 5, Nov. 17).

§ – See also Table **1145**.
⊖ – 2nd class only. For Dečín - Ústí nad Labem hlavní see Table **1100**.

1150 PRAHA - PARDUBICE - BRNO - BŘECLAV - WIEN / BRATISLAVA

km	FAST TRAINS	EC 271	EC 71	EC 71	EC 273	EC 73	EC 275		EC 75	EC 277	EC 103	EC 77	EC 171		IC 571	EC 173	EC 131	EC 279		EC 175	EC 105	IC 573	EC 177	
		✕	✕	✕	✕	🍷	✕		🍷	✕	✕	✕	✕		✕	✕	✕	✕		✕	✕	✕	✕	
			⚒n	§	◆	§			§		▽	§	b			◆	◆			b	▽		b	
0	**Praha** hlavní ▷ d.	...	0439	...	0539	0639	0739	...	0839	0939	...	1039	1139	...	1239	1339	...	1439	...	1539	...	1639	1739	...
62	Kolín ▷ d.	...	0520	...	0620	│	0820	...	│	1020	...	│	1220	...	│	1420	...	│	...	1620	...	│	1820	...
104	**Pardubice** ▷ d.	...	0541	...	0641	0741	0841	...	0941	1041	...	1141	1241	...	1341	1441	...	1541	...	1641	...	1741	1841	...
164	Česká Třebová ▷ d.	...	0618	...	0718	0818	0918	...	1018	1118	...	1218	1318	...	1418	1518	...	1618	...	1718	...	1818	1918	...
255	**Brno** hlavní a.	...	0719	...	0819	0919	1019	...	1119	1219	...	1319	1419	...	1519	1619	...	1719	...	1819	...	1919	2019	...
255	**Brno** hlavní **1159** d.	0622	0722	0722	0822	0922	1022	...	1122	1222	...	1322	1422	...	1522	1622	...	1722	...	1822	...	...	2022	...
314	**Břeclav** **1159** a.	0654	0754	0754	0854	0954	1054	...	1154	1254	...	1354	1454	...	1554	1654	...	1754	...	1854	...	...	2054	...
314	**Břeclav** d.	0657	0802	0802	0857	1002	1057	...	1202	1257	1302	1402	1457	...	...	1702	1657	1802	...	1857	1902	...	2057	...
	Wien Meidling **982** a.	│	0924	0924	│	1124	│	...	1324	│	1424	1524	│	...	...	1824	│	1922	...	│	2017	...	│	...
332	Kúty 🏛 d.	0713	...	...	0913	...	1113	...	...	1313	...	...	1513	...	...	...	1713	...	...	1913	...	...	2113	...
396	**Bratislava** hlavná a.	0750	...	...	0950	...	1150	...	...	1350	...	...	1550	...	...	...	1750	...	...	1950	...	...	2150	...
	Budapest Keleti **1175** a.	1035	...	...	1235	...	1435	...	...	1635	...	...	1835	...	...	...	2035	...	...	2235	...	...	...	...

		EC 79	EC 379	877		EN 477	477 407		
		✕	✕	🍷					
			b	Ⓑh		M	V		
Praha hlavní ▷ d.	...	1839	1939	2103	...	2345	2345	...	...
Kolín ▷ d.	...	│	2020	2146	...	│	│	...	...
Pardubice ▷ d.	...	1941	2041	2210	...	0103	0103	...	...
Česká Třebová ▷ d.	...	2018	2118	2249	...	│	│	...	...
Brno hlavní a.	...	2119	2219	2355	...	0244	0244	...	...
Brno hlavní **1159** d.	...	2122	...	...	...	0315	0315	...	...
Břeclav **1159** a.	...	2154	...	...	...	0354	0354	...	...
Břeclav d.	...	2202	...	...	...	0440	0449	...	...
Wien Meidling **982** a.	...	2303p	...	...	...	│	0617	...	...
Kúty 🏛 d.	...	...	...	...	...	0455	...	...	...
Bratislava hlavná a.	...	...	...	...	...	0536	...	...	...
Budapest Keleti **1175** a.	...	...	...	...	...	0835	...	...	...

		718	876		EC 176	IC 572		EC 378	EC 78	
			🍷		✕	✕		✕	✕	
			⚒n		b	⚒n		b		
Budapest Keleti **1175** d.	...	...	...	...	...	...	...	...	...	...
Bratislava hlavná d.	...	...	...	...	...	...	...	0610	...	...
Kúty 🏛 d.	...	...	...	...	...	...	...	0649	...	...
Wien Meidling **982** d.	...	...	...	...	...	...	...	│	0650p	...
Břeclav a.	...	...	...	...	...	...	...	0702	0753	...
Břeclav **1159** d.	...	...	...	...	...	...	...	0705	0805	...
Brno hlavní **1159** a.	...	...	...	...	...	...	...	0737	0837	...
Brno hlavní d.	...	...	0431	...	0539	0639	...	0739	0839	...
Česká Třebová ▷ d.	...	...	0541	...	0641	0741	...	0841	0941	...
Pardubice ▷ d.	...	0509	0618	...	0718	0818	...	0918	1018	...
Kolín ▷ d.	...	0537	│	...	0739	│	...	0939	│	...
Praha hlavní ▷ a.	...	0623	0721	...	0821	0921	...	1021	1121	...

	EC 104	EC 174	EC 278	EC 130	EC 172	IC 570	EC 170		EC 70	EC 102	EC 276	EC 72		EC 274	EC 74		EC 272	EC 76	EC 270		406 476	EN 476	476 718	
	✕	✕	✕	✕	✕	✕	✕		✕	✕	✕	🍷		✕	🍷		✕	✕	✕					
	▽	b	◆	◆	◆		b		§	▽		§			§		◆	§			V	N	P	
Budapest Keleti **1175** d.	...	0525	...	0725	...	...	0925	...	...	...	1125	...	...	1325	...	...	1525	...	1725	...	...	2005	2005	...
Bratislava hlavná d.	...	0810	...	1010	...	...	1210	...	...	...	1410	...	...	1610	...	...	1810	...	2010	...	...	2258	2258	...
Kúty 🏛 d.	...	0849	...	1049	...	...	1249	...	...	...	1449	...	...	1649	...	...	1849	...	2049	...	...	2340	2340	...
Wien Meidling **982** d.	0741	│	0824	│	0931	...	│	...	1231	1331	│	1431	...	│	1631	...	│	1831	│	...	2231	│	│	...
Břeclav a.	0853	0902	0953	1102	1053	...	1302	...	1353	1453	1502	1553	...	1702	1756	...	1902	1953	2102	...	2343	2353	2353	...
Břeclav **1159** d.	...	0905	1005	...	1105	1205	1305	...	1405	...	1505	1605	...	1705	1805	...	1905	2005	2105	...	0015	0015	0015	...
Brno hlavní **1159** a.	...	0937	1037	...	1137	1237	1337	...	1437	...	1537	1637	...	1737	1837	...	1937	2037	2137	...	0052	0052	0052	...
Brno hlavní d.	...	0939	1039	...	1139	1239	1339	...	1439	...	1539	1639	...	1739	1839	...	1939	2039	...	...	0103	0103	0103	...
Česká Třebová ▷ d.	...	1041	1141	...	1241	1341	1441	...	1541	...	1641	1741	...	1841	1941	...	2041	2141	...	...	│	│	│	...
Pardubice ▷ d.	...	1118	1218	...	1318	1418	1518	...	1618	...	1718	1818	...	1918	2018	...	2118	2218	...	...	0244	0244	0509	...
Kolín ▷ d.	...	1139	│	...	1339	│	1539	...	│	...	1739	│	...	1939	│	...	2139	2239	...	...	│	│	0537	...
Praha hlavní ▷ a.	...	1221	1321	...	1421	1521	1621	...	1721	...	1821	1921	...	2021	2121	...	2221	2321	...	...	0403	0403	0623	...

SEMI-FAST TRAINS PRAHA - ČESKÁ TŘEBOVÁ - BRNO

km		1973	861	863	865	867	1977	869	871	873	875	877
		Ⓐv	T				Ⓐ				Ⓑh	S
0	**Praha** hlavní ▷ d.	...	0552	0752	0952	1152	...	1352	1552	1752	1952	2103
62	Kolín ▷ d.	...	0637	0837	1037	1237	...	1437	1637	1837	2037	2146
104	**Pardubice** ▷ d.	...	0706	0906	1106	1306	...	1506	1706	1906	2106	2210
139	Choceň ▷ d.	...	0725	0925	1125	1325	1420	1525	1725	1925	2125	2226
154	Ústí nad Orlicí ▷ d.	...	0738	0938	1138	1338	1434	1538	1738	1938	2138	2238
164	**Česká Třebová** ▷ d.	0643	0749	0949	1149	1349	1447	1549	1749	1949	2148	2249
181	Svitavy d.	0659	0800	1000	1200	1400	1501	1600	1800	2000	...	2300
208	Letovice d.	0728	0821	1021	1221	1421	1529	1621	1821	2021	...	2317
233	Blansko d.	0749	0842	1042	1242	1442	1552	1642	1842	2042	...	2334
255	**Brno** hlavní a.	0812	0902	1102	1302	1502	1612	1702	1902	2102	...	2355

	878	876	874	872	870	868	866	864	862	860
	⚒n	⚒n					△	△	R	Ⓑh
Brno hlavní d.	...	0431	0657	0857	1057	1257	1457	1657	1857	2051
Blansko d.	...	0453	0718	0918	1118	1318	1518	1718	1918	2111
Letovice d.	...	0511	0739	0939	1139	1339	1539	1739	1939	2130
Svitavy d.	0500	0529	0800	1000	1200	1400	1600	1800	2000	2150
Česká Třebová ▷ d.	0511	0541	0811	1011	1211	1411	1611	1811	2011	2200
Ústí nad Orlicí ▷ d.	0521	│	0821	1021	1221	1421	1621	1821	2021	...
Choceň ▷ d.	0535	│	0835	1035	1235	1435	1635	1835	2035	...
Pardubice ▷ d.	0559	0618	0859	1059	1259	1459	1659	1859	2059	...
Kolín ▷ d.	0627	│	0927	1127	1327	1527	1727	1927	2127	...
Praha hlavní ▷ a.	0713	0721	1013	1213	1413	1613	1813	2013	2213	...

◆ – NOTES (LISTED BY TRAIN NUMBERS)

130/1 – VARSOVIA – [12] ✕ Warszawa - Katowice - Ostrava - Břeclav - Bratislava - Budapest and v.v.

172/3 – VINDOBONA – [12] ✕ Hamburg - Berlin - Praha - Wien - Villach and v.v.

272/3 – AVALA – [12] ✕ Praha - Bratislava - Budapest - Beograd and v.v.

278 – GUSTAV KLIMT – [12] ✕ Graz - Wien - Brno - Praha.

M – METROPOL – 🛏 1, 2 cl., ▬ 2 cl., [2] Berlin - Dresden - Praha - Bratislava - Budapest; 🛏 1, 2 cl., ▬ 2 cl. Praha - Bratislava - Budapest (also [2] June 13 - Sept. 13). For other cars Břeclav - Budapest see Tables **95** / **99**.

N – METROPOL – 🛏 1, 2 cl., ▬ 2 cl., [2] Budapest - Bratislava - Praha - Dresden - Berlin. For other cars Budapest - Břeclav see Tables **95** / **99**.

P – 🛏 1, 2 cl., ▬ 2 cl. Budapest - Bratislava - Pardubice (**718**) - Praha (also [2] June 14 - Sept. 14).

R – Daily Brno - Pardubice, ⑥⑦ to Praha (also Apr. 21, Oct. 28, Nov. 17; not Oct. 26).

S – Daily Praha - Česká Třebova, Ⓑ **h** to Brno.

T – From Praha on ① (also Apr. 22, Oct. 29, Nov. 18; not Apr. 21, Oct. 27, Nov. 17). From Pardubice on ①–⑥ **n**. Runs daily Česká Třebová - Brno.

V – 🛏 1, 2 cl., ▬ 2 cl., [2] Berlin - Dresden - Praha - Břeclav (**407/6**) - Wien Westbf and v.v. (arrive 0634, depart 2212).

b – From / to Berlin or Hamburg (Table **60**).

h – Ⓑ (not Apr. 20, Nov. 16).

n – ①–⑥ (not Apr. 21, July 5, Nov. 17).

p – Wien **Praterstern** (see Table **982**).

v – Additional trains: 0445 Ⓐ, 0545 ⚒ **n**.

▷ – See also Table **1160**.

△ – Other trains Brno - Česká Třebová: 1345 Ⓐ, 1545 Ⓐ, 1745 Ⓐ.

▽ – For origin / destination see Table **60**.

§ – To / from Wiener Neustadt.

FOR OTHER TRAIN NAMES SEE TABLE **60**

1151 PRAHA - HAVLIČKŮV BROD - BRNO

For fast trains Praha - Brno see Table **1150**

km		971	973	973	975	977	979	981	983	985	961	987	989	963	965
				⚒n					Ⓐ		Ⓑh		Ⓑh		
0	Praha Smichov d.	...	...	0547	0747	0942	1147	1347	1447	1547	1647	1747	1847	1947	2152
4	**Praha** hlavní ⊡ d.	...	...	0600	0800	1000	1200	1400	1500	1600	1700	1800	1900	2000	2204
66	Kolín ⊡ d.	...	...	0647	0847	1047	1247	1447	1547	1647	1747	1847	1947	2047	2250
77	Kutná Hora d.	...	...	0658	0858	1058	1258	1458	1558	1658	1758	1858	1958	2058	2300
86	Čáslav d.	...	...	0708	0908	1108	1308	1508	1608	1708	1808	1908	2008	2108	2309
140	**Havlíčkův Brod** d.	0603	0803	0803	1003	1203	1403	1603	1703	1803	1902	2003	2103	2200	2400r
	Jihlava **1152** a.	│	│	│	│	│	│	│	│	│	1924	│	│	...	...
173	Žďár nad Sázavou d.	0630	0830	0830	1030	1230	1430	1630	1730	1830	...	2030	2127z	...	...
261	**Brno** hlavní a.	0745	0941	0941	1141	1341	1541	1741	1841	1941	...	2144	2235z	...	...

	964	962	960	988	986	984	982	980	978	976	976	974	972	970	
	Ⓐ	⚒n		⚒n							Ⓑh		Ⓐ		
Brno hlavní d.	...	...	...	...	0620	0820	1020	1220	1420	1520	1520	1620	1720	1820	...
Žďár nad Sázavou d.	...	...	...	0632a	0732	0932	1132	1332	1532	1632	1632	1732	1832	1932	...
Jihlava **1152** d.	...	...	0533n	│	│	│	│	│	│	│	│	│	│	│	...
Havlíčkův Brod d.	...	0458	0558	0658	0758	0958	1158	1358	1558	1656	1658	1758	1856	1958	...
Čáslav d.	0447	0550	0650	0750	0850	1050	1250	1450	1650	...	1750	1850	...	2050	...
Kutná Hora d.	0457	0559	0659	0759	0859	1059	1259	1459	1659	...	1759	1859	...	2059	...
Kolín ⊡ d.	0508	0614	0714	0810	0910	1110	1310	1510	1710	...	1814	1910	...	2110	...
Praha hlavní ⊡ a.	0555	0701	0801	0902	1002	1157	1357	1602	1802	...	1901	2002	...	2202	...
Praha Smichov a.	0607	0717	0817	0917	1017	1212	1417	1617	1817	...	1917	2017	...	2217	...

PARDUBICE - HAVLIČKŮV BROD ⊖ 2nd class

km				Ⓐ		Ⓐ	
0	**Pardubice** d.	0937	1137	1303	1540	1619	185
11	Chrudim d.	1001	1204	1321	1603	1647	192
52	Hlinsko v Čech. a.	1052	1254	1404	1654	1743	201
52	Hlinsko v Čech. d.	1107	*1302*	1405	*1702*	1801	201
92	**Havlíčkův Brod** a.	1154	*1353*	1452	*1750*	1848	205

	Ⓐ						
Havlíčkův Brod d.	0813	1008x	*1208*	1408	1608h	1806	201
Hlinsko v Čech. a.	0901	1056	*1257*	1500	1658h	1857	211
Hlinsko v Čech. d.	0902	1100	1300	1501	1702	1858	213
Chrudim d.	0950	1148	1349	1550	1750	1949	222
Pardubice a.	1011	1213	1413	1613	1813	2013	224

a – Ⓐ only.
h – Ⓑ (not Apr. 20, Nov. 16).
n – ①–⑥ (not Apr. 21, July 5, Nov. 17).
r – ⑤⑥ (also Apr. 20, 30, May 7, Oct. 27, Nov. 16).
x – 1016 on Ⓒ.
z – Runs Havlíčkův Brod - Brno on ⑤ (also Oct. 27).

⊡ – See also Tables **1150** / **60**.
⊖ – Selected trains only - runs approx every 2 hours.

HAVLÍČKŮV BROD - JIHLAVA — 1152

2nd class

km			Ⓐ		R				Ⓐ		Ⓐ		Ⓐ		P	Ⓐ	
0	Havlíčkův Brod	d.	0448	0604	0647	0700	0805	1005	1205	1314	1405	1513	1605	1712	1805	1903	2005	2105
27	Jihlava	a.	0516	0632	0717	0723	0834	1034	1235	1346	1435	1544	1636	1744	1835	1924	2034	2134

			Q		Ⓐ				Ⓐ		Ⓐ		Ⓐ		Ⓐ		S	
Jihlava	d.	0519	0533	0605	0654	0726	0923	1122	1236	1324	1436	1522	1614	1722	1813	1925	2035	...
Havlíčkův Brod	a.	0548	0556	0643	0735	0752	0952	1152	1305	1354	1505	1552	1644	1752	1844	1953	2058	...

P – Ⓑ (not Apr. 20, Nov. 16). From Praha (Table **1151**).
Q – ①–⑥ (not Apr. 21, July 5, Nov. 17). To Praha (Table **1151**).
R – ①⑥ also Apr. 22, May 1, 8, Oct. 29, Nov. 18; not Apr. 21, May 3, 10, Oct. 27, Nov. 17. To Plzeň (Table **1135**).
S – ⑤⑦ also Apr. 21, 30, May 7, Oct. 28, Nov. 17; not Apr. 20, May 2, 9, Oct. 26, Nov. 16. From Plzeň (Tab **1135**).

BRNO - PŘEROV - OSTRAVA - BOHUMÍN — 1155

km			406 ♦	821 ⚒n	823 ⚒n	IC 531	825	EC 104 ♦	827	EC 130 ♦	829	831	833	835	EC 102 ♦	837	839	841	IC 100 M	843 Ⓑh	845	847 ⑦e	849	
0	**Brno** hlavní 1156	d.	...	0502	0602	...	0702	...	0902	...	1102	1202	1302	1402	...	1502	1602	1702	...	1802	1902	2002	2102	...
45	Vyškov na Moravě 1156	d.	...	0545	0645	...	0745	...	0945	...	1145	1245	1345	1445	...	1545	1645	1745	...	1845	1945	2045	2142	...
71	Kojetin	d.	...	0611	0711	...	0811	...	1011	...	1211	1311	1411	1511	...	1611	1711	1811	...	1911	2011	2111	2211	...
	Bratislava 1150	d.	...	|	|	...	|	...	|	1010	|	|	|	|	...	|	|	|	...	|	|	|	|	...
	Wien Meidling 1150	d.	2231	|	|	...	|	0741	|	|	|	|	|	|	1331	|	|	|	...	|	|	|	|	...
	Břeclav 1159	d.	0025	|	|	0710	|	0910	|	1107	|	|	|	|	1510	|	|	|	1823	|	|	|	|	...
88	**Přerov**	▽ d.	0119	0626	0726	0808	0826	1008	1026	1208	1226	1326	1426	1526	1608	1626	1726	1826	1918	1926	2026	2126	2226	...
117	Hranice na Moravě	▽ d.	|	0644	0744	0826	0844	1026	1044	1226	1244	1344	1444	1544	1626	1644	1744	1844	1936	1944	2044	2144	2244	...
167	Ostrava Svinov	▽ a.	0200	0716	0810	0850	0916	1050	1116	1250	1316	1410	1516	1610	1650	1716	1810	1916	2000	2010	2116	2210	2316	...
172	**Ostrava** hlavní	▽ a.	0209	0725	0819	0859	0925	1059	1125	1259	1325	1419	1525	1619	1659	1725	1819	1925	2009	2019	2125	2219	2325	...
180	Bohumín	▽ a.	0219	0734	0828	0908	0934	1108	1134	1308	1334	1428	1534	1628	1708	1734	1828	1934	2018	2028	2134	2228	2334	...

		407 ♦	848 ⚒n	846 Ⓐ	844	IC 101 M	842	840		838	EC 103 ♦	836	834	832	EC 131 ♦	830	828	EC 105 ♦	826 Ⓑh	824	IC 530	822 ⑦e	820	
Bohumín	▽ d.	0210	0430	0540	0630	0652	0740	0830	...	1030	1052	1230	1340	1430	1452	1540	1630	1652	1740	1830	1852	1940	2030	...
Ostrava hlavní	▽ d.	0219	0439	0549	0639	0701	0749	0839	...	1039	1101	1239	1349	1439	1501	1549	1639	1701	1749	1839	1901	1949	2039	...
Ostrava Svinov	▽ d.	0229	0447	0557	0647	0709	0757	0847	...	1047	1109	1247	1357	1447	1509	1557	1647	1709	1757	1847	1909	1957	2047	...
Hranice na Moravě	▽ d.	|	0523	0623	0723	0733	0823	0923	...	1123	1133	1323	1423	1523	1533	1623	1723	1733	1823	1923	1933	2023	2123	...
Přerov	▽ d.	0311	0542	0642	0742	0752	0842	0942	...	1142	1152	1342	1442	1542	1552	1642	1742	1752	1842	1942	1952	2042	2142	...
Břeclav 1159	a.	0405	|	|	|	0850	|	|	...	|	1250	|	|	|	1654	|	|	1850	|	|	2050	|	|	...
Wien Meidling 1150	a.	0617	|	|	|	...	|	|	...	|	1424	|	|	|	|	|	|	2017	|	|	...	|	|	...
Bratislava 1150	a.	...	|	|	|	...	|	|	...	|	...	|	|	|	1750	|	|	...	|	|	...	|	|	...
Kojetin	d.	...	0557	0657	0757	...	0857	0957	...	1157	...	1357	1457	1557	...	1657	1757	...	1857	1957	...	2057	2157	...
Vyškov na Moravě 1156	d.	...	0620	0720	0820	...	0920	1020	...	1220	...	1420	1520	1620	...	1720	1820	...	1920	2020	...	2120	2220	...
Brno hlavní 1156	d.	...	0658	0757	0857	...	0957	1057	...	1257	...	1459	1559	1659	...	1759	1859	...	1957	2056	...	2156	2256	...

102/3 – POLONIA – [12] ✕ Villach - Wien - Břeclav - Ostrava - Katowice - Warszawa and v.v.
104/5 – SOBIESKI – [12] ✕ Wien Westbf (d. 0718 / a. 2034) - Břeclav - Ostrava - Katowice - Warszawa and v.v.
130/1 – VARSOVIA – [12] ✕ Budapest - Bratislava - Břeclav - Ostrava - Katowice - Warszawa and v.v.
406/7 – CHOPIN – 🛏 1, 2 cl., ▬ 2 cl., [2] Wien Westbf (d. 2212 / a. 0634) - Bohumín - Warszawa and v.v.; 🛏 1, 2 cl. Wien - Bohumín (**403/2**) - Kraków and v.v. (also ▬ 2 cl. on dates in Table **99**); 🛏 1, 2 cl., ▬ 2 cl., [2] Budapest (**476/7**) - Bratislava - Břeclav (**406/7**) - Warszawa and v.v.; 🛏 1, 2 cl., ▬ 2 cl. Budapest (**476/7**) - Bratislava - Břeclav (**406/7**) - Bohumín (**403/2**) - Kraków and v.v.

M – MORAVIA – [12] Břeclav - Bohumín and v.v. Conveys on dates in Table **95** 🛏 1, 2 cl. Wien Westbf - Bohumín (**405/4**) - Minsk - Moskva / St Peterburg and v.v.
e – Also Apr. 21, Oct. 28, Nov. 17; not Apr. 20, Oct. 26, Nov. 16.
h – Not Apr. 20, Nov. 16.
n – ①–⑥ (not Apr. 21, July 5, Nov. 17).
▽ – See also Table **1160**.

BRNO - OLOMOUC - ŠUMPERK and JESENÍK — 1156

km			901 Ⓐ	1701 2Ⓐ	1701 2Ⓒ	1403 Ⓒ	1403 ⑥t	905	1405 2	907	1407 2	909	909 ⑤f	1703 2	911	1411 2	913	1413 2	915 v	1635	2Ⓐ	2	917	917 Ⓑh	2
0	**Brno** hlavní 1155	d.	0523	...	...	0628	0628	0718	...	0918	...	1118	1118	...	1318	...	1518	...	1718	...	...	...	1918	1918	...
45	Vyškov na Moravé 1155	d.	0602	...	...	0704	0704	0802	...	1002	...	1202	1202	...	1402	...	1602	...	1802	...	...	...	2002	2002	...
61	Nezamyslice	d.	0620	...	...	0720	0720	0820	...	1020	...	1220	1220	...	1420	...	1620	...	1820	...	...	...	2020	2020	...
80	Prostějov	d.	0635	...	...	0735	0735	0835	...	1035	...	1235	1235	...	1435	...	1635	...	1835	...	...	...	2035	2035	...
100	**Olomouc**	a.	0651	...	...	0751	0751	0851	...	1051	...	1251	1251	...	1452	...	1651	...	1851	...	...	...	2051	2051	...
100	**Olomouc** 1160	d.	0656	...	0656	...	0756	0856	...	1056	...	...	1256	*1231*	1456	...	1656	...	1856	...	1931	...	...	2056	2234
146	Zábřeh na Moravé 1160	a.	0723	...	0727	...	0823	0923	▽	1123	▽	...	1323	*1310*	1523	▽	1723	▽	1923	...	2010	...	...	2123	2310
146	Zábřeh na Moravé	d.	0726	0731	0731	...	0832	0926	0932	1126	1132	...	1326	1331	1526	1532	1726	1732	1926	...	2011	...	...	2126	2316
159	**Šumperk**	a.	0741	|	|	...	|	0940	|	1140	|	...	1340	|	1540	|	1740	|	1942	1928	2027	2057	...	2141	2332
171	Hanušovice	a.	...	0800	0800	...	0900	...	1000	...	1200	...	...	1400	...	1600	...	1800	...	2001	...	2135	...	...	...
203	Lipová Lázně	a.	...	0859	0859	...	0958	...	1059	...	1259	...	...	1459	...	1659	...	1859	...	2058	...	2227	...	...	...
207	**Jeseník**	a.	...	0910	0910	...	1005	...	1110	...	1310	...	...	1511	...	1710	...	1910	...	2105	...	2236	...	...	...

		1638 Ⓐ	914 ⚒n	914	1700 2⑦	1630 ⚒n	1412 2	912	1410 2	910	1702 2	908 ⑤f	908	1406 2	906	1404 2	904	1704 2Ⓒ	1706 2⚒	902 Ⓐ	1402 ⑦d	1402 Ⓒ	900 Ⓒ	1634 Ⓒv	2
eseník	d.	...	...	...	0453	0453	0652	...	0854	...	1054	...	...	1254	...	1454	...	1538	1654	...	1654	...	...	1844	...
ipová Lázně	d.	...	...	...	0501	0501	0701	...	0903	...	1103	...	...	1303	...	1503	...	1545	1703	...	1703	...	...	1854	...
anušovice	d.	...	...	...	0556	0556	0801	▽	1001	▽	1201	...	...	1401	▽	1601	▽	1654	1801	...	1801	...	...	1951	...
Šumperk	d.	0453	0613	...	|	0630	|	0809	|	1009	|	1219	...	|	1409	|	1609	|	|	1817	|	...	2014	2027	2031
ábřeh na Moravé	a.	0510	0630	...	0626	|	0828	0823	1028	1023	1229	1233	...	1428	1423	1628	1623	1723	1828	1832	1828	...	2032	...	2047
ábřeh na Moravé 1160	d.	0514	0632	...	*0649*	u	...	0836	...	1036	*1249*	1235	...	...	1436	...	1636	1728	*1849*	1835	1836	...	2035	...	2049
lomouc 1160	a.	0551	0702	...	*0727*	0734	...	0903	...	1103	*1325*	1303	...	...	1503	...	1703	1804	*1925*	1903	1903	...	2103	...	2125
lomouc	d.	0558	0707	0707	...	...	...	0907	...	1107	...	1307	1307	...	1507	...	1707	...	...	1907	1907	1907	2107	...	2130
rostějov	d.	0615	0725	0725	...	...	...	0925	...	1125	...	1325	1325	...	1525	...	1725	...	...	1925	1925	1925	2125	...	2156
ezamyslice	d.	0637	0739	0739	...	...	...	0939	...	1139	...	1339	1339	...	1539	...	1739	...	...	1939	1939	1939	2139	...	...
yškov na Moravé 1155	d.	0700	0802	0802	...	...	...	1002	...	1202	...	1402	1402	...	1602	...	1802	...	...	2002	2002	2002	2202	...	...
rno hlavní 1155	a.	0746	0842	0842	...	...	...	1042	...	1242	...	1443	1443	...	1643	...	1842	...	...	2039	2039	2039	2238	...	...

– Also Apr. 21, May 1, 8, Oct. 28, Nov. 17; not Apr. 20, Nov. 16.
– Also Apr. 30, May 7; not May 2, 9.
– Not Apr. 20, Nov. 16.
n – ①–⑥ (not Apr. 21, July 5, Nov. 17).
t – Also May 1, 8, Oct. 28.
u – Via Uničov.
v – Connection with train in next column is at Bludov (6 minutes before Šumperk).
▽ – On certain days conveys through carriage from train in previous column.

BRNO - UHERSKÉ HRADIŠTĚ - LUHAČOVICE / BYLNICE — 1157

2nd class only

km						⑤f					
0	**Brno** hlavní	d.	0735	0928	1128	1249	1328	1528	1728	1928	2128
67	Kyjov	d.	0837	1032	1232	1351	1432	1632	1832	2032	2232
90	Veselí nad Moravou	d.	0901	1101	1301	1415	1501	1701	1901	2101	2258
104	Kunovice	a.	|	|	|	1430	|	|	1918	2118	...
108	Uherské Hradiště	▷ a.	0919	1119	1319	*1439*	1519	1719	*1928*	*2122*	...
113	**Staré Město u Uh. H**	▷ a.	0927	1127	1327	...	1527	1727	*1935*	*2129*	...

		Ⓐ									⑦e
Staré Město u Uh. H.	▷ d.	*0533*	...	0835	1035	1235	1435	1635	1835	*2025*	...
Uherské Hradiště	▷ d.	*0539*	*0630*a	0841	1041	1241	1441	1641	1842	*2032*	*2038*
Kunovice	d.	0544	0636	|	|	|	|	|	|	|	2043
Veselí nad Moravou	d.	0601	0701	0901	1101	1301	1501	1701	1901	2101	2101
Kyjov	d.	0628	0728	0928	1128	1328	1528	1728	1928	2128	2128
Brno hlavní	a.	0733	0834	1033	1233	1433	1633	1833	2033	2233	2233

km			Ⓒ				Ⓐ	⑤f			
	Brno hlavní	▷ d.	...	...	...	...	...	1249	...	1728	1928
0	**Staré Město u Uh. H**	▷ d.	0635	0823	1005	1224	1334	*1405*	1605	*1855*	|
5	Uherské Hradiště	▷ d.	0644	0831	1031	1231	1343	*1431*	1631	*1918*	*2113*
7	Kunovice	d.	0647	0834	1034	1234	1346	1436	1634	1923	2123
22	Uherský Brod	▷ d.	0705	0855	1055	1255	1415	1455	1655	1945	2145
26	Újezdec u Luhačovic	a.	0709	0859	1059	1259	1419	1459	1659	1948	2149
36	Luhačovice	▷ a.	0726	*0916*	*1116*	*1316*	*1516*	*1516*	*1716*	*2018*x	*2206*
35	Bojkovice	a.	...	0915	1115	1315	1434	1515	1715	2002	2202
63	Bylnice	a.	...	0952	1155	1355	1515	1555	1755	2040*	2240
68	Vlárský průsmyk 🛂	a.	...	*1000*	...	...	1524	1604	...	...	...
90	**Trenčianska Teplá**	a.	...	...	...	...	...	*1622*	...	...	...

						Ⓐ	Ⓒ		⑦t	k	⑦e
Trenčianska Teplá	d.	...	...	...	...	...	...	...	*1737*	...	...
Vlárský průsmyk 🛂	d.	...	*0754*	*1002*	...	...	*1402*	*1545*a	*1755*	...	...
Bylnice	d.	...	0802	1010	1202	1402	1410	1602	1802	1802	1925
Bojkovice	d.	0645	0845	1047	1245	1445	1447	1645	1845	1845	2005
Luhačovice	▷ d.	*0642*	*0842*	*1042*	*1242*	*1442*	*1442*	*1642*	*1842*	*1842*v	*2002*
Újezdec u Luhačovic	d.	0700	0900	1100	1300	1500	1500	1700	1900	1900	2020
Uherský Brod	▷ d.	0708	0906	1106	1306	1506	1506	1706	1905	1905	2025
Kunovice	a.	0727	0926	1127	1326	1526	1526	1726	1923	1923	2042
Uherské Hradiště	▷ a.	0730	0930	1130	1330	1530	1530	1730	*1928*	1928	*2048*
Staré Město u Uh. H	▷ a.	*0750*	0937	1137	1351	1537	1537	1751	*1935*	1935	|
Brno hlavní	▷ a.	...	...	...	...	...	...	...	2103	...	2233

– Ⓐ only.
– Also Apr. 21, Oct. 28, Nov. 17; not Apr. 20, Oct. 26, Nov. 16.
f – Also Apr. 30, May 7; not May 2, 9, July 4 - Aug. 29.
k – ⚒ (daily June 28 - Aug. 30).
t – Also Apr. 21, Oct. 28, Nov. 17; not Apr. 20, June 29 - Aug. 24, Oct. 26, Nov. 16.
v – Ⓑ (not Apr. 20, Nov. 16).
x – ⑥ (also May 1, 8).
▷ – See also Table **1159**.
* – Not Apr. 20, Nov. 16.

1159 OLOMOUC - UHERSKÉ HRADIŠTĚ - BŘECLAV - BRNO

For direct services Olomouc - Brno see Table **1156**. For night train **406/7** Warszawa - Wien see Tables **99** and **1155** (also calls at Otrokovice: **406** at 0101, **407** at 0328)

km		816 ⚒n	881 Ⓐ	814	*IC* 101 ♦	883 ⊡	812	885	810	*EC* 103 ♦	887	808	889	806	*EC* 131 ♦	891	804	*EC* 105 ♦	893	♠ 1363	802	*IC* 530 b	*IC* 561 V	800 Ⓑr	*IC* 551 ✕
	Praha hlavní **1160** d.	...	...	...	...	...	...	0652z	...	...	...	...	1052z	...	...	1252z	...	...	1452z	1628	...	...	1711	...	1911
0	**Olomouc** ▽ d.	...	0555	0708	...	0755	0908	0955	1108	...	1155	1308	1355	1508	...	1555	1708	...	1755	1846	1908	...	1944	2108	2144
	Ostrava hlavní **1155** d.	...	|	|	0701	|	|	|	|	1101	|	|	|	|	1501	|	|	1701	|	|	|	1901	|	|	|
22	Přerov ▽ d.	...	0612	0724	0752	0812	0924	1012	1124	1152	1212	1324	1412	1524	1552	1612	1724	1752	1812	1902	1924	1952	2000	2124	2200
37	Hulín d.	...	0627	0735	|	0824	0935	1024	1135	|	1224	1335	1424	1535	|	1624	1735	|	1824	1912	1935	|	2010	2135	2210
50	Otrokovice ▷ d.	...	0637	0745	0809	0834	0945	1034	1145	1209	1233	1345	1434	1545	1611	1634	1745	1809	1834	1921	1945	2009	2020	2145	2229
61	**Zlín** střed ▷ a.	...	|	|	|	|	|	|	|	|	...	|	|	|	|	|	|	|	|	|	|	|	|	|	|	2242
68	Staré Město u U.H. ⊖ d.	...	0657	0756	0820	0853*	0956	1053*	1156	1220	...	1356	1453*	1556	1622	1653*	1756	1820	1845	1930	1956	2020	2043*	2156	...
73	Uherské Hradiště a.	...	0703	|	|	0859	|	1059	|	|	...	|	1459	|	|	1659	|	|	*1900*	...	|	|	2049	|	...
90	Uherský Brod a.	...	0722	|	|	0920	|	1120	|	|	...	|	1520	|	|	1720	|	|	...	...	|	|	...	|	...
104	**Luhačovice** a.	...	0741	|	|	0939	|	1139	|	|	...	|	1539	|	|	1739	|	|	...	...	|	|	...	|	...
102	Hodonin d.	0617	...	0817	0837	...	1017	...	1217	1237	...	1417	...	1617	1640	...	1817	1837	...	...	2017	2037	...	2217	...
122	**Břeclav** a.	0631	...	0831	0850	...	1031	...	1231	1250	...	1431	...	1631	1654	...	1831	1850	...	...	2031	2050	...	2231	...
122	**Břeclav** **1150** d.	0638	...	0838	...	...	1038	...	1238	*1305*	...	1438	...	1638	*1705*	...	1838	*1905*	...	...	2038	*2105*	...	...	...
181	**Brno** hlavní **1150** a.	0724	...	0924	...	...	1124	...	1324	*1337*	...	1524	...	1724	*1737*	...	1924	*1937*	...	...	2124	*2137*	...	...	...

	892	*IC* 550 ✕	♠ 1350	801 ⚒n	*IC* 560 V	*IC* 531	803	890 Ⓐ	*EC* 104 ♦	805	888	*EC* 130 ♦	807	886	809	884	*EC* 102 ♦	811	882	813	*IC* 100 ♦	880	815	2	817 Ⓑr
Brno hlavní **1150** d.	...	...	...	...	...	*0622*	0636	...	*0822*	0836	...	*1022*	1036	...	1236	...	*1422*	1436	...	1636	*1722*	...	1836	...	2036
Břeclav **1150** a.	...	...	...	...	...	*0654*	0721	...	*0854*	0921	...	*1054*	1121	...	1321	...	*1454*	1521	...	1721	*1754*	...	1921	...	2121
Břeclav d.	...	...	...	0528	...	0710	0728	...	0910	0928	...	1107	1128	...	1328	...	1510	1528	...	1728	1823	...	1928	2035	2128
Hodonin d.	...	...	...	0542	...	0724	0742	...	0924	0942	...	1122	1142	...	1342	...	1524	1542	...	1742	1836	...	1942	2056	2144
Luhačovice d.	...	...	...	|	...	|	|	0820	|	|	1020	|	|	...	|	1420	|	|	1620	|	|	1825	|	|	...
Uherský Brod d.	...	...	...	|	...	|	|	0838	|	|	1038	|	|	...	|	1438	|	|	1638	|	|	1843	|	|	...
Uherské Hradiště d.	...	...	...	|	0714	|	|	0900	|	|	1100	|	|	...	|	1500	|	|	1700	|	|	1901	|	|	...
Staré Město u U.H. ⊖ d.	0425	...	0550	0604	0730	0741	0804	0918*	0941	1004	1118*	1141	1204	...	1404	1518*	1541	1604	1718*	1804	1853	1918*	2004	2132	...
Zlín střed ▷ d.	|	0514	|	|	|	|	|	|	|	|	|	|	|	...	|	|	|	|	|	|	|	|	|	|	...
Otrokovice ▷ d.	0438	0538	0602	0615	0742	0752	0815	0930	0952	1015	1130	1152	1215	1330	1415	1530	1552	1615	1730	1815	1903	1930	2015	2210x	...
Hulín d.	0447	0547	0610	0625	0750	|	0825	0939	|	1025	1139	|	1225	1339	1425	1539	|	1625	1739	1825	|	1939	2025	2222	...
Přerov ▽ a.	0457	0558	0619	0635	0800	0806	0835	0949	1006	1035	1149	1207	1235	1349	1435	1549	1606	1635	1749	1835	1917	1949	2035	2236	...
Ostrava hlavní **1155** a.	|	|	|	|	|	0859	|	|	1059	|	|	1259	|	|	|	|	1659	|	|	|	2009	|	|	|	...
Olomouc ▽ a.	0520	0617	0635	0652	0817	b	0851	1006	...	1051	1206	...	1251	1406	1451	1606	...	1651	1806	1851	b	2006	2051	2258	...
Praha hlavní **1160** a.	0813	0853	0856	...	1053	...	...	...	...	...	1513z	...	...	1713z	...	1913z	...	...	2113z	...	...	...	...	...	...

100/1 – MORAVIA – 🚃12 Břeclav - Bohumín and v.v. Conveys on dates in Table **95** 🛏 1, 2 cl. Wien Bohumín (**405/4**) - Moskva / St Peterburg and v.v.
102/3 – POLONIA – 🚃12 ✕ Warszawa - Katowice - Ostrava - Břeclav - Wien - Villach and v.v.
104/5 – SOBIESKI – 🚃12 ✕ Warszawa - Katowice - Ostrava - Břeclav - Wien and v.v.

130/1 – VARSOVIA – 🚃12 ✕ Warszawa - Katowice - Ostrava - Břeclav - Bratislava - Budapest and v.v.
V – To / from Veseli nad Moravou (a. 2111 / d. 0659).
b – From / to Bohumín (Table **1155**).
n – ①–⑥ (not Apr. 21, July 5, Nov. 17).
r – Ⓑ (not Apr. 20, Nov. 16).
x – Arrive 2146.

z – For faster journey change at Olomouc – see Table **1160**.
♠ – *LEO EXPRESS* – *LE* train operated by Leo Express.
⊖ – Full name: Staré Město u Uherské Hradiště.
⊡ – From Hradec Králové via Pardubice (Table **1160**).
▽ – See also Table **1160**.
▷ – Local trains: 1 - 2 per hour (or trolleybus every 10 mins).
* – Arrives 8 - 12 minutes earlier.

1160 PRAHA - OLOMOUC - OSTRAVA - ŽILINA

For VLTAVA *EN* **404/5** Praha - Bohumín - Moskva see Table **95**

km		441 ♦	*EC** 141 ✕ H	♠ 1351 🅁🍷 Ⓐ	*EC** 121 ✕	*SC•* 501 🅁🍷 Ⓐ	♥ 1001 🅁🍷 ⚒	*EC** 143 ✕	♠ 1353 🅁🍷	*EC** 221 D	*SC•* 503 🅁🍷 ⚒n	♥ 1003 🅁🍷	*EC** 145 ✕	*EC** 123 🍷	*SC•* 505 🅁🍷	♥ 1005 🅁🍷	♠ 1355 🅁🍷	*EC** 147 ✕	*EC** 223 ✕ Du	*SC•* 507 🅁🍷 Ⓑh	♥ 1007 🅁🍷	♠ 1357 🅁🍷	*EC** 149 ✕	*EC** 125	*SC•* 509 🅁🍷
0	**Praha** hlavní △ d.	0004	0411	0506	0511	0536	0544	0611	0706	0711	0736	0744	0811	0911	0936	0944	1006	1011	1111	1136	1144	1206	1211	1311	1336
62	Kolín △ d.	0100	0455	|	0555	|	|	0655	|	0755	|	|	0855	0955	|	|	|	1055	1155	|	|	|	1255	1355	|
104	**Pardubice** △ d.	0124	0517	|	0617	0634	0646	0717	|	0817	0834	0846	0917	1017	1034	1046	|	1117	1217	1234	1246	|	1317	1417	1434
164	Česká Třebová △ d.	0204	0555	|	0655	|	0723	0755	|	0855	|	0923	0955	1055	|	1123	|	1155	1255	|	1323	|	1355	1455	|
206	Zábřeh na Moravé d.	|	0617	|	0717	|	0745	0817	|	0917	|	0945	1017	1117	|	1145	|	1217	1317	|	1345	|	1417	1517	|
252	**Olomouc** **1159** d.	0253	0643	0721	0743	0749	0811	0843	0921	0943	0949	1011	1043	1143	1149	1211	1221	1243	1343	1349	1411	1421	1443	1543	1549
	Přerov **1159** d.	0322	|	0739	|	|	|	|	0939	|	|	|	|	|	|	|	1239	|	|	|	|	1439	|	|	|
303	Hranice na Moravě ▷ d.	0341	0713	|	0813	|	0840	0913	|	1013	|	1040	1113	1213	|	1240	|	1313	1413	|	1440	|	1513	1616	|
353	Ostrava Svinov ▷ d.	0412	0740	0824	|	0835	0907	0940	1024	|	1035	1107	1140	|	1235	1307	1324	1340	|	1435	1507	1524	1540	|	1635
358	**Ostrava** hlavní ▷ a.	0419	0747	0831	|	0843	0914	0947	1031	|	1043	1114	1147	|	1243	1314	1331	1347	|	1443	1514	1531	1547	|	1643
358	**Ostrava** hlavní ⊙ d.	0422	0749	0833	|	...	0915	0949	1033	|	...	1115	1149	|	...	1315	1333	1349	|	...	1515	1533	1549	|	...
366	Bohumín d.	0441	0803	0839	|	...	|	1003	1039	|	...	|	1203	|	...	|	1339	1403	|	...	|	1539	1603	|	...
381	Karviná hlavní d.	0456	0818	...	|	...	|	1018	...	|	...	|	1218	|	...	|	...	1418	|	...	|	...	1618	|	...
376	Havířov ⊙ d.	|	|	...	|	...	0934	|	...	|	...	1134	|	|	...	1334	...	|	|	...	1534	...	|	|	...
397	**Český Těšín** ⊙ d.	0519	0839	...	|	...	...	1039	...	|	...	...	1239	|	...	...	...	1439	|	...	...	...	1639	|	...
404	Třinec d.	0527	0846	...	|	...	...	1046	...	|	...	...	1246	|	...	...	...	1446	|	...	...	...	1646	|	...
435	Čadca 🏛 d.	0553	0911	...	|	...	...	1111	...	|	...	...	1311	|	...	...	...	1511	|	...	...	...	1711	|	...
329	Valašské Meziříčí d.	|	|	...	0839	...	...	|	...	1039	...	...	|	1239	...	...	...	|	1439	...	...	...	|	1641	...
348	**Vsetín** d.	|	|	...	0858	...	...	|	...	1058	...	...	|	1258	...	...	...	|	1458	...	...	...	|	1659	...
366	Horní Lideč 🏛 d.	|	|	...	0917	...	...	|	...	1117	...	...	|	1317	...	...	...	|	1517	...	...	...	|	1717	...
394	Púchov d.	|	|	...	0941	...	...	|	...	1141	...	...	|	1341	...	...	...	|	1541	...	...	...	|	1741	...
406	Považská Bystrica d.	|	|	...	0957	...	...	|	...	1157	...	...	|	1357	...	...	...	|	1557	...	...	...	|	1757	...
△439	**Žilina** a.	0621	0938	...	1028	...	...	1138	...	1228	...	...	1338	1428	...	...	...	1538	1628	...	...	...	1738	1828	...
	Poprad Tatry **1180** a.	0835	...	...	...	...	...	...	...	...	...	...	...	1619	...	...	...	...	...	...	...	...	...	...	...
	Košice **1180** a.	0952	...	...	...	...	...	...	...	...	...	...	...	1732	...	...	...	...	...	...	...	...	...	...	...

	♥ 1009 🅁🍷	♠ 1359 🅁🍷	*EC** 151 ✕	*EC** 127	*SC•* 511 🅁🍷 ⊗	♥ 1011 🅁🍷	♠ 1361 🅁🍷	*EC** 153 ✕	♠ 1363 🅁🍷 ⊖	*SC•* 513 🅁🍷 ⑤⑦t	♥ 1013 🅁🍷 E	*IC* 561 V	*SC•* 515 🅁🍷 ⊗	♥ 1015 🅁🍷	*IC* 541 ✕ U	♠ 1365 🅁🍷	*IC* 551 ✕ Z	*SC•* 517 🅁🍷	♥ 1017 🅁🍷	*IC* 543 ✕	*SC•* 519 🅁🍷 ⑦e	♥ 1019 🅁🍷 ④–⑦	♠ 1367 🅁🍷 ⑤⑥‡	*EN* 445 ⛝ ♦	443 ♦
Praha hlavní △ d.	1344	1406	1411	1511	1536	1544	1606	1611	1628	1636	1644	1711	1736	1744	1811	1836	1911	1936	1944	2011	2036	2044	2136	2153	222
Kolín △ d.	|	|	1455	1555	|	|	|	1655	|	|	|	1755	|	|	1855	|	1955	|	|	2055	|	|	|	2246	231
Pardubice △ d.	1446	|	1517	1617	1634	1646	|	1717	|	1734	1746	1817	1834	1846	1917	|	2017	2034	2046	2117	2134	2146	|	2312	233
Česká Třebová △ d.	1523	|	1555	1655	|	1723	|	1755	|	|	1823	1855	|	1923	1955	|	2055	|	2123	2155	|	2223	|	|	001
Zábřeh na Moravé d.	1545	|	1617	1717	|	1745	|	1817	|	|	1845	1917	|	1945	2017	|	2117	|	2145	2217	|	2245	|	|	004
Olomouc **1159** d.	1611	1621	1643	1743	1749	1811	1821	1843	1846	1849	1911	1944	1949	2011	2043	2051	2144	2149	2211	2243	2249	2311	2351	0037	011
Přerov **1159** d.	|	1639	|	|	|	|	1839	|	1900	|	|	1958	|	|	|	2109	2158	|	|	|	|	|	0009	|	|
Hranice na Moravě ▷ d.	1640	|	1713	1813	|	1840	|	1916	...	|	1940	...	|	2040	2113	|	...	|	2240	2313	|	2340	|	|	|
Ostrava Svinov ▷ d.	1707	1724	1740	|	1835	1907	1924	1944	...	1935	2007	...	2035	2107	2147	2154	...	2235	2307	2347	2335	0007	0054	|	020
Ostrava hlavní ▷ a.	1714	1731	1747	|	1843	1914	1931	1951	...	1943	2014	...	2043	2114	2154	2201	...	2243	2314	2354	2343	0014	0101	0137	021
Ostrava hlavní ⊙ d.	1715	1733	1749	|	|	1915	1933	1953	...	|	2015	...	|	2115	2156	2203	...	|	2315	2356	|	0015	0103	0139	021
Bohumín d.	|	1739	1803	|	1852r	|	1941	2003	...	1953	|	...	2052	|	2205	2210	...	2252	|	0003	2352	|	0109	0229‡	023
Karviná hlavní d.	|	...	1818	|	...	|	1959	2018	...	2007s	|	...	...	|	2220	2226	...	...	|	...	...	|	...	|	025
Havířov ⊙ d.	1734	...	|	|	...	1935	...	|	...	...	2035	...	...	2135	|	...	...	...	2335	...	...	0035	...	|	|
Český Těšín ⊙ d.	...	...	1839	|	...	1954	...	2039	...	...	2054	...	...	2154	2241	...	...	...	2354	...	...	0054	...	|	031
Třinec d.	...	...	1846	|	...	2002	...	2046	...	...	2102	...	...	2202	2248	...	...	...	0002	...	...	0103	...	|	032
Čadca 🏛 d.	...	...	1911	|	...	2030	...	2111	...	...	...	...	...	...	...	...	...	...	...	...	...	...	...	|	034
Valašské Meziříčí d.	...	...	|	1839	...	|	...	|	...	...	...	...	...	...	...	...	...	...	...	...	...	...	...	|	|
Vsetín d.	...	...	|	1858	...	|	...	|	...	...	...	...	...	...	...	...	...	...	...	...	...	...	...	|	|
Horní Lideč 🏛 d.	...	...	|	1917	...	|	...	|	...	...	...	...	...	...	...	...	...	...	...	...	...	...	...	|	|
Púchov d.	...	...	|	1941	...	|	...	|	...	...	...	...	...	...	...	...	...	...	...	...	...	...	...	|	|
Považská Bystrica d.	...	...	|	1957	...	|	...	|	...	...	...	...	...	...	...	...	...	...	...	...	...	...	...	|	|
Žilina a.	...	...	1938	2028	...	2052	...	2138	...	...	...	...	...	...	...	...	...	...	...	...	...	...	...	0354	041
Poprad Tatry **1180** a.	...	...	...	...	...	...	...	...	...	...	...	...	...	...	...	...	...	...	...	...	...	...	...	0612	063
Košice **1180** a.	...	...	...	...	...	...	...	...	...	...	...	...	...	...	...	...	...	...	...	...	...	...	...	0741	075

ŽILINA - OSTRAVA - OLOMOUC - PRAHA 1160

	EN 444	442	SC• 518	IC 542	♥ 1000	SC• 516	IC 550	♠ 1350	♥ 1002	IC 540	SC• 514	♠ 1352	♥ 1004	SC• 512	IC 560	♠ 1354	EC* 152	♥ 1006	SC• 510	EC* 126	♠ 1356	EC* 150	♥ 1008	SC• 508	EC* 124
	⊠ ♦	♦	[R]🍷 F	✕	[R]🍷 ⚒	[R]🍷 ⚒n	✕ Z	[R]🍷 ⊖	[R]🍷	✕ T	[R]🍷 R	[R]🍷 ⚒b	[R]🍷	[R]🍷 ⊗	V	[R]🍷	✕	[R]🍷	[R]🍷	✕	[R]🍷	✕	[R]🍷	[R]🍷 Ⓑh	
Košice **1180** d.	2101	2208	...	...	...	...	...	...	...	...	...	...	...	...	...	...	...	...	...	...	...	...	...	...	...
Poprad Tatry **1180** d.	2234	2326	...	...	...	...	...	...	...	...	...	...	...	...	...	...	...	...	...	...	...	...	...	...	...
Žilina d.	0035	0135	...	...	...	...	...	...	...	...	...	...	...	...	...	...	0622	0706	...	0732	...	0822	...	...	0932
Považská Bystrica d.	|	|	...	...	...	...	...	...	...	...	...	...	...	...	...	...	|	|	...	0805	...	|	...	...	1005
Púchov d.	|	|	...	...	...	...	...	...	...	...	...	...	...	...	...	...	|	|	...	0818	...	|	...	...	1018
Horní Lideč 🏛 d.	|	|	...	...	...	...	...	...	...	...	...	...	...	...	...	...	|	|	...	0843	...	|	...	...	1043
Vsetín d.	|	|	...	...	...	...	...	...	...	...	...	...	...	...	...	...	|	|	...	0902	...	|	...	...	1102
Valašské Meziříčí d.	|	|	...	...	...	...	...	...	...	...	...	...	...	...	...	...	|	|	...	0921	...	|	...	...	1121
Čadca 🏛 d.	|	0203	...	...	...	...	...	...	...	...	...	...	...	...	...	...	0652	0732	...	|	...	0852	...	...	|
Trinec d.	|	0224	...	...	0358	...	...	...	0458	0513	...	...	0558	...	...	...	0714	0758	...	|	...	0914	0958z	...	|
Český Těšín ⊙ d.	|	0234	...	...	0406	...	...	...	0506	0522	...	...	0606	...	...	...	0723	0806	...	|	...	0923	1006z	...	|
Havířov ⊙ d.	|	|	...	...	0424	...	...	...	0524	|	...	...	0624	...	...	...	|	0824	...	|	...	|	1024	...	|
Karviná hlavní d.	|	0253	...	...	|	...	...	...	|	0542	0556	0601	|	...	...	0656	0742	|	...	|	...	0942	|	...	|
Bohumín d.	0259	0337	0411	0358	|	0511	...	...	|	0558	0611	0617	|	0711	...	0717	0805	|	0911c	|	0917	1005	|	...	|
Ostrava hlavní ⊙ a.	0305	0344	0417	0404	0444	0517	...	...	0544	0604	0617	0623	0644	0717	...	0723	0812	0844	0917c	|	0923	1012	1044	...	|
Ostrava hlavní ▷ d.	0307	0346	0419	0406	0445	0519	...	...	0545	0606	0619	0625	0645	0719	...	0725	0814	0845	0919	|	0925	1014	1045	1119	|
Ostrava Svinov ▷ d.	|	0355	0428	0414	0453	0528	...	...	0553	0614	0628	0633	0653	0728	...	0733	0823	0853	0928	|	0933	1023	1053	1128	|
Hranice na Moravě ▷ d.	|	|	|	0447	0519	|	...	...	0619	0647	|	|	0719	|	...	|	0848	0919	|	0947	|	1048	1119	|	1147
Přerov **1159** d.	|	|	|	|	|	|	0602	0621	|	|	|	0721	|	|	0802	0821	|	|	|	|	1021	|	|	|	|
Olomouc **1159** d.	0406	0452	0515	0519	0549	0615	0619	0637	0651	0719	0715	0737	0749	0815	0819	0837	0919	0949	1015	1019	1037	1119	1149	1215	1219
Zábřeh na Moravé d.	|	0518	|	0543	0614	|	0643	|	0714	0743	|	|	0814	|	0843	|	0943	1014	|	1043	|	1143	1214	|	1243
Česká Třebová △ d.	|	0544	|	0605	0636	|	0705	|	0736	0805	|	|	0836	|	0905	|	1005	1036	|	1105	|	1205	1236	|	1305
Pardubice △ d.	0529	0630	0627	0645	0714	0728	0745	|	0814	0845	0828	|	0914	0928	0945	|	1045	1114	1128	1145	|	1245	1314	1328	1345
Kolín △ d.	0554	0654	|	0707	|	|	0807	|	|	0907	|	|	|	|	1007	|	1107	|	|	1207	|	1307	|	|	1407
Praha hlavní △ a.	0649	0737	0727	0753	0816	0827	0853	0856	0916	0953	0927	0956	1016	1027	1053	1056	1153	1216	1227	1253	1256	1353	1416	1427	1453

	♠ 1358	EC* 148	♠ 1360	♥ 1010	SC• 506	EC* 222	EC* 146	♠ 1362	♥ 1012	SC• 504	EC* 122	EC* 144	♠ 1364	♥ 1014	SC• 502	EC* 220	EC* 142	♠ 1366	♥ 1016	SC• 500	EC* 120	EC* 140	EC* 140	♥ 1018	440
	[R]🍷 ⑦q	✕	[R]🍷	[R]🍷	[R]🍷	✕ Du	✕	[R]🍷	[R]🍷	[R]🍷	🍷	✕	[R]🍷	[R]🍷	[R]🍷	D	✕	[R]🍷	[R]🍷	[R]🍷 ⑦e	✕	✕	✕ ⑦e	[R]🍷 ④–⑦	♦k
Košice **1180** d.	...	...	...	...	...	...	...	...	...	...	1027	...	...	...	...	...	...	...	...	...	...	...	...	...	1808
Poprad Tatry **1180** d.	...	...	...	...	...	...	...	...	...	...	1141	...	...	...	...	...	...	...	...	...	...	...	...	...	1926
Žilina d.	...	1022	...	...	...	1132	1222	...	...	...	1332	1422	...	...	...	1532	1622	...	...	...	1732	1822	1822	...	2132
Považská Bystrica d.	...	|	...	...	...	1205	|	...	...	...	1405	|	...	...	...	1605	|	...	...	...	1805	|	|	...	|
Púchov d.	...	|	...	...	...	1218	|	...	...	...	1418	|	...	...	...	1618	|	...	...	...	1818	|	|	...	|
Horní Lideč 🏛 d.	...	|	...	...	...	1243	|	...	...	...	1443	|	...	...	...	1643	|	...	...	...	1843	|	|	...	|
Vsetín d.	...	|	...	...	...	1302	|	...	...	...	1502	|	...	...	...	1702	|	...	...	...	1902	|	|	...	|
Valašské Meziříčí d.	...	|	...	...	...	1321	|	...	...	...	1521	|	...	...	...	1721	|	...	...	...	1921	|	|	...	|
Čadca 🏛 d.	...	1052	...	...	...	|	1252	...	...	...	|	1452	...	...	...	|	1652	...	...	...	|	1852	1852	...	2203
Trinec d.	...	1114	...	...	...	|	1314	...	...	...	|	1514	...	...	...	|	1714	...	...	...	|	1914	1914	...	2226
Český Těšín ⊙ d.	...	1123	...	...	...	|	1323	...	...	...	|	1523	...	...	...	|	1723	...	...	...	|	1923	1923	...	2237
Havířov ⊙ d.	...	|	...	1224	...	|	|	...	1424	...	|	|	...	1624	...	|	|	...	1824	...	|	|	|	...	|
Karviná hlavní d.	1056	1142	...	|	...	|	1342	...	|	...	|	1542	...	|	...	|	1742	...	|	...	|	1942	1942	...	2258
Bohumín d.	1117	1205	1217	|	...	|	1405	1417	|	...	|	1605	1617	|	...	|	1805	1817	|	...	|	2005	2005	...	2322
Ostrava hlavní ⊙ a.	1123	1212	1223	1244	...	|	1412	1423	1444	...	|	1612	1623	1644	...	|	1812	1823	1844	...	|	2012	2012	...	2329
Ostrava hlavní ▷ d.	1125	1214	1225	1245	1319	|	1414	1425	1445	1519	|	1614	1625	1645	1719	|	1814	1825	1845	1919	|	...	2014	2045	2333
Ostrava Svinov ▷ d.	1133	1223	1233	1253	1328	|	1423	1433	1453	1528	|	1623	1633	1653	1728	|	1823	1833	1853	1928	|	...	2023	2053	2344
Hranice na Moravě ▷ d.	|	1248	|	1319	|	1347	1448	|	1519	|	1547	1648	|	1719	|	1747	1848	|	1919	|	1947	...	2048	2119	0012
Přerov **1159** d.	1221	|	1321	|	|	|	|	1521	|	|	|	|	1721	|	|	|	|	1921	|	|	|	...	|	|	0045
Olomouc **1159** d.	1237	1319	1337	1349	1415	1419	1519	1537	1549	1615	1619	1719	1737	1749	1815	1819	1919	1937	1949	2015	2021	...	2119	2149	0105
Zábřeh na Moravé d.	|	1343	|	1414	|	1443	1543	|	1614	|	1643	1743	|	1814	|	1843	1943	|	2014	|	2052	...	2143	2214	|
Česká Třebová △ d.	|	1405	|	1436	|	1505	1605	|	1636	|	1705	1805	|	1836	|	1905	2005	|	2036	|	2114	...	2205	2240	0151
Pardubice △ d.	|	1445	|	1514	1528	1545	1645	|	1714	1728	1745	1845	|	1914	1928	1945	2045	|	2114	2128	2156	...	2245	2318	0235
Kolín △ d.	|	1507	|	|	|	1607	1707	|	|	|	1807	1907	|	|	|	2007	2107	|	|	|	2221	...	2307	|	0300
Praha hlavní △ a.	1456	1553	1556	1616	1627	1653	1753	1756	1816	1827	1853	1953	1956	2016	2027	2053	2153	2156	2216	2227	2307	...	2353	0020	0355

SEMI-FAST TRAINS Faster connections may be available by changing at Olomouc (see above). Additional trains run Praha - Česká Třebova (see Table **1150**).

	883	885	1423	889	891	893	851	853	875	719
	⊡		⑥S			⊖			Ⓑh	
Praha hlavní △ d.	...	0652	0852	1052	1252	1452	1652	1852	1952	2311
Kolín △ d.	...	0737	0937	1137	1337	1537	1737	1937	2037	2355
Pardubice △ d.	0606	0806	1006	1206	1406	1606	1806	2006	2106	0020
Choceň △ d.	0625	0825	1025	1225	1425	1625	1825	2025	2125	...
Ústí nad Orlicí △ d.	0638	0838	1038	1238	1438	1638	1838	2038	2138	...
Česká Třebová △ d.	0650	0850	1050	1250	1450	1650	1850	2050	2148	...
Zábřeh na Moravé d.	0713	0913	|	1313	1513	1713	1913	2113	...	...
Olomouc a.	0752	0952	1133	1352	1552	1752	1952	2152	...	...
Olomouc d.	0755	0955	1135	1355	1555	...	1955	2155	...	...
Luhačovice **1159** a.	0939	1139	|	1539	1739	...	|	|	...	...
Hranice na Moravě d.	...	...	1207	...	...	...	2030	2230	...	...
Valašské Meziříčí d.	...	...	1232	...	...	...	2055	2255	...	...
Vsetín a.	...	...	1248	...	...	...	2112	2312	...	...

	718	892	852	850		888	886	884	882	
		⊖					Θ			2
Vsetín d.	...	...	0450	0652	...	...	...	...	...	...
Valašské Meziříčí d.	...	...	0508	0710	...	...	...	...	...	...
Hranice na Moravě d.	...	...	0532	0734	...	...	...	...	...	...
Luhačovice **1159** d.	...	...	|	|	...	1020	...	1420	1620	...
Olomouc a.	...	...	0602	0806	...	1206	...	1606	1806	...
Olomouc d.	...	0522	0609	0809	...	1209	1400	1609	1809	...
Zábřeh na Moravé d.	...	|	0648	0848	...	1248	1448	1648	1848	...
Česká Třebová △ d.	...	0611	0711	0911	...	1311	1511	1711	1911	2144
Ústí nad Orlicí △ d.	...	0621	0721	0921	...	1321	1521	1721	1921	2155
Choceň △ d.	...	0635	0735	0935	...	1335	1535	1735	1935	2210
Pardubice △ d.	0509	0659	0759	0959	...	1359	1559	1759	1959	2241
Kolín △ d.	0537	0727	0827	1027	...	1427	1627	1827	2027	...
Praha hlavní △ a.	0623	0813	0913	1113	...	1513	1713	1913	2113	...

♦ – **NOTES** (LISTED BY TRAIN NUMBER)

40/1 – EXCELSIOR – 🛏 1, 2 cl., ▬ 2 cl., (12) Cheb - Karlovy Vary - Praha - Košice and v.v.; 🛏 1, 2 cl. Cheb (**762/6**) - Plzeň - Praha (**441/0**) - Košice and v.v.

42/3 – ŠIRAVA – 🛏 1, 2 cl., ▬ 2 cl., (12) Praha - Bohumín - Košice - Humenné and v.v.; 🛏 1, 2 cl. Praha - Bohumín - Košice and v.v.; 🛏 1, 2 cl., (2) Praha - Bohumín (**403/2**) - Kraków and v.v. (also ▬ 2 cl. Apr. 16 - Nov. 3 from Praha, Apr. 17 - Nov. 4 from Kraków).

44/5 – SLOVAKIA – 🛏 1, 2 cl., ▬ 2 cl. Praha - Bohumín - Poprad Tatry - Košice and v.v.; 🛏 1, 2 cl. Praha - Bohumín - Poprad Tatry and v.v.; 🛏 1, 2 cl. Praha - Žilina (**1841/52**) - Banska Bystrica - Zvolen and v.v.; 🛏 1, 2 cl., (2) Praha - Bohumín (**406/7**) - Katowice - Warszawa and v.v. (also ▬ 2 cl. Apr. 16 - Nov. 3 from Praha, Apr. 15 - Nov. 2 from Warszawa).

– (12) Praha - Žilina - Banská Bystrica - Zvolen and v.v. (Table **1185**).
– Daily to Ostrava, ①②③ (daily from June 15) to Trinec.
– ① (also ②–⑤ to June 27 / from Sept. 1), also Apr. 17, 22, 30, May 7, Oct. 29, Nov. 18; not Apr. 21, May 2, 9, Oct. 27, Nov. 17.
– ① (also Apr. 22, Oct. 29, Nov. 18; not Apr. 21, Oct. 27, Nov. 17). Runs daily Ostrava - Žilina.
– From Karvina on ① (also Apr. 22, Oct. 29, Nov. 18; not Apr. 21, Oct. 27, Nov. 17); from Bohumín on ①–⑥ (not Apr. 21, May 3, 10, July 5, Oct. 28, Nov. 17).
– ⑥ Apr. 5 - Sept. 27 (also May 1, 8, Oct. 25, Nov. 15).
– ⚒**n** from Trinec; daily from Bohumin.
– Daily to Bohumin; Ⓑ**h** to Trinec.
– To / from Veseli nad Moravou (Table **1159**).
– To / from Zlín střed (Table **1159**).
– Also May 1, 8; not May 2, 3, 9, 10, Oct. 27.
– © only.
– ⑦ (also Apr. 21, Oct. 28, Nov. 17; not Apr. 20, Oct. 26, Nov. 16).
– Not Apr. 20, Nov. 16.
– Also conveys ▬ 2 cl. Košice - Pardubice (**718**) - Praha, arrive 0623.

n – ①–⑥ (not Apr. 21, July 5, Nov. 17).
q – Also Apr. 21, May 2, 3, 9, 10, Oct. 27, 28, Nov. 17.
r – ①–⑥ (also Apr. 20, Oct. 26, Nov. 16; not Apr. 21, Oct. 28, Nov. 17).
s – ⑤ (also Apr. 30, May 7; not May 2, 9).
t – Also ④ to June 26 / from Sept. 4 (also Apr. 16, 29 30, May 6, 7; not Apr. 20, May 1, 2, 8, 9, Oct. 26, Nov. 16).
u – Conveys (12) Praha - Žilina - Banská Bystrica - Zvolen (**836/1**) - Bratislava and v.v.
z – ⑦ (also Apr. 21, May 1, 8, Oct. 28, Nov. 17).

♥ – *REGIOJET – IC* train operated by RegioJet a.s. ČD tickets and passes not valid.
♠ – *LEO EXPRESS – LE* train operated by Leo Express a.s. ČD tickets and passes not valid.

‡ – Also Apr. 20, 30, May 7, Oct. 26, 27, Nov. 16.
• – *SUPERCITY PENDOLINO* train, reservation compulsory (reservation fee CZK 200). On journeys from Praha the last pick up point is Olomouc; on journeys to Praha the first set down point is Olomouc.
¦ – Arrive 0145.
⊙ – Additional trains Český Těšín - Havířov - Ostrava : from Český Těšín every 2 hours 0625 Ⓐ - 1825 Ⓐ, from Ostrava hlavní every 2 hours 0758 Ⓐ - 1958 Ⓐ, journey 45 minutes. Local trains run hourly Český Těšín - Havířov - Ostrava Svinov (jny 50 mins).
⊗ – From / to Františkovy Lázně via Cheb, Plzen (Table **1120**).
△ – See also Table **1150**.
▷ – See also Table **1155**.
⊡ – From Hradec Králové (depart 0529).
⊠ – International journeys only.
⊖ – To / from Staré Město u Uherské Hradiště (Table **1159**).
Θ – From Otrokovice (Table **1159**).
Δ – *466 km* via Ostrava.
* – Classified *Ex* in Slovakia.

OTHER TRAIN NAMES: **122/3** KOŠIČAN, **220/1** FATRA, **222/3** DETVAN.

1165 PARDUBICE - LETOHRAD - LICHKOV - KLODZKO

Most 2nd class only

km		1915 b			1917	893			1653	
	Praha hl **1150/60** ..▷ d.	...	...	...	*1211*r	1452	...	...	*1611*r	...
0	**Pardubice** ....▷ d.	...	...	...	1336	1606	...	...	1736	...
50	Ústi nad Orlici ....▷ d.	0747	*0943*	1243	1426	1637	1643	...	1835	...
64	Letohrad ....a.	0807	*1003*	1303	1441	...	1703	...	1856	...
64	Letohrad ....d.	0809	1005	1307	1443	...	1710	...	1857	...
85	Lichkov 🏛 ....d.	0838	1040	1334	1515	...	1736	1745	1918	1920
94	Miedzylesie ....a.	0846	1049	...	1523	...	...	1754	...	1929
94	Miedzylesie .... **1095** d.	0904	1050	...	1528	...	...	1802	...	1933
130	**Klodzko** Gj......... **1095** a.	0943	1133	...	1611	...	...	1853	...	2025
	Wroclaw **1095**..........a.	1138	...	...	...	...	...	2103	...	2230

	1652 Ⓐ	b		872				884	1916	864	1914 s
Wroclaw **1095** .... d.	...	0622	...	...	...	1220	...	...	...	...	1650
Klodzko Gj. ....**1095** d.	...	0816	...	...	1205	1430	...	...	1639	...	1843
Miedzylesie ....**1095** a.	...	0901	...	...	1250	1517	...	...	1722	...	1929
Miedzylesie 🏛 .... d.	...	0903	...	...	1251	1531	...	...	1725	...	1932
Lichkov........................ d.	0650	0912	...	...	1259	1540	1556	...	1733	...	1940
Letohrad...................... a.	0715	0941	...	...	1329	...	1624	...	1757	...	2001
Letohrad...................... d.	0718	...	0943	...	1343	...	1643	...	1758	...	2002
Ústi nad Orlici.......... ▷ a.	0735	...	1004	1021	1406	...	1706	1721	1818	1821	2019
Pardubice.............. ▷ a.	0825	...	...	1054	...	...	...	1754	...	1854	...
Praha hl **1150/60** . ▷ a.	...	...	...	1213	...	...	...	1913	...	2013	...

HRADEC KRALOVÉ - LETOHRAD

km		Ⓐ	Ⓒ					935		
	Praha hlavní **1145** ....d.	...	...	...	...	...	...	1511	...	...
0	**Hradec Králové**..........d.	0705	0705	0905	1105	1305	1505	1705	1905	...
21	Týniště nad Orlicí.........d.	0733	0733	0931	1131	1331	1531	1731	1931	...
36	Doudleby nad Orlici......d.	0752	0753	0951	1151	1351	1551	1751	1951	...
62	**Letohrad** ....a.	...	0828	1028	1233	1431	1631	1833	2028	...

	934	Ⓐ	Ⓒ								
Letohrad .... d.	0533	...	0730	0835	...	1133	1333	1533	1733	2006	...
Doudleby nad Orlici ..... d.	0610	0811	0811	0910	...	1210	1410	1610	1810	2056	2108
Týniště nad Orlicí .... d.	0630	0832	0832	0932	...	1232	1432	1632	1832	...	2133
Hradec Králové .... a.	0653	0854	0854	0954	...	1254	1454	1654	1854	...	2158
Praha hlavní **1145**.... a.	0845	...	...	...	...	...	...	...	...	...	...

b – Not Dec. 25, 26, Jan. 1.
r – Connection by *Ex* or *EC* train (1, 2 class).
s – Not Dec. 24, 25, 31.
▷ – See also Tables **1150** / **1160**.

Timings in Poland are subject to alteration from June 15.

1166 OLOMOUC / JESENIK - OPAVA - OSTRAVA

2nd class only

km			1121	1123			1125	1127		1129		1131		1133	1135	
0	**Olomouc**.................... d.	...	...	0707**n**	0859	...	...	1107	...	1307	...	1507	...	1707	1907	...
64	Bruntál......................... d.	...	...	0832**n**	1032	...	...	1232	...	1432	...	1632	...	1832	2032	...
• 58	**Jesenik**.................... d.	0530	...	|	|	0930	...	|	1330	|	...	|	1730a	|	|	...
• 38	Gjuchojazy (Poland) . d.	0613	...	|	|	1013	...	|	1413	|	...	|	1813	|	|	...
• 17	Tremešná ve Slezsku. d.	0642	...	|	|	1042	...	|	1442	|	1645	|	1842	|	|	...
87	Krnov............................. d.	0700	0706	0906	1057	1100	1106	1306	1500	1507	1704	1706	1900	1906	2057	*2105*
116	**Opava** východ .... ▷ d.	...	0746	0946	...	...	1146	1346	...	1546	...	1746	...	1946	...	2142
144	Ostrava Svinov .... ▷ a.	...	0807	1007	...	...	1207	1407	...	1607	...	1807	...	2007	...	2217
149	**Ostrava** hlavní......... ▷ a.	...	...	...	...	...	1223	1423	...	1623	...	...	...	...	...	...

	1134 ⚒n	1132		1130		1128			1126	1124		1122	1120	⑦e		
Ostrava hlavní.......... ▷ d.	...	...	...	...	...	...	...	...	...	1357	...	1557	1757	...	...	...
Ostrava Svinov .... ▷ d.	...	0609	...	0809	...	1009	...	...	1209	1409	...	1609	1809	...	...	...
Opava východ .... ▷ d.	*0425*	0633	...	0833	...	1033	...	...	1233	1433	...	1633	1833	...	...	*2028*
Krnov............................ d.	0509	0709**r**	0708	0909**r**	0908	1103	1109	1110	1309	1509**r**	1507	1709	1903	1906	1910	2107
Tremešná ve Slezsku.. a.	|	|	0727	|	0928	...	|	1127	|	|	1524	|	...	|	1927	|
Gjuchojazy (Poland) .. a.	|	|	0755	|	...	...	|	1155	|	|	1555	|	...	|	1955	|
Jesenik.................... a.	|	|	0842	|	...	...	|	1242	|	|	1642	|	...	|	2042	|
Bruntál......................... d.	0537	0736	...	0936	...	...	1137	...	1336	1536	...	1736	...	1932	...	2136
Olomouc.................... a.	0652	0852	...	1052	...	...	1254	...	1452	1652	...	1852	...	2056	...	2303

Additional trains **OPAVA - OSTRAVA**

	Ⓐ	FAST	Ⓐ		SLOW	⊖
Opava východ... d.	0519	every	1919	0430	every	2030
Ostrava Svinov.. a.	0545	2	1945	0502	hour	2102
Ostrava hlavní .. a.	0557	hrs	1957	...	until	...

	Ⓐ	FAST	Ⓐ		SLOW	▽
Ostrava hlavní .. d.	0709	every	1909	...	every	...
Ostrava Svinov.. d.	0722	2	1922	0446	hour	2046
Opava východ... a.	0745	hrs	1945	0518	until	2118

a – Ⓐ only.
e – Also Apr. 21, Oct. 28, Nov. 17; not Apr. 20, Oct. 26, Nov. 16.
n – ①–⑥ (not Apr. 21, July 5, Nov. 17).
r – Arrives 5 - 6 minutes earlier.

⊖ – Also at 2142, 2244.
▽ – Also at 2159, 2258, 0016.
▷ – For additional trains see panel on right.
• – Distance from Krnov.

1169 OTHER LOCAL SERVICES

2nd class

BŘECLAV - ZNOJMO *69 km* Journey 90 minutes

From Břeclav: every 2 hours 0931 - 1931, also 0731 **c**, 1233 Ⓐ, 1433 Ⓐ, 1633 Ⓐ, 2137 Ⓐ.
From Znojmo: every 2 hours 0855 - 1855, also 0658, 1155 Ⓐ, 1355 Ⓐ, 1555 Ⓑ, 1755 Ⓐ.

BRNO - ZNOJMO *89 km* Journey 2 hours Change at Miroslav and Hrušovany

From Brno: 0649 ⑥, 0849 Ⓒ, 1254 Ⓒ, 1454 **R**, 1654 Ⓒ.
From Znojmo: 0903 Ⓒ, 1303 Ⓒ, 1503 **R**, 1703 Ⓒ.

CHOCEŇ - LITOMYŠL *24 km* Journey 55 minutes

From Choceň: 0508 Ⓐ, 0629, 0839, 1039, 1239 Ⓒ, 1429 Ⓐ, 1539 Ⓒ, 1639 Ⓐ, 1839 Ⓒ.
From Litomyšl: 0444 Ⓐ, 0605 Ⓐ, 0719 Ⓒ, 0933, 1224 Ⓒ, 1244 Ⓐ, 1524, 1732, 1934 Ⓒ.
Change at Vysoké Myto město on certain journeys.

JINDŘICHŮV HRADEC - NOVÁ BYSTŘICE *33 km* Narrow gauge, 80 mins

Winter service: from Jindřichův Hradec 0925 Ⓒ, 1428; from Nová Bystřice 1058 Ⓒ, 1621.
May / June / Sept / Oct: 2 - 3 journeys. July / Aug: 6 journeys. Operator: JHMD www.jhmd.cz
Steam train June 30 - Aug. 30: from Jindřichův Hradec 0925, returning 1513 (also from Jindřichův Hradec 1050 returning 1420 on ⑥ May 3 - June 28, ⑥ Sept. 6 - 27, also Oct. 25).

KOJETIN - KROMĚŘÍŽ *9 km* Journey 12 minutes

From Kojetin: 0507 Ⓐ, 0624, 0724, 0814, 0911 ⑥, 0924 ⑦, 0939 Ⓐ, 1039, 1214, 1324, 1424 Ⓐ, 1524, 1624, 1724, 1824, 1924 Ⓑ, 2014, 2114 ⑦, 2214, 2259 Ⓐ.
From Kroměříž: 0450 Ⓐ, 0540 ⚒, 0605 ⑦, 0640 ⚒, 0700 ⑦, 0740, 0840, 0955, 1140, 1255 1340 Ⓐ, 1440, 1540, 1640, 1740, 1840 Ⓑ, 1940, 2003 ⑦, 2040 ⑦, 2140, 2240 Ⓐ.
Hulin - Kroměříž: 1 - 2 trains per hour connecting with trains in Table **1159**. *8 km*, 8 mins.

PRAHA - KARLŠTEJN *33 km* Journey 42 minutes

From Praha hlavní: hourly 0420 - 2320 (every 30 minutes 1220 - 1920). From Karlštejn: hour 0456 - 2256 (every 30 mins 1256 - 1956). Most trains continue to / from Beroun (10 mins).

TŘEMEŠNÁ VE SLEZSKU - OSOBLAHA *20 km* Narrow gauge, 45 minutes

From Třemešná: 0450 Ⓐ **n**, 0650 Ⓐ **n**, 0730 ⑥ **b**, 0915 **T**, 1045 **s**, 1130, 1527, 1930.
From Osoblaha: 0350 Ⓐ **n**, 0550 ⚒, 0950, 1350, 1400 **T**, 1455 **s**, 1750.

R – Ⓒ Apr. 19 - Sept. 28.
b – Also Ⓐ June 30 - Aug. 29.
n – Not June 30 - Aug. 29.
s – Ⓒ June 21 - Aug. 31 (also May 8, 31, Sept. 6, 13, 20). Steam journey; special fares.
T – ③④ June 4 - 19 (heritage unit).
c – Ⓒ (daily June 28 - Aug. 31).

SLOVAKIA

Operator: National railway operator is Železničná spoločnosť Slovensko (ŽSSK), www.slovakrail.sk, which runs on the network of Železnice Slovenskej Republiky (ŽSR), www.zsr.sk.

Services: All trains convey first and second class seating, **except** where shown otherwise in footnotes or by '2' in the train column, or where the footnote shows sleeping and/or couchett cars only. Descriptions of sleeping (🛏) and couchette (▬) cars appear on page 8.

Timings: Valid **December 15, 2013 - December 13, 2014**, incorporating amendments from March 2. Holiday cancellation dates of mainline trains are shown in the tables, but certain loca trains may also be cancelled during the period Dec. 24 - Jan. 1 and these cancellations may not be shown in the tables.

Supplements: A higher level of fares applies to travel by *EC* and *IC* trains. It is possible to reserve seats on most Express trains.

1170 BRATISLAVA - LEVICE - ZVOLEN

km		831 ⊖§	811	833 ⊖	813	835 ◇	815	*Ex* 531 Ⓐ	837	801 Ⓑ P
0	**Bratislava** hlavná . **1175** d.	0601	0801	1001	1201	1401	1601	1656	1801	2349
49	Galanta .... **1175** d.	0637	0837	1037	1237	1437	1637	|	1837	0027
60	Šal'a.................... **1175** d.	0647	0847	1047	1247	1447	1647	|	1847	0037
89	Šurany........................ d.	0709	0909	1109	1309	1509	1709	1752	1909	0101
132	Levice.......................... d.	0749	0949	1149	1349	1549	1749	1834	1949	0148
187	Žiar nad Hronom............ d.	0840	1040	1240	1440	1640	1840	1922	2040	0238
209	**Zvolen** osob. .... a.	0858	1058	1258	1458	1658	1858	1940	2058	0257
	Banská Bystrica **1185**. a.	0933	|	1333	|	1733	|	2000	2128	|
	Košice **1190** .... a.	...	1437	...	1837	...	2237	...	...	0700
	Prešov **1196**.............. a.	...	...	...	...	...	...	...	...	0740

	838 2 Ⓐ	*Ex* 530 Ⓐ	830 ◇	810	832 ◇	812	834 ⊖	814	836 ⊖§	800 Ⓑ P
Prešov **1196**.............. d.	...	...	...	...	...	...	...	...	...	212
Košice **1190** .... d.	...	...	...	0523	...	0923	...	1323	...	222
Banská Bystrica **1185**. d.	...	0535	0627	|	1027	|	1427	|	1827	|
Zvolen osob................. d.	...	0554	0702	0902	1102	1302	1502	1702	1902	021
Žiar nad Hronom .... d.	...	0613	0722	0922	1122	1322	1522	1722	1922	023
Levice .... d.	0547	0659	0813	1013	1213	1413	1613	1813	2013	033
Šurany .... d.	0627	0740	0851	1051	1251	1451	1651	1851	2051	041
Šal'a.................... **1175** d.	0651	|	0914	1114	1314	1514	1714	1914	2114	043
Galanta .... **1175** d.	0700	|	0925	1125	1325	1525	1725	1925	2125	044
Bratislava hlavná.. **1175** a.	0733	0836	0959	1159	1359	1559	1759	1959	2159	052

P – POL'ANA – from Bratislava and Prešov on Ⓑ (not Apr. 18, 20, Aug. 29, 31, Sept. 14, Nov. 16). 🛏 1, 2 cl. and [2] Bratislava - Košice - Prešov and v.v.
◇ – [12] Bratislava - Zvolen and v.v.; [2] Bratislava - Zvolen (**1841/45/50**) - Banská Bystrica - Žilina and v.v.
⊖ – [12] Bratislava - Zvolen and v.v.; [12] Bratislava - Zvolen (**220/1/2/3**) - Banská Bystrica Žilina - Praha and v.v.
§ – Also conveys [2] Bratislava - Zvolen (**821/0**) - Banská Bystrica - Brezno - Margecar and v.v. (Table **1190**).

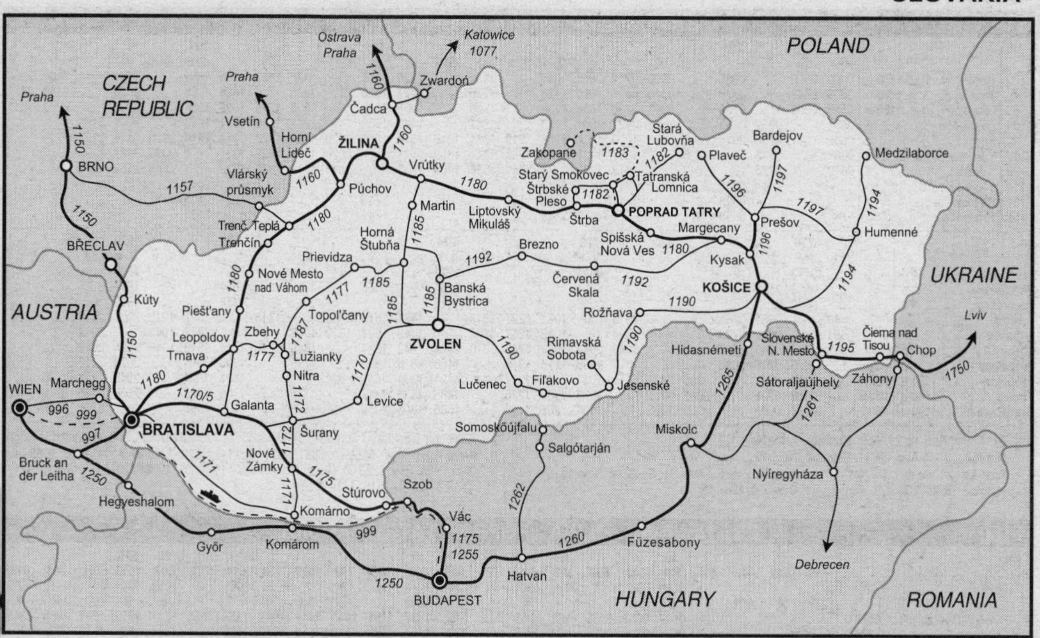

1171 BRATISLAVA - KOMÁRNO

2nd class

km	⊖	Ⓒ	Ⓐ						Ⓐ	Ⓐ
0	**Bratislava** hlavná........d.	0605	0705	0805	every	2005	2205	A	1513	1713
5	Bratislava Nové Mesto.d.	0613	0713	0813	**two**	2013	2213	L	1526	1726
42	Dunajská Streda..........d.	0711	0821	0911	hours ‡	2111	2307	S	1605	1805
94	**Komárno**....................a.	0813	0922	1013	until	2213	...	O	1704	1904

⊖	Ⓐ					Ⓐ	Ⓒ	Ⓐ	Ⓒ	Ⓐ	
Komárno.................. d.	0635	0743	0943	1143	1343	1435	1543	1635	1743	1835	1943
Dunajská Streda .... d.	0750	0850	1050	1250	1450	1550	1650	1750	1850	1950	2050
Bratislava Nové Mesto a.	0828	0942	1142	1342	1542	1642	1742	1842	1941	2042	2142
Bratislava hlavná .... a.	0837	0950	1150	1350	1550	1650	1750	1850	1950	2050	2150

km	△				Ⓐ		Ⓐ		Ⓐ		
0	Nové Zamky................d.	0852	1052	1252	1352	1452	1552	1652	1752	1852	2052
29	Komárno ....a.	0922	1122	1322	1422	1522	1622	1722	1822	1922	2122

▽	Ⓐ				Ⓐ		Ⓐ		Ⓐ		
Komárno......................d.	0737	0842	1042	1242	1342	1442	1542	1642	1742	1842	2042
Nové Zamky ....a.	0803	0908	1108	1308	1408	1508	1608	1708	1808	1908	2108

△ – Additional journeys: 0452, 0552 Ⓐ, 0652, 0735 Ⓐ.
▽ – Additional journeys: 0442, 0542 Ⓐ, 0642.
⊖ – Operator: Regiojet. Additional journeys run Bratislava - Dunajská Streda.
‡ – On Ⓐ the 1605 journey departs at 1613.

1172 NOVÉ ZAMKY - NITRA

2nd class

km	△		Ⓐ‡	‡	‡		Ⓐ	‡	Ⓐ			
0	**Nové Zamky** ....d.	0625	0723	0920	1120	1320	1424	1520	1615	1720	1815	1920
10	Šurany..............a.	0639	0734	0932	1132	1332	1436	1532	1627	1732	1827	1932
10	Šurany..............d.	0640	0741	0933	1133	1333	1437	1533	1633	1733	1833	1938
36	**Nitra**.................a.	0721	0816	1016	1216	1416	1512	1616	1716	1816	1916	2013

▽	‡			‡	Ⓐ	‡	Ⓐ	‡	Ⓐ		
Nitra.............d.	0632	0753	0953	1153	1253	1353	1450	1553	1653	1753	1853
Šurany...........a.	0703	0829	1025	1225	1325	1425	1529	1625	1725	1825	1925
Šurany...........d.	0710	0830	1028	1228	1333	1426	1533	1628	1733	1828	1933
Nové Zamky .a.	0722	0841	1040	1240	1346	1439	1545	1640	1746	1840	1946

‡ – To/from Prievidza (Table **1187**).
△ – Also at 0428, 0520, 2120, 2241.
▽ – Also at 0337, 0527, 2053, 2235.

1175 BRATISLAVA - ŠTÚROVO - BUDAPEST

km		*EN* 477	*EN* 477	*EC* 271	*EC* 273	*EC* 275	*EC* 277	*EC* 171	*EC* 131	*EC* 175
				✕	✕	✕	✕	✕	✕	✕
		M	**S**		**A**			**H**	**V**	**J**
	Praha hlavní **1150** ....d.	2345	2345	...	0539	0739	0939	1139	...	1539
	Brno hlavní **1150** ....d.	0315	0315	0622	0822	1022	1222	1422	...	1822
	Břeclav **1150** ....d.	0440	0440	0657	0857	1057	1257	1457	1657	1857
0	**Bratislava** hlavná ....d.	0548	0548	0753	0953	1153	1353	1553	1753	1953
91	Nové Zámky ....d.	0644	0644	0846	1046	1246	1446	1646	1846	2046
135	Štúrovo.................................a.	0710	0710	0911	1111	1311	1511	1711	1911	2111
135	Štúrovo 🏛 ....d.	0713	0713	0914	1114	1314	1514	1714	1914	2114
150	Szob 🏛 .... ▷ d.	|	|	0925	1125	1325	1525	1725	1925	2125
180	Nagymaros-Visegrád .... ▷ d.	|	|	0936	1136	1336	1536	1736	1936	2136
197	Vác...................................... ▷ d.	0750	0750	0950	1150	1350	1550	1750	1950	2150
214	**Budapest** Keleti .... ▷ a.	0835	0835	1035	1235	1435	1635	1835	2035	2235

	EC 174	*EC* 130	*EC* 170	*EC* 276	*EC* 274	*EC* 272	*EC* 270	*EN* 476	**476 718**
	✕	✕	✕	✕	✕	✕	✕		
	J	**V**	**H**			**B**		**M**	**S**
Budapest Keleti .... ▷ d.	0525	0725	0925	1125	1325	1525	1725	2005	2005
Vác.................................. ▷ d.	0610	0810	1010	1210	1410	1610	1810	2047	2047
Nagymaros-Visegrád .... ▷ d.	0624	0824	1024	1224	1424	1624	1824	|	|
Szob 🏛 .... ▷ d.	0636	0836	1036	1236	1436	1636	1836	|	|
Štúrovo 🏛 ....a.	0646	0846	1046	1246	1446	1649	1846	2121	2121
Štúrovo ....d.	0649	0849	1049	1249	1449	1649	1849	2124	2124
Nové Zámky ....d.	0716	0916	1116	1316	1516	1716	1916	2152	2152
Bratislava hlavná ....a.	0807	1007	1207	1407	1607	1807	2007	2246	2246
Břeclav **1150** ....a.	0902	1102	1302	1502	1702	1902	2102	2353	2353
Brno hlavní **1150** ....a.	0937	...	1337	1537	1737	1937	2137	0052	0052
Praha hlavní **1150** ....a.	1221	...	1621	1821	2021	2221	....	0403	0623

ADDITIONAL TRAINS BRATISLAVA - NOVÉ ZAMKY

2nd class

△						871	873		877	879		
		Ⓐ	Ⓒ		Ⓐ	Ⓐ	Ⓐ			Ⓐ		
atislava hl.... § d.	0707	0807	0907	1107	1207	1301	1501	1507	1701	1901	1907	2107
alanta........... § d.	0757	0857	0957	1157	1257	1337	1537	1557	1737	1937	1957	2157
al'a............... § d.	0807	0907	1007	1207	1307	1347	1547	1607	1747	1947	2007	2207
ové Zámky ..... a.	0836	0936	1036	1236	1336	1406	1609	1636	1809	2006	2036	2236

▽	872	874	876								
		Ⓐ	Ⓐ		Ⓐ						
Nové Zámky ... d.	0520	0553	0620	0646	0722	0922	1122	1322	1522	1722	1922
Šal'a .... § d.	0541	0614	0641	0716	0752	0952	1152	1352	1552	1752	1952
Galanta......... § d.	0552	0625	0652	0727	0809	1003	1203	1403	1603	1803	2003
Bratislava hl .. § a.	0626	0659	0726	0821	0857	1051	1251	1451	1651	1851	2051

– AVALA – 12 ✕ Praha - Bratislava - Budapest - Beograd. Conveys June 13 - Sept. 5 🛏 2 cl. Praha - Subotica - Bar (also 🛏 1, 2 cl. on ②③⑤⑥ June 13 - Sept. 5), Table **1360**.
– AVALA – 12 ✕ Beograd - Budapest - Bratislava - Praha. Conveys June 14 - Sept. 6 🛏 2 cl. Bar - Subotica - Praha (also 🛏 1, 2 cl. on ③④⑥⑦ June 14 - Sept. 6), Table **1360**.
– HUNGARIA – 12 ✕ Berlin - Dresden - Praha - Bratislava - Budapest and v.v.
– JÁN JESENIUS – 12 ✕ Hamburg - Berlin - Dresden - Praha - Budapest and v.v.
– METROPOL – 🛏 1, 2 cl., 🛏 2 cl., 2 Berlin - Dresden - Praha - Bratislava - Budapest and v.v.; 🛏 1, 2 cl., 🛏 2 cl., 2 Warszawa (**407/6**) - Břeclav (**477/6**) - Budapest and v.v.; 🛏 1, 2 cl., 🛏 2 cl. Kraków (**402/3**) - Bohumín (**407/6**) - Břeclav (**477/6**) - Budapest and v.v.
– 🛏 1, 2 cl., 🛏 2 cl. Praha - Budapest and v.v. (also 2 June 13 - Sept. 13 from Praha, June 14 - Sept. 14 from Budapest).

V – VARSOVIA – 12 ✕ Warszawa - Katowice - Ostrava - Břeclav - Bratislava - Budapest and v.v.

▷ – For local trains Szob - Budapest Nyugati see Table **1255**.
△ – Also at: 0444, 1307, 1407Ⓐ, 1607Ⓐ, 1707, 1807Ⓐ, 2307.
▽ – Also at: 0321, 0430 Ⓒ, 0438 Ⓐ, 1422 Ⓐ, 1622 Ⓐ.
§ – See also Table **1170**.

OTHER TRAIN NAMES:
270/1 PETROV, **274/5** JAROSLAV HAŠEK, **276/7** SLOVAN.

1177 BRATISLAVA - NITRA and PRIEVIDZA

2nd class

km					721					723					725					727					
		Ⓐ	Ⓐ				Ⓐ			Ⓑh	Ⓑh		Ⓑh	Ⓐ				Ⓐ		Ⓑd	Ⓑd	Ⓐ			
0	**Bratislava** hl. .... **1180** d.	0420	0500	...	0655	...	0800	0755	0955	1055	...	1155	...	1355	1455	...	1555	1655	1755	1855	...	1955	...	2100	2300
46	Trnava .... **1180** d.	0509	0549	...	0726	...	0849	0826	1026	1126	...	1226	...	1426	1526	...	1626	1726	1826	1926	...	2026	...	2149	2357
63	Leopoldov .... **1180** a.	0523	0603	...	0738	...	0903	0838	1038	1138	...	1238	...	1438	1538	...	1638	1738	1838	1938	...	2038	...	2203	0011
63	Leopoldov .... d.	0534	...	0632	0753	...	...	0927	1041	1153	...	1241	...	1441	1553	...	1641	1750	1841	1953	...	2041	2125	...	...
87	Zbehy .... d.	0602	...	0706	0816	0820	...	1000	1114	1216	1219	1314	1346	1514	1616	1620	1714	1823	1914	2016	2020	2114	2153	...	...
91	Lužianky .... a.	0607	...	0713	|	0826	...	1007	1121	|	1225	1321	1352	1521	|	1626	1721	1829	1921	|	2026	2121	2200	...	...
98	**Nitra** .... a.	0619	...	0726	|	0843	...	1019	1132	|	1251	1336	1403	1536	|	1643	1749	1850	1932	|	2045	2132	2212	...	...
114	Topoľčany .... ▷ a.	...	...	...	0840	...	...	...	...	1240	...	...	...	...	1640	...	...	...	...	2040	...	...	...	...	...
131	Partizánske .... ▷ a.	...	...	...	0915	...	...	...	...	1315	...	...	...	...	1715	...	...	...	...	2105	...	...	...	...	...
158	**Prievidza** .... ▷ a.	...	...	...	0949	...	...	...	...	1349	...	...	...	...	1749	...	...	...	...	2139	...	...	...	...	...

			720				600		722				724						726			1520			
		⚒b	⚒b	Ⓐ		Ⓐ						Ⓑh	Ⓑh		Ⓐ						⑦e	⑦e	Ⓒ		
Prievidza .... ▷ d.	...	...	0443	...	...	...	...	...	0821	...	...	...	1221	...	...	...	...	...	1621	...	...	1837	...	...	...
Partizánske .... ▷ d.	...	...	0517	...	...	...	...	...	0854	...	...	...	1254	...	...	...	...	...	1654	...	...	1911	...	...	...
Topoľčany .... ▷ d.	...	...	0540	...	...	...	...	...	0918	...	...	...	1318	...	...	...	...	...	1718	...	...	1935	...	...	...
Nitra .... d.	0423	0540	|	0631	0741	...	...	0918	|	1031	1227	1313	|	1431	1513	1618	...	1718	|	1827	1918	|	2018	...	...
Lužianky .... d.	0440	0551	|	0642	0753	...	...	0934	|	1042	1242	1334	|	1442	1527	1629	1642	1734	|	1842	1942	|	2042	...	...
Zbehy .... d.	0447	0558	0607	0649	0800	...	...	0940	0944	1049	1249	1340	1344	1449	1534	...	1649	1740	1744	1849	1948	2001	2049	...	...
Leopoldov .... a.	0515	...	0629	0716	0835	...	...	...	1006	1116	1316	...	1406	1516	1608	...	1716	...	1806	1916	...	2033	2116	...	...
Leopoldov .... **1180** d.	0521	...	0644	0721	...	0856	0921	...	1021	1121	1321	...	1421	1521	1656	...	1721	...	1821	1921	...	2040	2121	2156	...
Trnava .... **1180** d.	0535	...	0658	0735	...	0912	0935	...	1035	1135	1335	...	1435	1535	1712	...	1735	...	1835	1935	...	2056	2135	2240	...
Bratislava hl .... **1180** a.	0605	...	0734	0805	...	0959	1005	...	1105	1205	1405	...	1505	1605	1759	...	1805	...	1905	2005	...	2136	2205	2327	...

b – ①–⑥ (not Apr. 19, 21, Aug. 30, Sept. 1, 15, Nov. 17).
d – Not Apr. 18, 20, Aug. 29, 31, Sept. 14, Nov. 16.
e – Also Apr. 21, Sept. 1, 15, Nov. 17; not Apr. 20, July 6 - Aug. 31, Sept. 14, Nov. 16.
h – Not Apr. 18, 20, May 1, 8, Aug. 29, 31, Sept. 14, Nov. 16.

▷ – Additional local trains (journey 70 - 90 mins, see Table **1187** for trains continuing to Nitra): From Topoľčany: 0550 Ⓐ, 0651, 0920 Ⓐ, 1113, 1320, 1420 Ⓐ, 1519, 1720, 1833 (not ⑦**e**), 1937 ⑦**e**, 2223 Ⓐ. From Prievidza: 0415 Ⓐ, 0521, 0619, 0718 Ⓐ, 0941, 1121, 1324, 1424 Ⓐ, 1518, 1714 Ⓐ, 1837, 2231 Ⓐ.

1180 BRATISLAVA - ŽILINA - POPRAD TATRY - KOŠICE

km			EN			IC			IC		Ex		IC							IC	613			
		761	445	443	441	501	601	603	503	605	123	607	505	609	733	1505	735	611	701	507	1613	741	703	615
						✕R	✕	✕	✕R	✕	✕	✕	✕R	✕	2	2	2	✕	2	✕R	✕			2
		Ⓐ	♦	♦R	♦	b				♦			Ⓐd	△	Ⓐ	⑤f	Ⓐ		F	b	B	Ⓐ	R	♦
0	**Bratislava** hlavná .... **1177** d.	...	...	...	...	0537	0555	0755	0937	0955	...	1155	1337	1355	1441	1441	1541	1555	1655	1737	1755	1841	1955	2340
46	Trnava .... **1177** d.	...	...	...	...	0604	0626	0826	1004	1026	...	1226	1404	1426	1519	1519	1619	1626	1726	1804	1826	1919	2026	0011
63	Leopoldov .... **1177** d.	...	...	...	...	|	0640	0840	|	1040	...	1240	|	1440	1532	1532	1632	1640	1740	|	1840	1932	2040	0025
81	Piešťany .... d.	...	...	...	...	|	0652	0852	|	1052	...	1252	|	1452	1544	1544	1644	1652	1752	|	1852	1944	2052	0037
99	Nové Mesto nad Váhom .... d.	...	...	...	...	|	0705	0905	|	1105	...	1305	|	1505	1600	1600	1658	1705	1805	|	1905	1958	2105	0050
124	**Trenčín** .... d.	...	...	...	...	0645	0724	0924	1045	1124	...	1324	1445	1524	1619	1619	...	1724	1824	1845	1924	▬	2124	0109
132	Trenčianska Teplá .... d.	...	...	...	...	|	0734	0934	|	1134	...	1334	|	1534	1626	1627	...	1734	1834	|	1934	...	2134	0119
	Praha hlavní **1160** .... d.	...	2153	2226	0004	|	|	|	|	|	0911	|	|	|	...	|	...	|	|	|	|	...	|	|
159	Púchov .... **1160** d.	...	|	|	|	|	0757	0957	|	1157	1341	1357	|	1557	...	|	...	1757	1857	|	1957	...	2157	0142
171	Považská Bystrica .... d.	...	|	|	|	|	0810	1010	|	1210	1357	1410	|	1610	...	|	...	1810	1910	|	2010	...	2210	0155
203	**Žilina** .... **1160** a.	...	0354	0410	0621	0749	0841	1041	1149	1241	1428	1441	1549	1641	...	1723	...	1841	1941	1949	2041	...	2241	0226
203	**Žilina** .... **1185** d.	...	0423	0445	0645	0752	0845	1045	1152	1245	1440	1445	1552	1645	...	1726	...	1845	...	1952	2045	...	...	0245
224	Vrútky .... **1185** d.	...	|	0503	0703	|	0903	1103	|	1303	|	1503	|	1703	...	|	...	1903	...	|	2103	...	...	0303
242	Kraľovany .... d.	...	|	0517	0717	|	0917	1117	|	1317	|	1517	|	1717	...	1756	...	1917	...	|	2117	...	...	0317
260	Ružomberok .... d.	...	0508	0534	0734	|	0934	1134	|	1334	|	1534	|	1734	...	1812	...	1934	...	|	2134	...	...	0334
286	Liptovský Mikuláš .... d.	...	0531	0553	0753	0852	0953	1153	1252	1353	1538	1553	1652	1753	...	1831	...	1953	...	2052	2153	...	...	0353
325	Štrba .... d.	...	|	0622	0822	|	1022	1222	|	1422	1606	1622	|	1822	...	1901	...	2022	...	|	2222	2	...	|
344	**Poprad-Tatry** .... d.	0538	0622	0638	0838	0933	1038	1238	1333	1438	1621	1638	1733	1838	...	1917	...	2038	...	2133	2238	2242	...	0438
370	Spišská Nová Ves .... d.	0557	0641	0657	0857	|	1057	1257	|	1457	1640	1657	|	1857	...	1937	...	2057	...	|	2257	2310	...	0457
410	Margecany .... d.	0624	|	0724	0924	|	1124	1324	|	1524	|	1724	|	1924	...	2006	...	2124	...	|	2324	2353	...	0524
429	Kysak .... **1196** a.	0638	0719	0738	0938	1027	1138	1338	1427	1538	1717	1738	1827	1938	...	|	...	2138	...	2227	2338	...	...	0538
445	**Košice** .... **1196** a.	0652	0741	0752	0952	1041	1152	1352	1441	1552	1732	1752	1841	1952	...	◐	...	2152	...	2240	2352	...	...	0552
	Humenné **1194** .... a.	...	...	1034	...	...	...	...	...	1834	...	...	...	...	...	2209	...	...	...	...	...	...	...	0834

						IC			IC		Ex		IC				Ex			IC		EN		
	734	700	702	704	600	500	602	604	502	606	122	608	504	1508	610	760	1502	1504	612	506	440	444	442	614
	2	2				✕R	✕	✕	✕R	✕	✕	✕	✕R	2	✕	2	✕R	2	✕	✕R				
	Ⓐ	Ⓐ	S	Ⓐ	P			△	Ⓐ					⑦v		Ⓐ	⑦v	⑦e		b	♦	♦	♦S	♦
Humenné **1194** .... d.	...	...	...	...	...	...	...	...	...	...	...	...	...	...	...	1328	...	1415	...	...	...	...	1928	2128
Košice .... **1196** d.	...	...	...	...	0408	0520	0608	0808	0919	1008	1027	1208	1319	...	1408	1517	1519	◐	1608	1719	1808	2101	2208	2359
Kysak .... **1196** d.	...	...	...	...	0422	0534	0622	0822	0933	1022	1043	1222	1333	...	1422	1531	1533	|	1622	1733	1822	2115	2222	0014
Margecany .... d.	...	...	...	...	0437	|	0638	0838	|	1038	|	1238	|	...	1438	1547	|	1615	1638	|	1838	|	2238	0030
Spišska Nová Ves .... d.	...	...	...	...	0504	|	0705	0905	|	1105	1122	1305	|	...	1505	1615	|	1645	1705	|	1905	2155	2305	0057
Poprad-Tatry .... d.	...	...	...	...	0524	0630	0726	0926	1029	1126	1141	1326	1429	...	1526	1633	1629	1704	1726	1829	1926	2234	2326	0121
Štrba .... d.	...	...	...	...	0539	|	0742	0942	|	1142	1156	1342	|	...	1542	...	|	1719	1742	|	1942	|	2342	|
Liptovský Mikuláš .... d.	...	...	...	...	0610	0710	0810	1010	1110	1210	1224	1410	1510	...	1610	...	1710	1748	1810	1910	2010	2317	0010	0202
Ružomberok .... d.	...	...	...	...	0629	|	0829	1029	|	1229	|	1429	|	...	1629	...	|	1805	1829	|	2029	2336	0029	0221
Kraľovany .... d.	...	...	...	...	0644	|	0844	1044	|	1244	|	1444	|	...	1644	...	|	1823	1844	|	2044	|	0044	0236
Vrútky .... **1185** d.	...	...	...	...	0659	|	0859	1059	|	1259	|	1459	|	...	1659	...	|	1837	1859	|	2059	|	0059	0251
Žilina .... **1185** a.	...	...	...	...	0715	0808	0915	1115	1208	1315	1320	1515	1608	...	1715	...	1808	1853	1915	2008	2115	0018	0115	0307
Žilina .... **1160** d.	...	...	0519	...	0719	0811	0919	1119	1211	1319	1332	1519	1611	1620	1719	...	1811	1856	1919	2011	2132	0035	0135	0319
Považská Bystrica .... d.	...	...	0552	...	0752	|	0952	1152	|	1352	1405	1552	|	1655	1752	...	|	|	1952	|	|	|	|	0352
Púchov .... **1160** d.	...	...	0605	...	0805	|	1005	1205	|	1405	1418	1605	|	1708	1805	...	|	|	2005	|	|	|	|	0405
Praha hlavní **1160** .... a.	...	...	|	...	|	|	|	|	|	|	1853	|	|	|	|	...	|	|	|	|	0355	0649	0737	|
Trenčianska Teplá .... d.	0439	0527	0627	...	0827	|	1027	1227	|	1427	...	1627	|	1735	1827	...	|	|	2027	|	...	...	...	0427
Trenčín .... d.	0448	0537	0637	...	0837	0917	1037	1237	1317	1437	...	1637	1717	1745	1837	...	1917	2002	2037	2117	...	...	...	0437
Nové Mesto nad Váhom .... d.	0515	0555	0655	0755	0855	|	1055	1255	|	1455	...	1655	|	1806	1855	...	|	|	2055	|	...	...	...	0455
Piešťany .... d.	0530	0608	0708	0808	0908	|	1108	1308	|	1508	...	1708	|	1819	1908	...	|	|	2108	|	...	...	...	0508
Leopoldov .... **1177** d.	0544	0621	0721	0821	0921	|	1121	1321	|	1521	...	1721	|	1833	1921	...	|	|	2121	|	...	...	...	0521
Trnava .... **1177** d.	0558	0635	0735	0835	0935	0958	1135	1335	1358	1535	...	1735	1758	1848	1935	...	2003	2048	2135	2158	...	...	...	0535
Bratislava hlavná .... **1177** a.	0634	0705	0805	0905	1005	1023	1205	1405	1423	1605	...	1805	1823	1921	2005	...	2031	2119	2205	2223	...	...	...	0605

♦ – **NOTES** (LISTED BY TRAIN NUMBERS)

440/1 – EXCELSIOR – 🛏 1, 2 cl., ▬ 2 cl., [12] Cheb - Karlovy Vary - Praha - Žilina - Košice and v.v.; 🛏 1, 2 cl. Cheb (**767/6**) - Plzeň - Praha (**441/0**) - Žilina - Košice and v.v.

442/3 – ŠÍRAVA – 🛏 1, 2 cl., ▬ 2 cl., [12] Praha - Žilina - Košice - Humenné and v.v.

444 – SLOVAKIA – 🛏 1, 2 cl., ▬ 2 cl. Košice - Poprad Tatry - Praha; [2] Košice - Žilina; 🛏 1, 2 cl. Poprad Tatry - Praha. Not Dec. 24, 31.

445 – SLOVAKIA – 🛏 1, 2 cl., ▬ 2 cl. Praha - Poprad Tatry - Košice; 🛏 1, 2 cl. Praha - Poprad Tatry. Not Dec. 24, 31.

605 – DARGOV – [12] and ✕ Bratislava - Košice; [12] and ✕ Bratislava - Košice (**909**) - Humenné; [2] Bratislava - Košice (**965**) - Čierna nad Tisou.

614/5 – ZEMPLÍN – 🛏 1, 2 cl., ▬ 2 cl., [2] Bratislava - Humenné and v.v.

B – Daily Bratislava - Žilina; Ⓑ (not Apr. 18, 20, Aug. 29, 31, Sept. 14, Nov. 16) Žilina - Poprad Tatry; ⑤ (also Apr. 17, 30, May 7, Aug. 28; not Apr. 18, Aug. 29) Poprad Tatry - Košice. Train number **1613** on ⑤, **1615** on ⑥.

F – To Trenčianska Teplá on Ⓐ; to Žilina on ⑤ (also Apr. 17, Aug. 28; not Apr. 18, July 4 - Aug. 29).

P – From Košice on ①–⑥ (not Apr. 19, 21, Aug. 30, Sept. 1, 15, Nov. 17). Runs daily Žilina - Bratislava.

R – Also conveys 🛏 1, 2 cl. Bratislava (**703**) - Žilina (**443**) - Košice.

S – Also conveys 🛏 1, 2 cl. Košice (**442**) - Žilina (**702**) - Bratislava.

b – Not Apr. 20.
d – Also Apr. 20.
e – Also Apr. 21, Sept. 1, 15, Nov. 17; not Apr. 20, Aug. 31, Sept. 14, Nov. 16.
f – Also Apr. 17, Aug. 28; not Apr. 18, Aug. 29.
v – Also Apr. 21, Sept. 1, 15, Nov. 17; not Apr. 20, Aug. 31, Sept. 14, Nov. 16.

◐ – Via Prešov (train **1505** arrives 2034, **1504** departs 1545).
△ – Also conveys 🛏 1, 2 cl. Bratislava - Košice - Chop - Lviv - Kyïv - Moskva and v.v. (journey 2 nights, Table **97**).

OTHER TRAIN NAMES

122/3 – KOŠICAN
500 – TATRAN
501 – MARTINUS SK
502/7 – LYONESS
503/6 – UNION POISTOVNA
504 – KRIVAN
505 – DOXXBET

2nd class — LOCAL LINES IN POPRAD TATRY AREA — 1182

km					Ⓐ	Ⓐ		Ⓒ						Ⓐ		Ⓐ			Ⓐ	Ⓐ			
0	**Poprad Tatry** d.	0406	...	0546	...	0646	...	0746	...	0946	...	1146	...	1346	...	1446	1546	...	1646	...	1746	1846	...	2146
8	Studený Potok d.	0422	0427	0558	0602	0658	0702	0758	0802	0958	1002	1158	1202	1358	1402	1458	1558	1602	1658	1702	1758	1858	1902	2158
17	**Tatranská Lomnica** a.	|	0438	|	0613	|	0713	|	0813	|	1013	|	1213	|	1413	|	|	1613	|	1713	|	|	1913	|
14	Kežmarok d.	0448	...	0618	...	0712	...	0812	...	1012	...	1218	...	1412	...	1518	1612	...	1718	...	1812	1918	...	2218
44	**Stará Lubovňa** a.	0533	...	0703a	...	...	...	...	...	...	...	1303	...	...	...	1610	...	...	1803	...	...	2003r	...	2303

				Ⓐ	Ⓐ	Ⓒ						Ⓐ					Ⓐ	Ⓐ			Ⓐ			
Stará Lubovňa d.	...	...	0458	...	0558	...	...	...	0903	...	...	...	...	...	...	1458	...	...	1658	...	...	1858	...	2158r
Kežmarok d.	...	0450	0550	...	0650	...	0750	...	0950	...	1150	...	1350	...	1450	1550	...	1650	1750	...	1850	1950	...	2250
Tatranská Lomnica d.	0443	|	|	0643	|	0743	|	0943	|	1143	|	1343	|	1443	|	|	1643	|	|	1843	|	|	2203	|
Studený Potok d.	0456	0501	0601	0656	0701	0756	0801	0956	1001	1156	1201	1356	1401	1456	1501	1601	1656	1701	1801	1856	1901	2001	2217	2301
Poprad Tatry a.	...	0514	0614	...	0714	...	0814	...	1014	...	1214	...	1414	...	1514	1614	...	1714	1814	...	1914	2014	2230	2314

Poprad Tatry - Starý Smokovec (journey 25 minutes, *13* km, narrow gauge): 0504, 0604, 0629 Ⓐ, 0729, 0829, 0929, 1004 **S**, 1029, 1129 **N**, 1229, 1329, 1429, 1504, 1529, 1629, 1729, 1829, 1929, 2029 **S**, 2129, 2240. Most continue to Štrbské Pleso (see below).

Starý Smokovec - Štrbské Pleso (journey 41 minutes, *16* km, narrow gauge): 0531, 0631, 0701 Ⓐ, 0801, 0901, 1001, 1031 **S**, 1101, 1201 **N**, 1301, 1401, 1501, 1531, 1601, 1701, 1801, 1901, 2001, 2101 **S**, 2201, 2308. Most journeys start from Poprad Tatry (see above).

Starý Smokovec - Tatranská Lomnica (14 mins, *6* km, narrow gauge): 0416, 0556, 0656, 0802, 0902, 1002, 1102, 1202 **N**, 1302 and hourly to 2102, 2202 **d**.

Štrbské Pleso - Štrba (journey 18 minutes, *5* km, rack railway): 0517, 0620, 0720, 0814, 0914, 1014, 1114, 1214, 1254, 1344, 1444, 1544, 1644, 1744, 1844, 1944, 2244.

Starý Smokovec - Poprad Tatry (journey 23 minutes, *13* km, narrow gauge): 0437, 0555, 0655, 0735 Ⓐ, 0755, 0855, 0955, 1055, 1155 **N**, 1255, 1355, 1455, 1555, 1635 **S**, 1655, 1755, 1855, 1955, 2055, 2155 **b**, 2306. Most start from Štrbské Pleso (see below).

Štrbské Pleso - Starý Smokovec (journey 39 minutes, *16* km, narrow gauge): 0513, 0613, 0643 Ⓐ, 0713, 0813, 0913, 1013, 1113 **N**, 1213, 1313, 1413, 1513, 1543 **S**, 1613, 1713, 1813, 1913, 2013, 2113 **d**, 2213. Most journeys continue to Poprad Tatry (see above).

Tatranská Lomnica - Starý Smokovec (14 mins, *6* km, narrow gauge): 0514, 0614, 0714 **z**, 0834, 0934, 1034, 1134 **N**, 1234 and hourly to 2034, 2134 **b**, 2234.

Štrba - Štrbské Pleso (journey 15 minutes, *5* km, rack railway): 0456, 0556, 0656, 0746, 0836, 0946, 1036, 1146, 1236, 1326, 1426, 1516, 1626, 1716, 1826, 1916, 2026.

N – Dec. 15 - Apr. 22, May 19 - Sept. 21.
S – May 19 - Sept. 21.
a – Ⓐ only.
b – Tatranská Lomnica - Starý Smokovec - Poprad Tatry.
d – Štrbské Pleso - Starý Smokovec - Tatranská Lomnica.
r – Ⓑ (not holidays).
z – 0734 on Ⓒ (daily June 30 - Aug. 31).

STRAMA 🚌 — 🚌 POPRAD TATRY - ZAKOPANE — 1183

		S	W	S		W	S	S	
Poprad Tatry (Bus Stn stand 4) d.	...	0850	1150	1150	...	1650	1650	1850	...
Starý Smokovec (Bus Station) d.	...	0910	1210	1210	...	1710	1710	1910	...
Tatranská Lomnica (Bus Stn) d.	...	0924	1224	1224	...	1724	1724	1924	...
Zakopane (Bus Station) a.	...	1033	1333	1333	...	1833	1833	2033	...
Zakopane (ul Balzera Nosal) a.	...	1039	1339	1339	...	1839	1839	2039	...

		S	W	S		S	W	S	
Zakopane (ul Balzera Nosal) d.	...	0600	0900	0900	...	1100	1500	1600	...
Zakopane (Bus Stn stand 8) d.	...	0615	0915	0915	...	1115	1515	1615	...
Tatranská Lomnica (Bus Stn) d.	...	0727	1027	1027	...	1227	1627	1727	...
Starý Smokovec (Bus Station) d.	...	0737	1037	1037	...	1237	1637	1737	...
Poprad Tatry (Bus Station) a.	...	0753	1053	1053	...	1253	1653	1753	...

S – June 15 - Sept. 30.
W – Apr. 30 - May 5, also Oct. 1 - 15.

Operator: STRAMA, Zakopane. Rail tickets not valid. 🏛 = Lysa Polana.
Bus stations at Poprad Tatry and Zakopane are adjacent to the railway stations.

This service will recommence on June 15, 2014

2nd class ✤ — ŽILINA - VRÚTKY - MARTIN - BANSKÁ BYSTRICA - ZVOLEN — 1185

km		*Ex* 530		1841				1843		1845		1847		*Ex* 221			1851			820	*Ex* 223			1853		
		Ⓐ	Ⓐ	①–⑥		Ⓐ	Ⓐ					Ⓐ				Ⓐ	Ⓑ		Ⓐ				⚒			
		§		**P d** ◇			**u**	**R**		◇				**F**			**h**			**H**	**D**					**n**
	Praha hl. **1160** d.	...	...	2153	...	...	...	2153	...	...	...	...	...	0711	...	...	...	...	...	...	1111	...	...	...	...	...
0	**Žilina** 1180 d.	...	...	0454	0458	...	*0555*	0654	...	0854	...	1054	...	1254	...	...	1454	...	*1558*	...	1654	...	*1734*	1854	...	...
21	Vrútky 1180 a.	...	...	0511	0519	...	*0615*	0711	...	0911	...	1111	...	1311	...	...	1511	...	*1617*	...	1711	...	*1754*	1911	...	...
21	Vrútky d.	...	0452	0513	0520	...	0650	0713	0720	0913	0920	1113	1120	1313	1320	1450	1513	1520	1620	...	1713	1720	1820	1913	1920	2120
28	**Martin** d.	...	0501	0520	0529	...	0659	0720	0729	0920	0929	1120	1129	1320	1329	1459	1520	1529	1629	...	1720	1729	1829	1920	1929	2129
52	Turčianske Teplice d.	...	0529	0538	0558	0621	0728	0738	0758	0938	0958	1138	1158	1338	1358	1528	1538	1558	1658	...	1738	1758	1902	1938	1958	2158
61	Horná Štubňa d.	...	0540	|	0609	|	0738	|	0808	|	1008	|	1209	|	1408	1538	|	1609	1708	...	|	1808	1912	|	2008	2208
80	Kremnica d.	...	...	|	0636	|	...	|	...	|	...	|	1236	|	...	...	|	1636	...	...	|	...	...	|	2042r	...
97	**Banská Bystrica** ▶ d.	0535	...	0627	|	0704	...	0827	...	1027	...	1227	|	1427	...	...	1627	|	...	1812	1827	...	...	2027	|	...
•118	**Zvolen** osob. ▶ a.	0553	...	0651	0719	...	...	0851	...	1051	...	1251	1319	1451	...	...	1651	1719	...	1837	1851	...	...	2051	2125r	...

				1840			1842		*Ex* 222	821		1844		*Ex* 220			1848			1850	1852			*Ex* 531	837
		Ⓐ	Ⓒ	①–⑥	Ⓐ							Ⓐ				Ⓒ		Ⓐ		Ⓑ				Ⓐ	
				d					**D**	**H**				**F**						**h** ◇	**P**			§	§
Zvolen osob. ▶ d.	...	0425	...	0509	...	0618	0709	...	0909	0931	...	1109	...	1309	1425	...	1509	1525	...	1709	1909	1904	...	1942	2102
Banská Bystrica ▶ d.	...	|	...	0535	...	|	0735	...	0935	0959	...	1135	...	1335	|	...	1535	|	...	1735	1935	|	...	2000	2128
Kremnica d.	...	0515	...	|	...	0708	|	...	|	...	...	|	...	|	1510	...	|	1610	...	|	|	1947	...	...	...
Horná Štubňa d.	0452	0550	0550	|	0652	0752	|	0952	|	...	1152	|	1352	|	1552	1552	|	1652	1752	|	|	2020	...	...	...
Turčianske Teplice d.	0502	0600	0600	0621	0702	0802	0821	1002	1021	...	1202	1221	1402	1421	1602	1602	1621	1702	1802	1821	2021	2030	...	...	...
Martin d.	0532	0632	0632	0640	0732	0832	0840	1032	1040	...	1232	1240	1432	1440	1632	1632	1640	1732	1832	1840	2040	2100	...	...	...
Vrútky a.	0540	0640	0640	0647	0740	0840	0847	1040	1047	...	1240	1247	1440	1447	1640	1640	1647	1740	1840	1847	2047	2108	...	...	...
Vrútky 1180 d.	*0544*a	...	...	0649	*0744*	...	0849	...	1049	...	...	1249	...	1449	...	...	1649	...	...	1849	2049	2110	...	...	...
Žilina 1180 a.	*0604*a	...	...	0706	*0804*	...	0906	...	1106	...	...	1306	...	1506	...	...	1706	...	...	1906	2106	2131	...	...	...
Praha hl. **1160** a.	...	...	...	...	...	...	...	...	1653	...	...	...	...	2053	...	...	...	...	...	...	0649	...	...	...	...

ADDITIONAL TRAINS BANSKÁ BYSTRICA - ZVOLEN

		Ⓐ	Ⓒ	Ⓐ	◇		Ⓐ					Ⓒ	Ⓐ			Ⓐ u		Ⓐ	⑦ b						
Banská Bystrica d.	0432	0455	0521	0521	0627	0637	0710	0737	...	0937	1137	1209	1237	1337	1437	1508	1537	1637	1720	1737	1837	1937	2129	2235	...
Zvolen a.	0504	0535	0554	0605	0651	0708	0743	0808	...	1008	1208	1240	1308	1408	1508	1543	1608	1708	1747	1808	1908	2011	2200	2308	...

		Ⓐ		Ⓐ							Ⓐ u	Ⓐ			Ⓐ	◇									
Zvolen d.	0447	0518	0617	0652	0752	...	0952	1152	1252	1352	1417	1452	...	1552	1652	1709	1752	1852	...	1952	2112	...	2230	...	...
Banská Bystrica a.	0519	0555	0649	0722	0823	...	1023	1223	1323	1423	1449	1523	...	1623	1722	1733	1824	1923	...	2025	2141	...	2300	...	...

CONNECTIONS HORNÁ ŠTUBŇA - PRIEVIDZA

km											
0	Horná Štubňa d.	0417	0617	0817	...	1217	1417	1617	1817	2017	...
18	Handlová d.	0440	0640	0840	...	1240	1440	1640	1840	2040	...
37	Prievidza a.	0511	0711	0911	...	1311	1511	1711	1911	2111	...

									v	
Prievidza d.	0438	0638	0838	...	1238	1438	1638	1838	2145	...
Handlová d.	0521	0721	0921	...	1321	1521	1721	1921	2221	...
Horná Štubňa a.	0544	0744	0944	...	1344	1544	1744	1944	2244	...

– DETVAN – [12] Praha - Žilina - Zvolen and v.v.; [12] Praha - Žilina - Zvolen (**836/1**) - Bratislava and v.v.; ✕ Praha - Žilina and v.v.
– FATRA – [12] Praha - Žilina - Zvolen and v.v.; [12] Praha - Žilina - Zvolen (**834/3**) - Bratislava and v.v.
– HOREHRONEC – [2] Zvolen - Banská Bystrica - Brezno - Margecany and v.v. (Table **1190**); [2] Bratislava (**831/6**) - Zvolen (**821/0**) - Banská Bystrica - Brezno - Margecany and v.v.
– [2] Žilina - Zvolen and v.v.; 🛏 1, 2 cl. Praha (**445/4**) - Žilina - Zvolen and v.v.
– [2] Žilina - Zvolen; conveys 🛏 1, 2 cl. Praha (**445**) - Žilina - Zvolen on dates when train **1841** does not run.

a – Ⓐ only.
b – To Bratislava. For days of running see Table **1170**.
d – Not Apr. 19, 21, Sept. 1, 15, Nov. 17.
h – Not Apr. 18, 20, Aug. 31, Sept. 14, Nov. 16.
n – Runs one hour later on ⚒.
r – ⑤⑦ (also Apr. 17, 21, Sept. 1, 15, Nov. 17; not Apr. 18, 20, Aug. 31, Sept. 14, Nov. 16).
u – Not June 28 - Sept. 1.
v – Not Apr. 20.

▶ – For additional trains see panel below main table.
◇ – Conveys [2] Žilina - Banská Bystrica - Zvolen - Bratislava and v.v. (Table **1170**).
✤ – 2nd class only, except where shown in footnotes.
§ – To / from Bratislava (Table **1170**).
• – *117* km via Kremnica.

2nd class, *33 km* — NITRA - TOPOL'ČANY — 1187

			Ⓐ			◇	Ⓐ			Ⓐ	
Nové Zamky **1172** d.	0428	0520	0723	0920	1120	1320	...	1520	1720	*1920*	*2120*
Nitra d.	0524	0639	0818	1023	1218	1418	1502	1618	1818	2018	2240
Lužianky d.	0536	0650	0830	1035	1230	1430	1514	1630	1831	2033	2253
Topoľčany a.	0620	0730	0907	1111	1307	1510	1604	1707	1907	2113	2329
Prievidza **1177** a.	0805	...	1035	1217	1431	*1628*	...	1825	...	...	...

		Ⓐ	d	Ⓐ	▷			Ⓐ			
Prievidza **1177** d.	0415a	0521	0619	...	0941	1121	1324	*1424*	*1518*	...	*1837*
Topoľčany d.	0524	0625	0743	0845	1050	1245	1448	1542	1645	1845	1943
Lužianky d.	0617	0706	0831	0933	1134	1333	1533	1631	1737	1933	2033
Nitra a.	0627	0718	0843	0945	1146	1345	1545	1643	1749	1945	2045
Nové Zamky **1172** a.	0722	...	...	*1040*	1240	1439	1640	1746	*1840*	...	2146

a – Ⓐ only.
d – On Ⓒ Lužianky d. 0818, Nitra a. 0829.
◇ – Change at Nitra on Ⓐ.
▷ – Change at Nitra on Ⓒ.

1190 ZVOLEN - LUČENEC - KOŠICE

2nd class

km			931 ①–⑥		811			813		815		801 Ⓑ P
	Bratislava hl. **1170** .d.	...	...	...	0801	...	...	1201	...	1601	...	2349
0	**Zvolen** osob. d.	0610	0713	0923	1113	1211	1323	1513	1723	1913	2223	0316
54	Lučenec d.	0719	0801	1036	1201	1336	1436	1601	1836	2001	2336	0407
69	Fiľakovo d.	0741	0814	1054	1214	1354	1454	1614	1854	2014	2354	0421
98	Jesenské d.	...	0841	...	1241	...	...	1641	...	2041	...	0449
162	Rožňava d.	...	0939	...	1338	...	...	1736	...	2139	...	0550
202	Moldava nad Bodvou d.	...	1013	...	1411	...	...	1811	...	2212	...	0631
233	**Košice** a.	...	1037	...	1437	...	...	1837	...	2237	...	0700
	Prešov **1196** a.	...	...	...	...	...	...	...	...	...	...	0740

		810		812		814		930 Ⓑ			800 Ⓑ P
Prešov **1196** d.	...	...	...	...	...	...	...	...	...	...	2126
Košice d.	...	0523	...	0923	...	1323	...	1523	...	...	2220
Moldava nad Bodvou d.	...	0551	...	0948	...	1348	...	1547	...	...	2246
Rožňava d.	...	0623	...	1021	...	1421	...	1619	...	...	2325
Jesenské d.	...	0719	...	1119	...	1519	...	1719	...	...	0018
Fiľakovo d.	0700	0746	0910	1146	1310	1546	1710	1746	2020	...	0046
Lučenec d.	0729	0801	0929	1201	1329	1601	1729	1801	2037	2229	0059
Zvolen osob. a.	0840	0849	1040	1249	1440	1649	1840	1849	...	2340	0155
Bratislava hl. **1170** a.	...	1159	...	1559	...	1959	...	...	...	...	0525

CONNECTIONS TO RIMAVSKÁ SOBOTA

km	⊖											
0	Fiľakovo d.	0600	...	...	0856	1056	...	1456	...	1656	1856	...
29	Jesenské d.	0644	0725	0844	0944	1144	1244	1544	1644	1744	1940	2044
40	Rimavská Sobota a.	0658	0739	0858	0958	1158	1258	1558	1658	1758	1954	2058

⊖				Ⓐ							
Rimavská Sobota d.	0600	0701	0815	1015	1101	1215	1415	1501	1615	1701	1915
Jesenské a.	0615	0715	0834	1034	1115	1234	1434	1515	1634	1715	1934
Fiľakovo a.	0649	...	0908	1108	...	1308	1508	...	1708	...	2008

P – POĽANA – from Bratislava and Prešov on Ⓑ (not Apr. 18, 20, Aug. 29, 31, Sept. 14, Nov. 16). 🛏 1, 2 cl. and [2].

⊖ – Connections from / to Zvolen are made at Jesenské on certain journeys (see main table).

1192 ZVOLEN - BANSKÁ BYSTRICA - BREZNO - MARGECANY

2nd class

km		821 H	603
	Bratislava **1170** d.	0601	...
0	**Zvolen** ▷ d.	0931	...
21	**Banská Bystrica** ▷ d.	1001	...
64	Brezno d.	1047	...
107	Červená Skala d.	1138	...
135	Dedinky d.	1210	...
160	Nálepkovo d.	1237	...
192	Gelnica d.	1309	...
200	**Margecany** a.	1319	1324
	Košice **1180** a.	...	1352

	610	820 H
Košice **1180** d.	1408	...
Margecany d.	1436	1445
Gelnica d.	...	1454
Nálepkovo d.	...	1529
Dedinky d.	...	1558
Červená Skala d.	...	1630
Brezno d.	...	1721
Banská Bystrica ▷ a.	...	1810
Zvolen ▷ a.	...	1837
Bratislava **1170** a.	...	2159

△						
B. Bystrica d.	0614	0835	1035	1235	1435	1641
Brezno a.	0719	0937	1140	1337	1542	1747

▽						Ⓐ
Brezno d.	0721	1019	1219	1419	1515	1606
B. Bystrica a.	0822	1125	1325	1525	1617	1712

		N	⑦e	Ⓐ	N	⑦e
Brezno d.	0722	1144	1250	1420	1600	1755
Červená Skala d.	0822	1245	1351	1522	1714	1852

	Ⓐ		N	⑦e	Ⓐ	
Červená Skala d.	0434	0612	0910	1251	1408	1556
Brezno a.	0535	0714	1009	1352	1510	1701

	Ⓐ					
Červená Skala d.	...	0929	...	1543	...	1911r
Nálepkovo d.	0839	1039	1420	1658	1839	2017
Margecany a.	0952	1152	1552	1752	1952	2120

	Ⓐ	L				
Margecany d.	0407	0657	1208	1608	1808	2008
Nálepkovo d.	0536	0758	1338	1727	1905	2106
Červená Skala a.	0640	0903	1444	1833r	...	...

H – HOREHRONEC – [2] Zvolen - Margecany and v.v.; [2] Bratislava (**831/6**) - Zvolen (**821/0**) - Margecany and v.v.

L – Ⓒ (daily June 28 - Aug. 31).

N – ①–⑥ (not Apr. 21, Sept. 1, 15, Nov. 17).

e – Also Apr. 21, Sept. 1, 15, Nov. 17.

r – ⑦ (also Feb. 3, Apr. 22, Sept. 1, 15, Nov. 17; not Feb. 2, Mar. 2, Apr. 20, June 29 - Aug. 31, Sept. 14, Nov. 16).

▷ – For other trains see Table **1185**.

△ – Also at 0428, 1341 Ⓐ, 1528 Ⓐ, 1745, 1835, 1942 Ⓐ, 2035, 2230.

▽ – Also at 0418, 0502 Ⓐ, 0604, 0819, 1827, 2022, 2215.

1194 KOŠICE - HUMENNÉ - MEDZILABORCE

2nd class

km		615 Z	443 S	901	903 Ⓐ	905	907 Ⓐ	909 B	911	913	915
	Bratislava hl **1180** d.	2340	...	...	...	...	...	0955	...	...	...
0	**Košice** d.	0650	0850	1100	1300	1450	1537	1650	1850	2100	2250
68	Trebišov d.	0746	0946	1146	1346	1546	1638	1746	1946	2146	2346
88	Michalovce d.	0812	1012	1212	1412	1612	1659	1812	2012	2212	0012
112	**Humenné** a.	0834	1034	1234	1434	1634	1721	1834	2034	2234	0034

	900 Ⓐ	902 X	904	906 Ⓐ	908	910 b	912	914	442 S	614 Z
Humenné d.	0338	0528	0728	0928	1128	1328	1528	1728	1928	2128
Michalovce d.	0400	0550	0750	0950	1150	1350	1550	1750	1950	2150
Trebišov d.	0423	0623	0823	1013	1223	1423	1623	1813	2023	2223
Košice a.	0510	0710	0910	1100	1310	1510	1710	1900	2110	2310
Bratislava hl **1180** a.	...	...	...	...	...	...	...	...	...	0605

km					Ⓐ		Ⓐz			Ⓐ	
0	Humenné d.	0637	0837	1037	1317	1437	1530	1637	1837	2037	2237
41	Medzilaborce a.	0745	0945	1145	1415	1545	1625	1745	1945	2145	2337
43	Medzilaborce mesto a.	0751a	0951	1151	1419	1551	...	1751	1951	...	...

		Ⓐ				Ⓑ				
Medzilaborce mesto d.	0418	...	0618	0818a	1018	1202	1424	1618	1818	2018
Medzilaborce d.	0427	0500	0627	0827	1027	1211	1429	1629	1827	2027
Humenné a.	0525	0559	0725	0925	1125	1309	1525	1725	1925	2125

B – [12] and X Bratislava (**605**) - Žilina - Košice (**909**) - Humenné.

S – ŠIRAVA – 🛏 1, 2 cl., ▬ 2 cl. and [12] Praha - Humenné and v.v.

Z – ZEMPLÍN – 🛏 1, 2 cl., ▬ 2 cl., [2] Bratislava - Humenné and v.v.

a – Ⓐ only.

b – On Ⓐ conveys [2] Humenné - Košice (**760**) - Poprad Tatry.

z – Not Feb. 3, Mar. 3-7, Apr. 17-22, June 30 - Aug. 28, Oct. 30, 31.

1195 KOŠICE - ČIERNA NAD TISOU - CHOP

2nd class

km							Ⓐz	965 B	Ⓐ		8819 △	
0	**Košice** d.	0504	0704	1004	1204	1414	1514	1635	1704	1855	2026	2255
62	Slovenské N. Mesto d.	0610	0810	1110	1310	1520	1620	1727	1811	2001	2134	0001
95	**Čierna nad Tisou** a.	0649	0849	1149	1349	1559	1659	1806	1849	2040	2211	0040

		Ⓐ	964 ▽		Ⓐ				Ⓐz		
Čierna nad Tisou d.	0412	0512	0557	0712	1012	1212	1412	1512	1612	1812	2012
Slovenské N. Mesto d.	0450	0550	0636	0750	1050	1250	1450	1550	1650	1850	2050
Košice a.	0556	0656	0726	0856	1156	1356	1556	1656	1756	1956	2153

km			△
0	Čierna nad Tisou 🏛 d.	1410	2244
10	Chop 🏛 ⊕ a.	1552	0030

		▽
Chop 🏛 ⊕ d.	0510	1630
Čierna nad Tisou 🏛 a.	0516	1636

B – [2] Bratislava (**605**) - Košice - Čierna nad Tisou.

⊕ – East European time (one hour ahead).

△ – Conveys 🛏 Bratislava (**609**) - Košice (**8819**) - Cierna nad Tisou (**8860**) - Chop (**16**) - Moskva.

▽ – Conveys 🛏 Moskva (**15**) - Chop (**8861**) - Cierna nad Tisou (**964**) - Košice (**604**) - Bratislava.

z – Not Dec. 21 - Jan. 6.

1196 KOŠICE - PREŠOV - PLAVEČ

2nd class

km		①u				Ns						Ⓐ			Ⓑ	E						Ⓒ	Ⓐ		
0	**Košice** **1180** d.	...	0418	0535	0635	0708	0735	0835	*0927*	1018	*1127*	1235	1335	1435	1435	1435	1535	1635	1727	1735a	1818	*1927*	1935	*2127*	2215
16	Kysak **1180** d.	0023	0436	0553	0653	0723	0753	0853	0953	1044	1153	1253	1353	1453	1453	1453	1553	1653	1743	1753	1836	1953	1953	2153	2232
33	**Prešov** a.	0046	0459	0616	0716	0740	0816	0916	1016	1107	1216	1316	1416	1516	1516	1516	1616	1716	...	1816	1902	2016	2016	2216	2256
33	**Prešov** d.	...	0518	0636a	...	...	0818	...	1018	...	1218	...	1418	...	1518	1518	1618	...	...	1818	1918	...	2018	...	2258
65	Lipany a.	...	0556	0714a	...	...	0856	...	1056	...	1256	...	1456	...	1556	1556	1656	...	...	1856	1956	...	2056	...	2336
88	**Plaveč** a.	...	...	...	...	...	...	...	...	...	...	...	...	...	...	1628	...	...	...	...	...	...	...	...	...

	⚒			Ⓐ		Ⓐ			Ⓐ	Ⓒ							Ⓐ	Ⓒ	E				Ns		⑦e
Plaveč d.	...	...	...	...	...	...	...	...	...	...	...	...	...	...	...	...	...	...	1728	...	...	...	...	...	...
Lipany d.	...	0421	0501	0557	0646	...	0901	...	1101	...	1201	1301	...	1501	...	...	1701	...	1801	1801	...	2028	...	...	...
Prešov a.	...	0459	0539	0635	0725	...	0939	...	1139	...	1239	1339	...	1539	...	...	1739	...	1839	1839	...	2107	...	...	...
Prešov d.	0344	0501	0541	0641	0741	0855	0941	1017	1141	1141	1241	1341	1441	1541	...	1641	1741	1741	1841	1841	2041	...	2126	2141	234
Kysak **1180** a.	0407	0524	0606	0706	0806	0919	1006	1040	1206	1206	1306	1406	1506	1606	1616	1706	1806	1806	1906	1906	2106	...	2142	2206	001
Košice **1180** a.	0424	0542	0624	0724	0824	...	1024	...	1224	1224	1324	1424	1524	1624a	1632	1724	1824	*1832*	1924	1924	2124	...	2158	2224	...

E – ⑤⑦ (also Feb. 3, Apr. 16, 22, 30, May 7, Sept. 1, 15, Oct. 29, Nov. 17; not Feb. 2, Mar. 2, 7, Apr. 18, 20, June 29 - Aug. 31, Sept. 14, Oct. 31, Nov. 16).

N – Train **801/0** from / to Bratislava - for days of running see Table **1190**.

a – Ⓐ only.

e – Also Apr. 21, Sept. 1, 15, Nov. 17; not Apr. 21, Aug. 31, Sept. 14, Nov. 16.

s – Conveys 🛏 1, 2 cl. and [2].

u – Also Apr. 22, Sept. 2, 16, Nov. 18; not Ap 21, Sept. 1, 15, Nov. 17.

1197 PREŠOV - BARDEJOV and HUMENNÉ

2nd clas

km			Ⓐ	Ⓒ		Ⓐ						Ⓑh
0	Prešov d.	0421	0605	0627	0824	1024	1224	1424	1624	1824	2039	2300
45	Bardejov a.	0532	0713	0735	0932	1132	1332	1532	1732	1932	2142	0009

		Ⓐ	Ⓒ		Ⓐ						
Bardejov d.	0428	0609	0631	0828	1028	1228	1428	1628	1828	1954	221
Prešov a.	0535	0716	0738	0935	1135	1335	1535	1735	1935	2115	232

km							Ⓐ					⑤b
0	Prešov d.	0333	0504	0620	0844	1044	1244	1444	1644	1844	2048	2056
70	Humenné a.	0520	0651	0802	1022	1222	1422	1622	1822	2022	2222	2209

							⑦b				
Humenné d.	0350	0540	0740	0940	1140	1340	1415	1540	1740	1940	...
Prešov a.	0518	0730	0911	1111	1311	1511	1526	1711	1911	2115	...

b – To / from Bratislava. For days of running see Table **1180**.

h – Not Apr. 20, Aug. 31, Sept. 14, Nov. 16.

HUNGARY

Operator: MÁV-START (www.mav-start.hu) running on the network of MÁV (www.mav.hu). Certain services in the west are operated by Györ - Sopron - Ebenfurthi Vasút (GySEV).

Services: All trains convey first and second class seating, **except** where shown otherwise in footnotes or by '2' in the train column, or where the footnote shows sleeping- and / or couchette cars only. Descriptions of sleeping- (🛏) and couchette (▬) cars appear on page 8. Certain international services, as indicated in the tables, cannot be used for internal journeys in Hungary, whilst others generally convey dedicated carriages for internal journeys, which may be made without reservation.

Timings: Valid **December 15, 2013 - December 13, 2014** with amendments and summer timings from **June 21**. Amendments are incorporated into the tables when information is received. Certain trains are cancelled during the Christmas and New Year period (further details are given in the December and January editions).

Reservations: Most InterCity (*IC*) and Express (*Ex*) trains have **compulsory** reservation, as shown by 🅁 in the tables. *IC* trains also require a supplement; the amount depends on distance of the journey. Passengers having passes which include the supplement (e.g. Eurail) have to pay the reservation fee only. Higher supplements and reservation fees apply at peak times (Friday and Sunday afternoons), and if purchased on day of travel. For **domestic** journeys on **international** *EC* / *IC* / *RJ* / *EN* trains, a supplement is required (and seat reservation is compulsory where shown as 🅁 in tables). For **international** journeys on these trains the supplement does not apply but seat reservation is possible (and is **compulsory** where shown in the tables). If a seat reservation or supplement is not paid in advance, an additional supplement of 500 HUF must be paid on the train.

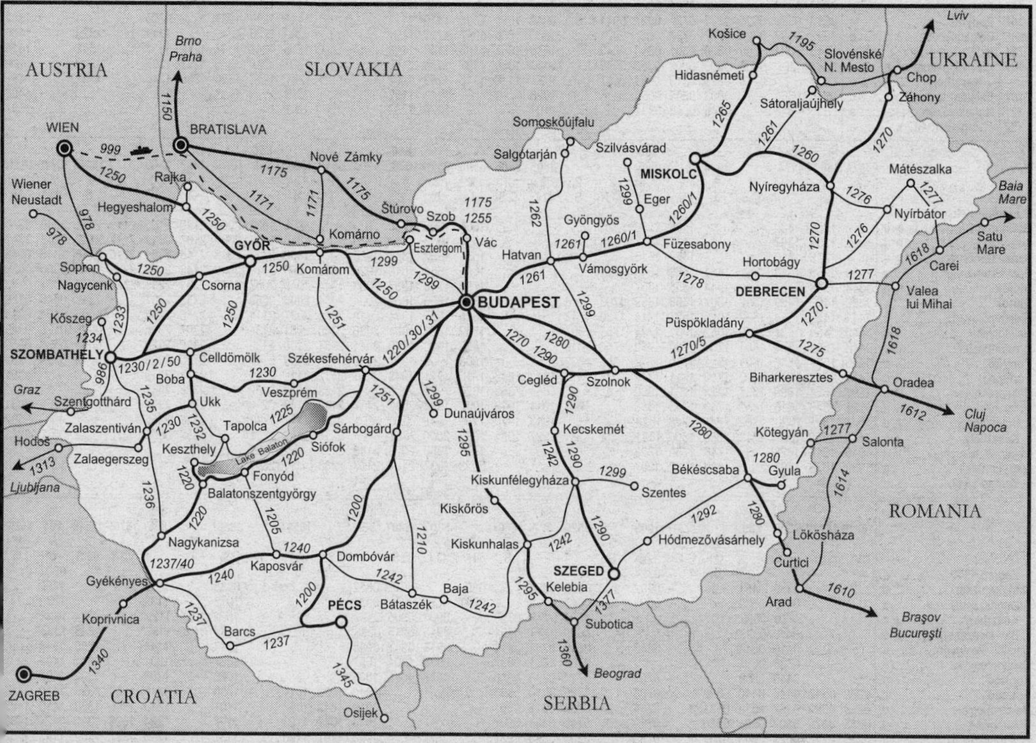

BUDAPEST - DOMBÓVÁR - PÉCS — 1200

km		*IC* 800 🅁 🍷	8002 2	*IC* 802 🅁	*IC* 812 🅁	*IC* 804 🅁	8004 2	*IC* 814 🅁	*IC* 204 ⊖ R	8006 2	*IC* 806 🅁 🍷	*IC* 816 🅁	*IC* 828 2🅁 n	8016 2	*IC* 808 🅁	*IC* 818 🅁
0	**Budapest** Keleti ..... d.	0545	...	0745	0945	1145	...	1345	1445	...	1545	1645	1645	...	1745	1945
•	**Budapest** Déli .... d.	|	0715	|	|	|	1315	|	|	1515	|	|	|	1715	|	|
13	Kelenföld .... d.	0559	0722	0759	0959	1159	1322	1359	1459	1522	1559	1659	1659	1722	1759	1959
93	Sárbogárd .... d.	0659	0831	0859	1059	1259	1431	1459	|	1631	1659	|	|	1831	1859	2059
173	Dombóvár .... a.	0753	0946	0953	1153	1353	1546	1553	1653	1746	1753	1853	1853	1946	1953	2153
173	Dombóvár .... d.	0755	1001	0955	1155	1355	1601	1555	....	1801	1755	1905	...	2001	1955	2155
218	Szentlörinc .... d.	0827	1044	1027	1227	1427	1644	1627	...	1844	1827	1943	...	2044	2027	2227
237	**Pécs** .... a.	0841	1103	1041	1241	1441	1703	1641	...	1903	1841	1957	...	2103	2041	2241

	IC 809 🅁	*IC* 819 🅁	*IC* 829 2🅁 n	*IC* 807 🅁	*IC* 817 🅁 🍷	*IC* 805 🅁	8007 2	*IC* 815 🅁	8005 2	*IC* 803 🅁	*IC* 813 🅁	8013 2	*IC* 205 ⊖ S	*IC* 801 🅁 🍷	8011 2 v	2
écs ....d.	0514	0603	...	0714	0914	1114	1050	1314	1250	1514	1714	1650	...	1914	1850	2050
zentlörinc..................d.	0528	0618	...	0728	0928	1128	1109	1328	1309	1528	1728	1709	...	1928	1909	2109
ombóvár....................a.	0559	0647	...	0759	0959	1159	1150	1359	1350	1559	1759	1750	...	1959	1950	2152
ombóvár....................d.	0601	0659	0659	0801	1001	1201	1207	1401	1407	1601	1801	1805	1855	2001	2007	...
árbogárd....................d.	0659	|	|	0859	1059	1259	1328	1459	1528	1659	1859	1928	|	2059	2128	...
elenföld ....a.	0800	0900	0900	1000	1200	1400	1434	1600	1634	1800	2000	2056	2100	2200	2256	...
udapest Déli ....a.	|	|	|	|	|	|	1444	|	1644	|	|	2104	|	|	2304	...
udapest Keleti ......a.	0815	0915	0915	1015	1215	1415	...	1615	...	1815	2015	...	2115	2215	...	...

– RIPPL-RÓNAI – [12] Budapest - Zagreb (**498**) - Ljubljana; [2] and 🍷 Budapest - Zagreb.
– RIPPL-RÓNAI – [12] and 🍷 Zagreb - Budapest.
– To / from Nagykanizsa (Table **1240**).

v – Change at Pusztaszabolcs (a. 2152 / d. 2204).
• – Budapest Déli - Kelenföld: *4 km.*
⊖ – 🅁 for domestic journeys within Hungary.

FONYÓD - PÉCS — 1205

km	2nd class	8807 Tc	18807 Su	8801 T	8801 S
	Tapolca **1232** ..... d.	0829	0829	...	1647
	Keszthely **1220**... d.	0904	0905	1706	1736
0	**Fonyód** .... ▶ d.	0950	1016	1831	1844
53	Kaposvár .... ▶ a.	1124	1135	1958	2002
82	Dombóvár alsó ...... d.	...	...	2055	2055
129	Szentlörinc............. d.	...	...	2130	2130
148	**Pécs** .... a.	...	...	2147	2147

	8802 S	8802 T		8806 Tc	18806 Su
Pécs........................ d.	0719	0719	...	...	...
Szentlörinc.................. d.	0733	0733	...	...	...
Dombóvár alsó .... d.	0826	0826	...	...	...
Kaposvár .... ▶ d.	0901	0917	...	1659	1705
Fonyód .... ▶ a.	1016	1032	...	1831	1837
Keszthely **1220**.... a.	1110	1118	...	1927	1931
Tapolca **1232** ...... a.	1155	...	...	2008	2008

S – June 21 - Aug. 31. **T** – Not June 21 - Aug. 31.
c – From / to Celldömölk (Table **1232**).
u – From / to Szombathely (Table **1232**).
▶ – **Additional trains Fonyód - Kaposvár**
Journey 80 - 90 minutes, *53* km.
From Fonyód 0331 ⚒, 0526, 0727 **S**, 0734 **T**, 1150, 1305 Ⓐ **T**, 1311 **S**, 1504 **T**, 1511 **S**, 1653 **T**, 1700 **S**, 2020 **T**, 2052 **S**.
From Kaposvár 0337, 0545, 0740, 1008 Ⓐ **T**, 1019 **S**, 1325, 1510 **T**, 1515 **S**, 1846, 2255 Ⓑ.

BUDAPEST - SÁRBOGÁRD - SZEKSZÁRD - BAJA — 1210

nd class (except *Ex* trains)

km		8310 Ⓐ	8300	*IR* 830 ⑥	*IR* 8302 ⚒	*IR* 834	Ⓐ	*IR* 836 E	*Ex* 1834 🅁 F	*Ex* 838 🅁	8318
0	**Budapest** Keleti .... ▷ d.	...	...	...	...	...	...	...	1340	1705	...
4	Kelenföld .... ▷ d.	...	...	...	...	...	...	...	1354	1719	...
84	**Sárbogárd** .... ▷ d.	0405	0548	0704	0904	1104	...	1504	1504	1817	2104
49	Szekszárd........................ a.	0512	0658	0818	1018	1200	1423	1600	1600	1911	2210
68	Bátaszék .... **1242** a.	0625	0725	0845	1045	1227	1447	1637	1637	1938	2301
88	**Baja** .... **1242** a.	0651	0747	0906	1106	1248	1508	1658	1658	1959	2323

	8319	*Ex* 839 🅁	*IR* 8307 Ⓐ	*IR* 837	*IR* 835	*IR* 18305 ⑦	8313 Ⓐ	*Ex* 1833 🅁 N	*IR* 831
Baja .... **1242** d.	0425	0611	0705	0909	1309	1511	1521	1704	1850
Bátaszék.............. **1242** d.	0445	0630	0727	0928	1328	1531	1541	1725	1909
Szekszárd.........................d.	0550	0700	0755	0955	1355	1602	1615	1752	1957
Sárbogárd................ ▷ a.	0654	0759	0852	1052	1452	1654	1733	1852	2052
Kelenföld .... ▷ a.	...	0905	...	...	...	...	...	2004	...
Budapest Keleti .... ▷ a.	...	0925	...	...	...	...	...	2020	...

– Daily, except when train **F** runs. **F** – ⑤ (not June 20 - Aug. 29). **N** – ⑦ (not June 15 - Aug. 31). ▷ – For connections see Table **1200**.

1220 BUDAPEST - SZÉKESFEHÉRVÁR - FONYÓD - KESZTHELY / NAGYKANIZSA

km		8530	8530	8612	8510	8510	IC 200		18700	850 860	8802	8802	18502	18502	8722	1872	852 862	Ex 15609	16809	Ex 1787		18702	5209 15209	15209	854 864
		2	2	2	2	2	⊖	2	2				2	2	2	2		⊕🅁	2△	2🅁	2	2	♥	♥	
		S	T		T	S	B	S	©S		KS	PT	Z	S	F	©S		S	S	©S	ⒶT	©S	M	S	
•	Budapest Keleti ▶ d.	...	...	...	...	...	...	...	...	...	...	...	...	...	...	...	...	...	...	...	...	...	1020	1020	...
0	Budapest Déli ▶ d.	...	...	...	0405	0405	0605	...	0700	0730	...	...	0805	0800	_0810_	0840	0930	...	...	⊡	...	1005	|	|	1130
4	Kelenföld ▶ d.	...	...	...	0412	0412	0612	...	0707	0737	...	...	0812	0807	_0817_	0847	0937	0930	0939	1007	...	1012	1036	1036	1137
67	Székesfehérvár ▶ a.	...	...	...	0511	0511	0651	...	0748	0816	...	...	0850	0848	_0910_	|	1016	1021	1026	1047	...	1053	1126	1128	1216
67	Székesfehérvár d.	...	...	...	0523	0523	0653	...	0751	0818	...	...	0851	0851	0913	|	1018	1023	1028	1050	...	1056	1128	1131	1218
115	Siófok a.	...	...	...	0618	0618	0737	...	0839	0857	...	...	0944	0948	1010	1003	1057	1102	1114	1135	...	1201	1211	1222	1257
115	Siófok d.	0410	0422	...	0622	0622	0739	0803	0841	0859	...	...	1005	1006	...	1004	1059	1104	1116	1137	...	1206	1213	1225	1259
130	Balatonföldvár d.	0430	0443	...	0649	0648	0753	0827	0903	0914	...	...	1026	1027	...	1018	1114	1122	1143	1153	...	1227	1229	1249	1314
146	Balatonlelle d.	0450	0508	...	0710	0709	0810	0851	0926	0934	...	...	1052	1053	...	1038	1134	1145	1204	1210	...	1251	1253	1312	1334
149	Balatonboglár d.	0457	0513	...	0715	0714	0818	0900	0931	0939	...	...	1058	1100	...	|	1139	1150	1223	1218	...	1300	1302	1317	1339
157	Fonyód a.	0507	0523	...	0724	0724	0826	0909	0940	0947	...	...	1108	1109	...	1050	1147	1200	1234	1227	...	1309	1311	1326	1347
157	Fonyód d.	0512	0528	0625	0727	0727	0827	0911	...	0949	1021	1036	1110	1111	...	1051	1149	1210	1237	1228	1300	...	1314	...	1349
165	Balatonfenyves d.	0522	0537	0635	0737	0737	|	0921	...	1000	1036	1047	1120	1121	...	|	1200	1220	1246	|	1311	...	1322	...	1400
181	Balatonszentgyörgy a.	0543	0601	0705	0800	0801	0848	0943	...	1016	1057	1106	1140	1143	...	|	1216	1241	1307	1249	1332	...	1341	...	1416
181	Balatonszentgyörgy ▲ d.	_0545_	|	0706	_0803_	_0802_	_0850_	0945	...	1020*	1058	1107	_1150_	_1150_	...	|	1220*	1246	1308	1253	1335	...	1346	...	1420*
	Keszthely ▲ a.	_0557_	|	0718	_0815_	_0813_	_0901_	0957	...	1031*	1110	1118	_1202_	_1202_	...	1121	1231*	1257	1320	1305	1346	...	1357	...	1431*
181	Balatonszentgyörgy d.	0545	0602	...	0803	0805	0850	...	...	1028	...	...	1143	1150	...	...	1228	...	...	...	...	...	...	...	1428
221	Nagykanizsa a.	0635	0646	...	0845	0848	0931	...	...	1107	...	...	1226	1232	...	...	1307	...	...	...	...	...	...	...	1507
352	_Zagreb_ 1340 a.	...	...	...	...	...	1250	...	...	...	...	...	...	...	...	...	...	...	...	...	...	...	...	...	...

	8514	18504	844 874		8524	18704	856 866			8806	8806	8506	8506	846 878	1204	8518	18608	858 868	18708	1868	1868		18748	18718	18610
	2	2		2	2	2		2	2	2	2	2	2			2	2		2			2	2	2	2
	T	S		©S	J	S		©R	S	QT	QS	T	S		A	T	S		S	G	S	T	S	U	U
Budapest Keleti ▶ d.	...	...	...	...	...	...	...	...	...	...	...	...	...	...	1815	...	...	...	...	...	...	...	...	...	...
Budapest Déli ▶ d.	...	1200	1330	...	...	1405	1530	...	...	...	...	1605	1605	1730	|	...	1805	1930	2000	2100	2105	_2110_	2140	2240	2340
Kelenföld ▶ d.	...	1207	1337	...	...	1412	1537	...	...	...	...	1612	1613	1737	1830	...	1813	1937	2007	2107	2112	_2117_	2147	2247	2347
Székesfehérvár ▶ a.	...	1248	1416	...	...	1452	1616	...	...	...	...	1653	1652	1816	1925	...	1852	2016	2048	2146	2151	_2210_	2246	2346	0046
Székesfehérvár d.	1250	1253	1418	...	1451	1453	1618	...	...	...	...	1655	1653	1818	1926	1850	1853	2018	2049	2148	2152	2235	2249	2350	0059
Siófok a.	1344	1348	1457	...	1544	1555	1657	...	...	...	...	1750	1748	1857	2003	1944	1948	2057	2140	2231	2235	2327	2339	0037	0153
Siófok d.	1350	1406	1459	1502	1607	1606	1659	1703	1718	...	...	1805	1806	1859	2004	2004	2006	2059	...	2232	2237	...	2345	0040	0159
Balatonföldvár d.	1411	1427	1514	1522	1628	1627	1714	1730	1743	...	...	1826	1827	1914	2018	2025	2027	2114	...	2248	2252	...	0006	0104	0219
Balatonlelle d.	1440	1451	1534	1549	1652	1651	1734	1751	1807	...	...	1852	1851	1934	2036	2048	2051	2134	...	2307	2315	...	0028	0125	0245
Balatonboglár d.	1446	1500	1539	1554	1701	1700	1739	1756	1818	...	...	1858	1900	1939	2041	2054	2100	2139	...	2312	2320	...	0033	0130	0250
Fonyód a.	1456	1509	1547	1604	1711	1709	1747	1805	1828	...	...	1908	1909	1947	2050	2104	2109	2147	...	2320	2328	...	0043	0139	0259
Fonyód d.	1458	1511	1549	1620	1713	1711	1749	...	...	1843	1848	1910	1911	1949	2051	2112	2111	2149	...	2321	2329	...	...	...	0301
Balatonfenyves d.	1508	1521	1600	1637	1723	1721	1800	...	...	1854	1859	1920	1921	2000	|	2123	2121	2159	...	2328	2337	...	...	...	0311
Balatonszentgyörgy a.	1528	1543	1616	1657	1743	1743	1816	...	...	1914	1919	1940	1943	2016	2117	2143	2143	2216	...	2345	2354	...	...	...	0331
Balatonszentgyörgy ▲ d.	_1548_	_1548_	1620*	1702	_1748_	_1748_	1820*	...	...	1915	1920	_1950_	_1948_	2020*	|	_2158_	2147	2220*	...	2346	2355	...	...	...	0332
Keszthely ▲ a.	_1559_	_1559_	1631*	1713	_1800_	_1800_	1831*	...	...	1927	1931	_2002_	_2000_	2031*	|	_2210_	2158	2231*	...	2357	0006	...	...	...	0343
Balatonszentgyörgy d.	1540	1546	1628	...	1746	1750	1828	...	...	...	...	1941	1950	2028	2118	2157	...	2227	...	...	...	...	...	...	...
Nagykanizsa a.	1630	1628	1707	...	1829	1832	1907	...	...	...	...	2023	2032	2107	2157	2238	...	2307	...	...	...	...	...	...	...
Zagreb 1340 a.	...	...	...	...	...	...	...	...	...	...	...	...	...	...	0001	...	...	...	...	...	...	...	...	...	...

	18719	18729	8509	859 869			1205		8529	847 877	18607		8807	18807	857 867		18517		18507		855 865	18705	18615	IC 201	15208
	2	2	2		2	2		2	2		2	2	2	2		2		2	2	2			2	⊖	♥
	V	L			Ⓐ	T	A	S			S	H	QT	QS		S	©R	T	S	T		©S	©S	C	S
Zagreb 1340 d.	...	...	...	...	...	...	0324	...	...	...	...	...	...	...	...	...	...	...	...	...	...	...	...	0957	...
Nagykanizsa d.	...	...	0335	0454	...	...	0602	...	0603	0654	...	0800	...	...	0852	...	...	...	0933	...	1050	...	...	1250	...
Balatonszentgyörgy a.	...	...	0415	0532	...	...	0639	...	0647	0732	...	0847	...	...	0932	...	...	...	1012	...	1132	...	...	1332	...
Keszthely ▲ d.	...	...	_0401_	0522*	...	...	|	...	_0628_	0722*	0750	...	0904	0905	0922*	...	...	...	_1002_	1006	1122*	...	1234	1322*	...
Balatonszentgyörgy ▲ a.	...	...	_0413_	0533*	...	...	|	...	_0640_	0733*	0801	...	0915	0916	0933*	...	...	...	_1014_	1018	1133*	...	1245	1333*	...
Balatonszentgyörgy d.	...	...	0416	0544	...	...	0642	...	0648	0744	0810	...	0916	0917	0944	...	...	...	1017	...	1144	...	1250	1344	...
Balatonfenyves d.	...	...	0436	0601	...	...	|	...	0708	0801	0837	...	0938	1004	1001	...	...	...	1037	...	1201	...	1311	1401	...
Fonyód a.	...	...	0446	0608	...	...	0702	...	0717	0808	0848	...	0948	1015	1008	...	...	...	1048	...	1208	...	1322	1408	...
Fonyód d.	0200	0312	0447	0610	0622	...	0703	...	0725	0810	0850	...	...	...	1010	1028	1044	...	1050	...	1210	1250	1326	1410	1414
Balatonboglár d.	0210	0322	0457	0619	0631	...	0714	...	0735	0819	0901	...	...	...	1019	1042	1058	...	1101	...	1219	1300	1338	1419	1425
Balatonlelle d.	0215	0327	0502	0624	0636	...	0719	...	0740	0824	0907	...	...	...	1024	1047	1103	...	1107	...	1224	1306	1343	1424	1430
Balatonföldvár d.	0235	0348	0523	0643	0701	...	0735	...	0804	0843	0937	...	...	...	1043	1107	1126	...	1137	...	1243	1337	1402	1443	1452
Siófok a.	0255	0409	0543	0659	0721	...	0752	...	0826	0859	0958	...	...	...	1059	1137	1151	...	1206	...	1259	1358	1425	1459	1520
Siófok d.	0257	0415	0545	0701	...	0737	0753	0808	...	0901	1008	...	...	...	1101	...	...	1154	1208	...	1301	1408	...	1501	1522
Székesfehérvár a.	0344	0507	0634	0739	...	0825	0830	0903	...	0939	1110	...	...	...	1139	...	...	1245	1303	...	1339	1501	...	1539	1607
Székesfehérvár ▶ d.	0346	0521	0636	0741	...	_0841_	0831	_0909_	...	0941	1111	...	...	...	1141	...	...	...	1304	...	1341	1504	...	1541	1610
Kelenföld ▶ a.	0440	0616	0721	0821	...	_0921_	0926	_0951_	...	1021	1151	...	...	...	1221	...	...	...	1346	...	1421	1546	...	1621	1708
Budapest Déli ▶ a.	0449	0629	0729	0829	...	_0929_	|	_0959_	...	1029	1159	...	...	...	1229	...	...	...	1354	...	1429	1554	...	1629	|
Budapest Keleti ▶ a.	...	...	...	...	...	...	0944	...	...	...	...	...	...	...	...	...	...	...	...	...	...	...	...	...	1727

	16806	8615	18605	18603	Ex 15608	853 863	15008 5008	8513	18503	18503	Ex 1786	18601	8801	851 861	8801	18701	18701	1871	8511	8511	1861	1861	8531	8531	1861
	2▽	2	2	2	⊕🅁			2	2	2	2🅁	2			2			2	2	2			2	2	2
	S	T	S	©S	S		N	D	W	S	©S	⑦S	PT		KS	⑦R	S	©S	T	S	G	S	T	S	U
Zagreb 1340 d.	...	...	...	...	...	...	...	...	...	...	...	...	...	...	...	...	...	...	...	...	...	...	...	...	...
Nagykanizsa d.	...	...	...	...	...	1450	...	1525	1525	1522	...	...	...	1650	...	...	...	...	1850	1926	...	...	2114	2130	...
Balatonszentgyörgy a.	...	...	...	...	...	1532	...	1608	1608	1608	...	...	...	1732	...	...	...	...	1935	2011	...	...	2156	2212	...
Keszthely ▲ d.	1336	1404	1402	...	1508	1522*	1535	_1601_	_1601_	_1601_	1650	...	1706	1722*	1736	_1803_	_1803_	1934	|	_2003_	2033	2107	_2143_	_2200_	232
Balatonszentgyörgy ▲ a.	1347	1416	1414	...	1519	1533*	1546	_1613_	_1613_	_1613_	1701	...	1718	1733*	1747	_1814_	_1814_	1945	|	_2015_	2044	2118	_2155_	_2212_	233
Balatonszentgyörgy d.	1355	1417	1417	...	1520	1544	1555	1617	1617	1617	1702	...	1720	1744	1751	1816	1817	1946	1940	2017	2045	2119	2157	2216	233
Balatonfenyves d.	1418	1437	1437	...	1545	1601	1619	1637	1637	1637	|	...	1806	1801	1820	|	1837	|	2001	2037	2104	2140	2219	2235	235
Fonyód a.	1426	1447	1448	...	1614	1608	1626	1647	1647	1648	1727	...	1816	1808	1831	1842	1844	2007	2011	2048	2111	2148	2229	2244	000
Fonyód d.	1427	1457	1450	1525	1616	1610	1628	1650	1650	1650	1728	1747	...	1810	—	1844	1850	2009	2012	2050	2112	2149	2234	2245	000
Balatonboglár d.	1437	1508	1501	1538	1626	1619	1638	1701	1701	1701	1738	1756	...	1819	...	1859	1901	2018	2022	2101	2121	2158	2243	2254	001
Balatonlelle d.	1442	1513	1507	1543	1631	1624	1643	1706	1706	1707	1743	1801	...	1824	...	1905	1907	2023	2027	2107	2126	2203	2248	2259	002
Balatonföldvár d.	1506	1538	1537	1602	1652	1643	1706	1741	1741	1737	1804	1819	...	1843	2	1938	1937	2040	2049	2129	2150	2222	2310	2319	004
Siófok a.	1535	1558	1558	1624	1715	1659	1727	1801	1801	1758	1823	1838	...	1859	T	1958	1958	2053	2115	2150	2205	2237	2328	2340	010
Siófok d.	1537	1623	1608	1626	1717	1701	1730	...	1805	1808	1826	1840	...	1901	2009	2009	2008	2055	2117	2153	2206	2238	...	...	010
Székesfehérvár a.	1625	1727	1703	1724	1754	1739	1821	...	1902	1902	1909	1924	...	1939	2104	2104	2103	2131	2205	2240	2241	2320	...	...	015
Székesfehérvár ▶ d.	1627	...	1704	1725	1756	1741	1823	...	1904	1904	1911	1926	...	1941	...	2107	2104	2132	2210	2246	2242	2321	...	...	015
Kelenföld ▶ a.	1725	...	1745	1811	1845	1821	1919	...	1945	1946	1951	2011	...	2021	...	2151	2146	2211	2250	2346	2321	0001	...	...	025
Budapest Déli ▶ a.	...	...	1754	1819	...	1829	|	...	1954	1954	⊡	2019	...	2029	...	2159	2154	2219	2259	2354	2329	0009	...	...	030
Budapest Keleti ▶ a.	...	...	...	...	...	...	1935	...	...	...	...	...	...	...	...	...	...	...	...	...	...	...	...	...	...

A – ADRIA – from Budapest ②⑤ June 13 - Aug. 29; from Split ③⑥ June 14 - Aug. 30 (next day from Zagreb). 1, 2 cl., 2 cl., (2) Ÿ Budapest - Zagreb - Split and v.v.; (2) Budapest - Nagykanizsa - Gyekenyes and v.v.; 1, 2 cl. Praha (**277/6**) - Budapest - Split and v.v.; 2 cl. Moskva - Budapest - Split and v.v. (Table **97**).
B – AGRAM – (12) Budapest - Gyekenyes - Zagreb; (2) Budapest - Gyekenyes.
C – AGRAM – (12) Ljubljana (**499**) - Zagreb (**201**) - Gyekenyes - Budapest; (12) Gyekenyes - Budapest.
D – Ⓐ to May 4; Ⓐ from Sept. 1.
F – Daily to Apr. 4; Ⓐ Apr. 5 - 30; Ⓐ Sept. 1 - Nov. 2; daily from Nov. 3.
G – ⑤⑥⑦ (and holidays) Apr. 30 - June 20.
H – © May 1 - June 20.
J – Ⓑ to Apr. 27; daily Apr. 28 - June 20; Ⓑ from Sept. 1.
K – Pécs - Fonyód - Tapolca and v.v. (Table **1205**).
L – June 21 - Sept. 1.
M – ⑥ to May 3; daily May 10 - June 20, Sept. 1 - 21; ⑥ from Sept. 27.
N – ⑦ to May 4; daily May 10 - June 20, Sept. 1 - 21; ⑦ from Sept. 28. To Miskolc (Table **1261**).
P – Pécs - Fonyód - Keszthely and v.v. (Table **1205**).
Q – (2) Kaposvár - Fonyód - Keszthely - Tapolca - Celldömölk (- Szombathely June 21 - Aug. 31) and v.v. (Table **1205**).
R – May 1 - June 20; Sept. 1 - 28.
S – June 21 - Aug. 31.
T – Dec. 15 - June 20, Sept. 1 - Dec. 13.
U – ④⑤⑥ June 20 - Aug. 30.
V – ⑤⑥⑦ June 21 - Aug. 31.
W – © Mar. 15 - May 4; daily May 5 - June 20; © Sept. -Nov. 2.
Z – © Apr. 5 - 27; daily May 1 - June 20; © Sept. 6 - Nov.
⊖ – 🅁 for domestic journeys within Hungary.
⊕ – From / to Miskolc (d. 0640 / a. 2118).
⊡ – From / to Szeged (0722/2224), Kecskemét (0834/2121
△ – From Nyíregyháza (0539), Debrecen (0624), Szolnok (081
▽ – To Szolnok (1845), Debrecen (2029), Nyíregyháza (211
♥ – From / to Sátoraljaújhely and Miskolc (Table **1261**).
▶ – See also Tables **1225** and **1230**.
▲ – See also Table **1232**. _Italic_ times: change at Balatonszentgyörgy.
• – Keleti - Kelenföld: _13 km_.
* – Portion is detached / attached at Balatonszentgyörgy.

BUDAPEST - SZÉKESFEHÉRVÁR - BALATONFÜRED - TAPOLCA 1225

km		9710	9720	9712	9700	972	1972	9722	19732	9702	19702	9714	9704	974	19704	9716	9706	976	19606	9726	19706	19608	9718	9708	19738	9738
		2	2	2	2		2	2		2	2	2	2		2	2	2		2	2	2	2	2	2	2	2
				T	S	T	S	F	E	S	SⒸ	T	S	T	S	T	S	T	S△	T	S	⑤V	T	S	S	b
0	**Budapest** Déli ▶ d.	...	*0405*	*0630*	0705	0735	0735	*0830*	0835	0905	0935	*1030*	1105	1235	1305	*1430*	1505	1535	1535	*1630*	1705	1800	*1830*	1905	*2010*	*2110*
4	Kelenföld ▶ d.	...	*0412*	*0637*	0712	0742	0742	*0837*	0842	0912	0944	*1037*	1112	1242	1312	*1437*	1512	1542	1542	*1637*	1712	1807	*1837*	1912	*2017*	*2117*
67	**Székesfehérvár** ▶ a.	...	*0511*	*0716*	0755	0822	0826	*0916*	0921	0955	1031	*1116*	1155	1330	1355	*1516*	1555	1621	1623	*1716*	1755	1848	*1916*	1955	*2110*	*2210*
67	**Székesfehérvár** d.	0422**z**	0522	0722	0756	0834	0840	0922	0922	0956	1044	1122	1156	1354	1356	1522	1556	1634	1640	1722	1756	1900	1922	1956	2122	2240
117	Balalatonalmádi d.	0524**z**	0624	0830	0846	0930	0943	1030	1030	1046	1144	1230	1246	1446	1446	1630	1646	1730	1743	1831	1846	1958	2030	2046	2230	2347
132	**Balatonfüred** a.	0545**z**	0645	0851	0900	0945	0958	1051	1051	1100	1201	1251	1300	1500	1500	1651	1700	1745	1758	1852	1900	2014	2051	2100	2250	0007
132	**Balatonfüred** d.	0546	0703	0903	0903	0947	1002	1103	1103	1103	1203	1303	1303	1503	1503	1703	1703	1747	1802	1903	1903	2016	2103	2103	...	...
157	Révfülöp d.	0625	0743	0943	0943	1018	1034	1143	1143	1143	1236	1343	1343	1543	1543	1743	1743	1818	1837	1943	1943	2048	2140	2140	...	...
168	Badacsonytomaj d.	0641	0801	1001	1001	1029	1045	1201	1201	1201	1251	1401	1401	1601	1601	1801	1801	1829	1853	2001	2001	2101	2201	2201	...	...
170	Badacsony d.	0644	0805	1004	1004	1032	1049	1204	1204	1204	1254	1404	1404	1604	1604	1804	1804	1832	1856	2004	2004	2104	2204	2208	...	...
184	**Tapolca** a.	0702	0822	1022	1022	1047	1105	1222	1222	1222	1316	1422	1422	1622	1622	1822	1822	1847	1914	2022	2022	2120	2222	2222	...	...

		9719	979	19707	9717	19607	9707	9727	19705	9715	9705	975	19703	19713	9713	1973	973	19701	9711	1971	9701	9721	19741	9721	9721	
	2	2		2	2	2	2	2	2	2	2		2		2	2		2	2	2	2	2	2	2	2	
	z			S	T	S△	S	T	S	T	S	T	S	E	F	S	T	S	T▽	SⒸ	S⑦		S	T⑧	S	
Tapolca d.	...	0432	0556	0740	0740	0847	0940	0940	1140	1140	1340	1340	1540	1540	1540	1656	1710	1740	1740	1852	1959	1940	...	1940	2140	...
Badacsony d.	...	0450	0611	0758	0758	0904	0958	0958	1158	1158	1358	1358	1558	1558	1558	1710	1724	1758	1758	1910	2017	1958	...	1958	2158	...
Badacsonytomaj d.	...	0453	0614	0801	0801	0907	1001	1001	1201	1201	1401	1401	1601	1601	1601	1713	1727	1801	1801	1913	2020	2001	...	2001	2201	...
Révfülöp d.	...	0507	0625	0815	0815	0923	1015	1018	1215	1215	1415	1415	1615	1615	1615	1724	1743	1815	1818	1924	2031	2015	...	2015	2218	...
Balatonfüred a.	...	0545	0652	0853	0853	0953	1053	1056	1253	1253	1453	1453	1653	1653	1653	1756	1814	1853	1856	1954	2100	2055	...	2053	2256	...
Balatonfüred d.	0340	0546	0654	0901	0910	1000	1101	1110	1301	1310	1501	1501	1701	1710	1710	1800	1816	1901	1910	2000	2101	...	2110	2110	2258	...
Balalatonalmádi d.	0358	0606	0710	0914	0930	1016	1114	1130	1314	1330	1514	1514	1714	1730	1730	1816	1831	1914	1930	2016	2114	...	2130	2130	2318	...
Székesfehérvár a.	0501	0714	0800	1000	1034	1119	1200	1234	1400	1434	1600	1600	1800	1834	1834	1914	1920	2000	2034	2111	2159	...	2234	2234	0018	...
Székesfehérvár ▶ d.	*0546*	*0741*	0812	1001	*1041*	1133	1201	*1241*	1401	*1441*	1601	1627	1801	1835	*1841*	1931	1932	2001	*2041*	2123	2211	...	2235	*2246*	...	...
Kelenföld ▶ a.	*0640*	*0821*	0851	1046	*1121*	1215	1246	*1321*	1446	*1521*	1646	1716	1846	1916	*1921*	2015	2015	2046	*2121*	2220	2251	...	2316	*2346*	...	...
Budapest Déli ▶ a.	*0649*	*0829*	0859	1054	*1129*	1224	1254	*1329*	1454	*1529*	1654	1724	1854	1924	*1929*	2024	2024	2054	*2129*	2229	2259	...	2324	*2354*	...	...

E – May 1 - June 20, Sept. 1 - Nov. 2.
F – Dec. 15 - Apr. 30; Nov. 3 - Dec. 13.
S – June 21 - Aug. 31.
T – Dec. 15 - June 20, Sept. 1 - Dec. 13.

V – ⑤ Apr. 30 - Aug. 29.
b – ⑧ (daily June 21 - Aug. 31).
z – ⚒ (daily June 21 - Aug. 31).

▶ – See also Tables **1220** and **1230**.
△ – To / from Szombathely (Table **1232**).
▽ – Through train to Budapest (a. 2124) on ⑦ May 4 - June 15.

BUDAPEST - SZÉKESFEHÉRVÁR - ZALAEGERSZEG and SZOMBATHELY 1230

For faster trains Budapest - Szombathely (via Győr) see Table **1250**. The section of line between Szombathely and Porpác (17 km) is operated by GySEV.

km		900	902	904	9004	*IC* 246	9006	906	*IC* 958	908	9008	1246
						C ⊖			🅁			K ⊖
0	**Budapest** Déli ▶ d.	0630	0830	1030	1230	1335	1430	1630	1735	1830	2030	2030
4	Kelenföld ▶ d.	0637	0837	1037	1237	1342	1437	1637	1742	1837	2037	2037
67	**Székesfehérvár** ▶ a.	0716	0916	1116	1316	1421	1516	1716	1821	1916	2117	2117
67	**Székesfehérvár** d.	0718	0918	1118	1318	1422	1518	1718	1822	1918	2118	2118
90	Várpalota d.	0735	0935	1134	1334	|	1535	1735	|	1934	2134	2134
112	Veszprém d.	0803	1003	1203	1403	1504	1603	1803	1904	2003	2158	2158
148	Ajka d.	0833	1033	1233	1433	1538	1633	1833	1938	2033	2232	2232
181	Boba a.	0900	1100	1300	1500	|	1700	1900	|	2100	2302	2302
	Zalaegerszeg a.	0956**z**	1156**z**	1356**z**	1556**z**	1641	1756**z**	1956**z**	2038	2156**z**	|	2355
181	Boba ▷ d.	0905	1105	1305	1505	...	1705	1905	...	2105	2306	...
191	Celldömölk ▷ d.	0914	1114	1314	1514	...	1714	1914	...	2114	2316	...
236	**Szombathely** ▷ a.	0947	1147	1347	1547	...	1747	1947	...	2156	...	...

	IC 959	1247	909	907	905	9005	9003	*IC* 247	903	901
	🅁	K ⊖						C ⊖		
Szombathely ▷ d.	...	...	0605	0807	1007	1207	1405	...	1607	1807
Celldömölk ▷ d.	...	...	0645	0843	1043	1243	1445	...	1643	1843
Boba ▷ a.	...	...	0653	0851	1051	1251	1453	...	1651	1851
Zalaegerszeg d.	0524	0524	0603**z**	0803**z**	1003**z**	1203**z**	1403**z**	1519	1603**z**	1803**z**
Boba d.	|	|	0701	0901	1101	1301	1501	|	1701	1901
Ajka d.	0624	0624	0726	0926	1126	1326	1526	1618	1726	1926
Veszprém d.	0654	0654	0800	1000	1200	1400	1600	1654	1800	2000
Várpalota d.	|	|	0820	1021	1221	1420	1620	|	1820	2021
Székesfehérvár a.	0734	0734	0839	1039	1239	1439	1639	1734	1839	2039
Székesfehérvár ▶ d.	0736	0736	0841	1041	1241	1441	1641	1736	1841	2041
Kelenföld ▶ d.	0817	0817	0922	1122	1322	1522	1722	1817	1922	2122
Budapest Déli ▶ a.	0824	0824	0929	1129	1329	1529	1729	1824	1929	2129

C – CITTADELLA – 🚃12 Budapest - Zalaegerszeg - Hodoš - Maribor and v.v.
K – ISTRIA – ①④ June 23 - Aug. 28 from Budapest, ②⑤ June 24 - Aug. 29 from Koper (next day from Zalaegerszeg). 🛏 1, 2 cl., 🛏 2 cl. 🚃12 Budapest - Zalaegerszeg - Hodoš - Ljubljana - Koper and v.v.; 🛏 1, 2 cl. Moskva - Budapest - Koper and v.v. Extends from / to Budapest Keleti (Keleti d. 1800, Déli a. 1909; Déli d. 0950. Keleti a. 1035).
z – 🚃2 Budapest - Zalaegerszeg and v.v. (train splits / joins at Boba). See Table **1232** for intermediate stations.

▶ – See also Tables **1220** and **1225**.
▷ – See also Tables **1232** and **1250**.
⊖ – 🅁 for domestic journeys within Hungary.

2nd class SZOMBATHELY - CELLDÖMÖLK - UKK - ZALAEGERSZEG and KESZTHELY 1232

km		9540	9510	907	950	905	952		9514	9005	954		9524	9003	9504	9516	903	9506	9526	901	956	9518	9021	9508	9528
					B		B				B				B			B			B			B	
0	**Szombathely** 1230 d.	...	...	0807	...	1007	...	1107	...	1207	...	1307	...	1405	...	*1507*	1607	...	*1707*	1807	...	...	2005	...	*2117*
45	Celldömölk 1230 d.	0452	0606	0843	...	1043	...	1149	1206	1243	...	1350	1406	1445	...	1606	1643	...	1806	1843	...	2006	2046	...	2206
55	Boba 1230 d.	0501	0615	0851	0909	1051	1109	...	1215	1251	1309	...	1415	1453	1509	1615	1651	1709	1815	1851	1909	2015	2055	2109	2215
73	**Ukk** a.	0518	0633	...	0923	...	1123	...	1233	...	1323	...	1433	...	1523	1633	...	1723	1833	...	1923	2033	...	2123	2233
73	**Ukk** d.	0525	0635	...	0924	...	1124	...	1235	...	1324	...	1435	...	1524	1635	...	1724	1835	...	1924	2038	...	2124	2235
104	Zalaszentiván a.	0558	0705	...	0947	...	1147	...	1305	...	1347	...	1505	...	1547	1705	...	1747	1905	...	1947	2105	...	2147	2305
113	**Zalaegerszeg** a.	0619	0714	...	0956	...	1156	...	1314	...	1356	...	1514	...	1556	1714	...	1756	1914	...	1956	2114	...	2156	2314

	9519	9509		9517		957	900	955	902	9505	904	9525		9503	9004	9513		953	9006	9523		951	906	9511	9521
		B				B		B		B				B				B				B			
Zalaegerszeg d.	0440	0603	...	0646	...	0803	...	1003	...	1203	...	1246	...	1403	...	1446	...	1603	...	1646	...	1803	...	1846	2043
Zalaszentiván d.	0448	0611	...	0654	...	0811	...	1011	...	1211	...	1254	...	1411	...	1454	...	1611	...	1654	...	1811	...	1854	2051
Ukk a.	0518	0634	...	0721	...	0834	...	1034	...	1234	...	1321	...	1434	...	1521	...	1634	...	1721	...	1834	...	1921	2121
Ukk d.	0523	0635	...	0723	...	0835	...	1035	...	1235	...	1323	...	1435	...	1523	...	1635	...	1723	...	1835	...	1923	2123
Boba 1230 d.	0541	0651	0701	0741	...	0851	0905	1051	1105	1251	1305	1341	...	1451	1505	1541	...	1651	1705	1741	...	1851	1905	1941	2141
Celldömölk 1230 a.	0552	...	0710	0752	0808	...	0913	...	1113	...	1313	1352	1408	...	1513	1552	1608	...	1713	1752	1808	...	1913	1952	2152
Szombathely 1230 a.	*0647*	...	0751	...	0847	...	0947	...	1147	...	1347	...	1447	...	1547	...	1647	...	1747	...	1847	...	1953	*2047*	*2246*

km			9619			8807	18807	19607	19809	9617	19807	19627				9615	9613	9601	8801	9623	9611	9621	9621	19631	
						Tk	Sk	S△	Sg		E	S	S	T				T	Sp			T	S	S	
0	**Szombathely** ▷ d.	...	...	...	...	...	0642	0725	...	...	0922	...	...	...	...	...	...	...	...	...	...	...	...	...	...
45	Celldömölk ▷ d.	...	...	...	...	0730	0730	0759	...	...	0956	...	...	...	...	1301	...	1500	...	...	...	...	...	...	...
55	Boba ▷ d.	...	...	...	...	0741	0741	|	0852	...	|	...	...	...	...	1314	...	1515	...	...	...	...	...	...	...
73	**Ukk** ▷ a.	...	...	...	...	0759	0759	|	|	...	|	...	...	...	...	1337	...	1537	...	...	...	...	...	...	...
73	**Ukk** d.	...	0521	...	0636	0800	0800	|	|	0940	|	1041	...	...	...	1338	1436	1538	...	1636	1836	2039	2039	...	...
81	Sümeg d.	...	0533	...	0648	0811	0811	0829	0915	0953	1025	1051	...	...	...	1352	1448	1551	...	1648	1847	2052	2052	...	...
101	**Tapolca** a.	...	0552	...	0707	0828	0828	0846	0931	1012	1043	1116	...	...	...	1413	1507	1612	...	1707	1906	2110	2110	...	...
101	**Tapolca** d.	0446	0555	0645	...	0829	0829	...	0935	1025	1052	1125	1235	1247	...	1434	1525	1632	1647	1717	1923	2111	2121	2224	...
126	**Keszthely** a.	0517	0626	0716	...	0859	0900	...	1000	1056	1116	1204	1307	1318	...	1505	1556	1703	1720	1748	1954	2142	2153	2255	...
126	**Keszthely** 1220 d.	...	0628	...	...	0904	0905	...	*1002*	...	...	1205	...	...	...	...	1601	...	1736	1803	2005	2143	2202	...	...
136	B'tonszentgyörgy 1220 a.	...	0640	...	...	0915	0916	...	*1014*	...	...	1217	...	...	...	...	1613	...	1747	1814	2017	2155	2214	...	...

	19610	9630	9620		19612	9612	19642	9602	8802	9614	9614	9624	9616	9626	19626	19804		9646	19808	19606	8806	18806	9618	19628	9658
	S				S		S	T	Sp	T	S			T	S	E			Sg	S△	Tk	Sk		S	
B'tonszentgyörgy 1220 d.	0345	...	0545**x**	...	0802	0850	...	...	1058	...	...	...	...	...	1548	...	...	1748	...	...	1915	1920	1948	2120	2158**t**
Keszthely 1220 a.	0357	...	0557**x**	...	0813	0901	...	...	1110	...	...	...	...	...	1559	...	...	1800	...	...	1927	1931	2002	2131	2210**t**
Keszthely d.	0358	...	0605	0655	0814	0902	1036	1120	1125	1235	1245	1400	1445	...	1600	1643	1700	1805	1839	...	1937	1937	2035	2132	2238
Tapolca a.	0429	...	0639	0729	0849	0933	1113	1151	1155	1309	1320	1431	1519	...	1630	1709	1738	1836	1906	...	2008	2008	2106	2206	2309
Tapolca d.	0435	0541	0641	...	0853	*1050*	...	1152	*1157*	...	...	1441	1545	1640	1640	1710	...	1838	1908	1917	2009	2009	...	2224	...
Sümeg d.	0456	0607	0706	...	0915	*1110*	...	1215	*1219*	...	...	1506	1611	1706	1706	1730	...	1905	1925	1936	2028	2028	...	2244	...
Ukk a.	0508	0617	0717	...	0923	*1121*	...	1229	*1233*	...	...	1517	1622	1717	1717	|	...	1916	|	|	2036	2036	...	2255	...
Ukk ▷ d.	...	0618	...	...	...	...	...	1242	*1242*	...	...	...	...	...	...	|	...	...	|	|	2037	2037	...	2256	...
Boba ▷ d.	...	0639	...	...	...	...	...	1308	*1308*	...	...	...	...	...	...	|	...	...	1947	|	2056	2056	...	2314	...
Celldömölk ▷ a.	...	0654	...	...	...	...	...	1319	*1319*	...	...	...	...	...	...	1802	...	...	...	2009	2107	2107	...	2324	...
Szombathely ▷ a.	...	...	...	...	...	...	...	...	...	...	...	...	...	...	...	1852	...	...	...	2102	...	2145	...	...	...

B – 🚃2 Budapest - Boba - Zalaegerszeg and v.v. (Table **1230**).
E – Ⓒ May 1 - Sept. 28 (daily June 21 - Aug. 31).
S – June 21 - Aug. 31.
T – Dec. 13 - June 20, Sept. 1 - Dec. 15.
g – From / to Győr (d. 0711 / a. 2113).
k – To / from Kaposvár (Table **1205**).
p – To / from Pécs (Table **1205**).
t – Not June 21 - Aug. 31.
x – 10 mins earlier until June 20.
△ – To / from Budapest (Table **1225**).
▷ – See also upper table.

1233 SOPRON - SZOMBATHELY
Operated by GySEV. 2nd class

km		◇	◇	◇			P				◇		◇	◇	◇	◇								
0	**Sopron** d.	0358	0458	0558	0658	...	0812	0922	...	1122	1222	...	1322	1422	1522	1622	1758	...	1925	2058	...	2228	...	...
38	Bük d.	0437	0537	0637	0737	...	0837	0958	...	1158	1258	...	1358	1458	1558	1658	1834	...	2003	2134	...	2302	...	...
62	**Szombathely** a.	0456	0556	0656	0756	...	0853	1017	...	1217	1317	...	1417	1517	1617	1717	1853	...	2022	2153	...	2321	...	...

	◇	◇	◇			◇				◇		◇		◇	◇	◇		P	◇		◇	◇		
Szombathely d.	0417	0517	0617	0717	...	0932	...	1132	1232	1332	1432	1532	...	1632	1728	1832	...	1908	1940	...	2112	2240	...	...
Bük d.	0442	0542	0642	0737	...	0955	...	1155	1255	1355	1455	1555	...	1655	1748	1852	...	1923	2002	...	2132	2301	...	...
Sopron a.	0521	0621	0721	0811	...	1031	...	1231	1331	1431	1531	1631	...	1731	1820	1925	...	1949	2035	...	2205	2337	...	...

P – To/from Pécs (Table **1237**). ◇ – To/from Szentgotthárd (Table **986**).

1234 SZOMBATHELY - KOSZEG
Operated by GySEV. 2nd class

From **Szombathely**: 0506, 0606, 0706, 0806, 0906, 1006, 1106, 1206 Ⓐ, 1306, 1406 Ⓐ, 1506, 1606, 1706, 1806, 1910, 2110, 2246 Ⓑ.
From **Köszeg**: 0432 ⚒, 0532, 0632, 0732, 0832, 0932, 1032, 1132 Ⓐ, 1232, 1332 Ⓐ, 1432, 1532, 1632, 1732, 1832, 2032, 2210.

18 km, journey time 20 - 25 minutes

1235 SZOMBATHELY - ZALASZENTIVÁN - ZALAEGERSZEG
MÁV-START / GySEV

km		8900						8902				8904									8906				
		△	2	2	2	2	2	2△	2	2	2	△	2	2	2	2	2	2	2Ⓐ	2	△	2	2	2	2
	Sopron 1233 d.	...	...	...	...	...	...	0812	...	...	...	...	...	...	...	...	...	...	...	...	...	...	...	...	...
0	**Szombathely** d.	0509	...	0611	...	0706	...	0908	...	1106	...	1308	...	1355	...	1431	...	1606	1631	...	1708	...	1806	1911	2230
24	Vasvár d.	0529	...	0635	...	0729	...	0928	...	1129	...	1329	...	1425	...	1456	...	1629	1656	...	1729	...	1829	1934	2254
49	Zalaszentiván a.	0552	...	0700	...	0754	...	0950	...	1154	...	1351	...	1451	...	1522	...	1654	1722	...	1751	...	1854	1959	2319
49	Zalaszentiván ▶ d.	...	0611	...	0706	...	0811	...	1011	...	1211	...	1411	...	1506	...	1548	1700	...	1748	...	1811	1859	2004	2324
58	**Zalaegerszeg** ▶ a.	...	0619	...	0714	...	0820	...	1020	...	1220	...	1420	...	1514	...	1556	1708	...	1756	...	1820	1908	2013	2333

								8909				8907								8905				8901	
	2⚒	2	2	2	2	2	2	△		2	2	△	2	2	2	2		2	2	2△		2	2	△	
Zalaegerszeg ▶ d.	0348	0440	...	0548	0730	...	0935	...	...	...	1335	...	1446	...	1535	...	...	1719	1735	...	...	1935	2135	...	...
Zalaszentiván ▶ a.	0357	0447	...	0557	0738	...	0944	...	...	...	1344	...	1453	...	1544	...	...	1728	1744	...	...	1944	2144	...	...
Zalaszentiván d.	0402	...	0455	0602	...	0802	...	1002	...	1202	...	1402	...	1502	...	1602	...	1733	...	1802	...	2002	...	2205	...
Vasvár d.	0428	...	0519	0626	...	0828	...	1029	...	1228	...	1429	...	1528	...	1628	...	1759	...	1829	...	2028	...	2226	...
Szombathely a.	0452	...	0545	0652	...	0852	...	1051	...	1252	...	1451	...	1552	...	1652	...	1826	...	1851	...	2052	...	2251	...
Sopron 1233 a.	...	...	...	...	...	...	...	...	...	...	...	...	...	...	...	...	...	...	...	1949	...	...	...	...	...

△ – To/from Pécs (Tables **1236/7**). ▶ – See also Tables **1232** and **1236**.

1236 ZALAEGERSZEG - ZALASZENTIVÁN - NAGYKANIZSA

km			8900		8902		8904			8906	
		2		2	2△	2		2	2		
	Szombathely 1235 d.	...	0509	...	0908	...	1308		...	1708	...
0	**Zalaegerszeg** ▶ d.	0548	|	0935	|	1335	|	1652	1735	|	...
9	Zalaszentiván ▶ a.	0557	0552	0944	0950	1344	1351	1700	1744	1751	...
9	Zalaszentiván d.	...	0600	...	1000	...	1400	1710	...	1800	...
61	**Nagykanizsa** a.	...	0652	...	1048	...	1448	1818	...	1848	...
	Pécs 1237 a.	...	0936	...	1336	...	1736	...	...	2142	...

		8909		8907		8905		8901	
	2		2		2	2▽	2		2
Pécs 1237 d.	...	0615	...	1015	...	1415	...	1815	...
Nagykanizsa d.	0609	0909	...	1309	...	1709	...	2109	...
Zalaszentiván a.	0709	0957	...	1357	...	1757	...	2201	...
Zalaszentiván ▶ d.	0712	1002	1011	1402	1411	1802	1811	2205	2204
Zalaegerszeg ▶ a.	0721	|	1020	|	1420	|	1820	|	2213
Szombathely 1235 a.	...	1051	...	1451	...	1851	...	2251	...

△ – From Sopron (depart 0812). ▽ – To Sopron (arrive 1949). ▶ – See also Tables **1232** and **1235**.

1237 NAGYKANIZSA - PÉCS

km			8900		8902		8904		8906	
		2		2Ⓐ	2△	2		2⑦		
	Szombathely 1235 d.	...	0509	...	0908	...	1308	...	1708	...
0	**Nagykanizsa** 1240 d.	0352	0653	...	1053	...	1453	...	1853	...
29	Gyékényes 1240 d.	0452	0720		1120	1255	1520	...	1920	...
84	Barcs d.	0612	0826	1012	1226	1412	1626	1812	2026	...
114	Szigetvár d.	0700	0857	1056	1257	1456	1657	1856	2106	...
129	Szentlőrinc d.	0729	0913	1129	1313	1529	1713	1915	2125	...
148	**Pécs** a.	0749	0936	1149	1336	1549	1736	1938	2142	...

	8909	8907		8905			8901		⊡
			2	2▽	2	2		2	2Ⓑ
Pécs d.	0615	1015	1212	1415	1455	1612	1815	2012	2225
Szentlőrinc d.	0639	1039	1238	1439	1518	1638	1839	2045	2251
Szigetvár d.	0655	1055	1258	1455	1536	1658	1855	2107	2309
Barcs d.	0726	1126	1337	1526	1615	1738	1926	2146	2348
Gyékényes 1240 a.	0838	1238	...	1638	...	1843	2038	...	...
Nagykanizsa 1240 a.	0905	1305	...	1705	...	1936	2105	...	...
Szombathely 1235 a.	1051	1451	...	1851	...	...	2251	...	...

△ – From Sopron (depart 0812). ▽ – To Sopron (arrive 1949). ⊡ – On ⑦ May 4 - Aug. 31 runs up to 15 minutes earlier.

1240 (BUDAPEST) - DOMBÓVAR - KAPOSVÁR - NAGYKANIZSA

km	*For Budapest - Nagykanizsa trains see Table 1220*					8202	*IC* 201	8212	8907	8234		8244	8905	8244		8226		*IC* 204	8206	*IC* 828		8218	8208	8208
		2	2 ⚒	2 †	2	2	⊖ Z	2		2	2 Ⓐb	2	2	2	2 Ⓐ	2	2	⊖ R	2	2 🅁	2	2	2 Ⓑ	2 ⑥
	Budapest Keleti 1200 d.	...	...	...	...	...	...	...	...	...	...	...	...	...	...	...	...	1445	...	1645	...	...	...	...
0	**Dombóvár** d.	...	0408	...	0602	0808	...	1008	...	1208	...	1408	...	...	...	1608	...	1655	1808	1857	...	2005	2208	2208
31	**Kaposvár** a.	...	0455	...	0652	0844	...	1055	...	1255	...	1455	...	...	...	1655	...	1736	1844	1938	...	2055	2244	2244
31	**Kaposvár** d.	...	0457	0457	0705	0905	...	1105	...	1305	1405	1505	...	...	1553	1700	...	1739	1905	1940	...	2105	2245	...
71	Somogyszob d.	...	0610	0610	0759	0959	...	1159	...	1359	1459	1559	...	...	1649	1759	...	1823	1959	2024	...	2214	2337	...
101	Gyékényes a.	...	0641	0641	0828	1028	...	1230	...	1428	1528	1630	...	←	1722	1828	...	1848	2030	2050	...	2243	0006	...
101	Gyékényes 1237 d.	0614	0720	0720	*0839*	...	1200	...	1239	1429	...	→	1639	1655	...	...	1858	...	*2039*	...	2059	...	...	...
130	**Nagykanizsa** 1237 a.	0648	0752	0752	*0905*	...	1235	...	1305	1507	...	...	1705	1732	...	...	1936	...	*2105*	...	2145	...	...	...

					IC 829	8239	8209	8900	8217	*IC* 200	8902	8205		8215	8235	8904	8235	*IC* 205	8233	8906	8201		8231	
	2 ⚒	2 †	2 Ⓐ	2	2 🅁	2	2		2	⊖ Z	2	2	2	2	2		2	⊖ S	2		2	2 Ⓑ	2 Ⓑ	2 ⑥
Nagykanizsa 1237 d.	...	...	...	0352	...	0502	0630	0653	...	0945	1053	...	1115	...	1427	1453	...	...	1633	1853	...	1917	2111	2111
Gyékényes 1237 a.	...	...	...	0450	...	0535	0708	0719	...	1010	1119	...	1148	...	1513	1519	←	...	1719	1919	...	1955	2143	2143
Gyékényes d.	0332	...	0417	...	0501	0536	0722	...	0929	...	...	1129	...	1327	→	...	1529	1644	1725	...	1923	...	2144	2144
Somogyszob d.	0404	...	0447	...	0528	0608	0759	...	0959	...	...	1159	...	1359	...	...	1559	1710	1757	...	1957	...	2214	2214
Kaposvár a.	0455	...	0541	...	0611	0659	0850	...	1050	...	...	1250	...	1450	...	...	1650	1802	1852	...	2053	...	2311	2305
Kaposvár d.	0503	0503	...	...	0613	0703	0914	...	1103	...	...	1314	...	1503	...	...	1657	1804	1858	...	2114	...	2312	...
Dombóvár a.	0550	0550	...	...	0649	0750	0950	...	1150	...	...	1350	...	1550	...	...	1744	1846	1945	...	2150	...	2359	...
Budapest Keleti 1200 a.	...	...	...	...	0915	...	...	...	...	...	...	...	...	...	...	...	...	2115	...	...	...	...	...	...

R – RIPPL-RÓNAI – 🛏12 Budapest - Zagreb (**498**) - Ljubljana; 🛏2 and 🍷 Budapest - Zagreb.
S – RIPPL-RÓNAI – 🛏12 and 🍷 Zagreb - Budapest.
Z – AGRAM, Budapest - Zagreb and v.v. – see Table **1220**.
b – Not Dec. 23 - Jan. 3, June 16 - Aug. 29.
⊖ – 🅁 for domestic journeys within Hungary.

1242 DOMBÓVAR - BAJA - KISKUNFÉLEGYHÁZA - KECSKEMÉT
2nd class

km						⚒	⑦			d	
0	**Dombóvár** d.	...	0610	...	...	1410	1410	1610	1810	...	...
60	Bátaszék 1210 d.	0521	0717	0726	...	1518	1532	1724	1923	1939	...
80	**Baja** 1210 a.	0542	...	0747	...	1543	1553	1745	...	1959	...

		Ⓐ	h							
Baja 1210 d.	0425	...	0611	...	...	1411	1613	...	1802**r**	...
Bátaszék 1210 d.	0444	0447	0629	0633	...	1433	1640	...	1840	...
Dombóvár a.	...	0554	...	0745	...	1545	1747	...	1947	...

km			Ⓐ						Ⓐ		
0	**Baja** d.	0413	0516	0609	0809	1009	1209	1409	1511	1609	1809
76	Kiskunhalas a.	0520	0630	0720	0920	1120	1320	1520	1630	1720	1920
76	Kiskunhalas d.	0532	0639	0732	0932	1132	1332	1532	...	1732	1932
122	Kiskunfélegyháza 1290 d.	0615	0721	0815	1015	1215	1415	1615	...	1815	2014
147	**Kecskemét** 1290 a.	0636	...	0836	1036	1236	1436	1636	...	1836	...

	Ⓐ						Ⓐ			
Kecskemét 1290 d.	...	0510	0722	0922	1122	1322	...	1522	1722	192[illegible]
Kiskunfélegyháza 1290 d.	...	0545	0745	0945	1145	1345	1438	1545	1745	194[illegible]
Kiskunhalas a.	...	0625	0825	1025	1225	1425	1518	1625	1825	202[illegible]
Kiskunhalas d.	0528	0637	0837	1037	1237	1437	1528	1637	1837	203[illegible]
Baja a.	0638	0742	0942	1142	1342	1542	1638	1742	1942	214[illegible]

d – Train *Ex* 838, 🅁. **h** – Train *Ex* 839, 🅁. **r** – Depart 1818 on certain dates.

BUDAPEST - GYÖR - SOPRON / SZOMBATHELY / WIEN 1250

km	FAST TRAINS	346	RJ 162	IC 910 IC 930	IC 910	RJ 60	IC 912 IC 942	IC 912	RJ 62	IC 922 IC 932	IC 922	RJ 64		RJ 66	IC 924 IC 934	IC 924	RJ 68	IC 916 IC 936	IC 916	RJ 42	IC 918 IC 938	IC 918	EN 466	EN 462
			✕	Ⓡ	Ⓡ	✕	Ⓡ	Ⓡ	✕	Ⓡ	Ⓡ	✕		✕	Ⓡ	Ⓡ	✕	Ⓡ		✕	Ⓡ	Ⓡ	✕	
		D	Z ⊖			M ⊖			M ⊖			M ⊖		F ⊖			M ⊖		G ⊖	S ⊖			W ⊖	K ⊖
0	**Budapest** Keleti ... d.	0510	0605	0610	0610	0710	0810	0810	0910	1010	1010	1110	...	1310	1410	1410	1510	1610	1610	1710	1810	1810	1910	2110
13	Kelenföld ... d.	0524	0619	0624	0624	0724	0824	0824	0924	1024	1024	1124	...	1324	1424	1424	1524	1624	1624	1724	1824	1824	1924	2124
75	Tatabánya ... d.	0558	|	0658	0658	0758	0858	0858	0958	1058	1058	1158	...	1358	1458	1458	1558	1658	1658	1758	1858	1858	1958	2158
141	**Györ** ... a.	0631	0728	0736	0736	0831	0936	0936	1031	1136	1136	1231	...	1431	1536	1536	1631	1736	1736	1831	1936	1936	2031	2231
141	**Györ** ... d.	0632	0729	0738	0738	0832	0938	0938	1032	1138	1138	1232	...	1432	1538	1538	1632	1738	1738	1832	1938	1938	2032	2232
172	Csorna ... d.	|	|	0802	0807	|	1002	1007	|	1202	1207	|	...	|	1602	1607	|	1802	1807	|	2002	2007	|	|
226	**Sopron** ... a.	|	|	0842	|	|	1042	|	|	1242	|	|	...	|	1642	|	|	1842	|	|	2042	|	|	|
244	**Szombathely** ... ◧ a.	|	|	...	0902	|	...	1102	|	...	1302	|	...	|	...	1702	|	...	1902	|	...	2102	|	|
	Graz **986** ... a.	|	|	...	...	|	...	...	|	...	...	|	...	|	...	...	|	...	2153	|	...	...	|	|
177	Mosonmagyaróvár ... d.	0650	0747	...	...	0850	...	...	1050	...	...	1250	...	1450	...	...	1650	...	...	1850	...	...	2050	2250
188	Hegyeshalom 🏛 ... d.	0702	0802	...	...	0902	...	...	1102	...	...	1302	...	1502	...	...	1702	...	...	1902	...	...	2102	2302
219	Bruck an der Leitha ... d.	|	|	...	...	|	...	...	|	...	...	|	...	|	...	...	|	...	...	|	...	...	|	|
261	**Wien** Meidling ... a.	0757	0857	...	...	0957	...	...	1157	...	...	1357	...	1557	...	...	1757	...	...	1957	...	...	2156	2356
272	**Wien** Westbahnhof ... a.	0814	0912	...	...	1012	...	...	1212	...	...	1412	...	1612	...	...	1812	...	...	2012	...	...	2216	...

FAST TRAINS	IC 919	IC 939 IC 919	EN 463	929	RJ 41	EN 467	IC 937 IC 917	IC 917	RJ 49		RJ 61	IC 935 IC 915	IC 915	RJ 63	IC 933 IC 913	IC 913	RJ 65	IC 943 IC 923	IC 923	RJ 67	IC 931 IC 911	IC 911	RJ 165	347
	Ⓡ	Ⓡ		2	✕	✕	Ⓡ	Ⓡ✕	✕		✕	Ⓡ	Ⓡ	✕	Ⓡ	Ⓡ	✕	Ⓡ	Ⓡ	✕	Ⓡ	Ⓡ	✕	
			K ⊖	Ⓐ	⊖	W ⊖		G ⊖	v ⊖		M ⊖			F ⊖			M ⊖			M ⊖			Z ⊖	D
Wien Westbahnhof ... d.	...	...	...	...	0648	0756	...	...	0948	...	1148	...	...	1348	...	...	1548	...	...	1748	...	...	1848	1948
Wien Meidling ... d.	...	...	0601	...	0702	|	...	...	1002	...	1202	...	...	1402	...	...	1602	...	...	1802	...	...	1902	2002
Bruck an der Leitha ... d.	...	...	|	...	|	|	...	...	|	...	|	...	...	|	...	...	|	...	...	|	...	...	|	|
Hegyeshalom 🏛 ... d.	...	...	0700	...	0758	0858	...	...	1058	...	1258	...	...	1458	...	...	1658	...	...	1858	...	...	1958	2058
Mosonmagyaróvár ... d.	...	...	0707	...	0805	0905	...	...	1105	...	1305	...	...	1505	...	...	1705	...	...	1905	...	...	2005	2105
Graz **986** ... d.	...	...	|	...	|	|	...	0608	|	...	|	...	...	|	...	...	|	...	...	|	...	...	|	|
Szombathely ... ◧ d.	0600	...	|	0700	|	|	...	0900	|	...	|	...	1300	|	...	1500	|	...	1700	|	...	1900	|	|
Sopron ... d.	|	0607	|	|	|	|	0907	|	|	...	|	1307	|	|	1507	|	|	1707	|	|	1907	|	|	|
Csorna ... d.	0659	0659	|	0759	|	|	0959	0959	|	...	|	1359	1359	|	1559	1559	|	1759	1759	|	1959	1959	|	|
Györ ... a.	0719	0719	0724	0819	0821	0921	1019	1019	1121	...	1321	1419	1419	1521	1619	1619	1721	1819	1819	1921	2019	2019	2024	2121
Györ ... d.	0720	0720	0725	...	0822	0922	1020	1020	1122	...	1322	1420	1420	1522	1620	1620	1722	1820	1820	1922	2020	2020	2025	2122
Tatabánya ... d.	0756	0756	0802	...	0856	0956	1056	1056	1156	...	1356	1456	1456	1556	1656	1656	1756	1856	1856	1956	2056	2056	|	2156
Kelenföld ... a.	0832	0832	0838	...	0932	1032	1132	1132	1232	...	1432	1532	1532	1632	1732	1732	1832	1932	1932	2032	2132	2132	2137	2232
Budapest Keleti ... a.	0849	0849	0854	...	0949	1049	1149	1149	1249	...	1449	1549	1549	1649	1749	1749	1849	1949	1949	2049	2149	2149	2154	2249

SLOWER SERVICES BUDAPEST - GYÖR

See above for faster services

km		9200	9292	9202	9304	9204	9404	9206	9406	9208	9408	△ 2
0	**Budapest** Keleti ... d.	0638	0838	1038	1238	1438	1538	1638	1738	1838	1938	...
	Budapest Déli ... d.	|	|	|	|	|	|	|	|	|	|	2120
13	Kelenföld ... d.	0652	0852	1052	1252	1452	1552	1652	1752	1852	1952	2128
75	Tatabánya ... △ d.	0730	0930	1130	1330	1530	1630	1730	1830	1930	2030	2213
84	Tata ... △ d.	0738	0938	1138	1338	1538	1638	1738	1838	1938	2038	2224
104	Komárom ... △ d.	0753	0953	1153	1353	1553	1653	1753	1853	1953	2053	2253
141	**Györ** ... a.	0826	1026	1226	1426	1626	1726	1826	1926	2026	2126	2323

	9409	9407	9209	9297	9207	9305	9303	9205	9203	9201	▽ 2
Györ ... d.	0544	0628	0728	0928	1128	1328	1428	1528	1728	1928	2031
Komárom ... ▽ d.	0610	0657	0757	0957	1157	1357	1457	1557	1757	1957	2110
Tata ... ▽ d.	0625	0713	0813	1013	1213	1413	1513	1613	1813	2013	2129
Tatabánya ... ▽ d.	0634	0723	0823	1023	1223	1423	1523	1623	1823	2023	2141
Kelenföld ... a.	0716	0804	0904	1104	1304	1504	1604	1704	1904	2104	2228
Budapest Déli ... a.	|	|	|	|	|	|	|	|	|	|	2239
Budapest Keleti ... a.	0731	0820	0920	1120	1320	1520	1620	1720	1920	2120	...

SLOWER SERVICES GYÖR - SOPRON / SZOMBATHELY

See above for faster services

km		2	2Y	2	2⚒	990	9200	2	9292	992	9202	2Y	2Ⓐ	2	2	2	9906	9204	2	9206	2X	998	2	9208	
	Budapest Keleti ★ ... d.	...	...	...	...	0638	0638	...	0838	1038	1038	...	...	...	...	...	1438	1438	...	1638	...	1838	...	1838	...
0	**Györ** ... d.	0405	0513	0554	0646	0842	0840	1037	1040	1242	1240	1330	1402	1440	1456	1603	1640	1640	1836	1840	1951	2043	...	2040	2240
31	Csorna ... d.	0435	0540	0624	0723	0909	|	1105	|	1309	|	1359	1431	1516	|	1634	1707	|	1906	|	2020	2112	2115	|	2310
85	**Sopron** ... a.	0528	0635	0726	0817	0953	|	1157	|	1354	|	1455	1525	1612	|	1725	1753	|	1955	|	2104	2156	|	|	0002
72	Celldömölk ... a.	...	...	...	...	...	0951	...	1151	...	1351	...	...	...	1635	...	...	1751	...	1951	...	...	|	2146	...
117	**Szombathely** ... ◧ a.	...	...	...	...	...	1047	...	1247	...	1447	...	...	...	...	...	...	1847	...	2047	...	...	2227	2246	...

	2	2⚒	2	9209		2	9297	997	9207	2	2		995	9205	2	2	9203	2		991	9201	2	2	2	
zombathely ... ◧ d.	...	...	...	0522	...	...	0707	...	0907	...	...	...	...	1307	...	...	1507	...	...	...	1707	...	...	...	...
elldömölk ... d.	...	...	...	0608	...	...	0808	...	1008	1124	...	...	...	1408	...	...	1608	...	...	...	1808	...	2118	...	...
Sopron ... d.	0343	0447	0549	|	...	0733	|	0954	|	|	1137	...	1359	|	1437	1527	|	1621	...	1754	|	1935	|	2230	...
sorna ... d.	0436	0543	0640	|	...	0832	|	1040	|	|	1231	...	1446	|	1533	1632	|	1721	...	1840	|	2034	|	2326	...
yör ... a.	0504	0613	0708	0716	...	0900	0916	1109	1116	1255	1259	...	1514	1516	1602	1659	1716	1752	...	1909	1916	2101	2243	2353	...
Budapest Keleti ★ ... a.	...	...	...	0920	...	...	1120	1320	1320	...	...	...	1720	1720	...	...	1920	...	...	2120	2120	...	...	...	...

2nd class

LOCAL TRAINS GYÖR - HEGYESHALOM - WIEN

See above for faster services

yör ... ☆ d.	0448	*0548*	0748	0948	1148	1348	1548	1748	1948
osonmagyaróvár ... ☆ d.	0514	*0614*	0814	1014	1214	1414	1614	1814	2014
egyeshalom 🏛 ... ☆ d.	0528	0628	0831	1026	1231	1431	1631	1831	2035
ruck an der Leitha ... **997** a.	0551	0651	0856	1056	1256	1456	1656	1856	2057
ien Hbf ... **997** a.	0623	0723	*0928*	*1128*	*1328*	*1528*	*1728*	*1928*	*2129*

Wien Hbf ... **997** d.	0635	0836	*1032*	*1232*	*1432*	*1636*	*1832*	*1932*	*2032*	...
Bruck an der Leitha ... **997** d.	0709	0907	1106	1306	1506	*1710*	1906	2006	2106	...
Hegyeshalom 🏛 ... ☆ d.	0736	0936	1136	1336	1536	1737	1936	2036	2136	2236
Mosonmagyaróvár ... ☆ d.	0744	0944	1144	1344	1544	1744	1944	2044	2144	2244
Györ ... ☆ a.	0810	1010	1210	1410	1610	1810	2010	2110	2210	2310

- – DACIA – 🛏 1, 2 cl., 🛌 2 cl., (2) 🍷 Wien - Budapest - Bucuresti and v.v.
- – (12) and ✕ München - Salzburg - Wien - Budapest and v.v. (Table **65**). Extended to / from Frankfurt on dates in Tables **912** / **930**.
- – (12) Budapest - Szombathely - Graz and v.v.
- – KÁLMÁN IMRE – 🛏 1, 2 cl., 🛌 2 cl., (2) München - Wien - Budapest and v.v.
- – (12) and ✕ München - Salzburg - Wien - Budapest and v.v. (Table **65**).
- – (12) and ✕ Salzburg - Wien - Budapest and v.v. (Table **65**).
- – WIENER WALZER – (12) ✕ Wien - Budapest and v.v.; 🛏 1, 2 cl., 🛌 2 cl., (2) Zürich - Wien - Budapest and v.v.
- – ⑦ (not June 22 - Aug. 31).
- – Ⓐ (not Dec. 23 - Jan. 3, June 16 - Aug. 29).
- – (12) and ✕ Zürich - Innsbruck - Salzburg - Wien - Budapest and v.v. (Table **86**).
- – From Innsbruck and Salzburg on dates in Table **86**.

◧ – For alternative services Budapest - Szombathely via Székesfehérvár see Table **1230**.
★ – See panel above. Faster journeys may be possible by changing at Györ (see top panel for fast services Budapest - Györ).
⊖ – Reservation compulsory for domestic journeys within Hungary.
△ – Local trains run at 0430 and hourly 0520 - 2320 Budapest Déli - Komárom (trains at 0430, 0520, 0720, 0920, 1120, 1320, 2020, 2120 extend to Györ).
▽ – Local trains run hourly 0710 - 2210 Komárom - Budapest Déli (also from Györ at 0831, 1031, 1231, 1631, 1831, 2031, 2131).
☆ – Local trains run hourly 0448 - 2248 Györ - Hegyeshalom and 0436 - 2236 Hegyeshalom - Györ. Trains from Györ at 0648, 1448, 1648 extend to Rajka, returning 0821, 1621, 1821 (15 mins later from Hegyeshalom).
RJ – *Railjet* service, first and economy (2nd) class. *Business class* also available to first class ticket holders (supplement payable).

nd class

KOMÁROM - SZÉKESFEHÉRVÁR - SÁRBOGÁRD 1251

km			S							
0	Komárom ... d.	...	0729	0830	...	...	1610	...	...	...
82	Székesfehérvár ... a.	...	0853	0954	...	...	1734	...	...	...
82	Székesfehérvár ... d.	...	...	...	...	1401	...	...	2001	...
21	Sárbogárd ... a.	...	...	...	...	1455	...	...	2055	...

								S	
Sárbogárd ... d.	...	0705	...	...	...	1505	...	...	...
Székesfehérvár ... a.	...	0759	...	...	...	1559	...	...	...
Székesfehérvár ... d.	0600	...	...	1425	...	...	...	2030	...
Komárom ... a.	0723	...	...	1548	...	...	...	2154	...

– June 21 - Aug. 31. From / to Györ (d. 0658 / a. 2226).

1255 BUDAPEST - VÁC - SZOB

Local trains, 2nd class

km										
0	**Budapest** Nyugati ..... d.	0048	0441	0541	0707	then	2107	2148	2248	2348
34	Vác ..... d.	0133	0533	0628	0734	hourly	2134	2233	2333	0033
51	Nagymaros-Visegrád ¶ d.	0149	0549	0644	0750	until	2150	2249	2349	0049
64	**Szob** ..... a.	0204	0604	0659	0805		2205	2304	0004	0104

Szob ..... d.	0455	0555	0655	then	1855	2000	2100	2200	2300
Nagymaros-Visegrád ¶ . d.	0510	0610	0710	hourly	1910	2015	2115	2215	2315
Vác ..... d.	0528	0628	0728	until	1928	2034	2134	2234	2334
Budapest Nyugati ..... a.	0554	0654	0754		1954	2117	2217	2317	0017

¶ – A ferry operates across the river to Visegrád.

For *EC* trains see Table **1175**.

1260 BUDAPEST - MISKOLC - NYÍREGYHÁZA

Fast trains

For slower trains Budapest - Miskolc see Table **1261**. Most *IC* trains continue beyond Debrecen to / from Budapest Nyugati. For trains Budapest - Debrecen - Nyiregyháza see Table **1270**

km		*IC* 560 🅁	*IC* 659 🅁	*EC* 532 ⊖ R	2	*IC* 657 🅁	*IC* 502 🅁	2	*IC* 564 🅁	*IC* 512 🅁	2	*IC* 655 🅁	*IC* 504 🅁	2	*IC* 566 🅁	*IC* 514 🅁	2	*IC* 653 🅁	*IC* 506 🅁	2	*IC* 568 🅁	*EC* 536 ⊖ H	2	*IC* 508 🅁	2	2 Ⓑ
0	**Budapest** Keleti . ▶ d.	...	...	0630	...	0730	0830	...	0930	1030	...	1130	1230	...	1330	1430	...	1530	1630	...	1730	1830	...	1930	...	...
126	Füzesabony ..... ▶ d.	...	...	0753	...	0853	0953	...	1053	1153	...	1253	1353	...	1453	1553	...	1653	1753	...	1853	1953	...	2053	...	...
183	**Miskolc** ..... ▶ a.	...	...	0829	...	0929	1029	...	1129	1229	...	1329	1429	...	1529	1629	...	1729	1829	...	1929	2029	...	2129	...	...
183	**Miskolc** ..... d.	0631	0731	...	*0836*	0931	...	*1036*	1131	...	*1236*	1331	...	*1436*	1531	...	*1636*	1731	...	*1836*	1931	...	*2036*	...	2136	2305
221	Szerencs ..... d.	0657	0757	...	0917	0957	...	1117	1157	...	1317	1357	...	1517	1557	...	1717	1757	...	1917	1957	...	2117	...	2217	2341
239	Tokaj ..... d.	0709	0809	...	0936	1009	...	1136	1209	...	1336	1409	...	1536	1609	...	1736	1809	...	1936	2009	...	2136	...	2236	2359
271	**Nyíregyháza** ..... a.	0730	0830	...	1015	1030	...	1215	1230	...	1415	1430	...	1615	1630	...	1815	1830	...	2015	2030	...	2215	...	2315	0033
	Debrecen **1270** .... a.	0802	0902	...	...	1102	...	...	1302	...	...	1502	...	...	1702	...	...	1902	...	...	2102	...	...	...	...	...

	529	*IC* 519 🅁	2	*EC* 537 ⊖ H	*IC* 569 🅁	2	*IC* 517 🅁	*IC* 650 🅁	2	*IC* 515 🅁	*IC* 567 🅁	2	*IC* 505 🅁	*IC* 652 🅁	2	*IC* 513 🅁	*IC* 565 🅁	2	*IC* 503 🅁	*IC* 654 🅁	2	*EC* 533 ⊖ R	*IC* 563 🅁	2	2	2
Debrecen **1270** ..... d.	...	...	...	...	0650	...	...	0854	...	...	1054	...	...	1254	...	...	1454	...	...	1654	...	...	1854	...	...	...
Nyíregyháza ..... d.	*0343*	0526	0539	...	0723	0739	...	0926	0939	...	1126	1139	...	1326	1339	...	1526	1539	...	1726	1739	...	1926	1939	2039	2239
Tokaj ..... d.	*0418*	0549	0621	...	0749	0821	...	0949	1021	...	1149	1221	...	1349	1421	...	1549	1621	...	1749	1821	...	1949	2021	2121	2321
Szerencs ..... d.	0446	0601	0641	...	0801	0840	...	1001	1040	...	1201	1240	...	1401	1440	...	1601	1640	...	1801	1840	...	2001	2040	2220**z**	2340
Miskolc ..... a.	0520	0625	0712	...	0825	*0920*	...	1025	*1120*	...	1225	*1320*	...	1425	*1520*	...	1625	*1720*	...	1825	*1920*	...	2025	*2120*	2255	...
Miskolc ..... ▶ d.	0535	0628	...	0728	0828	...	0928	1028	...	1128	1228	...	1328	1428	...	1528	1628	...	1728	1828	...	1928	...	...	...	...
Füzesabony ..... ▶ d.	0623	0707	...	0807	0907	...	1007	1107	...	1207	1307	...	1407	1507	...	1607	1707	...	1807	1907	...	2007	...	...	...	...
Budapest Keleti .. ▶ a.	0800	0830	...	0930	1030	...	1130	1230	...	1330	1430	...	1530	1630	...	1730	1830	...	1930	2030	...	2130	...	...	...	...

H – HERNÁD – 🚃12 and 🍷 Budapest - Miskolc - Košice and v.v.
R – RÁKÓCZI – 🚃12 Budapest - Miskolc - Košice and v.v.

z – Arrive 2140.

▶ – For slower services see Table **1261**.
⊖ – Compulsory reservation for domestic journeys within Hungary.

1261 BUDAPEST - MISKOLC - SÁTORALJAÚJHELY

Slower trains

For fast trains Budapest - Miskolc - Szerencs see Table **1260**. For faster journeys use *IC* train (Table **1260**) and change at Füzesabony (for Eger) or Szerencs (for Sátoraljaújhely).

km		2	2	2	5500 2	5200	542 2△	520	552 2△	522	544 2△	524	554 2△	526	546 2△	528	556 2△	1528 ⑤E	5208 k	5508 2	5008 k	5108	2	
0	**Budapest** Keleti ..... ▶ d.	...	...	...	0500	0600	0700	0800	0900	1000	1100	1200	1300	1400	1500	1600	1700	1755	1800	1900	2000	2200	2235	...
67	Hatvan ..... d.	...	...	*0505*	0554	0653	0753	0853	0953	1053	1153	1253	1353	1453	1553	1653	1753	|	1853	1955	2053	2253	2353	...
87	Vámosgyörk ⊡ ..... d.	...	...	*0520*	0609	0705	0805	0905	1005	1105	1205	1305	1405	1505	1605	1705	1805	|	1905	2010	2105	2305	0008	...
126	Füzesabony ..... ▶ a.	...	...	*0554*	0646	0729	0829	0929	1029	1129	1229	1329	1429	1529	1629	1729	1829	1920	1929	2043	2129	2329	0042	...
126	Füzesabony ..... ▶ d.	...	...	0602	0650	0732	0831	0932	1031	1132	1231	1332	1431	1532	1631	1732	1831	1922	1932	2108	2132	2332	...	...
143	**Eger** ⊙ ..... a.	...	...	|	0710	|	0850	|	1050	|	1250	|	1450	|	1650	|	1850	|	|	2125	|	|	...	...
139	Mezőkövesd ..... d.	...	...	0613	—	0743	...	0943	—	1143	—	1343	—	1543	—	1743	—	|	1943	—	2143	2343	...	...
183	**Miskolc** ..... ▶ a.	...	...	0652	2	0817	...	1017	2	1217	2	1417	2	1617	2	1817	2	2003	2017	2	2217	0017	...	...
183	**Miskolc** ..... ▶ d.	*0536*	*0636*	...	*0736*	0836	...	1036	*1136*	1236	*1336*	1436	*1536*	1636	*1736*	1836	*1936*	2016	2036	*2136*	...	...	...	...
221	Szerencs ..... ▶ d.	0613	0713	...	0813	0913	...	1113	1213	1313	1413	1513	1613	1713	1813	1913	2013	2045	2113	2224	...	...	...	...
257	Sárospatak ..... a.	0702	0802	...	0902	1002	...	1202	1302	1402	1502	1602	1702	1802	1902	2002	2102	2132	2202	2305	...	...	...	...
267	**Sátoraljaújhely** ..... a.	0711	0811	...	0911	1011	...	1211	1311	1411	1511	1611	1711	1811	1911	2011	2111	2141	2211	2314	...	...	...	...

	5009	5509	529	547 2△	5209 k	2	527	545 2△	525	2	5205	2	523	2	521	1521 ⑦G	541 2△	2	5201	2	2	2	2	2
Sátoraljaújhely ..... d.	...	...	0354	...	0549	0649	0749	...	0949	1049	1149	1249	1349	1449	1549	1621	...	1649	1749	1849	1949	...	2049	...
Sárospatak ..... d.	...	...	0404	...	0604	0704	0804	...	1004	1104	1204	1304	1404	1504	1604	1631	...	1704	1804	1904	2004	...	2104	...
Szerencs ..... ▶ d.	...	...	0446	...	0646	0744	0846	...	1046	1144	1246	1344	1446	1544	1646	1717	...	1744	1846	1944	2046	...	2144	...
Miskolc ..... ▶ a.	...	...	0520	...	0720	*0820*	0920	...	1120	*1220*	1320	*1420*	1520	*1620*	1720	1746	...	*1820*	1920	*2020*	2120	...	*2255*	...
Miskolc ..... ▶ d.	0328	...	0535	...	0735	—	0935	...	1135	—	1335	—	1535	—	1735	1750	...	...	1935	...	...	2200	...	2300
Mezőkövesd ..... d.	0406	...	0610	...	0810	2△	1010	...	1210	2△	1410	2△	1610	2△	1810	|	...	...	2010	...	...	2238	...	2338
Eger ⊙ ..... d.	|	0440	|	0704	|	0904	|	1104	|	1304	|	1504	|	1704	|	|	1904	...	|	...	...	|	...	|
Füzesabony ..... ▶ a.	0417	0457	0619	0721	0819	0922	1019	1122	1219	1322	1419	1522	1619	1722	1819	1832	1921	...	2019	...	...	2250	...	2350
Füzesabony ..... ▶ d.	0419	0506	0623	0723	0823	0923	1023	1123	1223	1323	1423	1523	1623	1723	1823	1834	1922	...	2023	...	...	...	...	...
Vámosgyörk ⊡ ..... d.	0454	0542	0651	0751	0851	0951	1051	1151	1251	1351	1451	1551	1651	1751	1851	|	1955	...	2051	...	...	...	...	...
Hatvan ..... d.	0513	0602	0706	0806	0906	1006	1106	1206	1306	1406	1506	1606	1706	1806	1906	|	2010	...	2106	...	...	...	...	...
Budapest Keleti ..... ▶ a.	0620	0715	0800	0900	1000	1100	1200	1300	1400	1500	1600	1700	1800	1900	2000	2005	2105	...	2200	...	...	...	...	...

E – ⑤ (not June 27 - Aug. 29). *IC* train, 🅁, 2nd class.
G – ⑦ (not June 22 - Aug. 31). *Ex* train, 🅁.
k – To / from Fonyód or Keszthely on dates in Table **1220**.
▶ – For faster trains see Table **1260**.
△ – Until June 20 classified *IC* with 🅁.

⊡ – Connecting trains **Vámosgyörk - Gyöngyös** and v.v. (journey 16 mins):
From Vámosgyörk: 0522, 0610, 0708, 0908, 1108, 1308, 1408, 1508, 1608, 1708, 1908.
From Gyöngyös: 0546, 0633, 0732, 0932, 1132, 1332, 1432, 1532, 1632, 1732, 1932.

⊙ – Additional local trains **Füzesabony - Eger** and v.v. (journey 17 minutes):
From Füzesabony: 0420, 0504, 0604, 0650, 0704, 0808 and hourly to 1808, 2008, 2208, 2308.
From Eger: 0331, 0440, 0531, 0631, 0731, 0831 and hourly to 2231.

1262 HATVAN - SALGÓTARJÁN - SOMOSKÖÚJFALU

2nd class

km										n	
0	Hatvan ..... d.	0410	0610	0810	1010	1210	1410	1610	1810	2010	2210
59	Salgótarján ..... a.	0540	0740	0940	1140	1340	1540	1740	1940	2140	2340
65	Somosköújfalu 🛃 ..... a.	0551	0751	0951	1151	1351	1551	1751	1951	2151	2351

						⑦b				
Somosköújfalu 🛃 ..... d.	0617	0817	1017	1217	1417	1600	1617	1817	2017	221
Salgótarján ..... d.	0629	0829	1029	1229	1429	1612	1629	1829	2029	222
Hatvan ..... a.	0750	0950	1150	1350	1550	1728	1750	1950	2150	235

b – To Budapest Keleti, arrive 1840.
n – On ⑦ starts from Budapest Keleti (depart 1905).

Additional journeys: Hatvan to Somosköújfalu: 0510 Ⓐ, 0710 Ⓐ, 1310 Ⓐ, 1510 Ⓐ, 1910 Ⓐ.
Somosköújfalu to Hatvan: 0317, 0417, 0517 Ⓐ, 0717 Ⓐ, 1317 Ⓐ, 1517 Ⓐ.

1265 MISKOLC - KOŠICE

km		2	*EC* 532 R⊖	2	2	2	2	2	*EC* 536 H⊖	2
	Budapest Keleti **1260/1** ..... d.	...	0630	...	...	...	...	...	1830	...
	Füzesabony **1260/1** ..... d.	0602	0753	0802	1002	1202	1402	1602	1953	2002
0	**Miskolc** ..... d.	0707	0833	0907	1107	1307	1507	1707	2033	2107
61	Hidasnémeti ..... a.	0813	0927	1013	1213	1413	1613	1813	2127	2213
61	Hidasnémeti 🛃 ..... d.	...	0937	...	...	...	...	...	2137	...
87	**Košice** ..... a.	...	0958	...	...	...	...	...	2158	...

	2	*EC* 537 H⊖	2	2	2	2	2	*EC* 533 R⊖	2
Košice ..... d.	...	0602	...	...	...	...	...	1802	...
Hidasnémeti 🛃 ..... a.	...	0623	...	...	...	...	...	1823	...
Hidasnémeti ..... d.	0547	0633	0947	1147	1347	1547	1647	1833	214
Miskolc ..... a.	0653	0726	1053	1253	1453	1653	1753	1926	225
Füzesabony **1260/1** ..... a.	0750	0806	...	1350	1550	1750	1850	2006	235
Budapest Keleti **1260/1** ... a.	...	0930	...	...	...	...	...	2130	...

H – HERNÁD – 🚃12 and 🍷 Budapest - Miskolc - Košice and v.v.
R – RÁKÓCZI – 🚃12 Budapest - Miskolc - Košice and v.v.

⊖ – Compulsoty reservation for domestic journeys within Hungary.
Other local trains run Miskolc - Hidasnémeti.

 Supplements are payable for domestic journeys on EC, EN and IC trains

BUDAPEST - DEBRECEN - NYÍREGYHÁZA - ZÁHONY - CHOP 1270

For trains to / from Romania see Table **1275**

km		IC 569 [R] ◇	IC 650 [R] ◇	IC 622 [R]	IC 567 [R] ◇	IC 612 [R]	IC 652 [R] ◇	IC 604 [R]	IC 565 [R] ◇	IC 614 [R]	IC 654 [R] ◇	IC 624 [R]	IC 563 [R] ◇	IC 626 [R]	IC 616 [R]	IC 16 [R] T	IC 608 [R]		Debrecen - Záhony runs approx hourly (connections available from IC at Nyíregyháza).							
0	**Budapest** Nyugati .. ◧ d.	...	0623	0723	0823	0923	1023	1123	1223	1323	1423	1523	1623	1723	1823	1840k	1923	S	...	0508	0628	E	1628	1828	2028	2228
11	Köbánya Kispest .... ◧ d.	...	0637	0737	0837	0937	1037	1137	1237	1337	1437	1537	1637	1737	1837	|	1937	L	...	0523	0642	V	1642	1842	2042	2242
18	Ferihegy ✈ .... ◧ d.	...	0643	0743	0843	0943	1043	1143	1243	1343	1443	1543	1643	1743	1843	|	1943	O	...	0531	0648	E	1648	1848	2048	2248
73	Cegléd .... ◧ d.	...	0718	0818	0918	1018	1118	1218	1318	1418	1518	1618	1718	1818	1918	|	2018	W	...	0624	0724	R	1724	1924	2124	2324
100	**Szolnok** .... ◧ d.	...	0738	0838	0938	1038	1138	1238	1338	1438	1538	1638	1738	1838	1938	2003	2038	E	0550	0650	0750	Y	1750	1950	2150	2350
177	Püspökladány .... d.	...	0824	0924	1024	1124	1224	1324	1424	1524	1624	1724	1824	1924	2024	2102	2124	R	0655	0755	0855		1855	2055	2255	0055
201	Hajdúszoboszló .... d.	...	0839	0939	1039	1139	1239	1339	1439	1539	1639	1739	1839	1939	2039	2120	2139		0714	0814	0914	2	1914	2114	2314	0114
221	**Debrecen** .... a.	...	0852	0952	1052	1152	1252	1352	1452	1552	1652	1752	1852	1952	2052	2134	2152	T	0729	0829	0929		1929	2129	2329	0129
221	**Debrecen** .... d.	0650	0854	0954	1054	1154	1254	1354	1454	1554	1654	1757	1854	1954	2054	2135	2154	R	0734	0834	0934	H	1934	2137	...	...
270	**Nyíregyháza** .... a.	0720	0924	1024	1124	1224	1324	1424	1524	1624	1724	1827	1924	2024	2124	2207	2224	A	0816	0916	1016	O	2016	2219	...	...
270	**Nyíregyháza** .... d.	*0748*	...	1031	...	...	...	...	...	1631	...	1831	...	2031r	...	2209	...	I	0848	0948	1048	U	2048	2248	...	...
313	Kisvárda .... d.	*0832*	...	1102	...	...	...	...	...	1702	...	1902	...	2102r	...	2240	...	N	0932	1032	1132	R	2132	2332	...	...
335	Záhony 🏛 .... ▶ a.	*0857*	...	1121	...	...	...	...	...	1721	...	1921	...	2121r	...	2258	...	S	0957	1057	1157	S	2157	2357	...	...
341	**Chop** 🏛 .... ⊙ ▶ a.	...	...	...	...	...	...	...	...	...	...	...	...	...	...	0113	...		...	...	...		...	...	...	...

	IC 609 [R]	IC 627 [R]	IC 560 [R] ◇	IC 15 [R] T	IC 659 [R] ◇	IC 607 [R]	IC 657 [R] ◇	IC 605 [R]	IC 564 [R] ◇	IC 615 [R]	IC 655 [R] ◇	IC 623 [R]	IC 566 [R] ◇	IC 621 [R]	IC 621 [R] ⑦	IC 653 [R] ◇	IC 568 [R] ◇		Záhony - Debrecen runs approx hourly (connections available into IC at Nyíregyháza).							
Chop 🏛 .... ⊙ ▶ d.	...	...	...	0540	...	...	...	...	...	...	...	...	...	...	...	...	...	S	...	...	...	...		...	...	...
Záhony 🏛 .... ▶ d.	...	0528	...	0632	...	...	...	...	...	...	...	1440	...	...	1627	...	...	L	...	...	...	0603	E	1603	1703	2003
Kisvárda .... d.	...	0547	...	0651	...	...	...	...	...	...	...	1459	...	...	1646	...	...	O	...	...	...	0628	V	1628	1728	2028
Nyíregyháza .... a.	...	0618	...	0724	...	...	...	...	...	...	...	1530	...	...	1717	...	...	W	...	...	...	0712	E	1712	1812	2112
Nyíregyháza .... d.	0532	0623	0732	0740	0832	0932	1032	1132	1232	1332	1432	1532	1632	1732	1732	1832	2032	E	...	...	0544	0744	R	1744	1844	2144
Debrecen .... a.	0602	0656	0802	0812	0902	1002	1102	1202	1302	1402	1502	1602	1702	1802	1802	1902	2102	R	...	...	0626	0826	Y	1826	1926	2226
Debrecen .... d.	0604	0704	0804	0816	0904	1004	1104	1204	1304	1404	1504	1604	1704	1804	1804	1904	...		0236	0409	0631	0831		1831	1931	▬
Hajdúszoboszló .... d.	0618	0718	0818	0831	0918	1018	1118	1218	1318	1418	1518	1618	1718	1818	1818	1918	...	T	0252	0425	0647	0847	2	1847	1947	...
Püspökladány .... d.	0634	0734	0834	0848	0934	1034	1134	1234	1334	1434	1534	1634	1734	1834	1834	1934	...	R	0313	0453	0708	0908		1908	2008	2
Szolnok .... ◧ d.	0722	0822	0922	0957	1022	1122	1222	1322	1422	1522	1622	1722	1822	1922	1922	2022	...	A	0425	0605	0815	1015	H	2015	2115	2225
Cegléd .... ◧ d.	0743	0843	0943	|	1043	1143	1243	1343	1443	1543	1643	1743	1843	1943	1943	2043	...	I	0448	0628	0838	1038	O	2038	2148	2248
Ferihegy ✈ .... ◧ d.	0815	0915	1015	|	1115	1215	1315	1415	1515	1615	1715	1815	1915	2015	2015	2115	...	N	0535	0715	0910	1110	U	2110	2240	2340
Köbánya Kispest .... ◧ a.	0820	0920	1020	|	1120	1220	1320	1420	1520	1620	1720	1820	1920	2020	2020	2120	...	S	0540	0720	0915	1115	R	2115	2248	2348
Budapest Nyugati .. ◧ a.	0837	0937	1037	1120k	1137	1237	1337	1437	1537	1637	1737	1837	1937	2037	2037	2137	...		0557	0737	0932	1132	S	2132	2305	0005

T – TISZA – 2 Budapest - Záhony and v.v.; 2 Záhony - Chop and v.v. 🛏 2 cl. Budapest - Kyïv / Moskva and v.v. (Table **97**); 🛏 2 cl. Beograd - Budapest - Moskva and v.v. (Table **97**). Conveys twice weekly in summer 🛏 2 cl. Bar - Beograd - Budapest - Moskva and v.v. (Table **1360**), 🛏 2 cl. Split / Koper - Zagreb - Budapest - Moskva and v.v. (Table **97**).

k – Budapest **Keleti**.

r – ⑤ only.

⊙ – Ukrainian (East European) time, one hour ahead of Hungarian time.

◧ – Also **1290** Budapest - Cegléd; **1280** Budapest - Szolnok. Ferihegy ✈ is served by 5 - 6 trains per hour.

◇ – To / from Miskolc, Table **1260** (most trains continue beyond Miskolc to / from Budapest Keleti).

▶ – Full service Záhony - Chop (2nd class):

						T							T
Záhony ... d.	0630	0815	1140	1532	2015	2356	Chop . ⊙ d.	0540	0827	1025	1408	1725	2220
Chop .. ⊙ a.	0748	0933	1258	1650	2133	0113	Záhony ... a.	0457	0745	0943	1326	1643	2138

BUDAPEST - BIHARKERESZTES - ORADEA 1275

km		2	IC* 367 H [R]	2	IC* 363 B [R]	2	2	IC* 365 A [R]	407 C [R]	2
0	**Budapest Keleti** .... ▷ d.	...	0640	...	0940	...	...	1440	1740	...
100	Szolnok .... ▷ d.	...	0804	...	1104	...	...	1604	1903	...
177	Püspökladány .... ▷ d.	0633	0910	1110	1210	1410	1610	1710	2010	2128
228	Biharkeresztes .... a.	0723	0958	1157	1258	1502	1656	1800	2059	2215
228	Biharkeresztes 🏛 .... d.	...	1023	...	1324	...	...	1824	2124	...
241	Episcopia Bihor 🏛 .... ⊙ a.	...	1138	...	1439	...	...	1939	2239	...
241	Episcopia Bihor .... ⊙ d.	...	1155	...	1500	...	...	1957	2256	...
247	**Oradea** .... ⊙ a.	...	1203	...	1508	...	...	2005	2304	...
	Cluj Napoca **1612** .... ⊙ a.	...	1437	...	1800	...	...	2246	0136	...

	406 C [R]	2	IC* 364 A [R]	2	IC* 366 H [R]	2	2	IC* 362 B [R]	2
Cluj Napoca **1612** .... ⊙ d.	0213	...	0720	...	1012	...	...	1507	...
Oradea .... ⊙ d.	0453	...	0957	...	1252	...	...	1751	...
Episcopia Bihor .... ⊙ a.	0501	...	1004	...	1300	...	...	1759	...
Episcopia Bihor 🏛 .... ⊙ d.	0521	...	1020	...	1320	...	...	1820	...
Biharkeresztes 🏛 .... a.	0436	...	0935	...	1235	...	...	1735	...
Biharkeresztes .... d.	0501	0646	1001	1200	1300	1504	1700	1802	1956
Püspökladány .... ▷ a.	0550	0736	1050	1247	1347	1551	1747	1848	2046
Szolnok .... ▷ a.	0657	...	1157	...	1457	...	...	1957	...
Budapest Keleti .... ▷ a.	0820	...	1320	...	1620	...	...	2120	...

A – ADY ENDRE – 12 🍷 Budapest - Cluj Napoca and v.v.

B – BIHAR – 12 🍷 Budapest - Cluj Napoca and v.v.

C – CORONA – 🛏 1, 2 cl., ▬ 2 cl., 12 🍷 Budapest - Cluj Napoca - Deda - Brasov and v.v.

H – HARGITA – 12 🍷 Budapest - Cluj Napoca - Deda - Brasov and v.v.; 2 Budapest - Cluj Napoca - Târgu Mures and v.v.

⊙ – Romanian (East European) time.

▷ – For connections see Table **1270**.

* – Classified *IC* in Hungary, *IR* in Romania.

2nd class DEBRECEN and NYÍREGYHÁZA - MÁTÉSZALKA 1276

km									△			Ⓑ
0	**Debrecen** .... d.	0508	0715	0915	1115	1315	1515	1715	1807	1920	2115	2246
58	Nyírbátor .... d.	0632	0832	1032	1232	1432	1632	1832	1908	2035	2232	0000
78	**Mátészalka** ...... a.	0656	0856	1056	1256	1456	1656	1856	1927	2058	2256	0024

			▽								
Mátészalka .... d.	0413	0458	0530	0703	0903	1103	1303	1503	1703	1900	2103
Nyírbátor .... d.	0437	0522	0551	0727	0927	1127	1327	1527	1727	1929	2127
Debrecen .... a.	0553	0635	0652	0840	1040	1240	1442	1642	1847	2045	2240

km		⚒				⚒	⑦					
0	**Nyíregyháza** .... d.	0530	...	0837	...	1437	1437	...	1637	...	...	...
38	Nyírbátor .... d.	0704	...	0959	...	1559	1559	...	1759	...	...	...
58	**Mátészalka** ...... a.	0728	...	1021	...	1621	1633	...	1821	...	...	...

		▽									
Mátészalka .... d.	...	0530	...	...	0734	...	1534	...	1725	...	...
Nyírbátor .... d.	...	0550	0553	...	0758	...	1558	...	1758	...	...
Nyíregyháza .. a.	...	...	0711	...	0922	...	1722	...	1916	...	...

△ – *IC* **624 / 638** from Budapest Nyugati, depart 1523, [R].

▽ – *IC* **639 / 627** to Budapest Nyugati, arrive 0937, [R].

DEBRECEN - ORADEA and BAIA MARE and other cross-border services 1277

km		6822 2	6814 2	6816 2
0	**Debrecen** .... d.	0912	1112	1512
30	Nyirábrány 🏛 .... a.	0951	1151	1551
39	Valea lui Mihai 🏛 . ⊙ a.	1123	1323	1723
39	Valea lui Mihai ...... ⊙ d.	1138	1338	1757
105	**Oradea** .... ⊙ a.	|	1456	|
70	Carei .... **1618** ⊙ a.	1214	...	1833
106	Satu Mare.... **1618** ⊙ a.	1258	...	1922
165	**Baia Mare** ... **1616** ⊙ a.	...	...	2212

	6817 2	6813 2	6811 2
Baia Mare ... **1616** ⊙ d.	0414	...	...
Satu Mare.... **1618** ⊙ d.	0620	1500	...
Carei........... **1618** ⊙ d.	0707	1544	...
Oradea .... ⊙ d.	|	|	1639
Valea lui Mihai ...... ⊙ a.	0745	1619	1821
Valea lui Mihai 🏛.. ⊙ d.	0837	1637	1837
Nyirábrány 🏛............ d.	0809	1609	1809
Debrecen .... a.	0848	1648	1848

km		2	2	
0	**Békéscsaba** .. **1280** d.	0639	1548	...
16	Gyula .... **1280** d.	0659	1606	...
36	Kötegyán 🏛 .... a.	0727	1633	...
50	**Salonta** 🏛 .... ⊙ a.	0900	1805	...

	2	2	
Salonta 🏛 .... ⊙ d.	0940	1830	...
Kötegyán 🏛 .... d.	0913	1813	...
Gyula .... **1280** d.	0948	1852	...
Békéscsaba .. **1280** a.	1008	1908	...

km		2	2	
0	**Mátészalka** .... d.	0535	1410	...
18	Tiborszállás 🏛 .... a.	0605	1440	...
18	Tiborszállás 🏛 .... d.	0620	1501	...
33	**Carei** .... ⊙ a.	0746	1627	...

	2	2	
Carei .... ⊙ d.	0927	1738	...
Tiborszállás 🏛........ a.	0853	1704	...
Tiborszállás 🏛........ d.	0908	1719	...
Mátészalka .... a.	0952	1803	...

– To Záhony, arrive 1853.

⊙ – Romanian (East European) time, one hour ahead of Hungarian time.

2nd class DEBRECEN - FÜZESABONY 1278

km										Ⓑ	
0	**Debrecen** .... d.	0450	0645	0845	1045	1245	1445	1645	1850	2000	2245
42	Hortobágy .... d.	0536	0736	0936	1136	1336	1536	1736	1936	2050	2331
73	Tiszafüred .... d.	0611	0811	1011	1211	1411	1611	1811	2011	2124	0005
103	**Füzesabony** .... a.	0644	0844	1044	1244	1444	1644	1844	2044	...	...

									Ⓑ	
Füzesabony .... d.	0502	0702	0902	1102	1302	1502	1702	1902	2102	2202
Tiszafüred .... d.	0536	0736	0936	1136	1336	1536	1736	1936	2135	2235
Hortobágy .... d.	0616	0816	1016	1216	1416	1616	1816	2016	...	...
Debrecen .... a.	0700	0900	1100	1300	1500	1700	1904	2100	...	...

ost journeys run Mátészalka (Table **1276**) - Debrecen - Füzesabony and v.v.

1280 BUDAPEST - BÉKÉSCSABA - LÖKÖSHÁZA - ARAD (- BUCURESTI)

km																							
					*IC**		*IC**		*IC*				*IC*		*IC**			*IC*	*IC*	*EN•*			•
				7400	**73**	**7402**	**373**	**7404**	**732**	**1471**	**1481**	**7304**	**734**	**7306**	**79**	**1696**	**7406**	**736**	**748**	**473**	**17408**		**347**
		2	2	2	[R]	2	[R]	2	2[R]			2	2[R]	2	[R]	[R]	2	2[R]	2[R]	[R]	2		[R]
		Ⓐ			T		R			N	A				K	Y				S	⑤		D
0	**Budapest** Keleti **1270** d.	...	...	0610	0710	0810	0910	1010	1110	1110	1110	1210	1310	1410	1510	...	1610	1710	1810	1910	2010	...	2330
100	Szolnok **1270** d.	0445	0545	0734	0834	0934	1034	1134	1234	1234	1234	1334	1434	1534	1634	...	1734	1834	1934	2034	2134	...	0055
141	Mezőtúr d.	0525	0625	0800	0900	1000	1100	1200	1300	1300	1300	1400	1500	1600	1700	...	1800	1900	2000	2100	2200	...	|
159	Gyoma d.	0547	0647	0813	0913	1013	1113	1213	1313	1313	1313	1413	1513	1613	1713	...	1813	1913	2013	2113	2213	...	|
196	**Békéscsaba** a.	0619	0719	0839	0939	1039	1139	1239	1339	1339	1339	1439	1539	1639	1739	...	1839	1939	2039	2139	2239	...	0152
196	**Békéscsaba** d.	0637	...	...	0944	...	1144	...	1344	1344	1344	1441	1541	1641	1744	...	...	1944	...	2144	...	...	0155
225	Lökösháza a.	0710	...	...	1006	...	1206	...	1406	1406	1406	1510	1610	1710	1810	...	...	2006	...	2206	...	...	0215
225	Lökösháza 🛃 d.	...	...	...	1035	...	1231	...	...	1432	1432	...	...	...	1835	...	...	...	...	2231	...	...	0240
236	Curtici 🛃 ⊙ d.	...	...	...	1210	...	1404	...	...	1612	1612	...	...	...	2008	...	...	...	...	0006	...	...	0420
253	**Arad** ⊙ a.	...	...	...	1231	...	1426	...	...	1634	1634	...	...	...	2030	...	...	...	...	0028	...	...	0442
	Timisoara **1614** ⊙ a.	...	...	...	1326	...	|	...	...	...	...	...	...	...	2123	2210	...	...	...	|	...	...	|
	Brasov **1600** ⊙ a.	...	...	...	|	...	2235	...	...	...	...	...	...	...	...	|	...	...	...	0934	...	...	1331
	Bucuresti Nord **1600** ⊙ a.	...	...	...	2245	...	...	...	...	...	...	...	...	...	...	0730	...	...	...	1210	...	...	1605

	•			*EN•*	*IC*			*IC**		*IC*		*IC*				*IC**		*IC**	*IC*		*IC*		
	346		**7309**	**472**	**739**	**7409**	**1695**	**78**	**7407**	**737**	**7405**	**735**	**7403**	**1470**	**1480**	**372**		**72**	**733**	**7301**	**731**		
	[R]		2	[R]	2[R]	2	[R]	[R]	2	2[R]	2	2[R]	2			[R]		[R]	2[R]	2	2[R]	2	2
	D			S			Y	K						N	A	R		T				④⑦	
Bucuresti Nord **1600** ⊙ d.	1300	...	...	1730	...	...	2145	...	...	...	...	...	...	...	...	...	...	0545	...	...	...	...	...
Brasov **1600** ⊙ d.	1537	...	...	2008	...	...	|	...	...	...	...	...	...	...	...	0600	...	|	...	...	...	...	...
Timisoara **1614** ⊙ d.	|	...	...	|	...	...	0702	0730	...	...	...	...	...	...	...	|	...	1425	...	...	...	...	...
Arad ⊙ d.	0104	...	...	0520	...	...	...	0825	...	...	...	...	...	1232	1232	1427	...	1521	...	...	...	...	...
Curtici 🛃 ⊙ a.	0124	...	...	0546	...	...	...	0847	...	...	...	...	...	1252	1252	1450	...	1543	...	...	...	...	...
Lökösháza 🛃 a.	0100	...	...	0525	...	...	...	0825	...	...	...	...	...	1229	1229	1414	...	1525	...	...	...	...	...
Lökösháza d.	0130	...	0455	0550	0650	...	...	0850	...	1050	...	1250	...	1315	1315	1450	...	1550	1650	1750	1850	...	...
Békéscsaba a.	0150	...	0517	0612	0712	...	...	0912	...	1112	...	1312	...	1335	1335	1512	...	1612	1712	1812	1912	...	...
Békéscsaba d.	0155	...	0530	0620	0720	0820	...	0920	1020	1120	1220	1320	1420	1420	1420	1520	...	1620	1720	1820	1920	2040	...
Gyoma d.	|	...	0559	0647	0747	0847	...	0947	1047	1147	1247	1347	1447	1447	1447	1547	...	1647	1747	1847	1947	2113	...
Mezőtúr d.	|	...	0614	0700	0800	0900	...	1000	1100	1200	1300	1400	1500	1500	1500	1600	...	1700	1800	1900	2000	2136	...
Szolnok **1270** d.	0257	...	0649	0727	0827	0927	...	1027	1127	1227	1327	1427	1527	1527	1527	1627	...	1727	1827	1927	2027	2215	2219
Budapest Keleti **1270** a.	0440	...	0815	0850	0950	1050	...	1150	1250	1350	1450	1550	1650	1650	1650	1750	...	1850	1950	2050	2150	...	0015

A – ALBENA – from Budapest ⑥ June 14 - Sept. 13 (next day from Varna): 🛏 1, 2 cl., ▬ 2 cl., (2) and ✕ Budapest - Craiova - Ruse - Varna and v.v.
D – DACIA – 🛏 1, 2 cl., ▬ 2 cl., (2) and 🍸 Wien - Budapest - Arad - Sighisoara - Brasov - Bucuresti and v.v.; (2) Budapest - Bucuresti and v.v.; (2) Budpaest - Lökösháza and v.v.
K – KÖRÖS / CRIS – (12) and 🍸 Budapest - Arad - Timisoara and v.v.
N – NESEBAR – from Budapest ②⑤ June 13 - Sept. 12 (next day from Burgas): 🛏 1, 2 cl., ▬ 2 cl., (2) and 🍸 Budapest - Craiova - Ruse - Burgas and v.v.
R – TRANSSYLVANIA – (12) ✕ Budapest - Arad - Simeria - Sibiu - Brasov and v.v.
S – ISTER – (12) Budapest - Lökösháza and v.v.; 🛏 1, 2 cl., ▬ 2 cl., (2) and 🍸 Budapest - Arad - Sigisoara - Brasov - Bucuresti and v.v.
T – TRAIANUS – (12) and 🍸 Budapest - Timisoara - Bucuresti and v.v.
Y – 🛏 1, 2 cl., ▬ 2 cl. and (12) Bucuresti - Timisoara and v.v.

b – Not ⑤.
s – To / from Szeged (Table **1292**).
⊙ – Romanian (East European) time.
• – Classified *IC* in Romania.
* – Classified *IR* in Romania.

Note: *IC* trains on this line have designated carriages for the use of passengers without seat reservations.

BÉKÉSCSABA - GYULA

2nd class. Journey 17 - 20 minutes

From **Békéscsaba**: 0522, 0639, 0748, 0948, 1148, 1248, 1348, 1425 Ⓐ, 1448, 1548, 1617 ⑦ **s**, 1648, 1748, 1948, 2048, 2230 **b**, 2243 ⑤.

From **Gyula**: 0458, 0548, 0618 Ⓐ, 0658, 0748, 0852, 0948, 1052, 1248, 1448, 1548, 1648, 1728 ⑦ **s**, 1748, 1852, 1948, 2048.

1290 BUDAPEST - KECSKEMÉT - SZEGED

km										
			IC	*IC*	*IC*		*IC*	*IC*		
		7010	**710**	**760**	**702**		**756**	**766**	**7008**	**7108**
		2	[R]	[R]	[R]		[R]	[R]		
0	**Budapest** Nyugati § d.	0405	0553	0653	0753		1753	1853	1953	2053
11	Köbánya Kispest § d.	0420	0607	0707	0807	and	1807	1907	2007	2107
18	Ferihegy ✈ § d.	0428	0613	0713	0813	hourly	1813	1913	2013	2113
73	Cegléd § d.	0531	0648	0748	0848	until	1848	1948	2048	2148
106	**Kecskemét** d.	0605	0711	0811	0911		1911	2011	2111	2213
131	Kiskunfélegyháza d.	0630	0730	0830	0930		1930	2030	2130	2230
191	**Szeged** a.	0715	0815	0915	1015		2015	2115	2215	2319

		IC	*IC*	*IC*		*IC*	*IC*	*IC*	
	7009	**709**	**719**	**707**		**753**	**763**	**701**	**7001**
	2	[R]	[R]	[R]		[R]	[R]	[R]	2
Szeged d.	0436	0547	0645	0745		1745	1845	1945	2045
Kiskunfélegyháza d.	0523	0631	0731	0831	and	1831	1931	2031	2131
Kecskemét d.	0539	0648	0748	0848	hourly	1848	1948	2048	2147
Cegléd § d.	0608	0713	0813	0913	until	1913	2013	2113	2218
Ferihegy ✈ § a.	0654	0744	0844	0944		1944	2044	2144	2250
Köbánya Kispest § a.	0700	0750	0850	0950		1950	2050	2150	2256
Budapest Nyugati § a.	0717	0807	0907	1007		2007	2107	2207	2312

§ – For additional trains see Table **1270**.

Note : *IC* trains on this line have designated carriages for the use of passengers without seat reservations.

1292 SZEGED - BÉKÉSCSABA

2nd class

km										
0	**Szeged** d.	0521	0621	0721	and	1721	1821	1921	2021	2221
31	Hódmezövásárhely d.	0601	0705	0801	hourly	1801	1905	2001	2105	2259
62	Orosháza d.	0631	0731	0831	until	1831	1931	2031	2133	2327
97	**Békéscsaba** a.	0712	0810	0910	△	1910	2010	2110	...	...

									z		
Békéscsaba d.	0547	0647	and	1347	1445	1547	1645	1747	1847	1947
Orosháza d.	0632	0732	hourly	1432	1532	1632	1732	1832	1932	2032
Hódmezövásárhely d.	0702	0802	until	1502	1602	1702	1802	1902	2002	2102
Szeged a.	0740	0840		1540	1640	1740	1840	1940	2040	2140

z – Starts from Gyula on ⑦ (Table **1280**).

△ – The 1421 from Szeged continues to Gyula on ⑦ (Table **1280**).

1295 BUDAPEST - KISKUNHALAS - KELEBIA

km											
						EC					
			790	**7900**	**792**	**273**	**794**	**796**	**798**		**341**
		2	2	2	2	A	2	2	2	2	B
0	**Budapest Keleti** d.	...	0605	0805	1005	1305	1405	1605	1805	1932r	2220
61	Kunszentmiklós-Tass d.	0510	0709	0909	1109	1359	1506	1709	1909	2050	2314
107	Kiskörös d.	0601	0801	1001	1201	1445	1601	1801	2001	2138	2358
134	Kiskunhalas a.	0633	0833	1033	1233	1515	1633	1833	2033	2209	0027
163	**Kelebia** 🛃 a.	0711	0911	1111	1311	1550	1711	1911	2111	...	0058
	Beograd **1360** a.	...	...	...	...	2050	...	...	...	...	0632

						EC			
	340	**7909**	**799**	**797**	**795**	**272**	**793**	**7903**	**791**
	B	2	2	2	2	A	2	2	2
Beograd **1360** d.	2145	...	...	...	...	0645	...	...	...
Kelebia 🛃 d.	0321	0448	0646	0846	1046	1210	1446	1646	1846
Kiskunhalas d.	0350	0525	0725	0925	1125	1241	1525	1725	1925
Kiskörös d.	0421	0600	0800	1000	1200	1312	1600	1800	2000
Kunszentmiklós-Tass d.	0505	0649	0850	1050	1250	1359	1650	1850	2050
Budapest Keleti a.	0604	0758	0954	1154	1354	1454	1754	1954	2154

A – AVALA – (12) and 🍸 Praha - Budapest - Beograd and v.v. ([R] for passengers joining at Beograd); 🛏 1, 2 cl. Moskva - Budapest - Beograd and v.v. For summer Praha / Budapest / Moskva - Bar and v.v. see Tables **1360/70**.

B – BEOGRAD – 🛏 1, 2 cl., ▬ 2 cl., (2) Budapest - Beograd and v.v.; (2) Budapest Kelebia and v.v. Conveys on ①④ June 19 - Aug. 28 ▬ 2 cl. Budapest - Skopje and v.v

r – Köbánya Kispest.

1299 OTHER LOCAL SERVICES

2nd class

BUDAPEST - DUNAÚJVÁROS — *80* km, journey 85 - 90 minutes

From **Budapest** Déli: 0555, 0655, 0855, 1055, 1255, 1355, 1455, 1555, 1655, 1855, 2055.

From **Dunaújváros**: 0332, 0432, 0532, 0632, 0732, 0832, 1037, 1232, 1437, 1537, 1637, 1732, 1837, 2032, 2237.

BUDAPEST - ESZTERGOM — *53 km*, journey 90 minutes

Due to track reconstruction the rail service is replaced by 🚌 until further notice, departing from Budapest Árpád hid bus station hourly 0435 - 2335, returning from Esztergom hourly 0301 - 2201. Journey by 🚌 takes 1 hour 25 minutes.

BUDAPEST - SZENTENDRE — *21 km*, journey time 41 minutes

HÉV suburban trains from Budapest Batthyány tér, every 20 - 30 minutes.

ESZTERGOM - KOMÁROM — *53 km*, journey time 90 minutes

From **Esztergom**: 0656, 1642. From **Komárom**: 0519, 1431.

EGER - SZILVÁSVÁRAD — *34 km*, journey time 65 minute

From **Eger**: 0445 Ⓐ, 0900 **E**, 1400 Ⓐ, 1500 **F**, 1750 Ⓐ.

From **Szilvásvárad**: 0555 Ⓐ, 1135 **G**, 1340 **F**, 1555 Ⓐ, 1755 Ⓒ, 1900 Ⓐ.

Via Szilvásvárad-Szalajkavölgy (for the forest railway), 5 minutes before Szilvásvárad.

HATVAN - SZOLNOK — *68 km*, journey 71 - 73 minute

From **Hatvan**: Ⓐ: hourly 0513 - 2213 (not 0913). Ⓒ: every 2 hours 0613 - 2213.

From **Szolnok**: Ⓐ: hourly 0431 - 2131 (not 0931). Ⓒ: every 2 hours 0431 - 2031, also 213

KISKUNFÉLEGYHÁZA - CSONGRÁD - SZENTES — *39 km*, journey time 53 minute

From **Kiskunfélegyháza**: 0534 Ⓐ, 0734, 0934, 1334, 1534, 1734, 1934, 2134.

From **Szentes**: 0428 Ⓐ, 0634, 0834, 1234, 1434, 1634, 1834 (calls Csongrád 18 mins later

E – ⑤–⑦ (daily Apr. 18 - Oct. 26).
F – Ⓒ Apr. 19 - Oct. 26.
G – ⑤ (Ⓐ Apr. 22 - Oct. 22).

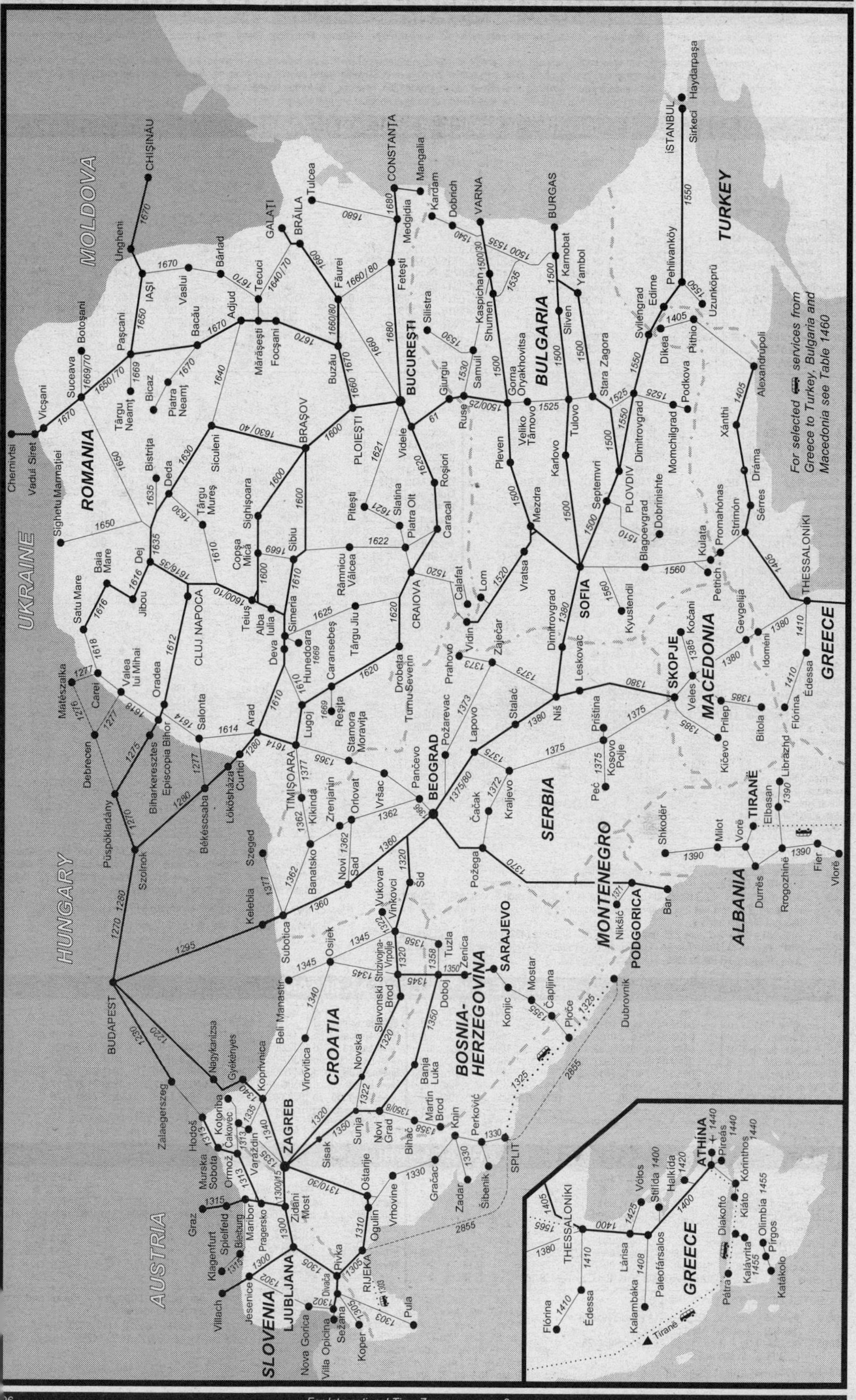

UKRAINE
MOLDOVA
ROMANIA
HUNGARY
AUSTRIA
SLOVENIA
CROATIA
BOSNIA-HERZEGOVINA
SERBIA
MONTENEGRO
BULGARIA
MACEDONIA
ALBANIA
GREECE
TURKEY
CHIŞINĂU
BUCUREŞTI
BUDAPEST
BEOGRAD
ZAGREB
LJUBLJANA
SARAJEVO
SOFIA
SKOPJE
TIRANË
PODGORICA
İSTANBUL
THESSALONÍKI
ATHÍNA
For selected services from Greece to Turkey, Bulgaria and Macedonia see Table 1460

SLOVENIA, CROATIA and BOSNIA-HERZEGOVINA

Operators: Slovenske Železnice (SŽ): www.slo-zeleznice.si; Hrvatske Železnice (HŽ): www.hznet.hr; Železnice Federacije Bosne i Hercegovine (ŽFBH): www.zfbh.ba; and Željeznice Republike Srpske (ŽRS): www.zrs-rs.com.

Services: All trains convey first and second class seating, **except** where shown otherwise in footnotes or by '2' in the train column, or where the footnote shows sleeping and / or couchette cars only. Descriptions of sleeping (🛏) and couchette (▬) cars appear on page 8. In Slovenia, travel by *ICS* train requires reservation and payment of a special fare.

Timings: Valid until **December 13, 2014** except where indicated otherwise. Readers should note, however, that further changes are possible.

Tickets: A supplement is payable for travel by internal express trains. Reservation of seats is possible on most express trains.

1300 VILLACH - JESENICE - LJUBLJANA - ZAGREB
SŽ, HŽ, ÖBB

km						499					415												EC 211		631		
		2 Ⓐ	2 Ⓐ	2		♦	2	2	2 Ⓐ	2 Ⓐ	♦	2 Ⓐ	2 Ⓐ	2 Ⓒ	2 Ⓐ		2	2 Ⓐ	2 Ⓐ	2 Ⓐ	2 Ⓐ	2 Ⓐ	✕ ♦	2 Ⓐ	2 Ⓐ	2	2
	München Hbf **890** d.	...	...	...	...	2340	...	...	...	...	...	...	...	...	...	...	...	...	...	...	...	...	...	...	...	...	...
	Salzburg Hbf **970** d.	...	...	...	...	0134	...	...	...	...	...	...	...	...	...	...	...	...	...	...	...	...	...	...	...	...	...
0	**Villach** Hbf d.	...	...	...	...	0415	...	...	...	...	0625	...	...	...	...	...	...	...	...	...	...	...	1253	...	...	...	...
38	**Jesenice** 🏛 a.	...	...	...	...	0455	...	...	...	...	0705	...	...	...	...	...	...	...	...	...	...	...	1333	...	...	...	...
38	**Jesenice 1302** d.	...	0433	...	...	0505	0531	...	0605	0625	0715	0733	...	0754	...	...	...	...	1105	...	...	1235	1340	...	...	1418	...
51	Lesce-Bled d.	...	0447	...	...	0518	0546	...	0620	0640	0731	0747	...	0813	...	...	...	...	1119	...	...	1249	1351	...	...	1435	...
74	Kranj d.	...	0510	...	...	0539	0611	...	0647	0708	0752	0814	...	0838	...	...	...	...	1143	...	...	1321	1411	...	...	1500	...
102	**Ljubljana** a.	...	0539	...	...	0559	0644	...	0722	0744	0811	0849	...	0907	...	...	...	...	1214	...	...	1352	1431	...	...	1531	...
102	**Ljubljana 1315** d.	0450	...	0555	...	0635	...	0650	...	...	0825	...	0853	...	0950	...	*1050*	1150	...	*1250*	*1350*	...	1445	1450	1535	...	1545
166	Zidani Most **1315** d.	0600	...	0659	...	0728	...	0755	...	...	0916	...	1000	...	1100	...	1155	1255	...	1400	1500	...	1540	1601	1634	...	1700
182	Sevnica **1315** d.	0620	...	0718	...	0744	...	0814	...	...	0932	...	1019	...	1119	...	1214	1315	...	1420	1520	...	1556	1621	1650	...	1719
215	Dobova **1315** 🏛 d.	0650	...	0748	...	0821	...	0844	...	...	1012	...	1050	...	1148	...	1243	1344	...	1450	1549	...	1641	1651	1720	...	1749
245	**Zagreb 1315** a.	...	...	...	...	0853	...	...	...	...	1044	...	...	...	...	...	...	...	...	...	...	...	1713	...	...	...	...
	Beograd **1320** a.	...	...	...	...	...	...	...	...	...	1732	...	...	...	...	...	...	...	...	...	...	...	...	...	...	...	...

				EC 213						
	2 Ⓐ	2 Ⓑ	2	♦	2	2	2	2 N	2 Ⓐ	
München Hbf **890** d.	...	...	...	1218	...	...	...	...	...	...
Salzburg Hbf **970** d.	...	...	...	1412	...	...	...	...	...	...
Villach Hbf d.	...	...	...	1653	...	...	...	...	...	...
Jesenice 🏛 a.	...	...	...	1733	...	...	...	...	...	...
Jesenice 1302 d.	1531	...	...	1740	...	1805	1910	2020	...	...
Lesce-Bled d.	1545	...	...	1751	...	1819	1924	2035	...	...
Kranj d.	1623	...	...	1812	...	1846	1951	2101	...	...
Ljubljana a.	1652	...	...	1831	...	1920	2022	2134	...	...
Ljubljana 1315 d.	...	1650	1755	1835	1855	...	...	...	2205	...
Zidani Most **1315** d.	...	1800	1903	1927	2000	...	...	...	2309	...
Sevnica **1315** d.	...	1819	1920	1942	2020	...	...	...	2327	...
Dobova **1315** 🏛 d.	...	1848	1949	2021	2049	...	...	...	2356	...
Zagreb 1315 a.	...	...	...	2053	...	...	...	...	...	...
Beograd **1320** a.	...	...	...	...	...	...	...	...	...	...

					630			632				EC 212	
	2 Ⓐ	2	2 Ⓐ	2	2 Ⓐ	2 Ⓒ N		2 Ⓐ	2	2 Ⓐ	2	♦	2
Beograd **1320** d.	...	...	...	...	...	...	...	...	...	...	...	...	...
Zagreb 1315 d.	...	...	...	...	...	...	...	...	...	...	...	0650	...
Dobova **1315** 🏛 d.	...	...	...	...	0450	...	...	0542	0600	...	0705	0738	...
Sevnica **1315** d.	...	0413	...	0500	0525	...	...	0610	0630	...	0736	0802	...
Zidani Most **1315** d.	...	0431	...	0520	0545	...	...	0627	0700	...	0755	0818	...
Ljubljana 1315 a.	...	0534	...	0626	0642	...	...	0720	0803	...	0902	0906	...
Ljubljana d.	0437	...	0610	...	...	0655	...	...	...	0819	...	0922	0945
Kranj d.	0510	...	0647	...	...	0725	...	...	...	0850	...	0942	1016
Lesce-Bled d.	0546	...	0712	...	...	0755	...	...	...	0914	...	1002	1040
Jesenice 1302 a.	0600	...	0725	...	...	0812	...	...	...	0927	...	1014	1053
Jesenice 🏛 d.	...	...	...	...	...	...	...	...	...	...	...	1017	...
Villach Hbf a.	...	...	...	...	...	...	...	...	...	...	...	1058	...
Salzburg Hbf **970** a.	...	...	...	...	...	...	...	...	...	...	...	1348	...
München Hbf **890** a.	...	...	...	...	...	...	...	...	...	...	...	1541	...

									EC 210														414			498	
	2 Ⓐ	2	2	2 Ⓐ	2 Ⓐ	2 ⑤y	2	2	✕ ♦	2	2 Ⓐ	2 Ⓐ	2 Ⓐ		2	2 Ⓐ	2	2	2 Ⓑ	2 Ⓐ	2	2	♦	2 Ⓑ	2 Ⓑ	♦	
Beograd **1320** d.	...	...	...	...	...	...	...	...	...	...	...	...	...	...	...	...	...	...	...	...	...	...	1100	...	...	...	...
Zagreb 1315 d.	...	...	...	...	...	...	...	...	1235	...	...	...	...	...	...	...	...	...	...	...	...	...	1837	...	...	2120	...
Dobova **1315** 🏛 d.	1010	...	1105	...	1211	...	...	1312	1338	...	...	1410	...	...	1510	...	...	1611	...	1705	1806	...	1925	1910	2011	2207	...
Sevnica **1315** d.	1040	...	1136	...	1241	...	...	1342	1402	...	...	1440	...	...	1539	...	...	1641	...	1736	1837	...	1949	1939	2041	2233	...
Zidani Most **1315** d.	1100	...	1155	...	1300	...	...	1400	1418	...	...	1500	...	...	1600	...	...	1700	...	1800	1857	...	2004	2007	2100	2248	...
Ljubljana 1315 a.	1202	...	1300	...	1402	...	...	1502	1505	...	...	1602	...	...	1702	...	...	1802	...	1902	2003	...	2053	2109	2202	2337	...
Ljubljana d.	...	1250	...	1332	...	1425	1445	...	1525	1532	1548	...	1621	...	...	1717	1752	...	1857	...	...	2025	2110	...	...	2355	...
Kranj d.	...	1321	...	1411	...	1500	1518	...	1553	1603	1623	...	1655	...	...	1749	1826	...	1931	...	...	2101	2131	...	...	0016	...
Lesce-Bled d.	...	1351	...	1435	...	1522	1545	...	1613	1627	1648	...	1719	...	...	1819	1849	...	1955	...	...	2125	2151	...	...	0036	...
Jesenice 1302 a.	...	1405	...	1448	...	1539	1559	...	1624	1640	1702	...	1732	...	...	1832	1901	...	2007	...	...	2137	2202	...	...	0047	...
Jesenice 🏛 d.	...	...	...	...	...	...	...	...	1627	...	...	...	...	...	...	...	...	...	...	...	...	...	2205	...	...	0050	...
Villach Hbf a.	...	...	...	...	...	...	...	...	1709	...	...	...	...	...	...	...	...	...	...	...	...	...	2243	...	...	0131	...
Salzburg Hbf **970** a.	...	...	...	...	...	...	...	...	...	...	...	...	...	...	...	...	...	...	...	...	...	...	...	...	...	0409	...
München Hbf **890** a.	...	...	...	...	...	...	...	...	...	...	...	...	...	...	...	...	...	...	...	...	...	...	...	...	...	0610	...

♦ – **NOTES** (LISTED BY TRAIN NUMBER)

210/1 – SAVA – [12] Vinkovci - Zagreb - Ljubljana - Villach and v.v.

212/3 – MIMARA – [12] Zagreb - Villach (**112/3**) - München - Frankfurt and v.v.

414/5 – ALPINE PEARLS – [2] Beograd - Zagreb - Ljubljana - Schwarzach-St Veit (**464/5**) - Zürich and v.v.; 🛏 1, 2 cl. and ▬ 2 cl. Zagreb - Schwarzach-St Veit - Zürich and v.v.; [12] and ✕ Beograd - Villach and v.v.

498 – LISINSKI – 🛏 1, 2 cl., ▬ 2 cl. and [2] Zagreb - Salzburg (**462**) - München; [12] Budapest (**204**) - Koprivnica (**782**) - Zagreb - Ljubljana. Conveys Mar. 20 - Oct. 7: ▬ 2 cl. (also 🛏 1, 2 cl. June 26 - Aug. 31) Rijeka (**480**) - Ljubljana - München.

499 – LISINSKI – 🛏 1, 2 cl., ▬ 2 cl. and [2] München (**463**) - Salzburg - Zagreb; [12] Ljubljana - Zagreb (**703**) - Koprivnica (**201**) - Budapest. Conveys Mar. 21 - Oct. 8: ▬ 2 cl. (also 🛏 1, 2 cl. June 27 - Sept. 1 from München): München - Ljubljana (**481**) - Rijeka.

N – Conveys on Ⓒ: [2] Ljubljana - Jesenice - Nova Gorica and v.v.

y – Not May 2, June 21 - Sept. 4, Oct. 31 (also Oct. 30).

1302 JESENICE - NOVA GORICA - SEŽANA
2nd class only SŽ

km		Ⓐ	q	t	Ⓐ	N			Ⓐ	Ⓐ		Ⓑ	
0	**Jesenice 1300** d.	...	0407	0407	0607	0819	1115	...	...	1433	1657	...	1903
10	Bled Jezero d.	...	0423	0423	0623	0835	1131	...	...	1449	1711	...	1919
28	Bohinjska Bistrica d.	...	0444	0444	0650	0902	1151	...	...	1509	1730	...	1939
56	Most na Soči d.	...	0519	0519	0726	0937	1226	...	...	1606	1806	...	2015
89	Nova Gorica a.	...	0557	0557	0816	1015	1305	...	...	1644	1843	...	2053
89	Nova Gorica d.	0455	0605	...	0912	...	...	1410	1530	...	...	1847	...
130	**Sežana 1305** a.	0554	0708	...	1010	...	...	1511	1628	...	...	1945	...

	Ⓐ							Ⓒ N	Ⓑ y	h	Ⓑ y	
Sežana 1305 d.	...	...	0627a	1018a	...	1431a	1640	...	...	2030	2050	...
Nova Gorica a.	...	...	0720a	1111a	...	1523a	1732	...	...	2121	2142	...
Nova Gorica d.	0322	0520	0737	1116	1445	1527	...	1805	1933	2124	...	...
Most na Soči d.	0357	0603	0816	1157	1524	1605	...	1851	2018	2204	...	...
Bohinjska Bistrica d.	0446	0648	0900	1248	1608	1648	...	1941	2101	2250	...	...
Bled Jezero d.	0506	0708	0921	1308	1629	1712	...	1959	2120	2312	...	...
Jesenice 1300 a.	0523	0723	0937	1325	1645	1729	...	2013	2136	2328	...	...

N – Conveys on Ⓒ: [2] Ljubljana - Jesenice - Nova Gorica and v.v.

a – Ⓐ only.

h – June 25 - Aug. 30.

q – Ⓐ (daily June 25 - Aug. 30).

t – ⑥ (not June 25 - Aug. 30).

y – Not June 25 - Aug. 30.

1303 DIVAČA - PULA
2nd class only HŽ, SŽ

km					1472	1474							
		Ⓐ		w	♦	♦		z	Ⓐ				
	Ljubljana **1305** d.	...	...	...	0611	0611	...	...	...	...	...	...	...
0	**Divača 1305** d.	...	...	...	0745	0750	...	...	...	1500	...	...	...
12	Hrpelje-Kozina d.	...	...	...	0804	0804	...	...	...	1518	...	...	...
30	Rakitovec 🏛 d.	...	...	...	0834	0834	...	...	...	1541	...	...	...
36	Buzet 🏛 d.	...	0518z	0710	0858	0858	1117y	1300	...	...	1556	...	1954r
43	Lupoglav ▲ d.	0445	0540	0732	0918	0918	1139	1322	1508	...	1618	...	2016
117	**Pula** a.	0620	0725	0908	1044	1044	1310	1458	1651	...	1752	...	2151

										1473	1475	
	Ⓐ	w	z					Ⓐ	v	♦	♦	
Pula d.	...	0505	0655	0915	1320	...	1427	1534	1720	1758	1758	1940
Lupoglav ▲ a.	...	0641	0833	1051	1500t	...	1609	1718	1902	1931	1931	2117
Buzet 🏛 d.	...	0703	...	1110	1528	...	...	...	...	2002	2002	...
Rakitovec 🏛 d.	0526	...	...	...	...	1609	...	...	...	2023	2023	...
Hrpelje-Kozina d.	0550	...	...	...	...	1634	...	...	...	2053	2050	...
Divača 1305 a.	0603	...	...	...	...	1647	...	...	...	2104	2101	...
Ljubljana **1305** a.	...	...	...	...	...	...	...	...	...	2239	2242	...

♦ – **NOTES** (LISTED BY TRAIN NUMBER)

1472/3 – June 25 - Aug. 30: [2] Pula - Hrpelje-Kozina (**1604/5**) - Ljubljana - Maribor and v.v.

1474/5 – Apr. 19 - May 4, June 21 - 24, Aug. 31 - Sept. 28: [2] Pula - Ljubljana and v.v.

r – Apr. 19 - May 4, June 21 - Sept. 28.

t – Depart 1510.

v – Ⓐ Dec. 15 - Apr. 18; daily Apr. 19 - May 4; Ⓐ May 5 - June 20; daily June 21 - Sept. 28; Ⓐ Sept. 29 - Dec. 12.

w – ⚒ Dec. 15 - Apr. 19; daily Apr. 20 - May 4; ⚒ May 5 - June 21; daily June 22 - Sept. 28; ⚒ Sept. 29 - Dec. 13.

y – Ⓒ Jan. 18 - Apr. 13; daily Apr. 14 - 21; Ⓒ Apr. 26 - June 8; daily June 14 - Aug. 31; Ⓒ Sept. 6 - Dec. 13.

z – Ⓐ Jan. 13 - Apr. 11, Apr. 22 - June 13, Sept. 1 - Dec. 12.

▲ – 🚌 service **Lupoglav - Rijeka and v.v.** Journey 40 minutes.
From Lupoglav: 0645⚒, 1110, 1620, 2120.
From Rijeka: 0600⚒, 1025, 1425Ⓐ, 1535Ⓒ, 1930

SŽ, HŽ 2nd class only except where shown — LJUBLJANA - RIJEKA, KOPER, SEŽANA and VILLA OPICINA — 1305

Services are currently severely disrupted owing to weather damage. Consult local information for latest schedules

km					1605	1474		481	ICS 29		ICS 35	IC 505							483		652		IC 509	ICS 33			
		Ⓐ	Ⓐ		♦	♦		♦	♦	Ⓐ	♦	♦		Ⓐ	Ⓐ		Ⓐ		♦		Ⓑ	Ⓐ	♦	♦		Ⓐ	
	Maribor 1315 d.	...	...	...	0340	...	...	...	0545	...	0745	0655	...	...	...	...	...	...	...	...	...	...	...	...	...	...	...
0	**Ljubljana** d.	0430	...	0555	0611	0611	...	0635	0741	0810	0942	0936	...	1040	1210	1312	...	1433	1510	1540	1608	1653	1745	1755	1854	1950	2100
67	Postojna d.	0538	...	0700	0711	0715	...	0734	0832	0919	1039	1039	...	1146	1318	1421	1455	1541	1613	1648	1711	1800	1848	1852	2002	2058	2207
80	Pivka ▲ d.	0551	...	0713	0724	0728	...	0747	0843	0932	1050	1051	...	1200	1331	1436	1508	1555	1626	1701	1723	1814	1900	1903	2015	2111	2220
	Ilirska Bistrica 🏛 ▲ d.	|	...	|	|	|	...	0814	|	|	|	|	...	|	|	|	1523	|	1650	|	|	|	|	|	|	|	|
	Šapjane 🏛 d.	|	...	|	|	|	...	0843	|	|	|	|	...	|	|	|	▬	|	1718	|	|	|	|	|	|	|	|
	Rijeka 1310 a.	|	...	|	|	|	...	0920	|	|	|	|	...	|	|	|	...	|	1755	|	|	|	|	|	|	|	|
104	Divača **1303** d.	0612	0615	0734	0745	0750	0756	...	0903	0954	1110	1113	1116	1222	1353	1458	1538	1617	...	1724	1743	1836	1921	1923	2037	2133	2242
116	Hrpelje-Kozina ⊡ d.	|	0629	|	|	0803	0809	...	0914	|	1122	1125	|	|	|	|	|	|	...	1737	|	|	1933	1935	|	|	|
153	**Koper** ⊡ a.	|	0706	|	0835	...	0845	...	0945	|	1153	1159	|	|	|	|	|	|	...	1813	|	|	2007	2005	|	|	|
113	**Sežana** 🏛 ▲ a.	0622	...	0744	...	...	...	...	...	1004	...	...	1126	1231	1403	1508	1548	1626	...	...	1752	1846	...	...	2047	2143	2252
	Villa Opicina **601** a.	...	...	...	...	...	...	...	...	1015	...	...	...	...	...	...	...	1637	...	...	...	...	...	...	...	...	...

km					ICS 32	IC 508						482					ICS 34	IC 504		ICS 28		653			1604	1475	480
		Ⓐ	Ⓐ	Ⓐ	♦	♦	Ⓐ		Ⓐ			♦	Ⓐ	Ⓐ	Ⓐ		♦	♦	Ⓐ	♦		Ⓑ			♦	♦	♦
	Villa Opicina **601** d.	...	...	...	...	...	...	...	...	1029a	...	...	...	...	...	...	...	...	...	...	1724	...	...	...	...	...	...
	Sežana 🏛 ▲ d.	0430	0510	0600	...	...	...	0710	0923	1040	...	...	1335	...	1433	1516	...	...	1645	...	1735	1820	1952	...	...	...	...
	Koper ⊡ d.	|	|	|	0530	0525	...	|	|	|	1003	...	|	...	|	|	1447	1445	|	1639	|	|	|	1917	2017	...	...
	Hrpelje-Kozina ⊡ d.	|	|	|	0601	0559	...	|	|	|	1036	...	|	...	|	|	1517	1518	|	1709	|	|	|	|	|	2050	...
	Divača **1303** d.	0440	0522	0610	0612	0613	...	0721	0933	1050	1058	...	1345	...	1443	1526	1529	1530	1655	1719	1745	1829	2002	2015	2107	2107	...
0	**Rijeka 1310** d.	|	|	...	|	|	...	|	|	...	|	1155	|	...	|	...	|	|	|	|	|	|	...	|	|	|	2040
28	Šapjane 🏛 d.	|	|	...	|	|	...	|	|	...	|	1250	|	...	|	...	|	|	|	|	|	|	...	|	|	|	2135
40	Ilirska Bistrica 🏛 d.	|	|	...	|	|	0632	|	|	...	|	1323	|	1415	|	...	|	|	|	|	|	|	...	|	|	|	2205
56	Pivka d.	0502	0544	...	0631	0637	0650	0743	0956	...	1121	1339	1408	1432	1506	...	1548	1551	1718	1738	1808	1850	...	2037	2128	2129	2221
	Postojna d.	0515	0557	...	0642	0649	0703	0757	1009	...	1135	1354	1421	1444	1519	...	1559	1603	1733	1749	1822	1902	...	2051	2140	2142	2233
	Ljubljana a.	0624	0705	...	0741	0751	0810	0902	1117	...	1241	1453	1529	...	1627	...	1658	1710	1840	1840	1929	2003	...	2159	2239	2242	2330
	Maribor 1315 a.	...	...	...	...	...	...	...	...	...	...	...	...	...	...	...	1903	1948	...	2043	...	...	...	...	0111	...	...

♦ – **NOTES** (LISTED BY TRAIN NUMBER)

28/9 – Ⓒ June 25 - Sept. 28: [12] and 🍷 Maribor - Ljubljana - Koper and v.v.
32 – June 26 - Aug. 31: [12] and 🍷 Koper - Ljubljana.
33 – June 25 - Aug. 30: [12] and 🍷 Ljubljana - Koper.
34/5 – Not Apr. 26 - Sept. 28: [12] and 🍷 Maribor - Ljubljana - Koper and v.v.
480 – OPATIJA – [12] Rijeka - Ljubljana. Conveys Mar. 20 - Oct. 7: ▬ 2 cl. (also 🛏 1, 2 cl. June 26 - Aug. 31) Rijeka - Ljubljana (**498**) - München.
481 – OPATIJA – [12] Ljubljana - Rijeka. Conveys Mar. 21 - Oct. 8: ▬ 2 cl. (also 🛏 1, 2 cl. June 27 - Sept. 1 from München, one day later from Ljubljana): München (**499**) - Ljubljana - Rijeka.
482/3 – LJUBLJANA – [12] Rijeka - Ljubljana and v.v.
504/5 – POHORJE – Apr. 26 - Sept. 28: [12] Maribor - Ljubljana - Koper and v.v.
508 – Not June 26 - Aug. 31: [12] Koper - Ljubljana.
509 – Not June 25 - Aug. 30: [12] Ljubljana - Koper.
1472/3 – June 25 - Aug. 30: [2] Pula - Hrpelje-Kozina (**1604/5**) - Ljubljana - Maribor and v.v.
1474/5 – Apr. 19 - May 4, June 21 - 24, Aug. 31 - Sept. 28: [2] Pula - Ljubljana and v.v.
1604 – ISTRA – June 25 - Aug. 30: [2] Koper - Ljubljana - Maribor. Conveys on ②⑤: 🛏 1, 2 cl., ▬ 2 cl., [2] and 🍷 Koper - Maribor (**1247**) - Hodoš - Zalaegerszeg (**959**) - Budapest.
1605 – ISTRA – June 25 - Aug. 30: [2] Maribor - Ljubljana - Koper. Conveys on ①④ (from Budapest): 🛏 1, 2 cl., ▬ 2 cl., [2] and 🍷 Budapest (**1246**) - Hodoš - Maribor - Koper.

a – Ⓐ only.

▲ – Local services **Pivka - Ilirska Bistrica and v.v.**: Journey 16 minutes.
From Pivka: 0555Ⓐ, 1206Ⓐ, 1339Ⓐ, 1508Ⓐ, 1725Ⓑ, 1820Ⓑ.
From Ilirska Bistrica: 0523Ⓐ, 0932Ⓐ, 1103Ⓐ, 1306Ⓐ, 1415Ⓐ, 1529Ⓐ, 1952Ⓑ.

⊡ – 🚌 service **Koper - Trieste and v.v.**: Journey 45 minutes.
From **Koper**: 0600⚒, 0642Ⓐ, 0700Ⓐ, 0730⚒, 1030⚒, 1200Ⓐ, 1400⚒, 1730⚒.
From **Trieste**: 0700⚒, 0900Ⓐ, 1115Ⓐ, 1230⚒, 1300⚒, 1400Ⓐ, 1530⚒, 1900⚒.
Service subject to alteration. No service on ⑦, Slovenian and Italian holidays.
Operator: Veolia Transport Slovenija.
An irregular 🚌 service also operates Trieste - Hrpelje-Kozina and v.v.

▲ – 🚌 service **Sežana - Trieste and v.v.**: Journey 30 – 45 minutes.
From **Sežana**: 0645⚒◧, 0750Ⓐ◧, 0820⚒♣, 1410⚒◧.
From **Trieste** Autostazione: 0730Ⓐ◧, 1245⚒◧, 1400⚒♣, 1445⚒◧.
Service subject to alteration. No service on ⑦, Slovenian and Italian holidays.
Operators: ◧ – Avrigo D.D., Nova Gorica; ♣ – Veolia Transport Slovenija, Ljubljana.

HŽ 2nd class only except where shown — RIJEKA - ZAGREB — 1310

km				703								701		
			Ⓐ	♦	⚒			Ⓐ			Ⓐ	♦		
0	**Rijeka 1305** d.	...	...	0540	...	0735	...	...	...	1345	1530	1710	...	1943
61	Delnice d.	...	...	0647	...	0847	...	...	...	1504	1642	1814	...	2101
90	Moravice d.	...	0610	0723	...	0926	...	...	...	1543	1725	1850	1942	2140
120	Ogulin **1330** d.	0405	0652	0754	0835	0959	1025	1200	...	1619	1757	1922	2020	2212
126	Oštarije **1330** d.	0411	0658	0801	0842	...	1032	1207	...	1626	...	|	2027	...
176	Karlovac **1330** d.	0523	0803	0850	0946	...	1136	1327	...	1739	...	2016	2127	...
229	**Zagreb 1330/40** a.	0619	0902	0931	1047	...	1239	1426	...	1832	...	2058	2224	...
	Osijek 1340 a.	...	...	1435	...	...	...	...	...	...	...	...	...	...

				700					702			
		Ⓐ		⚒	♦			Ⓐ		♦	Ⓐ		
Osijek 1340 d.	...	...	...	...	...	...	...	...	...	1203	...	...	...
Zagreb 1330/40 d.	...	...	0750	0950	1135	1315	...	1442	1533	1657	1718	...	2130
Karlovac **1330** d.	...	...	0851	1045	1215	1415	...	1537	1639	1738	1816	...	2223
Oštarije **1330** d.	...	...	1001	1149	|	1515	...	1640	1744	1830	1920	...	2324j
Ogulin **1330** d.	0400	0625	1008	1155	1310	1521	1540	1646	1758	1837	1935	...	2330j
Moravice d.	0433	0701	1041	...	1345	...	1619	...	1830	1912	...	...	...
Delnice d.	0512	0745	1121	...	1425	...	1700	...	...	1947	...	...	...
Rijeka 1305 a.	0626	0904	1235	...	1527	...	1815	...	...	2049	...	...	...

♦ – **NOTES** (LISTED BY TRAIN NUMBER)

700/1 – [12] Zagreb - Rijeka and v.v.
702 – [12] Osijek - Rijeka.
703 – [12] Rijeka - Zagreb - Osijek. Conveys [12] Ljubljana (**499**) - Zagreb - Koprivnica (**201**) - Budapest.

j – 8 minutes later June 27 - Aug. 30.

SŽ, MÁV 2nd class only except where shown — MARIBOR - ČAKOVEC, MURSKA SOBOTA and ZALAEGERSZEG — 1313

km		1247								640			247										1642			IC 518		642	
		♦	Ⓐ	Ⓐ	Ⓐ	Ⓐ	Ⓐ§	Ⓐ	Ⓒ		Ⓐ		♦	⚒	g	Ⓐ	Ⓐ		Ⓐ				j			♦	Ⓐ	♦	Ⓐ
	Ljubljana 1315 d.	2248	...	...	...	...	...	...	...	...	...	...	...	...	...	...	...	...	...	...	...	...	...	...	...	1515	...	...	...
0	**Maribor 1315** d.	0200	...	...	...	...	0700	...	0700	...	1020	...	1205	1225	1225	1325	...	1432	...	...	1525	...	...	...	...	|	1830	...	2205
19	Pragersko **1315** d.	|	...	...	...	0617	|	...	0731	1010	1050	...	|	1257	1257	|	...	1501	...	...	|	...	1604	...	...	1725	|	1940	2236
37	Ptuj d.	|	...	...	...	0646	0746	...	0756	1026	1111	...	1232	1321	1321	1408	...	1522	...	...	1612	...	1632	...	...	1740	1918	1954	2302
59	Ormož d.	|	0438	...	0531	0709	0810	0815	0819	1044	1133	...	1250	1346	1346	1433	...	1546	1550	...	1636	1640	1658	1735	...	1758	1942	2013	2326
	Središče 🏛 a.	|	0448	...	|	▬	|	0826	|	|	...	...	|	|	|	1444	...	|	1601	...	|	1651	|	1746	...	|	...	|	...
	Čakovec 1335 a.	|	...	...	|	...	|	...	|	|	...	...	|	|	|	...	...	|	...	...	|	...	|	...	...	|	...	|	...
98	**Murska Sobota** d.	|	...	0320	0621	...	0857	...	0906	1121	...	...	1332	1432	1433	...	1517	1633	...	...	1722	...	1747	...	...	1842	...	2103	...
127	Hodoš a.	0330	...	0349	...	...	...	...	...	...	...	...	1355	...	1500	...	1547	...	...	...	...	...	...	...	...	1909	...	2136	...
127	Hodoš 🏛 d.	0353	...	...	...	0620	...	...	...	...	...	...	1429	...	...	...	...	...	...	1619	...	...	...	...	1907	...	...	...	...
174	**Zalaegerszeg** a.	0431	...	...	...	0710	...	...	...	...	...	...	1507	...	...	...	...	...	...	1716	...	...	...	...	2006	...	...	...	...
	Budapest D 1230 a.	0824	...	...	...	...	...	...	...	...	...	...	1824	...	...	...	...	...	...	...	...	...	...	...	...	...	...	...	...

km			IC 519		643																1641			246	1643				1246
			♦	Ⓐ	♦	Ⓐ	Ⓐ		Ⓐ	Ⓐ	Ⓐ	Ⓐ	Ⓐ	⚒	g	Ⓐ	Ⓐ			Ⓐ	g			♦	g		Ⓐ		♦
	Budapest D 1230 d.	...	...	...	...	...	...	...	...	...	...	...	...	...	...	...	...	...	...	...	...	...	...	1335	...	...	...	...	2030
	Zalaegerszeg d.	...	...	...	...	...	...	0520	...	...	...	...	...	...	...	...	...	1445	...	...	...	...	1630	1653	...	...	...	...	0010
	Hodoš 🏛 a.	...	...	...	...	...	...	0610	...	...	...	...	...	...	...	...	...	1539	...	...	...	...	1720	1732	...	...	...	...	0048
	Hodoš d.	...	0420	...	0505	0558	...	...	...	...	...	...	...	...	...	...	...	...	...	1555	1610	...	...	1745	...	...	2015	...	0105
	Murska Sobota d.	...	0449	...	0540	0627	0630	...	...	0945	...	1148	...	1500	1500	...	...	...	...	1625	1641	...	...	1809	1820	1925	2043	...	|
0	**Čakovec 1335** d.	...	|	...	|	...	|	...	...	|	...	|	...	|	|	...	...	...	...	...	|	...	...	|	|	|	...	...	|
12	Središče 🏛 d.	0426	|	0541	|	...	|	...	1030	|	...	|	1505	|	|	1609	...	...	1713	...	|	1755	...	|	|	|	...	...	|
22	Ormož d.	0442	0526	0554	0627	...	0720	...	1041	1045	1205	1234	1516	1546	1546	1620	1710	...	1725	...	1732	1806	...	1844	1857	2012	...	...	|
	Ptuj d.	0507	0542	0620	0645	...	0746	...	...	1110	1231	1302	...	1613	1613	...	1739	...	...	...	1756	...	...	1902	1913	2038	...	...	|
	Pragersko **1315** d.	0539	0608	0655	0700	...	0818	...	...	1142	1301	1337	...	1658	1658	...	1801	...	...	...	1825	...	...	|	1927	|	...	...	|
	Maribor 1315 a.	0601	|	0717	...	...	0840	...	...	1204	1324	1400	...	1722	1722	...	...	...	...	...	|	...	...	1927	...	2123	...	...	0240
	Ljubljana 1315 a.	...	0809	...	...	...	...	...	...	...	...	...	...	...	...	...	...	...	...	...	2028	...	...	...	...	...	...	...	0606

♦ – **NOTES** (LISTED BY TRAIN NUMBER)

46/7 – CITADELLA – [12] Budapest - Maribor and v.v.
18/9 – PTUJ – Ⓐ: [2] Ljubljana - Hodoš and v.v.
42/3 – MURA – [12] Pragersko - Hodoš and v.v.
246 – ISTRA – ①④ June 23 - Aug. 28: 🛏 1, 2 cl., ▬ 2 cl., [2] and 🍷 Budapest - Hodoš - Maribor (**1605**) - Koper.
1247 – ISTRA – ②⑤ June 24 - Aug. 29: 🛏 1, 2 cl., ▬ 2 cl., [2] and 🍷 Koper (**1604**) - Maribor - Hodoš - Zalaegerszeg (**959**) - Budapest.

g – ⑦ until June 22, Aug. 31 - Dec. 7 (also Apr. 21; not Apr. 20, 27).
j – ⑤ until June 20, Sept. 5 - Dec. 12 (also Oct. 30; not May 2, Oct. 31).
§ – Subject to confirmation.

1315 LJUBLJANA and ZAGREB - MARIBOR - GRAZ

SŽ, HŽ, ÖBB

km				ICS 12		ICS 14	EC 158			ICS 18	IC 506			ICS 20		IC 518	EC 150	ICS 22	ICS 34		IC 502	IC 504	ICS 28	ICS 26		1604	604
		2 Ⓐ	2 Ⓐ	R	2	R	✕ ♦	2	2	R	Ⓐ	2 ⚒	2 Ⓐ	R	2	2 ♦	✕ ♦	R z	R ♦	2 y	♦	♦	R ♦	R	2	♦	2 w
	Koper **1305** d.	...	...	...	...	...	...	...	...	...	...	...	...	...	...	...	...	...	1447	...	...	1445	1639	...	...	2007	...
0	**Ljubljana 1300** d.	...	...	0545	...	0805	...	...	1250	1312	1345	1350	...	1512	...	1515	1600	1712	1712	...	1725	1725	1850	2012	2050	2248	2248
*	**Zagreb 1300** d.	...	...	|	...	|	0725	...	|	|	|	|	...	|	...	|	|	|	|	...	|	|	|	|	|	|	|
	Dobova **1300** ▦ d.	...	...	|	...	|	0812	...	|	|	|	|	...	|	...	|	|	|	|	...	|	|	|	|	|	|	|
	Sevnica **1300** d.	...	...	|	...	|	0839	...	|	|	|	|	...	|	...	|	|	|	|	...	|	|	|	|	|	|	|
64	Zidani Most **1300** d.	...	...	0630	0700	0850	|	1200	1402	1357	1442	1500	...	1557	1601	1608	1657	1757	1757	...	1824	1824	1935	2057	2153	2349	2354
89	Celje d.	...	...	0650	0725	0910	0918	1225	1427	1417	1509	1525	...	1617	1626	1638	1723	1818	1818	...	1850	1850	1956	2117	2219	0015	0019
137	Pragersko **1313** d.	...	...	0722	0810	0941	0959	1310	1512	1451	1550	1610	...	1651	1711	1719	1801	1852	1852	...	1932	1932	2031	2151	2303	0058	0059
156	**Maribor 1313** ▲ a.	...	...	0735	0828	0953	1014	1328	1530	1504	1606	1628	...	1704	1729	...	1816	1903	1903	...	1948	1948	2043	2204	2322	0111	0113
156	**Maribor** d.	0502	0620	...	0833	...	1019	1333	...	...	...	...	1635	...	1734	...	1819	...	...	1940	...	...	...	...	...	...	...
172	Spielfeld-Straß ▦ a.	0525	0643	...	0852	...	1036	1352	...	...	...	...	1658	...	1752	...	1836	...	...	2002	...	...	...	...	...	...	...
172	Spielfeld-Straß **980** ▦ d.	...	...	...	...	...	1048	...	...	...	...	...	...	...	...	...	1848	...	...	...	...	...	...	...	...	...	...
219	**Graz** Hbf **980** a.	...	...	...	...	...	1120	...	...	...	...	...	...	...	...	...	1920	...	...	...	...	...	...	...	...	...	...
	Wien Meidling **980** a.	...	...	...	...	...	1357	...	...	...	...	...	...	...	...	...	2157	...	...	...	...	...	...	...	...	...	...

		605	1605		ICS 11	ICS 29	IC 519		IC 503	IC 505	ICS 13	ICS 35		EC 151	ICS 17		ICS 19	1611		ICS 21	1615	1641		1643	ICS 23	EC 159	1613
	2 h	2 w	♦	2	R v	R ♦	2 ♦	2 Ⓐ	♦	♦	R t	R ♦	2	✕ ♦	R	2	R	2 g	2 Ⓐ	R x	2 g	2 ♦	2	2 ♦	R	✕ ♦	2 g
Wien Meidling **980** d.	...	...	...	...	...	...	...	...	...	...	...	...	...	0803	...	...	...	...	...	...	...	...	...	...	...	1603	...
Graz Hbf **980** d.	...	...	...	...	...	...	...	...	...	...	...	...	...	1038	...	...	...	...	...	...	...	...	...	...	...	1838	...
Spielfeld-Straß **980** ▦ a.	...	...	...	...	...	...	...	...	...	...	...	...	...	1108	...	...	...	...	...	...	...	...	...	...	...	1908	...
Spielfeld-Straß ▦ d.	...	...	...	...	...	...	...	0545	...	...	...	...	0903	1120	...	1405	...	...	1710	...	...	...	1758	...	...	1920	...
Maribor a.	...	...	...	...	...	...	...	0608	...	...	...	...	0923	1137	...	1422	...	...	1731	...	...	...	1818	...	...	1938	...
Maribor 1313 ▲ d.	0115	0340	0340	0420	0545	0545	...	...	0655	0655	0745	0745	0928a	1150	1245	1425	1545	1620	...	1745	1800	...	1823a	...	1945	1955	2005
Pragersko **1313** d.	0136	0357	0357	0440	0600	0600	0608	...	0714	0714	0759	0759	0948a	1206	1259	1446	1559	1639	...	1759	1818	1825	1843a	1931	1959	2011	2022
Celje d.	0213	0441	0441	0528	0635	0635	0652	...	0756	0756	0834	0834	1034a	1245	1334	1532	1634	1724	...	1834	1900	1909	1929a	2013	2034	2050	2104
Zidani Most **1300** d.	0236	0507	0507	0555	0654	0654	0718	...	0822	0822	0853	0853	1058a	1312	1354	1555	1654	1750	...	1854	1928	1934	1953a	2037	2054	|	2130
Sevnica **1300** d.	|	|	|	|	|	|	|	...	|	|	|	|	...	|	|	...	|	|	...	|	|	|	...	|	|	2129	|
Dobova **1300** ▦ d.	|	|	|	|	|	|	|	...	|	|	|	|	...	|	|	...	|	|	...	|	|	|	...	|	|	2211	|
Zagreb 1300 a.	|	|	|	|	|	|	|	...	|	|	|	|	...	|	|	...	|	|	...	|	|	|	...	|	|	2243	|
Ljubljana 1300 a.	0331	0606	0606	0659	0738	0738	0809	...	0919	0919	0937	0937	...	1408	1438	...	1738	1840	...	1938	2022	2028	...	2129	2138	...	2220
Koper **1305** a.	...	...	0835	...	...	0945	...	...	...	1159	...	1153	...	...	...	...	...	...	...	...	...	...	...	...	...	...	...

ADDITIONAL SERVICES MARIBOR - ZIDANI MOST and v.v.: 2nd class only

		Ⓐ	Ⓐ	Ⓐ		Ⓐ	Ⓐ	Ⓐ		Ⓐ		Ⓐ		Ⓑ
Maribor ▲ d.	0515	0615	0715	0820	1015	1120	1215	1320	1520	1620	1720	1920	2020	2100
Pragersko d.	0535	0635	0735	0840	1035	1140	1235	1340	1539	1639	1739	1939	2040	2119
Celje d.	0621	0722	0821	0926	1121	1226	1321	1426	1625	1725	1825	2025	2126	2207
Zidani Most d.	0645	0746	0845	0950	1145	1250	1345	1450	1648	1748	1849	2048	2149	2232

		Ⓐ	Ⓐ	Ⓐ	Ⓐ	Ⓐ	Ⓐ		Ⓐ			Ⓐ
Zidani Most d.	0500	0600	0800	0922	1000	1105	1304	1700	1801	1900	2006	2100
Celje d.	0525	0625	0825	0947	1025	1130	1329	1726	1826	1925	2031	2125
Pragersko d.	0612	0712	0910	1032	1109	1214	1415	1813	1919	2013	2117	2212
Maribor ▲ a.	0630	0730	0927	1050	1128	1233	1435	1832	1937	2033	2137	2232

♦ – **NOTES** (LISTED BY TRAIN NUMBER)

28/9 – Ⓒ June 25 - Sept. 28: [12] and 🍷 Maribor - Ljubljana - Koper and v.v.
34/5 – Not Apr. 26 - Sept. 28: [12] and 🍷 Maribor - Ljubljana - Koper and v.v.
150/1 – EMONA – [12] and ✕ Ljubljana - Wien and v.v.
158/9 – CROATIA – [12] and ✕ Zagreb - Wien and v.v.
502/3 – POHORJE – Not Apr. 26 - Sept. 28: [12] Ljubljana - Maribor and v.v.
504/5 – POHORJE – Apr. 26 - Sept. 28: [12] Maribor - Ljubljana - Koper and v.v.
518/9 – PTUJ – Ⓐ: [2] Ljubljana - Hodoš and v.v.
1604 – ISTRA – June 25 - Aug. 30: [2] Koper - Ljubljana - Maribor. Conveys on ②⑤: 🛏 1, 2 cl., ▬ 2 cl., [2] and 🍷 Koper - Maribor (**1247**) - Hodoš - Zalaegerszeg (**959**) - Budapest.
1605 – ISTRA – June 25 - Aug. 30: [2] Maribor - Ljubljana - Koper. Conveys on ①④ (from Budapest): 🛏 1, 2 cl., ▬ 2 cl., [2] and 🍷 Budapest (**1246**) - Hodoš - Maribor - Koper.
1641 – ⑦ until June 22, Aug. 31 - Dec. 7 (also Apr. 21; not Apr. 20, 27): [2] Hodoš - Ljubljana.
1643 – ⑦ until June 22, Aug. 31 - Dec. 7 (also Apr. 21; not Apr. 20, 27): [2] Murska Sobota - Zidani Most.

a – Ⓐ only.
g – ⑦ until June 22, Aug. 31 - Dec. 7 (also Apr. 21; not Apr. 20, 27).
h – June 8 - Sept. 28.

t – Apr. 26 - Sept. 28.
v – Not Ⓒ June 25 - Sept. 28.
w – Not June 25 - Aug. 30.
x – Not Ⓒ Apr. 26 - Sept. 28.
y – June 25 - Aug. 30 runs 13 minutes later.
z – Ⓐ Apr. 26 - Sept. 28.

▲ – For Maribor - Bleiburg (- Klagenfurt) services see panel below.

MARIBOR - BLEIBURG (- KLAGENFURT) and v.v.:

km		Ⓐ	Ⓐ		Ⓐ	Ⓐ
0	Maribor d.	0520	1445	*Klagenfurt* d.	*0806*	*1636*
87	Bleiburg ▦ a.	0730	1659	Bleiburg ▦ d.	0938	1732
126	*Klagenfurt* a.	*0837*	*1754*	Maribor a.	1139	1933

Other services are available Bleiburg - Klagenfurt and v.v.

* – Zagreb - Celje: *104 km*.

1320 ZAGREB - VINKOVCI - BEOGRAD

SŽ, HŽ, ŽS

km		741		415		743	745	EC 211		747
		♦	2	♦				✕ ♦	2 ⚒	
	Ljubljana **1300** d.	...	...	0825	...	...	...	1445	...	...
0	**Zagreb** d.	0624	0745	1115	...	1307	1520	1739	1851	2135
105	Novska d.	0812	1006	1309	...	1459	1714	1928	2114	2324
191	Slavonski Brod d.	0914	1126	1410	...	1600	1814	2028	2233	0028
224	Strizivojna-Vrpolje **1345** d.	0932	1157	1428	...	1619	1832	2046	...	0050
	Osijek **1345** a.	|	|	|	...	|	|	|	...	|
256	**Vinkovci** d.	0949	1222	1454	...	1636	1849	2103	...	0113
288	Šid ▦ a.	...	...	1518	...	...	...	...	...	...
407	**Beograd** a.	...	...	1732	...	...	...	...	...	...

	740	742	744	EC 210	746	414		748	750
				✕ ♦		♦		♦	†n
Beograd d.	...	...	...	...	...	1100	...	...	...
Šid ▦ d.	...	...	...	...	...	1355	...	...	...
Vinkovci d.	0248	0555	0733	0901	1217	1441	...	1713	1931
Osijek **1345** d.	|	|	|	|	|	|	...	|	|
Strizivojna-Vrpolje **1345** d.	0311	0613	0752	0920	1235	1500	...	1737	1949
Slavonski Brod d.	0335	0631	0811	0939	1255	1522	...	1801	2009
Novska d.	0440	0736	0909	1037	1355	1622	...	1905	2108
Zagreb a.	0637	0931	1056	1224	1543	1809	...	2101	2300
Ljubljana **1300** a.	...	...	...	1505	...	2053	...	...	...

♦ – **NOTES** (LISTED BY TRAIN NUMBER)

210/1 – SAVA – [12] Vinkovci - Zagreb - Ljubljana - Villach and v.v.
414/5 – ALPINE PEARLS – [2] Beograd - Zagreb - Ljubljana - Schwarzach-St Veit (**464/5**) - Zürich and v.v.; 🛏 1, 2 cl. and ▬ 2 cl. Zagreb - Schwarzach-St Veit - Zürich and v.v.; [12] and ✕ Beograd - Villach and v.v.

741 – [12] Zagreb - Vinkovci. Conveys June 28 - Aug. 31 (from Split, one day later from Zagreb): [2] Split (**1822**) - Zagreb - Vinkovci.
748 – [12] Vinkovci - Zagreb. Conveys June 27 - Aug. 30: [2] Vinkovci - Zagreb (**1823**) - Split.

n – Not Apr. 20, May 1, June 19, 25, Aug. 5, 15, Nov. 1.

1322 LOCAL SERVICES in Croatia

2nd class only HŽ

ZAGREB - SISAK CAPRAG and v.v.: Journey 60 – 75 minutes. All services call at Sisak (6 minutes from Sisak Caprag).
From Zagreb: 0437Ⓐ q, 0547Ⓐ, 0640, 0744Ⓐ, 1052, 1154Ⓐ, 1354, 1447Ⓐ, 1545, 1640Ⓐ, 1747Ⓐ, 1855, 1957, 2054Ⓐ, 2247.
From Sisak Caprag: 0415⚒, 0508, 0616, 0715Ⓐ, 0811Ⓐ, 1030⚒, 1215, 1408Ⓐ, 1518, 1613Ⓐ, 1708, 1812Ⓐ, 2005, 2115.

SISAK CAPRAG - SUNJA and v.v.: Journey 25 minutes.
From Sisak Caprag: 0337⚒, 0720⚒, 0754, 1216, 1459, 1700, 1901Ⓐ, 2006, 2348.
From Sunja: 0444⚒, 0552, 0651, 1151, 1255⚒, 1634, 1941, 2051, 2143Ⓐ.

SUNJA - NOVSKA and v.v.: Journey 70 minutes.
From Sunja: 0818, 1240Ⓐ q, 1533Ⓐ, 2040Ⓐ.
From Novska: 0442, 0541, 1041, 1403Ⓐ q, 1806Ⓐ.

VINKOVCI - VUKOVAR and v.v.: Journey 40 minutes.
From Vinkovci: 0405Ⓐ, 1021Ⓐ, 1341Ⓐ q, 1520, 1934Ⓐ.
From Vukovar: 0455Ⓐ, 0552Ⓐ q, 1111Ⓐ, 1432Ⓐ q, 1628 2021Ⓐ.

q – Not June 14 - Aug. 31.

1325 🚌 SPLIT - PLOČE - DUBROVNIK

🚌 SPLIT - DUBROVNIK: Up to 18 departures per day. Journey 4 hrs - 5 hrs 10 mins.
🚌 SPLIT - PLOČE: Up to 22 departures per day. Journey 2 hrs - 2 hrs 50 mins.
🚌 PLOČE - DUBROVNIK: Up to 17 departures per day. Journey 2 hrs - 2 hrs 20 mins.

Note: various operators run on these routes; tickets are not interchangeable.
Split and Ploče bus stations are situated adjacent to the railway stations.
Buses pass through Bosnia between Ploče and Dubrovnik (passports required).

HŽ 2nd class only except where shown ZAGREB - ZADAR, ŠIBENIK and SPLIT 1330

km	km			1204			ICN 521								ICN 523					1823			825		
							Ⓡ	🚌						🚌	Ⓡ										🚌
			⚒	♦	Ⓐ		Z		Ⓐq	⚒	⚒				Zy	Ⓐ	Ⓐ	⚒		♦			♦		h
0		**Zagreb 1310** d.	...	0015	...	...	0630	...	...	...	...	...	...	...	1250	...	...	...	...	2145	...	...	2305	...	...
53		Karlovac **1310** d.	...	|	...	...	0708	...	...	...	...	...	...	...	1326	...	...	...	...	2232	...	...	2345	...	...
103		Oštarije **1310** d.	...	|	...	...	0805	...	...	...	...	...	...	...	|	...	...	...	...	|	...	...	|	...	...
109		**Ogulin 1310** d.	...	0158	...	...	|	...	...	...	...	...	...	...	|	...	...	...	...	2340	...	...	0052	...	...
225		Gospić d.	...	|	...	...	0934	...	...	...	...	...	...	...	1547	...	...	...	...	0208	...	...	0307	...	...
269		Gračac d.	...	|	...	...	1007	...	...	...	...	...	...	...	1632	...	...	...	...	0243	...	...	0343	...	...
333		Knin a.	...	0623	...	...	1116	...	...	...	...	...	...	...	1737	...	...	...	...	0358	...	...	0457	...	...
333	0	Knin d.	...	0639	0750	...	1117	1120	...	...	...	1516	...	1715	1738	1936	...	...	...	0359	0411	...	0458	...	0505
	95	**Zadar** ⊡ a.	...	|	|	...	|	1340	...	...	...	|	...	1935	|	|	...	...	...	|	|	...	|	...	0725
387	—	Perković a.	...	0731	0857	...	1201	...	...	...	...	1623	...	...	1822	2043	...	...	...	0454	0518	...	0553	←	...
387	0	Perković d.	0713	0734	0905	0910	1202	...	1231	1311	1457	1626	1650	...	1823	2049	2053	2305	...	0502	→	0524	0558	0555	...
	22	**Šibenik** ⊡ a.	0741	|	0933	|	|	...	|	1339	1525	1654	|	...	|	2117	|	2330	...	|	...	|	|	0623	...
435		**Split** ⊡ a.	...	0824	...	1011	1244	...	1332	...	...	...	1753	...	1905	...	2154	...	...	0558	...	0625	0654	...	...

							ICN 520						ICN 522						1205				1822		824	
			🚌				Ⓡ						Ⓡ		🚌							🚌				
	Ⓐ	⚒	h				Zy			⚒	Ⓐq	Ⓐk	Z	Ⓐq		Ⓐ		Ⓐ	♦	Ⓐ			♦	⚒	♦	
Split ⊡ d.	...	...	...	0750	...	...	0820	...	...	...	1024	...	1340	...	...	...	1518	...	1837	1935	...	...	2104	...	2201	...
Šibenik ⊡ d.	0442	0630	...	|	...	0824	|	...	...	1047	|	1346	|	1410	...	1540	|	...	|	|	2010	...	|	2220	|	...
Perković a.	0516	0706	...	0852	...	0900	0903	←	...	1122	1126	1421	1423	1446	...	1616	1620	←	1942	2037	2046	...	2209	2255	2301	...
Perković d.	0521	...	...	...	...	→	0904	0915	...	...	...	...	1424	...	...	→	...	1625	1943	...	2048	...	2210	...	2302	...
Zadar ⊡ d.	|	...	0735	...	...	...	|	|	...	...	...	...	|	...	1440	...	...	|	|	...	|	2030	|	...	|	...
Knin a.	0635	...	0954	...	...	...	0949	1025	...	...	...	...	1508	...	1659	...	...	1734	2034	...	2157	2249	2305	...	2357	...
Knin d.	...	...	...	...	...	...	1000	...	...	...	...	...	1510	...	...	...	...	...	2048	...	...	...	2306	...	0008	...
Gračac d.	...	...	...	...	...	...	1104	...	...	...	...	...	1624	...	...	...	...	...	|	...	...	...	0027	...	0129	...
Gospić d.	...	...	...	...	...	...	1138	...	...	...	...	...	1658	...	...	...	...	...	|	...	...	...	0104	...	0206	...
Ogulin 1310 d.	...	...	...	...	...	...	|	...	...	...	...	...	|	...	...	...	...	...	0140	...	...	...	0356	...	0421	...
Oštarije **1310** d.	...	...	...	...	...	...	|	...	...	...	...	...	1827	...	...	...	...	...	|	...	...	...	|	...	|	...
Karlovac **1310** d.	...	...	...	...	...	...	1359	...	...	...	...	...	1914	...	...	...	...	...	|	...	...	...	0452	...	0519	...
Zagreb 1310 a.	...	...	...	...	...	...	1434	...	...	...	...	...	1948	...	...	...	...	...	0311	...	...	...	0531	...	0600	...

♦ – **NOTES** (LISTED BY TRAIN NUMBER)

824 – 🛏 1,2 cl. and [2] (also ▬ 2 cl. June 28 - Aug. 31) Split - Zagreb.
825 – 🛏 1,2 cl. and [2] (also ▬ 2 cl. June 27 - Aug. 30) Zagreb - Split.
1204 – ADRIA – ②⑤ June 13 - Aug. 29 (from Budapest, one day later from Zagreb): 🛏 1,2 cl., ▬ 2 cl., [2] and ✕ Budapest - Zagreb - Split; 🛏 1,2 cl. Praha (**277**) - Budapest - Split; 🛏 1,2 cl. Moskva (**15**) - Budapest - Split.
1205 – ADRIA – ③⑥ June 14 - Aug. 30: 🛏 1,2 cl., ▬ 2 cl., [2] and ✕ Split - Zagreb - Budapest; 🛏 1,2 cl. Split - Budapest (**276**) - Praha; 🛏 1,2 cl. Split - Budapest (**16**) - Moskva.
1822 – June 28 - Aug. 31: ▬ 2 cl. and [2] Split - Zagreb; [2] Split - Zagreb (**783**) - Osijek; [2] Split - Zagreb (**741**) - Vinkovci.
1823 – June 27 - Aug. 30: ▬ 2 cl. and [2] Zagreb - Split; [2] Osijek (**782**) - Zagreb - Split; [2] Vinkovci (**748**) - Zagreb - Split.

Z – [12] Zagreb - Split and v.v.
h – ⚒ (daily June 29 - Aug. 31).
k – June 14 - Aug. 31.
q – Not June 14 - Aug. 31.
t – © (daily June 14 - Aug. 31).
y – June 14 - Sept. 14.
⊡ – Frequent 🚌 services operate Zadar - Šibenik - Split and v.v.; some continue to Ploče and Dubrovnik (see Table **1325**). Bus station locations: Zadar, Split and Ploče are adjacent to rail station, Šibenik approximately 10 minutes walk.

HŽ, MÁV 2nd class only except where shown ZAGREB - VARAŽDIN - NAGYKANIZSA 1335

There is currently no service Kotoriba - Murakeresztúr and v.v.

km					990									992		790		IC 570								j		
				Ⓐ	⚒	⚒		⚒		⚒	Ⓐ	Ⓐ				Ⓐ		♦			Ⓐ	ⒶV	⚒	V				⚒
0	**Zagreb** d.	...	...	0429	0717	...	...	0930	...	1108	...	1313	...	1410	...	1512	1524	1631	...	...	1626	...	1818	...	1923	...	2101	2225
38	Zabok d.	...	...	0544	0809	...	...	1032	...	1212	...	1423	...	1512	...	1604	1634	k	←	...	1733	...	1928	...	2032	...	2215	2324
104	**Varaždin** ▲ d.	0539	...	0744	0940	1020	...	1206	1306	1420r	1515	1602	...	1643	...	1724	1816	1828	1909	...	1938	2010	2106	2115	2210	2218	2348	0055
115	Čakovec **1313** d.	0551	...	0754	0952	1031	...	...	1326	1433	1527	...	...	1656	...	1741	→	1838	1930	...	...	2022	...	2127	...	2230	2358	...
145	Kotoriba 🏛 d.	0629	...	...	1025	1104	...	...	1400	1516	1603	...	...	1733	...	1811	...	...	2006	...	...	2057	...	2205y	...	2307	...	...
151	Murakeresztúr 🏛 d.	...	0854	...	...	...	1254	...	...	...	...	...	1654	...	...	...	...	...	...	2054	...	...	...	...	...	...	...	...
165	**Nagykanizsa** a.	...	0905	...	...	...	1305	...	...	...	...	...	1705	...	...	...	...	...	...	2105	...	...	...	...	...	...	...	...

					991	IC 571										993						995		997			
		⚒	⚒	Ⓐ		♦		⚒			⚒	Ⓐ		ⒶV	⚒	†	⚒	⚒	⚒		Q		⚒			Ⓐ	
Nagykanizsa d.	...	...	...	...	...	...	...	...	0653	...	...	...	1053	...	...	...	...	...	...	1453	...	...	...	...	1853	...	...
Murakeresztúr 🏛 d.	...	...	...	...	...	...	...	...	0704	...	...	...	1104	...	...	...	...	...	...	1504	...	...	...	...	1904	...	...
Kotoriba 🏛 d.	...	...	...	0431	...	...	0539d	0633	...	0749	...	1109	...	1156	1246	...	...	1417a	1447	—	1612	1704	1817a	1912	...	2116	2220
Čakovec **1313** d.	...	...	...	0508	...	0522	0623d	0709	...	0824	1004a	1152	...	1234	1321	...	*1402a*	1458	1528	...	1657	1747	1855a	1957	...	2151	2254
Varaždin ▲ d.	0254	0340	0427	0518	0527	0534	0646	0719	...	0834	1022	1209	...	1244	1331	1334	1419	1508	1538	1547	1707	1800	1920	2009	...	2201	2304
Zabok d.	0429	0515	0627	...	0656	k	0840	...	...	...	1216	1351	...	...	...	1513	1605	...	...	1732	...	1927	2105	2143b	...	...	...
Zagreb a.	0529	0616	0729	...	0752	0722	0943	...	...	...	1324	1456	...	...	...	1605	1707	...	...	1831	...	2023	2205	2238b	...	...	...

▲ – **VARAŽDIN - KOPRIVNICA and v.v.** 2nd class only except where shown:

km			IC 571									
		⚒	♦	⚒	⚒	ⒶV	⑥t		⚒	Q		Ⓐ
0	Varaždin d.	0424	0534	0652	1026	1308	1308	1422	1605	1712	1908	2215
42	Koprivnica a.	0517	0611	0739	1115	1357	1357	1510	1654	1801	1956	2303

									IC 570				
	Ⓐ		⚒	⚒	⚒	Ⓐ		⚒	♦	⑦q	ⒶV	V	
Koprivnica d.	0429	0547	0830	1134	1307	1443	1537	1704	1749	1812	1908	2022	...
Varaždin a.	0521	0643	0919	1223	1400	1541	1633	1752	1826	1900	1959	2109	...

♦ – **NOTES** (LISTED BY TRAIN NUMBER)

70 – Ⓐ: [2] Zagreb - Koprivnica - Čakovec. Ⓡ.
71 – Ⓐ: [2] Čakovec - Koprivnica - Zagreb. Ⓡ.

Q – ⑦ (also Apr. 21; not June 20): [2] Kotoriba - Varaždin - Koprivnica.
V – [2] Koprivnica - Varaždin - Kotoriba and v.v.
a – Ⓐ only.
b – Ⓑ only.
d – ⚒ only.
j – Not ⑤⑥ and days before holidays.
k – Via Koprivnica.
q – Also Apr. 21; not June 20.
r – Arrive 1352.
t – Not Nov. 1.
y – ⑤ (also Apr. 30, June 18, Aug. 14; not May 2, June 20, Aug. 15).

HŽ, MÁV ZAGREB - KOPRIVNICA - NAGYKANIZSA and OSIJEK 1340

km			1205	783	703	201	981	205	IC 570	IC 581	971	
		2	♦	♦	♦	♦	2	♦	♦	Ⓡ🍷	2	2
	Rijeka **1310** d.	...	...	...	0540	...	...	...	...	...	...	...
0	**Zagreb** d.	...	0324	0706	1002	1002	1256	1436	1631	1704	1835	2022
57	Križevci d.	...	0413	0752	1048	1048	1352	1535	1718	1747	1930	2124
88	Koprivnica **1335** d.	...	0437	0825	1119	1122	1444	1613	1737	1820	2003	2155
03	Gyékényes 🏛 d.	...	0535	|	|	1200	|	1644	...	|	...	...
32	**Nagykanizsa** a.	...	0600	|	|	1235	|	|	...	|	...	...
	Budapest Déli **1220** a.	...	0944k	|	|	1629	|	2115k	...	|	...	...
53	Virovitica d.	0418	...	0931	1225	...	1602	...	...	1921	...	...
25	Našice d.	0538	...	1047	1350	...	1737	...	...	2031	...	...
75	**Osijek 1345** a.	0641	...	1130	1435	...	1830	...	...	2112	...	...

		IC 571	IC 580	200		702	204	782	1204		980
	2	♦	Ⓡ🍷	♦	2Ⓐ		♦	♦	♦	2	2
Osijek 1345 d.	...	...	0530	...	...	1203	...	1620	...	1933	2348
Našice d.	...	...	0612	...	...	1247	...	1705	...	2034	0035
Virovitica d.	...	...	0724	...	...	1403	...	1820	...	2154	0153
Budapest Déli **1220** d.	...	...	|	0605	...	|	1445k	|	1815k	...	|
Nagykanizsa d.	...	...	|	0945	...	|	|	|	2158	...	|
Gyékényes 🏛 d.	...	...	|	1047	...	|	1913	|	2242	...	|
Koprivnica **1335** d.	0500	0621	0837	1118	1400	1513	1941	1941	2258	...	0308
Križevci d.	0532	0641	0857	1150	1429	1536	2002	2002	2317	...	0344
Zagreb a.	0632	0722	0937	1247	1526	1620	2049	2049	0001	...	0440
Rijeka **1310** a.	...	...	...	...	...	2049	...	...	...	...	...

♦ – **NOTES** (LISTED BY TRAIN NUMBER)

0 – AGRAM – [12] Budapest - Koprivnica (**2206**) - Zagreb.
1 – AGRAM – [12] Ljubljana (**499**) - Zagreb (**703**) - Koprivnica - Budapest.
4 – [12] Budapest - Koprivnica (**782**) - Zagreb (**498**) - Ljubljana; ✕ Budapest - Zagreb.
5 – [12] and ✕ Zagreb (**2207**) - Koprivnica - Budapest.
0/1 – Ⓐ: [2] Zagreb - Koprivnica - Čakovec and v.v. Ⓡ.
3 – [12] Rijeka - Zagreb - Osijek. Conveys [12] Ljubljana (**499**) - Zagreb - Koprivnica (**201**) - Budapest.
2 – [12] Osijek - Zagreb; [12] Budapest (**204**) - Koprivnica - Zagreb (**498**) - Ljubljana). Conveys June 27 - Aug. 30: [2] Osijek - Zagreb (**1823**) - Split.
783 – [12] Zagreb - Osijek. Conveys June 28 - Aug. 31 (from Split, one day later from Zagreb: [2] Split (**1822**) - Zagreb - Osijek.
1204 – ADRIA – ②⑤ June 13 - Aug. 29: 🛏 1,2 cl., ▬ 2 cl., [2] and ✕ Budapest - Zagreb - Split; 🛏 1,2 cl. Praha (**277**) - Budapest - Split; 🛏 1,2 cl. Moskva (**15**) - Budapest - Split.
1205 – ADRIA – ③⑥ June 14 - Aug. 30 (from Split, one day later from Zagreb): 🛏 1,2 cl., ▬ 2 cl., [2] and ✕ Split - Zagreb - Budapest; 🛏 1,2 cl. Split - Budapest (**276**) - Praha; 🛏 1,2 cl. Split - Budapest (**16**) - Moskva.
k – Budapest **Keleti**.

1345 PÉCS - OSIJEK - DOBOJ

2nd class only except where shown HŽ, MÁV, ŽRS

There is currently no service Slavonski Šamac - Šamac and v.v.

km																												
			⚒	🚌 Ⓐ	Ⓐ		⚒	Ⓐ	⚒	⚒	⚒			⚒	Ⓐ		Ⓐ		🚌	⚒						Ⓐ	Ⓑ	Ⓐ
	Budapest Déli 1200 ..... d.	...	...	...	...	...	...	...	...	...	...	...	...	...	...	...	...	...	...	...	...	...	...	...	...	...	...	...
0	**Pécs** ..... d.	...	...	...	...	...	...	...	...	...	...	...	...	...	...	...	...	...	...	...	...	...	...	...	...	...	...	...
43	Magyarbóly ..... 🏛 d.	...	...	...	...	...	...	...	...	...	...	...	...	...	...	...	...	...	...	...	...	...	...	...	...	...	...	...
54	Beli Manastir ..... 🏛 d.	...	...	...	0543	0703	...	...	0822	...	...	1051	...	1223	...	...	1410	...	...	...	1615	...	1843	...	...	2005	...	2302
82	**Osijek 1340** ..... a.	...	...	...	0614	0734	...	...	0853	...	...	1122	...	1254	...	...	1441	...	...	...	1646	...	1914	...	...	2036	...	2333
82	**Osijek 1340** ..... d.	...	0418	...	...	...	0749	0805	...	0900	1053	...	...	...	1351	1406	...	1540	...	1623	...	1818	...	2000	2015	...	2220	...
	Vinkovci ..... a.	...	|	...	...	...	0832	|	...	|	1136	...	...	...	|	1449	...	|	...	1705	...	1901	...	|	2058	...	2303	...
130	Strizivojna-Vrpolje **1320** ... d.	...	0521	0527	...	...	...	0909	...	1004	...	...	...	...	1455	...	...	1641	1642	...	...	...	...	2103	...	...	...	...
150	Slavonski Šamac ..... 🏛 d.	...	...	0549	...	...	...	...	...	...	...	...	...	...	...	...	...	...	1705	...	...	...	...	...	...	...	...	...
154	Šamac ..... 🏛 d.	0450	...	...	...	...	...	...	...	...	...	...	...	...	...	...	...	...	...	...	...	...	...	...	...	...	...	...
226	**Doboj 1350** ..... a.	0625	...	...	...	...	...	...	...	...	...	...	...	...	...	...	...	...	...	...	...	...	...	...	...	...	...	...

km																												
			Ⓐ	⚒		Ⓐ	🚌 Ⓐ	⚒	⚒	⚒		Ⓐ	⚒	⚒		Ⓐ		⚒	Ⓐ			Ⓐ		🚌			Ⓑ	Ⓐ
	Doboj 1350 ..... d.	...	...	...	...	...	...	...	...	...	...	...	...	...	...	...	...	...	...	...	...	...	...	...	...	1920	...	...
	Šamac ..... 🏛 d.	...	...	...	...	...	...	...	...	...	...	...	...	...	...	...	...	...	...	...	...	...	...	...	...	2055	...	...
	Slavonski Šamac ..... 🏛 d.	...	...	...	...	...	0557	...	...	...	...	...	...	...	...	...	...	...	...	...	...	...	...	1712	...	...	...	...
	Strizivojna-Vrpolje **1320** ... d.	0055	...	...	...	0535	0618	0620	...	...	...	1011	...	1140	...	...	...	...	1650	...	...	...	...	1733	1858	...	...	...
0	Vinkovci ..... d.	|	...	0538	...	|	...	|	0642	...	...	|	...	|	1203	...	...	1517	|	...	1727	...	1909	...	|	...	2108	...
35	**Osijek 1340** ..... a.	0149	...	0621	...	0635	...	0721	0725	...	...	1111	...	1241	1245	...	...	1600	1751	...	1810	...	1952	...	1957	...	2151	...
	Osijek 1340 ..... d.	...	0502	...	0624	...	...	...	...	0741	1010	...	1142	...	...	1320	1527	...	...	1802	...	1924	...	...	...	...	...	2221
	Beli Manastir ..... 🏛 d.	...	0533	...	0655	...	...	...	...	0812	1041	...	1213	...	...	1351	1558	...	...	1833	...	1955	...	...	...	...	...	2252
	Magyarbóly ..... 🏛 d.	...	...	...	...	...	...	...	...	...	...	...	...	...	...	...	...	...	...	...	...	...	...	...	...	...	...	...
	Pécs ..... a.	...	...	...	...	...	...	...	...	...	...	...	...	...	...	...	...	...	...	...	...	...	...	...	...	...	...	...
	Budapest Déli 1200 ..... a.	...	...	...	...	...	...	...	...	...	...	...	...	...	...	...	...	...	...	...	...	...	...	...	...	...	...	...

1350 ZAGREB and BIHAĆ - DOBOJ - SARAJEVO

2nd class only except where shown HŽ, ŽFBH, ŽRS

Services between Bihać and Novi Grad are currently suspended

km				715													397								
0	**Zagreb 1322** ..... d.	...	...	...	...	...	...	...	...	...	...	...	...	...	...	...	0918	...	...	...	...	...	...	...	...
72	Sunja **1322** ..... ⊡ d.	...	...	...	...	...	...	...	...	...	...	...	...	...	...	...	1033	...	...	...	...	...	...	...	...
	Bihać 1358 ..... d.	...	...	...	...	...	...	...	...	...	...	...	...	...	...	...	|	...	...	...	...	...	...	...	...
	Blatna ..... d.	...	...	...	...	...	...	...	...	...	...	...	...	...	...	...	|	...	...	...	...	...	...	...	...
112	Novi Grad ..... ⊡ d.	...	...	...	...	...	...	...	...	0432	...	...	...	0710	...	...	1205	...	...	...	...	...	...	...	1905
214	Banja Luka ..... d.	...	...	...	...	...	0429	...	...	0629	0724	...	...	0917	...	...	1342	...	...	1532	...	...	...	1924	2110
324	**Doboj 1345** ..... a.	...	...	...	...	...	0637	...	...	...	0939	...	...	...	...	...	1509	...	...	1741	...	...	...	2139	...
324	**Doboj 1345** ..... d.	...	...	0425	...	...	...	...	...	...	...	...	...	...	...	...	1518	...	...	...	...	...	...	...	...
347	Maglaj ..... d.	...	...	0452	...	0515	...	...	...	...	...	0930	...	...	...	...	1545	...	...	...	1707	...	...	...	...
370	Zavidovici ..... d.	...	...	0513	...	0543	...	...	...	...	...	0958	...	...	...	...	1606	...	...	...	1735	...	...	...	...
419	Zenica ..... d.	0506	...	0608	...	0641	...	0747	...	...	...	1056	1106	...	1513	...	1653	...	...	...	1833	1918	...	...	...
447	Kakanj ..... d.	0539	...	0634	...	...	...	0826	...	...	...	...	1144	...	1546	...	1719	...	1736	...	...	1951	...	...	...
465	Visoko ..... d.	0600	...	0650	...	...	...	0847	...	...	...	...	1210	...	1612	...	1735	...	1803	...	...	2012	...	...	...
472	Podlugovi ..... d.	0609	...	0658	...	...	...	0856	...	...	...	...	1219	...	1620	...	1743	...	1812	...	...	2021	...	...	...
496	**Sarajevo 1355** ..... a.	0645	...	0728	...	...	...	0932	...	...	...	...	1255	...	...	...	1813	...	1848	...	...	2057	...	...	...

km										396									714						
	Sarajevo 1355 ..... d.	...	...	0447	...	...	...	0713	...	1046	...	...	1122	...	...	...	1524	...	1553	...	...	...	...	...	1924
	Podlugovi ..... d.	...	...	0524	...	...	...	0754	...	1117	...	...	1159	...	...	...	1601	...	1624	...	...	1724	...	...	2001
	Visoko ..... d.	...	...	0533	...	...	...	0803	...	1125	...	...	1208	...	...	...	1610	...	1632	...	...	1737	...	...	2014
	Kakanj ..... d.	...	...	0600	...	...	...	0824	...	1141	...	...	1229	...	...	...	1630	...	1648	...	...	1758	...	...	2035
	Zenica ..... d.	...	...	0637	...	0725	...	0856	...	1208	...	...	1301	...	1531	...	...	...	1721	...	...	1830	1925	...	2107
	Zavidovici ..... d.	...	...	...	...	0824	...	...	...	1254	...	...	...	...	1630	...	...	...	1807	...	...	...	2024	...	...
	Maglaj ..... d.	...	...	...	...	0851	...	...	...	1315	...	...	...	...	1657	...	...	...	1828	...	...	...	2051	...	...
	Doboj 1345 ..... a.	...	...	...	...	...	...	...	...	1341	...	...	...	...	...	...	...	...	1854	...	...	...	...	...	...
	Doboj 1345 ..... d.	0402	...	...	0732	...	...	...	...	1351	...	...	...	1525	...	...	...	...	...	...	1932	...	...	...	...
	Banja Luka ..... d.	0617	0730	...	0941	...	...	...	...	1527	...	1541	...	1747	...	...	...	1923	...	...	2141	...	...	...	...
0	Novi Grad ..... ⊡ d.	...	0936	...	...	...	...	...	...	1704	...	1739	...	...	...	...	...	2124	...	...	...	...	...	...	...
20	Blatna ..... d.	...	...	...	...	...	...	...	...	|	...	...	...	...	...	...	...	...	...	...	...	...	...	...	...
78	**Bihać 1358** ..... a.	...	...	...	...	...	...	...	...	|	...	...	...	...	...	...	...	...	...	...	...	...	...	...	...
	Sunja **1322** ..... ⊡ d.	...	...	...	...	...	...	...	...	1836	...	...	...	...	...	...	...	...	...	...	...	...	...	...	...
	Zagreb 1322 ..... a.	...	...	...	...	...	...	...	...	1951	...	...	...	...	...	...	...	...	...	...	...	...	...	...	...

⊡ – 🏛 at Volinja (Croatia) / Dobrljin (Bosnia-Herzegovina).

1355 SARAJEVO - PLOČE

Most services 2nd class only HŽ, ŽFBH

km				723						721	
		🚌 ⚒	🚌 ⚒			🚌 Ⓐ		🚌 ⚒			
	Zagreb 1350 ..... d.	...	...	...	...	...	...	...	...	...	...
0	**Sarajevo 1350** ..... d.	...	...	0651	0715	...	1530	...	...	1857	1921
67	Konjic ..... d.	...	...	0818	0859	...	1709	...	...	2024	2105
129	Mostar ..... d.	...	...	0928	...	...	...	...	...	2134	...
149	Žitomislići ..... d.	...	...	0947	...	...	...	...	...	2153	...
163	Čapljina ..... 🏛 d.	...	...	1003	...	...	...	...	...	2209	...
173	Metković ..... d.	0516	0633	...	...	1325	...	1705	...	...	...
194	**Ploče** ..... a.	0546	0703	...	...	1353	...	1733	...	...	...

			720							722
		🚌 ⚒				🚌 Ⓐ	🚌 ⚒			
Ploče ..... d.	...	0555	...	...	...	1243	1420	...	...	...
Metković ..... d.	...	0625	...	...	...	1311	1448	...	...	...
Čapljina ..... 🏛 d.	...	...	0630	...	...	...	...	...	...	1835
Žitomislići ..... d.	...	...	0647	...	...	...	...	...	...	1852
Mostar ..... d.	...	...	0707	...	...	...	...	...	...	1912
Konjic ..... d.	0501	...	0820	...	1121	...	...	1716	...	2027
Sarajevo 1350 ..... a.	0640	...	0946	...	1300	...	...	1855	...	2153
Zagreb 1350 ..... a.	...	...	...	...	...	...	...	...	...	...

1358 LOCAL SERVICES in Bosnia

2nd class only HŽ, ŽFBH, ŽRS

VINKOVCI - TUZLA and v.v. :

Services between Brčko and Tuzla are currently suspended

km		Ⓐ					Ⓐ	
0	Vinkovci ..... d.	0326	0952	...	1500	...	1933	...
49	Gunja ..... d.	0426	1053	...	1601	...	2034	...
53	Brčko ..... 🏛 d.	...	...	...	...	...	...	...
127	Tuzla ..... a.	...	...	...	...	...	...	...

	Ⓐ					Ⓐ	
Tuzla ..... d.	...	...	...	...	...	...	...
Brčko ..... 🏛 d.	...	...	...	...	...	...	...
Gunja ..... d.	0433	...	1100	1608	...	2041	...
Vinkovci ..... a.	0534	...	1200	1709	...	2142	...

TUZLA - DOBOJ and v.v. :

km				Ⓐ				
0	Tuzla ..... d.	...	1020	...	...	1709	...	...
32	Petrovo Novo . d.	0540	1104	1410	...	1753	2035	...
60	Doboj ..... a.	0628	1152	1458	...	1841	2123	...

				Ⓐ			
Doboj ..... d.	0442	0728	...	1315	1528	1930	...
Petrovo Novo d.	0530	0817	...	1403	1617	2018	...
Tuzla ..... a.	...	0900	...	...	1700	...	...

BIHAĆ - MARTIN BROD and v.v. :

km						
0	Bihać **1350** ... d.	...	...	...	...	...
38	Kulen Vakuf .. d.	...	...	...	...	...
48	Martin Brod .. a.	...	...	...	...	...

Martin Brod ..... d.	...	...	...	...	...
Kulen Vakuf ..... d.	...	...	...	...	...
Bihać **1350** ..... a.	...	...	...	...	...

SERBIA, MONTENEGRO and FYRO MACEDONIA

MAP PAGE 501

Operators: Železnice Srbije (ŽS): www.zeleznicesrbije.com; Železnice Crne Gore (ŽCG): www.zcg-prevoz.me; Makedonski Železnici (MŽ): www.mztransportad.com.mk; Trainkos (KŽ/HK): www.trainkos.com.

Services: All trains convey first- and second-class seating, except where shown otherwise in footnotes, by a '2' in the train column, or where the footnote shows that the train conveys sleeping- (🛏) and / or couchette (▬) cars only. Descriptions of sleeping- and couchette cars are given on page 8.

Timings: Valid until **December 13, 2014** except where indicated otherwise. Readers should note, however, that further changes are possible.
Services may be amended or cancelled at short notice and passengers are strongly advised to check locally before travelling.

Tickets: A supplement is payable for travel by internal express trains. Reservation of seats is possible on most express trains.

Visas: Most nationals do not require a visa to enter Serbia and Montenegro, but must obtain an entry stamp in their passport, sight of which will be required by officials on leaving the country. These must be obtained at a border crossing recognised by the authorities - this excludes Kosovo's external borders with Montenegro, Former Yugoslav Republic Of Macedonia (FYROM) and Albania. Note also that Serbia should not be entered from Kosovo unless initial travel into Kosovo was via Serbia. Visas are not required for entry into FYROM for most nationals.

Currency: Visitors must declare large amounts of foreign currency upon arrival; currently €2000 in Montenegro, and €10000 in Serbia and FYROM. It is reported, however, that FYROM may now be operating on a threshold of €2000. A certificate issued by the customs officer must be presented on departure, otherwise any funds held may be confiscated.

Security: Following the declaration of independence by Kosovo (which has not been recognised by Serbia) caution should be exercised when travelling in southern Serbia and northern Kosovo. Caution is also advised in the northern and western border regions of the Former Yugoslav Republic Of Macedonia.

ŽS (BUDAPEST -) KELEBIA - SUBOTICA - BEOGRAD 1360

km		341 ◐ B		2	2	2	IC 541 [R] 2 ◧		2		2	2		IC 547 [R] 2 ◧	2		743 Y	2	IC 273 ⚡ A		2	1137 P	2	2
	Budapest Keleti **1295** d.	2220	...	...	...	...	...	...	...	...	...	...	...	...	...	...	...	...	1305	...	...	...	...	...
0	**Kelebia** 🏛 d.	0140	...	...	...	...	...	...	...	...	...	...	...	...	...	...	...	...	1620	...	...	...	...	...
10	**Subotica 1362** 🏛 a.	0152	...	...	...	...	...	...	...	...	...	...	...	...	...	...	...	...	1632	...	...	...	...	...
10	**Subotica** d.	0230	...	...	0410	...	0545	...	0734	...	1015	...	...	...	...	...	1434	...	1700	...	...	1818	1930	...
108	Novi Sad **1362** a.	0451	...	...	0646	...	0800	...	1006	...	1243	...	...	...	...	...	1654	...	1913	...	...	2047	2200	...
108	Novi Sad d.	0500	...	0600	...	0723	0805	...	1017	...	...	1255	...	1415	1517	...	1724	1753	1920	...	2035	2117	...	2222
181	Novi Beograd d.	0620	...	0735	...	0855	0922	...	1156	...	...	1424	...	1539	1705	...	1850	1936	2038	...	2209	2237	...	2351
186	**Beograd** a.	0632	...	0747	...	0907	0934	...	1208	...	...	1436	...	1551	1717	...	1902	1948	2050	...	2221	...	...	0003

	2	2	2	1136 P		IC 272 ⚡ A		742 Y	2			IC 546 [R] 2 ◧		2		2		IC 540 [R] 2 ◧		2	2		340 ◐ B	
Beograd d.	...	0440	...	...	...	0645	...	0715	0815	...	1015	1115	...	1300	...	1525	...	1645	...	1800	2013	...	2145	...
Novi Beograd d.	...	0453	...	0517	...	0658	...	0728	0827	...	1028	1128	...	1313	...	1538	...	1658	...	1813	2025	...	2158	...
Novi Sad **1362** a.	...	0642	...	0657	...	0825	...	0903	0955	...	1204	1250	...	1454	...	1717	...	1815	...	1949	2156	...	2316	...
Novi Sad d.	0422	...	0706	0728	...	0834	...	0934	...	...	...	...	...	1516	...	...	...	1820	...	1952	...	...	2319	...
Subotica 1362 a.	0653	...	0936	1002	...	1053	...	1210	...	...	...	...	...	1809	...	...	...	2040	...	2236	...	...	0136	...
Subotica 🏛 d.	...	...	...	...	...	1128	...	...	...	...	...	...	...	...	...	...	...	...	...	...	...	...	0218	...
Kelebia 🏛 a.	...	...	...	...	...	1140	...	...	...	...	...	...	...	...	...	...	...	...	...	...	...	...	0230	...
Budapest Keleti **1295** a.	...	...	...	...	...	1454	...	...	...	...	...	...	...	...	...	...	...	...	...	...	...	...	0604	...

A – AVALA – [12] and ✕ Praha - Budapest - Beograd and v.v.; 🛏 1, 2 cl. Moskva (**15/6**) - Budapest - Beograd and v.v. Conveys ①③ June 11 - Sept. 3 (from Moskva); ④⑥ June 14 - Sept. 6 (from Bar): 🛏 1, 2 cl. Moskva (**15/6**) - Budapest - Subotica (**1136/7**) - Bar and v.v. Conveys ①⑤ June 13 - Sept. 5 (from Budapest); ②⑥ June 14 - Sept. 6 (from Bar): 🛏 1, 2 cl. and ▬ 2 cl. (also [2] July 4 - Aug. 29 from Budapest; July 5 - Aug. 30 from Bar) Budapest - Subotica (**1136/7**) - Bar and v.v. Conveys June 13 - Sept. 5 (from Praha); June 14 - Sept. 6 (from Bar): ▬ 2 cl. (also 🛏 1, 2 cl. ②③⑤⑥ from Praha, ③④⑥⑦ from Bar) Praha - Subotica (**1136/7**) - Bar and v.v.

B – BEOGRAD – 🛏 1, 2 cl., ▬ 2 cl. and [2] Beograd - Budapest and v.v.

P – PANONIJA – June 6 - Sept. 7 (from Subotica); June 7 - Sept. 8 (from Bar): 🛏 1, 2 cl., ▬ 2 cl. and [2] Subotica - Bar and v.v. Conveys ①⑤ June 13 - Sept. 5 (from Budapest); ②⑥ June 14 - Sept. 6 (from Bar): 🛏 1, 2 cl. and ▬ 2 cl. (also [2] July 4 - Aug. 29 from Budapest; July 5 - Aug. 30 from Bar) Budapest (**272/3**) - Subotica - Bar and v.v. Conveys June 13 - Sept. 5 (from Praha); June 14 - Sept. 6 (from Bar): ▬ 2 cl. (also 🛏 1, 2 cl. ②③⑤⑥ from Praha, ③④⑥⑦ from Bar) Praha (**272/3**) - Subotica - Bar and v.v. Conveys ①③ June 11 - Sept. 3 (from Moskva); ④⑥ June 14 - Sept. 6 (from Bar): 🛏 1, 2 cl. Moskva (**15/6**) - Budapest (**272/3**) - Subotica - Bar and v.v.

Y – [12] Beograd - Subotica and v.v. Conveys Dec. 15 - June 5, Sept. 8 - Dec. 12 (from Subotica and Novi Sad); Dec. 15 - June 6, Sept. 9 - Dec. 12 (from Bar): ▬ 2 cl. and [2] Subotica - Beograd (**432/3**) - Bar and v.v.; ▬ 2 cl. Novi Sad - Beograd (**432/3**) - Bar and v.v.

◧ – Train with 'global' price.
◐ – Supplement payable for travel in Serbia.
⚡ – Supplement payable for travel in Hungary and Serbia.

ŽS 2nd class only SUBOTICA - KIKINDA, ZRENJANIN, NOVI SAD and PANČEVO 1362

km												
	Subotica 1360 d.	...	0400	...	...	0705	...	...	1330	...	1618	...
	Senta d.	...	0516	...	...	0827	...	...	1444	...	1742	...
	Banatsko Miloševo d.	...	...	...	...	0918	...	...	...	...	1836j	...
0	**Kikinda 1377** d.	...	...	0430	...	0935	1110	...	...	1815	1853	...
19	Banatsko Miloševo d.	...	...	0448	...	...	1128	...	...	1833	...	...
71	**Zrenjanin** d.	0315	...	0633	0645	...	1313	1425	...	2018	...	2025
96	Orlovat stajalište d.	0408	...	...	0739	...	...	1519	...	...	...	2127
	Novi Sad **1360** a.	...	...	...	|	...	...	|	...	...	...	|
145	**Pančevo** glavna **1365/6** a.	...	...	...	0849	...	...	1631	...	...	...	2243

Pančevo glavna **1365/6** d.	...	...	...	...	...	1116	...	...	1756	...	2250
Novi Sad **1360** d.	...	...	...	...	...	|	...	...	|	...	|
Orlovat stajalište d.	0529	...	...	...	...	1226	...	...	1908	...	0006
Zrenjanin d.	0623	0700	...	...	...	1320	1410	...	2002	2030	0059
Banatsko Miloševo a.	▬	0846	...	...	...	...	1556	...	...	2216	...
Kikinda 1377 a.	...	0903	0947	...	...	...	1613	1905	...	2233	...
Banatsko Miloševo d.	...	...	1010	...	...	...	...	1930	...	...	...
Senta d.	0531	...	1100	...	1454	...	...	2022	...	...	...
Subotica 1360 a.	0645	...	1214	...	1608	...	...	2138	...	...	...

j – Arrive 1827.

ŽS, CFR 2nd class only except where shown BEOGRAD - VRŠAC - TIMISOARA 1365

km										
0	**Beograd** d.	...	...	...	...	...	...	...	...	...
6	Beograd Dunav d.	0720	...	...	1145	1550	...	...	2030	...
7	Pančevački Most d.	0724	...	...	1149	1554	...	...	2034	...
22	Pančevo glavna **1362/6** d.	0751	...	...	1216	1621	...	...	2101	...
89	Vršac a.	0905	...	...	1330	1735	...	...	2215	...
89	Vršac 🏛 d.	...	1038	...	...	...	1830	...	...	...
109	Stamora Moravita 🏛 § a.	...	1200	...	...	...	1952	...	...	...
109	Stamora Moravita § d.	...	1230	...	...	...	2029	...	...	...
165	**Timisoara** Nord § a.	...	1329	...	...	...	2129	...	...	...

Timisoara Nord § d.	...	...	0748	...	...	...	...	1613	...
Stamora Moravita § a.	...	...	0900	...	...	...	...	1727	...
Stamora Moravita 🏛 § d.	...	...	0930	...	...	...	...	1807	...
Vršac 🏛 a.	...	...	0852	...	...	...	...	1729	...
Vršac d.	0515	...	...	0940	...	1350	...	...	1800
Pančevo glavna **1362/6** d.	0631	...	...	1056	...	1506	...	...	1916
Pančevački Most d.	0658	...	...	1123	...	1533	...	...	1943
Beograd Dunav d.	0701	...	...	1126	...	1536	...	...	1946
Beograd a.	...	...	...	...	...	...	...	...	...

§ – Romanian (East European) time.

ŽS 2nd class only NOVI BEOGRAD - PANČEVO local services 1366

Novi Beograd d.	...	0715	...	0815	0915	...	1015	1115	1215	...	1315	1415	...	1515	1615	...	...	1715	1815	...	1915	2015	2100	...	2145	2230
Beograd centar d.	...	0721	...	0821	0921	...	1021	1121	1221	...	1321	1421	...	1521	1621	...	...	1721	1821	...	1921	2021	2106	...	2151	2236
Pančevački Most d.	0739	0731	0805	0831	0931	1020	1031	1131	1231	1235	1331	1431	1435	1531	1631	1637	1729	1731	1831	1922	1931	2031	2116	2130	2201	2246
Pančevo glavna **1362/5** d.	0806	...	0829	...	...	1043	...	...	...	1258	...	...	1459	...	...	1705	1756	...	...	1951	...	...	...	2154	...	...

Pančevo glavna **1362/5** d.	...	0716	...	...	0912	...	0932	...	...	1141	...	1336	...	...	...	1546	...	...	1832	...	...	2041	...	2236	...	...
Pančevački Most d.	0702	0742	0802	0902	0935	1002	0955	1102	1202	1207	1302	1357	1402	1502	1602	1612	1702	1802	1855	1902	2002	2108	2132	2257	2217	2302
Beograd centar d.	0713	...	0813	0913	...	1013	...	1113	1213	...	1313	...	1413	1513	1613	...	1713	1813	...	1913	2013	...	2143	...	2228	2313
Novi Beograd a.	0719	...	0819	0919	...	1019	...	1119	1219	...	1319	...	1419	1519	1619	...	1719	1819	...	1919	2019	...	2149	...	2234	2319

1370 BEOGRAD - PODGORICA - BAR

ŽCG, ŽS

km		2 Z	2	2	2	2	2	2 Z	2	431 T		2	2	IC 581 [R] 2 ◧ ⊗	2	IC 513 [R] 2 ◧	2	2	433 L		1343 A	2	2	1137 P
0	**Beograd** d.	...	...	0245	...	0705	...	...	...	0910	...	...	1035	1445	1505	1620	...	1905	2010	...	2110	...	...	2239n
93	Valjevo d.	...	...	0504	...	0920	...	...	...	1102	...	...	1242	1641	1716	1828	...	2114	2202	...	|	...	...	0033
	Kraljevo **1372/5** d.	...	...	|	...	|	...	...	...	|	...	...	|	|	|	|	...	|	|	...	|	...	...	|
159	Požega **1372** d.	...	...	0707	...	1057	...	...	...	1228	...	...	1419	1826	1856	1959	...	2250	2328	...	0030	...	...	0200
185	Užice d.	...	...	0747	...	1136	...	...	...	1301	...	...	1505	...	1936	2035	...	2319	0003	...	0109	...	...	0300
288	Prijepolje d.	...	...	1013	...	1358	...	...	...	1517	...	...	1736	...	2158	2244	...	...	0218	...	0430t	...	...	0523
338	Bijelo Polje ⊞ d.	...	0902	...	...	...	...	...	...	1721	...	1835	...	...	...	...	...	...	0415	...	0545	0630	...	0720
468	**Podgorica 1371** d.	1010	1130	...	1250	...	1520	1650	1800	1929	...	2110	...	...	...	...	0515	...	0627	...	0758	0853	0905	0955
524	**Bar** a.	1112	1226	...	1346	...	1620	1756	1856	2027	...	2206	...	...	...	...	0614	...	0728	...	0849	...	1008	1046

	IC 580 [R] 🍷 ◧ ⊗	IC 512 [R] 2 ◧	2	2	2	2	2		430 T	2	2	2	2	2	2	2	1136 P	2	2 Z	432 L	2		1342 A	2
Bar d.	...	...	...	...	0525	0635	...	...	0900	1020	1135	...	1405	...	1450	1640	1700	...	1830	1900	...	...	2000	2030
Podgorica 1371 d.	...	...	...	...	0625	0732	...	...	1000	1118	1234	...	1501	...	1550	1737	1801	1820	1928	2005	...	...	2105	2134
Bijelo Polje ⊞ d.	...	...	...	...	0843	...	...	...	1227	...	...	...	...	...	1812	...	2040	2049	...	2235	...	...	2335	...
Prijepolje d.	...	0301	0326	0731	...	...	1131	...	1358	...	...	1536	...	1956	...	...	2202	...	...	0001	...	...	0050t	...
Užice d.	...	0520	0600	1021	...	...	1410	...	1618	...	...	1815	...	2250	...	...	0050	...	...	0220	0230	...	0345	...
Požega **1372** d.	0459	0548	0631	1058	...	...	1441	...	1643	...	...	1856	...	...	...	...	0125	...	...	0245	0302	...	0434	...
Kraljevo **1372/5** a.	|	|	|	|	...	...	|	...	|	...	...	|	...	...	...	...	|	...	...	|	|	...	|	...
Valjevo d.	0626	0714	0809	1243	...	...	1619	...	1809	...	...	2033	...	...	...	...	0300	...	...	0411	0439	...	|	...
Beograd a.	0826	0904	1028	1451	...	...	1834	...	1958	...	...	2314	...	...	...	...	0515n	...	...	0601	0642	...	0753	...

A – AUTO-VOZ – June 6 - Sept. 7 (from Beograd); June 7 - Sept. 8 (from Bar): 🛏 1, 2 cl. and ━ 2 cl. Beograd - Bar and v.v.

L – LOVĆEN – 🛏 1, 2 cl., ━ 2 cl. and [2] Beograd - Bar and v.v. Conveys Dec. 15 - June 5, Sept. 8 - Dec. 12 (from Subotica and Novi Sad); Dec. 15 - June 6, Sept. 9 - Dec. 12 (from Bar): ━ 2 cl. and [2] Subotica (**742/3**) - Beograd - Bar and v.v.; ━ 2 cl. Novi Sad (**742/3**) - Beograd - Bar and v.v.

P – PANONIJA – June 6 - Sept. 7 (from Subotica); June 7 - Sept. 8 (from Bar): 🛏 1, 2 cl., ━ 2 cl. and [2] Subotica - Bar and v.v. Conveys ①⑤ June 13 - Sept. 5 (from Budapest); ②⑥ June 14 - Sept. 6 (from Bar): 🛏 1, 2 cl. and ━ 2 cl. (also [2] July 4 - Aug. 29 from Budapest; July 5 - Aug. 30 from Bar) Budapest (**272/3**) - Subotica - Bar and v.v. Conveys June 13 - Sept. 5 (from Praha); June 14 - Sept. 6 (from Bar): ━ 2 cl. (also 🛏 1, 2 cl. ②③⑤⑥ from Praha, ③④⑥⑦ from Bar) Praha (**272/3**) - Subotica - Bar and v.v. Conveys ①③ June 11 - Sept. 3 (from Moskva); ④⑥ June 14 - Sept. 6 (from Bar): 🛏 1, 2 cl. Moskva (**15/6**) - Budapest (**272/3**) - Subotica - Bar and v.v.

T – TARA – [12] Beograd - Bar and v.v.

Z – from / to Nikšić.

n – **Novi Beograd**.

t – Prijepolje **teretna**.

◧ – Train with 'global' price.

⊗ – Temporarily suspended.

1371 PODGORICA - NIKŠIĆ

ŽCG

km									B	
0	**Podgorica 1370** d.	0700	0805	1120	...	1400	1610	...	1935	2030
25	Danilovgrad d.	0732	0832	1145	...	1427	1642	...	2002	2055
61	**Nikšić** a.	0813	0920	1223	...	1508	1723	...	2043	2140

		B				B			
Nikšić d.	0625	0840	0950	...	1240	1535	1805	...	2100
Danilovgrad d.	0707	0922	1032	...	1319	1617	1847	...	2142
Podgorica 1370 a.	0735	0948	1058	...	1343	1643	1913	...	2206

B – From / to Bar.

1372 POŽEGA - KRALJEVO

2nd class only ŽS

tariff km							IC 581 [R] 2 ◧ ⊗				
0	**Požega 1370** d.	0605	0830	...	1255	1645	1828	...	2030	2120	...
45	Čačak d.	0647	0912	...	1337	1727	1856	...	2112	2202	...
83	**Kraljevo 1370/5** a.	0745	0958	...	1423	1813	2014	...	2158	2248	...
	Lapovo **1375/80** a.	...	...	...	...	...	...	...	...	...	...
	Niš **1373/80** a.	...	...	...	...	...	...	...	...	...	...

	IC 580 [R] 2 ◧ ⊗									
Niš **1373/80** d.	...	...	...	...	...	...	...	...	...	...
Lapovo **1375/80** d.	...	...	...	...	...	...	...	...	...	...
Kraljevo 1370/5 d.	0358	...	0412	0630	...	1050	...	1445	1635	1825
Čačak d.	0428	...	0459	0717	...	1137	...	1532	1732	1912
Požega 1370 a.	0456	...	0540	0758	...	1218	...	1613	1813	1953

◧ – Train with 'global' price.

⊗ – Temporarily suspended.

1373 BEOGRAD - ZAJEČAR - NIŠ

2nd class only except where shown ŽS

tariff km													
0	**Beograd** d.	...	...	...	0415	...	...	1025	...	...	...	...	1935
98	Požarevac ♣ d.	...	...	...	0636	...	...	1247	...	...	...	...	2147
199	Majdanpek ♣ d.	...	0400	...	▬	0915	...	...	...	1705	...	...	...
★	Prahovo pristanište d.	...	|	0400	0835	|	...	...	...	|	1750	...	...
296	**Zaječar** d.	0350	0615	0635f	1022	1125	1150	...	1505	1921	1937	1955	...
343	Knjaževac d.	0456	...	0739	...	...	1306	...	1609	...	...	2101	...
420	**Niš 1372/80** a.	0703	...	0954	...	...	1512	...	1818	...	...	2307	...

Niš 1372/80 d.	0240	...	...	0720	1051	...	...	1545	...	...	1845
Knjaževac d.	0502	...	...	0931	1300	...	...	1803	...	...	2107
Zaječar d.	0608	0630	0645	1035	1404	1430	1530	1909	2005	2025	2213
Prahovo pristanište a.	▬	0816	|	▬	▬	|	1716	▬	2151	|	...
Majdanpek ♣ d.	...	...	0855	...	...	1642	...	...	...	2235	...
Požarevac ♣ d.	0440	...	...	1055	1341	...	...	1942	...	...	...
Beograd a.	0701	...	...	1313	1601	...	...	2210	...	...	...

f – Arrive 0547.

★ – Prahovo - Zaječar: *81 km*.

♣ – Currently no service Požarevac - Majdanpek and v.v.

1375 LAPOVO and PRIŠTINA - KOSOVO POLJE - SKOPJE

2nd class only except where shown ŽS, KŽ

km					891 ⊠	⊠		⊠		761 ⊠		⊠	
	Beograd **1380** d.	...	...	...	...	...	...	...	...	...	...	...	...
0	**Lapovo 1380** d.	...	0325	...	...	...	1105	...	...	...	...	...	1840
28	**Kragujevac** d.	...	0424	...	...	...	1204	...	...	...	...	...	1939
82	Kraljevo **1370/2** d.	0240	0624	0655	...	...	1404	...	1500	...	...	...	2139
163	Raška d.	0419	...	0837	...	...	...	...	1642	...	...	...	...
180	Lešak d.	...	...	0910	...	...	...	...	1715	...	...	...	...
210	Zvečan ♣ d.	...	...	1021	...	...	...	...	1828	...	...	...	...
214	Mitrovica ♣ d.	...	...	...	...	...	...	...	...	...	...	...	...
	Priština d.	...	...	...	0710	0750	...	...	...	1630	...	...	...
247	**Kosovo Polje** ♣ d.	...	...	...	0722	0801	...	1605	...	1641	...	1848	...
*	Peć a.	...	...	...	|	0950	...	|	...	1826	...	|	...
276	Uroševac d.	...	...	...	0802	...	...	1649	...	...	...	1935	...
304	Deneral Janković ⊞ a.	...	...	...	0900	...	...	1730	...	...	...	2016	...
331	**Skopje 1380/5** a.	...	...	...	0952	...	...	...	...	...	...	...	...

	⊠		760 ⊠		⊠			⊠	892 ⊠		
Skopje 1380/5 d.	...	...	...	...	...	...	...	...	1620	...	...
Deneral Janković ⊞ d.	0548	...	...	...	1050	...	...	...	1745	...	...
Uroševac d.	0632	...	...	...	1135	...	...	...	1829	...	...
Peć d.	|	...	0532	...	|	...	...	1210	|	...	...
Kosovo Polje ♣ d.	0714	...	0721	...	1219	...	...	1359	1910	...	...
Priština a.	...	...	0732	...	...	...	...	1410	1920	...	...
Mitrovica ♣ d.	...	...	...	...	...	...	...	...	...	...	...
Zvečan ♣ d.	...	...	...	...	...	1045	...	...	...	1855	...
Lešak d.	...	...	...	...	...	1154	...	...	...	2004	...
Raška d.	...	0435	...	...	...	1229	...	...	...	2039	...
Kraljevo **1370/2** d.	...	0620	...	0646	...	1414	1455	...	...	2224	2235
Kragujevac d.	...	...	...	0847	...	...	1656	...	...	...	0036
Lapovo 1380 a.	...	...	...	0945	...	...	1754	...	...	...	0134
Beograd **1380** a.	...	...	...	...	...	...	...	...	...	...	...

⊠ – Service operated by KŽ (see country heading).

* – Kosovo Polje - Peć: *82 km*.

♣ – Currently no service Zvečan - Mitrovica - Kosovo Polje and v.v.

1377 MINOR BORDER CROSSINGS

2nd class only ŽS, MÁV, CFR

SUBOTICA - SZEGED and v.v.:

km				
0	Subotica d.	0728	1057	*1440*
24	Horgoš ⊞ d.	0833	1202	1543
31	Röszke ⊞ a.	0850	1219	1600
43	Szeged a.	*0930*	*1300*	1630

Szeged d.	*0822*	*1153*	1430
Röszke ⊞ d.	0907	1236	1500
Horgoš ⊞ d.	0939	1308	1517
Subotica a.	1030	1359	*1813*

KIKINDA - JIMBOLIA - TIMISOARA and v.v.:

km								
0	Kikinda **1362** d.	...	...	0945	...	...	1640	...
19	Jimbolia ⊞ § d.	0502	0844	1104	1229	1728	1759	2010
58	Timisoara § a.	0550	0932	...	1317	1816	...	2058

Timisoara § d.	0702	0817	...	1424	1617	...	1938
Jimbolia ⊞ § d.	0750	0927	1135	1534	1705	1820	2050
Kikinda **1362** a.	...	...	1054	...	...	1739	...

§ – East European time, one hour ahead of Central European time.

ŽS, MŽ, BDŽ — BEOGRAD - NIŠ - SOFIA, SKOPJE and THESSALONÍKI — 1380

km											337													335		293
		2	2	2	2	2	2⚒	2	2	2	S	2	2	2	2	2	2	2	2	2	2	2	2	H	2	N
0	**Beograd 1375** d.	...	...	...	...	...	...	0330	...	0720	0750	←	...	...	...	...	1010	...	...	...	...	1530	...	1845	1925	2150
110	Lapovo **1372/5** d.	...	0335	...	...	...	...	0611	...	0942	0948	0952	...	...	...	...	1254	1551	...	...	...	1813	...	2108	2155	2347
135	Jagodina d.	...	0401	...	...	...	...	0637	...	→	1008	1018	...	...	...	...	1320	1617	...	...	...	1839	...	2129	...	0007
155	Paraćin d.	...	0428	...	...	...	...	0704	...	...	1033	1045	...	...	...	...	1346	1644	...	...	...	1906	...	2156	...	0032
176	Stalać **1372** d.	...	0452	...	...	...	...	0729	...	...	1057	1110	...	...	...	...	...	1707	...	...	...	1931	...	2222	...	0055
244	**Niš 1372/3** a.	...	0620	...	...	...	...	0904	...	...	1159	1244	...	...	...	...	...	1843	...	...	...	2102	...	2325	...	0157
244	**Niš** d.	0340	...	...	0724	0725	...	...	...	...	1218	...	...	1520	1530	1550	...	...	...	...	1935	...	...	2341	...	0245
	Dimitrovgrad ▦ d.	|	...	...	|	1018	...	...	...	...	|	...	...	|	1823	|	...	...	...	...	|	...	...	|	...	0530
	Dragoman ▦ § d.	|	...	...	|	...	...	...	...	...	|	...	...	|	...	|	...	...	...	...	|	...	...	|	...	0726
	Sofia § a.	|	...	...	|	...	...	...	...	...	|	...	...	|	...	|	...	...	...	...	|	...	...	|	...	0813
288	Leskovac d.	0442	...	...	0826	...	...	...	...	...	1308	...	...	1622	...	1651	...	...	...	...	2036	...	...	0028	...	...
392	Preševo ▦ d.	0719	...	...	...	...	...	...	...	...	1600	...	...	1851	...	...	...	...	...	...	2313	...	...	0322	...	...
401	Tabanovci ▦ d.	...	...	0747	...	...	...	...	...	...	1640	...	1740	...	...	...	...	...	2011	...	...	...	0503	0402	...	...
462	**Skopje** a.	...	...	0845	...	...	...	...	...	...	1722	...	1835	...	...	...	...	...	2108	...	...	...	0555	0444	...	...
462	**Skopje 1375/85** d.	...	...	0900	...	...	1320	...	1650	...	...	...	...	...	...	...	...	...	...	2240	...	...	0605	0506	...	...
524	Veles **1385** d.	...	...	0952	...	...	1410	...	1741	...	...	...	...	...	...	...	...	...	...	2330	...	...	0656	0601	...	...
651	Gevgelija a.	...	...	1139	...	...	...	...	1923	...	...	...	...	...	...	...	...	...	...	...	...	...	0843	0749	...	...
651	Gevgelija ▦ d.	...	...	...	...	...	...	...	...	...	...	...	...	...	...	...	...	...	...	...	...	...	...	0830	...	...
654	Idoméni ▦ a.	...	...	...	...	...	...	...	...	...	...	...	...	...	...	...	...	...	...	...	...	...	...	0935	...	...
654	Idoméni d.	...	...	...	...	...	...	...	...	...	...	...	...	...	...	...	...	...	...	...	...	...	...	1010	...	...
730	**Thessaloníki 1400** § a.	...	...	...	...	...	...	...	...	...	...	...	...	...	...	...	...	...	...	...	...	...	...	1116	...	...

km											336											292			334	
		2	2	2	2	2	2⚒	2	2	2	S	2		2	2	2	2	2	2⚒	2	2	P	2	2	H	2
	Thessaloníki 1400 § d.	...	...	...	...	...	...	...	...	...	...	...	...	...	...	...	...	...	...	...	...	...	...	...	1552	...
	Idoméni a.	...	...	...	...	...	...	...	...	...	...	...	...	...	...	...	...	...	...	...	...	...	...	...	1659	...
	Idoméni ▦ d.	...	...	...	...	...	...	...	...	...	...	...	...	...	...	...	...	...	...	...	...	...	...	...	1732	...
	Gevgelija ▦ a.	...	...	...	...	...	...	...	...	...	...	...	...	...	...	...	...	...	...	...	...	...	...	...	1637	...
	Gevgelija d.	...	...	...	...	...	...	0449	...	...	...	...	...	0956	...	...	...	...	...	...	...	...	...	1700	1715	...
	Veles **1385** d.	...	...	...	0511	...	0610	0633	...	...	...	...	...	1150	...	...	...	...	1423	...	...	...	...	1848	1858	...
	Skopje 1375/85 a.	...	...	...	0603	...	0712	0726	...	...	...	...	...	1240	...	...	...	...	1519	...	...	...	...	1937	1950	...
	Skopje d.	...	...	...	0620	...	...	...	...	...	0820	...	...	▬	...	...	...	...	...	1620	...	...	1900	...	2010	2300
	Tabanovci ▦ a.	...	...	...	0720	...	...	...	...	...	0924	...	...	...	...	...	...	...	...	1720	...	...	1956	...	2124	0438
	Preševo ▦ d.	...	...	0250	...	...	...	...	...	0815	1000	...	...	...	...	...	...	...	...	...	1935	...	...	...	2205	...
	Leskovac d.	...	...	0527	...	...	...	...	...	1052	1228	...	1248	...	...	1720	...	...	...	...	2210	...	...	...	0027	...
0	**Sofia** § d.	...	...	|	...	...	...	...	...	|	|	...	|	...	...	|	...	...	...	...	|	2030	...	...	|	...
42	Dragoman ▦ § d.	...	...	|	...	...	...	...	...	|	|	...	|	2	...	|	...	2	...	...	|	2114	...	...	|	...
63	Dimitrovgrad ▦ d.	...	...	|	...	...	...	...	...	|	|	...	|	1130	...	|	...	1920	...	...	|	2120	...	...	|	...
161	**Niš 1372/3** a.	...	...	0628	...	...	...	...	...	1153	1311	...	1352	1423	...	1821	...	2213	...	...	2311	2340	...	...	0109	...
	Niš d.	...	0315	...	...	0735	...	...	1105	...	1321	...	...	...	1540	...	1920	...	...	...	...	0002	...	...	0121	...
	Stalać **1372** d.	...	0453	...	...	0909	...	...	1240	...	1424	...	...	...	1711	...	2055	...	...	...	...	0111	...	...	0224	...
	Paraćin d.	...	0515	...	...	0930	...	...	1301	...	1446	1500	...	...	1733	...	2117	...	...	...	...	0131	...	...	0244	...
	Jagodina d.	...	0540	...	...	0956	...	...	1328	...	1513	1526	...	...	1759	...	2144	...	...	...	...	0158	...	...	0311	...
	Lapovo **1372/5** d.	0350	0614	...	...	1030	...	...	1352	...	1534	1554	...	...	1833	...	2208	...	...	...	...	0219	...	...	0332	...
	Beograd 1375 a.	0626	0847	...	...	1257	...	...	...	...	1809	1823	...	...	2107	...	...	...	...	...	...	0454	...	...	0533	...

H – HELLAS – 🛏 2 cl. and 🚃2 Beograd - Skopje - Thessaloníki and v.v.
N – NUŠIĆ – 🛏 2 cl. and 🚃2 Beograd - Sofia. Conveys ⑤ June 20 - Aug. 29 (from Skopje): 🛏 2 cl. Skopje (**334**) - Niš (**293**) - Sofia (**3623**) - Burgas.
P – NUŠIĆ – 🛏 2 cl. and 🚃2 Sofia - Beograd. Conveys ⑦ June 22 - Aug. 31 (from Burgas and Sofia): 🛏 2 cl. Burgas (**3622**) - Sofia (**292**) - Niš (**335**) - Skopje.
S – 🚃2 Beograd - Skopje and v.v.

§ – East European time.

MŽ 2nd class only — BRANCH LINES in FYRO Macedonia — 1385

SKOPJE - KOČANI and BITOLA and v.v. :

km					🅁 §		
0	Skopje **1380** d.	0648	1430	1522	1710	1938	...
62	Veles **1380** d.	0753	1526	1621	1752	2027	...
★	Kočani a.	|	|	1814	|	|	...
170	Prilep d.	0939	1712	...	1926	2225	...
228	Bitola a.	1027	1800	...	2000	2313	...

		🅁 §				
Bitola d.	0310	0530	...	1245	1835	...
Prilep d.	0349	0610	...	1335	1924	...
Kočani d.	|	|	0550	|	|	...
Veles **1380** d.	0540	0730	0750	1525	2115	...
Skopje **1380** a.	0638	0811	0840	1616	2205	...

SKOPJE - KIČEVO and v.v. :

km				
0	Skopje d.	0805	1650	...
86	Tetovo d.	0911	1753	...
163	Kičevo a.	1012	1854	...

Kičevo d.	0533	1218	...
Tetovo d.	0633	1319	...
Skopje a.	0735	1422	...

§ – Also conveys 🚃1.
★ – Veles - Kočani : *110 km.*

ALBANIA

SEE MAP PAGE 501

Operator: Hekurudha Shqiptarë (HSH).
Services: Trains convey one class of accommodation only. Tickets are not sold in advance, only for the next available departure.
Timings: Timings have been compiled from the latest information received, but readers should be aware that timetable amendments usually come into effect at short notice, and are advised to check information locally before travelling.
Security: Most visits to Albania are reported to be trouble free, but travellers are advised to avoid the north-east of the country.

HSH One class only — ALBANIAN RAILWAYS — 1390

Tiranë - Vorë and v.v. is currently closed

km	km										
	0	**Shkodër** d.	...	...	0545	...	...	...	...	...	...
0		**Tiranë** d.	...	...	|	...	...	...	...	...	...
16	82	Vorë d.	...	...	0904	...	...	...	...	...	...
	98	**Tiranë** a.	...	...	|	...	...	...	...	...	...
36	—	**Durrës** a.	...	...	0940	...	...	...	...	...	...
—	0	**Durrës** d.	0720	...	...	...	1325	...	1510	...	...
		Rrogozhinë a.	0830	...	...	...	1435	...	1619	...	...
0	36	Rrogozhinë d.	0832	...	...	...	1453	...	1621	...	...
	77	Elbasan a.	1008	...	...	...	|	...	1755	...	...
	98	**Librazhd** a.	1100	...	...	...	|	...	...	...	...
17		Lushnjë a.	...	...	...	...	1530	...	...	...	...
49		Fier a.	...	...	...	...	1637	...	...	...	...
83		**Vlorë** a.	...	...	...	...	1816	...	...	...	...

Vlorë d.	...	...	0500	...	...	...	...	...	...
Fier d.	...	...	0639	...	...	...	...	...	...
Lushnjë d.	...	...	0746	...	...	...	...	...	...
Librazhd d.	...	...	|	...	...	...	1215	...	...
Elbasan d.	0600	...	|	...	...	...	1305	...	...
Rrogozhinë a.	0730	...	0822	...	...	...	1438	...	...
Rrogozhinë d.	0732	...	0837	...	...	...	1444	...	...
Durrës a.	0843	...	0945	...	...	...	1553	...	...
Durrës d.	...	...	...	...	1300	...	...	...	...
Tiranë d.	...	...	...	...	|	...	...	...	...
Vorë d.	...	...	...	...	1352	...	...	...	...
Tiranë a.	...	...	...	...	|	...	...	...	...
Shkodër a.	...	...	...	...	1705	...	...	...	...

GREECE

SEE MAP PAGE 501

Operator: TRAINOSE S.A., ΤΡΑΙΝΟΣΕ Α.Ε.: www.trainose.gr.

Services: All trains convey first and second class seating except where shown otherwise in footnotes or by '2' in the train column, or where the footnote shows sleeping and/or couchette cars only. Descriptions of sleeping (🛏) and couchette (🛏) cars appear on page 8. Services that convey catering may vary from day to day.

Timings: Timings have been compiled from the latest information received. Readers should be aware that timetable amendments may come into effect at short notice, and are advised to check information locally before travelling. There are currently no cross-border passenger trains serving Greece.

Tickets: Reservation of seats is possible (and recommended) on most express trains. *IC* trains carry a supplement which varies depending upon distance travelled. Break of journey is only permitted when tickets are so endorsed before travel with the station quoted.

1400 ATHÍNA - LÁRISA - THESSALONÍKI

km			**590**		*IC* **50**	**884**		**2590**	*IC* **52**		**3520**		*IC* **54**		*IC* **56**		*IC* **58**		*IC* **60**	**1510**		**3592**		**500**
		2		2	✕⚡	🍷	2	2	✕⚡	2	⑦		✕⚡	2	✕⚡	2	🍷⚡		✕⚡		2	2		🍷
0	**Athína** Lárisa **1420** d.	...	...	...	0718	0827	...	...	1018	...	1118	...	1218	...	1418	...	1615	...	1818	1917	...	...	...	2355
7	SKA (Acharnon) **1420/40** d.	...	...	...	0728	0836	...	...	1028	...	1127	...	1227	...	1427	...	1624	...	1827	1926	...	...	...	0005
61	Inói **1420** d.	...	...	...	0808	0916	...	...	1108	...	1206	...	1308	...	1508	...	1702	...	1908	2005	...	...	...	0047
89	Thíva d.	...	...	...	0824	0931	...	...	1124	...	1222	...	1324	...	1524	...	1716	...	1924	2021	...	...	...	0105
129	Levadiá d.	...	...	...	0843	0953	...	...	1143	...	1247	...	1343	...	1543	...	1736	...	1943	2046	...	...	...	0128
154	Tithoréa d.	...	...	...	|	1006	...	...	|	...	1308	...	|	...	1555	...	|	...	1955	2107	...	...	...	0142
169	Amfíklia d.	...	...	...	|	1019	...	...	|	...	1320	...	|	...	|	...	|	...	|	2119	...	...	...	|
210	Lianokládi d.	0515	...	0815	0941	1102	1115	...	1241	1315	1402	...	1441	1515	1641	1810	1838	...	2041	2202	2215	...	...	0230
	Lamia d.	0525	...	0825	|	|	1125	...	|	1325	...	...	|	1525	|	1820	|	...	|	...	2225	...	...	|
	Stilída a.	0548	...	0848	|	|	1148	...	|	1348	...	...	|	1548	|	1843	|	...	|	...	2248	...	...	|
291	Paleofársalos **1408** d.	...	0917	...	1100	1222r	...	1232	1400	...	...	...	1600	...	1805	...	1949	...	2200	...	...	...	...	0353
	Kalambáka **1408** a.	...	0819p	...	|	1318	...	|	|	...	...	...	|	...	|	...	|	...	|	...	...	...	...	|
333	**Lárisa 1425** ▲ d.	...	0941	...	1120	...	...	1252	1420	...	...	...	1619	...	1824	...	2009	...	2219	...	...	2337	...	0418
417	Kateríni ▲ d.	...	1031	...	1157	...	...	1338	1457	...	...	...	1657	...	1902	...	2046	...	2257	...	...	0023	...	0507
465	Platí **1410** ▲ d.	...	1057	...	1218	...	...	1402	1518	...	...	...	1718	...	1923	...	2107	...	2318	...	...	0048	...	0534
502	**Thessaloníki 1410** ▲ a.	...	1124	...	1241	...	...	1428	1541	...	...	...	1741	...	1946	...	2131	...	2341	...	...	0113	...	0601

km			**1511**		*IC* **51**		*IC* **53**			*IC* **55**			*IC* **57**		**3521**		*IC* **59**	**591**		**885**	*IC* **61**			**501**
		2			🍷⚡	2	✕⚡		2	✕⚡		2	✕⚡	2	⑦		✕⚡		2	🍷	✕⚡	2		🍷
	Thessaloníki 1410 ▲ d.	...	...	...	0511	...	0704	...	...	1004	...	...	1204	...	...	...	1504	1617	...	...	1804	...	...	2300
	Platí **1410** ▲ d.	...	...	...	0535	...	0728	...	...	1028	...	...	1228	...	...	...	1528	1645	...	...	1828	...	...	2328
	Kateríni ▲ d.	...	...	...	0556	...	0749	...	...	1049	...	...	1249	...	...	...	1549	1712	...	...	1849	...	...	2355
	Lárisa 1425 ▲ d.	...	...	...	0633	...	0826	...	...	1126	...	...	1326	...	...	...	1626	1801	...	...	1926	...	...	0043
	Kalambáka **1408** d.	...	...	...	|	...	|	...	...	|	...	...	|	...	...	...	|	1925p	...	1732	|	...	...	|
	Paleofársalos **1408** d.	...	...	...	0657	...	0845	...	...	1145	...	...	1345	...	...	...	1645	1824	...	1830	1945	...	...	0107
0	Stilída d.	0607	...	...	|	0857	|	...	1157	|	...	1357	|	1557	...	...	|	...	1857	|	|	2254	...	|
17	Lamia d.	0630	...	...	|	0920	|	...	1220	|	...	1420	|	1620	...	...	|	...	1920	|	|	2317	...	|
23	Lianokládi d.	0639	0649	...	0805	0929	1006	...	1229	1306	...	1429	1506	1629	1642	...	1803	...	1929	1943	2105	2326	...	0231
	Amfíklia d.	...	0729	...	|	...	|	...	...	|	...	...	|	...	1722	...	|	...	...	2025	|	...	...	|
	Tithoréa d.	...	0740	...	|	...	|	...	...	1350	...	...	|	...	1733	...	1850	...	...	2036	|	...	...	|
	Levadiá d.	...	0800	...	0906	...	1101	...	...	1401	...	...	1601	...	1753	...	1901	...	...	2048	2201	...	...	0331
	Thíva d.	...	0825	...	|	...	1121	...	...	1421	...	...	1622	...	1818	...	1921	...	...	2110	2221	...	...	0354
	Inói **1420** d.	...	0841	...	0940	...	1137	...	...	1437	...	...	1637	...	1834	...	1937	...	...	2125	2236	...	...	0412
	SKA (Acharnon) **1420/40** d.	...	0919	...	1018	...	1216	...	...	1516	...	...	1716	...	1912	...	2016	...	...	2204	2315	...	...	0452
	Athína Lárisa **1420** a.	...	0928	...	1026	...	1224	...	...	1524	...	...	1724	...	1921	...	2024	...	...	2212	2324	...	...	0501

▲ – Local service Thessaloníki - Litóhoro - Lárisa and v.v.:

Thessaloníki d.	0537	0640	0800	0920	1258	1425	1537	1714	1837	2045	2147
Platí d.	0604	0707	0827	0947	1325	1452	1604	1741	1904	2112	2214
Kateríni d.	0628	0731	0852	1011	1349	1516	1628	1805	1928	2136	2238
Litóhoro △ d.	0638	0741	0902	1021	1359	1526	1638	1815	1938	2146	2248
Lárisa a.	0712	0815	0936	1055	1433	1600	1712	1849	2012	2220	2322

Lárisa d.	0600	0720	0830	1046	1150	1450	1645	1738	1900	2109	2337
Litóhoro △ d.	0637	0757	0907	1123	1227	1527	1722	1815	1937	2146	0014
Kateríni d.	0646	0806	0916	1132	1236	1536	1731	1824	1946	2155	0023
Platí d.	0711	0831	0941	1157	1301	1601	1756	1849	2011	2220	0048
Thessaloníki a.	0736	0856	1006	1222	1326	1626	1821	1914	2036	2245	0113

FOR NOTES SEE TABLE 1405

1405 THESSALONÍKI - ALEXANDRÚPOLI - DÍKEA

OSE, BDZh

There are currently no cross-border services from / to Turkey

km		**1682**		**610**	**1684**		*IC* **90**	**1686**		
		2			2		⚡	2		
0	**Thessaloníki** d.	...	...	0711	...	...	1610	...	...	...
42	Kilkís d.	...	...	0755	...	...	1651	...	...	...
97	Rodópoli d.	...	...	0839	...	...	1725	...	...	...
130	Strimón d.	...	...	0908	...	...	|	...	...	...
162	Sérres d.	...	...	0930	...	...	1806	...	...	...
232	Dráma d.	...	...	1026	...	...	1856	...	...	...
327	Xánthi d.	...	...	1203	...	...	2031	...	...	...
374	Komotiní d.	...	...	1235	...	...	2059	...	...	...
	Alexandrúpoli a.	0754	...	1330	...	...	2150	2207	...	...
443	**Alexandrúpoli** Port d.	0803	...	1342	1442	...	2202	2216	...	...
	Alexandrúpoli d.	0808	...	1346	1447	...	2206	2221	...	...
556	Píthio d.	0954	...	...	1633	...	...	0007	...	...
*	*İstanbul Sirkeci* **1550** a.	|	...	...	|	...	...	|	...	...
574	Néa Orestiáda d.	1022	...	...	1701	...	...	0035	...	...
611	Díkea a.	1109	...	...	1748	...	...	0122	...	...

	IC **91**	**1681**		**1683**		**611**		**1685**	
	⚡	2		2				2	
Díkea d.	...	0426	...	1132	...	...	...	1822	...
Néa Orestiáda d.	...	0514	...	1220	...	...	...	1910	...
İstanbul Sirkeci **1550** d.	...	|	...	|	...	...	...	|	...
Píthio d.	...	0542	...	1248	...	...	...	1938	...
Alexandrúpoli a.	0716	0727k	...	1433	...	1534	...	2123	...
Alexandrúpoli Port d.	0725	0740	...	1438	...	1543	...	2133	...
Alexandrúpoli d.	0732	0744	...	...	...	1550	...	2147	...
Komotiní d.	0824	...	...	...	...	1645	...	...	...
Xánthi d.	0852	...	...	...	...	1717	...	...	...
Dráma d.	1025	...	...	...	...	1857	...	...	...
Sérres d.	1115	...	...	...	...	1951	...	...	...
Strimón d.	|	...	...	...	...	2013	...	...	...
Rodópoli d.	1156	...	...	...	...	2042	...	...	...
Kilkís d.	1229	...	...	...	...	2126	...	...	...
Thessaloníki a.	1308	...	...	...	...	2209	...	...	...

k – Connection available into train *IC* **91** at Alexandrúpoli (a. 0727, d. 0732).
p – Via Paleofársalos.
r – Arrive 1211.

⚡ – 🅁 with supplement payable. *Icity* train.
△ – Station for Mount Ólimbos.
* – Píthio - İstanbul: *268 km*.

1408 LÁRISA - PALEOFÁRSALOS - KALAMBÁKA

km		**880**	*IC* **51**	**882**		**884**		**886**	
		♦	🍷⚡	♦		🍷		♦	
	Thessaloníki **1400** d.	...	0511	...	...	...	...	1617	...
	Athína **1400** d.	...	|	...	...	0827	...	|	...
	Lárisa 1400 d.	0424	0633	0650	...	|	...	1801	...
0	Paleofársalos **1400** d.	0451	0651	0717	...	1222	...	1831	...
31	Kardítsa d.	0511	...	0737	...	1242	...	1851	...
60	Tríkala d.	0530	...	0756	...	1303	...	1910	...
82	**Kalambáka 1400** ⊡ a.	0545	...	0811	...	1318	...	1925	...

	883		**885**		**887**	*IC* **60**		
	♦		🍷		♦	✕⚡		
Kalambáka 1400 ⊡ d.	0819	...	1732	...	2058	...	...	...
Tríkala d.	0835	...	1748	...	2114	...	...	...
Kardítsa d.	0854	...	1809	...	2134	...	...	...
Paleofársalos **1400** a.	0913	...	1828	...	2152	2200	...	...
Lárisa 1400 a.	0941	...	|	...	2243	2219	...	...
Athína **1400** a.	|	...	2212	...	...	|	...	...
Thessaloníki **1400** a.	1124	...	...	...	...	2341	...	...

♦ – **NOTES** (LISTED BY TRAIN NUMBER)

880 – 12 Lárisa (**561**) - Paleofársalos - Kalambáka.
882 – 12 Lárisa (**563**) - Paleofársalos - Kalambáka.
883 – 12 Kalambáka - Paleofársalos (**590**) - Thessaloníki.
886 – 12 Thessaloníki (**591**) - Paleofársalos - Kalambáka.
887 – 12 Kalambáka - Paleofársalos (**562**) - Lárisa.

⚡ – 🅁 with supplement payable. *Icity* train.

⊡ – An infrequent bus service operates Kalambáka - Igumenítsa and v.v. (approximately *250 km*).

THESSALONÍKI - ÉDESSA - FLÓRINA 1410

km											
			IC 81			*IC* 83				*IC* 85	
		Ⓐ		Ⓐ			Ⓐ		Ⓐ		
0	**Thessaloníki 1400/05** d.	0430	0714	0820	1046	1223	1328	1547	1659	1930	2132
38	Platí **1400** d.	0459	0741	0849	1115	1250	1357	1616	1728	1957	2203
69	Véria d.	0532	0803	0918	1146	1311	1426	1645	1759	2018	2232
97	Skídra d.	0555	0822	0941	1209	1330	1449	1708	1822	2037	2255
112	**Édessa** a.	0609	0837	0955	1223	1345	1503	1722	1836	2052	2309
162	Amíndeo d.	...	0921	...	...	1429	...	...	...	2136	...
196	**Flórina** a.	...	0947	...	...	1455	...	...	...	2202	...

			IC 82		*IC* 84			*IC* 86		
		Ⓐ		Ⓐ			Ⓐ			Ⓐ
Flórina d.	...	...	0615	...	0959	...	...	1612	...	...
Amíndeo d.	...	...	0643	...	1026	...	...	1640	...	...
Édessa d.	0450	0616	0727	1004	1111	1233	1509	1724	1842	2056
Skídra d.	0505	0631	0742	1019	1126	1248	1524	1739	1857	2111
Véria d.	0528	0653	0802	1041	1145	1312	1546	1758	1919	2133
Platí **1400** d.	0556	0722	0822	1110	1205	1341	1617	1819	1948	2202
Thessaloníki 1400/05 a.	0625	0751	0848	1139	1231	1410	1646	1845	2017	2231

PIREÁS - ATHÍNA - HALKÍDA 1420

km																								
		Ⓐ													Ⓐ									
0	Pireás d.	...	...	0530	0630	0730	0830	0930	1030	1130	...	1230	1330	1430	...	1530	1630	1730	1830	1930	2030	2130	2230	...
10	**Athína** Lárisa **1400** d.	0433	0449	0550	0650	0750	0850	0950	1050	1150	...	1250	1350	1450	1519	1550	1650	1750	1850	1950	2050	2150	2250	...
17	SKA (Acharnon) **1400/40** d.	0441	0459	0600	0700	0800	0900	1000	1100	1200	...	1300	1400	1500	1529	1600	1700	1800	1900	2000	2100	2200	2300	...
71	Inói **1400** d.	0522	0552	0654	0752	0852	0952	1052	1152	1252	...	1352	1452	1552	1617	1652	1752	1852	1952	2052	2152	2250	2351	...
94	**Halkída** a.	...	0614	0716	0814	0914	1014	1114	1214	1314	...	1414	1514	1614	...	1714	1814	1914	2014	2114	2214	...	0013	...

	Ⓐ		Ⓐ		Ⓐ												Ⓐ						
Halkída d.	...	0527	...	0625	...	0728	0828	0928	1028	1128	1228	1328	1428	...	1528	1628	...	1728	1828	1928	2028	2128	...	2224
Inói **1400** d.	0529	0552	0622	0652	0720	0752	0852	0952	1052	1152	1252	1352	1452	...	1552	1652	1727	1752	1852	1952	2052	2152	...	2252
SKA (Acharnon) **1400/40** d.	0616	0641	0709	0741	0807	0841	0941	1041	1141	1241	1341	1441	1541	...	1641	1741	1814	1841	1941	2041	2141	2241	...	2341
Athína Lárisa **1400** a.	0635	0650	0723	0750	0816	0850	0950	1050	1150	1250	1350	1450	1550	...	1650	1750	1823	1850	1950	2050	2150	2250	...	2350
Pireás a.	...	0708	...	0810	...	0908	1008	1108	1208	1308	1413	1508	1608	...	1708	1811	...	1910	2008	2108	2208	2318	...	0008

LÁRISA - VÓLOS 1425

km												
0	Lárisa **1425** d.	0437	0637	0837	1130	...	1430	1630	1830	2018	2230	...
61	Vólos a.	0525	0725	0925	1218	...	1518	1718	1918	2106	2318	...

Vólos d.	0530	0730	1025	...	1225	1525	1725	1925	2125	2325	...
Lárisa **1425** a.	0618	0818	1113	...	1313	1613	1813	2013	2213	0013	...

2nd class — ATHÍNA AIRPORT ✈ and ATHÍNA - KÓRINTHOS - KIÁTO 1440

km	km										
0		**Athína** Airport ✈ ▲ d.	0526	...	0544	0611	and	2111	2126	...	2144
25		Neratziótissa ▲ d.	0548	...	0607	0634	at the	2134	2148	...	2207
	0	**Athína** Lárisa d.	|	0550	|	|	same	|	|	2150	|
31	7	SKA (Acharnon) **1400/20** d.	0555	0600	0613	0640	minutes	2140	2155	2200	2213
34		Ano Liosia d.	0558	...	0617	0643	past each	2143	2158	...	2217
104		**Kórinthos** d.	...	...	0706	...	hour	...	...	...	2306
125		**Kiáto 1450** a.	...	...	0719	...	until	...	...	...	2319

Kiáto 1450 d.	...	0525	...	...	and	...	...	2125	...
Kórinthos d.	...	0539	...	...	at the	...	...	2139	...
Ano Liosia d.	0602	0628	...	0647	same	2147	2202	2228	...
SKA (Acharnon) **1400/20** d.	0605	0632	0641	0650	minutes	2150	2205	2232	2241
Athína Lárisa a.	|	|	0650	|	past each	|	|	|	2250
Neratziótissa ▲ d.	0612	0638	...	0657	hour	2157	2212	2238	...
Athína Airport ✈ ▲ a.	0635	0701	...	0720	until	2220	2235	2301	...

▲ – Frequent Metro services operate as follows:
Line 1 (green): Pireás - Monastiraki - Omónia - Attiki - Neratziótissa - Kifissia.
Line 2 (red): Aghios Dimitrios - Syntagma - Omónia - Athína Lárisa (for **Athína** mainline station) - Attiki - Aghios Antonios.
Line 3 (blue): Egaleo - Monastiraki - Syntagma - Athína Airport ✈.
Operators: ISAP Line 1; Attiko Metro Lines 2 and 3.

Additional trains operate on Ⓐ Athína Airport - Neratziótissa and v.v.

KIÁTO - PÁTRA 🚌 services (including Pireás, Athína and Athína Airport connections) 1450

Pireás d.	0530	...	0730	...	1030	...	1330	...	1530	...	1730	...
Athína Lárisa d.	0550	...	0750	...	1150	...	1350	...	1550	...	1750	...
Athína Airport ✈ d.	|	0544	|	0744	|	1144	|	1344	|	1544	|	1744
Neratziótissa d.	|	0607	|	0807	|	1207	|	1407	|	1607	|	1807
SKA (Acharnon) d.	0600	0613	0800	0813	1200	1213	1400	1413	1600	1613	1800	1813
Kórinthos d.	...	0706	...	0906	...	1306	...	1506	...	1706	...	1906
Kiáto a.	...	0719	...	0919	...	1319	...	1519	...	1719	...	1919
change to bus												
		🚌		🚌		🚌		🚌		🚌		🚌
Kiáto 1440 d.	...	0725	...	0930	...	1330	...	1530	...	1730	...	1930
Xilókastro d.	...	|	...	0950	...	|	...	|	...	1750	...	|
Diakoftó **1455** d.	...	|	...	1055	...	1415	...	1615	...	1855	...	|
Pátra a.	...	0850	...	1200	...	1520	...	1720	...	2000	...	2100

	🚌		🚌		🚌		🚌		🚌		🚌	
Pátra d.	0650	...	0850	...	1130	...	1350	...	1630	...	1850	...
Diakoftó **1455** d.	0755	...	|	...	1220	...	1455	...	1720	...	|	...
Xilókastro d.	0900	...	|	...	|	...	1600	...	|	...	|	...
Kiáto 1440 a.	0920	...	1020	...	1320	...	1620	...	1820	...	2020	...
change to train												
Kiáto d.	0925	...	1025	...	1325	...	1625	...	1825	...	2025	...
Kórinthos d.	0939	...	1039	...	1339	...	1639	...	1839	...	2039	...
SKA (Acharnon) d.	1032	1041	1132	1141	1432	1541	1732	1741	1932	1941	2132	2141
Neratziótissa d.	1038	|	1138	|	1438	|	1738	|	1938	|	2138	|
Athína Airport ✈ a.	1101	|	1201	|	1501	|	1801	|	2001	|	2201	|
Athína Lárisa d.	...	1050	...	1150	...	1550	...	1750	...	1950	...	2150
Pireás a.	...	1108	...	1208	...	1608	...	1808	...	2008	...	2208

PELOPÓNNISOS narrow-gauge branches 1455

Diakoftó – Kalávrita

2nd class only, rack railway

km						
				Ⓒ		Ⓒ
0	Diakoftó **1450** d.	0845	1115	1233	1432	1550
23	Kalávrita a.	0952	1222	1343	1542	1700

			Ⓒ		Ⓒ
Kalávrita d.	0957	1227	1430	1550	1650
Diakoftó **1450** a.	1104	1337	1540	1700	1757

⊗ – Service currently suspended.

Katákolo – Pírgos – Olimbía

2nd class only

km											
					⊗	⊗			⊗	⊗	⊗
0	Katákolo d.	...	0840	...	1030	1211	...	...	1405	1550	1730
12	Pírgos a.	0700	0904	...	1050	1233	1235	...	1425	1610	1752
33	Olimbía a.	0728	0932	...	1112	...	1303	...	1447	1632	...

		⊗		⊗			⊗	⊗	⊗	
Olimbía d.	0733	...	0937	1120	...	1308	...	1500	1637	...
Pírgos d.	0804	1000	1005	1144	...	1336	1338	1524	1701	...
Katákolo a.	0826	1018	...	1202	...	...	1400	1542	1719	...

🚌 INTERNATIONAL BUS SERVICES 1460

A number of operators run long-distance 🚌 services to and from Greece, and selected services are listed below. Details should be checked with the relevant operator before travel. Rail tickets and passes are not valid. Further details about travelling to Greece by bus can be found on www.europebyrail.eu

ATHÍNA - ISTANBUL: Depart Athína 1700. Depart Istanbul 1800. Journey 16 hours. Operator: Metro www.metroturizm.com.tr

THESSALONIKI - ISTANBUL: Depart Thessaloniki 2100. Depart Istanbul 2100. Journey 10 - 11 hours. Operator: Simeonidis Tours www.simeonidistours.gr
Depart Thessaloniki 1000, 2200, 2330. Depart Istanbul 1000, 1800, 2200. Journey 10 - 11 hours. Operator: Metro www.metroturizm.com.tr

THESSALONIKI - SKOPJE: Depart Thessaloniki 1730 ①–⑥. Depart Skopje 0600 ①–⑥. Journey 4 - 5 hours. Operator: Simeonidis Tours www.simeonidistours.gr

THESSALONIKI - SOFIA: See Table **1565** for the 🚌 service operated in conjunction with Greek Railways. Other coaches are operated by Union Ivkoni (www.union-ivkoni.com) as follows:
Pireás (0730) → Athína (0830) → Thessaloniki (1530) → Sofia (2030) → Varna (0500).
Varna (2345) → Sofia (0800) → Thessaloniki (1300) → Athína (2000) → Pireás (2100).
Kórinthos → Pireás → Athína (1900) → Thessaloniki (0130) → Sofia (0645) → Plovdiv → Burgas.
Burgas → Plovdiv → Sofia (2000) → Thessaloniki (0100) → Athína (0800) → Pireás → Kórinthos.

BULGARIA and TURKEY IN EUROPE

SEE MAP PAGE 501

Operators: Bâlgarski Dârzhavni Zheleznitsi (BDZh) www.bdz.bg
Türkiye Cumhuryeti Devlet Demiryolları (TCDD) www.tcdd.gov.tr

Services: Trains convey first- and second-class seating, except where shown otherwise in footnotes or by '2' in the train column, or where the footnote shows sleeping and / or couchette cars only. Descriptions of sleeping (🛏) and couchette (▬) cars appear on page 8. Seat reservation is possible on most long-distance trains (compulsory on express trains).

Timings: BDŽ schedules are valid **until Dec. 13, 2014**. Timetable amendments are possible at short notice so it is advisable to confirm timings locally before travelling.
Please refer to Tables **61**, **98** and **99** for international through cars to / from Burgas and Varna (summer only). TCDD schedules are the latest available. For services in Asian Turkey see pages 514–516.

1500 SOFIA - RUSE, BURGAS and VARNA

km	km				2655			8631	8611	2611	3621		460	2613	3623	8601	2615	8613	4612	4640	3625	8641	2641	382	8637	2627	8627
									↯[R]	↯[R]			[R]								↯[R]		↯[R]	[R] E			
			⊙	⊙		⊙	⊙					⊙	A											L	Z	Z B	Z
0	0	**Sofia** 1520 ‡ d.	...	...	...	...	...	...	0630	0645	0705	...	0755	1030	1045	1035	1300	1325	1525	...	1620	1700	1740	1845	...	2235	2240
	103	Septemvri ‡ d.	...	...	...	...	...	...	0804	│	│	...	│	│	│	1222	│	1511	│	...	│	1842	│	│	...	│	0031
	119	Pazardzhik ‡ d.	...	...	...	...	...	...	0823	│	│	...	│	│	│	1241	│	1530	│	...	│	1906	│	│	...	│	0051
	156	**Plovdiv** ‡ a.	...	...	...	...	...	...	0907	│	│	...	│	│	│	1323	│	1612	│	...	│	2000	│	│	...	│	0133
	156	**Plovdiv** d.	...	...	...	...	...	0718	0910	│	│	...	│	│	│	1327	│	1614	│	...	│	2004	│	│	2315	│	0140
	262	Stara Zagora d.	...	...	...	...	...	0906	1052	│	│	...	│	│	│	1517	│	1803j	│	1615	│	2151	│	│	0102	│	0335
	340	Yambol d.	...	0630	...	...	...	1007	1150	│	│	...	│	│	│	│	│	1908	│	│	│	2250	│	│	0202	│	0437
		Karlovo d.	...	│	...	0555	...	│	│	│	0930	...	│	│	1311	│	│	│	│	│	1836	...	│	│	│	│	│
		Kazanlak d.	...	│	...	0710	...	│	│	│	1027	...	│	│	1411	│	│	│	│	│	1933	...	│	│	│	│	│
		Tulovo d.	...	│	...	0741j	...	│	│	│	1041	...	│	│	1425	│	│	│	│	1651	1947	...	│	│	│	│	│
		Sliven d.	0505	│	...	0904	0933	│	│	│	1158	1358	│	│	1537	1622	│	│	│	│	2057	...	│	│	│	│	│
	389	Karnobat a.	0604	0722	...	...	1032	1049	1227	│	1244	1457	│	│	1623	1704	│	1950	│	│	2140	...	│	│	0244	│	0518
	389	Karnobat 1535 d.	0605	0724	...	...	1055	1051	1228	│	1246	1458	│	│	1624	1706	│	1952	│	│	2141	...	│	│	0246	│	0519
	450	**Burgas** 1535 a.	0722	0840	...	...	1207	│	1312	│	1331	1613	│	│	1711	│	│	2037	│	◐	2225	...	│	│	│	│	0607
88		Mezdra 1520 d.	▬	▬	...	...	...	│	...	0812	▬	...	0925	1200	▬	│	1429	...	1657	│	...	...	1913	2016	│	0005	...
194		Pleven d.	...	...	0700	...	...	│	...	0922	...	...	1037	1316	...	│	1547	...	1812	│	...	...	2037	2132	│	0121	...
239		Levski d.	...	...	0731	...	...	│	...	0951	...	...	1106	1346	...	│	1616	...	1841	│	...	...	2107	2203	│	0152	...
294		Gorna Oryakhovitsa a.	...	...	0810	...	...	│	...	1030	...	...	1145	1425	...	│	1657	...	1921	1926	...	...	2147	2242	│	0235	...
294		Gorna Oryakhovitsa ‡ d.	...	...	0819	...	...	│	...	1035	Ⓐ	...	1158	1435	...	│	1704	...	1938	1940	...	...	...	2248	│	0245	...
405		**Ruse** 🏛 ‡ a.	⊙	R⊙	│	...	...	│	...	│	⊙	...	1355	│	⊙	│	│	...	2135	│	...	...	...	0045	│	│	...
435		Shumen 1535 d.	0653	0712	1009	...	...	│	...	1221	1432	...	...	1622	1710	│	1854	...	...	2133	...	...	...	...	│	0441	...
459		Kaspichan 1530/5 d.	0725	0743	1028	...	...	│	...	│	1459	...	...	1641	1737	│	1913	...	...	2151	...	...	...	...	│	0500	...
518		Povelyanovo 1530/5 d.	0828	...	1116	...	...	1247	...	1322	1604	...	...	1727	1841	1905	1959	...	...	2240	...	...	...	...	0446	0553	...
543	546	**Varna** 1530/5 a.	0859	...	1140	...	...	1312	...	1344	1635	...	...	1752	1912	1930	2023	...	...	2305	...	...	...	...	0510	0618	...

km		2640	383	3620	8640	4641	4611		2610	3622	8602			2612	3624	2614	461	8612		8632			2654		9646	2626	8636
		↯[R]	[R]	↯[R]					↯[R]								[R]	↯[R]	Ⓐ					Ⓑ r			
			E					⊙				⊙	R⊙				A		⊙		⊙	⊙		⊙	S	Z B	Z
	Varna 1530/5 d.	...	...	...	...	0450	...	0600	0715	...	1000	...	...	1105	...	1330	...	...	1415	1550	...	1650	1735	1950	...	2145	2320
	Povelyanovo 1530/5 d.	...	...	...	...	0516	...	0634	0738	...	1025	...	...	1131	...	1356	...	...	1446	1615	...	1723	1759	2023	...	2233	2344
	Kaspichan 1530/5 d.	...	...	...	...	0603	...	0735	│	...	│	...	1038	1218	...	1443	...	...	1550	│	...	1826	1849	2127	...	2319	│
	Shumen 1535 d.	...	...	...	...	0621	...	0800	0839	...	│	...	1106	1237	...	1504	...	...	1616	│	...	1850	1908	2153	...	2339	│
	Ruse 🏛 ‡ d.	...	0445	...	...	│	0612	▬	│	...	│	...	▬	│	...	│	1620	...	│	│	...	▬	│	▬	2324	│	│
	Gorna Oryakhovitsa ‡ a.	...	0643	...	...	0812	0812	...	1026	...	│	...	...	1424	...	1658	1817	...	*1858*	│	...	...	2058	...	0128	0132	│
	Gorna Oryakhovitsa d.	0500	0655	...	...	0826	0824	...	1031	...	│	...	...	1434	...	1710	1827	...	▬	│	...	...	2103	...	▬	0147	│
	Levski d.	0539	0738	...	...	│	0903	...	1110	...	│	...	...	1513	...	1751	1905	...	...	│	...	...	2142	...	...	0229	│
	Pleven d.	0608	0813	...	...	│	0934	**8610**	1141	...	│	...	...	1543	...	1824	1934	...	...	│	...	...	2213	...	**8626**	0303	│
	Mezdra 1520 d.	0722	0932	...	...	│	1050	X	1252	...	│	...	...	1705	...	1947	2050	...	⊙	│	...	⊙	...	⊙	Z	0427	│
0	**Burgas** 1535 d.	│	│	0525	...	◐	│	0645	│	0955	│	1110	...	│	1415	│	│	1455	1535	│	...	1740	...	1900	2240	│	│
61	Karnobat 1535 a.	│	│	0610	...	│	│	0730	│	1042	1233	1222	...	│	1503	│	│	1540	1649	1812	...	1855	...	2012	2327	│	0143
61	Karnobat d.	│	│	0611	...	│	│	0731	│	1043	1234	1250	⊙	│	1504	│	│	1541	1650	1813	...	1856	...	2013	2328	│	0145
119	Sliven d.	│	│	0652	...	│	│	│	│	1130	│	1349	1405	│	1558	│	│	│	│	│	1800	1955	...	│	│	│	│
195	Tulovo d.	│	│	0755	...	1053	│	│	│	1237	│	...	1533	│	1721	│	│	│	│	│	2005	...	...	│	│	│	│
210	Kazanlak d.	│	│	0809	...	│	│	│	│	1252	│	...	1549	│	1735	│	│	│	│	│	2022	...	...	│	│	│	│
269	Karlovo d.	│	│	0904	...	│	│	│	│	1356	│	...	1700	│	1837	│	│	│	│	│	2135	...	...	│	│	│	│
	Yambol d.	│	│	│	0530	│	│	0813	│	│	1316	...	...	│	│	│	│	1621	1742	1851	...	...	...	2105	0009	│	0228
	Stara Zagora d.	│	│	│	0634	1127	│	0927j	│	│	1423	...	...	│	│	│	│	1727	...	1957	...	...	...	...	0120	│	0345j
	Plovdiv a.	│	│	│	0817	...	│	1109	│	│	1607	...	...	│	│	│	│	1905	...	2135	...	...	...	...	0258	│	0528
	Plovdiv ‡ d.	│	│	│	0820	...	│	1112	│	│	1614	...	...	│	│	│	│	1910	...	...	...	...	...	...	0308	│	...
	Pazardzhik ‡ d.	│	│	│	0913	...	│	1203	│	│	1658	...	...	│	│	│	│	1958	...	...	...	...	...	...	0354	│	...
	Septemvri ‡ d.	│	│	│	0932	...	│	1222	│	│	1716	...	...	│	│	│	│	2024	...	...	...	...	...	...	0414	│	...
418	**Sofia** 1520 ‡ a.	0856	1110	1117	1125	...	1226	1415	1425	1620	1910	...	...	1840	2100	2122	2225	2207	...	...	...	...	...	...	0608	0610	...

Other trains **SOFIA - PLOVDIV**

			1621	1623		1625	491
	⊙	⊙			Ⓐ⊙	¶	T
Sofia d.	...	0715	0820	1145	1430	1530	1845
Septemvri d.	0533	0939j	1005	1332	1630	1717	2029
Pazardzhik d.	0556	1004	1024	1351	1700	1736	2049
Plovdiv a.	0649	1059	1110	1445	1755	1818	2132

	1620	1622		1624			1626
			⊙	¶	⊙	⊙	
Plovdiv d.	0600	0730	1200	1325	1345	1700	1820
Pazardzhik d.	0654	0824	1309	1417	1448	1801	1908
Septemvri d.	0721	0845	1333	1437	1525j	1823	1928
Sofia a.	0914	1030	1542	1629	1746	2038	2120

Other trains **GORNA ORYAKHOVITSA - RUSE**

	⊙	⊙		⊙	⊙
Gorna Oryakhovitsa d.	0824	1050	...	1440	1725
Ruse a.	1042	1309	...	1709	1958

	⊙	⊙	⊙		⊙
Ruse d.	0755	1135	1410	...	1825
Gorna Oryakhovitsa a.	1018	1411	1635	...	2050

A – ROMANIA – [2] Sofia - Bucuresti and v.v. See Table **61**.
B – Conveys 🛏 1, 2 cl. and [2] Sofia - Povelyanovo - Kardam and v.v.
E – BULGARIA EXPRESS – [12] Sofia - Bucuresti and v.v. See Table **61**.
L – Conveys 🛏 1, 2 cl. and [2] Sofia - Ruse (**9647**) - Silistra (Table **1530**).
R – To / from Ruse (Table **1530**).
S – From Silistra (Table **1530**). Conveys 🛏 1, 2 cl. and [2] (attached to train **2626** at Gorna Oryakhovitsa; see the following column).

T – BALKAN EXPRESS – [2] Sofia - Svilengrad; ▬ 2 cl. Sofia - Çerkezköy (see Table **1550**).
X – Conveys from Stara Zagora [2] Svilengrad - Sofia, also ▬ 2 cl. Çerkezköy - Sofia (see Table **1550**).
Z – Conveys 🛏 1, 2 cl. and [12].

j – Arrives 10–15 minutes earlier.

r – Not Mar. 2, Apr. 18, May 1–5.

◐ – Via Veliko Târnovo (Table **1525**).
¶ – Conveys [1] only.
↯ – Express train. Higher fare payable.
⊙ – Local stopping train. 2nd class only.
‡ – See also panel below main table.

1510 SEPTEMVRI - DOBRINISHTE

Narrow gauge; 2nd class only

km										
0	**Septemvri** d.	0230	...	0945	...	1344	...	1740	...	...
39	Velingrad d.	0424	...	1116	...	1518	...	1915	...	...
119	Bansko d.	0731	...	1434	...	1823	...	...	...	...
125	**Dobrinishte** a.	0743	...	1447	...	1835	...	...	...	...

Dobrinishte d.	...	...	0640	...	0920	...	1520	...	...	...
Bansko d.	...	...	0655	...	0937	...	1538	...	...	...
Velingrad d.	0545	...	0955	...	1250	...	1846	...	1950	...
Septemvri a.	0710	...	1126	...	1420	...	2010	...	2115	...

1520 SOFIA - VIDIN - CALAFAT - CRAIOVA

km		70100	7620	70222	7622	7624	7630
		2					
0	**Sofia** 1500 d.	...	0700	...	1200	1720	1930
88	Mezdra 1500 d.	0525	│	1305	│	│	2118
106	Vratsa d.	0544	0845	1322	1340	1902	2135
182	Brusartsi ⊖ d.	0724	1001	...	1457	2024	2253
204	Lom ⊖ a.	│	│	...	│	│	2320
269	**Vidin** ★ a.	0915	1140	...	1641	2207	...

	2660	7631	7621	7623	70101	70123	7625
	A				2	2	
Vidin ★ d.	...	...	0540	1155	1310	...	1720
Lom ⊖ d.	...	0540	│	│	│	1600	│
Brusartsi ⊖ d.	...	0610	0721	1335	1459	1631	1905
Vratsa d.	0510	0736	0839	1457	1627	1812	2021
Mezdra 1500 a.	0524	0751	│	1514	1645	1830	│
Sofia 1500 a.	0716	0945	1023	1706	*1840*	...	2208

km		①–⑥			⊡	⊡	
	Vidin 🏛 d.	...	...	...	1215	1740	...
0	**Calafat** ★ d.	0330	0630	...	│	│	...
107	**Craiova** a.	0630	0935	...	1535	2106	...

	⊡		⊡			Ⓑ	
Craiova d.	0800	...	1319	...	1700	2000	...
Calafat ★ a.	│	...	│	...	2002	2252	...
Vidin 🏛 a.	1100	...	1630	...	...	...	...

A – ①–⑥ (not Mar. 3, Apr. 19, May 2–6).
B – ①②③④⑦.
⊖ – Additional journeys Brusartsi - Lom and v.v. Journey time: 26–28 minutes. **From Brusartsi** at 0610①–⑤, 0730, 1005, 1345, 1510, 1756, 1910 and 2030. **From Lom** at 0648, 0923, 1300, 1425, 1834, 1950 and 2121 **B**.
⊡ – Timings are subject to confirmation (a change of train at Golenţi may be required).
★ – A new 2 km rail / road bridge links Vidin and Calafat. A toll is charged for motor vehicles, but is free for pedestrians and cyclists to cross.

RUSE - STARA ZAGORA - DIMITROVGRAD - MOMCHILGRAD - PODKOVA — 1525

Services Gorna Oryakhovitsa - Dimitrovgrad and v.v. are subject to alteration until Aug. 12 (overnight trains **464/5** are expected to be operated by 🚌 between Gorna and Dimitrovgrad).

km		2	Ⓐd 2J	4641 V	2	2	2	461/5 Ⓡ B	Ⓐ 2S	2
0	**Ruse** 1500 d.	...	...	*0612*	*0755*	*1135*	*1410*	1620	...	*1825*
111	Gorna Oryakhovitsa 1500 a.	...	...	*0812*	*1018*	*1411*	*1635*	1817	...	*2050*
111	Gorna Oryakhovitsa d.	0505	...	0826	1042	1437	1717	1910	...	2155
125	Veliko Târnovo d.	0522	...	0843	1102	1457	1737	1929	...	2213
226	Tulovo d.	0759	0940	1053	1326	1712	1959	|	2201	...
253	Stara Zagora d.	0838	1026	1127	1406	1751	2038	2159	2240	...
306	Dimitrovgrad Sever a.	...	1144	...	...	...	...	2301	...	...
310	**Dimitrovgrad** a.	...	...	...	...	...	...	2326	...	...

	2	2	464/0 Ⓡ B	2	Ⓐ 2L	2	2	Ⓐd 2K	4640 V	2
Dimitrovgrad d.	...	...	0629	...	...	...	...	...	...	...
Dimitrovgrad Sever d.	...	...	0725	...	...	...	...	1358	...	...
Stara Zagora d.	...	0650	0843r	0942	1135	...	1445	1534	1615	1904
Tulovo d.	...	0732	0919	1021	1216	...	1527	1614	1651	1956r
Veliko Târnovo d.	0645	1003	1120	1321	...	1626	1757	...	1906	2216
Gorna Oryakhovitsa a.	0703	1021	1135	1340	...	1645	1815	...	1926	2233
Gorna Oryakhovitsa 1500 d.	*0824*	*1050*	1158	*1440*	...	*1725*	...	...	*1938*	...
Ruse 1500 a.	*1042*	*1309*	1355	*1709*	...	*1958*	...	...	*2135*	...

km		2	2	2
0	**Dimitrovgrad** d.	0505	...	1510
23	Haskovo d.	0534	...	1540
87	Kârdzhali d.	0720	1310	1740
101	**Momchilgrad** a.	0740	1330	1753
119	**Podkova** a.	0805	1355	1825

	2	2	2	2
Podkova d.	0620	0815	1410	...
Momchilgrad d.	0645	0841	1435	1700
Kârdzhali d.	0740f	0900	...	1725
Haskovo d.	0939	...	...	1916
Dimitrovgrad a.	1008	...	...	1943

B – BOSPHOR – 2 Bucuresti - Dimitrovgrad and v.v.; conveys 🛏 1, 2 cl. and 🛌 2 cl. Bucuresti - Ruse - Çerkezköy and v.v.
J – From Karlovo (d. 0750) and Kazanlak (d. 0912).
K – To Kazanlak (a. 1642).
L – To Sliven (a. 1346).
S – From Sliven (d. 2023).
V – To / from Varna (Table **1520**).
d – Runs daily Stara Zagora - Dimitrovgrad Sever and v.v.
f – Arrives 0706.
r – Arrives 12 – 14 minutes earlier.

RUSE - SILISTRA and VARNA — 1530

km		9647 H	2	9621	S2	2655	2		9623	2	2
0	**Ruse** d.	0215	...	0630	0720	...	...	...	1605	1800	...
5	Ruse Razpr d.	0232	...	0638	0729	...	...	...	1613	1808	...
71	Razgrad d.	0340	...	0746	0847	...	...	...	1722	1930	...
93	Samuil d.	0414r	0455	0808	0909	...	0920	...	1743	1950	2013
	Silistra a.	0650	|	|	|	...	1150	...	|	...	2250
142	Kaspichan 1500 a.	...	0555	0906	1012	1028	...	...	1836	...	...
201	Povelyanovo 1500 a.	...	...	0957	...	1115	...	...	1924	...	...
226	**Varna** 1500 a.	...	...	1023	...	1140	...	...	1950	...	...

km		2	2	2	S2	2	9620	2	2	9622	9646 D
	Varna 1500 d.	...	...	0600	...	...	0920	...	...	1805	...
	Povelyanovo 1500 d.	...	...	0634	...	...	0945	...	...	1830	...
	Kaspichan 1500 d.	...	...	0734	0801	...	1033	...	1730	1917	...
0	**Silistra** d.	...	0440	...	|	...	|	1500	|	|	1910
113	Samuil d.	0505	0706	...	0911r	...	1127	1728	1841	2010	2140r
	Razgrad d.	0527	...	...	0932	...	1147	...	1904	2029	2200
	Ruse Razpr a.	0700	...	...	1050	1125	1255	...	2021	2135	2307
	Ruse a.	0708	...	...	...	1132	1304	...	2030	2143	2319

D – Conveys 🛏 1, 2 cl. and 2 Silistra - Gorna Oryakhovitsa (**2626**) - Sofia.
H – Conveys 🛏 1, 2 cl. and 2 Sofia (**382**) - Ruse - Silistra.
S – To / from Shumen (Table **1500**).
r – Arrives 10 – 15 minutes earlier.

VARNA and SHUMEN - BURGAS — 1535

km		2	8602	3621	2	2	2	8632	8613	2	2
	Varna 1500 d.	0612	1000	...	1025	1340	...	1550	...	1835	...
	Povelyanovo 1500 d.	0644	1025	...	1057	1413	...	1615	...	1908	...
0	**Shumen** d.	|	|	...	|	|	1345	|	...	|	1914
50	Komunari d.	0740	1109	...	1153	1508	1557	1657	...	2000	2025
133	Karnobat 1500 d.	0927r	1233	1246	1353r	1710j	...	1812	1952	2136	...
194	**Burgas** 1500 a.	1040	...	1331	1509	1827	...	...	2037	...	...

	2	2	2	3622	8631	2	2	2	8601	2
Burgas 1500 d.	...	...	0740	0955	...	...	1340	1535	...	1640
Karnobat 1500 d.	0300	...	0904r	1042	1051	...	1502r	1649	1706	1804r
Komunari d.	0436	0540	1048	...	1205	1515	1643	...	|	1944
Shumen a.	|	0651	|	...	|	1657	|	...	|	|
Povelyanovo 1500 a.	0532	...	1145	...	1247	...	1739	...	1905	2039
Varna 1500 a.	0605	...	1216	...	1312	...	1815	...	1930	2110

– Arrives 11 – 15 minutes earlier.
j – Arrives 1645.

VARNA - DOBRICH - KARDAM — 1540

km			D			
0	**Varna** 1500 d.	0450	...	1300	1610	1900
	Sofia 1500 d.	|	2235	|	|	|
25	Povelyanovo 1500 d.	0515	0615	1332	1643	1932
93	**Dobrich** a.	...	0732	1450	1804	2047
131	Kardam a.	...	0840	...	1912	...

				E
Kardam d.	...	0900	...	1932
Dobrich d.	0545	1007	1455	2052
Povelyanovo 1500 a.	0712	1126	1610	2210
Sofia 1500 a.	|	|	|	0610
Varna 1500 a.	0745	1205	1648	...

D – 🛏 1, 2 cl. and 2 Sofia (**2627**) - Povelyanovo (**2637**) - Kardam.
E – 🛏 1, 2 cl. and 2 Kardam (**2636**) - Povelyanovo (**2626**) - Sofia.

BDŽ; TCDD

(SOFIA -) PLOVDIV - SVILENGRAD - İSTANBUL — 1550

km	Bulgarian train number / Turkish train number	2	2	2	2	2	2	2	2	491 81031 Ⓡ A	461/5 81031 Ⓡ B	81721 ❦
	Bucureşti 61 d.	...	...	...	...	...	...	...	...	...	1255	...
0	*Sofia* 1500 d.	...	...	...	...	...	...	...	...	1845	|	...
56	**Plovdiv** d.	0617	*1010*	*1355*	...	*1620*	*1824*	...	*2015*	2143	|	...
02	Parvomaj d.	0706	1112	1442	...	1707	1917	...	2102	2215	|	...
34	Dimitrovgrad a.	0738	1145	1515	...	1738	1948	...	2133	2238	2326	...
34	Dimitrovgrad d.	0743	...	...	1630	...	...	2009	...	2256t	2327	...
99	Svilengrad a.	0905	...	...	1750	...	...	2129	...	0040	0040	...
99	Svilengrad 🛃 d.	...	...	...	...	...	...	...	...	0130	0130	...
18	**Kapıkule** 🛃 a.	...	...	...	...	...	...	...	...	0150	0150	...
18	**Kapıkule** d.	...	...	...	...	...	...	...	...	0255	0255	0700
38	Edirne d.	...	...	...	...	...	...	...	...	0320	0320	0733
	Uzunköprü d.	...	...	...	...	...	...	...	...	|	|	|
85	Pehlivanköy d.	...	...	...	...	...	...	...	...	|	|	0828
06	Alpullu d.	...	...	...	...	...	...	...	...	0424	0424	0852
06	Çerkezköy a.	...	...	...	...	...	...	...	...	0541	0541	1033
93	Halkalı ¶ a.	...	...	...	...	...	...	...	...	*0706**	*0706**	1216
21	**İstanbul** Sirkeci ¶ a.	...	...	...	...	...	...	...	...	*0752**	*0752**	...

km	Turkish train number / Bulgarian train number	81722 ❦	2	81032 492 Ⓡ A	81032 464/2 Ⓡ B	2	2	2	2	2	2
0	**İstanbul** Sirkeci ¶ d.	...	...	*2200**	*2200**	...	...	...	...	...	...
28	Halkalı ¶ d.	1602	...	*2238**	*2238**	...	...	...	...	...	...
115	Çerkezköy d.	1750	...	0005	0005	...	...	...	...	...	...
215	Alpullu d.	1935	...	0124	0124	...	...	...	...	...	...
237	Pehlivanköy d.	1956	...	|	|	...	...	...	...	...	...
258	Uzunköprü a.	|	...	|	|	...	...	...	...	...	...
	Edirne d.	2048	...	0230	0230	...	...	...	...	...	...
	Kapıkule a.	2115	...	0252	0252	...	...	...	...	...	...
	Kapıkule 🛃 d.	...	...	0405	0405	...	...	...	...	...	...
	Svilengrad 🛃 a.	...	...	0425	0425	...	...	...	...	...	...
	Svilengrad d.	...	0435	0515	0515	...	...	...	1500	...	1835
	Dimitrovgrad a.	...	0556	0628	0628	...	...	...	1619	...	2000
	Dimitrovgrad d.	...	0557	0629	0629	*0710*	*1020*	*1400*	1620	*1830*	2005
	Parvomaj d.	...	0626	◇	|	0755	1100	1445	1652	1910	2036
	Plovdiv a.	...	*0713*	1109	|	0838	1141	1528	*1746*	1951	*2142*
	Sofia 1500 a.	...	...	1415	|	...	...	...	...	...	...
	Bucureşti 61 a.	...	...	...	1729	...	...	...	...	...	...

– BALKAN EXPRESS – 🛌 2 cl. Sofia - Çerkezköy and v.v.; 2 Sofia - Svilengrad and v.v.
– BOSPHOR – Conveys 🛏 1, 2 cl. and 🛌 2 cl. Until Aug. 12 this service is expected to be operated by 🚌 between Gorna Oryakhovitsa and Dimitrovgrad (please confirm timings locally).
Departs Dimitrovgrad 2256, then calls at Dimitrovgrad Sever (a. 2303, d. 2318) to pick up Bucureşti cars (see following column), then calls at Dimitrovgrad again (a. 2326, d. 2327).

* – By 🚌 from / to Çerkezköy.
◇ – Via Stara Zagora (a. 0831, then conveyed on train **8610** to Sofia).
¶ – For İstanbul suburban services via the Marmaray tunnel see the panel in Table **1570**.
❦ – Suspended until further notice.

SOFIA - KYUSTENDIL, PETRICH, KULATA and THESSALONÍKI — 1560

km		2	Ⓑ2		2			2	361 Ⓡ	Ⓐ2		2	2
0	**Sofia** d.	...	0440	0700	0815	1000	1140	...	1530	...	1700	*1830*	2005
33	Pernik d.	...	0541	0746	0914	1050	1225	1325	1610	...	1747	1930	2101
48	Radomir d.	...	0610	0808	0938	1116	1247	1349	1630	1634	1808	2003	2123
2	**Kyustendil** a.	...	|	|	1105	|	|	1517	|	1800	|	2129	|
1	Dupnitsa d.	0558	0723	0851	—	1209	1327	—	1710	—	1850	—	2210
23	**Blagoevgrad** a.	0647	0800	0920	...	1245	1355	...	1737	...	1930	...	2238
3	**Blagoevgrad** d.	0655	—	*0925*	...	...	*1400*	...	1738	...	1931	...	...
6	Sandanski d.	0808	...	*1045*	...	...	*1518*	...	1832	...	2040	...	...
7	General Todorov. a.	0820	2	*1057*	2	...	*1530*	2	1841	...	2052	2	...
7	General Todorov. d.	0821	0830	*1107*	1115	...	*1542*	1535	1842	1850	2102	2100	...
7	**Petrich** a.	|	0843	*1120*	|	...	*1555*	|	|	1903	2115	|	...
0	Kulata 🛃 a.	0835	...	...	1130	...	...	1550	1853	...	...	2114	...
1	Promahónas 🛃 a.	...	...	...	...	...	...	...	1925	...	...	...	...
5	Strimón a.	...	...	...	...	...	...	...	2000	...	...	...	...
4	**Thessaloníki** a.	...	...	...	...	...	...	...	2222	...	...	...	...

	2		2	2	2	360 Ⓡ	2		2		2
Thessaloníki d.	...	...	...	...	...	0655	...	...	...	...	...
Strimón d.	...	...	...	...	...	0906	...	...	...	...	...
Promahónas 🛃 d.	...	...	...	...	...	0950	...	...	...	...	...
Kulata 🛃 d.	0505	...	0700	...	...	1020	1355	...	1625	...	1925
Petrich d.	|	0505	|	0700	1005	|	|	*1410*	|	*1625*	*1920*t
General Todorov a.	0521	0518	0715	0711	1018	1031	1410	*1424*	1640	*1638*	1939
General Todorov d.	—	0528	—	0725	—	1032	—	*1436*	—	*1648*	1940
Sandanski d.	...	0541	...	0739	...	1043	...	*1450*	...	*1701*	1954
Blagoevgrad a.	2	0650	...	0852	2	1136	...	*1605*	...	*1722*	2109
Blagoevgrad d.	0600	0651	...	0853	0930	1138	1332	1610	...	1844	2110
Dupnitsa d.	0632	0720	2	0939	1008	1207	1409	1645	2	1919	2148
Kyustendil d.	|	|	0710	...	|	|	|	|	1805	|	...
Radomir d.	0716	0801	0853	...	1103	1247	1505	1731	1933	1959	...
Pernik d.	0733	0819	0913	...	1123	1302	1527	1748	1954	2015	...
Sofia a.	0818	0909	1008	...	1213	1345	1624	1835	2042	2104	...

Additional journeys Radomir - Kyustendil and v.v.: **From Radomir** at 0720, 1125 and 1813. **From Kyustendil** at 0423, 0920, 1115, 1330 and 1613 Ⓐ. Journey: 86 – 96 minutes.

Change trains at General Todorov.

TURKEY IN ASIA

Operator: Türkiye Cumhuryeti Devlet Demiryolları (TCDD).

Services: *YHT* trains convey first and second class seating. Long distance trains convey a single class of seating known locally as 'Pullman' (shown as [1] in footnotes) and may also convey sleeping and/or couchette cars. Local trains convey 2nd class seating, shown as '2' in the train column. Descriptions of sleeping (🛏) and couchette (▬) cars appear on page 8. Reservation of seats (free of charge) is required for *YHT* and express trains.

Timings: Schedules are the latest available. Timetable amendments are possible at short notice so please confirm timings locally before travelling.

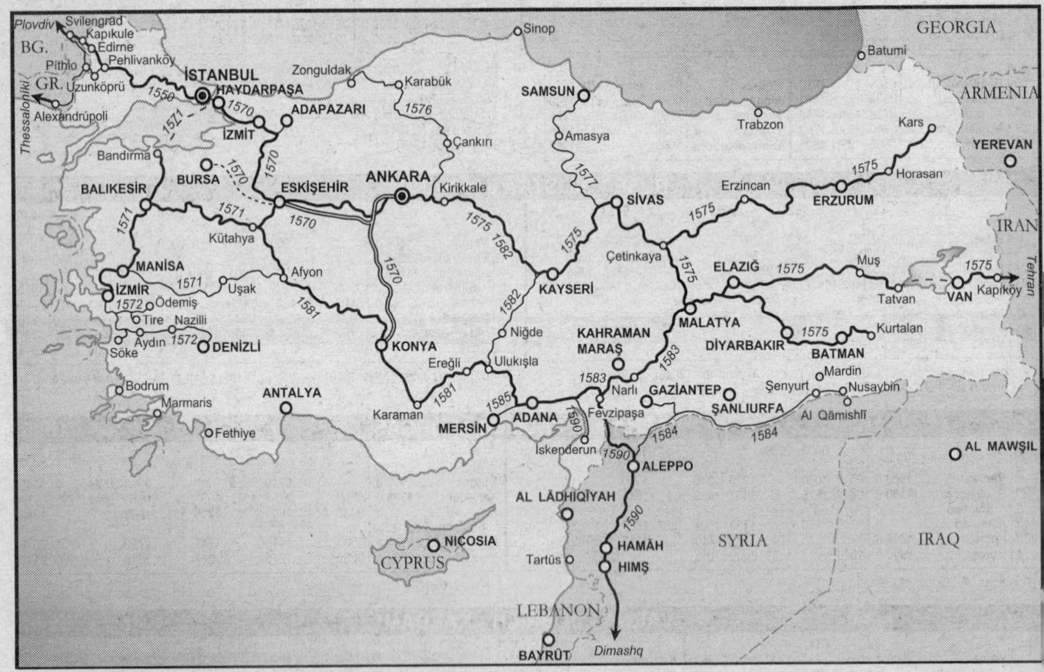

1570 HAYDARPAŞA - ESKIŞEHIR - KONYA and ANKARA — TCDD

km		*YHT* 91002 R	*YHT* 91202 R	*YHT* 91004 R	31129 B	*YHT* 91204 R	*YHT* 91302 R	*YHT* 91006 R	
0	**Haydarpaşa** △ d.	...	...	...	...	...	...	...	...
91	Izmit △ d.	...	...	...	...	...	...	...	...
132	Arifiye △ d.	...	...	...	...	...	...	...	...
	Adapazari △ a.	...	...	...	...	...	...	...	...
232	Bilecik △ d.	...	...	...	...	...	...	...	...
263	Bozüyük △ d.	...	...	...	...	...	...	...	...
313	**Eskişehir** △ a.	...	...	...	...	...	...	...	...
313	**Eskişehir** d.	0645	...	0745	0549	...	0800	0900	...
668	**Konya** a.	|	...	|	|	...	1000	|	...
	Konya d.	|	0700	|	|	0830	...	|	...
487	Polatli d.	0734	|	0834	0819	0940	...	0949	...
551	Sincan d.	0753	0829	0853	0929	1000	...	|	...
576	**Ankara** a.	0815	0850	0915	0953	1021	...	1030	...

km		*YHT* 91206 R	*YHT* 91008 R	*YHT* 91208 R	*YHT* 91010 R	*YHT* 91210 R	*YHT* 91014 R	*YHT* 91212 R	
0	**Haydarpaşa** △ d.	...	...	...	...	...	...	...	...
91	Izmit △ d.	...	...	...	...	...	...	...	...
132	Arifiye △ d.	...	...	...	...	...	...	...	...
	Adapazari △ a.	...	...	...	...	...	...	...	...
232	Bilecik △ d.	...	...	...	...	...	...	...	...
263	Bozüyük △ d.	...	...	...	...	...	...	...	...
313	**Eskişehir** △ a.	...	...	...	...	...	...	...	...
313	**Eskişehir** d.	...	1115	...	1245	...	1500	...	...
668	**Konya** a.	...	|	...	|	...	|	...	...
	Konya d.	1030	|	1215	|	1430	|	1600	...
487	Polatli d.	|	1205	|	|	1540	1550	|	...
551	Sincan d.	|	1224	1341	1354	1600	1609	|	...
576	**Ankara** a.	1215	1245	1402	1415	1621	1630	1745	...

km		*YHT* 91304 R	*YHT* 91016 R	*YHT* 91018 R	*YHT* 91214 R	*YHT* 91020 R	*YHT* 91216 R	*YHT* 9102 R
0	**Haydarpaşa** △ d.	...	...	...	...	...	...	...
91	Izmit △ d.	...	...	...	...	...	...	...
132	Arifiye △ d.	...	...	...	...	...	...	...
	Adapazari △ a.	...	...	...	...	...	...	...
232	Bilecik △ d.	...	...	...	...	...	...	...
263	Bozüyük △ d.	...	...	...	...	...	...	...
313	**Eskişehir** △ a.	...	...	...	...	...	...	...
313	**Eskişehir** d.	1600	1635	1815	...	1900	...	2100
668	**Konya** a.	1800	|	|	...	|	...	|
	Konya d.	...	|	|	1815	|	2030	|
487	Polatli d.	...	|	|	1925	1950	2140	|
551	Sincan d.	...	1744	1924	1945	2009	2200	220
576	**Ankara** a.	...	1805	1945	2006	2030	2221	223

km via HSL		*YHT* 91001 R	*YHT* 91201 R	*YHT* 91003 R	*YHT* 91005 R	*YHT* 91301 R	*YHT* 91203 R	*YHT* 91007 R	
0	**Ankara** d.	0645	0700	0810	0910	...	0935	1100	...
25	Sincan d.	0706	0721	0831	|	...	0956	1121	...
89	Polatlı d.	0724	|	0849	|	...	1017	1139	...
309	**Konya** a.	|	0852	|	|	...	1130	|	...
	Konya d.	|	...	|	|	0935	...	|	...
	Eskişehir a.	0815	...	0940	1040	1135	...	1230	...
	Eskişehir △ d.	...	...	...	...	...	...	...	...
	Bozüyük △ d.	...	...	...	...	...	...	...	...
	Bilecik △ d.	...	...	...	...	...	...	...	...
	Adapazari △ d.	...	...	...	...	...	...	...	...
	Arifiye △ d.	...	...	...	...	...	...	...	...
	Izmit △ d.	...	...	...	...	...	...	...	...
558	**Haydarpaşa** △ a.	...	...	...	...	...	...	...	...

km via HSL		*YHT* 91205 R	*YHT* 91009 R	*YHT* 91207 R	*YHT* 91013 R	*YHT* 91209 R	*YHT* 91015 R	*YHT* 91303 R	
0	**Ankara** d.	1120	1245	1300	1500	1530	1630	...	...
25	Sincan d.	|	1306	1321	1521	1551	1651	...	...
89	Polatlı d.	|	|	|	1539	|	|	...	...
309	**Konya** a.	1310	|	1452	|	1722	|	...	...
	Konya d.	...	|	...	|	...	|	1855	...
	Eskişehir a.	...	1415	...	1630	...	1800	2055	...
	Eskişehir △ d.	...	...	...	...	...	...	...	...
	Bozüyük △ d.	...	...	...	...	...	...	...	...
	Bilecik △ d.	...	...	...	...	...	...	...	...
	Adapazari △ d.	...	...	...	...	...	...	...	...
	Arifiye △ d.	...	...	...	...	...	...	...	...
	Izmit △ d.	...	...	...	...	...	...	...	...
558	**Haydarpaşa** △ a.	...	...	...	...	...	...	...	...

km via HSL		*YHT* 91211 R	*YHT* 91017 R	*YHT* 91213 R	*YHT* 91019 R	21130 B	*YHT* 91215 R	*YH* 910 R
0	**Ankara** d.	1700	1800	1830	1900	1820	2045	210
25	Sincan d.	|	1821	1851	1921	1849	2106	212
89	Polatlı d.	1739	|	1912	1939	1953	2127	|
309	**Konya** a.	1850	|	2025	|	|	2240	|
	Konya d.	...	|	...	|	|	...	|
	Eskişehir a.	...	1930	...	2030	2210	...	223
	Eskişehir △ d.	...	...	...	...	...	...	...
	Bozüyük △ d.	...	...	...	...	...	...	...
	Bilecik △ d.	...	...	...	...	...	...	...
	Adapazari △ d.	...	...	...	...	...	...	...
	Arifiye △ d.	...	...	...	...	...	...	...
	Izmit △ d.	...	...	...	...	...	...	...
558	**Haydarpaşa** △ a.	...	...	...	...	...	...	...

🚌 CONNECTIONS ESKIŞEHIR - BURSA AND V.V.

km										
0	**Eskişehir** d.	0830	0950	1045	1245	1430	1645	1815	1945	2100
	Bursa a.	1045	1205	1300	1500	1645	1900	2030	2200	2315

Bursa d.	0500	0615	0830	1000	1215	1335	1530	1630	18
Eskişehir a.	0730	0845	1100	1230	1445	1550	1800	1845	20

B – IZMIR MAVI TRENI – 🛏, [1] and ✕ Izmir - Eskişehir and v.v.

* – The Marmaray tunnel (13.6km from near Kazlıçeşme station to near Ayrılıkçeşmesi station) includes the world's deepest immersed tube tunnel at 60.46 metres below sea level (1.4km in length, between Sirkeci and Üsküdar).

△ – Service suspended due to engineering work.

The following 🚌 operators offer services to points on Table **1570**:

Kamil Koc Otobusleri: ✆ +90 (224) 224 2511. www.kamilkoc.com.tr
Metro Turizm: ✆ +90 (212) 658 3232. www.metroturizm.com.tr
Ulusoy: ✆ +90 (212) 682 1700. www.ulusoy.com.tr
Varan: ✆ +90 (212) 438 0000. www.varan.com.tr

'MARMARAY*' SUBURBAN SERVICES

Kazlıçeşme d.	0600	and	2350
Yenikapı d.	0605	every	2355
Sirkeci d.	0609	10	2359
Üsküdar d.	0613	minutes	0003
Ayrılıkçeşmesi a.	0618	until	0008

Ayrılıkçeşmesi d.	0600	and	23
Üsküdar d.	0605	every	23
Sirkeci d.	0609	10	23
Yenikapı d.	0613	minutes	00
Kazlıçeşme a.	0618	until	00

TCDD — ESKIŞEHIR, BANDIRMA and AFYON - IZMIR — 1571

km		71136	21316	32526	21130	31622	31002	71601	32528	31004	31620
							③–①				
		A			B		C			D	
	Ankara **1570** d.	...	...	...	1820	...	...	...	...	...	...
0	**Eskişehir** ♧ d.	...	...	...	2225	...	...	...	...	...	...
78	Kütahya ♧ d.	...	...	...	0001	...	...	...	...	...	...
128	Tavşanlı d.	...	...	...	|	...	...	...	...	...	...
‡	**Bandirma** Şehir d.	...	...	...	|	...	0700	...	...	1555	...
‡	**Bandirma** Gar d.	...	...	...	|	...	0703	...	...	1558	...
◇	**Afyon** Ali Çetinkaya d.	0025	...	...	0205	...	|	...	...	|	...
◇	Usak d.	0252	...	...	0435	0620	|	...	...	|	1620
◇	Alaşehir d.	0505	...	0530	0649	0839	|	...	1530	|	1840
331	Ballıkesir d.	|	0350	|	|	|	0849	1400	|	1743	|
413	Soma d.	|	0525	|	|	|	1020	1530	|	1912	|
454	Akhisar d.	|	0604	|	|	|	1101	1616	|	1952	|
506	Manisa d.	0631	0648	0728	0815	1037	1155	1712	1725	2036	2048
572	**Izmir** Alsancak a.	0745	0807	0850	0931	1155	1316	1833	...	2152	2212

	31603	31001	31619	32525	31621	31003	32527	31315	31129	31135
		③–①								
		C				D			B	A
Izmir Basmane d.	0650	0820	0735	1030	1508	1415	...	1745	1830	2035
Manisa d.	0816	0933	0901	1215	1635	1533	1820	1906	1950	2149
Akhisar d.	0918	1025	|	|	|	1615	|	1953	|	|
Soma d.	1019	1106	|	|	|	1654	|	2035	|	|
Ballıkesir d.	1150	1236	|	|	|	1825	|	2209	|	|
Alaşehir d.	...	|	1106	1414	1839	|	2019	...	2121	2314
Usak d.	...	|	1335	...	2108	|	...	...	2340	0123
Afyon Ali Çetinkaya a.	...	|	...	...	...	|	...	...	0221	0347
Bandirma Gar a.	...	1413	...	...	...	2002	...	...	|	...
Bandirma Şehir a.	...	1416	...	...	...	2005	...	...	|	...
Tavşanlı d.	...	...	...	...	...	...	...	...	|	...
Kütahya ♧ d.	...	...	...	...	...	...	...	...	0410	...
Eskişehir ♧ a.	...	...	...	...	...	...	...	...	0534	...
Ankara **1570** a.	...	...	...	...	...	...	...	...	0953	...

⛴ Istanbul - Bandirma — İstanbul Deniz Otobüsleri *

km	*Until June 15*										
						⑤					
0	**İstanbul** Yenikapi d.	0700	...	...	...	1200	...	...	...	1900	...
	Bandirma Şehir a.	0910	...	...	...	1410	...	...	...	2110	...

Until June 15	①–⑤			⑥			⑤⑦			
Bandirma Şehir d.	0730	...	...	0930	...	...	1530	...	...	1830
İstanbul Yenikapi a.	0940	...	...	1140	...	...	1740	...	...	2040

A – KONYA MAVI TRENI – sleeper, couchette, (1) and ✕ Konya - Izmir Basmane and v.v.
B – IZMIR MAVI TRENI – sleeper, (1) and ✕ Izmir - Eskişehir and v.v.
C – 6 EYLÜL EKSPRESI – (1) Bandirma - Izmir and v.v.
D – 17 EYLÜL EKSPRESI – (1) Bandirma - Izmir and v.v.

♧ – For local services see Table **1581**.
‡ – Bandirma Sehir - Bandirma Gar: *1 km.* Bandirma Sehir - Ballıkesir *101 km.*
◇ – Afyon - Manisa; *355 km.* Usak - Manisa: *220 km.* Alaşehir - Manisa: *122 km.*
* – İstanbul Deniz Otobüsleri ✆ +90 (212) 455 6900. www.ido.com.tr

TCDD 2nd class — IZMIR - TIRE, ÖDEMIŞ, SÖKE and DENIZLI — 1572

km																									
																									⑤⑥†
0	**Izmir** Basmane ⊡ d.	...	0620	0745	0923	...	0900	1010	1125	1220	...	1330	1355	...	1510	1540	1610	1630	1710	...	1815	1830	1910	1957	2130
18	Adnan Menderes ⊡ d.	...	0639	0806	0943	...	0921	1030	1145	1242	...	1351	1417	...	1529	1602	1631	1654	1730	...	1837	1853	1930	2018	2154
49	Torballı d.	...	0709	0833	1018	...	0950	1058	1212	1312	...	1418	1447	...	1603	1638	1705	1729	1800	...	1907	1927	2006	2053	2222
86	Çatal d.	...	0756	|	1104	...	|	1137	|	1348	...	|	1530	...	1652	|	1745	|	1843	1850	|	2008	|	2132	2300
96	**Tire** a.	...	|	|	|	...	|	1147	|	|	...	|	1540	...	|	|	1755	|	|	1900	|	2018	|	|	|
111	**Ödemiş** Gar a.	...	0825	|	1129	...	|	...	|	1413	...	|	...	...	1724	|	...	|	1909	...	|	...	|	2158	2325
112	**Ödemiş** Şehir a.	...	0828	|	1132	...	|	...	|	1416	...	|	...	...	1727	|	...	|	1912	...	|	...	|	2201	2328
77	Selçuk d.	...	...	0901	...	...	1018	...	1239	...	...	1443	...	...	...	1705	...	1757	...	...	1933	...	2043	...	...
	Söke d.	0630	...	|	...	1035	|	...	|	...	1400	|	...	1520	...	|	...	|	...	...	|	...	2132	...	...
100	Ortaklar d.	0658	...	0925	...	1107	1042	...	1305	...	1424	1507	...	1548	...	1729	...	1822	...	...	1957	...	...	...	...
130	Aydin d.	0729	...	0955	...	1144	1111	...	1342	...	1456	1538	...	1619	...	1759	...	1856	...	...	2027	...	...	...	...
175	Nazilli d.	0824	...	1043	...	1236	1158	...	1431	...	1547	1631	...	1718	...	1849	...	1945	...	...	2114	...	...	...	...
251	Goncali d.	0937	...	1150	...	...	1304	...	1538	...	...	...	...	1832	...	1954	...	2051	...	...	2221	...	...	...	...
260	**Denizli** a.	0948	...	1201	...	...	1315	...	1549	...	...	...	...	1843	...	2005	...	2102	...	...	2232	...	...	...	...

km																									
																								⑤⑥†	⑤⑥†
0	**Denizli** d.	...	...	...	...	0420	...	...	0545	...	0655	0820	1005	...	...	...	1250	...	1450	...	...	...	1715	...	...
9	Goncali d.	...	...	...	...	0433	...	...	0557	...	0708	0832	1018	...	...	...	1303	...	1503	...	...	...	1727	...	...
85	Nazilli d.	...	...	...	...	0540	...	...	0704	...	0822	0945	1133	...	1250	...	1409	...	1611	1645	...	1734	1847	...	...
130	Aydin d.	...	...	...	...	0626	...	...	0755	...	0914	1032	1228	...	1344	...	1457	...	1700	1740	...	1830	1940	...	...
160	Ortaklar d.	...	...	...	0619‡	0654	...	...	0824	...	0945	1100	1302	...	1423	...	1525	...	1728	1820	...	1859	2014	...	...
183	**Söke** a.	...	...	...	0555‡	|	...	...	|	...	1007	|	1324	...	1445	...	|	...	|	1842	...	|	|	...	...
183	Selçuk d.	...	...	...	0649	0722	...	...	0900	...	...	1128	▬	...	...	...	1553	...	1758	▬	...	1932	2044	...	...
	Ödemiş Şehir d.	...	0520	...	|	|	0658	...	|	0844	...	|	...	1205	...	1457	|	...	|	...	1743	|	|	...	1920
	Ödemiş Gar d.	...	0524	...	|	|	0703	...	|	0849	...	|	...	1210	...	1502	|	...	|	...	1747	|	|	...	1925
	Tire d.	0535	|	0620	|	|	|	0740	|	|	...	|	1155	|	...	|	|	1613	|	1805	|	|	|	1930	|
	Çatal d.	0545	0556	0631	|	|	0728	0755	|	0914	...	|	1206	1234	...	1526	|	1625	|	1815	1818	|	|	1940	1949
211	Torballı d.	...	0644	0710	0722	0747	0810	0838	0927	0955	...	1152	1244	1313	...	1606	1618	1706	1822	...	1906	2003	2112	...	2028
242	Adnan Menderes ⊡ a.	...	0714	0736	0758	0816	0837	0909	0959	1025	...	1219	1321	1346	...	1635	1646	1733	1849	...	1934	2031	2141	...	2058
260	**Izmir** Basmane ⊡ a.	...	0732	0754	0820	0839	0855	0930	1022	1043	...	1239	1342	1407	...	1655	1708	1754	1909	...	1954	2053	2203	...	2119

‡ – Calls at Söke then Ortaklar.

⊡ – Frequent local trains operate 0600 - 2300.

TCDD — ANKARA - KARS, KURTALAN, TATVAN and TEHRAN — 1575

km				11512	11532	11542			11410	21124	
				③	②⑦	△					
		2	2	A	B♤	C	2	2	D	E	2
0	**Ankara** 1582 d.	...	...	1025	1115	1115	...	1740	1605	1900	...
70	Irmak 1582 d.	...	...	|	1249	1249	...	1910	1739	2022	...
92	Kirikkale 1582 d.	...	...	|	1315	1315	...	1933	1803	2046	...
365	Boğazköprü 1582 d.	...	...	|	1756	1756	...	...	2236	0104	...
381	Kayseri d.	...	...	1730	1827	1827	...	...	2307	0136	...
603	Sivas d.	0845	1750	2136	2210	2210	...	...	0247	0512	...
715	Çetinkaya d.	1006	1908	|	0007	0007	...	...	0426	0702	...
779	Divriği d.	1112	2014	|	|	|	0504	...	0543	|	...
935	Erzincan d.	▬	...	|	|	|	0828	...	0842	|	...
1150	Erzurum d.	...	...	|	|	|	▬	...	1232	|	...
1235	Horasan d.	...	...	|	|	|	...	...	1402	|	...
1307	Sarkamıs d.	...	...	|	|	|	...	...	1549	|	...
1366	**Kars** a.	...	...	|	|	|	...	...	1703	|	...
854	Malatya d.	...	...	0302	0247	0247	...	...	...	0925	...
949	Yolçatı d.	2	...	|	0500	0450	...	...	...	...	...
1107	Diyarbakir d.	0730	...	|	|	0850	...	...	...	...	1758
1198	Batman d.	0950	...	|	|	1106	②⑤⑦	...	...	...	2017
267	**Kurtalan** a.	...	...	|	|	1246	2	...	...	...	▬
973	Elâzig d.	...	...	0631	0620	...	0705	...	...	...	...
201	Mus d.	...	...	1223	1219	...	1446	...	...	...	...
295	**Tatvan** Gar a.	...	...	1440	1437	...	1728	...	...	...	**51516**
300	**Tatvan** Iskele ♡ a.	...	...	1453	...	...	...	...	...	...	②
0	**Van** Iskele ♡ d.	...	...	2130	...	...	...	...	...	...	F
3	**Van** Gar d.	...	...	2154	...	...	...	...	...	...	2000
114	Kapiköy 🏛 d.	...	...	0130	...	...	...	...	...	...	2315
120	Razi d.	...	...	0235	...	...	...	...	...	...	0010
342	Tabriz a.	...	...	0635	...	...	...	...	...	...	0625
342	Tabriz d.	...	...	0823	...	...	...	...	...	...	...
078	**Tehran** a.	...	...	2020	...	...	...	...	...	...	...

		51123		41409		51511	51515	51541	51531	
					①③⑥	③	①	▽	②④	
	2	E	2	D	2	A	F	C	B♤	2
Tehran d.	...	...	...	...	...	2125	...	...	...	...
Tabriz a.	...	...	...	...	...	0926	...	...	...	...
Tabriz d.	...	...	...	...	...	1056	2230	...	...	...
Razi d.	...	...	...	...	...	1540	0400	...	...	...
Kapiköy 🏛 d.	...	...	...	...	...	1740	0415	...	...	...
Van Gar a.	...	...	...	...	...	1933	0606	...	...	...
Van Iskele ♡ a.	...	...	...	...	...	1956	...	...	...	...
Tatvan Iskele ♡ d.	...	...	...	...	...	0457	...	...	...	...
Tatvan Gar d.	...	...	...	...	0630	0715	...	...	0720	...
Mus d.	...	...	...	...	0946	0944	...	...	0943	...
Elâzig d.	...	...	...	...	1621	1545	...	...	1604	...
Kurtalan d.	...	...	...	...	...	|	...	0930	|	...
Batman d.	...	...	0504	...	...	|	...	1110	|	1500
Diyarbakir d.	...	...	0721	...	...	|	...	1314	|	1715
Yolçatı d.	...	...	▬	...	...	|	...	1637	1637	▬
Malatya d.	...	1530	...	...	...	1820	...	1849	1849	...
Kars d.	...	|	...	0945	...	|	...	|	|	...
Sarkamis d.	...	|	...	1102	...	|	...	|	|	...
Horasan d.	...	|	...	1245	...	|	...	|	|	...
Erzurum d.	...	|	2	1430	...	|	...	|	|	...
Erzincan d.	...	|	1400	1825	...	|	...	|	|	2
Divriği d.	1445	|	1723	2122	...	|	...	|	|	0600
Çetinkaya d.	1549	1757	▬	2245	...	|	...	2137	2137	0702
Sivas d.	1706	1947	...	0037	...	2255	...	2335	2335	0816
Kayseri d.	...	2318	...	0402	...	0241	...	0330	0330	...
Boğazköprü 1582 d.	...	2346	2	0427	...	|	...	0354	0354	...
Kirikkale 1582 d.	...	0415	0600	0900	...	|	...	0837	0837	...
Irmak 1582 d.	...	0439	0624	0926	...	|	...	0902	0902	...
Ankara 1582 a.	...	0610	0803	1102	...	0922	...	1037	1037	...

– TRANSASYA EKSPRESI – couchette and ✕ Ankara(**11512/51511**) - Tatvan and v.v.; couchette and ✕ Van (**11512/51511**) - Razi (**59/60**) - Tehrān and v.v.
– VAN GÖLÜ EKSPRESI – sleeper, couchette and (2) Ankara - Tatvan and v.v.
– GÜNEY EKSPRESI – sleeper, couchette and (2) Ankara - Kurtalan and v.v.
– DOĞU EKSPRESI – sleeper, couchette, (12) Ankara - Kars and v.v.
– 4 EYLÜL MAVI – (12), couchette and ✕ Ankara - Malatya and v.v.
– (2) and 🍷 Tabriz(**494/495**) - Kapiköy(**51515/51516**) - Van and v.v.

△ – ①③④⑤⑥.
▽ – ①③⑤⑥⑦.

♤ – Due to engineering work this train will terminate / start at Elâzig until July 25.

♡ – By ⛴ Tatvan - Van and v.v. Passengers must leave the train at Tatvan and rejoin it at Van. Note that different sets of coaching stock are used either side of the ferry.

1576 ANKARA - ZONGULDAK TCDD

km				①③⑤
0	**Ankara** d.	...	...	...
70	Irmak d.	...	...	...
172	Çankiri d.	...	...	1550
364	Karabük d.	0505	1815	1936
486	**Zonguldak** ♡ a.	0810	2119	...

	①③⑤		
Zonguldak ♡ d.	...	0640	1835
Karabük d.	0645	0949	2144
Çankiri d.	1031	...	...
Irmak d.	...	...	...
Ankara a.	...	...	...

Note: Services Çankiri - Zonguldak and v.v. are suspended for engineering work with no re-opening date given. Please check with operator before travelling.

♡ – Local service Zonguldak - Filyos and v.v. (journey 32 minutes). From Zonguldak at 0610, 0800, 1800. From Filyos at 0700, 1700, 1900.

1577 SIVAS - AMASYA - SAMSUN TCDD

km		2	2A	2
0	**Sivas** d.	...	...	0735
111	Yenice d.	...	...	⊖
181	Turhal d.	...	...	⊖
245	**Amasya** d.	0455	0800	1315
272	Suluova d.	0527	0841	⊖
292	Havza d.	0555	0916	⊖
378	**Samsun** a.	0805	...	1626

	2	2B	2
Samsun d.	⊖	...	1800
Havza d.	⊖	1656	2010
Suluova d.	⊖	1733	2037
Amasya d.	⊖	1812	2108
Turhal d.	⊖	...	...
Yenice d.	⊖	...	...
Sivas a.	⊖	...	...

A – Also at 1500.
B – Also at 0926.
⊖ – No information available at time of going to press.

1581 ESKIŞEHIR - KONYA - ADANA TCDD

km		71622 A	11126 E	2	21130 C	31135 F	2	71306 G	2	2
0	**Eskişehir** 1571 d.	1815	...	1940	2225	...	0900	...	1300	...
79	Kütahya 1571 d.	1945	...	2058	0001	...	1016	...	1415	...
163	Afyon Ali Çetinkaya d.	2127	...	...	0145	0356	...	...	...	...
261	Akşehir d.	...	...	...	...	0515	...	...	...	...
435	Konya d.	...	0630	...	...	0757	...	1500	...	1919
537	Karaman d.	...	0802	...	...	...	...	1624	...	2041
	Ereğli d.	...	0918	...	...	...	...	1739	...	2149
672	Ulukişla 1582 d.	...	1025	...	...	...	...	1843	...	...
781	Yenice 1582 d.	...	1241	...	...	...	...	2110	...	...
804	**Adana** 1582 d.	...	1300	...	...	...	...	2130	...	...

	2	2	61305 G	2	71136 F	61125 E	31129 C	2	71621 A
Adana 1582 d.	...	...	0701	...	...	1545	...	...	...
Yenice 1582 d.	...	...	0724	...	...	1606	...	...	...
Ulukişla 1582 d.	...	...	1016	...	...	1838	...	...	...
Ereğli d.	0553	...	1104	...	...	1929	...	...	...
Karaman d.	0703	...	1221	...	...	2005	...	...	...
Konya d.	0811	...	1339	...	2015	2217	...	...	...
Akşehir d.	...	...	...	...	2258	...	...	...	...
Afyon Ali Çetinkaya d.	...	...	...	...	0015	...	0221	...	0720
Kütahya 1571 d.	...	1110	...	1715	...	...	0410	0732	0921
Eskişehir 1571 a.	...	1228	...	1832	...	...	0534	0848	1050

km		E	2	2	2	2	G	2	2	2
0	Konya d.	0630	0710	0907	1205	1402	1500	1739	1919	2250
102	Karaman d.	0802	0825	1016	1314	1512	1624	1848	2028	2359

	2	2	2	2	G	2	2	2	E
Karaman d.	0010	0703	0900	1045	1221	1424	1700	1911	2005
Konya d.	0116	0811	1006	1150	1339	1531	1807	2017	2217

A – AFYON ESKIŞEHIR EKSPRES – Eskişehir - Afyon and v.v.
C – IZMIR MAVI TRENI – , and ✕ Izmir - Eskişehir and v.v.
E – ICANADOLU MAVI TRENI – , and ✕ Konya - Adana and v.v.
F – KONYA MAVI TRENI – , , and ✕ Konya - Izmir Basmane and v.v.
G – TOROS EKSPRESİ – Adana - Konya and v.v.

1582 ANKARA - ADANA TCDD

km		11512 ③A	11532 B△	11410 D	2	21124 E	21206 F	21302 G	11126 H	71306 J	
0	**Ankara** 1575 d.	1025	1115	1605	1727	1900	2005	...	...	...	...
70	Irmak 1575 d.	|	1249	1739	1859	2022	2125	...	...	...	...
92	Kirikkale 1575 d.	|	1315	1803	1933	2046	2148	...	...	...	...
365	Boğazköprü 1575 d.	|	1756	2236	...	0104	0217u	0721k	...	...	...
381	Kayseri 1575 d.	1730	1815	2256	...	0124	*0230**	0700k	...	...	...
479	*Niğde d.	...	...	...	...	...	0352	0856	...	...	...
542	Ulukışla 1581 d.	...	...	...	...	...	0502	1004	1025	1843	...
651	Yenice 1581 d.	...	...	...	...	...	0709	1212	1241	2110	...
674	**Adana** 1581 d.	...	...	...	...	...	0728	1234	1300	2130	...

	61125 H	61301 G	51123 E	61205 F	2	51511 ⑥A	51531 B▽	41409 D	61305 J	
Adana 1581 d.	1545	1645	...	1930	...	...	...	...	0701	...
Yenice 1581 d.	1606	1710	...	1951	...	...	...	...	0724	...
Ulukışla 1581 d.	1838	1936	...	2220	...	...	...	...	1016	...
Niğde d.	...	2041	...	2321	...	...	...	...	...	...
Kayseri 1575 d.	...	2233k	2318	*0040**	...	0241	0330	0402	...	...
Boğazköprü 1575 d.	...	2214k	2346	0057u	...	|	0354	0427	...	...
Kirikkale 1575 d.	...	...	0415	0539	0600	|	0837	0900	...	...
Irmak 1575 d.	...	...	0439	0605	0624	|	0902	0926	...	...
Ankara 1575 a.	...	...	0610	0735	0803	0922	1037	1102	...	...

A – TRANSASYA EKSPRESI – and ✕ Ankara(**11512/51511**) - Tatvan and v.v.; and ✕ Van(**11512/51511**) - Razi(**59/60**) - Tehrān and v.v.
B – VAN GÖLÜ EKSPRESI – and Haydarpaşa - Tatvan and v.v.
C – GÜNEY EKSPRESI – and Ankara - Kurtalan and v.v.
D – DOĞU EKSPRESI – Ankara - Kars and v.v.
E – 4 EYLÜL MAVI – and ✕ Ankara - Malatya and v.v.
F – CUKUROVA MAVI TREN – and Ankara - Adana and v.v.
G – ERCIYES EKSPRESI – Kayseri - Adana and v.v.
H – ICANADOLU MAVI TRENI – , and ✕ Konya - Adana and v.v.
J – TOROS EKSPRESİ – Adana - Konya and v.v.
k – Calls at Kayseri then Boğazköprü and v.v.
u – Boğazköprü Müselles.
* – Connection by 🚌 from / to Boğazköprü Müselles.
△ – Runs as **11542** on ①③④⑤⑥ (see note **C**).
▽ – Runs as **51541** on ①②④⑥⑦ (see note **C**).

1583 ADANA - ELAZIG TCDD

km		61502 A	2	
0	**Adana** d.	1100	1835	...
79	Toprakkale d.	1212	1942	...
142	Fevzipaşa d.	1358	2057	...
211	Narlı d.	1522	...	...
336	Doğansehir d.	1816	...	...
392	Malatya d.	1955	...	...
487	Yolçatı d.	2201	...	...
511	**Elăzig** a.	2221	...	...

	2	51501 A	
Elăzig d.	...	0735	...
Yolçatı d.	...	0801	...
Malatya d.	...	1016	...
Doğansehir d.	...	1131	...
Narlı d.	...	1418	...
Fevzipaşa d.	0738	1559	...
Toprakkale d.	0857	1716	...
Adana a.	1000	1823	...

A – FIRAT EKSPRESI – Elazig - Adana and v.v.

1584 GAZIANTEP - ALEPPO & NUSAYBIN TCDD

km		②④⑦ 2		
0	**Gaziantep** d.	1000	...	...
	Nizip d.	1123	...	...
88	Karkamiş d.	1233	...	...
143	Çöbanbey 🏛 d.	|	...	...
218	**Aleppo** a.	|	...	...
356	Şenyurt d.	1958	...	...
381	**Nusaybin** a.	2105	...	...

	①③⑤ 2		
Nusaybin d.	0700	...	...
Şenyurt d.	0808	...	...
Aleppo d.	|	...	...
Çöbanbey 🏛 d.	|	...	...
Karkamiş d.	1514	...	...
Nizip d.	1627	...	...
Gaziantep a.	1802	...	...

SERVICES SUSPENDED DUE TO ENGINEERING WORKS.

1585 MERSIN - ADANA TCDD

km																		J	K							
0	**Mersin** d.	0600	0637	0730	0800	0900	0930	1030	1100	1200	1230	1330	1420	1500	1610	1630	1705	1720	1750	1810	1840	1910	2005	2050	2133	2234
26	Tarsus d.	0618	0707	0748	0823	0918	0953	1048	1129	1218	1254	1348	1449	1518	1628	1659	1723	1749	1819	1839	1858	1939	2023	2113	2159	2300
43	Yenice d.	0629	0722	0759	0836	0929	1006	1059	1143	1229	1308	1359	1502	1529	1639	1712	1734	1804	1834	1852	1909	1955	2035	2126	2213	2314
67	**Adana** a.	0645	0746	0815	0856	0945	1026	1115	1206	1245	1328	1415	1526	1545	1655	1734	1750	1829	1857	1916	1925	2018	2051	2146	2236	2336

								K	J																
Adana d.	...	0600	0646	0738	0805	0820	0901	0932	1003	1100	1115	1200	1330	1420	1510	1600	1630	1710	1736	1813	1853	1910	2015	2115	2215	2315
Yenice d.	...	0617	0713	0755	0828	0844	0918	0957	1030	1117	1140	1217	1347	1445	1527	1618	1656	1728	1803	1839	1910	1936	2032	2137	2239	2340
Tarsus d.	...	0628	0727	0806	0842	0858	0929	1011	1044	1128	1153	1228	1358	1458	1538	1629	1709	1739	1818	1852	1921	1950	2043	2150	2253	2353
Mersin a.	...	0645	0754	0825	0904	0924	0946	1040	1113	1145	1218	1245	1415	1525	1555	1646	1734	1758	1846	1919	1938	2017	2100	2211	2319	0015

J – Islahiye - Adana - Mersin and v.v.
K – Iskenderun - Adana - Mersin and v.v.

1590 ADANA - ALEPPO - DIMASHQ CFS, TCDD

All trains in Syria are believed to have been withdrawn due to on-going hostilities.

km	*Turkish train number* / *Syrian train number*	2J	2K							
0	**Adana** d.	1835	1900	...	...	...	...	...	...	...
79	Toprakkale d.	1942	2008	...	...	...	...	...	...	...
138	Iskenderun a.	|	2115	...	...	...	...	...	...	...
142	Fevzipaşa d.	2057	...	...	...	...	...	...	...	...
	Islahiye d.	2109	...	...	...	...	...	...	...	...
174	Meydan Ekbez 🏛 a.	...	...	...	...	...	...	...	...	...
174	Meydan Ekbez 🏛 d.	...	...	...	...	...	...	...	...	...
274	**Aleppo** a.	...	...	...	...	...	...	...	...	...
274	**Aleppo** d.	...	...	...	...	...	...	...	...	...
418	Hamāh d.	...	...	...	...	...	...	...	...	...
479	Himş II d.	...	...	...	...	...	...	...	...	...
623	**Dimashq** Kadem a.	...	...	...	...	...	...	...	...	...

Turkish train number / *Syrian train number*	2K	2J							
Dimashq Kadem d.	...	...	...	...	...	...	...	...	...
Himş II d.	...	...	...	...	...	...	...	...	...
Hamāh d.	...	...	...	...	...	...	...	...	...
Aleppo a.	...	...	...	...	...	...	...	...	...
Aleppo d.	...	...	...	...	...	...	...	...	...
Meydan Ekbez 🏛 a.	...	...	...	...	...	...	...	...	...
Meydan Ekbez 🏛 d.	...	...	...	...	...	...	...	...	...
Islahiye d.	...	0723	...	...	...	...	...	...	...
Fevzipaşa d.	...	0738	...	...	...	...	...	...	...
Iskenderun a.	0715	|	...	...	...	...	...	...	...
Toprakkale d.	0822	0857	...	...	...	...	...	...	...
Adana a.	0932	1003	...	...	...	...	...	...	...

J – Islahiye - Adana - Mersin and v.v.
K – Iskenderun - Adana - Mersin and v.v.

ROMANIA

SEE MAP PAGE 501

Operator: Societatea Naţională de Transport Feroviar de Călători (CFR Călători): www.cfrcalatori.ro. Additionally, Regiotrans and Trans-Feroviar operate some services and these are identified in the relevant tables.

Services: Trains convey 1st- and 2nd-class seating accommodation unless otherwise indicated. Sleeping- (🛏) and couchette (▬) cars are described on page 8. Russian-type sleeping-cars, as used in trains to and from destinations in Belarus, Moldova, Russia and Ukraine, are described on page 530; these cars are not accessible to passengers making journeys wholly within Romania or between Romania and Bulgaria.

Timings: Valid from **June 8, 2014** unless stated otherwise. Alterations to schedules are possible at any time.

Tickets: Reservation is obligatory for travel by all CFR Călători services for which a train number is shown in the tables, and passengers boarding without a prior reservation are surcharged. Supplements are payable for travel by **Intercity** (*IC*) and most other fast trains. Trains shown without numbers are slow stopping-services calling at all, or most, stations.

♦ – **NOTES for all tables in Romania section** (LISTED BY TRAIN NUMBER)

72/3 – TRAIANUS – [12] and ✕ Bucureşti - Arad - Budapest and v.v.
346/7 – DACIA – 🛏 1,2 cl., ▬ 2 cl., [12] and ✕ Bucureşti - Budapest - Wien and v.v.
362/3 – BIHARIA – [12] and ✕ Cluj Napoca - Budapest and v.v.
364/5 – ADY ENDRE – [12] and ✕ Cluj - Budapest and v.v.
366/7 – HARGHITA – [12] and ✕ Braşov - Cluj - Budapest and v.v.; [2] Târgu Mureş (**368/9**) - Cluj - Budapest and v.v.
368/9 – HARGHITA – [2] Târgu Mureş - Cluj (**366/7**) - Budapest and v.v.
372/3 – TRANSILVANIA – [12] and ✕ Braşov - Budapest and v.v.
382 – BULGARIA EXPRES – 🛏 1,2 cl. and [12] Sofia (**1384**) - Ruse - Bucureşti - Vadul Siret (**60**) - Moskva. For other cars see Table **98**.
383 – BULGARIA EXPRES – 🛏 1,2 cl. Moskva (**59**) - Vadul Siret - Bucureşti (**1385**) - Ruse - Sofia. For other cars see Table **98**.
401/2 – PRIETENIA – 🛏 1,2 cl.. and [12] Bucureşti - Ungheni (**106/5**) - Chişinău and v.v.
406/7 – CORONA – 🛏 1,2 cl., ▬ 2 cl., [12] and ✕ Budapest - Cluj - Braşov and v.v.
472/3 – ISTER – 🛏 1,2 cl., ▬ 2 cl., [12] and ✕ Bucureşti - Budapest and v.v.
533 – [12] and ✕ Bucureşti (**346**) - Teiuş - Cluj Napoca.
1520 – [2] Sibiu (**1722**) - Râmnicu Vâlcea - Bucureşti.
1580/9 – [12] Braşov - Bucureşti - Constanţa and v.v.
1621/2 – [12] and ✕ Bucureşti - Timişoara and v.v.
1641 – 🛏 1,2 cl., ▬ 2 cl. and [12] Bucureşti - Dej Călători; 🛏 1,2 cl., ▬ 2 cl. and [2] Bucureşti - Sărăţel (**4116**) - Bistriţa; [2] Bucureşti - Dej Călători (**4090**) - Baia Mare - Satu Mare; [2] Bucureşti - Deda (**4541**) - Târgu Mureş.
1642 – 🛏 1,2 cl., ▬ 2 cl. and [12] Dej Călători - Bucureşti; 🛏 1,2 cl., ▬ 2 cl. and [2] Bistriţa (**4117**) - Sărăţel - Bucureşti; [2] Satu Mare (**4091**) - Baia Mare - Dej Călători - Bucureşti.
1643 – 🛏 1,2 cl., ▬ 2 cl. and [12] Bucureşti - Salva (**4133**) - Sighetu Marmaţiei.
1644 – 🛏 1,2 cl., ▬ 2 cl. and [12] Sighetu Marmaţiei - Salva (**4136**) - Bucureşti; [2] Târgu Mureş (**4546**) - Deda - Bucureşti.
1645/6 – [12] Bucureşti - Târgu Mureş and v.v.
1651/2 – [12] Bucureşti - Suceava and v.v.; [12] Bucureşti - Bacău (**5471/2**) - Piatra Neamţ and v.v.
1653/4 – 🛏 1,2 cl., ▬ 2 cl. and [12] Bucureşti - Suceava - Vatra Dornei Băi and v.v.
1657/8 – [12] Bucureşti - Bacău - Bicaz and v.v.
1722 – [2] Sibiu - Râmnicu Vâlcea (**1520**) - Bucureşti.
1724/5 – [2] Sibiu - Podu Olt - Craiova and v.v.; [2] Braşov (**2104/7**) - Podu Olt - Craiova and v.v.
1741 – 🛏 1,2 cl., ▬ 2 cl. and [12] Bucureşti - Cluj Napoca - Oradea - Satu Mare.
1742 – Dec. 14 - June 13, Sept. 15 - Dec. 12: 🛏 1,2 cl., ▬ 2 cl. and [12] Satu Mare - Oradea - Cluj Napoca - Bucureşti.
1743/4 – [2] Timişoara - Arad - Oradea - Baia Mare and v.v.
1765/6 – ▬ 2 cl. and [12] Iaşi - Cluj Napoca - Timişoara and v.v.
1821/2 – For days of running and composition – see Table **1680**.
1823 – [12] Bucureşti - Târgu Jiu - Simeria - Cluj Napoca; [12] Bucureşti - Simeria (**1829**) - Deva.
1824 – [12] Deva - Târgu Jiu - Craiova - Bucureşti.
1829 – [12] Bucureşti (**1823**) - Simeria - Deva.
1833/4 – [12] Iaşi - Cluj - Oradea - Timişoara and v.v.
1837/8 – 🛏 1,2 cl., ▬ 2 cl. and [12] Iaşi - Cluj Napoca - Timişoara and v.v.
1843/4 – [12] Sighetu Marmaţiei (**4134/5**) - Beclean pe Someş - Timişoara and v.v.
1861/2 – For days of running and composition – see Table **1680**.
1870/1 – [2] Galaţi - Constanţa and v.v.
1931/2 – For days of running and composition – see Table **1680**.
1934 – June 14 - Sept. 14: 🛏 1,2 cl., ▬ 2 cl. and [12] Satu Mare - Oradea - Cluj Napoca - Bucureşti.
1944/5 – For days of running and composition – see Table **1680**.
1946/7 – [12] Sighetu Marmaţiei - Beclean pe Someş (**1944/5**) - Mangalia and v.v.
2801/2 – For days of running and composition – see Table **1680**.
4116/7 – 🛏 1,2 cl., ▬ 2 cl. and [2] Bucureşti (**1641/2**) - Sărăţel - Bistriţa and v.v.
4541/6 – [2] Bucureşti (**1641/4**) - Deda (**4541/6**) - Târgu Mureş and v.v.
5471/2 – [12] Bucureşti (**1651/2**) - Bacău - Piatra Neamţ and v.v.
10191/2 – For days of running and composition – see Table **1680**.
10195/6 – [12] Deva - Craiova (**10191/2**) - Mangalia and v.v. See Table **1680** for dates.
10198/9 – [2] Reşiţa Nord - Caransebeş (**10191/2**) - Mangalia and v.v. See Table **1680** for dates.

♣ – Operated by Regiotrans. § – Operated by Transferoviar Grup SA.
□ – Operated by Softrans S.R.L.
• – Subject to cancellation for scheduled track maintenance.

Additional notes are shown in the relevant table.

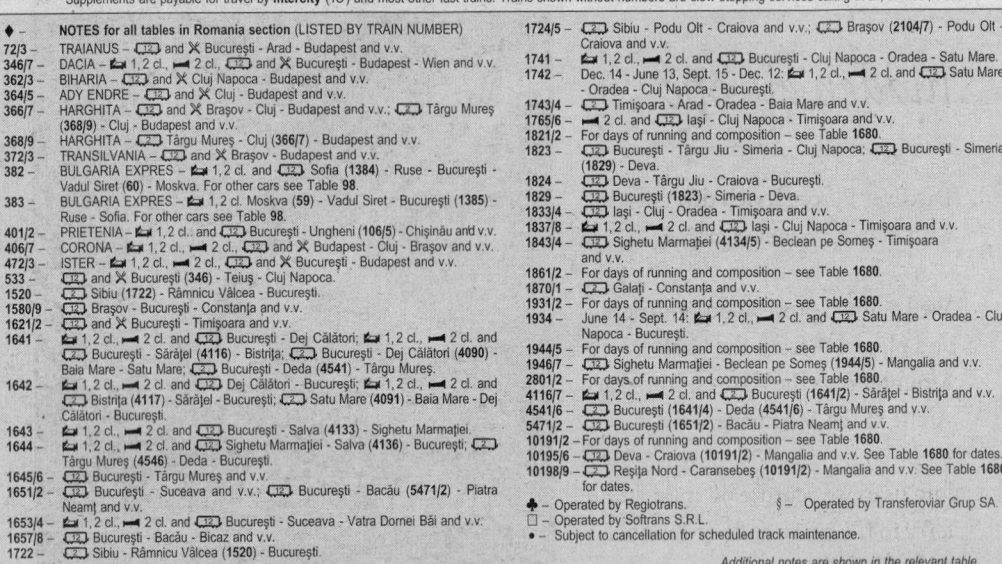

1600 BUCUREŞTI - BRAŞOV - SIBIU and CLUJ NAPOCA

km			372		1745	1637	1580	14091	1732	1621	1645			533	346	1725	1527	1633	472	1643	14031	1741	1945	1931	1641	14093
								♣						*IC*	*IC*				*IC*		♣					♣
			♦				♦	2C	g	♦	♦			♦	♦	♦			♦	♦	2	♦	♦	♦	♦	2CJ
	Constanţa **1680** d.	...	...	...	...	...	0530	...	...	...	...	...	...	...	...	...	...	...	...	...	...	...	1435	1720	...	...
0	**Bucureşti** Nord d.	...	...	...	0552	0700	0830	0850	...	1000	1110	...	...	1300	1300	...	1530	1645	1730	1805	1752	1840	|	2030	2110	2120
59	Ploieşti Vest d.	...	...	...	0635	0745	0913	0951	1013p	1048	1154	...	...	1342	1342	...	1613	1736	1812	1848	1855	1923	2033p	2114	2153	2222
92	Câmpina d.	...	...	...	0701	0811	0939	1023	1043	1114	1220	...	...	|	|	...	1638	1802	|	1914	1926	1949	2104	2141	2221	2251
121	Sinaia d.	...	...	...	0732	0837	1005	1054	1109	1143	1246	...	...	1430	1430	...	1705	1831	1901	1943	1955	2015	2132	2209	2247	2319
140	Predeal d.	...	...	...	0758	0904	1033	1121	1138	1209	1314	...	...	1452	1452	...	1733	1858	1925	2009	2022	2044	2200	2237	2314	2344
166	**Braşov** a.	...	...	...	0835	0940	1110	1158	1215	1246	1353	...	...	1528	1528	...	1810	1935	2000	2045	2100	2122	2236	2313	2351	0020
166	**Braşov** d.	0320	0600	0617	0845	...	...	...	...	1300	...	1425	...	1537	1537	1600	1825	...	2008	...	...	2131	2249	2328	0003	...
294	Sighişoara **1669** d.	|	|	|	1115	...	...	...	...	|	...	|	...	1757	1757	|	|	...	2227	...	...	2352	|	0149	|	...
332	Mediaş **1669** d.	|	|	|	1210	...	...	...	...	|	...	|	...	1850	1850	|	|	...	2320	...	...	0048	|	0250	|	...
343	Copşa Mică **1669** d.	|	|	|	1232	...	...	...	...	|	...	|	...	|	|	|	|	...	|	...	...	0109	|	0307	|	...
	Făgăraş d.	0449	0712	0750	|	...	...	...	...	1413	...	1556	...	|	|	1753	1938	...	|	...	...	|	|	|	|	...
	Podu Olt **1622** d.	0636	|	0926	|	...	...	...	...	|	...	1742	...	|	|	1906	|	...	|	...	...	|	|	|	|	...
	Sibiu **1622/69** a.	0711	0844	1001	|	...	...	...	...	1538	...	1816	...	|	|	1934	2123	...	|	...	...	|	|	|	|	...
373	Blaj d.	...	|	...	1320	...	...	...	...	...	...	...	...	1955	1955	...	...	...	0024	...	...	0154	◐	0355	◐	...
394	Teiuş **1610** d.	...	|	...	1355	...	...	...	...	...	...	...	...	2042	2047	...	...	...	|	...	...	0229	|	0429	|	...
407	Aiud **1610** d.	...	|	...	1407	...	...	...	...	...	...	...	...	|	|	...	...	...	|	...	...	0241	|	0441	|	...
427	Războieni **1610** d.	...	|	...	1426	...	...	...	...	...	...	...	...	2110	|	...	...	...	|	...	...	0301	|	0502	|	...
444	Câmpia Turzii **1610** d.	...	|	...	1442	...	...	...	...	...	...	...	...	2126	|	...	...	...	|	...	...	0317	|	0518	|	...
496	**Cluj Napoca** **1610** a.	...	|	...	1538	...	...	...	...	...	...	...	...	2222	|	...	...	...	|	...	...	0413	|	0615	|	...
	Oradea **1612** a.	...	|	...	|	...	...	...	...	...	...	...	...	...	|	...	...	...	|	...	...	0713	|	0924	|	...
	Baia Mare **1616** a.	...	|	...	2007	...	...	...	...	...	...	...	...	...	|	...	...	...	|	...	...	|	0835	...	0927	...
	Satu Mare **1616** a.	...	|	...	2158	...	...	...	...	...	...	...	...	...	|	...	...	...	|	...	...	0929	1020	...	...	...
	Arad **1610** a.	...	1415	...	...	...	...	...	...	...	...	...	...	...	0055	...	...	...	0511	...	...	...	...	...	...	...
	Budapest K **1280** a.	...	1750	...	...	...	...	...	...	...	...	...	...	...	0440	...	...	...	0850	...	...	...	...	...	...	...

km		1644	14092	1934	1634	1528	473	347	14030	1724	1636		14094	1746	1731	1589	1622		1646	532		373	1944	1642	1932	1742
			♣				*IC*	*IC*	♣				♣							*IC*						
		♦	2CJ	♦			♦	♦	2	♦•		2⚒	2C		g	♦	♦	2	♦			♦	♦	♦	♦	♦
	Budapest K **1280** d.	...	...	...	...	...	1910	2330	...	...	...	...	...	...	...	...	...	...	...	...	...	0910	...	...	...	...
	Arad **1610** d.	...	...	...	...	...	0033	0447	...	...	...	...	...	...	...	...	...	...	...	...	...	1436	...	...	...	...
	Satu Mare **1616** d.	...	...	1805	...	...	|	|	...	...	...	...	...	0340	...	...	...	...	...	...	...	|	1315	...	...	1650
	Baia Mare **1616** d.	...	...	|	...	...	|	|	...	...	...	...	...	0524	...	...	...	...	...	...	...	|	1507	1822	...	|
	Oradea **1612** d.	...	...	2039	...	...	|	|	...	...	...	...	...	|	...	...	...	...	...	...	...	|	|	|	1908	1908
	Cluj Napoca **1610** d.	...	...	2340	...	...	|	|	...	...	...	...	...	0930	...	...	...	...	...	1400	...	|	|	|	2200	2200
	Câmpia Turzii **1610** d.	...	...	0035	...	...	|	|	...	...	...	...	...	1024	...	...	...	...	...	1453	...	|	|	|	2254	2254
	Războieni **1610** d.	...	...	0054	...	...	|	|	...	...	...	...	...	1042	...	...	...	...	...	1511	...	|	|	|	2312	2312
	Aiud **1610** d.	...	...	0116	...	...	|	|	...	...	...	...	...	1102	...	...	...	...	...	|	...	|	|	|	2331	2331
	Teiuş **1610** d.	...	...	0133	...	...	|	|	...	...	...	...	...	1117	...	...	...	...	...	1544	...	|	|	|	2347	2347
	Blaj d.	...	...	0216	...	...	0522	0920	...	...	...	...	...	1148	...	...	...	...	...	1617	...	|	◐	◐	0023	0023
0	**Sibiu** **1622/69** d.	...	...	|	...	0605	|	|	...	1054	...	1202	...	|	...	...	1501	1440	...	|	1920	2004	|	|	|	|
22	Podu Olt **1622** d.	...	...	|	...	|	|	|	...	1138	...	1239	...	|	...	...	|	1532	...	|	2000	|	|	|	|	|
84	Făgăraş d.	...	...	|	...	0746	|	|	...	1239	...	1414	...	|	...	...	1627	1707	...	|	2150	2126	|	|	|	|
	Copşa Mică **1669** d.	...	...	0308	...	|	|	|	...	|	...	|	...	1231	...	...	|	|	...	1706	|	|	|	|	0108	010
	Mediaş **1669** d.	...	...	0325	...	|	0625	1022	...	|	...	|	...	1248	...	...	|	|	...	1723	|	|	|	|	0124	012
	Sighişoara **1669** d.	...	...	0421	...	|	0721	1116	...	|	...	|	...	1343	...	...	|	|	...	1826	|	|	|	|	0221	022
149	**Braşov** a.	...	...	0637	...	0907	0934	1331	...	1407	...	1544	...	1604	...	...	1740	1836	...	2038	2309	2235	0059	0328	0437	043
	Braşov d.	0530	0616	0647	0730	0919	0942	1340	1400	...	1420	...	1600	1616	1640	1710	1755	...	1840	2045	...	...	0111	0345	0450	045
	Predeal d.	0608	0648	0727	0805	0953	1015	1413	1433	...	1453	...	1632	1656	1713	1745	1828	...	1913	2117	...	...	0151	0427	0531	053
	Sinaia d.	0633	0710	0755	0832	1019	1038	1434	1457	...	1521	...	1656	1723	1738	1812	1855	...	1940	2138	...	...	0217	0450	0600	060
	Câmpina d.	0705	0740	0824	0906	1047	|	|	1529	...	1553	...	1727	1754	1807	1840	1925	...	2008	|	...	...	0245	0520	0632	063
	Ploieşti Vest d.	0731	0815	0851	0933	1113	1129	1523	1557	...	1620	...	1804	1822	1831	1906	1951	...	2035	2228	...	...	0313p	0552	0700	070
	Bucureşti Nord a.	0815	0901	0936	1028	1157	1210	1605	1648	...	1709	...	1850	1906	...	1950	2040	...	2120	2309	...	...	|	0637	0748	074
	Constanţa **1680** a.	...	...	...	...	...	...	...	...	...	...	...	...	...	...	2255	...	...	...	...	...	...	0827	...	1207	...

C – From/to Craiova (Table **1620**).
J – Also conveys [2] Braşov - Ploieşti Vest (**14068/9**) - Iaşi and v.v.
g – From/to Galaţi via Ploieşti Sud (Table **1660**).
p – Ploieşti Sud.
* – Subject to confirmation.
◐ – Via Miercurea Ciuc (Table **1630**).
For notes ♦, ♣, §, □ and • see heading.

For train list and additional notes see heading

CLUJ NAPOCA and SIBIU - DEVA - ARAD and TIMIŞOARA 1610

km		1765 ♦	1811 2	2			1821 ♦	1837 ♦	372 ♦	369 ♦	2	2	2		♣2 ①⑤
0	**Cluj Napoca** 1600 d.	0026	...	...	...	...	...	0440	...	...	...	0745	...	...	...
52	Câmpia Turzii 1600 d.	0119	...	...	...	...	...	0534	...	...	...	0901	...	...	...
	Târgu Mureş d.	|	...	...	0327	...	...	|	...	0712	...	|	...	...	...
	Luduş d.	|	...	...	0433	...	...	|	...	0807	...	|	...	...	...
69	Războieni 1600 d.	0138	...	...	0458	...	...	0553	...	0832	...	0926	...	...	...
90	Aiud 1600 d.	0158	...	...	0524	...	...	0615	...	...	...	0959	...	...	...
103	Teiuş 1600 d.	0214	...	...	0540	...	...	0631	...	...	...	1015	...	...	...
	Bucureşti Nord 1600 d.	|	...	...	|	...	2345	|	...	...	...	...	...	...	...
	Braşov 1600 d.	|	...	...	|	...	|	|	0600	...	...	...	...	...	0745
83∆	**Sibiu** d.	|	0308	...	|	...	|	|	0844	...	...	...	...	...	|
9∆	Sebeş Alba d.	|	0438	...	|	...	▽	|	1015	...	...	...	...	...	|
122	**Alba Iulia** d.	0248	|	...	0624	...	|	0706	|	...	...	...	...	...	1517
132	Vinţu de Jos d.	0305	0452	...	0640	...	|	0723	1031	...	...	...	...	...	1538
176	Simeria 1625 d.	0417	0601	0628	...	...	0755	0843	1146	...	1240	...	1535	...	1706
185	Deva 1625 d.	0429	0612	0640	...	...	0807	0855	1158	...	1251	...	1547	...	1717
208	Ilia d.	0455	0639	0719	...	...	0835	0923	|	...	1329	...	1622	...	1743
298	Radna d.	0614	|	0923	...	...	0952	|	|	...	1518	...	1806	...	1915
333	**Arad** a.	0714n	|	1012	...	...	1030	|	1415	...	1611	...	1854	...	2002
	Budapest Keleti 1280 a.	|	|	...	...	...	...	|	1750	...	...	...	...	...	|
291	Lugoj 1620 a.	|	0814	...	...	...	...	1106	...	...	...	...	...	...	|
355	**Timişoara** Nord 1620 a.	0808	0934	...	...	...	...	1226	...	...	...	...	...	...	2136

km		2	1621		2	368 ♦	2	1819 2		IC 346 ♦	2	2	2Ⓑ	IC 472 ♦	1844 ♦
0	**Cluj Napoca** 1600 d.	1207	...	...	...	1520	...	...	...	...	...	1952	...	...	2315
52	Câmpia Turzii 1600 d.	1323	...	...	...	1628	...	...	...	...	...	2109	...	...	0010
	Târgu Mureş d.	|	...	...	1415	|	1540	1733	...	...	1924	|	2222	...	|
	Luduş d.	|	...	...	1518	|	1634	1818	...	...	2020	|	2317	...	|
69	Războieni 1600 d.	1348	...	...	1541	1649	1658	1847	...	...	2044	2133	2340	...	0029
90	Aiud 1600 d.	1415	...	...	...	...	1724	1904	...	...	...	2204	...	...	0049
103	Teiuş 1600 d.	1429	...	...	...	...	1737	1919	...	...	...	2219	...	...	0106
	Bucureşti Nord 1600 d.	...	1000	...	...	...	...	|	...	1300	...	...	...	1730	|
	Braşov 1600 d.	...	1300	...	...	...	...	|	...	1537	...	...	...	2008	|
83∆	**Sibiu** d.	...	1546	1551	...	...	...	|	...	|	...	...	...	|	|
9∆	Sebeş Alba d.	...	1717	1755	...	...	...	|	...	|	...	...	...	|	|
122	**Alba Iulia** d.	...	|	|	...	...	...	1949	...	2119	...	...	...	0124	0140
132	Vinţu de Jos d.	...	1732	1809	...	...	...	2004	...	|	...	...	...	|	0200
176	Simeria 1625 d.	...	1856	...	...	...	...	2058	...	2234	...	...	...	0242	0321
185	Deva 1625 d.	...	1908	...	...	...	...	2108	...	2245	...	...	...	0252	0332
208	Ilia d.	...	1936	...	...	...	...	2133	...	|	...	...	...	|	0359
298	Radna d.	...	2054	...	...	...	...	|	...	|	...	...	...	|	0522
333	**Arad** a.	...	2145n	...	...	...	...	|	...	0055	...	...	...	0511	0609n
	Budapest Keleti 1280 a.	...	|	...	...	...	...	|	...	0440	...	...	...	0850	|
291	Lugoj 1620 a.	...	|	...	...	...	...	2308	...	...	...	...	...	...	|
355	**Timişoara** Nord 1620 a.	...	2239	...	...	...	...	0025	...	...	...	...	...	...	0705

	2	2	2		IC 347 ♦	369 ♦	1812 2	• 2⚒	2	2	♣2 ②⑥	1820 2	1622	368 ♦
Timişoara Nord 1620 d.	...	...	...	...	...	...	0506	...	...	...	0645	0757	0820	...
Lugoj 1620 d.	...	...	...	...	...	...	0626	...	...	...	|	0931	|	...
Budapest Keleti 1280 d.	...	...	...	...	2330	...	|	...	...	...	|	|	|	...
Arad d.	...	...	...	...	0447	...	|	...	...	0752	0825	|	0907n	...
Radna d.	...	...	...	...	|	...	|	...	...	0840	0906	|	|	...
Ilia d.	...	...	...	...	|	...	0816	...	...	1027	1037	1120	1109	...
Deva 1625 d.	...	...	...	...	0658	...	0839	...	...	1057	1104	1145	1135	...
Simeria 1625 d.	...	...	...	...	0715	...	0850	...	...	1109	1128	1156	1202	...
Vinţu de Jos d.	...	...	...	0645	|	...	0957	...	...	...	1235	1302	1308	...
Alba Iulia d.	...	...	...	|	0825	...	|	...	...	...	1253	1319	|	...
Sebeş Alba d.	...	...	...	0657	|	...	1009	...	...	...	|	|	1320	...
Sibiu a.	...	...	...	0859	|	...	1140	...	...	...	|	|	1501	...
Braşov 1600 a.	...	...	...	...	1331	...	...	...	...	...	2031	|	1740	...
Bucureşti Nord 1600 a.	...	...	...	...	1605	...	...	...	...	...	...	|	2040	...
Teiuş 1600 d.	...	0630	0843	...	...	...	...	...	1420	...	...	1350	...	...
Aiud 1600 d.	...	0643	0855	...	...	...	...	...	1431	...	...	1401	...	...
Războieni 1600 d.	0518	0706	0923	...	...	0840	...	1209	1458	...	...	1420	...	1715
Luduş d.	0548	0732	|	...	...	|	...	1237	|	...	...	1445	...	1742
Târgu Mureş a.	0649	0832	|	...	...	|	...	1335	|	...	...	1526	...	1841
Câmpia Turzii 1600 d.	...	...	0943	...	...	0856	...	...	1518	...	...	...	...	...
Cluj Napoca 1600 a.	...	...	1055	...	...	0948	...	...	1630	...	...	...	...	...

	2	2	373 ♦		1766 ♦	2	2 Ⓐ	2	2	1838 ♦	1822 ♦	1843 ♦	1823 ♦	IC 473 ♦
Timişoara Nord 1620 d.	...	...	...	...	1340	1345	...	...	...	1738	...	2124	...	...
Lugoj 1620 d.	...	...	...	...	|	|	...	...	...	1857	...	|	...	...
Budapest Keleti 1280 d.	...	...	0910	...	|	|	...	...	...	|	...	|	...	1910
Arad d.	...	...	1436	...	1435n	1510	1630	1735	...	|	1855	2216n	...	0033
Radna d.	...	...	|	...	1525	1557	1726	1823	...	|	1935	2257	...	|
Ilia d.	...	...	|	...	1645	1745	1939	2056	...	2041	2052	0014	...	|
Deva 1625 d.	1418	...	1650	...	1711	1818	2013	2130	...	2107	2118	0040	...	0250
Simeria 1625 d.	1430	...	1712	...	1724	1829	2025	2142	...	2130	2133	0051	0109	0309
Vinţu de Jos d.	1537	...	1816	1821	1835	...	...	...	...	2236	|	0203	0225	|
Alba Iulia d.	1554	...	|	1838	1853	...	...	...	...	2255	|	0224	0247	0426
Sebeş Alba d.	|	...	1828	|	|	...	...	...	...	|	▽	|	|	|
Sibiu a.	|	...	2004	|	|	...	...	...	...	|	|	|	|	|
Braşov 1600 a.	|	...	2235	|	|	...	...	...	...	|	|	|	|	0934
Bucureşti Nord 1600 a.	|	...	...	|	|	...	...	...	...	|	0540	|	|	1210
Teiuş 1600 d.	1634	1638	...	1917	1934	...	...	...	2026	2327	...	0305	0321	...
Aiud 1600 d.	...	1649	...	1928	1948	...	...	...	2038	2339	...	0317	0333	...
Războieni 1600 d.	...	1716	...	2011	2008	...	...	...	2114	2359	...	0337	0352	...
Luduş d.	...	|	...	2046	|	...	...	...	|	|	...	|	|	...
Târgu Mureş a.	...	|	...	2143	|	...	...	...	|	|	...	|	|	...
Câmpia Turzii 1600 d.	...	1735	...	...	2025	...	...	...	2135	0015	...	0353	0408	...
Cluj Napoca 1600 a.	...	1845	...	...	2121	...	...	...	2250	0111	...	0449	0504	...

n – Aradu **Nou**. ▽ – Via Craiova and Târgu Jiu (Table **1625**). ∆ – Distance from Vinţu de Jos. For notes ♦, ♣, §, ☐ and • see page 518.

CLUJ NAPOCA - ORADEA 1612

km		406 ♦	1741 ♦	1531 2t	1931 ♦	364 ♦	366 ♦		1533 •2	362 ♦	1833 ♦	1535 2
	Bucureşti N 1600 d.	...	1840	...	2030	...	...	...	...	...	...	...
	Braşov 1600/35 d.	1855	2131	...	2328	...	0255	...	...	...	...	...
0	**Cluj Napoca** d.	0213	0428	0545	0635	0720	1012	...	1345	1507	1545	2045
50	Huedin d.	0307	0524	0637	0731	0813	1106	...	1438	1602	1644	2137
153	**Oradea** a.	0449	0713	0825	0924	0954	1249	...	1627	1748	1841	2350
	Budapest K 1275 a.	0820	...	...	...	1320	1620	...	...	2120	...	...

	1532 2	1834 ♦	367 ♦	363 ♦	1534	1742 ♦	1932 ♦	365 ♦	1934 ♦	1536 •2t	407 ♦
Budapest K 1275 d.	...	...	0640	0940	...	...	...	1440	...	...	1740
Oradea d.	0608	0959	1205	1513	1701	1908	1908	2008	2039	2112	2306
Huedin d.	0755	1153	1347	1710	1855	2055	2055	2156	2230	2307	0049
Cluj Napoca a.	0845	1246	1437	1800	1942	2145	2145	2246	2322	2356	0136
Braşov 1600/35 a.	...	...	2215	...	...	0437	0437	...	0637	...	0853
Bucureşti N 1600 a.	...	...	...	...	...	0748	0748	...	0936	...	...

t – From/to Timişoara (Table **1614**). For notes ♦, ♣, §, ☐ and • see page 518.

ORADEA - ARAD - TIMIŞOARA 1614

km		1744 2m	2	1531 •2	73 ♦	2	2	79 T	1833 ♦	2	
	Cluj Napoca 1612 d.	...	...	0545	...	...	...	...	1545	...	...
0	**Oradea** d.	0315	0505	0828	...	...	1604	...	1845	2007	...
39	Salonta d.	0355	0553	0915	...	...	1651	...	1928	2105	...
121	**Arad** a.	0515	0731	1033	...	...	1837	...	2057	2300	...
121	**Arad** 1669 d.	0521	0734	1036	1235	1627	1842	2032	2107	2330j	...
178	**Timişoara** Nord 1669 a.	0615	0911	1126	1326	1747	1958	2123	2202	0042j	...

	2	1834 ♦	78 T		2	72 ♦	1743 2m	1536 •2	2	2
Timişoara Nord 1669 d.	0544	0625	0730	...	1306	1425	1550	1750	1735	2024
Arad 1669 a.	0703	0723	0822	...	1418	1516	1647	1841	1901	2151
Arad d.	0706	0737	...	...	1421	...	1653	1848	1911	...
Salonta d.	0843	0914	...	...	1619	...	1819	2028	2105	...
Oradea a.	0932	0953	...	...	1709	...	1902	2109	2152	...
Cluj Napoca 1612 a.	...	1246	...	...	...	...	...	2356	...	...

T – (12) Timişoara - Arad - Budapest and v.v. (Table **1280**).
j – Not nights of ⑤/⑥ and ⑥/⑦.
m – From/to Baia Mare (Table **1618**).
For Cluj - Timişoara via Teiuş see Table **1610**.
For notes ♦, ♣, §, ☐ and • see page 518.

CLUJ NAPOCA - BAIA MARE - SATU MARE 1616

km		D	1741 ♦	1945 ♦	1641 ♦	2		2	2	1745	2Ⓑ	1744 ♦
	Bucureşti N 1600 d.	...	1840	...	2110	...	...	...	...	0552	...	...
	Braşov 1600 d.	...	2131	2249	0003	...	...	...	...	0845	...	...
0	**Cluj Napoca** d.	...	0428	▽	▽	0540	...	1410	1410	1554	1822	...
59	Dej Călători d.	...	|	0545	0631	0727	...	1528	1528	1726	1952	...
135	Jibou d.	...	△	0725	0809	0907	...	1708	1714	1848	2127	...
193	**Baia Mare** a.	...	|	0835	0927	...	...	1819	|	2007	2234	...
193	**Baia Mare** 1669 d.	0414	|	0853	0947	...	...	...	◐	2021	...	2345
252	**Satu Mare** 1669 a.	0607	0929	1020	1114	...	...	...	1948	2158	...	0108

	1746	2	2	1944 ♦	2		1642 ♦	1742 ♦	D	1743 ♦
Satu Mare 1669 d.	0340	...	0733	1315	...	...	1610	1650	1953	2120
Baia Mare 1669 a.	0510	...	◧	1453	...	...	1759	|	2212	2244
Baia Mare d.	0524	0845	|	1507	1530	...	1822	|	...	...
Jibou d.	0640	1020	1020	1617	1641	...	1946	△	...	...
Dej Călători d.	0807	1149	1149	1802	1845	...	2116	|	...	...
Cluj Napoca a.	0914	1252	1252	▽	2013	...	▽	2200	...	...
Braşov 1600 a.	1622	...	...	0059	...	...	0328	0437	...	...
Bucureşti N 1600 a.	1906	...	...	...	...	...	0637	0748	...	...

D – From/to Debrecen (Table **1277**).
△ – Via Oradea (Tables **1612**/**1618**).
▽ – Via Miercurea Ciuc (Table **1630**).
◐ – Via Carei (a. 1912).
◧ – Via Carei (d. 0812).
For notes ♦, ♣, §, ☐ and • see page 518.

ORADEA - CAREI - SATU MARE 1618

km		2	1741 ♦	2	D	2•	2p	2q	D	D	1743 ♦	2
0	**Oradea** d.	0310	0725	0743	...	...	1535	1535	...	1639	1912	1940
66	Valea lui Mihai d.	0441	0830	0909	1138	1252	1710	1710	1757	1837	2020	2111
97	Carei d.	0518	0856	...	1215	1329	1746	1755	1840	...	2046	...
133	**Satu Mare** a.	0602	0929	...	1258	1414	1849	1840	1953	...	2115	...
	Baia Mare 1616 a.	...	...	...	...	...	...	...	2212	...	2244	...

	1744 ♦	2	D	2	D	D	2	1742 ♦	1934 ♦	2	
Baia Mare 1616 d.	2345	...	0414	...	...	...	...	...	...	...	...
Satu Mare d.	0113	...	0620	0740	...	1500	1551	1650	1805	1934	...
Carei d.	0142	...	0707	0857	...	1544	1633	1725	1838	2017	...
Valea lui Mihai d.	0206	0435	0837	0940	1338	1637	1711	1752	1905	2114	...
Oradea a.	0307	0602	...	1107	1456	...	1836	1858	2020	2238	...

D – From/to Debrecen (Table **1277**). p – June 14 - Sept. 15. q – Not June 14 - Sept. 15. For notes ♦, ♣, §, ☐ and • see page 518.

1620 BUCUREŞTI - CRAIOVA - TIMISOARA

km		1698		1827	72	1591	1593		♣ 14092	1521		1691	15901		1523	1825	1693	1823	1595	1525	♣ 14094	1597	10191	10191 10199	1821
		2	2	2	♦		h	2T	2B	2	•2		□	2	2R	2T		♦		2R	2B		♦	♦	♦
0	**Bucureşti** Nord ... d.	...	...	...	0545	0645	0745	0845	0920	0945	...	1045	1245	...	1345	1445	1545	1645	1745	1845	1905	1945	0017**b**	0017**b**	2345
51	Videle ... d.	...	...	...	0633	0733	0840	0936	1013	1033	...	1134	1335	...	1434	1534	1633	1732	1835	1934	1958	2035	0109	0109	0032
100	Roşiori Nord ... d.	...	...	...	0714	0815	0925	1030	1102	1115	...	1216	1417	...	1516	1616	1715	1815	1917	2016	2050	2118	|	|	0115
155	Caracal ... d.	...	...	0720	0759	0900	▬	1126	1211	1159	...	1305	1504	...	1600	1705	1801	1905	2006	2104	2150	2205	|	|	0205
209	**Craiova** ... a.	...	...	0807	0845	0946	...	1220	1307	...	...	1352	1550	...	...	1751	1847	1952	2052	...	2246	2251	0318	0318	0252
209	**Craiova** ... **1625** d.	...	0335	0810	0852	0948	...	1222	...	...	...	1400	...	...	...	1755	1855	2000	...	...	...	▬	0330	0330	0302
245	Filiaşi ... **1625** d.	...	0411	0835	0917	1012	...	1248	...	...	...	1425	...	...	...	1818	1920	2025	...	...	...	...	|	|	0328
323	Drobeta Turnu Severin ... d.	...	0615	▬	1043	1148	...	...	...	...	...	1558	...	...	...	...	2045	...	...	...	...	...	0533	0533	...
347	Orşova ... d.	...	0650	...	1113	...	...	...	...	...	1343	1629	...	...	...	...	2115	...	...	...	...	...	0604	0604	...
364	Băile Herculane ... d.	...	...	2	1137	...	2	...	...	...	1412	1654	...	...	...	...	2140	...	...	...	...	2⚒	0629	0629	...
435	Caransebeş ... d.	0640	...	0757	1302	...	1321	...	...	...	1632	1819	...	1926	...	...	2305	...	...	...	...	0502	0824	0845	...
	Reşiţa Nord **1669** ... a.	0533**r**	...	|	|	...	|	...	...	...	|	|	...	|	...	...	|	...	...	...	...	|	|	0930	...
474	Lugoj ... **1610** d.	0707	...	0842	1328	...	1411	...	...	...	1731	1845	...	2012	...	...	2333	...	...	...	...	0548	0858	...	...
533	**Timişoara** Nord ... **1610** a.	0755	...	0952	1415	...	1524	...	...	...	1856	1932	...	2120	...	...	0020	...	...	...	...	0656	0958	...	...

	♣ 14091	1594	1520	1826	15902	1692	1824	1596		1828	1522	1590		♣ 14093			73		1699	1822		9380 1592	10192	10198 10192	
	2B		R	2T	□		♦		2	2	R		2	2B	2	2	♦	2Ⓑ	2	♦	2	⚒	♦	♦	2
Timişoara Nord ... **1610** d.	...	...	...	...	...	0545	...	...	0756	...	...	...	...	...	...	1258	1400	1428	1621	...	1935	...	1905	...	2218
Lugoj ... **1610** d.	...	...	...	...	...	0635	...	...	0923	...	...	...	...	...	...	1410	1457	1540	1713	...	2049	...	2002	...	2334
Reşiţa Nord **1669** ... d.	...	...	...	...	...	|	...	...	|	...	...	...	...	...	...	|	|	|	1843**r**	...	|	...	|	1902	|
Caransebeş ... d.	...	...	...	...	...	0700	...	...	1014	...	...	...	...	...	...	1452	1524	1626	1750	...	2132	...	2041	2041	0017
Băile Herculane ... d.	...	...	...	...	...	0826	...	...	...	...	...	...	...	...	...	...	1655	1847	...	...	...	...	2228	2228	...
Orşova ... d.	...	...	...	...	...	0851	...	...	...	...	...	...	...	...	1558	...	1719	1915	...	...	...	...	2254	2254	...
Drobeta Turnu Severin ... d.	...	...	...	...	...	0920	...	...	...	...	...	1425	...	...	1640	...	1750	...	...	...	...	...	2335	2335	...
Filiaşi ... **1625** d.	...	...	...	0641	...	1049	1200	...	...	1512	...	1547	1625	...	1840	...	1910	...	...	0156	...	...	|	|	...
Craiova ... **1625** a.	...	...	...	0707	...	1114	1228	...	...	1538	...	1613	1651	...	1928	...	1936	...	...	0222	...	...	0132	0132	...
Craiova ... d.	0448	0500	...	0710	0840	1122	1235	1420	...	1540	...	1620	1655	1732	...	...	1945	...	...	0232	...	0255	0144	0144	...
Caracal ... d.	0536	0542	0715	0753	0921	1204	1318	1502	...	1621	1638	1702	1752	1820	...	...	2026	...	...	0315	...	0342	|	|	...
Roşiori Nord ... d.	0638	0630	0806	0842	1008	1252	1406	1550	...	...	1722	1745	1846	1916	...	...	2110	...	...	0404	...	0450	|	|	...
Videle ... d.	0738	0720	0855	0932	1057	1340	1455	1640	...	...	1816	1833	1945	2012	...	...	2158	...	...	0452	...	0542	0356	0356	...
Bucureşti Nord ... a.	0830	0806	0942	1020	1145	1428	1543	1729	...	...	1904	1920	2035	2102	...	...	2245	...	...	0540	...	0635	0450**b**	0450**b**	...

B – (12) From / to Braşov (Table **1600**).
R – From / to Râmnicu Vâlcea (Table **1622**).
T – From / to Târgu Jiu (Table **1625**).

b – Bucureşti **Băneasa**.
h – Not holidays.
r – Via Caransebeş.

For notes ♦, ♣, §, □ and • see page 518.

1621 BUCUREŞTI - PITESTI - CRAIOVA

2nd class only (except where shown)

km		1891	1781	1783	1893	1785	1895	1787	1897	1789	1791	1793	2802 ♦
0	**Bucureşti** Nord ... d.	0610	0710	0910	1310	1410	1510	1610	1710	1812	1910	2010	2310
108	Piteşti ... d.	0812	0901	1105	1515	1601	1710	1802	1915	2005	2102	2202	0140
189	Slatina ... d.	0927	...	...	1632	...	1834	...	2034	...	...	...	0255
206	Piatra Olt ... **1622** d.	0946	...	...	1652	...	1853	...	2053	...	...	...	0313
250	**Craiova** ... **1622** a.	1030	...	...	1805	...	1937	...	2137	...	...	...	...

	1780	1782	1890	1892	1784	1786	1788	1894	1790	1792	1896	2801 ♦
Craiova ... **1622** d.	...	...	0445	0645	...	...	...	1245	...	...	1624	...
Piatra Olt ... **1622** d.	...	...	0533	0731	...	...	...	1332	...	...	1631	2210
Slatina ... d.	...	...	0552	0750	...	...	...	1352	...	...	1750	2230
Piteşti ... d.	0520	0620	0720	0920	1120	1320	1420	1520	1620	1720	1920	0025
Bucureşti Nord ... a.	0654	0800	0854	1100	1254	1500	1554	1654	1754	1900	2054	0201

For notes ♦, ♣, §, □ and • see page 518.

1622 SIBIU - RÂMNICU VÂLCEA - CRAIOVA

2nd class only (except where shown)

km		1722	1520		1720		1736	1522			2107	1725	2801	
		♦	♦	2⚒	•	2⚒	⑥⑦		2⚒•	2	♦	♦t	♦	2
0	**Sibiu** ... **1600** d.	0250	...	0333	0638	0752	1156	...	...	1603	...	1830	1745	...
	Braşov **1600** ... d.	|	...	|	|	|	|	...	...	|	1600	|	|	...
22	Podu Olt ... **1600** d.	|	...	0403	|	0827	|	...	1300	1639	1910	1910	|	2002
83	Călimănesti ... d.	0448	...	0543	0828	1017	1339	1422	1443	1847	2038**j**	2038**j**	1946	2142
99	**Râmnicu Vâlcea** ... d.	0505	0515	0611	0848	1042	1359	1442	1510	1913	2105	2105	2014	2208
186	Piatra Olt ... **1621** d.	...	0635	0823	1007	...	...	1556	1750	2133	2221	2221	2210	...
*	Caracal ... a.	...	0709	...	|	...	...	1630	...	...	|	|	|	...
	Bucureşti N **1620** ... a.	...	0942	...	|	...	...	1904	...	...	|	|	0201	...
230	**Craiova** ... **1621** a.	...	...	...	1052	...	...	...	...	...	2305	2305	...	...

		2802		2104	1724	1521	1737		1721	1523	1723	1525
	2⚒	♦	2⚒	♦	♦		⑥⑦	2Ⓑ	•			
Craiova ... **1621** d.	...	...	...	0725	0725	...	...	...	1450	...	...	...
Bucureşti N **1620** .. d.	...	2310	...	|	|	0945	...	...	|	1345	...	1845
Caracal ... d.	...	|	...	|	|	1200	...	...	|	1605	1805	2105
Piatra Olt ... **1621** d.	...	0333	0400	0839	0839	1233	...	...	1558	1656	1858	2145
Râmnicu Vâlcea ... d.	0300	0510	0650	0953	0953	1346	1515	1605	1710	1815	2012	...
Călimănesti ... d.	0324	0528	0714	1009	1009	1401	1531	1629	1726	...	2028	...
Podu Olt ... **1600** a.	0534	|	0906	1128	1128	...	|	1809	|	...	2203	...
Braşov **1600** ... a.	|	|	...	1407	|	...	|	|	|	...	|	...
Sibiu ... **1600** a.	0612	0720	...	...	1201	...	1739	1847	1917	...	2236	...

j – Depart 2044 June 28 - Sept. 15.
t – Train **12725** June 28 - Sept. 15.

* – *32 km* from Piatra Olt.

For notes ♦, ♣, §, □ and • see page 518.

1625 CRAIOVA - TÂRGU JIU - DEVA

km		1821	10195		1827					1825	1829	1823	
		♦	♦	2	2•	2	2Ⓐ	2	2	2	♦	♦	2
	Bucureşti N **1620** ... d.	2345	0017**b**	...	...	0845	...	...	...	1445	1645	1645	...
0	**Craiova** ... **1620** d.	0302	0350	...	0810	1222	1415	...	1605	1755	2000	2000	...
36	Filiaşi ... **1620** d.	0329	0417	...	0836	1249	1513	...	1702	1820	2027	2027	...
107	**Târgu Jiu** ... d.	0445	0612	...	1000	1410	1705	...	1850	1945	2150	2150	2242
157	Petroşani ... a.	0555	0729	...	1120	...	1833	...	2015	...	2259	2259	0011
157	Petroşani ... d.	0600	0733	0740	...	...	...	1925	...	...	2303	2303	0014
237	Simeria ... **1610** d.	0755	0928	1026	...	...	...	2158	...	...	0106	0109	0231
246	**Deva** ... **1610** a.	0805	0938	1037	...	...	...	2208	...	...	0116	|	0241
	Cluj Napoca **1610** ... a.	|	...	|	...	...	...	...	...	...	...	0504	|
	Arad **1610** ... a.	1030	...	1340	...	...	...	...	...	...	...	...	0605

	1826			1824	1828						10196	1822
	2	2	2	♦	2•	2	2	2Ⓐ	2Ⓐ	2	♦	♦
Arad **1610** ... d.	...	...	...	...	...	...	...	...	...	1510	...	1855
Cluj Napoca **1610** ... d.	...	...	...	...	...	0625	...	...	...	|	...	|
Deva ... **1610** d.	...	...	...	0710	...	|	...	...	...	1818	1945	2118
Simeria ... **1610** d.	...	...	*0425*	0722	...	1118	...	...	...	1853	1958	2133
Petroşani ... a.	...	...	*0702*	0922	...	1320	...	...	...	2119	2147	2322
Petroşani ... d.	...	0440	0820	0925	1235	1325	...	1430	1915	2145	2150	2326
Târgu Jiu ... d.	0515	0628	0959	1040	1350	1435	1500	1620	2100	2328	2325	0040
Filiaşi ... **1620** a.	0639	0815	1138	1158	1511	...	1623	1803	2250	...	0053	0155
Craiova ... **1620** a.	0707	0922	1224	1228	1538	...	1651	1850	2336	...	0120	0222
Bucureşti N **1620** ... a.	1020	...	...	1543	...	...	2035	...	...	...	0450**b**	0540

b – Bucureşti **Băneasa**.

For notes ♦, ♣, §, □ and • see page 518.

1630 BRAŞOV - MIERCUREA CIUC - DEDA - TÂRGU MURES

km		366			1645		406	1643	1945	1641	4541
		♦	2•	2•		2	♦	♦	♦	♦	♦
	Bucureşti N **1600** ... d.	...	...	...	1110	...	...	1805	...	2110	2110
0	**Braşov** ... **1640** d.	0255	...	1200	1405	1717	1855	2057	2249	0003	0003
32	Sfântu Gheorghe . **1640** d.	0324	...	1242	1433	1803	1923	2125	2317	0031	0031
95	**Miercurea Ciuc** .. **1640** d.	0425	1207	1418	1534	1922	2024	2235	0023	0130	0130
	Galaţi **1640** ... d.	|	|	|	|	|	|	|	|	|	|
103	Siculeni ... **1640** d.	0433	1216	1426	1545	1939	2035	2247	0036	0142	0142
150	Gheorghieni ... d.	0521	1323	...	1636	2054	2123	2337	0136	0231	0231
184	Topliţa ... d.	0603	1405	...	1710	2140	2157	0018	0221	0305	0305
228	**Deda** ... a.	0659	1520	...	1808	...	2255	0116	0319	0401	0401
228	**Deda** ... **1635** d.	...	...	...	1820	...	...	...	...	...	0423
250	Reghin ... **1635** d.	...	...	...	1844	...	...	...	...	...	0455
282	**Târgu Mureş** ... **1635** a.	...	...	...	1921	...	...	...	...	...	0545

		407			1646		367	1944	1642	4546	1644
	2	♦	2⚒	2•		2	♦	♦	♦	♦	♦
Târgu Mureş ... **1635** d.	...	...	...	1120	1307	1423	...	...	...	2300	...
Reghin ... **1635** d.	...	...	...	1207	1344	1509	...	...	...	2346	...
Deda ... **1635** a.	...	...	...	1238	1406	1540	...	...	...	0017	...
Deda ... d.	...	0450	...	1250	1418	1553	1809	2029	2322	0100	0100
Topliţa ... d.	0435	0546	...	1406	1515	1711	1905	2137	0017	0203	0203
Gheorghieni ... d.	0522	0627	1251	1452	1552	1756	1942	2224	0054	0245	0245
Siculeni ... **1640** d.	0626	0713	1402	1604	1651	1906	2033	2323	0144	0335	0335
Galaţi **1640** ... a.	|	|	|	...	|	|	|	|	|	|	|
Miercurea Ciuc .. **1640** d.	0649	0723	1413	...	1701	1914	2044	2331	0153	0344	0344
Sfântu Gheorghe **1640** d.	0810	0827	1535	...	1802	...	2149	0032	0252	0453	0453
Braşov ... **1640** a.	0846	0853	1610	...	1828	...	2215	0059	0328	0519	0519
Bucureşti N **1600** ... a.	...	...	...	...	2120	...	...	...	0637	0815	0815

For notes ♦, ♣, §, □ and • see page 518.

DEDA and BISTRIŢA - DEJ - CLUJ NAPOCA 1635

km		1641 ◆	4116 ◆	366 ◆	2⚒	2•	2Ⓑ	2	406 ◆	1643 ◆	1945 ◆
	Bucureşti Nord **1600** d.	2110	2110	...	...	...	...	...	...	1805	...
	Braşov **1630** d.	0003	0003	0255	...	...	...	...	1855	2057	2249
0	**Deda** d.	0409	0409	0700	...	...	...	...	2256	0119	0327
Δ 10	**Bistriţa** Nord d.	|	0544j	|	0730	1010	1535	1905	|	|	|
47	Sărăţel d.	0521	0530	0751	0756	1025	1553	1920	2358	0209	0430
72	Beclean pe Someş **1650** d.	0549	...	0817	0831	1053	1631	1950	0023	0233	0504
97	Dej Călători **1616/50** d.	0631	...	0549	0913	1129	1708	2026	0055	...	0545
	Baia Mare **1616** a.	0927	...	|	|	|	|	|	|	...	0835
156	**Cluj Napoca** **1616/50** a.	...	...	0953	1040	1236	1835	2136	0159	...	...
	Budapest Keleti **1275** a.	...	...	1620	...	...	...	...	0820	...	...

	2•	2	367 ◆	2	1944 ◆	4117 ◆	1642 ◆	2Ⓑ	1644 ◆	407 ◆
Budapest Keleti **1275** d.	...	...	0640	...	...	...	...	...	...	1740
Cluj Napoca **1616/50** d.	0721	1127	1501	1530	...	...	...	1945	...	0148
Baia Mare **1616** d.	|	|	|	|	1507	...	1822	|	...	|
Dej Călători **1616/50** d.	0847	1305	1622	1653	1802	...	2116	2131	...	0305
Beclean pe Someş **1650** d.	0918	1342	1650	1733	1846	...	2144	2208	2256	0333
Sărăţel d.	0946	1416	1716	1802	1912	2205	2229	2241	2325	0359
Bistriţa Nord a.	1000	1434	|	1817	|	2150j	|	2258	|	|
Deda a.	...	...	1806	...	2002	2319	2319	...	0028	0449
Braşov **1630** a.	...	...	2215	...	0059	0328	0328	...	0519	0853
Bucureşti Nord **1600** a.	...	...	...	...	...	0637	0637	...	0815	...

j – Via Sărăţel. Δ – Distance from Sărăţel. For notes ◆, ♣, §, □ and • see page 518.

BRAŞOV - MIERCUREA CIUC - ADJUD - GALAŢI 1640

km		2	2⚒	2	2	2	2•	2	2	1541 •	2
0	**Braşov** **1630** d.	...	0430	...	...	...	1200	...	...	1612	*1717*
32	Sfântu Gheorghe **1630** d.	...	0510	...	...	...	1242	...	...	1649	*1803*
95	**Miercurea Ciuc** **1630** a.	...	0625	...	...	...	1402	...	...	1809	*1917*
95	**Miercurea Ciuc** **1630** d.	...	—	0722	...	...	1426	...	1555	1811	1935
	Târgu Mureş **1630** d.	...	...	|	...	...	|	...	|	|	|
103	Siculeni **1630** d.	...	2	0731	...	...	1426	...	1612	1823	1950
144	Ghimeş d.	...	0520	0853	...	...	—	1702	1750	1926	2107
179	Comăneşti d.	0409	0611	0944	1000	...	...	1751	1838	2007	2157
216	Oneşti d.	0508	0718	—	1059	1400	...	1845	1934	2049	2331
254	**Adjud** **1670** d.	0650	0830	...	1203	1450	...	1934	2028	2141	0026
279	Mărăşeşti **1670** a.	0724	0906	2	1237	1527	2	2005	2103	...	0100
279	Mărăşeşti d.	...	...	1115	...	...	1603	...	...	...	...
	Iaşi **1670** a.	...	...	|	...	...	|	...	...	...	...
298	Tecuci **1670** d.	...	...	1145	...	...	1630	...	...	...	...
383	**Galaţi** **1670** a.	...	...	1404	...	...	1846	...	...	...	...

	2	2•	2•	1540 •	2	2	2	2Ⓐj	2	2
Galaţi **1670** d.	...	...	...	...	0740	...	...	1425	...	1945
Tecuci **1670** d.	...	...	...	...	1000	...	...	1631	...	2214
Iaşi **1670** d.	...	...	...	...	|	...	...	|	...	|
Mărăşeşti a.	...	...	...	...	1026	...	...	1656	...	2240
Mărăşeşti **1670** d.	...	0420	0610	...	—	1222	1420	...	1722	...
Adjud **1670** d.	...	0511	0647	0823	...	1255	1453	...	1803	...
Oneşti d.	...	0559	0740	0901	...	1337	1536	...	1848	...
Comăneşti d.	0408	0658	0840	0948	...	1431	1632	...	2010	...
Ghimeş d.	0458	0749	0936	1029	2⚒	1518	1728	...	2056	...
Siculeni **1630** a.	0613	0906	...	1127	1402	...	1854	...	...	...
Târgu Mureş **1630** a.	|	|	...	|	|	...	|	...	...	...
Miercurea Ciuc **1630** a.	0628	0916	...	1138	1410	...	1903	...	...	...
Miercurea Ciuc **1630** d.	...	...	...	1140	1413	...	...	...	...	...
Sfântu Gheorghe **1630** d.	...	...	...	1241	1535	...	...	...	...	...
Braşov **1630** a.	...	...	...	1320	1610	...	...	...	...	...

j – Not July 1 - Aug. 31. For notes ◆, ♣, §, □ and • see page 518.

IAŞI - SUCEAVA - DEJ - CLUJ NAPOCA 1650

km		2Ⓐ	1653 ◆	1833	1947 ◆	1831 •	1844 ◆	1644 ◆	1765 ◆	1837 ◆
0	**Iaşi** d.	...	...	0605	...	1100	...	...	1515	1925
76	Paşcani **1670** d.	...	0330	0714	...	1208	...	...	1623	2033
122	Vereşti **1670** d.	...	0405	0748	...	1242	...	...	1657	2107
137	**Suceava** **1670** a.	...	0420	0803	...	1257	...	...	1713	2122
137	**Suceava** d.	...	0434	0817	...	1311	...	...	1727	2134
187	Gura Humorului Oraş d.	...	0521	0905	...	1359	...	...	1815	2221
219	Câmpulung Moldovenesc d.	...	0604	0948	...	1451	...	...	1906	2303
257	Vatra Dornei Băi d.	...	0710	1057	...	1603	...	...	2016	0012
351	Năsăud d.	...	...	1303	...	1808	...	...	2205	0206
Δ118	**Sighetu Marmaţiei** d.	0055	...	|	1424	|	1626	1746	|	|
Δ 61	Vişeu de Jos d.	0305	...	|	1608	|	1831	1954	|	|
357	Salva d.	0448	...	1312	1747	1816	2027	2146	2213	0215
379	Beclean pe Someş **1635** d.	0522	...	1338	1822	1842	2115	...	2238	0241
402	Dej Călători **1635** d.	0619	...	1412	...	1917	2152	...	2310	0318
460	**Cluj Napoca** **1635** a.	0730	...	1518	...	2022	2258	...	0014	0423
	Oradea **1612** a.	...	...	1841	...	...	|	...	|	|
	Timişoara N **1610/14** a.	...	...	2202	...	...	0705	...	0808	1226

	1643 ◆	1838 ◆	1946 ◆	1843 ◆	1832 •	1834	2Ⓐ	1654 ◆	1766 ◆
Timişoara N **1610/14** d.	...	1738	...	2134	...	0625	...	...	1340
Oradea **1612** d.	...	|	...	|	...	0959	...	...	|
Cluj Napoca **1635** d.	...	0126	...	0503	0912	1259	1540	...	2136
Dej Călători **1635** d.	...	0243	...	0623	1029	1416	1712	...	2257
Beclean pe Someş **1635** d.	0253	0310	0524	0702	1057	1444	1740	...	2325
Salva d.	0337	0335	0602	0745	1121	1508	1826	...	2349
Vişeu de Jos d.	0540	|	0744	0948	|	|	2046	...	|
Sighetu Marmaţiei a.	0730	|	0935	1149	|	|	2244	...	|
Năsăud d.	...	0345	...	...	1131	1517	...	...	2358
Vatra Dornei Băi d.	...	0539	...	...	1321	1711	...	2142	0152
Câmpulung Moldovenesc d.	...	0646	...	...	1432	1817	...	2244	0300
Gura Humorului Oraş d.	...	0729	...	...	1516	1902	...	2336	0345
Suceava a.	...	0816	...	...	1603	1949	...	0025	0432
Suceava **1670** d.	...	0828	...	...	1615	2001	...	0037	0444
Vereşti **1670** d.	...	0842	...	...	1628	2014	...	0050	0457
Paşcani **1670** d.	...	0923	...	...	1706	2052	...	0126	0536
Iaşi a.	...	1030	...	...	1812	2158	...	...	0642

Δ – Distance from Salva. For notes ◆, ♣, §, □ and • see page 518.

BUCUREŞTI - GALAŢI 1660

km		2	1671	1571	2	1673	2	15073 §	1871 ◆	2	1675	1731 V
0	**Bucureşti** Nord **1670** d.	...	0625	0820	...	1340	...	1530	...	...	1810	...
	Ploieşti Sud **1670** d.	...	|	0904	...	|	...	|	...	...	|	1842
**	Buzău **1670** d.	0210	|	1015	1307	|	1500	|	...	1840	|	1953
71	Urziceni d.	|	0733	|	|	1447	|	1642	...	|	1917	|
Δ	Feteşti d.	|	|	|	|	|	|	|	1711	|	|	|
138	Făurei d.	0401	0842	1143	1451	1556	1639	1753	1927	2042j	2026	2120
198	Brăila d.	0504	0933	1232	1551	1644	1741	1849	2017	2144	2116	2208
229	**Galaţi** a.	0550	1011	1310	1635	1723	1827	1927	2055	2230	2155	2246

	2	1670	1732 V	15072 §	1870 ◆	1672	2	1572	2	1674	2
Galaţi d.	0415	0450	0600	0725	0735	0925	0930	1340	1520	1740	1935
Brăila d.	0502	0530	0639	0806	0816	1005	1019	1420	1610	1820	2025
Făurei d.	0601	0619	0730	0857	0924	1057	1119	1511	1709	1912	2138
Feteşti a.	|	|	|	|	1040	|	|	|	|	|	|
Urziceni d.	|	0727	|	1010	...	1206	|	|	|	2029	|
Buzău **1670** d.	0743	|	0859	|	...	|	1300	1643	1850	|	2314
Ploieşti Sud **1670** d.	...	|	1011	|	...	|	...	1755	...	|	...
Bucureşti Nord **1670** a.	...	0832	...	1131	...	1312	...	1840	...	2134	...

V – From/to Braşov (Table **1600**). j – Arrive 2023. ** – Buzău - Făurei: *40 km*. Δ – Feteşti - Făurei: *89 km*. For notes ◆, ♣, §, □ and • see page 518.

LOCAL SERVICES 1669

Local trains, 2nd class only

ARAD (NOU) - TIMISOARA *57 km, ± 75 minutes*

rom Arad Nou: 0444⚒, 0624, 1354, 1456, 1624⑤⑦♣, 747Ⓐ, 2029①⑤♣.
rom Timişoara: 0434Ⓐ, 0645②⑥♣, 0831, 1345, 1622Ⓐ, 323Ⓑ.
or long-distance trains see Table **1614**.

BAIA MARE - SATU MARE *59 km, ± 110 minutes*

rom Baia Mare: 0737, 1219⚒•, 1545, 1928Ⓑ.
rom Satu Mare: 0429⚒, 0742, 1120⚒•, 1610.
or long-distance trains see Table **1616**.

BISTRIŢA - DEDA:

km			Ⓐ	⚒			
0	Bistriţa Nord d.	0426	0450	0730	1232	1543	1938
10	Sărăţel d.	0440	0504	0756	1249	1615	2012
57	Deda a.	...	...	...	...	1721	2115

						Ⓑ
eda d.	0500	...	...	...	1658	...
ărăţel d.	0620	0910	1416	1802	1822	2241
istriţa Nord a.	0635	0926	1434	1817	1837	2258

or long-distance trains see Table **1635**.

CLUJ NAPOCA - ORADEA *153 km, ± 200 minutes*

rom Cluj Napoca: 0325, 0741, 1414•, 1616.
rom Oradea: 0343, 1137, 1525, 1748.
All services operated by Transferoviar Grup SA.

PAŞCANI - TÂRGU NEAMT *31 km, ± 45 minutes*

From Paşcani: 0653, 0924, 1445**j**, 1630, 1830, 2020.
From Târgu Neamt: 0545, 0752, 1100, 1540, 1722, 1922.
All services operated by Regiotrans.

REŞIŢA - CARANSEBEŞ *43 km, ± 80 minutes*

From Reşiţa Nord: 0608, 1334, 1752, 2235.
From Caransebeş: 0436, 0556, 0735, 1630, 1930.
For long-distance trains see Table **1620**.

SIGHIŞOARA - SIBIU:

km		⚒						
0	**Sighişoara** d.	...	...	...	...	1500	...	...
39	Mediaş d.	0429	0530	...	1247	1626	...	2000
50	Copşa Mică d.	0451	0618	...	1310	1657	...	2032
95	**Sibiu** a.	0555	0722	...	1413	1809	...	2135

							Ⓐ
Sibiu d.	0723	...	1204	1543	...	1925	2322
Copşa Mică d.	0828	...	1309	1650	...	2030	0024
Mediaş d.	0847	...	1329	1710	...	2050	0043
Sighişoara a.	...	...	1442	...	...	...	...

SIMERIA - HUNEDOARA *16 km, ± 30 minutes*

From Simeria: 0604, 0716, 1127, 1310, 1525, 1640, 1834, 2030.
From Hunedoara: 0515, 0640, 1036, 1205, 1350, 1603, 1720, 1910.
All services operated by Regiotrans.

TÂRGU MUREŞ - RÂZBOIENI:

km					⚒			Ⓑ
0	**Târgu Mureş** d.	0327	0712	...	1415	1540	1924	2222
40	Luduş d.	0433	0807	...	1518	1634	2020	2317
59	**Războieni** a.	0456	0832	...	1541	1657	2044	2340

	⚒			⚒•			
Războieni d.	0401	0518	0706	1209	...	1715	2011
Luduş d.	0432	0548	0732	1237	...	1742	2046
Târgu Mureş a.	0533	0649	0832	1335	...	1841	2143

For long-distance trains see Table **1610**.

VEREŞTI - BOTOŞANI *44 km, ± 65 minutes*

From Vereşti: 0331, 0803**p**, 0904**q**, 1343, 1754, 1905.
From Botoşani: 0500, 0931, 1130, 1540, 1921**q**, 2030**p**, 2154.
For long-distance trains see Table **1670**.

h – Not during school holidays.
j – From Iaşi, d. 1319.
p – June 21 - Sept. 9.
q - Not June 21 - Sept. 9.
For notes ◆, ♣, §, □ and • see page 518.

1670 BUCUREŞTI - BUZĂU - BACĂU - IASI and SUCEAVA

km ☆		1861 ♦	1944 ♦	1661	382 ♦	1655	14069 ♣ J2•	2	□ 2	1753		1663	□ 2	1866 2	1651 ♦	1657 ♦	1665	1659	□ 2	402 ⊠ ♦	1551	1653 ♦		1667 ⊙	1755 ⊙
0	**Bucureşti** Nord .... **1660** d.	...	...	0545	0600	0730	...	0930	1020	1100	...	1200	1220	...	1400	1500	1600	1700	1736	1935	2000	2130	...	2300	2330
59	Ploieşti Sud .... **1660** d.	...	0313	0629	0653	0814	0829	1032	1125	1145	...	1245	1319	...	1445	1544	1645	1745	1835	2029	2049	2214	...	2344	0014
128	**Buzău** .... **1660/80** d.	0247	0420	0740	0803	0925	0940	1152	1235	1256	...	1356	1430	...	1556	1655	1756	1858	1944	2148	2158	2325	...	0055	0125
161	Râmnicu Sărat .... d.	0320	▬	0813	|	0959	1013	...	...	1329	...	1429	...	...	1629	1728	1830	|	...	|	▬	2359	...	0128	0158
199	Focşani .... d.	0400	...	0853	0918	1040	1054	...	...	1409	...	1509	...	...	1709	1808	1910	2008	...	2303	...	0040	...	0206	0237
219	Mărăşeşti .... **1640** d.	0434	...	|	|	1106	1123	...	...	1434	...	|	...	...	1734	1834	|	2034	...	|	...	0106	...	|	0302
244	Adjud .... **1640** d.	|	...	|	1015	1135	|	...	...	1502	...	|	...	...	1802	1901	|	2101	...	2357	...	0134	...	|	0329
303	**Bacău** .... d.	|	**1864**	|	1105	1216	|	...	...	1552	...	|	...	...	1857	1942	|	2144	...	0044	...	0225	...	|	0419
346	Roman .... d.	|	2•	|	1141	▬	|	...	...	1624	...	|	...	...	1931	...	|	2216	...	0118	...	0258	...	|	0451
	Galaţi .... **1640** d.	|	0608	|	|	...	|	...	...	|	...	|	...	1640	|	...	|	|	...	|	...	|	...	|	|
238	Tecuci .... **1640** d.	0459n	0749	0951	|	...	1149n	...	...	|	...	1611	...	1821	|	...	2009	|	...	|	...	|	...	0304	|
288	Bârlad .... d.	0541	0839	1035	|	...	1230	...	...	|	...	1654	...	1910	|	...	2100	|	...	|	...	|	...	0347	|
340	Vaslui .... d.	0647	0936	1132	|	...	1324	...	...	|	...	1754	...	2010	|	...	2158	|	...	|	...	|	...	0444	|
408	**Iaşi** .... a.	0812	1045	1243	|	2	1440	...	...	|	...	1905	...	2119	|	...	2306	|	...	0253	2	|	...	0554	|
408	**Iaşi** .... RO d.	...	...	...	|	1321	...	...	...	|	...	...	...	...	|	...	...	|	...	0317	0451	|	...	...	|
431	Ungheni **1730** .... 🛃 MD a.	...	...	...	|	1505	...	...	...	|	...	...	...	...	|	...	...	|	...	0502	0655	|	...	...	|
538	**Chişinău 1730** .... a.	...	...	...	|	...	...	...	...	|	...	...	...	...	|	...	...	|	...	0852	...	|	...	...	|
387	Paşcani .... **1650** d.	...	...	...	1217	...	...	...	...	1656	...	...	...	...	2003	...	...	2248	...	...	...	0330	...	...	0522
432	Vereşti .... **1650** a.	...	...	...	|	...	...	...	...	1738	...	...	...	...	2037	...	...	|	...	...	...	0405	...	...	0604
476	Botoşani **1669** .... a.	...	...	...	|	...	...	...	...	1856x	...	...	...	...	|	...	...	|	...	...	...	|	...	...	0722x
448	**Suceava** .... **1650** a.	...	...	...	1305	...	...	...	...	1754	...	...	...	...	2049	...	...	2330	...	...	...	0420	...	...	0620
450	**Suceava** Nord .... ▲ RO a.	...	...	...	1331	...	...	...	...	...	...	...	...	...	2059	...	...	...	...	...	...	...	...	...	...
539	Chernivtsi .... ▲ UA a.	...	...	...	1832	...	...	...	...	...	...	...	...	...	...	...	...	...	...	...	...	...	...	...	...

	1654 ♦	1550	□ 2	1658 ♦	1650	1662	1652 ♦	1863 2•	□ 2	2	□ 2	1752	1945 ♦	1656	1664	14068 ♣ J2•	383 ♦	1666	1865 2	2	1862 ♦	1754 ⊙	1668 ⊙	401 ⊠ ♦	
Chernivtsi .... ▲ UA d.	...	...	...	...	...	...	...	...	...	...	...	...	...	...	...	...	1034	...	...	...	...	...	...	...	...
Suceava Nord .... ▲ RO d.	...	...	...	...	...	...	0840	...	...	...	...	...	...	...	...	...	1542	...	...	...	...	...	...	...	...
Suceava .... **1650** d.	0037	...	...	...	0500	...	0846	...	...	...	...	1230	...	...	...	...	1605	...	...	...	...	2250	...	...	...
Botoşani **1669** .... d.	|	...	...	...	|	...	|	...	...	...	...	1130x	...	...	...	...	|	...	...	...	...	2154x	...	...	...
Vereşti .... **1650** d.	0050	...	...	...	|	...	0859	...	...	...	...	1258	...	...	...	...	|	...	...	...	...	2318	...	...	...
Paşcani .... **1650** d.	0128	...	...	...	0546	...	0936	...	...	...	...	1338	...	...	...	...	1655	...	...	...	...	2358	...	...	...
Chişinău 1730 .... d.	|	...	...	...	|	...	|	...	...	...	...	|	...	...	...	...	|	...	...	...	...	|	...	1635	...
Ungheni **1730** .... 🛃 MD d.	|	...	...	...	|	...	|	...	...	0755	...	|	...	...	...	...	|	...	...	1740	...	|	...	2023	...
Iaşi .... RO a.	|	...	...	...	|	...	|	...	...	0952	...	|	...	...	...	...	|	...	...	1925	...	|	...	2207	...
Iaşi .... d.	|	...	...	...	|	0600	|	0800	...	...	...	|	...	...	1420	1536	|	1635	1830	...	2205	|	2310	2225	...
Vaslui .... d.	|	...	...	...	|	0718	|	0912	...	...	...	|	...	...	1532	1654	|	1751	1941	...	2320	|	0027	|	...
Bârlad .... d.	|	...	...	...	|	0809	|	1002	...	...	...	|	...	...	1622	1741	|	1840	2031	...	0010	|	0117	|	...
Tecuci .... **1640** d.	|	...	...	...	|	0904	|	1053	...	...	...	|	...	...	1712n	1820n	|	1934	2115	...	0052n	|	0213	|	...
Galaţi .... **1640** a.	|	...	...	...	|	|	|	1234	...	...	...	|	...	...	|	|	|	|	2254	...	|	|	|	|	...
Roman .... d.	0157	...	...	...	0613	|	1005	...	...	...	...	1406	...	...	|	|	1728	|	...	...	|	0026	|	0001	...
Bacău .... d.	0239	...	...	0428	0647	|	1052	...	...	...	...	1447	...	1632	|	|	1807	|	...	...	|	0107	|	0041	...
Adjud .... **1640** d.	0319	...	...	0509	0727	|	1133	...	...	...	...	1528	...	1713	|	|	1855	|	...	...	|	0148	|	0130	...
Mărăşeşti .... **1640** d.	0347	...	...	0541	0756	|	1202	...	...	...	...	1556	...	1740	1752	1855	|	|	...	...	0138	0217	|	|	...
Focşani .... d.	0415	...	...	0609	0824	0954	1230	...	...	...	...	1624	...	1820	1820	1923	1949	2023	...	...	0206	0245	0303	0227	...
Râmnicu Sărat .... d.	0456	...	...	0651	0905	1036	1311	...	...	...	...	1705	...	1901	1901	2004	|	2104	...	...	0247	0327	0345	|	...
Buzău .... **1660/80** d.	0529	0650	0715	0724	0944	1109	1344	...	1455	...	1725	1738	1922	1934	1934	2037	2101	2136	...	...	0318	0401	0418	0346	...
Ploieşti Sud .... **1660** d.	0641	0801	0828	0836	1053	1223	1456	...	1604	...	1835	1850	2030	2046	2046	2147	2212	2247	...	...	...	0514	0531	0457	...
Bucureşti Nord .... **1660** a.	0725	0848	0930	0920	1137	1310	1540	...	1700	...	1930	1940	...	2130	2130	...	2302	2330	...	...	...	0600	0615	0550	...

BACĂU - PIATRA NEAMŢ - BICAZ

km		2	2	2		2	2		5471 ♦	1657 ♦	
	Bucureşti Nord .... d.	...	...	...	...	...	...	...	1400	1500	...
0	**Bacău** .... d.	0415	0525	0920	...	1413	1642	...	1912	1957	...
60	Piatra Neamţ .... d.	0544	0656	1100	...	1546	1818	...	2043	2107	...
86	**Bicaz** .... a.	0627	...	...	...	1629	...	...	...	2139	...

	1658 ♦	2 ⚒	2	5472 ♦		2	2	2		2
Bicaz .... d.	0230	...	0656	...	...	...	...	1653	...	...
Piatra Neamţ .... d.	0302	0457	0734	0919	...	1425	1623	1731	...	2110
Bacău .... a.	0414	0639	0902	1027	...	1602	1756	1859	...	2238
Bucureşti Nord .... a.	0920	...	...	1540	...	...	...	...	...	...

J – 🚃 Braşov (14092/3) - Ploieşti Vest (d. 0822; a. 2156) - Iaşi and v.v.

n – Tecuci **Nord**.

x – Portion attached to / detached from main train at Vereşti.

⊙ – Also conveys 🛏 1, 2 cl. and 🛌 2 cl.

⊠ – For international journeys only.

* – Subject to confirmation.

▲ – 🛃 : Vicşani (RO) / Vadul Siret (UA).

☆ – Tecuci - Galaţi *85 km*; Iaşi - Roman *114 km*.

MD Moldova. RO Romania. UA Ukraine.

For notes ♦, ♣, §, □ and • see page 518.

1680 BUCURESTI - CONSTANŢA - MANGALIA

Summer service 2014

km		2801 ♦	2	10192 ♦	1862 ♦		1944 ♦	1822 ♦		1681 2y	1981 y		1983 y	1870 ♦	1932 ♦		14081 ♣m	1583		1585	2	1587		1589 R
0	**Bucureşti** Nord .... d.	0230	...	0452b	...	...	...	0620	...	0640	0720	...	0820	...	0920	...	0935	1015	...	1400	...	1700	...	2015
	Buzău .... d.	|	...	|	0338	...	0422	|	...	|	|	...	|	...	|	...	|	|	...	|	...	|	...	|
	Făurei .... d.	|	...	|	0507	...	0550	|	...	|	|	...	|	0924	|	...	|	|	...	|	...	|	...	|
146	Feteşti .... d.	0432	...	0613	0633	...	0711	0753	...	0823	0852	...	|	1042	1054	...	1113	1149	...	1533	...	1834	...	2149
190	Medgidia .... d.	0530	0605	|	0719	...	0754	0834	...	0913	0929	...	|	1123	1136	...	1151	1231	...	1613	1820	1916	...	2231
334	**Tulcea** Oraş .... a.	|	0910	|	|	...	|	|	...	1200	|	...	|	|	|	...	|	|	...	|	2116	|	...	|
225	**Constanţa** .... a.	0621	...	0719	0748	...	0827	0905	...	...	0954	...	1045	1149	1207	...	1217	1256	...	1637	...	1941	...	2255
225	**Constanţa** .... d.	0636	...	0739	0805	...	0846	0924	...	...	1011	...	1100	...	1223	...	...	...	...	...	...	...	...	...
239	Eforie Nord .... d.	0705	...	0803	0829	...	0910	0948	...	...	1036	...	1124	...	1248	...	...	...	...	...	...	...	...	...
268	**Mangalia** .... a.	0808	...	0902	0928	...	1015	1054	...	...	1139	...	1229	...	1349	...	...	...	...	...	...	...	...	...

km		1580 R	2	1582		1584	1945 ♦	1980 y		1871 ♦	1586	1931 ♦	1682 2y	14082 ♣m		2802 ♦	1982 y	2802 ♦	2	1821 ♦		10191 ♦	1861 ♦	
	Mangalia .... d.	...	...	...	...	...	1242	1355	...	...	...	1540	...	...	...	1658	1750	...	...	1840	...	1945	2015	...
	Eforie Nord .... d.	...	...	...	...	...	1350	1456	...	...	...	1638	...	...	...	1807	1850	...	...	1946	...	2056	2115	...
	Constanţa .... a.	...	...	...	...	...	1418	1520	...	...	...	1705	...	...	...	1834	1914	...	...	2014	...	2114	2138	...
0	**Constanţa** .... d.	0530	...	0830	...	1400	1435	1535	...	1600	1650	1720	...	1815	...	1850	1930	...	...	2030	...	2135	2153	...
	Tulcea Oraş .... d.	|	0540	|	...	|	|	|	...	|	|	|	1535	|	...	|	|	...	1745	|	...	|	|	...
35	Medgidia .... d.	0557	0841	0857	...	1427	1504	|	...	1628	1717	1747	1821	1843	...	1939	1958	←	2053	2057	...	2202	2221	...
79	Feteşti .... d.	0638	...	0939	...	1509	1549	|	...	1711	1759	1829	1905	1921	...	→	2035	2046	...	2139	...	2246	2304	...
168	Făurei .... d.	|	...	|	...	|	1749	|	...	1907	|	|	|	|	...	...	|	|	...	|	...	|	0100	...
208	Buzău .... a.	|	...	|	...	|	1919	|	...	...	|	|	|	|	...	...	|	|	...	|	...	|	0229	...
	Bucureşti Nord .... a.	0809	...	1111	...	1641	...	1800	...	...	1931	2001	2047	2057	...	...	2204	2237	...	2311	...	0008b	...	...

♦ – NOTES (LISTED BY TRAIN NUMBER)

1821/2 – 🛏 1, 2 cl., 🛌 2 cl. and 🚃12 Arad - Craiova - Bucureşti and v.v. Train extended Bucureşti - Constanţa - Mangalia and v.v. June 13 - Sept. 12 (from Arad); June 14 - Sept. 13 (from Mangalia / Bucureşti).

1861/2 – 🚃12 Iaşi - Constanţa and v.v. Train extended Constanţa - Mangalia and v.v. June 14 - Sept. 13 (from Iaşi); June 15 - Sept. 14 (from Mangalia).

1870/1 – 🚃2 Galaţi - Constanţa and v.v.

1931/2 – June 14 - Sept. 13 (from Oradea); June 15 - Sept. 14 (from Mangalia): 🛏 1, 2 cl., 🛌 2 cl. and 🚃12 Oradea - Bucureşti - Constanţa - Mangalia and v.v.

1944/5 – June 14 - Sept. 13 (from Satu Mare and Sighetu Marmaţiei); June 15 - Sept. 14 (from Mangalia): 🚃12 Satu Mare - Mangalia and v.v.; 🚃12 Sighetu Marmaţiei (**1946/7**) - Beclean pe Someş - Mangalia and v.v.

2801/2 – June 28 - Sept. 15 (from Sibiu); June 27 - Sept. 14 (from Mangalia): 🚃12 Sibiu Mangalia and v.v.

10191/2 – June 14 - Sept. 13 (from Timişoara / Reşiţa / Deva); June 15 - Sept. 14 (from Mangalia): 🚃12 Timişoara - Mangalia and v.v.; 🚃2 Reşiţa Nord (**10198/9**) - Caransebeş Mangalia and v.v.; 🚃12 Deva (**10195/6**) - Craiova - Mangalia and v.v.

G – From / to Galaţi.

R – From / to Braşov.

b – Bucureşti **Băneasa**.

m – June 20 - Sept. 9.

y – June 14 - Sept. 13.

For notes ♦, ♣, §, □ and • see page 518.

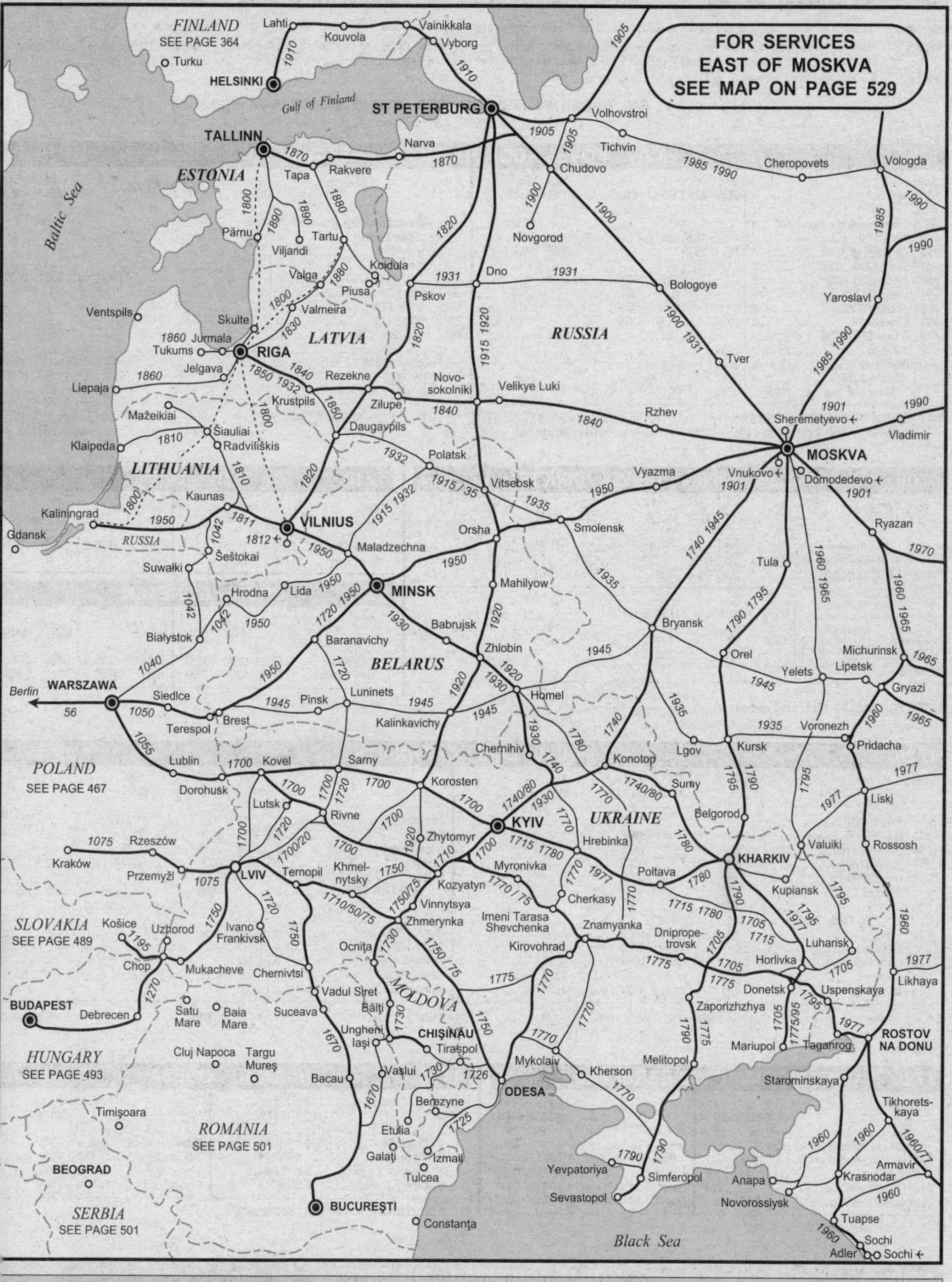
FOR SERVICES
EAST OF MOSKVA
SEE MAP ON PAGE 529
FINLAND
SEE PAGE 364
Turku
Lahti
Kouvola
Vainikkala
Vyborg
HELSINKI
Gulf of Finland
ST PETERBURG
Volhovstroi
Tichvin
Cheropovets
Vologda
Chudovo
Novgorod
TALLINN
Narva
Rakvere
Tapa
ESTONIA
Baltic Sea
Pärnu
Viljandi
Tartu
Koidula
Valga
Piusa
Pskov
Dno
Bologoye
Yaroslavl
Valmeira
Ventspils
Skulte
Jurmala
Tukums
RIGA
LATVIA
RUSSIA
Tver
Jelgava
Liepaja
Rezekne
Novo-
sokolniki
Velikye Luki
Zilupe
Krustpils
Rzhev
Sheremetyevo
Vladimir
Mažeikiai
Daugavpils
MOSKVA
Siauliai
Radviliškis
Klaipeda
Polatsk
Vnukovo
Domodedevo
Vyazma
LITHUANIA
Vitsebsk
Kaunas
Kaliningrad
Gdansk
RUSSIA
VILNIUS
Orsha
Smolensk
Ryazan
Maladzechna
Šeštokai
Suwałki
Tula
MINSK
Mahilyow
Hrodna
Lida
Białystok
Babrujsk
Bryansk
Baranavichy
Orel
Zhlobin
Michurinsk
BELARUS
Yelets
Lipetsk
WARSZAWA
Berlin
Siedlce
Gryazi
Pinsk
Luninets
Homel
Terespol
Brest
Kalinkavichy
Voronezh
POLAND
SEE PAGE 467
Chernihiv
Lgov
Kursk
Pridacha
Lublin
Kovel
Sarny
Konotop
Korosten
Sumy
Dorohusk
Liski
Lutsk
Rivne
KYIV
UKRAINE
Belgorod
Zhytomyr
Hrebinka
Valuiki
Rossosh
Rzeszów
Kraków
KHARKIV
Przemyžl
LVIV
Ternopil
Khmel-
nytsky
Myronivka
Kozyatyn
Poltava
Kupiansk
Vinnytsya
Cherkasy
SLOVAKIA
SEE PAGE 489
Košice
Uzhorod
Ivano
Frankivsk
Zhmerynka
Imeni Tarasa
Shevchenka
Znamyanka
Dniprope-
trovsk
Luhansk
Chop
Mukacheve
Chernivtsi
Ocniţa
Kirovohrad
Horlivka
Likhaya
Vadul Siret
Donetsk
Uspenskaya
BUDAPEST
Debrecen
Satu
Mare
Baia
Mare
Suceava
Bălţi
MOLDOVA
Zaporizhzhya
Ungheni
Iaşi
CHIŞINĂU
Tiraspol
Mariupol
Taganrog
ROSTOV
NA DONU
HUNGARY
SEE PAGE 493
Cluj Napoca
Targu
Mureş
Vaslui
Mykolaiv
Kherson
Melitopol
Bacau
ODESA
Starominskaya
Tikhorets-
kaya
Timişoara
Berezyne
ROMANIA
SEE PAGE 501
Etulia
Galaţi
Izmail
Tulcea
Yevpatoriya
Simferopol
Sevastopol
Anapa
Novorossiysk
Armavir
Krasnodar
BEOGRAD
Tuapse
SERBIA
SEE PAGE 501
BUCUREŞTI
Constanţa
Black Sea
Sochi
Adler
Sochi

UKRAINE and MOLDOVA

SEE MAP PAGE 523

Operators: **UZ**: Ukrzaliznytsya, www.uz.gov.ua **CFM**: Calea Ferată din Moldova, www.railway.md Other operators as indicated in the table headings and notes.

Timings: Valid from **June 1, 2014 until further notice**. Timings of international services to and from non-CIS countries should be verified from the international tables at the front of this book. Local time is used throughout: i.e. East European Time for Ukraine and Moldova – for other countries, see the time comparison chart on page **2**.

Tickets: Prior reservation is necessary except for travel by purely local trains.

SEE ALSO THE PANEL ***RAIL TRAVEL IN RUSSIA, BELARUS, UKRAINE, and MOLDOVA*** ON PAGE 530

1700 KYÏV - KOVEL - DOROHUSK - (WARSZAWA) — UZ, PKP

km		*Sko* 67*KJ* A	*Fir* 43*KJ* F	*Fir* 49*KJ*	*Fir* 84*LJ* w		*Sko* 111*OJ* H	*Fir* 77*MJ*	
	Moskva Kiyevskaya **1740** d.	...	...	...	...	...	...	1632	...
0	**Kyïv 1750** d.	1552	1830	2018	...	...	0404	0543	...
156	Korosten **1920** d.	1825	2049	|	...	...	0602	0752	...
311	Sarny **1720** d.	2134	|	|	...	...	|	|	...
159	Kozyatyn **1750** d.	|	|	2231	0230	...	|	|	...
391	Rivne **1720** d.	|	|	|	0647	...	|	1208	...
469	Lutsk **1720** d.	|	|	|	0829	...	|	1345	...
453	**Kovel 1720** d.	0035	|	|	1036	...	|	1530	...
652	**Lviv 1720 1750** a.	|	0252	0527	...	...	1328	...	...
512	Yahodyn 🏛 UA d.	0324	...	...	...	...	...	...	...
520	**Dorohusk** 🏛 PL a.	0236	...	...	...	...	...	...	...
	Lublin **1055** a.	0511	...	...	...	...	...	...	...
	Warszawa Centralna **1055** a.	0745	...	...	...	...	...	...	...

km		*Sko* 68*KJ* A		*Fir* 78*LJ*	*Fir* 84*LJ* w	*Sko* 112*LJ* H		*Fir* 50*LJ*	*Fir* 44*LJ* 43 F
	Warszawa Centralna **1055** d.	1650	...	...	...	...	...	...	
	Lublin **1055** d.	1916	...	...	...	...	...	...	...
0	**Dorohusk** 🏛 PL d.	2116	...	...	...	...	...	...	...
8	Yahodyn 🏛 UA d.	0025	...	...	...	...	...	...	...
	Lviv 1720 1750 d.	|	...	...	...	1736	...	2327	0050
67	**Kovel 1720** d.	0215	...	0823	1805	|	...	|	|
151	Lutsk **1720** d.	|	...	1046	2013	|	...	|	|
229	Rivne **1720** d.	|	...	1225	2135	|	...	|	|
461	Kozyatyn **1750** d.	|	...	|	0139	|	...	0650	|
	Sarny **1720** d.	0438	...	|	...	|	...	|	|
	Korosten **1920** d.	0817	...	|	...	0045	...	|	0642
	Kyïv 1750 a.	1035	...	1915	...	0242	...	0912	0846
	Moskva Kiyevskaya **1740** a.	...	...	1041	...	...	...	...	...

A – KYÏV EKSPRES / KIEV EXPRESS – 🛏 1, 2 cl. Kyïv - Warszawa and v.v.
F – To/from Ivano-Frankivsk (Table **1720**).
H – From/to Kharkiv (Table **1780**).
w – From/to Odesa (Table **1750**).
PL – Poland (Central European Time).
UA – Ukraine (East European Time).

1705 KHARKIV and DNIPROPETROVSK - DONETSK — Intercity trains

km	km		*IC* 170*PC*	*IC* 157*OJ*		*IC* 174*PC*	*IC* 171*PC*			
0		**Kharkiv** d.	...	0618	...	...	1507	...	...	...
	0	Dnipropetrovsk d.	0636	|	...	1541	|	...	...	...
362	269	**Donetsk** d.	0945	1021	...	1850	1910	...	...	...

	IC 172*KJ*	*IC* 169*DJ*		*IC* 1730*DJ*	*IC* 158*DJ*					
Donetsk d.	1024	1105	...	1926	1936	...	...	...	...	...
Dnipropetrovsk d.	|	1411	...	2232	|	...	...	...	...	...
Kharkiv a.	1430	...	...	...	2338	...	...	...	...	...

NOTES FOR TABLES 1705, 1710 and 1715

1710 KYÏV - LVIV — Intercity trains

km		*IC* 169			*IC* 170	
0	**Kyïv 1750** d.	1726	...	**Lviv 1750** d.	0550	...
572	**Lviv 1750** a.	2220	...	**Kyïv 1750** a.	1045	...

1715 KYÏV - DONETSK

km		154*OJ*	152*KJ*		152*DJ*	154*DJ*
0	Kyïv **1775** d.	0603	1534	Donetsk **1775** d.	0628	1647
744	Donetsk **1775** a.	1253	2237	**Kyïv 1750** a.	1320	2338

1720 MINSK - LVIV - CHERNIVTSI — LDZ, BCh, UZ

km			*Fir* 43*KJ*	*Pas* 371*BJ* E		*Pas* 608*LJ*		
0	**Minsk 1950** d.	...	...	1738	...	...	...	...
142	Baranavichy Polesskiye d.	...	...	1947	...	...	...	...
258	Luninets **1700** ‡ BY d.	...	...	2145	...	...	...	...
364	Sarny **1700** ‡ UA d.	...	...	0053	...	...	...	...
451	Rivne **1700** d.	...	...	0228	...	...	...	...
	Kovel d.	...	...	|	...	...	...	...
	Lutsk d.	...	...	|	...	...	...	...
	Kyïv **1700 1750** d.	...	1830	|	...	...	...	...
658	**Lviv** a.	...	0252	0552	...	...	...	...
658	**Lviv** d.	...	0312	0625	...	1712	...	...
799	Ivano-Frankivsk d.	...	0545	0859	...	2017	...	...
854	Kolomyya d.	...	...	1002	...	2135	...	...
925	**Chernivtsi** a.	...	...	1127	...	2250	...	...

	Pas 372*LJ* C	*Fir* 43*LJ*		*Sko* 608*KJ*			
Chernivtsi d.	1353	...	...	0028	...	...	...
Kolomyya d.	1517	...	...	0152	...	...	...
Ivano-Frankivsk d.	1629	2155	...	0323	...	...	...
Lviv a.	1928	0030	...	0616	...	...	...
Lviv d.	1948	0050	...	...	...	...	...
Kyïv **1700 1750** a.	|	0846	...	...	...	...	...
Lutsk a.	|	...	...	...	...	...	...
Kovel a.	|	...	...	...	...	...	...
Rivne **1700** d.	2309	...	...	...	...	...	...
Sarny **1700** ‡ UA d.	0047	...	...	...	...	...	...
Luninets **1700** ‡ BY d.	0427	...	...	...	...	...	...
Baranavichy Polesskiye d.	0701	...	...	...	...	...	...
Minsk 1950 a.	0903	...	...	...	...	...	...

E – Even dates.
C – Uneven dates [... *31*, *3* ...].
‡ – 🏛: Horyn (BY) / Udrytsk (UA).
BY – Belarus.
UA – Ukraine.

1725 ODESA - IZMAÏL and BEREZYNE — UZ

km		*Pas* 686*PC* P	*Pas* 686*OJ* P		*Pas* 686*SH* P	*Pas* 686*KJ* P
0	**Odesa** Holovna d.	1620	1620	**Izmaïl** d.	...	2359
85	Bilhorod-Dnistrovsky d.	1847	1847	Berezyne d.	2312	|
175	Artsyz d.	2041	2057	Artsyz d.	0239	0239
210	Berezyne a.	|	2252	Bilhorod-Dnistrovsky d.	0431	0431
282	**Izmaïl** a.	2256	...	**Odesa** Holovna a.	0650	0650

P – ③⑤⑦ (daily May 26 - Sept. 16).

1726 CHIŞINĂU - ODESA — UZ, CFM

km		*Pas* 642*SZ*			*Pas* 641*SH*	
0	**Chişinău** 1670 d.	0730	...	**Odesa** Holovna ◧ d.	1648	...
58	Tighina **II** d.	0924	...	Tiraspol ◧ d.	1920	...
71	Tiraspol ◧ d.	0944	...	Tighina **II** d.	2003	...
190	**Odesa** Holovna ◧ d.	1218	...	**Chişinău** 1670 a.	2144	...

◧ – 🏛: Novosavitskaya (CFM) / Kuchurhan (UZ).

1730 ETULIA - CHIŞINĂU - ZHMERYNKA — UZ, CFM

km		*Pas* 6654 ¶	*Pas* 6009 ¶	*Sko* 47*SZ* M	*Pas* 801	*Sko* 61*CJ* S	*Sko* 341*MZ* M			
0	**Etulia** d.	1422	...	...	...	...	...	...	...	...
136	Basarabeasca a.	1820	...	...	...	...	...	...	...	...
136	Basarabeasca d.	...	0245	...	...	...	...	...	...	...
331	**Chişinău** 1670 d.	...	0715	1300	1604	2049	2059	...	...	...
438	Ungheni 1670 d.	...	...	|	1830	|	2350	...	...	...
516	Bălti Oraş d.	...	...	1623	2030	0030	0202	...	...	...
614	Ocniţa 🏛 MD d.	...	...	1824	2214	0324	0423	...	...	...
768	**Zhmerynka** ‡ UA a.	...	...	2304	...	0747	0912	...	...	...
729	Mamalyha 🏛 UA a.	...	...	...	...	...	...	...	...	...
787	**Chernivtsi** a.	...	...	...	...	...	...	...	...	...

	Pas 6010 ¶	*Pas* 6653 ¶	*Sko* 341*FJ* M	*Sko* 47*MZ* M	*Sko* 61*MZ* S	*Pas* 802			
Chernivtsi d.	...	...	...	...	...	...	...	...	...
Mamalyha 🏛 UA d.	...	...	...	...	...	...	...	...	...
Zhmerynka ‡ UA d.	...	...	0601	1813	1909	...	...	...	...
Ocniţa 🏛 MD d.	...	...	1125	2318	2347	0408	...	...	...
Bălti Oraş d.	...	...	1415	0108	0232	0612	...	...	...
Ungheni 1670 d.	...	...	1627	|	|	0806	...	...	...
Chişinău 1670 d.	1853	...	1933	0432	0608	1018	...	...	...
Basarabeasca a.	2334	...	...	...	...	...	...	...	...
Basarabeasca d.	...	0820	...	...	...	...	...	...	...
Etulia a.	...	1212	...	...	...	...	...	...	...

M – To/from Moskva (Table **1750**).
S – To/from St Peterburg (Table **1920**).
‡ – 🏛: Mohyliv-Podilski (UA).
¶ – 4 only.
MD – Moldova.
UA – Ukraine.

RZhD, UZ

MOSKVA - BRYANSK - SUMY, CHERNIHIV and KYÏV 1740

km		Sko 59MJ A	Sko 33MJ U	Sko 341FJ	Fir 9CH ④⑤⑦	Sko 89VJ Z	Sko 73AJ	Fir 77MJ K	Sko 41VJ	Sko 41VJ C	Sko 55MJ L	Sko 117MJ	Sko 47MZ	Fir 5JA	Fir 23MJ	Fir 3MJ M	Sko 21MJ g	Fir 1JA 1VJ	Sko 15FJ S
0	**Moskva** Kiyevskaya d.	0930	1017	1243	1340	1348	1557	1632	1657	1657	1910	1731	0015	2025	2125	2132	2250	2317	2213§
387	Bryansk Orlovski d.	1416	1600	1919	1830	1943	2202	2322	2345	2345	0112	0022	0700	0220	0324	0357	0456	|	0426§
504	Suzemka 🏛 RU d.	|	|	|	...	2151	|	0125	|	|	|	|	|	0420	|	0557	|	|	0638
519	Zernove 🏛 UA d.	|	|	|	...	|	|	|	|	|	|	0130	|	|	|	|	|	|	|
651	Konotop **1780** d.	1657	1858	2230	...	2259	0120	0302	0226	0226	0345	0357	1035	0530	0600	0731	0804	|	0757
780	**Sumy 1780** d.	|	|	|	...	|	|	|	|	|	|	0633	|	|	|	|	|	|	|
829	**Chernihiv** a.	|	|	|	...	|	|	|	|	0515	|	...	|	|	|	|	|	|	|
872	**Kyïv** a.	1919	|	0115	...	0125	0358	0528	0522	...	0625	...	1331	0754	0847	1009	1126	0702	1037
	Odesa Holovna **1750 1770** a.	|	1101	|	...	...	|	...	...	...	...	...	|	...	1906	...	...	...	|
	Chişinău **1730 1750** a.	|	...	1920	...	...	|	...	...	...	...	...	0432	...	...	...	...	...	|
	Lviv **1750** a.	|	...	...	...	...	1344	...	...	...	...	...	...	...	...	...	...	...	2043
	Chernivtsi **1750** a.	0957	...	...	...	...	...	...	...	...	...	...	...	...	...	...	...	...	...

	Sko 55KJ L	Fir 24SH	Sko 47SZ	Sko 34SH G	Sko 60MJ B	Fir 10KH ④⑤⑦	Sko 341MZ	Sko 658KJ W	Sko 42KJ	Sko 22KJ h	Fir 2KJ 2LJ	Fir 6KJ	Sko 74LJ	Sko 117OJ	Sko 90KJ Z	Fir 78LJ K	Sko 16KH T	Fir 4KJ
Chernivtsi **1750** d.	...	...	...	...	1902	...	...	...	...	...	...	...	...	...	...	...	...	...
Lviv **1750** d.	...	...	...	...	2354	...	...	...	...	...	...	...	0741	...	...	...	1056	...
Chişinău **1730 1750** d.	...	...	1300	...	|	...	2059	...	...	...	...	...	|	...	...	...	|	...
Odesa Holovna **1750 1770** d.	...	1502	|	1803	|	...	|	...	...	...	...	...	|	...	...	...	|	...
Kyïv d.	2359	0115	0335	|	0948	...	1350	...	1438	1654	2052	1909	1716	...	1949	1934	2043	2138
Chernihiv d.	|	|	|	|	|	...	|	1443	|	|	|	|	|	...	|	|	|	|
Sumy 1780 d.	|	|	|	|	|	...	|	|	|	|	|	|	|	1914	|	|	|	|
Konotop **1780** d.	0303	0357	0625	1001	1242	...	1655	1808	1808	1952	|	|	2021	2212	2245	2253	2328	0017
Zernove 🏛 UA d.	|	|	|	|	|	...	|	|	|	|	|	|	|	0105	|	|	|	|
Suzemka 🏛 RU d.	|	0720	|	|	|	...	|	|	|	|	|	|	|	|	0211	|	|	0340
Bryansk Orlovski d.	0806	0910	1212	1505	1739‡	1930	2304	2339	2339	0046	|	0238	0256	0412	0322‡	0435	0428¦	0518
Moskva Kiyevskaya a.	1406	1516	1755	2050	2106	2359	0518	0533	0533	0616	0643	0859	0906	1004	0948	1041	0955¦	1050

FOR NOTES, SEE TABLE **1750** BELOW.

UZ, CFM

KYÏV - ODESA, CHERNIVTSI and LVIV / ODESA - CHERNIVTSI and LVIV 1750

km		Sko 341FJ	Sko 89VJ	Sko 111OJ	Sko 73AJ	175	Sko 55MJ	Fir 123KJ	Fir 23MJ	Sko 15FJ	Sko 15VJ D	Sko 15FJ S	Sko 47MZ R	Sko 61MZ	Fir 43KJ N	Sko 13DJ	Fir 108PC F	Sko 49KJ	Fir 26SH 26DJ	Sko 117MJ	Sko 59MJ A	Fir 91KJ	Fir 84LJ k	Sko 19AJ H	Sko 7KJ
	Moskva Kiyevskaya **1740** d.	1243	1348	...	1557	...	1910	...	2125	2215§	2215§	2215§	0015	...	...	...	...	...	...	...	0930	...	...	...	...
	Kharkiv **1780** d.	|	|	1851	|	...	|	...	|	|	|	|	|	...	...	...	...	...	...	...	|	...	...	...	...
0	**Kyïv 1700** d.	0135	0147	0404	0413	0630	0645	0821	0907	1105	1105	1105	1346	...	1830	2006	...	2018	...	1843	2010	2240	...	...	2313
	St Peterburg Vitebski **1920** d.	|	|	|	|	|	|	|	|	|	|	|	|	1621**r**	|	|	...	|	...	|	|	|	...	2359**q**	|
159	Kozyatyn **1700** d.	0352	0358	|	0626	0829	0916	1036	1116	1332	1332	1332	1558	1645	|	|	...	2231	...	2101	2218	|	0159	0223	0123
221	Vinnytsya d.	0455	0509	|	0724	0918	|	1155	1216	1426	1426	1426	1700	1742	|	|	...	2326	...	2156	2309	|	0307	0325	0220
	Odesa Holovna d.	|	|	|	|	|	|	|	|	|	|	|	|	|	|	|	1858	|	1828	|	|	|	|	|	|
268	Zhmerynka **1775** d.	0601	0555	|	|	|	|	1306	1323	|	|	|	1813	1848	|	|	0155	|	0036	|	|	|	0413	0431	|
654	**Odesa** Holovna a.	|	...	◧	|	|	|	1953	1906	|	|	|	|	|	◧	|	|	|	|	|	|	|	0959	1030	|
	Chişinău **1730** a.	1920	...	|	|	|	|	...	...	|	|	|	0432	0518	|	|	|	|	|	|	|	|	...	...	|
367	Khmelnytsky **1775** d.	...	...	|	0939	1102	1247	...	...	1639	1639	1639	...	...	|	|	0330	0132	0204	0005	0111	|	...	...	0434
486	Ternopil **1775** d.	...	...	|	1136	...	...	...	...	1835	1835	1835	...	...	|	|	0534	0323	0401	0215	0330	|	...	...	0625
627	**Lviv 1775** a.	...	...	1328	1344	...	...	...	...	2043	2043	2043	...	...	0252	0500	0748	0527	0610	|	|	0626	...	...	0828
627	**Lviv** d.	...	...	...	...	...	...	...	...	2114	2114	2114	...	...	...	0526	0814	...	...	|	|	...	...	...	0854
	Chernivtsi a.	...	...	...	...	...	...	...	...	|	|	|	...	...	...	|	|	...	...	0818	0957	...	...	...	1327
	Bucureşti Nord **1670** a.	...	...	...	...	...	...	...	...	|	|	|	...	...	...	|	|	...	...	...	2302	...	...	...	1420
	Sofiya **1500** a.	...	...	...	...	...	...	...	...	|	|	|	...	...	...	|	|	...	...	...	1110	...	...	...	...
852	Mukacheve d.	...	...	...	...	...	...	...	...	0156	0156	0156	...	...	...	0956	1249	...	...	...	...	...	...	...	...
893	**Chop** a.	...	...	...	...	...	...	...	...	0300	0300	0300	...	...	...	1050	1340	...	...	...	...	...	...	...	...
	Košice **1195** a.	...	...	...	...	...	...	...	...	|	0730	|	...	...	...	|	|	...	...	...	...	...	...	...	...
	Budapest Keleti **1270** a.	...	...	...	...	...	...	...	...	|	...	1120	...	...	...	|	|	...	...	...	...	...	...	...	...
915	**Uzhhorod** a.	...	...	...	...	...	...	...	...	0428	...	...	...	...	...	1148	1424	...	...	...	...	...	...	...	...

	Fir 107LJ R	Sko 8LJ	Sko 61CJ	Sko 341MZ	Sko 14LJ	Sko 74LJ	Sko 90KJ	Sko 16UJ D	Sko 16KH T	Sko 16LJ	176	Sko 55KJ	Fir 24SH	Sko 47SZ F	Sko 112LJ	Fir 84SH k	Sko 20LJ J	Fir 124SH	Fir 26LJ 26OJ	Sko 118MJ	Fir 44LJ N	Fir 92LJ	Sko 60MJ B
Uzhhorod d.	1748	...	...	...	2308	...	...	...	...	0135	...	...	...	...	...	...	...	...	...	...	...	...	...
Budapest Keleti **1270** d.	|	...	...	...	|	...	...	...	1840	|	...	...	...	...	...	...	...	...	...	...	...	...	...
Košice **1195** d.	|	...	...	...	|	...	...	2010	|	|	...	...	...	...	...	...	...	...	...	...	...	...	...
Chop d.	1840	1813	...	...	0010	...	...	0415	0415	0415	...	...	...	...	...	...	...	...	...	...	...	...	...
Mukacheve d.	1947	1919	...	...	0120	...	...	0527	0527	0527	...	...	...	...	...	...	...	...	...	...	...	...	...
Sofiya **1500** d.	|	|	...	...	|	...	...	|	|	|	...	...	...	...	...	...	...	...	...	...	...	...	1845
Bucureşti Nord **1670** d.	|	|	...	...	|	...	...	|	|	|	...	...	...	...	...	...	...	...	...	...	...	...	0600
Chernivtsi d.	|	|	...	...	|	...	...	|	|	|	...	...	...	...	...	...	...	...	...	1818	...	...	1902
Lviv a.	0019	2355	...	...	0557	...	...	1032	1032	1032	...	...	...	...	...	...	...	...	...	|	...	...	|
Lviv 1775 d.	0042	0032	...	...	0617	0844	...	1056	1056	1056	...	...	...	...	1736	...	...	...	2023	|	0050	2253	|
Ternopil **1775** d.	0250	0239	...	...	|	1103	...	1306	1306	1306	...	...	...	...	|	...	...	...	2242	0045	|	|	0157
Khmelnytsky **1775** d.	0454	0446	...	...	|	1308	...	1513	1513	1513	1646	1751	...	...	|	...	...	...	0105	0247	|	|	0411
Chişinău **1730** d.	|	|	2049	2059	|	|	...	|	|	|	|	|	...	1300	|	...	...	...	|	|	|	|	|
Odesa Holovna d.	|	|	|	|	|	|	...	|	|	|	|	|	1502	|	◧	1818	1840	1911	|	|	|	|	|
Zhmerynka **1775** d.	0643	|	0807	0935	|	|	1534	|	|	|	|	|	2107	2324	|	0021	0055	0227	0251	|	|	|	|
Odesa Holovna a.	1228	|	|	|	|	|	|	|	|	|	|	|	|	|	|	|	|	|	0836	|	|	|	|
Vinnytsya d.	...	0648	0857	1025	|	1511	1629	1708	1708	1708	1832	|	2156	0014	|	0117	0143	0327	...	0439	◧	|	0608
Kozyatyn **1700** d.	...	0742	1016	1120	|	1605	1725	1800	1800	1800	1926	2139	2251	0113	|	0210	0258	0428	...	0531	|	|	0704
St Peterburg Vitebski **1920** a.	...	|	1202**z**	|	|	|	|	|	|	|	|	|	|	|	|	...	0530**z**	|	...	|	|	|	|
Kyïv 1700 a.	...	1008	...	1330	1524	1824	1949	2003	2003	2003	2119	2339	0055	0320	0242	...	...	0703	...	0803	0846	0640	0913
Kharkiv **1780** a.	...	...	...	|	...	|	|	|	|	|	...	|	|	|	1120	...	...	...	...	...	...	...	|
Moskva Kiyevskaya **1740** a.	...	...	...	0518	...	0906	0948	0955¦	0955¦	0955¦	...	1406	1516	1755	...	...	...	...	...	...	...	...	2143

– BOLGARIYA EKSPRESS – 🛏 1, 2 cl. Moskva (**59**) - Kyïv - Vadul Siret (**383**) - Sofia. Conveys on ⑥ (②⑥ June 14 - Aug. 30): 🛏 2 cl. Minsk (**312 / 384**) - Homel (**54**) - Kyïv (**59**) - Vadul Siret (**1385**) - Sofia. Conveys (on dates shown in Table **98**) 🛏 2 cl. Moskva - Ruse - Varna and Burgas.

– BOLGARIYA EKSPRES – 🛏 1, 2 cl. Sofia (**382**) - Vadul Siret (**60**) - Kyïv - Moskva. Conveys on ② (②⑤ June 17 - Sept. 2) 🛏 2 cl. Sofia - Kyïv - Minsk. Conveys on dates shown in Table **98**: 🛏 2 cl. Varna and Burgas - Ruse - Moskva.

– Moskva (**41**) - Konotop - Nizhyn (**657**) - Chernihiv.

– 🛏 1, 2 cl. Moskva - Chop - Bratislava and v.v. (Table **96**).

– Conveys on even dates from Chişinău: 🛏 1, 2 cl. Chişinău - Zhmerynka - Lviv - Przemyśl (Tables **1730**, **1056**).

– Even dates (daily June 2 - Sept. 10, Dec. 26 - 31, Jan. 2 - 5, May 1 - 6, 8 - 25).

– From St Peterburg ①③④⑤⑥ (daily June 26 - Sept. 30).

– ①③⑤⑥⑦ (daily June 28 - Oct. 2).

– To / from Kovel (Table **1700**).

– To / from Khmelnytsky (Table **1750**).

– Daily May 28 - Oct. 1; even dates Oct. 2 - Jan. 30.

N – To / from Ivano-Frankivsk (Table **1720**).

R – Conveys on even dates from Przemyśl: 🛏 1, 2 cl. Przemyśl - Lviv - Zhmerynka - Chişinău (Tables **1056**, **1730**).

S – TISSA – 🛏 2 cl. Moskva - Kyïv - Záhony (**629**) - Budapest (**794**) - Kelebia (**345**) - Beograd. Conveys on dates shown in Table **97**: 🛏 1, 2 cl. Moskva - Skopje and 🛏 2 cl. Kyïv - Skopje.

T – TISSA – 🛏 2 cl. Beograd (**344**) - Kelebia (**793**) - Budapest (**628**) - Záhony - Kyïv - Moskva. Conveys on dates shown in Table **97**: 🛏 1, 2 cl. Skopje - Moskva and 🛏 2 cl. Skopje - Kyïv.

U – Uneven dates [*... 29, 1 ...*]; daily June 1 - Sept. 9, Dec. 25 - Dec. 30, Jan. 1 - 4, May 1 - 5, 7 - 25.

W – Chernihiv (**658**) - Nizhyn (**42**) - Konotop - Moskva.

Z – To / from Zhmerynka (Table **1750**).

g – Daily June 1 - Sept. 28; also Oct. 5, 12, 19, 26, Nov. 1, 2, Dec. 27 - 29, Jan. 1 - 4, Feb. 22, Mar. 7, Apr. 30 - May 3, May 8.

h – Daily June 2 - Sept. 29; also Oct. 6, 13, 20, 27, Nov. 2, 3, Dec. 28 - 30, Jan. 2 - 5, Feb. 23, Mar. 8, May 1 - 4, May 9.

k – To / from Kovel.

q – Two days earlier.

r – Previous day.

z – Next day.

RU – Russia (Moskva Time).

UA – Ukraine (East European Time).

◧ – Via Korosten (Table **1700**).

‡ – Bryansk Lgovski.

§ – From Oct. 26, 2014 depart Moskva 2336, Bryansk Orlovski 0518.

¦ – From Oct. 26, 2014 arrive Bryansk Orlovski 0525, Moskva 1130.

TRAIN NAMES:

176/175 PODILSKY EKSPRES

1770 KYÏV and ODESA - SEVASTOPOL — UZ

km		*Fir* 23MJ Z	*Fir* 61KH	*Fir* 40KJ	*Fir* 121KJ	*Fir* 12KJ S	*Fir* 298KJ P	*Fir* 310SH	*Sko* 33MJ C	
	Moskva Kiyevskaya **1740** d.	2125	1533	...	...	...	...	...	1017	...
0	Konotop d.	0600	0128	...	...	...	...	...	1858	...
414	Znamyanka d.	|	0949x	...	...	...	...	...	0425	...
	Kyïv 1775 d.	0907	|	1310	1814	2001	2301	...	|	...
	Myronivka **1775** d.	|	|	1447	|	|	|	...	|	...
	Im. T. Shevchenka **1775** d.	|	0802x	1621	2233	2228	0156	...	|	...
826	**Odesa** Holovna a.	1906	|	|	|	|	|	2359	1101	...
	Mykolaiv d.	...	1355	**d**	0353	**d**	0705	0432	...	...
	Kherson d.	...	...	|	...	|	0812	0550	...	...
	Simferopol **1775 1790** a.	...	...	0415	...	0925	1332	1152	...	...
	Sevastopol 1775 1790 a.	...	...	0620	...	...	1557	...	...	...

km		*Fir* 122SH	*Fir* 40PC	*Fir* 12PC S	*Fir* 310DJ	*Fir* 298PC Q		*Fir* 62OJ	*Fir* 24SH Z	*Sko* 34SH D
0	**Sevastopol 1775 1790** d.	...	1240	...	...	1820	...	...	...	...
78	Simferopol **1775 1790** d.	...	1450	1710	1645	2017	...	...	...	...
360	Kherson d.	...	|	|	2242	0103	...	...	...	...
415	Mykolaiv d.	2023	**d**	**d**	0007	0217	...	1045	...	...
	Odesa Holovna d.	|	|	|	0440	|	...	|	1502	1803
726	Im. T. Shevchenka **1775** d.	0213	0424	0418	...	0737	...	1714z	|	|
835	Myronivka **1775** d.	0342	|	|	...	|	...	|	|	|
942	**Kyïv 1775** a.	0618	0716	0655	...	1108	...	|	0055	|
	Znamyanka d.	...	...	...	...	...	...	1519z	|	0041
	Konotop a.	...	...	...	...	...	...	2339	0337	0925
	Moskva Kiyevskaya **1740** a.	...	...	...	...	...	...	1122	1516	2050

C – Uneven dates [... *29, 1* ...]; daily June 1 - Sept. 9, Dec. 25 - Dec. 30, Jan. 1-4, May 1-5, 7-25.
D – Even dates (daily June 2 - Sept. 10, Dec. 26-31, Jan. 2-5, May 1-6, 8-25).
P – May 27 - Aug. 31.
Q – May 27 - Sept. 1.
S – SLAVUTICH.
Z – Via Zhmerynka (Table **1750**).
d – Via Dnipropetrovsk (Table **1775**).
x – Calls at Im. T. Shevchenka before Znamyanka.
z – Calls at Znamyanka before Im. T. Shevchenka.

1775 LVIV and KYÏV - MARIUPOL and SEVASTOPOL — UZ

km		168	*Fir* 40KJ	166	*Fir* 84KJ	*Sko* 86LJ 86SH	*Fir* 12KJ	*Fir* 38KJ	*Fir* 72KJ	*Fir* 80KJ	*Sko* 70LJ
0	**Lviv 1750** d.	...	...	...	...	0938	...	...	...	...	1748
141	Ternopil **1750** d.	...	...	...	...	1144	...	...	...	...	2001
260	Khmelnytsky **1750** d.	...	...	...	...	1338	...	...	...	...	2205
359	Zhmerynka **1750** d.	...	...	...	...	1521	...	...	...	...	2357
468	Kozyatyn **1750** d.	...	...	...	...	1718	...	...	...	...	0201
	Kyïv 1770 d.	0715	1310	1740	1700	|	2001	2007	2036	2325	|
663	Myronivka **1770** d.	|	1447	|	|	1955	|	|	2213	|	0438
772	Im. T. Shevchenka **1770** d.	0916	1621	1941	|	2142	2228	2248	0003	0207	0626
864	Znamyanka d.	1016	1733	2041	|	2303	2335	2359	0115	0318	0749
973	Pyatykhatky d.	|	|	|	◧	|	|	|	0309	0510	0945
1052	Dniprodzerzhynsk d.	1206	|	2231	|	0156	|	|	0413	0613	1101
1088	**Dnipropetrovsk** Holovny d.	1246	2121	2256	|	0249	0302	0343	0510	0650	1157
1357	Donetsk a.	|	|	...	0635	|	|	0804	|	...	1623
1489	**Mariupol** a.	|	|	...	0915	|	|	...	|	...	1905
1214	Zaporizhzhya **I 1790** d.	1405	2318	...	...	0441	0449	...	0657	...	...
1326	Melitopol **1790** d.	...	0103	...	...	0634	0626	...	...	...	...
1570	Simferopol **1770 1790** a.	...	0415	...	...	0950	0925	...	...	...	...
1648	**Sevastopol 1770 1790** a.	...	0620	...	...	...	...	...	...	...	...

	165	168	*Sko* 70DJ	*Sko* 86DJ 86PC	*Fir* 72DJ	*Fir* 40PC	*Fir* 79PC	*Fir* 37DJ	*Fir* 12PC	*Fir* 84DJ
Sevastopol 1770 1790 d.	...	...	...	...	...	1240	...	...	...	...
Simferopol **1770 1790** d.	...	...	...	1310	...	1450	...	...	1710	...
Melitopol **1790** d.	...	...	...	1642	...	1900	...	...	2006	...
Zaporizhzhya **I 1790** d.	...	1559	...	1822	1927	2032	...	...	2135	...
Mariupol d.	...	|	1033	|	|	|	...	...	|	1617
Donetsk d.	...	|	1339	|	|	|	...	1941	|	1916
Dnipropetrovsk Holovny d.	0724	1736	1816	2024	2153	2249	2233	2353	2345	|
Dniprodzerzhynsk d.	0750	1801	1900	2101	2231	|	2310	|	|	|
Pyatykhatky d.	|	|	2052	|	2348	|	0041	|	|	◧
Znamyanka d.	0941	1952	2314	0008	0145	0257	0242	0334	0306	|
Im. T. Shevchenka **1770** d.	1036	2048	0046	0131	0309	0424	0406	0458	0418	|
Myronivka **1770** d.	|	|	0224	0253	0444	0556	|	|	|	|
Kyïv 1770 a.	1237	2249	|	|	0606	0716	0648	0741	0655	0904
Kozyatyn **1750** d.	...	...	0517	0550	...	...	...	...	...	...
Zhmerynka **1750** d.	...	...	0731	0810	...	...	...	...	...	...
Khmelnytsky **1750** d.	...	...	0905	0948	...	...	...	...	...	...
Ternopil **1750** d.	...	...	1109	1150	...	...	...	...	...	...
Lviv 1750 a.	...	...	1316	1356	...	...	...	...	...	...

◧ – Via Poltava (Table **1780**).

TRAIN NAMES: **12** SLAVUTICH **38/37** DONBAS **80/79** DNIPRO **166/165** STOLYCHNY EKSPRES

1780 KYÏV and HOMEL - KHARKIV and LUHANSK — BCh, UZ

km **		*Sko* 112LJ	*IC* 156	*Pas* 140BJ W❖	*Pas* 126KJ	*IC* 162	*Fir* 20KJ	*Fir* 84KJ m	*IC* 164	*Pas* 134KJ	*Sko* 100BJ R	*Fir* 64KJ
	Uzhhorod **1750** d.	...	...	...	...	...	...	...	...	...	...	...
	Lviv **1750** d.	1736	...	...	...	...	...	...	...	...	...	...
0	**Kyïv** d.	0302	0620	...	1432	1337	1900	1700	1808	1920	...	2223
148	Hrebinka d.	0451	|	...	|	|	2101	1850	|	2132	...	0011
333	**Poltava** Kyïvska d.	0832	0922	...	|	1637	0029	2241	2107	0127	...	0357
	Minsk **1930** d.	|	|	0059	|	|	|	▬	|	|	0900	|
	Homel § BY d.	|	|	0619	|	|	|	...	|	|	1400	|
	Konotop **1740** § UA d.	|	|	1252	1722	|	|	*Pas*	|	|	1948	|
	Sumy **1740** d.	|	|	1536	2000	|	|	**325**OJ	|	|	2215	|
491	**Kharkiv** a.	1120	1056	1915	0003	1811	|	2253	2241	|	0128	0646
	Simferopol **1790** a.	...	...	0508	|	...	|	|	...	|	1033	...
814	**Luhansk** a.	...	...	...	1048	...	1018	1038	...	1115	...	...

	Pas 326DJ	*Fir* 134DJ	*IC* 161	*IC* 163	*IC* 155	*Sko* 111OJ	*Fir* 63OJ	*Sko* 126DJ	*Sko* 100PC Q	*Fir* 20DJ	*Pas* 140PC U❖
Luhansk d.	1800	1948	...	...	...	...	...	1348	...	1720	...
Simferopol **1790** d.	|	|	...	...	...	...	...	|	1303	|	0755
Kharkiv d.	0453	|	0656	1321	1843	1851	2220	0015	2254	|	1749
Sumy **1740** d.	▬	|	|	|	|	|	|	0354	0218	|	2108
Konotop **1740** § UA d.	*Fir*	|	|	|	|	|	|	0632	0512	|	2337
Homel § BY a.	**84**DJ	|	|	|	|	|	|	|	1038	|	0509
Minsk **1930** a.	**m**	|	|	|	|	|	|	|	1608	|	0954
Poltava Kyïvska d.	0339	0515	0832	1458	2019	2201	0129	|	...	0245	...
Hrebinka d.	0655	0903	|	|	|	0150	0454	|	...	0618	...
Kyïv a.	0904	1102	1137	1757	2321	0346	0708	0939	...	0811	...
Lviv **1750** a.	...	...	...	...	...	1328	...	...	...	...	...
Uzhhorod **1750** a.	...	...	...	...	...	...	...	...	...	...	...

Q – Even dates (daily June 1 - Oct. 2).
R – Uneven dates [... *29, 1* ...] (daily May 31 - Oct. 1).
U – Uneven dates [... *31, 3* ...] June 16 - Sept. 21.
W – Even dates June 18 - Sept. 20.
m – To / from Mariupol (Table **1775**).
❖ – Subject to confirmation.
** – Homel - Konotop: *222 km*. Sumy - Kharkiv: *195 km*. Kharkiv - Luhansk: *439 km*.
§ – 🏛 : Terekowka (BY) / Khorobychi (UA).
BY – Belarus.
UA – Ukraine.

1790 MOSKVA - KHARKIV - SIMFEROPOL - SEVASTOPOL — RZhD, UZ

For additional trains Moskva - Kharkiv see Table **1795**

km		*Sko* 7AJ Fs	*Sko* 201MJ S	*Fir* 29JA A	*Sko* 100BJ R	*Fir* 15GJ	*Sko* 17JI	*IC* 152 V	*Sko* 67MJ
0	**Moskva** Kurskaya d.	0337	1120	0910	...	1455	1527	...	2305
194	Tula **I** d.	0552	1429	1134	...	1743	1848	...	0148
383	Orel d.	0823	1704	1405	...	2002	2126	...	0409
537	Kursk d.	1018	1910	1602	...	2157	2314	...	0613
697	Belgorod § RU d.	1357	2224	1926	...	0052	0218	...	0926
	Minsk **1780** d.	|	|	|	0900	|	|	...	|
781	**Kharkiv** § UA a.	1448	2317	1948	0128	0140	0311	...	1023
781	**Kharkiv** d.	1513	2340	2021	0150	0200	0332	...	1047
1081	Dnipropetrovsk Holovny a.	|	|	|	|	0650	|	0845	|
1108	Zaporizhzhya **I 1775** d.	1953	0354	0045	0604	...	0800	1005	1531
1220	Melitopol **1775** d.	2138	0532	0212	0743	...	0952	1120	1716
1464	**Simferopol 1775** a.	0050	|	0530	1033	...	1256	1340	2025
1464	**Simferopol 1770 1775** d.	0110	|	...	...	...	1320	...	...
1543	Yevpatoriya a.	|	0955	...	...	...	|	...	...
1542	**Sevastopol 1770 1775** a.	0245	...	...	...	...	1525	...	...

	Fir 16PC	*Sko* 68PC	*Sko* 100PC Q	*Fir* 30PC B	*Sko* 202PC T	*IC* 152 V	*Sko* 18PC	*Sko* 8PC Gs
Sevastopol 1770 1775 d.	...	...	...	...	...	...	1755	2205
Yevpatoriya d.	...	...	...	...	1633	...	|	|
Simferopol 1770 1775 a.	...	...	...	...	|	...	1924	0001
Simferopol 1775 d.	...	1215	1303	1535	|	1704	1939	0100
Melitopol **1775** d.	...	1537	1612	1851	2223	1928	2301	0435
Zaporizhzhya **I 1775** d.	...	1717	1742	2023	0002	2042	0038	0616
Dnipropetrovsk Holovny d.	1350	|	|	|	|	2159	|	|
Kharkiv a.	1905	2207	2234	0024	0438	...	0523	1110
Kharkiv § UA d.	1946	2239	2254	0054	0501	...	0550	1148
Minsk **1780** a.	|	|	1608	|	|	...	|	|
Belgorod § RU d.	2254	0136	...	0350	0833	...	0937	1453
Kursk d.	0127	0416	...	0638	1135	...	1206	1749
Orel d.	0320	0607	...	0841	1338	...	1359	200
Tula **I** d.	0535	0826	...	1107	1551	...	1614	223
Moskva Kurskaya a.	0903	1109	...	1407	1845	...	1901	010

A – Even dates (daily May 27 - Sept. 30, Dec. 26-30).
B – Uneven dates [... *31, 3* ...] (daily May 28 - Oct. 1, Dec. 27-31).
F – Even dates (daily Apr. 24 - Oct. 4, Dec. 22 - Jan. 10).
G – Even dates [... *30, 1, 4* ...] (daily Apr. 26 - Oct. 6, Dec. 24 - Jan. 12).
Q – Even dates (daily June 1 - Oct. 2).
R – Uneven dates [... *29, 1* ...] (daily May 31 - Oct. 1).
S – June 29 - Aug. 30.
T – June 30 - Aug. 31.
V – May 27 - Sept. 8.
s – From / to St Peterburg (Table **1900**).
RU – Russia (Moskva Time).
UA – Ukraine (East European Time).
§ – 🏛 : Krasny Khutor (RU) / Kozacha Lopan (UA

TRAIN NAME: **67/68** KRYM.

RZhD, UZ MOSKVA - KHARKIV - DONETSK - MARIUPOL 1795

For additional trains Moskva - Kharkiv see Table **1790**

km		**9**MJ	**77**GJ	**18**KJ	**26**KJ	**27**MJ	**179**DJ	**321**OJ	
		Sko	Sko	Sko	Sko	Sko	Fir	Sko	
				■(1)	●	S■(5)		●	
0	**Moskva** Kurskaya d.	1440	1625	...	...	2145	...	...	...
194	Tula **I** d.	1715	1930	...	...	0026	...	...	...
383	Orel d.	1941	2210	...	...	0245	...	...	...
537	Kursk d.	2133	0022	...	...	0442	...	...	...
697	Belgorod § RU d.	0037	0343	...	...	0826	...	...	...
781	**Kharkiv** § UA a.	0057	0405	...	...	0848	...	...	...
781	**Kharkiv** d.	0127	0445	...	...	0923	1401	2215	...
917	Izyum d.	|	0652	...	...	|	1608	0043	...
1055	Mikitivka d.	|	0956	...	...	1402	1834	0339	...
1163	**Luhansk** a.	|	|	...	...	|	2044	|	...
1061	Horlivka UA d.	|	1011	...	...	1414	...	0359	...
	Kyïv d.	|	|	2319	2319	|	...	|	...
	Dnipropetrovsk UA d.	|	|	0720	0720	|	...	|	...
1162	Uspenskaya ⊞ RU d.	|	|	1634	1634	1855	...	|	...
1227	Taganrog d.	|	|	1744	1744	2032	...	|	...
1294	**Rostov na Donu** a.	|	|	1844	1844	2143	...	|	...
1114	**Donetsk** a.	0655	1142	...	k	n	...	0553	...
1114	**Donetsk** d.	...	1152	...	...	...	...	0603	...
1246	**Mariupol** a.	...	1409	...	...	...	...	0831	...

	27SJ	**78**DJ	**10**DJ	**322**OJ	**180**DJ	**18**SJ	**25**SJ	
	Sko	Sko	Sko	Sko	Fir	Sko	Sko	
	T■(3)			■		■(3)	●(4)	
Mariupol d.	...	1146	...	1818	...	...	...	...
Donetsk a.	...	1411	...	2051	...	...	...	...
Donetsk d.	n	1421	1527	2101	...	...	k	...
Rostov na Donu d.	0704	|	|	|	...	2234	2234	...
Taganrog d.	0813	|	|	|	...	2345	2345	...
Uspenskaya ⊞ RU d.	1015	|	|	|	...	0144	0144	...
Dnipropetrovsk UA d.	|	|	|	|	...	0755	0755	...
Kyïv a.	|	|	|	|	...	1555	1555	...
Horlivka UA d.	1130	1554	|	2316	...	...	...	...
Luhansk d.	|	|	|	|	2235	...	...	...
Mikitivka d.	1142	1606	|	2344	0051	...	...	...
Izyum d.	|	|	1924	0234	0324	...	...	...
Kharkiv a.	1626	2111	2135	0500	0531	...	...	...
Kharkiv § UA d.	1649	2135	2205	...	...	...	...	...
Belgorod § RU d.	2039	0120	0101	...	...	...	...	...
Kursk d.	2327	0345	0332	...	...	...	...	...
Orel d.	0120	0545	0529	...	...	...	...	...
Tula **I** d.	0334	0800	0746	...	...	...	...	...
Moskva Kurskaya a.	0616	1049	1034	...	...	...	...	...

k – To / from Kislovodsk (Table **1960**).
n – To / from Kislovodsk (a. 0815, d. 2101; not shown in Table **1960**).

S – Uneven dates May 27 - Oct. 29.
T – From Kislovodsk (next day from Rostov) on uneven dates May 27 - Oct. 27.

● – Even dates. For ●(4) see page 530.
■ – Uneven dates. For ■(1), ■(3) and ■(5) see page 530.
⊙ – ⊞: Vystrjel (RU) / Hrakivka (UA).
§ – ⊞: Krasny Khutor (RU) / Kozacha Lopan (UA).
RU – Russia (Moskva Time).
UA – Ukraine (East European Time).

MOSKVA - LUHANSK

km		**11**GJ Sko		**11**DJ Sko
0	**Moskva** Pav. d.	2300	**Luhansk** d.	1933
426	Yelets d.	0640	Valuiki ⊙ d.	0230
757	Valuiki ⊙ d.	1405	Yelets d.	0923
1005	**Luhansk** a.	1801	**Moskva** Pav. a.	1627

LITHUANIA, LATVIA and ESTONIA

SEE MAP PAGE 523

Operators: Lithuania: **LG** (Lietuvos Geležinkeliai), www.litrail.lt Latvia: **LDz** (Latvijas Dzelzcelš), www.ldz.lv Estonia: **Elron** (except for international trains, which are operated by **GoRail**), www.edel.ee

Services: Trains convey first- and second-class seating unless indicated otherwise. International trains to and from CIS countries (Belarus, Russia, Ukraine) are composed of Russian-style sleeping-cars (for details of train types and classes of travel in the CIS, see the panel on page **530**).

Timings: Valid from **June 1, 2014 until further notice**. Timings are expressed in local time at the station concerned (time comparison chart: page **2**).

Reservations: Reservation is compulsory for travel by long-distance and international services – *i.e.* all those for which a train number is shown.

RIGA - TALLINN, ST PETERBURG, VILNIUS and KALININGRAD 1800

RIGA - TALLINN (**E**).
Journey time: 4 hours 25 mins.
From **Riga**: 0700, 0900, 1230, 1445, 1600, 1830, 2035, 0235.
From **Tallinn**: 0600, 0700, 0830, 1000, 1245, 1600, 1830, 2230.

RIGA - ST PETERBURG (**E**).
Journey time: 10 hours 35 mins.
From Riga: 0840, 1845, 2255.
From St Peterburg Baltiski: 1155, 2140, 0015.

RIGA - VILNIUS (**E**).
Journey time: 4 hours 30 mins.
From Riga: 0700, 0830, 1035, 1230, 1445, 1600, 1815, 2250, 0255.
From Vilnius: 0630, 0700, 1000, 1230, 1415, 1610, 1830, 2230.

RIGA - KALININGRAD (**E**) and (**T**).
Journey time: 9–10 hours.
From Riga: 1000 **B T**, 2210 **A T**, 2210 **E**.
From Kaliningrad: 0920 **B T**, 2100 **A T**, 2100 **E**.

A – Runs on uneven dates. **B** – Runs on even dates. **E** – Lux Express (www.luxexpress.eu). **T** – Toks or BAL (www.eurolines.lt).

LG VILNIUS - KLAIPEDA 1810

km			**17**		**781**			**23**		**21**	
		c	2	c	2	c	c	A 2	c x	2	c
0	**Vilnius 1042, 1811** d.	...	0645	...	1130	...	...	1420	...	1740	...
67	Kaišiadorys d.	...	0732	...	|	...	...	|	...	1827	...
192	Radviliškis d.	0610	0902	...	|	1430	1505	1635	1723	1957	...
212	Šiauliai d.	0635	0923	0945	1339	1504	1538	1654	1744	2018	2035
***	Mažeikiai a.	|	|	1100	|	1617	|	...	...	|	2150
376	**Klaipeda** a.	0928	1125	...	1510	...	1833	...	...	2220	...

		18			**780**	**24**				**22**
	c	2	c	c	2	A 2	c	c	c z	2
Klaipeda d.	...	0650	0822	...	1215	...	1524	...	...	1705
Mažeikiai d.	0710	|	|	1140	|	...	|	1655	...	|
Šiauliai d.	0823	0856	1120	1254	1352	1722	1820	1808	1850	1913
Radviliškis d.	...	0915	1154	1325	|	1742	1854	...	1911	1932
Kaišiadorys d.	...	1050	...	...	|	|	...	...	...	2106
Vilnius 1042, 1811 a.	...	1137	...	...	1555	2000	...	...	...	2157

A – ⑤⑦. **c** – 3rd class only. **x** – From Kaunas (depart 1521); *138 km* Kaunas - Radviliškis. **z** – To Kaunas (arrive 2118). *** *78 km* Šiauliai - Mažeikiai.

LG VILNIUS - KAUNAS 1811

km		Ⓐ																				Ⓑ	
0	**Vilnius** d.	0448	0456	0620	0730	0847	0945	1025	1113	1140	1225	...	1405	1450	...	1630	1645	1730	1752	1830	1952	2040	...
67	Kaišiadorys d.	0531	0600	0710	0820	0948	1026	1112	1200	1239	1306	...	1453	1550	1640	1711	1749	1815	1847	1934	2042	2132	...
104	**Kaunas** a.	0555	0638	0737	0849	1025	1050	1138	1229	1316	1330	...	1520	1627	1704	1735	1827	1839	1920	2012	2109	2209	...

	⚒		Ⓐ																			
Kaunas d.	0456	0533	0623	0705	0809	0906	1055	1208	...	1340	1440	1530	1632	1705	1720	1755	1841	1907	1944	2019	2128	...	...
Kaišiadorys d.	0525	0610	0652	0740	0836	0940	1132	1234	...	1411	1505	1605	1657	1730	1757	1821	1906	1941	2010	2054	2155	...	...
Vilnius a.	0630	0720	0738	0845	0923	1040	1242	1320	...	1515	1549	1712	1738	1816	1905	1911	1950	2048	2056	2145	2244	...	...

z – To / from Šiauliai (Table **1810**).

LG 3rd class VILNIUS - VILNIUS AIRPORT 1812

km			Ⓐ																				
0	**Vilnius** d.	0545	0620	0750	0850	0935	1050	1145	1250	1330	1400	1450	...	1600	1657	1745	...	1920	2010	2140	...	...	...
4	**Vilnius Airport** a.	0552	0627	0757	0857	0942	1057	1152	1257	1337	1407	1457	...	1607	1704	1752	...	1927	2017	2147	...	...	...

		Ⓐ																				
Vilnius Airport d.	0557	0709	0802	0902	0947	...	1102	1157	1302	1342	1412	1502	...	1612	1709	1757	1932	2022	2152	...	...	...	...
Vilnius a.	0605	0717	0810	0910	0955	...	1110	1205	1310	1350	1420	1510	...	1620	1717	1805	1940	2030	2200	...	...	...	...

LG 3rd class VILNIUS - TURMANTAS 1818

km						Ⓐ			
0	**Vilnius** d.	0540	0813	1144	1531	1635	1839	2100	...
101	Ignalina d.	0732	1000	1331	1718	1755	2020	2231	...
147	**Turmantas** a.	0814	1042	1413	1800	...	2059	...	...

							Ⓐ		
Turmantas d.	...	0435	0834	1206	1553	1815	...	...	...
Ignalina d.	0421	0511	0917	1248	1635	1857	2024	...	...
Vilnius a.	0600	0633	1101	1432	1820	2034	2148	...	...

NOTES FOR TABLES 1818 and 1820
B – BALTIYA – 🛏 1, 2 cl., ▬ 3 cl., [4], ✕.
w – Not Dec. 31.
x – One hour later from Oct. 26, 2014.

LT – Lithuania.
LV – Latvia (East European Time).
RU – Russia (Moskva Time).

LG, LDz, RZhD VILNIUS / RIGA - ST PETERBURG 1820

km		Pas **92**RJ	Fir **38**RJ
		w	B w
0	**Vilnius** d.	1950	...
	Riga **1840** d.	|	1835
173	Daugavpils ⊞ LV a.	2200	2138
173	Daugavpils d.	2241	2241
260	Rezekne I d.	0003	0003
304	Karsava ⊞ LV d.	0130	0130
337	Pytalovo ⊞ RU d.	0405x	0405x
431	Pskov d.	0540x	0540x
715	**St Peterburg** Vitebski a.	1025x	1025x

	Pas **91**RJ	Fir **37**RJ
	w	B w
St Peterburg Vitebski d.	1940x	1940x
Pskov d.	0034x	0034x
Pytalovo ⊞ RU d.	0301x	0301x
Karsava ⊞ LV d.	0320	0320
Rezekne I d.	0405	0405
Daugavpils a.	0522	0522
Daugavpils ⊞ LV d.	0550	0625
Riga **1840** a.	|	0930
Vilnius a.	0806	...

LATVIA and ESTONIA

1830 RIGA - CESIS - VALGA *LDz*

km				A						Ⓐ		
0	**Riga** 1880	d.	0620	0754	0910	1038	1255	1542	1730	1824	1935	2110	...
53	Sigulda	d.	0746	0911	1027	1152	1407	1659	1847	1927	2052	2223	...
93	Cesis	d.	0830	...	...	1237	1452	...	...	2013	...	2309	...
121	Valmiera	d.	0901	...	...	...	1524	...	...	2044	...	2340	...
164	Lugaži ... LV **1880**	a.	1002	...	...	...	1625	...	...	2144	...	...	...
168	**Valga** ... EE **1880**	a.	1010	...	...	...	1632	...	...	2151	...	...	...

				Ⓐ		A				Ⓑ	
Valga . EE **1880**	d.	...	0455	...	...	...	1143	...	...	...	1724	
Lugaži . LV **1880**	d.	...	0502	...	...	...	1150	...	...	...	1731	...
Valmiera	d.	0504	0602	...	...	...	1250	...	...	...	1831	...
Cesis	d.	0533	0632	...	...	...	1320	1509	...	...	1902	...
Sigulda	d.	0617	0716	0800	0957	1051	1405	1555	1737	1909	1947	2139
Riga 1880	a.	0729	0826	0914	1111	1204	1517	1706	1851	2019	2050	2251

A – ⑥⑦ Apr. 18 - Oct. 27. EE – Estonia. LV – Latvia.

1840 RIGA - REZEKNE - MOSKVA and ST PETERBURG *LDz, RZhD*

km				*Pas* 662*AJ* N w	Ⓒ		*Fir* 2*RJ* L w		*Fir* 38*RJ* B w	
0	**Riga 1850**	d.	0946	...	1140	...	1645	1652	1835	...
129	Krustpils (Jekabpils) **1850**	d.	1148	...	1323	...	1836	1857	2025	...
224	**Rezekne II**	d.	1326	...	1434	...	1955	2035	0003¶	...
	St Peterburg Vitebski **1820**	a.	|	...	...	...	|	|	1025y	...
279	Zilupe LV	d.	1429	...	...	...	2130	2138	...	...
305	Sebezh RU	d.	...	...	...	...	2348	...	...	...
416	Novosokolniki	d.	...	...	...	...	|	...	...	...
445	**Velikiye Luki**	a.	...	...	...	...	0144	...	...	...
445	**Velikiye Luki**	d.	...	2045	...	...	0207	...	...	...
686	Rzhev	d.	...	0219	...	...	0538	...	...	...
921	**Moskva** Rizhskaya	a.	...	0642	...	...	0942	...	...	...

			Fir 37*RJ* B w	*Fir* 1*RJ* L w	*Pas* 661*AJ* N w	Ⓒ			
Moskva Rizhskaya	d.	...	...	1900	2008	...	...	...	...
Rzhev	d.	...	...	2257	0040	...	...	...	...
Velikiye Luki	a.	...	...	0205	0650	...	...	...	...
Velikiye Luki	d.	...	...	0228	...	...	...	...	...
Novosokolniki	d.	...	...	|	...	...	...	...	...
Sebezh RU	d.	...	...	0525	...	...	...	...	...
Zilupe LV	d.	0330	...	0537	...	...	1510	...	...
St Peterburg Vitebski **1820**	d.	|	1940y	|	...	...	|	...	...
Rezekne II	d.	0435	0405¶	0632	...	1454	1616	...	...
Krustpils (Jekabpils) **1850**	d.	0611	0737	0747	...	1606	1808	...	...
Riga 1850	a.	0827	0930	0940	...	1800	2029	...	...

B – BALTIJA – 1, 2 cl., 3 cl., 4 ✕.
L – LATVIJAS EKSPRESIS – 1, 2 cl.
N – 2 cl., 3 cl.
w – Not Dec. 31.
y – One hour later Oct. 26, 2014 - Mar. 28, 2015.
¶ – Rezekne I.
LV – Latvia (East European Time).
RU – Russia (Moskva Time).

1850 RIGA - DAUGAVPILS - POLATSK *LDz, BCh*

km				Ⓒ		Ⓒ	Ⓒ					
0	**Riga 1840**	d.	0740	0830	0946	1140	1305	1525	1612	1652	1732	2110
129	Krustpils (Jekabpils) **1840**	d.	0958	1056	1148	1323	1504	1736	1759	1857	1942	2330
218	Daugavpils § LV	d.	1126	...	...	...	1639	...	1908	...	2107	...
379	**Polatsk** § BY	a.	...	...	...	...	...	...	...	...	...	...

						Ⓒ	Ⓒ	Ⓒ			
Polatsk § BY	d.	...	...	...	...	...	...	...	...	...	...
Daugavpils § LV	d.	...	...	0614	0733	...	1253	...	...	1715	...
Krustpils (Jekabpils) **1840**	d.	0452	0611	0724	0902	1149	1424	1606	1808	1857	...
Riga 1840	a.	0729	0827	0919	1113	1415	1635	1800	2029	2122	...

BY – Belarus. LV – Latvia. § – : Indra (LV) / Bihosava (BY).

1860 RIGA AREA local trains *LDz*

RIGA - JELGAVA and v.v. *43 km*
1-2 trains per hour. Journey ± 49 minutes.

RIGA - LIELVARDE and v.v. *51 km*
1-2 trains per hour. Journey ± 60 minutes. Certain of these trains continue to / start from **Aizkraukle** *82 km* ± 86 minutes.

RIGA - SAULKRASTI and v.v. *48 km*
1-2 trains per hour. Journey ± 60 minutes. Certain of these trains continue to / start from **Skulte** *56 km* ± 70 minutes.

RIGA - SLOKA (JURMALA) and v.v. *32 km*
1-2 trains per hour. Journey ± 52 minutes. Certain of these trains continue to / start from **Tukums i + II** *65 km* ± 84 minutes.

RIGA – LIEPAJA and v.v. *223 km*. Ekspresis KURZEME ⑤⑦ (also June 24, Nov. 18, 22): Riga dep. 1825, Liepaja arr. 2140; ①⑥ (also June 25, Nov. 19, 23): Liepaja dep. 0605, Riga arr. 0916.

1870 TALLINN - ST PETERBURG and MOSKVA *Elron, GoRail, RZhD*

km			🚌	810*RJ*	220 B	812*RJ* R	222 B	34*KH*	224 B		🚌
0	**Tallinn 1880**	d.	0800	0750	0850	1526	1551	1800z	1851	...	2340
77	Tapa **1880**	d.	|	0844	0951	1619	1652	1912z	1952	...	|
104	Rakvere	d.	|	0903	1009	1638	1710	1937z	2010	...	|
163	Jõhvi	d.	|	0945	1058	1719	1800	2024z	...	...	|
209	Narva EE	d.	|	1050	1132	1822	1834	2145z	...	...	|
380	**St Peterburg** Vitebski. RU	a.	|	1518x	...	2305	...	|	...	...	|
	St Peterburg Baltiski RU	a.	1610	...	...	...	...	|	...	...	0830
633	Bologoye **1900** RU	a.	...	...	...	...	...	0545	...	...	...
797	Tver **1900**	a.	...	...	...	...	...	0734	...	...	...
964	**Moskva** Oktyabrskaya **1900**	a.	...	...	...	...	...	0920	...	...	...

		221 B	34*RJ*	223 B	809*RJ* S	🚌	225 B	809*RJ*		🚌
Moskva Oktyabrskaya **1900**	d.	...	1805	...	...	...	...	...	...	...
Tver **1900**	d.	...	2002	...	...	...	...	...	...	...
Bologoye **1900** RU	d.	...	2228	...	...	...	...	...	...	...
St Peterburg Baltiski RU	d.	...	|	...	...	0900	...	...	...	2350
St Peterburg Vitebski RU	d.	...	|	...	0655	|	...	1733	...	|
Narva EE	d.	...	0515z	0705	1000	|	1623	2027z	...	0120
Jõhvi	d.	...	0558z	0740	1038	|	1658	2105z	...	|
Rakvere	d.	0615	0654z	0829	1121	|	1750	2148z	...	|
Tapa **1880**	d.	0635	0718z	0849	1141	|	1810	2208z	...	|
Tallinn 1880	a.	0735	0823z	0949	1232	1315	1910	2259z	...	0440

A – *Firmenny*. 1, 2 cl. Ⓡ.
B – (*tavaklassi*; general class).
R – ④⑤⑦: Mar. 30, 2014 - Oct. 25, 2014.
S – ①⑤⑥: Mar. 30, 2014 - Oct. 25, 2014.
z – 1 hour earlier Oct. 26, 2014 - Mar. 28, 2015.
x – 1 hour later Oct. 26, 2014 - Mar. 28, 2015.
EE – Estonia (East European Time).
RU – Russia (Moskva Time).
🚌 – Operated by Lux Express (www.luxexpress.eu). Timings apply to bus, not rail, stations except for St Peterburg Baltiski rail station.

1880 TALLINN - TARTU - ORAVA and VALGA *Elron, LDz*

km			210	10	330	380	12	332	14	334	382	214	16	216
0	**Tallinn 1870**	d.	0610	0816	...	...	1316	...	1535	...	...	1640	1729	1945
77	Tapa **1870**	d.	0711	0908	...	...	1407	...	1628	...	...	1741	1820	2046
142	Jõgeva	d.	0800	0948	...	...	1446	...	1707	...	...	1829	1903	2133
190	**Tartu**	a.	0841	1016	...	...	1514	...	1735	...	...	1904	1931	2209
190	**Tartu**	d.	...	...	1018	1026	▬	1516	...	1737	1745	...	...	...
233	Põlva	d.	...	...	|	1114	...	|	...	|	1833	...	...	...
262	**Orava**	d.	...	...	|	1140	...	|	...	|	1859	...	...	...
	Koidula	d.	...	...	|	1150	...	|	...	|	1909	...	...	...
	Piusa	a.	...	...	|	1208	**661**	|	...	|	...	...	...	...
215	Elva	d.	...	...	1046	...	**851**	1544	...	1806	...	...	...	...
273	**Valga**	a.	...	...	1132	...		1630	...	1852	...	...	...	...
0	**Valga** .. EE **1830**	d.	...	...	...	...	1143	...	...	...	...	...	...	...
4	Lugaži .. LV **1830**	d.	...	...	...	...	1150	...	...	...	...	...	...	...
168	**Riga** 1830	a.	...	...	...	...	1517	...	...	...	...	...	...	...

		211	385	331	11	13	333	15	383	854 664	335	17	217
Riga 1830	d.	...	...	...	...	...	...	...	...	1255	...	...	...
Lugaži LV **1830**	a.	...	...	...	...	...	...	...	...	1625	...	...	...
Valga EE **1830**	a.	...	...	...	...	...	...	...	...	1632	...	...	...
Valga	d.	...	...	0614	...	...	1400	...	...	▬	1642	...	...
Elva	d.	...	...	0701	...	...	1447	...	...	...	1729	...	...
Piusa	d.	...	...	|	...	...	|	...	1457	...	|	...	...
Koidula	d.	...	0558	|	...	...	|	...	1515	...	|	...	...
Orava	d.	...	0609	|	...	...	|	...	1526	...	|	...	...
Põlva	d.	...	0634	|	...	...	|	...	1551	**215**	|	...	...
Tartu	a.	...	0721	0729	...	...	1515	...	1638		1758	...	...
Tartu	d.	0622	...	...	0731	0822	...	1517	...	1648	...	1800	1947
Jõgeva	d.	0700	...	...	0800	0850	...	1547	...	1725	...	1829	2022
Tapa **1870**	d.	0749	...	...	0840	0932	...	1628	...	1820	...	1909	2111
Tallinn 1870	a.	0849	...	...	0928	1020	...	1716	...	1920	...	1957	2211

☛ All trains convey (*tavaklass*; general class).

☛ Express 🚌 services operate Tallinn - Tartu and v.v. 20+ times daily (journey: 2½ hrs).

1890 TALLINN - PÄRNU and VILJANDI *Elron*

km					z									
0	**Tallinn**	d.	0744	...	0939	1120	1420	1626	1720	...	1813	1934	2033	2220
54	Rapla	d.	0840	...	1040	1220	1522	1727	1813	...	1915	2036	2133	2321
72	Lelle	d.	0854	0858	1056	...	1538	1743	1830	1832	1931	2052	...	2337
98	Türi	a.	0917	|	1116	...	1559	1803	1851	|	1951	2113	...	2357
151	**Viljandi**	a.	0957	|	...	...	1639	...	1931	|	...	2153	...	...
136	**Pärnu**	a.	...	0959	...	...	...	...	...	1933	...	...	...	...

						Ⓐ	Ⓒ						Ⓐ	
Pärnu	d.	...	...	0631	...	...	...	...	...	...	1719	...	...	...
Viljandi	d.	...	...	|	0635	0841	0833	...	1327	...	|	1725	...	...
Türi	d.	0526	0624	|	0716	0915	0915	1259	1408	...	|	1806	1958	...
Lelle	d.	0547	0645	0732	0737	0934	0936	1320	1429	...	1820	1827	2019	...
Rapla	d.	0603	0701	...	0751	0948	0952	1336	1445	1739	...	1841	2036	2147
Tallinn	a.	0704	0802	...	0843	1040	1052	1437	1545	1841	...	1933	2136	2248

z – Runs 10–11 minutes later on Ⓒ.

☛ All trains convey (*tavaklass*; general class).

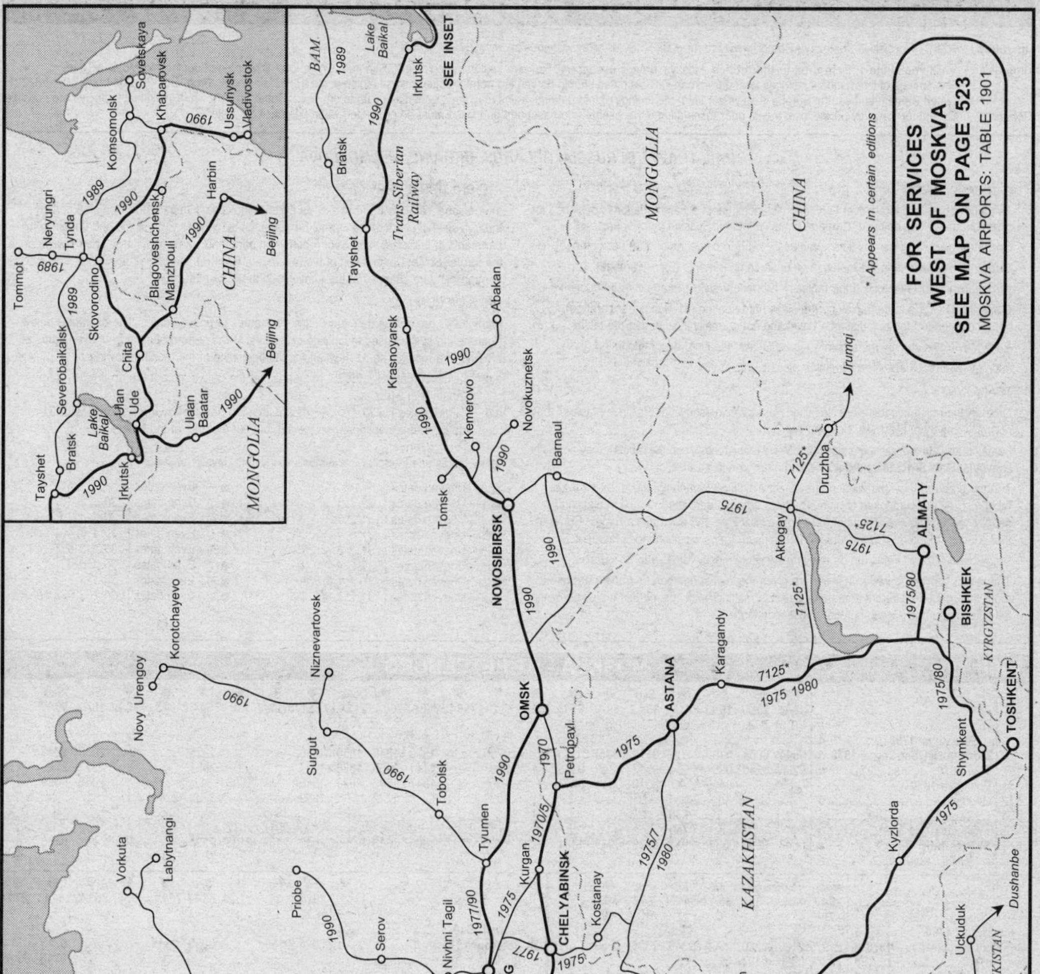
FOR SERVICES
WEST OF MOSKVA
SEE MAP ON PAGE 523
MOSKVA AIRPORTS: TABLE 1901
* Appears in certain editions
SEE INSET
FINLAND
SEE MAP PAGE 364
TURKEY
SEE MAP PAGE 514
RUSSIA
KAZAKHSTAN
MONGOLIA
CHINA
UKRAINE
BELARUS
LATVIA
ESTONIA
GEORGIA
ARMENIA
AZERBAIJAN
UZBEKISTAN
TURKMENISTAN
KYRGYZSTAN
Barents Sea
Beloe More
Gulf of Bothnia
Baltic Sea
Black Sea
Caspian Sea
Lake Baikal
BAM
Trans-Siberian Railway
MOSKVA
ST. PETERBURG
HELSINKI
TALLINN
RIGA
NIZHNI NOVGOROD
KAZAN
PERM
YEKATERINBURG
CHELYABINSK
UFA
SAMARA
SARATOV
VOLGOGRAD
ROSTOV NA DONU
OMSK
NOVOSIBIRSK
ASTANA
ALMATY
BISHKEK
TOSHKENT
BAKI
TBILISI
YEREVAN
Murmansk
Belomorsk
Petrozavodsk
Archangelsk
Konosha
Vologda
Kotlas
Mikun
Syktyvkar
Sosnogorsk
Vorkuta
Labytnangi
Kirov
Yaroslavl
Vladimir
Bologoye
Tver
Novgorod
Vyborg
Pskov
Dno
Velikiye Luki
Smolensk
Vitsebsk
Orsha
Minsk
Vilnius
Brest
Homel
Chişinău
Bryansk
Konotop
Kyiv
Sumy
Kharkiv
Kursk
Orel
Tula
Ryazan
Michurinsk
Tambov
Lipetsk
Yelets
Voronezh
Liski
Povorino
Penza
Saransk
Ulyanovsk
Toliatti
Luhansk
Likhaya
Horlivka
Donetsk
Mariupol
Melitopol
Simferopol
Sevastopol
Anapa
Novorossiysk
Krasnodar
Tuapse
Sochi
Adler
Sokhumi
Poti
Batumi
Armavir
Mineralnye Vody
Kislovodsk
Nalchik
Vladikavkaz
Groznyy
Makhachkala
Derbent
Astrakhan
Atyrau
Makat
Aktau
Oral
Orenburg
Orsk
Aktobe
Kandyagash
Kungrad
Uckuduk
Dushanbe
Kyzlorda
Shymkent
Magnitogorsk
Kostanay
Kurgan
Petropavl
Nivhni Tagil
Serov
Priobe
Tyumen
Tobolsk
Surgut
Niznevartovsk
Novy Urengoy
Korotchayevo
Karagandy
Aktogay
Druzhba
Urumqi
Barnaul
Tomsk
Kemerovo
Novokuznetsk
Abakan
Krasnoyarsk
Tayshet
Bratsk
Irkutsk
Severobaikalsk
Tynda
Neryungri
Tommot
Skovorodino
Chita
Ulan Ude
Ulaan Baatar
Beijing
Manzhouli
Harbin
Blagoveshchensk
Khabarovsk
Komsomolsk
Sovetskaya
Ussuriysk
Vladivostok

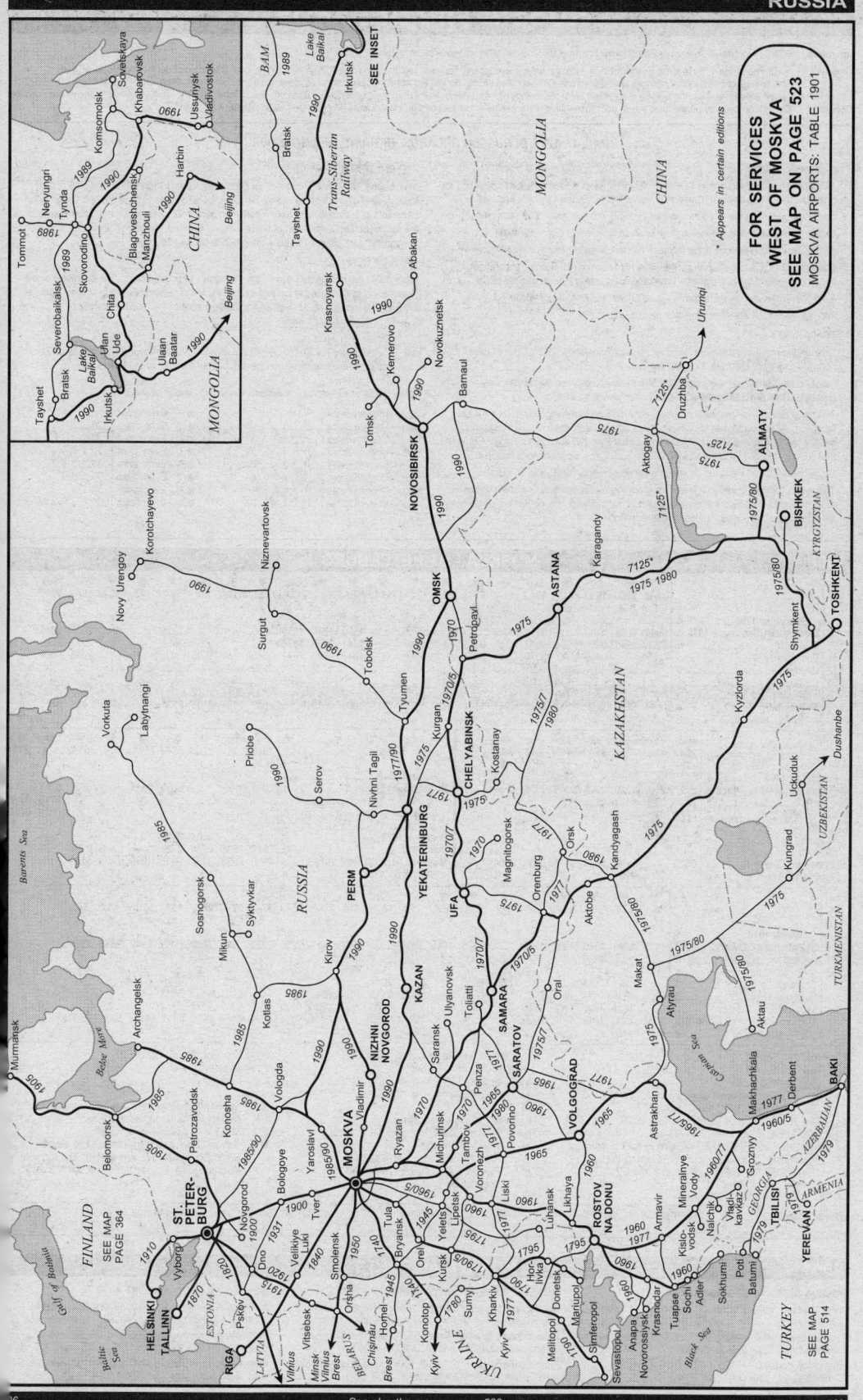

RUSSIA and BELARUS

SEE MAPS PAGES 523/529

Operators: **RZhD**: Rossiskiye Zheleznye Dorogi, www.rzd.ru – **BCh**: Belaruskaya Chyhunka, www.rw.by

Timings: Valid from **June 1, 2014 until further notice**. Moskva Time is used for all Russian stations (including Kaliningrad, where local time is one hour behind Moskva Time). The timings of international services to and from non-CIS countries should be verified from the international tables at the front of this book. From Oct. 26, 2014 until Mar. 28, 2015 (when western and central Europe is on winter time) the timings of international trains may vary, generally by up to one hour. Details are shown in individual tables where possible.

Tickets: Except for travel by purely local trains, prior reservation is necessary and passports and visas must be presented when purchasing tickets.

RAIL TRAVEL IN RUSSIA, BELARUS, UKRAINE, and MOLDOVA

CARRIAGE TYPES

As trains generally operate over very long distances, most accommodation is designed for overnight as well as day use. Carriage types (with their Russian names) are:

Spálny vagón CB (🛏 1 cl. in the tables) – 2-berth compartments (9 per carriage)

Kupéiny K (🛏 2 cl. in the tables) – 4-berth compartments (9 per carriage)

Platskártny ПЛ (🛏 3 cl. in the tables) – Dormitory-style carriage with 54 bunks

Óbshchi O (4 in the tables) – 4th-class hard seating (81 places per carriage), not recommended for long-distance travel and not normally indicated in the tables.

A few day trains convey more comfortable *Sidyáchi* (seating) accommodation.

Intercity (*IC* in tables) – New Ukrainian electric units.

TRAIN TYPES

Ordinary long-distance trains are classified *Passazhírsky* (shown as *Pas* in the tables): they normally convey at least 🛏 3 cl. and 🛏 2 cl.

Faster long-distance trains are classified *Skóry* (shown as *Sko* in the tables): they normally convey at least 🛏 3 cl. and 🛏 2 cl. and often also 🛏 1 cl.

The top grade of fast long-distance trains are classified *Firménny* (shown as *Fir* in the tables). They are composed of higher-quality carriages dedicated to a particular, and usually named, service. They normally convey 🛏 2 cl. and 🛏 1 cl. carriages. Some of these trains (marked ☆ in the tables) are premium trains with enhanced facilities.

High-speed *Sapsan* trains run on daytime services, mostly Moskva to St Peterburg.

The most important trains on a route are given the lowest numbers (numbers are used more than once in different areas). To assist in making bookings, certain tables show the full booking numbers (train number plus two letters).

INTERNATIONAL SERVICES

International services to, from and via Poland, Slovakia, Hungary and Romania convey through sleeping cars of the normal European ('RIC') types, with single and double compartments in first class, and 3- or 4-berth compartments in second class. The railways of the former Soviet Union being of broad gauge (1520mm), the bogies (trucks) of these through cars are changed at the frontier with these countries.

DAYS OF RUNNING

Many trains run on alternate days only: even dates or uneven dates. The examples below illustrate the system used to indicate exceptions to the pattern of even or uneven dates at the end of a month with 31 days and at the beginning of the month following:

e.g. "Uneven dates [... *29, 1* ...]" means that the train does not run on the 31st of a month with 31 days.

e.g. "Even dates [... *30, 1, 4* ...]" means that the train, **following a month with 31 days**, runs exceptionally on the 1st, but not the 2nd, of the month.

Many tables use the following symbols to indicate days of running:

■ – Uneven dates.	● – Even dates.
■(1) – Uneven dates [.. *29, 1* ..]	●(3) – Even dates [.. *30, 1, 3, 8* ..]
■(2) – Uneven dates [.. *31, 2, 3* ..]	●(4) – Even dates [.. *30, 1, 4* ..]
■(3) – Uneven dates [.. *31, 3* ..]	●(5) – Even dates [.. *30, 1, 3, 4* ..]
■(5) – Uneven dates [.. *31, 2, 5* ..]	●(6) – Even dates [.. *30, 1, 3, 6* ..]
■(7) – Uneven dates [.. *31, 2, 4, 7* ..]	●(7) – Even dates [.. *30, 1, 6* ..]
■(8) – Uneven dates [.. *31, 2, 4, 6, 8, 10, 11* ..]	●(8) – Even dates [.. *30, 1, 3, 5, 8* ..]
■(9) – Uneven dates [.. *31, 2, 4, 6, 9* ..]	●(9) – Even dates [.. *30, 1, 3, 5, 7, 10* ..]

1900 MOSKVA - ST PETERBURG

RZhD

km		*Fir* 38*AJ* T	*Fir* 20*UJ* q ✕	*Sko* 16*AJ* m t	≋ 874*JA*	*Sko* 30*AJ*	*Fir* 59*A* g	*Sko* 8*PC* M	♥ 752*AJ*	♥ 754*AJ* ①⑥	♥ 756*AJ* C	♥ 758*AJ*	♥ 760*AJ*	*Sko* 212*AJ* A m	♥ 762*AJ*	≋ 872*MJ*	≋ 712	♥ 764*AJ*	≋ 873	♥ 766*AJ*	*Sko* 18*AJ* p	*Sko* 56*AJ*	
	Sevastopol **1790** d.	...	...	...	...	...	...	2205x	...	...	...	...	...	...	...	...	...	...	...	...	...	...	...
0	**Moskva** Oktyabrskaya § **1870** d.	0044	0054	0100	...	0110	0135k	0128k	0645	0700	1115	1330	1345	1550	1630	...	...	1925	...	1945	2030	2040	...
167	Tver **1870** d.	0236	0250	0257	...	0312	0349	0333	|	0807	|	1441	1456	1826	1737	...	...	2031	...	|	2221	2255	...
331	Bologoye **1870** d.	|	|	0445	...	0510	0544	0548	|	|	|	1547	1602	2023	1840	...	1803	|	...	|	2358	0059	...
532	Chudovo d.	|	|	|	...	|	|	|	|	1009	|	|	1722	|	1952	...	|	2233	2244	|	...	|	...
606	Novgorod na Volkhove d.	|	|	|	0630	|	|	|	|	|	|	|	|	|	|	1845	|	|	2355	|	...	|	...
	Chudovo d.	|	|	|	0755	|	|	|	|	|	|	|	|	|	|	2017	2017	|	...	|	...	|	...
650	**St Peterburg** Glavny ‡ a.	0848	0900	0838c	0934	0939	0945	1001	1035	1100	1537	1800	1815	0156c	2040	2133	2133	2324	...	2335	...	0440	...
	Helsinki **1910** a.	...	...	...	...	...	...	...	...	...	...	...	...	...	...	...	...	...	...	...	...	...	...

	Fir 28*AJ* D	*Sko* 42*AJ*	*Fir* 32 L	*Fir* 26*AJ* Q	*Fir* 54*CH* ⊠	*Fir* 2*AJ* K	*Fir* 4*AJ* Ⓑ	
Sevastopol **1790** d.	...	...	...	...	...	...	...	...
Moskva Oktyabrskaya § **1870** d.	2127	2150	2250	2300	2340	2355	2359	...
Tver **1870** d.	2338	0030	0107	0115	|	|	|	...
Bologoye **1870** d.	0127	0236	|	|	|	|	|	...
Chudovo d.	|	0456	|	|	|	|	|	...
Novgorod na Volkhove d.	|	0610	|	|	|	|	|	...
Chudovo d.	|	...	|	|	|	|	|	...
St Peterburg Glavny ‡ a.	0517	...	0548c	0639	0835	0755	0800	...
Helsinki **1910** a.	...	...	1206	...	...	...	...	...

	Fir 19*UJ* q ✕	*Fir* 31 L	*Sko* 17*AJ* p	*Sko* 55*AJ*	♥ 751*AJ*	≋ 874	♥ 753*AJ*	≋ 171	≋ 871
Helsinki **1910** d.	...	1752	...	...	...	...	...	...	...
St Peterburg Glavny ‡ d.	0020	0158c	...	0050	0645	...	0700	0713	0713
Chudovo d.	|	|	...	|	|	...	|	0845	0840
Novgorod na Volkhove d.	|	|	...	|	|	0630	|	|	0954
Chudovo d.	|	|	...	|	|	0743	0750	|	...
Bologoye **1870** d.	|	|	0501	0450	|	...	|	1025	...
Tver **1870** d.	0626	0635	0705	0727	|	...	0953	...	...
Moskva Oktyabrskaya § **1870** a.	0900	0825	0906	0953	1035	...	1100	...	...
Sevastopol **1790** a.	...	...	...	...	...	...	...	...	...

km		♥ 755*AJ* C	♥ 757*AJ*	♥ 759*AJ* ⑤⑦	♥ 761*AJ*	*Fir* 59*A* g	≋ 872	♥ 763*AJ*	♥ 765*AJ*	*Sko* 7*AJ* M	*Sko* 42*CH*	≋ 873	*Sko* 211*AJ* B m	*Sko* 29*AJ*	*Fir* 37*AJ* S	*Fir* 27*AJ* E	*Fir* 25*AJ* Q	*Sko* 15*AJ* m	*Fir* 53*CH* ⊠	*Fir* 1*AJ* K	*Fir* 3*AJ* Ⓑ		
	Helsinki **1910** d.	...	...	...	...	...	...	...	...	...	...	...	...	...	...	...	...	...	...	...	...	...	...
0	**St Peterburg** Glavny ‡ d.	1115	1330	1345	1500	1722	...	1925	1945	2000	...	2057	...	2215	2222	2229	2300	2322c	2342	2355	2359	...	...
118	Chudovo d.	|	|	|	|	|	...	|	|	|	...	2244	...	|	|	|	|	|	|	|	|	...	...
192	Novgorod na Volkhove d.	|	|	|	|	|	1845	|	|	|	2120	2355	...	|	|	|	|	|	|	|	|	...	...
	Chudovo d.	|	|	1438	|	|	1955	2015	|	|	2244	...	...	|	|	|	|	|	|	|	|	...	...
	Bologoye **1870** d.	|	1539	1554	1659	2151	...	|	|	2355	0113	...	0040	|	|	0203	|	0313	|	|	|	...	...
	Tver **1870** d.	|	1651	1706	1804	2345	...	2218	|	0131	0309	...	0236	0330	0337	0352	0435	0451	|	|	|	...	...
	Moskva Oktyabrskaya § **1870** a.	1532	1800	1815	1910	0145k	...	2334	2335	0322k	0530	...	0444	0515	0524	0558	0715	0728	0838	0755	0800	...	...
	Sevastopol **1790** a.	...	...	...	...	...	...	...	...	0245z	...	...	...	...	...	...	...	...	...	...	...	...	...

A – May 29 - Sept. 1.
B – May 31 - Sept. 3.
C – June 12, 15, 21, 22.
D – May 27 - Oct 15 uneven dates [... *31, 3* ...]; also Oct. 19, 29, Nov. 3, 5, 9, 19, 23, Dec. 21, 27, 29.
E – May 28 - Oct 14 even dates; also Oct. 18, 28, Nov. 2, 4, 8, 18, 22, Dec. 20, 26, 28.
K – KRASNAYA STRELA (RED ARROW) - 🛏 1 cl. with ensuite, 🛏 1, 2 cl., ✕ Moskva - St Peterburg and v.v.
L – LEV TOLSTOI – 🛏 1 cl. with ensuite, 🛏 1, 2 cl., ✕ Moskva - Helsinki and v.v.

M – Runs on dates shown in Table **1790**.
Q – ①–⑥ (May 27 - Sept. 7).
S – Ⓑ (daily May 26 - Sept. 6).
T – ①–⑥ (daily May 26 - Sept. 7).

c – St Peterburg **Ladozhski**.
g – To/from Nizhni Novgorod (Table **1990**).
k – Moskva **Kurskaya**.
m – To/from Murmansk (Table **1905**).
p – To/from Petrozavodsk (Table **1905**).
q – Operated by Tverskoy Express.

t – Not Sept. 24, 30, Oct. 16, 22.
x – Two days earlier.
z – Next day.

≋ – *Swallow* high-speed train, special fares payable.
§ – Also known as *Leningradski vokzal.*
‡ – Also known as *Moskovski vokzal.*
♥ – *Sapsan* high-speed train, special fares payable. ✕ Ⓡ
⊠ – *Grand Express* 🛏 1 cl. with ensuite, shower, sofa, air conditioning, TV, DVD and wi-fi, 🛏 1, 2 cl., ✕.

Named trains:									
3/4	EKSPRESS	17/18	KARELIYA	25/26	SMENA	37/38	AFANASI NIKITIN	159/160	AVRORA
7/8	NEVA	19/20	MEGAPOLIS	31/32	LEV TOLSTOI	42	ILMEN	166/165	NEVSKY EXPRESS

1901 MOSKVA AIRPORTS ✈

MOSKVA DOMODEDOVO AIRPORT ✈

Aeroexpress rail service Moskva Paveletskaya - Moskva Domodedovo ✈. *35 km* Journey time 40 - 47 minutes.

From **Moskva Paveletskaya**: 0600, 0630, 0700, and every 30 minutes (not 1230) until 2330, 0000.

From **Domodedovo** ✈: 0600, 0700, 0730, 0800, and every 30 minutes (not 1230) until 2330, 0000.

MOSKVA SHEREMETYEVO AIRPORT ✈

Aeroexpress rail service Moskva Belorusskaya - Moskva Sheremetyevo ✈. *35 km* Journey time 35 minutes.

From **Moskva Belorusskaya**: 0530, 0600, 0630, and every 30 minutes (not 1300) until 2330, 0000, 0030.

From **Sheremetyevo** ✈: 0500, 0600, 0630, and every 30 minutes (not 1200) until 2330, 0000, 0030.

MOSKVA VNUKOVO AIRPORT ✈

Aeroexpress rail service Moskva Kiyevskaya - Moskva Vnukovo ✈. *28 km* Journey time 34 - 42 minutes.

From **Moskva Kiyevskaya**: 0600, 0700, and every 60 minutes (not 1200; also 1530, 1730, 1930) until 2300, 000

From **Vnukovo** ✈: 0600, 0700 and every 60 minutes (also 1630, 1830) until 2300, 0000.

RZhD — (MOSKVA and) ST PETERBURG - PETROZAVODSK - MURMANSK — 1905

km		*Sko* 18*AJ* Kf	*Sko* 92*AJ* y	*Sko* 16*AJ* t	*Sko* 212*AJ* B		*Sko* 22*CH*	*Pas* 658*AJ* f	
	Moskva Oktyabrskaya **1900** .. d.	2030	2220	0100	1550	...	...	...	...
0	**St Peterburg** Ladozhski .... d.	|	|	0911	0232	...	1720	2207	...
* 114	Volkhovstroi I .... d.	0424	|	1118	0431	...	1948	0028	...
394	**Petrozavodsk** .... d.	0903	1253	1646	0945	...	0114	0640	...
773	Belomorsk .... d.	...	2219	2348	1735	...	0805	...	...
1161	Kandalaksha .... d.	...	0552	0658	0019	...	1515	...	...
1438	**Murmansk** .... a.	...	1200	1232	0539	...	2053	...	...

	Sko 21*CH*		*Sko* 211*AJ* D	*Sko* 15*AJ* f	*Sko* 17*AJ* K	*Sko* 91*CH* w	*Pas* 657*AJ* f	
Murmansk .... d.	0910	...	1820	1925	...	2021	...	...
Kandalaksha .... d.	1447	...	0010	0048	...	0249	...	...
Belomorsk .... d.	2138	...	0643	0720	...	1030	...	...
Petrozavodsk .... d.	0448	...	1438	1505	1855	2036	2250	...
Volkhovstroi I .... d.	1006	...	|	2028	0043	|	0506	...
St Peterburg Ladozhski .... a.	1211	...	|	2244	|	|	0707	...
Moskva Oktyabrskaya **1900** .. a.	...	...	0444	0728	0906	1138	...	...

B – May 29 - Sept. 1.
D – May 31 - Sept. 3.
K – KARELIYA.
f – Not Sept. 25, Oct. 1, 17, 23, Dec. 31.
t – Not Sept. 24, 30, Oct. 16, 22, Dec. 31.
w – Not odd days Sept. 3 - Oct. 27, not Sept. 18, Oct 2, 16, 30, Dec. 4, 11, 18.
y – Not odd days Sept. 1 - Oct. 25, not Oct 14, 28, Dec. 9, 16.
* – Moskva - Vokhovstroi : *641 km.*

RZhD, VR — ST PETERBURG - HELSINKI — 1910

Service June 1 - October 25, 2014.

km		781 *AE*30 A	*Fir* 32*AJ* B	783 *AE*34 A	785 *AE*36 A	787 *AE*38 A	
	Moskva Okt. **1900** .... d.	...	2300	...	...	...	...
***	**St Peterburg** Ladozhski .... d.	...	0553	...	...	...	...
0	**St Peterburg** Finlyandski .. d.	0640	|	1125	1525	2025	...
129	Vyborg .... a.	0735	0754	1220	1620	2120	...
129	Vyborg .... 🏛 RU d.	0745	0844	1230	1630	2130	...
159	Vainikkala .... 🏛 FI a.	0714	0832	1159	1559	2059	...
159	Vainikkala .... d.	0721	0900	1206	1606	2106	...
250	**Kouvola 797** .... a.	0800	0959	1245	1645	2145	...
312	Lahti **797** .... a.	0826	1042	1311	1711	2211	...
400	Tikkurila **797** .... a.	0901	1142	1346	1746	2246	...
413	Pasila **797** .... a.	0910	1210	1355	1755	2255	...
416	**Helsinki 797** .... a.	0916	1217	1401	1801	2301	...

	*AE*33 782 A	*AE*35 784 A	*AE*37 786 A	*Fir* 31*AJ* B	*AE*39 788 A	
Helsinki 797 .... d.	0612	1000	1500	1752	1900	...
Pasila **797** .... d.	0618	1006	1506	1758	1906	...
Tikkurila **797** .... d.	0628	1016	1516	1809	1916	...
Lahti **797** .... d.	0702	1050	1550	1911	1950	...
Kouvola 797 .... d.	0728	1116	1616	1952	2016	...
Vainikkala .... a.	0807	1155	1655	2047	2055	...
Vainikkala .... 🏛 FI d.	0814	1202	1702	2112	2102	...
Vyborg .... 🏛 RU a.	0939	1327	1827	2253	2227	...
Vyborg .... d.	0944	1332	1832	2343	2232	...
St Peterburg Finlyandski a.	1048	1436	1936	|	2336	...
St Peterburg Ladozhski . a.	...	...	...	0121	...	...
Moskva Okt. **1900** .... a.	...	...	...	0824	...	...

ST PETERBURG - MALADZECHNA — 1915 — RZhD, BCh

km		*Sko* 79*CH* C
0	**St Peterburg** Vit. **1920** ...... d.	2010
245	Dno **1920** .... d.	2351
421	Novosokolniki **1920** .... ‡ RU d.	0303
568	**Vitsebsk 1920** .... ‡ BY d.	0509
670	Polatsk .... d.	0710
868	**Maladzechna** .... a.	0959
	Vilnius **1950** .... a.	1335z
	Kaliningrad **1950** .... a.	2114x

	Sko 80*CH* C
Kaliningrad **1950** .... d.	1002
Vilnius **1950** .... d.	1539
Maladzechna .... d.	1908
Polatsk .... d.	2246
Vitsebsk **1920** .... ‡ BY d.	0101
Novosokolniki **1920** .... ‡ RU d.	0448
Dno **1920** .... d.	0729
St Peterburg Vit. **1920** .... a.	1106

NOTES FOR TABLES 1910 AND 1915

A – *Allegro* (12) ✕ Ⓡ St Peterburg - Helsinki and v.v.
B – LEV TOLSTOI – 🛏 1 cl. with ensuite, 🛏 1, 2 cl., ✕ Moskva - Helsinki and v.v. (also **32** *VJ*).
C – Runs on dates shown in Table **1950**.
x – 2023 from Oct. 28, 2014.
z – 1155 from Oct. 28, 2014.
*** *143 km* St Peterburg Ladozhski - Vyborg.
‡ – 🏛: Yezyaryshcha (BY) / Zaverezhye (RU).
BY – Belarus (GMT + 3 hours, all year; see p 2).
FI – Finland (East European Time, GMT + 2 hours winter, GMT + 3 hours summer).
RU – Russia (Moskva Time).
§ – Finlyandski vokzal.
◧ – Ladozhski vokzal.

RZhD, BCh, UZ — ST PETERBURG - HOMEL and KOZYATYN — 1920

km		*Sko* 49*BJ* A	*Sko* 53*AJ*	*Sko* 61*MZ*	*Fir* 55*BJ*	*Sko* 83*AJ* K	*Fir* 51*BJ*	*Sko* 19*AJ* BR	
0	**St Peterburg** Vitebski **1915** ...... d.	1522	1600	1644	...	1747	1913	2359	...
245	Dno **1915** .... d.	1857	1955	2036	...	2131	2256	0355	...
421	Novosokolniki **1915** .... § RU d.	2202	2247	2350	...	0041	0154	0729	...
568	Vitsebsk .... § BY d.	2335	0038	0138	...	0252	0310	0922	...
	Moskva Belorusskaya **1950** .... d.	|	|	|	2119	|	|	|	...
652	**Orsha** Tsentralnaya .... a.	0057	0157	0256	0323	0412	0425	1045	...
652	**Orsha** Tsentralnaya .... d.	0123	0217	0318	0344	0441	0448	1108	...
	Minsk Passazhirski **1950** .... a.	0353	|	|	|	|	0714	|	...
	Brest Tsentralny **1950** .... a.	0824	|	|	|	|	...	|	...
726	Mahilyow I .... d.	...	0357	0506	0548	0626	...	1301	...
853	Zhlobin **1930** .... d.	...	0625	0738	0808	0905	...	1549	...
	Homel 1930 .... a.	...	0734	|	0931	1027	...	|	...
	Kyïv Passazhirski **1930** .... a.	...	1444x	|	...	...	...	|	...
954	Kalinkavichy **1700** .... ‡ BY d.	...	...	0913	...	...	...	1807	...
1109	Korosten **1700** .... ‡ UA d.	...	...	1324	...	...	...	2227	...
1191	Zhytomyr .... d.	...	...	1457	...	...	...	0018	...
1267	**Kozyatyn** .... a.	...	...	1635	...	...	...	0200	...
	Odesa Holovna **1750** .... a.	...	...	|	...	...	...	1030	...
	Chişinău **1750** .... a.	...	...	0608	...	...	...	...	...

	Sko 20*LJ* S	*Fir* 52*BJ* B	*Sko* 54*KJ*	*Sko* 61*CJ*	*Fir* 55*MZ*	*Sko* 83*MZ* E	*Sko* 22*GJ* A	
Chişinău **1750** .... d.	...	...	...	2049	...	...	...	...
Odesa Holovna **1750** .... d.	1840	...	...	|	...	...	...	...
Kozyatyn .... d.	0258	...	...	1016	...	...	...	...
Zhytomyr .... d.	0436	...	...	1151	...	...	...	...
Korosten **1700** .... ‡ UA d.	0626	...	...	1350	...	...	...	...
Kalinkavichy **1700** .... ‡ BY d.	1028	...	...	1747	...	...	...	...
Kyïv Passazhirski **1930** .... d.	|	...	1044x	|	...	...	...	...
Homel 1930 .... d.	|	...	1651	|	1842	1936	...	...
Zhlobin **1930** .... d.	1215	...	1806	1935	2017	2110	...	...
Mahilyow I .... d.	1500	...	2056	2225	2258	2324	...	...
Brest Tsentralny **1950** .... d.	|	...	|	|	|	|	1944	...
Minsk Passazhirski **1950** .... d.	|	1741	|	|	|	|	2338	...
Orsha Tsentralnaya .... a.	1623	2014	2217	2343	0018	0042	0157	...
Orsha Tsentralnaya .... d.	1644	2036	2233	0003	0037	0103	0402	...
Moskva Belorusskaya **1950** .... a.	|	|	|	|	0840	|	|	...
Vitsebsk .... § BY d.	1814	2202	0015	0133	...	0238	0526	...
Novosokolniki **1915** .... § RU d.	2157	0156	0404	0525	...	0626	1011	...
Dno **1915** .... d.	0124	0434	0647	0837	...	0913	1304	...
St Peterburg Vitebski **1915** ...... a.	0530	0816	1010	1202	...	1253	1640	...

A – Conveys (on dates shown in Table **95**) 🛏 1, 2 cl. St Peterburg - Orsha - Brest - Praha and v.v.
B – Conveys (on dates shown in Table **56**) 🛏 1, 2 cl. St Peterburg - Orsha - Berlin and v.v.
E – Even dates.
J – Uneven dates [... *29, 1* ...].
K – Uneven dates [... *31, 3* ...].
P – To / from Lviv (Table **1720**)
R – ①③④⑤⑥ (daily June 26 - Sept. 30).
S – ①③⑤⑥⑦ (daily June 28 - Oct. 2).
x – Up to 60 mins. earlier from Oct. 28.
BY – Belarus (GMT + 3 hours, all year, see p 2).
RU – Russia (Moskva Time).
UA – Ukraine.
§ – 🏛 : Yezyaryshcha (BY) / Zaverezhye (RU).
‡ – 🏛 : Slovechno (BY) / Berezhest (UA).

Named trains :
51 / 52 ZVYAZDA
53 / 54 LYBID
55 / 56 SOZH

BCh, UZ — MINSK - HOMEL - KYÏV — 1930

km		*Pas* 312*CH* E ❖	*Sko* 384*MZ* A	*Sko* 53*AJ*	*Sko* 100*BJ* C	*Sko* 94*BJ* D		*Sko* 86*BJ*	
	Kaliningrad **1950** .... d.	1401	...	...	...	...	...	...	...
	Vilnius **1950** .... d.	1858	...	...	...	...	...	...	...
0	**Minsk** Passazhirski .... d.	0059	2305	...	0900	1302	...	2120	...
	St Peterburg Vitebski **1920** .... d.	|	|	1600	|	|	...	|	...
214	Zhlobin **1920** .... d.	0425	0246	0625	1221	1615	...	0032	...
304	**Homel 1920** .... a.	0553	0406	0734	1340	1730	...	0136	...
304	**Homel** .... ‡ BY d.	0619	0800	0800	1400	1808	...	0156	...
	Kharkiv Passazhirski **1780** ..... a.	1921	|	|	0128	|	...	|	...
415	Chernihiv .... ‡ UA d.	...	1142	1143x	|	2158	...	0545	...
	Simferopol **1775 1790** .... a.	...	|	|	1033	|	...	|	...
624	**Kyïv** Passazhirski **1700 1720** .... a.	...	1856	1444x	...	0039	...	0836	...
	Odesa **1750** .... a.	...	...	...	...	1052	...	...	...

	Sko 94*SH* B	*Sko* 100*PC* J	*Pas* 311*DJ* C ❖	*Sko* 54*KJ*	*Sko* 54*KJ* A		*Sko* 86*KJ*	
Odesa **1750** .... d.	1442	...	...	...	...	...	...	...
Kyïv Passazhirski **1700 1720** .... d.	0045	...	...	1044x	1035x	...	2156	...
Simferopol **1775 1790** .... d.	|	1303	...	|	|	...	|	...
Chernihiv .... ‡ UA d.	0354	|	...	1340x	1226x	...	0101	...
Kharkiv Passazhirski **1780** ..... d.	|	2254	0050	|	|	...	|	...
Homel .... ‡ BY a.	0730	1038	1348	1626	1626	...	0407	...
Homel 1920 .... d.	0813	1113	1418	1651	1828z	...	0429	...
Zhlobin **1920** .... d.	0935	1241	1543	1806	2003	...	0540	...
St Peterburg Vitebski **1920** .... a.	|	|	|	1010	|	...	|	...
Minsk Passazhirski .... a.	1301	1608	1919	...	2310	...	0903	...
Vilnius **1950** .... a.	...	...	2355	...	...	...	...	...
Kaliningrad **1950** .... a.	...	...	0836	...	...	...	...	...

A – Conveys (on dates shown in Table **98**) 🛏 2 cl. Minsk - Kyïv - Sofiya and v.v.
B – Uneven dates [... *31, 3* ...] (daily June 11 - Oct. 1).
C – Uneven dates [... *29, 1* ...] (daily May 31 - Oct. 1).
D – Even dates (daily June 10 - Sept. 30).
E – Even dates.
J – Even dates (daily June 1 - Oct. 2).
x – Up to 60 mins earlier from Oct. 28.
z – Train **615***BJ* Homel - Minsk.
❖ – Subject to confirmation.
‡ – 🏛 : Teryukha (BY) / Hornostayivka (UA).
BY – Belarus.
UA – Ukraine.
Named trains : **86** BELY AIST, **53 / 54** LYBID

RZhD — MOSKVA - DNO - PSKOV — 1931

km		*Fir* E 10*AJ*
0	**Moskva** Okt ★ **1870** .... d.	1830
167	Tver **1870** .... d.	2121
331	Bologoye **1870** .... d.	2359
588	Dno .... d.	0546
687	**Pskov** .... a.	0730

	Fir E 10*CH*
Pskov .... d.	1805
Dno .... d.	2020
Bologoye **1870** .... d.	0211
Tver **1870** .... d.	0400
Moskva Okt ★ **1870** .... a.	0627

E – Not Dec. 31.
★ – Moskva **Oktyabrskaya**, also known as *Leningradski vokzal.*

LDz, BCh — RIGA - MINSK — 1932

km		*Sko* A 88*BJ*
0	**Riga 1850** .... d.	1835
218	Daugavpils **1850** .... § LV d.	2202
379	**Polatsk** .... § BY d.	0231
578	Maladzechna .... d.	0527
655	**Minsk** .... a.	0635

	Sko A 87*BJ*
Minsk .... d.	2130
Maladzechna .... d.	2308
Polatsk .... § BY d.	0205
Daugavpils **1850** .... § LV d.	0625
Riga 1850 .... a.	0930

A – ⑤⑦ (daily June 1 - Aug. 31) not Dec. 31 from Riga; not Jan. 1 from Minsk 🛏 2 cl., 🛏 3 cl., (2) Riga - Minsk and v.v.
§ – 🏛 : Indra (LV) / Bihosava (BY).

1935 VORONEZH - POLATSK RZhD, BCh

km		*Fir* 39*SZ* D	*Pas* 468*SJ* A
0	**Voronezh** d.	...	1630
246	Kursk d.	...	2235
324	Lgov d.	...	0015
541	Bryansk Orlovski a.	...	0440
541	Bryansk Orlovski d.	...	0515
	Moskva Beloruss. **1950** d.	2144	|
796	Smolensk a.	0323	1227
796	Smolensk d.	0357	...
937	Vitsebsk § RU d.	0555	...
1039	**Polatsk** § BY a.	0736	...

	Pas 468*MJ* B	*Fir* 39*BJ* D
Polatsk § BY d.	...	1758
Vitsebsk § RU d.	...	2010
Smolensk a.	...	2319
Smolensk d.	1105	2358
Moskva Beloruss. **1950** a.	|	0549
Bryansk Orlovski a.	1554	...
Bryansk Orlovski d.	1634	...
Lgov a.	2045	...
Kursk a.	2250	...
Voronezh a.	0410	...

1945 VORONEZH - HOMEL - BREST RZhD, BCh

km		*Sko* 75*FJ*	*Pas* 376*SJ* Y	*Pas* 603*BJ*
0	**Voronezh** d.	...	1800	...
**	Moskva Beloruss. d.	1553	|	...
548	Bryansk Orlovski d.	0045	0738	...
776	Zlynka 🏛 RU d.	0507	1224	...
802	Dobrush 🏛 BY d.	0433	1151	...
827	**Homel** a.	0500	1217	...
827	**Homel** d.	0543	...	2201
956	Kalinkavichy d.	0753	...	0024
1133	Luninets d.	1118	...	0329
1361	**Brest** Tsentralny a.	1509	...	0742

	Pas 376*FJ* Z	*Sko* 76*SZ*	*Pas* 604*BJ*
Brest Tsentralny d.	...	1012	1930
Luninets d.	...	1434	0025
Kalinkavichy d.	...	1739	0320
Homel a.	...	1938	0524
Homel d.	1740	2019	...
Dobrush 🏛 BY d.	1810	2049	...
Zlynka 🏛 RU d.	1937	2218	...
Bryansk Orlovski a.	0006	0240	...
Moskva Beloruss. a.	|	1140	...
Voronezh a.	1150	...	...

NOTES FOR TABLES 1935 and 1945:

A – June 26 - Sept. 28. Even dates. Also Aug. 1, Sept. 1; not Aug. 2, Sept. 2.

B – June 24 - Sept. 26. Even dates.

D – DVINA.

Y – Uneven dates [... *31, 2, 5* ...].

Z – Uneven dates [... *31, 3* ...].

** – Moskva - Bryansk: *485 km*.

§ – 🏛: Zavolsha (BY) / Rudnya (RU).

BY – Belarus (GMT+3 hours, all year; see page 2).

RU – Russia (Moskva Time).

1950 MOSKVA - MINSK, VILNIUS, KALININGRAD and BREST RZhD, BCh, LG

km		*Sko* 23*JI* M ♠	*Sko* 21*JA* V ♠	*Sko* 19*JA* J	*Sko* 21*JA* V ✣	*Sko* 23*JI* M ✣	*Pas* 807*BJ*	*Sko* 25*BJ*	*Sko* 115*BJ* ♠	*Sko* 115*BJ* ✣	*Fir* 29*CH* G	*Sko* 27*BJ*	*Sko* 47*AJ* R	*Sko* 9*JA* P ♠	*Sko* 9*JA* P ✣	*Fir* 77*SZ*	*Sko* 5*TJ*	*Sko* 147*CH* F	*Pas* 195*BJ*	*Fir* 55*BJ* X	*Fir* 39*SZ* D
0	**Moskva** Belorusskaya d.	0744	0744	...	0843	0843	...	0951	...	...	1420	1543	...	1650	1720	1708	1855	2144	1939	2119	2144
243	Vyazma d.	1036	1036	...	1136	1136	...	1407	...	...	1744	1915	...	1947	2036	2105	2217	0120	2349	0045	0116
419	Smolensk § RU d.	1223	1223	...	1323	1323	...	1615	...	...	1951	2139	...	2132	2220	2320	0012	0343	0238	0300	0323
	St Peterburg Vitebski ▲ d.	|	|	2359	|	|	...	|	...	...	|	|	0100	|	|	|	|	|	|	|	...
538	Orsha Tsentralnaya § BY a.	1235	1235	1045	1332	1332	...	1640	...	...	2016	2206	1211	2143	2231	2335	0030	0402	0308	0323	...
538	Orsha Tsentralnaya d.	1247	1247	1347	1347	1347	...	1709	...	...	2030	2219	1234	2154	2242	2347	0043	0414	0321	...	...
750	**Minsk** a.	1506	1506	1606	1606	1606	...	1953	...	...	2300	0049	1519	0010	0058	0206	0309	0645	0634	...	...
750	**Minsk** d.	1528	1528	1625	1625	1625	1850	...	2044	2144	2323	0119	1548	0022	0110	0233	0333	0711	0648	...	...
828	Maladzechna ‡ BY d.	|	|	|	|	|	1952	...	|	|	0033	|	|	|	|	0348	0443	0828	|	...	...
956	Lida d.	|	|	|	|	|	|	...	|	|	|	|	|	|	|	0616	|	|	|	...	...
1088	Hrodna a.	|	|	|	|	|	|	...	|	|	|	|	|	|	|	0831	|	|	|	...	...
944	**Vilnius** ‡ LT a.	|	|	|	|	|	2120	...	|	|	0349	|	|	|	|	...	0800	1152	|	...	...
944	**Vilnius** ¶ LT d.	|	|	|	|	|	...	...	|	|	0406	|	|	|	|	...	...	1209	|	...	...
1286	**Kaliningrad** ¶ Ka a.	|	|	|	|	|	...	...	|	|	1129	|	|	|	|	...	...	1940	|	...	...
892	Baranavichy Tsentralnye d.	1709	1709	1807	1807	1807	...	...	2228	2328	...	0303	1830**p**	|	|	...	...	...	0920**p**	...	...
	Lviv **1720** a.	|	|	|	|	|	...	...	|	|	...	|	0448	|	|	...	...	...	|	...	...
1094	**Brest** Tsentralny a.	1901	1901	1958	1958	1958	...	...	0030	0130	...	0530	...	0340	0440	...	...	...	1232	...	...
	Warszawa Wschodnia **1050** a.	2342	...	...	...	2342	...	...	0530	0530	...	...	...	0802	0802	...	...	...	...	...	...

	Fir 1*BJ*	*Fir* 3*BJ* E	*Fir* 7*MJ* R	*Pas* 805*BJ*	*Sko* 131*BJ*	*Sko* 79*CH* L	*Fir* 51*BJ*	*Pas* 803*BJ*	*Fir* 645*BJ*
Moskva Belorusskaya d.	2225	2311	2311	...	2334	...	...	...	...
Vyazma d.	0206	0155	0155	...	0253	...	...	...	...
Smolensk § RU d.	0420	|	|	...	0459	...	...	...	...
St Peterburg Vitebski ▲ d.	|	|	|	...	|	1640	1913	...	...
Orsha Tsentralnaya § BY a.	0443	0343	0343	...	0536	|	0425	...	...
Orsha Tsentralnaya d.	0455	0354	0354	...	0549	|	0448	...	...
Minsk a.	0728	0609	0609	...	0827	|	0714	...	...
Minsk d.	...	...	0623	0740	0846	|	...	1010	1638
Maladzechna ‡ BY d.	...	...	|	0840	|	0555	...	1109	|
Lida d.	...	...	|	|	|	|	...	|	|
Hrodna a.	...	...	|	|	|	|	...	|	|
Vilnius ‡ LT a.	...	...	|	1010	|	0907	...	1257	|
Vilnius ¶ LT d.	...	...	|	...	|	0924	...	...	|
Kaliningrad ¶ Ka a.	...	...	|	...	|	1650	...	...	|
Baranavichy Tsentralnye d.	...	...	0833	...	1035	...	...	...	1820
Lviv **1720** a.	...	...	|	...	|	...	...	...	|
Brest Tsentralny a.	...	...	1046	...	1253	...	...	...	2026
Warszawa Wschodnia **1050** a.	...	...	...	...	...	...	...	...	...

	Sko 132*BJ*	*Sko* 116*BJ* ♠	*Sko* 116*BJ* ✣	*Pas* 804*TJ*	*Fir* 646*BJ*	*Sko* 22*AJ* V ♠
Warszawa Wschodnia **1050** d.	...	2130	2130	...	...	...
Brest Tsentralny d.	0430	0410	0510	...	0630	0840
Lviv **1720** d.	|	|	|	...	|	|
Baranavichy Tsentralnye d.	0656	0630	0730	...	0837	1033
Kaliningrad ¶ Ka d.	|	|	|	...	|	|
Vilnius ¶ LT a.	|	|	|	...	|	|
Vilnius ‡ LT d.	|	|	|	0700	|	|
Hrodna d.	|	|	|	|	|	|
Lida d.	|	|	|	|	|	|
Maladzechna ‡ BY d.	|	|	|	0830	|	|
Minsk a.	0842	0807	0907	0930	1013	1212
Minsk d.	0859	...	...	...	...	1229
Orsha Tsentralnaya a.	1136	...	...	...	...	1458
Orsha Tsentralnaya § BY d.	1151	...	...	...	...	1516
St Peterburg Vitebski ▲ a.	|	...	...	...	...	|
Smolensk § RU d.	1413	...	...	...	...	1732
Vyazma d.	1645	...	...	...	...	1948
Moskva Belorusskaya a.	2021	...	...	...	...	2230

	Sko 48*LJ* E	*Sko* 20*GJ* J	*Sko* 22*AJ* V ✣	*Sko* 24*JI* S ♠	*Sko* 24*JI* S ✣	*Fir* 52*BJ*	*Pas* 808*RJ*	*Fir* 39*BJ* D	*Sko* 26*BJ*	*Sko* 50*BJ*	*Sko* 80*CH* C	*Fir* 4*BJ* R	*Fir* 8*BJ* E	*Fir* 2*BJ*	*Fir* 55*MZ* X	*Pas* 806*RJ*	*Sko* 6*TJ*	*Sko* 28*BJ*	*Fir* 30*CH* Y	*Fir* 78*BJ*	*Sko* 10*ZH* P ♠	*Sko* 10*ZH* P ✣	*Sko* 148*CH* A	*Pas* 196*BJ*
Warszawa Wschodnia **1050** d.	...	...	...	0426	0423	...	...	...	...	...	...	...	...	...	...	...	...	...	...	...	1610	1610	...	...
Brest Tsentralny d.	...	0940	0940	1110	1210	...	...	...	...	1405	...	...	1740	...	...	...	...	1750	...	...	2233	2333	...	2143
Lviv **1720** d.	2312	|	|	|	|	...	...	...	...	|	...	...	|	...	...	...	...	|	...	...	|	|	...	|
Baranavichy Tsentralnye d.	1031**p**	1133	1133	|	|	...	...	...	...	1640	...	...	1939	...	...	...	...	2020	...	...	|	|	...	0115**p**
Kaliningrad ¶ Ka d.	|	|	|	|	|	...	...	...	...	|	1018	...	|	...	...	...	...	|	1314	...	|	|	1656	|
Vilnius ¶ LT a.	|	|	|	|	|	...	...	...	...	|	1542	...	|	...	...	...	...	|	1845	...	|	|	2228	|
Vilnius ‡ LT d.	|	|	|	|	|	...	1458	...	...	|	1559	...	|	...	...	1814	1655	|	1902	...	|	|	2245	|
Hrodna d.	|	|	|	|	|	...	|	...	...	|	|	...	|	...	...	|	|	|	|	1656	|	|	|	|
Lida d.	|	|	|	|	|	...	|	...	...	|	|	...	|	...	...	|	|	|	|	1908	|	|	|	|
Maladzechna ‡ BY d.	|	|	|	|	|	...	1648	...	...	|	1919	...	|	...	...	1944	2032	|	2215	2148	|	|	0200	|
Minsk a.	1230	1314	1314	1436	1536	...	1745	...	...	1828	|	...	2122	...	...	2044	2147	2204	2321	2253	0155	0255	0305	0313
Minsk d.	1243	1329	1329	1454	1554	1741	...	...	1826	1848	|	2145	2145	2130	...	...	2209	2218	2347	2320	0207	0307	0331	0340
Orsha Tsentralnaya a.	1536	1558	1558	1712	1811	2014	...	...	2136	2115	|	0001	0001	2349	...	...	0035	0054	0208	0148	0423	0523	0559	0623
Orsha Tsentralnaya § BY d.	1555	1653	1616	1723	1823	2036	...	...	2149	2138	|	0011	0011	0001	0037	...	0049	0107	0219	0200	0433	0533	0616	0647
St Peterburg Vitebski ▲ a.	0522	0530	|	|	|	0816	...	...	|	0928	1107	|	|	|	|	...	|	|	|	|	|	|	|	|
Smolensk § RU d.	...	...	1832	1939	2039	...	...	2358	0015	...	...	|	|	0232	0259	...	0313	0334	0440	0447	0650	0750	0856	0935
Vyazma d.	...	...	2048	2143	2243	...	...	0235	0244	...	...	0427	0427	0448	0527	...	0535	0555	0639	0719	0855	0955	1148	1232
Moskva Belorusskaya a.	...	...	2320	2358	0058	...	...	0549	0556	...	...	0644	0644	0805	0840	...	0901	0920	0927	1026	1145	1253	1526	1623

A – Daily June 1 - Aug. 31; ②⑤⑦ Sept. 1 - 26; ⑤⑦ Sept. 26 - Dec. 13.

C – ②④⑥⑦ June 1 - Sept 12; ②④⑥ Sept. 13 - Dec. 27 (also Dec. 28, 30, Jan. 2, 4, 6, 8, 9); ②④⑥ Jan. 13 - May 30.

D – DVINA – to / from Polatsk (Table **1935**).

E – Even dates.

F – Daily June 1 - Sept. 1; ①③⑥ Sept. 2 - 27; ③⑥ Sept. 27 - Dec. 13.

G – Even dates (daily June 1 - Sept. 2; Dec. 26 - Jan. 2; also Nov. 1, Feb. 1, Mar. 1, Apr. 1).

H – Even dates [... *30, 1, 4* ...].

J – Conveys (on dates shown in Table 95) 🛏 2 cl. St Peterburg - Praha and Wien and v.v.

L – ①③⑤⑦ June 1 - Sept 13; ③⑤⑦ Sept. 14 - Dec. 28 (also Dec. 29, Jan. 1, 3, 5, 7, 9, 10); ③⑤⑦ Jan. 14 - May 31.

M – TRANSEUROPEAN EXPRESS ①②④⑥⑦ May 31 - Oct. 5; ①④⑦ Oct. 6 - Dec. 13: 🛏 1, 2 cl. Moskva (**23** *JI*) - Brest (**452**) - Berlin - Paris. ✕ (RZD) Moskva - Brest (Table **24**).

P – POLONEZ – 🛏 1, 2 cl., 🍸 Warszawa - Moskva and v.v. ✕ Brest - Moskva and v.v.

R – Uneven dates [... *29, 1* ...].

S – TRANSEUROPEAN EXPRESS ①②③④⑥ June 1 - Oct. 5; ②③⑥ Oct. 6 - Dec. 13: 🛏 1, 2 cl. Paris (**453**) - Berlin - Brest (**24** *JI*) - Moskva. ✕ (RZD) Brest - Moskva (Table **24**).

V – VLTAVA – Conveys (on dates shown in Table **95**) 🛏 1, 2 cl. Moskva - Warszawa - Cheb, Praha and Wien and v.v. ✕ Moskva - Brest.

X – SOZH – To / from Homel (Table **1920**).

Y – Uneven dates (daily June 1 - Sept. 1; Dec. 25 - Jan. 2).

p – Baranavichy Polesskiye.

✣ – Provisional timings for Oct. 26, 2014 - Mar. 28, 2015.

♠ – Mar. 30, 2014 - Oct. 25, 2014.

BY – Belarus (GMT+3 hours, all year; see page 2).

Ka – Kaliningrad region of Russia (Moskva Time).

LT – Lithuania (East European Time).

RU – Russia (Moskva Time).

§ – 🏛: Osinovka (BY) / Krasnoye (RU).

‡ – 🏛: Hudahai (BY) / Kena (LT).

¶ – 🏛: Kybartai (LT) / Nesterov (Ka).

▲ – See Tables **1915** and **1920**.

Other named trains:

1/2 BELORUSSIYA / BELARUS
3/4 MINSK
7/8 SLAVYANSKI EKSPRESS
29/30 YANTAR
77/78 NEMAN / NYOMAN
103/104 SUZORYE
105/106 BUH / BUG

MOSKVA - VORONEZH - ROSTOV NA DONU - SOCHI - ADLER 1960

km		49AJ	43SJ	87GJ	126EI	35AJ	70	4SJ	104MJ	12M	102MJ	30SJ	46VJ	20SJ	382JA	139NJ	305SJ	62CH	26KJ	34SJ	25JA	77CH	29MJ	156M	202MJ
		Sko	Fir	Sko	Sko	Fir	Fir	Fir	Fir	Fir	Fir	Fir	Sko	Fir	Pas	Sko	Pas	Sko	Sko	Sko	Fir	Sko	Fir	Sko	Sko
											C				■(3)				●			■(3)			
		L	J	E	N	Q				§	☆	☆		☆		Y	S							§	G
	St Peterburg Glavny .... d.	1409	1537	...	...	2007	...	...	...	...	...	...	...	...	...	...	...	...	...	...	...	...	...	...	...
	Bologoye .... d.	1838	1931	...	...	0004	...	...	...	...	...	...	...	...	...	...	...	...	...	...	...	...	...	...	...
	Tver .... d.	2014	2117	g	...	0146	...	...	...	...	...	...	...	...	...	...	...	...	...	...	...	...	...	...	...
0	**Moskva** Kazanskaya .... d.	2229r	|	|	0025	|	0810	0820	1010	1020	1330	1340	1520	1838	1438	...	1530r	1950	...	2152	...	...	...	2228	2350
0	**Moskva** Paveletskaya .... d.	|	|	|	|	|	|	|	|	|	|	|	|	|	|	...	|	|	...	|	2114	2104	2142	|	|
198	Ryazan II .... d.	|	0251	0424	0346	0657	1053	1103	1254	1304	1630	1640	1743	2141	1824	...	|	2314	...	0113	|	|	|	0146	0241
408	Michurinsk Uralski .... d.	|	0635	0733	0755	|	|	|	|	|	|	|	|	|	|	...	|	0236	...	0420	|	0616	|	|	|
412	Michurinsk Voronezhski .... d.	|	|	|	|	0952	1316	1331	1521	1531	1921	1931	2001	0015	2133	...	|	|	...	|	0441	|	|	0421	0535
426	Yelets .... d.	0623	|	|	|	|	|	|	|	|	|	|	|	|	|	...	0036	|	...	|	|	|	0549	|	|
504	Lipetsk .... d.	0739	|	|	|	|	|	|	|	|	|	|	|	|	|	...	0200	|	...	|	|	|	0705	|	|
469	Gryazi Voronezhski .... d.	|	0750	0838	0905	1056	1355	|	|	|	|	|	2040	0059	2253	...	|	0343	...	0525	0535	0732	...	0513	0633
588	**Voronezh** I .... d.	|	|	|	|	1258	1530	|	|	|	|	|	2205	|	0110	...	0528	|	...	|	0755	|	...	0757	|
591	**Voronezh** Pridacha .... d.	1107	1017	1042	1118	|	...	1545	1741	1755	2140	2157	...	0246	|	d	|	0548	...	0755	...	1001	...	|	0839
667	Liski .... d.	1240	1136	1207	1231	1445	...	1657	|	1912	2302	2312	...	0347	0310	0449	0712	0732	...	0918	...	1117	...	0947	0957
786	Rossosh .... d.	1504	1400	1419	1445	1722	...	1838	2041	2053	0039	0049	...	0526	0511	0706	0924	0959	...	1136	...	1329	...	1208	1200
1062	Likhaya .... d.	1945	2001	1850	1930	2146	...	2215	|	0016	|	0416	...	0943	1017	1201	1415	1429	k	1627	...	1840	...	1754	1602
1226	**Rostov na Donu** .... a.	2252	2321	2217	2235	0009	...	0028	0207	0230	0608	0624	...	1212	1417	1440	1730	1740	1844	1947	...	2205	...	2048	1917
1226	**Rostov na Donu** .... d.	2314	2341	2235	2257	0024	...	0046	0223	0253	0624	0640	...	...	1506	1520	1831	1814	1907	2019	...	2225	...	2110	1940
1405	Tikhoretskaya .... d.	0213	|	|	|	|	...	|	|	|	|	|	...	...	1750	1820	|	2048	2209	2307	...	0101	...	|	2230
1332	Starominskaya Tim. .... d.	|	0127	2357	0051	|	...	|	|	|	|	|	...	...	|	|	2012	|	|	|	...	u	...	2243	|
1510	**Krasnodar** I .... d.	|	0443	0251	|	0404	...	|	0537	|	|	0957	...	...	|	|	2307	|	|	|	...	...	...	|	|
1645	Novorossiysk .... a.	|	0805	|	0630	|	...	|	|	|	|	1300	...	...	|	|	|	|	|	|	...	...	...	|	|
1636	Anapa .... a.	|	...	|	...	|	...	|	|	1005	|	...	...	...	|	|	|	|	|	|	...	...	...	0510	|
1533	Armavir Rostovski .... d.	0443	...	|	...	|	...	0455	|	...	|	...	...	...	2027	2110t	|	2313	0031	0130	...	...	...	...	0114t
1721	Mineralnye Vody .... d.	0825	...	|	...	|	...	0743	|	...	|	...	...	...	2334	|	|	0238	0344	0437	...	...	...	...	|
1747	Pyatigorsk .... d.	0917	...	|	...	|	...	0820	|	...	|	...	...	...	|	|	|	m	0430	v	...	...	...	...	|
1785	**Kislovodsk** .... a.	1011	...	|	...	|	...	0914	|	...	|	...	...	...	○	|	|	...	0528	...	...	...	...	...	|
2051	Groznyy .... a.	...	...	|	...	|	...	...	|	...	|	...	...	...	0833	|	|	...	...	...	...	...	...	...	|
1658	Tuapse .... d.	...	...	0654	...	0724	...	...	0804	...	1207	...	...	...	...	0332	0304	...	...	...	...	...	...	...	0646
1738	**Sochi** .... a.	...	...	0854	...	0930	...	...	0947	...	1350	...	...	...	...	0541	0508	...	...	...	...	...	...	...	0845
1761	**Adler** .... a.	...	...	0937	...	1014	...	...	1034	...	1426	...	...	...	...	0625	0552	...	...	...	...	...	...	...	0929

	49CH	30JI	102SJ	44SJ	88SJ	36AJ	104SJ	3SJ	69B	77SJ	61SJ	140NJ	33SJ	202MJ	29VJ	25VJ	306SJ	382SJ	19SJ	155S	11	45VJ	126SJ	25SJ	
	Sko	Fir	Fir	Fir	Sko	Fir	Fir	Fir	Fir	Sko	Sko	Sko	Sko	Sko	Fir	Fir	Pas	Pas	Fir	Sko	Fir	Sko	Sko	Sko	
			D							■(1)								■(1)						●(4)	
	M	☆	☆	K	F	R						Z		G			S		☆	§	§		P		
Adler .... d.	...	...	1816	...	1526	1656	2010	...	...	...	...	1440	...	1716	...	...	2045	...	...	...	...	...	...	...	...
Sochi .... d.	...	...	1853	...	1611	1803	2057	...	...	...	...	1528	...	1811	...	...	2132	...	...	...	...	...	...	...	...
Tuapse .... d.	...	...	2048	...	1824	2005	2250	...	...	...	...	1743	...	2015	...	...	2335	...	...	...	...	...	...	...	...
Groznyy .... d.	...	...	|	...	|	|	|	...	...	...	..	|	...	|	...	...	|	1620	...	...	...	...	...	...	...
Kislovodsk .... d.	1346	...	|	...	|	|	|	1939	...	...	...	|	...	|	...	...	|	○	...	...	...	...	...	1121	...
Pyatigorsk .... d.	1443	...	|	...	|	|	|	2037	...	...	m	|	v	|	...	...	|	|	...	...	...	...	...	1219	...
Mineralnye Vody .... d.	1600	...	|	...	|	|	|	2137	...	...	2147	|	2237	|	...	...	|	0138	...	...	...	...	...	1421	...
Armavir Rostovski .... d.	1834	...	|	...	|	|	|	2355	...	...	0008	0018t	0121	0258t	...	...	|	0402	...	...	...	...	...	1709	...
Anapa .... d.	|	...	|	...	|	|	|	|	...	...	|	|	|	|	...	...	|	|	...	0910	1340	...	...	|	...
Novorossiysk .... d.	|	2000	|	1700	|	|	|	|	...	...	|	|	|	|	...	...	|	|	...	|	|	...	1400	|	...
Krasnodar I .... d.	|	2236	|	1957	2155	2314	0113	|	...	...	|	|	|	|	...	...	0355	|	...	|	|	...	|	|	...
Starominskaya Tim. .... d.	|	|	|	0002	0134	|	|	|	...	u	|	|	|	|	...	...	0739	|	...	1529	|	...	1944	|	...
Tikhoretskaya .... d.	2039	|	|	|	|	|	|	0205	...	0150	0226	0245	0338	0522	...	...	|	0629	...	|	|	...	|	1934	...
Rostov na Donu .... a.	2313	0211	0229	0142	0309	0240	0423	0431	...	0439	0500	0515	0622	0744	...	...	0911	0859	...	1652	2024	...	2112	2212	...
Rostov na Donu .... d.	2336	0229	0244	0201	0327	0256	0438	0446	...	0514	0543	0534	0714	0807	...	...	0930	0944	1420	1710	2047	...	2137	2233	...
Likhaya .... d.	0255	0447	|	0532	0635	0610	|	0702	...	0838	1002	0847	1103	1124	...	...	1333	1419	1710	2022	2309	...	0101	k	...
Rossosh .... d.	0736	0811	0821	0937	1125	1100	1014	1024	...	1315	1508	1326	1601	1545	...	...	1802	1926	2101	0046	0235	...	0522	...	...
Liski .... d.	0920	|	1012	1125	1309	1247	|	1205	...	1518	1705	1549	1845	1800	...	...	1941	2210	2236	0230	0424	...	0711	...	...
Voronezh Pridacha .... d.	1128	1059	1114	1232	1424	|	1303	1318	...	1625	1820	b	1951	1925	...	...	|	|	2337	|	0526	...	0822	...	...
Voronezh I .... d.	|	|	|	|	|	1454	|	|	1610	|	|	...	|	|	...	2125	2240	0035	|	0433	|	0732	|	...	...
Gryazi Voronezhski .... d.	|	|	|	1557	1633	1646	|	|	1744	1834	2103	...	2205	2130	...	2320	|	0210	0121	0710	0657	0853	1103	...	...
Lipetsk .... d.	1455	|	|	|	|	|	|	|	|	|	|	...	|	|	2035	|	0057	|	|	|	|	|	|	...	...
Yelets .... d.	1704	|	|	|	|	|	|	|	|	|	|	...	|	|	2233	|	0244	|	|	|	|	|	|	...	...
Michurinsk Voronezhski .... d.	|	1325	1339	|	|	1744	1526	1536	1829	|	|	...	|	2245	|	0039	|	0340	0215	0814	0753	0938	|	...	...
Michurinsk Uralski .... d.	|	|	|	1740	1812	|	|	|	|	2005	2230	...	2357	|	|	|	|	|	|	|	|	|	1259	...	...
Ryazan II .... d.	|	1550	1600	2153	2143	2103	1753	1803	2046	|	0209	...	0316	0143	|	|	|	0751	0444	1139	1027	1154	1642	...	...
Moskva Paveletskaya .... a.	|	|	|	|	|	|	|	|	|	0500	|	...	|	|	0615	0750	|	|	|	|	|	|	|	...	...
Moskva Kazanskaya .... a.	0155r	1831	1838	|	|	|	2035	2055	2330	...	0523	...	0628	0457	...	...	1105r	1052	0735	1510	1400	1417	1937	...	...
Tver .... a.	0435	...	...	0355	h	0219	...	...	...	...	...	...	...	...	...	...	...	...	...	...	...	...	...	...	...
Bologoye .... a.	0627	...	...	0552	...	0355	...	...	...	...	...	...	...	...	...	...	...	...	...	...	...	...	...	...	...
St Peterburg Glavny .... a.	1228	...	...	1007	...	0743	...	...	...	...	...	...	...	...	...	...	...	...	...	...	...	...	...	...	...

SARATOV - ADLER

km		14ZH Sko △		14SJ Sko ▽
0	**Saratov** I .... d.	0947	**Adler** .... d.	1837
429	Volgograd I .... d.	1654	**Sochi** .... d.	1924
964	Tikhoretskaya d.	0238	Tuapse .... d.	2145
1100	**Krasnodar** I .. d.	0522	**Krasnodar** I ... d.	0050
1248	Tuapse .... d.	0915	Tikhoretskaya. d.	0326
1328	**Sochi** .... a.	1145	Volgograd I .... d.	1414
1351	**Adler** .... a.	1229	**Saratov** I .... a.	2045

ROSTOV - BAKI

km		392SJ Pas ◧		391SZ Pas ◧
0	**Rostov na Donu**. d.	1807	**Baki** .... AZ d.	2150
307	Armavir Rostovski d.	2334	Derbent .... d.	0725
495	Mineralnye Vody .. d.	0222	Mahachkala .... d.	1018
773	Gudermes .... d.	0947	Gudermes .... d.	1520
896	Mahachkala .... d.	1407	Mineralnye Vody... d.	0017
1025	Derbent .... a.	1637	Armavir Rostovski d.	0250
1286	**Baki** .... AZ a.	0350	**Rostov na Donu**.. a.	0811

ADLER - SUKHUMI

km		305SJ S		306SJ S
	Moskva .... d.	1530r	**Sukhumi** .... d.	1503
0	**Adler** .... ◐ d.	0622	Gagra .... d.	1727
39	Gagra .... d.	0915	**Adler** .... ◐ a.	2013
112	**Sukhumi** .... a.	1125	*Moskva* .... a.	1105r

SOCHI - ADLER - KRASNAYA POLYANA

6 trains daily from Sochi, 10 from Adler

SOCHI - ADLER - SOCHI AIRPORT ✈

Sochi - Adler - Sochi Airport: 0700, 0800, 0950, 1050, 1230, 1423, 1554, 1802, 1857, 2050, 2206 (also **Adler - Sochi Airport** at 1119, 1225, 1425, 1725, 2031, 2325).
Sochi Airport - Adler - Sochi: 0001, 0800, 0900, 1100, 1300, 1330, 1600, 1750, 1900, 2100, 2200, 2300 (also **Sochi Airport - Adler** at 1000, 1200, 1500, 1700, 2000).
Journey Sochi - Sochi Airport 41 - 43 minutes, Adler - Sochi Airport 10 minutes.

C – June 1 - Oct. 1.
D – June 1 - Oct. 2.
E – June 1 - Oct. 8.
F – June 1 - Oct. 10.
G – Uneven dates ■(3) June 3 - Sept. 21.
J – Uneven dates ■(5) June 1 - Nov. 5.
K – Uneven dates ■(3) June 1 - Nov. 3.
L – Uneven dates ■(3) (daily June 1 - Sept. 7).
M – Uneven dates ■(5) (daily June 1 - Sept. 9).
N – Uneven dates ■(3) (daily June 1 - Oct. 3, Dec. 15 - Jan. 9).
P – Uneven dates (daily June 1 - Sept. 30, Dec. 13 - Jan. 7).
Q – Even dates ● (daily June 1 - Oct. 2).
R – Even dates ●(4) (daily June 1 - Oct. 4).
S – June 1 - Sept. 16 from Moskva; June 3 - Sept. 18 from Sukhumi. Journey 2 nights. For Sukhumi section see panel below main table.
Y – From Novosibirsk even dates June 2 - 20; daily June 22 - Aug. 30. Departs Liski on 4th day.

Z – Even dates June 2 - 24; daily June 26 - Sept. 4.

b – To Novosibirsk (Table **1990**). Via Penza (0309), Saransk (0613).
d – From Novosibirsk (Table **1990**). Via Saransk (1426), Penza (1808).
g – From Nizhni Novgorod (d. 1926) via Vladimir (d. 2250).
h – To Nizhni Novgorod (a. 0718) via Vladimir (a. 0408).
k – From / to Kyiv (Table **1795**).
m – To / from Nalchik (arrive 0550; depart 1745).
r – Moska **Kurskaya**.
t – Armavir **Tuapsinkii**.
u – To / from Stavropol (arrive 0602; depart 2117).
v – To / from Vladikavkaz (arrive 0920; depart 1746).

◐ – ▦ = Veseloe (Russia) / Tsandryphsh (Abkhazia Autonomous Region).
§ – Daily from June 1 (further dates to be advised).
△ – ■(3) (daily June 1 - Oct. 1).
▽ – ●(4) (Daily June 1 - Oct. 2.

☆ – Premium class train.
○ – Calls at Gudermes 0654 southbound, 1811 northbound.
● – Even dates. See page 530.
■ – Uneven dates. See page 530.
◧ – Runs approx every 4 days.
AZ – Azerbaijan (▦ = Yalama).

All dates in footnotes are subject to confirmation

1965 MOSKVA - SARATOV, VOLGOGRAD and BAKI

km ☆		79AJ	1IJ	9GJ	17MJ	15JI	95CH	86VJ	31CH	7CJ	5GJ
		Sko	Fir	Fir	Sko	Sko	Sko	Sko	Fir	Sko	Fir
		G				J	E			●(4)	
	St Peterburg Glavny d.	2020	...	...	...	...	...	...	...	...	...
	Tver d.	0154	...	...	...	...	...	...	...	...	...
0	**Moskva** Paveletskaya d.	0417r	1342	1750	1954	2004	2020r	2110k	2200	2255	2359
198	Ryazan II d.	|	|	|	|	|	△	0043	|	|	|
408	Michurinsk Uralski d.	|	|	0117	0328	|	|	0405	0600	0703	0906
	Michurinsk Voronezhski d.	|	2011	|	|	0356	|	|	|	|	|
426	Yelets d.	1338	|	|	|	|	0530	|	|	|	|
504	Lipetsk d.	1501	|	|	|	|	0807	|	|	|	|
541	Gryazi Voronezhski d.	1625	2138	|	|	0535	0933	|	|	|	|
481	Tambov I d.	|	|	0230	0440	|	|	0529	0720	0813	1027
861	**Saratov** I a.	|	|	0850	1141	|	|	1204	...	1429	1735
778	Povorino d.	2230	0206	...	...	1010	1405	|	...	a	|
1145	**Volgograd** I a.	0458	0825	...	...	1653	2030	|	...	...	|
1595	Astrakhan I a.	...	...	...	...	...	0451	2345	...	...	0610
*2083	Makhachkala a.	...	...	...	...	...	1610	1235	...	...	...
2212	Derbent a.	...	...	...	...	...	1905	...	...	...	...
2473	**Baki** AZ a.	...	...	...	...	...	0600	...	...	...	...

	9ZH	1ZH	17ZH	7RJ	15ZH	5ZH	79ZH	95SZ	85SJ	31VJ
	Fir	Fir	Sko	Sko	Sko	Fir	Sko	Sko	Sko	Fir
				■(1)	K		H	F		
Baki AZ d.	...	...	...	...	...	...	...	0030	...	...
Derbent d.	...	...	...	...	...	...	...	0835	...	...
Makhachkala d.	...	...	...	...	...	...	...	1113	1435	...
Astrakhan I d.	...	...	...	...	...	1445	...	2055	0148	...
Volgograd I d.	...	1514	...	...	1713	|	0107	0525	|	...
Povorino d.	...	2152	...	a	0013	|	0830	1255	|	...
Saratov I d.	1630	|	1903	1933	|	0317	|	|	1350	...
Tambov I d.	2249	|	0153	0214	|	1019	|	|	2035	2115
Gryazi Voronezhski d.	|	0227	|	|	0525	|	1445	1800	|	|
Lipetsk d.	|	|	|	|	|	|	1544	1855	|	|
Yelets d.	|	|	|	|	|	|	1800	2052	|	|
Michurinsk Voronezhski d.	|	0323	|	|	0617	1200	|	|	|	|
Michurinsk Uralski d.	0030	|	0333	0356	|	|	|	|	2240	2306
Ryazan II d.	|	|	|	|	|	|	|	▽	0219	|
Moskva Paveletskaya a.	0720	0958	1029	1038	1400	1910	0259r	0415r	0530k	0624
Tver a.	...	...	...	...	...	...	...	0528	...	...
St Peterburg Glavny a.	...	...	...	...	...	...	...	1254	...	...

E – ②⑤⑥ (train 55CH on ⑥).
F – ②④⑥ (train 55SZ on ④).
G – Even dates (daily June 1 - Sept. 6).
H – Uneven dates (daily June 1 - Sept. 5).
J – Uneven dates ■(3) (daily June 1 - Oct. 5, Dec. 20 - Jan. 10).
K – Even dates (daily June 1 - Oct. 4, Dec. 18 - Jan. 8).
a – To/from Almaty (Table **1975**).
k – Moskva **Kazanskaya**.
r – Moska **Kurskaya**.
* – *1537 km* via Saratov.
● – Even dates. See page 530.
■ – Uneven dates. See page 530.
△ – Via Tula I (2342). ▽ – Via Tula I (0124).
AZ – Azerbaijan (🚆 = Yalama).

1970 MOSKVA - SAMARA - UFA - CHELYABINSK

km		18SZ	55MJ	66JI	122B	32UJ	68JI	40JI	10	14EJ	6FJ	72/84
		Sko	Sko	Sko	Sko	Fir	Fir	Fir	Fir	Fir	Sko	Sko
		B			●	F	■	●			T	A
0	**Moskva** Kaz. d.	0040	1408	1610	1708	1716	1810	1810	2008	2124	2248	2310
197	Ryazan I d.	0347	1722	1944	2026	2036	2106	2106	2300	0041	0202	0231
601	Ruzayevka ⊡ d.	0955	2352	0203	0250	0235	0301	0301	0352	0555	0822	0901
712	Inza d.	1135	0144	0346	0424	|	0435	0435	|	|	1003	|
908	Syzran I d.	1434	0512	0717	0703	0649	0722	0722	0738	0948	1259	1334
1044	**Samara** a.	1710	0800	t	0908	0935	0945	0944	0918	1212	1538	1603
1044	**Samara** d.	1814	...	...	...	1035	...	1024	...	1253	1619	1658
1216	Buzuluk' d.	2135	...	...	...	1410	...	|	...	|	1935	|
1462	Orenburg a.	0138	...	...	...	1830	...	|	...	|	2332	|
1567	**Ufa** a.	...	...	...	...	...	...	1855	...	2113	...	0132
1933	Magnitogorsk a.	...	...	...	...	...	...	...	...	0732x	...	|
2048	**Chelyabinsk** a.	...	...	...	...	...	...	...	...	0617	...	1113

	121	55JI	13UJ	67JI	39JI	9JI	66EI	31UJ	5FJ	71/83	17SZ
	Sko	Sko	Fir	Sko	Fir	Fir	Sko	Fir	Sko	Sko	Sko
	■			●	■			G	T	A	B
Chelyabinsk d.	...	...	1950	...	...	...	...	...	...	0237	...
Magnitogorsk d.	...	...	1809x	...	...	...	...	...	...	|	...
Ufa d.	...	...	0453	...	0800	...	...	...	...	1225	...
Orenburg d.	...	...	|	...	|	...	...	0856	1155	|	1420
Buzuluk' d.	...	...	|	...	|	...	...	1333	1621	|	1826
Samara a.	...	...	1314	...	1601	...	...	1644	1915	2100	2126
Samara d.	1125	1233	1350	1642	1642	1840	t	1723	1954	2145	2205
Syzran I d.	1355	1522	1633	1917	1917	2020	1956	2035	2248	0043	0054
Inza d.	1640	1826	|	|	|	|	2311	|	0150	|	0343
Ruzayevka ⊡ d.	1901	2034	2138	2358	2358	0026	0110	0120	0346	0535	0546
Ryazan I d.	0118	0240	0308	0540	0540	0456	0643	0653	1017	1212	1222
Moskva Kaz. a.	0452	0546	0620	0908	0908	0755	1024	1029	1353	1520	1530

MOSKVA - PENZA, SARANSK, ULYANOVSK

km		22JI	132UJ	52JI	42JI
		Fir	Sko	Fir	Fir
0	**Moskva** Kaz d.	1908	1535	2040	2134
197	Ryazan I d.	2234	1854r	0006r	0051
313	Ryazhsk I d.	|	2033	0143	|
710	**Penza** I d.	|	0508	0755	|
601	Ruzayevka ⊡ d.	0437	n	...	0632
627	**Saransk** I a.	|	...	...	0705
712	Inza d.	0641	...	...	...
873	**Ulyanovsk** a.	0920	...	...	...

	41JI	131UJ	51JI	21JI
	Fir	Sko	Fir	Fir
Ulyanovsk d.	...	...	...	1920
Inza d.	...	...	...	2233
Saransk d.	2040	...	...	|
Ruzayevka ⊡ d.	2125	o	...	0045
Penza I d.	|	1912	2103	|
Ryazhsk I d.	|	0405	0315	|
Ryazan I d.	0258	0556r	0502r	0550
Moskva Kaz a.	0603	0938	0823	0930

PENZA - SAMARA - CHELYABINSK - OMSK

km		134JI	12UJ	
		Sko	Sko	
		v	c	
0	**Penza** I d.	1643	...	...
253	Syzran I d.	2033	...	...
389	**Samara** d.	2355	...	...
912	Ufa d.	0919	...	...
1393	**Chelyabinsk** d.	1853	2110	...
1651	Kurgan d.	2237	0109	...
1918	Petropavl § d.	0313	0546	...
2191	**Omsk** a.	0746	1013	...

	133EI	11UJ	
	Sko	Sko	
	w	d	
Omsk d.	0725	2300	...
Petropavl § d.	1240	0416	...
Kurgan d.	1708	0839	...
Chelyabinsk d.	2132	1226	...
Ufa d.	0732	...	...
Samara d.	1656	...	...
Syzran I d.	1925	...	...
Penza I a.	2315	...	...

A – To/from Astana (for days of running see Table **1975**).
B – To/from Bishkek (for days of running see Table **1975**).
F – Uneven dates (daily June 1 - Sept. 5, Dec. 21 - Jan. 15).
G – Even dates (daily June 1 - Sept. 4, Dec. 20 - Jan. 14).
T – To/from Toshkent (for days of running see Table **1975**).
c – From Chelyabinsk ■(1). To Chita (Table **1990**).
d – From Chita ■(5) (Table **1990**). Depart Omsk on 3rd day.
n – To Samara (a. 1242), Orenburg (a. 2118), Orsk (a. 0350).
o – From Orsk (d. 2040), Orenburg (d. 0310), Samara (d. 1140).
r – Ryazan II.
t – To/from Toliatti (a. 1030/d. 1630).
v – From Penza ■(9). To Vladivostok (Table **1990**).
w – From Vladivostok (Table **1990**). Runs even dates (uneven dates in Aug., Nov., Dec., Feb., Mar.). Depart Omsk on 6th day.
x – Portion detached or attached at Ufa.
⊡ – Also known as Saransk Gorod or Saransk II.
§ – Kazakhstan time (but Moskva time).
● – Even dates. See page 530.
■ – Uneven dates. See page 530.

1975 TRAINS TO KAZAKHSTAN AND BEYOND

km	TOSHKENT	6FJ	18SZ	381EI
		Sko	Sko	Pas
		T	n	②④⑥
0	*Moskva Kaz* ‡ d.	2248	0040	...
1044	**Samara** d.	1619	1814	...
	Ufa d.	|	|	1135
1462	Orenburg d.	0017	0250	2107
1734	Aktobe KA d.	1045	1328	0803
1828	Kandyagash KA d.	1224	1507	0953
2767	Kyzlorda KA d.	0420	0732	0338
3315	**Toshkent** UZ a.	1613	|	1853
3240	Shymkent KA d.	...	1557	...
3720	**Bishkek** II KY a.	...	0230	...

	5FJ	17SZ	381MZ
	Sko	Sko	Pas
	T	u	②④⑦
Bishkek II KY d.	...	1416	...
Shymkent KA d.	...	0441	...
Toshkent UZ d.	1900	|	0021
Kyzlorda KA d.	0959	1345	1810
Kandyagash KA d.	0224	0536	1318
Aktobe KA d.	0404	0716	1504
Orenburg d.	1155	1420	2232
Ufa a.	|	|	0711
Samara a.	1915	2126	...
Moskva Kaz ‡ a.	1353	1530	...

km	ALMATY	7CJ	34T	310KH
		Sko		Pas
		●(4)		
0	*Moskva Pav* § d.	2255	...	...
856	**Saratov** d.	1506	...	...
1291	Oral/Uralsk KA d.	0420	...	...
1750	**Aktobe** KA d.	1458	2246	0058
1844	Kandyagash KA d.	1651	0020	0323
2940	**Aktau** ⊙ KA a.	|	|	0555*
2783	Kyzlorda KA d.	0823	1633	...
3256	Shymkent KA d.	1712	0239	...
4008	**Almaty** I KA a.	0634	1533	...
4017	**Almaty** II KA a.	0708	1559	...

	309KH	7RJ	33
	Pas	Sko	
		■(1)	
Almaty II KA d.	...	0625	2133
Almaty I KA d.	...	0652	2202
Shymkent KA d.	...	2101	1135
Kyzlorda KA d.	...	0621	2122
Aktau ⊙ KA d.	1420	|	|
Kandyagash KA d.	1710*	2132	1343
Aktobe KA d.	1854	2342	1508
Oral/Uralsk KA d.	...	1010	...
Saratov a.	...	1854	...
Moskva Pav § a.	...	1038	...

km	ASTANA	90UJ	84CJ	72CJ	304CJ	306SZ	316
		Fir	Sko	Sko	Pas	Pas	Pas
		■(3)	B	■(3)	③⑤	④⑦	①
0	*Moskva Kaz* ‡ d.	1848	2310	2310	...	...	...
1044	**Samara** d.	|	1658	1658	...	...	...
2048	Chelyabinsk d.	▽	1148	1200	...	...	...
	Yekaterinburg d.	2158*	|	|	1754	1754	1754
2306	Kurgan d.	0440	1526	△	0152	0152	0152
2573	Petropavl KA d.	0945	2056	|	0811	0811	0811
3064	**Astana** KA a.	...	0705	1053	1927	1852	1852
3064	**Astana** KA d.	...	0735	...	1959	1922	1922
3305	Karagandy KA d.	...	1125	...	0022	0021	0021
4407	**Almaty** II KA a.	...	...	...	2049	|	|
4356	Bishkek II KY a.	...	...	...	...	2057	|
4522	Shymkent KA d.	...	...	...	...	...	0052*
4755	**Toshkent** UZ a.	...	...	...	...	...	0810

	89UJ	71CJ	83CJ	316	305SZ	303CJ
	Fir	Sko	Sko	Pas	Pas	Pas
	■(1)	■(1)	C	⑥	②⑤	①③
Toshkent UZ d.	...	...	...	0215	...	...
Shymkent KA d.	...	...	...	1201	...	...
Bishkek II KY d.	...	...	...	|	1115	...
Almaty II KA d.	...	...	...	|	|	1341
Karagandy KA d.	...	...	0650	1249*	1249*	1249
Astana KA a.	...	...	1025	1650	1650	1650
Astana KA d.	...	0810	1055	1722	1722	1722
Petropavl KA d.	1335	|	1805	0142	0142	0142
Kurgan d.	1859	△	2247	0800	0800	0800
Yekaterinburg a.	0059	|	|	1520	1520	1520
Chelyabinsk d.	▽	0237	0237	...	...	...
Samara a.	|	2100	2100	...	...	...
Moskva Kaz ‡ a.	0502*	1520	1520	...	...	...

km	DUSHANBE	320EI 330
		①③⑥
0	**Moskva** Kaz. d.	1216
198	Ryazan II d.	1536
409	Michurinsk Vor d.	1835
1073	**Volgograd** d.	1222
1802	Atyrau KA d.	0745
1932	Makat KA d.	1025
2639	Kungrad UZ d.	0325
3190	Uckuduk II UZ d.	1408
3467	Navoi UZ d.	1921
3712	Karshi UZ d.	2345
4044	Termez UZ d.	|
4269	**Dushanbe** I TA a.	1918

	319ZJ 329
	②④⑥
Dushanbe I TA d.	0332
Termez UZ d.	|
Karshi UZ d.	2152
Navoi UZ d.	0137
Uckuduk II UZ d.	0622
Kungrad UZ d.	1520
Makat KA d.	0806
Atyrau KA d.	1050
Volgograd d.	0256
Michurinsk Vor d.	1658
Ryazan II d.	2031
Moskva Kaz a.	0001

B – Even dates ●(4) June 2 - Aug. 30.
C – Even dates ● June 2 - Aug. 30.
T – ②③④⑥ from Moskva, ①③⑥⑦ from Toshkent.
b – Every 4 days (**369**/**389** runs on ■ to Almaty).
d – Every 4 days (**369**/**385** runs on ■ from Almaty).
n – ②⑤⑦ (arrive Bishkek on 4th day).
u – ①③⑤ (arrive Moskva on 4th day).
⊙ – Mangyshlak station (12 km from Aktau).
* – More than 24 hours after previous time shown.
▽ – Via Kazan (Table **1990**).
△ – Via Kostanay.
● – Even dates. See page 530.
■ – Uneven dates. See page 530.
§ – See Table **1965**.
‡ – See Table **1970**.
KA – Kazakhstan (GMT+6).
KY – Kyrgyzstan (GMT+6).
TA – Tajikistan (GMT+5).
UZ – Uzbekistan (GMT+5).

VIA AKTOGAY	369	389	301	325
	b	b	●	●
Novosibirsk d.	1051	1051	1402	1402
Barnaul a.	1652	1652	2014	2014
Aktogay KA d.	1645	1645	1940	1940
Almaty I KA a.	0414	0414	0738	0738
Almaty II KA a.	|	|	0841	...
Bishkek II KY a.	|	1644	...	...
Shymkent KA a.	1940	...	...	...
Toshkent UZ a.	0333	...	...	...

	326	302	369	385
	■	●	d	d
Toshkent UZ d.	...	...	1512	...
Shymkent KA d.	...	...	0117	...
Bishkek II KY d.	...	...	|	2317
Almaty II KA d.	...	1600	|	|
Almaty I KA d.	1525	1652	1652	1652
Aktogay KA d.	0230	0444	0444	0444
Barnaul d.	2235	0030	0030	0030
Novosibirsk a.	0338	0558	0558	0558

OTHER SERVICES TO BAKI AND ASTANA 1977

TYUMEN - BAKI

km		373 Pas ●		373 Pas ●
0	Tyumen d.	1741	**Baki** AZ d.	0550
326	**Yekaterinburg** a.	2306	Derbent d.	1340
326	**Yekaterinburg** d.	2356	Mahachkala d.	1635
578	Chelyabinsk d.	0805	Astrakhan d.	0301
1059	Ufa d.	1748	**Saratov** I a.	1502
1582	**Samara** d.	0312	**Saratov** I d.	1557
2019	**Saratov** I a.	1212	**Samara** d.	0135
2019	**Saratov** I d.	1300	Ufa d.	1054
2695	Astrakhan d.	0139	Chelyabinsk d.	2043
3183	Mahachkala d.	1143	**Yekaterinburg** a.	0256
3312	Derbent d.	1420	**Yekaterinburg** d.	0345
3573	**Baki** AZ a.	0055	Tyumen a.	0901

KHARKIV - BAKI

km		369OJ Pas ◧		369SZ Pas ◧
0	**Kharkiv** d.	0522	**Baki** AZ d.	2150
388	Uspenskaya 🏛 a.	1353	Derbent a.	0655
388	Uspenskaya 🏛 d.	1453	Derbent d.	0725
520	**Rostov n. D.** a.	1710	Mahachkala d.	1018
520	**Rostov n. D.** d.	1807	Gudermes d.	1520
827	Armavir Rost. d.	2334	Mineral. Vody d.	0017
1015	Mineral. Vody d.	0222	Armavir Rost. d.	0250
1293	Gudermes d.	0947	**Rostov n. D.** a.	0811
1416	Mahachkala d.	1407	**Rostov n. D.** d.	0916
1545	Derbent a.	1637	Uspenskaya 🏛 a.	1117
1545	Derbent d.	1858	Uspenskaya 🏛 d.	1217
1806	**Baki** AZ a.	0350	**Kharkiv** a.	1850

KIEV - SARATOV - ASTANA

km		108KJ Sko ④		107CJ Sko ①
0	**Kyïv** d.	1730	**Astana** KA d.	1741
150	Hrebinka d.	1955	Orsk d.	1027
335	Poltava Kyïvska. d.	2311	Orenburg d.	1552
489	**Kharkiv** d.	0223	Oral / Uralsk d.	0146
618	Kupiansk UA d.	0456	**Saratov** I d.	1101
857	Liski RU d.	1140	Povorino d.	1840
1082	Povorino d.	1528	Liski RU d.	2233
1462	**Saratov** I d.	2316	Kupiansk UA d.	0754
1897	Oral / Uralsk d.	1210	**Kharkiv** a.	0728
2238	Orenburg d.	1832	Poltava Kyïvska. a.	1036
2569	Orsk d.	2330	Hrebinka a.	1400
3644	**Astana** KA a.	2100	**Kyiv** a.	1556

◧ – Runs approx every 4 days. ● – Even dates. AZ – Azerbaijan (🏛 Yalama). KA – Kazakhstan (GMT + 6). RU – Russia (Moskva time). UA – Ukraine (East European Time).

GEORGIA 1979

GMT + 4. *Subject to alteration*

km		870	872	18	24	852	878	874	858	644	602	622
0	**Tbilisi** d.	0735	0820	0900	0900	1100	1525	1750	1815	2110	2110	2245
221	Kutaisi a.	|	|	1417	|	|	1925	|	|	0250	|	|
317	Zugdidi a.	1330	|	...	1725	|	...	|	|	...	0625	|
312	Poti a.	...	1345	...	...	|	...	2317	|	...	...	|
342	**Maxinjauri** § a.	...	...	...	...	1625	...	...	2339	...	...	0655

	877	873	857	23	17	871	869	851	601	643	621
Maxinjauri § d.	...	...	0755	...	...	...	...	1800	...	...	2210
Poti d.	...	0800	|	...	...	1740	...	|	...	...	|
Zugdidi d.	...	|	|	0955	...	|	1745	|	2130	...	|
Kutaisi d.	0730	|	|	|	1225	|	|	|	|	0020	|
Tbilisi a.	1130	1310	1322	1800	1800	2255	2325	2340	0635	0635	0700

km		37 🛏		38 🛏
0	Tbilisi d.	1630r	Baki AZ d.	2030
551	Baki AZ a.	0910	Tbilisi a.	1045r

km	🛏	372 W	202 S	🛏	201 S	371 Y
	Maxinjauri § d.	...	1525	Yerevan AR d.	1515	2130
0	Tbilisi d.	2020	2216	Tbilisi a.	0012	0750
374	Yerevan AR a.	0655	0735	Maxinjauri § a.	0725	...

S – Summer: mid June - late Sept.
W – ■(3) late Sept to mid June.
Y – ● late Sept. to mid June.
r – One hour later in winter.
§ – Station for Batumi.
AR – Armenia (GMT + 4).
AZ – Azerbaijan (GMT + 4 winter, + 5 summer).
● ■ See page 530.

KAZAKHSTAN and UZBEKISTAN 1980

KA	4	2	10	87 ■	80 ●
Astana d.	1325	1849	2218	2305	2350
Aktobe a.	|	|	|	1544	|
Karagandy d.	1706	2122	0155	...	0223
Almaty I a.	0755	|	1706	...	|
Almaty II a.	0831	0730	...	...	|
Shymkent a.	...	...	...	...	1525

KA	1	80 ■	3	88 ■	9
Shymkent d.	...	1655	...	...	...
Almaty II d.	1940	|	1259	...	...
Almaty I d.	|	|	1329	...	2110
Karagandy d.	0602	0633	0514	...	1225
Aktobe d.	|	|	|	2054	|
Astana a.	0825	0856	0940	1340	1542

KA	47 ●	37 ■
Astana d.	1140	1140
Kandyagash d.	1144*	1144*
Atyrau a.	2130	|
Aktau ⊙ a.	...	0810

KA	47 ●	37 ■
Aktau ⊙ d.	...	0915
Atyrau d.	2000	|
Kandyagash d.	0630	0630
Astana a.	0615	0615

UZ	160 ‡ ⑥⑦	162 ‡	10	56/58	662
Toshkent d.	0700	0800	0830	1930	2110
Samarkand a.	0908	1008	1157	2345	0138
Bukhara I a.	...	...	1528	...	0712

UZ	55/57	9	161 ‡	159 ‡ ⑥⑦	661
Bukhara I d.	...	0840	...	...	2040
Samarkand d.	0540	1203	1700	1800	0211
Toshkent a.	1028	1531	1910	2010	0630

⊙ – Mangyshlak station (12 km from Aktau).
‡ – AFROSIYOB – high-speed Talgo train.
* – More than 24 hours after previous time.
● – Even dates. ■ – Uneven dates.
KA – Kazakhstan (GMT + 6).
UZ – Uzbekistan (GMT + 5).

MOSKVA - ARCHANGELSK, LABYTNANGI and VORKUTA 1985

km		16JA Sko	388AJ Pas ■(5) △	34JA Sko v	224CH Sko ◧	10 Fir E	318MJ Pas ■	22JA Fir B	42VJ Sko	653SJ Pas	90GJ Sko ● n
0	**Moskva** Yarolslavsk d.	1005	...	1335	1335	...	1950	2035	2150	...	...
282	Yaroslavl d.	1452	...	1812	1812	...	0021	0048	0154	...	...
	St Peterburg Lad. ▷ d.	|	0950	|	|	1454	|	|	|	...	...
496	Vologda I ▷ d.	1909	|	2223	2223	|	0435	0510	0611	...	...
707	Konosha I d.	2223	0115	0130	0130	0503	0802	0828	0934	...	...
1134	**Archangelsk** a.	0632	|	|	|	1356	1821	|	|	...	...
825	Velsk d.	...	0345	0402	0402	...	...	1025	1130	...	...
1084	**Kotlas** Uzlovoy d.	...	0855	0831	0831	...	...	1434	1531	...	0855z
1325	Mikun d.	...	1437	1305	1345	...	...	1919	2033	...	1314
1412	Syktyvkar a.	...	1845x	1445	|	...	...	|	|	...	|
1571	Sosnogorsk d.	...	1949	...	1837	...	...	2359	0133	...	1806
2406	Labytnangi a.	...	|	...	...	...	...	1640	|	1045	|
2277	**Vorkuta** a.	...	1010	...	...	...	...	...	1403	2045	0840

	317MJ Pas ■(2)	223 Sko ◧	34M Sko v	41MJ Sko	15JA Sko	387JA Pas ■(3) △	9C Fir E	21NJ Fir C	653JA 653MJ	89GJ Sko ●(4) u
Vorkuta d.	...	...	...	1630	...	2053	...	...	0935	1320
Labytnangi d.	...	...	...	|	...	|	...	0750	2014	|
Sosnogorsk d.	...	0500	...	0559	...	1149	...	0057	...	0323
Syktyvkar d.	...	|	0745	|	...	0840x	...	|	...	|
Mikun d.	...	1007	1007	1101	...	1654	...	0532	...	0828
Kotlas Uzlovoy d.	...	1415	1415	1600	...	2223	...	1037	...	1247z
Velsk d.	...	1853	1853	2014	...	0346	...	1459	...	...
Archangelsk d.	0715	|	|	|	2008	|	2043	|	...	...
Konosha I d.	1810	2142	2142	2227	0435	0632	0612	1708	...	...
Vologda I ▷ d.	2153	0050	0050	0135	0800	|	|	2023	...	...
St Peterburg Lad ▷ a.	|	|	|	|	|	2152	2115	|	...	...
Yaroslavl d.	0221	0512	0512	0543	1213	...	...	0057	...	...
Moskva Yarolslavsk a.	0623	0912	0912	0958	1643	...	...	0446	...	...

B – ②⑤ (daily June 1 - Sept. 30). *Sko* number **210***CH* on certain dates.
C – ①⑤ (daily June 1 - Oct. 3). *Sko* number **209***MJ* on certain dates.
E – ①②④⑤ from St P'burg; ②③⑤⑥ from Archangelsk (daily July/Aug).
n – June 2 - Sept. 20. From Nizhni Novgorod (d. 1610), Kirov (d. 2352).
u – June 2 - Sept. 22. To Kirov (a. 2050), Nizhni Novgorod (a. 0415).
v – On certain dates is *Fir* numbered **224***CH* (**228** from Syktyvkar).
x – Carriage detaches / attaches at Mikun.
z – Kotlas **Yuzhny**.

△ – Dates vary in Oct., Feb - Apr.
▷ – See also Table **1990**.
● – Even dates. See page 530.
■ – Uneven dates. See page 530.
◧ – Runs 4 - 5 times per week.
‡ – Winter dates are subject to confirmation.

km		● ‡		■ ‡
0	**Murmansk** .. **1905** d.	1707	**Archangelsk** d.	2149
277	Kandalaksha **1905** d.	2343	Belomorsk **1905** d.	1222
665	Belomorsk **1905** d.	0834	Kandalaksha **1905** d.	2105
1151	**Archangelsk** a.	2322	**Murmansk** **1905** a.	0350

373*JA* / **672***JA* from Murmansk; **671***JA* / **374***JA* from Archangelsk.

NOVOSIBIRSK - SEVEROBAIKALSK - TYNDA - NERYUNGRI - TOMMOT 1989

km	*Baikal - Amur Magistrale (BAM)*	87IJ 348Y ●	348Y ●	71IJ Sko ■(3)		92IJ Sko n	76EI Sko ■(7) n	324	78EI Sko ■	
	Moskva Yar. **1990** d.	...	...	...	...	1245	1310r	...	...	...
0	**Novosibirsk** ▷ d.	...	...	...	...	1529	1504	...	2004	...
762	Krasnoyarsk ▷ d.	...	1800	...	...	0433	0318	...	0847	...
	Ulan Ude ▷ d.	...	|	1112	...	|	|	...	|	...
	Irkutsk ▷ d.	1338	|	1853	...	|	|	...	|	...
180	**Tayshet** a.	0133	0155	0600	...	1140	1012	...	1537	...
180	**Tayshet** d.	0248	0400	0630	...	1210	1052	...	1554	...
473	Bratsk d.	1023	1318	1318	...	1852	1653	...	|	...
2243	**Severobaikalsk** d.	0513	0513	0513	...	0823	0816	...	▽	...
972	Skovorodino d.	...	...	...	...	...	|	...	2216x	...
528	**Tynda** a.	...	...	...	...	...	1022*	...	0311	...
	Tynda d.	...	...	...	...	...	1152	...	0411	...
757	Neryungri d.	...	...	...	...	...	1715	0156	0932	...
125	Tommot a.	...	...	...	...	...	...	0945	...	...
493	**Yakutsk** ⊕ a.	...	...	...	...	...	...	...	...	...

	323	91IJ Sko s	75EI Sko ■(1) u	77EI Sko ■(3)		71Y Sko ■(3)	347Y 87Y ●(4)	347Y ●(4)	
Yakutsk ⊕ d.	...	...	...	...	...	...	...	...	...
Tommot d.	1306	...	...	...	...	...	...	...	...
Neryungri d.	2117	...	2302	0210	...	...	...	...	...
Tynda a.	...	...	0517	0721	...	...	...	...	...
Tynda d.	...	...	0656	0821	...	...	...	...	...
Skovorodino d.	...	...	|	1312	...	...	...	...	...
Severobaikalsk d.	...	0831	1121*	▽	...	1705	1705	1705	...
Bratsk d.	...	2230	0048	|	...	0744	0829	0829	...
Tayshet a.	...	0521	0656	1741z	...	1337	1825	1849	...
Tayshet d.	...	0551	0741	1743z	...	1415	1945	2014	...
Irkutsk ▷ a.	...	|	|	|	...	0126	0656	|	...
Ulan Ude ▷ a.	...	|	|	|	...	0912	...	|	...
Krasnoyarsk ▷ a.	...	1234	1415	0018	...	...	...	0343	...
Novosibirsk ▷ a.	...	0131	0255	1251	...	...	...	...	...
Moskva Yar. **1990** a.	...	0345	0442r	...	...	...	...	...	...

– Novosibirsk on 3rd day, Severobaikalsk on 5th day.
– Moskva Kazanskaya.
– Novosibirsk 3rd day, Moskva 5th day.
– Novosibirsk 5th day, Moskva 7th day.
– 4th day.
– 3rd day.
– Following day (more than 24 hours after previous time shown).

● – Even dates. See page 530.
■ – Uneven dates. See page 530.
▽ – Via Irkutsk (Table **1990**).
▷ – See also Table **1990**.
∆ – *4182* via Skovorodino.
⊕ – Under construction.

km		364	667		667	363
0	**Tynda** d.	1120	...	**Khabarovsk** d.	1415	...
951	Novy Urgal d.	1045	...	Komsomolsk d.	2350	1145
1469	Komsomolsk d.	2330	1400	Novy Urgal d.	...	0126
1857	**Khabarovsk** a.	...	2334	**Tynda** a.	...	0025

1990 MOSKVA - YEKATERINBURG - NOVOSIBIRSK - IRKUTSK - VLADIVOSTOK

km	*TransSiberian Railway*	14*AJ*	74*EJ*	140*NJ*	44*EI*	100*EI*	59*A*	64*BJ*	104	702*H*	732*H*	92*IJ*	76*EI*	82	118*EJ*	138	6*EI*	134*JI*	12*UJ*	78*EI*	70*CH*	2*MJ*	8*NJ*	84*MJ*	50*EJ*
		Fir	*Fir*	*Sko*	*Sko*	*Sko*	*Fir*	*Sko*	*Sko*	♥	❦	*Sko*	*Sko*	*Sko*	*Sko*	*Sko*	*Fir*	*Sko*	*Sko*	*Sko*	*Sko*	*Fir*	*Sko*	*Fir*	*Fir*
		●(6)	■(7)		■(9)	●(9)							■(7)	●(8)	■(5)	●(6)		■(9)	■(1)	■					
		V		Q		◇	d	C	D													MR	N	M	N
0	**Moskva** Yaroslavskaya ......d.	...	...	...	0035	0035	...	...	...	...	...	1245	...	...	...	...	...	...	...	...	1305	1350	...	1405	1405
	Moskva Kazanskaya..........d.	...	...	...	|	|	0200**k**	0335**r**	0335**r**	0645**k**	1100**k**	|	1310	1310	1320	1320	...	...	...	...	|	|	...	|	|
	Yaroslavl ....d.	...	...	...	0446	0446	|	|	|	|	|	|	|	|	|	|	...	...	...	...	1742	|	...	|	|
210	Vladimir...........................d.	...	...	...	|	|	0438	0650	0650	0832	1247	1609	|	|	|	|	...	...	...	...	|	1705	...	1716	1716
461	**Nizhni Novgorod** ⊡..........d.	...	...	...	|	|	0736	1120	1120	1040	1500	1931	|	|	|	|	...	...	...	...	|	2006	...	2014	2014
	St Peterburg Ladozhski .d.	1530	1530	...	|	|	...	|	|	...	...	|	|	|	|	|	...	...	...	...	|	|	...	|	|
	Vologda I.........................d.	0238	0238	...	|	|	...	|	|	...	...	|	|	|	|	|	...	...	...	...	|	|	...	|	|
917	**Kirov** ⊖...........................d.	1243	1243	...	1840	1840	...	1850	1850	...	...	0150	|	|	|	|	...	...	...	...	0605	0205	...	0215	0215
1397	Perm II.............................d.	2056	2056	...	0331	0331	...	0341	0341	...	...	0945	|	|	|	|	...	...	...	...	1411	0955	...	1032	1032
	Murom I............................d.	|	|	...	|	|	...	|	|	...	...	|	1749	1749	1800	1800	...	...	...	...	|	|	...	y	w
	Kazan ....d.	|	|	...	|	|	...	|	|	...	...	|	0200	0200	0210	0210	...	...	...	...	|	|	...	...	...
	Sarapul.............................d.	|	|	a	|	|	...	|	|	...	...	|	0759	0759	0809	0809	...	...	...	...	|	|	...	...	...
1778	**Yekaterinburg** ⊙ ....a.	0211	0211	0601	0913	0913	...	0922	0922	...	...	1503	1611	1611	1601	1601	...	...	...	...	1954	1511	...	...	...
1778	**Yekaterinburg** ⊙ ....d.	0238	0238	0628	1009	1009	...	1017	1017	...	...	1531	1701	1701	1643	1643	...	...	...	...	2021	1539	...	...	...
2104	Tyumen ....d.	0732	0701	1242	1548	1548	...	1558	1558	...	...	2024	2213	2213	2222	2222	...	h	c	...	0305	2014	...	...	...
2676	**Omsk** ....a.	1630	...	2044	2331	2331	...	0012	0012	...	...	0607	0538	0538	0617	0617	...	0746	1013	...	1150	0314	...	...	...
2676	**Omsk** ....d.	1704	...	2120	0003	0003	...	0047	0047	...	...	0640	0559	0559	0652	0652	...	0820	1029	...	1210	0330	...	...	...
3303	**Novosibirsk** ....a.	0048	...	0637	0832	0832	...	0844	0844	...	...	1440	1410	1410	1702	1500	...	1545	1908	...	1944	1113	...	...	...
3303	**Novosibirsk** ....d.	0137	...	...	0929	0929	...	...	...	...	...	1529	1504	1504	1752	1519	...	1604	2004	2004	2038	1132	1132	...	...
3532	Tayga ....d.	o	...	...	1327	1327	...	...	...	...	...	1926	1833	1833	o	1844	...	2049	0006	0006	0020	1448	1448	...	...
4065	**Krasnoyarsk** ....d.	...	...	...	2204	2204	...	...	...	...	...	0433	0318	0318	...	0330	...	0625	0847	0847	0917	2303	2303	...	...
4483	Tayshet.............................d.	...	...	...	0505	0505	...	...	...	...	...	1210	1052	1015	...	...	...	1321	1554	1554	1632	0541	0541	...	...
5152	**Irkutsk**.............................a.	...	...	...	1622	1622	...	...	...	...	...	x	u	2128	...	...	...	0029	0308	0308	0328	1557	1557	...	...
5152	**Irkutsk**.............................d.	...	...	...	1652	1652	...	...	...	...	...	...	...	2208	...	...	...	0059	0335	0335	0403	1620	1620	...	...
5608	Ulan Ude ....d.	...	...	...	0135	0135	...	...	...	...	...	...	...	0614	...	...	...	0924	1159	1159	1245	2318	2318	...	...
6165	Chita II..............................d.	...	...	...	1232	1232	...	...	...	...	...	...	...	...	...	...	...	2105	2336	0012	0023	0921	0921	...	...
7274	Skovorodino......................d.	...	...	...	1028	1028	...	...	...	...	...	...	...	...	...	...	...	1852	...	2216	...	0544	0544	...	...
8492	**Khabarovsk** ....d.	...	...	...	0655	0749	...	...	...	...	...	...	...	...	...	...	1410	1543	...	u	...	0125	0125	...	...
9147	Ussuriysk..........................d.	...	...	...	...	1816	...	...	...	...	...	...	...	...	...	...	2312	0124	...	...	...	1046	1046	...	...
9258	**Vladivostok**.......................a.	...	...	...	...	2013	...	...	...	...	...	...	...	...	...	...	0110	0320	...	...	...	1240	1240	...	...

local time ★		734*H*	736*H*	41*G*	56*Y*	16*EJ*	60*UJ*	8*JA*	12*JA*	90*UJ*	50*MJ*	704*H*	96*NJ*	32*GJ*	2*JI*	110*EI*	30*NJ*	38*NJ*	68*Y*	4*ZJ*	6	20*SZ*	36	98	140
		❦	❦	*Sko*	*Fir*	*Fir*	*Fir*	*Fir*	*Fir*	*Fir*	*Sko*	♥	*Sko*	*Fir*	*Fir*	*Sko*	*Fir*	*Fir*	*Sko*	*Sko*	*Sko*	*Sko*	*Fir*	*Fir*	*Fir*
					■(5)	☆				■(3)							■(7)	●(6)		②	③④	⑥			
						N	M	M	N				▽		☆		U	U		B‡	A‡	P‡			
	Moskva Yaroslavskaya ......d.	...	...	...	1620	...	...	1650	1650	...	...	...	...	2005	...	2235	2250	2250	2305	2345	2345	2345	2355	...	...
	Moskva Kazanskaya..........d.	1415**k**	1645**k**	...	|	1650	1650	|	|	1848	1920	1930**k**	1939	|	2208	|	|	|	|	|	|	|	|	0015	0140**k**
	Yaroslavl ....d.	|	|	...	|	|	|	|	|	|	|	|	|	|	|	|	|	|	0333	|	|	|	|	|	|
	Vladimir...........................d.	1602	1832	...	1949	|	|	1959	1959	|	|	2117	|	2317	|	0150	0200	0200	|	0253	0253	0253	0303	|	0428
	Nizhni Novgorod ⊡..........d.	1815	2045	2125	2245	|	|	2255	2255	|	|	2325	|	0217	|	0452	0502	0502	|	0548	0548	0548	0619	|	0752
	St Peterburg Ladozhski .d.	...	...	|	|	|	|	|	|	|	|	...	|	|	|	|	|	|	|	|	|	|	...	|	...
	Vologda I.........................d.	...	...	|	|	|	|	|	|	|	|	...	|	|	|	|	|	|	|	|	|	|	...	|	...
	Kirov ⊖...........................d.	...	...	|	0535	|	|	0545	0545	|	|	...	|	0833	|	1148	1203	1203	1422	1233	1233	1233	...	|	...
+2	Perm II.............................d.	...	...	|	1334	|	|	1321	1344	|	|	...	|	...	|	2007	1957	1957	2213	2017	2017	2017	...	|	...
	Murom I............................d.	...	...	|	|	2115	2115	...	|	0014	0030	...	0043	...	|	|	|	|	|	|	|	|	...	0515	...
	Kazan ....d.	...	...	0617	|	0504	0504	...	|	0743	0815	...	0806	...	0927	|	|	|	|	|	|	|	...	1333	...
	Sarapul.............................d.	...	...	...	|	1051	1051	...	|	1332	...	...	1343	...	...	|	|	|	|	|	|	|	...	...	...
+2	**Yekaterinburg** ⊙ ....a.	...	...	...	1859	1809	1809	...	1922	2131	...	...	2243	...	...	0122	0113	0113	0328	0132	0132	0132	...	...	...
+2	**Yekaterinburg** ⊙ ....d.	...	...	...	1930	...	1908	...	2010	2158	...	...	2314	...	...	0149	0140	0140	0358	0159	0159	0159	...	...	...
+2	Tyumen ....d.	...	...	...	0042	...	0218	...	0235	p	...	...	0442	...	...	0751	0742	0742	1008	0638	0638	0638	...	...	...
+3	**Omsk** ....a.	...	...	...	0758	...	n	...	t	...	...	...	1227	...	...	s	1555	1555	1837	1337	1337	1337	...	...	...
+3	**Omsk** ....d.	...	...	...	0835	...	...	...	...	...	...	...	1258	...	...	...	1611	1611	1857	1353	1353	1353	...	...	...
+3	**Novosibirsk** ....a.	...	...	...	1555	...	...	...	...	...	...	...	b	...	...	...	2347	2347	0211	2104	2104	2104	...	...	...
+3	**Novosibirsk** ....d.	...	...	...	1644	...	...	...	...	...	...	...	...	...	...	...	0036	0036	0300	2123	2123	2123	...	...	...
+3	Tayga ....d.	...	...	...	2020	...	...	...	...	...	...	...	...	...	...	...	m	0429	0640	0059	0059	0059	...	...	...
+4	**Krasnoyarsk** ....d.	...	...	...	0440	...	...	...	...	...	...	...	...	...	...	...	...	z	q	0907	0907	0907	...	...	...
+5	Tayshet.............................d.	...	...	...	...	...	...	...	...	...	...	...	...	...	...	...	...	...	...	|	|	|	...	...	...
+5	**Irkutsk**.............................a.	...	...	...	...	...	...	...	...	...	...	...	...	...	...	...	...	...	...	0228	0228	0228	...	...	...
+5	**Irkutsk**.............................d.	...	...	...	...	...	...	...	...	...	...	...	...	...	...	...	...	...	...	0253	0253	0253	...	...	...
+5	Ulan Ude ....d.	...	...	...	...	...	...	...	...	...	...	...	...	...	...	...	...	...	...	1052	1052	1122	...	...	...
+6	Chita II..............................d.	...	...	...	...	...	...	...	...	...	...	...	...	...	...	...	...	...	...	...	...	2223	...	...	...
+6	Skovorodino......................d.	...	...	...	...	...	...	...	...	...	...	...	...	...	...	...	...	...	...	...	...	...	...	...	...
+7	**Khabarovsk** ....d.	...	...	...	...	...	...	...	...	...	...	...	...	...	...	...	...	...	...	...	...	...	...	...	...
+7	Ussuriysk..........................d.	...	...	...	...	...	...	...	...	...	...	...	...	...	...	...	...	...	...	...	...	...	...	...	...
+7	**Vladivostok**.......................a.	...	...	...	...	...	...	...	...	...	...	...	...	...	...	...	...	...	...	...	...	...	...	...	...

ROSSIYA SUMMARY

km		2*MJ* *Fir* MR	
0	**Moskva** Yar. ....d.	1350	*1st day*
461	Nizhni Novgorod......d.	2006	*1st day*
917	Kirov ....d.	0205	*2nd day*
1778	Yekaterinburg ....d.	1539	*2nd day*
2676	Omsk ....d.	0330	*3rd day*
3303	Novosibirsk..............d.	1132	*3rd day*
4065	Krasnoyarsk ....d.	2303	*3rd day*
5152	Irkutsk ....d.	1620	*4th day*
5608	Ulan Ude..................d.	2318	*4th day*
8492	Khabarovsk ....d.	0125	*7th day*
9258	**Vladivostok**............a.	1240	*7th day*

MOSKVA - BEIJING via Ulaan Baatar

km	*Trans-Mongolian Railway*	362*Y* *Pas* e	4*ZJ* *Sko* ②	6*ZJ* *Sko* § ③	6*MZ* *Sko* ④	24 *Exp* ④ ◧
0	*Moskva Yar.* .... △ d.	...	2345 ②	2345 ③	2345 ④	...
3303	*Novosibirsk*...... △ d.	...	2123 ④	2123 ⑤	2123 ⑥	...
5152	**Irkutsk**....................d.	1702	0253 ⑥	0253 ⑦	0253 ①	...
5608	Ulan Ude ....d.	0224	1122 ⑥	1122 ⑦	1122 ①	...
5863	Naushki 🏛...............d.	1350	1723 ⑥	1723 ⑦	1723 ①	...
5886	Suche Bator 🏛 .. MO d.	2055	2355 ⑥	2355 ⑦	2355 ①	...
6265	**Ulaan Baatar**..... MO a.	0503	0635 ⑦	0635 ①	0635 ②	...
6265	**Ulaan Baatar**..... MO d.	...	0715 ⑦	...	...	0715 ④
6770	Dzamin Uud 🏛 .. MO d.	...	2035 ⑦	...	...	2035 ④
6780	Erlan 🏛 .... CH a.	...	2100 ⑦	...	...	2100 ④
7622	**Beijing** .... CH a.	...	1404 ①	...	...	1404 ⑤

MOSKVA - BEIJING via Harbin

km	*Trans-Manchurian Train name: Vostok*	20*SZ* *Sko* ⑥	602*CH* 654*JA* Y
0	*Moskva Yar.* .. △ d.	2345 ⑥	...
1778	*Yekaterinburg* △ d.	0159 ①	...
3303	*Novosibirsk*.... △ d.	2123 ①	...
5152	**Irkutsk**...................d.	0253 ③	...
6165	Chita II....................d.	2248 ③	1315
6625	Zabaikalsk 🏛 ....d.	1405 ④	0435
6637	Manzhouli 🏛.... CH d.	0010 ⑤	0900
7572	Harbin............. CH d.	1317 ⑤	...
7814	Changchun....... CH d.	1600 ⑤	...
8119	Shenyang......... CH a.	1933 ⑤	...
8961	**Beijing**............ CH a.	0546 ⑥	...

A – To Ulaanbaatar (see below main table).
B – To Ulaanbaatar and Beijing (see below main table).
C – ④⑦ from Minsk (d. 1533), Smolensk (d. 2110), Moskva next day.
D – ② from Brest (d. 1044), Minsk (d. 1533), Smolensk (d. 2110), Moskva next day. Also from Brest on ④ from July 3 (train **114**).
M – Uneven dates (even dates in Aug., Nov., Dec., Feb., Mar.).
N – Even dates (uneven dates in Aug., Nov., Dec., Feb., Mar.).
P – VOSTOK. To Beijing via Harbin (see below main table).
Q – From Adler even dates June 2 - 24; daily June 26 - Sept. 4 (depart Yekaterinburg on 3rd day).
R – ROSSIYA (see also summary below main table). Also conveys 🛏 Moskva - Tumangan (North Korea) 4 times per month.
U – June 1 - Oct. 5, Dec. 21 - Jan. 13 (dates subject to confirmation).
V – June 1 - Oct. 11, Dec. 24 - Jan. 21 (dates subject to confirmation).
Y – ④⑥ Chita to Manzhouli; daily to Zabaikalsk (arrive 0125).

a – From Adler, Sochi, Rostov (Table **1960**).
b – To Barnaul (a. 0518). On ■(5) to Barnaul (a. 0305), Biisk (0850).
c – From Chelyabinsk (Table **1970**), depart previous day.
d – From St Peterburg (Table **1900**).
e – Arrives Naushki 0848 (attaches to train **364**); arrives Suche Bator 1836 (attaches to train **264**).
h – From Penza and Samara (Table **1970**). Depart Omsk on 3rd day.
k – Moskva **Kurskaya**.
m – To Kemerovo (a. 0515).
n – To Tobolsk (a. 0550), Surgut (a. 1427) and Niznevartovsk (a. 2018).
o – To Novokuznetsk (train **14** a. 0830; train **118** a. 0222).
p – To Petropavl (Table **1975**).
q – To Abakan (a. 0200).
r – Moskva **Belorusskaya**.
s – To Tobolsk (a. 1053), Surgut (a. 2045), Korotchayevo (a. 1048), Novy Urengoy (a. 1250).
t – To Tobolsk (a. 0615), Surgut (a. 1642), Korotchayevo (a. 0547), Novy Urengoy (a. 0752).
u – To Neryungri (Table **1989**).
w – To Nivhni Tagil (a. 1932).
x – To Severobaikalsk (Table **1989**).
y – To Serov (a. 2245), Priobe (a. 1055).
z – To Tomsk II (a. 0634).

♥ – *Sapsan* high-speed train, special fares payable. 🅁
❦ – *Swallow* high-speed train, special fares payable. 🅁
★ – Shows the number of hours that local time is ahead of Moskva time (all timings within Russia are shown in Moskva time).
◧ – Confirm days of running when booking. May run twice-weekly in summer.
△ – For timings Moskva - Irkutsk see main table.
▽ – On ■(5) train number is **136***MJ*.
◇ – 7 nights Moskva - Vladivostok.

⊡ – Former name: Gorki.
⊙ – Former name: Sverdlovsk.
⊖ – Also known as Vyatka.
☆ – Premium class train.
§ – Operated by Mongolian Railways.
‡ – For international journeys only.

● – Even dates (see page 530).
●(3) – Even dates [.. *30, 1, 3, 8* ..]
●(4) – Even dates [.. *30, 1, 4* ..]
●(5) – Even dates [.. *30, 1, 3, 4* ..]
●(6) – Even dates [.. *30, 1, 3, 6* ..]
●(8) – Even dates [.. *30, 1, 3, 5, 8* ..]
●(9) – Even dates [.. *30, 1, 3, 5, 7, 10* ..]

■ – Uneven dates (see page 530).
■(1) – Uneven dates [.. *29, 1* ..]
■(3) – Uneven dates [.. *31, 3* ..]
■(5) – Uneven dates [.. *31, 2, 5* ..]
■(7) – Uneven dates [.. *31, 2, 4, 7* ..]
■(9) – Uneven dates [.. *31, 2, 4, 6, 9* ..]

CH – China (GMT + 8).
MO – Mongolia (GMT + 8).

VLADIVOSTOK - IRKUTSK - NOVOSIBIRSK - YEKATERINBURG - MOSKVA 1990

TransSiberian Railway		67*Y*	77*EI*	11*UJ*	701*H*	3*ZJ*	5	41	731*H*	37*NJ*	29*NJ*	139*NJ*	19*CH*	703*H*	733*N*	139*G*	69*JA*	63*BJ*	103	73*E*	13*NJ*	735*N*	59	133*EI*	91*IJ*
		Sko	*Sko*	*Sko*	♥	*Sko*	*Sko*	*Sko*	≋	*Fir*	*Fir*	*Sko*	*Sko*	♥	≋	*Fir*	*Sko*	*Sko*	*Sko*	*Fir*	*Fir*	≋	*Fir*	*Sko*	*Sko*
			■(3)	■(5)		⑤‡	③⑥‡			■(5)	●(4)		①‡					①③	⑤	■(3)	■(3)				
						B	**A**			**U**	**U**	**Q**	**P**					**C**	**D**		**V**		**d**	**N**	
Vladivostok	d.	...	...	...	...	...	...	...	...	...	...	...	...	...	...	...	...	...	...	...	...	...	...	1210	...
Ussuriysk	d.	...	...	...	...	...	...	...	...	...	...	...	...	...	...	...	...	...	...	...	...	...	...	1415	...
Khabarovsk	d.	...	**u**	...	...	...	...	...	...	...	...	...	...	...	...	...	...	...	...	...	...	...	...	0109	...
Skovorodino	d.	...	1312	...	...	...	...	...	...	...	...	...	...	...	...	...	...	...	...	...	...	...	...	2116	...
Chita II	d.	...	1137	1137	...	...	...	...	...	...	...	...	1833	...	...	...	1747	...	...	...	...	...	...	1945	...
Ulan Ude	d.	...	2138	2138	...	0244	0244	...	...	...	...	...	0520	...	...	...	0448	...	...	...	...	...	...	0530	...
Irkutsk	a.	...	0537	0537	...	1049	1049	...	...	...	...	...	1325	...	...	...	1253	...	...	...	...	...	...	1335	...
Irkutsk	d.	...	0605	0605	...	1114	1114	...	...	...	...	...	1355	...	...	...	1328	...	...	...	...	...	...	1405	**x**
Tayshet	d.	...	1743	1743	...	|	|	...	...	...	...	...	|	...	...	...	0058	...	...	...	...	...	...	0145	0551
Krasnoyarsk	d.	**q**	0055	0055	...	0415	0415	...	...	**z**	...	...	0714	...	...	...	0815	...	...	...	...	...	...	0911	1307
Tayga	d.	0857	0940	0940	...	1224	1224	...	...	1043	**m**	...	|	...	...	...	1700	...	...	...	**o**	...	...	1843	2130
Novosibirsk	a.	1223	1251	1251	...	1553	1553	...	...	1423	1423	...	1839	...	...	...	2036	...	...	...	2305	...	...	2226	0131
Novosibirsk	d.	1302	...	1349	...	1612	1612	...	...	1502	1502	1730	1858	...	...	...	2125	2327	2327	...	2350	...	...	2315	0217
Omsk	a.	2110	...	2232	...	2330	2330	...	...	2307	2307	0251	0314	...	...	...	0530	0702	0702	...	0726	...	...	0650	1049
Omsk	d.	2126	...	2300	...	2350	2350	...	...	2324	2324	0322	0332	...	...	...	0557	0736	0736	...	0800	...	...	0725	1105
Tyumen	d.	0452	...	**c**	...	0651	0651	...	...	0702	0702	1053	1038	...	...	...	1439	1535	1535	1547	1547	...	...	**h**	1755
Yekaterinburg ⊙	a.	1051	...	...	...	1115	1115	...	...	1202	1202	1545	1447	...	...	...	2007	2101	2101	2109	2109	...	...	...	2314
Yekaterinburg ⊙	d.	1124	...	...	...	1142	1142	...	...	1229	1229	1619	1514	...	...	...	2109	2128	2128	2136	2136	...	...	...	2341
Sarapul	d.	|	...	...	...	|	|	...	...	|	|	**a**	|	...	...	...	|	|	|	|	|	...	...	...	|
Kazan	d.	|	...	...	...	|	|	2207	...	|	|	...	|	...	...	...	|	|	|	|	|	...	...	...	|
Murom I	d.	|	...	...	...	|	|	|	...	|	|	...	|	...	...	...	|	|	|	|	|	...	...	...	|
Perm II	d.	1726	...	...	...	1736	1736	|	...	1856	1856	...	2115	...	...	...	0302	0322	0322	0333	0333	...	...	...	0533
Kirov ⊖	d.	0056	...	...	...	0106	0106	|	...	0323	0323	...	0506	...	...	...	1109	1135	1135	1157	1157	...	...	...	1407
Vologda I	d.	|	...	...	...	|	|	|	...	|	|	...	|	...	...	...	|	|	|	2235	2235	...	...	...	|
St Peterburg Ladozhski	a.	|	...	...	...	|	|	|	...	|	|	...	|	...	...	...	|	|	|	1000	1000	...	...	...	|
Nizhni Novgorod ⊡	d.	|	...	...	0645	0702	0702	0658	0945	0953	0953	...	1115	1445	1630	1655	|	1813	1813	...	...	1910	1925	...	2050
Vladimir	d.	|	...	...	0854	1043	1043	...	1157	1328	1328	...	1448	1654	1842	2020	|	2220	2220	...	...	2122	2300	...	0045
Yaroslavl	d.	1252	...	...	|	|	|	...	|	|	|	...	|	|	|	|	2354	|	|	...	...	|	|	...	|
Moskva Kazanskaya	a.	|	...	...	1040**k**	|	|	...	1345**k**	|	|	...	|	1840**k**	2030**k**	2242**k**	|	0120**r**	0120**r**	...	...	2310**k**	0120**k**	...	|
Moskva Yaroslavskaya	a.	1658	...	...	...	1358	1358	...	...	1630	1630	...	1758	...	...	...	0411	...	...	...	...	...	...	...	0345

		75*EI*	81	89*UJ*	95*NJ*	137	117*NJ*	9	11*E*	55*Y*	1*MJ*	7*NJ*	5*EI*	43*EI*	99*EI*	49*GJ*	35*GJ*	1*GJ*	59*EJ*	15*EJ*	97	31*GJ*	109*MJ*	49*EJ*	84*EJ*
		Sko	*Sko*	*Fir*	*Sko*	*Sko*	*Sko*	*Fir*	*Fir*	*Fir*	*Fir*	*Sko*	*Fir*	*Sko*	*Sko*	*Sko*	*Fir*	*Fir*	*Fir*	*Fir*	*Fir*	*Fir*	*Sko*	*Fir*	*Fir*
		■(1)	●	■(1)		■	●			●				●	●					☆					
					▽			**N**	**M**		**N R**	**M**			◇			☆	**N**	**N**				**M**	**M**
Vladivostok	d.	...	...	...	...	...	...	...	...	...	0430	0430	1415	...	1655	...	...	...	...	...	...	...	...	...	...
Ussuriysk	d.	...	...	...	...	...	...	...	...	...	0638	0638	1613	...	1911	...	...	...	...	...	...	...	...	...	...
Khabarovsk	d.	...	...	...	...	...	...	...	...	...	1649	1649	0115	0647	0647	...	...	...	...	...	...	...	...	...	...
Skovorodino	d.	...	...	...	...	...	...	...	...	...	1132	1132	...	0403	0403	...	...	...	...	...	...	...	...	...	...
Chita II	d.	...	...	...	...	...	...	...	...	...	0841	0841	...	0212	0212	...	...	...	...	...	...	...	...	...	...
Ulan Ude	d.	...	1059	...	...	...	...	...	...	...	1823	1823	...	1220	1220	...	...	...	...	...	...	...	...	...	...
Irkutsk	a.	...	1914	...	...	...	...	...	...	...	0124	0124	...	2010	2010	...	...	...	...	...	...	...	...	...	...
Irkutsk	d.	**u**	2002	...	...	...	...	...	...	...	0147	0147	...	2045	2045	...	...	...	...	...	...	...	...	...	...
Tayshet	d.	0741	0741	...	...	...	...	...	...	...	1240	1240	...	0816	0816	...	...	...	...	...	...	...	...	...	...
Krasnoyarsk	d.	1450	1450	...	...	1435	...	...	...	1800	1930	1930	...	1543	1543	...	...	...	...	...	...	...	...	...	...
Tayga	d.	2323	2323	...	...	2340	**o**	...	...	0223	0337	0337	...	0037	0037	...	...	...	...	...	...	...	...	...	...
Novosibirsk	a.	0255	0255	...	...	0313	0247	...	...	0600	0645	0645	...	0408	0408	...	...	...	...	...	...	...	...	...	...
Novosibirsk	d.	0346	0346	...	**b**	0336	0336	...	...	0650	0704	...	...	0505	0505	...	...	...	...	...	...	...	...	...	...
Omsk	a.	1148	1148	...	1041	1138	1138	...	...	1406	1505	...	...	1356	1356	...	...	...	...	...	...	...	...	...	...
Omsk	d.	1217	1217	...	1117	1208	1208	...	**t**	1444	1523	...	...	1428	1428	...	...	...	**n**	...	...	...	**s**	...	...
Tyumen	d.	1940	1940	**p**	1920	1930	1930	...	2017	2212	2232	...	...	2222	2222	...	...	...	0043	...	...	...	0034	...	...
Yekaterinburg ⊙	a.	0049	0049	0059	0109	0117	0117	...	0237	0312	0321	...	...	0247	0247	...	...	...	0724	...	...	...	0607	...	...
Yekaterinburg ⊙	d.	0122	0122	0132	0201	0209	0209	...	0322	0339	0349	...	...	0330	0330	...	...	...	0812	0812	...	...	0640	...	...
Sarapul	d.	0956	0956	1010	1020	1032	1032	...	|	|	|	...	...	|	|	...	...	...	1606	1606	...	...	|	...	...
Kazan	d.	1557	1557	1613	1633	1649	1649	...	|	|	|	...	...	|	|	1750	...	1945	2147	2147	2157	...	|	...	...
Murom I	d.	0007	0007	0019	0048	0108	0108	...	|	|	|	...	...	|	|	0121	...	|	0448	0448	0545	...	|	**w**	**y**
Perm II	d.	|	|	|	|	|	|	0908	0908	0926	0936	...	...	0918	0918	|	...	|	|	|	|	...	1248	1258	1258
Kirov ⊖	d.	|	|	|	|	|	|	1654	1654	1714	1724	...	...	1704	1704	|	...	|	|	|	|	2030	2114	2129	2129
Vologda I	d.	|	|	|	|	|	|	|	|	|	|	...	...	|	|	|	...	|	|	|	|	|	|	|	|
St Peterburg Ladozhski	a.	|	|	|	|	|	|	|	|	|	|	...	...	|	|	|	...	|	|	|	|	|	|	|	|
Nizhni Novgorod ⊡	d.	|	|	|	|	|	|	2255	2255	2310	2320	...	...	|	|	|	2330	|	|	|	|	0301	0321	0331	0331
Vladimir	d.	|	|	|	|	|	|	0221	0221	0248	0258	...	...	|	|	|	0325	|	|	|	|	0620	0703	0713	0713
Yaroslavl	d.	|	|	|	|	|	|	|	|	|	|	...	...	0653	0653	|	|	|	|	|	|	|	|	|	|
Moskva Kazanskaya	a.	0442	0442	0502	0538	0545	0545	|	|	|	|	...	...	|	|	0611	|	0710	0923	0923	1035	|	|	|	|
Moskva Yaroslavskaya	a.	...	...	...	...	...	...	0522	0522	0552	0601	...	...	1103	1103	...	0629	...	...	...	...	0943	1030	1038	1038

ROSSIYA SUMMARY

km			1*MJ* *Fir* **N R**	
0	**Vladivostok**	d.	0430	*1st day*
766	Khabarovsk	d.	1649	*1st day*
3650	Ulan Ude	d.	1823	*3rd day*
4106	Irkutsk	d.	0147	*4th day*
5193	Krasnoyarsk	d.	1930	*4th day*
5955	Novosibirsk	d.	0704	*5th day*
6582	Omsk	d.	1523	*5th day*
7480	Yekaterinburg	d.	0349	*6th day*
8341	Kirov	d.	1724	*6th day*
8797	Nizhni Novgorod	d.	2320	*6th day*
9258	**Moskva** Yar.	a.	0601	*7th day*

BEIJING - MOSKVA via Ulaan Baatar

km	*Trans-Mongolian Railway*		5*VJ* *Sko* ②	3*ZJ* *Sko* ③	5*SZ* *Sko* § ⑤	23 *Exp* ⑦◧	263 *Pas* **e**
0	**Beijing**	CH d.	...	0805 ③	...	0805 ⑦	...
842	Erlan ▦	CH d.	...	2359 ③	...	2359 ①	...
852	Dzamin Uud ▦	MO d.	...	0240 ④	...	0240 ①	...
1356	**Ulaan Baatar**	MO a.	...	1420 ④	...	1420 ②	...
1356	**Ulaan Baatar**	MO d.	1525 ②	1525 ④	1525 ⑤	...	2115
1735	Suche Bator ▦	MO d.	2305 ②	2305 ④	2305 ⑤	...	1000
1758	Naushki ▦	d.	2204 ②	2204 ④	2204 ⑤	...	1018
2013	Ulan Ude	d.	0244 ③	0244 ⑤	0244 ⑥	...	1725
2469	**Irkutsk**	a.	1049 ③	1049 ⑤	1049 ⑥	...	0215
4319	*Novosibirsk* △	a.	1553 ④	1553 ⑥	1553 ⑦	...	...
7622	*Moskva Yar.* △	a.	1358 ⑥	1358 ①	1358 ②	...	...

BEIJING - MOSKVA via Harbin

km	*Trans-Manchurian Train name: Vostok*		19*CH* *Sko* ⑥	**653** **601** **Y**
0	**Beijing**	CH d.	2300 ⑥	...
841	Shenyang	CH d.	0855 ⑦	...
1141	Changchun	CH d.	1214 ⑦	...
1388	Harbin	CH d.	1510 ⑦	...
2323	Manzhouli ▦	CH d.	0701 ①	1300
2335	Zabaikalsk ▦	d.	0803 ①	1419
2795	Chita II	d.	1833 ①	0213
3808	**Irkutsk**	a.	1325 ②	...
5658	*Novosibirsk* △	a.	1839 ③	...
7183	*Yekaterinburg* △	a.	1447 ④	...
8961	*Moskva Yar.* △	a.	1758 ⑤	...

– From Ulaanbaatar (see below main table).
– From Beijing and Ulaanbaatar (see below main table).
– To Smolensk a. 0752 ④⑥ and Minsk a. 1149 ④⑥.
– To Smolensk a. 0752 ①, Minsk a. 1149 ①, Brest a. 1638 ①. Also runs on ⑦ from June 29 (train **113**), Brest a. 1638 ③.
– Uneven dates (even dates in Aug., Nov., Dec., Feb., Mar.).
– Even dates (uneven dates in Aug., Nov., Dec., Feb., Mar.).
– VOSTOK. From Beijing via Harbin (see below main table).
– Even dates June 2 - 20; daily June 22 - Aug. 30 (arrive Adler on 5th day).
– ROSSIYA (see also summary below main table). Also conveys 🛏 Tumangan (North Korea) - Moskva 4 times per month.
– June 1 - Oct. 3, Dec. 19 - Jan. 11. Dates subject to confirmation.
– June 1 - Oct. 7, Dec. 21 - Jan. 17. Dates subject to confirmation.
– ⑤⑦ from Manzhouli (Zabaikalsk a. 0925); daily from Zabaikalsk.
– To Rostov, Sochi, Adler (Table **1960**).
– From Barnaul (d. 1845 on uneven dates, 2055 on even dates).
– To Chelyabinsk (Table **1970**).
– To St Peterburg (Table **1900**).
– Arrives Suche Bator 0512, Naushki 0705. Train number **361**/*J* from Naushki.
– To Samara and Penza (Table **1970**).
– Moskva **Kurskaya**.
– From Kemerovo (d. 0915).

n – From Niznevartovsk (d. 0530), Surgut (d. 1010), Tobolsk (1930).
o – From Novokuznetsk (train **13** d. 1624; train **117** d. 1718).
p – From Petropavl (Table **1975**)..
q – From Abakan (d. 1415 previous day).
r – Moskva **Belorusskaya**.
s – From Novy Urengoy (d. 1450), Korotchayevo (d. 1704), Surgut (d. 0812), Tobolsk (d. 1920).
t – From Novy Urengoy (d. 1000), Korotchayevo (d. 1235), Surgut (d. 0317), Tobolsk (d. 1505).
u – From Neryungri (Table **1989**). Train **75** departs Tayshet on 4th day.
w – From Nivhni Tagil (depart 0450).
x – From Severobaikalsk (Table **1989**), depart previous day.
y – From Priobe (d. 1300), Serov (d. 0145).
z – From Tomsk II (d. 0755).
♥ – *Sapsan* or *Swallow* high-speed train, special fares payable. Ⓡ
◧ – Confirm days of running when booking. May run twice-weekly in summer.
△ – For timings Irkutsk - Moskva see main table.
▽ – On even dates train number is **136**NJ.
◇ – Journey 7 nights Vladivostok - Moskva.
‡ – For international journeys only. For day of running from point of origin see below main table.
§ – Operated by Mongolian Railways.

⊡ – Former name: Gorki.
⊙ – Former name: Sverdlovsk.
⊖ – Also known as Vyatka.
☆ – Premium class train.

● – Even dates (see page 530).
●(2) – Even dates [.. *30, 2* ..]
●(3) – Even dates [.. *30, 1, 3, 8* ..]
●(4) – Even dates [.. *30, 1, 4* ..]
●(5) – Even dates [.. *30, 1, 3, 4* ..]
●(6) – Even dates [.. *30, 1, 3, 6* ..]
●(8) – Even dates [.. *30, 1, 3, 5, 8* ..]
●(9) – Even dates [.. *30, 1, 3, 5, 7, 10* ..]

■ – Uneven dates (see page 530).
■(1) – Uneven dates [.. *29, 1* ..]
■(3) – Uneven dates [.. *31, 3* ..]
■(5) – Uneven dates [.. *31, 2, 5* ..]
■(7) – Uneven dates [.. *31, 2, 4, 7* ..]
■(9) – Uneven dates [.. *31, 2, 4, 6, 9* ..]

CH – China (GMT + 8).
KO – North Korea (GMT + 9).
MO – Mongolia (GMT + 8).

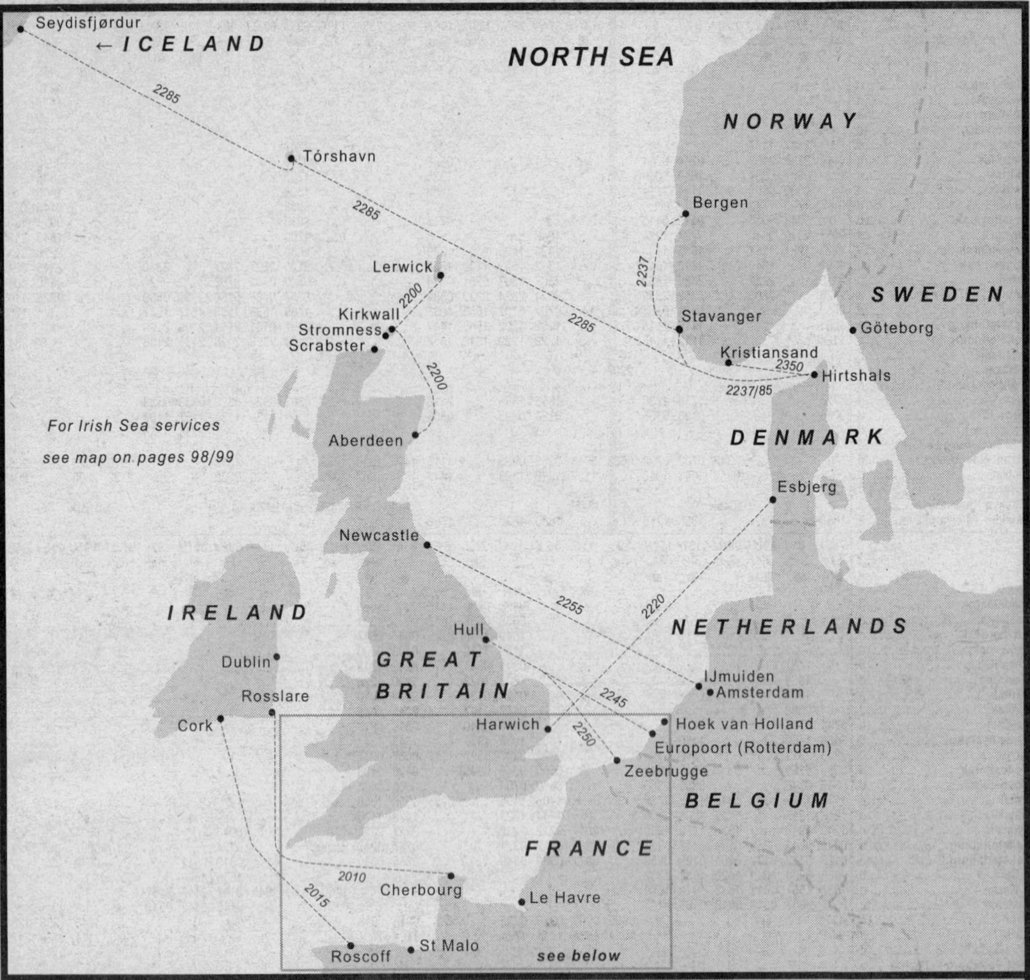
Seydisfjørdur
← ICELAND
NORTH SEA
2285
Tórshavn
NORWAY
2285
Bergen
Lerwick
2237
2200
Kirkwall
Stromness
Scrabster
2285
Stavanger
SWEDEN
Göteborg
Kristiansand
2350
Hirtshals
2237/85
2200
For Irish Sea services
see map on pages 98/99
Aberdeen
DENMARK
Esbjerg
Newcastle
2255
2220
IRELAND
NETHERLANDS
Hull
Dublin
GREAT
BRITAIN
IJmuiden
Amsterdam
Rosslare
2245
Cork
Harwich
Hoek van Holland
2250
Europoort (Rotterdam)
Zeebrugge
BELGIUM
FRANCE
2010
Cherbourg
2015
Le Havre
St Malo
Roscoff
see below

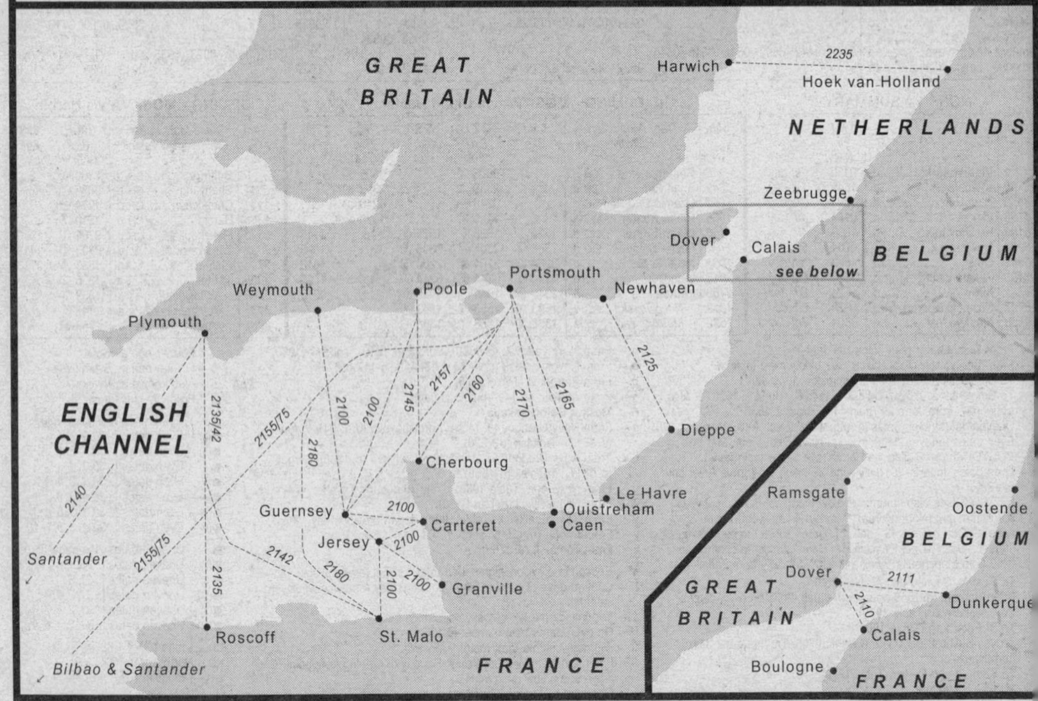
GREAT
BRITAIN
Harwich
2235
Hoek van Holland
NETHERLANDS
Zeebrugge
Dover
Calais
BELGIUM
see below
Weymouth
Poole
Portsmouth
Newhaven
Plymouth
2125
ENGLISH
CHANNEL
2135/42
2155/75
2180
2100
2100
2145
2157
2160
2170
2165
Dieppe
Cherbourg
Le Havre
Ouistreham
Caen
2140
Guernsey
2100
Carteret
Jersey
2100
Santander
2155/75
2142
2180
2100
2135
2100
Granville
Roscoff
St. Malo
Bilbao & Santander
FRANCE
Ramsgate
Oostende
BELGIUM
Dover
2111
GREAT
BRITAIN
2110
Dunkerque
Calais
Boulogne
FRANCE

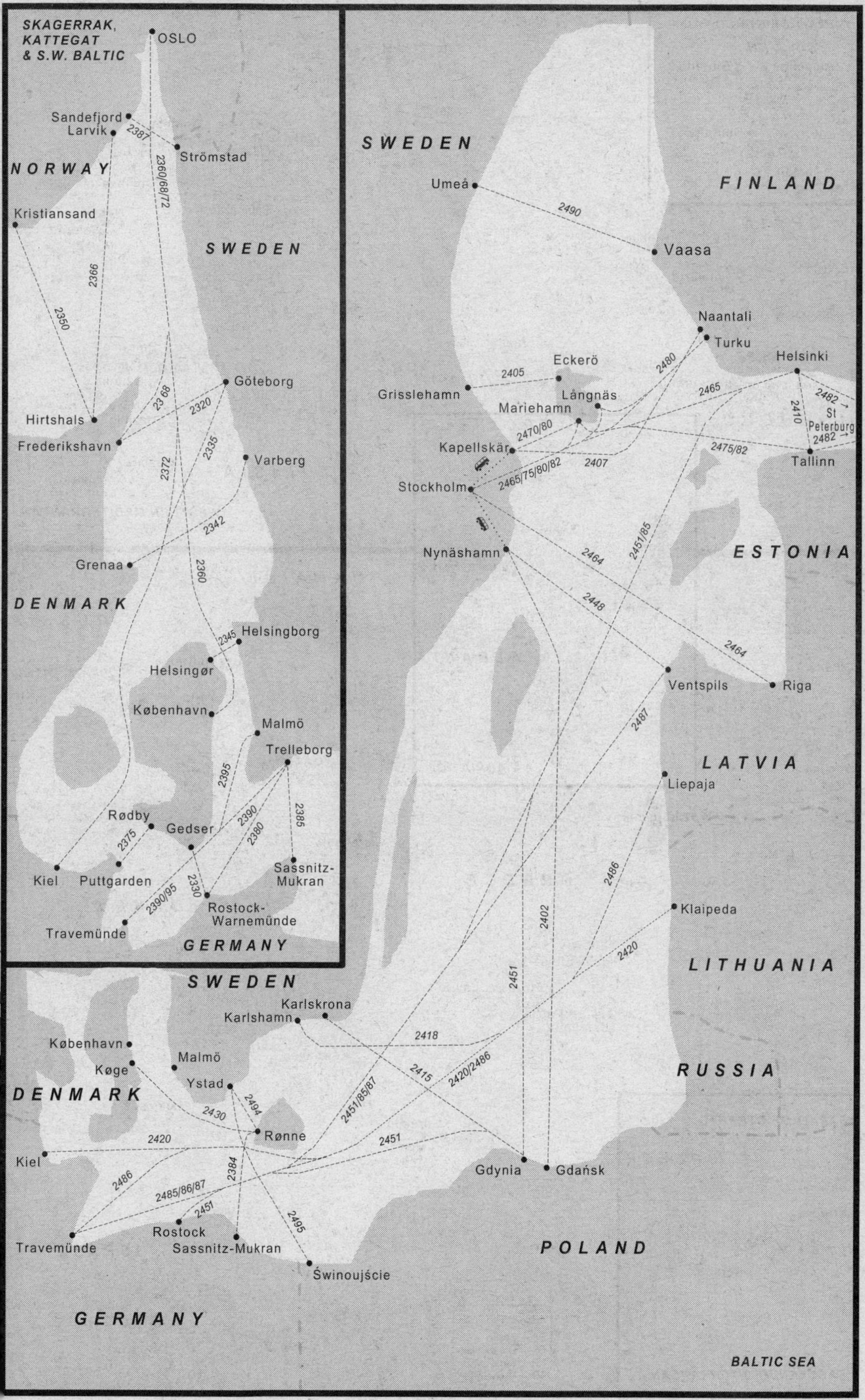
SKAGERRAK, KATTEGAT & S.W. BALTIC
OSLO
Sandefjord
Larvik
2387
Strömstad
2360/68/72
NORWAY
Kristiansand
SWEDEN
2366
2350
Göteborg
23 68
2320
Hirtshals
Frederikshavn
2335
Varberg
2372
2342
Grenaa
2360
DENMARK
2345
Helsingborg
Helsingør
København
Malmö
Trelleborg
2395
Rødby
Gedser
2390
2380
2385
2375
Kiel
Puttgarden
2330
Sassnitz-Mukran
2390/95
Rostock-Warnemünde
Travemünde
GERMANY
SWEDEN
Umeå
FINLAND
2490
Vaasa
Naantali
Turku
Eckerö
2405
2480
Helsinki
Grisslehamn
Långnäs
2465
2482
St Peterburg
Mariehamn
2410
2470/80
2482
2475/82
Kapellskär
2407
Tallinn
2465/75/80/82
Stockholm
Nynäshamn
2451/85
ESTONIA
2464
2448
2464
Ventspils
Riga
2487
LATVIA
Liepaja
2486
2402
Klaipeda
2451
2420
LITHUANIA
SWEDEN
Karlskrona
Karlshamn
2418
København
Køge
Malmö
2415
2420/2486
RUSSIA
DENMARK
Ystad
2451/85/87
2430
2494
Rønne
2420
2451
Kiel
2384
Gdynia
Gdańsk
2486
2485/86/87
2451
2495
Rostock
Travemünde
Sassnitz-Mukran
POLAND
Świnoujście
GERMANY
BALTIC SEA

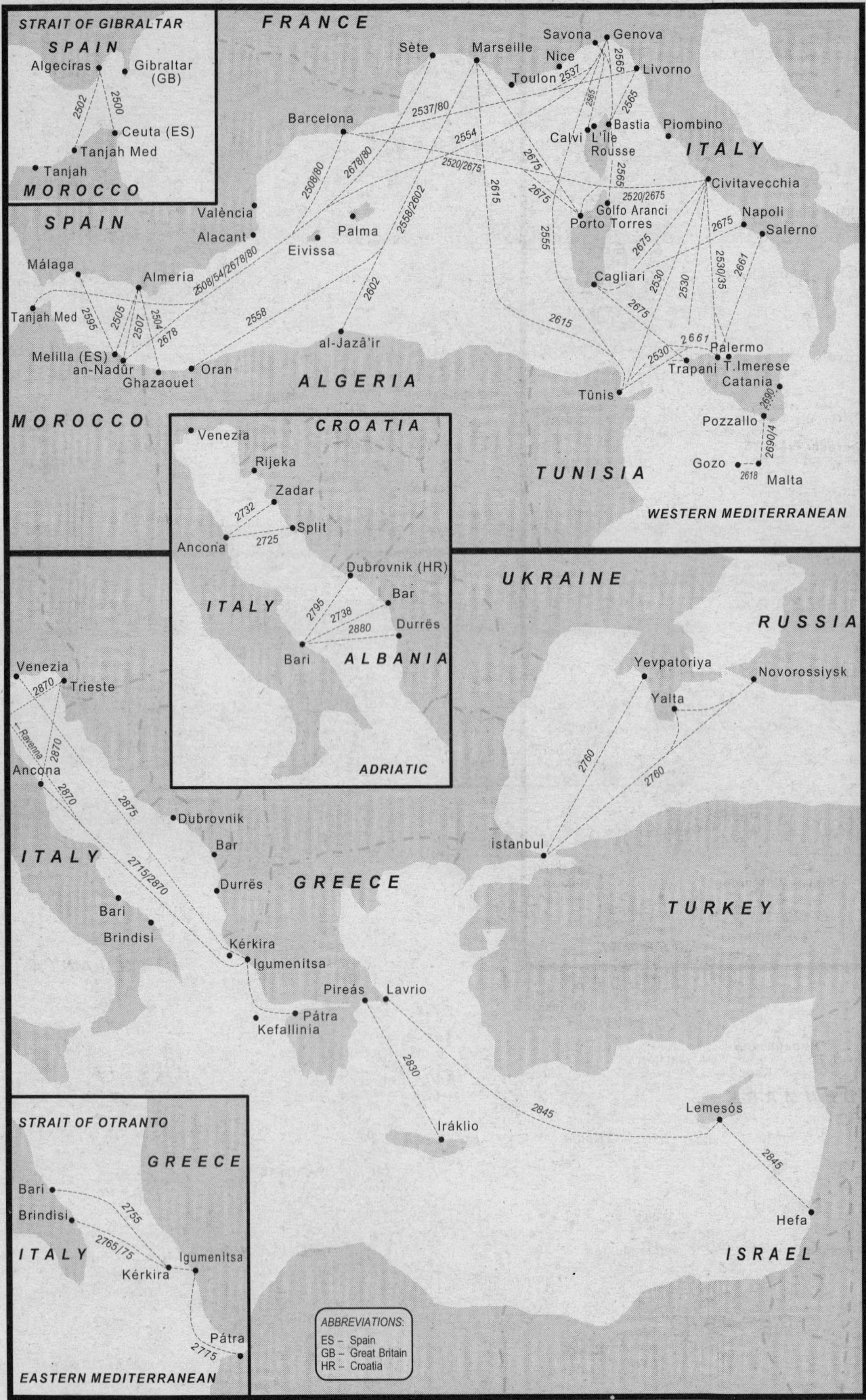
STRAIT OF GIBRALTAR
SPAIN
Algeciras
Gibraltar (GB)
2502
2500
Ceuta (ES)
Tanjah Med
Tanjah
MOROCCO
FRANCE
Sète
Marseille
Savona
Genova
Nice
Toulon
Livorno
Barcelona
Piombino
Bastia
Calvi
L'Île Rousse
ITALY
Civitavecchia
Golfo Aranci
Porto Torres
Napoli
Salerno
València
Alacant
Palma
Eivissa
SPAIN
Málaga
Almeria
Tanjah Med
Melilla (ES)
an-Nadûr
Ghazaouet
Oran
al-Jazâ'ir
ALGERIA
Cagliari
Palermo
Trapani
T.Imerese
Catania
Tûnis
Pozzallo
Gozo
Malta
TUNISIA
MOROCCO
WESTERN MEDITERRANEAN
2537/80
2537
2565
2554
2520/2675
2675
2615
2555
2508/80
2678/80
2558/2602
2508/54/2678/80
2558
2602
2595
2505
2507
2504
2678
2530
2530/35
2661
2690
2690/4
2618
Venezia
CROATIA
Rijeka
Zadar
2732
Split
Ancona
2725
Dubrovnik (HR)
Bar
ITALY
2795
2738
2880
Durrës
Bari
ALBANIA
ADRIATIC
UKRAINE
RUSSIA
Yevpatoriya
Novorossiysk
Yalta
2760
İstanbul
TURKEY
Venezia
Trieste
2870
Ravenna
Ancona
2875
Dubrovnik
Bar
ITALY
2715/2870
Durrës
GREECE
Bari
Brindisi
Kérkira
Igumenitsa
Pireás
Lavrio
Pátra
Kefallinia
2830
2845
Iráklio
Lemesós
Hefa
ISRAEL
STRAIT OF OTRANTO
GREECE
Bari
2755
Brindisi
2765/75
ITALY
Igumenitsa
Kérkira
Pátra
2775
EASTERN MEDITERRANEAN
ABBREVIATIONS:
ES – Spain
GB – Great Britain
HR – Croatia

SHIPPING CONTENTS

SHIPPING OPERATORS

ACCIONA TRASMEDITERRANEA www.trasmediterranea.es
Avda. de Europa 10, Parque Empresarial La Moraleja, C.P. 28108 Alcobendas, Madrid:
✆ +34 (0)91 423 85 00, fax +34 (0)91 423 85 55.
Reservations: ✆ +34(0) 902 45 46 45.
U.K. agent: Southern Ferries, 30 Churton Street, Victoria, London SW1V 2LP
✆ 0844 815 7785, fax 0844 815 7795.

A G EMS www.ag-ems.de
Postfach 11 54, 26691 Emden-Außenhafen: ✆ +49 (0)1805 180 182,
fax +49 21 89 07 405.

ALILAURO www.alilauro.it
Stazione Marittima, Piazzale Angioino, 80133 Napoli: ✆ +39 081 497 2222,
fax +39 081 497 2228. Reservations: ✆ +39 (0)81 497 2238.

ALSFÆRGENS www.faergen.dk
Færgen, Dampskibskajen 3, 3700 Rønne: ✆ +45 70 23 15 15.

ANEK LINES www.anek.gr
22 Akti Kondili Str., 18545 Pireás: ✆ +30 210 4197 420, +30 210 4197 430.
U.K. agent: Viamare Ltd., Suite 3, 447 Kenton Road, Harrow, HA3 0XY:
✆ 020 8206 3420, fax 020 8206 1332.

BALEÀRIA (EUROLÍNIES MARÍTIMES) www.balearia.com
Estació Marítima s/n, 03700 Dénia: ✆ +34 96 642 86 00; call centre: ✆ +34 96 642 87 00.

BLUE LINE www.bluferries.it
Postboks 36, Englandsvej 370, DK 2770 Kastrup, Denmark: ✆ +45 3672 6001.
Italy agent: ✆ +39 071 20 40 41, fax +39 071 20 26 18.
Croatia agent: ✆ +385 21 352 533, fax +385 21 352 482.
UK agent: Viamare (see Anek Lines).

BLUFERRIES www.blueline-ferries.com
✆ +39 090 6786 406, fax +39 090 6406 508.

BORNHOLMERFÆRGEN www.faergen.dk
Færgen, Dampskibskajen 3, 3700 Rønne: ✆ +45 70 23 15 15.

BRITTANY FERRIES www.brittany-ferries.co.uk
Millbay, Plymouth, PL1 3EW: ✆ 0871 244 1401.
Reservations: U.K. ✆ 0871 244 0744; France ✆ +33 825 828 828;
Spain ✆ +34 942 36 06 11.

BUMERANG SHIPPING COMPANY TOURISM TRAVEL & TRADE S.A.
Rihtim Cad. Veli Alemdar Han Kat. 6, 80030 Karaköy - Istanbul: ✆ +90 (0)212 251 7373,
fax +90 (0)212 251 1472.

CAREMAR www.caremar.it
See Tirrenia for details.

COLOR LINE www.colorline.com
Postboks 1422 Vika, N-0115 Oslo: ✆ + 47 22 94 44 00, fax +47 22 83 04 30.
Reservations: Norway ✆ +47 22 94 42 00; Denmark ✆ +45 99 56 19 77;
Germany ✆ +49 431 7300 300; Sweden ✆ +46 526 62 000.

COMARIT www.comarit.com
Avenue Mohamed VI, Tanjah: ✆ +212 539 32 00 32, fax +212 539 32 59 00.

COMPAGNIE TUNISIENNE DE NAVIGATION www.ctn.com.tn
5 Avenue Dag Hammarskjoeld, 1001 Tûnis: ✆ +216 (71) 341 777, fax +216 (71) 345 736.
Reservations: ✆ +33 825 88 80 88.
U.K. agent: Southern Ferries (see Acciona Trasmediterranea).

CONDOR FERRIES LTD. www.condorferries.co.uk
New Harbour Road South, Hamworthy, Poole, BH15 4AJ.
Reservations: ✆ 0845 609 1024.
Information: U.K. ✆ 01202 207 216; Jersey ✆ 01534 872 240; Guernsey 12023 (local calls only); St Malo ✆ (0)825 165 463; Cherbourg ✆ +33 2 33 88 44 88.

CORSICA FERRIES www.corsica-ferries.fr
5 bis Rue Chanoine Leschi, 20296 Bastia: ✆ +33 4 95 32 95 95, fax +33 4 95 32 14 71.

DESTINATION GOTLAND www.destinationgotland.se
Korsgatan 2, Box 1234, 621 23 Visby: ✆ +46 (0)498 20 18 00, fax +46 (0)498 20 18 90.
Reservations: ✆ +46 (0)771 22 33 00, fax +46 (0)498 20 13 90.

DFDS SEAWAYS www.dfdsseaways.co.uk
International Port, Parkeston, Harwich CO12 4SR.
International Passenger Terminal, Royal Quays, North Shields, Newcastle, NE29 6EE.
Reservations: U.K. ✆ 0871 522 9955; Denmark ✆ +45 33 42 30 00, +45 7917 7917;
Netherlands ✆ +31 255 54 66 66; Norway ✆ +47 21 62 10 00;
Ostuferhafen 15, 24149 Kiel: ✆ +49 (0)431 20976 420, fax +49 (0)431 20976 102;
Klaipeda: ✆ +370 46 395 051.

ECKERÖ LINE www.eckeroline.fi
Mannerheimintie 10, 00100 Helsinki: ✆ +358 6000 4300, fax +358 9 2288 5547.
Passanger Harbour, Sadama 29, 10111 Tallinn: ✆ +372 664 6000,
fax +372 631 8690.

ECKERÖ LINJEN www.eckerolinjen.fi
P.O. Box 158, Torggatan 2, AX-22101 Mariehamn, Åland: ✆ +358 (0)18 28 000,
fax +358 (0)18 28 380.
SE-760 45 Grisslehamn: ✆ +46 (0)175 258 00, fax +46 (0)175 330 54.
Berghamn, AX-22270 Eckerö, Åland: ✆ +358 (0)18 28 300, fax +358 (0)18 38 230.

ENDEAVOR LINES www.endeavor-lines.com
35 Posidonos Ave, 183 44 Moschato, Athína: ✆ +30 210 9405 222,
fax +30 210 9405 066.
Reservations: Nautilus Shipping Agencies, 72 Othonos Amalias Ave, 26221 Patras: ✆ +30 2610 620061, fax +30 2610 620031.
Brindisi: ✆ +39 0831 527667, fax +39 0831 564070; Igumenítsa ✆ +30 26650 26833, fax +30 26650 26111; Corfu: ✆ +30 26610 32467, fax +30 26610 33409.

E N T M V www.algerieferries.com
27, Boulevard des Dames, 13002 Marseille: ✆ +33 (0)4 91 90 64 70,
fax +33 (0)4 91 91 59 58. Reservations: ✆ +213 (021) 42 46 50.

EUROFERRIES www.euroferries.co.uk
The Ferry Terminal, Ramsgate Harbour, Ramsgate CT11 9FT.
✆ 0844 414 5355.

FANØFÆRGEN www.faergen.dk
Færgen, Dampskibskajen 3, 3700 Rønne: ✆ +45 70 23 15 15.

FASTNETLINE www.fastnetline.com
Ferry Port, Ringaskiddy, Cork: +353 (0) 21 437 8892.
U.K. reservations: ✆ 0844 576 8831.

FERRIMAROC www.ferrimaroc.com
Muelle de Ribera s/n, 04002 Almería: ✆ +34 9 50 27 48 00, fax +34 9 50 27 63 66.

FRED. OLSEN S.A. www.fredolsen.es
Polígono Industrial de Añaza s/n, 38109 Santa Cruz de Tenerife: ✆ +34 922 628 200,
fax +34 922 628 232. Reservation: ✆ +34 902 100 107.

F R S www.frs.es
Estación Maritima. P.O. / Apto de correos 13, E-11380 Tarifa - Cádiz: ✆ +34 956 68 18 30,
fax +34 956 62 71 80.

FINNLINES www.finnlines.com
Porkkalankatu 20A, FI-00180 Helsinki: ✆ +358 (0)10 343 4500, (0)10 343 4600.

FJORD LINE www.fjordline.com
Skoltegrunnskaien, N-5003, 5003 Bergen: ✆ +47 51 46 40 99, fax +47 55 31 88 00.
Reservations: ✆ +47 51 46 40 99.

FLAGGRUTEN www.flaggruten.no
Tide ASA, Postbox 6300, N-5893 Bergen: ✆ +47 55 23 87 00, fax +47 55 23 87 01.

FÖRDE REEDEREI SEETOURISTIK www.frs.de
Norderhofenden 19 - 20, D 24937 Flensburg: ✆ +49 (0)461 864 0, fax +49 (0)461 864 30.

GOZO CHANNEL www.gozochannel.com
Mgarr Harbour, Mgarr Gozo: ✆ +356 2210 9000, fax +356 2155 6743.

GRANDI NAVI VELOCI www3.gnv.it
Via Fieschi 17, 16121 Genova: ✆ +39 010 5509 465, fax +39 010 5509 301.
Contact centre: ✆ +39 010 2094 591.
U.K. agent: Viamare (see Anek Lines).

GRIMALDI LINES www.grimaldi-lines.com
Via Marchese Campodisola 13, 80133 Napoli: ✆ +39 081 496 444, fax +39 081 551 7716.
U.K. agent: Viamare (see Anek Lines).

HURTIGRUTEN (NORWEGIAN COASTAL VOYAGE) www.hurtigruten.no
Fredrik Langes gate 14, Postboks 6144, 9008 Tromsø: ✆ +47 970 57 030.
Reservations: ✆ +47 810 30 000.
U.K. reservations: ✆ 0203 603 6213.

INTERNATIONAL MARITIME TRANSPORT CORPORATION (I M T C) www.imtc.co.ma
50 Avenue Paster, 20 300 Casablanca: ✆ +212 (22) 437 620, fax +212 (22) 543 548.
Spain agent: Vapores Suardiaz Andalucia S.A. (VS), Avda. Del Puerto 1 - 6, SP-11006 Cádiz: ✆ +34 956 282 111, fax +34 956 282 846.

IRISH FERRIES www.irishferries.com
P.O. Box 19, Alexandra Road, Dublin 1: ✆ +353 (0)1 855 2222, fax +353 (0)1 855 2272.
Corn Exchange Building, Ground Floor, Brunswick Street, Liverpool L2 7TP:
✆ 08717 300 400, fax 0151 236 0562.
France reservations: ✆ +33 1 70 72 03 26, fax +33 1 70 72 03 27.

ISLE OF MAN STEAM PACKET CO. www.steam-packet.com
Sea Terminal, Douglas, Isle of Man IM1 2RF.
Reservations: ✆ 661 661; U.K. ✆ 08722 992 992; Ireland ✆ +44 8722 992 992.

ISLES OF SCILLY STEAMSHIP CO. www.islesofscilly-travel.co.uk
Travel Centre, Quay Street, Penzance, TR18 4BZ: ✆ 0845 710 5555, fax 01736 334 228.
Overseas reservations: ✆ +44 (0)1736 334 228.

JADROLINIJA www.jadrolinija.hr
Riva 16, 51000 Rijeka: ✆ +385 (51) 666 111, fax +385 (51) 213 116.
U.K. agent: Viamare (see Anek Lines).

KATTEGATRUTEN www.kattegat-ruten.dk
Sverigesgade 4, 8000 Århus: ✆ +45 38 111 222, fax +45 86 205 981.

L D LINES www.ldlines.co.uk
Continental Ferry Port, Wharf Road, Portsmouth, PO2 8QW: ✆ 0844 576 8836,
fax 01235 84 56 08.
Terminal de la Citadelle, BP 90746, F-76060 Le Havre: ✆ 0825 304 304.
Outside U.K. and France: ✆ +33 (0)2 32 14 52 09.

LINDA LINE OY www.lindaline.fi
Makasiiniterminaali, 00140 Helsinki: ✆ +358 (0)9 668 9700, fax +358 (0)9 668 97070.
Ädala 4a, 10614 Tallinn: ✆ +372 6 999 340, fax +372 6 999 340.
Tallinn port: ✆ +372 6 999 333, fax +372 6 999 330.
Reservations: ✆ +358 (0)600 0668970.

LNP www.lnp.hr
Linijska Nacionalna Plovidba d.d., Boktuljin put b.b., 21000 Split: ✆ +385 (0)21 338 310, fax +385 (0)21 352 447.

MANCHE ÎLES EXPRESS www.manche-iles-express.com
Albert Quay, St Helier, Jersey: ✆ 01534 880 756, fax 01534 880 314.
Terminal Building, New Jetty, White Rock, St Peter Port, Guernsey: ✆ 01481 701 316, fax 01481 701 319.

MEDMAR www.medmargroup.it
Terminal Porta di Massa, Napoli: ✆ +39 (0)81 333 44 11, fax +39 (0)81 333 44 36.

METROMARE DELLO STRETTO (CONSORZIO) www.metromaredellostretto.it
Via Calabria 1, 98100 Messina: ✆ +39 0923 873 813, fax +39 0923 593 200.

MINOAN LINES www.minoan.gr
17, 25th August Street, 712 02 Heraklion: ✆ +30 2810 399800, fax +30 2810 330308.
Reservations: ✆ +30 210 414 5700.
U.K. agent: Viamare (see Anek Lines).

MOBY LINES www.moby.it
Via Ninci 1, 57037 Portoferraio: ✆ +390 (565) 91 41 33, fax +390 (565) 91 76 52.
Outside Italy: ✆ +49 (0)611 14020, fax +49 (0)611 140 2244.
U.K. agent: Viamare (see Anek Lines).

MOLS-LINIEN www.mols-linien.dk
Færgehavnen, 8400 Ebeltoft: ✆ +45 89 52 52 00, fax +45 89 52 52 90.
Reservations: ✆ +45 70 10 14 18.

MONTENEGRO LINES www.montenegrolines.net
Barska Plovidba, Obala 13 jula bb, 85000 Bar: ✆ +382 30 312 366, fax +382 30 311 652.
Reservations: ✆ +382 30 303 469.

NAVIERA ARMAS www.naviera-armas.com
Juan Rejón 32 - 5 y 6, 35008 Las Palmas de Gran Canaria, España. ✆ +34 (928) 22 72 82, fax +34 (928) 46 99 91.
Call centre: ✆ +34 902 456 500.

NAVIGAZIONE LIBERA del GOLFO www.navlib.it
Molo Beverello, 80133 Napoli: ✆ +39 081 552 07 63, fax +39 081 552 55 89.

NORDIC FERRY SERVICES www.nordic-ferry.com
Damoskibskajen 3, DK-3700 Rønne: ✆ +45 70 23 15 15.

NORDLANDSEKSPRESSEN www.torghatten-nord.no
Postboks 2380, 9271 Tromsø: ✆/fax +47 906 20 700.

NORFOLK LINE www.norfolkline.com
Kranenburgweg 180, 2583 ER The Hague: ✆ + 31 70 35 27 400, fax +31 70 35 27 435.
Reservations: Dover - Dunkerque ✆ 0871 574 7235.
Irish Sea: ✆ 0871 200 0621, 01 800 806 118.

NORTHLINK FERRIES www.northlinkferries.co.uk
Ferry Road, Stromness, KW16 3BH, Orkney: ✆ 01856 88 55 00, fax 01856 85 17 95.
Reservations: ✆ 0845 6000 449.

P & O FERRIES www.poferries.com
Channel House, Channel View Road, Dover, CT17 9TJ: ✆ 08716 645 645; outside U.K.: ✆ +44 1304 863 000.
Belgium ✆ +32 070 70 77 71; France ✆ +33 0825 12 01 56;
Germany ✆ +49 0180 500 9437; Netherlands ✆ +31 020 200 8333;
Spain ✆ +34 902 02 04 61; other countries ✆ +352 34 20 80 82 94.

P & O IRISH SEA www.poirishsea.com
Arran House, 100 Port Ranald Drive, Troon, KA10 6HH.
Larne Harbour, Larne BT40 1AW.
Reservations: U.K. ✆ 0871 66 44 77; Dublin ✆ 01 407 34 34.

POLFERRIES www.polferries.pl
Polish Baltic Shipping Co., ul. Portowa 41, 78 100 Kolobrzeg: ✆ +48 94 35 52 102, fax +48 94 35 52 208.
Reservations: ✆ +48 94 35 52 119, +48 94 35 52 233.

POSEIDON LINES
32 Alkyonidon Avenue, 166 73 Voula, Athina: ✆ +30 210 965 8300, fax +30 210 965 8310.
U.K. agent: Viamare (see Anek Lines).

REEDEREI CASSEN EILS www.helgolandreisen.de
Bei der Alten Liebe 12, 27472 Cuxhaven: ✆ +49 (0)4721 35082, fax +49 (0)4721 31161.

ST PETER LINE
1, ul. Karavannaya, St Peterburg: ✆ +7 (812) 702 07 77. www.stpeterline.com

SALAMIS LINES www.salamisinternational.com
1, G. Katsounotos Str., P.O. Box 50531, 3607 Limassol: ✆ +357 258 60 600, fax +357 253 42 600.
Salamis Cruise Lines: ✆ +357 2586 0000, fax +357 2537 4437.

SAMSØFÆRGEN www.faergen.dk
Færgen, Dampskibskajen 3, 3700 Rønne: ✆ +45 70 23 15 15.

SARDINIA FERRIES www.corsica-ferries.fr
5 bis Rue Chanoine Leschi, 20296 Bastia: ✆ +33 4 95 32 95 95, fax +33 4 95 32 14 71.

SCANDLINES GmbH www.scandlines.de
Hochhaus am Fährhafen, 18119 Rostock: ✆ +49 (0)381 5435-0, fax +49 (0)381 5435-678.
Reservations: Germany ✆ +49 (0)1805 11 66 88; Denmark ✆ +45 33 15 15 15, fax +45 3529 02 01; Latvia ✆ +371 6362 07 83, fax +371 6362 06 90; Lithuania ✆/fax +370 46 310561.

SIREMAR
See Tirrenia for details.

SMYRIL LINE www.smyrilline.com
Yviri Vid Strond 1, Postboks 370, FO-110 Tórshavn: ✆ +298 34 59 00, fax +298 34 59 50.
Reservations: Iceland ✆ +354 570 8600, fax +354 552 9450;
Denmark ✆ +45 96 55 03 60, fax +45 96 55 03 61.
U.K. agent: The Travel Gateway, 2 Morrow Court, Appleford Road, Sutton Courtenay, OX14 4FH: ✆ 0844 576 5503, fax 01235 845108.

SNAV www.snav.it
Stazione Marittima, Molo Angioino, 80133 Napoli: ✆ +39 081 428 55 55, fax +39 081 428 52 59.
U.K. agent: Viamare (see Anek Lines).

SNCM www.sncm.fr
✆ +33 825 88 80 88.
Information: Bordeaux ✆ 05 56 44 46 07; Marseille ✆ 04 91 56 33 90; Nice ✆ 04 93 62 63 07; Toulon ✆ 04 94 16 66 62.
U.K. agent: Southern Ferries (see Acciona Trasmediterranea).

STENA LINE www.stenaline.com
Stena House, Station Approach, Holyhead, LL65 1DQ: ✆ 08447 70 70 70.
Reservations: Denmark ✆ +45 96 200 200; Germany ✆ +49 1805 91 66 66;
Ireland ✆ +353 (0)1204 7777; Netherlands ✆ +31 174 31 58 11;
Northern Ireland ✆ +44 8447 70 70 70; Norway ✆ +47 23 17 91 30;
Poland ✆ +48 58 660 92 00; Sweden ✆ +46 31 704 00 00.

SUPERFAST FERRIES www.superfast.com
123 - 125 Syngrou Av. & 3 Torva Str., 117 45, Athina: ✆ +30 210 891 9000, fax +30 210 891 9029.
Reservations: ✆ +30 210 891 9800; Germany ✆ +49 451 88 00 61 66, fax +49 451 88 00 61 29.
U.K. agents: The Travel Gateway (see Smyril Line); Viamare (see Anek Lines).

TALLINK SILJA www.tallinksilja.com
Keilaranta 9, 02151 Espoo: ✆ +358 9 180 41, fax +358 9 180 4402.
Södra Hamnvägen 50A, 10253 Stockholm: ✆ +46 8 666 3330.
Reservations: ✆ +358 600 174 552; rest of Europe ✆ +49 451 58 99 222, fax +49 451 58 99 203; outside Europe ✆ +358 600 15700.

TIRRENIA www.tirrenia.it
Rione Sirignano 2, Casella Postale 438, 80121 Napoli: ✆ +39 091 749 31 11, fax +39 091 749 33 66. Call centre: ✆ +39 02 2630 2803.
U.K. agent: The Travel Gateway (see Smyril Line).

TOREMAR www.toremar.it
Via Calafati 6, 57123 Livorno. Call centre: ✆ +39 02 2630 2803.
U.K. agent: S.M.S. Travel & Tourism, 40/42 Kenway Road, London, SW5 0RA: ✆ 020 7244 8422, fax 020 7244 9829.

TORGHATTEN NORD AS www.torghatten-nord.no
P.O. Box 2380, 9271 Tromsø: ✆ +47 906 20 700, fax +47 907 20 700.

TRANSEUROPA FERRIES www.transeuropaferries.com
Slijkensesteenweg 2, B-8400 Oostende: ✆ +32 (0)59 340 260, fax +32 (0)59 340 261.
Ferry Terminal, New Port, Ramsgate, CT11 9FT: ✆ 01843 595 522, fax 01843 594 663.

TRANSMANCHE FERRIES www.transmancheferries.com
Ferry Port, Railway Approach, Newhaven, BN9 0DF.
7 Quai Gaston Lalitte, 76200 Dieppe.
Reservations: ✆ 0844 576 8836, fax 01235 84 56 08; outside U.K. and France ✆ +33 (0)2 32 14 52 09.

TT-LINE www.ttline.com
Zum Hafenplatz 1, 23570 Lübeck-Travemünde: ✆ +49 (0)4502 801-81.
Rostock: ✆ +49 (0)381 67079-0; Trelleborg ✆ +46 (0)410 56-200.

UNITY LINE www.unityline.pl
Plac Rodja 8, 70-419, Szczecin: ✆ +48 (0)91 35 95 795, fax +48 (0)91 35 95 885.
Reservations: ✆ +48 (0)91 35 95 600.
Färjeterminalen, 271 39 Ystad: ✆ +46 (0)411 55 69 00, fax +46 (0)411 55 69 53.

USTICA LINES www.usticalines.it
Via Orlandini 48, 91100 Trapani: ✆ +39 0923 873 813, fax +39 0923 593 200.

VAASANLAIVAT www.vaasanlaivat.fi
Vaasanlaivat, Laivanvarustajankatu 3, FIN-65170 Vaasa.
Reservations: ✆ +358 (0)207 716 810.

VENTOURIS FERRIES www.ventouris.gr
17 Gr. Lampraki Str., 185 33 Pireás: ✆ +30 210 482 8001-4, fax +30 210 483 2909.
UK agent: Viamare (see Anek Lines).

VIKING LINE www.vikingline.fi
Lönnrotinkatu 2, FIN-00100 Helsinki: ✆ +358 (0)9 12 351, fax +358 (0)9 647 075.
U.K. agent: Emagine U.K. Ltd, Leigh, WN7 1AZ: ✆ 01942 262 662, fax 01942 606 500.

VIRTU FERRIES LTD www.virtuferries.com
Sea Passenger Terminal, Pinto Road, Valletta, FRN 1910, Malta: ✆ +356 2206 9022, fax +356 21 235 435.

TIME COMPARISON

COMPARAISON DES HEURES COMPARAZIONE DELLE ORE ZEITVERGLEICH COMPARACIÓN DE LAS HORAS

West European Time	*WINTER: GMT* *SUMMER: GMT +1*	Algeria, Morocco, Canaries, Tunisia, Faeroe Islands	East European Time	*WINTER: GMT +2* *SUMMER: GMT +3*	Cyprus
Central European Time	*WINTER: GMT +1* *SUMMER: GMT +2*	Israel			

Daylight Saving Time ('Summer Time') applies between 0100 GMT on March 30 and 0100 GMT on October 26, 2014 *(GMT = Greenwich Mean Time = UTC,*

Time comparison for countries with their own section in the ERT are shown on page 2

BELFAST - CAIRNRYAN 2002

Stena Line by ship — 2014 service
Sailings from Stranraer and Belfast. (No service Dec. 25)

Belfast		Cairnryan	
0330	→	0545	②③④⑤⑥
0730	→	0945	
1130	→	1345	
1530	→	1745	
1930	→	2145	
2300	→	0115	⑦
2330	→	0145	①②③④⑤⑥

Cairnryan		Belfast	
0400	→	0615	②③④⑤⑥
0530	→	0745	⑦
0730	→	0945	①②③④⑤⑥
1130	→	1345	
1530	→	1745	
1930	→	2145	
2330	→	0145	①②③④⑤⑥
2359	→	0215	⑦

Subject to alteration during Xmas/New Year period

CAIRNRYAN - LARNE 2005

P & O Irish Sea by ship Journey 2 hours — 2014 service

Until June 30 and from September 1
Depart Cairnryan and Larne: 0400①②③④⑤⑥, 0730, 1030①②③④⑤⑥, 1300⑦, 1330①②③④⑤⑥, 1630, 2000, 2300⑦, 2359①②③④⑤.

July 1 - August 31
Depart Cairnryan and Larne: 0400①②③④⑤⑥, 0730, 1030, 1330, 1630, 2000, 2300⑦, 2359①②③④⑤.

Subject to alteration during Easter and Xmas/New Year period.

CHERBOURG - ROSSLARE 2010

Celtic Link Ferries by ship — 2014 service
Sailings from Portsmouth Continental Ferry Port and Cherbourg.

Cherbourg		Rosslare
1600⑦	→	0900①
2100③	→	1500④
2100⑤	→	1200⑥

Rosslare		Cherbourg
1600⑥	→	1000⑦
2130②	→	1530③
2130④	→	1630⑤

Irish Ferries — 2014 service

Cherbourg		Rosslare	
1800	→	1130	May 12, 14, 20, 26, 28, June 3, 9, 11, 17, 23, 25, July 1, 7, 9, 13, 15, 21, 23, 27, 29, Aug. 2, 4, 6, 10, 12, 14, 18, 20, 24, 26, 28, Sept. 1, 3, 7, 9, 15, 17, 21, 23.
2000	→	1400	② Mar. 4 - May 6, Sept. 30 - Dec. 16.
2130	→	1430	⑥ Mar. 1 - May 3, Sept. 27 - Dec. 13.
2130	→	1530	④ Mar. 6 - May 8, Sept. 25 - Dec. 18.

Rosslare		Cherbourg	
1530	→	1100	May 11, 13, 19, 25, 27, June 2, 8, 10, 16, 22, 24, 30, July 6, 8, 12, 14, 20, 22, 26, 28, Aug. 1, 3, 5, 9, 11, 13, 17, 19, 23, 25, 25, 27, 31, Sept. 2, 6, 8, 14, 16, 20, 22.
1800	→	1400	⑦ Mar. 2 - May 4, Sept. 28 - Dec. 14.
2130	→	1630	⑤ Mar. 7 - May 2, Sept. 26 - Dec. 12.
2130	→	1700	③ Mar. 5 - May 7, Sept. 24 - Dec. 17.

CORK - ROSCOFF 2015

Brittany Ferries — Service to October 31, 2014 (No winter service)
Sailings from Cork (Ringaskiddy) and Roscoff.

Cork		Roscoff	
1600⑥	→	0700⑦§	Mar. 15 - Nov. 1.

Roscoff		Cork	
2030⑤	→	0930⑥	Mar. 14 - May 9, Sept. 26 - Oct. 31.
2130⑤¶	→	1000⑥	May 16 - Sept. 19.

§ – Arrive 0645 on May 25; 0620 on July 20.
¶ – Depart 2110 Sept. 5.

Times may vary owing to tidal conditions.

DOUGLAS - BELFAST 2020

Isle Of Man Steam Packet Co. by SeaCat — Service to September 30, 2014 (No winter service)
Sailings from Belfast Albert Quay.

Douglas		Belfast	
0500	→	0745	May 27 only.
0700	→	0945	See note **A**.
0945	→	1230	June 1 only.
1500	→	1745	Apr. 18 only.
1930	→	0015	See note **B**.

Belfast		Douglas	
0100	→	0545	See note **C**.
0930	→	1215	May 27 only.
1045	→	1330	See note **D**.
1145	→	1430	Aug. 20, 24 only.
1500	→	1745	June 1 only.
1845	→	2130	Apr. 18 only.

A – Apr. 23, 27, May 7, 13, 21, 27; ③⑦ June 15 - July 16; July 22, 27, 30, Aug. 13, 20, 24, 26, 31, Sept. 3, 10 (also June 10, July 11).
B – Apr. 19, July 19, Aug. 9, 16; ⑥ Sept. 6 - 27.
C – Apr. 20, July 20, Aug. 10, 17; ⑦ Sept. 7 - 28.
D – Apr. 23, 27, May 7, 13, 21; ③⑦ June 15 - July 16; July 22, 27, 30, Aug. 3, 6, 13, 26, 31, Sept. 3, 10 (also June 10, July 11).

A special service operates during the TT Race period

DOUGLAS - DUBLIN 2025

Isle Of Man Steam Packet Co. by SeaCat — Service to September 30, 2014 (No winter service)
Sailings from Dublin North Wall.

Douglas		Dublin	
0700	→	0955	See note **E**.
1800	→	2055	June 3 only.
1930	→	0015	July 5, 12, 26.

Dublin		Douglas	
0100	→	0545	July 6, 13, 27.
1045	→	1340	See note **G**.
1130	→	1415	May 25 only.
2200	→	0045	June 3 only.

E – Apr. 16, 20, May 25, June 11; ② June 17 - Aug. 12; Aug. 17, 27, Sept. 4 (also July 20, 23; not July 22).
F – July 5, 12, 26.
G – Apr. 16, 20, June 11; ② June 17 - Aug. 12; Aug. 17, 27, Sept. 4 (also July 20, 23; not July 22).

A special service operates during the TT Race period

FISHGUARD - ROSSLARE 2030

Stena Line by ship — 2014 service (No service Dec. 25, 26)

Fishguard		Rosslare
0245	→	0615
1430	→	1800

Rosslare		Fishguard
0900	→	1230
2100§	→	0015

§ – Dec. 24 depart 1900.

HEYSHAM - DOUGLAS 2035

Isle Of Man Steam Packet Co. — June 1 - September 30, 2014 (No service Dec. 25)
Sailings from Heysham Port and Douglas.

Heysham		Douglas	
0215	→	0545	Daily June 1 - 28; ①②③④⑤⑥ June 30 - Aug. 16; daily Aug. 18 - Sept. 6; ①②③④⑤⑥ Sept. 8 - 30 (not June 19 - 21).
1200	→	1400	June 19 - 21 only.
1415	→	1745	Daily June 1 - Sept. 30 (not June 19 - 21).

Douglas		Heysham	
0845	→	1045	June 19 - 21 only.
0845	→	1215	Daily June 1 - Sept. 30 (not June 19 - 21).
1945	→	2315	①②③④⑤⑦ June 1 - Sept. 30 (not June 18 - 20).
2000	→	2330	Aug. 23, 30 only.

A special service operates during the TT Race period (until June 9)

HOLYHEAD - DUBLIN 2040

Irish Ferries by ship — 2014 service (No service Dec. 25, 26)
Sailings from Holyhead and Dublin Ferryport.

Holyhead		Dublin	
0240	→	0555	Not Dec. 27.
0800	→	1130	②③④⑤⑥
1410	→	1725	
2000	→	2315	②③④⑤

Dublin		Holyhead	
0155	→	0525	②③④⑤⑥
0805	→	1130	
1415	→	1745	②③④⑤
2055	→	0020	Not Dec. 24.

Sailing times may vary owing to tidal conditions.
🚌 Dublin Ferryport - Dublin Busaras (Central Bus Station).

Irish Ferries by fast ferry Journey 2 hours — 2014 service (No service Dec. 25, 26)
Sailings from Holyhead and Dublin Ferryport.
Depart Holyhead: 1150, 1715 (not Dec. 24).
Depart Dublin: 0845, 1430 (not Dec. 24).
🚌 Dublin Ferryport - Dublin Busaras (Central Bus Station).

Stena Line by ship — 2014 service (No service Dec. 25, 26)
Sailings from Holyhead and Dublin Ferryport.

Holyhead		Dublin	
0230	→	0545	
0855§	→	1210	
1350	→	1705	
2030§	→	2345	Not Dec. 24.

Dublin		Holyhead	
0215§	→	0545	Not Dec. 27.
0820	→	1150	
1510§	→	1840	
1830	→	2200	Dec. 24 only.
2030	→	2400	Not Dec. 24.

Subject to alteration during Xmas/New Year period

§ – No foot passengers conveyed.

HOLYHEAD - DUN LAOGHAIRE 2045

Stena Line by *HSS* fast ferry — April 9 - September 9, 2014
Sailings from Holyhead and Dun Laoghaire.

Holyhead		Dun Laoghaire
1030	→	1245

Dun Laoghaire		Holyhead
1330	→	1545

🚌 Dun Laoghaire - Dublin Busaras (Central Bus Station).

2050 BIRKENHEAD (LIVERPOOL) - BELFAST

Stena Line — 2014 service (No service Dec. 25)

Sailings from Birkenhead Twelve Quays Terminal and Belfast Victoria Terminal.

Birkenhead		Belfast		Belfast		Birkenhead	
1030	→	1830	②③④⑤⑥⑦	1030	→	1830	②③④⑤⑥⑦
2200	→	0600	①	2200	→	0600	①
2230	→	0630	②③④⑤⑥⑦	2230	→	0630	②③④⑤⑥⑦

2052 LIVERPOOL - DUBLIN

P & O Irish Sea — 2014 service

Conveys passengers with vehicles only

Liverpool		Dublin		Dublin		Liverpool	
0300	→	1030	①②③④⑤⑥	0900	→	1700	②③④⑤⑥
0930	→	1730	②③④⑤⑥	1500	→	2330	①②③④⑤
2100	→	0500		1600	→	2359	⑦
				2130	→	0530	

Subject to alteration during holiday periods

2053 LIVERPOOL - DOUGLAS

Isle Of Man Steam Packet Co. — Service to September 30, 2014

Sailings from Liverpool Landing Stage and Douglas.

Liverpool		Douglas	
1115	→	1400	①⑤⑥ Mar. 28 - Apr. 28; ①④⑤⑥ June 16 - Sept. 22 (also Apr. 17, 22, 24, May 22 - 24, Sept. 2; not July 3, 11, Sept. 4, 11, 18).
1915	→	2200	Daily.
Douglas		**Liverpool**	
0730	→	1015	①⑤⑥ Mar. 28 - Apr. 28; ①④⑤⑥ June 16 - Sept. 22 (also Apr. 17, 22, 24, May 22 - 24, Sept. 2; not July 3, 11, Sept. 4, 11, 18).
1500	→	1745	Daily.

Sailing times may vary.

A special service operates during the TT Race period (May 25 - June 14, also Aug. 10 - 31)

2055 PEMBROKE - ROSSLARE

Irish Ferries — 2014 service (No service Dec. 25, 26)

Pembroke		Rosslare	Rosslare		Pembroke
0245	→	0645	0845	→	1245
1445	→	1845	2045	→	0045

Sailing times may vary owing to tidal conditions

2065 ROSSLARE - ROSCOFF

Irish Ferries — 2014 service (No winter service)

Rosslare		Roscoff		Roscoff		Rosslare	
1630	→	1030	See note **R**.	1830	→	1100	See note **S**.
1730	→	1100	May 9 only.	1900	→	1100	See note **T**.

R – May 15, 17, 21, 23, 29, 31, June 4, 6, 12, 14, 18, 20, 26, 28, July 2, 4, 10, 16, 18, 24, 30, Aug. 7, 15, 21, 29, Sept. 4, 10, 12, 18.

S – May 10, 22, 24, June 7, 13, 21, 27, 29, July 5, 11, 17, 19, 25, Aug. 8, 16, 22, 30, Sept. 5, 13, 19.

T – May 16, 18, 30, June 1, 5, 15, 19, July 3, 31, Sept. 11.

2080 TROON - LARNE

P & O Irish Sea — March 31 - October 6, 2014 (No winter service)

Troon		Larne	Larne		Troon
1100	→	1315	0745	→	1000
1930	→	2145	1615	→	1830

ENGLISH CHANNEL & BAY OF BISCAY

2100 CHANNEL ISLAND SERVICES

POOLE - GUERNSEY - JERSEY by fast ferry

Condor Ferries — 2014 service

Sailings from Poole, St Peter Port and St Helier Elizabeth Terminal.

Apr. - Oct.: 1 – 3 sailings per week (5 – 7 sailings in peak summer).

Departure times vary owing to tidal conditions.

WEYMOUTH and POOLE - GUERNSEY / JERSEY - ST MALO by fast ferry

Condor Ferries — 2014 service

Sailings by catamaran from St Helier Elizabeth Terminal or Albert Quay, St Malo Gare Maritime de la Bourse and St Peter Port.

1 – 3 sailings per week (5 – 7 sailings Apr. - Sept.). Journey 4½ – 5½ hours.

Most sailings from Weymouth. A change of vessel may be necessary in either Guernsey or Jersey (extended journey time).

Departure times vary owing to tidal conditions.

WEYMOUTH - GUERNSEY - JERSEY by fast ferry

Condor Ferries — 2014 service

Sailings by catamaran from Weymouth Quay, St Peter Port and St Helier Elizabeth Terminal.

①⑤⑥ Mar. 3 - 31; daily Apr. 2 - Sept. 28; ①③④⑤⑥⑦ Sept. 29 - Nov. 2; ①⑤ Nov. 3 - 28 (also Mar. 2; not Apr. 29).

Connections available Jersey - St Malo and v.v. most days.

Departure times vary owing to tidal conditions.

OTHER SERVICES:

Manche îles Express operate catamaran services in summer from Jersey to Carteret, Granville, Sark and Guernsey, and from Guernsey to Alderney and Diélette.

2110 DOVER - CALAIS

DFDS Seaways / LD Lines by ship — 2014 service

Sailings from Dover Eastern Docks and Calais Maritime. Journey 90 minutes

Conveys passengers with vehicles only.

Depart Dover: 0030, 0230①②③④⑤⑥, 0515①②③④⑤⑥, 0730, 1015, 1215, 1445, 1645, 1915, 2115.

Depart Calais: 0100①②③④⑤⑥, 0400①②③④⑤⑥, 0600, 0900, 1100, 1330, 1530, 1800, 2000, 2300.

P & O Ferries Journey 90 minutes — 2014 service

Sailings from Dover Eastern Docks and Calais Maritime. (No service Dec. 25)

On night services, conveys passengers with vehicles only. Timings subject to variation.

February 12 - 24

From Dover: 0050, 0220①②③④⑤⑥, 0320, 0420①②③④⑤⑥, 0640, 0735, 0825, 0925, 1015, 1110, 1205, 1255, 1355, 1445 1540, 1640, 1725, 1835, 1915, 2015, 2120①②③④⑤⑦, 2205, 2315.

From Calais: 0030①②③④⑤⑥, 0120, 0240①②③④⑤⑥, 0435, 0545①②③④⑤⑥, 0630⑦, 0645①②③④⑤⑥, 0745, 0850, 0950, 1045, 1135, 1235, 1325, 1420, 1520, 1605, 1715, 1755, 1850, 1955, 2035, 2145, 2335.

February 25 - March 13

From Dover: 0045, 0225, 0340, 0450, 0630, 0740, 0845, 0955, 1100, 1210, 1315, 1425, 1530, 1645, 1745, 1905, 2005, 2125, 2225, 2345.

From Calais: 0035, 0140, 0310, 0425, 0550, 0705, 0815, 0940, 1050, 1155, 1305, 1410, 1525, 1625, 1745, 1840, 2000, 2055, 2215, 2325.

March 14 - December 15

From Dover: 0050, 0220①②③④⑤⑥, 0320, 0420①②③④⑤⑥, 0640, 0735, 0825, 0925, 1015, 1110, 1205, 1255, 1355, 1445, 1540, 1640, 1725, 1835, 1915, 2015, 2120①②③④⑤⑦, 2205, 2315.

From Calais: 0030①②③④⑤⑥, 0120, 0240①②③④⑤⑥, 0435, 0545①②③④⑤⑥, 0630⑦, 0645①②③④⑤⑥, 0745, 0850, 0950, 1045, 1135, 1235, 1325, 1420, 1520, 1605, 1715, 1755, 1850, 1955, 2035, 2145, 2335.

▲ – A reduced service will operate Dec. 24 - 27 (no service on Dec. 25).

🚌 connections:

Dover Eastern Docks - Dover Priory station: from Dover Eastern Docks on arrival of ship; from Dover Priory station approximately every 20 minutes 0715 – 1930.

Calais Port - Calais Ville station 1100 – 1745; Calais Ville station - Calais Port 1030 – 1800.

DOVER - DUNKERQUE 2111

DFDS Seaways by ship **2014 service**

Sailings from Dover Eastern Docks and Dunkerque. Journey 2 hours

Conveys passengers with vehicles only

Depart Dover: 0200②③④⑤⑥, 0400①②③④⑤, 0600①②③④⑤⑥, 0800, 1000①②③④⑤⑥, 1200, 1400, 1600, 1800, 2000①②③④⑤⑦, 2200, 2359①②③④⑤⑦.

Depart Dunkerque: 0200①②③④⑤, 0400①②③④⑤⑥, 0600, 0800①②③④⑤⑥, 1000, 1200, 1400, 1600, 1800①②③④⑤⑦, 2000, 2200①②③④⑤⑦, 2359①②③④⑤.

NEWHAVEN - DIEPPE 2125

Transmanche Ferries / L D Lines **2014 service**

Sailings from Newhaven and Dieppe. **(No service Dec. 25)**

Newhaven		Dieppe	Dieppe		Newhaven
1000	→	1500	0530	→	0830
2300	→	0400	1800	→	2100

Newhaven ferry terminal is adjacent to Newhaven Town rail station.
For rail services see Table **101**.

Departure times may vary owing to tidal conditions.

PENZANCE - ST. MARY'S 2130

Isles Of Scilly Steamship Co. **2014 service**

Sailings from Penzance Lighthouse Pier and St Mary's. **(No winter service)**

Penzance		St Mary's		St Mary's		Penzance	
0630	→	0910	May 24.	0945	→	1225	May 24.
0700	→	0940	May 31.	1015	→	1255	May 31.
0915	→	1155	See note **A**.	1400	→	1640	See note **D**.
1030	→	1310	⑥⑦ June 29 - Sept. 7.	1500	→	1740	See note **B**.
1330	→	1610	May 24.	1630	→	1910	See note **C**.
1415	→	1655	May 31.	1645	→	1925	May 24.
				1730	→	2010	May 31.

A – ①③⑤⑥ Mar. 17-22; ①②③④⑤⑥ Mar. 24 - May 1; ①②③④⑤⑥ May 6-23; ①②③④⑤ May 26-30; ①②③④⑤⑥ June 2-28; ①②③④⑤ June 29 - Sept. 7; ①②③④⑤⑥ Sept. 8 - Oct. 11; ①③⑤⑥ Oct. 13 - Nov. 8.
B – ⑥⑦ June 29 - Sept. 7; ①③⑤⑥ Oct. 20 - Nov. 1.
C – ①③⑤⑥ Mar. 17-22; ①②③④⑤⑥ Mar. 24 - May 1; ①②③④⑤⑥ May 6-23; ①②③④⑤ May 26-30; ①②③④⑤⑥ June 2-28; ①②③④⑤ June 29 - Sept. 7; ①②③④⑤⑥ Sept. 8 - Oct. 11; ①③⑤⑥ Oct. 13-18.
D – ①③⑤⑥ Nov. 3-18.

Departure times may vary owing to tidal conditions.

PLYMOUTH - ROSCOFF 2135

Brittany Ferries Departure times vary **Service to October 31, 2014**

Sailings from Plymouth Millbay and Roscoff.

From Plymouth: Feb. 6, 7, 9-11, 13, 14, 16-18, 20-22, Mar. 13 - Oct. 31: 1–2 sailings daily (not Oct. 30).

From Roscoff: Feb. 7, 8, 10-12, 14, 15, 17-19, 21-23, Mar. 15-20, 22-27, 29-31, Apr. 1 - Oct. 31: 1–2 sailings daily (not Oct. 30).

PLYMOUTH - SANTANDER 2140

Brittany Ferries **Service to October 31, 2014**

Sailings from Plymouth Millbay and Santander. **(No winter service)**

Plymouth		Santander	
1545⑦	→	1215①	Mar. 16 - Oct. 26.
Santander		**Plymouth**	
1730③	→	1200④	Mar. 12 only.
2115③	→	1615④	Mar. 19 - Oct. 29.

PLYMOUTH - ST MALO 2142

Brittany Ferries **Service to October 31, 2014**
(No service Apr. - Oct.)

Sailings from Plymouth Millbay and St Malo Terminal Ferry du Naye.

Plymouth		St Malo	
2045	→	0820	Oct. 30 only.
2200	→	0800	Feb. 23 only.
St Malo		**Plymouth**	
2030	→	0800	Feb. 5, Oct. 30 only.

POOLE - CHERBOURG 2145

Brittany Ferries **Service to November 3, 2014**
(No winter service)

Poole		Cherbourg		Cherbourg		Poole	
0830	→	1345	Mar. 28 - Nov. 3.	1830	→	2145	See note **P**.
				2215	→	0700	See note **Q**.

P – ①④⑤⑥⑦ Mar. 27 - July 14; daily July 17 - Sept. 8; ①④⑤⑥⑦ Sept. 11 - Nov. 3.
Q – ②③ May 6 - July 16, Sept. 9 - Oct. 29.

🚌 Cherbourg Port - Cherbourg station (operated by Zéphir).

PORTSMOUTH - BILBAO 2155

Brittany Ferries **Service to November 3, 2014**

Conveys passengers with vehicles only

Portsmouth		Bilbao	
1145③	→	1245④	Mar. 19 - Oct. 29 (also Feb. 5).
1700⑤	→	1730⑥	Mar. 14 only.
2230⑦	→	0745②	Mar. 16 - Nov. 2 (also Feb. 2, 9).
Bilbao		**Portsmouth**	
1030②	→	0900③	Mar. 18 - Oct. 28 (also Feb. 4, 11).
1530④	→	1415⑤	Mar. 20 - Oct. 30 (also Feb. 6).
2030⑥	→	1945⑦	Mar. 15 only.

PORTSMOUTH - CHANNEL ISLANDS 2157

Condor Ferries by ship **2014 service**

Sailings from Portsmouth Continental Ferry Port, St Helier and St Peter Port.

Portsmouth		St Peter Port		St Helier	
0900	→	A	→	B	①②③④⑤⑥ Jan. 1 - Nov. 15; daily Nov. 17-30.
St Helier		**St Peter Port**		**Portsmouth**	
C	→	D	→	0630	①②③④⑤⑥ Jan. 1 - Nov. 15; daily Nov. 17-30.

A – Most arrivals 1600, but variations possible between 1555 and 2300.
B – Most arrivals 1920, but variations possible between 1705 and 2050.
C – Most departures 2120, but variations possible between 1835 and 2220.
D – Most departures 1720, but variations possible between 1720 and 2359.

Times may vary owing to tidal conditions.

PORTSMOUTH - CHERBOURG 2160

Brittany Ferries by fast ferry **2014 service**

Sailings from Portsmouth Continental Ferry Port and Cherbourg. **(No winter service)**

Portsmouth		Cherbourg	
0900	→	1300	Daily Apr. 17 - May 21; ①②③ May 26 - Sept. 9.
1600	→	2000	④⑤⑥⑦ May 22 - Sept. 7.
Cherbourg		**Portsmouth**	
1700	→	1900	Daily Apr. 17 - May 21; ①②③ May 26 - Sept. 8.
2045	→	2245	④⑤⑥⑦ May 22 - Sept. 7.

🚌 Cherbourg Port - Cherbourg station (operated by Zéphir).

Condor Ferries by ship **May 25 - September 7, 2014**

Sailings from Portsmouth Continental Ferry Port and Cherbourg. **(No winter service)**

Portsmouth		Cherbourg	Cherbourg		Portsmouth
0900⑦	→	1530⑦	1615⑦	→	2015⑦

PORTSMOUTH - LE HAVRE 2165

Brittany Ferries by fast ferry **May 22 - September 7, 2014**
(No winter service)

Sailings from Portsmouth Continental Ferry Port and Le Havre Terminal de la Citadelle.

Portsmouth		Le Havre		Le Havre		Portsmouth	
0700	→	1145	④⑤⑥⑦	1230	→	1515	④⑤⑥⑦

A shuttle 🚌 service operates between the terminal and railway station

L D Lines **2014 service**

Sailings from Portsmouth Continental Ferry Port and Le Havre Terminal de la Citadelle.

Portsmouth		Le Havre	Le Havre		Portsmouth
2300	→	0800	1700	→	2130

A shuttle 🚌 service operates between the terminal and railway station

2170 PORTSMOUTH - OUISTREHAM (CAEN)

Brittany Ferries by ship — **Service to November 3, 2014 (No service Dec. 25, Jan. 1)**

Sailings from Portsmouth Continental Ferry Port and Ouistreham.

Portsmouth		Ouistreham		Ouistreham		Portsmouth	
0815	→	1500	See note A.	0830	→	1315	See note F.
1445	→	2130	See note B.	1400	→	1915	See note G.
2200	→	0645	See note C.	1630	→	2115	See note H.
2200	→	0730	⑦ Sept. 14 - Oct. 26.	2300	→	0645	Daily (not Feb. 26).
2245	→	0645	See note D.				
2245	→	0730	See note E.				

A – ①②③④⑥⑦ Feb. 1 - May 18; ①②④⑤⑥⑦ May 19 - Sept. 9; daily Sept. 11 - Nov. 3 (not Feb. 26, Oct. 22).
B – Daily Feb. 1 - Sept. 13; ②③④⑥ Sept. 16 - Nov. 1 (also Oct. 24, Nov. 2, 3; not Feb. 3, 26).
C – ①⑤ Sept. 15 - Oct. 31.
D – ①②③⑤⑥⑦ Feb. 1 - May 18; ①③④⑤⑥⑦ May 19 - Sept. 12; ②③ Sept. 16 - Oct. 29 (also Oct. 23, Nov. 1, 2, 3; not Oct. 21).
E – ④ Feb. 6 - May 15; ② May 20 - Sept. 9; ④⑥ Sept. 13 - Oct. 30 (also Oct. 21; not Oct. 23).
F – ①②③④⑥⑦ Feb. 1 - May 18; ①②④⑤⑥⑦ May 19 - Sept. 13; ②③④⑥ Sept. 16 - Nov. 1 (also Nov. 2, 3).
G – ⑤ Feb. 28 - Mar. 7; ①⑤⑦ Sept. 14 - Oct. 31 (not Oct. 24).
H – Daily Feb. 1 - Sept. 13; ②③④⑥ Sept. 16 - Nov. 1 (also Oct. 24, Nov. 2, 3; not Feb. 26, 28, Mar. 7).

🚌 Ouistreham - Caen station (journey 45 minutes) to connect with most sailings.

2175 PORTSMOUTH - SANTANDER

Brittany Ferries Journey time 24 hours — **Service to November 1, 2014**

Sailings from Portsmouth Continental Ferry Port and Santander.

Portsmouth		Santander	
1100	→	1215	②⑤ Feb. 25 - Mar. 11.
1145	→	1245	Feb. 12, 19 only.
1700	→	1730	⑤ Feb. 7 - 21; ③ Mar. 21 - Oct. 31.
1715	→	1815	② Mar. 18 - Oct. 28.
2230	→	0745	⑦ Feb. 16 - 23.

Santander		Portsmouth	
1030	→	0900	Feb. 18 only.
1515	→	1415	① Mar. 17 - Oct. 27.
1530	→	1415	④ Feb. 13 - 20.
1730	→	1700	③⑥ Feb. 26 - Mar. 8.
2030	→	1915	Nov. 1 only.
2030	→	1945	⑥ Feb. 1 - 22; ⑥ Mar. 22 - Oct. 25.

2180 PORTSMOUTH - ST MALO

Brittany Ferries Departure times vary — **Service to November 3, 2014**

Sailings from Portsmouth Continental Ferry Port and St. Malo Terminal Ferry du Naye.

From Portsmouth: Feb. 2 - 5, 7, 9, 10, 12, 14, 16, 17, 19, 21, 24, 26, 28, Mar. 1 - 3, 5, 7 - 10, 12, 14, 16, 17, 19, 21, 23, 24, 26, 28, 30, 31; ①③④⑤⑥⑦ Apr. 2 - July 14; daily July 16 - Sept. 8; Sept. 10 - 15, 17, 19, 21, 22, 24, 26, 28, 29, Oct. 1, 3, 5, 6, 8, 10, 12, 13, 15, 17, 19, 20, 22 - 24, 26, 27, 29.

From St. Malo: Feb. 1, 3, 4, 6, 8, 10, 11, 13, 15, 17, 18, 20, 22, 24, 25, 27, Mar. 1 - 4, 6, 8 - 11, 13, 15, 17, 18, 20, 22, 24, 25, 27, 29, 31; ①②④⑤⑥⑦ Apr. 1 - July 15; daily July 17 - Sept. 9; Sept. 11 - 16, 18, 20, 22, 23, 25, 27, 29, 30, Oct. 2, 4, 6, 7, 9, 11, 13, 14, 16, 18, 20, 21, 23 - 25, 27, 28, 31, Nov. 3.

2195 SAINT-NAZAIRE - GIJÓN

L D Lines — **2014 service**

Conveys passengers with vehicles only

St-Nazaire		Gijón	Gijón		St-Nazaire
1800④	→	1000⑤	1700⑦	→	0800①
1900①	→	1100②	1900③	→	1100④
2200⑥	→	1300⑦	2200②	→	1400③

NORTH SEA

2200 ABERDEEN - KIRKWALL - LERWICK

NorthLink Ferries — **2014 service**

Aberdeen		Kirkwall		Kirkwall		Lerwick
January 2 - March 31 and November 1 - December 30						
1700④⑥⑦	→	2300④⑥⑦	→	2345④⑥⑦	→	0730⑤⑦①
1900①②③⑤	→	→	→	→	→	0730②③④⑥
April 1 - October 31						
1700②④⑥⑦	→	2300②④⑥⑦	→	2345②④⑥⑦	→	0730③⑤⑦①
1900①③⑤	→	→	→	→	→	0730②④⑥

Lerwick		Kirkwall		Kirkwall		Aberdeen
January 2 - March 31 and November 1 - December 30						
1730③⑤	→	2300③⑤	→	2345③⑤	→	0700④⑥
1900①②④⑥⑦	→	→	→	→	→	0700②③⑤⑦①
April 1 - October 31						
1730①③⑤	→	2300①③⑤	→	2345①③⑤	→	0700②④⑥
1900②④⑥⑦	→	→	→	→	→	0700③⑤⑦①

Subject to alteration during ship maintenance

A 🚌 transfer service is available Kirkwall - Stromness and v.v. in conjunction with evening sailings.

2220 HARWICH - ESBJERG

DFDS Seaways — **2014 service**

Sailings from Harwich International Port and Esbjerg Englandskajen.

Harwich		Esbjerg	
1745§	→	1300	③⑤⑦ Mar. 2 - May 17; uneven dates May 21 - 31; even dates June 2 - July 30; uneven dates Aug. 1 - 31; even dates Sept. 2 - 14; ③⑤⑦ Sept. 17 - Oct. 31; ③⑦ Nov. 2 - Dec. 28 (also Dec. 19, 23, 30; not Mar. 7, Dec. 24).

Esbjerg		Harwich	
1845⊡	→	1200	②④⑥ Mar. 1 - May 24; even dates May 26 - 30; uneven dates June 1 - July 31; even dates Aug. 2 - 30; uneven dates Sept. 1 - 13; ②④⑥ Sept. 16 - Oct. 30; ②⑥ Nov. 1 - Dec. 27 (also Dec. 18, 22, 29; not Mar. 6, Dec. 23).

§ – Depart 1715 on ⑦.
⊡ – Depart 1715 on Mar. 1, 8, and ⑥ Nov. 8 - Dec. 13.

Additional sailings available in peak summer

For rail services from / to London – see Table **200**

2235 HARWICH - HOEK VAN HOLLAND

Stena Line by ship — **2014 service (No service Dec. 24, 25)**

Sailings from Harwich International Port and Hoek van Holland.

Harwich		Hoek		Hoek		Harwich	
0900	→	1645	See note H.	1430	→	2000	Not Oct. 1 - 7, Dec. 26.
1000	→	1800	⑦	2130	→	0630	⑥⑦
2315	→	0745	Not Oct. 1 - 6, Dec. 31.	2230	→	0630	See note J.

H – ①②③④⑤⑥ (not Oct. 7, Dec. 26). J – ①②③④⑤ (not Dec. 31).

See Table **15a** for connecting rail services London - Harwich and v.v. and Hoek van Holland - Amsterdam and v.v.

2237 HIRTSHALS - STAVANGER - BERGEN

Fjord Line — **2014 service (No service Dec. 24, 25)**

Hirtshals		Stavanger		Bergen		Stavanger		Hirtshals
Until March 16								
2100⑥	→	0600⑦		...		1000⑦	→	1900⑦
2100②④⑦	→	0700③⑤①	→	1315 / 1430③⑤①	→	2100③⑤①	→	0700④⑥②
March 17 - August 31								
2130①	→	0700②		...		2100②	→	0730③
2130②	→	0700③	→	1300 / 1415③	→	2100③	→	0730④
2130③	→	0700④	→	1300 / 1415④	→	2100④	→	0730⑤
2130④	→	0700⑤	→	1300 / 1415⑤	→	2100⑤	→	0730⑥
2130⑤	→	0700⑥	→	1300 / 1415⑥	→	2100⑥	→	0730⑦
2130⑥	→	0700⑦	→	1300 / 1415⑦	→	2100⑦	→	0730①
2130⑦	→	0700①	→	1300 / 1415①	→	2100①	→	0730②

Subject to alteration during Xmas / New Year period

2239 LOFOTEN ISLANDS

Torghatten Nord by fast ferry — **Service to January 31, 2015**

BODØ - SVOLVÆR

Bodø		Svolvær		Svolvær		Bodø	
1715	→	2050	①②③④⑥	0630	→	1000	①②③④⑤⑥
1800	→	2135	⑤	1600	→	1930	⑦
2030	→	2330	⑦				

Torghatten Nord by ship — **Service to February 1, 2015**

BODØ - MOSKENES

Bodø		Moskenes		Moskenes		Bodø	
Until June 12 and August 18 - February 1							
0015	→	0330	②④⑤	0700	→	1015	①②③④⑤⑥
0130	→	0545	③	1200	→	1900	⑦
1300	→	1630	⑦	1700	→	2359	⑦
1530	→	1845	③	1900	→	2345	③
1630	→	1945	①②④⑤⑥	2030	→	2345	①②④
2100	→	0015	⑦				
June 13 - August 17							
0045	→	0415		0600	→	0915	
0430	→	0800	①②③④⑤⑥	1030	→	1430	
0600	→	1000		1400	→	1715	
1015	→	1330		1930	→	2330	
1500	→	1900		2115	→	0030	
1745	→	2100		2359	→	0330	①②③④⑤⑦

NORWEGIAN COASTAL SERVICES 2240

Hurtigruten — 2014 service

BERGEN - TRONDHEIM - TROMSØ - KIRKENES

NORTHBOUND

	WINTER ❖ arrive	*WINTER* ❖ depart	*SUMMER* ❖ arrive	*SUMMER* ❖ depart	day
Bergen ♣	...	2230◇	...	2000	A
Florø	0430	0445	0200	0215	B
Måløy	0715	0730	0415	0430	B
Torvik	1030	1045	0715	0730	B
Ålesund	1200‡	1500‡	0800	0845	B
Geiranger ▲	|	|	1325 g	1330 g	B
Urke ▲	|	|	1130 h	1500 h	B
Ålesund	1200‡	1500‡	1815¶	1900	B
Molde	1800	1830	2145	2215	B
Kristiansund	2215◇	2300◇	0145	0200	B/C
Trondheim	0600‡	1200‡	0830	1200	C
Rørvik	2045◇	2115◇	2045	2115	C
Brønnøysund	0045	0100	0045	0100	D
Sandnessjøen	0345	0415	0345	0415	D
Nesna	0525	0530	0525	0530	D
Ørnes	0915	0930	0915	0930	D
Bodø	1230‡	1500‡	1230	1500	D
Stamsund	1900	1930	1900	1930	D
Svolvaer	2100	2200	2100	2200	D
Stokmarknes	0100	0115	0100	0115	E
Sortland	0245	0300	0245	0300	E
Risøyhamn	0415	0430	0415	0430	E
Harstad	0645	0800	0645	0800	E
Finnsnes	1115	1145	1115	1145	E
Tromsø	1430‡◇	1830‡◇	1430	1830	E
Skjervøy	2230	2245	2230	2245	E
Øksfjord	0200	0215	0200	0215	F
Hammerfest	0515	0600	0515	0600	F
Havøysund	0845	0915	0845	0915	F
Honningsvåg	1145	1445	1115	1445	F
Kjøllefjord	1700‡	1715‡	1700	1715	F
Mehamn ⊗	1915	1930	1915	1930	F
Berlevåg	2145◇	2200◇	2145	2200	F
Båtsfjord	2345	0015	2345	0015	F/G
Vardø	0315	0330	0315	0330	G
Vadsø	0645	0715	0645	0715	G
Kirkenes	0900‡	...	0900	...	G

SOUTHBOUND

	ALL YEAR ❖ arrive	*ALL YEAR* ❖ depart	day
Kirkenes	...	1230	A
Vadsø	|	|	
Vardø	1545	1645	A
Båtsfjord	1945◇	2015◇	A
Berlevåg	2200	2215	A
Mehamn ⊗	0045	0100	B
Kjøllefjord	0245	0300	B
Honningsvåg	0530	0545	B
Havøysund	0745	0800	B
Hammerfest	1045‡	1245‡§	B
Øksfjord	1530§	1545§	B
Skjervøy	1915§	1945§	B
Tromsø	2345	0130	B/C
Finnsnes	0415	0445	C
Harstad	0800	0830	C
Risøyhamn	1045	1100	C
Sortland	1230	1300	C
Stokmarknes	1415	1515	C
Svolvaer	1830‡◇	2030‡◇	C
Stamsund	2200	2230	C
Bodø	0230	0415	D
Ørnes	0700	0715	D
Nesna	1100	1115	D
Sandnessjøen	1230‡	1300‡	D
Brønnøysund	1545	1700	D
Rørvik	2030◇	2130◇	D
Trondheim	0630	1000	E
Kristiansund	1630‡	1700‡	E
Molde	2100	2130	E
Ålesund	0030	0100	F
Urke ▲	|	|	
Geiranger ▲	|	|	
Ålesund	0030◇	0100◇	F
Torvik	0215	0230	F
Måløy	0515	0545	F
Florø	0745	0815	F
Bergen ♣	1430◇		F

A – 1st day .... G – 7th day.

g – June 2 - Sept. 1.
h – Sept. 2 - Nov. 1.

❖ – **Validity dates**:
Northbound (from Bergen): winter service valid **Jan. 1 - May 31** and **Nov. 1 - Dec. 31**; summer service valid **June 1 - Oct. 31**.
Southbound (from Kirkenes): all year service valid **Jan. 7 - Jan. 6, 2015**.

♣ – Sailings from Bergen Frilenesset.
▲ – Embarkation and disembarkation take place by tender - passengers are required to be at the quay 30 minutes before departure.
¶ – One hour earlier Sept. 2 - Nov. 1.
§ – One hour earlier Apr. 8 - June 7. Sails into Lyngenfjorden after Skjervøy.
⊗ – Currently no service.
‡ – Dec. 24 arrival: waits in port 24 hours and departs on Dec. 25.
◇ – Dec. 31 arrival: departure delayed until Jan. 1 (d. 0030 - 0130).

Variations:

Northbound (from Bergen): no sailings Jan. 4, 8, 19, 21, 28, 31, Feb. 8, 11, Oct. 29, Nov. 15, 26, 30, Dec. 7. Departure on Mar. 3 terminates at Svolvaer (Mar. 6), departure on Mar. 25 terminates at Honningsvåg (Mar. 30).

Southbound (from Kirkenes): no sailings Jan. 10, 14, 25, 27, Feb. 3, 6, 14, 17, Nov. 4, 21, Dec. 2, 6, 13. Departure on Mar. 9 originates at Brønnøysund (Mar. 12), departure on Mar. 31 originates at Brønnøysund (Apr. 3).

Additional Xmas/New Year holiday variations (no arrivals or departures from/to):

Dec. 24: *northbound*: Bergen, Ålesund, Molde, Kristiansund, Trondheim, Rørvik, Bodø, Stamsund, Svolvaer, Tromsø, Skjervøy, Mehamn and Berlevåg; *southbound*: Kirkenes, Vardø, Båtsfjord, Berlevåg, Hammerfest, Øksfjord, Skjervøy, Tromsø, Svolvaer, Stamsund, Brønnøysund, Rørvik, Molde and Bergen.

Dec. 25: *northbound*: Florø, Måløy, Torvik, Brønnøysund, Sandnessjøen, Nesna, Ørnes, Stokmarknes, Sortland, Risøyhamn, Harstad, Finnsnes, Øksfjord, Hammerfest, Havøysund, Honningsvåg, Båtsfjord, Vardø and Vadsø; *southbound*: Mehamn, Kjøllefjord, Honningsvåg, Havøysund, Tromsø, Finnsnes, Harstad, Risøyhamn, Sortland, Stokmarknes, Bodø, Ørnes, Nesna, Trondheim, Ålesund, Torvik, Måløy and Florø.

Dec. 31: *northbound*: Molde, Stamsund, Svolvaer, Skjervøy, Kjøllefjord and Mehamn; *southbound*: Berlevåg, Havøysund, Øksfjord, Skjervøy, Stamsund, Kristiansund and Molde.

Jan. 1: *northbound*: Florø, Måløy, Torvik, Brønnøysund, Sandnessjøen, Nesna, Ørnes, Øksfjord, Hammerfest, Havøysund, Kjøllefjord and Båtsfjord; *southbound*: Mehamn, Kjøllefjord, Honningsvåg, Ørnes, Nesna and Torvik.

HELGOLAND (Germany) services 2242

The following services operate:

Route:		Operator:
BREMERHAVEN - HELGOLAND	Summer only	Reederei Cassen Eils
BÜSUM - HELGOLAND	Summer only	Reederei Cassen Eils
CUXHAVEN - HELGOLAND	Summer service	Förde Reederei Seetouristik
	Winter service	Reederei Cassen Eils
HAMBURG - HELGOLAND	Summer service	Förde Reederei Seetouristik
WILHELMSHAVEN - HELGOLAND	Summer only	A G Ems

HULL - ROTTERDAM 2245

P & O Ferries — 2014 service
(No service Dec. 24, 25, 30, 31)

Sailings from Hull King George Dock and Rotterdam Europoort.

Hull		Rotterdam		Rotterdam		Hull
2030	→	0815§		2100⊡	→	0800

§ – On ⑥⑦ arrive 0900.
⊡ – On ⑥⑦ depart 2030.

Subject to alteration during Xmas/New Year period

🚌 connections (reservation recommended):
Hull railway station (depart 1715) - King George Dock and v.v.
Rotterdam Centraal Station (depart 1700) - Europoort and v.v.
Amsterdam Centraal Station (depart 1700) - Europoort and v.v.

HULL - ZEEBRUGGE 2250

P & O Ferries — 2014 service

Sailings from Hull King George Dock and Zeebrugge Leopold II Dam.

Hull		Zeebrugge		Zeebrugge		Hull
1830	→	0845§		1900	→	0830◇

§ – On ⑥⑦ arrive 0930. ◇ – On ⑥⑦ arrive 0900.

Subject to alteration during Xmas/New Year period

🚌 connections (reservation recommended):
Hull railway station (depart 1715) - King George Dock and v.v.
Brugge Station (depart 1730) - Zeebrugge and v.v.

NEWCASTLE - IJMUIDEN (AMSTERDAM) 2255

DFDS Seaways — 2014 service
(No service Dec. 24, 25)

Sailings from Newcastle International Ferry Terminal, Royal Quays and IJmuiden Felison Terminal.

Newcastle		IJmuiden		IJmuiden		Newcastle
1700	→	0930		1730	→	0900

🚌 connections:
Newcastle rail station - International Ferry Terminal (North Shields) and v.v.
(depart Newcastle station 2½ and 1¼ hours before sailing; depart Ferry Terminal following arrival of ship).
Victoria Hotel Amsterdam (near Centraal station) - IJmuiden and v.v.
(depart hotel every 10 minutes 1530 - 1630; depart Ferry Terminal following arrival of ship).

SCRABSTER - STROMNESS 2280

NorthLink Ferries Journey 1 hour 30 minutes — 2014 service

January 3 - June 12 and August 27 - December 31
From Scrabster: 0845①②③④⑤, 1200⑥⑦, 1900.
From Stromness: 0630①②③④⑤, 0900⑥⑦, 1645.

June 13 - August 26 ♦
From Scrabster: 0845①②③④⑤⑥, 1200⑦, 1315①②③④⑤⑥, 1900.
From Stromness: 0630①②③④⑤⑥, 0900⑦, 1100①②③④⑤⑥, 1645.

♦ – Also Mar. 31, Apr. 4, 7, 11, May 23, 26, 31, June 2, 3, 6, 7, 9, 10, Aug. 29, 30, Sept. 2, Oct. 13, 17, 20, 24.

Subject to alteration during Xmas/New Year period

ICELAND and the FAEROE ISLANDS 2285

Smyril Line — 2014 service

	arrive	*depart*	
Until March 28			
Hirtshals	1000⑥	1500⑥	
Tórshavn	0500①	2100④	Last sailing departs Tórshavn on Mar. 27.
March 29 - June 13			
Hirtshals	1000⑥	1500⑥	First sailing departs Hirtshals on Mar. 29.
Tórshavn	0500①	1400①	
Seydisfjördur	0900②	2000③	
Tórshavn	1500④	2100④	Last sailing departs Tórshavn on June 12.
June 14 - August 22 ▲			
Hirtshals	1230⑥	1530⑥	First sailing departs Hirtshals on June 14.
Tórshavn	2230⑦	2330⑦	
Hirtshals	0930②	1130②	
Tórshavn	1730③	1800③	
Seydisfjördur	0930④	1130④	
Tórshavn	0300⑤	0330⑤	Last sailing departs Tórshavn on Aug. 22.
August 23 - October 31 ▲			
Hirtshals	1000⑥	1500⑥	First sailing departs Hirtshals on Aug. 23.
Tórshavn	0500①	1400①	
Seydisfjördur	0900②	2000③	
Tórshavn	1500④	2100④	Last sailing departs Tórshavn on Oct. 30.
November 1 - December 22 ▲			
Hirtshals	1000⑥	1500⑥	First sailing departs Hirtshals on Nov. 1.
Tórshavn	0500①	2100④	Last sailing departs Tórshavn on Dec. 22.
December 23 - 31			
No sailings			

▲ – Variations: June 14 Hirtshals a. 1000 (not 1230); Aug. 23 Hirtshals a. 1230, d. 1630 (not 1000, 1500); Nov. 27 - 20 special Christmas sailing (no regular service to/from Hirtshals).

Tórshavn - Seydisfjördur and v.v. sailings also operate once per week in winter (not Mar. 17 - 21) weather permitting. These sailings cannot be booked in advance – contact operator for more details.

In poor weather conditions sailings may dock at Klaksvík or Kollafjördur (for Tórshavn), and Frederikshavn or Hanstholm (for Hirtshals).

2304 BØJDEN - FYNSHAV

AlsFærgen Journey 50 minutes **2014 service**

June 2 - 18

Depart Bøjden: 0700①②③④⑤⑥ **A**, 0900, 1000⑤⑥⑦ **B**, 1100, 1200⑤⑥⑦ **B**, 1300, 1400⑤⑥⑦ **B**, 1500, 1600⑤⑥⑦ **B**, 1700, 1900, 210①⑤⑥⑦ **C**.

Depart Fynshav: 0600①②③④⑤⑥ **A**, 0800, 1000, 1100⑤⑥⑦ **B**, 1200, 1300⑤⑥⑦ **B**, 1400, 1500⑤⑥⑦ **B**, 1600, 1700⑤⑥⑦ **B**, 1800, 2000⑤⑥⑦ **C**.

June 19 - August 31

Depart Bøjden: 0700①②③④⑤⑥, 0900, 1000 **D**, 1100, 1200 **D**, 1300, 1400 **D**, 1500, 1600 **D**, 1700, 1900, 2100 **D**.

Depart Fynshav: 0600, 0800, 1000, 1100 **D**, 1200, 1300 **D**, 1400, 1500 **D**, 1600, 1700 **D**, 1800, 2000 **D**.

A – Not June 9.
B – Also June 9.
C – Also June 9; not June 7.
D – Not Aug. 19, 20, 26, 27.

Subject to alteration on and around holidays

2310 EBELTOFT - SJÆLLANDS ODDE

Mols-Linien by catamaran **2014 service**

Journey 65 minutes

Ebeltoft - Sjællands Odde and v.v.: 6 - 13 sailings daily in summer; 2 - 9 in winter.

Subject to alteration during holiday periods

2312 ESBJERG - FANØ

FanøFærgen Journey 12 minutes **2014 service**

Up to 3 departures hourly: 0530 - 0015 from Esbjerg, 0510 - 0030 from Fanø.

Subject to alteration on and around holidays

2320 FREDERIKSHAVN - GÖTEBORG

Stena Line **2014 service**

Sailings from Frederikshavn Trafikhavn and Göteborg.

Frederikshavn		Göteborg		Göteborg		Frederikshavn	
February 1 - June 22 and August 11 - December 20							
0800	→	1125	②③④⑤⑥	0030	→	0400	②③④⑤⑥
1150	→	1515	①⑦	0800	→	1115	①⑦
1400	→	1725	②③④⑤⑥⑦	0915	→	1230	②③④⑤⑥⑦
2015	→	2350		1600	→	1925	
2230	→	0210	①②③④⑤⑦	1815	→	2145	①②③④⑤⑦
June 23 - August 10							
0345	→	0715		0800	→	1115	①③④⑤⑥⑦
1150	→	1515	①③④⑤⑥⑦	1000	→	1315	
1430	→	1755		1600	→	1915	
2000	→	2320		1845	→	2215	
2300	→	0240		2355	→	0310	

Subject to alteration on and around holidays

2330 GEDSER - ROSTOCK

Scandlines **2014 service**

Sailings from Rostock Überseehafen and Gedser.

Journey 1 hour 45 minutes

Depart Gedser: 0130①②③④⑥, 0330⑤, 0340①, 0700, 0900, 1115, 1330, 1530, 1745, 2000, 2215.

Depart Rostock: 0030⑤, 0130①, 0430①⑥, 0600, 0900, 1115, 1330, 1530, 1745, 2000, 2215.

Subject to alteration on and around holidays

2335 GÖTEBORG - KIEL

Stena Line **2014 service**

Sailings from Kiel Schwedenkai and Göteborg. **(No service Dec. 24, 25)**

Göteborg		Kiel	Kiel		Göteborg
1845	→	0915	1845	→	0915

Subject to alteration during Xmas/New Year period

2342 GRENAA - VARBERG

Stena Line Journey 4 - 5½ hours **2014 service**

Grenaa		Varberg		Varberg		Grenaa	
February 1 - June 22 and August 11 - December 20							
0100	→	0615	①②③④⑤	0850	→	1315	①②③④⑤
1420	→	1845	①②③④⑤⑦	1945	→	0005	①②③④⑤⑦
June 23 - August 10							
1315	→	1730		0805	→	1220	
2350	→	0445		1835	→	2250	

2345 HELSINGØR - HELSINGBORG

Scandlines Journey 20 minutes **2014 service**

From Helsingør and Helsingborg: Sailings every 15 minutes (every 30 minutes at night).

Subject to alteration on and around holidays

2350 HIRTSHALS - KRISTIANSAND

Color Line by ship **2014 service**

Hirtshals		Kristiansand		Kristiansand		Hirtshals	
February 1 - March 16							
1215	→	1530		0800	→	1115	
2045	→	2400		1630	→	1945	
March 17 - April 3							
2130	→	0045		0800	→	1115	
April 4 - December 23							
1215	→	1530	See note L.	0800	→	1115	See note L.
2045§	→	2400§		1630	→	1945	

L – Not Apr. 7, 28, May 12, 26, June 16, Aug. 25, Sept. 8, 22, Oct. 6, 20, Nov. 3, 17, Dec. 1, 15.
§ – June 30 - Aug. 11 depart 2145 (a. 0100).

Fjord Line by catamaran **2014 service**

Hirtshals		Kristiansand		Kristiansand		Hirtshals	
May 15 - June 19 and August 18 - 31							
1145	→	1400	See note P.	0830	→	1045	
1800	→	2015		1500	→	1715	See note P.
June 20 - August 17							
1000	→	1215		0645	→	0900	
1700	→	1915		1330	→	1545	
2330	→	0145	See note Q.	2015	→	2230	See note Q.

P – Not May 20, 27, June 3, 17, Aug. 26.
Q – Not June 24, 25, July 1, 2, 8, 9, 15, 16, Aug. 5, 6, 12, 13.

2355 KALUNDBORG - SAMSØ

SamsøFærgen **2014 service**

Journey 1 hour 50 minutes

May 26 - June 1

Depart Kalundborg: 0845③⑦, 0915①②④⑤⑥, 1315③⑦, 1515④⑤⑥, 1745③⑦, 1810①②, 1940④⑤⑥, 2205③⑦.

Depart Kolby Kås (Samsø): 0630③⑦, 0700①②④⑤⑥, 1100③⑦, 1300④⑤⑥, 1535③⑦, 1550①②, 1730④⑤⑥, 2000③⑦.

June 2 - 8

Depart Kalundborg: 0845⑤, 0915①②③④⑥⑦, 1315⑤, 1515①②③④⑥⑦, 1745⑤, 1940①②③④⑥⑦, 2205⑤.

Depart Kolby Kås (Samsø): 0630⑤, 0700①②③④⑥⑦, 1100⑤, 1300①②③④⑥⑦, 1535⑤, 1730①②③④⑥⑦, 2000⑤.

June 9 - 15

Depart Kalundborg: 0845①⑦, 0915②③④⑤⑥, 1315①⑦, 1515②③④⑤⑥, 1745①⑦, 1940②③④⑤⑥, 2205①⑦.

Depart Kolby Kås (Samsø): 0630①⑦, 0700②③④⑤⑥, 1100①⑦, 1300②③④⑤⑥, 1535①⑦, 1730②③④⑤⑥, 2000①⑦.

June 16 - August 17

Depart Kalundborg: 0215 (July 20, 21 only), 0845⑤⑥⑦, 0915①②③④, 1315⑤⑥⑦, 1515①②③④, 1745⑤⑥⑦, 1940①②③④, 2205⑤⑥⑦.

Depart Kolby Kås (Samsø): 0010 (July 20, 21 only), 0630⑤⑥⑦, 0700①②③④, 1100⑤⑥⑦, 1300①②③④, 1535⑤⑥⑦, 1730①②③④, 2000⑤⑥⑦.

August 18 - 31

Depart Kalundborg: 0845⑤⑦, 0915①②③④⑥, 1315⑤⑦, 1515①②③④⑥, 1745⑤⑦, 1940①②③④⑥, 2205⑤⑦.

Depart Kolby Kås (Samsø): 0630⑤⑦, 0700①②③④⑥, 1100⑤⑦, 1300①②③④⑥, 1535⑤⑦, 1730①②③④⑥, 2000⑤⑦.

Subject to alteration during holiday periods

2360 KØBENHAVN - OSLO

DFDS Seaways **2014 service**

Sailings from København Dampfærgevej and Oslo Vippetangen (Utstikker 2).

København		Oslo		Oslo		København	
1630	→	0945	Not Dec. 24.	1630	→	0945	Not Dec. 24.

2366 LARVIK - HIRTSHALS

Color Line **2014 service**

(No service Dec. 24)

Larvik		Hirtshals		Hirtshals		Larvik	
April 4 - June 24							
0800	→	1145	See note R.	1245	→	1630	See note R.
1730	→	2115		2215	→	0200	
June 25 - August 10							
0800	→	1145		1245	→	1630	
1730	→	2115	Not July 16.	2215	→	0200	Not July 16.
August 11 - December 23							
0800	→	1145	②③④⑤⑥⑦	1245	→	1630	②③④⑤⑥⑦
1730	→	2115		2215	→	0200	

P – ②③④⑤ (not Feb. 11, 25, Mar. 11).
Q – ①②③④⑤ (not Feb. 11, 25, Mar. 11).
R – ②③④⑤⑥⑦ (also Apr. 21, June 29; not Apr. 4).

2368 OSLO - FREDERIKSHAVN

Stena Line **2014 service**

Sailings from Oslo Vippetangen and Frederikshavn. **(No service Dec. 24, 25)**

Oslo		Frederikshavn		Frederikshavn		Oslo	
February 1 - June 16 and August 18 - December 31							
1900	→	0730	②③④⑤⑥⑦	0900	→	1830	③④⑤⑥⑦
				1830	→	0730	①
June 17 - August 17							
1900	→	0745		0915	→	1830	

Subject to alteration on and around holidays

For international shipping maps – see pages 538 - 540

OSLO - KIEL 2372

Color Line **2014 service**
(No service Dec. 31)

Sailings from Oslo Color Line Terminalen, Hjortnes and Kiel Oslo-Kai.

Oslo		Kiel	
1400	→	1000	See note **P**.

Kiel		Oslo	
1400	→	1000	See note **Q**.

P – Not Apr. 7, 9, 22, 24.

Q – Not Apr. 8, 10, 21, 23, 25.

🚌 Oslo Color Line Terminal - Oslo Sentral rail station.
Kiel Oslo-Kai - Hamburg ZOB (Central Bus Station).

PUTTGARDEN - RØDBY 2375

Scandlines Journey 45 minutes **2014 service**

Departures every 30 minutes (every 40 minutes at night and in winter).

Subject to alteration on and around holidays

ROSTOCK - TRELLEBORG 2380

Stena Line Journey 6 - 7½ hours **Service to September 30, 2014**

Sailings from Rostock Überseehafen and Trelleborg.

From Rostock: 0730②⑥, 0745①③④⑦, 0800⑤, 1500②③④⑤⑥⑦, 2245.
From Trelleborg: 0730③④⑥⑦, 0930②, 1500①②③④⑤⑦, 1515⑥, 2245.

Subject to alteration on and around holidays

TT Line by ship **2014 service**

Sailings from Rostock Überseehafen and Trelleborg.

Rostock		Trelleborg	
0730	→	1345	②⑥⑦
0800	→	1400	③④⑤
1000	→	1630	①
1345	→	1915	②③
1500	→	2100	④⑤⑥⑦
2300	→	0600	

Trelleborg		Rostock	
0045	→	0645	③④⑤
0730	→	1345	④⑥⑦
0925	→	1500	②③⑤
1515	→	2115	①②⑤⑥⑦
1530	→	2100	③④
2245	→	0615	⑥
2300	→	0600	①⑤⑦

Subject to alteration during holiday periods

SASSNITZ-MUKRAN - RØNNE 2384

BornholmerFærgen **2014 service**
(No winter service)

Sassnitz		Rønne		Rønne		Sassnitz	
April 5 - May 25							
1150	→	1510	See note **W**.	0800	→	1120	See note **W**.
1330	→	1730	See note **X**.	0900	→	1245	See note **X**.
May 26 - June 13							
1150	→	1510	See note **Y**.	0800	→	1120	See note **Y**.
1330	→	1730	⑥⑦ (also May 29).	0900	→	1245	⑥⑦ (also May 29).
June 14 - 25							
1150	→	1510	⑥	0730	→	1100	June 15 only.
1200	→	1530	June 15 only.	0800	→	1120	⑥
1330	→	1730	④⑥⑦ (not June 15).	0900	→	1245	④⑥⑦ (not June 15).
June 26 - September 7							
1150	→	1510	See note **Z**.	0800	→	1120	See note **Z**.
1330	→	1730	⑥⑦ (also Aug. 14).	0900	→	1245	⑥⑦ (also Aug. 14).

W – ④⑦ (also Apr. 5, 12, 21, May 3; not Apr. 6, 10, May 22).
X – ⑥ (also May 22; not Apr. 5, 12, May 3).
Y – ④ (also June 9; not May 29).
Z – ①②③④⑤⑥ (not Aug. 14).

SASSNITZ-MUKRAN - TRELLEBORG 2385

Stena Line Journey 4 hours **2014 service**

Sailings from Fährhafen Sassnitz-Mukran and Trelleborg.

Until June 4 and from September 1

From Sassnitz: 0800, 1615. From Trelleborg: 0815, 1745.

June 5 - August 31

From Sassnitz: 0745, 1300, 1815, 2315⑤⑥.
From Trelleborg: 0745, 1300, 1830, 2330⑤⑥.

Subject to alteration on and around holidays

STRÖMSTAD - SANDEFJORD 2387

Color Line Journey 2½ hours **2014 service**

January 31 - June 12

Depart Strømstad: 1100 **S**, 1330 **T**, 1730 **S**, 2000 **T**.
Depart Sandefjord: 0800 **S**, 1000 **T**, 1400 **S**, 1700 **T**.

June 13 - August 17

Depart Strømstad: 1100, 1330, 1800, 2000.
Depart Sandefjord: 0800, 1000, 1430, 1700.

August 18 - December 23

Depart Strømstad: 1100, 1330, 1730, 2000.
Depart Sandefjord: 0800, 1000, 1400, 1700.

S – Not Apr. 7, 8.
T – Not Apr. 22, 23.

TRAVEMÜNDE - TRELLEBORG 2390

TT Line **2014 service**

Sailings from Travemünde Skandinavienkai and Trelleborg.

Travemünde		Trelleborg		Trelleborg		Travemünde	
Until July 4							
0030	→	0830	⑦	0630	→	1515	②③④
0230	→	1000	②③④⑤⑥	0930	→	1700	②③⑤
0300	→	1030	①	1000	→	1730	④⑥⑦
0930	→	1700	②③	1300	→	2045	⑥
1000	→	1730	④⑤⑥⑦	1645	→	0045	①②③④⑤⑦
1545	→	2315	②③④	2200	→	0730	
2200	→	0730					
July 5 - 20 and August 9 - 17							
0030	→	0830	⑦	1000	→	1730	
0230	→	1000	②③④⑤⑥	1300	→	2045	⑥
0300	→	1030	①	1645	→	0045	①②③④⑤⑦
1000	→	1730		2200	→	0730	
2200	→	0730					
July 21 - August 8							
1000	→	1730		1000	→	1730	
2200	→	0730		2200	→	0730	

Subject to alteration during holiday periods

🚌 connection available Trelleborg - Malmö railway station and v.v. for certain sailings.

TRAVEMÜNDE - MALMÖ 2395

Finnlines **2014 service**

Travemünde		Malmö		Malmö		Travemünde	
0100	→	1015	⑦	1000	→	1900	②③④⑤⑥
0230	→	1115	②③④⑤	1330	→	2315	⑥
0300	→	1145	①⑥	1600	→	0045	①②③④⑤
1000	→	1900	②③④⑤	1600	→	0100	⑦
1100	→	2000	⑥	2200	→	0700	①②③④⑤⑦
2200	→	0700	Daily.	2300	→	0830	⑥

BALTIC SEA

GDAŃSK - NYNÄSHAMN 2402

Polferries **Service to January 31, 2015**

Gdańsk		Nynäshamn	
1800	→	1300	See note **A**.

Nynäshamn		Gdańsk	
1800	→	1300	See note **B**.

A – Mar. 1, 5, 8, 12, 15, 18, 20, 22, 25, 27, 29, Apr. 1, 3, 5, 8, 10, 12, 15, 17, 22, 24, 26, 29, May 1, 4, 6, 8, 10, 13, 15, 17, 20, 22, 24, 27, 29, 31, June 3, 5, 7, 10, 12, 14, 17, 19, 21, 23, 25, 27, 29, July 1, 3, 5, 7, 9, 11, 13, 15, 17, 19, 21, 23, 25, 27, 29, 31, Aug. 2, 4, 6, 8, 10, 12, 14, 16, 18, 20, 22, 24, 26, 28, 30, Sept. 2, 4, 6, 9, 11, 13, 16, 18, 20, 23, 25, 27, 30, Oct. 2, 4, 7, 9, 11, 14, 16, 18, 21, 23, 25, 28, 30, Nov. 2, 5, 8, 12, 15, 19, 22, 26, 29, Dec. 3, 6, 10, 13, 15, 17, 19, 21, 27, Jan. 2, 4, 6, 8, 10, 13, 15, 18, 20, 22, 25, 27, 29.

B – Mar. 3, 7, 10, 14, 17, 19, 21, 24, 26, 28, 31, Apr. 2, 4, 7, 9, 11, 14, 16, 18, 23, 25, 28, 30, May 3, 5, 7, 9, 12, 14, 16, 19, 21, 23, 26, 28, 30, June 2, 4, 6, 9, 11, 13, 16, 18, 20, 22, 24, 26, 28, 30, July 2, 4, 6, 8, 10, 12, 14, 16, 18, 20, 22, 24, 26, 28, 30, Aug. 1, 3, 5, 7, 9, 11, 13, 15, 17, 19, 21, 23, 25, 27, 29, Sept. 1, 3, 5, 8, 10, 12, 15, 17, 19, 22, 24, 26, 29, Oct. 1, 3, 6, 8, 10, 13, 15, 17, 20, 22, 24, 27, 29, 31, Nov. 3, 7, 10, 14, 17, 21, 24, 28, Dec. 1, 5, 8, 12, 14, 16, 18, 20, 22, 29, Jan. 3, 5, 7, 9, 12, 14, 16, 19, 21, 23, 26, 28, 30.

GRISSLEHAMN - ECKERÖ 2405

Eckerö Linjen **Service to January 11, 2015**
(No service Dec. 24, 25)

Stockholm (*by* 🚌)		Grisslehamn		Eckerö		Mariehamn (*by* 🚌)	
0730♦	→	1000	→	1300	→	*1350*♦	
1230♦	→	1500	→	1800	→	*1850*♦	
1730♦	→	2000	→	2245	→	*2330*♦	See note **C**.

Mariehamn (*by* 🚌)		Eckerö		Grisslehamn		Stockholm (*by* 🚌)	
0720♦	→	0830	→	0915	→	*1115*♦	See note **D**.
1220♦	→	1330	→	1430	→	*1645*♦	
1720♦	→	1830	→	1930	→	*2130*♦	

C – ④⑤⑥⑦ until June 12; daily June 13 - Aug. 17; ④⑤⑥⑦ Aug. 18 - Jan. 11 (not June 20).
D – ①⑤⑥⑦ until June 12; daily June 13 - Aug. 17; ①⑤⑥⑦ Aug. 18 - Jan. 11 (not June 21).
♦ – 🚌 connections: Stockholm Cityterminalen (near Central station) - Grisslehamn and v.v.; Eckerö - Mariehamn and v.v.

2407 NAANTALI - KAPELLSKÄR

Finnlines — 2014 service

Conveys passengers with vehicles only

Naantali		Kapellskär		Kapellskär		Naantali	
0930	→	1630	⑥⑦	0100	→	1000	②③④⑤⑥
0930	→	1715	①②③④⑤	0915	→	1815	⑥⑦
1630	→	2315	①②③④⑤	0915	→	1900	①②③④⑤
2230	→	0530		2145	→	0645	

Sailing times are subject to alteration

2410 HELSINKI - TALLINN

Eckerö Line by ship — 2014 service (No service Dec. 24, 25)

Sailings from Helsinki Länsiterminaali and Tallinn A-terminal.

Helsinki		Tallinn	Tallinn		Helsinki
0830	→	1100	1200	→	1430
1530	→	1745	1845	→	2115

Connection: Tram route 9 Helsinki railway sation - Länsiterminaali

Linda Line Oy by hydrofoil — 2014 service

Linda Line Express Journey 1 hour 30 minutes

Sailings from Helsinki Makasiiniterminaali and Tallinn Linnahalli.

April 4 - June 26

Depart Helsinki: 0800①②③④⑤⑥, 1000, 1200⑤⑥⑦, 1400①②③④⑤⑦, 1700, 1900, 2100 **C**

Depart Tallinn: 0800①②③④⑤⑥, 1000, 1200⑤⑦, 1500, 1700, 1900, 2100⑦.

June 27 - August 17

Depart Helsinki: 0800①②③④⑤⑥, 1000, 1200, 1400, 1700, 1900, 2100⑤⑦.

Depart Tallinn: 0800①⑥, 1000, 1200, 1500, 1700, 1900, 2100①②③④⑤⑦.

C – ⑦ from May 4.

Tallink Silja by ship — 2014 service

Sailings from Helsinki Länsiterminaali and Tallinn D-terminal.

Journey 2 hours (§ – 3½ hours)

Until March 2

Depart Helsinki: 0730①②③④⑤⑥, 0830⑥, 1030, 1330⑦, 1400①②③④⑤, 1430⑥, 1630⑦, 1730①②③④⑤⑥, 1830§**F**, 1930⑦, 2030①②③④⑤⑥, 2230⑦.

Depart Tallinn: 0730, 1030⑦, 1100①②③④⑤, 1130⑥, 1230§**F**, 1330⑦, 1400①②③④⑤⑥, 1630⑦, 1730①②③④⑤⑥, 1930⑦, 2100①②③④⑤⑥, 2230⑦.

March 3 - December 23

Depart Helsinki: 0730, 1030, 1330①③④⑤⑥⑦, 1630, 1830§**F**, 1930, 2230.

Depart Tallinn: 0730, 1030, 1230§**F**, 1330①③④⑤⑥⑦, 1630, 1930, 2230.

F – Not Feb. 14, 15, Mar. 24.

Connection: Tram route 9 Helsinki railway sation - Länsiterminaali

Viking Line by ship Journey 2½ hours — 2014 service (No service Dec. 24, 25)

Sailings from Helsinki Katajanokka terminal and Tallinn A-terminal.

Until June 11 and September 1 - December 31

Depart Helsinki: 1130, 2000⑦, 2130①②③④⑤⑥.

Depart Tallinn: 0800, 1630⑦, 1800①②③④⑤⑥.

June 12 - August 31

Depart Helsinki: 1000, 2130. Depart Tallinn: 0700, 1800.

2415 KARLSKRONA - GDYNIA

Stena Line — 2014 service

Karlskrona		Gdynia		Gdynia		Karlskrona	
0900	→	1930	②③④⑥⑦	0900	→	1900	⑥⑦
1930	→	0730	⑤	0900	→	1930	②③④
2000	→	1730	①⑥	1930	→	0745	①⑤
2000	→	0900	⑦	2100	→	0745	②③⑥
2100	→	0730	②③	2100	→	0900	④⑦
2100	→	0900	④				

Subject to alteration during Easter and Xmas / New Year periods

2418 KARLSHAMN - KLAIPEDA

DFDS Seaways — 2014 service

Sailings from Karlshamn Ferry Terminal and Klaipeda International Ferry Port.

Karlshamn		Klaipeda	Klaipeda		Karlsham
1800	→	0900	1800	→	0900

2420 KIEL - KLAIPEDA

DFDS Seaways — 2014 service

Sailings from Kiel Ostuferhafen and Klaipeda International Ferry Port.

Kiel		Klaipeda	Klaipeda		Kiel
1400①	→	1230②	1500①	→	1230②
1600②	→	1400③	1730②	→	1400③
1800③	→	1630④	1900③	→	1600④
2000④	→	1800⑤	2100④	→	1800⑤
2200⑤	→	2000⑥	2300⑤	→	1900⑥
2300⑥	→	2200⑦	0100⑦	→	2200⑦

Subject to alteration during Xmas / New Year period

2430 KØGE - RØNNE

BornholmerFærgen — 2014 service

Køge		Rønne	Rønne		Køge
0030	→	0600§	1700	→	2230

§ – Mar. 30 arrive 0700.

2445 NYNÄSHAMN - VISBY

Destination Gotland — 2014 service

Nynäshamn		Visby		Visby		Nynäshamn	
			May 5 - June 15				
0900	→	1220	① (not May 5).	0730	→	1050	①②③④⑤⑥
1130	→	1450	①②③④⑤⑥	0805	→	1120	⑦ (not June 1, 8).
1200	→	1515	⑦ (not June 1, 8).	0855	→	1210	June 1, 8 only.
1250	→	1605	June 1, 8 only.	1245	→	1600	See note **E**.
1635	→	1950	See note **E**.	1535	→	1850	June 1 only.
1945	→	2300	June 1 only.	1600	→	1915	⑤⑥⑦ (not June 1, 8).
2005	→	2320	⑤⑥⑦ (not June 1, 8).	1645	→	2000	See note **F**.
2105	→	0020	See note **F**.	1920	→	2235	⑦ (not June 1, 15).
			June 16 - 22				
0700	→	1015	④⑤	0730	→	1045	①②③④⑤⑦
1130	→	1450	①②③④⑤⑦	0855	→	1210	③⑤⑦
1245	→	1605	③⑤⑦	1045	→	1400	④⑥
1445	→	1800	④⑥	1245	→	1600	①②④⑥
1635	→	1950	①②④⑥	1345	→	1700	⑦
1735	→	2050	⑦	1520	→	1835	③④
1910	→	2225	③④	1535	→	1850	⑦
1945	→	2300	⑦	1645	→	2000	①②③
2105	→	0020	①②③	1900	→	2215	④
2320	→	0235	④	2345	→	0300	⑦
			June 23 - 29				
0730	→	1045	⑥⑦	0050	→	0405	⑥⑦
0900	→	1220	①	0705	→	1020	⑤⑥⑦
1055	→	1410	⑤⑥⑦	0730	→	1050	①②③④
1130	→	1450	①②③④	0835	→	1150	⑤
1230	→	1545	⑤	0850	→	1210	②③④⑥⑦
1245	→	1605	②③④⑥⑦	1055	→	1410	①
1445	→	1800	①	1445	→	1800	①⑤⑥⑦
1835	→	2150	①⑤⑥⑦	1645	→	2000	①②③④⑤
2105	→	0020	①②③④⑤	1910	→	2225	⑥⑦
2330	→	0245	⑥⑦				
			June 30 - August 11				
0450	→	0805	⑥⑦	0050	→	0405	
0700	→	1015	②③④⑤	0330	→	0645	①⑥⑦
0730	→	1045	①⑥⑦	0705	→	1020	
1055	→	1410		0845	→	1200	③④⑤ (not July 16).
1235	→	1550	③④⑤ (not July 16).	0850	→	1205	①⑥⑦
1250	→	①⑥⑦		1055	→	1410	②③④⑤
1450	→	1805	②③④⑤	1445	→	1800	
1835	→	2150		1910	→	2225	
2330	→	0245					

E – ⑤ (not May 30, June 6). **F** – ①②③④ (also June 8).

Additional services operate at peak times;
subject to alteration during Easter and Xmas / New Year periods

🚐 service Stockholm Cityterminalen - Nynäshamn connects with most sailings.

2448 NYNÄSHAMN - VENTSPILS

Stena Line — Service to September 30, 2014

Nynäshamn		Ventspils	Ventspils		Nynäshamn
1000①	→	2100①	0001②	→	1000②
1900②	→	0700③	1000③	→	1900③
2200③	→	1000④	2000④	→	0800⑤
2200⑤	→	1000⑥	1800⑥	→	0605⑦
0800⑦	→	1900⑦	2300⑦	→	0900①

2450 OSKARSHAMN - VISBY

Destination Gotland — 2014 service

Oskarshamn		Visby		Visby		Oskarshamn	
			May 5 - June 8				
1055	→	1355	②	0715	→	1015	②⑥
1540	→	1835	⑦ (not June 1).	1200	→	1455	⑦ (not June 1).
1715	→	2010	June 1 only.	1345	→	1640	June 1 only.
2010	→	2305	See note **H**.	1620	→	1915	⑤ (not June 6).
2035	→	2330	June 8 only.	1640	→	1935	⑦ (not June 1, 8).
2110	→	0005	See note **J**.	1700	→	1955	②
2115	→	0010	②	1705	→	2000	See note **K**.
			June 9 - 27				
1015	→	1310	June 22 only.	0645	→	0940	June 22 only.
1055	→	1355	See note **L**.	0715	→	1015	See note **L**.
2010	→	2305	See note **M**.	1620	→	1915	See note **M**.
2110	→	0005	See note **N**.	1700	→	1955	②
2115	→	0010	②	1705	→	2000	See note **N**.
			June 28 - August 11				
1050	→	1345	①⑥⑦ (not Aug. 11).	0720	→	1015	①⑥⑦ (not Aug. 11)
1105	→	1400	July 16 only.	0740	→	1035	July 16 only.
1310	→	1605	See note **P**.	0930	→	1225	See note **P**.
1510	→	1805	①⑥⑦	1130	→	1425	①⑥⑦
1645	→	1940	②	1315	→	1610	②
2110	→	0005	①③④⑤⑥⑦	1700	→	1955	②
2115	→	0010	②	1705	→	2000	①③④⑤⑥⑦

F – ② (also Apr. 18; not Mar. 4 - Apr. 8).
G – ②⑥ (also Apr. 18; not ② Mar. 4 - Apr. 8).
H – ⑤⑥⑦ (not June 1, 6, 8). **J** – ①③④ (also June 1, 6).
K – ①③④ (also June 1, 6, 8). **L** – Not June 11, 12, 21, 22.
M – ⑤⑥⑦ (not June 20, 22, 27). **N** – ①③④ (also June 22, 27).
P – ②③④⑤ (not July 16).

Additional services operate at peak times;
subject to alteration during Easter and Xmas / New Year periods

2451 ROSTOCK - GDYNIA - HELSINKI

Finnlines — 2014 servic

Sailings from Helsinki Vuosaaren satama.

Rostock		Gdynia		Helsinki
2100①	→	→	→	0900③

Helsinki		Gdynia		Rostock
2000⑤	→	→	→	1200⑦
1000⑥	→	→	→	2100⑦

Subject to alteration on and around German and Finnish holidays

For international shipping maps – see pages 538 - 540

STOCKHOLM - RIGA 2464

Tallink Silja — **2014 service**

Sailings from Stockholm Frihamnsterminalen and Riga passenger port.

Stockholm		Riga		Riga		Stockholm	
1700	→	1100	Not Apr. 3 - 11.	1730	→	1030§	Not Apr. 3 - 10.

§ – Arrive 0930 Apr. 9.

STOCKHOLM - MARIEHAMN - HELSINKI 2465

Tallink Silja — **2014 service** **(No service Dec. 24)**

Sailings from Stockholm Värtahamnen and Helsinki Olympiaterminaali.

Stockholm		Mariehamn		Helsinki		Helsinki		Mariehamn		Stockholm	
1700	→	2355	→	0955	Note **A**.	1700	→	0425	→	0930	Note **C**.
2000	→	0255	→	1255	Note **B**.						

A – Not May 25, Sept. 6 - Oct. 16 (from Stockholm).
B – May 25 only (from Stockholm).
C – Not Sept. 6 - Oct. 15.

🚌 Stockholm Värtahamnen - Ropsten metro station (for Stockholm Centralen).

Viking Line — **2014 service** **(No service Dec. 24, 25)**

Sailings from Stockholm Stadsgården and Helsinki Katajanokka.

Stockholm		Mariehamn		Helsinki
1630	→	2345	→	1010§

Helsinki		Mariehamn		Stockholm
1730◘	→	0430	→	1000

◘ – Depart 1815 June 12 - Aug. 31.
§ – Arrive 0950 June 12 - Aug. 31.

Connections:
🚌 Stockholm Cityterminalen (near Central station) - Slussen metro station - Viking Line terminal. Tram no. 4T runs daily from Helsinki city centre to the Viking Line Terminal.

(STOCKHOLM -) KAPELLSKÄR - MARIEHAMN 2470

Viking Line — **2014 service** **(No service Dec. 24, 25)**

Sailings from Kapellskär and Mariehamn.

Stockholm (by 🚌)		Kapellskär		Mariehamn		Mariehamn		Kapellskär		Stockholm (by 🚌)	
Until April 16 and August 25 - December 31											
1245♦	→	1445	→	1815		0745	→	0900	→	*1035*♦	
1810♦	→	2000	→	2325		1830	→	1945	→	*2120*♦	
April 17 - June 20											
0740♦	→	0930	→	1245	⑤⑥	0745	→	0900	→	*1035*♦	⑤⑥
1010♦	→	1200	→	1530	①②③④	0800	→	0930	→	*1105*♦	①②③④
1245♦	→	1445	→	1815	⑤⑥⑦	1300	→	1415	→	*1555*♦	⑤⑥⑦
1700♦	→	1900	→	2230	①②③④	1600	→	1730	→	*1910*♦	①②③④
1810♦	→	2000	→	2315	⑤⑥⑦	1830	→	1940	→	*2120*♦	⑤⑥⑦
June 21 - August 24											
0740♦	→	0930	→	1245		0745	→	0900	→	*1035*♦	
1245♦	→	1445	→	1815		1300	→	1415	→	*1555*♦	
1810♦	→	2000	→	2325		1830	→	1945	→	*2120*♦	

♦ – Connecting 🚌 service from / to Stockholm Cityterminalen (near Central station).

STOCKHOLM - TALLINN 2475

Tallink Silja — **2014 service**

Sailings from Stockholm Värtahamnen and Tallinn D-terminal.

Stockholm		Mariehamn		Tallinn	Tallinn		Mariehamn		Stockholm
Until March 1 and November 9 - December 31									
1745	→	0100	→	1045	1800	→	0500	→	1000
March 2 - November 8									
1745	→	0100	→	1000	1800	→	0500	→	1000

STOCKHOLM - TURKU via Mariehamn / Långnäs 2480

Tallink Silja — **2014 service**

Sailings from Stockholm Värtahamnen and Turku.

Stockholm		Mariehamn		Långnäs§		Turku	
0710	→	1345	→	→	→	1915	Not May 17 - 27.
1930	→	→	→	0255	→	0700	Not May 5 - 12.

Turku		Långnäs§		Mariehamn		Stockholm	
0815	→	→	→	1345	→	1815	Not May 6 - 13.
2015	→	0045	→	→	→	0610	Not May 17 - 27.

§ – Långnäs is 28km from Mariehamn.

Nearest metro station to Stockholm Värtahamnen is Gärdet (for Stockholm Centralen).

Viking Line — **2014 service** **(No service Dec. 24, 25)**

Sailings from Stockholm Stadsgården and Turku Linnansatama.

Stockholm		Mariehamn		Långnäs§		Turku
0745	→	1425	→	→	→	1950
2000	→	→	→	0320	→	0735

Turku		Långnäs§		Mariehamn		Stockholm
0845	→	→	→	1425	→	1855
2055	→	0110	→	→	→	0630

§ – Långnäs is 28km from Mariehamn.

🚌 connections: Stockholm Cityterminalen (near Central station) - Slussen metro station - Viking Line terminal; Turku city centre - harbour (bus no. 1).

ST PETERBURG - HELSINKI - STOCKHOLM - TALLINN 2482

St Peter Line — **2014 service**

	St Peterburg		Helsinki		Stockholm		Tallinn		St Peterburg
♣	1900 **A**	→	0800 **B** / 1600 **B**	→	0800 **C** / 1800 **C**	→	1130 **D** / 1900 **D**	→	0930§ **E**
♠	1900 **A**	→	0800 **B** / 1800 **B**	→	→	→	→	→	0930§ **C**

♣ – Sailings from St Peterburg: contact operator for sailing dates.
♠ – Sailings from St Peterburg: contact operator for sailing dates. No sailing Apr. 11 - 13.
A – 1st day; **B** – 2nd day; **C** – 3rd day; **D** – 4th day; **E** – 5th day.
§ – One hour later until Mar. 30 and from Oct. 27.

Subject to alteration during Easter and Xmas / New Year periods

TRAVEMÜNDE - HELSINKI 2485

Finnlines — **2014 service**

Sailings from Travemünde Skandinavienkai and Helsinki Vuosaaren satama.

Travemünde		Helsinki	Helsinki		Travemünde
0300②-⑤	→	0800③-⑥	1730①-⑥	→	2100②-⑦
0300⑦	→	0800①			
0400⑥	→	0900⑦			

Subject to alteration on and around German and Finnish holidays

TRAVEMÜNDE - LIEPAJA 2486

Stena Line — **2014 service**

Travemünde		Liepaja	Liepaja		Travemünde
1800②	→	2230③	0400②	→	0730③
2000④	→	2330⑤	0400④	→	0730⑤
2000⑤	→	2330⑥	1700⑥	→	1900⑦
2100⑦	→	0030①	0400⑦	→	0730①

Subject to alteration on and around holidays

TRAVEMÜNDE - VENTSPILS 2487

Stena Line — **Service to September 30, 2014**

Travemünde		Ventspils	Ventspils		Travemünde
0600④	→	0800⑤	0400③	→	0730④
1800⑥	→	2000⑦	1000⑤	→	1330⑥
2359①	→	0200③	2200⑦	→	0330②

Subject to alteration on and around holidays

VAASA - UMEÅ (HOLMSUND) 2490

Vaasanlaivat — **2014 service**

Vaasa		Umeå		Umeå		Vaasa	
Until April 30							
0800	→	1130	⑦	0900	→	1430	①②
0900	→	1230	④⑤⑥	1200	→	1730	③
2000	→	2300	①②⑦	1300	→	1830	⑦
				1800	→	2330	④⑤⑥
May 1 - September 30							
0800	→	1100	⑦	0800	→	1300	③
0900	→	1200	④⑤⑥	0900	→	1400	①②
1430	→	1730	③	1300	→	1800	⑦
2000	→	2300	①②⑦	1800	→	2300	④⑤⑥
				1900	→	2400	③

Subject to alteration Apr. 20, 21, 25, June 20, July 27

YSTAD - RØNNE 2494

BornholmerFærgen by fast ferry — **2014 service**

Up to 8 sailings daily, departure times vary, journey 75 minutes.

See Table **727** for rail connections Ystad - København and v.v.

(KØBENHAVN -) YSTAD - ŚWINOUJŚCIE 2495

Polferries — **2014 service**

København		Ystad		Świnoujście	Świnoujście		Ystad		København
1200▲	→	1400	→	2000	1200 Y	→	1900 Y	→	*2200*▲Y
1930▲Y	→	2130 Y	→	0600 Y	2230	→	0615	→	*0920*▲

Y – ①②③④⑤⑦ only.
▲ – 🚌 operates København railway station - Polferries Terminal and v.v. Times may vary.

No sailings Apr. 18 - 21, May 2, June 20, Dec. 24 - 31.

Unity Line — **2014 service** **(No service Dec. 24, 25, 31)**

Ystad		Świnoujście	Świnoujście		Ystad
1330	→	2000	1300	→	2015
2230	→	0645	2300	→	0630

A connecting 🚌 service operates Świnoujście terminal - Szczecin Hotel Radisson SAS and v.v.: Świnoujście depart 0730, Szczecin arrive 0900. Return journey Szczecin depart 1000, Świnoujście arrive 1130.

2500 ALGECIRAS - CEUTA

Acciona Trasmediterranea **by fast ferry** **Service to September 15, 2014**

Subject to alteration at Easter and Christmas. Journey 55 minutes

Depart Algeciras and Ceuta: 3–5 sailings daily, departure times vary.

Baleària (Eurolínies Marítimes) **by fast ferry** **Service to June 15, 2014**

Journey 30 minutes

Depart Algeciras: 0600, 0900①②③④⑤⑥, 1200, 1500, 1800, 2200.
Depart Ceuta: 0730, 1030①②③④⑤⑥, 1330, 1630, 1930, 2330.

2502 ALGECIRAS - TANJAH (TANGIERS) MED

Acciona Trasmediterranea Journey 2 hours **Service to September 15, 2014**

From Algeciras and Tanjah Med: 4–6 sailings daily, departure times vary.

Tanjah (Tangiers) Med port is located approximately 45 km east of Tanjah.
A connecting 🚌 operates between Tanjah Med and Tanjah.

2504 ALMERÍA - GHAZAOUET

Acciona Trasmediterranea **Service to August 31, 2014**

Almería		Ghazaouet	
2359	→	0800	② Mar. 11 - June 10; ①⑤ June 17 - Aug. 29.

Ghazaouet		Almeria	
1300	→	2200	②⑥ June 21 - Aug. 30.
1400	→	2200	③ Mar. 12 - June 11.

2505 ALMERÍA - MELILLA

Acciona Trasmediterranea Journey 6-8 hours **Service to July 28, 2014**
(No service Dec. 24, 25)

Depart Almería: 1630①, 2330②③④⑤⑥⑦.
Depart Melilla: 1300②③④⑤⑥, 2300①⑦.

Additional sailings by fast ferry in summer (journey 3 hours)

Subject to alteration during Easter and Xmas / New Year periods

2507 ALMERÍA - AN-NADÛR (NADOR)

Acciona Trasmediterranea Journey 5-8 hours **Service to September 9, 2014**

From Almeria and an-Nadûr: up to 3 sailings daily.

2508 BARCELONA - TANJAH (TANGIERS) MED

Grandi Navi Veloci Journey 27-32 hours **2014 service**

From Barcelona: 1000 **D**, 1200 **E**, 1600 **F**, 1700 **G**.
From Tanjah Med: 1600 **H**, 2300 **J**.

D – Mar. 21, Apr. 4, 18, 25, May 9, 23; ⑤ June 6 - Oct. 17; Oct. 31, Nov. 14, 28, Dec. 12, 19.
E – ②⑦ June 1 - Aug. 17; ②⑦ Sept. 21 - 30 (not June 3).
F – Mar. 16, 30, Apr. 13, May 4, 18; ⑦ June 1 - Oct. 12; Oct. 26, Nov. 9, 23, Dec. 7, 14, 21.
G – Mar. 11, 25, Apr. 8, 29, May 13, 27, Oct. 21, Nov. 4, 18, Dec. 2.
H – Mar. 22, Apr. 5, 19, 26, May 10, 24; ①⑥ Aug. 18 - Sept. 15; Oct. 18, Nov. 1, 15, 29, Dec. 13, 20.
J – Mar. 12, 17, 26, 31, Apr. 9, 14, 30, May 5, 14, 19, 28; ①③ June 2 - Oct. 13; Oct. 22, 27, Nov. 5, 10, 19, 24, Dec. 3, 8, 15.

Tanjah (Tangiers) Med port is located approximately 45 km east of Tanjah.
A connecting 🚌 operates between Tanjah Med and Tanjah.

2510 BALEARIC ISLANDS (see map page 321)

Acciona Trasmediterranea *All routes subject to alteration around holidays* **2014 services**

BARCELONA - EIVISSA (IBIZA) **by ship** Journey 8 - 14 hours

Depart Barcelona: **Mar. 11 - June 19**: 2230②④; **June 20 - Sept. 6**: 2230①②④⑤, 2300⑥.
Depart Eivissa: **Mar. 11 - June 19**: 1100③⑤; **June 20 - Sept. 7**: 1100②③⑤, 1700⑥, 1830⑦.

BARCELONA - MAÓ (MAHÓN) **by ship** Journey 8 - 9 hours

Depart Barcelona: **Mar. 11 - June 10**: 2300①③⑤; **June 17 - Aug. 31**: 2300①③④⑤⑥⑦.
Depart Maó: **Mar. 11 - June 10**: 1100②④, 1700⑥; **June 17 - Aug. 31**: 1100.

BARCELONA - PALMA **by ship** Journey 6½ - 8½ hours, departure times vary

Depart Barcelona: **Mar. 11 - June 19**: 2300①②③④⑤⑦; **June 21 - Sept. 12**: 2300; **Sept. 14 - 30**: 2300①②③④⑤⑦.
Depart Palma: **Mar. 11 - June 15**: 1200①②③④⑤, 2300⑥, 2330⑦; **June 16 - Sept. 12**: 1200①②③④⑤⑥, 2330⑥⑦; **Sept. 13 - 30**: 1200①②③④⑤, 2300⑥, 2330⑦.

PALMA - MAÓ (MAHÓN) **by ship** Journey 5½ hours

Depart Palma: **Mar. 16 - Sept. 30**: 0800⑦.
Depart Maó: **Mar. 16 - Sept. 30**: 1715⑦.

VALÈNCIA - MAÓ (MAHÓN) via Palma **by ship** Journey 14 - 15 hours

Depart València: **Mar. 15 - Sept. 30**: 2300⑥.
Depart Maó: **Mar. 16 - Sept. 30**: 1715⑦.

VALÈNCIA - PALMA **by ship** Journey 8 hours

Depart València: **Mar. 11 - Sept. 30**: 2300①②③④⑤⑥.
Depart Palma: **Mar. 11 - Sept. 30**: 1130②③④⑤⑥, 2345⑦.

Baleària (Eurolínies Marítimes) **Service to October 5, 2014**

DÉNIA - EIVISSA (IBIZA) - PALMA

Dénia		Eivissa		Palma
1700⑥⑦	→	2030 / 2130⑥⑦	→	0100⑦①
2000①②③④⑤	→	2330①②③④⑤ / 0030②③④⑤⑥	→	0400②③④⑤⑥

Palma		Eivissa		Dénia
0800	→	1130 / 1230	→	1600

OTHER SERVICES:

Dénia - Sant Antoni and v.v.:	1–2 sailings daily, journey 2–4 hours.
Formentera - Eivissa and v.v.:	frequent daily services (0700 - 2130).
València - Palma and v.v.:	6 sailings per week (daily in summer), journey 5–6 hours (some services via Eivissa).

2512 CANARY ISLANDS

Acciona Trasmediterranea **2014 service**

CÁDIZ - GRAN CANARIA - TENERIFE - PALMA - LANZAROTE - CÁDIZ

	arrive	*depart*
Cádiz	1230①	1700②
Lanzarote (Arrecife)	2300③	2359③
Gran Canaria (Las Palmas)	0800④	1255④
Tenerife (Santa Cruz)	1700④	2330④
Palma (Santa Cruz)	0800⑤	1600⑤
Tenerife (Santa Cruz)	2130⑤	2330⑤
Gran Canaria (Las Palmas)	0800⑥	1400⑥
Lanzarote (Arrecife)	2330⑥	0100⑦

Fred. Olsen **Inter-Island services** **2014 services**

Playa Blanca (Lanzarote) - Corralejo (Fuerteventura), journey 15 minutes;
Puerto del Rosario (Fuerteventura) - Morro del Jable (Fuerteventura), journey 80 minutes;
Morro del Jable - Las Palmas de Gran Canaria (Gran Canaria), journey 100 minutes;
Las Palmas de Gran Canaria - Agaete (by 🚌, journey 25 minutes);
Agaete (Gran Canaria) - Santa Cruz de Tenerife (Tenerife), journey 60 minutes;
Santa Cruz de Tenerife - Los Cristianos (by 🚌, journey 60 minutes);
Los Cristianos (Tenerife) - San Sebastián de la Gomera (La Gomera), journey 35 minutes;
San Sebastián de la Gomera - Santa Cruz de la Palma (La Palma), journey 90 minutes;
San Sebastián de la Gomera - Valverde (El Hierro), journey 90 minutes.

Naviera Armas **Inter-Island services** **2014 services** (subject to alteration)

Corralejo (Fuerteventura) - Playa Blanca (Lanzarote)	5–6 sailings daily.
Las Palmas (Gran Canaria) - Arrecife (Lanzarote)	5 sailings per week.
Las Palmas (Gran Canaria) - Morro Jable (Fuerteventura)	1 sailing daily.
Las Palmas (Gran Canaria) - Puerto del Rosario (Fuerteventura)	3 sailings per week.
Las Palmas (Gran Canaria) - Santa Cruz (Tenerife)	2–3 sailings daily.
Los Cristianos (Tenerife) - San Sebastián (La Gomera)	1–3 sailings daily.
Los Cristianos (Tenerife) - Valverde (El Hierro)	3 sailings per week.
Santa Cruz (La Palma) - San Sebastián (La Gomera)	unknown
Santa Cruz (Tenerife) - Arrecife (Lanzarote)	4 sailings per week.
Santa Cruz (Tenerife) - Morro Jable (Fuerteventura)	1 sailing per week.
Santa Cruz (Tenerife) - Valverde (El Hierro)	3 sailings per week.

2520 CIVITAVECCHIA - BARCELONA

Grimaldi Lines **2014 service**

Civitavecchia		Barcelona			Barcelona		Civitavecchia	
2215§	→	1815	①②③④⑤⑥		2215	→	1845	①②③④⑤⑥

§ – Apr. 27 depart 2100.

2530 CIVITAVECCHIA - SICILY - TÛNIS

Grandi Navi Veloci **2014 service**

Civitavecchia		Palermo		Tûnis		Palermo		Civitavecchia
2000⑤	→	0900⑥ / 1000⑥	→	2000⑥ / 2300⑥	→	0900⑦ / 2000⑦	→	0900①

Grimaldi Lines **2014 service**

Civitavecchia		Trapani		Tûnis		Trapani		Civitavecchia
1700③	→		→	1300④ / 1600②	→		→	1300③

2535 CIVITAVECCHIA - TERMINI IMERESE

Grandi Navi Veloci **2014 service**

Civitavecchia		Termini Imerese		Termini Imerese		Civitavecchia
2030①③	→	1130②④		0130⑤	→	1630⑤
				0200③	→	1700③

2537 GENOVA - BARCELONA

Grandi Navi Veloci **2014 service**

Genova		Barcelona			Barcelona		Genova	
1300	→	0700	See note **K**.		1300	→	0730	See note **N**.
1800	→	1100	See note **L**.		2300	→	1730	See note **P**.
2000	→	1300	See note **M**.					

K – Mar. 20, Apr. 3, 17, 24 May 8, 22; ④ June 5 - Oct. 16; Oct. 30, Nov. 13, 27, Dec. 11, 18.
L – Mar. 15, 29, Apr. 12, May 3, 17; ⑥ May 31 - Oct. 11; Oct. 25, Nov. 8, 22, Dec. 6, 13, 20.
M – Mar. 10, 24, Apr. 7, 28, May 12, 26, Oct. 20, Nov. 3, 17, Dec. 1.
N – Mar. 14, 19, 28, Apr. 2, 11, 16, May 2, 7, 16, 21, 30, June 4; ③⑤ June 11 - Oct. 15; Oct. 24, 29, Nov. 7, 12, 21, 26, Dec. 5, 10, 17.
P – Mar. 23, Apr. 6, 20, 27, May 1, 11, 25, Oct. 19, Nov. 2, 16, 30, Dec. 14, 21.

2547 GENOVA - PALERMO

Grandi Navi Veloci Journey 21 hours **2014 service**

From Genova: 2100 **P**, 2300 **Q**.
From Palermo: 2100 **R**, 2200 **S**, 2300 **T**, 2359 **V**.

P – Daily June 16 - Sept. 13 (also June 9, Dec. 13; not Aug. 15).
Q – ①②③④⑤⑥ Mar. 7 - June 14, Sept. 15 - Dec. 20 (also Dec. 21; not June 9, Dec. 13).
R – Daily June 16 - Sept. 13 (also June 10; not June 15).
S – Dec. 12 only.
T – ①②③④⑤ Mar. 7 - June 13, Sept. 15 - Dec. 19 (also Dec. 21; not June 10, Dec. 12).
V – ⑥ Mar. 8 - June 14, Sept. 20 - Dec. 20.

GENOVA - TANJAH (TANGIERS) MED 2554

Grandi Navi Veloci — 2014 service

Genova		Tanjah Med		Tanjah Med		Genova	
1300	→	1130	See note **F**.	1600	→	0030	See note **J**.
1800	→	1630	See note **G**.	2300	→	0730	See note **K**.
2000	→	1830	See note **H**.				

F – Mar. 20, Apr. 3, 17, 24, May 8, 22; ④ June 5 - Oct. 16; Oct. 30, Nov. 13, 27, Dec. 11, 18.
G – Mar. 15, 29, Apr. 12, May 3, 17; ⑥ May 31 - Oct. 11; Oct. 25, Nov. 8, 22, Dec. 6, 13, 20.
H – Mar. 10, 24, Apr. 7, 28, May 12, 26, Oct. 20, Nov. 3, 17, Dec. 1.
J – Mar. 8, 22, Apr. 5, 19, 26, May 10, 24, Oct. 18, Nov. 1, 15, 29, Dec. 13, 20.
K – Mar. 12, 17, 26, 31, Apr. 9, 14, 30, May 5, 14, 19, 28, June 2; ①③ June 9 - Oct. 13; Oct. 22, 27, Nov. 5, 10, 19, 24, Dec. 3, 8, 15.

Tanjah (Tangiers) Med port is located approximately 45 km east of Tanjah. A connecting 🚌 operates between Tanjah Med and Tanjah.

All sailings via Barcelona (see Table **2508**)

GENOVA - TÛNIS 2555

Compagnie Tunisienne de Navigation / S N C M — 2014 service
Departure times vary. Journey 20 - 24 hours
From Genova: ⑥ Apr. 5 - Dec. 27 (also June 18, 25, 30, July 2, 7, 9, 14, 16, 21, 24, 28, 31, Aug. 4, 7, 12, 14, 19, 25, 26, 28, Sept. 2, 4, 8, 11, 15, 17, 24, Oct. 1, Dec. 17, 24, 30).
From Tûnis: ⑤ Apr. 4 - Dec. 26 (also June 17, 24, 29, July 1, 6, 8, 13, 15, 20, 23, 27, 30, Aug. 3, 6, 11, 13, 18, 27, Sept. 1, 3, 7, 10, 14, 16, 23, 29, Dec. 15, 23, 29).

Grandi Navi Veloci Departure times vary. Journey 24 hours — 2014 service
From Genova: ③⑥ Mar. 12 - June 14; ①③⑥ June 16 - Aug. 11; ②⑤⑦ Aug. 15 - Sept. 14; ③⑥ Sept. 17 - Dec. 20.
From Tûnis: ④⑦ Mar. 13 - June 15; ②④⑦ June 17 - Aug. 12; ①③⑥ Aug. 16 - Sept. 15; ④⑦ Sept. 18 - Dec. 21.

MARSEILLE - ORAN 2558

E N T M V Journey 24 - 25 hours — 2014 service
Departures from Marseille: June 6, 13, 23, July 1, 5, 12, 19, 22, 26, 31, Aug. 6, 12, 16, 23, 28, Sept. 1, 7, 11, 15, 23, 29, Oct. 3, 14, 24.
Departures from Oran: June 3, 15, 24, July 1, 6, 13, 18, 22, 25, Aug. 1, 6, 9, 17, 23, 27, 31, Sept. 4, 9, 14, 23, 30, Oct. 8, 16, 26.

GULF OF NAPOLI (including Gulf of Salerno and Ponziane Islands) 2560

Alilauro — 2014 services (subject to confirmation)
Napoli Mergellina or Beverello - Capri: 5 - 11 sailings daily.
Napoli Beverello - Forio: 5 sailings daily (summer only).
Napoli Beverello - Ischia: 2 - 6 sailings daily by ship, 4 - 8 sailings daily by catamaran.
Napoli Mergellina or Beverello - Ischia: 4 - 7 sailings daily.
Napoli Mergellina or Beverello - Sorrento: 5 - 9 sailings daily.
Napoli - Sorrento - Positano - Amalfi: summer only, infrequent sailings.
Pozzuoli - Ischia: frequent service by ship.
Sorrento - Capri: 7 - 16 sailings daily by catamaran, also 1 - 6 sailings by ship.
Salerno - Amalfi - Positano - Capri: summer only, infrequent sailings by catamaran.
Additional infrequent services to Capri operate (summer only) from Ischia, Castellammare di Stábia, Torre Annunziata, Positano and Amalfi.

Caremar — 2014 services (subject to confirmation)
Napoli - Capri: 6 sailings daily by catamaran, 3 sailings by ship.
Napoli - Ischia: 9 sailings daily by catamaran, 5 sailings by ship.
Napoli - Procida: 8 sailings daily by catamaran, 5 sailings by ship.
Pozzuoli - Procida - Ischia: 1 sailing daily by catamaran, 3 sailings by ship.
Sorrento - Capri: 4 sailings daily by catamaran.
Additional infrequent services operate between Procida and Ischia, Formia and Ventotene, Formia and Ponza, Anzio and Ponza.

Medmar — 2014 services (subject to confirmation)
Napoli - Ischia: up to 7 sailings daily.
Ischia - Pozzuoli: up to 10 sailings daily.
Additional infrequent services operate between Pozzuoli, Procida and Ischia.

Navigazione Libera del Golfo by *Linea Jet* — 2014 services (subject to confirmation)
Napoli (Molo Beverello) - Capri: up to 9 sailings daily (more in summer). Journey 40 minutes.
Sorrento - Capri: 6 - 8 sailings daily (19 - 20 in summer). Journey 25 minutes.
Additional services operate (summer only) between Castellammare di Stábia and Capri.

SNAV Journey 40 minutes — 2014 service
Napoli (Beverello) - Capri: 0700, 0805, 0835, 0910, 0930, 1010, 1035, 1110, 1135, 1240, 1400, 1440, 1535, 1600, 1630, 1810⑤⑦, 2000.
Capri - Napoli (Beverello): 0650, 0805, 0910, 0935, 1010, 1035, 1135, 1215, 1240, 1340, 1440, 1525, 1630, 1705, 1710, 1810, 1910⑤⑦.

CORSICA 2565

Sailings from mainland FRANCE

MARSEILLE - AJACCIO — 2014 service
S N C M Journey 9 - 12 hours
From Marseille and Ajaccio: Feb. - Apr. 3 – 4 sailings per week; May - June: 3 – 5 sailings per week; July - Aug.: 5 – 8 sailings per week; Sept. - Oct.: 3 – 4 sailings per week.
Most sailings overnight, departure times vary.

MARSEILLE - BASTIA — 2014 service
S N C M Journey 10 - 13 hours
From Marseille and Bastia: Feb. - June: 4 – 6 sailings per week; July - Aug.: 6 – 9 sailings per week; Sept. - Oct.: 3 sailings per week.
Most sailings overnight, departure times vary.

MARSEILLE - L'ÎLE ROUSSE — 2014 service
S N C M Journey 8 - 11½ hours
From Marseille and L'Île Rousse: Apr. - Oct.: 3 sailings per week. Additional sailings in summer.
All sailings overnight, departure times vary.

MARSEILLE - PORTO VECCHIO — 2014 service
S N C M Journey 14 hours
From Marseille: Mar.: ③⑤; Apr. - Oct.: ①③⑤.
From Porto Vecchio: Mar.: ④⑥; Apr. - Oct.: ②④⑥.
All sailings overnight, departure times vary.

MARSEILLE - PROPRIANO — 2014 service
S N C M Journey 9½ - 12½ hours
From Marseille and Propriano: late-June - late-Aug.: 1 – 2 sailings per week.
Most sailings overnight, departure times vary.

NICE - AJACCIO — 2014 service
Corsica Ferries Journey 4½ - 9 hours
From Nice and Ajaccio: Apr. - June: 10 – 15 sailings per month; July - Aug.: 16 – 21 sailings per month; Sept.: 10 sailings per month.
Most sailings by day, departure times vary.

S N C M Journey 4½ - 9 hours
From Nice and Ajaccio: Mar. - July: 2 – 3 sailings per week; Aug.: 4 – 5 sailings per week; Sept - Oct.: 1 – 2 sailings per week.
Departure times vary.

NICE - BASTIA — 2014 service
Corsica Ferries Journey 5 - 6 hours
From Nice and Bastia: 3 – 5 sailings per week (daily June - Sept.).
Most sailings by day, departure times vary.

S N C M Journey 5 hours
From Nice and Bastia: Mar.: 2 sailings per week; Apr.: 3 – 4 sailings per week; May - June: 6 – 7 sailings per week; July - Sept.: 7 – 8 sailings per week; Oct.: 3 sailings per week.
All sailings by day, departure times vary.

NICE - CALVI — 2014 service
Corsica Ferries Journey 4 - 5½ hours
From Nice and Calvi: Apr. - May: 1 sailing per week; June: 5 – 7 sailings per week; July - Sept.: no sailings.
All sailings by day, departure times vary.

S N C M Journey 3 - 4 hours
From Nice and Calvi: Apr. - mid-May: 1 sailing per week; mid-May - mid-Sept.: 5 – 7 sailings per week; mid-Sept. - Oct.: 1 sailing per week.
All sailings by day, departure times vary.

NICE - L'ÎLE ROUSSE — 2014 service
Corsica Ferries Journey 5 - 5½ hours
From Nice and L'Île Rousse: May: occasional sailings; June: up to 3 sailings per week; July - Sept.: up to 8 sailings per week.
All sailings by day, departure times vary.

S N C M Journey 3 - 6½ hours (night sailings 12 hours)
From Nice and L'Île Rousse: late-May - June: up to 3 sailings per week; July - early-Sept.: up to 8 sailings per week; Sept.: 1 – 2 sailings per week.
Departure times vary.

TOULON - AJACCIO — 2014 service
Corsica Ferries Journey 6 - 10 hours
From Toulon and Ajaccio: Apr. - Sept.: 1 – 2 sailings daily.
Departure times vary.

TOULON - BASTIA — 2014 service
Corsica Ferries Journey 9 - 10 hours
From Toulon and Bastia: Daily Apr. 1 - Sept. 30.
Departure times vary.

TOULON - L'ÎLE ROUSSE — 2014 service
Corsica Ferries Journey 6 - 7 hours
From Toulon and L'Île Rousse: mid-Apr. - June: up to 2 sailings per week; July - Aug.: 3 – 6 sailings per week; Sept. 1 – 3 sailings per week.
All sailings by day, departure times vary.

2565 CORSICA continued

Sailings from ITALY

GENOVA - BASTIA — **2014 service**

Moby Lines

Genova		Bastia	
2200	→	0800§	①③⑤ May 2-26; daily May 28 - Sept. 15; ①③⑤ Sept. 17-26.

Bastia		Genova	
1100	→	1730	Daily May 29 - Sept. 15.
1200	→	1830	⑦ May 4-25 (also Sept. 21, 28).
2200	→	0730	②④ May 1-27; ②④ Sept. 16-25.

§ – Arrive 0730 in May.

LIVORNO - BASTIA — **2014 service**

Corsica Ferries Journey 4 hours (night sailings 7½ hours)

From Livorno and Bastia: Apr. - May: 1–2 sailings daily; June - Sept: up to 4 sailings daily. Most sailings by day, departure times vary.

Moby Lines

Livorno		Bastia	
0800	→	1205	Daily May 28 - Sept. 14.
1400	→	1805	②④⑥ May 1-27; ②④⑥ Sept. 16-27.

Bastia		Livorno	
0830	→	1235	②④⑥ May 1-27; ②④⑥ Sept. 16-27.
1400	→	1805	Daily May 28 - Sept. 14.

SAVONA - BASTIA — **2014 service**

Corsica Ferries Journey 6-10 hours

From Savona and Bastia: Apr. - May: 2–4 sailings per week; June: 1–2 sailings daily; July - Aug.: 2–3 sailings daily; Sept.: up to 3 sailings daily. Departure times vary.

SAVONA - CALVI — **2014 service**

Corsica Ferries

From Savona and Calvi: July - mid-Sept.: 1 sailing per week. Departure times vary.

CORSICA - SARDINIA

BONIFACIO - SANTA TERESA DI GALLURA — **2014 service**

Moby Lines Journey 60 minutes — **April 16 - Sept. 28 only**

From Bonifacio: 0830, 1200, 1700, 2000.
From Santa Teresa di Gallura: 0700, 1000, 1500, 1830.

Saremar Journey 1 hour

Up to 3 sailings per day.

2570 ITALIAN ISLAND SERVICES (Egadi, Eolie, Pantelleria, Pelagie and Ustica Islands)

Alilauro — **2014 service** (subject to confirmation)

Napoli Mergellina - Stromboli - Panarea - Salina - Vulcano - Lipari and v.v.: 2–3 sailings per week (daily in Aug.).

Siremar — **2014 services** (subject to confirmation)

NAPOLI - MILAZZO via Stromboli, Ginostra, Panarea, Lipari and Vulcano.
Also serves Rinella (on ②④) and S.M. Salina (on ①⑤). Journey 16-20 hours.
Sailings from Napoli: 2000②⑤.
Sailings from Milazzo: 1500①④ (depart 1350 Nov. - Mar.).

OTHER SERVICES:
Inter-island sailings operate, also from mainland Sicily to the islands. Services operate to differing frequencies (additional sailings in summer).

EOLIE ISLANDS:
Alicudi to Filicudi, Lipari, Milazzo, Rinella, Salina and Vulcano.
Filicudi to Alicudi, Lipari, Milazzo, Rinella, Salina and Vulcano.
Ginostra to Lipari, Milazzo, and Panarea.
Lipari to Alicudi, Filicudi, Ginostra, Milazzo, Panarea, Rinella, Salina, Stromboli and Vulcano.
Milazzo to Alicudi, Filicudi, Ginostra, Lipari, Panarea, Rinella, Salina, Stromboli and Vulcano.
Panarea to Filicudi, Ginostra, Lipari, Milazzo, Rinella, Salina, Stromboli and Vulcano.
Rinella to Alicudi, Filicudi, Lipari, Milazzo, Panarea, Salina, Stromboli and Vulcano.
Salina to Alicudi, Filicudi, Lipari, Milazzo, Panarea, Rinella, Stromboli and Vulcano.
Stromboli to Alicudi, Filicudi, Lipari, Milazzo, Panarea, Rinella, Salina and Vulcano.
Vulcano to Alicudi, Filicudi, Lipari, Milazzo, Panarea, Rinella, Salina and Stromboli.

EGADI ISLANDS:
Favignana to Levanzo, Marettimo and Trapani.
Levanzo to Favignana, Marettimo, and Trapani.
Marettimo to Favignana, Levanzo and Trapani.
Trapani to Favignana, Levanzo and Marettimo.

PANTELLERIA ISLAND:
Trapani - Pantelleria and v.v.

PELAGIE ISLANDS:
Porto Empedocle (Agrigento) - Linosa - Lampedusa and v.v.

USTICA ISLAND:
Palermo - Ustica and v.v.

Ustica Lines by hydrofoil — **2014 services**

EGADI & EOLIAN ISLANDS and USTICA

The Sicilian ports of Messina, Milazzo, Palermo and Trapani are linked by island-hopping services serving Alicudi, Favignana, Filicudi, Levanzo, Lipari, Marettimo, Panarea, Rinella, Salina, Stromboli, Ustica and Vulcano.

Services operate to differing frequencies (additional sailings in summer).

LAMPEDUSA - LINOSA - PORTO EMPEDOCLE (AGRIGENTO) by hydrofoil

June 20 - September 10

Lampedusa		Linosa		Porto Empedocle		Linosa		Lampedusa	
0730	→	0830/0845	→	1145/1500	→	1800/1815	→	1915	①③④⑤⑥⑦
0930	→	1030		...		1040	→	1140	②③④⑤⑥⑦
1730	→	1830		...		1845	→	1945	②③④⑤⑥⑦

TRAPANI - PANTELLERIA by hydrofoil — **June 20 - Sept. 10**

Journey 2½ hours.
Depart Trapani: 1320. Depart Pantelleria: 1610.

MILAZZO - VULCANO by hydrofoil Journey 50 minutes

January 1 - June 19
Depart Milazzo: 0720, 0930, 1430, 1800, 1900.
Depart Vulcano: 0805, 1235, 1335, 1550, 1715, 1935.

June 20 - September 10
Depart Milazzo: 0620, 0750, 0940, 1200, 1425, 1620, 1910.
Depart Vulcano: 0810, 1035, 1230, 1405, 1745, 1830, 1935.

MILAZZO - PALERMO by hydrofoil — **June 20 - Sept. 10**

Journey 2½ hours

Milazzo		Palermo		Milazzo	
0620	→	1135/1350	→	1915	Daily.

2580 LIVORNO - BARCELONA - TANJAH (TANGIERS) MED

Grimaldi Lines — **2014 service**

Livorno		Barcelona		Tanjah Med		Barcelona		Livorno
2330⑥	→	2000/2359⑦	→	1030/1700②	→	2000/2359③	→	1930④

Tanjah (Tangiers) Med port is located approximately 45 km east of Tanjah.
A connecting 🚌 operates between Tanjah Med and Tanjah.

2595 MÁLAGA - MELILLA

Acciona Trasmediterranea Journey 7-8 hours — **Service to September 10, 2014**

From Málaga: 1300②③④⑤⑥, 2300①⑦.
From Melilla: 1200①, 2330③④⑤⑥, 2359①.

Departure times may vary at peak times
Subject to alteration during Easter and Xmas/New Year periods

Also daily sailings by fast ferry in summer (journey 4 hours).

2602 MARSEILLE - AL-JAZÂ'IR (ALGIERS)

SNCM/ENTMV Journey 20 hours, departure times vary — **Service to October 31, 2014**

Departures from Marseille: June 2, 3, 7, 10, 14, 17, 21, 26, 28, July 1, 2, 5, 7, 9, 12, 14, 16, 17, 19, 22, 23, 24, 26, 28, 31, Aug. 2, 4, 6, 9, 11, 13, 16, 18, 21, 23, 25, 26, 27, 28, 30, 31, Sept. 1, 2, 3, 6, 7, 8, 9, 10, 13, 16, 17, 20, 23, 27, 29, Oct. 1, 3, 8, 11, 18, 25.

Departures from al-Jazâ'ir: June 2, 4, 5, 9, 11, 16, 18, 23, 25, 28, 30, July 2, 3, 6, 9, 10, 13, 15, 17, 18, 20, 23, 24, 25, 29, 30, Aug. 1, 3, 5, 7, 10, 12, 14, 17, 19, 22, 24, 26, 28, 29, 31, Sept. 1, 2, 3, 4, 7, 8, 9, 10, 11, 15, 17, 18, 22, 24, 28, 30, Oct. 2, 7, 9, 13, 20, 27.

Other services operate from Marseille to Annâbah, Bijâyah, Sakîkdah, Wâhran (Oran) and v.v.

2615 MARSEILLE - TÛNIS

Compagnie Tunisienne de Navigation/S N C M — **2014 service**

Departure times vary. Journey 20-24 hours

Departures from Marseille: ④ Apr. 3 - Dec. 25 (also July 1, 5, 8, 12, 14, 19, 21, 26, 28, 30, Aug. 2, 5, 9, 12, 17, 19, 22, 24, 26, 31, Sept. 2, 7, 9, 15, Dec. 21, 28; not July 31, Aug. 28).

Departures from Tûnis: ② Apr. 1 - June 24, Sept. 16 - Dec. 23 (also June 13, 20, 27, 30, July 2, 4, 7, 9, 11, 13, 16, 18, 20, 23, 25, 27, 29, Aug. 1, 4, 5, 8, 11, 13, 16, 18, 20, 21, 23, 25, 27, 28, 30, Sept. 1, 3, 6, 8, 10, 13, 19, 26, Dec. 20, 27).

2618 MGARR (Gozo) - CIRKEWWA (Malta)

Gozo Channel Co. Journey 25 minutes — **2014 service**

Until May 4
From Mgarr: 0130, 0330, 0500, 0600, 0630①, 0645②③④⑤⑥⑦, 0700①, 0730, 0815, 0900, 0945, 1030, 1115, 1200, 1245, 1330, 1415, 1500, 1545, 1630, 1715, 1800, 1915, 2045, 2200, 2345.
From Cirkewwa: 0200, 0400, 0545, 0630①, 0645②③④⑤⑥⑦, 0700①, 0730, 0815, 0900, 0945, 1030, 1115, 1200, 1245, 1330, 1415, 1500, 1545, 1630, 1715, 1800, 1845, 2000, 2120, 2235, 0020.

From May 5 (subject to alteration)
From Mgarr: 0045, 0200, 0330, 0500, 0600, 0630①②③④⑤, 0645⑥⑦, 0700①②③④⑤, 0730, 0815, 0900, 0945, 1030, 1115, 1200, 1245, 1330, 1415, 1500, 1545, 1630, 1715, 1800, 1845, 1930, 2015, 2100, 2145, 2300.
From Cirkewwa: 0115, 0235, 0400, 0545, 0630①②③④⑤, 0645⑥⑦, 0700①②③④⑤, 0730, 0815, 0900, 0945, 1030, 1115, 1200, 1245, 1330, 1415, 1500, 1545, 1630, 1715, 1800, 1845, 1930, 2015, 2100, 2145, 2215, 2345.

2625 NAPOLI - PALERMO

GNV — **Service to October 31, 2014**

Napoli		Palermo		Palermo		Napoli	
0900	→	1930	See note **N**.	0900	→	1930	See note **N**.
2000	→	0630	See note **P**.	2000	→	0630	See note **P**.
2100	→	0730	See note **N**.	2100	→	0730	See note **N**.

N – July 26, 27, Aug. 1-3, 7-9, 11, 14, 16-18, 22-24, 29-31.
P – Daily until July 25 and from Sept. 1 (also July 28-31, Aug. 4-6, 10, 12, 13, 15, 19-21, 25-28).

Tirrenia — **2014 service**

Napoli		Palermo	Palermo		Napoli
2015	→	0630	2015	→	0630

NAPOLI - TRAPANI 2630

Ustica Lines **by hydrofoil** **June 28 - August 30, 2014**
(No winter service)

⑥: Napoli 1500 → Ustica 1905/1925 → Favignana 2125/2135 → Trapani 2200.
⑥: Trapani 0615 → Favignana 0635/0640 → Ustica 0840/0900 → Napoli 1315.

REGGIO DI CALABRIA - MESSINA 2660

Metromare dello Stretto **by hydrofoil** Journey 30 minutes **2013 service**

From Reggio di Calabria: 0640①②③④⑤, 0740, 0800①②③④⑤, 0920, 1120①②③④⑤, 1250, 1320⑥⑦, 1410①②③④⑤, 1510①②③④⑤, 1730, 1850①②③④⑤, 1930⑥⑦, 2010①②③④⑤.
From Messina: 0600①②③④⑤, 0700, 0720①②③④⑤, 0840, 1040①②③④⑤, 1210, 1240⑥⑦, 1330①②③④⑤, 1430①②③④⑤, 1440⑥⑦, 1640①②③④⑤, 1810①②③④⑤, 1820⑥⑦, 1930①②③④⑤.

Ustica Lines **by hydrofoil** Journey 30 minutes **2014 service**

Until June 30

From Reggio di Calabria: 0640①②③④⑤, 0730⑥⑦, 0740①②③④⑤, 0805①②③④⑤, 0920, 1120, 1250, 1420①②③④⑤, 1525①②③④⑤, 1620⑥⑦, 1655①②③④⑤, 1820①②③④⑤, 1940⑥⑦, 1945⑥⑦.
From Messina: 0600①②③④⑤, 0650⑥⑦, 0700①②③④⑤, 0725①②③④⑤, 0840, 1040, 1210, 1340①②③④⑤, 1445①②③④⑤, 1540⑥⑦, 1615①②③④⑤, 1740①②③④⑤, 1900⑥⑦, 1905①②③④⑤.

July 1 - September 10

From Reggio di Calabria: 0920, 1250. From Messina: 0840, 1210.

SALERNO - PALERMO - TÛNIS 2661

Grimaldi Lines **2014 service**

Salerno		Palermo		Tûnis		Palermo		Salerno
1200①	→	2230①/0100②	→	1300②/1700④	→	0700⑤/0900⑤	→	1930⑤
2300⑤	→	0930⑥/1130⑥	→	2230⑥/0001⑦	→	1500⑦/1900⑦	→	0700①

SARDINIA 2675

Sailings from FRANCE

MARSEILLE - PORTO TORRES 2014 service

S N C M Journey 16 - 19 hours

From Marseille: 0930 ⑦ June 29 - Aug. 31; 2000 ⑤ Apr. 11 - June 20, Sept. 5 - 26.
From Porto Torres: 1500 ⑥ Apr. 12 - June 21, Sept. 6 - 27; 2130 ⑦ June 29 - Aug. 31.

Sailings from mainland ITALY

CIVITAVECCHIA - ARBATAX 2014 service

Tirrenia

Civitavecchia		Arbatax	Arbatax		Civitavecchia
1900③⑤	→	0500④⑥	2359③⑦	→	1000④①

CIVITAVECCHIA - CAGLIARI 2014 service

Tirrenia

Civitavecchia		Cagliari	Cagliari		Civitavecchia
1900①②④⑥⑦	→	0800②③⑤⑦①	1900①②④⑤⑥	→	0800②③⑤⑥⑦
1900③⑤	→	1000④⑥	1900③⑦	→	1000④①

CIVITAVECCHIA - OLBIA 2014 service

Moby Lines

Civitavecchia		Olbia		Olbia		Civitavecchia	
1530	→	2030	See note M.	0900	→	1430	See note M.

M – Daily May 29 - Sept. 14 (also Sept. 20 - 22, 27, 28).

Tirrenia Journey 5 hours (night sailings 8 hours)

From Civitavecchia and Olbia: night sailing every day (d. 2230). Additional day sailings in summer.

CIVITAVECCHIA - PORTO TORRES 2014 service

Grimaldi Lines

Civitavecchia		P. Torres	
2215	→	0530	①⑤ Apr. 15 - June 8; ①④⑤⑥ June 9 - 22; ①②④⑤⑥ June 23 - Sept. 7; ①④⑤⑥ Sept. 8 - 14; ①⑤ Sept. 15 - Oct. 5.
P. Torres		**Civitavecchia**	
1130	→	1845	②⑥ Apr. 15 - June 8; ②⑤⑥⑦ June 9 - 22; ②③⑤⑥⑦ June 23 - Sept. 7; ②⑤⑥⑦ Sept. 8 - 14; ②⑥ Sept. 15 - Oct. 5.

GENOVA - ARBATAX 2014 service

Tirrenia

Genova		Arbatax	
1945	→	1300	①⑤ Mar. 3 - July 18, Sept. 8 - Dec. 29.
2130	→	1300	①⑥ July 21 - Aug. 18; ①⑤ Aug. 22 - Sept. 5.
Arbatax		**Genova**	
1400	→	0730	②⑦ July 22 - Aug. 19; ②⑥ Aug. 23 - Sept. 6.
1400	→	0800	②⑥ Mar. 4 - July 19, Sept. 9 - Dec. 30.

GENOVA - OLBIA 2014 service

Moby Lines

Genova		Olbia	
0900	→	2000	⑥⑦ May 31 - July 20; July 26 - 28, 31, Aug. 1 - 4, 8 - 10, 15 - 17, 21 - 25, 28 - 31, Sept. 1, 4 - 8, 13, 14.
2130	→	0800§	Daily May 28 - Oct. 6 (also Oct. 8, 10).
Olbia		**Genova**	
0900	→	2000	⑥⑦ June 1 - July 27; July 28, 31, Aug. 1 - 4, 8 - 10, 15 - 17, 21 - 25, 28 - 31, Sept. 1, 4 - 8, 13, 14 (also May 30, June 6).
2100	→	0800	Daily May 28 - Oct. 7 (also Oct. 9, 11; not May 31).

§ – Arrive 0830 Aug. 1 - Sept. 30.

Tirrenia

Genova		Olbia	
0900	→	1900	③④⑦ Aug. 20 - Sept. 7.
1945	→	0800	①③⑤ Mar. 3 - July 18, Sept. 8 - Dec. 31.
2130	→	0730	①③④⑤⑥ July 21 - Aug. 16; ①⑤ Aug. 18 - Sept. 5.
Olbia		**Genova**	
0900	→	1900	④⑤⑥ July 24 - Aug. 16.
1945	→	0800	②④⑥ Mar. 4 - July 19, Sept. 9 - Dec. 30.
2130	→	0730	②⑦ July 22 - Aug. 17; ②③④⑥⑦ Aug. 19 - Sept. 7.

GENOVA - PORTO TORRES 2014 service

Grandi Navi Veloci Journey 10 – 12 hours

From Genova: 2030: even dates June 4 - July 30; uneven dates Aug. 1 - 31; even dates Sept. 2 - 12 (also May 30, June 1).
From Porto Torres: 2030: uneven dates June 5 - July 31; even dates Aug. 2 - 30; uneven dates Sept. 1 - 13 (also May 31, June 2).

Tirrenia

Genova		Porto Torres	Porto Torres		Genova
2030	→	0800	2030	→	0800

LIVORNO - GOLFO ARANCI 2014 service

Sardinia Ferries Journey 6½ – 10 hours. Departure times vary.

From Livorno and Golfo Aranci: Apr. - May: up to 7 sailings per week; June - Sept.: 1 – 2 sailings daily.

LIVORNO - OLBIA 2014 service

Moby Lines

Livorno		Olbia	
0800	→	1430	⑥ May 10 - 24; daily May 30 - Sept. 21 (also Sept. 27, 28).
2200	→	0700	May 19 - 23, 26 - 29; ② July 29 - Sept. 2; Sept. 22 - 26; daily Sept. 29 - Oct. 31.
2300	→	0700	June 2 - 6, 9 - 13, 16 - 18, 23 - 27, July 1, 3, 8, 9, 15, 22, Sept. 8 - 12, 15 - 19.
2350	→	0730	⑥⑦ May 17 - June 15; June 19 - 22, 28 - 30, July 2, 4 - 7; ①③④⑤⑥⑦ July 10 - Sept. 7; ⑥⑦ Sept. 13 - 28 (also May 30).
Olbia		**Livorno**	
1100	→	1800	② July 29 - Sept. 2.
1415	→	2115	June 2 - 5, 9 - 13, 16 - 18, 23 - 27, July 1, 3, 8, 9, 15, 22, Sept. 8 - 12, 15 - 19.
1545	→	2230	⑥ May 10 - 24; ⑥⑦ May 31 - June 15; June 19 - 22, 28 - 30, July 2, 4 - 7; ①③④⑤⑥⑦ July 10 - Sept. 7; ⑥⑦ Sept. 13 - 28 (also May 30).
2200	→	0700	①②③④⑤ May 19 - June 18; June 23 - 27, July 1, 3; ② July 8 - Sept. 2; Sept. 8 - 12, 15 - 19, 23 - 26; daily Sept. 29 - Oct. 31 (also July 9).
2230	→	0700	⑥⑦ May 17 - June 15; June 19 - 22, 28 - 30, July 2, 4 - 7; ①③④⑤⑥⑦ July 10 - Sept. 7; ⑥⑦ Sept. 13 - 28 (also Sept. 22).

NAPOLI - CAGLIARI 2014 service

Tirrenia

Napoli		Cagliari	Cagliari		Napoli
1900②④	→	0830③⑤	1900①③	→	0830②④

PIOMBINO - OLBIA 2014 service

Moby Lines

Piombino		Olbia	
0900	→	1400	Sept. 20, 21, 27, 28.
1200	→	1730	Sept. 15 - 19, 22 - 26.
1430	→	1930	⑥⑦ May 31 - June 15; June 19 - 22, 28 - 30, July 4 - 7, 11 - 14, 18 - 21; ①③④⑤⑥⑦ July 24 - Sept. 7 (also Sept. 13, 14).
Olbia		**Piombino**	
0815	→	1300	⑥⑦ May 31 - June 15; June 19 - 22, 28 - 30, July 4 - 7, 11 - 14, 18 - 21; ①③④⑤⑥⑦ July 24 - Sept. 7 (also Sept. 13, 14).
1430	→	1930	Sept. 20, 27.
2100	→	0530	Sept. 14 - 19, 21 - 26.

Sailings from SICILY

PALERMO - CAGLIARI 2014 service

Tirrenia

Palermo		Cagliari	Cagliari		Palermo
1930⑥	→	0700⑦	1930⑤	→	0700⑥

TRAPANI - CAGLIARI 2014 service

Tirrenia

Trapani		Cagliari	Cagliari		Trapani
2230⑦	→	0800①	1030⑦	→	2030⑦

For shipping operator details – see pages 541/542

2675 SARDINIA continued

Sailings from SPAIN

BARCELONA - PORTO TORRES — 2014 service

Grimaldi Lines

Barcelona		Porto Torres	Porto Torres		Barcelona
2215①②④⑤⑥	→	1030②③⑤⑥⑦	0630②③⑤⑥⑦	→	1815②③⑤⑥⑦

2678 SÈTE - AN-NADÛR (NADOR)

Grandi Navi Veloci — 2014 service

Sète		an-Nadûr		an-Nadûr		Sète	
1400③	→	1800④	May 28 - Oct. 8.	1000	→	1600*	See note **T**.
2100	→	0100§	See note **S**.	2359④	→	0600⑥	May 29 - Oct. 9 (also Oct. 15).

S – Mar. 15, 23, 31, Apr. 8, 16, 24, May 2, 10, 18, Oct. 13, 22, 30, Nov. 7, 15, 23, Dec. 1, 7, 15.
T – Mar. 17, 25, Apr. 2, 10, 18, 26, May 4, 12, 20, Oct. 24, Nov. 1, 9, 17, 25, Dec. 3, 9, 17.
* – Next day. § – Two days later.

2680 SÈTE - TANJAH (TANGIERS) MED

Grandi Navi Veloci — 2014 service

Sète		Tanjah Med		Tanjah Med		Sète	
2100	→	0700¶	See note **V**.	0100	→	1300*	See note **X**.
				1200	→	2359*	Oct. 15 only.
				1500	→	0300¶	See note **Y**.
				1600	→	0400¶	See note **Z**.
				1800	→	0600¶	See note **S**.
				2000	→	0800	See note **T**.

S – ⑥ June 7 - Aug. 16, Sept. 20 - Oct. 4.
T – ① June 2 - Aug. 11, Sept. 22 - 29 (also Oct. 11).
V – Mar. 7, 11, 15, 19, 23, 27, 31, Apr. 4, 8, 12, 16, 20, 24, 28, May 2, 6, 10, 14, 18, 22, 31; ①⑥ June 7 - Oct. 18; Oct.22, 26, 30, Nov. 3, 7, 11, 15, 19, 23, 27, Dec. 1, 5, 7.
X – Mar. 10, 18, 26, Apr. 3, 11, 19, 27, May 5, 13, 21, Oct. 25, Nov. 2, 10, 18, 26, Dec. 4, 10, 18.
Y – Mar. 13, 21, 29, Apr. 6, 14, 22, 30, May 8, 16, 24, Oct. 6, 13, 20, 28, Nov. 5, 13, 21, 29, Dec. 7, 13, 21.
Z – ①⑥ Aug. 18 - Sept. 15.
* – Next day. ¶ – Two days later.

Tanjah (Tangiers) Med port is located approximately 45 km east of Tanjah.
A connecting 🚌 operates between Tanjah Med and Tanjah.

2690 VALLETTA - CATANIA

Virtu Ferries by catamaran — Journey 4 hours — 2014 service

Apr. - May: ①⑤⑥; June: ①⑤⑥⑦; July: ①②④⑤⑥⑦; Aug.: daily; Sept.: ①②⑤⑥⑦; Oct. - Mar.: ①⑤⑥.

1 sailing per day. Departure times vary.

All sailings by catamaran Valletta - Pozzallo and v.v., then by 🚌 to/from Catania (see also Table **2694**).

Subject to alteration during Xmas/New Year period

2694 VALLETTA - POZZALLO

Virtu Ferries by catamaran — Journey 1½ hours — 2014 service

Apr. - June: 1–2 sailings on ①③⑤⑥⑦; July - Aug.: daily; Sept.: 1–2 sailings on ①②③⑤⑥⑦; Oct. - Mar.: 1–2 sailings on ①③⑤⑥⑦.

Departure times vary.

Subject to alteration during Xmas/New Year period

2695 VILLA SAN GIOVANNI - MESSINA

Bluferries by ship — Journey 30 minutes — 2014 service

From Villa San Giovanni:
①–⑥: 0035, 0215, 0400, 0500, 0530, 0700, 0835, 1015, 1200, 1305, 1330, 1500, 1635, 1815, 2000, 2110, 2130, 2300.
⑦: 0035, 0215, 0315, 0530, 0700, 0835, 1005, 1135, 1310, 1500, 1630, 1800, 1940, 2110, 2245, 2300.
From Messina:
①–⑥: 0125, 0310, 0420, 0445, 0615, 0745, 0925, 1110, 1220, 1245, 1415, 1545, 1725, 1910, 2020, 2045, 2215, 2345.
⑦: 0125, 0215, 0310, 0420, 0615, 0745, 0925, 1050, 1225, 1415, 1545, 1715, 1850, 2025, 2200, 2345.

Metromare dello Stretto by hydrofoil — 2013 service (subject to alteration)
Journey 20 minutes

From Villa San Giovanni: 0710①②③④⑤, 0740, 0815①②③④⑤, 0850①②③④⑤, 0915⑥⑦, 0945①②③④⑤, 1115①②③④⑤, 1140⑥⑦, 1220①②③④⑤, 1320①②③④⑤, 1420①②③④⑤, 1520⑥⑦, 1540①②③④⑤, 1640①②③④⑤, 1710①②③④⑤, 1820①②③④⑤, 2000.
From Messina: 0620, 0655①②③④⑤, 0745①②③④⑤, 0820①②③④⑤, 0845⑥⑦, 0905①②③④⑤, 1045①②③④⑤, 1110⑥⑦, 1150①②③④⑤, 1250①②③④⑤, 1340①②③④⑤, 1440⑥⑦, 1450①②③④⑤, 1550①②③④⑤, 1640①②③④⑤, 1735①②③④⑤, 1840⑥⑦, 1850①②③④⑤.

2699 OTHER SERVICES

Corsica Ferries by fast ferry — Journey 30 minutes — June 6 - September 15, 2014 (No winter service)

From Piombino and Portoferraio (Elba): up to 7 sailings daily.

Moby Lines — 2014 service (No service Dec. 25)

Piombino - Portoferraio (Elba): up to 15 sailings daily in high-summer, less frequent at other times; journey time 1 hour

Toremar — 2014 services

Services operate from Piombino to Cavo, Pianosa, Portoferraio and Rio Marina; from Livorno to Capraia and Gorgona; from Porto Santo Stefano to Isola del Giglio.

ADRIATIC / EASTERN MEDITERRANEAN / BLACK SEA

2715 ANCONA - PÁTRA via Igumenítsa

Anek Lines / Superfast Ferries — 2014 service

Ancona		Igumenítsa		Pátra	Pátra		Igumenítsa		Ancona
January 1 - June 27 and September 7 - December 31									
1330 **A**	→	0800 **B**	→	1430 **B**	1730 **C**	→	2359 **C**	→	1630 **A**
June 28 - September 6									
1330	→	0600	→	1130	1430	→	2000	→	1030
1630②④⑥	→	0900③⑤⑦	→	1430③⑤⑦	1730①③⑤	→	2300①③⑤	→	1330②④⑥

A – ②③④⑤⑥⑦ (not Jan. 1, 2). **B** – ③④⑤⑥⑦① (not Jan. 2, 3).
C – ①②③④⑤⑥ (not Jan. 1, 2).

Services on ②④ July 8 - Aug. 28 from Ancona; ①③ July 21 - Sept. 3 from Pátra sail via Kérkira.

🚌 connection Pátra - Pireás - Athína and v.v. operates most days in summer.

For international journeys only

Minoan Lines — 2014 service

Ancona		Igumenítsa		Pátra	Pátra		Igumenítsa		Ancona
January 1 - July 23 and September 11 - December 31									
1400①	→	0830②	→	1500②	1800①	→	2359①	→	1700②
1400②	→	0830③	→	1500③	1800②	→	2359②	→	1700③
1500③	→	0930④	→	1700④	1800④	→	2359④	→	1700⑤
1400⑤	→	0830⑥	→	1500⑥	1800⑤	→	2359⑤	→	1700⑥
1400⑥	→	0830⑦	→	1500⑦	1800⑥	→	2359⑥	→	1700⑦
1400⑦	→	0830①	→	1500①	1800⑦	→	2359⑦	→	1700①
July 24 - September 10 ♦									
1700①	→	0930②	→	1530②	1800①	→	2359①	→	1430②
1800②	→	1030③	→	1630③	1800②	→	2359②	→	1430③
1800③	→	1030④	→	1630④	1600④	→	2200④	→	1230⑤
1600⑤	→	0830⑥	→	1430⑥	1600⑤	→	2200⑤	→	1230⑥
1600⑥	→	0830⑦	→	1430⑦	1700⑥	→	2300⑥	→	1330⑦
1700⑦	→	0930①	→	1530①	1700⑦	→	2300⑦	→	1330①

♦ – A special service operates Aug. 6 - 20 – contact operator for details.

2725 ANCONA - SPLIT

Blue Line — 2014 service (No service Dec. 24, 25)

Ancona		Split	
1030	→	1900	⑦ Aug. 17 - Sept. 7.
2000	→	0700	①③⑤ Apr. 11 - July 25; ①②③④⑤⑦ July 27 - Aug. 16; ①②③④⑤⑥ Aug. 18 - Sept. 6; ①③⑤ Sept. 8 - Oct. 6 (also May 3 June 28, July 3, 5, Oct. 4; not May 2, June 27, July 2, 4, Oct. 3).
2100	→	0700	⑥ July 19 - Aug. 9.

Split		Ancona	
1030	→	1900	⑥ July 19 - Aug. 9.
2000	→	0700	②④⑦ Apr. 10 - July 22; ①②③④⑤⑦ July 24 - Aug. 15; ①②③④⑤⑥ Aug. 16 - Sept. 6; ②④⑦ Sept. 9 - Oct. 5 (also May 2 June 27, July 2, Oct. 3; not May 1, June 26, July 1, Oct. 2).
2100	→	0700	⑦ Aug. 17 - Sept. 7.

Jadrolinija — 2014 service

Ancona		Split		Split		Ancona	
January 2 - March 17 and November 2 - December 29							
2100	→	0700	①⑤	2100	→	0700	④⑦
March 18 - July 18 and September 1 - October 31							
2100	→	0700	①③⑤	2100	→	0700	②④⑦
July 19 - August 31							
1100	→	1830	⑦ Aug. 17 - 31.	1430	→	2230	⑥ July 19 - Aug. 9.
2100	→	0600	①③⑤	2100	→	0700	②④
2359	→	1130	⑥ July 19 - Aug. 9.	2100	→	0900	⑦
				2200	→	0940	⑥ Aug. 16 - 30.

SNAV by ship — 2014 service (No winter service

Ancona		Split	
2015	→	0700	Apr. 11, 14, 16, 18, 21, 23 - 25, 28 - 30, May 2, 3, 5 - 9, 12 - 17, 19 - 23, 26 - 30, June 1 - 4, 6, 9 - 13, 16 - 20, 23 - 25, 27 - 30, July 2 - 27, 29, 30 Aug. 1 - 31, Sept. 1 - 12, 15 - 19, 22 - 26, 29, 30, Oct. 1 - 4.
2115	→	0800	July 30, 31 only.
Split		**Ancona**	
1100	→	1900	July 30, 31 only.
2015	→	0700	Apr. 10, 13, 15, 17, 20, 22, 24, 27 - 30, May 1, 3, 4, 6 - 8, 10, 11, 13 - 1 18 - 23, 25, 27 - 29, 31, June 1 - 3, 5, 6, 8, 10 - 13, 15, 17 - 20, 22, 24, 2 27 - 29, July 1 - 28, 31, Aug. 1 - 31, Sept. 1 - 12, 14, 16 - 19, 21, 23 - 2 28, 30, Oct. 1 - 3, 5.

For international shipping maps – see pages 538 - 540

ANCONA - ZADAR 2732

Jadrolinija — **2014 service (No winter service)**

Ancona		Zadar	Zadar		Ancona
June 2 - July 3 and September 8 - 27▲					
2200②④⑥	→	0700③⑤⑦	2200①③⑤	→	0700②④⑥
July 4 - 24 and August 27 - September 5					
2200②④⑤⑥	→	0700③⑤⑥⑦	1200⑤⑥	→	1800⑤⑥
			2200①③	→	0700②④
July 25 - August 26					
1230⑦	→	1830⑦	0800⑥	→	1400⑥
1600⑥	→	2200⑥	1200②③④⑤	→	1800②③④⑤
2200⑤	→	0530⑥	2200⑦	→	0700①
2200①②③④	→	0600②③④⑤	2345⑥	→	0700⑦

▲ – June 13, Sept. 12: Zadar depart 1200, Ancona arrive 1930.

BARI - BAR 2738

Montenegro Lines — **2014 service**

Bari		Bar	
1200	→	2200	Aug. 15-19, 24-26, 29-31.
2300	→	0900	②⑤ Mar. 4 - June 6; ①③⑤ June 9 - July 18; ①③⑤⑥ July 21 - Aug. 13; ③⑤⑥ Aug. 20-27; ①③⑤ Sept. 1-29; ②⑤ Oct. 3 - Dec. 12 (also Apr. 26, Aug. 7; not Apr. 25).
Bar		**Bari**	
1200	→	2200	July 26, Aug. 2, 7-9.
2230	→	0830	④⑦ Mar. 2 - June 5; ②④⑦ June 8 - Aug. 12; ②④⑦ Sept. 2 - Oct. 5; ④⑦ Oct. 9 - Nov. 9 (also Apr. 21; not Apr. 20, Aug. 7).
2300	→	0900	①②④⑤⑥⑦ Aug. 14-31.

BARI - PÁTRA via Kérkira and Igumenítsa 2755

Superfast Ferries — **2014 service (No service Jan. 1, 2)**

Bari		Kérkira		Igumenítsa		Pátra
1330⑦	→	→	→	2300⑦	→	0700①
2000①–⑥	→	0500②–⑦§	→	0600②–⑦	→	1300②–⑦
Pátra		**Igumenítsa**		**Kérkira**		**Bari**
1800	→	0030	→	0200⊡	→	0930

§ – Kérkira sailings operate ④ June 5-26; ④⑤⑥ July 3 - Sept. 13; ④ Sept. 18-25 only.
⊡ – Kérkira sailings operate ③ June 4-25; ③⑥⑦ July 2 - Sept. 14; ③ Sept. 17-24 only.

Subject to alteration during ship maintenance periods

🚐 connection Pátra - Pireás - Athína and v.v.
Tickets available on-board ship and from 30 Amalías av., Síndagma, Athína.

BLACK SEA services 2760

Bumerang Shipping Company Tourism Travel & Trade S.A.

İSTANBUL - YALTA - NOVOROSSIYSK — **Irregular sailings, journey 30 hours**
İSTANBUL - YEVPATORIYA — **Journey 24 hours**

BRINDISI - IGUMENÍTSA 2765

Grimaldi Lines — **2014 service**

Brindisi		Igumenítsa	Igumenítsa		Brindisi
1300⑥⑦	→	2230⑥⑦	0100	→	0830
1630⑤	→	0100⑥	0130⑥	→	0930⑥
2000①②③④⑥	→	0430②③④⑤⑦			

BRINDISI - PÁTRA 2775

Grimaldi Lines — **2014 service**

Brindisi		Pátra	Pátra		Brindisi
1300⑦	→	0800①	1700①②③④⑤⑦	→	0830②③④⑤⑥①
2000①②③④⑥	→	1300②③④⑤⑦			

DUBROVNIK - BARI 2795

Jadrolinija — **2014 service (No winter service)**

Dubrovnik		Bari	
1200	→	1930	⑦ June 1-30; ⑤⑥⑦ July 1-28; ③④⑤⑥⑦ July 29 - Aug. 19; ⑦ Sept. 2-30.
2200	→	0800	①③⑤ Apr. 11 - June 30; ① July 29 - Aug. 19; ①③④⑤⑥⑦ Aug. 20 - Sept. 1; ①③⑤ Sept. 2-30; ①③ Oct. 1-30.
Bari		**Dubrovnik**	
1200	→	1930	①④⑤⑥⑦ Aug. 20 - Sept. 1.
2200	→	0700	②④⑥ Apr. 11 - May 31; ②④⑥⑦ June 1-30; ②④⑤⑥⑦ July 1-28; ②③④⑤⑥⑦ July 29 - Aug. 19; ② Aug. 20 - Sept. 1; ②④⑥⑦ Sept. 2-30; ②④ Oct. 1-30.

GREEK ISLANDS 2800

Summary table of regular ⛴ services to the Greek Islands.

Each route is operated by various shipping companies to differing schedules.
Additional inter-island routes are operated at less regular intervals.

Pireás to Égina, Póros, Ídra, Spétses, Kíthira, Andikíthira.
Pireás to Sérifos, Sífnos, Mílos, Folégandros.
Pireás to Páros, Íos, Thíra (Santoríni), Iráklio.
Pireás to Náxos, Amorgós, Astipálea.
Pireás to Pátmos, Léros, Kálimnos, Kos, Nísiros, Tílos, Sími, Ródos, Kárpathos, Kásos.
Pireás to Ikaría, Sámos, Híos, Lésvos.
Pireás and **Rafína** to Síros, Dílos, Míkonos, Tínos, Ándros.
Pátra to Zákinthos (Zante), Kefallinía, Itháki, Kérkira (Corfu), Igumenítsa.
Vólos, **Ágios Konstantínos** and **Kimi** to Skíathos, Skópelos, Alónissos, Skíros.
Kavála to Thásos, Samothráki, Límnos.

PIREÁS - IRÁKLIO 2830

Minoan Lines — **Service to November 30, 2014**

Pireás		Iráklio		Iráklio		Pireás	
2100	→	0600	Not July 1 - Aug. 31.	2130	→	0600	Not July 1 - Aug. 31.
2200	→	0630	July 1 - Aug. 31.	2200	→	0630	July 1 - Aug. 31.

Additional sailings in summer on some days at 1100 from Pireás and Iráklio

Anek Lines / Superfast Ferries — **2014 service (No service Dec. 24, 25, 31, Apr. 19, 20)**

Pireás		Iráklio	Iráklio		Pireás
2100	→	0600	2130	→	0600

Variations:
Apr. 18 depart Pireás and Iráklio 1500 (a. 2200)

LAVRIO - LEMESÓS (LIMASSOL) - HEFA 2845

Salamis Lines — **2014 service**

Weekly service – contact operator for details.

RIJEKA - SPLIT - DUBROVNIK 2855

Jadrolinija — **May 30 - September 28, 2014**

Rijeka		Split		Stari Grad		Korčula		Dubrovnik
1900①	→	0700/0730②	→	0915/0945②	→	1330/1400②	→	1730②
1900⑤	→	0700/0730⑥	→	0915/0945⑥	→	1330/1400⑥	→	1730⑥
Dubrovnik		**Korčula**		**Stari Grad**		**Split**		**Rijeka**
0900④	→	1230/1300④	→	1640/1700④	→	1840/1930④	→	0700⑤
0900⑦	→	1230/1300⑦	→	1640/1700⑦	→	1840/1930⑦	→	0700①

TRIESTE and RAVENNA - PÁTRA via Igumenítsa 2870

Minoan Lines — **2014 service**

Trieste		Ravenna		Ancona		Igumenítsa		Pátra
January 1 - July 23 and September 11 - December 31								
0530①⑥	→	→	→	1400①⑥	→	0830②⑦	→	1500②⑦
0630③	→	→	→	1500③	→	0930④	→	1700④
Pátra		**Igumenítsa**		**Ancona**		**Ravenna**		**Trieste**
1800①④⑥	→	2359①④⑥	→	1700②⑤⑦	→	→	→	0130③⑥①
July 24 - September 10								
Trieste		**Ravenna**		**Ancona**		**Igumenítsa**		**Pátra**
2300①③⑤	→	0730②④⑥	→	→	→	1030③⑤⑦	→	1900③⑤⑦
Pátra		**Igumenítsa**		**Ancona**		**Ravenna**		**Trieste**
2359①③⑥	→	0830②④⑦	→	→	→	1000③⑤①	→	1800③⑤①

For full service Ancona - Igumenítsa - Pátra and v.v. see Table **2715**.

VENEZIA - PÁTRA via Igumenítsa and Kérkira (Corfu) 2875

Anek Lines — **2014 service**

Venezia	Igumenítsa	Kérkira	Pátra	Pátra	Kérkira	Igumenítsa	Venezia
January 5 - April 28 and September 25 - December 31 (from Pátra, 2 days later from Venezia)							
1400② →	1700③ →	→	→ 2350③	2359① →	→	→ 0700② →	0800③
1400③ →	1700④ →	→	→ 2350④	2359④ →	→	→ 0700⑤ →	0800⑥
1200⑥ →	1500⑦ →	→	→ 2200⑦	2359⑤ →	→	→ 0700⑥ →	0800⑦
1200⑦ →	1500① →	→	→ 2200①	2359⑦ →	→	→ 0700① →	0800②
May 1 - September 22 (from Pátra, 2 days later from Venezia)							
1800② →	2200③ →	→	→ 0500④	2359① →	→	→ 0700② →	0800③
1800③ →	2200④ →	→	→ 0500⑤	2359④ →	→	→ 0700⑤ →	0800⑥
1200⑥ →	1500⑦ →	→	→ 2200⑦	2359⑤ →	→	→ 0700⑥ →	0800⑦
1200⑦ →	1500① →	→	→ 2200①	2359⑦ →	→	→ 0700① →	0800②

For international journeys only

BARI - DURRËS 2880

Ventouris Ferries — Journey 10 hours — **July 1 - September 30, 2014 (No winter service)**

Bari		Durres	
1200	→	2100	July 12, 19, 26, 27, Aug. 1-3, 8-10, 16, 17, 22-31, Sept. 5, 6.
2300	→	0800	
Durres		**Bari**	
1200	→	2100	July 12, 19, 26, 27, 31, Aug. 1-10, 16, 17, 22-25, 28-31, Sept. 5, 6.
2300	→	0800	

OTHER SERVICES 2899

Jadrolinija — **2014 services**
Many local services operate to the Islands along the Croatian coast.

LNP — **2014 services**
All-year services operate Split - Rogač, Šibenik - Kaprije - Žirje and Lopar - Valbiska.

Salamis Cruise Lines — **2014 services**
Cruises around Greece and the Greek Islands (2-8-days, May 30 - Oct. 20).

Venezia Lines — **2014 services**
Services operate Apr. 19 - Oct. 4 from Venezia to Mali Lošinj, Poreč, Pula and Rovinj.

280 (Summer) PARIS - LE MANS - RENNES and NANTES

TGV Atlantique

Service July 6 - Aug. 24. *For service to July 5/from Aug. 25 see page 184*

TGV trains convey 🍸. Many trains continue to destinations in Tables **281**, **284**, **285**, **288** and **293**. For other trains Massy - Nantes via St Pierre des Corps see Table **335**.

km	July 6 - Aug. 24	⚒ t	⑥	Ⓐ	Ⓐ D	TGV 8905 ①–⑥ k	TGV 8051 ①–⑥ k	Ⓐ	TGV 8807 ①–⑥ k	TGV 8081 ①–⑤	TGV 8053*	TGV 8911	TGV 8693 ①–④ m	TGV 8813		TGV 8715 j	TGV 5486 ☆		TGV 5471 ☆j	⑦ j	TGV 8915	TGV 8617 j	TGV 5214	TGV 5211 j
	Lille Europe **11** d.	...	...	...	...	...	...	...	...	...	...	...	...	...	...	...	...	...	...	...	...	...	0836	0836
	Charles de Gaulle ✈ d.	...	...	...	...	...	...	...	...	...	...	...	...	...	...	...	...	...	...	...	...	...	0949	0949
	Marne la Vallée § d.	...	...	...	...	...	...	...	...	...	...	...	...	...	...	...	0932	...	0932	...	...	...	1002	1002
0	**Paris** Montparnasse d.	...	...	...	...	0650	0701	...	0720	0734	0805	0849	0906	0950	...	1005	|	...	|	...	1051	1106	|	|
14	Massy TGV d.	...	...	...	...	0702	|	...	0732	0746	|	|	|	|	...	|	1006	...	1008	...	|	|	1037	1037
202	**Le Mans** d.	0612	0634	0650	0703	|	0802	0824	0831	|	0906	|	|	1051	...	|	1101	1105	1108	1138	|	1206	1130	1134
292	Laval d.	|	0729	|	0753	|	0847	|	|	|	0952	|	|	|	...	|	|	|	1152	1227	|	1249	|	|
327	Vitré d.	|	0753	|	0822	|	|	|	|	|	|	|	|	|	...	|	|	|	|	1250	|	1310	|	|
365	**Rennes** a.	|	0815	|	0848	|	0923	|	|	0954	1028	|	1114	|	...	1215	|	|	1228	1323	|	1330	|	1250
251	Sablé d.	0640	...	0713	...	|	...	0847	0855	...	...	|	...	|	...	...	|	1127	...	...	|	...	|	...
299	Angers St Laud **289** d.	0703	...	0738	...	|	...	0911	0919	...	...	1030	...	1133	...	...	1143	1151	...	...	|	...	1213	...
387	**Nantes 289** a.	0751	...	0820	...	0907	...	0950	0956	...	...	1106	...	1210	...	...	1218	1231	...	...	1259	...	1248	...

July 6 - Aug. 24	TGV 8817	TGV 8717 j	TGV 8975	TGV 5350 ♠	TGV 5365 ⑥ ♠t	TGV 8621 ⑤ f	TGV 8055 ⑥ t	TGV 5226 j	TGV 5225		TGV 8933*	TGV 8059* Ⓐ y	TGV 8629 Ⓒ j	TGV 8823 ⑤ f	⑤ n	⑤ f	TGV 8839* Ⓒ	TGV 8729*	TGV 5232	TGV 5209 Lm	TGV 8829 ⑤–⑦	TGV 8063* Ⓑ j	⚒ t	TGV 8831 ⑤ f
Lille Europe **11** d.	...	...	...	...	...	...	...	1106z	1106z	...	...	...	...	...	...	...	...	...	1352	1352	...	...	...	...
Charles de Gaulle ✈ d.	...	...	...	...	...	...	...	1249	1249	...	...	...	...	...	...	...	...	...	1449	1449	...	...	...	...
Marne la Vallée § d.	...	...	...	...	...	...	...	1302	1302	...	...	...	...	...	...	...	...	...	1502	1502	...	...	...	...
Paris Montparnasse d.	1149	1205	1220	...	...	1303	1305	|	|	...	1350	1358	1400	1419	...	...	1450	1505	|	|	1551	1559	...	1620
Massy TGV d.	|	|	|	1236	1236	|	|	1335	1335	...	|	|	|	|	...	...	|	|	1535	1535	|	|	...	|
Le Mans d.	|	1306	|	1331	1331	1406	1406	1431	1435	...	1450	|	|	1517	1535	1536	1550	|	1630	1630	|	|	1702	|
Laval d.	|	|	|	|	|	|	|	|	|	...	|	1547	1545	...	|	1626	|	|	|	|	|	|	|	|
Vitré d.	|	|	|	|	|	|	|	|	|	...	|	|	|	...	|	1644	|	|	|	|	|	|	|	|
Rennes a.	|	1422	|	1450	|	1522	1522	1546	|	...	|	1623	1622	...	|	1703	|	1715	1749j	|	|	1814	|	|
Sablé d.	|	...	1341	...	|	...	...	...	|	...	|	...	...	...	1557	...	|	...	...	|	|	...	1726	|
Angers St Laud **289** d.	1328	...	1405	...	1418	...	...	...	1518	...	1533	...	...	...	1620	...	1632	...	...	1712	1729	...	1750	1800
Nantes 289 a.	1411	...	1440	...	1454	...	...	...	1554	...	1609	...	...	...	1659	...	1714	...	...	1752	1811	...	1829	1837

July 6 - Aug. 24	TGV 8737* ①–⑤ q	Ⓐ	⑦ w	TGV 8833 Ⓐ	TGV 8747 ⑤		TGV 8743 Ⓒ j	TGV 8937* Ⓑ n	①–④ m	⑤ f	TGV 8649 ⑤ f	TGV 8939* ①–⑤ n	TGV 8841	TGV 5488 ④⑤ ☆n		TGV 8657	TGV 8943 ⑤⑥ d	TGV 8067 ⑦ p	TGV 8093* ①–⑤ fk	TGV 5372 ♠	TGV 5371 ♠	TGV 8845 ⑤ f	TGV 8979 A	TGV 8977 ⑤ f
Lille Europe **11** d.	...	...	...	...	...	...	...	...	...	...	...	...	...	...	...	...	...	...	...	...	...	...	...	...
Charles de Gaulle ✈ d.	...	...	...	...	...	...	...	...	...	...	...	...	...	...	...	...	...	...	...	...	...	...	...	...
Marne la Vallée § d.	...	...	...	...	...	...	...	...	...	...	...	...	...	1732	...	...	...	...	...	...	...	...	...	...
Paris Montparnasse d.	1638	...	...	1653	1658	...	1706	1720	...	...	1728	1746	1751	|	...	1808	1821	1838	1838	...	...	1846	1850	1850
Massy TGV d.	|	...	...	|	|	...	|	|	...	...	|	|	|	1805	...	|	|	|	|	1838	1838	|	|	|
Le Mans d.	1738	1742	1742	1750	|	...	1806	|	1821	1821	1838	|	1851	1857	...	|	|	|	|	1932	1938	|	1951	1951
Laval d.	1823	1831	|	|	|	...	1852	|	|	|	1924	|	|	|	...	|	|	2017	2017	|	2025	|	|	|
Vitré d.	|	1848	|	|	|	...	|	|	|	|	|	|	|	|	...	|	|	2038	2038	|	|	|	|	|
Rennes a.	1900	1910	|	|	1916	...	1930	|	|	|	1959	|	|	|	...	2017	|	2058	2058	|	2101	|	|	|
Sablé d.	...	...	1805	|	...	...	...	|	1844	1846	...	|	|	|	...	...	|	...	...	|	...	|	2013	2014
Angers St Laud **289** d.	...	...	1830	1833	...	...	...	|	1909	1911	...	|	1933	1944	...	...	|	...	...	2013	...	|	2038	2038
Nantes 289 a.	...	...	1910	1909	...	...	...	1928	1949	1952	...	2007	2010	2019	...	...	2032	...	...	2048	...	2101	2116c	2118

July 6 - Aug. 24	TGV 8665* j	Ⓑ n	TGV 5230	TGV 8761	TGV 8849 ⑦ w	TGV 8851 ①–④ e	TGV 8949 ⑤ f		TGV 5488 Ⓒ ☆	TGV 8071 ⑤–⑦ s	TGV 8097 ⑤ f	TGV 5387 ♣	TGV 8853*	TGV 8077 ⑥ t	TGV 8679 ⑤ f	TGV 8077 ①–④ m	TGV 8075 ⑦ p		TGV 5234 ⑤ f	TGV 8857 ⑦ w	TGV 8957 ⑤ f	TGV 8079 ⑦ p	TGV 8779 ⑤ n	
Lille Europe **11** d.	...	...	1752	...	...	...	...	...	...	...	...	...	...	...	...	...	...	...	1952	...	...	...	...	...
Charles de Gaulle ✈ d.	...	...	1848	...	...	...	...	...	...	...	...	...	...	...	...	...	...	...	2049	...	...	...	...	...
Marne la Vallée § d.	...	...	1901	...	...	...	...	...	1932	...	...	...	...	...	...	...	...	...	2103	...	...	...	...	...
Paris Montparnasse d.	1905	...	|	1938	1950	1950	1951	...	|	2000	2021	...	2050	2104	2104	2105	2105	...	|	2150	2150	2205	2157	...
Massy TGV d.	|	...	1936	|	|	|	|	...	2008	|	|	2046	|	|	|	|	|	...	2136	|	|	|	|	...
Le Mans d.	2006	2016	2031	|	|	2051	|	...	2100	2105	2120	2139	|	|	|	|	2205	...	2231	2250	2250	|	2306	...
Laval d.	|	|	|	|	|	|	|	...	|	2151	|	|	|	|	|	2244	2250	...	|	|	|	2344	2352	...
Vitré d.	|	|	|	|	|	|	|	...	|	|	|	|	|	|	2302	|	2312	...	|	|	|	|	|	...
Rennes a.	2122	|	|	2147	|	|	|	...	|	2227	2236	2303	|	2315	2322	2322	2332	...	|	|	|	0022	0027	...
Sablé d.	...	2038	|	...	|	|	|	...	|	...	...	...	|	...	...	...	...	...	|	...	...	...	...	...
Angers St Laud **289** d.	...	2101	2113	...	2129	2133	2131	...	2143	...	...	...	2228	...	...	...	...	...	2314	2333	2333	...	...	...
Nantes 289 a.	...	2144	2149	...	2210	2210	2207	...	2219	...	...	...	2309	...	...	...	...	...	2349	0009	0009	...	...	...

July 6 - Aug. 24	TGV 8800 ① g	TGV 8802 Ⓐ	TGV 8052 ①–⑤	TGV 8804 Ⓐ C	TGV 5252 ①–⑥ k	TGV 5254 ①–⑥ k	TGV 8906 ① g	TGV 8706* ①–⑥ k	TGV 8812 ① g	TGV 8912 ②–⑤ v	TGV 8810 ⑥ t	Ⓐ	TGV 8914 ① g	TGV 8814 B	TGV 8080* ①–⑥ t	TGV 5312 E ♠j	TGV 5314 ♠j	Ⓐ	TGV 8816	TGV 5478 N ☆	Ⓐ	TGV 8818 Ⓐ	TGV 8058 Ⓐ	TGV 8014 †
Nantes 289 d.	0500	0525	...	0600	0605	...	0630	...	...	0630	0630	0634	0700	0700	...	0705	...	...	0730	0735	0739	0800	...	...
Angers St Laud **289** d.	0542	0605	...	0640	0643	...	|	...	0713	0713	0708	0718	|	|	...	0743	...	...	0809	0814	0823	0839	...	...
Sablé d.	|	0630	...	|	|	...	|	...	|	|	|	0740	|	|	...	|	...	...	|	|	0848	|	...	...
Rennes d.	|	|	0525	|	|	0607	|	0625	|	|	|	|	|	|	0703	|	0707	0710	|	|	|	|	0803	080
Vitré d.	|	|	0548	|	|	|	|	|	|	|	|	|	|	|	|	|	|	0730	|	|	|	|	|	|
Laval d.	|	|	0608	|	|	|	|	0705	|	|	|	|	|	|	|	|	|	0748	|	|	|	|	|	084
Le Mans d.	0625	0653	0658	|	0733	0733	|	|	0801	0801	0750	0804	|	|	0821	0833	0833	0837	|	0857	0913	|	0923	092
Massy TGV a.	|	|	|	|	0824	0824	|	|	|	|	|	...	|	|	|	0923	0923	...	|	0947	...	|	|	|
Paris Montparnasse a.	0724	0751	0758	0818	|	|	0845	0853	0901	0901	0849	...	0910	0911	0925	...	...	...	0945	|	...	1015	1020	102
Marne la Vallée § a.	...	...	...	...	0857	0857	...	...	...	...	...	...	...	...	...	...	...	...	...	1027	...	...	...	...
Charles de Gaulle ✈ a.	...	...	...	...	0911	0911	...	...	...	...	...	...	...	...	...	...	...	...	...	...	...	...	...	...
Lille Europe **11** a.	...	...	...	...	1017	1017	...	...	...	...	...	...	...	...	...	...	...	...	...	...	...	...	...	...

July 6 - Aug. 24	TGV 8062* ⑥⑦ t	TGV 8618 Ⓐ	TGV 8822 Ⓒ	TGV 5318 ♣j	TGV 5326 ♣	TGV 8064 j	TGV 8824		TGV 5270	TGV 5272 j	TGV 8620 Ⓐ n	TGV 8926 Ⓐ	TGV 8622 Ⓒ j	TGV 5256 ⑦	⑦ w	TGV 8972 Ⓑ n	TGV 8974 ⑥ t	⚒ t		TGV 5324 L ♣	TGV 8084 ①–⑤ n	TGV 8932	TGV 8084 ⑥⑦ j	TGV 873 j
Nantes 289 d.	...	...	0900	...	0908	...	1000	...	1005	...	...	1105	...	...	1141	1200	1200	1204	...	...	...	1300	...	...
Angers St Laud **289** d.	...	...	0939	...	0946	...	1038	...	1043	...	...	1144	...	...	1223	1241	1239	1246	...	...	...	1339	...	...
Sablé d.	...	...	|	...	|	...	|	...	|	...	...	|	...	...	1247	|	|	1308	...	...	...	|	...	...
Rennes d.	0903	0903	|	0908	|	0933	|	...	|	1004	1033	|	1103	1114p	|	|	|	|	...	1210	1233	|	1303	140
Vitré d.	|	|	|	|	|	|	|	...	|	|	|	|	|	|	|	|	|	|	...	|	|	|	|	|
Laval d.	|	|	|	|	|	|	|	...	|	1042	1111	|	1140	|	|	|	|	|	...	|	1311	|	1341	|
Le Mans d.	|	1022	1022	1033	1033	|	|	...	1133	1133	1157	|	1227	1232	1310	|	1323	1333	...	1333	1357	1422	|	|
Massy TGV a.	|	|	|	1125	1125	|	|	...	1224	1224	|	|	|	1326	...	|	|	...	...	1423	|	|	|	|
Paris Montparnasse a.	1117	1121	1121	...	...	1144	1214	...	|	|	1256	1323	1326	|	...	1421	1421	...	...	...	1453r	1519	1524	161
Marne la Vallée § a.	...	...	...	...	...	...	...	...	1257	1257	...	...	...	1356	...	...	...	...	...	...	...	...	...	...
Charles de Gaulle ✈ a.	...	...	...	...	...	...	...	...	1311	1311	...	...	...	1411	...	...	...	...	...	...	...	...	...	...
Lille Europe **11** a.	...	...	...	...	...	...	...	...	1407	1407	...	...	...	1507	...	...	...	...	...	...	...	...	...	...

A – Daily **except** ⑤ (also Aug. 15).
B – July 8-11, Aug. 19-22.
C – July 11, Aug. 18-22.
D – July 7-18, Aug. 18-22.
E – Not Aug. 18-23.

G – Also July 14, Aug. 14; not July 13, Aug. 15.
L – ①②③④⑦ only.
N – ①⑤⑥⑦ (also Aug. 14).
c – Not July 6-20.
d – Also Aug. 14.

e – Not July 14, Aug. 14.
f – Also Aug. 14; not Aug. 15.
g – Also July 15; not July 14.
j – Not July 13.
k – Not July 14.

m – Not Aug. 14.
n – Not Aug. 15.
p – Also July 14; not July 13.
q – Also Aug. 15; not July 14, Aug. 14.

NOTES CONTINUED ON NEXT PAGE →

NANTES and RENNES - LE MANS - PARIS 280 (Summer)

Service July 6 - Aug. 24. *For service to July 5/from Aug. 25 see page 185*

July 6 - Aug. 24	*TGV* 8834	*TGV* 5278	*TGV* 5280	*TGV* 8836	*TGV* 5480	*TGV* 5460	*TGV* 8940	*TGV* 8640*			*TGV* 8646	*TGV* 5346		*TGV* 8752	*TGV* 8944		*TGV* 8978	*TGV* 8088	*TGV* 8088	*TGV* 8658	*TGV* 5288	*TGV* 5290	*TGV* 8846	*TGV* 8848
				⑤					Ⓑ	⑥			Ⓐ			⑦		Ⓐ	Ⓒ					⑦
				f	☆	☆j		j	n	t	j	♠j		j		w			j			j		w
Nantes 289 d.	1400	1404	...	...	1433	...	1500	...	1519	1539	...	...	...	...	1700	1705	1730	...	...	...	1755	...	1800	1830
Angers St Laud **289** d.	1439	1444	...	...	1511	...	|	...	1601	1620	...	...	...	...	1739	1746	|	...	...	...	1834	...	1840	|
Sablé d.	|	|	...	...	|	...	|	...	1625	1645	...	...	...	...	|	1809	|	...	...	...	|	...	1904	|
Rennes d.	|	|	1408j	...	|	1433	|	1503	|	|	1603	1607	1637	1703	|	|	|	1733	1733	1803	|	1807	|	|
Vitré d.	|	|	|	...	|	|	|	|	|	|	|	|	1659	|	|	|	|	|	|	|	|	|	|	|
Laval d.	|	|	|	...	|	1511	|	|	|	|	1641	1648	1717	|	|	|	|	1811	1812	|	|	|	|	|
Le Mans d.	1522	1525	1533	1541	1602	1602	|	1622	1648	1714	1726	1732	1806	|	1823	1832	|	1857	|	|	1932	1932	|	|
Massy TGV a.	|	1623	1623	|	1653	1653	|	|	...	...	|	1822	...	|	|	...	|	|	|	|	2022	2022	|	|
Paris Montparnasse a.	1620	|	|	1639	|	|	1712	1721	...	...	1825	...	...	1913	1923	...	1939	1955	1953	2014	|	|	2021	2039
Marne la Vallée § a.	...	1658	1658	...	1728	1728	...	...	...	...	...	...	...	...	...	...	...	...	...	...	2056	2056	...	...
Charles de Gaulle ✈ a.	...	1711	1711	...	...	...	...	...	...	...	...	...	...	...	...	...	...	...	...	...	2111	2111	...	...
Lille Europe **11** a.	...	1807	1807	...	...	...	...	...	...	...	...	...	...	...	...	...	...	...	...	...	2251z	2251z	...	...

July 6 - Aug. 24	*TGV* 8762	*TGV* 8762		*TGV* 8672*	*TGV* 8850*	*TGV* 5342	*TGV* 5344		*TGV* 8982	*TGV* 8676	*TGV* 8952*	*TGV* 8780	*TGV* 8090	*TGV* 8092	*TGV* 8688	*TGV* 8682*	*TGV* 8856		*TGV* 8076	*TGV* 8958	*TGV* 8686	*TGV* 8960	*TGV* 8796	
	①–⑤	Ⓒ	⑤			⑤⑦	⑤⑦	Ⓐ		⑦		①⑥	②–⑤	⑦	⑦		⑤⑦	Ⓒ	⑤⑦	⑦	⑦	⑦	⑦	
	n	j	n			♣G	♣G			p		x	v	p	p		fw		fp	w	p	w	p	
Nantes 289 d.	...	...	1839	...	1900	1905	...	1909	1930	...	2000	...	...	...	...	...	2100	2108	...	2200	...	2225	...	...
Angers St Laud **289** d.	...	...	1927	...	1940	1944	...	1954	|	...	2040	...	...	...	...	...	2139	2156	...	|	...	2304	...	...
Sablé d.	...	...	1950	...	|	|	...	2017	|	...	|	...	...	...	...	...	|	2220	...	|	...	|	...	...
Rennes d.	1833	1833	|	1902	|	|	1907	|	|	1933	|	2003	2003	2003	2033	2103	|	|	2133	|	2203	|	2233	...
Vitré d.	1855	1854	|	|	|	|	|	|	|	|	|	|	|	|	2055	|	|	|	|	|	|	|	|	...
Laval d.	|	|	|	|	|	|	|	|	|	|	|	2040	2040	2041	|	|	|	|	2211	|	|	|	2313	...
Le Mans d.	|	1957	2012	|	2022	2033	2033	2039	|	2052	|	|	|	|	|	|	2222	2243	2257	|	|	|	|	...
Massy TGV a.	|	|	...	|	|	2122	2122	...	|	|	|	|	|	|	|	|	|	|	|	0001	|	|	|	...
Paris Montparnasse a.	2054	2055	...	2112	2121	...	...	...	2142	2152	2218	2222	2226	2223	2254	2323	2321	...	2355	0009	0013	0041	0053	...
Marne la Vallée § a.	...	...	...	...	...	...	...	...	...	...	...	...	...	...	...	...	...	...	...	...	...	...	...	...
Charles de Gaulle ✈ a.	...	...	...	...	...	...	...	...	...	...	...	...	...	...	...	...	...	...	...	...	...	...	...	...
Lille Europe **11** a.	...	...	...	...	...	...	...	...	...	...	...	...	...	...	...	...	...	...	...	...	...	...	...	...

NOTES - CONTINUED FROM PREVIOUS PAGE

- **r** – Arrive 1506 on ⑤ (Le Mans d. 1406).
- **s** – Also July 14, Aug. 14, 15; not July 6, 12, 13.
- **t** – Also Aug. 15.
- **v** – Not July 15, Aug. 15.
- **w** – Also July 14.
- **x** – Also July 15, Aug. 15; not July 12, 14.
- **y** – Not days before holidays.
- **z** – Lille **Flandres**.

TGV – 🄡, supplement payable, 🍸.
§ – Marne la Vallée-Chessy (for Disneyland Paris).
♣ – From/to Lyon (Table **335**).
♠ – From/to Lyon and Marseille (Table **335**).
☆ – From/to Strasbourg (Table **391**).

*** – The train number shown is altered as below:**
8053 runs as 8091 on ⑥⑦.
8059 runs as 8625 on ①–④.
8062 runs as 8618 on ⑥.
8063 runs as 8633 on ⑤⑦.
8080 runs as 8056 on ⑥.
8093 runs as 8095 on ⑤.
8640 runs as 8744 on ⑥⑦.
8665 runs as 8663 on ⑤.
8672 runs as 8670 on ⑤–⑦.
8682 runs as 8794 on ⑦.
8706 runs as 8702 on ①.
8729 runs as 8087 on ⑤.
8737 runs as 8739 on ⑤.
8839 runs as 8927 on ⑥.
8850 runs as 8950 on ⑤⑦.
8853 runs as 8953 on ⑤.
8933 runs as 8821 on ⑤⑥.
8937 runs as 8935 on ⑤.
8939 runs as 8839 on ⑤.
8952 runs as 8852 on ⑤.

RENNES - ST MALO 281 (Summer)

Service July 6 - Aug. 24. *For service to July 5/from Aug. 25 see page 185*

km	*TGV trains,* 🄡	*TGV* 8081	*TGV* 8091	*TGV* 8085	*TGV* 5227	*TGV* 8089	*TGV* 8087	*TGV* 8093	*TGV* 8095	*TGV* 8099	*TGV* 8097
		①–⑤	†		Ⓑ		⑤	①–④	⑤	⑦	⑤
		n	q		w	A	f	m	f	y	f
	Paris M'parnasse **280** d.	0734	0805	...	...	...	1508	1838	1838	...	2021
	Lille Flandres **11** d.	|	|	...	1106	...	|	|	|	...	|
0	**Rennes 272** d.	0959	1034	1222	1549	1723	1724	2101	2100	2132	2243
58	Dol **272** d.	1032	1106	1256	|	|	|	|	2132	|	2314
81	**St Malo** a.	1046	1121	1310	1635	1806	1807	2143	2147	2212	2330

TGV trains, 🄡	*TGV* 8080	*TGV* 8084	*TGV* 8084	*TGV* 8088	*TGV* 5290	*TGV* 8094	*TGV* 8090	*TGV* 8092	*TGV* 8098
	①–⑤	①–⑤	⑥⑦		Ⓑ	⑥	①–⑤	⑦	⑦
	n	n	q	q	Lw	t	n	v	v
St Malo d.	0604	1140	1210	1640	1710	1908	1913	1910	2045
Dol **272** d.	0620	|	|	1656	|	1924	|	1926	|
Rennes 272 a.	0653	1228	1258	1728	1802	1955	1955	1958	2128
Lille Flandres **11** a.	|	|	|	|	...	...	|	|	|
Paris M'parnasse **280** a.	0917	1506	1524	1955	...	...	2226r	2223	2355

July 6 - Aug. 24	Ⓐ	Ⓐ	⑥	⑦	Ⓐ	⑥	Ⓐ	⑥	†	†	†	⚒	⚒	⑤	⑥	Ⓐ	Ⓐ	Ⓐ	⑥	Ⓐ		Ⓐ	⑥	†	⚒	⑤
						⊖t								f												f
Rennes 272 d.	0630	0730	0730	0930	0940	0940	1040	1100	1100	1130	1343	1343	1440	1535	1545	1636	1720	1730	1730	1800	1830	1930	1940	1945	2208	2248
Dol **272** d.	0711	0808	0814	1008	1018	1016	1114	1133	1149	1204	1420	1423	1516	1609	1620	1714	1737	1808	1810	1844	1910	2006	2028	2023	2246	2324
St Malo a.	0730	0825	0833	1022	1032	1030	1128	1148	1208	1218	1433	1442	1530	1623	1635	1730	1819	1828	1828	1903	1928	2020	2042	2037	2300	2339

July 6 - Aug. 24	⑥	Ⓐ	⑥	Ⓐ	Ⓐ	Ⓐ		Ⓐ	⑥	†		†	⚒		Ⓑ	⑤	†	⑥	†	Ⓐ	⑥	†		⑤		
				P	Q	P								Z		f					⊖t			f	M	
St Malo d.	0550	0620	0630	0650	0650	0720	0750	0930	0950	0950	...	1250	1250	1450	1550	1650	1720	1720	1750	1820	1820	1830	1955	2030	2050	...
Dol **272** d.	0604	0638	0649	0706	0708	0738	0805	0944	1004	1005	...	1304	1309	1505	1604	1704	1734	1740	1810	1838	1835	1844	2009	2044	2104	...
Rennes 272 a.	0641	0719	0740	0744	0749	0819	0845	1019	1039	1043	...	1341	1349	1537	1636	1736	1808	1823	1903	1920	1908	1916	2043	2117	2137	...

- **A** – Daily except ⑤ (also Aug. 15; not Aug. 14).
- **L** – To Le Mans.
- **M** – ①②③④⑥ (also Aug. 15; not July 14, Aug. 14).
- **P** – To July 18/from Aug. 18.
- **Q** – July 21 - Aug. 14.
- **Z** – ①②③④⑥ only.
- **f** – Also Aug. 14; not Aug. 15.
- **m** – Not Aug. 14.
- **n** – Not Aug. 15.
- **q** – Not July 13.
- **r** – Not ① (also July 15).
- **t** – Also Aug. 15.
- **v** – Also July 14; not July 13.
- **w** – Not July 13, Aug. 15.
- **y** – Also July 14.
- ⊖ – To/from Nantes (Table **287**).

DOL - DINAN 282 (Summer)

2nd class

Service July 6 - Aug. 24. *For service to July 5/from Aug. 25 see page 185*

July 6 - Aug. 24	Ⓐ	⑥	Ⓐ	Ⓒ	⚒	†	⑥		†	Ⓐ	⑥	†	Ⓐ	①–④	†	⑤		⑤⑥	
			⊙	⊙										m		f		f	
Dol d.	0702	0818	1037	1115	1305	1425	1521	...	1702	1730	1814	1815	1849	2016	2030	2136	...	2251	...
Dinan a.	0725	0841	1100	1138	1328	1448	1552	...	1732	1759	1842	1838	1919	2039	2053	2159	...	2314	...

July 6 - Aug. 24	Ⓐ	⚒		Ⓒ			①–④	⑥		⑤			†		Ⓐ	Ⓒ		Ⓐ	
							m			f									
Dinan d.	0630	0732	...	0927	1230	...	1435	1435	...	1535	...	1627	1740	...	1810	1855	...	1934	...
Dol a.	0657	0800	...	0957	1258	...	1458	1458	...	1558	...	1650	1803	...	1833	1918	...	1957	...

- **f** – Also Aug. 14; not Aug. 15.
- **m** – Not Aug. 14.
- ⊙ – To/from St Brieuc (Table **299**).

MORLAIX - ROSCOFF 283 (Summer)

2nd class

Service July 6 - Aug. 24. *For service to July 5/from Aug. 25 see page 185*

km	*July 6 - Aug. 24*	🚌 Ⓐ	🚌 ⚒	⑥	Ⓐ	†	🚌 †			🚌 ①–④	🚌 ⑤	🚌 ①–④	🚌 †	🚌 ⑥	🚌 ⑤	🚌 †	🚌 ①–④	🚌 ⑤
										n		n					n	
0	**Morlaix 284** d.	0730	0919	1021	1041	1100	1208	1255	1521	1634	1743	1833	1830	1833	2016	2024	2132	2150
28	**Roscoff** a.	0757	0954	1050	1110	1129	1238	1324	1550	1704	1813	1903	1905	1903	2048	2054	2207	2225

July 6 - Aug. 24	🚌 Ⓐ	🚌 Ⓒ	🚌 Ⓐ				🚌 Ⓐ	①–④		†	🚌 ①–④	⑥	⑤		🚌 Ⓐ	🚌 †	🚌 ⑤	
								n			n		f					
Roscoff d.	0633	0822	0827	1135	...	1339	1533	1640	...	1708	1726	1727	1737	...	1825	1928	2055	...
Morlaix 284 a.	0703	0857	0901	1203	...	1407	1608	1708	...	1736	1756	1755	1805	...	1900	1958	2130	...

- **f** – Also Aug. 14, 22; not Aug. 15.
- **n** – Not Aug. 14.

All services call at St Pol de Léon (*21 km/15 mins from Morlaix*).

🚌 call at Roscoff port on days of sailings. *Bus service is subject to alteration.*

284 (Summer) RENNES - ST BRIEUC - MORLAIX - BREST

Service July 6 - Aug. 24. *For service to July 5/from Aug. 25 see page 186*

km	TGV trains convey 🍸	Ⓐ	Ⓐ	Ⓐ	⑥	Ⓐ u	Ⓐ	⑥	55803 Ⓐ	Ⓐ	⑥	⚒	⚒	†	†	TGV 8609 ①–⑥ g		TGV 8613 ⑤–⑦ j	⚒	TGV 8693			TGV 8617 f	
	Paris Montparnasse **280** d.	...	...	...	...	...	...	...	...	...	...	...	...	...	...	0837	...	0906	...	0906	...	...	1105	...
0	**Rennes** d.	...	...	0612	...	...	0620	0640	0700	0720	0830	0945	...	0957	...	|	...	1117	...	1122	1238	...	1333	...
80	Lamballe **299** d.	...	...	0651	...	0703	0723	0745	|	0809	0906	1022	...	1034	...	|	...	|	...	1205	1315	...	|	...
101	**St Brieuc 299** d.	...	...	0704	0708	0723	0737	0800	0747	0823	0919	1036	...	1048	...	1136	...	|	...	1218	1328	...	1423	...
132	Guingamp d.	...	...	0721	0726	0746	...	...	|	...	0938	1054	1101	1105	...	1154	...	|	...	1235	1346	...	1442	1452
158	Plouaret-Trégor d.	...	...	0736	0741	0803	...	...	|	...	0953	|	1117	1121	1134	|	...	|	...	1250	1404	1410	|	1507
175	Lannion a.	...	...	|	|	0822	...	...	|	...	|	|	1136	|	1153	|	...	|	...	1309	|	1428	|	1526
189	Morlaix d.	0616	0637	0800	0803	...	...	...	0830	...	1012	1123	...	1140	...	1225	...	1244	1259	...	1424	...	1512	...
215	Landivisiau d.	0631	0700	0815	0820	...	...	...	|	...	1027	|	...	1155	...	|	...	|	1321	...	1439	...	|	...
230	Landerneau **286** d.	0641	0714	0828	0834	...	...	...	|	...	1037	|	...	1205	...	|	...	1308	1333	...	1449	...	|	...
248	**Brest 286** a.	0659	0733	0840	0846	...	...	...	0902	...	1049	1156	...	1217	...	1257	...	1319	1353	...	1501	...	1545	...

July 6 - Aug. 24		⑤ k	Ⓒ	TGV 8639 ①–④ m		TGV 8621 ⑤ k	Ⓐ	⑤ k	TGV 8625 ①–④ m	TGV 8629 Ⓒ f	TGV 8641 ⑥ t	⑤ k	Ⓒ	①–④ m	†	⚒	⚒	†	Ⓐ	Ⓐ E	Ⓐ F	TGV 8633 ⑤⑦ p	†	
Paris Montparnasse **280** d.	...	...	...	...	...	1303	...	...	1358	1400	...	...	...	...	...	...	...	...	...	...	...	1559	...	...
Rennes d.	1348	1435	1435	1429	...	1525	...	...	1625	1625	1630	1639	...	...	...	...	1700	1729	1744	...	...	1818	...	...
Lamballe **299** d.	1446	1515	1513	1508	...	1604	...	...	|	1704	1714	1717	...	...	...	...	1801	1808	1821	...	...	|	...	...
St Brieuc 299 d.	1501	1527	1526	1521	...	1619	...	...	1715	1718	1724	1729	...	...	...	1741	1815	1821	1834	...	...	1908	...	...
Guingamp d.	...	1545	1543	1539	...	1638	...	...	1733	1736	...	1746	...	...	1750	1806	...	1837	1851	...	...	1926	1932	...
Plouaret-Trégor d.	...	|	1557	|	...	|	...	1707	|	1751	...	1800	...	...	1807	1823	...	1851	1905	1924	1925	|	1949	...
Lannion a.	...	|	|	|	...	|	...	1726	|	|	...	|	...	...	1826	1842	...	|	|	1943	1944	|	2008	...
Morlaix d.	...	1614	1615	1610	...	1709	1725	...	1803	1810	...	1819	1817	1844	...	...	...	1908	1923	...	...	1956	...	...
Landivisiau d.	...	|	1631	|	...	|	1749	...	|	|	...	1833	1837	1903	...	...	...	1924	1940	...	...	|	...	...
Landerneau **286** d.	...	|	1641	|	...	|	1801	...	|	|	...	1843	1847	1913	...	...	...	1934	1950	...	...	2020	...	...
Brest 286 a.	...	1646	1656	1641	...	1740	1819	...	1836	1842	...	1855	1905	1928	...	...	...	1946	2002	...	...	2031	...	...

July 6 - Aug. 24	⑥	⑥	†	Ⓐ	TGV 8647 ⑤ k	TGV 8643 ①–④ m		⑤ k	Ⓐ	①–④ m	†	TGV 8649 ⑤ k	TGV 8691 ⑤ k		TGV 8657 f		TGV 8663 ⑤ k	TGV 8667 ⑤ k		TGV 8665 A		†	TGV 8679 ⑤ k	TGV 8689 ⑦ s
Paris Montparnasse **280** d.	...	...	...	...	1708	1705	...	...	...	...	...	1728	...	...	1808	...	1905	1905	...	1905	...	...	2104	2359
Rennes d.	1845	...	1838	1845	|	1925	...	1927	...	1935	1940	2002	2009	...	2020	...	2125	2130	...	2125	...	2240	2325	|
Lamballe **299** d.	1922	...	1937	1946	|	2004	...	2005	...	2027	2016	|	2050	...	|	...	|	2214	...	2206	...	2316	|	|
St Brieuc 299 d.	1935	...	1947	1957	2009	2018	...	2018	...	2038	2028	|	2103	...	2112	...	2215	2225	...	2221	...	2329	0015	0423
Guingamp d.	1951	...	...	...	|	2036	...	2036	...	...	2048	|	2120	...	2131	...	2233	...	...	2238	...	2348	0033	0440
Plouaret-Trégor d.	2006	2013	...	...	|	2052	...	2051	2057	...	|	|	2135	...	|	...	2248	...	...	2254	2303	0003	|	|
Lannion a.	|	2032	...	...	|	|	...	|	2116	...	|	|	2154	...	|	...	|	...	...	|	2322	|	|	|
Morlaix d.	2023	...	...	...	|	2112	...	2110	...	...	2118	2130	...	...	2200	...	2306	...	...	2312	...	0022	0101	0516
Landivisiau d.	2040	...	...	...	|	|	...	|	...	...	|	|	...	...	|	...	|	...	...	|	...	0037	|	|
Landerneau **286** d.	2050	...	...	...	|	|	...	2133	...	...	|	|	...	...	|	...	2331	...	...	2336	...	0047	|	0540
Brest 286 a.	2102	...	...	...	2121	2143	...	2145	...	...	2150	2201	...	...	2231	...	2342	...	...	2347	...	0059	0133	0552

July 6 - Aug. 24	②–⑤ x	① h	TGV 8612 ① h	⚒	① h	Ⓐ	Ⓐ	†	Ⓐ	TGV 8618 ⑥ t	TGV 8618 Ⓐ	Ⓐ	Ⓐ	Ⓒ	Ⓐ	TGV 8620 Ⓐ	Ⓒ	TGV 8622 Ⓒ f	†	⑥			TGV 8636 ⑤–⑦ q	TGV 8634 ①–④
Brest 286 d.	...	...	0445	...	...	0536	...	...	...	0640	0645	0749	...	...	...	0817	...	0843	1018	1040	1116	...	1140	1145
Landerneau **286** d.	...	...	|	...	...	0547	...	...	...	0653	0658	0806	...	...	...	|	...	|	1030	1051	1132	...	|	|
Landivisiau d.	...	...	|	...	...	0557	...	...	...	|	|	0819	...	...	...	|	...	|	1040	|	1144	...	|	|
Morlaix d.	...	...	0518	...	...	0614	...	...	...	0716	0721	0842	...	...	...	0849	...	0915	1055	1114	1208	...	1214	1218
Lannion d.	...	0506	|	...	0601	|	...	...	0654	|	|	...	...	...	0834	|	0907	|	|	|	...	1203	|	|
Plouaret-Trégor d.	...	0524	|	...	0620	0631	...	...	0711	|	|	...	...	...	0852	|	0925	0934	1112	|	...	1221	1232	1237
Guingamp d.	0541	0540	0548	...	...	0646	0702	0726	0731	0746	0751	...	...	...	0908	0920	...	0950	1127	1143	...	...	1248	1252
St Brieuc 299 d.	0558	...	0606	0633	...	0703	0725	0742	0751	0805	0810	...	0901	0936	...	0938	...	1008	1144	1200	...	...	1306	1310
Lamballe **299** d.	0610	...	0619	0644	...	0715	0740	0754	...	0819	|	...	0916	0951	...	|	...	|	1156	1212	...	...	1319	|
Rennes a.	0648	...	0657	0748	...	0753	0840	0850	...	0858	0858	...	1013	1048	...	1024	...	1054	1236	1252	...	...	1358	1358
Paris Montparnasse **280** a.	...	...	...	...	...	...	...	...	...	1117	1121	...	...	...	...	1256	...	1326	...	...	...	...	...	...

July 6 - Aug. 24	⑤ k	TGV 8640 Ⓐ		TGV 8646 f		A	†	⑤ k	⑤ k	TGV 8658 f	TGV 8662 ⑤–⑦ q	⑤ k	①–④ m	†	†	⑤ k	⑤ k	†	①–④ m		TGV 8672 ①–④ m	TGV 8670 ⑤–⑦ q	⑥	①–④ m
Brest 286 d.	1208	1247	...	1346	...	1432	...	...	1503	...	1545	...	...	...	1556	...	1606	...	...	...	1646	1653	...	...
Landerneau **286** d.	1220	|	...	|	...	1443	...	...	1514	...	|	...	...	...	1607	...	1617	...	...	...	|	|	...	...
Landivisiau d.	|	|	...	|	...	1453	...	...	1524	...	|	...	...	...	1617	...	1627	...	...	...	|	|	...	...
Morlaix d.	1243	1319	...	1420	...	1510	...	...	1540	...	1619	...	...	...	1632	...	1643	...	...	...	1719	|	...	...
Lannion d.	|	|	1346	|	...	|	...	1531	|	1559	|	...	...	1623	|	1628	|	1657	1706	...	|	|	...	1734
Plouaret-Trégor d.	|	|	1406	|	...	1528	...	1549	|	1620	|	...	...	1641	|	1646	1700	1715	1724	...	|	|	...	1753
Guingamp d.	1311	1349	1422	1449	...	1542	...	1603	1616	1635	|	...	...	1656	1708	...	1715	1730	1739	...	1749	1752	...	1808
St Brieuc 299 d.	1329	1408	...	1511	...	1558	1607	...	1633	1653	1707	1712	1713	...	1726	...	1732	...	1757	...	1807	1812	1825	1827
Lamballe **299** d.	1341	1421	...	|	...	1610	1621	...	1645	1707	|	1724	1726	...	1738	...	1744	...	1810	...	1821	|	1839	...
Rennes a.	1420	1458	...	1557	...	1650	1720	...	1723	1753	1757	1815	1829	...	1817	...	1823	...	1850	...	1858	1857	1942	...
Paris Montparnasse **280** a.	...	1721	...	1825	...	...	...	...	...	2014	2014	...	...	...	...	...	...	...	...	...	2112	2111	...	...

July 6 - Aug. 24	Ⓐ	TGV 8676 ⑦ s	Ⓐ	⑥	⑥	†	⑤ k	Ⓐ	†	Ⓐ E	†	TGV 8688 ⑦ s	⑥	Ⓐ F	Ⓐ	⑥		TGV 8682 ⑥ v	TGV 8696 ⑦ w	TGV 8682 Ⓐ	†	Ⓐ	TGV 8686 ⑦ s	⑤ k
Brest 286 d.	1704	1712	...	...	1725	1729	...	1740	...	1800	...	1813	...	1821	...	1822	...	1844	...	1848	1902	1933	1948	...
Landerneau **286** d.	1718	|	...	...	1736	1740	...	1751	...	1817	...	|	...	1838	...	1837	...	|	...	|	1913	1950	2001	...
Landivisiau d.	1727	|	...	...	1746	1750	...	|	...	1829	...	|	...	1851	...	1847	...	|	...	|	1923	2003	|	...
Morlaix d.	1743	1746	...	...	1803	1806	...	1814	...	1852	...	1847	...	1914	...	1902	...	1918	...	1922	1939	2018	2025	...
Lannion d.	|	|	...	1757	|	|	1755	|	...	|	1832	|	1859	...	1902	|	...	|	1916	|	|	...	|	2026
Plouaret-Trégor d.	1805	|	...	|	1821	1823	1814	|	...	1912	1850	|	1917	...	1920	1924	...	|	|	|	1955	...	|	2045
Guingamp d.	...	1815	...	1827	1842	1838	1828	1843	...	...	1906	1917	...	...	1935	1938	...	1948	1948	1952	2010	...	|	...
St Brieuc 299 d.	...	1833	1834	...	1859	1855	1849	1901	1907	...	...	1938	...	...	...	...	...	2006	2006	2011	2027	...	2108	...
Lamballe **299** d.	...	1846	1847	...	1911	1907	...	1912	1922	...	...	|	...	...	...	...	...	2019	2019	|	2039	...	|	...
Rennes a.	...	1924	1940	...	1949	1945	...	1950	2018	...	...	2028	...	...	...	...	...	2058	2058	2058	2115	...	2155	...
Paris Montparnasse **280** a.	...	2152	...	...	...	...	...	...	...	...	...	2254	...	...	...	...	...	2313	2313	2313	...	...	0013	...

A – Daily **except** ⑤ (also Aug. 15; not July 13, Aug. 14).
E – Ⓐ July 7 - 18, Aug. 18 - 22.
F – July 21 - Aug. 14.

f – Not July 13.
g – Not July 14.
h – Also July 15; not July 14.
j – Also Aug. 14; not July 13.
k – Also Aug. 14; not Aug. 15.
m – Not July 14, Aug. 14.
p – Also July 14, Aug. 14; not July 13, Aug. 15.

q – Also July 14, Aug. 14.
s – Also July 14; not July 13.
t – Also Aug. 15.
u – From/to Dinan, Table **299**.
v – Not July 12.
w – Also July 14.
x – Not July 15, Aug. 15.

TGV – 🅁, supplement payable, 🍸.

GUINGAMP - PONTRIEUX - PAIMPOL

Service July 6 - Aug. 24. *47 km.* Journey 45 minutes.

From Guingamp: 0702 Ⓐ, 1200 ⚒, 1237 †, 1448, 1742 Ⓐ, 1745 Ⓒ, 1955 ⑤ **k**, 2041 ①–④ **m**, 2153 ⑤ **k**.

From Paimpol: 0559 Ⓐ, 0805 Ⓐ, 0835 Ⓒ, 1340, 1637 Ⓐ, 1642 Ⓒ, 1846 Ⓒ, 1847 Ⓐ.

🚂 – A steam train operates between Paimpol and Pontrieux May 8 - Sept. 14 (not daily). www.vapeurdutrieux.com

RENNES and NANTES - QUIMPER 285 (Summer)

TGV trains convey 🍸

Service July 6 - Aug. 24. *For service to July 5/from Aug. 25 see page 187*

km	July 6 - Aug. 24	Ⓐ	Ⓐ	⑥	⑥	Ⓐ	Ⓐ	†	① k	⑥	①–⑥ p	①–⑥ p	⑦ ◇s	TGV 8701 j		† n	⑦ s	Ⓐ	⑥ t	⑥ t	TGV 8715 j	⑤ h	TGV 8719 Ⓐ	TGV 8721 ⑥ t	⑥ t
0	*Paris* ⊡ **280** d.	...	...	...	...	...	...	...	...	...	...	...	...	0823	...	...	...	...	...	...	1005	...	...	...	...
365	**Rennes 287** d.	...	...	...	0654	0710	...	0720	...	0830	0940	...	0938	|	...	...	1051	...	...	1133	1218	1302	1337	1337	...
	Nantes ◧ d.	...	...	...	|	|	0651	|	0730	|	|	0925	|	|	...	1007	|	1118	1118	|	|	|	|	|	1312
	Savenay ◧ d.	...	...	...	|	|	0714	|	0752	|	|	0947	|	|	...	1029	|	1141	1140	|	|	|	|	|	1336
437	Redon **287** ◧ d.	...	...	...	0735	0746	0752	0758	0827	0908	1018	1023	1021	|	...	1055	1126	1207	1216	1211	1255	1338	|	|	1403
492	Vannes d.	...	0700	0706	0804	...	0822	...	...	...	...	1052	1056	1143	...	...	1152	1235	1245	...	1322	1408	1438	1438	...
511	Auray d.	...	0713	0721	0817	...	0834	...	...	...	...	1104	1109	1157	...	...	1205	1248	1257	...	1335	1421	1451	1451	...
545	Lorient d.	0645	0743	0748	0836	...	0854	...	...	...	...	1125	...	1216	...	...	1225	1307	1317	...	1354	1439	1508	1511	...
565	Quimperlé d.	0700	0757	...	0848	...	0906	...	...	...	...	1137	...	|	...	...	1238	1319	1329	...	1408	1450	...	|	...
612	**Quimper** a.	0728	0825	...	0915	...	0933	...	...	...	...	1204	...	1250	...	...	1304	1346	1356	...	1437	1518	...	1544	...

July 6 - Aug. 24	Ⓒ	TGV 8717 j	Ⓒ	⑤ h	Ⓒ	①–④ m	13895	TGV 8723 ⑤ h	①–④ m	⑤ h	⑤ h	Ⓐ	①–④ m	† n	†	⑥ ⊖	①–④ m⊖	† ⊖		⑤ h	TGV 8729 A	①–④ m	⑤ h	†	Ⓐ
Paris ⊡ **280** d.	...	1205	...	...	...	...	...	1345	...	...	...	...	...	...	...	...	...	...	...	...	1505	...	...	...	...
Rennes 287 d.	1350	1425	...	1433	1433	1440	...	|	...	1610	...	...	1639	...	1641	...	...	...	...	1700	1718	...	...	1735	1756
Nantes ◧ d.	|	|	...	|	|	|	1520	|	...	|	...	1619	|	1620	|	1641	1649	1659	...	|	|	1724	1725	|	|
Savenay ◧ d.	|	|	...	|	|	|	|	|	...	|	...	1640	|	1642	|	|	|	|	...	|	|	1746	1747	|	|
Redon **287** ◧ d.	1429	|	...	1517	1518	1515	1602	|	...	1649	...	1709	1716	1710	1721	1725	1733	1742	...	1741	|	1821	1821	1828	1837
Vannes d.	1459	1525	...	...	...	...	1633	1653	1700	1720	1731	...	1743	...	1751	1751	1802	1810	...	1811	1821	...	...	1900	...
Auray d.	1512	1538	...	...	...	...	1646	1706	1714	1732	1745	...	1756	...	1804	|	|	|	...	1824	1835	...	...	1915	...
Lorient d.	1533	1558	1610	...	...	...	1708	1725	1746	1753	1817	...	1818	...	1825	1818	1830	1837	...	1845	1855	...	...	1940	...
Quimperlé d.	1544	|	1625	...	...	...	1721	|	1801	1805	1832	...	1830	...	1837	|	|	|	...	1856	|	...	...	...	...
Quimper a.	1612	1632	1655	...	...	...	1750	1800	1832	1832	1902	...	1857	...	1904	1852	1904	1911	...	1923	1930	...	...	...	...

July 6 - Aug. 24	⑥	⑤ h⊖	⑥	†	Ⓐ	Ⓐ	†	TGV 8737 ①–④ m	TGV 8739 ⑤ h	TGV 8747 ⑤	TGV 8743 Ⓒ j		3854 3855 ♠	TGV 8759 ①–④ m	Ⓐ	⑥	N	⑤ h	† n	TGV 8757 ⑤ h	L	TGV 8761 q	TGV 5237 ♥q	TGV 8775 ⑤ h	TGV 8779 ⑤ n
Paris ⊡ **280** d.	...	...	...	...	...	...	...	1638	1638	1658	1706	...	...	...	...	...	...	...	...	1855	...	1938	...	...	2157
Rennes 287 d.	...	...	1815	1826	...	1831	1858	1903	1903	1919	1930	...	...	2024	...	2030	2030	...	...	|	...	2150	2203	2239	0030
Nantes ◧ d.	1741	1809	|	|	1821	|	|	|	|	|	|	...	1905	|	1950	|	|	2025	2043	|	2126	|	|	|	|
Savenay ◧ d.	1803	|	|	|	1843	|	|	|	|	|	|	...	1929	|	2018	|	|	2047	2104	|	2147	|	|	|	|
Redon **287** ◧ d.	1842	1853	1855	1906	1912	1917	1937	1942	1942	|	2007	...	2014*	|	2045	2107	2111	2112	2131	|	2215	2227	2240	2316	|
Vannes d.	1913	1922	...	...	...	...	...	2008	2011	2019	2033	...	2045	2124	...	...	2140	...	...	2203	...	2254	2307	2342	0132
Auray d.	1925	1934	...	...	...	...	...	...	2025	2033	2046	...	2059	|	...	...	2153	...	...	2217	...	2307	2321	2355	0145
Lorient d.	1946	1956	...	...	...	...	...	...	2044	2053	2104	...	2120	2152	...	...	2214	...	...	2237	...	2326	2339	0014	0202
Quimperlé d.	1957	2007	...	...	...	...	...	...	|	2106	2117	...	|	|	...	...	2226	...	...	|	...	2339	2352	0028	...
Quimper a.	2025	2033	...	...	...	...	...	...	2119	2136	2146	...	2200	2226	...	...	2253	...	...	2312	...	0007	0020	0056	...

July 6 - Aug. 24	TGV 8702 ① k	TGV 8706 ②–⑥ B	Ⓐ	Ⓐ R	⑥ t	Ⓐ	Ⓐ	3830 3831 ♠	TGV 8718 ①–⑥ p	Ⓐ ⊖	Ⓐ	⑥	Ⓐ	TGV 5272 ♣j	Ⓐ R	TGV 8720 Ⓐ	Ⓐ ⊖	TGV 8722 Ⓒ t	①–⑥ p	† ⊖	† n	⑥ ⊖	Ⓐ	13894 ⑥	13894 Ⓑ
Quimper d.	0411	...	...	0530	...	0600	...	0620	0633	0704	...	0705	0717	0739	0754	0809	0833	0839	...	0917	...	0941	0958	1007	1011
Quimperlé d.	0441	...	...	0557	...	0627	...	|	0704	0734	...	0734	0744	0810	0823	0839	|	0909	...	|	...	|	1025	1036	1040
Lorient d.	0454	0458	...	0609	...	0640	...	0659	0719	0749	...	0748	0757	0823	0837	0854	0909	0924	...	0954	...	1017	1038	1048	1053
Auray d.	0513	|	...	0630	...	0700	...	0721	0739	...	...	...	0818	0842	0903	0914	|	0944	...	|	...	|	1100	1111	1117
Vannes d.	0527	0525	...	0643	...	0712	...	0736	0754	...	...	...	0831	0856	0918	0928	0937	0958	...	1022	...	1046	1112	1123	1130
Redon **287** d.	0553	0551	0648	0714	0741	0745	0750	0807	0819	...	0851	...	0902	0923	...	|	1006	|	1030	1050	1101	1112	1143	1154	1202
Savenay ◧ d.	|	|	0724	|	0810	|	0818	|	|	...	0922	...	|	|	...	|	|	|	|	|	|	|	|	1224	1229
Nantes ◧ a.	|	|	0745	|	0831	|	0840	0853	|	...	0945	...	|	|	...	|	1050	|	|	1133	|	1156	|	1247	1250
Rennes 287 ◧ a.	0628	0628	...	0753	...	0829	...	...	0855	...	...	...	0937	0959	...	1028	...	1058	1107	...	1151	...	1220	...	...
Paris ⊡ **280** a.	0853	0853	...	...	...	...	...	...	...	...	...	...	...	...	...	...	...	...	...	...	...	...	...	...	...

July 6 - Aug. 24	Ⓒ	TGV 8730 j	⑥	①–④ m	①–④ m		⑤ h	TGV 8744 Ⓒ j	Ⓐ	⑤ h	⑤ h	⑥	⑥	†	Ⓐ	Ⓒ	TGV 8752 j	† n	Ⓐ	†	⑤ h	①–④ m	†	TGV 8762 ①–④ m	TGV 8762 Ⓒ j
Quimper d.	1024	1142	...	1232	...	...	1238	1234	...	1316	...	1331	...	...	...	...	1433	...	1512	1530	1544	...	1600	1617	1617
Quimperlé d.	1052	|	...	1259	...	...	1306	1304	...	1343	...	1358	...	...	...	...	1503	...	1539	1558	1612	...	1627	|	|
Lorient d.	1104	1220	1300	1312	...	...	1318	1322	1332	1356	...	1410	...	...	...	...	1521	...	1552	1610	1631	...	1640	1657	1655
Auray d.	1127	1239	1327	1331	...	...	1337	1340	1358	1413	...	1432	...	...	...	...	1540	...	1614	1633	1653	...	1702	1716	1715
Vannes d.	1139	1254	1342	1344	...	...	1350	1354	1411	1426	...	1445	...	...	...	...	1554	...	1627	1646	1705	...	1714	1730	1730
Redon **287** d.	1210	1320	...	1418	1423	...	1418	1422	...	1459	1506	1518	1523	1526	1542	1550	1623	1657	1658	1717	1736	1743	1746	|	|
Savenay ◧ d.	|	|	...	|	1449	...	|	|	...	|	1529	|	1547	1549	|	|	|	1706	1722	|	|	1810	1813	|	|
Nantes ◧ a.	|	|	...	|	1511	...	|	|	...	|	1550	|	1608	1611	|	|	|	1750	1745	|	|	1833	1834	|	|
Rennes 287 ◧ a.	1248	1355	...	1453	...	...	1453	1458	...	1534	...	1553	...	...	1622	1628	1658	...	...	1753	1812	...	...	1828	1828
Paris ⊡ **280** a.	...	1613	...	...	...	...	...	1721	...	...	...	...	...	...	...	...	1913	...	...	...	...	...	...	2049	2055

July 6 - Aug. 24	TGV 8762 ⑤ h	Ⓐ	①–④ m	TGV 8774 ⑦ s	⑤ h	⑥	⑤ h	⑥	Ⓐ	TGV 8776 ⑦ v	TGV 8780 ①⑥ C	†	⑤ h	†	①–④ m	TGV 8794 ⑦ v	TGV 8790 D	②–④ f	⑤ h	Ⓐ R	TGV 8798 ⑦ s	† ◇	TGV 8796 ⑦ v	⑦ j	
Quimper d.	1617	...	1706	1715	1722	...	...	...	1727	1746	1746	1754	1800	...	1807	1834	1845	1846	...	1900	1947	...	...	2035	...
Quimperlé d.	|	...	1734	|	1750	...	...	...	1755	|	|	1821	1828	...	1836	1905	|	|	...	1927	|	...	...	2103	...
Lorient d.	1657	1713	1746	1751	1805	...	...	...	1807	1822	1824	1834	1839	...	1851	1919	1922	1921	...	1938	2025	...	2057	2117	...
Auray d.	1716	1741	1804	1811	1833	...	...	...	1831	1842	1845	1853	1901	...	1921	1939	1942	1942	...	...	2044	2052	2118	2136	...
Vannes d.	1730	1755	1817	1825	1846	...	...	...	1843	1857	1859	1907	1913	...	1934	1952	1957	1955	...	...	2058	2105	2131	2149	...
Redon **287** d.	|	...	1846	1851	...	1901	1908	1914	1926	|	|	1938	1940	1945	...	2019	|	|	2036	...	|	2140	|	2217	...
Savenay ◧ d.	|	...	|	|	...	1928	|	|	1954	|	|	|	|	2014	...	|	|	|	2102	...	|	|	|	|	...
Nantes ◧ a.	|	...	|	|	...	1950	|	|	2015	|	|	|	|	2034	...	|	|	|	2125	...	|	|	|	|	...
Rennes 287 ◧ a.	1828	...	1920	1928	...	...	1947	1950	...	|	1958	2012	2015	...	...	2055	2055	2053	...	...	2158	2223	2228	2251	...
Paris ⊡ **280** a.	2054	...	...	...	...	...	...	...	...	2207	2222	...	...	...	...	2313	...	...	...	...	...	...	0053	...	...

Auray - Quiberon *July 5 - Aug. 24* ❦

28 km				⚒t	⑦s						
Rennes (above) d.	...	...	...	...	0938	...	...	...	...	...	...
Auray d.	0800	0858	1008	1111	1111	1225	1350	1601	1735	1841	2055
Quiberon a.	0844	0949	1058	1202	1202	1315	1434	1652	1826	1931	2139

									⚒	†	
Quiberon d.	0854	1004	1107	1220	1437	1557	1731	1837	1941	1945	2149
Auray a.	0937	1048	1150	1303	1522	1640	1815	1924	2024	2028	2232
Rennes (above) a.	...	...	...	...	...	...	...	...	...	2223	...

– Daily **except** ⑤ (also Aug. 15; not July 13, Aug. 14).
– ②–⑥ July 12 - Aug. 23 (not July 15).
– ①⑥ (also July 15, Aug. 15; not July 12, 14).
– ①⑤⑥ (also July 15, Aug. 14; not July 14).
– ①②③④⑥ (also July 13, Aug. 15; not July 14, Aug. 14).
– ①②③④⑦ (also Aug. 15; not Aug. 14).
– July 7 - 18, Aug. 18 - 22.
Not July 15, Aug. 14.
– Also Aug. 14; not Aug. 15.
Not July 13.
– Also July 15; not July 14.

m – Not July 14, Aug. 14.
n – Not Aug. 15.
p – Not July 14.
q – Not July 12, 13.
s – Also July 14.
t – Also Aug. 15.
v – Also July 14; not July 13.
w – Until June 22.
y – Until July 4.
z – From Sept. 6.

TGV – Ⓡ, supplement payable, 🍸.
⊡ – Paris Montparnasse.
⊖ – To/from Brest (Table **286**).
◇ – To/from Quiberon (see below main table).
◧ – See also **287** Nantes - Redon, **287/8** Nantes - Savenay.
♥ – From Lille Europe (depart 1752, Table **11**).
♣ – To Lille Europe (arrive 1407, Table **11**).
♠ – To/from Bordeaux (Table **292**).
* – Arrive 1958.

❦ – **June 14 - 22, Sept. 6 - 14**:
From Auray: 1053Ⓒ, 1342Ⓒ**w**, 1345Ⓒ**z**, 1437Ⓒ**w**, 1545Ⓒ, 1840Ⓒ.
From Quiberon: 1148Ⓒ, 1440Ⓒ**z**, 1729Ⓒ**w**, 1740Ⓒ**z**, 1945Ⓒ.

June 28 - July 4, Aug. 25 - 31:
From Auray: 0800, 1111⚒, 1342**y**, 1601, 1841, 2055.
From Quiberon: 0854, 1220, 1437**y**, 1740, 1941⚒, 2149.

286 (Summer) BREST - QUIMPER

Service July 6 - Aug. 24. *For service to July 5/from Aug. 25 see page 188*

km		Ⓐ ⊖	⑥	Ⓐ	†	⑥	Ⓐ	⑥	†	†	Ⓐ	⑥	⑤ f	Ⓒ	Ⓐ	Ⓐ	†	⑥	⑤ f	†
0	**Brest 284** d.	0551	0707	0716	0810	0835	0842	0920	1011	1108	1159	1212	1535	1628	1725	1844	1851	1945	2012	2017
18	Landerneau **284** d.	0603	0720	0728	|	|	0854	0931	1025	1121	1211	1224	1547	1643	1740	1905	1903	2000	2027	2032
72	Châteaulin d.	0640	0800	0805	|	|	0929	1010	1101	1157	1247	1300	1624	1720	1821	1938	1939	2036	2104	2109
102	**Quimper** a.	0703	0823	0828	0915	0939	0953	1033	1124	1220	1310	1323	1649	1744	1845	2001	2002	2059	2127	2132
	Nantes **285** a.	...	...	1050	1133	1156	...	...	...	...	...	...	...	...	...	...	...	...	...	...

	Ⓐ	⑥	Ⓐ	†	⑥	Ⓐ		⑤ f	Ⓒ	Ⓐ	⑥	①–④ m	⑤ f	†		⑤ f	†	
Nantes **285** d.	...	...	...	...	...	...	...	...	...	...	1641	1649	...	1659		1809	...	
Quimper d.	0615	0734	0739	0922	0944	0959	1445	1558	1757	1755	1855	1911	1912	1913	...	2038	2043	...
Châteaulin d.	0642	0802	0808	0946	1012	1023	1508	1626	1821	1823	|	1940	1940	1941	...	2106	2111	...
Landerneau **284** d.	0723	0840	0843	1021	1048	1100	1544	1704	1859	1901	|	|	2014	2015	...	2142	2149	...
Brest 284 a.	0736	0853	0856	1034	1100	1112	1557	1720	1912	1914	2003	2025	2027	2027	...	2155	2203	...

f – Also Aug. 14; not Aug. 15.
m – Not July 14, Aug. 14.
⊖ – To Lorient (Table **285**).

CAT 🚌 *31*, journey 90 minutes.
Subject to alteration.
From Brest : 0700 Ⓐ, 0930 †, 1000 ⚒, 1415 †, 1440 ⚒, 1610 ⑤, 1800 Ⓐ.
From Quimper : 0710 Ⓐ, 1135 ⑤, 1245 †, 1255 ⚒, 1640 ⚒, 1730 Ⓐ, 1740 †.

287 (Summer) RENNES - REDON - NANTES

Service July 6 - Aug. 24. *For service to July 5/from Aug. 25 see page 188*

km		Ⓐ	⑥ t	Ⓐ	†	**3830**	Ⓐ	⑥	Ⓒ	Ⓐ	⑥ t	①–④ m	⑤ f		⑤ f	⑥	†	①–④ m	⑤ f	Ⓐ		⑤ f	①–④ m	⑥	†	Ⓐ
0	**Rennes** § d.	0629	...	...	0720	...	0745	0830	1000	1210	1229	...	1415	...	...	...	*1433*	1440	1535	...	...	1647	*1644*	1700	1729	1745
72	Redon § a.	0723	...	...	0758	...	|	0908	|	|	|	...	|	...	...	...	*1518*	1515	|	...	...	|	*1739*	|	|	|
72	Redon ◇ d.	...	0741	0750	...	0807	|	...	|	|	|	1423	|	...	1506	1523	1526	1523	|	1658	...	|	1743	|	|	|
106	Savenay ◇ d.	...	0810	0818	...	|	|	...	|	|	|	1449	|	...	1529	1547	1549	|	|	1722	...	|	1810	|	|	|
145	**Nantes** ◇ a.	...	0831	0840	...	0853	0902	...	1115	1324	1349	1511	1529	...	1550	1608	1611	1607	1650	1745	...	1805	1833	1815	1845	1900

	Ⓐ	⑥	†	Ⓐ	†		⑥ s	①–④ m	⑤ f	†	⑥	
Rennes § d.	...	1815	1826	1831	1858	...	1920	1927	...	1948	2030	...
Redon § a.	...	1855	1906	1917	1937	...	|	|	...	|	2107	...
Redon ◇ d.	1841	1901	...	1926	1945	...	|	|	2036	|	...	...
Savenay ◇ d.	1908	1928	...	1954	2014	...	|	|	2102	|	...	...
Nantes ◇ a.	1931	1950	...	2015	2034	...	2035	2044	2125	2105	...	...

	⑥	Ⓐ	Ⓐ a	⑥ s	⚒ t	† n	⑥	Ⓐ	⑥ t
Nantes ◇ d.	...	0651	0724	0820	0925	1007	1118	1229	1256
Savenay ◇ d.	...	0714	|	|	0947	1029	1141	|	|
Redon ◇ a.	..	0741	|	|	1012	1055	1205	|	|
Redon § d.	0734	...	|	|	*1030*	1101	...	|	|
Rennes § a.	0820	...	0842	0934	*1107*	1151	...	1345	1410

	Ⓐ	⑥	⑤ f	①–④ m	⑤ f	①–④ m	† n	Ⓒ	⑤ f	Ⓐ	†	Ⓐ	⑥ ⊖	⑤ f	Ⓐ	⑥	**3855**		⑤ f	Ⓐ	⑤ f	† n	⑤⑦ E	L	
Nantes ◇ d.	1440	1503	1535	1602	1619	1620	1620	...	1648	1724	1758	1759	1803	...	1821	...	1905	1925	...	1950	2025	2043	2105	2126	...
Savenay ◇ d.	|	|	|	|	1640	1641	1642	...	|	1746	|	|	|	...	1842	...	1929	|	...	2018	2047	2104	2129	2147	...
Redon ◇ a.	|	|	|	|	1707	1709	1710	...	|	1821	|	|	|	...	1913	...	1958	|	...	2045	2112	2131	2158	2215	...
Redon § d.	|	|	|	|	...	*1724*	...	1729	|	...	|	|	|	1908	...	1934	...	|	2029	...	2119	...	2227	2229	...
Rennes § a.	1602	1617	1650	1717	...	*1822*	...	1823	1806	...	1912	1913	1917	1947	...	2013	...	2044	2116	...	2201	...	2307	2306	...

E – Also July 14, Aug. 14; not July 13, Aug! 15. From Bordeaux (train **3857/6**).
L – ①②③④⑥ (also July 13, Aug. 15; not July 14, Aug. 14).
a – From Angers (depart 0618).
f – Also Aug. 14; not Aug. 15.
m – Not July 14, Aug. 14.
n – Not Aug. 15.
s – Also Aug. 15. To/from St Malo (Table **281**).
t – Also Aug. 15.
⊖ – From Tours (Table **289**).
§ – For other trains Rennes - Redon see Table **285**.
◇ – For other trains Redon - Nantes see Table **285**, for Savenay - Nantes see Tables **285** and **288**.

288 (Summer) NANTES - ST NAZAIRE - LE CROISIC

Service July 6 - Aug. 24. *For service to July 5/from Aug. 25 see page 188*

km	*July 6 - Aug. 24*	Ⓐ	Ⓐ	Ⓐ	⑥ t	Ⓐ	①–⑥ v	⑦ s	*TGV* **8905** ⚒ t	⑦ O s	*TGV* **8911**	①–⑥ v	Ⓐ	† n	*TGV* **8915**	Ⓐ	Ⓒ	*TGV* **8919** ⑤ f	*TGV* **8921** L	Ⓐ	*TGV* **8927** ⑥ t	Ⓐ	⑥ t	Ⓐ T
	Paris ⊡ **280** d.	...	...	...	...	...	...	...	0650	...	0849	...	...	...	1051	...	...	...	1350	...	1453	...	...	...
0	**Nantes 285/7** d.	0616	0642	0656	0719	0753	0800	0903	0911	1002	1110	1150	1200	1223	1303	1428	1433	1445	1613	1643	1712	1719	1729	1805
39	Savenay **285/7** d.	0649	0706	0720	0743	0820	0834	0931	|	1026	|	1211	1231	1244	|	1450	1455	|	|	1704	|	1741	1753	|
64	**St Nazaire** d.	0711	0726	0739	0801	0835	0859	0945	0947	1052	1145	1226	1246	1301	1341	1505	1516	1520	1649	1728	1748	1757	1808	1847
79	Pornichet d.	...	...	0753	0812	...	0910	0955	1000	1107	|	1239	...	1312	1353	1516	1527	|	|	1741	|	1809	1819	1858
83	La Baule Escoublac d.	...	...	0800	0822	...	0915	1003	1008	1116	1202	1246	...	1321	1402	1522	1534	1537	1708	1748	1804	1817	1826	1907
90	**Le Croisic** a.	...	...	0815	0835	...	0926	1016	1021	1132	1211	1259	...	1333	1415	1538	1547	1546	1717	1802	1813	1832	1839	1920

July 6 - Aug. 24	† T	Ⓐ	⑥ t	⑦ s	①–④ m	*TGV* **8937** L	*TGV* **8935** ⑤ f	①–④ m		⑥ O t	⑤ O f		*TGV* **8939** ①–④ m	*TGV* **8943** ⑤⑥ w	⑥ t	*TGV* **5231** ♥	*TGV* **8949** ⑤ f	①–④ m	† n		*TGV* **8953** ⑤ f	† n	⑤⑥ w	*TGV* **8957** ⑤ f
Paris ⊡ **280** d.	...	...	...	...	...	1722	1723	...	...	...	...	...	1746	1821	...	...	1953	...	...	...	2050	...	...	2150
Nantes 285/7 d.	1805	1841	1839	1900	1909	1933	1932	...	...	1946	1946	...	2006	2036	2132	2153	2211	2222	2222	...	2308	2325	2325	0013
Savenay **285/7** d.	1831	1916	1914	1921	1943	|	|	←	...	|	|	...	|	|	2159	|	|	2249	2249	...	|	2346	2354	|
St Nazaire d.	1847	1931	1942*	1942	2002	2008	2009	2019	...	2022	2021	...	2045	2112	2213	2229	2248	2303	2302	...	2348	0002	0008	0049
Pornichet d.	1858	1942	1952	1952	→	...	2021	2031	...	2033	2035	...	|	|	...	2242	2300	2314	...	...	|	0013	0019	|
La Baule Escoublac d.	1907	1949	2002	2002	...	...	2028	2040	...	2041	2043	...	2101	2127	...	2250	2307	2321	...	...	0001	0020	0026	0105
Le Croisic a.	1920	2002	2015	2015	...	...	2042	2052	...	2055	2056	...	2110	2137	...	2303	2320	2334	...	...	0010	0033	0037	0114

July 6 - Aug. 24	Ⓐ	*TGV* **8906** ① k	*TGV* **8912** ②–⑤ p	*TGV* **8914** ① k		Ⓐ	Ⓐ	Ⓐ	Ⓒ	Ⓐ	Ⓒ O	Ⓐ	*TGV* **5270** ♥		*TGV* **8926** Ⓐ	*TGV* **8928** Ⓒ	Ⓐ	⑥ t	*TGV* **8932**		Ⓐ	*TGV* **8940**	Ⓐ	
Le Croisic d.	0512	...	...	0554	...	...	0634	...	0710	0730	0806	0829	0850	...	0958	1025	1036	1035	1147	1219	...	1352	...	...
La Baule Escoublac d.	0525	...	...	0605	...	...	0646	...	0722	0744	0820	0842	0903	...	1010	1037	1048	1053	1201	1231	...	1403	...	...
Pornichet d.	0532	...	...	|	...	...	0653	...	0730	0751	0825	0847	0911	...	|	|	1056	1103	1207	1238	...	|	...	...
St Nazaire d.	0542	0547	0551	0621	...	0626	0705	0742	0741	0807	0837	0859	0924	...	1026	1053	1107	1114	1221	1248	1352	1419	1520	...
Savenay **285/7** d.	...	0603	|	|	...	0645	0729	0758	0755	0825	0851	0913	|	...	|	|	1122	1129	|	1311	1408	|	1533	...
Nantes 285/7 a.	...	0625	0625	0655	...	0720	0750	0820	0820	0848	0913	0934	1000	...	1100	1126	1143	1150	1255	1345	1439	1455	1600	...
Paris ⊡ **280** a.	...	0845	0901	0910	...	...	...	...	...	...	...	...	...	...	1323	1344	...	...	1519	...	...	1712	...	...

July 6 - Aug. 24	Ⓑ	*TGV* **8944**	Ⓐ	⑥ t	⑦ s	①–④ O m	⑤ O f	*TGV* **8950** ⑤⑦ q	①–④ m	⑦ s		Ⓐ	*TGV* **8952** A	Ⓐ	Ⓒ O	①–④ m	⑤ f	⑦ s	⑥ t	*TGV* **8958** ⑦ s	Ⓐ	*TGV* **8960** ⑦ s	⑤ f	
Le Croisic d.	1520	1553	...	1628	1652	...	...	1746	...	1759	...	1815	1855	...	1902	2010	2012	2025	2026	2053	...	2112	...	...
La Baule Escoublac d.	1536	1604	...	1644	1706	...	...	1801	...	1812	...	1827	1906	...	1921	2023	2027	2037	2039	2104	...	2126	...	...
Pornichet d.	1542	|	...	1651	1713	...	...	1808	...	1819	...	1834	|	...	1930	2032	2034	2043	2048	|	...	2133	...	...
St Nazaire d.	1552	1621	1613	1701	1725	1736	1736	1821	1829	1831	...	1846	1922	1926	1945	2042	2052	2055	2058	2121	2116	2146	2214	...
Savenay **285/7** d.	1609	|	1648	1714	1742	1752	1752	|	1848	1847	...	1915	|	1940	|	2057	2109	2114	2112	|	2134	|	2232	...
Nantes 285/7 a.	1630	1655	1711	1741	1813	1812	1814	1855	1917	1920	...	1945	1955	2005	2019	2119	2130	2141	2133	2155	2201	2220	2252	...
Paris ⊡ **280** a.	...	1923	...	...	...	...	...	2121	...	...	...	...	2218	...	...	...	...	...	...	0009	...	0041	...	...

A – Daily **except** ⑤ (also Aug. 15; not Aug. 14).
L – ①②③④⑦ (not Aug. 14).
O – To/from Orléans (Table **289**).
T – To/from Tours (Table **289**).
f – Also Aug. 14; not Aug. 15.
k – Also July 15; not July 14.
m – Not July 14, Aug. 14.
n – Not Aug. 15.
p – Not July 15, Aug. 15.
q – Also July 14; not Aug. 15.
s – Also July 14.
t – Also Aug. 15.
v – Not July 14.
w – Also Aug. 14.
TGV – Ⓡ, supplement payable, 🍸.
♥ – From/to Lille Europe (Table **11**), d. 1752, a. 140
⊡ – Paris Montparnasse.
⊖ – From Le Mans (Table **280**).
* – Arrive 1927.

HAMBURG - KIEL — 820

RE services except where shown

Regional services valid JULY 14 - AUG. 24. For *ICE* services see main table on page 387.

		⚒							
Hamburg Hbf .... 823 d.	0028	0520	0620	0700	0805		2205	2323	...
Hamburg Altona ...... d.	|	|	|	0726	0826	and	2226	|	...
Elmshorn .... 823 d.	0100	0551	0650	0750	0850	hourly	2250	2353	...
Neumünster .... 823 d.	0133	0618	0716	0816	0916	until	2316	0019	...
Kiel Hbf .... a.	0200	0638	0737	0827	0927		2337	0039	...

	Ⓐ		Ⓐ						
Kiel Hbf .... d.	0404	0521	...	0621		2021	2121	2221	2323
Neumünster .... 823 d.	0425	0542	...	0642	and	2042	2142	2242	2343
Elmshorn .... 823 d.	0457	0609	0613	0709	hourly	2109	2209	2309	0009
Hamburg Altona .... a.	|	0631	|	0731	until	2131	|	|	|
Hamburg Hbf .... 823 a.	0531	0701c	0650	0751		2151	2237	2337	0038

c – Ⓒ only.

Local services OFFENBURG - FREIBURG - BASEL — 912

SERVICE UNTIL SEPTEMBER 28. See pages 426 and 428 for service from September 29. See also note ⊠.

	†z	Ⓐt	Ⓐt	Ⓐt	⑥	⚒	⑥	Ⓐt		⚒t	Ⓐt		⊗				⊖	⊖		Ⓒz	Ⓐt		⑥	†z	Ⓐt	Ⓒz
Offenburg .... d.	0049	0428	...	0525	...	0549	...	0634	...	0706	...	0807	0907	1007	1107	1204	1307	1404	1507	...	1534	1607	...	...	1707	1707
Freiburg (Brsg) Hbf .... a.	0131	0528	...	0625	...	0649	...	0729	...	0756	...	0855	0955	1055	1155	1250	1355	1450	1555	...	1633	1656	...	...	1756	1756
Freiburg (Brsg) Hbf .... d.	0132	0529	0618	0628	0632	0710	...	0734	0815	0815	...	0915	1015	1115	1215	1315	1415	1515	1615	...	1635	1715	...	...	1815	1815
Müllheim (Baden) ... ⊠ d.	0152	0550	0651	0655	0659	0731	...	0751	0835	0835	0839	0935	1035	1135	1235	1337	1435	1535	1635	...	1702	1735	...	...	1835	1835
Schliengen .... a.	|	0556	|	...	|	0736	🚌	|	0841	0841	|	0941	1041	1141	1241	1342	1441	1541	1641	🚌	|	1741	🚌	🚌	|	1841
Schliengen .... d.	|	...	|	...	|	...	0809	|	0853*	0853*	|	0959*	1059*	1159*	1259*	1359*	1453*	1551*	...	1659	|	...	1749	1759	|	...
Basel Bad Bf ▦ .... ⊠ a.	0220	...	0711	...	0722	...	0910	0813	0954*	0954*	0902	1100*	1200*	1300*	1400*	1500*	1554*	1652*	...	1800	1729	...	1850	1900	1859	...
Basel SBB .... a.	...	...	0720	...	0754	...	...	0820	...	...	0924	...	...	...	...	...	...	...	...	...	1754	...	...	...	1924	...

	⑥	†z		⚒t	†z				
Offenburg .... d.	...	...	1807	...	...	1907	2007	2043	2244
Freiburg (Brsg) Hbf .... a.	...	...	1856	...	...	1955	2055	2142	2342
Freiburg (Brsg) Hbf .... d.	...	...	1915	...	...	2015	...	2145	2343
Müllheim (Baden) ... ⊠ d.	...	...	1935	...	...	2035	...	2212	0009
Schliengen .... a.	🚌	🚌	1941	🚌	🚌	2041	...	2217	...
Schliengen .... d.	1853	1859	...	1950	1959	2053*	...	2235*	...
Basel Bad Bf ▦ .... ⊠ a.	1954	2000	...	2051	2100	2154*	...	2336*	...
Basel SBB .... a.	...	...	...	...	...	...	...	...	...

		⚒t		Ⓐt	Ⓐt	⑥	Ⓒz	⚒t		Ⓐt	⑥		Ⓑ
Basel SBB .... d.	...	...	...	0608	...	0638	...	...	...	0737	0738	...	...
Basel Bad Bf ▦ . ⊠ d.	...	0505*	...	0625	...	0657	...	0648*	...	0757	0757	...	0759*
Schliengen .... a.	...	0558*	...	|	...	|	...	0741*	...	|	|	...	0852*
Schliengen .... d.	...	0614	...	|	0644	|	...	0751	...	|	|	...	0902
Müllheim (Baden) ⊠ d.	...	0620	0620	0645	0650	0718	0718	0759	...	0818	0823	0829	0906
Freiburg (Brsg) Hbf. a.	...	0646	0646	...	0718	0744	0744	0822	...	...	0844	0851	0934
Freiburg (Brsg) Hbf. d.	0555	0656	0656	...	0722	0803	0803	0825	0825	...	0903	0903	...
Offenburg .... a.	0645	0745	0745	...	0814	0851	0851	0921	0921	...	0953	0953	...

	Ⓐt	⑥	Ⓒz					Ⓐt		⊡	⊡	⊡	Ⓐt	Ⓒz	Ⓐt	†z	⑥	Ⓒz	⚒t		†z	A				B
Basel SBB .... d.	0837	...	🚌	...	...	...	...	1308	...	...	...	...	1738	...	...	🚌	🚌	...	...	...	...	1938	...	...	...	...
Basel Bad Bf ▦ .... ⊠ d.	0858	...	0905	...	1005*	1105*	1205*	1330	1305*	1409*	1509*	1609*	1759	1705*	...	1805	1813	1813*	1848*	...	1905*	1959	...	...	2136*	...
Schliengen .... a.	|	...	0958	...	1058*	1158*	1258*	|	1358*	1502*	1602*	1702*	|	1758*	...	1858	1906	1906*	1941*	...	1958*	|	...	...	2229*	...
Schliengen .... d.	|	0916	▬	1016	1116	1216	1316	|	1416	1516	1616	1716	|	1816	1850	...	...	1916	1949	...	2016	|	...	...	2239	...
Müllheim (Baden) ... ⊠ d.	0923	0923	...	1023	1123	1223	1323	1355	1423	1523	1623	1723	1823	1823	1855	...	...	1923	1955	...	2023	2023	2054	2158	2245	...
Freiburg (Brsg) Hbf .... a.	0944	0944	...	1044	1144	1244	1344	1423	1444	1544	1644	1744	1844	1844	1923	...	...	1944	2021	...	2044	2044	2122	2219	2307	...
Freiburg (Brsg) Hbf .... d.	...	...	1003	1103	1203	1307	1403	1427	1507	1603	1703	1803	1903	1903	1925	...	...	2003	...	2028	...	...	2125	2225	...	2325
Offenburg .... a.	...	...	1053	1153	1253	1353	1450	1521	1553	1650	1751	1850	1949	1949	2021	...	...	2050	...	2124	...	...	2221	2318	...	0019

A – ①–④ (not May 1, 29, June 9, 19).
B – ③–⑦ (also June 9).
D – ①–⑤ (not Apr. 22, May 1, 29, June 9).
E – ①–⑥ (not June 9).
n – Not July 31 - Sept. 14.
t – Not June 19.

z – Also June 19.
* – By 🚌.
⊗ – Change trains at Freiburg on ⚒ (not June 19).
⊖ – 🚌 connection runs 6–8 minutes later on Ⓒz.
⊡ – 🚌 connection runs 4 minutes **earlier** on Ⓒz.

⊠ – Selected *ICE* services call additionally at Müllheim during the period Apr. 22 - Sept. 28. Holders of regional tickets may use these trains between Müllheim and Basel Bad Bf only. Journey time: 15–16 minutes. Timings may vary by a few minutes July 31 - Sept. 14.
From Müllheim at 0039 **D**, 0819 **E**, 1022 **n**, 1219, 1311, 1419, 1511, 1619 **n**, 1719 **n**, 1819, 1919 **n**, 2019 and 2234 **E**. **From Basel Bad Bf** at 0722 **E**, 0823, 1023, 1228, 1428, 1523, 1623 **n**, 1723 **n**, 1823, 1923 and 2023.

TRIER - LUXEMBOURG — 915

SERVICE MAY 2 - JUNE 27. All services are operated by 🚌 Trier - Wasserbillig and v.v. See page 432 for service until May 1.

km	▦ at Igel	①–⑤ t	①–⑤ t	①–⑤ t	①–⑤ t	⑦ v	①–⑤ t					①–⑥													①–⑤ t	
0	Trier Hbf .... 🚌 d.	0527	0613	0631	0645	0654	0713	0741	0843	0854	0954	1040	1054	1154	1254	1354	1454	1554	1654	1754	1854	1954	2054	2141	2154	2254
	Wasserbillig ...... 🚌 a.	0554	0640	0658	0712	0721	0740	0808	0910	0921	1021	1107	1121	1221	1321	1421	1521	1621	1721	1821	1921	2021	2121	2208	2221	2321
	Wasserbillig .... d.	0559	0645	0703	0717	0726	0745	0813	0915	0926	1026	1112	1126	1226	1326	1426	1526	1626	1726	1826	1926	2026	2126	2213	2226	2326
51	Luxembourg .... a.	0633	0724	0747	0753	0807	0824	0850	0947	1007	1107	1144	1207	1307	1407	1507	1607	1707	1807	1907	2007	2107	2207	2245	2312	0012

▦ at Wasserbillig	①–⑤ t	①–⑤ t	①–⑥ t	①–⑤ t														①–⑤ t	①–⑤ t		①–⑤ t	①–⑤ t				
Luxembourg .... d.	0440	0505	0548	0634	0648	0710	0748	0848	0948	1048	1148	1248	1314	1348	1448	1548	1648	1708	1738	1748	1808	1838	1848	1948	2048	2250z
Wasserbillig .... a.	0521	0536	0632	0713	0732	0745	0832	0932	1032	1132	1232	1332	1345	1432	1532	1632	1732	1743	1812	1832	1843	1912	1932	2032	2132	2332
Wasserbillig .... 🚌 d.	0539	0635	0648	0718	0737	0835	0848	0937	1037	1137	1237	1337	1435	1448	1537	1637	1737	1748	1817	1837	1848	1917	1937	2037	2137	2337
Trier Hbf .... 🚌 a.	0607	0702	0715	0745	0804	0902	0915	1004	1104	1204	1304	1404	1502	1515	1604	1704	1804	1815	1844	1904	1915	1944	2004	2104	2204	0004

t – Not May 29, June 9, 23.
v – Also May 29, June 9, 23.
z – 2248 on ⑥⑦ (also May 29, June 9, 23).

FRANKFURT - MAINZ - IDAR OBERSTEIN - SAARBRÜCKEN — 917

RB / *RE* services

SERVICE JULY 28 - SEPT. 4. Trains are replaced by 🚌 Neubrücke (*km149*) - Türkismühle - St Wendel and v.v. See page 433 for service to July 27 / from Sept. 5.

km		Ⓐ	Ⓐw	⚒w	⚒											⑤			①–④					Ⓐ	⑤–⑦
0	Frankfurt (Main) Hbf .... ‡ d.	...	...	...	...	...	0725	0825	...	1025	...	1225	...	1425	...	1529	1625	...	1734	1825	...	2025	...	2225	...
11	Frankfurt Flughafen ✈ § .... ‡ d.	...	...	...	...	...	0737	0837	...	1037	...	1237	...	1437	...	|	1638	...	|	1837	...	2037	...	2237	...
39	Mainz Hbf .... ‡ d.	...	0510	...	b	0655	0800	0900	1000	1100	1155	1300	1355	1500	1555	1608	1700	1755	1808	1900	1955	2100	2205	2300	2338
80	Bad Kreuznach .... d.	0501	0542	...	0632e	0737	0826	0926	1026	1126	1225	1326	1424	1526	1624	1645	1726	1824	1845	1926	2024	2126	2244	2326	0019
102	Bad Sobernheim .... d.	0523	0603	...	0654	0755	0844	0944	1044	1144	1245	1344	1445	1544	1645	1708	1744	1845	1908	1944	2045	2144	2307	2344	0042
117	Kirn .... d.	0540	0619	...	0712	0805	0854	0954	1054	1154	1255	1354	1455	1554	1655	1727	1754	1855	1927	1954	2055	2154	2323	2354	0058
131	Idar-Oberstein .... d.	0558	0635	0635	0729	0816	0905	1005	1105	1205	1307	1405	1506	1605	1706	1744	1805	1906	1944	2005	2106	2205	2340	0005	0115
149	Neubrücke .... a.	0619	0654	0654	0750	0831	0920	1020	1120	1220	1321	1420	1520	1620	1720	...	1820	1920	...	2020	2120	2220	...	0020	...
149	Neubrücke .... 🚌 d.	0632*	0659*	0659*	0759*	0843*	0943*	1043*	1143*	1243*	1343*	1443*	1543*	1643*	1743*	...	1843*	1943*	...	2043*	2143*	2245*	...	0030*	...
155	Türkismühle .... 🚌 d.	0644*	|	|	0811*	0855*	0955*	1055*	1155*	1255*	1355*	1455*	1555*	1655*	1755*	...	1855*	1955*	...	2055*	2155*	2257*	...	0042*	...
170	St Wendel .... 🚌 a.	0718*	0732*	0732*	0845*	0929*	1029*	1129*	1229*	1329*	1429*	1529*	1629*	1729*	1829*	...	1929*	2029*	...	2129*	2229*	2331*	...	0116*	...
170	St Wendel .... d.	0723	0740	0740	0850	0938	1038	1138	1238	1340	1438	1538	1638	1738	1838	...	1938	2038	...	2138	2238	2341	...	0121	...
179	Ottweiler (Saar) .... d.	0733	0749	0749	0858	0945	1045	1145	1245	1347	1445	1545	1645	1745	1845	...	1945	2045	...	2145	2245	2351	...	0128	...
184	Neunkirchen (Saar) .... d.	0740	0757	0757	0905	0952	1052	1152	1252	1353	1452	1552	1652	1752	1852	...	1952	2052	...	2152	2252	0000	...	0134	...
205	Saarbrücken Hbf .... a.	0800	0823	0823	0924	1011	1111	1211	1311	1413	1511	1611	1711	1811	1911	...	2012	2111	...	2212	2311	0026	...	0154	...

		Ⓐ	Ⓐ	⚒																	🚌				
Saarbrücken Hbf .... d.	0115	0305	...	0348	0450	0546	0651	0749	0851	0949	1051	1149	1251	1349	1451	1549	1651	1749	1849	1935	...	2035	2135	2210	2343
Neunkirchen (Saar) .... d.	0144	0321	...	0404	0517	0602	0708	0807	0908	1008	1108	1208	1308	1408	1508	1608	1708	1808	1908	2004	...	2108	2214j	2240	0010
Ottweiler (Saar) .... d.	0151	0327	...	0410	0523	0608	0713	0813	0913	1013	1113	1213	1313	1413	1513	1613	1713	1813	1913	2010	...	2115	2221	2247	0017
St Wendel .... a.	0202	0333	...	0416	0531	0615	0720	0820	0920	1020	1120	1220	1320	1420	1520	1620	1720	1820	1920	2020	...	2124	2232	2258	0028
St Wendel .... 🚌 d.	...	0340*	...	0426*	0537*	0635*	0725*	0826*	0926*	1026*	1123*	1226*	1326*	1426*	1526*	1626*	1726*	1826*	1940*	▬	2026	2129*	...	2303*	...
Türkismühle .... 🚌 d.	...	0415*	...	0501*	0612*	0710*	0800*	0901*	1001*	1101*	1158*	1301*	1401*	1501*	1601*	1701*	1801*	1901*	2015*	...	2101	2203*	...	2337*	...
Neubrücke .... 🚌 a.	...	0426*	...	0512*	0623*	0721*	0811*	0912*	1012*	1112*	1209*	1312*	1412*	1512*	1612*	1712*	1812*	1912*	2026*	...	2112	...	...	...	...
Neubrücke .... d.	...	0433	...	0533	0633	0737	0836	0937	1037	1137	1237	1337	1437	1537	1637	1737	1837	1937	2043	...	2112	...	...	...	...
Idar-Oberstein .... d.	...	0449	...	0549	0648	0752	0852	0952	1052	1152	1252	1352	1452	1552	1652	1752	1852	1952	2103	...	2211	...	...	...	...
Kirn .... d.	...	0500	0505	0600	0659	0803	0903	1003	1103	1203	1303	1403	1503	1603	1703	1803	1903	2003	2117	...	...	...	...	...	...
Bad Sobernheim .... d.	...	0509	0523	0610	0709	0812	0913	1012	1112	1212	1312	1412	1512	1612	1712	1812	1912	2012	2131	...	...	...	...	...	...
Bad Kreuznach .... d.	...	0528	0602	0631	0731	0832	0934	1032	1133	1232	1333	1432	1533	1632	1733	1832	1933	2033	2152	2247	...	...	...	...	...
Mainz Hbf .... ‡ a.	...	0557	0639	0657	0757	0857	1005	1057	1205	1257	1405	1457	1605	1657	1805	1857	2005	2105	2219	2324	...	...	...	...	...
Frankfurt Flughafen ✈ § .... ‡ a.	...	0620	|	0720	0820	0920	...	1120	...	1320	...	1520	...	1720	...	1920	...	...	...	...	...	...	...	...	...
Frankfurt (Main) Hbf .... ‡ a.	...	0636	0724	0736	0836	0936	...	1136	...	1336	...	1536	...	1736	...	1936	...	...	...	...	...	...	...	...	...

– From Bingen (Table **918**).
– Ⓐ (not June 19).
j – Arrives 2204.
w – Does not run on Aug. 15 Neubrücke - Saarbrücken.
* – By 🚌.

BEYOND EUROPE
North America

Introduction

The Beyond Europe section covers principal rail services in a different area of the world each month. There are six areas, each appearing twice yearly as follows:

India:	January and July editions
South East Asia and Australasia:	February and August editions
China:	March and September editions
Japan:	April and October editions
Africa and the Middle East:	May and November editions
North America:	June and December editions

The months have been chosen so that we can bring you up-to-date information for those countries which make seasonal changes.

Limited details of services in South America can be found in the European Rail Timetable Summer and Winter editions.

Contents

INDEX OF PLACES

by table number

CANADA

Capital: **Ottawa** (GMT -5). 2014 Public Holidays: Jan. 1, Apr. 18, 21, May 19, July 1, Sep. 1, Oct. 13, Nov. 11, Dec. 25, 26.

The principal operator in Canada is Via Rail (Via Rail ✆ 1 888 842 7245. www.viarail.ca). Timings shown are the most recently available and are subject to alteration at any time, but especially around public holidays. Details of other operators can be found in relevant tables. Unless otherwise noted all trains carry first and second class seated accomodation. In Canada first class is called 'Via1' and second class is called 'Economy'. Most very long distance trains convey sleeping cars, and where this is the case it is detailed in the footnotes. Almost all sleeping car accommodation in North America has two berths per compartment, some of which are en-suite, although the exact product offering varies by operator and route. Most trains also convey some form of catering, but again the actual service offered varies considerably. Tickets are available from staffed stations, websites and through authorised ticketing agents. A reservation is neccessary for travel on very long distance Via Rail trains, but generally not for corridor services such as Montréal - Ottawa/Toronto and Toronto - Windsor/London/Sarnia.

Via Rail offers the 'Canrailpass'. There are two options, 'System' valid for twenty one days on the whole Via Rail network, and 'Corridor' which is valid for seven days on the Québec City - Montréal - Ottawa - Toronto - Windsor corridor. Both Canrailpass options comprise of seven credits, each of which is valid for a one-way journey in Second class between two stations. Upgrades to other classes of service are not permitted. One complimentary stopover is allowed on each trip. In the case of multiple stopovers, the stopover of longest duration will be considered to be the complimentary stopover. All travel must be reserved in advance. Other terms and conditions apply. For full details see the Via Rail website (www.viarail.ca). Prices: Adult Corridor CA$498, Adult System High Season (June 1 - Oct. 15) CA$1159, Adult System Low Season CA$725. Discounted passes are available to Youths (12 - 25), Children, and Seniors (60+).

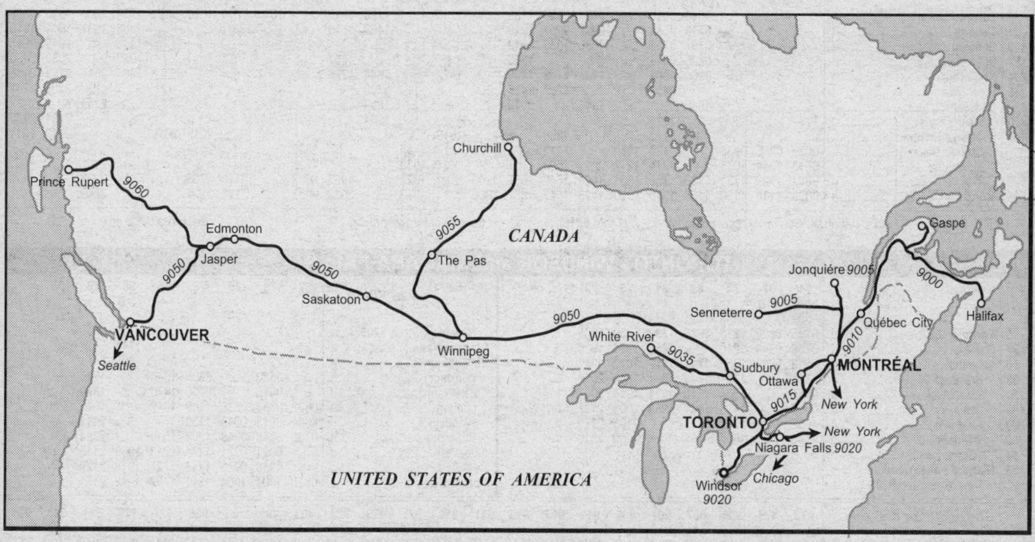

Via Rail — GASPÉ and HALIFAX — 9000

km		15	17
		R	R
		③⑤⑦	③⑤⑦
		A	Z B
1099	**Halifax** d.	1100	...
996	Truro d.	1231	...
872	Amherst d.	1408	...
795	**Moncton** d.	1517	...
795	**Moncton** d.	1532	...
666	Miramichi d.	1808	...
494	Campbellton d.	2149	...
800	**Gaspé** d.	|	1420
737	Percé d.	|	1539
618	Bonaventure d.	|	1830
475	Matapédia d.	2149	2149
325	Mont Joli d.	0024	0024
296	Rimouski d.	0059	0059
192	Rivière du Loup d.	0251	0251
0	**Sainte Foy 9010** a.	0502	0502
	Montréal Central **9010** a.	0915	0915

	16	14
	R	R
	③⑤⑦	③⑤⑦
	Z B	A
Montréal Central **9010** d.	1855	1855
Sainte Foy 9010 d.	2227	2227
Rivière du Loup d.	0055	0055
Rimouski d.	0243	0243
Mont Joli d.	0321	0321
Matapédia d.	0615	0621
Bonaventure d.	0909	|
Percé d.	1158	|
Gaspé a.	1317	|
Campbellton d.	...	0759
Miramichi d.	...	1136
Moncton a.	...	1407
Moncton d.	...	1422
Amherst d.	...	1526
Truro d.	...	1707
Halifax a.	...	1838

A – OCEAN – [2] Montréal - Halifax and v.v.
B – [2] Montréal - Gaspé and v.v.
Z – During infrastructure work currently in progress, trains 16 and 17 will not be operating and train services between Matapédia and Gaspé will be suspended. As an alternative you can travel on trains 14 and 15 between Montréal and Matapédia.

Via Rail — JONQUIÈRE and SENNETERRE — 9005

km		604	600
		R	R
		2	2
		②④⑦	②④⑦
717	**Senneterre** d.	0545**h**	...
561	Clova d.	0750**h**	...
495	Parent d.	0850**h**	...
297	La Tuque d.	1153**h**	...
510	**Jonquière** d.	|	0810**h**
444	Chambord d.	|	0911**h**
341	Lac Édouard d.	|	1105**h**
251	Rivière à Pierre d.	|	1240**h**
217	**Hervey** a.	1325**h**	1350**h**
217	**Hervey** d.	1400**h**	1400**h**
170	Shawinigan d.	1448**h**	1448**h**
0	**Montréal** Central a.	1715**h**	1715**h**

	601	603
	R	R
	2	2
	①③⑤	①③⑤
Montréal Central d.	0815	0815
Shawinigan d.	1043	1043
Hervey a.	1130	1130
Hervey d.	1140	1200
Rivière à Pierre d.	1234	|
Lac Édouard d.	1408	|
Chambord d.	1605	|
Jonquière a.	1710	|
La Tuque d.	...	1318
Parent d.	...	1625
Clova d.	...	1721
Senneterre a.	...	1940

h – 3 hours later on ⑦.

Via Rail — QUÉBEC CITY - MONTRÉAL — 9010

km		15	17	33	23	25	625	27		
		2	2							
		①③⑥	①③⑥	①–⑤			①–⑤			
		A *	B *	C						
0	**Québec City** Palais ▽ d.	...	...	0535	0745	1245	1500	1745	...	...
21	Ste. Foy ▽ d.	0517	0517	0600	0810	1310	1525	1810	...	...
26	Charny ▽ d.	|	|	|	0816**u**	|	|	|	...	...
172	Drummondville d.	0739	0739	0718	0938	1448	1658	1941	...	...
219	St. Hyacinthe d.	0827	0827	|	1025	|	|	2023	...	...
265	St. Lambert ▽ d.	0902	0902	0817	1054	1542	1802	2049	...	...
272	**Montréal** Central ▽ a.	0915	0915	0832	1104	1552	1813	2100	...	...

	20	622	22	24	28	628	16	14	
					C		2	2	
	①–⑤			①–⑤	①–⑤	⑥⑦	③⑤⑦	③⑤⑦	
					C		B *	A *	
Montréal Central ▽ d.	0615	0900	1300	1610	1815	1825	1855	1855	...
St. Lambert ▽ d.	0628	0922	1313	1622	1838	1838	1920	1920	...
St. Hyacinthe d.	0656	0948**u**	|	|	1906	1906	1953	1953	...
Drummondville d.	0722	1023	1407	1723	1950	1950	2035	2025	...
Charny ▽ d.	|	|	1553	|	|	|	|	|	...
Ste. Foy ▽ d.	0901	1156	1600	1905	2112	2112	2212**a**	2212**a**	...
Québec City Palais ▽ a.	0924	1219	1622	1927	2135	2135	...	...	...

A – OCEAN – [2] Montréal Central - Halifax and v.v. (Table **9000**).
B – [2] Montréal Central - Gaspé and v.v. (Table **9000**).
C – [12] Québec City Palais - Montréal Central - Ottawa Union and v.v. (Table **9015**).

– Arrival time.
– Request stop. Calls to pick up only.
– Calls to set down only.

* – A shuttle operates between Sainte-Foy and Québec City Palais R required.
▽ – Local traffic not carried Montréal Cenrtal - St Lambert and v.v., or Québec City Palais - Charny and v.v.

9015 MONTRÉAL - OTTAWA - TORONTO *Via Rail*

km		651 2 ①–⑤	655 2 ⑥	41 ①–⑤	641 ⑥	43 ①–⑤	51 ①–⑤	53 ①–⑥	643 ⑥⑦	33 A ①–⑤	633 ⑥⑦	57		61	45	657 ⑦–⑤	59 ⑦–⑤	65	659	67 ⑦–⑤	37 ①–⑤	639 ⑥⑦	69 ⑤⑦	39 ①–④
0	**Montréal** Central d.	...	...	...	...	...	0620	0645	...	0847	0857	1010	...	1150	...	1250	1455	1540	1600	1700	1705	1750	1830	1915
19	Dorval d.	...	...	...	...	...	0644	0711	...	0919	0919	1035	...	1214	...	1314	1518	1604	1623	1724	1727	1812	1854	1948
100	Alexandria d.	...	...	...	...	...	0734	│	...	1004	1004	│	...	│	...	1359	│	│	│	│	1810	1858	│	2036
187	**Ottawa** Union a.	...	...	...	...	...	0817	│	...	1055	1055	│	...	│	...	1451	1647	│	1802	│	1852	1945	│	2123
187	**Ottawa** Union d.	...	...	0530	0640	0730	0832	│	0900	...	...	│	...	│	1230	1506	1702	│	1817	│	...	...	│	...
253	Smiths Falls d.	...	...	0622	0725	│	0920	│	0948	...	...	│	...	│	│	│	│	│	1909	│	...	...	│	...
	Cornwall d.	...	...	│	│	│	│	0801	│	...	...	1129	...	1305	│	│	│	1655	│	│	...	...	1946	...
298	Brockville d.	...	...	0652	0756	│	0949	│	1021	...	...	1216	...	│	1352	1625	│	│	1943	│	...	...	│	...
378	**Kingston** d.	0532	0645	0735	0839	0922	1033	0926	1104	...	...	1302	...	1431	1438	1709	│	1821	2025	│	...	...	2111	...
451	Belleville d.	0614	0724	0817	0920	│	│	│	1148	...	...	1345	...	│	1525	│	│	│	2106	│	...	...	│	...
520	Cobourg d.	0659	0806	0851	0954	│	1144	│	1221	...	...	1425	...	│	│	1820	│	│	2144	│	...	...	│	...
581	Oshawa d.	0739	0841	0928	1030	│	│	1110	1301	...	...	1501	...	│	1632	1853s	│	2005	2217s	2114s	...	...	2255	...
633	**Toronto** Union a.	0825	0912	1002	1104	1134	1249	1139	1333	...	...	1535	...	1644	1708	1925	2101	2034	2249	2143	...	...	2323	...

km		30 ①–⑤	32 ①–⑤	632 ⑥⑦	52 ①–⑥	50 ①–⑥	634 2 ⑦	56	54	60	28 ①–⑤	44 ①–⑤	38 ①–⑤	644	64	638 ⑥⑦	46 ⑦–⑤	66 ⑦–⑤	656 ⑦–④	646 ⑤	650 ①–⑤	68 ⑤⑦	48 ①–⑥	648 ⑦
0	**Toronto** Union d.	...	...	...	0640	0640	...	0925	0925	1135	...	1215	...	1425	1515	...	1530	1700	1620	1620	1735	1800	1835	1835
51	Oshawa d.	...	...	...	0718	0718	...	0957	0957	1213	...	│	...	1459	1549	...	1607	1731u	│	│	1808	1831	1911	1910
113	Cobourg d.	...	...	...	0751	0751	...	1030	1030	1249	...	│	...	│	│	...	1640	│	│	│	1843	│	1949	1947
182	Belleville d.	...	...	...	0826	0826	...	│	│	1328	...	│	...	│	1657	...	│	│	│	│	1923	│	2032	2030
254	**Kingston** d.	...	...	...	0908	0908	...	1143	1143	1409	...	1422	...	1644	1736	...	1752	│	│	│	2003	2014	2113	2115
335	Brockville d.	...	...	...	│	0959	...	│	1239	1456	...	│	...	1730	│	...	1837	│	│	│	...	│	2201	2202
428	Cornwall d.	...	...	...	1046	│	...	1316	│	1545	...	│	...	1808	1903	...	│	│	│	│	...	2141	│	│
380	Smiths Falls d.	...	...	...	│	1029	...	│	│	│	...	│	...	1904	│	...	│	│	│	│	...	│	2231	2232
446	**Ottawa** Union a.	...	...	...	│	1112	...	│	1358	│	...	1619	...	...	│	...	1951	│	2019	2019	...	│	2313	2314
	Ottawa Union d.	0629	0955	0955	│	1127	1130	│	1413	│	1610	...	1735	...	│	1830	...	│	2034	...	...	│	...	...
	Alexandria d.	0713	1044	1045	│	1214	1217	│	1503	│	│	...	1835	...	│	1925	...	│	│	...	...	│	...	...
520	Dorval d.	0804	1129	1131	1136	1259	1301	1404	1548	1637	1741	...	1923	...	1953	2013	...	2119	2205	...	...	2230	...	...
539	**Montréal** Central a.	0823	1148	1150	1155	1318	1320	1423	1607	1657	1800	...	1943	...	2012	2033	...	2138	2224	...	...	2249	...	...

A – (12) Québec City Palais - Montréal Central - Ottawa Union and v.v. (Table **9010**). s – Calls to set down only. u – Calls to pick up only.

9020 TORONTO - WINDSOR and NIAGARA FALLS *GO Transit, Via Rail*

km	*Via Rail*	71	97 Ⓡ B	73	83 ①–⑤	81 ⑤⑥	75 ⑦–④	79		
0	**Toronto** Union d.	0735	0820	1215	1635	1730	1730	1905	...	...
34	Oakville d.	0759	0844	1240	│	1756	1756	1928	...	...
56	Aldershot d.	0813	0859	1258	1711	1812	1812	1941	...	...
96	Brantford d.	0843	│	1327	1741	1844	1844	2009	...	...
139	Woodstock d.	0910	│	1354	1810	1914	1914	2037	...	...
185	London d.	0950	│	1433	1847	1955	2001	2117	...	...
290	Chatham d.	1052	│	1536	...	...	2105	2219	...	...
360	**Windsor** a.	1143	│	1626	...	...	2159	2310	...	...
114	St. Catharines d.	...	0954	...	...	...	...	...	...	...
133	**Niagara Falls** (Canada) a.	...	1016	...	...	...	...	...	...	...
	New York Penn ***9205*** a.	...	2150	...	...	...	...	...	...	...

Via Rail	82 ①–⑤	70 ①–⑤	80 ⑥⑦	72	76	98 Ⓡ B	78		
New York Penn ***9205*** d.	...	...	...	...	...	0715	...	...	...
Niagara Falls (Canada) d.	...	...	...	...	...	1745	...	...	...
St. Catharines d.	...	...	...	...	...	1808	...	...	...
Windsor d.	...	0530	...	0905	1345	│	1745	...	...
Chatham d.	...	0619	...	0950	1430	│	1830	...	...
London d.	0625	0736	0736	1100	1542	│	1940	...	...
Woodstock d.	0654	0813	0813	1130	│	│	2011	...	...
Brantford d.	0725	0848	0848	1203	1640	│	2044	...	...
Aldershot d.	│	0921	0921	1234	1713	1903	2115	...	...
Oakville d.	│	0938	0938	1248	1727	1918	2129	...	...
Toronto Union a.	0835	1004	1004	1311	1752	1942	2151	...	...

km	*GO Transit - 2nd class only*	473 ①–⑤	475 ①–⑤	905 ⑥⑦	907 ⑥⑦	907 ①–⑤	909	911	913 ⑥⑦	915	917	919	921 ⑥⑦	479 ①–⑤	923 ⑥⑦	493 ①–⑤	495 ①–⑤		925 ⑥⑦	927	929 ⑥⑦	931	933 ⑥⑦	935
0	**Toronto** Union d.	0613	0655	0743	0843	0846	0943	1043	1143	1243	1343	1443	1543	1610	1643	1702	1734	...	1743	1843	1943	2043	2143	2243
34	Oakville d.	0651	0733	0822	0922	0922	1022	1122	1222	1322	1422	1522	1622	1639	1722	1734	1806	...	1822	1922	2022	2122	2222	2322
51	Burlington a.	0710	0752	0842	0941	0941	1042	1142	1242	1342	1442	1542	1642	1658	1742	1754	1826	...	1842	1942	2042	2142	2242	2342
114	St. Catharines a.	*0808**	*0850**	*0940**	*1040**	*1040**	*1140**	*1240**	*1340**	*1440**	*1540**	*1640**	*1740**	*1801**	*1840**	*1852**	*1924**	...	*1940**	*2040**	*2140**	*2240**	*2340**	*0040**
133	**Niagara Falls** (Canada) a.	*0835**	*0917**	*1007**	*1107**	*1107**	*1207**	*1307**	*1407**	*1507**	*1607**	*1707**	*1807**	*1828**	*1907**	*1919**	*1951**	...	*2007**	*2107**	*2207**	*2307**	*0007**	*0107**

GO Transit - 2nd class only		490 ①–⑤	492 ①–⑤	474 ①–⑤	908 ⑥⑦	476 ①–⑤	910 ⑥⑦	912	914	916	918 ⑥⑦	920	922 ⑥⑦	922 ①–⑤	924 ⑥⑦	482 ①–⑤	926 ⑥⑦	928 ①–⑤	928 ⑥⑦	930	932 ⑥⑦	934	936 ⑥⑦	938
Niagara Falls (Canada) d.	...	*0458**	*0518**	*0619**	*0635**	*0709**	*0735**	*0835**	*0935**	*1035**	*1135**	*1235**	*1335**	*1345**	*1435**	*1507**	*1535**	*1631**	*1635**	*1735**	*1835**	*1935**	*2035**	*2135**
St. Catharines d.	...	*0518**	*0538**	*0639**	*0655**	*0729**	*0755**	*0855**	*0955**	*1055**	*1155**	*1255**	*1355**	*1405**	*1455**	*1527**	*1555**	*1651**	*1655**	*1755**	*1855**	*1955**	*2055**	*2155**
Burlington d.	...	0633	0653	0754	0810	0844	0910	1010	1110	1210	1310	1410	1510	1520	1610	1642	1710	1806	1810	1910	2010	2110	2210	2310
Oakville d.	...	0655	0715	0814	0828	0900	0928	1028	1128	1228	1328	1428	1528	1538	1628	1658	1728	1824	1828	1928	2028	2128	2228	2328
Toronto Union a.	...	0725	0743	0852	0910	0933	1010	1111	1211	1311	1410	1511	1610	1623	1711	1741	1810	1907	1910	2011	2110	2211	2310	0011

B – THE MAPLE LEAF – (12) and 🍸 Toronto (**97/98**) - Niagara Falls (**64/63**) - New York and v.v. (Table **9205**). * – Connection by 🚌.

9025 TORONTO - COCHRANE *Ontario Northland*

km		421 ①–⑤ C	🚌
0	**Toronto** Bay Street d.	...	0915
143	Washago d.	...	1145
164	Gravenhurst d.	...	1220
219	Huntsville d.	...	1315
351	**North Bay** a.	...	1450
351	**North Bay** d.	...	1615*
513	Cobalt d.	...	1755
529	New Liskeard d.	...	1825
571	Engleheart d.	...	1920
643	Swastika d.	...	r
677	Matheson d.	...	2115*
754	**Cochrane** a.	...	2230
754	**Cochrane** d.	0900	...
	Fraserdale d.	r	...
	Moose River d.	r	...
1053	**Moosonee** a.	1350	...

	🚌	422 ①–⑤ C
Moosonee d.	...	1700
Moose River d.	...	r
Fraserdale d.	...	r
Cochrane a.	...	2142
Cochrane d.	0830	...
Matheson d.	1000*	...
Swastika d.	r	...
Engleheart d.	1145	...
New Liskeard d.	1245	...
Cobalt d.	1310	...
North Bay a.	1500	...
North Bay d.	1600*	...
Huntsville d.	1740	...
Gravenhurst d.	1850	...
Washago d.	1910	...
Toronto Union a.	2145	...

C – POLAR BEAR EXPRESS – (2) and 🍸 Cochrane - Moosonee and v.v. Ⓡ also ⑦ in summer. r – Calls on request. * - Change buses

9040 HEARST - SAULT STE MARIE *Algoma Central*

km		632 2D ②⑤⑦	632 2E ②⑤⑦
0	**Hearst** d.	0800	0830
82	Oba d.	0915	0945
126	Mosher d.	0955	1030
162	Franz d.	1045	1115
211	Hawk Junction d.	1150	1225
282	Eton d.	1310	1340
292	Agawa Canyon d.	1325	1355
475	**Sault Ste. Marie** a.	1740	1810

	631 2D ①④⑥	631 2E ①④⑥
Sault Ste. Marie d.	0900	0920
Agawa Canyon d.	1305	1325
Eton d.	1320	1340
Hawk Junction d.	1500	1520
Franz d.	1545	1605
Mosher d.	1630	1650
Oba d.	1710	1730
Hearst a.	1840	1900

D – Oct. 30, 2013 - May 6, 2014. E – May 8 - Nov. 4, 2014.

9030 TORONTO - SARNIA *2nd class Via Rail*

km		85	87
0	**Toronto** Union d.	1055	1740
34	Brampton d.	1131	1816
47	Georgetown d.	1142	1827
79	Guelph d.	1208	1852
101	Kitchener d.	1236	1920
143	Stratford d.	1313	1956
195	London d.	1419	2112
290	**Sarnia** a.	...	2218

	84	88
Sarnia d.	0611	...
London d.	0733	1951
Stratford d.	0834	2058
Kitchener d.	0910	2135
Guelph d.	0942	2207
Georgetown d.	1010	2236
Brampton d.	1020	2251
Toronto Union a.	1050	2320

9035 WHITE RIVER - SUDBURY *Via Rail*

km		186 2 ③⑤⑦	
0	**White River** d.	0900	...
79	Franz d.	1020	...
209	Chapleau d.	1315	...
341	Biscotasing d.	1515	...
484	**Sudbury** § a.	1830	...

	185 2 ②④⑥	
Sudbury § d.	0900	...
Biscotasing d.	1130	...
Chapleau d.	1415	...
Franz d.	1630	...
White River a.	1745	...

§ – Sudbury is 10 km from Sudbury Junction (Table **9050**).

9045 THE PAS - PUKATAWAGAN *Keewatin Railway*

km		291 F ①④	
0	**The Pas** d.	1115	...
88	Cranberry Portage d.	1415	...
251	**Pukatawagan** a.	2000	...

	290 F ②⑤	
Pukatawagan d.	1030	...
Cranberry Portage d.	1715	...
The Pas a.	1900	...

F – Operated by Keewatin Railway Company. To book ✆ 204 623 5255.

Via Rail TORONTO - VANCOUVER 9050

km			1 ® A				2 ® A	
0	**Toronto** Union	d.	2200	②⑥	**Vancouver** Pacific	a.	2030	②⑤
143	Washago	d.	0040	③⑦	Agassiz	a.	2233	:
241	Parry Sound	d.	0242	:	**Kamloops** North	a.	0600	③⑥
422	Sudbury Junction	§ d.	0513	:	**Kamloops** North	d.	0635	:
444	**Capreol**	a.	0538	:	Valemount	d.	1250	:
444	**Capreol**	d.	0608	:	**Jasper**	a.	1600	:
683	Foleyet	d.	1059	:	**Jasper**	d.	1730	:
859	Oba	d.	1351	:	Edson	d.	2020	:
921	Hornepayne	d.	1520	:	**Edmonton**	a.	2300	:
1084	Longlac	d.	1749	:	**Edmonton**	d.	2359	:
1537	Sioux Lookout	d.	0009	①④	Wainwright	d.	0315	④⑦
1652	Red Lake Road	d.	0209	:	Biggar	d.	0645	:
1943	**Winnipeg**	a.	0800	:	**Saskatoon**	a.	0800	:
1943	**Winnipeg**	d.	1145	:	**Saskatoon**	d.	0825	:
2032	Portage la Prairie	d.	1309	:	Melville	d.	1240	:
2173	Rivers	d.	1458	:	Rivers	d.	1645	:
2394	Melville	d.	1727	:	Portage la Prairie	d.	1930	:
2702	**Saskatoon**	a.	2207	:	**Winnipeg**	a.	2045	:
2702	**Saskatoon**	d.	2232	:	**Winnipeg**	d.	2230	:
2792	Biggar	d.	2359	:	Red Lake Road	d.	0251	①⑤
3017	Wainwright	d.	0300	②⑤	Sioux Lookout	d.	0542	:
3221	**Edmonton**	a.	0622	:	Longlac	d.	1303	:
3221	**Edmonton**	d.	0737	:	Hornepayne	d.	1610	:
3430	Edson	d.	1013	:	Oba	d.	1710	:
3600	**Jasper**	a.	1300	:	Foleyet	d.	1958	:
3600	**Jasper**	d.	1430	:	**Capreol**	a.	0018	②⑥
3721	Valemount	d.	1607	:	**Capreol**	d.	0048	:
4052	**Kamloops** North	a.	2309	:	Sudbury Junction	§ d.	0117	:
4052	**Kamloops** North	d.	2344	:	Parry Sound	d.	0433	:
4360	Agassiz	d.	|	①③	Washago	d.	0649	:
4466	**Vancouver** Pacific	a.	0942	:	**Toronto** Union	a.	0930	:

A – THE CANADIAN – 1 cl., (2) and ✕ Toronto - Vancouver and v.v. From Toronto on ②⑥ (also ④ Apr. 27 - Oct. 31). From Vancouver on ②⑤ (also ⑦ Apr. 28 - Oct. 31).
r – Request stop.
§ – Sudbury Junction is 10 km from Sudbury (Table **9040**).

Via Rail WINNIPEG - CHURCHILL 9055

km			693 ® B ②④⑦				692 ® B ②④⑥	
0	**Winnipeg**	d.	1205	②⑦	**Churchill**	d.	1930	②④⑥
88	Portage la Prairie	d.	1315r	:	Herchmer	d.	0003	③⑤⑦
283	Dauphin	d.	1706r	:	Giliam (Nelson River)	d.	0530	:
484	Canora	d.	2046	:	**Thompson**	a.	1130	:
549	Endeavour	d.	2154r	:	**Thompson**	d.	1400	:
635	Hudson Bay	d.	2332r	:	Thicket Potage	d.	1622	:
777	**The Pas**	a.	0145	①⑤	Wabowden	d.	1811	:
777	**The Pas**	d.	0230	①③⑤	Cormorant	d.	2147	:
843	Cormorant	d.	0412	:	**The Pas**	a.	2330	③⑤⑦
996	Wabowden	d.	0748	:	**The Pas**	d.	0315	①⑥
1073	Thicket Potage	d.	0937	:	Hudson Bay	d.	0527r	:
1149	**Thompson**	a.	1200	:	Endeavour	d.	0655r	:
1149	**Thompson**	d.	1700	:	Canora	d.	0818	:
1401	Giliam (Nelson River)	d.	2330	:	Dauphin	d.	1206	:
1540	Herchmer	d.	0426	②④⑥	Portage la Prairie	d.	1537r	:
1697	**Churchill**	a.	0900	②④⑥	**Winnipeg**	a.	1645	①⑥

B – 1 cl., (2) and ✕ Churchill - Winnipeg and v.v.
r – Request stop.

Via Rail PRINCE RUPERT - JASPER 9060

km			5 ® C ③⑤⑦				6 ® C ③⑤⑦	
0	**Jasper**	d.	1245	③⑤⑦	**Prince Rupert**	d.	0800	③⑤⑦
174	McBride	d.	1444	:	Terrace (Kitimat)	d.	1025	:
409	**Prince George**	a.	1908	:	New Hazelton	d.	1230r	:
409	**Prince George**	d.	0800	①④⑥	Smithers	d.	1424	:
560	Fort Fraser	d.	1032r	:	Fort Fraser	d.	1757r	:
795	Smithers	d.	1420	:	**Prince George**	a.	2029	:
869	New Hazelton	d.	1537r	:	**Prince George**	d.	0945	①④⑥
1007	Terrace (Kitimat)	d.	1805	:	McBride	d.	1348	:
1160	**Prince Rupert**	a.	2025	:	**Jasper**	a.	1830	:

C – (2) and 🍸 (Also (1) and ✕, June 15, 20, 25, 29, Jul. 4, 9, 13, 18, 23, 27, Aug.1, 6, 10, 15, 20, 24, 29, Sep. 3, 7, 12, 17, 21, 26). Compulsory overnight stop in Prince George. Passengers must arrange their own accommodation.
r – Request stop.

RMR ROCKY MOUNTAINEER TOURS 9065

		D	E	F	G			G	E	D	F
Vancouver ‡	d.	0730	0730	...	...	**Calgary**	d.	...	...	0615	...
N. Vancouver	d.	|	|	0730	...	Banff	d.	...	...	0830	...
Whistler	a.	|	|	1130	...	Lake Louise	d.	...	...	0945	
Whistler	d.	|	|	...	0715	**Jasper**	d.	0700	0815	|	...
Quesnel ♥	a.	|	|	...	2030	Kamloops ♥	a.	|	1800	2000	...
Quesnel ♥	d.	|	|	...	0715	Kamloops ♥	d.	|	0730	0730	...
Kamloops ♥	a.	1830	1830	...	|	Quesnel ♥	a.	1930	|	|	...
Kamloops ♥	d.	0630	0745	...	|	Quesnel ♥	d.	0715	|	|	...
Jasper	a.	|	1900	...	2100	Whistler	a.	2030	|	|	...
Lake Louise	a.	1930	...	...	...	Whistler	d.	...	|	|	1500
Banff	a.	2030	...	...	...	**N. Vancouver**	a.	...	|	|	1900
Calgary	a.	2215	...	...	...	**Vancover** ‡	a.	...	1830	1830	...

D – FIRST PASSAGE TO THE WEST – For 2014 dates contact operator.
E – JOURNEY THROUGH THE CLOUDS – For 2014 dates contact operator.
F – WHISTLER SEA TO SKY CLIMB – For 2014 dates contact operator.
G – RAINFOREST TO GOLD RUSH – For 2014 dates contact operator.
‡ – Vancouver Cottrell Street.
♥ – Compulsory overnight stop.
Operator: Rocky Mountaineer Railtours (www.rockymountaineer.com)

West Coast VANCOUVER - MISSION CITY 9070

km			①-⑤	①-⑤		①-⑤	①-⑤		①-⑤	
0	**Vancouver** Waterfront	d.	1550	1620	...	1650	1730	...	1820	...
26	Coquitlam	d.	1619	1649	...	1719	1759	...	1849	...
68	**Mission City**	a.	1705	1735	...	1805	1845	...	1935	...

			①-⑤	①-⑤		①-⑤	①-⑤		①-⑤	
Mission City	d.	...	0525	0555	...	0625	0655	...	0725	...
Coquitlam	d.	...	0610	0640	...	0710	0740	...	0810	...
Vancouver Waterfront	a.	...	0640	0710	...	0740	0810	...	0840	...

Operator: West Coast Express ✆ 604 488 8906.

Greyhound CALGARY - EDMONTON 9090

km			5200	5204	5206	5208	5210	5214	5216 ⑤⑦	5218	5222 ⑤⑦	5224
0	**Calgary**	d.	0030	0700	0800	1201	1300	1600	1700	1800	1900	2000
303	**Edmonton**	a.	0605	1030	1150	1530	1720	1950	2030	2150	2230	2350

			5201	5205	5207	5211	5209	5215	5217 ⑤⑦	5219	5223 ⑤⑦	5225
Edmonton	d.	...	0045	0700	0800	1300	1400	1600	1700	1800	1900	2000
Calgary	a.	...	0610	1020	1150	1720	1750	1930	2030	2150	2230	2350

UNITED STATES OF AMERICA

Capital: **Washington DC** (GMT -5, add one hour in summer). 2014 Public Holidays: Jan. 1, 20, Feb. 17, May 26, July 4, Sep. 1, Oct. 13, Nov. 11, 27, Dec. 25.

The principal operator in the USA is Amtrak (✆ 1 800 872 7245. www.amtrak.com). Details of other operators can be found in relevant tables. Unless otherwise noted all trains carry first and second class seated accomodation known as 'Business' and 'Coach' class respectively. Acela Express trains running between Boston, New York and Washington convey business class and an enhanced seated accommodation, confusingly called 'First Class'. Most very long distance trains convey sleeping cars, and where this is the case it is detailed in the footnotes. Almost all sleeping car accommodation in North America has two berths per compartment, some of which are en-suite, although the exact product offering varies by operator and route. Most trains also convey some form of catering, but again the actual service offered varies considerably. Timings shown are the latest available and are subject to alteration around public holidays and it is recommended that you confirm all timings locally as short notice changes are possible. Tickets are available from staffed stations, websites and through authorised ticketing agents. Amtrak requires reservations on practically all of its services, and also requires that you have identity documents available for inspection.

Amtrak offers the 'USA Rail Pass' It is available to both US citizens and foreign nationals and has the option of three validity periods: 15 day/8 segments of travel, 30 day/12 segments of travel and 45 day/18 segments of travel. The pass is valid in coach class on the entire Amtrak system. Be warned though: this program is now revenue/capacity managed and may not be available on all trains all the time. The pass allows travel from the USA to Vancouver in British Columbia and to Montréal in Quebec, but the pass is not valid on services to Toronto. The pass is also not valid on the Autotrain, Acela Express trains or on certain Thruway buses. The pass alone is not valid for travel; tickets and where neccessary reservations, must be obtained for each segment of travel. Upgrades to higher levels of accommodation may be possible subject to capacity and the payment of relevant supplements. Travel is limited to no more than four one-way journeys over any given route segment. A segment is any time you get on and then get off a train or bus, regardless of the length of that journey. For full details see the Amtrak website (www.amtrak.com).

White Pass and Yukon Railroad SKAGWAY - WHITEHORSE 9100

km			1 A	🚌			🚌	2 A
0	**Skagway** Shops	d.	0730	1400	**Whitehorse**	d.	0730	...
22	White Pass	🚌 d.	|	|	Carcross	a.	0845	...
41	Fraser	a.	0900	1445	Carcross	d.	0845	1130
41	Fraser	d.	0900	1500	Bennett	a.	|	1255
65	Bennett	a.	1015	|	Bennett	d.	|	1410
65	Bennett	d.	1130	|	Fraser	a.	1000	1500
108	Carcross	a.	1300	1600	Fraser	d.	1000	1505
108	Carcross	d.	...	1600	White Pass	🚌 d.	|	|
177	**Whitehorse**	a.	...	1730	**Skagway** Shops	a.	1100	1645

☛ For services crossing the US / Canadian border passengers must provide proof of citizenship. All services ®. All times shown are Alaska time. Additional excursions such as Skagway - Fraser and v.v. and White Pass Summit are available.

A – May 28 - Sept. 5. From Skagway ③④⑥. From Carcross ②⑤.

Operator: White Pass & Yukon Railroad ✆ Skagway 907 983 2217. www.wpyr.com

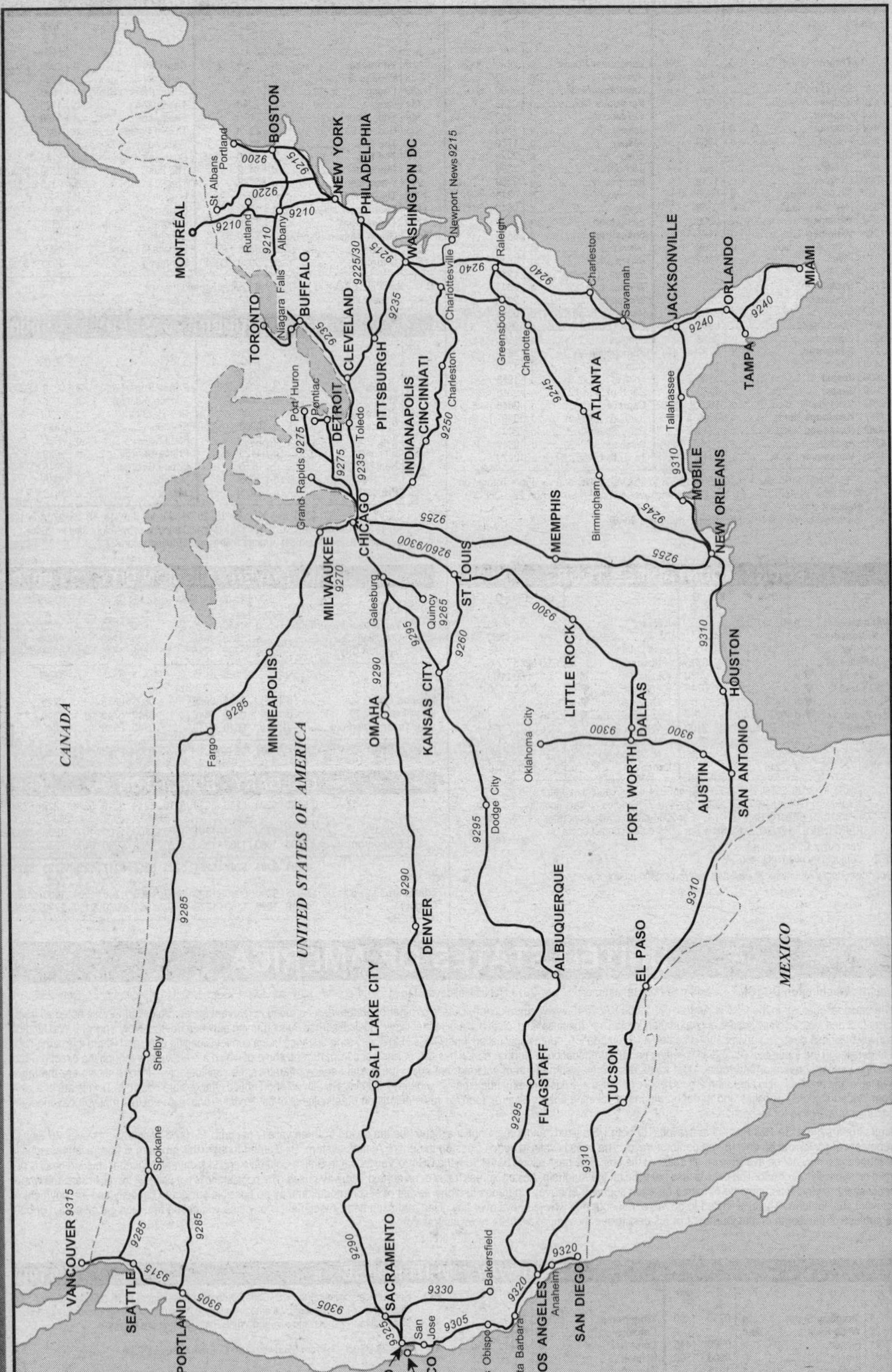
CANADA
UNITED STATES OF AMERICA
MEXICO
MONTRÉAL
St Albans
Portland
BOSTON
NEW YORK
PHILADELPHIA
WASHINGTON DC
Newport News
Rutland
Albany
TORONTO
Niagara Falls
BUFFALO
CLEVELAND
PITTSBURGH
Toledo
DETROIT
Pontiac
Port Huron
Grand Rapids
CHICAGO
INDIANAPOLIS
CINCINNATI
Charlottesville
Charleston
Raleigh
Greensboro
Charlotte
Savannah
JACKSONVILLE
ORLANDO
MIAMI
TAMPA
Tallahassee
ATLANTA
Birmingham
MOBILE
NEW ORLEANS
MEMPHIS
MILWAUKEE
ST LOUIS
Galesburg
Quincy
KANSAS CITY
LITTLE ROCK
DALLAS
FORT WORTH
Oklahoma City
HOUSTON
AUSTIN
SAN ANTONIO
MINNEAPOLIS
Fargo
OMAHA
Dodge City
DENVER
ALBUQUERQUE
EL PASO
SALT LAKE CITY
FLAGSTAFF
TUCSON
Shelby
Spokane
VANCOUVER
SEATTLE
PORTLAND
SACRAMENTO
OAKLAND
SAN FRANCISCO
San Jose
Bakersfield
San Luis Obispo
Santa Barbara
LOS ANGELES
Anaheim
SAN DIEGO
9200
9210
9215
9220
9225/30
9235
9240
9245
9250
9255
9260
9260/9300
9265
9270
9275
9285
9290
9295
9300
9305
9310
9315
9320
9325
9330

Alaska Railroad — ALASKA — 9105

km			D	E	Ab	Ba	B	C
						④	⑦	④–⑦
0	**Fairbanks**	d.	...	...	0815	...	0830	...
195	Denali	d.	...	...	1230	...	1230	...
305	Hurricane	d.	...	...	|	1445	1445	1600
392	Talkeetna	d.	...	...	1655	1650	1650	1900
498	Wasilla	d.	...	...	1815	1825	1825	...
572	**Anchorage**	a.	...	...	2000	2000	2000	...
572	**Anchorage**	d.	0645	0945	...	...	...	...
636	Girdwood	d.	0800	1100	...	...	...	...
652	**Portage**	a.	|	1130	...	...	...	...
20a	Whittier	d.	|	1245	...	...	...	...
652	**Portage**	d.	|	1325	...	...	...	...
666	Spencer	a.	|	1345	...	...	...	...
666	Spencer	d.	|	1355	...	...	...	...
683	Grandview	a.	|	1520	...	...	...	...
750	**Seward**	a.	1105	...	...	...	...	...

		Aa	B	Ba	C	E	D
			⑥	④	④–⑦		
Seward	d.	...	...	...	...	...	1800
Grandview	d.	...	...	...	...	1530	|
Spencer	a.	...	...	...	...	1630	|
Spencer	d.	...	...	...	...	1640	|
Portage	a.	...	...	...	...	1715	|
Whittier	d.	...	...	...	...	1845	|
Portage	d.	...	...	...	...	1920	|
Girdwood	d.	...	...	...	...	1940	2055
Anchorage	a.	...	...	...	...	2115	2215
Anchorage	d.	0815	0830	0830	....	...	...
Wasilla	d.	0935	0950	0950	....	...	...
Talkeetna	d.	1120	1125	1125	1245	...	...
Hurricane	a.	|	1340	1340	1500	...	...
Denali	d.	1600	1555	...	...	...	...
Fairbanks	a.	2000	2000	...	....	...	...

A – DENALI STAR – [2] and ✕ (**Aa** May 14 - Sep. 13. **Ab** May 15 - Sep. 14)
B – [2] Sep 21 - May 5.
Ba 1st ④ of every month Oct 3. - May 1.
C – HURRICANE TURN – [2] May 15 - Sept. 14.
D – COASTAL CLASSIC – [2] and ✕ May 10 - Sep. 14.
E – GLACIER DISCOVERY – [2] and ✕ June 1 - Sep. 14.
a – Kms from Portage.
Operator : Alaska Railroad ✆ Anchorage 907 265 2620. Fax 907 265 2323.

Amtrak — BRUNSWICK - PORTLAND - BOSTON — 9200

km			680	690	682	692	684	694	686	696	688	698
			①–⑤	⑥⑦	①–⑤	⑥⑦	①–⑤	⑥⑦	①–⑤	⑥⑦	①–⑤	⑥⑦
0	**Brunswick**	d.	...	...	0705	0705	...	...	...	...	1755	1755
	Freeport	d.	...	...	0720	0720	...	...	...	...	1810	1810
47	Portland	d.	0520	0535	0800	0800	1245	1245	1435	1450	1850	1850
66	Old Orchard Beach ≪	d.	0535	0550	0815	0815	1300	1300	1450	1505	1905	1905
72	Saco	d.	0542	0557	0822	0822	1307	1307	1457	1512	1912	1912
98	Wells	d.	0559	0614	0839	0839	1324	1324	1514	1529	1929	1929
124	Dover	d.	0617	0632	0857	0857	1342	1342	1533	1547	1947	1947
133	Durham	d.	0625	0639	0905	0905	1350	1350	1540	1555	1955	1955
151	Exeter	d.	0639	0652	0918	0918	1403	1403	1553	1608	2008	2008
178	Haverhill	d.	0700	0712	0939	0939	1424	1424	1614	1629	2029	2029
232	**Boston** North	a.	0750	0800	1030	1030	1515	1515	1705	1720	2120	2120

		681	691	693	683	685	695	687	697	699	689
		①–⑤	⑥⑦	⑥⑦	①–⑤	①–⑤	⑥⑦	①–⑤	⑥⑦	⑥⑦	①–⑤
Boston North	d.	0905	0905	1135	1135	1700	1700	1740	1930	2320	2320
Haverhill	d.	0953	0953	1223	1223	1748	1748	1827	2018	0007r	0008r
Exeter	d.	1014	1014	1244	1244	1809	1809	1847	2039	0027r	0029r
Durham	d.	1027	1027	1257	1257	1822	1822	1900	2052	0040r	0042r
Dover	d.	1035	1035	1304	1305	1830	1830	1907	2059	0047r	0050r
Wells	d.	1053	1053	1321	1323	1848	1848	1925	2116	0105r	0108r
Saco	d.	1110	1110	1338	1340	1905	1905	1945	2133	0121r	0124r
Old Orchard Beach ≪	d.	1115	1115	1343	1345	1910	1910	1950	2138	0123r	0126r
Portland	a.	1140	1140	1400	1405	1935	1935	2010	2155	0145	0145
Freeport	a.	1210	1210	...	...	2005	2005	...	...	...	...
Brunswick	a.	1225	1225	...	...	2020	2020	...	...	...	...

r – Calls on request. ≪ – Seasonal stop. Station open mid-June to mid-October.

Amtrak — NEW YORK - ALBANY - RUTLAND, MONTREÁL and NIAGARA FALLS — 9210

km			63	69	281	233	283	235	291	255	49	237	253	239	293	241	243	259	245	261
								①–⑤	⑥–④	⑤		①–⑤	⑥⑦	①–④	⑤		①–⑤	⑥⑦	①–⑤	⑥⑦
			F	2H	J		J		K		G				K					
0	**New York** Penn ▼	d.	0715	0815	1020	1120	1320	1420	1515	1515	1540	1640	1715	1747	1747	1915	2055	2115	2245	2335
24	Yonkers ▼	d.	0739	0844	|	1144	1344	1444	1539	1539	|	|	1739	|	|	1939	2119	2139	|	|
54	Croton Harmon ▼	d.	0759	0903	1101	1203	1403	1503	1558	1558	1626u	|	1758	1832	1830	1958	2138	2158	2326	0016
118	Poughkeepsie ▼	d.	0840	0943	1143	1245	1445	1545	1640	1640	1710u	|	1840	1922	1911	2040	2220	2240	0008	0058
142	Rhinecliff Kingston	d.	0855	0957	1158	1300	1500	1600	1655	1655	|	1813	1855	1932	1932	2055	2236	2255	0023	0113
184	Hudson	d.	0915	1020	1218	1320	1520	1620	1715	1715	|	1833	1915	1953	1953	2115	2256	2315	0043	0134
229	**Albany** Rensselaer	a.	0945	1050	1245	1350	1545	1650	1745	1745	1820u	1900	1945	2015	2015	2145	2325	2345	0115	0205
229	**Albany** Rensselaer	d.	1000	1105	1300	...	1600	...	1800	...	1905u	...	...	...	2025	...	...	...	...	...
258	Schenectady	d.	1024	1129	1323	...	1623	...	1824	...	1931	...	...	...	2049	...	...	...	...	...
288	Saratoga Springs	d.	|	1157	|	...	|	...	1850	...	|	...	...	...	2115	...	...	...	...	...
391	**Rutland**	a.	|	|	|	...	|	...	2048	...	|	...	...	...	2313	...	...	...	...	...
436	Westport	d.	|	1408	|	...	|	...	...	...	|	...	...	...	...	...	...	...	...	...
500	Plattsburgh	d.	|	1512	|	...	|	...	...	...	|	...	...	...	...	...	...	...	...	...
617	**Montréal** Central	a.	|	1906	|	...	|	...	...	...	|	...	...	...	...	...	...	...	...	...
382	Utica	d.	1141	...	1440	...	1744	...	...	...	2044	...	...	...	...	...	...	...	...	...
459	Syracuse	d.	1243	...	1540	...	1852	...	...	...	2141	...	...	...	...	...	...	...	...	...
597	Rochester	d.	1357	...	1659	...	2006	...	...	...	2300	...	...	...	...	...	...	...	...	...
706	Buffalo Exchange St.	a.	1514	...	1824	...	2131	...	...	...	2359d	...	...	...	...	...	...	...	...	...
745	**Niagara Falls** USA	a.	1623	...	1940	...	2240	...	...	...	...	...	...	...	...	...	...	...	...	...
	Toronto Union **9020**	a.	1942	...	...	...	...	...	...	...	...	...	...	...	...	...	...	...	...	...

		230	232	250	234	252	236	280	254	290	238	284	256	292	242	48	244	68	64	296	288
		①–⑤	①–⑤	⑥⑦	①–⑤	⑥		①–⑥	⑦	①–⑤			⑦	⑥	①–⑤					⑦	⑦
								J		K		J		K		G		2H	F	K	J
Toronto Union **9020**	d.	...	...	...	...	...	...	...	...	...	...	...	...	...	...	...	...	...	0820	...	...
Niagara Falls USA	d.	...	...	...	...	...	...	0345	...	...	...	0635	...	...	...	...	...	...	1230	...	1450
Buffalo Exchange St	d.	...	...	...	...	...	...	0410	...	...	...	0710	...	...	...	0908d	...	...	1305	...	1526
Rochester	d.	...	...	...	...	...	...	0531	...	...	...	0821	...	...	...	1008	...	...	1413	...	1637
Syracuse	d.	...	...	...	...	...	...	0653	...	...	...	0945	...	...	...	1138	...	...	1528	...	1757
Utica	d.	...	...	...	...	...	...	0748	...	...	...	1040	...	...	...	1242	...	...	1629	...	1852
Montréal Central	d.	...	...	...	...	...	...	|	...	...	...	|	...	...	...	|	...	0930	|	...	|
Plattsburgh	d.	...	...	...	...	...	...	|	...	...	...	|	...	...	...	|	...	1235	|	...	|
Westport	d.	...	...	...	...	...	...	|	...	...	...	|	...	...	...	|	...	1340	|	...	|
Rutland	d.	...	...	...	...	...	...	|	...	0800	...	|	...	1100	...	|	...	|	|	1705	|
Saratoga Springs	d.	...	...	...	...	...	...	|	...	0937	...	|	...	1236	...	|	...	1548	|	1847	|
Schenectady	d.	...	...	...	...	...	...	0925	...	1023	...	1225	...	1315	...	1400	...	1645	1827	1928	2032
Albany Rensselaer	a.	...	...	...	...	...	...	0955	...	1053	...	1255	...	1345	...	1450s	...	1715	1855	1953	2105
Albany Rensselaer	d.	0505	0555	0615	0655	0715	0820	1010	1010	1115	1210	1310	1415	1415	1510	1545s	1610	1740	1915	2015	2115
Hudson	d.	0530	0620	0640	0720	0740	0845	1035	1035	1140	1236	1335	1440	1440	1536	|	1635	1805	1940	2040	2140
Rhinecliff Kingston	d.	0550	0640	0701	0742	0801	0906	1056	1056	1201	1257	1355	1500	1500	1558	1631s	1657	1828	2001	2101	2201
Poughkeepsie ▼	d.	|	|	0715	|	0815	0920	1115	1115	1215	1315	1415	1515	1515	1615	1649s	1715	1845	2015	2115	2215
Croton Harmon ▼	d.	0643	0731	0755	|	0855	0958	1155	1155	1255	1355	1455	1555	1555	1655	1735s	1755	1925	2055	2155	2255
Yonkers ▼	d.	|	|	0816	|	0916	1019	|	|	1316	1416	1516	1616	1616	1715	|	|	1946	2116	2216	|
New York Penn ▼	a.	0730	0815	0850	0920	0950	1050	1250	1250	1350	1450	1550	1650	1650	1746	1823	1850	2020	2145	2250	2345

– THE MAPLE LEAF – [12] and 🍷 Toronto (**97/98**) - Niagara Falls (**64/63**) - New York and v.v. (Table **9020**).
– LAKE SHORE LIMITED – 🛏 1, 2 cl., [2] and ✕ New York - Albany - Chicago and v.v.
– ADIRONDACK – [2] and 🍷 New York - Montréal and v.v.
– EMPIRE SERVICE – [12] and 🍷 New York - Niagara Falls and v.v.
– ETHAN ALLEN EXPRESS – [12] and 🍷 New York - Rutland and v.v.

d – Buffalo **Depew**.
s – Calls to set down only.
u – Calls to pick up only.
▼ – Local traffic not carried. Frequent services are operated by Metro North Railroad.

9215 BOSTON - NEW YORK - WASHINGTON - NEWPORT NEWS

Most trains 🍸 Amtrak

km						*Acela*						*Acela*			*Acela*	*Acela*			*Acela*	*Acela*			*Acela*	*Acela*
		67	**151**	**111**	**121**	**2103**	**181**	**89**	**131**	**51**		**2107**	**79**	**183**	**2109**	**2203**	**153**	**185**	**2151**	**2205**	**155**	**141**	**2153**	**2207**
			①–⑤	①–⑤	⑥	①–⑤	①–⑤		⑥⑦	③⑤⑦		①–⑤		①–⑤	①–⑤	⑥	⑥⑦	①–⑤	①–⑤	⑦	⑥⑦	①–⑤	①–⑤	⑥
								♦		♦			♦											
0	**Boston** South d.	2130	...	...	...	...	...	...	...	...	...	...	...	...	...	...	...	...	0505	...	...	...	0605	...
69	Providence d.	2222	...	...	...	...	...	...	...	...	...	...	...	...	...	...	...	...	0540	...	...	...	0643	...
169	New London d.	2331	...	...	...	...	...	...	...	...	...	...	...	...	...	...	...	...	0624	...	...	...	|	...
	Springfield MA d.	|	...	...	...	...	...	...	...	...	...	...	...	...	...	...	...	...	|	...	...	0555	|	...
	Hartford d.	|	...	...	...	...	...	...	...	...	...	...	...	...	...	...	...	...	|	...	...	0635	|	...
251	New Haven d.	0035	...	...	...	...	...	...	...	...	...	...	...	...	...	...	...	...	0706	...	...	0737	0814	...
301	Stamford d.	0121	...	...	...	...	...	...	...	...	...	...	...	...	...	...	...	...	0752	...	...	0827	|	...
373	**New York** Penn a.	0215	...	...	...	...	...	...	...	...	...	...	...	...	...	...	...	...	0844	...	...	0921	0945	...
373	**New York** Penn d.	0300	0440	0530	0545	0600	0610	0605	0645	0645	...	0700	0705	0717	0800	0800	0805	0810	0900	0900	0905	0935	1000	1000
389	Newark NJ d.	0320	0456	0546u	0601u	0615u	0626	0622u	0701	0705u	...	0715u	0724u	0733	0815u	0814	0821u	0826	0915	0914u	0921	0951	1015	1014u
519	**Philadelphia** 30th Street d.	0440	0605	0655	0710	0720	0745	0732u	0813	0815u	...	0817	0835	0845	0912	0912	0933	0939	1010	1012	1030	1110	1110	1112
670	Baltimore Penn d.	0610	0732	0800	0822	0820	0859	0850u	0930	0929u	...	0917	0945	0951	1012	1015	1043	1045	1111	1115	1140	1217	1210	1215
687	BWI Airport d.	0623	0746	0813	0834	|	0911	|	0943	|	...	|	|	1004	|	1027	1055	1057	1124	1127	1152	1229	1222	1227
735	**Washington** Union a.	0657	0815	0845	0910	0855	0950	0955u	1016	1105u	...	0958	1025	1040	1058	1052	1130	1135	1158	1152	1225	1300	1245	1252
735	**Washington** Union d.	0730	...	...	...	...	...	0955u	...	1105u	...	...	1055	...	...	...	...	...	...	...	...	...	...	...
822	Fredricksburg d.	0835	...	...	...	...	...	|	...	|	...	...	1157	...	...	...	...	...	...	...	...	...	...	...
911	Richmond d.	0945	...	...	...	...	...	1150	...	|	...	...	1302	...	...	...	...	...	...	...	...	...	...	...
1042	**Newport News** a.	1150	...	...	...	...	...	...	...	|	...	...	...	...	...	...	...	...	...	...	...	...	...	...
1092	Norfolk a.	*1250**	...	...	...	...	...	...	...	|	...	...	...	...	...	...	...	...	...	...	...	...	...	...
	Virgina Beach a.	*1330**	...	...	...	...	...	...	...	|	...	...	...	...	...	...	...	...	...	...	...	...	...	...
915	Charlottesville d.	...	...	...	...	...	...	...	...	1355	...	...	...	...	...	...	...	...	...	...	...	...	...	...
1012	**Lynchburg** a.	...	...	...	...	...	...	...	...	...	...	...	...	...	...	...	...	...	...	...	...	...	...	...

				Acela	*Acela*					*Acela*	*Acela*	*Acela*						*Acela*		*Acela*				
	143	**495**	**95**	**2155**	**2211**	**91**	**405**	**195**	**125**	**2117**	**2251**	**2213**	**147**	**157**	**145**	**171**	**99**	**2159**	**133**	**2121**	**493**	**401**	**93**	**83**
	⑥⑦	①–⑤	①–⑤	①–⑤	⑦		⑥⑦	⑥⑦	①–⑤	①–⑤	⑥	⑦	⑥	⑦	⑦	①–⑤	⑥⑦	①–⑤	⑤	①–⑤	①–⑤	⑥⑦	①–④	⑤
		2				♦	2														2	2		
Boston South d.	...	...	0610	0715	...	...	...	0640	...	...	0810	...	...	...	...	0815	0840	0915	...	...	...	...	0930	0930
Providence d.	...	...	0650	0750	...	...	...	0720	...	...	0845	...	...	...	...	0854	0919	0950	...	...	...	...	1011	1011
New London d.	...	...	0745	|	...	...	...	0817	...	...	|	...	...	...	...	0945	1019	|	...	...	...	...	1112	1112
Springfield MA d.	0630	0710	|	|	...	...	0730	|	...	...	|	...	0800	...	0905	|	|	|	...	...	1030	1040	|	|
Hartford d.	0708	0745	|	|	...	...	0805	|	...	...	|	...	0837	...	0941	|	|	|	...	...	1103	1114	|	|
New Haven d.	0809	0835	0843	|	...	...	0855	0909	...	...	1013	...	0939	...	1039	1040	1109	1113	...	...	1150	1200	1209	1209
Stamford d.	0858	...	0930	0954	...	...	...	0958	...	...	1058	...	1028	...	1128	1129	1158	1158	...	...	...	...	1258	1258
New York Penn a.	0950	...	1021	1045	...	...	...	1050	...	...	1145	...	1125	...	1225	1220	1252	1245	...	...	...	...	1348	1348
New York Penn d.	1005	...	1035	1100	1100	1102	...	1105	1135	1200	1200	1200	1205	1205	1255	1235	1317	1300	1309	1400	...	...	1402	1402
Newark NJ d.	1021	...	1051	1115	1114u	1122u	...	1122	1151	1215u	1214	1214u	1221	1221	1311	1251	1334	1315	1325u	1415u	...	...	1418	1418
Philadelphia 30th Street d.	1133	...	1200	1212	1212	1235u	...	1234	1313	1312	1312	1312	1333	1333	1417	1408	1448	1408	1429	1508	...	...	1527	1527
Baltimore Penn d.	1243	...	1314	1312	1315	1355u	...	1340	1422	1415	1415	1415	1443	1443	1525	1530	1553	1508	1540	1608	...	...	1634	1634
BWI Airport d.	1255	...	1327	|	1327	|	...	1352	1435	|	1426	1427	1455	1455	1537	1544	1605	1521	1552	1620	...	...	1646	1646
Washington Union a.	1330	...	1400	1345	1352	1505u	...	1425	1505	1455	1452	1452	1530	1530	1612	1620	1635	1558	1625	1655	...	...	1720	1720
Washington Union d.	...	...	1430	...	...	1505u	...	1450	1555	...	...	...	1600	1600	1650	1650	1700	...	...	...	...	...	1750	1750
Fredricksburg d.	...	...	1539	...	...	|	...	1600	1713	...	...	...	|	1711	|	|	1807	...	...	...	...	...	1858	1858
Richmond d.	...	...	1645	...	...	1709	...	1705	1826	..	...	...	|	1824	|	|	1910	...	...	...	...	...	2007	2010
Newport News a.	...	...	1850	...	...	...	...	...	|	...	...	...	|	|	|	|	2110	...	...	...	...	...	...	2210
Norfolk a.	...	...	*1950**	...	...	...	...	...	2050	...	...	...	|	2048	|	|	*2155**	...	...	...	...	...	...	*2255**
Virgina Beach a.	...	...	*2030**	...	...	...	...	...	...	...	...	...	|	...	|	|	*2225**	...	...	...	...	...	...	*2325**
Charlottesville d.	...	...	...	...	...	...	...	...	...	...	...	...	1826	...	1916	1923	...	...	...	...	...	...	...	...
Lynchburg a.	...	...	...	...	...	...	...	...	...	...	...	...	1939	...	2029	2036	...	...	...	...	...	...	...	...

			Acela	*Acela*							*Acela*	*Acela*				*Acela*	*Acela*			*Acela*	*Acela*			
	161	**19**	**2253**	**2163**	**85**	**87**	**71**	**97**	**173**	**463**	**2165**	**2221**	**127**	**163**	**129**	**2167**	**2255**	**159**	**193**	**2119**	**2225**	**135**	**137**	**55**
	⑥⑦		⑥⑦	①–⑤	①–⑤	⑦	⑥		①–⑤	⑥⑦	①–⑤	⑦	①–⑤	⑥⑦	①–⑤	①–⑤	⑦	⑥⑦	①–⑤	①–⑤	⑦	⑥⑦	①–⑤	①–⑤
		♦						♦		2														♦
Boston South d.	0940	...	1110	1110	...	...	...	...	1115	...	1210	...	...	1140	...	1310	1310	...	...	...	...	1340	1340	...
Providence d.	1020	...	1144	1146	...	...	...	...	1156	...	1246	...	...	1220	...	1346	1344	...	...	...	...	1419	1421	...
New London d.	1115	...	|	|	...	...	...	...	1248	...	|	...	...	1318	...	|	|	...	...	...	...	1513	1514	...
Springfield MA d.	|	...	|	|	...	...	...	...	|	1240	|	...	...	|	...	|	|	...	...	...	...	|	|	1450
Hartford d.	|	...	|	|	...	...	...	...	|	1316	|	...	...	|	...	|	|	...	...	...	...	|	|	1532
New Haven d.	1209	...	1313	1313	...	...	...	...	1340	1405	1413	...	...	1409	...	1513	1513	...	...	...	...	1609	1609	1639
Stamford d.	1258	...	1358	1356	...	...	...	...	1429	...	1458	...	...	1458	...	1558	1558	...	...	...	...	1658	1658	1728
New York Penn a.	1352	...	1445	1445	...	...	...	...	1520	...	1545	...	...	1550	...	1645	1645	...	...	...	...	1750	1800	1825
New York Penn d.	1405	1415	1500	1500	1505	1504	1504	1515	1535	...	1600	1600	1605	1605	1642	1700	1700	1705	1739	1800	1800	1805	1825	1845
Newark NJ d.	1421	1437u	1514	1515	1522	1520	1520	1538u	1551	...	1615	1614u	1622	1621	1658u	1715	1714	1721	1756	1815u	1814u	1821	1841	1903
Philadelphia 30th Street d.	1533	1555u	1617	1608	1630	1635	1635	1658u	1655	...	1708	1712	1733	1735	1809	1808	1812	1833	1904	1908	1912	1933	1954	2010
Baltimore Penn d.	1645	1712u	1718	1708	1742	1748	1748	1814u	1802	...	1810	1815	1840	1844	1924	1908	1915	1940	2021	2008	2015	2050	2100	2120
BWI Airport d.	1657	|	1730	1720	1755	1759	1759	|	1814	...	1822	1827	1852	1856	1936	1920	1927	1952	2033	2020	2027	2102	2112	|
Washington Union a.	1730	1830u	1755	1745	1825	1835	1835	1930u	1845	...	1848	1852	1925	1930	2005	1945	1952	2026	2105	2045	2052	2135	2145	2159
Washington Union d.	...	1830u	...	...	1905	1900	1900	1930u	...	...	...	...	...	...	...	...	...	...	...	...	...	...	...	...
Fredricksburg d.	...	|	...	...	2018	2014	2011	|	...	...	...	...	...	...	...	...	...	...	...	...	...	...	...	...
Richmond d.	...	|	...	...	2118	2125	2124	2140	...	...	...	...	...	...	...	...	...	...	...	...	...	...	...	...
Newport News a.	...	|	...	...	...	...	|	...	...	...	...	...	...	...	...	...	...	...	...	...	...	...	...	...
Norfolk a.	...	|	...	...	...	...	2348	...	...	...	...	...	...	...	...	...	...	...	...	...	...	...	...	...
Virgina Beach a.	...	|	...	...	...	...	...	...	...	...	...	...	...	...	...	...	...	...	...	...	...	...	...	...
Charlottesville d.	...	2052	...	...	...	...	...	...	...	...	...	...	...	...	...	...	...	...	...	...	...	...	...	...
Lynchburg a.	...	2200	...	...	...	...	...	...	...	...	...	...	...	...	...	...	...	...	...	...	...	...	...	...

	Acela	*Acela*							*Acela*	*Acela*				*Acela*		*Acela*								
	2171	**2257**	**57**	**465**	**475**	**165**		**175**	**2259**	**2173**	**467**	**167**		**2297**	**123**	**2175**	**187**	**177**		**139**	**479**	**497**	**169**	**179**
	①–⑤	⑦	⑥⑦	⑦	①–⑤	⑥⑦		①–⑤	⑦	①–⑤	⑥	⑥		⑦	⑦	①–⑤	①–⑤	①–⑤		⑦	①–⑤	⑦	⑥⑦	①–⑤
			♦	2	2						2										2	2		
Boston South d.	1510	1510	...	...	...	1500	...	1520	1610	1615	...	1635	...	1710	...	1720	...	1735	...	1740	...	...	1840	184
Providence d.	1545	1546	...	...	...	1549	...	1601	1644	1650	...	1714	...	1748	...	1755	...	1814	...	1820	...	...	1920	192
New London d.	|	|	...	...	...	1649	...	1657	|	|	...	1813	...	|	...	|	...	1915	...	1915	...	...	2016	201
Springfield MA d.	|	|	1450	1610	1605	|	...	|	|	|	1725	|	...	|	...	|	...	|	...	|	1925	1940	|	|
Hartford d.	|	|	1526	1647	1642	|	...	|	|	|	1804	|	...	|	...	|	...	|	...	|	2001	2015	|	|
New Haven d.	1713	1713	1639	1731	1735	1737	...	1745	1813	1816	1900	1909	...	1913	...	1920	...	2013	...	2009	2050	2100	2109	211
Stamford d.	1759	1758	1728	...	...	1828	...	1833	1858	1901	...	1958	...	1958	...	2005	...	2103	...	2058	...	...	2158	215
New York Penn a.	1845	1845	1825	...	...	1927	...	1925	1945	1945	...	2050	...	2045	...	2050	...	2151	...	2150	...	...	2250	225
New York Penn d.	1900	1900	1901	...	...	2001	...	1940	2000	2000	...	2105	...	...	2105	2105	2120	2205	...	2205	...	...	2305	...
Newark NJ d.	1915	1914	1918	...	...	2017	...	1957	2014	2015	...	2121	...	...	2121u	2120	2136	2221	...	2221	...	...	2321	...
Philadelphia 30th Street d.	2008	2012	2028	...	...	2129	...	2115	2112	2110	...	2233	...	...	2233	2215	2245	2330	...	2333	...	...	0030	...
Baltimore Penn d.	2108	2115	2136	...	...	2239	...	2220	2215	2210	...	2343	...	...	2343	2315	2351	0040	...	0043	...	...	0140	...
BWI Airport d.	2120	2126	2148	...	...	2251	...	2233	2226	2222	...	2355	...	...	2355	|	0003	0052	...	0055	...	...	0152	...
Washington Union a.	2148	2152	2225	...	...	2325	...	2305	2252	2250	...	0029	...	...	0029	2350	0035	0125	...	0129	...	...	0225	...
Washington Union d.	...	...	...	...	...	...	...	...	...	...	...	...	...	...	...	...	...	...	...	...	...	...	...	...
Fredricksburg d.	...	...	...	...	...	...	...	...	...	...	...	...	...	...	...	...	...	...	...	...	...	...	...	...
Richmond d.	...	...	...	...	...	...	...	...	...	...	...	...	...	...	...	...	...	...	...	...	...	...	...	...
Newport News a.	...	...	...	...	...	...	...	...	...	...	...	...	...	...	...	...	...	...	...	...	...	...	...	...
Norfolk a.	...	...	...	...	...	...	...	...	...	...	...	...	...	...	...	...	...	...	...	...	...	...	...	...
Virgina Beach a.	...	...	...	...	...	...	...	...	...	...	...	...	...	...	...	...	...	...	...	...	...	...	...	...
Charlottesville d.	...	...	...	...	...	...	...	...	...	...	...	...	...	...	...	...	...	...	...	...	...	...	...	...
Lynchburg a.	...	...	...	...	...	...	...	...	...	...	...	...	...	...	...	...	...	...	...	...	...	...	...	...

♦ – NOTES, LISTED BY TRAIN NUMBER:

- **19/20** – CRESCENT – 🛏 1, 2 cl., (2) and ✕ New York - Washington - New Orleans and v.v.
- **50/51** – CARDINAL – 🛏 1, 2 cl., (2) and 🍸 Chicago - Washington - New York and v.v.
- **54/55** – VERMONTER – (12) and 🍸 Washington - New York - New Haven - St Albans and v.v.
- **56/57** – VERMONTER – (12) and 🍸 Washington - New York - New Haven - St Albans and v.v.
- **79/80** – CAROLINIAN – (12) and 🍸 New York - Washington - Charlotte and v.v.
- **89/90** – PALMETTO – (12) and 🍸 New York - Washington - Savannah and v.v.

Amtrak Most trains 🍷

NEWPORT NEWS - WASHINGTON - NEW YORK - BOSTON 9215

km		66	2190	190	490	150	450		110	2150	2290	170	470		160	460	180	2100	162	130	2154	98	172	54
			Acela							Acela	Acela							Acela			Acela			
			①–⑤	①–⑤	①–⑤	⑥⑦	⑥⑦		①–⑤	①–⑤	⑥	①–⑤	①–⑤		⑥⑦	⑥⑦	①–⑤	①–⑤	⑥⑦	①–⑤	①–⑤		①–⑤	⑥⑦
					2		2						2									♦		♦
	Lynchburg d.	...	...	...	...	...	...	...	...	...	...	...	...	...	...	...	...	...	...	...	...	...	...	...
	Charlottesville d.	...	...	...	...	...	...	...	...	...	...	...	...	...	...	...	...	...	...	...	...	...	...	...
	Virginia Beach d.	*1430**	...	...	...	...	...	...	...	...	...	...	...	...	...	...	...	...	...	...	...	...	...	...
	Norfolk d.	*1515**	...	...	...	...	...	...	...	...	...	...	...	...	...	...	...	...	...	...	...	...	...	...
	Newport News d.	1720	...	...	...	...	...	...	...	...	...	...	...	...	...	...	...	...	...	...	...	...	...	...
	Richmond d.	1900	...	...	...	...	...	...	...	...	...	...	...	...	...	...	...	...	...	...	...	0435	...	...
	Fredericksburg d.	1957	...	...	...	...	...	...	...	...	...	...	...	...	...	...	...	...	...	...	...	|	...	...
	Washington Union a.	2120	...	...	...	...	...	...	...	...	...	...	...	...	...	...	...	...	...	...	...	0721s	...	...
	Washington Union d.	2210	...	0315	...	0315	...	...	0400	0500	...	0452	...	...	0525	...	0530	0600	0620	0630	0700	0721s	0725	0730
	BWI Airport d.	2240	...	0339	...	0338	...	...	0425	|	...	0520	...	...	0552	...	0557	0621	0647	0657	0721	|	0753	0755
	Baltimore Penn d.	2256	...	0354	...	0354	...	...	0441	0530	...	0535	...	...	0609	...	0613	0634	0704	0714	0734	0816s	0809	0812
	Philadelphia 30th Street d.	0013	...	0515	...	0515	...	...	0550	0630	...	0646	...	...	0719	...	0724	0735	0819	0828	0835	0931s	0918	0920
	Newark NJ d.	0132	...	0622	...	0622	...	...	0704	0728	...	0757	...	...	0827	...	0824s	0832s	0924	0942	0931	1047s	1026	1025
	New York Penn a.	0150	...	0640	...	0640	...	...	0722	0745	...	0815	...	...	0845	...	0844	0849	0942	1000	0948	1106	1044	1043
	New York Penn d.	0240	0620	0655	...	0700	...	...	...	0803	0803	0830	...	...	0900	...	...	...	1000	...	1003	...	1100	1130
	Stamford d.	0325	0705	0747	...	0748	...	...	...	0847	0848	0919	...	...	0948	...	...	...	1048	...	1048	...	1148	1218
0	New Haven d.	0440	0758	0837	0840	0840	0842	...	...	0936	0937	1013	1030	...	1044	1046	...	...	1144	...	1137	...	1244	1323
60	Hartford d.	|	|	|	0929	|	0923	...	...	|	|	|	1114	...	|	1128	...	...	|	...	|	...	|	1411
101	**Springfield** MA a.	|	|	|	1010	|	1003	...	...	|	|	|	1153	...	|	1205	...	...	|	...	|	...	|	1458
	New London d.	0534	0837	0926	...	0929	...	...	...	|	|	1100	...	...	1129	...	...	...	1232	...	|	...	1332	...
	Providence d.	0656	0911	1017	...	1025	...	...	...	1046	1050	1158	...	...	1225	...	...	...	1328	...	1248	...	1423	...
	Boston South a.	0758	1005	1105	...	1115	...	...	...	1140	1145	1245	...	...	1315	...	...	...	1420	...	1340	...	1515	...

	2104	56	152		86	2158	2250	184	164	464	20	2160	2208	174	82	154	2110	2252	84	88	488		2164	2212
	Acela					Acela	Acela					Acela	Acela				Acela	Acela					Acela	Acela
	①–⑤	①–⑤	⑥⑦		①–⑤	①–⑤	⑥⑦	①–⑤	⑥⑦	⑥⑦		①–⑤	⑦	①–⑤	⑥	⑦	①–⑤	⑦	①–⑤	⑥⑦	⑥⑦		①–⑤	⑥⑦
		♦									♦													
Lynchburg d.	...	...	...	...	...	...	...	...	...	...	0556	...	...	...	...	...	...	...	...	...	...	...	...	...
Charlottesville d.	...	...	...	...	...	...	...	...	...	...	0709	...	...	...	...	...	...	...	...	...	...	...	...	...
Virginia Beach d.	...	...	...	...	...	...	...	...	...	...	|	...	...	...	...	...	...	...	...	...	...	...	...	...
Norfolk d.	...	...	...	...	...	...	...	...	...	...	|	...	...	0500	...	...	...	...	...	0605	...	...	...	...
Newport News d.	...	...	...	...	...	...	...	...	...	...	|	...	...	|	...	...	...	...	...	|	...	...	...	...
Richmond d.	...	...	...	...	0600	...	...	...	0635	...	|	...	...	0710	0735	...	...	...	0800	0825	...	...	...	...
Fredericksburg d.	...	...	...	...	0700	...	...	...	0734	...	|	...	...	0810	0833	...	...	...	0858	0925	...	...	...	...
Washington Union a.	...	...	...	...	0815	...	...	...	0900	...	0953s	...	...	0944	0944	...	...	...	1015	1055	...	...	...	...
Washington Union d.	0800	0810	0810	...	0840	0900	0900	0920	0925	...	0953s	1000	1000	1020	1020	1020	1100	1100	1102	1125	...	...	1200	1200
BWI Airport d.	0821	0837	0837	...	0907	0921	0921	0948	0952	...	|	1021	1021	1047	1047	1047	1121	1121	1127	1152	...	...	|	1221
Baltimore Penn d.	0834	0854	0854	...	0923	0934	0934	1004	1010	...	1055s	1034	1034	1104	1104	1104	1134	1134	1144	1209	...	...	1230	1234
Philadelphia 30th Street d.	0935	0959	1012	...	1038	1035	1037	1115	1119	...	1208s	1135	1137	1216	1219	1219	1235	1237	1254	1319	...	...	1330	1337
Newark NJ d.	1029s	1103	1125s	...	1147	1130	1137	1222	1229	...	1325s	1230	1237s	1326	1328	1328	1330s	1337	1359	1428	...	...	1429	1437s
New York Penn a.	1046	1121	1145	...	1205	1146	1153	1240	1247	...	1346	1246	1255	1344	1346	1346	1350	1353	1420	1446	...	...	1445	1455
New York Penn d.	...	1133	...	...	1230	1203	1203	...	1300	...	...	1303	...	1400	1400	...	...	1403	...	1500	...	...	1503	...
Stamford d.	...	1246	...	...	1318	1248	1248	...	1348	...	...	1348	...	1448	1448	...	...	1448	...	1548	...	...	1546	...
New Haven d.	...	1325	...	...	1410	1337	1337	...	1444	1450	...	1437	...	1544	1544	...	...	1537	...	1644	1650	...	|	...
Hartford d.	...	1413	...	...	|	|	|	...	|	1541	...	|	...	|	|	...	...	|	...	|	1736	...	|	...
Springfield MA a.	...	1500	...	...	|	|	|	...	|	1616	...	|	...	|	|	...	...	|	...	|	1815	...	|	...
New London d.	...	...	...	...	1452	|	|	...	1532	...	...	|	...	1635	1634	...	...	|	...	1733	...	...	|	...
Providence d.	...	...	...	...	1547	1447	1451	...	1630	...	...	1547	...	1730	1726	...	...	1650	...	1827	...	...	1744	...
Boston South a.	...	...	...	...	1635	1542	1547	...	1720	...	...	1640	...	1830	1816	...	...	1746	...	1920	...	...	1840	...

	176	476	140	2166	2254		186	194	2168	2216	94	494	156	2170	2256	148	92	168	132	432	134	2172	2220	2258
				Acela	Acela				Acela	Acela				Acela	Acela							Acela	Acela	Acela
	①–⑤	①–⑤	⑥⑦	①–⑤	⑦		①–⑤	⑥⑦	①–⑤	⑥	①–⑤	①–⑤	⑥⑦	①–⑤	⑦	①–⑤		⑥	⑦	⑦	④⑤	①–⑤	⑥	⑦
																	♦							
Lynchburg d.	0738	...	...	...	...	...	...	...	...	...	...	...	0959	...	...	...	...	...	...	...	...	...	...	...
Charlottesville d.	0852	...	...	...	...	...	...	...	...	...	...	...	1113	...	...	...	...	...	...	...	...	...	...	...
Virginia Beach d.	|	...	...	...	...	...	...	*0610**	...	...	*0700**	...	|	...	...	...	...	...	...	...	...	...	...	...
Norfolk d.	|	...	...	...	...	...	...	*0650**	...	...	*0740**	...	|	...	...	...	...	...	...	...	...	...	...	...
Newport News d.	|	...	...	...	...	...	...	0815	...	...	0915	...	|	...	...	...	...	...	...	...	...	...	...	...
Richmond d.	|	...	...	...	...	...	...	0955	...	...	1104	...	|	...	...	...	1230	...	...	...	...	...	...	...
Fredericksburg d.	|	...	...	...	...	...	...	1054	...	...	1204	...	|	...	...	...	|	...	...	...	...	...	...	...
Washington Union a.	1120	...	...	...	...	...	...	1219	...	...	1335	...	1335	...	...	...	1514s	...	...	...	...	...	...	...
Washington Union d.	1202	...	1225	1300	1300	...	1302	1305	1400	1400	1402	...	1420	1500	1500	1502	1514s	1525	1525	...	1530	1600	1600	1600
BWI Airport d.	1229	...	1252	|	1321	...	1329	1332	|	1421	1430	...	1447	1521	1521	1529	|	1552	1552	...	1554	|	1621	1621
Baltimore Penn d.	1245	...	1309	1330	1334	...	1345	1351	1430	1434	1446	...	1504	1534	1535	1545	1615s	1609	1609	...	1609	1630	1634	1634
Philadelphia 30th Street d.	1355	...	1419	1430	1437	...	1500	1502	1530	1537	1557	...	1619	1635	1637	1700	1735s	1719	1719	...	1733	1730	1737	1737
Newark NJ d.	1501	...	1528	1529	1537	...	1612	1615	1629	1634s	1704	...	1726	1730	1736	1810	1854s	1828	1828	...	1838s	1829	1835s	1836
New York Penn a.	1519	...	1546	1545	1553	...	1630	1635	1645	1655	1721	...	1746	1747	1752	1830	1918	1846	1846	...	1857	1845	1852	1852
New York Penn d.	1530	...	1630	1600	1603	...	...	1700	1700	...	1742	...	...	1800	1803	1845	...	1900	1930	...	...	1900	...	1903
Stamford d.	1618	...	1718	|	1648	...	...	1748	1745	...	1831	...	...	1847	1848	1940	...	1948	2018	...	...	1948	...	1948
New Haven d.	1714	1720	1826	1733	1737	...	...	1840	1834	...	1932	1930	...	1936	1937	2049	...	2044	2114	2120	...	2037	...	2037
Hartford d.	|	1810	1919	|	|	...	...	|	|	...	|	2016	...	|	|	2136	...	|	|	2210	...	|	...	|
Springfield MA a.	|	1850	2000	|	|	...	...	|	|	...	|	2055	...	|	|	2225	...	|	|	2250	...	|	...	|
New London d.	1817	...	...	|	|	...	...	1932	|	...	2024	...	...	|	|	...	...	2135	2207	...	...	2116	...	|
Providence d.	1919	...	...	1847	1849	...	...	2025	1949	...	2116	...	...	2047	2048	...	...	2235	2302	...	...	2150	...	2147
Boston South a.	2012	...	...	1940	1946	...	...	2115	2043	...	2210	...	...	2140	2145	...	...	2326	2355	...	...	2245	...	2246

		178	146		126	80	2122	2222	136	196	192		166	2124	138	50	158	2126	188	182	90	2128	2228	198
							Acela	Acela						Acela				Acela				Acela	Acela	
		①–⑤	⑥		⑦		①–⑤	⑦	⑤	①–④	⑥		⑦	①–⑤	①–⑤	③⑤⑦	⑥⑦	①–⑤	①–⑤	⑥⑦		①–⑤	⑦	
						♦										♦					♦			
Lynchburg d.	...	...	...	...	...	...	...	...	...	...	...	...	...	...	...	...	...	...	...	...	...	...	...	...
Charlottesville d.	...	...	...	...	...	...	...	...	...	...	...	...	...	...	...	1458	...	...	...	...	...	...	...	...
Virginia Beach d.	...	...	...	...	...	...	...	...	...	...	...	...	...	...	...	|	...	...	...	...	...	...	...	...
Norfolk d.	...	...	...	...	...	...	...	...	...	...	...	...	...	...	...	|	...	...	...	...	...	...	...	...
Newport News d.	...	...	...	...	...	...	...	...	...	...	...	...	...	...	...	|	...	...	...	...	...	...	...	...
Richmond d.	...	...	...	...	...	1412	...	...	...	...	...	...	...	...	...	|	...	...	...	...	1725	...	...	...
Fredericksburg d.	...	...	...	...	...	1512	...	...	...	...	...	...	...	...	...	|	...	...	...	...	|	...	...	...
Washington Union a.	...	...	...	...	...	1637s	...	...	...	...	...	...	...	...	...	1806s	...	...	...	...	1957s	...	...	...
Washington Union d.	...	1602	1625	...	1625	1637s	1700	1700	1705	1705	1720	...	1720	1800	1805	1806s	1820	1900	1910	1920	1957s	2000	2000	2105
BWI Airport d.	...	1629	1652	...	1652	|	|	1721	1732	1732	1747	...	1747	|	1833	|	1847	|	1937	1947	|	|	2021	2132
Baltimore Penn d.	...	1645	1710	...	1710	1751s	1730	1734	1748	1748	1804	...	1804	1830	1850	1905s	1904	1930	1954	2004	2050s	2030	2034	2148
Philadelphia 30th Street d.	...	1755	1820	...	1820	1907s	1830	1837	1900	1900	1919	...	1919	1930	2000	2020s	2015	2030	2109	2119	2207s	2132	2137	2304
Newark NJ d.	...	1902	1926	...	1924s	2027s	1927s	1937s	2022	2022s	2028	...	2028	2027s	2112	2135s	2124s	2130s	2214s	2227	2327s	2227s	2237s	0010s
New York Penn a.	...	1920	1946	...	1946	2047	1947	1955	2041	2041	2047	...	2047	2045	2130	2156	2145	2148	2234	2249	2347	2245	2255	0030
New York Penn d.	...	1950	2000	...	...	...	...	...	2057	...	...	...	2100	...	...	...	...	...	...	...	...	...	...	...
Stamford d.	...	2045	2048	...	...	...	...	...	2149	...	...	...	2148	...	...	...	...	...	...	...	...	...	...	...
New Haven d.	...	2142	2154	...	...	...	...	...	2259	...	...	...	2241	...	...	...	...	...	...	...	...	...	...	...
Hartford d.	...	|	2242	...	...	...	...	...	2347	...	...	...	|	...	...	...	...	...	...	...	...	...	...	...
Springfield MA a.	...	|	2320	...	...	...	...	...	0030	...	...	...	|	...	...	...	...	...	...	...	...	...	...	...
New London d.	...	2235	...	...	...	...	...	...	...	...	...	...	2331	...	...	...	...	...	...	...	...	...	...	...
Providence d.	...	2337	...	...	...	...	...	...	...	...	...	...	0020	...	...	...	...	...	...	...	...	...	...	...
Boston South a.	...	0030	...	...	...	...	...	...	...	...	...	...	0110	...	...	...	...	...	...	...	...	...	...	...

91/92 – SILVER STAR – 🛏 1, 2 cl., (2) and ✕ New York - Washington - Tampa - Miami and v.v.
97/98 – SILVER METEOR – 🛏 1, 2 cl., (2) and ✕ New York - Washington - Orlando - Miami and v.v.

s – Calls to set down only.
u – Calls to pick up only.
* - Connection by 🚌

9220 ST ALBANS - SPRINGFIELD Amtrak

km		55 ①–⑤ A	57 ⑥⑦ A
0	**St. Albans** d.	0858	0858
38	Burlington Essex Jct. d.	0927	0927
70	Waterbury d.	0952	0952
90	Montpelier d.	1005	1005
133	Randolph d.	1038	1038
189	White River Jct. d.	1115	1115
205	Windsor VT d.	1132	1132
225	Claremont d.	1142	1142
252	Bellows Falls d.	1203	1203
291	Brattleboro d.	1234	1234
355	Amherst d.	1319	1319
397	**Springfield** MA a.	1440	1440
	New York Penn **9215** a.	1825	1825
	Washington U **9215** a.	2159	2225

	54 ⑥⑦ A	56 ①–⑤ A
Washington U **9215** d.	0730	0810
New York P **9215** d.	1130	1133
Springfield MA d.	1515	1515
Amherst d.	1620	1620
Brattleboro d.	1710	1710
Bellows Falls d.	1740	1740
Claremont d.	1759	1759
Windsor VT d.	1808	1808
White River Jct. d.	1829	1829
Randolph d.	1905	1905
Montpelier d.	1938	1938
Waterbury d.	1950	1950
Burlington Essex Jct. d.	2017	2017
St. Albans a.	2057	2057

A – VERMONTER – (12) and 🍸 Washington - New York - New Haven - St Albans and v.v.

9225 HARRISBURG - PITTSBURGH Amtrak

km		43 B	
	New York Penn **9215** d.	1052	...
	Philadelphia **9215** d.	1242	...
0	**Harrisburg** d.	1436	...
95	Lewistown d.	1546	...
154	Huntingdon d.	1622	...
186	Tyrone d.	1648r	...
213	Altoona d.	1706	...
275	Johnstown d.	1800	...
334	Latrobe d.	1841r	...
346	Greensburg d.	1852	...
401	**Pittsburgh** a.	2005	...

	42 B	
Pittsburgh d.	0730	...
Greensburg d.	0811	...
Latrobe d.	0821r	...
Johnstown d.	0904	...
Altoona d.	1001	...
Tyrone d.	1017r	...
Huntingdon d.	1044	...
Lewistown d.	1121	...
Harrisburg a.	1255	...
Philadelphia **9215** a.	1455	...
New York Penn **9215** a.	1650	...

B – PENNSYLVANIAN – (12) and 🍸 Pittsburgh - Harrisburg - New York and v.v.
r – Calls on request.

9230 NEW YORK - PHILADELPHIA - HARRISBURG Amtrak

km		601 ①–⑤	605 ①–⑤	607 ①–⑤	611 ⑥	661 ⑥⑦	641 ①–⑤	609 ①–⑤	663 ⑥⑦	643 ①–⑤	43 B		645 ①–⑤	615 ⑦	665 ⑥⑦	647 ①–⑤	649 ①–⑤	667 ⑥⑦	651 ①–⑤	653 ①–⑤	669 ⑥⑦	655 ①–⑤	671 ⑥⑦	619 ①–⑤
0	**New York** Penn **9215** d.	*0300*	*0440*	*0530*	*0545*	0700	0725	*0810*	0909	0930	1052	...	1205	*1205*	1305	1411	1444	1513	1603	1710	1717	1835	1953	*2105*
16	Newark NJ **9215** d.	*0320*	*0456*	*0546*r	*0601*	0717u	0742u	*0826*	0927u	0946u	1109u	...	1222u	*1221*	1323u	1428u	1459u	1532u	1620u	1727	1734u	1852u	2009u	*2120*
146	**Philadelphia** 30th Street d.	0525	0625	0725	0725	0835	0900	1000	1055	1100	1242	...	1335	1355	1445	1545	1645	1655	1735	1842	1855	2015	2145	2259
178	Paoli d.	0551	0651	0751	0750	0900	0923	1023	1120	1123	1312	...	1359	1420	1510	1610	1711	1722	1802	1907	1922	2040	2210	2324
255	Lancaster d.	0635	0735	0830	0834	0945	1005	1103	1203	1206	1352	...	1443	1504	1555	1650	1758	1807	1847	1951	2007	2125	2255	0009
300	Elizabethtown d.	0651	0751	0845	0850	1001	1020	1119	1220	1220	1406	...	1500	1521	1611	1704	1814	1823	1903	2007	2023	2141	2311	0025
315	**Harrisburg** a.	0710	0810	0905	0910	1020	1040	1140	1240	1240	1426	...	1520	1540	1630	1725	1835	1845	1925	2035	2045	2200	2330	0045

	640 ①–⑤	600 ①–⑤	660 ⑥⑦	642 ①–⑤	662 ⑥	644 ①–⑤	664 ⑥⑦	646 ①–⑤	648 ①–⑤	666 ⑥⑦	650 ①–⑤	42 B	670 ⑥⑦	652 ①–⑤	654 ①–⑤	672 ⑥⑦	656 ①–⑤	618 ①–④	658 ⑤	674 ⑦	610 ⑥	620 ①–⑤	612 ⑦	622 ①–⑤
Harrisburg d.	0500	0630	0720	0800	0820	0900	0930	1000	1100	1120	1200	1305	1405	1520	1630	1705	1735	1840	1840	1905	1905	2015	2020	2115
Elizabethtown d.	0517	0647	0737	0816	0837	0917	0947	1016	1117	1137	1217	1323	1422	1537	1647	1722	1752	1857	1857	1922	1922	2032	2037	2132
Lancaster d.	0535	0706	0755	0832	0855	0933	1005	1032	1134	1155	1235	1340	1440	1554	1705	1740	1810	1912	1912	1940	1940	2047	2055	2147
Paoli d.	0619	0753	0841	0910	0941	1016	1046	1110	1217	1241	1316	1424	1528	1637	1750	1825	1855	1955	1955	2025	2025	2129	2140	2229
Philadelphia 30th Street a.	0645	0819	0905	0935	1005	1041	1110	1135	1242	1305	1345	1455	1555	1705	1825	1850	1923	2020	2020	2050	2050	2155	2210	2255
Newark NJ a.	0812	*1026*	1031	1046	1142	1157	1231	1252	1403	1440	1508	1630s	1713	1833	1954	2014	2045	*2214*	2142	2214s	*2227*	*0010*	*0010*	*0132*
New York Penn a.	0830	*1044*	1049	1104	1159	1215	1249	1310	1422	1457	1526	1650	1732	1853	2012	2034	2103	*2234*	2200	2234	*2249*	*0030*	*0030*	*0150*

B – PENNSYLVANIAN – see Table **9225**.
f – ⑤ only.
s – Calls to set down only.
u – Calls to pick up only.

9235 BOSTON - CHICAGO Amtrak

km		449 C	29 E	49 D
0	**Boston** South d.	1155	...	...
70	Worcester d.	1258	...	...
157	Springfield MA d.	1415	...	...
242	Pittsfield d.	1536	...	...
	New York **9205** d.	|	...	1540
320	**Albany** R'laer d.	1735	...	1905
349	Schenectady d.	...	...	1931
558	Syracuse d.	...	...	2141
686	Rochester d.	...	...	2300
784	Buffalo Depew d.	...	...	2359
931	Erie d.	...	...	0136
◇	**Washington** U d.	...	1605	|
◇	Harper's Ferry d.	...	1716	|
◇	Martinsburg d.	...	1745	|
◇	Cumberland d.	...	1924	|
◇	Pittsburgh d.	...	2359	|
◇	Alliance d.	...	0139	|
1083	**Cleveland** d.	...	0259	0345
1179	Sandusky d.	...	0402	0455
1254	Toledo d.	...	0522	0615
1379	Waterloo d.	...	0636	0733
1467	Elkhart d.	...	0729	0825
1494	South Bend d.	...	0751	0849
1629	**Chicago** Union a.	...	0845	0945

	30 E	48 D	448 C
Chicago Union d.	1840	2130	...
South Bend d.	2109	2359	...
Elkhart d.	2129	0022	...
Waterloo d.	2023	0115	...
Toledo d.	2349	0320	...
Sandusky d.	0040	0412	...
Cleveland d.	0154	0550	...
Alliance d.	0305	|	...
Pittsburgh d.	0520	|	...
Cumberland d.	0931	|	...
Martinsburg d.	1100	|	...
Harper's Ferry d.	1125	|	...
Washington U a.	1310	|	...
Erie d.	...	0722	...
Buffalo Depew d.	...	0908	...
Rochester d.	...	1008	...
Syracuse d.	...	1138	...
Schenectady d.	...	1400	...
Albany R'laer a.	...	1450	1525
New York **9205** a.	...	1823	|
Pittsfield d.	...	...	1629
Springfield MA d.	...	...	1753
Worcester d.	...	...	1857s
Boston South a.	...	...	2110

9240 WASHINGTON - MIAMI Amtrak

km		89 F	91 G	97 H
0	**New York** Penn d.	0605	1102	1515
16	Newark NJ d.	0622u	1122u	1538u
146	Philadelphia 30th St d.	0732u	1235u	1658u
297	Baltimore Penn d.	0850u	1355u	1814u
362	**Washington** Union d.	0955u	1505u	1930u
536	Richmond d.	1202	1719	2150
581	Petersburg d.	1232	1757	2224
738	Rocky Mount d.	1402	1929	2356
852	**Raleigh** d.	|	2113	|
882	Fayetteville d.	1544	|	0134
1015	Florence d.	1728	|	0328
1167	Charleston SC d.	1915	|	0506
1328	Savannah d.	2103	0434	0650
1565	**Jacksonville** a.	...	0655	0923
1565	**Jacksonville** d.	...	0715	0948
1792	Winter Park d.	...	0954	1227
1800	Orlando d.	...	1031	1310
1829	Kissimmee d.	...	1055	1332
1959	**Tampa** d.	...	1245	|
	Winter Haven d.	...	1343	1424
1955	Sebring d.	...	1424	1505
2120	West Palm Beach a.	...	1613s	1654s
2189	Fort Lauderdale a.	...	1712s	1802s
2224	**Miami** Amtrak a.	...	1805	1855

	98 H	92 G	90 F
Miami Amtrak d.	0820	1150	...
Fort Lauderdale d.	0900u	1230u	...
West Palm Beach d.	0957u	1327u	...
Sebring d.	1124	1459	...
Winter Haven d.	1210	1544	...
Tampa d.	|	1717	...
Kissimmee d.	1256	1840	...
Orlando d.	1335	1924	...
Winter Park d.	1352	1941	...
Jacksonville a.	1648	2237	...
Jacksonville d.	1708	2257	...
Savannah d.	1938	0130	0820
Charleston SC d.	2123	|	1000
Florence d.	2320	|	1139
Fayetteville d.	0045	|	1304
Raleigh d.	|	0854	|
Rocky Mount d.	0217	1015	1459
Petersburg d.	0341	1152	1631
Richmond d.	0435	1230	1725
Washington Union a.	0721s	1514s	1957s
Baltimore Penn a.	0816s	1615s	2050s
Philadelphia 30th St a.	0931s	1735s	2207s
Newark NJ a.	1047s	1854s	2327s
New York Penn a.	1106s	1918s	2347s

Notes for Table **9235** and **9240**.

C – 🛏 1, 2 cl., (2) and 🍸 Boston(**449/448**) - Albany(**48/49**) - Chicago and v.v.
D – LAKE SHORE LIMITED – 🛏 1, 2 cl., (2) and ✕ New York(**49/48**) - Albany(**49/48**) - Chicago and v.v.; conveys 🛏 1, 2 cl., (2) and 🍸 Boston(**449/448**) - Albany(**48/49**) - Chicago and v.v.
E – CAPITOL LIMITED – 🛏 1, 2 cl., (2) and ✕ Washington - Chicago and v.v.
F – PALMETTO – (12) and 🍸 New York - Washington - Savannah and v.v.
G – SILVER STAR – 🛏 1, 2 cl., (2) and ✕ New York - Washington - Tampa - Miami and v.v.
H – SILVER METEOR – 🛏 1, 2 cl., (2) and ✕ New York - Washington - Orlando - Miami and v.v.

s – Calls to set down only.
u – Calls to pick up only.
◇ – Washington - Cleveland distances : Washington *0 km*, Harper's Ferry *88 km*, Martinsburg *118 km*, Cumberland *234 km*, Pittsburgh *478 km*, Alliance *613 km*, Cleveland *702 km*.

9245 WASHINGTON - CHARLOTTE - NEW ORLEANS Amtrak

km		73 2	75 2	79 A	19 B
	New York Penn **9215** d.	...	...	0705	1415
0	**Washington** Union d.	...	...	1055	1830
174	Richmond d.	...	...	1310	|
219	Petersburg d.	...	...	1343	|
376	Rocky Mount d.	...	...	1513	|
490	**Raleigh** d.	0645	1145	1650	|
619	Greensboro d.	0818	1318	1832	0022
645	High Point d.	0834	1334	1848	0039
699	Salisbury d.	0908	1408	1924	0117
766	**Charlotte** a.	0955	1455	2012	0245
890	Spartanburg d.	...	...	...	0414
940	Greenville d.	...	...	...	0501
1102	Gainesville d.	...	...	...	0658
1179	**Atlanta** d.	...	...	...	0838
1344	Anniston d.	...	...	...	1000
1447	Birmingham d.	...	...	...	1208
1536	Tuscaloosa d.	...	...	...	1307
1692	Meridian d.	...	...	...	1504
1829	Hattiesburg d.	...	...	...	1638
2018	**New Orleans** a.	...	...	...	1932

	20 B	80 A	74 2	76 2
New Orleans d.	0700	...	...	...
Hattiesburg d.	0930	...	...	...
Meridian d.	1107	...	...	...
Tuscaloosa d.	1244	...	...	...
Birmingham d.	1424	...	...	...
Anniston d.	1559	...	...	...
Atlanta d.	2004	...	...	...
Gainesville d.	2059	...	...	...
Greenville d.	2258	...	...	...
Spartanburg d.	2339	...	...	...
Charlotte d.	0146	0700	1200	1715
Salisbury d.	0232	0743	1241	1756
High Point d.	0317	0817	1314	1829
Greensboro d.	0344	0839	1334	1849
Raleigh d.	|	1025	1511	2026
Rocky Mount d.	|	1152	...	...
Petersburg d.	|	1320	...	...
Richmond d.	|	1412	...	...
Washington Union a.	0953	1637	...	...
New York Penn **9215** a.	1346	2047	...	...

A – CAROLINIAN – (12) and 🍸 New York - Washington - Charlotte and v.v.
B – CRESCENT – 🛏 1, 2 cl., (2) and ✕ New York - Washington - New Orleans and v.v.

Amtrak WASHINGTON - CHICAGO 9250

km		51 ③⑤⑦ A	851 B
	New York P **9215** d.	0645	...
0	**Washington** Union d.	1105	...
109	Culpeper d.	1230	...
181	Charlottesville d.	1355	...
338	Clifton Forge d.	1610	...
393	White Sulpher Springs d.	1702	...
528	Charleston WV d.	2016	...
606	Huntington d.	2145	...
678	South Portsmouth d.	2251	...
872	Cincinnati d.	0123	...
1069	**Indianapolis** a.	0457	...
1069	**Indianapolis** d.	0600	0600
1144	Crawfordsville d.	0658r	0658r
1187	Lafayette d.	0733	0733
1383	**Chicago** Union a.	1005	1005

	50 ②④⑥ A	851 B
Chicago Union d.	1745	1745
Lafayette d.	2200	2200
Crawfordsville d.	2230r	2230r
Indianapolis a.	2350	2350
Indianapolis d.	2359	...
Cincinnati d.	0327	...
South Portsmouth d.	0542	...
Huntington d.	0710	...
Charleston WV d.	0820	...
White Sulpher Spings d.	1131	...
Clifton Forge d.	1223	...
Charlottesville d.	1458	...
Culpepper d.	1611	...
Washington Union a.	1806	...
New York P **9215** a.	2156	...

A – CARDINAL – 1,2 cl., (2) and Chicago - New York and v.v.
B – HOOSIER STATE – (2) Chicago - Indianapolis and v.v.
r – Request stop.

Amtrak CHICAGO - NEW ORLEANS 9255

km		391 D	393 E	59 C
0	**Chicago** Union d.	0815	1605	2005
92	Kankakee d.	0922	1712	2123r
208	Champaign ‡ d.	1025	1815	2234
323	Effingham d.	1129	1919	2337r
408	Centralia d.	1216	2006	0025r
498	Carbondale d.	1345	2135	0126
725	Newbern d.	...	...	0356r
850	Memphis d.	...	...	0650
1051	Greenwood d.	...	...	0900
1136	Yazoo City d.	...	...	0951r
1207	Jackson d.	...	...	1120
1334	McComb d.	...	...	1240r
1419	Hammond d.	...	...	1328
1503	**New Orleans** a.	...	...	1532

	58 C	390 D	392 E
New Orleans d.	1345	...	...
Hammond d.	1445	...	...
McComb d.	1532r	...	...
Jackson d.	1744	...	...
Yazoo City d.	1842r	...	...
Greenwood d.	1937	...	...
Memphis d.	2240	...	...
Newbern d.	0022r	...	...
Carbondale d.	0316	0730	1615
Centralia d.	0410r	0823	1708
Effingham d.	0457r	0907	1752
Champaign ‡ d.	0610	1014	1859
Kankakee d.	0713r	1115	2000
Chicago Union a.	0900	1300	2145

C – CITY OF NEW ORLEANS – 1,2 cl., (2) and Chicago - New Orleans and v.v.
D – SALUKI – (12) and Chicago - Carbondale and v.v.
E – ILLINI – (12) and Chicago - Carbondale and v.v.
r – Request stop.
‡ – Champaign Urbana

Amtrak CHICAGO - ST. LOUIS - KANSAS CITY 9260

km		311 F	301 G	303 G	313 F	21 H	3 J	305 G	307 G	
0	**Chicago** Union d.	...	0700	0925	...	1345	1500	1715	1900	...
60	Joliet Union d.	...	0757	1015	...	1440u	|	1805	1950	...
148	Pontiac d.	...	|	1106	...	1527	|	1856	2041	...
204	Bloomington d.	...	0914	1139	...	1604	|	1929	2114	...
252	Lincoln d.	...	|	1210	...	1637	|	2002	2147	...
298	Springfield IL d.	...	1015	1250	...	1714	|	2039	2224	...
360	Carlinville d.	...	|	1328	...	1749r	|	2119	2304	...
414	Alton d.	...	1122	1359	...	1822	|	2150	2335	...
457	**St. Louis** d.	0915	1220	1500	1600	1921	|	2245	0030	...
480	Kirkwood d.	0944	...	...	1629	...	|	...	...	...
658	Jefferson City d.	1136	...	...	1822	...	|	...	...	...
760	Sedalia d.	1246	...	...	1939	...	|	...	...	...
866	Lee's Summit d.	1404	...	...	2050	...	|	...	...	...
912	**Kansas City** a.	1455	...	...	2140	...	2211	...	...	...

	300 G	302 G	22 H	314 F	4 J	304 G	306 G	316 F	
Kansas City d.	...	...	...	0815	0743	...	...	1600	...
Lee's Summit d.	...	...	...	0851	|	...	...	1636	...
Sedalia d.	...	...	...	1004	|	...	...	1749	...
Jefferson City d.	...	...	...	1118	|	...	...	1903	...
Kirkwood d.	...	...	...	1313	|	...	...	2058	...
St. Louis d.	0435	0640	0755	1355	|	1500	1730	2140	...
Alton d.	0520	0725	0843	...	|	1545	1815	...	...
Carlinville d.	0550	0755	0915r	...	|	1614	1845	...	...
Springfield IL d.	0632	0837	0955	...	|	1656	1932	...	...
Lincoln d.	0700	0905	1025	...	|	1724	2000	...	...
Bloomington d.	0731	0946	1108	...	|	1756	2036	...	...
Pontiac d.	0759	1014	1139	...	|	1823	2104	...	...
Joliet Union d.	0859	1119	1256s	...	|	1926	2202	...	...
Chicgo Union a.	1000	1220	1352	...	1515	2040	2310	...	...

F – RIVER RUNNER – (12) and St Louis - Kansas City and v.v.
G – LINCOLN SERVICE – (12) and Chicago - St. Louis and v.v.
H – TEXAS EAGLE. See Table **9300**.
J – SOUTHWEST CHIEF. See Table **9295**.
r – Request stop.
s – Calls to set down only.
u – Calls to pick up only.

Amtrak CHICAGO - QUINCY 9265

km		381 A	5 C	3 D	383 B					
0	**Chicago** Union d.	0735	1400	1500	1755	...	...	...	...	...
166	Princeton d.	0921	1544	1646	1941	...	...	...	...	...
259	Galesburg d.	1022	1638	1738	2042	...	...	...	...	...
413	**Quincy** a.	1203	...	...	2223	...	...	...	...	...

	380 B	4 D	382 A						
Quincy d.	0612	...	1730	...	...	...	...	...	...
Galesburg d.	0738	1208	1856	...	...	...	...	...	...
Princeton d.	0835	1258	1953	...	...	...	...	...	...
Chicago Union a.	1040	1515	2158	...	...	...	...	...	...

A – CARL SANDBURG – (12) and Chicago Union - Quincy and v.v.
B – ILLINOIS ZEPHYR – (12) and Chicago Union - Quincy and v.v.
C – CALIFONIA ZEPHYR – See Table **9290**.
D – SOUTHWEST CHIEF – See Table **9295**.

Amtrak 2nd class CHICAGO - MILWAUKEE 9270

km		329 ①–⑥	331	333	335	337	339	341		
0	**Chicago** Union d.	0610	0825	1020	1305	1515	1708	2005	...	...
100	Sturtevant d.	0710	0925	1120	1405	1615	1814	2105	...	...
125	**Milwaukee Airport** a.	0724	0939	1134	1419	1629	1828	2119	...	...
138	**Milwaukee** a.	0739	0954	1149	1434	1644	1845	2134	...	...

	330 ①–⑥	332	334	336	338	340	342		
Milwaukee d.	0615	0805	1100	1300	1500	1745	1935	...	...
Milwaukee Airport d.	0626	0815	1110	1310	1510	1755	1945	...	...
Sturtevant d.	0643	0828	1123	1323	1523	1808	1958	...	...
Chicago Union a.	0757	0934	1229	1429	1629	1914	2104	...	...

Amtrak CHICAGO - GRAND RAPIDS, PORT HURON, DETROIT and PONTIAC 9275

km		350 K	Bus	352 K	Bus	364 L	Bus	370 M	354 K	Bus
0	**Chicago** Union CT d.	0720	...	1250	...	1600	...	1655	1800	...
140	Benton Harbour ET d.	|	...	|	...	|	...	1938	|	...
282	**Grand Rapids** ET a.	|	...	|	1630	|	1923	2155	|	...
34	Michigan City CT d.	|	...	1358	|	|	|	...	1900	...
141	Niles ET d.	1007	...	1533	|	1833	|	...	2035	...
221	Kalamazoo d.	1055	...	1608	1725	1912	2020	...	2110	...
258	Battle Creek d.	1127	1215	1640	...	1945	...	...	2147	2230
335	East Lansing d.	|	1350	|	...	2054	...	...	|	2345
382	Durand d.	|	|	|	...	2131	...	...	|	|
409	Flint d.	|	1545	|	...	2202	...	...	|	0040
513	**Port Huron** a.	|	...	|	...	2338	...	...	|	...
331	Jackson d.	1218	...	1733	...	...	...	...	2237	...
390	Ann Arbor d.	1305	...	1816	...	...	...	...	2320	...
439	Dearborn d.	1335	...	1846	...	...	...	...	2351	...
450	**Detroit** a.	1404	...	1913	...	...	...	...	0018	...
494	**Pontiac** a.	1503	...	2012	...	...	...	...	0119	...

	371 M	351 K	365 L	Bus	Bus	353 K	Bus	Bus	355 K
Pontiac d.	...	0545	...	...	...	1035	...	...	1740
Detroit d.	...	0628	...	...	...	1120	...	...	1823
Dearborn d.	...	0651	...	...	...	1143	...	...	1845
Ann Arbor d.	...	0726	...	...	...	1217	...	...	1921
Jackson d.	...	0808	...	...	...	1258	...	...	2001
Port Huron d.	...	|	0620	...	...	|	...	...	|
Flint d.	...	|	0732	...	0840	|	...	1625	|
Durand d.	...	|	0804	...	|	|	...	|	|
East Lansing d.	...	|	0845	...	0945	|	...	1730	|
Battle Creek d.	...	0902	0952	...	1125	1354	...	|	2055
Kalamazoo d.	...	0935	1025	1045	...	1425	1530	2020	2126
Niles ET d.	...	|	1103	|	...	1458	|	...	2203
Michigan City CT d.	...	|	|	|	...	|	|	...	2134
Grand Rapids ET d.	0740	|	|	1135	...	|	1620	...	|
Benton Harbour ET d.	0944	|	|	...	...	|	...	...	|
Chicago Union CT a.	1038	1047	1145	...	...	1558	...	...	2257

K – WOLVERINE – (12) and Chicago - Pontiac and v.v.
L – BLUE WATER – (12) and Chicago - Port Huron and v.v.
M – PERE MARQUETTE – (2) Chicago - Grand Rapids and v.v.
CT – Central Time.
ET – Eastern Time.

Greyhound SELECTED BUS ROUTES 9280

km	*Greyhound service*	1529	1535	1539	1537	1511			
0	**Nashville** d.	0315	0645	1110	1700	2235	...	...	...
337	**Memphis** a.	0700	1045	1510	2055	0220	...	...	...

Greyhound service	1502	1510	1514	1508	1504			
Memphis d.	0500	0920	1340	2030	2300	...	...	...
Nashville a.	0855	1315	1740	0015	0255	...	...	...

km	*Greyhound service*	6025	6001	6027	6021	6023	6005	6009	6029	6013	6017 ⑤⑦
0	**Las Vegas** NV d.	2330	0135	0325	0700	0800	0915	1201	1505	1700	1930
501	**Los Angeles** a.	0430	0825	0835	1440	1325	1600	1710	2205	2215	0105

Greyhound service	6034	6002	6016	6006	6012	6010	6014	6044 ⑤⑦	6018	6048
Los Angeles d.	0030	0615	0830	1000	1215	1415	1500	1815	1830	2245
Las Vegas NV a.	0530	1410	1340	1655	1730	2140	2020	2330	0045	0415

9285 CHICAGO - SEATTLE — Amtrak

km			7 A	27 B			28 B	8 A
0	**Chicago** Union	d.	1415	...	**Portland**	d.	1645	...
137	Milwaukee	d.	1555u	...	Vancouver WA	d.	1707	...
241	Columbus	d.	1705	...	Pasco	d.	2057	...
314	Wisconsin Dells	d.	1752	...	**Seattle** King Street	d.	|	1640
386	Tomah	d.	1830	...	Everett	d.	|	1739
452	La Crosse	d.	1914	...	Wenatchee	d.	|	2042
673	**Minneapolis / St Paul**	a.	2203	...	**Spokane**	a.	0013	0045
673	**Minneapolis / St Paul**	d.	2210	...	**Spokane**	d.	...	0130
773	St. Cloud	d.	0040	...	Sandpoint	d.	...	0235
1058	Fargo	d.	0335	...	Whitefish	d.	...	0746
1194	Grand Forks	d.	0452	...	Essex	d.	...	0855r
1332	Devils Lake	d.	0613	...	Shelby	d.	...	1143
1522	Minot	d.	0906	...	Havre	d.	...	1332
2072	Malta	d.	1325	...	Malta	d.	...	1452
2212	Havre	d.	1504	...	Minot	d.	...	2142
2381	Shelby	d.	1722	...	Devils Lake	d.	...	2332
2537	Essex	d.	1941r	...	Grand Forks	d.	...	0057
2624	Whitefish	d.	2116	...	Fargo	d.	...	0213
2924	Sandpoint	d.	2349	...	St. Cloud	d.	...	0514
3030	**Spokane**	a.	0140	...	**Minneapolis / St Paul**	a.	...	0752
3030	**Spokane**	d.	0215	0245	**Minneapolis / St Paul**	d.	...	0800
3306	Wenatchee	d.	0535	|	La Crosse	d.	...	1047
3501	Everett	d.	0838	|	Tomah	d.	...	1126
3554	**Seattle** King Street	a.	1025	|	Wisconsin Dells	d.	...	1208
3265	Pasco	d.	...	0535	Columbus	d.	...	1257
3621	Vancouver WA	d.	...	0918	Milwaukee	d.	...	1407s
3638	**Portland**	a.	...	1010	**Chicago** Union	a.	...	1555

A – EMPIRE BUILDER – 🛏 1, 2 cl., [2] and 🍸 Chicago - Spokane - Seattle and v.v.
B – EMPIRE BUILDER – 🛏 1, 2 cl., [2] Chicago - Spokane - Portland and v.v.
s – Calls to set down only.
u – Calls to pick up only.

9290 CHICAGO - SAN FRANCISCO — Amtrak

km			5 C	🚌			🚌	6 C
0	**Chicago** Union	d.	1400	...	**San Francisco** ‡	d.	0750	...
261	Galesburg	d.	1638	...	Emeryville	d.	0825	0910
330	Burlington	d.	1725	...	Martinez	d.	...	0954
450	Ottumwa	d.	1853	...	Sacramento	d.	...	1109
806	**Omaha**	a.	2255	...	Truckee	d.	...	1438
806	**Omaha**	d.	2305	...	Reno	d.	...	1606
892	Lincoln	d.	0014	...	Winnemucca	d.	...	1908
1049	Hastings	d.	0147	...	Elko	d.	...	2131
1261	McCook	d.	0343	...	**Salt Lake City**	a.	...	0305
1668	**Denver** Union	a.	0715	...	**Salt Lake City**	d.	...	0330
1668	**Denver** Union	d.	0805	...	Provo	d.	...	0435
1770	Winter Park	d.	1007	...	Green River	d.	...	0759
1791	Granby	d.	1037	...	Grand Junction	d.	...	1023
1966	Glenwood Springs	d.	1353	...	Glenwood Springs	d.	...	1210
2109	Grand Junction	d.	1610	...	Granby	d.	...	1512
2279	Green River	d.	1758	...	Winter Park	d.	...	1550
2516	Provo	d.	2126	...	**Denver** Union	a.	...	1838
2587	**Salt Lake City**	a.	2305	...	**Denver** Union	d.	...	1910
2587	**Salt Lake City**	d.	2330	...	McCook	d.	...	2349
3010	Elko	d.	0303	...	Hastings	d.	...	0142
3232	Winnemucca	d.	0540	...	Lincoln	d.	...	0326
3514	Reno	d.	0836	...	**Omaha**	a.	...	0459
3569	Truckee	d.	0937	...	**Omaha**	d.	...	0514
3785	Sacramento	d.	1413s	...	Ottumwa	d.	...	0909
3879	Martinez	d.	1526s	...	Burlington	d.	...	1036
3922	Emeryville	a.	1610	1625	Galesburg	d.	...	1131s
3936	**San Francisco** ‡	a.	...	1705	**Chicago** Union	a.	...	1450

C – CALIFORNIA ZEPHYR – 🛏 1, 2 cl., [2] and 🍸 Chicago - Emeryville and v.v.
s – Calls to set down only.
‡ – San Francisco Ferry Building Amtrak Station.

9295 CHICAGO - LOS ANGELES — Amtrak

km			3 D				4 D	
0	**Chicago** Union	d.	1500	...	**Los Angeles** Union	d.	1815	...
261	Galesburg	d.	1738	...	San Bernardino	d.	1959	...
329	Fort Madison	d.	1842	...	Victorville	d.	2110	...
677	**Kansas City**	a.	2211	...	Barstow	d.	2156	...
677	**Kansas City**	d.	2245	...	Needles	d.	0023	...
783	Topeka	d.	0029	...	Kingman	d.	0133*	...
1001	Newton	d.	0245	...	Williams Junction	d.	0250*	...
1247	Dodge City	d.	0525	...	**Flagstaff**	d.	0441*	...
1488	Lamar	d.	0659	...	Winslow	d.	0539*	...
1572	La Junta	d.	0830	...	Gallup	d.	0821	...
1704	Trinidad	d.	0950	...	**Abuquerque**	a.	1142	...
1741	Raton	d.	1056	...	**Abuquerque**	d.	1210	...
1918	Las Vegas NM	d.	1238	...	Lamy	d.	1317	...
2022	Lamy	d.	1424	...	Las Vegas NM	d.	1503	...
2132	**Abuquerque**	a.	1555	...	Raton	d.	1650	...
2132	**Abuquerque**	d.	1645	...	Trinidad	d.	1749	...
2391	Gallup	d.	1908	...	La Junta	d.	1941	...
2595	Winslow	d.	1950*	...	Lamar	d.	2240	...
2690	**Flagstaff**	d.	2057*	...	Dodge City	d.	0027	...
2768	Williams Junction	d.	2133*	...	Newton	d.	0259	...
2967	Kingman	d.	2346*	...	Topeka	d.	0518	...
3067	Needles	d.	0049	...	**Kansas City**	a.	0724	...
3337	Barstow	d.	0339	...	**Kansas City**	d.	0743	...
3398	Victorville	d.	0418	...	Fort Madison	d.	1109	...
3472	San Bernardino	d.	0532	...	Galesburg	d.	1208	...
3588	**Los Angeles** Union	a.	0815	...	**Chicago** Union	a.	1515	...

D – SOUTHWEST CHIEF – 🛏 1, 2 cl., [2] and 🍸 Chicago - Los Angeles and v.v.
* - Do not observe DST, schedule times will be one hour later from November 2 2014.

9300 CHICAGO - SAN ANTONIO — Amtrak

km			821 2 E	21 F			22 F	822 2 E
0	**Chicago** Union	d.	...	1345	**Los Angeles** Union	d.	2200b	...
148	Pontiac	d.	...	1527	**San Antonio**	a.	0450b	...
298	Springfield IL	d.	...	1714	**San Antonio**	d.	0700	...
457	**St. Louis**	a.	...	1921	San Marcos	d.	0832	...
457	**St. Louis**	d.	...	2000	Austin	d.	0931	...
717	Poplar Bluff	d.	...	2342	Taylor	d.	1022	...
813	Walnut Ridge	d.	...	0037	Temple	d.	1125	...
1007	Little Rock	d.	...	0310	**Fort Worth**	a.	1358	...
1127	Arkadelphia	d.	...	0420r	**Fort Worth**	d.	1420	1725
1240	Texarkana	d.	...	0558	Gainesville	d.	|	1831
1384	Longview	d.	...	0828	Ardmore	d.	|	1912
1588	**Dallas**	a.	...	1130	**Oklahoma City**	d.	|	2123
1588	**Dallas**	d.	...	1150	**Dallas**	a.	1520	...
336c	**Oklahoma City**	d.	0825	|	**Dallas**	d.	1540	...
172c	Ardmore	d.	1023	|	Longview	d.	1815	...
109c	Gainesville	d.	1105	|	Texarkana	d.	2043	...
1638	**Fort Worth**	a.	1223	1325	Arkadelphia	d.	2202r	...
1638	**Fort Worth**	d.	...	1410	Little Rock	d.	2339	...
1844	Temple	d.	...	1643	Walnut Ridge	d.	0141	...
1906	Taylor	d.	...	1736	Poplar Bluff	d.	0244	...
1962	Austin	d.	...	1830	**St. Louis**	a.	0719	...
2011	San Marcos	d.	...	1912	**St. Louis**	d.	0755	...
2060	**San Antonio**	a.	...	2155	Springfield IL	d.	0955	...
2060	**San Antonio**	d.	...	0245a	Pontiac	d.	1139	...
4389	**Los Angeles** Union	a.	...	0535a	**Chicago** Union	a.	1352	...

E – HEARTLAND FLYER – [2]
F – TEXAS EAGLE – 🛏 1, 2 cl., [2] and 🍸 Chicago (21/22) - San Antonio (421/422) - Los Angeles and v.v.
a – San Antonio - Los Angeles ②④⑦ only. Arrives Los Angeles ①③⑤. See Table 9310.
b – Los Angeles - San Antonio ③⑤⑦ only. Arrives San Antonio ①④⑥. See Table 9310.
c – km from Fort Worth.
r – Stops on request.

9305 SEATTLE - LOS ANGELES — Amtrak

km			11 G	🚌			🚌	14 G
	Vancouver BC	d.	...	0530	**Los Angeles** Union	d.	...	1010
0	**Seattle** King Street	d.	0935	0900	Santa Barbara	d.	...	1240
64	Tacoma	d.	1021	...	San Luis Obispo	d.	...	1535
114	Olympia	d.	1111	...	Paso Robles	d.	...	1637
151	Centralia	d.	1135	...	Salinas	d.	...	1828
219	Kelso Longview	d.	1219	...	San Jose	d.	...	2023
282	Vancouver WA	d.	1258	...	**Oakland**	a.	...	2124
298	**Portland**	a.	1350	...	**Oakland**	d.	...	2139
298	**Portland**	d.	1425	...	**San Francisco** ‡	d.	2110	|
382	Salem	d.	1537	...	Emeryville	a.	2145	2154
496	Eugene	d.	1710	...	Emeryville	d.	...	2204
691	Chemult	d.	2008	...	Martinez	d.	...	2246
808	Klamath Falls	d.	2200	...	**Sacramento**	d.	...	2359
976	Dunsmuir	d.	0035	...	Chico	d.	...	0147
1067	Redding	d.	0221	...	Redding	d.	...	0306
1186	Chico	d.	0350	...	Dunsmuir	d.	...	0456
1320	**Sacramento**	d.	0635	...	Klamath Falls	d.	...	0817
1397	Martinez	d.	0734	...	Chemult	d.	...	0932
1441	Emeryville	a.	0810	...	Eugene	d.	...	1236
1441	Emeryville	d.	0820	0825	Salem	d.	...	1355
	San Francisco ‡	a.	|	0900	**Portland**	a.	...	1532
1449	**Oakland**	a.	0835	...	**Portland**	d.	...	1612
1449	**Oakland**	d.	0850	...	Vancouver WA	d.	...	1628
1573	San Jose	d.	1007	...	Kelso Longview	d.	...	1706
1624	Salinas	d.	1148	...	Centralia	d.	...	1749
1780	Paso Robles	d.	1338	...	Olympia	d.	...	1814
1835	San Luis Obispo	d.	1520	...	Tacoma	d.	...	1903
2025	Santa Barbara	d.	1802	...	**Seattle** King Street	a.	2115	2037
2190	**Los Angeles** Union	a.	2100	...	Vancouver	a.	0020	...

G – COAST STARLIGHT – 🛏 1, 2 cl., [2] and 🍸 Seattle - Los Angeles and v.v.
‡ – San Francisco Ferry Building Amtrak Station.
NOTE: Due to extensive trackwork schedules are subject to change.

9310 NEW ORLEANS - LOS ANGELES — Amtrak

km			1563 🚌 J	1 ①③⑥ H			2 ③⑤⑦ H	1562 🚌 J
0	Orlando	d.	...	...	**Los Angeles** Union	d.	2200	...
235	**Jacksonville**	d.	2145	...	Pomona	d.	2241	...
509	Tallahasse	d.	0115	...	Palm Springs	d.	0036	...
998	Mobile	d.	0535	...	Yuma *	d.	0247	...
1230	**New Orleans**	a.	0755	...	Maricopa *	d.	0540	...
1230	**New Orleans**	d.	...	0900	Tucson *	d.	0815	...
1434	New Iberia	d.	...	1156r	Benson *	d.	0915r	...
1462	Lafeyette	d.	...	1224	Lordsburg	d.	1215r	...
1581	Lake Charles	d.	...	1355	**El Paso**	a.	1510	...
1678	Beaumont	d.	...	1548	**El Paso**	d.	1535	...
1810	Houston	d.	...	1855	Alpine	d.	2045	...
2146	**San Antonio**	a.	...	0005	Del Rio	d.	0102	...
2146	**San Antonio**	d.	...	0245	**San Antonio**	a.	0450	...
2418	Del Rio	d.	...	0549	**San Antonio**	d.	0625	...
2765	Alpine	d.	...	1038	Houston	d.	1210	...
3114	**El Paso**	a.	...	1322	Beaumont	d.	1405	...
3114	**El Paso**	d.	...	1347	Lake Charles	d.	1529	...
3350	Lordsburg	d.	...	1613r	Lafeyette	d.	1715	...
3539	Benson*	d.	...	1718r	New Iberia	d.	1741r	...
3619	Tucson*	d.	...	1845	**New Orleans**	a.	2140	...
3757	Maricopa*	d.	...	2102	**New Orleans**	d.	...	1030
4021	Yuma*	d.	...	2349	Mobile	d.	...	1350
4253	Palm Springs	d.	...	0202	Tallahasse	a.	...	2320
4371	Pomona	d.	...	0404s	**Jacksonville**	a.	...	0200
4422	**Los Angeles** Union	a.	...	0535	Orlando	a.	...	...

H – SUNSET LIMITED – 🛏 1, 2 cl., [2] and 🍸; Conveys TEXAS EAGLE (421/2) San Antonio - Los Angeles and v.v.
J – Operated by Greyhound USA. Change at Mobile and Tallahasse.
r – Calls on request.
s – Calls to set down only.
* - Do not observe DST, schedule times will be one hour later from November 2 2014.

Amtrak Most trains 🍷 VANCOUVER - SEATTLE - PORTLAND - EUGENE 9315

km		503	🚌	505	501	11	513	507	🚌	509	🚌	517
		①-⑤		⑥⑦								
		A	D	A	A	B	A	A		A		A
0	**Vancouver** (Canada) d.	...	...	...	...	0530*	0640	0900*	...	1130*	1700	1745
93	Bellingham d.	...	...	...	...	|	0845	|	...	|	|	1949
135	Mount Vernon d.	...	...	...	...	|	0915	|	...	|	|	2019
198	Everett d.	...	...	...	...	|	1002	|	...	|	|	2109
251	**Seattle** King Street a.	...	...	...	...	0900*	1105	1245*	...	1530*	2045	2210
251	**Seattle** King Street d.	...	...	...	0730	0935	1125	1400	...	1730	▬	...
315	Tacoma d.	...	...	...	0813	1021	1208	1443	...	1813	...	...
365	Olympia d.	...	...	...	0850	1111	1245	1520	...	1850	...	...
402	Centralia d.	...	...	...	0911	1135	1306	1541	...	1911	...	...
470	Kelso Longview d.	...	...	...	0952	1219	1347	1622	...	1952	...	...
533	Vancouver WA d.	...	...	...	1030	1258	1425	1700	...	2030	...	...
549	**Portland** a.	...	...	...	1120	1350	1515	1750	...	2120	🚌	...
549	**Portland** d.	0600	0700	0830	1140*	1425	1535*	1805	1900	...	2130	...
633	Salem d.	0707	0820	0937	1240*	1537	1645*	1912	2005t	...	2255t	...
678	Albany d.	0736	0855	1006	1315*	1610	1720*	1941	2040t	...	2335t	...
747	**Eugene** a.	0835	0945	1105	1405*	1703	1810*	2040	2130	...	0025	...

	510	🚌	500	🚌	506	516	14	🚌	508	🚌
	A		A		A	A	B	C	A	
Eugene d.	...	...	0530	0720	0840*	1140*	1236	1315	1600	1730
Albany d.	...	...	0613	0810	0935*	1235*	1322	1405	1643	1825
Salem d.	...	...	0642	0850	1015*	1305*	1355	1440	1712	1855
Portland a.	...	...	0805	1010	1145*	1415*	1532	1545	1835	2025
Portland d.	...	...	0820	▬	1215	1445	1612	...	1850	...
Vancouver WA d.	...	...	0835	...	1230	1500	1628	...	1905	...
Kelso Longview d.	...	...	0910	...	1305	1535	1706	...	1940	...
Centralia d.	...	...	0951	...	1346	1616	1749	...	2021	...
Olympia d.	...	...	1012	...	1407	1637	1814	...	2042	...
Tacoma d.	...	...	1054	...	1449	1719	1903	...	2124	...
Seattle King Street a.	...	...	1210	🚌	1605	1835	2037	...	2230	...
Seattle King Street d.	0740	1045	1240*	1345	1645*	1850	2130*	...	...	...
Everett d.	0831	|	1325*	|	|	1942	|	...	...	...
Mount Vernon d.	0921	|	1410*	|	|	2027	|	...	...	...
Bellingham d.	0952	|	1440*	|	|	2100	|	...	...	...
Vancouver (Canada) a.	1140	1415	...	1715	2015*	2250	0030*	...	...	...

A – CASCADES – (12) and 🍷.
B – COAST STARLIGHT – Table **9305**.
C – Additional trip 1445.
D – Additional trip 1040.
t – Paid ticket required to board.
* – Connection by 🚌.

Amtrak Most trains 🍷 SAN LUIS OBISPO - LOS ANGELES - SAN DIEGO 9320

km		🚌	562	564	566			🚌	768	🚌	768	572	572	774	580	🚌	582	🚌	784		790	1790	🚌	796
								A	A	B	B	A	B								①-⑤	⑥⑦		
0	**San Luis Obispo** d.	...	...	...	...	...	...	0350	....	0310	....	...	...	0655	...	...	...	1030	...	...	1335	1355	1540	...
40	Santa Maria d.	...	...	...	...	...	...	0440	....	0410	....	...	...	0730	...	...	...	1120u	...	...	1411	1431	1635	...
190	Santa Barbara d.	...	...	...	...	...	...	0630	0648	0600	0613	...	...	0926	...	1255	...	1345	1403	...	1612	1635	1840	1858
248	Oxnard d.	...	...	...	...	...	...	...	0742	...	0707	...	...	1017	...	1350	...	...	1456	...	1707	1730	...	1950
355	**Los Angeles** Union a.	...	...	...	...	...	...	...	0935	...	0900	...	...	1215	...	1535	...	...	1655	...	1910	1915	...	2145
355	**Los Angeles** Union d.	0230	0615	0725	0830	...	...	...	0950	...	0920	1115	1110	1230	1500	...	1610	...	1710	...	1930	1930	...	2210
406	Anaheim d.	|	0652	0803	0908	...	...	...	1030	...	1005	1153	1148	1308	1538	...	1648	...	1748	...	2011	2011	...	2248
448	San Juan Capistrano d.	0355s	0726	0841	0947	...	...	...	1107	...	1107	1233	1236	1343	1611	...	1722	...	1822	...	2048	2048	...	2321
495	Oceanside d.	0430s	0809	0916	1024	...	...	...	1141	...	1142	1308	1318	1418	1645	...	1756	...	1903	...	2119	2119	...	2352
560	**San Diego** a.	0515	0900	1010	1122	...	...	...	1235	...	1241	1403	1424	1515	1747	...	1903	...	2007	...	2225	2224	...	0100

		761	1761	763	🚌	565	567	769	🚌		573	777	579	583	583		785	🚌	591	🚌	591	🚌	595	🚌
		①-⑤	⑥⑦											A	B				A	A	B	A		
San Diego d.	...	...	...	0605	...	0705	0824	0925	...	...	1042	1200	1340	1440	1500	...	1600	...	1845	...	1845	...	2105	2215
Oceanside d.	...	...	...	0701	...	0755	0925	1017	...	...	1146	1252	1431	1540	1551	...	1659	...	1937	...	1943	...	2204	2315
San Juan Capistrano d.	...	...	...	0734	...	0829	0957	1048	...	...	1217	1324	1504	1619	1624	...	1732	...	2007	...	2013	...	2236	2350
Anaheim d.	...	...	...	0807	...	0904	1034	1123	...	...	1253	1359	1538	1654	1704	...	1808	...	2047	...	2053	...	2309	|
Los Angeles Union a.	...	...	...	0850	...	0950	1118	1210	...	...	1338	1445	1625	1740	1750	...	1855	...	2135	...	2145	...	2355	0130
Los Angeles Union d.	...	0735	0750	0905	...	...	...	1225	...	...	...	1500	...	...	...	...	1910	...	...	2150	...	2200	...	...
Oxnard d.	...	0921	0921	1037	...	...	...	1359	...	...	...	1632	...	...	...	...	2040	...	...	2345	...	2355	...	...
Santa Barbara d.	...	1022	1022	1140	1145	...	...	1500	1510	...	...	1742	...	...	...	...	2145	2155	...	0035	...	0045	...	...
Santa Maria d.	...	1216	1216	...	1315	...	...	...	1635	...	...	1936	...	...	...	...	...	2325	...	...	...	...	...	...
San Luis Obispo a.	...	1300	1300	...	1410	...	...	...	1715	...	...	2030	...	...	...	...	...	0015	...	...	...	...	...	...

A – Will not run on ⑥⑦ from Jul. 19 - Aug. 31 and Sept. 1
B – Will only run on ⑥⑦ from Jul. 19 - Aug. 31 and Sept. 1
s – Calls to set down only.

Amtrak 2nd class Most trains 🍷 SAN JOSE and SAN FRANCISCO - SACRAMENTO 9325

km		520	522	720	524	724	526	528	728	530	732	532	734	534	736	536	538	738	540	542	742	544*	746	546	548	748
		①-⑤	①-⑤	⑥⑦	①-⑤	⑥⑦	①-⑤	①-⑤	⑥⑦	①-⑤	⑥⑦	①-⑤	⑥⑦	①-⑤	⑥⑦	①-⑤	①-⑤	⑥⑦	①-⑤	①-⑤	⑥⑦		⑥⑦	①-⑤	①-⑤	⑥⑦
0	**San Jose** d.	...	...	...	0640	0750	...	0905	0950	...	...	1220	1250	...	1420	...	1510	...	...	1620	1625	1750	...	1915	...	2110
75	Oakland JLS ¶ d.	0525	0625	0720	0745	0855	0915	1015	1055	1215	1225	1325	1355	1450	1525	1530	1620	1625	1650	1730	1730	1855	1955	2020	2205	2215
	San Francisco ‡ d.	0515e	0605e	0700e	0710e	0825e	0845e	0945e	1025e	1145e	1155e	1255e	1325e	1420e	1455e	1500e	1540e	1555e	1620e	1655e	1655e	1815e	1925e	1955e	2135e	2145e
83	Emeryville d.	0535	0635	0730	0755	0905	0925	1025	1105	1225	1235	1335	1405	1500	1535	1540	1630	1635	1700	1745	1740	1905	2005	2030	2215	2225
128	Martinez d.	0614	0714	0809	0834	0944	1004	1104	1144	1304	1314	1414	1444	1539	1614	1619	1709	1714	1739	1824	1819	1944	2044	2109	2254	2304
219	**Sacramento** a.	0723	0823	0918	0948	1058	1113	1218	1258	1413	1423	1528	1558	1648	1726	1722	1823	1823	1848	1938	1922	2058	2153	2228	0003	0013

	521	523	723	525	527	727	529	531	729	533	535	733	537	737	541	741	543	743	545	745	747	547	549	749	551	751
	①-⑤	①-⑤	⑥⑦	①-⑤	①-⑤	⑥⑦	①-⑤	①-⑤	⑥⑦	①-⑤	①-⑤	⑥⑦	①-⑤	⑥⑦	①-⑤	⑥⑦	①-⑤	⑥⑦	①-⑤	⑥⑦	⑥⑦	①-⑤	①-⑤	⑥⑦	①-⑤	⑥⑦
Sacramento d.	0430	0530	0540	0620	0700	0740	0740	0820	0910	0920	1010	1040	1210	1210	1410	1415	1535	1535	1640	1640	1740	1740	1850	1910	2110	2110
Martinez d.	0530	0630	0640	0720	0800	0840	0840	0920	1010	1020	1110	1140	1310	1310	1510	1515	1635	1635	1740	1740	1840	1840	1950	2010	2210	2210
Emeryville d.	0610	0710	0720	0800	0840	0920	0920	1000	1050	1100	1150	1220	1350	1350	1550	1555	1715	1715	1820	1820	1920	1920	2030	2050	2250	2250
San Francisco ‡ a.	0640e	0755e	0755e	0840e	0920e	0950e	0950e	1035e	1115e	1135e	1225e	1255e	1425e	1425e	1620e	1625e	1750e	1750e	1845e	1845e	1950e	1950e	2100e	2125e	2320e	2320e
Oakland JLS ¶ a.	0621	0721	0731	0818	0851	0931	0938	1018	1108	1118	1201	1231	1401	1401	1608	1606	1726	1726	1838	1838	1931	1931	2048	2108	2308	2308
San Jose a.	0738	0838	0848	...	1013	1048	...	...	...	...	1318	1348	1518	1518	...	1723	1848	1848	...	...	2048	2058	2355b	2359b	...	...

b – Connection by 🚌, change at **Emeryville**.
e – Connection by 🚌 San Francisco - Emeryville and v.v.
‡ – San Francisco Ferry Building Amtrak Station.
¶ – Oakland Jack London Square.
* – Train **744** on ⑥⑦.

Amtrak 2nd class Most trains 🍷 OAKLAND and SAN FRANCISCO - BAKERSFIELD 9330

km		🚌	702	712	714	716	🚌	704	718		
		◧					◧				
0	**Oakland** JLS ¶ d.	0530	...	0730	1005	1315	1515	...	1750	...	...
	San Francisco ‡ d.	0450	...	0700e	0935e	1245e	1435	...	1715e	...	...
8	Emeryville d.	0515	...	0740	1015	1325	1500	...	1800	...	...
53	Martinez d.	|	...	0819	1054	1404	|	...	1839	...	...
90	**Sacramento** d.	|	0640	|	|	|	|	1655	|	...	...
148	Lodi d.	|	0718	|	|	|	|	1733	|	...	...
167	Stockton San Joaquin d.	0715d	0735d	0917	1149	1503	1720d	1750d	1934	...	...
215	Modesto d.	...	0809	0945	1217	1531	...	1824	2007	...	...
271	Merced d.	...	0851	1031	1259	1613	...	1906	2047	...	...
329	Madera d.	...	0919	1059	1333	1646	...	1934	2120	...	...
364	Fresno d.	...	0955	1135	1410	1720	...	2006	2155	...	...
412	Hanford d.	...	1028	1209	1444	1754	...	2039	2228	...	...
542	**Bakersfield** a.	...	1202	1341	1611	1926	...	2207	2356	...	...
704	Los Angeles a.	...	1430*	1610*	1840*	2150*	...	0030*	0220*	...	...

	711	701	🚌	713	715	717	703	🚌		
			◧					◧		
Los Angeles d.	0145*	0410*	...	0735*	1045*	1305*	1510*	...	...	...
Bakersfield d.	0455	0715	...	1005	1320	1545	1820	...	...	...
Hanford d.	0612	0832	...	1126	1442	1706	1940	...	...	...
Fresno d.	0650	0910	...	1205	1520	1745	2018	...	...	...
Madera d.	0714	0937	...	1229	1544	1809	2042	...	...	...
Merced d.	0748	1008	...	1308	1622	1842	2115	...	...	...
Modesto d.	0828	1049	...	1342	1657	1925	2152	...	...	...
Stockton S.Joaquin d.	0901	1120d	1130d	1418	1733	2003	2225d	2235d	...	...
Lodi d.	|	1134	|	|	|	|	2239	|	...	...
Sacramento a.	|	1230	|	|	|	|	2330	|	...	...
Martinez d.	1003	...	|	1519	1828	2056	...	|	...	...
Emeryville d.	1048s	...	1300	1603s	1913s	2143s	...	0010	...	...
San Francisco ‡ a.	1120e	...	1320	1640e	1945e	2215e	...	0035	...	...
Oakland JLS ¶ a.	1100	...	1250	1615	1925	2155	...	2355	...	...

d – Stockton **Downtown**. Also known as ACE station.
e – Connection by 🚌 San Francisco - Emeryville and v.v.
s – Calls to set down only.
* – Connection by 🚌.
◧ – Calling order is San Francisco - Emeryville - Oakland and v.v.
‡ – San Francisco Ferry Building Amtrak Station
¶ – Oakland Jack London Square.

What's new this month *(continued from page 3)*

BULGARIA

As mentioned earlier, the Thessaloníki – Kulata – Sofia service made a welcome return in May with one daily train being provided in each direction. Please be aware that seating capacity is limited (there are only two through coaches) and reservation is compulsory. There have also been a number of alterations to domestic services between Sofia and Kulata and full details of these will be found in Table **1560**.

A brand new international service commenced on May 10 between Vidin and Craiova, the first scheduled passenger services using the recently completed Danube bridge. There are two daily return journeys and timings will be found in Table **1520**. These appear to be through services, although some reports suggest that a change of train at Golenţi may be required.

LITHUANIA

A number of additional services have been introduced between Vilnius and Kaunas (Table **1811**).

ESTONIA

From June 1 *Elron* has introduced additional services on the Tallinn – Tartu – Valga route. The express train service between Tallinn and Tartu has doubled from two to four, and a third train is now running between Tartu and Valga (Table **1880**).

RUSSIA

Amongst the many changes in the new timetable is an increase in the high-speed service between Moskva and Nizhni Novgorod (Table **1990**), which now sees three *Swallow* units each way (previously one) as well as the two *Sapsan* trains. The withdrawal of train **1248/9** Berlin to Saratov at the end of last year has allowed space to expand our coverage of services to and within Kazakhstan (Tables **1975** and **1980**).

SHIPPING

DFDS Seaways is to cease operation of its Harwich – Esbjerg route on September 29 (Table **2220**). This crossing, the last remaining passenger ferry between Great Britain and Scandinavia, was inaugurated as long ago as 1875.

BEYOND EUROPE

This month's Beyond Europe section covers North America with Tables numbered **9000** upwards.

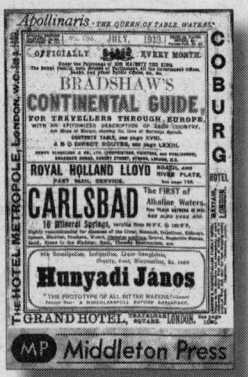

As an added extra for readers of this seasonal Summer edition we are including the remaining five BEYOND EUROPE sections, in addition to the pages for **North America** which appear in the preceding pages.

The tables covering **Africa and the Middle East, India, South East Asia, Australia and New Zealand**, **China** and **Japan** appear in our monthly editions. Limited updates have been made to these tables for this seasonal edition.

As a further bonus we are also including a small section for **South America**, which does not appear in the monthly editions.

BEYOND EUROPE
Africa and the Middle East

Introduction

The Beyond Europe section covers principal rail services in a different area of the world each month. There are six areas, each appearing twice yearly as follows:

India:	January and July editions
South East Asia and Australasia:	February and August editions
China:	March and September editions
Japan:	April and October editions
Africa and the Middle East:	May and November editions
North America:	June and December editions

The months have been chosen so that we can bring you up-to-date information for those countries which make seasonal changes.

Limited details of services in South America can be found in the European Rail Timetable Summer and Winter editions.

Contents

INDEX OF PLACES

by table number

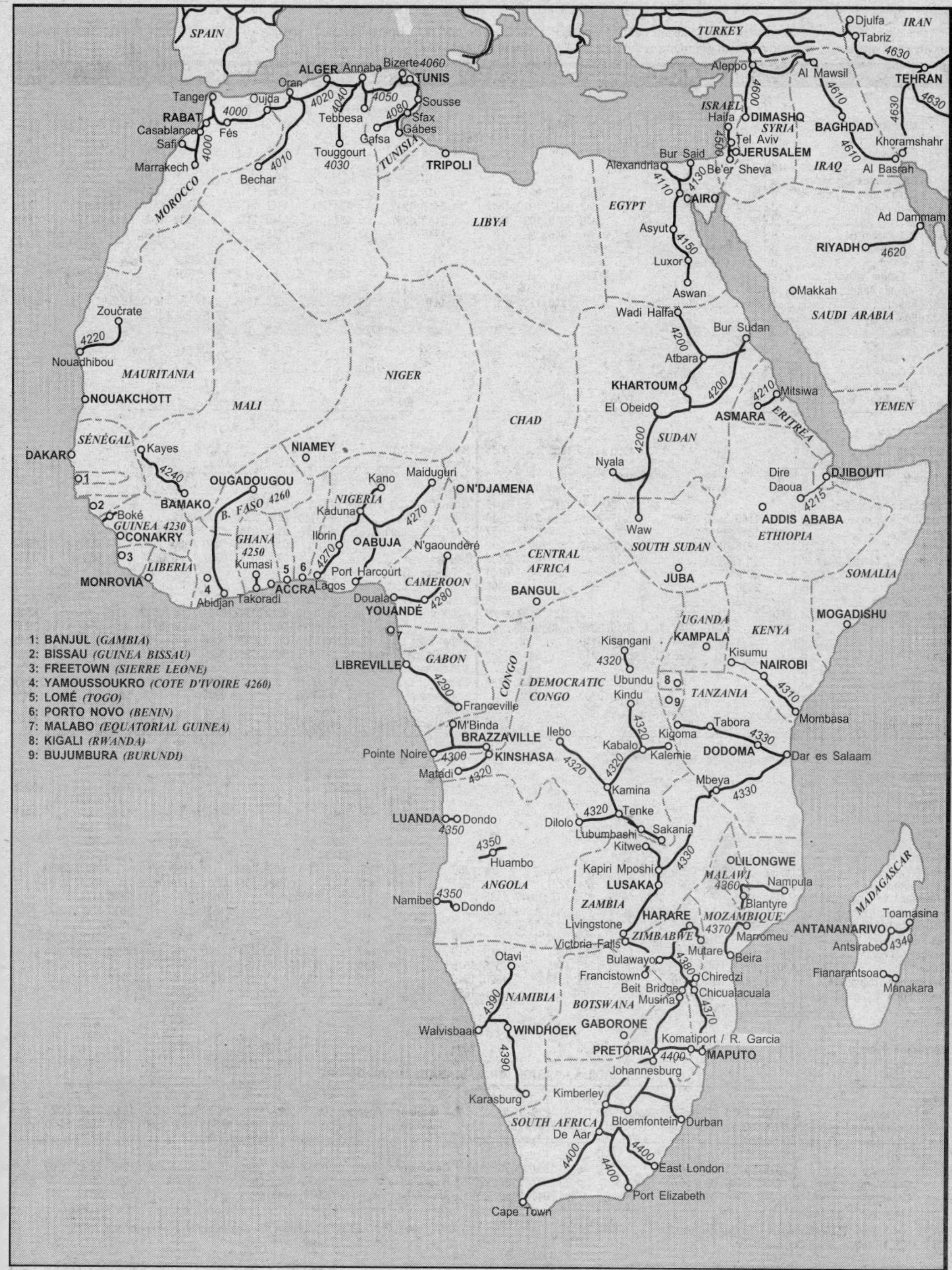
SPAIN
TURKEY
IRAN
Djulfa
Tabriz
4630
TEHRAN
ALGER
Annaba
Bizerte
4060
TUNIS
Tanger
Oran
Oujda
RABAT
4000
Casablanca
Safi
Fés
Marrakech
4020
4040
4050
Tebbesa
Sousse
4080
Sfax
Gafsa
Gabes
Touggourt
4030
TUNISIA
TRIPOLI
Bechar
4010
MOROCCO
Aleppo
Al Mawsil
4600
4610
ISRAEL
Haifa
DIMASHQ
SYRIA
BAGHDAD
Tel Aviv
4500
JERUSALEM
Khoramshahr
Bur Said
Alexandria
Be'er Sheva
IRAQ
Al Basrah
4110
4130
CAIRO
EGYPT
LIBYA
Asyut
4150
Luxor
Aswan
Ad Dammam
RIYADH
4620
Makkah
SAUDI ARABIA
Zoučrate
4220
Nouadhibou
MAURITANIA
NOUAKCHOTT
MALI
NIGER
Wadi Halfa
4200
Bur Sudan
Atbara
KHARTOUM
El Obeid
ASMARA
4210
Mitsiwa
ERITREA
YEMEN
CHAD
SUDAN
SÉNÉGAL
DAKAR
Kayes
4240
NIAMEY
OUGADOUGOU
Kano
Maiduguri
N'DJAMENA
Nyala
Dire Daoua
DJIBOUTI
4215
BAMAKO
B. FASO 4260
NIGERIA
Kaduna
4270
Boké
GUINEA 4230
CONAKRY
GHANA
4250
Ilorin
ABUJA
N'gaounderé
ADDIS ABABA
ETHIOPIA
Waw
SOUTH SUDAN
Kumasi
Port Harcourt
CAMEROON
CENTRAL AFRICA
JUBA
SOMALIA
LIBERIA
MONROVIA
Abidjan
Takoradi
ACCRA
Lagos
Douala
YOUANDÉ
4280
BANGUL
UGANDA
KAMPALA
KENYA
MOGADISHU
Kisangani
4320
Ubundu
Kisumu
NAIROBI
LIBREVILLE
GABON
4290
Franceville
CONGO
DEMOCRATIC CONGO
Kindu
TANZANIA
4310
Mombasa
M'Binda
BRAZZAVILLE
Pointe Noire
4300
KINSHASA
Matadi
Ilebo
Kabalo
Kigoma
Kalemie
Tabora
4330
DODOMA
Dar es Salaam
Kamina
Mbeya
LUANDA
Dondo
4350
Dilolo
Tenke
Lubumbashi
Sakania
Huambo
Kitwe
Kapiri Mposhi
LILONGWE
MALAWI
4360
Nampula
Blantyre
ANGOLA
LUSAKA
Namibe
Dondo
ZAMBIA
HARARE
MOZAMBIQUE
MADAGASCAR
Toamasina
ANTANANARIVO
Antsirabe
4340
Livingstone
ZIMBABWE
4370
Marromeu
Victoria Falls
Mutare
Beira
Bulawayo
Otavi
4380
Chiredzi
Francistown
Fianarantsoa
Manakara
Beit Bridge
Chicualacuala
Musina
NAMIBIA
BOTSWANA
4390
Walvisbaai
WINDHOEK
GABORONE
Komatiport / R. Garcia
PRETORIA
4400
MAPUTO
Johannesburg
Karasburg
Kimberley
SOUTH AFRICA
Bloemfontein
Durban
De Aar
East London
Port Elizabeth
Cape Town
1: BANJUL (GAMBIA)
2: BISSAU (GUINEA BISSAU)
3: FREETOWN (SIERRE LEONE)
4: YAMOUSSOUKRO (COTE D'IVOIRE 4260)
5: LOMÉ (TOGO)
6: PORTO NOVO (BENIN)
7: MALABO (EQUATORIAL GUINEA)
8: KIGALI (RWANDA)
9: BUJUMBURA (BURUNDI)

MOROCCO

Capital: **Rabat** (GMT + 0). 2014 Public Holidays: Jan. 1, 11, 13, May 1, July 28, Aug. 14, 20, 21, Oct. 3, 24, Nov. 6, 18.

Rail services in Morocco are operated by Office National des Chemins de Fer (ONCF. www.oncf.ma). Unless indicated trains convey 1st and 2nd class seating. Trains may also convey couchette and/or sleeping cars and where this is the case it will be noted in the footnotes.

4000 MARRAKECH - CASABLANCA - FÈS - OUJDA and BENI NSAR — ONCF

km														B		B									
0	**Marrakech** Guéliz d.	...	...	...	...	...	...	0455	...	...	...	0655	...	...	...	...	0855	...	...	...	1055	...	...	...	1255
**	**Safi** d.	...	...	...	...	...	...	|	...	...	0545	|	...	...	...	...	|	...	...	...	|	...	...	...	|
74	Benguerir d.	...	...	...	...	...	...	0546	...	...	0744	0750	...	...	...	...	1002	...	...	...	1150	...	...	...	1402
174	Settat d.	...	...	...	...	...	...	0716	...	...	...	0916	...	...	...	...	1116	...	...	...	1316	...	...	...	1516
257	**Casablanca** Voyageurs a.	...	...	...	...	...	...	0810	...	...	...	1010	...	...	...	...	1210	...	...	...	1410	...	...	...	1610
257	**Casablanca** Voyageurs d.	0515	0545	0615	0715	...	0745	0815	0915	0945	...	1015	1115	...	1145	...	1215	1315	...	1345	1415	1515	1545	...	1615
346	Rabat Ville d.	0612	0647	0717	0812	...	0847	0917	1012	1047	...	1117	1212	...	1247	...	1317	1412	...	1447	1517	1612	1647	...	1717
386	Kenitra d.	0637	0716	0749	0837	...	0916	0949	1037	1116	...	1149	1237	...	1316	...	1349	1437	...	1516	1549	1637	1716	...	1749
471	Sidi Kacem d.	|	|	0845	|	...	|	1045	|	|	...	1245	|	1332	|	1435	1445	|	...	|	1645	|	|	1835	1845
	Mechraa Bel Ksiri d.	|	0814	|	|	...	1014	|	|	1214	...	|	|	|	1414	1511	|	|	...	1614	|	|	1814	1911	|
	Asilah d.	|	0938	|	|	...	1142	|	|	1338	...	|	|	|	1538	1639	|	|	...	1738	|	|	1931	2041	|
620	**Tanger** Ville a.	|	1030	|	|	...	1230	|	|	1430	...	|	|	|	1630	1725	|	|	...	1830	|	|	2020	2125	|
526	Meknes Amir d.	0803	...	0934	1007	...	...	1134	1203	...	...	1334	1403	1424	...	...	1534	1603	...	...	1734	1803	...	...	1934
582	**Fès** a.	0835	...	1010	1035	...	...	1210	1235	...	...	1410	1435	1500	...	...	1610	1635	...	...	1810	1835	...	...	2010
582	**Fès** d.	...	...	1055	...	...	...	...	...	...	...	...	...	1525	...	...	...	...	1715	...	...	...	...	...	...
701	Taza d.	...	...	1306	...	...	...	...	...	...	...	...	...	1729	...	...	...	...	1915	...	...	...	...	...	...
	Guercif d.	...	...	1401	...	...	...	...	...	...	...	...	...	1824	...	...	...	...	2014	...	...	...	...	...	...
818	Taourirt d.	...	...	1446	...	1520	...	...	...	...	...	...	...	1908	...	...	...	...	2130	...	...	...	...	...	...
935	**Oujda** a.	...	...	1635	...	|	...	...	...	...	...	...	...	2100	...	...	...	...	|	...	...	...	...	...	...
	Nador d.	...	...	...	...	1703	...	...	...	...	...	...	...	...	...	...	...	...	2313	...	...	...	...	...	...
	Beni Nsar Port a.	...	...	...	...	1723	...	...	...	...	...	...	...	...	...	...	...	...	2333	...	...	...	...	...	...

			C							A
Marrakech Guéliz d.	...	...	1455	...	...	1655	...	1855	...	2055
Safi d.	...	...	|	...	1545	|	...	|	...	|
Benguerir d.	...	...	1550	...	1744	1802	...	1951	...	2150
Settat d.	...	...	1716	...	...	1916	...	2116	...	2314
Casablanca Voyageurs a.	...	...	1810	...	...	2010	...	2210	...	0010
Casablanca Voyageurs d.	1715	1745	1815	1945	...	2015	2115	2215	2245	0045
Rabat Ville d.	1812	1847	1917	2048	...	2117	2222	2317	2347	0157
Kenitra d.	1837	1916	1948	2121	...	2148	2249	2352	0020	0232
Sidi Kacem d.	|	|	2044	2210	...	2239	|	0043	0108	0405
Mechraa Bel Ksiri d.	|	2014	|	|	...	|	|	|	|	0441
Asilah d.	|	2136	|	|	...	|	|	|	|	0608
Tanger Ville a.	|	2225	|	|	...	|	|	|	|	0700
Meknes Amir d.	2007	...	2133	2304	...	2331	|	0131	0157	▬
Fès a.	2035	...	2210	2340	...	0010	0048	0210	0230	...
Fès d.	...	...	...	0015	...	...	0110	...	0250	...
Taza d.	...	...	...	0225	...	...	0316	...	0443	...
Guercif d.	...	...	...	0323	...	...	0416	...	0536	...
Taourirt d.	...	...	...	|	...	...	0503	...	0622	0745
Oujda a.	...	...	...	|	...	...	0700	...	0810	|
Nador d.	...	...	...	0600	...	...	...	...	...	0932
Beni Nsar Port a.	...	...	...	0625	...	...	...	...	...	0953

	A	C								
Beni Nsar Port d.	...	1925	...	...	...	...	...	...	...	...
Nador d.	...	1943	...	...	...	...	...	...	...	...
Oujda d.	...	|	2000	...	2110	...	...	...	...	...
Taourirt d.	...	|	2151	...	2250	...	...	...	...	...
Guercif d.	...	2201	2235	...	2332	...	...	...	...	...
Taza d.	...	2259	2336	...	0032	...	...	...	...	...
Fès a.	...	0100	0147	...	0240	...	...	...	...	...
Fès d.	...	0145	0210	0230	0300	0450	...	0550	...	0650
Meknes Amir d.	...	0220	0243	0307	|	0524	...	0621	...	0724
Tanger Ville d.	2135	|	|	|	|	|	...	|	0535	|
Asilah d.	2225	|	|	|	|	|	...	|	0612	|
Mechraa Bel Ksiri d.	2351	|	|	|	|	|	...	|	0729	|
Sidi Kacem d.	0110	0313	0342	0404	|	0612	...	|	|	0812
Kenitra d.	0225	0425	0445	0505	0530	0710	...	0747	0840	0908
Rabat Ville d.	0315	0515	0530	0545	0615	0745	...	0815	0915	0945
Casablanca Voyageurs a.	0430	0615	0630	0645	0715	0845	...	0910	1020	1045
Casablanca Voyageurs d.	0450	...	...	0650	...	0850	...	...	...	1050
Settat d.	0541	...	...	0741	...	0941	...	...	...	1141
Benguerir d.	0659	...	...	0900	...	1106	1200	...	...	1300
Safi a.	|	...	...	|	...	|	1402	...	...	|
Marrakech Guéliz a.	0800	...	...	1000	...	1200	...	...	...	1400

									B				B												
Beni Nsar Port d.	...	...	...	...	...	...	...	...	...	...	...	...	...	...	0825	...	...	...	...	...	...	1210	...	...	1745
Nador d.	...	...	...	...	...	...	...	...	...	...	...	...	...	...	0843	...	...	...	...	...	...	1228	...	...	1803
Oujda d.	...	...	...	...	...	...	...	...	...	...	...	...	0710	...	|	...	...	...	...	...	...	|	1300	...	|
Taourirt d.	...	...	...	...	...	...	...	...	...	...	...	...	0854	...	1045	...	...	...	...	...	...	1412	1447	...	1947
Guercif d.	...	...	...	...	...	...	...	...	...	...	...	...	0936	...	1130	...	...	...	...	...	...	▬	1529	...	...
Taza d.	...	...	...	...	...	...	...	...	...	...	...	...	1034	...	1227	...	...	...	...	...	...	...	1625	...	...
Fès a.	...	...	...	...	...	...	...	...	...	...	...	...	1235	...	1440	...	...	...	...	...	...	...	1830	...	...
Fès d.	0750	...	0850	0950	...	...	1050	1150	...	...	1250	...	1305	1350	...	...	1450	1550	...	1650	1750	...	1850	2050	...
Meknes Amir d.	0821	...	0924	1021	...	...	1124	1221	...	...	1324	...	1342	1421	...	...	1524	1621	...	1724	1821	...	1924	2124	...
Tanger Ville d.	|	0735	|	|	0825	0935	|	|	1040	1135	|	...	|	|	...	1335	|	|	1535	|	|	1735	|	|	...
Asilah d.	|	0812	|	|	0904	1014	|	|	1113	1213	|	...	|	|	...	1413	|	|	1611	|	|	1813	|	|	...
Mechraa Bel Ksiri d.	|	0929	|	|	1040	1129	|	|	1240	1329	|	...	|	|	...	1530	|	|	1729	|	|	1930	|	|	...
Sidi Kacem d.	|	|	1012	|	1121	|	1212	|	1321	|	1412	...	1433	|	...	|	1612	|	|	1812	|	|	2012	2212	...
Kenitra d.	0947	1040	1110	1147	...	1240	1310	1347	...	1440	1510	...	...	1547	...	1640	1710	1747	1840	1910	1947	2038	2105	2305	...
Rabat Ville d.	1015	1115	1145	1215	...	1315	1345	1415	...	1515	1545	...	...	1615	...	1715	1745	1815	1915	1945	2015	2115	2145	2345	...
Casablanca Voyageurs a.	1110	1220	1245	1310	...	1420	1445	1510	...	1620	1645	...	...	1710	...	1820	1845	1910	2020	2045	2110	2220	2245	0045	...
Casablanca Voyageurs d.	...	...	1250	...	...	...	1450	...	...	...	1650	...	...	...	...	...	1850	...	...	2050	...	...	...	...	...
Settat d.	...	...	1341	...	...	...	1541	...	...	...	1741	...	...	...	...	...	1941	...	...	2141	...	...	...	...	...
Benguerir d.	...	...	1506	...	...	...	1700	...	...	...	1906	2000	...	...	...	...	2059	...	...	2259	...	...	...	...	...
Safi a.	...	...	|	...	...	...	|	...	...	...	|	2202	...	...	...	...	|	...	...	|	...	...	...	...	...
Marrakech Guéliz a.	...	...	1600	...	...	...	1800	...	...	...	2005	...	...	...	...	...	2203	...	...	2359	...	...	...	...	...

EL JADIDA - CASABLANCA - CASABLANCA AIRPORT

km		①–⑥									
0	**El Jadida** d.	0630	0830	1030	1130	1230	1430	1730	1830	1930	...
123	**Casablanca** V'geurs a.	0751	0951	1151	1315	1351	1551	1851	2005	2051	...

	①–⑥									
Casablanca V'geurs d.	0627	0827	0920	1027	1227	1427	1627	1727	1927	...
El Jadida a.	0750	0950	1045	1150	1350	1550	1750	1850	2050	...

km										
0	Ain Seeba d.	0257	0430	0557	0657		1857	1957	2057	2157
	Casablanca V'geurs d.	0307	0440	0607	0707	and hourly	1907	2007	2107	2207
	Casablanca Airport a.	0340	0513	0640	0740	until	1940	2040	2140	2240

Casablanca Airport d.	0000	0400	0600	0700	and hourly	1900	2000	2100	2200
Casablanca V'geurs a.	0032	0432	0632	0732	until	1932	2032	2132	2232
Ain Seeba a.	0043	0443	0643	0743	_	1943	2043	2143	2243

A – 1, 2 cl., [12] Marrakech - Tanger and v.v.
B – [12] Tanger - Fés - Oudja and v.v.
C – 1, 2 cl., [12] Casablanca V. - Fès - Beni Nsar Port and v.v.
** – Safi - Benguerir: *142 km.*

4005 CASABLANCA - RABAT - KENITRA — ONCF

km	↓		⚒	A	⚒	⚒	C																			
93	**Casablanca** Port d.	0630	0700	0730	0800	0900	0930	1030	1100	1130	1200	1230	1330	1400	1430	1500	1530	1600	1630	1700	1730	1800	1830	1900	1930	2000
	Ain Seeba d.	0639	0709	0739	0809	0909	0939	1039	1109	1139	1209	1239	1339	1409	1439	1509	1539	1609	1639	1709	1739	1809	1839	1909	1939	2009
0	**Rabat** Ville d.	0742	0757	0842	0902	0957	1037	1142	1157	1232	1302	1342	1432	1502	1542	1557	1632	1702	1742	1757	1837	1902	1942	2002	2042	2102
7	Salé Ville d.	0750	0805	0850	0910	1005	1045	1150	1205	1240	1310	1350	1440	1510	1550	1605	1640	1710	1750	1805	1845	1910	1950	2010	2050	2110
40	**Kenitra** a.	0812	0826	...	0932	1026	1103	1209	1226	1303	1334	1412	1505	1534	1609	1628	1703	1729	1809	1826	1903	1932	2009	2032	2109	2132

↓		⚒	⚒		⚒		⚒	B																	D
Kenitra d.	0555	0610	0625	0655	0725	0800	0830	....	0925	1025	1055	1200	1227	1255	1325	1400	1455	1525	1600	1627	1655	1725	1800	1827	1855	1925
Salé Ville d.	0617	0632	0647	0717	0747	0820	0850	0919	0948	1046	1117	1220	1248	1316	1347	1420	1516	1547	1620	1648	1717	1747	1820	1848	1916	1947
Rabat Ville d.	0630	0645	0700	0730	0800	0830	0900	0930	1000	1100	1130	1230	1300	1330	1400	1430	1530	1600	1630	1700	1730	1800	1830	1900	1930	2000
Ain Seeba a.	0729	0735	0753	0829	0850	0929	0950	1029	1050	1150	1220	1339	1350	1420	1450	1528	1620	1650	1729	1750	1829	1850	1929	1950	2029	2050
Casablanca Port a.	0740	0745	0803	0840	0900	0940	1000	1040	1100	1200	1230	1340	1400	1430	1500	1540	1630	1700	1740	1800	1840	1900	1940	2000	2040	2100

A – Additional trips: 0830, 1000, 1300. B – Additional trips: 1019, 1149, 1447. C – Additional trips: 2030,2130, 2200. D – Additional trips: 2027,2125.

ALGERIA

Capital: **Alger** (GMT +1). 2014 Public Holidays: Jan. 1, 13, May 1, July 5, 28, Oct. 4, 24, Nov. 1, 3, 25.

Rail services are operated Société Nationale des Transports Ferroviaires (SNTF. www.sntf.dz). Unless otherwise noted, trains convey first and second class seated accommodation. Long distance overnight trains may convey sleeping cars and/or couchettes and where this is the case it will be shown in the footnotes. Timings are the most recent available and are subject to alteration at any time.

SNTF 2nd class unless indicated — ORAN - GHAZAOUET and BÉCHAR — 4010

km			2	2	2	2		✕A			
0	**Oran**	d.	0730	1250	...	1700	...	2030	...	...	...
76	Sidi bel Abbès	d.	0835	1355	...	1822	...	2134	...	...	...
163	Tlemcen	d.	0956	1512	1700	1942	...	|	...	...	...
219	Maghnia	d.	1105	1622	1823	...	...	|	...	...	...
284	**Ghazaouet**	d.	...	...	2010	...	...	|	...	...	...
350	Naâma	a.	...	...	...	...	...	0130	...	...	...
676	**Béchar**	a.	...	...	...	...	...	0546	...	...	...

		✕A	2	2	2	2	2			
Béchar	d.	2000	...	...	...	...	...	...	...	...
Naâma	d.	0009	...	...	...	...	...	...	...	...
Ghazout	d.	|	...	...	0430	...	...	...	...	...
Maghnia	d.	|	...	0445	0618	...	1405	...	...	...
Tlemcen	d.	|	...	0550	0740	1030	1510	...	...	...
Sidi bel Abbès	d.	0349	0540	0706	...	1145	1629	...	...	...
Oran	a.	0500	0655	0809	...	1249	1726	...	...	...

A – 🛏, (12) and ✕ Oran - Béchar and v.v.

SNTF — ORAN - ALGER — 4020

km				2	✕	✕	✕	✕	2	2	
0	**Oran**	d.	...	...	0625	0800	1230	1500	1615	1715	...
77	Mohammadia	d.	...	...	0716	|	1320	|	1700	1813	...
126	Relizane	d.	...	...	0750	0903	1354	1607	1731	1847	...
213	Chlef	d.	...	0530	0846	0953	1448	1653	1829	...	...
303	Khémis Miliana	d.	...	0625	0954	|	1554	|	...	...	...
354	El Affroun ☆	d.	0550	|	1038	|	1645	|	...	...	...
372	Blida ☆	d.	0604	0759	1051	1129	1658	1829	...	...	...
421	**Alger** Agha ☆	a.	0655	0757	1129	1200	1737	1900	...	...	...

		2	2	2✕	✕	✕	✕	✕	2	2
Alger Agha ☆	d.	...	...	...	0625	0800	1230	1500	1658	1830
Blida ☆	d.	...	...	...	0700	0829	1305	1529	1732	|
El Affroun ☆	d.	...	...	...	0713	|	1318	|	|	1910
Khémis Miliana	d.	...	...	...	0756	|	1401	|	1800	...
Chlef	d.	...	0540	0650	0854	1004	1503	1704	1932	...
Relizane	d.	0525	0635	0745	1001	1051	1604	1751	...	...
Mohammadia	d.	0600	0708	0823	1034	|	1642	|	...	...
Oran	a.	0717	0756	0911	1130	1200	1736	1900	...	...

☆ – Additional local trains available.

SNTF 2nd class only — TEBESSA, TOUGGOURT and M'SILA — 4030

km											
0	**Constantine**	d.	...	...	0515	0545	...	...	...	...	...
49	Aïn M'Lila	d.	...	...	0601	|	...	...	...	...	...
115	Oum el Bouaghi	d.	...	...	0658	|	...	...	...	...	...
212	Sidi Yahia	d.	...	...	0837	|	...	...	...	...	...
258	**Tebessa**	a.	...	...	0916	|	...	...	...	...	...
118	Batna	d.	0430	...	...	0724	...	...	...	...	...
151	Aïn Touta	d.	|	...	...	|	...	...	...	...	...
238	Biskra	d.	|	1530	...	0921	2000	...	...	...	...
403	Djamâa	d.	|	1843	...	...	2310	...	...	...	...
455	**Touggourt**	a.	|	1946	...	...	0016	...	...	...	...
202	Barika	d.	0530	...	...	...	...	...	...	...	...
299	**M'Sila**	a.	0651	...	...	...	...	...	...	...	...

M'Sila	d.	...	...	...	...	1642	...	...	...	...
Barika	d.	...	...	...	...	1807	...	...	...	...
Touggourt	d.	...	0100	...	0600	|	...	...	...	...
Djamâa	d.	...	0158	...	0659	|	...	...	...	...
Biskra	d.	...	0512	...	1013	|	...	...	1625	...
Aïn Touta	d.	...	...	...	...	1843	...	...	1756	...
Batna	d.	...	...	...	...	1909	...	...	1821	...
Tebessa	d.	...	...	...	...	...	...	1510	|	...
Sidi Yahia	d.	...	...	...	...	...	...	1548	|	...
Oum el Bouaghi	d.	...	...	...	...	...	...	1726	|	...
Aïn M'Lila	d.	...	...	...	...	...	...	1821	|	...
Constantine	a.	...	...	...	...	...	...	1908	2006	...

SNTF 2nd class unless indicated — ALGER - CONSTANTINE - TEBESSA — 4040

km					✕B							✕C
0	**Alger** ☆	d.	...	...	0725	...	1230	1430	1530	1620	1645	1940
54	Thénia ☆	d.	...	...	0811	...	|	|	|	1705	1736	2026
123	Bouira	d.	...	...	0940	...	1412	1612	1713	1824	1906	2138
171	Beni Mansour	d.	...	0540	1026	1040	1451	1652	|	—	...	2225
259	**Béjaïa**	a.	...	0728	|	1229	|	1829	|	...	...	|
237	Bordj Bou Arreridj	d.	0615	...	1143	—	1553	...	1850	1640	...	2330
289	**M'Sila**	a.	0703	...	|	...	1642	...	|	|	...	|
308	Setif	d.	—	...	1230	...	...	...	1932	1720	...	0021
464	**Constantine**	a.	...	...	1430	...	...	...	...	1924	...	0251
464	**Constantine**	d.	...	...	—	1455	...	...	...	...	...	0251
521	El Harrouch	d.	...	...	...	1541	...	...	...	...	...	0354
582	El Milia	d.	...	...	...	1658	...	...	...	...	...	|
620	**Jijel**	a.	...	...	...	1739	...	...	...	...	...	|
532	Ramdane Djamel	d.	...	...	...	—	...	...	...	...	...	0410
550	**Skikda**	a.	...	...	...	...	...	...	...	...	...	|
557	Azzaba	d.	...	...	...	...	...	...	...	...	...	0435
631	**Annaba**	a.	...	...	...	...	...	...	...	...	...	0538
631	**Annaba**	d.	...	...	...	1640	...	...	...	...	...	...
686	Bouchegouf	d.	...	...	...	1752	...	...	...	...	...	...
721	Mechrouha	d.	...	...	...	1848	...	...	...	...	...	...
738	Souk Ahras	d.	0600	...	1335	1910	...	...	...	...	...	...
787	**Sidi El Hémissi**	a.	0709	...	1444	|	...	...	...	...	...	...
762	Dreá	d.	...	...	...	1957	...	...	...	...	...	...
794	Oued Kéberit	d.	...	...	...	2036	...	...	...	...	...	...
862	**Tebessa**	a.	...	...	...	2149	...	...	...	...	...	...

		✕B						✕C			
Tebessa	d.	...	...	...	...	0430	...	...	...	...	...
Oued Kéberit	d.	...	...	...	...	0541	...	...	...	...	...
Dreá	d.	...	...	...	...	0618	...	...	...	...	...
Sidi El Hémissi	d.	...	...	...	...	|	...	...	...	0719	1602
Souk Ahras	d.	...	...	...	...	0656	...	...	...	0828	1714
Mechrouha	d.	...	...	...	...	0722	...	...	...	—	—
Bouchegouf	d.	...	...	...	...	0810	...	...	...	...	...
Annaba	a.	...	...	...	...	0932	...	...	...	...	...
Annaba	d.	1920	...	...	...	—	...	...	...	...	...
Azzaba	d.	2016	...	...	...	...	...	...	...	...	...
Skikda	d.	|	...	...	...	...	...	...	...	...	...
Ramdane Djamal	d.	2041	...	...	...	...	...	...	...	...	...
Jijel	d.	|	...	...	...	...	...	...	...	0645	...
El Milia	d.	|	...	...	...	...	...	...	...	0725	...
El Harrouch	d.	|	...	...	...	...	...	...	...	0843	...
Constantine	a.	2154	...	...	...	...	...	...	...	0941	...
Constantine	d.	2154	...	...	...	...	...	0640	0741	—	...
Setif	d.	0019	0540	...	...	...	...	0845	1007	...	...
M'Sila	d.	|	|	...	0651	...	...	|	|	...	1700
Bordj Bou Arreridj	d.	0111	0620	...	0740	...	...	0929	1050	...	1748
Béjaïa	d.	|	|	0635	|	0800	...	|	...	1650	—
Beni Mansour	d.	0226	|	0808	0844	0959	...	1037	...	1850	...
Bouira	d.	0318	0757	0849	0933	...	1015	1121	...	...	1720
Thénia ☆	d.	0441	|	|	|	...	1133	1230	...	...	1838
Alger ☆	a.	0544	0942	1033	1115	...	...	1315	...	...	...

B – (1) and ✕ Alger - Constantine and v.v.   C – 🛏 (12) and ✕ Alger - Annaba and v.v.   ☆ – Additional local trains available.

TUNISIA

Capital: **Tunis** (GMT +1). 2014 Public Holidays: Jan. 1, 13, Mar. 20, 21 Apr. 9, May 1, July 25, 28, 29, 30 Oct. 4, Nov. 7.

Rail services are operated Société Nationale des Chemins de Fer Tunisiens (SNCFT. www.sncft.com). Unless otherwise noted, trains convey first and second class seated accommodation. Long distance overnight trains may convey sleeping cars and/or couchettes and where this is the case it will be shown in the footnotes. Timings are the most recent available and are subject to alteration at any time.

SNCFT offers the **Carte Bleue** pass. The pass allows unlimited travel on all scheduled SNCFT services (except the Lézard Rouge tourist train) for a period of 7, 15, or 21 days, and are available for each of the three classes of accommodation. Supplements are payable in advance for using certain services. For more information, please visit the website of the European agent www.fahrplancenter.com

SNCFT — GHARDIMAOU - TUNIS — 4050

km			①–⑥	①–⑥					①–⑤		
0	**Ghardimaou**	d.	...	...	0505	1020	1245	1525	...	...	...
34	Jendouba	d.	...	...	0533	1048	1308	1548	...	...	...
92	Béja	d.	...	0510	0624	1144	1354	1636	...	...	...
177	Tebourba	d.	0605	|	0741	|	1459	1743	1850	...	...
211	**Tunis** Ville	a.	0646	0700	0816	1330	1533	1816	1927	...	...

		①–⑥				⑥		①–⑤		①–⑤
Tunis Ville	d.	0510	0615	0925	1300	1440	1700	1745	...	1840
Tebourba	d.	0545	0649	|	1335	1518	1744	1827	...	1916
Béja	d.	...	0757	1103	1454	1632	1858	...	...	2030
Jendouba	d.	...	0844	1148	1540	...	1950	...	...	...
Ghardimaou	a.	...	0905	1208	1616	...	2016	...	...	...

SNCFT — BIZERTE - TUNIS — 4060

km			①–⑥								
0	**Bizerte**	d.	0530	0820	1425	1805	...	...	...	...	...
34	Mateur	d.	0609	0854	1500	1837	...	...	...	...	...
98	**Tunis** Ville	a.	0724	1000	1614	1944	...	...	...	...	...

		①–⑥		⑥	⑦–⑤					
Tunis Ville	d.	0555	1215	1420	1545	1820	...	...	...	...
Mateur	d.	0701	1328	1527	1644	1932	...	...	...	...
Bizerte	a.	0732	1403	1558	1715	2007	...	...	...	...

4070 KALAÂ KASBAH - TUNIS SNCFT

km		⊡	1	⊡	1	⊡				
	El Kef d.	...	0550	...	...	...	...	...	...	...
0	**Kalaâ Kasbah** d.	...	|	0600a	...	1345	...	...	...	...
44	Dahmani d.	0400	|	0703	1305	1449	...	...	...	...
63	Le Sers d.	0428	0607	0722	1324	1428	...	...	...	...
115	Gaafour d.	0524	0713	0832	1410	1618	...	...	...	...
175	Pont du Fahs d.	0615	|	0922	1447	1712	...	...	...	...
235	**Tunis** Ville a.	0732	0839	1038	1538	1829	...	...	...	...

	⊡	1	⊡	1	⊡					
Tunis Ville d.	0555	1030	1410	1620	1805	...	...	...	...	...
Pont du Fahs d.	0715	1121	1528	1710	1922	...	...	...	...	...
Gaafour d.	0806	1158	1617	1746	2011	...	...	...	...	...
Le Sers d.	0903	1243	1714	1831	2107	...	...	...	...	...
Dahmani d.	0932	1303	1744	|	2134	...	...	...	...	...
Kalaâ Kasbah a.	1034	...	1845a	|	...	...	...	...	...	...
El Kef a.	...	...	...	1907	...	...	...	...	...	...

a – June 1 - Sep. 30.

⊡ – Supplement payable.

4080 TUNIS - SOUSSE - SFAX - TOZEUR SNCFT

km		1	⊡	1		⊡	⊡			⊡	⊡	1	⑥1	⚒⊡	1	⚒1	1	⊡	①-⑤	⊡	⊡	⊡	🚌	
0	**Tunis** Ville d.	0550	0600	0800	...	0830	0930	...	...	1235	1305	1400	1430	1545	1620	1730	1750	1800	1815	1845	2045	2215	...	...
59	Bir Bou Rekba ◇ d.	0635	0653	0846	...	0923	1023	...	...	1321	1356	1447	1533	1639	|	1818	1832	1853	1915	1939	2138	2307	...	...
64	Hammamet ◇ d.	|	|	|	...	|	|	...	...	|	|	|	1540	|	|	1824	|	|	1926	|	|	|	...	...
76	**Nabeul** ◇ a.	|	|	|	...	|	|	...	...	|	|	|	1559	|	|	1838	|	|	1945	|	|	|	...	...
142	Kalaâ Séghira d.	0723	|	0932	...	|	|	...	...	|	1454	|	...	1745	1802	...	|	1952	...	2045	|	|	...	...
149	**Sousse** d.	0729	0810	|	...	1045	1137	...	...	1422	|	1540	...	1752	|	...	1930	|	...	2052	2250	0020	...	...
174	Monastir d.	...	|	|	...	1124	|	...	...	1508	|	...	...	...	|	...	2005	|	...	...	|	|	...	...
217	**Mahdia** a.	...	|	|	...	...	|	...	...	1604	|	...	...	...	|	...	...	|	...	...	|	|	...	...
215	El Jem d.	...	0907	1013	...	...	1234	...	...	...	1548	...	...	...	|	...	...	2042	...	...	2347	0117	...	...
278	**Sfax** d.	...	1000	1050	...	...	1327	...	...	...	1643	...	...	...	1935	...	...	2131	...	...	0040	0215	...	...
340	Ghraïba d.	...	1052	...	...	...	1418	...	...	...	1735	...	...	...	|	...	...	...	...	...	0134	|	...	...
422	**Gabès** a.	...	1204	...	...	...	|	...	...	...	1843	...	...	...	2125	...	...	...	...	...	|	0413	0420	...
	Tataouine a.	...	...	...	...	...	|	...	...	...	...	...	...	...	...	...	...	...	...	...	|	...	0645	...
482	Gafsa d.	...	...	...	...	...	1634	...	...	...	...	...	...	...	...	...	...	...	...	...	0347	...	...	...
521	Metlaoui d.	...	...	...	...	...	1711	...	...	...	...	...	...	...	...	...	...	...	...	...	0424	...	...	...
574	**Tozeur** a.	...	...	...	...	...	1759	...	...	...	...	...	...	...	...	...	...	...	...	...	0512	...	...	...

		⊡	🚌	⊡	⚒1	⊡	⚒⊡	⚒1	1	⊡	1	1	⊡		⊡	⊡	1		1		⊡		⊡	
Tozeur d.	...	2030	...	...	...	...	...	...	...	...	...	...	0630	...	...	...	...	...	...	...	...	...	...	...
Metlaoui d.	...	2121	...	...	...	...	...	...	...	...	...	...	0721	...	...	...	...	...	...	...	...	...	...	...
Gafsa d.	...	2200	...	...	...	...	...	...	...	...	...	...	0800	...	...	...	...	...	...	...	...	...	...	...
Tataouine d.	...	|	2100	...	...	...	...	...	...	...	...	...	|	...	...	...	...	...	...	...	...	...	...	...
Gàbes d.	...	|	2355	0005	...	...	...	...	...	...	0500	...	|	...	...	1115	...	...	...	...	...	...	1605	...
Ghraïba d.	...	0011	...	|	...	...	...	...	...	...	|	...	1011	...	...	1229	...	...	...	...	...	...	1717	...
Sfax d.	...	0115	...	0210	...	...	...	...	...	0530	0653	...	1110	...	...	1330	...	...	1610	...	...	...	1825	...
El Jem d.	...	0209	...	0258	...	...	...	...	...	0620	|	...	1158	...	...	1420	...	...	1649	...	...	...	1916	...
Mahdia d.	...	|	...	|	...	...	...	...	...	|	|	...	|	...	...	|	...	...	|	...	1700	...	|	...
Monastir d.	...	|	...	|	...	...	...	...	0645	|	|	...	|	...	1305	|	...	...	|	...	1754	...	|	...
Sousse d.	...	0315	...	0405	...	0520	0615	...	|	0730	|	0955	1304	...	1400	|	1550	...	|	...	1837	...	2025	...
Kalaâ Seghira d.	...	|	...	|	...	0528	|	...	0722	|	0820	|	|	...	|	1509	|	...	1729	...	|	...	|	...
Nabeul ◇ d.	...	|	...	|	0530	|	|	0725	|	|	|	|	|	...	|	|	|	...	|	...	|	...	|	...
Hammamet ◇ d.	...	|	...	|	0547	|	|	0739	|	|	|	|	|	...	|	|	|	...	|	...	|	...	|	...
Bir Bou Rekba ◇ d.	...	0418	...	0508	0553	0632	0721	0745	0810	0834	|	1047	1407	...	1507	1605	1644	...	1815	...	1931	...	2129	...
Tunis Ville a.	...	0515	...	0601	0703	0730	0819	0829	0859	0930	1003	1129	1502	...	1605	1700	1729	...	1902	...	2015	...	2223	...

⊡ – Supplement payable. ◇ – Additional services available with connections from/to Tunis.

4090 SOUSSE - MONASTIR AIRPORT - MAHDIA SNCFT

km		⚒				⚒																		
0	**Sousse** Bab El Jedid d.	0540	0630	0710	0740	0820	0915	1010	1040	1115	1150	1230	1315	1400	1450	1550	1620	1705	1750	1835	1915	1950	...	...
3	**Sousse** Sud d.	0556	0636	0721	0746	0826	0921	1016	1046	1121	1156	1236	1321	1406	1456	1556	1626	1711	1756	1841	1921	1956	...	...
15	Monastir Airport ✈ d.	0600	0650	0735	0800	0840	0935	1030	1100	1135	1210	1250	1335	1420	1510	1610	1640	1725	1810	1855	1935	2010	...	...
24	Monastir d.	0620	0710	0755	0820	0850	1000	1050	1110	1150	1230	1315	1355	1440	1530	1630	1700	1745	1830	1915	1950	2025	...	...
47	Moknine d.	0651	0743	0830	0851	...	1031	1121	...	1221	1306	1350	1432	1515	1601	1700	1731	1816	1915	1950	2021	2056	...	...
73	**Mahdia** a.	0735	0825	0850	0935	...	1108	1158	...	1258	1341	1425	1508	1553	1645	...	1806	1858	2005	2022	2055	2130	...	...

		⚒				⚒																	
Mahdia d.	...	0445	0530	0605	0640	...	0750	0840	0945	1015	...	1125	1225	1310	1350	1435	1520	1610	...	1715	1825	1910	...	...
Moknine d.	...	0520	0605	0640	0715	0740	0825	0915	1020	1100	...	1205	1305	1348	1430	1514	1555	1645	1745	1805	1909	1945	...	...
Monastir d.	...	0605	0650	0725	0800	0825	0910	0955	1105	1145	1220	1250	1350	1430	1510	1555	1640	1730	1825	1850	1955	2030	...	...
Monastir Airport ✈ d.	...	0617	0700	0735	0810	0835	0920	1005	1115	1155	1230	1300	1400	1440	1520	1605	1650	1740	1835	1900	2005	2040	...	...
Sousse Sud d.	...	0630	0715	0750	0825	0850	0935	1020	1130	1210	1245	1315	1415	1455	1535	1620	1705	1755	1850	1915	2020	2055	...	...
Sousse Bab El Jedid a.	...	0635	0720	0755	0830	0855	0940	1025	1135	1215	1250	1320	1420	1500	1540	1625	1710	1800	1855	1920	2025	2100	...	...

EGYPT

Capital: **Cairo** (GMT +2). 2014 Public Holidays: Jan. 7, 13, 25, Apr. 21, 25, May 1, July 23, 28, 29, 30, Oct. 6, 7, 25.

Rail services are operated Egyptian National Railways (ENR. www.enr.gov.eg). Unless otherwise noted, trains convey first and second class seated accommodation. Long distance overnight trains may convey sleeping cars and/or couchettes and where this is the case it will be shown in the footnotes. Timings are the most recent available and are subject to alteration at any time.

4100 MERSA MATRUH - CAIRO and ALEXANDRIA Egyptian National Railways

km		2	A	2	B					
0	**Mersa Matruh** d.	0705	1335	1545	2300	...	...	...	...	...
84	El Alamein d.	1024	1620	1830	|	...	...	...	...	...
311	**Alexandria** a.	1330	|	2115	|	...	...	...	...	...
509	**Cairo** Main a.	...	2135	...	0600	...	...	...	...	...

	2	A	2	B					
Cairo Main d.	...	0640	...	2300	...	...	...	...	...
Alexandria d.	0640	|	1330	|	...	...	...	...	...
El Alamein d.	0924	1145	1717	|	...	...	...	...	...
Mersa Matruh a.	1205	1415	2020	0600	...	...	...	...	...

A – June - Sept. only.

B – 🛏 (1, 2 class). June 15 - Sept. 15. From Mersa on ②④⑦, from Cairo on ①③⑥.

4110 CAIRO - ALEXANDRIA Egyptian National Railways

km		**903**	**905**	**901**		**909**	**911**	**89**		**913**	**917**	**919**		**915**	**923**	**925**		**921**	**927**	**931**		**1919**	**935**	
0	**Cairo** Main d.	0600	0800	0815	...	0900	1000	1100	...	1200	1400	1410	...	1515	1600	1715	...	1800	1900	2015	...	2100	2230	...
45	Benha d.	0636	|	0881	...	|	1036	|	...	1236	|	1445	...	1551	1636	1751	...	|	|	2050	...	|	|	...
86	Tanta d.	0720	|	0923	...	|	1108	1205	...	1308	|	1528	...	1623	1720	1832	...	1903	|	2124	...	|	2335	...
147	Damanhūr d.	0815	|	1007	...	|	1153	|	...	1352	|	1620	...	1708	1813	1918	...	|	|	2216	...	|	|	...
208	**Alexandria** a.	0915	1030	1100	...	1130	1250	1340	...	1445	1630	1720	...	1805	1920	2015	...	2030	2130	2315	...	2330	0120	...

		902	**906**		**904**	**900**		**910**	**912**		**914**	**916**		**918**	**922**		**88**	**928**		**926**	**930**		**934**	
Alexandria d.	...	0600	0700	...	0800	0815	...	1000	1200	...	1300	1400	...	1500	1530	...	1645	1800	...	1900	2000	...	2200	...
Damanhūr d.	...	0700	|	...	|	0920	...	1100	|	...	1400	|	...	|	1635	...	|	|	...	|	2105	...	|	...
Tanta d.	...	0800	|	...	|	1008	...	1144	1330	...	1500	|	...	|	1725	...	1825	1930	...	|	2155	...	2330	...
Benha d.	...	0845	|	...	|	1042	...	1227	|	...	1542	|	...	|	1757	...	|	|	...	|	2227	...	|	...
Cairo Main a.	...	0920	0940	...	1040	1115	...	1300	1430	...	1615	1630	...	1730	1830	...	1925	2030	...	2130	2300	...	0030	...

ALEXANDRIA and CAIRO - DUMYAT — 4120

Egyptian National Railways 2nd class only

km										
240	**Alexandria** d.	...	...	1815	...	...	...	...	...	...
205	**Cairo** Main d.	0515	0725	|	1935	...	...	...	...	...
0	**Dumyat** a.	1015	1125	2230	2355	...	...	...	...	...

Dumyat d.	0640	0715	1315	1630	...	...	...	...	...
Cairo Main a.	1005	|	1800	2020	...	...	...	...	...
Alexandria a.	...	1210	...	...	...	...	...	...	...

☛ All services are subject to confirmation.

ALEXANDRIA and CAIRO - BÛR SA'ÎD — 4130

Egyptian National Railways 2nd class only

km										
334	**Alexandria** d.	...	0430	...	...	1530	...	...	...	...
236	**Cairo** Main d.	0615	|	1345	1440	|	1945	...	...	...
0	**Bûr Sa'îd** a.	1015	1110	1800	1905	2210	2350	...	...	...

Bûr Sa'îd d.	0530	0725	0930	1300	1730	1825	1815	...	...
Cairo Main a.	0945	|	1335	1710	2135	|	0050	...	...
Alexandria a.	...	1330	...	...	...	0035	...	...	...

☛ All services are subject to confirmation.

CAIRO - EL SUWEIS — 4140

Egyptian National Railways 2nd class only

km										
0	**Cairo** Ain Shams d.	0630	0510n	0920	1310	1615	1845	2145	...	...
127	**El Suweis** a.	0840	0950	1135	1520	1830	2100	2400	...	...

El Suweis d.	0600	1010	1310	1525	1550	1900	2125	...	...
Cairo Ain Shams a.	0815	1215	1525	2005n	1805	2110	2335	...	...

☛ All services are subject to confirmation.

n – Cairo Main.

CAIRO - ASWÂN — 4150

Egyptian National Railways

km		1902	934	980	982	986	988	88	976	996	886
0	**Cairo** Main ◇ d.	0005	0100	0800	1200	1300	1900	2000	2100	2200	2315
13	El Giza ◇ d.	0030	0130	0825	1225	1325	1925	2025	2125	2230	2340
124	Béni Suef ◇ d.	|	0250	0940	1350	1443	2045	2147	2243	2348	0100
247	El Menya ◇ d.	|	0425	1110	1520	1630	2220	2330	0015	0120	0235
375	Asyût ◇ d.	0455	0620	1300	1715	1830	0010	0125	0215	0310	0430
467	Sohâg ◇ d.	0625	0740	1430	1850	2000	0125	0250	0340	0435	0545
609	Qena ◇ d.	0845	1000	1710	2120	2235	0340	0525	0605	0655	0805
671	Luxor d.	0950	1055	1825	2235	...	0445	0640	0705	0800	0910
879	**Aswân** a.	1305	...	2200	0205	...	0800	1015	...	1120	1230

	981	983	935	887	977	1903	997	89	989	987
Aswân d.	0530	0700	...	1500	...	1615	1945	2000	2130	...
Luxor d.	0915	1035	1200	1820	1900	1945	2320	2345	0100	...
Qena ◇ d.	1025	1145	1305	1920	2005	2045	0020	0055	0200	0600
Sohâg ◇ d.	1310	1430	1530	2145	2225	2300	0245	0340	0420	0850
Asyût ◇ d.	1440	1610	1610	2305	2350	0030	0405	0515	0540	1025
El Menya ◇ d.	1630	1805	1845	0055	0140	|	0555	0710	0730	1225
Béni Suef ◇ d.	1805	1940	2225	0230	0315	|	0740	0850	0905	1405
El Giza ◇ d.	1930	2104	|	0355	0435	0525	0900	|	1025	1530
Cairo Main ◇ a.	1950	2125	2205	0415	0455	0545	0920	1035	1045	1550

◇– Additional services available.

OTHER AFRICAN STATES

For details of capital cities and public holiday dates please see individual tables.

Unless otherwise noted, trains convey first and second class seated accommodation. Some operators also offer third class seating. This will not normally be mentioned in the tables, and where it is the only class available will be noted as second class. Long distance overnight trains may convey sleeping cars and/or couchettes. As a general rule, first class sleepers have two berths per cabin, whilst second class has four. The standard of accommodation varies widely with no two countries beng the same. Timings are the latest available and are valid until further notice, but may change at any time so we suggest you confirm them locally before travelling. In Muslim countries a different timetable may be operated during the festival of Ramadan.

SUDAN and SOUTH SUDAN — 4200

Sudan Railways Corporation

Sudan: **Khartoum** (GMT +3). 2014 Public Holidays: Jan. 1, 7, 13, June 30, Jul. 28, Oct. 4, 25, Dec. 25.
South Sudan: **Juba** (GMT +3). 2014 Public Holidays: Apr. 18 -21, May 1, 16, Jul. 9, 28, 30, Oct. 4, Dec. 1, Dec. 25.

km		222 ②	101 ④A	212 E	551 B	202 ④C	D01 ④D			
926	**Wadi Halfa** d.	1800b	...	...	...	0200d	...	...	...	...
576	Abu Hamed d.	0600c	...	...	...	0800e	...	...	...	...
551	Dagash d.	...	...	...	...	1030e	...	...	...	...
351	Berber d.	...	...	...	...	2300e	...	...	...	...
810	**Bûr Sûdan** d.	...	1530d	...	...	|	...	...	...	...
	Sinkat d.	...	2000d	...	...	|	...	...	...	...
720	Gebeit d.	...	2240d	...	...	|	...	...	...	...
620	Haiya Junction d.	...	0445e	...	...	|	...	...	...	...
310	**Atbara** a.	...	1255e	...	...	2345e	...	...	...	...
310	**Atbara** d.	...	...	2130	...	0200f	...	...	...	...
295	Ed Dâmer d.	...	...	2300	...	0300g	...	...	...	...
170	Shendî d.	...	...	0300	...	0930g	...	...	...	...
0	**Khartoum** Bahri a.	...	...	0730	...	1700g	...	...	...	...
0	**Khartoum** Bahri d.	...	...	...	...	...	2000d	...	...	...
270	Sennâr Junction d.	...	...	...	...	...	0600e	...	...	...
383	Kôsti d.	...	...	...	...	...	1030e	...	...	...
470	Tendelti d.	...	...	...	...	...	1500e	...	...	...
605	Er Rahad d.	...	...	...	⊖	...	2100e	...	...	...
629	**El Obeid** a.	...	...	...	|	...	2230e	...	...	...
983	Babanusa d.	...	...	...	⊖	...	...	...	...	...
	El Daien d.	...	...	...	⊖	...	...	...	...	...
1318	**Nyâlâ** a.	...	...	...	⊖	...	...	...	...	...

	552 B	221 ④	201 ①C	502 ①D	102 ①A	211 E			
Nyâlâ d.	⊖	...	...	...	...	...	...	...	...
El Daien d.	⊖	...	...	...	...	...	...	...	...
Babanusa d.	⊖	...	...	...	...	...	...	...	...
El Obeid d.	|	...	...	0700a	...	...	...	...	...
Er Rahad d.	⊖	...	...	0830a	...	...	...	...	...
Tendelti d.	...	...	...	1445a	...	...	...	...	...
Kôsti d.	...	...	...	1930a	...	...	...	...	...
Sennâr Junction d.	...	...	...	0000b	...	...	...	...	...
Khartoum Bahri a.	...	...	...	1030b	...	...	...	...	...
Khartoum Bahri d.	...	...	0800a	...	...	2130	...	...	...
Shendî d.	...	...	1545a	...	...	0200	...	...	...
Ed Dâmer d.	...	...	2200a	...	...	0600	...	...	...
Atbara a.	...	...	2300a	...	...	0730	...	...	...
Atbara d.	...	...	0100b	...	2000a	...	...	...	...
Haiya Junction d.	...	...	|	...	0415b	...	...	...	...
Gebeit d.	...	...	|	...	1015b	...	...	...	...
Sinkat d.	...	...	|	...	1120b	...	...	...	...
Bûr Sûdan a.	...	...	|	...	1545b	...	...	...	...
Berber d.	...	...	0345b	...	...	...	...	...	...
Dagash d.	...	...	1530b	...	...	...	...	...	...
Abu Hamed d.	...	1730d	1745b	...	...	...	...	...	...
Wadi Halfa a.	...	0545e	2230b	...	...	...	...	...	...

A – 12 From Bûr Sûdan 1st and 3rd ④ of each month, from Atbara on following ①. Service temporarily withdrawn March 2014
B – 1 cl., 2. From El Rahad/ Nyâlâ every two weeks day and time not fixed.
C – 1 cl., 2. From Khartoum on 1st and 3rd ① of each month, from Wadi Halfa on following ④. Service temporarily withdrawn March 2014
D – 1 cl., 2 cl., 3 and 🍸. From Khartoum on 2nd ④ of each month, from El Obeid on following ①. Service temporarily withdrawn March 2014 Not operated by SRC.
E – 1 cl., 23

a – ①. b – ②. c – ③. d – ④. e – ⑤. f – ⑥. g – ⑦. ⊖ – No timings available.

ERITREA — 4210

Chemins de Fer d'Eritrea

km		①–⑥ 2	A	⑦ B
0	**Mitsiwa** d.	⊖	⊖	...
5	Otumlo d.	⊖	|	...
8	Moncullo d.	...	⊖	...
70	Ghinda d.	...	⊖	...
92	Nefasit d.	...	⊖	1000
118	**Asmara** a.	...	⊖	1200

	①–⑥ 2	A	⑦ B
Asmara d.	...	⊖	0800
Nefasit d.	...	⊖	0915
Ghinda d.	...	⊖	...
Moncullo d.	...	⊖	...
Otumlo d.	⊖	|	...
Mitsiwa a.	⊖	⊖	...

Capital: **Asmara** (GMT +3).

2014 Public Holidays: Jan. 1, 13, 19, Feb. 10, Mar. 8, Apr. 21, May 1, 24, June 20, Jul. 28, Sep. 1, Oct. 4, Dec. 25.

A – No regular service. Charter service available.
B – Minimum 10 passengers required.
⊖ – No information available.

ETHIOPIA — 4215

Chemins de Fer Djibouti Ethiopien

km		②④⑥	
0	**Diré Daoua** d.	0600	...
210	Dewelé 🏛 a.	1400	...
228	Ali Sabieh 🏛 d.	1530	...
318	**Djibouti** a.	2000	...

	①③⑥	
Djibouti d.	0600	...
Ali Sabieh 🏛 d.	1000	...
Dewelé 🏛 a.	1130	
Diré Daoua a.	2000	

apital: **Addis Abeba** (GMT +3). 2014 Public Holidays: Jan. 7, 13, 19, Mar. 2, Apr. 18, 20, ay 1, 5, 28, July 28, 29, Sept. 11, 27, Oct. 4.

ibouti Tourist Office claims that the train trip to Dire Daoua is amongst the most dangerous in e world!

MAURITANIA — 4220

SNIM 2nd class only

km			
0	**Nouadhibou** d.	1450	...
652	**Zouèrate** a.	0540	...

Zouèrate d.	1215	...
Nouadhibou a.	0618	...

Capital: **Nouakchott** (GMT +0).

2014 Public Holidays: Jan. 1, 13, May 1, 25, July 28, 29, Oct. 4, 25, Nov. 3.

SNIM – Société Nationale Industrielle et Minière

4230 GUINEA

2nd class only   Chemins de Fer Guinea, Chemins de Fer de Boké

km		①–⑤	①–⑤	①–⑤		①–⑤	①–⑤	①–⑤
0	**Conakry** Portovoya d.	...	0847	1725	**Halte Km 36** d.	0645	...	1916
	Simbaya d.	0600	0940	1829	Simbaya d.	0730	1630	1950
36	**Halte Km 36** a.	0640	...	1906	**Conakry** P'voya a.	0837	1710	...

km		B				B		
0	**Kamsar** d.	0930	...	...	**Sangaredi** d.	1415	...	...
55	Boké d.	1130	...	...	Boké d.	1630	...	...
136	**Sangaredi** a.	1345	...	...	**Kamsar** a.	1830	...	...

Capital: **Conakry** (GMT +0).

2014 Public Holidays: Jan. 1, 13, Apr. 3, 9, May 1, 25, Jul,. 24, 29, Aug. 15, Oct. 2, 4, Nov. 1, Dec. 25.

A – ①–⑤

B – ①④⑤⑦.

4240 MALI

2nd class only   Transrail

km		B				A		
0	**Kayes** d.	0715	...	...	**Bamako** d.	0715	...	...
160	Bafoulabé d.	1130	...	...	Kati d.	0815	...	...
308	Kita d.	1805	...	...	Kita d.	1300	...	...
468	Kati d.	2250	...	...	Bafoulabé d.	1935	...	...
493	**Bamako** a.	2345	...	...	Kayes d.	2350	...	...

Capital: **Bamako** (GMT +0).

2014 Public Holidays: Jan. 1, 20, Feb. 4. Mar. 26, Apr. 9, May 1, 25, Jul. 29, Sep. 22, Oct. 4, Dec. 25.

A – ①②④⑥

B – ②③⑤⑦.

4250 GHANA

Ghana Railway Corporation

km		A				A		
0	**Takoradi** d.	2030	...	...	**Kumasi** d.	2030	...	...
276	**Kumasi** a.	0830	...	...	**Takoradi** a.	0830	...	...

km		2B	2B	2B		2B	2B	2B
0	**Accra** d.	0740	1000	1400	**Nsawam** d.	0600	1140	1220
40	**Nsawam** a.	0920	1140	1540	**Accra** a.	0740	1320	1400

km		①–⑥	①–⑥			①–⑥	①–⑥	
0	**Accra** d.	0715	1754	...	**Asoprochona** d.	0615	1212	...
31	**Asoprochona** a.	0800	1839	...	**Accra** a.	0700	1257	...

Capital: **Accra** (GMT +0).

2014 Public Holidays: Jan. 1, Mar. 6, Apr. 18, 21, May, 1, 25, Jul. 1, Sep. 21, Oct. 5, Dec. 5, 25, 26.

A – Service operates 3 days a week. Trains tend to run late.

B – ①–⑥. Additional trains from Accra at 1900, from Nsawam at 1910.

4260 BURKINA FASO - CÔTE D'IVOIRE

Sitarail

km		②④⑥ 2	②④⑥ A		①③⑤ 2	②④⑥ A
0	**Ouagadougou** d.	...	0730	**Abidjan** Treichville d.	0900	1030
93	Koudougou d.	...	⊖	**Abidjan** Plateau d.	0920	⊖
349	Bobo Dioulasso d.	...	⊖	Anyama d.	1015	⊖
446	Banfora d.	...	⊖	Agboville d.	1240	⊖
495	Niangoloko ▦ d.	...	⊖	Dimbokro d.	1615	⊖
539	Ouangolodougou d.	...	⊖	Bouaké d.	...	⊖
576	Ferkessédougou d.	...	⊖	Katiola d.	...	⊖
658	Tafiré d.	...	⊖	Tafiré d.	...	⊖
769	Katiola d.	...	⊖	Ferkessédougou d.	...	⊖
820	Bouaké d.	...	⊖	Ouangolodougou d.	...	⊖
958	Dimbokro d.	0900	⊖	Niangoloko ▦ d.	...	⊖
1064	Agboville d.	1255	⊖	Banfora d.	...	⊖
1115	Anyama d.	1515	⊖	Bobo Dioulasso d.	...	⊖
1141	**Abidjan** Plateau a.	1610	⊖	Koudougou d.	...	⊖
1143	**Abidjan** Treichville a.	1625	⊖	**Ouagadougou** a.	...	⊖

Capitals: **Ouagadougou** (Burkina Faso, GMT +0), **Yamoussoukro** (Côte d'Ivoire, GMT +0).

2014 Public Holidays:

Burkina Faso: Jan. 1, 3, 13, Mar. 8, Apr. 21, May 1, 29, Jul. 28, Aug. 4, 5, 8, 15, Oct. 15, 25, Nov. 1, 4, Dec. 11, 25.

Côte d'Ivoire: Jan. 1, 14, Apr. 21, May 1, 29, June 9, Jul. 28, Aug. 7, 15, Oct. 15, Nov. 1, 15, Dec. 25.

A – [12] and 🍸 Abidjan - Ouagadougou and v.v. Journey time 43 - 48 hours.

⊖ – No timings available.

4270 NIGERIA

Nigerian Railways Corporation

Capital: **Abuja** (GMT +1). 2014 Public Holidays: Jan. 1, 13, Apr. 18, 21, May 1, Jul. 29, Aug. 8, Oct. 1, 5, Dec. 25, 26.

km		⑤A	⑤B		①A	⑤B
0	**Lagos** Terminal d.	1200	...	**Kano** d.	0900	⊖
14	Agege d.	⊖	...	Zaria d.	⊖	⊖
91	Abeokuta d.	⊖	...	**Kaduna** Junction d.	⊖	⊖
193	Ibadan d.	⊖	...	Minna d.	⊖	...
280	Ede d.	⊖	...	Zungeru d.	⊖	...
295	Oshogbo d.	⊖	...	Jebba d.	⊖	...
391	Ilorin d.	⊖	...	Ilorin d.	⊖	...
488	Jebba d.	⊖	...	Oshogbo d.	⊖	...
685	Zungeru d.	⊖	...	Ede d.	⊖	...
744	Minna d.	⊖	...	Ibadan d.	⊖	...
902	**Kaduna** Junction d.	⊖	⊖	Abeokuta d.	⊖	...
986	Zaria d.	⊖	⊖	Agege d.	⊖	...
1126	**Kano** a.	1701a	⊖	**Lagos** Terminal a.	1424a	...

km		C	⑤B		C	⑤B
0	**Port Harcourt** New d.	⊖	⊖	**Maiduguri** d.	⊖	...
63	Aba d.	⊖	⊖	Buni d.	⊖	...
113	Umuahia Ibeku d.	⊖	⊖	Gombe d.	⊖	...
243	Enugu d.	⊖	⊖	Bauchi d.	⊖	...
375	Oturkpo d.	⊖	⊖	**Kaduna** Junction d.	⊖	⊖
463	Makurdi d.	⊖	⊖	Kafanchan d.	⊖	⊖
565	Lafia d.	⊖	⊖	Lafia d.	⊖	⊖
737	Kafanchan d.	⊖	⊖	Makurdi d.	⊖	⊖
916	**Kaduna** Junction d.	⊖	⊖	Oturkpo d.	⊖	⊖
1333	Bauchi d.	⊖	...	Enugu d.	⊖	⊖
1499	Gombe d.	⊖	...	Umuahia Ibeku d.	⊖	⊖
1658	Buni d.	⊖	...	Aba d.	⊖	⊖
1801	**Maiduguri** a.	⊖	...	**P Harcourt** New a.	⊖	⊖

A – Conveys 🛏 (1 cl.), [2] and ✕.

B – Port Harcourt - Kaduna - Kano and v.v.

C – Port Harcourt - Kaduna - Maiduguri and v.v. Once per week in each direction. Subject to confirmation.

⊖ – No timings available.

a – Next day.

4280 CAMEROON

Camrail

Capital: **Youandé** (GMT +1). 2014 Public Holidays: Jan. 1, 13, Feb. 11, Apr. 18, May 1, 20, 21, 29, Jul. 29, Aug. 15, Oct. 1, 4, Dec. 25.

km		151 A	181	103 ①③⑤	191 B	153 A	②④⑥ 2				
0	**Douala** Bessengué d.	0600	0730	0900	...	1445	...	...	...	...	...
72	Edéa d.	|	0910	1210	...	|	...	...	...	...	...
152	Eséka d.	|	1050	1510	...	|	...	...	...	...	...
220	Ngoumou d.	|	1230	1720	...	|	...	...	...	...	...
263	**Yaoundé** d.	0945	1315	1810	1910	1830	...	...	...	...	...
477	Nanga Eboko d.	...	...	...	2300	...	...	...	...	...	...
582	Belabo d.	...	...	...	0230	...	0830	...	...	...	...
686	Mbitom d.	...	...	...	0450	...	1115	...	...	...	...
910	**N'gaoundéré** a.	...	...	...	1000	...	1800	...	...	...	...
km											
	Douala Bonaberi d.	...	...	...	...	...	...	...	...	...	...
	Mbanga d.	...	...	0920	1300	1730	...	...	...	...	...
	Kumba a.	...	...	1030	1410	1840	...	...	...	...	...

	184	①③⑤ 2	②④⑥	192 B	152 A	154 A			
N'gaoundéré d.	...	0800	...	1915	...	...	...	...	...
Mbitom d.	...	1140	...	0000	...	...	...	...	...
Belabo d.	...	1730	...	0230	...	...	...	...	...
Nanga Eboko d.	...	...	...	0600	...	...	...	...	...
Yaoundé d.	0800	...	0915	1000	1025	1920	...	...	...
Ngoumou d.	0855	...	1030	...	|	|	...	...	...
Eséka d.	1045	...	1250	...	|	|	...	...	...
Edéa d.	1225	...	1600	...	|	|	...	...	...
Douala Bessengué a.	1350	...	1910	...	1410	2305	...	...	...
Kumba d.	...	...	...	0750	1130	1530	...	...	...
Mbanga d.	...	...	...	0900	1240	1640	...	...	...
Douala Bonaberi a.	...	...	...	...	...	...	...	...	...

A – Conveys [1] and ✕. B – Conveys [12] 🛏 2 cl. (2 & 4 berth) 🍸.

☛ – Note: All intermediate and arrival times are approximate.

4290 GABON

Chemins de Fer Trans Gabonnais

Capital: **Libreville** (GMT +1). 2014 Public Holidays: Jan. 1, Apr. 17, 21, May 1, 29, June 9, July 28, Aug. 15, 16, Oct. 15, Nov. 1, Dec. 25.

km		②	⑤	④	⑦					
0	**Owendo** (Libreville) d.	2000	2000	2000	2000	...	...	...	...	...
183	Ndjole d.	2310	2305	2330	2330	...	...	...	...	...
340	Booué d.	0245	0240	0255	0255	...	...	...	...	...
485	Lastourville d.	0510	0510	0535	0535	...	...	...	...	...
625	Moanda d.	0715	0720	0805	0805	...	...	...	...	...
670	**Franceville** a.	0750	0755	0840	0840	...	...	...	...	...

	③	⑦	②	⑤					
Franceville d.	2100	2100	2100	2100	...	...	...	...	...
Moanda d.	2145	2145	2145	2145	...	...	...	...	...
Lastourville d.	0010	0000	0015	0015	...	...	...	...	...
Booué d.	0250	0250	0250	0250	...	...	...	...	...
Ndjole d.	0550	0555	0600	0600	...	...	...	...	...
Owendo (Libreville) a.	0850	0855	0920	0920	...	...	...	...	...

CONGO — 4300

Chemins de Fer Congo Océan

km		②④⑥ A	②④⑥ B	②⑤
0	**Brazzaville** d.	...	1100	1200
137	Mindouli d.	...	1600	1750
190	Loutété d.	0700	1845	2050
261	Nkayi d.	1015	2140	...
342	Dolisie d.	1450	0130	...
509	**Pointe Noire** a.	2210	0740	...

	①③⑤ A	①③⑤ B	①④
Pointe Noire d.	0600	1100	...
Dolisie d.	1310	1720	...
Nkayi d.	1735	2100	...
Loutété d.	2020	2350	0400
Mindouli d.	...	0230	0700
Brazzaville a.	...	0730	1245

Capital: **Brazzaville** (GMT +1).
2014 Public Holidays: Jan. 1, Apr. 21, May 1, 29, June 9, 10, Aug. 15, Nov. 1, 28, Dec. 25.

A – [12] and ✕.
B – ▬ [12] and ✕.

KENYA — 4310

Kenya Railways

km		②④⑦ A	①③⑤	
0	**Mombasa** d.	1900	...	...
164	Voi d.	2320	...	...
263	Mtito Andei d.	0150	...	...
337	Makindu d.	0350	...	...
530	**Nairobi** a.	1000	...	...
0	**Nairobi** d.	...	1830	...
183	Nakuru d.	...	0105	...
400	**Kisumu** a.	...	0920	...

	②④⑦	①③⑤ A	
Kisumu d.	1830	...	...
Nakuru d.	0255	...	...
Nairobi a.	0900	...	...
Nairobi d.	...	1900	...
Makindu d.	...	2315	...
Mtito Andei d.	...	0111	...
Voi d.	...	0400	...
Mombasa a.	...	1000	...

Capital: **Nairobi** (GMT +3).
2014 Public Holidays: Jan. 1, Apr. 18, 21, May, 1, June 1, Oct. 5, 20, Dec. 12, 25, 26.

A – JAMBO KENYA DELUXE – [12] and ✕.

DEMOCRATIC CONGO — 4320

Société Nationale des Chemins de Fer du Congo

Capital: **Kinshasa** (GMT +1). 2014 Public Holidays: Jan. 1, 4, 16, 17, Apr. 20, 30, May 1, 17, June 30, Aug. 1, Dec. 25.

km		2A	C	B	2D	2E	2			
255	**Sakania** d.	...	...	...	...	⊖	...	...	...	...
0	Lubumbashi d.	0300	0700	0700	1300	⊖	...	...	...	...
237	Tenke d.	1500	2000	2000	0200	...	...	...	...	...
757	**Dilolo** d.	|	|	|	2200	...	...	...	...	...
600	Kamina d.	1300	1600	2000	...	...	...	...	...	...
1047	Kabalo d.	2000	|	|	...	...	⊖	...	...	...
1583	Kindu a.	...	|	|	...	...	⊖	...	...	...
1320	Kalemie a.	...	|	|	...	...	...	...	...	...
913	Mwene Ditu d.	...	1000	2000	...	...	...	...	...	...
1156	Kananga d.	...	...	2200	...	...	...	...	...	...
1578	**Ilebo** a.	...	...	0900	...	...	...	...	...	...

	2D	C	B	2A	2E	2			
Ilebo d.	...	...	1600	...	...	...	...	...	...
Kananga d.	...	...	0500	...	...	...	...	...	...
Mwene Ditu d.	...	1600	0700	...	...	...	...	...	...
Kalemie d.	...	|	|	...	...	...	...	...	...
Kindu d.	...	|	|	...	...	⊖	...	...	...
Kabalo d.	...	|	|	0600	...	⊖	...	...	...
Kamina d.	...	1100	1100	1400	...	...	...	...	...
Dilolo d.	1500	|	|	|	...	...	...	...	...
Tenke d.	1400	1200	1400	1600	...	...	...	...	...
Lubumbashi a.	0300	1900	2100	2300	⊖	...	...	...	...
Sakania a.	...	...	...	...	⊖	...	...	...	...

km		②⑥2	③2	
0	**Kinshasa** Est d.	0730	0730	...
366	**Matadi** a.	1930	2330	...

	④2	③⑦2	
Matadi d.	0500	0600	...
Kinshasa Est a.	2110	1800	...

km		2		
0	**Kisangani** d.	F	...	...
125	**Ubundu** a.	F	...	...

	2		
Ubundu d.	F	...	...
Kisangani a.	F	...	...

☛ All timings are approximate.
A – From Lubumbashi 2nd and 4th ⑥ of each month. From Kabalo 1st and 3rd ④.
B – From Lubumbashi 1st ⑥ of each month. From Ilebo on following ①.
C – From Lubumbashi 1st and 3rd ① of each month. From Mwene on following ④.
D – From Lubumbashi 1st and 3rd ④. From Dilolo on following ⑦.
E – One train per week.
F – A service runs approximately every 2 months. No schedule available.
⊖ – No information available.

TANZANIA and ZAMBIA — 4330

Tanzania Railways, TAZARA, Zambian Railways

Capitals: **Dodoma** (Tanzania, GMT +3), **Lusaka** (Zambia, GMT +2).
2014 Public Holidays: Tanzania: Jan. 1, 12, 13, Apr. 21, 26, May 1, July 7, Aug. 8, Oct. 4, 14, 15, Dec. 9, 25, 26.
2014 Public Holidays: Zambia: Jan. 1, Mar. 12, Apr. 18, 21, May 1, 25, July 7, 8, Aug. 4, Oct. 24, Dec. 25.

km	*Tanzania Railways*	②⑤ A	B
0	**Dar es Salaam** ◧ d.	1700	...
78	Ruvu d.	1931	...
203	Morogoro d.	0015	...
290	Kilosa d.	0235	...
465	Dodoma d.	0810	...
578	Manyoni d.	1214	...
637	Itigi d.	1318	...
840	**Tabora** a.	1825	...
840	**Tabora** d.	2010	2100
975	Kaliua d.	2305	0045
1051	**Mpanda** a.	|	1030
1144	Uvinza d.	0330	...
1256	**Kigoma** a.	0725	...

	B	④⑦ A
Kigoma d.	...	1700
Uvinza d.	...	2112
Mpanda d.	1300	|
Kaliua d.	2310	0136
Tabora a.	0245	0430
Tabora d.	...	0725
Itigi d.	...	1315
Manyoni d.	...	1417
Dodoma d.	...	1840
Kilosa d.	...	2340
Morogoro d.	...	0215
Ruvu d.	...	0616
Dar es Salaam ◧ a.	...	0850

km	*TAZARA*	⑤ C	② C
0	**Dar es Salaam** ◧ d.	1350	1550
226	Kisaki d.	1910	2013
360	Ifakara d.	2230	2258
496	Mlimba d.	0140	0152
652	Makambako d.	0803	0746
849	Mbeya d.	1440	1325
969	Tunduma 🛃 d.	1813	1717
970	Nakonde 🛃 d.	1818	1647
1226	Kasama d.	0031	2227
1412	Mpika d.	0445	0148
1652	Serenje d.	0931	0556
1761	Mkushi Boma d.	1143	0753
1852	**Kapiri Mposhi** ⊡ a.	1337	0926

	⑤ C	② C
Kapiri Mposhi ⊡ d.	1400	1600
Mkushi Boma d.	1538	1743
Serenje d.	1817	1947
Mpika d.	2318	0010
Kasama d.	0309	0319
Nakonde d.	0925	0909
Tunduma 🛃 d.	1045	1029
Mbeya 🛃 d.	1500	1428
Makambako d.	2129	2015
Mlimba d.	0351	0208
Ifakara d.	0659	0512
Kisaki d.	1035	0757
Dar es Salaam ◧ a.	1546	1235

km	*Zambia Railways*	①⑤ 2	②④ 2
0	**Kitwe** d.	0845	...
66	Ndola d.	1130	...
199	Kapiri Mposhi ⊡ d.	1642	...
262	Kabwe d.	1940	...
331	Chisamba d.	2217	...
384	**Lusaka** a.	2350	...
384	**Lusaka** d.	0030	1800
432	Kafue d.	0300	2021
481	Mazabuka d.	0510	2215
540	Monze d.	0720	0021
577	Pemba d.	0850	|
643	Choma d.	1125	0215
713	Kalomo d.	1359	0510
851	**Livingstone** a.	2000	0910

	③⑦ 2	①⑤ 2
Livingstone d.	1800	2000
Kalomo d.	2226	0100
Choma d.	0031	0345
Pemba d.	|	0550
Monze d.	0315	0730
Mazabuka d.	0520	0930
Kafue d.	0730	1140
Lusaka a.	0910	1320
Lusaka d.	...	1420
Chisamba d.	...	1555
Kabwe d.	...	1900
Kapiri Mposhi ⊡ d.	...	2145
Ndola d.	...	0330
Kitwe a.	...	0600

km	*Zambia Railways*	⑤ 2	
0	**Mulobezi** d.	1000	...
85	Ngwezi d.	1900	...
163	**Livingstone** a.	0500	...

	② 2	
Livingstone d.	0700	...
Ngwezi d.	1700	...
Mulobezi a.	0200	...

A – 🛏 1, 2 cl., [2] and ✕ Dar es Salaam - Kigoma and v.v. Subject to confirmation.
B – Once per week, subject to confirmation.
C – 🛏 1, 2 cl., ▬ 1, 2 cl., [2] and ✕.
◧ – Stations are approximately 8 km from each other.
⊡ – Stations are approximately 2 km from each other.

MADAGASCAR — 4340

Chemins de Fer Fianarantsoa-Côte Est / Madarail

Capital: **Antananarivo** (GMT +3).
2014 Public Holidays: Jan. 1, Mar. 29, Apr. 21, May 1, 29, June 26, Aug. 15, Nov. 1, Dec, 25.

km	*Madarail*	⑤ 2	② 2
0	**Toamasina** d.	...	0820
43	Tampolo d.	...	0951
86	Ambila-Lemaitso d.	0800	1125
162	Lohariandava d.	1150	1515
223	Andasibe ◇ d.	1515	1725
249	**Moramanga** a.	1740	1855

	① 2	④ 2
Moramanga d.	0700	1500
Andasibe ◇ d.	0830	1600
Lohariandava d.	1050	1820
Ambila-Lemaitso d.	1340	2200
Tampolo d.	1520	...
Toamasina a.	1650	...

km	*CFFCE*	②④⑥ A	
0	**Fianarantsoa** d.	0700	...
39	Ranomena d.	0825	...
62	Tolongoina d.	0940	...
79	Manampatrana d.	1045	...
118	Sahasinaka d.	1230	...
163	**Manakara** a.	1400	...

	③⑤⑦ A	
Manakara d.	0645	...
Sahasinaka d.	0819	...
Manampatrana d.	1032	...
Tolongoina d.	1157	...
Ranomena d.	1342	...
Fianarantsoa a.	1500	...

A – Subject to confirmation.

◇ – Special tour trains using Michelin railcars run Andasibe - Antananarivo and v.v., and Antananarivo - Antsirabe and v.v. For dates contact operator.

4350 ANGOLA — INCFA

km		③	⑥	①-⑤		①-⑤	
0	**Luanda** ⊗ d.	0610	0700	0800	1530	1655	...
23	Viana ⊗ d.	0710	0758	0854	1625	1748	...
65	Catete d.	0754	0841	0942	1715	1838	...
135	Zenza d.	0857	0951	...	...	...	...
190	**Dondo** (Cuanza) a.	|	1051	...	...	...	...
241	N'dalatando d.	1218	...	...	...	...	...
424	**Malange** a.	1644	...	...	...	...	...

	①-⑤	⑥	⑥	④	①-⑤	
Malange d.	...	...	...	0700	...	...
N'dalatando d.	...	...	...	1136	...	...
Dondo (Cuanza) d.	...	...	1330	|	...	...
Zenza d.	...	...	1440	1540	...	...
Catete d.	1000	1200	1542	1552	1850	...
Viana ⊗ d.	1052	1112	1633	1652	1959	...
Luanda ⊗ a.	1141	1202	1714	1747	2047	...

Capital: **Luanda** (GMT +1).

2014 Public Holidays: Jan. 1, 4, Feb. 4, Mar. 8, 29, Apr. 4, 18, 21, May 1, 25, June 1, Sep. 17, Nov. 1, 11, Dec. 25, 26.

⊗ – Additional local trains available.
✣ – Service suspended.
♥ – 4 trains weekly days and timings to be confirmed. This service daily from August 2014
a – timings to be confirmed
◧ – Services dep. Lobita and Benguela at 0600, 1700 journey time 65 min.

km		①-⑤	①-⑤	①a
0	**Lobito** ◧ d.	...	...	0530
33	Benguela ◧ a.	...	...	|
395	**Caála** d.	0630	...	|
408	Dango d.	0730	...	|
423	Huambo d.	0755	1000	1845
453	Cambuio d.	...	1100	|
478	**Katchiungo** a.	...	1155	|
1016	Luena d.	...	...	0300
1332	Luau a.	...	...	...

	①-⑤	①-⑤	④a
Luau d.	...	...	...
Luena d.	...	...	2100
Katchiungo d.	1300	...	|
Cambuio d.	1355	...	|
Huambo d.	1455	1600	0700
Dango d.	...	1622	|
Caála a.	...	1730	|
Benguela ◧ d.	...	...	|
Lobita ◧ a.	...	...	1648

km		✣		♥
0	**Namibe** d.	...	...	0600
162	Bibala d.	...	...	0845
246	Lubango d.	0600	...	1010
424	Matala d.	1040	...	1300
509	**Dondo** (Lubango) a.	1240	...	|
756	Menongue a.	...	...	1800

	♥		✣
Menongue d.	0900	...	...
Dondo (Lubango) a.	|	...	1715
Matala d.	1100	...	1910
Lubango d.	1400	...	2340
Bibala d.	1530	...	...
Namibe a.	1810	...	...

4360 MALAWI — 2nd class only — Central East African Railway

km		⑥	④	⑤
0	**Balaka** d.	...	0600	0600
16	Nkaya d.	...	0658	1028
42	Liwonde d.	...	0816	|
114	**Nayuchi** a.	...	1137	|
104	Blantyre d.	...	...	1733
112	Limbe d.	0900	...	1815
233	**Makhanga** a.	1715	...	...

	③	⑦	④
Makhanga d.	...	0700	...
Limbe d.	0700	1645	...
Blantyre d.	0750	...	...
Nayuchi d.	|	...	1245
Liwonde d.	|	...	1635
Nkaya d.	1315	...	1740
Balaka a.	1735	...	1855

Capital: **Lilongwe** (GMT +2).

2014 Public Holidays: Jan. 1, 2, 3, 15, Mar. 3, Apr. 18, 21, May 1, 14, June 14, July 6, 7, Oct. 15, Dec. 25, 26.

4370 MOÇAMBIQUE — 2nd class only — CD do Norte / CF Moçambique

Capital: **Maputo** (GMT +2). 2014 Public Holidays: Jan. 1, Feb. 3, Apr. 7, May 1, June 25, Sep. 7, 25, Oct. 4, Dec. 25.

km			A	
0	**Nampula** d.	0500	...	...
173	Iapala d.	0910	...	...
252	Malema d.	1145	...	...
302	Mutuáli d.	1315	...	...
356	Cuamba d.	1500	⊖	...
464	Mitande d.	...	⊖	...
541	**Nayuci** a.	...	⊖	...

		A	
Nayuci d.	...	⊖	...
Mitande d.	...	⊖	...
Cuamba d.	0530	⊖	...
Mutuáli d.	0715	...	...
Malema d.	0845	...	...
Iapala d.	1150	...	...
Nampula a.	1600	...	...

km		⑥	②	
0	**Beira** d.	0600	1850	...
28	Dondo d.	0736	2026	...
128	Muanza d.	1019	2309	...
150	Inhaminga d.	1218	0106	...
175	Inhamitanga d.	1259	0147	...
255	Marromeu a.	1610	|	...
320	**Nhamalabue** a.	...	0523	...
577	Maotize a.	...	1349	...

	⑦	④	
Moatize d.	...	0700	...
Nhamalabue d.	...	1610	...
Marromeu d.	0800	|	...
Inhamitanga d.	1110	1947	...
Inhaminga d.	1151	2028	...
Muanza d.	1358	2300	...
Dondo d.	1651	0153	...
Beira a.	1807	0309	...

km		⑥⑦	⑥	③
0	**Maputo** d.	0730	0955	1300
208	Chókwe d.	1212	1901	1951
534	**Chicualacuala** a.	...	0349	0342

	④	⑦	⑥⑦
Chicualacuala d.	1300	1015	...
Chókwe d.	2258	2145	1420
Maputo a.	0549	0810	1906

km		①-⑤	⑥	⑥⑦ B
0	**Maputo** d.	0745	0800	1030
53	Moambe d.	0908	0933	1159
88	**Ressano Garcia** a.	1020	1045	1253

	①-⑤ C	⑦	⑥⑦
Ressano Garcia d.	1205	1225	1640
Moambe d.	1319	1339	1726
Maputo a.	1511	1535	1857

A – Once a week. Day of operation varies.
B – Additional trip ①-⑤ 1810.
C – Additional trip ⑥⑦ 0300.
⊖ – No information available.

4380 ZIMBABWE — National Railways of Zimbabwe

Capital: **Harare** (GMT +2). 2014 Public Holidays: Jan. 1, Apr. 18, 21, May 1, Aug. 11, 12, Dec. 22, 25, 26.

km		①④⑥ A		
0	**Mutare** d.	2100	...	...
77	Nyazura d.	2307	...	...
99	Rusape d.	0010	...	...
166	Macheke d.	0239	...	...
201	Marondera d.	0345	...	...
273	**Harare** a.	0605	...	...

	③⑤⑦ A		
Harare d.	2130	...	...
Marondera d.	2345	...	...
Macheke d.	0100	...	...
Rusape d.	0320	...	...
Nyazura d.	0409	...	...
Mutare a.	0600	...	...

km		B		
0	**Bulawayo** d.	1930	...	...
126	Gwayi d.	2310	...	...
266	Dete d.	0200	...	...
339	Hwange d.	0347	...	...
351	Thomson Junction d.	0455	...	...
472	**Victoria Falls** a.	0800	...	...

	B		
Victoria Falls d.	1900	...	...
Thomson Jct d.	2230	...	...
Hwange d.	2303	...	...
Dete d.	0110	...	...
Gwayi d.	0340	...	...
Bulawayo a.	0805	...	...

km		②⑤⑦ A	①③⑤	
0	**Harare** d.	2000	...	...
44	Norton d.	2120	...	...
127	Chegutu d.	2227	...	...
160	Kadoma d.	2320	...	...
237	Kwekwe d.	0054	...	...
**	Masvingo d.	|	2000	...
302	Gweru d.	0242	0345	...
336	Somabhula d.	|	...	...
369	Shangani d.	|	...	...
486	**Bulawayo** a.	0700	...	...

	①④⑥ A	①③⑤	
Bulawayo d.	2000	...	...
Shangani d.	|	...	...
Somabhula d.	|	...	...
Gweru d.	0030	0245	...
Masvingo a.	|	0955	...
Kwekwe d.	0227	...	...
Kadoma d.	0412	...	...
Chegutu d.	0502	...	...
Norton d.	0620	...	...
Harare a.	0730	...	...

km		③ A	⑦ A	
0	**Bulawayo** d.	1215	1730	...
113	Shangani d.	1513	2045	...
150	Somabhula d.	1607	2140	...
229	Bannockburn d.	1755	2335	...
309	Ngezi d.	1941	0135	...
401	Rutenga d.	2300	0455	...
433	Lundi d.	|	0636	...
500	**Chicualacuala** a.	0251a	|	...
499	Triangle d.	...	0720	...
523	**Chiredzi** a.	...	0758	...

	④ A	① A	
Chiredzi d.	...	1530	...
Triangle d.	...	1620	...
Chicualacuala d.	1520a	|	...
Lundi d.	|	1701	...
Rutenga d.	2000	2000	...
Ngezi d.	2255	2255	...
Bannockburn d.	0135	0135	...
Somabhula d.	0450	0450	...
Shangani d.	0552	0556	...
Bulawayo a.	0910	0910	...

km		④⑦ 2		
0	**Bulawayo** d.	1800	...	...
	Beit Bridge a.	0540	...	...

	①⑤ 2		
Beit Bridge d.	2100	...	...
Bulawayo a.	0845	...	...

km		①⑤ 2		
0	**Bulawayo** ‡ d.	0900	...	...
196	**Francistown** ‡ a.	1425	...	...

	②⑥ 2		
Francistown ‡ d.	1230	...	...
Bulawayo ‡ a.	1715	...	...

A – 🛏 1, 2 cl. and (2) Ⓡ.
B – 🛏 1 cl., 2 cl. and (2).
a – Sango Halt.
⊖ – No information available.
** – Masvingo - Gweru *199 km*.
‡ – 🛃 is Plumtree.

4390 NAMIBIA — Starline

Capital: **Windhoek** (GMT +1). 2014 Public Holidays: Jan. 1, Mar. 21, Apr. 18, 21, May 1, 4, 9, 25, 29, Aug. 26, Dec. 10, 25, 26.

km		①③ 2△	⑧ 2	⑥ A
412	**Walvisbaai** d.	...	1900	...
373	Swakopmund d.	...	2045	1500
222	Usakos d.	...	0045	|
419	**Otjiwarongo** d.	1540	|	|
282	Omaruru d.	1930	|	|
210	Kranzberg d.	2150	0135	|
191	Karibib d.	2220	0220	|
70	Okahandja d.	0140	0510	|
0	**Windhoek** a.	0320	0700	1030

	⑤ A	①③ 2△	⑧ 2
Windhoek d.	1200a	1545	1955
Okahandja d.	|	1805	2205
Karibib d.	|	2040	0040
Kranzberg d.	|	2140	0130
Omaruru d.	|	2335	|
Otjiwarongo d.	|	0220	|
Usakos d.	|	...	0150
Swakopmund d.	1000	...	0530
Walvisbaai a.	...	...	0715

km		⑧	③⑥ 2	
0	**Windhoek** d.	1940	...	...
97	Rehoboth d.	2210	...	...
192	Kalkrand d.	0000	...	...
274	Mariental d.	0220	...	...
423	Tses d.	0510	...	...
505	**Keetmanshoop** a.	0700	...	...
505	**Keetmanshoop** d.	...	0850	...
681	Grünau d.	...	1310	...
732	**Karasburg** a.	...	1430	...

	④⑦ 2	⑧	
Karasburg d.	1120	...	...
Grünau d.	1225	...	...
Keetmanshoop a.	1630	...	...
Keetmanshoop d.	...	1850	...
Tses d.	...	2040	...
Mariental d.	...	0020	...
Kalkrand d.	...	0230	...
Rehoboth d.	...	0425	...
Windhoek a.	...	0700	...

A – DESERT EXPRESS – 🛏, (coach) and ✕. Special service including meals and excursions.
a – departs 1300 in the summer.
△ – Subject to confirmation.

Metrorail / Shosholoza Meyl

SOUTH AFRICA 4400

Capital: **Pretoria** (GMT +2). 2014 Public Holidays: Jan. 1, Mar. 21 Apr. 18, 20, 27, 28 May 1, 7, June 16, Aug. 9, Sep. 24, Dec. 16, 25, 26.

km			③⑤⑦ ⚡ 2	A	③⑤⑦ B	③⑤⑦ C	⑤ 2	④ D	E	F	
0	**Johannesburg**	d.	...	1230	1315	1420	...	1500	1830	1820	...
14	Germiston	d.	...	|	1350	|	...	|	1903	|	...
172	Standerton	d.	...	|	|	|	...	|	2120	|	...
315	Newcastle	d.	...	|	|	|	...	|	2330	|	...
438	Ladysmith	d.	...	|	|	|	...	|	0130	|	...
617	Pietermaritzburg	d.	...	|	|	|	...	|	0458	0605	...
722	**Durban**	a.	...	|	|	|	...	|	0710	0830	...
75	Vereeniging	d.	...	|	1455	1600	...	|	...	...	...
210	Kroonstad	d.	...	|	1725	1832	...	|	...	...	...
407	**Bloemfontein**	a.	...	|	2020	2115	...	|	...	...	...
407	**Bloemfontein**	d.	1715	|	2030	2135	...	|	...	...	...
664	Burgersdorp	d.	|	|	|	0305	1741↓	|	...	...	...
809	Queenstown	d.	|	|	|	0610	1445	|	...	...	...
1023	**East London**	a.	|	|	|	1020	|	|	...	...	...
835	Cradock	d.	|	|	0445	...	|	|	...	...	...
1112	**Port Elizabeth**	a.	|	|	0915	...	|	|	...	...	...
186	Klerksdorp	d.	|	1625	...	...	|	|	...	...	...
495	Kimberley	d.	1958	2120	...	...	|	2303	...	...	...
908	De Aar	d.	...	0135	...	...	0100	|	...	...	...
988	Beaufort West	d.	...	0600	...	...	0440	0720	...	...	...
1355	Worcester	d.	...	1205	...	...	0440	|	...	...	...
1511	Bellville	d.	...	1500	...	...	1335	|	...	...	...
1530	**Cape Town**	a.	...	1530	...	...	1410	1615	...	...	...

		F	E	③⑤⑦ C	② D	③⑤⑦ B	①④⑥ ⚡ 2	A	④ 2	
Cape Town	d.	...	...	...	0905	...	...	1000	1025	...
Belleville	d.	...	...	...	|	...	...	1035	1105	...
Worcester	d.	...	...	...	|	...	...	1330	1355	...
Beaufort West	d.	...	...	...	1845	...	...	1950	2005	...
De Aar		...	...	...	|	...	...	2345	0010	...
Kimberley	d.	...	...	...	0300	...	0500	0346	|	...
Klerksdorp	d.	...	...	...	|	...	|	0826	|	...
Port Elizabeth	d.	...	...	...	|	1500	|	|	|	...
Cradock	d.	...	...	...	|	1932	|	|	|	...
East London	d.	...	...	1415	|	|	|	|	|	...
Queenstown	d.	...	...	1900	|	|	|	|	1002	...
Burgersdorp	d.	...	...	2156	|	|	|	|	0717↑	...
Bloemfontein	a.	...	...	0341	|	0426	0742	|	...	...
Bloemfontein	d.	...	...	0401	|	0446	...	|	...	...
Kroonstad	d.	...	...	0708	|	0752	...	|	...	...
Vereeniging	d.	...	...	0929	|	1010	...	|	...	...
Durban	d.	1730	1915	|	|	|	...	|	...	...
Pietermaritzburg	d.	2008	2136	|	|	|	...	|	...	...
Ladysmith	d.	|	0042	|	|	|	...	|	...	...
Newcastle	d.	|	0240	|	|	|	...	|	...	...
Standerton		|	0510	|	|	|	...	|	...	...
Germiston	d.	|	0723	|	|	1112	...	|	...	...
Johannesburg	a.	0630	0745	1050	1103	1135	...	1215	...	

km			③⑤ G	③⑤ H	
0	**Johannesburg**	d.	1810	1900	...
14	Germiston	d.	1837	1940	...
70	Pretoria	d.	1940	2056	...
183	Witbank	d.	2225	|	...
218	Middelburg	d.	2320	|	...
422	Nelspruit	d.	0415	|	...
461	Kaapmuiden	d.	0515	|	...
530	**Komatipoort** ▼	a.	0638	|	...
292	Mokopane	d.	...	0228	...
357	Polokwane	d.	...	0430	...
504	Makhado	d.	...	0759	...
633	**Musina** ▶	a.	...	1115	...

		④⑦ H	④⑦ G	
Musina ▶	d.	1525	...	...
Makhado	d.	1815	...	...
Polokwane	d.	2235	...	...
Mokopane	d.	2345	...	...
Komatipoort ▼	d.	|	1800	...
Kaapmuiden	d.	|	1936	...
Nelspruit	d.	|	2040	...
Middelburg	d.	|	0139	...
Witbank	d.	|	0229	...
Pretoria	d.	0425	0500	...
Germiston	d.	0523	0557	...
Johannesburg	a.	0545	0620	...

Johannesburg - Pretoria and v.v. 70 km. Journey 100 minutes. Operator: Metrorail.

From **Johannesburg**: Trains call at Germiston ± 30 minutes, and Isando* ± 45 minutes later.

Ⓐ: 0247, 0321, 0347, 0432, 0505, 0530, 0550, 0605, 0635, 0650, 0705, 0725, 0735, 0815, 0835, 0905, 0955, 1040, 1125, 1210, 1306, 1339, 1406, 1436, 1502, 1538, 1611, 1620, 1636, 1713, 1747, 1808, 1835, 1851, 1926.

⑥: 0410, 0525, 0625, 0725, 0825, 0925, 1028, 1133, 1233, 1325, 1533, 1628, 1735, 1848.

⑦: 0430, 0529, 0735, 0935, 1035, 1135, 1235, 1435, 1635, 1740, 1915.

From **Pretoria**: Trains call at Isando* ± 55 minutes, and Germiston ± 75 minutes later.

Ⓐ: 0305, 0335, 0413, 0430, 0450, 0505, 0520, 0540; 0545, 0600, 0605, 0620, 0630, 0645, 0710, 0730, 0750, 0830, 0900, 0935, 0955, 1040; 1125, 1230, 1325, 1405, 1443, 1515, 1535, 1550, 1620, 1640, 1715, 1735, 1805, 1835, 1925.

⑥: 0505, 0605, 0720, 0820, 0920, 1020, 1120, 1225, 1325, 1430, 1530, 1650, 1805, 1930.

⑦: 0445, 0645, 0845, 0945, 1045, 1145, 1245, 1345, 1530, 1645, 1845.

A – TRANS KAROO – 🛏, [2] [car] and ✕ Johannesburg - Cape Town and v.v. From Johannesburg ②③⑤⑦. From Cape Town ③④⑤⑦
B – ALGOA – 🛏, [2] and ✕ Johannesburg - Port Elizabeth and v.v. Conveys PREMIER CLASSE – 🛏 (1 cl.) [1] and ✕ Johannesburg - Port Elizabeth and v.v.
C – AMATOLA – 🛏, [2] and ✕ Johannesburg - East London and v.v.
D – PREMIER CLASSE – 🛏 (1 cl.) [1] and ✕ Johannesburg - Cape Town and v.v.
E – TRANS NATAL – 🛏, [2] [car] and ✕ Durban - Johannesburg and v.v. From Johannesburg and Durban on ①③⑤⑦.
F – PREMIER CLASSE – 🛏 (1 cl.) [1] and ✕ Johannesburg - Durban and v.v. From Johannesburg on last ⑤ of each month, from Durban on following ⑦.
G – KOMATI – [2] and 🍸 Johannesburg - Komatipoort and v.v.
H – BOSVELDER – [2] and 🍸 Johannesburg - Musina and v.v.

▶ – Musina - Beit Bridge (Zimbabwe): *12 km.* ▼ – Komatipoort - Ressano Garcia (Mozambique): *5 km.* ⚡ – Service suspended. * – For OR Tambo Airport.

LUXURY and CRUISE TRAINS

THE BLUE TRAIN:
A luxury cruise train running regularly between Pretoria and Cape Town with excursions along the way. Also occasional trips from Pretoria to Durban. ✆ +27 12 334 8459. Fax +27 12 334 8464. www.bluetrain.co.za.

ROVOS RAIL:
Luxury cruise train running regularly between Pretoria and Cape Town. Once a week the return from Cape Town goes on to Victoria Falls. Also run annual trips to Swakopmund and Dar es Salaam. Most tours feature haulage by the company's preserved steam locomotives. ✆ +27 12 315 8242. Fax +27 12 323 0843. www.rovos.co.za.

SHONGOLOLO EXPRESS:
Various 16 day train journeys throughout Southern Africa with excursions along the way. Tours start from Johannesburg or Cape Town and destinations include Dar es Salaam, Victoria Falls and Swakopmund. ✆ +27 86 177 7014. Fax +27 11 486 4057. www.shongololo.com.

ISRAEL

Capital: **Jerusalem** (GMT +2, add 1 hour in summer). 2014 Public Holidays: Mar. 16, Apr. 15, 21, 27, May 5, 6, Jun. 4, Aug. 5, Sep. 25, 26, Oct. 4, 9, 17, Dec. 17.

Rail services are operated Israel Railways (www.rail.co.il). All services convey a single class of seated accommodation. Timings are the most recent available and are subject to alteration at any time, particularly around religious holidays. Tickets and reservations may be purchased up to 7 days in advance of travel at stations or through the website.

Israel Railways

NAHARIYYA - TEL AVIV 4500

km			⑦–⑤	⑦–⑤	⑦–⑤	⑦–⑤	⑦–⑤	⑦–④	⑤	⑦–④	⑤	⑦–④	⑤		⑦–④	⑤	⑦–④	⑤	⑤	⑦–④	⑤		⑤	⑦–④	⑤
0	**Nahariyya**	d.	0013	0113	0213	0313	0413	0454	0457	0529	0531	0554	0557	and at	0929	0931	0954	0957	1031	1054	1057	and at	1331	1354	1357*
	Akko	d.	0020	0120	0220	0320	0420	0501	0504	0536	0538	0601	0604	the same	0936	0938	1001	1004	1038	1101	1104	the same	1338	1401	1404*
20	Qiryat Motzkin	d.	0029	0129	0229	0329	0429	0511	0514	0546	0548	0611	0614	minutes	0946	0948	1011	1014	1048	1111	1114	minutes	1348	1411	1414*
38	Haifa Hof HaKarmel	d.	0048	0148	0248	0348	0448	0536	0539	0616	0613	0636	0639	past each	1016	1013	1036	1039	1113	1136	1139	past each	1413	1436	1439*
71	Binyamina	d.	0106	0206	0306	0406	0506	0556	0602	|	0632	0656	0702	hour until	|	1032	1056	1102	1132	1156	1202	hour until	1432	1456	1502*
123	**Tel Aviv** Savidor C	a.	0146	0246	0346	0446	0546	0628	0634	0704	0703	0728	0734		1104	1103	1128	1134	1203	1228	1234		1503	1528	1534*

			⑦–④	⑤	⑦–④	⑤	⑦–④	⑦–④	⑦–④	⑦–④	⑦–④	⑦–④	⑥	⑦–④	⑥	⑦–④	⑦–④	⑥	⑦–④	⑥	⑦–④	⑥	⑥④	⑥	⑦–④		ex⑤
Nahariyya	d.	...	1429	1431*	1454	1457*	1529	1554	1629	1654	1729	1754	...	1829	1855	1854	1929	1926	1954	1951	2054	2026	2051	2151	2154	...	2313
Akko	d.	...	1436	1438*	1501	1504*	1536	1601	1636	1701	1736	1801	...	1836	1902	1901	1936	1933	2001	1958	2101	2033	2058	2158	2201	...	2320
Qiryat Motzkin	d.	...	1446	1448*	1511	1514*	1546	1614	1646	1711	1746	1811	...	1846	1912	1911	1946	1943	2011	2008	2111	2043	2108	2208	2211	...	2329
Haifa Hof HaKarmel	d.	...	1516	1513*	1536	1539*	1616	1636	1716	1736	1816	1836	1913	1916	1939	1936	2016	2013	2036	2039	2136	2113	2139	2239	2236	...	2348
Binyamina	d.	...	|	1532*	1556	1602*	|	1656	|	1756	|	1856	1932	|	2002	1956	|	2032	2056	2102	2156	2132	2202	2302	2256	...	0006
Tel Aviv Savidor C	a.	...	1614	1603*	1628	1634*	1704	1728	1758	1828	1904	1928	2004	2004	2034	2028	2104	2104	2128	2134	2228	2204	2251	2518	2343	...	0046

		⑦–⑤	⑦–⑤	⑦–⑤	⑦–⑤	⑦–⑤	⑦–④	⑤	⑦–④	⑤	⑤	⑦–④		⑦–④	⑤	⑤	⑦–④	⑤	⑤	⑦–④		⑤	⑤	⑦–④	
Tel Aviv Savidor C	d.	0119	0219	0319	0419	0519	0559	0552	0623	0623	0652	0659	and at	0923	0923	0952	0959	1023	1052	1059	and at	1323	1352	1359	...
Binyamina	d.	0155	0255	0355	0455	0555	0630	0623	|	0853	0723	0730	the same	|	0953	1023	1030	1053	1123	1130	the same	1353	1423	1430	...
Haifa Hof HaKarmel	d.	0213	0313	0413	0513	0613	0649	0647	0708	0712	0747	0749	minutes	1008	1012	1047	1049	1112	1147	1149	minutes	1412	1447	1449	...
Qiryat Motzkin	d.	0232	0332	0432	0532	0632	0715	0713	0740	0738	0813	0815	past each	1040	1038	1113	1115	1138	1213	1215	past each	1438	1513	1515	...
Akko	a.	0241	0341	0441	0541	0641	0724	0722	0750	0747	0822	0824	hour until	1050	1047	1122	1124	1147	1222	1224	hour until	1447	1522*	1524	...
Nahariyya	a.	0249	0349	0449	0549	0649	0733	0731	0759	0756	0831	0833		1059	1056	1131	1133	1156	1231	1233		1456	1531*	1533	...

		⑦–④	⑤	⑦–④	⑦–④	⑦–④	⑦–④	⑦–④	⑦–④	⑦–④	⑦–④	⑦–④	⑥	⑦–④	⑥	⑦–④	⑦–④	⑥	⑥	⑦–④	⑥	⑦–④	⑥	⑦–④	⑥	⑦–④	⑦
Tel Aviv Savidor C	d.	1423	1423	1459	1523	1559	1623	1659	1723	1759	1823	1859	1923	1923	1952	1959	2023	2023	2052	2059	2152	2159	2252	2259	2352	2359	0119
Binyamina	d.	|	1453	1530	|	1630	|	1730	|	1830	|	1930	1954	|	2023	2030	|	2053	2123	2130	2237	2230	2337	2330	0037	0041	0155
Haifa Hof HaKarmel	d.	1508	1512	1549	1608	1649	1708	1749	1808	1849	1908	1949	2012	2008	2047	2049	2108	2112	2147	2149	2301	2249	0001	2349	0101	0100	0213
Qiryat Motzkin	d.	1540	1538*	1615	1640	1715	1740	1815	1840	1915	1940	2018	2041	2040	2118	2115	2140	2141	2218	2217	2332	2317	0032	0017	0132	0128	0232
Akko	a.	1550	1547*	1624	1650	1724	1750	1824	1850	1924	1950	2024	2050	2050	2127	2124	2150	2150	2227	2226	2341	2326	0041	0026	0141	0137	0241
Nahariyya	a.	1559	1556*	1633	1659	1733	1759	1833	1859	1933	1959	2033	2059	2059	2136	2133	2159	2159	2236	2235	2350	2335	0050	0035	0150	0146	0249

* Summer only.

4510 TEL AVIV - BEN GURION AIRPORT - MODI'IN, JERUSALEM and BE'ER SHEVA

Israel Railways

km			⑦–⑤	⑦–⑤	⑦–⑤	⑦–⑤	⑦–⑤	⑤	⑦–⑤	⑦–④	⑦–④	⑦–④	⑤		⑦–④	⑤	⑦–④	⑤	⑦–④	⑤	⑦–④	⑤	⑦–④	⑤	⑦–④	⑤
0	**Tel Aviv** Savidor Center	d.	0048	0148	0248	0348	0448	0514	0539	0544	0601	0607	0614	...	0631	0637	0644	0644	0701	0706	0707	0714	0731	0737	0737	0744
14	Ben Gurion Airport	a.	0101	0201	0301	0401	0501	|	0558	|	0619	|	|	...	0649	0655	|	0702	0719	|	|	|	0749	0755	|	0802
35	**Modi'in** Center	a.	...	...	...	...	...	|	...	|	0643	|	|		0713	0719	|	|	0743	|	|	|	0813	0819	|	|
20	Lod	d.	...	...	...	...	...	0534	...	0604	...	0627	0634		...	...	0704	0713	...	0726	0727	0734	...	...	|	0813
51	Bet Shemesh	a.	...	...	...	...	...	0559	...	0629	...	|	0659		...	...	0729	|	...	|	|	0759	...	...	|	|
82	**Jerusalem** Malha	a.	...	...	...	...	...	0639	...	0709	...	|	0739		...	...	0810	|	...	|	|	0840	...	...	|	|
63	Kiryat Gat	d.	...	...	...	...	...	...	...	...	...	0654	...		...	...	...	0738	...	0751	0754	...	...	...	0819	0838
107	**Be'er Sheva** Center	a.	...	...	...	...	...	...	...	...	...	0729	...		...	...	...	0814	...	0827	0829	...	...	...	0854	0914

		⑦–④	⑦–④	⑤	⑦–④	⑤	⑦–④	⑦–④	⑤	⑦–④	⑤	⑦–④	⑤	⑦–④	⑤	⑦–④	⑦–④	⑤	⑦–④	⑤	⑦–④	⑤	⑦–④	⑤	⑦–④	⑤
Tel Aviv Savidor Center	d.	0744	0801	0806	0807	0814	0831	0837	0837	0844	0844	0901	0906	0907	0914	0931	0937	0937	0944	0944	1001	1006	1007	1014	1031	1037
Ben Gurion Airport	a.	|	0819	|	|	|	0849	|	0855	|	0902	0919	|	|	|	0949	|	0955	|	1002	1019	|	|	|	1049	1055
Modi'in Center	a.	|	0843	|	|	|	0913	|	0919	|	|	0943	|	|	|	1013	|	1019	|	|	1043	|	|	|	1113	1119
Lod	d.	0804	...	0826	0827	0834	...	|	...	0904	0913	...	0926	0927	0934	...	|	...	1004	1013	...	1026	1027	1034	...	...
Bet Shemesh	a.	0829	...	|	|	0839	...	|	...	0929	|	...	|	|	0959	...	|	...	1029	|	...	|	|	1059	...	...
Jerusalem Malha	a.	0910	...	|	|	0940	...	|	...	1010	|	...	|	|	1040	...	|	...	...	|	...	|	|	1140	...	...
Kiryat Gat	d.	...	...	0851	0854	...	...	0919	...	...	0938	...	0951	0954	...	...	1019	...	...	1038	...	1051	1054	...	...	...
Be'er Sheva Center	a.	...	...	0927	0929	...	...	0954	...	...	1014	...	1027	1029	...	...	1054	...	...	1114	...	1127	1129	...	...	...

		⑦–④	⑦–④	⑤	⑦–④	⑤	⑦–④	⑤	⑦–④	⑤	⑦–④	⑤	⑦–④	⑤	⑦–④	⑤	⑦–④	⑤	⑦–④	⑤	⑦–④	⑤	⑦–④	⑤	⑦–④	⑤
Tel Aviv Savidor Center	d.	1037	1044	1044	1101	1106	1107	1114	1131	1137	1144	1144	1201	1206	1207	1214	1231	1237	1244	1244	1301	1306	1307	1314	1331	1337
Ben Gurion Airport	a.	|	|	1102	1119	|	|	|	1149	1155	|	1202	1219	|	|	|	1249	1255	|	1302	1319	|	|	|	1349	1355
Modi'in Center	a.	|	|	|	1143	|	|	|	1213	1219	|	|	1243	|	|	|	1313	1319	|	|	1343	|	|	|	1413	1419
Lod	d.	|	1104	1113	...	1126	1127	1134	...	...	1204	1213	...	1226	1227	1234	...	...	1304	1313	...	1326	1327	1334	...	...
Bet Shemesh	a.	|	1129	|	...	|	|	1159	...	...	1229	|	...	|	|	1259	...	...	1329	|	...	|	|	1359	...	...
Jerusalem Malha	a.	|	1210	|	...	|	|	1239	...	...	...	|	...	|	|	1339	...	...	1409	|	...	|	|	1439	...	...
Kiryat Gat	d.	1118	...	1138	...	1151	1154	...	...	...	...	1238	...	1251	1254	...	...	...	...	1338	...	1351	1354	...	...	...
Be'er Sheva Center	a.	1150	...	1214	...	1227	1229	...	...	...	...	1314	...	1327	1329	...	...	...	...	1414	...	1427	1429	...	...	...

		⑦–④	⑤	⑤	⑤ s	⑦–④	⑦–④	⑤	⑦–④	⑦–④	⑤ s	⑦–④	⑤ s	⑦–④	⑦–④	⑦–④	⑦–④	⑦–④	⑦–④	⑦–④	⑦–④	⑦–④	⑦–④	⑦–④	⑦–④	⑦–④
Tel Aviv Savidor Center	d.	1344	1344	1406	1414	1401	1407	1437	1431	1444	1444	1501	1506	1507	1531	1544	1601	1607	1613	1631	1637	1644	1701	1707	1713	1731
Ben Gurion Airport	a.	|	1402	|	|	1419	|	1455	1449	|	1502	1519	|	|	1549	|	1619	|	1630	1649	|	|	1719	|	1731	1749
Modi'in Center	a.	|	|	|	|	1443	|	1519	1513	|	|	1543	|	|	1613	|	1643	|	|	1713	|	|	1743	|	1755	1813
Lod	d.	1404	1413	1426	1434	...	1427	...	...	1504	1513	...	1526	1527	...	1604	...	1627	1641	...	|	1704	...	1727	...	...
Bet Shemesh	a.	1429	|	|	1459	...	|	...	...	1529	|	...	|	|	...	1629	...	|	|	...	|	1729	...	|	...	...
Jerusalem Malha	a.	...	|	|	1533	...	|	...	...	1609	|	...	|	|	...	...	...	|	|	...	|	1809	...	|	...	...
Kiryat Gat	d.	...	1438	1453	...	...	1454	...	...	...	1538	...	1553	1554	...	...	...	1654	1705	...	1719	...	...	1754	...	...
Be'er Sheva Center	a.	...	1514	1530	...	...	1529	...	...	...	1614	...	1630	1629	...	...	...	1729	1740	...	1754	...	...	1829	...	...

		⑦–④	⑦–④	⑦–④	⑦–④	⑦–④	⑦–④	⑦–④	⑥ w	⑦–④	⑦–④	⑦–④	⑦–④	⑦–④	⑦–④	⑥ w	⑦–④	⑥ w	⑦–④	⑥ w	⑦–④	⑦–④	⑥	⑦–④	⑦–④	⑥
Tel Aviv Savidor Center	d.	1737	1744	1801	1807	1831	1837	1844	1907	1901	1907	1931	1937	1944	2001	2007	2007	2014	2031	2037	2044	2101	2107	2107	2131	2137
Ben Gurion Airport	a.	|	|	1819	|	1849	|	|	|	1919	|	1949	|	|	2019	|	|	|	2049	2055	|	2119	|	|	2149	2155
Modi'in Center	a.	|	|	1843	|	1913	|	|	|	1943	|	2013	|	|	2043	|	|	|	2113	2119	|	2143	|	|	2213	2219
Lod	d.	|	1804	...	1827	...	|	1904	1927	...	1927	...	|	2004	...	2027	2027	2034	...	...	2104	...	2127	2127	...	...
Bet Shemesh	a.	|	1829	...	|	...	|	1929	|	...	|	...	|	2029	...	|	|	2059	...	...	2129	...	|	|	...	...
Jerusalem Malha	a.	|	1909	...	|	...	|	2009	|	...	|	...	|	2109	...	|	|	2139	...	...	...	...	|	|	...	...
Kiryat Gat	d.	1818	...	...	1854	...	1918	...	1952	...	1954	...	2018	...	...	2052	2054	...	...	...	...	...	2152	2154	...	...
Be'er Sheva Center	a.	1850	...	...	1929	...	1950	...	2028	...	2029	...	2050	...	...	2128	2129	...	...	...	...	...	2228	2229	...	...

		⑦–④	⑦–④	⑥	⑦–④	⑦–④	⑦–④	⑥ w	⑦–④	⑦–④	⑦
Tel Aviv Savidor Center	d.	2144	2201	2207	2207	2231	2244	2254	2307	2346	0007
Ben Gurion Airport	a.	|	2219	|	|	2349	|	2312	|	0004	0024
Modi'in Center	a.	|	2243	|	|	2313	|	2336	|	0028	...
Lod	d.	2204	...	2227	2227	...	2304	...	2327	...	...
Bet Shemesh	a.	2229	...	|	|	...	2329	...	|	...	...
Jerusalem Malha	a.	...	...	|	|	...	...	...	|	...	...
Kiryat Gat	d.	...	...	2252	2254	...	...	...	2354	...	...
Be'er Sheva Center	a.	...	...	2328	2329	...	...	...	0029	...	...

		⑦–⑤	⑦–⑤	⑦–⑤	⑦–⑤	⑦–⑤	⑤	⑦–④	⑦–⑤	⑤	⑦–④
Be'er Sheva Center	d.	...	...	...	......	...	...	...	0459	0501	...
Kiryat Gat	d.	...	...	...	...	...	...	...	0532	0535	...
Jerusalem Malha	d.	...	...	...	...	...	...	...	|	|	...
Bet Shemesh	d.	...	...	...	...	...	...	...	|	|	...
Lod	d.	...	...	...	...	...	...	...	0559	0559	...
Modi'in Center	d.	...	...	...	...	...	0510	0517	|	|	0547
Ben Gurion Airport	d.	0102	0202	0302	0402	0502	0528	0535	|	|	0605
Tel Aviv Savidor Center	a.	0114	0214	0314	0414	0514	0549	0556	0620	0620	0626

		⑦–④	⑤	⑦–④	⑦–④	⑦–④	⑤	⑦–④	⑤	⑦–④	⑦–④	⑤	⑤	⑦–④	⑦–④	⑤	⑦–④	⑤	⑦–④	⑦–④	⑤	⑤	⑦–④	⑦–④	⑦–④	⑤
Be'er Sheva Center	d.	...	...	...	0547	0559	...	...	0601	...	0638	...	0628	...	0659	...	...	0701	...	...	...	0728	0738	...	...	...
Kiryat Gat	d.	...	...	...	0620	0632	...	...	0635	...	0708	...	0702	...	0732	...	...	0735	...	...	...	0802	0808	...	...	...
Jerusalem Malha	d.	0517	...	...	|	|	0547	...	|	0617	|	...	|	...	|	0647	...	|	...	0717	...	|	|	...	...	0747
Bet Shemesh	d.	0559	...	...	|	|	0629	...	|	0659	|	...	|	...	|	0729	0730	|	...	0759	...	|	|	...	...	0829
Lod	d.	0623	...	...	0645	0659	0653	...	0659	0723	|	...	0726	...	0759	0753	0753	0759	...	0823	...	0826	|	...	...	0853
Modi'in Center	d.	|	0610	0617	|	|	|	0647	|	|	|	0710	|	0717	|	|	|	|	0747	|	0810	|	|	0817	0835	|
Ben Gurion Airport	d.	|	0628	0635	0655	|	|	0705	|	|	|	0728	0736	0735	|	|	|	|	0805	|	0828	|	|	0835	0853	|
Tel Aviv Savidor Center	a.	0644	0649	0656	0714	0720	0714	0726	0720	0744	0750	0749	0755	0756	0812	0814	0814	0820	0826	0844	0849	0855	0850	0856	0914	0914

		⑦–④	⑤	⑦–④	⑦–④	⑤	⑤	⑦–④	⑦–④	⑤	⑦–④	⑤	⑦–④	⑤	⑤	⑦–④	⑦–④	⑤	⑦–④	⑤	⑦–④	⑦–④	⑤	⑤	⑦–④	⑤
Be'er Sheva Center	d.	0759	0801	...	...	...	0828	0838	...	...	0859	0901	...	...	0928	...	...	...	0959	1001	...	...	...	1028	...	...
Kiryat Gat	d.	0832	0835	...	...	...	0902	0908	...	...	0932	0935	...	...	1002	...	...	...	1032	1035	...	...	...	1102	...	...
Jerusalem Malha	d.	|	|	...	0817	...	|	|	...	0847	|	|	...	...	|	0917	...	0947	|	|	...	...	...	|	...	1046
Bet Shemesh	d.	|	|	...	0859	...	|	|	...	0959	|	|	...	...	|	0959	...	1029	|	|	...	1100	...	|	...	1129
Lod	d.	0859	0859	...	0923	...	0926	|	...	0953	0959	0959	...	...	1026	1023	...	1053	1059	1059	...	1123	...	1126	...	1153
Modi'in Center	d.	|	|	0847	|	0910	|	|	0917	|	|	|	0947	1010	|	|	1017	|	|	|	1047	|	1110	|	1117	|
Ben Gurion Airport	d.	|	|	0905	|	0928	|	|	0935	|	|	|	1005	1028	|	|	1035	|	|	|	1105	|	1128	|	1135	|
Tel Aviv Savidor Center	a.	0920	0920	0926	0944	0949	0955	0950	0956	1014	1020	1020	1026	1049	1055	1044	1056	1114	1120	1120	1126	1144	1149	1155	1156	1214

		⑦–④	⑤	⑦–④	⑦–④	⑤	⑤	⑦–④	⑤	⑦–④	⑤	⑦–④	⑦–④	⑤	⑦–④	⑤	⑤	⑦–④	⑤	⑦–④	⑤	⑤	⑦–④	⑦–④	⑤	⑦–④
Be'er Sheva Center	d.	1059	1101	...	...	...	1128	...	...	1159	1201	...	...	...	...	1228	...	1259	1301	...	...	1328	...	...	...	1359
Kiryat Gat	d.	1132	1135	...	...	...	1202	...	...	1232	1235	...	...	...	...	1302	...	1332	1335	...	...	1402	...	...	...	1432
Jerusalem Malha	d.	|	|	...	1117	...	|	...	1146	|	|	...	...	...	...	|	1246	|	|	...	...	|	1316	...	1346	|
Bet Shemesh	d.	|	|	...	1159	...	|	...	1229	|	|	...	1300	...	...	|	1329	|	|	...	...	|	1359	...	1429	|
Lod	d.	1159	1159	...	1223	...	1226	...	1253	1259	1259	...	1323	...	...	1326	1353	1359	1359	...	...	1426	1423	...	1459	1459
Modi'in Center	d.	|	|	1147	|	1210	|	1217	|	|	|	1247	|	1310	1317	|	|	|	|	1347	1410	|	|	1417	|	|
Ben Gurion Airport	d.	|	|	1205	|	1228	|	1235	|	|	|	1305	|	1328	1335	|	|	|	|	1405	1428	|	|	1435	|	|
Tel Aviv Savidor Center	a.	1220	1220	1226	1244	1249	1255	1256	1314	1320	1320	1326	1344	1349	1356	1355	1414	1420	1420	1426	1449	1455	1444	1456	1514	1520

		⑦–④	⑦–④	⑤ s	⑦–④	⑦–④	⑦–④	⑦–④	⑦–④	⑦–④	⑦–④	⑦–④	⑦–④	⑦–④	⑦–④	⑦–④	⑦–④	⑦–④	⑦–④	⑦–④	⑦–④	⑦–④	⑥	⑦–④	⑦–④	⑥ w
Be'er Sheva Center	d.	...	...	...	1438	...	1459	...	...	1538	...	1559	...	...	1638	...	1659	...	...	1738	...	1758	...	...	...	...
Kiryat Gat	d.	...	...	...	1508	...	1532	...	...	1608	...	1632	...	...	1708	...	1732	...	...	1808	...	1832	...	...	...	...
Jerusalem Malha	d.	...	...	...	|	...	|	...	1516	|	...	|	...	1616	|	...	|	...	1716	|	...	|	...	...	1816	...
Bet Shemesh	d.	...	1500	...	|	...	|	...	1559	|	...	|	...	1659	|	...	|	...	1759	|	...	|	...	...	1859	...
Lod	d.	...	1523	...	|	...	1559	...	1623	|	...	1659	...	1723	|	...	1759	...	1823	|	...	1859	1901	...	1923	...
Modi'in Center	d.	1447	|	1510	|	1517	|	1547	|	|	1617	|	1647	|	|	1717	|	1747	|	|	1817	|	|	1847	|	1910
Ben Gurion Airport	d.	1505	|	1528	|	1535	|	1605	|	|	1635	|	1705	|	|	1735	|	1805	|	|	1835	|	|	1905	|	1928
Tel Aviv Savidor Center	a.	1526	1544	1549	1550	1556	1620	1626	1644	1650	1656	1720	1726	1744	1750	1756	1820	1826	1844	1850	1856	1920	1920	1926	1944	1949

		⑦–④	⑦–④	⑦–④	⑥ w	⑦–④	⑦–④	⑦–④	⑦–④	⑥ w	⑥ w	⑥ w	⑦–④	⑦–④	⑥	⑦–④	⑦–④	⑥	⑦–④	⑥	⑦–④	⑦–④	⑥ s	⑦–④	⑦–④	⑥
Be'er Sheva Center	d.	1838	...	1859	1901	...	...	...	1958	...	...	2001	...	...	...	...	2059	2101	...	...	...	2159	2201	...	2259	...
Kiryat Gat	d.	1908	...	1932	1935	...	...	...	2032	...	...	2035	...	...	...	...	2132	2135	...	...	...	2232	2235	...	2332	...
Jerusalem Malha	d.	|	...	|	|	...	1916	...	|	...	1950	|	...	2017	...	...	|	|	2117	...	...	|	|	...	|	...
Bet Shemesh	d.	|	...	|	|	...	1959	...	|	...	2028	|	...	2059	...	...	|	|	2159	...	...	|	|	...	|	...
Lod	d.	|	...	1959	1959	...	2023	...	2059	...	2052	2059	...	2123	...	...	2159	2159	2223	...	...	2259	2259	...	2359	...
Modi'in Center	d.	|	1917	|	|	1947	|	2017	|	2010	|	|	2047	|	2110	2117	|	|	|	2210	2217	|	|	2317	|	2310
Ben Gurion Airport	d.	|	1935	|	|	2005	|	2035	|	2028	|	|	2105	|	2128	2135	|	|	|	2228	2235	|	|	2335	|	2328
Tel Aviv Savidor Center	a.	1950	1956	2020	2020	2026	2044	2056	2120	2049	2113	2120	2126	2144	2149	2156	2220	2220	2244	2249	2256	2320	2220	2356	0020	2349

s – Summer only. w – Winter only.

SYRIA 4600

Chemins de fer Syriens Services suspended due to hostilities

Capital: **Dimashq** (GMT +2, add 1 hour in summer). 2014 Public Holidays:

km										
0	**Al Qamishli** d.	...	...	...	...	...	...	...	...	...
81	Al Hasakah d.	...	...	...	...	...	...	...	...	...
210	Dayr az Zawr d.	...	...	...	...	...	...	...	...	...
346	Ar Raqqah d.	...	...	...	...	...	...	...	...	...
550	**Aleppo** (Halab) a.	...	...	...	...	...	...	...	...	...
550	**Aleppo** (Halab) d.	...	...	...	...	...	...	...	...	...
694	Hamah d.	...	...	...	...	...	...	...	...	...
755	Hims 2 d.	...	...	...	...	...	...	...	...	...
899	**Dimashq** Kadem a.	...	...	...	...	...	...	...	...	...

Dimashq Kadem d.	...	...	...	...	...	...	...	...	...
Hims 2 d.	...	...	...	...	...	...	...	...	...
Hamah d.	...	...	...	...	...	...	...	...	...
Aleppo (Halab) a.	...	...	...	...	...	...	...	...	...
Aleppo (Halab) d.	...	...	...	...	...	...	...	...	...
Ar Raqqah d.	...	...	...	...	...	...	...	...	...
Dayr az Zawr d.	...	...	...	...	...	...	...	...	...
Al Hasakah d.	...	...	...	...	...	...	...	...	...
Al Qamishli a.	...	...	...	...	...	...	...	...	...

km										
0	**Aleppo** (Halab) d.	...	...	...	...	...	...	...	...	...
68	Bismaron d.	...	...	...	...	...	...	...	...	...
95	Jisr ash Shughur d.	...	...	...	...	...	...	...	...	...
199	**Al Ladhiqyah** a.	...	...	...	...	...	...	...	...	...
199	**Al Ladhiqyah** d.	...	...	...	...	...	...	...	...	...
280	Tartus d.	...	...	...	...	...	...	...	...	...
382	Hims 2 d.	...	...	...	...	...	...	...	...	...
526	**Dimashq** Kadem a.	...	...	...	...	...	...	...	...	...

Dimashq Kadem d.	...	...	...	...	...	...	...	...	...
Hims 2 d.	...	...	...	...	...	...	...	...	...
Tartus d.	...	...	...	...	...	...	...	...	...
Al Ladhiqyah a.	...	...	...	...	...	...	...	...	...
Al Ladhiqyah d.	...	...	...	...	...	...	...	...	...
Jisr ash Shughur d.	...	...	...	...	...	...	...	...	...
Bismaron d.	...	...	...	...	...	...	...	...	...
Aleppo (Halab) a.	...	...	...	...	...	...	...	...	...

IRAQ 4610

Iraq Railways

km		2C	21 B
609	Umm Qasr d.	1130	...
541	**Al Basrah** Ma'qil d.	1400	1800
370	An Nasiriyah (for Ur) d.	▬	|
182	Ad Dawanyah d.	...	|
107	Al Hillah (for Babylon) d.	**11**	|
0	**Baghdad** West a.	**A**	0615
0	**Baghdad** West d.	1920	...
117	Samarra d.	2310	...
171	Tikrit d.	|	...
211	Ba'iji d.	|	...
406	**Al Mawsil** a.	0755	...

	20 B	12 A
Al Mawsil d.	...	1900
Ba'iji d.	...	|
Tikrit d.	...	|
Samarra d.	...	0400
Baghdad West a.	...	0800
Baghdad West d.	1700	▬
Al Hillah (for Babylon) d.	|	...
Ad Dawanyah d.	|	...
An Nasiriyah (for Ur) d.	|	**2C**
Al Basrah Ma'qil a.	0520	0800
Umm Qasr a.	...	1025

Capital: **Baghdad** (GMT +3).

2014 Public Holidays: Jan. 1, 6, 13, May 1, July 14, 28, 29, Aug. 8, Oct. 3, 5, 6, 25, Nov. 3.

Rail services in Iraq are operated by Iraq Railways. Trains convey second class seating and also sleeping cars where indicated. Information regarding rail services is still very hard to obtain and the schedules shown should be treated as subject to confirmation.

A – 🛏 2 cl. Runs when required.
B – 🛏 2 cl.
C – Runs once per week. Days of operation unknown.

SAUDI ARABIA 4620

Saudi Railways Organization

Capital: **Riyadh** (GMT +3). 2014 Public Holidays: July 28 - Aug. 3, Sep. 23, 30, Oct. 1 - 10.

Rail services are operated by the Saudi Railways Organization (www.saudirailways.org). Trains convey first (called Premium or Al-Rihab) and second class (Standard or Al-Taleaa) seating. Reservations are available from 6 months until 1 hour before departure time

km									
0	**Ad Dammam** d.	0520	0906	...	1302	1655	...	2005	...
74	Abqaiq d.	0601	0947	...	1343	1739	...	2048	...
139	Al Hufuf d.	0654	1050	...	1441	1834	...	2140	...
449	**Ar Riyad** a.	0940	1326	...	1722	2115	...	0020	...

Ar Riyad d.	...	0700	1058	...	1331	1732	...	1955	...
Al Hufuf d.	...	0948	1345	...	1616	2011	...	2243	...
Abqaiq d.	...	1027	1424	...	1655	2052	...	2322	...
Ad Dammam a.	...	1120	1518	...	1751	2152	...	0015	...

IRAN 4630

Raja Trains

Capital: **Tehran** (GMT +3.5, add 1 hour in summer).
2014 Public Holidays: Jan. 2, 19, Feb. 11, Mar. 20 - 24,Apr. 1,2, 4, May 13, 27, June 14, July 19, 29, Aug. 22, Oct. 5, 13, Nov. 2, 3, Dec. 13, 22.

Rail services are operated by Raja Trains, an associate of Islamic Republic of Iran Railways (www.raja.ir). Except where noted as convey 2nd class only, all trains convey sleeping cars which convert to seating for daytime travel.

km					2																			
0	Tehran d.	...	0630	0650	0710	...	1630	1650	...	1710	1730	...	...	1750	1830	1940	...	...	2025	2050	...	...	...	...
926	Mashhad a.	...	1445	1540	1620	...	0220	0240	...	0435	0455	...	...	0515	0600	0715	...	...	0755	0820	...	...	...	...

							2					●												
Mashhad d.	...	...	...	0610	...	0630	0650	...	...	1750	1810	1830	...	1850	1910	1930	...	1930	2010	2050	...	2110	...	...
Tehran a.	...	...	...	1435	...	1610	1630	...	...	0550	0605	0455	...	0530	0545	0610	...	0610	0745	0825	...	0840	...	...

km			
0	**Tehran** d.	1840	1935
736	**Tabriz** a.	0740	0815

Tabriz d.	1720	1845
Tehran a.	0605	0745

km		A	
0	**Tabriz** d.	0745	...
	Djulfa a.	1030	...

	A	
Djulfa d.	1545	...
Tabriz a.	1830	...

km			
0	**Tehran** d.	1330	1500
1329	**Bandar e Abbas** a.	0820	0825

Bandar e Abbas d.	1230	1430
Tehran a.	0745	0910

km				
0	**Tehran** d.	2010	...	2220
494	**Eşfahan** d.	0400	0450	0525
	Shiraz a.	1110	1235	...

Shiraz d.	...	1525	1735
Eşfahan d	2130	2250	0055
Tehran a.	0405	0620	...

km			
0	**Tehran** d.	1310	...
924	**Khorramshahr** a.	0640	...

Khorramshahr d.	1115	1410
Tehran a.	0425	0845

km			
0	**Tehran** d.	1140	...
	Zahedan a.	0950z	...

Zahedan d.	1525	...
Tehran a.	1255z	...

km			
0	**Mashhad** d.	1050	2020
165	**Sarakhs** a.	1340	2310

Sarakhs d.	0640	1510
Mashhad a.	0925	1800

km			
0	**Mashhad** d.	1515	1625
	Eşfahan a.	1015	0910

Eşfahan d.	1545	1755
Mashhad a.	0835	1045

km			
0	**Mashhad** d.	1250	...
	Shiraz a.	1155	...

Shiraz d.	1735	...
Mashhad a.	1750	...

A – ①③⑥
z – Next day (more than 24 hours after previous time). ● – Even dated days.

ZAHEDAN - QUETTA 4640

km		404 A	
0	**Zahedan** d.	1000	...
84	Mirjawa 🏛 a.	1220	...
84	Mirjawa 🏛 d.	1300	...
100	Kuhi Taftan a.	1540	...
100	Kuhi Taftan d.	1710	...
222	Nok Kundi d.	2152	...
389	Dalbandin d.	0545	...
578	Nushki d.	1302	...
689	Wali Khan d.	1802	...
712	Spezand d.	1935	...
737	**Quetta** a.	2020	...

	403 B	
Quetta d.	0800	...
Spezand d.	0920	...
Wali Khan d.	1016	...
Nushki d.	1510	...
Dalbandin d.	2240	...
Nok Kundi d.	0557	...
Kuhi Taftan a.	1100	...
Kuhi Taftan d.	1230	...
Mirjawa 🏛 a.	1505	...
Mirjawa 🏛 d.	1515	...
Zahedan a.	1740	...

NOTE: Pakistan Railways and Raja Trains give different schedules for this train. This table shows the Pakistan Railways version. The Raja version is: Quetta d. 0830 - Zahedan a. 1335 / Zahedan d. 0800 - Quetta a. 1515.

A – 🛏12 departs on 3rd and 17th of the month.
B – 🛏12 departs on 1st and 15th of the month.

QUETTA - AMRITSAR 4650

km		39 A	402 ①④	14002 ①④
0	**Quetta** d.	0945	...	...
131	Sibi d.	1440	...	...
296	Jacobabad d.	1725	...	...
385	Rohri d.	1945	...	...
840	Khanewal d.	0350	...	...
1127	**Lahore** Junction a.	0905	...	...
1127	**Lahore** Junction d.	...	0800	...
	Wagah a.	...	0835	...
	Wagah d.	...	1130	...
1147	Atari 🏛 a.	...	1150	...
1147	Atari 🏛 d.	...	...	2015
1173	**Amritsar** a.	...	...	2037

	14001 ①④	401 ①④	24 A
Amritsar d.	0650	...	...
Atari 🏛 a.	0715	...	...
Atari 🏛 d.	...	1100	...
Wagah a.	...	1410	...
Wagah d.	...	1610	...
Lahore Junction a.	...	1645	...
Lahore Junction d.	...	...	1700
Khanewal d.	...	...	2150
Rohri d.	...	...	0610
Jacobabad d.	...	...	0820
Sibi d.	...	...	1125
Quetta a.	...	...	1625

A – AKBAR EXPRESS
NOTE: Timings are subject to confirmation and connections are not guaranteed.

BEYOND EUROPE
India

Introduction

The Beyond Europe section covers principal rail services in a different area of the world each month. There are six areas, each appearing twice yearly as follows:

India:	January and July editions
South East Asia and Australasia:	February and August editions
China:	March and September editions
Japan:	April and October editions
North America:	May and November editions
Africa and the Middle East:	June and December editions

The months have been chosen so that we can bring you up-to-date information for those countries which make seasonal changes.

Limited details of services in South America can be found in the European Rail Timetable Summer and Winter editions.

Contents

INDEX OF PLACES

by table number

INDIA

Capital: **New Delhi** (GMT +5.5). 2014 Public Holidays: Jan. 14, 26, Feb. 27, Mar. 16, Apr. 8, 13, 18, May 14, Aug. 15, 17, Oct. 2, 5, 6, 23 Nov. 4, 6, Dec. 25.

Rail services in India are operated by Indian Railways. Most trains convey a selection of first and second class accommodation from the several available. Trains which conve second class only are noted in either the column head or footnotes. Note that Rajdhani and Shatabdi trains convey first class accommodation only. The exact carriage type available on each train varies. A brief summary of train types and accommodation follows:

Rajdhani (shown as *RDi* in column heads). Air-conditioned first class night trains. Special fares payable. Conveys First Class 2 or 4-berth sleepers (code 1A); two-tier (code 2A or three-tier (code 3A) first class open plan berths. **Shatabdi** (shown as *SDi* in column heads). Air-conditioned first class daytime trains. Special fares payable. Conveys Cha Class seats (code CC); Executive Chair Class. **Duronto** (shown in column heads as *Duro*). Non-stop trains. Conveys first class sleeping accommodation (codes 1A, 2A, 3A a above); second class non air-conditioned 6-berth (code SL). **Express** (shown in column heads as *Exp*). Most services convey first class air conditioned two-tier (code 2A) c three-tier (code 3A) open plan berths; second class 'Sleeper Class' non air-conditioned six-berth (code SL); non air-conditioned second class seats (code 2S). **Yuva** (shown i column heads as *Yuva*). Low-cost air-conditioned train. Seating accommodation only. During the day, all sleepers and berths convert to seated accommodation. The code shown are those used by Indian Railways.

Timings are valid until further notice. Short notice changes are possible, especially around religious festivals and during monsoon seasons. Tickets can be purchased fro stations or through authorised agents. Reservations are required for travel on all trains shown in this section.

For multiple journies the best value ticket is the Indrail Pass. This is only available to foreign nationals and non-resident Indians. It is personal and non-transferable. Holde should always have their passports ready for inspection. Holders of Indrail Passes are exempted from all reservation fees, sleeping car charges and can travel as they like, fro any point in any train in the class it is issued for, within the period of validity. Reservations are essential, particularly on overnight journeys and are allocated on a first come firs served basis and can be made up to 360 days in advance. There is a maximum luggage allowance of 70Kgs. The exact amount depends upon the type of pass or class of trave Prices for AC CLASS Adult pass: ½ day US$57, 1 day US$95, 2 days US$160, 4 days US$220, 7 days US$270, 15 days US$370, 21 days US$396, 30 days US$495, 60 day US$800, 90 days US$1060. A Child pass is available at half price.

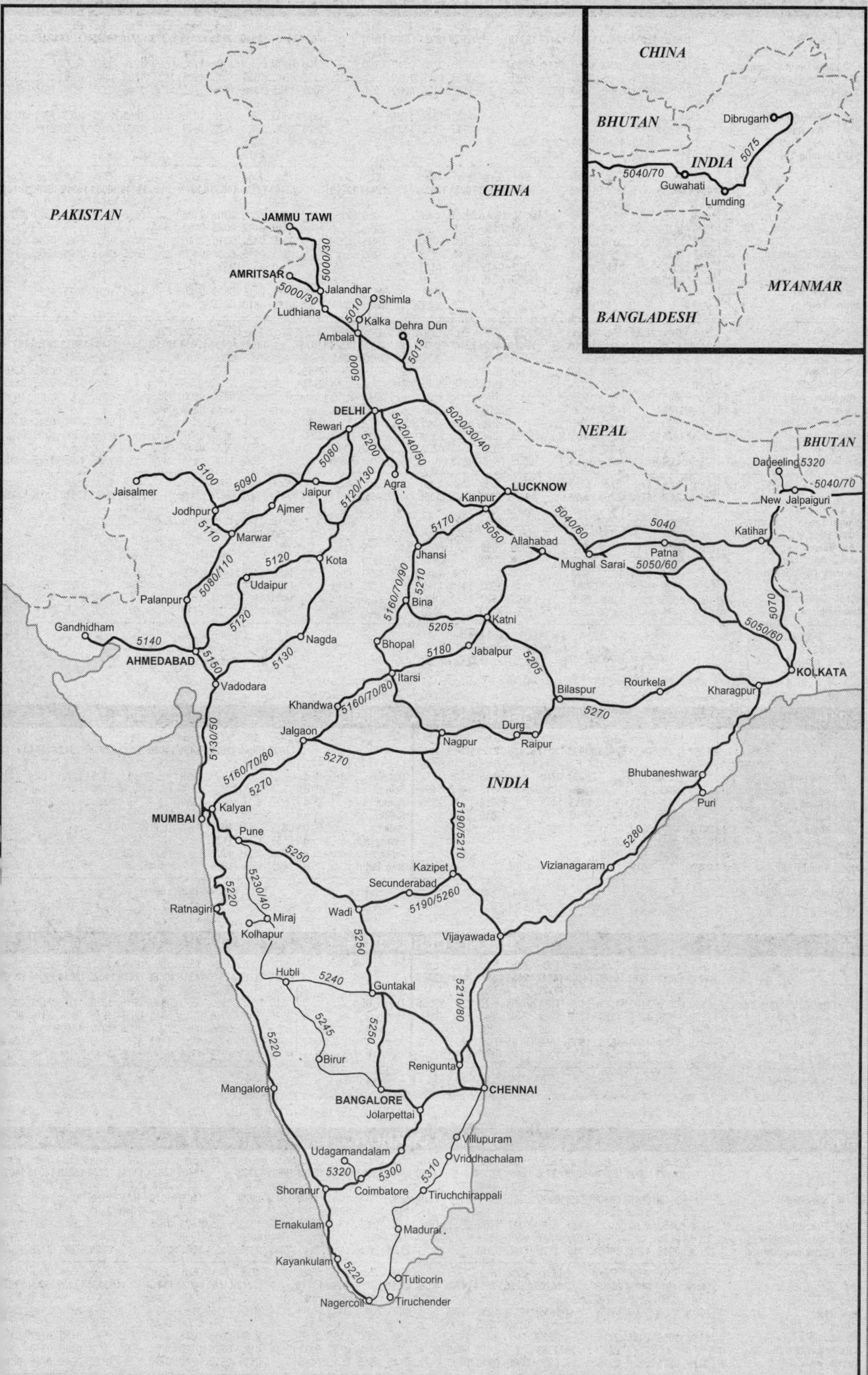
CHINA
BHUTAN
INDIA
Dibrugarh
5075
5040/70
Guwahati
Lumding
MYANMAR
BANGLADESH
PAKISTAN
CHINA
NEPAL
BHUTAN
JAMMU TAWI
5000/30
AMRITSAR
5000/30
Jalandhar
Shimla
Ludhiana
5010
Kalka
Dehra Dun
Ambala
5015
5000
DELHI
Rewari
5020/40/50
5020/30/40
5200
5080
Agra
LUCKNOW
5100
5090
Jaipur
5120/130
Kanpur
Jaisalmer
Jodhpur
Ajmer
5110
Marwar
5170
5050
5040/60
Allahabad
Mughal Sarai
5040
Patna
5050/60
Katihar
Darjeeling
5320
5040/70
New Jalpaiguri
5120
Kota
Jhansi
Udaipur
5080/110
Palanpur
5120
5160/70/90
5210
Bina
5205
Katni
5070
5050/60
Gandhidham
5140
AHMEDABAD
5150
5130
Nagda
Bhopal
5180
Jabalpur
5205
KOLKATA
Vadodara
Itarsi
Bilaspur
Rourkela
Kharagpur
5270
Khandwa
5160/70/80
Jalgaon
Durg
Raipur
Nagpur
5130/50
5270
5160/70/80
5270
INDIA
Bhubaneshwar
Puri
MUMBAI
Kalyan
Pune
5190/5210
5250
Kazipet
Secunderabad
5280
Vizianagaram
5230/40
5220
Ratnagiri
Miraj
Kolhapur
Wadi
5190/5260
Vijayawada
5250
Hubli
5240
Guntakal
5210/80
5245
5250
5220
Birur
Renigunta
Mangalore
CHENNAI
BANGALORE
Jolarpettai
Villupuram
Udagamandalam
Vriddhachalam
5320
5300
5310
Shoranur
Coimbatore
Tiruchchirappali
Ernakulam
Madurai
Kayankulam
5220
Tuticorin
Nagercoil
Tiruchender

5000 DELHI - AMRITSAR and JAMMU TAWI — Indian Railways

km		Exp	Exp	Exp	Exp	Exp	Exp		SDi	SDi	Exp	SDi		Exp	Exp	Exp	Exp	Exp	Exp	Exp	Exp	Exp	Exp	Exp
		15707	12471	12473	12475	12477	12919		12029	12031	12497	12037 12043		14037	11057	12549	12925	12483	12379	12715	19325	12203	12459	12421
			A	⑦	④	③			ex ④	④				②⑤⑦		③		⑤	⑥		③	①②⑤		④
0	**New Delhi** d.	0325j	0450	0450	0450	0450	0530	...	0720	0720	0640	0700	...	0800	0430	0930f	1105	1130	1215j	1230	1130h	1405	1330	1340
191	Ambala Cantonment d.	0700	0805	0805	0805	0805	0905	...	0957	0957	1015	|	...	1125	0940	1310	1455	1505	1525	1550	1640	1655	1715	|
304	Ludhiana d.	0855	0950	0950	0950	0950	1055	...	1127	1127	1200	1225	...	1305	1335	1510	1645	1705	1705	1745	1830	1830	1915	1935
356	Jalandhar Cantonment d.	|	1045	1045	1045	1045	1150	...	|	|	|	...	...	|	1443	1610	1736	|	|	|	|	|	|	|
361	Jalandhar City d.	1005	|	|	|	|	|	...	1222	1222	1557	...	...	1358	1500	|	1750	1810	1810	1855	1925	1925	2022	2035
440	**Amritsar** a.	1230	|	|	|	|	|	...	1335	1325	1420	...	...	1520	1630	|	1920	1945	1945	2020	2100	2100	2145	2205
468	Chakki Bank ♥ d.	...	1230	1230	1230	1230	1350	...	...	...	...	...	...	p	...	1755	...	...	...	...	...	...	...	...
568	**Jammu Tawi** a.	...	1445	1445	1445	1445	1605	...	...	...	...	...	...	...	...	2110	...	...	...	...	...	...	...	...

	Exp	Exp		Exp	Exp		SDi	Exp	Exp	RDi		Exp	Duro		Exp	Exp	Exp	Exp		Exp	Exp	Exp	Exp	Exp
	14649	14673		18507	14645		12013	12903	18237	12425		12445	12265		22401	12413	14033	11077		11449	16031	16317	16687	18101
	①③⑥	B		③⑥⑦									②⑤⑦		①③⑥					③	②⑤⑥	①	④	
New Delhi d.	1245j	1245j	...	1515	1550j	...	1630	1905h	2015h	2040	...	2050	2215a	...	2215a	2225j	2010j	2105	...	0010	0010	0010	0010	2200j
Ambala Cantonment d.	1630	1630	...	1845	2145	...	1905	0100	0215	|	...	2358	|	...	0110	0142	0025	0132	...	|	|	|	|	0245
Ludhiana d.	1940	1940	...	2015	0005	...	2032	0300	0400	0055	...	0135	0255	...	0245	0320	0210	0345	...	0700	0700	0700	0700	0505
Jalandhar Cantonment d.	2042	2042	...	|	0100	...	|	0359	0545	|	...	0230	|	...	0340	0415	0306	0445	...	0805	0805	0805	0805	0616
Jalandhar City d.	2055	2055	...	2135	|	...	2122	0415	0600	|	...	|	|	...	|	|	0330	|	...	|	|	|	|	0630
Amritsar a.	2325	2325	...	2355	|	...	2235	0545	0810	|	...	|	|	...	|	|	|	|	...	|	|	|	|	0750
Chakki Bank ♥ d.	...	...	...	...	0300	...	...	...	...	0335	...	0425	|	...	0525	0615	0550	0705	...	1035	1035	1035	1035	|
Jammu Tawi a.	...	...	...	...	0515	...	...	...	...	0540	...	0635	0715	...	0715	0810	0915	1000	...	1310	1310	1310	1310	1410

	Exp	Exp	Duro	Exp	Exp		RDi	Exp	Exp	Exp		Exp	Exp	Exp		Exp	Exp	SDi	Exp		Exp	Exp	Exp	Exp
	12414	18238	12266	22402	18110		12426	14034	12446	12904		18508	19326	11078		14646	12204	12014	12716		11450	16032	16318	16318
			①③⑥	②④⑦								③⑥⑦	④				③⑥⑦				③	②⑤⑥	①	④
Jammu Tawi d.	1815	...	1920	1905	1430	...	1940	1615	2105	...	...	...	...	2145	...	2045	...	...	...	...	2345	2345	2345	2345
Chakki Bank ♥ d.	2000	...	|	2050	|	...	2110	1915	2248	...	...	...	...	2345	...	2305	...	...	...	...	0133	0133	0133	0133
Amritsar d.	|	1615	|	|	1935	...	|	|	|	2125	...	2345	2315	|	...	|	0430	0500	0535	...	|	|	|	|
Jalandhar City d.	|	1735	|	|	2050	...	|	2200	|	2233	...	0055	0030	|	...	|	0537	0603	0640	...	|	|	|	|
Jalandhar Cantonment d.	2200	1750	|	2230	2106	...	|	2218	0033	2248	...	|	|	0145	...	0125	|	|	|	...	0340	0340	0340	0340
Ludhiana d.	2255	1915	2330	2315	2205	...	0005	2335	0125	2350	...	0215	0140	0300	...	0230	0630	0657	0745	...	0500	0500	0500	0500
Ambala Cantonment d.	0100	2220	|	0120	0040	...	|	0150	0340	0200	...	0420	0410	0514	...	0500	0820	0837	1000	...	|	|	|	|
New Delhi a.	0355j	0415h	0420a	0420a	0430j	...	0505	0545j	0650	0710h	...	0750	0950h	1000	...	1055j	1100	1115	1300	...	1325	1315	1315	1315

	Exp	Exp	Exp	Exp	Exp		Exp	Exp	Exp	Exp		Exp	Exp		Exp	Exp	Exp	Exp		SDi	Exp	SDi	SDi	Exp
	12484	12460	15708	12250	12926		14038	12380	12920	11058		14650	14674		12472	12474	12476	12478		12038 12044	12498	12030	12032	12422
	⑦			④			①③⑥	⑦				①③⑥	B		C	④	①	⑦				⑤–③	④	①
Jammu Tawi d.	...	...	...	0500	...	...	...	...	0900	...	...	...	...	...	1115	1115	1115	1115	...	...	...	...	...	...
Chakki Bank ♥ d.	...	...	...	0635	...	...	...	...	1040	...	...	...	...	...	1300	1300	1300	1300	...	...	...	...	...	...
Amritsar d.	0555	0615	0715	|	0810	...	0930	1055	|	0830	...	1155	1155	...	|	|	|	|	...	...	1510	1655	1655	1430
Jalandhar City d.	0700	0722	0835	|	0915	...	1040	1203	|	0955	...	1310	1310	...	|	|	|	|	...	...	1615	1758	1758	1535
Jalandhar Cantonment d.	|	0735	0848	0825	0928	...	|	|	1238	1013	...	1323	1323	...	1450	1450	1450	1450	...	...	|	|	|	|
Ludhiana d.	0805	0835	0955	0930	1025	...	1145	1300	1340	1130	...	1425	1425	...	1550	1550	1550	1550	...	1640	1718	1853	1853	1645
Ambala Cantonment d.	1015	1055	1200	1145	1305	...	1355	1520	1540	1550	...	1710	1710	...	1800	1800	1800	1800	...	|	1920	2032	2032	|
New Delhi a.	1325	1415	1505j	1520f	1625	...	1725j	1820j	1900	2020	...	2045j	2045j	...	2130	2130	2130	2130	...	2210	2250	2305	2305	2320

A – ①②⑤⑥.
B – ②④⑤⑦.
C – ②③⑤⑥.

a – Delhi Sarai Rohilla.
f – Delhi Safdarjang.
h – Delhi Hazrat Nizamuddin.

j – Delhi Junction.
p – To Pathankot arr.1820.
♥ – Pathankot Cantonment.

5010 DELHI - KALKA - SHIMLA — Indian Railways

km			Exp	Duro	Exp	Exp	SDi	Exp	Exp	SDi	SDi
		52457	12311	52451	52453	14095	12011	52455	12925	12005	12045
											①–⑥
0	**New Delhi** d.	...	2125j	...	...	0545a	0740	...	1105	1715	1915
191	Ambala Cantonment d.	...	0220	...	...	0950	1030	...	1515	1957	2155
268	Chandigarh d.	...	0350	...	...	1033	1113	...	1612	2048	2235
305	**Kalka** a.	...	0430	...	...	1110	1145	...	1645	2120	...
305	**Kalka** ¶ d.	0400	...	0530	0600	...	...	1210	...	...	...
347	Barog ¶ d.	0625	...	|	0815	...	...	1425	...	...	...
351	Solan ¶ d.	0639	...	|	0829	...	...	1439	...	...	...
401	**Shimla** ¶ a.	0920	...	1015	1105	...	...	1720	...	...	...

	SDi	SDi	Exp	Exp	Exp	SDi		Duro	Exp	Exp
	12006	12046	22926	52456	14096	12012	52458	52542	52454	12312
		①–⑥								
Shimla ¶ d.	...	...	...	1030	...	...	1425	1740	1815	...
Solan ¶ d.	...	...	...	1314	...	...	1725	|	2050	...
Barog ¶ d.	...	...	...	1340	...	...	1750	|	2110	...
Kalka ¶ a.	...	...	...	1610	...	...	2010	2225	2320	...
Kalka d.	0615	...	1020	...	1650	1745	...	...	...	2355
Chandigarh d.	0653	1200	1120	...	1728	1823	...	...	...	0110
Ambala Cantonment d.	0738	1240	1305	...	1830	1905	...	...	...	0220
New Delhi a.	1025	1520	1625	...	2240a	2155	...	...	...	0630j

a – Delhi Sarai Rohilla.
j – Delhi Junction.
¶ – Narrow gauge railway.

5015 DELHI - DEHRA DUN — Indian Railways

km		Exp	SDi	Exp	Exp	Exp	Exp	SDi	Exp	Exp	Exp
		19019	12017	12287	19565	14309	14317	12055	12687	14041	12205
				⑦	⑥	④⑤	①⑦		⑤		
0	**Delhi** H. Nizamuddin d.	0550	0650n	1100	1100n	1130	1130	1525n	2110	2220j	2355n
76	Meerut City d.	0830	0808	1228	1228	1252	1252	1638	2243	|	0118
190	Saharanpur d.	1245	1010	|	|	1535	1535	|	0205	|	|
271	Haridwar d.	1515	1130	1600	1655	1655	1655	1940	0325	0625	0400
323	**Dehra Dun** a.	1735	1240	1810	1900	1905	1905	2110	0500	0810	0540

	SDi	Exp	Exp	Exp	Exp	Exp	Exp	SDi	Exp	Exp
	12056	12288	14310	14318	19566	12688	19020	12018	14042	1220
		①	②③	⑤⑥	⑦	①				
Dehra Dun d.	0510	0550	0550	0550	0550	0645	1035	1700	2125	2330
Haridwar d.	0625	0745	0745	0745	0745	0830	1245	1813	2315	0055
Saharanpur d.	|	|	0955	0955	|	1050	1605	1950	|	|
Meerut City d.	0942	1127	1130	1130	1127	1220	1920	2116	|	0342
Delhi H. Nizamuddin a.	1110n	1315	1315	1315	1310n	1415	2115	2245n	0740j	0515

j – Delhi Junction.
n – New Delhi.

5020 DELHI - LUCKNOW — Indian Railways

km		Exp	SDi	Exp	Exp	RDi	RDi	Exp		Exp	Exp	Exp	Exp	Exp	Exp	Exp		Exp	Exp	SDi	Exp	Exp	Exp	Exp
		19403	12004	12876	15610	12236	12436	12204		14258	12420	12392	12566	12558	19601	12372		19407	12524	12034	15708	15280	14018	1401
		③		②⑤⑦		②	④⑦	③⑥⑦							⑥	④		⑤	③⑦	①–⑥		①⑤	③	⑤⑦
0	**New Delhi** d.	0040j	0615	0630	0745j	0930	0930	1115	...	1140	1230	1315	1420	1450v	1505j	1505j	...	1505j	1510	1555	1520j	1655j	1620j	1620
	Kanpur Central d.	|	1125	1240	|	|	|	|	...	|	1955	|	2020	|	|	|	...	|	|	2040	2300	|	|	|
167	Moradabad d.	0350	|	|	1120	1217	1217	1402	...	1515	|	1605	|	1740	1825	1825	...	1825	1825	...	|	2030	1950	1950
258	Bareilly Junction d.	0525	|	|	1305	1347	1347	1521	...	1653	|	1732	|	|	|	1955	...	1955	|	...	|	2215	|	|
493	**Lucknow** Junction a.	0945	1230	1405	1745	1725	1725	1840	...	2135	2125	2115	2145	2240	2335	2335	...	2335	2335	...	0025	0200	0325	032

	Exp	Exp	Exp	Exp		Exp	Exp	Exp	Exp		Exp	Exp	Exp	Exp		Exp	Exp	Exp	Exp		Exp	Exp	Exp	Duro
	14008	14014	14004	22408		14206	12226	12554	14208		12556	15716	19269	15716		12212	14650	14674	13414		13484	12230	12234	1227
	②④	①⑥	④⑦	①③⑤								①②④	⑤⑥	①		③	①③⑥	A	①③⑥		A		①③⑥	②⑤
New Delhi d.	1620j	1620j	1805	1815v	...	1835j	1920j	1950	1950j	...	2025	2040j	2040j	2040j	...	2100v	2115j	2115j	2150j	...	2150j	2210	2330	233
Kanpur Central d.	|	|	|	|	...	|	0140	0225	|	...	0315	|	|	|	...	|	|	|	0545	...	0545	|	|	|
Moradabad d.	1950	1950	2115	2115	...	2225	|	|	2305	...	|	2350	2350	2350	...	2350	0045	0045	|	...	|	0120	0222	|
Bareilly Junction d.	|	|	2240	2240	...	2358	|	|	0040	...	|	0115	0115	0115	...	0125	0220	0220	|	...	|	0255	0346	|
Lucknow Junction a.	0325	0325	0225	0225	...	0350	0300	0345	0420	...	0445	0515	0515	0515	...	0515	0610	0610	0720	...	0720	0645	0710	071

For footnotes and return service see next page ▷ ▷ ▷

Indian Railways — LUCKNOW - DELHI — 5020

km		14205	22407	12371	12033	14649		14673	12523	19602	12211	19270		15715	12203	12419	15279	14003	15609	12235	12435	12203	12875	12003
		Exp	Exp	Exp	SDi	Exp		Exp	Exp	Exp	Exp	Exp		Exp	Exp	Exp	Exp	Exp	Exp	RDi	RDi	Exp	Exp	SDi
			①③⑤	②	①-⑥	①③⑥		A	③⑦	②	⑥	①②		①③⑥	①②⑤		①⑤	③⑦		⑥	③⑦	①②⑤	①③⑥	
0	**Lucknow** Junction d.	0055	0130	0130	...	0115	...	0115	0330	0330	0430	0430	...	0455	0610	0525	0320	0550	0535	0610	0610	0610	1345	1535
	Bareilly Junction d.	0435	0505	0505	...	0535	...	0535	|	|	0805	0805	...	0825	0933	|	0718	0958	0919	0931	0931	0931	|	|
	Moradabad d.	0620	0655	0655	...	0730	...	0730	0900	0900	0945	0945	...	1005	1107	|	0900	1140	1125	1107	1107	1107	|	|
72	Kanpur Central d.	|	|	|	0600	|	...	|	|	|	|	|	...	|	|	0700	|	|	|	|	|	|	1525	1650
511	**New Delhi** a.	0935j	1005v	1020j	1115	1155j	...	1155j	1210	1210	1225v	1240j	...	1310j	1350	1400	1415	1440	1505j	1350	1350	1350	2140	2205

	15707	14017	14007	14015		14013	13413	13483	12391		14257	19408	19404	12565		14207	12555	12229	12553		12225	12557	12233	12271
	Exp	Exp	Exp	Exp		Exp	Exp	Exp	Exp		Exp	Exp	Exp	Exp		Exp	Exp	Exp	Exp		Exp	Exp	Exp	Duro
		⑤	④⑥	①③		②⑦	②⑤⑦	B				⑥	③										②⑤⑦	①④⑥
Lucknow Junction d.	1820	1850	1850	1850	...	1850	1935	1935	2030	...	2045	2130	2130	2120	...	2140	2150	2215	2225	...	2315	2340	2330	2330
Bareilly Junction d.	|	|	|	|	...	|	|	|	0012	...	0047	0108	0108	|	...	0127	|	0157	|	...	|	|	0245	|
Moradabad d.	|	0125	0125	0125	...	0125	|	|	0155	...	0235	0300	0300	|	...	0325	|	0350	|	...	|	0450	0425	|
Kanpur Central d.	2000	|	|	|	...	|	2115	2115	|	...	|	|	|	2258	...	|	2328	|	2359	...	0050	|	|	|
New Delhi a.	0250j	0450j	0450j	0450j	...	0450j	0430j	0430j	0510	...	0610	0620j	0620j	0530	...	0650j	0550	0710	0630	...	0700j	0750v	0730	0730

A – ②④⑤⑦. B – ①③④⑥. j – Delhi Junction. v – Delhi Anand Vihar Terminal.

Indian Railways — JAMMU TAWI and AMRITSAR - LUCKNOW — 5030

km		15708	18104	14650	14674		12238	15934	13050	13006		12356	12588	15652	15654		15098	12332	13152	12204		12318	12358	
		Exp	Exp	Exp	Exp		Exp	Exp	Exp	Exp		Exp	Exp	Exp	Exp		Exp	Exp	Exp	Exp		Exp	Exp	
			③⑤	①③⑥	A			⑤				③⑦	⑥	③	⑤		②	①④⑦		③⑥⑦		②⑤	①④	
0	**Jammu Tawi** d.	...	...	...	...	...	1400	...	...	...	...	2010	2245	2245	2245	...	2245	2245	1855	...	...	...	...	...
100	Chakki Bank ♥ d.	...	...	...	...	...	1540	...	...	...	...	2145	0025	0025	0025	...	0025	0025	2205	...	...	...	...	...
**	**Amritsar** d.	0715	1235	1155	1155	...	|	1550	1810	1845	...	|	|	|	|	...	|	|	|	0430	...	0605	0605	...
**	Jalandhar City d.	0835	1350	1310	1310	...	|	1658	1923	1957	...	|	|	|	|	...	|	|	|	0537	...	0705	0705	...
213	Jalandhar Cantonment d.	0848	|	1323	1323	...	1730	|	1938	2007	...	2332	0215	0215	0215	...	0215	0215	0005	|	...	|	|	...
265	Ludhiana d.	0955	1500	1425	1425	...	1825	1800	2040	2120	...	0025	0320	0320	0320	...	0320	0320	0155	0630	...	0805	0805	...
378	Ambala Cantonment d.	1200	1655	1710	1710	...	2100	2020	2310	2330	...	0235	0525	0525	0525	...	0525	0525	0430	0820	...	1015	1015	...
460	Saharanpur d.	|	1830	|	|	...	2225	2200	0055	0115	...	0405	0700	0700	0700	...	0700	0700	0620	|	...	1145	1145	...
652	Moradabad d.	|	2130	0045	0045	...	0135	0100	0420	0505	...	0705	1005	1005	1005	...	1005	1005	1045	1402	...	1450	1450	...
743	Bareilly Junction d.	|	2258	0220	0220	...	|	0235	|	0635	...	0833	1133	1133	1133	...	1133	1133	1230	1521	...	1620	|	...
978	**Lucknow** Junction a.	0025	0240	0610	0610	...	0745	0800	1145	1035	...	1225	1520	1520	1520	...	1520	1520	1705	1840	...	2005	2005	...

		12317	12357	12203	15933		14649	14673	13151	18103		13005	13049	12355	12237		15707	12331	15097	15651		15563	12587	
		Exp	Exp	Exp	Exp		Exp	Exp	Exp	Exp		Exp	Exp	Exp	Exp		Exp	Exp	Exp	Exp		Exp	Exp	
		①④	③⑦	①②⑤	④		①③⑥	A		②④				②⑥				③⑥⑦	⑤	②		④	①	
Lucknow Junction d.	...	0225	0225	0610	0610	...	0115	0115	1040	1520	...	1545	1610	1735	1815	...	1825	1950	1940	1940	...	1940	1940	...
Bareilly Junction d.	...	0622	|	0933	0933	...	0535	0535	1525	1853	...	1937	|	2053	|	...	|	2328	2328	2328	...	2328	2328	...
Moradabad d.	...	0805	0805	1107	1107	...	0730	0730	1725	2035	...	2125	2255	2235	2315	...	|	0110	0110	0110	...	0110	0110	...
Saharanpur d.	...	1130	1130	|	1450	...	|	|	2130	2350	...	0125	0305	0145	0230	...	|	0420	0420	0420	...	0420	0420	...
Ambala Cantonment d.	...	1300	1300	1655	1615	...	1630	1630	2310	0120	...	0315	0445	0325	0420	...	0700	0548	0548	0548	...	0548	0548	...
Ludhiana d.	...	1440	1440	1830	1805	...	1940	1940	0150	0358	...	0545	0713	0533	0630	...	0855	0730	0730	0730	...	0730	0730	...
Jalandhar Cantonment d.	...	|	|	|	|	...	2042	2042	0255	|	...	0647	0815	0628	0725	...	|	0830	0830	0830	...	0830	0830	...
Jalandhar City d.	...	1543	1543	1925	1910	...	2055	2055	|	0505	...	0700	0830	|	|	...	1025	|	|	|	...	|	|	...
Amritsar a.	...	1715	1715	2100	2100	...	2325	2325	|	0630	...	0855	1010	|	|	...	1230	|	|	|	...	|	|	...
Chakki Bank ♥ d.	...	...	...	...	...	...	...	...	0500	...	...	...	...	0810	0915	...	...	1015	1015	1015	...	1015	1015	...
Jammu Tawi a.	...	...	...	...	...	...	...	...	0830	...	...	...	...	1025	1125	...	...	1230	1230	1230	...	1230	1230	...

A – ②④⑤⑦.

♥ – Pathankot Cantonment.
** – Amritsar - Jalandhar Cantonment : *84 km*. Jalandhar City - Jalandhar Cantonment : *5 km*.

Indian Railways — DELHI - GUWAHATI — 5040

via Kanpur

km		12506	12424	12502
		Exp	RDi	Exp
				③④⑦
0	**New Delhi** d.	0650v	1400	2345
440	Kanpur Central d.	1300	1829	0620
634	Allahabad d.	1552	2032	0900
787	Mughal Sarai d.	1825	2255	|
999	Patna Junction d.	2220	0210	|
1109	Barauni d.	0105	0445	|
1288	Katihar d.	0455	0750	2050
1471	New Jalpaiguri d.	0835	1105	0020
1723	New Bongaigaon d.	1350	1502	0452
1879	**Guwahati** a.	1645	1720	0815

	12501	12423	12505
	Exp	RDi	Exp
	②③⑥		
Guwahati d.	0600	0705	0945
New Bongaigaon d.	0858	0920	1245
New Jalpaiguri d.	1335	1315	1715
Katihar d.	1705	1625	2110
Barauni d.	|	1920	0025
Patna Junction d.	|	2150	0305
Mughal Sarai d.	|	0107	0720
Allahabad d.	0425	0256	0940
Kanpur Central d.	0650	0508	1250
New Delhi a.	1300	1010	1915v

j – Delhi Junction.

via Lucknow

km		15610	12436	12236
		Exp	RDi	RDi
			④⑦	②
0	**New Delhi** d.	0745j	0930	0930
167	Moradabad d.	1120	1217	1217
258	Bareilly Junction d.	1305	1347	1347
493	Lucknow Junction d.	1810	1735	1735
981	Chhapra d.	0405	0200	0200
1128	Barauni d.	0905	0505	|
1308	Katihar d.	1345	0845	0845
1491	New Jalpaiguri d.	1810	1205	1205
1742	New Bongaigaon d.	2330	1605	1605
1899	**Guwahati** a.	0300	1900	1900

	12235	12435	15609
	RDi	RDi	Exp
	⑤	②⑥	
Guwahati d.	0555	0555	2200
New Bongaigaon d.	0813	0813	0105
New Jalpaiguri d.	1215	1215	0620
Katihar d.	1525	1605	1045
Barauni d.	|	1900	1425
Chhapra d.	2155	2155	1945
Lucknow Junction d.	0610	0610	0535
Bareilly Junction d.	0933	0933	0919
Moradabad d.	1107	1107	1125
New Delhi a.	1350	1350	1505j

v – Delhi Anand Vihar Terminal.

Indian Railways — DELHI - PATNA - KOLKATA — 5050

km		12506	12324	12274	12312	12488	15484		12332	12424	12368	12034		12302	12314	12250	12260		12306	12024	12570	22406	12316	12318
		Exp	Exp	Duro	Exp	Exp	Exp		Exp	RDi	Exp	SDi		RDi	RDi	Yuva	Duro		RDi	SDi	Exp	Exp	Exp	Exp
			④⑦	②⑥					②③⑥			①-⑥		⑥-④		⑦	C		⑤	①-⑥	②⑥	①③⑤	②	③⑥
0	**New Delhi** d.	0650v	0700	1300	0700j	0740v	0640j	...	...	1400	1440v	1555	...	1700	1630	1945	2005	...	1700	...	1700v	1700v	...	...
440	Kanpur Central d.	1300	1340	|	1430	1355	1520	...	...	1839	|	2040	...	2132	2115	0022	0039	...	2132	...	2207	2207	...	...
634	Allahabad Junction d.	1552	1645	|	1730	1700	1805	...	...	2032	|	...	...	2325	|	0224	|	...	2335	...	0009	0009	...	...
787	Muhgal Sarai d.	1825	1940	|	2025	2005	2115	...	...	2255	|	...	...	0155	0138	0438	0439	...	0155	...	0232	0232	...	...
	Patna Junction d.	2155	|	|	|	2325	0035	...	0150	0200	0645	...	...	|	|	|	|	...	0455	0545	0555	0555	0615	0615
1189	Dhanbad d.	...	0200	|	0325	...	...	...	|	...	...	...	...	0645	0628	0900	0858	...	|	|	...	...	|	|
1247	Asansol d.	...	0300	|	0440	...	...	...	0820	...	...	...	...	|	0719	00956	|	...	|	1047	...	...	1159	1159
1447	**Kolkata** Howrah a.	...	0600	0610	0755	...	...	...	1130	...	...	...	...	0955	1015e	1235	1230e	...	1235	1325	...	...	1510	1510

	12326	12372	12388	12304	12382	12310		12394	12330	12380	11106	12402	12276		14056	12350	12370	12328	12360	22214		12352	13112	12334
	Exp	Exp	Exp	Exp	Exp	RDI		Exp	Exp	Exp	Exp	Exp	Duro		Exp	Exp	Exp	Exp	Exp	Duro		Exp	Exp	Exp
	⑦	④		A	①②⑤				③	⑦	⑥		③⑤⑦				E	④⑦	③⑤⑦	②④⑥				
New Delhi d.	...	1505j	1520v	1620	1620	1720	...	1730	1910j	1910j	...	2010	2240	...	2340j	2345	...	...	...	...	...	...	2050j	...
Kanpur Central d.	...	|	|	2340	2340	2152	...	|	0115	0115	...	0235	|	...	0555	0620	...	...	...	...	...	...	0650	...
Allahabad Junction d.	...	|	|	0210	0245	2359	...	|	|	|	...	0513	0610	...	0835	0900	...	...	...	...	...	...	1058	...
Muhgal Sarai d.	...	0635	|	0455	0635	0215	...	|	|	|	...	0755	...	...	1130	|	...	...	...	...	...	...	1415	...
Patna Junction d.	0615	|	0735	0805	|	0540	...	0655	|	|	1050	1130	...	...	1445	1500	1800	1800	2010	2040	...	2110	1935	2235
Dhanbad d.	|	1218	...	|	1218	...	...	...	1245	1245	|	...	...	...	...	...	|	|	|	|	...	|	|	|
Asansol d.	1159	1322	...	1341	1341	...	...	...	1357	1357	1710	...	...	...	...	...	0006	0006	0207	|	...	0333	0315	0423
Kolkata Howrah a.	1515	1630	...	1655	1655	...	...	...	1725e	1725e	2145c	...	...	...	...	...	0315	0315	0515c	0540h	...	0635	0730	0730

A – ③④⑥⑦.
B – ①②⑤⑥.
C – ①②④⑤.
D – ①③④⑦.
E – ①②③⑤⑥.
F – ①③④⑥⑦.
c – Kolkata Chitpur.
h – Kolkata Shalimar.
j – Delhi Junction.
e – Kolkata Sealdah.
v – Delhi Anand Vihar Terminal.

For return service see next page ▷ ▷ ▷

5050 KOLKATA - PATNA - DELHI

Indian Railways

km		Exp	Duro	Duro	Exp	Exp	Exp	Exp	Exp	Exp	RDi	Exp	Exp	Exp	Exp	Exp	Exp	Exp	Exp	RDI	Exp	RDi
		12391	12273	12275	14055	12317	12325	12303	12381	11105	12309	12367	12387	12569	22405	12393	12327	12315	12369	12305	12301	12423
			①⑤	②④⑥		③⑦	④	B	③④⑦	⑦				①⑤	②④⑥		②⑤	④	F	⑦	①–⑥	
0	**Kolkata** Howrah d.	...	1250	...	...	0740	0740c	0805	0815	0725c	...	...	...	...	...	...	1310	1310e	1310	1405	1655	...
200	Asansol d.	...	|	...	...	1040	1040	1040	1053	1104	...	...	...	...	...	...	1534	1605	1534	|	|	...
	Dhanbad d.	...	|	...	...	|	|	|	1205	|	...	...	...	...	...	...	|	|	|	|	2005	...
532	**Patna** Junction d.	1050	|	...	1315	1605	1605	1615	|	1810	1925	1705	1645	1915	1915	1800	2100	2150	2100	2125	|	2150
744	Mughal Sarai d.	1427	|	...	1657	...	...	1947	1802	...	2235	|	|	2300	2300	|	...	...	...	0055	0057	0107
896	Allahabad Junction d.	|	|	2240	1925	...	...	2205	2200	...	0028	|	|	0055	0055	|	...	...	...	0246	0243	0256
1091	Kanpur Central d.	|	|	|	2155	...	...	0032	0032	...	0235	|	|	0300	0300	|	...	...	...	0453	0453	0508
1530	**New Delhi** a.	0510	0605	0605	0605j	...	...	0720	0720	...	0735	0740v	0810v	0825v	0825v	0835	...	...	...	0955	0955	1010

	Exp	SDI	RDi	Yuva	Duro	SDi	Exp	Exp	Exp	Exp	Exp	Exp	Exp	Exp	Exp	Exp	Exp	Exp	Exp	Duro	Exp
	12371	12023	12313	12249	12259	12033	12401	12329	12379	12349	12323	15483	12505	13005	12311	12333	12487	13111	12351	22213	12331
	①	①–⑥		④	D	①–⑥		②	⑤		②⑤									①③⑤	②⑤⑥
Kolkata Howrah d.	0815	1405	1650e	1840	1830e	...	...	1310e	1310e	...	1850	...	...	1910	1940	2000	...	2015c	2035	2205h	2355
Asansol d.	1053	1642	1920	2052	|	...	...	1605	1605	...	2118	...	...	2154	2217	2238	...	2332	2322	0111	0236
Dhanbad d.	1205	|	2020	2156	2156	...	...	1715	1715	...	2250	...	...	|	2336	|	...	|	|	|	|
Patna Junction d.	|	2215	|	|	|	...	1810	|	|	2235	|	2345	0305	0410	|	0425	0520	0700	0605	0640	1000
Mughal Sarai d.	1817	...	0117	0232	0235	...	2217	|	|	|	0520	0400	0720	...	0630	...	0937	1227	...	...	...
Allahabad Junction d.	|	...	|	0420	|	...	0045	|	|	0425	0740	0635	0940	...	0930	...	1155	1530	...	...	...
Kanpur Central d.	|	...	0518	0625	0615	0600	0325	0400	0400	0650	1020	0920	1250	...	1240	...	1425	1905	...	...	...
New Delhi a.	1020j	...	1020	1125	1125	1115	1145	1205j	1205j	1300	1700	1810j	1915v	...	2045j	...	2050v	0310j	...	...	...

For footnotes and return service see previous page.

5060 LUCKNOW - MUGHAL SARAI - PATNA - KOLKATA

Indian Railways

km		Exp	Exp	Exp	Exp	Exp	Exp	Exp	Exp	Exp	Exp	Exp	Exp
		12354	12328	12370	13010	13006	12332	12358	12318	12326	13050	13152	12372
		⑦	④⑦	A			①②⑤	①④	②⑤	⑥			④
0	**Lucknow** Junction d.	0125	0900	0900	0835	1050	1530	2015	2015	2015	1210	1720	2345
127	Faizabad d.	|	|	|	1110	|	|	|	|	|	|	2025	|
134	Ayodhya d.	|	|	|	1132	|	|	|	|	|	|	2053	|
283	Varanasi Junction d.	0720	1325	1325	1610	1655	2115	0110	0115	0115	1915	0130	0520
300	**Mughal Sarai** d.	0835	1425	1425	1730	1815	2215	0220	0245	0245	2040	0300	0635
512	**Patna** Junction d.	|	1800	1800	|	2155	0150	|	0615	0615	0230	|	|
***	Dhanbad d.	1445	|	|	0120	|	|	0730	|	|	|	1032	1218
843	Asansol d.	1550	0006	0006	0225	0404	0820	0825	1159	1159	1105	1149	1322
1055	**Kolkata** Howrah a.	1855	0315	0315	0655	0720	1130	1120k	1510e	1515k	1545	1550k	1630

	Exp	Exp	Exp	Exp	Exp	Exp	Exp	Exp	Exp	Exp	Exp	Exp
	12353	12371	12317	12325	12357	12327	12369	13151	13005	13049	13009	12331
	⑤	①	③⑦	④	②⑥	②⑤	B					②⑤⑥
Kolkata Howrah d.	0815	0815	0740e	0740k	1220k	1310	1310	1145k	1910	1350	2030	2355
Asansol d.	1053	1053	1040	1040	1459	1534	1530	1520	2154	1811	0016	0236
Dhanbad d.	1205	1205	|	|	1602	|	|	1657	|	|	0130	|
Patna Junction d.	|	|	1615	1615	|	2110	2110	|	0420	0215	|	1015
Mughal Sarai d.	1817	1817	1947	1947	2122	0047	0047	0152	0827	0737	0937	1402
Varanasi Junction d.	1930	1930	2040	2040	2200	0155	0155	0250	0927	0845	1030	1447
Ayodhya d.	|	|	|	|	|	|	|	0555	|	|	1413	|
Faizabad d.	|	|	|	|	|	|	|	0625	|	|	1449	|
Lucknow Junction a.	0120	0120	0210	0210	0245	0715	0715	1030	1520	1545	1820	1940

A – ①②③⑤⑥.
B – ①③④⑥⑦.

e – Kolkata Sealdah.
k – Kolkata.

*** – Mughal Sarai - Dhanbad: *402 km*.
Dhanbad - Asansol: *58 km*.

5070 KOLKATA - NEW JALPAIGURI - GUWAHATI

Indian Railways

km		Exp	Exp	SDi	Exp	Exp	Exp	Exp	Exp	Exp
		15657	12509	12041	12507	15901	12345	15959	12517	15611
			A	①–⑥	④	③			④⑦	④
0	**Kolkata** Howrah d.	0635e	1115	1415	1415	1425	1550	1735	2140k	2155
213	Rampurhat d.	1050	1428	|	1743	1743	1859	|	|	0210
335	Malda Town d.	1355	1730	1910	2015	2015	2145	0210	0410	0520
480	Kishanganj d.	1617	1933	2100	2206	2206	2337	0425	0603	|
567	**New Jalpaiguri** d.	1830	2145	2220	0010	0010	0200	0630	0800	0930
819	New Bongaigaon d.	0040	0225	...	0435	0455	0627	1150	1237	1625
975	**Guwahati** a.	0430	0550	...	0755	0815	0930	1545	1540	1915

	Exp	Exp	Exp	Exp	Exp	SDi	Exp	Exp	Exp
	15902	12508	12510	15960	12346	12042	15612	12518	15658
	⑥	⑤	①B			①–⑥	⑥	③⑥	
Guwahati d.	0515	0630	0630	0750	1245	...	1845	2100	2230
New Bongaigaon d.	0825	0940	0940	1130	1530	...	2140	2350	0210
New Jalpaiguri d.	1425	1425	1425	1645	1925	0535	0320	0350	0750
Kishanganj d.	1536	1536	1536	1802	2034	0643	|	0458	0901
Malda Town d.	1845	1845	1845	2210	2340	0850	0750	0825	1235
Rampurhat d.	2110	2110	2110	|	0158	|	1020	|	1501
Kolkata Howrah a.	0045	0045	0045	0545	0510	1335	1410	1500k	1925e

A – ①②⑤⑥⑦. Runs as **12513** on ① and as **12515** on ②.
B – ①②③④⑦. Runs as **12514** on ④ and as **12516** on ③.

e – Kolkata Sealdah.
k – Kolkata.

5075 GUWAHATI - DIBRUGARH

Indian Railways

km		Exp	Exp	Exp	Exp	Exp	RDi	RDi	Exp	Exp	RDi
		15929	15927	15901	15905	14056	12424	12236	15959	15904	12436
		⑦	③⑤⑦	④	②			③		⑤	①⑤
0	**Guwahati** d.	0510	0715	0835	1400	1440	1745	1925	1605	1845	1925
87	Chaparmukh d.	0715	0842	|	|	1617	|	|	1755	|	|
184	Lumding d.	0920	1055	1225	1720	1910	2102	2232	2015	2215	2232
250	Dimapur d.	1050	1225	1400	1855	2055	2225	0010	2145	2343	0010
323	Furkating d.	1232	1357	1612	2027	2232	|	|	2345	0127	|
358	Mariani d.	1328	1440	1655	2120	2325	0047	0225	0110	0210	0225
513	New Tinsukia d.	1640	|	|	0210	0245	0340t	|	0430	0500	0515t
561	**Dibrugarh** a.	1800	1815	2020	0330	0400	0450	0530	0545	0615	0615

	Exp	Exp	Exp	RDi	RDi	RDi	Exp	Exp	Exp	Exp
	15928	15903	15902	12435	12235	12423	15960	14055	15906	15930
		①	⑤	①⑤	④				⑥	⑦
Dibrugarh d.	0600	0840	1830	1920	1925	2035	1825	2310	2345	2345
New Tinsukia d.	|	0955	|	2025	|	2140	1940	0025	0055	0055
Mariani d.	0925	1230	2145	2240	2240	0012	2325	0325	0355	0420
Furkating d.	1012	1332	|	|	|	|	0030	0417	0445	0522
Dimapur d.	1135	1440	2345	0040	0040	0200	0225	0535	0600	0655
Lumding d.	1315	1615	0130	0217	0217	0322	0415	0730	0740	0850
Chaparmukh d.	1447	|	|	|	|	|	0546	0920	|	1100
Guwahati a.	1650	1945	0455	0530	0530	0640	0735	1130	1200	1440

t – Tinsukia Junction.

5080 DELHI - JAIPUR - AHMEDABAD

Indian Railways

km		Exp	SDi	Exp	Exp	Exp	Exp	Exp	RDi	Exp
		19708	12015	19264	12215	14311	19270	12916	12958	19106
				①④	A	④⑤⑦	①②			
0	**Delhi** Junction d.	...	0605n	0820a	0920a	1140	1255	1520	1955n	2220
83	Rewari d.	...	0745	1000	1045	1345	1452	1705	|	0025
157	Alwar d.	...	0840	1107	1142	1452	1545	1803	|	0134
308	**Jaipur** d.	0845	1035	1325	1425	1800	1850	2035	0035	0425
444	Ajmer d.	1115	1245	1600	1640	2035	2140	2250	0234	0650
749	Abu Road d.	1655	...	2135	2120	0132	0253	0340	0610	1155
801	Palanpur d.	1820	...	2315	2215	0242	0420	0500	0704	1313
866	Mahesana d.	1940	...	0018	|	0410	|	0600	0809	1426
934	**Ahmedabad** a.	2205	...	0210	0120	0615	0715	0740	0935	1655

	Exp	Exp	Exp	Exp	Exp	Exp	Exp	SDI	Exp
	19105	12957	12915	12216	14312	19263	19269	12016	19707
				B	②④⑦	③⑦	⑤⑥		
Ahmedabad d.	1005	1745	1830	1940	2020	0050	0050	...	0525
Mahesana d.	1158	1855	1948	|	2148	0240	|	...	0652
Palanpur d.	1352	2002	2109	2248	2340	0419	0419	...	0903
Abu Road d.	1451	2054	2205	2344	0036	0538	0538	...	1010
Ajmer d.	2050	0055	0230	0505	0610	1105	1105	1545	1635
Jaipur d.	2315	0250	0440	0720	0845	1320	1320	1750	1855
Alwar d.	0136	|	0640	0916	1100	1543	1540	1934	...
Rewari d.	0320	|	0825	1045	1235	1802	1730	2100	...
Delhi Junction a.	0505	0730n	1010	1210a	1435	1940a	2000	2240n	...

A – ①②④⑥.
B – ②③⑤⑦.

a – Delhi Sarai Rohilla.
n – New Delhi.

Indian Railways DELHI - JODHPUR 5090

km		Exp 14659	Exp 12461	Exp 12463 ③⑤⑦
0	**Delhi** Junction .... d.	1730	2115	2225a
83	Rewari .... d.	1945	2322	|
157	Alwar .... d.	2055	0014	0049
308	Jaipur .... d.	2345	0245	0315
471	Degana .... d.	0236	0513	0549
516	Merta Road .... d.	0340	0552	0630
620	**Jodhpur** .... a.	0505	0745	0825

	Exp 12464 ②④⑥	Exp 12462	Exp 14660
Jodhpur .... d.	1900	2000	2300
Merta Road .... d.	2040	2124	0028
Degana .... d.	2112	2200	0113
Jaipur .... d.	0025	0100	0500
Alwar .... d.	0230	0310	0714
Rewari .... d.	|	0455	0915
Delhi Junction .... a.	0535a	0645	1110

a – Delhi Sarai Rohilla.

Indian Railways JODHPUR - JAISALMER 5100

km		Exp 14659	54820	Exp 14810
0	**Jodhpur** .... d.	0530	0745	2345
65	Osian .... d.	0633	0908	0050
137	Phalodi .... d.	0738	1035	0151
184	Ramdevra .... d.	0816	1124	0247
194	Pokaran .... d.	0855	1220	0330
198	Ashapura .... d.	0901	1228	0337
301	**Jaisalmer** .... a.	1115	1500	0530

	54819	Exp 14660	Exp 14809
Jaisalmer .... d.	0830	1715	2330
Ashapura .... d.	0958	1832	0045
Pokaran .... d.	1030	1905	0115
Ramdevra .... d.	1044	1917	0129
Phalodi .... d.	1153	2001	0236
Osian .... d.	1310	2100	0332
Jodhpur .... a.	1500	2225	0520

Indian Railways JODHPUR - AHMEDABAD 5110

km		Exp 16311 ③	Exp 19028 ②	Exp 16507 ④⑥	Exp 16533 ③	Exp 19224	Exp 14707	Exp 12479	Exp 19066 ⑥	Exp 16126 ①	Exp 17038 ⑤⑦
0	**Jodhpur** .... d.	0130	0335	0540	0540	0555	1445	1845	1920	2115	2115
31	Luni .... d.	0207	0403	0613	|	0624	1514	1915	|	2154	2154
103	Marwar Junction .... d.	0337	0600	0745	0745	0800	1705	2035	2119	2310	2310
268	Abu Road .... d.	0650	0850	1033	1033	1057	1940	2338	0030	0217	0217
321	Palanpur .... d.	0747	1025	1150	|	1210	2133	0053	|	0322	0322
386	Mahesana .... d.	0842	1134	1307	|	1333	2245	0150	0306	0428	0428
459	**Ahmedabad** .... a.	1045	1335	1430	1430	1500	0035	0330	0435	0625	0625

	Exp 14708	Exp 17037 ④⑤	Exp 16125 ①	Exp 16312 ①	Exp 16508 ③⑤	Exp 16534 ②	Exp 19065 ⑥	Exp 19223	Exp 19027 ⑥	Exp 12480
Ahmedabad .... d.	0010	0100	0100	0735	0705	0705	0805	1120	1955	2135
Mahesana .... d.	0154	0302	0302	0920	0920	|	1008	1240	2123	2243
Palanpur .... d.	0325	0500	0500	1050	1050	|	|	1423	2248	0031
Abu Road .... d.	0431	0605	0605	1155	1155	1155	1234	1522	2344	0136
Marwar Junction .... d.	0800	0908	0908	1455	1455	1455	1515	1815	0245	0437
Luni .... d.	0911	1018	1018	1555	1555	|	|	1915	0345	0539
Jodhpur .... a.	0950	1050	1100	1630	1633	1633	1700	2000	0420	0630

Indian Railways DELHI and JAIPUR - UDAIPUR - AHMEDABAD 5120

km		Exp 12992	Exp 12315 ⑤	Exp 19665	Exp 12963 A	Exp 12981	52927	Exp 19943			
0	**Delhi** Sarai Rohilla ...... d.	...	...	...	1900h	1940	...	...	...	...	...
83	Rewari .... d.	...	...	...	|	2107	...	...	...	...	...
**	**Jaipur** .... d.	1400	1715	2245	|	|	...	...	...	...	...
373	Ajmer .... d.	1610	1945	0110	|	0210	...	...	...	...	...
559	Chittaurgarh .... d.	1925	0020	0425	0505	0533	...	...	...	...	...
673	**Udaipur** City .... d.	2130	0300	0645	0720	0750	0810	1745	...	...	...
883	Himmatnagar .... d.	...	...	...	...	...	1810	0155	...	...	...
971	**Ahmedabad** .... a.	...	...	...	...	...	2125	0425	...	...	...

	Exp 12316 ①	Exp 12991	Exp 19944	Exp 12982	Exp 12964 B	52928	Exp 19666			
Ahmedabad .... d.	...	...	2300	...	...	0710	...	...	...	...
Himmatnagar .... d.	...	...	0150	...	...	1025	...	...	...	...
Udaipur City .... d.	0025	0600	0920	1715	1815	1900	2220	...	...	...
Chittaurgarh .... d.	0240	0820	...	1930	2050	...	0035	...	...	...
Ajmer .... d.	0630	1130	...	2245	|	...	0350	...	...	...
Jaipur .... a.	0845	1325	...	|	|	...	0600	...	...	...
Rewari .... d.	...	...	...	0343	|	...	...	...	...	...
Delhi Sarai Rohilla ... a.	...	...	...	0510	0630h	...	...	...	...	...

A – Via Mathura (d. 2110), Sawai Madhopur (d. 2350) and Kota (d. 0125).
B – Via Kota (d. 2355), Sawai Madhopur (d. 0108) and Mathura (d. 0430).
h – Delhi Hazrat Nizamuddin.
** – Jaipur - Ajmer: *136 km*.

Indian Railways DELHI and JAIPUR - MUMBAI 5130

km		Exp 12904	Exp 19708	Exp 12956	Exp 12215 D	Exp 12910 ③⑤⑦	RDi 12952	Yuva 12248 ⑥	RDi 12954	Duro 12240 ②④	Exp 12980 ①③⑤	Exp 12926	Duro 22210 ②⑥	Exp 12908 ①④	Exp 12472 A	Exp 19024	Exp 19020	
0	**Delhi** H Nizamuddin ... d.	0740	...	...	0920	1540h	1630n	1540	1655	...	...	1650n	2330n	2135	2150n	1351	2155	...
124	Mathura .... d.	1000	...	...	|	1712	|	1712	1840	...	...	1915	|	|	0010	1705	0145	...
	Jaipur .... d.	|	0845	1410	1425	|	|	|	|	1910	2025	|	|	|	|	|	|	...
340	Sawai Madhopur .... d.	1305	|	1610	|	|	|	|	2038	|	2245	2205	|	|	0229	2110	0525	...
448	Kota Junction .... d.	1435	△	1735	△	2015	2115	2015	2155	|	0010	2345	|	0310	0400	2320	0750	...
673	Nagda .... d.	1757	|	2105	|	|	|	|	0024	|	0308	0320	|	|	0727	0445	1315	...
714	Ratlam .... d.	1910	|	2150	|	2325	0005	2325	0053	|	0350	0420	|	|	0820	0600	1435	...
976	Vadodara .... d.	2315	0030	0145	0310	0310	0341	0315	0430	|	0803	0825	|	1110	1215	1100	2005	...
1104	Surat .... d.	0120	0222	0335	0450	0450	0518	0502	0615	|	1013	1025	|	|	1410	1335	2238	...
1340	Borivali .... d.	0424	0543	0642	0724	0724	|	|	0907	|	1329	1354	|	1551	1722	1840	0332	...
1360	**Mumbai** Bandra .... a.	0520c	0635	0740c	0810	0810	0835c	0920	1000c	1140c	1420	1445	1615c	1635	1805	2010c	0420	...

km		Exp 19019	Exp 19023	Exp 12471 B	Exp 12925	Exp 12216 C	Exp 12979 ②④⑥	RDi 12951	Exp 12907 ③⑦	Exp 12909 ②④⑥	Yuva 12247 ⑤	RDi 12953	Exp 12955	Exp 19707	Exp 12903	Duro 12239 ②⑦	Duro 22209 ①⑤	
0	**Mumbai** Bandra .... d.	0005	0725c	0755	1135	1255	1545	1640c	1650	1655	1655	1740c	1850c	2100	2130c	2315c	2315c	...
19	Borivali .... d.	0040	0807	0828	1214	1323	1627	|	1724	1726	|	1819	1930	2141	2206	|	|	...
252	Surat .... d.	0445	1349	1147	1547	1606	2035	1942	|	2007	2007	2104	2245	0102	0115	|	|	...
381	Vadodara .... d.	0645	1615	1345	1740	1748	2238	2117	2255	2142	2142	2245	0040	0253	0303	|	|	...
642	Ratlam .... d.	1250	2110	1805	2200	|	0300	0040	|	0110	0110	0220	0440	|	0720	|	|	...
684	Nagda .... d.	1425	2225	1905	2325	△	0355	|	|	|	|	0312	0538	△	0815	|	|	...
909	Kota Junction .... d.	1930	0245	2140	0215	|	0635	0330	0635	0355	0355	0525	0850	|	1115	|	|	...
1017	Sawai Madhopur .... d.	2115	0410	2257	0350	|	0835	|	|	|	|	0628	1040	|	1230	|	|	...
1148	**Jaipur** .... a.	|	|	|	|	0705	1045	|	|	|	|	|	1250	1855	|	1435	|	...
	Mathura .... d.	0230	0945	0205	0750	|	...	|	|	0727	0727	0902	...	...	1625	...	|	...
	Delhi H Nizamuddin ... a.	0525	1218	0408	1040n	1210h	...	0830n	1345	0940	0940	1055	...	...	1835	...	1655n	...

A – ②③⑤⑥.
B – ①④⑤⑦.
C – ②③⑤⑦.
D – ①②④⑥.

c – Mumbai Central.
h – Delhi Sarai Rohilla.
n – New Delhi.

△ – Via Ahmedabad (Table **5080**).

Indian Railways GANDHIDHAM - AHMEDABAD 5140

km		Exp 16335 ⑤	Exp 19452 ④	Exp 16505 ②	Exp 11091 ③	Exp 14312 ②④⑦	Exp 15667 ⑥	Exp 12937 ⑥	Exp 19132	Exp 12993 ⑤	Exp 19116
0	**Gandhidham** .... d.	0530	0630	0900	1005	1410	1315	1700	2115	2245	2340
53	Samakhiali .... d.	0632	0732	0956	1107	1515	1420	1756	2219	2352	0045
94	Maliya Miyana .... d.	0712	0814	|	|	|	1507	|	2256	|	0123
170	Dhrangadhra .... d.	0818	|	1136	1302	1702	|	1944	0008	0131	0235
236	Viramgam .... d.	0952	1241	1305	1421	1835	1941	|	0125	|	0350
301	**Ahmedabad** .... a.	1105	1350	1430	1530	1940	2105	2300	0235	0410	0505

	Exp 19131	Exp 14311 ①⑤⑥	Exp 16336 ④	Exp 16506 ①	Exp 12994 ③	Exp 11092 ②	Exp 12938 ③	Exp 19451 ⑤	Exp 15668 ⑤	Exp 19115
Ahmedabad .... d.	0200	0645	0735	0740	0745	0805	1105	0825	1930	2359
Viramgam .... d.	0306	0800	0839	0849	|	0918	|	0944	2035	0108
Dhrangadhra .... d.	0413	0910	0952	0947	0947	1015	1306	|	|	0208
Maliya Miyana .... d.	0524	|	1056	|	|	|	|	1502	0157	0335
Samakhiali .... d.	0616	1114	1146	1147	1210	1224	1517	1604	0245	0430
Gandhidham .... a.	0715	1215	1320	1320	1320	1330	1645	1720	0400	0530

Indian Railways AHMEDABAD - MUMBAI 5150

km		Exp 12215 A	Exp 22452 ①④	Exp 14707	Exp 12972	Exp 19132	Exp 12479	Exp 12489 ③⑦	Exp 12960 ②⑤	Exp 12934	Exp 12990 ①④⑥	Exp 19066 ⑦	Exp 22473 ②	Exp 12932 ①–⑥	Exp 19116	Exp 19012	Exp 19030 ⑤	Exp 19216	SDi 12010 ①–⑥	Exp 19028 ②	Exp 19018	Exp 19144	Duro 12268	Exp 12902	Exp 19708	Exp 19006
0	**Ahmedabad** .... d.	0130	0130	0100	0212	0300	0350	0440	0440	0455	0455	0455	0455	0600	0525	0700	0930	0710	1430	1400	2030	2105	2345	2200	2240	2250
64	Anand .... d.	|	0225	0202	0316	0410	0455	0542	0542	0559	0612	|	0614	0658	0637	0817	1041	0841	1530	1545	2147	2217	|	2316	2342	2352
100	Vadodara .... d.	0310	0315	0255	0400	0500	0542	0630	0630	0645	0700	0705	0700	0745	0725	0905	1135	0940	1617	1635	2245	2305	|	0011	0030	0045
229	Surat .... d.	0445	0502	0442	0555	0705	0735	0820	0820	0840	0855	0855	0855	0927	1000	1120	1322	1230	1802	1835	0055	0105	|	0205	0220	0235
462	Borivali .... d.	0724	0831	0851	0925	1038	1046	1123	|	1152	1159	1159	1202	1221	1323	1520	1624	1807	2045	2142	0447	0503	|	0516	0543	0607
480	**Mumbai** Bandra .... a.	0810	0920	0940	1020	1125	1135	1200d	1200d	1235c	1240d	1245	1245	1300c	1405	1625c	1710	1915c	2135c	2225	0540	0555	0600c	0625c	0635	0710c

		Exp 12959 ③⑥	SDi 12009 ①–⑥	Exp 19011	Exp 19215	Exp 19027 ⑥	Exp 22451 ①④	Exp 19029 ③	Exp 12216 A	Exp 12480	Exp 12933	Exp 12931 ①–⑥	Exp 12490 ③⑦	Exp 12989 ①④⑥	Exp 22474 ②	Exp 19115	Exp 14708	Exp 19131	Exp 19017	Exp 19143	Exp 19005	Exp 19707	Exp 12971	Duro 12267	Exp 12901	Exp 19065 ⑤
Mumbai Bandra .... d.	...	0005d	0625c	0545c	0820c	1205	1205	1225	1255	1330	1340c	1420c	1435d	1435d	1435	1450	1505	1710	1735	1940	2025c	2100	2130	2325c	2200c	2325
Borivali .... d.	...	|	0659	0627	0902	1240	1240	1303	1323	1400	1417	1500	1506	1506	1509	1519	1546	1747	1820	2019	2116	2141	2208	|	2253	0002
Surat .... d.	...	0420	0945	1033	1415	1600	1600	1650	1606	1728	1740	1800	1827	1827	1827	1906	1925	2145	2205	0027	0042	0102	0140	|	0215	0355
Vadodara .... d.	...	0610	1120	1245	1700	1748	1748	1857	1748	1925	1930	1940	2020	2020	2020	2130	2145	2350	0010	0227	0235	0253	0330	|	0422	0550
Anand .... d.	...	0645	1152	1321	1748	1820	1824	1931	|	1958	2007	2019	2052	2052	2054	2209	2222	0026	0044	0259	0308	0331	0403	|	0454	|
Ahmedabad .... a.	...	0805	1310	1455	1940	1930	1930	2040	1930	2115	2125	2140	2210	2210	2210	2340	2350	0140	0210	0435	0445	0505	0525	0550	0635	0745

A – ②③⑤⑦.
c – Mumbai Central.
d – Mumbai Dadar.

5160 DELHI - PUNE and MUMBAI

Indian Railways

km		Exp 12172 ③⑥	Exp 12138	Duro 12264 ①④	Exp 12148 ④	Exp 12782 ①	Exp 12630 ③⑤	Exp 11078	Exp 12780	Exp 11058	
0	**Delhi** H Nizamuddin d.	0010	0515n	1100	0555	0555	0855	1020n	1505	2105	...
134	Mathura Junction d.	|	0753	|	0815	0815	|	1250	1650	2340	...
188	Agra Cantonment d.	0310	0855	|	0915	0915	|	1355	1750	0103	...
306	Gwalior d.	|	1040	|	1110	1110	|	1540	1935	0258	...
403	Jhansi d.	0600	1235	|	1245	1245	1505	1723	2122	0500	...
556	Bina d.	|	1455	|	1515	1515	|	2005	|	0855	...
694	Bhopal d.	1040	1655	|	1710	1710	1925	2210	0115	1120	...
786	Itarsi d.	|	1850	▽	1910	1910	|	0005	0255	1330	...
969	Khandwa d.	|	2145	|	2200	2200	|	0325	0535	1645	...
1093	Bhusaval d.	1645	2345	|	0010	0010	|	0515	0730	1855	...
1277	Manmad d.	|	0210	|	0250	0250	|	0815	1015	2150	...
1513	Daund d.	|	|	|	0755	0755	|	1310	1500	|	...
1589	**Pune** a.	|	|	0710	0915	0915	1105	1435	1620	|	...
1484	Kalyan d.	2300	0625	...	...	...	...	...	...	0245	...
1521	**Mumbai** LTT a.	2345	0735h	...	...	...	...	...	...	0350	...

	Exp 11057	Exp 12779	Exp 12171 ①④	Duro 12263 ②⑤	Exp 12629 ③⑤	Exp 12147 ②	Exp 12781 ⑥	Exp 11077	Exp 12137	
Mumbai LTT d.	2345	...	0755	...	...	...	...	...	1940h	...
Kalyan d.	0035	...	0830	...	...	...	...	...	2040	...
Pune d.	|	0410	|	1110	0900	1610	1610	1720	|	...
Daund d.	|	0550	|	|	|	1745	1745	1850	|	...
Manmad d.	0410	1020	|	|	|	2155	2155	2330	0030	...
Bhusaval d.	0650	1255	1420	|	|	0025	0025	0235	0305	...
Khandwa d.	0940	1510	|	|	|	0235	0235	0440	0510	...
Itarsi d.	1255	1740	|	▽	|	0500	0500	0720	0750	...
Bhopal d.	1510	1935	2045	|	0045	0635	0635	0915	0940	...
Bina d.	1745	|	|	|	|	0835	0835	1130	1215	...
Jhansi d.	2040	0004	0042	|	0613	1038	1038	1345	1430	...
Gwalior d.	2218	0122	|	|	|	1203	1203	1520	1605	...
Agra Cantonment d.	0018	0305	0405	|	|	1405	1405	1710	1755	...
Mathura Junction d.	0120	0402	|	|	|	1505	1505	1807	1850	...
Delhi H Nizamuddin a.	0410n	0615	0715	0655	1300	1705	1705	2016	2051	...

d – Mumbai Dadar. h – Mumbai CST. n – New Delhi. ▽ – Via Kota and Vadodara, but makes no passenger stops.

5170 LUCKNOW - PUNE and MUMBAI

Indian Railways

km		Exp 11016	Exp 12541	Exp 12144 ②	Exp 12174 ②④	Exp 12104 ⑦	Exp 15101 ③	Exp 12533	Exp 12108 ②④⑦		
0	**Lucknow** Junction d.	0040	0355	0240	0550	0630	0630	1945	2245	...	...
72	Kanpur Central d.	0235	0535	0425	0800	0800	0800	2132	0020	...	...
292	Jhansi d.	0725	0955	1035	1205	1205	1205	0150	0400	...	...
445	Bina d.	1000	|	1300	|	1420	|	|	|	...	...
583	Bhopal d.	1205	1355	1455	1635	1635	1635	0610	0815	...	...
674	Itarsi d.	1410	1530	|	|	1830	1830	0750	|	...	...
858	Khandwa d.	1720	1810	1845	|	2105	2105	1030	|	...	...
981	Bhusaval d.	1920	1955	2035	2255	2255	2255	1220	1500	...	...
1166	Manmad d.	2220	|	2255	|	0135	0110	1430	|	...	...
1402	Daund d.	|	|	|	|	0620	|	|	|	...	...
1477	**Pune** a.	|	|	|	|	0805	|	|	|	...	...
1372	Kalyan d.	0315	|	|	0500	...	|	1845	2140	...	...
1409	**Mumbai** LTT a.	0420	0400	0410	0605	...	0615h	2005h	2245	...	...

	Exp 12534	Exp 12542	Exp 15102 ⑤	Exp 12173 ②⑦	Exp 12107 ①③⑥	Exp 12103 ⑤	Exp 12143 ⑦	Exp 11015		
Mumbai LTT d.	0820h	1110	1535h	1625	1625	...	1640	2245	...	...
Kalyan d.	0915	|	|	1710	1710	...	|	2330	...	...
Pune d.	|	|	|	|	|	1615	|	|	...	...
Daund d.	|	|	|	|	|	1745	|	|	...	...
Manmad d.	1245	|	2118	|	|	2155	2155	0330	...	...
Bhusaval d.	1510	1805	2330	2250	2250	0025	0025	0610	...	...
Khandwa d.	1725	2120	0250	|	|	0235	0250	0915	...	...
Itarsi d.	1930	2340	0535	|	|	0510	|	1200	...	...
Bhopal d.	2115	0125	0735	0510	0510	0705	0735	1400	...	...
Bina d.	|	|	|	|	|	0910	0950	1655	...	...
Jhansi d.	0220	0535	1230	0935	0935	1120	1230	1930	...	...
Kanpur Central d.	0700	0955	1715	1335	1350	1545	1545	0020	...	...
Lucknow Junction a.	0840	1125	1905	1455	1510	1710	1715	0145	...	...

h – Mumbai CST.

5180 MUGHAL SARAI and ALLAHABAD - MUMBAI

Indian Railways

km		Exp 11062 A	Exp 22104 ③	Exp 15267 ⑦	Exp 12545 ⑤	Exp 12361 ①	Exp 19050 ④	Exp 12321	Exp 13201	Exp 18609 ④	Exp 12168	Exp 11094	Duro 12294 ②⑥	Exp 12142	Exp 11060 ①④⑥	Exp 11056 B	Exp 15018	Exp 12335 ②⑤⑦	Exp 15646 ①④	Exp 15648 ③	Exp 11070 ①③Z	Exp 11068 ④⑦	Exp 12166 ②⑤⑥	Exp 11072 X
	Mughal Sarai d.	...	...	...	0532	0532	0307	0827	0422	0700	...	...	...	1450	...	...	...	1755	1755	1755	...	...	...	...
	Varanasi d.	2320	...	0345	|	|	|	|	|	0800	1025	1120	...	|	...	...	1115	|	|	|	...	...	2020	1550
0	**Allahabad** Junction d.	0315	0650	0748	|	|	|	1142	0825	1220	|	|	1930	|	1702	1702	1630	|	|	|	1615	2108	2325	1945
103	Manikpur d.	0510	0900	|	|	|	|	1335	1050	|	1430	1710	|	|	|	|	1832	|	|	|	1800	2300	|	2135
216	Maihar d.	0722	|	|	|	|	|	1525	1250	|	|	1855	|	|	|	|	2025	|	|	|	|	|	|	2320
278	Katni d.	0820	1135	1210	1210	1210	0920	1620	1350	1705	1725	1950	|	|	|	|	2120	0030	0030	0030	|	0140	|	0025
369	Jabalpur d.	1000	1315	1355	1355	1355	1110	1805	1530	1930	1950	2130	|	2310	2320	2332	2350	0210	0210	0210	|	0315	0500	|
614	Itarsi d.	1405	1720	|	1805	1805	|	2225	2045	2350	0030	0130	|	|	0350	0350	0435	0725	0725	0725	0805	0805	0905	0940
791	Khandwa d.	1700	|	2045	2045	2045	|	0105	0035	0235	0310	0415	|	|	|	|	0820	1005	1005	1005	1130	1130	|	1250
915	Bhusaval d.	1900	|	2230	2230	2230	2200	0300	0235	0420	0455	0615	|	0755	0810	0810	1020	1205	1205	1205	1350	1350	1350	1445
1099	Manmad d.	2115	|	|	0120	0120	|	0540	0455	0640	|	0850	|	0955	|	|	1255	1450	1450	1450	1600	1600	1600	1740
1306	Kalyan d.	0235	0410	0510	0500	0500	|	1020	1025	1100	1135	1300	|	1420	1505	1505	1730	1905	1905	1905	2035	2035	2035	2200
1349	**Mumbai** LTT a.	0340	0500	0605	0605	0615h	0920b	1125h	1130	1205	1230d	1415h	1450	1530h	1605	1605	1840	2000	2000	2000	2140	2140	2140	2305

		Exp 12167	Exp 11093	Exp 11067 ③⑥	Exp 12165 ①④⑤	Exp 15017	Exp 11069 ②⑦Y	Exp 12336 ②④⑦	Exp 15645 ③⑥	Exp 15647 ⑤	Exp 11055 C	Exp 12362 ③	Exp 12546 ①	Exp 11061 D	Exp 11065 ②④⑦	Exp 22103 ①	Duro 12293 ①⑤	Exp 11071 W	Exp 19049 ①	Exp 15268 ②	Exp 18610 ⑥	Exp 12322	Exp 12141	Exp 13202
Mumbai LTT d.	...	0035	0010h	0520	0520	0635	0520	0805	0805	0805	1055	1105h	1120	1215	1215	1430	1725	1240	1545b	1550	1550	2125h	2325h	2215
Kalyan d.	...	0125	0115	0610	0610	0723	0610	0840	0840	0840	1138	1200	1200	1300	1300	1510	|	1330	|	1635	1635	2230	0023	2300
Manmad d.	...	|	0515	0940	0940	1120	0940	1230	1230	1230	|	1550	1550	1635	1635	|	|	1650	|	|	2118	0213	0400	0305
Bhusaval d.	...	0745	0735	1200	1230	1350	1200	1455	1455	1455	1740	1815	1815	1910	1910	|	|	1945	0420	2330	2330	0435	0620	0530
Khandwa d.	...	1030	1015	1435	|	1645	1435	1740	1740	1740	|	2050	2050	2140	2140	|	|	2200	|	0250	0250	0705	|	0815
Itarsi d.	...	1315	1240	1710	1710	2120	1710	2010	2010	2010	2230	2320	2320	0025	0025	0130	|	0025	|	|	0520	0940	|	1140
Jabalpur d.	...	1650	1630	2115	2115	0120	|	2345	2345	2345	0155	0250	0250	0405	0405	0450	|	|	1245	0915	0915	1335	1440	1610
Katni d.	...	1800	1740	2230	|	0235	|	0055	0055	0055	|	0400	0400	0515	0515	0600	|	1010	1355	1035	1035	1445	|	1725
Maihar d.	...	|	1840	|	|	0323	|	|	|	|	|	|	|	0614	0614	|	|	1106	|	|	|	1532	|	1818
Manikpur d.	...	2212	2155	0145	|	0555	0650	|	|	|	|	|	|	0855	0855	0947	|	1330	|	|	|	1812	|	2120
Allahabad Junction a.	...	|	0015	0350	0350	0810	0850	|	|	|	0950	|	|	1040	1040	1140	1225	1530	|	1550	1550	2025	|	2355
Varanasi a.	...	0350	0440	...	0705	1240	...	|	|	|	...	|	|	1400	1400	...	...	1925	|	1945	1945	|	|	|
Mughal Sarai a.	...	...	...	...	...	...	...	0855	0855	0855	...	1215	1215	...	...	...	...	...	2330	...	2040	0002	0030	0355

A – Runs as **11066** on ②④⑥.
B – ②③⑤⑦.
C – Runs as **11059** on ②④⑥.
D – ①③⑤⑥.
W – Via Bhopal (d. 0310) and Bina (d. 0545).
Y – Via Bhopal (d. 1850), Bina (d. 2150) and Jhansi (d. 0030).
X – Via Bina (d. 0540) and Bhopal (d. 0740).
Z – Via Jhansi (d. 0030), Bina (d. 0255) and Bhopal (d. 0505).
b – Mumbai Bandra.
d – Mumbai Dadar.
h – Mumbai CST.

5190 DELHI - SECUNDERABAD - TIRUPATI and BANGALORE

Indian Railways

km		Exp 12650 A	Exp 12708 ③⑤⑦	Exp 12648 ③	Duro 12286 ①⑤	RDi 12438 ⑦	Exp 12724	RDi 22692 C	RDi 22694 ③④⑦	Duro 12214 ①△	Exp 12722
0	**Delhi** H Nizamuddin d.	0645	0720	0840	1550	1600	1730n	2050	2050	2300h	2300
134	Mathura Junction d.	|	|	1035	|	|	1944	|	|	|	0105
188	Agra Cantonment d.	|	|	1135	|	|	2040	|	|	|	0215
306	Gwalior d.	|	|	1308	|	|	2210	|	|	|	0353
403	Jhansi d.	1215	1345	1445	|	2040	2342	0120	0120	|	0530
556	Bina d.	|	|	1715	|	|	|	|	|	|	0810
694	Bhopal d.	1615	1750	1915	|	0005	0330	0450	0450	|	1015
786	Itarsi d.	|	|	2110	|	|	|	|	|	|	1230
1083	Nagpur d.	2220	0015	0150	|	0535	0950	1025	1025	|	1745
1528	Kazipet d.	|	0650	0932	|	1127	1647	1607	1607	|	0140
1660	**Secunderabad** a.	|	0915	|	1400	1400	1915	1835	1835	|	0405
***	**Secunderabad** d.	|	0930	|	...	...	...	1850	1850	|	...
1666	Kacheguda d.	0715	0945	1235	...	...	...	|	|	|	...
1772	Mahabubnagar d.	|	1124	1400	...	...	...	|	|	|	...
1902	Kurnool Town d.	|	1338	1610	...	...	...	|	|	|	...
1956	Dhone d.	|	1515	1745	...	...	...	|	|	|	...
2292	Renigunta d.	|	2102	|	...	...	...	|	|	|	...
2302	**Tirupati** a.	|	2135	|	...	...	...	|	|	|	...
2101	Dharmavaram d.	1520	...	2055	...	...	...	0330	|	|	...
2290	**Bangalore** City a.	1910y	...	0030y	...	...	...	0640	0640	0730y	...

	RDI 22691 D	RDi 22693 ②⑤⑥	Duro 12213 ⑥△	Exp 12723	Exp 12649 B	RDi 12437 ③	Duro 12285 ④⑦	Exp 12647 ⑦	Exp 12707 ①③⑤	Exp 12721
Bangalore City d.	2020	2020	2340y	...	2210y	...	...	2340y	...	...
Dharmavaram d.	2322	|	|	...	0045	...	...	0245	...	...
Tirupati d.	|	|	|	...	|	...	...	|	0545	...
Renigunta d.	|	|	|	...	|	...	...	|	0602	...
Dhone d.	|	|	|	...	|	...	...	0545	1210	...
Kurnool Town d.	|	|	|	...	|	...	...	0635	1304	...
Mahabubnagar d.	|	|	|	...	|	...	...	0835	1506	...
Kacheguda d.	|	|	|	...	0835	...	...	1045	1650	...
Secunderabad a.	0735	0735	|	...	|	...	...	|	1725	...
Secunderabad d.	0750	0750	|	0650	|	1245	1330	|	1755	2255
Kazipet d.	0930	0930	|	0842	|	1447	|	1320	1950	0130
Nagpur d.	1535	1535	|	1555	1715	2045	|	2110	0210	0925
Itarsi d.	|	|	|	|	|	|	|	0155	|	1455
Bhopal d.	2135	2135	|	2210	2315	0220	|	0330	0815	1650
Bina d.	|	|	|	|	|	|	|	0535	|	1915
Jhansi d.	0056	0056	|	0220	0300	0531	|	0745	1210	2130
Gwalior d.	|	|	|	0338	|	|	|	0915	|	2250
Agra Cantonment d.	|	|	|	0528	|	|	|	1125	|	0050
Mathura Junction d.	|	|	|	0620	|	|	|	1220	|	0145
Delhi H Nizamuddin a.	0550	0550	0650h	0838	0915	1020	1035	1415	1800	0400

A – ①②④⑥⑦.
B – ①③⑤⑥⑦.
C – ①②⑤⑥.
D – ①③④⑦.
h – Delhi Sarai Rohilla.
n – New Delhi.
y – Bangalore Yesvantpur Junction.
△ – Journey 31 - 32 hours.
*** – Secunderabad - Kacheguda: 7 *km*.

Indian Railways

DELHI - AGRA 5200

km		Exp	SDi	Exp	Exp	Exp	Exp	Exp	Exp	Exp	Exp	Exp	Exp	Exp	Exp	Exp	Exp	Exp	Exp	Exp	Exp	Exp	Exp	Exp
		12172	12002	18238	12138	12148	12644	12646	12782	12804	12280	12642	12648	12808	18508	13008	12618	11078	12626	18478	14010	19326	12716	14310
		③⑥				④	⑤	②	①	③⑦		①⑥	③	A	①④⑦							④		②③
0	**Delhi** Hazrat Nizamuddin d.	0010	0600n	0440	0515n	0555	0555	0555	0555	0555	0710	0720	0840	0840	0850	0700n	0920	1020n	1130n	1205	1220h	1010	1320n	1345
134	Mathura Junction d.	|	0729	0710	0753	0815	0815	0815	0815	0815	0911	|	1035	1035	1035	1050	1125	1250	1333	1435	1525	1157	1538	1600
188	**Agra** Cantonment a.	0305	0806	0830	0850	0910	0910	0910	0910	0910	1005	1023	1130	1130	1145	1210	1220	1350	1425	1550	1615	1315	1630	1655

	Exp	Exp	Exp	Exp	Exp	Exp	Exp	Exp	Exp	RDi	Exp	Exp	Exp	Exp	Exp	Exp	Exp	Exp	Exp	Exp	Exp	Exp	Exp	Exp
	14318	12191	12780	11450	16032	16318	16688	12688	12550	12434	12612	12190	12724	12616	14212	12920	12448	12156	12628	11058	12622	12722	12486	12422
	⑤⑥			④	③⑥⑦	②	⑤	①	④	③⑤	①						④–②						②⑤⑥	①
Delhi Hazrat Nizamuddin d.	1345	1421	1505	1447	1447	1447	1447	1447	1535f	1600	1600	1610	1730n	1840n	1800	1920n	2015	2100	2115n	2105	2230n	2300	2350	2350
Mathura Junction d.	1600	1620	1650	1730	1730	|	|	|	|	|	|	1820	1944	2055	2036	2148	2217	|	2310	2340	|	0105	0155	|
Agra Cantonment a.	1655	1710	1745	1830	1830	1830	1830	1830	1905	1808	1808	1922	2037	2145	2155	2240	2315	2335	0002	0055	0107	0210	0250	0250

	Exp	Exp	Exp	Exp	Exp	Exp	Exp	Exp	Exp	Exp	Exp	Exp	Exp	Exp	Exp	Exp	Exp	Exp	Exp	Exp	RDi	Exp	Exp	Exp
	11057	12721	12919	22181	12447	12615	14009	12779	12621	12171	12155	12723	12549	14211	12627	14309	14317	19325	12192	12611	12433	12189	12715	12485
					⑥–④					②⑤			③			④⑤	①⑦	③		⑦	①⑥			①②⑤
Agra Cantonment d.	0018	0050	0125	0210	0225	0250	0155	0305	0353	0405	0450	0523	0536	0600	0645	0708	0623	0625	0735	0757	0757	0823	0840	0915
Mathura Junction d.	0125	0145	0218	0305	0320	0350	0250	0402	|	|	|	0608	|	0702	0737	0810	0810	0810	0835	|	|	0920	0930	1010
Delhi Hazrat Nizamuddin a.	0345	0400	0435	0520	0530	0557	0615h	0615	0637	0715	0805	0838	0929f	0943	0953	1110	1110	1110	1117	1020	1020	1135	1145	1310n

	Exp	Exp	Exp	Exp	Exp	Exp	Exp	Exp	Exp	Exp	Exp	Exp	Exp	Exp	Exp	Exp	Exp	Exp	Exp	Exp	Exp	Exp	SDi	Exp
	12421	12617	12625	18477	12647	18507	12807	12781	12643	12803	12147	12645	12641	13007	18237	11077	16787	12687	12317	16031	11449	12279	12001	22403
	④				②	③⑥⑦	B	⑦	④	②⑥	③	①	⑤⑦				③⑦	⑤		①④⑤	②			④
Agra Cantonment d.	0915	1015	1025	1053	1125	1130	1345	1405	1405	1405	1405	1405	1515	1530	1608	1712	1730	1730	1755	1833	1833	1855	2035	2350
Mathura Junction d.	|	1105	1115	1152	1220	1220	1440	1505	1505	1505	1505	1505	|	1635	1710	1807	|	|	1850	2000	2000	1955	2113	0050
Delhi Hazrat Nizamuddin a.	1310n	1310	1317	1405	1415	1415	1645	1705	1705	1705	1705	1705	1800	1915	1945	2016	2040	2040	2051	2220	2220	2200	2245n	0355n

A – ①②④⑤⑥.
B – ①③④⑤⑦.
f – Delhi Safdarjang.
h – Delhi Sarai Rohilla.
n – New Delhi.

Indian Railways

DELHI - BILASPUR 5205

km	km		SDi	Exp	Exp	Exp	Exp	Exp	Exp	RDi	
			12002	18508	18478	18238	12410	12550	12824	12442	
				①④⑦			A	④	②⑤⑦	②⑥	
0	0	**Delhi** Hazrat Nizamuddin d.	0600	0850	1205	0440	1525	1535f	1725	1545n	...
135	135	Mathura Junction d.	0729	1035	1430	0710	1740	|	|	|	...
189	189	Agra Cantonment d.	0811	1150	1600	0840	1851	1910	|	|	...
307	307	Gwalior d.	0935	1320	1745	1035	2035	|	|	|	...
404	404	Jhansi d.	1053	1502	1928	1320	2205	2240	2330	2040	...
557	557	Bina d.	|	1735	2230	1640	0020	|	|	|	...
	632	Saugor d.	|	1855	2355	|	|	0210	0240	|	...
	819	Katni Murwara d.	|	2205	0410	|	|	0540	0610	|	...
	985	Anupper d.	|	0110	0750	|	|	0835	0900	|	...
695		Bhopal d.	1405	|	|	1850	0225	|	|	0005	...
788		Itarsi d.	...	|	|	2125	0410	|	|	|	...
1085		Nagpur d.	...	|	|	0355	0940	|	|	0545	...
1215		Gondia d.	...	|	|	0556	1123	|	|	0725	...
1387		Raipur Junction d.	...	|	|	0955	1415	|	|	1015	...
1498	1136	**Bilaspur** a.	...	0430	1055	1220	1645	1115	1150	1200	...

	Exp	Exp	Exp	RDi	Exp	Exp	Exp	SDi	
	12409	12823	12549	12441	18477	18507	18237	12001	
	B	①④⑥	②	①④		②⑤⑥			
Bilaspur d.	0555	1450	1450	1400	1525	1905	1415	...	...
Raipur Junction d.	0745	|	|	1540	|	|	1620	...	...
Gondia d.	1039	|	|	1825	|	|	1923	...	...
Nagpur d.	1305	|	|	2045	|	|	2205	...	...
Itarsi d.	1800	|	|	|	|	|	0440	...	...
Bhopal d.	1950	|	|	0220	|	|	0650	1445	...
Anupper d.	|	1720	1720	|	1825	2145	|	|	...
Katni Murwara d.	|	2045	2045	|	2310	0135	|	|	...
Saugor d.	|	2320	2320	|	0200	0420	|	|	...
Bina d.	2215	|	|	|	0425	0620	0930	|	...
Jhansi d.	0041	0240	0238	0531	0645	0830	1200	1759	...
Gwalior d.	0230	|	|	|	0845	0950	1355	1910	...
Agra Cantonment d.	0418	|	0536	|	1055	1130	1610	2035	...
Mathura Junction d.	0503	|	|	|	1200	1220	1710	2113	...
Delhi Hazrat Nizamuddin a.	0725	0905	0929f	1045n	1405	1415	1945	2245	...

A – ①②③④⑥.
B – ①③④⑤⑥.
f – Delhi Safdarjang.
n – New Delhi.

Indian Railways

DELHI - TIRUPATI and CHENNAI 5210

km		Exp	Exp	Exp	Exp	Exp	Exp	Exp	Exp	Exp	RDi	Duro	RDi	RDi	Exp	Exp	Exp	Exp	Exp	RDi	RDi	Exp	Exp	Exp	Exp	Exp
		12650	12804	12644	12646	12642	12652	12708	18238	12626	12442	12270	12438	12434	12612	12688	16318	16688	12724	12430	22694	16032	12616	12622	12722	22404
		C	③⑦	⑤	②	①⑥	②④	③⑤⑦			②⑥	②⑥	⑦	③⑤	①	①	②	⑤		A	③④⑦	③⑥⑦				⑦
0	**Delhi** H Nizamuddin d.	0645	0555	0555	0555	0720	0720	0720	0440	1130n	1545n	1550	1600	1600	1600	1447	1450	1455	1730n	2050	2050	1447	1840n	2230n	2300	2350
135	Mathura Junction d.	|	0815	0815	0815	|	|	|	0710	1333	|	|	|	|	|	|	|	|	1944	|	|	1730	2055	|	0105	0155
189	Agra Cantonment d.	|	0915	0915	0915	1028	|	|	0840	1430	|	|	|	1810	1810	1835	1838	1910	2040	|	|	1835	2150	0110	0215	0255
307	Gwalior d.	|	1110	1110	1110	|	|	|	1035	1602	|	|	|	1925	1925	2020	2020	2055	2210	|	|	2015	2336	0239	0353	|
404	Jhansi d.	1215	1245	1245	1245	1345	1345	1345	1320	1734	2045	|	2040	2040	2040	2145	2152	2240	2342	0120	0120	2208	0108	0412	0530	0627
557	Bina d.	|	1515	1515	1515	|	|	|	1640	1950	|	|	|	|	|	|	|	|	|	|	|	0110	0330	|	0810	|
695	Bhopal d.	1615	1710	1710	1710	1750	1750	1750	1845	2140	0005	|	0005	0005	0005	0150	0150	0300	0330	0450	0450	0300	0525	0800	1015	1100
788	Itarsi d.	|	1910	1910	1910	1945	|	|	2125	2335	|	|	|	|	|	|	0345	0530	|	|	|	0530	0735	0953	1230	1315
1085	Nagpur d.	2210	2325	2325	2325	0015	0015	0015	0330	0400	0530	|	0525	0535	0535	0840	0840	1045	0940	1015	1015	1045	1230	1430	1735	1845
1298	Balharshah d.	...	0305	0305	0305	0340	|	|	...	0747	...	|	...	|	0830	1200	1200	1440	...	...	...	1440	1605	1735	...	2250
1543	Warangal d.	...	0632	0632	0632	|	|	S	...	1107	...	|	...	1126	|	1533	1533	1843	...	...	...	1843	1935	2050	...	0302
1752	Vijayawada d.	...	1105	1115	1115	1050	1050	|	...	1500	...	|	...	1430	1430	1920	1920	2345	...	...	...	0100	2325	0025	...	0730
2046	Gudur d.	...	...	1535	1535	1505	|	|	...	1930	...	|	...	|	1825	|	2343	0430	...	...	...	0740	0400	|	...	1200
2122	Renigunta a.	...	...	1645	1645	|	|	2100	...	2040	...	|	...	|	|	|	0055	0550	...	...	...	|	|	|	...	|
2132	**Tirupati** a.	...	...	1710	1710	|	|	2135	...	2105	...	|	...	|	|	|	0120	0605	...	...	...	|	|	|	...	|
2184	**Chennai** Central a.	...	...	...	...	1805e	1805e	...	...	...	...	2010‡	...	2015	2015	0215	...	...	...	...	...	1010	0615	0715	...	1425e

		Exp	Exp	RDi	RDi	Exp	Exp	Exp	Exp	RDi	RDi	Exp	Duro	RDi	Exp	Exp	Exp	Exp	Exp	Exp	Exp	Exp	Exp	Exp	Exp	Exp
		22403	12721	12429	22693	12615	12621	12723	12649	12437	12433	12611	12269	12441	12625	12643	12645	12803	12641	12651	12707	18237	16687	16317	12687	16031
		③		B	③⑥⑦				D	③	⑤⑦	⑥	①⑤	①④		③	⑦	①⑤	④⑥	②⑦	①③⑤		②	⑥	④	③④⑦
Chennai Central d.	...	1315e	...	...	...	1915	2200	...	...	...	0610	0610	0640	...	...	...	...	...	0905e	0905e	...	...	...	...	0945	0515
Tirupati d.	...	|	...	...	...	|	|	...	...	...	|	|	|	...	0357	0735	0735	...	|	|	0545	...	0910	0910	|	|
Renigunta d.	...	|	...	...	...	|	|	...	...	...	|	|	|	...	0420	0800	0800	...	|	|	0602	...	0940	0940	|	|
Gudur d.	...	1552	...	...	...	2132	|	...	...	...	|	0801	|	...	0557	0942	0942	...	|	|	|	...	1125	1125	|	0817
Vijayawada d.	...	2020	...	...	...	0205	0420	...	...	...	1200	1200	|	...	1015	1435	1435	1435	1610	1610	|	...	1620	1620	1700	1450
Warangal d.	...	2355	...	...	...	0505	0705	...	...	...	1440	|	|	...	1305	1735	1735	1735	|	|	S	...	1945	1945	2035	1800
Balharshah d.	...	0420	...	...	...	0855	1110	...	...	...	|	1800	|	...	1710	2125	2125	2125	2315	|	|	...	2340	2340	0040	2250
Nagpur d.	...	0745	0925	1535	1535	1225	1420	1555	1715	2045	2045	2045	|	2045	2025	0030	0030	0030	0210	0210	0210	2205	0255	0255	0350	0245
Itarsi d.	...	1310	1455	|	|	1735	1853	|	|	|	|	|	|	|	0120	0500	0500	0455	0640	|	|	0440	0740	0740	|	0810
Bhopal d.	...	1455	1650	2135	2135	1930	2035	2210	2315	0220	0220	0220	|	0220	0300	0635	0635	0635	0815	0815	0815	0650	0935	0935	1000	1010
Bina d.	...	|	1915	|	|	2135	|	|	|	|	|	|	|	|	0505	0835	0835	0835	|	|	|	0930	|	|	|	1245
Jhansi d.	...	1930	2130	0056	0056	2342	0027	0220	0300	0531	0531	0531	|	0531	0707	1038	1038	1038	1210	1210	1210	1200	1400	1405	1405	1455
Gwalior d.	...	|	2250	|	|	0102	0145	0338	|	|	0638	0638	|	|	0830	1203	1203	1203	|	|	|	1355	1535	1535	1535	1620
Agra Cantonment d.	...	2350	0050	|	|	0250	0353	0528	|	|	0757	0757	|	|	1028	1405	1405	1405	1515	|	|	1610	1730	1730	1730	1835
Mathura Junction d.	...	0050	0145	|	|	0350	|	0620	|	|	|	|	|	|	1123	1505	1505	1505	|	|	|	1710	|	|	|	2010
Delhi H Nizamuddin a.	...	0355n	0400	0550	0550	0557	0637	0838	0915	1020	1020	1020	1035‡	1045n	1317	1705	1705	1705	1800	1800	1800	1945	2040	2040	2040	2220

– ①②⑤⑥.
– ①②④⑤.
C – ①②④⑥⑦.
D – ①②④⑥⑦.
S – Via Secunderabad (Table **5190**).
e – Chennai Egmore.
n – New Delhi.
‡ – Next day (more than 24 hours after previous time).

5220 DELHI, AHMEDABAD and MUMBAI - GOA - MANGALORE - TRIVANDRUM

Indian Railways

km		Exp	Exp	Exp	Exp	Exp	Exp	Exp	Exp	Exp	RDi	Exp	SDi	Exp	Exp	Exp	Exp	Exp	Exp	Exp	Exp	Duro	Exp	Exp	Duro
		22150	**12133**	**16333**	**16335**	**16348**	**16311**	**10111**	**16603**	**16630**	**12432**	**12450**	**12051**	**10103**	**12218**	**16649**	**12484**	**12288**	**19578**	**16345**	**16605**	**12284**	**12619**	**12201**	**12223**
		③⑦ **A**		④	⑤		③				②③⑦	①⑥			③		⑦	①	⑥⑦			⑥ **z**		①⑤	②⑥
0	**Delhi** Hazrat Nizamuddin ....d.	...	...	...	...	...	...	...	...	...	1100	0730	...	...	1400	...	1400	1400	...	...	...	2135	...	...	...
458	Kota Junction ....d.	...	...	...	...	...	...	...	...	...	1540	1320	...	...	1955	...	1955	1955	...	...	...	|	...	...	...
****	**Ahmedabad** ....d.	...	...	1125	1125	...	1110	...	...	...	|	|	...	...	|	...	|	|	0327	...	...	|	...	...	...
986	Vadodara Junction ....d.	...	...	1312	1312	...	1322	...	...	...	2235	2150	...	...	0405	...	0357	0405	0520	...	...	|	...	...	...
***	**Mumbai** CST ....d.	...	2210	|	|	...	|	2305	...	...	|	|	0525d	0710	|	...	|	|	|	1140t	...	|	1520t	1655t	2050
1397	Panvel ....d.	2125	2320	2205	2205	...	2205	0030	...	...	0510	0510	0638	0830	1230	...	1230	1230	1315	1255	...	|	1625	1810	|
1678	Ratnagiri ....d.	0200	0345	0255	0225	...	0255	0530	...	...	0945	0945	1045	1315	|	...	|	|	1935	1900	...	|	2135	2305	|
1917	**Madgaon** ....d.	0555	0710	0740	0740	...	0740	1045	...	...	1305	1315	1410	1845	2105	...	2220	2220	2345	2310	...	|	0135	0225	|
2166	Udupi ....d.	1000	1112	1156	1156	...	1156	...	...	...	1620	...	...	...	0042	...	|	|	0402	0302	...	|	0538	0622	|
2234	**Mangalore** Junction ....d.	1120	1240	1340	1340	1420c	1340	...	1745c	1820c	1800	...	...	...	0225	0450c	0310	0310	0605	0450	0720c	|	0730c	0815	|
2365	Cannanore ....d.	1330	...	1605	1605	1705	1605	...	2025	2120	2010	...	...	...	0430	0720	0520	0520	0850	0740	0955	|	...	1025	|
2455	Calicut ....d.	1505	...	1745	1745	1850	1745	...	2210	2305	2130	...	...	...	0600	0905	0655	0655	1030	0925	1140	|	...	1150	|
2541	Shoranur ....d.	1645	...	2005	2005	2110	2005	...	0015	0125	2300	...	...	...	0805	1115	0840	0840	1220	1140	1400	|	...	1345	|
2574	Trichur ....d.	1720	...	2053	2053	2201	2053	...	0100	0210	2343	...	...	...	0840	1154	0920	0920	1300	1220	1435	|	...	1420	|
2645	**Ernakulam** Town ....d.	1850j	...	2215	2215	2340	2215	...	0230j	0345	0105j	...	...	...	1030j	1340	1100j	1042	1450j	1420j	1620j	1525j	...	1540	1745j
2762	Kayankulam ....d.	...	...	|	|	0215	0024	...	0450	0610	|	...	...	...	1232	1602	1310	|	1732	1622	1837	...	...	1805	...
2789	Quilon ....d.	...	...	0125	0125	0310	0125	...	0545	0715	0335	...	...	...	1320	1710	1400	1400	1830	1720	2000	...	...	1855	...
2866	**Trivandrum** Central ....a.	...	...	0245	0240	0445	0245k	...	0705	0900	0445	...	...	...	1445k	1835	1515k	1515k	1940	1840	2105	...	...	2030k	...

		Duro	Exp	RDi	Exp	Exp	Exp	Duro	Exp	Exp	Exp	SDi	Exp	Exp	Exp	Exp	Exp	Exp	Exp	Exp	Exp	Exp	Exp	Exp	Exp
		12224	**10104**	**12431**	**16312**	**16336**	**16334**	**12283**	**16604**	**16629**	**16347**	**12052**	**12449**	**10112**	**22149**	**12134**	**12620**	**16606**	**16650**	**12202**	**12287**	**12217**	**12483**	**19578**	**16346**
		③⑦		②④⑤	⑥	②	①	② **z**					②③		②⑤ **B**					④⑦	⑤	⑥	③	①②	
Trivandrum Central ....d.	...	...	...	1915	1535k	1535	1535	...	1930	1830	2040	...	...	...	...	...	...	0350	0625	0850k	0850k	0915k	0915k	1055	0950
Quilon ....d.	...	...	...	2010	1635	1635	1635	...	2035	1955	2200	...	...	...	...	...	...	0455	0730	0950	0950	1015	1015	1200	1055
Kayankulam ....d.	...	...	...	|	1712	|	|	...	2120	2050	2247	...	...	...	...	...	...	0530	0822	1020	|	1050	1050	1235	1137
Ernakulam Town ....d.	...	2130j	...	2230j	2010	2010	2010	2330j	2330j	2358	0130	...	...	...	0515j	...	...	0810j	1105	1300	1300	1255j	1255j	1440j	1405j
Trichur ....d.	...	|	...	2350	2125	2125	2125	|	0105	0130	0305	...	...	...	0628	...	...	0935	1240	1420	1420	1420	1420	1600	1533
Shoranur ....d.	...	|	...	0040	2230	2230	2230	|	0205	0255	0410	...	...	...	0720	...	...	1040	1345	1515	1515	1515	1515	1715	1655
Calicut ....d.	...	|	...	0210	0030	0030	0030	|	0345	0450	0610	...	...	...	0850	...	...	1240	1545	1645	1645	1645	1645	1840	1910
Cannanore ....d.	...	|	...	0330	0205	0205	0205	|	0525	0640	0755	...	...	...	1020	...	...	1425	1740	1815	1815	1815	1815	2005	2050
Mangalore Junction ....d.	...	|	...	0540	0500	0500	0500	|	0800c	1005c	1055c	...	...	...	1235	1355	1435c	1720c	2030c	2040	2040	2040	2040	2230	2330
Udupi ....d.	...	|	...	0658	0622	0622	0622	|	...	...	...	...	...	...	1350	1506	1558	...	...	2146	|	2146	|	2340	0054
Madgaon ....d.	...	|	0930	1010	1105	1105	1105	|	...	...	...	1430	1120	1800	1710	1850	2040	...	...	0130	0130	0130	0130	0400	0510
Ratnagiri ....d.	...	|	1425	1355	1615	1615	1615	|	...	...	...	1750	1505	2305	2045	2220	0030	...	...	0505	|	|	|	0810	0920
Panvel ....d.	...	|	1925	1810	2125	2125	2125	|	...	...	...	2150	1955	0410	0230	0250	0515	...	...	1020	1100	1100	1100	1345	1515
Mumbai CST ....a.	...	1815t	2140	|	|	|	|	|	...	...	...	2305d	|	0550	...	0425	0635t	...	...	1145t	|	|	|	|	1640t
Vadodara Junction ....d.	...	...	...	0026	0522	0522	0522	|	...	...	...	...	0218	...	...	...	...	...	...	...	1816	1816	1816	2125	...
Ahmedabad ....a.	...	...	...	|	0735	0715	0715	|	...	...	...	...	|	...	...	...	...	...	...	...	|	|	|	2310	...
Kota Junction ....d.	...	...	...	0650	...	...	...	|	...	...	...	...	1010	...	...	...	...	...	...	...	0255	0255	0255	...	...
Delhi Hazrat Nizamuddin ....a.	...	...	...	1240	...	...	...	1930	...	...	...	...	1750	...	...	...	...	...	...	...	1040	1040	1105	...	...

A – From Pune (d. 1845 ③⑦).
B – To Pune (a. 0550 ③⑥).
c – Mangalore Central.
d – Mumbai Dadar.
j – Ernakulam Junction.
k – Trivandrum Kochuveli.
t – Mumbai Lokmaniya Tilak Terminus.
z – Journey time 42 - 44 hours.
*** – Mumbai CST - Panvel: *68 km*.
**** – Ahmedabad - Vadodara: *100 km*.

5230 MUMBAI - PUNE - KOLHAPUR

Indian Railways

km		Exp	Exp	Exp	Exp	Exp	Exp	Exp	Exp	Exp	Exp	Exp	Exp	Exp	Exp	Exp	Exp	Exp	Exp	Exp	Exp	Exp	Exp	Exp
		11049	**22105**	**12148**	**12127**	**11007**	**11301**	**11029**	**16331**	**17031**	**11041**	**11009**	**11019**	**16381**	**11046**	**12125**	**12123**	**11023**	**11011**	**22107**	**12701**	**12115**	**11027**	**11040**
		①		⑤					**A**						③									
0	**Mumbai** CST ....d.	...	0540	...	0645	0700	0805	0840	1205	1245	1400	1430	1510	1545	...	1625	1710	1750	2023	2100	2150	2242	2345	...
54	Kalyan ....d.	0520	0637	...	|	0800	0858	0935	1310	1345	1505	1530	1610	1640	...	|	|	1850	2125	2153	2240	2340	0040	...
192	**Pune** ....a.	0810	0908	0930	0957	1105	1140	1240	1545	1630	1800	1840	1900	1915	1930	1950	2025	2155	0010	0030	0120	0210	0325	0450
471	Miraj ....a.	1407	...	1437	...	...	...	1905	...	...	...	...	...	...	0225	...	...	0440	0552	...	...	...	...	1115
518	**Kolhapur** ....a.	1525	...	1620	...	...	...	2025	...	...	...	...	...	...	0345	...	...	0605	0720	...	...	...	...	1245

		Exp	Exp	Exp	Exp	Exp	Exp	Exp	Exp	Exp	Exp	Exp	Exp	Exp	Exp	Exp	Exp	Exp	Exp	Exp	Exp	Exp	Exp	Exp
		16382	**12702**	**12116**	**17412**	**22108**	**11010**	**12124**	**12126**	**11024**	**11045**	**17032**	**11042**	**11008**	**11302**	**11030**	**12147**	**16332**	**12128**	**22106**	**11050**	**11039**	**11028**	**11020**
											④						②	**B**			⑥			
Kolhapur ....d.	...	...	...	...	2030	...	...	...	...	2250	2345	...	...	...	...	0755	0905	...	...	...	1250	1530	...	...
Miraj ....d.	...	...	...	...	2138	...	...	...	...	0005	0045	...	...	...	...	0910	1020	...	...	...	1345	1640	...	...
Pune ....d.	...	0050	0115	0310	0335	0415	0605	0715	0750	0700	0725	0910	0935	1530	1555	1545	1555	1640	1755	1835	1950	2305	2340	2350
Kalyan ....d.	...	0340	0355	0540	0615	0645	0847	|	|	1040	...	1155	1225	1825	1840	1920	...	1940	|	2052	2220	...	0230	0240
Mumbai CST ....a.	...	0450	0505	0650	0725	0805	0953	1025	1115	1155	...	1305	1345	1940	1955	2035	...	2050	2105	2155	...	...	0345	0355

A – Runs as **16339** on ③④⑤⑦ and as **16351** on ②⑥.
B – Runs as **16340** on ②③④⑥ and as **16352** on ①⑤.

5240 MUMBAI - PUNE - HUBLI

Indian Railways

km		Exp	Exp	Exp	Exp	Exp	Exp	Exp	Exp	
		16531	**16533**	**16209**	**16507**	**16505**	**11005**	**11035**	**11021**	
		②	④	①⑥	⑤⑦	③	①⑤⑦	④	②③⑥	
0	**Mumbai** Dadar ....d.	...	...	...	...	...	2130	2130	2130	...
54	Kalyan ....d.	0110	0110	0110	0110	0110	2210	2210	2210	...
192	**Pune** ....d.	0420	0420	0420	0420	0420	0110	0110	0110	...
338	Satara ....d.	0713	0713	0713	0713	0713	0400	0400	0400	...
472	Miraj ....d.	1035	1035	1035	1035	1035	0655	0655	0655	...
610	Belgaum ....d.	1330	1330	1330	1330	1330	0905	0905	0905	...
661	Londa ....d.	1417	1417	1417	1417	1417	1000	1000	1000	...
731	Dharwad ....d.	1555	1555	1625	1625	1625	1127	1127	1127	...
751	**Hubli** ....a.	1645	1645	1730	1730	1730	1230	1230	1230	...

	Exp	Exp	Exp	Exp	Exp	Exp	Exp	Exp	
	16532	**16534**	**16210**	**16506**	**16508**	**11006**	**11036**	**11022**	
	⑥	①	③⑤	⑦	②④	①③④	⑦	②⑤⑥	
Hubli ....d.	0635	0635	0635	0635	0635	1515	1515	1515	...
Dharwad ....d.	0700	0700	0712	0712	0712	1535	1535	1535	...
Londa ....d.	0825	0825	0835	0835	0835	1655	1655	1655	...
Belgaum ....d.	0940	0940	0940	0940	0940	1800	1800	1800	...
Miraj ....d.	1245	1245	1245	1245	1245	2050	2050	2050	...
Satara ....d.	1503	1503	1503	1503	1503	2308	2308	2308	...
Pune ....d.	1850	1850	1850	1850	1850	0220	0220	0220	...
Kalyan ....d.	2140	2140	2140	2140	2140	0455	0455	0455	...
Mumbai Dadar ....a.	...	...	...	...	...	0550	0550	0550	...

5245 HUBLI - BANGALORE

Indian Railways

km		Exp	Exp	Exp	Exp	Exp		SDi	Exp	Exp	Exp	Exp		Exp	Exp	Exp	Exp	Exp		Exp	Exp	Exp	Exp	
		17310	**12726**	**12777**	**11005**	**11021**		**12080**	**17315**	**16507**	**16505**	**16209**		**16531**	**16533**	**17312**	**17314**	**16591**		**19406**	**12630**	**16590**	**16536**	
		②⑦		③	①②⑥	③④⑦			①	⑤⑦	③	①⑥		②	④	④	⑥			⑦	④⑥			
0	**Hubli** ....d.	0200	0600	0650	1240	1240	...	1400	1440	1740	1740	1740	...	1655	1655	2025	2025	1800	...	2145	2220	2245	2320	...
129	Harihar ....d.	0450	0755	0852	1450	1450	...	1552	|	2010	2010	2010	...	|	|	2128	2128	|	...	|	|	0047	0140	...
258	Birur ....d.	0650	0945	1055	1700	1700	...	1732	1906	2210	2210	2210	...	|	|	0042	0042	|	...	|	|	0250	0350	...
303	Arsikere ....d.	0750	1040	1200	1800	1800	...	1820	2000	2305	2305	2305	...	|	|	0135	0135	|	...	0315	|	0350	0440	...
393	Tumkur ....d.	0940	1230	|	1930	1930	...	2002	2140	0130	0130	0130	...	|	|	0335	0345	|	...	|	0455	0540	0630	...
469	**Bangalore** City ....a.	1125y	1405	1500y	2050y	2050y	...	2125	2310y	0315	0315	0315	...	0445	0445	0515y	0515y	0610	...	0620y	0620y	0700	0810	...

			Exp	SDi	Exp	Exp		Exp	Exp	Exp	Exp	Exp		Exp	Exp	Exp	Exp	Exp		Exp	Exp	Exp	Exp	
			12778	**12079**	**11006**	**11022**		**19405**	**12629**	**12725**	**17309**	**16535**		**16589**	**16532**	**16534**	**17311**	**17313**		**16508**	**16210**	**16506**	**16592**	
			⑤		①③④	②⑤⑥		①	②④		②⑦				⑤	⑦	⑤	⑦		①③	②④	⑥		
Bangalore City ....d.	...	...	0440y	0600	0630y	0630y	...	1045	1350y	1300	1445y	1850	...	2115	1700	1720	2155y	2155y	...	2155	2155	2155	2200	...
Tumkur ....d.	...	...	|	0705	0732	0732	...	|	1450	1405	1550	2035	...	2225	|	|	2305	2305	...	2305	2305	2305	|	...
Arsikere ....d.	...	...	0725	0835	0935	0935	...	1320	|	1540	1735	2205	...	0006	|	|	0050	0050	...	0050	0050	0050	|	...
Birur ....d.	...	...	0810	0917	1022	1022	...	|	|	1625	1822	2252	...	0100	|	|	0140	0140	...	0140	0140	0140	|	...
Harihar ....d.	...	...	1017	1107	1225	1225	...	|	|	1825	|	0110	...	0255	|	|	|	0350	...	0350	0350	0350	|	...
Hubli ....a.	...	...	1240	1325	1505	1505	...	1925	2140	2110	2340	0400	...	0535	0625	0625	0635	0625	...	0625	0625	0625	1100	...

y – Bangalore Yesvantpur Junction.

Indian Railways — MUMBAI - PUNE - SECUNDERABAD, BANGALORE and CHENNAI — 5250

km		Exp	Exp	Exp	Exp	Exp	Exp		Exp	Exp	Exp	Exp	Exp	Exp	Exp	Exp	Exp	Exp	Exp	Duro		Exp	Exp	SDi
		11301	**16331**	**16339**	**16351**	**17222**	**17031**		**11041**	**11019**	**16381**	**19568**	**16613**	**17203**	**17017**	**19202**	**12163**	**12701**	**11013**	**12219**		**11043**	**11027**	**12025**
			①	**A**	②⑥	④⑦						⑤	⑦	⑥	①③④	②				③⑥		⑤		③–①
0	**Mumbai** CST d.	0805	1205	1205	1205	1225**t**	1245	...	1400	1510	1545	...	...	...	...	...	2030**d**	2150	2235**t**	2305**t**	...	0015**t**	2345	...
54	Kalyan d.	0900	1310	1310	1310	|	1345	...	1505	1610	1640	1945	1945	1945	1945	1945	2115	2240	2318	|	...	0100	0040	...
192	**Pune** d.	1145	1550	1550	1550	1535	1635	...	1810	1905	1925	2230	2230	2230	2230	2230	0010	0125	0155	|	...	0358	0335	0550
263	Daund d.	1310	1705	1705	1705	|	1815	...	1930	2040	2055	|	2355	2355	2355	2355	|	|	|	|	...	0530	0515	|
456	Solapur d.	1620	2025	2025	2025	1945	2225	...	2325	0025	0055	0300	0300	0300	0300	0300	0405	0535	0635	|	...	0845	0925	0913
568	Gulbarga d.	1844	2230	2230	2230	2150	0030	...	0110	0233	0300	0453	0453	0453	0453	0453	0610	0720	0848	|	...	1055	1130	1042
605	Wadi d.	1955	2330	2330	2330	2250	0155	...	0235	0400	0420	0610	0610	0610	0610	0610	0720	0850	1010	|	...	1215	1255	1135
717	Vikarabad d.	|	|	|	|	0030	0359	...	|	|	|	|	|	|	|	|	|	1035	|	|	...	|	|	1250
800	**Secunderbad** a.	|	|	|	|	0200	0555**h**	...	|	0745	|	|	|	1030	1030	1030	|	1210**h**	|	1105	...	|	|	1420
713	Raichur d.	2145	0110	0110	0110	...	...	...	0410	...	0552	0730	0730	...	...	...	0850	...	1145	...	...	1335	1455	...
783	Adoni d.	2300	0245	0245	0245	...	...	...	0525	...	0702	|	0840	...	...	...	1000	...	1250	...	...	1452	1700	...
834	Guntakal d.	0010	0405	0405	0405	...	...	...	0630	...	0820	0955	0955	...	...	...	1115	...	1410	...	...	1630	1815	...
863	Gooty d.	0055	0450	0450	0440	...	...	...	0655	...	0845	|	1050	...	...	...	1142	...	1440	...	...	1702	1842	...
913	Anantapur d.	0240	0550	0550	|	...	...	...	|	...	|	1200	1200	...	...	...	|	...	1542	...	...	|	|	...
942	Dharmavaram d.	0415	0700	0700	|	...	...	...	|	...	|	1305	1305	...	...	...	|	...	1655	...	...	|	|	...
1041	Hindupur d.	0550	0820	0820	|	...	...	...	|	...	|	1420	1420	...	...	...	|	...	1830	...	...	|	|	...
1177	**Bangalore** City a.	0850	1025**k**	1025**k**	|	...	...	...	|	...	|	1620**k**	1620**k**	...	...	...	|	...	2150	...	...	|	|	...
1017	Cuddapah d.	...	...	...	0720	...	...	...	1005	...	1135	...	...	...	...	...	1410	...	...	...	...	1925	2135	...
1142	Renigunta d.	...	...	...	0958	...	...	...	1345	...	1435	...	...	...	...	...	1705	...	...	...	...	2245	0100	...
1152	**Tirupati** a.	...	...	...	...	...	...	...	|	...	1510	...	...	...	...	...	|	...	...	...	...	|	|	...
1214	Arakkonam d.	...	...	...	...	...	...	...	1505	...	...	...	...	...	...	...	1805	...	...	...	...	0003	0225	...
1283	**Chennai** Central a.	...	...	...	...	...	...	...	1645	...	...	...	...	...	...	...	1945**e**	...	...	...	...	...	0415	...

		Exp	Exp	SDi	Exp	Exp	Exp	Exp		Exp	Exp	Exp	Exp	Exp	Exp		Duro	Exp	Exp	Exp	Exp	Exp	Exp	Exp
		11028	**11020**	**12026**	**16382**	**12702**	**19201**	**17018**		**17204**	**16614**	**11044**	**12164**	**19567**	**22819**		**12220**	**17032**	**11042**	**11014**	**11302**	**16332**	**16340**	**16352**
				③–①			③	①②⑥		④	⑤	⑦		①	③⑥		②⑤					⑥	**B**	④⑦
Chennai Central d.	...	2250	...	...	...	...	...	...	...	...	...	...	0650**e**	...	...	...	...	...	1155	...	...	...	...	...
Arakkonam d.	...	0005	...	...	...	...	...	...	...	...	...	0430	|	...	...	...	...	...	1300	...	...	...	...	...
Tirupati d.	...	|	...	...	0340	...	...	...	...	...	...	|	|	...	...	...	...	...	|	...	...	...	...	...
Renigunta d.	...	0220	...	...	0420	...	...	...	...	...	...	0730	0935	...	...	...	...	...	1445	...	...	...	...	2205
Cuddapah d.	...	0435	...	...	0630	...	...	...	...	...	...	0940	1130	...	...	...	...	...	1705	...	...	...	...	0015
Bangalore City d.	...	|	...	...	|	...	...	...	...	...	0720**k**	|	|	1130**k**	...	...	...	...	|	1600	2000	2135**k**	2135**k**	|
Hindupur d.	...	|	...	...	|	...	...	...	...	...	0950	|	|	1305	...	...	...	...	|	1810	2230	2330	2330	|
Dharmavaram d.	...	|	...	...	|	...	...	...	...	...	1145	|	|	1435	...	...	...	...	|	2020	0025	0125	0125	|
Anantapur d.	...	|	...	...	|	...	...	...	...	...	1220	|	|	1522	...	...	...	...	|	2105	0110	0215	0215	|
Gooty d.	...	0800	...	...	1000	...	...	...	...	...	1320	1245	1415	|	...	...	...	...	2010	2220	0250	0345	0345	0345
Guntakal d.	...	0850	...	...	1115	...	...	...	...	...	1420	1330	1500	1720	...	...	...	...	2055	2250	0320	0420	0420	0420
Adoni d.	...	1000	...	...	1150	...	...	...	...	...	1500	1405	1540	|	...	...	...	...	2138	2335	0410	0455	0455	0500
Raichur d.	...	1155	...	...	1340	...	...	...	...	...	1610	1530	1650	1915	...	...	...	...	2320	0045	0540	0630	0630	0630
Secunderabad d.	...	|	1145	1445	|	1445**h**	1500	1500	...	1500	|	|	|	|	2110	...	2305	2040**h**	|	|	|	|	|	|
Vikarabad d.	...	|	|	1541	|	1602	|	|	...	1619	|	|	|	|	2215	...	|	2203	|	|	|	|	|	|
Wadi d.	...	1500	1610	1725	1740	1810	1845	1845	...	1845	1845	1845	1910	2145	0035	...	|	0050	0145	0305	0800	0905	0905	0905
Gulbarga d.	...	1545	1655	1756	1818	1850	1930	1930	...	1930	1930	1930	1950	2230	|	...	|	0130	0235	0343	0850	0943	0943	0943
Solapur d.	...	1820	1855	1940	2020	2100	2125	2125	...	2125	2125	2125	2200	0015	0310	...	|	0350	0440	0600	1120	1150	1150	1140
Daund d.	...	2155	2230	|	2320	|	0030	0030	...	0030	0030	0030	|	|	|	...	|	0735	0805	0930	1425	1510	1510	1510
Pune d.	...	2340	2350	2310	0055	0115	0205	0205	...	0205	0205	0205	0235	0505	0755	...	|	0910	0935	1045	1555	1640	1640	1640
Kalyan d.	...	0230	0240	...	0340	0355	0445	0445	...	0445	0445	0450	0505	0747	|	...	|	1155	1225	1325	1840	1940	1940	1940
Mumbai CST a.	...	0345	0355	...	0450	0505	...	...	...	...	...	0545	0600**d**	...	1105	...	1105**t**	1305	1345	1430**t**	1955	2050	2050	2050

A – ③④⑤⑦.
B – ①②③⑤.
a – Calls at Renigunta, then Tirupati.
d – Mumbai Dadar.
e – Chennai Egmore.
h – Hyderabad.
k – Bangalore Krishnarajapuram.
t – Mumbai Lokmaniya Tilak Terminus.

Indian Railways — SECUNDERABAD - TIRUPATI and CHENNAI — 5260

km		Exp	Exp	Exp	Exp	Exp	Exp			
		17406	**17230**	**12604**	**12734**	**12764**	**12760**			
						④–①				
0	**Secunderabad** d.	0605	1225	1720	1805	1830	1855	...	...	...
132	Kazipet d.	0820	|	|	|	2020	2055	...	...	...
351	Vijayawada d.	1315	|	|	|	0040	0110	...	...	...
	Guntur d.	|	1740	2225	2310	|	|	...	...	...
382*	Tenali d.	1400	1822	2312	0002	0108	0138	...	...	...
643	Gudur d.	1910	2240	0320	0415	0510	0540	...	...	...
726	Renigunta d.	2040	0005	|	0532	0632	|	...	...	...
736	**Tirupati** a.	2125	0030	|	0605	0700	|	...	...	...
793	**Chennai** Central a.	...	...	0555	...	...	0815	...	...	...

	Exp	Exp	Exp	Exp	Exp	Exp			
	12603	**12763**	**12733**	**12759**	**17229**	**17405**			
		⑤–②							
Chennai Central d.	1645	...	...	1810	...	...	...	...	...
Tirupati d.	|	1700	1825	|	0035	0525	...	...	...
Renigunta d.	|	1717	1842	|	0100	0542	...	...	...
Gudur d.	1918	1857	2017	2045	0247	0742	...	...	...
Tenali d.	2320	2208	0010	0015	0647	1150	...	...	...
Guntur d.	0010	|	0105	|	0735	|	...	...	...
Vijayawada d.	|	2335	|	0120	|	1330	...	...	...
Kazipet d.	|	0250	|	0442	|	1720	...	...	...
Secunderabad a.	0515	0550	0625	0715	1310	2040	...	...	...

B – ①②⑤⑥⑦.
* – *311 km* via Guntur.

Indian Railways — MUMBAI and PUNE - KOLKATA — 5270

km		Exp	Exp	Duro	Duro	Exp	Duro	Exp	Exp	Exp	Exp
		12859	**12869**	**12261**	**12221**	**15611**	**12289**	**12101**	**12129**	**12809**	**18029**
			⑦	**C**	①⑥	③		**A**			
0	**Mumbai** CST d.	0600	1105	1715	...	1125**t**	2015	2035**t**	...	2035	2155**t**
53	Kalyan d.	0700	1200	|	...	1210	|	2120	...	2140	2245
	Pune d.	|	|	|	1515	|	|	|	1825	|	|
260	Manmad d.	|	|	|	|	1620	|	|	0035	0122	0250
420	Jalgaon d.	1220	|	|	|	|	|	|	0235	0310	0445
441	Bhusaval d.	1300	1815	|	|	1845	|	0315	0330	0400	0520
584	Akola d.	1455	2010	|	|	2040	|	0505	0535	0610	0755
663	Badnera d.	1625	2215	|	|	|	|	0700	0715	0800	0955
759	Wardha d.	1732	|	|	|	|	|	|	0840	0928	1130
837	Nagpur d.	1905	0135	|	|	0135	0720	1000	1020	1125	1330
967	Gondia d.	2048	0313	|	|	0313	...	1138	1203	1316	1555
139	Raipur Junction d.	2335	0600	|	|	0600	...	1430	1455	1615	1935
250	Bilaspur d.	0130	0800	|	|	0830	...	1625	1650	1815	2225
454	Jharsuguda d.	0427	1057	|	|	1207	...	|	1947	2140	0205
554	Raurkela d.	0550	1227	|	|	1340	...	2056	2120	2311	0342
718	Tatanagar d.	0830	1500	|	|	1645	...	2335	2355	0150	0710
853	Kharagpur d.	1025	1650	|	|	1927	...	0130	0147	0340	0930
969	**Kolkata** Howrah a.	1230	1930	1940‡	1940‡	2130	...	0335	0350	0550	1215**h**

	Duro	Duro	Exp	Exp	Exp	Exp	Exp	Exp	Exp	Duro
	12262	**12222**	**12860**	**15612**	**12870**	**18030**	**12810**	**12130**	**12102**	**12290**
	D	④⑥		⑦	⑤				**B**	
Kolkata Howrah d.	0820	0820	1350	1435	1435	1500**h**	2015	2155	2255	...
Kharagpur d.	|	|	1535	1620	1620	1750	2200	2340	0040	...
Tatanagar d.	|	|	1732	1810	1810	2015	2352	0137	0235	...
Raurkela d.	|	|	2000	2045	2045	2312	0225	0405	0500	...
Jharsuguda d.	|	|	2143	2215	2215	0055	0400	0552	|	...
Bilaspur d.	|	|	0045	0120	0120	0445	0725	0915	0940	...
Raipur Junction d.	|	|	0225	0305	0305	0645	0910	1055	1130	...
Gondia d.	|	|	0515	0555	0600	1015	1200	1339	1415	...
Nagpur d.	|	|	0730	0830	0830	1340	1420	1550	1630	2040
Wardha d.	|	|	0835	|	|	1505	1533	1646	|	|
Badnera d.	|	|	1018	|	1125	1705	1753	1828	1915	|
Akola d.	|	|	1115	1224	1224	1810	1855	1925	2010	|
Bhusaval d.	|	|	1330	1425	1425	2045	2130	2140	2205	|
Jalgaon d.	|	|	1354	|	|	2110	2155	2210	|	|
Manmad d.	|	|	|	1645	|	2315	2345	0030	|	|
Pune a.	|	1135‡	|	|	|	|	|	0650	|	|
Kalyan d.	|	...	2010	2210	2210	0345	0415	...	0450	|
Mumbai CST a.	1030‡	...	2120	2315	2330	0450**t**	0525	...	0545**t**	0755

– ①②⑤⑥.
– ①③④⑦.
C – ②③④⑦.
D – ①②③⑤.
h – Kolkata Shalimar.
t – Mumbai Lokmaniya Tilak Terminus.
‡ – Next day (more than 24 hours after previous time).

5280 KOLKATA - PURI, SECUNDERABAD, TIRUPATI and CHENNAI

Indian Railways

km		Exp 12514 ⑤	Exp 12508 ⑥	Exp 12510 A	Exp 12821	Duro 22203 ②④⑦	Exp 12703	Exp 18645	Exp 22825 ②	SDi 12073 ①–⑥	SDi 12277 ④–②	Exp 12841	Exp 12663 C	Duro 22201 ①③⑤	Exp 18409	Exp 12863	Exp 12881 ②④	Exp 12887 ①	Exp 12895 ⑤	Exp 12837	Exp 16324 ②⑦	Exp 12660 ③	Exp 15644 ⑤	Exp 15228 ①	Exp 12867 ⑦	Exp 12839
0	**Kolkata** Howrah d.	0105	0105	0105	0600	...	0725	1145	1220h	1325	1425	1450	1610	2000d	1900	2035	2055	2055	2055	2235	2245h	2300h	2315	2315	2330	2345
116	Kharagpur d.	0300	0300	0300	0745	...	0910	1352	1405	1515	1610	1635	1800	|	2052	2230	2250	2250	2250	0025	0145	0145	0115	0145	0115	0130
232	Balasore d.	0427	0427	0427	0930	...	1037	1550	1540	1644	1737	1802	1927	|	2303	2357	0027	0027	0027	0155	0329	0329	|	0329	0242	0300
409	Cuttack d.	0657	0657	0657	1207	...	1315	1915	1805	1928	1954	2045	|	|	0155	0225	0310	0310	0310	0430	0555	0555	0515	0555	|	0540
437	Bhubaneswar d.	0750	0750	0750	1250	...	1355	1955	1850	2020	2027	2125	2240	|	0235	0315	0345	0345	0345	0515	0640	0640	0555	0640	0555	0620
456	Khurda Road d.	0845	0845	0845	1320	...	1440	2035	1940	...	|	2215	2330	|	0330	0350	0435	0435	0435	0550	0730	0730	0635	0730	0645	0710
500	**Puri** a.	|	|	|	1430	...	|	|	|	...	2210	|	|	0400	0445	|	0555	0555	0555	0730	|	|	0800	|	|	|
819	Vizianagram d.	1405	1405	1405	...	...	2005	0235	0100	...	...	0012	|	...	...	0920	...	...	...	...	1305	1305	...	1305	1200	1247
879	Visakhapatanam d.	1550	1550	1550	...	2230	2130	0405	0250	...	...	0445	0615	...	...	1100	...	...	...	...	1440	1440	...	1440	|	1410
1081	Rajahmundry d.	|	1855	1855	...	|	0031	0744	0554	...	...	0733	0922	...	...	1357	...	...	...	...	1750	1750	...	1750	|	1734
1259	Vijayawada d.	2155	2155	2155	...	|	0335	1120	0850	...	...	1035	1225	...	...	1700	...	...	...	...	2055	2055	...	2055	1905	2045
	Guntur d.	|	|	|	...	|	0425	|	|	...	...	|	|	...	...	|	...	...	...	...	|	|	...	|	|	|
1574	**Secunderabad** a.	0420	|	|	...	0800	0935	1800	|	...	...	|	|	...	...	|	...	...	...	...	|	|	...	|	|	|
1637	Renigunta d.	...	|	|	...	...	...	...	|	...	...	|	|	...	...	2315	...	...	...	...	|	0330	...	|	0105	|
1647	**Tirupati** a.	...	|	|	...	...	...	...	|	...	...	|	|	...	...	2340	...	...	...	...	|	0345	...	|	0120	|
1691	**Chennai** Central a.	...	0415	0415	...	...	...	...	1700	...	...	1715	2000e	...	...	...	...	...	...	...	0355	...	...	0355	...	0350

		Exp 12664 D	Duro 22202 ②④⑥	Exp 12840	Exp 12838	Exp 12864	Exp 12888 ⑦	Exp 12896 ④	Exp 15643 ⑥	Exp 12882 ①③	Exp 18410	Exp 12509 B	Exp 12513 ⑦	Exp 12842	SDi 12074 ①–⑥	Sdi 12278 ④–②	Exp 12659 ①	Exp 16323 ⑤⑦	Exp 12507 ③	Exp 15227 ④	Exp 18646	Exp 12704	Duro 22204 ①③⑥	Exp 12822	Exp 22826 ④	Exp 12868 ③
Chennai Central d.	...	2230e	...	2340	...	...	...	...	...	...	...	0620	...	0845	...	...	...	1000	1000	1000	...	...	...	...	1620	...
Tirupati d.	...	|	...	|	...	0235	...	...	...	...	...	|	...	|	...	...	0910	|	|	|	...	...	...	...	|	1950
Renigunta d.	...	|	...	|	...	0300	...	...	...	...	...	|	...	|	...	...	0940	|	|	|	...	...	...	...	|	2015
Secunderabad d.	...	|	...	|	...	|	...	...	...	...	...	|	0730	|	...	...	|	|	|	|	1025	1600	2030	...	|	|
Guntur d.	...	|	...	|	...	|	...	...	...	...	...	|	|	|	...	...	|	|	|	|	|	2035	|	...	|	|
Vijayawada d.	...	0540	...	0640	...	0940	...	...	...	...	...	1320	1320	1525	...	...	1620	1700	1700	1700	1650	2140	|	...	2350	0300
Rajahmundry d.	...	0753	...	0914	...	1205	...	...	...	...	...	1529	|	1742	...	...	1845	1912	1912	1912	1927	0003	|	...	0203	|
Visakhapatanam d.	...	1205	...	1320	...	1615	...	...	...	...	...	1945	1945	2210	...	...	2325	2325	2325	2325	2355	0350	0605	...	0635	|
Vizianagram d.	...	|	...	1420	...	1712	...	...	...	...	...	2042	2042	|	...	...	0022	0022	0022	0022	0112	0450	...	...	0745	0940
Puri d.	...	|	1945	|	2000	|	2215	2215	2215	2215	2230	|	|	|	...	0600	|	|	|	|	|	|	...	1150	|	|
Khurda Road d.	...	1825	|	2010	2115	2230	2315	2315	2315	2315	2330	0200	0200	0415	...	|	0550	0550	0550	0550	0720	1025	...	1250	1340	|
Bhubaneswar d.	...	1850	|	2040	2147	2255	2345	2345	2345	2345	2355	0225	0225	0440	0600	0705	0620	0620	0620	0620	0745	1055	...	1320	1410	1515
Cuttack d.	...	|	|	2115	2225	2330	0020	0020	0020	0020	0035	0315	0315	0512	0632	0737	0705	0705	0705	0705	0822	1130	...	1355	1455	|
Balasore d.	...	2249	|	0012	0103	0216	0251	0251	|	0251	0338	0623	0623	0805	0903	1017	0947	0947	0947	0947	1142	1352	...	1620	1732	1833
Kharagpur d.	...	0100	|	0152	0240	0355	0445	0445	0445	0445	0600	0830	0830	0948	1050	1155	1140	1140	1140	1140	1348	1530	...	1808	1932	2023
Kolkata Howrah a.	...	0320	0400d	0410	0450	0610	0705	0705	0705	0705	0810	1055	1055	1150	1240	1345	1350h	1350h	1355	1355	1610	1745	...	2015	2130h	2225

A – ①②③④. Runs as **12516** on ④.
B – ①④⑤⑥. Runs as **12515** on ①.
C – ①④⑦. Runs as **12665** on ①.
D – ②⑤⑥. Runs as **12666** on ⑥.
d – Kolkata Sealdah.
e – Chennai Egmore.
h – Kolkata Shalimar.

5290 CHENNAI - BANGALORE

Indian Railways

km		Exp 15228 ③	Exp 12510 ②③④	SDi 12007 ④–②		Exp 12639	Exp 12609	Exp 12296		Exp 17311 ⑤	Exp 17313 ⑦	Exp 12577 ④		Exp 12607	SDi 12027 ③–①	Exp 16222		Exp 12657	Exp 12691 ⑤	Exp 22682 ④		Exp 12292 ⑥		
0	**Chennai** Central d.	0415	0440	0600	...	0750	1335	1355	...	1410	1410	1440	...	1535	1730	2130	...	2315	2330	2330	...	2330	...	...
68	Arakkonam d.	0525	0555	|	...	0855	1440	1505	...	1515	1515	1540	...	1640	|	2235	...	0015	0030	0030	...	0030	...	...
130	Katpadi d.	0625	0655	|	...	0955	1545	1600	...	1610	1610	1630	...	1745	1905	2345	...	0110	0125	0120	...	|	...	...
214	Jolarpettai d.	0740	0820	|	...	1107	1708	1730	...	1745	1745	1745	...	1855	|	0102	...	0225	0245	0240	...	0245	...	...
350	Krishnarajapuram d.	1000	1045	|	...	1257	1915	1938	...	2010	2010	|	...	2055	|	0315	...	|	0445	0445	...	0445	...	...
361	**Bangalore** City a.	1120y	1150	1050	...	1400	2005	2020	...	2135y	2135y	2055	...	2135	2230	0400	...	0510	0525	0530	...	0600y	...	...

		SDi 12028 ③–①	Exp 17312 ⑤	Exp 17314 ⑦		Exp 12608	Exp 12610	Exp 12295		Exp 12578 ⑥	Exp 12640	SDi 12008 ④–②		Exp 12658	Exp 12291 ⑤	Exp 12692 ⑦		Exp 22681 ③	Exp 12509 ③④⑤	Exp 16221		Exp 15227 ③		
Bangalore City d.	...	0600	0530y	0530y	...	0630	0800	0900	...	1010	1510	1625	...	2240	2245y	2300	...	2300	2330	2345	...	2355	...	...
Krishnarajapuram d.	...	|	0610	0610	...	0653	0824	0928	...	|	1533	|	...	|	2326	2326	...	2326	2356	0015	...	0045	...	...
Jolarpettai d.	...	|	0825	0825	...	0845	1030	1130	...	1220	1725	|	...	0105	0132	0132	...	0132	0210	0300	...	0425	...	...
Katpadi d.	...	0900	0930	0930	...	0950	1150	1235	...	1325	1840	|	...	0210	|	0245	...	0245	0320	0410	...	0705	...	...
Arakkonam d.	...	|	1025	1025	...	1045	1300	1335	...	1420	1935	|	...	0300	0340	0340	...	0340	0410	0525	...	0805	...	...
Channai Central a.	...	1100	1155	1155	...	1215	1430	1505	...	1555	2115	2125	...	0440	0515	0515	...	0515	0540	0725	...	0930	...	..

y – Bangalore Yesvantpur Junction.

5300 CHENNAI and BANGALORE - TRIVANDRUM

Indian Railways

km		Exp 16324 ②④	Exp 12516 ⑤	Duro 12243 ③–①	Exp 22619 ③	Duro 22207 ②⑤	Exp 15906 ②	Exp 12697 ⑦	Exp 12777 ③	Exp 12695	Exp 16315 ③⑤⑦	Exp 16381	Exp 16321 ④	Exp 12644 ⑥	Exp 12623	Exp 12257 ②④⑦	Exp 12626	Exp 16526	Exp 16325 ②	Exp 12511 ①⑤⑥	Exp 16327 ④⑦	Exp 17230	Exp 16318 ④	Exp 12660 ⑤
0	**Chennai** Central d.	0415	0440	0715	...	1630	...	1515	...	1525	...	...	...	...	1945	...	...	...	2345	2345	2345	...	...	...
	Tirupati d.	|	|	|	...	|	...	|	...	|	...	1515	...	1712	|	...	2107	...	|	|	|	0035	0122	0347
130	Katpadi d.	0625	0655	|	1135	|	1610	1705	...	1720	...	1800	...	1935	2130	...	2330	...	0150	0150	0150	0240	0350	0550
214	Jolarpettai d.	0740	0830	|	|	|	1755	1820	...	1840	...	1930	...	|	|	...	0045	...	0320	0320	0320	0350	0505	0655
	Bangalore City d.	|	|	|	|	|	|	|	1520y	|	1715	|	1715	|	|	2100y	|	2140	|	|	|	|	|	|
	Krishanrajapuram d.	|	|	|	|	|	|	|	|	|	|	|	1742	|	|	|	|	2210	|	|	|	|	|	|
	Bangarapet d.	|	|	|	|	|	|	|	1640	|	|	|	1830	|	|	|	|	2310	|	|	|	|	|	|
335	Salem Junction d.	0920	0955	|	1420	|	1940	1950	1950	2010	2125	2105	2125	2210	0010	0130	0215	0230	0450	0450	0450	0530	0640	0830
394	Erode Junction d.	1045	1120	|	1540	|	2040	2050	2055	2125	2225	2210	2225	2325	0110	0230	0325	0345	0615	0615	0615	0645	0815	0950
494	Coimbatore Junction d.	1240	1320	1405	1720	|	2235	|	|	2310	0020	2350	0020	0120	|	0415	0510	0525	0800	0800	0800	0830	1000	1130
548	Palghat Junction d.	1400	1450	...	1840	|	2355	2335	2335	0035	0155	0125	0155	0245	0340	0535	0630	0650	0910	0910	0915	0955	1115	1245
626	Trichur d.	1530	1620	...	1955	|	0110	0045	0045	0135	0310	0253	0313	0403	0450	0643	0755	0817	1120	1120	1120	1205	1245	1408
697	Ernakulam Town d.	1735j	1745	...	2135	|	0240	0215	0215	0310	0445j	0435	0510j	0600j	0625	0815	0945j	1010	1257	1257	1300	1350	1420	1540
814	Kayankulam d.	1950	2020	...	2325	|	|	|	|	0518	|	0705	0732	0852	0905	1030	1215	1242	1525	1525	1525	1632	1650	1800
842	Quilon d.	2055	2110	...	0025	|	0525	0510	0510	0610	0740	0815	0837	0945	1000	1120	1310	1340	1610	1610	1610	1730	1745	1850
919	**Trivandrum** Central a.	2230	2230	...	0130	0545	0705	0635	0630k	0735	0925k	0930	1030	1105	1125	1235k	1435	1540	1730	1730	1730	1855	1925	2015

km		Exp 22620 ⑦	Duro 12244 ③–①	Exp 16326 ⑥	Exp 16328 ①④	Exp 12512 ②③⑦	Exp 17229	Exp 16382	Exp 12625	Exp 12778 ④	Exp 12515 ⑦	Exp 16525	Exp 12643 ②	Exp 12624	Exp 16316 ②④⑥	Exp 16317 ⑤	Exp 12659 ⑦	Exp 16323 ④⑥	Exp 16322 ③	Exp 15905 ⑥	Exp 12258 ①③⑤	Exp 12696	Duro 22208 ③⑥	Exp 1269 ⑥
0	**Trivandrum** Central d.	0430	...	0615	0545	0615	0715	0805	1115	1250k	1250	1300	1420	1430	1605k	1600	1600	1635	1635	1655	1700k	1720	2130	2020
77	Quilon d.	0535	...	0715	0645	0715	0820	0920	1220	1350	1350	1415	1520	1535	1710	1700	1705	1735	1735	1800	1800	1825	|	2123
105	Kayankulam d.	0610	...	0755	0722	0755	0902	1000	1255	|	1425	1500	1555	1610	|	1740	1740	1825	1825	|	1835	1905	|	|
222	Ernakulam Town d.	0830j	...	1010j	1015	1010j	1150	1330	1550j	1715	1715	1755	1900	1920	2035	2040	2040	2055j	2035j	2115	2115	2150	|	0025
293	Trichur d.	1000	...	1150	1150	1150	1315	1505	1715	1835	1835	1950	2020	2040	2205	2203	2203	2220	2203	2245	2245	2313	|	0200
371	Palghat Junction d.	1220	...	1405	1405	1405	1520	1645	1840	2010	2010	2130	2155	2210	2340	2345	2340	0010	2340	0025	0025	0045	|	0340
425	Coimbatore Junction d.	1330	1520	1525	1525	1525	1635	1805	2005	|	2140	2255	2345	|	0100	0100	0100	0130	0100	0145	0145	0210	|	|
525	Erode Junction d.	1520	|	1715	1715	1715	1830	2000	2200	2245	2325	0035	0120	0050	0240	0310	0310	0310	0240	0320	0320	0350	|	0600
584	Salem Junction d.	1620	|	1810	1810	1810	1930	2100	2300	2345	0025	0135	0220	0145	0340	0410	0410	0410	0340	0415	0420	0445	|	0655
	Bangarapet d.	|	|	|	|	|	|	|	|	0240	|	0440	|	|	|	|	|	|	0645	|	|	|	|	|
	Krishnarajapuram d.	|	|	|	|	|	|	|	|	|	|	0545	|	|	|	|	|	|	0745	|	|	|	|	|
853	**Bangalore** City a.	|	|	|	|	|	|	|	|	0430y	|	0655	|	|	0835	|	|	|	0835	|	0905y	|	|	|
705	Jolarpettai d.	|	|	1950	1950	1950	2125	2320	0045	...	0210	...	|	|	...	0610	0610	0600	...	0615	...	0620	|	085
789	Katpadi d.	1903	|	2055	2055	2055	2247	0050	0202	...	0320	...	0530	0430	...	0725	0725	0705	...	0723	...	0730	|	100
912	**Tirupati** a.	...	|	|	|	|	0030	0335	0355	...	|	...	0730	|	...	0933	0933	|	...	...	...	|	|	|
919	**Chennai** Central a.	...	2215	2305	2305	2305	...	...	...	...	0540	...	...	0655	...	...	...	0930	...	...	...	0950	1030	122

k – Trivandrum Kochuveli.
y – Bangalore Yesvantpur Junction.

Indian Railways

CHENNAI - SENGOTTAI, TUTICORIN, TIRUCHENDER and NAGERCOIL 5310

km		56765	56768	16127	56735	12635	12633	16612	16735	12667	12642	12652	56761	12693	16723	12661	12631	12637	12665	56763	22205	56731	56767	16236	22623	56733
				Exp		Exp	Exp	Exp	Exp	Exp	Exp	Exp		Exp	Exp	Exp	Exp	Exp	Exp		Duro			Exp	Exp	
		2	2		2					④	②⑦	③⑤	2						②	2	①③	2	2		⑤⑦	2
0	**Chennai** Egmore ...... d.	...	...	0740	...	1320	1730	...	1605	1850	1830	1830	...	1915	1935	2005	2050	2120	2020	...	2230c	...	...	...	2245	...
56	Chengalpattu .... d.	...	...	0835	...	1415	1825	...	1700	1945	1925	1925	...	2010	2030	2100	2145	2215	2115	...	|	...	...	...	2340	...
159	Villupuram .... d.	...	...	1035	...	1555	2015	...	1905	2125	2125	2125	...	2205	2225	2240	2330	2345	2255	...	|	...	...	...	0120	...
214	Vriddhachalam Jct..... d.	...	...	1112	...	1635	2057	...	|	2212	2212	2212	...	2247	2312	2322	0012	0027	2337	...	|	...	...	...	|	...
340	Tiruchchirappalli Jct... d.	...	...	1315	...	1835	2305	...	2340	0050	0050	0050	...	0115	0225	0155	0240	0315	0340	...	|	...	...	...	0600	...
433	Dindigul.................... d.	...	...	1510	...	2005	0045	0100	0150	0220	0220	0220	...	0247	0400	0330	0407	0445	0507	...	|	...	...	0610	0730	...
495	Madurai Junction....... d.	...	...	1635	1715	2125	0200	0205	0300	0325	0325	0345	...	0350	0500	0435	0525	0620	0635	...	0700	0715	...	0725	0850	1125
538	Virudunagar .... d.	...	...	1715	1812	...	0240	0250	0342	0412	0412	...	...	0435	0540	0517	0612	—	0717	...	...	0802	...	0807	...	1220
662	Tenkasi .... d.	...	...	|	2042	...	|	|	|	|	|	...	...	|	|	0735	|	**56828**	|	...	...	1010	...	|	...	1431
670	**Sengottai**............. a.	...	...	|	2105	...	|	|	|	|	|	...	...	|	|	0815	|	2	|	...	...	1045	...	|	...	1500
623	Vanchi Maniyachchi .. d.	...	1720	1840	...	...	|	0510	0510	|	0530	...	...	0601	0700	...	|	0720	0846	...	...	...	1000	1000	...	...
656	**Tuticorin**.............. a.	...	1845	|	...	...	|	0610	|	|	|	...	...	0710	|	...	|	0930	|	...	...	...	|	1110	...	...
652	Tirunelveli Junction ... d.	1840	...	1930	...	...	0455	...	0610	0630	0630	...	0720	...	0825	...	0830	...	0940	0935	...	...	1115	...	...	...
714	**Tiruchender**.......... a.	2040	...	|	...	...	|	...	0800	|	|	...	0910	...	|	...	...	...	|	1125	...	...	1310	...	...	...
726	**Nagercoil** Junction ... a.	...	...	2140	...	...	0610	...	...	0805	0810	...	...	...	0151	...	...	...	1100	...	...	...	...	...	...	...

	56734	56736	56768	16235	12638	56827	56764	12668	12632	12634	12662	22206	22624	12694	56766	16724	12641	12651	16736	16611	12636	56732	16128	56767	56762	12666
				Exp	Exp			Exp	Exp	Exp	Exp	Duro	Exp	Exp		Exp	Exp	Exp	Exp	Exp	Exp		Exp			Exp
	2	2	2			2	2	⑤				②④	④⑥		2		③⑤	①⑥				2		2	2	⑥
Nagercoil Junction .... d.	...	...	...	...	...	...	...	1705	...	1740	...	...	...	...	...	1805	1940	...	...	...	...	...	0535	...	...	0815
Tiruchender .... d.	...	...	1435	...	...	...	1630	|	...	|	...	...	...	...	1755	|	|	...	1945	...	...	...	|	...	0705	|
Tirunelveli Junction .... d.	...	...	1620	...	...	...	1810	1820	1850	1905	...	...	...	...	1940	1950	2055	...	2115	...	...	...	0745	...	0855	0940
Tuticorin .... d.	...	...	|	1635	...	1750	...	|	|	|	...	...	...	1950	...	|	|	...	|	2130	...	...	|	0845	...	|
Vanchi Maniyachchi ... d.	...	...	1705	1713	...	1850	...	|	|	|	...	...	...	2023	...	2035	2121	...	2141	2230	...	...	0835	0945	...	1015
Sengottai.............. d.	1200	1600	...	|	...	...	...	|	|	|	1900	...	...	|	...	|	|	...	|	|	...	0700	|	...	...	|
Tenkasi .... d.	1215	1612	...	|	...	...	...	|	|	|	1918	...	...	|	...	|	|	...	|	|	...	0713	|	...	...	|
Virudunagar .... d.	1430	1825	...	1837	...	...	...	2017	2037	2105	2120	...	...	2145	...	2210	2247	...	2307	0005	...	0930	1000	...	...	1140
Madurai Junction .... d.	1550	1935	...	1950	2035	...	...	2115	2125	2150	2210	2240	2115	2250	...	2300	2355	2355	0015	0105	0650	1045	1110	...	...	1250
Dindigul .... d.	...	...	...	2115	2145	...	...	2212	2230	2252	2315	|	2212	2355	...	0010	0055	0055	0117	0225	0740	...	1215	...	...	1350
Tiruchchirappalli Jct ... d.	...	...	...	...	2315	...	...	2355	0020	0035	0105	|	2350	0130	...	0200	0300	0300	0330	...	0900	...	1410	...	...	1600
Vriddhachalam Jct ..... d.	...	...	...	...	0104	...	...	0155	0215	0240	0245	|	|	0320	...	0336	0450	0450	|	...	1045	...	1620	...	...	1757
Villupuram .... d.	...	...	...	...	0220	...	...	0302	0325	0335	0355	|	0410	0425	...	0510	0540	0540	0835	...	1142	...	1720	...	...	1855
Chengalpattu .... d.	...	...	...	...	0415	...	...	0445	0515	0525	0540	|	0555	0615	...	0700	0730	0730	1025	...	1320	...	1930	...	...	2030
Chennai Egmore .... a.	...	...	...	...	0535	...	...	0605	0640	0650	0705	0710c	0720	0745	...	0840	0850	0850	1140	...	1440	...	2115	...	...	2210

c – Chennai Central.

Indian Railways

HILL and MOUNTAIN RAILWAYS 5320

KANGRA VALLEY RAILWAY

km		52464	52466	18110	52472	14034	52468	14036	52474	52470
		2	2		2		2	②④⑥	2	2
0	**Joginder Nagar** ....d.	...	...	...	0720	...	...	...	1220	...
34	Baijnath Paprola ....d.	0400	0720	...	1050	...	1410	...	1555	1735
54	Palampur Himachal..............d.	0438	0800	...	1130	...	1451	...	1641	1813
99	Kangra Mandir ....d.	0550	0946	...	1246	...	1605	...	1756	1946
246	**Pathankot** ....a.	1050	1420	...	1730	...	2025	...	2235	2355
246	Pathankot Junction ....‡ d.	...	...	1645	...	1905	...	2130	...	...
800	Delhi Junction................‡ a.	...	...	0430	...	0545	...	0745	...	...

	52471	52463	14033	56465	14035	52473	18101	52467	52469
	2	2		2	①③⑤	2		2	2
Delhi Junction ....‡ d.	...	...	2010	...	2245	...	2200	...	...
Pathankot Junction...........‡ d.	...	...	0610	...	0820	...	1100	...	...
Pathankot............................ d.	0215	0400	...	0645	...	1000	...	1320	1550
Kangra Mandir........................ d.	0647	0843	...	1110	...	1503	...	1858	2032
Palampur Himachal .... d.	0806	1001	...	1310	...	1634	...	2014	2139
Baijnath Paprola .... d.	0950	1045	...	1400	...	1805	...	2055	2230
Joginder Nagar .... a.	1125	...	...	...	...	1945	...	...	...

MATHERAN HILL RAILWAY

km		52101	11007	52103	11029	52105	95107	52107	52109	52109
							2			
	Mumbai CST .... ♥ d.	...	0710	...	0840	...	0930	...	...	...
	Neral .... ♥ a.	...	0828	...	1003	...	1109	...	...	...
0	**Neral** ....d.	0730	...	0900	...	1035	...	1140	1250	1705
21	**Matheran** ....a.	0929	...	1110	...	1230	...	1344	1505	1900

	52102	11024	52104	95122	52106	95128	52110	52108	52112
				2		2			
Matheran .... d.	0700	...	0950	...	1235	...	1350	1515	1630
Neral...................................... a.	0835	...	1135	...	1400	...	1525	1650	1810
Neral.............................. ♥ d.	...	1010	...	1223	...	1547	...	...	...
Mumbai CST.................. ♥ a.	...	1155	...	1402	...	1729	...	...	...

NILGIRI MOUNTAIN RAILWAY

km		56141	12671	56136	56143	56138
0	Chennai Central ....‡ d.	...	2115	...	...	...
530	Mettupalaiyam ....‡ a.	...	0615	...	...	...
0	**Mettupalaiyam**....................d.	...	...	0710	...	...
28	Coonor ....d.	0745	...	1040	1235	1630
46	**Udagamandalam** (Ooty)......a.	0905	...	1200	1350	1745

	56139	56142	56137	12672	56140
Udagamandalam (Ooty) .... d.	0915	1215	1400	...	1800
Coonor .... d.	1025	1320	1515	...	1910
Mettupalaiyam...................... a.	...	...	1745	...	...
Mettupalaiyam.................‡ d.	...	...	...	1945	...
Chennai Central ....‡ a.	...	...	...	0505	...

DARJEELING HIMALAYAN RAILWAY

km		52543	52587	52546	52548	52549	52545
				🚂	🚂	🚂	
0	**New Jalpaiguri** Junction......d.	0830	...	...	...	...	...
8	Siliguri Junction......................d.	0855	...	...	...	...	...
18	Sukna ....d.	0923	...	...	...	...	...
26	Rangtong..................................d.	0955	...	...	...	...	...
32	Chunbhati ....d.		...	...	...	...	...
38	Tindharia ....d.	1059	...	...	...	...	...
50	Mahanadi..................................d.	1208	...	...	...	...	...
57	Kurseong..................................d.	1300	0700	...	...	...	1500
65	Tung...d.	...	0735	...	...	...	1536
73	Sonada......................................d.	...	0812	...	...	...	1617
82	Ghum ....d.	...	0900	0920	1200	1440	1708
88	**Darjeeling** ....a.	...	0945	1000	1240	1530	1750

	52546	52544	52548	52549	52542	52588
	🚂		🚂	🚂		
Darjeeling.............................. d.	0800	1015	1040	1320	...	1600
Ghum .... d.	0850	1050	1130	1400	...	1635
Sonada...................................... d.	...	1134	...	...	...	1722
Tung .... d.	...	1215	...	...	...	1802
Kurseong.................................. d.	...	1310	...	...	1430	1840
Mahanadi .... d.	...	...	...	...	1501	...
Tindharia .... d.	...	...	...	...	1551	...
Chunbhati................................. d.	...	...	...	...	|	...
Rangtong.................................. d.	...	...	...	...	1639	...
Sukna....................................... d.	...	...	...	...	1710	...
Siliguri Junction .... d.	...	...	...	...	1753	...
New Jalpaiguri Junction .... a.	...	...	...	...	1810	...

* – Next day (more than 24 hours after previous time).
‡ – By main-line train (*Exp*).
♥ – By main-line train. Frequent additional trains (2 cl. only) are available. Journey 2 hours.

Indian / Pakistan Rlys

LAHORE - DELHI 5400

km		402	14002
			Exp
		①④	①④
0	**Lahore** Jct .... d.	0800	...
	Wagah.............................. a.	0835	...
	Wagah.............................. d.	1130	...
20	Atari 🏛........................... a.	1150	...
20	Atari 🏛........................... d.	...	2015
46	**Delhi** Junction .... a.	...	0320

	14001	401
	Exp	
	③⑥	①④
Delhi Junction .... d.	2305	...
Atari 🏛........................... a.	0715	...
Atari 🏛........................... d.	...	1100
Wagah.............................. a.	...	1410
Wagah.............................. d.	...	1610
Lahore Jct...................... a.	...	1645

NOTE: Timings are subject to confirmation and connections are not guaranteed.

Bangladesh / Indian Rlys

KOLKATA - DHAKA 5450

km		13108 3109	
		Exp	
		⑥	
0	**Kolkata** Chitpur .... d.	0710	...
122	Gede .... a.	|	...
122	Gede .... d.	|	...
	Darsana 🏛 .... a.	|	...
540	**Dhaka** Cantonment .... a.	1800	...

	3110 13109	
	Exp	
	②	
Dhaka Cantonment....... d.	0710	...
Darsana 🏛 .... d.	|	...
Gede .... a.	|	...
Gede .... d.	|	...
Kolkata Chitpur .... a.	1800	...

NOTE: Timings are subject to confirmation.

BEYOND EUROPE
South East Asia, Australia and New Zealand

Introduction

The Beyond Europe section covers principal rail services in a different area of the world each month. There are six areas, each appearing twice yearly as follows:

India:	January and July editions
South East Asia and Australasia:	February and August editions
China:	March and September editions
Japan:	April and October editions
Africa and the Middle East:	May and November editions
North America:	June and December editions

The months have been chosen so that we can bring you up-to-date information for those countries which make seasonal changes.

Limited details of services in South America can be found in the European Rail Timetable Summer and Winter editions.

Contents

INDEX OF PLACES

by table number

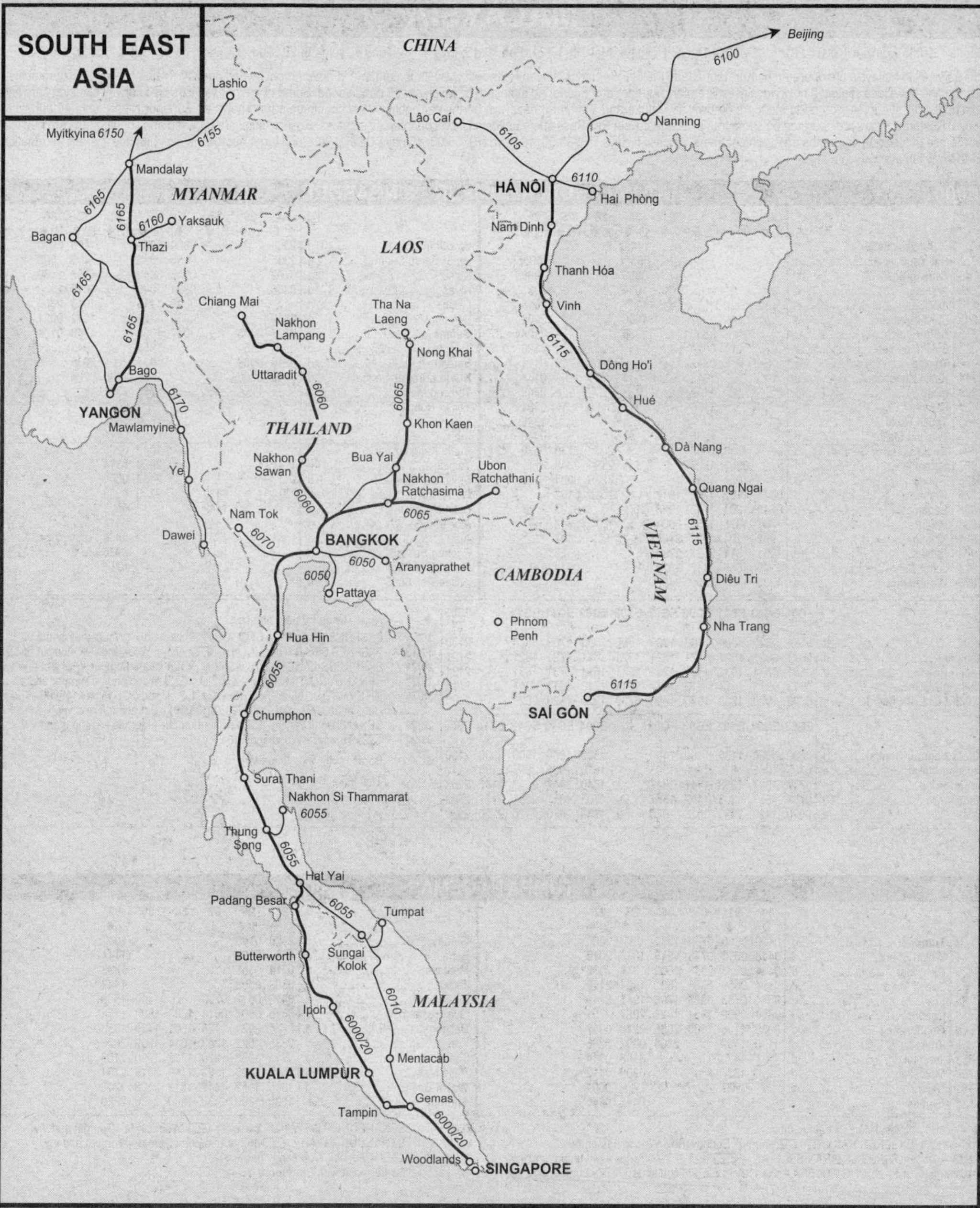
SOUTH EAST ASIA
CHINA
Beijing
6100
Lashio
Myitkyina 6150
6155
Mandalay
MYANMAR
6165
6165
6160
Yaksauk
Bagan
Thazi
6165
6165
Bago
YANGON
6170
Mawlamyine
Ye
Dawei
Lào Cai
6105
Nanning
HÁ NÔI
6110
Hai Phòng
Nam Dinh
Thanh Hóa
Vinh
LAOS
Chiang Mai
Nakhon Lampang
Uttaradit
6060
THAILAND
Nakhon Sawan
6060
Tha Na Laeng
Nong Khai
6065
Khon Kaen
Bua Yai
Nakhon Ratchasima
Ubon Ratchathani
6065
6115
Dông Ho'i
Hué
Dà Nang
Quang Ngai
6115
Diêu Tri
Nha Trang
VIETNAM
Nam Tok
6070
BANGKOK
6050
Aranyaprathet
6050
Pattaya
CAMBODIA
Phnom Penh
Hua Hin
6055
6115
SAÍ GÔN
Chumphon
Surat Thani
Nakhon Si Thammarat
6055
Thung Song
6055
Hat Yai
Padang Besar
6055
Tumpat
Sungai Kolok
Butterworth
6010
MALAYSIA
Ipoh
6000/20
Mentacab
KUALA LUMPUR
Gemas
Tampin
6000/20
Woodlands
SINGAPORE

PHILIPPINES
Kota Kinabalu
6015
Sabah
Tenom
BRUNEI
MALAYSIA
SEE ABOVE
Medan
Tanjung Balai
6200
Pematangsiantar
KUALA LUMPUR
Rantau Prapat
SINGAPORE
MALAYSIA
Sarawak
Kalimantan
Pariaman
6200
Sumatra
Padang
INDONESIA
Sulawesi
Lubuk Linggau
Palembang
6200
6200
Panjang
JAKARTA
6210
Semarang
6205
6215
Surabaja
Bandung
6220
Solo
Malang
Lombok
Flores
Java
Bali
Timor

MALAYSIA

Capital: **Kuala Lumpur** (GMT +8). 2014 Public Holidays: Jan. 1, 14 31, Feb. 1, 15, May 1, 13, June 7, July 28, 29, Aug. 31, Sept. 1, 16, Oct. 5, 23, 25, Dec. 25.

Rail services in Malaysia are operated by Keretapi Tanah Melayu Berhad (Malayan Railways, www.ktmb.com.my), a government owned agency. Trains convey a mixture of first, second and thirdclass seating (known locally as Premier, Superior and Economy) almost all of which are air conditioned. Some overnight services also convey sleeping cars and couchettes. First and second class sleepers (known as Deluxe and Standard) have two berths per cabin, whilst couchette cars (known as Superior Night) have 40 curtained bunks. Restaurant cars are operated on some trains. The Malaysia Rail Pass offers unlimited travel on Intercity services. Reservations are required and supplements are payable for the use of sleeping car berths on overnight trains. Prices: 5 days US$35.00, 10 days US$55.00, 15 days US$70.00. Child fares approximately half price. For full information go to www.ktmintercity.com.my.

6000 HAT YAI - KUALA LUMPUR - SINGAPORE

Keretapi Tanah Melayu Berhad

km		27	13	1	91	35	28	25	21	
		R ◆	R ◆	R ◆	2 ◆	R ◆	R ◆	R ◆	R ◆	
	Bangkok **6055** d.	...	...	...	...	1445t	...	...	...	...
0	**Hat Yai** Junction d.	...	...	...	...	0650t	...	...	1600t	...
45	Padang Besar d.	...	...	...	...	0855	...	...	1900	...
76	Arau d.	...	...	...	...	1034	...	...	1937	...
114	Alor Setar d.	...	...	...	...	1117	...	...	2018	...
205	Bukit Mertajam d.	...	...	...	...	1306	...	...	2201	...
216	**Butterworth** d.	...	...	0800	...	1330	...	...	2228	...
227	Bukit Mertajam d.	...	...	0820	...	...	...	...	2320	...
312	Taiping d.	...	...	0942	...	...	...	...	0111	...
344	Kuala Kangsar d.	...	...	1013	...	...	...	...	0147	...
398	**Ipoh** d.	...	...	1102	...	...	...	...	0249	...
434	Kampar d.	...	...	1135	...	...	...	...	0331	...
450	Tapah Road d.	...	...	|	...	...	...	...	0346	...
517	Tanjong Malim d.	...	...	1236	...	...	...	...	0448	...
604	**Kuala Lumpur** Sentral d.	...	0830	1400	...	...	2030	2230	0630	...
677	Seremban d.	...	0953	1527	...	...	2150	2348	...	...
726	Tampin d.	...	1037	1616	...	...	2236	0034	...	...
779	**Gemas** d.	0646	1122	1706	1812	...	2325	0123	...	...
805	Segamat d.	0745	1201	1743	1928	...	...	0227	...	...
864	Paloh d.	|	1325	1853	2034	...	...	0348	...	...
891	Kluang d.	0922	1354	1921	2101	...	...	0417	...	...
942	Kulai d.	1051	1511	2022	2234	...	...	0525	...	...
974	Johor Bahru Sentral d.	1145	1605	2117	2323	...	...	0618	...	...
978	**Woodlands** ◇ a.	1230	1630	2200	2400	...	...	0700	...	...

	24	29	36	92	2	20	12	26	
	R ◆	R ◆	R ◆	2 ◆	R ◆	R ◆	R ◆	R ◆	
Woodlands ◇ d.	2330	...	...	0600	0830	...	1400	2000	...
Johor Bahru Sentral d.	2335	...	...	0605	0835	...	1405	2005	...
Kulai d.	0102	...	...	0716	0942	...	1507	2130	...
Kluang d.	0206	...	...	0821	1046	...	1615	2238	...
Paloh d.	|	...	...	0849	1115	...	1643	2307	...
Segamat d.	0348	...	...	1010	1227	...	1812	0021	...
Gemas d.	0427	0445	...	1047	1306	...	1848	0100	...
Tampin d.	0524	0554	...	...	1353	...	1943	...	...
Seremban d.	0610	0639	...	...	1437	...	2035	...	...
Kuala Lumpur Sentral d.	0730	0800	...	...	1550	2130	2200	...	...
Tanjong Malim d.	...	...	...	...	1733	2314	...	...	...
Tapah Road d.	...	...	...	...	|	0021	...	...	...
Kampar d.	...	...	...	...	1830	0037	...	...	...
Ipoh d.	...	...	...	...	1902	0111	...	...	...
Kuala Kangsar d.	...	...	...	...	1949	0236	...	...	...
Taiping d.	...	...	...	...	2020	0314	...	...	...
Bukit Mertajam d.	...	...	...	...	2137	0501	...	...	...
Butterworth d.	...	...	1430	...	2200	0530	...	...	...
Bukit Mertajam d.	...	...	1449	...	...	0625	...	...	...
Alor Setar d.	...	...	1641	...	...	0814	...	...	...
Arau d.	...	...	1723	...	...	0856	...	...	...
Padang Besar d.	...	...	1800	...	...	0930	...	...	...
Hat Yai Junction a.	...	...	2109t	...	...	1030t	...	...	...
Bangkok **6055** a.	...	...	1330t	...	...	...	...	...	...

	EG01	EG03	ES01	EG05	EG07	ES03	EG09	EG11	EG13		ES05
Ipoh d.	0500	0800	1000	1100	1200	1500	1600	1700	1800	...	2100
Kampar d.	0521	0821	1021	1121	1221	1521	1621	1721	1821	...	2121
Tapah Road d.	0531	0831	1031	1131	1231	1531	1631	1731	1831	...	2131
Tanjong Malim d.	0613	0913	1114	1213	1313	1614	1713	1813	1913	...	2214
Kuala Lumpur Sentral a.	0720	1020	1230	1320	1420	1730	1820	1920	2020	...	2330

	EG02	EG04	ES02	EG06	EG08		ES04	EG10	EG12	EG14	ES06
Kuala Lumpur Sentral d.	0600	0900	1100	1300	1400	...	1500	1800	1900	2000	2100
Tanjong Malim d.	0705	1005	1210	1405	1505	...	1610	1905	2005	2105	2210
Tapah Road d.	0747	1047	1253	1447	1547	...	1640	1947	2047	2147	2253
Kampar d.	0757	1057	1303	1457	1557	...	1703	1957	2057	2157	2303
Ipoh a.	0820	1120	1330	1520	1620	...	1730	2020	2120	2220	2330

◆ – Notes, listed by train number.
1/2 – EKSPRES RAKYAT – [12] and 🍸 Butterworth - Woodlands and v.v.
12/13 – EKSPRES SINARAN SELATAN – [12] and 🍸 Woodlands - K. Lumpur and v.v.
20/21 – EKSPRESS LANGKAWI – 🛏 2 cl., [2] Kuala Lumpur - Hat Yai and v.v.
26/27 – SENANDUNG TIMURAN – 🛏 2 cl., [2] Woodlands - Tumpat and v.v.
35/36 – INTERNATIONAL EXPRESS – 🛏 1, 2 cl. and ✕ Bangkok (**49/48**) - Hat Yai and v.v.; 🛏 2 cl. Hat Yai (**35/36**) - Butterworth and v.v.
28/29 – SENANDUNG WAU – [2] Kuala Lumpur - Gemas - Tumpat and v.v.
91/92 – [2] Tumpat - Woodlands and v.v.
◇ – Border point with Singapore.
t – Thai time.

6010 TUMPAT - GEMAS

Keretapi Tanah Melayu Berhad

km		81	91	83	85	29	27			
		3	2 ◆	3	3	R ◆	R ◆			
0	**Tumpat** d.	0400	0600	0730	1530	1800	2000	...	...	...
14	Wakaf Bharu d.	0418	0616	0748	1546	1817	2019	...	...	...
25	Pasir Mas d.	0434	0633	0804	1602	1835	2038	...	...	...
53	Tanah Mera d.	0504	0659	0835	1631	1904	2110	...	...	...
85	Krai d.	0544	0733	0923	1708	1943	2149	...	...	...
135	Dabong d.	0654	0909	1054	1822	2057	2301	...	...	...
206	Gua Masang d.	0936	1106	1300	2035	2213	0017	...	...	...
300	Kuala Lipis d.	1130	1307	...	2300	0002	0206	...	...	...
353	Jerantut d.	...	1420	...	...	0108	0314	...	...	...
406	Mentakab d.	...	1537	...	...	0205	0412	...	...	...
492	Bahau d.	...	1727	...	...	|	0601	...	...	...
528	**Gemas** a.	...	1812	...	...	0445	0646	...	...	...

	28	26	82	84	86	92			
	R ◆	R ◆	3	3	3	2 ◆			
Gemas d.	2325	0100	...	...	...	1047	...	...	...
Bahau d.	|	0154	...	...	...	1147	...	...	...
Mentakab d.	0214	0355	...	...	...	1333	...	...	...
Jerantut d.	0309	0508	...	...	...	1431	...	...	...
Kuala Lipis d.	0418	0612	0730	...	1400	1539	...	...	...
Gua Masang d.	0615	0807	0914	1330	1600	1734	...	...	...
Dabong d.	0734	0921	1126	1501	1720	1853	...	...	...
Krai d.	0835	1022	1243	1614	1900	2028	...	...	...
Tanah Mera d.	0915	1058	1320	1712	1950	2103	...	...	...
Pasir Mas d.	0947	1125	1353	1749	2016	2154	...	...	...
Wakaf Bharu d.	1008	1142	1412	1812	2108	2213	...	...	...
Tumpat a.	1030	1200	1430	1900	2130	2230	...	...	...

◆ – Notes, listed by train number.
1/2 – EKSPRES RAKYAT – [12] and 🍸 Butterworth - Woodlands and v.v.
12/13 – EKSPRES SINARAN SELATAN – [12] and 🍸 Woodlands - K. Lumpur and v.v.
24/25 – SENANDUNG SUTERA – 🛏 1, 2 cl., [2] Woodlands - Kuala Lumpur and v.v.
26/27 – SENANDUNG TIMURAN – 🛏 2 cl., [2] Woodlands - Tumpat and v.v.
28/29 – SENANDUNG WAU – [2] Kuala Lumpur - Gemas - Tumpat and v.v.
91/92 – [2] Tumpat - Woodlands and v.v.
◇ – Border point with **Singapore**.

6015 TENOM - TANJONG ARU

JKNS

km		201		502		508		504	
						⑦		①–⑥	
0	**Tenom** d.	...	...	0730	...	1230	...	1300	...
49	Beaufort a.	...	...	0951	...	1455	...	1545	...
49	Beaufort d.	0500	...	1101	...	1630	...	1700	...
101	Papar d.	0611	...	1216	...	1750	...	1828	...
134	**Tanjong Aru** ◐ a.	0657	...	1310	...	1845	...	1910	...

		101A	101		106A	102A		103	104
					⑦	①–⑥			⑦
Tanjong Aru ◐ d.	...	...	0745	...	...	...	...	1340	1725
Papar d.	...	...	0829	...	...	...	...	1428	1823
Beaufort a.	...	...	0940	...	...	...	...	1542	1934
Beaufort d.	...	0750	...	...	1300	1330	...	...	...
Tenom a.	...	1013	...	...	1510	1555	...	...	...

◐ – Kota Kinabalu.
Operator: Jabatan Keretapi Negeri Sabah (Sabah State Railways).

6020 BANGKOK - WOODLANDS

EOE

km		★	
0	**Bangkok** Hua Lampong. d.	1750	day 1
	Wang Po a.	0510	day 2
	Wang Po d.	0630	:
133	Kanchanaburi a.	0900	:
133	Kanchanaburi d.	1100	:
1161	Butterworth a.	1400	day 3
1161	Butterworth d.	1700	:
1549	Kuala Lumpur Sentral a.	2355	:
1549	Kuala Lumpur Sentral d.	0045	day 4
1923	**Woodlands** ◇ a.	1145	:

	★	
Woodlands ◇ d.	1600	day 1
Kuala Lumpur Sentral a.	2340	:
Kuala Lumpur Sentral d.	0200	day 2
Butterworth a.	0854	:
Butterworth d.	1130	:
Kanchanaburi a.	0925	day 3
Kanchanaburi d.	1215	:
Wang Po a.	|	:
Wang Po d.	|	:
Bangkok H. Lampong a.	1645	:

★ – EASTERN AND ORIENTAL EXPRESS – Luxury cruise train.
2014 departure dates:
From **Bangkok** on Jan. 3, 27, Feb. 5, Mar. 3, 12, 21, 30, Apr. 27, May. 6, Jun. 17, Jul. 29, Aug. 26, Sep. 26, Oct. 14, 27, Nov. 5, 21, 30, Dec. 23.
From **Woodlands** on Jan. 23, Feb. 1, 10, 19, Mar. 8, 17, 26, Apr. 3, 23, May. 2, Jun. 3, Jul. 25, Aug. 22, Sep. 20, Oct. 3, Nov. 1, 10, 26, Dec. 19.
Operator: Eastern and Oriental Express ✆ London 0845 217 0799.
◇ – Border point with Singapore.

THAILAND

Capital: **Bangkok** (GMT +7). 2014 Public Holidays: Jan. 1, Feb. 14, Apr. 6, 13, 14, 15, 16, May 1, 5, July 1, 11, Aug. 12, Oct. 23, Dec. 5, 10, 31.

Rail services are operated by State Railway of Thailand (www.railway.co.th). Trains may convey any combination of first, second or third class seating as shown in either columns or footnotes. Overnight trains may also convey sleeping cars or couchettes. Sleeping cars have lockable two berth compartments which convert into seats during the day. Couchettes are arranged 'open plan' along the coach and during the day the bottom bunks are used as seats. Dining cars are operated on all important trains. The Thailand Rail Pass offers twenty days unlimted travel in seated accommodation. Two passes are available. Pass A costs 1550 Baht and does not include supplements for express trains or sleeping cars. Pass B costs 3000 Baht and includes all supplements.

State Railway of Thailand — BANGKOK - BAN PLU TA LUANG and ARANYAPRATHET — 6050

km	3rd class only		275	283	281	367	389	279	277	391	371
										A	
0	**Bangkok** Hua Lampong	d.	0555	0655	0800	1010	1210	1305	1525	1635	1740
5	Makkasan	d.	0620	0716	0816	1030	1228	1317	1545	1654	1802
31	Hua Takhe ‡	d.	0703	0814	0857	1109	1304	1348	1618	1730	1842
61	Chachoengsao Junction	d.	0740	0859	0932	1145	1330	1421	1644	1755	1924
131	Si Racha Junction	d.	|	1013a	|	...	...	|	|	...	|
155	Pattaya	d.	|	1035a	|	...	...	|	|	...	|
184	**Ban Plu Ta Luang**	a.	|	1120a	|	...	...	|	|	...	|
122	Prachin Buri	d.	0858	...	1046	...	...	1522	1741	...	2032
161	Kabin Buri	d.	0948	...	1135	...	...	1612	1820	...	...
255	**Aranyaprathet**	a.	1135	...	...	...	...	1735	...	...	...

3rd class only		372	278	280	368	390	282	284	276	386
						B				①–⑤
Aranyaprathet	d.	...	...	0640	...	...	...	...	1355	...
Kabin Buri	d.	...	0630	0823	...	...	1225	...	1539	...
Prachin Buri	d.	0500	0719	0921	...	...	1316	...	1630	...
Ban Plu Ta Luang	d.	|	|	|	...	...	|	1335a	|	...
Pattaya	d.	|	|	|	...	...	|	1421a	|	...
Si Racha Junction	d.	|	|	|	...	...	|	1452a	|	...
Chachoengsao Junction	d.	0619	0831	1022	1235	1405	1429	1620	1800	2005
Hua Takhe ‡	d.	0701	0911	1107	1316	1435	1500	1711	1855	2038
Makkasan	d.	0751	0958	1148	1354	1512	1546	1807	1940	2116
Bangkok Hua Lampong	a.	0815	1015	1205	1410	1525	1600	1825	1955	2130

A – Also at 1700 Ⓐ, 1825.
B – Also at 0545 Ⓐ, 0705.
a – ①–⑤ only.
‡ – For Suvarnabhumi International Airport.

State Railway of Thailand — BANGKOK - HAT YAI - SUNGAI KOLOK — 6055

km			453	175	43	261		171	35	37	463	169	451		83	173	447	167	85	39	41		455	445	457
			3	23	2 🍷	3		C	A	B	3	C	3		B	C	3	C	B	2 🍷	2 🍷		3	3	3
0	**Bangkok** Hua Lampong	d.	...	...	0805	0920	...	1300	1445	1510	...	1535	...	...	1705	1735	...	1830	1930	2250	2250	...	...	...	...
117	Rachaburi	d.	...	...	1004	1145	...	1526	1701	1730	...	1820	...	...	1924	2007	...	2050	2150	0052	0052	...	...	...	...
229	Hua Hin	d.	...	...	1129	1335	...	1717	1845	1913	...	2010	...	...	2110	2154	...	2234	2336	0224	0224	...	...	...	...
377	Bang Saphan Yai	d.	...	...	1321	...	...	1946	2107	2143	...	2249	...	...	2341	0048	...	0111	0232	0433	0433	...	...	...	...
485	Chumphon	d.	...	...	1441	...	...	2121	2245	2324	...	0052	...	...	0127	0258	...	0328	0423	0559	0559	...	...	0630	...
651	Surat Thani ♥	d.	...	...	1645	...	...	0027	0126	0203	...	0348	...	...	0427	0603	0613	0628	0716	0805	0815	...	...	0946	...
773	Thung Song Junction	d.	...	...	...	...	...	0239	0322	0400	...	0556	...	...	0635	0832	0907	0855	0932	...	0954	...	...	1219	...
832	**Nakhon Si Thammarat**	a.	...	...	...	...	...	|	|	|	...	|	0600	...	|	0955	|	|	1055	...	|	...	0958	|	1415
845	Trang	a.	...	...	...	...	...	|	|	|	...	|	|	...	0805	...	|	1036	...	...	|	...	|	|	|
866	**Kantang**	a.	...	...	...	...	...	|	|	|	...	|	|	...	...	...	|	1120	...	...	|	...	|	|	|
862	Phatthalung	d.	...	...	...	...	...	0422	0506	0548	0602	0738	0822	...	...	...	1123	...	...	...	1112	...	1224	1420	1655
943	Hat Yai Junction	d.	...	0630	...	...	...	0645	0700	0735	0755	0930	1018	...	...	...	1312	...	...	...	1250	...	1433	1650	...
1009	Pattani	d.	...	0739	...	...	...	0810	...	0858	0919	1050	1145	...	...	...	1448	...	...	...	1404	...	1616	...	...
1055	Yala	d.	0630	0806	...	...	...	0848	...	0929	0958	1120	1227	...	...	...	1545	...	...	...	1430	...	1710	...	...
1159	**Sungai Kolok**	a.	0840	1000	...	...	...	1045	...	1120	1210	...	1450	...	...	...	1800	...	...	...	...	...	...	...	...

		458	262	40	446		174	456	168	448		86	452	170	42	44		84	172	464		38	176	36	454
		3	3	2 🍷	2		C	3	C	3		B	3	C	2 🍷	2 🍷		B	C	3		B	2	A	2
Sungai Kolok	d.	...	...	...	...	...	...	...	...	0630	...	...	0855	...	...	...	...	...	1130	1225	...	1420	1455	...	1525
Yala	d.	...	...	...	...	...	...	0635	...	0828	...	...	1122	1235	1455	...	...	...	1326	1432	...	1609	1637	...	1740
Pattani	d.	...	...	...	...	...	...	0716	...	0920	...	...	1206	1306	1519	...	...	...	1405	1528	...	1640	1704	...	...
Hat Yai Junction	d.	...	...	...	0640	...	...	0918	...	1058	...	...	1350	1445	1623	...	...	...	1539	1705	...	1810	1815	1845	...
Phatthalung	d.	0600	...	...	0853	...	...	1118	...	1300	...	...	1534	1623	1736	...	...	...	1713	1850	...	1947	...	2019	...
Kantang	d.	|	...	...	|	...	...	|	1240	|	...	...	|	|	|	...	...	...	|	...	...	|	...	|	...
Trang	d.	|	...	...	|	...	...	|	1329	|	...	...	|	|	|	...	...	1725	|	...	...	|	...	|	...
Nakhon Si Thammarat	d.	0830	...	...	|	...	1300	1355	|	|	...	1500	1805	|	|	...	...	|	|	...	...	|	...	|	...
Thung Song Junction	d.	...	...	...	1058	...	1424	...	1517	1531	...	1620	...	1813	1903	...	...	1912	1927	...	...	2138	...	2207	...
Surat Thani ♥	d.	...	...	1040	1325	...	1647	...	1738	1755	...	1837	...	2014	2041	2041	...	2104	2126	...	...	2328	...	2357	...
Chumphon	d.	...	...	1246	1630	...	1936	...	2031	...	...	2122	...	2323	2249	2249	...	2359	0044	...	...	0206	...	0234	...
Bang Saphan Yai	d.	...	...	1407	...	...	2128	...	2216	...	...	2308	...	0112	0019	0019	...	0148	0219	...	...	0336	...	0404	...
Hua Hin	d.	...	1410	1601	...	...	0045	...	0116	...	...	0147	...	0428	0222	0222	...	0415	0456	...	...	0605	...	0629	...
Rachaburi	d.	...	1600	1741	...	...	0244	...	0306	...	...	0404	...	0625	0350	0350	...	0608	0649	...	...	0749	...	0813	...
Nakhon Pathom	d.	...	1716	1826	...	...	0340	...	0405	...	...	0500	...	0726	0438	0438	...	0704	0744	...	...	0842	...	0903	...
Bangkok Hua Lampong	a.	...	1900	1945	...	...	0510	...	0535	...	...	0630	...	0900	0555	0555	...	0835	0915	...	...	1010	...	1030	...

A – INTERNATIONAL EXPRESS – See Table **6003**.
B – 🛏 1, 2 cl., [23].
C – 🛏 2 cl., [23].
♥ – Station is at Phun Phin, 13 km away.

State Railway of Thailand — BANGKOK - CHIANG MAI — 6060

km			403	407	401	409		111	9	201	3		209	211	109	207		1	13	105	107		51		
			3	3	3	3		23 🍴	2 🍷	23	2 🍷		3	23	B 🍴	3		A 🍴	A 🍴	23 🍷	B 🍴		B 🍴		
0	**Bangkok** Hualampong	d.	...	...	...	...	...	0700	0830	0925	1050	...	1120	1255	1245	1405	...	1810	1935	1950	2010	...	2200	...	...
58	Bang Pa In	d.	...	...	...	...	...	0823	|	1111	|	...	1251	1417	|	1537	...	|	|	2100	|	...	|	...	...
71	Ayutthaya	d.	...	...	...	0600	...	0837	0943	1126	1215	...	1305	1429	1418	1552	...	1945	2101	2114	2142	...	2230	...	...
133	Lop Buri	d.	...	...	0600	0715	...	0944	1029	1237	1300	...	1421	1539	1519	1721	...	2041	2155	2207	2236	...	0027	...	...
246	Nakhon Sawan	d.	...	0500	0807	...	...	1127	1138	1503	1407	...	...	1751	1713	1915	...	2213	2355	2336	0003	...	0212	...	...
319	Taphan Hin	d.	...	0624	0923	...	...	1257	1222	1635	1458	...	...	1915	1816	...	...	|	|	0052	0136	...	0328	...	...
389	Phitsanulok	d.	0555	0730	1050	...	...	1414	1319	1750	1600	...	...	...	1921	...	...	0011	0150	0205	0249	...	0441	...	...
485	Uttaradit	d.	0736	0912	...	...	...	1600	1445	...	1910	...	...	...	2113	...	...	|	0313	0352	0446	...	0620	...	...
488	Sila At	d.	0740	0923	...	...	...	1604	1452	...	1915	...	...	...	2127	...	...	0157	0327	0400	0507	...	0641	...	...
534	Den Chai	d.	...	1018	...	...	...	1720	1553	...	...	...	...	...	2302	...	...	0303	0433	...	0615	...	0746	...	...
642	Nakhon Lampang	d.	...	1241	...	...	...	...	1811	...	...	...	...	...	0047	...	...	0529	0707	...	...	...	1037	...	...
683	Khun Tan	d.	...	1335	...	...	...	...	|	...	...	...	...	...	0246	...	...	0640	0821	...	...	...	1144	...	...
729	Lamphun	d.	...	1422	...	...	...	...	2005	...	...	...	...	...	0338	...	...	0740	0924	...	...	...	1237	...	...
751	**Chiang Mai**	a.	...	1447	...	...	...	...	2030	...	...	...	...	...	0405	...	...	0815	0955	...	...	...	1305	...	...

			208	212	202		106	112	210		102	12	402		408	410	4		108	14	2		52		
			3	3	23		23 🍷	23 🍴	3		B 🍴	2 🍷	3		3	3	2 🍷		B 🍴	A 🍴	A 🍴		B 🍴		
Chiang Mai	d.	...	...	...	...	...	...	...	...	...	0545	0845	...	...	0920	...	...	...	...	1600	1700	...	1730	...	...
Lamphun	d.	...	...	...	...	...	...	...	...	...	0610	0913	...	...	0952	...	...	...	...	1624	1723	...	1753	...	...
Khun Tan	d.	...	...	...	...	...	...	...	...	...	0714	|	...	...	1039	...	...	...	...	1724	1824	...	1854	...	...
Nakhon Lampang	d.	...	...	...	...	...	...	...	...	...	0832	1054	...	...	1132	...	...	...	...	1830	1919	...	2000	...	...
Den Chai	d.	...	...	...	...	...	...	0720	...	...	1056	1253	...	...	1340	...	...	...	1905	|	2134	...	2228	...	...
Sila At	d.	...	...	...	...	...	0730	0832	...	...	1202	1346	...	...	1453	1630	1950	...	2010	2156	2234	...	2339	...	...
Uttaradit	d.	...	...	...	...	...	0735	0840	...	...	1210	1353	...	...	1459	1634	2000	...	2017	2204	|	...	2346	...	...
Phitsanulok	d.	...	...	...	0605	...	0859	1018	...	...	1401	1508	1345	...	1652	1810	2140	...	2206	2339	0009	...	0131	...	...
Taphan Hin	d.	...	...	0530	0722	...	0955	1133	...	...	1507	|	1500	...	1811	...	2238	...	2328	|	|	...	0247	...	...
Nakhon Sawan	d.	...	0500	0701	0839	...	1052	1252	...	...	1611	1652	1626	...	1945	...	0004	...	0033	0200	0212	...	0356	...	...
Lop Buri	d.	...	0705	0919	1104	...	1227	1448	1727	...	1755	1805	1835	...	...	...	0137	...	0216	0341	0354	...	0540	...	...
Ayutthaya	d.	...	0827	1028	1218	...	1328	1605	1847	...	1914	1853	...	...	...	...	0233	...	0314	0445	0459	...	0645	...	...
Bang Pa In	d.	...	0842	1040	1232	...	1340	1620	1901	...	|	|	...	...	...	...	|	...	|	|	|	...	|	...	...
Bangkok Hualampong	a.	...	1020	1210	1405	...	1505	1800	2035	...	2110	2025	...	...	...	...	0400	...	0510	0630	0650	...	0830	...	...

A – Conveys 🛏 1, 2 cl.
B – Conveys 🛏 2 cl., [23].

6065 BANGKOK - NONG KHAI and UBON RATCHATHANI — State Railway of Thailand

km		425	421	415	431	917	21	419	135	75	71	427	417	233	145	77	139	69	913	67	133	73	141
		3	3	3	3	3	2 🍷	3	23 ✕	23 🍷	23 🍷	3	3	3	23 ✕	23 🍷	B ✕	A ✕	3	A ✕	B ✕	23 🍷	23 ✕
0	**Bangkok** Hua Lampong d.	...	...	...	...	...	0545	...	0640	0820	1005	...	...	1140	1520	1835	1855	2000	...	2030	2045	2150	2225
71	Ayutthaya d.	...	...	...	...	...	0658	...	0825	0940	1124	...	...	1306	1650	2000	2025	2141	...	2151	2217	2309	2351
113	Saraburi d.	...	...	...	...	...	0733	...	0909	1018	1203	...	...	1352	1800	2038	2109	2224	...	2232	2302	2345	0032
125	Kaeng Khoi Junction d.	...	...	...	0500	...	0741	...	0922	1030	1214	...	...	1405	1813	2050	2122	2239	...	2252	2318	2355	0053
180	Pak Chong d.	...	...	...	0618	...	0852	...	1052	|	1325	...	...	1522	1944	|	2246	|	...	0024	|	0105	0226
264	Nakhon Ratchasima d.	...	0610	0620	0759	...	1001	1100	1212	|	1427	1422	1600	1650	2115	|	0007	|	...	0153	|	0231	0349
346	Bua Yai Junction d.	...	|	0758	0936	...	|	|	|	1448	|	|	1741	|	|	0106	|	0314	...	|	0424	|	|
450	Khon Kaen d.	...	|	0942	1120	...	|	|	|	1618	|	|	1903	|	|	0233	|	0455	...	|	0618	|	|
569	Udon Thani d.	...	|	1144	...	...	|	|	|	1805	|	|	2102	|	|	0430	|	0656	...	|	0844	|	|
621	**Nong Khai** a.	...	|	1225	...	1600	|	|	|	...	|	|	...	|	|	0515	|	0825	0910	|	0935	|	|
627	**Tha Na Laeng** (Laos) a.	...	|	...	...	1615	|	|	|	...	|	|	...	|	|	...	|	...	0920	|	...	|	|
376	Buri Ram d.	...	0836	...	...	...	1134	1300	1419	...	1614	1630	...	1910	2338	...	0222	...	...	0344	...	0428	0605
420	Surin d.	0535	0938	...	...	...	1209	1345	1507	...	1708	1718	...	2000	0030	...	0315	...	...	0432	...	0519	0701
515	Si Sa Ket d.	0712	1130	...	...	...	1318	1600	1700	...	1840	1903	...	...	0219	...	0507	...	...	0618	...	...	0900
575	**Ubon Ratchathani** a.	0825	1231	...	...	...	1400	1710	1800	...	...	2015	...	...	0335	...	0615	...	...	0725	...	...	1020

	234	424	72	416	76	428	136	146	432	426	22	914	418	142	74	78	68	420	918	70	140	134
	3	3	23 🍷	3	23 🍷	3	23 ✕	23 ✕	3	3	2 🍷	3	3	23 ✕	23 ✕	23 ✕	A ✕	3	3	A ✕	B ✕	B ✕
Ubon Ratchathani d.	...	...	...	...	...	0618	0700	0845	...	1233	1450	...	...	1650	...	...	1830	1845	...	...	1930	...
Si Sa Ket d.	...	...	...	...	...	0716	0804	0951	...	1330	1531	...	...	1757	1905	...	1930	1948	...	...	2028	...
Surin d.	0518	0704	0755	...	...	0912	0939	1130	...	1509	1641	...	...	1931	2025	...	2059	2122	...	...	2202	...
Buri Ram d.	0606	0756	0835	...	...	0957	1027	1226	...	1556	1715	...	...	2028	2110	...	2143	...	...	...	2250	...
Tha Na Laeng (Laos) d.	|	|	|	...	...	|	|	|	...	|	|	0950	...	|	|	...	|	...	1700	...	|	...
Nong Khai d.	|	|	|	...	0600	|	|	|	...	|	|	1000	1303	|	|	...	|	...	1715	1820	|	1915
Udon Thani d.	|	|	|	0550	0654	|	|	|	...	|	|	...	1349	|	|	1840	|	...	...	1920	|	2010
Khon Kaen d.	|	|	|	0801	0832	|	|	|	1355	|	|	...	1554	|	|	2011	|	...	...	2105	|	2216
Bua Yai Junction d.	|	|	|	0940	1015	|	|	|	1545	|	|	...	1742	|	|	2133	|	...	...	2253	|	0012
Nakhon Ratchasima d.	0822	0955	1018	1115	|	1155	1233	1454	1734	1815	1847	...	1925	2232	2254	|	2337	...	...	|	0051	|
Pak Chong d.	1009	...	1127	...	|	...	1400	1635	1913	...	1948	...	...	0003	0026	|	0127	...	...	|	0228	|
Kaeng Khoi Junction d.	1136	...	1228	...	1441	...	1530	1750	2030	...	2053	...	...	0132	0158	0208	0246	...	...	0257	0352	0445
Saraburi d.	1151	...	1241	...	1454	...	1545	1805	...	...	2106	...	...	0148	0210	0222	0304	...	...	0313	0413	0500
Ayutthaya d.	1240	...	1317	...	1535	...	1637	1905	...	...	2146	...	...	0237	0254	0305	0355	...	...	0404	0525	0550
Bangkok Hua Lampong a.	1415	...	1450	...	1710	...	1840	2100	...	...	2315	...	...	0425	0435	0450	0550	...	...	0600	0730	0800

A – Conveys 🛏 1, 2 cl., (23). B – Conveys 🛏 2 cl., (23).

6070 BANGKOK - NAM TOK — State Railway of Thailand

km	3rd class only	485	909	257	259
			Ⓒ A		
0	**Bangkok** Thon Buri d.	...	0630h	0750	1335
47	Nakhon Pathom d.	...	0820	0902	1503
63	Nong Pla Duk Junction d.	0435	0836	0922	1522
116	Kanchanaburi d.	0607	0927	1035	1626
193	**Nam Tok** a.	0820	...	1235	1830

3rd class only	260	258	910	486
			Ⓒ A	
Nam Tok d.	0520	1255	1425	1530
Kanchanaburi d.	0719	1448	1653	1741
Nong Pla Duk Junction d.	0835	1602	1755	1850
Nakhon Pathom d.	0921	1631	1809	...
Bangkok Thon Buri a.	1025	1740	1925h	...

A – Tourist train to River Khwae Bridge (a. 0935) and allied war cemetery at Kanchanaburi. Conveys (2). Ⓡ. Special fare payable.
h – Bangkok Hua Lampong.

6075 BANGKOK - SUVARNABHUMI INTERNATIONAL AIRPORT — Airport Rail Link

Bangkok Makksan - Suvarnabhumi International Airport (jouney 20 minutes):
0600, 0645, 0730, 0815, 0900, then every 45 minutes until 2100, 2145, 2230, 2315, 2400.

Suvarnabhumi International Airport - Bangkok Makksan (jouney 20 minutes):
0625, 0710, 0755, 0840, 0925, then every 45 minutes until 2125, 2210, 2255, 2340.

VIÊT NAM

Capital: **Há Nôi** (GMT +7). 2014 Public Holidays: Jan. 1, 30, 31, Feb. 1-5, Apr. 9, 30, May 1, Sep. 2.

Rail services are operated by Duóng Sát Viêt Nam (Viêt Nam Railways, www.vr.com.vn). Unless stated trains convey first and second class accommodation. First class has fou berth compartments, whilst second class has six. Dining facilities (meals brought to your seats) are provided on some trains.

6100 HÁ NOI - BEIJING — Duóng Sát Viêt Nam

km		DD3	M3	M1	T6	MR1	T190
		2		②⑤ A		B	
0	**Há Nôi** Gia Lam d.	0600	1355b	1830h	...	2140	...
162	Dong Dang a.	1135	1905	2240	...	0200	...
162	Dong Dang 🛃 d.	...	...	2359	...	0300	...
207	Pingxiang 🛃 a.	...	...	0141	...	0441	...
207	Pingxiang d.	...	...	0325	...	0641	...
430	Nanning a.	...	...	0635	...	1012	...
430	Nanning d.	...	...	0805	0805	...	1030
861	Guilin d.	...	...	1305	1305	...	1541
1409	Changsha d.	...	...	2039	2039	...	2244
1771	Wuhan Wuchang d.	...	...	0013	0013	...	0217
2307	Zhengzhou d.	...	...	0542	0542	...	0732
2996	**Beijing** xi a.	...	...	1208	1208	...	1422

	MR2	T5	M2	T189	M4	DD4
	B		④⑦ A			2
Beijing xi d.	...	1545	1545	1817	...	...
Zhengzhou d.	...	2216	2216	0110	...	...
Wuhan Wuchang d.	...	0330	0330	0623	...	...
Changsha d.	...	0654	0654	0951	...	...
Guilin d.	...	1429	1429	1746	...	...
Nanning a.	...	2015	2015	2330	...	...
Nanning d.	1820	...	2115	...	...	...
Pingxiang a.	2111	...	0030	...	...	...
Pingxiang 🛃 d.	2241	...	0240	...	...	...
Dong Dang 🛃 a.	2322	...	0221	...	...	...
Dong Dang d.	0022	...	0350	...	0520	1305
Há Nôi Gia Lam a.	0445	...	0810h	...	1040b	1902

A – 🛏 (4 berth) Beijing (**T5/6**) - Dong Dang (**M2/1**) - Há Nôi and v.v.
B – 🛏 1, 2 cl. Nanning (**T8701/2**) - Pingxiang (**MR2/1**) - Há Nôi and v.v.
b – Há Nôi Long Bien.
h – Há Nôi.

6105 HÁ NOI - LÂO CAÍ — Duóng Sát Viêt Nam

km		LC3	SP5	SP7	SP1	SP3	LC1	LC5	LC7
				B	A	A	A		
0	**Há Nôi** d.	0610	1940	2035	2110	2150	2200	2235	2305
6	**Há Nôi** Gia Lâm d.	0628	1958	2053	|	|	2218	2253	2323
155	Yên Bái d.	1056	2345	0035	0120	0205	0253	0337	0427
	Phō Lu d.	1508	0314	0344	0425	0506	0613	0657	0747
296	**Lâo Caí** a.	1635	0422	0435	0535	0615	0720	0805	0905

	LC4	LC6	LC2	SP8	SP2	SP4	SP6	LC8
			A	B	A	A		
Lâo Caí d.	0915	1805	1845	1930	2015	2100	2130	2210
Phō Lu d.	1050	1915	1957	2043	2125	2210	2240	2320
Yên Bái d.	1512	|	2325	2355	0033	0124	0341	0256
Há Nôi Gia Lâm a.	2000	0303	0348	0404	|	|	0637	0717
Há Nôi a.	2012	...	0405	0420	0455	0515	0655	...

A – 🛏 1, 2 cl., (12) Há Nôi - Lâo Caí and v.v.
B – Conveys private sleeping cars operated by Livitrans: www.livitrans.com

6110 HÁ NOI - HAI PHÒNG — Duóng Sát Viêt Nam

km		HP1	LP3	LP5	LP7
				2	
0	**Há Nôi** Long Bien d.	0600h	0930	1535	1810
6	**Há Nôi** Gia Lâm d.	0615	0950	1548	1825
57	Hai Duong d.	0717	1110	1659	1935
	Phú Thái d.	0745	1139	1728	2004
102	**Hai Phòng** a.	0815	1210	1800	2035

	LP2	LP6	LP8	HP2
		2		
Hai Phòng d.	0610	0855	1510	1840
Phú Thái d.	0643	0928	1543	|
Hai Duong d.	0715	0957	1615	1938
Gia Lâm d.	0830	1107	1730	2051
Há Nôi Long Bien a.	0840	1118	1740	2105h

HÁ NÔI - SAÍ GÔN 6115

Duóng Sắt Việt Nam

km		SE5 A	TN1 B	SE1 A	SE3 A	SE7 A♣
0	**Hà Nôi** d.	0900	1315	1900	2300	0615
87	Nam Dinh d.	1043	1514	2038	|	0756
116	Ninh Binh d.	1117	1549	|	|	0830
175	Thanh Hóa d.	1239	1727	2221	|	0940
319	Vinh d.	1503	2002	0056	0400	1156
522	Dông Ho'i d.	1925	0110	0455	0749	1543
688	Hué d.	2224	0428	0753	1039	1907
791	Dà Nang d.	0133	0739	1036	1309	2141
928	Quang Ngai d.	0404	1031	1326	|	0035
1095	Diêu Tri d.	0728	0347	1626	1811	0323
1315	Nha Trang d.	1118	1750	2026	2143	0737
1726	**Saí Gôn** (Ho Chi Minh) a.	1837	0305	0346	0430	1505

	SE8 A♣		SE6 A	TN2 B	SE2 A	SE4 A
Saí Gôn (Ho Chi Minh) d.	0630	...	0900	1315	1900	2300
Nha Trang d.	1328	...	1637	2147	0236	0536
Diêu Tri d.	1725	...	2048	0143	0619	0910
Quang Ngai d.	2034	...	2335	0500	0906	|
Dà Nang d.	2327	...	0236	0756	1155	1404
Hué d.	0212	...	0511	1117	1435	1628
Dông Ho'i d.	0533	...	0848	1436	1753	1928
Vinh d.	0931	...	1312	1953	2146	2313
Thanh Hóa d.	1159	...	1543	2300	0024	|
Ninh Binh d.	1310	...	1658	0029	|	|
Nam Dinh d.	1344	...	1332	0116	0215	|
Hà Nôi a.	1528	...	1926	0300	0351	0430

A – Conveys 1, 2 cl., and ✕. B – Conveys 2 cl., . ♣ – Runs only at peak periods.

MYANMAR

Capital: **Yangon** (GMT +6½). 2014 Public Holidays: Jan. 4, Feb. 12, Mar. 2, 7, 27, Apr. 13 -17, May 1, July 19, Aug. 2, Oct. 30, Nov. 28, Dec. 8, 25.

Rail service in Myanmar is provided by Myanmar Railways Corporation (MRC). Unless noted all trains convey first and second class seating (known locallly as upper and ordinary). All seating is allocated on purchase of tickets. Sleeping cars are operated on overnight trains and bedding is supplied. Sleepers have 6 compartments comprising 4 x 4-berth and 2 x 2-berth.

MYITKYINA - MANDALAY 6150

Myanmar Railways

km		37	56	42 B	34	58
0	**Myitkyina** d.	0430	0745	0910	1350	1510
299	Kawlin d.	1431	1919	0025	2355	0336
	Shwebo d.	⊖	⊖	⊖	⊖	⊖
529	Sagaing d.	⊖	⊖	⊖	⊖	⊖
539	**Mandalay** a.	2200	0415	1120	0720	1220

	37	33	55	57	41 B
Mandalay d.	0430	1300	1410	1620	1945
Sagaing d.	⊖	⊖	⊖	⊖	⊖
Shwebo d.	⊖	⊖	⊖	⊖	⊖
Kawlin d.	1107	1933	2208	0057	0608
Myitkyina a.	2200	0630	1045	1330	2105

B – and Myitkyina - Mandalay and v.v. ⊖ – Information unavailable at press date.

LASHIO - MANDALAY 6155

Myanmar Railways

km		132	
0	**Lashio** d.	0500	...
74	Hsipaw d.	0940	...
	Kyaukme d.	1125	...
	Gokteik d.	1325	...
213	Pyin Oo Lwin a.	1605	...
213	Pyin Oo Lwin d.	1740	...
280	**Mandalay** a.	2240	...

	131	
Mandalay d.	0400	...
Pyin Oo Lwin a.	0752	...
Pyin Oo Lwin d.	0822	...
Gokteik d.	1108	...
Kyaukme d.	1339	...
Hsipaw d.	1515	...
Lashio a.	1935	...

THAZI - YAKSAUK 6160

Myanmar Railways

km		141	143
0	**Thazi** d.	z	0600
197	Kalaw d.	1106	1252
	Aungban d.	1145	1342
	Heho d.	1343	1518
247	Shwenyaung a.	1445	1618
	Shwenyaung d.	...	1658
	Yaksauk a.	...	2015

	142	144
Yaksauk d.	...	0730
Shwenyaung a.	...	1015
Shwenyaung d.	0930	1045
Heho d.	1045	1155
Aungban d.	1215	1334
Kalaw d.	1304	1419
Thazi a.	z	2145

z – From / to Naypyitaw (Table **6165**).

MANDALAY - BAGAN - YANGON 6165

Myanmar Railways

km		8	6 A	4 A	120	62 B	142	32	12	
0	**Mandalay** d.	...	1500	1700	2100	...	...	...	0600	...
129	Thazi d.	...	1756	2001	|	...	z	...	0906	...
	Naypyitaw d.	2000	2059	2319	|	...	0036	0800	1219	...
***	**Bagan** a.	|	|	|	0450	...	|	|	|	...
***	**Bagan** d.	|	|	|	...	1700	|	|	|	...
335	Taungoo d.	2251	2357	0217	...	|	0515	1056	1527	...
548	Bago d.	0337	0428	0713	...	|	1209	1537	2022	...
622	**Yangon** a.	0530	0630	0915	...	1030	1440	1730	2230	...

	11	31	141	5 A	61 B	3 A	7	119	
Yangon d.	0600	0800	1100	1500	1600	1700	2030	...	...
Bago d.	0759	0959	1313	1654	|	1859	2229	...	...
Taungoo d.	1304	1443	1951	2135	|	0004	0318	...	...
Bagan a.	|	|	|	|	0930	|	|	...	...
Bagan d.	|	|	|	|	...	|	|	0700	...
Naypyitaw d.	1552	1730	0053	0013	...	0243	0600	|	...
Thazi d.	1901	...	z	0312	...	0557	...	|	...
Mandalay a.	2230	...	...	0630	...	0915	...	1430	...

A – and Yangon - Mandalay and v.v.
B – and Runs via Pyay line.
y – From Kalaw (Table **6160**), a. 1249.
z – To Kalaw (Table **6160**), a. 1051.
*** – Yangon - Bagan: *644 km*. Mandalay - Bagan: *179 km*.

YANGON - MAWLAMYINE - DAWEI 6170

Myanmar Railways

km		⑥	89	175	35
0	**Yangon** d.	0625	0715	1825	2100
78	Bago d.	⊖	0904	2019	2250
	Kyaikto d.	1100	1157	2320	0130
281	**Mawlamyine** a.	...	1650	0400	0600
281	**Mawlamyine** d.	...	...	0430	...
	Ye d.	...	...	1025	...
	Dawei Port a.	...	...	1900	...

	90	⑦	36	176
Dawei Port d.	...	...	...	0540
Ye d.	...	...	...	1438
Mawlamyine a.	...	...	...	2025
Mawlamyine d.	0800	...	1930	2055
Kyaikto d.	1233	⊖	2355	0130
Bago d.	1524	⊖	0245	0413
Yangon a.	1730	⊖	0445	0620

⊖ – Information unavailable at press date.

INDONESIA

apital: **Jakarta** (GMT +7). 2014 Public Holidays: Jan. 1, 14, 31, Mar. 31, Apr. 18, May 1, 15, 27, 29, July 28, 29, Aug. 17, Oct. 5, 25, Dec. 25.

ail services in Indonesia are operated by PT Kereta Api (Indonesian Railways, www.kereta-api.co.id). Trains may convey any of three classes of seated accommodation which e known locally as Eksekutif, Bisnis and Ekonomi, shown in the tables as 1, 2 and 3.

SUMATRA 6200

PT Kereta Api

Medan - Pematangsiantar: *127 km* Journey 4 hours

edan depart:
ematangsiantar depart:

Medan - Rantau Prapat: *266 km* Journey 5½ - 6 hours

edan depart: 0747, 1017, 1544, 2303.
antau Prapat depart: 0752, 1458, 1718, 2313.

Medan - Tanjung Balai: *173 km* Journey 4½ hours

edan depart:
njung Balai depart:

Padang - Pariaman: Journey 2 hours.

Padang depart:
Pariaman depart:

Palembang - Lubuk Linggau: *305 km* Journey 7 - 8½ hours

Palembang Kertapati depart: 0930◐, 2100.
Lubuk Linggau depart: 0930◐, 2100.

Palembang - Panjang ♠: *401 km* Journey 8 - 8½ hours

Palembang Kertapati depart: 0830◐, 2000.
Panjang depart: 0830◐, 2000.

- Tourist train. ◐ – Conveys 3rd class only. ♠ – Panjang is also known as Tanjungkarang Telukbetang.

6205 JAKARTA - BANDUNG

PT Kereta Api

km		20	22	24	26	28	30			
		12	12	12	12	12	12			
0	**Jakarta** Gambir d.	0545	0820	1050	1535	1805	1940	...	...	...
12	**Jakarta** Jatinegara d.	|	|	|	|	|	|	...	...	...
173	**Bandung** a.	0845	1116	1342	1847	2101	2240	...	...	...

	19	21	23	25	27	29			
	12	12	12	12	12	12			
Bandung d.	0500	0715	1205	1435	1615	1950	...	...	...
Jakarta Jatinegara a.	0749	1019	1502	1720	1900	2250	...	...	...
Jakarta Gambir a.	0759	1029	1512	1730	1910	2300	...	...	...

6210 JAKARTA - SEMARANG - SURABAJA

PT Kereta Api

km		48	14	108	16	2		50	52	54	120	106	64			12	18	44	56		36	92	4	140
		12	1	3	1	1		12	12	12	3	3	12			1	1	1♣	12		1	2	1	3
	Jakarta Pasar Senen d.	0600g	0730g	0745	0900g	0930g	...	0900g	1100g	1330g	1410	1515	1545	...	...	1645g	1725g	1745g	1840g	...	1930g	1950	2130g	2210
0	**Jakarta** Jatinegara d.	0609	|	|	0910	0939	...	0954	1109	1339	|	1524	1554	...	...	|	1735	1754	1849	...	1939	1959	2139	|
212	Cirebon d.	0851	1016	1045p	1142	1213	...	1234	1405	1628	1712p	1812p	1840	...	...	1940	2012	2039	2150	...	2220	2243	0013	0110p
288	Tegal d.	...	1121	1157	...	|	...	...	1532	...	1835	1930	2002	...	...	2047	...	2148	2309	...	2329	0005	|	0250
348	Pekalongan d.	...	1210	1253	...	1359	...	...	...	...	1939	2030	2055	...	...	2137	...	2240	...	...	0024	0115	|	0355
443	**Semarang** Tawang d.	...	1342	1429	...	1520	...	...	...	...	2148n	2220	2250	...	...	2259	...	0115	...	...	0205	0239	0317	0516n
644	Madiun d.	...	...	...	...	|	...	...	...	...	|	0215	|	...	...	...	...	0445	...	...	|	...	|	...
714	Kertosono d.	...	...	...	...	|	...	...	...	...	|	|	|	...	...	...	...	0543	...	...	|	...	|	...
737	Kediri d.	...	...	...	...	|	...	...	...	...	|	0405	|	...	...	...	...	...	...	...	|	...	|	...
881	**Malang** a.	...	...	...	...	|	...	...	...	...	|	0743	|	...	...	...	...	...	...	...	|	...	|	...
573	Cepu d.	...	...	...	...	|	...	...	...	...	0106	...	0130	...	...	...	...	...	...	...	0403	...	|	...
610	Bojonegoro d.	...	...	...	...	|	...	...	...	...	0143	...	0212	...	...	...	...	...	...	...	0440	...	|	...
713	**Surabaja** Pasar Turi a.	...	...	...	...	1913	...	...	...	...	0325	...	0406	...	...	...	...	...	...	...	0625	...	0710	...

		15	47	49	147	11		51	91	17	1	53	55		13	139	119	107	43		63	105	35	3
		1	12	12	3	1		12	2	1	1	12	12		1	3	3	3	1♥		12	3	1	1
Surabaja Pasar Turi d.	...	...	...	...	...	...	...	...	...	...	0815	...	...	...	...	...	1500	...	...	...	1700	...	1825	2015
Bojonegoro d.	...	...	...	...	...	...	...	...	...	...	|	...	...	...	...	...	1645	...	...	...	1845	...	2015	|
Cepu d.	...	...	...	...	...	...	...	...	...	...	|	...	...	...	...	...	1734	...	...	...	1925	...	2056	|
Malang d.	...	...	...	...	...	...	...	...	...	...	|	...	...	...	...	...	|	...	...	...	|	1345	|	|
Kediri d.	...	...	...	...	...	...	...	...	...	...	|	...	...	...	1600	...	|	...	...	...	|	1704	|	|
Kertosono d.	...	...	...	...	...	...	...	...	...	...	|	...	...	...	1723	...	|	...	1617	...	|	|	|	|
Madiun d.	...	...	...	...	...	...	...	...	...	...	|	...	...	...	1814	...	|	...	1730	...	|	1858	|	|
Semarang Tawang d.	...	...	...	...	...	0530	...	...	0800	...	1158	...	...	...	1920	1900n	1933n	2000	2103	...	2126	2222	2302	2358
Pekalongan d.	...	...	...	...	...	0653	...	...	0930	...	1356	...	...	...	2154	2033	2121	2200	2312	...	2336	0006	0029	|
Tegal d.	...	...	...	0600	0625	0744	...	...	1030	...	|	...	1620	...	2204g	2132	2216	2257	0007	...	0028	0105	0122	|
Cirebon d.	...	0455	0615	0740	0800p	0850	...	1000	1152	1400	1503	1515	1815	...		2248p	2356p	0043p	0144	...	0208	0220p	0238	0300
Jakarta Jatinegara a.	...		0858	1023	1100	1124	...	1238	1433	1640	1723	1755	2053			0134	0241	0325	0416	...	0444	0459	0511	0530
Jakarta Pasar Senen a.	...	0743g	0910g	1035g	1112	1134g	...	1250g	1445	1652g	1758g	1807g	2108g		...	0146	0253	0337	0443g	...	0456	0526	0538g	0557g

g – Jakarta Gambir. n – Semerang Poncol. p – Cirebon Prujakan. ♣ – To Jombang (a. 0615). ♥ – From Jombang (d. 1600).

6215 JAKARTA - YOGYAKARTA - SURABAJA

PT Kereta Api

km		134	112	72	98	102	10	40	76	116	126	88	114	118	34	32	100	110	8	104	42	96	128	74
		3	3	12	2	12	1	1	12	3	3	12	3	3	1	1	2	3	1	12	1	2	3	12
	Jakarta Pasar Senen d.	0530	0610	0630g	0650	0710	0800g	0830g	...	1130k	1300	...	1340	1610	1700g	1820g	1830	1855	2020g	2030	2100g	2115	2200	...
0	**Jakarta** Jatinegara d.	|	|	0639	|	0719	0809	0839	...	|	1309	...	|	|	|	|	1839	1904	2029	2039	2109	2124	2209	...
212	Cirebon d.	0845p	0906p	0923	0942	1004	1055	1122	...	1505p	1600p	...	1648p	1921p	1949	2108	2127	2151p	2310	2322	2348	0007	0100p	...
343	Purwokerto d.	1046	1118	1133	1152	1222	1301	1348	...	1727	1808	...	|	|	2202	2316	2338	0010	0119	0142	0212	0238	0348	...
370	Kroya d.	1123	1153	1207	|	1252	|	|	...	1801	|	...	|	|	|	|	|	0101	|	0210	|	|	|	...
445	Kutoarjo d.	1307	1321	...	1349	1424	|	1518	...	1946	2046	...	|	|	|	0114	|	0218	|	0338	|	0405	0525	...
508	**Yogyakarta** d.	...	1430	...	1457	...	1526	1605	1615	|	|	2215	|	|	0035	0206	0228	0328	0339	...	0422	0504	...	0725
568	Solo Balapan d.	...	...	...	...	...	1629	...	1705	2155j	2250j	2310	0011j	0311j	0125	0255	...	...	0442	...	...	0556	...	0820
663	Madiun d.	...	...	...	...	...	...	...	1823	2325	...	0028	0135	0503	0245	0415	...	...	...	...	...	...	...	0942
756	Kediri d.	...	...	...	...	...	...	...	|	|	...	0201	0312	0655	|	0552	...	...	...	...	...	...	...	|
826	Blitar d.	...	...	...	...	...	...	...	|	|	...	0321	0442	...	|	0712	...	...	...	...	...	...	...	|
900	**Malang** a.	...	...	...	...	...	...	...	|	|	...	0514	0654	...	|	0919	...	...	...	...	...	...	...	|
750	Jombang d.	...	...	...	...	...	...	...	2008	0045	...	...	...	...	0400	...	...	...	...	...	...	...	...	1101
831	**Surabaja** Gubeng a.	...	...	...	...	...	...	...	2127	0150	...	...	...	...	0515	...	...	...	...	...	...	...	...	1204

		101	97	109	7	39	73	87	127	133	125	71	117	115	103	111	99	95	41	75	9	31	33	113
		12	2	3	1	1	12	12	3	3	3	12	3	3	12	3	2	2	1	12	1	1	1	3
Surabaja Gubeng d.	...	...	...	...	...	...	0800	...	...	...	...	...	...	1200	...	...	...	...	...	1545	...	...	1815	...
Jombang d.	...	...	...	...	...	...	0902	...	...	...	...	...	...	1309	...	...	...	...	...	1647	...	...	1923	...
Malang d.	...	...	...	...	...	...	|	0800	...	...	...	...	...	|	...	...	...	...	...	|	...	1500	|	1600
Blitar d.	...	...	...	...	...	...	|	1002	...	...	...	...	...	|	...	...	...	...	...	|	...	1657	|	1080
Kediri d.	...	...	...	...	...	...	|	1125	...	...	...	...	1200	|	...	...	...	...	...	|	...	1818	|	1927
Madiun d.	...	...	...	...	...	...	1030	1258	...	...	...	...	1356	1433	...	...	...	...	...	1826	...	2000	2042	2107
Solo Balapan d.	...	...	...	...	0800	...	1147	1415	...	...	1530j	...	1546j	1611j	...	...	...	1800	...	1943	2000	2120	2205	2231
Yogyakarta d.	...	...	0715	0735	0856	1000	1252	1501	...	...	|	...	|	|	...	1800	1830	1902	1945	2029	2056	2210	2300	|
Kutoarjo d.	...	0700	0810	0833	|	1050	...	...	1629	1700	1734	...	|	1809	1830	1858	1931	1954	|	...	|	2305	|	|
Kroya d.	...	0815	|	0942	|	|	...	...	1756	1826	|	1913	|	1925	1950	2010	|	|	|	...	|	|	|	|
Purwokerto d.	...	0845	0941	1013	1116	1221	...	...	1835	1858	1926	1943	|	2003	2025	2040	2102	2132	2210	...	2315	0043	0113	|
Cirebon d.	...	1123	1230	1247p	1330	1434	...	...	2053p	2135p	2157p	2221	2257p	2254p	2312	2348p	0016	0038	0107	...	0130	0308	0325	0630
Jakarta Jatinegara a.	...	1402	1510	1528	1603	1706	...	...	2337	0019	0041	0051	0112	0142	0154	0227	0247	0316	0340	...	0403	0540	0557	0915
Jakarta Pasar Senen a.	...	1429	1522	1555	1630g	1718g	...	...	2349	0031	0053	0059g	0124	0214k	0221	0254	0309	0328	0352g	...	0430g	0607g	0624g	0927

j – Solo Jebres. k – Jakarta Kota. g – Jakarta Gambir. p – Cirebon Prujakan.

6220 BANDUNG - SURABAYA

PT Kereta Api

km		66	6	86	94	68	38			
		12	1	123	2	12	1			
0	**Bandung** d.	0700	0800	1535	1700	1900	2000	...	...	...
124	Tasikmalaya d.	0945	1043	1827	1957	2145	2245	...	...	...
156	Banjar d.	1036	1133	1917	2051	2235	2339	...	...	...
249	Kroya d.	|	1328	|	|	|	0120	...	...	...
324	Kutoarjo d.	1336	|	2235	|	0156	0234	...	...	...
387	**Yogyakarta** d.	1436	1515	2330	0112	0255	0330	...	...	...
447	Solo Balapan d.	1541	1604	0025	0205	0345	0420	...	...	...
542	Madiun d.	...	1720	0155	0325	...	0535	...	...	...
612	Kertosono d.	...	|	|	...	...	|	...	...	...
635	Kediri d.	...	|	0339	...	...	|	...	...	...
705	Blitar d.	...	|	0507	...	...	|	...	...	...
779	**Malang** a.	...	|	0726	...	...	|	...	...	...
629	Jombang d.	...	1835	...	0445	...	0650	...	...	...
710	**Surabaya** Gubeng a.	...	1928	...	0602	...	0810	...	...	...

	65	5	67	85	93	37			
	12	1	12	123	2	1			
Surabaya Gubeng d.	...	0730	...	...	1700	1900	...	...	...
Jombang d.	...	0826	...	...	1802	2009	...	...	...
Malang d.	...	|	...	1245	|	|	...	...	...
Blitar d.	...	|	...	1443	|	|	...	...	...
Kediri d.	...	|	...	1606	|	|	...	...	...
Kertosono d.	...	|	...	|	1822	|	...	...	...
Madiun d.	...	0945	...	1755	1930	2130	...	...	...
Solo Balapan d.	0700	1101	1900	1928	2050	2248	...	...	...
Yogyakarta d.	0800	1155	2000	2022	2144	2337	...	...	...
Kutoarjo d.	0858	|	2100	2116	|	|	...	...	...
Kroya d.	|	1344	|	|	|	0147	...	...	...
Banjar d.	1205	1519	2341	0027	0155	0321	...	...	...
Tasikmalaya d.	1300	1609	0033	0117	0251	0412	...	...	...
Bandung a.	1541	1843	0327	0410	0545	0702	...	...	...

AUSTRALIA

Capital: **Canberra** (GMT +10). 2014 Public Holidays: Jan. 1, 26, Apr. 18, 21, 25, June 9, Dec. 25, 26.

Interstate trains are operated by Great Southern Rail (www.gsr.com.au). Intrastate services are operated by Government owned agencies NSW Train Link (New South Wales, www.nswtrainlink.info), Queensland Rail (Queensland, www.qr.com.au), V/Line (Victoria, www.vline.com.au) and Transwa (Western Australia, www.transwa.wa.gov.au). Unless indicated all trains convey first and second class seated accommodation. On longer distance and overnight trains the first class accommodation is usually a private compartment which converts to sleeping berths for night time travel. The exact offering varies by operator and by train. Most longer distance trains also convey a refreshment facility. Due to the low frequency of trains reservations are recommended, even if they are not always compulsory. A national rail pass called the Ausrail Pass offers six months unlimited travel on CountryLink, GSR and most Queensland Rail train services. Reservations are required for all journeys and supplements may also be payable. Prices: 3 months AU$722.00, 6 months AU$990. See www.railaustralia.com.au/ausrail.php

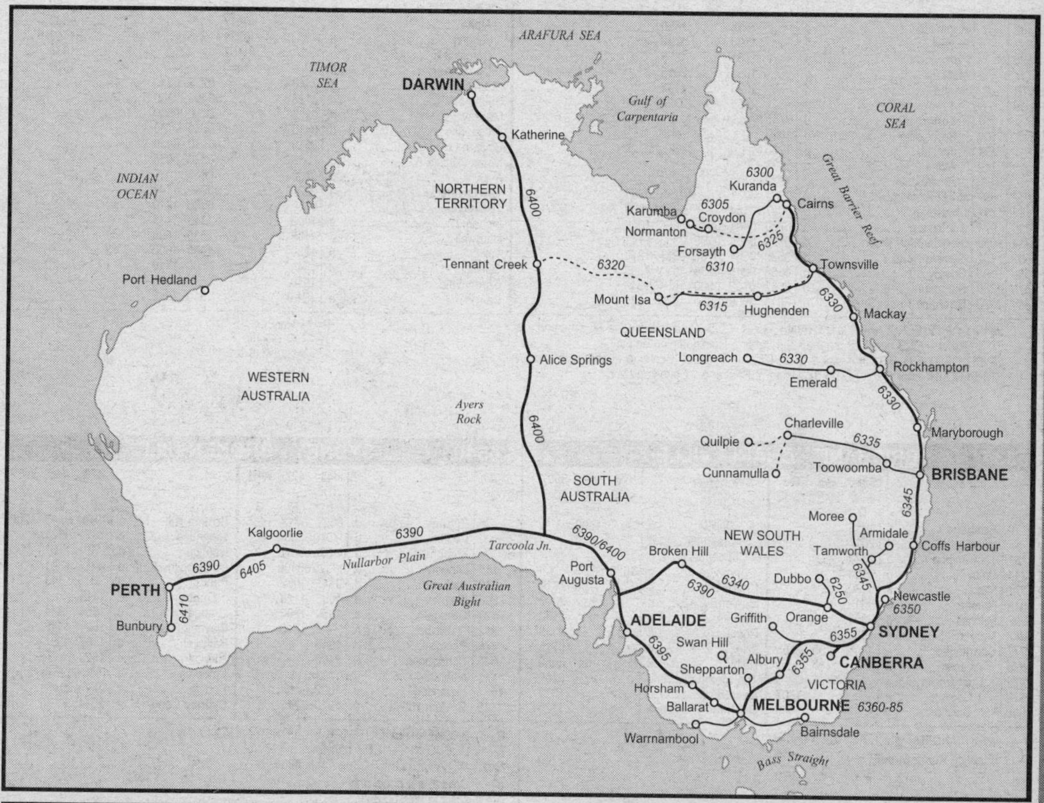

Queensland Rail — CAIRNS - KURANDA — 6300

km	From September 2	3K30 2a	3K32 2a	From September 2	3C61 2a	3C65 2a
0	**Cairns** d.	0830	0930	**Kuranda** d.	1400	1530
	Freshwater d.	0850	0950	Freshwater d.	1532	1702
33	**Kuranda** a.	1025	1125	**Cairns** a.	1555	1725

a – Not Apr. 7, 8, May 1, 2, Oct. 20, 21, Nov. 6, 7, Dec. 4, 5, 25.

CKST — CAIRNS - FORSAYTH — 6310

km		4 ③B	4 ④B		5 ⑤B	5 ⑥B
0	**Cairns** d.	0630	...	**Forsayth** d.	0830	...
33	Kuranda d.	0810	...	Einasleigh d.	1215	...
74	Mareeba d.	0930	...	Mount Suprise a.	1415	...
194	Almaden a.	1315	...	Mount Suprise d.	...	0815
194	Almaden d.	...	0800	Almaden a.	...	1145
302	Mount Suprise a.	...	1130	Almaden d.	...	1215
302	Mount Suprise d.	...	1215	Mareeba d.	...	|
357	Einasleigh d.	...	1445	Kuranda a.	...	1650
423	**Forsayth** a.	...	1730	**Cairns** a.	...	1830

B – SAVANNAHLANDER – [2]. Mar. 7 - Dec. 12.
Operator: Cairns Kuranda Steam Ltd ✆ +61 7 4053 6848.

Greyhound — TOWNSVILLE - TENNANT CREEK — 6320

km		481 🚌D	484 🚌D		884 🚌E	482 🚌D
0	**Townsville** d.	0700	...	**Tennant Creek** d.	2200	...
135	Charters Towers d.	0840	...	Barkly Homestead d.	0030	...
378	Hughenden a.	1135	...	Camooweal d.	0355	...
378	Hughenden d.	1210	...	**Mount Isa** a.	0600	...
490	Richmond d.	1335	...	**Mount Isa** d.	...	0710
634	Julia Creek a.	1520	...	Cloncurry d.	...	0836
634	Julia Creek d.	1600	...	Julia Creek a.	...	1010
768	Cloncurry d.	1745	...	Julia Creek d.	...	1040
886	**Mount Isa** a.	1905	...	Richmond d.	...	1215
886	**Mount Isa** d.	...	1930	Hughenden a.	...	1340
1074	Camooweal d.	...	2215	Hughenden d.	...	1415
1353	Barkly Homestead d.	...	0040	Charters Towers d.	...	1710
1547	**Tennant Creek** a.	...	0250	**Townsville** a.	...	1855

D – ②④⑤⑦. E – ①③⑤⑥. Operator: Greyhound Australia ✆ 07 3258 1600.

Queensland Rail — NORMANTON - CROYDON — 6305

km		③ A			④ A	
0	**Normanton** d.	0830	...	**Croydon** d.	0830	...
90	Blackbull a.	1115	...	Blackbull a.	1015	...
152	**Croydon** a.	1330	...	**Normanton** a.	1330	...

A – GULFLANDER – [2]. Services usually suspended mid Dec. - mid Feb.

Queensland Rail — TOWNSVILLE - MOUNT ISA — 6315

km	From September 2	3M34 ④⑦C		From September 2	3231 ①⑤C	
0	**Townsville** d.	1240	...	**Mount Isa** d.	1330	...
138	Charters Towers d.	1543	...	Duchess d.	1515	...
388	Hughenden d.	2019	...	Cloncurry d.	1745	...
502	Richmond d.	2246	...	Julia Creek d.	2100	...
648	Julia Creek d.	0211	...	Richmond d.	0005	...
780	Cloncurry d.	0520	...	Hughenden d.	0240	...
890	Duchess d.	0744	...	Charters Towers d.	0705	...
977	**Mount Isa** a.	0935	...	**Townsville** a.	1010	...

C – INLANDER – 🛏 1, 2 cl., [2] and 🍸 Townsville - Mount Isa and v.v. Ⓡ.

Trans North Bus — CAIRNS - KARUMBA — 6325

km		🚌 ①③⑤			🚌 ②④⑥	
0	**Cairns** Central d.	0630	...	**Karumba** d.	0630	...
33	Kuranda d.	0705	...	Normanton d.	0725	...
75	Mareeba d.	0740	...	Croydon d.	0925	...
109	Atherton d.	0820	...	Georgetown d.	1055	...
140	Herberton d.	0835	...	Mount Surprise d.	1240	...
160	Ravenshoe d.	0945	...	Undara d.	1305	...
211	Mount Garnet d.	1015	...	Mount Garnet d.	1355	...
287	Undara d.	1105	...	Ravenshoe d.	1450	...
321	Mount Surprise d.	1130	...	Herberton d.	1520	...
422	Georgetown d.	1325	...	Atherton d.	1540	...
579	Croydon d.	1505	...	Mareeba d.	1615	...
744	Normanton d.	1645	...	Kuranda d.	1640	...
820	**Karumba** a.	1730	...	**Cairns** Central a.	1730	...

Operator: Trans North Bus and Coach ✆ 07 4095 8644.

6330 CAIRNS, TOWNSVILLE and LONGREACH - BRISBANE

Queensland Rail

km	km	From September 2		A960	V9Q4	Q904	3936	Q902
				①④	③⑦	▽	②④⑥	
				C	A	B	D	B
0		**Cairns**	d.	...	0805	...	0715	...
23		Gordonvale	d.	...	0835	...	0748	...
87		Innisfail	d.	...	0955	...	0911	...
135		Tully	d.	...	1108	...	1025	...
178		Cardwell	d.	...	1153	...	1115	...
232		Ingham	d.	...	1243	...	1217	...
340		**Townsville**	a.	...	1428	...	1355	...
340		**Townsville**	d.	...	1428	...	1420	...
421		Ayr	d.	...	1543	...	1551	...
432		Home Hill	d.	...	1558	...	1610	...
531		Bowen	d.	...	1708	...	1733	...
596		Proserpine	d.	...	1758	...	1825	...
717		Mackay	d.	...	1953	...	2055	...
754		Sarina	d.	...	2023	...	2132	...
869		St Lawrence	d.	...	2153	...	2324	...
	0	**Longreach**	d.	0755	|	...	|	...
	108	Barcaldine	d.	1022	|	...	|	...
	194	Jericho	d.	1200	|	...	|	...
	249	Alpha	d.	1313	|	...	|	...
	422	Emerald	d.	1723	|	...	|	...
1042	687	Rockhampton	d.	2231	0037	...	0255	0750
1152	797	Gladstone	d.	0027	0154	...	0430	0900
1330	975	Bundaberg	d.	0250	0401	0515	0654	1042
1414	1059	Maryborough West	d.	0359	0454	0605	0803	1141
1507	1152	Gympie North	d.	0530	0604	0705	0934	1246
1550	1195	Cooroy	d.	0558	0645	0738	1021	1326
1575	1220	Nambour	d.	0647	0708	0800	1054	1349
1681	1326	**Brisbane** Roma Street	a.	0915	0900	0950	1335	1555

From September 2		AC37	Q301	AW57	VCQ5	AC37	Q303	Q303	AW57
		⑦	ex③	⑥	①⑤	②④	△	②⑦	②
		D	B	C	A	D	B	B	C
Brisbane Roma Street	d.	0900	1100	1310	1545	1325	1655	1655	1810
Nambour	d.	1110	1235	1515	1745	1535	1841	1841	2026
Cooroy	d.	1135	1258	1536	1807	1600	1859	1859	2047
Gympie North	d.	1230	1331	1630	1846	1655	1933	1933	2140
Maryborough West	d.	1410	1435	1755	1956	1820	2035	2035	2305
Bundaberg	d.	1600	1535	1905	2053	1930	2130	2140	0015
Gladstone	d.	1830	1715	2135	2240	2200	...	2320	0245
Rockhampton	d.	2050	1825	2320	0002	2355	...	0030	0435
Emerald	d.	|	...	0413	|	|	...	...	0928
Alpha	d.	|	...	0817	|	|	...	...	1332
Jericho	d.	|	...	0931	|	|	...	...	1443
Barcaldine	d.	|	...	1107	|	|	...	...	1636
Longreach	a.	|	...	1400	|	|	...	...	1900
St Lawrence	d.	2340	...	...	0222	0245	...	...	...
Sarina	d.	0125	...	...	0400	0430	...	...	...
Mackay	d.	0225	...	...	0450	0530	...	...	...
Proserpine	d.	0415	...	...	0630	0730	...	...	...
Bowen	d.	0510	...	...	0710	0830	...	...	...
Home Hill	d.	0635	...	...	0820	0955	...	...	...
Ayr	d.	0700	...	...	0835	1020	...	...	...
Townsville	a.	0825	...	...	0945	1145	...	...	...
Townsville	d.	0850	...	...	0955	1210	...	...	...
Ingham	d.	1045	...	...	1140	1415	...	...	...
Cardwell	d.	1135	...	...	1236	1505	...	...	...
Tully	d.	1230	...	...	1400	1600	...	...	...
Innisfail	d.	1340	...	...	1500	1710	...	...	...
Gordonvale	d.	1510	...	...	1615	1840	...	...	...
Cairns	a.	1545	...	...	1640	1915	...	...	...

A – SPIRIT OF QUEENSLAND TILT TRAIN – [bed] R, [2] and 🍸 Brisbane - Cairns and v.v.
B – TILT TRAIN – [12] and 🍸 Brisbane - Bundaberg, Rockhampton and v.v.
C – SPIRIT OF THE OUTBACK – [sleeper] 1, 2 cl., [2] [car] and 🍸 Brisbane - Longreach and v.v.
D – SUNLANDER – [sleeper] 1, 2 cl., [2] [car] and 🍸 Brisbane - Cairns and v.v.

R – RailBed
△ – ①③④⑤.
▽ – ①②④⑤⑥.

6335 BRISBANE - CHARLEVILLE

Queensland Rail

km	From September 2		3S86	🚌	🚌
			②④	③⑤	③⑤
			D		
0	**Brisbane** ‡	d.	1915	...	...
38	Ipswich	d.	2014	...	...
161	Toowoomba	d.	2320	...	...
244	Dalby	d.	0120	...	...
371	Miles	d.	0330	...	...
512	Roma	d.	0615	...	...
597	Mitchell	d.	0805	...	...
687	Morven	d.	1000	...	...
777	**Charleville**	a.	1145	1155	1155
875	Wyandra	a.	...	1315	|
972	Cunnamulla	a.	...	1425	|
876	Cooladdi	a.	...	...	1305
998	Quilpie	a.	...	...	1430

From September 2		🚌	🚌	3907
		③⑤	③⑤	③⑤
				D
Quilpie	d.	...	1500	...
Cooladdi	d.	...	1640	...
Cunnamulla	d.	1500	|	...
Wyandra	d.	1625	|	...
Charleville	d.	1735	1740	1815
Morven	d.	...	...	2000
Mitchell	d.	...	...	2150
Roma	d.	...	...	2335
Miles	d.	...	...	0215
Dalby	d.	...	...	0450
Toowoomba	d.	...	...	0700
Ipswich	d.	...	...	1015
Brisbane ‡	a.	...	...	1125

D – WESTLANDER – [sleeper] 1, 2 cl., [2] and 🍸. [R].
‡ – Brisbane **Roma Street**.

6340 SYDNEY - BROKEN HILL

NSW Train Link

km			445	427	WE1
			①		③
			E	F	G
0	**Sydney** Central	d.	0620	0718	1455
	Penrith	d.	0704u	0806u	|
	Katoomba	d.	0759u	0859u	|
155	Lithgow	d.	0839u	0940u	|
240	Bathurst	d.	0947	1052	|
290	Blayney	d.	1035	1138	|
323	Orange	d.	1059	1202	|
462	**Dubbo**	a.	|	1345	|
446	Parkes	d.	1248	|	|
546	Condobolin	d.	1400	|	|
816	Ivanhoe	d.	1631	|	|
1017	Menindee	d.	1822	|	|
1125	**Broken Hill**	a.	1910	*2245**	0630

		428	446	WE2
			②	②
		F	E	G
Broken Hill	d.	*0345**	0745	1900
Menindee	d.	|	0924	|
Ivanhoe	d.	|	1107	|
Condobolin	d.	|	1341	|
Parkes	d.	|	1443	|
Dubbo	d.	1415	|	|
Orange	d.	1554	1644	|
Blayney	d.	1621	1716	|
Bathurst	d.	1707	1801	|
Lithgow	d.	1623	1913s	|
Katoomba	d.	1905s	1954s	|
Penrith	d.	1956s	2045s	|
Sydney Central	a.	2044	2130	1015

E – BROKEN HILL OUTBACK EXPLORER – [2] and 🍸.
F – DUBBO XPT – [12] and 🍸.
G – INDIAN PACIFIC – See Table **6350**.
s – Calls to set down only.
u – Calls to pick up only.
* – Connection by 🚌.

6345 BRISBANE, ARMIDALE and MOREE - SYDNEY

NSW Train Link

km	km			036	244	224	032	034
				H	J	K	L	M
0		**Brisbane** Roma Street	d.	...	...	...	0555	*1510**
182		Casino	d.	...	...	...	0820	1930
291		Grafton City	d.	0515	...	...	0953	2058
379		Coffs Harbour	d.	0626	...	...	1105	2210
		Nambucca Heads	d.	0708	...	...	1147	2251r
		Macksville	d.	0721	...	...	1200	2305r
483		Kempsey	d.	0805	...	...	1243	2347
532		Wauchope	d.	0844	...	...	1322	0024
608		Taree	d.	0952	...	...	1441	0131
	0	**Armidale**	d.	|	...	0840	|	|
	124	Tamworth	d.	|	...	1027	|	|
	◐	**Moree**	d.	|	0805	|	|	|
	◐	Narrabri	d.	|	0910	|	|	|
	◐	Gunnedah	d.	|	1014	|	|	|
	168	Werris Creek	d.	|	1107	1107	|	|
	264	Scone	d.	|	1228	1228	|	|
	290	Muswellbrook	d.	|	1248	1248	|	|
794	387	Maitland	d.	1253	1355	1355	1732	0410
824	416	Broadmeadow	d.	1319	1419	1419	1754	0433
897	499	Gosford	d.	1419s	1521s	1521s	1855s	0538s
953	545	Hornsby	d.	1459s	1603s	1603s	1936s	0622s
987	579	**Sydney** Central	a.	1539	1638	1638	2012	0659

		033	243	223	035	031
		M	J	K	H	L
Sydney Central	d.	0711	0929	0929	1141	1441
Hornsby	d.	0750u	1005u	1005u	1220u	1520u
Gosford	d.	0832u	1044u	1044u	1300u	1601u
Broadmeadow	d.	0936	1145	1145	1405	1704
Maitland	d.	1000	1210	1210	1429	1727
Muswellbrook	d.	|	1316	1316	|	|
Scone	d.	|	1337	1337	|	|
Werris Creek	d.	|	1457	1457	|	|
Gunnedah	d.	|	1545	|	|	|
Narrabri	a.	|	1652	|	|	|
Moree	a.	|	1800	|	|	|
Tamworth	a.	|	...	1537	|	|
Armidale	a.	|	...	1735	|	|
Taree	d.	1241	...	...	1725	2008
Wauchope	d.	1348	...	...	1831	2113
Kempsey	d.	1426	...	...	1910	2152
Macksville	d.	1507	...	...	1955	2234
Nambucca Heads	a.	1519	...	...	2009	*2305**
Coffs Harbour	d.	1558	...	...	2050	2335
Grafton City	d.	1712	...	...	2215	0049
Casino	a.	1841	...	...	...	0219
Brisbane Roma Street	a.	*2234**	...	...	...	0453

H – GRAFTON XPT – [12]. [R].
J – MOREE EXPLORER – [12] and 🍸. [R].
K – ARMIDALE XPLORER – [12] and 🍸. [R].
L – BRISBANE XPT – [12] Brisbane - Sydney; [sleeper] 1 cl., [2] Sydney - Brisbane. [R].
M – CASINO XPT – [sleeper] 1 cl., [2] Casino - Sydney; [12] Sydney - Casino. [R].

r – Calls on request.
s – Calls to set down only.
u – Calls to pick up only.
* – Connection by 🚌.
◐ – Moree - Narrabri: *97 km*. Moree - Gunnedah: *190 km*. Moree - Werris Creek: *255 km*.

Sydney Trains — NEWCASTLE - SYDNEY — 6350

km			Ⓐ	Ⓐ	Ⓐ	Ⓐ	Ⓐ	Ⓐ	Ⓐ	Ⓐ	Ⓐ	Ⓐ	Ⓐ	and at the same minutes past each hour until	Ⓐ	Ⓐ	Ⓐ	Ⓐ	Ⓐ	Ⓐ	Ⓐ	Ⓐ	Ⓐ	Ⓐ
0	**Newcastle** d.	Ⓐ	0226	0419	0433	0518	0545	0618	0638	0718	0729	0819	0829		1319	1329	1416	1430	1510	1529	1619	1629	1719	1819
88	Gosford d.		0357	0536	0606	0635	0705	0735	0806	0835	0900	0936	1000		1436	1500	1533	1601	1638	1700	1736	1800	1836	1936
161	**Sydney** Central a.		0527	0656	0712	0756	0826	0855	0926	0955	1025	1056	1126		1556	1626	1659	1729	1759	1826	1856	1926	1956	2056

	Ⓐ	Ⓐ	Ⓐ	Ⓐ	Ⓐ		Ⓒ	Ⓒ	Ⓒ	Ⓒ	Ⓒ	Ⓒ	Ⓒ	Ⓒ	Ⓒ	Ⓒ	Ⓒ	Ⓒ	Ⓒ	Ⓒ	Ⓒ	Ⓒ	Ⓒ	Ⓒ	Ⓒ
Newcastle d.	1829	1919	1929	2029	2129	Ⓒ	0241	0432	0523	0632	0723	0833	0923	1033	1123	1233	1323	1433	1523	1633	1723	1833	1906	2007	2137
Gosford d.	2000	2036	2101	2200	2302		0414	0551	0651	0751	0851	0951	1051	1151	1251	1351	1451	1551	1651	1751	1851	1951	2039	2140	2313
Sydney Central a.	2126	2156	2226	2325	0029		0541	0710	0810	0910	1010	1110	1210	1310	1410	1510	1610	1710	1810	1910	2010	2110	2210	2310	*0045*

		Ⓐ	Ⓐ	Ⓐ	Ⓐ	Ⓐ	Ⓐ	Ⓐ	Ⓐ	Ⓐ	Ⓐ	and at the same minutes past each hour until	Ⓐ	Ⓐ	Ⓐ	Ⓐ	Ⓐ	Ⓐ	Ⓐ	Ⓐ	Ⓐ	Ⓐ	Ⓐ	Ⓐ
Sydney Central d.	Ⓐ	0145	0345	0445	0515	0545	0615	0645	0715	0745	0815		1315	1345	1415	1515	1545	1615	1645	1715	1745	1815	1915	2015
Gosford d.		0311	0512	0612	0635	0712	0735	0812	0841	0912	0935		1435	1513	1536	1635	1705	1735	1805	1833	1905	1935	2035	2135
Newcastle a.		0447	0642	0742	0751	0842	0904	0942	1002	1042	1051		1604	1647	1710	1751	1825	1851	1925	1949	2025	2051	2204	2304

	Ⓐ	Ⓐ	Ⓐ	Ⓐ		⑥	Ⓒ	Ⓒ	Ⓒ	Ⓒ	Ⓒ	Ⓒ	Ⓒ	Ⓒ	Ⓒ	Ⓒ	Ⓒ	Ⓒ	Ⓒ	Ⓒ	Ⓒ	Ⓒ	Ⓒ	Ⓒ	Ⓒ
Sydney Central d.	2115	2145	2245	2345	Ⓒ	0145	0445	0545	0715	0815	0915	1015	1115	1215	1315	1415	1515	1615	1715	1815	1915	2015	2145	2245	2345
Gosford d.	2235	2313	0015	0115		0311	0615	0717	0841	0936	1036	1136	1236	1336	1436	1536	1636	1736	1836	1936	2036	2142	2315	0015	0115
Newcastle a.	0004	0047	0149	0249		0447	0746	*0848*	0958	1103	1153	1303	1353	1503	1553	1703	1754	1903	1953	2103	2159	2313	0046	0146	0246

Operator: Sydney Trains ✆ 02 8202 2200.

NSW Train Link — SYDNEY - CANBERRA, GRIFFITH and MELBOURNE — 6355

km		631 ⑥⑦A	641 ⑥B	631 ⒶA	623 C	633 A	635 A	621 D			
0	**Sydney** Central d.	0657	0657	0704	0732	1208	1812	2032	...	...	...
143	Moss Vale d.	0839	0839	0854	0921	1354	2004	2218	...	...	...
222	Goulburn d.	0929	0929	0944	1012	1444	2054	2309	...	...	...
318	Queanbeyan d.	1051	|	1106	|	1606	2216	|	...	...	...
326	**Canberra** a.	1107	|	1122	|	1622	2230	|	...	...	...
320	Yass Junction d.	...	1053	...	1120	...	...	0017r	...	...	...
383	Harden d.	...	1144r	...	1211r	...	...	0107r	...	...	...
427	Cootamundra d.	...	1217	...	1246	...	...	0142	...	...	...
483	Junee d.	...	1258	...	1327	...	...	0220	...	...	...
580	Narrandera d.	...	1414	...	|	...	...	|	...	...	...
658	**Griffith** a.	...	1520	...	|	...	...	|	...	...	...
518	Wagga Wagga a.	...	...	...	1354	...	...	0247	...	...	...
547	The Rock d.	...	...	...	1414r	...	...	0305r	...	...	...
594	Culcairn d.	...	...	...	1441r	...	...	0332r	...	...	...
643	**Albury** 6301 a.	...	...	...	1511	...	...	0403	...	...	...
727	Wangaratta 6301 d.	...	...	...	1553	...	...	0445	...	...	...
765	Benalla 6301 d.	...	...	...	1617	...	...	0509	...	...	...
961	**Melbourne** S Cross a.	...	...	...	1830	...	...	0725	...	...	...

	632 A	642 ⑦B	634 ⑥⑦A	634 ⒶA	624 C	636 ⑥⑦A	636 ⒶA	622 D		
Melbourne S Cross d.	...	...	...	...	0830	...	...	1950	...	...
Benalla 6301 d.	...	...	...	...	1041	...	...	2154	...	...
Wangaratta 6301 d.	...	...	...	...	1106	...	...	2220	...	...
Albury 6301 d.	...	...	...	...	1149	...	...	2305	...	...
Culcairn d.	...	...	...	...	1221r	...	...	2334r	...	...
The Rock d.	...	...	...	...	1249r	...	...	0002r	...	...
Wagga Wagga d.	...	...	...	...	1307	...	...	0022	...	...
Griffith d.	...	0720	...	...	|	...	...	|	...	...
Narrandera d.	...	0821	...	...	|	...	...	|	...	...
Junee d.	...	0941	...	...	1351	...	...	0048	...	...
Cootamundra d.	...	1032	...	...	1438	...	...	0135	...	...
Harden d.	...	1108r	...	...	1514r	...	...	0241r	...	...
Yass Junction d.	...	1159	...	...	1605	...	...	0305r	...	...
Canberra d.	0650	|	1140	1153	|	1720	1725	|	...	...
Queanbeyan d.	0659	|	1149	1202	|	1729	1734	|	...	...
Goulburn d.	0820	1313	1310	1323	1715	1851	1856	0413	...	...
Moss Vale d.	0913	1413	1413	1415	1804	1944	1950	0502	...	...
Sydney Central a.	1056	1556	1556	1559	1953	2125	2137	0653	...	...

A – CANBERRA XPLORER – (12) and 🍷.
B – GRIFFITH XPLORER – (12) and 🍷.
C – MELBOURNE XPT – (12) and 🍷.
D – MELBOURNE XPT – 🛏 1 cl., (12) and ✕.
b – 1432 on ⑥⑦.
r – Calls on request.

V/Line — MELBOURNE - SHEPPARTON — 6360

km		①–⑤	⑥	⑦	①–⑤	①–⑤	①–⑤	⑦	①–⑤	①–⑤	⑥⑦
0	**Melbourne** S Cross d.	0701	0912	0930	0932	1252	1432	1512	1631	1822	1832
99	Seymour a.	0833	1027	1052	1053	1410	1554	1632	1808	1945	1951
99	Seymour d.	0845*	1032	1057	1058	1415	1605*	1640*	1815*	1950	1956
147	Murchison East d.	|	1107	1132	1133	1450	|	|	|	2025	2031
	Murchison d.	|	|	|	|	|	1653*	1728*	1903*	|	|
182	**Shepparton** a.	0955*	1141	1206	1207	1523	1723*	1800*	1935*	2059	2105

	①–⑤	⑥⑦ E	①–⑤	①–⑤	①–⑤	⑦	⑥	①–⑤	⑦	⑤
Shepparton d.	0631	0704	0850*	1040*	1250	1342*	1605	1606	1705	1800*
Murchison d.	|	|	0920*	1107*	|	1407*	|	|	|	1832*
Murchison East d.	0659	0732	|	|	1317	|	1633	1633	1733	|
Seymour d.	0734	0807	1015*	1155*	1352	1457*	1708	1708	1808	1920*
Seymour d.	0736	0809	1034	1214	1354	1512	1710	1710	1810	1947
Melbourne S Cross a.	0910	0928	1154	1335	1515	1635	1829	1835	1929	2140

E – 10 - 12 minutes later on ⑦.
* – By 🚌.

V/Line — MELBOURNE - ALBURY — 6365

km			C		①–⑤		D				
0	**Melbourne** S Cross d.	0710	0830	1200	1432	1801	1950	...	...	...	...
99	Seymour a.	0824	|	1314	1554	1930	|	...	...	...	...
99	Seymour d.	0826	0948u	1316	1605*	1932	2059u	...	...	...	...
196	Benalla d.	0930	1041	1420	1720*	2036	2154	...	...	...	...
234	Wangaratta d.	0955	11061	1445	1755*	2101	2220	...	...	...	...
301	Wodonga d.	1043	|	1533	1840*	2149	|	...	...	...	...
318	**Albury** a.	1055	1149	1545	1850*	2200	2305	...	...	...	...

	D		①–⑤		C					
Albury d.	0403	0635	0900*	1245	1511	1720	...	...	...	...
Wodonga d.	|	0645	0910*	1255	|	1730	...	...	...	...
Wangaratta d.	0445	0731	1000*	1341	1553	1816	...	...	...	...
Benalla d.	0509	0758	1035*	1408	1617	1843	...	...	...	...
Seymour d.	0605s	0900	1200*	1510	|	1945	...	...	...	...
Seymour d.	|	0902	1214	1512	|	1947	...	...	...	...
Melbourne S Cross a.	0725	1025	1335	1635	1830	2140	...	...	...	...

C – MELBOURNE XPT – (12) and 🍷 Sydney Central - Melbourne Southern Cross and v.v.
D – MELBOURNE XPT – 🛏 1 cl., (12) and ✕ Sydney Central - Melbourne Southern Cross and v.v.
s – Calls to set down only.
u – Calls to pick up only.
* – By 🚌.

V/Line — MELBOURNE - WARRNAMBOOL — 6370

km		①–⑤	⑥	⑦	①–⑤	⑥	⑦	①–⑤	①–⑤	⑥⑦	
0	**Melbourne** S Cross d.	0719	0800	0900	1300	1300	1600	1619	1900	1900	...
73	Geelong a.	0822	0855	0955	1352	1355	1655	1726	1957	1955	...
73	Geelong d.	0827	0900	1000	1357	1400	1710*	1735*	2002	2000	...
133	Colac d.	0926	1000	1100	1457	1500	1815*	1905*	2108	2102	...
267	**Warrnambool** a.	1045	1116	1218	1614	1617	1950*	...	2225	2220	...

	①–⑤	⑥	⑦		①–⑤	⑥	⑦		①–⑤	⑥⑦
Warrnambool d.	0530	0632	0710	...	1129	1143	1210*	...	1716	1725
Colac d.	0654	0751	0829	...	1250	1300	1405*	...	1835	1844
Geelong a.	0754	0850	0928	...	1348	1358	1520*	...	1934	1944
Geelong d.	0756	0852	0930	...	1350	1400	1535	...	1936	1946
Melbourne S Cross a.	0905	0954	1030	...	1454	1503	1634	...	2045	2049

☛ Additional trains are available Melbourne - Geelong and v.v.
* – By 🚌.

V/Line — MELBOURNE - TRARALGON - BAIRNSDALE — 6375

km		①–⑤ [R]	⑥ [R]	⑦ [R]	⑦ [R]	⑥ [R]	①–⑤ [R]	⑥⑦	①–⑤	⑥⑦ [R]	①–⑤ [R]
0	**Melbourne** S Cross d.	0712	0725	0804	1025	1156	1328	1336	1529	1816	1835
32	Dandenong d.	0755u	0800u	0840u	1100u	1239u	1406u	1419u	1609u	1859u	1917u
101	Warragul d.	0845	0859	0929	1152	1333	1455	1513	1700	1951	2007
131	Moe d.	0904	0918	0948	1213	1352	1514	1531	1718	2010	2026
145	Morwell d.	0922	0932	1001	1223	1404	1527	1541	1728	2023	2039
159	**Traralgon** a.	0932	0942	1011	1235	1414	1537	1553	1741	2033	2049
207	Sale d.	1012	1023	1052	1400*	1454	1617	1700*	1835*	2114	2129
276	**Bairnsdale** a.	1109	1118	1147	1500*	1546	1712	...	...	2209	2223

	①–⑤ [R]	⑥ [R]	①–⑤	⑦ [R]	⑥ [R]	①–⑤ [R]	⑦ [R]	⑥	⑥⑦ [R]	①–⑤ [R]
Bairnsdale d.	0610	0625	...	0745	1217	1230	1255*	...	1632	1800
Sale d.	0701	0717	0755*	0837	1309	1322	1415	1520*	1724	1852
Traralgon d.	0739	0755	0910	0916	1348	1402	1454	1629	1803	1932
Morwell d.	0752	0806	0919	0927	1359	1415	1503	1638	1814	1943
Moe d.	0804	0817	0929	0938	1413	1427	1512	1647	1825	1954
Warragul d.	0823	0836	0949	0957	1432	1446	1533	1708	1844	2016
Dandenong d.	0917s	0928s	1046s	1046s	1524s	1539s	1626s	1804s	1934s	2117s
Melbourne S Cross a.	0957	1006	1127	1130	1610	1625	1710	1850	2019	2206

☛ Additional trains are available Melbourne - Traralgon and v.v.
s – Calls to set down only.
u – Calls to pick up only.
* – By 🚌.

6380 MELBOURNE - BENDIGO - SWAN HILL and ECHUCA — V/Line

km		①-⑤	①-⑤ R	⑥⑦ R	⑥⑦ R	①-⑤	⑥⑦	①-⑤	⑥⑦	①-⑤	①③⑤ 🚌	②④ 🚌	①-⑤ R	⑥⑦ R	①-⑤ R	⑥⑦ R	①-⑤	⑤ 🚌	①-⑤	⑦	⑥	①-⑤	①-⑤	⑥⑦	⑤	⑥
0	**Melbourne** S Cross .. d.	0612	0742	0836	0936	1015	1036	1215	1216	1315	...	...	1515	1716	1820	1836	1920	...	2022	2020	2050	2122	2222	2220	2349	2350
38	Sunbury d.	0652u	|	|	1011u	1048u	1109u	1248u	1251u	1351u	...	...	1553u	1749u	|	|	1952u	...	2053u	2053u	2123u	2153u	2253u	2253u	0021u	0023u
78	Woodend d.	0720	0850	0939	1039	1109	1130	1309	1319	1419	...	...	1621	1817	1932	1942	2020	...	2121	2121	2151	2222	2321	2321	0049	0051
92	Kyneton d.	0728	0900	0949	1046	1117	1137	1317	1326	1426	...	...	1628	1824	1942	1952	2027	...	2128	2128	2158	2228	2328	2328	0056	0058
125	Castlemaine d.	0747	0926	1011	1109	1134	1155	1334	1345	1446	...	...	1647	1844	2006	2014	2044	...	2147	2147	2217	2245	2347	2347	0115	0117
162	**Bendigo** ☛ a.	0816	0954	1040	1131	1204	1219	1404	1409	1512	1530	1530	1710	1907	2034	2038	2109	2120	2212	2211	2241	2310	0012	0011	0140	0141
289	Kerang a.	|	1126	1212	|	1356*	1406*	|	|	...	|	1757	|	|	2208	2212	...	2340	...	...	...	...	...	...	...	...
345	**Swan Hill** a.	|	1208	1254	|	1439*	1448*	|	|	...	1840	1840	|	|	2251	2255	...	0025	...	...	...	...	...	...	...	...
222	Rochester a.	0940*	...	...	1232	...	...	1510*	1515*	...	...	...	1811	2008	...	...	...	...	...	...	...	...	...	...	...	...
248	**Echuca** a.	1003*	...	...	1257	...	...	1533*	1538*	...	...	...	1836	2033	..	...	...	...	...	...	...	...	...	...	...	...

	⑥	①-⑤	⑦	⑥ R	①-⑤ R	①-⑤ R	⑥⑦ R	①-⑤	⑥	⑦ R	①③⑤ 🚌	②④ 🚌	①-⑤	⑥	①-⑤	⑦	①-⑤	①-⑤ R	⑦	⑥ R	⑥⑦ R	⑥	⑦ R	⑤	①-⑤	⑥⑦
Echuca d.	...	...	...	0705	0720	...	...	0855*	0855*	0905	...	...	...	...	...	1250*	1255*	...	...	...	1610	...	...	...	...	...
Rochester d.	...	...	...	0728	0743	...	...	0920*	0920*	0928	...	...	...	...	...	1315*	1320*	...	...	...	1633	...	...	...	...	...
Swan Hill d.	...	...	...	|	|	0711	0710	|	|	|	0900	0900	...	1000*	1050*	|	|	1250	1305*	1330	|	...	1627	1525*	...	...
Kerang d.	...	...	...	|	|	0752	0751	|	|	|	|	0950	...	1046*	1136*	|	|	1330	1351*	1410	|	...	1707	1605*	...	...
Bendigo ☛ d.	0730	0745	0800	0829	0845	0921	0923	1030	1030	1030	1215	1215	1230	1232	1336	1424	1430	1503	1537	1544	1735	1840	1840	1847	2038	2046
Castlemaine d.	0751	0806	0821	0850	0908	0948	0947	1051	1053	1053	...	...	1251	1253	1357	1446	1451	1530	1558	1608	1756	1906	1907	1859	2101	2107
Kyneton d.	0811	0825	0841	0910	0930	1013	1012	1111	1113	1113	...	...	1311	1313	1416	1505	1511	1554	1617	1631	1816	1929	1935	1924	2121	2127
Woodend d.	0819	0833	0849	0918	0939	1024	1023	1120	1121	1121	...	...	1320	1321	1425	1513	1520	1604	1625	1641	1824	1937	1945	1942	2129	2135
Sunbury d.	0850s	0858s	0919s	0950s	1011s	|	|	1152s	1153s	1153s	...	...	1352s	1353s	1450s	1545s	1552s	|	1651s	|	1856s	2002s	|	2014s	2201s	2208s
Melbourne S Cross ... a.	0926	0931	0951	1023	1048	1134	1131	1228	1226	1226	...	...	1428	1426	1528	1623	1629	1711	1723	1743	1930	2034	2045	2049	2234	2241

☛ Additional trains are available Melbourne - Bendigo and v.v. s – Calls to set down only. u – Calls to pick up only. * – By 🚌.

6385 MELBOURNE - MARYBOROUGH and ARARAT — V/Line

km		①-⑤ R	⑥ R	⑦ R	②⑥ A	①-⑤	⑥	⑥ 🚌	①-⑤ R	⑥	①-④	①②④ 🚌	⑦	⑦	①-⑤	①-⑤	⑤ 🚌	①-⑤	⑥⑦ R	①-⑤ R	⑦	①-⑤	⑥⑦	①-⑤ 🚌	①-⑤
0	**Melbourne** S Cross .... d.	0804	0808	0828	0805	0906	0908	...	1208	1208	1308	...	1328	1508	1600	1638	...	1740	1808	1825	1912	2024	2047	2125	2154
41	Melton d.	0838	0836	0856	|	0942	0942	...	1236	1242	1343	...	1402	1542	|	|	...	|	1836	1858	1946	2058	2121	|	2228
53	Bacchus Marsh d.	0847	0854	0905	|	0954	0955	...	1253	1251	1355	...	1411	1551	|	|	...	|	1852	1908	1959	2107	2130	|	2237
82	Ballan d.	0909	0911	0922	|	1011	1012	...	1310	1308	1412	...	1428	1608	|	1729	...	1840	1909	1925	2016	2124	2147	|	2254
122	**Ballarat** a.	0934	0935	0940	|	1033	1034	1045	1333	1334	1428	1450	1450	1634	1714	1745	1755	1856	1929	1941	2032	2140	2203	2255	2310
180	**Maryborough** a.	|	|	|	|	|	...	1151	|	|	|	1557	|	|	1812	|	1902	|	|	|	|	...	...	...	...
210	**Ararat** a.	1034	1033	1038	1138	1216*	...	...	1434	1507*	1606*	...	1632*	1815*	...	1914*	...	2016*	2027	2040	2202*	...	...	...	...

		①-⑥ 🚌	①-⑤	⑥	⑥	⑥ R	①-⑤	①-⑤ R	①-⑥	⑦	⑦ R	D	①-⑤	⑥	⑥	①-⑤	⑦	①-⑤ R	⑥⑦	①⑤ A	⑥⑦ R	①-⑤ R	⑦	①-⑤	⑥⑦
Ararat d.	...	...	...	...	...	0710	...	0735	...	...	0815	...	0817*	0825*	0922*	1026*	1126*	1210	1525*	1531	1605	1654	1740*	1730*	...
Maryborough d.	...	0400	...	...	0706	|	0731	|	...	0811	|	0829	|	|	|	|	|	|	|	|	|	|	|	|	...
Ballarat d.	...	0510	0531	0614	0757	0813	0822	0837	0911	0902	0917	0938	1012	1012	1131	1212	1311	1312	1707	|	1707	1757	1911	1922	2113
Ballan d.	...	|	0547	0630	...	0829	...	0853	0927	...	0939	...	1028	1028	1147	1228	1327	1328	1729	|	1729	1819	1933	1944	2129
Bacchus Marsh d.	...	|	0604	0647	...	0846	...	0910	0944	...	0956	...	1045	1045	1204	1245	1344	1345	1746	|	1746	1848	1950	2001	2150
Melton d.	...	|	0613	0656	...	0854	...	0918	0954	...	1011	...	1053	1053	1212	1253	1352	1355	1754	|	1754	1858	1959	2014	2158
Melbourne S Cross ..... a.	...	0640	0648	0732	...	0923	...	0952	1029	...	1045	...	1133	1129	1248	1335	1430	1431	1827	1850	1827	1936	2035	2052	2234

☛ Additional trains are available Melbourne - Ballarat and v.v. A – See Table **6395**. D – ①②④⑤⑥.

6390 SYDNEY - PERTH — Great Southern Rail

km		WE1 R ③A			WE2 R ⑦A	
0	**Sydney** Central d.	1455	③	East **Perth** d.	1155	⑦
1125	Broken Hill a.	0640	④	Kalgoorlie a.	2230	:
1125	Broken Hill d.	0820	:	Kalgoorlie d.	0120	①
1688	**Adelaide** Parklands a.	1505	:	**Adelaide** Parklands a.	0720	②
1688	**Adelaide** Parklands d.	1840	:	**Adelaide** Parklands d.	1015	:
3690	Kalgoorlie a.	1910	⑤	Broken Hill a.	1725	:
3690	Kalgoorlie d.	2240	:	Broken Hill d.	1940	:
4343	East **Perth** a.	0910	⑥	**Sydney** Central a.	1110	③

For footnotes see Table **6400**.

6395 MELBOURNE - ADELAIDE — Great Southern Rail

km		8701 R B ②⑥			8702 R B ①⑤	
0	**Melbourne** S Cross d.	0805	...	**Adelaide** Parklands d.	0745	...
74	Geelong North Shore d.	0942	...	Murray Bridge d.	0949	...
265	Ararat d.	1140	...	Nhill d.	1305	...
381	Horsham d.	1255	...	Dimboola d.	1334	...
416	Dimboola d.	1318	...	Horsham d.	1358	...
454	Nhill d.	1343	...	Ararat d.	1531	...
734	Murray Bridge d.	1605	...	Geelong North Shore ... d.	1738	...
828	**Adelaide** Parklands a.	1750	...	**Melbourne** S Cross a.	1850	...

For footnotes see Table **6400**.

6400 DARWIN - ADELAIDE — Great Southern Rail

km		8506 R ③C			8505 R ⑦C	
0	**Darwin** △ d.	1000	③	**Adelaide** Parklands d.	1220	⑦
310	Katherine a.	1340	:	Snowtown d.	1446	:
310	Katherine d.	1820	:	Crystal Brook d.	1520	:
	Newcastle Waters d.	2220	:	Coonamia ◇ d.	1536	:
947	Tennant Creek a.	0253	④	Port Augusta a.	1645	:
947	Tennant Creek d.	0427	:	Port Augusta d.	1700	:
1414	**Alice Springs** a.	0910	:	**Alice Springs** a.	1345	①
1414	**Alice Springs** d.	1245	:	**Alice Springs** d.	1800	:
2661	Port Augusta a.	0648	⑤	Tennant Creek a.	2300	:
2661	Port Augusta d.	0730	:	Tennant Creek d.	0105	②
2751	Coonamia ◇ d.	0825	:	Newcastle Waters d.	0445	:
2775	Crystal Brook d.	0845	:	Katherine a.	0900	:
2827	Snowtown d.	0925	:	Katherine d.	1300	:
2973	**Adelaide** Parklands a.	1230	:	**Darwin** △ a.	1730	:

A – INDIAN PACIFIC – 🛏 1 cl., 12 and ✕ Sydney - Adelaide - Perth and v.v. From Sydney on ③ (also ⑥ Aug. 31 - Nov. 15). From Perth on ⑦ (also ③ Sep. 3 - Nov. 19 but runs to a different timetable. Departs Perth at 1155, Kalgoorlie 0140 ④, Adelaide 1000 ⑤, Broken Hill 1830 ⑤ arrives Sidney 1015 ⑥).

B – THE OVERLAND – 12 and 🍸 Melbourne - Adelaide and v.v.

C – THE GHAN – 🛏 1 cl., 2, ✕ (in 1st class) and 🍸 Darwin - Adelaide and v.v From Adelaide on ⑦ (also ③ May 21 - Aug. 20) From Darwin on ③ (also ⑥ May 24 - Aug. 23 but runs to a different time table. Departs Darwin at 0900, Katherine at 1645, Alice Springs at 1445 on ⑦, arrives Adelaide 1230 on ①.

△ – Darwin station is in the suburb of Berrimah. 🚌 connections to and from Darwin city centre are provided by the operator.

◇ – For Port Pirie.

6405 KALGOORLIE - PERTH — All trains 2 cl. and R — TransWA

km				KPA ①-⑤	KPA6 ⑥				KPA4 ⑦	KPL2 ①	KPL4 ⑤
0	**Kalgoorlie** d.	...	...	0705	0705	...	...	...	1405	1500	1500
250	Southern Cross d.	...	...	0912	0917	...	...	...	1612	1707	1715
371	Merredin d.	...	...	1023	1028	...	...	...	1723	1818	1829
427	Kellerberrin d.	...	...	1102	1107	...	...	...	1802	1857	1908
531	Northam d.	...	...	1209	1212	...	...	...	1907	2002	2013
641	Midland d.	...	...	1323	1323	...	...	...	2020	2115	2125
653	East **Perth** a.	...	...	1345	1345	...	...	...	2040	2135	2145

		PKA F	PKA1 ④⑤			PKA4 ⑥	PKL1 ①	PKL3 ⑤		
East **Perth** d.	...	0710	0710	...	...	1410	1515	1515	...	...
Midland d.	...	0727	0727	...	...	1427	1533	1532	...	...
Northam d.	...	0850	0850	...	...	1547	1645	1655	...	...
Kellerberrin d.	...	0956	0956	...	...	1653	1750	1800	...	...
Merredin d.	...	1027	1027	...	...	1728	1821	1831	...	...
Southern Cross d.	...	1144	1144	...	...	1845	1938	1948	...	...
Kalgoorlie a.	...	1400	1405	...	...	2100	2150	2205	...	...

F ①②③⑥

6410 PERTH - BUNBURY — All trains 2 cl. and R — TransWA

km		103	105								
0	**Perth** City d.	0930	1755	...	...	...	...	...	...	...	...
30	Armadale d.	0956	1825	...	...	...	...	...	...	...	...
85	Pinjarra d.	1042	1911	...	...	...	...	...	...	...	...
111	Waroona d.	1100	1929	...	...	...	...	...	...	...	...
136	Harvey d.	1121	1950	...	...	...	...	...	...	...	...
157	Brunswick Junction d.	1136	2005	...	...	...	...	...	...	...	...
183	**Bunbury** a.	1155	2024	...	...	...	...	...	...	...	...

	102	108								
Bunbury d.	0600	1445	...	...	...	...	...	...	...	...
Brunswick Junction d.	0617	1502	...	...	...	...	...	...	...	...
Harvey d.	0632	1517	...	...	...	...	...	...	...	...
Waroona d.	0656	1538	...	...	...	...	...	...	...	...
Pinjarra d.	0712	1555	...	...	...	...	...	...	...	...
Armadale d.	0755	1639	...	...	...	...	...	...	...	...
Perth City a.	0830	1712	...	...	...	...	...	...	...	...

NOTE: Trains will only call at intermediate stations if bookings are made in advance.

NEW ZEALAND

Capital: **Wellington** (GMT +12, add one hour in Summer). 2014 public holidays: Jan. 1, 2, Feb. 6, Apr. 18, 21, 25, June 2, Oct. 27, Dec. 25, 26.

Long distance rail services are operated by Tranz Scenic (www.tranzscenic.co.nz). Only one class of accommodation is offered, which is referred to in the tables as second class. All services operated by TranzScenic require compulsory reservation. The Scenic Rail Pass offers unlimited travel on the TranzScenic network (not the Capital Connection) and also allows one journey on the Interislander ferry service. Prices: 7 days NZ$599, 14 days NZ$699, 21 days NZ$799. For full information go to www.kiwirailscenic.co.nz.

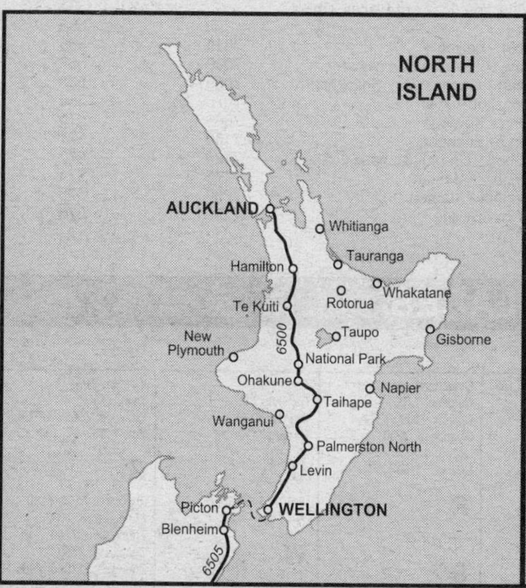

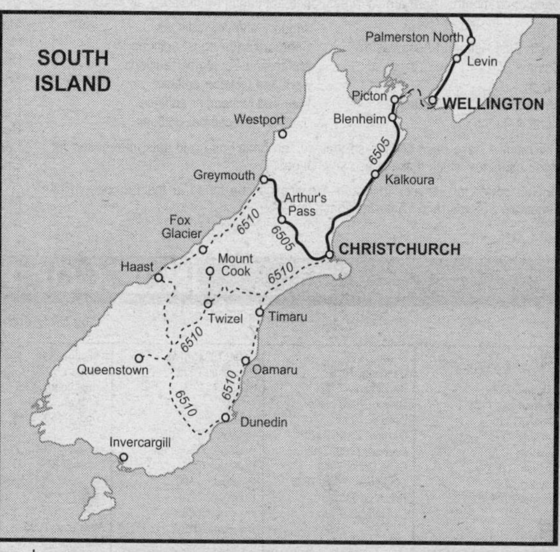

KiwiRail Scenic — AUCKLAND - WELLINGTON — 6500

km		1203	0201
			R
		①–⑤	①④⑥
		B	A
0	**Auckland** d.	...	0750
34	Papakura d.	...	0840
139	Hamilton d.	...	1015
183	Otorohanga d.	...	1054
334	National Park d.	...	1315
364	Ohakune d.	...	1345
544	**Palmerston North** d.	0615	1620
590	Levin d.	0653	|
632	Paraparaumu d.	0732	1730
681	**Wellington** ⊡ a.	0820	1825

	0200	1205
	R	
	②⑤⑦	①–⑤
	A	B
Wellington ⊡ d.	0755	1715
Paraparaumu d.	0845	1803
Levin d.	|	1842
Palmerston North d.	1000	1920
Ohakune d.	1245	...
National Park d.	1315	...
Otorohanga d.	1545	...
Hamilton d.	1630	...
Papakura d.	1755	...
Auckland a.	1850	...

Note: Trains are permitted to depart from intermediate stations earlier than advertised provided that all pre-booked passengers are on board.

A – NORTHERN EXPLORER – [2] and 🍸. Not Dec. 25.
B – CAPITAL CONNECTION – [2] and 🍸. Not Dec. 25.
– Calls to set down only.
– Calls to pick up only.
⊡ – See Table **6405**.

KiwiRail Scenic — PICTON - CHRISTCHURCH — 6505

km		803	0701
		R	R
		D	C
0	**Picton** ⊡ d.	...	1300
28	Blenheim d.	...	1333
157	Kaikoura d.	...	1528
285	Waipara d.	...	1730
318	Rangiora d.	...	1757
348	**Christchurch** a.	...	1821
348	**Christchurch** d.	0815	...
417	Springfield d.	0915	...
484	Arthur's Pass d.	1042	...
498	Otira d.	1103	...
	Moana d.	1147	...
565	Brunner d.	1221	...
579	**Greymouth** a.	1245	...

	0700	0804
	R	R
	C	D
Greymouth d.	...	1345
Brunner d.	...	1405
Moana d.	...	1442
Otira d.	...	1533
Arthur's Pass d.	...	1557
Springfield d.	...	1712
Christchurch a.	...	1805
Christchurch d.	0700	...
Rangiora d.	0728	...
Waipara d.	0756	...
Kaikoura d.	0954	...
Blenheim d.	1146	...
Picton ⊡ a.	1213	...

Note: Trains are permitted to depart from intermediate stations earlier than advertised provided that all pre-booked passengers are on board.

C – COASTAL PACIFIC – [2] and 🍸. Not May 7 - Sep. 26, Dec. 25.
D – THE TRANZALPINE – [2] and 🍸. Not Dec. 25.

⊡ – Wellington - Picton ⛴ service ('Interislander'). Journey 3½ hours.
From Wellington: 0700, 0900, 1500, 1700*, 2000.
From Picton: 0905*, 1100, 1400, 1900.
Temporay Timetable to Mar. 31 2014. * – No walk-on passengers
Operator: Interislander ✆ +64 4 498 3302.

SELECTED SOUTH ISLAND BUS SERVICES — 6510

km	Operator	AS	IC	IC	AS	NM	IC	AS	IC	
									⑤⑦	
0	**Christchurch** d.	0730	0730	0745	0800	0830	1400	1500	1715	...
82	Ashburton d.	0845	0850	0915	0920	0950	1525	1630	1850	...
160	Timaru d.	|	|	1030	1025	|	1700	1800	2030	...
240	Oamaru d.	|	|	1205	1200	|	1815	1910	2135	...
366	**Dunedin** a.	|	|	1345	1350	|	1950	2045	2305	...
144	Geraldine d.	0925	1000	...	...	1045	...	...	...	...
191	Fairlie d.	1000	1025	...	...	1125	...	...	...	...
341	**Mount Cook** a.	|	1300	...	...	|	...	...	...	...
341	**Mount Cook** d.	|	1425	...	...	|	...	...	...	...
281	Twizel d.	1120	1515	...	...	1330	...	...	...	...
435	Cromwell d.	1340	1715	...	...	1530	...	...	...	...
496	**Queenstown** a.	1430	1830	...	...	1630	...	...	...	...

Operator	IC	AS	NM	IC	IC	AS	AS	IC	
								⑤⑦	
Queenstown d.	...	...	0805	0745	...	...	1500	...	...
Cromwell d.	...	...	0910	0920	...	...	1555	...	...
Twizel d.	...	...	1110	1130	...	...	1805	...	...
Mount Cook a.	...	...	|	1230	...	...	|	...	...
Mount Cook d.	...	...	|	1345	...	...	|	...	...
Fairlie d.	...	...	1315	1550	...	...	1920	...	...
Geraldine d.	...	...	1410	1655	...	...	2000	...	...
Dunedin d.	0745	0800	|	|	1250	1430	|	1715	...
Oamaru d.	0930	1000	|	|	1500	1635	|	1855	...
Timaru d.	1120	1110	|	|	1620	1740	|	2030	...
Ashburton d.	1225	1210	1455	1735	1730	1845	2040	2135	...
Christchurch a.	1345	1350	1630	1855	1855	2000	2145	2250	...

km	Operator	IC	AS	AS	IC
0	**Greymouth** d.	...	...	...	1330
41	Hokitika d.	...	...	...	1455
89	Franz Josef d.	...	...	0800	1705
13	**Fox Glacier** d.	...	...	0845	1740
	Paringa d.	...	...	1005	...
31	Haast d.	...	...	1120	...
76	Wanaka d.	...	...	1435	...
93	**Queenstown** d.	0745	1500	1615	...
54	Cromwell d.	0850	1555	...	...
85	Alexandra d.	0920	1630	...	...
27	Roxburgh d.	0955	1715	...	...
17	Milton d.	1130	1830	...	...
73	**Dunedin** a.	1225	1930	...	...

Operator	IC	AS	AS	IC
Dunedin d.	...	...	1000	1355
Milton d.	...	...	1040	1445
Roxburgh d.	...	...	1220	1605
Alexandra d.	...	...	1250	1640
Cromwell d.	...	...	1340	1705
Queenstown d.	...	0810	1430	1815
Wanaka d.	...	0945	...	...
Haast d.	...	1250	...	...
Paringa d.	...	1435	...	...
Fox Glacier d.	0830	1525	...	...
Franz Josef d.	0915	1610	...	...
Hokitika d.	1230	...	...	...
Greymouth a.	1315	...	...	...

– Atomic Travel. ✆ 03 349 0697. IC – Intercity Coachlines. ✆ 09 583 5780. NM – Newmans. ✆ 09 583 5780.

BEYOND EUROPE
China

Introduction

The Beyond Europe section covers principal rail services in a different area of the world each month. There are six areas, each appearing twice yearly as follows:

India:	January and July editions
South East Asia and Australasia:	February and August editions
China:	March and September editions
Japan:	April and October editions
Africa and the Middle East:	May and November editions
North America:	June and December editions

The months have been chosen so that we can bring you up-to-date information for those countries which make seasonal changes.

Limited details of services in South America can be found in the European Rail Timetable Summer and Winter editions.

Contents

INDEX OF PLACES

by table number

China

Capital: Beijing (GMT + 8). 2014 Public Holidays: Jan. 1, 31, Feb. 1, Apr. 5, 6, 7, May 1, 2, 3, 31, June 1, 2, Sep. 8, Oct. 1, 2, 3.

Rail services in the People's Republic are generally operated by Chinese Railways. High-speed services are operated by China Rail High Speed. All times shown are Beijing tir unless otherwise stated. Schedules in this section are as per the latest information available and are liable to change at any time.

Trains are numbered using a combination of letters and numbers, with the letter indicating the type of train. The fastest trains carry prefixes **C** and **G**. These use the new hig speed railways and run at speeds up to 300 km/h on routes such as Wuhan to Guangzhou and Beijing to Tianjin. Other high-speed trains running at speeds of up to 200 km/h a prefixed with the letter **D** and **Z**. These trains use both dedicated high-speed railways and normal lines. Ordinary long distance trains are prefixed **T** or **K**. **T** trains make few stops and thus are considerably quicker than **K** trains. Most **K** trains in this section are only shown to highlight additional connections between major points and may not be show in their entirety. Also shown are a few trains without prefix letters. These are essentially similar to **K** trains but are slower still and are only shown in this section where there are higher category trains.

In total seven classes of accommodation are available, but not all will be available on every train. Seated accommodation can be either Hard, Soft, Second or First class. Ha seats are generally padded plastic seats. This is the cheapest class available and is often very busy. Soft seats are cloth covered and generally can be reclined. Second cla seats have five seats per row and are similar to economy class seating on an aeroplane. First class has four seats per row. Sleeping accommodation is available in either Ha Soft or Deluxe Soft classes. Hard sleepers consist of cabins of six berths (upper, middle and lower), with three beds attached to the wall on either side. The cabin is open and h no door. Soft sleepers have four berths and a sliding door. Deluxe Soft cabins have two berths and an en-suite bathroom. Generally **K**, **T** and **Z** trains convey Soft and Ha sleepers, and Hard Seats whilst **C**, **D** and **G** trains convey First and Second class seats. Exact train compositions are **not** shown in the tables.

All travel should be reserved in advance either at stations or through an agent. At many stations you may find it possible to only book for trains calling there, however in ma cities such as Beijing, Shanghai and Guangzhou you may be able to purchase all tickets. Some major stations may have English speakers available at ticket desks. Reservatio for **Z** and **D** usually open 10 - 21 days in advance. Other classes of train are only usually available 7 - 10 days before departure. In peak seasons such as Spring Festival holida reservations may only open 5 days before departure. Identity documents, such as passports for most foreigners or ID cards for Chinese citizens, are required to buy tickets and to board **C**, **D** and **G** trains.

More comprehensive train schedules are available (in Chinese!) from Chinese Railways official websites: www.chinamor.cn.net and www.tielu.org. Other unofficial websites su as www.cnvol.com and www.chinatravelguide.com offer timetable search facilities in English. A printed English language timetable is available at www.chinatt.org.

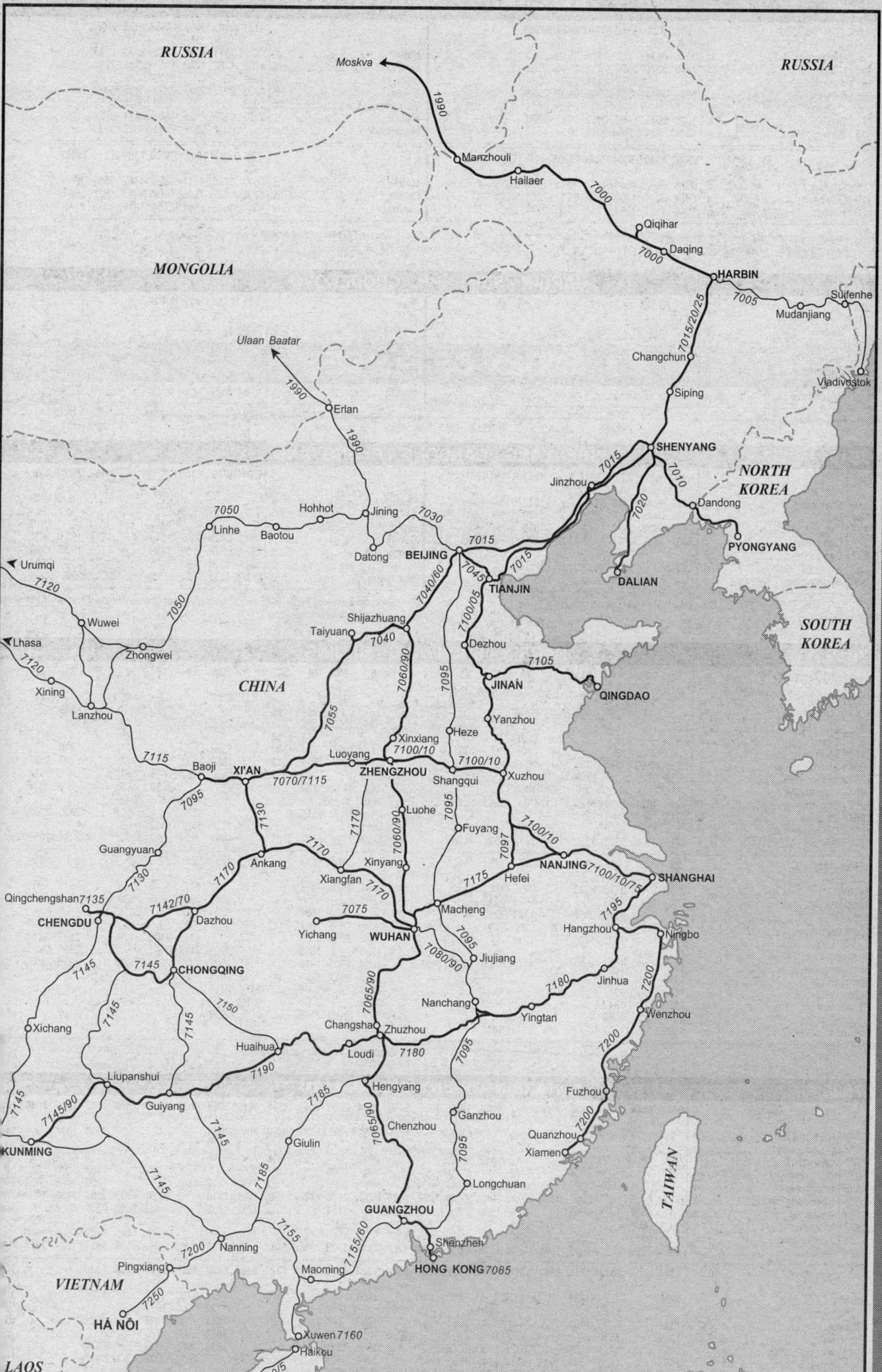
RUSSIA
Moskva
1990
Manzhouli
Hailaer
7000
Qiqihar
Daqing
HARBIN
7005
Suifenhe
Mudanjiang
Vladivostok
7015/20/25
Changchun
Siping
SHENYANG
MONGOLIA
Ulaan Baatar
Erlan
NORTH KOREA
Jinzhou
7010
7020
Dandong
PYONGYANG
DALIAN
7050
Linhe
Baotou
Hohhot
Jining
7030
Datong
BEIJING
7015
7045
TIANJIN
Urumqi
7120
Wuwei
Zhongwei
Lhasa
Xining
Lanzhou
Shijiazhuang
Taiyuan
7040
7040/60
7100/05
Dezhou
SOUTH KOREA
CHINA
7060/90
7095
7105
JINAN
QINGDAO
Yanzhou
7055
Xinxiang
Heze
7115
Baoji
XI'AN
Luoyang
ZHENGZHOU
7100/10
Shangqui
Xuzhou
7070/7115
7095
7130
7170
Luohe
Fuyang
7097
Guangyuan
Ankang
Xinyang
Xiangfan
Hefei
NANJING
7100/10/75
SHANGHAI
Qingchengshan
7135
7142/70
7175
Macheng
7195
CHENGDU
Dazhou
7075
Yichang
WUHAN
Hangzhou
Ningbo
CHONGQING
7080/90
Jiujiang
Jinhua
7200
7150
7065/90
Nanchang
7180
Yingtan
Wenzhou
Xichang
Changsha
Zhuzhou
Huaihua
Loudi
7190
Liupanshui
Guiyang
Hengyang
Fuzhou
7185
Ganzhou
Chenzhou
Quanzhou
Xiamen
KUNMING
7145/90
Giulin
TAIWAN
Longchuan
GUANGZHOU
7155
Shenzhen
Nanning
Pingxiang
7155/60
Maoming
HONG KONG
7085
VIETNAM
7250
HÀ NÔI
Xuwen
7160
Haikou
LAOS
7160/5
Sanya

7000 MANZHOULI and QIQHAR - HARBIN

Chinese Railways

km		20 ⑤A	K20 B	4192	K7092	2624	K7058			
0	**Manzhouli** d.	0034	0034	...	1805	1914	2050	...	...	...
186	Hailaer d.	0246	0246	0854	2031	2144	2321	...	...	...
289	Yakeshi d.	|	|	1018	2144	2301	0034	...	...	...
396	Boketu d.	0544	0544	1224	2342	0107	0235	...	...	...
	Qiqihar d.	|	|	|	|	0555	0714	...	...	...
776	Daqing d.	1049	1049	1959	0452	0721	0925	...	...	...
935	**Harbin** a.	1244	1244	2328**d**	0643	0934	1144	...	...	...

	4191	19 ⑦A	K19 B	K7057	2623	K7091			
Harbin d.	0836**d**	1511	1511	1758	2033	2115	...	...	...
Daqing d.	1052	1702	1702	1954	2235	2258	...	...	...
Qiqihar d.	1231	|	|	2153	0012	|	...	...	...
Boketu d.	1728	2217	2217	0234	0428	0408	...	...	...
Yakeshi d.	1937	|	|	0432	0628	0604	...	...	...
Hailaer d.	2101	0126	0126	0601	0811	0728	...	...	...
Manzhouli a.	...	0328	0328	0823	1032	0932	...	...	...

km		T5002	T310	T5004	T5006	T5008	T48 C	T312		
0	**Qiqihar** d.	0726	0832	1044	1501	1811	1855	2038	...	...
129	Daqing d.	0854	0944	1209	1623	1947	2001	2148	...	...
288	**Harbin** a.	1044	1131	1357	1811	2135	2144	2333	...	...

	T47 C	T5001	T5003	T5005	T309	T311	T5007		
Harbin d.	0530	0700	1111	1424	1442	1633	1840	...	...
Daqing d.	0706	0852	1308	1609	1651	1835	2021	...	...
Qiqihar a.	0817	1015	1441	1751	1819	1959	2145	...	...

A – Beijing - Moscow and v.v. For details see Table **1990**.
B – Beijing(**K19/20**) - Manzhouli and v.v.
C – Beijing(**T47/48**) - Qiqihar and v.v.
d – Harbin dong.

7005 HARBIN - SUIFENHE - GRODEKOVO

Chinese Railways

km			K7023	402 2	2727	310 2					
0	**Harbin** d.	...	2048	...	2258	...	...	...	...	...	...
161	Yimianpo d.	...	|	...	|	...	...	...	...	...	...
355	Mudanjiang a.	...	0251	...	0429	...	...	...	...	...	...
648	**Suifenhe** a.	...	0707	...	0912	...	...	...	...	...	...
648	**Suifenhe** 🏛 d.	...	...	0930	...	1311	...	...	...	...	...
669	**Grodekovo** ◐ a.	...	...	0653	...	1035	...	...	...	...	...

	309 2	2728	401 2	K7024						
Grodekovo ◐ d.	0551	...	0943	...	...	...	...	...	...	...
Suifenhe 🏛 a.	1110	...	1504	...	...	...	...	...	...	...
Suifenhe d.	...	1254	...	2110	...	...	...	...	...	...
Mudanjiang d.	...	1728	...	0139	...	...	...	...	...	...
Yamianpo d.	...	2031	...	0427	...	...	...	...	...	...
Harbin a.	...	2321	...	0715	...	...	...	...	...	...

d – Harbin dong.
◐ – Moscow time (GMT +4). Operator in Russia is **RZhD**.

7010 SHENYANG - DANDONG - PYONGYANG

Chinese Railways

km		K189	K27	K27 A	K7317		K957	K7591	K7315	
0	**Shenyang** d.	0101	0340	0340	0740	...	1318	1354	1649	...
84	Muxi d.	0239	0449	0449	0900	...	1429	1508	1801	...
217	Fengcheng d.	0420	0630	0630	1044	...	1620	1754	1951	...
277	**Dandong** a.	0507	0717	0717	1138	...	1730	1903	2050	...
277	**Dandong** d.	...	...	0935	...	...	...	...	...	...
282	Sinuiji 🏛 ⊗ d.	...	...	1346	...	...	...	...	...	...
506	**Pyongyang** ⊗ a.	...	...	1930	...	...	...	...	...	...

	K7316	K7592	K190	K7318		K958	K28	K28 A	
Pyongyang ⊗ d.	...	...	...	...	...	...	...	1010	...
Sinuiji 🏛 ⊗ d.	...	...	...	...	...	...	...	|	...
Dandong a.	...	...	...	...	...	...	...	1510	...
Dandong d.	0542	0723	0802	1345	...	1621	1831	1831	...
Fengcheng d.	0634	0829	0856	1439	...	1730	1920	1920	...
Muxi d.	0847	1110	1045	1628	...	1941	2104	2104	...
Shenyang a.	1002**b**	1233	1223	1755**b**	...	2042	2205	2205	...

A – ①③④⑥. Beijing(**K27/28**) - Dandong(**6/5**) - Pyongyang and v.v.
b – Shenyang bei.
⊗ – Korean Standard Time (GMT +9, 1 hour ahead of Chinese time). Times in North Korea are subject to confirmation.

7015 HARBIN - SHENYANG - BEIJING

China Rail High Speed

km	All trains prefix 'D'	12	4	14	10	2	24	52	28			6	26	74	20		102	16	18	30		22	8	
0	**Harbin** xi d.	...	...	...	...	...	...	...	0650	...	...	...	0928	...	...	...	1022	...	...	1426	...	...	...	...
**	Changchun d.	...	...	...	...	...	0740	...	|	...	...	...	|	1054	1117	...	|	...	...	|	...	1549	...	...
240	Changchun xi d.	...	...	...	...	...	|	...	0824	...	...	...	1050	|	|	...	1200	...	...	1547	...	|	...	...
358	Siping dong d.	...	...	...	...	...	0825	...	|	...	...	...	|	|	1208	...	|	...	...	1625	...	|	...	...
538	**Shenyang** bei a.	...	...	...	...	...	0925	...	1001	...	...	...	1233	1251	1308	...	1332	...	...	1731	...	1740	...	...
538	**Shenyang** bei d.	0718	0800	0830	0856	0920	0928	0942	1003	...	...	1213	1237	1255	1312	...	1335	1432	1512	1734	...	1742	1837	...
761	Jinzhou nan d.	0839	0921	|	1109	|	|	|	1120	...	...	1338	|	|	|	...	1456	1557	1633	1851	...	|	1956	...
804	Huludao bei d.	0856	|	|	|	1050	1058	|	|	...	...	|	1412	1430	|	...	|	|	1650	|	...	|	2034	...
926	Shanhaiguan d.	0945	1021	1049	1118	|	|	1243	1218	...	...	1443	|	|	|	...	1553	1659	1734	1948	...	|	|	...
964	Beidaihe d.	1018	|	|	1151	|	|	|	1250	...	...	|	|	1515	|	...	1626	1732	|	|	...	2030	2126	...
1090	Dangshan bei d.	|	1151	1218	|	1256	1306	1417	1346	...	...	1611	|	|	|	...	1721	1827	1902	|	...	|	|	...
1241	**Beijing** a.	1219	1300	1328	1352	1406	1417	1531	1455		...	1723	1728	1747	1753	...	1831	1936	2012	2222	...	2231	2330	...

All trains prefix 'D'		29	5	21	15		17	25	11	9		101	19	73		27	23	51	7	1		3	13	
Beijing d.	...	0700	0705	0713	0731	...	0915	1002	1240	1321	...	1351	1418	1428	...	1515	1533	1713	1745	1808	...	1819	1851	...
Dangshan bei d.	...	|	0815	0823	|	...	1025	1112	|	|	...	1501	|	|	...	|	1643	1825	1855	1920	...	1929	2001	...
Beidaihe d.	...	|	|	0919	0938	...	1121	1208	1442	|	...	|	1624	1630	...	1721	|	|	|	2016	...	|	|	...
Shanhaiguan d.	...	0935	|	|	|	...	|	1241	|	1556	...	|	|	1703	...	1753	|	2007	|	|	...	|	2130	...
Huludao bei d.	...	|	|	1031	1100	...	1233	|	1554	|	...	|	1735	|	...	1837	|	2055	2103	2129	...	2137	2213	...
Jinzhou nan d.	...	1032	1039	|	|	...	|	1342	1612	1657	...	1733	|	1800	...	|	1905	2112	2121	|	...	2155	2231	...
Shenyang bei a.	...	1148	1155	1201	1234	...	1412	1458	1728	1822	...	1854	1909	1916	...	2011	2022	2323	2244	2307**y**	...	2315	2353**y**	...
Shenyang bei d.	...	1152	...	1204	...	...	...	1501	...	...	...	1856	1911	1920	...	2013	2028	...	...	...	...	...	...	...
Siping dong d.	...	1253	...	1311	...	...	...	1614	...	...	...	2003	|	|	...	2114	2135	...	...	...	...	...	...	...
Changchun xi d.	...	1338	...	1349	...	...	...	1653	...	...	...	2042	|	|	...	2152	|	...	...	...	...	...	...	...
Changchun a.	...	|	...	1359	...	...	...	|	...	...	...	|	2100	2109	...	|	2217	...	...	...	...	...	...	...
Harbin xi a.	...	1509	...	...	...	...	...	1817	...	...	...	2213	...	...	...	2311	...	...	...	...	...	...	...	...

y – Shenyang.
** – Changhcun *0 km* - Siping dong *130 km*.

7020 HARBIN - SHENYANG - DALIAN

China Rail High Speed

km	All trains prefix 'D'	8042	8044		8046	8048	8002	8004	1302	8006	8050	1304	8008	8052	1306	8010	1308	8030	8054	8056	1310	1312	8058	135
0	**Harbin** xi d.	...	...	...	...	...	...	...	0705	...	...	0739	...	...	0829	...	0914	...	...	...	0948	1037	...	114
**	Changchun d.	...	...	...	...	...	0704	0800	|	0834	...	|	0923	...	|	1013	|	1135	...	...	|	|	...	|
240	Changchun xi d.	...	...	...	...	...	|	0812	0832	|	...	0912	|	...	0956	|	1040	|	...	...	1115	1218	...	130
358	Siping dong d.	...	...	...	...	...	0749	|	0910	|	...	|	1006	...	|	1059	|	1220	...	...	1153	|	...	|
538	**Shenyang** bei a.	...	...	...	...	...	0904**y**	0949	1014**y**	1024	...	1054**y**	1107	...	1150**y**	1158	1212	1325	...	...	1259	1402	...	144
538	**Shenyang** bei d.	0700	0728	...	0800	0830	0908**y**	0952	1017**y**	1027	1036	1058**y**	1110	1128**y**	1156**y**	1201	1216	...	1230	1325	1302	1405	1433	..
638	Anshan xi d.	|	0822	...	0853	|	|	1039	|	|	1117	|	1151	|	|	1248	1303	...	|	1402	1349	|	|	..
677	Haicheng xi d.	|	0838	...	|	0927	0955	|	|	1118	|	|	|	|	|	|	|	...	|	|	|	|	1538	..
715	Yinkou dong d.	|	0856	...	0921	|	1013	|	1122	|	1145	|	|	|	|	1316	|	...	1352	1430	1417	1508	1556	..
921	**Dalian** bei a.	0940**d**	1004	...	1035	1104	1130**d**	1215	1230	1244	1253	1311	1333	1346**d**	1406	1500	1457	...	1523**d**	1555	1531	1628	1721	..

All trains prefix 'D'		1314		8012	1316	8060	1318	8014	1320	8062	8034	1322	8016	8064	1324	8066	8032	1326	8018	8068	1328			13
Harbin xi d.	...	1200	...	...	1234	...	1317	...	1400	...	...	1454	...	...	1606	...	...	1700	...	...	1755	...	...	19
Changchun d.	...	|	...	1225	|	...	|	1448	|	...	1954	|	1630	...	|	...	1732	|	1823	...	|	...	...	|
Changchun xi d.	...	1321	...	|	1401	...	1444	|	1520	...	|	1627	|	...	1627	...	1744	1827	1836	...	1922	...	...	21
Siping dong d.	...	1359	...	1310	|	...	|	1539	|	...	2030	|	1715	...	|	...	1828	|	1920	...	|	...	...	|
Shenyang bei a.	...	1459	...	1421	1539	...	1632**y**	1638	1652	...	2135	1805	1820	...	1905	...	1933	2005	2019	...	2104**y**	...	...	22
Shenyang bei d.	...	1503	...	1425	1543	1617	1636**y**	1641	1655	1744**y**	...	1808	1824	1849**y**	1908	1930**y**	...	2009	2023	2052**y**	2108**y**	...	...	
Anshan xi d.	...	1544	...	1506	|	|	1713	1722	1742	1821	...	1855	1905	1932	|	2007	...	|	|	|	2145	...	...	
Haicheng xi d.	...	|	...	|	|	|	|	|	|	|	...	|	|	|	|	2023	...	|	2120	2145	2201	...	...	
Yinkou dong d.	...	|	...	|	|	1726	|	1756	|	|	...	|	|	|	|	|	...	|	|	|	|	...	...	
Dalian bei a.	...	1726	...	1654	1800	1834	1849	1922	1924	2008	...	2031	2041	2108	2125	2149	...	2232	2258**d**	2305	2321	...	...	

For footnotes and return service see next page.

China Rail High Speed — DALIAN - SHENYANG - HARBIN — 7020

All trains prefix 'D'		1351	8029	1353	8001	1301	8041	1303	1305	8043	8003	8045	1307	8047	8005	1309	8049		8031	1311	8007	1313	1315	8009	
Dalian bei	d.	...	...	...	0707	0733	0740	0804	0854	0820	0823	0903	0951	1000	1024	1055	1124	...	...	1147	1155	1235	1258	1313	...
Yinkou dong	d.	...	...	...	│	│	0855	0919	│	│	0945	│	1112	1128	│	1216	1246	...	...	│	│	│	│	1422	...
Haicheng xi	d.	...	...	...	│	│	0913	│	│	│	1003	1037	│	│	│	│	1304	...	...	1314	│	│	1425	1440	...
Anshan xi	d.	...	...	...	│	0906	│	│	1025	0957	│	│	│	1156	1207	1244	│	...	...	1330	1345	│	1441	│	...
Shenyang bei	a.	...	...	...	0936	0945	1010	1023y	1101y	1039y	1048y	1138	1214	1231y	1249y	1320y	1359	...	...	1406y	1426y	1452	1521y	1530	...
Shenyang bei	d.	0720	0742	0839	0939	0948	...	1026y	1104y	...	1051y	...	1218	...	1252y	1323y	...	...	1353	1409y	1429y	1455	1525y	1534	...
Siping dong **	d.	0827	0833	0946	1046	│	...	│	1215	...	1202	...	│	...	1403	│	...	...	1500	│	1540	│	│	│	...
Changchun xi	d.	0906	│	1031	│	1134	...	1210	1253	...	│	...	1404	...	│	1513	...	...	│	1553	│	1635	1705	│	...
Changchun	a.	│	0943	│	1129	│	...	│	│	...	1251	...	│	...	1451	│	...	...	1542	│	1623	│	│	1729	...
Harbin xi	a.	1037	...	1202	...	1253	...	1334	1418	...	...	...	1529	...	...	1638	...		...	1724	...	1800	1830	...	

All trains prefix 'D'		8051	1355	1317	8011	1319	8053	1321	8013	8055	1323	8057	1325	8015		8059		1327	8017	8061	8063	8065	8067		
Dalian bei	d.	1334	...	1345	1354	1430	1447	1518	1527	1545	1616	1616	1715	1716	...	1745	...	1748	1823	1855	1922	1950	2028	...	...
Yinkou dong	d.	1443	...	│	│	1545	│	1639	│	1714	1731	1750	│	│	...	│	...	1909	1938	│	│	2112	│	...	...
Haicheng xi	d.	1501	...	│	│	│	│	│	1707	│	│	1809	1842	1856	...	│	...	│	1956	│	│	2130	│	...	...
Anshan xi	d.	│	...	1528	1538	│	│	1707	1723	│	1759	1825	│	│	...	1947	...	1937	2012	│	2105	│	2219	...	...
Shenyang bei	a.	1557	...	1608	1613y	1653	1724y	1747	1758y	1817y	1841y	1906	1932	1941y	...	2022y	...	2017	2052	2119	2145	2225	2300	...	...
Shenyang bei	d.	...	1550	1611	1616y	1656	...	1750	1801y	...	1845y	...	1935	1944y	...	...	...	2020	2055	...	...	...	...	...	...
Siping dong	d.	...	1657	│	1727	1803	...	1857	1912	...	│	...	│	2049	...	...	...	│	2202	...	...	...	...	...	...
Changchun xi	d.	...	1736	1751	│	1842	...	1936	│	...	2029	...	2121	2128	...	...	...	2200	│	...	...	...	...	...	...
Changchun	a.	...	│	│	1810	│	...	│	1955	...	│	...	│	2138	...	...	...	│	2244	...	...	...	...	...	...
Harbin xi	a.	...	1902	1916	...	2001	...	2101	...	...	2200	...	2240	...	...	...	...	2319	...	...	...	...	...	...	...

d – Dalian.
y – Shenyang.

** – Changhcun *0 km* - Siping dong *130 km*.

Chinese Railways — HARBIN - TIANJIN and BEIJING — 7025

km			T188 ♦	K20 ♦	Z62	K28 ♦	T238 ♦	T244	T122 ♦	T18	T48 ♦	T272	T318	T184	T158
0	**Harbin**	d.	...	1317	...	...	1907	1916	...	2107	2209	...	0625	0910	1048
51	Changchun	d.	...	1600	2015	...	2128	2134	2117	│	│	2355	0935	1142	1258
546	**Shenyang** bei	a.	...	1918y	│	...	0005	0013	0021	0217	0257	0234	1213	1433	1523
546	**Shenyang** bei	d.	1725	1933y	│	2222y	0013	0020	0028	0223	0303	0242	1224	1439	1534
934	Shanhaiguan	d.	2336	0022	│	0305	0358	0405	0421	│	│	0643	1638	1810	│
972	Beidaihe	d.	│	│	│	0335	│	│	0504	│	│	│	│	1845	│
1235	**Tianjin**	a.	0257	0348	│	0648	0704	0710	0743	│	│	│	│	2130	│
1249	**Beijing**	a.	...	0546	0608	0831	...	...	...	0836	0914	0952	2020	...	2108

			T47 ♦	K27 ♦	T271	T237 ♦	Z61	T17	T121 ♦	T187 ♦	K19 ♦	T243	T157	T183	T317
Beijing	d.	...	1644	1727	1905	...	2210	2123	...	...	2300	...	0626	...	0936
Tianjin	d.	...	│	1906	│	1935	│	│	2010	2204	0041	0356	│	0559	│
Beidiahe	d.	...	1911	2159	2139	│	│	│	2238	│	│	0631	│	0850	1242
Shanhaiguan	d.	...	│	2243	2222	2255	│	│	2320	0119	0413	│	│	1015	1328
Shenyang bei	a.	...	0025	0321y	0142	0208	│	0336	0342	0647	0847y	1028	1221	1347	1758
Shenyang bei	d.	...	0031	...	0148	0216	│	0342	0356	...	0855y	1039	1227	1355	1806
Changchun	d.	...	│	...	0442	0532	0633	│	0705	...	1214	1331	1455	1649	2140
Harbin	a.	...	0515	...	...	0743	...	0826	...	...	1449	1545	1653	1906	0022

Chinese Railways — BEIJING - HOHHOT — 7030

km			K217	K43	K1177	T315	T177 ♦	K263	K597	K573	K89	K617	K273		
0	**Beijing**	d.	0035x	1055	1338	1529x	1518	1950	2025x	2038x	2215x	2249	2347b	...	...
196	Zhangjiakou nan	d.	0410	1435	1739	1856	1839	2326	2346	0012	0136	0220	0350	...	...
	Datong	d.	0700	1736	│	│	│	│	0234	0302	│	│	│	...	...
374	Jining nan	d.	0854	1929	2009	2032	2108	0234	0426	0456	0447	0507	0640	...	...
524	**Hohhot** dong	a.	1037	2118h	2201	2413	2231	0431h	0609	0654h	0636	0700	0823	...	...

km			T178 ♦	K1178	T316	K44	K618	K218	K598	K274	K264	K90	K574		
0	**Hohhot** dong	d.	0221	0200	0825h	0929h	1425	1812	1932	2120	2237h	2315	2259h	...	...
150	Jining nan	d.	0359	0428	0933	1133	1556	2003	2109	2351	0034	0110	0052	...	...
277	Datong	d.	│	│	│	1340	│	2156	2304	│	│	│	0307	...	...
455	Zhangjiakou nan	d.	0623	0717	1112	1615	1813	0043	0140	0224	0328	0407	0537	...	...
651	**Beijing**	a.	0941	1118	1424x	1942	2139	0411x	0458x	0707b	0715	0720	0910x	...	...

Chinese Railways — BEIJING - BADALING — 7035

km			S201	S203	S205	S207	S209	S211	S213	S215	S217	S219	S221	S223	
0	**Beijing** bei	d.	0612	0758	0834	0902	1057	1242	1314	1335	1524	1711	1741	2128	...
82	**Badaling** △	a.	0731	0920	0947	1015	1213	1401	1425	1450	1643	1830	1857	2244	...

			S208	S210	S212	S214	S216	S218	S220	S222	S224	S226	S228	S232	
Badaling △	d.	...	0823	1051	1119	1150	1340	1508	1552	1621	1733	1934	2006	2133	...
Beijing bei	a.	...	0947	1212	1240	1312	1500	1643	1725	1739	1854	2111	2143	2303	...

China Rail High Speed — BEIJING - TAIYUAN — 7040

km			D2001	G601	G91	G603	G605	G607	D2003	G609	D2005	G611	G613	G615	
0	**Beijing** xi	d.	0710	0735	0830	0915	1015	1132	1319	1510	1521	1700	1756	2021	...
244	Shijiazhuang	d.	0910	0857	0939	1044	1144	1254	1528	1639	1723	1829	1918	2150	...
384	Yangquan bei	d.	0955	0942	│	1129	1229	1339	│	1724	1808	1914	2004	2235	...
505	**Taiyuan**	a.	1033	1020	1100	1208	1307	1417	1645	1803	1845	1952	2043	2313	...

			G602	G92	D2002	G604	D2004	G606	G608	G610	G635	G612	D2006	G614	G616
Taiyuan	d.	...	0707	0830	0910	1143	1111	1240	1343	1438	1616	1806	1715	1920	2013
Yangquan bei	d.	...	0748	│	0950	1224	1152	1320	1424	1519	1657	1847	1757	2001	2054
Shijiazhuang	d.	...	0834	0950	1037	1311	1240	1406	1512	1605	1805	1933	1844	2048	2140
Beijing xi	a.	...	0953	1100	1256	1435	1456	1525	1638	1724	...	2052	2105	2207	2309

China Rail High Speed — BEIJING - TIANJIN — 7045

High-speed '**C**' trains (numbers **C20xx**, **C21xx** and **C22xx**). *120 km.* Journey 33 - 38 minutes.

Beijing nan depart: 0630, 0645, 0705, 0725, 0735, 0745, 0755, 0805, 0820, 0830, 0845, 0900, 0920, 0930, 0940, 0950, 1000, 1010, 1030, 1040, 1055, 1110, 1125, 1135, 1145, 1155, 1220, 1240, 1255, 1305, 1310, 1315, 1330, 1340, 1405, 1415, 1425, 1445, 1455, 1515, 1525, 1535, 1550, 1555, 1605, 1615, 1620, 1630, 1640, 1650, 1700, 1720, 1740, 1805, 1825, 1835, 1905, 1915, 1930, 1940, 1955, 2010, 2030, 2040, 2050, 2100, 2115, 2130, 2140, 2155, 2210, 2225, 2300.

Tianjin depart: 0625, 0640, 0650, 0710, 0720, 0740, 0755, 0800, 0810, 0825, 0840, 0845, 0905, 0910, 0925, 0935, 0955, 1010, 1020, 1035, 1045, 1100, 1120, 1125, 1130, 1150, 1200, 1220, 1225, 1245, 1310, 1325, 1350, 1405, 1410, 1425, 1435, 1440, 1450, 1500, 1510, 1515, 1520, 1535, 1555, 1605, 1615, 1630, 1645, 1705, 1725, 1735, 1750, 1800, 1815, 1830, 1850, 1910, 1930, 1940, 2005, 2015, 2020, 2030, 2055, 2105, 2120, 2135, 2150, 2200, 2215, 2245.

CR* — HOHHOT - LANZHOU — 7050

km			1717	2635	K43	K43B	T177 ♦
0	**Hohhot**	d.	1348	1433	2143	2143	2256d
165	Baotou	d.	1622	1703	0001	0001	0053
383	Linhe	d.	1935	2006	0248	0248	0317
676	Yinchuan	d.	0021	0112	0718	0718	0708
838	Zhongwei	d.	0305	0358	1000	1000	0939
1095	**Wuwei**	a.	│	│	1409	│	1332
970	Jingtai	d.	0541	0609	...	1237	...
1057	Beiyin xi	d.	0712	0741	...	1405	...
1144	**Lanzhou**	a.	0901	0926	...	1619	...

			T178 ♦	1718	2636	K44	K44B
Lanzhou	d.	...	...	0846	1146	...	1526
Beiyin xi	d.	...	...	1034	1320	...	1701
Jingtai	d.	...	...	1210	1458	...	1833
Zhongwei	d.	...	...	1453	1747	...	2059
Wuwei	d.	...	1039	│	│	1649	│
Yinchuan	d.	...	1742	1818	2043	0001	0001
Linhe	d.	...	2127	0005	0112	0401	0401
Baotou	d.	...	2351	0344	0418	0703	0703
Hohhot	a.	...	0156d	0600	0630	0903	0906

CR* — BEIJING - LANZHOU — 7055

km			T69 ♦	T175 ♦	T75	T41	Z55	T7 ♦	T27 ♦
0	**Beijing** xi	d.	1001	1156	1425	1443	1620	1712	2000
291	Shijiazhuang bei	d.	1302	1451	1658	1732	1859	2017	2239
395	Yangquan bei	d.	1416	1615	│	1846	│	2133	│
516	**Taiyuan**	a.	1518	1717	│	2011	2129	2236	0050
516	**Taiyuan**	d.	1528	1724	│	2019	2138	2246	0056
701	Lvliang	d.	1723	1918	│	2226	│	0042	│
790	Suide	d.	1823	2018	│	2350	│	│	│
1283	**Xi'an**	a.	│	│	0200	0502	│	0703	│
1267	Zhongwei	d.	2309	0119	│	...	0442	...	0751
1524	**Wuwei**	a.	0240	│	│	...	│	...	│
1573	**Lanzhou**	a.	...	0620	0853	...	0957	...	1302

		T28 ♦	T42	T176 ♦	T8 ♦	T76	Z56	T70 ♦
Lanzhou	d.	1510	...	1421	...	1752	2133	...
Wuwei	d.	│	...	│	...	│	│	0345
Zhongwei	d.	2019	...	2051	...	│	0242	0719
Xi'an	d.	│	1818	│	2234	0157	│	│
Suide	d.	│	0019	0217	│	│	│	1146
Lvliang	d.	│	0121	0329	0520	│	│	1251
Taiyuan	a.	0317	0332	0528	0706	│	0926	1437
Taiyuan	d.	0323	0344	0538	0715	│	0933	1447
Yangquan bei	d.	│	│	│	0828	│	│	1556
Shijiazhuang bei	d.	0540	0619	0755	0953	1214	1159	1721
Beijing xi	a.	0819	0908	1048	1240	1449	1435	2010

♦ – **NOTES** for Tables **7025 - 7055** (by train number):

T7/8 – Beijing xi(**T7/8**) - Chengdu and v.v.
K19/20 – Beijing(**K19/20**) - Manzhouli and v.v.
K27/28 – ①③④⑥. Beijing(**K27/28**) - Dandong(**6/5**) - Pyongyang and v.v.
T27/28 – Beijing xi(**T27/28**) - Lhasa and v.v.
T47/48 – Qiqihar(**T48/47**) - Beijing.
T69/70 – Beijing xi(**T69/70**) - Urumqi and v.v.
T121/122 – Changchun(**T122/21**) - Tianjin(**T123/24**) - Guangzhou and v.v.
T175/176 – Beijing xi(**T175/176**) - Xining xi and v.v.
T177/178 – Beijing(**T177/178**) - Urümqi and v.v.
T187/188 – Shenyang bei(**T188/87**) - Tianjin(**T185/86**) - Shenzhen and v.v.
T237/238 – Harbin(**T238/37**) - Tianjin(**T235/36**) - Guangzhou and v.v.

b – Beijing bei.
d – Hohhot dong.
h – Hohhot.
x – Beijing xi.
y – Shenyang.

△ – For Great Wall of China.

* – Operator: Chinese Railways.

7060 BEIJING - WUHAN (- GUANGZHOU)

China Rail High Speed

km	All trains prefix 'G'	93	551	541	507	651	501	821	71	531	653	509	83	95	73	571	511	79	825	655	831	513	545	621	553	75
0	**Beijing** xi d.	...	...	...	0700	0705	0730	...	0800	...	0821	0843	0900	...	...	0927	0937	1000	...	1005	...	1046	...	...	...	...
281	Shijiazhuang d.	...	...	...	0823	0828	0852	...	0922	0915	0949	1017	1009	...	...	1050	1059	1109	...	1134	...	1210	...	1233	...	...
403	Xingtai dong d.	...	...	...	|	0858	0922	...	|	0952	|	|	|	...	...	1120	|	|	...	|	...	|	...	|	...	...
456	Handan dong d.	...	...	...	0904	0916	|	...	1003	1010	|	|	|	...	...	1145	|	|	...	1215	...	1252	...	1314	...	...
516	Anyang dong d.	...	...	...	|	|	|	...	|	1030	1039	1110	|	...	...	|	|	|	...	|	...	|	...	1333	...	...
626	Xinxiang dong d.	...	...	...	0952	|	1012	...	|	|	1117	|	|	...	...	|	1230	|	...	1255	...	|	...	|	...	...
	Xi'an bei **7070** d.	...	...	...	|	|	|	0800	|	|	|	|	|	0948	...	|	|	|	1044	|	1120	|	...	|	...	...
693	**Zhengzhou** dong a.	...	...	...	1013	1019	1033	1022	1104	1112	1138	1150	1130	1150**z**	...	1239	1251	1230	1315**z**	1316	1343**z**	1346	...	1422	...	...
693	**Zhengzhou** dong d.	0800**z**	...	0830	1022	1026	1036	1042	1107	1117	1143	1154	1133	1153**z**	1209	1242	1254	1233	1318**z**	1320	1347**z**	1350	1410	1426	...	1435
	Xi'an bei **7070** a.	|	...	|	|	1249	|	|	|	|	1413	|	|	|	|	|	|	|	|	1543	|	|	|	|	...	|
848	Luohe xi d.	|	...	0906	|	...	|	1123	|	|	...	|	|	|	1251	|	1329	|	1404	...	|	|	1445	1504	...	1517
1030	Xinyang dong d.	|	0900	0953	|	...	1151	1204	|	1240	...	1311	|	|	1340	1355	|	|	1445	...	|	1505	|	|	1532	1604
1229	**Wuhan** a.	0955	1002	1036	1223	...	1235	1248	1306	1326	...	1400**h**	1318	1348	1423	...	1452**h**	1417	1528	...	1605	1549	1615	1628	1639	1650
	Changsha nan **7065** a.	1116	1131	1206	...	...	1412	1416	1434	1447	...	...	1440	1509	1552	...	...	1538	1657	...	1735	...	1744	1758	1807	1813
	Guangzhou nan **7065** a.	1339	1416	1446	...	...	...	1654	1738	1746	...	...	...	1730	1831	...	...	1759	1935	...	2016	...	2023	2048	2053	2058
	Shenzhen bei **7065** a.	...	...	...	...	...	...	1734	1816	...	...	...	...	...	1906	...	...	...	2016	...	...	...	...	...	...	2139

All trains prefix 'G'	835	659	517	839	855	81	89	87	547	855	503	661	851	663	521	505	665	523	635	525	669	527	561	563	565	567
Beijing xi d.	...	1208	1228	...	1300	1305	1330	1400	...	...	1437	1442	...	1447	1527	1540	1600	1618	...	1714	1738	1804	1811	1823	1910	1955
Shijiazhuang d.	...	1332	1352	...	1410	1427	1439	|	...	...	1600	1605	...	1624	1649	1709	1729	1742	1805	1836	1900	1927	1941	1952	2040	2118
Xingtai dong d.	...	1402	|	...	|	|	|	|	...	...	|	1635	...	1701	|	|	1759	|	|	1906	|	|	|	|	2110	2148
Handan dong d.	...	|	1433	...	|	1516	|	|	...	...	1641	1653	...	|	1730	1751	|	1823	1846	|	1941	2008	2022	2033	|	2206
Anyang dong d.	...	1432	|	...	|	|	|	|	...	...	1700	1712	...	1731	1749	|	|	|	|	1936	2000	|	|	2113	2142	2225
Xinxiang dong d.	...	|	|	...	|	|	|	|	...	...	|	|	...	1801	1817	|	|	|	|	2011	2028	|	2121	|	2223	2253
Xi'an bei **7070** d.	1219	|	|	1257	|	|	|	|	...	1511	|	|	1529	|	|	|	|	|	|	|	|	|	|	|	|	|
Zhengzhou dong a.	1449**z**	1514	1527	1528**z**	1534	1617	1600	1624	...	1727**z**	1749	1801	1758	1822	1838	1852	1907	1924	1940	2302	2049	2109	2142	2134	2244	2314
Zhengzhou dong d.	1454**z**	1521	1530	1532**z**	1537	1620	...	1627	1645	1730**z**	1753	1803	1813	1824	1841	1856	1915	1928	1944	2036	2052	2113	...	...	...	...
Xi'an bei **7070** a.	|	1736	|	|	|	|	...	1842	|	|	|	2043	|	2111	|	|	2152	|	|	|	2308	|	...	...	...	...
Luohe xi d.	|	...	|	|	|	|	...	...	|	|	1829	...	|	...	1937	|	...	|	|	2118	...	|	...	...	...	...
Xinyang dong d.	1615	...	|	|	1645	|	...	...	|	1857	|	...	1935	...	2017	|	...	2036	2059	|	...	2228	...	...	...	...
Wuhan a.	1705	...	1737	1743	1729	1812	...	...	1851	1940	1947	...	2019	...	2106**h**	2055	...	2120	2150	2247**h**	...	2312	...	...	...	...
Changsha nan **7065** a.	1838	...	...	1927	...	1935	...	...	2027	...	2122	...	2201	...	...	2231	...	...	...	...	...	...	...	...	...	...
Guangzhou nan **7065** a.	2120	...	...	2206	...	2232	...	...	2313	...	...	...	...	...	...	...	...	...	...	...	...	...	...	...	...	...
Shenzhen bei **7065** a.	...	...	...	...	...	...	...	...	...	...	...	...	...	...	...	...	...	...	...	...	...	...	...	...	...	...

All trains prefix 'G'	562	90	508	564	652	502	654	84	512	856	852	656	632	514	94	516	832	660	622	518	556	96	88	80	66	72
Shenzhen bei **7065** d.	...	...	...	...	...	...	...	...	...	...	...	...	...	...	...	...	...	...	...	...	...	...	...	...	...	0756
Guangzhou nan **7065** d.	...	...	...	...	...	...	...	...	...	...	...	...	...	...	0800	...	0718	...	0753	...	...	0900	...	1000	1000	0830
Changsha nan **7065** d.	...	...	...	...	...	0730	...	0900	...	...	0810	...	...	...	1022	...	0954	...	1040	...	...	1119	...	1220	1220	1111
Wuhan d.	...	...	0722	...	...	0912	...	1020	0933**h**	0923	0950	...	1000	1030	1143	1140**h**	1130	...	1210	1300	1216	1240	...	1341	1341	1250
Xinyang dong d.	...	...	0808	...	...	|	...	|	|	1015	1038	...	|	|	|	1233	|	...	1257	1345	|	|	...	|	|	|
Luohe xi d.	...	...	0855	...	...	|	...	|	|	1109	|	...	|	1155	|	1314	|	...	1337	|	|	|	...	|	|	1423
Xi'an bei **7070** d.	...	...	|	...	0748	|	0850	|	|	|	|	1003	|	|	|	|	|	1101	|	|	|	|	1309	|	|	|
Zhengzhou dong a.	...	...	0929	...	1011	1058	1119	1205	1134	1201**z**	1200	1225	1219	1236	1328	1348	1351**z**	1340	1411	1453	1417	1435**z**	1517	1526	1526	1457
Zhengzhou dong d.	0806	0900	0932	0940	1014	1101	1124	1208	1139	1205**z**	1228	1230	1112	1244	...	1351	1356**z**	1343	1414	1456	1426	1438**z**	1520	1529	1529	1500
Xi'an bei **7070** a.	|	|	|	|	|	|	|	|	|	1432	1506	|	|	|	...	|	1623	|	|	|	|	1642	|	|	|	|
Xinxiang dong d.	0829	|	|	1002	1036	1123	|	|	1201	...	...	|	|	|	...	|	...	1411	1436	|	|	...	|	|	|	|
Anyang dong d.	0903	|	|	1030	|	|	|	|	1229	...	...	|	1306	|	...	|	...	|	|	|	|	...	|	|	|	|
Handan dong d.	0924	|	|	|	|	|	|	|	|	...	...	|	|	1341	...	|	...	1439	1517	|	|	...	|	|	|	1620
Xingtai dong d.	|	|	1047	|	|	1218	|	|	1310	...	...	1345	|	|	...	|	...	|	|	|	|	...	|	|	|	|
Shijiazhuang d.	1006	1023	1118	1131	1158	1248	1301	1332	1342	...	...	1416	1427	1424	...	1524	...	1535	1556	1623	1611	...	|	1652	1653	1702
Beijing xi a.	1124	1130	1237	1250	1317	1407	1420	1440	1501	...	...	1537	1547	1550	...	1650	...	1717	...	1735	1730	...	1750	1759	1800	1821

All trains prefix 'G'	574	74	566	542	520	532	822	522	662	836	664	568	68	504	666	524	506	70	82	840	826	528	670	844	76	548
Shenzhen bei **7065** d.	...	0850	...	...	...	...	1000	...	...	...	...	...	...	...	...	...	...	...	...	...	1300	...	...	...	1550	...
Guangzhou nan **7065** d.	...	0930	...	0944	...	1024	1040	...	...	1135	...	...	1115	...	...	...	...	1250	1243	1227	1342	...	...	1350	1630	1622
Changsha nan **7065** d.	...	1210	...	1235	...	1308	1324	...	...	|	...	...	1403	1436	...	...	1508	1534	1535	1514	1621	...	...	1635	1908	1920
Wuhan d.	...	1351	...	1411	1425**h**	1439	1453	1512**h**	...	1550	...	...	1535	1612	...	1634	1643	1707	1707	1655	1751	1800	...	1809	2031	2049
Xinyang dong d.	1425	1436	...	1457	|	1524	1545	|	...	|	...	...	1620	1657	...	|	|	1752	1752	1741	1836	1846	...	1854	|	|
Luohe xi d.	1507	|	...	1543	|	1606	|	|	...	1715	...	...	1709	|	...	|	1808	|	|	|	1916	|	...	|	2156	2214
Xi'an bei **7070** d.	|	|	...	|	|	|	|	|	1142	|	1437	...	|	|	1602	|	|	|	|	|	|	|	1753	|	|	|
Zhengzhou dong a.	1548	1557	...	1623	1634	1648	1710**z**	1713	1404	1804**z**	1718	...	1750	1807	1817	1827	1850	1906	1906	1907**z**	1957	2004	2006	2018	2131	2256
Zhengzhou dong d.	1553	...	1618	...	1637	1654	1714**z**	1716	1407	1809**z**	1722	1723	1753	1811	1820	1830	1853	1911	1911	1912**z**	2012	2008	2015	2034	...	...
Xi'an bei **7070** a.	|	...	|	...	|	|	1944	|	|	2029	|	|	|	|	|	|	|	|	|	2138	2233	|	|	2256	...	...
Xinxiang dong d.	|	...	1642	...	|	1716	...	|	1429	...	1744	1808	|	|	1842	1852	|	|	|	...	...	|	2037	...	...	...
Anyang dong d.	1650	...	|	...	|	|	...	1759	|	...	|	1835	1841	|	|	|	|	1954	1954	...	...	|	|	...	...	...
Handan dong d.	|	...	1724	...	1741	|	...	|	|	...	|	|	1902	|	|	1934	|	2013	|	...	...	|	2119	...	...	...
Xingtai dong d.	1723	...	|	...	|	1809	...	|	1522	...	1837	|	|	|	1935	|	2002	2031	2026	...	...	2124	|	...	...	...
Shijiazhuang d.	1754	...	1806	...	1823	1837	...	1900	1553	...	1912	1939	1950	1947	2006	2017	2032	2102	2057	...	...	2155	2201	...	...	...
Beijing xi a.	1919	...	1925	...	1941	...	...	2019	1712	...	2033	2057	2109	2113	2132	2143	2151	2221	2223	...	...	2314	2320	...	...	...

h – Wuhan Hankou. z – Zhengzhou.

7065 (BEIJING -) WUHAN - GUANGZHOU - SHENZHEN

China Rail High Speed

km	All trains prefix 'G'	6011	6101	1103	1001	1105	1111	77	1003	93	551	541	1005	1007	1009	501	821	71	531	83	1011	73	95	79
	Beijing xi **7060** d.	...	...	...	...	...	...	...	...	...	...	...	...	...	...	0730	...	0800	...	0900	...	...	...	1000
	Xi'an bei **7070** d.	...	...	...	...	...	...	...	...	...	...	...	...	...	...	|	0800	|	...	|	...	...	0948	|
	Zhengzhou dong **7060** d.	...	...	...	...	...	...	...	...	0800z	...	0830	...	...	...	1036	1042	1107	1117	1133	...	1209	1153	1233
0	**Wuhan** d.	...	...	0715	0728	0745	0826	0900	0950	0958	1006	1041	1050	1145	1213	1238	1251	1309	1329	1321	1342	1427	1351	1420
209	Yueyang dong d.	...	...	0806	|	0836	|	|	1048	|	1057	|	1148	|	1311	|	1342	1400	|	|	1441	1533	|	|
347	**Changsha** nan a.	...	...	0840	0853	0910	0951	1018	1122	1116	1131	1206	1222	1317	1345	1412	1416	1434	1447	1440	1515	1552	1509	1538
347	**Changsha** nan d.	0700	0706	0843	0856	0915	0954	1021	1125	1119	1134	1210	1225	1320	1348	...	1419	1438	1452	...	1518	1556	1512	1541
387	Zhuzhou xi d.	|	|	0900	|	|	|	|	|	|	1151	|	1242	|	|	...	|	|	1514	...	|	|	|	|
496	Hengyang dong d.	0739	0745	|	|	0954	1033	|	1204	|	|	1249	|	1359	|	...	1458	1524	1549	...	1557	|	|	|
628	Chenzhou xi d.	0814	0820	|	1010	1029	|	|	1239	|	1248	|	|	1434	1502	...	|	1617	|	...	1632	1703	|	|
758	Shaoguan d.	0847	0853	1030	1043	|	1134	|	|	|	1321	1351	1412	|	|	...	1559	|	1653	...	|	|	|	|
968	**Guangzhou** nan a.	0941	0955	1132	1138	1157	1236	1241	1407	1339	1416	1446	1507	1602	1630	...	1654	1738	1746	...	1806	1831	1730	1759
1070	**Shenzhen** bei a.	1020	...	...	1218	...	...	1313	1448	...	...	...	1544	1637	1713	...	1734	1816	...	...	1853	1906	...	...

All trains prefix 'G'	1013	825	1015	831	545	621	553	75	1017	835	1145	1147	1149	6027	839	81	1153	1155	547	1159	6123	503	851	505
Beijing xi **7060** d.	...	...	...	...	...	...	...	...	...	...	...	...	...	...	...	1305	...	...	...	...	...	1437	...	1540
Xi'an bei **7070** d.	...	1044	...	1120	...	...	...	...	...	1219	...	...	...	...	1257	|	...	...	...	...	...	|	1529	|
Zhengzhou dong **7060** d.	...	1318**z**	...	1347**z**	1410	1426	...	1435	...	1454**z**	...	...	...	...	1532**z**	1620	...	...	1645	...	...	1753	1813	1856
Wuhan d.	1444	1532	1549	1610	1619	1633	1642	1655	1706	1713	1720	1727	1736	...	1747	1817	1824	1832	1855	1920	...	1950	2022	2059
Yueyang dong d.	1536	1623	|	1702	|	1724	1733	|	1757	1804	|	|	1835	...	|	|	|	1938	1946	2025	...	2048	2121	2158
Changsha nan a.	1610	1657	1714	1735	1744	1758	1807	1813	1831	1838	1845	1852	1909	...	1927	1935	1958	2012	2027	2059	...	2122	2201	2231
Changsha nan d.	1614	1700	1718	1739	1747	1804	1811	1816	1834	1844	1849	1855	1912	1922	1930	1939	2003	2016	2031	2102	2115	...	...	...
Zhuzhou xi d.	|	|	|	|	|	|	|	1833	1851	|	|	|	1929	|	|	1956	|	2033	|	|	|	...	...	...
Hengyang dong d.	|	|	1757	1819	1827	1843	|	1902	|	|	1928	1926	|	2001	2009	2035	|	2102	2110	2141	2154	...	...	...
Chenzhou xi d.	|	1814	1832	1854	1901	1918	|	|	1948	|	|	2009	2026	|	|	|	2120	2137	2145	2216	2229	...	...	...
Shaoguan d.	1801	|	|	|	|	1952	1958	2003	|	2025	2030	|	2059	2104	2111	2137	2157	|	2218	2249	|	...	...	...
Guangzhou nan a.	1856	1935	2000	2016	2023	2048	2053	2058	2116	2120	2125	2137	2154	2211	2206	2232	2252	2305	2313	2344	2350	...	...	...
Shenzhen bei a.	1938	2016	2040	...	...	...	...	2139	2156	...	...	...	...	2252	...	...	...	...	...	...	...	...	...	...

For footnotes and return service see next page

China Rail High Speed — SHENZHEN - GUANGZHOU - WUHAN (- BEIJING) — 7065

All trains prefix 'G'	502	852	84	1102	832	1002	622	94	72	96	1004	74	542	66	1006	532	822	1008	504	68	836	1124	1010	1126
Shenzhen bei d.	...	...	...	...	...	0700	...	...	0756	...	0830	0850	...	...	0922	...	1000	1025	...	...	...	...	1120	...
Guangzhou nan d.	...	...	...	0700	0718	0733	0753	0800	0830	0900	0910	0930	0944	1000	1006	1024	1040	1106	...	1115	1135	1146	1201	1220
Shaogun d.	...	...	...	|	|	0826	0852	|	|	|	1003	1024	1052	|	|	|	1133	1200	...	1208	1229	|	1255	1313
Chenzhou xi d.	...	...	...	0819	0837	|	|	|	|	|	|	|	|	|	1136	1151	1206	1233	...	1241	1302	1312	|	1346
Hengyang dong d.	...	...	...	0854	0912	0927	|	|	|	|	|	|	1153	|	1211	1226	1242	1308	...	|	1337	|	1357	|
Zhuzhou xi d.	...	...	...	0923	|	|	1017	|	1053	|	|	1149	|	|	|	|	|	1337	...	1338	|	1409	1426	|
Changsha nan a.	...	...	...	0940	0951	1006	1034	1019	1108	1116	1144	1206	1232	1217	1250	1305	1321	1354	...	1357	1416	1426	1444	1454
Changsha nan d.	0730	0810	0900	0944	0954	1012	1040	1022	1111	1119	1148	1210	1235	1220	1255	1308	1324	1359	1436	1403	1421	1430	1447	1459
Yueyang dong d.	0805	0855	|	1020	1030	|	1117	|	1157	|	|	1255	|	|	|	1346	1400	|	|	|	1457	1507	|	1536
Wuhan a.	0909	0945	1017	1111	1127	1152	1207	1140	1247	1237	1322	1348	1408	1338	1422	1436	1450	1526	1609	1532	1547	1559	1621	1628
Zhengzhou dong **7060** a.	1058	1200	1205	...	1351**z**	...	1411	1328	1457	1435**z**	...	1557	1623	1526	...	1648	1710**z**	...	1807	...	1804**z**	...	...	...
Xi'an bei **7070** a.	|	1504	|	...	1623	...	...	...	|	1642	...	...	...	|	...	...	1944	...	|	...	2029	...	...	...
Beijing xi **7060** a.	1407	...	1440	...	...	...	...	...	1821	...	...	...	...	1800	...	...	...	...	2113	...	...	...	...	...

All trains prefix 'G'	506	840	70	82	1012	826	844	544	546	78	1138	1140	1142	1144	1014	548	76	1146	1016	1148	1150	1152	1018	1154	1158
Shenzhen bei d.	...	...	...	...	1238	1250	...	...	...	1400	...	...	...	...	1520	...	1550	...	1620	...	...	...	1800	...	...
Guangzhou nan d.	...	1227	1250	1243	1318	1331	1350	1400	1410	1433	1440	1517	1540	1546	1604	1622	1630	1645	1700	1725	1735	1748	1839	1803	1910
Shaogun d.	...	1320	1343	1336	|	1425	1443	1454	1503	|	1534	1610	1633	|	|	1728	|	1745	|	1818	|	1841	1932	1856	2003
Chenzhou xi d.	...	|	1416	1409	1444	1458	|	1527	1536	|	|	1650	|	1713	1731	|	1749	|	1826	1851	|	1914	|	1929	2036
Hengyang dong d.	...	|	1451	1444	1519	|	|	1602	|	|	1635	|	1734	|	1806	|	1824	|	1901	1926	|	1949	|	2026	2111
Zhuzhou xi d.	...	1454	|	|	|	|	|	|	1640	|	1704	|	|	|	1835	|	|	1909	|	|	|	|	2103	|	|
Changsha nan a.	...	1511	1530	1530	1558	1614	1630	1641	1657	1652	1721	1757	1813	1827	1852	1915	1903	1926	1940	2005	2015	2028	2120	2043	2150
Changsha nan d.	1508	1514	1534	1537	1604	1621	1635	1646	1702	1655	1725	1802	1817	1832	1855	1920	1908	1931	1943	2008	2018	2031	2123	2046	2153
Yueyang dong d.	1543	1551	1610	1613	1644	1658	|	|	1738	|	1808	|	1853	1908	1931	1956	|	2007	2019	2044	2101	2107	2159	|	2229
Wuhan a.	1640	1650	1704	1704	1742	1748	1802	1820	1830	1813	1900	1928	1950	2005	2021	2046	2028	2057	2116	2141	2151	2204	2249	2219	2319
Zhengzhou dong **7060** a.	1850	1907**z**	1906	1906	...	1957	2018	2025	2101**z**	...	...	...	...	...	...	2256	2231	...	...	...	...	...	...	...	...
Xi'an bei **7070** a.	|	2138	|	|	...	2233	2256	...	...	...	...	...	...	...	...	...	...	...	...	...	...	...	...	...	...
Beijing xi **7060** a.	2151	...	2221	2223	...	...	...	...	...	...	...	...	...	...	...	...	...	...	...	...	...	...	...	...	...

z – Zhengzhou.

China Rail High Speed — ZHENGZHOU - XI'AN — 7070

km	Prefix 'G' unless noted	2002	652	824	654	98	656	2006	828	834	660	838	D1002	842	88	662	858	854	664	2012	666	670	D1004	D308 A
0	**Xi'an** Bei d.	0740	0748	0800	0850	0948	1003	1018	1044	1120	1101	1219	1235	1257	1309	1142	1511	1529	1437	1639	1602	1753	1836	2101
121	Huashan bei d.	|	0825	0836	0926	|	1040	1055	1120	1156	|	1255	1319	1348	|	|	|	1605	1515	1715	1638	1829	1919	2141
257	Sanmenxia nan d.	0842	|	|	1006	|	|	1128	|	|	1206	1335	1423	|	|	1244	1613	1638	|	|	|	|	2002	2218
380	Luoyang Longmen d.	0919	0928	0939	|	|	1143	1205	1231	1306	1243	1412	1512	1451	|	1321	1650	|	1617	1825	|	|	2051	2301
505	**Zhengzhou** a.	0946	|	|	|	1150	|	1242	1315	1343	|	1449	1623	1528	|	|	1727	|	1655	1905	1817	|	2140	2344
523	**Zhengzhou** dong a.	...	1011	1022	1119	|	1225	...	|	|	1343	|	...	|	1517	1404	|	1758	1718	...	1820	2006	...	...
	Wuhan **7060** a.	...	|	1248	|	1348	|	...	1528	1605	|	1705	...	1743	|	|	1940	2019	|	...	|	|	...	...
	Changsha nan **7065** a.	...	|	1416	|	1509	|	...	1657	1735	|	1838	...	1927	|	|	...	2201	|	...	|	|	...	...
	Gaungzhou nan **7065** a.	...	|	1654	|	1730	|	...	1935	2016	|	2120	...	2206	|	|	...	...	|	...	|	|	...	...
	Shenzhen bei **7065** a.	...	|	1734	|	...	|	...	2016	...	|	...	...	...	|	|	...	...	|	...	|	|	...	...
	Beijing xi **7060** a.	...	1317	...	1420	...	1535	...	...	...	1717	...	...	...	1750	1712	...	...	2033	...	2132	2320	...	...

Prefix 'G' unless noted	D307 A	2001	D1001	651	653	857	853	655	2007	833	97	D1003	659	87	823	837	661	841	663	2011	665	827	845	669
Beijing xi **7060** d.	...	...	...	0705	0821	...	...	1005	...	...	...	...	1208	1400	...	...	1442	...	1447	...	1600	...	...	1738
Shenzhen bei **7065** d.	...	...	...	|	|	...	...	|	...	...	...	...	|	|	1000	...	|	...	|	...	|	1300	...	|
Guangzhou nan **7065** d.	...	...	...	|	|	...	...	|	...	0718	0900	...	|	|	1040	1135	|	1227	|	...	|	1342	1350	|
Changsha nan **7065** d.	...	...	...	|	|	...	0810	|	...	0954	1119	...	|	|	1324	1421	|	1514	|	...	|	1621	1635	|
Wuhan **7060** d.	...	...	...	|	|	0923	0950	|	...	1130	1240	...	|	|	1453	1550	|	1655	|	...	|	1751	1809	|
Zhengzhou dong d.	...	...	...	1026	1143	|	1228	1320	...	|	|	...	1521	1627	|	|	1803	|	1824	...	1915	2012	2034	2052
Zhengzhou d.	0556	0800	0900	|	|	1205	|	|	1307	1356	1438	1452	|	|	1714	1809	1823	1912	1844	1940	|	|	|	|
Luoyang Longmen d.	0640	0839	0949	1109	1226	1244	1311	1403	1346	1435	|	1541	1604	|	1754	1848	|	1951	1923	2019	2005	|	2119	2206
Sanmenxia nan d.	0724	0916	1039	|	1303	1322	|	|	1423	|	|	1642	|	|	|	|	1932	2028	2000	2056	|	|	2156	|
Huashan bei d.	0803	|	1124	1214	|	|	1423	1508	1522	1540	|	1727	|	|	1907	1954	2008	|	|	|	|	|	|	|
Xi'an Bei a.	0848	1030	1210	1249	1413	1432	1506	1543	1557	1623	1642	1812	1736	1842	1944	2029	2043	2138	2111	2210	2152	2235	2256	2308

A – Shanghai(**D306/305**) - Zhengzhou(**D307/308**) - Xi'an bei.

China Rail High Speed — WUHAN - YICHANG — 7075

km	All trains prefix 'D'	5811	5813	5883	5815	5817	5819	5833	5821	5853	3077	3253	5801	5857	3073	5825	5877	5827	5863	5845	3257	5867	3081	3007	5873
	Shanghai Hongqiao **7175** d.	...	...	...	...	...	...	...	...	...	...	...	...	...	0642	...	...	...	...	...	...	...	...	1354	...
	Nanjing nan **7175** d.	...	...	...	...	...	...	...	...	...	0720	...	...	...	0902	...	...	...	...	...	...	...	1510	|	...
	Nanchang **7080** d.	...	...	...	...	...	...	...	...	...	|	0844	...	...	|	...	...	...	...	...	1506	...	|	|	...
0	**Wuhan** Hankou d.	0620	0625	0656	0720	0735	0824	0906	0956	1050	1118	1146	1206	1238	1257	1448	1458	1521	1620	1710	1817	1829	1902	1948	2010
83	Tianmen nan d.	|	0709	0742	|	0812	0901	0950	|	1129	|	1224	|	|	1335	|	1543	|	1658	|	|	1907	1947	|	2055
114	Xiantao xi d.	|	|	0759	0813	|	0916	1007	|	|	1206	1241	|	1325	|	|	|	1608	|	|	|	1923	|	|	|
134	Qianjiang (Hubei) d.	0713	0732	|	|	|	|	1020	|	1151	1219	|	|	1338	1358	1541	|	|	1721	1803	1913	|	|	2041	|
204	Jingzhou d.	0741	0801	0836	0848	0857	0951	1049	1109	1220	1248	1316	1328	1407	1427	1609	1629	1643	1750	1833	1942	1958	2032	2110	2139
292	**Yichang** dong a.	0820	0833	0908	0920	0936	1023	1127	1140	1252	1319	1348	1405	1440	1457	1647	1700	1720	1828	1905	2021	2030	2111	2142	2211

All trains prefix 'D'		3008	5854	5812	3082	3258	5858	5814	5878	5802	5818	5864	3074	3254	5846	5868	3078	5820	5874	5824	5826	5834	5884	5828	5832
Yichang dong d.	...	0710	0730	0810	0840	0900	0945	1000	1040	1230	1305	1310	1340	1410	1430	1525	1535	1600	1705	1750	1900	1935	2050	2100	2100
Jingzhou d.	...	0745	0807	0845	0922	0943	1020	1035	1121	1305	1340	1352	1415	1445	1505	1600	1611	1641	1740	1835	1942	2020	2134	2142	2205
Qianjiang (Hubei) d.	...	0814	0836	0914	|	1012	|	|	|	1334	|	|	1444	|	1548	1629	1640	|	1809	|	|	2048	|	|	|
Xiantao xi d.	...	0827	0849	|	|	1025	|	|	|	|	1415	1427	|	1520	|	|	1653	|	|	1910	|	2102	|	|	|
Tianmen nan d.	...	0844	0906	0936	1007	|	1105	|	|	1357	|	|	1507	1537	|	|	|	1726	1832	|	2026	2218	|	|	|
Wuhan Hankou a.	...	0918	1005	1010	1048	1116	1204	1145	1240	1431	1505	1512	1541	1611	1645	1726	1737	1800	1907	2000	2100	2159	2247	2254	2317
Nanchang **7080** a.	...	|	...	...	|	1445	...	...	...	...	...	...	|	1925	...	...	|	...	...	...	...	...	...	...	...
Nanjing nan **7175** a.	...	|	...	...	1449	...	...	...	...	...	...	...	1938	...	...	...	2137	...	...	...	...	...	...	...	...
Shanghai Hongqiao **7175** a.	...	1517	...	...	...	...	...	...	...	...	...	...	2156	...	...	...	...	...	...	...	...	...	...	...	...

China Rail High Speed — WUHAN - NANCHANG — 7080

km		D3221	D3258	D3248		T127 ♦		D3254		
	Yichang dong **7075** d.	...	0900	...	...	...	...	1410	...	...
0	**Wuhan** Hankou d.	0826	1121	1533	...	1546**g**	...	1614	...	...
118	Huangshi d.	0946	1241	1640	...	|	...	|	...	...
368	**Nanchang** a.	1147	1445	1845	...	1918	...	1925	...	...

	D3222	D3253		D3247		D3257		T128 ♦	
Nanchang d.	0800	0844	...	1207	...	1505	...	2203	...
Huangshi d.	|	|	...	1406	...	1707	...	|	...
Wuhan Hankou a.	1052**g**	1143	...	1513	...	1814	...	0121	...
Yichang dong **7075** a.	...	1348	...	...	...	2021	...	...	...

T127/28 – Chengdu(**T126/25**) - Wuhan Wuchang(**T127/28**) - Dongguan dong and v.v.

g – Wuhan Wuchang.

7085 BEIJING, SHANGHAI and GUANGZHOU - SHENZHEN and HONG KONG

GUANGZHOU DONG - SHENZHEN via Dongguan — China Rail High Speed

High-speed '**D**' trains (numbers **D70xx** and **D71xx**). *139 km.* Journey 70 minutes. Trains call at **Dongguan** 34–37 minutes after Guangzhou and 28–32 minutes after Shenzhen.

Guangzhou dong depart: 0615, 0630, 0651, 0700, 0708, 0716, 0724, 0733, 0750, 0800, 0808, 0816, 0824, 0841, 0851, 0901, 0917, 0932, 0948, 1000, 1010, 1018, 1029, 1037, 1053, 1103, 1111, 1119, 1127, 1143, 1153, 1206, 1219, 1227, 1237, 1255, 1312, 1320, 1330, 1339, 1355, 1402, 1410, 1421, 1429, 1445, 1457, 1510, 1521, 1531, 1539, 1556, 1607, 1622, 1632, 1641, 1649, 1705, 1714, 1722, 1731, 1741, 1758, 1810, 1825, 1833, 184, 1858, 1907, 1920, 1934, 1943, 1951, 1959, 2016, 2024, 2033, 2041, 2049, 2110, 2126, 2143, 2200, 2213, 2232, 2240.

Shenzhen depart: 0620, 0640, 0653, 0710, 0720, 07307, 0746, 0801, 0822, 0831, 0839, 0847, 0855, 0904, 0921, 0931, 0939, 0947, 0955, 1012, 1022, 1035, 1048, 1103, 1120, 1131, 1141, 1149, 1200, 1208, 1224, 1234, 1242, 1250, 1258, 1314, 1324, 1337, 1350, 1358, 1408, 1425, 1443, 1451, 1501, 1510, 1526, 1533, 1541, 1551, 1600, 1616, 1628, 1640, 1654, 1702, 1710, 1727, 1738, 1753, 1803, 1812, 1820, 1836, 1845, 1853, 1902, 1912, 1929, 1940, 1956, 2004, 2012, 2029, 2037, 2051, 2105, 2114, 2122, 2130, 2147, 2155, 2204, 2212, 2220, 2240.

GUANGZHOU NAN - SHENZHEN BEI — China Rail High Speed

High-speed '**G**' trains (numbers **G62xx**). *102 km.* Journey 36 - 44 minutes.

Guangzhou nan depart: 0700, 0714, 0800, 0835, 0900, 0925, 0944, 1013, 1025, 1046, 1110, 1142, 1232, 1244, 1258, 1323, 1350, 1412, 1436, 1455, 1515, 1535, 1608, 1637, 1658, 1723, 1747, 1803, 1816, 1836, 1848, 1902, 1920, 1940, 2004, 2040, 2103, 2120, 2135, 2152, 2216, 2256.

Shenzhen bei depart: 0700, 0712, 0734, 0756, 0812, 0830, 0850, 0922, 0938, 1000, 1025, 1040, 1120, 1219, 1200, 1215, 1238, 1300, 1335, 1400, 1412, 1430, 1500, 1520, 1535, 1550, 1620, 1635, 1655, 1740, 1800, 1820, 1836, 1920, 1945, 2010, 2030, 2100, 2200, 2230, 2300.

Certain trains continue from/to Changsha, Wuhan, Xi'an and Beijing. See Tables **7060**, **7065** and **7070**.

GUANGZHOU - KOWLOON — MTR Corporation

km		T801	T807	T813	T823	T817	T809	T825	T815	T803	T819	T827	T811
0	**Guangzhou** dong ... d.	0819	0904	0955	1037	1203	1404	1538	1614	1733	1820	2030	2132
82	Dongguan ... d.	0903	0948	1039	1121	|	1448	1622	1658	1817	1904	2114	|
174	**Kowloon** Hung Hom ... a.	1017	1102	1153	1233	1356	1602	1734	1812	1931	2018	2226	2325

		T812	T824	T820	T804	T808	T814	T826	T818	T810	T828	T816	T802
Kowloon Hung Hom ... d.	...	0725	0815	0924	1052	1132	1223	1311	1432	1635	1800	1844	2004
Dongguan ... d.	...	0837	0925	1036	1204	|	|	1421	1544	1747	1910	1956	2113
Guangzhou dong ... a.	...	0924	1012	1123	1251	1326	1417	1508	1631	1834	1957	2043	2200

BEIJING & SHANGHAI - KOWLOON — Chinese Railways

	T97 A	T99 B
Beijing xi ... d.	1308	...
Shanghai ... d.	|	1820
Kowloon Hung Hom . a.	1256	1256

	T100 A	T98 B
Kowloon Hung Hom d.	1515	1515
Shanghai ... a.	1000	|
Beijing xi ... a.	...	1451

Note: Trains make no intermediate passenger stops.

A – Even dates in Feb., Mar., Jun., Jul.,Sep., Oct.; Odd dates in Jan., Apr., May., Aug., Nov., Dec.

B – Even dates in Jan., Apr., May., Aug, Nov., Dec.; Odd dates in Feb., Mar., Jun., Jul., Sep., Oct.

7090 BEIJING and TIANJIN - WUHAN - NANCHANG and GUANGZHOU — Chinese Railways

km		T95	T15	T235	T255	T123	T145	T97	T89	T167	T13	T9	T5	T253	T1	T87	T61	T151	T201	T179	T189		T37	T263
				♦		♦						♦	♦			♦	♦	♦	♦		♦		♦	♦
0	**Beijing** xi ... d.	...	1101	...	...	...	1209**b**	1308	...	1410	1500**b**	1516	1548	...	1555**b**	1556	1631	1637	1811	...	2209	...	...	...
	Tianjin ... d.	...	|	0712	...	0753	|	|	...	|	|	|	|	1315	|	|	|	|	|	...	|	...	...	...
281	Shijiazhuang ... d.	...	|	1140	...	1236	1507	|	1620	1708	1738	1800	1829	1821	1905	1853	1915	1928	2041	...	0100	...	...	...
689	Zhengzhou ... d.	...	1640	1555	1602	1653	1937	1846	1955	2134	2056	2214	2216	2236	2249	2257	2322	A	2354	...	0443	...	0245	0335
1225	**Wuhan** Wuchang ... a.	...	2110	2104	2156	2213	0100	2318	0027	0250	0138	...	0314	0331	0348	0359	0447	...	0423	...	0959	...	0756	0805
1225	**Wuhan** Wuchang ... d.	1735	2116	2122	2216	2229	0120	2335	0041	0310	0150	...	0330	0341	0359	0415	0459	...	0435	0631	1015	...	0807	0818
1587	Changsha ... a.	2115	0029	0044	0148	0206	0459	0300	0354	|	0508	...	0646	0702	0721	0807	0815	...	0750	0952	1343	...	1138	1155
1587	Changsha ... d.	2121	0035	0055	0154	0214	0514	0306	0400	|	0520	...	...	0708	...	...	...	...	0756	0958	...	...	1148	1201
1639	Zhuzhou ... d.	|	|	0136	|	0252	0558	|	|	|	|	...	...	0746	...	...	...	...	|	1044	...	...	1226	|
2006	**Nanchang** ... a.	|	|	|	|	|	1039	|	|	0811	|	...	...	|	...	...	...	...	|	|	...	...	|	|
2297	**Guangzhou** ... a.	0431**f**	0732	0841**d**	0900	0930	...	1010**d**	1108	...	1243**d**	...	...	1427	...	...	...	...	1504	1725	...	...	1923	1905

km		T202	T146	T264	T10	T62	T168		T6	T88	T90	T2	T190	T16	T14	T98	T236	T254	T124	T96	T152		T180	T38
		♦		♦	♦	♦			♦	♦			♦				♦		♦		♦			♦
0	**Guangzhou** ... d.	0947	...	1207	...	...	...	...	...	...	1405	...	...	1643	1624**d**	1800	1817**d**	1820	1904	1923	...	...	2112	2348
	Nanchang ... d.	|	1310	|	...	...	1938	...	...	...	|	...	...	|	|	|	|	|	|	|	...	...	|	|
655	Zhuzhou ... d.	|	1739	|	...	...	|	...	...	...	|	...	...	|	|	|	0108	0114	0138	|	...	...	0402	0635
707	Changsha ... a.	1653	1815	1914	...	...	|	...	...	...	2116	...	...	2343	2349	0107	0144	0150	0214	0243	...	...	0439	0715
707	Changsha ... d.	1659	1825	1920	...	1943	|	...	2039	2028	2122	2210	0213	2349	0006	0113	0150	0200	0224	0253	...	...	0445	0721
1069	**Wuhan** Wuchang ... a.	2010	2149	2234	...	2258	2310	...	0001	2352	0039	0136	0535	0303	0326	0425	0515	0529	0550	0626	...	...	0808	1042
1069	**Wuhan** Wuchang ... d.	2016	2157	2246	...	2312	2325	...	0013	0001	0049	0148	0552	0309	0338	0437	0527	0541	0558	...	...	...	...	1054
1605	Zhenghzou ... d.	0102	0330	0343	0436	0450	0535	...	0541	0521	0529	0703	1111	0752	0828	0921	1057	1105	1127	...	B	...	...	1624
2017	Shijiazhuang ... d.	0415	0747	...	0827	0834	0942	...	0930	0923	0905	1052	1455	|	1141	|	1513	1505	1540	...	1207	...	...	...
2436	**Tianjin** ... a.	|	|	...	|	|	|	...	|	|	...	|	|	|	|	|	1916	2018	1953	...	|	...	...	...
2297	**Beijing** xi ... a.	0642	1051**b**	...	1106	1112	1255	...	1208	1215	...	1355**b**	1740	1327	1414**b**	1456	...	...	...	...	1450	...	...	...

♦ – **NOTES** (by train number):
- **T5/6** – Beijing(**T5/6**) - Nanning and v.v.
- **T9/10** – Beijing(**T9/10**) - Chongqing bei and v.v.
- **T37/38** – Urumqi(**T36/35**) - Zhengzhou(**T37/38**) - Guangzhou and v.v.
- **T61/62** – Beijing(**T61/62**) - Kunming and v.v.
- **T87/88** – Beijing xi(**T87/88**) - Guiyang and v.v.
- **T123/124** – Changchun(**T122/121**) - Tianjin(**T123/124**) - Guangzhou and v.v.
- **T151/152** – Beijing xi(**T151/152**) - Xining xi and v.v.
- **T189/190** – Beijing(**T189/190**) - Nanning and v.v.
- **T201/202** – Beijing(**T201/202**) - Sanya and v.v.
- **T235/236** – Harbin(**T238/237**) - Tianjin(**T235/36**) - Guangzhou and v.v.
- **T263/264** – Lhasa(**T266/265**) - Zhengzhou(**T263/64**) - Shanghai and v.v.

A – Via Xi'an (Table **7115**. a. 0523). **B** – Via Xi'an (Table **7115**. d. 0126).

b – Beijing. **d** – Guangzhou dong. **f** – To Shenzhen arr. 0613

7095 BEIJING - NANCHANG - SHENZHEN — Chinese Railways

km		T159	Z133	Z65	Z67	T107	K105	T185	K1619	T127
		♦						♦		♦
0	**Beijing** xi ... d.	...	1945	2000	2006	2012	2345	...	...	...
* *	**Tianjin** ... d.	...	|	|	|	|	|	0314	2210	...
147	Renqiu ... d.	...	|	|	|	|	0119	0511	0032	...
274	Hengshui ... d.	...	2150	|	|	2240	0252	0638	0202	...
426	Liaocheng ... d.	...	2310	|	|	0008	0440	0828	0347	...
582	Heze ... d.	...	|	|	|	|	|	|	|	...
687	Shangqiu nan ... d.	...	|	|	|	|	0728	1108	0648	...
* * *	**Jinan** ... d.	1206	|	|	|	|	|	|	|	...
* * *	Xuzhou ... d.	1611	|	|	|	|	|	|	|	...
855	Fuyang ... d.	2015	|	|	|	0400	0930	1252	0903	...
1091	Macheng ... d.	2240	|	|	|	|	1200	1509	1226	...
1314	Jiujiang ... d.	|	0610	0618	0628	|	1421	1715	1553	...
1449	**Nanchang** ... a.	0157	0714	0722	0732	0931	1541	1833	1712	...
1449	**Nanchang** ... d.	0213	0728	...	...	0949	1557	1847	1732	1931
1675	Ji'an ... d.	0434	0940	...	...	1209	1848	2112	2034	2152
1861	Ganzhou ... d.	0636	...	...	...	1411	2109	2314	2248	2354
2102	Longchuan ... d.	0934	...	...	...	1649	0058	0157	0221	0244
2248	Huizhou ... d.	1123	...	...	...	1830	0251	0344	0407	0433
2310	Dongguan dong ... d.	1208	...	...	...	|	0350	0429	|	0516
2396	**Guangzhou** dong ... a.	1258	...	...	...	|	|	|	|	...
2372	**Shenzhen** ... a.	...	...	...	...	1945	0502	0513	0628**d**	...

	Z66	Z68	Z134	T128	K1620	T108	K106	T160	T186
				♦				♦	♦
Shenzhen ... d.	...	...	...	...	0818**d**	1425	1054	...	2008
Guangzhou dong ... d.	...	...	...	...	|	|	|	1521	|
Dongguan dong ... d.	...	...	...	1202	|	|	|	1617	2056
Huizhou ... d.	...	...	...	1253	1022	1544	1235	1701	2139
Longchuan ... d.	...	...	...	1450	1300	1728	1434	1850	2335
Ganzhou ... d.	...	...	...	1731	1631	2007	1803	2137	0214
Ji'an ... d.	...	...	1735	1931	1910	2208	2025	2341	0415
Nanchang ... a.	...	...	1958	2151	2209	0026	2319	0156	0630
Nanchang ... d.	2006	2012	2020	...	2226	0040	2333	0212	0650
Jiujiang ... d.	|	2120	2131	...	2356	|	0057	|	0819
Macheng ... d.	|	|	|	...	0236	|	|	0544	1025
Fuyang ... d.	|	|	|	...	0530	0643	0628	0814	1247
Xuzhou ... d.	|	|	|	...	|	|	|	1147	|
Jinan ... a.	|	|	|	...	|	|	|	1526	|
Shangqiu nan ... d.	|	|	|	...	0739	|	0841	...	1425
Heze ... d.	|	|	|	...	|	0911	0955	...	|
Liaocheng ... d.	|	|	0426	...	1042	1030	1127	...	1653
Hengshui ... d.	|	|	0545	...	1243	|	1320	...	1824
Renqiu ... d.	|	|	|	...	|	|	1439	...	1937
Tianjin ... a.	|	|	|	...	1606	|	|	...	2151
Beijing xi ... a.	0732	0738	0803	...	...	1413	1618	...	...

♦ – **NOTES** (by train number):
- **T127/28** – Chengdu(**T126/25**) - Wuhan Wuchang(**T127/28**) - Dongguan dong and v.v.
- **T159/60** – Guangzhou dong(**T160/59**) - Jinan(**T161/62**) - Qingdao and v.v.
- **T185/86** – Shenyang bei(**T188/87**) - Tianjin(**T185/86**) - Shenzhen and v.v.

d – Shenzhen dong.

* * – Tianjin *0 km* - Renqiu *142 km*. * * * – Jinan *0 km* - Xuzhou *319 km* - Fuyang *542 km*.

7097 BEIJING - BENGBU - HEFEI — China Rail High Speed

km	All trains prefix '**G**'	7281	261	263	265	7285	7287	29	245	267	271
0	**Beijing** nan ... d.	...	0715	0755	1010	...	...	1335	...	1438	1827
406	Jinan xi ... d.	...	0903	0938	|	...	...	1517	1611**j**	1625	2015
692	Xuzhou dong ... d.	....	|	|	1309	...	...	|	1715	1749	|
848	**Bengbu** nan ... d.	0713	1053	1129	|	1415	1653	|	1818	1830	2159
911	Huainan dong ... d.	0731	|	1147	1400	|	1711	|	1837	1848	|
980	**Hefei** ... a.	0805	1138	1224	1427	1512	1753	1726	1903	1925	2244

	246	262	264	266	268	7284	30	7286	7288	272
Hefei ... d.	0700	0730	0826	0927	1246	1305	1338	1538	1750	1828
Huainan dong ... d.	0728	0758	|	|	1314	1340	|	1606	1825	|
Bengbu nan ... d.	0748	0817	0916	1012	1333	1357	|	1623	1842	1910
Xuzhou dong ... d.	0826	|	0955	1056	1411	...	|	...	...	|
Jinan xi ... d.	0951**j**	1007	1108	1221	1523	...	1550	...	...	2054
Beijing nan ... a.	...	1145	1246	1407	1709	...	1728	...	...	2232

j – Jinan.

China Rail High Speed

BEIJING and NANJING - SHANGHAI and NINGBO 7100

km		G7342	G7631	G7601	G7603	G7581	G7589	G7635	G7609	G61	D5431	D361	G63	G51	G101	G57	G105	G11	G31	G221 Q	G55 A	G107	D315	G109	G111
0	**Beijing** nan d.	...	...	...	...	...	...	...	...	...	...	...	...	0705T	0700	0725	0736	0800	0830	...	0813	0808	0818	0835	0840
314	Dezhou dong d.	...	...	...	...	...	...	...	...	...	...	...	...	0803	|	0847	|	|	|	...	0943	0930	1012	0949	0955
406	Jinan xi d.	...	...	...	...	...	...	...	...	0715	...	0705	0750	0829	0840	0913	0924	0934	1004	0940j	1009	0958	1055	1015	1031
692	Xuzhou dong d.	...	...	...	...	...	0710	...	...	0834	0811	0850	0917	0942	0959	1025	|	|	|	1058	1121	1106	1249	|	|
848	Bengbu nan d.	...	...	...	...	...	0801	...	...	0918	0901	0934	|	|	|	|	|	|	|	|	1238	|	1353	|	|
1023	**Nanjing** nan d.	0641	0702	0726	0739	0739	0852	0859	0945	1002	1008	1024	1034	1059	1115	1149	1200	1155	1218	1214	|	1224	1513	1252	1259
1088	Zhenjiang nan d.	|	|	|	|	|	|	|	|	|	|	1046	|	|	|	|	|	|	|	1234	|	|	1553	|	|
1153	Changzhou bei d.	|	|	|	|	0834	0933	|	|	|	1057	1114	|	|	1136	|	|	1229	|	|	|	|	1615	|	1333
1210	Wuxi dong d.	|	|	|	|	0850	0952	|	|	|	1117	1143	|	|	|	|	|	|	|	1306	|	|	1635	1338	|
1237	Suzhou bei d.	|	|	|	|	0908	1004	|	|	|	1130	1156	|	|	1213	|	1258	|	|	|	|	|	1655	|	1357
1318	**Shanghai** Hongqiao a.	0948	|	|	|	0944	1033	|	|	|	1202	1227	|	|	1236	|	1321	1309	|	1334	|	1339	1733	1413	1420
1279	Hangzhou dong a.	...	0828	0901	0915	1047	1141	1029	1140	1125	...	...	1158	1228	|	1306	...	...	1332	...	1405	...	...	...	...
1439	Ningbo a.	...	0926	...	...	1154	1243	1137	...	...	...	...	1259	1328	|	1414	...	...	...	...	1203k	...	...	...	...

	G1	G113	G115	G211	G41	G7639	G13	G119	G121	G229 Q	G213	G15	G35	G125	G127	D319	G129	G7617	G131	G133	G137	G135	G59	G3	G43
Beijing nan d.	0900	0905	0916	0931T	0933	...	1000	1045	1105	...	1051T	1100	1505	1135	1150	1140	1204	...	1228	1249	1306	1307	1340	1400	1405
Dezhou dong d.	|	1020	1038	1025	1055	...	|	|	|	...	1145	|	1620	1300	|	1348	|	...	|	1410	|	|	|	|	|
Jinan xi d.	|	1046	1105	1051	1121	...	1134	1226	1253	1208j	1211	1234	1647	1336	1332	1416	1352	...	1409	1436	1447	1448	1532	|	1545
Xuzhou dong d.	|	1151	|	|	1237	...	|	1343	|	1336	1316	|	1806	1437	1450	1606	1457	...	1527	1541	1559	|	1644	|	1656
Bengbu nan d.	|	|	1250	|	|	...	|	|	|	|	|	|	|	|	|	1739	|	...	|	|	1644	1631	|	|	|
Nanjing nan d.	1241	1308	1334	1313	1354	1400	1348	1506	1521	1453	1432	1448	1923	1559	1606	1856	1620	1605	1650	1657	1728	1723	1801	1741	1812
Zhenjiang nan d.	|	|	|	1334	|	|	|	|	|	|	|	|	|	|	|	1918	1641	|	|	|	|	|	|	|	|
Changzhou bei d.	|	1342	|	|	|	|	|	|	1555	1526	|	|	|	|	1640	1943	|	|	|	|	|	1757	|	|	|
Wuxi dong d.	|	|	1420	1406	|	|	|	|	|	|	1532	|	|	1645	|	2008	1713	|	|	1743	|	|	|	|	1858
Suzhou bei d.	|	1406	|	|	|	|	|	1556	|	1550	|	|	|	|	1704	2021	|	|	1741	|	1830	1821	|	|	1910
Shanghai Hongqiao a.	1348	1429	1448	1434	1508	|	1455	1619	1642	1613	1600	1555	|	1713	1727	2052	1741	|	1804	1818	1853	1844	|	1848	1934
Hangzhou dong a.	...	...	...	...	1617	1530	...	...	...	...	...	...	2045	...	...	...	...	1740	...	...	...	...	1923	...	2039
Ningbo a.	...	...	...	...	...	1633	...	...	...	...	...	...	...	...	...	...	...	...	...	...	...	...	2037	...	...

	G139	G7619	G141	G215	G143	G7641	G17	G225 Q	G53	G7351	G145	G19	G147	G149		G37	G21	G39	G153	G157	G155	G233 Q		G201	
Beijing nan d.	1416	...	1422	1442T	1443	...	1500	...	1535T	...	1529	1600	1610	1615	...	1605	1700	1643	1705	1732	1740	...	...	1755	...
Dezhou dong d.	|	...	1536	|	1604	...	|	...	|	...	1644	1715	|	|	...	1720	|	|	1827	1851	1855	...	...	|	...
Jinan xi d.	1551	...	1602	1601	1638	...	1634	1636j	1656	...	1710	1741	1752	1756	...	1746	1843	1831	1853	1917	1921	1920j	...	1936	...
Xuzhou dong d.	1703	...	|	1715	1756	...	|	1755	1814	...	1822	1846	|	1908	...	1851	|	|	2005	|	2033	2039	...	2055	...
Bengbu nan d.	|	...	|	|	|	...	|	|	|	...	1901	|	|	1955	...	|	|	|	|	|	|	2117	...	|	...
Nanjing nan d.	1819	1839	1840	1833	1912	1907	1850	1913	1930	1848	1946	2003	2028	2040	...	2008	2108	2055	2121	2136	2150	2201	...	2210	...
Zhenjiang nan d.	1840	|	|	|	|	|	|	|	|	|	|	|	|	|	...	|	|	|	|	2159	|	|	...	...	...
Changzhou bei d.	1900	|	|	|	|	|	|	|	|	|	2020	|	|	|	...	|	|	|	|	2219	2224	|	...	...	...
Wuxi dong d.	|	|	1926	1919	1958	|	|	|	|	|	|	|	|	2126	...	|	2154	|	2207	|	|	|	...	...	...
Suzhou bei d.	1924	|	|	1931	|	|	|	2003	|	|	|	|	2119	|	...	|	2206	|	|	|	2248	|	...	...	...
Shanghai Hongqiao a.	1947	|	1955	1955	2027	|	1959	2027	|	|	2107	2112	2142	2201	...	|	2229	|	2242	2259	2311	2308	...	...	...
Hangzhou dong a.	...	2014	...	...	...	2036	...	...	2059	2029	...	...	...	...	...	2131	...	2217	...	...	...	...	...	...	...
Ningbo a.	...	...	...	...	...	2139	...	...	...	...	...	...	...	...	...	...	...	...	...	...	...	...	...	...	...

	D352	G202	G102	G222 Q	G104	G106	G12	G108	G32	D316	G34	G2	G112	G212	G58	G36	G114	G230 Q	G54	G116	G14	G118	G120	D320	
Ningbo d.	...	...	...	...	...	...	...	...	...	...	...	...	...	...	0743	...	...	...	...	...	...	...	...	...	...
Hangzhou dong d.	...	...	...	...	...	...	...	...	0830	...	0720	...	...	...	0853	0953	...	...	0930	...	...	...	...	...	...
Shanghai Hongqiao d.	...	...	0700	0705	0710	0725	0800	0807	|	0817	|	0900	0910	0905	|	|	0920	0915	|	0945	1000	1010	1015	1023	...
Suzhou bei d.	...	...	|	|	0734	|	|	0832	|	|	|	|	0934	|	|	|	0952	0939	|	|	|	1035	|	|	...
Wuxi dong d.	...	...	|	0734	|	0802	0830	|	|	0900	|	|	|	0934	|	|	|	|	|	1015	|	|	|	1107	...
Changzhou bei d.	...	...	0742	|	|	|	|	|	|	0921	|	|	|	|	|	|	1016	1003	|	|	|	|	|	|	...
Zhenjiang nan d.	...	...	|	0805	0810	|	|	|	|	|	|	|	|	1005	|	|	|	|	|	|	|	|	1104	|	...
Nanjing nan d.	...	0700	0816	0826	0831	0850	0916	0923	0942	1000	0845	1009	1031	1026	1019	1120	1050	1037	1055	1101	1109	1133	1139	1159	...
Bengbu nan d.	...	|	|	|	|	0935	|	|	|	1214	|	|	|	|	|	|	|	|	|	1151	|	|	1224	|	...
Xuzhou dong d.	0705	0821	|	0944	0949	1016	1032	1045	|	1309	1012	|	|	1142	1135	|	1206	1201	1222	1230	|	1249	|	1426	...
Jinan xi d.	0858	0940	1043	1053j	1103	1129	1144	1201	1157	1450	1124	|	1300	1252	1248	1348	1318	1317j	1334	1342	1323	1401	1410	1639	...
Dezhou dong d.	0928	|	|	...	|	1155	|	|	|	|	|	|	1324	|	|	1414	|	...	|	|	|	|	|	1708	...
Beijing nan a.	1110	1133	1221	...	1242	1308	1316	1355	1328	1043	1303	1348	1439	1405T	1426	1527	1450	...	1444T	1521	1455	1543	1550	1916	...

	G42	G122	G16	G124	G214	G126	D318	G128	G130	G132	G178	G134	G56 A	G38	G136	G138	G140	G4	G226 Q	G64	G142	G144	G216	G18	G146
Ningbo d.	...	...	...	...	...	...	...	...	...	...	...	...	1151	...	...	...	...	...	...	1321	...	...	...	...	...
Hangzhou dong d.	0930	...	...	...	...	...	...	...	...	...	...	...	1255	1147	...	...	...	...	...	1425	...	...	...	...	...
Shanghai Hongqiao d.	1031	1044	1100	1110	1110	1115	0931	1137	1203	1218	1235	1310	|	|	1317	1329	1341	1400	1405	|	1430	1435	1454	1500	1505
Suzhou bei d.	|	1109	|	1135	1135	1147	|	|	|	1243	1300	|	|	|	|	1354	1405	|	1429	|	|	1505	1522	|	1530
Wuxi dong d.	1101	|	|	|	|	|	|	1207	1233	|	1312	|	|	|	|	|	1417	|	1441	|	1500	|	|	|	1542
Changzhou bei d.	|	1140	|	|	|	|	1041	1226	|	1307	|	|	|	|	1405	1418	|	|	|	|	|	1529	|	|	|
Zhenjiang nan d.	1133	|	|	|	|	|	|	|	|	|	|	|	|	|	1425	|	1453	|	|	|	1532	|	|	|	1614
Nanjing nan d.	1154	1214	1209	1226	1226	1238	1125	1300	1326	1342	1358	1427	1421	1314	1446	1452	1514	1509	1527	1545	1553	1603	1624	1609	1636
Bengbu nan d.	|	|	|	|	|	|	1307	|	|	|	|	1511	|	1358	|	|	|	|	|	|	|	|	|	|	|
Xuzhou dong d.	|	1331	|	1342	1342	|	1352	1416	1451	|	1535	1557	1539	1436	1602	|	|	|	1650	1701	1709	|	1748	|	1753
Jinan xi d.	1416	1443	1423	1501	1502	1512	1621	1535	1602	1610	1651	1702	1657	1554	1708	1728	1742	|	1813j	1825	1834	1841	1904	1823	1911
Dezhou dong d.	|	|	|	1528	1528	1539	1651	|	1628	1638	...	1728	|	|	1740	|	|	|	...	...	|	|	|	|	|
Beijing nan a.	1606	1624	1555	1648	1619T	1652	1825	1714	1741	1751	...	1853	1836	1733	1905	1908	1921	1848	...	...	2006	2013	2021T	1955	2050

	G148	G52	G44	G7341	G20	G150	G152	G234 Q	G218	G7610	G22	G154	G40	G156	G60	G158	G160	G7612	G7636	D362	G62	G7590	G7638	G7640	G7616
Ningbo d.	...	1349	...	...	...	...	...	...	...	1541	...	...	...	...	1435	...	...	...	1723	...	...	1652	1918	1944	...
Hangzhou dong d.	...	1454	1412	...	...	...	...	...	...	1645	...	...	1726	...	1545	...	...	1800	1826	...	1744	1801	2028	2055	2106
Shanghai Hongqiao d.	1518	|	1524	1541	1600	1605	1620	1631	1638	|	1700	1714	|	1719	|	1743	1755	|	|	1807	|	1910	|	|	|
Suzhou bei d.	1543	|	1556	|	|	1630	|	|	1703	|	|	1739	|	|	|	1808	|	|	|	1840	|	1942	|	|	|
Wuxi dong d.	|	|	|	|	1630	|	|	|	|	|	1730	|	|	1756	|	|	|	|	|	1852	|	1954	|	|	|
Changzhou bei d.	1607	|	1620	|	|	|	|	|	1727	|	|	|	|	|	|	1832	|	|	|	1913	|	2013	|	|	|
Zhenjiang nan d.	|	|	|	|	|	|	|	1725	|	|	|	1816	|	|	|	|	|	|	|	|	|	|	|	|	|
Nanjing nan d.	1642	1619	1654	1846	1716	1727	1735	1746	1801	1813	1816	1838	1859	1843	1703	1906	1912	1928	1954	1956	1925	2047	2156	2223	2241
Bengbu nan d.	|	1701	|	...	|	|	|	|	|	...	|	|	|	1926	1747	|	1956	...	...	2046	|	2138	...	...	...
Xuzhou dong d.	|	1741	1810	...	|	|	1851	1902	1924	...	1932	|	2015	|	1830	2022	2038	...	...	2136	2050	2215	...	...	...
Jinan xi d.	1917	1848	1929	...	1937	1955	2004	2017j	2036	...	2044	2105	2122	2110	1950	2140	|	...	...	2306	2200	...	...	...	...
Dezhou dong d.	1943	1914	2001	...	|	2021	2030	...	|	...	|	|	|	2135	|	|	2211	...	...	...	...	...	...	...	...
Beijing nan a.	2056	2004T	2114	...	2109	2141	2158	...	2159T	...	2216	2243	2300	2255	2135	2319	2324	...	...	...	...	...	...	...	...

km		D629	D651	D625	D291	D621	D281	D285		
0	**Zhengzhou** d.	0330	0350	0753	0900	1202	1420	1509	...	...
203	Shangqiu d.	0512	0529	0928	1039	1335	1555	1640	...	...
349	Xuzhou dong d.	0702	0729	1141	1221	1629	1739	1828	...	...
520	Bengbu nan d.	0746	0828	|	|	1813	|	1927	...	...
695	**Nanjing** nan d.	0837	0917	1340	1414	1913	1951	2017	...	...
760	Zhenjiang nan d.	|	0939	1414	|	1943	2022	2046	...	...
825	Changzhou bei d.	0914	1001	|	1451	2004	2042	2111	...	...
882	Wuxi dong d.	|	1021	1449	1511	2024	2102	2134	...	...
909	Suzhou bei d.	0941	1034	1502	1524	2043	|	2148	...	...
990	**Shanghai** Hongqiao a.	1007	1059	1600	1550	2134h	2148	2224	...	...

	D618	D622	D282	D286	D292	D630	D652		
Shanghai Hongqiao d.	0206h	0521h	0630	0734	1610	2004	2026	...	...
Suzhou bei d.	|	|	0656	0807	1637	|	2052	...	...
Wuxi dong d.	0558	0558	0707	|	1659	2038	|	...	...
Changzhou bei d.	0619	0619	0728	|	|	2059	|	...	...
Zhenjiang nan d.	|	|	|	0908	|	|	2134	...	...
Nanjing nan d.	0657	0657	0805	0930	1751	2138	2156	...	...
Bengbu nan d.	|	|	|	|	1857	2228	|	...	...
Xuzhou dong d.	0845	0845	1031	1124	1953	2322	2341	...	...
Shangqiu d.	1010	1010	1159	1257	2122	|	0130	...	...
Zhengzhou a.	1141	1141	1336	1429	2255	0258	0306	...	...

– Beijing nan(**G55/56**) - Fuzhou and v.v.

Q – To/from Qingdao (Table **7105**).

h –Shanghai. **j** –Jinan. **k**–Ningbo

7105 BEIJING - JINAN - QINGDAO

Chinese Railways, China Rail High Speed

km		D6001	D6003	D6005	D331	G185	G247	D6007	G223	D333	D6009	D341	D335	D6011	G231	D337	D6013	G187	G189	G171	G193	D6015	G243	G191
									S						S									
0	**Beijing** nan ... d.	...	...	...	0710	0730	...	...	...	0823	...	...	1030	...	...	1124	...	1233	1259	...	1427	...	...	1318
122	Tianjin nan ... d.	...	...	...	0746	|	...	...	...	0921	...	1044x	1112	...	...	1206	...	|	1335	1448x	|	...	...	|
314	Dezhou dong ... d.	...	...	...	0832	|	...	...	...	1043	...	1153	|	...	...	1320	...	1402	1427	1542	|	...	...	1440
426	**Jinan** ... d.	0720	0815	0840	0923	0936	0951	1043	1055	1129	1239	1248	1308	1328	1320	1411	1402	1447	1512	1627	1620	1946	1740	1525
536	Zibo ... d.	0803	0904	0924	1007	1020	1035	1126	1139	1212	1328	1337	1352	1411	1403	1455	1446	1533	1556	1711	1723	1734	1826	1610
636	Weifang ... d.	0840	0952	1001	1106	1056	1125	1208	1215	1251	1406	1420	1430	1450	1440	1538	1529	|	1634	1749	1800	1816	1904	1646
819	**Qingdao** ... a.	0959	1106	1115	1225	1210	1247	1323	1329	1405	1526	1534	1544	1604	1554	1659	1643	1720	1748	1908	1915	1930	2023	1800

	T161	G227	D339	G195	G197	D6017	G235		
	A	S					S		
Beijing nan ... d.	...	...	1546	1638	1716	...	...	...	...
Tianjin nan ... d.	...	...	1649	|	1757	...	...	...	...
Dezhou dong ... d.	...	...	1742	1800	1843	...	...	...	...
Jinan ... d.	1540	1816	1833	1849	1909	2013	2021	...	...
Zibo ... d.	1641	1900	1922	1932	2012	2056	2105	...	...
Weifang ... d.	1737	1944	2017	2009	2050	2134	2149	...	...
Qingdao ... a.	2008	2059	2136	2123	2204	2253	2303	...	...

	D6002	T162	G224	D332	G186	G188	G190	G244	G172
		A	S						
Qingdao ... d.	0550	0642	0656	0703	0726	0802	0822	0832	0906
Weifang ... d.	0700	0857	0805	0818	0836	0912	0931	0942	1016
Zibo ... d.	0738	1036	0848	0902	0914	0949	1009	1020	1054
Jinan ... d.	0831	1154	0936	0952	1004	1039	1059	1108	1145
Dezhou dong ... d.	...	...	...	1054	1042	1117	|	...	|
Tianjin nan ... a.	...	...	...	1145	|	|	1221	...	1331x
Beijing nan ... a.	...	...	...	1225	1201	1237	1256	...	...

	D6004	G232	D6006	D334	G192	G194		D336	G248	G196	G228	D6008		D338	D342	G198	D6010		D6014	G236	D6012	D340	D6016	D6018
		S									S									S				
Qingdao ... d.	0914	0926	1020	1012	1137	1213	...	1230	1313	1327	1355	1343	...	1430	1612	1606	1627	...	1633	1635	1710	1722	1845	2000
Weifang ... d.	1030	1040	1129	1137	1246	1322	...	1345	1429	1437	1504	1453	...	1539	1726	1715	1736	...	1746	1751	1825	1832	1953	2110
Zibo ... d.	1108	1118	1212	1220	1324	1359	...	1428	1518	|	1546	1537	...	1622	1808	1752	1813	...	1826	1830	1903	1915	2036	2154
Jinan ... d.	1215	1206	1300	1310	1414	1449	...	1518	1609	1559	1634	1625	...	1712	1858	1842	1906	...	1919	1918	1951	2005	2124	2242
Dezhou dong ... d.	...	...	...	|	|	1534	...	1620	...	1643	...	...	...	1814	1949	|	...	...	...	...	...	2043	...	...
Tianjin nan ... a.	...	...	...	1431	|	|	...	1704	...	1727	...	...	...	1905	2039x	|	...	...	...	...	...	2133	...	...
Beijing nan ... a.	...	...	...	1514	1616	1647	...	1746	...	1809	...	...	...	1946	...	2038	...	...	...	...	...	2221	...	...

A – Guangzhou dong(**T160/59**) - Jinan(**T161/62**) - Qingdao and v.v. S – To/from Shanghai Hongqiao (Table **7100**). x – Tianjin xi.

7110 SHANGHAI - NANJING - ZHENGZHOU

Chinese Railways

km		K290	T112	T116	T138	K152	T164	T52	D306	K282
		♦	♦	♦	♦		♦	♦	♦	♦
0	**Shanghai** ... d.	0843	1154n	1542	1552	1643	1936	2025	2200	2032
84	Suzhou ... d.	0955	1323	1638	1645	1748	|	2127	2244	2140
126	Wuxi ... d.	1027	1352	1707	1714	1820	2042	2155	|	2222
165	Changzhou ... d.	1058	1421	1734	1741	1851	|	2223	2325	2258
237	Zhenjiang ... d.	1146	1507	1816	1823	1938	|	|	|	2346
301	**Nanjing** ... a.	1243	1548	1856	1903	2022	2205	2350	0031	0044
301	**Nanjing** ... d.	1251	1607	1904	1910	2031	2216	2356	0035	0050
485	Bengbu ... d.	1511	1751	2045	2051	2235	0005	0142	|	0254
649	Xuzhou ... d.	1729	1936	2224	2233	|	0129	0329	|	0510
795	Shangqiu ... d.	1915	|	2348	2359	0442	|	0453	|	0653
998	**Zhengzhou** ... a.	2130	2248	0149	0201	0745	0412	0641	0553	0902

	T137	T163	T115	T51	T111	K289	K151	K284	D305
	♦	♦	♦	♦	♦	♦		♦	♦
Zhengzhou ... d.	0233	0257	0308	0418	0437	1747	1841	1938	2348
Shangqiu ... d.	|	|	0456	0602	|	2002	2100	2155	|
Xuzhou ... d.	0609	0551	0632	0735	0752	2150	|	2342	|
Bengbu ... d.	0751	0716	0809	0928	0934	2343	0036	0135	|
Nanjing ... d.	0928	0846	1000	1105	1111	0141	0234	0333	0507
Nanjing ... d.	0934	0855	1006	1111	1117	0149	0242	0342	0511
Zhenjiang ... d.	1013	|	|	1150	1156	0232	0325	|	|
Changzhou ... d.	1109	|	|	1238	1244	0320	0413	|	0615
Wuxi ... d.	1136	1017	1144	1305	1311	0351	0444	|	|
Suzhou ... d.	1204	|	1212	1333	1339	0423	0516	|	0656
Shanghai ... a.	1258	1125	1305	1431	1455n	0527	0630	0757	0748

For footnotes see Table **7120**.

7115 ZHENGZHOU - XI'AN - LANZHOU

Chinese Railways

km		K131	T35	K889		K1351	T197	K377		T193	T113	T151	T23	T223	K621	K1027	T117	T139	K595		K419	T265	T165	T53
			♦	♦			♦			♦	♦	♦	♦	♦			♦	♦				♦	♦	♦
0	**Zhengzhou** ... d.	1528	1635	1731	...	1929	2122	2150	...	2247	2301	...	...	...	2344	0104	0155	0222	0306	...	0406	0349	0420	0651
124	Luoyang ... d.	1715	1809	1908	...	2107	2256	2323	...	0017	0032	0045	...	...	0118	0249	|	|	0458	...	0541	|	|	|
512	**Xi'an** ... a.	2238	2255	0020	...	0248	0333	0430	...	0456	0508	0523	...	...	0640	0811	0750	0821	1024	...	1046	0954	1009	1245
512	**Xi'an** ... d.	2252	2310	0032	...	0300	0341	0442	...	0508	0516	0533	...	0559	0700	0821	0802	...	1033	...	1100	1009	1017	1253
685	Baoji ... d.	0117	0103	0233	...	0501	0527	0640	...	0656	0703	0721	0822	0822	0902	1033	0950	...	1240	...	1301	|	|	1441
840	Tianshui ... d.	0304	0243	0414	...	0645	0706	0841	...	0833	0841	0856	|	|	1100	1216	1123	...	1421	...	1442	|	|	1616
1188	**Lanzhou** ... a.	0721	0628	0818	...	1114	1051	1318	...	1210	1240	1248	1354	1354	1517	1632	1505	...	1827	...	1904	1638	1647	1951

		K378	K132	K420		T140	K596	T36		T118	T24	T224	T166	T266	T54	T114	T194	T198	T152		K1352	K890	K1028	K622
						♦		♦		♦	♦	♦	♦	♦	♦	♦	♦	♦	♦					
Lanzhou ... d.	...	0122	0910	0946	...	...	1156	1211	...	1230	1244	1239	1312	1336	1405	1413	1543	1606	1644	...	2154	2313	2336	2344
Tianshui ... d.	...	0544	1332	1416	...	...	1645	1609	...	1632	|	|	|	|	1753	1819	1934	2004	2054	...	0206	0339	0419	0352
Baoji ... d.	...	0831	1613	1700	...	...	1932	1846	...	1906	2012	2018	|	|	2030	2056	2212	2246	2335	...	0451	0620	0700	0637
Xi'an ... a.	...	1025	1810	1852	...	...	2144	2020	...	2042	...	2213	2049	2120	2205	2230	2344	0018	0112	...	0647	0845	0857	0827
Xi'an ... d.	...	1038	1824	1906	...	2002	2156	2028	...	2104	...	...	2058	2140	2217	2240	2354	0028	0126	...	0701	0903	0912	0841
Luoyang ... d.	...	1539	2312	0002	...	|	0314	0112	...	|	...	...	|	|	|	0308	0433	0513	0609	...	1208	1425	1545	1353
Zhengzhou ... a.	...	1709	0050	0134	...	0216	0448	0239	...	0252	...	...	0245	0325	0412	0429	0554	0639	...	...	1349	1608	1746	1536

For footnotes see Table **7120**.

7120 LANZHOU - ÜRÜMQI and LHASA

km		T35	T177	T197	T193	T295	T53	T69		
		♦	♦	♦	♦		♦	♦		
	Zhongwei ... d.	...	0939	...	...	...	...	2309	...	...
0	**Lanzhou** ... d.	0640	|	1103	1220	1601	2001	|	...	...
303	Wuwei ... d.	1002	1338	1425	1542	1929	2323	0246	...	...
770	Jiayuguan ... d.	1517	1842	1918	2043	0036	0415	0747	...	...
1067	Liuyuan ... d.	1920	2157	|	2341	0340	0717	1051	...	...
1339	Hami nan ... d.	2324	0122	0147	0306	0705	1042	1416	...	...
1749	Turpan ... d.	0433	0545	0610	0729	1128	1505	1839	...	...
1892	**Ürümqi** ... a.	0635	0739	0804	0923	1322	1659	2033	...	...

	T70	T36	T296	T178	T54	T194	T198		
	♦	♦		♦	♦	♦	♦		
Ürümqi ... d.	1003	1519	1540	1701	1711	1849	1900	...	...
Turpan ... d.	1145	1701	1724	1842	1855	2033	2045	...	...
Hami nan ... d.	1608	2124	2147	2305	2316	0056	0111	...	...
Liuyuan ... d.	1927	0043	0106	0226	0235	0417	|	...	...
Jiayuguan ... d.	2242	0347	0416	0539	0547	0723	0743	...	...
Wuwei ... d.	0345	0850	0924	1039	1048	1226	1247	...	...
Lanzhou ... a.	|	1159	1239	|	1355	1535	1556	...	...
Zhongwei ... a.	0711	...	...	1456	...	...	...	...	...

km		T175	K889	T151	T27	T23	T223	T265	T165	
		♦	♦	♦	♦	♦	♦	♦	♦	
0	**Zhongwei** ... d.	0119	...	...	0751	...	...	...	...	...
306	**Lanzhou** ... d.	0632	0830	1259	1319	1409	1409	1653	1702	...
534	Xining xi ... d.	0910	1135	1558	1610	1715	1715	1945	2015	...
1352	Golmud ... d.	...	...	...	0202	0307	0307	0518	0559	...
2172	Naqu ... d.	...	...	...	1114	1218	1218	1459	1605	...
2449	**Lhasa** ... a.	...	...	...	1540	1635	1635	1920	2015	...

	T24	T224	T166	T266	T28	T176	T152	K890	
	♦	♦	♦	♦	♦	♦	♦	♦	
Lhasa ... d.	1000	1000	1130	1208	1348	...	...	...	...
Naqu ... d.	1413	1413	1501	1614	1717	...	...	...	...
Golmud ... d.	2357	2357	0051	0144	0308	...	...	...	...
Xining xi ... d.	0935	0935	1000	1052	1220	1125	1350	2000	...
Lanzhou ... a.	1226	1219	1253	1321	1455	1407	1632	2301	...
Zhongwei ... a.	...	...	...	...	2010	2026	...	...	...

♦ – **NOTES** for Tables **7110**, **7115** and **7120** (by train number):

T23/24 – Chengdu(**T22/21**) - Lanzhou(**T23/24**) - Lhasa and v.v.
T27/28 – Beijing xi(**T27/28**) - Lhasa and v.v.
T35/36 – Urumqi(**T36/35**) - Zhengzhou(**T37/38**) - Guangzhou and v.v.
T51/52 – Urumqi(**T54/53**) - Zhengzhou(**T51/52**) - Shanghai and v.v.
T53/54 – Urumqi(**T54/53**) - Zhengzhou(**T51/52**) - Shanghai and v.v.
T69/70 – Beijing xi(**T69/70**) - Urumqi and v.v.
T111/112 – Lanzhou(**T114/13**) - Zhengzhou(**T111/12**) - Shanghai and v.v.
T113/114 – Lanzhou(**T114/13**) - Zhengzhou(**T111/12**) - Shanghai and v.v.
T115/116 – Lanzhou(**T118/17**) - Zhengzhou(**T115/16**) - Shanghai and v.v.
T117/118 – Lanzhou(**T118/17**) - Zhengzhou(**T115/16**) - Shanghai and v.v.
T137/138 – Xian(**T140/139**) - Zhengzhou(**T137/138**) - Shanghai and v.v.
T139/140 – Xian(**T140/139**) - Zhengzhou(**T137/138**) - Shanghai and v.v.
T151/152 – Beijing xi(**T151/152**) - Xining xi and v.v.
T163/164 – Lhasa(**T166/165**) - Zhengzhou(**T163/164**) - Shanghai and v.v.
T165/166 – Lhasa(**T166/165**) - Zhengzhou(**T163/164**) - Shanghai and v.v.
T175/176 – Beijing xi(**T175/176**) - Xining xi and v.v.
T177/178 – Beijing(**T177/78**) - Urumqi and v.v.
T193/194 – Zhengzhou(**T193/194**) - Urumqi and v.v.
T197/198 – Zhengzhou(**T197/198**) - Urumqi and v.v.
T223/224 – Lhasa(**T224/223**) - Xian(**T221/222**) - Chongqing and v.v.
T265/266 – Lhasa(**T266/265**) - Zhengzhou(**T263/64**) - Shanghai and v.v.
K282/284 – Shanghai(**K282/284**) - Zhengzhou(**K283/281**) - - Chengdu and v.v.
K289/290 – Shanghai(**K290/289**) - Zhengzhou(**K291/292**) - - Chengdu and v.v.
D305/306 – Shanghai(**D306/305**) - Zhengzhou(**D307/308**) - Xi'an bei.
K889/890 – Zhengzhou(**K889/890**) - Xining xi and v.v.

n – Shanghai nan.

ÜRÜMQI - ALMATY - ASTANA 7125

km		5801	13* ②⑦	13/53 ②
0	**Ürümqi** d.	2358	0021	0021
144	Shihezi d.	0322	|	|
241	Kuitun d.	0525	|	|
477	Alashankou a.	1016	0900	0900
477	Alashankou 🏢 d.	...	1100	1100
493	Druzhba 🏢 a.	...	0920	0920
493	Druzhba d.	...	1240	1240
654	Beskol' d.	...	1540	1540
797	**Aktogay** a.	...	1737	1737
797	**Aktogay** d.	...	1817	1855
1051	Ush Tobe d.	...	2251	|
1283	Qapshaghay d.	...	0319	|
1354	**Almaty** I a.	...	0438	|
1363	**Almaty** II a.	...	0538	|
2465	Qaraghandy a.	...	...	0900
2706	**Astana** a.	...	...	1218

	5802	54/14 ⑦	14* ②⑦
Astana d.	...	1715	...
Qaraghandy d.	...	2150	...
Almaty II d.	...	|	0020
Almaty I d.	...	|	0107
Qapshaghay d.	...	|	0222
Ush Tobe d.	...	|	0711
Aktogay a.	...	1036	1106
Aktogay d.	...	1146	1146
Beskol' d.	...	1401	1401
Druzhba a.	...	1635	1635
Druzhba 🏢 d.	...	1950	1950
Alashankou 🏢 a.	...	2210	2210
Alashankou d.	2122	2350	2350
Kuitun d.	0213	|	|
Shihezi d.	0415	|	|
Ürümqi a.	0908	0950	0950

* – Train number: **13** *CJ* on ②, **13** *KH* on ⑦; from Almaty **14** *CJ* on ②, **14** *TJ* on ⑦.

For connections to Moscow see Table **1975**.

Operators: Chinese Railways and Kazakstan Temir Zholy.

XI'AN - CHENGDU 7130

Chinese Railways

km		K291 C	K245	T7 A	K5	T24 B	K879	K385	K869	K165 D
	Zhengzhou d.	2139	2323	...	...	...	...	1343	1337	...
0	**Xi'an** d.	0436	0625	0736	1320	...	1945	2038	2128	2218
173	Baoji d.	0704	0846	0929	1548	2042	2211	2250	2332	0039
523	Guangyuan d.	1535	1702	1608	0016	0342	0654	0732	0821	0934
727	Mianyang d.	1902	2027	1922	0341	|	1016	1054	1142	1255
842	**Chengdu** a.	2040	2210	2050	0508	0816	1150	1240	1336	1430

		T8 A	K880	K166 D	K870	K292 C	K386	T22 B	K6	K246
Chengdu d.	...	0945	1250	1326	1441	1650	1750	2045	2115	2138
Mianyang d.	...	1118	1432	1510	1644	1830	1937	|	2253	2317
Guangyuan d.	...	1441	1833	1843	2114	2208	2312	0137	0223	0250
Baoji d.	...	2049	0346	0411	0630	0720	0745	0759	1014	1046
Xi'an a.	...	2221	0540	0601	0901	0930	0943	...	1215	1249
Zhengzhou a.	...	...	...	...	1636	1716	1614	...	...	1934

A – Bejing xi(**T7/8**) - Chengdu and v.v.
B – Chengdu(**T22/21**) - Lanzhou(**T23/24**) - Lhasa and v.v.
C – Shanghai(**K290/289**) - Zhengzhou(**K291/292**) - - Chengdu and v.v.
D – Xi'an(**K165/66**) - Kunming and v.v.

CHENGDU - QINGCHENGSHAN 7135

China Rail High Speed

km	All trains prefix 'D'	6103		6101	6105			6109	6113	6181	6107			6119		6111	6123		6115	6127		6117	6129	6131
0	**Chengdu** d.	0730	...	0832	0834	...	...	0931	1148	1225	1317	...	...	1417	...	1534	1647	...	1733	1841	...	1852	1932	2017
57	Dujiangyan d.	0807	...	0919	0916	...	...	1013	1218	1258	1350	...	...	1459	...	1612	1724	...	1815	1916	...	2034	2014	2054
65	**Qingchengshan** a.	0815	...	0927	0924	...	...	1021	1226	1306	1358	...	...	1507	...	1620	1732	...	1823	1926	...	2042	2022	2102

All trains prefix 'D'			6104		6102	6106		6110	6114		6116	6108		6120		6112	6124			6128		6132	6118	6134
Qingchengshan d.	...	...	0827	...	0941	0942	...	1035	1245	...	1317	1421	...	1540	...	1632	1742	...	...	1936	...	2039	2054	2114
Dujiangyan d.	...	...	0837	...	0951	0952	...	1045	1255	...	1327	1431	...	1551	...	1641	1752	...	...	1946	...	2049	2104	2124
Chengdu a.	...	...	0916	...	1027	1027	...	1125	1335	...	1402	1515	...	1632	...	1718	1827	...	...	2025	...	2128	2139	2159

CHENGDU - CHONGQING 7140

Chinese Railways

km	All trains prefix 'D'	5102		5104	5106		5108	5110	5112	5134	5114	5116		5118	5166	5120	5122	5124	5138	5126	5128	5130	5140	5132
0	**Chengdu** dong d.	0800h	...	0856h	0910h	...	1042	1117	1204	0928	1310	1410	...	1431	1458	1534	1642	1704	1729	1845h	1857	1942	2006h	2110h
146	Suining d.	0903	...	|	|	...	|	1224	|	1027	|	|	...	|	|	1632	|	|	|	|	1955	|	2121	|
198	Tongnan d.	0934	...	|	1040	...	|	1255	|	1058	1435	|	...	1548	|	1703	|	1821	|	|	2026	2059	2157	2234
247	Hechuan d.	1000	...	|	1106	...	|	1321	|	1124	1501	|	...	1614	|	1729	1820	1847	1906	|	2053	2125	2231	2300
313	**Chongqing** bei a.	1027	...	1100	1133	...	1241	1348	1403	1156	1528	1609	...	1641	1657	1756	1847	1914	1933	2049	2120	2152	2320	2327

All trains prefix 'D'			5101	5103	5105	5107	5109		5111	5133	5113	5115	5117		5119	5121	5123	5135	5125	5127	5129	5137	5131	5139
Chongqing bei d.	...	...	0800	0853	0930	1050	1122	...	1200	1219	1303	1409	1428	...	1553	1629	1701	1537	1816	1905	1952	1958	2110	2115
Hechuan d.	...	...	0830	|	1000	|	1152	...	1230	1249	|	1440	|	...	1623	1659	1732	|	1846	1936	2022	2029	|	|
Tongnan d.	...	...	0856	|	|	|	1218	...	|	1315	|	1506	|	...	1649	|	1758	|	...	2002	2048	|	|	|
Suining d.	...	...	0926	|	|	|	1248	...	|	|	|	|	|	...	1719	|	|	|	|	|	|	|	2230	2232
Chengdu dong a.	...	...	1022	1053	1144	1250	1352	...	1406	1430	1511	1621	1628	...	1820h	1834	1922	1937h	2035h	2131h	2208h	2218h	2331h	2333h

– Chengdu.

CHENGDU - DAZHOU 7142

Chinese Railways

km	All trains prefix 'D'	5182	5184	5186	5196	5192	5188	5190		
0	**Chengdu** dong d.	0809h	1036	1418	1450	1647	1650	2029	...	...
146	Suining d.	0912	|	|	1548	1745	1757	2127	...	...
213	Nanchong d.	0949	1204	1547	1624	|	1834	2204	...	...
372	**Dazhou** a.	1100	1313	1656	1738	1937	1944	2317	...	...

All trains prefix 'D'	5181	5183	5185	5187	5195	5191	5189		
Dazhou d.	0735	1120	1339	1720	1757	1905	2022	...	...
Nanchong d.	0851	1234	1451	1835	1916	2031	2137	...	...
Suining d.	|	|	|	|	|	|	2211	...	...
Chengdu dong a.	1014	1358	1615	1958	2039	2200h	2312h	...	...

– Chengdu.

CHENGDU - NANNING and KUNMING 7145

Chinese Railways

km		K1273	K853	K9465	K829 B	K1139	K485	K1223	T8897	K139
0	**Chengdu** dong d.	0830h	0844	1005	1132	1459	1754	1700h	1905	2141
217	Neijiang d.	1302	1325	1436	1641	1904	|	2109	|	0133
337	Yibin d.	1524	1620	1721	1908	2124	|	2325	|	|
744	Liupanshui d.	2225	0157	0302	0417	0540	|	0718	|	|
502	Chongqing d.	|	|	|	|	|	2239b	|	|	0756
810	Zunyi d.	|	|	|	|	|	0633	|	0504	1503
65*	Guiyang d.	0323	|	0730	0818	|	1003	1139	0735	1804
424	Jinchengjiang d.	▬	|	...	1438	|	1538	1653	▬	2347
585	Liuqiao d.	**K482**	|	...	1720	|	1830	1919	**K364**	0229
720	Litang d.	**B**	|	...	...	|	...	...	**B**	|
840	**Nanning** a.	0955	┘	...	...	|	...	...	0240	0715
914	Qujing d.	|	0534	...	...	1110	...	...	|	...
71	**Kunming** a.	2300	0733	...	...	1301	...	...	1502	...

	K854	K363 B	K486	K481 B	K1224	K830 B	K1274	K1140	K140
Kunming d.	0838	1210	...	1730	...	...	...	1648	...
Qujing d.	1100	|	...	|	...	...	...	1848	...
Nanning d.	|	0015	...	0525	...	...	...	|	1200
Litang d.	|	▬	...	▬	...	...	...	|	1321
Liuqiao d.	|	**T8898**	0653	**K9466**	0638	0722	...	|	1515
Jinchengjiang d.	|		1016		0933	0949	...	|	1844
Guiyang d.	|	2011	1751	1515	1601	1635	1715	|	0016
Zunyi d.	|	2259	2121	|	|	|	|	|	0322
Chongqing d.	|	|	|	|	|	|	|	|	0952
Liupanshui d.	1423	|	|	1922	2022	2045	2100	0043	|
Yibin d.	2359	|	|	0257	0400	0434	0556	0826	|
Neijiang d.	0216	|	|	0519	0620	0648	0824	1114	1537
Chengdu dong a.	0633	0712	0756	0954h	1025	1032	1345h	1631	2026

km		K853	K113	K165 D	K145	K117	K673			
0	**Chengdu** d.	0844	1301	1502	1357	1613	1915	...	...	...
57	Xichang d.	|	2309	0018	0041	0128	0520	...	...	...
49	Panzhihua d.	|	0215	0428	0446	0500	0928	...	...	...
00	**Kunming** a.	0733	0743	0956	1040	...	1633	...	...	...

	K114			K146	K674	K166 D		K118	
Kunming d.	0917	...	...	1655	1819	1848	...	...	...
Panzhihua d.	1548	...	...	2256	2347	0035	...	1201	...
Xichang d.	1831	...	...	0204	0304	0331	...	1450	...
Chengdu a.	0533	...	...	1210	1223	1248	...	2325	...

– To / from Guangzhou (Table **7155**).
– Xi'an(**K165/66**) - Kunming and v.v.
b – Chongqing bei. **h** – Chengdu.
* – *993 km* via Yibin.

CHONGQING - ZHUZHOU - GUANGZHOU 7150

Chinese Railways

km			K194	K72	K204	K686	K578	K778	K334	K426
0	**Chongqing** bei d.	...	1420	0802	1247	1420	1532	1600	1911	2345
00	Fuling d.	...	1600	0916	1409	1533	1700	1723	2059	0103
80	Qianjiang (Chongqing) d.	...	1816	1134	1630	1735	1918	2007	2324	0408
02	Huaihua d.	...	2335	1603	2100	2122	2345	0036	0451	1240
17	Loudi d.	...	0336	2007	|	0122	0350	|	0903	1716
42	**Zhuzhou** a.	...	0528	2204	0257	0304	0542	0620	1115	1935
23	Chenzhou d.	...	0912	...	0613	0633	...	0936	...	...
97	**Guangzhou** a.	...	1342	...	1049	1031	...	1351	...	...

	K777	K71	K193	K577	K333	K425	K685	K203	
Guangzhou d.	1656	...	0832	...	...	...	1610	1547	...
Chenzhou d.	2112	...	1227	...	...	...	2007	1946	...
Zhuzhou d.	0038	0420	1552	1544	1626	2203	2340	2334	...
Loudi d.	|	0601	1733	1742	1808	2353	0111	|	...
Huaihua d.	0638	1014	2155	2214	2228	0445	0510	0557	...
Qianjiang (Chongqing) d.	1111	1504	0213	0247	0314	1129	0931	1016	...
Fuling d.	1313	1808	0418	0514	0527	1342	1150	1243	...
Chongqing bei a.	1443	1927	0526	0630	0639	1503	1302	1359	...

7155 NANNING - GUANGZHOU — Chinese Railways

km		K829 A	K363 B	K481 B
0	**Nanning** d.	...	0030	0540
**	**Liuqiao** d.	1733	|	|
120	Litang d.	|	|	|
263	Yuli d.	2130	0351	0902
438	Maoming dong d.	0122	0637	1306
700	Zhaoqing d.	0441	1021	1725
787	Fuoshan d.	0622	1141	1918
809	**Guangzhou** a.	0654	1208	2008

	K364 B	K830 A	K482 B
Guangzhou d.	1358	1922	2108
Fuoshan d.	1441	1952	2137
Zhaoqing d.	1612	2117	2302
Maoming dong d.	2009	0051	0336
Yuli d.	2255	0344	0614
Litang d.	|	|	|
Liuqiao a.	|	0707	|
Nanning a.	0225	...	0940

A – To / from Chendgu (Table **7145**).
B – To / from Kunming (Table **7145**).
** – Liuqiao - Litang: *135 km*.

7160 GUANGZHOU - SANYA — Chinese Railways

km		K407	T201 B	K1167
0	**Guangzhou** d.	0551	1516	1908
22	Fuoshan d.	0621	1542	1938
109	Zhaoqing d.	0753	1657	2054
361	Maoming dong d.	1118	1939	0012
488	Zhanjiang xi d.	1306	2129	|
601	Xunwen d.	|	2248	0453
794	Haikou d.	1731	0158	0813
1157	**Sanya** a.	...	0550	...

	K408	K1168	T202 B
Sanya d.	...	...	1838
Haikou d.	1125	2038	2228
Xunwen d.	1431	2339	0140
Zhanjiang xi d.	1605	0103	|
Maoming dong d.	1757	0315	0505
Zhaoqing d.	2117	0625	0753
Fuoshan d.	2229	0801	0859
Guangzhou a.	2256	0842	0925

B – Beijing(**T201/02**) - Sanya and v.v.

7165 HAIKOU - SANYA — China Rail High Speed

High-speed '**D**' trains (numbers **D73xx**). *284 km.* Journey 2 - 2¼ hours.

Haikou dong depart (* trains originate at Haikou, departing 15 - 25 minutes earlier): 0700, 0735, 0812*, 0848, 0920, 1010, 1035*, 1058, 1125, 1150, 1235, 1310, 1400, 1414*, 1440, 1513, 1550, 1620, 1650, 1740, 1827*, 1920, 1946, 2003, 2035, 2100*, 2130, 2155*.

Sanya depart (* trains continue to Haikou, arriving 21 minutes after Haikou dong): 0635, 0700, 0730*, 0758, 0823, 0900, 0930, 1000, 1040, 1110*, 1140, 1210, 1300, 1325, 1400, 1430, 1500, 1535*, 1610, 1637, 1700, 1735*, 1820, 1840, 1920*, 2010*, 2110, 2200.

7170 ZHENGZHOU and WUHAN - CHENGDU and CHONGQING — Chinese Railways

km		K389	K257	K1269	K507	K205	K351	K805	T247	K283 D	T221 A		K909	K15	K817	K819	K745	T125 B	K1063	K117	K1075	K357	K291	T9 C	K1257
	Zhengzhou d.	...	0412	...	0540	0624	...	...	...	0920	...	...	1357	1557	1722	1816	1702	...	1949	2017	...	...	2139	2226	...
0	**Wuhan** Wuchang d.	0444	|	0450	|	|	0900	1010	1649	|	...	...	|	|	|	|	|	0133	|	|	2306	2337	|	|	1128
165	Suizhou d.	0718	|	|	|	|	1148	1221	1857	|	...	...	|	|	|	|	|	0321	|	|	0114	|	|	|	|
334	Xiangfan d.	0912**y**	1122	|	1246	1316	1343**y**	1455**y**	2052	1630	...	...	2246	2301	|	|	0110	|	0241	0304	0305**y**	|	|	0502	|
500	Shiyan d.	1148	1338	|	1517	1551	1636	1828	2256	1859	...	...	0133	0143	|	|	|	0645	0507	0532	0545	|	|	0657	|
**	**Xi'an** d.	|	|	|	|	|	|	|	|	|	2228	...	|	|	|	|	|	|	|	|	|	|	0436	|	|
702	Ankang d.	1501	1666	|	1803	1854	1943	2131	0136	2155	|	...	0425	0429	0451	0531	|	0920	0753	0819	0833	|	|	0930	|
978	Dazhou d.	|	|	2029	2155	|	2325	0200	0447	|	0545	...	0751	0808	0809	0844	1304	1244	1126	1139	1150	1229	|	1253	0303
1137	Nanchong d.	|	|	|	|	|	0129	|	0632	|	|	...	|	|	1003	|	1510	1458	|	1325	|	|	|	|	0512
1204	Suining d.	|	|	|	|	|	0230	|	0717	|	|	...	|	|	1046	|	1556	1548	|	1412	|	|	|	|	0559
1375	**Chengdu** a.	0441	0558	|	|	0832	0430	|	0845**d**	1140	|	...	|	|	1231	|	1724**d**	1725	|	1543	|	|	2040	|	0728
1233	**Chongqing** bei a.	...	...	2357	0036	...	...	0456	...	...	0825	...	1053	1114	...	1206	...	...	1452	...	1430	1508	...	1543	...

		K806	K1270	K508	T10 C	K1022	K16		K910	T248	K390	T222 A	K818	K820	K258	K292	K1064	K206	K746	K281 D	T126 B	K1258	K358	K118	K352
Chongqing bei d.	...	0825	0955	...	1133	1145	1229	...	1336	...	...	2018	...	2025	...	...	2157	...	...	...	...	...	2314	...	...
Chengdu d.	...	|	|	...	|	|	|	...	|	1032	1014	|	1715	|	1355	1650	|	1740	1842**d**	1830	2239	0833**d**	|	2359	2348
Suining d.	...	|	|	...	|	|	|	...	|	1247	|	|	1921	|	|	|	|	|	2040	|	0034	1113	|	0148	0129
Nanchong d.	...	|	|	...	|	|	|	...	|	1349	|	|	2012	|	|	|	|	|	2128	|	0128	1213	|	0243	0225
Dazhou d.	...	1140	1300	1236	1413	1444	1506	...	1642	1701	|	2311	2224	2318	|	|	0108	|	2345	|	0333	1408	0214	0456	0448
Ankang d.	...	1611	|	1607	1723	|	1814	...	2002	2051	2252	|	0128	0211	0321	|	0500	0601	|	0614	0654	|	|	0801	0824
Xi'an a.	...	|	|	|	|	|	|	...	|	|	|	0539	|	|	|	0947	|	|	|	|	|	|	|	|	|
Shiyan d.	...	1922	|	1911	2000	|	2101	...	2306	2325	0128	...	|	|	0600	|	0811	0916	|	0907	0940	|	|	1059	1135
Xiangfan d.	...	2233**y**	|	2213	2222	|	2344	...	0210	0159	0331**y**	...	|	|	0840	|	1115	1216	1146	1253	|	|	|	1347	1500**y**
Suizhou d.	...	0014	|	|	|	|	|	...	|	0321	0509	...	|	|	|	|	|	|	|	|	1330	|	|	|	1642
Wuhan Wuchang a.	...	0219	0010	|	|	0508	|	...	|	0525	0812	...	|	|	|	|	|	|	|	|	1531	0606	1701	|	1933
Zhengzhou a.	...	...	...	0533	0423	...	0630	...	1128	...	...	...	1254	1331	1543	1716	1844	1856	2100	1917	...	...	...	2100	...

A – Lhasa(**T224/23**) - Xian(**T221/22**) - Chongqing.
B – Chengdu(**T126/25**) - Wuhan Wuchang(**T127/28**) - Dongguan dong and v.v.
C – Beijing(**T9/10**) - Chongqing.
D – Shanghai(**K282/284**) - Zhengzhou(**K283/281**) - - Chengdu and v.v.
d – Chengdu dong.
y – Xiangfan dong.
** – Xian *0 km* - Dazhou *535 km*.

7175 SHANGHAI - NANJING - WUHAN — China Rail High Speed

km	All trains prefix '**D**'	3077	3003	3073	3057	5479	2212	3065	3022	3091	3061	3069	5467	3081	5483	3027	3094	3007	3011	3033	3015	3043	3087	3047
0	**Shanghai** Hongqiao d.	...	0633	0642	0706	0720	0733	0803	0845	0843	0927	1020	1145	...	1252	1331	1427	1354	1452	1510	1605	1704	1652	1747
84	Suzhou d.	...	0709	0718	0742	0756	0809	0840	0929**y**	0910**b**	1003	1056	1244	...	1335	1406	|	1434	1532	1545	1641	1740	|	1832
126	Wuxi d.	...	0726	0735	0759	0823	0832	0857	0955	|	1031	1113	1301	...	1353	1423	|	1451	1549	1601	1658	1757	|	1849
165	Changzhou d.	...	0743	0752	0816	0845	0849	0914	1012	|	1054	1130	1334	...	1410	1439	|	1509	1605	1618	1715	1814	|	1906
237	Zhenjiang d.	...	0823	0830	0842	0911	0924	0947	1045	|	|	1156	1405	...	1442	1504	|	1535	1631	|	1747	1840	|	|
301	**Nanjing** nan d.	0720	0853	0902	0913	0942	0957	1019	1117	1107	1203	1228	1439	1510	1515	1537	1637	1607	1702	1719	1820	1912	1846	1957
457	Hefei d.	0837	1005	1014	1025	1106	1111	1137	1232	1215	1309	1342	1553	1624	1629	1645	1746	1714	1809	1825	1927	2024	1954	2105
549	Liuan d.	0919	1048	1057	1109	1148	1159	1220	|	|	1353	1424	...	1706	1711	1729	|	|	1853	1910	2010	2107	2037	|
821	**Wuhan** Hankou a.	1114	1230**h**	1252	1308	...	1343	1418	1517**g**	1437	1550	1634**g**	...	1858	...	1922	2019	1944	2051	2112	2156	2257	2241	232
	Yichang dong **7075** a.	1319	...	1457	...	...	...	...	...	...	...	...	...	2111	...	...	...	2142	...	...	...	...	...	...

All trains prefix '**D**'	5680	3028	3016	3093	3012	3034	3008	3054	3044	5484	3082	3088	3048	3004	3058	2211	3066	3092	3074	5488	3024	3062	3070	307
Yichang dong **7075** d.	...	...	...	...	...	...	0710	...	...	...	0840	...	...	...	...	...	...	...	1340	...	...	...	...	153
Wuhan Hankou d.	...	0708	0723	0807	0813**g**	0840	0922	0920	0928**g**	...	1054	1029	1115**g**	1308**h**	1330	1430	1450	1525	1548	...	1553**g**	1630	1718	174
Liuan d.	...	0904	0918	1001	1013	|	|	|	1141	1220	1251	1211	1333	1457	1530	1626	1646	|	1739	1746	1808	1825	|	193
Hefei d.	0803	0952	1006	1050	1102	1122	1158	1208	1229	1307	1340	1300	1422	1546	1618	1717	1734	1806	1829	1839	1856	1913	1956	202
Nanjing nan d.	0913	1106	1120	1204	1215	1227	1313	1325	1338	1425	1449	1419	1535	1701	1732	1821	1839	1922	1944	1957	2007	2027	2104	213
Zhenjiang d.	0944	1136	1149	|	1245	1258	1343	|	1421	|	...	|	|	1731	1802	1850	1910	|	2021	2027	2042	|	2134	...
Changzhou d.	1013	1202	1220	|	1317	1329	1410	|	1458	1519	...	|	1624	1803	1834	1916	1946	|	2047	2101	2108	2125	2201	...
Wuxi d.	1030	1219	1237	|	1334	1345	1427	|	1510	1547	...	|	1640	1820	1902	1933	2004	|	2105	2119	2126	2142	2217	...
Suzhou d.	1048	1237	1255	|	1352	1407	1444	|	1533	1608	...	|	1658	1838	1920	1952	2023	|	2123	2137	2144	2159	2235	...
Shanghai Hongqiao a.	1115	1311	1329	1402	1426	1444	1517	1518	1607	1637	...	1608	1725	1924	1949	2052	2058	2119	2156	2210	2217	2232	2303	...

g – Wuhan Wuchang.
h – Wuhan.
y – Shuzhou Yuanqu.

7180 SHANGHAI - NANCHANG and ZHUZHOU - GUANGZHOU — Chinese Railways

km		D97	K1185	T169	T81 A	D91	D93	T77 B	T99	K11	K527
0	**Shanghai** nan d.	0740**h**	0907	1113	1302	1449**h**	1612**h**	1618	1820**a**	1920	1929
80	Jiaxing d.	0820**n**	1011	1202	|	|	1646**n**	1709	|	2020	2030
188	Hangzhou nan d.	0853	1121	1307	1447	1620	1737	1816	|	2128	2141
312	Yiwu d.	0959	1245	1415	1614	1718	|	1928	|	2256	2304
360	Jinhua xi d.	1035	1340	1500	1702	1751	1904	2028	2123	2343	2347
446	Quzhou d.	1116	1441	1551	1759	1833	|	2121	|	0039	0046
557	Shangrao d.	1207	1612	1701	1911	1928	2043	2228	|	|	0239
673	Yingtan d.	1301	1749	1820	2040	2023	2137	0006	|	0355	0400
813	**Nanchang** a.	1406	2008	|	|	2129	2242	|	|	0545	|
1044	Pingxiang d.	...	...	2150	0039	...	...	|	|	...	0844
1125	**Zhuzhou** a.	...	...	2238	0143	...	...	0435	0330	...	0956
1125	**Zhuzhou** d.	...	...	2253	0201	...	...	0450	0345	...	1011
1259	Hengyang d.	...	...	|	0324	...	...	0613	|	...	1139
1406	Chenzhou d.	...	...	0145	...	...	...	...	|	...	1325
1559	Shaoguan dong d.	...	...	0327	...	...	...	...	|	...	1525
1780	**Guangzhou** a.	...	...	0548	...	...	...	...	1021**d**	...	1811

	K528	K1186	K12	T170	T100	T82 A	D92	T78 B	D94	D9
Guangzhou d.	0800	...	...	1353	1806**d**	...	...	...	...	...
Shaogun dong d.	1016	...	...	1608	|	...	...	...	...	...
Chenzhou d.	1157	...	...	1744	|	...	...	...	...	...
Hengyang d.	1350	...	...	1933	|	2041	...	0133	...	...
Zhuzhou a.	1515	...	...	2049	0041	2157	...	0249	...	...
Zhuzhou d.	1528	...	...	2102	0053	2212	...	0259	...	...
Pingxiang d.	1628	...	...	2153	|	2303	...	|	...	...
Nanchang d.	|	1759	2120	|	|	|	0810	|	0858	143
Yingtan d.	2046	2007	2306	0131	|	0256	0917	0728	1005	154
Shangrao d.	2206	2149	|	|	|	|	1013	0840	1101	163
Quzhou d.	2324	2341	0152	0414	|	0545	|	0952	|	|
Jinhua xi d.	0025	0042	0253	0517	0700	0639	1142	1055	1234	18
Yiwu d.	0103	0120	0330	0557	|	0712	|	1134	1302	18
Hangzhou nan d.	0224	0241	0458	0718	|	0850	1309	1250	1411	19
Jiaxing d.	|	0344	0611	0830	|	0953	|	1351	1511**n**	|
Shanghai Nan a.	0409	0511	0719	0940	1008**a**	1104	1426**h**	1505	1544**h**	205

A – Shanghai nan(**T81/82**) - Nanning and v.v.
B – Shanghai nan(**T77/78**) - Guilin and v.v.
a – Shanghai.
d – Guangzhou dong.
h – Shanghai Hongqiao.
n – Jiaxing nan.

Chinese Railways — NANCHANG, CHANGSHA and ZHUZHOU - NANNING — 7185

km		K315	K1191	K779	K581	T81 A	K1137	T77 B	T5 C	K181	T189 D
0	**Nanchang** d.	...	0643	...	...	...	1359	...	...	...	...
231	Pingxiang d.	...	1041	...	2128	0039	1827	...	...	0513	...
* *	**Changsha** d.	1313	|	1910	|	|	|	...	0652	|	1352
312	**Zhuzhou** a.	1353	1155	1950	2227	0143	1959	...	|	0622	|
312	**Zhuzhou** d.	1359	1210	2002	2242	0201	2020	0450	|	0638	|
437	Loudi d.	|	1403	|	0027	|	2223	|	|	|	|
446	Hengyang d.	1541	|	2210	|	0339	|	0627	0900	0816	1615
808	Guilin d.	2228	2344	0442	0748	1022	0717	1216	1429	1546	2301
989	Liuqiao d.	0116	0221	0708	1031	1319	1200	...	1654	1809	0137
1124	Litang d.	|	|	0856	|	|	1400	...	|	|	|
1244	**Nanning** a.	0500	0615	1050	1410	1640	1555	...	2015	2140	0535

	K182	T6 C	T82 A	T190 D	K316	T78 B	K1192	K780	K582	K1135
Nanning d.	0600	0805	0905	1250	1120	...	1225	1835	2150	2350
Litang d.	|	|	|	|	1242	...	1346	2004	2322	0114
Liuqiao d.	0859	1058	1207	1548	1430	...	1530	2212	0114	0307
Guilin d.	1138	1305	1458	1827	1729	1907	1840	0106	0332	0717
Hengyang d.	2003	1842	2041	0014	0107	0133	|	0850	|	|
Loudi d.	|	|	|	|	|	|	0320	|	1329	1621
Zhuzhou a.	2128	|	2157	|	|	0249	0526	1024	1546	1815
Zhuzhou d.	2146	|	2212	|	|	...	0550	1052	1605	1830
Changsha a.	|	2031	|	0207	0306	...	|	1132	|	|
Pingxiang a.	2237	...	2259	...	...	...	0642	...	1657	1929
Nanchang a.	...	...	...	...	...	...	1032	...	...	2254

A – Shanghai nan(**T81/82**) - Nanning and v.v.
B – Shanghai nan(**T77/78**) - Guilin and v.v.
C – Beijing(**T5/6**) - Nanning and v.v.
D – Beijing xi(**T189/90**) - Nanning and v.v.
* * – Changsha *0 km* - Zhuzhou *52 km*.

Chinese Railways — CHANGSHA and ZHUZHOU - KUNMING — 7190

km		K491	K337	T87 A	T61 B	K79	K739	K1201	K471	K109	K1235
* *	**Changsha** d.	...	0850	0822	0830	...	...	1448	1505	2337	...
0	**Zhuzhou** d.	0647	|	|	|	0858	1108	|	|	|	0023
145	Loudi d.	0834	1105	1027	1040	1047	1249	1709	1719	0154	0210
440	Huaihua d.	1308	1507	1433	1447	1455	1710	2234	2144	0612	0628
709	Kaili d.	1712	1908	1826	1843	1937	2106	0224	|	1017	1031
917	**Guiyang** a.	1940	2134	2041	2058	2201	2323	0446	0405	1239	1258
917	**Guiyang** d.	1956	2149	...	2117	2236	2344	...	0420	1306	1324
948	Anshun d.	2120	2310	...	2240	2356	|	...	0536	1425	1451
1146	Liupanshui d.	0028	0200	...	0132	0238	0338	...	0814	1707	1739
1378	Qujing d.	0313	0445	...	0418	0525	0627	...	1335	1957	2023
1525	**Kunming** a.	0520	0640	...	0609	0708	0800	...	1525	2142	2206

	K1202	K472	K1236	K492	K80	K338	T62 B	T88 A	K740	K110
Kunming d.	...	1120	1140	1233	1914	1942	2150	...	2250	2310
Qujing d.	...	1306	1325	1417	2100	2128	2344	...	0038	0048
Liupanshi d.	...	1851	1642	1750	2358	0041	0330	...	0519	0348
Anshun d.	...	2057	1846	2004	0158	0244	0521	...	0720	0559
Guiyang a.	...	2230	1954	2145	0306	0352	0638	...	0900	0712
Guiyang d.	1428	2245	2015	2200	0318	0410	0652	0800	0930	0726
Kaili d.	1708	0112	|	0033	0544	0652	0918	1025	1152	1002
Huaihua d.	2113	0512	0257	0444	0954	1130	1318	1427	1625	1502
Loudi d.	0114	0941	0707	0856	1347	1615	1724	1818	2059	2000
Zhuzhou a.	|	|	0917	1136	1532	|	|	|	0018	|
Changsha a.	0349	1220	...	...	...	1923	1931	2016	...	2335

A – Beijing xi(**T87/88**) - Guiyang and v.v.
B – Beijing(**T61/62**) - Kunming and v.v.
* * – Changsha *0 km* - Loudi *177 km*.

China Rail High Speed — SHANGHAI - HANGZHOU - NINGBO — 7195

High-speed '**G**' trains (numbers **G73xx**) *169 km*. Journey 71–72 minutes. Trains call at **Jiaxing nan** 21–30 minutes after Shanghai and 28–35 minutes after Hangzhou.
Shanghai Hongqiao depart: 0730, 0830, 0836, 0930 and hourly until 1830, 1834, 1930, 2100, 2131. **Hangzhou** depart: 0610, 0700 and hourly until 1600, 1618, 1700, 1800, 1900, 2000, 2149

km		7503	7505	7507	7509	7511	7513	7515	7517	7519	7525	7527
0	**Shanghai** Hongqiao d.	0800	0900	1000	1100	1200	1300	1400	1500	1600	1900	2000
84	Jiaxin nan d.	0828	|	|	1129	|	|	1430	|	1634	1936	2029
159	**Hangzhou** dong d.	0855	0947	1101	1204	1301	1401	1502	1547	1701	2001	2101
314	**Ningbo** a.	0954	1037	1159	1301	1359	1458	1600	1637	1758	2058	2205

	7502	7504	7506	7508	7510	7512	7514	7518	7520	7522	7524
Ningbo d.	0716	0830	0930	1030	1130	1230	1330	1530	1630	1730	1830
Hangzhou dong d.	0829	0923	1039	1139	1239	1339	1430	1637	1729	1829	1932
Jiaxin nan d.	0901	|	|	|	1304	1404	|	|	|	1853	|
Shanghai Hongqiao d.	0935	1015	1131	1237	1337	1431	1529	1730	1829	1927	2025

China Rail High Speed — SHANGHAI - HANGZHOU - FUZHOU - XIAMEN - LONGYAN — 7200

km	All trains prefix '**D**'	3231	3111	3203	377	3105	3201	3213	3113	3107	379	3205	3207	3135	3209	3119	5431	3117	G55	3121	3101	381		3103
	Nanjing nan d.	...	...	...	...	...	...	0757	...	...	...	...	...	0808	...	...	...	1139	...	...	...	...	...	...
0	**Shanghai** Hongqiao d.	...	...	0630	...	0748	0753	|	0812	0939	0705	0920	1135	1043	1215	1245	1205	|	...	1339	1505	1521	...	1540
80	Jiaxing nan d.	...	...	0704	...	|	0841	|	0846	1033	0745	1016	|	1135	|	1319	1241	|	...	|	1549	1604	...	1626
173	**Hangzhou** dong d.	0715	0730	0748	0805	0904	0914	1012	0931	1111	0818	1032	1252	1213	1329	1422	1315	1429	1405	1451	1623	1644	...	1712
332	Ningbo d.	0835	0850	0911	0925	1025	1051	1139	1107	1232	0944	1212	1427	1328	1448	1541	1441	1550	1507	1616	1742	1811	...	1832
484	Taizhou d.	0937	0945	|	1032	1125	|	1240	1226	1327	1045	1313	1522	1423	1543	1642	|	1657	1602	1724	1843	1912	...	1927
607	Wenzhou nan d.	1029	1043	1111	1124	1224	1238	1333	1324	1431	1137	1405	1620	1521	1635	1740	1626	1749	1654	1809	1935	2004	...	2025
901	**Fuzhou** nan d.	1238	1248	1315	1327	1423	1453	1535	1504	1624	1345	1614	1830	1729	1844	1943	...	1952	1858f	2013	2140f	2209	...	2224
1056	Quanzhou d.	1339	...	1419	1426	...	1546	1632	...	...	1445	1712	|	1833	1951	|	...	2057	...	...	...	...	...	...
1123	**Xiamen** bei a.	1405	...	1445	1457	...	1617	1713	...	...	1518	1738	1956	1858	2017	2114	...	2123	...	...	...	...	...	...

All trains prefix '**D**'	5482	3122	3102	G56	382	3104	3118	3120	3208	3136	3214	3210	3108	3132	3206	3114	3202	3204	3106	378		3112	380	3232
Xiamen bei d.	...	...	...	...	...	...	0730	0800	0903	0931	1014	1028	...	1213	1306	...	1331	1350	...	1442	...	...	1526	1608
Quanzhou d.	...	...	...	...	...	...	0757	0833	0930	1004	1042	1101	...	1245	1333	...	1403	1417	...	1509	...	...	1552	1642
Fuzhou nan d.	...	0650	0710f	0800f	0740	0830	0902	0942	1037	1120	1143	1143	1342	1351	1442	1445	1508	1520	1557	1618	...	1650	1701	1750
Wenzhou nan d.	0747	0850	0922	1003	0950	1036	1115	1143	1244	1325	1357	1415	1544	1558	1647	1703	1711	1727	1756	1826	...	1902	1910	1951
Taizhou d.	0843	0941	|	1053	1035	|	1159	1238	1334	1420	|	1506	1641	1654	|	1754	1801	1817	1853	1916	...	1953	2000	2053
Ningbo d.	0951	1046	1113	1151	1140	1235	1308	1344	1440	1522	1551	1601	1748	1754	1841	1859	1908	1935	2000	2022	...	2059	2100	2153
Hangzhou dong d.	1111	1210	1230	1249	1315	1352	1426	1515	1555	1631	1709	1723	1859	1937	2010	2025	2044	2057	2117	2200	...	2215	2221	2303
Jiaxing nan d.	1150	|	|	...	|	|	|	|	1626	1715	|	|	|	|	2052	2108	|	|	|	2237	...	...	...	...
Shanghai Hongqiao a.	1225	1320	1353	...	1440	1512	|	1638	1707	1749	|	1843	2020	2047	2125	2141	2200	2207	2237	2310	...	...	...	...
Nanjing nan a.	...	...	...	...	...	...	1626	...	...	2029	1912	...	...	...	...	...	...	...	...	...	...	...	...	...

km	All trains prefix '**D**'	6211	6213	6215	6217	6219	6221	6223	6225	6227	6201	6229	6231 A	6233	6235	6237	6451	6239	6241	6203	6243	6245	6413	6247	6249	6251	6253
0	**Fuzhou** d.	0630	0640	0705n	0750	0810	0835n	0855	0913	0955	0940	1010	1125	1224	1316	1333	1400	1413	1532	1540	1614	1644	1652	1744	1850	1910	2030
174	Quanzhou d.	0742	0756	0809	0907	0925	0938	1012	1030	1012	|	1131	1248	1349	1436	1455	1527	|	1702	|	1738	1801	1813	1908	2013	|	2146
276	**Xiamen** a.	0832	0823b	0840b	1001	0952b	1006b	1058	1057b	1202	1123	1221	1397	1439	1525	1558	1553b	1630	1751	1723	1827	1853	1839b	1958	2057	2117	2230

All trains prefix '**D**'	6212	6214	6421	6202	6216	6218	6220	6222	6224	6226	6228	6230	6204	6232	6234	6236 B	6238	6240	6242	6244	6246	6248	6250	6252	6254
Xiamen d.	0718	0807	0909b	0940	1027	1113	1142	1227	1248	1301	1431	1455	1540	1613	1710	1754b	1743	1845	1916	1927	2019b	2025b	2015	2055b	2100
Quanzhou d.	0814	0903	0937	|	1124	1158	1234	1320	1339	1351	1516	1545	|	1708	1801	1823	1840	1934	2008	2019	2046	2052	|	2127	2145
Fuzhou a.	0936	1025	1106	1123	1240	1314	1351	1441	1505	1517	1642	1700	1723	1828	1926	1932	2000	2056	2124	2134	2155	2149n	2226	2244n	2300

km	All trains prefix '**D**'	6472	6474	6476	6478	6480	6482	6484	6413	3135	6486
0	**Xiamen** d.	0705	0930	1050	1205	1339	1600	1753	1841b	1859b	2004
55	Zhangzhou d.	0741	0958	1118	1235	1410	1636	1823	1906	1919	2034
169	**Longyan** a.	0837	1050	1216	1325	1500	1726	1913	1957	2009	2124

All trains prefix '**D**'	6471	6421	3136	6473	6475	6477	6479	6481	6483	6485
Longyan d.	0735	0750	0820	1010	1148	1353	1615	1752	1928	2042
Zhangzhou d.	0831	0847	0911	1107	1245	1444	1706	1847	2014	2111
Xiamen a.	0906	0905b	0929b	1135	1313	1512	1734	1924	2042	2207

f –Fuzhou. **h** –Hangzhou. **n** –Fuzhou nan. **x** –Xiamen.

Chinese Railways, Duóng Sát Viêt Nam — HÁ NOI - BEIJING — 7250

km		DD3 2	M3	M1 ②⑤A	T6	MR1 B	T190				
0	**Há Nôi** Gia Lam d.	0600	1355b	1830h	...	2140	...	...	...	...	...
162	Dong Dang a.	1135	1905	2240	...	0200	...	...	...	...	...
162	Dong Dang d.	...	...	2359	...	0300	...	...	...	...	...
207	Pingxiang a.	...	...	0141	...	0441	...	...	...	...	...
207	Pingxiang d.	...	...	0325	...	0631	...	...	...	...	...
430	Nanning a.	...	...	0635	...	1030	...	...	...	...	...
430	Nanning d.	...	...	0805	0805	...	1250	...	...	...	...
861	Guilin d.	...	...	1305	1305	...	1827	...	...	...	...
1409	Changsha d.	...	...	2039	2039	...	0213	...	...	...	...
1771	Wuhan Wuchang d.	...	...	0013	0013	...	0552	...	...	...	...
2307	Zhengzhou d.	...	...	0541	0541	...	1111	...	...	...	...
2996	**Beijing** xi a.	...	...	1208	1208	...	1740	...	...	...	...

	MR2 B	T5	M2 ④⑦A	T189	M4	DD4 2			
Beijing xi d.	...	1548	1548	2209	...	...	...	...	...
Zhengzhou d.	...	2216	2216	0443	...	...	...	...	...
Wuhan Wuchang d.	...	0330	0330	1015	...	...	...	...	...
Changsha d.	...	0652	0652	1352	...	...	...	...	...
Guilin d.	...	1429	1429	2301	...	...	...	...	...
Nanning a.	...	2015	2015	0535	...	...	...	...	...
Nanning d.	1820	...	2115	...	...	...	...	...	...
Pingxiang a.	2211	...	0030	...	...	...	...	...	...
Pingxiang d.	2241	...	0240	...	...	...	...	...	...
Dong Dang a.	2322	...	0221	...	...	...	...	...	...
Dong Dang d.	0022	...	0350	...	0520	1305	...	...	...
Há Nôi Gia Lam a.	0445	...	0810h	...	1040b	1902	...	...	...

A – (4 berth) Beijing (**T5/6**) - Dong Dang (**M2/1**) - Há Nôi and v.v.
B – 1, 2 cl. Nanning (**T8701/2**) - Pingxiang (**MR2/1**) - Há Nôi and v.v.
b –Há Nôi Long Bien. **h** –Há Nôi.

BEYOND EUROPE
Japan

Introduction

The Beyond Europe section covers principal rail services in a different area of the world each month. There are six areas, each appearing twice yearly as follows:

India:	January and July editions
South East Asia and Australasia:	February and August editions
China:	March and September editions
Japan:	April and October editions
Africa and the Middle East:	May and November editions
North America:	June and December editions

The months have been chosen so that we can bring you up-to-date information for those countries which make seasonal changes.

Limited details of services in South America can be found in the European Rail Timetable Summer and Winter editions.

Contents

INDEX OF PLACES

by table number

JAPAN

Capital: Tokyo (GMT + 9). 2014 Public Holidays: Jan. 1, 13, Feb. 11, Mar, 21, Apr. 29, May 4, 5, 6, July 21, Sep. 15, 23, Oct. 13, Nov. 3, 24, Dec. 23.

Operators: Most rail services in Japan are operated by the six private regional railway companies which are marketed as a whole as Japan Railways (JR); there are also a number of private railways, some quite large, which are not shown in this section. The six regional operators are JR Central (jr-central.co.jp), JR East (www.jreast.co.jp), JR Hokkaido (www.jrhokkaido.co.jp), JR Kyushu (www.jrkyushu.co.jp), JR Shikoku (www.jr-shikoku.co.jp) and JR West (www.westjr.co.jp).

Services: Except where noted, all trains convey first and second class seated accommodation (known locally as "Green" and "Standard" respectively). Seat reservation is obligatory in first class and a supplement must be paid. No trains convey restaurant cars, but nearly all main-line services have some kind of refreshment service available, often in the form of box-meals or in vending machines. The few remaining overnight trains have one or two berths in first class and 2 or 4 berths in second. Trains are very punctual and delays are rare.

Timings: The latest available timings are shown. The availability of english language timetable information varies by operator. An english language booklet of timetables for high-speed and principal long distance trains is available on application from the Japan National Tourism Organization in London (✆ 020 7398 5678 or www.seejapan.co.uk), however it does not list all stations. Much more detailed information can be obtained using the Hyperdia Timetable and Route Search website, which is also available in english (www.hyperdia.com/en).

Tickets: Tickets can be purchased from windows or machines at stations. A basic one-class fare structure applies according to the distance travelled. Rural lines have a slightly higher fare. Supplements are payable for travel on high-speed and express services, for the use of first class, and in some cases where a JR group train uses the line of a private operator.

Passes: The Japanese Railways Group offers the Japan Rail Pass. To qualify for a pass you must enter the country under the status of "temporary visitor" and your passport must be endorsed with this stamp. When you purchase your pass, which cannot be done in Japan, you will receive an Exchange Order which must be exchanged, within 3 months, for an actual pass. This is done at any of 43 JR stations most of which do not open until 1000. The JR Pass is not valid on Nozomi and Mizuho trains and a supplement is payable for any sleeping berths, but it is valid for all other JR Group Railways, some JR buses and the JR ferry from Miyajima to Miyajimaguchi. You can travel in a higher class by paying the relevant supplements. The pass is valid from the date it is first used. Ages for the child pass are from 6 to 11. A variety of more region specific passes are available. Prices: Adult first class 7 Day ¥37800/14 Day ¥ 61200/21 Day ¥79600, Adult second class 7 Day ¥28300/14 Day ¥45100/21 Day ¥57700, Child first class 7 Day ¥18900/14 Day ¥30600/21 Day ¥39800, Child second class 7 Day ¥14150/14 Day ¥22550/21 Day ¥28850.

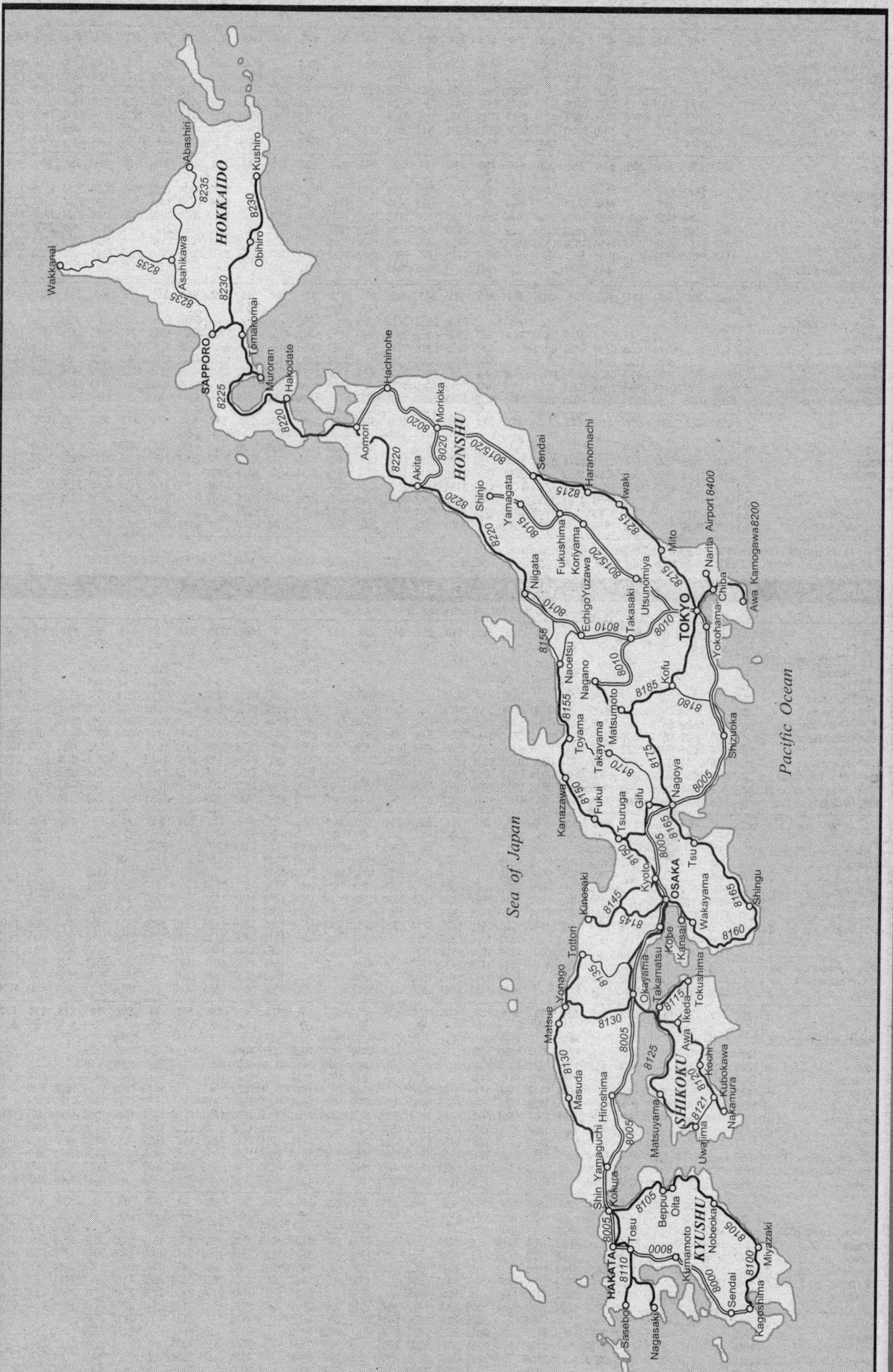
HOKKAIDO
HONSHU
SHIKOKU
KYUSHU
Sea of Japan
Pacific Ocean
Wakkanai
Abashiri
Asahikawa
Kushiro
Obihiro
SAPPORO
Tomakomai
Muroran
Hakodate
Aomori
Hachinohe
Morioka
Akita
Shinjo
Yamagata
Sendai
Haranomachi
Fukushima
Koriyama
Iwaki
Niigata
Mito
Utsunomiya
Takasaki
EchigoYuzawa
Narita Airport
Chiba
Awa Kamogawa
TOKYO
Yokohama
Naoetsu
Nagano
Kofu
Matsumoto
Shizuoka
Toyama
Takayama
Kanazawa
Fukui
Gifu
Nagoya
Tsuruga
Kyoto
OSAKA
Tsu
Shingu
Wakayama
Kinosaki
Kobe
Kansai
Tottori
Yonago
Matsue
Okayama
Takamatsu
Tokushima
Awa Ikeda
Kochi
Kubokawa
Nakamura
Matsuyama
Uwajima
Masuda
Hiroshima
Shin Yamaguchi
Kokura
HAKATA
Tosu
Beppu
Oita
Nobeoka
Miyazaki
Kumamoto
Sendai
Kagoshima
Sasebo
Nagasaki
8235
8230
8225
8220
8020
8015/20
8215
8015
8010
8400
8200
8155
8185
8180
8175
8170
8150
8005
8165
8160
8145
8135
8130
8115
8125
8120
8121
8105
8000
8110
8100

8000 KAGOSHIMA - HAKATA

JR Kyushu

Kyushu Shinkansen high-speed line

km		540	302	304	400	308	600	310	542	314	602	544	604	316	546	318	548	402	320	550	552	554	404	556	406
			A				✤				✤		✤												
0	**Kagoshima** Chuo d.	...	...	...	0609	0632	0700	...	0703	0730	0800	0803	0856	...	0903	...	0942	0950	...	1040	1110	1142	1150	1240	1256
36	Sendai (Kyushu) d.	...	...	...	0621	0645	|	...	0715	0743	|	0816	|	...	0916	...	0954	1002	...	1052	1122	1154	1202	1253	1308
158	Kumamoto d.	0610	0625	0640	0706	0729	0744	0747	0800	0827	0844	0900	0940	0925	1000	1009	1029	1047	1108	1128	1207	1229	1247	1329	1353
224	Kurume d.	0641	0655	0711	0727	0800	|	0818	0824	0900	|	0924	|	0955	1024	1039	1050	1108	1138	1149	1228	1250	1307	1350	1414
230	Shin Tosu d.	0645	0700	0715	0731	0807	|	0823	0828	0908	|	0929	|	1004	1029	1043	1054	1113	1143	1154	1233	1254	1312	1354	1418
256	**Hakata** a.	0658	0712	0728	0745	0820	0817	0836	0841	0921	0917	0941	1013	1017	1041	1056	1107	1125	1155	1207	1246	1307	1325	1407	1432
	Shin Osaka **8005** a.	0944	...	...	...	...	1044	...	1124	...	1144	1224	1244	...	1324	...	1344	...	...	1444	1524	1544	...	1644	...

	326	558	408	328	560	562	330	410	606	332	564	566	568	340	608	570	344	572	412	348	610	458	352	354	414
									✤						✤						✤				
Kagoshima Chuo d.	...	1342	1356	...	1442	1502	...	1531	1600	...	1607	1636	1703	1727	1800	1803	...	1829	1904	1932	1949	2008	2054	2139	2220
Sendai (Kyushu) d.	...	1354	1408	...	1454	1514	...	1544	|	...	1620	1649	1715	1740	|	1815	...	1841	1917	1945	|	2021	2107	2152	2233
Kumamoto d.	1409	1429	1453	1504	1529	1559	1604	1618	1644	1649	1704	1723	1800	1824	1844	1900	1937	1925	2001	2040	2033	2105	2151	2236	2317
Kurume d.	1440	1450	1514	1534	1550	1620	1634	1639	|	1719	1725	1744	1820	1855	|	1920	2007	1947	2022	2111	|	2126	2122	2307	2338
Shin Tosu d.	1444	1454	1518	1542	1554	1624	1638	1643	|	1724	1729	1748	1825	1900	|	1925	2012	1951	2027	2115	|	2130	2226	2311	2342
Hakata a.	1457	1507	1532	1555	1607	1637	1651	1656	1717	1738	1742	1801	1837	1912	1917	1937	2024	2004	2039	2128	2106	2143	2239	2324	2355
Shin Osaka **8005** a.	...	1744	...	...	1845	1924	...	...	1944	...	2026	2045	2121	...	2142	2221	...	2249	...	...	2337	...	...	...	...

	303	305	307	401	403	405	313	601	451	541	543	545	603	319	547	407	605	323	549	551	325	409	553	327	411
								✤					✤	B			✤								
Shin Osaka **8005** d.	...	...	...	...	...	...	...	0600	...	0625	0650	0715	0753	...	0807	...	0859	...	0918	0959	...	...	1059	...	...
Hakata d.	...	...	0610	0645	0721	0749	0810	0829	0857	0909	0932	0958	1020	1013	1045	1103	1128	1147	1206	1236	1247	1320	1336	1347	1420
Shin Tosu d.	...	...	0624	0658	0737	0803	0823	|	0910	0922	0946	1012	|	1033	1058	1116	|	1201	1220	1250	1304	1334	1350	1401	1434
Kurume d.	...	...	0628	0703	0741	0807	0828	|	0915	0927	0950	1016	|	1037	1103	1121	|	1206	1225	1254	1309	1338	1354	1406	1438
Kumamoto d.	0611	0639	0700	0723	0804	0829	0909	0908	0936	0947	1011	1037	1054	1107	1124	1142	1202	1235	1245	1315	1338	1359	1415	1435	1459
Sendai (Kyushu) d.	0656	0724	0744	0808	0848	0913	0953	|	1010	1032	1045	1121	|	...	1158	1226	|	...	1329	1349	...	1443	1449	...	1543
Kagoshima Chuo a.	0708	0736	0756	0819	0900	0925	1005	0948	1022	1043	1057	1133	1137	...	1210	1238	1245	...	1341	1401	...	1454	1501	...	1554

	555	413	331	557	415	333	559	417	335	561	563	339	565	567	343	607	569	347	609	571	573	353	355	611	377
																✤			✤					✤	
Shin Osaka **8005** d.	1159	...	...	1259	...	...	1359	...	...	1459	1520	...	1559	1620	...	1659	1720	...	1759	1820	1859	...	...	1959	...
Hakata d.	1436	1520	1547	1536	1621	1644	1636	1707	1720	1736	1802	1818	1836	1902	1919	1932	2002	2017	2027	2102	2136	2151	2232	2227	2308
Shin Tosu d.	1450	1533	1600	1550	1634	1657	1650	1721	1734	1750	1818	1831	1850	1916	1934	|	2016	2031	|	2116	2150	2204	2245	|	2321
Kurume d.	1454	1538	1605	1554	1639	1702	1654	1726	1738	1754	1822	1836	1854	1920	1938	|	2020	2036	|	2120	2154	2209	2250	|	2326
Kumamoto d.	1515	1559	1634	1615	1659	1731	1715	1747	1808	1815	1847	1906	1915	1944	2014	2006	2044	2109	2101	2143	2215	2239	2319	2301	2355
Sendai (Kyushu) d.	1552	1643	...	1650	1743	...	1749	1831	...	1849	1931	...	1949	2028	...	|	2128	...	|	2217	2249	2324	...	|	...
Kagoshima Chuo a.	1605	1654	...	1701	1755	...	1801	1843	...	1901	1943	...	2001	2040	...	2049	2140	...	2144	2239	2301	2335	...	2344	...

✤ – NOT available to holders of Japan Rail Pass. To use these trains you must pay the full fare.
A – Additional services 0713, 0811, 1309, 1735, 1804, 1908, 2016, 2120. B – Additional services: 0700, 0732, 0840, 0918, 1057, 1446, 1754, 1845, 1945, 2044, 2122.

8005 HAKATA - OSAKA - TOKYO

JR Central, JR West

Sanyo and *Tokkaido Shinkansen* high-speed lines

km		200	100	102	504	104	506	106	108	508	110	214	510	112	512	2	4	460	120	514	6	540	8	462	516	10
		✤	✤	✤		✤		✤	✤		✤	✤		✤		✤	✤		✤		✤	k	✤			✤
	Kagoshima C **8000** d.	...	...	...	...	...	...	...	...	...	...	...	...	...	...	...	...	...	...	...	...	...	...	...	...	...
0	**Hakata** d.	...	...	...	...	...	...	...	...	...	...	...	...	...	...	0605	0629	...	...	...	0705	0700	0729	...	...	0749
56	Kokura d.	...	...	...	...	...	...	...	...	...	...	...	...	...	...	0622	0646	...	...	...	0722	0717	0746	...	...	0806
248	Hiroshima d.	...	...	...	...	...	...	...	0600	...	0619	...	...	0640	...	0713	0737	0613	0800	...	0812	0818	0837	...	...	0852
393	Okayama d.	...	...	...	...	0600	...	0620	0641	...	0700	...	...	0723	...	0749	0814	0727	0840	...	0849	0858	0914	0831	...	0934
521	Shin Kobe d.	...	0609	0619	...	0636	...	0656	0716	...	0736	...	...	0756	...	0822	0846	0826	0916	...	0922	0931	0946	0925	...	1006
554	Shin **Osaka** d.	0600	0623	0633	0608	0650	0627	0710	0730	0717	0750	0800	0726	0810	0816	0837	0900	0840	0930	0916	0937	0944	1000	0940	1015	1020
593	Kyoto d.	0614	0638	0648	0623	0705	0642	0726	0745	0732	0805	0816	0742	0826	0833	0854	0916	0856	0945	0933	0954	...	1016	0956	1033	1035
727	Nagoya d.	0650	0715	0724	0718	0742	0734	0803	0822	0827	0842	0853	0834	0903	0927	0932	0953	0934	1022	1027	1032	...	1053	1034	1127	1112
1044	Shin Yokohama a.	0808	0834	0844	0852	0904	0922	0924	0944	0952	1004	1014	1022	1024	1052	1055	1114	1122	1144	1152	1155	...	1214	1222	1252	1234
1063	**Tokyo** Shinagawa a.	0819	0846	0856	0903	0916	0933	0936	0956	1003	1016	1026	1033	1036	1103	1106	1126	1133	1156	1203	1206	...	1226	1233	1303	1246
1069	**Tokyo** a.	0826	0853	0903	0910	0923	0940	0943	1003	1010	1023	1033	1040	1043	1110	1113	1133	1140	1203	1210	1213	...	1233	1240	1310	1253

	600	14	464	124	518	542	16	602	18	466	126	520	544	20	604	546	22	468	128	522	548	24	26	470	130	524
	✤	✤		✤			✤	✤	✤		✤			✤	✤		✤		✤			✤	✤		✤	
Kagoshima C **8000** d.	0700	...	...	...	...	0703	...	0800	...	...	...	...	0803	...	0856	0903	...	...	...	...	0942	...	...	...	...	...
Hakata d.	0819	0829	...	...	...	0843	0905	0919	0929	...	...	...	0943	1005	1015	1043	1029	...	...	...	1109	1104	1129	...	...	...
Kokura d.	0836	0846	...	...	...	0901	0922	0936	0946	...	...	...	1001	1022	1032	1101	1046	...	...	...	1126	1121	1146	...	...	...
Hiroshima d.	0922	0937	...	0947	...	0953	1012	1022	1037	...	1049	...	1053	1108	1118	1153	1137	...	1149	...	1217	1213	1232	...	1252	...
Okayama d.	0958	1014	0929	1028	...	1034	1049	1058	1114	1024	1128	...	1134	1149	1154	1234	1214	1124	1228	...	1258	1249	1314	1224	1328	...
Shin Kobe d.	1031	1046	1025	1106	...	1111	1122	1131	1146	1125	1206	...	1211	1222	1232	1311	1246	1225	1306	...	1331	1322	1346	1325	1406	...
Shin **Osaka** d.	1044	1100	1040	1120	1116	1124	1137	1144	1200	1140	1220	1216	1224	1237	1244	1324	1300	1240	1320	1316	1344	1337	1400	1340	1420	1416
Kyoto d.	...	1116	1056	1135	1133	...	1154	...	1216	1156	1235	1233	...	1254	...	...	1316	1256	1335	1333	...	1354	1416	1356	1435	1433
Nagoya d.	...	1153	1134	1212	1227	...	1232	...	1253	1234	1312	1327	...	1332	...	...	1353	1334	1412	1427	...	1432	1453	1434	1512	1527
Shin Yokohama a.	...	1314	1322	1334	1352	...	1355	...	1414	1422	1434	1452	...	1455	...	...	1514	1522	1534	1552	...	1555	1614	1622	1634	1652
Tokyo Shinagawa a.	...	1326	1333	1346	1403	...	1406	...	1426	1433	1446	1503	...	1506	...	...	1526	1533	1546	1603	...	1606	1626	1633	1646	1703
Tokyo a.	...	1333	1340	1353	1410	...	1413	...	1433	1440	1453	1510	...	1513	...	...	1533	1540	1553	1610	...	1613	1633	1640	1653	1710

	28	550	30	472	132	526	552	32	554	34	474	134	528	36	556	38	476	40	136	530	42	558	44	478	138	532
	✤		✤		✤			✤		✤		✤		✤		✤		✤	✤		✤		✤		✤	
Kagoshima C **8000** d.	...	1040	...	...	...	...	1110	...	1142	...	...	...	...	...	1240	...	...	...	...	...	...	1342	...	...	...	...
Hakata d.	1204	1209	1229	...	...	...	1248	1304	1309	1329	...	...	...	1404	1409	1429	...	1448	...	...	1504	1509	1529	...	...	...
Kokura d.	1221	1226	1246	...	...	...	1306	1321	1326	1346	...	...	...	1421	1426	1446	...	1505	...	...	1521	1526	1546	...	...	...
Hiroshima d.	1313	1317	1332	...	1352	...	1358	1413	1417	1432	...	1452	...	1513	1517	1532	...	1552	1601	...	1613	1617	1637	...	1701	...
Okayama d.	1349	1358	1414	1324	1428	...	1434	1449	1458	1514	1424	1528	...	1549	1558	1614	1524	1628	1642	...	1649	1658	1714	1624	1742	...
Shin Kobe d.	1422	1431	1446	1425	1506	...	1511	1522	1531	1546	1525	1606	...	1622	1631	1646	1625	1706	1715	...	1722	1731	1746	1725	1815	...
Shin **Osaka** d.	1437	1444	1500	1440	1520	1516	1524	1537	1544	1600	1540	1620	1616	1637	1644	1700	1640	1720	1730	1716	1737	1744	1800	1740	1830	1816
Kyoto d.	1454	...	1516	1456	1535	1533	...	1554	...	1616	1556	1635	1633	1654	...	1716	1656	1735	1745	1733	1754	...	1816	1756	1845	1833
Nagoya d.	1532	...	1553	1534	1612	1627	...	1632	...	1653	1634	1712	1727	1732	...	1753	1734	1812	1822	1827	1832	...	1853	1834	1922	1927
Shin Yokohama a.	1655	...	1714	1722	1734	1752	...	1755	...	1814	1822	1834	1852	1855	...	1914	1922	1934	1944	1952	1955	...	2014	2022	2044	2052
Tokyo Shinagawa a.	1706	...	1726	1733	1746	1803	...	1806	...	1826	1833	1846	1903	1906	...	1926	1933	1946	1956	2003	2006	...	2026	2033	2056	2103
Tokyo a.	1713	...	1733	1740	1753	1810	...	1813	...	1833	1840	1853	1910	1913	...	1933	1940	1953	2003	2010	2013	...	2033	2040	2103	2110

	48	560	50	480	52	534	562	54	606	254	56	482	536	564	538	60	566	62	568	64	608	96	98	570	572	610
	✤		✤		✤			✤	✤	✤	✤					✤		✤		✤	✤	✤	✤			✤
Kagoshima C **8000** d.	...	1442	...	...	...	...	1502	...	1600	...	...	...	...	1607	...	...	1636	...	1703	...	1800	...	...	1803	1829	1949
Hakata d.	1605	1609	1629	...	1648	...	1639	1705	1719	...	1729	...	...	1744	...	1809	1803	1829	1839	1855	1919	1929	2000	1939	2006	2108
Kokura d.	1622	1626	1646	...	1705	...	1656	1722	1736	...	1746	...	...	1801	...	1826	1820	1846	1856	1912	1935	1946	2017	1957	2023	2126
Hiroshima d.	1713	1717	1737	...	1752	...	1748	1808	1822	...	1837	...	...	1856	...	1912	1917	1932	1947	1958	2022	2037	2103	2048	2120	2213
Okayama d.	1749	1758	1814	1724	1828	...	1834	1849	1858	...	1914	1824	...	1937	...	1954	1958	2008	2028	2033	2058	2114	2144	2131	2201	2249
Shin Kobe d.	1822	1831	1846	1825	1906	...	1911	1922	1931	...	1946	1925	...	2013	...	2026	2031	2046	2109	2105	2130	2146	2216	2208	2237	2325
Shin **Osaka** d.	1837	1845	1900	1840	1920	1916	1924	1937	1944	1950	2000	1940	2026	2026	2037	2040	2045	2100	2121	2120	2142	2200	2230	2221	2249	2337
Kyoto d.	1854	...	1916	1856	1935	1933	...	1954	...	2005	2016	1956	2042	...	2053	2056	...	2116	...	2134	...	2215	2246	...	...	...
Nagoya d.	1932	...	1953	1934	2012	2027	...	2032	...	2042	2053	2034	2125	...	2129	2132	...	2153	...	2210	...	2250	2320	...	...	...
Shin Yokohama a.	2055	...	2114	2122	2134	2152	...	2155	...	2204	2214	2222	2251	...	2307	2254	...	2314	...	2327	...	...	...	...	...	...
Tokyo Shinagawa a.	2106	...	2126	2133	2146	2203	...	2206	...	2216	2226	2233	2303	...	2319	2306	...	2325	...	2338	...	...	...	...	...	...
Tokyo a.	2113	...	2133	2140	2153	2210	...	2213	...	2223	2233	2240	2310	...	2326	2313	...	2332	...	2345	...	...	...	...	...	...

For return service and footnotes see next page ▷ ▷ ▷

JR Central, JR West

HAKATA - OSAKA - TOKYO

8005

Sanyo and *Tokkaido Shinkansen* high-speed lines

	601 ✣	541	543	95 ✣	545	603 ✣	97 ✣	547	99 ✣	1 ✣	3 ✣	605 ✣	501	5 ✣	549	7 ✣	461	9 ✣	551	11 ✣	503	13 ✣	463	15 ✣	553	17 ✣
Tokyo d.	...	...	...	...	...	...	...	...	...	0600	0616	...	0626	0630	...	0650	0703	0710	...	0730	0733	0750	0803	0810	...	0830
Tokyo Shinagawa d.	...	...	...	...	...	...	...	...	0600	0607	0623	...	0634	0637	...	0657	0710	0717	...	0737	0740	0757	0810	0817	...	0837
Shin Yokohama d.	...	...	...	...	...	...	...	...	0611	0618	0634	...	0646	0649	...	0709	0722	0729	...	0749	0752	0809	0822	0829	...	0849
Nagoya d.	...	...	...	0620	...	...	0706	...	0730	0737	0754	...	0821	0812	...	0835	0911	0852	...	0912	0919	0932	1011	0952	...	1013
Kyoto d.	...	...	...	0656	...	...	0743	...	0806	0812	0830	...	0916	0849	...	0913	0948	0930	...	0952	1013	1010	1048	1029	...	1052
Shin **Osaka** d.	0600	0625	0650	0712	0715	0753	0759	0807	0821	0827	0845	0859	0930	0905	0918	0929	1005	0945	0959	1009	1026	1025	1105	1045	1059	1109
Shin Kobe d.	0613	0638	0703	0725	0729	0806	0812	0820	0835	0841	0859	0913	...	0919	0932	0942	1019	0959	1012	1023	...	1039	1119	1059	1112	1123
Okayama d.	0651	0716	0742	0757	0807	0839	0844	0857	0907	0913	0931	0946	...	0951	1011	1019	1120	1031	1046	1056	...	1116	1220	1131	1146	1156
Hiroshima d.	0727	0757	0823	0838	0848	0915	0920	0939	0943	0954	1007	1023	...	1032	1051	1055	...	1107	1127	1132	...	1152	...	1207	1227	1232
Kokura d.	0813	0851	0914	0925	0940	1002	1012	1026	1034	1040	1059	1110	...	1119	1147	1143	...	1159	1218	1223	...	1238	...	1259	1318	1323
Hakata a.	0829	0907	0930	0941	0956	1018	1028	1043	1051	1056	1114	1126	...	1134	1204	1159	...	1214	1234	1239	...	1254	...	1314	1334	1339
Kagoshima C **8000** a.	0948	1043	1057	...	1133	1137	...	1210	...	...	...	1245	...	...	1341	...	...	...	1401	...	...	...	...	...	1501	...

	505	103 ✣	465	19 ✣	555	21 ✣	507	105 ✣	467	23 ✣	557	25 ✣	509	107 ✣	469	27 ✣	559	29 ✣	511	109 ✣	471	31 ✣	561	33 ✣	563	513
Tokyo d.	0833	0850	0903	0910	...	0930	0933	0950	1003	1010	...	1030	1033	1050	1103	1110	...	1130	1133	1150	1203	1210	...	1230	...	1233
Tokyo Shinagawa d.	0840	0857	0910	0917	...	0937	0940	0957	1010	1017	...	1037	1040	1057	1110	1117	...	1137	1140	1157	1210	1217	...	1237	...	1240
Shin Yokohama d.	0852	0909	0922	0929	...	0949	0952	1009	1022	1029	...	1049	1052	1109	1122	1129	...	1149	1152	1209	1222	1229	...	1249	...	1252
Nagoya d.	1019	1033	1111	1052	...	1113	1119	1133	1211	1152	...	1213	1219	1233	1311	1252	...	1313	1319	1333	1411	1352	...	1413	...	1419
Kyoto d.	1113	1110	1148	1129	...	1152	1213	1210	1248	1229	...	1252	1313	1310	1348	1329	...	1352	1413	1410	1448	1429	...	1452	...	1513
Shin **Osaka** d.	1126	1125	1205	1145	1159	1209	1226	1225	1305	1245	1259	1309	1326	1325	1405	1345	1359	1409	1426	1425	1505	1445	1459	1509	1520	1526
Shin Kobe d.	...	1139	1219	1159	1212	1223	...	1239	1319	1259	1312	1323	...	1339	1419	1359	1412	1423	...	1439	1519	1459	1512	1523	1534	...
Okayama d.	...	1216	1320	1231	1246	1256	...	1316	1420	1331	1346	1356	...	1416	1520	1431	1446	1456	...	1516	1620	1531	1546	1556	1612	...
Hiroshima d.	...	1252	...	1312	1327	1332	...	1352	...	1412	1427	1432	...	1452	...	1512	1527	1532	...	1552	...	1612	1627	1632	1653	...
Kokura d.	...	...	...	1359	1418	1423	...	...	...	1459	1518	1523	...	...	...	1559	1618	1623	...	...	...	1659	1718	1723	1744	...
Hakata a.	...	...	...	1414	1434	1439	...	...	...	1514	1534	1539	...	...	...	1614	1634	1639	...	...	...	1714	1734	1739	1800	...
Kagoshima C **8000** a.	...	...	...	...	1605	...	...	...	...	...	1701	...	...	...	...	...	1801	...	...	...	...	...	1901	...	1943	...

	111 ✣	473	35 ✣	565	37 ✣	567	515	113 ✣	475	39 ✣	607 ✣	41 ✣	569	517	115 ✣	477	43 ✣	609 ✣	45 ✣	519	571	117 ✣	479	47 ✣	573	49 ✣
Tokyo d.	1250	1303	1310	...	1330	...	1333	1350	1403	1410	...	1430	...	1433	1450	1503	1510	...	1530	1533	...	1550	1603	1610	...	1630
Tokyo Shinagawa d.	1257	1310	1317	...	1337	...	1340	1357	1410	1417	...	1437	...	1440	1457	1510	1517	...	1537	1540	...	1557	1610	1617	...	1637
Shin Yokohama d.	1309	1322	1329	...	1349	...	1352	1409	1422	1429	...	1449	...	1452	1509	1522	1529	...	1549	1552	...	1609	1622	1629	...	1649
Nagoya d.	1433	1511	1452	...	1513	...	1519	1533	1611	1552	...	1613	...	1619	1633	1711	1652	...	1713	1719	...	1733	1811	1752	...	1813
Kyoto d.	1510	1548	1529	...	1552	...	1613	1610	1648	1629	...	1652	...	1713	1710	1748	1729	...	1752	1813	...	1810	1848	1829	...	1852
Shin **Osaka** d.	1525	1605	1545	1559	1609	1620	1626	1625	1705	1645	1659	1709	1720	1726	1725	1805	1745	1759	1809	1826	1820	1825	1905	1845	1859	1909
Shin Kobe d.	1539	1619	1559	1612	1623	1634	...	1639	1719	1659	1712	1723	1734	...	1739	1819	1759	1813	1823	...	1834	1839	1919	1859	1912	1923
Okayama d.	1616	1720	1631	1646	1656	1712	...	1716	1820	1731	1750	1756	1812	...	1816	1920	1831	1846	1856	...	1912	1916	2020	1931	1946	1956
Hiroshima d.	1656	...	1712	1727	1732	1753	...	1756	...	1812	1826	1832	1853	...	1856	...	1912	1922	1932	...	1953	1956	...	2007	2027	2032
Kokura d.	...	...	1759	1818	1823	1844	...	...	...	1859	1913	1923	1944	...	...	...	1959	2009	2023	...	2044	...	...	2059	2118	2123
Hakata a.	...	...	1814	1834	1839	1900	...	...	...	1914	1930	1939	2000	...	...	...	2014	2025	2039	...	2100	...	...	2114	2134	2139
Kagoshima C **8000** a.	...	...	...	2001	...	2040	...	...	...	...	2049	...	2140	...	...	...	...	2144	...	...	2239	...	...	...	2301	...

	521	51 ✣	481	53 ✣	611 ✣	55 ✣	523	119 ✣	765	121	57 ✣	123 ✣	527	59 ✣	529	125 ✣	127 ✣	531	129 ✣	259 ✣	533	131 ✣	133 ✣	135 ✣	263 ✣	265 ✣
Tokyo d.	1633	1650	1703	1710	...	1730	1733	1750	...	1800	1810	1830	1833	1850	1903	1910	1930	1933	1950	2000	2003	2010	2030	2050	2100	2120
Tokyo Shinagawa d.	1640	1657	1710	1717	...	1737	1740	1757	...	1807	1817	1837	1840	1857	1910	1917	1937	1940	1957	2007	2010	2017	2037	2057	2107	2127
Shin Yokohama d.	1652	1709	1722	1729	...	1749	1752	1809	...	1819	1829	1849	1852	1909	1922	1929	1949	1952	2009	2019	2022	2029	2049	2109	2119	2138
Nagoya d.	1819	1833	1911	1852	...	1913	1919	1933	...	1942	1952	2013	2019	2033	2111	2052	2113	2119	2133	2142	2210	2152	2212	2233	2242	2257
Kyoto d.	1913	1910	1948	1929	...	1952	2013	2010	...	2019	2030	2052	2113	2110	2203	2129	2152	2213	2210	2219	2302	2229	2250	2309	2319	2332
Shin **Osaka** d.	1926	1925	2005	1945	1959	2009	2026	2026	2040	2035	2045	2109	2126	2126	2216	2145	2209	2226	2226	2233	2316	2245	2306	2325	2332	2345
Shin Kobe d.	...	1939	2019	1959	2013	2023	...	2039	2054	2048	2059	2122	...	2139	...	2158	2222	...	2239	...	...	2258	2320	2339	...	...
Okayama d.	...	2016	2111	2031	2046	2056	...	2116	2151	2122	2131	2200	...	2213	...	2235	2259	...	2313	...	...	2335	2357	...	...	...
Hiroshima d.	...	2052	...	2112	2122	2132	...	2156	...	...	2206	2240	...	2250	...	2315	...	...	2354	...	...	...	...	...	...	...
Kokura d.	...	2140	...	2159	2209	2223	...	...	...	...	2257	...	...	2341	...	...	...	...	...	...	...	...	...	...	...	...
Hakata a.	...	2155	...	2214	2225	2239	...	...	...	...	2313	...	...	2356	...	...	...	...	...	...	...	...	...	...	...	...
Kagoshima C **8000** a.	...	...	...	...	2344	...	...	...	...	...	...	...	...	...	...	...	...	...	...	...	...	...	...	...	...	...

k – To/from Kumamoto (Table **8000**).

✣ – NOT available to holders of Japan Rail Pass. To use these trains you must pay the full fare.

8010

TOKYO - NAGANO and NIIGATA

JR East

Nagano and *Joetsu Shinkansen* high-speed lines

km		301	501	401	503	303	305	505	307	507	403	309	509	311	313	511	315	405	513	317	515	517	407	319
0	**Tokyo** 8015 8020 d.	0608	0624	0636	0652	0700	0708	0724	0748	0752	0804	0824	0836	0852	0912	0920	0928	0944	0952	1016	1024	1044	1056	1116
4	**Tokyo** Ueno 8015 8020 d.	0614	0630	0642	0658	0706	0714	|	0754	0758	0810	0830	0842	0858	|	0926	0934	0950	0958	1022	1030	1050	1102	1122
31	Omiya 8015 8020 d.	0634	0650	0702	0718	0726	0734	0748	0814	0818	0830	0850	0902	0918	0935	0946	0954	1010	1018	1042	1050	1110	1122	1142
109	Takasaki d.	0658	0716	0737	0750	|	0811	|	0839	0850	0903	0921	0930	0951	|	1010	|	1046	|	1107	|	1138	1155	1207
151	Karuizawa d.	|	0733	|	0811	|	|	|	|	0911	|	|	0946	|	|	1031	|	|	1055	|	1127	1159	|	|
169	Sakudaira d.	|	0741	|	0820	|	|	|	|	0920	|	|	0955	|	|	1040	|	|	1104	|	|	1208	|	|
194	Ueda d.	|	0751	|	0830	|	|	0837	|	0930	|	|	1005	|	|	1050	|	|	1114	|	|	1218	|	|
226	**Nagano** a.	|	0803	|	0842	|	|	0848	|	0942	|	|	1017	|	|	1102	|	|	1126	|	1150	1230	|	|
183	Echigo Yuzawa d.	0724	...	0806	...	0812	0841	...	0905	...	0932	0947	...	1025	|	...	1039	1116	...	1133	...	...	1224	1233
245	Nagaoka d.	0749	...	...	...	0834	0906	...	0927	...	...	1013	...	1045	|	...	1105	...	...	1158	...	...	...	1258
269	Tsubame Sanjo d.	0759	...	...	...	0845	0916	...	0938	...	...	1024	...	|	|	...	1116	...	...	1208	...	...	...	1308
301	**Niigata** a.	0812	...	...	...	0858	0928	...	0951	...	...	1037	...	1104	1049	...	1129	...	...	1221	...	...	...	1321

	519	521	409	321	523	323	525	325	413	527	327	415	529	329	331	531	417	333	533	335	535	419	337	537
okyo 8015 8020 d.	1124	1144	1152	1216	1224	1232	1308	1316	1340	1408	1416	1440	1508	1516	1532	1540	1552	1616	1624	1632	1640	1652	1716	1724
okyo Ueno 8015 8020 d.	1130	1150	1158	1222	1230	1238	1314	1322	1346	1414	1422	1446	1514	1522	1538	1546	1558	1622	1630	1638	1646	1658	1722	1730
miya 8015 8020 d.	1150	1210	1218	1242	1250	1258	1334	1342	1406	1434	1442	1506	1534	1542	1558	1606	1618	1642	1650	1658	1706	1718	1742	1750
akasaki d.	|	1235	1251	|	1315	1327	1359	1406	1439	1503	1506	1539	1559	|	1627	1631	1651	1706	|	1727	1734	1751	1806	|
Karuizawa d.	1227	1251	|	|	1331	|	1420	|	|	1519	|	|	1615	|	|	1652	|	|	1727	|	1755	|	|	1827
Sakudaira d.	|	1300	|	|	1340	|	1428	|	|	1528	|	|	1624	|	|	1700	|	|	1736	|	1804	|	|	1836
Ueda d.	|	1310	|	|	1350	|	1438	|	|	1538	|	|	1634	|	|	1710	|	|	1746	|	1814	|	|	1846
Nagano a.	1250	1322	|	|	1402	|	1450	|	|	1550	|	|	1646	|	|	1722	|	|	1758	|	1826	|	|	1858
chigo Yuzawa d.	...	...	1320	1327	...	|	...	1434	1508	...	1532	1608	...	1627	|	...	1720	1732	...	|	...	1820	1832	...
agaoka d.	...	...	...	1348	...	1413	...	1454	...	...	1557	...	...	1652	1713	...	...	1753	...	1813	...	...	1857	...
subame Sanjo d.	...	...	...	1358	...	1423	...	1504	...	...	1607	...	...	1702	1723	...	...	1803	...	|	...	...	1907	...
iigata a.	...	...	...	1411	...	1436	...	1517	...	...	1620	...	...	1715	1736	...	...	1816	...	1832	...	...	1920	...

	339	539	421	341	423	541	425	343	543	427	545	345	547	429 Ⓐ	347	349	549	351	473	553	353	555	431	475
okyo 8015 8020 d.	1732	1740	1752	1812	1816	1824	1832	1852	1908	1912	1924	1932	1944	1952	2012	2024	2036	2052	2112	2128	2140	2204	2224	2300
okyo Ueno 8015 8020 d.	1738	1746	1758	1818	1822	1830	1838	1858	1914	1918	1930	1938	1950	1958	|	2030	2042	2058	2118	2134	2146	2210	2230	2306
miya 8015 8020 d.	1758	1806	1818	1838	1842	1850	1858	1918	1934	1938	1950	1958	2010	2018	2036	2050	2102	2118	2138	2154	2206	2230	2250	2326
akasaki d.	1831	1835	1851	1903	1915	1919	1931	1948	1959	2011	2015	2029	2038	2051	|	2123	2127	2151	2210	2219	2239	2258	2323	2358
Karuizawa d.	|	1856	|	|	|	1940	|	|	2015	|	2032	|	2059	|	|	|	2143	|	...	2236	|	2319	|	...
Sakudaira d.	|	1905	|	|	|	1949	|	|	2024	|	2041	|	2108	|	|	|	2152	|	...	2245	|	2328	|	...
Ueda d.	|	1915	|	|	|	1959	|	|	2034	|	2051	|	2118	|	|	|	2202	|	...	2255	|	2338	|	...
Nagano a.	|	1927	|	|	|	2011	|	|	2046	|	2103	|	2130	|	|	|	2214	|	...	2307	|	2350	|	...
chigo Yuzawa d.	1901	...	1920	1930	1944	...	2002	2017	...	2040	...	2055	...	2125	2121	2154	...	2221	...	...	2309	...	2352	...
agaoka d.	1926	...	...	1953	...	...	...	2042	...	...	...	2117	...	...	2142	2220	...	2243	...	...	2334	...	...	...
subame Sanjo d.	1936	...	...	2003	...	...	...	2052	...	...	...	2128	...	...	2152	2231	...	2254	...	...	2344	...	...	...
igata a.	1949	...	...	2016	...	...	...	2104	...	...	...	2141	...	...	2204	2244	...	2307	...	...	2357	...	...	...

r return service and footnotes see next page ▷ ▷ ▷

8010 TOKYO - NAGANO and NIIGATA

JR East

Nagano and *Joetsu Shinkansen* high-speed lines

	470	400	500	472	300	504	402	302	506	304	404	508	306	510	308	310	512	514	312	314	406	516	316	518
Niigata d.	...	...	...	...	0605	...	...	0629	...	0657	...	...	0715	...	0745	0800	...	...	0833	0904	...	...	0913	...
Tsubame Sanjo d.	...	...	...	...	0617	...	...	0642	...	0709	...	...	0727	...	0758	0812	...	...	0845	|	...	...	0926	...
Nagaoka d.	...	...	...	...	0628	...	...	0653	...	0720	...	...	0738	...	0809	0823	...	...	0856	|	...	...	0937	...
Echigo Yuzawa d.	...	0607	...	...	|	...	0710	0720	...	|	0744	...	0804	...	0836	0849	...	...	0917	|	0921	...	1004	...
Nagano d.	...	|	0600	...	|	0642	|	|	0706	|	|	0740	|	0803	|	|	0826	0900	|	|	|	0931	|	1011
Ueda d.	...	|	0615	...	|	0654	|	|	0718	|	|	0752	|	0815	|	|	0838	0912	|	|	|	0943	|	|
Sakudaira d.	...	|	0625	...	|	0704	|	|	0728	|	|	|	|	0825	|	|	0848	0922	|	|	|	0953	|	|
Karuizawa d.	...	|	0635	...	|	0713	|	|	0737	|	|	|	|	0834	|	|	0857	|	|	|	|	1002	|	|
Takasaki d.	0618	0637	0650	0653	0713	0733	0740	0748	0757	0802	0814	|	0834	0850	0906	|	0917	|	0946	|	0951	1018	1030	|
Omiya 8015 8020 d.	0651	0710	0715	0727	0747	0759	0815	0823	0827	0835	0851	0843	0907	0915	0939	|	0947	1007	1015	1020	1027	1047	1055	1109
Tokyo Ueno 8015 8020 d.	0711	0731	0735	0747	0807	0819	0835	0843	0847	0855	0911	0903	0927	0935	0959	|	1007	1027	1035	|	1047	1107	1115	|
Tokyo 8015 8020 a.	0716	0736	0740	0752	0812	0824	0840	0848	0852	0900	0916	0908	0932	0940	1004	0955	1012	1032	1040	1043	1052	1112	1120	1131

	318	408	520	320	410	522	322	412	524	324	414	526	326	528	416	530	328	532	418	330	534	332	536	420
Niigata d.	0945	...	...	1015	...	...	1113	...	...	1213	...	...	1313	...	...	...	1407	...	...	1456	...	1523	...	...
Tsubame Sanjo d.	0957	...	...	1027	...	...	1126	...	...	1226	...	...	1326	...	...	...	1421	...	...	1508	...	1535	...	...
Nagaoka d.	1008	...	...	1038	...	...	1137	...	...	1237	...	...	1337	...	...	...	1432	...	...	1519	...	1546	...	...
Echigo Yuzawa d.	|	1028	...	1105	1112	...	1204	1209	...	1304	1309	...	1404	...	1409	...	1500	...	1509	|	...	1608	...	1612
Nagano d.	|	|	1030	|	|	1115	|	|	1218	|	|	1310	|	1352	|	1430	|	1501	|	|	1530	|	1552	|
Ueda d.	|	|	1042	|	|	1127	|	|	1230	|	|	1322	|	1404	|	1442	|	|	|	|	1542	|	1604	|
Sakudaira d.	|	|	1052	|	|	1137	|	|	1240	|	|	1332	|	1415	|	1452	|	|	|	|	1552	|	1615	|
Karuizawa d.	|	|	1102	|	|	1147	|	|	1250	|	|	1342	|	1424	|	1502	|	1524	|	|	1602	|	1624	|
Takasaki d.	1050	1101	1121	|	1142	1203	1230	1242	1306	1330	1342	1402	1430	|	1442	1522	1526	|	1542	1606	1622	|	|	1642
Omiya 8015 8020 d.	1115	1135	1147	1155	1215	1231	1255	1315	1331	1355	1415	1431	1455	1503	1515	1547	1555	1603	1615	1635	1647	1655	1703	1715
Tokyo Ueno 8015 8020 d.	1135	1155	1207	1215	1235	1251	1315	1335	1351	1415	1435	1451	1515	1523	1535	1607	1615	1623	1635	1655	1707	1715	1723	1735
Tokyo 8015 8020 a.	1140	1200	1212	1220	1240	1256	1320	1340	1356	1420	1440	1456	1520	1528	1540	1612	1620	1628	1640	1700	1712	1720	1728	1740

	334	538	336	540	422	338	542	340	424	544	342	344	546	426	346	548	348	550	428	350	552	430	554	352
Niigata d.	1548	...	1620	...	...	1645	...	1720	...	...	1751	1816	...	...	1843	...	1925	...	...	2019	...	...	...	2135
Tsubame Sanjo d.	1601	...	1632	...	...	1657	...	1732	...	...	1803	1828	...	...	1855	...	1937	...	...	2032	...	...	...	2147
Nagaoka d.	1612	...	1643	...	...	1708	...	1743	...	...	1814	1839	...	...	1906	...	1948	...	...	2043	...	...	...	2158
Echigo Yuzawa d.	1639	...	1704	...	1708	1736	...	1804	1812	...	1840	1901	...	1910	1932	...	2009	...	2022	2109	...	2139	...	2224
Nagano d.	|	1623	|	1649	|	|	1730	|	|	1811	|	|	1846	|	|	1933	|	2027	|	|	2106	|	2146	|
Ueda d.	|	1635	|	1701	|	|	1742	|	|	1823	|	|	1858	|	|	1945	|	2039	|	|	2118	|	2158	|
Sakudaira d.	|	1645	|	1711	|	|	1752	|	|	1833	|	|	1908	|	|	1955	|	2049	|	|	2128	|	2208	|
Karuizawa d.	|	1654	|	1720	|	|	1802	|	|	1843	|	|	1918	|	|	2005	|	2059	|	|	2138	|	2218	|
Takasaki d.	1709	1714	1730	|	1742	1805	1822	1830	1842	1859	1910	|	1934	1940	2002	2025	|	2118	2056	2138	2154	2209	2234	2250
Omiya 8015 8020 d.	1735	1747	1755	1803	1815	1835	1847	1855	1915	1931	1935	1947	1959	2015	2035	2051	2055	2147	2131	2203	2219	2243	2259	2315
Tokyo Ueno 8015 8020 d.	1755	1807	1815	1823	1835	1855	1907	1915	1935	1951	1955	2007	2019	2035	2055	2111	2115	2207	2151	2223	2239	2303	2319	2335
Tokyo 8015 8020 a.	1800	1812	1820	1828	1840	1900	1912	1920	1940	1956	2000	2012	2024	2040	2100	2116	2120	2212	2156	2228	2244	2308	2324	2340

8015 TOKYO - SHINJO and MORIOKA

JR East

Yamagata and *Tohoku Shinkansen* high-speed line

km		41	121	201	203	123	123	125	205	127	127	43	129	129	131	131	45	133	133	47	135	135	49	137	137	51
0	**Tokyo** 8010/20 d.	0604	0612	0620	0640	0712	0712	0732	0744	0808	0808	0848	0856	0856	0924	0924	0940	1000	1000	1036	1100	1100	1136	1200	1200	1236
4	**Tokyo** Ueno 8010/20 d.	0610	0618	0626	0646	0718	0718	0738	0750	0814	0814	0854	0902	0902	|	|	0946	1006	1006	1042	1106	1106	1142	1206	1206	1242
31	Omiya 8010/20 d.	0630	0638	0646	0706	0738	0738	0758	0810	0834	0834	0914	0922	0922	0948	0948	1006	1026	1026	1102	1126	1126	1202	1226	1226	1302
109	Utsunomiya d.	0654	0702	0719	0737	0806	0806	0821	0844	0905	0905	0939	0946	0946	|	|	1031	1050	1050	1128	1150	1150	1229	1250	1250	1331
226	Koriyama d.	0725	0731	0757	0822	0834	0834	0856	0926	0933	0933	1007	1017	1017	|	|	1059	1119	1119	1157	1219	1219	1257	1319	1319	1402
272	Fukushima d.	0740	0747	0815	0841	0850	0853	0915	0940	0949	0950	1025	1033	1034	1048	1051	1114	1135	1138	1217	1235	1238	1317	1335	1338	1417
295	Yonezawa d.	|	0820	|	|	0926	|	|	|	1025	|	|	1105	|	1121	|	|	1210	|	|	1307	|	|	1409	|	|
342	Yamagata d.	|	0859	|	|	1007	|	|	|	1104	|	|	1137	|	1152	|	|	1246	|	|	1344	|	|	1444	|	|
369	Murayama d.	|	0927	|	|	1031	|	|	|	...	|	|	...	|	1212	|	|	1308	|	|	...	|	|	1507	|	|
404	**Shinjo** a.	|	0955	|	|	1054	|	|	|	...	|	|	...	|	1235	|	|	1331	|	|	...	|	|	1530	|	|
351	Sendai (Honshu) d.	0802	...	0841	0902	...	0919	0938	1006	...	1011	1049	...	1100	...	1114	1136	...	1204	1239	...	1304	1339	...	1404	1439
497	**Morioka** a.	0919	...	...	...	...	...	...	...	...	...	1207	...	...	...	...	1254	...	...	1354	...	...	1454	...	...	1554

	139	139	53	141	141	55	143	143	57	145	145	147	149	149	151	153	153	157	157	219	59	159	159	221	223
Tokyo 8010 8020 d.	1300	1300	1336	1400	1401	1436	1500	1500	1536	1600	1600	1636	1700	1700	1728	1800	1800	1916	1916	1928	2020	2044	2044	2056	2144
Tokyo Ueno 8010 8020 d.	1306	1306	1342	1406	1406	1442	1506	1506	1542	1606	1606	1642	1706	1706	1734	1806	1806	1922	1922	1934	2026	2050	2050	2102	2150
Omiya 8010 8020 d.	1326	1326	1402	1426	1426	1502	1526	1526	1602	1626	1626	1702	1726	1726	1754	1826	1826	1942	1942	1954	2046	2110	2110	2122	2210
Utsunomiya d.	1350	1350	1431	1450	1450	1531	1550	1550	1631	1650	1650	1731	1750	1750	1818	1850	1850	2008	2008	2026	2110	2134	2134	2150	2235
Koriyama d.	1419	1419	1502	1519	1519	1602	1619	1619	1702	1719	1719	1822	1819	1819	1855	1919	1919	2038	2038	2103	2138	2203	2203	2228	2308
Fukushima d.	1435	1438	1517	1535	1538	1617	1635	1638	1717	1735	1738	1818	1836	1838	1910	1936	1937	2056	2057	2117	2156	2219	2220	2243	2322
Yonezawa d.	1512	|	|	1611	|	|	1707	|	|	1808	|	↓	1909	|	|	2012	|	2128	|	|	|	2251	|	|	|
Yamagata d.	1550	|	|	1650	|	|	1746	|	|	1844	|	|	1945	|	|	2047	|	2159	|	|	|	2326	|	|	|
Murayama d.	...	|	|	1714	|	|	...	|	|	1906	|	|	...	|	|	...	|	2221	|	|	|	...	|	|	|
Shinjo a.	...	|	|	1740	|	|	...	|	|	1929	|	|	...	|	|	...	|	2245	|	|	|	...	|	|	|
Sendai (Honshu) d.	...	1504	1539	...	1604	1639	...	1704	1739	...	1804	1842	...	1904	1930	...	1958	...	2123	2143	2220	...	2246	2303	2347
Morioka a.	...	...	1654	...	...	1754	...	...	1854	...	...	...	...	...	...	...	...	...	...	...	2331	...	...	...	...

	202	204	120	120	122	122	124	126	128	128	210	130	132	132	134	136	136	42	138	138	212	44	140	140		46
Morioka d.	...	...	...	...	...	0631	...	...	...	...	...	...	...	...	...	...	...	1007	...	...	...	1107	...	...	...	1207
Sendai (Honshu) d.	0606	0624	...	0712	...	0743	0805	0824	...	0844	0906	0924	...	0941	1024	...	1041	1124	...	1144	1200	1224	...	1244	...	1324
Shinjo d.	|	|	0541	|	...	|	|	|	0716	|	|	|	...	|	|	0916	|	|	...	|	|	|	1117	|	...	|
Murayama d.	|	|	0604	|	...	|	|	|	0740	|	|	|	...	|	|	0940	|	|	...	|	|	|	1140	|	...	|
Yamagata d.	|	|	0625	|	0708	|	|	|	0802	|	|	|	0903	|	|	1001	|	|	1057	|	|	|	1208	|	...	|
Yonezawa d.	|	|	0703	|	0738	|	|	|	0840	|	|	|	0937	|	|	1037	|	|	1136	|	|	|	1238	|	...	|
Fukushima d.	0633	0646	0739	0739	0814	0814	0835	0846	0916	0916	0929	0951	1013	1013	1049	1116	1116	1150	1216	1216	1223	1250	1316	1316	...	1350
Koriyama d.	0647	0704	0753	0753	|	|	0849	0902	0930	0930	0948	1006	1027	1027	1104	1130	1130	1205	1230	1230	1239	1305	1330	1330	...	1405
Utsunomiya d.	0723	0742	0822	0822	|	|	0918	0934	0958	0958	1030	1038	1058	1058	1134	1158	1158	1234	1258	1258	1320	1334	1358	1358	...	1434
Omiya 8010 8020 d.	0751	0811	0847	0847	0913	0913	0943	0959	1023	1023	1059	1103	1123	1123	1159	1223	1223	1259	1323	1323	1351	1359	1423	1423	...	1459
Tokyo Ueno 8010 8020 d.	0811	0831	0907	0907	|	|	1003	1019	1043	1043	1119	1123	1143	1143	1219	1243	1243	1319	1343	1343	1411	1419	1443	1443	...	1519
Tokyo 8010 8020 a.	0816	0836	0912	0912	0935	0935	1008	1024	1048	1048	1124	1128	1148	1148	1224	1248	1248	1324	1348	1348	1416	1424	1448	1448	...	1524

	142	142	214	48	144	144	50	146	146	52	148	148	150	150	152	154	154	156	156	54	56	158	158	58	160	60
Morioka d.	...	...	...	1307	...	...	1407	...	...	1507	...	...	...	...	...	...	...	...	...	1754	1840	...	...	1940	...	202
Sendai (Honshu) d.	...	1344	1400	1424	...	1444	1524	...	1544	1624	...	1634	...	1644	1725	...	1744	...	1844	1910	2000	...	2017	2054	...	214
Shinjo d.	...	|	|	|	1318	|	|	...	|	|	...	|	1517	|	|	...	|	1711	|	|	|	1843	|	|	1957	|
Murayama d.	...	|	|	|	1342	|	|	...	|	|	...	|	1542	|	|	...	|	1737	|	|	|	1906	|	|	2021	|
Yamagata d.	1304	|	|	|	1404	|	|	1504	|	|	1546	|	1607	|	|	1705	|	1803	|	|	|	1931	|	|	2043	|
Yonezawa d.	1340	|	|	|	1438	|	|	1540	|	|	1623	|	1638	|	|	1741	|	1838	|	|	|	2012	|	|	2117	|
Fukushima d.	1416	1416	1423	1450	1516	1516	1550	1616	1616	1650	1701	1701	1716	1716	1750	1816	1816	1916	1916	1933	2023	2049	2049	2124	2155	220
Koriyama d.	1430	1430	1439	1505	1530	1530	1605	1630	1630	1705	1715	1715	1730	1730	1805	1830	1830	1930	1930	1947	2042	2104	2104	2138	2209	222
Utsunomiya d.	1458	1458	1520	1534	1558	1558	1631	1658	1658	1734	1746	1716	1758	1758	1834	1859	1859	1959	1959	2022	2110	2134	2134	2206	2238	225
Omiya 8010 8020 d.	1523	1523	1551	1559	1623	1623	1659	1723	1723	1759	1811	1811	1823	1823	1859	1923	1923	2023	2023	2047	2135	2159	2159	2231	2303	231
Tokyo Ueno 8010 8020 d.	1543	1543	1611	1619	1643	1643	1719	1743	1743	1819	1831	1831	1843	1843	1919	1943	1943	2043	2043	2107	2155	2219	2219	2251	2323	233
Tokyo 8010 8020 a.	1548	1548	1616	1624	1648	1648	1724	1748	1748	1824	1836	1836	1848	1848	1924	1948	1948	2048	2048	2112	2200	2224	2224	2256	2328	234

JR East

TOKYO - AKITA and AOMORI 8020

Akita and *Tohoku Shinkansen* high-speed lines

km		93	95	95	1 [R]	1	111	3	3	101	5 [R]	7	7 [R]	9	9	11 [R]	13	13	15		17	15 [R]	19	19
0	**Tokyo** 8010 8015 d.	...	...	...	0632	0632	0716	0736	0736	0756	0820	0840	0840	0908	0908	0936	1020	1020	1040	...	1120	1120	1220	1220
4	**Tokyo** Ueno 8010 8015 d.	...	...	...	0638	0638	0722	0742	0742	0802	|	0846	0846	0914	0914	|	1026	1026	1046	...	1126	1126	1226	1226
31	Omiya 8010 8015 d.	...	...	...	0658	0658	0742	0802	0802	0822	0844	0906	0906	0933	0933	1000	1046	1046	1106	...	1146	1146	1246	1246
325	Sendai (Honshu) d.	...	0640	0640	0806	0806	0858	0912	0912	0936	0952	1016	1016	1042	1042	1108	1154	1154	1217	...	1254	1254	1354	1354
497	Morioka d.	0654	0758	0800	0849	0848	1011	0954	0956	1049	1032	1057	1059	1123	1125	1148	1235	1237	1301	...	1335	1337	1435	1437
537	Tazawako d.	|	0831	|	|	0922	...	1025	|	...	|	1129	|	1159	|	|	1311	|	...	...	1407	|	1511	|
555	Kakunodate d.	|	0845	|	|	0935	...	1039	|	...	|	1143	|	1216	|	|	1325	|	...	...	1421	|	1525	|
572	Omagari d.	|	0859	|	|	0947	...	1052	|	...	|	1157	|	1228	|	|	1337	|	...	...	1433	|	1537	|
624	**Akita** a.	|	0932	|	|	1025	...	1125	|	...	|	1230	|	1301	|	|	1408	|	...	...	1504	|	1608	|
593	Hachinohe d.	0727	...	0836	0922	...	...	...	1032	...	|	...	1127	...	1202	|	...	1305	...	...	...	1414	...	1505
675	Shin **Aomori** a.	0755	...	0904	0950	...	...	...	1100	...	1119	...	1251	...	1229	1235	...	1329	...	...	...	1443	...	1529

		21	21	23	23	25	25	27	27	113	29	29	115	31	31	103	33	33		105	35	35 [R]		37 [R]
Tokyo 8010 8015 d.	...	1320	1320	1420	1420	1520	1520	1620	1620	1656	1720	1720	1756	1820	1820	1856	1920	1920	...	1940	2016	2016	...	2136
Tokyo Ueno 8010 8015 d.	...	1326	1326	1426	1426	1526	1526	1626	1626	1702	1726	1726	1802	1826	1826	1902	1926	1926	...	1946	|	|	...	|
Omiya 8010 8015 d.	...	1346	1346	1446	1446	1546	1546	1646	1646	1722	1746	1746	1822	1846	1846	1922	1946	1946	...	2006	2040	2040	...	2200
Sendai (Honshu) d.	...	1454	1454	1554	1554	1654	1654	1754	1754	1839	1854	1854	1939	1954	1954	2030	2055	2055	...	2115	2148	2148	...	2307
Morioka d.	...	1535	1537	1635	1637	1735	1937	1835	1837	1954	1935	1937	2054	2035	2037	2143	2136	2138	...	2223	2230	2231	...	...
Tazawako d.	...	1607	|	1712	|	1809	|	1913	|	...	2008	|	...	2113	|	...	2208	|	...	...	|	|	...	...
Kakunodate d.	...	1621	|	1728	|	1823	|	1928	|	...	2022	|	...	2126	|	...	2221	|	...	...	|	|	...	...
Omagari d.	...	1633	|	1741	|	1835	|	1942	|	...	2034	|	...	2139	|	...	2234	|	...	...	2323	|	...	...
Akita a.	...	1708	|	1812	|	1906	|	2013	|	...	2105	|	...	2209	|	...	2304	|	...	...	2353	|	...	...
Hachinohe d.	...	...	1614	...	1705	...	1814	...	1909	...	...	2014	...	...	2109	...	...	2206	...	...	...	2308	...	...
Shin **Aomori** a.	...	...	1643	...	1729	...	1843	...	1937	...	...	2042	...	...	2137	...	...	2230	...	...	...	2336	...	...

	2 [R]	102	4 [R]	112	6		8	114	10	10	116	12	12		14	14	16	16	18	18		20	20	
Shin **Aomori** d.	...	...	0617	...	...	...	0649	...	...	0743	...	...	0837	...	...	0952	...	1039	...	1152	...	...	1239	...
Hachinohe d.	...	...	0641	...	...	...	0717	...	...	0811	...	...	0905	...	...	1016	...	1107	...	1216	...	...	1307	...
Akita d.	...	...	|	...	0605	...	|	...	0714	|	...	0810	|	...	0912	|	1006	|	1106	|	...	1212	|	...
Omagari d.	...	...	|	...	0640	...	|	...	0747	|	...	0842	|	...	0949	|	1038	|	1141	|	...	1246	|	...
Kakunodate d.	...	...	|	...	|	...	|	...	0757	|	...	0855	|	...	0959	|	1054	|	1153	|	...	1257	|	...
Tazawako d.	...	...	|	...	|	...	|	...	0810	|	...	0908	|	...	1013	|	1108	|	1209	|	...	1311	|	...
Morioka d.	...	0610	0711	0716	0736	...	0800	0804	0850	0850	0857	0950	0950	...	1050	1050	1150	1150	1250	1250	...	1350	1350	...
Sendai (Honshu) d.	0636	0721	0752	0833	0816	...	0855	0915	0930	0930	1013	1030	1030	...	1130	1130	1230	1230	1330	1330	...	1430	1430	...
Omiya 8010 8015 d.	0744	0831	0900	0951	0925	...	1003	1031	1039	1039	1131	1139	1139	...	1239	1239	1339	1339	1439	1439	...	1539	1539	...
Tokyo Ueno 8010 8015 a.	|	0851	|	1011	|	...	1023	1051	1059	1059	1151	1159	1159	...	1259	1259	1359	1359	1459	1459	...	1559	1559	...
Tokyo 8010 8015 a.	0807	0856	0923	1016	0947	...	1028	1056	1104	1104	1156	1204	1204	...	1304	1304	1404	1404	1504	1504	...	1604	1604	...

	22	22		24	24 [R]	118	26	26	104	28	28 [R]		30	30	32	32	34 [R]	36	36	38	38 [R]		96	96
Shin **Aomori** d.	...	1352	...	...	1438	...	...	1552	...	...	1638	...	...	1722	...	1744	1824	...	1838	...	1944	...	...	2040
Hachinohe d.	...	1416	...	...	1506	...	...	1616	...	...	1706	...	...	|	...	1812	|	...	1906	...	2012	...	...	2108
Akita d.	1306	|	...	1412	|	...	1506	|	...	1612	|	...	1634	|	1710	|	|	1816	|	1911	|	...	2016	|
Omagari d.	1339	|	...	1447	|	...	1539	|	...	1647	|	...	1708	|	1743	|	|	1849	|	1944	|	...	2049	|
Kakunodate d.	1350	|	...	1458	|	...	1551	|	...	1658	|	...	1718	|	1754	|	|	1859	|	1954	|	...	2059	|
Tazawako d.	1408	|	...	1512	|	...	1608	|	...	1712	|	...	1734	|	1810	|	|	1913	|	2010	|	...	2113	|
Morioka d.	1450	1450	...	1550	1550	1554	1650	1650	1706	1750	1750	...	1815	1815	1850	1850	1913	1950	1950	2050	2050	...	2151	2151
Sendai (Honshu) d.	1530	1530	...	1630	1630	1709	1730	1730	1819	1830	1830	...	1857	1857	1930	1930	1953	2030	2030	2130	2130	...	2301	2301
Omiya 8010 8015 d.	1639	1639	...	1739	1739	1827	1839	1839	1927	1939	1939	...	2007	2007	2039	2039	2101	2139	2139	2239	2239	...	...	...
Tokyo Ueno 8010 8015 a.	1659	1659	...	1759	1759	1847	1859	1859	1947	1959	1959	...	2027	2027	2059	2059	|	2159	2159	2259	2259	...	...	...
Tokyo 8010 8015 a.	1704	1704	...	1804	1804	1852	1904	1904	1952	2004	2004	...	2032	2032	2104	2104	2123	2204	2204	2304	2304	...	...	...

JR Kyushu

MIYAZAKI - KAGOSHIMA 8100

km											
0	**Miyazaki** d.	0553	0718	0815	0921	1018	1229	1415	1619	1736	1855
50	Miyakonojo d.	0646	0807	0906	1008	1106	1315	1503	1708	1827	1942
123	**Kagoshima** d.	0803	0921	1018	1119	1221	1424	1618	1826	1938	2101
126	**Kagoshima** Chuo a.	0807	0925	1022	1123	1225	1428	1622	1830	1942	2105

Kagoshima Chuo d.	0600	0737	0848	0958	1150	1419	1623	1720	1828	2023
Kagoshima d.	0604	0742	0853	1003	1154	1424	1627	1724	1833	2027
Miyakonojo d.	0726	0906	1008	1120	1304	1532	1737	1840	1950	2138
Miyazaki a.	0822	0959	1057	1209	1355	1618	1825	1932	2038	2228

JR Kyushu

HAKATA - MIYAZAKI 8105

km																									
0	**Hakata** d.	...	...	...	...	...	...	0623	...	0700	0733	0802	0823	0902	...	0921	0957	...	1019	1057	...	1119	1157	...	1219
67	Kokura d.	...	...	...	...	...	0639	0715	...	0800	0834	0857	0917	0948	...	1009	1040	...	1109	1139	...	1209	1239	...	1309
186	Beppu d.	...	...	...	...	0744	0804	0833	...	0922	0951	1014	1034	1057	...	1128	1150	...	1225	1249	...	1327	1349	...	1428
198	Oita d.	...	...	...	0700	0758	0816	0843	0910	0932	1006	1024	1044	1106	1112	1138	1200	1207	1235	1258	1304	1336	1359	1406	1437
322	Nobeoka d.	0649	0712	0808	0912	...	1028	...	1106	...	1208	...	...	...	1309	...	...	1409	...	...	1511	...	...	1614	...
405	**Miyazaki** a.	0759	0830	0917	1015	...	1134	...	1209	...	1307	...	...	...	1411	...	...	1512	...	...	1616	...	...	1721	...
412	**Miyazaki** Airport a.	0814	0841	0930	1029	...	1147	...	1219	...	1317	...	...	...	1421	...	...	1523	...	...	1631	...	...	1731	...

Hakata d.	1257	...	1319	1357	...	1419	1457	...	1519	1557	...	1619	1657	...	1719	1757	...	1819	1857	1920	1959	2020	2103	2205	2257
Kokura d.	1339	...	1409	1439	...	1509	1539	...	1609	1639	...	1709	1739	...	1809	1839	...	1909	1941	2012	2047	2115	2153	2304	2352
Beppu d.	1450	...	1525	1549	...	1627	1649	...	1727	1751	...	1827	1852	...	1924	1952	...	2035	2051	2135	2205	2238	2314	0027	0110
Oita d.	1500	1506	1535	1558	1606	1636	1658	1707	1736	1801	1805	1837	1901	...	1934	2001	2019	2044	2101	2145	2215	2248	2324	0036	0120
Nobeoka d.	...	1732	...	...	1814	...	...	1909	...	...	2013	...	...	2126	...	...	2225	...	...	...	...	...	...	...	...
Miyazaki a.	...	1836	...	...	1923	...	...	2014	...	...	2119	...	...	2234	...	...	2327	...	...	...	...	...	...	...	...
Miyazaki Airport a.	...	1846	...	...	1935	...	...	...	...	...	...	...	...	...	...	...	...	...	...	...	...	...	...	...	...

Miyazaki Airport d.	...	...	...	...	...	...	...	...	...	...	...	...	...	...	...	...	...	...	0925	...	...	1020	...	...	1126
Miyazaki d.	...	...	...	...	...	...	...	...	0600	...	...	0702	...	...	0807	...	...	...	0937	...	...	1031	...	...	1136
Nobeoka d.	...	...	...	...	...	...	...	...	0709	...	...	0809	...	...	0912	...	...	...	1039	...	...	1141	...	...	1242
Oita d.	0445	0523	0559	0641	0713	0746	0810	0842	0908	0910	0939	1005	1011	1045	1106	1111	1145	1210	1239	1245	1311	1339	1345	1411	1440
Beppu d.	0453	0531	0607	0649	0722	0755	0818	0851	...	0919	0947	...	1020	1053	...	1120	1153	1218	...	1253	1320	...	1353	1420	...
Kokura a.	0614	0650	0731	0810	0844	0919	0939	1005	...	1042	1105	...	1141	1205	...	1241	1305	1341	...	1405	1441	...	1505	1541	...
Hakata a.	0716	0749	0830	0855	0940	1003	1022	1047	...	1128	1148	...	1228	1247	...	1328	1346	1428	...	1446	1528	...	1547	1628	...

Miyazaki Airport d.	...	...	1220	...	...	1322	...	...	1415	...	...	1525	...	1624	...	...	1719	1754	1828	...	1936	2023	...	2107	...	...
Miyazaki d.	...	...	1229	...	...	1331	...	...	1433	...	...	1535	...	1638	...	...	1731	1803	1842	...	1944	2039	...	2120	2235	2350
Nobeoka d.	...	...	1340	...	...	1441	...	...	1541	...	...	1641	...	1744	...	...	1840	1917	1946	...	2049	2145	...	2225	2341	0053
Oita d.	1445	1511	1540	1545	1610	1641	1645	1710	1738	1745	1811	1842	1912	1939	1942	2012	2055	...	2142	2144	...	...	2254	...	...	...
Beppu d.	1453	1520	...	1553	1618	...	1653	1718	...	1753	1820	1851	1921	...	1950	2020	2104	...	...	2153	...	...	2303	...	...	...
Kokura a.	1605	1641	...	1705	1741	...	1805	1841	...	1905	1943	2006	2041	...	2112	2139	2228	...	...	2311	...	...	...	...	...	...
Hakata a.	1647	1728	...	1748	1829	...	1847	1929	...	1947	2030	2057	2128	...	2201	2227	2323	...	...	2359	...	...	...	...	...	...

Some trains run on a different schedule on ©.

8110 HAKATA - SASEBO and NAGASAKI

JR Kyushu

km																								
0	**Hakata** d.	0600	0634	0717	0730	0754	0814	0834	0856	0915	0931	0955	...	1015	1032	1055	1115	1132	1155	1232	1255	1332	1355	1432
29	Tosu d.	0621	0656	0740	0757	0816	0838	0857	0916	0938	0957	1016	...	1038	1058	1115	1138	1158	1215	1258	1315	1358	1415	1458
54	Saga d.	0638	0713	0801	0815	0833	0856	0915	0934	0956	1017	1033	...	1056	1116	1133	1156	1216	1233	1316	1333	1416	1433	1516
117	**Sasebo** a.	|	|	|	0925	|	...	1024	|	|	1125	|	...	|	1227	|	|	1324	|	1425	|	1524	|	1625
154	**Nagasaki** a.	0801	0835	0926	...	0950	...	...	1048	1122	...	1148	...	1221	...	1249	1322	...	1348	...	1448	...	1548	...

Hakata d.	1455	1515	1532	1555	1615	1632	...	1655	1715	1733	1755	1815	1833	1900	1933	2000	2033	...	2100	2132	2210	2232	2256	2335
Tosu d.	1515	1538	1558	1615	1638	1658	...	1715	1739	1758	1815	1837	1858	1920	1957	2021	2058	...	2120	2158	2229	2256	2317	2358
Saga d.	1533	1556	1616	1633	1656	1716	...	1733	1756	1816	1833	1857	1916	1937	2016	2038	2116	...	2138	2217	2246	2313	2335	0016
Sasebo a.	|	|	1724	|	|	1826	...	|	|	1925	|	|	2023	|	2128	|	2227	...	|	2320	|	...	0038	...
Nagasaki a.	1650	1723	...	1753	1821	...	...	1850	1925	...	1952	2023	...	2055	...	2156	...	...	2256	...	2358	...	...	...

Nagasaki d.	...	...	0600	...	0628	...	0729	...	...	0829	...	0846	0920	...	...	0950	1020	...	1053	1120	...	1220	...	1320
Sasebo d.	...	...	|	0624	|	0711	|	0808	...	|	0847	|	|	...	0944	|	|	1043	|	|	1144	|	1244	|
Saga d.	0627	0707	0718	0731	0756	0820	0845	0912	0926	0945	0953	1013	1035	...	1053	1113	1135	1153	1213	1235	1252	1335	1353	1435
Tosu d.	0646	0723	0735	0749	0813	0839	0902	0932	0944	1002	1012	1031	1052	...	1112	1130	1152	1212	1230	1252	1312	1351	1412	1452
Hakata a.	0707	0747	0759	0815	0835	0904	0920	0953	1005	1021	1034	1052	1112	...	1134	1152	1213	1234	1252	1313	1334	1412	1434	1513

Nagasaki d.	...	1420	...	1453	1520	...	...	1553	1620	...	1650	1720	...	1750	1821	...	1855	1922	...	...	2023	...	2130	...
Sasebo d.	1344	|	1444	|	|	...	1544	|	|	1643	|	|	1745	|	|	1845	|	|	...	1952	|	2100	|	...
Saga d.	1453	1535	1552	1613	1635	...	1653	1713	1736	1753	1814	1836	1853	1914	1936	1954	2018	2039	...	2057	2141	2211	2245	2321
Tosu d.	1512	1552	1613	1630	1652	...	1712	1730	1752	1812	1831	1852	1912	1931	1953	2013	2035	2055	...	2113	2158	2228	2301	2338
Hakata a.	1534	1613	1636	1651	1713	...	1734	1753	1814	1834	1852	1914	1935	1951	2013	2038	2055	2114	...	2135	2218	2249	2320	2358

8115 TAKAMATSU - TOKUSHIMA

JR Shikoku

km																								
									a											a				
0	**Takamatsu** d.	...	0706	0823	0910	1011	...	1107	1206	1312	...	1412	1512	1612	...	1714	1812	...	1916	2005	2119	...	2222	2329
10	Yashima d.	...	0716	0833	0920	1022	...	1117	|	1322	...	1423	1522	1622	...	1724	1822	...	1926	2015	2129	...	2233	2238
64	Ikenotani d.	...	0804	0924	1009	1115	...	1204	|	1407	...	|	1612	|	...	1814	|	...	2016	2106	2224	...	|	0028
75	**Tokushima** a.	...	0814	0936	1018	1125	...	1212	1304	1415	...	1520	1620	1716	...	1823	1924	...	2026	2114	2233	...	2332	0038

				b											b								
Tokushima d.	0543	0701	...	0823	0922	...	1028	1131	1224	...	1325	1426	...	1528	1646	1728	...	1830	1932	2033	...	2159	...
Ikenotani d.	0553	0712	...	0834	0932	...	|	1140	1233	...	|	1436	...	1537	|	1737	...	1838	|	|	...	2209	...
Yashima d.	0642	0804	...	0920	1022	...	|	|	1322	...	1423	1522	...	1622	|	1822	...	1926	2028	2129	...	2305	...
Takamatsu a.	0653	0813	...	0931	1032	...	1138	1234	1331	...	1433	1532	...	1632	1744	1832	...	1936	2037	2138	...	2315	...

a – From Okayama (dep. 1 hour earlier).

b – To Okayama (arr. 1 hour later).

8118 TOKUSHIMA - AWA IKEDA

JR Shikoku

km													
0	**Tokushima** a.	0648	0903	0948	1201	1317	1500	1656	1757	1927	2017	2235	...
74	**Awa Ikeda** a.	0810	1014	1140	1315	1515	1616	1829	1916	2116	2131	0014	...

Awa Ikeda d.	0648	0652	0834	0937	1125	1237	1333	1539	1637	1951	1855	2140
Tokushima d.	0803	0855	0947	1128	1236	1423	1445	1720	1746	2104	2157	2333

8120 OKAYAMA and TAKAMATSU - KOCHI - NAKAMURA

JR Shikoku

km																									
0	**Okayama** d.	...	...	...	...	*0708*	...	0851	1005	1105	...	1205	*1305*	1405	1505	...	*1605*	1705	...	1805	1905	...	2005	...	2138
	Takamatsu d.	...	0604	...	0720	|	0825	|	|	|	...	|	|	|	|	1624	|	|	...	|	|	...	|	2027	|
97	Awa Ikeda d.	...	0706	...	0829	*0829*	0924	1020	1122	1234	...	1332	*1425*	1523	1630	1734	*1734*	1834	...	1935	2029	...	2138	2138	2257
179	**Kochi** ‡ a.	...	0809	0820	0931	0953	1030	1130	1229	1340	1350	1442	1543	1639	1741	1836	1855	1945	1953	2049	2145	2155	2249	2242	0004
251	Kubokawa ‡ d.	...	...	0927	...	1057	...	1249	...	...	1454	...	1651	1806	...	...	2010	...	2104			2305	...		...
294	**Nakamura** ‡ a.	...	...	1004	...	1132	...	1324	...	...	1531	...	1727	1846	...	...	2049	...	2139	...	...	2341	...	...	...

km																									
	Nakamura ‡ d.	...	...	...	...	0608	0700	...	...	0924	...	1111	...	...	1324	...	...	1510	...	1647	...	...	*1745*	1934	...
	Kubokawa ‡ d.	...	...	...	...	0648	0740	...	...	1004	...	1157	...	...	1402	...	...	1551	...	1730	...	...	*1824*	2012	...
0	**Kochi** ‡ d.	0500	0600	0700	0700	0801	0902	0913	1013	1113	1213	1304	1313	1413	1504	1513	1613	1713	1713	1834	1837	1934	1934	2115	2120
82	Awa Ikeda d.	0607	0709	0813	0813	0907	...	1020	1122	1223	1322	...	1424	1523	...	1620	1719	1823	1823	...	1947	2040	2040	...	2227
158	**Takamatsu** a.	0704	|	0921	|	|	...	|	|	|	|	...	|	|	...	|	|	|	1925	...	|	2141	|	...	2324
	Okayama a.	...	0838	...	0938	1033	...	1140	1241	1341	1441	...	1541	1641	...	1741	1846	1941	...	...	2110	...	2157	...	...

‡ – Japan Rail Pass holders must pay a supplement to travel between these stations.

8121 UWAJIMA - KUBOKAWA

JR Shikoku

km											
0	**Uwajima** ‡ d.	...	0611	0939	1137	1537	1739	1825	...	...	...
82	**Kubokawa** ‡ a.	...	0847	1147	1345	1750	1945	2040	...	...	...

Kubokawa ‡ d.	0627	1004	1320	1510	1658	1824	2019	...	...	...
Uwajima ‡ d.	0830	1217	1528	1724	1902	2037	2223	...	...	...

‡ – Japan Rail Pass holders must pay a supplement to travel between these stations.

8125 OKAYAMA and TAKAMATSU - MATSYUAMA and UWAJIMA

JR Shikoku

km																									
72	**Okayama** d.	...	...	...	...	...	...	...	0723	...	...	0832	...	...	0925	...	...	1034	...	...	1134	...	...	1235	...
0	**Takamatsu** d.	...	...	...	0517	...	0600	...	|	0737	...	|	0845	...	|	0940	...	|	1047	...	|	1150	...	|	1250
46	Utazu d.	...	...	...	|	...	|	...	0802	0802	...	0913	0913	...	1006	1006	...	1116	1113	...	1214	1214	...	1314	1314
164	Imabari d.	...	...	0629	0711	...	0756	...	0930	0930	...	1041	1041	...	1135	1135	...	1241	1241	...	1339	1339	...	1443	1443
214	**Matsuyama** a.	0549	0649	0710	0758	0808	0836	0903	1005	1005	1014	1115	1115	1125	1210	1210	1227	1315	1315	1324	1413	1413	1428	1517	1517
311	**Uwajima** a.	0713	0813	...	...	0930	...	1024	...	...	1131	...	...	1244	...	...	1350	...	...	1446	...	...	1551	...	...

Okayama d.	...	1335	...	...	1435	...	...	1535	...	...	1635	...	...	1735	...	1834	...	...	1935	...	...	2038	...	...	2159
Takamatsu d.	...	|	1350	...	|	1450	...	|	1550	...	|	1650	...	|	1750	|	1848	...	|	1952	...	|	2059	2220	|
Utazu d.	...	1414	1414	...	1515	1515	...	1615	1615	...	1715	1715	...	1814	1814	1912	1917	...	2009	2012	...	2114	2117	2239	2235
Imabari d.	...	1541	1541	...	1645	1645	...	1745	1745	...	1847	1847	...	1947	1947	2052	2052	...	2156	2156	...	2255	2255	0019	0019
Matsuyama a.	1527	1616	1616	1632	1724	1724	1730	1826	1826	1842	1924	1924	1936	2028	2028	2131	2131	2148	2235	2235	2244	2330	2330	0054	0054
Uwajima a.	1650	...	...	1749	...	...	1857	...	...	2009	...	...	2056	2204	...	...	...	2306	...	...	0003	...	...	...	...

Uwajima d.	...	...	...	...	...	...	0533	...	...	0635	0635	0739	...	...	0839	...	...	0949	...	...	1042	...	...	1155	...
Matsuyama d.	...	0505	0505	...	0613	0613	0658	0720	0720	0810	0810	0903	0915	0915	1007	1021	1021	1118	1123	1123	1213	1220	1220	1316	132[illegible]
Imabari d.	0437	0541	0541	...	0650	0650	...	0756	0756	0847	0847	...	0957	0957	...	1059	1059	...	1202	1202	...	1259	1259	...	140[illegible]
Utazu d.	0606	0715	0714	0753	0827	0826	...	0926	0925	1020	1021	...	1133	1132	...	1234	1233	...	1335	1334	...	1435	1434	...	153[illegible]
Takamatsu a.	|	|	0737	0811	|	0844	...	|	0944	1038	|	...	|	1154	...	|	1254	...	|	1355	...	|	1455	...	|
Okayama a.	0643	0751	...	...	0859	...	...	0959	...	...	1058	...	1211	...	...	1311	...	...	1410	...	...	1511	...	...	161[illegible]

Uwajima d.	1155	...	1256	...	...	1359	...	...	1456	...	...	1603	...	...	1709	...	...	1808	...	1905	...	2016	...	2116	...
Matsuyama d.	1316	1326	1413	1423	1423	1520	1528	1528	1618	1628	1628	1726	1737	1737	1834	1841	1841	1929	1933	2027	2034	2135	2139	2239	230[illegible]
Imabari d.	...	1405	...	1501	1501	...	1606	1606	...	1704	1704	...	1813	1813	...	1919	1919	...	2009	...	2111	...	2215	...	234[illegible]
Utazu d.	...	1534	...	1635	1636	...	1736	1735	...	1836	1835	...	1939	1938	...	2052	2051	...	|	...	|	...	|	...	...
Takamatsu a.	...	1555	...	1655	|	...	|	1754	...	|	1854	...	|	1956	...	|	2109	...	2155	...	2258	...	0002	...	...
Okayama a.	...	...	...	...	1711	...	1811	...	...	1911	...	...	2011	...	...	2128	...	...	...	...	...	...	...	...	...

JR West — TOTTORI and OKAYAMA - IZUMOSHI - YAMAGUCHI — 8130

km	Station																									
	Tottori d.	...	0704	...	0824	...	0944	...	...	1123	...	...	1342	...	...	1517	...	...	1742	...	1844	...	...	2049	...	...
	Kurayoshi d.	...	0733	...	0858	...	1012	...	...	1151	...	...	1411	...	...	1550	...	...	1811	...	1914	...	...	2122	...	...
0	**Okayama** d.	...	|	0705	|	0805	|	0905	1005	|	1105	1205	|	1305	1405	|	1505	1605	|	1705	|	1805	1905	|	2005	2140
80	Niimi d.	...	|	0809	|	0907	|	1010	1108	|	1207	1310	|	1412	1509	|	1609	1707	|	1808	|	1908	2007	|	2110	2243
159	Yonago d.	0552	0808	0916	0930	1015	1049	1116	1214	1224	1315	1415	1443	1518	1616	1625	1721	1817	1845	1918	1948	2021	2121	2155	2216	2347
188	Matsue d.	0615	0836	0942	...	1037	1111	1139	1237	1248	1338	1438	1504	1540	1639	1650	1745	1840	1907	1944	...	2044	2146	...	2238	0009
220	**Izumoshi** d.	0640	0906	1010	...	1103	1136	1207	1305	1310	1410	1504	1528	1605	1705	1717	1813	1913	1933	2012	...	2111	2210	...	2304	0033
	Hamada d.	0806	1014	...	...	...	1250	...	...	1417	▬	...	1641	...	...	1832	...	...	2046	...	...	...	...	...	...	...
	Masuda d.	0840	1051	...	...	...	1325	...	...	1452	1616	...	1718	...	...	1905	...	...	2118	...	...	...	...	...	...	...
	Tsuwano a.	0910	*1205*	...	...	...	1356	...	...	...	1656	...	1749	...	...	...	...	...	...	...	...	...	...	...	...	...
	Yamaguchi a.	*1137*	*1316*	...	...	...	...	...	...	...	1818	...	*2044*	...	...	...	...	...	...	...	...	...	...	...	...	...
	Shin **Yamaguchi** a.	*1216*	*1354*	...	...	...	...	...	...	...	1841	...	*2109*	...	...	...	...	...	...	...	...	...	...	...	...	...

km	Station																									
0	Shin **Yamaguchi** d.	...	...	...	...	...	...	...	...	...	...	...	...	...	...	*0912*	...	...	...	...	...	...	*1329*	...	...	...
13	Yamaguchi d.	...	...	...	...	...	...	...	...	...	...	...	...	...	...	0946	...	...	...	...	...	...	1358	...	...	...
63	Tsuwano d.	...	...	...	...	...	...	...	...	...	...	...	...	*0958*	...	1110	...	...	...	1356	...	...	1519	...	...	...
94	Masuda d.	...	...	...	...	...	0552	...	0702	...	...	...	...	*1031*	...	1150	1217	...	...	1432	...	...	1600	1608	...	...
135	Hamada d.	...	...	...	...	...	0624	...	0738	...	...	...	...	*1103*	...	...	1251	...	...	1506	...	...	...	1641	...	...
224	**Izumoshi** d.	0447	0533	...	0628	0724	0737	0832	0855	0934	1033	...	1135	1235	1333	...	1401	1430	1533	1614	1631	1717	...	1748	1835	...
256	Matsue d.	0512	0558	...	0659	0751	0800	0858	0924	1001	1058	...	1203	1301	1359	...	1427	1459	1601	1642	1659	1743	...	1814	1901	...
285	Yonago d.	0536	0624	0700	0725	0819	0825	0923	0950	1027	1126	1219	1227	1326	1428	...	1453	1527	1627	1711	1724	1814	...	1841	1925	2040
	Niimi d.	0641	0729	|	0834	0933	|	1036	|	1134	1234	|	1336	1436	15364	...	|	1636	1735	|	1835	1924	...	|	2034	|
	Okayama a.	0741	0834	|	0938	1035	|	1138	|	1238	1338	|	1438	1538	1638	...	|	1738	1838	|	1938	2023	...	|	2135	|
338	Kurayoshi d.	...	...	0733	...	...	0858	...	1027	...	...	1251	...	...	...	...	1524	...	...	1743	...	...	...	1914	...	2112
378	**Tottori** a.	...	...	0804	...	...	0927	...	1058	...	...	1319	...	...	...	...	1553	...	...	1816	...	...	...	1943	...	2140

JR West — KYOTO and OKAYAMA - KURAYOSHI — 8135

km	Station																							
0	**Kyoto** d.	...	0706	...	...	0852	...	...	1052	...	...	1252	...	1452	...	...	1656	...	...	1932	...	...	...	...
39	Shin Osaka d.	...	0730	...	...	0916	...	...	1116	...	...	1316	...	1516	...	...	1719	...	...	1957	...	...	...	...
43	Osaka d.	...	0737	...	...	0924	...	...	1124	...	...	1324	...	1524	...	...	1726	...	...	2005	...	...	...	...
131	Himeji d.	...	0837	...	...	1022	...	...	1220	...	...	1420	...	1620	...	...	1821	...	...	2106	...	...	...	...
	Okayama d.	*0647*	|	...	*0914*	|	...	*1105*	|	...	*1343*	|	...	|	*1724*	...	|	*1946*	...	|	...	...	...	...
166	Kamigori ‡ d.	0725	0902	...	0950	1048	...	1142	1243	...	1419	1444	...	1644	1803	...	1845	2022	...	2130	...	...	...	...
222	Chizu ‡ d.	0811	0944	...	1036	1130	...	1226	1323	...	1501	1524	...	1725	1845	...	1931	2104	...	2214	...	...	...	...
254	Tottori d.	0838	1014	...	1104	1159	...	1253	1353	...	1533	1556	...	1753	1917	...	2001	2130	...	2242	...	...	...	...
294	**Kurayoshi** a.	...	1044	...	...	1231	...	...	1423	...	...	1623	...	...	...	...	2032	...	...	...	...	...	...	...

km	Station																							
0	**Kurayoshi** d.	0608	...	...	0817	...	...	1014	...	1222	...	...	1425	...	...	1624	...	...	...	...	...	...	...	...
40	Tottori d.	0639	...	0705	0853	...	1002	1046	...	1254	1400	...	1454	1621	...	1654	1840	...	1858	2035	...	...	...	...
72	Chizu ‡ d.	0708	...	0734	0921	...	1033	1115	...	1322	1427	...	1522	1652	...	1724	1908	...	1932	2103	...	...	...	...
128	Kamigori ‡ d.	0751	...	0820	1003	...	1115	1202	...	1401	1510	...	1600	1733	...	1804	1947	...	2014	2148	...	...	...	...
182	**Okayama** a.	|	...	*0857*	|	...	*1148*	|	...	|	*1545*	...	|	*1811*	...	|	|	...	*2048*	*2222*	...	...	...	...
	Himeji d.	0815	...	...	1025	...	...	1225	...	1425	...	...	1625	...	...	1829	2010	...	...	...	...	...	...	...
	Osaka d.	0924	...	...	1120	...	...	1321	...	1521	...	...	1719	...	...	1936	2105	...	...	...	...	...	...	...
	Shin Osaka d.	0929	...	...	1124	...	...	1326	...	1526	...	...	1724	...	...	1942	2111	...	...	...	...	...	...	...
	Kyoto a.	0952	...	...	1147	...	...	1348	...	1548	...	...	1748	...	...	2005	2137	...	...	...	...	...	...	...

‡ – Japan Rail Pass holders must pay a supplement to travel between these stations.

JR West — KYOTO and OSAKA - KINOSAKI — 8145

km	Station																							
0	**Kyoto** d.	0836	0925	...	1025	1125	...	1225	1325	...	1425	1525	...	1625	1729	...	1829	1929	...	2037	...	2137	...	...
76	Ayabe d.	0945	1032	...	1135	1231	...	1340	1432	...	1535	1631	...	1735	1841	...	1945	2045	...	2149	...	2243	...	...
89	Fukuchiyama d.	0954	1041	...	1144	1245	...	1349	1444	...	1545	1640	...	1743	1854	...	1954	2057	...	2158	...	2252	...	...
148	Toyooka d.	...	...	...	...	1340	...	...	1541	...	...	...	...	...	1950	...	...	2152	...	...	...	...	...	...
158	**Kinosaki** Onsen a.	...	...	...	...	1349	...	...	1549	...	...	...	...	...	...	...	...	...	...	...	...	...	...	...

Kinosaki Onsen d.	...	...	...	...	...	...	...	...	...	...	1039	...	...	1232	...	...	...	...	...	1612	...	...	...	...
Toyooka d.	...	...	...	...	...	0742	...	...	...	...	1049	...	...	1242	...	...	...	...	...	1622	...	...	...	...
Fukuchiyama d.	...	0602	0655	...	0743	0838	...	0948	1041	...	1145	1242	...	1343	1440	...	1543	1642	...	1728	1822	...	1929	...
Ayabe d.	...	0612	0712	...	0753	0855	...	0958	1059	...	1156	1300	...	1356	1458	...	1556	1659	...	1740	1842	...	1942	...
Kyoto a.	...	0719	0821	...	0859	1006	...	1106	1206	...	1305	1406	...	1505	1605	...	1706	1808	...	1849	1953	...	2048	...

km	Station																							
0	Shin **Osaka** d.	0808	...	0904	1005	...	1105	...	1205	1305	...	1405	...	1505	1705	...	1801	...	1906	2005	...	2105	...	2205
4	**Osaka** d.	0814	...	0910	1011	...	1111	...	1211	1311	...	1411	...	1511	1711	...	1811	...	1912	2012	...	2112	...	2212
118	Fukuchiyama d.	0956	...	1048	1146	...	1243	...	1350	1442	...	1546	...	1647	1852	...	2002	...	2055	2155	...	2255	...	2355
178	Toyooka d.	1050	...	1144	1242	...	...	...	1445	...	...	1641	...	1747	...	...	2056	...	...	...	...	...	...	...
188	**Kinosaki** Onsen a.	1058	...	1152	1250	...	...	...	1454	...	...	1650	...	1756	...	...	...	...	...	...	...	...	...	...

Kinosaki Onsen d.	...	...	...	...	...	...	...	...	...	...	0925	...	1133	...	1330	...	1435	...	1530	...	...	1702	...	1818
Toyooka d.	...	...	0550	...	...	...	...	...	...	...	0935	...	1143	...	1339	...	1445	...	1540	...	...	1712	...	1828
Fukuchiyama d.	...	0551	0521	...	0745	...	0840	...	0949	...	1046	...	1245	...	1442	...	1545	...	1646	...	1723	1815	...	1926
Osaka a.	...	0735	0839	...	0926	...	1019	...	1123	...	1223	...	1423	...	1621	...	1720	...	1820	...	1855	1947	...	2100
Shin **Osaka** a.	...	0743	0846	...	0933	...	1025	...	1129	...	1229	...	1429	...	1627	...	1726	...	1828	...	1901	1953	...	2106

JR West — OSAKA and NAGOYA - TOYAMA — 8150

km	Station																							
0	**Osaka** d.	...	...	0709	...	0740	...	0810	0840	...	...	0912	0942	...	1012	1042	...	...	1142	...	1212	1242	...	1342
4	Shin **Osaka** d.	...	...	0714	...	0744	...	0818	0844	...	...	0917	0946	...	1016	1046	...	...	1146	...	1216	1246	...	1346
43	Kyoto d.	...	...	0738	...	0811	...	0841	0909	...	...	0942	1010	...	1040	1110	...	...	1210	...	1240	1310	...	1410
	Nagoya d.	...	...	|	...	|	0750	|	|	...	0850	|	|	0948	|	|	...	...	|	1148	|	|	...	|
	Gifu d.	...	...	|	...	|	0810	|	|	...	0911	|	|	1012	|	|	...	...	|	1212	|	|	...	|
	Maibara d.	...	...	|	0809	|	0859	|	|	...	0956	|	|	1056	|	|	...	1156	|	1256	|	|	1356	|
137	Tsuruga d.	...	...	0829	0840	0902	0928	0938	|	...	1026	1035	|	1125	1134	|	...	1225	1302	1326	|	1402	1426	1502
191	Fukui d.	0700	0730	0902	0916	0937	1002	1013	1031	...	1100	1111	1133	1200	1209	1232	...	1300	1335	1401	1408	1435	1501	1536
268	Kanazawa d.	0748	0820	0946	1006	1029	1050	1103	1121	...	1148	1200	1218	1249	1257	1322	...	1348	1423	1449	1453	1527	1549	1625
308	Takaoka d.	...	0844	1011	...	1053	1114	...	1145	...	...	...	1244	1313	...	1349	...	...	1447	1514	...	1552	...	1652
327	**Toyama** a.	...	0855	1022	...	1105	1127	...	1157	...	...	...	1256	1325	...	1401	...	...	1501	1526	...	1604	...	1704

km	Station																							
	Osaka d.	...	1442	...	1542	...	...	1612	1642	...	1712	1742	...	...	1812	1842	...	1927	...	2007	...	2056	...	...
	Shin **Osaka** d.	...	1446	...	1546	...	...	1616	1646	...	1716	1746	...	...	1816	1846	...	1931	...	2012	...	2101	...	...
	Kyoto d.	...	1510	...	1610	...	...	1640	1709	...	1740	1809	...	...	1840	1909	...	1954	...	2037	...	2124	...	...
0	**Nagoya** d.	1348	|	...	|	1548	...	|	|	...	|	|	...	1748	|	|	...	|	...	|	2003	|	...	...
30	Gifu d.	1410	|	...	|	1611	...	|	|	...	|	|	...	1811	|	|	...	|	...	|	2024	|	...	...
80	Maibara d.	1456	|	1556	|	1656	...	|	|	1756	|	|	...	1856	|	|	1956	|	...	|	2105	|	2156	2248
126	Tsuruga d.	1525	1602	1626	1702	1724	...	1732	|	1825	1835	|	...	1927	1936	2006	2025	2049	...	2133	2138	2217	2225	2317
180	Fukui d.	1600	1635	1701	1736	1759	...	1805	1830	1859	1910	1931	...	2002	2011	2037	2100	2123	...	2208	2213	2249	2259	2351
257	Kanazawa d.	1651	1724	1751	1828	1849	...	1852	1918	1951	1958	2023	...	2050	2100	2122	2151	2214	...	2257	2303	2335	2347	0039
297	Takaoka d.	1716	1751	...	1852	1915	...	...	1943	...	...	2046	...	2116	...	2147	...	2239	...	...	2329	0000	...	...
316	**Toyama** a.	1729	1804	...	1903	1926	...	...	1954	...	...	2059	...	2128	...	2200	...	2253	...	...	2341	0012	...	...

For return service see next page ▷ ▷ ▷

8150 TOYAMA - NAGOYA and OSAKA — JR West

Toyama d.	...	0456	0508	...	...	...	0612	...	0709	...	0725	...	...	0818	...	0909	0914	...	...	1010	...	1106	1116	...
Takaoka d.	...	0508	0520	...	...	...	0626	...	0722	...	0737	...	...	0830	...	0921	0927	...	...	1022	...	1118	1129	...
Kanazawa d.	0500	0535	0547	0611	0643	...	0702	0711	0749	...	0805	0815	0848	0903	...	0948	0953	1048	...	1055	1124	1145	1156	1249
Fukui d.	0549	0620	0636	0701	0733	...	0747	0800	0838	...	0848	0905	0937	0947	...	1037	1042	1136	...	1142	1209	1235	1244	1337
Tsuruga d.	0621	0653	0710	0738	0811	...	0817	0838	0912	...	|	0939	1010	|	...	1110	1116	1209	...	1216	|	1310	1316	1411
Maibara d.	0656	|	0752	|	0844	...	|	|	0950	...	|	|	1044	|	...	1150	|	1244	...	|	|	1350	|	1444
Gifu d.	...	|	0829	|	...	...	|	|	1026	...	|	|	...	|	...	1227	|	...	...	|	|	1427	|	...
Nagoya a.	...	|	0851	|	...	...	|	|	1048	...	|	|	...	|	...	1248	|	...	...	|	|	1448	|	...
Kyoto a.	...	0751	...	0837	...	...	0911	0934	...	...	1011	1037	...	1109	...	...	1209	...	...	1309	1337	...	1409	...
Shin **Osaka** a.	...	0817	...	0901	...	...	0934	0958	...	...	1035	1101	...	1132	...	...	1232	...	...	1332	1401	...	1432	...
Osaka a.	...	0822	...	0906	...	...	0939	1003	...	...	1039	1106	...	1137	...	...	1237	...	...	1337	1406	...	1437	...

Toyama d.	1208	1306	1310	...	...	1419	...	...	...	1522	...	1611	1616	...	1711	1756	1813	...	...	...	1956	...	2149	...
Takaoka d.	1221	1318	1322	...	...	1431	...	...	...	1535	...	1623	1628	...	1723	1809	1826	...	...	...	2008	...	2202	...
Kanazawa d.	1253	1345	1356	1417	1446	1457	1519	1548	...	1601	1613	1648	1654	1748	1756	1842	1851	1943	...	2005	2035	2143	2229	...
Fukui d.	1342	1435	1443	1506	1536	1543	1607	1637	...	1644	1706	1737	1744	1837	1842	1928	1941	2032	...	2055	2120	2231	2316	...
Tsuruga d.	1416	1510	1516	1541	1610	|	1642	1710	...	|	1741	1810	1815	1911	1915	2001	2014	2106	...	2129	2150	...	...	...
Maibara d.	|	1550	|	|	1650	|	|	1744	...	|	|	1850	|	1944	|	|	2051	|	...	2201	|	...	...	...
Gifu d.	|	1626	|	|	1726	|	|	...	...	|	|	1925	|	...	|	|	2124	|	...	...	|	...	...	...
Nagoya a.	|	1649	|	|	1749	|	|	...	...	|	|	1946	|	...	|	|	2146	|	...	...	|	...	...	...
Kyoto a.	1509	...	1609	1637	...	1707	1739	...	...	1809	1838	...	1908	...	2009	2054	...	2202	...	...	2244	...	...	...
Shin **Osaka** a.	1532	...	1632	1701	...	1730	1803	...	...	1832	1902	...	1932	...	2032	2117	...	2225	...	...	2307	...	...	...
Osaka a.	1537	...	1637	1706	...	1735	1809	...	...	1837	1907	...	1937	...	2037	2122	...	2230	...	...	2312	...	...	...

8155 ECHIGO YUZAWA and NIIGATA - KANAZAWA — JR East

km																								
0	**Echigo Yuzawa** ‡ d.	0820	...	0914	1048	...	...	1140	1240	1334	...	...	1439	...	1539	...	1636	1739	...	1838	...	1939	2130	...
	Niigata d.	|	0754	|	|	...	1012	|	|	|	...	1302	|	...	|	1520	|	|	...	|	1813	|	|	...
	Nagaoka d.	|	0847	|	|	...	1103	|	|	|	...	1356	|	...	|	1611	|	|	...	|	1905	|	|	...
84	**Naoetsu** ‡ d.	0907	0938	1010	1138	...	1154	1233	1330	1425	...	1447	1526	...	1631	1703	1729	1832	...	1935	1957	2036	2217	...
123	Itoigawa d.	|	1002	1033	|	...	1220	1256	1353	|	...	1513	1549	...	1656	1728	1752	1854	...	1958	2021	2059	2240	...
202	Toyama d.	1016	1053	1123	1246	...	1315	1343	1440	1532	...	1603	1638	...	1743	1820	1841	1941	...	2047	2112	2149	2327	...
221	Takaoka d.	1028	1106	1135	1258	...	1328	1355	1452	1545	...	1616	1650	...	1755	1833	1854	1954	...	2059	2126	2202	2339	...
262	**Kanazawa** a.	1053	1131	1159	1323	...	1353	1420	1516	1609	...	1641	1715	...	1820	1901	1918	2018	...	2123	2154	2227	0003	...

km																								
0	**Kanazawa** d.	0608	0638	0710	0820	...	0913	1016	1034	1116	...	1207	1315	...	1338	1416	1512	1620	...	1646	1717	1823	1854	...
41	Takaoka d.	0632	0704	0735	0844	...	0937	1041	1103	1140	...	1231	1339	...	1404	1440	1537	1644	...	1712	1741	1847	1922	...
60	Toyama d.	0644	0718	0748	0856	...	0949	1053	1116	1153	...	1243	1351	...	1417	1452	1549	1656	...	1725	1753	1859	1934	...
139	Itoigawa d.	|	0810	0838	0943	...	1036	1141	1206	|	...	1330	1440	...	1509	1539	1637	|	...	1819	1843	|	2027	...
178	**Naoetsu** ‡ d.	0753	0835	0901	1006	...	1100	1205	1232	1302	...	1353	1503	...	1534	1602	1701	1803	...	1844	1906	2008	2052	...
	Nagaoka d.	|	0928	|	|	...	|	|	1324	|	...	|	|	...	1627	|	|	|	...	1936	|	|	2144	...
314	**Niigata** a.	|	1018	|	|	...	|	|	1419	|	...	|	|	...	1720	|	|	|	...	2027	|	|	2233	...
	Echigo Yuzawa ‡ a.	0841	...	0954	1054	...	1153	1255	...	1354	...	1451	1558	...	...	1656	1752	1853	...	...	2000	2059	...	...

‡ – Japan Rail Pass holders must pay a supplement to travel between these stations.

8160 OSAKA - SHINGU — JR West

km																								
	Kyoto d.	...	0836	...	...	0932	...	...	...	...	...	...	...	...	...	1732	...	...	...	...	...	...	...	...
0	Shin **Osaka** d.	0733	0903	0932	...	1002	1100	1200	...	1300	1400	1500	...	1600	1703	1803	...	1904	2003	2103	...	2146	...	2244
14	**Osaka** Tennoji d.	0759	0921	0949	...	1020	1117	1217	...	1317	1417	1517	...	1617	1720	1821	...	1923	2020	2124	...	2204	...	2306
75	Wakayama d.	0853	1006	1036	...	1105	1200	1302	...	1401	1503	1602	...	1702	1806	1917	...	2013	2111	2211	...	2252	...	0008
181	Shirahama d.	1012	1130	1203	...	1227	1317	1429	...	1519	1635	1719	...	1832	1932	2043	...	2139	2238	...	...	...	...	...
234	Kushimoto d.	1103	1221	...	...	...	1412	...	...	1612	...	1816	...	...	2023	...	...	2237	...	...	...	...	...	...
261	**Kii Katsuura** d.	1134	1253	...	...	...	1442	...	...	1644	...	1847	...	...	2054	...	...	2312	...	...	...	...	...	...
276	**Shingu** a.	1149	1309	...	...	...	1457	...	...	1659	...	1902	...	...	2109	...	...	2328	...	...	...	...	...	...

Shingu d.	...	...	...	...	...	...	0646	...	0837	...	...	1031	...	...	1244	...	...	...	1428	1542	...	...	1745	...
Kii Katsuura d.	...	...	...	...	...	...	0700	...	0854	...	...	1046	...	...	1300	...	...	...	1448	1557	...	...	1800	...
Kushimoto d.	...	...	...	...	...	...	0731	...	0926	...	...	1119	...	...	1331	...	...	...	1521	1629	...	...	1832	...
Shirahama d.	...	...	...	0638	0712	...	0827	0920	1028	...	1118	1230	1320	...	1430	1446	1524	...	1625	1732	1815	...	1930	...
Wakayama d.	0454	0604	0626	0808	0843	...	0950	1049	1150	...	1249	1349	1449	...	1547	1615	1647	...	1747	1850	1946	...	2049	...
Osaka Tennoji a.	0559	0658	0723	0858	0931	...	1033	1133	1234	...	1334	1434	1534	...	1629	1700	1730	...	1832	1934	2030	...	2131	...
Shin **Osaka** a.	0621	0720	0751	0922	0951	...	1050	1150	1250	...	1350	1450	1550	...	1650	1720	1750	...	1852	1951	2050	...	2151	...
Kyoto a.	...	...	...	...	1017	...	...	...	...	...	...	...	...	...	...	...	1819	...	...	2019	...	...	...	...

8165 NAGOYA - SHINGU — JR Central

km											
0	**Nagoya** d.	0805	1001	1258	1947	...	...	...	...	...	...
37	Yokkaichi ‡ d.	0837	1036	1337	2019	...	...	...	...	...	...
48	Suzuka ‡ d.	0845	1045	1345	2027	...	...	...	...	...	...
66	Tsu ‡ d.	0901	1101	1400	2041	...	...	...	...	...	...
86	Matsusaka d.	0916	1116	1416	2056	...	...	...	...	...	...
93	Taki d.	0924	1129	1424	2103	...	...	...	...	...	...
206	Kumano Shi d.	1114	1318	1605	2253	...	...	...	...	...	...
228	**Shingu** a.	1134	1337	1624	2313	...	...	...	...	...	...
244	**Kii Katsuura** a.	1156	1357	1642	...	...	...	...	...	...	...

Kii Katsuura d.	...	0855	1223	1710	...	...	...	...	...	...
Shingu d.	0620	0913	1244	1728	...	...	...	...	...	...
Kumano Shi d.	0640	0933	1305	1748	...	...	...	...	...	...
Taki d.	0819	1118	1448	1929	...	...	...	...	...	...
Matsusaka d.	0826	1126	1456	1937	...	...	...	...	...	...
Tsu ‡ d.	0841	1142	1512	1953	...	...	...	...	...	...
Suzuka ‡ d.	0854	1154	1525	2006	...	...	...	...	...	...
Yokkaichi ‡ d.	0904	1204	1534	2014	...	...	...	...	...	...
Nagoya a.	0941	1241	1610	2048	...	...	...	...	...	...

‡ – Japan Rail Pass holders must pay a supplement to travel between these stations.

8170 NAGOYA - TOYAMA — JR Central

km											
0	**Nagoya** d.	0745	0843	0993	1048	1143	1248	1448	1543	1743	1943
30	Gifu d.	0805	0903	1010	1108	1206	1308	1508	1606	1805	2006
58	Mino Ota d.	0826	0923	1032	1129	1226	1328	1529	1629	1829	2030
119	Gero d.	0919	1014	1130	1222	1324	1424	1626	1733	1933	2124
167	Takayama d.	1002	1100	1220	1315	1408	1510	1715	1817	2018	2207
182	Hida Furukawa d.	...	1113	1233	1328	...	1524	1731	...	...	...
256	**Toyama** a.	...	1226	...	1444	...	1642	1852	...	...	...

Toyama d.	...	...	0800	...	...	...	1302	...	1510	1710
Hida Furukawa d.	...	...	0918	...	...	1306	1419	...	1624	1825
Takayama d.	0646	0800	0938	1124	1233	1330	1439	1536	1644	1845
Gero d.	0731	0845	1026	1211	1318	1418	1525	1621	1727	1928
Mino Ota d.	0827	0948	1119	1316	1420	1519	1619	1715	1819	2020
Gifu d.	0852	1012	1141	1341	1441	1541	1641	1741	1841	2043
Nagoya a.	0913	1033	1202	1402	1502	1602	1702	1802	1903	2102

JR Central — NAGOYA - NAGANO — 8175

km																								
0	**Nagoya** d.	0700	0800	...	0900	1000	...	1100	1200	...	1300	1400	...	1500	1600	...	1740	1840	...	1940	...	...	...	...
80	Nakatsugawa d.	0750	0850	...	0950	1050	...	1150	1250	...	1350	1449	...	1549	1649	...	1830	1930	...	2032	...	...	...	...
133	Kiso Fukushima d.	0830	0926	...	1026	1126	...	1226	1326	...	1426	1525	...	1625	1725	...	1907	2005	...	2110	...	...	...	...
175	Shiojiri d.	0858	0956	...	1054	1154	...	1254	1354	...	1454	1554	...	1654	1754	...	1936	2033	...	2138	...	...	...	...
188	Matsumoto d.	0909	1007	...	1105	1205	...	1305	1404	...	1504	1604	...	1705	1806	...	1946	2043	...	2149	...	...	...	...
251	**Nagano** a.	1001	1058	...	1157	1254	...	1353	1453	...	1555	1655	...	1753	1858	...	2039	2133	...	2239	...	...	...	...

Nagano d.	...	0609	0744	...	0900	1000	...	1100	1200	...	1300	1400	...	1500	1600	...	1700	1811	...	1940	...	...	...	...
Matsumoto d.	...	0704	0836	...	0952	1050	...	1151	1253	...	1352	1453	...	1553	1653	...	1751	1906	...	2031	...	...	...	...
Shiojiri d.	...	0714	0845	...	1003	1101	...	1201	1303	...	1403	1503	...	1603	1703	...	1802	1919	...	2041	...	...	...	...
Kiso Fukushima d.	...	0742	0913	...	1030	1130	...	1230	1330	...	1430	1530	...	1630	1730	...	1830	1948	...	2109	...	...	...	...
Nakatsugawa d.	...	0822	0950	...	1106	1206	...	1306	1406	...	1506	1607	...	1709	1809	...	1909	2026	...	2144	...	...	...	...
Nagayo a.	...	0917	1045	...	1201	1301	...	1401	1501	...	1601	1701	...	1805	1905	...	2005	2121	...	2234	...	...	...	...

JR Central — SHIZUOKA - KOFU — 8180

km										
0	**Shizuoka** d.	0816	0940	1140	1340	1540	1740	1940	...	...	...
34	Fuji d.	0844	1014	1211	1411	1611	1811	2011	...	...	...
131	**Kofu** a.	1028	1208	1403	1602	1802	1959	2204	...	...	...

Kofu d.	0624	0843	1042	1237	1435	1636	1836	...	...	...
Fuji d.	0811	1037	1234	1429	1629	1828	2032	...	...	...
Shizuoka a.	0837	1102	1301	1456	1656	1855	2059	...	...	...

JR East — TOKYO - MATSUMOTO — 8185

km																								
0	**Tokyo** Shinjuku d.	0700	0730	0800	0830	...	0900	1000	1100	1200	...	1300	1400	...	1500	1600	1700	1730	...	1800	1900	2000	2100	...
37	Hachioji d.	0729	0803	0834	0908	...	0939	1034	1130	1231	...	1331	1430	...	1531	1631	1734	1808	...	1837	1935	2034	2133	...
124	Kofu d.	0829	0908	0929	1016	...	1039	1129	1232	1329	...	1431	1524	...	1632	1728	1834	1915	...	1936	2036	2131	2240	...
185	Chino d.	0908	0952	1007	1059	...	1124	1204	1314	1407	...	1515	1600	...	1716	1804	1916	1958	...	2012	2121	2208	2324	...
192	Kami Suwa d.	0915	0957	1012	1104	...	1130	1209	1319	1412	...	1521	1605	...	1722	1809	1922	2004	...	2017	2126	2214	2329	...
212	Shiojiri d.	0931	1015	1029	1119	...	1146	|	1336	1426	...	1537	|	...	1738	1825	1940	2021	...	2036	2143	2229	2346	...
225	**Matsumoto** a.	0939	1023	1038	1128	...	1156	1231	1346	1435	...	1546	1626	...	1748	1834	1950	2031	...	2047	2152	2238	2355	...

Matsumoto d.	...	0608	0651	0800	0851	...	0914	0954	1108	1200	...	1302	1347	...	1449	1519	1547	1658	...	1718	1835	1921	2000	...
Shiojiri d.	...	0617	0659	0809	0900	...	0924	1003	|	1208	...	1311	1356	...	1458	1527	1555	1707	...	1727	1843	1930	2008	...
Kami Suwa d.	...	0634	0713	0825	0915	...	0941	1021	1130	1225	...	1328	1413	...	1512	1544	1615	1722	...	1744	1859	1946	2025	...
Chino d.	...	0639	0719	0831	0921	...	0946	1026	1135	1230	...	1333	1419	...	1518	1550	1620	1728	...	1750	1905	1951	2031	...
Kofu d.	...	0724	0756	0910	1003	...	1031	1106	1211	1312	...	1409	1503	...	1555	1632	1702	1805	...	1833	1942	2030	2109	...
Hachioji d.	...	0830	0851	1005	1104	...	1133	1204	1305	1410	...	1504	1601	...	1650	1732	1801	1902	...	1934	2036	2135	2206	...
Tokyo Shinjuku a.	...	0913	0926	1038	1133	...	1204	1233	1333	1441	...	1533	1634	...	1726	1807	1836	1935	...	2007	2106	2207	2236	...

Some trains run on a slightly different schedule on Ⓒ.

JR East — TOKYO - IZUKYU SHIMODA and SHUZENJI — 8195

km											
0	**Tokyo** d.	0900	0900	0925j	1000	1100	1200	1200	1300	...	...
29	Yokohama d.	0923	0923	0958	1023	1123	1223	1223	1323	...	...
84	Odawara d.	1001	1001	|	1101	|	1300	1300	|	...	...
105	Atami d.	1022	1024	1056	1122	1219	1322	1324	1419	...	...
122	Ito ‡ d.	1045	|	1117	1146	1240	1346	|	1442	...	...
168	**Izukyu Shimoda** ‡ a.	1136	|	1212	1246	1329	1448	|	1541	...	...
121	Mishima ‡ d.	...	1040	...	...	...	...	1340	...	...	...
141	**Shuzenji** ‡ a.	...	1108	...	...	...	...	1406	...	...	...

	Ⓒ									
Shuzenji ‡ d.	...	...	...	1235	...	...	...	1539	...	...
Mishima ‡ d.	...	...	...	1305	...	...	...	1606	...	...
Izukyu Shimoda ‡ d.	...	1008	1213	|	1302	1416	1508	|	1605	...
Ito ‡ d.	1005	1105	1306	|	1404	1509	1600	|	1659	...
Atami d.	1033	1129	1332	1332	1428	1532	1628	1628	1724	...
Odawara d.	1050	1146	1350	1350	1445	|	1645	1645	|	...
Yokohama d.	1127	1222	1427	1427	1522	1624	1722	1722	1824	...
Tokyo a.	1149	1242	1449	1449	1545	1645	1744	1744	1856j	...

j – Tokyo **Shinjuku**.

‡ – Japan Rail Pass holders must pay a supplement to travel between these stations.

JR East — TOKYO - AWA KAMOGAWA — 8200

km												
0	**Tokyo** d.	0715	0900	1000	1100	1300	1400	1500	1700	1900	2100	2200
43	Soga d.	0753	0935	1033	1134	1334	1434	1534	1733	1935	2134	2232
62	Oami d.	0805	0947	1045	1146	1346	1446	1546	1745	1949	2148	2246
74	Mobara d.	0813	0955	1053	1154	1353	1453	1553	1753	1957	2158	2254
82	Kazusa Ichinomiya d.	0820	1001	1105	1201	1401	1501	1601	1800	2008	2206	2301
110	Katsuura a.	0846	1030	1129	1230	1430	1526	1625	1831	2033	2230	2326
133	**Awa Kamogawa** a.	...	1053	1154	...	1459	1551	1649	...	...	...	...

Awa Kamogawa d.	...	0737	...	...	1135	...	1440	1532	1637	1747	...
Katsuura d.	0726	0808	0908	1009	1205	1410	1505	1559	1705	1811	2006
Kazusa Ichinomiya d.	0753	0833	0933	1034	1234	1435	1534	1631	1738	1836	2038
Mobara d.	0759	0839	0939	1040	1241	1441	1541	1638	1744	1842	2044
Oami d.	0810	0847	0947	1049	1249	1449	1548	1646	1752	1850	2053
Soga d.	0824	0902	1002	1102	1302	1502	1601	1700	1805	1903	2106
Tokyo a.	0859	0934	1036	1135	1335	1535	1634	1734	1840	1936	2139

JR East — TOKYO - MANZA KAZAWAGUCHI and MAEBASHI — 8205

km											
		Ⓒ					Ⓐ	Ⓒ	Ⓐ	Ⓐ	Ⓐ
0	**Tokyo** Ueno d.	0900	1000	1210	1900	2000	2100	2104j	2103j	2200	2250
27	Omiya d.	0926	1026	1235	1925	2025	2124	2135	2135	2227	2314
62	Kumagaya d.	0952	1052	1302	1950	2053	2150	2202	2205	2252	2339
102	Takasaki d.	1021	1123	1334	2024	2127	2223	2234	2234	2324	0009
173	**Manza Kazawaguchi** a.	1139	1243	1455	|	|	|	|	|	|	...
112	**Maebashi** a.	...	...	...	*2041*a	2140	*2236*	2245	2245	2336	...

	Ⓐ	Ⓐ	Ⓒ		Ⓒ		Ⓒ		Ⓐ	Ⓐ
Maebashi d.	0726	*0748*	*0755*	0833	0908	...	...	...	1752k	*2047*
Manza Kawaguchi d.	|	|	|	|	|	1049	1340	1525	|	|
Takasaki d.	0739	0819	0819	0850	0921	1206	1501	1645	1759	2104
Kumagaya d.	0810	0850	0851	0920	0952	1238	1530	1715	1829	2146
Omiya d.	0840	0919	0920	0951	1022	1306	1600	1744	1854	2225
Tokyo Ueno a.	0911j	0947	0946	1014	1054j	1331	1624	1810	1919	2257

a – 2046 on Ⓒ

j – Tokyo **Shinjuku**.

JR East — TOKYO - NIKKO — 8210

km											
0	**Tokyo** Shinjuku d.	0730	1031	1301	1732	...	...	...	...	...	...
27	Omiya d.	0802	1102	1332	1802	...	...	...	...	...	...
135	**TobuNikko** ‡ d.	0929	|	|	|	...	...	...	...	...	...
140	**Kinugawa** Onsen ‡ a.	...	1238	1512	1940	...	...	...	...	...	...

Kinugawa Onsen ‡ d.	0813	1038	1505	...	...	...	...	...	...	...
TobuNikko ‡ d.	|	|	|	1639	...	...	...	...	...	...
Omiya d.	0949	1217	1646	1804	...	...	...	...	...	...
Tokyo Shinjuku a.	1018	1248	1719	1836	...	...	...	...	...	...

‡ – Japan Rail Pass holders must pay a supplement to travel to / from this station.

8215 TOKYO - SENDAI

JR East

km																								
0	**Tokyo** Ueno d.	0700	0730	0800	...	0830	0900	0930	1000	...	1030	1100	1130	...	1200	1230	1300	1330	...	1400	1430	1500	...	1530
67	Tsuchiura d.	0742	0818	0850	...	0918	|	1016	|	...	1115	|	1215	...	|	1313	|	1413	...	|	1513	|	...	1613
118	Mito d.	0813	0850	0919	...	0950	1016	1048	1106	...	1148	1207	1248	...	1307	1345	1407	1445	...	1507	1545	1607	...	1646
124	Katsuta d.	0818	0855	0925	...	0955	1022	1053	1112	...	1153	1212	1252	...	1312	1350	1412	1450	...	1513	1550	1612	...	1651
150	Hitachi d.	0834	0915	0941	...	...	1042	...	1127	...	1213	1231	...	...	1330	...	1431	1509	...	1529	...	1631	...	1709
212	Iwaki △ d.	0918	...	1022	...	...	1126	...	1207	...	...	1314	...	...	1414	...	1511	...	...	1613	...	1712	...	...
290	Haranomachi △ d.	...	...	...	...	...	...	...	...	...	...	...	...	...	...	...	...	...	...	...	...	...	...	...
361	**Sendai** (Honshu) △ a.	...	...	...	...	...	...	...	...	...	...	...	...	...	...	...	...	...	...	...	...	...	...	...

Tokyo Ueno d.	...	1600	1630	1700	1730	...	1800	1815	1830	1900	...	1915	1930	2000	2015	2030	2100	2115	2130	...	2200	2215	2230	2300
Tsuchiura d.	...	|	1714	|	1816	...	1839	1905	1915	1939	...	2008	2015	2041	2106	2116	2142	2208	2216	...	2253	2309	2321	2353
Mito d.	...	1707	1747	1807	1848	...	1909	...	1947	2011	...	...	2050	2111	2140	2149	2212	...	2250	...	2325	2345	2355	0025
Katsuta d.	...	1712	1751	1813	1853	...	1914	...	1952	2017	...	...	2055	2118	2145	2155	2217	...	2256	...	2330	2350	2359	0030
Hitachi d.	...	1727	...	1831	...	...	1933	...	2013	2035	...	...	...	2136	...	2213	2235	...	2316	...	...	...	...	...
Iwaki △ d.	...	1808	...	1914	...	...	2018	...	...	2117	...	...	...	2217	...	2256	2321	...	...	...	...	...	...	...
Haranomachi △ d.	...	...	...	...	...	...	...	...	...	...	...	...	...	...	...	...	...	...	...	...	...	...	...	...
Sendai (Honshu) △ a.	...	...	...	...	...	...	...	...	...	...	...	...	...	...	...	...	...	...	...	...	...	...	...	...

Sendai (Honshu) △ d.	...	...	...	...	...	...	...	...	...	...	...	...	...	...	...	...	...	...	...	...	...	...	...	...
Haranomachi △ d.	...	...	...	...	...	...	...	...	...	...	...	...	...	...	...	...	...	...	...	...	...	...	...	...
Iwaki △ d.	...	...	...	...	...	...	...	0613	...	...	0658	0727	0802	...	...	0919	...	1016	...	...	1120	...	...	1220
Hitachi d.	...	...	...	...	0543	...	...	0700	0720	...	0740	0813	0847	...	...	1001	1027	1100	...	...	1201	...	...	1301
Katsuta d.	...	...	0539	0553	0602	0620	0700	0720	0741	...	0759	0831	0908	...	0946	1020	1046	1120	...	1146	1220	1246	...	1320
Mito d.	...	...	0545	0559	0608	0626	0706	0726	0747	...	0805	0838	0915	...	0952	1027	1052	1127	...	1152	1227	1252	...	1327
Tsuchiura d.	...	0605	0620	0631	0640	0700	0739	0758	0819	...	0834	0909	0946	...	1025	|	1123	1155	...	1223	|	1323	...	|
Tokyo Ueno a.	...	0706	0724	0734	0746	0804	0843	0859	0911	...	0925	0959	1028	...	1106	1136	1206	1235	...	1306	1335	1406	...	1435

Sendai (Honshu) △ d.	...	...	...	...	...	...	...	...	...	...	...	...	...	...	...	...	...	...	...	...	...	...	...	...
Haranomachi △ d.	...	...	...	...	...	...	...	...	...	...	...	...	...	...	...	...	...	...	...	...	...	...	...	...
Iwaki △ d.	...	...	1320	...	...	1416	...	1517	...	...	...	1616	...	1720	...	...	...	1820	...	1916	...	...	2018	...
Hitachi d.	...	1325	1402	...	...	1500	...	1600	...	1625	...	1700	...	1802	...	1826	...	1900	...	1959	...	...	2100	...
Katsuta d.	...	1346	1420	1446	...	1520	1546	1620	...	1646	...	1720	1746	1820	...	1846	...	1920	1946	2020	...	2046	2120	2146
Mito d.	...	1352	1427	1452	...	1527	1552	1627	...	1652	...	1727	1752	1827	...	1852	...	1927	1952	2027	...	2052	2127	2152
Tsuchiura d.	...	1423	|	1523	...	1555	1623	1655	...	1723	...	|	1823	|	...	1923	...	|	2023	|	...	2123	2156	2223
Tokyo Ueno a.	...	1506	1535	1606	...	1636	1708	1738	...	1807	...	1835	1908	1936	...	2004	...	2035	2104	2134	...	2204	2236	2305

△ – Limited Express services Iwaki - Sendai and v.v. are suspended due to earthquake damage. Some local services may be available.

8220 NIIGATA - HAKODATE

JR East

km																									
0	**Niigata** d.	...	...	...	...	...	...	...	...	...	...	...	0827	...	...	1058	...	...	1229	...	1532	...	1738	1849	2116
168	Sakata d.	...	...	0536	...	0636	...	...	...	...	...	...	1039	...	...	1307	...	...	1443	...	1739	...	1946	2058	2323
273	Akita d.	...	...	0726	0705	0829	...	0854	...	...	...	...	1202	1310	...	...	...	...	1613	1731	1902	1929	▬	*2305*	...
421	Hirosaki d.	...	...	...	0913	...	...	1102	...	...	...	...	...	1516	...	...	...	...	...	1936	...	2133	...	...	...
455	Shin Aomori d.	0808	0912	...	0940	...	1017	1135	1130	1245	1451	1539	...	1545	1653	...	1853	1947	...	2006	...	2202	...	...	...
459	Aomori d.	0824	0929	...	0946	...	1030	1141	1150	1300	1506	1601	...	1551	1709	...	1905	2000	...	2012	...	2208	2218	...	...
623	**Hakodate** a.	1026	1140	...	...	...	1222	...	1342	1458	1702	1755	...	...	1908	...	2056	2154	...	...	...	...	0144	...	...

Hakodate d.	...	0322	...	...	...	...	...	0724	...	...	0808	1021	...	1119	...	...	1204	...	1403	...	1556	...	1707	1821	1932
Aomori d.	...	0539	...	...	...	0543	...	0928	0951	...	1011	1220	...	1323	1336	...	1418	1558	1603	...	1756	1846	1913	2023	2129
Shin Aomori d.	...	...	...	...	...	0549	...	0933	0958	...	1016	1225	...	1328	1343	...	1423	1604	1608	...	1801	1855	1919	2028	2134
Hirosaki d.	...	...	...	...	...	0616	...	...	1025	...	...	...	...	...	1412	...	...	1633	...	...	...	1927	...	...	...
Akita d.	...	...	...	...	...	0823	0912	...	1233	1257	...	...	...	...	1620	1636	...	1846	...	2044	...	2133	...	...	...
Sakata d.	...	...	0544	0645	0858	...	1047	...	...	1426	...	...	1553	...	...	1801	...	...	...	2226	...	...	...	...	...
Niigata a.	...	...	0749	0852	1100	...	1256	...	...	1631	...	...	1805	...	...	2010	...	...	...	...	...	...	...	...	...

8225 TOKYO, HAKODATE and MURORAN - SAPPORO

JR Hokkaido

km																								
				②⑤⑦ A			B																	
0	**Tokyo** Ueno d.	...	...	1620	...	...	1903	...	...	...	...	...	...	...	...	...	...	...	...	...	...	...	...	...
27	Omiya d.	...	...	1645	...	...	1930	...	...	...	...	...	...	...	...	...	...	...	...	...	...	...	...	...
269	Fukushima d.	...	...	1952	...	...	2229	...	...	...	...	...	...	...	...	...	...	...	...	...	...	...	...	...
348	Sendai (Honshu) d.	...	...	2059	...	...	2330	...	...	...	...	...	...	...	...	...	...	...	...	...	...	...	...	...
896	**Hakodate** a.	...	...	0502	...	...	0635	...	...	...	...	...	...	...	...	...	...	...	...	...	...	...	...	...
896	**Hakodate** d.	0123	...	0508	...	0704	0643	...	0830	...	...	...	1230	...	...	1413	1518	...	...	...	1711	...	1941	...
1050	Toya d.	|	...	0713	...	0843	0859	...	1010	...	...	...	1410	...	...	1608	1658	...	...	...	1912	...	2124	...
	Muroran d.	|	0659	|	0819	|	|	...	|	...	...	1322	|	...	1625	|	|	...	1825	...	|	...	|	...
1086	Higashi-Muroran d.	0417	0711	0746	0831	0910	0937	...	1036	...	...	1336	1436	...	1638	1643	1724	...	1838	...	1941	...	2150	...
1103	Noboribetsu d.	|	0726	0801	0846	0921	0949	...	1048	...	...	1351	1448	...	1652	1656	1736	...	1853	...	1954	...	2202	...
1144	Tomakomai d.	0501	0751	0834	0910	0945	1020	...	1112	...	...	1417	1512	...	1717	1722	1800	...	1917	...	2019	...	2225	...
1171	Minami Chitose d.	0525	0808	0856	0928	1001	1041	...	1127	...	...	1435	1527	...	1735	1741	1815	...	1935	...	2041	...	2242	...
1215	**Sapporo** a.	0607	0837	0932	0958	1030	1115	...	1158	...	...	1506	1558	...	1807	1814	1846	...	2006	...	2116	...	2317	...

km																								
															①③⑥ A		B							
0	**Sapporo** d.	0636	0730	...	0834	1022	1113	...	1213	...	1351	...	1606	...	1612	1651	1712	...	1844	...	1929	2033	2200	...
44	Minami Chitose d.	0708	0801	...	0908	1052	1146	...	1245	...	1420	...	1635	...	1646	1719	1746	...	1916	...	2000	2102	2241	...
71	Tomakomai d.	0725	0819	...	0926	1109	1203	...	1302	...	1438	...	1653	...	1706	1735	1806	...	1933	...	2017	2120	2304	...
112	Noboribetsu d.	|	0845	...	0953	1132	1226	...	1326	...	1503	...	1718	...	1737	1759	1835	...	1959	...	2040	2145	2335	...
129	Higashi-Muroran d.	0801	0859	...	1007	1144	1245	...	1338	...	1518	...	1734	...	1757	1812	1851	...	2015	...	2052	2200	2352	...
136	**Muroran** a.	|	|	...	|	|	1256	...	|	...	1530	...	1746	...	|	|	|	...	2026	...	|	2211	|	...
	Toya d.	|	0927	...	1034	1211	...	...	1403	...	...	...	...	...	1843	1837	1926	...	...	...	2118	...	|	...
	Hakodate a.	1014	1135	...	1236	1354	...	...	1546	...	...	...	...	...	2106	2028	2138	...	...	...	2301	...	0252	...
	Hakodate d.	...	...	...	...	...	...	...	...	...	...	...	...	...	2112	...	2149	...	...	...	...	...	...	...
	Sendai (Honshu) a.	...	...	...	...	...	...	...	...	...	...	...	...	...	0436	...	0451	...	...	...	...	...	...	...
	Fukushima a.	...	...	...	...	...	...	...	...	...	...	...	...	...	0536	...	0553	...	...	...	...	...	...	...
	Omiya a.	...	...	...	...	...	...	...	...	...	...	...	...	...	0900	...	0932	...	...	...	...	...	...	...
	Tokyo Ueno a.	...	...	...	...	...	...	...	...	...	...	...	...	...	0925	...	1005	...	...	...	...	...	...	...

A – CASSIOPEIA. B – HOKUTOSEI.

8230 SAPPORO - KUSHIRO

JR Hokkaido

km												
0	**Sapporo** d.	0702	0802	0851	1018	1151	1307	1420	1628	1758	1945	2105
44	Minami Chitose d.	0732	0829	0922	1046	1222	1338	1452	1700	1832	2015	2132
220	Obihiro d.	0927	1036	1128	1259	1423	1544	1704	1920	2033	2221	2337
349	**Kushiro** a.	1101	...	1301	...	1558	...	1842	2104	...	2356	...

Kushiro d.	...	...	0714	0824	...	1120	...	1333	...	1617	1900
Obihiro d.	0649	0758	0849	0958	1133	1301	1333	1507	1605	1750	2033
Minami Chitose d.	0902	1004	1059	1158	1332	1503	1542	1712	1804	1947	2235
Sapporo a.	0935	1031	1129	1228	1401	1536	1614	1744	1836	2019	2310

SAPPORO - WAKKANAI and ABASHIRI — 8235

JR Hokkaido

km											
0	**Sapporo** d.	0721	0748	0941	...	1508	1730	1749	...	...	...
	Takikawa d.	0820	0842	1039	...	1604	1829	1839	...	...	...
137	Asahikawa d.	0901	0916	1119	...	1642	1908	1913	...	...	...
396	**Wakkanai** a.	|	1300	|	...	|	|	2247	...	...	...
185	Kamikawa d.	0942	...	1201	...	1731	1952	...	...	...	...
375	**Abashiri** a.	1246	...	1509	...	2037	2258	...	...	...	...

Abashiri d.	0623	...	0930	1329	...	...	1718	...	...	...
Kamikawa d.	0925	...	1231	1632	...	...	2020	...	...	...
Wakkanai d.	|	0710	|	|	...	1651	|	...	...	...
Asahikawa d.	1011	1045	1313	1713	...	2032	2100	...	...	...
Takikawa d.	1047	1118	1349	1749	...	2104	2139	...	...	...
Sapporo a.	1146	1214	1445	1847	...	2155	2238	...	...	...

SHIN CHITOSE AIRPORT - SAPPORO - ASAHIKAWA — 8240

JR Hokkaido

km																								
0	**Shin Chitose Airport** d.	...	...	...	...	...	...	...	1019	1119	1219	1319	...	1419	1519	...	1619	1719	...	1819	...	1919	2019	2116	...
3	Minami Chitose d.	...	...	...	...	...	...	...	1022	1122	1222	1322	...	1422	1522	...	1622	1722	...	1822	...	1922	2022	2120	...
47	**Sapporo** d.	0651	0800	0825	0900	0930	1000	...	1100	1200	1300	1400	1430	1500	1600	1630	1700	1800	1830	1900	1930	2000	2100	2200	2305
	Takikawa d.	0743	0852	0917	0952	1022	1052	...	1152	1252	1352	1452	1522	1552	1652	1722	1752	1852	1922	1952	2022	2052	2152	2252	2357
184	**Asahikawa** a.	0816	0925	0950	1025	1055	1125	...	1225	1325	1429	1529	1559	1629	1725	1759	1829	1925	1959	2025	2055	2125	2225	2325	0030

Asahikawa d.	...	0518	0600	0645	0719	0755	0825	0855	...	0955	1055	1155	1255	1355	1425	1455	1525	1555	1625	1655	1755	1825	1855	1955	2155
Takikawa d.	...	0550	0632	0717	0751	0827	0857	0927	...	1027	1127	1227	1327	1427	1457	1527	1557	1627	1657	1727	1827	1857	1927	2027	2227
Sapporo a.	...	0643	0734	0826	0846	0920	0950	1020	...	1120	1220	1320	1420	1520	1550	1620	1650	1720	1750	1820	1920	1950	2020	2120	2320
Minami Chitose a.	...	...	...	...	0928	0958	...	1058	...	1158	1258	1358	1458	1558	...	1658	...	1758	...	1858	1958	...	2058	...	...
Shin Chitose Airport a.	...	...	...	...	0931	1001	...	1101	...	1201	1301	1401	1501	1601	...	1701	...	1801	...	1901	2001	...	2101	...	...

SUMMARY OF OVERNIGHT TRAINS — 8300

				A						
Takamatsu d.	...	...	2126	...	...	...	...	...	...	...
Izumoshi d.	...	1855	|	...	...	...	...	...	...	...
Matsue d.	...	1927	|	...	...	...	...	...	...	...
Yonago d.	...	1956	|	...	...	...	...	...	...	...
Niimi d.	...	2120	|	...	...	...	...	...	...	...
Okayama d.	...	2233	2233	...	...	...	...	...	...	...
Osaka d.	...	0034	0034	1150	...	...	...	...	...	...
Shin **Osaka** d.	...	|	|	1156	...	...	...	...	...	...
Kyoto d.	...	|	|	1225	...	...	...	...	...	...
Tsuruga d.	...	|	|	1348	...	...	...	...	...	...
Yokohama d.	...	0645	0645	|	...	...	...	...	...	...
Tokyo a.	...	0708	0708	|	...	...	...	...	...	...
Tokyo Ueno d.	...	...	...	|	2116	...	...	...	...	...
Omiya d.	...	...	...	|	2142	...	...	...	...	...
Fukui d.	...	...	...	1440	|	...	...	...	...	...
Kanazawa d.	...	...	...	1540	|	...	...	...	...	...
Takaoka d.	...	...	...	1614	|	...	...	...	...	...
Toyama d.	...	...	...	1631	|	...	...	...	...	...
Naoetsu d.	...	...	...	1759	|	...	...	...	...	...
Nagaoka d.	...	...	...	1858	|	...	...	...	...	...
Niitsu d.	...	...	...	1939	|	...	...	...	...	...
Sakata a.	...	...	...	|	0500	...	...	...	...	...
Akita a.	...	...	...	|	0638	...	...	...	...	...
Aomori a.	2218	...	...	|	0952	...	...	...	...	...
Hakodate a.	0123	...	...	|	...	...	...	...	...	...
Noboribetsu a.	|	...	...	0811	...	...	...	...	...	...
Tomakomai a.	0501	...	...	0850	...	...	...	...	...	...
Minami Chitose a.	0524	...	...	0910	...	...	...	...	...	...
Sapporo a.	0607	...	...	0952	...	...	...	...	...	...

A – ①③⑤⑥.

		B								
Sapporo d.	...	1405	2200	...	...	...	...	...	...	...
Minami Chitose d.	...	1439	2241	...	...	...	...	...	...	...
Tomakomai d.	...	1500	2304	...	...	...	...	...	...	...
Noboribetsu d.	...	1532	2335	...	...	...	...	...	...	...
Hakodate d.	...	|	0322	...	...	...	...	...	...	...
Aomori d.	1823	|	0539	...	...	...	...	...	...	...
Akita d.	2123	|	...	...	...	...	...	...	...	...
Sakata d.	2301	|	...	...	...	...	...	...	...	...
Niitsu d.	0134	0440	...	...	...	...	...	...	...	...
Nagaoka d.	|	0529	...	...	...	...	...	...	...	...
Naoetsu d.	|	0627	...	...	...	...	...	...	...	...
Toyama d.	|	0803	...	...	...	...	...	...	...	...
Takaoka d.	|	0818	...	...	...	...	...	...	...	...
Kanazawa d.	|	0851	...	...	...	...	...	...	...	...
Fukui d.	|	0956	...	...	...	...	...	...	...	...
Omiya a.	0629	|	...	...	...	...	...	...	...	...
Tokyo Ueno a.	0658	|	...	...	...	...	...	...	...	...
Tokyo d.	...	|	...	2200	2200	...	...	...	...	...
Yokohama d.	...	|	...	2224	2224	...	...	...	...	...
Tsuruga d.	...	1052	...	|	|	...	...	...	...	...
Kyoto a.	...	1215	...	|	|	...	...	...	...	...
Shin **Osaka** a.	...	1247	...	|	|	...	...	...	...	...
Osaka a.	...	1253	...	|	|	...	...	...	...	...
Okayama a.	...	...	...	0627	0627	...	...	...	...	...
Niimi a.	...	...	...	|	0742	...	...	...	...	...
Yonago a.	...	...	...	|	0903	...	...	...	...	...
Matsue a.	...	...	...	|	0930	...	...	...	...	...
Izumoshi a.	...	...	...	|	0958	...	...	...	...	...
Takamatsu a.	...	...	...	0727.	...	...	...	...	...	...

B – ②④⑥⑦.

AIRPORT RAIL LINKS — 8400

CHUBU CENTRAL JAPAN INTERNATIONAL AIRPORT

SKY' Limited Express service Meitetsu Nagoya - Central Japan International Airport and v.v. *44 km*. Journey 30 minutes. Operator: Meitetsu.
From Meitetsu Nagoya at 0600Ⓐ, 0602Ⓒ, 0628Ⓐ, 0630Ⓒ, 0648Ⓐ, 0653Ⓒ, 0720, 0750, 0820Ⓒ, 0823Ⓐ, 0850, 0920, 0950, 1020, 1050, 1120, 1150, 1220, 1250, 1320, 1350, 1420, 1450, 1520, 1550, 1620, 1650, 1719, 1749, 1819, 1849, 1919, 1949, 2019, 2049, 2119. Frequent additional slower trains are available.
From Central Japan International Airport at 0703Ⓐ, 0713Ⓒ, 0726Ⓐ, 0729Ⓒ, 0759, 0829Ⓒ, 0834Ⓐ, 0907, 0937, 1007, 1037, 1107, 1137, 1207, 1237, 1307, 1337, 1407, 1437, 1507, 1537, 1607, 1637, 1706, 1736, 1806, 1836, 1906, 1936, 2007, 2037, 2107, 2137, 2207. Frequent additional slower trains are available.

KANSAI AIRPORT

HARUKA' Limited Express service Kyoto - Shin Osaka ■ - Kansai Airport and v.v. *100 km*. Journey 80 - 90 minutes. Operator: JR West.
From Kyoto at 0546, 0622, 0645, 0715, 0745Ⓐ, 0749Ⓒ, 0817, 0850, 0915, 0945, 1015, 1045, 1115, 1215, 1315, 1415, 1515, 1615, 1645, 1715, 1745, 1815, 1845, 1915, 1945, 2015.
From Kansai Airport at 0630Ⓐ, 0640Ⓒ, 0727Ⓐ, 0742Ⓒ, 0755Ⓐ, 0806Ⓒ, 0844Ⓒ, 0846Ⓐ, 0916, 0946, 1016 and at hourly until 1616, 1646, 1716, 1746, 1816, 1846, 1916, 1946, 2016, 2046, 2124, 2216.
■ – Trains call at Shin Osaka 28 - 33 minutes after Kyoto and 45 - 50 minutes after Kansai Airport.

TOKYO HANEDA AIRPORT

Limited Express service Tokyo Shinagawa - Haneda Airport International Terminal △ and v.v. *14 km*. Journey 20 minutes. Operator: Keikyu Railway.
From Tokyo Shinagawa at 0551 and every 10 - 15 minutes until 2300.
From Haneda Airport International Terminal at 0530 and every 10 - 15 minutes until 2330.
△ – Most trains continue to/from Haneda Aiport Domestic Terminal, journey 3 minutes.

TOKYO NARITA AIRPORT

NARITA EXPRESS' Limited Express service Tokyo - Narita Airport Terminal 1 ▽ and v.v. *79 km*. Journey 55 minutes. Operator: JR East.
From Tokyo at 0618, 0631, 0700, 0715, 0731, 0800, 0830, 0900, 1003, 1033, 1103, 1203, 1233, 1303, 1333, 1403, 1433, 1503, 1533, 1603, 1633, 1703, 1733, 1803, 1833, 1903, 2003.
From Narita T1 at 0730, 0744, 0813, 0850, 0915, 0945, 1015, 1045, 1114, 1145, 1219, 1314, 1345, 1418, 1444, 1514, 1544, 1618, 1644, 1716, 1744, 1815, 1848, 1912, 1946, 2044, 2144.
▽ – Trains also call at Narita Aiport Terminal 2, 2 minutes before/after Terminal 1.

SKYLINER' Limited Express service Tokyo Ueno Keisei - Narita Airport Terminal 1 ▷ and v.v. *69 km*. Journey 45 minutes. Operator: Keisei Electric Railway.
From Tokyo Ueno Keisei at 0558, 0630, 0650Ⓐ, 0654Ⓒ, 0710Ⓐ, 0716Ⓒ, 0732Ⓐ, 0736Ⓒ, 0752Ⓐ, 0756Ⓒ, 0817Ⓐ, 0819Ⓒ, 0843Ⓐ, 0846Ⓒ, 0920, 1000, 1040, 1100, 1140, 1220, 1300, 1340, 1400, 1440, 1500, 1520, 1540, 1600, 1620, 1640, 1700, 1740Ⓒ, 1745Ⓐ.
From Narita Airport Terminal 1 at 0816Ⓒ, 0817Ⓐ, 0915Ⓒ, 0924Ⓐ, 0958, 1038, 1118, 1158, 1258, 1338, 1418, 1438, 1458, 1518, 1538, 1558, 1618, 1638, 1658, 1718, 1740, 1810Ⓐ, 1818Ⓒ, 1849Ⓐ, 1858Ⓒ, 1930Ⓐ, 1938Ⓒ, 2010, 2038Ⓒ, 2043Ⓐ, 2109, 2149, 2230.
▷ – Trains also call at Narita Airport Terminal 2, 3 minutes before/after Terminal 1. Additional slower trains are available.

BEYOND EUROPE - SOUTH AMERICA

9900 MEXICO — Ferromex

km		①④⑥ A	B
0	**Chihuahua** d.	0600	0600
132	Cuauhtémoc d.	0825	0825
295	Creel d.	1120	1147
355	Divisadero d.	1304	1341
	Posada Barrancas d.	1311	1352
370	San Rafael d.	1337	1416
	Bahuichivo d.	1428	1512
440	Témoris d.	1525	1612
570	El Fuerte d.	1823	1919
655	**Los Mochis** a.	2022	2128

	②⑤⑦ A	B
Los Mochis d.	0600	0600
El Fuerte d.	0816	0819
Témoris d.	1120	1124
Bahuichivo d.	1220	1224
San Rafael d.	1325	1328
Posada Barrancas d.	1343	1346
Divisadero d.	1422	1414
Creel d.	1544	1539
Cuauhtémoc d.	1837	1907
Chihuahua a.	2054	2134

km		⑥⑦ C	
0	**Guadalajara** d.	1100	...
	Amatitán a.	1300	...

	⑥⑦ C	
Amatitán d.	1800	...
Guadalajara a.	2000	...

A – EL CHEPE – [1] and ✕.
B – EL TARAHUMARA – [2] and 🍸.
C – TEQUILA EXPRESS – [1]. also runs ⑤ in Jul, Aug.

9905 HONDURAS — FC de Honduras

km		①–⑤	①–⑤	①–⑤	①–⑤	①–⑤	①–⑤	①–⑤	①–⑤	①–⑤
0	**S Pedro Sula** Est d.	0730	0830	0930	1030	1130	1230	1330	1430	1530
3	**S Pedro Sula** Central a.	0750	0850	0950	1050	1150	1250	1350	1450	1550

		①–⑤	①–⑤	①–⑤	①–⑤	①–⑤	①–⑤	①–⑤	①–⑤	①–⑤
S Pedro Sula Central d.	...	0800	0900	1000	1100	1200	1300	1400	1500	1600
S Pedro Sula Est a.	...	0820	0920	1020	1120	1220	1320	1420	1520	1620

9910 PANAMA — Panama Canal Rly

km		①–⑤	
0	**Ciudad Panama** d.	0715	...
77	**Colon** a.	0815	...

	①–⑤	
Colon d.	1715	...
Ciudad Panama a.	1815	...

9915 COSTA RICA — INCOFER

km		①–⑤	①–⑤	①–⑤	①–⑤	①–⑤	①–⑤	①–⑤	①–⑤	①–⑤	①–⑤	①–⑤	①–⑤	①–⑤
0	**San José** Pacifico d.	0500	0601	0617	0635	0728	0805	1612	1611	1707	1738	1739	1755	1910
8	Pavas Metropolis III d.	0535	|	0648	|	|	|	|	1651	|	|	1816	|	|
10	**S Antonio de Belén** a.	...	0635	...	0710	0803	0840	1643	...	1742	1814	...	1830	1945

	①–⑤	①–⑤	①–⑤	①–⑤	①–⑤	①–⑤	①–⑤	①–⑤	①–⑤	①–⑤	①–⑤	①–⑤	①–⑤	①–⑤
S Antonio de Belén d.	...	0558	0640	...	0715	0805	0842	1621	1645	...	1800	...	1830	1900
Pavas Metropolis III d.	0537	|	|	0649	|	|	|	|	|	1655	|	1818	|	|
San José Pacifico a.	0615	0633	0715	0728	0755	0840	0917	1655	1720	1739	1830	1900	1905	1935

km		①–⑤	①–⑤	①–⑤	①–⑤	①–⑤
0	**Freses de Curidabat** d.	0651	0801	1705	1811	1925
4	Universidad Costa Rica d.	0700	0808	1714	1819	1934
15	**San José** Pacifico a.	0728	0832	1739	1841	1953

		①–⑤	①–⑤	①–⑤	①–⑤	①–⑤
San José Pacifico d.	...	0617	0728	1628	1739	1900
Universidad Costa Rica d.	...	0641	0750	1654	1800	1919
Freses de Curidabat a.	...	0650	0759	1701	1807	1925

km		①–⑤	①–⑤	①–⑤	①–⑤	①–⑤	①–⑤	①–⑤	①–⑤	①–⑤	①–⑤	△
0	**San José** Atlantico d.	0530	0600	0630	0700	0730	0800	1530	1600	1630	1700	1730
10	**Heredia** a.	0600	0630	0700	0730	0800	0830	1600	1630	1700	1730	1800

	①–⑤	①–⑤	①–⑤	①–⑤	①–⑤	①–⑤	①–⑤	①–⑤	①–⑤	①–⑤	▽
Heredia d.	0600	0630	0700	0730	0800	0830	1600	1630	1700	1730	1800
San José Atlantico a.	0630	0700	0730	0800	0830	0900	1630	1700	1730	1800	1830

△ – ①–⑤. Also at 1800①–⑤, 1830①–⑤, 1900①–⑤, 1930①–⑤.

▽ – ①–⑤. Also at 1830①–⑤, 1900①–⑤, 1930①–⑤, 2000①–⑤.

9920 CUBA — Unión de los Ferrocarriles Cubanos

km		19 2 ◧	2 ◧	2 ◧	D ◧	2 ◧	2 ◧			
0	**Habana** Central d.	0740	0840	1515	1800	2030	2200	...	...	...
90	Matanzas d.	|	|	|	|	|	|	...	...	...
286	Santa Clara d.	1200	1325	2000	|	|	0205	...	...	...
	Sancti Spiritus d.	1320	|	2120	|	0125	0325	...	...	...
436	Ciego de Avila d.	1525	|	2245	|	0245	0445	...	...	...
538	Camagüey d.	1720	1735	0035	0150	0435	0640	...	...	...
714	Bayamo d.	|	|	|	|	|	|	...	...	...
770	**Manzanillo** a.	|	|	|	|	|	|	...	...	...
652	Las Tunas d.	2000	|	0245	|	0635	0855	...	...	...
729	Cacocúm d.	|	|	|	|	|	|	...	...	...
806	Combinado d.	|	|	|	|	|	|	...	...	...
	Holguim d.	|	2035	0350	|	0745	|	...	...	...
884	**Guantanamo** a.	|	...	|	|	...	|	1640	...	...
854	**Santiago de Cuba** a.	2340	...	0720	0710	...	1235	1820	...	...

	2 ◧	2 ◧	20 2 ◧	D ◧	2 ◧	◧	2 ◧		
Santiago de Cuba d.	0735	...	0800	1515	1845	...	2200	...	...
Guantanamo d.	0930	...	|	|	|	...	|	...	...
Holguim d.	...	0840	1135	1930	|	2035	|	...	...
Combinado d.	...	|	|	|	|	|	|	...	...
Cacocúm d.	...	|	|	|	|	|	|	...	...
Las Tunas d.	...	0955	1330	2045	|	2150	0145	...	...
Manzanillo d.	...	|	|	|	|	|	|	...	...
Bayamo d.	...	|	|	|	|	|	|	...	...
Camagüey d.	...	1150	1530	2245	0115	2345	0345	...	...
Ciego de Avila d.	...	1425	1725	0040	|	0140	0540	...	...
Sancti Spiritus d.	...	1545	1845	0200	|	0300	0700	...	...
Santa Clara d.	...	1705	|	0320	|	|	0845	...	...
Matanzas d.	...	|	|	|	|	|	|	...	...
Habana Central a.	...	2050	0030	0705	0700	0625	1220		...

D – [1] Habana Central - Santiago de Cuba and v.v.

◧ – Subject to confirmation.

9925 VENEZUELA

km		①–⑤	①–⑤	①–⑤		①–⑥	①–⑥	①–⑥	①–⑥	①–⑥	①–⑥		①–⑥	①–⑥	①–⑥	①–⑤	①–⑤	①–⑤		①–⑤	①–⑤	①–⑤
0	**Caracas** d.	0500	0520	0540	and every	0900	1000	1100	1200	1300	1400	...	1500	1600	1700	1720	1740	1800	and every	2020	2040	2100
24	Charallave Norte d.	0517	0537	0557	20 minutes	0917	1017	1117	1217	1317	1417	...	1517	1617	1717	1737	1757	1817	20 minutes	2037	2057	2117
32	Charallave Sur d.	0522	0542	0602	until	0922	1022	1122	1222	1322	1422	...	1522	1622	1722	1742	1802	1822	until	2042	2002	2122
41	**Cúa** a.	0531	0551	0611		0931	1031	1131	1231	1331	1431	...	1531	1631	1731	1751	1811	1831		2051	2011	2131

		①–⑤	①–⑤	①–⑤		①–⑥	①–⑥	①–⑥	①–⑥	①–⑥	①–⑥		①–⑥	①–⑥	①–⑥	①–⑤	①–⑤	①–⑤		①–⑤	①–⑤	①–⑤
Cúa d.	...	0500	0520	0540	and every	0900	1000	1100	1200	1300	1400	...	1500	1600	1700	1720	1740	1800	and every	2020	2040	2100
Charallave Sur d.	...	0509	0529	0549	20 minutes	0909	1009	1109	1209	1309	1409	...	1509	1609	1709	1729	1749	1809	20 minutes	2029	2049	2109
Charallave Norte d.	...	0514	0534	0554	until	0914	1014	1114	1214	1314	1414	...	1514	1614	1714	1734	1754	1814	until	2034	2054	2114
Caracas a.	...	0531	0551	0611		0931	1031	1131	1231	1331	1431	...	1531	1631	1731	1751	1811	1831		2054	2011	2131

9930 COLOMBIA

BARRANCABERMEJA — Coopsercol Ltda

km										
0	**Puerto Parra** d.	...	...	0510	...	...	...	...	...	...
65	Barrancabermeja d.	0600	...	0725	...	1130	...	1430	...	1700
95	**García Cardena** a.	0700	...	...	...	1230	...	1530	...	1800

García Cardena d.	...	0700	...	...	...	1230	...	1530	...	1800
Barrancabermeja d.	...	0800	...	1300	...	1330	...	1630	...	1900
Puerto Parra a.	...	...	...	1515	...	...	...	...	...	...

BOGOTÁ - ZAPAQUIRÁ — Turistren

km		⑥⑦	
0	**Bogotá Sabana** d.	0830	...
15	Usaquen d.	0930	...
34	La Caro d.	1035	...
40	Cajicá d.	|	...
53	**Zapaquirá** a.	1130	...

	⑥⑦	⑥⑦
Zapaquirá d.	1230	...
Cajicá d.	1310	1515
La Caro d.	...	1540
Usaquen d.	...	1650
Bogotá Sabana a.	...	1740

9935 ECUADOR — FC del Ecuador

km	All trains 🄁	24 ④–⑦	32 ④–⑦	
0	**Quito** d.	0815	0815	...
45	Machachi d.	1000	1000	...
62	El Boliche (Mt. Cotopaxi) d.	|	1045	...
80	Lasso d.	1105	...	...
110	**Latacunga** a.	1215	...	...

All trains 🄁	23 ⑥⑦	31 ④–⑦	25 ④–⑦
Latacunga d.	...	...	1330
Lasso d.	...	...	1430
El Boliche (Mt Cotopaxi) d.	1315	1345	|
Machachi d.	1400	1430	1615
Quito a.	...	1615	1815

km		A ②–⑦	⑤⑥⑦	A ④–⑦
0	**Riobamba** d.	...	...	1200
41	Colta d.	...	...	1340
98	Alausi d.	0800	0900	...
111	Sibambe d.	0900	1000	...
154	**Bucay** a.	...	...	...

All trains 🄁	B ②–⑦	⑤⑥⑦	④–⑦
Bucay d.	...	...	...
Sibambe d.	0930	1030	...
Alausi d.	1030	1130	...
Colta d.	...	...	143
Riobamba a.	...	...	161

A– Additional trips 1100, 1500.
B– Additional trips 1230, 1630.

PERU 9940

POROY - MACHU PICCHU — Perurail

	71	81	301	83	31	501	33	203	11	73	303	603	75	51
	B	B	A	B	A	A	B	A	C	B	A	A	B	B
	...	...	...	...	0640	...	0742	0825	0905	...	...	...	...	...
	0507	0610	0705	0745	|	0853	|	1032	|	1258	1327	1537	1900	2100
	0634	0740	0827	0915	0952	1024	1051	1211	1224	1424	1449	1702	2043	2250

	50	72	302	204	74	32	304	504	34	604	12	606	84	76
	B	B	A	A	B	A	A	A	B	A	C	A	B	B
	0535	0853	1055	1337	1455	1520	1548	1622	1643	1727	1750	1810	1845	2145
	0744	1052	1232	1504	1631	|	1729	1801	|	1856	|	1945	2018	2316
	...	...	...	...	...	1905	...	...	2023	2050	2116	...	...	...

A – VISTADOME – [1] and 🍸.
B – EXPEDITION – [2] and 🍸.
C – HIRAM BINGHAM – [1] and ✕.
D – 2014 Jun. 27, Jul. 26, Aug. 29, Oct. 8. 31.
E – 2014 Jun. 30, Jul. 29, Sept. 1, Oct. 11, Nov. 3.
△ – Poroy is *13 km* from **Cusco**. Connecting bus service operates.

…O

…*rney 10 hours.*
… Apr. - Oct.).
… Apr. - Oct.).
…rator: Perurail.

LIMA - HUANCAYO

TREN DE LA SIERRA. *332 km. Journey 12 hours.*
From Lima at 0700 on dates in note **D**.
From Huancayo at 0700 on dates in note **E**.
Trains convey [12] and ✕. Operator: FC Central Andino.

TACNA - ARICA

62 km. Journey 2 hours. 2nd class.
From Tacna .
From Arica.
Service suspended. Operator: FC Tacna Arica.

BOLIVIA 9945

…aria Oriental

…UIJARRO - SANTA CRUZ DA LA SIERRA — FO

	9	13	7		10	14	8
	①③⑤	②④⑦	①③⑤		②④⑥	①③⑤	②④⑦
	1100	1600	1830	**SC da la Sierra** .. d.	1145	1600	1830
	1405	1836	2049	Pozo del Tigre .... d.	1456	|	|
…d.	1757	2141	2324	San José Chiquitos d.	1828	2150	2339
…d.	2308	0153	0231	Roboré .... d.	2306	0147	0258
..... d.	0240	|	|	Rivero Torrez...... d.	0256	0503	0536
.... a.	0638	0800	0755	**Puerto Quijarro** . a.	0620	0800	0756

SANTA CRUZ DE LA SIERRA - YACUIBA — FO

km		2				1		
		④				⑤		
0	**SC de la Sierra**..... a.	1530	...	...	**Yacuíba**............. d.	1700	...	...
115	Cabezas .... d.	1840	...	...	Villa Montes .... d.	1948	...	...
239	Charaguá .... d.	2312	...	...	Boyuibe .... d.	2235	...	...
360	Boyuibe .... d.	0219	...	...	Charaguá............. d.	0135	...	...
434	Villa Montes........... d.	0503	...	...	Cabezas .... d.	0604	...	...
533	**Yacuíba** .... a.	0755	...	...	**SC de la Sierra** .. a.	0935	...	...

…OURO - VILLAZÓN — FA

km		2	16	68		1	15	67
		②⑤	③⑦	①④		③⑥	①④	①④
	… d.	1530	1900	...	**Villazón**............. d.	1530	1530	...
	…yuni.................. d.	2240	0250	0330	Tupiza .... d.	1825	1905	...
	Avaroa .... a.	|	|	0930	Atocha .... d.	2145	2300	...
404	Atocha.................. d.	0055	0520	...	**Avaroa**............ d.	|	|	1200
501	Tupiza .... d.	0410	0905	...	Uyuni.................. d.	0005	0145	1810
602	**Villazón** .... a.	0705	1205	...	**Oruro** .... a.	0700	0910	...

OTHER SERVICES IN BOLIVIA — FA

km		②④⑥				③⑤⑦		
0	**Cochabamba** .... d.	0800	...	...	**Aiquille** .... d.	0800	...	...
216	**Aiquille** .... a.	1645	...	...	**Cochabamba** ..... a.	1645	...	...

km		②④⑥				①③⑤		
0	**Potosí** .... d.	0800	...	...	**Sucre** El Tejar .... d.	0800	...	...
171	**Sucre** El Tejar .... a.	1400	...	...	**Potosí** .... a.	1400	...	...

BRAZIL 9950

Estrada de Ferro do Carajás / Estrada de Ferro Vitória a Minas

SÃO LUIS - PARAUAPEBAS — EFC

km		①④⑥ 12				②⑤⑦ 12		
0	**São Luis**.............. d.	0800	...	...	**Parauapebas** ..... d.	0600	...	...
126	Arari .... d.	1016	...	...	Itainopolis .... d.	0731	...	...
145	Vitória do Mearim .. d.	1040	...	...	Marabá .... d.	0829	...	...
213	Santa Inês .... d.	1156	...	...	São Pedro .... d.	0956	...	...
264	Alto Alegre............ d.	1256	...	...	Acailandia .... d.	1219	...	...
281	Mineirinho............. d.	1319	...	...	Nova Vida............ d.	1429	...	...
299	Auzilândia............. d.	1340	...	...	Presa de Porco ... d.	1525	...	...
315	Altamira................ d.	1402	...	...	Altamira .... d.	1551	...	...
334	Presa de Porco...... d.	1430	...	...	Auzilândia .... d.	1613	...	...
384	Nova Vida .... d.	1526	...	...	Mineirinho .... d.	1634	...	...
513	Acailandia.............. d.	1741	...	...	Alto Alegre .... d.	1659	...	...
650	São Pedro.............. d.	1957	...	...	Santa Inês .... d.	1804	...	...
738	Marabá.................. d.	2131	...	...	Vitória do Mearim d.	1913	...	...
785	Itainopolis .... d.	2222	...	...	Arari .... d.	1941	...	...
861	**Parauapebas** .... a.	2350	...	...	**São Luis** .... a.	2200	...	...

BELO HORIZONTE - VITÓRIA — EFVM

km		2				2		
0	**Belo Horizonte** ..... d.	0730	...	...	**Vitória**................ d.	0700	...	...
71	Dois Irmãos .... d.	0903	...	...	Flexal................... d.	0715	...	...
97	Rio Piracicaba .... d.	1002	...	...	Fundão .... d.	0802	...	...
149	Drumond .... d.	1048	...	...	Piraqueacú .... d.	0829	...	...
173	Antonio Dias .... d.	1116	...	...	Colatina .... d.	0927	...	...
	Mario Carvalho ...... d.	1152	...	...	Aimorés .... d.	1026	...	...
286	Periquito................ d.	1315*	...	...	Conselheiro Pena d.	1125	...	...
339	G Valadares .... d.	1420	...	...	G Valadares.......... d.	1314	...	...
415	Conselheiro Pena .. d.	1547	...	...	Periquito .... d.	1405	...	...
484	Aimorés.................. d.	1704	...	...	Mario Carvalho ..... d.	1532	...	...
532	Colatina .... d.	1804	...	...	Antonio Dias .... d.	1605	...	...
588	Piraqueacú .... d.	1859	...	...	Drumond .... d.	1639	...	...
612	Fundão .... d.	1926	...	...	Rio Piracicaba....... d.	1732	...	...
657	Flexal .... d.	2012	...	...	Dois Irmãos .... d.	1830	...	...
664	**Vitória**................... a.	2030	...	...	**Belo Horizonte** .. a.	2010	...	...

URUGUAY 9955

Ferrocarriles del Estado

km		①-⑤	①-⑤	⑥	⑥	①-⑤	⑥	①-⑤	①-⑤	⑥	①-⑤	⑥	①-⑤	①-⑤	⑥	①-⑤	⑥	①-⑤	①-⑤	⑥			
0	**Montevideo** Nueva Terminal .... d.	0625	0725	0805	0900	0940	1035	1115	1330	1350	1500	1520	1540	1730	1740	1750	1810	1845	1930	1935	...	...	...
8	Sayago .... d.	0638	0738	0818	0916	0953	1048	1128	1343	1403	1513	1533	1554	1743	1754	1804	1823	1859	1943	1952	...	...	...
19	Las Piedras .... d.	0701	0803	0841	0939	1016	1111	1151	1408	1426	1538	1556	1618	1810	1819	1828	1846	1922	2006	2016	...	...	...
26	Progreso... d.	0715	...	...	0953	...	...	...	...	...	...	...	1632	1824	1834	...	...	1936	...	2041	...	...	...
42	Canalones .... d.	...	...	...	1016	...	...	...	...	...	...	...	...	1847	1857	...	...	1959	...	2052	...	...	...
63	**25 de Augosto**............................... a.	...	...	...	1047	...	...	...	...	...	...	...	...	1917	1927	...	...	2029	...	2123	...	...	...

		①-⑤	①-⑤	⑥	①-⑤	⑥	①-⑤	①-⑤	⑥	①-⑤	⑥	①-⑤	①-⑤	⑥	⑥	①-⑤	⑥	①-⑤	⑥				
25 de Augosto............................ d.	...	0400	...	0530	0530	0635	...	...	...	...	...	...	...	...	...	...	1715	...	...	...	...	...	...
Canalones .... d.	...	0431	...	0600	0559	0705	...	...	...	...	...	...	...	...	...	...	1744	...	...	...	...	...	...
Progreso...................................... d.	...	0453	...	0623	0623	0728	0730	...	...	...	...	...	...	...	...	1700	1806	...	...	...	...	...	...
Las Piedras .... d.	...	0509	0600	0638	0638	0743	0742	0810	0950	1025	1125	1200	1415	1435	1610	1714	1818	1840	1930	...	...	...	...
Sayago .... d.	...	0530	0622	0701	0705	0806	0807	0932	1012	1047	1145	1222	1436	1459	1632	1735	1850	1902	1952	...	...	...	...
Montevideo N Terminal................. a.	...	0546	0636	0717	0721	0822	0822	0846	1026	1101	1159	1236	1450	1511	1646	1750	1907	1916	2006	...	...	...	...

ARGENTINA 9960

BUENOS AIRES - MAR DEL PLATA — Ferrobaires

km		315	301			316	1316	302
		①③⑤	⑤			②④	⑦	⑦
0	**Buenos Aires** ‡ .... d.	1522	1802	...	**Mar del Plata** ..... d.	1504	1521	1620
114	Chascomús .... d.	1711	|	...	Maipú .... d.	1707	1717	|
204	Dolores.................. d.	1836	|	...	Dolores .... d.	1801	1815	|
271	Maipú .... d.	1946	|	...	Chascomús......... d.	1915	1930	|
399	**Mar del Plata** .... a.	2137	2343	...	**Buenos Aires** ‡.. a.	2104	2121	2205

‡ – Buenos Aires Plaza Constitución.

BUENOS AIRES - TANDIL — Ferrobaires

km		333					334	
		②⑤					③⑦	
0	**Buenos Aires** ‡ .... d.	1650	...	...	**Tandil**................ d.	...	2240	...
64	Cañuelas .... d.	1805	...	...	Rauch.................. d.	...	0000	...
107	Monte.................... d.	1854	...	...	Las Flores........... d.	...	0157	...
179	Las Flores .... d.	2024	...	...	Monte .... d.	...	0327	...
269	Rauch.................... d.	2222	...	...	Cañuelas .... d.	...	|	...
330	**Tandil** .... a.	2341	...	...	**Buenos Aires** ‡.. a.	...	0530	...

‡ – Buenos Aires Plaza Constitución.

BUENOS AIRES - BAHÍA BLANCA — Ferrobaires

km		1351	351			352	1352	
		①③⑤	②④			③⑤	②④⑦	
0	**Buenos Aires** ‡ .... d.	1945	1945	...	**B. Blanca** Sud.... d.	1935	1940	...
64	Cañuelas .... d.	|	|	...	Tornquist .... d.	|	2128	...
	Monte.................... d.	2152	2152	...	Pigüé .... d.	|	2234	...
179	Las Flores .... d.	2324	2324	...	Coronel Suárez... d.	|	2340	...
289	Azul....................... d.	0121	0121	...	Pringles.......... d.	2349	|	...
332	Olavarria............... a.	0230	0230	...	Laprida........... d.	0102	|	...
332	Olavarria............... d.	0246	0246	...	Olavarria............ a.	0246	0246	...
420	Laprida............. d.	|	0424	...	Olavarria............ d.	0300	0300	...
490	Pringles............ d.	|	0538	...	Azul.................... d.	0412	0412	...
488	Coronel Suárez...... d.	0555	|	...	Las Flores.......... d.	0614	0614	...
538	Pigüé.................... d.	0655	|	...	Monte .... d.	0756	0756	...
	Tornquist .... d.	0756	|	...	Cañuelas .... d.	0850	0850	...
680*	**Bahía Blanca** Sud. a.	0941	0950	...	**Buenos Aires** ‡.. a.	1020	1020	...

* – *640 km* via Pringles.
‡ – Buenos Aires Plaza Constitución.

9960 ARGENTINA

BUENOS AIRES - GENERAL ALVEAR

km		383 ⑦	377 ⑦	375 ⑤	381 ⑤
0	**B. Aires** Plaza Constitución .. d.	1645	1830	1915	2025
98	Empalme Lobos d.	1904	2047	2126	2249
136	Roque Pérez d.	2030	2213	2252	0015
185	Saladillo a.	2207	2350	0030	0152
233	**General Alvear** a.	0020	...	...	0405

	378 ①	376 ⑥	384 ①
General Alvear d.	...	...	0110
Saladillo d.	0230	0315	0322
Roque Pérez d.	0408	0453	0500
Empalme Lobos d.	0535	0619	0627
B. Aires Plaza Constitución . a.	0752	0845	0845

BUENOS AIRES - LINCOLN / REALICÓ / PEHUAJO

km		1331 ①–⑤	115 ①–⑤	115 ①②⑥	115 ③	115 ④	153 ⑤	2153 ⑥	111 ⑤
0	**Buenos Aires** Once d.	1730	1835	1835	1835	1835	1950	...	2105
98	Mercedes DFS d.	2003	2040	2103	2103	2103	2217	...	2332
158	Chivilcoy Sud d.	...	2148	2231	2231	2231	2346	...	0101
209	Bragado a.	...	2246	2349	2349	2349	0106	...	0219
209	Bragado d.	...	...	0013	0013	...	...	0130	0240
263	Los Toldos d.	...	...	|	|	...	...	0347	|
313	**Lincoln** d.	...	...	|	|	...	...	0535	|
336	General Pinto d.	...	...	|	|	...	...	0640	|
390	Ameghino d.	...	...	|	|	...	...	0840	|
446	General Villegas d.	...	...	|	|	...	...	1002	|
559	**Realicó** a.	...	...	|	|	...	...	1300	|
261	9 de Julio d.	...	...	0111	0111	...	...	...	0338
310	Carlos Casares a.	...	...	0155	0155	...	...	...	0422
363	**Pehuajo** a.	...	...	0307	...	...	...	...	0534

	156 ⑦	1546 ①	1332 ①–⑤		
Pehuajo d.	...	...	...		
Carlos Casares d.	...	...	...		
9 de Julio d.	...	...	...		
Realicó d.	1351	...	...		
General Villegas d.	1650	...	...		
Ameghino d.	1812	...	...		
General Pinto d.	2012	...	...		
Lincoln d.	2117	...	...		
Los Toldos d.	2305	...	...		
Bragado a.	0120	...	...	...	063
Bragado d.	...	0200	...	...	07
Chivilcoy Sud d.	...	0314	...	...	08
Mercedes DFS d.	...	0439	0610	...	094
Buenos Aires Once a.	...	0703	0849	...	121

BASAVILBASO - CONCORDIA — SOFSA

km		①–⑤	①⑤	
0	**Basavilbaso** d.	0700	...	...
56	Villaguay Este d.	0831	...	...
61	Villaguay Central ... a.	0852	...	...
	Villaguay Central ... d.	...	0926	...
56	Villaguay Este d.	...	0947	...
171	**Concordia** a.	...	1236	...

	①⑤	①–⑤	
Concordia d.	1300	...	...
Villaguay Este d.	1549	...	...
Villaguay Central a.	1610	...	...
Villaguay Central d.	...	1628	...
Villaguay Este d.	...	1648	...
Basavilbaso a.	...	1820	...

VIEDMA - BARILOCHE

km				⑤
0	**Viedma** ◧ d.	...	...	1800
189	San Antonio Oeste d.	...	...	2200
625	Ing Jacobacci d.	...	...	0655
819	**Bariloche** a.	...	...	1135

Bariloche d.	
Ing Jacobacci d.	
S Antonio Oeste . d.	
Viedma ◧ a.	

◧ – 🚌 connections available to / from B. Blanca and Buenos Aires (operator E

PARANÁ - CONCEPCIÓN DEL URUGUAY — UEFER

km		2302 ⑤		
0	**Paraná** d.	1300	...	...
46	Crespo d.	1415	...	...
120	Nogoyá d.	1600	...	...
216	Basavilbaso d.	1830	...	...
280	**C del Uruguay** a.	2010	...	...

	2303 ⑦		
C del Uruguay ... d.	1300	...	...
Basavilbaso d.	1430	...	...
Nogoyá d.	1710	...	...
Crespo d.	1900	...	...
Paraná a.	2010	...	...

BUENOS AIRES - TUCUMÁN — Ferrocentral

km		265 ①⑤	273 ①⑤	
0	**B. Aires** Retiro c.	0728	1413	...
314	Rosario Norte c.	1455	2154	...
523	Rafaela d.	2009	...	...
684	Ceres d.	2343	...	...
791	Pinto d.	0149	...	...
858	Colonia Dora d.	0311	...	...
1020	La Banda d.	0619	...	...
1170	**Tucumán** a.	0958	...	...

	266 ③	266 ⑥	274 ④⑦
Tucumán d.	1552	1900	...
La Banda d.	1951	2259	...
Colonia Dora d.	2244	0152	...
Pinto d.	0003	0311	...
Ceres d.	0227	0535	...
Rafaela d.	0546	0854	...
Rosario Norte d.	1115	1408	2219
B. Aires Retiro ... a.	2000	2308	0740

BUENOS AIRES - ALBERDI — Ferrobaires

km			513 ①⑤	
0	**B. Aires** Retiro d.	...	1812	...
111	Mercedes d.	...	2038	...
209	Chacabuco d.	...	2224	...
255	Junin a.	...	2312	...
336	**Alberdi** a.	...	...	...

	514 ①②		
Alberdi d.	...	...	...
Junin d.	0405	...	...
Chacabuco d.	0458	...	...
Mercedes d.	0701	...	...
B. Aires Retiro ... a.	0938	...	...

BUENOS AIRES - CÓRDOBA — Ferrocentral

km		215 ①②	215 ⑥	269 ①⑤
0	**B. Aires** Retiro d.	*	**	2035
314	Rosario Norte d.	...	...	0402
384	Cañada de Gómez d.	...	...	0607
566	Villa Maria d.	0545	0700	0941
708	**Córdoba** Mitre a.	0953	1108	1342

	268 ③⑦		216 ①⑤⑦
Córdoba Mitre d.	1439	...	1700
Villa Maria d.	1850	...	2108
C de Gómez d.	2219	...	...
Rosario Norte d.	0022	...	...
B. Aires Retiro ... a.	0907	...	...

*– Not holiday ①
**– Runs holiday ①

SALTA - SOCOMPA — Tren a las Nubes

km		809 ⑥a	
0	**Salta** d.	0705b	...
53	El Alisal d.	0909	...
68	Chorillos d.	0943	...
218	Viaducto La Polvorilla a.	1510	...
570	**Socompa** a.	...	...

	810 ⑥a	
Socompa d.	...	...
Viaducto La Polvorilla d.	1530	...
Chorillos d.	2121	...
El Alisal d.	2156	...
Salta a.	2348	...

a – From May 3 to Dec 6 ex Jun.28, Nov 29. b - Passengers should arrive at 0615

9965 CHILE

Empresa de los Ferrocarriles del Estado

SANTIAGO - CHILLÁN

km		22001	601 ①–⑤	553 ⑥⑦	6731	22011	20201	503 ①-⑤	603 ⑥⑦	605 ①-⑤	507 ①–⑤	509 ①-⑤	511	513
0	**Santiago** Alameda d.	0840	0905	0900	...	1800	1815	1830	1830	1845	1900	1930	2000	2145
	San Bernardo d.	0905	0931	0925	...	1826	|	1855	1855	1910	1925	1955	2025	2210
85	Rancagua d.	0957	1045	1034	1730	1914	|	2002	2004	2019	2032	2102	2132	2317
138	San Fernando d.	1034	...	1116	1812	1953	1938	...	2046	2101	...	...	...	...
191	Curicó d.	1108	...	...	...	2027	2018	...	...	...	...	...	...	...
	Molina d.	1119	...	...	...	2038	2053	...	...	...	...	...	...	...
258	**Talca** d.	1155	...	...	...	2114	2104	...	...	...	...	...	...	...
278	San Javier d.	1214	...	...	...	2133	2140	...	...	...	...	...	...	...
308	Linares d.	1233	...	...	...	2152	2159	...	...	...	...	...	...	...
348	Parral d.	1304	...	...	...	2223	2217	...	...	...	...	...	...	...
382	San Carlos d.	1328	...	...	...	2247	...	...	...	...	...	...	...	...
400	**Chillán** a.	1345	...	...	...	2304	...	...	...	...	...	...	...	...

	500 ①–⑤	502 ①–⑤	504 ①–⑤	506 ①–⑤	508 ①–⑤	610	22202	672	512 ⑥⑦	614 ①-⑤	514 ①-⑤	654 ⑥⑦	22014	22016 ⑦
Chillán d.	...	...	...	...	...	...	...	...	...	...	...	...	1645	1810
San Carlos d.	...	...	...	...	...	...	...	...	...	...	...	...	1703	1828
Parral d.	...	...	...	...	...	...	...	...	...	...	...	...	1727	1852
Linares d.	...	...	...	...	...	...	0630	...	...	...	...	...	1758	1923
San Javier d.	...	...	...	...	...	...	0649	...	...	...	...	...	1816	1941
Talca d.	...	...	...	...	...	...	0708	...	...	...	...	...	1833	1958
Molina d.	...	...	...	...	...	...	0744	...	...	...	...	...	1909	2038
Curicó d.	...	...	...	...	...	...	0755	...	...	...	...	...	1920	2052
San Fernando d.	...	...	...	...	...	0610	0829	1200	...	1858	...	1900	1953	2125
Rancagua d.	0540	0555	0610	0625	0640	0654	0910	1242	1820	1940	1945	1945	2030	2202
San Bernardo d.	0648	0703	0718	0733	0748	0802	1022	...	1928	...	2053	2053	2117	2249
Santiago Alameda a.	0712	0727	0742	0757	0812	0826	1055	...	1952	...	2117	2117	2142	2314

VICTORIA - TEMUCO

km		22931 ①–⑤	22933	22935
0	**Victoria** d.	0630	1130	1800
44	Lautaro d.	0717	1217	1847
73	**Temuco** a.	0757	1257	1906

	22932 ①–⑤	22934	22936
Temuco d.	0930	1630	2000
Lautaro d.	1010	1710	2040
Victoria a.	1057	1757	2127

TALCA - CONSTITUCIÓN

km		20701		20703
0	**Talca** d.	0730	...	1645
	Gonzalez Bastias ... d.	0913	...	1828
89	**Constitución** a.	1114	...	2029

	20702		2070
Constitución d.	0730	...	1625
Gonzalez Bastias . d.	0916	...	1831
Talca a.	1054	...	2009